International GAAP® 2021

Generally Accepted Accounting Practice
under International Financial Reporting Standards

Cullum Allen	Lennart Hoogerwaard	Tina Patel
Jeremy Barnes	Jane Hurworth	Claire Patra
Anne-Cathrine Bernhoft	Ted Jones	Michael Pratt
Martin Beyersdorff	Heather de Jongh	Matthew Richardson
Mike Bonham	Parbin Khatun	Tim Rogerson
David Bradbery	Maria Kingston	Vadim Shelaginov
Rob Carrington	Bernd Kremp	Yuta Shimomura
Jessica Cayadi	Dean Lockhart	Anna Sirocka
Victor Chan	Sharon MacIntyre	Kirsty Smith
Wei Li Chan	Anna Malcolm	Sharanya Sreedaran
Larissa Connor	Amanda Marrion	David Stolker
Pieter Dekker	Emily Moll	Michael Varila
Tim Denton	Richard Moore	Aikaterini Vatzaki
Alicia Edelstein	Ayesha Moosa	Jane Watson
Prahalad Halgeri	Tom Mullins	
Andrea Holmes	Mqondisi Ndlovu	

This edition first published in 2021 by John Wiley & Sons Ltd.
Cover, cover design and content copyright © 2021 Ernst & Young LLP.
The United Kingdom firm of Ernst & Young LLP is a member of Ernst & Young Global Limited.
International GAAP® is a registered trademark of Ernst & Young LLP.

This publication contains copyright © material and trademarks of the IFRS Foundation®. All rights reserved. Reproduced by Ernst & Young LLP with the permission of the IFRS Foundation. Reproduction and use rights are strictly limited. For more information about the IFRS Foundation and rights to use its material please visit www.ifrs.org. Disclaimer: To the extent permitted by applicable law the Board and the IFRS Foundation expressly disclaims all liability howsoever arising from this publication or any translation thereof whether in contract, tort or otherwise (including, but not limited to, liability for any negligent act or omission) to any person in respect of any claims or losses of any nature including direct, indirect, incidental or consequential loss, punitive damages, penalties or costs.

Registered office
John Wiley & Sons Ltd, The Atrium, Southern Gate, Chichester, West Sussex, PO19 8SQ, United Kingdom

For details of our global editorial offices, for customer services and for information about how to apply for permission to reuse the copyright material in this book please see our website at www.wiley.com

The right of the author to be identified as the author of this work has been asserted in accordance with the Copyright, Designs and Patents Act 1988.

All rights reserved. No part of this publication may be reproduced, stored in a retrieval system, or transmitted, in any form or by any means, electronic, mechanical, photocopying, recording or otherwise, except as permitted by the UK Copyright, Designs and Patents Act 1988, without the prior permission of the publisher.

Wiley publishes in a variety of print and electronic formats and by print-on-demand. Some material included with standard print versions of this book may not be included in e-books or in print-on-demand. If this book refers to media such as a CD or DVD that is not included in the version you purchased, you may download this material at http://booksupport.wiley.com. For more information about Wiley products, visit www.wiley.com.

Designations used by companies to distinguish their products are often claimed as trademarks. All brand names and product names used in this book are trade names, service marks, trademarks or registered trademarks of their respective owners. The publisher is not associated with any product or vendor mentioned in this book.

Limit of Liability/Disclaimer of Warranty: While the publisher and author have used their best efforts in preparing this book, they make no representations or warranties with respect to the accuracy or completeness of the contents of this book and specifically disclaim any implied warranties of merchantability or fitness for a particular purpose. It is sold on the understanding that the publisher is not engaged in rendering professional services and neither the publisher nor the author shall be liable for damages arising herefrom. If professional advice or other expert assistance is required, the services of a competent professional should be sought.

This publication has been carefully prepared, but it necessarily contains information in summary form and is therefore intended for general guidance only, and is not intended to be a substitute for detailed research or the exercise of professional judgement. The publishers, Ernst & Young LLP, Ernst & Young Global Limited or any of its Member Firms or partners or staff can accept no responsibility for loss occasioned to any person acting or refraining from action as a result of any material in this publication. On any specific matter, reference should be made to the appropriate adviser.

ISBN 978-1-119-77243-9 (paperback)
[EY personnel only ISBN 978-1-119-77244-6]
ISBN 978-1-119-77245-3 (ebk)
ISBN 978-1-119-77266-8 (ebk)

A catalogue record for this book is available from the British Library.

Printed and bound by CPI Group (UK) Ltd, Croydon, CR0 4YY.

This book is printed on acid-free paper, responsibly manufactured from well-managed FSC®-certified forests and other controlled sources.

Preface

The IASB noted in its 2018 analysis of the use of IFRS around the world that, other than China, India, Japan and the United States, the vast majority of the 166 jurisdictions they have researched require the use of IFRS for all or most domestic publicly accountable entities (listed companies and financial institutions) in their capital markets. Maintaining the current international alignment of accounting standards requires an ongoing commitment on the part of all jurisdictions involved, but the benefits of IFRS are clear when looking at the way in which the IASB was able to consider the impact of the coronavirus pandemic on financial reporting.

The coronavirus outbreak was first reported near the end of 2019, with the virus subsequently spreading worldwide. On 11 March 2020, the World Health Organisation classified the outbreak as a pandemic. While the coronavirus outbreak is first and foremost a public health concern, it has significantly impacted the world economy and, indirectly, financial reporting and the work of the IASB itself.

In response to the development, the IASB issued Amendments to IFRS 16 – *Leases: Covid-19-Related Rent Concessions*, deferred the effective date of Amendments to IAS 1 – *Presentation of Financial Statements: Classification of Liabilities as Current or Non-current*, decided to extend the consultation period of several consultation documents by three months, and decided to monitor the situation with a view to making further changes to its timelines, if necessary. As a result, the next milestones of many of the IASB's projects have been pushed out to accommodate the exceptional circumstances.

The economic impacts of the coronavirus outbreak can also be seen in the financial reports of companies where it has affected the accounting for and disclosure of going concern issues, impairment testing, government grants, leases, onerous contracts, income taxes and fair value measurement. While the economic uncertainty increased the need for the careful exercise of judgement, IFRS has offered an accounting framework that provides the necessary guidance to deal even with these unusual circumstances.

New standards

IFRS 16 became effective in 2019 and its interactions with other standards has given rise to a number of challenging implementation questions that continue to be addressed. The Interpretations Committee has published agenda decisions on the treatment of subsurface rights, determining the incremental borrowing rate, the definition of a lease and the interaction between the lease term and useful life of leasehold improvements. The IASB continues to work on its project that deals with the application of IAS 12 – *Income Taxes* – to right-of-use assets and lease liabilities, while the Interpretations

Committee is currently considering the accounting for the sale and leaseback of an asset in a single-asset entity.

IFRS 17 – *Insurance Contracts* – was amended in June 2020 and has an effective date of 1 January 2023. The IASB amended IFRS 17 in response to matters of concern raised primarily in Europe regarding the concepts and practical implementation of the standard that were raised by stakeholders. IFRS 17, together with IFRS 9 – *Financial Instruments*, will result in profound changes to the accounting in IFRS financial statements for insurance companies. This will also have a significant impact on data, systems and processes used to produce information for financial reporting purposes. The new model is likely to have a significant impact on the profit and total equity of some insurance entities, but IFRS 17 has been welcomed by the user community as it is expected to improve comparability between insurers and increase the transparency around the drivers of performance and source of earnings.

Current work plan

The IASB has deferred its agenda consultation until 2021 and is currently still working on the projects in its work plan for the period from 2017 until 2021. The work plan can be divided into three elements: the standard-setting and maintenance projects, the research projects, and the Better Communication in Financial Reporting initiative.

The IASB's standard-setting and maintenance agenda focuses almost exclusively on narrow scope projects that address certain aspects of existing standards. The exposure draft on the rate-regulated activities project – a more comprehensive project but limited in impact as it is industry-specific – was delayed by almost a year and is now expected to be published in early 2021.

As part of its active research agenda, the IASB's core model for dynamic risk management and discussion paper on business combinations under common control are expected in late 2020, while the comment period on the discussion paper on goodwill and impairment was extended to December 2020. The IASB is currently considering the direction on the projects on financial instruments with characteristics of equity and extractive activities. Although these technically complex but important projects are taking longer than expected, we encourage the IASB to continue its work as they deal with issues that have been the source of many accounting questions.

The IASB expects to publish, in late 2020, its request for information on the Post-Implementation Review of IFRS 10 – *Consolidated Financial Statements*, IFRS 11 – *Joint Arrangements* – and IFRS 12 – *Disclosure of Interests in Other Entities*. The Interpretations Committee has often discussed requests regarding the interpretation of IFRS 11 and it seems likely that the Post-Implementation Review will similarly give rise to questions from constituents.

Better communication and sustainability reporting

The IASB continues to work on the various aspects of its Better Communication in Financial Reporting initiative, such as the primary financial statements, management commentary and the taxonomy. The project to update the Management Commentary Practice Statement, for which an exposure draft is expected early in 2021, is seen by the

IASB as the cornerstone of the notion of 'broader financial information'. That said, there is an ongoing debate as to how 'broad' annual reporting, and by extension the IASB's own remit, should be.

In November 2019, Hans Hoogervorst, the Chairman of the IASB, noted in a speech that 'The popularity of non-GAAP has risen sharply and there is growing interest in broader reporting, particularly in the area of sustainability. [...] In the light of these developments, the IASB constantly asks itself how it can strengthen the relevance of IFRS Standards in this changing world.'[1] Sue Lloyd, the Vice-Chair of the IASB, noted in December 2019 that '[...] the IASB exists to write Standards that result in investors getting the information they need to make their investment decisions. We know that in order to make informed investment decisions, investors need information that goes beyond the boundaries of that captured within the traditional financial statements. Investors need information about items that are not recognised and measured for accounting purposes, but that can affect the company's future cash flows and the value of its equity.'[2]

Many of the non-financial issues that interest investors can be characterised as externalities, which are commonly defined as consequences of an industrial or commercial activity that affect other parties without being reflected in market prices. Traditional financial reporting has focused on how companies are affected by externalities that are inflicted upon them (i.e. the investor perspective), but far less on how their actions affect others (i.e. the societal perspective). In addressing these considerations, the IASB faces the challenge that it does not have the breadth of expertise that would allow it to cover the entire field of non-financial reporting and that its resources are limited.

In September 2020, Erik Thedéen, the Chair of IOSCO's Task Force on Sustainable Finance, noted in a speech that IOSCO is engaging with two initiatives that 'are both very interesting and very promising'.[3] Firstly, an alliance of five framework- and standard-setting institutions of international significance – CDP, the Climate Disclosure Standards Board (CDSB), the Global Reporting Initiative (GRI), the International Integrated Reporting Council (IIRC) and the Sustainability Accounting Standards Board (SASB) – announced a commitment to working towards a comprehensive corporate reporting system. Secondly, a working group of IFRS trustees is considering what role the IFRS Foundation can play in setting standards for sustainability reporting. The Trustees of the IFRS Foundation published a consultation paper on sustainability reporting to assess if there is sufficient demand for global sustainability standards and, if so, whether the development of a sustainability standards board under the governance structure of the IFRS Foundation would be an appropriate approach to achieving further consistency and global comparability in sustainability reporting.

---

1 Speech by Hans Hoogervorst, 5 November 2019 (IASB Chair delivers keynote at Eumedion Annual Symposium, Netherlands). IFRS Foundation website: http://www.ifrs.org/news-and-events/2019/11/the-iasb-from-financial-to-integrated-standard-setter/
2 Speech by Sue Lloyd, 9 December 2019 (Enhancing relevance in 2020 and beyond). IFRS Foundation website: http://www.ifrs.org/news-and-events/2019/12/enhancing-relevance-in-2020-and-beyond/
3 Speech by Erik Thedéen, 1 October 2020 (speech at the conference Driving Global Standards on Sustainable Finance). Swedish Finansinspektionen website: https://www.fi.se/en/published/presentations/2020/erik-thedeens-speech-at-driving-global-standards-on-sustainable-finance/

We commend the initiative of the Trustees of the IFRS Foundation in taking an active role in the efforts to improve the broader financial report, as non-financial reporting provides important information that allows users to put the financial statements in context and helps them in assessing future risks and opportunities. In addition to IOSCO, the International Federation of Accountants (IFAC) has also expressed support for the creation of a new sustainability standards board that would exist alongside the IASB under the IFRS Foundation. However, as legislators in some jurisdictions have already taken steps to ensure a minimum level of communication about sustainability issues, we believe it is crucial in the interest of broad acceptance to build as broad a base of support as possible.

This edition of *International GAAP®* covers the many interpretations, practices and solutions that have now been developed based on our work with clients, and discussions with regulators, standard-setters and other professionals. In particular, the edition has been revised to consider the many financial reporting issues that have arisen in the context of the coronavirus pandemic. We believe that *International GAAP®*, now in its sixteenth edition, plays an important role in ensuring consistent application of IFRS and helping companies as they address emerging issues (e.g. interest rate benchmark reform, application of IFRS 16 and implementation of IFRS 17). These issues are complex and give rise to many practical questions about the recognition, measurement, presentation and disclosure requirements.

Our team of authors and reviewers hails from all parts of the world and includes not only our global technical experts but also senior client-facing professionals. This gives us an in-depth knowledge of practice in many different countries and industry sectors, enabling us to go beyond mere recitation of the requirements of standards to explaining their application in many varied situations.

We are deeply indebted to many of our colleagues within the global organisation of EY for their selfless assistance and support in the publication of this book. It has been a truly international effort, with valuable contributions from EY people around the globe.

Our thanks go particularly to those who reviewed and edited the drafts, most notably: Elisa Alfieri, Mark Barton, Christian Baur, Paul Beswick, Silke Blaschke, Linzi Carr, Patrick Cavanagh, Larissa Clark, Tony Clifford, Angela Covic, Josh Forgione, Peter Gittens, Archibald Groenewald, Paul Hebditch, Lara Iob, Guy Jones, Steinar Kvifte, Michiel van der Lof, James Luke, Kerri Madden, Mark Mahar, Fernando Marticorena, John Offenbacher, John O'Grady, Christiana Panayidou, Pierre Phan Van Phi, Christoph Piesbergen, George Prieksaitis, Takeshi Saida, Gerard van Santen, Nicola Sawaki, Rachel Simons, Alison Spivey, Leo van der Tas, Daniel Trotman, Hans van der Veen, Tracey Waring, Arne Weber, Clare Wong and Luci Wright.

Our thanks also go to everyone who directly or indirectly contributed to the book's creation, including the following members of EY's IFRS desks: Thato Lengana, Steve Mwereria, Teresia Ng'ang'a, Anna Pickup and Tanay Rai.

We also thank Jeremy Gugenheim for his assistance with the production technology throughout the period of writing.

London,
October 2020

Cullum Allen
Jeremy Barnes
Anne-Cathrine Bernhoft
Martin Beyersdorff
Mike Bonham
David Bradbery
Rob Carrington
Jessica Cayadi
Victor Chan
Wei Li Chan
Larissa Connor
Pieter Dekker
Tim Denton
Alicia Edelstein
Prahalad Halgeri
Andrea Holmes

Lennart Hoogerwaard
Jane Hurworth
Ted Jones
Heather de Jongh
Parbin Khatun
Maria Kingston
Bernd Kremp
Dean Lockhart
Sharon MacIntyre
Anna Malcolm
Amanda Marrion
Emily Moll
Richard Moore
Ayesha Moosa
Tom Mullins
Mqondisi Ndlovu

Tina Patel
Claire Patra
Michael Pratt
Matthew Richardson
Tim Rogerson
Vadim Shelaginov
Yuta Shimomura
Anna Sirocka
Kirsty Smith
Sharanya Sreedaran
David Stolker
Michael Varila
Aikaterini Vatzaki
Jane Watson

Lists of chapters

Volume 1

1. International GAAP 1
2. The IASB's Conceptual Framework 39
3. Presentation of financial statements and accounting policies 109
4. Non-current assets held for sale and discontinued operations 187
5. First-time adoption 217
6. Consolidated financial statements 385
7. Consolidation procedures and non-controlling interests 491
8. Separate and individual financial statements 571
9. Business combinations 633
10. Business combinations under common control 761
11. Investments in associates and joint ventures 807
12. Joint arrangements 887
13. Disclosure of interests in other entities 941
14. Fair value measurement 995
15. Foreign exchange 1175
16. Hyperinflation 1249
17. Intangible assets 1285
18. Property, plant and equipment 1381
19. Investment property 1437
20. Impairment of fixed assets and goodwill 1511
21. Capitalisation of borrowing costs 1643
22. Inventories 1673

Index of extracts from financial statements .... *index* 1
Index of standards .... *index* 7
Index .... *index* 111

The lists of chapters in volumes 2 and 3 follow overleaf.

Volume 2

23	Leases	1701
24	Government grants	1821
25	Service concession arrangements	1847
26	Provisions, contingent liabilities and contingent assets	1923
27	Revenue: Introduction and scope	2015
28	Revenue: Identify the contract and performance obligations	2045
29	Revenue: Determine and allocate the transaction price	2157
30	Revenue: Recognition	2253
31	Revenue: Licences, warranties and contract costs	2313
32	Revenue: Presentation and disclosure	2387
33	Income taxes	2441
34	Share-based payment	2623
35	Employee benefits	2887
36	Operating segments	2973
37	Earnings per share	3017
38	Events after the reporting period	3071
39	Related party disclosures	3093
40	Statement of cash flows	3131
41	Interim financial reporting	3189
42	Agriculture	3269
43	Extractive industries	3325

Index of extracts from financial statements	*index* 1
Index of standards	*index* 7
Index	*index* 111

The list of chapters in volume 3 follows overleaf.

Volume 3

44	Financial instruments: Introduction	3571
45	Financial instruments: Definitions and scope	3579
46	Financial instruments: Derivatives and embedded derivatives	3615
47	Financial instruments: Financial liabilities and equity	3657
48	Financial instruments: Classification	3767
49	Financial instruments: Recognition and initial measurement	3839
50	Financial instruments: Subsequent measurement	3865
51	Financial instruments: Impairment	3905
52	Financial instruments: Derecognition	4079
53	Financial instruments: Hedge accounting	4173
54	Financial instruments: Presentation and disclosure	4399
55	Insurance contracts (IFRS 4)	4525
56	Insurance contracts (IFRS 17)	4669

Index of extracts from financial statements	*index* 1
Index of standards	*index* 7
Index	*index* 111

Abbreviations

The following abbreviations are used in this book:

Professional and regulatory bodies:

AASB	Australian Accounting Standards Board
AcSB	Accounting Standards Board of Canada
AICPA	American Institute of Certified Public Accountants
AOSSG	Asian-Oceanian Standard-Setters Group
APB	Accounting Principles Board (of the AICPA, predecessor of the FASB)
ARC	Accounting Regulatory Committee of representatives of EU Member States
ASAF	Accounting Standards Advisory Forum
ASB	Accounting Standards Board in the UK
ASBJ	Accounting Standards Board of Japan
ASU	Accounting Standards Update
CASC	China Accounting Standards Committee
CESR	Committee of European Securities Regulators, an independent committee whose members comprised senior representatives from EU securities regulators (replaced by ESMA)
CICA	Canadian Institute of Chartered Accountants
EC	European Commission
ECB	European Central Bank
ECOFIN	The Economic and Financial Affairs Council
EDTF	Enhanced Disclosure Task Force of the (FSB)
EFRAG	European Financial Reporting Advisory Group
EITF	Emerging Issues Task Force in the US
EPRA	European Public Real Estate Association
ESMA	European Securities and Markets Authority (see CESR)
EU	European Union
FAF	Financial Accounting Foundation
FASB	Financial Accounting Standards Board in the US
FCAG	Financial Crisis Advisory Group
FEE	Federation of European Accountants

FSB	Financial Stability Board (successor to the FSF)
FSF	Financial Stability Forum
G4+1	The (now disbanded) group of four plus 1, actually with six members, that comprised an informal 'think tank' of staff from the standard setters from Australia, Canada, New Zealand, UK, and USA, plus the IASC
G7	The Group of Seven Finance Ministers (successor to G8)
G8	The Group of Eight Finance Ministers
G20	The Group of Twenty Finance Ministers and Central Bank Governors
GPPC	Global Public Policy Committee of the six largest accounting networks
HKICPA	Hong Kong Institute of Certified Public Accountants
IASB	International Accounting Standards Board, or the Board
IASC	International Accounting Standards Committee. The former Board of the IASC was the predecessor of the IASB
IASCF	International Accounting Standards Committee Foundation (predecessor of the IFRS Foundation)
ICAEW	Institute of Chartered Accountants in England and Wales
ICAI	Institute of Chartered Accountants of India
ICAS	Institute of Chartered Accountants of Scotland
IFAC	International Federation of Accountants
IFASS	International Forum of Accounting Standard Setters
IFRIC	The IFRS Interpretations Committee (formerly the International Financial Reporting Interpretations Committee) of the IASB
IGC	Implementation Guidance Committee on IAS 39 (now disbanded)
IOSCO	International Organisation of Securities Commissions
IPSASB	International Public Sector Accounting Standards Board
IPTF	International Practices Task Force (a task force of the SEC Regulations Committee)
ISDA	International Swaps and Derivatives Association
IVSC	International Valuation Standards Council
KASB	Korea Accounting Standards Board
RICS	Royal Institution of Chartered Surveyors
SAC	Standards Advisory Council, predecessor of the IFRS Advisory Council which provides advice to the IASB on a wide range of issues
SEC	Securities and Exchange Commission (the US securities regulator)
SIC	Standing Interpretations Committee of the IASC (replaced by IFRIC)
TEG	Technical Expert Group, an advisor to the European Commission
TRG	Joint Transition Resource Group for Revenue Recognition

Accounting related terms:

ADS	American Depositary Shares
AFS	Available-for-sale investment
ARB	Accounting Research Bulletins (issued by the AICPA)
ARS	Accounting Research Studies (issued by the APB)
ASC	Accounting Standards Codification®. The single source of authoritative US GAAP recognised by the FASB, to be applied to non-governmental entities for interim and accounting periods ending after 15 September 2009
ASU	Accounting Standards Update
BCUCC	Business Combinations Under Common Control
CCIRS	Cross Currency Interest Rate Swap
CDO	Collateralised Debt Obligation
CLO	Collateralized Loan Obligation
CF	Conceptual Framework
CGU	Cash-generating Unit
CU	Currency Unit
DD&A	Depreciation, Depletion and Amortisation
DPF	Discretionary Participation Feature
E&E	Exploration and Evaluation
EBIT	Earnings Before Interest and Taxes
EBITDA	Earnings Before Interest, Taxes, Depreciation and Amortisation
EIR	Effective Interest Rate
EPS	Earnings per Share
FAS	Financial Accounting Standards (issued by the FASB). Superseded by Accounting Standards Codification® (ASC)
FC	Foreign currency
FICE	Financial Instruments with the Characteristics of Equity
FIFO	First-In, First-Out basis of valuation
FRS	Financial Reporting Standard (issued by the ASB)
FTA	First-time Adoption
FVLCD	Fair value less costs of disposal
FVLCS	Fair value less costs to sell (following the issue of IFRS 13, generally replaced by FVLCD)
FVPL	Fair value through profit and loss
FVOCI	Fair value through other comprehensive income

GAAP	Generally accepted accounting practice (as it applies under IFRS), or generally accepted accounting principles (as it applies to the US)	
HTM	Held-to-maturity investment	
IAS	International Accounting Standard (issued by the former board of the IASC)	
IBOR	Interbank Offered Rate	
IBNR	Incurred but not reported claims	
IFRS	International Financial Reporting Standard (issued by the IASB)	
IFRS for SMEs	International Financial Reporting Standard for Small and Medium-sized Entities	
IGC Q&A	Implementation guidance to the original version of IAS 39 (issued by the IGC)	
IPO	Initial Public Offering	
IPR&D	In-process Research and Development	
IPSAS	International Public Sector Accounting Standard	
IRR	Internal Rate of Return	
IRS	Interest Rate Swap	
JA	Joint Arrangement	
JCA	Jointly Controlled Asset	
JCE	Jointly Controlled Entity	
JCO	Jointly Controlled Operation	
JO	Joint Operation	
JV	Joint Venture	
LAT	Liability Adequacy Test	
LC	Local Currency	
LIBOR	London Inter Bank Offered Rate	
LIFO	Last-In, First-Out basis of valuation	
NBV	Net Book Value	
NCI	Non-controlling Interest	
NPV	Net Present Value	
NRV	Net Realisable Value	
OCI	Other Comprehensive Income	
PP&E	Property, Plant and Equipment	
R&D	Research and Development	
SCA	Service Concession Arrangement	
SE	Structured Entity	
SFAC	Statement of Financial Accounting Concepts (issued by the FASB as part of its conceptual framework project)	

SFAS	Statement of Financial Accounting Standards (issued by the FASB). Superseded by Accounting Standards Codification® (ASC)
SME	Small or medium-sized entity
SPE	Special Purpose Entity
SPE-PRMS	Society of Petroleum Engineers – Petroleum Resources Management System
SV	Separate Vehicle
TSR	Total Shareholder Return
VIU	Value In Use
WACC	Weighted Average Cost of Capital

References to IFRSs, IASs, Interpretations and supporting documentation:

AG	Application Guidance
AV	Alternative View
BCZ	Basis for Conclusions on IASs
BC	Basis for Conclusions on IFRSs and IASs
DI	Draft Interpretation
DO	Dissenting Opinion
DP	Discussion Paper
ED	Exposure Draft
IE	Illustrative Examples on IFRSs and IASs
IG	Implementation Guidance
IN	Introduction to IFRSs and IASs
PIR	Post-implementation Review

Authoritative literature

The content of this book takes into account all accounting standards and other relevant rules issued up to September 2020. Consequently, it covers the IASB's *Conceptual Framework for Financial Reporting* and authoritative literature listed below.

References in the main text of each chapter to the pronouncements below are generally to the versions of those pronouncements as approved and expected to be included in the Blue Book edition of the Bound Volume 2021 International Financial Reporting Standards – IFRS – Consolidated without early application – Official pronouncements applicable on 1 January 2021, to be published by the IASB.

References to those pronouncements below which have an effective date after 1 January 2021 (such as IFRS 17 – *Insurance contracts*) are to the versions of those pronouncements that are expected to be included in the Red Book edition of the Bound Volume 2021 International Financial Reporting Standards – IFRS – Official pronouncements issued at 1 January 2021, to be published by the IASB.

US GAAP accounting standards are organised within a comprehensive FASB Accounting Standards Codification©, which is now the single source of authoritative US GAAP recognised by the FASB to be applied to non-governmental entities and has been applied in this publication.

† The standards and interpretations marked with a dagger have been withdrawn or superseded.

		IASB Framework
		The Conceptual Framework for Financial Reporting
		International Financial Reporting Standards (2021 Bound Volume)
	IFRS 1	First-time Adoption of International Financial Reporting Standards
	IFRS 2	Share-based Payment
	IFRS 3	Business Combinations
†	IFRS 4	Insurance Contracts
	IFRS 5	Non-current Assets Held for Sale and Discontinued Operations
	IFRS 6	Exploration for and Evaluation of Mineral Resources
	IFRS 7	Financial Instruments: Disclosures
	IFRS 8	Operating Segments
	IFRS 9	Financial Instruments
	IFRS 10	Consolidated Financial Statements

IFRS 11	Joint Arrangements	
IFRS 12	Disclosure of Interests in Other Entities	
IFRS 13	Fair Value Measurement	
IFRS 14	Regulatory Deferral Accounts	
IFRS 15	Revenue from Contracts with Customers	
IFRS 16	Leases	

International Financial Reporting Standards (mandatory after 1 January 2023)

IFRS 17	Insurance Contracts	

International Accounting Standards (2021 Bound Volume)

IAS 1	Presentation of Financial Statements
IAS 2	Inventories
IAS 7	Statement of Cash Flows
IAS 8	Accounting Policies, Changes in Accounting Estimates and Errors
IAS 10	Events after the Reporting Period
IAS 12	Income Taxes
IAS 16	Property, Plant and Equipment
IAS 19	Employee Benefits
IAS 20	Accounting for Government Grants and Disclosure of Government Assistance
IAS 21	The Effects of Changes in Foreign Exchange Rates
IAS 23	Borrowing Costs
IAS 24	Related Party Disclosures
IAS 26	Accounting and Reporting by Retirement Benefit Plans
IAS 27	Separate Financial Statements
IAS 28	Investments in Associates and Joint Ventures
IAS 29	Financial Reporting in Hyperinflationary Economies
IAS 32	Financial Instruments: Presentation
IAS 33	Earnings per Share
IAS 34	Interim Financial Reporting
IAS 36	Impairment of Assets
IAS 37	Provisions, Contingent Liabilities and Contingent Assets
IAS 38	Intangible Assets
IAS 39	Financial Instruments: Recognition and Measurement
IAS 40	Investment Property
IAS 41	Agriculture

Chapter 1   International GAAP

1   WHY INTERNATIONAL FINANCIAL REPORTING STANDARDS MATTER 3
2   THE IFRS FOUNDATION AND THE IASB 4
    2.1   The standard-setting structure 4
    2.2   The IFRS Foundation 4
    2.3   The Monitoring Board 6
    2.4   The International Accounting Standards Board (IASB) 8
    2.5   The IFRS Interpretations Committee (the Interpretations Committee) 9
         2.5.1   Agenda decisions 10
    2.6   The Due Process Handbook 11
    2.7   The IFRS Advisory Council (the Advisory Council) 12
    2.8   Accounting Standards Advisory Forum (ASAF) 13
    2.9   Other advisory bodies 14
3   THE IASB'S TECHNICAL AGENDA AND CONVERGENCE WITH US GAAP 15
    3.1   The IASB's current priorities and future agenda 15
    3.2   IFRS/US GAAP convergence 16
4   THE ADOPTION OF IFRS AROUND THE WORLD 16
    4.1   Worldwide adoption 16
    4.2   Europe 19
         4.2.1   EU 19
                 4.2.1.A   Endorsed IFRS standards 21
                 4.2.1.B   Evaluation of the Regulation 22
         4.2.2   Russia 25
         4.2.3   United Kingdom 26
    4.3   Americas 27

			4.3.1	US	27
			4.3.2	Canada	27
			4.3.3	Brazil	28
	4.4	Asia			28
		4.4.1	China		28
			4.4.1.A	Mainland China	28
			4.4.1.B	Hong Kong	30
		4.4.2	Japan		30
		4.4.3	India		31
	4.5	Australia			32
	4.6	South Africa			33
5	CONSISTENCY IN APPLICATION OF IFRS				33
6	SUMMARY				35

Chapter 1   International GAAP

1   WHY INTERNATIONAL FINANCIAL REPORTING STANDARDS MATTER

With globalisation has come the increasing integration of world markets for goods, services and capital – with the result that companies that traditionally were reliant on their domestic capital markets for financing now have substantially increased access to debt and equity capital, both inside and outside their national borders.

Yet – perhaps not entirely surprisingly – the world of financial reporting was slow to respond reflecting, no doubt, a widespread nationalism in respect of countries' own standards.

Undoubtedly, one of the main advantages of a single set of global accounting standards is that it would enable the international capital markets to assess and compare inter-company performance in a much more meaningful, effective and efficient way. This should increase companies' access to global capital and ultimately reduce the cost thereof. Thus the request for global standards came both from regulatory bodies and from preparers of financial statements. As early as 1989 the International Organisation of Securities Commissions (IOSCO), the world's primary forum for co-operation among securities regulators, prepared a paper noting that cross border security offerings would be facilitated by the development of internationally accepted standards. For preparers, greater comparability in financial reporting with their global peers had obvious attractions.

Notwithstanding these anticipated benefits, it has only been since 2000 that there has been a serious effort made toward such global standards. This came about largely as a result of the European Commission's announcement in June 2000 that it would present proposals to introduce the requirement that all listed European Union (EU) companies report in accordance with International Accounting Standards by 2005. This requirement not only changed the face of European financial reporting, but global reporting as well after many other countries followed Europe's lead. Indeed, the IFRS Foundation reports that 144 jurisdictions require IFRS standards for all or most domestic publicly accountable entities (listed companies) in their capital markets.[1]

Thus global financial reporting has ceased to be characterised by numerous disparate national systems to the point at which there are today essentially only two – IFRS and US GAAP.

2 THE IFRS FOUNDATION AND THE IASB

2.1 The standard-setting structure

The diagram below illustrates the structure within which standards are set by the International Accounting Standards Board (IASB).

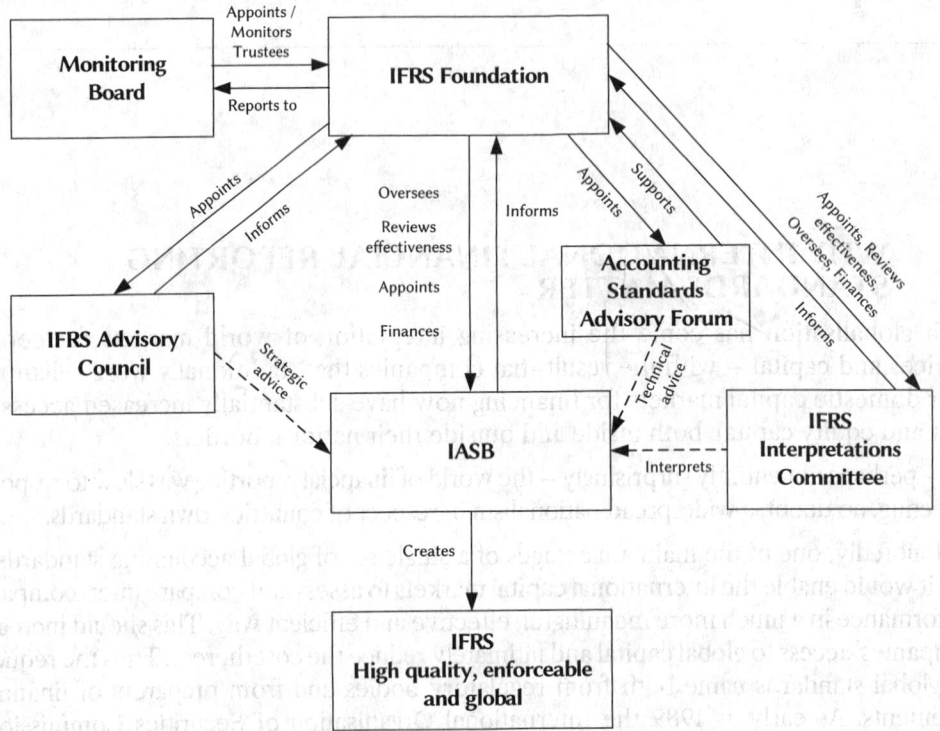

The various elements of the structure are discussed further below.

Unless indicated otherwise, references to IFRS include the following:
- International Financial Reporting Standards – standards developed by the IASB;
- International Accounting Standards (IAS) – standards developed by the International Accounting Standards Committee (IASC), the predecessor to the IASB;
- Interpretations developed by the IFRS Interpretations Committee (Interpretations Committee) or its predecessor, the Standing Interpretations Committee (SIC); and
- International Financial Reporting Standards for Small and Medium-sized Entities (IFRS for SMEs) – a stand-alone standard for general purpose financial statements of small and medium-sized entities (as defined).

2.2 The IFRS Foundation

The governance of the IFRS Foundation primarily rests with the Trustees of the IFRS Foundation (Trustees) who, in turn, act under the terms of the IFRS Foundation Constitution (the Constitution).[2] Section 17 of the Constitution requires a review, every five years, of the structure and effectiveness of the IFRS Foundation. The last review was completed in 2016 and, as a result, the Constitution was revised in the same year. In October 2018, the Trustees approved a narrow-scope amendment to the Constitution to extend the term of the Trustee Chair and Vice-Chairs up to a maximum of nine years, taking into account any previous term already served as Trustee, Vice-Chair or Chair, as the case may be. The Trustees also approved an amendment to allow for the Trustee Chair to be appointed from among the Trustees or to be recruited externally. In August 2020, as a result of the amendments to the Due Process Handbook (the Handbook) (see 2.6 below), an amendment was made to the Constitution to reflect that the IFRS Advisory Council (the Advisory Council) advises the Board (and Trustees) on strategic matters and, especially since the establishment and activity of the Accounting Standards Advisory Forum (ASAF), it no longer functions as a technical consultative body.[3]

The 2020 Agenda Consultation was initiated in September 2019. At the time of writing, the Board is discussing the content of a Request for Information. To assist stakeholders affected by the coronavirus pandemic, the publication of the Request for Information will be postponed to the first half of 2021 (estimated March 2021).[4]

It is a requirement of the Constitution that, in order to ensure a broad international basis, there must be:[5]

- six Trustees appointed from the Asia/Oceania region;
- six Trustees appointed from Europe;
- six Trustees appointed from the Americas;
- one Trustee appointed from Africa; and
- three Trustees appointed from any area, subject to maintaining overall geographical balance.

The appointment of Trustees to fill vacancies caused by routine retirement or other reasons is the responsibility of the remaining Trustees but subject to the approval of the Monitoring Board as discussed at 2.3 below. The appointment of the Trustees is normally for a term of three years, renewable once.[6]

The Constitution requires that the Trustees comprise individuals that, as a group, provide a balance of professional backgrounds, and have an interest in promoting and maintaining transparency in corporate reporting globally. This includes individuals with global experience at a senior level in securities market regulators, firms representing investors, international audit networks, preparers, users, academics and officials serving the public interest. To achieve such a balance, Trustees are selected after consultation with the accounting and audit profession, the securities market and other public interest bodies, regulators, investors, preparers, users and academics. The Trustees are required to establish procedures for inviting suggestions for appointments from these relevant organisations and for allowing individuals to put forward their own names, including advertising vacant positions.[7]

The Constitution provides that 'all Trustees shall be required to show a firm commitment to the IFRS Foundation and the IASB as a high quality global standard-setter, to be financially knowledgeable, and to have an ability to meet the time commitment. Each Trustee shall have an understanding of, and be sensitive to, the challenges associated with the adoption and application of high quality global accounting standards developed for use in the world's capital markets and by other users'.[8]

The Trustees are responsible also for appointing the members of the IASB, Interpretations Committee, IFRS Advisory Council (the Advisory Council)[9] and the Accounting Standards Advisory Forum (ASAF).[10] In addition, their duties include the following:[11]

- appointing the Executive Director, in consultation with the IASB Chair, and establishing his or her contract of service and performance criteria;
- reviewing annually the strategy of the IFRS Foundation and the IASB and its effectiveness, including consideration, but not determination, of the IASB's agenda;
- assuming responsibility for establishing and maintaining appropriate financing arrangements;
- approving annually the budget of the IFRS Foundation and determining the basis for funding;
- reviewing broad strategic issues affecting financial reporting standards, promoting the IFRS Foundation and its work and promoting the objective of rigorous application of IFRS, provided that the Trustees are excluded from involvement in technical matters relating to financial reporting standards;
- establishing or amending operating procedures for the Trustees;
- establishing and amending operating procedures, consultative arrangements and due process for the IASB, the Interpretations Committee and the Advisory Council and reviewing their compliance;
- approving amendments to the Constitution after following a due process, including consultation with the Advisory Council and publication of an exposure draft for public comment and subject to the voting requirements given in the Constitution;
- exercising all powers of the IFRS Foundation except for those expressly reserved to the IASB, the Interpretations Committee and the Advisory Council;
- fostering and reviewing the development of educational programmes and materials that are consistent with the IFRS Foundation's objectives; and
- publishing an annual report on the IFRS Foundation's activities, including audited financial statements and priorities for the coming year.

The IFRS Foundation's funding is derived primarily from voluntary contributions from jurisdictions that have put in place national financing regimes. While funding mechanisms differ, most jurisdictions have established either a levy on companies or a system of publicly supported financing. The IFRS Foundation is continuing its work towards a global funding system characterised by a long-term commitment by jurisdictions, public sponsorship (either direct or implicit governmental or regulatory support), flexibility, proportionally allocated contributions and public accountability in the budget process.[12] In 2019, the major funders of the IFRS Foundation were the international accounting firms, the European Commission, Japan and China.[13]

2.3 The Monitoring Board

The Monitoring Board was created to address a perceived lack of accountability and responsiveness by the IASB and the IFRS Foundation to the concerns of its constituents.

The Monitoring Board provides a formal link between the Trustees and public authorities. This relationship seeks to replicate, on an international basis, the link between accounting standard-setters and those public authorities that have generally overseen accounting standard-setters.[14]

The Charter of the Monitoring Board notes that the Monitoring Board's mission is:[15]

- to cooperate to promote the continued development of IFRS as a high quality set of global accounting standards;
- to monitor and reinforce the public interest oversight function of the IFRS Foundation, while preserving the independence of the IASB. In that regard;
  - to participate in the selection and approval of the Trustee appointments;
  - to advise the Trustees with respect to the fulfilment of their responsibilities, in particular with respect to regulatory, legal and policy developments that are pertinent to the IFRS Foundation's oversight of the IASB and appropriate sources of IFRS Foundation funding; and
  - to discuss issues and share views relating to IFRS, as well as regulatory and market developments affecting the development and functioning of these standards.

The responsibilities of the Monitoring Board are to:[16]

- participate in the process for appointing Trustees and approve the appointment of Trustees;
- review and provide advice to the Trustees on the fulfilment of their responsibilities – there is an obligation on the Trustees to report annually to the Monitoring Board; and
- meet with the Trustees or a sub-group thereof at least annually; the Monitoring Board has the authority to request meetings with the Trustees or separately with the chair of the Trustees and with the chair of the IASB to discuss any area of the work of the Trustees or the IASB.

At the time of writing, the Monitoring Board comprises representatives of:[17]

- the IOSCO Board;
- the Securities and Exchange Commission (SEC), United States of America;
- the European Commission;
- the Financial Services Agency, Japan;
- the IOSCO Growth and Emerging Markets Committee;
- the Comissão de Valores Mobiliários, Brazil;
- the Financial Services Commission, Republic of Korea;
- the Ministry of Finance, People's Republic of China;
- the Basel Committee on Banking Supervision (observer);
- the IOSCO Africa and Middle-East Regional Committee (observer); and
- the IOSCO Inter-American Regional Committee (observer).

The current chairman is the representative of the IOSCO Board.

Membership of the Monitoring Board is assessed based on the following criteria:[18]

- the member must be a capital market authority responsible for setting the form and content of financial reporting in its jurisdiction;
- the jurisdiction has made a clear commitment to moving towards application of IFRS and promoting global acceptance of a single set of high-quality international accounting standards as the final goal;
- the IFRS standards to be applied should be essentially aligned with IFRS standards developed by the IASB;
- the jurisdiction can be regarded as a major market for capital-raising based on the size of market capitalization, the number of listed companies and capital market activity;
- the jurisdiction makes financial contributions to setting IFRS;
- the jurisdiction has a robust enforcement mechanism to ensure proper implementation of relevant accounting standards; and
- the relevant national or regional standard-setting body is committed to contributing actively to the development of IFRS.

Historically the motivation for the use of IFRS was to facilitate cross-border capital raising and, therefore, the membership of the Monitoring Board was focused on capital markets authorities that were committed to the development of high-quality global accounting standards. While this continues to be a criterion for membership, beginning with the 2016 review of its members, the Monitoring Board will evaluate the integration of IFRS for domestic issuers in that member's jurisdiction.[19]

2.4   The International Accounting Standards Board (IASB)

The members of the IASB are appointed by the Trustees.[20] Currently, the IASB comprises 13 members while the Constitution provides for 14 members. The main qualifications for membership of the IASB are professional competence and recent relevant professional experience.[21]

The Trustees are required to select IASB members so that the IASB, as a group, will comprise the best available combination of technical expertise and diversity of international business and market experience, including auditors, preparers, users, academics and market and/or financial regulators. No individual should be both a Trustee and a member of the IASB at the same time.[22] Furthermore, the IASB, in consultation with the Trustees, is expected to establish and maintain liaison with national standard-setters and other official bodies concerned with standard-setting to assist in the development of IFRS and to promote the convergence of national accounting standards and IFRS.[23]

The IASB will normally be required to comprise:[24]

- four members from Asia/Oceania;
- four members from Europe;
- four members from the Americas;
- one member from Africa; and
- one member appointed from any area, subject to maintaining overall geographical balance.

The responsibilities of the IASB are listed in Section 36 of the Constitution. Its primary role is to have complete responsibility for all IASB technical matters including preparing and issuing IFRS standards (other than interpretations) and exposure drafts, each of which is required to include any dissenting opinions; and final approval of and issuing interpretations developed by the Interpretations Committee.[25]

Approval by at least eight members of the IASB is required for the publication of an exposure draft and IFRS (which includes final interpretations of the Interpretations Committee), if there are fewer than 14 members of the IASB. If there are 14 members, approval is required by at least nine members.[26] Other decisions of the IASB, including the publication of a discussion paper, require a simple majority of the members present at a meeting that is attended by at least 60% of the members.[27] The IASB has full discretion over its technical agenda and over project assignments on technical matters. It must, however, consult the Trustees on its agenda, and the Advisory Council on major projects, agenda decisions and work priorities. In addition, the IASB is required to carry out public consultation every five years in developing its technical agenda.[28] The most recent agenda consultation took place in August 2015. In November 2016, the IASB published the *IASB® Work Plan 2017-2021 (Feedback Statement on the 2015 Agenda Consultation)* on its agenda consultation and its five-year plan. The IASB adopted a central theme for its activities: 'Better Communication in Financial Reporting'.[29]

The IASB meets monthly, but not in August. These meetings are open to the public and meeting materials are available on the IASB's website.

2.5 The IFRS Interpretations Committee (the Interpretations Committee)

For IFRS to be truly global standards, consistent application and interpretation is required. The Interpretations Committee assists the Board in improving financial reporting through timely assessment, discussion and resolution of financial reporting issues identified within the IFRS framework.[30]

The national accounting standard-setting bodies and regional bodies involved with accounting standard-setting are often consulted on issues referred to the Interpretations Committee.[31] The Interpretations Committee is expected to address issues:[32]

'(a) that have widespread effect and have, or are expected to have, a material effect on those affected;

(b) where financial reporting would be improved through the elimination, or reduction, of diverse reporting methods;

(c) that can be resolved efficiently within the confines of existing IFRS standards and the *Conceptual Framework for Financial Reporting;* and

(d) the matter is sufficiently narrow in scope that the Board or the Interpretations Committee can address it in an efficient manner, but not so narrow that it is not cost-effective for the Board or the Interpretations Committee and stakeholders to undertake the due process required to change a standard.'

The Board may seek the assistance of the Interpretations Committee in developing narrow-scope amendments (which include annual improvements), drawing on the Interpretations Committee's experience of the application of IFRS standards.[33]

If the Interpretations Committee does not plan to add an item to its work programme, it publishes a tentative agenda decision in the *IFRIC Update* and on the IFRS Foundation website and requests comments on the matter. The comment period for tentative agenda decisions is normally at least 60 days. After considering comments received, the Interpretations Committee will either confirm its decision and publish an agenda decision, revise its tentative agenda decision and re-expose for comment a revised tentative agenda decision, add the issue to its work programme or refer the matter to the IASB.[34]

Before an agenda decision is published, the Board is asked –at its first public meeting at which it is practicable to present the agenda decision –whether it objects to the agenda decision. Specifically, Board members are asked whether they object to (a) the Interpretations Committee's decision that a standard-setting project should not be added to the work plan, and (b) the Interpretations Committee's conclusion that the agenda decision does not add or change requirements in IFRS standards. If four or more Board members object, the agenda decision is not published and the Board decides how to proceed.[35]

The Interpretations Committee has 14 voting members. The chair, who is appointed by the Trustees, is a member of the IASB, the Director of Technical Activities or an appropriately qualified individual. The chair does not have the right to vote. The Trustees may appoint representatives of regulatory organisations, who have the right to attend and speak at meetings but not the right to vote.[36] Currently, the Basel Committee on Banking Supervision, European Commission and IOSCO have observer status. The quorum for a meeting is 10 members,[37] and approval of draft or final interpretations requires that not more than four voting members vote against the draft or final interpretation.[38]

The Interpretations Committee meets six times a year. All technical decisions are taken at sessions that are open to public observation. Although the Interpretations Committee develops interpretations, because they are part of the respective IFRS standards, they must be ratified by the IASB.[39]

2.5.1 Agenda decisions

An agenda decision explains why a standard-setting project has not been added to the work plan and, in many cases, includes explanatory material.[40] It cannot add or change requirements in IFRS standards. Instead, explanatory material explains how the applicable principles and requirements in IFRS standards apply to the transaction or fact pattern described in the agenda decision.[41] Explanatory material derives its authority from the standards themselves. Accordingly, an entity is required to apply the applicable IFRS standard(s), reflecting the explanatory material in an agenda decision.[42]

In December 2018, the Board discussed the timing of application of accounting policy changes that result from an agenda decision published by the Interpretations Committee and confirmed its view that it expects companies to be entitled to sufficient time to implement changes in accounting policy.

In March 2019, the Board further explained its position on agenda decisions. Firstly, the Board acknowledged that agenda decisions often provide new information that should be seen as helpful and persuasive. It follows that a company does not make an error simply because its application of IFRS was inconsistent with an agenda decision. Secondly, regarding how quickly companies are expected to implement an accounting policy change that results from an agenda decision, the Board formally acknowledged that it may take time to implement such an accounting policy change. The Board believes that this reflects its expectations of what is reasonable for preparers, assists companies in implementing any such change, and ultimately supports consistent application of IFRS by facilitating accounting policy changes. What constitutes 'sufficient time' would depend on the particular facts and circumstances, taking into account the accounting policy change and the reporting entity and would require judgement. What the Board had in mind was 'a matter of months rather than years'. However, it is not expected that sufficient time would include the time needed to undertake related steps, such as changing affected covenants in documents nor the time to wait to see whether any of the Board's projects could remove the need to make an accounting policy change (to avoid two changes in accounting in a short period of time).[43] The Board also made it clear that companies need to consider agenda decisions and implement any necessary accounting policy changes on a timely basis (i.e. as soon and as quickly as possible). If necessary, companies should be in a position to explain their implementation process and, if material, consideration should be given to whether disclosure related to the accounting policy change is required.[44] The Due Process Handbook has also been amended in August 2020 to reflect this.[45]

2.6 The Due Process Handbook

The Trustees' Due Process Oversight Committee (DPOC) is responsible for overseeing the due process procedures of the IASB and Interpretations Committee throughout all the development stages of a standard, the IFRS Taxonomy or an interpretation, including agenda-setting and post-implementation reviews (PIRs).[46] The Foundation published the revised Handbook in August 2020. The main changes are:[47]

- clarifying the authority of agenda decisions published by the Interpretations Committee and their role in supporting consistent application of IFRS standards and enhancing the related due process by formally involving the Board in their finalisation; and
- reflecting recent developments in the Board's effect analysis process – assessing the likely effects of a new or amended IFRS standard – that emphasise the role of such analyses in standard-setting and make it clear that such analyses take place at all stages of standard-setting.

In addition, the amendments enhance and streamline the consultation requirements for adding major projects to the Board's work plan; update and enhance the minimum amount of review required for educational material produced by the Foundation; and clarify the DPOC's role in overseeing the IFRS Taxonomy due process.

The Handbook describes the due process requirements of the IASB and Interpretations Committee.[48] The requirements are built on the following principles:[49]

- transparency – the IASB and the Interpretations Committee conduct their standard-setting process in a transparent manner;
- full and fair consultation – considering the perspectives of stakeholders globally; and
- accountability – the IASB analyses the potential effects of its proposals on affected parties and explains the rationale for why it made the decisions it reached in developing or amending a standard.

In order to gain a wide range of views from interested parties throughout all stages of the development of IFRS, the Trustees and the IASB have established consultative procedures with the objective of ensuring that, in exercising its independent decision-making, the IASB conducts its standard-setting process in a transparent manner.[50] The Handbook specifies some minimum steps that the IASB and the Interpretations Committee are required to follow before a standard or interpretation can be issued.[51] The following due process steps are mandatory:[52]

- debating any proposals in one or more public meetings;
- exposing for public comment a draft of any proposed new standard, proposed amendment to a standard or proposed interpretation with minimum comment periods;
- considering in a timely manner those comment letters received on the proposals;
- considering whether the proposals should be exposed again;
- consulting the IFRS Advisory Council (see 2.7 below) and the Accounting Standards Advisory Forum (see 2.8 below) on the work plan, major projects, project proposals and work priorities; and
- ratification of an interpretation by the IASB in a public Board meeting.

The steps specified in the Constitution that are 'non-mandatory' include:[53]

- publishing a discussion document (for example, a discussion paper) before an exposure draft is developed;
- establishing consultative groups or other types of specialist advisory groups;
- holding public hearings; and
- undertaking fieldwork.

If the IASB decides not to undertake any of the non-mandatory steps, it is required to inform the DPOC of its decision and reason (known as the 'comply or explain' approach). Those explanations must be published in the decision summaries and in the Basis for Conclusions with the exposure draft or IFRS in question.[54]

Although not mandatory, the IASB conducts public meetings and roundtables to ensure that it has appropriate input from its constituents.

The IASB normally allows a minimum period of 120 days for comment on an exposure draft. If the matter is narrow in scope and urgent, the IASB may consider a comment period of no less than 30 days, but it will only set a period of less than 120 days after consulting, and obtaining approval from, the DPOC.[55]

Under a 'fast track' comment process, if the matter is exceptionally urgent, and only after formally requesting and obtaining prior approval from 75% of the Trustees, 'the IASB may reduce the period for public comment on an exposure draft to below 30 days but may not dispense with a comment period'.[56]

2.7 The IFRS Advisory Council (the Advisory Council)

The Advisory Council (whose members are appointed by the Trustees) provides a forum for geographically and functionally diverse organisations and individuals with an interest in international financial reporting to:

- provide input on the IASB's agenda, project timetable and project priorities; and
- give advice on projects, with emphasis on application and implementation issues, including matters that may warrant the attention of the Interpretations Committee.[57]

A secondary objective of the Advisory Council is 'to encourage broad participation in the development of IFRS as high-quality, globally-accepted standards.'[58]

The Advisory Council comprises thirty or more members, having a diversity of geographical and professional backgrounds. The chair of the Council is appointed by the Trustees, and may not be a member of the IASB or a member of its staff.[59] The Advisory Council normally meets at least two times a year, and its meetings are open to the public. The matters on the agenda for the Advisory Council's meetings will include those strategic matters and other priorities identified through consultation with the chair of the Advisory Council and representatives of the Trustees and the Board. In addition, the IASB must consult the Advisory Council in advance of any proposed changes to the Constitution.[60]

Members are appointed for an initial term of three years and may be asked to remain for up to three additional years.[61]

2.8 Accounting Standards Advisory Forum (ASAF)

The ASAF, established in 2013, is an advisory group consisting of national accounting standard-setters and regional bodies, the purpose of which is to provide technical advice and feedback to the IASB.

The membership of the ASAF consists of 12 non-voting members (appointed by the Trustees), plus the chair, who is the IASB chair or vice-chair. To ensure a broad geographical representation, the members are from the following geographic regions:[62]

- one member from Africa;
- three members from the Americas (North and South);
- three members from the Asia/Oceania region;
- three members from Europe (including non-EU); and
- two members appointed from any area of the world at large, subject to maintaining overall geographic balance.

The ASAF meets four times a year, and its meetings are open to the public.

The objective of the ASAF is 'to provide an advisory forum where members can constructively contribute towards the achievement of the IASB's goal of developing globally accepted high-quality accounting standards.' The ASAF was established to:[63]

- support the IFRS Foundation in its objectives, and contribute towards the development, in the public interest, of a single set of high quality understandable, enforceable and globally accepted financial reporting standards to serve investors and other market participants in making informed resource allocations and other economic decisions;
- formalise and streamline the IASB's collective engagement with the global community of national standard-setters and regional bodies in its standard setting process to ensure that a broad range of national and regional input on major technical issues related to the IASB's standard setting activities are discussed and considered; and
- facilitate effective technical discussions on standard-setting issues, primarily on the IASB's work plan but which may include other issues that have major implications for the IASB's work, in sufficient depth, with representatives at a high level of professional capability and with a good knowledge of their jurisdictions/regions.

As required by the ASAF's Terms of Reference, the Trustees completed their second review of the ASAF in 2018, following the first review undertaken in 2015. There was very positive feedback from the review, highlighting that the ASAF continues to be a key component of the IFRS Foundation's engagement strategy with national standard-setters. Actions taken following the 2015 review have resulted in positive change and there were improvements made to the 'feedback loop' between the Board and the ASAF. As a result of the review, the Trustees have decided not to incorporate consultation with the ASAF as a mandatory due process step in the Handbook. The Trustees also found no compelling reason to amend the Constitution to incorporate an explicit reference to the ASAF. The Trustees are amending the Terms of Reference to permit one ASAF meeting a year to be held via videoconference. In addition, the Trustees decided that formal three-yearly reviews of ASAF are no longer necessary and will amend the ASAF Terms of Reference accordingly.[64]

2.9 Other advisory bodies

In addition to the Advisory Council and the ASAF, discussed in 2.7 and 2.8 above, respectively, above, the IASB has a number of other formal advisory bodies that provide input on its work and resources to consult. Meetings with the advisory bodies are held in public and meeting materials are available on the IASB's website.

The IASB's other advisory bodies are as follows:[65]

- Capital Markets Advisory Committee – provides the IASB with regular input from the international community of users of financial statements;
- Emerging Economies Group – enhances the participation of emerging economies in the development of IFRS standards;
- Global Preparers Forum – provides the IASB with input from companies preparing financial statements;
- IFRS Taxonomy Consultative Group – helps develop the IFRS Taxonomy;
- Islamic Finance Consultative Group – focuses on potential challenges in applying IFRS to Shariah-compliant instruments and transactions;
- SME Implementation Group – supports the international adoption of the *IFRS for SMEs* and monitors its implementation;
- World Standard-setters Conferences – helps achieve the G20-endorsed objective of global accounting standards;
- Transition Resource Group for IFRS 17 Insurance Contracts – aids the implementation of IFRS 17 – *Insurance Contracts*;
- Consultative Group for Rate Regulation – informs the project on rate regulation; and
- Management Commentary Consultative Group – informs the project on management commentary.

3 THE IASB'S TECHNICAL AGENDA AND CONVERGENCE WITH US GAAP

3.1 The IASB's current priorities and future agenda

The IASB's 2020 activities focused on:[66]

- assessing whether it would be feasible to permit subsidiaries that are small and medium enterprises to apply the recognition and measurement requirements of IFRS standards and the disclosure requirements of the *IFRS for SMEs* standard with minimal tailoring of those disclosure requirements;
- proposing new requirements for presentation and disclosure in financial statements, with a focus on the statement of profit or loss;
- developing an accounting model that will require rate-regulated companies to provide information about their incremental rights to add amounts, and incremental obligations to deduct amounts, in determining the future rates to be charged to customers as a result of goods or services already supplied;
- discussing whether it can develop requirements that would improve the comparability and transparency of accounting for combinations under common control to help investors compare and better understand information that companies provide in financial statements about such transactions;
- exploring whether it can develop an accounting model that would enable investors to understand a company's dynamic risk management activities and to evaluate the effectiveness of those activities;
- exploring amendments to IAS 32 – *Financial Instruments: Presentation* – to address common accounting challenges that arise in practice when applying the standard;
- assessing whether it would be feasible to eliminate measurement inconsistencies by capping asset returns used in estimates of pension benefits that depend on asset returns, without changing other aspects of IAS 19 – *Employee Benefits*; and
- performing the post-implementation review of IFRS 10 – *Consolidated Financial Statements*, IFRS 11 – *Joint Arrangements* – and IFRS 12 – *Disclosure of Interests in Other Entities*.

At the time of writing, the IASB's work plan reflects that work on a number of these projects will continue into 2021 and beyond.

The IASB conducted its most recent agenda consultation in August 2015, the outcome of which set the technical priorities until 2021. The work plan has been revised in response to feedback received during the agenda consultation. The IASB has adopted the theme 'Better Communication in Financial Reporting' and much of the work will focus on making the financial information more relevant and improving the communication of that information. See 2.2 above for information on the next agenda consultation.

3.2 IFRS/US GAAP convergence

'Convergence' is a term used to describe the coming together of national systems of financial reporting and IFRS. Between 2002 and 2013, the IASB and FASB had various projects to both improve IFRS and US GAAP, respectively, and to achieve their convergence. In addition, the US Securities and Exchange Commission (SEC) have taken some steps towards the acceptance of IFRS in the US. In 2007, the SEC began permitting foreign private issuers to file IFRS financial statements without reconciliation to US GAAP. In 2008, the SEC set out a proposed roadmap outlining the milestones and conditions that, if met, could lead to the use of IFRS in the US by domestic registrants. In 2011, the SEC staff issued a work plan to explore the incorporation of IFRS into the US financial reporting system. The SEC staff has since published its final report on the IFRS work plan that raised significant concerns about the further incorporation of IFRS in the US capital markets.

In 2013, the convergence process between the IASB and the FASB largely came to an end. One of the messages the IASB staff received from respondents outside of the US to the 2011 agenda consultation was for the IASB to consider whether convergence should continue to be a priority. Ultimately, developing 'a single set of high-quality, understandable, enforceable and globally accepted financial reporting standards' has largely superseded convergence as a significant driver of the IASB's agenda setting process. In fact, the Handbook, which was revised in 2013, removed convergence from the list of factors that are influential in setting the agenda.

4 THE ADOPTION OF IFRS AROUND THE WORLD

4.1 Worldwide adoption

Since 2001, there has been a tremendous increase in the adoption of IFRS around the world. The precise way in which this has happened has varied among jurisdictions. This section sets out a brief description of how a number of key jurisdictions in each continent have approached the adoption. Some have adopted full IFRS, i.e. IFRS as issued by the IASB. Other jurisdictions have converged, or have a plan to converge, their standards with IFRS.

An entity is required to apply IFRS 1 – *First-time Adoption of International Financial Reporting Standards* – when it first asserts compliance with IFRS. The IASB has, therefore, established unambiguously the principle that full application of its standards and related interpretations is necessary for an entity to be able to assert that its financial statements comply with IFRS (as issued by the IASB). Consequently, it is necessary for countries that align their national standards with IFRS to require the application of IFRS 1 so that entities reporting under those standards can assert compliance with IFRS. In addition, an entity that applies IFRS as amended by a local authority cannot assert compliance with IFRS.

The following table summarises IFRS adoption (generally for consolidated financial statements) in jurisdictions with domestic market capitalisation exceeding US$500 billion as at 30 June 2020. For further details on selected locations, see 4.2 to 4.6 below. In addition, the IFRS Foundation is developing profiles of application of IFRS. At the time of writing, profiles for 166 jurisdictions have been completed and are available on the IASB's website.

Jurisdiction	IFRS Status	IFRS Permitted
Australia	Required for all publicly accountable entities, and any entities preparing general purpose financial statements that elect not to apply the framework under the Reduced Disclosure Requirements (RDR). Non-publicly accountable reporting entities are required to apply IFRS recognition and measurement requirements, but can provide simplified disclosures under the RDR.	
Brazil	Required for regulated public companies, with exemptions for banks and real estate companies; other companies must follow converged national standards.	
Canada	Required for publicly accountable entities.	Permitted for all other entities.
Mainland China	Substantially converged national standards.	
European Union	IFRS as adopted by the European Union (EU) (EU IFRS – see 4.2.1 below) required for consolidated financial statements of all EU companies listed on an EU regulated market. Exemption for non-EU companies applying for listing on an EU regulated market that apply certain GAAPs determined by the European Commission to be equivalent to EU IFRS.	EU member states may permit or require the application of EU IFRS by unlisted companies and in separate financial statements.
France	See European Union.	EU IFRS permitted for the consolidated financial statements of non-listed entities.
Germany	See European Union.	EU IFRS permitted for the consolidated financial statements of non-listed entities.
Hong Kong	HKFRS (converged with IFRS) is required for all Hong Kong incorporated companies (listed and non-listed).	Permitted for listed companies incorporated overseas.
India	IFRS converged Indian Accounting Standards (Ind AS), with some mandatory and numerous optional departures from IFRS, to apply in phases from financial years beginning on or after 1 April 2016.	Until Ind AS was introduced, listed companies with subsidiaries were permitted to apply IFRS in consolidated financial statements. This option is no longer available.
Italy	See European Union. EU IFRS is required in the separate financial statements of companies on the Italian regulated stock exchange except insurance companies. Scope of EU IFRS extended to certain financial institutions.	EU IFRS permitted in the statutory separate and consolidated financial statements of all other non-listed entities and non-regulated enterprises (except SMEs).

Jurisdiction	IFRS Status	IFRS Permitted
Japan	Mandatory adoption has been put on hold for the time being.	Permitted for most companies that are listed or planning to be listed on a domestic stock exchange.
Korea	IFRS as adopted by Korea without modification (K-IFRS) is required for all listed entities, unlisted financial institutions and state-owned entities.	K-IFRS permitted for non-listed entities.
Russia	Required for banks, insurance entities, non-state pension funds, clearing institutions, certain investment management entities, listed companies and for some state unitary enterprises and state-owned public joint-stock companies. Substantially converged national standards applicable to stand-alone financial statements.	
Saudi Arabia	IFRS (as adopted by the local regulators – mainly with some additional disclosure requirements) is required for banks, insurance companies and listed entities.	Non-listed entities have the option to adopt either full IFRS or IFRS for SMEs. Self-regulated entities can choose, but are not required, to adopt IFRS.
Singapore	Singapore incorporated entities listed on the Singapore Exchange are required to file financial statements prepared in accordance with converged national standards equivalent to IFRS (Singapore Financial Reporting Standards (International) – SFRS(I)). Foreign entities that are listed on the Singapore Exchange are required to file financial statements prepared in accordance with SFRS(I), IFRS or US GAAP.	Singapore incorporated entities are permitted to file IFRS financial statements with approval.
South Africa	Required for all listed companies. Non-listed companies generally use either IFRS or IFRS for SMEs.	
Spain	See European Union.	EU IFRS permitted for non-listed groups for consolidated financial statements; no reversion to local GAAP once an entity has applied EU IFRS.
Switzerland	Issuers of equity securities that are incorporated in Switzerland and listed under the International Standard on the SIX Swiss Exchange (SIX) must apply either IFRS or US GAAP. Other listed entities incorporated in Switzerland must apply IFRS, US GAAP or Swiss GAAP-FER. Entities not incorporated in Switzerland must apply IFRS, US GAAP or a national GAAP deemed by the SIX to be equivalent.	IFRS permitted in consolidated statutory financial statements of non-listed entities.

Taiwan	Standards and interpretations endorsed by the local regulators apply for financial statements beginning on or after 1 January 2020. The effective dates for standards and interpretations for Taiwan IFRS are mostly aligned with global effective dates; however, early adoption is generally not permitted.	IFRS permitted for foreign issuers, with reconciliation to 'Taiwan-IFRS'.
United Kingdom	See European Union. In addition, EU IFRS is mandatory when a company admitted to the UK Alternative Investment Market (AIM) is incorporated in the European Economic Area (EEA) unless such company is not a parent company. As a result of the UK's withdrawal from the EU, UK companies should apply UK-adopted international accounting standards (UK-adopted IAS) rather than EU IFRS for financial years beginning on or after 31 December 2020. This is discussed further at 4.2.3 below.	EU IFRS or UK-adopted IAS permitted for all companies, except in the charities sector; restrictions on reversion to local GAAP once an entity has adopted EU IFRS or UK-adopted IAS.
United States	Substantial convergence of selected standards.	Permitted for foreign private issuers preparing financial statements in accordance with IFRS as issued by the IASB. There is no endorsement process in the US.

4.2 Europe

4.2.1 EU

In July 2002, the European Parliament adopted Regulation No. 1606/2002 (the Regulation), which required publicly traded EU incorporated companies[67] to prepare, by 2005 at the latest, their consolidated financial statements under IFRS 'adopted' (as discussed further below) for application within the EU. Although an EU regulation has direct effect on companies, without the need for national legislation, the Regulation provides an option for EU member states to permit or require the application of adopted IFRS in the preparation of annual unconsolidated financial statements and to permit or require the application of adopted IFRS by unlisted companies. This means that EU member states can require the uniform application of adopted IFRS by important sectors, such as banking or insurance, regardless of whether companies are listed. An analysis of the implementation of the Regulation published in 2012 shows that nearly all EU member states use the option to permit the application of adopted IFRS in the consolidated accounts of some or all types of unlisted companies. More than half of the EU member states also permit the application of adopted IFRS in the annual financial statements of some or all types of unlisted companies.[68]

The Regulation established the basic rules for the creation of an endorsement mechanism for the adoption of IFRS, the timetable for implementation and a review clause to permit an assessment of the overall approach proposed. The European Commission took the view that an endorsement mechanism was needed to provide the necessary public oversight. The European Commission considered also that it was not appropriate, politically or legally, to delegate accounting standard-setting unconditionally and irrevocably to a private organisation over which the European Commission had no influence. In addition, the endorsement mechanism is responsible for examining whether the standards adopted by the IASB satisfy relevant EU public policy criteria.

The role of the endorsement mechanism is not to reformulate or replace IFRS, but to oversee the adoption of new standards and interpretations, intervening only when they contain material deficiencies or have failed to cater for features specific to the EU economic or legal environments. The central task of this mechanism is to confirm that IFRS provides a suitable basis for financial reporting by listed EU companies. The mechanism is based on a two-tier structure, combining a regulatory level with an expert level, to assist the European Commission in its endorsement role.

The recitals to the Regulation state that the endorsement mechanism should act expeditiously and also be a means to deliberate, reflect and exchange information on international accounting standards among the main parties concerned, in particular national accounting standard setters, supervisors in the fields of securities, banking and insurance, central banks including the European Central Bank (ECB), the accounting profession and users and preparers of accounts. The mechanism should be a means of fostering common understanding of adopted international accounting standards in the EU community.[69]

The European Commission is advised on IFRS by the European Financial Reporting Advisory Group (EFRAG). In addition to EFRAG, the European Commission seeks approval from its member states through the Accounting Regulatory Committee. EFRAG is a private sector body established by the European organisations prominent in European capital markets, e.g. Accountancy Europe and the European Banking Federation. In addition to advising the European Commission on endorsement of IFRS, EFRAG is the mechanism by which Europe as a whole can participate in the global debate on accounting standards and it coordinates European responses to IASB proposals. EFRAG plays a proactive role issuing discussion papers, field-test reports and feedback statements on outreach events. The objective of the proactive work is to involve European stakeholders at an early stage in identifying necessary improvements to financial reporting to influence the IASB. EFRAG's activities also include assessments of whether the IASB's proposals and IFRS requirements are conducive to the European public good. This includes the interaction with economic concerns, such as financial stability and growth.

The EFRAG Board includes, in equal numbers, representatives of European stakeholder organisations and national standard setters and is led by the President of the EFRAG Board, who is nominated by the European Commission. The EFRAG Board is responsible for all EFRAG positions and operates on the basis of a consensus-based decision-making process with the objective of Europe speaking with one voice. The European Commission, the European supervisory authorities and the ECB participate in the EFRAG Board in an observer capacity. The EFRAG Board takes all its decisions after considering the advice of the EFRAG Technical Expert Group and the results of

EFRAG's due process, and after hearing from the Accounting Regulatory Committee and making all assessments deemed relevant from the political perspective.

The EU endorsement process is only completed when the standard, interpretation or amendment is published in the Official Journal of the European Union. The advice from EFRAG and the vote by the ARC are not sufficient to adopt a standard, interpretation or an amendment.

4.2.1.A Endorsed IFRS standards

To date, apart from the carve out from IAS 39 – *Financial Instruments: Recognition and Measurement* – and the decision not to endorse IFRS 14 – *Regulatory Deferral Accounts*, all IASB standards which are currently effective have ultimately been endorsed.[70]

IAS 39 as endorsed for use in the EU is currently different in one important respect from the version published by the IASB. Certain text has been carved out so that, essentially, the EU version allows the use of macro fair value hedge accounting in situations that the full version of IAS 39 does not. The European Commission has continued to emphasise the need for the IASB and representatives of European banks to find an appropriate technical solution to allow the removal of the carve-out as rapidly as possible. However, there have been only limited signs of progress on this issue and IFRS 9 – *Financial Instruments* – does not remove the reasons for the carve-out (see Chapter 44 at 5). Consequently the carve-out continues to be available for entities that prepare their financial statements in accordance with IFRS as endorsed for use in the EU and continue to apply the macro fair value hedge accounting requirements of IAS 39.

The July 2014 version of IFRS 9, the October 2017 amendments to IFRS 9 and, the amendments to IFRS 4 – *Insurance Contracts* – delaying the application of IFRS 9 for certain insurers until 2021 were endorsed for use in the EU in time for companies to adopt in the 2018 reporting season. However, the European Commission considered that the amendments are not sufficiently broad in scope to meet the needs of all significant insurance entities in the European Union. Consequently, for those entities that prepare financial statements in accordance with IFRS as adopted by the EU, the following modification applies:

'A financial conglomerate as defined in Article 2(14) of Directive 2002/87/EC may elect that none of its entities operating in the insurance sector within the meaning of Article 2(8)(b) of that Directive apply IFRS 9 in the consolidated financial statements for financial years the commencement of which precedes 1 January 2021 where all of the following conditions are met:

(a) no financial instruments are transferred between the insurance sector and any other sector of the financial conglomerate after 29 November 2017 other than financial instruments that are measured at fair value with changes in fair value recognised through the profit or loss account by both sectors involved in such transfers;

(b) the financial conglomerate states in the consolidated financial statements which insurance entities in the group are applying IAS 39;

(c) disclosures requested by IFRS 7 – *Financial Instruments: Disclosures* – are provided separately for the insurance sector applying IAS 39 and for the rest of the group applying IFRS 9'.[71]

The purpose of (a) above is to prevent a group transferring financial instruments between different 'sectors' (i.e. between insurance and non-insurance subsidiaries) with the purpose of either avoiding measurement of those financial instruments at fair value through profit or loss in the group financial statements or recognising previously unrecognised fair value gains or losses in profit or loss.

A financial conglomerate (as defined above) which takes advantage of this 'top-up' to use a mixed IFRS 9/IAS 39 measurement model for financial instruments in its consolidated financial statements should not make an explicit and unreserved statement that those consolidated financial statements comply with IFRS as issued by the IASB. *[IAS 1.16]*. Similarly, depending on local regulations, use of the 'top-up' may affect the ability of subsidiaries of the financial conglomerate that are parent entities from using the exemption from preparing consolidated financial statements discussed in Chapter 6 at 2.2.1.D. We expect this 'top up' to be added to the 2020 amendments, but at the time of writing, this has not yet been finalised.

The September 2019 amendments to IAS 39 and IFRS 9 addressing IBOR reform were endorsed in January 2020, in time for companies to adopt the amendments in the 2019 reporting season, but at the time of writing neither IFRS 17 nor the amendments to IFRS 4, extending the delayed application of IFRS 9 for certain insurers until 2023, have been endorsed.

Previously, there were standards and a number of Interpretations Committee interpretations that have had delayed application dates. The most notable is the effective date for IFRS 10, IFRS 11, IFRS 12, IAS 27 – *Separate Financial Statements* – and IAS 28 – *Investments in Associates and Joint Ventures* – for which the European Commission permitted a one-year deferral to the mandatory effective date set by the IASB.

Although issued by the IASB in May 2017, IFRS 17 has not yet been endorsed and, at the time of writing, the timeline for endorsement was still unclear.[72] In the process of preparing a draft endorsement advice, EFRAG has conducted significant outreach with constituents, including users. Constituents have raised a number of concerns during the course of the outreach. Several topics identified as meriting further consideration by the IASB were communicated by the EFRAG Board to the IASB in 2018. In a letter to the IASB in March 2020, the EFRAG Board however regretted that some of the Board's conclusions deviate from EFRAG's recommendations, in particular the annual cohort requirement. EFRAG noted that, without addressing this issue, the resulting standard would not be aligned with the insurance market and would not meet the required cost/benefits trade-off.[73] The final amendments to IFRS 17, issued in June 2020, did not include any changes to the annual cohort requirement.

4.2.1.B Evaluation of the Regulation

In 2014, the European Commission started an evaluation of the Regulation on the application of IFRS to assess whether:

- the Regulation achieved its objective in an efficient and effective manner;
- the criteria that all new IFRS should meet to become EU law are appropriate and whether the process for adoption of standards works properly; and
- the governance structure of the bodies developing the standards and advising the European Commission is appropriate.

The evaluation mainly included a public consultation, an informal expert group, and a review of literature on the impact of the mandatory adoption of IFRS in the EU and on the performance of IFRS during the financial crisis. The results were included in a report issued in 2015. The key findings showed that IFRS was successful in creating a common accounting language for capital markets and that there is still no well-defined alternative to IFRS. The evidence from the evaluation also showed that the objectives of the Regulation remain relevant. Companies that responded to the public consultation were mostly positive about their experience of using IFRS and in most cases, benefits outweighed costs. Investors also largely supported IFRS for improving the transparency and comparability of financial statements. Most stakeholders considered that the process through which IFRS become part of EU law works well.

However, the report identified room for improvement in some areas. Amongst others, it was noted that the coherence of standards with EU laws should continue to be assessed during standard development and endorsement. In addition, the European Commission announced that it will look at whether the powers of the European supervisory authorities are sufficient and will consider measures to simplify the endorsement process. Furthermore, the European Commission suggested that the IASB strengthen its impact analysis and consider the needs of long-term investors when developing standards.

On 31 January 2018, the High-Level Expert Group (HLEG) on Sustainable Finance, established by the European Commission, published its final report setting out strategic recommendations for a financial system that supports sustainable investments.[74]

In this report, the HLEG recommends the European Commission to change the Regulation:

- 'to specify that international accounting standards should only be adopted if they are conducive to the European public good, including its sustainability and long-term investment objectives; and
- to provide the power to the EU to adjust specific aspects of IFRS standards adopted by the IASB before transposing them into EU law. This would remove the anomaly of the EU being the only constituency currently forgoing such a possibility and can be confined to cases where key overarching EU policy goals would otherwise be compromised.'

Reference to the HLEG report has been made when the European Commission launched in March 2018 a consultation document *Fitness Check on the EU Framework for Public Reporting by Companies* (the Consultation Document) which generally sought stakeholder views on whether the EU framework for public reporting by companies is fit for purpose.[75] The objectives of this fitness check were:

- to assess whether the EU public reporting framework is overall still relevant for meeting the intended objectives, adds value at the European level, is effective, internally consistent, coherent with other EU policies, efficient and not unnecessarily burdensome;
- to review specific aspects of the existing legislation as required by EU law; and
- to assess whether the EU public reporting framework is fit for new challenges (such as sustainability and digitalisation).

The Consultation Document stated that the above-mentioned European Commission's evaluation of the Regulation in 2015 showed that the use of IFRS in the EU has significantly increased the credibility of IFRS and its use worldwide.

However, the current level of commitment to IFRS by third country jurisdictions would differ significantly and that very few of the major capital markets and large jurisdictions have made the use of IFRS as issued by the IASB mandatory. The European Commission then concluded that as a result, the level of global convergence achieved were suboptimal compared to the initial objective on global use. The Consultation Document also addressed the issue that the current endorsement process would prevent the EU from modifying the content of the standards issued by the IASB. The European Commission claimed this fact had raised concerns, citing the report of the HLEG, that this lack of flexibility would prevent the EU from reacting if these standards were to pose an obstacle to broader EU policy goals such as long-term investments and sustainability. The questionnaire in the Consultation Document therefore asked respondents whether it is still appropriate that the Regulation prevents the European Commission from modifying the content of IFRS, given the different levels of commitment to require IFRS as issued by the IASB around the globe. Responses were due by July 2018; in October 2018 the European Commission published a summary report of the contributions to the public consultation.[76]

Stakeholders from 23 Member States and 25 third countries submitted 338 responses on the public consultation and most responses were submitted by entities from Belgium, France, Germany and the United Kingdom. Most respondents commented that the EU framework for public reporting overall brings added value and is coherent, effective and relevant for achieving its main intended objectives of safeguarding stakeholders' interests, ensuring financial stability, developing the internal market, integrated EU capital markets and promoting sustainability. In terms of developing the internal market and promoting integrated EU capital markets, IFRS standards were considered effective as they helped reduce the cost of capital and increase investments in the EU. Concerning the potential impact of IFRS standards on sustainable investments; whilst a few believed IFRS standards had led to pro-cyclicality and short-termism, most respondents said that (to their knowledge) there was no evidence of such impacts. Several respondents pointed out that the broad criterion of 'being conducive to the EU public good' should allow the European Commission to adequately consider sustainability and long-term investment concerns during the endorsement process, though few saw a need to spell out specific sustainability and long-term investments endorsement criteria.

Most respondents supported the status quo about the EU IFRS endorsement process and cautioned against 'EU carve-ins' that could lead to 'EU-IFRSs', a situation that could be detrimental to EU companies active globally and to foreign investments into the EU. Those who were in favour of 'EU carve-ins' did not see why the EU should not enjoy this power whilst other jurisdictions do. Some of them argued that 'carve-in' powers would increase the European Union's ability to influence the IASB standard-setting process compared to the current 'yes-no' endorsement process.

In connection with the HLEG report, the European Commission has issued its action plan for financing sustainable growth in March 2018 where it committed to request EFRAG, where appropriate, to assess the impact of new or revised IFRS standards on sustainable investments.[77] As a result, the European Commission requested EFRAG in June 2018 to consider alternative accounting treatments for equity instruments as required by IFRS 9. Possible accounting treatments should properly portray the performance and risk of long-term investment business models for those equity and equity type investments that are much needed for achieving the UN Sustainable Development Goals and the goals of the Paris Agreement on climate change. The request addresses concerns that neither of the accounting treatments in IFRS 9 for equity instruments is attractive for long-term investors and that this might create a disincentive to hold equity instruments on a long-term basis which might in turn curb financing for sustainable projects. In May 2019, EFRAG launched a public consultation to gather constituents' views on whether alternative accounting treatments to those in IFRS 9 are needed whereby the consultation is intended to complement previous EFRAG discussions and consultations on the accounting treatment for financial instruments.[78] In January 2020, EFRAG provided its advice to the European Commission together with the Feedback Statement from the public consultation and a supporting paper. EFRAG advised, in particular, that the European Commission recommend to the IASB an expeditious review of the non-recycling treatment of equity instruments within IFRS 9.[79]

4.2.2 Russia

Stand-alone financial statements are required to be prepared by all legal entities in accordance with Russian Accounting Principles (RAP). Most of RAP are substantially based on IFRS, although some IFRS standards have no comparable RAP standard and some RAP standards that are based on IFRS have not been updated for recent changes.

However, Russian Federal Law on consolidated financial statements (the Law) requires mandatory application of IFRS for the preparation and presentation of consolidated financial statements by certain Russian entities, including credit institutions, insurance companies, listed companies, non-state pension funds, management companies of investment funds, mutual funds and non-state pension funds, and clearing institutions. In addition, pursuant to the Law, the Russian government issued a regulation that required certain state unitary enterprises and state-owned public joint stock companies to present their consolidated financial statements in accordance with IFRS. Russian entities that are otherwise in the scope of the Law but have no subsidiaries (except for banks that hold only a basic license) are also required to present their IFRS financial statements in addition to their single entity financial statements prepared under RAP. Credit institutions and listed companies are required to present their half-year interim consolidated financial statements under IFRS for interim purposes.

Credit institutions and listed companies are also required to present their half-year interim consolidated financial statements under IFRS for interim purposes.

There is an IFRS endorsement process in Russia. Individual IFRS standards (including interpretations) become mandatory starting from the effective date specified in the IFRS or from the date of its endorsement if it is later. IFRS standards can be voluntarily applied after they are endorsed but before their effective date. In practice, the time period between the IASB issuing a new or amended standard and its endorsement in

Russia is not significant, which allows Russian companies to early adopt IFRS standards and amendments.

The IFRS endorsement process involves an analysis of the Russian language text of an IFRS, provided by the IFRS Foundation, by the National Organization for Financial Accounting and Reporting Standards Foundation (NOFA), an independent, non-commercial organisation identified by the Ministry of Finance of the Russian Federation (Ministry of Finance). NOFA performs an analysis of an individual IFRS's suitability for the Russian financial reporting system. NOFA advises the Ministry of Finance whether an IFRS should be endorsed as issued by the IASB or whether certain requirements should be 'carved out' to meet the needs of the financial reporting system in Russia. The Ministry of Finance, after consultation with the Central Bank of the Russian Federation, makes the final decision on endorsement and publication of an IFRS.

At the time of writing, the Ministry of Finance has endorsed, without any 'carve outs', all IFRS standards effective from 1 January 2020. IFRS 17 has also been endorsed and, therefore, are available for early adoption by Russian companies.

4.2.3 United Kingdom

On 31 January 2020, the United Kingdom (UK) ceased to be a member of the EU. A Withdrawal Agreement with the EU was enacted into UK law by the European Union (Withdrawal Agreement) Act 2020 and entered into force. That agreement established a transition period ending on the implementation period completion day (defined as 31 December 2020), during which the UK continues to be subject to the EU legislative framework. After the implementation period completion day, the UK will no longer be a part of the EU Single Market or the EU Customs Union and will acquire 'third country' status, the terms of which will be defined in a new arrangement. At the time of writing, this new arrangement has yet to be determined and the UK government has indicated that the transition period will not be extended.

On the implementation period completion day, existing IFRS standards as adopted by the EU will be incorporated into UK law with effect from that date by way of the 'International Accounting Standards and European Public Limited-Liability Company (Amendment etc.) (EU Exit) Regulations 2019' No 685 (IAS EU Exit Regulation). These standards will form 'UK-adopted IAS' which will replace EU IFRS for UK companies. The IAS EU Exit Regulation will give power to the Secretary of State for Business, Energy and Industrial Strategy (BEIS) to endorse new or amended standards, which would then form part of UK-adopted IAS, and to delegate this responsibility to an endorsement body. The intention is to delegate these functions to a newly-formed independent UK endorsement body.

For financial years beginning after the implementation period completion day, UK incorporated companies that do not apply UK GAAP will use UK-adopted IAS rather than EU IFRS. On the implementation period completion day, UK-adopted IAS will be identical to EU IFRS, but there is the potential for divergence if different endorsement decisions are made. UK incorporated entities with securities admitted to trading in the EEA may need to confirm they have followed both frameworks.

Until then, companies that are required or choose to apply EU IFRS will in general continue to apply those standards. Any new or amended standards adopted by the EU during the transition period can continue to be used, but not those adopted afterwards. However, where a company is due to file its accounts for the relevant financial year after the transition period, that company may choose to apply UK-adopted IAS, including any new or amended accounting standards adopted by either the BEIS Secretary of State, or the UK endorsement body. If a company takes advantage of this option, it will be required to clearly state this fact when preparing its accounts for that financial year.

The above is based on existing legislation as at the time of writing, however there may be some further changes during the transition period as a result of any subsequent agreements reached between the UK and the EU or decisions taken under UK and/or EU law.

4.3 Americas

4.3.1 US

See 3.2 above for a discussion of the status of US adoption of IFRS.

4.3.2 Canada

For publicly accountable enterprises, the Accounting Standards Board (AcSB) adopted IFRS as Canadian GAAP for fiscal years beginning on or after 1 January 2011, with some deferrals for certain types of entities, which have now expired, and with the exception of pension plans and benefit plans that have characteristics similar to pension plans. Such plans follow the accounting standards for pension plans issued by the AcSB as of 1 January 2011, rather than IAS 26 – *Accounting and Reporting by Retirement Benefit Plans.*

The definition of 'publicly accountable enterprises' is essentially the same as 'publicly accountable entity' in IFRS for SMEs. Canadian publicly accountable enterprises that are registered with the US SEC are permitted to apply US accounting standards rather than IFRS. Securities regulators have indicated that they will consider permitting the use of US standards by Canadian rate-regulated entities that file with Canadian securities commissions even if they are not SEC registered. A number of these entities have been granted permission to use US standards.

For non-publicly accountable enterprises and not-for-profit organisations, the AcSB has developed new bases of accounting that are derived from Canadian standards rather than IFRS, although IFRS is also available for use by those entities on a voluntary basis.

The adoption of IFRS in Canada for publicly accountable enterprises means that the AcSB has effectively ceased to make final decisions on most matters affecting the technical content and timing of implementation of standards applied to publicly accountable enterprises in Canada. The AcSB's plans for incorporating new or amended IFRS into Canadian standards include reviewing all IASB documents issued for comment. As part of this process, the AcSB seeks the input of Canadian stakeholders by issuing its own 'wraparound exposure draft' of the IASB proposals, together with a document highlighting the key elements of the IASB proposals that are particularly relevant to Canadian stakeholders. In addition, the AcSB may perform outreach activities such as public roundtables. Any changes to IFRS must be approved by the AcSB before becoming part of Canadian GAAP.

While the AcSB retains the power to modify or add to the requirements of IFRS, it intends to avoid changing IFRS when adopting them as Canadian GAAP. Accordingly, the AcSB does not expect to eliminate any options within existing IFRS. As issues relevant to Canadian users of financial information arise in the future, the AcSB will work to resolve them through the Interpretations Committee or the IASB. In the event that a resolution by the Interpretations Committee or IASB is not possible, the AcSB will stand ready to develop additional temporary guidance.

The AcSB has an IFRS Discussion Group to provide a public forum to discuss the application of IFRS in Canada and to identify matters that should be forwarded to the Interpretations Committee for further consideration. The Group does not interpret IFRS or seek consensus on its application in Canada. It meets in public up to four times per year and has generated several submissions for the Interpretations Committee's agenda.

4.3.3 Brazil

Local accounting standards in Brazil (CPCs) have been converged with IFRS since 2010 and public companies regulated by the 'Comissão de Valores Mobiliários' (CVM) are also required to make a formal statement of compliance with IFRS as issued by the IASB for their consolidated financial statements. The previous exception for homebuilding companies, which were temporarily permitted to continue to apply IAS 11 – *Construction Contracts* – rather than IAS 18 – *Revenue* – under IFRIC 15 – *Agreements for the Construction of Real Estate*, was eliminated with the adoption of IFRS 15 – *Revenue from Contracts with Customers*. However, at the time of writing local regulators are still discussing how IFRS 15 should be applied for the homebuilding industry and the financial statements of entities in the industry do not refer to IFRS as issued by the IASB as the basis of preparation.

Banks are regulated by the Brazilian Central Bank, which continues to require preparation of financial statements under its pre-existing rules. However, larger companies, as defined by law, including banks, are also required to prepare annual financial statements in accordance with IFRS since 2010, which must be made publicly available. Insurance companies were required to adopt the local CPCs, and hence IFRS, in 2011.

Non-public companies outside financial services are required to apply the CPCs. Smaller non-public companies are permitted to apply CPCs for SMEs which is an equivalent of IFRS for SMEs.

4.4 Asia

4.4.1 China

4.4.1.A Mainland China

The Ministry of Finance in China (the MOF) – through its Accounting Regulatory Department – is responsible for the promulgation of accounting standards, which are applicable to various business enterprises.

Representatives of the China Accounting Standards Committee (CASC), which falls under the Accounting Regulatory Department of the MOF, and the IASB met in Beijing in November 2005 to discuss a range of issues relating to the convergence of Chinese accounting standards with IFRS. At the conclusion of the meeting, the two delegations released a joint statement (2005 Beijing Joint Statement) setting out key points of agreement, including the following:

- the CASC stated that convergence is one of the fundamental goals of its standard-setting programme, with the intention that an enterprise applying Chinese accounting standards should produce financial statements that are the same as those of an enterprise that applies IFRS; and
- the delegation acknowledged that convergence with IFRS will take time and how to converge with IFRS is a matter for China to determine.

Since February 2006, the MOF issued a series of new and revised Accounting Standards for Business Enterprises (ASBE), which included the Basic Standard and 41 specific accounting standards. In April 2010, the MOF issued the *Road Map for Continual Convergence of the ASBE with IFRS* (the MOF Road Map), which requires the application of ASBE by all listed companies, some non-listed financial enterprises and central state-owned enterprises, and most large and medium-sized enterprises. The MOF Road Map also states that ASBE will continue to maintain convergence with IFRS.

In November 2015, representatives of the Trustees of the IFRS Foundation and the MOF held a bilateral meeting in Beijing, China. During the meeting, both parties noted the success of 2005 Beijing Joint Statement, between CASC and IASB. It is the view of both parties that 2005 Beijing Joint Statement has achieved its objectives. In particular, the ASBE is now substantially converged with IFRS and the use of those standards has significantly enhanced the quality and transparency of financial reporting in China. Recognising these developments, both parties updated the 2005 Beijing Joint Statement to reflect progress made in China and set out the following bases for future cooperation:

- reaffirming the goal of full convergence;
- enhancing continued cooperation; and
- establishing a joint working group for further cooperation.

To maintain continuous convergence with IFRS, during the period from July 2019 to June 2020, the MOF released (1) application guidance for non-monetary transactions and debt restructurings, which are based on the general principles of IFRS; (2) interpretations for clarified definition of related party, new definition of business and introduction of optional concentration test, which are consistent with IFRS; and (3) regulation on the accounting for coronavirus-related rent concessions, which is generally consistent with *Covid-19-Related Rent Concessions – Amendment to IFRS 16* released on 28 May 2020, except that practical expedient is also granted to lessors, but entities with securities listed on markets other than Mainland China are not allowed to apply the relief to lessor accounting.

ASBE, to a large extent, represents convergence with IFRS, with due consideration being given to specific situations in China. ASBE covers the recognition, measurement, presentation and disclosure of most transactions and events, financial reporting, and nearly all the topics covered by current IFRS. Most of ASBE is substantially in line with the corresponding IFRS, with a more simplified form of disclosures. ASBE and IFRS can be largely harmonised by selecting appropriate accounting policies with supplemental disclosures which satisfy the requirements of both sets of accounting standards.

However, there are ASBE standards that do not have an IFRS equivalent, such as accounting for common control business combinations, and there are certain standards that restrict or eliminate measurement alternatives that exist in IFRS. For example, the ASBE on investment property permits the use of the fair value model only when certain strict criteria are met. Furthermore, the more significant divergence from IFRS is that the ASBE on impairment of assets prohibits the reversal of an impairment loss for long-lived assets in all situations.

4.4.1.B Hong Kong

The Hong Kong Institute of Certified Public Accountants (HKICPA) is the principal source of accounting principles in Hong Kong. These include a series of Hong Kong Financial Reporting Standards, accounting standards referred to as Hong Kong Accounting Standards (HKAS) and Interpretations issued by the HKICPA. The term 'Hong Kong Financial Reporting Standards' (HKFRS) is deemed to include all of the foregoing.

HKFRS was fully converged with IFRS (subject to the exceptions discussed below) with effect from 1 January 2005. The HKICPA Council supports the integration of its standard-setting process with that of the IASB.

Although the HKICPA Council has a policy of maintaining convergence of HKFRS with IFRS, the HKICPA Council may consider it appropriate to include additional disclosure requirements in an HKFRS or, in some exceptional cases, to deviate from an IFRS. Each HKFRS contains information about the extent of compliance with the equivalent IFRS. When the requirements of an HKFRS and an IFRS differ, the HKFRS is required to be followed by entities reporting within the area of application of HKFRS. However in practice, exceptions to IFRS are few and relate to certain transitional provisions.

Certain smaller companies or groups meeting the necessary requirements and size criteria are permitted (but not required) to adopt the HKICPA's locally developed small and medium-sized financial reporting framework and financial reporting standards.

4.4.2 Japan

Gradual convergence of Japanese GAAP and IFRS has been ongoing for a number of years; however, full mandatory adoption of IFRS in Japan has been put on hold for the time being.

In June 2009, the Business Advisory Council (BAC), a key advisory body to the Financial Services Agency, approved a roadmap for the adoption of IFRS in Japan. This roadmap gives the option of voluntary adoption to companies that meet certain conditions.

In June 2013, the BAC published the Interim Policy Relating to IFRS (the Policy), which further encourages the voluntary adoption of IFRS. The Policy states that although it is not yet the right time to determine whether or not to require mandatory implementation of IFRS in Japan, the BAC recognises that it is important to expand greater voluntary adoption of IFRS in Japan. Accordingly, conditions for voluntary adoption of IFRS have been relaxed, and some other measures have been taken to make the dual reporting of IFRS in consolidated financial statements and Japanese GAAP in standalone financial statements less of a burden on preparers.

The ruling Liberal Democratic Party (LDP) issued the Statement on Approach to IFRS (the Statement) in June 2013. In contrast to the Policy issued by the BAC, the Statement puts more emphasis on preparation for the future adoption of IFRS. The Statement highlights key points to expand greater voluntary adoption of IFRS in Japan.

IFRS as issued by the IASB is the basis of voluntary adoption of IFRS in Japan, but a further endorsement mechanism was put in place in 2015. It is contemplated that under this endorsement mechanism, each IFRS would be reviewed and amended only after careful consideration of situations specific to Japan. However, the endorsement mechanism has also been used to introduce a 'carved-out version' of IFRS to make transition to IFRS as issued by the IASB easier for Japanese companies. In June 2015, Japan's Modified International Standards (JMIS): Accounting Standards Comprising IFRS standards and the ASBJ Modifications were issued by the Accounting Standards Board of Japan (ASBJ). Since then JMIS has been periodically updated and the latest endorsement was finalised in December 2018 taking into account IFRS issued by the IASB until 31 December 2017, but excluding IFRS 17. JMIS differs from IFRS in that it requires goodwill to be amortised and requires all items recorded in other comprehensive income be recycled to profit or loss eventually. At the time of writing, no Japanese companies have announced plans to apply JMIS. It should be noted that despite the introduction of JMIS, there is no change in the option of Japanese companies to be able to use IFRS as issued by the IASB if they so elect.

As a result, the number of the companies adopting IFRS in Japan voluntarily (including those who have officially announced their plan to adopt IFRS in the future) increased to 223 as of July 2020, mostly larger companies. Although a small percentage of listed companies, the companies that have adopted or officially announced that they will adopt IFRS represent a significant and growing part of the market capitalisation of the Tokyo Stock Exchange, accounting for around 40% of the total market capitalisation at the time of writing.

4.4.3   India

Accounting standards in India are formulated by the Institute of Chartered Accountants of India (ICAI). The central government prescribes the standards of accounting or any addendum thereto, as recommended by the ICAI, in consultation with and after examination of the recommendations made by the National Financial Reporting Authority (NFRA). The Ministry of Corporate Affairs (MCA) notifies the standards under the Companies Act by publishing them in the Gazette of India. Notified standards are authoritative under Indian law. Until the financial year ended 31 March 2016, all companies registered under the Companies Act were required to follow local GAAP known as Accounting Standards (ASs), which are based on old versions of IFRS and contain many key differences from IFRS.

In February 2015, the MCA notified the Companies (Indian Accounting Standards) Rules, 2015 laying down the roadmap for application of IFRS converged standards, known as Indian Accounting Standards (Ind AS), to Indian companies other than banking companies, insurance companies and non-banking finance companies (NBFCs). The Ind AS standards have also been notified.

In January 2016, the MCA issued the phasing-in dates of Ind AS applicability for NBFCs. The Reserve Bank of India also issued the Ind AS applicability dates in phases for banks starting from 1 April 2018. However, pending necessary legislative amendments and considering the level of preparedness of many banks, implementation of Ind AS to the banks has been deferred till further notice. The Insurance Regulatory and Development Authority of India initially expected Ind AS to be applied to insurers from the same date as banks. However, due to the issuance of IFRS 17 by the IASB, it was decided that the effective date of implementation will be decided after the finalisation of IFRS 17 by the IASB. All companies applying Ind AS are required to present comparative information according to Ind AS for at least one year. Ind AS will apply to both standalone financial statements and consolidated financial statements of companies covered under the roadmap.

Companies not covered under the roadmap can either apply Ind AS voluntarily or continue applying existing standards, i.e. ASs. If Ind ASs are applied voluntarily, this option will be irrevocable. Voluntary adoption of Ind AS is permitted for all companies other than NBFCs. In 2009, the Securities and Exchange Board of India, the securities regulator in India, permitted listed companies with subsidiaries to submit their consolidated financial statements in accordance with IFRS as issued by the IASB. Few companies in India have availed themselves of this option, which is no longer available for companies.

4.5 Australia

Australia has a regime in which IFRS standards are issued under its legal framework as Australian Accounting Standards (AAS). These are essentially word-for-word copies of IFRS ('IFRS equivalent'). AAS also include some additional Australian specific paragraphs for not-for-profit and public sector entities.

In addition to the IFRS equivalent AAS, there are some additional Australian specific standards for entities such as superannuation entities, general insurance and life insurance entities (the insurance standards will be replaced by AASB 17 – *Insurance Contracts*, which is equivalent to IFRS 17, once effective), not-for-profit entities and public sector entities and some additional disclosures exist within certain standards.

Compliance by Australian private sector for-profit entities with AAS will result in compliance with IFRS as issued by the IASB, unless they are not publicly accountable and elect to apply the Reduced Disclosure Requirements (RDR) framework. Explicit statements of compliance with IFRS – when they are compliant – are required to be made by the preparers (in the notes to the financial statements and in the Directors' Declaration required by the Corporations Act), as well by the auditors in their reports. Not-for-profit and public sector entities cannot make an explicit statement of compliance with IFRS, as they have other Australian specific accounting standards and Australian specific paragraphs to comply with in preparing financial statements.

Australia has not adopted the *IFRS for SMEs* standard, and it is unlikely to do so in the near future because of measurement differences and the removal of options as compared to IFRS. Australia has a RDR framework for reporting entities that are not publicly accountable (per the IFRS for SMEs definition). This framework requires such entities to apply all recognition and measurement requirements of AAS, but provide

RDR disclosures. The RDR disclosures are specified and were chosen based on the principles adopted by the IASB in its development of the *IFRS for SMEs* standard. Financial statements prepared under the RDR are general purpose financial statements, but will not be in compliance with IFRS as issued by the IASB. From 1 July 2021, the RDR framework will be replaced by the Simplified Disclosure Standard (SDS). SDS is more closely based on the disclosures of the *IFRS for SMEs* standard, with an overlay of certain Australian specific disclosures.

Australia also permits non-reporting entities (as defined by AAS) to prepare special purpose financial statements. Preparers are encouraged to follow the recognition and measurement requirements of AAS but have flexibility as to the level of disclosure they choose to provide. From 1 July 2021, the ability for private sector entities to prepare special purpose financial statements will be removed when financial statements are required by either Australian legislation to comply with AAS or 'accounting standards'; or another means (e.g. constitution) to comply with AAS. These entities will be required to prepare general purpose financial statements.

4.6 South Africa

For periods beginning on or after 1 January 2005, the South African securities exchange, JSE Limited (JSE), has required that all listed companies prepare financial statements under IFRS.

Effective 1 May 2011, the South African Companies Act permits different accounting frameworks to apply to different categories of companies based on their 'public interest score'. Listed companies are required to use IFRS, however other companies (depending on their public interest score) may apply IFRS, IFRS for SMEs, or in certain situations (introduced, in particular, for micro-entities) entity specific accounting policies as determined by themselves.

In addition to the disclosure requirements of IFRS and IFRS for SMEs, the South African Companies Act and the JSE impose certain additional disclosure requirements on reporting entities. Further, the previous South African standard setter – the Accounting Practices Board – has issued three Financial Reporting Guides. While these interpretations are specific to issues in the South African environment, IFRS reporters in South Africa make use of them as they are based on a framework equivalent to that used for IFRS. These are updated for developments in IFRS.

5 CONSISTENCY IN APPLICATION OF IFRS

The use of a consistent set of accounting standards by companies throughout the world has the potential to improve the comparability and transparency of financial information. The provision of higher quality information has been shown to reduce financial statement preparation costs and, it is believed, to enable capital markets participants to make better decisions. The global adoption of IFRS is a necessary condition for global comparability, but, on its own, it is insufficient. Global comparability cannot be achieved without a rigorous and consistent application of the standards. However, consistent application of the standards cannot be achieved unless countries adopt IFRS without modifying the standards issued by the IASB.

Studies into the impact of the use of IFRS indicate reduced cost of capital and improvements in share prices and trading, resulting in part from increased disclosure and enhanced information comparability. However, the research concludes that these improvements occur in countries with strong legal enforcement.[80] The adoption of IFRS alone is, therefore, unlikely to produce uniform financial reporting. The standards need to be applied, audited and enforced on a consistent basis in order to get the most out of comparability.[81]

Practitioners and regulators agree that enforcement of accounting standards is an integral part of achieving accounting quality under IFRS. With this in mind, ESMA has agreed on common enforcement priorities and has made the consistent application of IFRS one of its primary objectives. In December 2014, ESMA's guidelines on enforcement of financial information (the Guidelines) became effective. They replace earlier versions of the guidelines from ESMA and its predecessor, the Council of European Securities Regulators (CESR). The Guidelines apply to all EU national competent authorities and other bodies in the EU that undertake enforcement responsibilities. The Guidelines build on a common approach to the enforcement of financial information and reinforce coordination among European enforcers. In addition, the Guidelines codify European common enforcement priorities and include a requirement to discuss views on accounting matters prior to taking enforcement decisions.[82]

In addition to enforcement, ESMA contributes to the standard-setting process by engaging with the IASB and the Interpretations Committee by submitting comment letters and identifying areas of diversity in practice (including areas in which a lack of clarity in standards could lead to diversity in practice). In addition, the IFRS Foundation and ESMA have entered into a joint Statement of Protocols, which reaffirms the cooperation between the two entities as well as describes additional areas of cooperation including electronic reporting, the implementation of new standards and emerging financial reporting issues.[83]

The IFRS Foundation and IOSCO have entered into a joint Statement of Protocols to facilitate consistency in the application of IFRS. This is in addition to the memorandum of understanding between the capital markets authorities that formed the Monitoring Board (see 2.3 above) and the IFRS Foundation.[84]

The SEC stresses the importance of enforcing IFRS, not only through its filing review process of foreign private issuers, but also through its collaboration with foreign counterparts bilaterally and through IOSCO.[85]

Although consistent application of IFRS is not the primary responsibility of the IASB, it understandably takes a keen interest. The ASAF was established (see 2.8 above) to coordinate interaction with national and regional standard-setting bodies to, among other things, identify where divergence occurs across borders.[86] The post-implementation reviews of all major standards and interpretations are intended to identify and rectify difficulties in consistency that are identified only after the standard is used. The Interpretations Committee plays a key role as well.

Much has been written about consistency in IFRS, but a recurring message is that it requires a coordinated effort by standard-setters, preparers, regulators and auditors.

6 SUMMARY

IFRS is now, together with US GAAP, one of the two globally recognised financial reporting frameworks. Although the goal of a single set of high-quality global accounting standards has not been fulfilled, given the number of countries that have adopted or converged with IFRS or have plans to in the future, it is safe to say that IFRS has become 'International GAAP'.

References

1. IFRS Foundation website https://www.ifrs.org/-/media/feature/around-the-world/adoption/use-of-ifrs-around-the-world-overview-sept-2018.pdf (accessed 17 August 2020).
2. IFRS Foundation Constitution, August 2020, Section 3.
3. IFRS Foundation website, https://www.ifrs.org/about-us/who-we-are/#constitution (accessed 25 August 2020).
4. IFRS Foundation website, https://www.ifrs.org/projects/work-plan/2020-agenda-consultation/#current-stage (Accessed 17 August 2020).
5. IFRS Foundation Constitution, August 2020, Section 6.
6. IFRS Foundation Constitution, August 2020, Section 8.
7. IFRS Foundation Constitution, August 2020, Section 7.
8. IFRS Foundation Constitution, August 2020, Section 6.
9. IFRS Foundation Constitution, August 2020, Sections 15(a) and (c).
10. Accounting Standards Advisory Forum: Terms of Reference/Charter.
11. IFRS Foundation Constitution, August 2020, Sections 13 and 15.
12. IFRS Foundation website, https://www.ifrs.org/about-us/who-we-are/#funding (accessed 17 August 2020).
13. *IFRS Foundation Annual Report 2019*, IFRS Foundation, 2020.
14. IFRS Foundation Constitution, August 2020, Section 18.
15. Charter of the IFRSF Monitoring Board, February 2016.
16. IFRS Foundation Constitution, August 2020, Section 19.
17. IOSCO website, https://www.iosco.org/about/?subSection=monitoring_board&subSection1=members (accessed 17 August 2020).
18. Charter of the IFRSF Monitoring Board, February 2016, Appendix A.
19. IFRS Foundation Monitoring Board Press Release, *Monitoring Board finalizes assessment approach for membership criteria and announces Chair selection*, 1 March 2013.
20. IFRS Foundation Constitution, August 2020, Section 24.
21. IFRS Foundation Constitution, August 2020, Section 25.
22. IFRS Foundation Constitution, August 2020, Section 25.
23. IFRS Foundation Constitution, August 2020, Section 27.
24. IFRS Foundation Constitution, August 2020, Section 26.
25. IFRS Foundation Constitution, August 2020, Section 36(a).
26. IFRS Foundation Constitution, August 2020 Section 35.
27. IFRS Foundation Constitution, August 2020, Section 35.
28. IFRS Foundation Constitution, August 2020, Section 36(d), (e) and (h).
29. IFRS Foundation website, https://www.ifrs.org/projects/better-communication/ (accessed on 17 August 2020).
30. Due Process Handbook. August 2020, para. 1.3.
31. Due Process Handbook. August 2020, para. 5.15.
32. Due Process Handbook. August 2020, para. 5.16.
33. Due Process Handbook. August 2020, para. 5.18.
34. Due Process Handbook. August 2020, para. 8.2.
35. Due Process Handbook. August 2020, para. 8.7.
36. IFRS Foundation Constitution, August 2020, Section 39.
37. Due Process Handbook. August 2020, para. 3.18.
38. IFRS Foundation Constitution, August 2020, Section 41.
39. Due Process Handbook. August 2020, para. 7.23.
40. Due Process Handbook. August 2020, para. 8.3.
41. Due Process Handbook. August 2020, para. 8.4.

Chapter 1

42 Due Process Handbook. August 2020, para. 8.5.
43 IFRS Foundation website, https://www.ifrs.org/news-and-events/2019/03/time-is-of-the-essence/ (accessed 17 August 2020).
44 IFRS Foundation website, https://www.ifrs.org/news-and-events/2019/03/time-is-of-the-essence/ (accessed 17 August 2020).
45 Due Process Handbook. August 2020, para. 8.6.
46 Due Process Handbook. August 2020, para 2.4.
47 IFRS Foundation website, https://www.ifrs.org/news-and-events/2020/08/ifrs-foundation-publishes-revised-due-process-handbook/ (accessed on 21 August 2020).
48 Due Process Handbook. August 2020, para. 1.5.
49 Due Process Handbook. August 2020, para. 3.1.
50 Due Process Handbook. August 2020, para. 1.2.
51 Due Process Handbook. August 2020 para. 3.43.
52 Due Process Handbook. August 2020, para. 3.44.
53 Due Process Handbook. August 2020, para. 3.45.
54 Due Process Handbook. August 2020, para. 3.46.
55 Due Process Handbook. August 2020, para. 6.7.
56 Due Process Handbook. August 2020, para. 6.8.
57 IFRS Advisory Council, Terms of reference and operating procedures, July 2014.
58 IFRS Advisory Council, Terms of reference and operating procedures, July 2014.
59 IFRS Foundation Constitution, August 2020, Section 44.
60 IFRS Foundation Constitution, August 2020, Section 45.
61 IFRS Advisory Council, Terms of reference and operating procedures, July 2014.
62 Accounting Standards Advisory Forum: Terms of Reference/Charter.
63 Accounting Standards Advisory Forum: Terms of Reference/Charter.
64 Feedback Statement, *Review of the Accounting Standards Advisory Forum 2018*, June 2018.
65 IFRS Foundation website, https://www.ifrs.org/about-us/consultative-bodies/ (accessed 17 August 2020).
66 IFRS Foundation website, https://www.ifrs.org/projects/work-plan/ (accessed on 17 August 2020).
67 This means those with their securities admitted to trading on a regulated market within the meaning of Article 1(13) of Council Directive 93/22/EEC (on investment services in the securities field) or those offered to the public in view of their admission to such trading under Council Directive 80/390/EEC (coordinating the requirements for the drawing up, scrutiny and distribution of the listing particulars to be published for the admission of securities to official stock exchange listing).

68 European Commission, Implementation of the IAS Regulation (1606/2002) in the EU and EEA, 7 February 2012.
69 European Commission, Regulation (EC) No 1606/2002 of the European Parliament and of the Council of 19 July 2002, Recital 11.
70 European Financial Reporting Advisory Group website, http://www.efrag.org/Activities/286/IFRS-14-Regulatory-Deferral-Accounts# (accessed 17 August 2020).
71 Commission Regulation (EU) 2017/1988 of 3 November 2017 amending Regulation (EC) No 1126/2008 adopting certain international accounting standards in accordance with Regulation (EC) No 1606/2002 of the European Parliament and of the Council as regards International Financial Reporting Standard 4, Official Journal of the European Union, 9 November 2017.
72 European Financial Reporting Advisory Group website, http://www.efrag.org/News/Public-244/EFRAG-Endorsement-Status-Report Update (accessed 17 August 2020).
73 European Financial Reporting Advisory Group website, http://www.efrag.org/Assets/Download?assetUrl=/sites/webpublishing/SiteAssets/Letter+to+IASB+Board+-+IFRS+17+-+24+March+2020.pdf (accessed 17 August 2020).
74 European Union High-Level Expert Group on Sustainable Finance, Financing a Sustainable European Economy, 31 January 2018.
75 European Commission, *Consultation Document Fitness Check on the EU Framework for Public Reporting by EU Companies*, 21 March 2018.
76 European Commission, *Summary Report of the Public Consultation on the Fitness Check on the EU framework for public reporting by companies (21 March 2018 - 31 July 2018)*, 31 October 2018.
77 European Commission, Action Plan: Financing Sustainable Growth, March 2018.
78 European Financial Reporting Advisory Group, *Request for Feedback, Equity Instruments – Research on Measurement*, May 2019.
79 European Financial Reporting Advisory Group website, http://www.efrag.org/News/Project-401/EFRAGs-advice-to-the-European-Commission-on-the-measurement-of-long-term-investments-in-equity-instruments- (accessed 17 August 2020).
80 Li, S. (2010) *Does mandatory adoption of International Financial Reporting Standards in the European Union reduce the cost of equity capital?* The Accounting Review, 85(2), 607-636.

81 Speech by Hans Hoogervorst, 'The Search for Consistency in Financial Reporting', Ernst & Young/Cass Business School, 17 January 2013.
82 European Securities and Markets Authority, *ESMA Report on Enforcement and Regulatory Activities of Accounting Enforcers in 2014*, 31 March 2015.
83 IFRS Foundation and ESMA Press Release, *IFRS Foundation and ESMA sign joint Statement of Protocols*, 15 July 2014.
84 IOSCO and IFRS Foundation, Statement of Protocols for Cooperation on International Financial Reporting Standards, 16 September 2013.
85 Speech by Mary Jo White, 'Regulation in a Global Financial System', Investment Company Institute General Membership Meeting, 1 May 2013.
86 IFRS Foundation, *Report of the Trustees' Strategy Review 2011, IFRSs as the Global Standards: Setting a Strategy for the Foundation's Second Decade*, February 2012.

Chapter 2   The IASB's Conceptual Framework

1   INTRODUCTION 43
     1.1   What is a conceptual framework? 44
     1.2   Why is a conceptual framework necessary? 44

2   DEVELOPMENT OF THE IASB'S CONCEPTUAL FRAMEWORK AND EFFECTIVE DATE 46

3   CONTENTS, PURPOSE AND SCOPE OF THE IASB'S CONCEPTUAL FRAMEWORK 47
     3.1   Contents of the Conceptual Framework 47
     3.2   Status and purpose of the Conceptual Framework 48

4   CHAPTER 1: THE OBJECTIVE OF GENERAL PURPOSE FINANCIAL REPORTING 48
     4.1   Objective, usefulness and limitations of general purpose financial reporting 49
            4.1.1   Objective and usefulness 49
            4.1.2   Limitations 50
     4.2   Information about the economic resources of an entity and the use made of them, claims against the entity, and changes in resources and claims 50
            4.2.1   Economic resources and claims 51
            4.2.2   Changes in economic resources and claims 51
            4.2.3   Information about the use of economic resources (stewardship) 52

5   CHAPTER 2: QUALITATIVE CHARACTERISTICS OF USEFUL FINANCIAL INFORMATION 52
     5.1   Fundamental qualitative characteristics 53
            5.1.1   Relevance (including materiality) 54

		5.1.2	Faithful representation	54
		5.1.3	Applying the fundamental qualitative characteristics	56
	5.2	Enhancing qualitative characteristics		56
		5.2.1	Comparability	56
		5.2.2	Verifiability	57
		5.2.3	Timeliness	57
		5.2.4	Understandability	58
		5.2.5	Applying the enhancing qualitative characteristics	58
	5.3	The cost constraint		58
6	CHAPTER 3: FINANCIAL STATEMENTS AND THE REPORTING ENTITY			59
	6.1	Financial statements		59
		6.1.1	Objective and scope of financial statements	59
		6.1.2	Reporting period and comparative information	60
		6.1.3	Perspective adopted in financial statements	60
		6.1.4	Going concern assumption	60
	6.2	The reporting entity		60
		6.2.1	Consolidated and unconsolidated financial statements	61
7	CHAPTER 4: THE ELEMENTS OF FINANCIAL STATEMENTS			62
	7.1	Matters concerning both assets and liabilities		63
		7.1.1	Unit of account	63
		7.1.2	Executory contracts	65
		7.1.3	Substance of contractual rights and contractual obligations	65
	7.2	Definition of assets		66
		7.2.1	Rights	66
		7.2.2	Potential to produce economic benefits	68
		7.2.3	Control	69
	7.3	Definition of liabilities		70
		7.3.1	Obligation	70
		7.3.2	Transfer an economic resource	71
		7.3.3	Present obligation existing as a result of past events	72
	7.4	Definition of equity		72
	7.5	Definition of income and expenses		73
8	CHAPTER 5: RECOGNITION AND DERECOGNITION			73
	8.1	The recognition process		74
	8.2	Recognition criteria		75
		8.2.1	Relevance	76
			8.2.1.A Existence uncertainty	76

		8.2.1.B	Low probability of an inflow or outflow of economic benefits.. 77
	8.2.2	Faithful representation... 77
		8.2.2.A	Measurement uncertainty.. 77
		8.2.2.B	Other factors.. 79
8.3	Derecognition.. 79

9 **CHAPTER 6: MEASUREMENT**.. 81

9.1	Measurement bases 82
	9.1.1 Historical cost 82
	9.1.2 Current value 83
	9.1.2.A Fair value.. 84
	9.1.2.B Value in use and fulfilment value 85
	9.1.2.C Current cost 85
9.2	Information provided by different measurement bases 86
	9.2.1 Historical cost 90
	9.2.2 Current value 91
	9.2.2.A Fair value.. 91
	9.2.2.B Value in use and fulfilment value 91
	9.2.2.C Current cost 92
9.3	Factors to consider in selecting measurement bases 92
	9.3.1 Relevance 93
	9.3.1.A Characteristics of the asset or liability..................... 93
	9.3.1.B Contribution to future cash flows 94
	9.3.2 Faithful representation... 94
	9.3.3 Enhancing characteristics and the cost constraint.................. 95
	9.3.3.A Historical cost 96
	9.3.3.B Current value 96
	9.3.4 Factors specific to initial measurement.................................... 97
	9.3.5 More than one measurement basis 98
9.4	Measurement of equity.. 99
9.5	Cash-flow-based measurement techniques 100

10 **CHAPTER 7: PRESENTATION AND DISCLOSURE**... 101

10.1	Presentation and disclosure objectives and principles 101
10.2	Classification.. 102
	10.2.1 Classification of assets and liabilities 102
	10.2.1.A Offsetting... 102
	10.2.2 Classification of equity 102
	10.2.3 Classification of income and expenses 103
	10.2.3.A Profit or loss and other comprehensive income 103

10.3 Aggregation 104
11 CHAPTER 8: CONCEPTS OF CAPITAL AND CAPITAL MAINTENANCE 104
    11.1 Financial capital maintenance 105
    11.2 Physical capital maintenance 106
12 MANAGEMENT COMMENTARY 106
    12.1 The IASB's practice statement 106
    12.2 Possible future changes to the practice statement 107

Chapter 2 The IASB's Conceptual Framework

1 INTRODUCTION

There have been numerous attempts over many decades to define the purpose and nature of accounting. Perhaps not surprisingly, most of the earlier studies were carried out by individual academics and academic committees in the US; for example, the writings in 1940 of Paton and Littleton[1] were intended to present a framework of accounting theory that would be regarded as a coherent and consistent foundation for the development of accounting standards, whilst the studies carried out over the years by various committees of the American Accounting Association have made a significant contribution to accounting theory.[2] In addition to the research carried out by individuals and academic committees, professional accounting bodies around the world have also, from time to time, issued statements that deal with various aspects of accounting theory. These can be seen as the first attempts at developing some form of conceptual framework.

With the globalisation of business and the increased access to the world's capital markets that goes with it, there are essentially only two truly global systems of financial reporting – IFRS and US GAAP.

In 2004 the IASB and FASB began a joint project to develop a single conceptual framework, the first phase of which was completed in September 2010. This version of the IASB's conceptual framework (the 2010 *Framework*) comprised two sections finalised in this first phase of the joint project with the FASB, together with other material carried forward from the conceptual framework issued by the former IASC in 1989 ('the 1989 *Framework*'), which was originally intended to be replaced in a second phase of the joint framework project. The 1989 *Framework*, although not jointly developed with the FASB, nevertheless drew heavily on the FASB's then current conceptual framework. No further joint work was undertaken by the two boards and in September 2012 the IASB decided to restart the project as an IASB project.

In July 2013 the IASB published a discussion paper[3] which was followed by an exposure draft of an updated framework in May 2015.[4]

In March 2018 the IASB published *Conceptual Framework for Financial Reporting* (the *Framework*).

This chapter discusses the *Framework* as published in 2018. Readers interested in predecessor versions should refer to earlier editions of International GAAP. The effective date for the revised *Framework* for preparers of financial statements is, broadly speaking, January 2020, although there are some exceptions to this. Furthermore, certain IFRS make reference to earlier versions of the *Framework*. This is discussed at 2 below.

Relevant chapters in this book will discuss, as appropriate, references to the *Framework* in the standards with which they deal.

1.1 What is a conceptual framework?

In general terms, a conceptual framework is a statement of generally accepted theoretical principles which form the frame of reference for a particular field of enquiry. In terms of financial reporting, these theoretical principles provide the basis for both the development of new reporting practices and the evaluation of existing ones. Since the financial reporting process is concerned with the provision of information that is useful in making business and economic decisions, a conceptual framework will form the theoretical basis for determining which events should be accounted for, how they should be measured and how they should be communicated. Therefore, although it is theoretical in nature, a conceptual framework for financial reporting has a highly practical end in view.

1.2 Why is a conceptual framework necessary?

A conceptual framework for financial reporting should be a theory of accounting against which practical problems can be tested objectively, and the utility of which is decided by the adequacy of the practical solutions it provides. However, the various standard-setting bodies around the world initially often attempted to resolve practical accounting and reporting problems through the development of accounting standards, without such an accepted theoretical frame of reference. The end result was that standard-setters determined the form and content of external financial reports, without resolving such fundamental issues as:

- What are the objectives of these reports?
- Who are the users of these reports?
- What are the informational needs of these users?
- What types of report will best satisfy their needs?

Consequently, standards were often produced on a haphazard and 'fire-fighting' basis with the danger of mutual inconsistencies. By contrast, an agreed framework would, in principle, provide standard-setters with a basis for designing standards that facilitate more consistent external financial reports that meet the needs of the user.

The main role of a conceptual framework is to assist the standard-setter and this is the focus of the discussion in the remainder of this section.

Experience of the last thirty years also shows that, in the absence of an agreed comprehensive conceptual framework, the same theoretical issues were revisited on numerous occasions by different standard-setting bodies. This inevitably sometimes resulted in the development of standards that were internally inconsistent and inconsistent with each other, or which were founded on incompatible concepts. For example, inconsistencies and conflicts have existed between and within individual standards concerning the emphasis placed on substance versus form; neutrality versus prudence; and whether earnings should be determined through balance sheet measurements or by matching costs and revenue. Some standard-setters have permitted two or more methods of accounting for the same set of circumstances, whilst others permitted certain accounting practices to be followed on an arbitrary or unspecified basis. These inconsistencies and irrationalities perhaps reflect the fundamental difficulty of determining what is required in order to give a faithful representation of economic phenomena.

Standard setters have adopted different approaches to the realisation of their conceptual frameworks in specific accounting standards. This can be seen by comparing the standards issued by the FASB with those issued by the IASB. In the US the FASB, in spite of its pioneering work on a conceptual framework, has produced a large number of highly detailed accounting rules. The IASB, on the other hand has tended to produce less detailed standards, relying on preparers and auditors to consider the general principles on which they are based in applying them to specific situations. Clearly, the proliferation of accounting standards in the US stems from many factors, not least the legal and regulatory environment. However, a more satisfactory conceptual framework might reduce the need for such a large number of highly detailed standards, since the emphasis would be on general principles rather than specific rules. Indeed this change of emphasis has been specifically considered by the US authorities following the financial reporting problems that led, in the US, to the Sarbanes-Oxley Act and the establishment of the Public Company Accounting Oversight Board. This is not to say that the IASB's more general 'principles-based' approach to standard setting is necessarily more satisfactory than the FASB's; rather, the legal and regulatory environment within which non-US businesses habitually work is quite different from that of the US.

The political and economic environment influences not only the approach taken to standard setting, but also the nature of the conceptual framework on which standards are based. Following the widespread incorporation of IFRS into the national GAAPs of many other countries, the IASB is faced with many stakeholders with a variety of needs and expectations. These different stakeholders often express differing views on proposals issued by the IASB and expect their views to be taken into account. Under these circumstances, an agreed conceptual framework is of great value, although the best defence against undue interference in the standard-setting process is the need of the capital markets for financial reporting that provides a sound basis for decision making, which in turn implies a system of financial reporting characterised by relevance, faithful representation, practicality and understandability. While it is probable that these characteristics are more likely to be achieved using a sound theoretical foundation, the converse also applies: namely that the framework must result in standards that account appropriately for actual business practice and economic reality. Otherwise how, for example, is an industry to be persuaded that a particular accounting treatment perceived as adversely affecting its economic interests is better than one which does not?

An agreed framework is therefore not the panacea for all accounting problems. Nor does it obviate the need for judgement to be exercised in the process of resolving accounting issues. What it can provide is a framework within which those judgements can be made. Indeed this is happening, as the principles expressed in the IASB's framework are frequently referred to in IFRSs and during the process of their development. Unfortunately, there is also evidence of the IASB issuing standards that contravene its own conceptual framework. For example, IAS 38 – *Intangible Assets* – requires the capitalisation of goodwill as an asset, despite the fact that goodwill does not meet the definition of an asset in the IASB's framework. Similarly IAS 12 – *Income Taxes* – requires recognition of deferred tax assets and liabilities that arguably do not meet the definitions of asset and liability under the framework.

2 DEVELOPMENT OF THE IASB'S CONCEPTUAL FRAMEWORK AND EFFECTIVE DATE

The IASB issued *Conceptual Framework for Financial Reporting 2010* in September 2010. This was effectively work-in-progress, comprising two chapters developed in the first phase of the then joint project of the IASB and FASB to develop an agreed framework (see 1 above), together with material carried forward from the former IASC's 1989 *Framework* (which was adopted in 2001 by the then newly-constituted IASB).

Following the completion of the first phase in 2010, the joint project with the FASB stalled somewhat until, in 2012, the IASB indicated that it no longer saw convergence between IFRS and US GAAP in the area of the conceptual framework as a primary objective and, moreover, that active work on the conceptual framework would resume shortly. This resulted in the publication by the IASB in July 2013 of a discussion paper DP/2013/1 – *A Review of the Conceptual Framework for Financial Reporting*. The discussion paper noted this was no longer a joint project with the FASB, but the IASB's own project.[5] The IASB followed the discussion paper with an exposure draft of an updated framework in May 2015 (*Exposure Draft ED/2015/3: Conceptual Framework for Financial Reporting*).

In March 2018 the IASB published *Conceptual Framework for Financial Reporting* (the *Framework*). This fully revised document replaced the sections of the 2010 version previously carried-forward from the 1989 *Framework* and also made amendments to the sections produced in 2010.

This chapter discusses the *Framework* as published in 2018. Readers interested in predecessor versions should refer to earlier editions of International GAAP.

The *Framework* itself has no explicit effective date. However:

- The Board and Interpretations Committee commenced using the 2018 *Framework* immediately it was issued. If, when developing a draft Interpretation, the Interpretations Committee is faced with an inconsistency between a standard (including any standard developed on the basis of the 1989 *Framework* or the 2010 *Framework*) and the concepts in the 2018 *Framework*, it will refer the issue to the Board, as required by the IFRS Foundation Due Process Handbook. *[CF BC0.27].*

- Preparers of financial statements could be affected by the changes to the *Framework* if they need to use it to develop an accounting policy when no standard applies to a particular transaction or other event or when a standard allows a choice of accounting policy (see Chapter 3 at 4.3). To achieve transition to the *Framework* for such entities, the Board issued *Amendments to References to the Conceptual Framework in IFRS Standards* in March 2018 (CF References). Where appropriate, that document updates references in standards to refer to the new *Framework* and updates related quotations. *[CF BC0.28]*. These changes are effective for periods beginning on or after 1 January 2020.[6]

Relevant chapters in this publication will discuss, as appropriate, references to the *Framework* in the standards with which they deal. At a more general level, it should be noted that not all such references have been changed to refer to the new *Framework*; some continue to refer to previous versions as discussed below.

The following continue to refer to the version of the framework in effect when they were developed:

- IFRIC 12 – *Service Concession Arrangements* – and IFRIC 19 – *Extinguishing Financial Liabilities with Equity Instruments* – continue to refer to the 1989 *Framework*; [IFRIC 12 references, BC20: IFRIC 19 references, BC16]
- IFRS 14 – *Regulatory Deferral Accounts*, IFRIC 20 – *Stripping Costs in the Production Phase of a Surface Mine* – and IFRIC 22 – *Foreign Currency Transactions and Advance Consideration* – continue to refer to the 2010 *Framework*; [IFRS 14.13, BC10: IFRIC 20 references, BC7: IFRIC 22 references, BC17] and
- IFRS 3 – *Business Combinations* – continues to refer to the 2010 *Framework* until, at the latest, periods beginning on or after 1 January 2022.[7] For subsequent periods, references in IFRS 3 are to the new *Framework* (see Chapter 9 at 1.1). *[IFRS 3.11, IFRS 14.13]*.

3 CONTENTS, PURPOSE AND SCOPE OF THE IASB'S CONCEPTUAL FRAMEWORK

3.1 Contents of the Conceptual Framework

The *Framework* comprises an introductory section dealing with its status and purpose (discussed at 3.2 below), followed by eight chapters and an appendix of defined terms. The appendix is an editorial device which extracts (or derives) definitions from the *Framework* itself. As these are dealt with in this chapter in the relevant sections the appendix is not reproduced.

The chapters are as follows:

- Chapter 1 – The objective of general purpose financial reporting (discussed at 4 below);
- Chapter 2 – Qualitative characteristics of useful financial information (discussed at 5 below);
- Chapter 3 – Financial statements and the reporting entity (discussed at 6 below);
- Chapter 4 – The elements of financial statements (discussed at 7 below);
- Chapter 5 – Recognition and derecognition (discussed at 8 below);
- Chapter 6 – Measurement (discussed at 9 below);
- Chapter 7 – Presentation and disclosure (discussed at 10 below); and
- Chapter 8 – Concepts of capital and capital maintenance (discussed at 11 below).

3.2 Status and purpose of the Conceptual Framework

The purpose of the *Framework* is to assist:

- the Board to develop IFRSs that are based on consistent concepts. However, the Board notes that to meet the objective of general purpose financial reporting, it may sometimes specify requirements that depart from aspects of the *Framework*. If it does so, it will explain the departure in the basis for conclusions on that standard; *[SP1.3]*
- preparers of financial statements to develop consistent accounting policies when no standard applies to a particular transaction or other event, or when a standard allows a choice of accounting policy (see Chapter 3 at 4.3); and
- all parties to understand and interpret IFRS.

The *Framework* describes the objective of, and the concepts for, general purpose financial reporting. *[SP1.1]*. It is not a standard, and nothing in it overrides any specific standard or any requirement of one. *[SP1.2]*.

The *Framework* may be revised from time to time in light of the IASB's experience of working with it. Revisions to it will not automatically lead to changes to the standards; any decision to amend a standard would require the Board to go through its normal due process. *[SP1.4]*.

The Board states that its work serves the public interest by fostering trust, growth and long-term financial stability in the global economy and that the *Framework* contributes to the development of standards that bring transparency, accountability and efficiency to financial markets. The IASB describes its *Framework* as providing the foundation for standards that:

- contribute to transparency by enhancing the international comparability and quality of financial information, enabling investors and other market participants to make informed economic decisions;
- strengthen accountability by reducing the information gap between the providers of capital and the people to whom they have entrusted their money. Standards based on the *Framework* provide information needed to hold management to account. As a source of globally comparable information, those standards are also of vital importance to regulators around the world; and
- contribute to economic efficiency by helping investors to identify opportunities and risks across the world, thus improving capital allocation. For businesses, the use of a single, trusted accounting language derived from standards based on the *Framework* lowers the cost of capital and reduces international reporting costs. *[SP 1.5]*.

4 CHAPTER 1: THE OBJECTIVE OF GENERAL PURPOSE FINANCIAL REPORTING

Chapter 1 of the *Framework* discusses the objective of general purpose financial reporting, which – in the IASB's view – forms the foundation of the *Framework*. Other aspects of the *Framework* (a reporting entity concept, the qualitative characteristics of, and the constraint on, useful financial information, elements of financial statements, recognition and derecognition, measurement, presentation and disclosure) flow logically from the objective. *[CF 1.1]*.

The Chapter is divided into three main sections dealing with:

- the objective, usefulness and limitations of general purpose financial reporting;
- information about a reporting entity's economic resources, claims, and changes in resources and claims; and
- information about an entity's use of such resources.

The first of these is discussed at 4.1 below; 4.2 below deals together with the other two items.

4.1 Objective, usefulness and limitations of general purpose financial reporting

4.1.1 Objective and usefulness

The *Framework* defines the objective of general purpose financial reporting as being:

> 'to provide financial information about the reporting entity that is useful to existing and potential investors, lenders and other creditors in making decisions relating to providing resources to the entity. Those decisions involve decisions about: buying, selling or holding equity and debt instruments; providing or settling loans and other forms of credit; or exercising rights to vote on, or otherwise influence, management's actions that affect the use of the entity's economic resources.' *[CF 1.2]*.

Existing and potential investors, lenders and other creditors (collectively, 'users' or 'primary users') cannot generally require reporting entities to provide information directly to them and must rely on general purpose financial reports for much of the financial information they need. Consequently, they are the primary users to whom general purpose financial reports are directed. *[CF 1.5]*. Moreover, financial reports are prepared for users with a reasonable knowledge of business and economic activities who can review and analyse the information diligently. *[CF 2.36]*.

Other parties, such as regulators and members of the public, may also find general purpose financial reports useful. However, those reports are not primarily directed to these other groups. *[CF 1.10]*. This draws out an interesting facet of the Board's objective for financial reporting being restricted to the information needs of those providing resources to a reporting entity. It excludes other common uses of financial information, notably the levying of corporation taxes and restrictions on distribution to members. These two very important areas of corporate activity will typically take as a starting point a measure of profit as reported in the entity's financial reports. Self-evidently, if these uses are not considered in the development of accounting requirements, there is a risk that financial statements will be less suitable for these purposes.

The decisions described in the objective depend on the returns that existing and potential investors, lenders and other creditors expect, for example, dividends, principal and interest payments or market price increases. Investors', lenders' and other creditors' expectations about returns depend on their assessment of the amount, timing and uncertainty of (the prospects for) future net cash inflows to the entity and on their assessment of management's stewardship of the entity's economic resources.

Existing and potential investors, lenders and other creditors need information to help them make those assessments. *[CF 1.3]*.

In doing so, users need information about: *[CF 1.4]*

- the economic resources of the entity, claims against the entity and changes in those resources and claims (see 4.2 below); and
- how efficiently and effectively the entity's management and governing board have discharged their responsibilities to use the entity's economic resources (see 4.2.3 below).

4.1.2   Limitations

The *Framework* acknowledges that general purpose financial reports do not, and cannot, provide all of the information needed by providers of capital. Users of financial reports need to consider other pertinent information, such as general economic and political conditions, and industry and company outlooks. Moreover, general purpose financial reports are not designed to show the value of a reporting entity, but to provide information to allow users to estimate it for themselves. *[CF 1.6, 1.7]*.

General purpose financial reports are focused on meeting the needs of the maximum number of primary users, who may have different, and possibly conflicting, needs for information. However, this does not preclude a reporting entity from including additional information that is most useful to a particular subset of primary users. *[CF 1.8]*. It should be noted, however, that IAS 1 – *Presentation of Financial Statements* – contains the requirement that the understandability of financial statements should not be reduced by obscuring material information with immaterial information. *[IAS 1.30A]*. Management of an entity need not rely on general purpose financial reports, since the relevant information can be obtained internally. *[CF 1.9]*.

The IASB notes that, to a large extent, financial reports are based on estimates, judgements and models rather than exact depictions. The *Framework* establishes the concepts that underlie those estimates, judgements and models. The concepts should be seen as a goal which the IASB and preparers should strive towards, but are unlikely to achieve in full, at least in the short term, because it takes time to understand, accept and implement new ways of analysing transactions and other events. Nevertheless, the IASB believes that setting such a goal is essential if financial reporting is to evolve so as to improve its usefulness. *[CF 1.11]*.

4.2   Information about the economic resources of an entity and the use made of them, claims against the entity, and changes in resources and claims

General purpose financial reports provide information about:

- the financial position of a reporting entity (the economic resources of, and claims against, the entity) – see 4.2.1 below; and
- the effects of transactions and other events that change the economic resources of, and claims against, the entity – see 4.2 below.

Both types of information provide useful input for decisions about providing resources to an entity. *[CF 1.12]*.

4.2.1 Economic resources and claims

Information about the nature and amounts of a reporting entity's economic resources and claims can help users to:

- identify the entity's financial strengths and weaknesses;
- assess the entity's liquidity and solvency, its needs for additional financing and how successful it is likely to be in obtaining that financing; and
- assess management's stewardship of the entity's economic resources.

Information about the priorities and payment requirements of existing claims helps users to predict how future cash flows will be distributed among lenders and creditors. *[CF 1.13]*.

Different types of economic resources affect a user's assessment of the entity's prospects for future cash flows in different ways. Some future cash flows result directly from existing economic resources, such as accounts receivable. Other cash flows result from the entity using several resources in combination to produce and market goods or services to customers. Although those cash flows cannot be identified with individual economic resources (or claims), users need to know the nature and amount of the resources available for use in an entity's operations. *[CF 1.14]*.

4.2.2 Changes in economic resources and claims

Changes in a reporting entity's economic resources and claims result from that entity's financial performance and from other events or transactions such as issuing debt or equity instruments. In order to assess properly the prospects for future cash flows of the entity and management's stewardship of resources, users need to know the extent to which the reporting entity has increased its available economic resources, and thus its capacity for generating net cash inflows through its operations rather than by obtaining additional resources directly from providers of capital. *[CF 1.15, 1.18, 1.21]*.

Information about a reporting entity's financial performance helps users to understand the return that the entity has produced on its economic resources. Information about the return can help users to assess management's stewardship of the entity's economic resources. Information about the variability and components of that return is also important, especially in assessing the uncertainty of future cash flows. Information about a reporting entity's past financial performance and how its management discharged its stewardship responsibilities is usually helpful in predicting the entity's future returns on its economic resources. *[CF 1.16]*.

Financial performance is reflected by changes in the entity's economic resources and claims other than by obtaining additional resources directly from providers of capital. *[CF 1.15, 1.18]*. This is sometimes described as a 'balance sheet approach' to recording financial performance, whereby financial performance for a period is essentially derived as part of the overall movement in the entity's financial position during that period. This is discussed more explicitly in the section of the *Framework* dealing with the elements of financial statements (see 7 below).

Consistent with this 'balance sheet approach', financial performance is based on accrual accounting, which depicts the effects of transactions and other events and circumstances on a reporting entity's economic resources and claims in the periods in which those effects occur, even if the resulting cash receipts and payments occur in a different period. This provides a better basis for assessing the entity's past and future performance than information based solely on cash flows. *[CF 1.17]*.

Information about an entity's financial performance may also indicate the extent to which events such as changes in market prices or interest rates have changed the entity's economic resources and claims, thereby affecting the entity's ability to generate net cash inflows. *[CF 1.19]*. Nevertheless, information about an entity's cash flows during a period also helps users to assess the entity's ability to generate future net cash inflows, understand the entity's operations, evaluate its financing and investing activities, assess its liquidity or solvency, assess management stewardship and interpret other information about financial performance. *[CF 1.20]*.

4.2.3 Information about the use of economic resources (stewardship)

Management is responsible for the use of an entity's economic resources – for example, by protecting those resources from unfavourable effects of economic factors, such as price and technological changes, and ensuring that the entity complies with applicable laws, regulations and contractual provisions. *[CF 1.23]*.

Information about how efficiently and effectively the reporting entity's management has discharged its responsibilities to use the entity's economic resources helps users to assess management's stewardship of those resources. Such information is also useful for predicting how efficiently and effectively management will use the entity's economic resources in future periods. Hence, it can be useful for assessing the entity's prospects for future net cash inflows. *[CF 1.22]*.

5 CHAPTER 2: QUALITATIVE CHARACTERISTICS OF USEFUL FINANCIAL INFORMATION

The *Framework* states that the types of information likely to be most useful to providers of capital are identified by various qualitative characteristics, *[CF 2.1]*, comprising:

- two 'fundamental qualitative characteristics' (see 5.1 below):
  - relevance; and
  - faithful representation; *[CF 2.5]* supplemented by
- four 'enhancing qualitative characteristics' (see 5.2 below):
  - comparability;
  - verifiability;
  - timeliness; and
  - understandability. *[CF 2.23]*.

Chapter 3 of the *Framework* also notes the role of cost as a 'pervasive constraint' on a reporting entity's ability to provide useful financial information. *[CF 2.39]*. This is discussed further at 5.3 below.

The relationship between the objective, fundamental characteristics, enhancing characteristics and the pervasive cost constraint can be represented diagrammatically:

Figure 2.1   Components of the Conceptual Framework

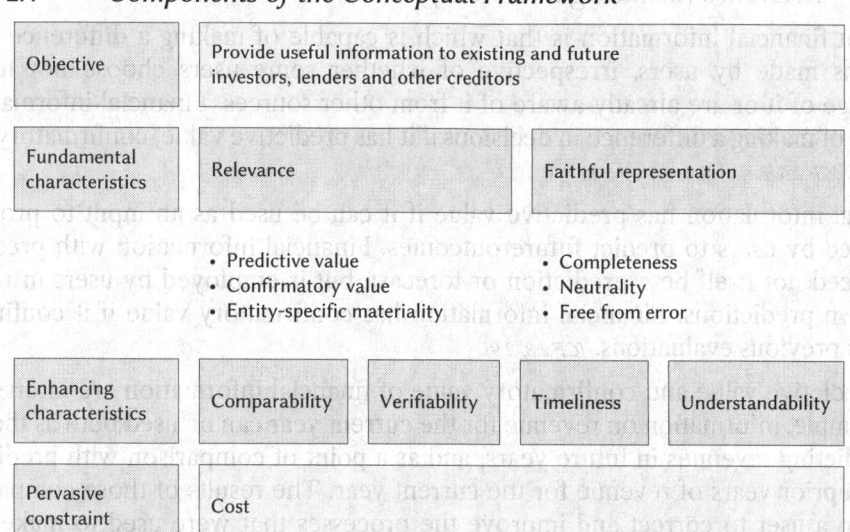

Monetary amounts in financial reports will not always be observed directly and must instead be estimated; in such cases measurement uncertainty arises. The use of reasonable estimates is an essential part of the preparation of financial information and does not undermine the usefulness of the information if the estimates are clearly and accurately described and explained. Even a high level of measurement uncertainty does not necessarily prevent such an estimate from providing useful information. This is discussed further at 5.1.3 below. *[CF 2.19]*.

Financial reports provide information about the reporting entity's economic resources, claims against the reporting entity and the effects of transactions and other events and conditions that change those resources and claims (collectively referred to in the *Framework* as 'the economic phenomena'). Some financial reports also include explanatory material about management's expectations and strategies for the reporting entity, and other types of forward-looking information. *[CF 2.2]*. The IASB's work on management reports is discussed at 12 below.

The qualitative characteristics of useful financial information apply to all financial information, whether provided in financial statements or in other ways. All financial information is also subject to a pervasive cost constraint on the reporting entity's ability to provide useful financial information. However, the considerations in applying the qualitative characteristics and the cost constraint may be different for different types of information. For example, applying them to forward-looking information may be different from applying them to information about existing economic resources and claims and to changes in those resources and claims. *[CF 2.3]*.

5.1   Fundamental qualitative characteristics

In order to be useful, financial information must be relevant (see 5.1.1 below) and faithfully represent what it purports to represent (see 5.1.2 below). *[CF 2.4]*.

5.1.1 Relevance (including materiality)

Relevant financial information is that which is capable of making a difference to the decisions made by users, irrespective of whether some users choose not to take advantage of it or are already aware of it from other sources. Financial information is capable of making a difference in decisions if it has predictive value, confirmatory value or both. *[CF 2.6, 2.7]*.

Financial information has predictive value if it can be used as an input to processes employed by users to predict future outcomes. Financial information with predictive value need not itself be a prediction or forecast, but is employed by users in making their own predictions. Financial information has confirmatory value if it confirms or changes previous evaluations. *[CF 2.8, 2.9]*.

The predictive value and confirmatory value of financial information are interrelated. For example, information on revenue for the current year can be used both as the basis for predicting revenues in future years, and as a point of comparison with predictions made in prior years of revenue for the current year. The results of those comparisons can help a user to correct and improve the processes that were used to make those previous predictions. *[CF 2.10]*.

The *Framework* refers to materiality as 'an entity-specific aspect of relevance based on the nature or magnitude, or both, of the items to which the information relates in the context of an individual entity's financial report'. In other words, information is material (and therefore relevant) if omitting it, misstating it, or obscuring it could reasonably be expected to influence the decisions of users of financial information about a specific reporting entity. Because of the specificity of materiality to a particular reporting entity, the IASB cannot specify a uniform quantitative threshold for materiality or predetermine what could be material in a particular situation. *[CF 2.11]*.

5.1.2 Faithful representation

The *Framework* observes that financial reports represent economic phenomena in words and numbers. To be useful, financial information must not only represent relevant phenomena, but it must also faithfully represent the substance of the phenomena that it purports to represent. In many circumstances, the substance of an economic phenomenon and its legal form are the same. If they are not the same, providing information only about the legal form would not faithfully represent the economic phenomenon (see 7.1.3 below). *[CF 2.12]*.

A perfectly faithful representation would be:
- complete,
- neutral, and
- free from error.

The IASB's objective is to maximise those qualities to the extent possible, while acknowledging that perfection is seldom, if ever, achievable. *[CF 2.13]*.

A complete depiction includes all information, including all necessary descriptions and explanations, necessary for a user to understand the phenomenon being depicted. For example, a complete depiction of a group of assets would include, at a minimum:

- a description of the nature of the assets;
- a numerical depiction of the assets; and
- a description of what the numerical depiction represents (for example, historical cost or fair value).

For some items, a complete depiction may also entail explanations of significant facts about the quality and nature of those items, factors and circumstances that might affect their quality and nature, and the process used to determine the numerical depiction. *[CF 2.14]*.

A neutral depiction is one without bias in the selection or presentation of financial information. A neutral depiction is not slanted, weighted, emphasised, de-emphasised or otherwise manipulated to increase the probability that financial information will be received favourably or unfavourably by users. That is not to imply that neutral information has no purpose or no influence on behaviour. On the contrary, relevant financial information is, by definition, capable of making a difference in users' decisions. *[CF 2.15]*.

The *Framework* has a discussion of the word 'prudence', the exercise of which is considered by the Board to support neutrality. The IASB considers prudence to be the exercise of caution when making judgements under conditions of uncertainty. This is said to mean that:

- assets and income are not overstated and liabilities and expenses are not understated; but also that
- the exercise of prudence does not allow for the understatement of assets or income or the overstatement of liabilities or expenses.

Such misstatements can lead to the overstatement or understatement of income or expenses in future periods. *[CF 2.16]*.

This is not, perhaps, a universally accepted view of the meaning of the word prudence – which to many may mean a more cautious approach to recognising gains and assets and a less cautious approach to recognising losses and liabilities.

The IASB addresses this by stating that the exercise of prudence does not imply a need for asymmetry, for example, a systematic need for more persuasive evidence to support the recognition of assets or income than the recognition of liabilities or expenses. Such asymmetry is not considered by the Board to be a qualitative characteristic of useful financial information. Nevertheless, particular standards may contain asymmetric requirements if this is a consequence of decisions intended to select the most relevant information that faithfully represents what it purports to represent. *[CF 2.17]*.

The *Framework* stresses that the term 'free from error' does not necessarily imply that information is accurate in all respects. Rather, information is 'free from error' if there are no errors or omissions either in the description of the economic phenomenon being depicted or in the selection or application of the process used to produce the reported information. For example, an estimate of an unobservable price or value cannot be determined to be accurate or inaccurate. However, a representation of that estimate can be faithful if the amount is described clearly and accurately as being an estimate, the nature and limitations of the estimating process are explained, and no errors have been made in selecting and applying an appropriate process for developing the estimate. *[CF 2.18]*.

5.1.3 Applying the fundamental qualitative characteristics

In order to be useful, information must be both relevant and provide a faithful representation. In the IASB's words 'neither a faithful representation of an irrelevant phenomenon nor an unfaithful representation of a relevant phenomenon helps users make good decisions'. *[CF 2.20]*.

The most efficient and effective process for applying the fundamental qualitative characteristics would, subject to the effects of the enhancing qualitative characteristics (see 5.2 below) and the cost constraint (see 5.3 below), usually be as follows:

- identify an economic phenomenon, information about which is capable of being useful to users of the reporting entity's financial information;
- identify the type of information about that phenomenon that would be most relevant; and
- determine whether that information is available and whether it can provide a faithful representation of the economic phenomenon.

If so, the process of satisfying the fundamental qualitative characteristics ends at that point. If not, the process is repeated with the next most relevant type of information. *[CF 2.21]*.

The *Framework* notes that, potentially, a trade-off between the fundamental qualitative characteristics may need to be made in order to meet the objective of financial reporting, which is to provide useful information about economic phenomena. This is illustrated by reference to estimation which, as noted at 5 above, is an essential part of the preparation of financial information and does not undermine the usefulness of it. The example given is where the most relevant information about a phenomenon may be a highly uncertain estimate. In some cases, the level of measurement uncertainty involved in making that estimate may be so high that it may be questionable whether the estimate would provide a sufficiently faithful representation of that phenomenon. In some such cases, the most useful information may be the highly uncertain estimate, accompanied by a description of the estimate and an explanation of the uncertainties that affect it. In other such cases, if that information would not provide a sufficiently faithful representation of that phenomenon, the most useful information may include an estimate of another type that is slightly less relevant but is subject to lower measurement uncertainty. In limited circumstances, there may be no estimate that provides useful information. In those limited circumstances, it may be necessary to provide information that does not rely on an estimate. *[CF 2.22]*.

5.2 Enhancing qualitative characteristics

The usefulness of relevant and faithfully represented financial information is enhanced by the characteristics of comparability (see 5.2.1 below), verifiability (see 5.2.2 below), timeliness (see 5.2.3 below) and understandability (see 5.2.4 below). These enhancing characteristics may also help determine which of two ways should be used to depict a phenomenon if both are considered equally relevant and faithfully represented. *[CF 2.4, 2.23]*.

5.2.1 Comparability

The IASB notes that decisions made by users of financial information involve choices between alternatives, such as selling or holding an investment, or investing in one entity or another. Consequently, information about a reporting entity is more useful if it can be compared with similar information about other entities, and about the same entity for another period or as at another date. *[CF 2.24]*.

Comparability is the qualitative characteristic that enables users to identify and understand similarities in, and differences among, items. Unlike the other qualitative characteristics, comparability does not relate to a single item, since – by definition – a comparison requires at least two items. The IASB clarifies that, for information to be comparable, like things must look alike and different things must look different, adding that 'comparability of financial information is not enhanced by making unlike things look alike any more than it is enhanced by making like things look different.' *[CF 2.25-2.27]*. Although a single economic phenomenon can be faithfully represented in more than one way, permitting alternative accounting methods for the same economic phenomenon diminishes comparability. *[CF 2.29]*.

The *Framework* stresses that consistency (that is, the use of the same methods for the same items, either from period to period within a reporting entity or in a single period across entities) helps to achieve comparability, but is not the same as comparability. The IASB adds that comparability is not the same as uniformity, but without any definition of 'uniformity' or clarification of how it differs from comparability. Some degree of comparability is likely to be attained simply by satisfying the fundamental qualitative characteristics. In other words, a faithful representation of a relevant economic phenomenon by one entity should naturally be comparable with a faithful representation of a similar relevant economic phenomenon by another entity. *[CF 2.26-2.28]*.

5.2.2 Verifiability

Verifiability helps assure users that information faithfully represents the economic phenomena that it purports to depict. Verifiability means that different knowledgeable and independent observers could reach a consensus, although not necessarily complete agreement, that a particular depiction is a faithful representation. Quantified information need not be a single point estimate to be verifiable. A range of possible amounts and their related probabilities can also be verified. *[CF 2.30]*.

The IASB notes that verification can be direct or indirect. Direct verification means verifying an amount or other representation through direct observation. Indirect verification means checking the inputs to a model, formula or other technique and recalculating the outputs using the same methodology. Some explanations and forward-looking financial information may not be verifiable until a future period, if at all. To help users decide whether to use such information, it would normally be necessary to disclose the assumptions, other factors and circumstances underlying the information, together with the methods of compiling the information. *[CF 2.31, 2.32]*.

5.2.3 Timeliness

Timeliness means that information is available to decision-makers in time to be capable of influencing their decisions. Generally, the older the information is the less useful it is. However, some information may continue to be timely long after the end of a reporting period, for example because some users may need to identify and assess trends. *[CF 2.33]*.

5.2.4 Understandability

Information is made understandable by classifying, characterising and presenting it clearly and concisely. *[CF 2.34]*. The IASB concedes that some phenomena are so inherently complex and difficult to understand that financial reports might be easier to understand if information about those phenomena were excluded. However, reports prepared without that information would be incomplete and therefore possibly misleading. Moreover, financial reports are prepared for users with a reasonable knowledge of business and economic activities who can review and analyse the information diligently. Even such users, however, may need to seek specialist advice in order to understand information about complex economic phenomena. *[CF 2.35, 2.36]*.

5.2.5 Applying the enhancing qualitative characteristics

The *Framework* stresses that, while the enhancing qualitative characteristics should be maximised to the extent possible, they cannot, either individually or as a group, make information useful if that information is irrelevant or does not give a faithful representation. *[CF 2.37]*.

Applying the enhancing qualitative characteristics is an iterative process that does not follow a prescribed order. Sometimes, one enhancing qualitative characteristic may have to be diminished in order to maximise another. For example, applying a new standard prospectively (that is, with no restatement of prior periods) will reduce comparability in the short term. However, that may be a price worth paying for improved relevance or faithful representation in the longer term. Appropriate disclosures may partially compensate for the lack of comparability. *[CF 2.38]*.

5.3 The cost constraint

The IASB acknowledges that cost is a pervasive constraint on the information provided by financial reporting, and that the cost of producing information must be justified by the benefits that it provides. Interestingly, the IASB argues that, while there is clearly an explicit cost to the preparers of financial information, the cost is ultimately borne by users, since any cost incurred by the reporting entity reduces the returns earned by users. In addition, users incur costs not only in analysing and interpreting any information that is provided, but also in obtaining or estimating any information that is not provided. *[CF 2.39, 2.40, 2.42]*.

Relevant and faithfully representative financial information helps users to make decisions with more confidence, resulting in a more efficient functioning of capital markets and a lower cost of capital for the economy as a whole. An individual provider of capital also receives benefits by making more informed decisions. However, it is not possible for general purpose financial reports to provide all information relevant to every user. *[CF 2.41]*.

In assessing whether the benefits of reporting particular information are likely to justify the cost, the IASB seeks information from providers of financial information, users, auditors, academics and others about the expected nature and quantity of the benefits and costs of that standard. In most situations, assessments are based on a combination of quantitative and qualitative information, and will normally be considered in relation to financial reporting generally, and not in relation to individual reporting entities. However, an assessment of costs and benefits will not always justify the same reporting requirements for all entities. Differences may be appropriate because of different sizes of entities, different ways of raising capital (publicly or privately), different needs of users or other factors. *[CF 2.42, 2.43]*.

6 CHAPTER 3: FINANCIAL STATEMENTS AND THE REPORTING ENTITY

Chapter 3 of the *Framework* deals with two questions:
- what are financial statements (discussed at 6.1 below); and
- what is the 'reporting entity' which prepares financial statements? (discussed at 6.2 below). *[CF 3.1, 3.10]*.

6.1 Financial statements

Financial statements provide information about economic resources of the reporting entity, claims against the entity, and changes in those resources and claims, that meet the definitions of the elements of financial statements (discussed at 7 below). *[CF 3.1]*.

6.1.1 Objective and scope of financial statements

The objective of financial statements is to provide financial information about the reporting entity's assets, liabilities, equity, income and expenses that is useful to users of financial statements in assessing the prospects for future net cash inflows to the reporting entity and in assessing management's stewardship of the entity's economic resources (discussed at 4 above). *[CF 1.1-1.2, 3.2]*.

That information is provided:
- in the statement of financial position, by recognising assets, liabilities and equity;
- in the statement(s) of financial performance, by recognising income and expenses; and
- in other statements and notes, by presenting and disclosing information about:
  - recognised assets, liabilities, equity, income and expenses, including information about their nature and about the risks arising from those recognised assets and liabilities;
  - assets and liabilities that have not been recognised, including information about their nature and about the risks arising from them;
  - cash flows;
  - contributions from holders of equity claims and distributions to them; and
  - the methods, assumptions and judgements used in estimating the amounts presented or disclosed, and changes in those methods, assumptions and judgements. *[CF 3.3]*.

The subject of presentation and disclosure is discussed at 10 below; recognition and derecognition is discussed at 8 below.

6.1.2 Reporting period and comparative information

Financial statements are prepared for a specified period of time (reporting period) and provide information about:
- assets and liabilities (including unrecognised assets and liabilities) and equity that existed at the end of the reporting period, or during the reporting period; and
- income and expenses for the reporting period. *[CF 3.4]*.

To help users of financial statements to identify and assess changes and trends, financial statements also provide comparative information for at least one preceding reporting period. *[CF 3.5]*.

Information about possible future transactions and other possible future events (forward-looking information) is included in financial statements if it:
- relates to the entity's assets or liabilities (including unrecognised assets or liabilities) or equity that existed at the end of the reporting period, or during the reporting period, or to income or expenses for the reporting period; and
- is useful to users of financial statements.

For example, if an asset or liability is measured by estimating future cash flows, information about those estimated future cash flows may help users of financial statements to understand the reported measures. Financial statements do not typically provide other types of forward-looking information, for example, explanatory material about management's expectations and strategies for the reporting entity. *[CF 3.6]*.

Financial statements include information about transactions and other events that have occurred after the end of the reporting period if providing that information is necessary to meet the objective of financial statements (see 4 above). *[CF 3.7]*.

6.1.3 Perspective adopted in financial statements

Financial statements provide information about transactions and other events viewed from the perspective of the reporting entity as a whole, not from the perspective of any particular group of the entity's existing or potential investors, lenders or other creditors. *[CF 3.8]*.

6.1.4 Going concern assumption

Financial statements are normally prepared on the assumption that the reporting entity is a going concern and will continue in operation for the foreseeable future. Hence, it is assumed that the entity has neither the intention nor the need to enter liquidation or to cease trading. If such an intention or need exists, the financial statements may have to be prepared on a different basis. If so, the financial statements describe the basis used. *[CF 3.9]*.

6.2 The reporting entity

A reporting entity is an entity that is required, or chooses, to prepare financial statements. A reporting entity can be a single entity or a portion of an entity or can comprise more than one entity. A reporting entity is not necessarily a legal entity. *[CF 3.10]*.

Sometimes one entity (parent) has control over another entity (subsidiary). If a reporting entity comprises both the parent and its subsidiaries, the reporting entity's financial statements are referred to as 'consolidated financial statements'. If a reporting entity is the parent alone, the reporting entity's financial statements are referred to as 'unconsolidated financial statements' (see 6.2.1 below). *[CF 3.11]*.

If a reporting entity comprises two or more entities that are not all linked by a parent-subsidiary relationship, the reporting entity's financial statements are referred to as 'combined financial statements'. *[CF 3.12]*.

Determining the appropriate boundary of a reporting entity can be difficult if the reporting entity:

- is not a legal entity; and
- does not comprise only legal entities linked by a parent-subsidiary relationship. *[CF 3.13]*.

In such cases, determining the boundary of the reporting entity is driven by the information needs of the primary users of the reporting entity's financial statements. Those users need relevant information that faithfully represents what it purports to represent. Faithful representation requires that:

- the boundary of the reporting entity does not contain an arbitrary or incomplete set of economic activities;
- including that set of economic activities within the boundary of the reporting entity results in neutral information; and
- a description is provided of how the boundary of the reporting entity was determined and of what constitutes the reporting entity. *[CF 3.14]*.

Without being explicit, this discussion in the *Framework* seems to confirm that combined financial statements can be said to comply with IFRS (subject, of course, to the matters in the bullets above and to compliance generally with IFRS for the 'combined' reporting entity).

The Basis for Conclusions, however, suggests a certain hesitancy by the Board. It articulates that the IASB is of the opinion that combined financial statements 'can provide useful information to users of financial statements in some circumstances' and for this reason the *Framework* 'acknowledges the concept of combined financial statements.'

This view is somewhat attenuated by the Board stating that the *Framework* 'does not discuss when or how entities could prepare combined financial statements' and that 'such discussion would be best developed if the Board decides in the future to develop a Standard on this topic'. *[CF BC3.21]*.

The *Framework* remains silent on a similar matter regarding what is frequently called 'carve-out' accounting. This is where a reporting entity is determined to be part of a legal entity. In our view, similar considerations should apply to financial statements prepared on this basis.

6.2.1 Consolidated and unconsolidated financial statements

Consolidated financial statements provide information about the assets, liabilities, equity, income and expenses of both the parent and its subsidiaries as a single reporting entity.

That information is useful for existing and potential investors, lenders and other creditors of the parent in their assessment of the prospects for future net cash inflows to the parent. This is because net cash inflows to the parent include distributions to the parent from its subsidiaries, and those distributions depend on net cash inflows to the subsidiaries. *[CF 3.15]*.

Consolidated financial statements are not designed to provide separate information about the assets, liabilities, equity, income and expenses of any particular subsidiary. A subsidiary's own financial statements are designed to provide that information. *[CF 3.16]*.

Unconsolidated financial statements are designed to provide information about the parent's assets, liabilities, equity, income and expenses, and not about those of its subsidiaries. That information can be useful to existing and potential investors, lenders and other creditors of the parent because:

- a claim against the parent typically does not give the holder of that claim a claim against subsidiaries; and
- in some jurisdictions, the amounts that can be legally distributed to holders of equity claims against the parent depend on the distributable reserves of the parent.

Another way to provide information about some or all assets, liabilities, equity, income and expenses of the parent alone is to present it in the notes to consolidated financial statements. *[CF 3.17]*.

Information provided in unconsolidated financial statements is typically not sufficient to meet the information needs of existing and potential investors, lenders and other creditors of the parent. Accordingly, when consolidated financial statements are required, unconsolidated financial statements cannot serve as a substitute for consolidated financial statements. Nevertheless, a parent may be required, or choose, to prepare unconsolidated financial statements in addition to consolidated financial statements. *[CF 3.18]*.

7 CHAPTER 4: THE ELEMENTS OF FINANCIAL STATEMENTS

As discussed at 4 above, it is the central tenet of the *Framework* that users of financial information require information concerning:

- the economic resources of and claims against an entity; and
- changes in those resources and claims.

These are described in the *Framework* as being linked to the 'elements' of financial statements which are: assets, liabilities, equity, income and expense.

They are analysed as follows. *[CF 4.1-4.4, 4.26, 4.63, 4.68, 4.69]*.

Economic resources are rights which have the potential to produce economic benefits.

Assets are present economic resources controlled by an entity as a result of past events (discussed at 7.2 below);

Claims against an entity comprise:

- *Liabilities*, which are present obligations to transfer economic resources as a result of past events (discussed at 7.3 below);
- *Equity* is the residual interest in the assets in an entity after deducting all its liabilities (discussed at 7.4 below).

Changes in economic resources and claims comprise:
- *Income* and *expenses* (discussed at 7.5 below); and
- *Other changes*.

Income is increases in assets, or decreases in liabilities, that result in increases in equity, other than those relating to contributions from holders of equity claims.

Expenses are decreases in assets, or increases in liabilities, that result in decreases in equity, other than those relating to distributions to holders of equity claims.

Other changes are:
- exchanges of assets or liabilities that do not result in increases or decreases in equity; and
- contributions from and distributions to holders of equity claims.

The recognition and derecognition of elements is discussed at 8 below. Measurement of the elements is discussed at 9 below and presentation at 10 below.

It is apparent that the approach to the elements of financial statements reflects what is sometimes described as a 'balance sheet approach' to recording financial performance, whereby financial performance for a period is essentially derived as part of the overall movement in the entity's financial position during that period. What this means is that all non-owner changes in equity comprise 'performance' in its broadest sense. A difficulty for the Board in developing the *Framework* is that there is in financial reporting a well-established idea of profit (and hence, a profit and loss account) which contains only a subset of all such performance. The provisions of the *Framework* in this regard are discussed at 10.2.3 below.

7.1 Matters concerning both assets and liabilities

The *Framework* discusses three concepts which will apply both to assets and liabilities and are relevant for accounting purposes. These are: unit of account, executory contracts and the substance of arrangements. These are discussed in turn below.

7.1.1 Unit of account

The unit of account is the right or the group of rights, the obligation or the group of obligations, or the group of rights and obligations, to which recognition criteria and measurement concepts are applied. *[CF 4.48]*.

A unit of account is selected for an asset or liability when considering how recognition criteria and measurement concepts will apply to that asset or liability and to the related income and expenses. In some circumstances, it may be appropriate to select one unit of account for recognition and a different unit of account for measurement. For example, contracts may sometimes be recognised individually but measured as part of a portfolio of contracts. For presentation and disclosure, assets, liabilities, income and expenses may need to be aggregated or separated into components. *[CF 4.49]*.

If an entity transfers part of an asset or part of a liability, the unit of account may change at that time, so that the transferred component and the retained component become separate units of account (derecognition is discussed at 8.3 below). *[CF 4.50]*.

A unit of account is selected to provide useful information, which implies that:
- the information provided about the asset or liability and about any related income and expenses must be relevant. Treating a group of rights and obligations as a single unit of account may provide more relevant information than treating each right or obligation as a separate unit of account if, for example, those rights and obligations:
  - cannot be or are unlikely to be the subject of separate transactions;
  - cannot or are unlikely to expire in different patterns;
  - have similar economic characteristics and risks and hence are likely to have similar implications for the prospects for future net cash inflows to the entity or net cash outflows from the entity; or
  - are used together in the business activities conducted by an entity to produce cash flows and are measured by reference to estimates of their interdependent future cash flows;
- the information provided about the asset or liability and about any related income and expenses must faithfully represent the substance of the transaction or other event from which they have arisen. Therefore, it may be necessary to treat rights or obligations arising from different sources as a single unit of account, or to separate the rights or obligations arising from a single source. Equally, to provide a faithful representation of unrelated rights and obligations, it may be necessary to recognise and measure them separately. *[CF 4.51]*.

Also relevant here is the discussion in the *Framework* of the substance of rights and obligations – see 7.1.3 below.

Just as cost constrains other financial reporting decisions, it also constrains the selection of a unit of account. Hence, in selecting a unit of account, it is important to consider whether the benefits of the information provided to users of financial statements by selecting that unit of account are likely to justify the costs of providing and using that information. In general, the costs associated with recognising and measuring assets, liabilities, income and expenses increase as the size of the unit of account decreases. Hence, in general, rights or obligations arising from the same source are separated only if the resulting information is more useful and the benefits outweigh the costs. *[CF 4.52]*.

Sometimes, both rights and obligations arise from the same source. For example, some contracts establish both rights and obligations for each of the parties. If those rights and obligations are interdependent and cannot be separated, they constitute a single inseparable asset or liability and hence form a single unit of account. For example, this is the case with executory contracts (see 7.1.2 below). Conversely, if rights are separable from obligations, it may sometimes be appropriate to group the rights separately from the obligations, resulting in the identification of one or more separate assets and liabilities. In other cases, it may be more appropriate to group separable rights and obligations in a single unit of account treating them as a single asset or a single liability. *[CF 4.53]*.

Treating a set of rights and obligations as a single unit of account differs from offsetting assets and liabilities (see 10.2.1.A below). *[CF 4.54]*.

Possible units of account include:
- an individual right or individual obligation;
- all rights, all obligations, or all rights and all obligations, arising from a single source, for example, a contract;
- a subgroup of those rights or obligations, or both, for example, a subgroup of rights over an item of property, plant and equipment for which the useful life and pattern of consumption differ from those of the other rights over that item;
- a group of rights or obligations, or both, arising from a portfolio of similar items;
- a group of rights or obligations, or both, arising from a portfolio of dissimilar items (for example, a portfolio of assets and liabilities to be disposed of in a single transaction); and
- a risk exposure within a portfolio of items; if a portfolio of items is subject to a common risk, some aspects of the accounting for that portfolio could focus on the aggregate exposure to that risk within the portfolio. *[CF 4.55]*

7.1.2 Executory contracts

An executory contract is a contract, or a portion of a contract, that is equally unperformed. That is, either: neither party has fulfilled any of its obligations, or both parties have partially fulfilled their obligations to an equal extent. *[CF 4.56]*

An executory contract establishes a combined right and obligation to exchange economic resources. The right and obligation are interdependent and cannot be separated. Hence, the combined right and obligation constitute a single asset or liability. The entity has an asset if the terms of the exchange are currently favourable; it has a liability if the terms of the exchange are currently unfavourable. Whether such an asset or liability is included in the financial statements depends on both the recognition criteria (see 8 below) and the measurement basis (see 9 below) selected for the asset or liability, including, if applicable, any test for whether the contract is onerous. *[CF 4.57]*

To the extent that either party fulfils its obligations under the contract, the contract is no longer executory. If the reporting entity performs first under the contract, that performance is the event that changes the reporting entity's right and obligation to exchange economic resources into a right to receive an economic resource. That right is an asset. If the other party performs first, that performance is the event that changes the reporting entity's right and obligation to exchange economic resources into an obligation to transfer an economic resource. That obligation is a liability. *[CF 4.58]*

7.1.3 Substance of contractual rights and contractual obligations

The terms of a contract create rights and obligations for an entity that is a party to that contract. To represent those rights and obligations faithfully (discussed at 5.1.2 above), financial statements report their substance. In some cases, the substance of the rights and obligations is clear from the legal form of the contract. In other cases, the terms of the contract or a group or series of contracts require analysis to identify the substance of the rights and obligations. *[CF 4.59]*

All terms in a contract, whether explicit or implicit, are considered unless they have no substance. Implicit terms could include, for example, obligations imposed by statute, such as statutory warranty obligations imposed on entities that enter into contracts to sell goods to customers. *[CF 4.60]*.

Terms that have no substance are disregarded. A term has no substance if it has no discernible effect on the economics of the contract. Terms that have no substance could include, for example:

- terms that bind neither party; or
- rights, including options, that the holder will not have the practical ability to exercise in any circumstances. *[CF 4.61]*.

A group or series of contracts may achieve or be designed to achieve an overall commercial effect. To report the substance of such contracts, it may be necessary to treat rights and obligations arising from that group or series of contracts as a single unit of account. For example, if the rights or obligations in one contract merely nullify all the rights or obligations in another contract entered into at the same time with the same counterparty, the combined effect is that the two contracts create no rights or obligations. Conversely, if a single contract creates two or more sets of rights or obligations that could have been created through two or more separate contracts, an entity may need to account for each set as if it arose from separate contracts in order to represent faithfully the rights and obligations (see the discussion of unit of account at 7.1.1 above). *[CF 4.62]*.

7.2 Definition of assets

As noted at 7 above, the definition of an asset is an economic resource subject to three criteria: it is a right of the entity; it has the potential to produce economic benefits; and it is controlled by the entity. Each is discussed in turn in the following sections. *[CF 4.5]*.

7.2.1 Rights

It is observed that rights that have the potential to produce economic benefits take many forms, including:

- rights that correspond to an obligation of another party (see 7.3.2 below), for example, rights to:
  - receive cash;
  - receive goods or services;
  - exchange economic resources with another party on favourable terms. Such rights include, for example, a forward contract to buy an economic resource on terms that are currently favourable or an option to buy an economic resource; and
  - benefit from an obligation of another party to transfer an economic resource if a specified uncertain future event occurs;
- rights that do not correspond to an obligation of another party, for example, rights:
  - over physical objects, such as property, plant and equipment or inventories. Examples of such rights are a right to use a physical object or a right to benefit from the residual value of a leased object; and
  - to use intellectual property. *[CF 4.6]*.

Many rights are established by contract, legislation or similar means. For example, an entity might obtain rights from owning or leasing a physical object, from owning a debt instrument or an equity instrument, or from owning a registered patent. However, an entity might also obtain rights in other ways, for example:

- by acquiring or creating know-how that is not in the public domain (see discussion of control at 7.2.3 below); or
- through an obligation of another party that arises because that other party has no practical ability to act in a manner inconsistent with its customary practices, published policies or specific statements – that is, a constructive obligation discussed at 7.3.1 below. *[CF 4.7]*.

Some goods or services, for example, employee services, are received and immediately consumed. An entity's right to obtain the economic benefits produced by such goods or services exists momentarily until the entity consumes the goods or services. *[CF 4.8]*.

Not all of an entity's rights are assets of that entity; to be assets the rights must also satisfy the other two criteria noted above (the potential to produce economic benefits, discussed at 7.2.2 below; and, control, discussed at 7.2.3 below). For example, rights available to all parties without significant cost – for instance, rights of access to public goods, such as public rights of way over land, or know-how that is in the public domain – are typically not assets for the entities that hold them. *[CF 4.9]*.

An entity cannot have a right to obtain economic benefits from itself. Accordingly:

- debt instruments or equity instruments issued by the entity and repurchased and held by it (for example, treasury shares) are not economic resources of that entity; and
- if a reporting entity comprises more than one legal entity, debt instruments or equity instruments issued by one of those legal entities and held by another of those legal entities are not economic resources of the reporting entity. *[CF 4.10]*.

In principle, each of an entity's rights is a separate asset. However, for accounting purposes, related rights are often treated as a single unit of account that is a single asset (unit of account is discussed at 7.1.1 above). For example, legal ownership of a physical object may give rise to several rights, including:

- the right to use the object;
- the right to sell rights over the object;
- the right to pledge rights over the object; and
- other rights. *[CF 4.11]*.

In many cases, the set of rights arising from legal ownership of a physical object is accounted for as a single asset. Conceptually, the economic resource is the set of rights, not the physical object. Nevertheless, describing the set of rights as the physical object will often provide a faithful representation of those rights in the most concise and understandable way. *[CF 4.12]*.

In some cases, it is uncertain whether a right exists. For example, an entity and another party might dispute whether the entity has a right to receive an economic resource from that other party. Until that existence uncertainty is resolved, for example, by a court ruling, it is uncertain whether the entity has a right and, consequently, whether an asset exists (see 8.2.1.A below). *[CF 4.13]*.

7.2.2 Potential to produce economic benefits

An economic resource is a right that has the potential to produce economic benefits. For that potential to exist, it does not need to be certain, or even likely, that the right will produce economic benefits. It is only necessary that the right already exists and that, in at least one circumstance, it would produce for the entity economic benefits beyond those available to all other parties. *[CF 4.14]*.

A right can meet the definition of an economic resource, and hence can be an asset, even if the probability that it will produce economic benefits is low. Nevertheless, that low probability might affect decisions about what information to provide about the asset and how to provide that information, including decisions about whether the asset is recognised (see 8.2.1.B below) and how it is measured (see 9 below). *[CF 4.15]*.

An economic resource could produce economic benefits for an entity by entitling or enabling it to do, for example, one or more of the following:

- receive contractual cash flows or another economic resource;
- exchange economic resources with another party on favourable terms;
- produce cash inflows or avoid cash outflows by, for example:
  - using the economic resource either individually or in combination with other economic resources to produce goods or provide services;
  - using the economic resource to enhance the value of other economic resources; or
  - leasing the economic resource to another party;
- receive cash or other economic resources by selling the economic resource; or
- extinguish liabilities by transferring the economic resource. *[CF 4.16]*.

Although an economic resource derives its value from its present potential to produce future economic benefits, the economic resource is the present right that contains that potential, not the future economic benefits that the right may produce. For example, a purchased option derives its value from its potential to produce economic benefits through exercise of the option at a future date. However, the economic resource is the present right, that is the right to exercise the option at a future date. The economic resource is not the future economic benefits that the holder will receive if the option is exercised. *[CF 4.17]*.

There is a close association between incurring expenditure and acquiring assets, but the two do not necessarily coincide. Hence, when an entity incurs expenditure, this may provide evidence that the entity has sought future economic benefits, but does not provide conclusive proof that the entity has obtained an asset. Similarly, the absence of related expenditure does not preclude an item from meeting the definition of an asset. Assets can include, for example, rights that a government has granted to the entity free of charge or that another party has donated to the entity. *[CF 4.18]*.

7.2.3 Control

Control links an economic resource to an entity. Assessing whether control exists helps to identify the economic resource for which the entity accounts. For example, an entity may control a proportionate share in a property without controlling the rights arising from ownership of the entire property. In such cases, the entity's asset is the share in the property, which it controls, not the rights arising from ownership of the entire property, which it does not control. *[CF 4.19]*.

An entity controls an economic resource if it has the present ability to direct the use of the economic resource and obtain the economic benefits that may flow from it. Control includes the present ability to prevent other parties from directing the use of the economic resource and from obtaining the economic benefits that may flow from it. It follows that, if one party controls an economic resource, no other party controls that resource. *[CF 4.20]*.

An entity has the present ability to direct the use of an economic resource if it has the right to deploy that economic resource in its activities, or to allow another party to deploy the economic resource in that other party's activities. *[CF 4.21]*.

Control of an economic resource usually arises from an ability to enforce legal rights. However, control can also arise if an entity has other means of ensuring that it, and no other party, has the present ability to direct the use of the economic resource and obtain the benefits that may flow from it. For example, an entity could control a right to use know-how that is not in the public domain if the entity has access to the know-how and the present ability to keep the know-how secret, even if that know-how is not protected by a registered patent. *[CF 4.22]*.

For an entity to control an economic resource, the future economic benefits from that resource must flow to the entity either directly or indirectly rather than to another party. This aspect of control does not imply that the entity can ensure that the resource will produce economic benefits in all circumstances. Instead, it means that if the resource produces economic benefits, the entity is the party that will obtain them either directly or indirectly. *[CF 4.23]*.

Having exposure to significant variations in the amount of the economic benefits produced by an economic resource may indicate that the entity controls the resource. However, it is only one factor to consider in the overall assessment of whether control exists. *[CF 4.24]*.

Sometimes one party (a principal) engages another party (an agent) to act on behalf of, and for the benefit of, the principal. For example, a principal may engage an agent to arrange sales of goods controlled by the principal. If an agent has custody of an economic resource controlled by the principal, that economic resource is not an asset of the agent. Furthermore, if the agent has an obligation to transfer to a third party an economic resource controlled by the principal, that obligation is not a liability of the agent, because the economic resource that would be transferred is the principal's economic resource, not the agent's. *[CF 4.25]*.

7.3 Definition of liabilities

As noted at 7 above, the *Framework* defines a liability as a present obligation of the entity to transfer an economic resource as a result of past events. *[CF 4.2, 4.26]*.

For a liability to exist, three criteria must all be satisfied:
- the entity has an obligation;
- the obligation is to transfer an economic resource; and
- the obligation is a present obligation that exists as a result of past events. *[CF 4.27]*.

These criteria are discussed in turn below.

7.3.1 Obligation

The first criterion for a liability is that the entity has an obligation. An obligation is a duty or responsibility that an entity has no practical ability to avoid. An obligation is always owed to another party (or parties). The other party (or parties) could be a person or another entity, a group of people or other entities, or society at large. It is not necessary to know the identity of the party (or parties) to whom the obligation is owed. *[CF 4.28, 29]*.

If one party has an obligation to transfer an economic resource, it follows that another party (or parties) has a right to receive that economic resource. However, a requirement for one party to recognise a liability and measure it at a specified amount does not imply that the other party (or parties) must recognise an asset or measure it at the same amount. For example, particular standards may contain different recognition criteria or measurement requirements for the liability of one party and the corresponding asset of the other party (or parties) if those different criteria or requirements are a consequence of decisions intended to select the most relevant information that faithfully represents what it purports to represent. *[CF 4.30]*.

Many obligations are established by contract, legislation or similar means and are legally enforceable by the party (or parties) to whom they are owed. Obligations can also arise, however, from an entity's customary practices, published policies or specific statements if the entity has no practical ability to act in a manner inconsistent with those practices, policies or statements. The obligation that arises in such situations is sometimes referred to as a 'constructive obligation'. *[CF 4.31]*.

In some situations, an entity's duty or responsibility to transfer an economic resource is conditional on a particular future action that the entity itself may take. Such actions could include operating a particular business or operating in a particular market on a specified future date, or exercising particular options within a contract. In such situations, the entity has an obligation if it has no practical ability to avoid taking that action. *[CF 4.32]*.

A conclusion that it is appropriate to prepare an entity's financial statements on a going concern basis also implies a conclusion that the entity has no practical ability to avoid a transfer that could be avoided only by liquidating the entity or by ceasing to trade. *[CF 4.33]*.

The factors used to assess whether an entity has the practical ability to avoid transferring an economic resource may depend on the nature of the entity's duty or responsibility. For example, in some cases, an entity may have no practical ability to avoid a transfer if any action that it could take to avoid the transfer would have economic consequences significantly more adverse than the transfer itself. However, neither an intention to make a transfer, nor a high likelihood of a transfer, is sufficient reason for concluding that the entity has no practical ability to avoid a transfer. *[CF 4.34]*.

In some cases, it is uncertain whether an obligation exists. For example, if another party is seeking compensation for an entity's alleged act of wrongdoing, it might be uncertain whether the act occurred, whether the entity committed it or how the law applies. Until that existence uncertainty is resolved, for example, by a court ruling, it is uncertain whether the entity has an obligation to the party seeking compensation and, consequently, whether a liability exists (see 8.2.1.A below). *[CF 4.35]*.

7.3.2 Transfer an economic resource

The second criterion for a liability is that the obligation is to transfer an economic resource. To satisfy this criterion, the obligation must have the potential to require the entity to transfer an economic resource to another party (or parties). For that potential to exist, it does not need to be certain, or even likely, that the entity will be required to transfer an economic resource; the transfer may, for example, be required only if a specified uncertain future event occurs. It is only necessary that the obligation already exists and that, in at least one circumstance, it would require the entity to transfer an economic resource. *[CF 4.36, 37]*.

An obligation can meet the definition of a liability even if the probability of a transfer of an economic resource is low. Nevertheless, that low probability might affect decisions about what information to provide about the liability and how to provide that information, including decisions about whether the liability is recognised (see 8.2.1.B below) and how it is measured (discussed at 9 below). *[CF 4.38]*.

Obligations to transfer an economic resource include, for example, obligations to:
- pay cash;
- deliver goods or provide services;
- exchange economic resources with another party on unfavourable terms. Such obligations include, for example, a forward contract to sell an economic resource on terms that are currently unfavourable or an option that entitles another party to buy an economic resource from the entity;
- transfer an economic resource if a specified uncertain future event occurs; and
- issue a financial instrument if that financial instrument will oblige the entity to transfer an economic resource. *[CF 4.39]*.

Instead of fulfilling an obligation to transfer an economic resource to the party that has a right to receive that resource, entities sometimes decide to, for example:
- settle the obligation by negotiating a release from the obligation;
- transfer the obligation to a third party; or
- replace that obligation to transfer an economic resource with another obligation by entering into a new transaction.

    In these situations, an entity has the obligation to transfer an economic resource until it has settled, transferred or replaced that obligation. *[CF 4.40, 4.41]*.

7.3.3 Present obligation existing as a result of past events

The third criterion for a liability is that the obligation is a present obligation that exists as a result of past events. That is:

- the entity has already obtained economic benefits or taken an action; and
- as a consequence, the entity will or may have to transfer an economic resource that it would not otherwise have had to transfer. [CF 4.42, 43].

The economic benefits obtained could include, for example, goods or services. The action taken could include, for example, operating a particular business or operating in a particular market. If economic benefits are obtained, or an action is taken, over time, the resulting present obligation may accumulate over that time. [CF 4.44].

If new legislation is enacted, a present obligation arises only when, as a consequence of obtaining economic benefits or taking an action to which that legislation applies, an entity will or may have to transfer an economic resource that it would not otherwise have had to transfer. The enactment of legislation is not in itself sufficient to give an entity a present obligation. Similarly, an entity's customary practice, published policy or specific statement of the type mentioned at 7.3.1 above gives rise to a present obligation only when, as a consequence of obtaining economic benefits, or taking an action, to which that practice, policy or statement applies, the entity will or may have to transfer an economic resource that it would not otherwise have had to transfer. [CF 4.45].

A present obligation can exist even if a transfer of economic resources cannot be enforced until some point in the future. For example, a contractual liability to pay cash may exist now even if the contract does not require a payment until a future date. Similarly, a contractual obligation for an entity to perform work at a future date may exist now even if the counterparty cannot require the entity to perform the work until that future date. [CF 4.46].

An entity does not yet have a present obligation to transfer an economic resource if it has not yet obtained economic benefits, or taken an action, that would or could require the entity to transfer an economic resource that it would not otherwise have had to transfer. For example, if an entity has entered into a contract to pay an employee a salary in exchange for receiving the employee's services, the entity does not have a present obligation to pay the salary until it has received the employee's services. Before then the contract is executory; the entity has a combined right and obligation to exchange future salary for future employee services (executory contracts are discussed at 7.1.2 above). [CF 4.47].

7.4 Definition of equity

As noted as 7 above, equity is the residual interest in the assets of the entity after deducting all its liabilities; accordingly, equity claims are claims on this residual interest. Put another way, equity claims are claims against the entity that do not meet the definition of a liability. Such claims may be established by contract, legislation or similar means, and include, to the extent that they do not meet the definition of a liability:

- shares of various types, issued by the entity; and
- some obligations of the entity to issue another equity claim. [CF 4.63, 64].

Different classes of equity claims, such as ordinary shares and preference shares, may confer on their holders different rights, for example, rights to receive some or all of the following from the entity:

- dividends, if the entity decides to pay dividends to eligible holders;
- the proceeds from satisfying the equity claims, either in full on liquidation, or in part at other times; or
- other equity claims. *[CF 4.65]*.

Sometimes, legal, regulatory or other requirements affect particular components of equity, such as share capital or retained earnings. For example, some such requirements permit an entity to make distributions to holders of equity claims only if the entity has sufficient reserves that those requirements specify as being distributable. *[CF 4.66]*.

Business activities are often undertaken by entities such as sole proprietorships, partnerships, trusts or various types of government business undertakings. The legal and regulatory frameworks for such entities are often different from frameworks that apply to corporate entities. For example, there may be few, if any, restrictions on the distribution to holders of equity claims against such entities. Nevertheless, the *Framework* makes clear that the definition of equity applies to all reporting entities. *[CF 4.67]*.

7.5 Definition of income and expenses

Income and expenses are the elements of financial statements that relate to an entity's financial performance. Users of financial statements need information about both an entity's financial position and its financial performance. Hence, although income and expenses are defined in terms of changes in assets and liabilities, information about income and expenses is just as important as information about assets and liabilities. *[CF 4.71]*.

Those terms are defined as follows:

- income is increases in assets, or decreases in liabilities, that result in increases in equity, other than those relating to contributions from holders of equity claims;
- expenses are decreases in assets, or increases in liabilities, that result in decreases in equity, other than those relating to distributions to holders of equity claims;

A consequence of these definitions is that:

- contributions from holders of equity claims are not income; and
- distributions to holders of equity claims are not expenses. *[CF 4.68-70]*.

Different transactions and other events generate income and expenses with different characteristics. Providing information separately about income and expenses with different characteristics can help users of financial statements to understand the entity's financial performance (see 10.2.3.A below). *[CF 4.72]*.

8 CHAPTER 5: RECOGNITION AND DERECOGNITION

Recognition is described in the *Framework* as the process of capturing for inclusion in the statement of financial position or the statement(s) of financial performance an item that meets the definition of one of the elements of financial statements (that is, an asset, a liability, equity, income or expenses).

8.1 The recognition process

Recognition involves depicting the item in one of those statements (either alone or in aggregation with other items) in words and by a monetary amount, and including that amount in one or more totals in that statement. The amount at which an asset, a liability or equity is recognised in the statement of financial position is referred to as its 'carrying amount'. [CF 5.1].

The statement of financial position and statement(s) of financial performance depict an entity's recognised assets, liabilities, equity, income and expenses in structured summaries that are designed to make financial information comparable and understandable. An important feature of the structures of those summaries is that the amounts recognised in a statement are included in the totals and, if applicable, subtotals that link the items recognised in the statement. [CF 5.2].

Recognition links the elements, the statement of financial position and the statement(s) of financial performance as follows:

- in the statement of financial position at the beginning and end of the reporting period, total assets minus total liabilities equal total equity; and
- recognised changes in equity during the reporting period comprise:
  - income minus expenses recognised in the statement(s) of financial performance; plus
  - contributions from holders of equity claims, minus distributions to holders of equity claims. [CF 5.3].

This is illustrated diagrammatically in Figure 2.2 below.

Figure 2.2 How recognition links the elements of financial statements

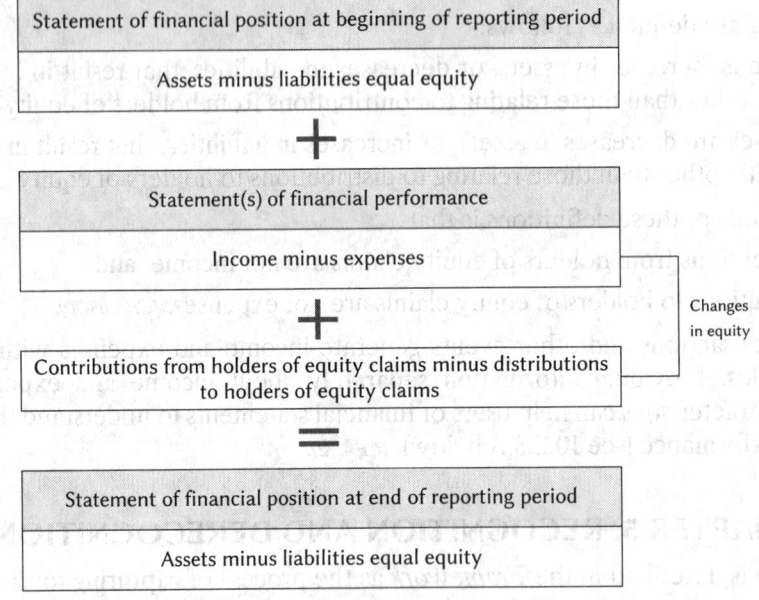

The statements of financial position and performance are linked because the recognition of one item (or a change in its carrying amount) requires the recognition or derecognition of one or more other items (or changes in the carrying amount of one or more other items). This is the familiar concept of 'double-entry' and the *Framework* provides the following description:

- the recognition of income occurs at the same time as:
  - the initial recognition of an asset, or an increase in the carrying amount of an asset; or
  - the derecognition of a liability, or a decrease in the carrying amount of a liability;
- the recognition of expenses occurs at the same time as:
  - the initial recognition of a liability, or an increase in the carrying amount of a liability; or
  - the derecognition of an asset, or a decrease in the carrying amount of an asset.

[CF 5.4].

The initial recognition of assets or liabilities arising from transactions or other events may result in the simultaneous recognition of both income and related expenses. For example, the sale of goods for cash results in the recognition of both income (from the recognition of one asset, being the cash) and an expense (from the derecognition of another asset, being the goods sold). The simultaneous recognition of income and related expenses is sometimes referred to as the matching of costs with income. Application of the concepts in the *Framework* leads to such matching when it arises from the recognition of changes in assets and liabilities. However, matching of costs with income is not an objective of the *Framework*. The *Framework* does not allow the recognition in the statement of financial position of items that do not meet the definition of an asset, a liability or equity. [CF 5.5].

8.2 Recognition criteria

Only items that meet the definition of an asset, a liability or equity are recognised in the statement of financial position. Similarly, only items that meet the definition of income or expenses are recognised in the statement(s) of financial performance. However, not all items that meet the definition of one of those elements are recognised. [CF 5.6].

Not recognising an item that meets the definition of one of the elements makes the statement of financial position and the statement(s) of financial performance less complete and can exclude useful information from financial statements. On the other hand, in some circumstances, recognising some items that meet the definition of one of the elements would not provide useful information. An asset or liability is recognised only if recognition of that asset or liability and of any resulting income, expenses or changes in equity provides users of financial statements with information that is useful; that is, with:

- relevant information about the asset or liability and about any resulting income, expenses or changes in equity (see 8.2.1 below); and
- a faithful representation of the asset or liability and of any resulting income, expenses or changes in equity (see 8.2.2 below). [CF 5.7].

Just as cost constrains other financial reporting decisions, it also constrains recognition decisions. There is a cost to recognising an asset or liability. Preparers of financial statements incur costs in obtaining a relevant measure of an asset or liability. Users of financial statements also incur costs in analysing and interpreting the information provided. An asset or liability is recognised if the benefits of the information provided to users of financial statements by recognition are likely to justify the costs of providing and using that information. In some cases, the costs of recognition may outweigh its benefits. *[CF 5.8]*.

It is not possible to define precisely when recognition of an asset or liability will provide useful information to users of financial statements, at a cost that does not outweigh its benefits. What is useful to users depends on the item and the facts and circumstances. Consequently, judgement is required when deciding whether to recognise an item, and thus recognition requirements may need to vary between and within standards. *[CF 5.9]*.

It is important when making decisions about recognition to consider the information that would be given if an asset or liability were not recognised. For example, if no asset is recognised when expenditure is incurred, an expense is recognised. Over time, recognising the expense may, in some cases, provide useful information, for example, information that enables users of financial statements to identify trends. *[CF 5.10]*.

Even if an item meeting the definition of an asset or liability is not recognised, an entity may need to provide information about that item in the notes. It is important to consider how to make such information sufficiently visible to compensate for the item's absence from the structured summary provided by the statement of financial position and, if applicable, the statement(s) of financial performance. *[CF 5.11]*.

8.2.1 Relevance

Information about assets, liabilities, equity, income and expenses is relevant to users of financial statements. However, recognition of a particular asset or liability and any resulting income, expenses or changes in equity may not always provide relevant information. That may be the case if, for example:

- it is uncertain whether an asset or liability exists (see 8.2.1.A below); or
- an asset or liability exists, but the probability of an inflow or outflow of economic benefits is low (see 8.2.1.B below). *[CF 5.12]*.

The presence of one or both of the factors described above does not lead automatically to a conclusion that the information provided by recognition lacks relevance. Moreover, factors other than these may also affect the conclusion. It may be a combination of factors and not any single factor that determines whether recognition provides relevant information. *[CF 5.13]*.

8.2.1.A Existence uncertainty

Sometimes it is uncertain whether an asset or liability exists. In some cases, that uncertainty, possibly combined with a low probability of inflows or outflows of economic benefits and an exceptionally wide range of possible outcomes, may mean that the recognition of an asset or liability, necessarily measured at a single amount, would not provide relevant information. Whether or not the asset or liability is recognised, explanatory information about the uncertainties associated with it may need to be provided in the financial statements. *[CF 5.14]*.

8.2.1.B   Low probability of an inflow or outflow of economic benefits

An asset or liability can exist even if the probability of an inflow or outflow of economic benefits is low (see 7.2.2 and 7.3.2 above). *[CF 5.15]*.

If the probability of an inflow or outflow of economic benefits is low, the most relevant information about the asset or liability may be information about the magnitude of the possible inflows or outflows, their possible timing and the factors affecting the probability of their occurrence. The typical location for such information is in the notes. *[CF 5.16]*.

Even if the probability of an inflow or outflow of economic benefits is low, recognition of the asset or liability may provide relevant information beyond the information described above. Whether that is the case may depend on a variety of factors. For example:

- if an asset is acquired or a liability is incurred in an exchange transaction on market terms, its cost generally reflects the probability of an inflow or outflow of economic benefits. Thus, that cost may be relevant information, and is generally readily available. Furthermore, not recognising the asset or liability would result in the recognition of expenses or income at the time of the exchange, which might not be a faithful representation of the transaction (see 8.2.2.B below);
- if an asset or liability arises from an event that is not an exchange transaction, recognition of the asset or liability typically results in recognition of income or expenses. If there is only a low probability that the asset or liability will result in an inflow or outflow of economic benefits, users of financial statements might not regard the recognition of the asset and income, or the liability and expenses, as providing relevant information. *[CF 5.17]*.

8.2.2   Faithful representation

Recognition of a particular asset or liability is appropriate if it provides not only relevant information, but also a faithful representation of that asset or liability and of any resulting income, expenses or changes in equity. Whether a faithful representation can be provided may be affected by the level of measurement uncertainty associated with the asset or liability or by other factors. *[CF 5.18]*.

8.2.2.A   Measurement uncertainty

For an asset or liability to be recognised, it must be measured. In many cases, such measures must be estimated and are therefore subject to measurement uncertainty. As noted at 5.1.2 above, the use of reasonable estimates is an essential part of the preparation of financial information and does not undermine the usefulness of the information if the estimates are clearly and accurately described and explained. Even a high level of measurement uncertainty does not necessarily prevent such an estimate from providing useful information. *[CF 5.19]*.

In some cases, the level of uncertainty involved in estimating a measure of an asset or liability may be so high that it may be questionable whether the estimate would provide a sufficiently faithful representation of that asset or liability and of any resulting income, expenses or changes in equity. The level of measurement uncertainty may be so high if, for example, the only way of estimating that measure of the asset or liability is by using cash-flow-based measurement techniques and, in addition, one or more of the following circumstances exists:

- the range of possible outcomes is exceptionally wide and the probability of each outcome is exceptionally difficult to estimate;
- the measure is exceptionally sensitive to small changes in estimates of the probability of different outcomes, for example if the probability of future cash inflows or outflows occurring is exceptionally low, but the magnitude of those cash inflows or outflows will be exceptionally high if they occur; or
- measuring the asset or liability requires exceptionally difficult or exceptionally subjective allocations of cash flows that do not relate solely to the asset or liability being measured. *[CF 5.20]*.

In some of these cases, the most useful information may be the measure that relies on the highly uncertain estimate, accompanied by a description of the estimate and an explanation of the uncertainties that affect it. This is especially likely to be the case if that measure is the most relevant measure of the asset or liability. In other cases, if that information would not provide a sufficiently faithful representation of the asset or liability and of any resulting income, expenses or changes in equity, the most useful information may be a different measure (accompanied by any necessary descriptions and explanations) that is slightly less relevant but is subject to lower measurement uncertainty. *[CF 5.21]*.

In limited circumstances, all relevant measures of an asset or liability that are available (or can be obtained) may be subject to such high measurement uncertainty that none would provide useful information about the asset or liability (and any resulting income, expenses or changes in equity), even if the measure were accompanied by a description of the estimates made in producing it and an explanation of the uncertainties that affect those estimates. In those limited circumstances, the asset or liability would not be recognised. *[CF 5.22]*.

Whether or not an asset or liability is recognised, a faithful representation of the asset or liability may need to include explanatory information about the uncertainties associated with the asset or liability's existence or measurement, or with its outcome, that is, the amount or timing of any inflow or outflow of economic benefits that will ultimately result from it (measurement uncertainty is discussed at 9.3.2 below). *[CF 5.23]*.

8.2.2.B   Other factors

Faithful representation of a recognised asset, liability, equity, income or expense involves not only recognition of that item, but also its measurement as well as presentation and disclosure of information about it (measurement is discussed at 9 below; presentation and disclosure is discussed at 10 below). *[CF 5.24]*.

Accordingly, when assessing whether the recognition can provide a faithful representation of an asset or liability, it is necessary to consider not merely its description and measurement in the statement of financial position, but also:

- the depiction of resulting income, expenses and changes in equity. For example, if an entity acquires an asset in exchange for consideration, not recognising the asset would result in recognising expenses and would reduce the entity's profit and equity. In some cases, for example, if the entity does not consume the asset immediately, that result could provide a misleading representation that the entity's financial position has deteriorated;
- whether related assets and liabilities are recognised. If they are not recognised, recognition may create a recognition inconsistency (accounting mismatch). That may not provide an understandable or faithful representation of the overall effect of the transaction or other event giving rise to the asset or liability, even if explanatory information is provided in the notes; and
- presentation and disclosure of information about the asset or liability, and resulting income, expenses or changes in equity. A complete depiction includes all information necessary for a user of financial statements to understand the economic phenomenon depicted, including all necessary descriptions and explanations. Hence, presentation and disclosure of related information can enable a recognised amount to form part of a faithful representation of an asset, a liability, equity, income or expenses. *[CF 5.25]*.

8.3   Derecognition

Derecognition is the removal of all or part of a recognised asset or liability from an entity's statement of financial position. Derecognition normally occurs when that item no longer meets the definition of an asset or of a liability:

- for an asset, derecognition normally occurs when the entity loses control of all or part of the recognised asset; and
- for a liability, derecognition normally occurs when the entity no longer has a present obligation for all or part of the recognised liability. *[CF 5.26]*.

Accounting requirements for derecognition aim to represent faithfully both:

- any assets and liabilities retained after the transaction or other event that led to the derecognition (including any asset or liability acquired, incurred or created as part of the transaction or other event); and
- the change in the entity's assets and liabilities as a result of that transaction or other event. *[CF 5.27]*.

These aims are normally achieved by:
- derecognising any assets or liabilities that have expired or have been consumed, collected, fulfilled or transferred, and recognising any resulting income and expenses (transferred component);
- continuing to recognise the assets or liabilities retained (retained component), if any. That retained component becomes a unit of account separate from the transferred component. Accordingly, no income or expenses are recognised on the retained component as a result of the derecognition of the transferred component, unless the derecognition results in a change in the measurement requirements applicable to the retained component; and
- applying one or more of the following procedures, if that is necessary to achieve one or both of those aims:
  - presenting any retained component separately in the statement of financial position;
  - presenting separately in the statement(s) of financial performance any income and expenses recognised as a result of the derecognition of the transferred component; or
  - providing explanatory information. *[CF 5.28]*.

In some cases, an entity might appear to transfer an asset or liability, but that asset or liability might nevertheless remain an asset or liability of the entity. For example, as discussed at 7.2.3 above:
- if an entity has apparently transferred an asset but retains exposure to significant positive or negative variations in the amount of economic benefits that may be produced by the asset, this sometimes indicates that the entity might continue to control that asset; or
- if an entity has transferred an asset to another party that holds the asset as an agent for the entity, the transferor still controls the asset. *[CF 5.29]*.

In these cases, derecognition of that asset or liability is not appropriate because it would not achieve a faithful representation of either the retained elements or the change in assets or liabilities. *[CF 5.27, 5.30]*.

When an entity no longer has a transferred component, derecognition of the transferred component faithfully represents that fact. However, in some of those cases, derecognition may not faithfully represent how much a transaction or other event changed the entity's assets or liabilities, even when supported by appropriate presentation and disclosure. In those cases, derecognition of the transferred component might imply that the entity's financial position has changed more significantly than it has. This might occur, for example:
- if an entity has transferred an asset and, at the same time, entered into another transaction that results in a present right or present obligation to reacquire the asset. Such present rights or present obligations may arise from, for example, a forward contract, a written put option, or a purchased call option; or

- if an entity has retained exposure to significant positive or negative variations in the amount of economic benefits that may be produced by a transferred component that the entity no longer controls. *[CF 5.31]*.

If derecognition is not sufficient to achieve a faithful representation of the retained elements and the change in assets or liabilities (even when supported by appropriate presentation and disclosure) those two aims might sometimes be achieved by continuing to recognise the transferred component. This would have the following consequences:

- no income or expenses are recognised on either the retained component or the transferred component as a result of the transaction or other event;
- the proceeds received (or paid) upon transfer of the asset (or liability) are treated as a loan received (or given); and
- separate presentation of the transferred component in the statement of financial position, or provision of explanatory information, is needed to depict the fact that the entity no longer has any rights or obligations arising from the transferred component. Similarly, it may be necessary to provide information about income or expenses arising from the transferred component after the transfer. *[CF 5.32]*.

One case in which questions about derecognition arise is when a contract is modified in a way that reduces or eliminates existing rights or obligations. In deciding how to account for contract modifications, it is necessary to consider which unit of account provides users of financial statements with the most useful information about the assets and liabilities retained after the modification, and about how the modification changed the entity's assets and liabilities:

- if a contract modification only eliminates existing rights or obligations, the discussion of derecognition above is considered in deciding whether to derecognise those rights or obligations;
- if a contract modification only adds new rights or obligations, it is necessary to decide whether to treat the added rights or obligations as a separate asset or liability, or as part of the same unit of account as the existing rights and obligations (see 7.1.1 above); and
- if a contract modification both eliminates existing rights or obligations and adds new rights or obligations, it is necessary to consider both the separate and the combined effect of those modifications. In some such cases, the contract has been modified to such an extent that, in substance, the modification replaces the old asset or liability with a new asset or liability. In cases of such extensive modification, the entity may need to derecognise the original asset or liability, and recognise the new asset or liability. *[CF 5.33]*.

9 CHAPTER 6: MEASUREMENT

As discussed at 8 above, elements recognised in financial statements are quantified in monetary terms. This requires the selection of a measurement basis, which is defined in the *Framework* as an identified feature (for example, historical cost, fair value or fulfilment value) of the item being measured. Applying a measurement basis to an asset or liability creates a measure for that asset or liability and for related income and expenses. *[CF 6.1]*.

The *Framework* does not provide detailed guidance on when a particular measurement basis would be suitable. Rather, it describes various measurement bases, the information they provide and the factors to consider in their selection (discussed further at 9.1 below). *[CF BC6.1]*. This approach reflects the belief of the Board that in different circumstances:

- different measurement bases may provide information relevant to users of financial statements; and
- a particular measurement basis may be:
  - easier to understand and implement than another;
  - more verifiable, less prone to error or subject to a lower level of measurement uncertainty than another; or
  - less costly to implement than another. *[CF BC6.10]*.

Consideration of the qualitative characteristics of useful financial information and of the cost constraint is likely to result in the selection of different measurement bases for different assets, liabilities, income and expenses. *[CF 6.2]*.

A standard may need to describe how to implement the measurement basis selected in that standard. That description could include:

- specifying techniques that may or must be used to estimate a measure applying a particular measurement basis;
- specifying a simplified measurement approach that is likely to provide information similar to that provided by a preferred measurement basis; or
- explaining how to modify a measurement basis, for example, by excluding from the fulfilment value of a liability the effect of the possibility that the entity may fail to fulfil that liability (own credit risk). *[CF 6.3]*.

The contents of Chapter 6 of the *Framework* are discussed in this section as follows:

- Measurement bases (such as historical cost and current value) – discussed at 9.1 below.
- Information provided by different measurement bases – discussed at 9.2 below.
- Factors to consider in selecting measurement bases – discussed at 9.3 below.
- Measurement of equity – discussed at 9.4 below.
- Cash-flow-based measurement techniques – discussed at 9.5 below.

9.1 Measurement bases

9.1.1 Historical cost

Historical cost measures provide monetary information about assets, liabilities and related income and expenses, using information derived, at least in part, from the price of the transaction or other event that gave rise to them. Unlike current value, historical cost does not reflect changes in values, except to the extent that those changes relate to impairment of an asset or a liability becoming onerous. *[CF 6.4]*.

The historical cost of an asset when it is acquired or created is the value of the costs incurred in acquiring or creating the asset, comprising the consideration paid to acquire or create the asset plus transaction costs. The historical cost of a liability when it is incurred or taken on is the value of the consideration received to incur or take on the liability minus transaction costs. *[CF 6.5]*.

When an asset is acquired or created, or a liability is incurred or taken on, as a result of an event that is not a transaction on market terms, it may not be possible to identify a cost, or the cost may not provide relevant information about the asset or liability. In some such cases, a current value of the asset or liability is used as a deemed cost on initial recognition and that deemed cost is then used as a starting point for subsequent measurement at historical cost (see 9.3.4 below). [CF 6.6].

The historical cost of an asset is updated over time to depict, if applicable:

- the consumption of part or all of the economic resource that constitutes the asset (depreciation or amortisation);
- payments received that extinguish part or all of the asset;
- the effect of events that cause part or all of the historical cost of the asset to be no longer recoverable (impairment); and
- accrual of interest to reflect any financing component of the asset. [CF 6.7].

The historical cost of a liability is updated over time to depict, if applicable:

- fulfilment of part or all of the liability, for example, by making payments that extinguish part or all of the liability or by satisfying an obligation to deliver goods;
- the effect of events that increase the value of the obligation to transfer the economic resources needed to fulfil the liability to such an extent that the liability becomes onerous. A liability is onerous if the historical cost is no longer sufficient to depict the obligation to fulfil the liability; and
- accrual of interest to reflect any financing component of the liability. [CF 6.8].

One way to apply a historical cost measurement basis to financial assets and financial liabilities is to measure them at amortised cost. The amortised cost of a financial asset or financial liability reflects estimates of future cash flows, discounted at a rate determined at initial recognition. For variable rate instruments, the discount rate is updated to reflect changes in the variable rate. The amortised cost of a financial asset or financial liability is updated over time to depict subsequent changes, such as the accrual of interest, the impairment of a financial asset and receipts or payments. [CF 6.9].

9.1.2 Current value

Current value measures provide monetary information about assets, liabilities and related income and expenses, using information updated to reflect conditions at the measurement date. Because of the updating, current values of assets and liabilities reflect changes, since the previous measurement date, in estimates of cash flows and other factors reflected in those current values. Unlike historical cost, the current value of an asset or liability is not derived, even in part, from the price of the transaction or other event that gave rise to the asset or liability. [CF 6.10].

Current value measurement bases include:

- fair value (discussed at 9.1.2.A below);
- value in use for assets and fulfilment value for liabilities (discussed at 9.1.2.B below); and
- current cost (discussed at 9.1.2.C below). [CF 6.11].

9.1.2.A Fair value

Fair value is the price that would be received to sell an asset, or paid to transfer a liability, in an orderly transaction between market participants at the measurement date. *[CF 6.12]*.

Fair value reflects the perspective of market participants; that is, participants in a market to which the entity has access. The asset or liability is measured using the same assumptions that market participants would use when pricing the asset or liability if those market participants act in their economic best interest. *[CF 6.13]*.

In some cases, fair value can be determined directly by observing prices in an active market. In other cases, it is determined indirectly using measurement techniques, for example, cash-flow-based measurement techniques (discussed at 9.5 below), reflecting all the following factors:

(a) estimates of future cash flows;

(b) possible variations in the estimated amount or timing of future cash flows for the asset or liability being measured, caused by the uncertainty inherent in the cash flows;

(c) the time value of money;

(d) the price for bearing the uncertainty inherent in the cash flows (a risk premium or risk discount). The price for bearing that uncertainty depends on the extent of that uncertainty. It also reflects the fact that investors would generally pay less for an asset (and generally require more for taking on a liability) that has uncertain cash flows than for an asset (or liability) whose cash flows are certain; and

(e) other factors, for example, liquidity, if market participants would take those factors into account in the circumstances. *[CF 6.14]*.

The factors mentioned in (b) and (d) above include the possibility that a counterparty may fail to fulfil its liability to the entity (credit risk), or that the entity may fail to fulfil its liability (own credit risk). *[CF 6.15]*.

Because fair value is not derived, even in part, from the price of the transaction or other event that gave rise to the asset or liability, fair value is not increased by the transaction costs incurred when acquiring the asset and is not decreased by the transaction costs incurred when the liability is incurred or taken on. In addition, fair value does not reflect the transaction costs that would be incurred on the ultimate disposal of the asset or on transferring or settling the liability. *[CF 6.16]*.

9.1.2.B Value in use and fulfilment value

Value in use is the present value of the cash flows, or other economic benefits, that an entity expects to derive from the use of an asset and from its ultimate disposal. Fulfilment value is the present value of the cash, or other economic resources, that an entity expects to be obliged to transfer as it fulfils a liability. Those amounts of cash or other economic resources include not only the amounts to be transferred to the liability counterparty, but also the amounts that the entity expects to be obliged to transfer to other parties to enable it to fulfil the liability. *[CF 6.17]*. Value in use and fulfilment value cannot be observed directly and are determined using cash-flow-based measurement techniques (see 9.5 below). *[CF 6.20]*.

Because value in use and fulfilment value are based on future cash flows, they do not include transaction costs incurred on acquiring an asset or taking on a liability. However, value in use and fulfilment value include the present value of any transaction costs an entity expects to incur on the ultimate disposal of the asset or on fulfilling the liability. *[CF 6.18]*.

Value in use and fulfilment value reflect entity-specific assumptions rather than assumptions by market participants. Nonetheless, they do reflect the factors set out in (a)-(e) at 9.1.2.A above. In practice, there may sometimes be little difference between the assumptions that market participants would use and those that an entity itself uses. *[CF 6.19, 6.20]*.

9.1.2.C Current cost

The current cost of an asset is the cost of an equivalent asset at the measurement date, comprising the consideration that would be paid at the measurement date plus the transaction costs that would be incurred at that date. The current cost of a liability is the consideration that would be received for an equivalent liability at the measurement date minus the transaction costs that would be incurred at that date. Current cost, like historical cost, is an entry value: it reflects prices in the market in which the entity would acquire the asset or would incur the liability. Hence, it is different from fair value, value in use and fulfilment value, which are exit values. However, unlike historical cost, current cost reflects conditions at the measurement date. *[CF 6.21]*.

In some cases, current cost cannot be determined directly by observing prices in an active market and must be determined indirectly by other means. For example, if prices are available only for new assets, the current cost of a used asset might need to be estimated by adjusting the current price of a new asset to reflect the current age and condition of the asset held by the entity. *[CF 6.22]*.

9.2 Information provided by different measurement bases

When selecting a measurement basis, it is important to consider the nature of the information that the measurement basis will produce in both the statement of financial position and the statement(s) of financial performance. The *Framework* summarises that information in a table which is reproduced in Figure 2.3 below. *[CF 6.23]*. This is followed by some further discussion at 9.2.1 and 9.2.2 below.

Figure 2.3   Summary of information provided by particular measurement bases

Assets

	Statement of financial position			
	Historical cost	**Fair value** (market-participant assumptions)	**Value in use** (entity-specific assumptions)[a]	**Current cost**
Carrying amount	Historical cost (including transaction costs), to the extent unconsumed or uncollected, and recoverable. (Includes interest accrued on any financing component.)	Price that would be received to sell the asset (without deducting transaction costs on disposal).	Present value of future cash flows from the use of the asset and from its ultimate disposal (after deducting present value of transaction costs on disposal).	Current cost (including transaction costs), to the extent unconsumed or uncollected, and recoverable.
Initial recognition[b]	–	Difference between consideration paid and fair value of the asset acquired.[c] Transaction costs on acquiring the asset.	Difference between consideration paid and value in use of the asset acquired. Transaction costs on acquiring the asset.	–
Sale or consumption of the asset[d, e]	Expenses equal to historical cost of the asset sold or consumed. Income received. (Could be presented gross or net.) Expenses for transaction costs on selling the asset.	Expenses equal to fair value of the asset sold or consumed. Income received. (Could be presented gross or net.) Expenses for transaction costs on selling the asset.	Expenses equal to value in use of the asset sold or consumed. Income received. (Could be presented gross or net.)	Expenses equal to current cost of the asset sold or consumed. Income received. (Could be presented gross or net.) Expenses for transaction costs on selling the asset.

	Statement(s) of financial performance			
Event	Historical cost	Fair value (market-participant assumptions)	Value in use (entity-specific assumptions)[a]	Current cost
Interest income	Interest income, at historical rates, updated if the asset bears variable interest.	Reflected in income and expenses from changes in fair value. (Could be identified separately.)	Reflected in income and expenses from changes in value in use. (Could be identified separately.)	Interest income, at current rates.
Impairment	Expenses arising because historical cost is no longer recoverable.	Reflected in income and expenses from changes in fair value. (Could be identified separately.)	Reflected in income and expenses from changes in value in use. (Could be identified separately.)	Expenses arising because current cost is no longer recoverable.
Value changes	Not recognised, except to reflect an impairment. For financial assets, income and expenses from changes in estimated cash flows.	Reflected in income and expenses from changes in fair value.	Reflected in income and expenses from changes in value in use.	Income and expenses reflecting the effect of changes in prices (holding gains and holding losses).

(a) This column summarises the information provided if value in use is used as a measurement basis. However, as noted at 9.3.3.B below, value in use may not be a practical measurement basis for regular remeasurements.
(b) Income or expenses may arise on the initial recognition of an asset not acquired on market terms.
(c) Income or expenses may arise if the market in which an asset is acquired is different from the market that is the source of the prices used when measuring the fair value of the asset.
(d) Consumption of the asset is typically reported through cost of sales, depreciation or amortisation.
(e) Income received is often equal to the consideration received but will depend on the measurement basis used for any related liability.

Liabilities

	Statement of financial position			
	Historical cost	Fair value (market-participant assumptions)	Fulfilment value (entity-specific assumptions)	Current cost
Carrying amount	Consideration received (net of transaction costs) for taking on the unfulfilled part of the liability, increased by excess of estimated cash outflows over consideration received. (Includes interest accrued on any financing component.)	Price that would be paid to transfer the unfulfilled part of the liability (not including transaction costs that would be incurred on transfer).	Present value of future cash flows that will arise in fulfilling the unfulfilled part of the liability (including present value of transaction costs to be incurred in fulfilment or transfer).	Consideration (net of transaction costs) that would be currently received for taking on the unfulfilled part of the liability, increased by excess of estimated cash outflows over that consideration.
Initial recognition[a]	–	Difference between consideration received and the fair value of the liability.[b] Transaction costs on incurring or taking on the liability.	Difference between consideration received and the fulfilment value of the liability. Transaction costs on incurring or taking on the liability.	–
Fulfilment of the liability	Income equal to historical cost of the liability fulfilled (reflects historical consideration). Expenses for costs incurred in fulfilling the liability. (Could be presented net or gross.)	Income equal to fair value of the liability fulfilled. Expenses for costs incurred in fulfilling the liability. (Could be presented net or gross. If gross, historical consideration could be presented separately.)	Income equal to fulfilment value of the liability fulfilled. Expenses for costs incurred in fulfilling the liability. (Could be presented net or gross. If gross, historical consideration could be presented separately.)	Income equal to current cost of the liability fulfilled (reflects current consideration). Expenses for costs incurred in fulfilling the liability. (Could be presented net or gross. If gross, historical consideration could be presented separately.)

	Statement(s) of financial performance			
Event	Historical cost	Fair value (market-participant assumptions)	Fulfilment value (entity-specific assumptions)	Current cost
Transfer of the liability	Income equal to historical cost of the liability transferred (reflects historical consideration). Expenses for costs paid (including transaction costs) to transfer the liability. (Could be presented net or gross.)	Income equal to fair value of the liability transferred. Expenses for costs paid (including transaction costs) to transfer the liability. (Could be presented net or gross.)	Income equal to fulfilment value of the liability transferred. Expenses for costs paid (including transaction costs) to transfer the liability. (Could be presented net or gross.)	Income equal to current cost of the liability transferred (reflects current consideration). Expenses for costs paid (including transaction costs) to transfer the liability. (Could be presented net or gross.)
Interest expenses	Interest expenses, at historical rates, updated if the liability bears variable interest.	Reflected in income and expenses from changes in fair value. (Could be identified separately.)	Reflected in income and expenses from changes in fulfilment value. (Could be identified separately.)	Interest expenses, at current rates.
Effect of events that cause a liability to become onerous	Expenses equal to the excess of the estimated cash outflows over the historical cost of the liability, or a subsequent change in that excess.	Reflected in income and expenses from changes in fair value. (Could be identified separately.)	Reflected in income and expenses from changes in fulfilment value. (Could be identified separately.)	Expenses equal to the excess of the estimated cash outflows over the current cost of the liability, or a subsequent change in that excess.
Value changes	Not recognised except to the extent that the liability is onerous. For financial liabilities, income and expenses from changes in estimated cash flows.	Reflected in income and expenses from changes in fair value.	Reflected in income and expenses from changes in fulfilment value.	Income and expenses reflecting the effect of changes in prices (holding gains and holding losses).

(a) Income or expenses may arise on the initial recognition of a liability incurred or taken on not on market terms.
(b) Income or expenses may arise if the market in which a liability is incurred or taken on is different from the market that is the source of the prices used when measuring the fair value of the liability.

9.2.1 Historical cost

Information provided by measuring an asset or liability at historical cost may be relevant to users of financial statements, because historical cost uses information derived, at least in part, from the price of the transaction or other event that gave rise to the asset or liability. *[CF 6.24]*.

Normally, if an entity acquired an asset in a recent transaction on market terms, the entity expects that the asset will provide sufficient economic benefits that the entity will at least recover the cost of the asset. Similarly, if a liability was incurred or taken on as a result of a recent transaction on market terms, the entity expects that the value of the obligation to transfer economic resources to fulfil the liability will normally be no more than the value of the consideration received minus transaction costs. Hence, measuring an asset or liability at historical cost in such cases provides relevant information about both the asset or liability and the price of the transaction that gave rise to that asset or liability. *[CF 6.25]*.

Because historical cost is reduced to reflect consumption of an asset and its impairment, the amount expected to be recovered from an asset measured at historical cost is at least as great as its carrying amount. Similarly, because the historical cost of a liability is increased when it becomes onerous, the value of the obligation to transfer the economic resources needed to fulfil the liability is no more than the carrying amount of the liability. *[CF 6.26]*.

If an asset other than a financial asset is measured at historical cost, consumption or sale of the asset, or of part of the asset, gives rise to an expense measured at the historical cost of the asset, or of part of the asset, consumed or sold. *[CF 6.27]*.

The expense arising from the sale of an asset is recognised at the same time as the consideration for that sale is recognised as income. The difference between the income and the expense is the margin resulting from the sale. Expenses arising from consumption of an asset can be compared to related income to provide information about margins. *[CF 6.28]*.

Similarly, if a liability other than a financial liability was incurred or taken on in exchange for consideration and is measured at historical cost, the fulfilment of all or part of the liability gives rise to income measured at the value of the consideration received for the part fulfilled. The difference between that income and the expenses incurred in fulfilling the liability is the margin resulting from the fulfilment. *[CF 6.29]*.

Information about the cost of assets sold or consumed, including goods and services consumed immediately (see 7.2.1 above), and about the consideration received, may have predictive value. That information can be used as an input in predicting future margins from the future sale of goods (including goods not currently held by the entity) and services and hence to assess the entity's prospects for future net cash inflows. To assess an entity's prospects for future cash flows, users of financial statements often focus on the entity's prospects for generating future margins over many periods, not just on its prospects for generating margins from goods already held. Income and expenses measured at historical cost may also have confirmatory value because they may provide feedback to users of financial statements about their previous predictions of cash flows or of margins. Information about the cost of assets sold or consumed may also help in an assessment of how efficiently and effectively the entity's management has discharged its responsibilities to use the entity's economic resources. *[CF 6.30]*.

For similar reasons, information about interest earned on assets, and interest incurred on liabilities, measured at amortised cost may have predictive and confirmatory value. *[CF 6.31]*.

9.2.2 Current value

9.2.2.A Fair value

Information provided by measuring assets and liabilities at fair value may have predictive value because fair value reflects market participants' current expectations about the amount, timing and uncertainty of future cash flows. These expectations are priced in a manner that reflects the current risk preferences of market participants. That information may also have confirmatory value by providing feedback about previous expectations. *[CF 6.32]*.

Income and expenses reflecting market participants' current expectations may have some predictive value, because such income and expenses can be used as an input in predicting future income and expenses. Such income and expenses may also help in an assessment of how efficiently and effectively the entity's management has discharged its responsibilities to use the entity's economic resources. *[CF 6.33]*.

A change in the fair value of an asset or liability can result from various factors set out in (a)-(e) at 9.1.2.A above. When those factors have different characteristics, identifying separately income and expenses that result from those factors can provide useful information to users of financial statements (see 10.2.3 below). *[CF 6.34]*.

If an entity acquired an asset in one market and determines fair value using prices in a different market (the market in which the entity would sell the asset), any difference between the prices in those two markets is recognised as income when that fair value is first determined. *[CF 6.35]*.

Sale of an asset or transfer of a liability would normally be for consideration of an amount similar to its fair value, if the transaction were to occur in the market that was the source for the prices used when measuring that fair value. In those cases, if the asset or liability is measured at fair value, the net income or net expenses arising at the time of the sale or transfer would usually be small, unless the effect of transaction costs is significant. *[CF 6.36]*.

9.2.2.B Value in use and fulfilment value

Value in use provides information about the present value of the estimated cash flows from the use of an asset and from its ultimate disposal. This information may have predictive value because it can be used in assessing the prospects for future net cash inflows. *[CF 6.37]*.

Fulfilment value provides information about the present value of the estimated cash flows needed to fulfil a liability. Hence, fulfilment value may have predictive value, particularly if the liability will be fulfilled, rather than transferred or settled by negotiation. *[CF 6.38]*.

Updated estimates of value in use or fulfilment value, combined with information about estimates of the amount, timing and uncertainty of future cash flows, may also have confirmatory value because they provide feedback about previous estimates of value in use or fulfilment value. *[CF 6.39]*.

9.2.2.C Current cost

Information about assets and liabilities measured at current cost may be relevant because current cost reflects the cost at which an equivalent asset could be acquired or created at the measurement date or the consideration that would be received for incurring or taking on an equivalent liability. *[CF 6.40]*.

Like historical cost, current cost provides information about the cost of an asset consumed or about income from the fulfilment of liabilities. That information can be used to derive current margins and can be used as an input in predicting future margins. Unlike historical cost, current cost reflects prices prevailing at the time of consumption or fulfilment. When price changes are significant, margins based on current cost may be more useful for predicting future margins than margins based on historical cost. *[CF 6.41]*.

To report the current cost of consumption (or current income from fulfilment), it is necessary to split the change in the carrying amount in the reporting period into the current cost of consumption (or current income from fulfilment), and the effect of changes in prices. The effect of a change in prices is sometimes referred to as a 'holding gain' or a 'holding loss'. *[CF 6.42]*.

9.3 Factors to consider in selecting measurement bases

In selecting a measurement basis it is necessary to consider not just the nature of the information that it will produce (discussed at 9.2 above), but also other factors (including the qualitative characteristics discussed at 5 above). *[CF 6.43]*. These other factors set out in the *Framework* are discussed in this section and comprise:

- relevance (see 9.3.1 below);
- faithful representation (see 9.3.2 below);
- enhancing characteristics and the cost constraint (see 9.3.3 below);

    These discussions focus on the factors to be considered in selecting a measurement basis for recognised assets and recognised liabilities. Some of those discussions may also apply in selecting a measurement basis for information provided in the notes, for recognised or unrecognised items. *[CF 6.47]*.

- factors specific to initial measurement (see 9.3.4 below); and
- the use of more than one measurement basis (see 9.3.5 below).

In most cases, no single factor will determine which measurement basis should be selected. The relative importance of each factor will depend on facts and circumstances. *[CF 6.44]*.

The information provided by a measurement basis must be useful to users of financial statements. To achieve this, the information must be relevant and it must faithfully represent what it purports to represent. In addition, the information provided should be, as far as possible, comparable, verifiable, timely and understandable. *[CF 2.4, 6.45]*.

As noted at 5.1.3 above, the *Framework* states that the most efficient and effective process for applying the fundamental qualitative characteristics would usually be to identify the most relevant information about an economic phenomenon. If that information is not available or cannot be provided in a way that faithfully represents the economic phenomenon, the next most relevant type of information is considered. The role played in the selection of a measurement basis by the fundamental qualitative characteristics is discussed at 9.3.1 and 9.3.2 below. That played by the enhancing characteristics and the cost constraint is discussed at 9.3.3 below. *[CF 6.46]*.

Additional factors to consider in selecting a measurement basis on initial recognition are discussed at 9.3.4 below. If the initial measurement basis is inconsistent with the subsequent measurement basis, income and expenses might be recognised at the time of the first subsequent measurement solely because of the change in measurement basis. Recognising such income and expenses might appear to depict a transaction or other event when, in fact, no such transaction or event has occurred. Hence, the choice of measurement basis for an asset or liability, and for the related income and expenses, is determined by considering both initial measurement and subsequent measurement. *[CF 6.48, 6.77]*.

9.3.1 Relevance

The relevance of information provided by a measurement basis for an asset or liability and for the related income and expenses is affected by:

- the characteristics of the asset or liability (see 9.3.1.A below); and
- how that asset or liability contributes to future cash flows (see 9.3.1.B below). *[CF 6.49]*.

9.3.1.A Characteristics of the asset or liability

The relevance of information provided by a measurement basis depends partly on the characteristics of the asset or liability, in particular, on the variability of cash flows and on whether the value of the asset or liability is sensitive to market factors or other risks. *[CF 6.50]*.

If the value of an asset or liability is sensitive to market factors or other risks, its historical cost might differ significantly from its current value. Consequently, historical cost may not provide relevant information if information about changes in value is important to users of financial statements. For example, amortised cost cannot provide relevant information about a financial asset or financial liability that is a derivative. *[CF 6.51]*.

Furthermore, if historical cost is used, changes in value are reported not when that value changes, but when an event such as disposal, impairment or fulfilment occurs. This could be incorrectly interpreted as implying that all the income and expenses recognised at the time of that event arose then, rather than over the periods during which the asset or liability was held. Moreover, because measurement at historical cost does not provide timely information about changes in value, income and expenses reported on that basis may lack predictive value and confirmatory value by not depicting the full effect of the entity's exposure to risk arising from holding the asset or liability during the reporting period. *[CF 6.52]*.

Changes in the fair value of an asset or liability reflect changes in expectations of market participants and changes in their risk preferences. Depending on the characteristics of the asset or liability being measured and on the nature of the entity's business activities, information reflecting those changes may not always provide predictive value or confirmatory value to users of financial statements. This may be the case when the entity's business activities do not involve selling the asset or transferring the liability, for example, if the entity holds assets solely for use or solely for collecting contractual cash flows or if the entity is to fulfil liabilities itself. *[CF 6.53]*.

9.3.1.B   Contribution to future cash flows

As noted at 4.2.1 above, some economic resources produce cash flows directly; in other cases, economic resources are used in combination to produce cash flows indirectly. How economic resources are used, and hence how assets and liabilities produce cash flows, depends in part on the nature of the business activities conducted by the entity. *[CF 6.54]*.

When a business activity of an entity involves the use of several economic resources that produce cash flows indirectly, by being used in combination to produce and market goods or services to customers, historical cost or current cost is likely to provide relevant information about that activity. For example, property, plant and equipment is typically used in combination with an entity's other economic resources. Similarly, inventory typically cannot be sold to a customer, except by making extensive use of the entity's other economic resources (for example, in production and marketing activities). The manner in which measuring such assets at historical cost or current cost can provide relevant information that can be used to derive margins achieved during the period is discussed at 9.2.1 and 9.2.2 above. *[CF 6.55]*.

For assets and liabilities that produce cash flows directly, such as assets that can be sold independently and without a significant economic penalty (for example, without significant business disruption), the measurement basis that provides the most relevant information is likely to be a current value that incorporates current estimates of the amount, timing and uncertainty of the future cash flows. *[CF 6.56]*.

When a business activity of an entity involves managing financial assets and financial liabilities with the objective of collecting contractual cash flows, amortised cost may provide relevant information that can be used to derive the margin between the interest earned on the assets and the interest incurred on the liabilities. However, in assessing whether amortised cost will provide useful information, it is also necessary to consider the characteristics of the financial asset or financial liability. Amortised cost is unlikely to provide relevant information about cash flows that depend on factors other than principal and interest. *[CF 6.57]*.

9.3.2   Faithful representation

When assets and liabilities are related in some way, using different measurement bases for those assets and liabilities can create a measurement inconsistency (accounting mismatch). If financial statements contain measurement inconsistencies, those financial statements may not faithfully represent some aspects of the entity's financial position and financial performance. Consequently, in some circumstances, using the same measurement basis for related assets and liabilities may provide users of financial statements with information that is more useful than the information that would result from using different measurement bases. This may be particularly likely when the cash flows from one asset or liability are directly linked to the cash flows from another asset or liability. *[CF 6.58]*.

As noted at 5.1.2 above, although a perfectly faithful representation is free from error, this does not mean that measures must be perfectly accurate in all respects. *[CF 6.59]*.

When a measure cannot be determined directly by observing prices in an active market and must instead be estimated, measurement uncertainty arises. The level of measurement uncertainty associated with a particular measurement basis may affect whether information provided by that measurement basis provides a faithful representation of an entity's financial position and financial performance. A high level of measurement uncertainty does not necessarily prevent the use of a measurement basis that provides relevant information. However, in some cases the level of measurement uncertainty is so high that information provided by a measurement basis might not provide a sufficiently faithful representation (see 5.1.3 above). In such cases, it is appropriate to consider selecting a different measurement basis that would also result in relevant information. *[CF 6.60]*.

Measurement uncertainty is different from both outcome uncertainty and existence uncertainty:

- outcome uncertainty arises when there is uncertainty about the amount or timing of any inflow or outflow of economic benefits that will result from an asset or liability.
- existence uncertainty arises when it is uncertain whether an asset or a liability exists (see 8.2.1.A above). *[CF 6.61]*.

The presence of outcome uncertainty or existence uncertainty may sometimes contribute to measurement uncertainty. However, outcome uncertainty or existence uncertainty does not necessarily result in measurement uncertainty. For example, if the fair value of an asset can be determined directly by observing prices in an active market, no measurement uncertainty is associated with the measurement of that fair value, even if it is uncertain how much cash the asset will ultimately produce and hence there is outcome uncertainty. *[CF 6.62]*.

9.3.3 Enhancing characteristics and the cost constraint

The enhancing qualitative characteristics of comparability, understandability and verifiability, and the cost constraint, have implications for the selection of a measurement basis (discussed at 5.2 above). The enhancing qualitative characteristic of timeliness has no specific implications for measurement. *[CF 6.63]*.

Just as cost constrains other financial reporting decisions, it also constrains the selection of a measurement basis. Hence, in selecting a measurement basis, it is important to consider whether the benefits of the information provided to users of financial statements by that measurement basis are likely to justify the costs of providing and using that information. *[CF 6.64]*.

Consistently using the same measurement bases for the same items, either from period to period within a reporting entity or in a single period across entities, can help make financial statements more comparable. *[CF 6.65]*.

A change in measurement basis can make financial statements less understandable. However, a change may be justified if other factors outweigh the reduction in understandability, for example, if the change results in more relevant information. If a change is made, users of financial statements may need explanatory information to enable them to understand the effect of that change. *[CF 6.66]*.

Understandability depends partly on how many different measurement bases are used and on whether they change over time. In general, if more measurement bases are used in a set of financial statements, the resulting information becomes more complex and, hence, less understandable and the totals or subtotals in the statement of financial position and the statement(s) of financial performance become less informative. However, it could be appropriate to use more measurement bases if that is necessary to provide useful information. *[CF 6.67]*.

Verifiability is enhanced by using measurement bases that result in measures that can be independently corroborated either directly, for example, by observing prices, or indirectly, for example, by checking inputs to a model. If a measure cannot be verified, users of financial statements may need explanatory information to enable them to understand how the measure was determined. In some such cases, it may be necessary to specify the use of a different measurement basis. *[CF 6.68]*.

9.3.3.A   Historical cost

In many situations, it is simpler, and hence less costly, to measure historical cost than it is to measure a current value. In addition, historical cost is generally well understood and, in many cases, verifiable. *[CF 6.69]*.

However, estimating consumption and identifying and measuring impairment losses or onerous liabilities can be subjective. Hence, the historical cost of an asset or liability can sometimes be as difficult to measure or verify as a current value. *[CF 6.70]*.

Using a historical cost measurement basis, identical assets acquired, or liabilities incurred, at different times can be reported in the financial statements at different amounts. This can reduce comparability, both from period to period for a reporting entity and in a single period across entities. *[CF 6.71]*.

9.3.3.B   Current value

Because fair value is determined from the perspective of market participants, not from an entity-specific perspective, and is independent of when the asset was acquired or the liability was incurred, identical assets or liabilities measured at fair value will, in principle, be measured at the same amount by entities that have access to the same markets. This can enhance comparability both from period to period for a reporting entity and in a single period across entities. In contrast, because value in use and fulfilment value reflect an entity-specific perspective, those measures could differ for identical assets or liabilities in different entities. Those differences may reduce comparability, particularly if the assets or liabilities contribute to cash flows in a similar manner. *[CF 6.72]*.

If the fair value of an asset or liability can be determined directly by observing prices in an active market, the process of fair value measurement is low-cost, simple and easy to understand; and the fair value can be verified through direct observation. *[CF 6.73]*.

Valuation techniques, sometimes including the use of cash-flow-based measurement techniques, may be needed to estimate fair value when it cannot be observed directly in an active market and are generally needed when determining value in use and fulfilment value. Depending on the techniques used:

- estimating inputs to the valuation and applying the valuation technique may be costly and complex; and
- the inputs into the process may be subjective and it may be difficult to verify both the inputs and the validity of the process itself. Consequently, the measures of identical assets or liabilities may differ. That would reduce comparability. *[CF 6.74]*.

In many cases, value in use cannot be determined meaningfully for an individual asset used in combination with other assets. Instead, the value in use is determined for a group of assets and the result may then need to be allocated to individual assets. This process can be subjective and arbitrary. In addition, estimates of value in use for an asset may inadvertently reflect the effect of synergies with other assets in the group. Hence, determining the value in use of an asset used in combination with other assets can be a costly process and its complexity and subjectivity reduces verifiability. For these reasons, value in use may not be a practical measurement basis for regular remeasurements of such assets. However, it may be useful for occasional remeasurements of assets, for example, when it is used in an impairment test to determine whether historical cost is fully recoverable. *[CF 6.75]*.

Using a current cost measurement basis, identical assets acquired or liabilities incurred at different times are reported in the financial statements at the same amount. This can enhance comparability, both from period to period for a reporting entity and in a single period across entities. However, determining current cost can be complex, subjective and costly. For example, as noted at 9.1.2.C above, it may be necessary to estimate the current cost of an asset by adjusting the current price of a new asset to reflect the current age and condition of the asset held by the entity. In addition, because of changes in technology and changes in business practices, many assets would not be replaced with identical assets. Thus, a further subjective adjustment to the current price of a new asset would be required in order to estimate the current cost of an asset equivalent to the existing asset. Also, splitting changes in current cost carrying amounts between the current cost of consumption and the effect of changes in prices (see 9.2.2.C above) may be complex and require arbitrary assumptions. Because of these difficulties, current cost measures may lack verifiability and understandability. *[CF 6.76]*.

9.3.4 Factors specific to initial measurement

At initial recognition, the cost of an asset acquired, or of a liability incurred, as a result of an event that is a transaction on market terms is normally similar to its fair value at that date, unless transaction costs are significant. Nevertheless, even if those two amounts are similar, it is necessary to describe what measurement basis is used at initial recognition. If historical cost will be used subsequently, that measurement basis is also normally appropriate at initial recognition. Similarly, if a current value will be used subsequently, it is also normally appropriate at initial recognition. Using the same measurement basis for initial recognition and subsequent measurement avoids recognising income or expenses at the time of the first subsequent measurement solely because of a change in measurement basis (see 9.3 above). *[CF 6.78]*.

When an entity acquires an asset, or incurs a liability, in exchange for transferring another asset or liability as a result of a transaction on market terms, the initial measure of the asset acquired, or the liability incurred, determines whether any income or expenses arise from the transaction. When an asset or liability is measured at cost, no income or expenses arise at initial recognition, unless income or expenses arise from the derecognition of the transferred asset or liability, or unless the asset is impaired or the liability is onerous. *[CF 6.79]*.

Assets may be acquired, or liabilities may be incurred, as a result of an event that is not a transaction on market terms. For example:

- the transaction price may be affected by relationships between the parties, or by financial distress or other duress of one of the parties;
- an asset may be granted to the entity free of charge by a government or donated to the entity by another party;
- a liability may be imposed by legislation or regulation; or
- a liability to pay compensation or a penalty may arise from an act of wrongdoing. *[CF 6.80]*.

In such cases, measuring the asset acquired, or the liability incurred, at its historical cost may not provide a faithful representation of the entity's assets and liabilities and of any income or expenses arising from the transaction or other event. Hence, it may be appropriate to measure the asset acquired, or the liability incurred, at deemed cost, as noted at 9.1.1 above. Any difference between that deemed cost and any consideration given or received would be recognised as income or expenses at initial recognition. *[CF 6.81]*.

When assets are acquired, or liabilities incurred, as a result of an event that is not a transaction on market terms, all relevant aspects of the transaction or other event need to be identified and considered. For example, it may be necessary to recognise other assets, other liabilities, contributions from holders of equity claims or distributions to holders of equity claims to represent faithfully the substance of the effect of the transaction or other event on the entity's financial position (see 7.1.3 above) and any related effect on the entity's financial performance. *[CF 6.82]*.

9.3.5 More than one measurement basis

Sometimes, consideration of the factors described at 9 above may lead to the conclusion that more than one measurement basis is needed for an asset or liability and for related income and expenses in order to provide relevant information that faithfully represents both the entity's financial position and its financial performance. *[CF 6.83]*.

In most cases, the most understandable way to provide that information is:

- to use a single measurement basis both for the asset or liability in the statement of financial position and for related income and expenses in the statement(s) of financial performance; and
- to provide in the notes additional information applying a different measurement basis. *[CF 6.84]*.

However, in some cases, information is more relevant, or results in a more faithful representation of both the entity's financial position and its financial performance, through the use of:

- a current value measurement basis for the asset or liability in the statement of financial position; and
- a different measurement basis for the related income and expenses in the statement of profit or loss – as distinct from the statement(s) of financial performance (see 10.2.3 below).

In selecting those measurement bases, it is necessary to consider the factors discussed at 9.3-9.3.4 above. *[CF 6.85]*.

In such cases, the total income or total expenses arising in the period from the change in the current value of the asset or liability is separated and classified (see 10.2.3 below) so that:

- the statement of profit or loss includes the income or expenses measured applying the measurement basis selected for that statement; and
- other comprehensive income includes all the remaining income or expenses. As a result, the accumulated other comprehensive income related to that asset or liability equals the difference between:
  - the carrying amount of the asset or liability in the statement of financial position; and
  - the carrying amount that would have been determined applying the measurement basis selected for the statement of profit or loss. *[CF 6.86]*.

9.4 Measurement of equity

The total carrying amount of equity (total equity) is not measured directly. It equals the total of the carrying amounts of all recognised assets less the total of the carrying amounts of all recognised liabilities. *[CF 6.87]*.

Because general purpose financial statements are not designed to show an entity's value, the total carrying amount of equity will not generally equal:

- the aggregate market value of equity claims on the entity;
- the amount that could be raised by selling the entity as a whole on a going concern basis; or
- the amount that could be raised by selling all of the entity's assets and settling all of its liabilities. *[CF 6.88]*.

Although total equity is not measured directly, it may be appropriate to measure directly the carrying amount of some individual classes of equity and some components of equity (see 7.4 above). Nevertheless, because total equity is measured as a residual, at least one class of equity cannot be measured directly. Similarly, at least one component of equity cannot be measured directly. *[CF 6.89]*.

Moreover, some initial recognition of equity will be a consequence of the initial recognition of an asset. Measurement on initial recognition is discussed at 9.3.4 above.

The total carrying amount of an individual class of equity or component of equity is normally positive, but can be negative in some circumstances. Similarly, total equity is generally positive, but it can be negative, depending on which assets and liabilities are recognised and on how they are measured. *[CF 6.90]*.

9.5 Cash-flow-based measurement techniques

When a measure cannot be observed directly, one way to estimate the measure is by using cash-flow-based measurement techniques. Such techniques are not measurement bases. They are techniques used in applying a measurement basis. Hence, when using such a technique, it is necessary to identify which measurement basis is used and the extent to which the technique reflects the factors applicable to that measurement basis. For example, if the measurement basis is fair value, the applicable factors are those described at 9.1.2.A above. *[CF 6.91]*.

Cash-flow-based measurement techniques can be used in applying a modified measurement basis, for example, fulfilment value modified to exclude the effect of the possibility that the entity may fail to fulfil a liability (own credit risk). Modifying measurement bases may sometimes result in information that is more relevant to the users of financial statements or that may be less costly to produce or to understand. However, modified measurement bases may also be more difficult for users of financial statements to understand. *[CF 6.92]*.

Outcome uncertainty (see 9.3.2 above) arises from uncertainties about the amount or timing of future cash flows. Those uncertainties are important characteristics of assets and liabilities. When measuring an asset or liability by reference to estimates of uncertain future cash flows, one factor to consider is possible variations in the estimated amount or timing of those cash flows (see (b) at 9.1.2.A above). Those variations are considered in selecting a single amount from within the range of possible cash flows. The amount selected is itself sometimes the amount of a possible outcome, but this is not always the case. The amount that provides the most relevant information is usually one from within the central part of the range (a central estimate). Different central estimates provide different information. For example:

- the expected value (the probability-weighted average, also known as the statistical mean) reflects the entire range of outcomes and gives more weight to the outcomes that are more likely. The expected value is not intended to predict the ultimate inflow or outflow of cash or other economic benefits arising from that asset or liability;
- the maximum amount that is more likely than not to occur (similar to the statistical median) indicates that the probability of a subsequent loss is no more than 50% and that the probability of a subsequent gain is no more than 50%; and
- the most likely outcome (the statistical mode) is the single most likely ultimate inflow or outflow arising from an asset or liability. *[CF 6.93]*.

A central estimate depends on estimates of future cash flows and possible variations in their amounts or timing. It does not capture the price for bearing the uncertainty that the ultimate outcome may differ from that central estimate (that is, the factor noted in (d) at 9.1.2.A above). *[CF 6.94]*.

As no central estimate gives complete information about the range of possible outcomes, users may need information about the range of possible outcomes. *[CF 6.95]*.

10 CHAPTER 7: PRESENTATION AND DISCLOSURE

Financial statements are viewed in the *Framework* as a communication tool wherein an entity presents and discloses information about its assets, liabilities, equity, income and expenses. *[CF 7.1].*

As discussed at 8.1 above:

- recognised assets, liabilities and equity are depicted in an entity's statement of financial position (discussed at 10.2.1 and 10.2.2 below); and
- income and expenses are depicted in an entity's statement(s) of financial performance (discussed at 10.2.3 below).

  These are structured summaries that are designed to make financial information comparable and understandable. An important feature of the structures of those summaries is that the amounts recognised in a statement are included in the totals and, if applicable, subtotals that link the items recognised in the statement. *[CF 5.2].*

Typically, the statement of financial position and the statement(s) of financial performance provide summarised information and more detailed information is provided in the notes. *[CF 7.22].*

Effective communication of information in financial statements makes that information more relevant and contributes to a faithful representation of an entity's assets, liabilities, equity, income and expenses. It also enhances the understandability and comparability of information in financial statements. Effective communication of information in financial statements requires:

- focusing on presentation and disclosure objectives and principles rather than focusing on rules (discussed at 10.1 below);
- classifying information in a manner that groups similar items and separates dissimilar items (discussed at 10.2 below); and
- aggregating information in such a way that it is not obscured either by unnecessary detail or by excessive aggregation (discussed at 10.3 below). *[CF 7.2].*

Just as cost constrains other financial reporting decisions, it also constrains decisions about presentation and disclosure. Hence, in making decisions about presentation and disclosure, it is important to consider whether the benefits provided to users of financial statements by presenting or disclosing particular information are likely to justify the costs of providing and using that information. *[CF 7.3].*

10.1 Presentation and disclosure objectives and principles

To facilitate effective communication of information in financial statements, when developing presentation and disclosure requirements in standards a balance is needed between:

- giving entities the flexibility to provide relevant information that faithfully represents the entity's assets, liabilities, equity, income and expenses; and
- requiring information that is comparable, both from period to period for a reporting entity and in a single reporting period across entities. *[CF 7.4].*

Including presentation and disclosure objectives in standards supports effective communication in financial statements because such objectives help entities to identify useful information and to decide how to communicate that information in the most effective manner. *[CF 7.5]*.

Effective communication in financial statements is also supported by considering the following principles:
- entity-specific information is more useful than standardised descriptions, sometimes referred to as 'boilerplate'; and
- duplication of information in different parts of the financial statements is usually unnecessary and can make financial statements less understandable. *[CF 7.6]*.

10.2 Classification

Classification is the sorting of assets, liabilities, equity, income or expenses on the basis of shared characteristics for presentation and disclosure purposes. Such characteristics include, but are not limited to, the nature of the item, its role (or function) within the business activities conducted by the entity, and how it is measured. *[CF 7.7]*.

Classifying dissimilar assets, liabilities, equity, income or expenses together can obscure relevant information, reduce understandability and comparability and may not provide a faithful representation of what it purports to represent. *[CF 7.8]*.

10.2.1 Classification of assets and liabilities

Classification is applied to the unit of account selected for an asset or liability (see 7.1.1 above). However, it may sometimes be appropriate to separate an asset or liability into components that have different characteristics and to classify those components separately. That would be appropriate when classifying those components separately would enhance the usefulness of the resulting financial information. For example, it could be appropriate to separate an asset or liability into current and non-current components and to classify those components separately. *[CF 7.9]*.

10.2.1.A Offsetting

Offsetting occurs when an entity recognises and measures both an asset and liability as separate units of account, but groups them into a single net amount in the statement of financial position. Offsetting classifies dissimilar items together and therefore is generally not appropriate. *[CF 7.10]*.

Offsetting assets and liabilities differs from treating a set of rights and obligations as a single unit of account (see 7.1.1 above). *[CF 7.11]*.

10.2.2 Classification of equity

To provide useful information, it may be necessary to classify equity claims separately if those equity claims have different characteristics (equity is discussed at 7.4 above). *[CF 7.12]*.

Similarly, to provide useful information, it may be necessary to classify components of equity separately if some of those components are subject to particular legal, regulatory or other requirements. For example, in some jurisdictions, an entity is permitted to make distributions to holders of equity claims only if the entity has sufficient reserves specified as distributable. Separate presentation or disclosure of those reserves may provide useful information. *[CF 7.13]*.

10.2.3 Classification of income and expenses

Classification is applied to:

- income and expenses resulting from the unit of account selected for an asset or liability; or
- components of such income and expenses if those components have different characteristics and are identified separately. For example, a change in the current value of an asset can include the effects of value changes and the accrual of interest (see Figure 2.3 at 9.2 above). It would be appropriate to classify those components separately if doing so would enhance the usefulness of the resulting financial information. *[CF 7.14]*.

Recognised changes in equity during the reporting period comprise:

- income minus expenses recognised in the statement(s) of financial performance; and
- contributions from, minus distributions to, holders of equity claims. *[CF 5.3]*.

A particularly important facet of classification is determining whether items of financial performance should be considered part of profit and loss or as other comprehensive income.

10.2.3.A Profit or loss and other comprehensive income

Income and expenses are classified and included either:

- in the statement of profit or loss; or
- outside the statement of profit or loss, in other comprehensive income. *[CF 7.15]*.

The statement of profit or loss is the primary source of information about an entity's financial performance for the reporting period. That statement contains a total for profit or loss that provides a highly summarised depiction of the entity's financial performance for the period. Many users of financial statements incorporate that total in their analysis either as a starting point for that analysis or as the main indicator of the entity's financial performance for the period. Nevertheless, understanding an entity's financial performance for the period requires an analysis of all recognised income and expenses, including income and expenses included in other comprehensive income, as well as an analysis of other information included in the financial statements. *[CF 7.16]*.

Because the statement of profit or loss is the primary source of information about an entity's financial performance for the period, all income and expenses are, in principle, included in that statement. Indeed, the Board observes that its intention in establishing this principle was to emphasise that the statement of profit or loss is the default location for income and expenses. *[CF 7.17, BC7.24]*.

However, in developing standards, the Board may decide in exceptional circumstances that income or expenses arising from a change in the current value of an asset or liability are to be included in other comprehensive income when doing so would result in the statement of profit or loss providing more relevant information, or providing a more faithful representation of the entity's financial performance for that period. *[CF 7.17]*.

Income and expenses that arise on a historical cost measurement basis (see Figure 2.3 at 9.2 above) are included in the statement of profit or loss. That is also the case when income and expenses of that type are separately identified as a component of a change in the current value of an asset or liability. For example, if a financial asset is measured at current value and if interest income is identified separately from other changes in value, that interest income is included in the statement of profit or loss. *[CF 7.18]*. This use of more than one measurement basis is discussed at 9.3.5 above.

In the view of the Board, if the statement of profit or loss is the primary source of information about financial performance for a period, the cumulative amounts included in that statement over time need to be as complete as possible. As a consequence, income and expenses can only be excluded permanently from the statement of profit or loss if there is a compelling reason in to do so in any particular case. *[CF BC7.29]*. In principle, therefore, income and expenses included in other comprehensive income in one period are reclassified from other comprehensive income into the statement of profit or loss in a future period when doing so results in the statement of profit or loss providing more relevant information, or providing a more faithful representation of the entity's financial performance for that future period.

However, if, for example, there is no clear basis for identifying the period in which reclassification would have that result, or the amount that should be reclassified, the Board may, in developing standards, decide that income and expenses included in other comprehensive income are not to be subsequently reclassified. *[CF 7.19]*.

10.3 Aggregation

Aggregation is the adding together of assets, liabilities, equity, income or expenses that have shared characteristics and are included in the same classification. *[CF 7.20]*.

Aggregation makes information more useful by summarising a large volume of detail. However, aggregation conceals some of that detail. Hence, a balance needs to be found so that relevant information is not obscured either by a large amount of insignificant detail or by excessive aggregation. *[CF 7.21]*.

Different levels of aggregation may be needed in different parts of the financial statements. For example, typically, the statement of financial position and the statement(s) of financial performance provide summarised information and more detailed information is provided in the notes. *[CF 7.22]*.

11 CHAPTER 8: CONCEPTS OF CAPITAL AND CAPITAL MAINTENANCE

The concept of capital maintenance is concerned with how an entity defines the capital that it seeks to maintain. It is a prerequisite for distinguishing between an entity's return *on* capital (that is, profit) and its return *of* capital. In general terms, an entity has maintained its capital if it has as much capital at the end of the period as it had at the beginning of the period. Any amount over and above that required to maintain the capital at the beginning of the period is profit. *[CF 8.4, 8.6]*.

The *Framework* identifies two broad concepts of capital maintenance:
- financial capital maintenance (see 11.1 below); and
- physical capital maintenance (see 11.2 below).

The principal difference between the two concepts of capital maintenance is the treatment of the effects of changes in the prices of assets and liabilities of the entity. *[CF 8.6]*. The selection of the appropriate concept of capital by an entity should be based on the needs of the users of its financial statements. *[CF 8.2]*.

The concept of capital maintenance chosen by an entity will determine the accounting model used in the preparation of its financial statements. Most entities adopt a financial concept of capital. It is explained that different accounting models exhibit different degrees of relevance and reliability, and it is for management to seek a balance between relevance and reliability (see 5 above for a discussion of the qualitative characteristics of useful financial information). *[CF 8.9]*. This use in Chapter 8 of the *Framework* of the term 'reliability' seems to be a drafting error – the term was used in the *1989 Framework* but was replaced in the *2010 Framework* with the term 'faithful representation'. As the text concerned has been carried forward unchanged from the *1989 Framework* to the current one, the failure to update this reference seems to us to be an oversight. The *Framework* notes that the IASB does not prescribe a particular model other than in exceptional circumstances, such as in a hyperinflationary economy (see Chapter 16). This intention will, however, be reviewed in the light of world developments. *[CF 8.1, 8.9]*.

The *Framework* notes that the revaluation or restatement of assets and liabilities gives rise to increases or decreases in equity that meet the definition of income and expenses, but – under certain concepts of capital maintenance – are included in equity as capital maintenance adjustments or revaluation reserves. *[CF 8.10]*.

11.1 Financial capital maintenance

Under a financial concept of capital, such as invested money or invested purchasing power, capital is synonymous with the net assets or equity of the entity. Under this concept a profit is earned only if the financial (or money) amount of the net assets at the end of the period exceeds the financial (or money) amount of net assets at the beginning of the period, after excluding any distributions to, and contributions from, owners during the period. *[CF 8.1, 8.3(a)]*.

Financial capital maintenance can be measured in either nominal monetary units or units of constant purchasing power. *[CF 8.3(a)]*. The financial capital maintenance concept does not require a particular measurement basis to be used. Rather, the basis selected depends upon the type of financial capital that the entity is seeking to maintain. *[CF 8.5]*.

Where capital is defined in terms of nominal monetary units, profit represents the increase in nominal money capital over the period. This has the implication that increases in the prices of assets held over the period, conventionally referred to as holding gains, are conceptually profits. They may not be recognised as such, however, until the assets are disposed of in an exchange transaction. *[CF 8.7]*.

When the concept of financial capital maintenance is defined in terms of constant purchasing power units, profit represents the increase in invested purchasing power over the period. Thus, only that part of the increase in the prices of assets that exceeds the increase in the general level of prices is regarded as profit. The rest of the increase is treated as a capital maintenance adjustment and, hence, as part of equity. [CF 8.7].

11.2 Physical capital maintenance

Under this concept a profit is earned only if the physical productive capacity (or operating capability) of the entity (or the resources or funds needed to achieve that capacity) at the end of the period exceeds the physical productive capacity at the beginning of the period, after excluding any distributions to, and contributions from, owners during the period. [CF 8.3(b)]. The physical capital maintenance concept requires the current cost basis of measurement to be adopted. [CF 8.5].

Because capital is defined in terms of the physical productive capacity, profit represents the increase in that capital over the period. Price changes affecting the assets and liabilities of the entity are changes in the measurement of the physical productive capacity of the entity, which are therefore treated as capital maintenance adjustments within equity and not as profit. [CF 8.8].

12 MANAGEMENT COMMENTARY

Over a number of years, a number of individual countries have issued regulations or guidance requiring or encouraging the preparation of narrative 'management commentary' to accompany the financial statements.

12.1 The IASB's practice statement

In December 2010 the IASB published its first guidance on management commentary – *Management Commentary – A Framework for Presentation* – as a non-binding 'IFRS Practice Statement'. The introduction to the Practice Statement clarifies that it is neither an IFRS nor part of the *Framework*. However, it has been prepared on the basis that management commentary meets the definition of other financial reporting in the *Preface to International Financial Reporting Standards*, and is therefore within the scope of the *Framework*. Consequently, the Statement should be read 'in the context of' the *Framework*. [MC.IN2, IN4].

Management commentary is described as a narrative report that relates to financial statements that have been prepared in accordance with IFRSs. Management commentary provides users with historical explanations of the amounts presented in the financial statements, specifically the entity's financial position, financial performance and cash flows. It also provides commentary on an entity's prospects and other information not presented in the financial statements. Management commentary also serves as a basis for understanding management's objectives and its strategies for achieving those objectives. [MC Appendix]. For many entities, management commentary is already an important element of their communication with the capital markets, supplementing as well as complementing the financial statements. [MC.IN3].

The Practice Statement is intended to set out a broad framework for the preparation of management commentaries, to be applied by management of individual reporting entities to their own specific circumstances. *[MC.IN5]*. The statement indicates that management commentary should be consistent with the following principles:

- to provide management's view of the entity's performance, position and progress; and
- to supplement and complement information presented in the financial statements. *[MC.12]*.

Management commentary should include information that is forward-looking and has the qualitative characteristics referred to in the *Framework*. *[MC.13]*.

The IASB also envisages that any management commentary will include the following elements:

- the nature of the business;
- management's objectives and strategies for meeting those objectives;
- the entity's most significant resources, risks and relationships;
- the results of operations and prospects; and
- the critical performance measures and indicators that management uses to evaluate the entity's performance against stated objectives. *[MC.24]*.

12.2 Possible future changes to the practice statement

At the time of writing the Board is pursuing a project to update the practice statement; an exposure draft is expected to be published in the first half of 2021. The project is intended to help entities prepare management commentaries that better meet the information needs of the primary users of financial reports.

The website of the IASB states that the update to the statement 'is expected to:

- consolidate innovations in narrative reporting since the publication of the Practice Statement in 2010;
- address gaps in reporting practice, such as the short-term focus in reporting and failure to identify and discuss matters that are specific and important to an entity; and
- remain principles-based but contain sufficient detail to support rigorous application of the Practice Statement by preparers and the effective review of entities' management commentaries by auditors or other providers of assurance.

In particular, the revised Practice Statement is expected to provide guidance on explaining an entity's business model, strategy and its performance, position and progress, incorporating a discussion of the long-term drivers of the entity's success and of risks, trends and factors in the operating environment that can affect the entity.

To help close the gaps in current reporting practice, the Board will focus on developing guidance on:

- identifying and reporting matters that are specific to the circumstances of the entity and underpin the entity's long-term success. For some entities, these matters could include intangible resources and relationships and environmental, social and governance (ESG) matters; and
- providing a coherent discussion of matters reported.'[8]

References

1. W. A. Paton and A. C. Littleton, *An Introduction to Corporate Accounting Standards*, Monograph No. 3, American Accounting Association, 1940.
2. See, for example: American Accounting Association, Executive Committee, 'A Tentative Statement of Accounting Principles Affecting Corporate Reports', *Accounting Review*, June 1936, pp.187-191; American Accounting Association, Executive Committee, 'Accounting Principles Underlying Corporate Financial Statements', *Accounting Review*, June 1941, pp.133-139; American Accounting Association, Committee to Prepare a Statement of Basic Accounting Theory, *A Statement of Basic Accounting Theory*, 1966; American Accounting Association, Committee on Concepts and Standards for External Financial Reports, *Statement on Accounting Theory and Theory Acceptance*, 1977. The 1977 report concluded that closure on the debate was not feasible, which is perhaps indicative of the complexity of the problem.
3. Discussion Paper – *A Review of the Conceptual Framework for Financial Reporting*, IASB, July 2013.
4. *Exposure Draft ED/2015/3: Conceptual Framework for Financial Reporting*, IASB, July 2013.
5. Discussion Paper – *A Review of the Conceptual Framework for Financial Reporting*, IASB, July 2013, para. 1.5.
6. *Conceptual Framework*, References: Introduction and other sections.
7. *Reference to the Conceptual Framework, Amendments to IFRS 3, paragraph 64Q, IASB, May 2020*.
8. *IASB website*, August 2020.

Chapter 3 Presentation of financial statements and accounting policies

1	INTRODUCTION			113
	1.1	Objective and scope of IAS 1		113
	1.2	Objective and scope of IAS 8		114
2	THE PURPOSE AND COMPOSITION OF FINANCIAL STATEMENTS			115
	2.1	The purpose of financial statements		115
	2.2	Frequency of reporting and period covered		116
	2.3	The components of a complete set of financial statements		116
	2.4	Comparative information		117
	2.5	Identification of the financial statements and accompanying information		119
		2.5.1	Identification of financial statements	119
		2.5.2	Statement of compliance with IFRS	120
3	THE STRUCTURE OF FINANCIAL STATEMENTS			121
	3.1	The statement of financial position		122
		3.1.1	The distinction between current/non-current assets and liabilities	122
		3.1.2	Non-current assets and disposal groups held for sale or distribution	123
		3.1.3	Current assets	124
		3.1.4	Current liabilities	124
			3.1.4.A Requirements for periods beginning before 1 January 2023	124
			3.1.4.B Changes to IAS 1 for periods beginning on or after 1 January 2023	126
			3.1.4.C Practical illustrations of the requirements	127

		3.1.5	Information required on the face of the statement of financial position 128
		3.1.6	Information required either on the face of the statement of financial position or in the notes 130
		3.1.7	Illustrative statements of financial position 131
	3.2	The statement of comprehensive income and the statement of profit or loss 133	
		3.2.1	Profit and loss and comprehensive income 133
		3.2.2	Information required on the face of the statement of profit or loss 135
			3.2.2.A Operating profit 137
		3.2.3	Classification of expenses recognised in profit or loss by nature or function 137
			3.2.3.A Analysis of expenses by nature 138
			3.2.3.B Analysis of expenses by function 140
		3.2.4	The statement of comprehensive income 140
			3.2.4.A The face of the statement of comprehensive income 140
			3.2.4.B Reclassification adjustments 144
			3.2.4.C Tax on items of other comprehensive income 145
		3.2.5	Discontinued operations 147
		3.2.6	Material and extraordinary items 148
			3.2.6.A Material items 148
			3.2.6.B Ordinary activities and extraordinary items 148
	3.3	The statement of changes in equity 148	
	3.4	The notes to the financial statements 151	
4	ACCOUNTING POLICIES 152		
	4.1	General principles 152	
		4.1.1	Fair presentation 152
			4.1.1.A Fair presentation and compliance with IFRS 152
			4.1.1.B The fair presentation override 153
		4.1.2	Going concern 155
		4.1.3	The accrual basis of accounting 156
		4.1.4	Consistency 156
		4.1.5	Materiality, aggregation and offset 157
			4.1.5.A Materiality and aggregation 157
			4.1.5.B Offset 159
		4.1.6	Profit or loss for the period 160
		4.1.7	Practice Statement 2 – Making Materiality Judgements 160
			4.1.7.A General characteristics of materiality 161
			4.1.7.B Making materiality judgements 162

			4.1.7.C	Specific topics	162
	4.2	The distinction between accounting policies and accounting estimates			163
	4.3	The selection and application of accounting policies			164
	4.4	Changes in accounting policies			166
	4.5	Changes in accounting estimates			167
	4.6	Correction of errors			168
	4.7	Impracticability of restatement			170
		4.7.1	Impracticability of restatement for a change in accounting policy		172
		4.7.2	Impracticability of restatement for a material error		173
5	DISCLOSURE REQUIREMENTS				174
	5.1	Disclosures relating to accounting policies			174
		5.1.1	Disclosure of accounting policies		174
			5.1.1.A	Summary of significant accounting policies	174
			5.1.1.B	Judgements made in applying accounting policies	175
		5.1.2	Disclosure of changes in accounting policies		175
			5.1.2.A	Accounting policy changes pursuant to the initial application of an IFRS	175
			5.1.2.B	Voluntary changes in accounting policy	176
			5.1.2.C	Future impact of a new IFRS	176
	5.2	Disclosure of estimation uncertainty and changes in estimates			177
		5.2.1	Sources of estimation uncertainty		177
		5.2.2	Changes in accounting estimates		179
	5.3	Disclosure of prior period errors			179
	5.4	Disclosures about capital			180
		5.4.1	General capital disclosures		180
		5.4.2	Puttable financial instruments classified as equity		182
	5.5	Other disclosures			182
6	FUTURE DEVELOPMENTS				183
	6.1	Standard-setting projects			183
		6.1.1	Management commentary		183
		6.1.2	Primary financial statements		183
	6.2	Maintenance projects			184
		6.2.1	Distinction between a change in an accounting policy and a change in an accounting estimate		184
		6.2.2	Accounting policy disclosure		184
		6.2.3	Disclosure Initiative – Targeted Standards-level Review of Disclosures		185

List of examples

Example 3.1:	Determining whether liabilities should be presented as current or non-current	127
Example 3.2:	Illustrative statement of financial position	132
Example 3.3:	Example of classification of expenses by nature	138
Example 3.4:	Illustrative statement of profit or loss with expenses classified by nature	139
Example 3.5:	Example of classification of expenses by function	140
Example 3.6:	Presentation of comprehensive income in one statement and the classification of expenses by function	142
Example 3.7:	Note disclosure of components of other comprehensive income	144
Example 3.8:	Statement of comprehensive income illustrating the presentation of comprehensive income in two statements with note disclosure of the tax effects relating to components of other comprehensive income	146
Example 3.9:	Statement of changes in equity	150
Example 3.10:	Retrospective restatement of errors	169
Example 3.11:	Prospective application of a change in accounting policy when retrospective application is not practicable	172
Example 3.12:	Illustrative capital disclosures: An entity that is not a regulated financial institution	181
Example 3.13:	Illustrative capital disclosures: An entity that has not complied with externally imposed capital requirements	182

Chapter 3 Presentation of financial statements and accounting policies

1 INTRODUCTION

There is no single IFRS dealing with the form, content and structure of financial statements and the accounting policies to be applied in their preparation. The subject of just what financial statements are, their purpose, contents and presentation is addressed principally by the following standards.

IAS 1 – *Presentation of Financial Statements* – is the main standard dealing with the overall requirements for the presentation of financial statements, including their purpose, form, content and structure. IAS 8 – *Accounting Policies, Changes in Accounting Estimates and Errors* – deals with the requirements for the selection and application of accounting policies. It also deals with the requirements as to when changes in accounting policies should be made, and how such changes should be accounted for and disclosed. IAS 7 – *Statement of Cash Flows* – deals with the presentation of the statement of cash flows and related disclosures. IFRS 5 – *Non-current Assets Held for Sale and Discontinued Operations* – deals with the classification and presentation of non-current assets held for sale in the statement of financial position, and the presentation of the results of discontinued operations; it also sets out the measurement requirements for such items. This chapter deals with the requirements of IAS 1 and IAS 8. Chapter 40 discusses the requirements of IAS 7 and Chapter 4 discusses the requirements of IFRS 5.

1.1 Objective and scope of IAS 1

IAS 1 deals with the components of financial statements, fair presentation, fundamental accounting concepts, disclosure of accounting policies, and the structure and content of financial statements.

IAS 1 applies to what it calls 'general purpose financial statements' (financial statements), that is those intended to meet the needs of users who are not in a position to require an entity to prepare reports tailored to meet their particular information needs, and it should be applied to all such financial statements prepared in accordance with International Financial

Reporting Standards (IFRSs). *[IAS 1.2, 7]*. The meaning of 'users' of financial statements is expanded upon in IAS 1 as it deals with the concept of materiality; this is discussed at 4.1.5.A below. Although International Financial Reporting Standards is probably a self-explanatory phrase, both IAS 1 and IAS 8 define it as 'Standards and Interpretations issued by the International Accounting Standards Board (IASB). They comprise:

(a) International Financial Reporting Standards;
(b) International Accounting Standards;
(c) IFRIC Interpretations; and
(d) SIC Interpretations'. *[IAS 1.7, IAS 8.5]*.

An important point here is that implementation guidance for standards issued by the IASB does not form part of those standards, and therefore does not contain requirements for financial statements. *[IAS 8.9]*. Accordingly, the often voluminous implementation guidance accompanying standards is not, strictly speaking, part of 'IFRS'. We would generally be surprised, though, at entities not following such guidance.

The standard applies equally to all entities including those that present consolidated financial statements and those that present separate financial statements (discussed in Chapter 8 at 1.1). IAS 1 does not apply to the structure and content of condensed interim financial statements prepared in accordance with IAS 34 – *Interim Financial Reporting* (discussed in Chapter 41 at 3.2), although its general principles as discussed at 4.1 below do apply to such interims. *[IAS 1.4]*.

The objective of the standard is to prescribe the basis for presentation of general purpose financial statements, and by doing so to ensure comparability both with the entity's financial statements of previous periods and with the financial statements of other entities. The standard sets out overall requirements for the presentation of financial statements, guidelines for their structure and minimum requirements for their content. The recognition, measurement and disclosure of specific transactions and other events are dealt with in other standards and in interpretations. *[IAS 1.1, 3]*.

IAS 1 is primarily directed at profit oriented entities (including public sector business entities), and this is reflected in the terminology it uses and its requirements. It acknowledges that entities with not-for-profit activities in the private sector, public sector or government may apply the standard and that such entities may need to amend the descriptions used for particular line items in the financial statements and for the financial statements themselves. *[IAS 1.5]*. Furthermore, IAS 1 is a general standard that does not address issues specific to particular industries. It does observe, though, that entities without equity (such as some mutual funds) or whose share capital is not equity (such as some co-operative entities) may need to adapt the presentation of members' or unit holders' interests. *[IAS 1.6]*.

1.2 Objective and scope of IAS 8

IAS 8 applies to selecting and applying accounting policies, and accounting for changes in accounting policies, changes in accounting estimates and corrections of prior period errors. *[IAS 8.3]*. Its objective is to prescribe the criteria for selecting and changing accounting policies, together with the accounting treatment and disclosure of changes in accounting policies, changes in accounting estimates and corrections of errors. The intention is to

Presentation of financial statements and accounting policies 115

enhance the relevance and reliability of an entity's financial statements and the comparability of those financial statements over time and with the financial statements of other entities. *[IAS 8.1]*.

Two particular issues which one might expect to be dealt with regarding the above are discussed in other standards and cross-referred to by IAS 8:

- disclosure requirements for accounting policies, except those for changes in accounting policies, are dealt with in IAS 1; *[IAS 8.2]* and
- accounting and disclosure requirements regarding the tax effects of corrections of prior period errors and of retrospective adjustments made to apply changes in accounting policies are dealt with in IAS 12 – *Income Taxes* (discussed in Chapter 33 at 10.2). *[IAS 8.4]*.

2 THE PURPOSE AND COMPOSITION OF FINANCIAL STATEMENTS

What financial statements are and what they are for are important basic questions for any body of accounting literature, and answering them is one of the main purposes of IAS 1.

2.1 The purpose of financial statements

IAS 1 describes financial statements as a structured representation of the financial position and financial performance of an entity. It states that the objective of financial statements is to provide information about the financial position, financial performance and cash flows of an entity that is useful to a wide range of users in making economic decisions. A focus on assisting decision making by the users of financial statements is seeking (at least in part) a forward looking or predictive quality. This is reflected by some requirements of accounting standards. For example: the disclosure of discontinued operations (discussed in Chapter 4 at 3); the use of profit from continuing operations as the 'control number' in calculating diluted earnings per share (discussed in Chapter 37 at 6.3.1); and also, the desire of some entities to present performance measures excluding what they see as unusual or infrequent items (discussed at 3.2.6 below).

IAS 1 also acknowledges a second important role of financial statements. That is, that they also show the results of management's stewardship of the resources entrusted to it.

To meet this objective for financial statements, IAS 1 requires that they provide information about an entity's:

(a) assets;
(b) liabilities;
(c) equity;
(d) income and expenses, including gains and losses;
(e) contributions by owners and distributions to owners in their capacity as owners (owners being defined as holders of instruments classified as equity); *[IAS 1.7]* and
(f) cash flows.

The standard observes that this information, along with other information in the notes, assists users of financial statements in predicting the entity's future cash flows and, in particular, their timing and certainty. *[IAS 1.9]*.

2.2 Frequency of reporting and period covered

IAS 1 requires that a complete set of financial statements (including comparative information, see 2.4 below) be presented 'at least annually'. Whilst this drafting is not exactly precise, it does not seem to mean that financial statements must never be more than a year apart (which is perhaps the most natural meaning of the phrase). This is because the standard goes on to mention that the end of an entity's reporting period may change, and that the annual financial statements are therefore presented for a period longer or shorter than one year. When this is the case, IAS 1 requires disclosure of, in addition to the period covered by the financial statements:

(a) the reason for using a longer or shorter period; and
(b) the fact that amounts presented in the financial statements are not entirely comparable. *[IAS 1.36]*.

Normally financial statements are consistently prepared covering a one year period. Some entities, particularly in the retail sector, traditionally present financial statements for a 52-week period. IAS 1 does not preclude this practice. *[IAS 1.37]*.

2.3 The components of a complete set of financial statements

A complete set of financial statements under IAS 1 comprises the following, each of which should be presented with equal prominence: *[IAS 1.10-11]*

(a) a statement of financial position as at the end of the period;
(b) a statement of profit or loss and other comprehensive income for the period to be presented either as:
   (i) one single statement of comprehensive income with a section for profit and loss followed immediately by a section for other comprehensive income; or
   (ii) a separate statement of profit or loss and statement of comprehensive income. In this case, the former must be presented immediately before the latter;
(c) a statement of changes in equity for the period;
(d) a statement of cash flows for the period;
(e) notes, comprising significant accounting policies and other explanatory information;
(f) comparative information in respect of the preceding period; and
(g) a statement of financial position as at the beginning of the preceding period when:
   (i) an accounting policy has been applied retrospectively; or
   (ii) a retrospective restatement has been made; or
   (iii) items have been reclassified.

The titles of the statements need not be those used in the standard (shown above).

The standard explains that notes contain information in addition to that presented in the statements above, and provide narrative descriptions or disaggregations of items presented in those statements and information about items that do not qualify for recognition in those statements. *[IAS 1.7]*.

In addition to information about the reporting period, IAS 1 also requires information about the preceding period. Comparative information is discussed at 2.4 below.

Financial statements are usually published as part of a larger annual report, with the accompanying discussions and analyses often being more voluminous than the financial statements themselves. IAS 1 acknowledges this, but makes clear that such reports and statements (including financial reviews, environmental reports and value added statements) presented outside financial statements are outside the scope of IFRS. *[IAS 1.14]*.

Notwithstanding that this type of information is not within the scope of IFRS, IAS 1 devotes two paragraphs to discussing what this information may comprise, observing that:

- a financial review by management may describe and explain the main features of the entity's financial performance and financial position and the principal uncertainties it faces and that it may include a review of:
  - the main factors and influences determining financial performance, including changes in the environment in which the entity operates, the entity's response to those changes and their effect, and the entity's policy for investment to maintain and enhance financial performance, including its dividend policy;
  - the entity's sources of funding and its targeted ratio of liabilities to equity (IAS 1 itself requires certain disclosures about capital. These are discussed at 5.4 below); and
  - the entity's resources not recognised in the statement of financial position in accordance with IFRS; *[IAS 1.13]*.
- reports and statements such as environmental reports and value added statements may be presented, particularly in industries in which environmental factors are significant and when employees are regarded as an important user group. *[IAS 1.14]*.

The IASB has published a practice statement on management commentary. The practice statement is a broad, non-binding framework for the presentation of narrative reporting to accompany financial statements prepared in accordance with IFRS.

Although management commentaries add helpful and relevant information beyond what is included in the financial statements, IFRS requires the financial statements to provide a fair presentation of the financial position, financial performance and cash flows of an entity on a stand-alone basis.

The Board continues to consider wider aspects of corporate reporting and has added to its agenda a project to revise and update the practice statement (see 6.1 below).

2.4 Comparative information

IAS 1 requires, except when IFRSs permit or require otherwise, comparative information to be disclosed in respect of the previous period for all amounts reported in the current period's financial statements. *[IAS 1.38]*. If any information is voluntarily presented, there will by definition be no standard or interpretation providing a dispensation from comparatives. Accordingly, comparative information is necessary for any voluntarily presented current period disclosure.

The above requirement for two sets of statements and notes represents the minimum which is required in all circumstances. *[IAS 1.38A]*.

An entity may present comparative information in addition to the minimum comparative financial statements required by IFRS, as long as that information is prepared in accordance with IFRSs. This comparative information may consist of one or more primary statements, but need not comprise a complete set of financial statements. When this is the case, IAS 1 requires an entity to present related note information for those additional statements. *[IAS 1.38C]*.

For example, an entity may present a third statement of profit or loss and other comprehensive income (thereby presenting the current period, the preceding period and one additional comparative period). In such circumstances, IAS 1 does not require a third statement of financial position, a third statement of cash flows or a third statement of changes in equity (that is, an additional comparative financial statement). The entity is required to present, in the notes to the financial statements, the comparative information related to that additional statement of profit or loss and other comprehensive income. *[IAS 1.38D]*.

However, further comparative information is required by IAS 1 in certain circumstances. Whenever an entity:

(a) applies an accounting policy retrospectively; or

(b) makes a retrospective restatement; or

(c) reclassifies items in its financial statements;

an additional statement of financial position is required as at the beginning of the preceding period if the change has a material effect on that additional statement. *[IAS 1.40A]*. The standard describes this as an 'additional' statement because the minimum requirement is for one comparative statement of financial position. Should an entity already have a policy of presenting two comparative statements this requirement would not necessarily require a fourth statement. Only if the second comparative statement is not essentially the same as one drawn-up 'as at the beginning of the preceding period', would a financial position as at the beginning of the preceding period be required. As such restatements are considered, by the IASB, narrow, specific and limited, no notes are required for this additional statement of financial position. *[IAS 1.40C, BC32C]*.

It is important to note that 'reclassifies', as that word is used by IAS 1 in this context (at (c) above), is not referring to a 'reclassification adjustment'. 'Reclassification adjustments' is a term defined by IAS 1 which describes the recognition of items in profit or loss which were previously recognised in other comprehensive income (often referred to as 'recycling'). IAS 1 applies this definition when setting out the required presentation and disclosure of such items (see 3.2.4.B below).

Comparative information is also required for narrative and descriptive information when it is relevant to an understanding of the current period's financial statements. *[IAS 1.38]*. The standard illustrates the current year relevance of the previous year's narratives with a legal dispute, the outcome of which was uncertain at the previous period and is yet to be resolved (the disclosure of contingent liabilities is discussed in Chapter 26 at 7.2). It observes that users benefit from information that the uncertainty existed at the end of the previous period, and about the steps that have been taken during the period to resolve the uncertainty. *[IAS 1.38B]*.

Another example would be the required disclosure of material items (see 3.2.6 below). IAS 1 requires that the nature and amount of such items be disclosed separately. *[IAS 1.97]*. Often a simple caption or line item heading will be sufficient to convey the 'nature' of material items. Sometimes, though, a more extensive description in the notes may be needed to do this. In that case, the same information is likely to be relevant the following year.

As noted at 1.1 above, one of the objectives of IAS 1 is to ensure the comparability of financial statements with previous periods. The standard notes that enhancing the inter-period comparability of information assists users in making economic decisions, especially by allowing the assessment of trends in financial information for predictive purposes. *[IAS 1.43]*. Requiring the presentation of comparatives allows such a comparison to be made within one set of financial statements. For a comparison to be meaningful, the amounts for prior periods need to be reclassified whenever the presentation or classification of items in the financial statements is amended. When this is the case, disclosure is required of the nature, amount and reasons for the reclassification (including as at the beginning of the preceding period). *[IAS 1.41]*.

The standard acknowledges, though, that in some circumstances it is impracticable to reclassify comparative information for a particular prior period to achieve comparability with the current period. For these purposes, reclassification is impracticable when it cannot be done after making every reasonable effort to do so. *[IAS 1.7]*. An example given by the standard is that data may not have been collected in the prior period(s) in a way that allows reclassification, and it may not be practicable to recreate the information. *[IAS 1.43]*. When it proves impracticable to reclassify comparative data, IAS 1 requires disclosure of the reason for this and also the nature of the adjustments that would have been made if the amounts had been reclassified. *[IAS 1.42]*.

As well as reclassification to reflect current period classifications as required by IAS 1, a change to comparatives as they were originally reported could be necessary:

(a) following a change in accounting policy (discussed at 4.4 below);
(b) to correct an error discovered in previous financial statements (discussed at 4.6 below); or
(c) in relation to discontinued operations (discussed in Chapter 4 at 3.2).

2.5 Identification of the financial statements and accompanying information

2.5.1 Identification of financial statements

It is commonly the case that financial statements will form only part of a larger annual report, regulatory filing or other document. As IFRS only applies to financial statements, it is important that the financial statements are clearly identified so that users of the report can distinguish information that is prepared using IFRS from other information that may be useful but is not the subject of those requirements. *[IAS 1.49-50]*.

This requirement will be particularly important in those instances in which standards allow for disclosure of information required by IFRS outside the financial statements.

As well as requiring that the financial statements be clearly distinguished, IAS 1 also requires that each financial statement and the notes be identified clearly. Furthermore, the following is required to be displayed prominently, and repeated when that is necessary for the information presented to be understandable:

(a) the name of the reporting entity or other means of identification, and any change in that information from the end of the preceding period;

(b) whether the financial statements are of an individual entity or a group of entities;

(c) the date of the end of the reporting period or the period covered by the set of financial statements or the notes (presumably whichever is appropriate to that component of the financial statements);

(d) the presentation currency, as defined in IAS 21 – *The Effects of Changes in Foreign Exchange Rates* (discussed in Chapter 15 at 3); and

(e) the level of rounding used in presenting amounts in the financial statements. *[IAS 1.51]*.

These requirements are met by the use of appropriate headings for pages, statements, notes, and columns etc. The standard notes that judgement is required in determining the best way of presenting such information. For example, when the financial statements are presented electronically, separate pages are not always used; the above items then need to be presented to ensure that the information included in the financial statements can be understood. *[IAS 1.52]*. IAS 1 considers that financial statements are often made more understandable by presenting information in thousands or millions of units of the presentation currency. It considers this acceptable as long as the level of rounding in presentation is disclosed and material information is not omitted. *[IAS 1.53]*.

2.5.2 Statement of compliance with IFRS

As well as identifying which particular part of any larger document constitutes the financial statements, IAS 1 also requires that financial statements complying with IFRS make an explicit and unreserved statement of such compliance in the notes. *[IAS 1.16]*. As this statement itself is required for full compliance, its absence would render the whole financial statements non-compliant, even if there was otherwise full compliance. The standard goes on to say that 'an entity shall not describe financial statements as complying with IFRSs unless they comply with all the requirements of IFRSs.' *[IAS 1.16]*.

The note containing this statement of compliance is also usually where entities provide any other compliance statement required by local regulation. For example, entities required to comply with IFRS as adopted for use in the EU would typically state compliance with that requirement alongside the statement of compliance with IFRS itself (assuming, of course, that the financial statements were in full compliance with both).

3 THE STRUCTURE OF FINANCIAL STATEMENTS

As noted at 2.3 above, a complete set of financial statements under IAS 1 comprises the following, each of which should be presented with equal prominence: *[IAS 1.10-11]*

(a) a statement of financial position as at the end of the period;
(b) a statement of profit or loss and other comprehensive income for the period to be presented either as:
   (i) one single statement of comprehensive income with a section for profit and loss followed immediately by a section for other comprehensive income; or
   (ii) a separate statement of profit or loss and statement of comprehensive income. In this case, the former must be presented immediately before the latter;
(c) a statement of changes in equity for the period;
(d) a statement of cash flows for the period;
(e) notes, comprising significant accounting policies and other explanatory information; and
(f) a statement of financial position as at the beginning of the preceding period in certain circumstances (see 2.4 above). *[IAS 1.10-10A]*.

The standard adopts a generally permissive stance, by setting out minimum levels of required items to be shown in each statement (sometimes specifically on the face of the statement, and sometimes either on the face or in the notes) whilst allowing great flexibility of order and layout. The standard notes that sometimes it uses the term 'disclosure' in a broad sense, encompassing items 'presented in the financial statements'. It observes that other IFRSs also require disclosures and that, unless specified to the contrary, they may be made 'in the financial statements'. *[IAS 1.48]*. This begs the question: if not in 'the financial statements' then where else could they be made? We suspect this stems from, or is reflective of, an ambiguous use of similar words and phrases. In particular, 'financial statements' appears to be restricted to the 'primary' statements (statement of financial position, statement of profit or loss and other comprehensive income, statement of changes in equity and statement of cash flows) when describing what a 'complete set of financial statements' comprises (see 2.3 above). This is because a complete set also includes notes. For the purposes of specifying where a particular required disclosure should be made, we consider the term 'in the financial statements' is intended to mean anywhere within the 'complete set of financial statements' – in other words the primary statements or notes.

IAS 1 observes that cash flow information provides users of financial statements with a basis to assess the ability of the entity to generate cash and cash equivalents and the needs of the entity to utilise those cash flows. Requirements for the presentation of the statement of cash flows and related disclosures are set out IAS 7. *[IAS 1.111]*. Statements of cash flows are discussed in Chapter 40; each of the other primary statements listed above is discussed in the following sections.

3.1 The statement of financial position

3.1.1 The distinction between current/non-current assets and liabilities

In most situations (but see the exception discussed below, and the treatment of non-current assets held for sale discussed in Chapter 4 at 2.2.4) IAS 1 requires statements of financial position to distinguish current assets and liabilities from non-current ones. *[IAS 1.60]*. The standard uses the term 'non-current' to include tangible, intangible and financial assets of a long-term nature. It does not prohibit the use of alternative descriptions as long as the meaning is clear. *[IAS 1.67]*.

The standard explains the requirement to present current and non-current items separately by observing that when an entity supplies goods or services within a clearly identifiable operating cycle, separate classification of current and non-current assets and liabilities on the face of the statement of financial position will provide useful information by distinguishing the net assets that are continuously circulating as working capital from those used in long-term operations. Furthermore, the analysis will also highlight assets that are expected to be realised within the current operating cycle, and liabilities that are due for settlement within the same period. *[IAS 1.62]*. The distinction between current and non-current items therefore depends on the length of the entity's operating cycle. The standard states that the operating cycle of an entity is the time between the acquisition of assets for processing and their realisation in cash or cash equivalents. However, when the entity's normal operating cycle is not clearly identifiable, it is assumed to be twelve months. *[IAS 1.68, 70]*. The standard does not provide any guidance on how to determine if an entity's operating cycle is 'clearly identifiable'. In some businesses the time involved in producing goods or providing services varies significantly from one customer project to another. In such cases, it may be difficult to determine what the normal operating cycle is. In the end, management must consider all facts and circumstances and judgment to determine whether it is appropriate to consider that the operating cycle is clearly identifiable, or whether the twelve months default is to be used.

Once assets have been classified as non-current they should not normally be reclassified as current assets until they meet the criteria to be classified as held for sale in accordance with IFRS 5 (see Chapter 4 at 2.1). However, an entity which routinely sells items of property plant and equipment previously held for rental should transfer such items to inventory when they cease to be rented and become held for sale. *[IAS 16.68A]*. Assets of a class that an entity would normally regard as non-current that are acquired exclusively with a view to resale also should not be classified as current unless they meet the criteria in IFRS 5. *[IFRS 5.3]*.

The basic requirement of the standard is that current and non-current assets, and current and non-current liabilities, should be presented as separate classifications on the face of the statement of financial position. *[IAS 1.60]*. The standard defines current assets and current liabilities (discussed at 3.1.3 and 3.1.4 below), with the non-current category being the residual. *[IAS 1.66, 69]*. Example 3.2 at 3.1.7 below provides an illustration of a statement of financial position presenting this classification.

An exception to this requirement is when a presentation based on liquidity provides information that is reliable and is more relevant. When that exception applies, all assets and liabilities are required to be presented broadly in order of liquidity. *[IAS 1.60]*. The reason for this exception given by the standard is that some entities (such as financial institutions) do not supply goods or services within a clearly identifiable operating cycle, and for these entities a presentation of assets and liabilities in increasing or decreasing order of liquidity provides information that is reliable and more relevant than a current/non-current presentation. *[IAS 1.63]*.

The standard also makes clear that an entity is permitted to present some of its assets and liabilities using a current/non-current classification and others in order of liquidity when this provides information that is reliable and more relevant. It goes on to observe that the need for a mixed basis of presentation might arise when an entity has diverse operations. *[IAS 1.64]*.

Whichever method of presentation is adopted, IAS 1 requires for each asset and liability line item that combines amounts expected to be recovered or settled:

(a) no more than twelve months after the reporting period; and

(b) more than twelve months after the reporting period;

disclosure of the amount expected to be recovered or settled after more than twelve months. *[IAS 1.61]*.

The standard explains this requirement by noting that information about expected dates of realisation of assets and liabilities is useful in assessing the liquidity and solvency of an entity. In this vein, IAS 1 asserts that IFRS 7 – *Financial Instruments: Disclosures* – requires disclosure of the maturity dates of financial assets (including trade and other receivables) and financial liabilities (including trade and other payables). This assertion in IAS 1 is not strictly correct, as IFRS 7 in fact only requires a maturity analysis (rather than maturity dates) and only requires this for financial liabilities (see Chapter 54 at 5.4.2). Similarly, IAS 1 views information on the expected date of recovery and settlement of non-monetary assets and liabilities such as inventories and provisions as also useful, whether assets and liabilities are classified as current or as non-current. An example of this given by the standard is that an entity should disclose the amount of inventories that are expected to be recovered more than twelve months after the reporting period. *[IAS 1.65]*.

3.1.2 Non-current assets and disposal groups held for sale or distribution

The general requirement to classify items as current or non-current (or present them broadly in order of liquidity) is overlaid with further requirements by IFRS 5 regarding non-current assets and disposal groups held for sale or distribution (discussed in Chapter 4 at 3). The aim of IFRS 5 is that entities should present and disclose information that enables users of the financial statements to evaluate the financial effects of disposals of non-current assets (or disposal groups). *[IFRS 5.30]*. In pursuit of this aim, IFRS 5 requires:

- non-current assets and the assets of a disposal group classified as held for sale or distribution to be presented separately from other assets in the statement of financial position; and

- the liabilities of a disposal group classified as held for sale or distribution to be presented separately from other liabilities in the statement of financial position.

These assets and liabilities should not be offset and presented as a single amount. In addition:

(a) major classes of assets and liabilities classified as held for sale or distribution should generally be separately disclosed either on the face of the statement of financial position or in the notes (see 3.1.6 below). However, this is not necessary for a disposal group if it is a subsidiary that met the criteria to be classified as held for sale or distribution on acquisition; and

(b) any cumulative income or expense recognised in other comprehensive income relating to a non-current asset (or disposal group) classified as held for sale or distribution should be presented separately. *[IFRS 5.38-39]*.

3.1.3 Current assets

IAS 1 requires an asset to be classified as current when it satisfies any of the following criteria, with all other assets classified as non-current. The criteria are:

(a) it is expected to be realised in, or is intended for sale or consumption in, the entity's normal operating cycle (discussed at 3.1.1 above);

(b) it is held primarily for the purpose of trading;

(c) it is expected to be realised within twelve months after the end of the reporting period; or

(d) it is cash or a cash equivalent (as defined in IAS 7, see Chapter 40 at 1.1) unless it is restricted from being exchanged or used to settle a liability for at least twelve months after the end of the reporting period. *[IAS 1.66]*.

As an exception to this, deferred tax assets are never allowed to be classified as current. *[IAS 1.56]*.

Current assets include assets (such as inventories and trade receivables) that are sold, consumed or realised as part of the normal operating cycle even when they are not expected to be realised within twelve months after the reporting period. Current assets also include assets held primarily for the purpose of being traded, for example, some financial assets that meet the definition of held for trading in IFRS 9 – *Financial Instruments* – and the current portion of non-current financial assets. *[IAS 1.68]*.

3.1.4 Current liabilities

3.1.4.A Requirements for periods beginning before 1 January 2023

IAS 1 requires a liability to be classified as current when it satisfies any of the following criteria, with all other liabilities classified as non-current. The criteria for classifying a liability as current are:

(a) it is expected to be settled in the entity's normal operating cycle (discussed at 3.1.1 above);

(b) it is held primarily for the purpose of trading;

(c) it is due to be settled within twelve months after the end of the reporting period; or

(d) the entity does not have an unconditional right to defer settlement of the liability for at least twelve months after the end of the reporting period. Terms of a liability that could, at the option of the counterparty, result in its settlement by the issue of equity instruments do not affect its classification. *[IAS 1.69]*.

Notwithstanding the foregoing, deferred tax liabilities are never allowed to be classified as current. *[IAS 1.56]*.

The requirements at (d) above are discussed by the IASB in its Basis for Conclusions which can be summarised as follows. According to the *Conceptual Framework*, conversion of a liability into equity is a form of settlement. The Board concluded, as part of its improvements project in 2007, that classifying a liability on the basis of the requirements to transfer cash or other assets rather than on settlement better reflects the liquidity and solvency position of an entity. In response to comments received, the Board decided to clarify that the exception to the unconditional right to defer settlement of a liability for at least twelve months criterion in (d) above only applies to the classification of a liability that can, at the option of the counterparty, be settled by the issuance of the entity's equity instruments. Thus the exception does not apply to all liabilities that may be settled by the issuance of equity. *[IAS 1.BC 38L-P]*.

In an agenda decision of November 2010 the Interpretations Committee reconfirmed (d) above by stating that a debt scheduled for repayment after more than a year which is, however, payable on demand of the lender is a current liability.

The standard notes that some current liabilities, such as trade payables and some accruals for employee and other operating costs, are part of the working capital used in the entity's normal operating cycle. Such operating items are classified as current liabilities even if they are due to be settled more than twelve months after the end of the reporting period. *[IAS 1.70]*.

However, neither IAS 19 – *Employee Benefits* – nor IAS 1 specifies where in the statement of financial position an asset or liability in respect of a defined benefit plan should be presented, nor whether such balances should be shown separately on the face of the statement or only in the notes – this is left to the judgement of the reporting entity (see 3.1.5 below). When the format of the statement of financial position distinguishes current assets and liabilities from non-current ones, the question arises as to whether this split needs also to be made for defined benefit plan balances. IAS 19 does not specify whether such a split should be made, on the grounds that it may sometimes be arbitrary. *[IAS 19.133, BC200]*. In practice few, if any, entities make this split.

Some current liabilities are not settled as part of the normal operating cycle, but are due for settlement within twelve months after the end of the reporting period or held primarily for the purpose of being traded. Examples given by the standard are some (but not necessarily all) financial liabilities that meet the definition of held for trading in accordance with IFRS 9, bank overdrafts, and the current portion of non-current financial liabilities, dividends payable, income taxes and other non-trade payables. Financial liabilities that provide financing on a long-term basis (and are not, therefore, part of the working capital used in the entity's normal operating cycle) and are not due for settlement within twelve months after the end of the reporting period are non-current liabilities. *[IAS 1.71]*.

126 *Chapter 3*

The assessment of a liability as current or non-current is applied very strictly in IAS 1. In particular, a liability should be classified as current:

(a) when it is due to be settled within twelve months after the end of the reporting period, even if:

   (i) the original term was for a period longer than twelve months; and

   (ii) an agreement to refinance, or to reschedule payments, on a long-term basis is completed after the period end and before the financial statements are authorised for issue (although disclosure of the post period end refinancing would be required); *[IAS 1.72, 76]* or

(b) when an entity breaches a provision of a long-term loan arrangement on or before the period end with the effect that the liability becomes payable on demand. This is the case even if the lender agreed, after the period end and before the authorisation of the financial statements for issue, not to demand payment as a consequence of the breach (although the post period end agreement would be disclosed). The meaning of the term 'authorised for issue' is discussed in Chapter 38 at 2.1.1. The standard explains that the liability should be classified as current because, at the period end, the entity does not have an unconditional right to defer its settlement for at least twelve months after that date. *[IAS 1.74, 76]*. However, the liability would be classified as non-current if the lender agreed by the period end to provide a period of grace ending at least twelve months after the reporting period, within which the entity can rectify the breach and during which the lender cannot demand immediate repayment. *[IAS 1.75]*.

The key point here is that for a liability to be classified as non-current requires that the entity has at the end of the reporting period an unconditional right to defer its settlement for at least twelve months thereafter. Accordingly, the standard explains that liabilities would be non-current if an entity expects, and has the discretion, to refinance or roll over an obligation for at least twelve months after the period end under an existing loan facility, even if it would otherwise be due within a shorter period. However, when refinancing or rolling over the obligation is not at the discretion of the entity the obligation is classified as current. *[IAS 1.73]*.

3.1.4.B Changes to IAS 1 for periods beginning on or after 1 January 2023

In January 2020 the IASB published *Classification of Liabilities as Current or Non-current – Amendments to IAS 1*. The amendments makes some changes to the requirements, as set out below. The amendments are effective for periods beginning on or after 1 January 2023; early adoption is permitted if disclosed. *[IAS 1(2023).139U]*.

The changes to the provisions of IAS 1 are:

(a) References to 'an unconditional right' in paragraphs 69 and 74 (discussed at 3.1.4.A above) are replaced with references to 'a right'.

(b) A new paragraph 72A has been added clarifying that a right to defer settlement of a liability for at least twelve months must have substance and must exist at the end of the reporting period. If the right is subject to compliance with specified conditions, the right exists at the end of the reporting period only if the entity complies with those conditions at the end of the reporting period. The conditions must be complied with at the end of the reporting period even if the lender does not test compliance until a later date.

(c) A new paragraph 75A is added to stipulate that a liability must be shown as non-current if there is a right to defer payment for at least twelve months. This is so irrespective of the likelihood of that right being exercised. Furthermore, any liability meeting the criteria to be classified as non-current must be classified as such, notwithstanding: any intention or expectation of the entity that it will be settled within twelve months; or, actual settlement before the accounts are authorised for issue.

(d) New paragraphs 76A and 76B have been introduced, which deal with the meaning of the 'settlement' of a liability in equity of the reporting entity. In circumstances where a counterparty has the option to require settlement in equity of the reporting entity of a liability within twelve months, the liability would be classified as current unless the entity classifies the option as an equity instrument, recognising it separately from the liability as an equity component of a compound financial instrument. (See Chapter 47 at 4).

Some of these amendments will require changes to current practices, for some entities. For instance, some entities may, under current practice, consider management intentions or expectations about future covenant breaches or settlements as relevant when assessing the appropriate classification. Others may consider that a right to defer settlement at least twelve months only needs to exist at agreed upon testing dates, not necessarily at the end of the reporting period (if not a testing date), in order to classify a liability as non-current. Still others may consider that the exception in the current standard applicable to convertible instruments applies regardless of whether the embedded derivative is accounted for as an equity or liability component of a compound financial instrument.

3.1.4.C Practical illustrations of the requirements

Some common scenarios involving debt covenants are illustrated in the following example.

Example 3.1: **Determining whether liabilities should be presented as current or non-current**

Scenario 1

An entity has a long-term loan arrangement containing a debt covenant. The specific requirements in the debt covenant have to be met as at 31 December every year. The loan is due in more than 12 months. The entity breaches the debt covenant at or before the period end. As a result, the loan becomes payable on demand.

Scenario 2

Same as scenario 1, but the loan arrangement stipulates that the entity has a grace period of 3 months to rectify the breach and during which the lender cannot demand immediate repayment.

Scenario 3

Same as scenario 1, but the lender agreed not to demand repayment as a consequence of the breach. The entity obtains this waiver:

(a) at or before the period end and the waiver is for a period of more than 12 months after the period end;

(b) at or before the period end and the waiver is for a period of less than 12 months after the period end;

(c) after the period end but before the financial statements are authorised for issue.

Scenario 4

An entity has a long-term loan arrangement containing a debt covenant. The loan is due in more than 12 months. At the period end, the debt covenants are met. However, circumstances change unexpectedly and the entity breaches the debt covenant after the period end but before the financial statements are authorised for issue.

As discussed in Chapter 54 at 4.4.9, IFRS 7 requires the following disclosures for any loans payable recognised at the reporting date:
- details of any defaults during the period of principal, interest, sinking fund, or redemption terms;
- the carrying amount of the loans payable in default at the reporting date; and
- whether the default was remedied, or the terms of the loans payable were renegotiated, before the financial statements were authorised for issue.

If, during the period, there were breaches of loan agreement terms other than those described above, the same information should be disclosed if those breaches permitted the lender to demand accelerated repayment (unless the breaches were remedied, or the terms of the loan were renegotiated, on or before the reporting date).

As noted at 5.5 below, IAS 1 requires certain disclosures of refinancing and rectification of loan agreement breaches which happen after the end of the reporting period and before the accounts are authorised for issue.

The table below sets out whether debt is to be presented as current or non-current and whether the above disclosures are required.

	Scenario 1	Scenario 2	Scenario 3(a)	Scenario 3(b)	Scenario 3(c)	Scenario 4
At the period end, does the entity have an unconditional right to defer the settlement of the liability for at least 12 months?	no	no	yes	no	no	yes
Classification of the liability	current	current	non-current	current	current	non-current
Are the above IFRS 7 disclosures required?	yes	yes	no	yes	yes	no
Are the disclosures in IAS 1 required?	no	no	no	no	yes	no

3.1.5 Information required on the face of the statement of financial position

IAS 1 does not contain a prescriptive format or order for the statement of financial position. *[IAS 1.57]*. Rather, it contains two mechanisms which require certain information to be shown on the face of the statement. First, it contains a list of specific items for which this is required, on the basis that they are sufficiently different in nature or function to warrant separate presentation. *[IAS 1.54, 57]*. Second, it stipulates that: additional line items (including the disaggregation of those items specifically required), headings and subtotals should be presented on the face of the statement of financial position when such presentation is relevant to an understanding of the entity's financial position. *[IAS 1.55]*. Clearly this is a highly judgemental decision for entities to make when preparing a statement of financial position, and allows a wide variety of possible presentations. The judgement as to whether additional items should be presented separately is based on an assessment of:

(a) the nature and liquidity of assets;
(b) the function of assets within the entity; and
(c) the amounts, nature and timing of liabilities. *[IAS 1.58]*.

IAS 1 indicates that the use of different measurement bases for different classes of assets suggests that their nature or function differs and, therefore, that they should be presented as separate line items. For example, different classes of property, plant and equipment can be carried at cost or revalued amounts in accordance with IAS 16 – *Property, Plant and Equipment*. *[IAS 1.59]*.

The face of the statement of financial position should include line items that present the following amounts: *[IAS 1.54]*

(a) property, plant and equipment;
(b) investment property;
(c) intangible assets;
(d) financial assets (excluding amounts shown under (f), (i) and (j));
(e) groups of contracts within the scope of IFRS 17 – *Insurance Contracts* – that are assets arising from each of:
   (i) insurance contracts; and
   (ii) reinsurance contracts;
(f) investments accounted for using the equity method;
(g) biological assets;
(h) inventories;
(i) trade and other receivables;
(j) cash and cash equivalents;
(k) the total of assets classified as held for sale and assets included in disposal groups classified as held for sale in accordance with IFRS 5;
(l) trade and other payables;
(m) provisions;
(n) groups of contracts within the scope of IFRS 17 that are liabilities arising from each of:
   (i) insurance contracts; and
   (ii) reinsurance contracts;
(o) financial liabilities (excluding amounts shown under (l) and (m));
(p) liabilities and assets for current tax, as defined in IAS 12;
(q) deferred tax liabilities and deferred tax assets, as defined in IAS 12;
(r) liabilities included in disposal groups classified as held for sale in accordance with IFRS 5;
(s) non-controlling interests, presented within equity; and
(t) issued capital and reserves attributable to owners of the parent.

The standard notes that items above represent a list of items that are sufficiently different in nature or function to warrant separate presentation on the face of the statement of financial position. In addition:

(a) line items should be included when the size, nature or function of an item or aggregation of similar items is such that separate presentation is relevant to an understanding of the entity's financial position; and
(b) the descriptions used and the ordering of items or aggregation of similar items may be amended according to the nature of the entity and its transactions, to provide information that is relevant to an understanding of the entity's financial position. For example, a financial institution may amend the above descriptions to provide information that is relevant to the operations of a financial institution. *[IAS 1.57]*.

As noted above, when relevant to an understanding of financial position, additional line items and subtotals should be presented. Regarding subtotals, IAS 1 requires that they should:

(a) be comprised of line items made up of amounts recognised and measured in accordance with IFRS;

(b) be presented and labelled in a manner that makes the line items that constitute the subtotal clear and understandable;

(c) be consistent from period to period (see 4.1.4 below); and

(d) not be displayed with more prominence than the subtotals and totals required in IFRS for the statement of financial position. *[IAS 1.55A, BC38G]*.

The distinction between trade and financial liabilities in certain supplier finance arrangements is discussed in Chapter 52 at 6.5.

3.1.6 Information required either on the face of the statement of financial position or in the notes

IAS 1 requires further sub-classifications of the line items shown on the face of the statement of financial position to be presented either on the face of the statement or in the notes. The requirements for these further sub-classifications are approached by the standard in a similar manner to those for line items on the face of the statement of financial position. There is a prescriptive list of items required (see below) and also a more general requirement that the sub-classifications should be made in a manner appropriate to the entity's operations. *[IAS 1.77]*. The standard notes that the detail provided in sub-classifications depends on the requirements of IFRSs (as numerous disclosures are required by other standards) and on the size, nature and function of the amounts involved. *[IAS 1.78]*.

Aside of the specific requirements, deciding what level of detailed disclosure is necessary is clearly a judgemental exercise. As is the case for items on the face of the statement of financial position, IAS 1 requires that the judgement as to whether additional items should be presented separately should be based on an assessment of:

(a) the nature and liquidity of assets;

(b) the function of assets within the entity; and

(c) the amounts, nature and timing of liabilities. *[IAS 1.58, 78]*.

The disclosures will also vary for each item, examples given by the standard are:

(a) items of property, plant and equipment are disaggregated into classes in accordance with IAS 16;

(b) receivables are disaggregated into amounts receivable from trade customers, receivables from related parties, prepayments and other amounts;

(c) inventories are disaggregated, in accordance with IAS 2 – *Inventories*, into classifications such as merchandise, production supplies, materials, work in progress and finished goods;

(d) provisions are disaggregated into provisions for employee benefits and other items; and

(e) equity capital and reserves are disaggregated into various classes, such as paid-in capital, share premium and reserves. *[IAS 1.78]*.

IAS 1 specifically requires the following information regarding equity and share capital to be shown either on the face of the statement of financial position or in the notes:

(a) for each class of share capital:
   (i) the number of shares authorised;
   (ii) the number of shares issued and fully paid, and issued but not fully paid;
   (iii) par value per share, or that the shares have no par value;
   (iv) a reconciliation of the number of shares outstanding at the beginning and at the end of the period;
   (v) the rights, preferences and restrictions attaching to that class including restrictions on the distribution of dividends and the repayment of capital;
   (vi) shares in the entity held by the entity or by its subsidiaries or associates; and
   (vii) shares reserved for issue under options and contracts for the sale of shares, including the terms and amounts; and

(b) a description of the nature and purpose of each reserve within equity. *[IAS 1.79]*.

An entity without share capital (such as a partnership or trust) should disclose information equivalent to that required by (a) above, showing changes during the period in each category of equity interest, and the rights, preferences and restrictions attaching to each category of equity interest. *[IAS 1.80]*.

IAS 32 – *Financial Instruments: Presentation* – allows two specific classes of liabilities to be reported as equity. These are:

- puttable financial instruments; and
- instruments that impose on the entity an obligation to deliver to another party a *pro rata* share of the net assets of the entity only on liquidation.

Both terms are defined and discussed at length in IAS 32 (see Chapter 47 at 4.6).

If an entity reclassifies one of these items between financial liabilities and equity, IAS 1 requires disclosure of:

- the amount reclassified into and out of each category (financial liabilities or equity); and
- the timing and reason for that reclassification. *[IAS 1.80A]*.

3.1.7 Illustrative statements of financial position

The implementation guidance accompanying IAS 1 provides an illustration of a statement of financial position presented to distinguish current and non-current items. It makes clear that other formats may be equally appropriate, as long as the distinction is clear. *[IAS 1.IG3]*. As discussed in Chapter 4 at 2.2.4, IFRS 5 provides further guidance relating to the presentation of non-current assets and disposal groups held for sale. *[IAS 1.IG Part I]*.

Example 3.2: Illustrative statement of financial position

XYZ GROUP – STATEMENT OF FINANCIAL POSITION AS AT 31 DECEMBER 2021

(in thousands of currency units)

	2021	2020
ASSETS		
Non-current assets		
Property, plant and equipment	350,700	360,020
Goodwill	80,800	91,200
Other intangible assets	227,470	227,470
Investments in associates	100,150	110,770
Investments in equity instruments	142,500	156,000
	901,620	945,460
Current assets		
Inventories	135,230	132,500
Trade receivables	91,600	110,800
Other current assets	25,650	12,540
Cash and cash equivalents	312,400	322,900
	564,880	578,740
Total assets	1,466,500	1,524,200
EQUITY AND LIABILITIES		
Equity attributable to owners of the parent		
Share capital	650,000	600,000
Retained earnings	243,500	161,700
Other components of equity	10,200	21,200
	903,700	782,900
Non-controlling interests	70,050	48,600
Total equity	973,750	831,500
Non-current liabilities		
Long-term borrowings	120,000	160,000
Deferred tax	28,800	26,040
Long-term provisions	28,850	52,240
Total non-current liabilities	177,650	238,280

	2021	2020
Current liabilities		
Trade and other payables	115,100	187,620
Short-term borrowings	150,000	200,000
Current portion of long-term borrowings	10,000	20,000
Current tax payable	35,000	42,000
Short-term provisions	5,000	4,800
Total current liabilities	315,100	454,420
Total liabilities	492,750	692,700
Total equity and liabilities	1,466,500	1,524,200

3.2 The statement of comprehensive income and the statement of profit or loss

3.2.1 Profit and loss and comprehensive income

The IASB regards all changes in net assets (other than the introduction and return of capital) and not just more traditional realised profits, as 'performance' in its widest sense. Accordingly, IAS 1 requires a performance statement showing such changes and calls it a statement of comprehensive income.

Total comprehensive income is defined by IAS 1 as the change in equity during a period resulting from transactions and other events, other than those changes resulting from transactions with owners in their capacity as owners. It comprises all components of 'profit or loss' and of 'other comprehensive income'. These two terms are defined as follows:

- profit or loss is the total of income less expenses, excluding the components of other comprehensive income; and
- other comprehensive income comprises items of income and expense (including reclassification adjustments) that are not recognised in profit or loss as required or permitted by other IFRSs. *[IAS 1.7]*.

What this means is that profit and loss is the default category – all comprehensive income is part of profit and loss unless a provision of IFRS requires or permits it to be 'other' comprehensive income. *[IAS 1.88]*.

The use of a variety of terminology is recognised by IAS 1 which notes the following. 'Although this Standard uses the terms "other comprehensive income", "profit or loss" and "total comprehensive income", an entity may use other terms to describe the totals as long as the meaning is clear. For example, an entity may use the term "net income" to describe profit or loss.' *[IAS 1.8]*.

IAS 1 sets out the following items which are included in other comprehensive income:

(a) changes in revaluation surplus relating to property, plant and equipment and intangible assets;

(b) remeasurements on defined benefit plans in accordance with IAS 19;

(c) gains and losses arising from translating the financial statements of a foreign operation;

(d) gains and losses from investments in equity instruments designated at fair value through other comprehensive income;

(e) gains and losses on financial assets measured at fair value through other comprehensive income;

(f) the effective portion of gains and losses on hedging instruments in a cash flow hedge and the gains and losses on hedging instruments that hedge investments in equity instruments measured at fair value through other comprehensive income;

(g) for particular liabilities designated as at fair value through profit and loss, the amount of the fair value changes attributable to changes in the liability's credit risk;

(h) changes in the value of the time value of options when separating the intrinsic value and time value of an option contract and designating as the hedging instrument only the changes in the intrinsic value;

(i) changes in the value of the forward elements of forward contracts when separating the forward element and spot element of a forward contract and designating as the hedging instrument only the changes in the spot element, and changes in the value of the foreign currency basis spread of a financial instrument when excluding it from the designation of that financial instrument as the hedging instrument; and

(j) insurance finance income and expenses related to insurance or reinsurance contracts which is excluded from profit or loss in certain circumstances in accordance with IFRS 17. *[IAS 1.7]*.

IAS requires that all items of income and expense be presented either:

(a) in a single statement of profit or loss and other comprehensive income (with a separate section for each in the order stated); or

(b) in two separate statements:
  (i) a statement of profit or loss; and
  (ii) a statement of comprehensive income beginning with profit and loss and containing components of other comprehensive income. *[IAS 1.10A]*.

If the approach in (b) is followed, the statement of profit or loss must be displayed immediately before the statement of comprehensive income. *[IAS 1.10A]*.

In addition to this choice, IAS 1 provides that different titles may be used for these statements. *[IAS 1.10]*.

Many entities continue to present a separate statement of profit or loss (often titled 'income statement'), and this section is structured in these terms. However, the requirements are the same whether total comprehensive income is presented in one or two statements.

IAS 1 adopts an essentially permissive approach to the format of the statement of profit or loss and statement of comprehensive income. It observes that, because the effects of an entity's various activities, transactions and other events differ in frequency, potential for gain or loss and predictability, disclosing the components of financial performance assists users in understanding the financial performance achieved and in making projections of future performance. *[IAS 1.86]*. In other words, some analysis of the make-up of net profit and other comprehensive income is needed, but a wide variety of presentations would all be acceptable.

IAS 1 requires certain specific items to appear on the face of the statement(s) and then supplements this with a more general requirement that:

- additional line items be presented (including the disaggregation of those specifically required) on the face of the statement(s); and
- the descriptions used and the ordering of items be amended;

when this is relevant to an understanding of the entity's financial performance. *[IAS 1.85-86]*.

Presentation of financial statements and accounting policies 135

The standard explains that additional line items should be included, and the descriptions used and the ordering of items amended when this is necessary to explain the elements of financial performance. Factors to be considered would include materiality and the nature and function of the items of income and expense. An example of this is that a financial institution may amend the descriptions to provide information that is relevant to the operations of a financial institution. *[IAS 1.86]*.

When additional subtotals are presented, line items should be given that reconcile those subtotals with the subtotals or totals required in IFRS. *[IAS 1.85B]*.

When such additional subtotals are presented, they should:

(a) be comprised of line items made up of amounts recognised and measured in accordance with IFRS;

(b) be presented and labelled in a manner that makes the line items that constitute the subtotal clear and understandable;

(c) be consistent from period to period (see 4.1.4 below); and

(d) not be displayed with more prominence than the subtotals and totals required in IFRS for the statement(s) presenting profit or loss and other comprehensive income. *[IAS 1.85A]*.

3.2.2 Information required on the face of the statement of profit or loss

As is the case for the statement of financial position, IAS 1 sets out certain items which must appear on the face of the statement of profit or loss and other required disclosures which may be made either on the face or in the notes.

The face of the statement of profit or loss should include, in addition to items required by other IFRSs, line items that present the following amounts (although as noted above, the order and description of the items should be amended as necessary): *[IAS 1.82]*

(a) revenue, presenting separately:
   (i) interest revenue calculated using the effective interest method; and
   (ii) insurance revenue under IFRS 17;

(b) gains and losses from the derecognition of financial assets measured at amortised cost;

(c) insurance service expenses from contracts issued in accordance with of IFRS 17;

(e) income or expenses from reinsurance contracts held in accordance with of IFRS 17;

(f) finance costs;

(g) impairment losses (including reversals of impairment losses or impairment gains) determined under IFRS 9;

(h) insurance finance income or expenses from contracts issued in accordance with of IFRS 17;

(i) finance income or expenses from reinsurance contracts held in accordance with of IFRS 17;

(j) share of the profit or loss of associates and joint ventures accounted for using the equity method;

(k) any difference between fair value and the previous carrying amount at the date of reclassification when a financial asset is reclassified out of the amortised cost category to be measured at fair value through profit or loss;

(l) any accumulated gain or loss previously recognised in other comprehensive income that is reclassified to profit or loss when a financial asset is reclassified out of the fair value through other comprehensive income category so that it is measured at fair value through profit or loss;

(m) tax expense;

(n) a single amount comprising the total of:
  (i) the post-tax profit or loss of discontinued operations; and
  (ii) the post-tax gain or loss recognised on the measurement to fair value less costs to sell or on the disposal of the assets or disposal group(s) constituting the discontinued operation; *[IFRS 5.33(a)(ii)]*

(o) profit or loss; *[IAS 1.81A]* and

(p) the following as allocations of profit or loss for the period:
  (i) profit or loss attributable to non-controlling interests; and
  (ii) profit or loss attributable to owners of the parent. *[IAS 1.81B]*.

It should be noted that (with the exception of (n) above) this provision of the standard does not require a single line item for each of the above. Indeed, in some circumstances a single line item may not be possible.

As discussed at 3.2.3 below, an analysis of expenses is required based either on their nature or their function. IAS 1 encourages, but does not require this to be shown on the face of the statement of profit or loss. *[IAS 1.99-100]*. The specific items listed above essentially identify the results of transactions by their nature (that is to say, not by their function in the business). Accordingly, those entities categorising expenses by function and also following the 'encouragement' to display this on the face of the statement could be required to present one or more of the above in more than one place within the statement. This may be particularly relevant to entities choosing to differentiate between 'operating' items and other items in the statement of profit or loss (which is a quite common practice and one acknowledged by the IASB – discussed at 3.2.2.A below) as some items in the list above may contain the results of transactions from operating and non-operating activities. By way of example, items (g) and (j) above could encompass both operating and non-operating items.

In practice judgement will be required when applying these provisions of the standard along with the more general requirements on: additional line items and subtotals; and, the ordering and description of line items, discussed at 3.2.1 above.

The implementation guidance accompanying the standard provides an illustrative example of a statement of profit or loss (see Example 3.4 at 3.2.3.A below).

3.2.2.A Operating profit

The current IAS 1 has omitted the requirement in the 1997 version to disclose the results of operating activities as a line item on the face of the statement of profit or loss. The reason given for this in the Basis for Conclusions to the standard because 'Operating activities' are not defined in the standard, and the Board decided not to require disclosure of an undefined item. *[IAS 1.BC55]*.

The Basis for Conclusions to IAS 1 goes on to state that

'The Board recognises that an entity may elect to disclose the results of operating activities, or a similar line item, even though this term is not defined. In such cases, the Board notes that the entity should ensure the amount disclosed is representative of activities that would normally be considered to be "operating".

'In the Board's view, it would be misleading and would impair the comparability of financial statements if items of an operating nature were excluded from the results of operating activities, even if that had been industry practice. For example, it would be inappropriate to exclude items clearly related to operations (such as inventory write-downs and restructuring and relocation expenses) because they occur irregularly or infrequently or are unusual in amount. Similarly, it would be inappropriate to exclude items on the grounds that they do not involve cash flows, such as depreciation and amortisation expenses.' *[IAS 1.BC56]*.

IAS 1 requires the face of the statement of profit or loss to show the share of the profit or loss of associates and joint ventures accounted for using the equity method.

For entities presenting a measure of operating profit, as noted at 3.2.2 above, in our view it is acceptable for an entity to determine which such investments form part of its operating activities and include their results in that measure, with the results of non-operating investments excluded from it.

3.2.3 Classification of expenses recognised in profit or loss by nature or function

IAS 1 states that components of financial performance may differ in terms of frequency, potential for gain or loss and predictability, and requires that expenses should be sub-classified to highlight this. *[IAS 1.101]*. To achieve this, the standard requires the presentation of an analysis of expenses (but only those recognised in profit or loss) using a classification based on either their nature or their function within the entity, whichever provides information that is reliable and more relevant. *[IAS 1.99]*. It is because each method of presentation has merit for different types of entities, that the standard requires management to make this selection. *[IAS 1.105]*. As noted at 3.2.2 above IAS 1 encourages, but does not require the chosen analysis to be shown on the face of the statement of profit or loss. *[IAS 1.100]*. This means that entities are permitted to disclose the classification on the face on a mixed basis, as long as the required classification is provided in the notes. Indeed, the IASB itself produces an example of such a statement of profit or loss in an illustrative example to IAS 7. *[IAS 7.IE A]*.

The standard also notes that the choice between the function of expense method and the nature of expense method will depend on historical and industry factors and the nature of the entity. Both methods provide an indication of those costs that might vary, directly or indirectly, with the level of sales or production of the entity. However, because information on the nature of expenses is useful in predicting future cash flows, additional disclosure is required when the function of expense classification is used (see 3.2.3.B below). *[IAS 1.105]*.

3.2.3.A Analysis of expenses by nature

For some entities, this 'reliable and more relevant information' may be achieved by aggregating expenses for display in profit or loss according to their nature (for example, depreciation, purchases of materials, transport costs, employee benefits and advertising costs), and not reallocating them among various functions within the entity. IAS 1 observes that this method may be simple to apply because no allocations of expenses to functional classifications are necessary. The standard illustrates a classification using the nature of expense method as follows: *[IAS 1.102]*

Example 3.3: *Example of classification of expenses by nature*

Revenue	x
Other income	x
Changes in inventories of finished goods and work in progress	x
Raw materials and consumables used	x
Employee benefits expense	x
Depreciation and amortisation expense	x
Other expenses	x
Total expenses	(x)
Profit before tax	x

The implementation guidance accompanying the standard provides a further example of a statement of profit or loss analysing expenses by nature. Whilst very similar to the above, it is expanded to show further captions as follows: *[IAS 1.IG Part I]*

Example 3.4: Illustrative statement of profit or loss with expenses classified by nature

XYZ GROUP – STATEMENT OF PROFIT OR LOSS FOR THE YEAR ENDED 31 DECEMBER 2021

(in thousands of currency units)

	2021	2020
Revenue	390,000	355,000
Other income	20,667	11,300
Changes in inventories of finished goods and work in progress	(115,100)	(107,900)
Work performed by the entity and capitalised	16,000	15,000
Raw material and consumables used	(96,000)	(92,000)
Employee benefits expense	(45,000)	(43,000)
Depreciation and amortisation expense	(19,000)	(17,000)
Impairment of property, plant and equipment	(4,000)	–
Other expenses	(6,000)	(5,500)
Finance costs	(15,000)	(18,000)
Share of profit of associates	35,100	30,100
Profit before tax	161,667	128,000
Income tax expense	(40,417)	(32,000)
Profit for the year from continuing operations	121,250	96,000
Loss for the year from discontinued operations	–	(30,500)
Profit for the year	121,250	65,500
Profit attributable to:		
Owners of the parent	97,000	52,400
Non-controlling interests	24,250	13,100
	121,250	65,500
Earnings per share (currency unit)		
Basic and diluted	0.46	0.30

A footnote to the illustrative examples explains that 'share of profits of associates' means share of the profit attributable to the owners of the associates and hence is after tax and non-controlling interests in the associates.

Example 3.4 above is an example of presenting comprehensive income in two statements. Example 3.6 below illustrates the presentation of comprehensive income in a single statement. An entity using the approach above would need to give a second statement presenting items of other comprehensive income – this would simply be the bottom portion of Example 3.6, starting with 'Profit for the year' and omitting earnings per share and the analysis of profit between owners and non-controlling interests. This is illustrated in Example 3.8 below.

3.2.3.B Analysis of expenses by function

For some entities, 'reliable and more relevant information' may be achieved by aggregating expenses for display purposes according to their function for example, as part of cost of sales, the costs of distribution or administrative activities. Under this method, IAS 1 requires as a minimum, disclosure of cost of sales separately from other expenses. The standard observes that this method can provide more relevant information to users than the classification of expenses by nature, but that allocating costs to functions may require arbitrary allocations and involve considerable judgement. An example of classification using the function of expense method given by the standard is set out below. [IAS 1.103].

Example 3.5: Example of classification of expenses by function

Revenue	×
Cost of sales	(×)
Gross profit	×
Other income	×
Distribution costs	(×)
Administrative expenses	(×)
Other expenses	(×)
Profit before tax	×

Entities classifying expenses by function are required by IAS 1 to disclose additional information on the nature of expenses. The standard highlights that this requirement also applies to depreciation and amortisation expense and employee benefits expense, [IAS 1.104], which seems a redundant considering that the disclosure of these items (broken down into their components) is specifically required by IAS 16, IAS 19 and IAS 38 – *Intangible Assets*.

The standard gives another illustration of expenses classified by function in the profit and loss section of the single statement of comprehensive income – see Example 3.6 below.

3.2.4 The statement of comprehensive income

3.2.4.A The face of the statement of comprehensive income

Whether presented as a separate statement or as a section of a combined statement (see 3.2.1 above), the face of the statement of comprehensive income should set out the items below. The items in (b) and, separately, the items in (c) should be presented in two groups, one including items which may subsequently be reclassified into profit or loss and another including items which will not: [IAS 1.7, 81A, 82A, 91]

(a) profit or loss (if two statements are presented this will be a single line item);
(b) each item of comprehensive income, classified by nature, which include:
  (i) changes in revaluation surplus relating to property, plant and equipment and intangible assets;
  (ii) remeasurements on defined benefit plans in accordance with IAS 19;
  (iii) gains and losses arising from translating the financial statements of a foreign operation;

Presentation of financial statements and accounting policies   141

(iv) gains and losses from investments in equity instruments designated at fair value through other comprehensive income;

(v) gains and losses on financial assets measured at fair value through other comprehensive income;

(vi) the effective portion of gains and losses on hedging instruments in a cash flow hedge and the gains and losses on hedging instruments that hedge investments in equity instruments measured at fair value through other comprehensive income;

(vii) for particular liabilities designated as at fair value through profit and loss, fair value changes attributable to changes in the liability's credit risk;

(viii) changes in the value of the time value of options when separating the intrinsic value and time value of an option contract and designating as the hedging instrument only the changes in the intrinsic value;

(ix) changes in the value of the forward elements of forward contracts when separating the forward element and spot element of a forward contract and designating as the hedging instrument only the changes in the spot element, and changes in the value of the foreign currency basis spread of a financial instrument when excluding it from the designation of that financial instrument as the hedging instrument;

(x) insurance finance income and expenses related to insurance or reinsurance contracts which is excluded from profit or loss in certain circumstances in accordance with IFRS 17;

(xi) the aggregate amount of tax relating to components of comprehensive income, unless the components are shown individually net of tax (see 3.2.4.C below). Tax should be allocated between the two groups mentioned above;

(c) share of the items of other comprehensive income of associates and joint ventures accounted for using the equity method;

(d) reclassification adjustments, unless the components of comprehensive income are shown after any related reclassification adjustments (see B below); *[IAS 1.94]* and

(e) total comprehensive income.

In a separate statement of other comprehensive income IAS 1 also requires an analysis of total comprehensive income for the period between that attributable to:

(a) non-controlling interests, and

(b) owners of the parent. *[IAS 1.81B]*.

In a combined statement of total comprehensive income, the equivalent analysis of profit and loss would also be required as would earnings per share disclosures (discussed in Chapter 37 at 7). When two separate statements are presented, these would appear on the statement of profit or loss. *[IAS 33.67A]*.

IAS 1 provides an illustration of both the 'one statement' and 'two statement' approach in its implementation guidance. An illustration of a single statement of comprehensive income is given in Example 3.6 below. *[IAS 1 IG Part I]*. An illustration of a separate statement of profit or loss is given in Example 3.4 above and an illustrative separate statement of other comprehensive income is given in Example 3.8 below.

Example 3.6: Presentation of comprehensive income in one statement and the classification of expenses by function

XYZ Group – Statement of profit or loss and other comprehensive income for the year ended 31 December 2021

(in thousands of currency units)

	2021	2020
Revenue	390,000	355,000
Cost of sales	(245,000)	(230,000)
Gross profit	145,000	125,000
Other income	20,667	11,300
Distribution costs	(9,000)	(8,700)
Administrative expenses	(20,000)	(21,000)
Other expenses	(2,100)	(1,200)
Finance costs	(8,000)	(7,500)
Share of profit of associates[1]	35,100	30,100
Profit before tax	161,667	128,000
Income tax expense	(40,417)	(32,000)
Profit for the year from continuing operations	121,250	96,000
Loss for the year from discontinued operations	–	(30,500)
PROFIT FOR THE YEAR	121,250	65,500
Other comprehensive income:		
Items that will not be reclassified to profit or loss:		
Gains on property revaluation	933	3,367
Investments in equity instruments	(24,000)	26,667
Remeasurements of defined benefit pension plans	(667)	1,333
Share of other comprehensive income of associates[2]	400	(700)
Income tax relating to items that will not be reclassified[3]	5,834	(7,667)
	(17,500)	23,000
Items that may be reclassified subsequently to profit or loss:		
Exchange differences on translating foreign operations[4]	5,334	10,667
Cash flow hedges[4]	(667)	(4,000)
Income tax relating to items that may be reclassified[3]	(1,167)	(1,667)
	3,500	5,000
Other comprehensive income for the year, net of tax	(14,000)	28,000
TOTAL COMPREHENSIVE INCOME FOR THE YEAR	107,250	93,500

	2021	2020
Profit attributable to:		
Owners of the parent	97,000	52,400
Non-controlling interests	24,250	13,100
	121,250	65,500
Total comprehensive income attributable to:		
Owners of the parent	85,800	74,800
Non-controlling interests	21,450	18,700
	107,250	93,500
Earnings per share (in currency units):		
Basic and diluted	0.46	0.30

Alternatively, items of other comprehensive income could be presented in the statement of profit or loss and other comprehensive income net of tax.

	2021	2020
Other comprehensive income for the year, after tax:		
Items that will not be reclassified to profit or loss:		
Gains on property revaluation	600	2,700
Investments in equity instruments	(18,000)	20,000
Remeasurements of defined benefit pension plans	(500)	1,000
Share of other comprehensive income of associates	400	(700)
	(17,500)	23,000
Items that may be reclassified subsequently to profit or loss:		
Exchange differences on translating foreign operations	4,000	8,000
Cash flow hedges	(500)	(3,000)
	3,500	5,000
Other comprehensive income for the year, net of tax[3]	(14,000)	28,000

(1) This means the share of associates' profit attributable to owners of the associates, i.e. it is after tax and non-controlling interests in the associates.
(2) This means the share of associates' other comprehensive income attributable to owners of the associates, i.e. it is after tax and non-controlling interests in the associates. In this example, the other comprehensive income of associates consists only of items that will not be subsequently reclassified to profit or loss. Entities whose associates' other comprehensive income includes items that may be subsequently reclassified to profit or loss are required to present that amount in a separate line.
(3) The income tax relating to each item of other comprehensive income is disclosed in the notes.
(4) This illustrates the aggregated presentation, with disclosure of the current year gain or loss and reclassification adjustment presented in the notes. Alternatively, a gross presentation can be used.

The illustrative examples in the standard all use the option, which is discussed at 3.2.4.B below, to present components of other comprehensive income net of related reclassification adjustments. The disclosure of those reclassification adjustments in a note is reproduced in Example 3.7 below. This note also demonstrates a reclassification not to profit and loss but to the statement of financial position. Whilst not addressed explicitly by the standard, evidently these items (like reclassifications to profit or loss) need not be shown on the face of the statement.

3.2.4.B Reclassification adjustments

'Reclassification adjustments' are items recognised in profit or loss which were previously recognised in other comprehensive income (commonly referred to as 'recycling') and IAS 1 requires their disclosure. [IAS 1.7, 92-93, 95]. Examples include adjustments arising in relation to the disposal of a foreign operation and hedged forecast transactions affecting profit or loss.

The standard allows a choice of how reclassification adjustments are presented. They may either be presented 'gross' on the face of the statement, or alternatively shown in the notes. In the latter case, components of comprehensive income on the face of the statement are shown net of any related reclassification adjustments. [IAS 1.94].

IAS 1 illustrates this requirement as follows: [IAS 1 IG Part I]

Example 3.7: Note disclosure of components of other comprehensive income

XYZ Group

Disclosure of components of other comprehensive income [1]
Notes – Year ended 31 December 2021
(in thousands of currency units)

	2021	2020
Other comprehensive income		
Exchange differences on translating foreign operations [2]	5,334	10,667
Investments in equity instruments	(24,000)	26,667
Cash flow hedges:		
Gains (losses) arising during the year	(4,667)	(4,000)
Less: reclassification adjustments for gains (losses) included in profit or loss	4,000	–
	(667)	(4,000)
Gains on property revaluation	933	3,367
Remeasurements of defined benefit pension plans	(667)	1,333
Share of other comprehensive income of associates	400	(700)
Other comprehensive income	(18,667)	37,334
Income tax relating to components of other comprehensive income [3]	4,667	(9,334)
Other comprehensive income for the year	(14,000)	28,000

(1) When an entity chooses an aggregated presentation in the statement of comprehensive income, the amounts for reclassification adjustments and current year gain or loss are presented in the notes.

(2) There was no disposal of a foreign operation. Therefore, there is no reclassification adjustment for the years presented.

(3) The income tax relating to each component of other comprehensive income is disclosed in the notes.

Some IFRSs require that gains and losses recognised in other comprehensive income should not be 'recycled' to profit and loss, and hence will not give rise to reclassification adjustments. IAS 1 gives the following examples:
(a) revaluation surpluses for revalued property, plant and equipment, and intangible assets;
(b) remeasurements on defined benefit plans; and
(c) amounts that are removed from the cash flow hedge reserve or a separate component of equity and included directly in the initial cost or other carrying amount of an asset or a liability in accordance with IFRS 9 in respect of a cash flow hedge or the accounting for the time value of an option (or the forward element of a forward contract or the foreign currency basis spread of a financial instrument). These amounts are directly transferred to assets or liabilities.

The standard observes that whilst items in (a) are not reclassified to profit or loss they may be transferred to retained earnings as the assets concerned are used or derecognised. *[IAS 1.96]*. This is illustrated in Example 3.9 below.

3.2.4.C Tax on items of other comprehensive income

IAS 1 requires disclosure of the amount of income tax relating to each item of other comprehensive income, including reclassification adjustments, either on the face of the statement or in the notes. *[IAS 1.90]*. This may be done by presenting the items of other comprehensive income either:
(a) net of related tax effects; or
(b) before related tax effects with one amount shown for the aggregate amount of income tax relating to those items.

If the alternative at (b) is selected, the tax should be allocated between the items that might be reclassified subsequently to profit and loss and those that will not. *[IAS 1.91]*.

The reference to reclassification adjustments here and in the definition of other comprehensive income (see 3.2.1 above) seems to suggest that such adjustments are themselves 'components' of other comprehensive income. That would mean that the standard requires disclosure of tax related to reclassification adjustments. The implementation guidance, however, suggests this is not required because the note illustrating the presentation in (b) above allocates tax only to items of comprehensive income themselves net of related reclassification adjustments.

Chapter 3

IAS 1 provides an illustration of both approaches in its implementation guidance.

The statement of comprehensive income and related note analysing tax are illustrated in Example 3.8 below (the related separate statement of profit or loss is shown in Example 3.4 above). [IAS 1 IG Part I].

Example 3.8: Statement of comprehensive income illustrating the presentation of comprehensive income in two statements with note disclosure of the tax effects relating to components of other comprehensive income

XYZ Group – Statement of profit or loss and other comprehensive income for the year ended 31 December 2021

(in thousands of currency units)	2021	2020
Profit for the year	121,250	65,500
Other comprehensive income:		
Items that will not be reclassified to profit or loss:		
Gains on property revaluation	933	3,367
Remeasurements of defined benefit pension plans	(667)	1,333
Share of other comprehensive income of associates[1]	400	(700)
Income tax relating to items that will not be reclassified[2]	(166)	(1,000)
	500	3,000
Items that may be reclassified subsequently to profit or loss:		
Exchange differences on translating foreign operations	5,334	10,667
Investments in equity instruments	(24,000)	26,667
Cash flow hedges	(667)	(4,000)
Income tax relating to items that may be reclassified[2]	4,833	(8,334)
	(14,500)	25,000
Other comprehensive income for the year, net of tax	(14,000)	28,000
TOTAL COMPREHENSIVE INCOME FOR THE YEAR	107,250	93,500

(in thousands of currency units)	2021	2020
Total comprehensive income attributable to:		
Owners of the parent	85,800	74,800
Non-controlling interests	21,450	18,700
	107,250	93,500

Disclosure of tax effects relating to each component of other comprehensive income

Notes	2021			2020		
	Before-tax amount	Tax (expense) benefit	Net-of-tax amount	Before-tax amount	Tax (expense) benefit	Net-of-tax amount
Exchange differences on translating foreign operations	5,334	(1,334)	4,000	10,667	(2,667)	8,000
Investments in equity instruments	(24,000)	6,000	(18,000)	26,667	(6,667)	20,000
Cash flow hedges	(667)	167	(500)	(4,000)	1,000	(3,000)
Gains on property revaluation	933	(333)	600	3,367	(667)	2,700
Remeasurements of defined benefit pension plans	(667)	167	(500)	1,333	(333)	1,000
Share of other comprehensive income of associates	400	–	400	(700)	–	(700)
Other comprehensive income	(18,667)	4,667	(14,000)	37,334	(9,334)	28,000

(1) This means the share of associates' other comprehensive income attributable to owners of the associates, i.e. it is after tax and non-controlling interests in the associates. In this example, the other comprehensive income of associates consists only of items that will not be subsequently reclassified to profit or loss. Entities whose associates' other comprehensive income includes items that may be subsequently reclassified to profit or loss are required to present that amount in a separate line.

(2) The income tax relating to each item of other comprehensive income is disclosed in the notes.

3.2.5 Discontinued operations

As discussed in Chapter 4 at 3.2, IFRS 5 requires the presentation of a single amount on the face of the statement of profit or loss relating to discontinued operations, with further analysis either on the face of the statement or in the notes.

3.2.6 Material and extraordinary items

3.2.6.A Material items

IAS 1 requires that when items of income or expense (a term covering both profit and loss, and other comprehensive income) are material, their nature and amount should be disclosed separately. *[IAS 1.97]*. Materiality is discussed at 4.1.5.A below. The standard goes on to suggest that circumstances that would give rise to the separate disclosure of items of income and expense include:

(a) write-downs of inventories to net realisable value or of property, plant and equipment to recoverable amount, as well as reversals of such write-downs;

(b) restructurings of the activities of an entity and reversals of any provisions for the costs of restructuring;

(c) disposals of items of property, plant and equipment;

(d) disposals of investments;

(e) discontinued operations;

(f) litigation settlements; and

(g) other reversals of provisions. *[IAS 1.98]*.

This information may be given on the face of the statement of profit or loss, on the face of the statement of comprehensive income or in the notes. In line with the permissive approach taken to the format of the performance statements discussed above, the level of prominence given to such items is left to the judgement of the entity concerned. However, regarding (e) above, IFRS 5 requires certain information to be presented on the face of the statement of profit or loss (see Chapter 4 at 3.2).

3.2.6.B Ordinary activities and extraordinary items

IAS 1 states that an entity 'shall not present any items of income or expense as extraordinary items, in the statement(s) presenting profit or loss and other comprehensive income, or in the notes.' *[IAS 1.87]*.

This derives from the fact that earlier versions of the standard required a distinction to be made between ordinary activities (and the results of them) and extraordinary items.

The basis for conclusions to IAS 1 explains that the removal of this distinction, and the prohibition on the presentation of extraordinary items, was made to avoid arbitrary segregation of an entity's performance. *[IAS 1.BC64]*.

3.3 The statement of changes in equity

IAS 1 requires the presentation of a statement of changes in equity showing: *[IAS 1.106]*

(a) total comprehensive income for the period (comprising profit and loss and other comprehensive income – see 3.2.1 above) showing separately the total amounts attributable to owner of the parent and to non-controlling interests;

(b) for each component of equity, the effects of retrospective application or retrospective restatement recognised in accordance with IAS 8 (discussed at 4.4 and 4.6 below); and

(c) for each component of equity, a reconciliation between the carrying amount at the beginning and the end of the period, separately disclosing changes resulting from:
   (i) profit or loss;
   (ii) other comprehensive income; and
   (iii) transactions with owners in their capacity as owners, showing separately contributions by and distributions to owners and changes in ownership interests in subsidiaries that do not result in a loss of control.

The reconciliation in (c)(ii) above must show each item of other comprehensive income, although that detail may be shown in the notes. *[IAS 1.106A]*.

The amounts of dividends shown as distributions to owners and the amounts of dividends per share should be shown either on the face of the statement or in the notes. *[IAS 1.107]*.

It can be seen that (a) above is effectively a sub-total of all the items required by (c)(i) and (c)(ii).

For these purposes, 'components' of equity include each class of contributed equity, the accumulated balance of each class of other comprehensive income and retained earnings. *[IAS 1.108]*.

This analysis reflects the focus of the IASB on the statement of financial position – whereby any changes in net assets (aside of those arising from transactions with owners) are gains and losses, regarded as performance. In this vein, IAS 1 observes that changes in an entity's equity between two reporting dates reflect the increase or decrease in its net assets during the period. Except for changes resulting from transactions with owners acting in their capacity as owners (such as equity contributions, reacquisitions of the entity's own equity instruments and dividends) and transaction costs directly related to such transactions, the overall change in equity during a period represents the total amount of income and expenses, including gains and losses, generated by the entity's activities during that period. *[IAS 1.109]*. After taking account of total gains and losses and owner transactions in this way, any other changes in equity will result from the restatement of prior periods. Point (b) above reflects this. IAS 8 requires retrospective adjustments to effect changes in accounting policies, to the extent practicable, except when the transitional provisions in another IFRS require otherwise. IAS 8 also requires that restatements to correct errors are made retrospectively, to the extent practicable. These are discussed at 4 below. IAS 1 observes that retrospective adjustments and retrospective restatements 'are not changes in equity but they are adjustments to the opening balance of retained earnings, except when an IFRS requires retrospective adjustment of another component of equity.' Point (b) above therefore requires disclosure in the statement of changes in equity of the total adjustment to each component of equity resulting, separately, from changes in accounting policies and from corrections of errors. These adjustments should be disclosed for each prior period and the beginning of the period. *[IAS 1.110]*.

Chapter 3

The illustrative statement from the implementation guidance accompanying IAS 1 is set out below. [IAS 1 IG Part I].

Example 3.9: Statement of changes in equity

XYZ Group – Statement of changes in equity for the year ended 31 December 2021

(in thousands of currency units)

	Share capital	Retained earnings	Translation of foreign operations	Investments in equity instruments	Cash flow hedge	Revaluation surplus	Total	Non-controlling interest	Total equity
Balance at 1 January 2020	600,000	118,100	(4,000)	1,600	2,000	–	717,700	29,800	747,500
Changes in accounting policy	–	400	–	–	–	–	400	100	500
Restated balance	600,000	118,500	(4,000)	1,600	2,000	–	718,100	29,900	748,000
Changes in equity for 2020									
Dividends	–	(10,000)	–	–	–	–	(10,000)	–	(10,000)
Total comprehensive income for the year[(1)]	–	53,200	6,400	16,000	(2,400)	1,600	74,800	18,700	93,500
Balance at 31 December 2020	600,000	161,700	2,400	17,600	(400)	1,600	782,900	48,600	831,500
Changes in equity for 2021	Share capital	Retained earnings	Translation of foreign operations	Investments in equity instruments	Cash flow hedge	Revaluation surplus	Total	Non-controlling interest	Total equity
Issue of share capital	50,000	–	–	–	–	–	50,000	–	50,000
Dividends	–	(15,000)	–	–	–	–	(15,000)	–	(15,000)
Total comprehensive income for the year[(2)]	–	96,600	3,200	(14,400)	(400)	800	85,800	21,450	107,250
Transfer to retained earnings	–	200	–	–	–	(200)	–	–	–
Balance at 31 December 2021	650,000	243,500	5,600	3,200	(800)	2,200	903,700	70,050	973,750

(1) The amount included in retained earnings for 2020 of 53,200 represents profit attributable to owners of the parent of 52,400 plus remeasurements of defined benefit pension plans of 800 (1,333, less tax 333, less non-controlling interest 200).

The amount included in the translation, investments in equity instruments and cash flow hedge reserves represent other comprehensive income for each component, net of tax and non-controlling interest, e.g. other comprehensive income related to investments in equity instruments for 2021 of 16,000 is 26,667, less tax 6,667, less non-controlling interest 4,000.

The amount included in the revaluation surplus of 1,600 represents the share of other comprehensive income of associates of (700) plus gains on property revaluation of 2,300 (3,367, less tax 667, less non-controlling interest 400). Other comprehensive income of associates relates solely to gains or losses on property revaluation.

(2) The amount included in retained earnings of 2021 of 96,600 represents profit attributable to owners of the parent of 97,000 less remeasurements of defined benefit pension plans of 400 (667, less tax 167, less non-controlling interest 100).

The amount included in the translation, investments in equity instruments and cash flow hedge reserves represent other comprehensive income for each component, net of tax and non-controlling interest, e.g. other comprehensive income related to the translation of foreign operations for 2021 of 3,200 is 5,334, less tax 1,334, less non-controlling interest 800.

The amount included in the revaluation surplus of 800 represents the share of other comprehensive income of associates of 400 plus gains on property revaluation of 400 (933, less tax 333, less non-controlling interest 200). Other comprehensive income of associates relates solely to gains or losses on property revaluation.

3.4 The notes to the financial statements

IAS 1 requires the presentation of notes to the financial statements that:

(a) present information about the basis of preparation of the financial statements and the specific accounting policies used (see 5.1 below);

(b) disclose the information required by IFRS that is not presented elsewhere in the financial statements; and

(c) provide additional information that is not presented elsewhere in the financial statements, but is relevant to an understanding of any of them. *[IAS 1.112]*.

The notes should, as far as practicable, be presented in a systematic manner, determined in consideration of its effect on the understandability and comparability of the financial statements. Each item on the face of the primary statements should be cross-referenced to any related information in the notes. *[IAS 1.113]*.

There is, perhaps, a trade-off to be made between understandability and comparability, in that allowing entities to structure their notes to, for instance, reflect their business model or perceived importance may reduce the comparability between one entity and another. The standard does not prescribe a specific order, but in the Basis for Conclusions the consistency dimension of comparability is highlighted, and it is clarified that the ordering of the notes generally is not expected to be changed frequently. *[IAS 1.BC76D]*.

Examples given in the standard of the systematic ordering or grouping of the notes are as follows:

(a) giving prominence to the areas of its activities that the entity considers to be most relevant to an understanding of its financial performance and financial position, such as grouping together information about particular operating activities;

(b) grouping together information about items measured similarly such as assets measured at fair value; or

(c) following the order of the line items in the statement(s) of profit or loss and other comprehensive income and the statement of financial position, such as:

   (i) a statement of compliance with IFRS (see 2.5.2 above);

   (ii) significant accounting policies applied (see 5.1.1 below);

   (iii) supporting information for items presented on the face of the primary statements, in the order in which each statement and each line item is presented; and

   (iv) other disclosures, including: contingent liabilities, unrecognised contractual commitments and non-financial disclosures such as financial risk management objectives and policies. *[IAS 1.114]*.

The standard also allows that notes providing information about the basis of preparation of the financial statements and specific accounting policies may be presented as a separate section of the financial statements. *[IAS 1.116]*.

4 ACCOUNTING POLICIES

The selection and application of accounting policies is obviously crucial in the preparation of financial statements. As a general premise, the whole purpose of accounting standards is to specify required accounting policies, presentation and disclosure. However, judgement will always remain; many standards may allow choices to accommodate different views, and no body of accounting literature could hope to prescribe precise treatments for all possible situations.

In the broadest sense, accounting policies are discussed by both IAS 1 and IAS 8. Whilst, as its title suggests, IAS 8 deals explicitly with accounting policies, IAS 1 deals with what one might describe as overarching or general principles.

4.1 General principles

IAS 1 deals with some general principles relating to accounting policies, with IAS 8 discussing the detail of selection and application of individual accounting policies and their disclosure.

The general principles discussed by IAS 1 can be described as follows:

- fair presentation and compliance with accounting standards;
- going concern;
- the accrual basis of accounting;
- consistency;
- materiality and aggregation;
- offsetting; and
- profit or loss for the period.

These are discussed in 4.1.1-4.1.6 below.

In September 2017 the IASB published Practice Statement 2 – *Making Materiality Judgements*. This is a non-mandatory statement and does not form part of IFRS. An overview of its contents is given at 4.1.7 below.

4.1.1 Fair presentation

4.1.1.A Fair presentation and compliance with IFRS

Consistent with its objective and statement of the purpose of financial statements, IAS 1 requires that financial statements present fairly the financial position, financial performance and cash flows of an entity. Fair presentation for these purposes requires the faithful representation of the effects of transactions, other events and conditions in accordance with the definitions and recognition criteria for assets, liabilities, income and expenses set out in the *Conceptual Framework* (discussed in Chapter 2).

The main premise of the standard is that application of IFRS, with additional disclosure when necessary, is presumed to result in financial statements that achieve a fair presentation. *[IAS 1.15]*. As noted at 1.1 above, an important point here is that implementation guidance for standards issued by the IASB does not form part of those standards (unless they are explicitly 'scoped-in'), and therefore does not contain requirements for financial statements. *[IAS 8.8]*. In contrast, any application guidance appended to a standard forms an integral part of that standard.

Accordingly, the often voluminous implementation guidance accompanying standards is not, strictly speaking, part of IFRS. We would generally be surprised, though, at entities not following such guidance. The presumption that application of IFRS (with any necessary additional disclosure) results in a fair presentation is potentially rebuttable, as discussed at 4.1.1.B below.

A fair presentation also requires an entity to:

(a) select and apply accounting policies in accordance with IAS 8, which also sets out a hierarchy of authoritative guidance that should be considered in the absence of an IFRS that specifically applies to an item (see 4.3 below);

(b) present information, including accounting policies, in a manner that provides relevant, reliable, comparable and understandable information; and

(c) provide additional disclosures when compliance with the specific requirements in IFRS is insufficient to enable users to understand the impact of particular transactions, other events and conditions on the entity's financial position and financial performance. *[IAS 1.17]*.

However, the standard makes clear that inappropriate accounting policies are not rectified either by disclosure of the accounting policies used or by notes or explanatory material. *[IAS 1.18]*. As discussed at 4.1.1.B below, it is possible that an extremely rare circumstance arises where departure from a provision of IFRS is needed to achieve fair presentation. This is only allowed by IAS 1, however, if permitted by such a regulatory framework.

4.1.1.B   The fair presentation override

The presumption that the application of IFRS, with additional disclosure when necessary, results in financial statements that achieve a fair presentation is a rebuttable one, although the standard makes clear that in virtually all situations a fair presentation is achieved through compliance.

The standard observes that an item of information would conflict with the objective of financial statements when it does not represent faithfully the transactions, other events and conditions that it either purports to represent or could reasonably be expected to represent and, consequently, it would be likely to influence economic decisions made by users of financial statements. When assessing whether complying with a specific requirement in an IFRS would be so misleading that it would conflict with the objective of financial statements, IAS 1 requires consideration of:

(a) why the objective of financial statements is not achieved in the particular circumstances; and

(b) how the entity's circumstances differ from those of other entities that comply with the requirement. If other entities in similar circumstances comply with the requirement, there is a rebuttable presumption that the entity's compliance with the requirement would not be so misleading that it would conflict with the objective of financial statements. *[IAS 1.24]*.

In the extremely rare circumstances in which management concludes that compliance with a requirement in an IFRS would be so misleading that it would conflict with the objective of financial statements, IAS 1 requires departure from that requirement. However, this is only permitted if the 'relevant regulatory framework requires, or otherwise does not prohibit, such a departure', which is discussed further below. [IAS 1.19].

When the relevant regulatory framework allows a departure, an entity should make it and also disclose:

(a) that management has concluded that the financial statements present fairly the entity's financial position, financial performance and cash flows;

(b) that it has complied with applicable IFRSs, except that it has departed from a particular requirement to achieve a fair presentation;

(c) the title of the IFRS from which the entity has departed, the nature of the departure, including:

　(i) the treatment that the IFRS would require;

　(ii) the reason why that treatment would be so misleading in the circumstances that it would conflict with the objective of financial statements set out in the *Framework*; and

　(iii) the treatment adopted;

(d) for each period presented, the financial impact of the departure on each item in the financial statements that would have been reported in complying with the requirement; and

(e) when there has been a departure from a requirement of an IFRS in a prior period, and that departure affects the amounts recognised in the financial statements for the current period, the disclosures set out in (c) and (d) above. [IAS 1.20-21].

Regarding (e) above, the standard explains that the requirement could apply, for example, when an entity departed in a prior period from a requirement in an IFRS for the measurement of assets or liabilities and that departure affects the measurement of changes in assets and liabilities recognised in the current period's financial statements. [IAS 1.22].

When the relevant regulatory framework does not allow a departure from IFRS, IAS 1 accepts that, notwithstanding the failure to achieve fair presentation, that it should not be made. Although intended to occur only in extremely rare circumstances, this is a very important provision of the standard as it allows a 'relevant regulatory framework' to override the requirement of IFRS to achieve a fair presentation. In that light, it is perhaps surprising that there is no definition or discussion in the standard of what a relevant regulatory framework is.

When a departure otherwise required by IAS 1 is not allowed by the relevant regulatory framework, the standard requires that the perceived misleading aspects of compliance are reduced, to the maximum extent possible, by the disclosure of:

(a) the title of the IFRS in question, the nature of the requirement, and the reason why management has concluded that complying with that requirement is so misleading in the circumstances that it conflicts with the objective of financial statements set out in the *Framework*; and

(b) for each period presented, the adjustments to each item in the financial statements that management has concluded would be necessary to achieve a fair presentation. [IAS 1.23].

Overall, this strikes us as a fairly uncomfortable compromise. However, the rule is reasonably clear and in our view such a circumstance will indeed be a rare one.

4.1.2 Going concern

When preparing financial statements, IAS 1 requires management to make an assessment of an entity's ability to continue as a going concern. This term is not defined, but its meaning is implicit in the requirement of the standard that financial statements should be prepared on a going concern basis unless management either intends to liquidate the entity or to cease trading, or has no realistic alternative but to do so. The standard goes on to require that when management is aware, in making its assessment, of material uncertainties related to events or conditions that may cast significant doubt upon the entity's ability to continue as a going concern, those uncertainties should be disclosed. Beyond requiring disclosure of the uncertainties, the standard does not specify more precisely what information should be disclosed. The Interpretations Committee recommended, in January 2013, that the IASB make a narrow-scope amendment to IAS 1 that would address when these disclosures should be made and what information should be disclosed. Although the IASB acknowledged that more prescriptive requirements would lead to useful information to investors and creditors, it also had the expectation that such requirements may result in 'boilerplate' disclosures that would obscure relevant disclosures about going concern and thus would contribute to disclosure overload. It also observed that this is a topic that is better handled through local regulator or audit guidance.[1]

When financial statements are not prepared on a going concern basis, that fact should be disclosed, together with the basis on which the financial statements are prepared and the reason why the entity is not regarded as a going concern. [IAS 1.25].

In assessing whether the going concern assumption is appropriate, the standard requires that all available information about the future, which is at least, but is not limited to, twelve months from the end of the reporting period should be taken into account. The degree of consideration required will depend on the facts in each case. When an entity has a history of profitable operations and ready access to financial resources, a conclusion that the going concern basis of accounting is appropriate may be reached without detailed analysis. In other cases, management may need to consider a wide range of factors relating to current and expected profitability, debt repayment schedules and potential sources of replacement financing before it can satisfy itself that the going concern basis is appropriate. [IAS 1.26].

There is no guidance in the standard concerning what impact there should be on the financial statements if it is determined that the going concern basis is not appropriate. Accordingly, entities will need to consider carefully their individual circumstances to arrive at an appropriate basis.

4.1.3 The accrual basis of accounting

IAS 1 requires that financial statements be prepared, except for cash flow information, using the accrual basis of accounting. *[IAS 1.27]*. No definition of this is given by the standard, but an explanation is presented that 'When the accrual basis of accounting is used, items are recognised as assets, liabilities, equity, income and expenses (the elements of financial statements) when they satisfy the definitions and recognition criteria for those elements in the *Conceptual Framework*.' *[IAS 1.28]*.

The *Conceptual Framework* explains the accruals basis as follows. 'Accrual accounting depicts the effects of transactions and other events and circumstances on a reporting entity's economic resources and claims in the periods in which those effects occur, even if the resulting cash receipts and payments occur in a different period. This is important because information about a reporting entity's economic resources and claims and changes in its economic resources and claims during a period provides a better basis for assessing the entity's past and future performance than information solely about cash receipts and payments during that period.' *[CF 1.17]*.

The requirements of the *Conceptual Framework* are discussed in more detail in Chapter 2.

4.1.4 Consistency

As noted at 1.1 and 1.2 above, one of the objectives of both IAS 1 and IAS 8 is to ensure the comparability of financial statements with those of previous periods. To this end, each standard addresses the principle of consistency.

IAS 1 requires that the 'presentation and classification' of items in the financial statements be retained from one period to the next unless:

(a) it is apparent, following a significant change in the nature of the entity's operations or a review of its financial statements, that another presentation or classification would be more appropriate having regard to the criteria for the selection and application of accounting policies in IAS 8 (see 4.3 below); or

(b) an IFRS requires a change in presentation. *[IAS 1.45]*.

The standard goes on to amplify this by explaining that a significant acquisition or disposal, or a review of the presentation of the financial statements, might suggest that the financial statements need to be presented differently. An entity should change the presentation of its financial statements only if the changed presentation provides information that is reliable and is more relevant to users of the financial statements and the revised structure is likely to continue, so that comparability is not impaired. When making such changes in presentation, an entity will need to reclassify its comparative information as discussed at 2.4 above. *[IAS 1.46]*.

IAS 8 addresses consistency of accounting policies and observes that users of financial statements need to be able to compare the financial statements of an entity over time to identify trends in its financial position, financial performance and cash flows. For this reason, the same accounting policies need to be applied within each period and from one period to the next unless a change in accounting policy meets certain criteria (changes in accounting policy are discussed at 4.4 below). *[IAS 8.15]*. Accordingly, the standard requires that accounting policies be selected and applied consistently for similar transactions, other events and conditions, unless an IFRS specifically requires or permits categorisation of items for which different policies may be appropriate. If an IFRS requires or permits such categorisation, an appropriate accounting policy should be selected and applied consistently to each category. *[IAS 8.13]*.

4.1.5 Materiality, aggregation and offset

4.1.5.A Materiality and aggregation

Financial statements result from processing large numbers of transactions or other events that are aggregated into classes according to their nature or function. The final stage in the process of aggregation and classification is the presentation of condensed and classified data, which form line items in the financial statements, or in the notes. *[IAS 1.30]*. The extent of aggregation versus detailed analysis is clearly a matter of judgement, with either extreme eroding the usefulness of the information.

IAS 1 resolves this issue with the concept of materiality, by requiring:

- each material class of similar items to be presented separately in the financial statements; and
- items of a dissimilar nature or function to be presented separately unless they are immaterial. *[IAS 1.29]*.

The standard also states when applying IAS 1 and other IFRSs an entity should decide, taking into consideration all relevant facts and circumstances, how it aggregates information in the financial statements, which include the notes. In particular, the understandability of financial statements should not be reduced by obscuring material information with immaterial information or by aggregating material items that have different natures or functions. *[IAS 1.30A]*.

Materiality is defined in IAS 1 and IAS 8 (by cross reference to IAS 1) as follows. *[IAS 1.7, IAS 8.5]*. 'Information is material if omitting, misstating or obscuring it could reasonably be expected to influence decisions that the primary users of general purpose financial statements make on the basis of those financial statements, which provide financial information about a specific reporting entity.'

The terms 'primary users' and 'users' are intended to be synonyms and are used interchangeably in IAS 1. *[IAS 1.BC13Q]*.

The standard goes on to observe that materiality depends on the nature or magnitude of information, or both. An entity assesses whether information, either individually or in combination with other information, is material in the context of its financial statements taken as a whole.

Information is considered to be obscured if it is communicated in a way that would have a similar effect for primary users of financial statements to omitting or misstating that information. The following are given as examples of circumstances that may result in material information being obscured:

(a) information regarding a material item, transaction or other event is disclosed in the financial statements but the language used is vague or unclear;

(b) information regarding a material item, transaction or other event is scattered throughout the financial statements;

(c) dissimilar items, transactions or other events are inappropriately aggregated;

(d) similar items, transactions or other events are inappropriately disaggregated; and

(e) the understandability of the financial statements is reduced as a result of material information being hidden by immaterial information to the extent that a primary user is unable to determine what information is material.

At a general level, applying the concept of materiality means that a specific disclosure required by an IFRS to be given in the financial statements (including the notes) need not be provided if the information resulting from that disclosure is not material. This is the case even if the IFRS contains a list of specific requirements or describes them as minimum requirements. On the other hand, the provision of additional disclosures should be considered when compliance with the specific requirements in IFRS is insufficient to enable users of financial statements to understand the impact of particular transactions, other events and conditions on the entity's financial position and financial performance. *[IAS 1.31]*.

IAS 1 goes on to observe that assessing whether information could reasonably be expected to influence economic decisions made by the primary users of a specific reporting entity's general purpose financial statements requires an entity to consider the characteristics of those users along with its own circumstances. For these purposes primary users of general purpose financial statements:

- are existing and potential investors, lenders and other creditors that cannot require reporting entities to provide information directly to them and must rely on general purpose financial statements for much of the financial information they need; and

- have a reasonable knowledge of business and economic activities and review and analyse the information diligently.

It is noted in the standard, though, that at times even well-informed and diligent users may need to seek the aid of an adviser to understand information about complex economic phenomena. *[IAS 1.7]*.

Regarding the presentation of financial statements, IAS 1 requires that if a line item is not individually material, it should be aggregated with other items either on the face of those statements or in the notes. The standard also states that an item that is not sufficiently material to warrant separate presentation on the face of those statements may nevertheless be sufficiently material for it to be presented separately in the notes. *[IAS 1.30]*.

In September 2017 the IASB published Practice Statement 2 – *Making Materiality Judgements*. This is a non-mandatory statement and does not form part of IFRS. An overview of its contents is given at 4.1.7 below.

4.1.5.B Offset

IAS 1 considers it important that assets and liabilities, and income and expenses, are reported separately. This is because offsetting in the statement of profit or loss or statement of comprehensive income or the statement of financial position, except when offsetting reflects the substance of the transaction or other event, detracts from the ability of users both to understand the transactions, other events and conditions that have occurred and to assess the entity's future cash flows. It clarifies, though, that measuring assets net of valuation allowances – for example, obsolescence allowances on inventories and doubtful debts allowances on receivables – is not offsetting. *[IAS 1.33]*.

Accordingly, IAS 1 requires that assets and liabilities, and income and expenses, should not be offset unless required or permitted by an IFRS. *[IAS 1.32]*.

Just what constitutes offsetting, particularly given the rider noted above of 'reflecting the substance of the transaction', is not always obvious. IAS 1 expands on its meaning as follows. It notes that:

(a) IFRS 15 – *Revenue from Contracts with Customers* – defines revenue from contracts with customers and requires it to be measured at the amount of consideration to which the entity expects to be entitled in exchange for transferring promised goods or services, taking into account the amount of any trade discounts and volume rebates allowed by the entity – in other words a notional 'gross' revenue and a discount should not be shown separately. Revenue from contracts with customers is discussed in Chapters 27 to 32; Chapter 29 addresses the determination of transaction price;

(b) entities can undertake, in the course of their ordinary activities, other transactions that do not generate revenue but are incidental to the main revenue-generating activities. The results of such transactions should be presented, when this presentation reflects the substance of the transaction or other event, by netting any income with related expenses arising on the same transaction. For example:

  (i) gains and losses on the disposal of non-current assets, including investments and operating assets, should be reported by deducting from the proceeds on disposal the carrying amount of the asset and related selling expenses; and

  (ii) expenditure related to a provision that is recognised in accordance with IAS 37 – *Provisions, Contingent Liabilities and Contingent Assets* – and reimbursed under a contractual arrangement with a third party (for example, a supplier's warranty agreement) may be netted against the related reimbursement; *[IAS 1.34]* and

(c) gains and losses arising from a group of similar transactions should be reported on a net basis, for example, foreign exchange gains and losses or gains and losses arising on financial instruments held for trading. However, such gains and losses should be reported separately if they are material. *[IAS 1.35]*.

4.1.6 Profit or loss for the period

The final provision of IAS 1 which we term a general principle is a very important one. It is that, unless an IFRS requires or permits otherwise, all items of income and expense recognised in a period should be included in profit or loss. *[IAS 1.88]*. This is the case whether one combined statement of comprehensive income is presented or whether a separate statement of profit or loss is presented (discussed at 3.2.1 above).

Income and expense are not defined by the standard, but they are defined by the *Conceptual Framework* as follows:

(a) income is increases in assets, or decreases in liabilities, that result in increases in equity, other than those relating to contributions from holders of equity claims; and

(b) expenses are decreases in assets, or increases in liabilities, that result in decreases in equity, other than those relating to distributions to holders of equity claims. *[CF 4.68, 4.49]*.

These definitions clearly suggest that the terms do not have what many would consider their natural meaning, as they encompass all gains and losses (for example, capital appreciation in a non-current asset like property). There is a somewhat awkward compromise with various gains and losses either required or permitted to bypass profit or loss and be reported instead in 'other comprehensive income'. Importantly, as discussed at 3.2.1 above, profit and loss, and other comprehensive income may each be reported as a separate statement.

IAS 1 notes that some IFRSs specify circumstances when an entity recognises particular items outside profit or loss, including the effect of changes in accounting policies and error corrections (discussed at 4.4 and 4.6 below). *[IAS 1.89]*. Other IFRSs deal with items that may meet the *Framework's* definitions of income or expense but are usually excluded from profit or loss. Examples given by IAS 1 are shown at 3.2.4.A above.

4.1.7 Practice Statement 2 – Making Materiality Judgements

In September 2017 the IASB published Practice Statement 2 – *Making Materiality Judgements* (Statement 2). This is a non-mandatory statement and does not form part of IFRS, its application is not, therefore, required to state compliance with IFRS. *[PS 2.2]*.

Notwithstanding the above, preparers of financial statements may wish to consider the practice statement and an overview of it is given below.

Statement 2 addresses three main areas:

- the general characteristics of materiality;
- a four-step process that may be applied in making materiality judgements when preparing financial statements (the 'materiality process'); and
- guidance on how to make materiality judgements in relation to the following:
  - prior period information;
  - errors;
  - information about covenants; and
  - interim reporting.

There is also a discussion of the interaction between the materiality and local laws and regulations. Local laws and regulations may specify additional requirements that can affect the information included in the financial statements. IFRS permits the disclosure of such additional information in order to meet local legal or regulatory requirements, although not material from an IFRS perspective, as long as it does not obscure information that is material (see 4.1.5.A above). *[PS 2.28, IAS 1.30A, BC13L, BC30F]*.

4.1.7.A General characteristics of materiality

The Practice Statement explores materiality by considering the following characteristics:

- *Definition of material*

    The objective of financial statements is to provide financial information about the reporting entity that is useful to primary users. An entity identifies the information necessary to meet the objective by making appropriate materiality judgements. The definition of material is discussed at 4.1.5.A above. *[PS 2.5-7]*.

- *Materiality judgements are pervasive*

    Materiality judgements are pervasive to the preparation of financial statements. Entities make materiality judgements in decisions about recognition and measurement as well as presentation and disclosure. Requirements in IFRS only need to be applied if their effect is material to the complete set of financial statements. However, it is inappropriate to make, or leave uncorrected, immaterial departures from IFRS to achieve a particular presentation. The Practice Statement reiterates that, as discussed at 4.1.5.A above, an entity does not need to provide a disclosure specified by IFRS if the information resulting from that disclosure is not material, even if IFRS contains a list of specific disclosure requirements or describes them as minimum requirements. *[PS 2.8-10]*.

- *Judgement*

    Materiality judgements require consideration of both the entity's circumstances (and how they have changed compared to prior periods) and how the information responds to the information needs of its primary users. *[PS 2.11-12]*.

- *Primary users and their information needs*

    When making materiality judgements, an entity needs to take into account how information could reasonably be expected to influence the primary users of its financial statements and what decisions they make on the basis of the financial statements. Primary users are existing and potential investors, existing and potential lenders and existing and potential other creditors. They are expected to have a reasonable knowledge of business and economic activities and to review and analyse the information included in the financial statements diligently. Since financial statements cannot provide all the information that primary users need, entities aim to meet the common information needs of their primary users and not, therefore, needs that are unique to particular users or to niche groups. *[PS 2.13-23]*.

- *Impact of publicly-available information*

    Financial statements must be capable of standing-alone. Therefore, entities make the materiality assessment regardless of whether information is publicly available from another source. *[PS 2.24-26]*.

4.1.7.B Making materiality judgements

The Practice Statement sets out a four-step process to help preparers making materiality judgements. This process describes how an entity may assess whether information is material for the purposes of recognition, measurement, presentation and disclosure.

The materiality process considers potential omissions and misstatements as well as unnecessary inclusion of immaterial information. In all cases, an entity focuses on how the information could reasonably be expected to influence the decisions of users of financial statements. *[PS 2.29-32]*.

The steps are as follows:

- *Step 1 – Identify*

    Identify information about transactions, other events and conditions that has the potential to be material considering the requirements of IFRS and the entity's knowledge of its primary users' common information needs. *[PS 2.35-39]*.

- *Step 2 – Assess*

    Determine whether the information identified in Step 1 is material considering quantitative (size of the impact of the information against measures of the financial statements) and qualitative (characteristics of the information making it more likely to influence decisions of the primary users) factors in the context of the financial statements as a whole. *[PS 2.40-55]*.

- *Step 3 – Organise*

    Organise material information within the draft financial statements in a way that communicates the information clearly and concisely (for example, by emphasising material matters, tailoring information to the entity's own circumstances, highlighting relationships between different pieces of information). *[PS 2.56-59]*.

- *Step 4 – Review*

    Review the draft financial statements to determine whether all material information has been identified and consider the information provided from a wider perspective and in aggregate, on the basis of the complete set of financial statements. *[PS 2.60-65]*.

4.1.7.C Specific topics

The Practice Statement provides guidance on how to make materiality judgements in the following specific circumstances:

- *Prior period information*

    Entities are required to provide prior period information if it is relevant to understand the current period financial statements, regardless of whether it was included in the prior period financial statements (discussed at 2.4 above). This might lead an entity to include prior period information that was not previously provided (if necessary to understand the current period financial statements) or to summarise prior period information, retaining only the information necessary to understand the current period financial statements. *[PS 2.66-71]*.

- *Errors*

    An entity assesses the materiality of an error (omissions or misstatements or both) on an individual and collective basis and corrects all material errors, as well as any immaterial financial reporting errors made intentionally to achieve a particular presentation of its financial statements (discussed at 4.6 below). When assessing whether cumulative errors (that is, errors that have accumulated over several periods) have become material an entity considers whether its circumstances have changed or further accumulation of a current period error has occurred. Cumulative errors must be corrected if they have become material to the current-period financial statements. *[PS 2.72-80]*.

- *Loan covenants*

    When assessing whether information about a covenant in a loan agreement is material, an entity considers the impact of a potential covenant breach on the financial statements and the likelihood of the covenant breach occurring. *[PS 2.81-83]*.

- *Materiality judgements for interim reporting*

    An entity considers the same materiality factors for the interim report as in its annual assessment. However, it takes into consideration that the time period and the purpose of interim financial statements (that is, to provide an update on the latest complete set of annual financial statements) differ from those of the annual financial statements. Interim financial statements are discussed in Chapter 41. *[PS 2.84-88]*.

4.2 The distinction between accounting policies and accounting estimates

IAS 8 defines accounting policies as 'the specific principles, bases, conventions, rules and practices applied by an entity in preparing and presenting financial statements.' *[IAS 8.5]*. In particular, IAS 8 considers a change in 'measurement basis' to be a change in accounting policy (rather than a change in estimate – see 6.2.1 below for information about the Board's proposals in these areas). *[IAS 8.35]*. Although not a defined term, IAS 1 (when requiring disclosure of them) gives examples of measurement bases as follows:

- historical cost;
- current cost;
- net realisable value;
- fair value; and
- recoverable amount. *[IAS 1.118]*.

'Accounting estimates' is not a term defined directly by the standards. However, it is indirectly defined by the definition in IAS 8 of a change in an accounting estimate as follows. A change in accounting estimate is an adjustment of the carrying amount of an asset or a liability, or the amount of the periodic consumption of an asset, that results from the assessment of the present status of, and expected future benefits and obligations associated with, assets and liabilities. Changes in accounting estimates result from new information or new developments and, accordingly, are not corrections of errors. *[IAS 8.5]*. Examples given by the IASB are estimates of bad debts and the estimated useful life of, or the expected pattern of consumption of the future economic benefits embodied in, a depreciable asset. *[IAS 8.38]*.

The standard also notes that corrections of errors should be distinguished from changes in accounting estimates. Accounting estimates by their nature are approximations that may need revision as additional information becomes known. For example, the gain or loss recognised on the outcome of a contingency is not the correction of an error. *[IAS 8.48]*.

The distinction between an accounting policy and an accounting estimate is particularly important because a very different treatment is required when there are changes in accounting policies or accounting estimates (discussed at 4.4 and 4.5 below). When it is difficult to distinguish a change in an accounting policy from a change in an accounting estimate, IAS 8 requires the change to be treated as a change in an accounting estimate. *[IAS 8.35]*.

4.3 The selection and application of accounting policies

Entities complying with IFRS (which is a defined term, discussed at 1.1 above) do not have a free hand in selecting accounting policies; indeed the very purpose of a body of accounting literature is to confine such choices.

IFRSs set out accounting policies that the IASB has concluded result in financial statements containing relevant and reliable information about the transactions, other events and conditions to which they apply. *[IAS 8.8]*.

To this end, the starting point in IAS 8 is that when an IFRS specifically applies to a transaction, other event or condition, the accounting policy or policies applied to that item should be determined by applying the IFRS and considering any relevant implementation guidance issued by the IASB for the IFRS. *[IAS 8.7]*. This draws out the distinction that IFRS must be applied whereas implementation guidance (which, as discussed at 1.1 above, is not part of IFRS) must be considered. As noted earlier, though, we would generally be surprised at entities not following such guidance.

Those policies need not be applied when the effect of applying them is immaterial. However, it is inappropriate to make, or leave uncorrected, immaterial departures from IFRS to achieve a particular presentation of an entity's financial position, financial performance or cash flows (see 4.6 below). *[IAS 8.8]*. The concept of materiality is discussed at 4.1.5 above.

There will be circumstances where a particular event, transaction or other condition is not specifically addressed by IFRS. When this is the case, IAS 8 sets out a hierarchy of guidance to be considered in the selection of an accounting policy.

The primary requirement of the standard is that management should use its judgement in developing and applying an accounting policy that results in information that is:

(a) relevant to the economic decision-making needs of users; and
(b) reliable, in that the financial statements:
    (i) represent faithfully the financial position, financial performance and cash flows of the entity;
    (ii) reflect the economic substance of transactions, other events and conditions, and not merely the legal form;
    (iii) are neutral, that is, free from bias;
    (iv) are prudent; and
    (v) are complete in all material respects. *[IAS 8.10]*.

Prudence and neutrality are not defined or otherwise discussed by IAS 8. They are, however, discussed in the IASB's *Conceptual Framework* as follows (see Chapter 2 for a discussion of the *Framework* and specifically at 5.1.2 regarding faithful representation).

A neutral depiction is one without bias in the selection or presentation of financial information. A neutral depiction is not slanted, weighted, emphasised, de-emphasised or otherwise manipulated to increase the probability that financial information will be received favourably or unfavourably by users. That is not to imply that neutral information has no purpose or no influence on behaviour. On the contrary, relevant financial information is, by definition, capable of making a difference in users' decisions. *[CF 2.15]*.

The *Conceptual Framework* has a discussion of the word 'prudence', the exercise of which is considered by the Board to support neutrality. The IASB considers prudence to be the exercise of caution when making judgements under conditions of uncertainty. This is said to mean that:

- assets and income are not overstated and liabilities and expenses are not understated; but also that
- the exercise of prudence does not allow for the understatement of assets or income or the overstatement of liabilities or expenses. Such misstatements can lead to the overstatement or understatement of income or expenses in future periods. *[CF 2.16]*.

The standard gives guidance regarding the primary requirement for exercising judgement in developing and applying an accounting policy. This guidance comes in two 'strengths' – certain things which management is required to consider, and others which it 'may' consider, as follows.

In making its judgement, management *shall* refer to, and consider the applicability of, the following sources in descending order:

(a) the requirements and guidance in IFRSs dealing with similar and related issues; and

(b) the definitions, recognition criteria and measurement concepts for assets, liabilities, income and expenses in the *Framework*; *[IAS 8.11]* and

in making this judgement, management may also consider the most recent pronouncements of other standard-setting bodies that use a similar conceptual framework to develop accounting standards, other accounting literature and accepted industry practices, to the extent that these do not conflict with the sources in (a) and (b) above. *[IAS 8.12]*. If an entity considers pronouncements of other standard-setting bodies in making its judgement in developing and applying an accounting policy, it should, in our view, consider all the contents of the pronouncements that are relevant to the issue. In other words, it should not adopt a selective or 'cherry-picking' approach.

In an agenda decision of March 2011, the Interpretations Committee noted the following. 'The Committee observed that when management develops an accounting policy through analogy to an IFRS dealing with similar and related matters, it needs to use its judgement in applying all aspects of the IFRS that are applicable to the particular issue.' The committee concluded that the issue of developing accounting policies by analogy requires no further clarification, so did not add the matter to its agenda.

4.4 Changes in accounting policies

As discussed at 4.1.4 above, consistency of accounting policies and presentation is a basic principle in both IAS 1 and IAS 8. Accordingly, IAS 8 only permits a change in accounting policies if the change:

(a) is required by an IFRS; or

(b) results in the financial statements providing reliable and more relevant information about the effects of transactions, other events or conditions on the entity's financial position, financial performance or cash flows. *[IAS 8.14]*.

IAS 8 addresses changes of accounting policy arising from three sources:

(a) the initial application (including early application) of an IFRS containing specific transitional provisions;

(b) the initial application of an IFRS which does not contain specific transitional provisions; and

(c) voluntary changes in accounting policy.

Policy changes under (a) should be accounted for in accordance with the specific transitional provisions of that IFRS.

A change of accounting policy under (b) or (c) should be applied retrospectively, that is applied to transactions, other events and conditions as if it had always been applied. *[IAS 8.5, 19-20]*. The standard goes on to explain that retrospective application requires adjustment of the opening balance of each affected component of equity for the earliest prior period presented and the other comparative amounts disclosed for each prior period presented as if the new accounting policy had always been applied. *[IAS 8.22]*. The standard observes that the amount of the resulting adjustment relating to periods before those presented in the financial statements (which is made to the opening balance of each affected component of equity of the earliest prior period presented) will usually be made to retained earnings. However, it goes on to note that the adjustment may be made to another component of equity (for example, to comply with an IFRS). IAS 8 also makes clear that any other information about prior periods, such as historical summaries of financial data, should be also adjusted. *[IAS 8.26]*.

The Interpretation Committee discussed the circumstance where an entity might determine that it needs to change an accounting policy as a result of an agenda decision issued by the Committee.

The particular point of discussion was the timing of such a change in accounting policy. In announcing its decision not to add the matter to its agenda it stated the following.

'The Board expects that an entity would be entitled to sufficient time to make that determination and implement any change (for example, an entity may need to obtain new information or adapt its systems to implement a change).'[2]

Frequently it will be straightforward to apply a change in accounting policy retrospectively. However, the standard accepts that sometimes it may be impractical to do so. Accordingly, retrospective application of a change in accounting policy is not required to the extent that it is impracticable to determine either the period-specific effects or the cumulative effect of the change. *[IAS 8.23]*. This is discussed further at 4.7 below. As noted at 4.3 above, in the absence of a specifically applicable IFRS an entity may apply an accounting policy from the most recent pronouncements of another standard-setting body that use a similar conceptual framework. The standard makes clear that a change in accounting policy reflecting a change in such a pronouncement is a voluntary change in accounting policy which should be accounted for and disclosed as such. *[IAS 8.21]*.

The standard clarifies that the following are not changes in accounting policy:

- the application of an accounting policy for transactions, other events or conditions that differ in substance from those previously occurring; and
- the application of a new accounting policy for transactions, other events or conditions that did not occur previously or were immaterial. *[IAS 8.16]*.

Furthermore, the standard requires that a change to a policy of revaluing intangible assets or property plant and equipment in accordance with IAS 38 and IAS 16 respectively is not to be accounted for under IAS 8 as a change in accounting policy. Rather, such a change should be dealt with as a revaluation in accordance with the relevant standards (discussed in Chapters 17 at 8.2 and 18 at 6). *[IAS 8.17-18]*. What this means is that it is not permissible to restate prior periods for the carrying value and depreciation charge of the assets concerned. Aside of this particular exception, the standard makes clear that a change in measurement basis is a change in an accounting policy, and not a change in an accounting estimate. However, when it is difficult to distinguish a change in an accounting policy from a change in an accounting estimate, the standard requires it to be treated as a change in an accounting estimate, discussed at 4.5 below. *[IAS 8.35]*.

4.5 Changes in accounting estimates

The making of estimates is a fundamental feature of financial reporting reflecting the uncertainties inherent in business activities. IAS 8 notes that the use of reasonable estimates is an essential part of the preparation of financial statements and it does not undermine their reliability. Examples of estimates given by the standard are:

- bad debts;
- inventory obsolescence;
- the fair value of financial assets or financial liabilities;
- the useful lives of, or expected pattern of consumption of the future economic benefits embodied in, depreciable assets; and
- warranty obligations. *[IAS 8.32-33]*.

Of course there are many others, some of the more subjective relating to share-based payments and post-retirement benefits.

Estimates will need revision as changes occur in the circumstances on which they are based or as a result of new information or more experience. The standard observes that, by its nature, the revision of an estimate does not relate to prior periods and is not the correction of an error. *[IAS 8.34]*. Accordingly, IAS 8 requires that changes in estimate be accounted for prospectively; defined as recognising the effect of the change in the accounting estimate in the current and future periods affected by the change. *[IAS 8.5, 36]*. The standard goes on to explain that this will mean (as appropriate):

- adjusting the carrying amount of an asset, liability or item of equity in the statement of financial position in the period of change; and
- recognising the change by including it in profit and loss in:
  - the period of change, if it affects that period only (for example, a change in estimate of bad debts); or
  - the period of change and future periods, if it affects both (for example, a change in estimated useful life of a depreciable asset or the expected pattern of consumption of the economic benefits embodied in it). *[IAS 8.36-38]*.

4.6 Correction of errors

As with all things, financial reporting is not immune to error and sometimes financial statements can be published which, whether by accident or design, contain errors. IAS 8 defines prior period errors as omissions from, and misstatements in, an entity's financial statements for one or more prior periods (including the effects of mathematical mistakes, mistakes in applying accounting policies, oversights or misinterpretations of facts, and fraud) arising from a failure to use, or misuse of, reliable information that:

(a) was available when financial statements for those periods were authorised for issue; and

(b) could reasonably be expected to have been obtained and taken into account in the preparation and presentation of those financial statements. *[IAS 8.5]*.

Errors can arise in respect of the recognition, measurement, presentation or disclosure of elements of financial statements. IAS 8 states that financial statements do not comply with IFRS if they contain errors that are:

(a) material; or

(b) immaterial but are made intentionally to achieve a particular presentation of an entity's financial position, financial performance or cash flows. *[IAS 8.41]*.

The concept in (b) is a little curious. As discussed at 4.1.5.A above, an error is material if it could influence the economic decisions of users taken on the basis of the financial statements. We find it difficult to imagine a scenario where an entity would deliberately seek to misstate its financial statements to achieve a particular presentation of its financial position, performance or cash flows but only in such a way that did not influence the decisions of users. In any event, and perhaps somewhat unnecessarily, IAS 8 notes that potential current period errors detected before the financial statements are authorised for issue should be corrected in those financial statements. This requirement is phrased so as to apply to all potential errors, not just material ones. *[IAS 8.41]*. The standard notes that corrections of errors are distinguished from changes in accounting estimates. Accounting estimates by their nature are approximations that may need revision as additional information becomes known. For example, the gain or loss recognised on the outcome of a contingency is not the correction of an error. *[IAS 8.48]*.

When it is discovered that material prior period errors have occurred, IAS 8 requires that they be corrected in the first set of financial statements prepared after their discovery. *[IAS 8.42]*. The correction should be excluded from profit or loss for the period in which the error is discovered. Rather, any information presented about prior periods (including any historical summaries of financial data) should be restated as far back as practicable. *[IAS 8.46]*. This should be done by:

(a) restating the comparative amounts for the prior period(s) presented in which the error occurred; or

(b) if the error occurred before the earliest prior period presented, restating the opening balances of assets, liabilities and equity for the earliest prior period presented. *[IAS 8.42]*.

This process is described by the standard as retrospective restatement, which it also defines as correcting the recognition, measurement and disclosure of amounts of elements of financial statements as if a prior period error had never occurred. *[IAS 8.5]*.

The implementation guidance accompanying the standard provides an example of the retrospective restatement of errors as follows: *[IAS 8.IG1]*

Example 3.10:   Retrospective restatement of errors

During 2021, Beta Co discovered that some products that had been sold during 2020 were incorrectly included in inventory at 31 December 2020 at £6,500.

Beta's accounting records for 2021 show sales of £104,000, cost of goods sold of £86,500 (including £6,500 for the error in opening inventory), and income taxes of £5,250.

In 2020, Beta reported:

	£
Sales	73,500
Cost of goods sold	(53,500)
Profit before income taxes	20,000
Income taxes	(6,000)
Profit	14,000

The 2020 opening retained earnings was £20,000 and closing retained earnings was £34,000.

Beta's income tax rate was 30 per cent for 2021 and 2020. It had no other income or expenses.

Beta had £5,000 of share capital throughout, and no other components of equity except for retained earnings. Its shares are not publicly traded and it does not disclose earnings per share.

Beta Co
Extract from the statement of comprehensive income

	2021 £	(restated) 2020 £
Sales	104,000	73,500
Cost of goods sold	(80,000)	(60,000)
Profit before income taxes	24,000	13,500
Income taxes	(7,200)	(4,050)
Profit	16,800	9,450

Beta Co
Statement of Changes in Equity

	Share capital £	Retained earnings £	Total £
Balance at 31 December 2019	5,000	20,000	25,000
Profit for the year ended 31 December 2020 as restated	–	9,450	9,450
Balance at 31 December 2020	5,000	29,450	34,450
Profit for the year ended 31 December 2021	–	16,800	16,800
Balance at 31 December 2021	5,000	46,250	51,250

Extracts from the Notes

1. Some products that had been sold in 2020 were incorrectly included in inventory at 31 December 2020 at £6,500. The financial statements of 2020 have been restated to correct this error. The effect of the restatement on those financial statements is summarised below. There is no effect in 2021.

	Effect on 2020 £
(Increase) in cost of goods sold	(6,500)
Decrease in income tax expense	1,950
(Decrease) in profit	(4,550)
(Decrease) in inventory	(6,500)
Decrease in income tax payable	1,950
(Decrease) in equity	(4,550)

As is the case for the retrospective application of a change in accounting policy, retrospective restatement for the correction of prior period material errors is not required to the extent that it is impracticable to determine either the period-specific effects or the cumulative effect of the error. *[IAS 8.43]*. This is discussed further at 4.7 below.

4.7 Impracticability of restatement

As noted at 4.4 and 4.6 above, IAS 8 does not require the restatement of prior periods following a change in accounting policy or the correction of material errors if such a restatement is impracticable.

The standard devotes a considerable amount of guidance to discussing what 'impracticable' means for these purposes.

The standard states that applying a requirement is impracticable when an entity cannot apply it after making every reasonable effort to do so. It goes on to note that, for a particular prior period, it is impracticable to apply a change in an accounting policy retrospectively or to make a retrospective restatement to correct an error if:

(a) the effects of the retrospective application or retrospective restatement are not determinable;

(b) the retrospective application or retrospective restatement requires assumptions about what management's intent would have been in that period; or

(c) the retrospective application or retrospective restatement requires significant estimates of amounts and it is impossible to distinguish objectively information about those estimates that:
  (i) provides evidence of circumstances that existed on the date(s) as at which those amounts are to be recognised, measured or disclosed; and
  (ii) would have been available when the financial statements for that prior period were authorised for issue from other information. *[IAS 8.5]*.

An example of a scenario covered by (a) above given by the standard is that in some circumstances it may impracticable to adjust comparative information for one or more prior periods to achieve comparability with the current period because data may not have been collected in the prior period(s) in a way that allows either retrospective application of a new accounting policy (or its prospective application to prior periods) or retrospective restatement to correct a prior period error, and it may be impracticable to recreate the information. *[IAS 8.50]*.

IAS 8 observes that it is frequently necessary to make estimates in applying an accounting policy and that estimation is inherently subjective, and that estimates may be developed after the reporting period. Developing estimates is potentially more difficult when retrospectively applying an accounting policy or making a retrospective restatement to correct a prior period error, because of the longer period of time that might have passed since the affected transaction, other event or condition occurred.

However, the objective of estimates related to prior periods remains the same as for estimates made in the current period, namely, for the estimate to reflect the circumstances that existed when the transaction, other event or condition occurred. *[IAS 8.51]*. Hindsight should not be used when applying a new accounting policy to, or correcting amounts for, a prior period, either in making assumptions about what management's intentions would have been in a prior period or estimating the amounts recognised, measured or disclosed in a prior period. For example, if an entity corrects a prior period error in calculating its liability for employees' accumulated sick leave in accordance with IAS 19, it would disregard information about an unusually severe influenza season during the next period that became available after the financial statements for the prior period were authorised for issue. However, the fact that significant estimates are frequently required when amending comparative information presented for prior periods does not prevent reliable adjustment or correction of the comparative information. *[IAS 8.53]*.

Therefore, retrospectively applying a new accounting policy or correcting a prior period error requires distinguishing information that:

(a) provides evidence of circumstances that existed on the date(s) as at which the transaction, other event or condition occurred; and

(b) would have been available when the financial statements for that prior period were authorised for issue,

from other information. The standard states that for some types of estimates (for example, a fair value measurement that uses significant unobservable inputs), it is impracticable to distinguish these types of information. When retrospective application or retrospective restatement would require making a significant estimate for which it is impossible to distinguish these two types of information, it is impracticable to apply the new accounting policy or correct the prior period error retrospectively. [IAS 8.52].

IAS 8 addresses the impracticability of restatement separately (although similarly) for changes in accounting policy and the correction of material errors.

4.7.1 Impracticability of restatement for a change in accounting policy

When retrospective application of a change in accounting policy is required, the change in policy should be applied retrospectively except to the extent that it is impracticable to determine either the period-specific effects or the cumulative effect of the change. [IAS 8.23]. When an entity applies a new accounting policy retrospectively, the standard requires it to be applied to comparative information for prior periods as far back as is practicable. Retrospective application to a prior period is not practicable for these purposes unless it is practicable to determine the cumulative effect on the amounts in both the opening and closing statement of financial position for that period. [IAS 8.26].

When it is impracticable to determine the period-specific effects of changing an accounting policy on comparative information for one or more prior periods presented:

- the new accounting policy should be applied to the carrying amounts of assets and liabilities as at the beginning of the earliest period for which retrospective application is practicable; and
- a corresponding adjustment to the opening balance of each affected component of equity for that period should be made.

The standard notes that this may be the current period. [IAS 8.24].

When it is impracticable to determine the cumulative effect, at the beginning of the current period, of applying a new accounting policy to all prior periods, the standard requires an adjustment to the comparative information to apply the new accounting policy prospectively from the earliest date practicable. [IAS 8.25]. Prospective application is defined by the standard as applying the new accounting policy to transactions, other events and conditions occurring after the date as at which the policy is changed. [IAS 8.5]. This means that the portion of the cumulative adjustment to assets, liabilities and equity arising before that date is disregarded. Changing an accounting policy is permitted by IAS 8 even if it is impracticable to apply the policy prospectively for any prior period. [IAS 8.27].

The implementation guidance accompanying the standard illustrates the prospective application of a change in accounting policy as follows: [IAS 8.IG3]

Example 3.11: Prospective application of a change in accounting policy when retrospective application is not practicable

During 2021, Delta Co changed its accounting policy for depreciating property, plant and equipment, so as to apply much more fully a components approach, whilst at the same time adopting the revaluation model.

In years before 2021, Delta's asset records were not sufficiently detailed to apply a components approach fully. At the end of 2020, management commissioned an engineering survey, which provided information on the components held and their fair values, useful lives, estimated residual values and depreciable amounts at the beginning of 2021. However, the survey did not provide a sufficient basis for reliably estimating the cost of those components that had not previously been accounted for separately, and the existing records before the survey did not permit this information to be reconstructed.

Delta's management considered how to account for each of the two aspects of the accounting change. They determined that it was not practicable to account for the change to a fuller components approach retrospectively, or to account for that change prospectively from any earlier date than the start of 2021. Also, the change from a cost model to a revaluation model is required to be accounted for prospectively (see 4.4 above). Therefore, management concluded that it should apply Delta's new policy prospectively from the start of 2021.

Additional information:

Delta's tax rate is 30 per cent.

	$
Property, plant and equipment at the end of 2020:	
Cost	25,000
Depreciation	(14,000)
Net book value	11,000
Prospective depreciation expense for 2021 (old basis)	1,500
Some results of the engineering survey:	
Valuation	17,000
Estimated residual value	3,000
Average remaining asset life (years)	7
Depreciation expense on existing property, plant and equipment for 2021 (new basis)	2,000

Extract from the Notes

1   From the start of 2021, Delta changed its accounting policy for depreciating property, plant and equipment, so as to apply much more fully a components approach, whilst at the same time adopting the revaluation model. Management takes the view that this policy provides reliable and more relevant information because it deals more accurately with the components of property, plant and equipment and is based on up-to-date values. The policy has been applied prospectively from the start of 2021 because it was not practicable to estimate the effects of applying the policy either retrospectively, or prospectively from any earlier date. Accordingly, the adoption of the new policy has no effect on prior years. The effect on the current year is to increase the carrying amount of property, plant and equipment at the start of the year by $6,000; increase the opening deferred tax provision by $1,800; create a revaluation surplus at the start of the year of $4,200; increase depreciation expense by $500; and reduce tax expense by $150.

4.7.2   Impracticability of restatement for a material error

IAS 8 requires that a prior period error should be corrected by retrospective restatement except to the extent that it is impracticable to determine either the period-specific effects or the cumulative effect of the error. *[IAS 8.43]*.

When it is impracticable to determine the period-specific effects of an error on comparative information for one or more prior periods presented, the opening balances of assets, liabilities and equity should be restated for the earliest period for which retrospective restatement is practicable (which the standard notes may be the current period). *[IAS 8.44]*.

When it is impracticable to determine the cumulative effect, at the beginning of the current period, of an error on all prior periods, the comparative information should be restated to correct the error prospectively from the earliest date practicable. *[IAS 8.45]*.

The standard explains that this will mean disregarding the portion of the cumulative restatement of assets, liabilities and equity arising before that date. *[IAS 8.47]*.

5 DISCLOSURE REQUIREMENTS

5.1 Disclosures relating to accounting policies

5.1.1 Disclosure of accounting policies

5.1.1.A Summary of significant accounting policies

IAS 1 makes the valid observation that it is important for users to be informed of the measurement basis or bases used in the financial statements (for example, historical cost, current cost, net realisable value, fair value or recoverable amount) because the basis on which the financial statements are prepared significantly affects their analysis. *[IAS 1.118]*.

Accordingly, the standard requires disclosure of significant accounting policies comprising:

(a) the measurement basis (or bases) used in preparing the financial statements; and

(b) the other accounting policies used that are relevant to an understanding of the financial statements. *[IAS 1.117]*.

When more than one measurement basis is used in the financial statements, for example when particular classes of assets are revalued, it is sufficient to provide an indication of the categories of assets and liabilities to which each measurement basis is applied. *[IAS 1.118]*.

It is clearly necessary to apply judgement when deciding on the level of detail required in the disclosure of accounting policies. Of particular note, is that the decision as to whether to disclose a policy should not just be a function of the magnitude of the sums involved. The standard states that an accounting policy may be significant because of the nature of the entity's operations even if amounts for current and prior periods are not material. It is also appropriate to disclose each significant accounting policy that is not specifically required by IFRS, but is selected and applied in accordance with IAS 8 (discussed at 4.3 above). *[IAS 1.121]*. Moreover, the relevance of the disclosure of accounting policies is improved if it specifically addresses how the entity has applied the requirements of IFRS, rather than a giving summary of those requirements.

In deciding whether a particular accounting policy should be disclosed, IAS 1 requires consideration of whether disclosure would assist users in understanding how transactions, other events and conditions are reflected in the reported financial performance and financial position. In doing so, each entity should consider the nature of its operations and the policies that the users of its financial statements would expect to be disclosed for that type of entity. The standard observes that disclosure of particular accounting policies is especially useful to users when those policies are selected from alternatives allowed in IFRSs – although the required disclosures are not restricted to such policies. An example is disclosure of the choice between the cost and fair value models in IAS 40 – *Investment Property*.

Some standards specifically require disclosure of particular accounting policies, including choices made by management between different policies they allow. For example IAS 16 requires disclosure of the measurement bases used for classes of property, plant and equipment (discussed in Chapter 18 at 8). *[IAS 1.119]*.

5.1.1.B Judgements made in applying accounting policies

The process of applying an entity's accounting policies requires various judgements, apart from those involving estimations, that can significantly affect the amounts recognised in the financial statements. For example, judgements are required in determining:

(a) when substantially all the significant risks and rewards of ownership of financial assets and, for lessors, assets are transferred to other entities;

(b) whether, in substance, particular sales of goods are financing arrangements and therefore do not give rise to revenue; and

(c) whether the contractual terms of a financial asset give rise on specified dates to cash flows that are solely payments of principal and interest on the principal amount outstanding. *[IAS 1.123]*.

IAS 1 requires disclosure, along with its significant accounting policies or other notes, of the judgements (apart from those involving estimations, see 5.2.1 below) management has made in the process of applying the entity's accounting policies that have the most significant effect on the amounts recognised in the financial statements. *[IAS 1.122]*.

Some of these disclosures are required by other standards. For example:

- IFRS 12 – *Disclosure of Interests in Other Entities*, requires disclosure of the judgements made in determining if control is present.
- IAS 40 requires disclosure of the criteria developed by the entity to distinguish investment property from owner-occupied property and from property held for sale in the ordinary course of business, when classification of the property is difficult. *[IAS 1.124]*.
- IFRS 15 requires disclosures of the judgments made in applying the standard that significantly affect the determination of the amount and timing of revenue from contracts with customers. *[IFRS 15.123]*.

5.1.2 Disclosure of changes in accounting policies

IAS 8 distinguishes between accounting policy changes made pursuant to the initial application of an IFRS and voluntary changes in accounting policy (discussed at 4.4 above). It sets out different disclosure requirements for each, as set out in 5.1.2.A and 5.1.2.B below. Also, if an IFRS is in issue but is not yet effective and has not been applied certain disclosures of its likely impact are required. These are set out in 5.1.2.C below.

5.1.2.A Accounting policy changes pursuant to the initial application of an IFRS

When initial application of an IFRS has an effect on the current period or any prior period, would have such an effect except that it is impracticable to determine the amount of the adjustment, or might have an effect on future periods, an entity should disclose:

(a) the title of the IFRS;

(b) when applicable, that the change in accounting policy is made in accordance with its transitional provisions;

(c) the nature of the change in accounting policy;

(d) when applicable, a description of the transitional provisions;

(e) when applicable, the transitional provisions that might have an effect on future periods;
(f) for the current period and each prior period presented, to the extent practicable, the amount of the adjustment:
   (i) for each financial statement line item affected; and
   (ii) if IAS 33 – *Earnings per Share* – applies to the entity, for basic and diluted earnings per share;
(g) the amount of the adjustment relating to periods before those presented, to the extent practicable; and
(h) if retrospective application required by IAS 8 is impracticable for a particular prior period, or for periods before those presented, the circumstances that led to the existence of that condition and a description of how and from when the change in accounting policy has been applied.

Impracticability of restatement is discussed at 4.7 above. Financial statements of subsequent periods need not repeat these disclosures. *[IAS 8.28]*.

5.1.2.B Voluntary changes in accounting policy

When a voluntary change in accounting policy has an effect on the current period or any prior period, would have an effect on that period except that it is impracticable to determine the amount of the adjustment, or might have an effect on future periods, an entity should disclose:

(a) the nature of the change in accounting policy;
(b) the reasons why applying the new accounting policy provides reliable and more relevant information;
(c) for the current period and each prior period presented, to the extent practicable, the amount of the adjustment:
   (i) for each financial statement line item affected; and
   (ii) if IAS 33 applies to the entity, for basic and diluted earnings per share;
(d) the amount of the adjustment relating to periods before those presented, to the extent practicable; and
(e) if retrospective application is impracticable for a particular prior period, or for periods before those presented, the circumstances that led to the existence of that condition and a description of how and from when the change in accounting policy has been applied.

Impracticability of restatement is discussed at 4.7 above. Example 3.11 therein illustrates the above disclosure requirements. Financial statements of subsequent periods need not repeat these disclosures. *[IAS 8.29]*.

5.1.2.C Future impact of a new IFRS

When an entity has not applied a new IFRS that has been issued but is not yet effective, it should disclose:

(a) that fact; and

(b) known or reasonably estimable information relevant to assessing the possible impact that application of the new IFRS will have on the financial statements in the period of initial application. *[IAS 8.30]*.

In producing the above disclosure, the standard requires that an entity should consider disclosing:

(a) the title of the new IFRS;
(b) the nature of the impending change or changes in accounting policy;
(c) the date by which application of the IFRS is required;
(d) the date as at which it plans to apply the IFRS initially; and
(e) either:
   (i) a discussion of the impact that initial application of the IFRS is expected to have on the entity's financial statements; or
   (ii) if that impact is not known or reasonably estimable, a statement to that effect. *[IAS 8.31]*.

5.2 Disclosure of estimation uncertainty and changes in estimates

5.2.1 Sources of estimation uncertainty

Determining the carrying amounts of some assets and liabilities requires estimation of the effects of uncertain future events on those assets and liabilities at the end of the reporting period. Examples given by IAS 1 are that (in the absence of fair values in an active market for identical items used to measure them) the following assets and liabilities require future-oriented estimates to measure them:

- the recoverable amount of classes of property, plant and equipment;
- the effect of technological obsolescence on inventories;
- provisions subject to the future outcome of litigation in progress; and
- long-term employee benefit liabilities such as pension obligations.

These estimates involve assumptions about such items as the risk adjustment to cash flows or discount rates used, future changes in salaries and future changes in prices affecting other costs. *[IAS 1.126]*.

In light of this, IAS 1 requires disclosure of information about the assumptions concerning the future, and other major sources of estimation uncertainty at the end of the reporting period, that have a significant risk of resulting in a material adjustment to the carrying amounts of assets and liabilities within the next financial year. In respect of those assets and liabilities, the notes must include details of:

(a) their nature; and
(b) their carrying amount as at the end of the reporting period. *[IAS 1.125]*.

IAS 1 goes on to observe that these assumptions and other sources of estimation uncertainty relate to the estimates that require management's most difficult, subjective or complex judgements. As the number of variables and assumptions affecting the possible future resolution of the uncertainties increases, those judgements become more subjective and complex, and the potential for a consequential material adjustment to the carrying amounts of assets and liabilities normally increases accordingly. *[IAS 1.127]*.

The disclosures are required to be presented in a manner that helps users of financial statements to understand the judgements management makes about the future and about other key sources of estimation uncertainty. The nature and extent of the information provided will vary according to the nature of the assumption and other circumstances. Examples given by the standard of the types of disclosures to be made are:

(a) the nature of the assumption or other estimation uncertainty;

(b) the sensitivity of carrying amounts to the methods, assumptions and estimates underlying their calculation, including the reasons for the sensitivity;

(c) the expected resolution of an uncertainty and the range of reasonably possible outcomes within the next financial year in respect of the carrying amounts of the assets and liabilities affected; and

(d) an explanation of changes made to past assumptions concerning those assets and liabilities, if the uncertainty remains unresolved. *[IAS 1.129]*.

The disclosure of some of these key assumptions is required by other standards. IAS 1 notes the following examples:

- IAS 37 requires disclosure, in specified circumstances, of major assumptions concerning future events affecting classes of provisions; and
- IFRS 13 – *Fair Value Measurement* – requires disclosure of significant assumptions (including the valuation technique(s) and inputs) used when measuring the fair values of assets and liabilities (not just financial ones) that are carried at fair value. *[IAS 1.133]*.

Other examples would include:

- IAS 19 requires disclosure of actuarial assumptions;
- IFRS 2 – *Share-based Payment* – requires disclosure, in certain circumstances, of: the option pricing model used, and the method used and the assumptions made to incorporate the effects of early exercise; and
- IAS 36 – *Impairment of Assets* – requires disclosure, in certain circumstances, of each key assumption on which management has based its cash flow projections.

These assumptions and other sources of estimation uncertainty are not required to be disclosed for assets and liabilities with a significant risk that their carrying amounts might change materially within the next financial year if, at the end of the reporting period, they are measured at fair value based on a quoted price in an active market for an identical asset or liability. *[IAS 1.128]*.

Also, it is not necessary to disclose budget information or forecasts in making the disclosures. *[IAS 1.130]*. Furthermore, the disclosures of particular judgements management made in the process of applying the entity's accounting policies (discussed at 5.1.1.B above) do not relate to the disclosures of sources of estimation uncertainty. *[IAS 1.132]*.

When it is impracticable to disclose the extent of the possible effects of an assumption or another source of estimation uncertainty at the end of the reporting period, the entity should disclose that it is reasonably possible, based on existing knowledge, that outcomes within the next financial year that are different from assumptions could require a material adjustment to the carrying amount of the asset or liability affected. In all cases, the entity should disclose the nature and carrying amount of the specific asset or liability (or class of assets or liabilities) affected by the assumption. [IAS 1.131].

In our view, these requirements of IAS 1 represent potentially highly onerous disclosures. The extensive judgements required in deciding the level of detail to be given has resulted in a wide variety of disclosure in practice. The Basis for Conclusions to the standard reveals that the Board was aware that the requirement could potentially require quite extensive disclosures and explains its attempt to limit this as follows. 'IAS 1 limits the scope of the disclosures to items that have a significant risk of causing a material adjustment to the carrying amounts of assets and liabilities within the next financial year. The longer the future period to which the disclosures relate, the greater the range of items that would qualify for disclosure, and the less specific are the disclosures that could be made about particular assets or liabilities. A period longer than the next financial year might obscure the most relevant information with other disclosures.' [IAS 1.BC84]. Careful judgement will be required to provide useful and compliant information without reducing the understandability of the financial statement by obscuring material information with immaterial information.

5.2.2 Changes in accounting estimates

IAS 8 requires disclosure of the nature and amount of a change in an accounting estimate that has an effect in the current period or is expected to have an effect in future periods, except for the disclosure of the effect on future periods when it is impracticable to estimate that effect. [IAS 8.39]. If the amount of the effect in future periods is not disclosed because estimating it is impracticable, that fact should be disclosed. [IAS 8.40].

5.3 Disclosure of prior period errors

When correction has been made for a material prior period error, IAS 8 requires disclosure of the following:

(a) the nature of the prior period error;
(b) for each prior period presented, to the extent practicable, the amount of the correction:
   (i) for each financial statement line item affected; and
   (ii) if IAS 33 applies to the entity, for basic and diluted earnings per share;
(c) the amount of the correction at the beginning of the earliest prior period presented; and
(d) if retrospective restatement is impracticable for a particular prior period, the circumstances that led to the existence of that condition and a description of how and from when the error has been corrected.

Financial statements of subsequent periods need not repeat these disclosures. [IAS 8.49]. Example 3.10 at 4.6 above illustrates these disclosure requirements.

5.4 Disclosures about capital

5.4.1 General capital disclosures

The IASB believes that the level of an entity's capital and how it manages it are important factors for users to consider in assessing the risk profile of an entity and its ability to withstand unexpected adverse events. Furthermore, the level of capital might also affect the entity's ability to pay dividends. [IAS 1.BC86]. For these reasons, IAS 1 requires disclosure of information that enables users of financial statements to evaluate an entity's objectives, policies and processes for managing capital. [IAS 1.134].

To achieve this, IAS 1 requires disclosure of the following, which should be based on the information provided internally to the entity's key management personnel: [IAS 1.135]

(a) qualitative information about its objectives, policies and processes for managing capital, including:
  (i) a description of what it manages as capital;
  (ii) when an entity is subject to externally imposed capital requirements, the nature of those requirements and how those requirements are incorporated into the management of capital; and
  (iii) how it is meeting its objectives for managing capital;

(b) summary quantitative data about what it manages as capital;

  Some entities regard some financial liabilities (for example, some forms of subordinated debt) as part of capital. Other entities regard capital as excluding some components of equity (for example, components arising from cash flow hedges);

(c) any changes in (a) and (b) from the previous period;

(d) whether during the period it complied with any externally imposed capital requirements to which it is subject; and

(e) when the entity has not complied with such externally imposed capital requirements, the consequences of such non-compliance.

IAS 1 observes that capital may be managed in a number of ways and be subject to a number of different capital requirements. For example, a conglomerate may include entities that undertake insurance activities and banking activities, and those entities may also operate in several jurisdictions. When an aggregate disclosure of capital requirements and how capital is managed would not provide useful information or distorts a financial statement user's understanding of an entity's capital resources, the standard requires disclosure of separate information for each capital requirement to which the entity is subject. [IAS 1.136].

Examples 3.12 and 3.13 below are based on the illustrative examples of capital disclosures contained in the implementation guidance accompanying IAS 1. [IAS 1.IG10-11].

Presentation of financial statements and accounting policies

Example 3.12: *Illustrative capital disclosures: An entity that is not a regulated financial institution*

The following example illustrates the application of the requirements discussed above for an entity that is not a financial institution and is not subject to an externally imposed capital requirement. In this example, the entity monitors capital using a debt-to-adjusted capital ratio. Other entities may use different methods to monitor capital. The example is also relatively simple. An entity should decide, in the light of its circumstances, how much detail to provide.

Facts

Group A manufactures and sells cars. It includes a finance subsidiary that provides finance to customers, primarily in the form of leases. Group A is not subject to any externally imposed capital requirements.

Example disclosure

The Group's objectives when managing capital are:

- to safeguard the entity's ability to continue as a going concern, so that it can continue to provide returns for shareholders and benefits for other stakeholders; and
- to provide an adequate return to shareholders by pricing products and services commensurately with the level of risk.

The Group sets the amount of capital in proportion to risk. The Group manages the capital structure and makes adjustments to it in the light of changes in economic conditions and the risk characteristics of the underlying assets. In order to maintain or adjust the capital structure, the Group may adjust the amount of dividends paid to shareholders, return capital to shareholders, issue new shares, or sell assets to reduce debt.

Consistently with others in the industry, the Group monitors capital on the basis of the debt-to-adjusted capital ratio. This ratio is calculated as net debt ÷ adjusted capital. Net debt is calculated as total debt (as shown in the statement of financial position) less cash and cash equivalents. Adjusted capital comprises all components of equity (i.e. share capital, share premium, non-controlling interests, retained earnings, and revaluation surplus) other than amounts accumulated in equity relating to cash flow hedges, and includes some forms of subordinated debt.

During 2021, the Group's strategy, which was unchanged from 2020, was to maintain the debt-to-adjusted capital ratio at the lower end of the range 6:1 to 7:1, in order to secure access to finance at a reasonable cost by maintaining a BB credit rating. The debt-to-adjusted capital ratios at 31 December 2021 and at 31 December 2020 were as follows:

	2021 €million	2020 €million
Total debt	1,000	1,100
Less: cash and cash equivalents	(90)	(150)
Net debt	910	950
Total equity	110	105
Add: subordinated debt instruments	38	38
Less: amounts accumulated in equity relating to cash flow hedges	(10)	(5)
Adjusted capital	138	138
Debt-to-adjusted capital ratio	6.6	6.9

The decrease in the debt-to-adjusted capital ratio during 2021 resulted primarily from the reduction in net debt that occurred on the sale of subsidiary Z. As a result of this reduction in net debt, improved profitability and lower levels of managed receivables, the dividend payment was increased to €2.8 million for 2021 (from €2.5 million for 2020).

Example 3.13: *Illustrative capital disclosures: An entity that has not complied with externally imposed capital requirements*

The following example illustrates the application of the requirement to disclose when an entity has not complied with externally imposed capital requirements during the period. Other disclosures would be provided to comply with the other requirements relating to capital.

Facts

Entity A provides financial services to its customers and is subject to capital requirements imposed by Regulator B. During the year ended 31 December 2021, Entity A did not comply with the capital requirements imposed by Regulator B. In its financial statements for the year ended 31 December 2021, Entity A provides the following disclosure relating to its non-compliance.

Example disclosure

Entity A filed its quarterly regulatory capital return for 30 September 2021 on 20 October 2021. At that date, Entity A's regulatory capital was below the capital requirement imposed by Regulator B by $1 million. As a result, Entity A was required to submit a plan to the regulator indicating how it would increase its regulatory capital to the amount required. Entity A submitted a plan that entailed selling part of its unquoted equities portfolio with a carrying amount of $11.5 million in the fourth quarter of 2021. In the fourth quarter of 2021, Entity A sold its fixed interest investment portfolio for $12.6 million and met its regulatory capital requirement.

5.4.2 Puttable financial instruments classified as equity

IAS 32 allows certain liabilities called 'puttable financial instruments' to be classified as equity. Puttable financial instrument is a term defined and discussed at length in IAS 32 (see Chapter 47 at 4.6). The IASB observes that 'Financial instruments classified as equity usually do not include any obligation for the entity to deliver a financial asset to another party. Therefore, the Board concluded that additional disclosures are needed in these circumstances.' *[IAS 1.BC100B]*.

The required disclosure for puttable financial instruments classified as equity instruments is as follows:

(a) summary quantitative data about the amount classified as equity;

(b) its objectives, policies and processes for managing its obligation to repurchase or redeem the instruments when required to do so by the instrument holders, including any changes from the previous period;

(c) the expected cash outflow on redemption or repurchase of that class of financial instruments; and

(d) information about how the expected cash outflow on redemption or repurchase was determined. *[IAS 1.136A]*.

5.5 Other disclosures

IAS 1 also requires disclosure:

(a) in the notes of:

    (i) the amount of dividends proposed or declared before the financial statements were authorised for issue but not recognised as a distribution to owners during the period, and the related amount per share; and

    (ii) the amount of any cumulative preference dividends not recognised; *[IAS 1.137]*

(b) in accordance with IAS 10 – *Events after the Reporting Period* – the following non-adjusting events in respect of loans classified as current liabilities, if they occur

between the end of the reporting period and the date the financial statements are authorised for issue (see Chapter 38 at 2.1.1):
(i) refinancing on a long-term basis;
(ii) rectification of a breach of a long-term loan arrangement; and
(iii) the granting by the lender of a period of grace to rectify a breach of a long-term loan arrangement ending at least twelve months after the reporting period;[3] *[IAS 1.76]*

(c) the following, if not disclosed elsewhere in information published with the financial statements:
(i) the domicile and legal form of the entity, its country of incorporation and the address of its registered office (or principal place of business, if different from the registered office);
(ii) a description of the nature of the entity's operations and its principal activities;
(iii) the name of the parent and the ultimate parent of the group; and
(iv) if it is a limited life entity, information regarding the length of its life. *[IAS 1.138]*.

6 FUTURE DEVELOPMENTS

The IASB is pursuing a number of matters which relate to the subjects discussed in this chapter.

The Board groups its projects into four categories: standard-setting, maintenance, research and other. We discuss below the current projects relevant to this chapter under these headings.[4]

6.1 Standard-setting projects

6.1.1 *Management commentary*

In November 2017, the Board added a project to its agenda to revise and update IFRS Practice Statement 1 – *Management Commentary* – issued in 2010 (see 2.3 above). In undertaking the project, the Board will consider how broader financial reporting could complement and support IFRS financial statements. To support the Board's work on updating the Practice Statement, the Board established the Management Commentary Consultative Group.

The Board has completed an initial round of consultations with its consultative bodies, including the Management Commentary Consultative Group, and is currently discussing what guidance to provide in the revised Practice Statement. The Board expects to publish an Exposure Draft in the first quarter of 2021.[5]

6.1.2 *Primary financial statements*

The IASB is developing what it describes as improvements to 'how information is communicated in the financial statements, with a focus on the statement(s) of financial performance'.[6]

At its meeting in May 2019 the IASB decided the consultation document for this project would be an exposure draft which would not be preceded by a discussion paper.

The Exposure Draft *General Presentation and Disclosures* was published in December 2019.[7] The deadline for comments on the draft was September 2020 and the Board will consider feedback on it in developing its final requirements.

The Exposure Draft sets out proposals for a new accounting standard on presentation and disclosures in financial statements that, when finalised, would replace IAS 1. It also sets out proposed amendments to other standards.

The IASB describes the proposal as follows.

'In the Exposure Draft the Board proposes:

- requiring additional subtotals in the statement of profit or loss. These subtotals would provide relevant information and create a more consistent structure to the statement of profit or loss, thereby improving comparability among companies.
- requiring disaggregation to help a company to provide relevant information. The Board proposes disaggregation principles, disaggregation of operating expenses either by nature or by function in the statement of profit or loss, a requirement for disaggregation of large "other" balances, a requirement to disaggregate information about unusual income and expenses and additional minimum line items in the statement of financial position.
- requiring disclosure of some management-defined performance measures – that is, performance measures not specified by IFRS Standards. To promote transparency, the Board proposes reconciliations between some management-defined performance measures and subtotals specified by IFRS Standards.
- limited changes to the statement of cash flows to improve consistency in classification by removing options.'

6.2 Maintenance projects

6.2.1 Distinction between a change in an accounting policy and a change in an accounting estimate

The IASB is considering amending IAS 8 to clarify the existing distinction between a change in accounting policy and a change in accounting estimate.

The Exposure Draft *Accounting Policies and Accounting Estimates* was published in September 2017. At the time of writing the Board's website indicates that the next milestone is an amendment to the standard the fourth quarter of 2020.

6.2.2 Accounting policy disclosure

In August 2019 the IASB published Exposure Draft ED/2019/6 – *Disclosure of Accounting Policies, Proposed amendments to IAS 1 and IFRS Practice Statement 2*.

The Board stated that the proposed amendments 'are intended to help entities:

- identify and disclose all accounting policies that provide material information to primary users of financial statements; and
- identify immaterial accounting policies and eliminate them from their financial statements.'[8]

The Board met in June 2020 and discussed the feedback received on the ED. At this meeting it tentatively decided:
- all types of accounting policy information should be subject to materiality judgements. The concept of materiality would therefore apply when deciding whether to disclose accounting policy information that is standardised, or that duplicates or summarises the requirements in IFRS Standards;
- at times, accounting policy information that is standardised, or that duplicates or summarises the requirements in IFRS Standards, can be material and should be disclosed;
- to add an example to IAS 1 to clarify that material accounting policy information could include standardised information or information that duplicates or summarises the requirements in IFRS Standards when the accounting required for a material transaction, other event or condition is complex and may not otherwise be understood by users of financial statements;
- to add:
    (a) an explanatory paragraph to the proposed amendments to IAS 1. This paragraph would:
        (i) clarify that entities are permitted to provide immaterial accounting policy information as long as it does not obscure material accounting policy information; and
        (ii) prompt entities to consider whether they are obscuring material accounting policy information with immaterial accounting policy information; and
    (b) further guidance to the proposed amendments to IFRS Practice Statement 2 relating to the amendments to IAS 1 described in (a).

The Board expects to issue a revision to the standard and practice statement in the fourth quarter of 2020.[9]

6.2.3 Disclosure Initiative – Targeted Standards-level Review of Disclosures

On 21 March 2018, the Board added a project to its agenda to perform a targeted standards-level review of disclosure requirements.

The Board is:
- developing guidance for it to use when developing and drafting disclosure requirements; and
- testing that guidance by applying it to the disclosure requirements in IAS 19 and IFRS 13 (discussed respectively in Chapters 35 and 14).

At the time of writing, the website of the IASB states 'The Board completed technical decisions on these elements in Q1 2020. To assist stakeholders affected by the coronavirus pandemic, the publication of an Exposure Draft of amendments to the disclosure sections of IAS 19 and IFRS 13 will be postponed to H1 2021 (estimated March 2021).'

References

1 *IFRIC Update*, January 2014.
2 *IFRIC Update*, March 2019.
3 With effect, at the latest, for periods beginning on or after 1 January 2022, IAS 1.76 is amended to require disclosure of the settlement of non-current liabilities after the end of the reporting period and before the accounts are authorised for issue.
4 *IASB website*, IASB work-plan, https://www.ifrs.org/projects/work-plan/ (accessed 7 September 2020).
5 *IASB website*, IASB work-plan, https://www.ifrs.org/projects/work-plan/ (accessed 7 September 2020).
6 *IASB website,* IASB work-plan, https://www.ifrs.org/projects/work-plan/ (accessed 7 September 2020).
7 Exposure Draft ED/2019/7 *General Presentation and Disclosures*, IASB, December 2019.
8 ED/2019/6 Introduction.
9 *IASB website,* IASB work-plan, https://www.ifrs.org/projects/work-plan/ (accessed 7 September 2020).

Chapter 4   Non-current assets held for sale and discontinued operations

1 OBJECTIVE AND SCOPE OF IFRS 5 189
2 NON-CURRENT ASSETS (AND DISPOSAL GROUPS) HELD FOR SALE OR HELD FOR DISTRIBUTION TO OWNERS 189
    2.1 Classification of non-current assets (and disposal groups) held for sale or held for distribution to owners 189
        2.1.1 The concept of a disposal group 190
        2.1.2 Classification as held for sale or as held for distribution to owners 191
            2.1.2.A Meaning of available for immediate sale 192
            2.1.2.B Meaning of highly probable 193
            2.1.2.C Abandonment 196
        2.1.3 Partial disposals of operations 196
            2.1.3.A Loss of control of a subsidiary 196
            2.1.3.B Partial disposal of an associate or joint venture 197
    2.2 Measurement of non-current assets (and disposal groups) held for sale 198
        2.2.1 Scope of the measurement requirements 198
        2.2.2 Measurement of non-current assets and disposal groups held for sale 198
            2.2.2.A Measurement on initial classification as held for sale 198
            2.2.2.B Subsequent remeasurement 199
        2.2.3 Impairments and reversals of impairment 200
        2.2.4 Presentation in the statement of financial position of non-current assets and disposal groups held for sale 202
        2.2.5 Changes to a plan of sale or to a plan of distribution 205

| | | 2.2.5.A | Assets (or disposal groups) to be retained by the entity | 205 |
| | | 2.2.5.B | Change in method of disposal | 206 |

3 DISCONTINUED OPERATIONS 206
   3.1 Definition of a discontinued operation 207
   3.2 Presentation of discontinued operations 208
   3.3 Trading between continuing and discontinued operations 210

4 COMPARATIVE INFORMATION 211
   4.1 Treatment of comparative information on initial classification as held for sale..211
      4.1.1 The statement of comprehensive income 211
      4.1.2 The statement of financial position..211
   4.2 Treatment of comparative information on the cessation of classification as held for sale.. 212

5 DISCLOSURE REQUIREMENTS 213
   5.1 Requirements of IFRS 5 213
   5.2 Disclosures required by standards other than IFRS 5........................... 214

6 POSSIBLE FUTURE DEVELOPMENTS 214

List of examples

Example 4.1:	Meaning of 'available for immediate sale'	192
Example 4.2:	Exceptions to the 'one year rule'	195
Example 4.3:	Measuring and presenting subsidiaries acquired with a view to sale and classified as held for sale	199
Example 4.4:	Allocation of impairment loss to the components of a disposal group	200
Example 4.5:	Presenting non-current assets or disposal groups classified as held for sale	203
Example 4.6:	Discontinued operation arising from abandonment	207
Example 4.7:	Presenting discontinued operations	209

Chapter 4 Non-current assets held for sale and discontinued operations

1 OBJECTIVE AND SCOPE OF IFRS 5

The objective of IFRS 5 – *Non-current Assets Held for Sale and Discontinued Operations* – is to specify the accounting for assets held for sale, and the presentation and disclosure of discontinued operations. In particular, the standard requires that non-current assets (and, in a 'disposal group', related liabilities and current assets, discussed at 2.1.1 below) meeting its criteria to be classified as held for sale be:

(a) measured at the lower of carrying amount and fair value less costs to sell, with depreciation on them ceasing; and

(b) presented separately on the face of the statement of financial position with the results of discontinued operations presented separately in the statement of comprehensive income. *[IFRS 5.1]*.

The classification and presentation requirements apply to all recognised non-current assets and disposal groups, while there are certain exceptions to the measurement provisions of the standard. *[IFRS 5.2, 5]*. These issues are discussed further at 2.2 below.

The classification, presentation and measurement requirements of IFRS 5 applicable to assets (or disposal groups) classified as held for sale also apply to those classified as held for distribution to owners acting in their capacity as owners. *[IFRS 5.5A]*. This is discussed at 2.1.2 below.

2 NON-CURRENT ASSETS (AND DISPOSAL GROUPS) HELD FOR SALE OR HELD FOR DISTRIBUTION TO OWNERS

2.1 Classification of non-current assets (and disposal groups) held for sale or held for distribution to owners

IFRS 5 frequently refers to current assets and non-current assets. It provides a definition of each term as follows:

'An entity shall classify an asset as current when:

(a) it expects to realise the asset, or intends to sell or consume it in its normal operating cycle;

(b) it holds the asset primarily for the purpose of trading;

(c) it expects to realise the asset within twelve months after the reporting period; or

(d) the asset is cash or a cash equivalent (as defined in IAS 7 – *Statement of Cash Flows*) unless the asset is restricted from being exchanged or used to settle a liability for at least twelve months after the reporting period.'

A non-current asset is 'an asset that does not meet the definition of a current asset'. *[IFRS 5 Appendix A]*.

These definitions are the same as those in IAS 1 – *Presentation of Financial Statements* (discussed in Chapter 3 at 3.1.1).

2.1.1 The concept of a disposal group

As its title suggests, IFRS 5 addresses the accounting treatment of non-current assets held for sale, that is assets whose carrying amount will be recovered principally through sale rather than continuing use in the business. *[IFRS 5.6]*. However, the standard also applies to certain liabilities and current assets where they form part of a 'disposal group'.

The standard observes that sometimes an entity will dispose of a group of assets, possibly with some directly associated liabilities, together in a single transaction. *[IFRS 5.4]*. A common example would be the disposal of a subsidiary. For these circumstances, IFRS 5 introduces the concept of a disposal group, which it defines as a group of assets to be disposed of, by sale or otherwise, together as a group in a single transaction, and liabilities directly associated with those assets that will be transferred in the transaction. The group includes goodwill acquired in a business combination if the group is a cash-generating unit to which goodwill has been allocated in accordance with the requirements of IAS 36 – *Impairment of Assets* (discussed in Chapter 20) or if it is an operation within such a cash-generating unit. *[IFRS 5 Appendix A]*.

The use of the phrase 'together in a single transaction' indicates that the only liabilities that can be included in the group are those assumed by the purchaser. Accordingly, any borrowings of the entity which are to be repaid out of the sales proceeds would be excluded from the disposal group.

The standard goes on to explain that a disposal group:

- may be a group of cash-generating units, a single cash-generating unit, or part of a cash-generating unit. Once the cash flows from an asset or group of assets are expected to arise principally from sale rather than continuing use, they become less dependent on cash flows arising from other assets, and a disposal group that was part of a cash-generating unit becomes a separate cash-generating unit; and

- may include any assets and any liabilities of the entity, including current assets, current liabilities and assets outside the scope of the measurement requirements of IFRS 5 (see 2.2 below). *[IFRS 5.4]*.

Discontinued operations are discussed at 3 below. As noted there, it seems highly unlikely that the definition of a discontinued operation would ever be met by a single non-current asset. Accordingly, a discontinued operation will also be a disposal group.

2.1.2 Classification as held for sale or as held for distribution to owners

IFRS 5 requires a non-current asset (or disposal group) to be classified as held for sale if its carrying amount will be recovered principally through a sale transaction rather than through continuing use. *[IFRS 5.6]*. For these purposes, sale transactions include exchanges of non-current assets for other non-current assets when the exchange has commercial substance in accordance with IAS 16 – *Property, Plant and Equipment* (discussed in Chapter 18 at 4.4). *[IFRS 5.10]*. For assets classified according to a liquidity presentation (see Chapter 3 at 3.1.1), non-current assets are taken to be assets that include amounts expected to be recovered more than twelve months after the reporting date. *[IFRS 5.2]*.

Determining whether (and when) an asset stops being recovered principally through use and becomes recoverable principally through sale is the critical distinction, and much of the standard is devoted to explaining how to make the determination.

For an asset (or disposal group) to be classified as held for sale:

(a) it must be available for immediate sale in its present condition, subject only to terms that are usual and customary for sales of such assets (or disposal groups);

(b) its sale must be highly probable; *[IFRS 5.7]* and

(c) it must genuinely be sold, not abandoned. *[IFRS 5.13]*.

These criteria are discussed further below. If an asset (or disposal group) has been classified as held for sale, but these criteria cease to be met, an entity should cease to classify the asset (or disposal group) as held for sale. *[IFRS 5.26]*. Changes in disposal plans are discussed at 2.2.5 below.

Slightly different criteria apply when an entity acquires a non-current asset (or disposal group) exclusively with a view to its subsequent disposal. In that case it should only classify the non-current asset (or disposal group) as held for sale at the acquisition date if:

- the 'one-year requirement' is met subject to its one exception (this is part of being 'highly probable', discussed at 2.1.2.B below); and

- it is highly probable that any other criteria in (a) and (b) above that are not met at that date will be met within a short period following the acquisition (usually within three months). *[IFRS 5.11]*.

The standard also makes it clear that the criteria in (a) and (b) above must be met at the reporting date for a non-current asset (or disposal group) to be classified as held for sale in those financial statements. However, if those criteria are met after the reporting date but before the authorisation of the financial statements for issue, the standard requires certain additional disclosures (discussed at 5 below). *[IFRS 5.12]*.

The classification, presentation and measurement requirements of IFRS 5 applicable to assets (or disposal groups) classified as held for sale also apply to those classified as held for distribution to owners acting in their capacity as owners. *[IFRS 5.5A]*. This applies when an entity is committed to distribute the asset (or disposal group) to its owners.

For this to be the case, the assets must be available for immediate distribution in their present condition and the distribution must be highly probable.

2.1.2.A Meaning of available for immediate sale

To qualify for classification as held for sale, a non-current asset (or disposal group) must be available for immediate sale in its present condition subject only to terms that are usual and customary for sales of such assets (or disposal groups). This is taken to mean that an entity currently has the intention and ability to transfer the asset (or disposal group) to a buyer in its present condition. The standard illustrates this concept with the following examples. *[IFRS 5.IG1-3]*.

Example 4.1: Meaning of 'available for immediate sale'

1 Disposal of a headquarters building

An entity is committed to a plan to sell its headquarters building and has initiated actions to locate a buyer.

(a) The entity intends to transfer the building to a buyer after it vacates the building. The time necessary to vacate the building is usual and customary for sales of such assets. The criterion of being available for immediate sale would therefore be met at the plan commitment date.

(b) The entity will continue to use the building until construction of a new headquarters building is completed. The entity does not intend to transfer the existing building to a buyer until after construction of the new building is completed (and it vacates the existing building). The delay in the timing of the transfer of the existing building imposed by the entity (seller) demonstrates that the building is not available for immediate sale. The criterion would not be met until construction of the new building is completed, even if a firm purchase commitment for the future transfer of the existing building is obtained earlier.

2 Sale of a manufacturing facility

An entity is committed to a plan to sell a manufacturing facility and has initiated actions to locate a buyer. At the plan commitment date, there is a backlog of uncompleted customer orders.

(a) The entity intends to sell the manufacturing facility with its operations. Any uncompleted customer orders at the sale date will be transferred to the buyer. The transfer of uncompleted customer orders at the sale date will not affect the timing of the transfer of the facility. The criterion of being available for immediate sale would therefore be met at the plan commitment date.

(b) The entity intends to sell the manufacturing facility, but without its operations. The entity does not intend to transfer the facility to a buyer until after it ceases all operations of the facility and eliminates the backlog of uncompleted customer orders. The delay in the timing of the transfer of the facility imposed by the entity (seller) demonstrates that the facility is not available for immediate sale. The criterion would not be met until the operations of the facility cease, even if a firm purchase commitment for the future transfer of the facility were obtained earlier.

3 Land and buildings acquired through foreclosure

An entity acquires through foreclosure a property comprising land and buildings that it intends to sell.

(a) The entity does not intend to transfer the property to a buyer until after it completes renovations to increase the property's sales value. The delay in the timing of the transfer of the property imposed by the entity (seller) demonstrates that the property is not available for immediate sale. The criterion of being available for immediate sale would therefore not be met until the renovations are completed.

(b) After the renovations are completed and the property is classified as held for sale but before a firm purchase commitment is obtained, the entity becomes aware of environmental damage requiring remediation. The entity still intends to sell the property. However, the entity does not have the ability to transfer the property to a buyer until after the remediation is completed. The delay in the timing of the transfer of the property imposed by others *before* a firm purchase commitment is obtained demonstrates that the property is not available for immediate sale (different requirements could apply if this happened after a firm commitment is obtained, as illustrated in scenario (b) of Example 4.2 below). The criterion that the asset be available for immediate sale would not continue to be met. The property would be reclassified as held and used in accordance with the requirements discussed at 2.2.5 below.

2.1.2.B   Meaning of highly probable

Many observers may consider the meaning of 'highly probable' to be reasonably self-evident, albeit highly judgemental. However, IFRS 5 provides extensive discussion of the topic. As a first step, the term is defined by the standard as meaning 'significantly more likely than probable'. This is supplemented by a second definition – probable is defined as 'more likely than not'. *[IFRS 5 Appendix A]*. Substituting the latter into the former leads to a definition of highly probable as meaning 'significantly more likely than more likely than not'.

The standard goes on to elaborate as follows:

For the sale to be highly probable:

- the appropriate level of management must be committed to a plan to sell the asset (or disposal group);
- an active programme to locate a buyer and complete the plan must have been initiated;
- the asset (or disposal group) must be actively marketed for sale at a price that is reasonable in relation to its current fair value;
- the sale should be expected to qualify for recognition as a completed sale within one year from the date of classification (although in certain circumstances this period may be extended as discussed below); and
- actions required to complete the plan should indicate that it is unlikely that significant changes to the plan will be made or that the plan will be withdrawn. *[IFRS 5.8]*.

As noted above, the classification, presentation and measurement requirements of IFRS 5 applicable to assets (or disposal groups) classified as held for sale also apply to those classified as held for distribution to owners acting in their capacity as owners (see 2.1.2 above). *[IFRS 5.5A]*.

For the distribution to be highly probable, actions to complete the distribution must have been initiated and should be expected to be completed within one year from the date of classification. Actions required to complete the distribution should indicate that it is unlikely that significant changes to the distribution will be made or that the distribution will not be completed. Whilst judgement will be needed in individual circumstances, relevant actions to consider could include: the steps taken by management to prepare for the distribution, board decisions illustrating the commitment to the planned distribution, and steps taken to organise the meeting of shareholders, if their approval is required. The probability of shareholders' approval, if this is required, should be considered as part of the assessment of whether the distribution is highly probable. *[IFRS 5.12A]*.

The basic rule above that for qualification as held for sale the sale should be expected to qualify for recognition as a completed sale within one year from the date of classification (the 'one year rule') is applied quite strictly by the standard. In particular, IFRS states that this 'criterion would not be met if:

(a) an entity that is a commercial leasing and finance company is holding for sale or lease equipment that has recently ceased to be leased and the ultimate form of a future transaction (sale or lease) has not yet been determined;

(b) an entity is committed to a plan to "sell" a property that is in use as part of a sale and leaseback transaction, but the sale does not qualify to be accounted for as a sale ...' in accordance with IFRS 16 – *Leases*. *[IFRS 5.IG4]*.

In (a), the entity does not yet know whether the asset will be sold at all and hence may not presume that it will be sold within a year.

In (b), whilst in legal form the asset has been sold it will not be recognised as sold in the financial statements. Sale and leaseback transactions are discussed in Chapter 23 at 8.

As indicated above, the standard contains an exception to the one year rule. It states that events or circumstances may extend the period to complete the sale beyond one year. Such an extension would not preclude an asset (or disposal group) from being classified as held for sale if the delay is caused by events or circumstances beyond the entity's control and there is sufficient evidence that the entity remains committed to its plan to sell the asset (or disposal group). This will be the case in the following situations: *[IFRS 5.9]*

(a) at the date an entity commits itself to a plan to sell a non-current asset (or disposal group) it reasonably expects that others (not a buyer) will impose conditions on the transfer of the asset (or disposal group) that will extend the period required to complete the sale, and:

　(i) actions necessary to respond to those conditions cannot be initiated until after a firm purchase commitment is obtained; and

　(ii) a firm purchase commitment is highly probable within one year;

(b) an entity obtains a firm purchase commitment and, as a result, a buyer or others unexpectedly impose conditions on the transfer of a non-current asset (or disposal group) previously classified as held for sale that will extend the period required to complete the sale, and

　(i) timely actions necessary to respond to the conditions have been taken; and

　(ii) a favourable resolution of the delaying factors is expected;

(c) during the initial one year period, circumstances arise that were previously considered unlikely and, as a result, a non-current asset (or disposal group) previously classified as held for sale is not sold by the end of that period, and

　(i) during the initial one year period the entity took action necessary to respond to the change in circumstances;

　(ii) the non-current asset (or disposal group) is being actively marketed at a price that is reasonable, given the change in circumstances; and

　(iii) the non-current asset (or disposal group) remains available for immediate sale and the sale is highly probable. *[IFRS 5 Appendix B]*.

Firm purchase commitment is a defined term in IFRS 5, meaning an agreement with an unrelated party, binding on both parties and usually legally enforceable, that:
- specifies all significant terms, including the price and timing of the transactions; and
- includes a disincentive for non-performance that is sufficiently large to make performance highly probable. *[IFRS 5 Appendix A]*.

The word 'binding' in this definition seems to envisage an agreement still being subject to contingencies. The standard provides an example where a 'firm purchase commitment' exists but is subject to regulatory approval (see scenario (a) in Example 4.2 below). In our view, to be 'binding' in this sense a contingent agreement should be only subject to contingencies outside the control of both parties.

The standard illustrates each of these exceptions to the one year rule with the following examples. *[IFRS 5.IG5-7]*.

Example 4.2: Exceptions to the 'one year rule'

Scenario illustrating (a) above

An entity in the power generating industry is committed to a plan to sell a disposal group that represents a significant portion of its regulated operations. The sale requires regulatory approval, which could extend the period required to complete the sale beyond one year. Actions necessary to obtain that approval cannot be initiated until after a buyer is known and a firm purchase commitment is obtained. However, a firm purchase commitment is highly probable within one year. In that situation, the conditions for an exception to the one year requirement would be met.

Scenario illustrating (b) above

An entity is committed to a plan to sell a manufacturing facility in its present condition and classifies the facility as held for sale at that date. After a firm purchase commitment is obtained, the buyer's inspection of the property identifies environmental damage not previously known to exist. The entity is required by the buyer to make good the damage, which will extend the period required to complete the sale beyond one year. However, the entity has initiated actions to make good the damage, and satisfactory rectification of the damage is highly probable. In that situation, the conditions for an exception to the one year requirement would be met.

Scenario illustrating (c) above

An entity is committed to a plan to sell a non-current asset and classifies the asset as held for sale at that date.

(a) During the initial one year period, the market conditions that existed at the date the asset was classified initially as held for sale deteriorate and, as a result, the asset is not sold by the end of that period. During that period, the entity actively solicited but did not receive any reasonable offers to purchase the asset and, in response, reduced the price. The asset continues to be actively marketed at a price that is reasonable given the change in market conditions, and the criteria regarding availability for immediate sale which is highly probable are therefore met. In that situation, the conditions for an exception to the one year requirement would be met. At the end of the initial one year period, the asset would continue to be classified as held for sale.

(b) During the following one year period, market conditions deteriorate further, and the asset is not sold by the end of that period. The entity believes that the market conditions will improve and has not further reduced the price of the asset. The asset continues to be held for sale, but at a price in excess of its current fair value. In that situation, the absence of a price reduction demonstrates that the asset is not available for immediate sale. In addition, to meet the condition that a sale be highly probable also requires an asset to be marketed at a price that is reasonable in relation to its current fair value. Therefore, the conditions for an exception to the one year requirement would not be met. The asset would be reclassified as held and used in accordance with the requirements discussed at 2.2.5 below.

2.1.2.C Abandonment

IFRS 5 stipulates that a non-current asset (or disposal group) that is to be abandoned should not be classified as held for sale. This includes non-current assets (or disposal groups) that are to be used to the end of their economic life and non-current assets (or disposal groups) that are to be closed rather than sold. The standard explains that this is because its carrying amount will be recovered principally through continuing use. *[IFRS 5.13]*.

If the disposal group to be abandoned meets the criteria for being a discontinued operation the standard requires it to be treated as such in the period in which the abandonment occurs. *[IFRS 5.13]*. This is discussed at 3.1 below. However, a non-current asset that has been temporarily taken out of use should not be accounted for as if it had been abandoned. *[IFRS 5.14]*. An example given by the standard is of a manufacturing plant that ceases to be used because demand for its product has declined but which is maintained in workable condition and is expected to be brought back into use if demand picks up. The plant is not regarded as abandoned. *[IFRS 5.IG8]*. However, in these circumstances an impairment loss may need to be recognised in accordance with IAS 36 (discussed in Chapter 20).

2.1.3 Partial disposals of operations

2.1.3.A Loss of control of a subsidiary

The standard provides that when an entity is committed to a sale plan involving loss of control of a subsidiary it should classify all the assets and liabilities of that subsidiary as held for sale when the relevant criteria are met (see 2.1 above). This is regardless of whether it will retain a non-controlling interest in the former subsidiary after the sale, such as for instance an interest in an associate or a joint venture. *[IFRS 5.8A]*.

If the retained interest represents a joint operation, it could be argued that, since the entity retains a direct interest in the underlying assets and obligations for the liabilities after the disposal, the transaction is in substance a sale of parts of the underlying assets and liabilities. On that basis, only the disposed of parts of the assets and liabilities would be classified as held for sale. The counter argument is that the requirement in IFRS 5 does not scope out situations in which the retained interest represents a joint operation. Furthermore, the loss of control of a subsidiary is a significant economic event in that it changes the relationship between the entity and the investee fundamentally, and therefore it would be appropriate to classify all assets and liabilities of the subsidiary as held for sale. Some further argue that classification as held for sale will depend on whether the operation of the joint operation represents a business. If it does, it could be argued that the principles of IFRS 3 – *Business Combinations* – should be applied, which demonstrates that effectively all assets and liabilities of the subsidiary are being disposed of. On that analysis, classification of all assets and liabilities of the subsidiary as held for sale is appropriate. However, as the standard is not explicit, judgement will be required.

If the subsidiary in question meets the definition of a discontinued operation, the standard's presentation and disclosure requirements for discontinued operations apply (see 3.2 below). *[IFRS 5.36A]*.

IFRS 5 does not explicitly extend these requirements to loss of control of a subsidiary in other ways. Given the alignment of the rules on sales with distributions to owners, it seems clear that partial distributions triggering loss of control would result in held for distribution classification.

However, control may be lost in other ways. Examples would include a subsidiary issuing shares to third parties, or control established by contract coming to an end.

The Basis for Conclusions on the standard sheds some light on the views of the Board. In particular, the following:

'At the date control is lost, all the subsidiary's assets and liabilities are derecognised and any investment retained in the former subsidiary is recognised. Loss of control is a significant economic event that changes the nature of an investment. The parent-subsidiary relationship ceases to exist and an investor-investee relationship begins that differs significantly from the former parent-subsidiary relationship. Therefore, the new investor-investee relationship is recognised and measured initially at the date when control is lost.

'The Board concluded that, under the sale plan described above, the controlling interest in the subsidiary is, in substance, exchanged for a non-controlling interest. Therefore, in the Board's view, being committed to a plan involving loss of control of a subsidiary should trigger classification as held for sale.' *[IFRS 5.BC24B-24C]*.

This, and the fact that the standard applies to assets held for distribution to owners, may suggest that the explicit rules for partial *sales* of assets resulting in loss of control should also apply to loss of control from other causes. However, the standard is not explicit, and the IFRIC concluded in January 2016[1] that it could not resolve the issue, and decided it should be considered for a broad-scope project on IFRS 5 (future developments of IFRS 5 are discussed at 6 below). In the meantime, judgement will be required.

2.1.3.B   Partial disposal of an associate or joint venture

In accordance with IAS 28 – *Investments in Associates and Joint Ventures*, IFRS 5 will apply to an investment, or a portion of an investment, in an associate or a joint venture that meets the criteria to be classified as held for sale (see 2.1.2 above and also Chapter 11 at 6). Any retained portion of such an investment that has not been so classified should be accounted for using the equity method until disposal of the portion that is classified as held for sale takes place. After the disposal takes place, any retained interest should be accounted for in accordance with IFRS 9 – *Financial Instruments* – unless the retained interest continues to be an associate or a joint venture, in which case the equity method should be used.

If such an investment ceases to be classified as held for sale, it should be accounted for using the equity method retrospectively from the date of its original classification as held for sale. Financial statements for the periods since classification as held for sale should be amended accordingly. *[IAS 28.20, 21]*.

2.2 Measurement of non-current assets (and disposal groups) held for sale

2.2.1 Scope of the measurement requirements

IFRS 5's classification and presentation requirements apply to all recognised non-current assets (which is defined in the same way as in IAS 1, discussed at 2.1 above) and disposal groups. However, the measurement provisions of the standard do not apply to the following assets (which remain covered by the standards listed) either as individual assets or as part of a disposal group: [IFRS 5.2, 5]

(a) deferred tax assets (dealt with in IAS 12 – *Income Taxes*);
(b) assets arising from employee benefits (dealt with in IAS 19 – *Employee Benefits*);
(c) financial assets within the scope of IFRS 9;
(d) non-current assets that are accounted for in accordance with the fair value model in IAS 40 – *Investment Property;*
(e) non-current assets that are measured at fair value less costs to sell in accordance with IAS 41 – *Agriculture;* and
(f) contractual rights under insurance contracts as defined in IFRS 4 – *Insurance Contracts.* For periods beginning on or after 1 January 2021 this becomes 'groups of contracts within the scope of IFRS 17 – *Insurance Contracts*'.

2.2.2 Measurement of non-current assets and disposal groups held for sale

2.2.2.A Measurement on initial classification as held for sale

IFRS 5 requires that immediately before the initial classification of an asset (or disposal group) as held for sale, the carrying amount of the asset (or all the assets and liabilities in the group) should be measured in accordance with applicable IFRSs. [IFRS 5.18]. In other words, an entity should apply its usual accounting policies up until the criteria for classification as held for sale are met.

Thereafter a non-current asset (or disposal group) classified as held for sale should be measured at the lower of its carrying amount and fair value less costs to sell. [IFRS 5.15]. IFRS 13 – *Fair Value Measurement* – defines fair value as 'the price that would be received to sell an asset or paid to transfer a liability in an orderly transaction between market participants at the measurement date' (see Chapter 14). [IFRS 13.9]. Costs to sell are defined as 'the incremental costs directly attributable to the disposal of an asset (or disposal group), excluding finance costs and income tax expense.' [IFRS 5 Appendix A]. When the sale is expected to occur beyond one year, the costs to sell should be measured at their present value. Any increase in the present value of the costs to sell that arises from the passage of time should be presented in profit or loss as a financing cost. [IFRS 5.17]. For disposal groups, the standard adopts a portfolio approach. It requires that if a non-current asset within the scope of its measurement requirements is part of a disposal group, the measurement requirements should apply to the group as a whole, so that the group is measured at the lower of its carrying amount and fair value less costs to sell. [IFRS 5.4]. It will still be necessary to apportion any write down to the underlying assets of the disposal group, but no element is apportioned to items outside the scope of the standard's measurement provisions. This is discussed further at 2.2.3 below.

Items held for distribution to owners should be measured at the lower of carrying amount and fair value less costs to distribute. Costs to distribute are incremental costs directly attributable to the distribution, excluding finance costs and income tax expense. *[IFRS 5.15A]*.

If a newly acquired asset (or disposal group) meets the criteria to be classified as held for sale (which, as discussed at 2.1.2 above, are subtly different for assets acquired exclusively with a view to subsequent disposal), applying the above requirements will result in the asset (or disposal group) being measured on initial recognition at the lower of its carrying amount had it not been so classified (for example, cost) and fair value less costs to sell. This means that if the asset (or disposal group) is acquired as part of a business combination, it will be measured at fair value less costs to sell. *[IFRS 5.16]*.

The implementation guidance accompanying the standard provides the following illustration of a subsidiary acquired with a view to sale. *[IFRS 5.IG13]*.

Example 4.3: Measuring and presenting subsidiaries acquired with a view to sale and classified as held for sale

Entity A acquires an entity H, which is a holding company with two subsidiaries, S1 and S2. S2 is acquired exclusively with a view to sale and meets the criteria to be classified as held for sale. Accordingly, S2 is also a discontinued operation (see 3.1 below).

The fair value less costs to sell of S2 is £135. A accounts for S2 as follows:

- initially, A measures the identifiable liabilities of S2 at fair value, say at £40;
- initially, A measures the acquired assets as the fair value less costs to sell of S2 (£135) plus the fair value of the identifiable liabilities (£40), i.e. at £175;
- at the reporting date, A remeasures the disposal group at the lower of its cost and fair value less costs to sell, say at £130. The liabilities are remeasured in accordance with applicable IFRSs, say at £35. The total assets are measured at £130 + £35, i.e. at £165;
- at the reporting date, A presents the assets and liabilities separately from other assets and liabilities in its consolidated financial statements as illustrated in Example 4.5 at 2.2.4 below; and
- in the statement of comprehensive income, A presents the total of the post-tax profit or loss of S2 and the post-tax gain or loss recognised on the subsequent remeasurement of S2, which equals the remeasurement of the disposal group from £135 to £130.

Further analysis of the assets and liabilities or of the change in value of the disposal group is not required.

The final sentence in the above example says no further analysis of the assets and liabilities is required. This must refer to there being no such disclosure requirement for financial statements. A detailed purchase price analysis and tracking of the acquired entity may still be needed, notwithstanding a partial relaxation of what is required to be disclosed by IFRS 5. This may be needed to be able to determine the split between gross assets and liabilities and how movements in the carrying amounts are reflected in profit or loss, or other comprehensive income.

2.2.2.B   Subsequent remeasurement

While a non-current asset is classified as held for sale or while it is part of a disposal group classified as held for sale it should not be depreciated or amortised. Interest and other expenses attributable to the liabilities of a disposal group classified as held for sale should continue to be recognised. *[IFRS 5.25]*.

On subsequent remeasurement of a disposal group, the standard requires that the carrying amounts of any assets and liabilities that are not within the scope of its measurement requirements, be remeasured in accordance with applicable IFRSs before the fair value less costs to sell of the disposal group is remeasured. *[IFRS 5.19]*.

2.2.3 Impairments and reversals of impairment

The requirement to measure a non-current asset or disposal group held for sale at the lower of carrying amount and fair value less costs to sell may give rise to a write down in value (impairment loss) and possibly its subsequent reversal. As noted above, the first step is to account for any items outside the scope of the standard's measurement rules in the normal way. After that, any excess of carrying value over fair value less costs to sell should be recognised as an impairment. *[IFRS 5.20]*.

Any subsequent increase in fair value less costs to sell of an asset up to the cumulative impairment loss previously recognised either in accordance with IFRS 5 or in accordance with IAS 36 should be recognised as a gain. *[IFRS 5.21]*. In the case of a disposal group, any subsequent increase in fair value less costs to sell should be recognised:

(a) to the extent that it has not been recognised under another standard in relation to those assets outside the scope of IFRS 5's measurement requirements; but

(b) not in excess of the cumulative amount of losses previously recognised under IFRS 5 or before that under IAS 36 in respect of the non-current assets in the group which are within the scope of the measurement rules of IFRS 5. *[IFRS 5.22]*.

Any impairment loss (or any subsequent gain) recognised for a disposal group should be allocated to the non-current assets in the group that are within the scope of the measurement requirements of IFRS 5. The order of allocation should be:

- first, to reduce the carrying amount of any goodwill in the group; and
- then, to the other non-current assets of the group *pro rata* on the basis of the carrying amount of each asset in the group. *[IFRS 5.23]*.

This is illustrated by the standard with the following example: *[IFRS 5.IG10]*

Example 4.4: Allocation of impairment loss to the components of a disposal group

An entity plans to dispose of a group of its assets (as an asset sale). The assets form a disposal group, and are measured as follows:

	Carrying amount at the reporting date before classification as held for sale ₹	Carrying amount as remeasured immediately before classification as held for sale ₹
Goodwill	1,500	1,500
Property, plant and equipment (carried at revalued amounts)	4,600	4,000
Property, plant and equipment (carried at cost)	5,700	5,700
Inventory	2,400	2,200
Investments in equity instruments	1,800	1,500
Total	16,000	14,900

The entity recognises the loss of ₹1,100 (₹16,000 – ₹14,900) immediately before classifying the disposal group as held for sale. The entity measures the fair value less costs to sell of the disposal group as ₹13,000. Because an entity measures a disposal group classified as held for sale at the lower of its carrying amount and fair value less costs to sell, the entity recognises an impairment loss of ₹1,900 (₹14,900 – ₹13,000) when the group is initially classified as held for sale. The impairment loss is allocated to non-current assets to which the measurement requirements of the IFRS are applicable. Therefore, no impairment loss is allocated to inventory and investments in equity instruments. The loss is allocated to the other assets in the order of allocation described above.

The allocation can be illustrated as follows:

First, the impairment loss reduces any amount of goodwill. Then, the residual loss is allocated to other assets *pro rata* based on the carrying amounts of those assets.

	Carrying amount as remeasured immediately before classification as held for sale ₹	Allocated impairment loss ₹	Carrying amount after allocation of impairment loss ₹
Goodwill	1,500	(1,500)	–
Property, plant and equipment (carried at revalued amounts)	4,000	(165)	3,835
Property, plant and equipment (carried at cost)	5,700	(235)	5,465
Inventory	2,200	–	2,200
Investments in equity instruments	1,500	–	1,500
Total	14,900	(1,900)	13,000

In the first table of this example, it is not particularly clear what the meaning and purpose of the left-hand column is. The fact that some of the figures are different in each column, seems to indicate that the column header 'Carrying amount at the reporting date before classification as held for sale' is referring to the opening statement of financial position at the beginning of the period in which the classification is made. As noted at 2.2.2.A above, an entity is required to remeasure the assets as normal under the relevant standards immediately before classifying them as held for sale. This would mean the difference of ₹1,100 reflects routine accounting entries (such as depreciation and revaluation) from the start of the period to the date of classification as held to sale. Also worthy of note is that the example does not say where the entity recognises the loss of ₹1,100. Given that the disposal group contains investments in equity instruments, some of this amount might be recorded in other comprehensive income rather than in profit or loss. Similarly, movements in property plant and equipment held at revalued amounts may be recorded directly in other comprehensive income.

One thing which the example above fails to illustrate is that the measurement requirements of the standard are incomplete. It is quite possible that the required impairment exceeds the carrying value of the non-current assets within the scope of the standard's measurement rules. IFRS 5 is silent on what to do in such circumstances. Possible approaches would be:

(a) to apply the impairment to current assets;
(b) to apply the impairment to non-current assets outside the scope of the standard's measurement rules;
(c) to recognise a separate provision; or
(d) restrict the impairment to the carrying value of the non-current assets within the scope of the standard's measurement requirements.

For the present, entities will need to apply judgement based on individual circumstances. This issue was brought to the attention of the Interpretations Committee which referred it to the IASB. The IASB intended to address the issue through a future amendment to IFRS 5. The Board decided tentatively to consider amending IFRS 5 as a matter of priority and to work with the FASB to ensure IFRS 5 remains aligned with US GAAP.[2] However, at its December 2009 meeting, the IASB 'decided not to add a project to its agenda to address the impairment measurement and reversal issues at this time.'[3] Possible future developments are discussed at 6 below.

The standard contains a reminder that requirements relating to derecognition are set out in IAS 16 for property, plant and equipment (discussed in Chapter 18 at 7), and IAS 38 – *Intangible Assets* – for intangible assets (discussed in Chapter 17 at 9.5) and notes that a gain or loss not previously recognised by the date of the sale of a non-current asset (or disposal group) should be recognised at the date of derecognition. *[IFRS 5.24]*. This may happen, for example, if the fair value less costs to sell of an asset classified as held for sale at the end of the previous period falls during the current period.

2.2.4 Presentation in the statement of financial position of non-current assets and disposal groups held for sale

The general requirement, discussed in Chapter 3 at 3.1.1, to classify items in the statement of financial position as current or non-current (or present them broadly in order of liquidity) is overlaid with further requirements by IFRS 5 regarding non-current assets held for sale and disposal groups. IFRS 5's aim is that entities should present and disclose information that enables users of the financial statements to evaluate the financial effects of disposals of non-current assets (or disposal groups). *[IFRS 5.30]*. In pursuit of this aim, IFRS 5 requires:

- non-current assets classified as held for sale and the assets of a disposal group classified as held for sale to be presented separately from other assets in the statement of financial position; and
- the liabilities of a disposal group classified as held for sale to be presented separately from other liabilities in the statement of financial position.

These assets and liabilities should not be offset and presented as a single amount. In addition:

(a) major classes of assets and liabilities classified as held for sale should generally be separately disclosed either on the face of the statement of financial position or in the notes. However, this is not necessary for a disposal group if it is a subsidiary that met the criteria to be classified as held for sale on acquisition; and

(b) any cumulative income or expense recognised directly in other comprehensive income relating to a non-current asset (or disposal group) classified as held for sale should be presented separately. *[IFRS 5.38, 39].*

The requirement in (b) was included in response to comments made to the IASB during the development of the standard. The Board describes the development as follows: 'Respondents to ED 4 noted that the separate presentation within equity of amounts relating to assets and disposal groups classified as held for sale (such as, for example, unrealised gains and losses on available-for-sale assets and foreign currency translation adjustments) would also provide useful information. The Board agreed and has added such a requirement to the IFRS.' *[IFRS 5.BC58].* On that basis, it might be considered that any non-controlling interest within equity relating to non-current assets (or disposal groups) held for sale should also be presented separately as it would seem to represent equally useful information about amounts within equity. However, such disclosure of non-controlling interests is not specifically required by the standard so would remain a matter of judgement. As noted at 3.2 below, the standard requires an analysis of the income for the period attributable to owners between continuing and discontinued operations.

IFRS 5 is silent as to whether the information specified in (b) above should be on the face of the statement of financial position or in a note. However, the implementation guidance to IFRS 5 shows a caption called 'Amounts recognised in other comprehensive income and accumulated in equity in relation to non-current assets held for sale' and illustrates the requirements as follows: *[IFRS 5.IG12]*

Example 4.5: *Presenting non-current assets or disposal groups classified as held for sale*

At the end of 2021, an entity decides to dispose of part of its assets (and directly associated liabilities). The disposal, which meets the criteria to be classified as held for sale, takes the form of two disposal groups, as follows:

	Carrying amount after classification as held for sale	
	Disposal group I €	Disposal group II €
Property, plant and equipment	4,900	1,700
Investments in equity instruments	*1,400	–
Liabilities	(2,400)	(900)
Net carrying amount of disposal group	3,900	800

* An amount of €400 relating to these assets has been recognised in other comprehensive income and accumulated in equity.

The presentation in the entity's statement of financial position of the disposal groups classified as held for sale can be shown as follows:

	2021 €	2020 €
ASSETS		
Non-current assets		
AAA	x	x
BBB	x	x
CCC	x	x
	x	x
Current assets		
DDD	x	x
EEE	x	x
	x	x
Non-current assets classified as held for sale	8,000	–
Total assets	x	x

	2021 €	2020 €
EQUITY AND LIABILITIES		
Equity attributable to equity holders of the parent		
FFF	x	x
GGG	x	x
Amounts recognised in other comprehensive income and accumulated in equity relating to non-current assets held for sale	400	–
	x	x
Non-controlling (or minority) interests	x	x
Total equity	x	x
Non-current liabilities		
HHH	x	x
III	x	x
JJJ	x	x
	x	x
Current liabilities		
KKK	x	x
LLL	x	x
MMM	x	x
	x	x
Liabilities directly associated with non-current assets classified as held for sale	3,300	–
	x	x
Total liabilities	x	x
Total equity and liabilities	x	x

The presentation requirements for assets (or disposal groups) classified as held for sale at the end of the reporting period do not apply retrospectively. The comparative statements of financial position for any previous periods are therefore not re-presented.

Non-current assets held for sale and discontinued operations

The implementation guidance accompanying IFRS 5 provides the following illustration of the presentation of discontinued operations. *[IFRS 5.IG11]*. (Note that the illustrative example assumes that the entity did not recognise any components of other comprehensive income in the periods presented.)

Example 4.7: Presenting discontinued operations

XYZ GROUP – STATEMENT OF COMPREHENSIVE INCOME FOR THE YEAR ENDED 31 DECEMBER 2021 (illustrating the classification of expenses by function)

(in thousands of Euros)

	2021	2020
Continuing operations		
Revenue	X	X
Cost of sales	(X)	(X)
Gross profit	X	X
Other income	X	X
Distribution costs	(X)	(X)
Administrative expenses	(X)	(X)
Other expenses	(X)	(X)
Finance costs	(X)	(X)
Share of profit of associates	X	X
Profit before tax	X	X
Income tax expense	(X)	(X)
Profit for the period from continuing operations	X	X
Discontinued operations		
Profit for the period from discontinued operations*	X	X
Profit for the period	X	X
Attributable to:		
Owners of the parent		
Profit for the period from continuing operations	X	X
Profit for the period from discontinued operations	X	X
Profit for the period attributable to owners of the parent	X	X
Non-controlling interest		
Profit for the period from continuing operation	X	X
Profit for the period from discontinued operations	X	X
Profit for the period attributable to non-controlling interests	X	X
	X	X

* The required analysis would be given in the notes.

The above reflects the requirement to disclose the amount of income from continuing operations and discontinued operations attributable to owners of the parent. It is noteworthy that the standard's illustrative example goes beyond what is strictly required by also giving an equivalent analysis for income attributable to non-controlling interests.

Adjustments in the current period to amounts previously presented in discontinued operations that are directly related to the disposal of a discontinued operation in a prior period should be classified separately in discontinued operations. The nature and amount of the adjustments should be disclosed. Examples given by the standard of circumstances in which these adjustments may arise include the following:

(a) the resolution of uncertainties that arise from the terms of the disposal transaction, such as the resolution of purchase price adjustments and indemnification issues with the purchaser;

(b) the resolution of uncertainties that arise from and are directly related to the operations of the component before its disposal, such as environmental and product warranty obligations retained by the seller; and

(c) the settlement of employee benefit plan obligations, provided that the settlement is directly related to the disposal transaction. *[IFRS 5.35]*.

In addition, IFRS 5 requires disclosure of the net cash flows attributable to the operating, investing and financing activities of discontinued operations. The standard allows that these disclosures may be presented either in the notes or on the face of the financial statements. These disclosures are not required for disposal groups that are newly acquired subsidiaries that meet the criteria to be classified as held for sale on acquisition (see 2.2.2 above). *[IFRS 5.33(c)]*.

As a discontinued operation will also be a disposal group, the requirements regarding presentation of disposal groups in the statement of financial position (discussed at 2.2.4 above) also apply to discontinued operations.

3.3 Trading between continuing and discontinued operations

Notwithstanding the one-line presentation discussed above, discontinued operations remain consolidated in group financial statements. That means any transactions between discontinued and continuing operations are eliminated as usual in the consolidation. As a consequence, the amounts ascribed to the continuing and discontinued operations will be income and expense only from transactions with counterparties external to the group. Importantly, this means that (unless additional disclosure is presented) the results presented on the face of the statement of comprehensive income will not necessarily represent the activities of the operations as individual entities, particularly when there has been significant trading between the continuing and discontinued operations. Some might consider the results for the continuing and discontinued operations on this basis to be of little use to readers of accounts. An argument could be made that allocating external transactions to or from the discontinued operation would yield more meaningful information.

The Interpretation Committee discussed this matter and published its agenda decision in January 2016.[5] In that decision the committee includes the following: 'The Interpretations Committee noted that neither IFRS 5 nor IAS 1 includes requirements regarding the presentation of discontinued operations that override the consolidation requirements in IFRS 10 – *Consolidated Financial Statements*. The Interpretations Committee also noted that paragraph B86(c) of IFRS 10 requires elimination of, among other things, income and expenses relating to intragroup transactions, and not merely intragroup profit. Consequently, the Interpretations Committee observed that not eliminating intragroup transactions would be inconsistent with the elimination requirements of IFRS 10.'

The Committee went on to observe: 'The Interpretations Committee also noted that paragraph 30 of IFRS 5 requires an entity to present and disclose information that enables users of the financial statements to evaluate the financial effects of discontinued operations and disposal activity. In the light of this objective, the Interpretations Committee observed that, depending on the particular facts and circumstances, an entity may have to provide additional disclosures in order to enable users to evaluate the financial effects of discontinued operations.'

4 COMPARATIVE INFORMATION

As discussed in Chapter 3 at 2.4, IAS 1 requires the presentation of comparative information. IFRS 5 deals with the particular requirements for non-current assets held for sale (and disposal groups) and discontinued operations.

Entities will need to consider whether any (and, if so, what) changes are necessary to comparative information as previously reported whenever:

- non-current assets or disposal groups first become classified as such; and
- that classification ceases.

4.1 Treatment of comparative information on initial classification as held for sale

4.1.1 The statement of comprehensive income

For non-current assets and disposal groups not qualifying as discontinued operations there are no special requirements relating to presentation in the statement of comprehensive income, accordingly no restatement of comparative amounts would be relevant.

When a component of an entity becomes classified as a discontinued operation, separate presentation of the total of its results for the period and any gain or loss on remeasurement is required on the face of the statement (see 3.2 above). IFRS 5 requires that these disclosures be re-presented for prior periods presented in the financial statements so that the disclosures relate to all operations that have been discontinued by the reporting date for the latest period presented. *[IFRS 5.34]*. Accordingly, adjustments to the comparative information as originally reported will be necessary for those disposal groups categorised as discontinued operations.

4.1.2 The statement of financial position

IFRS 5 states that an entity shall not reclassify or re-present amounts presented for non-current assets or for the assets and liabilities of disposal groups classified as held for sale in the statements of financial position for prior periods to reflect the classification in the statement of financial position for the latest period presented. *[IFRS 5.40]*. The standard has no separate requirements relating to the statement of financial position for a disposal group also qualifying as a discontinued operation and accordingly comparatives are not adjusted.

4.2 Treatment of comparative information on the cessation of classification as held for sale

As discussed at 2.2.5 above, when a non-current asset ceases to be classified as held for sale the measurement basis for it reverts to what it would have been if it had not been so classified at all (or recoverable amount if lower). Typically this would require a 'catch-up' depreciation charge as depreciation would not have been accounted for while it was held for sale. The standard explicitly requires this to be a current year charge. *[IFRS 5.28].* This seems to indicate that for non-current assets and disposal groups ceasing to be so classified the measurement of items in comparative information (statement of comprehensive income and statement of financial position) should not be revisited. This requirement applies equally to discontinued operations.

The above is supplemented with the following. 'Financial statements for the periods since classification as held for sale shall be amended accordingly if the disposal group or non-current asset that ceases to be classified as held for sale is a subsidiary, joint operation, joint venture, associate, or a portion of an interest in a joint venture or an associate. The entity shall present that adjustment in the same caption in the statement of comprehensive income' within continuing operations used to record any gains and losses on non-current assets (or disposal groups) held for sale. *[IFRS 5.28, 37].*

IAS 28 clarifies that, as regards associates and joint ventures, the amendment of financial statements 'for the periods since classification as held for sale' means retrospectively from the date of its original classification as held for sale. *[IAS 28.21].* This clarification is not repeated in IFRS 10 or IFRS 11 – *Joint Arrangements*. However, we believe the clarification should apply to assets or disposal groups within the scope of those standards. As a result, when a disposal group or non-current asset that was classified as held for sale represented an entire subsidiary, joint operation, joint venture or associate or was a portion of an interest in a joint venture or associate, and subsequently no longer qualifies as held for sale, financial statements must be amended retrospectively as though the disposal group or non-current asset never qualified as held for sale.

This area has been considered by the Interpretations Committee. The committee decided not to add it to its agenda, noting that IFRS 5 is a possible subject for a research project by the IASB which would examine a number of areas (possible future developments of IFRS 5 are discussed at 6 below). In its agenda decision the Committee observed the following: 'paragraph 28 requires the effects of a remeasurement (upon ceasing to be classified as held for sale) of a non-current asset to be recognised in profit or loss in the current period. Paragraph 28 also requires financial statements for the periods since classification as held for sale or as held for distribution to owners to be "amended accordingly" if the disposal group or non-current asset that ceases to be classified as held for sale or as held for distribution to owners is a subsidiary, joint operation, joint venture, associate, or a portion of an interest in a joint venture or an associate. The issue relates to a situation in which a disposal group that consists of both a subsidiary and other non-current assets ceases to be classified as held for sale. In such a situation, should an entity recognise the remeasurement adjustments relating to the subsidiary and the other non-current assets in different accounting periods, and should any amendment apply to presentation as well as to measurement?'[6] This articulation of the question by the Committee suggests that, until any amendment to the standard is made, judgement may be required.

Regarding the treatment of discontinued operations in the statement of comprehensive income, the standard states that if an entity ceases to classify a component as held for sale, the results of operations of the component previously presented in discontinued operations should be reclassified and included in income from continuing operations for all periods presented. The amounts for prior periods should be described as having been re-presented. *[IFRS 5.36]*.

As discussed at 4.1.2 above, the amounts presented for non-current assets or for the assets and liabilities of disposal groups classified as held for sale in the comparative statement of financial position should not be reclassified or re-presented.

5 DISCLOSURE REQUIREMENTS

5.1 Requirements of IFRS 5

As discussed at 2.2.4 and 3.2 above, IFRS 5 sets out detailed requirements for the prominent presentation of amounts relating to non-current assets held for sale, disposal groups and discontinued operations. In particular, and as discussed at 3.2 above, the single amount reflecting the income from discontinued operations must be analysed into its components, either on the face of the statement of comprehensive income or in the notes. In addition, disclosure is required in the notes in the period in which a non-current asset (or disposal group) has been either classified as held for sale or sold:

(a) a description of the non-current asset (or disposal group);

(b) a description of the facts and circumstances of the sale, or leading to the expected disposal, and the expected manner and timing of that disposal;

(c) the gain or loss recognised as a result of measuring the non-current asset (or disposal group) at fair value less costs to sell (discussed at 2.2 above) and, if not separately presented on the face of the statement of comprehensive income, the caption in the statement that includes that gain or loss; and

(d) if applicable, the segment in which the non-current asset (or disposal group) is presented in accordance with IFRS 8 – *Operating Segments* (discussed in Chapter 36 at 3.1). *[IFRS 5.41]*.

If a non-current asset (or disposal group) meets the criteria to be classified as held for sale after the reporting date but before the financial statements are authorised for issue, the information specified in (a), (b) and (d) above should also be disclosed in the notes. *[IFRS 5.12]*.

Further, should:

- a non-current asset (or disposal group) cease to be classified as held for sale; or
- an individual asset or liability be removed from a disposal group,

then IFRS 5 requires disclosure of, in the period of the decision to change the plan to sell the non-current asset (or disposal group), a description of the facts and circumstances leading to the decision and the effect of the decision on the results of operations for the period and any prior periods presented. *[IFRS 5.42]*.

5.2 Disclosures required by standards other than IFRS 5

IFRS 5 explains that disclosures in other IFRSs do not apply to non-current assets (or disposal groups) classified as held for sale or discontinued operations unless those IFRSs require:

- specific disclosures in respect of non-current assets (or disposal groups) classified as held for sale or discontinued operations; or
- disclosures about the measurement of assets and liabilities within a disposal group that are not within the scope of the measurement requirement of IFRS 5 and such disclosures are not already provided in the other notes to the financial statements.

The requirement in the second bullet above reflects the fact that such assets continue to be measured in accordance with the specific IFRS dealing with them. In practice, much of the requirement will be satisfied by the disclosure of accounting policies. The requirement for other disclosures will depend on the standard concerned. An example would be actuarial assumptions used to measure a pension plan as the surplus or deficit is not within the measurement scope of IFRS 5.

IFRS 12 – *Disclosure of Interests in Other Entities* – clarifies that all the disclosures of that standard apply to interests that are classified as held-for-sale, with the exception only of those disclosures (summarised financial information) identified by IFRS 12 as not being required. *[IFRS 12.5A, B17]*.

The standard goes on to say that additional disclosures about non-current assets (or disposal groups) classified as held for sale or discontinued operations may be necessary to comply with the general requirements of IAS 1, in particular paragraphs 15 and 125 of that Standard. *[IFRS 5.5B]*. Those provisions deal with fair presentation and estimation uncertainty and are discussed in Chapter 3 at 4.1.1 and at 5.2.1.

6 POSSIBLE FUTURE DEVELOPMENTS

The IASB has, over recent years, discussed a number of issues related to IFRS 5, as set out below.[7]

(a) The scope of held-for-sale classification;
(b) Accounting for disposal groups consisting mainly of financial instruments;
(c) The 'excess impairment' issue discussed at 2.2.3 above;
(d) The reversal of goodwill impairments in a disposal group;
(e) The allocation of impairments within a disposal group;
(f) The definition of discontinued operation and disclosures;
(g) The presentation of other comprehensive income of disposal groups;
(h) The application of the term 'major line of business';
(i) The treatment of intragroup transactions between continuing and discontinued operations;

(j)   The application of the presentation requirements in the standard to a disposal group consisting of a subsidiary and other non-current assets in the case of a change to a plan of sale; and

(k)   The applicability of the disclosure requirements in IFRS 12 to a subsidiary classified as held-for-sale.

Item (i) above was referred to the Interpretations Committee for consideration. It published an agenda decision in January 2016, which is discussed at 3.3 above. As regards item (k) above, the Board has amended IFRS 12 (see 5.2 above).

With regard to the rest of the items, the IASB included a reference to them in its request for views in its 2015 Agenda Consultation. In November 2016, the Board published *IASB Work Plan 2017-2021: Feedback Statement on the 2015 Agenda Consultation.* This document notes: 'The Board agreed that the best way to start a review of these issues would be through a post-implementation review of IFRS 5. The Board intends to carry out that review after the forthcoming post-implementation reviews of IFRS 13 and of IFRS Standards 10–12.'

The Board completed its post-implementation review of IFRS 13 in December 2018.[8] At the time of writing, the Board's post-implementation review of IFRS 10, IFRS 11 and IFRS 12 is in the first phase (of two), which involves an initial identification and assessment of the matters to be examined. The Board expects to publish a request for information for the post-implementation review in the fourth quarter of 2020.[9]

The IASB's 2020 Agenda Consultation was initiated in September 2019 when the approach to the consultation was discussed by the Board and the IFRS Advisory Council. That approach was refined in Q4 2019 and will continue to be further refined in 2020 with a view to publishing a Request for Information in H1 2021.

Time will tell whether the Board will conduct a review of IFRS 5 and, if it does, which, if any, of the matters discussed above will be addressed.

References

1   *IASB Update*, January 2016.
2   *IASB Update*, July 2009.
3   *IASB Update*, December 2009.
4   *IFRIC Update*, January 2016.
5   *IFRIC Update*, January 2016.
6   *IFRIC Update*, January 2016.
7   IASB meeting July 2015, Agenda Paper 12C.
8   *Project Report and Feedback Statement, Post-implementation Review of IFRS 13 Fair Value Measurement*, IASB, December 2018.
9   IASB website, *IASB work-plan*, https://www.ifrs.org/projects/work-plan/ (accessed 7 September 2020).

Chapter 5 — First-time adoption

1 INTRODUCTION 227
   1.1   Objectives of first-time adoption 227
   1.2   Authoritative literature 228
   1.3   Defined terms 228
   1.4   Future developments 229

2 WHO IS A FIRST-TIME ADOPTER? 229
   2.1   The first IFRS financial statements in scope of IFRS 1 229
   2.2   When should IFRS 1 be applied? 232
         2.2.1   Repeat application of IFRS 1 233
   2.3   Determining the previous GAAP 234
         2.3.1   Transition to IFRSs from a similar GAAP 235

3 OPENING IFRS STATEMENT OF FINANCIAL POSITION 236
   3.1   First-time adoption timeline 237
   3.2   Opening IFRS statement of financial position and accounting policies 238
   3.3   Fair value and deemed cost 240
   3.4   Transitional provisions in other standards 240
   3.5   Departures from full retrospective application 241

4 EXCEPTIONS TO THE RETROSPECTIVE APPLICATION OF OTHER IFRSs 243
   4.1   Introduction 243
   4.2   Estimates 244
   4.3   Derecognition of financial assets and financial liabilities 247
   4.4   Hedge accounting: general 248
         4.4.1   Paragraphs B5 and B6 of IFRS 1 when applying IFRS 9 248
         4.4.2   Applicability of IAS 39 hedge requirements 249

4.5	Hedge accounting in the opening IFRS statement of financial position			249
	4.5.1	Measurement of derivatives and elimination of deferred gains and losses		249
	4.5.2	Hedge relationships reflected in the opening IFRS statement of financial position		252
		4.5.2.A	Prohibition on retrospective designation	252
		4.5.2.B	Designation in anticipation of adoption of IFRSs	253
	4.5.3	Reflecting cash flow hedges in the opening IFRS statement of financial position		253
	4.5.4	Reflecting fair value hedges in the opening IFRS statement of financial position		254
	4.5.5	Reflecting foreign currency net investment hedges in the opening IFRS statement of financial position		255
	4.5.6	'Costs of hedging' (where excluded from the hedge relationship under previous GAAP)		255
4.6	Hedge accounting: subsequent treatment			256
	4.6.1	Discontinuation of a hedge relationship		256
	4.6.2	Ineffectiveness of cash flow and foreign currency net investment hedges in continuing hedge relationships		257
	4.6.3	Ineffectiveness of fair value hedges in continuing hedge relationships		258
	4.6.4	'Costs of hedging' (where excluded from the hedge relationship under previous GAAP)		259
4.7	Hedge accounting: examples			259
4.8	Non-controlling interests			262
4.9	Classification and measurement of financial instruments under IFRS 9			262
	4.9.1	Classification of financial instruments		262
		4.9.1.A	Assessment of a modified time value of money element	262
		4.9.1.B	Assessment of whether the fair value of a prepayment feature is insignificant	263
	4.9.2	Measurement of financial instruments measured at amortised cost		263
	4.9.3	Transition adjustments		263
4.10	Impairment of financial instruments under IFRS 9			264
4.11	Embedded derivatives			264
4.12	Government loans			265
4.13	Insurance contracts			266

5	OPTIONAL EXEMPTIONS FROM THE REQUIREMENTS OF CERTAIN IFRSs		266
	5.1	Introduction	266
	5.2	Business combinations and acquisitions of associates and joint arrangements	266
		5.2.1 Definition of a 'business' under IFRS 3	267
		5.2.1.A Asset acquisitions	268
		5.2.2 Option to restate business combinations retrospectively	268
		5.2.2.A Associates and joint arrangements	271
		5.2.3 Classification of business combinations	271
		5.2.4 Assets and liabilities to be recognised in the opening IFRS statement of financial position	271
		5.2.4.A Assets and liabilities to be excluded	271
		5.2.4.B Recognition of assets and liabilities	272
		5.2.4.C Previous GAAP carrying amount as deemed cost	274
		5.2.4.D In-process research and development	275
		5.2.4.E Subsequent measurement under IFRSs not based on cost	276
		5.2.4.F Example of recognition and measurement requirements	276
		5.2.5 Restatement of goodwill	277
		5.2.5.A Prohibition of other adjustments to goodwill	280
		5.2.5.B Derecognition of negative goodwill	281
		5.2.5.C Goodwill previously deducted from equity	281
		5.2.6 Currency adjustments to goodwill	282
		5.2.7 Previously unconsolidated subsidiaries	283
		5.2.8 Previously consolidated entities that are not subsidiaries	285
		5.2.9 Measurement of deferred taxes and non-controlling interests	285
		5.2.10 Transition accounting for contingent consideration	287
	5.3	Share-based payment transactions	287
		5.3.1 Use of previously published fair values	290
		5.3.2 Restatement of costs recognised under previous GAAP	290
	5.4	Insurance contracts	290
	5.5	Deemed cost	291
		5.5.1 Fair value or revaluation as deemed cost	292
		5.5.1.A Determining deemed cost	293
		5.5.1.B Deemed cost determined before the date of transition to IFRSs	295
		5.5.2 Event-driven fair value measurement as deemed cost	295
		5.5.2.A 'Push down' accounting	296

		5.5.2.B	'Fresh start' accounting 297
		5.5.2.C	Exemption for event-driven revaluations after the date of transition 297
	5.5.3		Deemed cost for oil and gas assets 297
	5.5.4		Deemed cost for assets used (or previously used) in operations subject to rate regulation 299
	5.5.5		Summary 301
5.6	Leases 302
5.7	Cumulative translation differences 304
	5.7.1		Gains and losses arising on related hedges 305
5.8	Investments in subsidiaries, joint ventures and associates 305
	5.8.1		Consolidated financial statements: subsidiaries and structured entities 305
	5.8.2		Separate financial statements: Cost of an investment in a subsidiary, joint venture or associate 306
5.9	Assets and liabilities of subsidiaries, associates and joint ventures 307
	5.9.1		Subsidiary becomes a first-time adopter later than its parent 308
		5.9.1.A	Cumulative translation differences 310
	5.9.2		Parent becomes a first-time adopter later than its subsidiary 311
	5.9.3		Implementation guidance on accounting for assets and liabilities of subsidiaries, associates and joint ventures 312
	5.9.4		Adoption of IFRSs on different dates in separate and consolidated financial statements 313
	5.9.5		Application to investment entities under IFRS 10 313
		5.9.5.A	Subsidiary adopts IFRSs after investment entity parent 313
		5.9.5.B	Non-investment entity parent adopts IFRSs after investment entity subsidiary 314
5.10	Compound financial instruments 314
5.11	Designation of previously recognised financial instruments 314
	5.11.1		Designation of financial asset as measured at fair value through profit or loss 314
	5.11.2		Designation of financial liability at fair value through profit or loss 315
	5.11.3		Designation of investment in an equity instrument 315
	5.11.4		Determination of an accounting mismatch for presenting a gain or loss on financial liability 315
5.12	Fair value measurement of financial assets or financial liabilities at initial recognition 315

5.13	Decommissioning liabilities included in the cost of property, plant and equipment	316
	5.13.1 IFRIC 1 exemption	316
	5.13.2 IFRIC 1 exemption for oil and gas assets at deemed cost	319
5.14	Financial assets or intangible assets accounted for in accordance with IFRIC 12	319
5.15	Borrowing costs	320
	5.15.1 Borrowing cost exemption	320
	5.15.2 Interaction with other exemptions	320
5.16	Extinguishing financial liabilities with equity instruments	321
5.17	Severe hyperinflation	321
5.18	Joint arrangements	322
5.19	Stripping costs in the production phase of a surface mine	322
5.20	Regulatory deferral accounts	322
	5.20.1 Defined terms in IFRS 14	322
	5.20.2 Scope	323
	5.20.3 Continuation of previous GAAP accounting policies (temporary exemption from paragraph 11 of IAS 8)	324
	5.20.4 Recognition of regulatory deferral account balances	324
	5.20.5 Changes in accounting policies	325
	5.20.6 Presentation	326
	5.20.6.A Presentation of deferred tax balances	326
	5.20.6.B Presentation of earnings per share amounts	327
	5.20.6.C Presentation of discontinued operations and disposal groups	327
	5.20.6.D Illustrative presentation of financial statements	328
	5.20.7 Disclosures	331
	5.20.7.A Explanation of activities subject to rate regulation	331
	5.20.7.B Explanation of recognised amounts	332
	5.20.8 Interaction with other standards	333
	5.20.8.A Application of IAS 10	333
	5.20.8.B Application of IAS 12	334
	5.20.8.C Application of IAS 36	334
	5.20.8.D Application of IFRS 3	334
	5.20.8.E Application of IFRS 5	334
	5.20.8.F Application of IFRS 10 and IAS 28	335
5.21	IFRS 15 – *Revenue from Contracts with Customers*	335
	5.21.1 Definition of a completed contract	337
	5.21.2 Implementation questions on definition of a completed contract	338

		5.21.2.A	Elements in a contract to be considered	338
		5.21.2.B	Identification of a contract under previous GAAP	339
		5.21.2.C	Some or all of revenue has not been recognised under previous GAAP	340
		5.21.2.D	Accounting for completed contracts excluded from transition	341

    5.22 Foreign currency transactions and advance consideration 341

    5.23 Designation of contracts to buy or sell a non-financial item 342

6 PRESENTATION AND DISCLOSURE 342

    6.1 Comparative information 342

    6.2 Non-IFRS comparative information and historical summaries 343

    6.3 Explanation of transition to IFRSs 343

        6.3.1 Disclosure of reconciliations 345

            6.3.1.A Reconciliation by a first-time adopter that continues to publish previous GAAP financial statements 347

        6.3.2 Line-by-line reconciliations and detailed explanations 348

        6.3.3 Recognition and reversal of impairments 356

        6.3.4 Inclusion of IFRS 1 reconciliations by cross reference 356

    6.4 Disclosure of financial instruments 356

        6.4.1 Designation of financial instruments 356

        6.4.2 Classification of financial instruments 356

    6.5 Disclosures regarding deemed cost 357

        6.5.1 Use of fair value as deemed cost 357

        6.5.2 Use of deemed cost for investments in subsidiaries, joint ventures and associates in separate financial statements 357

        6.5.3 Use of deemed cost for oil and gas assets 357

        6.5.4 Use of deemed cost for assets used in operations subject to rate regulation 357

        6.5.5 Use of deemed cost after severe hyperinflation 358

    6.6 Interim financial reports 358

        6.6.1 Reconciliations in the interim financial reports 358

        6.6.2 Disclosures in the interim financial report 360

    6.7 Disclosure of IFRS information before adoption of IFRSs 361

7 ACCOUNTING POLICIES AND PRACTICAL APPLICATION ISSUES 363

    7.1 IAS 7 – *Statement of Cash Flows* 363

    7.2 IAS 8 – *Accounting Policies, Changes in Accounting Estimates and Errors* 364

		7.2.1	Changes in IFRS accounting policies during the first IFRS reporting period 364

- 7.2.1 Changes in IFRS accounting policies during the first IFRS reporting period 364
- 7.2.2 Changes in estimates and correction of errors 365
- 7.3 IAS 12 – *Income Taxes* 365
  - 7.3.1 Previous revaluation of plant, property and equipment treated as deemed cost on transition 366
  - 7.3.2 Share-based payment transactions subject to transitional provisions of IFRS 1 367
  - 7.3.3 Retrospective restatements or applications 367
  - 7.3.4 Defined benefit pension plans 368
- 7.4 IAS 16 – *Property, Plant and Equipment* – and IAS 40 – *Investment Property* (cost model) 369
  - 7.4.1 Depreciation method and rate 369
  - 7.4.2 Estimates of useful life and residual value 370
  - 7.4.3 Revaluation model 370
  - 7.4.4 Parts approach 371
- 7.5 IFRS 16 – *Leases* 371
- 7.6 IFRS 15 – *Revenue from Contracts with Customers* 371
- 7.7 IAS 19 – *Employee Benefits* 372
  - 7.7.1 Sensitivity analysis for each significant actuarial assumption 372
  - 7.7.2 Full actuarial valuations 372
  - 7.7.3 Actuarial assumptions 372
  - 7.7.4 Unrecognised past service costs 373
- 7.8 IAS 21 – *The Effects of Changes in Foreign Exchange Rates* 373
  - 7.8.1 Functional currency 373
- 7.9 IAS 28 – *Investments in Associates and Joint Ventures* 374
  - 7.9.1 Impairment review at date of transition to IFRSs 374
- 7.10 IAS 29 – *Financial Reporting in Hyperinflationary Economies* 375
- 7.11 IFRS 11 – *Joint Arrangements* 375
- 7.12 IAS 36 – *Impairment of Assets* 376
- 7.13 IAS 37 – *Provisions, Contingent Liabilities and Contingent Assets* 377
- 7.14 IAS 38 – *Intangible Assets* 378

8 REGULATORY ISSUES 379
- 8.1 First-time adoption by foreign private issuers that are SEC registrants 379
  - 8.1.1 SEC guidance 379
  - 8.1.2 IPTF guidance 380
- 8.2 Disclosure of IFRS information in financial statements for periods prior to an entity's first IFRS reporting period 382

	8.2.1	IFRS guidance...382
	8.2.2	Disclosure of expected changes in accounting policies...383

List of examples

Example 5.1:	Scope of application of IFRS 1	230
Example 5.2:	Entity applying national GAAP and IFRSs	230
Example 5.3:	First IFRS financial statements outside the annual report or statutory financial statements	231
Example 5.4:	Repeated application of IFRS 1 when an entity does not apply IFRSs for one year	233
Example 5.5:	Determining the date of transition to IFRSs	237
Example 5.6:	Prohibition from applying superseded standards	239
Example 5.7:	Order of application of exemptions	243
Example 5.8:	Application of IFRS 1 to estimates	246
Example 5.9:	Unrecognised gains and losses on existing cash flow hedge	254
Example 5.10:	Pre-transition cash flow hedges	259
Example 5.11:	Existing fair value hedges	260
Example 5.12:	Government loan with below-market interest rate	265
Example 5.13:	Acquisition of assets	268
Example 5.14:	Restructuring provision	272
Example 5.15:	Items not recognised under previous GAAP	273
Example 5.16:	Lease in which the acquiree was a lessee not capitalised in accordance with previous GAAP	273
Example 5.17:	Provisionally determined fair values	274
Example 5.18:	Items measured on a cost basis	275
Example 5.19:	Items not measured at original cost	276
Example 5.20:	Business combination example	276
Example 5.21:	Recognition and derecognition of acquired intangible assets	278
Example 5.22:	Impairment testing of goodwill on first-time adoption	278
Example 5.23:	Previous GAAP impairment of goodwill embedded in equity method investment	279
Example 5.24:	Adjusting goodwill	280
Example 5.25:	Goodwill deducted from equity and treatment of related intangible assets	281
Example 5.26:	Goodwill related to foreign net investments	282
Example 5.27:	Adjustments made during measurement period to provisional amounts	282
Example 5.28:	Subsidiary not consolidated under previous GAAP	284
Example 5.29:	Calculation of deemed cost of goodwill	285

Example 5.30:	Restatement of intangible assets, deferred tax and non-controlling interests 286
Example 5.31:	Deemed cost of property, plant and equipment 295
Example 5.32:	Determining whether an arrangement contains a lease...............302
Example 5.33:	Parent adopts IFRSs before subsidiary...308
Example 5.34:	Interaction between paragraph D16(a) of IFRS 1 and the business combination exemptions applied by its parent.............309
Example 5.35:	Subsidiary adopts IFRSs before parent 311
Example 5.36:	Limited ability to choose first-time adoption exemptions........... 312
Example 5.37:	Decommissioning component in property, plant and equipment...317
Example 5.38:	Illustrative presentation of financial statements for regulatory deferral account balances..328
Example 5.39:	Transition practical expedient for contract modifications..........336
Example 5.40:	Definition of completed contract: contract duration...................339
Example 5.41:	Reconciliations to be presented in first IFRS financial statements...346
Example 5.42:	Reconciliations to be presented in IFRS half-year reports..........359
Example 5.43:	Reconciliations to be presented in IFRS quarterly reports.........360
Example 5.44:	Remeasurement of deferred tax asset recognised as the result of retrospective application..368
Example 5.45:	Revaluation reserve under IAS 16 370

Chapter 5 — First-time adoption

1 INTRODUCTION

1.1 Objectives of first-time adoption

In principle, a first-time adopter should prepare financial statements as if it had always applied IFRSs. Although entities routinely have to apply new accounting standards by way of prior year adjustment, adopting IFRSs, a new basis of accounting, is a challenging undertaking and poses a distinct set of problems. One cannot underestimate the magnitude of the effort involved in adopting a large number of new accounting standards. The requirements of individual standards will often differ significantly from those under an entity's previous GAAP and information may need to be collected that was not required under the previous GAAP.

IFRS 1 – *First-time Adoption of International Financial Reporting Standards* – has a rather limited objective, to ensure that an entity's first IFRS financial statements, and its interim financial reports for part of the period covered by those first IFRS financial statements, contain high quality financial information that: *[IFRS 1.1]*

- is transparent for users and comparable over all periods presented;
- provides a suitable starting point for accounting in accordance with IFRSs; and
- can be generated at a cost that does not exceed the benefits.

It is important for users to be mindful of this objective as it provides the principal rationale underlying many of the decisions reflected in the standard, in particular the various exceptions that require, and exemptions that allow, a first-time adopter to deviate from the general rule (i.e. a retrospective application).

Although IFRS 1 owes its existence to the 2005 adoption of IFRSs by EU companies whose securities are traded on an EU regulated market,[1] one of the IASB's aims was 'to find solutions that would be appropriate for any entity, in any part of the world, regardless of whether adoption occurs in 2005 or at a different time'. *[IFRS 1.BC3]*. IFRS 1 had to be written in a way that completely ignores a first-time adopter's previous GAAP. This means that first-time adoption exemptions are made available to all first-time adopters, including those whose previous GAAP was very close to IFRSs. A first-time adopter that so desires will be able to make considerable adjustments to its opening IFRS statement of financial position, using the available exemptions in IFRS 1, even if the differences between its previous GAAP and IFRSs were only minor. Yet, it may also be required to make considerable adjustments due to the requirement to use the same IFRS standards for all periods presented in the first IFRS financial statements.

Another issue is the potential for lack of comparability between different first-time adopters, and between first-time adopters and entities already applying IFRSs. *[IFRS 1.BC9]*. The IASB ultimately decided that it was more important to achieve 'comparability over time within a first-time adopter's first IFRS financial statements and between different entities adopting IFRSs for the first time at a given date; achieving comparability between first-time adopters and entities that already apply IFRSs is a secondary objective.' *[IFRS 1.BC10]*.

A revised IFRS 1 was issued in November 2008, which retains the substance of the previous version of the standard but within a changed structure. *[IFRS 1.BC3B]*. The standard has been further amended as a result of the IASB's annual improvements process, consequential amendments resulting from issuance of new standards, as well as to provide limited exceptions and exemptions that address specific matters. This approach always carried the risk that its complexity might eventually overwhelm its practical application. All these amendments are incorporated into the applicable sections of this chapter.

1.2 Authoritative literature

This chapter generally discusses the requirements of IFRS 1 for accounting periods beginning on or after 1 January 2021 unless otherwise stated and reflects the amendments to the original version of IFRS 1 referred to at 1.1 above.

This chapter does not deal with the first-time adoption of the earlier versions of IFRS 1. A detailed discussion of the first-time adoption using the earlier versions of the standard can be found in Chapter 5 of *International GAAP 2020* and prior editions. Especially, entities (e.g. insurance companies) that elect to continue applying IAS 39 – *Financial Instruments: Recognition and Measurement* – should refer to previous editions of *International GAAP*, specifically *International GAAP 2018*, for guidance.

1.3 Defined terms

IFRS 1 defines the following terms in connection with the transition to IFRSs: *[IFRS 1 Appendix A]*

- *Date of transition to IFRSs:* The beginning of the earliest period for which an entity presents full comparative information under IFRSs in its first IFRS financial statements.
- *First IFRS financial statements:* The first annual financial statements in which an entity adopts International Financial Reporting Standards, by an explicit and unreserved statement of compliance with IFRSs.
- *First IFRS reporting period:* The latest reporting period covered by an entity's first IFRS financial statements.
- *First-time adopter:* An entity that presents its first IFRS financial statements.
- *International Financial Reporting Standards (IFRSs):* Standards and Interpretations issued by the International Accounting Standards Board (IASB). They comprise:

(a) International Financial Reporting Standards;
(b) International Accounting Standards;
(c) IFRIC Interpretations (Interpretations developed by the IFRS Interpretations Committee); and
(d) SIC Interpretations (Interpretations of the former Standing Interpretations Committee).

Opening IFRS statement of financial position: An entity's statement of financial position (i.e. balance sheet) at the date of transition to IFRSs.

Previous GAAP: The basis of accounting that a first-time adopter used immediately before adopting IFRSs.

1.4 Future developments

As at the time of writing, there was no specific project dealing with IFRS 1. However, the IASB is currently pursuing a number of projects. Consideration will be given at the time of deliberations to how new standards or amendments may impact a first-time adopter of IFRSs and resulting consequential amendments to IFRS 1 will be included in the new standards or amendments. Entities contemplating conversion to IFRSs should monitor the IASB's agenda in order to anticipate how future standards or amendments may affect their conversions.

2 WHO IS A FIRST-TIME ADOPTER?

2.1 The first IFRS financial statements in scope of IFRS 1

An entity's first IFRS financial statements are the first annual financial statements in which the entity adopts IFRSs, by making in those financial statements an explicit and unreserved statement of compliance with IFRSs. *[IFRS 1.3, Appendix A]*. The standard provides description of the circumstances in which an entity is a first-time adopter and therefore is within the scope of this standard. These circumstances are discussed below.

An entity's financial statements are considered its first IFRS financial statements, and thus fall within the scope of IFRS 1, when it presented, for example, its most recent previous financial statements: *[IFRS 1.3(a)]*

(i) in accordance with national requirements that are not consistent with IFRSs in all respects;
(ii) in conformity with IFRSs in all respects, except that the financial statements did not contain an explicit and unreserved statement that they complied with IFRSs;
(iii) containing an explicit statement of compliance with some, but not all, IFRSs;
(iv) in accordance with national requirements inconsistent with IFRSs, but using some individual IFRSs to account for items for which national requirements did not exist; or
(v) in accordance with national requirements, with a reconciliation of some amounts to the amounts determined in accordance with IFRSs.

An entity whose most recent previous financial statements contained an explicit and unreserved statement of compliance with IFRSs can never be considered a first-time adopter. This is the case even in the following circumstances: *[IFRS 1.4]*

- the entity presented financial statements containing an explicit and unreserved statement of compliance with IFRSs despite the fact that the auditors issued a qualified audit report on those IFRS financial statements. By contrast, an entity that makes a statement of compliance that excludes any IFRSs will still be a first-time adopter (see Example 5.1 below);
- the entity presented financial statements claiming to comply both with national GAAP and IFRSs; or
- the entity stops presenting a separate set of financial statements under national requirements, which was previously presented in addition to its IFRS financial statements (see Example 5.2 below).

The IASB could have introduced special rules that would have required an entity that significantly departed from IFRSs to apply IFRS 1. However, the IASB considered that such rules would lead to 'complexity and uncertainty'. *[IFRS 1.BC5]*. In addition, this would have given entities applying 'IFRS-lite' (entities not applying IFRSs rigorously in all respects e.g. applying IFRSs except for certain standards and interpretations) an option to side step the requirements of IAS 8 – *Accounting Policies, Changes in Accounting Estimates and Errors* – to disclose departures from IFRSs as errors. *[IFRS 1.BC6]*.

The following examples illustrate certain scenarios in connection with determining whether an entity is a first-time adopter.

Example 5.1:   Scope of application of IFRS 1

Entity A applied IFRSs in its previous financial statements, but stated that it 'applied IFRSs except for IFRS 2 – *Share-based Payment*.'

Entity A is a first-time adopter because its financial statements did not contain an unreserved statement of compliance with IFRSs. It is irrelevant whether the auditors' report was qualified or not.

Entity B applied IFRSs in its previous financial statements and stated that 'the financial statements are prepared in conformity with IFRSs.' Despite that statement, Entity B had not applied IFRS 2.

Entity B is not a first-time adopter because its financial statements contained an unreserved statement of compliance with IFRSs. Even if the auditors had qualified their report, the entity would still not be a first-time adopter.

It is clear that the scope of IFRS 1 is very much rules-based, which, as the example above illustrates, can lead to different answers in similar situations and sometimes to counter-intuitive answers.

Example 5.2:   Entity applying national GAAP and IFRSs

Entity C prepares two sets of financial statements, one set of financial statements based on its national GAAP and the other set based on IFRSs. The IFRS financial statements contained an explicit and unreserved statement of compliance with IFRSs and were made available externally. From 2021 onwards, Entity C stops presenting financial statements based on its national GAAP.

Entity C is not a first-time adopter because it already published financial statements that contained an explicit and unreserved statement of compliance with IFRSs.

Example 5.3: **First IFRS financial statements outside the annual report or statutory financial statements**

Entity D prepared financial statements under its previous GAAP for the period ending 31 December 2020. In connection with its initial public offering, Entity D published an offering document that includes IFRS financial statements that contain an unreserved statement of compliance with IFRSs. The date of transition to IFRSs for the purposes of those financial statements, which cover the most recent three financial years, was 1 January 2018.

Entity D's annual report (or statutory financial statements) are prepared under IFRSs for the first time for the period ending 31 December 2021.

The IFRS financial statements included in Entity D's offering document were its first IFRS financial statements, containing an unreserved statement of compliance with IFRSs. Therefore, Entity D should not apply IFRS 1 in its first annual report (or statutory financial statements) prepared under IFRSs as it is not a first-time adopter. Although not required by IFRSs, Entity D may want to repeat information about its transition to IFRSs in its annual report (or statutory financial statements) for the year ended 31 December 2021.

If, however, Entity D had included financial statements in its offering document that did not contain an unreserved statement of compliance with IFRSs then the annual report (or statutory financial statements) for 2021 would need to be prepared in accordance with IFRS 1. If those financial statements only included comparative information for the year ended 31 December 2020 then Entity D's date of transition would be 1 January 2020.

An entity will be a first-time adopter if it has previously prepared financial statements in accordance with IFRSs but only for internal purposes. The entity may have: *[IFRS 1.3(b)-(c)]*

- prepared financial statements in accordance with IFRSs for internal use only, without making them available to the entity's owners or any other external users;
- prepared a reporting package in accordance with IFRSs for consolidation purposes without preparing a complete set of financial statements as defined in IAS 1 – *Presentation of Financial Statements*.

Where previous financial statements containing an explicit and unreserved statement of compliance with IFRSs have been authorised for issue, but are subject to restrictions for specific use or that limited the distribution to certain users, these restrictions will need to be evaluated to determine whether or not those previous financial statements were general-purpose financial statements. If the previous financial statements were general-purpose financial statements made available to the entity's owners or any other external users, the entity is not a first-time adopter.

IFRSs are intended to be applied in the preparation of general-purpose financial statements, i.e. those intended to meet the needs of users who are not in a position to require an entity to prepare reports tailored to their particular information needs. Many existing and potential investors, lenders and other creditors ('the primary users') cannot require reporting entities to provide information directly to them and must rely on general purpose financial statements for much of the financial information they need. *[IAS 1.2, 7]*. The objective of general-purpose financial reporting is to provide financial information about the reporting entity that is useful to the primary users in making decisions relating to providing resources to the entity. *[CF 1.2]*. Management of an entity need not rely on general-purpose financial reports, since the relevant information can be obtained internally (see Chapter 2 at 4.1.1 and 4.1.2 and Chapter 3 at 1.1). *[CF 1.9]*.

Judgement is required in making the determination of whether or not the previous financial statements were general-purpose financial statements in accordance with IFRSs, based on the specific facts and circumstances. Factors to consider include the purpose and intended use for which the financial statements have been prepared (including the nature of any restrictions over their use), the extent to which the financial statements have been made available to owners or other external users, whether or not the recipients are permitted to make the financial statements available to other users, and whether the financial statements have been authorised for issue by the relevant body. In our view, availability does not require active distribution of the financial statements. If the financial statements could be requested by owners or other external users (and there is a mechanism publicised by which such requests could be made), the financial statements would be available.

A restriction of the distribution (or over the use) of the financial statements authorised for issue does not necessarily mean the financial statements are not general-purpose financial statements. For example, if a set of financial statements that includes an explicit and unreserved statement of compliance with IFRSs was made available to an external party (such as a bank for the purposes of a lending decision) and the information has not specifically been tailored for the bank's needs, the financial statements would generally be regarded as general-purpose financial statements. *[IFRS 1.3(b)]*. Where such a set of financial statements was made available only to an entity's board members, CEO or CFO who are also entity's shareholders but not to other owners, however, there may be a question over whether these are general-purpose financial statements. Accordingly, it would be necessary to understand the full facts and circumstances in making this determination, taking into account the above factors.

An entity that is a subsidiary of an IFRS reporting parent may be able to use the amounts reported for it in the group's financial statements when it adopts IFRSs for its own financial statements (see 5.9.1 below).

Finally, IFRS 1 applies also to a first-time adopter that did not present financial statements for previous periods. *[IFRS 1.3(d)]*. For example, when an entity transfers its operations into a new company prior to an issue to the public, the new company would be a first-time adopter if the entity never applied IFRSs in the past.

An entity that is already applying IFRSs in preparing its financial statements must not apply IFRS 1 to changes in its accounting policies. Instead, such an entity should apply: *[IFRS 1.5]*

- the requirements of IAS 8; and
- specific transitional requirements in other IFRSs.

2.2 When should IFRS 1 be applied?

An entity that presents its first IFRS financial statements is a first-time adopter, *[IFRS 1 Appendix A]*, and should apply IFRS 1 in preparing those financial statements. *[IFRS 1.2(a)]*. It should also apply the standard in each interim financial report that it presents in accordance with IAS 34 – *Interim Financial Reporting* – for a part of the period covered by its first IFRS financial statements. *[IFRS 1.2(b)]*. Therefore, a first-time adopter does not apply IFRS 1 to a 'trading statement', an 'earnings press release' or other financial report issued at its interim reporting date that is not described as complying with IAS 34 or IFRSs. In Extract 5.1 below, AGF Mutual Funds described its adoption of IFRSs in its interim or semi-annual financial statements.

> **Extract 5.1: AGF Mutual Funds (2014)**
> Notes to Financial Statements (UNAUDITED) [extract]
> 2. SUMMARY OF ACCOUNTING POLICIES: [extract]
> **Basis of presentation and adoption of International Financial Reporting Standards**
>
> These financial statements have been prepared in compliance with International Financial Reporting Standards ("IFRS") applicable to the preparation of interim financial statements, including International Accounting Standard ("IAS") 34, *Interim Financial Reporting* and IFRS 1, *First-time Adoption of International Financial Reporting Standards*. The Funds adopted this basis of accounting effective October 1, 2014 as required by Canadian securities legislation and the Canadian Accounting Standards Board. Previously, the Funds prepared their financial statements in accordance with Canadian generally accepted accounting principles as defined in Part V of the CPA Handbook ("Canadian GAAP"). The Funds have consistently applied the accounting policies used in the preparation of their opening IFRS statements of financial position as at October 1, 2013 and throughout all periods presented, as if these policies had always been in effect. Note 10 includes disclosures of the impact of the transition to IFRS on the Funds' reported financial position and financial performance, including the nature and effect of significant changes in accounting policies from those used in the Funds' financial statements for the year ended September 30, 2014 prepared under Canadian GAAP.

2.2.1 Repeat application of IFRS 1

Sometimes an entity may meet the criteria for applying IFRS 1 (see 2.1 above) but has applied IFRSs in a previous reporting period. The IASB explained this issue with an example of an entity that had applied IFRS 1 in connection with a foreign listing, subsequently delisted from the foreign exchange and no longer presented IFRS financial statements, but is now adopting IFRSs again together with other entities in its local jurisdiction – see Example 5.4 below.

IFRS 1 does not prohibit an entity from applying IFRS 1 more than once. *[IFRS 1.2-3]*. In May 2012, IFRS 1 was amended to clarify that an entity that stopped applying IFRSs in the past and chooses, or is required, to resume preparing IFRS financial statements has the option to apply IFRS 1 again. *[IFRS 1.4A]*. The Board reasoned that the entity should on cost-benefit grounds be allowed, rather than required, to apply IFRS 1 again. *[IFRS1.BC6C]*. If the entity chooses not to reapply IFRS 1, it must retrospectively restate its financial statements in accordance with IAS 8 as if it had never stopped applying IFRSs while disclosing (in addition to the disclosures required by IAS 8) the reasons why it stopped applying IFRSs and why it resumed applying IFRSs, as well as the reasons for choosing the retrospective restatement method. *[IFRS 1.4B, 23A, 23B]*.

Example 5.4: *Repeated application of IFRS 1 when an entity does not apply IFRSs for one year*

Entity E prepared IFRS financial statements for 2018 and 2019 that contained an explicit and unreserved statement of compliance with IFRSs. However, in 2020 Entity E did not make an unreserved statement of compliance with IFRSs (i.e. Entity E did not issue IFRS compliant financial statements in 2020).

If Entity E resumes presenting financial statements in accordance with IFRSs, it may choose to apply IFRSs as a first-time adopter or it may elect to restate its financial statements retrospectively as if it had never stopped producing IFRS financial statements.

If it elects to apply IFRSs as a first-time adopter for the purposes of its 2021 financial statements, there is no requirement under IFRS 1 for Entity E to base its first IFRS financial statements in 2021 on the IFRS information that it produced before 2021. Therefore, Entity E is able to apply the IFRS 1 exemptions without regard to the elections it made in its first IFRS financial statements in 2018. In fact, in this case, Entity E is unable to apply certain IFRS 1 exemptions by reference to the date of transition that it used in its 2018 financial statements (see 3.5 below).

2.3 Determining the previous GAAP

An entity may prepare two complete sets of financial statements, e.g. one set of financial statements based on its national GAAP and another set for distribution to foreign investors based on US GAAP. Applying the definition of 'previous GAAP' (i.e. 'the basis of accounting that a first-time adopter used immediately before adopting IFRSs' *[IFRS 1 Appendix A]*) to such a dual reporting entity is not straightforward, as the examples below illustrate:

(a) *A dual reporting entity adopts IFRSs and at the same time stops presenting financial statements under its national GAAP and US GAAP:* Both national GAAP and US GAAP meet the definition of 'previous GAAP'. However, the entity can only present one set of IFRS financial statements. Therefore, the entity must choose a 'previous GAAP'. While, at least in theory, this appears to be a free choice there are a number of limiting constraints that should be taken into account:

(i) national legislation and regulatory requirements may restrict an entity's options and require either national GAAP or US GAAP to be designated as the previous GAAP;

(ii) comparability with other entities in the same jurisdiction may be increased if all entities in that jurisdiction use the same GAAP as their previous GAAP; and

(iii) one set of financial statements may be considered to be the 'main' set of financial statements, for example:

- if the national GAAP financial statements received very limited circulation then they are clearly not the entity's 'main' financial statements. Conversely, if the US GAAP financial statements are only prepared for a specific purpose (e.g. to obtain a bank loan) then they may not be the entity's 'main' financial statements; or
- the relative dominance of shareholder groups might provide an indication as to which set of financial statements is considered to be the 'main' set of financial statements.

An entity should apply judgement when the constraints above do not all identify the same GAAP as the previous GAAP.

IFRS 1 only requires disclosure of reconciliations between an entity's previous GAAP and IFRSs. However, it will be advisable for an entity to provide disclosures, on a voluntary basis, that contain sufficient information to enable users to understand the material reconciling items between the IFRS financial statements and the financial statements that were not prepared under its previous GAAP. Some national regulators (e.g. the US Securities and Exchange Commission), in fact, expect such disclosures (see 8.1.2 below).[2]

(b) *A dual reporting entity adopts IFRSs and at the same time continues to present financial statements under its national GAAP but stops presenting financial statements under US GAAP:* While one might expect US GAAP to be treated as the previous GAAP, both national GAAP and US GAAP meet the definition of 'previous GAAP'. An entity should therefore consider the criteria (i) to (iii) under (a) above in determining its previous GAAP.

If an entity treats its national GAAP as its previous GAAP then it may want or need to present an explanation of the differences between US GAAP and IFRSs to aid former users of the US GAAP financial statements.

As illustrated in Extract 5.2 below, when Infosys adopted IFRSs it treated Indian GAAP as its previous GAAP even though it continued to report under Indian GAAP for statutory purposes. However, Infosys provided additional reconciliations between US GAAP and its previous GAAP.

(c) *A dual reporting entity adopts IFRSs and at the same time stops presenting financial statements under US GAAP. Several years later it stops presenting financial statements under its national GAAP:* The entity is not a first-time adopter when it ceases to present financial statements under its national GAAP, even if the entity treated US GAAP (rather than its national GAAP) as its previous GAAP when it adopted IFRSs. *[IFRS 1.4(a)].* However, the entity may want or need to present an explanation of the differences between its national GAAP and IFRSs to aid former users of its national GAAP financial statements.

Extract 5.2: Infosys Technologies Limited (2009)

2 Notes to the consolidated financial statements [extract]

2.1 Transition to IFRS reporting [extract]

The financial statements of Infosys Technologies Limited and its subsidiaries have been prepared in accordance with IFRS. Infosys Technologies Limited and its subsidiaries adopted all IFRS standards and the adoption was carried out in accordance to IFRS 1, using April 1, 2007 as the transition date. The transition was carried out from Indian GAAP, which was considered as the Previous GAAP. The effect of adopting IFRS has been summarized in the reconciliations provided. The transition to IFRS reporting has resulted in changes in the reported financial statements, notes thereto and accounting principles compared to what had been presented previously. Until the adoption of IFRS, the financial statements included in the Annual Reports on Form 20-F and Quarterly Reports on Form 6-K were prepared in accordance with accounting principles generally accepted in the United States of America (U.S. GAAP) under the historical cost convention on the accrual basis. However, for the purposes of the transition, such transition was carried out from Indian GAAP, which has been considered as the Previous GAAP. The reconciliation statements provided in Note 2.2 describe the differences between IFRS and Indian GAAP. In addition, reconciliations from U.S. GAAP to Indian GAAP have been provided in Note 2.3 for the periods presented.

The Group's financial statements for the year ending March 31, 2009 are the first annual financial statements to comply with IFRS.

2.3 The following voluntary reconciliations provide a quantification of reconciliation items between U.S. GAAP and Previous GAAP: [extract]

• equity as at April 1, 2007 (Note 2.3.1)
• equity as at March 31, 2008 (Note 2.3.2)
• equity as at March 31, 2009 (Note 2.3.3)
• net income for the year ended March 31, 2008 (Note 2.3.4)
• net income for the year ended March 31, 2009 (Note 2.3.5)

2.3.1 Transition to IFRSs from a similar GAAP

One consequence of the ongoing harmonisation of accounting standards around the world is that many national GAAPs are now virtually identical to IFRSs. However, differences between these national GAAPs and IFRSs often exist regarding the scope, transitional provisions, effective dates and actual wording of standards. In addition, some national GAAPs contain accounting alternatives not permitted by IFRSs.

When an entity reporting under such a national GAAP (e.g. Singapore GAAP) adopts IFRSs there will often not be major changes required in its accounting policies to comply with IFRSs. A similar situation may arise where an entity reporting under the IFRS for SMEs adopts full IFRSs, for example, due to an IPO. However, under IFRS 1 it is not relevant whether or not a previous GAAP was very similar to IFRSs. Therefore, regardless of the absence of significant differences in accounting policies, that entity would be a first-time adopter when it includes an explicit and unreserved statement of compliance with IFRSs for the first time. So, even if the entity's accounting policies were already fully aligned with IFRSs:

(a) it would be permitted to apply the IFRS 1 exemptions and required to apply the IFRS 1 exceptions;

(b) it would need to restate items for which the applicable first-time adoption exceptions differ from the transitional rules applicable to ongoing reporters (e.g. classification and measurement of financial assets);

(c) it would not be permitted to apply different versions of IFRSs that were effective at earlier dates; and

(d) it would need to explain the transition to IFRSs.

Notwithstanding the above, we believe an entity that:

- reported under a national GAAP that is identical with IFRSs in all respects;
- applied the national GAAP equivalent of IFRS 1 when the entity adopted that national GAAP;
- made an explicit and unreserved statement of compliance with that national GAAP in its most recent financial statements; and
- could have made an explicit and unreserved statement of compliance with IFRSs in those financial statements, if required,

does not have to reapply IFRS 1 the first time that it makes an explicit and unreserved statement of compliance with IFRSs.

For example, if an entity that meets the requirements described above decides to make an explicit and unreserved statement of compliance with IFRSs for the first time, either voluntarily or required to do so by a regulatory requirement related to an IPO, the entity would not be required to reapply IFRS 1.

3 OPENING IFRS STATEMENT OF FINANCIAL POSITION

At the date of transition to IFRSs, an entity should prepare and present an opening IFRS statement of financial position that is the starting point for its accounting under IFRSs. *[IFRS 1.6]*. The date of transition to IFRSs is the beginning of the earliest period for which an entity presents full comparative information under IFRSs in its first IFRS financial statements. *[IFRS 1 Appendix A]*. Therefore, the date of transition for an entity reporting under IFRSs for the first time at 31 December 2021 and presenting one year of comparative figures is 1 January 2020. For entities that adopt IFRSs at the beginning of a year, it is recommended that they consider the filing requirements for interim financial reports that a regulator in their jurisdiction may impose. For example, a regulator may require the opening IFRS statement of financial position to be presented in the first IFRS interim financial report even though this is not an IFRS 1 presentation requirement (see 6.6 below).

3.1 First-time adoption timeline

An entity's first annual IFRS financial statements must include at least three statements of financial position (i.e. balance sheets), two statements of profit or loss and other comprehensive income, two separate statements of profit or loss (if presented), two statements of cash flows and two statements of changes in equity and related notes, including comparative information for all statements presented. *[IFRS 1.21]*. The beginning of the earliest comparative period for which the entity presents full comparative information under IFRSs will be treated as its date of transition to IFRSs. The diagram below shows how for an entity with a December year-end the above terms are related:

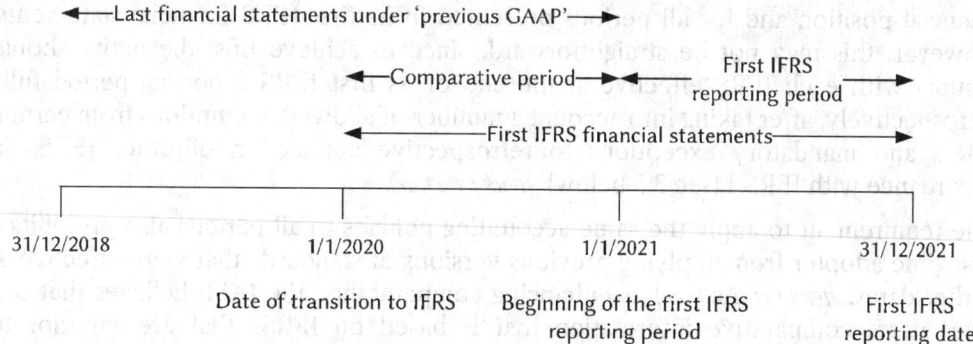

The diagram above also illustrates that there is a period of overlap, for the financial year 2020, which is reported first under the entity's previous GAAP and then as a comparative period under IFRSs. The following example illustrates how an entity should determine its date of transition to IFRSs.

Example 5.5: Determining the date of transition to IFRSs

Entity A's year-end is 31 December and it presents financial statements that include one comparative period. Entity A is required (e.g. by national legislation) to produce IFRS financial statements for the first annual accounting period starting on or after 1 January 2021.

A's first IFRS financial statements are for the period ending on 31 December 2021. Its date of transition to IFRSs is 1 January 2020, which is the beginning of the single comparative period included in its first IFRS financial statements.

Entity B's year-end is 31 July and it presents financial statements that include two comparative periods. Entity B is required to produce IFRS financial statements for the first annual accounting period starting on or after 1 January 2021.

B's first IFRS financial statements are for the period ending on 31 July 2022. Its date of transition to IFRSs is 1 August 2019, which is the beginning of the earliest period for which full comparative information is included in its first IFRS financial statements.

Entity C's most recent financial statements, under its previous GAAP, are for the period from 1 July 2019 to 31 December 2020. Entity C presents its first IFRS financial statements (that include one comparative period) for the period ending 31 December 2021.

C's date of transition is 1 July 2019. While IFRSs require presentation of at least one comparative period, the comparative period is not required to be equal in length to the current period. *[IFRS 1.21, IAS 1.38]*. Thus, the entity's date of transition will be the beginning of the earliest comparative period, irrespective of the length of that period. However, an entity must disclose the reason why the comparative period is not equal in length and the fact that the periods presented are not entirely comparable. *[IAS 1.36]*.

Similarly, it is generally not considered to be a problem if the current or comparative period in an entity's first IFRS financial statements only covers a 52-week period, because IAS 1 does not preclude the practice of presenting financial statements for 52-week financial periods. *[IAS 1.37]*.

3.2 Opening IFRS statement of financial position and accounting policies

The fundamental principle of IFRS 1 is to require full retrospective application of the standards effective at the end of an entity's first IFRS reporting period, but with limited exceptions for the opening IFRS statement of financial position. IFRS 1 requires a first-time adopter to use the same accounting policies in its opening IFRS statement of financial position and for all periods presented in its first IFRS financial statements. However, this may not be straightforward, since to achieve this, the entity should comply with each IFRS effective at the end of its first IFRS reporting period fully retrospectively, after taking into account a number of allowed exemptions from certain IFRSs and mandatory exceptions to retrospective application of other IFRSs in accordance with IFRS 1 (see 3.5 below). *[IFRS 1.7, 13, 18]*.

The requirement to apply the same accounting policies to all periods also prohibits a first-time adopter from applying previous versions of standards that were effective at earlier dates. *[IFRS 1.8]*. As well as enhancing comparability, the IASB believes that this gives users comparative information that is based on IFRSs that are superior to superseded versions of those standards and avoids unnecessary costs. *[IFRS 1.BC11]*.

For similar reasons, IFRS 1 also permits an entity to choose to apply either the current standard or a new standard that is not yet mandatory if that standard allows early application. *[IFRS 1.8]*. Whichever standard is selected it would need to be applied consistently throughout the periods presented in its first IFRS financial statements on a retrospective basis, unless IFRS 1 provides an exemption or an exception that permits or requires otherwise. *[IFRS 1.BC11A]*. The diagram below summarises these requirements in IFRS 1.

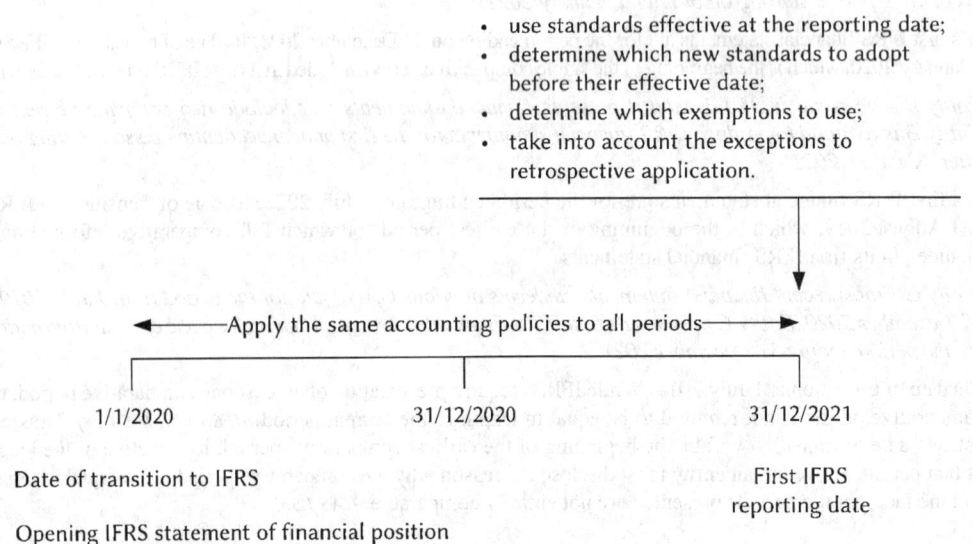

It should be noted that depending on the end of its first IFRS reporting period, an entity may or may not have the option to choose which version of a particular standard it may apply, as can be seen in the example below.

Example 5.6: Prohibition from applying superseded standards

Entity A's date of transition to IFRSs is 1 July 2019 and its first IFRS reporting period ends on 30 June 2021. How should Entity A apply the amendments to IFRS 16 – *Covid-19-Related Rent Concessions – Amendments to IFRS 16*, which are effective for annual periods beginning 1 July 2020, in its first IFRS financial statements?

IFRS 1 requires Entity A to apply the amendments to IFRS 16 because they are effective in its first IFRS reporting period. Since IFRS 1 prohibits an entity from applying a superseded standard to transactions that occurred before 1 July 2020 while applying the amended standard in the period beginning 1 July 2020, Entity A has to apply the above-mentioned amendments to IFRS 16 for all periods presented.

Except to the extent that the exceptions and exemptions at 3.5 below apply, in preparing its opening IFRS statement of financial position, an entity should: *[IFRS 1.10]*

(a) recognise all assets and liabilities whose recognition is required by IFRSs;

(b) not recognise assets or liabilities if IFRSs do not permit such recognition;

(c) reclassify items recognised under previous GAAP as one type of asset, liability or component of equity, but are a different type of asset, liability or component of equity in accordance with IFRSs; and

(d) apply IFRSs in measuring all recognised assets and liabilities.

Any change in accounting policies on adoption of IFRSs may cause changes in the amounts recorded under previous GAAP in respect of events and transactions that occurred before the date of transition. The effects of these changes should be recognised at the date of transition to IFRSs in retained earnings or, if appropriate, in another category of equity. *[IFRS 1.11]*. For example, an entity that applies the revaluation model under IAS 16 – *Property, Plant and Equipment* – (see Chapter 18 at 6) in its first IFRS financial statements would recognise the difference between cost and the revalued amount of property, plant and equipment in a revaluation reserve. By contrast, an entity that had applied a revaluation model under its previous GAAP, but decided to apply the cost model under IAS 16, would reallocate the revaluation reserve to retained earnings or a separate component of equity not described as a revaluation reserve (see 7.4.3 below).

A first-time adopter is under no obligation to ensure that its IFRS accounting policies are similar to or as close as possible to its previous GAAP accounting policies. Therefore, for example, a first-time adopter could adopt the IAS 16 revaluation model despite the fact that it applied a cost model under its previous GAAP or *vice versa*. However, a first-time adopter would need to take into account the guidance in IAS 8 to ensure that its choice of accounting policy results in information that is relevant and reliable. *[IAS 8.8, 10-12]*.

The requirement to prepare an opening IFRS statement of financial position and 'reset the clock' at that date poses a number of challenges for first-time adopters. Even a first-time adopter that already applies a standard that is directly based on IFRSs may need to or decide to restate items in its opening IFRS statement of financial position (see 2.3.1 above). For example, an entity applying a property, plant and equipment standard under previous GAAP that is based on IAS 16 may decide to use a deemed cost exemption for certain of its assets as allowed by IFRS 1.

3.3 Fair value and deemed cost

Some exemptions in IFRS 1 refer to 'fair value' and 'deemed cost', which the standard defines as follows: *[IFRS 1 Appendix A]*

- *Deemed cost:* An amount used as a surrogate for cost or depreciated cost at a given date. Subsequent depreciation or amortisation assumes that the entity had initially recognised the asset or liability at the given date and that its cost was equal to the deemed cost.
- *Fair value:* The price that would be received to sell an asset or paid to transfer a liability in an orderly transaction between market participants at the measurement date (see Chapter 14 and IFRS 13 – *Fair Value Measurement*).

The fair values determined by a first-time adopter should reflect the conditions that existed at the date for which they were determined, i.e. the first-time adopter should not apply hindsight in measuring the fair value at an earlier date.

3.4 Transitional provisions in other standards

The transitional provisions in other standards only apply to entities that already report under IFRSs. Therefore, a first-time adopter is not able to apply those transitional provisions (unless specified by the requirements in paragraphs 14 to 17 and Appendices B to E of IFRS 1). *[IFRS 1.9, 13, 18]*. The exceptions and the exemptions to this general rule are covered in the later parts of this chapter that deal with the exceptions to the retrospective application of other IFRSs (see 4 below) and the exemptions from other IFRSs (see 5 below).

It is important to note that the transition rules for first-time adopters and entities that already report under IFRSs may differ significantly.

The IASB considers 'case by case when it issues a new IFRS whether a first-time adopter should apply that IFRS retrospectively or prospectively. The Board expects that retrospective application will be appropriate in most cases, given its primary objective of comparability over time within a first-time adopter's first IFRS financial statements. However, if the Board concludes in a particular case that prospective application by a first-time adopter is justified, it will amend the IFRS on first-time adoption of IFRSs.' *[IFRS 1.BC14]*.

IAS 8 allows exceptions from retrospective application for entities that cannot apply a requirement after making every reasonable effort to do so. There is no such relief in IFRS 1. The Interpretations Committee agreed 'that there were potential issues, especially with respect to "old" items, such as property, plant and equipment. However, those issues could usually be resolved by using one of the transition options available in IFRS 1' (see 3.5 below).[3] For example, an entity could elect to use fair value as deemed cost at the date of transition if an entity is unable to apply IAS 36 – *Impairment of Assets* – on a fully retrospective basis (see 7.12 below). Therefore no 'impracticability relief' was added to the standard for first-time adopters. The transition options usually involve using certain surrogate values as deemed cost and are discussed at 5.5 below.

3.5 Departures from full retrospective application

IFRS 1 establishes two types of departure from the principle of full retrospective application of standards in force at the end of the first IFRS reporting period: *[IFRS 1.12]*

- it prohibits retrospective application of some aspects of other standards (the 'mandatory exceptions'); and
- it grants a number of exemptions from some of the requirements of other standards ('optional exemptions').

Mandatory exceptions: IFRS 1 prohibits retrospective application of IFRSs in some areas, particularly where this would require judgements by management about past conditions after the outcome of a particular transaction is already known. The mandatory exceptions in the standard cover the following situations: *[IFRS 1.13-17, Appendix B]*

- estimates (see 4.2 below);
- derecognition of financial assets and financial liabilities (see 4.3 below);
- hedge accounting (see 4.4 to 4.7 below);
- non-controlling interests (see 4.8 below);
- classification and measurement of financial instruments (see 4.9 below);
- impairment of financial instruments (see 4.10 below)
- embedded derivatives (see 4.11 below)
- government loans (see 4.12 below); and
- insurance contracts (see 4.13 below).

The reasoning behind most of the exceptions is that retrospective application of IFRSs in these situations could easily result in an unacceptable use of hindsight and lead to arbitrary or biased restatements, which would be neither relevant nor reliable. *[IFRS 1.BC12(b)].*

Optional exemptions: In addition to the mandatory exceptions, IFRS 1 grants limited optional exemptions from the general requirement of full retrospective application of the standards in force at the end of an entity's first IFRS reporting period, considering the fact that the cost of complying with them would be likely to exceed the benefits to users of financial statements. *[IFRS 1.BC12(a)].* The standard provides exemptions in relation to: *[IFRS 1 Appendix C, D]*

- business combinations (see 5.2 below);
- share-based payment transactions (see 5.3 below);
- insurance contracts (see 5.4 below);
- deemed cost (see 5.5 below);
- leases (see 5.6 below);
- cumulative translation differences (see 5.7 below);
- investments in subsidiaries, joint ventures and associates (see 5.8 below);
- assets and liabilities of subsidiaries, associates and joint ventures (see 5.9 below);
- compound financial instruments (see 5.10 below);
- designation of previously recognised financial instruments (see 5.11 below);
- fair value measurement of financial assets or financial liabilities at initial recognition (see 5.12 below);
- decommissioning liabilities included in the cost of property, plant and equipment (see 5.13 below);
- financial assets or intangible assets accounted for in accordance with IFRIC 12 – *Service Concession Arrangements* (see 5.14 below);
- borrowing costs (see 5.15 below);
- extinguishing financial liabilities with equity instruments (see 5.16 below);
- severe hyperinflation (see 5.17 below);
- joint arrangements (see 5.18 below);
- stripping costs in the production phase of a surface mine (see 5.19 below);
- regulatory deferral accounts (see 5.20 below);
- revenue from contracts with customers (see 5.21 below);
- foreign currency transactions and advance consideration (see 5.22 below); and
- designation of contracts to buy or sell a non-financial item (see 5.23 below).

In addition to the above, IFRS 1 grants certain exemptions that are intended to have short-term applications. These are included in Appendix E to the standard. At the time of this update, there are no short-term exemptions that apply where entity's first IFRS reporting period begins on or after 1 January 2021 (and therefore the requirements of Appendix E are not discussed in this chapter). However, the short-term exemptions may still be relevant for certain earlier reporting periods (where the first IFRS reporting period begins before 1 January 2019). First-time adopters should monitor IFRS developments for any new short-term exemptions that may be issued after the publication of this edition.

It is specifically prohibited under IFRS 1 to apply exemptions by analogy to other items. *[IFRS 1.18].*

Application of these exemptions is entirely optional, i.e. a first-time adopter can pick and choose the exemptions that it wants to apply. Importantly, the IASB did not establish a hierarchy of exemptions. Therefore, when an item is covered by more than one exemption, a first-time adopter has a free choice in determining the order in which it applies the exemptions.

Example 5.7: Order of application of exemptions

Entity A acquired a building in a business combination. If Entity A were to apply the business combinations exemption described at 5.2 below, it would at the date of transition recognise the building at the acquisition date value net of subsequent depreciation and impairment of €120. However, if it were to use the fair value as the deemed cost of the building it would have to recognise it at €150. Which value should Entity A use?

Entity A can choose whether it wants to recognise the building at €120 or €150 in its opening IFRS statement of financial position. The fact that Entity A uses the business combinations exemption does not prohibit it from also applying the 'fair value as deemed cost' exemption in relation to the same assets. Also, Entity A is not required to apply the 'fair value as deemed cost' exemption to all assets or to all similar assets as entities can choose to which assets they want to apply this exemption (see 5.5 below).

4 EXCEPTIONS TO THE RETROSPECTIVE APPLICATION OF OTHER IFRSs

4.1 Introduction

IFRS 1 provides a number of mandatory exceptions that specifically prohibit retrospective application of some aspects of other IFRSs as listed in 3.5 above. Each of the exceptions is explained in detail below.

4.2 Estimates

IFRS 1 requires an entity to use estimates under IFRSs that are consistent with the estimates made for the same date under its previous GAAP – after adjusting for any difference in accounting policy – unless there is objective evidence that those estimates were in error in accordance with IAS 8. *[IFRS 1.14, IAS 8.5]*.

Under IFRS 1, an entity must not apply hindsight and make 'better' estimates when it prepares its first IFRS financial statements. This also means that an entity is not allowed to consider subsequent events that provide evidence of conditions that existed at that date, but that came to light after the date its previous GAAP financial statements were finalised. If an estimate made under previous GAAP requires adjustment because of new information after the relevant date, an entity treats this information in the same way as a non-adjusting event after the reporting period under IAS 10 – *Events after the Reporting Period*. Effectively, the IASB wishes to prevent entities from using hindsight to 'clean up' their balance sheets as part of the preparation of the opening IFRS statement of financial position. In addition, the exception also ensures that a first-time adopter need not conduct a search for, and change the accounting for, events that might have otherwise qualified as adjusting events. *[IFRS 1.BC84]*.

IFRS 1 provides the following guidance on estimates:

- When previous GAAP required estimates of similar items for the date of transition to IFRSs, an entity can be in one of the following two positions: *[IFRS 1.IG3]*
    - its previous GAAP accounting policy was consistent with IFRSs, in which case the estimates under IFRS need to be consistent with those made for that date under previous GAAP, unless there is objective evidence that those estimates were in error under IAS 8; *[IAS 8.5]* or
    - its previous GAAP accounting policy was not consistent with IFRSs, in which case it adjusts the estimate only for the difference in accounting policies (unless there is objective evidence that those estimates were in error).

    In both situations, it accounts for the revisions to those estimates in the period in which it makes the revisions in the same way as a non-adjusting event after the reporting period under IAS 10. *[IFRS 1.15, IG3, IAS 10.10]*.

- When an entity needs to make estimates under IFRSs at the date of transition to IFRSs that were not required under its previous GAAP, those estimates should reflect conditions that existed at that date. This is consistent with the distinction in IAS 10 between adjusting events and non-adjusting events after the reporting period. In particular, estimates of market prices, interest rates or foreign exchange rates should reflect market conditions at that date. *[IFRS 1.16, IG3]*. Entities that are preparing for transition to IFRSs should consider gathering the data necessary for the estimate at the date of transition to make the transition easier and to ensure that hindsight is not incorporated into the estimate.

The requirements above apply both to estimates made in respect of the date of transition to IFRSs and to those in respect of any of the comparative periods presented, in which case the reference to the date of transition to IFRSs above are replaced by references to the end of that comparative period. *[IFRS 1.17]*.

The flowchart below shows the decision-making process that an entity needs to apply in dealing with estimates at the date of transition and during any of the comparative periods included in its first IFRS financial statements.

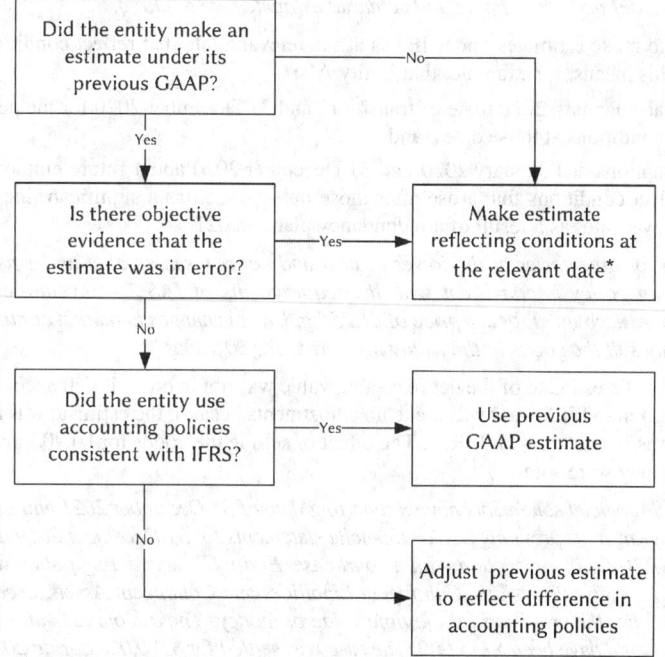

* The relevant date is the date to which the estimate relates

The general prohibition in IFRS 1 on the use of hindsight in making estimates about past transactions does not override the requirements in other IFRSs that base classifications or measurements on circumstances existing at a particular date, e.g. the distinction between finance leases and operating leases for a lessor. *[IFRS 1.IG4]*.

IFRS 1 requires an entity that is unable to determine whether a particular portion of an adjustment is a transitional adjustment or a change in estimate to treat that portion as a change in accounting estimate under IAS 8, with appropriate disclosures as required by IAS 8. *[IFRS 1.IG58B, IAS 8.32-40]*. The distinction between changes in accounting policies and changes in accounting estimates is discussed in detail in Chapter 3 at 4.2.

If a first-time adopter concludes that estimates under previous GAAP were made in error, it should distinguish the correction of those errors from changes in accounting policies in its reconciliations from previous GAAP to IFRSs (see 6.3.1 below). *[IFRS 1.26]*.

The example below illustrates how an entity should deal with estimates on the date of transition and in comparative periods included in its first IFRS financial statements. [IFRS 1.IG Example 1].

Example 5.8: Application of IFRS 1 to estimates

Entity A's first IFRS financial statements have a reporting date of 31 December 2021 and include comparative information for one year. In its previous GAAP financial statements for 31 December 2020, Entity A accounted for its pension plan on a cash basis. However, under IAS 19 – Employee Benefits – the plan is classified as a defined benefit plan and actuarial estimates are required.

Entity A will need to make estimates under IFRSs at the relevant date that reflect conditions that existed at the relevant date. This means, for example, that Entity A's:

- discount rates at 1 January 2020 (date of transition) and 31 December 2020 for the pension plan should reflect market conditions at those dates; and
- actuarial assumptions at 1 January 2020 and 31 December 2020 about future employee turnover rates should not reflect conditions that arose after those dates – such as a significant increase in estimated employee turnover rates as a result of a redundancy plan in 2021.

Entity B accounted for inventories at the lower of cost and net realisable value under its previous GAAP. Entity B's accounting policy is consistent with the requirements of IAS 2 – Inventories. Under previous GAAP, the goods were accounted for at a price of £1.25/kg. Due to changes in market circumstances, Entity B ultimately could only sell the goods in the following period for £0.90/kg.

Assuming that Entity B's estimate of the net realisable value was not in error, it will account for the goods at £1.25/kg upon transition to IFRSs and will make no adjustments because the estimate was not in error and its accounting policy was consistent with IFRSs. The effect of selling the goods for £0.90/kg will be reflected in the period in which they were sold.

Entity C's first IFRS financial statements have a reporting date of 31 December 2021 and include comparative information for one year. In its previous GAAP financial statements for 31 December 2019, Entity C accounted for a provision of $150,000 in connection with a court case. Entity C's accounting policy was consistent with the requirements of IAS 37 – Provisions, Contingent Liabilities and Contingent Assets, except for the fact that Entity C did not discount the provision for the time value of money. The discounted value of the provision at 31 December 2019 would have been $135,000. The case was settled for $190,000 during 2020.

In its opening IFRS statement of financial position at 1 January 2020, Entity C will measure the provision at $135,000. IFRS 1 does not permit an entity to adjust the estimate itself, unless it was in error, but does require an adjustment to reflect the difference in accounting policies. The unwinding of the discount and the adjustment due to the under-provision will be included in the comparative statement of profit and loss and other comprehensive income for 2020.

Entity D's first IFRS financial statements have a reporting date of 31 December 2021 and include comparative information for one year. In its previous GAAP financial statements for 31 December 2020, Entity D did not recognise a provision for a court case arising from events that occurred in September 2020. When the court case was concluded on 30 June 2021, Entity D was required to pay €1,000,000 and paid this on 10 July 2021.

In preparing its comparative statement of financial position at 31 December 2020, the treatment of the court case at that date depends on the reason why Entity D did not recognise a provision under its previous GAAP at that date.

Scenario 1 – Previous GAAP was consistent with IAS 37. At the date of preparing its 2020 financial statements, Entity D concluded that the recognition criteria were not met. In this case, Entity D's assumptions under IFRSs are to be consistent with its assumptions under previous GAAP. Therefore, Entity D does not recognise a provision at 31 December 2020 and the effect of settling the court case is reflected in the 2021 statement of profit or loss and other comprehensive income.

Scenario 2 – Previous GAAP was not consistent with IAS 37. Therefore, Entity D develops estimates under IAS 37, which requires that an entity determines whether a present obligation exists at the end of the reporting period by taking account of all available evidence, including any additional evidence provided by events after the end of the reporting period. Similarly, under IAS 10, the resolution of a court case after the end of the reporting period is an adjusting event if it confirms that the entity had a present obligation at that date. In this instance, the resolution of the court case confirms that Entity D had a liability in September 2020 (when the events occurred that gave rise to the court case). Therefore, Entity D recognises a provision at 31 December 2020. Entity D measures that provision by discounting the €1,000,000 paid on 10 July 2021 to its present value, using a discount rate that complies with IAS 37 and reflects market conditions at 31 December 2020.

Some of the potential consequences of applying IAS 37 resulting in changes in the way an entity accounts for provisions are addressed at 7.13 below.

4.3 Derecognition of financial assets and financial liabilities

IFRS 1 requires a first-time adopter to apply the derecognition requirements in IFRS 9 – *Financial Instruments* – prospectively to transactions occurring on or after the date of transition to IFRSs but a first-time adopter need not apply them retrospectively to transactions occurring before that date. For example, if a first-time adopter derecognised non-derivative financial assets or non-derivative financial liabilities under its previous GAAP as a result of a transaction that occurred before the date of transition to IFRSs, the entity shall not recognise those assets or liabilities under IFRSs unless they qualify for recognition as a result of a later transaction or event. *[IFRS 1.B2]*. However, a first-time adopter may apply the derecognition requirements in IFRS 9 retrospectively from a date of the entity's choosing, provided that the information needed to apply IFRS 9 to financial assets and financial liabilities derecognised as a result of past transactions was obtained at the time of initially accounting for those transactions. *[IFRS 1.B3]*. This will effectively prevent most first-time adopters from restating transactions that occurred before the date of transition to IFRSs.

A first-time adopter that derecognised non-derivative financial assets and financial liabilities before the date of transition to IFRSs and chose not to apply IFRS 9's derecognition requirements retrospectively from an earlier date does not recognise these items under IFRSs even if they meet the IFRS 9 recognition criteria. *[IFRS 1.IG53]*. An entity does not recognise financial assets and financial liabilities in its opening statement of financial position that do not qualify for recognition in accordance with IFRS 9, or have already qualified for derecognition in accordance with IFRS 9 through the application of paragraph B3 of IFRS 1. *[IFRS 1.B2, B3, IG54]*.

However, IFRS 1 contains no specific exceptions and exemptions to retrospective application of IFRS 10 – *Consolidated Financial Statements* – except for those for non-controlling interests (see 4.8 below). Accordingly, its consolidation requirements should be applied fully retrospectively by first-time adopters. For example, an entity may have derecognised, under its previous GAAP, non-derivative financial assets and financial liabilities when they were transferred to a structured entity as part of a securitisation programme. If that entity is considered to be a controlled entity under IFRS 10, those assets and liabilities will be re-recognised on transition to IFRSs by way of the application of IFRS 10 rather than through application of IFRS 9. Of course, if the structured entity itself then subsequently achieved derecognition of the items concerned under the entity's previous GAAP (other than by transfer to another structured entity or member of the entity's group), then the items remain derecognised on transition. Some arrangements for the transfer of assets, particularly securitisations, may last for some time, with the result that transfers might be made both before and after (or on) the date of transition to IFRSs under the same arrangement. IFRS 1 clarifies that transfers made under such arrangements fall within the first-time adoption exception only if they occurred before the date of transition to IFRSs. Transfers on or after the date of transition to IFRSs are subject to the full requirements of IFRS 9. *[IFRS 1.IG53]*.

4.4 Hedge accounting: general

From 4.4 to 4.7 below, we discuss the hedge accounting treatment for first-time adopters under IFRS 9.

First-time adoption issues relating to hedge accounting in the opening IFRS statement of financial position are discussed at 4.5 below and subsequent measurement issues are discussed in 4.6 below. Hedge accounting is dealt with comprehensively in Chapter 53.

Summary:

- If designated as a hedge relationship under previous GAAP and the hedge relationship is of a type that qualifies for hedge accounting under IFRS 9, which consists only of eligible hedging instruments and eligible hedged items in paragraph 6.4.1(a) of IFRS 9: *[IFRS 9.6.4.1(a)]*
  - an entity is required to reflect the hedge relationship in its opening IFRS statement of financial position irrespective of whether the hedge designation, documentation and effectiveness criteria for hedge accounting under IFRS 9 (paragraphs 6.4.1(b), (c)) are met on or before the date of transition; *[IFRS 1.B5, IFRS 9.6.4.1(b), 6.4.1(c)]* but
  - if the hedge designation, documentation or effectiveness criteria are not met by the date of transition, an entity must apply the requirements in IFRS 9 to discontinue hedge accounting subsequently. *[IFRS 1.B6, IFRS 9.6.5.6, 6.5.7]*.
- If designated as a hedge relationship under previous GAAP, but the hedge relationship is of a type that does not qualify for hedge accounting under IFRS 9: *[IFRS 1.B5, IFRS 9.6.4.1(a)]*
  - an entity is required to remove that relationship from its opening IFRS statement of financial position (except for the exception relating to certain net positions designated as a hedged item under previous GAAP – see 4.5.2 below).
- Regardless of the designation under previous GAAP, if the qualifying criteria for hedge accounting that comply with paragraph 6.4.1 of IFRS 9 (including hedge designation, documentation and effectiveness) are met prior to the date of transition: *[IFRS 1.B6, IG60, IFRS 9.6.4.1]*
  - hedge accounting is required from the date the qualifying criteria are met; but
  - retrospective designation under IFRS is not permitted.

4.4.1 Paragraphs B5 and B6 of IFRS 1 when applying IFRS 9

Paragraphs B5 and B6 of IFRS 1 refer to a 'hedging relationship of a type that does not qualify for hedge accounting' and the 'conditions for hedge accounting' when specifying the recognition (or otherwise) of hedge relationships in the opening IFRS statement of financial position and subsequent accounting, respectively. These descriptions were not modified to reflect requirements of IFRS 9. However, IFRS 9 does not set out hedge relationship types or conditions for hedge accounting. Instead, it sets out qualifying criteria which consist of (a) eligibility, (b) formal designation and documentation, and (c) hedge effectiveness. *[IFRS 9.6.4.1]*.

Therefore, the wording in paragraphs B5 and B6 of IFRS 1 has not been updated for IFRS 9, and IFRS 1 is relatively unclear as to whether the same two-step approach above (i.e. 'type' test and 'condition' test) continues to apply.

In our view, the IASB did not intend to change the requirements of IFRS 1 for recognising a hedging relationship in the opening IFRS statement of financial position or the subsequent accounting upon issuance of IFRS 9 and we believe that the reference to 'a hedging relationship of a type that does not qualify for hedge accounting' in paragraph B5 of Appendix B to IFRS 1 relates only to the qualifying criterion in paragraph 6.4.1(a) of IFRS 9 (i.e. eligible hedging instruments and hedged items) and the 'conditions for hedge accounting' in paragraph B6 of Appendix B to IFRS 1 relate to the qualifying criteria in paragraphs 6.4.1(b)-(c) of IFRS 9. Discussions in 4.4 to 4.7 below are based on this view.

4.4.2 Applicability of IAS 39 hedge requirements

A transition requirement of IFRS 9 for hedge accounting permits an existing IFRS user to choose as its accounting policy to continue to apply the hedge accounting requirements of IAS 39 to all of its hedge relationships instead of the requirements in Chapter 6 of IFRS 9. *[IFRS 9.7.2.21]*. First-time adopters do not have this choice because IFRS 1 prohibits first-time adopters from applying the transition provisions in other IFRSs, except as specified in Appendices B-E. *[IFRS 1.9]*. Further, paragraphs B4 to B6 of IFRS 1 contain mandatory exceptions for hedge accounting, but they do not refer to the transition requirements of IFRS 9, and the basis for conclusion attached to IFRS 9 under the heading 'Transition related to the hedge accounting requirements' states 'The IASB decided not to change the requirements of IFRS 1 for hedge accounting. The IASB noted that a first-time adopter would need to look at the entire population of possible hedging relationships and assess which ones would meet the qualifying criteria of the new hedge accounting model'. *[IFRS 9.BC7.52]*. Accordingly, a first-time adopter is not allowed to apply IAS 39 to a macro-hedging arrangement and its various components would have to be separately accounted for under IFRS 9. This is in contrast to an existing IFRS user, who would be permitted to continue to apply IAS 39 hedge accounting.

4.5 Hedge accounting in the opening IFRS statement of financial position

4.5.1 Measurement of derivatives and elimination of deferred gains and losses

Under its previous GAAP an entity's accounting policies might have included a number of accounting treatments for derivatives that formed part of a hedge relationship. For example, accounting policies might have included those where the derivative was:

- not explicitly recognised as an asset or liability (e.g. in the case of a forward contract used to hedge an expected but uncontracted future transaction);
- recognised as an asset or liability but at an amount different from its fair value (e.g. a purchased option recognised at its original cost, perhaps less amortisation; or an interest rate swap accounted for by accruing the periodic interest payments and receipts); or
- subsumed within the accounting for another asset or liability (e.g. a foreign currency denominated monetary item and a matching forward contract or swap accounted for as a 'synthetic' functional currency denominated monetary item).

Whatever the previous accounting treatment, a first-time adopter must isolate and separately account for all derivatives in its opening IFRS statement of financial position as assets or liabilities measured at fair value. *[IFRS 1.B4(a)]*.

All derivatives are measured at fair value through profit or loss, other than those that are financial guarantee contracts, a commitment to provide a loan at a below-market interest rate, a loan commitment that is subject to the impairment requirements of IFRS 9, or those that are designated and effective as hedging instruments. Accordingly, the difference between the previous carrying amount of these derivatives (which may have been zero) and their fair value should be recognised as an adjustment of the balance of retained earnings at the date of transition to IFRSs. *[IFRS 1.IG58A]*. If an entity is unable to determine whether a particular portion of an adjustment is a transition adjustment (i.e. a change in accounting policy) or a change in estimate, it must treat that portion as a change in accounting estimate, with the appropriate disclosures. *[IFRS 1.IG58B, IAS 8.32-40]*. The distinction between changes in accounting policies and changes in accounting estimates is discussed in detail in Chapter 3 at 4.2.

Hedge accounting policies under an entity's previous GAAP might also have included one or both of the following accounting treatments:

- derivatives were measured at fair value but, to the extent they were regarded as hedging future transactions, the gain (or loss) arising was reported as a liability (or asset) such as deferred (or accrued) income;
- realised gains or losses arising on the termination of a previously unrecognised derivative used in a hedge relationship (such as an interest rate swap hedging a borrowing) were included in the statement of financial position as deferred or accrued income and amortised over the remaining term of the hedged exposure.

In all cases, an entity is required to eliminate deferred gains and losses arising on derivatives that were reported in accordance with previous GAAP as if they were assets or liabilities. *[IFRS 1.B4(b)]*. In contrast to adjustments made to restate derivatives at fair value, the implementation guidance does not specify in general terms how to deal with adjustments to eliminate deferred gains or losses, i.e. whether they should be taken to retained earnings or a separate component of equity.

The requirement to eliminate deferred gains and losses does not appear to extend to those that have been included in the carrying amount of other assets or liabilities that will continue to be recognised under IFRSs. For example, under an entity's previous GAAP, the carrying amount of non-financial assets such as inventories or property, plant and equipment might have included the equivalent of a basis adjustment (i.e. hedging gains or losses were considered an integral part of the asset's cost). Of course, entities should also consider any other provisions of IFRS 1 that apply to those hedged items, e.g. whether any of the exemptions such as those for business combinations (see 5.2 below) or deemed cost (see 5.5 below) will be used.

The following diagram illustrates the treatment of hedge accounting in the opening IFRS statement of financial position and subsequent periods. Hedge accounting in the opening IFRS statement of financial position will be discussed in the sub-sections following the diagram and hedge accounting after transition to IFRSs is dealt with at 4.6 below.

First-time adoption 251

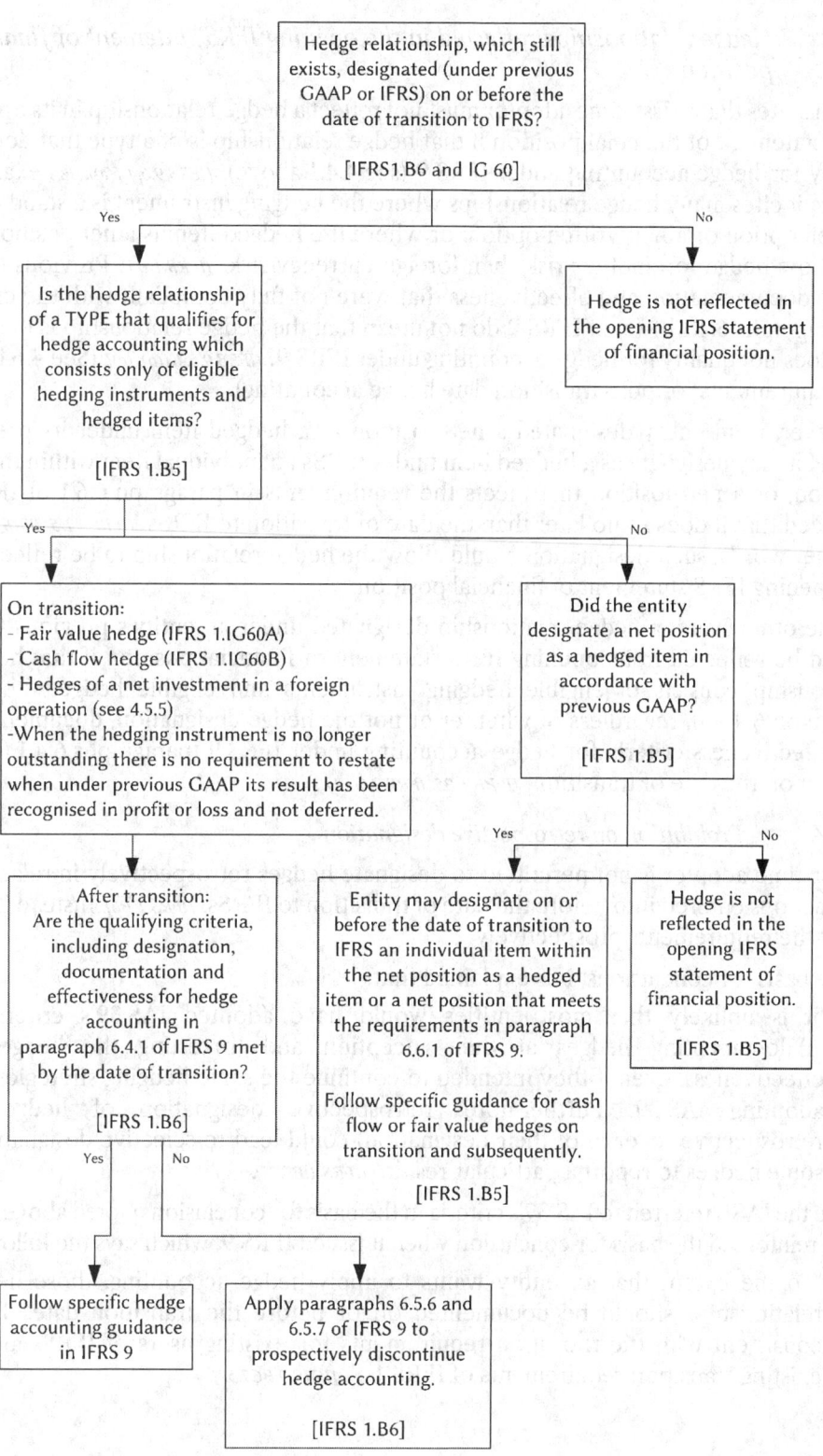

4.5.2 Hedge relationships reflected in the opening IFRS statement of financial position

IFRS 1 states that a first-time adopter must not reflect a hedge relationship in its opening IFRS statement of financial position if that hedge relationship is of a type that does not qualify for hedge accounting under IFRS 9 (see 4.4.1 above). *[IFRS 9.6.4.1(a)]*. As examples of this, it cites many hedge relationships where the hedging instrument is a stand-alone written option or a net written option; or where the hedged item is a net position in a cash flow hedge for another risk than foreign currency risk. *[IFRS 1.B5]*. Previous GAAP hedge documentation and effectiveness that were not fully compliant with the criteria in paragraphs 6.4.1(b)-(c) of IFRS 9 do not mean that the hedge relationship is of a type that does not qualify for hedge accounting under IFRS 9. *[IFRS 9.6.4.1(b), (c)]*. (See 4.6 below for requirements for post-transition date hedge accounting).

However, if an entity designated a net position as a hedged item under its previous GAAP, it may designate as a hedged item under IFRSs an individual item within that net position, or a net position that meets the requirements in paragraph 6.6.1 of IFRS 9, provided that it does so no later than the date of transition to IFRSs. *[IFRS 1.B5, IFRS 9.6.6.1]*. In other words, such designation would allow the hedge relationship to be reflected in the opening IFRS statement of financial position.

On the other hand, a hedge relationship designated under an entity's previous GAAP should be reflected in its opening IFRS statement of financial position if that hedging relationship consists of eligible hedging instruments and eligible hedged items in paragraph 6.4.1(a), regardless of whether or not the hedge designation, documentation and effectiveness criteria for hedge accounting under IFRS 9 (paragraphs 6.4.1 (b)-(c)) are met on the date of transition. *[IFRS 1.B5, IFRS 9.6.4.1]*.

4.5.2.A Prohibition on retrospective designation

A first-time adopter is not permitted to designate hedges retrospectively in relation to transactions entered into before the date of transition to IFRSs. *[IFRS 1.B6]*. Instead it must apply the requirements prospectively.

In the basis for conclusions, it is explained that:

> 'it is unlikely that most entities would have adopted IAS 39's criteria for (a) documenting hedges at their inception and (b) testing the hedges for effectiveness, even if they intended to continue the same hedging strategies after adopting IAS 39. Furthermore, retrospective designation of hedges (or retrospective reversal of their designation) could lead to selective designation of some hedges to report a particular result.' *[IFRS 1.BC75]*.

While the IASB referred to IAS 39's criteria in the basis for conclusion quoted above, it has since reinforced the basis for conclusion when it issued IFRS 9, which says the following:

> 'To the extent that an entity wants to apply hedge accounting, those hedging relationships should be documented on or before the transition date. This is consistent with the transition requirements for existing users of IFRSs and the existing transition requirements of IFRS 1...'. *[IFRS 9.BC7.52]*.

4.5.2.B Designation in anticipation of adoption of IFRSs

If a first-time adopter, in anticipation of the adoption of IFRSs, decides to designate a transaction as a hedge under IFRS 9 and completes the required documentation sometime before the date of transition to IFRS, some have questioned whether upon adoption of IFRS hedge accounting should be applied prior to the date of transition. In our view, as long as the hedge is properly designated and documented in accordance with IFRS 9.6.4.1 prior to the date of transition, the first-time adopter should apply hedge accounting from the date that it met the requirement. As explained in 4.5.2.A above, a first-time adopter cannot designate a transaction retrospectively as a hedge under IFRS. *[IFRS 1.B6]*.

4.5.3 Reflecting cash flow hedges in the opening IFRS statement of financial position

A first-time adopter may have deferred gains and losses on a cash flow hedge of a forecast transaction under its previous GAAP. If, at the date of transition, the hedged forecast transaction is not highly probable, but is expected to occur, the entire deferred gain or loss should be recognised in the cash flow hedge reserve within equity. *[IFRS 1.IG60B]*. This is consistent with the treatment required for deferred gains or losses on cash flow hedges applicable after the transition to IFRSs (other than losses not expected to be recovered) (see Chapter 53 at 7.2.1). *[IFRS 9.6.5.12]*.

How should an entity deal with such a hedge if, at the date of transition to IFRSs, the forecast transaction *is* highly probable? It would make no sense if the hedge of the transaction that is expected to occur were required to be reflected in the opening IFRS statement of financial position, but the hedge of the highly probable forecast transaction (which is clearly a 'better' hedge) were not.

Therefore, it must follow that a cash flow hedge should be reflected in the opening IFRS statement of financial position in the way set out above if the hedged item is a forecast transaction that is highly probable (see Example 5.9 below). Similarly, it follows that a cash flow hedge of the variability in cash flows attributable to a particular risk associated with a recognised asset or liability (such as all or some future interest payments on variable rate debt) should also be reflected in the opening IFRS statement of financial position. To do otherwise would allow an entity to choose not to designate (in accordance with IFRS 9) certain cash flow hedges, say those that are in a loss position, until one day after its date of transition, thereby allowing associated hedging losses to bypass profit or loss completely. However, this would effectively result in the retrospective de-designation of hedges to achieve a desired result, thereby breaching the general principle of IFRS 1 (i.e. a first-time adopter cannot designate a hedge relationship retrospectively).

If, at the date of transition to IFRSs, the forecast transaction was not expected to occur, consistent with the requirements of paragraphs 6.5.6-6.5.7 and 6.5.12(b) of IFRS 9, a first-time adopter should reclassify any related deferred gains and losses that are not expected to be recovered into retained earnings. *[IFRS 1.IG60B, IFRS 9.6.5.6-7, 6.5.12(b)]*.

Example 5.9: Unrecognised gains and losses on existing cash flow hedge

Entity A has the euro as its functional currency. In September 2019 it entered into a forward currency contract to sell dollars for euros in twelve months to hedge dollar denominated sales that it forecasts are highly probable to occur in September 2020. Entity A will apply IFRS 9 from 1 January 2020, its date of transition to IFRSs. The historical cost of the forward contract is €nil and at the date of transition it had a positive fair value of €100.

Case 1: Gains and losses deferred: Under Entity A's previous GAAP, until the sales occurred the forward contract was recognised in the statement of financial position at its fair value and the resulting gain or loss was deferred in the statement of financial position as a liability or an asset. When the sale occurred, any deferred gain or loss was recognised in profit or loss as an adjustment to the revenue recognised on the hedged sale.

This relationship must be reflected in Entity A's opening IFRS statement of financial position whether or not the hedge designation, documentation and effectiveness criteria for hedge accounting under IFRS 9 (paragraphs 6.4.1(b)-(c)) are met on the date of transition: the deferred gain should be reclassified to the cash flow hedge reserve within equity and there is no adjustment to the carrying amount of the forward contract. *[IFRS 1.IG60B]*.

Case 2: Gains and losses unrecognised: Under Entity A's previous GAAP the contract was not recognised in the statement of financial position. When the sale occurred, any unrecognised gain or loss was recognised in profit or loss as an offset to the revenue recognised on the hedged sale.

Although this Case is more problematic, we consider that it should be accounted for in the same way as Case 1. The difference between the previous carrying amount of a derivative and its fair value would be recognised in the cash flow hedge reserve within equity.

Many existing hedge relationships that were acceptable under previous GAAP may not meet the full hedge accounting requirements of paragraph 6.4.1 of IFRS 9 although the hedge relationship is of a type that qualified for hedge accounting under paragraph 6.4.1(a) of IFRS 9 and is therefore reflected in the opening IFRS statement of financial position. Also, in many such cases hedge ineffectiveness will not previously have been assessed or separately recognised in profit or loss. For cash flow hedges, ineffectiveness is not recognised in opening retained earnings but is deferred, as part of the cash flow hedge reserve within equity. As noted above, the entire unrecognised portion of the fair value of the hedging instrument is recognised in the cash flow hedge reserve in equity in the opening IFRS statement of financial position. There is no reference to the effective portion. *[IFRS 1.IG60B]*.

4.5.4 Reflecting fair value hedges in the opening IFRS statement of financial position

If a first-time adopter has, under its previous GAAP, deferred or not recognised gains and losses on a fair value hedge of a hedged item that is not measured at fair value, the entity should adjust the carrying amount of the hedged item at the date of transition. The adjustment, which is essentially the effective part of the hedge that was not recognised in the carrying amount of the hedged item under the previous GAAP, should be calculated as the lower of: *[IFRS 1.IG60A]*

(a) that portion of the cumulative change in the fair value of the hedged item that was not recognised under previous GAAP; and

(b) that portion of the cumulative change in the fair value of the hedging instrument and, under previous GAAP, was either (i) not recognised or (ii) deferred in the statement of financial position as an asset or liability.

Therefore, an entity may be required to recognise some ineffectiveness in retained earnings in the opening statement of financial position for fair value hedges, if the cumulative change in the fair value of the hedged item is lower than the unrecognised cumulative change in fair value of the hedging instrument. However, if the hedged item fair value adjustment on the date of transition is restricted by the change in fair value of the hedging instrument (i.e. where the cumulative change in the fair value of the hedged item is higher than the cumulative change in fair value of the hedging instrument), any ineffectiveness is not recognised on the date of transition.

4.5.5 Reflecting foreign currency net investment hedges in the opening IFRS statement of financial position

IFRS 1 does not provide explicit guidance on reflecting foreign currency net investment hedges in the opening IFRS statement of financial position. However, IFRS 9 requires that ongoing IFRS reporting entities account for those hedges similarly to cash flow hedges. *[IFRS 9.6.5.13]*. It follows that the first-time adoption provisions regarding cash flow hedges (see 4.5.3 above) also apply to hedges of foreign currency net investments.

Specifically, the entire deferred or unrecognised gain or loss on the hedging instrument is recognised in the currency translation adjustment on transition. This will result in some previously deferred or unrecognised gains or losses on hedging instruments not being recognised in profit or loss until the foreign operation is disposed of.

A first-time adopter that applies the exemption to reset cumulative translation differences to zero (see 5.7 below) should not reclassify pre-transition gains and losses on the hedging instruments that were recognised in equity under previous GAAP to profit or loss upon disposal of a foreign operation. Instead, those pre-transition gains and losses should be recognised in the opening balance of retained earnings to avoid a disparity between the treatment of the gains and losses on the hedged item and the hedging instrument. This means that the requirement to reset the cumulative translation differences also applies to related gains and losses on hedging instruments.

4.5.6 'Costs of hedging' (where excluded from the hedge relationship under previous GAAP)

The time value of options, forward points of forward contracts and foreign currency basis spreads (referred to as 'costs of hedging') may not have been accounted for in the manner permitted by IFRS 9. For instance, they may have been amortised under previous GAAP, regardless of the type of hedged item, being either a transaction related or a time-period related hedge. Also, the amount deferred under previous GAAP might not represent the 'aligned' value of 'costs of hedging' if the critical terms of the hedging instrument are not fully aligned with those of the hedged item (see Chapter 53 at 7.5.1.A).

By separately accruing the option time value or forward points, for example, under previous GAAP and only locking in the intrinsic or spot value of the hedged item, an entity has made a clear intention that only the intrinsic or spot value forms part of the hedge. Therefore, the special cash flow hedging rules in paragraph IG60B of the implementation guidance in IFRS 1 (see 4.5.3 above) apply purely to the full unrecognised intrinsic or spot value. *[IFRS 1.IG60B]*. Similarly, if the 'costs of hedging' had been excluded from a fair value hedge relationship, they would not form part of the adjustment to the hedging instrument taken to retained earnings required by paragraph IG60A of the implementation guidance in IFRS 1 (see 4.5.4 above).

IFRS 1 does not provide specific guidance on how to account for those 'costs of hedging' on transition to IFRSs. In our view, the same approach as applied to cash flow hedges (i.e. paragraph IG60B of the implementation guidance in IFRS 1) should also be applied to the 'costs of hedging'. *[IFRS 1.IG60B]*. The same accounting applies to 'costs of hedging' excluded from cash flow and fair value hedge relationships.

Accordingly, any previously unrecognised amount of the fair value of the option time value, forward points or foreign currency basis spread would be recognised in a separate component of equity recognised at the date of transition. Therefore, the 'costs of hedging' excluded from the hedge relationship under previous GAAP are neither recognised in the cash flow hedge reserve nor retained earnings.

In many cases, the amount of 'costs of hedging' that was amortised or deferred under previous GAAP and is recognised as a separate component of equity on transition includes accumulated differences due to the different accounting treatments under previous GAAP compared to IFRS 9 (rather than, say, representing only the aligned time value of the option, forward element or foreign currency basis spread). Any such accumulated differences are included in the amount deferred under previous GAAP and recognised in equity.

If the 'costs of hedging' were not excluded from the hedge relationship under previous GAAP, the above accounting does not apply but instead they give rise to ineffectiveness. The treatment of ineffectiveness for cash flow hedges, fair value hedges and foreign currency net investment hedges is explained in 4.5.3 to 4.5.5 above.

4.6 Hedge accounting: subsequent treatment

The implementation guidance explains that hedge accounting can be applied prospectively only from the date the hedge relationship is fully designated and documented. In other words, after the transition to IFRSs, hedge accounting under IFRS 9 can be applied only if the qualifying criteria in paragraph 6.4.1 of IFRS 9 are met. *[IFRS 9.6.4.1, 6.5.1]*. Therefore, if the hedging instrument is still held at the date of transition to IFRSs, the designation, documentation and effectiveness of a hedge relationship must be completed on or before that date if the hedge relationship is to qualify for hedge accounting from that date. *[IFRS 1.IG60]*. For further discussion on measuring ineffectiveness, see Chapter 53 at 7.4.

4.6.1 Discontinuation of a hedge relationship

Before the date of transition to IFRSs an entity may have designated as a hedge a transaction under previous GAAP that is of a type that qualifies for hedge accounting under IFRS 9, which consists only of eligible hedging instruments and eligible hedged items in paragraph 6.4.1(a), but does not meet other qualifying criteria in IFRS 9 (i.e. paragraphs 6.4.1 (b)-(c)) at the date of transition. *[IFRS 9.6.4.1]*. In this case, the entity should follow the general requirements in paragraphs 6.5.6 and 6.5.7 of IFRS 9 for discontinuing hedge accounting subsequent to the date of transition to IFRSs – these are dealt with in Chapter 53 at 8.3. *[IFRS 1.B6, IFRS 9.6.5.6-6.5.7]*.

For cash flow hedges, any net cumulative gain or loss that was reclassified to the cash flow hedge reserve on the date of transition to IFRS (see 4.5.3 above) should remain there until: *[IFRS 1.IG60B]*

(a) the forecast transaction subsequently results in the recognition of a non-financial asset or non-financial liability;
(b) the forecast transaction affects profit or loss; or
(c) subsequently circumstances change and the forecast transaction is no longer expected to occur, in which case any related net cumulative gain or loss that had been reclassified to the cash flow hedge reserve on the date of transition to IFRS is reclassified to profit or loss.

The requirements above do little more than reiterate the general requirements of IFRS 9, i.e. that hedge accounting can only be applied prospectively if the qualifying criteria are met, and entities should experience few interpretative problems in dealing with this aspect of the hedge accounting requirements.

4.6.2 Ineffectiveness of cash flow and foreign currency net investment hedges in continuing hedge relationships

Hedge accounting in accordance with IFRS 9 is applied prospectively from the date the hedge accounting is fully designated and documented. *[IFRS 1.IG60]*. Accounting for ongoing cash flow hedges and foreign currency net investment hedges is discussed in more detail in Chapter 53 at 7.2 and 7.3.

As noted at 4.5.3 and 4.5.5 above, ineffectiveness relating to cash flow and foreign currency net investment hedges reflected in the opening statement of financial position is not recognised in the opening retained earnings but is deferred, as part of the cash flow hedge reserve (or cumulative translation reserve) within equity. The entity does not recognise any past ineffectiveness deferred in equity on transition in profit or loss as ineffectiveness in subsequent periods. Rather, the entity measures ineffectiveness in subsequent periods by reference to cumulative changes in the fair value of the hedging instrument and hedged item subsequent to the date of transition (if that is the date from which the hedge relationship qualifies under IFRS 9). In order to capture the appropriate cumulative change in fair value of the hedged item, where a hypothetical derivative is used to measure ineffectiveness, the ineffectiveness recognised in profit or loss on the continuing hedge relationship is determined by reference to the hypothetical derivative where terms were set at inception of the hedge relationship, rather than on the date of transition to IFRSs. This means that the fair value movements arising on the hedged item which are used in calculating the ongoing adjustments required to the cash flow hedge reserve derive from the hypothetical derivative whose terms were set at the inception of the hedge relationship (designated under previous GAAP).

Any ineffectiveness deferred in equity on transition (as part of, say, the cash flow hedge reserve) is not subsequently recognised as ineffectiveness in the following periods. This amount will remain in equity until (a) the forecast transaction subsequently results in the recognition of a non-financial asset or non-financial liability (when the amount deferred in equity is included directly in the initial cost or other carrying amount of the asset or liability), (b) the forecast transaction affects profit or loss, or (c) subsequently circumstances change and the forecast transaction is no longer expected to occur, in which case the amount is reclassified from equity to profit or loss.

This deferral implies a discrepancy between the profit or loss impact of the hedged item and the amounts reclassified from cash flow hedge reserves under paragraphs 6.5.11(d)-6.5.12 of IFRS 9. Therefore, when the hedged item affects several periods (e.g. a hedge of variable interest on a debt instrument), it is necessary to recognise this mismatch appropriately over the hedging period.

In certain cases, no deferral of ineffectiveness will occur, (e.g. where on transition the change in fair value of the hedged item exceeds the change in fair value of the hedging derivative). In those circumstances, subsequent changes in fair value of the hedging instrument that are effective are deferred in the cash flow hedge reserve (or for a foreign currency net investment hedge, the cumulative translation reserve).

4.6.3 Ineffectiveness of fair value hedges in continuing hedge relationships

Hedge accounting in accordance with IFRS 9 is applied prospectively from the date the hedge accounting is fully designated and documented. *[IFRS 1.IG60]*. Accounting for ongoing fair value hedges is discussed in more detail in Chapter 53 at 7.1.

As noted at 4.5.4 above, if the cumulative change in the fair value of the hedged item is lower than the unrecognised cumulative change in fair value of the hedging instrument, ineffectiveness relating to fair value hedges is recognised in retained earnings on transition. However, if the hedged item fair value adjustment on transition is restricted by the change in fair value of the hedging instrument (i.e. where the cumulative change in the fair value of the hedged item is higher than the cumulative change in fair value of the hedging instrument), any ineffectiveness is not recognised on transition. This ineffectiveness not recognised on transition is not subsequently recognised in profit or loss through the next revaluation of the hedged item. For example, at the date of transition, the cumulative change in the fair value of the hedged item is £100,000 whereas the cumulative change in fair value of the hedging instrument is £80,000 (and therefore, the fair value adjustment to the hedged item is restricted to the change in fair value of the hedging instrument, i.e. £80,000). Following the date from when the hedge relationship is designated under IFRS 9, subsequent changes in the fair value of the hedged item attributable to the hedged risk and changes in the fair value of the hedging instrument would be recognised in profit or loss (without reference to the adjustment made to the hedged item on transition). *[IFRS 9.6.5.8]*. As time passes, the mechanics of fair value hedge accounting would normally result in an automatic unwinding of 100% of the cumulative fair value changes attributable to the hedged risk so that the carrying amount of the hedged item would, at any point in time, reflect fair value adjustments attributable to the hedged risk that are consistent with the remaining term of the hedge relationship. However, because at the date of transition, some of the cumulative changes in the fair value of the hedged item were not recognised, total fair value changes unwound, at any point in time, would outpace the cumulative adjustments applied to the hedged item up to that point. In this example, the hedged item carrying amount at maturity would be less than its nominal amount by £20,000 since the original adjustment on transition was £80,000 but the subsequent cumulative net change in fair value that would be recognised in profit or loss would be £100,000. In order to deal with this difference, the £20,000 would need to be amortised over the term of the hedge in profit or loss. For interest bearing hedged items, this would typically be achieved using the effective interest rate method. *[IFRS 9.6.5.10]*.

4.6.4 'Costs of hedging' (where excluded from the hedge relationship under previous GAAP)

As explained at 4.5.6 above, 'costs of hedging' that were amortised or deferred under previous GAAP, are recognised as a separate component of equity rather than retained earnings on transition, including any accumulated difference in the amount deferred under previous GAAP and the amount in accordance with IFRSs.

While IFRS 1 does not provide specific guidance on how to account for 'costs of hedging', including the difference arising on transition in subsequent periods, in our view, the same approach as applied to cash flow hedges (see 4.6.2 above) should also be applied to the 'costs of hedging'. In cases where the hedge relationship is transaction related, any amount of 'costs of hedging' on transition deferred in equity will be included directly in the initial cost or other carrying amount of a non-financial asset or a non-financial liability on its initial recognition, or reclassified to profit or loss as a reclassification adjustment in the same period or periods during which the hedged expected future cash flows affect profit or loss, depending on whether the hedged item results in a non-financial item or not. If the hedged item is time-period related, the difference will be amortised on a systematic and rational basis over the remaining hedging periods.

If the first-time adopter excludes the time value of options, forward element of forward contracts or foreign currency basis spread from the designation of the hedge relationship, prospectively under IFRS 9, and the entity is required (in the case of time value of options) or chooses (in the case of the forward element of forward contracts and foreign currency basis spreads) to apply the 'costs of hedging' guidance in IFRS 9, the 'costs of hedging' will subsequently be accounted for in accordance with paragraphs 6.5.15 and 6.5.16 of IFRS 9 and paragraphs B6.5.29-B6.5.39 of the Application Guidance to IFRS 9. If the 'costs of hedging' guidance is not chosen to apply to the forward element of forward contracts or foreign currency basis spread, movements in the fair value of the forward element or foreign currency basis spread are recognised in profit or loss. *[IFRS 9.6.5.15, 6.5.16, B6.5.29-B6.5.39].* If the first-time adopter does not exclude the 'costs of hedging' from the designation of the hedge relationship prospectively under IFRS 9, normal hedge accounting is applied but this designation will give rise to ineffectiveness to be accounted for in profit or loss. Any amounts deferred in equity for 'costs of hedging' at the date of transition (see 4.5.6 above) will be accounted for as described above. See Chapter 53 at 7.5 for further discussion of accounting for 'cost of hedging' under IFRS 9.

4.7 Hedge accounting: examples

The following examples illustrate the guidance considered at 4.5 to 4.6 above. In order to simplify the examples, these examples ignore any effects of Interbank Offered Rates (IBOR) reform.

Example 5.10:   Pre-transition cash flow hedges

Case 1: All hedge accounting qualifying criteria met from date of transition and thereafter

In 2013 Entity A borrowed €10m from a bank. The terms of the loan provide that a coupon of 3 month LIBOR plus 2% is payable quarterly in arrears and the principal is repayable in 2028. In 2016, Entity A decided to 'fix' its coupon payments for the remainder of the term of the loan by entering into a twelve-year pay-fixed, receive-floating interest rate swap. The swap has a notional amount of €10m and the floating leg resets quarterly based on 3 month LIBOR.

In Entity A's final financial statements prepared under its previous GAAP, the swap was clearly identified as a hedging instrument in a hedge of the loan and was accounted for as such. The fair value of the swap was not recognised in Entity A's statement of financial position and the periodic interest settlements were accrued and recognised as an adjustment to the loan interest expense. On 1 January 2020, Entity A's date of transition to IFRSs, the loan and the swap were still in place and the swap had a positive fair value of €1m and a €nil carrying amount. In addition, Entity A met all the qualifying criteria in IFRS 9 to permit the use of hedge accounting for this arrangement throughout 2020 and 2021.

In its opening IFRS statement of financial position Entity A should:

- recognise the interest rate swap as an asset at its fair value of €1m; and
- credit €1m to a separate component of equity, to be reclassified to profit or loss as the hedged transactions (future interest payments on the loan) affect profit or loss.

In addition, hedge accounting would be applied throughout 2020 and 2021.

Case 2: Hedge terminated prior to date of transition

The facts are as in Case 1 except that in April 2019 Entity A decided to terminate the hedge and the interest rate swap was settled for its then fair value of €1.5m. Under its previous GAAP, Entity A's stated accounting policy in respect of terminated hedges was to defer any realised gain or loss on terminated hedging instruments where the hedged exposure remained. These gains or losses would be recognised in profit or loss at the same time as gains or losses on the hedged exposure. At the end of December 2019, A's statement of financial position included a liability (unamortised gain) of €1.4m.

IFRS 1 does not explicitly address hedges terminated prior to the date of transition. However, because the terminated hedge relates to a transaction that has an ongoing risk exposure, the provisions of IFRS 9 on hedge discontinuance should be applied to this relationship. Accordingly, in its opening IFRS statement of financial position Entity A should:

- remove the deferred gain of €1.4m from the statement of financial position; and
- credit €1.4m to a separate component of equity, to be reclassified to profit or loss as the hedged transactions (future interest payments on the loan) affect profit or loss.

Example 5.11:   Existing fair value hedges

Case 1: All hedge accounting qualifying criteria met from date of transition and thereafter (1)

On 15 November 2019, Entity B entered into a forward contract to sell 50,000 barrels of crude oil to hedge all changes in the fair value of certain inventory. Entity B will apply IFRS 9 from 1 January 2020, its date of transition to IFRSs. The historical cost of the forward contract is $nil and at the date of transition the forward had a negative fair value of $50.

In Entity B's final financial statements prepared under its previous GAAP, the forward contract was clearly identified as a hedging instrument in a hedge of the inventory and was accounted for as such. The contract was recognised in the statement of financial position as a liability at its fair value and the resulting loss was deferred in the statement of financial position as an asset. In the period between 15 November 2019 and 1 January 2020 the fair value of the inventory increased by $47. In addition, Entity B met all the qualifying criteria in IFRS 9 to permit the use of hedge accounting for this arrangement throughout 2020 until the forward expired.

In its opening IFRS statement of financial position Entity B should:

- continue to recognise the forward contract as a liability at its fair value of $50;
- derecognise the $50 deferred loss asset on the forward contract;
- recognise the crude oil inventory at its historical cost plus $47 (the lower of the change in fair value of the crude oil inventory, $47, and that of the forward contract, $50); and
- record the net adjustment of $3 in retained earnings.

In addition, hedge accounting would be applied throughout 2020 until the forward contract expired.

Case 2: All hedge accounting qualifying criteria met from date of transition and thereafter (2)

In 2013 Entity C borrowed €10m from a bank. The terms of the loan provide that a coupon of 8% is payable quarterly in arrears and the principal is repayable in 2028. In 2016, Entity C decided to alter its coupon payments for the remainder of the term of the loan by entering into a twelve-year pay-floating, receive-fixed interest rate swap. The swap has a notional amount of €10m and the floating leg resets quarterly based on 3 month LIBOR.

In Entity C's final financial statements prepared under its previous GAAP, the swap was clearly identified as a hedging instrument in a hedge of the loan and accounted for as such. The fair value of the swap was not recognised in Entity C's statement of financial position and the periodic interest settlements on the swap were accrued and recognised as an adjustment to the loan interest expense.

On 1 January 2020, Entity C's date of transition to IFRSs, the loan and the swap were still in place and the swap had a negative fair value of €1m and a €nil carrying amount. The cumulative change in the fair value of the loan attributable to changes in 3 month LIBOR was €1.1m, although this change was not recognised in Entity C's statement of financial position because the loan was accounted for at amortised cost. In addition, Entity C met all the qualifying criteria in IFRS 9 to permit the use of hedge accounting for this arrangement throughout 2020 and 2021.

In its opening IFRS statement of financial position Entity C should:

- recognise the interest rate swap as a liability at its fair value of €1m; and
- reduce the carrying amount of the loan by €1m (the lower of the change in its fair value attributable to the hedged risk, €1.1m, and that of the interest rate swap, $1m) to €9m.

In addition, hedge accounting would be applied throughout 2020 and 2021.

Case 3: Hedge terminated prior to date of transition

The facts are as in Case 2 above except that in April 2019 Entity C decided to terminate the fair value hedge and the interest rate swap was settled for its then negative fair value of €1.5m. Under its previous GAAP, Entity C's stated accounting policy in respect of terminated hedges was to defer any gain or loss on the hedging instrument as a liability or an asset where the hedged exposure remained and this gain or loss was recognised in profit or loss at the same time as the hedged exposure. At the end of December 2019 the unamortised loss recognised as an asset in Entity C's statement of financial position was €1.4m. The cumulative change through April 2019 in the fair value of the loan attributable to changes in 3 month LIBOR that had not been recognised was €1.6m.

In its opening IFRS statement of financial position Entity C should:

- remove the deferred loss asset of €1.4m from the statement of financial position; and
- reduce the carrying amount of the loan by €1.4m (the lower of the change in its fair value attributable to the hedged risk, €1.6m, and the change in value of the interest rate swap that was deferred in the statement of financial position, €1.4m).

The €1.4m adjustment to the loan would be amortised to profit or loss over its remaining term.

Case 4: Documentation completed after the date of transition

The facts are as in Case 2 above except that, at the date of transition, Entity C had not prepared documentation that would allow it to apply hedge accounting under IFRS 9. Hedge documentation was subsequently prepared as a result of which the hedge qualified for hedge accounting with effect from the beginning of July 2020 and through 2021.

As in Case 2, in its opening IFRS statement of financial position Entity C should:

- recognise the interest rate swap as a liability at its fair value of €1m; and
- reduce the carrying amount of the loan by €1m (the lower of the change in its fair value attributable to the hedged risk, €1.1m, and that of the interest rate swap, €1m), because the loan was clearly identified as a hedged item.

For the period from January 2020 to June 2020, hedge accounting would not be available. Accordingly, the interest rate swap would be remeasured to its fair value and any gain or loss would be recognised in profit or loss with no offset from remeasuring the loan. The €1m adjustment to the loan would be amortised to profit or loss over its remaining term (the amortisation may begin as soon as an adjustment exists and must begin no later than when the hedged item ceases to be adjusted for hedging gains and losses). With effect from July 2020 hedge accounting would be applied prospectively.

4.8 Non-controlling interests

A first-time adopter must apply IFRS 10 retrospectively, except for the following requirements that apply prospectively from its date of transition to IFRSs: *[IFRS 1.B7]*

(a) the requirement that total comprehensive income is attributed to the owners of the parent and to the non-controlling interests even if this results in the non-controlling interests having a deficit balance; *[IFRS 10.B94]*

(b) the requirements on accounting for changes in the parent's ownership interest in a subsidiary that do not result in a loss of control; *[IFRS 10.23, B96]* and

(c) the requirements on accounting for a loss of control over a subsidiary, and the related requirements in paragraph 8A of IFRS 5 – *Non-current Assets Held for Sale and Discontinued Operations* – to classify all assets and liabilities of that subsidiary as held for sale. *[IFRS 10.B97-B99, IFRS 5.8A]*.

However, if a first-time adopter restates any business combination that occurred prior to its date of transition to comply with IFRS 3 – *Business Combinations* – it must also apply IFRS 10, including these requirements, from that date onwards (see 5.2.2 below). *[IFRS 1.C1]*.

4.9 Classification and measurement of financial instruments under IFRS 9

4.9.1 Classification of financial instruments

IFRS 9 requires a financial asset to be measured at amortised cost if it meets two tests that deal with the nature of the business model that holds the financial asset and the contractual cash flow characteristics of the financial asset. *[IFRS 9.4.1.2]*. Also, the standard requires a financial asset to be measured at fair value through other comprehensive income if certain conditions are met. *[IFRS 9.4.1.2A]*. These are described in detail in Chapter 48. Paragraph B8 of IFRS 1 requires a first-time adopter to assess whether a financial asset meets the conditions on the basis of the facts and circumstances that exist at the date of transition to IFRSs. *[IFRS 1.B8]*. The resulting classifications are applied retrospectively. *[IFRS 1.IG56]*.

4.9.1.A Assessment of a modified time value of money element

If it is impracticable to assess a modified time value of money element under paragraphs B4.1.9B-B4.1.9D of IFRS 9 on the basis of the facts and circumstances that exist at the date of transition, the first-time adopter should assess the contractual cash flow characteristics of that financial asset on the basis of the facts and circumstances that existed at that date of transition without taking into account the requirements related to the modification of the time value of money element in paragraphs B4.1.9B-B4.1.9D of IFRS 9.

In this case, the entity should also apply paragraph 42R of IFRS 7 – *Financial Instruments: Disclosures* – and disclose the carrying amount at the reporting date of the financial assets whose contractual cash flow characteristics have been assessed based on the facts and circumstances that existed at the date of transition without taking into account the requirements related to the modification of the time value of money element in paragraphs B4.1.9B-B4.1.9D of IFRS 9 until those financial assets are derecognised (see 6.4.2 below). *[IFRS 1.B8A, IFRS 7.42R, IFRS 9.B4.1.9B-B4.1.9D]*.

4.9.1.B Assessment of whether the fair value of a prepayment feature is insignificant

Similarly, if it is impracticable to assess whether the fair value of a prepayment feature is insignificant under paragraph B4.1.12(c) of IFRS 9 on the basis of the facts and circumstances that exist at the date of transition, paragraph B8B of IFRS 1 requires an entity to assess the contractual cash flow characteristics of that financial asset on the basis of the facts and circumstances that existed at that date of transition without taking into account the exception for prepayment features in paragraph B4.1.12 of IFRS 9 (see Chapter 48 at 6.4.4).

In this case, the entity should also apply paragraph 42S of IFRS 7 and disclose the carrying amount at the reporting date of the financial assets whose contractual cash flow characteristics have been assessed based on the facts and circumstances that existed at the date of transition without taking into account the exception for prepayment features in paragraph B4.1.12 of IFRS 9 until those financial assets are derecognised (see 6.4.2 below). *[IFRS 1.B8B, IFRS 7.42S, IFRS 9.B4.1.12].*

4.9.2 Measurement of financial instruments measured at amortised cost

For those financial assets and financial liabilities measured at amortised cost in the opening IFRS statement of financial position, an entity determines the gross carrying amount of the financial assets and the amortised cost of the financial liabilities on the basis of circumstances existing when the assets and liabilities first satisfied the recognition criteria in IFRS 9. However, if the entity acquired those financial assets and financial liabilities in a past business combination to which the entity elects not to apply IFRS 3 retrospectively, their carrying amount in accordance with previous GAAP immediately following the business combination is their deemed cost in accordance with IFRSs at that date. *[IFRS 1.C4(e), IG57].*

Paragraph B8C of IFRS 1 states that if it is impracticable (as defined in IAS 8) for an entity to apply retrospectively the effective interest method in IFRS 9, the fair value of the financial asset or the financial liability at the date of transition to IFRSs should be the new gross carrying amount of that financial asset or the new amortised cost of that financial liability at the date of transition to IFRSs. *[IFRS 1.B8C].*

4.9.3 Transition adjustments

An entity should treat an adjustment to the carrying amount of a financial asset or financial liability as a transition adjustment to be recognised in the opening balance of retained earnings (or another component of equity, as appropriate) at the date of transition to IFRSs only to the extent that it results from adopting IFRS 9. *[IFRS 1.IG58A].*

An investment may have been measured at fair value under previous GAAP (with revaluation gains recognised outside profit or loss). If the investment is classified as at fair value through profit or loss under IFRS 9, the pre-IFRS 9 revaluation gain that had been recognised outside profit or loss is reclassified into retained earnings on initial application of IFRS 9. If, on initial application of IFRS 9, the investment is measured at fair value through other comprehensive income in accordance with paragraph 4.1.2A of IFRS 9 or is designated at fair value through other comprehensive income in accordance with paragraph 5.7.5 of IFRS 9, then the pre-IFRS 9 revaluation gain is recognised in a separate component of equity. Subsequently, the entity recognises gains and losses on these financial assets in accordance with IFRS 9. *[IFRS 1.IG59, IFRS 9.4.1.2A, 5.7.5].*

4.10 Impairment of financial instruments under IFRS 9

Paragraph B8D of IFRS 1 requires a first-time adopter to apply the impairment requirements in Chapter 5.5 of IFRS 9 retrospectively subject to paragraphs B8E-B8G of IFRS 1. *[IFRS 1.B8D]*.

At the date of transition to IFRSs, paragraph B8E of IFRS 1 requires a first-time adopter to use reasonable and supportable information that is available without undue cost or effort (see Chapter 51 at 5.9) to determine the credit risk at the date that the financial instruments were initially recognised (or for loan commitments and financial guarantee contracts the date that the entity became a party to the irrevocable commitment in accordance with paragraph 5.5.6 of IFRS 9) and compare that to the credit risk at the date of transition to IFRSs. *[IFRS 1.B8E, IFRS 9.5.5.6, B7.2.2-B7.2.3]*.

In order to determine the loss allowance on financial instruments initially recognised (or loan commitments or financial guarantee contracts to which the entity became a party to the contract) prior to the date of transition to IFRSs, both on the transition and until the derecognition of those items an entity should consider information that is relevant in determining or approximating the credit risk at initial recognition. In order to determine or approximate the initial credit risk, an entity may consider internal and external information, including portfolio information, in accordance with paragraphs B5.5.1–B5.5.6 of IFRS 9 (see Chapter 51). *[IFRS 9.B5.5.1-B5.5.6, B7.2.3]*.

A first-time adopter may apply the following guidance to determine whether there has been a significant increase in credit risk since initial recognition: *[IFRS 1.B8F]*

(a) the requirements (on financial instruments determined to have low credit risk) in paragraphs 5.5.10 and B5.5.22–B5.5.24 of IFRS 9 (see Chapter 51 at 6.4.1); *[IFRS 9.5.5.10, B5.5.22-B5.5.24]* and

(b) the rebuttable presumption in paragraph 5.5.11 of IFRS 9 for contractual payments that are more than 30 days past due if an entity will apply the impairment requirements by identifying significant increases in credit risk since initial recognition for those financial instruments on the basis of past due information (see Chapter 51 at 6.2.2). *[IFRS 9.5.5.11]*.

A first-time adopter would not be required to make that assessment if that would require undue cost or effort. In such a case, paragraph B8G of IFRS 1 requires a first-time adopter to recognise a loss allowance at an amount equal to lifetime expected credit losses at each reporting date until that financial instrument is derecognised (unless that financial asset is low credit risk at a reporting date, in which case, paragraph B8F(a) of IFRS 1 applies and the entity may assume that the credit risk has not increased significantly since initial recognition (see Chapter 51 at 6.4.1)). *[IFRS 1.B8F(a), B8G, IFRS 9.5.5.10, 7.2.19(a), 7.2.20, B5.5.22-B5.5.24, B7.2.2]*.

4.11 Embedded derivatives

When IFRS 9 requires an entity to separate an embedded derivative from a host contract, the initial carrying amounts of the components at the date the instrument first satisfied the recognition criteria in IFRS 9 should reflect circumstances that existed at that date. If the initial carrying amounts of the embedded derivative and host contract cannot be determined reliably, the entire combined contract should be designated at fair value through profit or loss. *[IFRS 1.IG55, IFRS 9.4.3.3, 4.3.6]*.

Paragraph B9 of IFRS 1 requires a first-time adopter to assess whether an embedded derivative should be separated from the host contract and accounted for as a derivative based on conditions that existed at the later of the date it first became a party to the contract and the date a reassessment is required by IFRS 9. *[IFRS 1.B9, IFRS 9.B4.3.11]*. It should be noted that IFRS 9 does not permit embedded derivatives to be separated from host contracts that are financial assets (see Chapter 46 at 4).

4.12 Government loans

It is common practice in certain countries for the government to grant loans to entities at below-market interest rates in order to promote economic development. A first-time adopter may not have recognised and measured such loans in its previous GAAP financial statements on a basis that complies with IFRSs. IAS 20 – *Accounting for Government Grants and Disclosure of Government Assistance* – requires such loans to be recognised at fair value with the effect of the below-market interest rate separately accounted for as a government grant (see Chapter 24 at 3.4). *[IAS 20.10A]*. The IASB has provided transition relief to first-time adopters in the form of an exception that requires government loans received to be classified as a financial liability or an equity instrument in accordance with IAS 32 – *Financial Instruments: Presentation* – and to apply the requirements in IFRS 9 and IAS 20 prospectively to government loans existing at the date of transition to IFRSs. Therefore, a first-time adopter will not recognise the corresponding benefit of the government loan at a below-market rate of interest as a government grant. A first-time adopter that did not, under its previous GAAP, recognise and measure a government loan at a below-market rate of interest on a basis consistent with IFRS requirements will use its previous GAAP carrying amount of the loan at the date of transition as the carrying amount of the loan in the opening IFRS statement of financial position and apply IFRS 9 to the measurement of such loans after the date of transition to IFRSs. *[IFRS 1.B10]*.

Alternatively, an entity may apply the requirements in IFRS 9 and IAS 20 retrospectively to any government loan originated before the date of transition, provided the information needed to do so had been obtained when it initially accounted for the loan under previous GAAP. *[IFRS 1.B11]*.

The requirements and guidance above do not preclude an entity from designating previously recognised financial instruments at fair value through profit or loss (see 5.11 below). *[IFRS 1.B12, D19-D19C]*.

The requirements that a government loan with a below-market interest rate is not restated from its previous GAAP amount are illustrated in the following example. *[IFRS 1.IG Example 12]*.

Example 5.12: Government loan with below-market interest rate

A government provides loans at a below-market rate of interest to fund the purchase of manufacturing equipment.

Entity S's date of transition to IFRSs is 1 January 2020.

In 2017, Entity S received a loan of £100,000 at a below-market rate of interest from the government. Under its previous GAAP, Entity S accounted for the loan as equity and the carrying amount was £100,000 at the date of transition. The amount repayable at 1 January 2023 will be £103,030.

No other payment is required under the terms of the loan and there are no future performance conditions attached to it. The information needed to measure the fair value of the loan was not obtained at the time it was initially accounted for.

The loan meets the definition of a financial liability in accordance with IAS 32. Entity S therefore reclassifies it from equity to liability. It also uses the previous GAAP carrying amount of the loan at the date of transition as the carrying amount of the loan in the opening IFRS statement of financial position. It calculates the effective interest rate starting at 1 January 2020 at 1%. The opening balance of £100,000 will accrete to £103,030 at 31 December 2022 and interest of £1,000, £1,010 and £1,020 will be charged to interest expense in each of the three years ended 31 December 2020, 2021 and 2022.

4.13 Insurance contracts

IFRS 17 – *Insurance Contracts* – was issued in May 2017 and will be effective for annual reporting periods beginning on or after 1 January 2023 (this date has been deferred from 1 January 2021, following amendments to IFRS 17 issued in June 2020). Early application is permitted for entities that apply IFRS 9 and IFRS 15 – *Revenue from Contracts with Customers* – on or before the date of initial application of IFRS 17.

An entity must apply the transition provisions in paragraphs C1 to C24 and C28 in Appendix C of IFRS 17 to contracts within the scope of IFRS 17 (see Chapter 56 at 17). The references in those paragraphs in IFRS 17 to the date of transition must be read as the date of transition to IFRSs. *[IFRS 1.B13]*. Therefore, first time adopters and entities moving from IFRS 4 – *Insurance Contracts* – will apply the same transition rules. This is because the Board saw no reason to give different transition approaches to first-time adopters of IFRSs from other entities. The Board decided not to give any additional relief on the restatement of comparative amounts from that already in IFRS 1. *[IFRS 17.BC407]*.

5 OPTIONAL EXEMPTIONS FROM THE REQUIREMENTS OF CERTAIN IFRSs

5.1 Introduction

As noted at 3.5 above, IFRS 1 grants limited optional exemptions from the general requirement of full retrospective application of the standards effective at the end of an entity's first IFRS reporting period. *[IFRS 1.7, 12(b)]*. Each of these exemptions, which are set out in Appendices C and D of IFRS 1 is explained in detail below.

5.2 Business combinations and acquisitions of associates and joint arrangements

The business combinations exemption in IFRS 1 is probably the single most important exemption in the standard, as it permits a first-time adopter not to restate business combinations that occurred prior to its date of transition to IFRSs. The detailed guidance on the application of the business combinations exemption is contained in Appendix C to IFRS 1 and is organised in the sections as follows: *[IFRS 1 Appendix C]*

- option to restate business combinations retrospectively (see 5.2.2 below);
- classification of business combinations (see 5.2.3 below);
- recognition and measurement of assets and liabilities (see 5.2.4 below);
- restatement of goodwill (see 5.2.5 below);
- currency adjustments to goodwill (see 5.2.6 below);
- previously unconsolidated subsidiaries (see 5.2.7 below);

- previously consolidated entities that are not subsidiaries (see 5.2.8 below);
- measurement of deferred taxes and non-controlling interests (see 5.2.9 below); and
- transition accounting for contingent consideration (see 5.2.10 below).

In our view, the business combinations exemption applies only to business combinations that occurred before the date of transition to IFRSs and only to business combinations as defined under IFRS 3 (see 5.2.1 below). *[IFRS 1 Appendix C]*. Therefore, it does not apply to a transaction that, for example, IFRSs treat as an acquisition of an asset (see 5.2.1.A below).

5.2.1 Definition of a 'business' under IFRS 3

As noted above, the business combinations exemption applies only to business combinations as defined under IFRS 3. Therefore, a first-time adopter needs to consider whether past transactions would qualify as business combinations under IFRS 3. That standard defines a business combination as 'a transaction or other event in which an acquirer obtains control of one or more businesses. Transactions sometimes referred to as "true mergers" or "mergers of equals" are also business combinations as that term is used in this IFRS.' *[IFRS 3 Appendix A]*. The definition of a business, which was amended in 2018, is 'an integrated set of activities and assets that is capable of being conducted and managed for the purpose of providing goods or services to customers, generating investment income (such as dividends or interest) or generating other income from ordinary activities.' *[IFRS 3 Appendix A]*. In addition, IFRS 3 states that 'if the assets acquired are not a business, the reporting entity shall account for the transaction or other event as an asset acquisition' (see 5.2.1.A below). *[IFRS 3.3]*. Distinguishing a business combination from an asset acquisition is described in detail in Chapter 9 at 3.

In October 2012, the IASB issued *Investment Entities (Amendments to IFRS 10, IFRS 12 and IAS 27)* (see 5.9.5 below). Amongst other changes, the amendment also stated that Appendix C of IFRS 1, which deals with the business combinations exemption, should be applied only to business combinations within the scope of IFRS 3. *[IFRS 1 Appendix C]*. In our view, the purpose of this change is to preclude the application of Appendix C to the acquisition by an investment entity, as defined in IFRS 10, of an investment in subsidiary that is required to be measured at fair value through profit or loss. *[IFRS 3.2A]*.

Therefore, we believe that the exemption is still available to transactions that meet the definition of a business combination under IFRS 3, even if the business combination is outside the scope of IFRS 3 (such as a combination of entities or businesses under common control).

However, the business combinations exemption does not apply to transactions which are not business combinations as defined in IFRS 3 (even if the transactions were accounted for as business combinations under previous GAAP). Examples of transactions that are not business combinations would include asset transactions (see 5.2.1.A below) or continuations (such as where a new holding company is inserted above an existing group). A first-time adopter which had such transactions under previous GAAP should retrospectively apply IFRSs applicable to those transactions. If transactions which are not business combinations as defined in IFRS 3 are combinations of entities under common control, there is no specific guidance under IFRS on accounting for them. We discuss this issue in Chapter 10 at 1.2, 1.3, 2 and 4.

5.2.1.A   Asset acquisitions

Because IFRS 3 provides such a specific definition of a business combination (as described in Chapter 9 at 3), it is possible that under some national GAAPs, transactions that are not business combinations under IFRS 3, e.g. asset acquisitions, may have been accounted for as if they were business combinations. If so, a first-time adopter will need to restate such transactions, as discussed in the following example.

Example 5.13:   Acquisition of assets

Entity A acquired a company that held a single asset at the time of acquisition. That company had no employees and the asset itself was not in use at the date of acquisition. Entity A accounted for the transaction under its previous GAAP using the purchase method, which resulted in goodwill. Can Entity A apply the business combinations exemption to the acquisition of this asset?

If Entity A concludes that the asset is not a business as defined in IFRS 3, it will not be able to apply the business combinations exemption. Instead, Entity A should account for such transaction as an asset acquisition (see Chapter 9 at 2.2.2). Entity A may consider applying other applicable optional exemptions under IFRS 1.

If, in the example above, the entity had accounted for the transaction as an asset acquisition rather than a business combination under previous GAAP, it would need to determine whether the transaction meets the definition of a business combination in IFRS 3 in order to qualify for use of the exemption.

5.2.2   Option to restate business combinations retrospectively

A first-time adopter must account for business combinations occurring after its date of transition under IFRS 3, i.e. any business combinations during the comparative periods presented need to be restated in accordance with IFRS 3.

A first-time adopter may elect not to apply IFRS 3 retrospectively to business combinations occurring before the date of transition. However, if a first-time adopter does restate a business combination occurring prior to its date of transition to comply with IFRS 3 it must also restate any subsequent business combinations under IFRS 3 and apply IFRS 10 from that date onwards. *[IFRS 1.C1]*. In other words, as shown on the timeline below, a first-time adopter is allowed to choose any date in the past from which it wants to account for all business combinations under IFRS 3 and would not restate business combinations that occurred prior to such date. It must be noted that a first-time adopter availing itself of this option is required to apply the version of IFRS 3 effective at the end of its first IFRS reporting period to any retrospectively restated business combinations. *[IFRS 1.7]*.

If any pre-transition business combinations are restated, the first-time adopter must also apply IFRS 10's requirements on: the attribution of total comprehensive income to the owners of the parent and to the non-controlling interests; accounting for changes in the parent's ownership interest in a subsidiary without loss of control; and accounting for a loss of control of a subsidiary (and the related IFRS 5 requirements on classification of the disposal group as 'held for sale') from the date of the earliest business combination that is restated (see 4.8 above). *[IFRS 1.B7, C1]*.

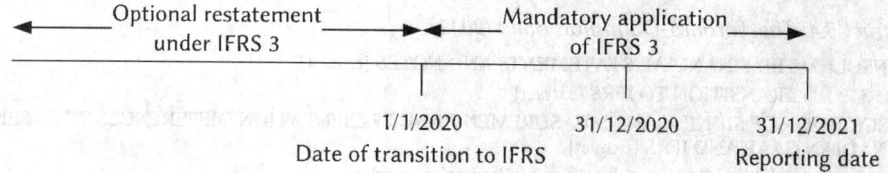

Even if a first-time adopter elects not to restate certain business combinations, it may still need to restate the carrying amounts of the acquired assets and assumed liabilities, as described at 5.2.4 below.

Although there is no restriction that prevents retrospective application by a first-time adopter of IFRS 3 to all past business combinations, in our opinion, a first-time adopter should not restate business combinations under IFRS 3 that occurred before the date of transition when this would require use of hindsight.

Extract 5.3 below and Extract 5.12 at 6.3 below illustrate the typical disclosure made by entities that opted not to restate business combinations that occurred before their date of transition to IFRSs, while Extract 5.4 below illustrates disclosures by an entity that chose to restate certain business combinations that occurred prior to its date of transition.

Extract 5.3: Husky Energy Inc. (2011)

Notes to the Consolidated Financial Statements[extract]

Note 26 First-Time Adoption of International Financial Reporting Standards [extract]

Key First-Time Adoption Exemptions Applied [extract]

IFRS 1, "First-Time Adoption of International Financial Reporting Standards," allows first-time adopters certain exemptions from retrospective application of certain IFRSs.

The Company applied the following exemptions: [extract]

[...]

- IFRS 3, "Business Combinations," was not applied to acquisitions of subsidiaries or interests in joint ventures that occurred before January 1, 2010.

[...]

i) IFRS 3 Adjustments – *Business Combinations* [extract]

Given that the Company elected to apply the IFRS 1 exemption which permits no adjustments to amounts recorded for acquisitions that occurred prior to January 1, 2010, no retrospective adjustments were required. The Company acquired the remaining interest in the Lloydminster Upgrader from the Government of Alberta in 1995 and is required to make payments to Natural Resources Canada and Alberta Department of Energy from 1995 to 2014 based on average differentials between heavy crude oil feedstock and the price of synthetic crude oil sales. Under IFRS, the Company is required to recognize this contingent consideration at its fair value as part of the acquisition and record a corresponding liability. Under Canadian GAAP, any contingent consideration was not required to be recognized unless amounts were resolved and payable on the date of acquisition. On transition to IFRS, Husky recognized a liability of $85 million, based on the fair value of remaining upside interest payments, with an adjustment to opening retained earnings. For the year ended December 31, 2010, the Company recognized pre-tax accretion of $9 million in finance expenses under IFRS. Changes in forecast differentials used to determine the fair value of the remaining upside interest payments resulted in the recognition of a pre-tax gain of $41 million for the year ended December 31, 2010.

Extract 5.4: The Toronto-Dominion Bank (2011)
CONSOLIDATED FINANCIAL STATEMENTS AND NOTES [extract]
Note 34   TRANSITION TO IFRS [extract]
DESCRIPTION OF SIGNIFICANT MEASUREMENT AND PRESENTATION DIFFERENCES BETWEEN CANADIAN GAAP AND IFRS [extract]
(d)   *Business Combinations: Elective Exemption* [extract]

As permitted under IFRS transition rules, the Bank has applied IFRS 3, *Business Combinations* (IFRS 3) to all business combinations occurring on or after January 1, 2007. Certain differences exist between IFRS and Canadian GAAP in the determination of the purchase price allocation. The most significant differences are described below.

Under Canadian GAAP, an investment in a subsidiary which is acquired through two or more purchases is commonly referred to as a "step acquisition". Each transaction is accounted for as a step-by-step purchase, and is recognized at the fair value of the net assets acquired at each step. Under IFRS, the accounting for step acquisitions differs depending on whether a change in control occurs. If a change in control occurs, the acquirer remeasures any previously held equity investment at its acquisition-date fair value and recognizes any resulting gain or loss in the Consolidated Statement of Income. Any transactions subsequent to obtaining control are recognized as equity transactions.

Under Canadian GAAP, shares issued as consideration are measured at the market price over a reasonable time period before and after the date the terms of the business combination are agreed upon and announced. Under IFRS, shares issued as consideration are measured at their market price on the closing date of the acquisition.

Under Canadian GAAP, an acquirer's restructuring costs to exit an activity or to involuntarily terminate or relocate employees are recognized as a liability in the purchase price allocation. Under IFRS, these costs are generally expensed as incurred and not included in the purchase price allocation.

Under Canadian GAAP, costs directly related to the acquisition (i.e. finder fees, advisory, legal, etc.) are included in the purchase price allocation, while under IFRS these costs are expensed as incurred and not included in the purchase price allocation.

Under Canadian GAAP, contingent consideration is recorded when the amount can be reasonably estimated at the date of acquisition and the outcome is determinable beyond reasonable doubt, while under IFRS contingent consideration is recognized immediately in the purchase price equation at fair value and marked to market as events and circumstances change in the Consolidated Statement of Income.

The impact of the differences between Canadian GAAP and IFRS to the Bank's IFRS opening Consolidated Balance Sheet is disclosed in the table below.

Business Combinations: Elective Exemption

(millions of Canadian dollars)	As at Nov. 1, 2010
Increase/(decrease) in assets:	
Available-for-sale securities	(1)
Goodwill	(2,147)
Loans – residential mortgages	22
Loans – consumer instalment and other personal	–
Loans – business and government	–
Intangibles	(289)
Land, buildings and equipment and other depreciable assets	2
Deferred tax assets	(12)
Other assets	104
(Increase)/decrease in liabilities:	
Deferred tax liabilities	102
Other liabilities	37
Subordinated notes and debentures	2
Increase/(decrease) in equity	(2,180)

The total impact of business combination elections to the Bank's IFRS opening equity was a decrease of $2,180 million, comprised of a decrease to common shares of $926 million, a decrease to contributed surplus of $85 million and a decrease to retained earnings of $1,169 million.

5.2.2.A Associates and joint arrangements

The exemption for past business combinations applies also to past acquisitions of investments in associates, interests in joint ventures and interests in joint operations (in which the activity of the joint operation constitutes a business, as defined in IFRS 3). The date selected for the first restatement of business combinations will also be applied to the restatement of these other acquisitions. *[IFRS 1.C5]*.

The application of the business combination exemptions in IFRS 1 has the following consequences for that business combination (see 5.2.3 to 5.2.10 below).

5.2.3 Classification of business combinations

IFRS 3 mandates a business combination to be accounted for either as an acquisition or reverse acquisition. *[IFRS 3.4, 5, B19]*. An entity's previous GAAP may be based on a different definition of, for example, a business combination, an acquisition, a uniting of interests (or merger) and a reverse acquisition. An important benefit of the business combinations exemption is that a first-time adopter will not have to determine the classification of past business combinations in accordance with IFRS 3. *[IFRS 1.C4(a)]*. For example, a business combination that was accounted for as a merger (or uniting of interests) using the pooling-of-interests method under an entity's previous GAAP will not have to be reclassified and accounted for under the acquisition method, nor will a restatement be required if the business combination would have been classified under IFRS 3 as a reverse acquisition by the acquiree. However, an entity may still elect to do so if it so wishes without using hindsight (see 5.2.2 above). *[IFRS 1.C1]*.

5.2.4 Assets and liabilities to be recognised in the opening IFRS statement of financial position

In its opening IFRS statement of financial position, a first-time adopter should recognise all assets acquired and liabilities assumed in a past business combination, with the exception of: *[IFRS 1.C4(b)]*

- certain financial assets and liabilities that were derecognised in accordance with previous GAAP and that fall under the derecognition exception (see 4.3 above); *[IFRS 1.B2]* and
- assets (including goodwill) and liabilities that were not recognised in the acquirer's consolidated statement of financial position under its previous GAAP and that would not qualify for recognition under IFRSs in the separate statement of financial position of the acquiree (see 5.2.4.B and Example 5.15 below).

The entity must exclude items it recognised under its previous GAAP that do not qualify for recognition as an asset or liability under IFRSs (see 5.2.4.A and Example 5.14 below).

5.2.4.A Assets and liabilities to be excluded

If the first-time adopter recognised under its previous GAAP items that do not qualify for recognition under IFRSs, these must be excluded from the opening IFRS statement of financial position.

An intangible asset, acquired as part of a business combination, that does not qualify for recognition as an asset under IAS 38 – *Intangible Assets* – should be derecognised, with the related deferred tax and non-controlling interests, with an offsetting change to goodwill, unless the entity previously deducted goodwill directly from equity under its previous GAAP (see 5.2.5 below).

All other changes resulting from derecognition of such assets and liabilities should be accounted for as adjustments of retained earnings or another category of equity, if appropriate. *[IFRS 1.C4(c)]*. For example:

- Any restructuring provisions recognised under previous GAAP and which remain at the date of transition to IFRS will need to be assessed against the IFRS recognition criteria. If the criteria are not met, then the provisions must be reversed against retained earnings.
- If an entity has deferred transaction costs (for which the services were received) relating to a business combination that has not been finalised under previous GAAP at the date of transition to IFRS, these deferred transaction costs would need to be recognised in retained earnings as they do not qualify for deferral under IFRSs.
- Assets and liabilities of a structured entity required to be consolidated under previous GAAP but that does not qualify for consolidation under IFRS 10 must be deconsolidated.

Example 5.14 below, which is based on one within the implementation guidance in IFRS 1, illustrates the exclusion of a restructuring provision that did not comply with IFRSs from the opening statement of financial position. *[IFRS 1.IG Example 3]*.

Example 5.14: Restructuring provision

Background

Entity A's first IFRS financial statements are for a period that ends on 31 December 2021 and include comparative information for 2020 only. It chooses not to restate previous business combinations under IFRSs. On 1 July 2019, Entity A acquired 100 per cent of Entity B. Under its previous GAAP, Entity A recognised an (undiscounted) restructuring provision of ¥100 million that would not have qualified as an identifiable liability under IFRS 3. The recognition of this restructuring provision increased goodwill by ¥100 million. At 1 January 2020 (date of transition to IFRSs), Entity A:

(a) had paid restructuring costs of ¥60 million; and
(b) estimated that it would pay further costs of ¥40 million in 2020 and that the effects of discounting were immaterial. At 1 January 2020, those further costs did not qualify for recognition as a provision under IAS 37.

Application of requirements

In its opening IFRS statement of financial position, Entity A:

(a) does not recognise a restructuring provision in respect of the outstanding ¥40 million provision under previous GAAP. The adjustment is recognised in retained earnings. *[IFRS 1.C4(c)]*.
(b) does not adjust the amount assigned to goodwill. However, Entity A tests the goodwill for impairment under IAS 36 and recognises any resulting impairment loss. *[IFRS 1.C4((g)]*.

5.2.4.B Recognition of assets and liabilities

An asset acquired or a liability assumed in a past business combination may not have been recognised under the entity's previous GAAP. However, this does not mean that such items have a deemed cost of zero in the opening IFRS statement of financial position. Instead, the acquirer recognises and measures those items in its opening IFRS statement of financial position on the basis that IFRSs would require in the statement of financial position of the acquiree. *[IFRS 1.C4(f)]*.

For example, if the acquirer had not recognised an assumed contingent liability under its previous GAAP that still exists at the date of transition to IFRSs, the acquirer should recognise that contingent liability at that date unless IAS 37 would prohibit its recognition in the financial statements of the acquiree. *[IFRS 1.C4(f)].*

The change resulting from the recognition of such assets and liabilities should be accounted for as an adjustment of retained earnings or another category of equity, if appropriate. However, if the change results from the recognition of an intangible asset that was previously subsumed within goodwill, it should be accounted for as an adjustment of that goodwill (and of the related deferred tax and non-controlling interests, if any) (see 5.2.5 below). *[IFRS 1.C4(b), C4(g)(i), C4(k)].*

Intangible assets acquired as part of a business combination that were not recognised under a first-time adopter's previous GAAP will rarely be recognised in the opening IFRS statement of financial position because either: (1) they cannot be capitalised in the acquiree's own statement of financial position under IAS 38; or (2) capitalisation would require the use of hindsight which is not permitted under IAS 38 (see 7.14 below).

Example 5.15:   Items not recognised under previous GAAP

Entity A acquired Entity B but did not recognise Entity B's right-of-use assets and internally generated customer lists under its previous GAAP.

Upon first-time adoption of IFRSs, Entity A recognises the right-of-use assets in its opening IFRS statement of financial position using the amounts that Entity B would recognise in its separate statement of financial position. The resulting adjustment to the net assets at the date of transition is reflected in retained earnings; goodwill is not restated to reflect the net assets that would have been recognised at the date of acquisition (see 5.2.5 below). However, Entity A does not recognise the customer lists in its opening IFRS statement of financial position, because Entity B is not permitted to capitalise internally generated customer lists under IAS 38. Any value that might have been attributable to the customer lists would remain subsumed in goodwill in A's opening IFRS statement of financial position.

Entity C acquired Entity D but did not recognise Entity D's brand name as a separate intangible asset under its previous GAAP.

Upon first-time adoption of IFRSs, Entity C will not recognise D's brand name in its opening IFRS statement of financial position because Entity D would not have been permitted under IAS 38 to recognise it as an asset in its own separate statement of financial position. Again, any value that might have been attributable to the brand name would remain subsumed in goodwill in Entity C's opening IFRS statement of financial position.

Example 5.16 below, which is based on one within the implementation guidance in IFRS 1, illustrates the capitalisation of leases that would be required under IFRS 16, but were not capitalised under the previous GAAP. *[IFRS 1.IG Example 7].*

Example 5.16:   Lease in which the acquiree was a lessee not capitalised in accordance with previous GAAP

Entity E's date of transition to IFRSs is 1 January 2020. Entity E acquired Entity F on 15 January 2014 and did not capitalise leases in which Entity F was a lessee. If Entity F prepared financial statements in accordance with IFRSs, it would recognise lease liabilities of £300,000 and right-of-use assets of £250,000 at 1 January 2020.

Entity E has elected not to apply the transition reliefs in paragraphs D9 and D9B–D9E of IFRS 1. *[IFRS 1.D9, D9B-D9E].* In its consolidated opening IFRS statement of financial position, Entity E recognises lease liabilities of £300,000 and right-of-use assets of £250,000, and charges £50,000 to retained earnings. *[IFRS 1.C4(f)].*

5.2.4.C Previous GAAP carrying amount as deemed cost

For assets and liabilities that are accounted for on a cost basis under IFRSs, the carrying amount in accordance with previous GAAP of assets acquired and liabilities assumed in that business combination is their deemed cost immediately after the business combination. This deemed cost is the basis for cost-based depreciation or amortisation from the date of the business combination. *[IFRS 1.C4(e)].*

The standard does not specifically define 'immediately after the business combination', but it is commonly understood that this takes account of the final determination of the purchase price allocation and final completion of purchase accounting. In other words, a first-time adopter would not use the provisionally determined fair values of assets acquired and liabilities assumed in applying the business combinations exemption.

Example 5.17: Provisionally determined fair values

Entity A acquired Entity B in August 2019 and made a provisional assessment of Entity B's identifiable net assets in its 31 December 2019 consolidated financial statements under its previous GAAP. In its 31 December 2020 consolidated financial statements – its last financial statements under previous GAAP – Entity A completed the initial accounting for the business combination and adjusted the provisional values of the identifiable net assets and the corresponding goodwill. Upon first-time adoption of IFRSs, Entity A elects not to restate past business combinations.

In preparing its opening IFRS statement of financial position as of 1 January 2020, Entity A should use the adjusted carrying amounts of the identifiable net assets as determined in its 2020 financial statements rather than the provisional carrying amounts of the identifiable net assets and goodwill at 31 December 2019.

IFRS 1 is silent as to whether the relevant carrying amounts of the identifiable net assets and goodwill are those that appeared in the financial statements drawn up immediately before the date of transition or any restated balance appearing in a later set of previous GAAP accounts. Since the adjustments that were made under previous GAAP effectively resulted in a restatement of the balances at the date of transition in a manner that is consistent with the approach permitted by IFRSs, it is in our view appropriate to reflect those adjustments in the opening IFRS statement of financial position. Since the adjustments are effectively made as at the date of transition, it is also appropriate to use the window period permitted by previous GAAP provided that this does not extend into the first IFRS reporting period. This is because any restatements in that period can only be made in accordance with IFRS 3. In effect, the phrase 'immediately after the business combination' in paragraph C4(e) of IFRS 1 should be interpreted as including a window period allowed by the previous GAAP that ends at the earlier of the end of the window period and the beginning of the first IFRS reporting period.

Although the use of cost-based measurements under previous GAAP might be considered inconsistent with the requirements of IFRSs for assets and liabilities that were not acquired in a business combination, the IASB did not identify any situations in a business combination in which it would not be acceptable to bring forward cost-based measurements made under previous GAAP. *[IFRS 1.BC36].* For example, assume an entity that adopts IFRSs with a date of transition of 1 January 2020 and, as required, applies IFRS 3 to business combinations occurring on or after 1 January 2020. Under the entity's previous GAAP, it acquired a business in 2014 and the purchase accounting resulted in negative goodwill. At that time, the negative goodwill was eliminated by reducing the amounts assigned to long-lived assets (PP&E and intangible assets) on a *pro rata* basis.

In this situation, the negative goodwill adjustment to PP&E and intangible assets is 'grandfathered' and is not adjusted in the opening IFRS statement of financial position. The negative goodwill adjustment to PP&E and intangible assets was part of the original purchase accounting and is not a subsequent measurement difference between completing the purchase price allocation and 1 January 2020 and therefore the adjustment forms part of the deemed cost of PP&E and intangible assets.

By contrast, under previous GAAP, the entity may have recognised amortisation of intangible assets from the date of acquisition. If this amortisation is not in compliance with IAS 38, it is not 'grandfathered' under the business combination exemption and therefore should be amended to the amount that complies with IFRSs on transition (note that the adjusted carrying amount should be tested for impairment if there are impairment indicators pursuant to the requirements of IAS 36 at the date of transition; see 7.12 below).

Example 5.18: Items measured on a cost basis

Entity C applies the business combination exemption under IFRS 1. In a business combination Entity C acquired property, plant and equipment, inventory and accounts receivable. Under its previous GAAP, Entity C initially measured these assets at cost (i.e. their fair value at the date originally acquired).

Upon adoption of IFRSs, Entity C determines that its accounting policy for these assets under its previous GAAP complied with the requirements of IFRSs. Therefore, property, plant and equipment, inventory and accounts receivable are not adjusted but recognised in the opening IFRS statement of financial position at the carrying amount under the previous GAAP.

5.2.4.D In-process research and development

IFRS 1 makes it clear that in-process research and development (IPR&D) that was included within goodwill under an entity's previous GAAP should not be recognised separately upon transition to IFRSs unless it qualifies for recognition under IAS 38 in the statement of financial position of the acquiree. *[IFRS 1.C4(h)(i)]*. However, IFRS 1 is silent on the treatment of IPR&D that was identified separately by an entity under the business combinations accounting standard of its previous GAAP, but which was immediately written off to profit or loss.

There are two possible scenarios. If previous GAAP requires IPR&D to be written off as an integral part of the business combination accounting under that GAAP then the carrying amount of IPR&D 'immediately after the business combination' would be zero. While we understand that there may be different views, it is our view that IFRS 1 does not allow reinstatement of the amount of IPR&D that was previously written off under this scenario.

However, if that write-off is not an integral part of the business combination accounting (e.g. the previous GAAP merely requires accelerated amortisation) then the carrying amount 'immediately after the business combination' would be the amount allocated to IPR&D by the business combinations standard under previous GAAP. In our view, reinstatement of the amount of IPR&D that was written off under this scenario is appropriate.

The above distinction may be largely irrelevant if the business combination takes place several years before the transition to IFRSs because, in practice, the IPR&D may have been amortised fully or may be impaired before the date of transition.

5.2.4.E Subsequent measurement under IFRSs not based on cost

IFRSs require subsequent measurement of some assets and liabilities on a basis other than original cost, such as fair value for certain financial instruments or on specific measurement bases for share-based payments (IFRS 2) and employee benefits (IAS 19). Even if a first-time adopter does not apply IFRS 3 retrospectively to a business combination, such assets and liabilities must be measured on that other basis in its opening IFRS statement of financial position. Any change in the carrying amount of those assets and liabilities should be accounted for as an adjustment of retained earnings, or other appropriate category of equity, rather than as an adjustment of goodwill. [IFRS 1.C4(d)].

Example 5.19: Items not measured at original cost

Entity A acquired in a business combination a trading portfolio of equity securities and a number of investment properties. Under its previous GAAP, Entity A initially measured these assets at historical cost (i.e. their fair value at the date of original acquisition).

Upon adoption of IFRSs, Entity A measures the trading portfolio of equity securities and the investment properties at fair value in its opening IFRS statement of financial position. The resulting adjustment to these assets at the date of transition is reflected in retained earnings.

5.2.4.F Example of recognition and measurement requirements

The following example, which is based on one within the implementation guidance in IFRS 1, illustrates many of the requirements discussed above. [IFRS 1.IG Example 2].

Example 5.20: Business combination example

Background

Entity A's first IFRS financial statements are for a reporting period that ends on 31 December 2021 and include comparative information for 2020 only. On 1 July 2017, Entity A acquired 100 per cent of Entity B. Under its previous GAAP, Entity A:

(a) classified the business combination as an acquisition by Entity A;

(b) measured the assets acquired and liabilities assumed at the following amounts under previous GAAP at 1 January 2020 (date of transition to IFRSs):

  (i) identifiable assets less liabilities for which IFRSs require cost-based measurement at a date after the business combination: €200 (with a tax base of €150 and an applicable tax rate of 30 per cent);

  (ii) pension liability (for which the present value of the defined benefit obligation measured under IAS 19 is €130 and the fair value of plan assets is €100): €nil (because Entity A used a pay-as-you-go cash method of accounting for pensions under its previous GAAP). The tax base of the pension liability is also €nil;

  (iii) goodwill: €180;

(c) did not, at the date of acquisition, recognise deferred tax arising from temporary differences associated with the identifiable assets acquired and liabilities assumed.

In its opening (consolidated) IFRS statement of financial position, Entity A decided to apply the business combination exemptions and as a result:

(i) classifies the business combination as an acquisition by Entity A even if the business combination would have qualified under IFRS 3 as a reverse acquisition by Entity B; [IFRS 1.C4(a)]

(ii) does not adjust the accumulated amortisation of goodwill. Entity A tests the goodwill for impairment under IAS 36 and recognises any resulting impairment loss, based on conditions that existed at the date of transition to IFRSs. If no impairment exists, the carrying amount of the goodwill remains at €180; [IFRS 1.C4(g)]

(iii) for those net identifiable assets acquired for which IFRSs require cost-based measurement at a date after the business combination, treats their carrying amount under previous GAAP immediately after the business combination as their deemed cost at that date; *[IFRS 1.C4(e)]*

(iv) does not restate the accumulated depreciation and amortisation of the net identifiable assets in (iii) above, unless the depreciation methods and rates under previous GAAP result in amounts that differ materially from those required under IFRSs (for example, if they were adopted solely for tax purposes and do not reflect a reasonable estimate of the asset's useful life under IFRSs). If no such restatement is made, the carrying amount of those assets in the opening IFRS statement of financial position equals their carrying amount under previous GAAP at the date of transition to IFRSs (€200); *[IFRS 1.IG7]*

(v) if there is any indication that identifiable assets are impaired, tests those assets for impairment, under IAS 36, based on conditions that existed at the date of transition to IFRSs (see 7.12 below);

(vi) recognises the pension liability, and measures it, at the present value of the defined benefit obligation (€130) less the fair value of the plan assets (€100), giving a carrying amount of €30, with a corresponding debit of €30 to retained earnings. *[IFRS 1.C4(d)]*. However, if Entity B had already adopted IFRSs in an earlier period, Entity A would measure the pension liability at the same amount as in Entity B's individual financial statements; *[IFRS 1.D17, IG Example 9]*

(vii) recognises a net deferred tax liability of €6 (€20 at 30 per cent) arising from:

(a) the taxable temporary difference of €50 (€200 less €150) associated with the identifiable assets acquired and non-pension liabilities assumed; less

(b) the deductible temporary difference of €30 (€30 less €nil) associated with the pension liability.

Entity A recognises the resulting increase in the deferred tax liability as a deduction from retained earnings. *[IFRS 1.C4(b), (k)]*. If a taxable temporary difference arises from the initial recognition of the goodwill, Entity A does not recognise the resulting deferred tax liability. *[IAS 12.15(a)]*.

5.2.5 Restatement of goodwill

Under the business combinations exemption, a first-time adopter takes the carrying amount of goodwill under its previous GAAP at the date of transition to IFRSs as a starting point and only adjusts it as follows: *[IFRS 1.C4(g)]*

(a) goodwill is increased by the carrying amount of any intangible asset acquired in a business combination under its previous GAAP (less any related deferred tax and non-controlling interests), that does not meet the recognition criteria under IFRSs. The first-time adopter accounts for the change in classification prospectively and does not, for example, reverse the cumulative amortisation on the item that it recognised as an intangible asset under its previous GAAP (see 5.2.4.A above); *[IFRS 1.C4(c)(i)]*

(b) goodwill is decreased if a first-time adopter is required to recognise an intangible asset under IFRSs that was subsumed in goodwill under its previous GAAP. It adjusts deferred tax and non-controlling interests accordingly (see 5.2.4.B above); *[IFRS 1.C4(f), (k)]* and

(c) goodwill must be tested for impairment at the date of transition to IFRSs in accordance with IAS 36 regardless of whether there is any indication that the goodwill may be impaired (see Chapter 20 at 2); any resulting impairment loss is recognised in retained earnings unless IAS 36 requires it to be recognised in a revaluation surplus (see Chapter 20 at 11). The impairment test must be based on conditions at the date of transition to IFRSs.

Application of the above guidance may sometimes be more complicated than expected as is illustrated in the example below.

Example 5.21:   Recognition and derecognition of acquired intangible assets

Before its date of transition to IFRSs, Entity A acquired an online retailer, Entity B. Under its previous GAAP, Entity A recognised an intangible asset of ¥1,200 related to 'deferred marketing costs', which does not meet the recognition criteria under IFRSs. Entity A also acquired customer relationships with a fair value of ¥900 that do meet the recognition criteria under IFRS 3, but which it did not recognise as an intangible asset under its previous GAAP.

Upon adoption of IFRSs, Entity A is required to derecognise the 'deferred marketing costs' intangible asset and increase the carrying amount of goodwill for a corresponding amount. It adjusts deferred tax and non-controlling interests accordingly. *[IFRS 1.C4(c)(i), C4(g)(i), C4(k)].* Nevertheless, the customer relationship intangible asset that is subsumed in goodwill cannot be recognised as its carrying amount in the statement of financial position of the acquiree, Entity B, would have been nil under IFRS. *[IFRS 1.C4(b)(ii), C4(f)].*

In economic terms it might be contended that the 'deferred marketing costs' intangible asset in the example above comprises the value that would have been attributable under IFRSs to the acquired customer relationships. However, unless Entity A concluded that not recognising the customer relationship intangible asset was an error under its previous GAAP, it would not be able to recognise the customer relationship intangible asset upon adoption of IFRSs.

Under IFRS 1, assets acquired and liabilities assumed in a business combination prior to the date of transition to IFRSs are not necessarily valued on a basis that is consistent with IFRSs. This can lead to 'double counting' in the carrying amount of assets and goodwill as is illustrated in the example below.

Example 5.22:   Impairment testing of goodwill on first-time adoption

Entity C acquired a business before its date of transition to IFRSs. The cost of acquisition was €530 and Entity C allocated the purchase price as follows:

	€
Properties, at carry-over cost	450
Liabilities, at amortised cost	(180)
Goodwill	260
Purchase price	530

The goodwill under Entity C's previous GAAP relates entirely to the properties that had a fair value at the date of acquisition that was significantly in excess of their value on a carry-over cost basis. In Entity C's opening IFRS statement of financial position the same assets, liabilities and goodwill are valued as follows:

	€
Properties, at fair value	750
Liabilities, at amortised cost	(180)
Provisional IFRS goodwill (before impairment test)	260
Total carrying amount	830

Entity C used the option to measure the properties at fair value at its date of transition in its opening IFRS statement of financial position. However, IFRS 1 does not permit goodwill to be adjusted to reflect the extent to which the increase in fair value relates to other assets recognised at the time of the acquisition. The total carrying amount of the acquired net assets including goodwill of €830 may now exceed the recoverable amount. When Entity C tests the 'provisional IFRS goodwill' for impairment on first-time adoption of IFRSs, the recoverable amount of the business is determined to be €620. Accordingly, it will have to recognise an impairment of goodwill of €210 and disclose this impairment under IFRS 1.

In some cases, the write-off will completely eliminate the goodwill and thereby any 'double counting'. However, in this particular case the remaining goodwill of €50 in truth represents goodwill that was internally generated between the date of acquisition and the date of transition to IFRSs.

The IASB accepted that IFRS 1 does not prevent the implicit recognition of internally generated goodwill that arose after the date of the business combination. It concluded that attempts to exclude such internally generated goodwill would be costly and lead to arbitrary results. *[IFRS 1.BC39]*.

As the business combinations exemption also applies to associates and joint arrangements (see 5.2.2.A above), *[IFRS 1.C5]*, a transition impairment review should be carried out on investments in associates and joint arrangements if they include an element of goodwill. However, the goodwill embedded in the amount of an investment in an associate or an investment in a joint venture will not be subject to a separate impairment test. Rather the entire carrying amount of the investment is reviewed for impairment following the requirements of IAS 36. In performing this impairment review of the investment in associate or joint venture, in our view, an investor does not reverse a previous GAAP impairment that was recognised separately on the notional goodwill element embedded in the investment. However, if the previous GAAP impairment had been recognised as a reduction of the entire investment (without attribution to any particular embedded account), the first-time adopter is able to reverse such impairment if it is assessed to no longer be necessary. Consider the two scenarios below:

Example 5.23:   Previous GAAP impairment of goodwill embedded in equity method investment

Scenario 1 – Impairment was recognised on the notional goodwill element embedded in the investment under previous GAAP

On 1 January 2014, Entity A acquired an investment in Entity B, which it accounts for using the equity method (the investment would qualify as an associate under IFRSs). The cost of investment was €1,500 compared to B's identifiable net assets of €500; therefore, notional goodwill of €1,000 was included in the carrying value of the investment at that time. The previous GAAP required the entity to:

- Amortise the notional goodwill of the associate on a straight-line basis.
- Test the equity accounted investment for impairment at the investment level.
- Allocate and recognise the impairment loss (if any) against notional goodwill.
- Goodwill impairments (including those on notional goodwill) are not permitted to be reversed and therefore affect future amortisation.

Therefore, under its previous GAAP, Entity A tested its investment in Entity B for impairment and recognised an impairment loss of €500 in the year ended 31 December 2014. This reduced the notional goodwill to €500, which Entity A amortises over 10 years (€50 annually). By its date of transition to IFRS, 1 January 2020, notional goodwill had been amortised by 5 years × €50 (€250), reducing notional goodwill to €250. Net assets are unchanged since acquisition, leaving the investment with a carrying value of €750.

Entity A applies the exemption from retrospective restatement for past acquisitions of investments in associates. *[IFRS 1.C5]*. Therefore, at 1 January 2020, its date of transition, Entity A also tests the investment for impairment in accordance with IAS 36. At 1 January 2020, the value of the investment in Entity B recovered, and is €1,500 based on its current listed share price. Under this scenario, the previous impairment to notional goodwill is not reversed, since the use of the business combination exemption as it applies to associates means that the goodwill determined under the previous GAAP acquisition accounting together with the subsequent accounting up to the date of transition is effectively grandfathered in a similar way to a subsidiary's goodwill under the business combinations exemption. *[IFRS 1.C4(g), (h)]*. Therefore, the carrying value of the notional goodwill as determined under previous GAAP becomes the embedded notional goodwill at transition unless specifically required to be adjusted.

Scenario 2 – Impairment was recognised at the investment level under previous GAAP

The same as Scenario 1, except that Entity A's previous GAAP impairment test was performed at the investment level, using a test similar to that required under IAS 36. Because of applying this approach, when Entity A recognised an impairment loss of €500 in the year ended 31 December 2014, the carrying amount of the investment was €1,000. Similar to Scenario 1, at 1 January 2020, the value of the investment in Entity B has recovered and is €1,500 based on its current listed share price.

Under this scenario, the previous impairment of notional goodwill, which is embedded in the full amount of the investment, is reversed. However, the impairment can only be reversed up to the pre-impairment equity accounted value that results from the application of the business combination exemption.

5.2.5.A Prohibition of other adjustments to goodwill

IFRS 1 prohibits restatement of goodwill for most other adjustments reflected in the opening IFRS statement of financial position. Therefore, a first-time adopter electing not to apply IFRS 3 retrospectively is not permitted to make any adjustments to goodwill other than those described at 5.2.5 above. *[IFRS 1.C4(h)]*. For example, a first-time adopter cannot restate the carrying amount of goodwill:

(i) to exclude in-process research and development acquired in that business combination (unless the related intangible asset would qualify for recognition under IAS 38 in the statement of financial position of the acquiree);

(ii) to adjust previous amortisation of goodwill;

(iii) to reverse adjustments to goodwill that IFRS 3 would not permit, but were made under previous GAAP because of adjustments to assets and liabilities between the date of the business combination and the date of transition to IFRSs.

Differences between the goodwill amount in the opening IFRS statement of financial position and that in the financial statements under previous GAAP may arise, for example, because:

(a) goodwill may have to be restated as a result of a retrospective application of IAS 21 – *The Effects of Changes in Foreign Exchange Rates* (see 5.2.6 below);

(b) goodwill in relation to previously unconsolidated subsidiaries will have to be recognised (see 5.2.7 below);

(c) goodwill in relation to transactions that do not qualify as business combinations under IFRSs must be derecognised (see 5.2.1 above); and

(d) 'negative goodwill' that may have been included within goodwill under previous GAAP should be derecognised under IFRSs (see 5.2.5.B below).

Example 5.24: Adjusting goodwill

Entity A acquired Entity B but under its previous GAAP it did not recognise the following items:

- Entity B's customer lists which had a fair value of ¥1,100 at the date of the acquisition and ¥1,500 at the date of transition to IFRSs; and
- Deferred tax liabilities related to the fair value adjustment of Entity B's property, plant and equipment, which amounted to ¥9,500 at the date of the acquisition and ¥7,800 at the date of transition to IFRSs.

What adjustment should Entity A make to goodwill to account for the customer lists and deferred tax liabilities at its date of transition to IFRSs?

As explained at 5.2.4.B above, Entity A cannot recognise the customer lists (internally generated intangible assets of acquiree) when it uses the business combinations exemption. Accordingly, Entity A cannot adjust goodwill for the customer lists. *[IFRS 1.C4(b)(ii), C4(f)]*.

Entity A must recognise, under IAS 12 – *Income Taxes* – the deferred tax liability at its date of transition because there is no exemption from recognising deferred taxes under IFRS 1. However, Entity A is not permitted to adjust goodwill for the deferred tax liability that would have been recognised at the date of acquisition. Instead, Entity A should recognise the deferred tax liability of ¥7,800 with a corresponding charge to retained earnings or other category of equity, if appropriate. *[IFRS 1.C4(b), C4(h), C4(k)].*

5.2.5.B   Derecognition of negative goodwill

Although IFRS 1 does not specifically address accounting for negative goodwill recognised under a previous GAAP, negative goodwill should be derecognised by a first-time adopter because it is not permitted to recognise items as assets or liabilities if IFRSs do not permit such recognition. *[IFRS 1.10].* Negative goodwill clearly does not meet the definition of a liability under the IASB's *Conceptual Framework* and its recognition is not permitted under IFRS 3. While not directly applicable to a first-time adopter, the transitional provisions of IFRS 3 specifically require that any negative goodwill is derecognised upon adoption. *[IFRS 3.B69(e)].*

5.2.5.C   Goodwill previously deducted from equity

If a first-time adopter deducted goodwill from equity under its previous GAAP then it should not recognise that goodwill in its opening IFRS statement of financial position. Also, it should not reclassify that goodwill to profit or loss if it disposes of the subsidiary or if the investment in the subsidiary becomes impaired. *[IFRS 1.C4(i)(i)].* Effectively, under IFRSs such goodwill ceases to exist, as is shown in the following example based on the implementation guidance in IFRS 1. *[IFRS 1.IG Example 5].*

Example 5.25:   Goodwill deducted from equity and treatment of related intangible assets

Entity A acquired a subsidiary before the date of transition to IFRSs. Under its previous GAAP, Entity A:
(a) recognised goodwill as an immediate deduction from equity;
(b) recognised an intangible asset of the subsidiary that does not qualify for recognition as an asset under IAS 38; and
(c) did not recognise an intangible asset of the subsidiary that would qualify under IAS 38 for recognition as an asset in the financial statements of the subsidiary. The subsidiary held the asset at the date of its acquisition by Entity A and at the date of transition to IFRSs.

In its opening IFRS statement of financial position, Entity A:
(a) does not recognise the goodwill, as it did not recognise the goodwill as an asset under previous GAAP; *[IFRS 1.C4(i)]*
(b) does not recognise the intangible asset that does not qualify for recognition as an asset under IAS 38. Because Entity A deducted goodwill from equity under its previous GAAP, the elimination of this intangible asset reduces retained earnings (see 5.2.4.A above); *[IFRS 1.C4(c)]* and
(c) recognises the intangible asset that qualifies under IAS 38 for recognition as an asset in the financial statements of the subsidiary, even though the amount assigned to it under previous GAAP in Entity A's consolidated financial statements was nil (see 5.2.4.B above). *[IFRS 1.C4(b)(ii), C4(f)].* The recognition criteria in IAS 38 include the availability of a reliable measurement of cost, *[IAS 38.21]*, and Entity A measures the asset at cost less accumulated depreciation and less any accumulated impairment losses identified under IAS 36 (see 7.12 below). Because Entity A deducted goodwill from equity under its previous GAAP, the recognition of this intangible asset increases retained earnings. *[IFRS 1.C4(c)(ii)].* However, if this intangible asset had been subsumed in goodwill recognised as an asset under previous GAAP, Entity A would have decreased the carrying amount of that goodwill accordingly (and, if applicable, adjusted deferred tax and non-controlling interests) (see 5.2.5 above). *[IFRS 1.C4(b)(ii), C4(f), C4(g)(i)].*

The prohibition on reinstating goodwill that was deducted from equity may have a significant impact on first-time adopters that hedge their foreign net investments.

Example 5.26: Goodwill related to foreign net investments

Entity B, which uses the euro (€) as its functional currency, acquired a subsidiary in the United States whose functional currency is the US dollar ($). The goodwill on the acquisition of $2,100 was deducted from equity. Under its previous GAAP Entity B hedged the currency exposure on the goodwill because it would be required to recognise the goodwill as an expense upon disposal of the subsidiary.

IFRS 1 does not permit reinstatement of goodwill deducted from equity nor does it permit transfer of goodwill to profit or loss upon disposal of the investment in the subsidiary. *[IFRS 1.C4(i)(i)]*. Under IFRSs, goodwill deducted from equity ceases to exist and Entity B can no longer hedge the currency exposure on that goodwill. Therefore, exchange gains and losses relating to the hedge will no longer be classified in currency translation difference but recognised in profit and loss after adoption of IFRSs.

If a first-time adopter deducted goodwill from equity under its previous GAAP, adjustments resulting from the subsequent resolution of a contingency affecting the purchase consideration, at or before the date of transition to IFRSs, should be recognised in retained earnings. *[IFRS 1.C4(i)(ii)]*. Effectively, the adjustment is being accounted for in the same way as the original goodwill that arose on the acquisition, rather than having to be accounted for in accordance with IFRS 3. This requirement could affect, for example, the way a first-time adopter accounts for provisional amounts relating to business combinations prior to its date of transition to IFRSs.

Example 5.27: Adjustments made during measurement period to provisional amounts

Entity C acquired Entity D on 30 September 2019. Entity C sought an independent valuation for an item of property, plant and equipment acquired in the combination. However, the valuation was not completed by the date of transition to IFRS (1 January 2020). Under Entity C's previous GAAP, any goodwill was written off against equity as incurred. Five months after the acquisition date (and after the date of transition), Entity C received the independent valuation.

In preparing its opening IFRS statement of financial position, Entity C should use the adjusted carrying amounts of the identifiable net assets (see 5.2.4.C above) with the corresponding adjustment being recognised in retained earnings.

5.2.6 Currency adjustments to goodwill

A first-time adopter need not apply IAS 21 retrospectively to fair value adjustments and goodwill arising in business combinations that occurred before the date of transition to IFRSs. *[IFRS 1.C2, IG21A]*. This exemption is different from the 'cumulative translation differences' exemption, which is discussed at 5.7 below.

IAS 21 requires any goodwill arising on the acquisition of a foreign operation and any fair value adjustments to the carrying amounts of assets and liabilities arising on the acquisition of that foreign operation to be treated as assets and liabilities of the foreign operation. Thus they are expressed in the functional currency of the foreign operation and are translated at the closing rate in accordance with the requirements discussed in Chapter 15 at 6.5. *[IAS 21.47]*. For a first-time adopter it may be impracticable, especially after a corporate restructuring, to determine retrospectively the currency in which goodwill and fair value adjustments should be expressed. If IAS 21 is not applied retrospectively, a first-time adopter should treat such fair value adjustments and goodwill as assets and liabilities of the entity rather than as assets and liabilities of the acquiree. As a result, those goodwill and fair value adjustments are either already expressed in the entity's functional currency or are non-monetary foreign currency items that are reported using the exchange rate applied in accordance with previous GAAP. *[IFRS 1.C2]*.

If a first-time adopter chooses not to take the exemption mentioned above, it must apply IAS 21 retrospectively to fair value adjustments and goodwill arising in either: *[IFRS 1.C1, C3]*

(a) all business combinations that occurred before the date of transition to IFRSs; or

(b) all business combinations that the entity elects to restate to comply with IFRS 3.

In practice the exemption may be of limited use for a number of reasons:

First, the exemption permits 'goodwill and fair value adjustments' to be treated as assets and liabilities of the entity rather than as assets and liabilities of the acquiree. Implicit in the exemption is the requirement to treat both the goodwill and the fair value adjustments consistently. However, the IASB apparently did not consider that many first-time adopters, under their previous GAAPs, will have treated fair value adjustments as assets or liabilities of the acquiree, while at the same time treating goodwill as an asset of the acquirer. As the exemption under IFRS 1 did not foresee this particular situation, those first-time adopters will need to restate either their goodwill or fair value adjustments. In many cases restatement of goodwill is less onerous than restatement of fair value adjustments.

Secondly, the paragraphs in IFRS 1 that introduce the exemption were drafted at a later date than the rest of the Appendix of which they form part. Instead of referring to 'first-time adopter' these paragraphs refer to 'entity'. Nevertheless, it is clear from the context that 'entity' should be read as 'first-time adopter'. This means that the exemption only permits goodwill and fair value adjustments to be treated as assets and liabilities of the first-time adopter (i.e. the ultimate parent in the reporting group). In practice, however, many groups have treated goodwill and fair value adjustments as assets and liabilities of an intermediate parent in the reporting group. Where the intermediate parent has a functional currency that is different from that of the ultimate parent or the acquiree, it will be necessary to restate goodwill and fair value adjustments.

The decision to treat goodwill and fair value adjustments as either items denominated in the parent's or the acquiree's functional currency will also affect the extent to which the net investment in those foreign subsidiaries can be hedged (see also 4.5.5 above).

5.2.7 Previously unconsolidated subsidiaries

Under its previous GAAP a first-time adopter may not have consolidated a subsidiary acquired in a past business combination. In that case, a first-time adopter applying the business combinations exemption should measure the carrying amounts of the subsidiary's assets and liabilities in its consolidated financial statements at the date of transition at either: *[IFRS 1.IG27(a)]*

(a) if the subsidiary has adopted IFRSs, the same carrying amounts as in the IFRS financial statements of the subsidiary, after adjusting for consolidation procedures and for the effects of the business combination in which it acquired the subsidiary; *[IFRS 1.D17]* or

(b) if the subsidiary has not adopted IFRSs, the carrying amounts that IFRSs would require in the subsidiary's statement of financial position. *[IFRS 1.C4(j)]*.

The deemed cost of goodwill is the difference at the date of transition between: *[IFRS 1.C4(j)]*
(i) the parent's interest in those adjusted carrying amounts; and
(ii) the cost in the parent's separate financial statements of its investment in the subsidiary.

The cost of an investment in a subsidiary in the parent's separate financial statements will depend on which option the parent has taken to measure the cost under IFRS 1 (see 5.8.2 below).

A first-time adopter is precluded from calculating what the goodwill would have been at the date of the original acquisition. The deemed cost of goodwill is capitalised in the opening IFRS statement of financial position. The following example, which is based on one within the implementation guidance in IFRS 1, illustrates this requirement. *[IFRS 1.IG Example 6]*.

Example 5.28:   Subsidiary not consolidated under previous GAAP

Background

Entity A's date of transition to IFRSs is 1 January 2020. Under its previous GAAP, Entity A did not consolidate its 75 percent interest in Entity B, which it acquired in a business combination on 15 July 2017. On 1 January 2020:

(a) the cost of Entity A's investment in Entity B is $180; and
(b) under IFRSs, Entity B would measure its assets at $500 and its liabilities (including deferred tax under IAS 12) at $300. On this basis, Entity B's net assets are $200 under IFRSs.

Application of requirements

Entity A consolidates Entity B. The consolidated statement of financial position at 1 January 2020 includes:

(a) Entity B's assets at $500 and liabilities at $300;
(b) non-controlling interests of $50 (25 per cent of [$500 – $300]); and
(c) goodwill of $30 (cost of $180 less 75 per cent of [$500 – $300]). Entity A tests the goodwill for impairment under IAS 36 (see 7.12 below) and recognises any resulting impairment loss, based on conditions that existed at the date of transition to IFRSs.

If the cost of the subsidiary (as measured under IFRS 1, see 5.8.2 below) is lower than the proportionate share of net asset value at the date of transition to IFRSs, the difference is taken to retained earnings, or other category of equity, if appropriate.

Slightly different rules apply to all other subsidiaries (i.e. those not acquired in a business combination but created) that an entity did not consolidate under its previous GAAP, the main difference being that goodwill should not be recognised in relation to those subsidiaries (see 5.8 below). *[IFRS 1.IG27(c)]*.

Note that this exemption requires the use of the carrying value of the investment in the separate financial statements of the parent prepared using IAS 27 – *Separate Financial Statements*. Therefore, if a first-time adopter, in its separate financial statements, does not opt to measure its cost of investment in a subsidiary at its fair value or previous GAAP carrying amount at the date of transition, *[IFRS 1.D15]*, it is required to calculate the deemed cost of the goodwill by comparing the cost of the investment (as determined in accordance with IAS 27) to its share of the carrying amount of the net assets determined on a different date. In the case of a highly profitable subsidiary this could give rise to the following anomaly:

Example 5.29: Calculation of deemed cost of goodwill

Entity C acquired Entity D before the date of transition for $500. The net assets of Entity D would have been $220 under IFRSs at the date of acquisition. Entity D makes on average an annual net profit of $60, which it does not distribute to Entity C.

At the date of transition to IFRSs, the cost of Entity C's investment in Entity D is still $500. However, the net assets of Entity D have increased to $460. Therefore, under IFRS 1 the deemed cost of goodwill is $40.

The deemed cost of goodwill is much lower than the goodwill that was paid at the date of acquisition because Entity D did not distribute its profits. In fact, if Entity D had distributed a dividend to its parent just before its date of transition, the deemed cost of goodwill would have been significantly higher.

5.2.8 Previously consolidated entities that are not subsidiaries

A first-time adopter may have consolidated an investment under its previous GAAP that does not meet the definition of a subsidiary under IFRSs. In this case the entity should first determine the appropriate classification of the investment under IFRSs and then apply the first-time adoption rules in IFRS 1. Generally, such previously consolidated investments should be accounted for as either:

- *an associate, a joint venture or a joint operation:* First-time adopters applying the business combinations exemption should also apply that exemption to past acquisitions of investments in associates, interests in joint ventures or interests in joint operations in which the activity of the joint operation constitutes a business, as defined in IFRS 3. *[IFRS 1.C5]*. If the business combinations exemption is not applicable or the entity did not acquire (i.e. created) the investment in the associate or joint venture, IAS 28 – *Investments in Associates and Joint Ventures* – should be applied retrospectively unless the entity applies the joint arrangements exemption. *[IFRS 1.D31]*. (See 5.18 below);

- *an investment under IFRS 9* (see 5.11 below); or

- *an executory contract or service concession arrangement:* There are no first-time adoption exemptions that apply; therefore, IFRSs should be applied retrospectively. However, a practical relief is provided for a service concession arrangement if retrospective application is impracticable (see 5.14 below).

5.2.9 Measurement of deferred taxes and non-controlling interests

Deferred tax is calculated based on the difference between the carrying amounts of assets and liabilities and their respective tax bases. Therefore, deferred taxes should be recalculated after all assets acquired and liabilities assumed have been adjusted under IFRS 1. *[IFRS 1.C4(k)]*.

IFRS 10 defines non-controlling interest as the 'equity in a subsidiary not attributable, directly or indirectly, to a parent.' *[IFRS 10 Appendix A]*. This definition is discussed in Chapter 7 at 5.1. Non-controlling interests should be calculated after all assets acquired, liabilities assumed and deferred taxes have been adjusted under IFRS 1. *[IFRS 1.C4(k)]*.

Any resulting change in the carrying amount of deferred taxes and non-controlling interests should be recognised by adjusting retained earnings (or, if appropriate, another category of equity), unless they relate to adjustments to intangible assets that are adjusted against goodwill. See Example 5.30 below. *[IFRS 1.IG Example 4]*.

In terms of the treatment of deferred tax in relation to recognised intangible assets, there is a difference depending on whether the first-time adopter previously recognised acquired intangible assets in accordance with its previous GAAP or whether it had subsumed the intangible asset into goodwill (in both cases, a deferred tax liability was not recognised under its previous GAAP but is required to be recognised under IFRSs). In the first case, the first-time adopter must recognise a deferred tax liability and adjust non-controlling interests and opening reserves accordingly. *[IFRS 1.C4(b), C4(k)]*. By contrast, in the second case it would have to decrease the carrying amount of goodwill, recognise the intangible assets and a deferred tax liability and adjust non-controlling interests as necessary, as discussed at 5.2.5 above. *[IFRS 1.C4(b), C4(f), C4(g)(i), C4(k)]*. The IASB discussed this issue in October 2005, but decided not to propose an amendment to address this inconsistency, i.e. the difference in the treatment of deferred tax depending on whether acquired intangible assets were recognised separately or subsumed within goodwill under previous GAAP.[4]

Example 5.30 below illustrates how to account for restatement of intangible assets, deferred tax and non-controlling interests where previous GAAP requires deferred tax to be recognised. *[IFRS 1.IG Example 4]*.

Example 5.30: Restatement of intangible assets, deferred tax and non-controlling interests

Entity A's first IFRS financial statements are for a period that ends on 31 December 2021 and include comparative information for 2020 only. On 1 July 2017, Entity A acquired 75% of subsidiary B. Under its previous GAAP, Entity A assigned an initial carrying amount of £200 to intangible assets that would not have qualified for recognition under IAS 38. The tax base of the intangible assets was £nil, giving rise to a deferred tax liability (at 30%) of £60. Entity A measured non-controlling interests as their share of the fair value of the identifiable net assets acquired. Goodwill arising on the acquisition was capitalised as an asset in Entity A's consolidated financial statements.

On 1 January 2020 (the date of transition to IFRSs), the carrying amount of the intangible assets under previous GAAP was £160, and the carrying amount of the related deferred tax liability was £48 (30% of £160).

Under IFRS 1, Entity A derecognises intangible assets that do not qualify for recognition as separate assets under IAS 38, together with the related deferred tax liability of £48 and non-controlling interests, with a corresponding increase in goodwill (see 5.2.5 above). The related non-controlling interests amount to £28 (25% of £112 (£160 minus £48)). Entity A makes the following adjustment in its opening IFRS statement of financial position:

	£ DR	£ CR
Goodwill	84	
Deferred tax liability	48	
Non-controlling interests	28	
Intangible assets		160

Entity A tests the goodwill for impairment under IAS 36 and recognises any resulting impairment loss, based on conditions that existed at the date of transition to IFRSs.

5.2.10 Transition accounting for contingent consideration

The business combination exemption does not extend to contingent consideration that arose from a transaction that occurred before the date of transition, even if the acquisition itself is not restated due to the use of the exemption. Therefore, such contingent consideration, other than that classified as equity under IAS 32, is recognised at its fair value at the date of transition, regardless of the accounting under previous GAAP. If the contingent consideration was not recognised at fair value at the date of transition under previous GAAP, the resulting adjustment is recognised in retained earnings or other category of equity, if appropriate. Subsequent adjustments will be recognised following the provisions of IFRS 3. *[IFRS 3.40, 58]*.

5.3 Share-based payment transactions

IFRS 2 applies to accounting for the acquisition of goods or services in equity-settled share-based payment transactions, cash-settled share-based payment transactions and transactions in which the entity or the counterparty has the option to choose between settlement in cash or equity. There is no exemption from recognising share-based payment transactions that have not yet vested at the date of transition to IFRSs. The exemptions in IFRS 1 clarify that a first-time adopter is not required to apply IFRS 2 fully retrospectively to equity-settled share-based payment transactions that have already vested at the date of transition to IFRSs. IFRS 1 contains the following exemptions and requirements regarding share-based payment transactions:

(a) only if a first-time adopter has disclosed publicly the fair value of its equity instruments, determined at the measurement date, as defined in IFRS 2, then it is encouraged to apply IFRS 2 to: *[IFRS 1.D2]*

    (i) equity instruments that were granted on or before 7 November 2002 (i.e. the date the IASB issued ED 2 – *Share-based Payment*);

    (ii) equity instruments that were granted after 7 November 2002 but vested before the date of transition to IFRSs.

Many first-time adopters that did not use fair value-based share-based payment accounting under previous GAAP will not have published the fair value of equity instruments granted and are, therefore, not allowed to apply IFRS 2 retrospectively to those share-based payment transactions;

(b) for all grants of equity instruments to which IFRS 2 has not been applied, a first-time adopter must still make the disclosures relating to the nature and extent of share-based payments required by paragraphs 44 and 45 of IFRS 2; *[IFRS 1.D2, IFRS 2.44, 45]*

(c) if a first-time adopter modifies the terms or conditions of a grant of equity instruments to which IFRS 2 has not been applied, the entity is not required to apply the requirements of IFRS 2 (in paragraphs 26-29) if the modification occurred before the date of transition to IFRSs; *[IFRS 1.D2, IFRS 2.26-29]* and

(d) a first-time adopter is 'encouraged, but not required, to apply IFRS 2 to liabilities arising from share-based payment transactions that were settled before the date of transition to IFRSs'. *[IFRS 1.D3]*.

There are a number of interpretation issues concerning these exemptions and requirements:

- *Meaning of 'disclosed publicly' under (a) above*

    IFRS 1 only permits retrospective application of IFRS 2 if the entity has 'disclosed publicly' the fair value of the equity instruments concerned, but IFRSs do not define what is meant by 'disclosed publicly'. While IFRS 1 does not specifically require public disclosure of the fair value of an entity's share-based payment transactions in its previous financial statements, it is clear that IFRS 1 requires fair value to have been published contemporaneously. In addition, the requirements in IFRS 1 to disclose publicly the fair value of share-based payment transactions can be met even if the fair value is only disclosed in aggregate rather than for individual awards.

- *First-time adopters encouraged to apply IFRS 2 under (a) and (d) above*

    The 'date of transition to IFRSs' to which those exemptions refer is the first day of the earliest comparative period presented in a first-time adopter's first IFRS financial statements. This effectively means that an entity could accelerate the vesting of an award that was otherwise due to vest after the date of transition to IFRSs in order to avoid applying IFRS 2 to that award.

- *Consistent selection of the exemptions under (a) and (d) above*

    A first-time adopter can choose which of the exemptions under (a) and (d) it wants to apply, i.e. there is no specific requirement to select the exemptions in a consistent manner.

- *Meaning of 'encouraged' under (a) and (d) above*

    Under IFRS 1, a first-time adopter is 'encouraged', but not required, to apply IFRS 2 to certain categories of share-based payment transactions (see (a) and (d) above). IFRS 1 does not specifically prohibit a literal reading of 'encouraged', which could, for example, allow a first-time adopter to decide to apply IFRS 2 only to some share-based payment transactions granted before 7 November 2002. We believe that it would generally be acceptable for a first-time adopter to apply IFRS 2 only to share-based payment transactions:

    (1) after an earlier date chosen by the entity (e.g. 1 January 2001), while not applying it to earlier transactions;

    (2) for which fair values were disclosed publicly.

- *Treatment of modifications, cancellations and settlements under (c) above*

    There is a slight ambiguity concerning the interpretation of the exemption under (c) above, because paragraph D2 of IFRS 1 refers only to the modification of awards. This could allow a literal argument that IFRS 1 does not prescribe any specific treatment when an entity cancels or settles, as opposed to modifying, an award to which IFRS 2 has not been applied. However, paragraph D2 also requires an entity to apply paragraphs 26-29 of IFRS 2 to 'modified' awards. These paragraphs deal not only with modification but also with cancellation and settlement (see Chapter 34 at 7); indeed paragraphs 28 and 29 are not relevant to modifications at all. This makes it clear that the IASB intended IFRS 2 to be applied not only to modifications, but also to any cancellation or settlement of an award to which IFRS 2 has not been applied, unless the modification, cancellation or settlement occurs before the date of transition to IFRSs. *[IFRS 1.D2, IFRS 2.26-29].*

- *Transactions where the counterparty has a choice of settlement method*

  These are not specifically addressed in the first-time adoption rules. It therefore appears that, where such transactions give rise to recognition of both an equity component and a liability component, the equity component is subject to the transitional rules for equity-settled transactions and the liability component to those for cash-settled transactions. This could well mean that the liability component of such a transaction is recognised in the financial statements, whilst the equity component is not.

- *Application of IFRS 2 to cash-settled transactions settled before the date of transition to IFRSs under (d) above*

  It is not entirely clear what lies behind the exemption under (d) above, since a first-time adopter would never be required to report a share-based payment transaction (or indeed any transaction) settled before the date of transition.

Extract 5.5 from Manulife Financial Corporation (Manulife) provides an illustration of typical disclosures made by entities that applied the share-based payments exemption. In the extract below, Manulife applied the exemption not to apply IFRS 2 to share-based payment transactions that were fully vested at the date of transition. The extract also illustrates the implicit limitation of the share-based payment exemption for awards that were granted after 7 November 2002 and that were still vesting at the date of transition to IFRS.

> *Extract 5.5: Manulife Financial Corporation (2011)*
> **Notes to Consolidated Financial Statements** [extract]
>
> **Note 25 First-time Adoption of IFRS** [extract]
>
> As outlined in note 1, the Company has adopted IFRS as a replacement of previous Canadian GAAP effective January 1, 2011. References to Canadian GAAP throughout this note relate to Canadian GAAP prior to the adoption of IFRS. The Company's opening Consolidated Statement of Financial Position was prepared at January 1, 2010, the Company's date of transition to IFRS (the "Transition Date") in accordance with the requirements of IFRS 1 "First-Time Adoption of International Financial Reporting Standards". This note explains the principal adjustments made by the Company in preparing the opening IFRS Consolidated Statement of Financial Position as at January 1, 2010 compared to the Consolidated Balance Sheet as at December 31, 2009 under Canadian GAAP and the required adjustments between IFRS and previous Canadian GAAP to total equity and total comprehensive income for the 2010 comparative year.
>
> IFRS has been applied retrospectively, except for certain optional and mandatory exemptions from full retrospective application provided for under IFRS 1, as detailed below.
>
> **(a) First-time adoption elections** [extract]
>
> **Optional exemptions** [extract]
>
> *Share-based payment transactions* – The Company elected to apply IFRS 2 "Share-based Payments" to all equity instruments granted after November 7, 2002 that had not vested by the Transition Date. The Company applied IFRS 2 for all liabilities arising from share-based payment transactions that existed at the Transition Date.

5.3.1 Use of previously published fair values

There is no explicit requirement in IFRS 1 or IFRS 2 that any voluntary retrospective application of IFRS 2 must be based on the fair value previously published. This might appear to allow a first-time adopter the flexibility of using a different valuation for IFRS 2 purposes than that previously used for disclosure purposes. However, the requirements of IFRS 1 in relation to estimates under previous GAAP (see 4.2 above) mean that the assumptions used in IFRS must be consistent with those used in the originally disclosed valuation. The entity will also need to consider the implications of the assertion, in effect, that there is more than one fair value for the same transaction.

5.3.2 Restatement of costs recognised under previous GAAP

A first-time adopter may elect to take advantage of the transitional provisions in IFRS 1 which allow it not to apply IFRS 2 to equity-settled share-based payment transactions that were vested before the date of transition to IFRS, despite having recognised a cost for those transactions in accordance with its previous GAAP. Neither IFRS 1 nor IFRS 2 clearly indicates the appropriate treatment of the costs of share-based payment transactions that were recognised under the previous GAAP. There are mixed views on this issue in different jurisdictions, some of which are being driven by local regulatory expectations. In practice, either of the following approaches is considered acceptable, provided that the treatment chosen is disclosed in the financial statements if the previously recognised costs are material:

- *not to change expense previously recognised under previous GAAP for equity instruments subject to transitional relief under IFRS 1.* This approach is consistent with the approach for cash-settled share-based payment transactions that are settled prior to the date of transition to IFRSs, since the entity must reflect the reduction in cash that was actually paid (and therefore the reduction in retained earnings) in the first IFRS financial statements; or

- *to derecognise share-based payment expense under previous GAAP for equity instruments subject to transitional relief under IFRS 1.* In other words, reverse cumulative amounts recognised in the retained earnings and equity accounts of the opening IFRS statement of financial position.

5.4 Insurance contracts

A first-time adopter may apply the transitional provisions in IFRS 4. *[IFRS 1.D4, IFRS 4.40-45]*. IFRS 4 restricts changes in accounting policies for insurance contracts, including changes made by a first-time adopter (see Chapter 55 at 8). *[IFRS 1.D4, 21-30]*.

The claims development information (see Chapter 55 at 11.2.5) need not be disclosed for claims development that occurred more than five years before the end of the first IFRS reporting period. For entities taking advantage of this relief, the claims development information will be built up from five to ten years in the five years following adoption of IFRSs. Additionally, if it is 'impracticable' for a first-time adopter to prepare information about claims development that occurred before the beginning of the earliest period for which full comparative information is presented, this fact should be disclosed. *[IFRS 4.44]*.

Furthermore, the IASB issued the amendments to IFRS 4 – *Applying IFRS 9 – Financial Instruments – with IFRS 4 Insurance Contracts* – in September 2016. The amendments permit insurers to either defer the application of IFRS 9 or use an 'overlay approach'. *[IFRS 4.46-49]*. See Chapter 55 at 10 for more details of these approaches and Chapter 55 at 10.1.3 and 10.2.2 for treatments for first-time adopters. *[IFRS 4.20L-20N, 35N]*.

As discussed in 4.13 above, IFRS 17 may be adopted prior to its mandatory effective date of 1 January 2023. IFRS 17 supersedes IFRS 4. Accordingly, this exemption does not apply to entities that choose early adoption of IFRS 17.

5.5 Deemed cost

IFRS 1 requires full retrospective application of standards effective at the end of a first-time adopter's first IFRS reporting period. *[IFRS 1.7]*. Therefore, in the absence of the deemed cost exemption, the requirements of, for example, IAS 16, IAS 38, IAS 40 – *Investment Property* – and IFRS 6 – *Exploration for and Evaluation of Mineral Resources* – would have to be applied as if the first-time adopter had always applied these standards. This could be quite onerous because:

- these items are long-lived which means that accounting records from the time of acquisition may not be available anymore. In the case of formerly state-owned businesses, the required accounting records possibly never even existed;
- the entity may have revalued the items in the past as a matter of accounting policy or because this was required under national law; or
- even if the items were carried at depreciated cost, the accounting policy for recognition and depreciation may not have been IFRS compliant.

Given the significance of items like property, plant and equipment in the statement of financial position of most first-time adopters and the sheer number of transactions affecting property, plant and equipment, restatement is not only difficult but would often also involve huge cost and effort. Therefore, the IASB decided to introduce the notion of a 'deemed cost' that is not the 'true' IFRS compliant cost basis of an asset, but a surrogate that is deemed to be a suitable starting point.

There are seven separate deemed cost exemptions in IFRS 1:

- fair value or revaluation as deemed cost (see 5.5.1 below);
- event-driven fair value measurement as deemed cost (see 5.5.2 below);
- deemed cost for oil and gas assets (see 5.5.3 below);
- deemed cost for assets used (or previously used) in operations subject to rate regulation (see 5.5.4 below);
- deemed cost for assets acquired or liabilities assumed in a business combination not restated under IFRSs (see 5.2 above);
- deemed cost for a right-of-use asset for a lessee based on certain exemptions in IFRS 1 (see 5.6 below); and
- deemed cost in determining the cost of an investment in a subsidiary, joint venture or associate (see 5.8.2 below).

5.5.1 Fair value or revaluation as deemed cost

To deal with the problem of restatement of long-lived assets upon first-time adoption of IFRSs, the standard permits a first-time adopter – for the categories of assets listed below – to measure an item in its opening IFRS statement of financial position using an amount that is based on its deemed cost: *[IFRS 1.D5, D6, D7]*

- property, plant and equipment, including bearer plants (see 7.4 below); *[IFRS 1.D5, D6]*
- investment property, if an entity elects to use the cost model in IAS 40. *[IFRS 1.D7]*. The fact that the exemption can only be applied to investment property accounted for under the cost model will not pose any problems in practice as the fair value model under IAS 40 requires an entity to measure its investment property at fair value at its date of transition to IFRSs;
- right-of-use assets under IFRS 16 – *Leases; [IFRS 1.D7]* and
- intangible assets (see 7.14 below) that meet: *[IFRS 1.D7]*
    - the recognition criteria in IAS 38 (including reliable measurement of original cost); and
    - the criteria in IAS 38 for revaluation (including the existence of an active market).

A first-time adopter cannot use this deemed cost approach by analogy for any other assets or for liabilities. *[IFRS 1.D7]*.

The use of fair value or revaluation as deemed cost for intangible assets will be very limited in practice because of the definition of an active market in IFRS 13. An active market is defined as one in which transactions for the item take place with sufficient frequency and volume to provide pricing information on an ongoing basis. *[IFRS 13 Appendix A]*. It is therefore unlikely that a first-time adopter will be able to apply this exemption to any intangible assets (see Chapter 17 at 8.2).

It is important to note that this exemption does not take classes or categories of assets as its unit of measure, but refers to 'an item of property, plant and equipment,' and similarly for investment property, right-of-use assets under IFRS 16 and intangible assets. *[IFRS 1.D5, D7]*. IAS 16 does not 'prescribe the unit of measure for recognition, i.e. what constitutes an item of property, plant and equipment. Thus, judgement is required in applying the recognition criteria to an entity's specific circumstances' (see Chapter 18 at 3.1). *[IFRS 1.IG12, IAS 16.9]*. A first-time adopter may therefore apply the deemed cost exemption to only some of its assets. For example, it could apply the exemption only to:

- a selection of properties;
- part of a factory; or
- some of the right-of-use asset leased under a single lease agreement.

The IASB argued that it is not necessary to restrict application of the exemption to classes of assets to prevent arbitrarily selective revaluations, because IAS 36 'requires an impairment test if there is any indication that an asset is impaired. Thus, if an entity uses fair value as deemed cost for assets whose fair value is above cost, it cannot ignore indications that the recoverable amount of other assets may have fallen below their carrying amount. Therefore, the IFRS does not restrict the use of fair value as deemed cost to entire classes of asset.' *[IFRS 1.BC45]*. Nevertheless, it seems doubtful that the quality of financial information would benefit from a revaluation of a haphazard selection of items of property, plant and equipment. Therefore, a first-time adopter should exercise judgement in selecting the items to which it believes it is appropriate to apply the exemption.

Extracts 5.6 and 5.7 below are typical disclosures of the use of the 'fair value or revaluation as deemed cost' exemption.

Extract 5.6: Suncor Energy Inc (2011)

Notes to the consolidated financial statements [extract]

6. First-Time Adoption of IFRS [extract]

Explanation of Significant Adjustments [extract]

(9) *Fair Value as Deemed Cost* [extract]

The company has applied the IFRS 1 election to record certain assets of property, plant and equipment at fair value on the Transition Date. The exemption has been applied to refinery assets located in Eastern Canada and certain natural gas assets in Western Canada. When estimating fair value, market information for similar assets was used, and where market information was not available, management relied on internally generated cash flow models using discount rates specific to the asset and long-term forecasts of commodity prices and refining margins. The aggregate of these fair values was $1.370 billion, resulting in a reduction of the carrying amount of property, plant and equipment as at January 1, 2010. Under Previous GAAP, impairment losses were recorded in the third quarter of 2010 for certain of these natural gas properties. There were no impairment losses recognized during 2010 under IFRS, as these properties were adjusted to fair value at the Transition Date. The impacts on the financial statements were as follows:

($ millions)	As at and for the year ended Dec 31, 2010
Property, plant and equipment, net	(527)
Retained earnings	(527)
Depreciation, depletion, amortization and impairment	(379)

Extract 5.7: Nexen Inc. (2011)

Notes to Consolidated Financial Statements [extract]

Note 26 Transition to IFRS [extract]

Elected Exemptions from Full Retrospective Application [extract]

In preparing these Consolidated Financial Statements in accordance with IFRS 1 First-time Adoption of International Financial Reporting Standards (IFRS 1), we applied the following optional exemptions from full retrospective application of IFRS.

(II)   FAIR VALUE OR REVALUATION AS DEEMED COST

We elected to measure certain producing oil and gas properties at fair value as at the transition date and use that amount as its deemed cost in the opening IFRS balance sheet.

5.5.1.A   Determining deemed cost

The deemed cost that a first-time adopter uses is either:

(a)   the fair value of the item at the date of transition to IFRSs; *[IFRS 1.D5]* or

(b)   a previous GAAP revaluation at or before the date of transition to IFRSs, if the revaluation was, at the date of the revaluation, broadly comparable to: *[IFRS 1.D6]*

  (i)   fair value; or

  (ii)   cost or depreciated cost in accordance with IFRSs, adjusted to reflect, for example, changes in a general or specific price index.

The revaluations referred to in (b) above need only be 'broadly comparable to fair value or reflect an index applied to a cost that is broadly comparable to cost determined in accordance with IFRSs'. *[IFRS 1.BC47]*. It appears that in the interest of practicality the IASB is allowing a good deal of flexibility in this matter. The IASB explains in the basis for conclusions that 'it may not always be clear whether a previous revaluation was intended as a measure of fair value or differs materially from fair value. The flexibility in this area permits a cost-effective solution for the unique problem of transition to IFRSs. It allows a first-time adopter to establish a deemed cost using a measurement that is already available and is a reasonable starting point for a cost-based measurement.' *[IFRS 1.BC47]*.

IFRS 1 describes the revaluations referred to in (b) above as a 'previous GAAP revaluation'. Therefore, in our view, such revaluations can be used as the basis for deemed cost only if they were recognised in the first-time adopter's previous GAAP financial statements. A previous GAAP impairment (or reversal of an impairment) that resulted in the recognition of the related assets at fair value in the previous GAAP financial statements may be recognised as a previous GAAP revaluation for the purposes of applying this exemption only if it is broadly comparable to the fair value under IFRS 13 or cost (or depreciated cost) in accordance with IFRSs, adjusted to reflect, for example, changes in a general or specific price index and not another measure such as fair value less costs of disposal. Moreover, when the previous GAAP impairment was determined for a group of impaired assets (e.g. a cash generating unit as defined in IAS 36, see Chapter 20 at 3), the recognised value of an individual asset needs to be broadly comparable to the specific asset's fair value under IFRS 13 or cost (or depreciated cost) in accordance with IFRSs, adjusted to reflect, for example, changes in a general or specific price index and not another measure such as fair value less costs of disposal or an allocation thereof for the purposes of this exemption.

If revaluations under previous GAAP did not satisfy the criteria in paragraphs D6 or D8 of IFRS 1, a first-time adopter measures the revalued assets within the scope of IAS 16 in its opening IFRS statement of financial position on one of the following bases: *[IFRS 1.D5-D8, IG11]*

(a) cost (or deemed cost) less any accumulated depreciation and any accumulated impairment losses under the cost model in IAS 16;

(b) deemed cost, being the fair value at the date of transition to IFRSs; or

(c) revalued amount, if the entity adopts the revaluation model in IAS 16 as its accounting policy under IFRSs for all items of property, plant and equipment in the same class.

The elections in paragraphs D6 or D8 of IFRS 1 are also available for use for investment property (measured under the cost model), right-of-use assets and intangible assets meeting certain criteria (see 5.5.1 above). *[IFRS 1.D7]*. If the elections in paragraphs D6 or D8 of IFRS 1 are not permitted for such assets, a first-time adopter should measure the asset in its opening IFRS statement of financial position on one of the bases above, i.e. applying the cost model, deemed cost or a revalued amount in accordance with relevant IFRSs. *[IFRS 1.D5-D8]*. A right-of-use asset recognised by a lessee under IFRS 16 may also be measured at a carrying amount based on certain exemptions in IFRS 1 (see 5.6 below).

A first-time adopter that uses fair value as deemed cost is required to disclose the resulting IFRS 1 adjustment separately (see 6.5.1 below). *[IFRS 1.30]*.

5.5.1.B   Deemed cost determined before the date of transition to IFRSs

If the deemed cost of an asset was determined before the date of transition then an IFRS accounting policy needs to be applied to that deemed cost in the intervening period to determine what the carrying amount of the asset is in the opening IFRS statement of financial position. This means that a first-time adopter that uses previous GAAP revaluation as the deemed cost of an item of property, plant and equipment will need to start depreciating the item from the date when the entity established the previous GAAP revaluation and not from its date of transition to IFRSs. *[IFRS 1.IG9]*. The example below illustrates the application of this requirement.

Example 5.31:   Deemed cost of property, plant and equipment

Entity A used to revalue items of property, plant and equipment to fair value under its previous GAAP, but changed its accounting policy on 1 January 2014 when it adopted a different accounting policy. Under that accounting policy, Entity A did not depreciate the asset and only recognised the maintenance costs as an expense. Entity A's date of transition to IFRSs is 1 January 2020.

In its balance sheet under previous GAAP the carrying amount of the asset is £80,000 at the date of transition to IFRSs, which is equal to the last revaluation. Entity A can use the last revalued amount as the deemed cost of the asset on 1 January 2014. However, Entity A will need to apply IAS 16 to the period after 1 January 2014 because the accounting policy under its previous GAAP is not permitted under IFRSs. Assuming that the economic life of the asset is 40 years from 2014 and that the residual value is nil, Entity A would account for the asset at £68,000 in its opening IFRS statement of financial position, which represents the deemed cost minus 6 years of depreciation.

5.5.2   Event-driven fair value measurement as deemed cost

A first-time adopter may use fair value measurements that arose from an event such as a privatisation or initial public offering as deemed cost for IFRSs at the date of that measurement. *[IFRS 1.D8]*.

IFRS 1 describes these revaluations as 'deemed cost in accordance with previous GAAP'. Therefore, to the extent that they related to an event that occurred prior to its date of transition or during the period covered by the first IFRS financial statements, they can be used as the basis for deemed cost only if they were recognised in the first-time adopter's previous GAAP financial statements. As discussed in 5.5.2.C below, a first-time adopter is also allowed to use event-driven fair values resulting from such events that occurred subsequent to the first-time adopter's date of transition to IFRSs, but during the period covered by the first IFRS financial statements.

The 'fair value or revaluation as deemed cost' exemption discussed at 5.5.1 above only applies to items of property, plant and equipment, investment property, right-of-use assets under IFRS 16 and certain intangible assets. *[IFRS 1.D5-D7]*. The event-driven deemed cost exemption, however, is broader in scope because it specifies that when a first-time adopter established a deemed cost in accordance with previous GAAP *for some or all of its assets and liabilities* [emphasis added] by measuring them at their fair value at one particular date because of an event such as a privatisation or initial public offering, the entity may use such event-driven fair value measurements as deemed cost for IFRSs at the date of that measurement. *[IFRS 1.D8]*.

There are two important limitations in the scope of this exemption:
- while it applies, in principle, to all assets and liabilities of an entity, it does not override the recognition criteria in IFRSs (see 3.2 above). *[IFRS 1.10]*. Consequently, a first-time adopter should derecognise goodwill, assets (e.g. certain intangible assets such as brand names and research) and liabilities that do not qualify for recognition under IFRSs in the statement of financial position of the entity; and
- it cannot be used if the event-driven revaluation did not result in a re-measurement to full fair value (i.e. it cannot be used in the case of a partial step-up towards fair value).

If revaluations under previous GAAP did not satisfy the criteria in paragraphs D6 or D8 of IFRS 1, a first-time adopter measures the revalued assets within the scope of IAS 16 in its opening IFRS statement of financial position on one of the following bases: *[IFRS1.D5-D8, IG11]*

(a) cost (or deemed cost) less any accumulated depreciation and any accumulated impairment losses under the cost model in IAS 16;

(b) deemed cost, being the fair value at the date of transition to IFRSs; or

(c) revalued amount, if the entity adopts the revaluation model in IAS 16 as its accounting policy under IFRSs for all items of property, plant and equipment in the same class.

Similarly, the elections in paragraphs D6 or D8 of IFRS 1 are also available for use for investment property (measured under the cost model), right-of-use assets and intangible assets meeting certain criteria (see 5.5.1 above). *[IFRS 1.D7]*. The accounting options where paragraphs D6 or D8 of IFRS 1 are not permitted for such assets are the same as those explained at 5.5.1.A above. *[IFRS 1.D5-D8, IG11]*.

A first-time adopter that uses fair value as deemed cost is required to disclose the resulting IFRS 1 adjustment separately (see 6.5.1 below). *[IFRS 1.30]*.

Finally, although a first-time adopter may use an event-driven fair value measurement as deemed cost for any asset or liability, it does not have to use them for all assets and liabilities that were revalued as a result of the event.

5.5.2.A 'Push down' accounting

Under some previous GAAPs an entity may have prepared its financial statements using 'push down' accounting, that is, the carrying amount of its assets and liabilities is based on their fair value at the date it became a subsidiary of its parent. If such a subsidiary subsequently adopts IFRSs, it will often require a very significant effort to determine the carrying amount of those assets and liabilities on a historical cost basis at the date of transition.

The event-driven deemed cost exemption applies to events 'such as a privatisation or initial public offering.' *[IFRS 1.D8]*. This list of events is clearly not meant to be exhaustive, but rather describes events that result in re-measurement of some or all assets and liabilities at their fair value. An acquisition that results in an entity becoming a subsidiary is a change of control event similar to a privatisation or an initial public offering. In our view, the application of 'push down' accounting results in event-driven fair value measurements that may be used as deemed cost for IFRSs at the date of that measurement.

The exemption can only be used, however, if 'push down' accounting resulted in the recognition of the related assets and liabilities at their fair value. For example, previous GAAP may not have required remeasurement to full fair value in the case of a partial acquisition or a step-acquisition, or if there was a bargain purchase that was allocated, for example, to reduce the fair values of long-lived assets. In these cases, the entity would not qualify for the event-driven deemed cost exemption, since the event did not result in the measurement of its assets and liabilities at their fair value.

5.5.2.B   'Fresh start' accounting

Some previous GAAPs require an entity that emerges from bankruptcy or undertakes a legal reorganisation to apply 'fresh start' accounting, which involves recognition of assets and liabilities at their fair value at that date.

In our view, the application of 'fresh start' accounting results in an event-driven fair value measurement that may be used as deemed cost for IFRSs at the date of that measurement. *[IFRS 1.D8]*. The use of the exemption is limited to instances that resulted in the recognition of the related assets and liabilities at their full fair value (i.e. it cannot be used in the case of a partial step-up towards fair value).

5.5.2.C   Exemption for event-driven revaluations after the date of transition

The event-driven revaluation exemption allows a first-time adopter to recognise in its first IFRS financial statements fair values arising from events whose measurement date is after the date of transition to IFRSs but during the periods covered by the first IFRS financial statements. The event-driven fair value measurements are recognised as deemed cost at the date that the event occurs. An entity should recognise the resulting adjustments directly in retained earnings (or if appropriate, another category of equity) at the measurement date. *[IFRS 1.D8(b)]*.

The Board explicitly considered whether to allow a first-time adopter that uses a revaluation subsequent to the date of transition to 'work back' to the deemed cost on the date of transition to IFRSs by adjusting the revaluation amounts to exclude any depreciation, amortisation or impairment between the date of transition to IFRSs and the date of that measurement. The Board rejected this approach 'because making such adjustments would require hindsight and the computed carrying amounts on the date of transition to IFRSs would be neither the historical costs of the revalued assets nor their fair values on that date.' *[IFRS 1.BC46B]*. Accordingly, at the date of transition to IFRSs, the entity should either establish the deemed cost by applying the criteria in paragraphs D5 to D7 of IFRS 1 (see 5.5.1 above) or measure assets and liabilities under the other requirements in IFRS 1. *[IFRS 1.D8(b)]*.

5.5.3   Deemed cost for oil and gas assets

It is common practice in some countries to account for exploration and development costs for oil and gas properties in development or production phases in cost centres that include all properties in a large geographical area, e.g. under the 'full cost accounting' method. However, this method of accounting generally uses a unit of account that is much larger than that is acceptable under IFRSs. Applying IFRSs fully retrospectively would pose significant problems for first-time adopters because it would also require amortisation at the IFRS unit of account level to be calculated (on a unit of production basis) for each year, using a reserves base that has changed over time because of changes in factors such as geological understanding and prices for oil and gas. In many cases, particularly for older assets, this information may not be available. Even when such information is available, the effort and cost to determine the opening balances at the date of transition would usually be very high.' *[IFRS 1.BC47A]*.

For these entities, use of the fair value as deemed cost exemption (see 5.5.1 above), however, was not considered to be suitable because: *[IFRS 1.BC47B]*

> 'Determining the fair value of oil and gas assets is a complex process that begins with the difficult task of estimating the volume of reserves and resources. When the fair value amounts must be audited, determining significant inputs to the estimates generally requires the use of qualified external experts. For entities with many oil and gas assets, the use of this fair value as deemed cost alternative would not meet the Board's stated intention of avoiding excessive cost.'

The IASB therefore decided to grant an exemption for a first-time adopter that accounted under its previous GAAP for 'exploration and development costs for oil and gas properties in the development or production phases ... in cost centres that include all properties in a large geographical area.' *[IFRS 1.D8A]*. Under the exemption, a first-time adopter may elect to measure oil and gas assets at the date of transition to IFRSs on the following basis: *[IFRS 1.D8A]*

(a) exploration and evaluation assets at the amount determined under the entity's previous GAAP; and

(b) assets in the development or production phases at the amount determined for the cost centre under the entity's previous GAAP. This amount must be allocated to the cost centre's underlying assets *pro rata* using reserve volumes or reserve values as of that date.

For this purpose, oil and gas assets comprise only those assets used in the exploration, evaluation, development or production of oil and gas. *[IFRS 1.D8A]*.

A first-time adopter that uses the exemption under (b) above should disclose that fact and the basis on which carrying amounts determined under previous GAAP were allocated (see 6.5.3 below). *[IFRS 1.31A]*.

To avoid the use of deemed costs resulting in an oil and gas asset being measured at more than its recoverable amount, the Board also decided that oil and gas assets that were valued using this exemption must be tested for impairment at the date of transition to IFRSs as follows: *[IFRS 1.D8A, BC47D]*

- exploration and evaluation assets must be tested for impairment under IFRS 6; and
- assets in the development and production phases must be tested for impairment under IAS 36.

The deemed cost amounts are reduced to take account of any impairment charge. *[IFRS 1.D8A]*.

Finally, a first-time adopter that applies the deemed cost exemption for oil and gas assets in the development or production phases in (b) above must also apply paragraph D21A of IFRS 1 to the related decommissioning and restoration obligation (see 5.13.2 below). This is required instead of applying paragraph D21 of IFRS 1 (see 5.13.1 below) or IFRIC 1 – *Changes in Existing Decommissioning, Restoration and Similar Liabilities*. *[IFRS 1.D21A]*.

Extract 5.8 below presents disclosure of the use of the 'deemed cost for oil and gas assets' exemption.

> **Extract 5.8: Zargon Oil & Gas Ltd. (2011)**
> Notes to the Consolidated Financial Statements [extract]
> 27   Reconciliation of Transition from Canadian GAAP to IFRS [extract]
> Explanatory notes [extract]
> (b) The Company elected under IFRS 1 to deem the Canadian GAAP carrying value of its oil and gas assets accounted for under the full cost method as at January 1, 2010 as their deemed cost under IFRS as at that date. As such, the Canadian GAAP full cost pool was reallocated upon transition to IFRS and the 2010 comparatives were restated to reflect the new IFRS accounting policies as follows:
> i. In accordance with IAS 16, IAS 38 and IFRS 6 on January 1, 2010 the Company reallocated costs of $24.37 million relating to unproved properties from property, plant and equipment to exploration and evaluation assets.
> ii. Under Canadian GAAP, all costs incurred prior to having obtained licence rights and lease expiries were included within property, plant and equipment. Under IFRS, such expenditures are expensed as incurred. There was no impact on adoption of IFRS due to the full cost as deemed cost exemption. However, the comparative 2010 balances were restated at December 31, 2010 resulting in a reduction in property, plant and equipment and retained earnings of $2.81 million, and an increase in exploration and evaluation expenses for the year of the same amounts.
> iii. The remaining full cost pool was allocated to the developed and producing assets pro rata using reserve values.
> iv. Under IFRS, impairment tests must be performed at a more lower reporting level than was required under Canadian GAAP. The Canadian GAAP "ceiling test" incorporated a 2-step approach for testing impairment, while IFRS uses a 1-step approach. Under Canadian GAAP, a discounted cash flow analysis was not required if the undiscounted cash flows from proved reserves exceeded the carrying amount (step 1). If the carrying amount exceeded the undiscounted future cash flows, then a prescribed discounted cash flow test was performed (step 2). Under IFRS, impairment testing is based on discounted cash flows and is calculated at the CGU level. Impairment tests are required to be performed at the transition date, and as at January 1, 2010 no impairment was identified. At December 31, 2010 an impairment test was performed and four of the Company's CGUs were found to have impairment.

5.5.4 Deemed cost for assets used (or previously used) in operations subject to rate regulation

Entities that hold items of property, plant and equipment, right-of-use assets under IFRS 16, or intangible assets that are used, or were previously used, in operations subject to rate regulation might have capitalised, as part of the carrying amounts, amounts that do not qualify for capitalisation in accordance with IFRSs. For example, when setting rates, regulators often permit entities to capitalise an allowance for the cost of financing the asset's acquisition, construction or production. This allowance typically includes an imputed cost of equity. IFRSs do not permit an entity to capitalise an imputed cost of equity. [IFRS 1.BC47F]. The IASB decided to permit a first-time adopter with operations subject to rate regulation to elect to use the previous GAAP carrying amount of such an item at the date of transition to IFRSs as deemed cost. [IFRS 1.D8B]. In the Board's view, this exemption is consistent with other exemptions in IFRS 1 in that it 'avoids excessive costs while meeting the objectives of the IFRS.' [IFRS 1.BC47I].

Operations are subject to rate regulation if they are governed by a framework for establishing the prices that can be charged to customers for goods or services and that framework is subject to oversight and/or approval by a rate regulator (as defined in IFRS 14 – *Regulatory Deferral Accounts*). [IFRS 1.D8B, IFRS 14 Appendix A].

Without this exemption, a first-time adopter with operations subject to rate regulation would have had either to restate those items retrospectively to remove the non-qualifying amounts, or to use fair value as deemed cost (see 5.5.1 above). Both alternatives, the Board reasoned, pose significant practical challenges, the cost of which can outweigh the benefits. *[IFRS 1.BC47G]*. Typically, once amounts are included in the total cost of an item of property, plant and equipment, they are no longer tracked separately. Therefore, their removal would require historical information that, given the typical age of some of the assets involved, is probably no longer available and would be difficult to estimate. For many of these assets, it may be impractical to use the exemption to use a deemed cost equal to transition-date fair value (paragraph D5 of IFRS 1) as such information may not be readily available. *[IFRS 1.BC47H]*.

A first-time adopter that applies this exemption to an item need not apply it to all items. At the date of transition to IFRSs, the first-time adopter must test for impairment in accordance with IAS 36 each item for which it used the exemption. *[IFRS 1.D8B]*.

If a first-time adopter uses the exemption for assets used in operations subject to rate regulation, it must disclose that fact and the basis on which carrying amounts were determined under previous GAAP. *[IFRS 1.31B]*.

Extract 5.9 below illustrates disclosure of the use of the deemed cost exemption for property, plant and equipment and intangible assets used in operations subject to rate regulation although IFRS 14 is not applied.

Extract 5.9: Enersource Corporation (2012)

Notes to Consolidated Financial Statements [extract]

Note 5 First-time adoption of IFRS: [extract]

(a) Previous Canadian GAAP carrying amount as deemed costs for PP&E and intangible assets. [extract]

Entities with operations subject to rate regulations may hold items of PP&E or intangible assets where the carrying amount of such items might include amounts that were determined under previous Canadian GAAP but do not qualify for capitalization in accordance with IFRS. If this is the case, a first-time adopter may elect to use the previous Canadian GAAP carrying amount of such an item at the date of transition to IFRS as deemed cost. An entity shall apply this exemption for annual periods beginning on or after 1 January 2011, but earlier application is permitted.

Entities are subject to rate regulation if they provide goods or services to customers at prices (i.e. rates) established by an authorized body empowered to establish rates that bind the customers and that are designed to recover the specific costs the entity incurs in providing the regulated goods or services and to earn a specified return.

Under this exemption the deemed cost at the date of transition becomes the new IFRS cost basis. The accumulated amortization recognized under previous Canadian GAAP prior to the transition date has been included as part of the deemed cost so that the net book values will not be affected.

At the date of transition to IFRS, an entity shall also test for impairment, each item for which this exemption is used.

This exemption does not only apply to individual entities with rate regulated activities but also to the consolidated financial statements of their parent companies.

Based on the definition above, the Corporation qualifies for this IFRS 1 exemption as Enersource Hydro is subject to rate regulations and accordingly the Corporation elected to use the deemed cost election for opening balance sheet values for its PP&E and intangible assets.

At the date of transition, the Corporation's gross book value, accumulated depreciation and net book value for PP&E was $872,359, $422,992 and $449,367 respectively. The gross book value, accumulated amortization and net book value for intangible assets was $18,389, $2,806 and $15,583 respectively.

The Corporation reviewed the additional requirements against the information provided in IAS 36 Impairment of Assets and determined that no impairments would be recorded.

While the current exemption in paragraph D8B of IFRS 1 provides a one-time relief to determine the transition-date balances of the eligible property, plant and equipment, right-of-use assets under IFRS 16 and intangible assets, IFRS 14 is wider in scope (see 5.20 below).

5.5.5 Summary

At its date of transition to IFRSs, a first-time adopter is allowed under IFRS 1 to measure the following assets and liabilities using a deemed cost:

- an item of property, plant and equipment, an investment property, a right-of-use asset under IFRS 16 and an intangible asset meeting certain criteria:
    - at fair value at the date of transition to IFRSs (see 5.5.1 above);
    - using a previous GAAP revaluation amount (at or before the date of transition) that is broadly comparable to (see 5.5.1 above):
        - fair value at the date of revaluation; or
        - cost or depreciated cost under IFRSs adjusted to reflect, for example, changes in a general or specific price index as a deemed cost as at the date of the revaluation;
- a right-of-use asset for a lessee, at a carrying amount based on certain exemptions in IFRS 1 (see 5.6 below);
- some or all of its assets and liabilities, based on a previous GAAP measure of deemed cost at one particular date that arose from an event-driven fair value, for example, at the date of an initial public offering or privatisation (see 5.5.2 above);
- assets acquired or liabilities assumed in a business combination not restated under IFRSs (see 5.2 above):
    - using a deemed cost, as at the date of the business combination, equal to the carrying amount under previous GAAP immediately after that business combination; or
    - if the item was not recognised under previous GAAP, using the carrying amount at the date of transition on the basis that IFRSs would require in the separate statement of financial position of the acquiree;
- certain oil and gas assets at a deemed cost at the date of transition based on the previous GAAP carrying amount (see 5.5.3 above);
- certain assets used or previously used in operations subject to rate regulation, at a deemed cost at the date of transition based on the previous GAAP carrying amount (see 5.5.4 above); and
- an investment in a subsidiary, joint venture or associate in separate financial statements (see 5.8.2 below).

The fact that IFRS 1 offers so many different bases for measurement does not disturb the IASB as it reasons that 'cost is generally equivalent to fair value at the date of acquisition. Therefore, the use of fair value as the deemed cost of an asset means that an entity will report the same cost data as if it had acquired an asset with the same remaining service potential at the date of transition to IFRSs. If there is any lack of comparability, it arises from the aggregation of costs incurred at different dates, rather than from the targeted use of fair value as deemed cost for some assets. The Board regarded this approach as justified to solve the unique problem of introducing IFRSs in a cost-effective way without damaging transparency.' *[IFRS 1.BC43]*. Although this is valid, it still means that an individual first-time adopter can greatly influence its future reported performance by carefully making decision on whether to apply these exemptions for the valuation of its assets. Users of the financial statements of a first-time adopter should therefore be mindful that historical trends under the previous GAAP might no longer be present in an entity's IFRS financial statements.

Where IFRSs require subsequent measurement of an asset or liability on a basis that is not based on original cost, for example, fair value, the asset or liability must be measured as at the date of transition on that basis. *[IFRS 1.7]*. This does not mean that a deemed cost may not be used. For example, where a class of property, plant and equipment is measured using the revaluation model, its carrying amount reflects the revalued amount under IAS 16 but the revaluation surplus is based on the difference between the revalued amount and the deemed cost (or historical cost) as at the date of transition. See 7.4.3 below.

5.6   Leases

IFRS 1 (paragraphs D9-D9E) provide first-time adopters with some exemptions from full retrospective application of IFRS 16.

Firstly, a first-time adopter may assess whether a contract existing at the date of transition contains a lease by applying paragraphs 9 to 11 of IFRS 16 to these contracts on the basis of facts and circumstances existing at that date. *[IFRS 1.D9, IFRS 16.9-11]*.

Example 5.32:   Determining whether an arrangement contains a lease

Entity A's first IFRS financial statements are for a period that ends on 31 December 2021 and include comparative information for 2020 only. Its date of transition to IFRSs is 1 January 2020.

On 1 January 2009, Entity A entered into a take-or-pay arrangement to supply gas. On 1 January 2014, there was a change in the contractual terms of the arrangement.

On 1 January 2020, Entity A may determine whether the arrangement contains a lease under IFRS 16 on the basis of facts and circumstances existing on that date. Alternatively, Entity A may apply the criteria in IFRS 16 on the basis of facts and circumstances existing on 1 January 2009 but will need to reassess the arrangement on 1 January 2014 in respect of the changes made on that date. *[IFRS16.11]*.

In addition, a first-time adopter that is a lessee may apply the following approach to all of its leases (subject to the practical expedients described in paragraph D9D of IFRS 1, as detailed below): *[IFRS 1.D9B]*

(a)   Measure a lease liability at the date of transition. A lessee must measure the lease liability at the present value of the remaining lease payments, discounted using the lessee's incremental borrowing rate at the date of transition.

(b) Measure a right-of-use asset at the date of transition by choosing, on a lease-by-lease basis, either:
 (i) its carrying amount as if IFRS 16 had been applied since the commencement date of the lease, but discounted using the lessee's incremental borrowing rate at the date of transition; or
 (ii) an amount equal to the lease liability, adjusted by the amount of any prepaid or accrued lease payments relating to that lease recognised in the statement of financial position immediately before the date of transition.
(c) Apply IAS 36 to right-of-use assets at the date of transition.

Notwithstanding the exemption above, a first-time adopter that is a lessee should measure the right-of-use asset at fair value at the date of transition for leases that meet the definition of investment property in IAS 40 and are measured using the fair value model in IAS 40 from the date of transition. *[IFRS 1.D9C]*.

Additionally, a first-time adopter that is a lessee may apply one or more of the following practical expedients at the date of transition (applied on a lease-by-lease basis): *[IFRS 1.D9D]*

(a) apply a single discount rate to a portfolio of leases with reasonably similar characteristics (e.g. a similar remaining lease term for a similar class of underlying asset in a similar economic environment);
(b) elect not to apply paragraph D9B of IFRS 1 to leases for which the lease term ends within 12 months of the date of transition. Instead, the entity must account for (including disclosure of information about) these leases as if they were short-term leases accounted for under paragraph 6 of IFRS 16; *[IFRS 1.D9B, IFRS 16.6]*
(c) elect not to apply paragraph D9B of IFRS 1 to leases for which the underlying asset is of low value (as described in paragraphs B3-B8 of IFRS 16). Instead, the entity must account for (including disclosure of information about) these leases under paragraph 6 of IFRS 16; *[IFRS 1.D9B, IFRS 16.6, B3-B8]*
(d) exclude initial direct costs from the measurement of the right-of-use asset at the date of transition; and
(e) use hindsight, such as in determining the lease term if the contract contains options to extend or terminate the lease.

Lease payments, lessee, lessee's incremental borrowing rate, commencement date of the lease, initial direct costs and lease term are defined in IFRS 16 and are used in IFRS 1 with the same meaning (see Chapter 23 at 2.4 and 4). *[IFRS 1.D9E, IFRS 16 Appendix A]*.

5.7 Cumulative translation differences

IAS 21 requires that an entity recognise some translation differences in other comprehensive income and accumulate these in a separate component of equity. On disposal of a foreign operation, the cumulative amount of the exchange differences deferred in the separate component of equity relating to that foreign operation (which includes, for example, the cumulative translation difference for that foreign operation, the exchange differences arising on certain translations to a different presentation currency and any gains and losses on related hedges) must be reclassified to profit or loss when the gain or loss on disposal is recognised. This also applies to exchange differences arising on monetary items that form part of a reporting entity's net investment in a foreign operation in its consolidated financial statements. *[IAS 21.32, 39, 48, IFRS 1.D12]*.

Full retrospective application of IAS 21 would require a first-time adopter to restate all financial statements of its foreign operations to IFRSs from their date of inception or later acquisition onwards, and then determine the cumulative translation differences arising in relation to each of these foreign operations. A first-time adopter need not comply with these requirements for cumulative translation differences that existed at the date of transition. If it uses this exemption: *[IFRS 1.D13]*

(a) the cumulative translation differences for all foreign operations are deemed to be zero at the date of transition to IFRSs; and

(b) the gain or loss on a subsequent disposal of any foreign operation must exclude translation differences that arose before the date of transition but must include later translation differences.

If a first-time adopter chooses to use this exemption, it must apply it to all foreign operations at its date of transition, which will include any foreign operations that became first-time adopters before their parent. Any existing separate component of the first-time adopter's equity relating to such translation differences would be transferred to retained earnings at the date of transition.

A subsidiary, an associate or a joint venture which becomes a first-time adopter later than its parent is also allowed to use this exemption even if paragraph D16(a) of IFRS 1 is applied (see 5.9.1 below). However, in May 2020, the IASB issued *Annual Improvements to IFRS Standards 2018-2020* and IFRS 1 was amended to introduce a further option for measurement of the cumulative translation differences at the date of transition for such entities (see 5.9.1.A below). *[IFRS 1.D13A, D16(a)]*.

An entity may present its financial statements in a presentation currency that differs from its functional currency. IFRS 1 is silent on whether the cumulative translation differences exemption should be applied to all translation differences or possibly separately to differences between the parent's functional currency and the presentation currency. However, IAS 21 does not distinguish between the translation differences arising on translation of subsidiaries into the functional currency of the parent and those arising on the translation from the parent's functional currency to the presentation currency. In our opinion, the exemption should therefore be applied consistently to both types of translation differences.

Since there is no requirement to justify the use of the exemption on grounds of impracticality or undue cost or effort, an entity that already has a separate component of equity and the necessary information to determine how much of it relates to each foreign operation in accordance with IAS 21 (or can do so without much effort) is still able to use the exemption. Accordingly, an entity that has cumulative exchange losses in respect of foreign operations may consider it advantageous to use the exemption if it wishes to avoid having to recognise these losses in profit or loss if the foreign operation is sold at some time in the future.

The extract below illustrates how companies typically disclose the fact that they have made use of this exemption.

> Extract 5.10: Coca-Cola FEMSA S.A.B. de C.V. (2012)
> NOTE 27 First-time adoption of IFRS [extract]
> 27.3 Explanation of the effects of the adoption of IFRS [extract]
> h) Cumulative Translation Effects [extract]
> The Company decided to use the exemption provided by IFRS 1, which permits it to adjust at the transition date all the translation effects it had recognized under Mexican FRS to zero and begin to record them in accordance with IAS 21 on a prospective basis. The effect was Ps. 1,000 at the transition date, net of deferred income taxes of Ps. 1,887.

5.7.1 Gains and losses arising on related hedges

Although IFRS 1 is not entirely clear whether this exemption extends to similar gains and losses arising on related hedges, we believe it is entirely appropriate for this exemption to be applied to net investment hedges as well as the underlying gains and losses.

Paragraph D13, which contains the exemption, explains that a first-time adopter need not comply with 'these requirements.' *[IFRS 1.D13]*. The requirements referred to are those summarised in paragraph D12 which explain that IAS 21 requires an entity: *[IFRS 1.D12]*

(a) to recognise some translation differences in other comprehensive income and accumulate these in a separate component of equity; and

(b) on disposal of a foreign operation, to reclassify the cumulative translation difference for that foreign operation (*including, if applicable, gains and losses on related hedges*) [our emphasis] from equity to profit or loss as part of the gain or loss on disposal.

The problem arises because paragraph D12 does not refer to the recognition of hedging gains or losses in other comprehensive income and accumulation in a separate component of equity (only the subsequent reclassification thereof). Accordingly, a very literal reading of the standard might suggest that an entity is required to identify historical gains and losses on such hedges. However, even if this position is accepted, the basis on which this might be done is not at all clear.

It is clear that the reasons cited by the IASB for including this exemption apply as much to related hedges as they do to the underlying exchange differences. The fact that IFRS 1 can be read otherwise might be seen as little more than poor drafting.

5.8 Investments in subsidiaries, joint ventures and associates

5.8.1 Consolidated financial statements: subsidiaries and structured entities

A first-time adopter must consolidate all subsidiaries (as defined in IFRS 10) unless IFRS 10 requires otherwise. *[IFRS 1.IG26]*. First-time adoption of IFRSs may therefore result in the consolidation for the first time of a subsidiary not consolidated under previous GAAP, either because the subsidiary was not regarded as such before, or because the parent did not prepare consolidated financial statements. If a first-time adopter did not consolidate a subsidiary under its previous GAAP, it must recognise the assets and liabilities of that subsidiary in its consolidated financial statements at the date of transition at either: *[IFRS 1.IG27(a)]*

(a) if the subsidiary has adopted IFRSs, the same carrying amounts as in the IFRS financial statements of the subsidiary, after adjusting for consolidation procedures and for the effects of the business combination in which it acquired the subsidiary; *[IFRS 1.D17]* or

(b) if the subsidiary has not adopted IFRSs, the carrying amounts that IFRSs would require in the subsidiary's statement of financial position. *[IFRS 1.C4(j)]*.

If the newly-consolidated subsidiary was acquired in a business combination before the date of the parent's transition to IFRSs, goodwill is the difference between the parent's interest in the carrying amount determined under either (a) or (b) above and the cost in the parent's separate financial statements of its investment in the subsidiary. This is no more than a pragmatic 'plug' that facilitates the consolidation process but does not represent the true goodwill that might have been recorded if IFRSs had been applied to the original business combination (see 5.2.7 above). *[IFRS 1.C4(j), IG27(b)]*. Therefore, if the first-time adopter accounted for the investment as an associate under its previous GAAP, it cannot use the notional goodwill previously calculated under the equity method as the basis for goodwill under IFRSs.

If the parent did not acquire the subsidiary, but established it, it does not recognise goodwill. *[IFRS 1.IG27(c)]*. Any difference between the carrying amount of the subsidiary and the identifiable net assets as determined in (a) or (b) above would be treated as an adjustment to retained earnings, representing the accumulated profits or losses that would have been recognised as if the subsidiary had always been consolidated.

The adjustment of the carrying amounts of assets and liabilities of a first-time adopter's subsidiaries may affect non-controlling interests and deferred tax, as discussed at 5.2.9 above. *[IFRS 1.IG28]*.

5.8.2 Separate financial statements: Cost of an investment in a subsidiary, joint venture or associate

When an entity prepares separate financial statements, IAS 27 requires a first-time adopter to account for its investments in subsidiaries, joint ventures and associates either: *[IFRS 1.D14]*

- at cost;
- in accordance with IFRS 9; or
- using the equity method as described in IAS 28.

However, if a first-time adopter measures such an investment at cost then it can elect to measure that investment at one of the following amounts in its separate opening IFRS statement of financial position: *[IFRS 1.D15]*

(a) cost determined in accordance with IAS 27; or
(b) deemed cost, which is its:
 (i) fair value at the entity's date of transition to IFRSs in its separate financial statements; or
 (ii) previous GAAP carrying amount at that date.

A first-time adopter may choose to use either of these bases to measure its investment in each subsidiary, joint venture or associate where it elects to use a deemed cost. *[IFRS 1.D15]*.

For a first-time adopter that chooses to account for such an investment using the equity method procedures in accordance with IAS 28: *[IFRS 1.D15A]*

(a) the first-time adopter applies the exemption for past business combinations in IFRS 1 (Appendix C) to the acquisition of the investment (see 5.2 above); *[IFRS 1 Appendix C]*
(b) if the entity becomes a first-time adopter for its separate financial statements earlier than for its consolidated financial statements and:
 (i) later than its parent, the entity would apply paragraph D16 of IFRS 1 in its separate financial statements (see 5.9.1 below); *[IFRS 1.D16]*
 (ii) later than its subsidiary, the entity would apply paragraph D17 of IFRS 1 in its separate financial statements (see 5.9.2 below). *[IFRS 1.D17]*.

A first-time adopter that applies the exemption should disclose certain additional information in its financial statements (see 6.5.2 below).

5.9 Assets and liabilities of subsidiaries, associates and joint ventures

Within groups, some subsidiaries, associates and joint ventures may have a different date of transition to IFRSs than the parent/investor, for example, because national legislation required IFRSs after, or prohibited IFRSs at, the date of transition of the parent/investor. As this could have resulted in permanent differences between the IFRS figures in a subsidiary's own financial statements and those it reports to its parent, the IASB introduced a special exemption regarding the assets and liabilities of subsidiaries, associates and joint ventures.

IFRS 1 contains detailed guidance on the approach to be adopted when a parent adopts IFRSs before its subsidiary (see 5.9.1 below) and when a subsidiary adopts IFRSs before its parent (see 5.9.2 below).

These provisions also apply when IFRSs are adopted at different dates by an investor in an associate and the associate, or a venturer in a joint venture and the joint venture. *[IFRS 1.D16-D17]*. In the discussion that follows 'parent' includes an investor in an associate or a venturer in a joint venture, and 'subsidiary' includes an associate or a joint venture. References to consolidation adjustments include similar adjustments made when applying equity accounting. IFRS 1 also addresses the requirements for a parent that adopts IFRSs at different dates for the purposes of its consolidated and its separate financial statements (see 5.9.4 below).

5.9.1 Subsidiary becomes a first-time adopter later than its parent

If a subsidiary becomes a first-time adopter later than its parent, it must in its financial statements measure its own assets and liabilities at either: *[IFRS 1.D16]*

(a) the carrying amounts that would be included in the parent's consolidated financial statements, based on the parent's date of transition, if no adjustments were made for consolidation procedures and for the effects of the business combination in which the parent acquired the subsidiary; or

(b) the carrying amounts required by the rest of IFRS 1, based on the subsidiary's date of transition. These carrying amounts could differ from those described in (a) when:

    (i) the exemptions in IFRS 1 result in measurements that depend on the date of transition;

    (ii) the subsidiary's accounting policies are different from those in the consolidated financial statements. For example, under IAS 16 the subsidiary may carry property at cost while the group uses the revaluation model, or *vice versa*.

IFRS 1 does not elaborate on exactly what constitutes 'consolidation procedures' but in our view it would encompass adjustments required in order to harmonise a subsidiary's accounting policies with those of the group, as well as purely 'mechanical' consolidation adjustments such as the elimination of intragroup balances, profits and losses.

The following example, which is based on the implementation guidance in IFRS 1, illustrates how an entity should apply these requirements. *[IFRS 1.IG Example 8]*.

Example 5.33: Parent adopts IFRSs before subsidiary

Entity A presents its (consolidated) first IFRS financial statements in 2014. Its foreign subsidiary B, wholly owned by Entity A since formation, prepares information under IFRSs for internal consolidation purposes from that date, but Subsidiary B will not present its first IFRS financial statements until 2021.

If Subsidiary B applies option (a) above, the carrying amounts of its assets and liabilities are the same in both its opening IFRS statement of financial position at 1 January 2020 and Entity A's consolidated statement of financial position (except for adjustments for consolidation procedures) and are based on Entity A's date of transition.

Alternatively, Subsidiary B may apply option (b) above, and measure all its assets or liabilities based on its own date of transition to IFRSs (1 January 2020). However, the fact that Subsidiary B becomes a first-time adopter in 2021 does not change the carrying amounts of its assets and liabilities in Entity A's consolidated financial statements.

Under option (b) a subsidiary would prepare its own IFRS financial statements, completely ignoring the IFRS elections that its parent used when it adopted IFRSs for its consolidated financial statements.

Under option (a) the numbers in a subsidiary's IFRS financial statements will be as close to those used by its parent as possible. However, differences other than those arising from business combinations will still exist in many cases, for example:

- a subsidiary may have hedged an exposure by entering into a transaction with a fellow subsidiary. Such transaction could qualify for hedge accounting in the subsidiary's own financial statements but not in the group's consolidated financial statements; or
- a pension plan may have to be classified as a defined contribution plan from the subsidiary's point of view, but is accounted for as a defined benefit plan in the group's consolidated financial statements.

The IASB seems content with the fact that the exemption will ease some practical problems, *[IFRS 1.BC62]*, though it will rarely succeed in achieving more than a moderate reduction of the number of reconciling differences between a subsidiary's own reporting and the numbers used by its parent.

More importantly, the choice of option (a) prevents the subsidiary from electing to apply any of the other voluntary exemptions offered by IFRS 1, since the parent had already made the choices for the group at its date of transition. Therefore, option (a) may not be appropriate for a subsidiary that prefers to use a different exemption (e.g. fair value as deemed cost) for property, plant and equipment due, for example, to a tax reporting advantage. Also, application of option (a) would allow the subsidiary to adopt a new IFRS that becomes effective during any of the periods presented in the same manner it was adopted by the parent. Option (a) is more difficult when a parent and its subsidiary have different financial years. In that case, IFRS 1 would seem to require the IFRS information for the subsidiary to be based on the parent's date of transition to IFRSs, which may not even coincide with an interim reporting date of the subsidiary; the same applies to any joint venture or associate.

Example 5.34 below explains the interaction between paragraph D16(a) of IFRS 1 (i.e. option (a) above) and the business combination exemptions in Appendix C of IFRS 1 applied by its parent.

Example 5.34:   Interaction between paragraph D16(a) of IFRS 1 and the business combination exemptions applied by its parent

Entity S has been a subsidiary of Entity P since 2014. Entity G was acquired by Entity S in 2016 and Entity S accounted for the acquisition under its previous GAAP. Entity P transitioned from previous GAAP to IFRSs in 2017 and decided to apply the business combination exemption in Appendix C of IFRS 1 to this acquisition. Entity S adopted IFRSs from its date of transition of 1 January 2020 and chose to apply paragraph D16(a) of IFRS 1.

Can Entity S apply IFRS 3 retrospectively to the acquisition of Entity G in its first IFRS financial statements?

In our opinion, Entity S cannot apply IFRS 3 to the acquisition of Entity G because, applying paragraph D16(a) of IFRS 1, a subsidiary which becomes a first-time adopter later than its parent measures its assets and liabilities at the carrying amount that would be included in the parent's consolidated financial statements, based on the parent's date of transition to IFRSs. Therefore, Entity S cannot apply IFRS 3 retrospectively, meeting the primary objective of using the paragraph D16(a) election in keeping one set of books.

A subsidiary may become a first-time adopter later than its parent, because it previously prepared a reporting package under IFRSs for consolidation purposes but did not present a full set of financial statements under IFRSs. The above election of paragraph D16(a) of IFRS 1 may be relevant not only when a subsidiary's reporting package complies fully with the recognition and measurement requirements of IFRSs, but also when it is adjusted centrally for matters such as review of events after the reporting period and central allocation of pension costs. Adjustments made centrally to an unpublished reporting package are not considered to be corrections of errors for the purposes of the disclosure requirements in IFRS 1. However, a subsidiary is not permitted to ignore misstatements that are immaterial to the consolidated financial statements of the group but material to its own financial statements. *[IFRS 1.IG31]*.

If a subsidiary was acquired after the parent's date of transition to IFRSs then it cannot apply option (a) because there are no carrying amounts included in the parent's consolidated financial statements, based on the parent's date of transition. Therefore, the subsidiary is unable to use the values recognised in the group accounts when it was acquired, since push-down of the group's purchase accounting values is not allowed in the subsidiary's financial statements. However, if the subsidiary had recognised those amounts in its previous GAAP financial statements, it may be able to use the same amounts as deemed costs under IFRSs pursuant to the 'event-driven' deemed cost exemption (see 5.5.2 above).

The exemption is also available to associates and joint ventures. This means that in many cases an associate or joint venture that wants to apply option (a) will need to choose which shareholder it considers its 'parent' for IFRS 1 purposes if more than one investor/joint venturer have already applied IFRS and determine the IFRS carrying amount of its assets and liabilities by reference to that parent's date of transition to IFRSs.

A subsidiary that adopts IFRSs after its investment entity parent is not permitted to use option (a) (see 5.9.5.A below).

5.9.1.A Cumulative translation differences

The IFRS Interpretations Committee considered whether a subsidiary that becomes a first-time adopter later than its parent and has foreign operations can recognise the cumulative translation differences at an amount that would be included in the parent's consolidated financial statements, based on the parent's date of transition to IFRSs, when it applies paragraph D16(a) of IFRS 1.

In September 2017, the Committee reached the conclusion that the cumulative translation differences are neither assets nor liabilities whereas the requirement in paragraph D16(a) applies to assets and liabilities. Hence, the requirement does not permit the subsidiary to recognise the cumulative translation differences at the amount as above. The Committee also concluded that the requirement cannot be applied to the cumulative translation differences by analogy because paragraph 18 of IFRS 1 clearly prohibits an entity from applying the exemptions in IFRS 1 by analogy to other items.[5]

However, in May 2020, the IASB issued *Annual Improvements to IFRS Standards 2018-2020* and IFRS 1 was amended. The amendment permits a subsidiary that applies paragraph D16(a) of IFRS 1 to measure cumulative translation differences at the carrying amount that would be included in its parent's consolidated financial statements, based on the parent's date of transition to IFRSs (if no adjustments were made for consolidation procedures and for the effects of the business combination in which the parent acquired the subsidiary). A similar election is available to an associate or joint venture that uses the exemption in paragraph D16(a) of IFRS 1. *[IFRS 1.D13A]*. The amendment is effective for annual reporting periods beginning on or after 1 January 2022. Earlier application is permitted with disclosing the fact. The subsidiary still has the option to apply IAS 21 retrospectively or apply paragraph D13 of IFRS 1 and deem the cumulative translation differences for all foreign operations to be zero at the date of transition to IFRSs (see 5.7 above). *[IFRS 1.D12, D13, D13A, BC55C]*.

5.9.2 Parent becomes a first-time adopter later than its subsidiary

If a parent becomes a first-time adopter later than its subsidiary, the parent must, in its consolidated financial statements, measure the subsidiary's assets and liabilities at the same carrying amounts that are in the subsidiary's financial statements, after adjusting for consolidation adjustments and for the effects of the business combination in which the entity acquired the subsidiary. The same applies for associates or joint ventures, substituting equity accounting adjustments. *[IFRS 1.D17]*.

Unlike other first-time adoption exemptions, this exemption does not offer a choice between different accounting alternatives. In fact, while a subsidiary that adopts IFRSs later than its parent can choose to prepare its first IFRS financial statements by reference to its own date of transition to IFRSs or that of its parent, the parent itself must use the IFRS measurements already used in the subsidiary's financial statements, adjusted as appropriate for consolidation procedures and the effects of the business combination in which it acquired the subsidiary. *[IFRS 1.BC63]*. However, this exemption does not preclude the parent from adjusting the subsidiary's assets and liabilities for a different accounting policy, e.g. cost model or revaluation model for accounting for property, plant and equipment.

The following example, which is based on the implementation guidance in IFRS 1, illustrates how an entity should apply these requirements. *[IFRS 1.IG Example 9]*.

Example 5.35: Subsidiary adopts IFRSs before parent

Entity C presents its (consolidated) first IFRS financial statements in 2021. Its foreign subsidiary D, wholly owned by Entity C since formation, presented its first IFRS financial statements in 2016. Until 2021, Subsidiary D prepared information for internal consolidation purposes under Entity C's previous GAAP.

The carrying amounts of Subsidiary D's assets and liabilities at 1 January 2020 are the same in both Entity C's (consolidated) opening IFRS statement of financial position and Subsidiary D's own financial statements (except for adjustments for consolidation procedures) and are based on Subsidiary D's date of transition to IFRSs. The fact that Entity C becomes a first-time adopter in 2021 does not change the carrying amounts of Subsidiary D's assets and liabilities in the group's first IFRS consolidated financial statements.

When a subsidiary adopts IFRSs before its parent, this will limit the parent's ability to choose first-time adoption exemptions in IFRS 1 freely as related to that subsidiary, as illustrated in the example below. However, this does not mean that the parent's ability to choose first-time adoption exemptions will always be limited. For example, a parent may still be able to deem a subsidiary's cumulative translation differences to be zero because IFRS 1 specifically states that under the option 'the cumulative translation differences for *all* [emphasis added] foreign operations are deemed to be zero at the date of transition to IFRSs' (see 5.7 above). *[IFRS 1.D13]*.

Example 5.36:   Limited ability to choose first-time adoption exemptions

Entity E will adopt IFRSs for the first time in 2021 and its date of transition is 1 January 2020. Subsidiary F adopted IFRSs in 2016 and its date of transition was 1 January 2015:

(a) *Subsidiary F and Entity E both account for their property, plant and equipment at historical cost under IAS 16.*

Upon first-time adoption, Entity E may only adjust carrying amounts of Subsidiary F's assets and liabilities to adjust for the effects of consolidation and business combinations. Entity E can therefore not apply the exemption to use fair value as deemed cost for Subsidiary F's property, plant and equipment as at its own date of transition (1 January 2020);

(b) *Subsidiary F accounts for its property, plant and equipment at revalued amounts under IAS 16, while Entity E accounts for its property, plant and equipment at historical cost under IAS 16.*

In this case, Entity E would not be allowed to apply the exemption to use fair value as deemed cost of Subsidiary F's property, plant and equipment because paragraph D17 of IFRS 1 would only permit adjustments for the effects of consolidation and business combinations. Although a consolidation adjustment would be necessary, this would only be to adjust Subsidiary F's revalued amounts to figures based on historical cost.

(c) *Subsidiary F may have deemed the cumulative translation difference for all its foreign subsidiaries to be zero at its date of transition (i.e. 1 January 2015).*

When Entity E adopts IFRSs it can deem Subsidiary F's cumulative translation differences to be zero at its date of transition (1 January 2020). This is because those cumulative translation differences result from translation of Subsidiary F's financial statements into Entity E's presentation currency.

The case where a non-investment entity parent adopts IFRSs after its investment entity subsidiary is discussed at 5.9.5.B below.

5.9.3 Implementation guidance on accounting for assets and liabilities of subsidiaries, associates and joint ventures

The requirements of IFRS 1 for a parent and subsidiary with different dates of transition do not override the following requirements of IFRS 1: *[IFRS 1.IG30]*

- the parent's election to use the business combinations exemption in Appendix C discussed at 5.2 above, which applies to assets and liabilities of a subsidiary acquired in a business combination that occurred before the parent's date of transition to IFRSs. However, the rules summarised at 5.9.2 above (parent adopting IFRSs after subsidiary) apply to assets acquired and liabilities assumed by the subsidiary after the business combination and still held and owned by it at the parent's date of transition to IFRSs;

- to apply the requirements in IFRS 1 in measuring items in the financial statements for which the provisions in paragraphs D16 and D17 of IFRS 1 are not relevant (for example, the use of the exemption in paragraph D16(a) to measure assets and liabilities at the carrying amounts in the parent's consolidated financial statements does not affect the use of the exemption in paragraph D13 of IFRS 1 to deem the cumulative translation differences for all foreign operations are zero at its date of transition, discussed in 5.7 above, since this is neither an asset nor a liability. However, the subsidiary also has an option to measure the cumulative translation differences at the carrying amount that would be included in its parent's consolidated financial statements, based on the parent's date of transition to IFRSs (if no adjustments were made for consolidation procedures and for the effects of the business combination in which the parent acquired the subsidiary). See 5.9.1.A above; *[IFRS 1.D13, D13A]* and

- a first-time adopter must give all the disclosures required by IFRS 1 as of its own date of transition to IFRSs – see 6 below.

5.9.4 Adoption of IFRSs on different dates in separate and consolidated financial statements

An entity may sometimes become a first-time adopter for its separate financial statements earlier or later than for its consolidated financial statements. Such a situation may arise, for example, when a parent avails itself of the exemption under paragraph 4 of IFRS 10 from preparing consolidated financial statements and prepares its separate financial statements under IFRSs (see Chapter 6 at 2.2). *[IFRS 10.4]*. Subsequently, the parent may cease to be entitled to the exemption or may choose not to use it and would, therefore, be required to apply IFRS 1 in its first IFRS consolidated financial statements.

Another example might be that, under local law, an entity is required to prepare its consolidated financial statements under IFRSs, but is required (or permitted) to prepare its separate financial statements under local GAAP. Subsequently the parent chooses, or is required, to prepare its separate financial statements under IFRSs.

If a parent becomes a first-time adopter for its separate financial statements earlier or later than for its consolidated financial statements, it must measure its assets and liabilities at the same amounts in both financial statements, except for consolidation adjustments. *[IFRS 1.D17]*. As drafted, the requirement is merely that the 'same' amounts be used, without being explicit as to which set of financial statements should be used as the benchmark. However, it seems clear from the context that the IASB intends that the measurement basis used in whichever set of financial statements first comply with IFRSs must also be used when IFRSs are subsequently adopted in the other set.

5.9.5 Application to investment entities under IFRS 10

IFRS 10 requires a parent that is an 'investment entity' as defined in the standard (see Chapter 6 at 10) to account for most of its subsidiaries at fair value through profit or loss in its consolidated financial statements rather than through consolidation. *[IFRS 10.31, Appendix A]*. This exception from normal consolidation procedures does not apply to:

- a parent entity that owns a subsidiary which is an investment entity but the parent itself is not an investment entity; *[IFRS 10.33]* or
- a parent that is an investment entity in accounting for subsidiary that is not itself an investment entity and whose main purpose and activities are providing services that relate to the investment entity's investment activities. *[IFRS 10.32]*.

In IFRS 1, there are exemptions relating to a parent adopting IFRSs earlier or later than its subsidiary. Below, we deal with situations where:

- a subsidiary that is required to be measured at fair value through profit or loss adopts IFRSs after its parent which is an investment entity (see 5.9.5.A below); or
- a parent that is not an 'investment entity' adopts IFRSs after a subsidiary which is an investment entity (see 5.9.5.B below).

5.9.5.A Subsidiary adopts IFRSs after investment entity parent

In this case, the subsidiary that is required to be measured at fair value through profit or loss must measure its assets and liabilities under the general provisions of IFRS 1, based on its own date of transition to IFRSs (i.e. option (b) in 5.9.1 above), *[IFRS 1.D16(a)]*, rather than (as would generally be permitted under option (a) in 5.9.1 above) by reference to the carrying amounts of its assets and liabilities in the consolidated financial statements of its parent, which are based on the fair value of the subsidiary's equity. This effectively prevents the accounting anomaly of the subsidiary measuring its net assets at the fair value of its own equity on transition to IFRSs.

5.9.5.B Non-investment entity parent adopts IFRSs after investment entity subsidiary

In this case, the parent is required to consolidate its subsidiaries and is not able to use the exception to consolidation in IFRS 10 (used by its investment entity subsidiaries). *[IFRS 1.D17]*. If the provisions in 5.9.2 above were to be applied, the effect would be that the parent would bring any investments in subsidiaries accounted for at fair value through profit or loss by the subsidiary into the parent's consolidated statement of financial position at their fair value. This would be contrary to the intention of the investment entities concept that such an accounting treatment is applied only by a parent that is itself an investment entity and paragraph D17 of IFRS 1 specifically prohibits this.

5.10 Compound financial instruments

IAS 32 requires compound financial instruments (e.g. many convertible bonds) to be split at inception into separate equity and liability components on the basis of facts and circumstances existing when the instrument was issued. *[IAS 32.15, 28]*. If the liability component is no longer outstanding, a full retrospective application of IAS 32 would involve identifying two components, one representing the original equity component and the other (retained earnings) representing the cumulative interest accreted on the liability component, both of which are accounted for in equity (see Chapter 47 at 6). A first-time adopter does not need to make this possibly complex allocation if the liability component is no longer outstanding at the date of transition to IFRSs. *[IFRS 1.D18]*. For example, in the case of a convertible bond that has been converted into equity, it is not necessary to make this split.

However, if the liability component of the compound instrument is still outstanding at the date of transition to IFRSs then a split is required to be made (see Chapter 47 at 6). *[IFRS 1.IG35-IG36]*.

5.11 Designation of previously recognised financial instruments

The following discusses the application of the exemption in paragraphs D19 to D19C of IFRS 1 regarding designation of previously recognised financial instruments to certain financial assets and financial liabilities.

5.11.1 Designation of financial asset as measured at fair value through profit or loss

IFRS 9 permits a financial asset to be designated as measured at fair value through profit or loss if the entity meets the criteria in paragraph 4.1.5 of IFRS 9 at the date the entity becomes a party to the financial instrument (see Chapter 48 at 7). *[IFRS 9.4.1.5]*.

Paragraph D19A of IFRS 1 allows a first-time adopter to designate a financial asset as measured at fair value through profit or loss in accordance with paragraph 4.1.5 of IFRS 9 on the basis of the facts and circumstances that exist at the date of transition to IFRSs. *[IFRS 1.D19A]*. If this exemption is used, IFRS 1 requires certain additional disclosures (see 6.4 below). *[IFRS 1.29]*.

5.11.2 Designation of financial liability at fair value through profit or loss

IFRS 9 permits a financial liability to be designated as a financial liability at fair value through profit or loss if the entity meets the criteria in paragraph 4.2.2 of IFRS 9 at the date the entity becomes a party to the financial instrument (see Chapter 48 at 7). *[IFRS 9.4.2.2]*.

Paragraph D19 of IFRS 1 allows a first-time adopter to designate, at the date of transition, a financial liability as measured at fair value through profit or loss provided the liability meets the criteria in paragraph 4.2.2 of IFRS 9 at that date. *[IFRS 1.D19]*. If this exemption is used, IFRS 1 requires certain additional disclosures (see 6.4 below). *[IFRS 1.29A]*.

Where a financial liability is designated at fair value through profit or loss, the first-time adopter is also required to determine whether the accounting required by paragraph 5.7.7 of IFRS 9 would create or enlarge an accounting mismatch in profit or loss on the basis of the facts and circumstances that exist at the date of transition to IFRSs (see 5.11.4 below). *[IFRS 1.D19C, IFRS 9.5.7.7-5.7.8]*.

5.11.3 Designation of investment in an equity instrument

At initial recognition, an entity may make an irrevocable election to designate an investment in an equity instrument (that is neither held for trading nor contingent consideration recognised by an acquirer in a business combination to which IFRS 3 applies) as at fair value through other comprehensive income in accordance with IFRS 9 (see Chapter 48 at 8). *[IFRS 9.5.7.5]*.

Paragraph D19B of IFRS 1 allows a first-time adopter to designate an investment in such an equity instrument as at fair value through other comprehensive income in accordance with paragraph 5.7.5 of IFRS 9 on the basis of the facts and circumstances that exist at the date of transition to IFRSs. *[IFRS 1.D19B]*.

5.11.4 Determination of an accounting mismatch for presenting a gain or loss on financial liability

IFRS 9 requires a fair value gain or loss on a financial liability that is designated as at fair value through profit or loss to be presented as follows unless this presentation creates or enlarges an accounting mismatch in profit or loss: *[IFRS 9.5.7.7-5.7.8]*

- the amount of change in the fair value of the financial liability that is attributable to changes in the credit risk of that liability must be presented in other comprehensive income; and
- the remaining amount of change in the fair value of the liability must be presented in profit or loss.

Paragraph D19C of IFRS 1 requires a first-time adopter to determine whether the treatment in paragraph 5.7.7 of IFRS 9 would create or enlarge an accounting mismatch in profit or loss on the basis of the facts and circumstances that exist at the date of transition to IFRSs (see Chapter 48 at 3 and Chapter 50 at 2.4). *[IFRS 1.D19C]*.

5.12 Fair value measurement of financial assets or financial liabilities at initial recognition

First-time adopters are granted similar transition relief in respect of the 'day 1' gain or loss recognition requirements of IFRS 9 as is available to existing IFRS reporters in response to concerns raised by constituents that retrospective application of the requirements would be difficult and expensive to implement, and might require subjective assumptions about what was observable and what was not. *[IFRS 1.BC83A]*. Consequently, first-time adopters may apply the requirements of paragraph B5.1.2A(b) of IFRS 9 about a deferral of the 'day 1' gain/loss prospectively to transactions entered into on or after the date of transition to IFRSs (see Chapter 49 at 3.3). *[IFRS 1.D20, IFRS 9.B5.1.2A(b)]*.

5.13 Decommissioning liabilities included in the cost of property, plant and equipment

5.13.1 IFRIC 1 exemption

Under IAS 16, the cost of an item of property, plant and equipment includes 'the initial estimate of the costs of dismantling and removing the item and restoring the site on which it is located, the obligation for which an entity incurs either when the item is acquired or as a consequence of having used the item during a particular period for purposes other than to produce inventories during that period.' *[IAS 16.16(c)]*. Therefore, a first-time adopter needs to ensure that property, plant and equipment cost includes an item representing the decommissioning provision as determined under IAS 37. IAS 37 requires the liability, both initially and subsequently, to be measured at the amount required to settle the present obligation at the end of the reporting period, reflecting a current market-based discount rate. *[IFRS 1.IG201]*.

An entity should apply IAS 16 in determining the amount to be included in the cost of the asset, before recognising depreciation and impairment losses which cause differences between the carrying amount of the decommissioning liability and the amount related to decommissioning costs to be included in the carrying amount of the asset. *[IFRS 1.IG13]*.

An entity accounts for changes in decommissioning provisions in accordance with IFRIC 1 which requires that, subject to specified conditions, changes in an existing decommissioning, restoration or similar liability are added to or deducted from the cost of the related asset. The resulting depreciable amount of the asset is depreciated over its useful life, and the periodic unwinding of the discount on the liability is recognised in profit or loss as it occurs. However, paragraph D21 of IFRS 1 provides an exemption for changes in such liabilities that occurred before the date of transition to IFRSs and prescribes an alternative treatment if the exemption is used. *[IFRS 1.D21, IG13, IG201-IG203, IFRIC 1]*.

In such cases, a first-time adopter must: *[IFRS 1.D21]*

(a) measure the decommissioning liability as at the date of transition in accordance with IAS 37;

(b) to the extent that the liability is within the scope of IFRIC 1, estimate the amount that would have been included in the cost of the related asset when the liability first arose, by discounting the liability to that date using its best estimate of the historical risk-adjusted discount rate(s) that would have applied for that liability over the intervening period; and

(c) calculate the accumulated depreciation on that amount, as at the date of transition to IFRSs, on the basis of the current estimate of the useful life of the asset, using the entity's IFRS depreciation policy.

Example 5.37:   Decommissioning component in property, plant and equipment

Entity A's date of transition to IFRSs is 1 January 2020 and the end of its first IFRS reporting period is 31 December 2021. Entity A built a factory that was completed and ready for use on 1 January 2015. Under its previous GAAP, Entity A accrued a decommissioning provision over the expected life of the factory. The facts can be summarised as follows:

Cost of the factory	€1,400
Residual value	€200
Economic life	20 years
Original estimate of decommissioning cost in year 20	€175
Revised estimate on 1 January 2017 of decommissioning cost in year 20	€300
Discount rate applicable to decommissioning liability (the discount rate is assumed to be constant)	5.65%
Discounted value of original decommissioning liability on 1 January 2015	€58
Discounted value on 1 January 2015 of revised decommissioning liability	€100
Discounted value on 1 January 2020 of revised decommissioning liability	€131

If Entity A applies the exemption from full retrospective application, what are the carrying amounts of the factory and the decommissioning liability in Entity A's opening IFRS statement of financial position?

The tables below show how Entity A accounts for the decommissioning liability and the factory under its previous GAAP, under IFRS 1 using the exemption and under IFRS 1 applying IFRIC 1 retrospectively.

	Decommissioning liability		
	Previous GAAP	IFRS 1 Exemption	Retrospective application of IFRIC 1
1 January 2015		100	58
Decommissioning costs €175 ÷ 20 years × 2 =	17.5		
Decommissioning costs €100 × (1.0565² – 1) =		12	
Decommissioning costs €58 × (1.0565² – 1) =			7
1 January 2017	17.5	112	65
Revised estimate of decommissioning provision	12.5		47
1 January 2017	30	112	112
Decommissioning costs €300 ÷ 20 years × 3 =	45		
Decommissioning costs €112 × (1.0565³ – 1) =		19	
Decommissioning costs €112 × (1.0565³ – 1) =			19
1 January 2020	75	131	131
Decommissioning costs €300 ÷ 20 years × 2 =	30		
Decommissioning costs €131 × (1.0565² – 1) =		16	
Decommissioning costs €131 × (1.0565² – 1) =			16
31 December 2021	105	147	147

In calculating the decommissioning provision, it makes no difference whether Entity A goes back in time and tracks the history of the decommissioning provision or whether it just calculates the decommissioning provision at its date of transition to IFRSs. This is not the case for the calculation of the related asset, as can be seen below.

	Factory		
	Previous GAAP	IFRS 1 Exemption	Retrospective application of IFRIC 1
1 January 2015	1,400	1,500	1,458
Depreciation (€1,400 – €200) ÷ 20 years × 2 =	(120)		
Depreciation (€1,500 – €200) ÷ 20 years × 2 =		(130)	
Depreciation (€1,458 – €200) ÷ 20 years × 2 =			(126)
1 January 2017			1,332
Revised estimate of decommissioning provision			47
1 January 2017			1,379
Depreciation (€1,400 – €200) ÷ 20 years × 3 =	(180)		
Depreciation (€1,500 – €200) ÷ 20 years × 3 =		(195)	
Depreciation (€1,379 – €200) ÷ 18 years × 3 =			(197)
1 January 2020	1,100	1,175	1,182
Depreciation (€1,400 – €200) ÷ 20 years × 2 =	(120)		
Depreciation (€1,500 – €200) ÷ 20 years × 2 =		(130)	
Depreciation (€1,379 – €200) ÷ 18 years × 2 =			(131)
31 December 2021	980	1,045	1,051

As can be seen above, a full retrospective application of IFRIC 1 would require an entity to go back in time and account for each revision of the decommissioning provision in accordance with IFRIC 1. In the case of a long-lived asset there could be a significant number of revisions that a first-time adopter would need to account for. It should also be noted that despite the significant revision of the decommissioning costs, the impact on the carrying amount of the factory is quite modest.

At its date of transition to IFRSs (1 January 2020), Entity A makes the following adjustments:

- the decommissioning liability is increased by €56 (= €131 – €75) to reflect the difference in accounting policy, irrespective of whether Entity A applies the exemption or not; and
- if Entity A applies the exemption it increases the carrying amount of the factory by €75. Whereas if Entity A applies IFRIC 1 retrospectively, the carrying amount of the factory would increase by €82.

It is important to note that in both cases the decommissioning component of the factory's carrying amount will be significantly lower than the decommissioning liability itself.

From the above example, it is clear that the exemption reduces the amount of effort required to restate items of property, plant and equipment with a decommissioning component. In many cases the difference between the two methods will be insignificant, except where an entity had to make major adjustments to the estimate of the decommissioning costs near the end of the life of the related assets.

A first-time adopter that elects the deemed cost approaches discussed in 5.5 above and elects to use the IFRIC 1 exemption to recognise its decommissioning obligation should be aware of the interaction between these exemptions that may lead to a potential overstatement of the underlying asset. In determining the deemed cost of the asset, the first-time adopter would need to make sure that the fair value of the asset is exclusive of the decommissioning obligation in order to avoid the potential overstatement of the value of the asset that might result from the application of the IFRIC 1 exemption.

5.13.2 IFRIC 1 exemption for oil and gas assets at deemed cost

A first-time adopter that applies the deemed cost exemption for oil and gas assets in the development or production phases accounted for in cost centres that include all properties in a large geographical area under previous GAAP (see 5.5.3 above) must not apply the IFRIC 1 exemption (see 5.13.1 above) or IFRIC 1 itself, but instead: *[IFRS 1.D21A]*

(a) measure decommissioning, restoration and similar liabilities as at the date of transition in accordance with IAS 37; and

(b) recognise directly in retained earnings any difference between that amount and the carrying amount of those liabilities at the date of transition determined under previous GAAP.

The IASB introduced this requirement because it believed that the existing IFRIC 1 exemption would require detailed calculations that would not be practicable for entities that apply the deemed cost exemption for oil and gas assets. *[IFRS 1.BC63CA]*.

5.14 Financial assets or intangible assets accounted for in accordance with IFRIC 12

Service concession arrangements are contracts between the public and private sector to attract private sector participation in the development, financing, operation and maintenance of public infrastructure (e.g. roads, bridges, tunnels, prisons, hospitals, airports, water distribution facilities, energy supply and telecommunication networks). *[IFRIC 12.1, 2]*.

IFRS 1 allows a first-time adopter to apply the transitional provision in IFRIC 12. *[IFRS 1.D22]*. IFRIC 12 requires retrospective application unless it is, for any particular service concession arrangement, impracticable for the operator to apply IFRIC 12 retrospectively at the start of the earliest period presented, in which case it must: *[IFRIC 12.29, 30]*

(a) recognise financial assets and intangible assets that existed at the start of the earliest period presented, which will be the date of transition for a first-time adopter;

(b) use the previous carrying amounts of those financial and intangible assets (however previously classified) as their carrying amounts as at that date; and

(c) test financial and intangible assets recognised at that date for impairment, unless this is not practicable, in which case the amounts must be tested for impairment at the start of the current period, which will be the beginning of the first IFRS reporting period for a first-time adopter.

This exemption was used by many Brazilian companies with service concession arrangements and a typical disclosure of the use of the exemption is given in Extract 5.11 below from the financial statements of Eletrobras:

> **Extract 5.11: Centrais Elétricas Brasileiras S.A. – Eletrobras (2010)**
> **Explanatory Notes to the Consolidated Financial Statements** [extract]
> 6   Transition to IFRS [extract]
> 6.1   Basis of transition to IFRS
> d)   Exemption for initial treatment of IFRIC 12
>
> Exemption for initial treatment of IFRIC 12. The Company has chosen to apply the exemption provided for in IFRS 1 related to the infrastructure of assets classified as concession assets on the transition date and made the corresponding reclassifications based on the residual book value on January 1, 2009, due to the concession contracts of the Company being substantially old without any possibility to perform a retrospective adjustment.

5.15 Borrowing costs

5.15.1 Borrowing cost exemption

For many first-time adopters, full retrospective application of IAS 23 – *Borrowing Costs* – would be problematic as the adjustment would be required in respect of any asset held that had, at any point in the past, satisfied the criteria for capitalisation of borrowing costs. To avoid this problem, IFRS 1 allows a modified form of the transitional provisions set out in IAS 23, which means that the first-time adopter can elect to apply the requirements of IAS 23 from the date of transition or from an earlier date as permitted by paragraph 28 of IAS 23. *[IFRS 1.D23]*.

From the date on which an entity that applies this exemption begins to apply IAS 23, the entity: *[IFRS 1.D23]*

- must not restate the borrowing cost component that was capitalised under previous GAAP and that was included in the carrying amount of assets at that date; and
- must account for borrowing costs incurred on or after that date in accordance with IAS 23, including those borrowing costs incurred on or after that date on qualifying assets already under construction.

IAS 23 applies to borrowing costs that are directly attributable to the acquisition, construction or production of a qualifying asset, as defined in IAS 23. If a first-time adopter established a deemed cost for an asset (see 5.5 above) then it cannot capitalise borrowing costs incurred before the measurement date of the deemed cost (see 5.15.2 below). *[IFRS 1.IG23]*. IAS 23 requires disclosure of interest capitalised during the period. Neither IAS 23 nor IFRS 1 requires disclosure of the cumulative amount capitalised. *[IFRS 1.IG24, IAS 23.26]*.

5.15.2 Interaction with other exemptions

There are limitations imposed on capitalised amounts under IAS 23. IAS 23 states that when the carrying amount of a qualifying asset exceeds its recoverable amount or net realisable value, the carrying amount is written down or written off in accordance with the requirement of other standards. *[IAS 23.16]*. Once an entity uses the 'fair value as deemed cost exemption' described at 5.5 above and has recognised an asset at fair value, in our view, the entity should not increase that value to capitalise interest incurred before that date. Interest incurred subsequent to the date of transition may be capitalised on a qualifying asset, subject to the requirements of IAS 23 (see Chapter 21).

5.16 Extinguishing financial liabilities with equity instruments

IFRIC 19 – *Extinguishing Financial Liabilities with Equity Instruments* – deals with accounting for transactions whereby a debtor and creditor might renegotiate the terms of a financial liability with the result that the debtor extinguishes the liability fully or partially by issuing equity instruments to the creditor (see Chapter 47 at 7). *[IFRIC 19.2]*. However, an entity should not apply IFRIC 19 to transactions in situations where: *[IFRIC 19.3]*

- the creditor is also a direct or indirect shareholder and is acting in its capacity as a direct or indirect existing shareholder;
- the creditor and the entity are controlled by the same party or parties before and after the transaction and the substance of the transaction includes an equity distribution by, or contribution to, the entity; or
- extinguishing the financial liability by issuing equity shares is in accordance with the original terms of the financial liability.

The transitional provisions of IFRIC 19 require retrospective application only from the beginning of the earliest comparative period presented. *[IFRIC 19.13]*. The Interpretations Committee concluded that application to earlier periods would result only in a reclassification of amounts within equity. *[IFRIC 19.BC33]*.

The Board provided similar transition relief to first-time adopters, effectively requiring application of IFRIC 19 from the date of transition to IFRSs. *[IFRS 1.D25]*.

5.17 Severe hyperinflation

If an entity has a functional currency that was, or is, the currency of a hyperinflationary economy, it must determine whether it was subject to severe hyperinflation before the date of transition to IFRSs. *[IFRS 1.D26]*. A currency of a hyperinflationary economy has been subject to severe hyperinflation if it has both of the following characteristics: *[IFRS 1.D27]*

- a reliable general price index is not available to all entities with transactions and balances in the currency; and
- exchangeability between the currency and a relatively stable foreign currency does not exist.

The functional currency of an entity ceases to be subject to severe hyperinflation on the 'functional currency normalisation date', when the functional currency no longer has either, or both, of these characteristics, or when there is a change in the entity's functional currency to a currency that is not subject to severe hyperinflation. *[IFRS 1.D28]*.

If the date of transition to IFRSs is on, or after, the functional currency normalisation date, the first-time adopter may elect to measure all assets and liabilities held before the functional currency normalisation date at fair value on the date of transition and use that fair value as the deemed cost in the opening IFRS statement of financial position. *[IFRS 1.D29]*.

Preparation of information in accordance with IFRSs for periods before the functional currency normalisation date may not be possible. Therefore, entities may prepare financial statements for a comparative period of less than 12 months if the functional currency normalisation date falls within a 12-month comparative period, provided that a complete set of financial statements is prepared, as required by paragraph 10 of IAS 1, for that shorter period. *[IFRS 1.D30]*. It is also suggested that entities disclose non-IFRS comparative information and historical summaries if they would provide useful information to users of financial statements – see 6.7 below. The Board noted that an entity should clearly explain the transition to IFRSs in accordance with IFRS 1's disclosure requirements. *[IFRS 1.BC63J, IFRS 1.23-28]*. See Chapter 16 regarding accounting during periods of hyperinflation.

5.18 Joint arrangements

A first-time adopter may apply the transitional provisions in Appendix C of IFRS 11 – *Joint Arrangements* (see Chapter 12) with the following exceptions: *[IFRS 1.D31, IFRS 11 Appendix C]*

- a first-time adopter must apply these transitional provisions at the date of transition to IFRSs;
- when changing from proportionate consolidation to the equity method, a first-time adopter must test the investment for impairment in accordance with IAS 36 as at the date of transition to IFRSs, regardless of whether there is any indication that it may be impaired. Any resulting impairment must be recognised as an adjustment to retained earnings at the date of transition to IFRSs.

5.19 Stripping costs in the production phase of a surface mine

In surface mining operations, entities may find it necessary to remove mine waste materials ('overburden') to gain access to mineral ore deposits. This waste removal activity is known as 'stripping'. A mining entity may continue to remove overburden and to incur stripping costs during the production phase of the mine. IFRIC 20 – *Stripping Costs in the Production Phase of a Surface Mine* – considers when and how to account separately for the benefits arising from a surface mine stripping activity, as well as how to measure these benefits both on initial recognition and subsequently. *[IFRIC 20.1, 3, 5]*.

First-time adopters may apply the transitional provisions set out in IFRIC 20, *[IFRIC 20 Appendix A]*, except that the effective date is deemed to be the beginning of the first IFRS reporting period. *[IFRS 1.D32]*.

5.20 Regulatory deferral accounts

IFRS 14 gives a first-time adopter that is a rate-regulated entity the option to continue with the recognition of rate-regulated assets and liabilities under previous GAAP on transition to IFRSs. IFRS 14 provides entities with an exemption from compliance with other IFRSs and the conceptual framework on first-time adoption and subsequent reporting periods, until the comprehensive project on rate regulation is completed. First-time adopters, whose previous GAAP prohibited the recognition of rate-regulated assets and liabilities, will not be allowed to apply IFRS 14 on transition to IFRSs. We discuss the requirements of IFRS 14 in detail below.

5.20.1 Defined terms in IFRS 14

IFRS 14 defines the following terms in connection with regulatory deferral accounts. *[IFRS 14 Appendix A]*.

Rate-regulated activities: An entity's activities that are subject to rate regulation.

Rate regulation: A framework for establishing the prices that can be charged to customers for goods or services and that framework is subject to oversight and/or approval by a rate regulator.

Rate regulator: An authorised body that is empowered by statute or regulation to establish the rate or a range of rates that bind an entity. The rate regulator may be a third-party body or a related party of the entity, including the entity's own governing board, if that body is required by statute or regulation to set rates both in the interest of the customers and to ensure the overall financial viability of the entity.

Regulatory deferral account balance: The balance of any expense (or income) account that would not be recognised as an asset or a liability in accordance with other IFRSs, but that qualifies for deferral because it is included, or is expected to be included, by the rate regulator in establishing the rate(s) that can be charged to customers.

5.20.2 Scope

An entity is permitted to apply IFRS 14 in its first IFRS financial statements, if and only if the entity conducts rate-regulated activities and recognised amounts that qualify as regulatory deferral account balances in its financial statements under its previous GAAP. *[IFRS 14.5]*. IFRS 14 applies only to the rate-regulated activities that are subject to statutory or regulatory restrictions through the actions of a rate regulator. *[IFRS 14.B1]*. IFRS 14 does not allow entities to recognise regulatory deferral account balances if those entities have a dominant position in a market and decide to self-regulate to avoid the potential government intervention that might occur if it were perceived to be abusing its dominant position. Instead, it requires there to be a formal rate regulator involved to ensure that the rate-regulatory mechanism in place is supported by statute or regulation and that the regulatory mechanism binds the entity. *[IFRS 14.BC22]*. Therefore, an entity cannot apply IFRS 14 to activities that are self-regulated, i.e. activities that are not subject to a pricing framework that is overseen and/or approved by a rate regulator. This does not prevent the entity from being eligible to apply IFRS 14 when: *[IFRS 14.B2, BC23]*

- the entity's own governing body or a related party establishes rates both in the interest of the customers and to ensure the overall financial viability of the entity within a specified pricing framework; and
- the framework is subject to oversight and/or approval by an authorised body that is empowered by statute or regulation.

An entity that is within the scope of, and that elects to apply, IFRS 14 must apply all of its requirements to all regulatory deferral account balances that arise from all of the entity's rate-regulated activities. *[IFRS 14.8]*.

An entity that elected to apply IFRS 14 in its first IFRS financial statements must apply IFRS 14 also in its financial statements for subsequent periods. In addition, an entity must not apply IFRS 14 in subsequent periods if it does not apply the standard when first adopting IFRSs. *[IFRS 14.6]*.

5.20.3 Continuation of previous GAAP accounting policies (temporary exemption from paragraph 11 of IAS 8)

In some cases, other IFRSs explicitly prohibit an entity from recognising, in the statement of financial position, regulatory deferral account balances that might be recognised, either separately or included within other line items such as property, plant and equipment, in accordance with previous GAAP accounting policies. However, an entity that elects to apply IFRS 14 in its first IFRS financial statements applies the exemption from paragraph 11 of IAS 8 (see Chapter 3 at 4.3) to its accounting policies for the recognition, measurement, impairment and derecognition of regulatory deferral account balances. *[IFRS 14.9-10, B4, IAS 8.11]*. The IASB decided that an entity could continue to follow those previous GAAP accounting policies, provided that they satisfy the requirements of paragraphs 10 and 12 of IAS 8 (see Chapter 3 at 4.3). This should help to ensure that those policies are generally accepted in the local jurisdiction, either because the local GAAP allows the use of another standard-setter's pronouncement or because of accepted industry practice. *[IFRS 14.BC32]*.

Consequently, on initial application of IFRS 14, an entity should continue to apply its previous GAAP accounting policies for the recognition, measurement, impairment, and derecognition of regulatory deferral account balances – provided that they satisfy the requirements of paragraphs 10 and 12 of IAS 8 (see Chapter 3 at 4.3) – except for any changes permitted by paragraphs 13 to 15 of IFRS 14 and subject to any presentation changes required by paragraphs 18 to 19 of IFRS 14. *[IFRS 14.9, 11, 13-15, 18-19, BC32, IAS 8.10, 12]*.

Such previous GAAP accounting policies may include, for example, the following practices: *[IFRS 14.B4]*

- recognising a regulatory deferral account debit balance when the entity has the right, as a result of the actual or expected actions of the rate regulator, to increase rates in future periods in order to recover its allowable costs (i.e. the costs for which the regulated rate(s) is intended to provide recovery);
- recognising, as a regulatory deferral account debit or credit balance, an amount that is equivalent to any loss or gain on the disposal or retirement of both items of property, plant and equipment and of intangible assets, which is expected to be recovered or reversed through future rates;
- recognising a regulatory deferral account credit balance when the entity is required, as a result of the actual or expected actions of the rate regulator, to decrease rates in future periods in order to reverse over-recoveries of allowable costs (i.e. amounts in excess of the recoverable amount specified by the rate regulator); and
- measuring regulatory deferral account balances on an undiscounted basis or on a discounted basis that uses an interest or discount rate specified by the rate regulator.

The accounting policy for the regulatory deferral account balances, as explained above, must, of course, be consistent from period to period unless there is an appropriate change in accounting policies (see 5.20.5 below). *[IFRS 14.12-15]*.

5.20.4 Recognition of regulatory deferral account balances

The regulatory deferral account balances to be recognised are restricted to the incremental amounts from what are permitted or required to be recognised as assets and liabilities under other IFRSs. *[IFRS 14.7]*. Therefore, the measurement of these balances effectively entails a two-step process:

(a) An entity would first determine the carrying amount of its assets and liabilities under IFRSs, excluding IFRS 14.

(b) These amounts would then be compared with the assets and liabilities determined under the entity's previous GAAP (i.e. its rate-regulated balances).

The differences would represent the regulatory deferral account debit or credit balances to be recognised by the entity under IFRS 14.

Some items of expense (income) may be outside the regulated rate(s) because, for example, the amounts are not expected to be accepted by the rate regulator or because they are not within the scope of the rate regulation. Consequently, such an item is recognised as income when earned or expense as incurred, unless another standard permits or requires it to be included in the carrying amount of an asset or liability. *[IFRS 14.B3]*.

The following are examples of the types of costs that rate regulators might allow in rate-setting decisions and that an entity might, therefore, recognise in regulatory deferral account balances: *[IFRS 14.B5]*

- volume or purchase price variances;
- costs of approved 'green energy' initiatives (in excess of amounts that are capitalised as part of the cost of property, plant and equipment in accordance with IAS 16);
- non-directly-attributable overhead costs that are treated as capital costs for rate regulation purposes (but are not permitted, in accordance with IAS 16, to be included in the cost of an item of property, plant and equipment);
- project cancellation costs;
- storm damage costs; and
- deemed interest (including amounts allowed for funds that are used during construction that provide the entity with a return on the owner's equity capital as well as borrowings).

5.20.5 Changes in accounting policies

An entity should not change its accounting policies in order to start to recognise regulatory deferral account balances. *[IFRS 14.13]*. Also, changes in its accounting policies for the recognition, measurement, impairment and derecognition of regulatory deferral account balances are only allowed if they would result in financial statements that are more relevant to the economic decision-making needs of users and no less reliable, or more reliable and no less relevant to those needs. The judgement of relevance and reliability is made using the criteria in IAS 8. *[IFRS 14.13, BC33, IAS 8.10]*. As explained in 5.20.3 above, IFRS 14 does not exempt entities from applying paragraphs 10 and 12 of IAS 8 when developing their accounting policies. *[IFRS 14.9]*. It should also be noted that IFRS 14 does not exempt entities from applying paragraphs 10 or 14-15 of IAS 8 (see Chapter 3 at 4.3 and 4.4) to changes in accounting policy. *[IFRS 14.14, IAS 8.10, 12, 14-15]*. These requirements apply both to changes in accounting policies made on initial application of IFRS 14 and to changes made in subsequent reporting periods. *[IFRS 14.15]*.

The application guidance in IFRS 14 clarifies that regulatory deferral account balances usually represent timing differences between the recognition of items of income or expenses for regulatory purposes and the recognition of those items for financial reporting purposes. When an entity changes an accounting policy on the first-time adoption of IFRSs or on the initial application of a new or revised standard, new or revised timing differences may arise that create new or revised regulatory deferral account balances. The prohibition in paragraph 13 of IFRS 14 that prevents an entity from changing its accounting policy in order to start to recognise regulatory deferral account balances does not prohibit the recognition of the new or revised regulatory deferral account balances that are created because of other changes in accounting policies required by IFRSs. This is because the recognition of regulatory deferral account balances for such timing differences would be consistent with the existing recognition policy and would not represent the introduction of a new accounting policy. Similarly, paragraph 13 of IFRS 14 does not prohibit the recognition of regulatory deferral account balances arising from timing differences that did not exist immediately prior to the date of transition to IFRSs but are consistent with the entity's accounting policies established in accordance with paragraph 11 of IFRS 14 (see 5.20.3 above), for example, storm damage costs. *[IFRS 14.11, 13, B6]*.

5.20.6 Presentation

IFRS 14 requires an entity to present the total of all regulatory deferral account debit balances and the total of all regulatory deferral account credit balances as separate line items in the statement of financial position. The totals of regulatory deferral account balances must not be classified as current or non-current. The separate line items in the statement of financial position must instead be distinguished from other items that are presented under other IFRSs by the use of sub-totals, which are drawn before the regulatory deferral account balances are presented. *[IFRS 14.20, 21, IE1]*.

Similarly, IFRS 14 requires an entity to present the net movement in those balances as separate line items in the statement(s) of profit or loss and other comprehensive income. The net movement in all regulatory deferral account balances for the reporting period that relate to items recognised in other comprehensive income must be presented in the other comprehensive income section of the statement of profit or loss and other comprehensive income. Separate line items must be used for the net movement related to items that, in accordance with other IFRSs, either will not or will be reclassified subsequently to profit or loss when specific conditions are met. *[IFRS 14.22, IE1]*. The remaining net movement in all regulatory deferral balances (excluding movements not reflected in profit or loss, such as amounts acquired) is presented as a separate line item, distinguished from the income and expenses that are presented in accordance with other IFRSs by the use of a sub-total drawn before that line item, in the profit or loss section of the statement of profit or loss and other comprehensive income. *[IFRS 14.23, IE1]*.

5.20.6.A Presentation of deferred tax balances

In relation to a deferred tax asset or deferred tax liability that is recognised as a result of recognising regulatory deferral account balances, the entity must not include that deferred tax amount within the total deferred tax asset (liability) balances. Instead, an entity is required to present the deferred tax asset or liability either: *[IFRS 14.24, B11]*

(a) with the line items that are presented for the regulatory deferral account debit balances and credit balances; or
(b) as a separate line item alongside the related regulatory deferral account debit balances and credit balances.

Similarly, when an entity recognises the movement in a deferred tax asset (liability) that arises as a result of recognising regulatory deferral account balances, the entity must not include the movement in that deferred tax amount within the tax expense (income) line item that is presented in the statement(s) of profit or loss and other comprehensive income under IAS 12. Instead, the entity must present the movement either: *[IFRS 14.24, B12]*

(a) with the line items that are presented in the statement(s) of profit or loss and other comprehensive income for the movements in regulatory deferral account balances; or
(b) as a separate line item alongside the related line items that are presented in the statement(s) of profit or loss and other comprehensive income for the movements in regulatory deferral account balances.

5.20.6.B Presentation of earnings per share amounts

IFRS 14 requires additional earnings per share amounts to be presented. When an entity presents earnings per share in accordance with IAS 33 – *Earnings per Share*, IFRS 14 requires the entity to present additional basic and diluted earnings per share calculated using the earnings amounts required by IAS 33 but excluding the movements in regulatory deferral account balances. This additional measure is required for each earnings per share amount presented. Furthermore, the earnings per share amount under IFRS 14 has to be presented with equal prominence to the earnings per share required by IAS 33 for all periods presented. *[IFRS 14.26, B14]*.

5.20.6.C Presentation of discontinued operations and disposal groups

When an entity applying IFRS 14 presents a discontinued operation, paragraph B20 of IFRS 14 requires the movement in regulatory deferral account balances that arose from the rate-regulated activities of the discontinued operation to be excluded from the line items required by paragraph 33 of IFRS 5 (see Chapter 4 at 3.2). *[IFRS 5.33]*. Instead, the movement must be presented either (a) within the line item that is presented for movements in the regulatory deferral account balances related to profit or loss; or (b) as a separate line item alongside the related line item that is presented for movements in the regulatory deferral account balances related to profit or loss. *[IFRS 14.25, B20]*.

Similarly, notwithstanding the requirements of paragraph 38 of IFRS 5 (see Chapter 4 at 2.2.4), when an entity presents a disposal group, the total of the regulatory deferral account debit balances and credit balances that are part of the disposal group are presented either (a) within the line items that are presented for the regulatory deferral account debit balances and credit balances; or (b) as separate line items alongside the other regulatory deferral account debit balances and credit balances. *[IFRS 14.25, B21]*.

If an entity chooses to include the regulatory deferral account balances and movements in those balances that are related to the disposal group or discontinued operation within the related regulated deferral account line items, it may be necessary to disclose them separately as part of the analysis of the regulatory deferral account line items described by paragraph 33 of IFRS 14 (see 5.20.7.B). *[IFRS 14.33, B22]*.

5.20.6.D Illustrative presentation of financial statements

As discussed in 5.20.6 to 5.20.6.C above, IFRS 14 requires an entity to present regulatory deferral account debit balances and credit balances and any related deferred tax asset (liability) as separate line items in the statement of financial position and the net movement in those balances as separate line items in the statement(s) of profit or loss and other comprehensive income. Sub-totals are to be drawn before the regulatory line items are presented in the statement of financial position and the profit and loss section of the statement(s) of profit or loss and other comprehensive income. *[IFRS 14.20-24].* In addition, an entity that presents earnings per share in accordance with IAS 33 is required to present additional basic and diluted earnings per share, which are calculated excluding the net movement in regulatory deferral account balances. *[IFRS 14.26].* Example 5.38 below, which is based on one in the Illustrative Examples to IFRS 14, illustrates how these requirements might be met, but is not intended to illustrate all aspects of IFRS 14 or IFRSs more generally. *[IFRS 14.IE1].* Note that in this case, the deferred tax amounts are included within the separate line items (see 5.20.6.A above).

The Illustrative Examples to IFRS 14 also illustrate a situation where the entity has a rate-regulated subsidiary presented as a disposal group and discontinued operation. In that example (which is not included in this chapter), the entity has instead chosen to present the regulatory deferral account balances included in the disposal group and the related deferred tax asset balance (and movement therein) as separate line items (see 5.20.6.A and 5.20.6.C above). *[IFRS 14.IE2].*

Example 5.38: *Illustrative presentation of financial statements for regulatory deferral account balances*

XYZ GROUP – STATEMENT OF FINANCIAL POSITION AS AT 31 DECEMBER 2021

($)	2021	2020
ASSETS		
Non-current assets		
Property, plant and equipment	350,700	360,020
Goodwill	80,800	91,200
Other intangible assets	227,470	227,470
Investments in associates	100,150	110,770
Investments in equity instruments	129,790	146,460
	888,910	935,920
Current assets		
Inventories	135,230	132,500
Trade receivables	91,600	110,800
Other current assets	25,650	12,540
Cash and cash equivalents	212,160	220,570
	464,640	476,410
Total assets	1,353,550	1,412,330
Regulatory deferral account debit balances and related deferred tax asset	112,950	111,870
Total assets and regulatory deferral account debit balances	1,466,500	1,524,200

Note: The aggregated total that is presented for regulatory deferral account debit balances and the related deferred tax asset includes the sum of the regulatory deferral account debit balances of $100,240 (2020 – $102,330) plus the deferred tax asset that is related to the recognition of regulatory deferral account balances of $12,710 (2020 – $9,540). This aggregated presentation is permitted by paragraphs 24 and B11 of IFRS 14. [IFRS 14.IE1].

XYZ GROUP – STATEMENT OF FINANCIAL POSITION AS AT 31 DECEMBER 2021 (Continued)

($)

	2021	2020
EQUITY AND LIABILITIES		
Equity attributable to owners of the parent		
Share capital	650,000	600,000
Retained earnings	243,500	164,500
Other components of equity	10,200	21,200
	903,700	785,700
Non-controlling interests	70,050	45,800
Total equity	973,750	831,500
Non-current liabilities		
Long-term borrowings	120,000	160,000
Deferred tax	28,800	26,040
Long-term provisions	28,850	52,240
	177,650	238,280
Current liabilities		
Trade and other payables	87,140	111,150
Short-term borrowings	80,000	200,000
Current portion of long-term borrowings	10,000	20,000
Current tax payable	35,000	42,000
Short-term provisions	5,000	4,800
	217,140	377,950
Total liabilities	394,790	616,230
Total equity and liabilities	1,368,540	1,447,730
Regulatory deferral account credit balances	97,960	76,470
Total equity, liabilities and regulatory deferral account credit balances	1,466,500	1,524,200

Note: Regulatory deferral account balances are not described as assets or liabilities for the purposes of IFRS 14. The sub-totals described as 'Total assets' and 'Total liabilities' are comparable to those that would be presented if the regulatory deferral account balances were not recognised. The difference between these two sub-totals represents the net balance of all regulatory deferral account balances recognised and any related deferred tax asset (liability) that arises as a result of recognising regulatory deferral account balances, which would otherwise be recognised within retained earnings or other components of equity.

XYZ Group – Statement of profit or loss and other comprehensive income for the year ended 31 December 2021

(illustrating the presentation of profit or loss and other comprehensive income in one statement and the classification of expenses within profit or loss by function)

($)

	2021	2020
Revenue	390,000	358,784
Cost of sales	(237,062)	(230,000)
Gross profit	152,938	128,784
Other income	44,247	16,220
Distribution costs	(9,000)	(13,700)
Administrative expenses	(20,000)	(21,000)
Other expenses	(2,100)	(1,200)
Finance costs	(8,000)	(7,500)
Share of profit of associates	35,100	15,100
Profit before tax	193,185	106,204
Income tax expense	(43,587)	(44,320)
Profit for the year before net movements in regulatory deferral account balances	149,598	61,884
Net movement in regulatory deferral account balances related to profit or loss and the related deferred tax movement	(27,550)	3,193
Profit for the year and net movements in regulatory deferral account balances	122,048	65,077
Other comprehensive income: Items that will not be reclassified to profit or loss		
Remeasurements of defined benefit pension plans	(7,938)	(3,784)
Net movement in regulatory deferral account balances related to other comprehensive income	7,140	4,207
Other comprehensive income for the year, net of income tax	(798)	423
TOTAL COMPREHENSIVE INCOME FOR THE YEAR	121,250	65,500
Profit and net movements in regulatory deferral account balances attributable to		
Owners of the parent	97,798	51,977
Non-controlling interests	24,250	13,100
	122,048	65,077
Total comprehensive income attributable to:		
Owners of the parent	97,000	52,400
Non-controlling interests	24,250	13,100
	121,250	65,500
Earnings per share (in $):		
Basic and diluted	0.61	0.35
Basic and diluted including net movement in regulatory deferral account balances	0.46	0.30

Notes:

(1) To simplify the example, it is assumed that all regulatory deferral account balances relate to activities that are carried out in wholly-owned subsidiaries and thus no amounts are attributable to non-controlling interests.

(2) The aggregated total that is presented for the net movement in regulatory deferral account balances related to profit or loss and the related deferred tax movement includes the net movement in regulatory deferral account balances of $30,720 (2020 – $9,127) and the movement in the related deferred tax asset that is related to the recognition of regulatory deferral account balances, which is $3,170 (20X6 – $12,320). This aggregated presentation is permitted by paragraphs 24 and B12 of IFRS 14. *[IFRS 14.24, B12]*.

5.20.7 Disclosures

IFRS 14 requires an entity to disclose information that enables users to assess: *[IFRS 14.27]*

- the nature of, and risks associated with, the rate regulation that establishes the price(s) that the entity can charge customers for the goods or services it provides; and
- the effects of that rate regulation on the entity's financial position, financial performance and cash flows.

Any of the disclosure requirements set out in 5.20.7.A and 5.20.7.B below may be omitted if not considered relevant to meet the disclosure objective. Where those disclosures are insufficient to meet the disclosure objective, an entity should provide additional information necessary to meet the disclosure objective. *[IFRS 14.28]*.

To meet the disclosure objective above, an entity should consider all of the following: *[IFRS 14.29]*

- the level of detail that is necessary to satisfy the disclosure requirements;
- how much emphasis to place on each of the various requirements;
- how much aggregation or disaggregation to undertake; and
- whether users of financial statements need additional information to evaluate the quantitative information disclosed.

5.20.7.A   Explanation of activities subject to rate regulation

In order to help users of the financial statements assess the nature of, and the risks associated with, an entity's rate-regulated activities, an entity is required to disclose the following for each type of rate-regulated activity: *[IFRS 14.30]*

(a) a brief description of the nature and extent of the rate-regulated activity and the nature of the regulatory rate-setting process;

(b) the identity of the rate regulator(s). If the rate regulator is a related party (as defined in IAS 24 – *Related Party Disclosures* (see Chapter 39 at 2.2)), the entity must disclose that fact, together with an explanation of how it is related;

(c) how the future recovery of each class (i.e. each type of cost or income) of regulatory deferral account debit balance or reversal of each class of regulatory deferral account credit balance is affected by risks and uncertainty, for example:

- demand risk (for example, changes in consumer attitudes, the availability of alternative sources of supply or the level of competition);
- regulatory risk (for example, the submission or approval of a rate-setting application or the entity's assessment of the expected future regulatory actions); and
- other risks (for example, currency or other market risks).

The disclosures required above may be provided in the notes to the financial statements or incorporated by cross-reference from the financial statements to some other statement such as a management commentary or a risk report that is available to users of the financial statements on the same terms as the financial statements and at the same time. *[IFRS 14.31]*.

5.20.7.B Explanation of recognised amounts

IFRS 14 also requires entities to explain the basis on which regulatory deferral account balances are recognised and derecognised, and how they are measured initially and subsequently, including how regulatory deferral account balances are assessed for recoverability and how impairment losses are allocated. *[IFRS 14.32]*.

Furthermore, for each type of rate-regulated activity, an entity is required to disclose the following information for each class of regulatory deferral account balance:

(a) a reconciliation of the carrying amount at the beginning and the end of the period, in a table unless another format is more appropriate. The entity must apply judgement in deciding the level of detail necessary, *[IFRS 14.29(a)]*, but the following components would usually be relevant: *[IFRS 14.33]*

- the amounts that have been recognised in the current period in the statement of financial position as regulatory deferral account balances;
- the amounts that have been recognised in the statement(s) of profit or loss and other comprehensive income relating to balances that have been recovered (sometimes described as amortised) or reversed in the current period; and
- other amounts, separately identified, that affected the regulatory deferral account balances, such as impairments, items acquired or assumed in a business combination, items disposed of, or the effects of changes in foreign exchange rates or discount rates;

(b) the rate of return or discount rate (including a zero rate or a range of rates, when applicable) used to reflect the time value of money that is applicable to each class of regulatory deferral account balance; and

(c) the remaining periods over which the entity expects to recover (or amortise) the carrying amount of each class of regulatory deferral account debit balance or to reverse each class of regulatory deferral account credit balance.

When rate regulation affects the amount and timing of an entity's income tax expense (income), the entity must disclose the impact of the rate regulation on the amounts of current and deferred tax recognised. In addition, the entity must separately disclose any regulatory deferral account balance that relates to taxation and the related movement in that balance. *[IFRS 14.34]*.

It is also important to note that when an entity provides disclosures in accordance with IFRS 12 – *Disclosure of Interests in Other Entities* – for an interest in a subsidiary, associate or joint venture (see Chapter 13) that has rate-regulated activities and for which regulatory deferral account balances are recognised in accordance with IFRS 14, the following disclosures are required:

- for each of the entity's subsidiaries with material non-controlling interests, the net movement in regulatory deferral account balances that is included within the profit or loss allocated to non-controlling interests; *[IFRS 12.12(e), IFRS 14.35, B25]*

- the amounts that are included for the regulatory deferral account debit and credit balances and the net movement in those balances (split between amounts recognised in profit or loss and amounts recognised in other comprehensive income) for each entity for which IFRS 12 disclosures are required; *[IFRS 12.12, 21, B10, B12-13, B16, IFRS 14.35, B26-B27]*
- in addition to the IFRS 12 disclosures concerning a gain or loss on losing control of a subsidiary during the reporting period, the portion of that gain or loss that is attributable to derecognising regulatory deferral account balances in the former subsidiary at the date when control is lost. *[IFRS 12.19, IFRS 14.35, B28]*.

When an entity concludes that a regulatory deferral account balance is no longer fully recoverable or reversible, it must disclose that fact, the reason why it is not recoverable or reversible and the amount by which the regulatory deferral account balance has been reduced. *[IFRS 14.36]*.

The Illustrative Examples to IFRS 14 include an example of the reconciliation of movements in regulatory balances by class, as required at (a) above (not shown in this chapter), for the regulatory deferral account balances illustrated in Example 5.38 at 5.20.6.D above. *[IFRS 14.IE1]*.

5.20.8 Interaction with other standards

Any specific exception, exemption or additional requirements related to the interaction of IFRS 14 with other standards are contained within IFRS 14. In the absence of any such exception, exemption or additional requirements, other standards must apply to regulatory deferral account balances in the same way as they apply to assets, liabilities, income and expenses that are recognised in accordance with other standards. *[IFRS 14.16]*. In some situations, another standard might need to be applied to a regulatory deferral account balance that has been measured in accordance with an entity's accounting policies established under paragraphs 11 and 12 of IFRS 14 (see 5.20.3 above) in order to reflect that balance appropriately in the financial statements. For example, the entity might have rate-regulated activities in a foreign country for which the transactions and regulatory deferral account balances are denominated in a currency that is not the functional currency of the reporting entity. The regulatory deferral account balances and the movements in those balances are translated by applying IAS 21 (see Chapter 15 at 5). *[IFRS 14.17, IAS 21.21, 23]*.

The following sections outline how some other IFRSs interact with the requirements of IFRS 14. In particular, the following sections clarify specific exceptions to, and exemptions from, other IFRSs and additional presentation and disclosure requirements that are expected to be applicable. *[IFRS 14.16, IFRS 14.B7-B28]*.

5.20.8.A Application of IAS 10

An entity may need to use estimates and assumptions in the recognition and measurement of its regulatory deferral account balances. For events that occur between the end of the reporting period and the date when the financial statements are authorised for issue, an entity has to apply IAS 10 to identify whether those estimates and assumptions should be adjusted to reflect those events. *[IFRS 14.B8]*.

5.20.8.B Application of IAS 12

Entities are required to apply the requirements of IAS 12 to rate-regulated activities, to identify the amount of income tax to be recognised. *[IFRS 14.B9]*. In some rate-regulatory schemes, rate regulators may permit or require an entity to increase its future rates in order to recover some or all of the entity's income tax expense. In such circumstances, this might result in the entity recognising a regulatory deferral account balance in the statement of financial position related to income tax, in accordance with its accounting policies established in accordance with paragraphs 11-12 of IFRS 14 (see 5.20.3 above). *[IFRS 14.11, 12]*. The recognition of this regulatory deferral account balance that relates to income tax might itself create an additional temporary difference for which a further deferred tax amount would be recognised. *[IFRS 14.B10]*.

5.20.8.C Application of IAS 36

As a rate-regulated entity is allowed to continue applying previous GAAP accounting policies (see 5.20.3 above), the requirements under IAS 36 do not apply to the separate regulatory deferral account balances recognised. *[IFRS 14.11, 12, B15]*. However, IAS 36 may require an entity to perform an impairment test on a CGU that includes regulatory deferral account balances. An impairment test would be required if: *[IFRS 14.B15-B16]*

- the CGU contains goodwill; or
- one or more of the impairment indicators described in IAS 36 have been identified relating to the CGU.

In such situations, the requirements under IAS 36, for identifying the recoverable amount and the carrying amount of a CGU (see Chapter 20 at 4 and 5) must be applied to decide whether any of the regulatory deferral account balances recognised are included in the carrying amount of the CGU for the purpose of the impairment test. *[IAS 36.74-79]*. The remaining requirements of IAS 36 should then be applied to any impairment loss that is recognised as a result of this test (see Chapter 20). *[IFRS 14.B16]*.

5.20.8.D Application of IFRS 3

If an entity acquires a business, paragraph B18 of IFRS 14 provides an exception to the core principle of IFRS 3 (that is, to recognise the assets acquired and liabilities assumed at their acquisition-date fair values) for the recognition and measurement of an acquiree's regulatory deferral account balances at the date of acquisition. In other words, the acquiree's regulatory deferral account balances are recognised in the consolidated financial statements of the acquirer in accordance with the acquirer's policies for the recognition and measurement of regulatory deferral account balances, irrespective of whether the acquiree recognises those balances in its own financial statements. *[IFRS 14.B17-B18]*.

5.20.8.E Application of IFRS 5

Since a rate-regulated entity is allowed to continue applying previous GAAP accounting policies (see 5.20.3 above), *[IFRS 14.11, 12]*, the measurement requirements of IFRS 5 do not apply to the regulatory deferral account balances recognised. *[IFRS 14.B19]*. The presentation of discontinued operations and disposal groups for an entity applying IFRS 14 is discussed in 5.20.6.C above.

5.20.8.F   Application of IFRS 10 and IAS 28

If a parent entity recognises regulatory deferral account balances in its consolidated financial statements under IFRS 14, the same accounting policies have to be applied to the regulatory deferral account balances arising in all of its subsidiaries. This requirement applies irrespective of whether the subsidiaries recognise those balances in their own financial statements. *[IFRS 14.8, B23, IFRS 10.19].*

Similarly, accounting policies for the recognition, measurement, impairment and derecognition of regulatory deferral account balances of an associate or joint venture will have to conform to those of the investing entity in applying the equity method. *[IFRS 14.B24, IAS 28.35-36].*

5.21   IFRS 15 – *Revenue from Contracts with Customers*

The requirements of IFRS 15 are discussed in Chapters 27 to 32.

Under the full retrospective method, entities had to apply IFRS 15 as if it had been applied since the inception of all its contracts with customers that are presented in the financial statements. However, to ease the potential burden of applying it on a fully retrospective basis, the IASB provided the optional practical expedients included in paragraph C5 of IFRS 15 to a first-time adopter. A first-time adopter is permitted to use one or more of the following practical expedients when applying this standard retrospectively and not to restate contracts that were completed before the earliest period presented (see 5.21.1 below). *[IFRS 1.D34, D35].*

Here are the practical expedients in paragraph C5 of IFRS 15: *[IFRS 15.C5, IFRS 1.D34]*

- for completed contracts, an entity need not restate contracts that:
    - begin and end within the same annual reporting period; or
    - are completed contracts at the beginning of the earliest period presented; *[IFRS 1.D35]*
- for completed contracts that have variable consideration, an entity may use the transaction price at the date the contract was completed rather than estimating variable consideration amounts in the comparative reporting periods;
- for contracts that were modified before the beginning of the earliest period presented, an entity need not retrospectively restate the contract for those contract modifications in accordance with paragraphs 20-21 of IFRS 15 (see Chapter 28 at 2.4). Instead, an entity must reflect the aggregate effect of all of the modifications that occur before the beginning of the earliest period presented when: *[IFRS 15.20-21]*
    - identifying the satisfied and unsatisfied performance obligations;
    - determining the transaction price; and
    - allocating the transaction price to the satisfied and unsatisfied performance obligations; and
- for all reporting periods presented before the beginning of the first IFRS reporting period, an entity need not disclose the amount of the transaction price allocated to the remaining performance obligations and an explanation of when the entity expects to recognise that amount as revenue (see paragraph 120 of IFRS 15). *[IFRS 15.120].*

For the purposes of IFRS 15, paragraph D35 of IFRS 1 defines a completed contract as a contract for which the entity has transferred all of the goods or services as identified in accordance with previous GAAP. *[IFRS 1.D35]*.

A first-time adopter may elect to apply one, some or all of these expedients. However, if an entity elects to use any of them, it must apply that expedient consistently to all contracts within all reporting periods presented. In addition, an entity is required to disclose the following information: *[IFRS 15.C6, IFRS 1.D34]*

- the expedients that have been used; and
- to the extent reasonably possible, a qualitative assessment of the estimated effect of applying each of those expedients.

Although IFRS 1 provides the practical expedients, adoption of IFRS 15 by a first-time adopter may be challenging. For example, determination of completed contracts may be challenging if its previous GAAP was not clear about when the goods or services had been transferred (see 5.21.1 and 5.21.2 below for discussion on the definition of a completed contract).

While the practical expedients provided some relief, first-time adopters will still need to use judgement and make estimates. For example, first-time adopters will need to use judgement in estimating stand-alone selling prices if there has been a wide range of selling prices and when allocating the transaction price to satisfied and unsatisfied performance obligations if there have been several performance obligations or contract modifications over an extended period. Furthermore, if a first-time adopter applies the practical expedient for contract modifications, it still has to apply the standard's contract modification requirements (see Chapter 28 at 2.4) to modifications made after the date of initial application.

Example 5.39:   Transition practical expedient for contract modifications

Entity A entered into a contract with a customer to sell equipment for $1 million and provide services for five years for $20,000 annually.

The equipment was delivered on 1 January 2016 and the service contract commenced at that time. The equipment and the service contract are separate performance obligations.

In 2018, the contract was modified to extend it by five years and to provide an additional piece of equipment for $1 million. The additional equipment will be delivered during 2021 and is a separate performance obligation.

Entity A adopts IFRSs on 1 January 2021 and, as part of adopting IFRS 15, it applies the practical expedient on contract modifications in accordance with paragraph C5(c) of IFRS 15. *[IFRS 15.C5(c)]*.

The total transaction price for the modified contract is $2,200,000 [$1 million (equipment) + $1 million (equipment) + (10 years × $20,000 (service))], which is allocated to the two products and the service contract based on the relative stand-alone selling price of each performance obligation. See Chapter 29 at 3 for discussion on allocating the transaction price to performance obligations.

The transaction price allocated to the second piece of equipment and the remaining unperformed services would be recognised when or as they are transferred to the customer.

When adopting IFRS 15 as part of its transition to IFRSs, a first-time adopter needs to analyse each of its contracts to determine the appropriate timing and pattern of recognition, considering the specific criteria and requirements of the standard. In some instances, this could result in a change in the timing and/or pattern of revenue recognition compared to its previous GAAP. An example of such a change in the timing of revenue recognition would be a contract manufacturer that produces goods designed to a customer's unique specifications where the goods do not have an alternative use. If the manufacturer also has an enforceable right to payment for performance completed to date, the third criterion in IFRS 15 to recognise revenue over time would be met, *[IFRS 15.35(c)]*, (see Chapter 30 at 2 for further discussion), even though the manufacturer might have recognised revenue at a point in time under its previous GAAP (e.g. based on the number of units produced or units delivered).

Other application issues that may make adopting IFRS 15 as part of transitioning to IFRS difficult and/or time-consuming, include the following:

- A first-time adopter will have to perform an allocation of the transaction price because of changes to the identified deliverables, the transaction price or both. If its previous GAAP required a method that is similar to the requirements in IFRS 15, this step may be straightforward. Regardless, a first-time adopter is required to determine the stand-alone selling price of each performance obligation as at inception of the contract. Depending on the age of the contract, this information may not be readily available and the prices may differ significantly from current stand-alone selling prices. While the practical expedients in paragraph C5 of IFRS 15 are clear about when it is acceptable to use hindsight in respect of variable consideration to determine the transaction price (see Chapter 29 at 2.2 for a discussion on variable consideration), the practical expedients are silent on whether the use of hindsight is acceptable for other aspects of the model (e.g. for the purpose of allocating the transaction price) or whether it is acceptable to use current pricing information if that were the only information available.

- Estimating variable consideration for all contracts for prior periods is likely to require significant judgement. The standard is clear that hindsight cannot be used for contracts that are not completed. As a result, entities must make this estimate based only on information that was available at contract inception. Contemporaneous documentation clarifying what information was available to management, and when it was available, is likely to be needed to support these estimates. In addition to estimating variable consideration using the expected value or a most likely amount method, a first-time adopter has to make conclusions about whether such variable consideration is subject to the constraint (see Chapter 29 at 2.2.3 for further discussion).

Finally, a first-time adopter needs to consider a number of other issues as it prepares to adopt IFRS 15 as part of its adoption of IFRSs. For example, a first-time adopter with significant deferred revenue balances under its previous GAAP may experience what some refer to as 'lost revenue' if those amounts were deferred at the date of transition to IFRSs and, ultimately, are reflected in the restated prior periods or as part of the cumulative adjustment upon transition, but are never reported as revenue in a current period within the financial statements.

5.21.1 Definition of a completed contract

For the purposes of IFRS 1, a completed contract is a contract for which the entity has transferred all of the goods or services identified in accordance with previous GAAP. *[IFRS 1.D35]*.

Depending on the practical expedients a first-time adopter chooses to apply, it may not need to apply IFRS 15 to contracts if it has completed performance before the date of transition to IFRSs, even if it has not yet received the consideration and that consideration is still subject to variability.

The IASB noted in the Basis for Conclusions that 'transferred all of the goods or services' is not meant to imply that an entity would apply the 'transfer of control' notion in IFRS 15 to goods or services that have been identified in accordance with previous GAAP. Rather it is performance in accordance with previous GAAP. *[IFRS 15.BC441]*. For example, if the previous GAAP has similar requirements to legacy revenue requirements in IFRS (i.e. IAS 11 – *Construction Contracts*, IAS 18 – *Revenue* and related Interpretations), in many situations the term 'transferred' would mean 'delivered' within the context of contracts for the sale of goods and 'performed' within the context of contracts for rendering services and construction contracts. In some situations, the entity would use judgement when determining whether it has transferred goods or services to the customer. *[IFRS 15.BC445D]*.

As discussed at 5.21 above, determining which contracts were completed before the earliest period presented may require significant judgement, particularly if a first-time adopter's previous GAAP did not provide detailed requirements that indicated when goods had been delivered or services performed.

5.21.2 Implementation questions on definition of a completed contract

5.21.2.A Elements in a contract to be considered

When determining whether a contract meets the definition of a completed contract, a first-time adopter must consider all of the elements (or components) in a contract that give rise to revenue in its previous GAAP. It should not consider the elements of a contract that do not result in recognition of revenue when assessing whether a contract is completed.

For example, under its previous GAAP, an entity may have accounted for a financing component (i.e. separating the interest income or expense from the revenue). Doing so effectively splits the contract into a revenue component and a financing component. In our view, the financing component generally would not be considered in determining whether the goods or services have transferred to the customer (i.e. it would generally not affect the assessment of whether the contract meets the definition of a completed contract).

In addition, income elements that are not within the scope of IFRS 15 need not be considered even if they were covered by revenue requirements in previous GAAP. For example, none of the following would be considered when determining whether a contract meets the definition of a completed contract because they are within the scope of IFRS 9, not IFRS 15:

- dividends (see Chapter 50 at 2); *[IFRS 9.5.7.1A, 5.7.6]*
- fees integral to the issuance of a financial instrument (see Chapter 50 at 3.1); *[IFRS 9.B5.4.1-3]* or
- interest income that is accounted for in accordance with the effective interest method (see Chapter 50 at 3). *[IFRS 9 Appendix A, IFRS 9.5.4.1, IFRS 9.B5.4.1-7]*.

5.21.2.B Identification of a contract under previous GAAP

When determining whether a contract is completed, a first-time adopter considers the requirements of its previous GAAP and not IFRS 15. In order to determine whether a contract is completed, a first-time adopter needs to determine the boundaries of a contract, including the term of the contract, whether it was combined with other contracts, whether it was modified, etc. That is, a first-time adopter must identify what is the contract in order to assess if it meets the definition of a completed contract.

IFRS 15 provides detailed requirements to assist entities in identifying a contract, including determining the contract duration. Considering the requirements of IFRS 15 could lead to different outcomes from previous GAAP (e.g. an entity may conclude a contract is of a shorter duration than the stated contractual term in certain circumstances under IFRS 15. See Chapter 28 at 2.2 for further discussion).

While a first-time adopter's previous GAAP may not have provided detailed requirements for identifying the contract, accounting policies and its past practice may be informative in identifying the contract, including determining: (a) what the first-time adopter considered the contract to be (e.g. master supply agreement or individual purchase orders); and (b) the contract duration (i.e. the stated contractual term or a shorter period). Consider the following examples.

Example 5.40: Definition of completed contract: contract duration

Scenario 1

On 30 June 2019, Entity A entered into a contract with a customer to provide services for 24 months. The customer was required to pay a fixed monthly fee of £150, which remained constant during the contract term of 24 months, regardless of the time needed to provide the services or the actual usage from the customer each day. The customer could cancel the contract at any time without penalty by giving Entity A one month's notice. Entity A had not received any cancellation notice up to 1 January 2020 and, based on past experience, Entity A did not expect customers to cancel within the first year. For this contract, Entity A had concluded that the contract duration under its previous GAAP was the stated contractual term of 24 months.

Entity A's accounting policy for these types of contracts under its previous GAAP stated that revenue from providing monthly services to customers was recognised over the service period, on a monthly basis. While not explicitly stated in its accounting policy, Entity A had typically treated the stated contractual term as the duration of the contract (unless the customer cancelled or the contract was modified), and considered this to be the period over which the contractual rights and obligations were enforceable.

Assume that Entity A adopts IFRSs on 1 January 2021. Entity A uses the practical expedient in paragraph C5(a)(ii) of IFRS 15 not to restate contracts that are completed contracts at the beginning of the earliest period presented (i.e. 1 January 2020; Entity A presents one comparative period only) (see 5.21 above). *[IFRS 15.C5(a)(ii)].*

Under IFRS 15, Entity A is likely to conclude that the contract is a month-to-month contract. However, when determining whether the contract is completed, Entity A only considers the requirements of its previous GAAP. Entity A might have noted that its previous accounting policy did not focus on the identification of contract duration and, therefore, perhaps the contract is neither a 24-month contract nor a month-to-month contract. Entity A had accounted for this type of service contract based on monthly invoicing and, arguably, that accounting treatment is similar to the accounting treatment of a month-to-month contract. However, while not explicitly stated, Entity A had generally viewed the stated contractual term as the period over which the rights and obligations are enforceable.

Furthermore, Entity A cannot cancel the contract with the customer and is obliged to render services for the entire contract period of 24 months, unless a termination notice is provided by the customer which would limit Entity A's obligation to provide services for the next 30 days from the notification date. Since no cancellation notice had been submitted by the customer at least one month before 1 January 2020, approximately 18 months of services still had to be provided as at the beginning of the earliest period presented (i.e. 1 January 2020). Therefore, Entity A concludes that the contract does not meet the definition of a completed contract and would need to be transitioned to IFRS 15.

Scenario 2

Assume the same facts as Scenario 1, with the exception that the customer submitted an early termination notice on 30 November 2019.

Similar to Scenario 1, the contract duration under previous GAAP would have been the stated contractual term of 24 months. However, in this scenario, the customer has submitted the termination notice on 30 November 2019. Therefore, Entity A concludes that the term of the contract ceased on 31 December 2019.

Entity A cannot cancel the contract with the customer and is obliged to render services for the entire contract period of 24 months, unless a termination notice is provided by the customer which limits Entity A's obligation to provide service to the next 30 days from the notification date. Since Entity A had provided all services prior to 31 December 2019, Entity A concludes that the contract is a completed contract. Entity A continues to apply its previous accounting policy to any remaining consideration still to be recognised.

Scenario 3

Assume the same facts as Scenario 1, with the exception that the customer was required to pay a non-refundable upfront fee of £50 at commencement of the contract (in addition to the monthly fixed fee). The customer can cancel the contract at any time without penalty, with a month's notice period. The customer cancelled the contract on 30 November 2019.

In its financial statements, Entity A's accounting policy for these types of contracts under its previous GAAP stated that revenues from non-refundable upfront fees were deferred over the average customer retention period. The customer retention period was estimated to be two years, and the deferred revenue was recognised as revenue on a straight-line basis over the next 24 months.

Similar to Scenario 2, the contract duration under its previous GAAP would have been the stated contractual term of 24 months. However, the customer had submitted the termination notice on 30 November 2019 and, therefore, Entity A concludes that the term of the contract ceases on 31 December 2019.

Entity A's previous accounting policy for the non-refundable upfront fee referred to recognition of deferred income over the average customer retention period, not the contractual term. The definition of a completed contract is not dependent on all revenue being recognised, but rather on all goods and services being transferred to the customer. Furthermore, the period over which revenue is recognised does not affect the contract duration. As such, recognition of this upfront fee is not relevant in determining whether the contract is a completed contract. All previously contracted services had been provided to the customer up to the date of cancellation. Therefore, the contract is a completed contract.

Entity A continues applying its previous accounting policy to any remaining consideration still to be recognised. However, given that the customer has terminated the contract early, Entity A needs to reassess, in line with the requirements of its previous GAAP, the period over which this remaining revenue arising from the non-refundable upfront fee would be recognised.

5.21.2.C   Some or all of revenue has not been recognised under previous GAAP

If some or all of revenue has not been recognised under a first-time adopter's previous GAAP, this could possibly prevent the contract from being completed.

The definition of a completed contract is not dependent on a first-time adopter having recognised all related revenue. However, the requirements in its previous GAAP with respect to the timing of recognition may provide an indication of whether the goods or services have been transferred.

For example, previous GAAP may, like IAS 18, have required an entity to have transferred to the buyer the significant risks and rewards of ownership of the goods as the most crucial of criteria which needed to be satisfied in order to recognise revenue from the sale of goods. In the following four examples of situations, an entity may have retained the significant risks and rewards of ownership and revenue may not have been recognised: *[IAS 18.16]*

- when the entity retained an obligation for unsatisfactory performance not covered by normal warranty provisions;
- when the receipt of the revenue from a particular sale was contingent on the derivation of revenue the buyer from its sale of the goods;
- when the goods were shipped subject to installation and the installation was a significant part of the contract which had not yet been completed by the entity; and
- when the buyer had the right to rescind the purchase for a reason specified in the sales contract and the entity was uncertain about the probability of return.

Understanding the reasons for the accounting treatment under previous GAAP may, therefore, assist a first-time adopter in determining whether the goods or services have been transferred and the completed contract definition has been met. However, judgement may be needed in respect of some goods or services. Assume, for example, that a first-time adopter sells products, but cannot recognise revenue immediately. The delayed recognition of revenue may be because of factors related to the timing of transfer, such as a bill-and-hold arrangement, or because the goods or services have been transferred, but not all of the criteria for recognition have been met.

5.21.2.D   Accounting for completed contracts excluded from transition

Depending on the practical expedients a first-time adopter applies, it may be able to exclude contracts that meet the definition of a completed contract from the population of contracts to be transitioned to IFRS 15 (i.e. it would not need to restate those contracts) (see Example 5.40 above).

IFRS 15 clarifies that if an entity chooses not to apply IFRS 15 to completed contracts, the entity would continue to account for the completed contracts in accordance with its accounting policies based on its previous GAAP.

Therefore, if a first-time adopter applies the practical expedient in paragraph C5(a)(ii) of IFRS 15 not to restate contracts that are completed contracts at the beginning of the earliest period presented, the first-time adopter also would not record an asset for incremental costs to obtain contracts under IFRS 15 (see Chapter 31 at 5.1) that meet the definition of a completed contract as at the beginning of the earliest period presented. Furthermore, any assets or liabilities related to completed contracts that are on the balance sheet prior to the date of the earliest period presented would continue to be accounted for under its previous accounting policy after the adoption of IFRSs. *[IFRS 15.C5(a)(ii)]*.

5.22   Foreign currency transactions and advance consideration

IFRIC 22 – *Foreign Currency Transactions and Advance Consideration* applies (with certain exceptions) to a foreign currency transaction (or part of it) when an entity recognises a non-monetary asset or non-monetary liability arising from the payment or receipt of advance consideration before the entity recognises the related asset, expense or income (or part of it). *[IFRIC 22.4]*. The Interpretation addresses how to determine the date of the transaction for the purpose of determining the exchange rate to use on initial recognition of the related asset, expense or income (or part of it) on the derecognition of a non-monetary asset or non-monetary liability arising from the payment or receipt of advance consideration in a foreign currency. *[IFRIC 22.7]*.

The Interpretation explains that the date of the transaction for this purpose is the date on which an entity initially recognises the non-monetary asset or non-monetary liability arising from the payment or receipt of advance consideration. If there are multiple payments or receipts in advance, a date of transaction is determined for each payment or receipt of advance consideration (see Chapter 15 at 5.1.2). *[IFRIC 22.8-9]*.

A first-time adopter need not apply the Interpretation to assets, expenses and income in the scope of the Interpretation that were initially recognised before the date of transition to IFRSs. *[IFRS 1.D36]*.

5.23 Designation of contracts to buy or sell a non-financial item

IFRS 9 allows some contracts to buy or sell a non-financial item to be designated at inception as measured at fair value through profit or loss (see Chapter 45 at 4.2.6). *[IFRS 9.2.5]*. Despite this requirement, paragraph D33 of IFRS 1 allows an entity to designate, at the date of transition to IFRSs, contracts that already exist on that date as measured at fair value through profit or loss but only if they meet the requirements of paragraph 2.5 of IFRS 9 at that date and the entity designates all similar contracts at fair value through profit or loss. *[IFRS 1.D33]*.

6 PRESENTATION AND DISCLOSURE

An entity's first IFRS financial statements should include at least three statements of financial position, two statements of profit or loss and other comprehensive income, two separate statements of profit or loss (if presented), two statements of cash flows and two statements of changes in equity and related notes, including comparative information for all statements presented. *[IFRS 1.21]*.

A first-time adopter is required to present notes supporting its opening IFRS statement of financial position. This was clarified as a part of the *Annual Improvements to IFRSs 2009-2011 Cycle* issued in May 2012. The Board explained that a first-time adopter should not be exempted from presenting three statements of financial position and related notes because it might not have presented this information previously on a basis consistent with IFRSs. *[IFRS 1.BC89B]*.

IFRS 1 does not exempt a first-time adopter from any of the presentation and disclosure requirements in other IFRSs, *[IFRS 1.20]*, with the exception of certain presentation and disclosures regarding:

- claims development information under IFRS 4 (see 5.4 above); and
- recognised regulatory deferral account balances under IFRS 14 (see 5.20 above).

6.1 Comparative information

IAS 1 requires, except where a standard or interpretation permits or requires otherwise, comparative information in respect of the previous period for all amounts reported in the current period's financial statements and comparative information for narrative and descriptive information when it is relevant to an understanding of the current period's financial statements. *[IAS 1.38]*.

6.2 Non-IFRS comparative information and historical summaries

Normally IFRSs require comparative information that is prepared on the same basis as information relating to the current reporting period. However, if an entity presents historical summaries of selected data for periods before the first period for which it presents full comparative information under IFRSs, e.g. information prepared under its previous GAAP, IFRS 1 does not require such summaries to comply with the recognition and measurement requirements of IFRSs. Furthermore, some entities present comparative information under previous GAAP in addition to the comparative information required by IAS 1. *[IFRS 1.22]*.

If an entity presents, in the IFRS financial statements, historical summaries or comparative information under its previous GAAP, it must: *[IFRS 1.22]*

(a) label the previous GAAP information prominently as not being prepared in accordance with IFRSs; and

(b) disclose the nature of the main adjustments that would make it comply with IFRSs. Those adjustments need not be quantified.

As an entity is only allowed to apply IFRS 1 in its first IFRS financial statements, a literal reading of IFRS 1 would seem to suggest that the above guidance is not available to an entity that prepares its second IFRS financial statements. In practice this need not cause a significant problem because this type of information is generally presented outside the financial statements, where it is not covered by the requirements of IFRSs.

Although IFRS 1 does not specifically require disclosure of the information in (a) and (b) above when the historical summaries or comparative information are presented outside the financial statements, these explanations would clearly be of benefit to users.

6.3 Explanation of transition to IFRSs

A first-time adopter is required to explain how the transition from its previous GAAP to IFRSs affected its reported financial position, financial performance and cash flows. *[IFRS 1.23]*. The IASB decided 'that such disclosures are essential, in the first (annual) IFRS financial statements as well as in interim financial reports (if any), because they help users understand the effect and implications of the transition to IFRSs and how they need to change their analytical models to make the best use of information presented using IFRSs.' *[IFRS 1.BC91]*.

As discussed at 3.5 and 5 above, IFRS 1 offers a wide range of exemptions that a first-time adopter may elect to apply. However, perhaps surprisingly, the standard does not explicitly require an entity to disclose which exemptions it has applied and how it applied them. In the case of, for example, the exemption relating to cumulative translation differences, it will be rather obvious whether or not an entity has chosen to apply the exemption. In other cases, users will have to rely on a first-time adopter disclosing those transitional accounting policies that are relevant to an understanding of the financial statements. In practice most first-time adopters voluntarily disclose which

IFRS 1 exemptions they elected to apply and which exceptions apply to them, as is illustrated below by Extract 5.12.

Extract 5.12: Bombardier Inc. (2011)
NOTES TO CONSOLIDATED FINANCIAL STATEMENTS [extract]
For the fiscal years ended December 31, 2011 and January 31, 2011
36.   ADOPTION OF IFRS [extract]

The Corporation has adopted IFRS effective for its annual consolidated financial statements beginning February 1, 2011. These consolidated financial statements are the Corporation's first annual consolidated financial statements prepared in accordance with IFRS. For all periods up to and including the fiscal year ended January 31, 2011, the Corporation prepared its consolidated financial statements in accordance with previous Canadian GAAP.

This note explains how the transition from previous Canadian GAAP to IFRS affected the Corporation's reported equity as at February 1, 2010 and January 31, 2011, as well as net income, comprehensive income and cash flows for the fiscal year ended January 31, 2011. References to Canadian GAAP in this note refer to Canadian GAAP applicable to the Corporation for reporting periods up to and including the fiscal year ended January 31, 2011.

IFRS 1, *First-time Adoption of International Financial Reporting Standards*, requires a first-time adopter to retrospectively apply all IFRS effective as at the end of its first annual reporting period (December 31, 2011 for the Corporation). IFRS 1 also provides a first-time adopter certain optional exemptions and requires certain mandatory exemptions from full retrospective application. Most of these exemptions, if elected or mandatory, must be applied as at the beginning of the required comparative period (the transition date). The Corporation's transition date to IFRS is February 1, 2010.

The Corporation has not modified the choices made with regard to elections under IFRS 1 or its accounting policies under IFRS during the fiscal year ended December 31, 2011, except for the additional exemption for retirement benefits to recognize all cumulative actuarial gains and losses as at February 1, 2010 in retained earnings as described in the following section.

EXEMPTIONS FROM FULL RETROSPECTIVE APPLICATION OF IFRS

In accordance with the mandatory exemptions from retrospective application of IFRS, the consolidated statement of financial position as at February 1, 2010 does not reflect any hedge relationships which did not satisfy the hedge accounting criteria in IAS 39, *Financial Instruments: Recognition and Measurement*, as of the transition date.

Under IFRS 1, the Corporation elected to apply the following optional exemptions in preparing its opening statement of financial position as at the transition date.

1. *Business combinations* – The Corporation elected to apply IFRS prospectively for business combinations from the date of transition to IFRS. Accordingly, the Corporation has not restated the accounting for acquisitions of subsidiaries, interests in joint ventures or associates that occurred before February 1, 2010.

2. *CCTD* – At the transition date, the Corporation transferred all cumulative foreign exchange losses, amounting to $117 million, from CCTD to retained earnings. There was no impact on equity as at February 1, 2010 as a result of this election.

3. *Borrowing costs* – The Corporation elected to begin capitalization of borrowing costs to qualifying assets under IFRS effective February 19, 2007, the launch date of the *CRJ1000 NextGen* aircraft program. Borrowing costs of $32 million, capitalized under Canadian GAAP prior to that date, were derecognized and applied against retained earnings at the transition date.

4. *Share-based compensation* – The Corporation did not apply IFRS 2, *Share-based payment*, to equity instruments granted prior to November 7, 2002 and those that have vested before February 1, 2010. At transition date, there was no adjustment related to these instruments as a result of this election.

5. *Retirement benefits* – The Corporation elected to disclose the defined benefit obligations, plan assets, deficit and experience adjustments on retirement benefit liabilities and assets prospectively from the date of transition, progressively building the data to present the four years of comparative information required under IFRS.

6. *Retirement benefits* – The Corporation elected to recognize all cumulative actuarial gains and losses as at February 1, 2010 in retained earnings.

If a first-time adopter did not present financial statements for previous periods, this fact should be disclosed. *[IFRS 1.28]*. The standard acknowledges that there are cases in which disclosure of how the transition to IFRSs affected the entity's reported financial position, financial performance and cash flows cannot be presented, because relevant comparative information under the entity's previous GAAP does not exist. In practice this may apply to entities that did not prepare consolidated accounts under their previous GAAPs or for a newly established entity. However, if the new entity is established by transferring a pre-existing business from a non-IFRS adopter to it and the new entity is determined to be a continuation of the pre-existing business, the entity would be expected to disclose the explanation of its transition to IFRSs.

6.3.1 Disclosure of reconciliations

A first-time adopter is required to present:

- reconciliations of its equity reported under previous GAAP to its equity under IFRSs at: *[IFRS 1.24(a)]*
  - the date of transition to IFRSs; and
  - the end of the latest period presented in the entity's most recent annual financial statements under previous GAAP;
- a reconciliation to its total comprehensive income under IFRSs for the latest period in the entity's most recent annual financial statements. The starting point for that reconciliation should be total comprehensive income under previous GAAP for the same period or, if an entity did not report such a total, profit or loss under previous GAAP; *[IFRS 1.24(b)]* and
- an explanation of the material adjustments to the statement of cash flows, if it presented one under its previous GAAP. *[IFRS 1.25]*.

These reconciliations should be sufficiently detailed to enable users to understand the material adjustments to the statement of financial position, statement of profit or loss (if presented) and statement of profit or loss and other comprehensive income. *[IFRS 1.25]*.

If a first-time adopter becomes aware of errors made under previous GAAP, it should distinguish the correction of errors from changes in accounting policies in the above reconciliations. *[IFRS 1.26]*. This means that the adoption of IFRSs should not be used to mask the error.

While the standard does not prescribe a layout for these reconciliations, the implementation guidance contains an example of a line-by-line reconciliation of the statement of financial position, statement of profit or loss and other comprehensive income. *[IFRS 1.IG Example 11]*. This presentation may be particularly appropriate when a first-time adopter needs to make transitional adjustments that affect a significant number of line items in the primary financial statements. If the adjustments are less pervasive a straightforward reconciliation of equity, total comprehensive income and/or profit or loss may provide an equally effective explanation of how the adoption of IFRSs affects the reported financial position, financial performance and cash flows.

The example below illustrates how these requirements apply to an entity whose first IFRS financial statements are for the period ending on 31 December 2021 and whose date of transition to IFRSs is 1 January 2020.

Example 5.41:   Reconciliations to be presented in first IFRS financial statements

Entity A's date of transition to IFRSs is 1 January 2020 and the end of its first IFRS reporting period is 31 December 2021. Entity A should present the following primary financial statements and reconciliations in its first IFRS financial statements.

	1 January 2020	31 December 2020	31 December 2021
Statement of financial position	●	●	●
Reconciliation of equity	●	●	‡
For the period ending			
Statement of profit or loss and other comprehensive income *		●	●
Statement of cash flows		●	●
Statement of changes in equity		●	●
Reconciliation of total comprehensive income †		●	‡
Explanation of material adjustments to the statement of cash flows		●	‡

*   Alternatively, the entity should present two statements: a statement of profit or loss and a statement of comprehensive income.
†   If an entity did not previously report total comprehensive income, then a reconciliation from profit or loss under previous GAAP to total comprehensive income under IFRSs should be presented.
‡   A first-time adopter that ceases to publish financial statements under previous GAAP is not required to present reconciliations of equity and total comprehensive income at the end of the first IFRS reporting period. However, a first-time adopter that continues to publish previous GAAP financial statements may have to reconcile the equity and total comprehensive income and explain material cash flow adjustments as of and for the end of the first IFRS financial reporting period. See 6.3.1.A below for further discussion.

First-time adopters do not apply the requirements of IAS 8 relating to the changes in accounting policies in their first IFRS financial statements. This is because that standard does not apply to the changes in accounting policies an entity makes when it adopts IFRSs or changes in those policies until after it presents its first IFRS financial statements. *[IFRS 1.27].*

A first-time adopter should explain changes in accounting policies or in its use of exemptions during the period between its first IFRS interim financial report and its first IFRS annual financial statements (see 6.6 below) and update the reconciliations of equity and total comprehensive income discussed herein. *[IFRS 1.27A]*. This requirement is necessary in order to explain the transition to IFRSs, *[IFRS 1.23]*, since the first-time adopter is exempt from the requirements of IAS 8 concerning reporting of such changes. *[IFRS 1.BC97]*.

6.3.1.A   Reconciliation by a first-time adopter that continues to publish previous GAAP financial statements

A first-time adopter that continues to publish financial statements under previous GAAP after adopting IFRSs must consider carefully the starting point of the reconciliations required by IFRS 1 in the first IFRS financial statements because the requirements to produce reconciliations do not consider this situation. Paragraph 24 of IFRS 1 results in different applications depending on the timing of issuance of the previous GAAP financial statements in relation to the first-time adopter's first IFRS reporting period. We believe a first-time adopter, that continues to publish previous GAAP financial statements and has already issued those financial statements for the first IFRS reporting period prior to the issuance of the first IFRS financial statements, has a choice of presenting reconciliations of equity and total comprehensive income:

(a)   respectively as at the end of, and for, the first IFRS reporting period;
(b)   respectively as at the end of, and for, both the first IFRS reporting period, and the comparative period; or
(c)   respectively as at the end of, and for, the comparative period.

In each case above, the reconciliation of equity as at the date of transition to IFRSs must be disclosed.

However, if the first IFRS financial statements were issued prior to the previous GAAP financial statements for the period, then IFRS 1 can only mean the previous GAAP financial statements for the immediate preceding year.

6.3.2 Line-by-line reconciliations and detailed explanations

The extract below from the 2011 financial statements of Bombardier Inc. complies with the versions of IFRS 1 and IAS 1 that were effective in 2011. However, it still provides a good example of an entity that not only provides summary reconciliations of equity and profit or loss, but also line-by-line reconciliations, as suggested by the implementation guidance in IFRS 1, and detailed explanations of the reconciling items.

The exceptions and exemptions used by Bombardier on transition to IFRSs are shown in Extract 5.12 above. The following extract does not include all of Bombardier's detailed explanations of the reconciling items.

Extract 5.13: Bombardier Inc. (2011)

NOTES TO CONSOLIDATED FINANCIAL STATEMENTS [extract]

For the fiscal years ended December 31, 2011 and January 31, 2011

(Tabular figures are in millions of U.S. dollars, unless otherwise indicated)

36. ADOPTION OF IFRS [extract]

RECONCILIATIONS OF EQUITY AND NET INCOME FROM CANADIAN GAAP TO IFRS

The following reconciliations illustrate the measurement and recognition differences in restating equity and net income reported under Canadian GAAP to IFRS for the dates and period indicated.

RECONCILIATION OF EQUITY

	Item	January 31, 2011	February 1, 2010
Equity under Canadian GAAP (as reported)		$ 4,352	$ 3,769
Measurement and recognition differences:			
Retirement benefits	A	(2,110)	(2,198)
Revenues	B	(552)	(554)
Aerospace program tooling	C	(195)	(246)
Sale and leaseback obligations	D	(1)	(6)
Other		(92)	(12)
		(2,950)	(3,016)
Income tax impact of all restatements	E	119	207
Total restatements		(2,831)	(2,809)
Equity under IFRS		$ 1,521	$ 960

RECONCILIATION OF EBIT, NET INCOME AND DILUTED EPS

Fiscal year ended January 31, 2011

	Item	BA	BT	EBIT	Net financing expense	Net income
As reported under Canadian GAAP		$448	$602	$1,050	$ (119)	$769 [1]
Reclassifications		1	–	1	(1)	–
Restatements to income before income taxes						
Retirement benefits	A	31	66	97	(44)	53
Revenues	B	24	(15)	9	(7)	2
Aerospace program tooling	C	55	–	55	(4)	51
Sale and leaseback obligations	D	10	–	10	(5)	5
Other		(15)	(2)	(17)	(28)	(45)
		105	49	154	(88)	66
Income tax impact of all restatements	E					(60)
Total restatements		105	49	154	(88)	6
As restated under IFRS		$554	$651	$1,205	$ (208)	$775
Diluted EPS under Canadian GAAP (as reported)						$0.42
Impact of IFRS restatements to net income						–
Diluted EPS under IFRS						$0.42

(1) Net of income taxes of $162 million.

The following items explain the most significant restatements to equity and net income resulting from the change in accounting policies upon adoption of IFRS.

A. RETIREMENT BENEFITS

The equity adjustment before income taxes was as follows as at February 1, 2010:

Net unrecognized actuarial loss recorded in deficit	$ (1,826)
Vested past service credits	(32)
Asset ceiling and additional liability test	(97)
Measurement date	(227)
Allocation of retirement benefit costs to inventories and aerospace program tooling	(16)
Equity adjustment, before income taxes	**$ (2,198)**

The transition date adjustments related to net unrecognized actuarial loss, change of measurement date and asset ceiling and additional liability test, net of income taxes of $177 million, totalled $1,973 million and have been presented as a separate item of the deficit as at February 1, 2010. Cumulative net actuarial gains and losses since February 1, 2010 are also presented in this separate item of the deficit.

The impact on EBT for the fiscal year ended January 31, 2011 was as follows:

Increase in EBIT	$ 97
Increase in net financing expense	(44)
Increase in EBT	**$ 53**

Actuarial gains and losses
Under Canadian GAAP, actuarial gains and losses were amortized through net income using a corridor approach over the estimated average remaining service life ("EARSL") of employees. Under IFRS, the Corporation has elected to recognize all actuarial gains and losses in OCI as incurred. As a result of this election, foreign exchange gains and losses on the translation of plan assets and liabilities are also recorded in OCI under IFRS.

Vested past service costs (credits)
Under Canadian GAAP, vested past service costs (credits) of defined benefit plans were amortized over the EARSL of plan participants from their grant date. Under IFRS, vested past service costs (credits) of defined benefit plans must be recognized in net income immediately as granted.

Asset ceiling and additionally liability test
Under IFRS, IFRIC 14, *The limit on a defined benefit asset, minimum funding requirements and their interaction*, requires entities to consider minimum funding requirements when assessing the financial position of defined benefit plans. This interpretation may require either a reduction of the retirement benefit asset or the recognition of an additional liability. Canadian GAAP also set limits on the recognition of the retirement benefit asset, but did not consider minimum funding requirements and as such could not create an additional liability.

Under Canadian GAAP, an adjustment arising from the asset ceiling was recognized in net income. Since the Corporation has elected to recognize all actuarial gains and losses in OCI under IFRS, variations arising from this test are also recognized in OCI in the period in which they occur.

Measurement date
Canadian GAAP allowed entities to use a measurement date for defined benefit obligations and plan assets up to three months prior to the financial year-end date. December 31 was used as the measurement date for all of the Corporation's defined benefit plans under Canadian GAAP.

Measurement of the defined benefit obligations and plan assets is performed at the reporting date under IFRS. Accordingly, defined benefit plans at BA and Corporate Office were measured using a January 31 measurement date under IFRS during the fiscal year ended January 31, 2011. Defined benefit plans at BT continued to use a December 31 measurement date as this is the financial year-end date of BT.

Allocation of retirement benefit costs to inventories and aerospace program tooling
The adjustment to inventories and aerospace program tooling arises from changes in the presentation of retirement benefit costs. The Corporation elected to segregate retirement benefit costs into three components under IFRS:
- retirement benefit expense (including current and past service costs or credits) recorded in EBIT;
- accretion on retirement benefit obligations and expected return on retirement plan assets recorded in financing expense and financing income; and
- actuarial gains and losses, asset ceiling and additional liability test and gains and losses on foreign exchange recorded in OCI.

Under Canadian GAAP these three components were eventually all recorded in EBIT. As a result, only current service costs are considered for capitalization in aerospace program tooling and inventories under IFRS, whereas under Canadian GAAP all three components were considered for capitalization.

[...]

C. AEROSPACE PROGRAM TOOLING

Restatements related to aerospace program tooling are attributed to the following three elements.

Government refundable advances

As an incentive to stimulate R&D, some governments provide advances during the development period, which are usually conditionally repaid upon delivery of the related product.

Under Canadian GAAP, contingently repayable advances received were deducted from aerospace program tooling or R&D expenses, and any repayments were recorded as an expense in cost of sales upon delivery of the aircraft. Under IFRS, a liability is recorded for the expected repayment of advances received if it is probable that the conditions for repayment will be met. Repayments are recorded as a reduction of the liability. Revisions to the estimate of amounts to be repaid result in an increase or decrease in the liability and aerospace program tooling or R&D expense, and a cumulative catch-up adjustment to amortization is recognized immediately in net income.

As a result, aerospace program tooling is recorded gross of government refundable advances under IFRS, resulting in a higher amortization expense in the earlier stages of an aircraft program's life. Recording of government refundable advances as a liability at transition decreased equity by $148 million as a significant portion of the related aerospace program tooling was amortized prior to February 1, 2010 under IFRS.

R&D expenditures incurred by vendors on behalf of the Corporation

As a new aircraft is developed, some vendors invest in the development of new technology (vendor non-recurring costs or "VNR costs"). These costs may be repaid to the vendor as part of the purchase price of the vendor's product, and the technology is transferred to the Corporation once an agreed amount is repaid.

Under Canadian GAAP, the amounts repaid to vendors were recognized as aerospace program tooling ratably as the vendor developed product was purchased. Under IFRS, upon evidence of successful development, which generally occurs at a program's entry-into-service, such VNR costs must be recognized as a liability based on the best estimate of the amount to be repaid to the vendor, with a corresponding increase in aerospace program tooling.

As a result, VNR costs are recorded earlier under IFRS, based on the present value of the best estimate of the amounts repayable, with consequential higher amortization of aerospace program tooling early in the program life. Repayments to vendors are recorded as a reduction of the liability.

The adjustment at transition decreased equity by $70 million as a significant portion of the related aerospace program tooling was amortized prior to February 1, 2010.

[...]

COMBINED IMPACT ON EBT OF ADJUSTMENTS TO AEROSPACE PROGRAM TOOLING

Increase (decrease) in EBT	Fiscal year ended January 31, 2011
Decrease in amortization resulting from overall lower aerospace program tooling balance	$ 33
Repayments of government refundable advances no longer recorded in EBIT	47
Change in estimates of the liability for government refundable advances	(14)
Foreign exchange loss upon translation of the liability for government refundable advances	(11)
Accretion expense on the liability for government refundable advances	(19)
Additional capitalization of borrowing costs due to a higher capitalization base for programs under development	15
	$ 51

[...]

E. INCOME TAX IMPACT OF ALL RESTATEMENTS

The restatements to equity as at February 1, 2010 totalling $3,016 million affected the accounting values of assets and liabilities but not their tax bases. Applying the Canadian statutory tax rate of 31.3% to these restatements would trigger the recognition of a deferred income tax asset of $944 million at the transition date. However, IFRS allows recognition of a deferred income tax asset only to the extent it is probable that taxable profit will be available against which the deductible temporary differences or unused income tax losses can be utilized. The deferred income tax asset has not been fully recognized under IFRS, as some of the income tax benefits are expected to materialize in periods subsequent to the period meeting the probability of recovery test necessary to recognize such assets. In connection with IFRS restatements to equity at transition, $207 million of additional deferred income tax assets were recognized.

Applying the Canadian statutory tax rate of 30.0% to the IFRS adjustments for the fiscal year ended January 31, 2011 would result in an income tax expense of $20 million. However, the probable future taxable profit that will be available to utilize operating losses and deductible temporary differences is lower under IFRS mainly due to the change in revenue recognition policy for medium and large business aircraft, which delays revenue recognition until completion of the aircraft. As a result, less deferred income tax benefits were recognized under IFRS during the fiscal year ended January 31, 2011. The additional income tax expense as a result of all restatements for the fiscal year ended January 31, 2011 was $60 million.

RECONCILIATIONS OF STATEMENTS OF FINANCIAL POSITION AND INCOME FROM CANADIAN GAAP TO IFRS

The following reconciliations illustrate the reclassifications and restatements from Canadian GAAP to IFRS to the opening statement of financial position and to the statement of income for the fiscal year ended January 31, 2011.

CONSOLIDATED STATEMENT OF FINANCIAL POSITION AS AT FEBRUARY 1, 2010

Canadian GAAP line items	Cdn GAAP	Reclassi- fications	Restate- ments	Items	IFRS	IFRS line items
Assets						**Assets**
Cash and cash equivalents	3,372				3,372	Cash and cash equivalents
Invested collateral	682	(682)				
Receivables	1,897	(137)	(619)	B	1,141	Trade and other receivables
Aircraft financing	473	(473)				
Inventories	5,268	62	2,300	A, B, D	7,630	Inventories
		547	(10)		537	Other financial assets
		500	19	B	519	Other assets
	11,692	(183)	1,690		13,199	Current assets

Canadian GAAP line items	Cdn GAAP	Reclassi- fications	Restate- ments	Items	IFRS	IFRS line items
		682	–		682	Invested collateral
PP&E	1,643	46	(15)		1,674	PP&E
		1,439	(54)	(1), C	1,385	Aerospace program tooling
Intangible assets	1,696	(1,696)				
Fractional ownership deferred costs	271	(271)				
Deferred income taxes	1,166		207	E	1,373	Deferred income taxes
Accrued benefit assets	1,070	(44)	(1,026)	A		
Derivative financial instruments	482	(482)				
Goodwill	2,247				2,247	Goodwill
		1,003			1,003	Other financial assets
Other assets	1,006	(455)	6	C, D	557	Other assets
	9,581	222	(882)		8,921	Non-current assets
	21,273	39	808		22,120	

First-time adoption

Canadian GAAP line items	Cdn GAAP	Reclassi-fications	Restate-ments	Items	IFRS	IFRS line items
Liabilities						**Liabilities**
Accounts payable and accrued liabilities	7,427	(4,230)	(152)	B, D	3,045	Trade and other payables
		1,180	(40)	B	1,140	Provisions
Advances and progress billings in excess of related long-term contract costs	1,899				1,899	Advances and progress billings in excess of related long-term contract inventories
Advances on aerospace programs	2,092	(1,374)	2,337	B	3,055	Advances on aerospace programs
Fractional ownership deferred revenues	346	(346)				
		359	178	D	537	Other financial liabilities
		1,989	(2)	D	1,987	Other liabilities
	11,764	(2,422)	2,321		11,663	Current liabilities
		677	(2)		675	Provisions
		1,373			1,373	Advances on aerospace programs
Deferred income taxes	65	(65)				
Long-term debt	4,162	(11)	(17)		4,134	Non-current portion of long-term debt
Accrued benefit liabilities	1,084	(59)	1,156	A	2,181	Retirement benefits
Derivative financial instruments	429	(429)				
		358	200	C	558	Other financial liabilities
		617	(41)		576	Other liabilities
	5,740	2,461	1,296		9,497	Non-current liabilities
	17,504	39	3,617		21,160	
Preferred shares	347				347	Preferred shares
Common shares	1,324				1,324	Common shares
Contributed surplus	132				132	Contributed surplus
Retained earnings	2,087		(937)	A-E	1,150	Deficit – Other earnings
			(1,973)	A, E	(1,973)	Deficit – Net actuarial losses
Accumulated OCI – AFS and cash flow hedges	(72)		(6)		(78)	Accumulated OCI – AFS and cash flow hedges
Accumulated OCI – CTA	(117)		117	(1)	–	Accumulated OCI – CCTD
Equity attributable to equity holders of Bombardier Inc.	3,701		(2,799)		902	Equity attributable to equity holders of Bombardier Inc.
Equity attributable to NCI	68		(10)		58	Equity attributable to NCI
	3,769		(2,809)		960	
	21,273	39	808		22,120	

(1) Restatements include effect of IFRS 1 optional exemptions.

CONSOLIDATED STATEMENT OF INCOME FOR THE FISCAL YEAR ENDED JANUARY 31, 2011

Canadian GAAP line items	Cdn GAAP	Reclassi-fications	Restate-ments	Items	IFRS	IFRS line items
Revenues	17,712		180	B, D	17,892	Revenues
Cost of sales	14,668	249	38	A-D	14,955	Cost of sales
	3,044	(249)	142		2,937	Gross margin
SG&A	1,369	7	1	A, B	1,377	SG&A
R&D	193	160	(34)	A, C	319	R&D
Other expense (income)	22	(7)	21	C	36	Other expense (income)
Amortization	410	(410)				
EBIT	1,050	1	154		1,205	EBIT
Financing income	(137)	3	(342)	A	(476)	Financing income
Financing expense	256	(2)	430	A-D	684	Financing expense
EBT	931	–	66		997	EBT
Income taxes	162		60	E	222	Income taxes
Net income	769	–	6		775	Net income
Attributable to shareholders of Bombardier	755		7		762	Attributable to equity holders of Bombardier
Attributable to NCI	14		(1)		13	Attributable to NCI
Basic EPS	0.42		0.01		0.43	Basic EPS
Diluted EPS	0.42		–		0.42	Diluted EPS

RECLASSIFICATIONS FROM CANADIAN GAAP REPORTING TO IFRS

A classified statement of financial position has been presented under IFRS, based on the operating cycle for operating items and based on a 12-month period for non-operating items.

The following are mandatory reclassifications of items in the statement of financial position upon transition to IFRS:
- Financial assets and financial liabilities are presented separately from non-financial assets and non-financial liabilities.
- Provisions are presented separately from other payables.
- Other long-term employment benefits, such as long-term disability and service awards, are segregated from retirement benefits and are presented in other liabilities.

The Corporation has also made the following elective reclassification of items in the statements of financial position to place focus on key accounts under IFRS:
- Aerospace program tooling is presented separately from goodwill and other intangibles.
- *Flexjet* fractional ownership deferred costs and fractional ownership deferred revenues are no longer presented separately and are included in other assets and other liabilities, respectively.
- Aircraft financing is no longer presented separately and is included in other financial assets, except for assets under operating leases which are presented as non-financial assets classified according to their nature.
- Derivative financial instruments are no longer presented separately and are included in other financial assets and other financial liabilities.

The Corporation has made the following mandatory reclassification of items in the statement of income:
- Amortization expense is no longer presented separately and is classified between cost of sales, SG&A and R&D based on the function of the underlying assets.

The Corporation has made the following elective reclassifications of items in the statement of income:
- Expected return on pension plan assets and accretion on retirement benefit obligations are presented in financing expense and financing income and are no longer included in EBIT.
- Other income and expenses related to operations, such as foreign exchange gains and losses, are no longer included in other expense (income) and are instead classified as cost of sales unless the item is unusual and material.
- Under Canadian GAAP, changes in valuation of credit and residual value guarantees, loans and lease receivables, lease subsidies, investments in financing structures and servicing fees are presented in cost of sales or other expense (income). Under IFRS, changes in the value of these items are presented in financing expense or financing income if the changes arise from variation in interest rates. Other changes in valuation of these items are presented in other expense (income) under IFRS.

RECONCILIATION OF COMPREHENSIVE INCOME FROM CANADIAN GAAP TO IFRS

The following reconciliation illustrates the restatements to comprehensive income reported under Canadian GAAP to IFRS for the fiscal year ended January 31, 2011.

RECONCILIATION OF COMPREHENSIVE INCOME

	Item	
Comprehensive income under Canadian GAAP (as reported)		$ 799
Differences on net income		6
Differences on OCI		
Retirement benefits	A	35
Other		(35)
Income tax impact of all restatements	E	(28)
		(28)
Comprehensive income under IFRS		$ 777

The following items explain the significant restatements to OCI resulting from the change in accounting policies upon adoption of IFRS.

A. RETIREMENT BENEFITS

A net actuarial gain of $35 million was recognized during the fiscal year ended January 31, 2011. This net actuarial gain was comprised of:

Actuarial gains, mainly due to changes in discount rates	$ 161
Loss arising from variations in the asset ceiling and additional liability	(70)
Foreign exchange losses on the translation of plan assets and liabilities	(56)
Net actuarial gain	$ 35

Actuarial gains and losses are recognized in OCI under IFRS in accordance with the Corporation's choice of accounting policy.

[...]

E. INCOME TAX IMPACT OF ALL RESTATEMENTS

The related deferred income tax assets have not been fully recognized in some countries, as it is not probable that all of the income tax benefits will be realized, and additional income tax expense was recorded in other counties.

6.3.3 Recognition and reversal of impairments

If a first-time adopter recognised or reversed any impairment losses on transition to IFRSs it should disclose the information that IAS 36 would have required if the entity had recognised those impairment losses or reversals in the period beginning with the date of transition to IFRSs (see Chapter 20 at 13). *[IFRS 1.24(c)]*. This provides transparency about impairment losses recognised on transition that might otherwise receive less attention than impairment losses recognised in earlier or later periods. *[IFRS 1.BC94]*.

6.3.4 Inclusion of IFRS 1 reconciliations by cross reference

The reconciliation disclosures required by IFRS 1 are generally quite lengthy. While IFRS 1 allows an entity's first interim report under IAS 34 to give certain of these disclosures by way of cross-reference to another published document, *[IFRS 1.32-33]*, there is no corresponding exemption for disclosure in the entity's first annual IFRS financial statements. Therefore, a first-time adopter should include all disclosures required by IFRS 1 within its first annual IFRS financial statements in the same way it would need to include other lengthy disclosures such as those on business combinations, financial instruments and employee benefits. Any additional voluntary information regarding the conversion to IFRSs that was previously published but that is not specifically required by IFRS 1 need not be repeated in the first IFRS financial statements.

6.4 Disclosure of financial instruments

6.4.1 Designation of financial instruments

If, on transition, a first-time adopter designates a previously recognised financial asset or financial liability as a 'financial asset or financial liability at fair value through profit or loss' (see 5.11.1 and 5.11.2 above), it must disclose: *[IFRS 1.29-29A, D19, D19A]*

- the fair value of financial assets or financial liabilities so designated at the date of designation; and
- their classification and carrying amount in the previous GAAP financial statements.

6.4.2 Classification of financial instruments

An entity should disclose the carrying amount at the reporting date of the financial assets whose contractual cash flow characteristics have been assessed based on the facts and circumstances that existed at the date of transition without taking into account the requirements related to the modification of the time value of money element in paragraphs B4.1.9B-B4.1.9D of IFRS 9 until those financial assets are derecognised. *[IFRS 1.B8A, IFRS 7.42R, IFRS 9.B4.1.9B-B4.1.9D]*. See 4.9.1.A above.

An entity should disclose the carrying amount at the reporting date of the financial assets whose contractual cash flow characteristics have been assessed based on the facts and circumstances that existed at the date of transition without taking into account the exception for prepayment features in paragraph B4.1.12 of IFRS 9 until those financial assets are derecognised. *[IFRS 1.B8B, IFRS 7.42S, IFRS 9.B4.1.12].* See 4.9.1.B above.

6.5 Disclosures regarding deemed cost

6.5.1 Use of fair value as deemed cost

If a first-time adopter uses fair value as deemed cost for any item of property, plant and equipment, investment property, right-of-use asset under IFRS 16 or an intangible asset in its opening IFRS statement of financial position (see 5.5.1 above), it must disclose for each line item in the opening IFRS statement of financial position: *[IFRS 1.30. D5, D7]*

- the aggregate of those fair values; and
- the aggregate adjustment to the carrying amounts reported under previous GAAP.

This disclosure is illustrated in Extract 5.6 at 5.5.1 above.

6.5.2 Use of deemed cost for investments in subsidiaries, joint ventures and associates in separate financial statements

If a first-time adopter uses deemed cost in its opening IFRS financial statement of financial position for an investment in a subsidiary, joint venture or associate in its separate financial statements (see 5.8.2 above), the entity's first IFRS separate financial statements must disclose: *[IFRS 1.31, D15]*

(a) the aggregate deemed cost of those investments for which deemed cost is their previous GAAP carrying amount;

(b) the aggregate deemed cost of those investments for which deemed cost is fair value; and

(c) the aggregate adjustment to the carrying amounts reported under previous GAAP.

6.5.3 Use of deemed cost for oil and gas assets

If a first-time adopter uses the deemed cost exemption in paragraph D8A(b) of IFRS 1 for oil and gas assets (see 5.5.3 above), it must disclose that fact and the basis on which carrying amounts determined under previous GAAP were allocated. *[IFRS 1.31A, D8A(b)].*

6.5.4 Use of deemed cost for assets used in operations subject to rate regulation

If a first-time adopter uses the exemption for assets used in operations subject to rate regulation (see 5.5.4 above), it must disclose that fact and the basis on which carrying amounts were determined under previous GAAP. *[IFRS 1.31B, D8B].*

6.5.5 Use of deemed cost after severe hyperinflation

If a first-time adopter uses the exemption to elect fair value as the deemed cost in its opening IFRS statement of financial position for assets and liabilities because of severe hyperinflation (see 5.17 above), it must disclose an explanation of how, and why, the first-time adopter had, and then ceased to have, a functional currency that has both of the following characteristics: *[IFRS 1.31C, D26-D30]*

(a) a reliable general price index is not available to all entities with transactions and balances in the currency; and

(b) exchangeability between the currency and a relatively stable foreign currency does not exist.

6.6 Interim financial reports

6.6.1 Reconciliations in the interim financial reports

If a first-time adopter presents an interim financial report under IAS 34 for part of the period covered by its first IFRS financial statements:

(a) Each such interim financial report must, if the entity presented an interim financial report for the comparable interim period of the immediately preceding financial year, include: *[IFRS 1.32(a)]*

- a reconciliation of its equity under previous GAAP at the end of that comparable interim period to its equity under IFRSs at that date; and
- a reconciliation to its total comprehensive income under IFRSs for that comparable interim period (current and year to date). The starting point for that reconciliation is total comprehensive income under previous GAAP for that period or, if an entity did not report such a total, profit or loss under previous GAAP.

(b) In addition, the entity's first interim financial report under IAS 34 for part of the period covered by its first IFRS financial statements must include the reconciliations described at 6.3.1 above, *[IFRS 1.24(a), (b), 25, 26]*, or a cross-reference to another published document that includes these reconciliations. *[IFRS 1.32(b)]*.

For an entity presenting annual financial statements under IFRSs, it is not compulsory to prepare interim financial reports under IAS 34. Therefore, the above requirements only apply to first-time adopters that prepare interim reports under IAS 34 on a voluntary basis or that are required to do so by a regulator or other party. *[IFRS 1.IG37]*.

Examples 5.42 and 5.43 below show which reconciliations should be included in half-year reports and quarterly reports, respectively.

Example 5.42: **Reconciliations to be presented in IFRS half-year reports**

As in Example 5.41 at 6.3.1 above, Entity A's date of transition to IFRSs is 1 January 2020, the end of its first IFRS reporting period is 31 December 2021 and it publishes a half-year report as at 30 June 2021 under IAS 34. Which primary financial statements and reconciliations must Entity A present in its first IFRS half-year report?

	1 January 2020	30 June 2020	31 December 2020	30 June 2021
Statement of financial position			●	●
Reconciliation of equity	●‡	●	●‡	
For the period ending				
Statement of profit or loss and other comprehensive income *		●		●
Statement of cash flows		●		●
Statement of changes in equity		●		●
Reconciliation of total comprehensive income †		●	●‡	
Explanation of material adjustments to the statement of cash flows			●‡	

*   Alternatively, the entity should present two statements: a statement of profit or loss and a statement of comprehensive income.
†   If an entity did not previously report total comprehensive income then a reconciliation from profit or loss under previous GAAP to total comprehensive income under IFRSs is presented.
‡   These additional reconciliations are required under paragraphs 24(a) and (b) and 25 of IFRS 1. The reconciliations must distinguish corrections of errors from changes in accounting policies (see 6.3.1 above).

The IAS 34 requirements regarding the disclosure of primary financial statements in interim reports are discussed in Chapter 41 at 5.

As can be seen from the tables in Example 5.42 above, the additional reconciliations and explanations required under (b) above would be presented out of context without the statement of financial position, statement of profit or loss (if presented), statement of profit or loss and other comprehensive income and statement of cash flows to which they relate. For this reason, we believe a first-time adopter should either (1) include the primary financial statements to which these reconciliations relate or (2) refer to another published document that includes these primary financial statements. The following example showing the various reconciliations to be included in the financial statements of a first-time adopter is based on the Illustrative Examples of IFRS 1: *[IFRS 1.IG Example 10]*

Example 5.43: Reconciliations to be presented in IFRS quarterly reports

Entity B's date of transition to IFRSs is 1 January 2020, the end of its first IFRS reporting period is 31 December 2021 and it publishes quarterly reports under IAS 34. Which reconciliations should Entity B present in its 2021 interim IFRS reports and in its first IFRS financial statements?

	Reconciliation of equity	Reconciliation of total comprehensive income or profit or loss †	Explanation of material adjustments to statement of cash flows
First quarter			
1 January 2020	○		
31 December 2020	○	○	○
31 March 2020			
– 3 months ending	●	●	
Second quarter			
30 June 2020			
– 3 months ending		●	
– 6 months ending	●	●	
Third quarter			
30 September 2020			
– 3 months ending		●	
– 9 months ending	●	●	
First IFRS financial statements			
1 January 2020	●		
31 December 2020	●	●	●

○ These reconciliations are only required to be presented in an entity's *first* interim financial report under IAS 34 and may be included by way of a cross-reference to another published document in which these reconciliations are presented. The reconciliations must distinguish corrections of errors from changes in accounting policies.

† If an entity did not previously report total comprehensive income, a reconciliation from profit or loss under previous GAAP to total comprehensive income under IFRSs must be presented.

If a first-time adopter issues interim financial report in accordance with IAS 34 for part of the period covered by its first IFRS financial statements and changes its accounting policies or its use of exemptions contained in IFRS 1, the first-time adopter is required to explain the changes in each such interim financial report in accordance with paragraph 23 and update the reconciliations at (a) and (b) above. *[IFRS 1.23, 32]*.

6.6.2 Disclosures in the interim financial report

Interim financial reports under IAS 34 contain considerably less detail than annual financial statements because they assume that users of the interim financial report also have access to the most recent annual financial statements. However, they would be expected to provide disclosure relating to material events or transactions to allow users to understand the current interim period. Therefore, a first-time adopter needs to consider what IFRS disclosures are material to an understanding of the current interim period. If the most recent annual financial statements under previous GAAP did not disclose information material to an understanding of the current interim period, the interim financial report must disclose that information (or include a cross reference to another published document that contains that information). *[IFRS 1.33, IAS 34.15-15A]*. A full set of IFRS accounting policy disclosures and related significant judgements and estimates should be included as well as information on the IFRS 1 exemptions employed. In addition, consideration should be given to both new disclosures not previously required under previous GAAP, and disclosures made under previous GAAP but for which the amounts contained therein have changed significantly due to changes in accounting policies resulting from the adoption of IFRSs.

It is also important to note that such disclosures apply to balances in both the opening and comparative year-end statement of financial position, each of which could be included in the first IFRS interim financial report (see 6.6.1 above). First-time adopters should expect to include significantly more information in their first IFRS interim report than would normally be included in an interim report (alternatively, it could cross refer to another published document that includes such information). *[IFRS 1.33]*.

Examples of additional annual disclosures under IFRSs to be included in the entity's first IAS 34 compliant interim financial report could include disclosures relating to retirement benefits, income taxes, goodwill and provisions, amongst other items that significantly differ from previous GAAP and those required IFRS disclosures that are more substantial than previous GAAP.

6.7 Disclosure of IFRS information before adoption of IFRSs

As the adoption of IFRSs may have a significant impact on their financial statements, many entities will want to provide information on its expected impact. There are certain difficulties that arise as a result of the application of IFRS 1 when an entity decides to quantify the impact of the adoption of IFRSs. In particular, IFRS 1 requires an entity to draw up an opening IFRS statement of financial position at its date of transition based on the standards that are effective at the end of its first IFRS reporting period. Therefore, it is not possible to prepare IFRS financial information – and assess the full impact of IFRSs – until an entity knows its date of transition to IFRSs and exactly which standards will be effective at the end of its first IFRS reporting period.

If an entity wanted to quantify the impact of the adoption of IFRSs before its date of transition, it would not be able to do this in accordance with IFRS 1. While an entity would be able to select a date and apply by analogy the requirements of IFRS 1 to its previous GAAP financial information as of that date, it would not be able to claim that such additional information complied with IFRSs. An entity should avoid presenting such additional information if it is believed that the information, despite being clearly marked as not IFRS compliant, would be misleading or misunderstood.

If an entity wants to quantify the impact of the adoption of IFRSs in advance of the release of its first IFRS financial statements but after its date of transition, there may still be some uncertainty regarding the standards that apply. If so, an entity should disclose the nature of the uncertainty and consider describing the information as 'preliminary' IFRS information. Extract 5.14 below is an example of an entity presenting information about the effect of adopting IFRSs in advance of its first IFRS financial statements. The extract complies with the versions of IFRS 1 and IAS 19 that were effective in 2011.

> **Extract 5.14: Canadian Imperial Bank of Commerce (CIBC) (2011)**
>
> Notes to the consolidated financial statements [extract]
>
> **Note 32 Transition to International Financial Reporting Standards** [extract]
>
> Publicly accountable enterprises are required to adopt IFRS for annual periods beginning on or after January 1, 2011. As a result, our audited consolidated financial statements for the year ending October 31, 2012 will be the first annual financial statements that comply with IFRS, including the application of IFRS 1 "First-time Adoption of International Financial Reporting Standards". IFRS 1 requires an entity to adopt IFRS in its first annual financial statements prepared under IFRS by making an explicit and unreserved statement of compliance with IFRS in those financial statements. We will make this statement of compliance when we issue our 2012 annual consolidated financial statements.
>
> IFRS 1 also requires that comparative financial information be provided. As a result, the first day at which we applied IFRS was as at November 1, 2010 (the Transition Date), and our consolidated opening IFRS balance sheet was prepared as at this date. The opening IFRS balance sheet represents our starting point for financial reporting under IFRS.
>
> In accordance with IFRS 1, we have retrospectively applied our IFRS accounting policies in the preparation of our opening IFRS balance sheet as at November 1, 2010. These IFRS accounting policies are those that we expect to apply in our first annual IFRS financial statements for the year ending October 31, 2012, although IFRS 1 provides certain optional exemptions and mandatory exceptions from retrospective application of IFRS, as described in Section A, Exemptions and exceptions from retrospective application of IFRS.
>
> The following information is provided to allow users of the financial statements to obtain a better understanding of the effect of the adoption of IFRS on our consolidated financial statements. The information below includes our opening IFRS balance sheet as at November 1, 2010, based on the IFRS optional exemptions and accounting policies that we expect to apply in our first annual IFRS financial statements. A description of the differences in accounting policies under IFRS and Canadian GAAP that resulted in transition adjustments as at November 1, 2010 is provided in Section B, Differences in accounting policies. [...]
>
> **Notes to the opening IFRS consolidated balance sheet**
>
> A. Exemptions and exceptions from retrospective application of IFRS
>
> Set forth below are the applicable IFRS 1 optional exemptions and mandatory exceptions from retrospective application of IFRS accounting policies that have been applied in the preparation of the opening IFRS balance sheet.
>
> *IFRS optional exemptions* [extract]
>
> *1. Actuarial gains and losses for post-employment defined benefit plans* – Retrospective application of the 'corridor approach' under IAS 19 "Employee Benefits" would require us to restate the accounting for our post-employment defined benefit plans, including unamortized actuarial gains and losses, from the inception or acquisition of the plans until the Transition Date as if IAS 19 had always been applied. However, IFRS 1 permits entities to instead recognize all unamortized actuarial gains and losses as at the Transition Date in opening retained earnings, except those related to subsidiaries that have applied IFRS in their own financial statements prior to their parent. We elected to apply this 'fresh-start' election, which resulted in the recognition of $1,150 million of after-tax unamortized net actuarial losses on our defined benefit plans that existed under Canadian GAAP as at November 1, 2010 through retained earnings. This amount excludes the unamortized actuarial losses related to CIBC FirstCaribbean which adopted IFRS prior to CIBC. This transition adjustment, together with the other employee benefits IFRS adjustments (see Section B.1), resulted in a decrease in after-tax retained earnings of $1,080 million.

7 ACCOUNTING POLICIES AND PRACTICAL APPLICATION ISSUES

The exceptions and exemptions of IFRS 1 are explained at 4 and 5 above, respectively. This section provides an overview of the detailed application guidance in IFRS 1 (to the extent that it is not covered in 4 and 5 above) and some of the practical application issues that are not directly related to any of the exceptions or exemptions. These issues are discussed on a standard by standard basis as follows:

- IAS 7 – *Statement of Cash Flows* (see 7.1 below);
- IAS 8 – *Accounting Policies, Changes in Accounting Estimates and Errors* (see 7.2 below);
- IAS 12 – *Income Taxes* (see 7.3 below);
- IAS 16 – *Property, Plant and Equipment* – and IAS 40 – *Investment Property* (cost model) (see 7.4 below);
- IFRS 16 – *Leases* (see 7.5 below);
- IFRS 15 – *Revenue from Contracts with Customers* (see 7.6 below);
- IAS 19 – *Employee Benefits* (see 7.7 below);
- IAS 21 – *The Effects of Changes in Foreign Exchange Rates* (see 7.8 below);
- IAS 28 – *Investments in Associates and Joint Ventures* (see 7.9 below);
- IAS 29 – *Financial Reporting in Hyperinflationary Economies* (see 7.10 below);
- IFRS 11 – *Joint Arrangements* (see 7.11 below);
- IAS 36 – *Impairment of Assets* (see 7.12 below);
- IAS 37 – *Provisions, Contingent Liabilities and Contingent Assets* (see 7.13 below); and
- IAS 38 – *Intangible Assets* (see 7.14 below).

7.1 IAS 7 – *Statement of Cash Flows*

A statement of cash flows prepared under IAS 7 may differ in the following ways from the one prepared under an entity's previous GAAP:

- The definition of cash and cash equivalents under IAS 7 may well differ from the one used under previous GAAP. *[IAS 7.6-8]*. In particular, IAS 7 includes within cash and cash equivalents those bank overdrafts that are repayable on demand and that form an integral part of an entity's cash management. *[IAS 7.8]*.
- The layout and definition of the categories of cash flows (i.e. operating, investing and financing) is often different from previous GAAP. In addition, IAS 7 contains specific requirements about the classification of interest, dividends and taxes.
- Differences in accounting policies between IFRSs and previous GAAP often have a consequential impact on the statement of cash flows.

IFRS 1 requires disclosure of an explanation of the material adjustments to the statement of cash flows, if a first-time adopter presented one under its previous GAAP (see 6.3.1 above). *[IFRS 1.25]*. The extract below illustrates how an IFRS statement of cash flows may differ from the one under previous GAAP.

Extract 5.15: Bombardier Inc. (2011)

NOTES TO CONSOLIDATED FINANCIAL STATEMENTS [extract]

For the fiscal years ended December 31, 2011 and January 31, 2011

(Tabular figures are in millions of U.S. dollars, unless otherwise indicated)

36. ADOPTION OF IFRS [extract]

CHANGES TO THE STATEMENT OF CASH FLOWS FROM CANADIAN GAAP TO IFRS

The net impact on the statement of cash flows as a result of adoption of IFRS was as follows for the fiscal year ended January 31, 2011:

Cash flows from operating activities	$ 14
Cash flows from investing activities	(52)
Cash flows from financing activities	38
	$ —

The following items explain the most significant restatements to the statement of cash flows, resulting from the changes in accounting policies upon adoption of IFRS:

- Under Canadian GAAP, payments to and from sale and leaseback facilities for pre-owned aircraft were classified as cash flows from operating activities. Under IFRS, such payments are treated as financing transactions and are classified as cash flows from financing activities. For the fiscal year ended January 31, 2011, cash flows from financing activities increased by $38 million as amounts received from these facilities exceeded repayments to the facilities.

- Under Canadian GAAP, inflows from government refundable advances were netted against additions to PP&E and intangible assets and classified as cash flows from investing activities, with any repayments classified as cash flows from operating activities. Under IFRS, all transactions related to the government refundable advances are classified as cash flows from operating activities. During the fiscal year ended January 31, 2011, $52 million in government refundable advances was received and classified as cash flows from operating activities under IFRS.

7.2 IAS 8 – Accounting Policies, Changes in Accounting Estimates and Errors

Normally when an entity that is already using IFRS changes an accounting policy, it should apply IAS 8 to such a change. IFRS 1 requires that a first-time adopter should apply the same accounting policies in its opening IFRS statement of financial position and throughout all periods presented in its first IFRS financial statements. *[IFRS 1.7]*. Therefore, the change in accounting policies should be treated as a change in the entity's opening IFRS statement of financial position and the policy should be applied consistently in all periods presented in its first IFRS financial statements.

7.2.1 Changes in IFRS accounting policies during the first IFRS reporting period

A first-time adopter may find that it needs to change IFRS accounting policies after it has issued an IFRS interim report but before issuing its first IFRS financial statements. Such a change in accounting policies could relate either to the ongoing IFRS accounting policies or to the selection of IFRS 1 exemptions.

IAS 8 does not apply to the changes in accounting policies an entity makes when it adopts IFRSs or to changes in those policies until after it presents its first IFRS financial statements. *[IFRS 1.27]*. Therefore, 'if during the period covered by its first IFRS financial statements an entity changes its accounting policies or its use of the exemptions contained in this IFRS', it must explain the changes between its first IFRS interim financial report and its first IFRS financial statements in accordance with paragraph 23 of IFRS 1, i.e. the disclosure objective to explain the transition (see 6.3 above) and update the reconciliations required by paragraphs 24(a) and (b) of IFRS 1 (see 6.3.1 above). *[IFRS 1.23, 24(a)-(b), 27A]*. A similar requirement applies to the disclosures in a first-time adopter's interim financial reports (see 6.6 above). *[IFRS 1.23, 32(c)]*.

The distinction between changes in accounting policies and changes in accounting estimates is discussed in detail in Chapter 3 at 4.2.

7.2.2 Changes in estimates and correction of errors

An entity that adopts IFRSs needs to assess carefully the impact of information that has become available since it prepared its most recent previous GAAP financial statements because the new information:

- may be a new estimate that should be accounted for prospectively (see 4.2 above); *[IFRS 1.14-17]* or

- may expose an error in the previous GAAP financial statements due to mathematical mistakes, error in applying accounting policies, oversights or misinterpretations of facts and fraud. *[IAS 8.5]*. In the reconciliation from previous GAAP to IFRSs such errors should be disclosed separately from the effect of changes in accounting policies (see 6.3.1 above). *[IFRS 1.26]*.

7.3 IAS 12 – *Income Taxes*

There are no particular provisions in IFRS 1 with regard to the first-time adoption of IAS 12, although the implementation guidance notes that IAS 12 requires entities to provide for deferred tax on temporary differences measured by reference to enacted or substantively enacted legislation by the end of the reporting period. Therefore, entities need to account for the effect of changes in tax rates and tax laws when those changes are enacted or substantively enacted. *[IFRS 1.IG5-IG6]*.

The full retrospective application of IAS 12 poses several problems that may not be immediately obvious. First, IAS 12 does not require an entity to account for all temporary differences. For example, an entity is not permitted under IAS 12 to recognise deferred tax on:

- taxable temporary differences arising on the initial recognition of goodwill; *[IAS 12.15]* and
- taxable and deductible temporary differences arising on the initial recognition of an asset or liability in a transaction that is not a business combination and that, at the time of the transaction, affected neither accounting profit nor taxable profit. *[IAS 12.15, 24]*.

In addition, a change in deferred tax should be accounted for in other comprehensive income or equity, instead of profit or loss, when the tax relates to an item that was originally accounted for in other comprehensive income or equity. *[IAS 12.61A]*.

Therefore, full retrospective application of IAS 12 requires a first-time adopter to establish the history of the items that give rise to temporary differences because, depending on the type of transaction, it may not be necessary to account for deferred tax, or changes in the deferred tax may need to be accounted for in other comprehensive income or equity.

The main issue for many first-time adopters of IFRSs will be that their previous GAAPs either required no provision for deferred tax, or required provision under a timing difference approach. They also need to be aware that many of the other adjustments made to the statement of financial position at the date of transition will also have a deferred tax effect that must be accounted for – see, for example, the potential deferred tax consequences of recognising or derecognising intangible assets where an entity uses the business combinations exemption, described at 5.2.4.A, 5.2.4.B, 5.2.5 and 5.2.9 above. Entities that reported under US GAAP must also bear in mind that IAS 12, though derived from FASB's Accounting Standard Codification 740 – *Income Taxes*, is different in a number of important respects.

7.3.1 Previous revaluation of plant, property and equipment treated as deemed cost on transition

In some cases, IFRS 1 allows an entity, on transition to IFRSs, to treat the carrying amount of plant, property or equipment revalued under its previous GAAP as its deemed cost as of the date of revaluation for the purposes of IFRSs (see 5.5.1 above).

Where an asset is carried at deemed cost on transition but the tax base of the asset remains at original cost, or an amount based on original cost, the previous GAAP revaluation will give rise to a temporary difference which is typically a taxable temporary difference associated with the asset. IAS 12 requires deferred tax to be recognised at transition on any such temporary difference (see Chapter 33 at 10.10).

If, after transition, the deferred tax is required to be remeasured, e.g. because of a change in tax rate, or a re-basing of the asset for tax purposes, the entity elects the cost model of IAS 16 and the asset concerned was revalued outside profit or loss under previous GAAP, the question arises as to whether the resulting deferred tax income or expense should be recognised in, or outside, profit or loss.

In our view, either approach is acceptable, so long as it is applied consistently.

The essence of the argument for recognising such income or expense in profit or loss is whether the reference in paragraph 61A of IAS 12 to the tax effects of 'items recognised outside profit or loss' means items recognised outside profit or loss under IFRSs, or whether it can extend to the treatment under previous GAAP. *[IAS 12.61A]*.

Those who argue that it must mean solely items recognised outside profit or loss under IFRSs note that an asset carried at deemed cost on transition is not otherwise treated as a revalued asset for the purposes of IFRSs. For example, any impairment of such an asset must be accounted for in profit or loss. By contrast, any impairment of plant, property or equipment treated as a revalued asset under IAS 16 would be accounted for outside profit or loss – in other comprehensive income – up to the amount of the cumulative revaluation gain previously recognised.

Those who hold the contrary view that it need not be read as referring only to items recognised outside profit or loss under IFRSs may do so in the context that the entity's previous GAAP required tax income and expense to be allocated between profit or loss, other comprehensive income and equity in a manner similar to that required by IAS 12. It is argued that it is inappropriate that the effect of transitioning from previous GAAP to IFRSs should be to require recognition in profit or loss of an item that would have been recognised outside profit or loss under the ongoing application of either previous GAAP or IFRSs. The counter-argument to this is that there are a number of other similar inconsistencies under IFRS 1.

A more persuasive argument for the latter view might be that, whilst IFRSs do not regard such an asset as having been revalued, it does allow the revalued amount to stand. IFRSs are therefore recognising an implied contribution by owners in excess of the original cost of the asset which, although it is not a 'revaluation' under IFRSs, would nevertheless have been recognised in equity on an ongoing application of IFRSs.

7.3.2 Share-based payment transactions subject to transitional provisions of IFRS 1

While IFRS 1 provides exemptions from applying IFRS 2 to share-based payment transactions that were fully vested prior to the date of transition to IFRSs, there are no corresponding exemptions from the provisions of IAS 12 relating to the tax effects of share-based payment transactions. Therefore, the provisions of IAS 12 relating to the tax effects of share-based payments apply to all share-based payment transactions, whether they are accounted for in accordance with IFRS 2 or not. *[IAS 12.68A-68C]*. IAS 12 effectively considers the cumulative expense associated with share-based payment transactions as an asset that has been fully expensed in the financial statements in advance of being recognised for tax purposes, thus giving rise to a deductible temporary difference (see Chapter 33 at 10.8).

This means that on transition to IFRSs, and subject to the restrictions on recognition of deferred tax assets, *[IAS 12.24-31]*, (see Chapter 33 at 7.4), a deferred tax asset should be established for all share-based payment awards outstanding at that date, including those not accounted for under the transitional provisions.

Where such an asset is remeasured or recognised after transition to IFRSs, the general rule regarding the 'capping' of the amount of any tax relief recognised in profit or loss to the amount charged to the profit or loss applies (see Chapter 33 at 10.8.1). Therefore, if there was no profit or loss charge for share-based payment transactions under the previous GAAP, all tax effects of share-based payment transactions not accounted for under IFRS 2 should be dealt with within equity. *[IAS 12.68C]*.

7.3.3 Retrospective restatements or applications

The adjustments arising from different accounting policies under previous GAAP and IFRSs should be recognised directly in retained earnings (or, if appropriate, another category of equity) at the date of transition to IFRSs. *[IFRS 1.11]*.

Because IAS 12 requires tax relating to an item that has been recognised outside profit or loss to be treated in the same way, any tax effect of a retrospective restatement or retrospective application on the opening comparative statement of financial position is dealt with as an adjustment to equity also. *[IAS 12.61A]*. This could be taken by some to mean that any subsequent remeasurement of tax originally recognised in equity as part of an adjustment at the date of transition to IFRSs should be accounted for in equity also. In our view, such an assertion fails to reflect the true nature of retrospective application, which is defined in IAS 8 as the application of a new accounting policy 'to transactions, other events and conditions *as if that policy had always been applied* (our emphasis), *[IAS 8.5]*, and under IFRS 1 'arise from events and transactions before the date of transition to IFRSs'. *[IFRS 1.11]*. This is illustrated by Example 5.44 below.

Example 5.44: Remeasurement of deferred tax asset recognised as the result of retrospective application

Entity A's date of transition to IFRSs was 1 January 2020. After applying IAS 37, its opening IFRS statement of financial position shows an additional liability for environmental remediation costs of €5 million as an adjustment to retained earnings, together with an associated deferred tax asset at 40% of €2 million.

The environmental liability does not change substantially over the next accounting period, but during the year ended 31 December 2021 the tax rate falls to 30%. This requires the deferred tax asset to be remeasured to €1.5 million giving rise to tax expense of €500,000. Should this expense be recognised in profit or loss for the period or in retained earnings?

IAS 8 defines retrospective application as the application of a new accounting policy 'to transactions, other events or conditions as if that policy had always been applied' and the treatment required by IFRS 1 is based on the fact that an entity is restating amounts that arise from events and transactions before the date of transition to IFRSs. Accordingly, if the item that gave rise to the deferred tax would have been recognised in profit or loss in the normal course of events had the new accounting policies (or IFRSs) always been applied, the effect of subsequent re-measurement is also recognised in profit or loss. In the fact pattern (Example 5.44 above), if IFRSs had always been applied, all the charge for environmental costs (and all the related deferred tax) would have been reflected in profit or loss in previous income statements. Therefore, the effect of the change in the tax rate is recognised in profit or loss.

Where the retrospective restatement giving rise to a deferred tax asset or liability directly in equity represented the cumulative total of amounts that would have been recognised ordinarily in other comprehensive income or directly in equity in previous periods if the new accounting policy had always been applied (e.g. deferred tax relating to the revaluation of property, plant, or equipment), any subsequent re-measurement of the deferred tax is also accounted for in the same manner, i.e. in other comprehensive income or directly in equity. Remeasurement of deferred tax relating to an asset that is measured at deemed cost on transition to IFRSs but where the tax base of the asset remains at original cost, or is an amount based on original cost is discussed in 7.3.1 above.

Retrospective restatements or applications are discussed in detail in Chapter 33 at 10.2.

7.3.4 Defined benefit pension plans

IAS 19 requires an entity, in accounting for a post-employment defined benefit plan, to recognise actuarial gains and losses relating to the plan in other comprehensive income. At the same time, service cost and net interest on the net defined benefit liability (asset) is recognised in profit or loss.

In many jurisdictions, tax relief for post-employment benefits is given on the basis of cash contributions paid to the plan fund (or benefits paid when a plan is unfunded).

This significant difference between the way in which defined benefit plans are treated for tax and financial reporting purposes can make the allocation of tax between profit or loss and other comprehensive income somewhat arbitrary.

The issue is of particular importance when a first-time adopter has large funding shortfalls on its defined benefit schemes and at the same time can only recognise part of its deferred tax assets. In such a situation the method of allocation may well affect the after-tax profit in a given year. In our view (see Chapter 33 at 10.7), these are instances of the exceptional circumstances envisaged by IAS 12 when a strict allocation of tax between profit or loss and other comprehensive income is not possible. Accordingly, any reasonable method of allocation may be used, provided that it is applied on a consistent basis.

One approach might be to compare the funding payments made to the scheme in a few years before the adoption of IFRSs with the charges that would have been made to profit or loss under IAS 19 in those periods. If, for example, it is found that the payments were equal to or greater than the charges to profit or loss, it could reasonably be concluded that any surplus or deficit on the statement of financial position is broadly represented by items that have been accounted for in other comprehensive income.

7.4 IAS 16 – *Property, Plant and Equipment* – and IAS 40 – *Investment Property* (cost model)

The implementation guidance discussed in this section applies to property, plant and equipment as well as investment properties that are accounted for under the cost model in IAS 40. *[IFRS 1.IG62].*

7.4.1 Depreciation method and rate

If a first-time adopter's depreciation methods and rates under its previous GAAP are acceptable under IFRSs then it accounts for any change in estimated useful life or depreciation pattern prospectively from when it makes that change in estimate (see 4.2 above). *[IFRS 1.14-15, IAS 16.51, 61].* However, if the depreciation methods and rates are not acceptable and the difference has a material impact on the financial statements, a first-time adopter should adjust the accumulated depreciation in its opening IFRS statement of financial position retrospectively. *[IFRS 1.IG7].* Additional differences may arise from the requirement in IAS 16 to review the residual value and the useful life of an asset at least each financial year end, *[IAS 16.51],* which may not be required under a first-time adopter's previous GAAP (see 7.4.2 below).

If a restatement of the depreciation methods and rates would be too onerous, a first-time adopter could opt instead to use fair value as the deemed cost. However, application of the deemed cost exemption is not always the only approach available. In practice, many first-time adopters have found that, other than buildings, there are generally few items of property, plant and equipment that still have a material carrying amount after more than 30 or 40 years of use. Therefore, the carrying value that results from a fully retrospective application of IAS 16 may not differ much from the carrying amount under an entity's previous GAAP.

7.4.2 Estimates of useful life and residual value

An entity may use fair value as deemed cost for an item of property, plant and equipment still in use that it had depreciated to zero under its previous GAAP (i.e. the asset has already reached the end of its originally assessed economic life). Although IFRS 1 requires an entity to use estimates made under its previous GAAP, paragraph 51 of IAS 16 would require the entity to re-assess the remaining useful life and residual value at least annually. *[IAS 16.51].* Therefore, the asset's deemed cost should be depreciated over its re-assessed economic life and taking into account its re-assessed residual value.

The same applies when an entity does not use fair value or revaluation as deemed cost. If there were indicators in the past that the useful life or residual value changed but those changes were not required to be recognised under previous GAAP, the IFRS carrying amount as of the date of transition should be determined by taking into account the re-assessed useful life and the re-assessed residual value. Often, this is difficult, as most entities would not have re-assessed the useful lives contemporaneously with the issuance of the previous GAAP financial statements. Accordingly, the fair value as deemed cost exemption might be the most logical choice.

7.4.3 Revaluation model

A first-time adopter that chooses to account for some or all classes of property, plant and equipment under the revaluation model needs to present the cumulative revaluation surplus as a separate component of equity. IFRS 1 requires that 'the revaluation surplus at the date of transition to IFRSs is based on a comparison of the carrying amount of the asset at that date with its cost or deemed cost.' *[IFRS 1.IG10].*

A first-time adopter that uses fair value as the deemed cost for those classes of property, plant and equipment would be required to reset the cumulative revaluation surplus to zero. Therefore, any previous GAAP revaluation surplus related to assets valued at deemed cost cannot be used to offset a subsequent impairment or revaluation loss under IFRSs. The following example illustrates the treatment of the revaluation reserve at the date of transition based on different deemed cost exemptions applied under IFRS 1.

Example 5.45: Revaluation reserve under IAS 16

An entity with a date of transition to IFRSs of 1 January 2020 has freehold land classified as property, plant and equipment. The land was measured under previous GAAP using a revaluation model that is comparable to that required by IAS 16. The previous GAAP carrying amount is €185,000, being the revaluation last determined in April 2019. The cost of the land under IFRSs as at 1 January 2020 is €90,000. The fair value of the land on 1 January 2020 is €200,000. The entity elects to apply the revaluation model under IAS 16 to the asset class that includes the land.

The revaluation reserve at the date of transition would depend on the exemption applied by the entity:

- if the entity chooses to use the transition date fair value as deemed cost, the IFRS revaluation reserve is zero (€200,000 – €200,000);
- if the entity chooses to use the previous GAAP revaluation as deemed cost, the IFRS revaluation reserve is €15,000 (€200,000 – €185,000);
- if the entity does not use the deemed cost exemption under IFRS 1, the IFRS revaluation reserve is €110,000 (€200,000 – €90,000).

7.4.4 Parts approach

IAS 16 requires a 'parts approach' to the recognition of property, plant and equipment. Thus a large item such as an aircraft is recognised as a series of 'parts' that may have different useful lives. An engine of an aircraft may be a part. IAS 16 does not prescribe the physical unit of measure (the 'part') for recognition i.e. what constitutes an item of property, plant and equipment. *[IFRS 1.IG12]*. Instead the standard relies on judgement in applying the recognition criteria to an entity's specific circumstances. *[IAS 16.9]*. However, the standard does require an entity to:

- apply a very restrictive definition of maintenance costs or costs of day-to-day servicing which it describes as 'primarily the costs of labour and consumables, and may include the cost of small parts. The purpose of these expenditures is often described as for the "repairs and maintenance" of the item of property, plant and equipment'; *[IAS 16.12]*
- derecognise the carrying amount of the parts that are replaced; *[IAS 16.13]* and
- depreciate separately each part of an item of property, plant and equipment with a cost that is significant in relation to the total cost of the item. *[IAS 16.43]*.

Based on this, it is reasonable to surmise that parts can be relatively small units. Therefore, it is possible that even if a first-time adopter's depreciation methods and rates are acceptable under IFRSs, it may have to restate property, plant and equipment because its unit of measure under previous GAAP was based on physical units significantly larger than parts as described in IAS 16. Accounting for parts is described in detail in Chapter 18 at 3.2.

In practice, however, there is seldom a need to account for every single part of an asset separately. Very often there is no significant difference in the reported amounts once all significant parts have been identified. Furthermore, as explained in Chapter 18 at 3.2, an entity may not actually need to identify the parts of an asset until it incurs the replacement expenditure.

7.5   IFRS 16 – *Leases*

Other than the exemption in paragraph D9 of IFRS 1 (concerning the assessment of whether a contract existing at the date of transition contains a lease – see 5.6 above), there are no exemptions regarding lease accounting available to a first-time adopter that is a lessor. Therefore, at the date of transition to IFRSs, a lessor classifies a lease as operating or financing on the basis of circumstances existing at the inception of the lease. *[IFRS 16.66]*. Lease classification is reassessed only if there is a lease modification. Changes in estimates (for example, changes in estimates of the economic life or the residual value of the underlying asset) or changes in circumstances (for example, default by the lessee) do not give rise to a new classification of a lease. *[IFRS 1.IG14]*. See Chapter 23 at 5.5 for further discussion about modifying lease terms under IFRS 16.

7.6   IFRS 15 – *Revenue from Contracts with Customers*

The exemptions in paragraphs D34 and D35 of IFRS 1 allow a first-time adopter not to restate contracts that were completed before the earliest period presented or completed contracts that begin and end within the same annual reporting period (see 5.21 above). *[IFRS 1.D34, D35]*.

However, where IFRS 15 is applied to a contract, a first-time adopter that has received amounts that do not yet qualify for recognition as revenue under IFRS 15 (e.g. the proceeds of a sale that does not qualify for revenue recognition) must recognise those amounts as a liability in its opening IFRS statement of financial position and adjust the liability for any significant financing component as required by IFRS 15. [IFRS 1.IG17]. It is therefore possible that revenue that was already recognised under a first-time adopter's previous GAAP will need to be deferred in its opening IFRS statement of financial position and recognised again (this time under IFRSs) as revenue at a later date.

Conversely, it is possible that revenue deferred under a first-time adopter's previous GAAP cannot be recognised as a contract liability in the opening IFRS statement of financial position. A first-time adopter would not be able to report such revenue deferred under its previous GAAP as revenue under IFRSs at a later date. See Chapters 27 to 32 for matters relating to revenue recognition under IFRS 15.

7.7 IAS 19 – *Employee Benefits*

7.7.1 Sensitivity analysis for each significant actuarial assumption

IAS 19 requires the disclosures set out below about sensitivity of defined benefit obligations. Therefore, for an entity's first IFRS financial statements careful preparation is needed to compile the information required to present the sensitivity disclosure for the current and comparative periods. IAS 19 requires an entity to disclose: [IAS 19.145]

(a) a sensitivity analysis for each significant actuarial assumption as of the end of the reporting period, showing how the defined benefit obligation would have been affected by changes in the relevant actuarial assumption that were reasonably possible at that date;

(b) the methods and assumptions used in preparing the sensitivity analyses required by (a) and the limitations of those methods; and

(c) changes from the previous period in the methods and assumptions used in preparing the sensitivity analyses, and the reasons for such changes.

7.7.2 Full actuarial valuations

An entity's first IFRS financial statements reflect its defined benefit liabilities or assets on at least three different dates, that is, the end of the first IFRS reporting period, the end of the comparative period and the date of transition to IFRSs (four different dates if it presents two comparative periods). If an entity obtains a full actuarial valuation at one or two of these dates, it is allowed to roll forward (or roll back) to another date but only as long as the roll forward (or roll back) reflects material transactions and other material events (including changes in market prices and interest rates) between those dates. [IFRS 1.IG21, IAS 19.59].

7.7.3 Actuarial assumptions

A first-time adopter's actuarial assumptions at its date of transition should be consistent with the ones it used for the same date under its previous GAAP (after adjustments to reflect any difference in accounting policies), unless there is objective evidence that those assumptions were in error (see 4.2 above). The impact of any later revisions to those assumptions is an actuarial gain or loss of the period in which the entity makes the revisions. [IFRS 1.IG19].

If a first-time adopter needs to make actuarial assumptions at the date of transition that were not necessary for compliance with its previous GAAP, those actuarial assumptions should not reflect conditions that arose after the date of transition. In particular, discount rates and the fair value of plan assets at the date of transition should reflect the market conditions at that date. Similarly, the entity's actuarial assumptions at the date of transition about future employee turnover rates should not reflect a significant increase in estimated employee turnover rates as a result of a curtailment of the pension plan that occurred after the date of transition. *[IFRS 1.IG20].*

If there is a material difference arising from a change in assumptions at the date of transition, consideration needs to be given to whether there was an error under previous GAAP. Errors cannot be recognised as transition adjustments (see 6.3.1 above).

7.7.4 Unrecognised past service costs

IAS 19 requires immediate recognition of all past service costs. *[IAS 19.103].* Accordingly, a first-time adopter that has unrecognised past service costs under previous GAAP must recognise such amount in retained earnings at the date of transition, regardless of whether the participants are fully vested in the benefit.

7.8 IAS 21 – *The Effects of Changes in Foreign Exchange Rates*

7.8.1 Functional currency

A first-time adopter needs to confirm whether all entities included within the financial statements have appropriately determined their functional currency. IAS 21 defines an entity's functional currency as 'the currency of the primary economic environment in which the entity operates' and contains detailed guidance on determining the functional currency. *[IAS 21.8-14].* See Chapter 15 at 4.

If the functional currency of an entity is not readily identifiable, IAS 21 requires consideration of whether the activities of the foreign operation are carried out as an extension of the reporting entity, rather than being carried out with a significant degree of autonomy. *[IAS 21.11].* This requirement often leads to the conclusion under IFRSs that intermediate holding companies, treasury subsidiaries and foreign sales offices have the same functional currency as their parent (see Chapter 15 at 4.2).

Many national GAAPs do not specifically define the concept of functional currency, or they may contain guidance on identifying the functional currency that differs from that in IAS 21. Consequently, a first-time adopter that measured transactions in a currency that was not its functional currency under IFRSs would need to restate its financial statements because IFRS 1 does not contain an exemption that would allow it to use a currency other than the functional currency in determining the cost of assets and liabilities in its opening IFRS statement of financial position. While there is the exemption that allows a first-time adopter to reset the cumulative exchange differences in equity to zero (see 5.7 above), a first-time adopter should recognise and measure its assets or liabilities in its functional currency retrospectively in accordance with IAS 21 (see Chapter 15 at 5). *[IAS 21.21, 23].* The IFRIC considered whether a specific exemption should be granted to first-time adopter to permit entities to translate all assets and liabilities at the transition-date exchange rate rather than applying the functional currency approach in IAS 21 but declined to offer first-time adopters any exemptions on transition on the basis that the position under IFRS 1 and IAS 21 was clear.[6]

The principal difficulty relates to non-monetary items that are measured on the basis of historical cost, particularly property, plant and equipment, since these will need to be re-measured in terms of the IAS 21 functional currency at the rates of exchange applicable at the date of acquisition of the assets concerned, and recalculating cumulative depreciation charges accordingly. It may be that, to overcome this difficulty, an entity should consider using the option in IFRS 1 whereby the fair value of such assets at the date of transition is treated as being their deemed cost (see 5.5.1 above).

7.9 IAS 28 – *Investments in Associates and Joint Ventures*

There are a number of first-time adoption exemptions that have an impact on the accounting for investments in associates and joint ventures:

- the business combinations exemption, which also applies to past acquisitions of investments in associates and interests in joint ventures (see 5.2.2.A above);
- an exemption in respect of determining the cost of an associate and a joint venture within any separate financial statements that an entity may prepare (see 5.8.2 above); and
- separate rules that deal with situations in which an investor or a joint venturer adopts IFRSs before or after an associate or a joint venture does so (see 5.9 above).

Otherwise there are no specific first-time adoption provisions for IAS 28, which means that a first-time adopter of IFRSs is effectively required to apply IAS 28 as if it had always done so. For some first-time adopters, this may mean application of the equity method for the first time. For the majority of first-time adopters, however, the issue is likely to be that they are already applying the equity method under their previous GAAPs and will now need to identify the potentially significant differences between the methodologies of the equity method under their previous GAAPs and under IAS 28.

In particular there may be differences between:

- the criteria used to determine which investments are associates or joint ventures;
- the elimination of transactions between investors or joint venturers and associates or joint ventures;
- the treatment of loss-making associates or joint ventures;
- the permitted interval between the reporting dates of an investor or a joint venturer and an associate or joint ventures with non-coterminous year-ends;
- the treatment of investments in entities formerly classified as associates or joint venture; and
- the requirement for uniform accounting policies between the investor or joint venturer and the associate or joint venture.

7.9.1 Impairment review at date of transition to IFRSs

A first-time adopter of IFRSs is required by IFRS 1 to perform an impairment test in accordance with IAS 36 to any goodwill recognised at the date of transition to IFRSs, regardless of whether there is any indication of impairment, unless a first-time adopter applies IFRS 3 retrospectively to the related past business combinations. *[IFRS 1.C4(g)(ii)]*. IFRS 1 specifically notes that its provisions with regard to past business combinations apply also to past acquisitions of investments in associates, interests in joint ventures and interests in joint operations (in which the activity of the joint operation constitutes a business, as defined in IFRS 3). *[IFRS 1.C5]*. Therefore, an impairment review for investments in associates or joint ventures whose carrying value includes an element of goodwill must be undertaken as at the date of transition. This impairment review will, however, need to be carried out on the basis required by IAS 28 as described in Chapter 11 at 8. See also 5.2.5 and Example 5.23 above.

7.10 IAS 29 – *Financial Reporting in Hyperinflationary Economies*

The IASB decided not to exempt first-time adopters from retrospective application of IAS 29 because hyperinflation can make unadjusted financial statements meaningless or misleading. *[IFRS 1.BC67]*.

Therefore, in preparing its opening IFRS statement of financial position a first-time adopter should apply IAS 29 to any periods during which the economy of the functional currency or presentation currency was hyperinflationary. *[IFRS 1.IG32]*. However, to make the restatement process less onerous, a first-time adopter may want to consider using fair value as deemed cost for property, plant and equipment (see 5.5.1 above). *[IFRS 1.D5, IG33]*. This exemption is also available to other long-lived assets such as investment properties, right-of-use assets under IFRS 16 and certain intangible assets. *[IFRS 1.D7]*. If a first-time adopter applies the exemption to use fair value or a revaluation as deemed cost, it applies IAS 29 to periods after the date for which the revalued amount or fair value was determined. *[IFRS 1.IG34]*.

7.11 IFRS 11 – *Joint Arrangements*

The 'business combinations' exemption described at 5.2 above is also applicable to past acquisitions of interests in joint ventures and interests in joint operations in which the activity of the joint operation constitutes a business, as defined by IFRS 3 (see 5.2.2.A above). *[IFRS 1.C5]*. Therefore, an impairment review for investments in joint ventures whose carrying value includes an element of goodwill must be undertaken as at the date of transition (see 5.2.5 above). *[IFRS 1.C4(g)(ii)]*. This impairment review will, however, need to be carried out on the basis required by IAS 28 as described in Chapter 11 at 8. See also 5.2.5 and Example 5.23 above.

In addition, the first-time adoption exemptions that are available for investments in associates can be applied to investments in joint ventures (see 7.9 above).

With respect to interests in joint operations, the requirements of IFRS 11 may well result in the 're-recognition' of assets that were transferred to others and therefore not recognised under previous GAAP. A joint operator is required to recognise its assets and liabilities, including its share of those assets that are jointly held and liabilities that are jointly incurred, based on the requirements of IFRSs applicable to such assets or liabilities. *[IFRS 11.20-23]*.

7.12 IAS 36 – *Impairment of Assets*

As far as goodwill is concerned, first time adopters of IFRSs that make use of the business combinations exemption are required by IFRS 1 to subject all goodwill carried in the statement of financial position at the date of transition to an impairment test, regardless of whether there are any indicators of impairment (see 5.2.5 above). *[IFRS 1.C4(g)(ii)]*.

While IFRS 1 does not specifically call for an impairment test of other assets, a first-time adopter should be mindful that there are no exemptions in IFRS 1 from full retrospective application of IAS 36. The implementation guidance reminds a first-time adopter to: *[IFRS 1.IG39]*

(a) determine whether any impairment loss exists at the date of transition to IFRSs; and

(b) measure any impairment loss that exists at that date, and reverse any impairment loss that no longer exists at that date. An entity's first IFRS financial statements include the disclosures that IAS 36 would have required if the entity had recognised those impairment losses or reversals in the period beginning with the date of transition to IFRSs. *[IFRS 1.24(c)]*. See 6.3.3 above.

As impairment losses for non-financial long-lived assets other than goodwill can be reversed under IAS 36, in many instances, there will be no practical difference between applying IAS 36 fully retrospectively and applying it at the date of transition. Performing the test under IAS 36 at the date of transition should result in re-measuring any previous GAAP impairment to comply with the approach in IAS 36 and recognition of any additional impairment or reversing any previous GAAP impairment that is no longer necessary.

The estimates used to determine whether a first-time adopter recognises an impairment loss or provision at the date of transition to IFRSs should be consistent with estimates made for the same date under previous GAAP (after adjustments to reflect any difference in accounting policies), unless there is objective evidence that those estimates were in error. *[IFRS 1.IG40]*. If a first-time adopter needs to make estimates and assumptions that were not necessary under its previous GAAP, they should not reflect conditions that arose after the date of transition to IFRSs. *[IFRS 1.IG41]*. See 4.2 above.

If a first-time adopter's opening IFRS statement of financial position reflects impairment losses, it recognises any later reversal of those impairment losses in profit or loss unless IAS 36 requires that reversal to be treated as a revaluation. This applies to both impairment losses recognised under previous GAAP and additional impairment losses recognised on transition to IFRSs. *[IFRS 1.IG43, IAS 36.119]*.

An impairment test might be more appropriate if a first-time adopter makes use of any of the deemed cost exemptions. In arguing that it is not necessary to restrict application of the deemed cost exemption to classes of assets to prevent selective revaluations, the IASB effectively relies on IAS 36 to avoid overvaluations:

> 'IAS 36 *Impairment of Assets* requires an impairment test if there is any indication that an asset is impaired. Thus, if an entity uses fair value as deemed cost for assets whose fair value is above cost, it cannot ignore indications that the recoverable amount of other assets may have fallen below their carrying amount. Therefore, IFRS 1 does not restrict the use of fair value as deemed cost to entire classes of asset.' *[IFRS 1.BC45]*.

Where a first-time adopter uses any of the deemed cost exemptions at the date of transition (see 5.5 above), any previous impairment reflected in the deemed cost is effectively subsumed into the new costs and could not subsequently be separated (and hence could never be reversed). While the example below refers to impairment of exploration and evaluation assets, the same considerations apply where a deemed cost is used for other assets, such as property, plant and equipment.

For example, if a first-time adopter applies the deemed cost exemption in paragraph D8A of IFRS 1 to exploration and evaluation assets which were previously partly impaired (see 5.5.3 above), the first-time adopter recognises the previously impaired exploration and evaluation assets (which nevertheless still have a net book value) in the opening statement of financial position on a 'net basis' (i.e. with accumulated depreciation of 'zero'). In this case, the previous impairment effectively becomes part of the new cost and hence could never be reversed. However, if a first-time adopter does not elect to use any deemed cost exemptions to the exploration and evaluation assets, it must identify exploration and evaluation assets that were previously expensed, impaired, or written off (whichever terminology was used under previous GAAP) but that are recognised under IFRSs. The entity recognises both the gross cost and impairment provision in the opening statement of financial position. Exploration and evaluation assets that have previously been derecognised on the basis that no future economic benefits were expected cannot be re-recognised.

7.13 IAS 37 – *Provisions, Contingent Liabilities and Contingent Assets*

The main issue for a first-time adopter in applying IAS 37 is that IFRS 1 prohibits retrospective application of some aspects of IFRSs relating to estimates. *[IFRS 1.14]*. This is discussed in detail at 4.2 above. Briefly, the restrictions are intended to prevent an entity from applying hindsight and making 'better' estimates as at the date of transition. Unless there is objective evidence that those estimates were in error, recognition and measurement are to be consistent with estimates made under previous GAAP, after adjustments to reflect any difference in accounting policies. The entity has to report the impact of any later revisions to those estimates as an event of the period in which it makes the revisions. *[IFRS 1.IG40]*. An entity cannot use hindsight in determining the provisions to be included under IAS 37 at the end of the comparative period within its first IFRS financial statements as these requirements also apply at that date. *[IFRS 1.14-17]*.

At the date of transition, an entity may also need to make estimates that were not necessary under its previous GAAP. Such estimates and assumptions must not reflect conditions that arose after the date of transition to IFRSs. *[IFRS 1.IG41]*.

If application of IAS 37 changes the way an entity accounts for provisions it needs to consider whether there are any consequential changes, for example:

- derecognition of a provision for general business risks may mean that assets in the related cash-generating unit are impaired; and
- remeasurement of a decommissioning provision may indicate that the decommissioning component of the corresponding asset needs to be reconsidered (see Chapter 26 at 6.3).

The above list is not exhaustive and a first-time adopter should carefully consider whether changes in other provisions have a consequential impact.

7.14 IAS 38 – *Intangible Assets*

An entity's opening IFRS statement of financial position: *[IFRS 1.IG44]*

(a) excludes all intangible assets and other intangible items that do not meet the criteria for recognition under IAS 38 at the date of transition to IFRSs; and

(b) includes all intangible assets that meet the recognition criteria in IAS 38 at that date, except for intangible assets acquired in a business combination that were not recognised in the acquirer's consolidated statement of financial position under previous GAAP and also would not qualify for recognition under IAS 38 in the acquiree's separate statement of financial position (see 5.2.4.B above). *[IFRS 1.C4(b)(ii), C4(f)]*.

IAS 38 imposes a number of criteria that restrict capitalisation of internally generated intangible assets. An entity is prohibited from using hindsight to conclude retrospectively that the recognition criteria are met, thereby capitalising an amount previously recognised as an expense. *[IAS 38.71]*. A first-time adopter of IFRSs must be particularly careful that, in applying IAS 38 retrospectively as at the date of transition, it does not capitalise costs incurred before the standard's recognition criteria were met. Therefore, a first-time adopter is only permitted to capitalise the costs of internally generated intangible assets when it: *[IFRS 1.IG46]*

(a) concludes, based on an assessment made and documented at the date of that conclusion, that it is probable that future economic benefits from the asset will flow to the entity; and

(b) has a reliable system for accumulating the costs of internally generated intangible assets when, or shortly after, they are incurred.

In other words, it is not permitted under IFRS 1 to reconstruct retrospectively the costs of intangible assets.

If an internally generated intangible asset qualifies for recognition at the date of transition, it is recognised in the entity's opening IFRS statement of financial position even if the related expenditure had been expensed under previous GAAP. If the asset does not qualify for recognition under IAS 38 until a later date, its cost is the sum of the expenditure incurred from that later date. *[IFRS 1.IG47]*. However, a first-time adopter that did not capitalise internally generated intangible assets is unlikely to have the type of documentation and systems required by IAS 38 and will therefore not be able to capitalise these items in its opening IFRS statement of financial position. Going forward, a first-time adopter will need to implement internal systems and procedures that enable it to determine whether or not any future internally generated intangible assets should be capitalised (for example, in the case of development costs).

Capitalisation of separately acquired intangible assets will generally be easier because there is usually contemporaneous documentation prepared to support the investment decisions. *[IFRS 1.IG48]*. However, if an entity that used the business combinations exemption did not recognise an intangible asset acquired in a business combination under its previous GAAP, it would only be able to do so upon first-time adoption if the intangible asset were to qualify for recognition under IAS 38 in the acquiree's statement of financial position (see 5.2.4.B above). *[IFRS 1.C4(b)(ii), C4(f), IG49]*.

If a first-time adopter's amortisation methods and rates under previous GAAP are acceptable under IFRSs, the entity does not restate the accumulated amortisation in its opening IFRS statement of financial position. Instead, the entity accounts for any change in estimated useful life or amortisation pattern prospectively from the period when it makes that change in estimate. *[IFRS 1.14, IAS 38.104].* If an entity's amortisation methods and rates under previous GAAP differ from those acceptable in accordance with IFRSs and those differences have a material effect on the financial statements, the entity would adjust the accumulated amortisation in its opening IFRS statement of financial position. *[IFRS 1.14, IG51].*

The useful life and amortisation method of an intangible asset should be reviewed at least each financial year end (see Chapter 17 at 9.2.3), which is often something that is not required under a first-time adopter's previous GAAP. *[IAS 38.104].*

8 REGULATORY ISSUES

8.1 First-time adoption by foreign private issuers that are SEC registrants

8.1.1 SEC guidance

A foreign private issuer that is registered with the US Securities and Exchange Commission (SEC) is normally required to present two comparative periods for its statement of profit or loss and other comprehensive income (or statement of profit or loss, if presented), statement of cash flows and statement of changes in equity. Converting two comparative periods to IFRSs was considered to be a significant burden to companies. Therefore, in April 2005, the SEC published amendments to Form 20-F that provided for a limited period a two-year accommodation for foreign private issuers that were first-time adopters of IFRSs.[7] In March 2008, the SEC extended indefinitely the two-year accommodation to all foreign private issuers that are first-time adopters of IFRSs as issued by the IASB.[8]

The amendment states that 'an issuer that changes the body of accounting principles used in preparing its financial statements presented pursuant to Item 8.A.2 of its Form 20-F ("Item 8.A.2") to International Financial Reporting Standards ("IFRS") issued by the International Accounting Standards Board ("IASB") may omit the earliest of three years of audited financial statements required by Item 8.A.2 if the issuer satisfies the conditions set forth in the related Instruction G. For purposes of this instruction, the term "financial year" refers to the first financial year beginning on or after January 1 of the same calendar year.' The accommodation only applies to an issuer that (a) adopts IFRSs for the first time by an explicit and unreserved statement of compliance with IFRSs as issued by the IASB and (b) the issuer's most recent audited financial statements are prepared in accordance with IFRSs.

First-time adopters that rely on the accommodation are allowed, but not required, to include any financial statements, discussions or other financial information based on their previous GAAPs. If first-time adopters do include such information, they should prominently disclose cautionary language to avoid inappropriate comparison with information presented under IFRSs. The SEC did not mandate a specific location for any previous GAAP information but did prohibit presentation of previous GAAP information in a side-by-side columnar format with IFRS financial information.

In addition, the accommodation only requires entities to provide selected historical financial data based on IFRSs for the two most recent financial years instead of the normal five years. Selected historical financial data based on US GAAP is not required for the five most recent financial years. Although the SEC does not prohibit entities from including selected financial data based on previous GAAP in their annual reports, side-by-side presentation of data prepared under IFRSs and data prepared under previous GAAP is prohibited. In addition, inclusion of previous GAAP selected financial data will trigger the requirement for the corresponding reconciled US GAAP selected financial data.[9]

Where a narrative discussion of its financial condition is provided, the accommodation requires management to focus on the financial statements prepared under IFRSs as issued by the IASB for the past two financial years.

IFRS 1 requires a first-time adopter to present reconciliations from its previous GAAP to IFRSs in the notes to its financial statements and allows certain exemptions from full retrospective application of IFRSs in deriving the relevant data. Under the SEC's accommodation, any issuer relying on any of the elective exemptions or mandatory exceptions from IFRSs that are contained within IFRS 1 will have to disclose additional information which includes:

- to the extent the primary financial statements reflect the use of exemptions permitted or required by IFRS 1:
  - detailed information for each exemption used, including:
    - an indication of the items or class of items to which the exemption was applied; and
    - a description of what accounting principle was used and how it was applied; and
  - where material, qualitative disclosure of the impact on financial condition, changes in financial condition and results of operations that the treatment specified by IFRSs would have had absent the election to rely on the exemption.

8.1.2 IPTF guidance

In November 2008, the Center for Audit Quality SEC Regulations Committee's International Practices Task Force ('IPTF') provided guidance as to the reconciliation requirements of an SEC foreign private issuer the first time it presents IFRS financial statements in its Form 20-F, when that issuer previously used US GAAP for its primary financial statements filed with the SEC.[10] Among others, the IPTF guidance addresses the concern that the reconciliations called for by IFRS 1, which are prepared using the issuer's local GAAP rather than US GAAP, would not have sufficient information to help US investors to bridge from the prior US GAAP financial statements filed with the SEC to IFRSs. Accordingly, the IPTF guidance requires additional detailed reconciliations in these circumstances from US GAAP to IFRSs either in a one step or a two-step format (see below).

The reconciliation requirements for each of the scenarios are described below:

- *SEC foreign private issuers that currently report under their local GAAP and provide a reconciliation from their local GAAP to US GAAP* – In the year of adoption of IFRSs, these entities will be allowed to file two years rather than three years of profit or loss statements, shareholders' equity and cash flows prepared in accordance with IFRSs. As part of the IFRS transition, these entities will provide the disclosures and reconciliations required under IFRS 1 including:
    - an equity reconciliation as at the date of the transition and as at the comparative year-end;
    - a comprehensive income (or statement of profit or loss, if presented) reconciliation for the comparative year; and
    - an explanation of material adjustments to the statement of cash flows for the comparative year.

    If the IFRS 1 disclosures and reconciliations are prepared using the local GAAP as the issuer's previous GAAP rather than US GAAP, no additional US GAAP to IFRSs or US GAAP to local GAAP reconciliations will be required.

- *SEC foreign private issuers that currently report under US GAAP only* – Some SEC foreign private issuers currently use US GAAP as their primary GAAP in both their home jurisdiction and the United States without reconciliation. These registrants would also be eligible to file two years rather than three years of statements of profit or loss and other comprehensive income, shareholders' equity and cash flows in their first set of IFRS financial statements. In the year of adoption of IFRSs, these entities will be required to provide the IFRS 1 disclosures and reconciliations described above. Such disclosures will be prepared using US GAAP as the issuer's previous GAAP.

- *SEC foreign private issuers that currently report under local GAAP for local reporting and under US GAAP in their SEC Form 20-F filings (assuming these issuers adopt IFRSs in the current period for both local and SEC reporting purposes)* – These registrants would also be eligible to file two years rather than three years of statements of profit or loss and other comprehensive income, shareholders' equity and cash flows in their first set of IFRS financial statements. Under IFRS 1, such entities might conclude their local GAAPs are their previous GAAPs and their IFRS 1 disclosures and reconciliations would be prepared on that basis. As no reconciliation from the local GAAP to US GAAP was previously provided, the SEC will require additional disclosure in the Form 20-F to enable investors to understand material reconciling items between US GAAP and IFRSs in the year of adoption. Two possible forms of disclosure are acceptable:
    - *One-Step Format* – Registrants can provide an analysis of the differences between US GAAP and IFRSs in a tabular format (consistent with Item 17 of Form 20-F) for the same time period and dates that the IFRS 1 reconciliations are required. The registrant must provide this disclosure for equity as at the beginning and end of the most recent comparative period to the year of adoption and of comprehensive income (or profit or loss) for the most recent comparative year. A description of the differences between US GAAP and IFRSs for the

statement of cash flows is not necessary because registrants are not required to reconcile IAS 7 statements of cash flows to those prepared under US GAAP.

- *Two-Step Format* – Registrants can choose to disclose a two-step reconciliation which would include a quantitative analysis of the differences between US GAAP and their local GAAP and between their local GAAP to IFRSs. The registrant must provide these reconciliations for equity as of the beginning and end of the most recent comparative period to the year of adoption of IFRSs and for comprehensive income (or profit or loss) for the most recent comparative year. Registrants will also be required to provide an explanation of the material differences between the statement of cash flows under US GAAP and the statement of cash flows under their local GAAP for the most recent comparative period to the year of adoption of IFRSs.

- *SEC foreign private issuers that currently report under IFRSs for local reporting and under US GAAP in their SEC Form 20-F filings (assuming these issuers adopted IFRSs for local reporting in a period that preceded the earliest period for which audited financial statements are required in their SEC filing)* – These registrants would not be eligible to file two years of statements of profit or loss and other comprehensive income, shareholders' equity and cash flows the first time they file IFRS financial statements with the SEC, since they are not first-time adopters of IFRSs. Rather, they are required to present a complete set of IFRS financial statements for all periods required by the Form 20-F. In addition, these issuers will be required to present a reconciliation that enables US investors to bridge their previous US GAAP to IFRSs. Such a reconciliation will be similar to the One-Step Format described above, except that the periods presented will be for equity as of the most recent comparative period presented and for comprehensive income (or profit or loss) for the two most recent comparative periods. However, if the issuers are required to present a statement of financial position as of the end of the earliest comparative period, the reconciliation will also be required of the equity as of the end of that period.

8.2 Disclosure of IFRS information in financial statements for periods prior to an entity's first IFRS reporting period

8.2.1 IFRS guidance

Although IFRS 1 provides detailed rules on disclosures to be made in an entity's first IFRS financial statements and in interim reports covering part of its first IFRS reporting period, it does not provide any guidance on presenting a reconciliation to IFRSs in financial reports before the start of the first IFRS reporting period. An entity wishing to disclose information on the impact of IFRSs in its last financial statements under its previous GAAP cannot claim that such information is prepared and presented in accordance with IFRSs because it does not disclose all information required in full IFRS financial statements and it does not disclose comparative information.

As the extract below illustrates, in practice, some entities get around this problem by disclosing pro forma IFRS information and stating that the pro forma information does not comply with IFRSs.

Chapter 6

Consolidated financial statements

1 INTRODUCTION 391
    1.1   Background 391
    1.2   Development of IFRS 10 392
    1.3   Consolidation procedures 393
    1.4   Disclosure requirements 393
2 OBJECTIVE AND SCOPE OF IFRS 10 394
    2.1   Objective 394
    2.2   Scope 394
        2.2.1   Exemption from preparing consolidated financial statements by an intermediate parent 395
            2.2.1.A   Condition (a) – consent of non-controlling shareholders 395
            2.2.1.B   Condition (b) – securities not traded in a public market 396
            2.2.1.C   Condition (c) – not filing financial statements for listing securities 396
            2.2.1.D   Condition (d) – parent's IFRS financial statements are publicly available and include subsidiaries that are consolidated or measured at fair value through profit or loss in accordance with IFRS 10 397
        2.2.2   Employee benefit plans and employee share trusts 398
        2.2.3   Investment entity exception 399
        2.2.4   Entity no longer a parent at the end of the reporting period ... 399
        2.2.5   Interaction of IFRS 10 and EU law 400
        2.2.6   Combined and carve-out financial statements 400
            2.2.6.A   Common control 401

	2.2.6.B	Purpose and users of combined financial statements	402
	2.2.6.C	Preparation of combined financial statements	402
	2.2.6.D	When combined financial statements are not general purpose	404
	2.2.6.E	The reporting entity in combined financial statements and in consolidated financial statements	404

3 CONTROL 405
   3.1 Assessing control 406
   3.2 Purpose and design of an investee 407

4 POWER OVER AN INVESTEE 408
   4.1 Relevant activities 409
       4.1.1 More than one relevant activity 409
       4.1.2 No relevant activities 411
       4.1.3 Single asset, single lessee vehicles 412
       4.1.4 Management of assets in the event of default 413
   4.2 Existing rights 413
       4.2.1 Evaluating whether rights are substantive 414
       4.2.2 Evaluating whether rights are protective 416
            4.2.2.A Veto rights 417
            4.2.2.B Franchises 417
            4.2.2.C Budget approval rights 419
            4.2.2.D Independent directors 419
       4.2.3 Incentives to obtain power 420
   4.3 Voting rights 420
       4.3.1 Power with a majority of the voting rights 421
       4.3.2 A majority of voting rights without power 421
            4.3.2.A Evaluating voting rights during bankruptcy ... 422
       4.3.3 Power without a majority of voting rights (de facto control) 422
       4.3.4 Potential voting rights 428
            4.3.4.A Exercise price or conversion price 430
            4.3.4.B Financial ability 431
            4.3.4.C Exercise period 432
       4.3.5 Contractual arrangement with other vote holders 433
       4.3.6 Additional rights from other contractual arrangements ... 433
   4.4 Contractual arrangements 434
       4.4.1 Structured entities 435
   4.5 Other evidence of power 436

	4.6	Determining whether sponsoring (designing) a structured entity gives power		438
5	EXPOSURE TO VARIABLE RETURNS			439
	5.1	Exposure to variable returns can be an indicator of power		440
	5.2	Returns that appear fixed can be variable		440
	5.3	Evaluating whether derivatives provide an exposure to variable returns		440
		5.3.1	Plain vanilla foreign exchange swaps and interest rate swaps	442
		5.3.2	Total return swaps	443
	5.4	Exposures to variable returns not directly received from an investee		444
	5.5	Exposure to variable returns in bankruptcy filings		444
	5.6	Interaction of IFRS 10 with the derecognition requirements in IFRS 9		445
	5.7	Reputational risk		445
6	LINK BETWEEN POWER AND RETURNS: PRINCIPAL-AGENCY SITUATIONS			445
	6.1	Delegated power: principals and agents		446
	6.2	Scope of decision-making		448
		6.2.1	Involvement in design	448
		6.2.2	Assessing whether the scope of powers is narrow or broad	449
	6.3	Rights held by other parties		449
		6.3.1	Evaluating whether a removal right is substantive	451
		6.3.1.A	Available replacements	451
		6.3.1.B	Exercise period	452
		6.3.2	Liquidation rights and redemption rights	452
	6.4	Remuneration		452
		6.4.1	Evaluating remuneration in the asset management industry	453
		6.4.2	Evaluating remuneration in other industries	453
	6.5	Exposure to variability of returns from other interests		454
		6.5.1	Evaluating returns received via an indirect investment in another entity	455
	6.6	Application examples in IFRS 10		456
	6.7	Other illustrative examples		460
7	RELATED PARTIES AND *DE FACTO* AGENTS			462
	7.1	Customer-supplier relationships		463
	7.2	Non-controlling interests when there is a *de facto* agent		463
8	CONTROL OF SPECIFIED ASSETS			464

	8.1	Identifying a silo	465
		8.1.1 Identifying silos in the insurance industry	465
		8.1.2 Identifying silos in the investment funds industry	466
	8.2	Evaluating control of a silo	466
	8.3	Consolidation of a silo	467
9	CONTINUOUS ASSESSMENT		467
	9.1	Changes in market conditions	468
	9.2	Bankruptcy filings and troubled debt restructurings	470
	9.3	Control reassessment as a result of action by others	471
10	INVESTMENT ENTITIES		472
	10.1	Definition of an investment entity	473
	10.2	Determining whether an entity is an investment entity	474
		10.2.1 Business purpose	474
		10.2.1.A Entities that provide investment-related services	475
		10.2.1.B Entities that are intermediate holding companies established for tax optimisation purposes	476
		10.2.2 Exit strategies	477
		10.2.3 Earnings from investments	477
		10.2.4 Fair value measurement	479
		10.2.5 Holding more than one investment	480
		10.2.6 Having more than one investor	480
		10.2.7 Unrelated investors	481
		10.2.8 Ownership interests	481
		10.2.9 Investment entity illustrative examples	482
		10.2.10 Multi-layered fund structures	485
	10.3	Accounting by an investment entity	485
		10.3.1 Accounting for a change in investment entity status	488
		10.3.1.A Becoming an investment entity	488
		10.3.1.B Ceasing to be an investment entity	488
	10.4	Accounting by a parent of an investment entity	489
11	FUTURE DEVELOPMENTS		490
	11.1	Post-Implementation Review of IFRS 10	490

List of examples

Example 6.1:	Consent for not preparing consolidated financial statements (1)	396
Example 6.2:	Consent for not preparing consolidated financial statements (2)	396
Example 6.3:	Preparation of consolidated financial statements after combined financial statements	405
Example 6.4:	Identifying relevant activities in life sciences arrangements	410
Example 6.5:	Identifying relevant activities in an investment vehicle	411
Example 6.6:	Identifying relevant activities in a structured entity	411
Example 6.7:	Rights exercisable when decisions need to be made	415
Example 6.8:	Rights held by franchisor	418
Example 6.9:	Less than a majority of voting rights (1)	424
Example 6.10:	Less than a majority of voting rights (2)	424
Example 6.11:	Less than a majority of voting rights (3)	425
Example 6.12:	Less than a majority of voting rights (4)	426
Example 6.13:	Less than a majority of voting rights (5)	426
Example 6.14:	Potential voting rights (1)	429
Example 6.15:	Potential voting rights (2)	429
Example 6.16:	Potential voting rights (3)	431
Example 6.17:	Potential voting rights (4)	432
Example 6.18:	Less than a majority of voting rights combined with additional rights under a contractual arrangement	434
Example 6.19:	Power through contractual arrangements	436
Example 6.20:	Derivatives that create risk for an investee	442
Example 6.21:	Structured entity that enters into foreign currency and interest rate swaps	443
Example 6.22:	Structured entity that enters into a total return swap	443
Example 6.23:	Structured entity that enters into a total return swap with the transferor	445
Example 6.24:	Link between power and returns is essential for control	446
Example 6.25:	Illustration of exposure to variability of returns through other interests	454
Example 6.26:	Illustration of exposure to variability of returns through indirect interests	456
Example 6.27:	Determining whether a decision-maker is a principal or agent (1)	457
Example 6.28:	Determining whether a decision-maker is a principal or agent (2)	457
Example 6.29:	Determining whether a decision-maker is a principal or agent (3)	458
Example 6.30:	Determining whether a decision-maker is a principal or agent (4)	458

Example 6.31:	Determining whether a decision-maker is a principal or agent (5)	458
Example 6.32:	Determining whether a decision-maker is a principal or agent (6)	459
Example 6.33:	Determining whether a decision-maker is a principal or agent (7)	460
Example 6.34:	Determining whether a bank is a principal or agent in relation to a securitisation	461
Example 6.35:	Control evaluation and consolidation with a de facto agent	464
Example 6.36:	Providing seed money for a fund	468
Example 6.37:	Value of option changes from 'in-the-money' to 'out-of-the-money'	469
Example 6.38:	Structured entity reassessments	469
Example 6.39:	Investee loses money due to change in market conditions	470
Example 6.40:	Bankruptcy filing	470
Example 6.41:	Troubled debt restructuring	470
Example 6.42:	Control reassessment without being involved	471
Example 6.43:	A limited partnership that is an investment entity	482
Example 6.44:	Start-up high technology fund that is not an investment entity	483
Example 6.45:	Master and feeder funds that are investment entities	484

Chapter 6 Consolidated financial statements

1 INTRODUCTION

1.1 Background

An entity may conduct its business not only directly, but also through strategic investments in other entities. IFRS broadly distinguishes between three types of such strategic investments:
- entities controlled by the reporting entity (subsidiaries);
- entities or activities jointly controlled by the reporting entity and one or more third parties (joint arrangements); and
- entities that, while not controlled or jointly controlled by the reporting entity, are subject to significant influence by it (associates).

The first type of investment is accounted for in accordance with IFRS 10 – *Consolidated Financial Statements*.

The revised *Conceptual Framework for Financial Reporting* ('2018 *Conceptual Framework*'), which was issued in March 2018, defines a reporting entity as an entity that is required, or chooses, to prepare financial statements. A reporting entity can be a single entity or a portion of an entity or can comprise more than one entity. A reporting entity is not necessarily a legal entity. *[CF 3.10, Appendix]*. The 2018 *Conceptual Framework* was effective immediately for the IASB and the IFRS Interpretations Committee. For preparers who develop accounting policies based on the 2018 *Conceptual Framework*, it is effective for annual periods beginning on or after 1 January 2020, with earlier application permitted. There are a few exceptions from applying the 2018 *Conceptual Framework*, for some areas of IFRS. The requirements of the 2018 *Conceptual Framework* are dealt with more fully in Chapter 2.

IFRS 10 establishes a single control model that applies to all entities, including 'structured entities' ('special purpose entities' and 'variable interest entities' under the previous IFRS standards and US GAAP, respectively). In addition, IFRS 10 deals with accounting for subsidiaries by investment entities.

This chapter discusses the requirements of IFRS 10, principally relating to which entities are controlled by a parent and therefore consolidated into the financial statements prepared by that parent (except for certain subsidiaries of investment entities). The requirements of IFRS 10 dealing with consolidation procedures and non-controlling interests are summarised briefly at 1.3 below and dealt with more fully in Chapter 7.

When management concludes that an entity does not have control of an investee, the requirements of IFRS 11 – *Joint Arrangements* – and IAS 28 – *Investments in Associates and Joint Ventures* – must be considered to determine whether it has joint control or significant influence, respectively, over the investee. The requirements of IFRS 11 and IAS 28 are dealt with in Chapter 12 and Chapter 11, respectively. The diagram below summarises the identification and accounting for each type of investment, as well as the interaction between IFRS 10, IFRS 11, IFRS 12 – *Disclosure of Interests in Other Entities* – and IAS 28.

Figure 6.1: Interaction between IFRS 10, IFRS 11, IFRS 12 and IAS 28

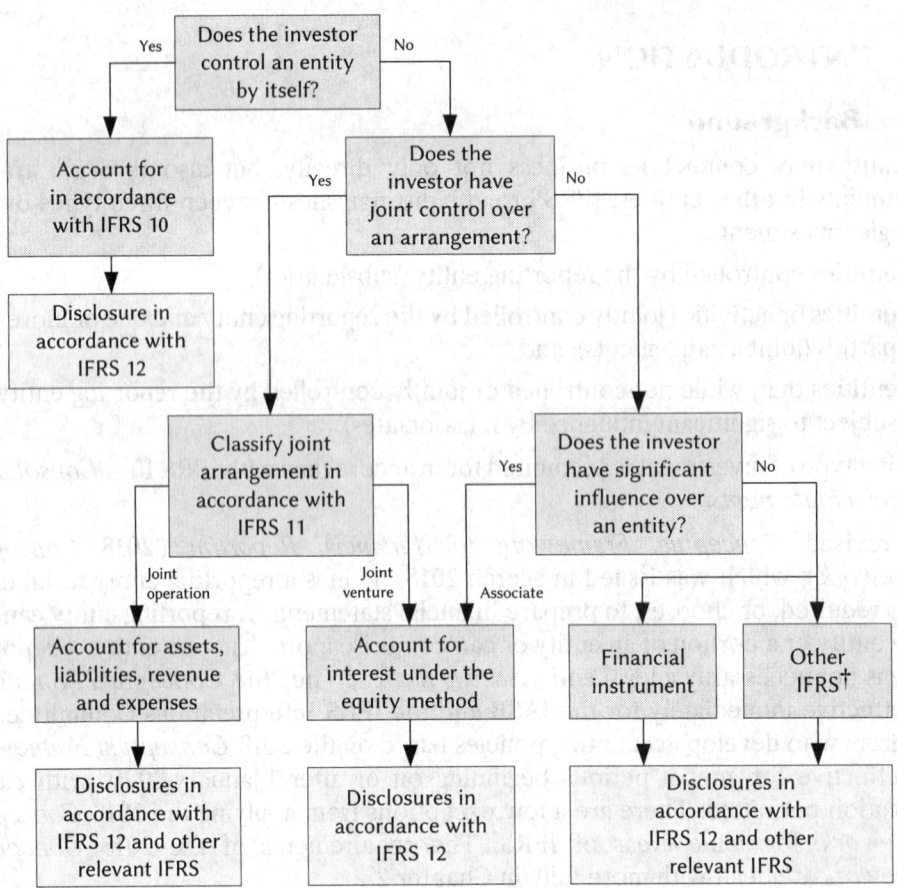

† This would be the case, for example, if an entity has control over (or simply rights to) assets and obligations for liabilities, but *not* control of an entity. In this case, the entity would account for these assets and obligations in accordance with the relevant IFRS.

1.2 Development of IFRS 10

IFRS 10 was issued in May 2011, together with an amended version of IAS 27 with a new title of *Separate Financial Statements* and IFRS 12. In addition, as a result of its project on joint ventures, the IASB issued, at the same time, IFRS 11 and an amended IAS 28. These standards were mandatory for annual periods beginning on or after 1 January 2013. *[IFRS 10.C1A]*.

In October 2012, the IASB issued *Investment Entities (Amendments to IFRS 10, IFRS 12 and IAS 27)* which introduced an exception to the principle that all subsidiaries shall be consolidated. The amendments defined an investment entity and required a parent that is an investment entity to measure its investments in subsidiaries at fair value through profit or loss, with limited exceptions. This amendment applied for annual periods beginning on or after 1 January 2014 but could be adopted early. *[IFRS 10.C1B]*. The investment entity exception is discussed at 10 below.

In December 2014, the IASB issued *Investment Entities: Applying the Consolidation Exception (Amendments to IFRS 10, IFRS 12 and IAS 28)* which clarifies two aspects of the investment entity exception. These amendments applied for annual periods beginning on or after 1 January 2016 but could be adopted earlier. *[IFRS 10.C1D]*. These amendments are discussed at 10 below.

1.3 Consolidation procedures

When an investor determines that it controls an investee, the investor (the parent) consolidates the investee (the subsidiary). The requirements of IFRS 10 relating to consolidation procedures, non-controlling interests and accounting for loss of control are dealt with in Chapter 7.

A parent consolidates a subsidiary from the date on which the parent first obtains control and continues consolidating that subsidiary until the date on which control is lost. IFRS 3 – *Business Combinations* – defines the date of acquisition, that is, the date on which control is first obtained. *[IFRS 3.8, Appendix A]*. The term 'date of acquisition' is used even if a parent gains control without acquiring an interest, or taking any action, as discussed at 9.3 below. IFRS 10 deals with consolidation thereafter (see Chapter 7).

When a parent gains control of a group of assets or an entity that is not a business, such transactions are excluded from the scope of IFRS 3. *[IFRS 3.2(b)]*. This is often the case when a parent gains control of a structured entity. Business combinations under common control are also excluded from the scope of IFRS 3, *[IFRS 3.2(c)]*, which means that if a parent gains control of a subsidiary (as defined in IFRS 10) that was previously controlled by an entity under common control, IFRS 3 also does not apply (see Chapter 10).

A parent consolidates all subsidiaries and recognises non-controlling interests for any interests held by investors outside of the group.

1.4 Disclosure requirements

IFRS 10 does not contain any disclosure requirements regarding an entity's interests in subsidiaries included in the consolidated financial statements or its interests in structured entities (whether consolidated or unconsolidated). Such disclosure requirements are contained within IFRS 12.

IFRS 12 contains all disclosure requirements related to an entity's interests in subsidiaries, joint arrangements, associates and structured entities. IFRS 12 requires disclosure of the judgements that were made in determining whether it controls another entity. Even if management concludes that it does not control an entity, the information used to make that judgement will be transparent to users of the financial statements. The required disclosures should also assist users of the financial statements to make their own assessment of the financial impact were management to reach a different conclusion regarding consolidation – by providing information about certain unconsolidated entities. The requirements of IFRS 12 are dealt with in Chapter 13.

2 OBJECTIVE AND SCOPE OF IFRS 10

2.1 Objective

The objective of IFRS 10 is to establish principles for the presentation and preparation of consolidated financial statements when an entity controls one or more other entities. *[IFRS 10.1]*.

To meet this objective, the standard:

(a) requires an entity (the parent) that controls one or more other entities (subsidiaries) to present consolidated financial statements;

(b) defines the principle of control, and establishes control as the basis for consolidation;

(c) sets out how to apply the principle of control to identify whether an investor controls an investee and therefore must consolidate the investee;

(d) establishes the accounting requirements for the preparation of consolidated financial statements; and

(e) defines an investment entity and the criteria that must be satisfied for the investment entity exception to be applied. *[IFRS 10.2]*.

This chapter deals with (a), (b), (c) and (e). The accounting requirements mentioned in (d) are dealt with in Chapter 7.

IFRS 10 also states that it does not deal with the accounting requirements for business combinations and their effect on consolidation, including goodwill arising on a business combination; these are covered by IFRS 3 (see Chapter 9). *[IFRS 10.3]*.

2.2 Scope

IFRS 10 requires that a parent (unless exempt or an investment entity as discussed below) shall present consolidated financial statements. This means that the financial statements of the group in which the assets, liabilities, equity, income, expenses and cash flows of the parent and its subsidiaries are included, should be presented as those of a single economic entity. A group consists of a parent and its subsidiaries (i.e. entities that the parent controls). *[IFRS 10.4, Appendix A]*.

Under IFRS 10, an entity must assess whether it controls the other entities in which it has an interest (the investees) – see 3 below. This applies to all types of investees including corporations, partnerships, limited liability corporations, trusts, and other types of entities. However, there is a scope exemption for post-employment benefit plans or other long-term employee plans to which IAS 19 – *Employee Benefits* – applies (see 2.2.2 below). In addition, an investment entity generally does not consolidate its subsidiaries (see 2.2.3 below).

IFRS 10 also provides an exemption from preparing consolidated financial statements for entities that are not an ultimate parent, if they meet certain criteria (see 2.2.1 below).

2.2.1 Exemption from preparing consolidated financial statements by an intermediate parent

A parent that prepares financial statements in accordance with IFRS is exempt from presenting (i.e. need not present) consolidated financial statements if it meets all of the following conditions:

(a) it is a wholly-owned subsidiary, or is a partially-owned subsidiary of another entity and all its other owners, including those not otherwise entitled to vote, have been informed about, and do not object to, the parent not presenting consolidated financial statements;

(b) its debt or equity instruments are not traded in a public market (a domestic or foreign stock exchange or an over-the-counter market, including local and regional markets);

(c) it did not file, nor is it in the process of filing, its financial statements with a securities commission or other regulatory organisation for the purpose of issuing any class of instruments in a public market; and

(d) its ultimate or any intermediate parent produces financial statements that are available for public use and comply with IFRSs, in which subsidiaries are consolidated or are measured at fair value through profit or loss in accordance with IFRS 10. *[IFRS 10.4(a)]*.

Where an entity uses this exemption, it may, but is not required to, prepare separate financial statements (see Chapter 8) as its only financial statements. *[IAS 27.8]*. However, if separate financial statements are prepared, they must comply with IAS 27. *[IAS 27.2]*.

The conditions for exemption from preparing consolidated financial statements raise the following interpretation issues.

2.2.1.A Condition (a) – consent of non-controlling shareholders

It is not clear whether a parent is required to obtain explicit consent that the owners of a reporting entity do not object to the use of the exemption.

IFRS 10 requires that, where the parent is itself a partly-owned subsidiary, any non-controlling shareholders must be informed of the parent's intention not to prepare consolidated financial statements. Since IFRS 10 does not expressly require obtaining explicit consent, the non-controlling shareholders may not have to give explicit consent, i.e. the absence of dissent is sufficient. However, parents that are partly-owned subsidiaries and wish to use the exemption from preparing consolidated financial statements are advised to obtain explicit written consent from non-controlling shareholders in advance. This is because IFRS 10 sets no time limit on when the non-controlling shareholders can register any objection. Thus, it is possible for the non-controlling shareholders to object to a parent's proposed use of the exemption just before the separate financial statements are printed and even after they have been issued.

IFRS 10 also requires all non-controlling owners 'including those not otherwise entitled to vote' to be informed of the parent's intention not to prepare consolidated financial statements. *[IFRS 10.4(a)]*. Thus, for example, the holders of any voting or non-voting preference shares must be notified of, and consent (or not object) to, the entity's intention to use the exemption.

In our view, the requirement to inform the non-controlling shareholders where the parent 'is a partially-owned subsidiary of another entity' is ambiguous, as illustrated by Examples 6.1 and 6.2 below.

Example 6.1: Consent for not preparing consolidated financial statements (1)

A parent (P) wishing to use the exemption is owned 60% by entity A and 40% by entity B. Entity A and entity B are both wholly-owned by entity C. In this case, P is not obliged to inform its non-controlling shareholder B of its intention not to prepare consolidated financial statements since, although it is a partly-owned subsidiary of A, it is a wholly-owned subsidiary of C (and therefore satisfies condition (a) without regard to its immediate owners).

Example 6.2: Consent for not preparing consolidated financial statements (2)

The facts are the same as in Example 6.1 above, except that A and B are both owned by an individual (Mr. X). P is not a wholly-owned subsidiary of any other entity, and therefore the rules applicable to partly-owned subsidiaries apply. Thus, P is required to inform B of any intention not to prepare consolidated financial statements.

2.2.1.B Condition (b) – securities not traded in a public market

It is not clear exactly what constitutes a 'public market'. It is clear that, where quoted prices are available for any of the parent's securities on a generally recognised share exchange, the parent is required to prepare consolidated financial statements, and cannot use the exemption. However, when there are no quoted prices, but the parent's shares are occasionally traded, for example, on a matched bargain basis through an exchange (as opposed to by private treaty between individual buyers and sellers), it is not clear whether this would meet the definition of a 'public market' for this condition.

In our view, any security that is traded in circumstances where it is necessary to have filed financial statements with a securities commission or regulator is regarded as 'traded in a public market' for condition (b). It is clear that the IASB regarded conditions (b) and (c) above as linked; in other words, that an entity would fall within (c) before falling within (b). *[IFRS 10.BCZ18]*. Condition (c) refers to the filing of financial statements with a securities commission or regulator as a precursor to public listing of securities, and this forms the basis for our view. The meaning of 'public market' is discussed in more detail in Chapter 36 at 2.2.1.

2.2.1.C Condition (c) – not filing financial statements for listing securities

It is not clear whether the 'financial statements' referred to are only those prepared under IFRS, or include those prepared under local GAAP.

In our view, the test is whether the entity currently has, or shortly will have, an ongoing obligation to file financial statements with a regulator in connection with the public trading of any of its securities – whether under IFRS or local GAAP. This conclusion is based on our view that the phrase 'financial statements' means any financial statements filed in connection with the public trading of securities. The IASB's view is that the information needs of users of financial statements of entities whose debt or equity instruments are traded in a public market are best served when investments in subsidiaries, associates, and jointly controlled entities are accounted for in accordance with IFRS 10, IAS 28, and IFRS 11 respectively. The Board therefore decided that the exemption from preparing such consolidated financial statements is not available to such entities or to entities in the process of issuing instruments in a public market. *[IFRS 10.BCZ18]*.

2.2.1.D Condition (d) – parent's IFRS financial statements are publicly available and include subsidiaries that are consolidated or measured at fair value through profit or loss in accordance with IFRS 10

The first part of this condition means that the exemption can be used either where a parent of the reporting entity prepares financial statements under IFRS that are publicly available through a regulatory filing requirement, or where those financial statements are available on request. An entity that uses the exemption from preparing consolidated financial statements must disclose the source for obtaining the financial statements of the relevant parent of the reporting entity (see Chapter 8 at 3.1). *[IAS 27.16(a)]*. For example, this information can be provided by providing:

- contact details of a person or an e-mail address from which a hard copy of the document can be obtained; or
- a website address where the financial statements can be found and downloaded.

This condition requires that the parent's financial statements comply with IFRS. There are a number of jurisdictions that have a national GAAP which is virtually identical to IFRS. However, differences between these national GAAPs and IFRS often exist regarding the scope, transitional provisions, effective dates and actual wording of standards. In addition, some national GAAPs contain accounting alternatives not permitted by IFRS. The question arises as to whether a reporting entity, that is a parent entity preparing IFRS financial statements, can claim exemption for the requirement to prepare consolidated accounts on the grounds that it has an ultimate or intermediate parent that produces consolidated financial statements under a national GAAP which is similar to IFRS (e.g. European Union (EU) adopted IFRS). In our view, if the ultimate or intermediate parent:

- reports under a national GAAP that is identical with IFRS in all respects;
- applied the national GAAP equivalent of IFRS 1 – *First-time Adoption of International Financial Reporting Standards* – when it adopted that national GAAP;
- makes an explicit and unreserved statement of compliance with that national GAAP in its most recent consolidated financial statements; and
- could have made an explicit and unreserved statement of compliance with IFRS in those consolidated financial statements, if required,

then the exemption from preparing consolidated financial statements is permitted for the reporting entity.

The second part of condition (d) above confirms that the exemption from preparing consolidated financial statements set out in (a) to (d) above is available to an intermediate parent entity that is a subsidiary of an investment entity. The exemption is available even though the investment entity parent may not prepare consolidated financial statements or consolidate the intermediate parent entity subsidiary. *[IFRS 10.BC28A-B]*. This condition was added by an amendment applicable for accounting periods beginning on or after 1 January 2016. *[IFRS 10.C1D]*.

In making its decision, the IASB observed that, when an investment entity measures its interest in a subsidiary at fair value, the disclosures required by IFRS 12 are supplemented by those required by IFRS 7 – *Financial Instruments: Disclosures* – and IFRS 13 – *Fair Value Measurement*. Accordingly, the IASB decided that this combination of information was sufficient to support the decision to retain an exemption from presenting consolidated financial statements for a subsidiary of an investment entity that is itself a parent entity. The IASB further noted that requiring an intermediate parent that is a subsidiary of an investment entity to prepare consolidated financial statements could result in significant additional costs, without commensurate benefit and this would be contrary to its intention in requiring investment entities to measure investments at fair value, which was to provide more relevant information at a reduced cost. *[IFRS 10.BC28D]*.

However, local law or regulations may conflict with this exemption if it is required that an entity has to be included within the consolidated financial statements of a parent by full consolidation in order to obtain the exemption.

2.2.2 Employee benefit plans and employee share trusts

IFRS 10 exempts post-employment benefit plans or other long-term employee benefit plans to which IAS 19 applies. *[IFRS 10.4A]*. However, it is not clear whether this means that an employee benefit plan that controls an investee is not required to consolidate that investee in its financial statements, or whether an investor that controls an employee benefit plan need not consolidate the plan itself.

In our view, the latter was intended: a sponsor of an employee benefit plan need not evaluate whether it controls that employee benefit plan, and, therefore, need not consolidate it. However, the employee benefit plan would need to apply IFRS 10 if it is preparing financial statements under IAS 26 – *Accounting and Reporting by Retirement Benefit Plans*. These employee benefit plans are referred to as 'Employee benefit plan (EBP) trust' in Figure 6.2 below.

In contrast, employee benefit trusts (or similar entities) established for employee share option plans, employee share purchase plans and other share-based payment programmes are not excluded from the scope of IFRS 10. This is because these are outside the scope of IAS 19. These trusts are referred to as 'Employee stock ownership plan (ESOP) trust' in Figure 6.2 below. The sponsoring entity of these trusts needs to evaluate whether it controls (and therefore consolidates) the trusts. If the trust is treated as an extension of the employer or sponsoring entity (see Chapter 34 at 12.3), its assets and liabilities will already be included in the financial statements of the employer entity that are used for preparing the consolidated financial statements of the group. If the trust is not accounted for as an extension of the employer or sponsoring entity, the parent will need to assess whether the trust, as a separate vehicle, needs to be consolidated according to the control criteria of IFRS 10.

The diagram below illustrates what is in scope and out of scope of IFRS 10.

Figure 6.2:   Understanding scope in employee benefit plans and employee stock ownership plans

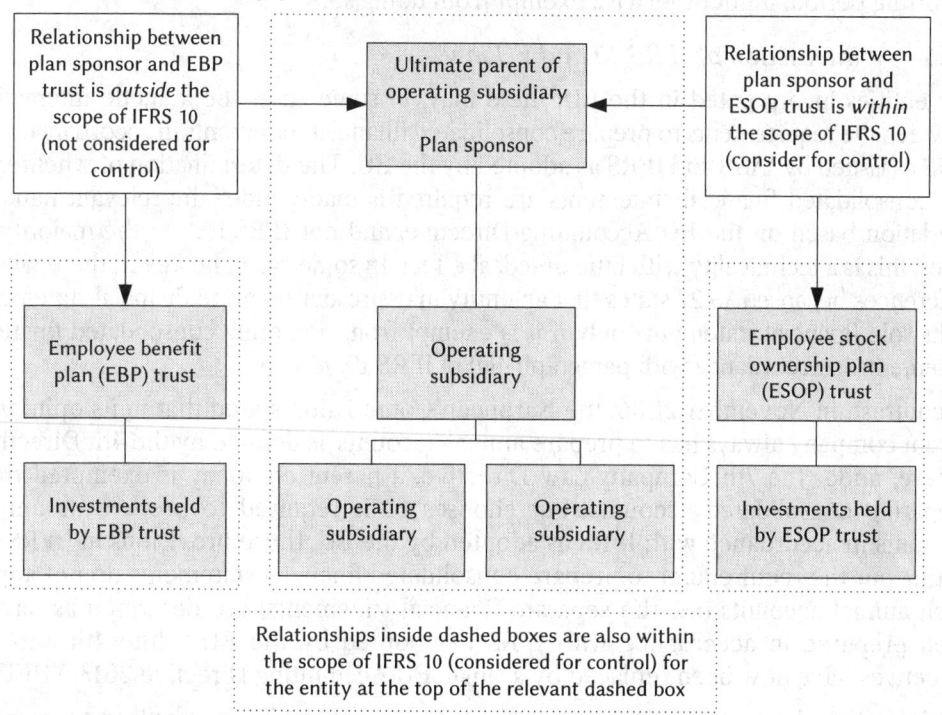

2.2.3   Investment entity exception

As an exception to the consolidation rule, a parent that is an investment entity shall not present consolidated financial statements if it is required to measure all of its subsidiaries at fair value through profit or loss. *[IFRS 10.4B]*. This is discussed at 10.3 below.

2.2.4   Entity no longer a parent at the end of the reporting period

It is not clear whether IFRS 10 requires an entity to prepare consolidated financial statements only if it is a parent at the end of the reporting period or also if it was a parent at any time during the reporting period.

In our view, consolidated financial statements must be prepared by an entity that was a parent during the reporting period, even if that entity is no longer a parent at the end of the reporting period (e.g. because it disposed of all its subsidiaries). IFRS 10 requires a parent to consolidate a subsidiary until the date on which the parent ceases to control the subsidiary. *[IFRS 10.20]*. This means that if a parent does not prepare consolidated financial statements pursuant to a concession in local law (see 2.2.5 below), the parent may not present separate financial statements in compliance with IFRS.

Likewise, we believe that an entity that had an associate, or an interest in a joint venture, during the reporting period but no longer does so at end of the reporting period, must apply IAS 28 and/or IFRS 11 to those investments in its financial statements for the reporting period, if not otherwise exempt from doing so.

2.2.5 Interaction of IFRS 10 and EU law

For entities incorporated in the EU, there may, in some cases, be a subtle interaction between the requirements to prepare consolidated financial statements in accordance with IFRS as issued by IASB and IFRS as adopted by the EU. The determination of whether or not consolidated financial statements are required is made under the relevant national legislation based on the EU Accounting Directive, and not IFRS 10.[1] In the majority of cases, this is a technicality with little practical effect. In some cases, however, there will be differences because IAS 27 states that an entity may present separate financial statements as its sole financial statements only if it is exempt from preparing consolidated financial statements in accordance with paragraph 4(a) of IFRS 10. *[IAS 27.8]*.

In contrast, in November 2006, the European Commission stated that in its opinion 'a parent company always has to prepare annual accounts as defined by the 4th Directive. Where, under the 7th Company Law Directive, a parent company is exempted from preparing consolidated accounts, but chooses or is required to prepare its annual accounts in accordance with IFRS as adopted by the EU, those provisions in [IFRS 10] setting out the requirement to prepare consolidated financial statements do not apply. Such annual accounts (i.e. the separate financial statements) are described as having been prepared in accordance with IFRS as adopted by the EU'[2] (the 4th and 7th Directives have now been replaced by a single EU Accounting Directive 2013/34/EU[3]).

Applying the above discussions, when an entity is not explicitly required to prepare consolidated financial statements under national legislation based on the EU Accounting Directive, even though IFRS 10 would oblige it to do so, it will not meet the criterion for exemption under paragraph 4(a) of IFRS 10. Consequently, when that entity presents separate financial statements, such financial statements must be described as having been prepared in accordance with 'IFRS as adopted by the EU' rather than 'IFRS as issued by the IASB'. An example of this situation would be an entity that has an investment in an entity that is not a 'subsidiary undertaking' under the EU Accounting Directive 2013/34/EU, but is a subsidiary under IFRS 10.

2.2.6 Combined and carve-out financial statements

Combined or carve-out financial statements are sometimes prepared under IFRS for a 'reporting entity' that does not comprise a group under IFRS 10. Although some GAAPs draw a distinction between combined and carve-out financial statements, in our view, the determination of whether these financial statements are permitted to be prepared in accordance with IFRS is the same. Accordingly, where the term 'combined' financial statements is used below, the views apply equally to carve-out financial statements.

The 2018 *Conceptual Framework* defines 'combined financial statements' as financial statements of a reporting entity that comprises two or more entities that are not all linked by a parent-subsidiary relationship. *[CF Appendix]*. However, the 2018 *Conceptual Framework* does not discuss when or how entities could prepare combined financial statements.

The IASB concluded that such discussion would be best developed if the IASB decides in the future to develop a Standard on this topic. *[CF 3.12, BC3.21]*.

Examples of when combined or carve-out financial statements might be requested include the following:

- two or more legal entities under common control of the same individual or group of individuals (e.g. 'horizontal' groups); or
- a group of business units that are intended to become a group in the future (e.g. following an initial public offering or demerger), which may or may not be separate legal entities.

In 2009, the Interpretations Committee received a request for guidance on whether a reporting entity may, in accordance with IFRS, present financial statements that include a selection of entities that are under common control, rather than being restricted to a parent/subsidiary relationship as defined by IFRS. The Interpretations Committee noted that the ability to include entities within a set of IFRS financial statements depends on the interpretation of 'reporting entity' in the context of common control. The Interpretations Committee decided not to add these issues on to its agenda.[4]

In our view, there are limited circumstances in which such combined financial statements can give a true and fair view in accordance with IFRS and be presented as 'general purpose' financial statements. As a minimum, there must be both of the following:

- common control for the full or a portion of the reporting period (see 2.2.6.A below); and
- a clear purpose for which the combined financial statements will be used by clearly identified intended users (see 2.2.6.B below).

In addition, the preparer must be able to coherently describe the various legal entities, segments, reportable segments, branches, divisions, geographical jurisdictions, or other 'units' that will be included in the combined financial statements. Careful consideration is required when concluding that it is appropriate to exclude any 'units' from the combined financial statements (such as unprofitable operations) that are similar to the 'units' that are being included in the combined financial statements. Such exclusion must be appropriate when considered in the context of the purpose of the financial statements, the intended users, and the terms and conditions of any relevant agreements (e.g. acquisitions, spin-offs). Other practical considerations related to the preparation of combined financial statements are noted in 2.2.6.C below.

Although IFRS is unclear on this issue, we believe that the fact that *IFRS for Small and Medium-sized Entities* specifically permits the preparation of combined financial statements, and the fact that the 2018 *Conceptual Framework* refers to combined financial statements, together provide a basis for preparing combined financial statements in appropriate circumstances.

2.2.6.A Common control

Determining whether common control exists can be difficult, and requires judgement based on the facts and circumstances (see Chapter 10 at 2.1.1). In our view, general purpose combined financial statements can only be prepared if the entities are under common control for the full or a portion of the reporting period. Furthermore, the financial results of each combined entity can only be included in the general purpose combined financial statements for the period in which that entity was under common control. Events that occur after the end of a reporting period that result in common control are non-adjusting events (see Chapter 38 at 2.1.3).

2.2.6.B Purpose and users of combined financial statements

A reporting entity is an entity that is required, or chooses, to prepare financial statements. *[CF 3.10, Appendix]*. Therefore, it is a matter of judgement of whether it is appropriate to prepare general purpose combined financial statements, depending upon the facts and circumstances related to both the purpose and the users of the financial statements, considerations that are interrelated.

For example, the facts and circumstances usually indicate that it is appropriate to prepare general purpose combined financial statements when required by regulators on behalf of investors. This is because the regulators purport to represent the needs of a wide range of users (investors) for a general purpose, for which the investors cannot otherwise command the financial information. Situations where regulators typically require combined financial statements include:

- carve-out transactions;
- spin-off transactions;
- financing transactions that require approval by a broad group of investors;
- transactions in which the combined entity will become the predecessor financial statements of a new entity; or
- transactions in which the combined entity will be a material acquisition (for the acquirer).

In addition, there may be circumstances when several third parties (banks, acquirers in a private bidding process) all request financial statements that combine the same entities – that is, the same combined financial statements. In such cases, the combined financial statements might be 'general purpose', because they are used by a wide range of users.

2.2.6.C Preparation of combined financial statements

Combined financial statements must include all normal consolidation entries (such as elimination of group transactions, unrealised profit elimination, etc.). In our view, the combined financial statements should disclose:

- the fact that the financial statements are combined financial statements;
- the reason why combined financial statements are prepared;
- the basis for determining which 'units' are included in the combined financial statements;
- the basis of preparation of the combined financial statements; and
- the related party disclosures required by IAS 24 – *Related Party Disclosures*.

Determining the appropriate boundary of a reporting entity can be difficult if the reporting entity: (a) is not a legal entity; and (b) does not comprise only legal entities linked by a parent-subsidiary relationship. In such cases, determining the boundary of the reporting entity is driven by the information needs of the primary users of the

reporting entity's financial statements. Those users need relevant information that faithfully represents what it purports to represent. Faithful representation requires that:
- the boundary of the reporting entity does not contain an arbitrary or incomplete set of economic activities;
- including that set of economic activities within the boundary of the reporting entity results in neutral information; and
- a description is provided of how the boundary of the reporting entity was determined and of what constitutes the reporting entity. *[CF 3.13-14]*.

In addition, management should consider who has the appropriate knowledge and authority to authorise the general purpose combined financial statements for issue (see Chapter 38 at 2.4).

While regulators may require combined or carve-out financial statements, IFRS does not describe how to prepare such information. Accordingly, practical issues frequently arise when preparing financial statements on a combined or carve-out basis, including the items below:
- *Management judgement and hindsight*: Absent clear legal boundaries, determining whether certain items are part of a combined reporting entity often requires significant management judgement and possibly the use of hindsight;
- *Comparative periods:* There is a risk that comparative information is prepared on a basis that reflects the impact of events before they actually occur (e.g. disposals of assets). Once it is determined what 'units' are being included in the combined financial statements, the comparative information presented is the comparative information for such units;
- *Allocation of overhead costs*: Combined reporting entities that are part of a larger group often benefit from certain overheads (e.g. legal or administrative);
- *Transfers of assets*: The group that owns the combined reporting entity may have been reorganised, resulting in the transfer of assets between 'units'. This raises questions about recognising gains or losses on disposals and the appropriate cost basis of assets acquired;
- *Financing costs*: It is often not clear how to allocate a group's liabilities and equity to the individual 'units' that it owns. The individual 'units' may differ considerably in nature, e.g. a group may own both low-risk established 'units' and a high-risk new venture. Therefore, it is not clear how to allocate interest expenses and other aspects of an entity's funding structure (e.g. embedded derivatives and compound financial instruments);
- *Taxation and employee benefits*: Legal and other requirements often create practical issues when determining the amount of the tax or employee benefit liabilities that are recognised in combined or carve-out financial statements; and
- *Designation*: Accounting under IFRS sometimes relies on management's stated intent and other designations (e.g. financial instrument and hedge designations, intent regarding assets held for sale and designation of groups of cash-generating units). It is often not clear how to reflect management's intent and designations in combined or carve-out financial statements.

There is a risk that an inappropriate allocation could result in a set of financial statements that does not offer a 'true and fair view' of the reporting entity. Preparation of financial information on a combined or carve-out basis generally requires a substantial number of adjustments and allocations to be made, and draws heavily on pronouncements of other standard-setting bodies that are referred to by the hierarchy of authoritative guidance in IAS 8 – *Accounting Policies, Changes in Accounting Estimates and Errors*.

Absent clarification by the IASB or the Interpretations Committee, diversity in practice will continue to exist. Therefore, the basis of preparation should disclose:
- which accounting standards have been applied; and
- the significant accounting judgements that were made, including the adjustments and allocations.

2.2.6.D   When combined financial statements are not general purpose

In our view, it is generally not appropriate to present 'general purpose' combined financial statements when requested by parties that can obtain the desired combined financial information through other means. In such cases, the combined financial statements are often deemed 'special purpose'. Examples of such parties include:
- lenders (banks) for the purpose of approving a loan or ensuring covenant compliance;
- governments and their agencies other than investor regulators (e.g. tax authorities);
- a single potential acquirer; or
- a board of directors or management.

When a group of family members prepares combined financial statements, judgement is required to assess the facts and circumstances, as to whether such combined financial statements are 'general purpose' or 'special purpose', depending on the purpose for which the family intends to use the combined financial statements.

Where it is not appropriate to present combined financial statements as 'general purpose', either because they are requested by a party that has the ability to otherwise command the information, or because there are deviations from IFRS as issued by the IASB due to the specific nature and purpose of the combined or carved-out financial statements, alternative options might include preparing:
- financial statements of each of the entities that would have been included in the combined financial information; or
- special purpose financial statements.

2.2.6.E   The reporting entity in combined financial statements and in consolidated financial statements

In certain circumstances, entities prepare general purpose combined financial statements in compliance with IFRS followed by consolidated financial statements in accordance with IFRS. Sometimes, group entities may be excluded from a parent's combined financial statements despite the fact that they are controlled by the parent, and would otherwise be consolidated by the parent under IFRS 10. For example, a subsidiary that will not form part of a sub-group to be listed may be excluded from the combined financial statements. In our view, the subsequent consolidated financial statements must be prepared according to IFRS 10 and therefore must include all subsidiaries controlled by a parent. This is because IFRS 10 defines consolidated financial statements as those including assets, liabilities, equity, income, expenses and cash flows of the parent and its subsidiaries. *[IFRS 10 Appendix A]*. A subsidiary is derecognised at the date that control is lost. *[IFRS 10.20, 25]*. IFRS 10 does not provide any exceptions to these requirements. Example 6.3 below illustrates the differences in the scope of consolidation that can arise where an entity prepares both combined and consolidated financial statements.

Example 6.3:   Preparation of consolidated financial statements after combined financial statements

In 2021, intermediate parent (P), which has three subsidiaries (S1, S2 and S3), is preparing for an IPO. P has historically not prepared consolidated financial statements as it has applied the exemption in IFRS 10.4(a). One of the subsidiaries, S3, is to be transferred to the ultimate parent prior to the listing and will not form part of the sub-group to be listed. In the prospectus, combined financial statements are presented including P, S1 and S2 for the annual periods ending 31 December 2019 and 2020. The combined financial statements are deemed to be general purpose financial statements in compliance with IFRS, as the combined entities have been under common control for the entire reporting period, and the combined financial statements are required by the regulator on behalf of investors, representing a wide range of users. The transfer of S3 to the ultimate parent occurred in August 2021 and P group was listed in October 2021.

When preparing the 2021 consolidated financial statements, should (now listed) P:

(a) present consolidated financial statements for 2021 (P+S1+S2+S3), showing comparatives for 2020 and consolidating S3 until August 2021; or

(b) present consolidated financial statements for 2021 excluding S3 (P1+S1+S2), showing comparative information for 2020 for only P1+S1+S2, as per the combined financial statements?

The consolidated financial statements must be prepared according to IFRS 10 and therefore the 2021 consolidated financial statements of P must include S3 in the 2020 comparatives and until control ceased in August 2021 (option (a) above).

3   CONTROL

An investor, regardless of the nature of its involvement with an entity (the investee), determines whether it is a parent by assessing whether it controls the investee. *[IFRS 10.5]*.

An investor controls an investee when it is exposed, or has rights, to variable returns from its involvement with the investee and has the ability to affect those returns through its power over the investee. *[IFRS 10.6]*.

Thus, an investor controls an investee if and only if the investor has all of the following:

(a) power over the investee;

(b) exposure, or rights, to variable returns from its involvement with the investee; and

(c) the ability to use its power over the investee to affect the amount of the investor's returns. *[IFRS 10.7]*.

Although not a defined term, IFRS 10 uses the term 'investor' to refer to a reporting entity that potentially controls one or more other entities, and 'investee' to refer to an entity that is, or may potentially be, the subsidiary of a reporting entity. Ownership of a debt or equity interest may be a key factor in determining whether an investor has control. However, it is also possible for a party to be an investor and potentially control an investee, without having an equity or debt interest in that investee.

An investor has to consider all facts and circumstances when assessing whether it controls an investee. *[IFRS 10.8]*.

Only one party, if any, can control an investee. *[IFRS 10.BC69]*. However, IFRS 10 notes that two or more investors collectively can control an investee. To control an investee collectively, investors must act together to direct the relevant activities (see 4.1 below). In such cases, because no investor can direct the activities without the co-operation of the others, no investor individually controls the investee. Each investor would account for its interest in the investee in accordance with the relevant IFRSs, such as IFRS 11, IAS 28 or IFRS 9 – *Financial Instruments*. *[IFRS 10.9]*.

3.1 Assessing control

Detailed application guidance is provided by IFRS 10 with respect to the assessment of whether an investor has control over an investee. To determine whether it controls an investee, an investor assesses whether it has all three elements of control described at 3 above. *[IFRS 10.B2]*.

Each of the three control criteria are explored in more detail at 4, 5 and 6 below, respectively.

IFRS 10 notes that consideration of the following factors may assist in making that determination:

(a) the purpose and design of the investee (see 3.2 below);

(b) what the relevant activities are and how decisions about those activities are made (see 4.1 below);

(c) whether the rights of the investor give it the current ability to direct the relevant activities (see 4.2 to 4.6 below);

(d) whether the investor is exposed, or has rights, to variable returns from its involvement with the investee (see 5 below); and

(e) whether the investor has the ability to use its power over the investee to affect the amount of the investor's returns (see 6 below). *[IFRS 10.B3]*.

In addition, when assessing control of an investee, an investor considers the nature of its relationship with other parties (see 7 below). *[IFRS 10.B4]*.

In many cases, when decision-making is controlled by voting rights that also give the holder exposure to variable returns, it is clear that whichever investor holds a majority of those voting rights controls the investee. *[IFRS 10.B6]*. However, in other cases (such as when there are potential voting rights, or an investor holds less than a majority of the voting rights), it may not be so clear. In those instances, further analysis is needed, and the criteria need to be evaluated based on all facts and circumstances (considering the factors listed above), to determine which investor, if any, controls an investee. *[IFRS 10.8]*. The diagram below illustrates this assessment.

The control principle outlined above applies to all investees, including structured entities. A structured entity is defined in IFRS 12 as 'an entity that has been designed so that voting or similar rights are not the dominant factor in deciding who controls the entity, such as when any voting rights relate to administrative tasks only and the relevant activities are directed by means of contractual arrangements'. *[IFRS 12 Appendix A]*.

There are no bright lines to determine whether an investor has an exposure, or has rights, to variable returns from its involvement with a structured entity, or whether it has the ability to affect the returns of the structured entity through its power over the structured entity. Rather, as with all investees, all facts and circumstances are considered when assessing whether the investor has control over an investee that is a structured entity. That is, the process outlined in the diagram below is used for structured entities, although the relevant facts and circumstances may differ from when voting rights are a more important factor in determining control.

Figure 6.3: Assessing control

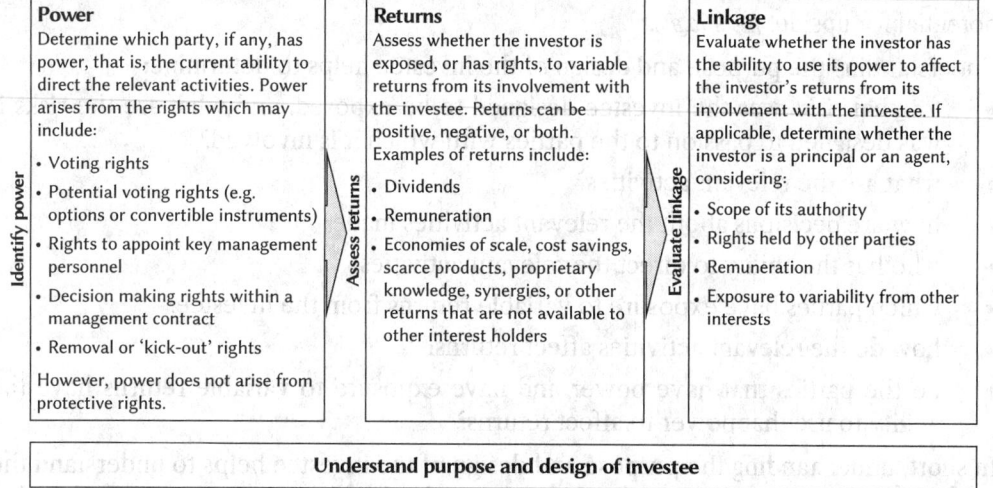

When management concludes that an entity does *not* have control, the requirements of IFRS 11 and IAS 28 must be considered to determine whether it has joint control or significant influence, respectively, over the investee, as shown in the diagram at 1.1 above.

3.2 Purpose and design of an investee

When assessing control of an investee, an investor considers the purpose and design of the investee in order to identify the relevant activities, how decisions about the relevant activities are made, who has the current ability to direct those activities and who receives returns from those activities. *[IFRS 10.B5]*. Understanding the purpose and design of an investee is therefore critical when identifying who has control.

When an investee's purpose and design are considered, it may be clear that an investee is controlled by means of equity instruments that give the holder proportionate voting rights, such as ordinary shares in the investee. In this case, in the absence of any additional arrangements that alter decision-making, the assessment of control focuses on which party, if any, is able to exercise voting rights (see 4.3 below) sufficient to determine the investee's operating and financing policies.

In the most straightforward case, the investor that holds a majority of those voting rights, in the absence of any other factors, controls the investee. *[IFRS 10.B6]*.

To determine whether an investor controls an investee in more complex cases, it may be necessary to consider some or all of the other factors listed at 3.1 above. *[IFRS 10.B7]*.

IFRS 10 notes that an investee may be designed so that voting rights are not the dominant factor in deciding who controls the investee, such as when any voting rights relate to administrative tasks only and the relevant activities are directed by means of contractual arrangements (this is the same wording that IFRS 12 uses in defining a structured entity – see 3.1 above). In such cases, an investor's consideration of the purpose and design of the investee shall also include consideration of the risks to which the investee was designed to be exposed, the risks it was designed to pass on to the parties involved with the investee and whether the investor is exposed to some or all of those risks. Consideration of the risks includes not only the downside risk, but also the potential for upside. *[IFRS 10.B8]*.

Understanding the purpose and design of the investee helps to determine:

- to what risks was the investee designed to be exposed, and what are the risks it was designed to pass on to the parties with which it is involved?
- what are the relevant activities?
- how are decisions about the relevant activities made?
- who has the ability to direct the relevant activities?
- which parties have exposure to variable returns from the investee?
- how do the relevant activities affect returns?
- do the parties that have power and have exposure to variable returns have the ability to use that power to affect returns?

In short, understanding the purpose and design of the investee helps to understand the goal of each investor; that is, why they are involved with the investee, and what that involvement is.

4 POWER OVER AN INVESTEE

The first criterion to have control relates to power. An investor has power when it has existing rights that give it the current ability to direct the relevant activities. *[IFRS 10.10, B9]*. Therefore, when assessing whether an investor has power, there are two critical concepts:

- relevant activities; and
- existing rights.

These concepts are discussed at 4.1 and 4.2 below, respectively. Power may be achieved through voting rights (see 4.3 below) or through rights arising from contractual arrangements (see 4.4 below). We also discuss other evidence of power (see 4.5 below) and determining whether sponsoring (designing) a structured entity gives power (see 4.6 below).

An investor can have power over an investee even if other entities have existing rights that give them the current ability to participate in the direction of the relevant activities. This may occur when another entity has significant influence, *[IFRS 10.14]*, i.e. 'the power to participate in the financial and operating policy decisions of the investee but is not control or joint control over those policies'. *[IAS 28.3]*.

4.1 Relevant activities

In many cases, it is clear that control of an investee is held through voting rights. However, when it is not clear that control of an investee is held through voting rights, a crucial step in assessing control is identifying the relevant activities of the investee and the way decisions about such activities are made. *[IFRS 10.B10]*. Relevant activities are the activities of the investee that significantly affect the investee's returns. *[IFRS 10.10]*.

For many investees, a range of activities significantly affect their returns. Examples of relevant activities, and decisions about them, include, but are not limited to:

- determining or changing operating and financing policies (which might include the items below);
- selling and purchasing goods and/or services;
- managing financial assets during their life (and/or upon default);
- selecting, acquiring or disposing of assets;
- researching and developing new products or processes;
- determining a funding structure or obtaining funding;
- establishing operating and capital decisions of the investee, including budgets; and
- appointing, remunerating or terminating the employment of an investee's service providers or key management personnel. *[IFRS 10.B6, B11-B12]*.

4.1.1 More than one relevant activity

In many cases, more than one activity will significantly affect an investee's returns.

Under IFRS 10, if two or more unrelated investors each have existing rights that give them the unilateral ability to direct different relevant activities, the investor that has the current ability to direct the activities that most significantly affect the returns of the investee has power over the investee. *[IFRS 10.13]*.

In some situations, activities that occur both before and after a particular set of circumstances or events may be relevant activities. When two or more investors have the current ability to direct relevant activities and those activities occur at different times, the investors shall determine which investor is able to direct the activities that most significantly affect those returns consistently with the treatment of concurrent decision-making rights. The investors reconsider this assessment over time if relevant facts or circumstances change. *[IFRS 10.B13]*.

Therefore, when there is more than one activity that significantly affects an investee's returns, and these activities are directed by different investors, it is important to determine which activities most significantly affect the investee's returns. This is illustrated in Example 6.4 below, which is from IFRS 10. *[IFRS 10.B13 Example 1]*.

Example 6.4:   Identifying relevant activities in life sciences arrangements

Two investors form an investee to develop and market a medical product. One investor is responsible for developing and obtaining regulatory approval of the medical product – that responsibility includes having the unilateral ability to make all decisions relating to the development of the product and to obtaining regulatory approval. Once the regulator has approved the product, the other investor will manufacture and market it – this investor has the unilateral ability to make all decisions about the manufacture and marketing of the product. If all the activities – developing and obtaining regulatory approval as well as manufacturing and marketing of the medical product – are relevant activities, each investor needs to determine whether it is able to direct the activities that most significantly affect the investee's returns. Accordingly, each investor needs to consider whether developing and obtaining regulatory approval or the manufacturing and marketing of the medical product is the activity that most significantly affects the investee's returns and whether it is able to direct that activity. In determining which investor has power, the investors would consider:

(a) the purpose and design of the investee;

(b) the factors that determine the profit margin, revenue and value of the investee as well as the value of the medical product;

(c) the effect on the investee's returns resulting from each investor's decision-making authority with respect to the factors in (b); and

(d) the investors' exposure to variability of returns.

In this particular example, the investors would also consider:

(e) the uncertainty of, and effort required in, obtaining regulatory approval (considering the investor's record of successfully developing and obtaining regulatory approval of medical products); and

(f) which investor controls the medical product once the development phase is successful.

In this example, IFRS 10 does not conclude which of the activities is the most relevant activity (i.e. the activity that most significantly affects the investee's returns). If it were concluded that the most relevant activity is:

- developing and obtaining regulatory approval of the medical product – then the investor that has the power to direct that activity would have power from the date of entering into the arrangement; or

- manufacturing and marketing the medical product – then the investor that has the power to direct that activity would have power from the date of entering into the arrangement.

To determine whether either investor controls the arrangement, the investors would also need to assess whether they have exposure to variable returns from their involvement with the investee (see 5 below) and the ability to use their power over the investee to affect the amount of the investor's returns (see 6 below). *[IFRS 10.7, B2]*. The investors are required to reconsider this assessment over time if relevant facts or circumstances change. *[IFRS 10.8]*.

Example 6.4 above illustrates a situation when two different activities that significantly affect an investee's returns are directed by different investors. Thus, it is important to identify the activity that *most* significantly affects returns, as part of assessing which investor, if any, has power. This differs from joint control, defined as the contractually agreed sharing of control of an arrangement, which exists only when decisions about the relevant activities require the unanimous consent of the parties sharing control. *[IFRS 11 Appendix A]*. Joint control is discussed in more detail in Chapter 12 at 4.

A second example, also provided by IFRS 10, is reproduced in Example 6.5 below. *[IFRS 10.B13 Example 2]*.

Example 6.5: Identifying relevant activities in an investment vehicle

An investment vehicle (the investee) is created and financed with a debt instrument held by an investor (the debt investor) and equity instruments held by a number of other investors. The equity tranche is designed to absorb the first losses and to receive any residual return from the investee. One of the equity investors who holds 30% of the equity is also the asset manager. The investee uses its proceeds to purchase a portfolio of financial assets, exposing the investee to the credit risk associated with the possible default of principal and interest payments of the assets. The transaction is marketed to the debt investor as an investment with minimal exposure to the credit risk associated with the possible default of the assets in the portfolio because of the nature of these assets and because the equity tranche is designed to absorb the first losses of the investee.

The returns of the investee are significantly affected by the management of the investee's asset portfolio, which includes decisions about the selection, acquisition and disposal of the assets within portfolio guidelines and the management upon default of any portfolio assets. All those activities are managed by the asset manager until defaults reach a specified proportion of the portfolio value (i.e. when the value of the portfolio is such that the equity tranche of the investee has been consumed).

From that time, a third-party trustee manages the assets according to the instructions of the debt investor. Managing the investee's asset portfolio is the relevant activity of the investee. The asset manager has the ability to direct the relevant activities until defaulted assets reach the specified proportion of the portfolio value; the debt investor has the ability to direct the relevant activities when the value of defaulted assets surpasses that specified proportion of the portfolio value. The asset manager and the debt investor each need to determine whether they are able to direct the activities that *most* significantly affect the investee's returns, including considering the purpose and design of the investee as well as each party's exposure to variability of returns.

Example 6.6 below illustrates a structured entity in which there is more than one activity that affects the investee's returns.

Example 6.6: Identifying relevant activities in a structured entity

A structured entity buys dollar-denominated assets, issues euro-denominated notes, and hedges the cash flow differences through currency and interest rate swaps. The activities that affect the structured entity's returns include:

- sourcing the assets from the market;
- determining the types of assets that are purchased;
- deciding how the structure is hedged; and
- managing the assets in the event of default.

If each of these activities is managed by different investors (e.g. one investor manages the assets in the event of default, but a different investor determines the types of assets that are purchased), it is necessary to determine which activity most significantly affects the structured entity's returns.

When there are multiple activities that significantly affect an investee's returns, but those activities are all directed by the same investor(s) (which is frequently the case when those activities are directed by voting rights), it is not necessary to determine which activity most significantly affects the investee's returns because the power assessment would be the same in each case.

4.1.2 No relevant activities

We believe that structured entities for which there is no substantive decision making are rare. That is, we believe virtually all structured entities have some level of decision-making and few, if any, are on 'autopilot'. Even if a structured entity operates on 'autopilot', there may be decisions outside the predetermined parameters that may need to be taken if an expected return fails to materialise which could significantly affect the returns of the entity and therefore be relevant activities.

In practice, many entities that may initially have few if any relevant activities can be terminated by at least one of the parties involved in the structure. In this case, the choice of whether to terminate may often be viewed as the relevant activity. IFRS 10 would most likely result in such entities being consolidated by an investor that has the power to dissolve the entity, if this power would affect its variable returns. See 4.6 below for additional guidance on evaluating relevant activities for structured entities and 6.3.2 below for additional guidance on liquidation and redemption rights.

However, if a structured entity truly has no decision-making, then no investor controls that structured entity. This is because no investor has power over the structured entity, that is, no investor has the current ability to direct the activities that significantly affect the structured entity's returns if there are no relevant activities after inception significantly affecting those returns. As discussed above, we believe that such situations where there is no substantive decision-making are rare. An example of a structured entity over which no investor had power was included in the IASB's publication, *Effect analysis: IFRS 10 – Consolidated Financial Statements and IFRS 12 – Disclosure of Interests in Other Entities.* However, this example caused controversy and the Effect Analysis was re-issued in 2013 with the example deleted.[5]

4.1.3 Single asset, single lessee vehicles

Some structured entities are single asset, single lease vehicles created to lease a single asset to a single lessee. Between November 2014 and May 2015, the Interpretations Committee discussed requests for clarification about the interaction of IFRS 10 and IAS 17 – *Leases* – in two situations which involved the establishment of a structured entity to lease a single asset to a single lessee.

In the first situation, the lease between the structured entity and the lessee was an operating lease and the question was whether the lessee should consolidate the structured entity. In the second situation, the lease between the structured entity and the lessee was a finance lease, and the question was whether the junior lender of the structured entity should consolidate the structured entity. In both situations, the consolidation decision would be based on an assessment of whether the entity controls the structured entity. The Interpretations Committee was asked whether the lessee's use of the leased asset was a relevant activity of the structured entity when assessing power over the structured entity.

The Interpretations Committee was of the view that the lessee's right to use the asset for a period of time would not, in isolation, typically give the lessee decision-making rights over the relevant activities of the structured entity and hence would not typically be a relevant activity of the structured entity. This is because on entering into a lease, regardless of whether it is a finance lease or an operating lease, the structured entity (lessor) would have two rights – a right to receive lease payments and a right to the residual value of the leased asset at the end of the lease. Consequently, the activities that would affect the structured entity's returns would relate to managing the returns derived from those rights; for example, managing the credit risk associated with the lease payments or managing the leased asset at the end of the lease term (for example, managing its sale or re-leasing). How the decision-making relating to those activities would significantly affect the structured entity's returns would depend on the particular facts and circumstances.

The Interpretations Committee noted that its conclusion does not mean that a lessee can never control the lessor. For example, a parent that controls another entity for other reasons can lease an asset from that entity. Further, in assessing control, an entity would consider all of the rights that it has in relation to the investee to determine whether it has power over that investee. This would include rights in contractual arrangements other than the lease contract, such as contractual arrangements for loans made to the lessor, as well as rights included within the lease contract, including those that go beyond simply providing the lessee with the right to use the asset.

As a result, the Interpretations Committee concluded that the principles and guidance within IFRS 10 would enable a determination of control to be made based on the relevant facts and circumstances of the scenario and it is not its practice to give case-by-case advice on individual fact patterns. Consequently, the Interpretations Committee concluded that neither an Interpretation nor an amendment to a Standard was required and decided not to add these issues to its agenda.[6]

We believe the discussions above also apply to leases as defined in IFRS 16 – *Leases*.

4.1.4 Management of assets in the event of default

The management of defaults on assets held by a structured entity will frequently be a relevant activity for that entity (see Example 6.5 at 4.1.1 above). However, in practice, if the assets held by the structured entity are bonds, the activities of a decision-maker that is contracted to manage any defaults may be limited to voting at creditors' meetings, as an independent administrator would be appointed to manage the bond default on behalf of all bond holders. Whether the decision-maker has power (i.e. the current ability to direct the management of defaults) or not will probably depend on the size of the structured entity's holding in the individual bonds that have defaulted. The greater the holding, the more likely the decision-maker may be able to control decision-making in a creditors' meeting.

4.2 Existing rights

Once the relevant activities are identified, the next step is to determine which investor, if any, has the current ability to direct those activities (i.e. who has the power). Sometimes, assessing power is straightforward, such as when power over an investee is obtained directly and solely from the voting rights that stem from holding voting interests (e.g. shares), and can be assessed by considering the voting rights from those shareholdings. In other cases, the assessment is more complex and requires many factors to be considered (e.g. instances when power is embedded in one or more contractual arrangements). *[IFRS 10.11]*.

Power arises from rights. To have power over an investee, an investor must have existing rights that give the investor the current ability to direct the relevant activities. The rights that may give an investor power can differ between investees. *[IFRS 10.B14]*.

Examples of rights that, either individually or in combination, can give an investor power include but are not limited to:

(a) rights in the form of voting rights (or potential voting rights) of an investee;
(b) rights to appoint, reassign or remove members of an investee's key management personnel who have the ability to direct the relevant activities;
(c) rights to appoint or remove another entity that directs the relevant activities;
(d) rights to direct the investee to enter into, or veto any changes to, transactions for the benefit of the investor; and
(e) other rights (such as decision-making rights specified in a management contract) that give the holder the ability to direct the relevant activities. *[IFRS 10.B15]*.

Generally, when an investee has a range of operating and financing activities that significantly affect the investee's returns and when substantive decision-making with respect to these activities is required continuously, it will be voting or similar rights that give an investor power, either individually or in combination with other arrangements. *[IFRS 10.B16]*.

4.2.1 Evaluating whether rights are substantive

For a right to convey power, it must provide the current ability to direct the relevant activities. An investor, in assessing whether it has power, considers only substantive rights relating to the investee (held by the investor and others). For a right to be substantive, the holder must have the practical ability to exercise the right. *[IFRS 10.B22]*. An investor that holds only protective rights (see 4.2.2 below) does not have power over an investee, and consequently does not control the investee. *[IFRS 10.14]*. Whether rights are substantive depends on facts and circumstances. The table below (although not exhaustive) describes the factors that should be considered. *[IFRS 10.B23]*.

Figure 6.4: Factors to consider in assessing whether a right is substantive

Factors	Examples
• Are there barriers (economic, operational or otherwise) that would prevent (or deter) the holder(s) from exercising their right(s)?	• Financial penalties • High exercise or conversion price • Narrow exercise periods • Absence of a mechanism to exercise • Lack of information to exercise • Lack of other parties willing or able to take over or provide specialist services • Legal or regulatory barriers (e.g. where a foreign investor is prohibited from exercising its rights)
• Do the holders have the practical ability to exercise their rights, when exercise requires agreement by more than one investor?	• The more parties necessary to come together to exercise this right, the less likely that the right is substantive • A mechanism is in place that provides those parties with the practical ability to exercise their rights collectively if they choose to do so • An independent board of directors may serve as a mechanism for numerous investors to act collectively in exercising their rights
• Would the investor that holds the rights benefit from their exercise or conversion?	• A potential voting right is in-the-money • An investor would obtain benefits from synergies between the investor and the investee

To be substantive, rights also need to be exercisable when decisions about the direction of the relevant activities need to be made. Usually, to be substantive, the rights need to be currently exercisable. However, sometimes rights can be substantive, even though the rights are not currently exercisable. *[IFRS 10.B24]*. This is illustrated by IFRS 10, *[IFRS 10.B24 Example 3-3D]*, as reflected in Example 6.7 below.

Example 6.7:   Rights exercisable when decisions need to be made

An investee has annual shareholder meetings at which decisions to direct the relevant activities are made. The next scheduled shareholders' meeting is in eight months. However, shareholders that individually or collectively hold at least 5% of the voting rights can call a special meeting to change the existing policies over the relevant activities, but a requirement to give notice to the other shareholders means that such a meeting cannot be held for at least 30 days. Policies over the relevant activities can be changed only at special or scheduled shareholders' meetings. This includes the approval of material sales of assets as well as the making or disposing of significant investments.

The above fact pattern applies to each scenario described below. Each scenario is considered in isolation.

Scenario A

An investor holds a majority of the voting rights in the investee. The investor's voting rights are substantive because the investor is able to make decisions about the direction of the relevant activities when they need to be made. The fact that it takes 30 days before the investor can exercise its voting rights does not stop the investor from having the current ability to direct the relevant activities from the moment the investor acquires the shareholding.

Scenario B

An investor is party to a forward contract to acquire the majority of shares in the investee. The forward contract's settlement date is in 25 days. The existing shareholders are unable to change the existing policies over the relevant activities because a special meeting cannot be held for at least 30 days, at which point the forward contract will have been settled. Thus, the investor has rights that are essentially equivalent to the majority shareholder in scenario A above (i.e. the investor holding the forward contract can make decisions about the direction of the relevant activities when they need to be made). The investor's forward contract is a substantive right that gives the investor the current ability to direct the relevant activities even before the forward contract is settled.

Scenario C

An investor holds a substantive option to acquire the majority of shares in the investee that is exercisable in 25 days and is deeply in the money. The same conclusion would be reached as in scenario B.

Scenario D

An investor is party to a forward contract to acquire the majority of shares in the investee, with no other related rights over the investee. The forward contract's settlement date is in six months. In contrast to the scenarios A to C above, the investor does not have the current ability to direct the relevant activities. The existing shareholders have the current ability to direct the relevant activities because they can change the existing policies over the relevant activities before the forward contract is settled.

This example illustrates that an investor with the current ability to direct the relevant activities has power even if its rights to direct have yet to be exercised. Evidence that the investor has been directing relevant activities can help determine whether the investor has power, but such evidence is not, in itself, conclusive in determining whether the investor has power over an investee. *[IFRS 10.12]*.

It should be noted that an investor in assessing whether it has power needs to consider substantive rights held by other parties. Substantive rights exercisable by other parties can prevent an investor from controlling the investee to which those rights relate. Such substantive rights do not require the holders to have the ability to initiate decisions. As long as the rights are not merely protective (see 4.2.2 below), substantive rights held by other parties may prevent the investor from controlling the investee even if the rights give the holders only the current ability to approve or block decisions that relate to the relevant activities. *[IFRS 10.B25]*.

It is important to remember that the purpose and design of an investee is critical when assessing whether a right is substantive. For example, the following should be considered when evaluating whether an investor's rights are substantive:

- Why were the rights granted?
- What compensation was given (or received) for the right? Does that compensation reflect fair value?
- Did other investors also receive this right? If not, why?

These questions should be considered both when a right is first granted, but also if an existing right is modified.

To be substantive and convey power, a right must give the investor the 'current ability' to direct the investee's relevant activities. However, 'current ability' does not always mean 'able to be exercised this instant'. The concept of 'current ability' is discussed more in the context of potential voting rights at 4.3.4 below.

4.2.2 Evaluating whether rights are protective

In evaluating whether rights give an investor power over an investee, the investor has to assess whether its rights, and rights held by others, are protective rights. *[IFRS 10.B26]*.

Under IFRS 10, protective rights are defined as 'rights designed to protect the interest of the party holding those rights without giving that party power over the entity to which those rights relate'. *[IFRS 10 Appendix A]*.

Since power is an essential element of control, protective rights do not provide the investor control over the investee. *[IFRS 10.14]*. In addition, holding protective rights cannot prevent another investor from having power over an investee. *[IFRS 10.B27]*.

Protective rights are typically held to prohibit fundamental changes in the activities of an investee that the holder does not agree with and usually only apply in exceptional circumstances (i.e. upon a contingent event). However, the fact that the right to make decisions is contingent upon an event occurring does not mean that the right is always a protective right. *[IFRS 10.B26]*.

Examples of protective rights include (but are not limited to) the right to:

- restrict an investee from undertaking activities that could significantly change the credit risk of the investee to the detriment of the investor;
- approve an investee's capital expenditures (greater than the amount spent in the ordinary course of business);
- approve an investee's issuance of equity or debt instruments;
- seize assets if an investee fails to meet specified loan repayment conditions; *[IFRS 10.B28]* and
- veto transactions between the investee and a related party.

In some cases, a right might be deemed protective, such as the ability to sell assets of the investee if an investee defaults on a loan, because default is considered an exceptional circumstance. However, in the event that the investee defaults on a loan (or, say, breaches a covenant), the investor holding that right will need to reassess whether that right has become a substantive right that gives the holder power (rather than merely a protective right), based on the change in facts and circumstances. This issue has been raised with the Interpretations Committee which, in September 2013, concluded that reassessment of control is required when facts and circumstances change in such a way that rights, previously determined to be protective, change (for example upon the breach of a covenant in a borrowing arrangement that causes the borrower to be in default). The Interpretations Committee observed that it did not expect significant diversity in practice to develop on this matter and decided not to add the issue to its agenda. In making its conclusion, the Interpretations Committee observed that:

- paragraph 8 of IFRS 10 requires an investor to reassess whether it controls an investee if facts and circumstances indicate that there are changes to one or more of the three elements of control;
- a breach of a covenant that results in rights becoming exercisable constitutes such a change;
- IFRS 10 does not include an exemption for any rights from this need for reassessment; and
- the IASB's redeliberations of this topic during the development of IFRS 10 concluded that rights initially determined to be protective should be included in a reassessment of control whenever facts and circumstances indicate that there are changes to one or more of the three elements of control.[7]

4.2.2.A   Veto rights

Whether veto rights held by an investor are merely a protective right or a right that may convey power to the veto holder will depend on the nature of the veto rights. If the veto rights relate to changes to operating and financing policies that significantly affect the investee's returns, the veto right may not merely be a protective right.

Other veto rights that are common, and are typically protective (because they rarely significantly affect the investee's returns) include veto rights over changes to:

- amendments to articles of incorporation;
- location of investee headquarters;
- name of investee;
- auditors; and
- accounting principles for separate reporting of investee operations.

4.2.2.B   Franchises

Many have questioned how to consider franchise rights, and whether they give power (to the franchisor), or whether they are merely protective rights. IFRS 10 notes that a franchise agreement for which the investee is the franchisee often gives the franchisor rights that are designed to protect the franchise brand. Franchise agreements typically give franchisors some decision-making rights with respect to the operations of the franchisee. *[IFRS 10.B29]*.

The standard goes on to say that, generally, franchisors' rights do not restrict the ability of parties other than the franchisor to make decisions that have a significant effect on the franchisee's returns. Nor do the rights of the franchisor in franchise agreements necessarily give the franchisor the current ability to direct the activities that significantly affect the franchisee's returns. [IFRS 10.B30].

It is necessary to distinguish between having the current ability to make decisions that significantly affect the franchisee's returns and having the ability to make decisions that protect the franchise brand. The franchisor does not have power over the franchisee if other parties have existing rights that give them the current ability to direct the relevant activities of the franchisee. [IFRS 10.B31].

By entering into the franchise agreement, the franchisee has made a unilateral decision to operate its business in accordance with the terms of the franchise agreement, but for its own account. [IFRS 10.B32].

Control over such fundamental decisions as the legal form of the franchisee and its funding structure often are not made by the franchisor and may significantly affect the returns of the franchisee. The lower the level of financial support provided by the franchisor and the lower the franchisor's exposure to variability of returns from the franchisee the more likely it is that the franchisor has only protective rights. [IFRS 10.B33].

When analysing whether a franchisor has power over a franchisee, it is necessary to consider the purpose and design of the franchisee. The assessment of whether a franchisor has power hinges on the determination of the relevant activities, and which investor (the franchisor or owner of the franchisee) has the current ability to direct that activity through its rights. The rights held by the franchisor must be evaluated to determine if they are substantive, (i.e. the franchisor has the practical ability to exercise its rights when decisions of the relevant activities need to be made so that it has the current ability to direct the relevant activities), or whether they are merely protective rights. A determination will need to be made in each case, based on the specific facts and circumstances. This is illustrated in Example 6.8 below.

Example 6.8: Rights held by franchisor

A franchisor has certain rights that are designed to protect its brand when it is being licensed by a franchisee. Activities that significantly affect the franchisee's returns include:

- determining or changing its operating policies;
- setting its prices for selling goods;
- selecting suppliers;
- purchasing goods and services;
- selecting, acquiring or disposing of equipment;
- appointing, remunerating or terminating the employment of key management personnel; and
- financing the franchise.

If certain of the activities above are directed by one investor (e.g. the owners of the franchisee), and other activities are directed by another investor (e.g. the franchisor), then the investors will need to determine which activity most significantly affects the franchisee's returns, as discussed at 4.1 above.

4.2.2.C Budget approval rights

Approval rights over budgets are fairly common in shareholders' agreements and form part of the assessment as to the level of power held by investors. If the budget approval rights held by a shareholder (or other investor) are viewed as substantive, that might indicate that the entity having those rights has power over an investee.

However, the purpose and design of arrangements is key to the analysis of who has power. Therefore, the right to approve budgets should not automatically be considered substantive but should be based on a careful consideration of the facts and circumstances. Factors to consider in assessing whether budget approval rights are substantive or protective include (but are not limited to):

- the level of detail of the budget that is required to be approved;
- whether the budget covers the relevant activities of the entity;
- whether previous budgets have been challenged and if so, the practical method of resolution;
- whether there are any consequences of budgets not being approved (e.g. may the operator/directors be removed?);
- whether the entity operates in a specialised business for which only the operator/directors have the specialised knowledge required to draw up the budget;
- who appoints the operator and/or key management personnel of the investee; and
- the nature of the counterparty with budget approval rights and their practical involvement in the business.

4.2.2.D Independent directors

In some jurisdictions, there are requirements that an entity appoints directors who are 'independent'. The phrase 'independent director' has a variety of meanings in different jurisdictions but generally means a director who is independent of a specific shareholder. In some situations, a majority of directors of an entity may be 'independent'.

The fact that a majority of directors of an entity are 'independent' does not mean that no shareholder controls an entity. IFRS 10 requires that all facts and circumstances be considered and in the context of an entity with independent directors it is necessary to determine the role that those directors have in decisions about the relevant activities of the entity. The power to appoint and remove independent directors should be considered as part of this assessment.

Similarly, an entity may have more than one governing body and it should not be assumed that because one body (which may consist of a majority of independent directors) has oversight of another this means that the supervisory body is the one that makes decisions about the relevant activities of the entity.

4.2.3 Incentives to obtain power

There are many incentives to obtain rights that convey power; generally, the more exposure to variable returns (whether positive or negative), the greater that incentive. IFRS 10 notes this in two contexts:

- the greater an investor's exposure, or rights, to variability of returns from its involvement with an investee, the greater the incentive for the investor to obtain rights sufficient to give it power. Therefore, having a large exposure to variability of returns is an indicator that the investor may have power. However, the extent of the investor's exposure is not determinative regarding whether an investor has power over the investee; *[IFRS 10.B20]* and

- an investor may have an explicit or implicit commitment to ensure that an investee continues to operate as designed. Such a commitment may increase the investor's exposure to variability of returns and thus increase the incentive for the investor to obtain rights sufficient to provide it with power. Therefore, a commitment to ensure that an investee operates as designed may be an indicator that the investor has power, but does not, by itself, give an investor power, nor does it prevent another party from having power. *[IFRS 10.B54].*

Thus, even though there may be an incentive to obtain rights that convey power when there is an exposure to variable returns, that incentive, by itself, does not represent power. Rather, the investor must analyse whether it actually does have power through existing rights, which might be in the form of voting rights, or rights through a contractual agreement, as discussed at 4.3 and 4.4 below, respectively.

4.3 Voting rights

Power stems from existing rights. Often an investor has the current ability, through voting or similar rights, to direct the relevant activities. *[IFRS 10.B34].*

In many cases, assessing power can be straightforward. This is often the case when, after understanding the purpose and design of the investee, it is determined that power over an investee is obtained directly and solely from the proportionate voting rights that stem from holding equity instruments, such as ordinary shares in the investee. In this case, in the absence of evidence to the contrary, the assessment of control focuses on which party, if any, is able to exercise voting rights sufficient to determine the investee's operating and financing policies. In the most straightforward case, the investor that holds a majority of those voting rights, in the absence of any other factors, controls the investee. *[IFRS 10.B6].*

Nevertheless, when taking into account other factors relating to voting rights, an investor can have power even if it holds less than a majority of the voting rights of an investee. An investor can have power with less than a majority of the voting rights of an investee, for example, through:

(a) a contractual arrangement between the investor and other vote holders (see 4.3.5 below);
(b) rights arising from other contractual arrangements (see 4.3.6 below);
(c) the investor's voting rights being sufficient (see 4.3.3 below);
(d) potential voting rights (see 4.3.4 below); or
(e) a combination of (a)-(d). [IFRS 10.B38].

If the relevant activities of an investee are directed through voting rights, an investor needs to consider the requirements of IFRS 10 in relation to such matters as discussed at 4.3.1 to 4.3.6 below. [IFRS 10.B34].

See 4.4 below for a discussion of cases when voting rights are *not* the right that gives power over an investee.

4.3.1 Power with a majority of the voting rights

In many cases, the legal environment or corporate structure dictate that the relevant activities are directed by the agreement of shareholders who hold more than half of the voting rights of the investee. Alternatively, a governing body, e.g. a Board of Directors, might make decisions regarding the investee and that Board might be appointed by whoever has the majority of the voting rights to direct an investee's relevant activities. In both cases, when one investor has more than half the voting rights, it has power, assuming that no other facts and circumstances are relevant. [IFRS 10.B35].

However, there may be other facts and circumstances that are relevant, as discussed at 4.3.2 below. In addition, any potential voting rights need to be considered (see 4.3.4 below).

4.3.2 A majority of voting rights without power

In some cases, voting rights do *not* provide the holder the power to direct the relevant activities. This might be the case, when:

- relevant activities are directed by another party with existing rights under a contract, and that party is not an agent of the investor (see 4.4 below); [IFRS 10.B36]
- voting rights are not substantive (see 4.2.1 above). For example, if the relevant activities are directed by government, judiciary, administrator, receiver, liquidator, or regulator (see 4.3.2.A below); [IFRS 10.B37]
- voting rights have been delegated to a decision-maker, which then holds the voting rights as an agent (see 6 below); or
- voting rights are held as a *de facto* agent of another investor (see 7 below).

4.3.2.A   Evaluating voting rights during bankruptcy

Many jurisdictions have laws that offer protection from creditors when an entity is in financial difficulty. For example, an investee in such a position might be placed in the hands of liquidators, receivers or court-appointed managers under a reorganisation plan. Evaluating whether an investor holding the majority of voting rights still has power over an investee in such situations requires the exercise of judgement based on the facts and circumstances. It also requires assessing whether the holder of the voting rights continues to have the current ability to direct the activities that most significantly affect the investee's returns.

In this evaluation, it should be determined whether the shareholders (who hold voting rights) can still direct the operating and financial policies of the investee (assuming that this is the relevant activity), once the investee enters into bankruptcy proceedings. Alternatively, the bankruptcy court (or trustee, or administrator) may direct operating and financial policies. Consideration should be given to the following:

- Who appoints management during the bankruptcy period?
- Who directs management (e.g. the shareholders, or a trustee for the creditors)?
- Does management have to seek approval from parties besides the shareholders (e.g. for significant and/or unusual transactions)?
- Who negotiates the plan of reorganisation?

Even if it appears that the shareholders retain power once the investee enters bankruptcy (i.e. they retain the current ability to direct the relevant activities), this does not mean that a majority shareholder automatically controls the investee. This is because the shareholder may not have any exposure to variable returns (see 5 below), or the ability to affect its returns through its power (see 6 below), which are the other two criteria for having control. Depending on the facts and circumstances, a shareholder might lose power (or control) when the investee files for bankruptcy protection, or when the investee exits from bankruptcy. Determining the appropriate method of accounting for the interest in the investee upon loss of power (or control) requires careful consideration of the nature of the rights and interests, such as whether the shareholder has significant influence over the investee, in which case it would apply the equity method under IAS 28 – see Chapter 11. Alternatively, if the investor does not have significant influence, it would likely account for its investment in the investee as a financial instrument under IFRS 9.

When an investee files for bankruptcy, parties holding other rights with respect to that investee might also have to consider whether the control assessment has changed. For example, a right that was previously deemed protective (such as the right to appoint an administrator in the event of a bankruptcy – a right that is frequently held by creditors), may be considered to be a right that now gives power. Alternatively, the trustee itself might have power, through its ability to direct the activities of the investee in bankruptcy.

4.3.3   Power without a majority of voting rights (de facto control)

An investor might have control over an investee even when it has less than a majority of the voting rights of that investee if its rights are sufficient to give it power, because such rights give the investor the practical ability to direct the relevant activities unilaterally (a concept known as '*de facto* control'). *[IFRS 10.B41]*.

When assessing whether an investor's voting rights are sufficient to give it power, an investor considers all facts and circumstances, including:

(a) the size of the investor's holding of voting rights relative to the size and dispersion of holdings of the other vote holders, noting that:

   (i) the more voting rights an investor holds, the more likely the investor is to have existing rights that give it the current ability to direct the relevant activities;

   (ii) the more voting rights an investor holds relative to other vote holders, the more likely the investor is to have existing rights that give it the current ability to direct the relevant activities; and

   (iii) the more parties that would need to act together to outvote the investor, the more likely the investor is to have existing rights that give it the current ability to direct the relevant activities;

(b) potential voting rights held by the investor, other vote holders or other parties;

(c) rights arising from other contractual arrangements; and

(d) any additional facts and circumstances that indicate the investor has, or does not have, the current ability to direct the relevant activities at the time that decisions need to be made, including voting patterns at previous shareholders' meetings. *[IFRS 10.B42]*.

In addition, IFRS 10 states that if it is not clear that the investor has power, having considered the factors above, then the investor does not control the investee. *[IFRS 10.B46]*.

Whether an investor should include voting rights held by related parties not controlled by the investor (e.g. shareholdings held by its parent, sister companies, associates or shareholdings held by key management personnel or other individuals who are related parties) would depend on the specific facts and circumstances (i.e. whether the related parties are *de facto* agents of the investor). See 7 below.

Potential voting rights and rights arising from other contractual arrangements are discussed at 4.3.4 to 4.3.6 below, respectively. *De facto* control is discussed in more detail below.

IFRS 10 includes several examples illustrating the assessment of power when an investor has less than a majority of voting rights. Some of these are summarised in Examples 6.9 to 6.12 below. Our variation on the examples provided in IFRS 10 is introduced in Example 6.13 below. In each of the examples, it is assumed that, after understanding the purpose and design of the investee:

- voting rights give an investor the ability to direct activities that most significantly affect the investee's returns (i.e. voting rights give power);
- none of the shareholders has arrangements to consult any of the other shareholders or make collective decisions;
- decisions require the approval of a majority of votes cast at the shareholders' meeting; and
- no other facts or circumstances are relevant.

When the direction of relevant activities is determined by majority vote and an investor holds significantly more voting rights than any other party, and the other shareholdings are widely dispersed, it may be clear, after considering the factors listed in (a)-(c) above alone, that the investor has power over the investee. [IFRS 10.B43]. This is illustrated in Example 6.9 below (although factors (b) and (c) are not applicable).

Example 6.9: Less than a majority of voting rights (1)

A holds 48% of the voting rights of B; the remaining 52% of B is widely held by thousands of shareholders (none of whom individually holds more than 1% of the voting rights, and none of the shareholders has any arrangements to consult any of the others or make collective decisions).

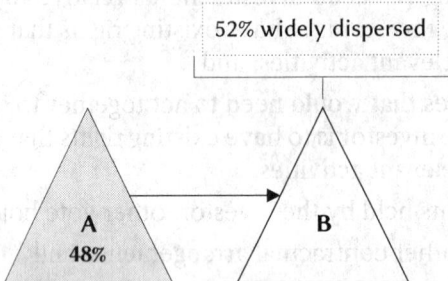

A has power over B, because A has a dominant voting interest (based on the absolute size of its holding, and relative to other shareholders), and a large number of shareholders would have to agree to outvote A. [IFRS 10.B43 Example 4].

In other situations, it may be clear after considering the factors listed in (a)-(c) above alone that an investor does not have power. [IFRS 10.B44]. This is illustrated in Example 6.10 below (although factors (b) and (c) are not applicable).

Example 6.10: Less than a majority of voting rights (2)

C holds 45% of the voting rights in D. Two other investors each hold 26% of the voting rights (total 52%), with the remaining 3% held by three other shareholders, each holding 1%. There are no other arrangements that affect decision-making.

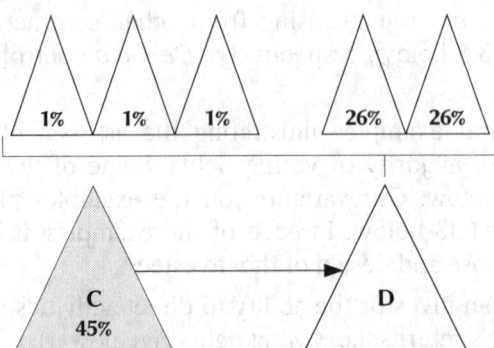

C does *not* have power over D, because the two remaining significant shareholders (i.e. a relatively small number) could easily cooperate to outvote C. The size of C's holding, and size of that holding relative to other shareholders, would *not* give it power. [IFRS 10.B44 Example 6].

However, the factors listed in (a)-(c) above alone may not be conclusive. If an investor, having considered those factors, is unclear whether it has power, it considers additional facts and circumstances, such as whether other shareholders are passive in nature as demonstrated by voting patterns at previous shareholders' meetings. *[IFRS 10.B45].*

When evaluating past voting patterns, significant judgement will be required to determine how far back to review. Judgement will also be required to determine whether past voting patterns may have been influenced by conditions that existed at a point in time, such as how well the entity was operating during the periods reviewed. For example, if an entity was profitable and operating smoothly, other shareholders may have been less motivated to exercise their voting rights. The fewer voting rights the investor holds, and the fewer parties that would need to act together to outvote the investor, the more reliance would be placed on the additional facts and circumstances to assess whether the investor's rights are sufficient to give it power. *[IFRS 10.B45].*

Consideration of additional facts and circumstances, referred to in paragraph B45 of the standard, includes the assessment of the factors that provide evidence of the practical ability to direct the relevant activities of the investee (paragraph B18), and the indicators that the investor may have power as a result of any special relationship with the investee (paragraph B19) or due to the extent of its exposure to variability of returns (paragraph B20), which are discussed at 4.5 below. When the facts and circumstances in paragraphs B18-B20 are considered together with the investor's rights, greater weight shall be given to the evidence of power in paragraph B18 than to the indicators of power in paragraphs B19 and B20. *[IFRS 10.B45].*

Example 6.11 below illustrates a situation where the factors in (a)-(c) above alone are not conclusive, and therefore facts and circumstances would need to be considered.

Example 6.11: Less than a majority of voting rights (3)

E holds 45% of the voting rights in F. The rest of F is dispersed among 11 investors, who each hold 5%. None of the shareholders has contractual arrangements to consult any of the others or make collective decisions.

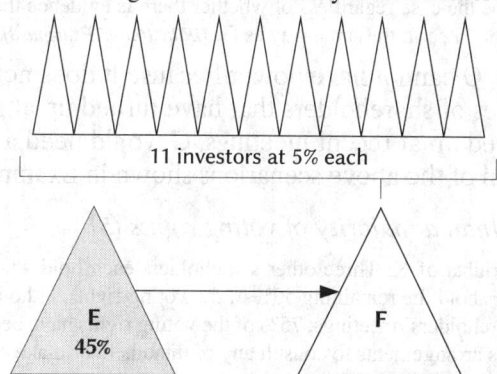

The size of E's holding and the dispersion of the other shareholders are *not* conclusive in determining whether E has power over F. Other relevant facts and circumstances (such as those discussed at 4.5 below) would be considered to determine whether E has power over F. *[IFRS 10.B45 Example 7].*

Comparing Examples 6.10 and 6.11 above illustrates the judgement that will need to be applied in determining whether an investor has power. The IASB considers that it may be easy for two other shareholders to act together to outvote an investor (as in Example 6.10 above), but that it may be more difficult for 11 other shareholders to act together to outvote an investor (as in Example 6.11 above). Where is the line between these two situations?

Example 6.12 below illustrates a situation where additional facts and circumstances need to be considered. For example, this may include whether other shareholders are passive in nature as demonstrated by voting patterns at previous shareholders' meetings.

Example 6.12:   Less than a majority of voting rights (4)

G holds 35% of the voting rights in H. Three other shareholders each hold 5% of the voting rights of H. The remaining 50% of the voting rights are held by numerous other shareholders, none individually holding more than 1% of the voting rights. None of the shareholders has arrangements to consult any of the others or make collective decisions. At recent shareholders' meetings, 75% of the voting rights have been represented (including G).

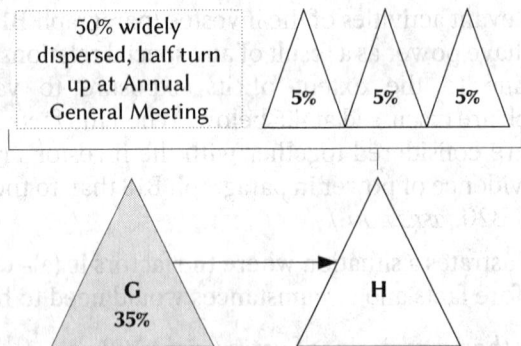

G does not have power over H because the size of G's holding relative to other shareholders, when considering their active participation at recent shareholders' meetings, does not give G the current ability to direct the activities of H. This would be the case regardless of whether there is evidence that G directed H in the past, or whether other shareholders voted in the same way as G. *[IFRS 10.B45 Example 8].*

In Example 6.12 above, G cannot have power because it does not have, at a minimum, more than half the votes of shareholders that have turned up at recent meetings. That is, since 75% have turned up at recent meetings, G would need a minimum of 37.5% to have power. A variation of the above scenario is shown in Example 6.13 below.

Example 6.13:   Less than a majority of voting rights (5)

J holds 38% of the voting rights of K. Three other shareholders each hold 4% of the voting rights of K. Numerous other shareholders hold the remaining 50% of the voting rights, although none individually holds more than 1%. At recent shareholders' meetings, 75% of the voting rights have been represented, including J. None of the shareholders has arrangements to consult any of the others or make collective decisions.

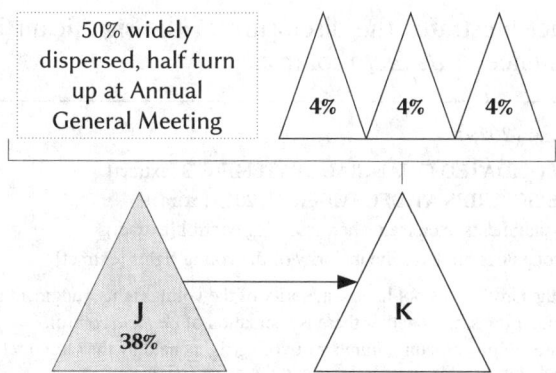

There are diverse views regarding the conclusion on this fact pattern, and judgement will need to be applied in practice. Some believe that J has power, because it has more than half the voting rights of those who have turned up at recent shareholder meetings. (J has more than half the voting rights, because J holds 38%, which is more than 37.5%, or half of 75%). Others believe that it is inconclusive whether J has power, because, while J has more than half the voting rights of those who have turned up at recent shareholder meetings, this is just barely the case. Contrast this fact pattern with Example 6.9 above, where IFRS 10 concludes that, after all relevant facts and circumstances have been considered, holding 48% in combination with remaining ownership that is widely dispersed results in an entity (A) having power.

Applying the concept of *de facto* control in the absence of 'bright lines' will require significant judgement of the facts and circumstances. For example:

- How large does an investor's interest need to be relative to others?
- How widely dispersed are the other investors? Could three shareholders easily act together?
- Are past voting patterns expected to be indicative of future voting patterns? How much history would be needed to make an assessment?
- Are there other relevant agreements between shareholders?

Generally, the lower the percentage held by one investor (the dominant shareholder, in Examples 6.9 to 6.13 above), the less likely that investor has *de facto* control.

Although perhaps rare, an investor could find itself in control of an investee simply because of circumstances that exist at a point in time, rather than because of deliberate action (see 9.3 below). In addition, while it may be easy to use hindsight to determine whether an investor had (or has) control, it might be difficult to apply this principle on a real-time basis. Information will need to be gathered and analysed (e.g. how widely dispersed are the other shareholders), so that management can reach a timely conclusion. It will also be necessary to monitor the changes in the profile of the other shareholders as this could mean that the investor has gained or lost power over the investee (see 9.3 below).

The following extract illustrates the disclosure of the significant judgements used in determining the existence of *de facto* control.

> **Extract 6.1: ENGIE SA (2019)**
> NOTES TO THE CONSOLIDATED FINANCIAL STATEMENTS [extract]
> NOTE 2   MAIN SUBSIDIARIES AT DECEMBER 31, 2019 [extract]
> 2.2   Significant judgments exercised when assessing control [extract]
> **Entities in which the Group does not have the majority of the voting rights** [extract]
>
> In the entities in which the Group does not have a majority of the voting rights, judgment is exercised with regard to the following items, in order to assess whether there is a situation of *de facto* control:
> - dispersion of the shareholding structure: number of voting rights held by the Group relative to the number of rights held respectively by the other vote holders and their dispersion;
> - voting patterns at shareholders' meetings: the percentages of voting rights exercised by the Group at shareholders' meetings in recent years;
> - governance arrangements: representation in the governing body with strategic and operational decision-making power over the relevant activities;
> - rules for appointing key management personnel;
> - contractual relationships and material transactions.
>
> The main fully consolidated entities in which the Group does not have the majority of the voting rights are Compagnie Nationale du Rhône (49.98%) and Gaztransport & Technigaz (40.4%).
>
> **Compagnie Nationale du Rhône ("CNR" – France excluding Infrastructures): 49.98%**
>
> The Group holds 49.98% of the share capital of CNR, with CDC holding 33.2%, and the balance (16.82%) being dispersed among around 200 local authorities. In view of the current provisions of the French "Murcef" law, under which a majority of CNR's share capital must remain under public ownership, the Group is unable to hold more than 50% of the share capital. However, the Group considers that it exercises *de facto* control as it holds the majority of the voting rights exercised at shareholders' meetings due to the widely dispersed shareholding structure and the absence of evidence of the minority shareholders acting in concert.
>
> **Gaztransport & Technigaz ("GTT" – Others): 40.4%**
>
> Since GTT's initial public offering in February 2014, ENGIE has been the largest shareholder in the company with a 40.4% stake, the free float representing around 49% of the share capital. The Group holds the majority of the voting rights exercised at shareholders' meetings in view of the widely dispersed shareholding structure and the absence of evidence of minority shareholders acting in concert. ENGIE also holds the majority of the seats on the Board of Directors. The Group considers that it exercises *de facto* control over GTT, based on an IFRS 10 criteria.

4.3.4   Potential voting rights

When assessing whether it has power over an investee, an investor also considers the potential voting rights that it holds, as well as potential voting rights held by others. Common examples of potential voting rights include options, forward contracts, and conversion features of a convertible instrument. Those potential voting rights are considered only if the rights are substantive (see 4.2.1 above). *[IFRS 10.B47].* In the remainder of this section, reference is made to 'options', but the concepts apply to all potential voting rights.

When considering potential voting rights, an investor considers the purpose and design of the entity, including the rights associated with the instrument, as well as those arising from any other involvement the investor has with the investee. This includes an assessment of the various terms and conditions of the instrument as well as the investor's apparent expectations, motives and reasons for agreeing to those terms and conditions. *[IFRS 10.B48].*

If the investor also has voting or other decision-making rights relating to the investee's activities, the investor assesses whether those rights, in combination with potential voting rights, give the investor power. *[IFRS 10.B49].*

Substantive potential voting rights alone, or in combination with other rights, may provide an investor the current ability to direct the relevant activities. *[IFRS 10.B50].* For example, if an investor has less than a majority of voting rights, but holds a substantive option that, if exercised, would give the investor a majority of voting rights, that investor would likely have power. *[IFRS 10.B42, B50].* Example 6.14 below illustrates when holding an option would likely give an investor power.

Example 6.14: Potential voting rights (1)

A holds 40% of the voting rights of B, and holds a currently exercisable in-the-money option to acquire a further 20% of the voting rights of B.

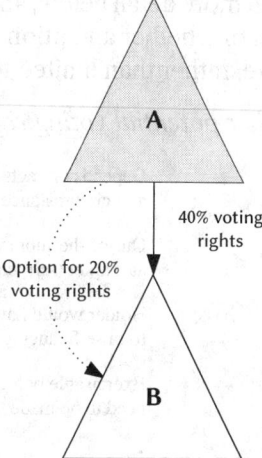

Assuming that voting rights give power over B, the option is substantive, and no other facts and circumstances are relevant to this assessment, A would likely have power over B, because A can currently exercise its right to obtain a majority of B's voting shares at any time.

The opposite is also true. If an investor holds a majority of the voting rights, but those voting rights are subject to a substantive option held by another investor, the majority shareholder would likely not have power.

Another example provided by IFRS 10 of a situation where substantive potential voting rights, in combination with other rights, can give an investor the current ability to direct the relevant activities is reflected in Example 6.15 below.

Example 6.15: Potential voting rights (2)

Investor A and two other investors each hold a third of the voting rights of an investee. The investee's business activity is closely related to investor A. In addition to its equity instruments, investor A also holds debt instruments that are convertible into ordinary shares of the investee at any time for a fixed price that is out of the money (but not deeply out of the money). If the debt were converted, investor A would hold 60% of the voting rights of the investee. Investor A would benefit from realising synergies if the debt instruments were converted into ordinary shares. Investor A has power over the investee because it holds voting rights of the investee together with substantive potential voting rights that give it the current ability to direct the relevant activities. *[IFRS 10.B50 Example 10].*

IFRS 10 is silent on whether the intention of the holder (i.e. whether the holder intends to exercise the option or not) is considered in the assessment of potential voting rights. However, IFRS 10 is clear that power arises from rights *per se* and the ability those rights give the investor to direct the relevant activities. *[IFRS 10.B14]*. Therefore, an option is only considered in the assessment of power if it is substantive (i.e. the holder has the practical ability to exercise the option when decisions about the direction of relevant activities need to be made). *[IFRS 10.B22, B24, B47]*. As discussed at 4.2.1 above, whether an option is substantive depends on facts and circumstances. Common factors to consider when evaluating whether an option is substantive include:

- exercise price or conversion price, relative to market terms;
- ability to obtain financing; and
- timing and length of exercise period.

These factors are each discussed in more detail below, and their implications are indicated in the table below. The evaluation of whether an option is substantive should consider all the factors discussed at 4.2.1 above, rather than limited to only one of the factors.

Figure 6.5: *Evaluating whether potential voting rights are substantive*

Evaluation	Non-substantive	Depends on facts and circumstances	Substantive
Exercise price	Deeply-out-of-the-money	Out-of-the-money or at market (fair value)	In-the-money
Financial ability to exercise	Holder has no financial ability	Holder would have to raise financing	Holder has cash or financing readily available
Exercise period	Not exercisable	Exercisable before decisions need to be made	Currently exercisable

4.3.4.A Exercise price or conversion price

IFRS 10 is clear that the exercise price (or conversion price) can and should be considered, in evaluating whether an option can give power, because it might represent a barrier to exercise. *[IFRS 10.B23(a)(ii)]*. Factors to consider are:

- deeply-out-of-the-money – Generally, these would be considered non-substantive;
- out-of-the-money (but not deeply) – Judgement will be needed to assess whether the cost of paying more than fair value is worth the potential benefits of exercise, including the exposures to variable returns that are associated with exercising that option (see 5 below for examples of exposures to variable returns);
- at market (fair value) – Consideration should be given as to whether the option conveys rights that differ from those that would be available to third parties in an open market; or
- in-the-money – Generally, in-the-money options would be considered substantive.

IFRS 10 does not define 'deeply-out-of-the-money' or provide a list of indicators for management to consider when exercising judgement in determining whether an option is deeply-out-of-the-money (as opposed to merely out-of-the-money). A call option with a strike price significantly above the value of the underlying interest is normally considered to be deeply-out-of-the-money.

When evaluating the exercise price, consideration is given as to whether the nature of the exercise price (e.g. deeply-out, out, or in-the-money) is expected to remain so for the entire exercise period, or whether the nature of the exercise price may change in the future. That is, the evaluation is not solely based on the nature of the option at inception or as of the end of the reporting period. This is because to convey power, an option must give an investor the current ability to direct the relevant activities when the decisions need to be made. Thus, for example, if an option was deeply-out-of-the-money at the reporting date, but the exercise price was subject to decrease such that the option was expected to become in-the-money before the relevant activities of the investee need to be directed, then the option may be substantive (or *vice versa*). This evaluation will require the exercise of judgement based on all relevant facts and circumstances. As noted above, the evaluation is not solely based on the nature of the option as of the end of the reporting period, i.e. whether a potential voting right is substantive is not based solely on a comparison of the strike or conversion price of the instrument and the then current market price of its underlying share. Although the strike or conversion price is one factor to consider, determining whether potential voting rights are substantive requires a holistic approach, considering a variety of factors. This includes assessing the purpose and design of the instrument, considering whether the investor can benefit for other reasons such as by realising synergies between the investor and the investee, and determining whether there are any barriers (financial or otherwise) that would prevent the holder of potential voting rights from exercising or converting those rights. Accordingly, a change in market conditions (i.e. the market price of the underlying shares) alone would not typically result in a change in the consolidation conclusion. *[IFRS 10.BC124]*.

Example 6.16 below reflects an example from IFRS 10 of an option that is currently exercisable, but is deeply-out-of-the-money and is expected to remain so for the whole of the exercise period. *[IFRS 10.B50 Example 9]*.

Example 6.16:   Potential voting rights (3)

Investor A holds 70% of the voting rights of an investee. Investor B has 30% of the voting rights of the investee as well as an option to acquire half of investor A's voting rights. The option is exercisable for the next two years at a fixed price that is deeply out of the money (and is expected to remain so for that two-year period). Investor A has been exercising its votes and is actively directing the relevant activities of the investee. In such a case, investor A is likely to meet the power criterion because it appears to have the current ability to direct the relevant activities. Although investor B has currently exercisable options to purchase additional voting rights (that, if exercised, would give it a majority of the voting rights in the investee), the terms and conditions associated with those options are such that the options are not considered substantive.

4.3.4.B   Financial ability

The financial ability of an investor to pay the exercise price should be considered when evaluating whether an option is substantive, because this could be an 'economic barrier' as contemplated by IFRS 10. *[IFRS 10.B23(a)]*. For example, if there is evidence that an investor cannot obtain financing to exercise an in-the-money option, this might indicate that the option is not substantive. However, financial ability is generally considered to be linked to the exercise price, because an investor should be able to obtain financing for an in-the-money option. As such, instances in which an investor would be unable to obtain financing for in-the-money options are expected to be uncommon.

In contrast, it is probably more common that the holder has the financial ability to exercise an option that is out-of-the-money (but not deeply so) and would consider exercising that option to benefit from synergies. This might be the case when the investee has strategic importance to the option holder.

4.3.4.C Exercise period

To have power over an investee, an investor must have existing rights that give the investor the current ability to direct an investee's relevant activities. *[IFRS 10.10]*. This would imply that an option needs to be currently exercisable to give power. However, under IFRS 10, an option can give an investor the current ability to direct an investee's relevant activities even when it is not currently exercisable. Although 'current' often means 'as of today' or 'this instant' in practice, the IASB's use of the term in IFRS 10 broadly refers to the ability to make decisions about an investee's relevant activities when they need to be made. *[IFRS 10.B24]*. This is illustrated in Example 6.17 below.

Example 6.17: Potential voting rights (4)

An investee holds annual shareholder meetings, at which decisions to direct the relevant activities are made. An investor holds an option to acquire the majority of shares in the investee, which is not currently exercisable. However, the option is exercisable before the next scheduled shareholder meeting, and before the next special shareholder meeting could be held (based on the investee's governance policies).

When considering solely the exercise period, the investor's option would be a substantive right that gives the investor power (since it would give the holder a majority of shares). This is because the investor *does have* the current ability to direct the investee's relevant activities when decisions need to be made, i.e. at the next scheduled shareholder meeting or next special shareholder meeting.

However, when concluding whether an investor has power over the investee in real fact patterns, all relevant facts and circumstances would be considered, to evaluate whether the option is substantive, not solely the exercise period.

In contrast, if the next shareholders' meeting occurs (or could be held) before the option is exercisable, that option would not be a right that would give the holder the current ability to direct the investee's activities (and therefore would not give the holder power). This is consistent with the conclusion for Scenario D in Example 6.7 at 4.2.1 above.

IFRS 10 does not contain separate requirements for different types of potential voting rights; that is, employee options are subject to the same requirements as those that are held by a third party. However, it would be unlikely that an option held by an employee would give that employee power (or control) over an investee in practice, usually because the employee options represent a small percentage of the outstanding shares, even if exercised. However, in a very small, privately owned entity it would be possible for an employee (such as a member of management) to have power, if an option gives the employee the current ability to direct the relevant activities, or if the employee has other interests in the investee.

It should be noted that the IASB considered, but did not change, similar requirements in IAS 28 related to how options are considered when evaluating whether an investor has significant influence. That is, IAS 28 does not incorporate the IFRS 10 concept of evaluating whether an option is substantive (see Chapter 11 at 4.4). Accordingly, an option might give power under IFRS 10, but the same option might not result in significant influence under IAS 28.

Simply holding a currently exercisable option that, if exercised, would give the investor more than half of the voting rights in an investee is not sufficient to demonstrate control of the investee. All facts and circumstances must be considered to assess whether an investor has power over an investee, including whether an option is substantive (including, but not limited to consideration of the exercise period). This may require considerable judgement to be exercised.

4.3.5 Contractual arrangement with other vote holders

A contractual arrangement between an investor and other vote holders can give the investor the right to exercise voting rights sufficient to give the investor power, even if the investor does not have voting rights sufficient to give it power without the contractual arrangement. However, a contractual arrangement might ensure that the investor can direct enough other vote holders on how to vote to enable the investor to make decisions about the relevant activities. *[IFRS 10.B39]*.

It should be noted that the contractual arrangement has to ensure that investor can direct the other party to vote as required. Where the arrangement is merely that the parties agree to vote the same way, that would only represent joint control; defined as the contractually agreed sharing of control of an arrangement, which exists only when decisions about the relevant activities require the unanimous consent of the parties sharing control. *[IFRS 11 Appendix A]*. Joint control is discussed in more detail in Chapter 12 at 4.

In some jurisdictions, investors holding a certain number of issued shares of a public company may be able to obtain proxy votes from other shareholders by public request or other means for voting at shareholder meetings. The question as to whether the investor has the ability to obtain a majority of votes (and hence power over an investee) through control of proxy votes will depend on the specific facts and circumstances of the process such as, for example, the investor's freedom to use the proxy vote and whether any statements of voting intent must be provided by the investor as a condition of obtaining the proxy vote. A situation where, for example, proxies must be requested each year would make it more difficult to demonstrate that the investor had power as a result of its ability to obtain proxy votes.

4.3.6 Additional rights from other contractual arrangements

Other decision-making rights, in combination with voting rights, can give an investor the current ability to direct the relevant activities. For example, the rights specified in a contractual arrangement in combination with voting rights may be sufficient to give an investor the current ability to direct the manufacturing processes of an investee or to direct other operating or financing activities of an investee that significantly affect the investee's returns. However, in the absence of any other rights, economic dependence of an investee on the investor (such as relations of a supplier with its main customer) does not lead to the investor having power over the investee. *[IFRS 10.B40]*.

Example 6.18 below reflects an example from IFRS 10 of a situation where an investor with less than a majority of the voting rights is considered to have power of the investee, taking into account rights under a contractual arrangement. *[IFRS 10.B43 Example 5]*.

Example 6.18:   *Less than a majority of voting rights combined with additional rights under a contractual arrangement*

Investor A holds 40% of the voting rights of an investee and twelve other investors each hold 5% of the voting rights of the investee. A shareholder agreement grants investor A the right to appoint, remove and set the remuneration of management responsible for directing the relevant activities. To change the agreement, a two-thirds majority vote of the shareholders is required. In this case, investor A concludes that the absolute size of the investor's holding and the relative size of the other shareholdings alone are not conclusive in determining whether the investor has rights sufficient to give it power. However, investor A determines that its contractual right to appoint, remove and set the remuneration of management is sufficient to conclude that it has power over the investee. The fact that investor A might not have exercised this right or the likelihood of investor A exercising its right to select, appoint or remove management shall not be considered when assessing whether investor A has power.

4.4   Contractual arrangements

Power stems from existing rights. Sometimes, the relevant activities are not directed through voting rights, but rather, are directed by other means, such as through one or more contractual arrangements. *[IFRS 10.11]*. For example, an investor might have the contractual ability to direct manufacturing processes, operating activities, or determine financing of an investee through a contract or other arrangement.

Similarly, when voting rights cannot have a significant effect on an investee's returns, such as when voting rights relate to administrative tasks only and contractual arrangements determine the direction of the relevant activities, the investor needs to assess those contractual arrangements in order to determine whether it has rights sufficient to give it power over the investee. To determine whether an investor has rights sufficient to give it power, the investor considers the purpose and design of the investee (see paragraphs B5-B8 of IFRS 10 discussed at 3.2 above) and the requirements in paragraphs B51-B54 (discussed below) together with paragraphs B18-B20 (see 4.5 below). *[IFRS 10.B17]*.

When these contractual arrangements involve activities that are closely related to the investee, then these activities are, in substance, an integral part of the investee's overall activities, even though they may occur outside the legal boundaries of the investee. Therefore, explicit or implicit decision-making rights embedded in contractual arrangements that are closely related to the investee need to be considered as relevant activities when determining power over the investee. *[IFRS 10.B52]*.

When identifying which investor, if any, has power over an investee, it is important to review the contractual arrangements that the investor and the investee entered into. This analysis should include the original formation documents and governance documents of the investee, as well as the marketing materials provided to investors and other contractual arrangements entered into by the investee.

It is common that the relevant activities of a structured entity are directed by contractual arrangement. This is discussed further at 4.4.1 below.

4.4.1 Structured entities

IFRS 12 defines a structured entity as an entity that has been designed so that voting or similar rights are not the dominant factor in deciding who controls the entity, such as when any voting rights relate to administrative tasks only and the relevant activities are directed by means of contractual arrangements. *[IFRS 12 Appendix A]*. Therefore, an entity that is controlled by voting rights is not a structured entity. Accordingly, although it might be thought that an entity that receives funding from third parties following a restructuring is a structured entity, this would not be the case, if that entity continues to be controlled by voting rights after the restructuring. *[IFRS 12.B24]*.

A structured entity often has some or all of the following features:
- restricted activities;
- a narrow and well-defined objective, such as:
  - holding a tax-efficient lease;
  - carrying out research and development activities;
  - funding an entity; or
  - providing investment opportunities for investors by passing on risks and rewards associated with assets to investors;
- insufficient equity to finance its activities without subordinated financial support; and
- financing in the form of multiple contractually-linked instruments to investors that create concentrations of credit or other risks (tranches). *[IFRS 12.B22]*.

Examples of structured entities include:
- securitisation vehicles;
- asset-backed financings; and
- some investment funds. *[IFRS 12.B23]*.

Management needs to evaluate whether it controls a structured entity using the same approach as for 'traditional entities' (those that are controlled through voting rights). That is, management evaluates whether an investor has power over the relevant activities, exposure to variable returns and the ability to affect those returns through its power over the structured entity, as shown in the diagram at 3.1 above. Frequently, as discussed above, the relevant activities of a structured entity are directed by contractual arrangement.

For some investees, relevant activities occur only when particular circumstances arise or events occur. The investee may be designed so that the direction of its activities and its returns are predetermined unless and until those particular circumstances arise or events occur. In this case, only the decisions about the investee's activities when those circumstances or events occur can significantly affect its returns and thus be relevant activities. The circumstances or events need not have occurred for an investor with the ability to make those decisions to have power. The fact that the right to make decisions is contingent on circumstances arising or an event occurring does not, in itself, make those rights protective. *[IFRS 10.B53]*.

This is illustrated in Example 6.19 below, which is summarised from an example included in IFRS 10. *[IFRS 10.B53 Example 11].*

Example 6.19: Power through contractual arrangements

An investee's only business activity, as specified in its founding documents, is to purchase receivables and service them on a day-to-day basis for its investor. The servicing includes collecting the principal and interest payments as they fall due and passing them on to the investor. For any receivable in default, the investee is required to automatically put the receivable in default to the investor, as contractually agreed in the put agreement between the investor and the investee.

The relevant activity is managing the receivables in default because it is the only activity that can significantly affect the investee's returns. Managing the receivables before default is not a relevant activity because it does not require substantive decisions to be made that could significantly affect the investee's returns – the activities before default are predetermined and amount only to collecting cash flows as they fall due and passing them on to investors.

The purpose and design of the investee gives the investor decision-making authority over the relevant activity. The terms of the put agreement are integral to the overall transaction and the establishment of the investee. Therefore, the put agreement, together with the founding documents of the investee, gives the investor power over the investee. This is the case, even though:

- the investor takes ownership of the receivables only in the event of default; and
- the investor's exposures to variable returns are *not* technically derived from the investee (because the receivables in default are no longer owned by the investee and are managed outside the legal boundaries of the investee).

To conclude whether the investor has control, it would also need to assess whether the other two criteria are met, i.e. it has exposure to variable returns from its involvement with the investee (see 5 below) and the ability to use its power over the investee to affect the amount of its returns (see 6 below). *[IFRS 10.7, B2].*

IFRS 10 also includes a much simpler example where the only assets of an investee are receivables and when the purpose and design of the investee are considered, it is determined that the only relevant activity is managing the receivables upon default. In this situation, the party that has the ability to manage the defaulting receivables has power over the investee, irrespective of whether any of the borrowers have defaulted. *[IFRS 10.B53 Example 12].*

An investor may have an explicit or implicit commitment to ensure that an investee continues to operate as designed. Such a commitment may increase the investor's exposure to variability of returns and thus increase the incentive for the investor to obtain rights sufficient to give it power. Therefore, a commitment to ensure that an investee operates as designed may be an indicator that the investor has power, but does not, by itself, give an investor power, nor does it prevent another party from having power. *[IFRS 10.B54].*

Notwithstanding the fact that the same approach is used to evaluate control for structured entities and traditional entities, it is still important to identify which entities are structured entities. This is because certain disclosure requirements of IFRS 12 apply only to structured entities, as discussed in Chapter 13.

4.5 Other evidence of power

In some circumstances, it may be difficult to determine whether an investor's rights give it power over an investee. In such cases, the investor considers other evidence that it has the current ability to direct an investee's relevant activities unilaterally. Consideration is given, but is not limited, to the following factors, which, when considered together with its rights, the indicators of a special relationship with the investee and the extent of the investor's exposure to variability of returns (see below), may provide evidence that the investor's rights are sufficient to give it power over the investee:

- the investor can, without having the contractual right to do so, appoint, approve or nominate the investee's key management personnel (or Board of Directors) who have the ability to direct the relevant activities;
- the investor can, without having the contractual right to do so, direct the investee to enter into, or veto any changes to, significant transactions for the benefit of the investor;
- the investor can dominate either the nominations process for electing members of the investee's governing body, or obtaining proxies from other holders of voting rights;
- the investee's key management personnel are related parties of the investor (for example, the chief executive officer of the investee and the chief executive officer of the investor are the same person); or
- the majority of the members of the investee's governing body are related parties of the investor. [IFRS 10.B18].

When the above factors and the indicators set out below are considered together with an investor's rights, IFRS 10 requires that greater weight is given to the evidence of power described above. [IFRS 10.B21]. Sometimes, there will be indications that an investor has a special relationship with the investee, which suggests that the investor has more than a passive interest in the investee. The existence of any individual indicator, or a particular combination of indicators, does not necessarily mean that the power criterion is met. However, having more than a passive interest in an investee may indicate that the investor has other rights that give it power over the investee or provide evidence of existing power over the investee. For example, IFRS 10 states that this might be the case when the investee:

- is directed by key management personnel who are current or previous employees of the investor;
- has significant:
  - obligations that are guaranteed by the investor; or
  - activities that either involve or are conducted on behalf of the investor;
- depends on the investor for:
  - funds for a significant portion of its operations;
  - licenses, trademarks, services, technology, supplies or raw materials that are critical to the investee's operations; or
  - key management personnel, such as when the investor's personnel have specialised knowledge of the investee's operations; or
- the investor's exposure, or rights, to returns from its involvement with the investee is disproportionately greater than its voting or other similar rights. For example, there may be a situation in which an investor is entitled, or exposed, to more than half of the returns of the investee but holds less than half of the voting rights of the investee. [IFRS 10.B19].

As noted at 4.2.3 above, the greater an investor's exposure, or rights, to variability of returns from its involvement with an investee, the greater is the incentive for the investor to obtain rights sufficient to give it power. Therefore, having a large exposure to variability of returns is an indicator that the investor may have power. However, the extent of the investor's exposure does not, in itself, determine whether an investor has power over the investee. *[IFRS 10.B20]*.

4.6 Determining whether sponsoring (designing) a structured entity gives power

IFRS 10 discusses whether sponsoring (that is, designing) a structured entity gives an investor power over the structured entity.

In assessing the purpose and design of an investee, an investor considers the involvement and decisions made at the investee's inception as part of its design and evaluate whether the transaction terms and features of the involvement provide the investor with rights that are sufficient to give it power. Being involved in the design of an investee alone is not sufficient to give an investor control. However, involvement in the design may indicate that the investor had the opportunity to obtain rights that are sufficient to give it power over the investee. *[IFRS 10.B51]*.

An investor's involvement in the design of an investee does not mean that the investor necessarily has control, even if that involvement was significant. Rather, an investor has control of an investee when all three criteria of control are met (see 3.1 above), considering the purpose and design of the investee. Thus, an investor's involvement in the design of an investee is part of the context when concluding if it controls the investee, but is not determinative.

In our view, there are relatively few structured entities that have no substantive decision-making. That is, virtually all structured entities have some level of decision-making and few, if any, are on 'autopilot' (see 4.1.2 above). In such cases, if that decision-making can significantly affect the returns of the structured entity, the investor with the rights to make those decisions would have power. This is because IFRS 10 clarifies that an investor has power when it has existing rights that give it the current ability to direct the relevant activities, even if those relevant activities only occur when particular circumstances arise or specific events occur (see 4.1.1 above).

However, a structured entity with limited decision-making requires additional scrutiny to determine which investor, if any, has power (and possibly control) over the structured entity, particularly for the investors that have a potentially significant explicit or implicit exposure to variable returns. Careful consideration is required regarding the purpose and design of the structured entity.

In addition, the evaluation of power may require an analysis of the decisions made at inception of the structured entity, including a review of the structured entity's governing documents, because the decisions made at formation may affect which investor, if any, has power.

For a structured entity with a limited range of activities, such as certain securitisation entities, power is assessed based on which activities, if any, significantly affect the structured entity's returns, and if so, which investor, if any, has existing rights that give it the current ability to direct those activities. The following considerations may also be relevant when determining which investor, if any, has power (and possibly control):

- an investor's ability to direct the activities of a structured entity only when specific circumstances arise or events occur may constitute power if that ability relates to the activities that most significantly affect the structured entity's returns (see 4.1.1 above);
- an investor does not have to actively exercise its power to have power over a structured entity (see 4.2.1 above); or
- an investor is more incentivised to obtain power over a structured entity the greater its obligation to absorb losses or its right to receive benefits from the structured entity (see 4.2.3 above).

5 EXPOSURE TO VARIABLE RETURNS

The second criterion for assessing whether an investor has control of an investee is determining whether the investor has an exposure, or has rights, to variable returns from its involvement with the investee. *[IFRS 10.B55]*. An investor is exposed, or has rights, to variable returns from its involvement with the investee when the investor's returns from its involvement have the potential to vary as a result of the investee's performance. Returns can be positive, negative or both. *[IFRS 10.15]*.

Although only one investor can control an investee, more than one party can share in the returns of an investee. For example, holders of non-controlling interests can share in the profits or distributions of an investee. *[IFRS 10.16]*.

Variable returns are returns that are not fixed and have the potential to vary as a result of the performance of an investee. As discussed at 5.2 below, returns that appear fixed can be variable. *[IFRS 10.B56]*.

Examples of exposures to variable returns include:

- dividends, fixed interest on debt securities that expose the investor to the credit risk of the issuer (see 5.2 below), variable interest on debt securities, other distributions of economic benefits and changes in the value of an investment in an investee;
- remuneration for servicing an investee's assets or liabilities, fees and exposure to loss from providing credit or liquidity support, residual interests in the investee's assets and liabilities on liquidation of that investee, tax benefits and access to future liquidity that an investor has from its involvement with the investee; and
- economies of scale, cost savings, scarce products, proprietary knowledge, synergies, or other exposures to variable returns that are not available to other investors. *[IFRS 10.B57]*.

Simply having an exposure to variable returns from its involvement with an investee does not mean that the investor has control. To control the investee, the investor would also need to have power over the investee, and the ability to use its power over the investee to affect the amount of the investor's returns. *[IFRS 10.7]*. For example, it is common for a lender to have an exposure to variable returns from a borrower through interest payments that it receives from the borrower, that are subject to credit risk.

However, the lender would not control the borrower if it does not have the ability to affect those interest payments (which is frequently the case).

It should be emphasised that with respect to this criterion, the focus is on the existence of an exposure to variable returns, not the amount of the exposure to variable returns.

5.1 Exposure to variable returns can be an indicator of power

Exposure to variable returns can be an indicator of power by the investor. This is because the greater an investor's exposure to the variability of returns from its involvement with an investee, the greater the incentive for the investor to obtain rights that give the investor power. However, the magnitude of the exposure to variable returns is not determinative of whether the investor holds power. *[IFRS 10.B20]*.

When an investor's exposure, or rights, to variable returns from its involvement with the investee are disproportionately greater than its voting or other similar rights, this might be an indicator that the investor has power over the investee when considered with other rights. *[IFRS 10.B19, B20]*.

5.2 Returns that appear fixed can be variable

An investor assesses whether exposures to returns from an investee are variable, based on the substance of the arrangement (regardless of the legal form of the returns). Even a return that appears fixed may actually be variable.

IFRS 10 gives the example of an investor that holds a bond with fixed interest payments. The fixed interest payments are considered an exposure to variable returns, because they are subject to default risk and they expose the investor to the credit risk of the issuer of the bond. How variable those returns are depends on the credit risk of the bond. The same logic would extend to the investor's ability to recover the principal of the bond. *[IFRS 10.B56]*.

Similarly, IFRS 10 also explains that fixed performance fees earned for managing an investee's assets are considered an exposure to variable returns, because they expose the investor to the performance risk of the investee. That is, the amount of variability depends on the investee's ability to generate sufficient income to pay the fee. *[IFRS 10.B56]*. Performance fees that vary based on the value of an investee's assets are also an exposure to variable returns using the same reasoning.

In contrast, a non-refundable fee received up-front (wherein the investor does not have exposure to credit risk or performance risk) would likely be considered a fixed return.

5.3 Evaluating whether derivatives provide an exposure to variable returns

Investors need to evaluate whether being party to a derivative gives them an exposure to a variable return.

As indicated at 3.2 above, an investee may be designed so that voting rights are not the dominant factor in deciding who controls the investee, such as when any voting rights relate to administrative tasks only and the relevant activities are directed by means of contractual arrangements. In such cases, an investor's consideration of the purpose and design of the investee shall also include consideration of the risks to which the investee was designed to be exposed, the risks that it was designed to pass on to the parties involved with the investee and whether the investor is exposed to some or all of these risks. Consideration of the risks includes not only the downside risk, but also the potential for upside. *[IFRS 10.B8]*.

When evaluating whether being party to a derivative is an exposure to a variable return, it is helpful to follow these steps:

- analyse the nature of the risks in the investee – for example, assess whether the purpose and the design of the investee exposes the investor to the following risks:
  - credit risk;
  - interest rate risk (including prepayment risk);
  - foreign currency exchange risk;
  - commodity price risk;
  - equity price risk; and
  - operational risk;
- determine the purpose(s) for which the investee was created – for example, obtain an understanding of the following:
  - activities of the investee;
  - terms of the contracts the investee has entered into;
  - nature of the investee's interests issued;
  - how the investee's interests were negotiated with or marketed to potential investors; and
  - which investors participated significantly in the design or redesign of the entity; and
- determine the variability that the investee is designed to create and pass along to its interest holders – considering the nature of the risks of the investee and the purposes for which the investee was created.

Some might argue that any derivative creates an exposure to variable returns, even if that exposure is only a positive exposure. However, we do not believe that this was the IASB's intention, given the following comments made by the IASB in both the Basis for Conclusions accompanying IFRS 10 and the Application Guidance of IFRS 12.

'Some instruments are designed to transfer risk from a reporting entity to another entity. During its deliberations, the Board concluded that such instruments create variability of returns for the other entity but do not typically expose the reporting entity to variability of returns from the performance of the other entity. For example, assume an entity (entity A) is established to provide investment opportunities for investors who wish to have exposure to entity Z's credit risk (entity Z is unrelated to any other party involved in the arrangement). Entity A obtains funding by issuing to those investors notes that are linked to entity Z's credit risk (credit-linked notes) and uses the proceeds to invest in a portfolio of risk-free financial assets. Entity A obtains exposure to entity Z's credit risk by entering into a credit default swap (CDS) with a swap counterparty. The CDS passes entity Z's credit risk to entity A, in return for a fee paid by the swap counterparty. The investors in entity A receive a higher return that reflects both entity A's return from its asset portfolio and the CDS fee. The swap counterparty does not have involvement with entity A that exposes it to variability of returns from the performance of entity A because the CDS transfers variability to entity A, rather than absorbing variability of returns of entity A.' [IFRS 10.BC66, IFRS 12.B9].

This principle is applied in the following example.

Example 6.20:   Derivatives that create risk for an investee

A structured entity (Entity A) enters into a CDS whereby a bank passes the credit risk of a reference asset to the structured entity and, hence, to the investors of that structured entity. In this example, if the bank has the power to amend the referenced credit risk in the CDS, it would have power over a relevant activity. However, as the bank, through the CDS, creates rather than absorbs risk, the bank is not exposed to a variable return. Consequently, the bank would not be able to use its power to affect its variable returns and so would not control the structured entity.

In our view, a derivative that introduces risk to an investee (e.g. a structured entity) would not normally be considered an exposure to variable returns under IFRS 10. Only a derivative that exposes a counterparty to risks that the investee was designed to create and pass on would be considered an exposure to variable returns under IFRS 10. This view is consistent with the IASB's intentions.

5.3.1   Plain vanilla foreign exchange swaps and interest rate swaps

It is important to consider the purpose and design of the entity when evaluating whether a plain vanilla foreign exchange or interest rate swap should be considered a creator or absorber of variable returns. It is our view that an exposure to variable returns generally absorbs the variability created by the investee's assets, liabilities or other contracts, and the risks the investee was designed to pass along to its investors. Therefore, if a derivative is entered into to reduce the variability of a structured entity's cash flows (such as might arise from movements in foreign currency or interest rates), it is not intended to absorb the cash flows of the entity. Instead, the derivative is entered into to align the cash flows of the assets of the structured entity with those of the investors and so reduce the risks to which the investors in the structured entity are exposed. Accordingly, the counterparty would not have an exposure to a variable return.

Meanwhile, a counterparty to a foreign exchange or interest rate swap typically has a senior claim on any cash flows due under the swap relative to any note holders. Consequently, it is unlikely to be exposed to the credit risk of the assets held by the structured entity, or else that risk will be deemed to be insignificant (i.e. losses on the assets would need to be so large that there would be insufficient funds in the structured entity to settle the derivatives).

However, if payments on a swap were subordinate to the rights of note holders, or contractually referenced to the performance of the underlying assets in the structured entity, the counterparty is exposed to the risk associated with the performance of the underlying assets (i.e. the risk that the structured entity may be unable to fulfil its obligations under the swap). In that case, if the swap counterparty had power over the structured entity because it has the ability to manage its assets, it is likely that it would be deemed to have the ability to affect its variable returns and so would control the structured entity.

The above principles are illustrated in Example 6.21 below.

Example 6.21: **Structured entity that enters into foreign currency and interest rate swaps**

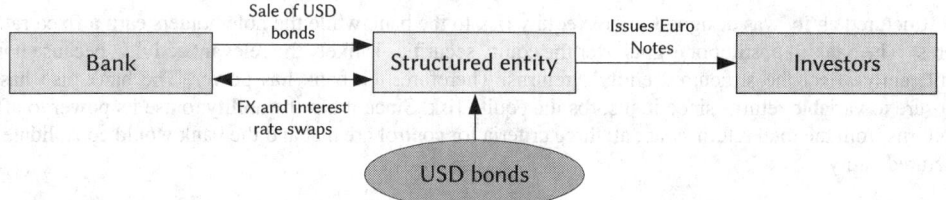

A bank designs a structured entity to meet the requirements of European investors, who wish to be exposed to US corporate bonds without the foreign exchange risk. The structured entity buys dollar-denominated debt securities through the bank, issues Euro-denominated notes and hedges the cash flow differences through a series of swaps entered into with the bank. Subsequently, the structured entity collects and pays the resultant cash flows. The bonds will be held by the structured entity until maturity and cannot be substituted. The bank manages the assets, including in the event of their default and earns a fixed fee for its services. The right to receive the fee ranks more senior than the notes.

Most of the activities of the structured entity are predetermined. It is possible that the relevant activity is the management of the assets in the event of default as discussed at 4.1.4 above. If this is the case, power is held by the bank, since it has the existing rights that give it the current ability to direct this activity. In evaluating the bank's exposure to variable returns from its involvement with the structured entity:

- the foreign currency and interest rate risks were not risks that the structured entity was designed to be exposed to or to pass on to the bank;
- the bank's exposure to movements in foreign exchange and interest rate risks is not affected by its power over the relevant activity;
- the fixed fee that the bank earns is not considered a variable return as its payment is unlikely to be affected by the credit risk of the bonds; and
- the bank's exposure to potential credit risk on its derivatives is considered insignificant, as that risk would only arise if losses on the bonds were so large that there were insufficient funds in the structured entity to settle the derivatives.

In conclusion, even if the bank has power by virtue of managing the defaults (i.e. the relevant activity), the bank has no exposure to variable returns, and thus does not control the structured entity and so would not consolidate it.

5.3.2 Total return swaps

The principles discussed at 5.3.1 above are also relevant where a structured entity enters into a total return swap, since the swap creates an equal, but opposite risk to each party, as illustrated in Example 6.22 below.

Example 6.22: **Structured entity that enters into a total return swap**

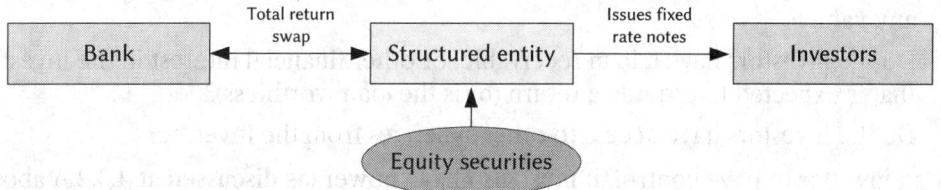

A structured entity acquires a portfolio of equity securities from the market, issues fixed rate notes to investors and hedges the mismatch in cash flows between the equity securities and the notes through entering into a total return swap with a bank. The choice of equity securities that make up the portfolio is pre-agreed by the bank and the note investors. However, the bank also has substitution rights over the equity securities held by the structured entity within certain parameters. The terms of this swap are that the structured entity pays the bank any increase in value of the securities and any dividends received from them, while the bank pays the structured entity any decline in the value of the securities and interest at a fixed rate.

The structured entity was designed to give equity risk to the bank while the note holders earn a fixed rate of interest. The bank's substitution rights over the equity securities is likely the relevant activity, because it may significantly affect the structured entity's returns. Therefore, the bank has power. The bank also has an exposure to variable returns since it absorbs the equity risk. Since it has the ability to use its power to affect its returns from the total return swap, all three criteria for control are met and the bank would consolidate the structured entity.

5.4 Exposures to variable returns not directly received from an investee

When identifying an exposure to variable returns, an investor must include all variable returns resulting from its investment including not only those directly received from the investee but also returns generated as a result of the investment that are not available to other interest holders. *[IFRS 10.B57]*.

Generally, the focus is on the variable returns that are generated by the investee. However, depending on the purpose and design of the arrangements and the investee, when the investor receives variable returns that are not generated by the investee, but stem from involvement with the investee, these variable returns are also considered.

Examples of such variable returns include using assets in combination with the assets of the investee, such as combining operating functions to achieve economies of scale, cost savings, sourcing scarce products, gaining access to proprietary knowledge or limiting some operations or assets, to enhance the value of the investor's other assets. *[IFRS 10.B57(c)]*.

5.5 Exposure to variable returns in bankruptcy filings

As discussed at 4.3.2.A above, evaluating whether an investor has control when its investee files for bankruptcy requires the exercise of judgement based on the facts and circumstances. Part of the assessment includes an evaluation of whether the investor has an exposure to variable returns from the investee once the investee files for bankruptcy. For example, based on the requirements for the particular type of bankruptcy in the relevant jurisdiction:

- Is the investee restricted from paying dividends to the investors upon filing for bankruptcy?
- Are the investors exposed to a variable return through their interests in the investee, notwithstanding the bankruptcy (e.g. do shares in the investee retain any value)?
- Do the investors have a loan receivable, or other financial interest in the investee, that is expected to provide a return (or is the loan worthless)?
- Do the investors have access to other synergies from the investee?

For an investor to have control, it must also have power (as discussed at 4.3.2.A above) and the ability to use its power over the investee to affect the amount of the investor's returns (see 6 below).

5.6 Interaction of IFRS 10 with the derecognition requirements in IFRS 9

In evaluating whether an entity has an exposure to the variable returns of a structured entity, it is also necessary to consider the interaction with the derecognition requirements set out in IFRS 9 (see Chapter 52). Specifically, it is relevant to consider the impact of whether or not the transfer criteria have been satisfied by the transferor on whether a transferor has exposure to variable returns arising from its involvement with a structured entity. The following example will help illustrate this issue.

Example 6.23: Structured entity that enters into a total return swap with the transferor

Assume the same facts as in Example 6.22 at 5.3.2 above, except that the bank originally sold the equity securities to the structured entity (rather than the structured entity acquired the equity securities from the market).

As the bank has, through the total return swap, retained substantially all of the risks and rewards of ownership of the securities, it would not derecognise them. Consequently, the structured entity would not recognise the securities but, instead recognises a loan to the bank, collateralised by the securities. As the bank has not derecognised the securities, it has no variable return from its involvement with the structured entity. Hence, it does not have control of the structured entity and would not consolidate it. The investors have no power over the structured entity, so none of the investors would consolidate it either.

5.7 Reputational risk

The term 'reputational risk' often refers to the risk that failure of an entity could damage the reputation of an investor or sponsor. To protect its reputation, the investor or sponsor might be compelled to provide support to the failing entity, even though it has no legal or contractual obligation to do so. During the financial crisis, some financial institutions stepped in and provided financing for securitisation vehicles that they sponsored, and in some cases took control of these vehicles. The IASB concluded that reputational risk is not an indicator of power in its own right, but may increase an investor's incentive to secure rights that give the investor power over an investee. Accordingly, reputational risk alone would not be regarded as a source of variable returns and so would not require a bank to consolidate a structured entity that it sponsors. *[IFRS 10.BC37-BC39]*.

6 LINK BETWEEN POWER AND RETURNS: PRINCIPAL-AGENCY SITUATIONS

The third criterion for having control is that the investor must have the ability to use its power over the investee to affect the amount of the investor's returns. *[IFRS 10.7]*. An investor controls an investee if the investor not only has power over the investee and exposure or rights to variable returns from its involvement with the investee, but also has the ability to use its power to affect the investor's returns from its involvement with the investee. *[IFRS 10.17]*.

Thus, an investor with decision-making rights shall determine whether it is a principal or an agent. An investor that is an agent in accordance with paragraphs B58-B72 of IFRS 10 does not control an investee when it exercises decision-making rights delegated to it. *[IFRS 10.18]*. This is discussed further at 6.1 below.

In January 2015, the Interpretations Committee noted that a fund manager that concludes that it is an agent in accordance with IFRS 10 should then assess whether it has significant influence in accordance with the guidance in IAS 28.[8] See Chapter 11 at 4.

The link between power over an investee and exposure to variable returns from involvement with the investee is essential to having control. An investor that has power over an investee, but cannot benefit from that power, does not control that investee. An investor that has an exposure to a variable return from an investee, but cannot use its power to direct the activities that most significantly affect the investee's returns, does not control that investee. This is illustrated in Example 6.24 below.

Example 6.24: Link between power and returns is essential for control

A structured entity is created and financed by debt instruments held by a senior lender and a subordinated lender and a minimal equity investment from the sponsor. The subordinated lender transferred receivables to the structured entity. Managing the receivables in default is the only activity of the structured entity that causes its returns to vary, and this power has been given to the subordinated lender by contract. The subordinated loan is designed to absorb the first losses and to receive any residual return from the structured entity. The senior lender has exposure to variable returns due to the credit risk of the structured entity.

When analysing which investor, if any, has control the first step is to identify the relevant activities. In this example, managing the receivables in default is the only activity of the structured entity that causes its returns to vary. Therefore, it would be the relevant activity. The next step is to determine which investor, if any, has the current ability to direct that relevant activity. In this example, the subordinated lender has the power that it was granted by contract. The subordinated lender is exposed to variable returns from its involvement with the structured entity through its subordinated debt. The subordinated lender has the ability to affect those returns through its power to manage the receivables in default. Since all three elements of control are present, the subordinated lender has control over the structured entity. This evaluation is made in the context of understanding the structured entity's purpose and design.

While the senior lender's exposure to variable returns is affected by the structured entity's activities, the senior lender has no power to direct those activities. Thus, the senior lender does *not* control the structured entity, because it is missing two of the elements of control.

6.1 Delegated power: principals and agents

When decision-making rights have been delegated or are being held for the benefit of others, it is necessary to assess whether the decision-maker is a principal or an agent to determine whether it has control. This is because if that decision-maker has been delegated rights that give the decision-maker power, it must be assessed whether those rights give the decision-maker power for its own benefit, or merely power for the benefit of others. An agent is a party primarily engaged to act on behalf of another party or parties (the principal(s)), and therefore does not control the investee when it exercises its decision-making powers. *[IFRS 10.B58]*. As an agent does not control the investee, it does not consolidate the investee. *[IFRS 10.18]*.

While principal-agency situations often occur in the asset management and banking industries, they are not limited to those industries. Entities in the construction, real estate and extractive industries also frequently delegate powers when carrying out their business. This is especially common when an investee is set up and one of the investors (often the lead investor) is delegated powers by the other investors to carry out activities for the investee. Assessing whether the lead investor is making decisions as a principal, or simply carrying out the decisions made by all the investors (i.e. acting as an agent) will be critical to the assessment.

An investor may delegate decision-making authority to an agent on some specific issues or on all relevant activities, but, ultimately, the investor as principal retains the power. This is because the investor treats the decision-making rights delegated to its agent as held by the investor directly. *[IFRS 10.B59]*. Accordingly, a decision-maker that is not an agent is a principal. However, it should be noted that:

- a decision-maker is not an agent simply because others benefit from the decisions that it makes; *[IFRS 10.B58]* and
- an obligation to act in the best interest of those who have delegated the power does not prevent the decision-maker from being a principal.

The terms and conditions of the arrangement are considered to assess whether an entity is an agent or a principal. The determination of whether a decision-maker is an agent or a principal is made based on the following:

- scope of decision-making authority;
- rights held by other parties (e.g. existence of removal rights);
- remuneration of the decision-maker; and
- exposure to variability of returns through other interests. *[IFRS 10.B60]*.

Each of these factors is discussed in more detail below. When reaching a conclusion, each of the factors is weighted according to the facts and circumstances of each case, *[IFRS 10.B60]*, which will require judgement. The only situation that is conclusive by itself is when removal rights are held by a single investor and the decision-maker can be removed without cause. *[IFRS 10.B61]*. This is discussed in more detail at 6.3 below. Accordingly, although each of the factors are discussed in isolation below, a conclusion should be based on all of the factors considered together. Of the four factors that need to be considered when assessing whether the decision-maker is acting as principal or agent, generally it will be the rights held by third parties to remove the decision-maker (see 6.3 below) and the exposure to variability of returns (see 6.5 below) that will require careful consideration.

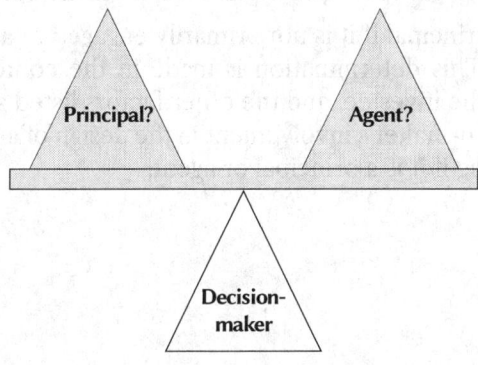

6.2 Scope of decision-making

To assess whether a decision-maker is a principal or an agent, the scope of its authority is evaluated by considering both:

- the activities that the decision-maker is permitted to direct (e.g. by agreement or by law); and
- the discretion that the decision-maker has when making decisions about those activities. [IFRS 10.B62].

It is implicit in the definition of control that, for a decision-maker to control the entity over which it has been delegated decision-making authority, the decision-maker must have power. This means that it must have been delegated the rights that give the current ability to direct the relevant activities (the activities that most significantly affect that investee's returns). If a decision-maker has been delegated rights that do not relate to the relevant activities, it would not have control over the investee.

For this reason, it is imperative to understand the purpose and design of the investee, the risks to which it was designed to be exposed and the risk it was designed to pass on to the other parties involved. Understanding the purpose and design of the investee often helps in assessing which rights were delegated, why they were delegated, and which rights have been retained by other parties, and why those rights were retained.

6.2.1 Involvement in design

IFRS 10 requires that a decision-maker considers the purpose and design of the investee, the risks to which the investee was designed to be exposed, the risks it was designed to pass on to the parties involved and the level of involvement the decision-maker had in the design of an investee. For example, if a decision-maker is significantly involved in the design of the investee (including in determining the scope of decision-making authority), that involvement may indicate that the decision-maker had the opportunity and incentive to obtain rights that result in the decision-maker having the ability to direct the relevant activities. [IFRS 10.B63].

However, a decision-maker's involvement in the design of an investee does not mean that decision-maker necessarily is a principal, even if that involvement was significant.

A decision-maker is a principal if it is not primarily engaged to act on behalf of and for the benefit of others. This determination is made in the context of considering the purpose and design of the investee, and the other factors listed at 6.1 above. While not determinative, a decision-maker's involvement in the design of an investee is part of the context when concluding if it is a principal or agent.

In our view, similar to the considerations for structured entities discussed at 4.6 above, when a decision-maker sponsors an investee and establishes certain decisions in the governing documents of the investee, there should be increased scrutiny as to whether that decision-maker is a principal or an agent with respect to the investee, particularly if the other factors are indicative of the decision-maker being a principal. However, when there are many parties involved in the design of an investee, the decisions established in the governing documents might be less relevant.

6.2.2 Assessing whether the scope of powers is narrow or broad

When evaluating whether a decision-maker is a principal or an agent, in considering the scope of its decision-making authority, it appears that a relevant factor is whether the scope of powers that have been delegated (and the discretion allotted) is narrow or broad. In an example in IFRS 10 where a decision-maker (fund manager) establishes, markets and manages a publicly traded, regulated fund according to narrowly defined parameters set out in the investment mandate, it is stated that this is a factor that indicates that the fund manager is an agent. *[IFRS 10.B72 Example 13]*. In another example, where the decision-maker (fund manager) has wide decision-making authority, it is implied that the extensive decision-making authority of the fund manager would be an indicator that it is a principal. *[IFRS 10.B72 Example 14-14A]*. This suggests that where the scope of powers is broad, this would be an indicator that the decision-maker is a principal. However, to conclude whether a decision-maker is an agent or a principal, the scope of power needs to be evaluated with the other three factors in totality.

6.3 Rights held by other parties

The decision-maker may be subject to rights held by other parties that may affect the decision-maker's ability to direct the relevant activities of the investee, such as rights of those parties to remove the decision-maker. Rights to remove are often referred to as 'kick-out' rights. Substantive removal rights may indicate that the decision-maker is an agent. *[IFRS 10.B64]*. Liquidation rights and redemption rights held by other parties, which may in substance be similar to removal rights, are discussed at 6.3.2 below.

Other substantive rights held by other parties that restrict a decision-maker's discretion are considered similarly to removal rights when evaluating whether the decision-maker is an agent. For example, a decision-maker that is required to obtain approval from a small number of other parties for its actions is generally an agent. *[IFRS 10.B66]*.

Figure 6.6: Evaluating rights to remove without cause

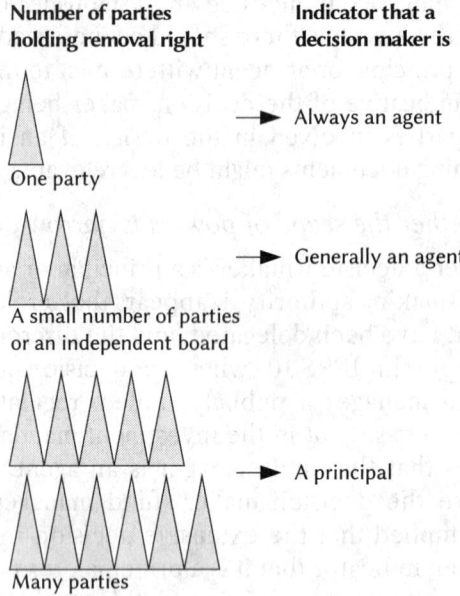

As shown in the diagram above, when a single investor holds substantive rights to remove the decision-maker without cause, that fact in isolation is sufficient to conclude that the decision-maker is an agent. *[IFRS 10.B65]*. That is, the decision-maker does not consolidate the entity.

However, if multiple investors hold such rights (i.e. no individual investor can remove the decision-maker without cause without the others), these rights would not, in isolation, determine whether a decision-maker is an agent or a principal. That is, all other facts and circumstances would need to be considered. The more parties that must act together to remove a decision-maker and the greater the magnitude of, and variability associated with, the decision-maker's other economic interests, the less weighting that is placed on the removal right. *[IFRS 10.B65]*. This is reflected in an example provided by IFRS 10 where there is a large number of widely dispersed unrelated third party investors. Although the decision-maker (the asset manager) can be removed, without cause, by a simple majority decision of the other investors, this is given little weighting in evaluating whether the decision-maker is a principal or agent. *[IFRS 10.B72 Example 15]*.

If an independent Board of Directors (or governing body), which is appointed by the other investors, holds a right to remove without cause, that would be an indicator that the decision-maker is an agent. *[IFRS 10.B23(b), B67]*. This is the position taken in an example in IFRS 10 (see Example 6.31 at 6.6 below) where a fund has a Board of Directors, all of whose members are independent of the decision-maker (the fund manager) and are appointed by the other investors. The Board of Directors appoints the fund manager annually. The example explains that the Board of Directors provides a mechanism to ensure that the investors can remove the fund manager if they decide to do so.

6.3.1 Evaluating whether a removal right is substantive

When evaluating removal rights, it is important to determine whether they are substantive, as discussed at 4.2.1 above. If the removal right is substantive, this may be an indicator that the decision-maker is an agent. [IFRS 10.B64]. On the other hand, if the removal right is not substantive, this may be an indicator that the decision-maker is a principal, but this indicator should be given less weight. The determination of whether the decision-maker is a principal needs to be based on the three other factors, i.e. scope of decision-making authority, remuneration and exposure to variability of returns through other interests.

Some of the criteria that might be more relevant when evaluating whether a removal right is substantive are shown in the diagram below. However, all of the factors noted at 4.2.1 above and IFRS 10 must be considered in this evaluation.

Figure 6.7:   Evaluating whether removal rights are substantive

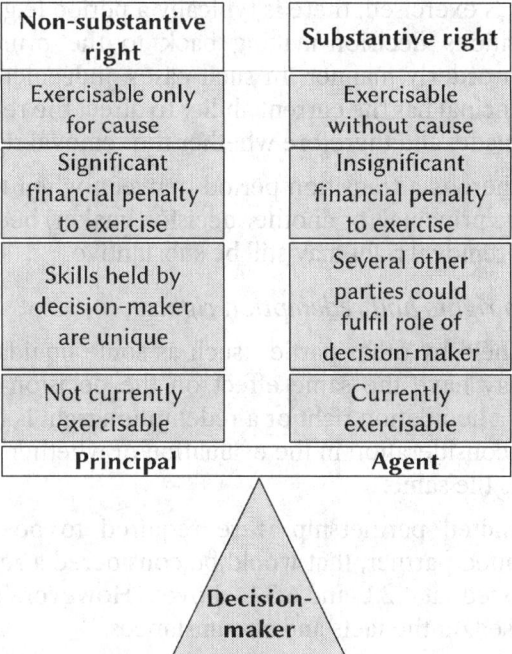

Evaluating whether a removal right is substantive will depend on facts and circumstances. [IFRS 10.B23].

6.3.1.A   Available replacements

When evaluating whether a removal right is substantive, consideration is given as to whether suitable replacements exist. This is because if there are no (or few) suitable replacements for the decision-maker, this would be an operational barrier that would likely prevent the parties holding the removal right from exercising that removal right. [IFRS 10.B23(a)(vi)].

In the asset management industry, suitable replacements are generally available. However, in other industries (e.g. construction, real estate, extractive), it is more common for the decision-maker to possess unique traits. For example, the decision-maker may have experience with a particular geographic location, local government, or proprietary intellectual property or tools. That might make it more difficult to assess whether there are other parties that could replace the decision-maker if the parties wanted to remove the decision-maker. However, regardless of the industry, an assessment of whether there are available replacements depends upon the specific facts and circumstances, and will require judgement.

6.3.1.B   Exercise period

A removal right may not be exercisable until a date in the future. In such cases, judgement must be exercised to determine whether (or when) that right becomes substantive. Similarly, when a removal right can only be exercised during a narrow period (e.g. for one day on the last day of the reporting period), judgement is necessary to determine whether the right is substantive.

When a removal right is exercised, there is typically a period (e.g. six months) until the decision-maker transitions decision-making back to the principal (or to another decision-maker) in an orderly manner. In such cases, judgement will be required to assess whether the principal has the current ability to direct the relevant activities when decisions need to be made, and therefore whether the removal right is substantive.

In our view, even if there is a transition period between when the decision-maker is removed and when the principal (or another decision-maker) becomes responsible for making decisions, the removal right may still be substantive.

6.3.2   Liquidation rights and redemption rights

In some cases, rights held by other parties (such as some liquidation rights and some redemption rights) may have the same effect on the decision-maker's authority as removal rights. When a liquidation right or a redemption right is in substance the same as a removal right, its consideration in the evaluation of whether a decision-maker is a principal or an agent is the same.

For example, if a limited partnership were required to be liquidated upon the withdrawal of one limited partner, that would be considered a removal right if it were substantive (as discussed at 4.2.1 and 6.3.1 above). However, such rights must be analysed carefully, based on the facts and circumstances.

6.4   Remuneration

The third factor to evaluate when assessing whether a decision-maker is a principal or an agent is remuneration.

The greater the magnitude of, and variability associated with, the decision-maker's remuneration relative to the returns expected from the activities of the investee, the more likely the decision-maker is a principal. *[IFRS 10.B68]*. Therefore, when determining if a decision-maker is a principal or an agent, the magnitude and variability of exposure to returns through remuneration are always considered. This applies even if the remuneration is at market rates. However, as discussed at 6.4.1 below, IFRS 10 does not include any examples of remuneration arrangements where it is clear the remuneration is of such significance that it, in isolation, indicates that the decision maker is a principal.

In determining whether it is a principal or an agent, the decision-maker also considers whether the following conditions exist:

(a) The remuneration of the decision-maker is commensurate with the services provided.

(b) The remuneration agreement includes only terms, conditions or amounts that are customarily present in arrangements for similar services and level of skills negotiated on an arm's length basis. *[IFRS 10.B69]*.

IFRS 10 states that a decision-maker cannot be an agent unless the conditions set out in (a) and (b) above are present. However, meeting those conditions in isolation is not sufficient to conclude that a decision-maker is an agent. *[IFRS 10.B70]*.

6.4.1 Evaluating remuneration in the asset management industry

When evaluating whether a decision-maker is a principal or an agent, an entity is required to evaluate the magnitude and the variability of the remuneration relative to the expected returns from the investee. In examples related to the asset management industry, IFRS 10 describes three common remuneration structures:

- 1% of net assets under management; *[IFRS 10.B72 Example 13]*
- 1% of assets under management and performance-related fees of 10% of profits if the investee's profits exceed a specified level; *[IFRS 10.B72 Example 15]* and
- 1% of assets under management and 20% of all the fund's profits if a specified profit level is achieved. *[IFRS 10.B72 Example 14]*.

In each case, the examples assume that the remuneration is commensurate with the services provided. In addition, the remuneration aligns the interests of the decision-maker with those of other investors. However, IFRS 10 concludes for each of these cases that the level of remuneration does not create an exposure to variable returns that is of such significance that, in isolation, it indicates that the fund manager is a principal. IFRS 10 does not include any examples of remuneration arrangements where the remuneration is of such significance that, in isolation, it does indicate that the fund manager is a principal. Additionally, IFRS 10 does not provide any examples of remuneration arrangements that are not market-based although this would always need to be assessed.

In our experience, in most asset management scenarios involving retail investors, management will be able to conclude that the remuneration is commensurate with services provided and only includes market terms. This is because otherwise, retail investors would take their business elsewhere.

As discussed at 6.4 above, a decision-maker cannot be an agent unless conditions (a) and (b) are met. However, meeting both criteria is not conclusive. The decision-maker must evaluate whether the magnitude and exposure to variable returns received through the remuneration, together with other factors, indicates that it is an agent or a principal.

6.4.2 Evaluating remuneration in other industries

IFRS 10 does not include any examples of principal-agency evaluations in the construction, real estate and extractive industries. In our view, in these industries, it is more common for the decision-maker to possess unique traits (see 6.3.1.A above). That might make it more difficult to assess whether the remuneration is commensurate with the skills provided and includes only market terms.

6.5 Exposure to variability of returns from other interests

When an investor has exposure to variable returns from its involvement with an investee (e.g. an investment in that investee, or provides a guarantee), and has been delegated decision-making authority by other parties, the investor considers that exposure to variable returns when assessing whether it has control over that investee. *[IFRS 10.B59, B71]*. This is illustrated in Example 6.25 below as well as in the examples provided by IFRS 10 reproduced at 6.6 below.

Example 6.25:   Illustration of exposure to variability of returns through other interests

A parent of a fund manager has a 20% direct interest in a fund. The other 80% of the fund is held by third party investors, who have delegated their rights with respect to the fund to the fund manager. When evaluating whether the parent controls the fund, it assesses whether the fund manager (which the parent controls) would use the power that has been delegated to it by the third parties holding the 80% interest, to benefit the parent, since the parent has a 20% direct interest in the fund and could benefit from that power.

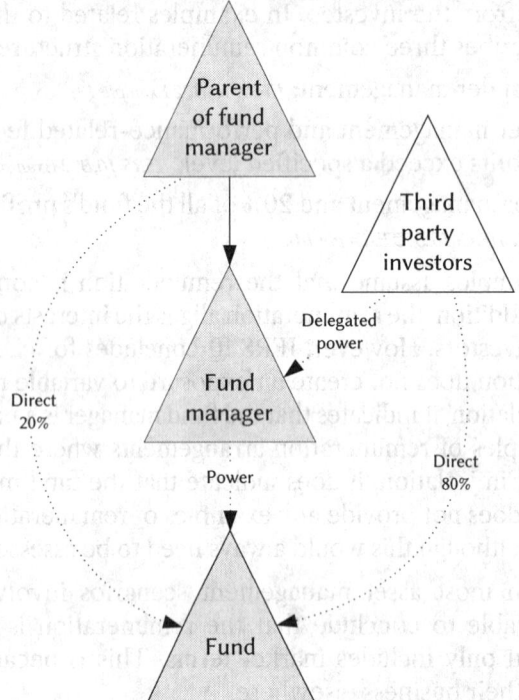

As discussed at 5 above, being an 'investor' and having an 'interest' in an investee is not limited to holding equity or debt instruments. A variety of exposures to variable returns can represent an 'interest' and any potential controlling party is referred to as an 'investor.'

IFRS 10 states that if a decision-maker has interests in an investee, just by virtue of holding those other interests, the decision-maker may be a principal. *[IFRS 10.B71]*. In the Basis for Conclusions accompanying IFRS 10, the IASB notes that a decision-maker might use its decision-making authority primarily to affect its exposure to variable returns from that interest. That is, the decision-maker would have power for its own benefit. *[IFRS 10.BC132]*. The IASB also notes in its Basis for Conclusions that it would be inappropriate to conclude that every decision-maker that is obliged, by law or contract (i.e. having any fiduciary responsibility) to act in the best interests of other parties is always an agent. This is because it would assume that a decision-maker that is legally or contractually obliged to act in the best interests of other parties will always do so, even if that decision-maker receives the vast majority of the returns that are influenced by its decision-making. *[IFRS 10.BC130]*. Accordingly, IFRS 10 requires an entity to evaluate the magnitude and variability of its other interests when determining if it is a principal or an agent, notwithstanding its fiduciary responsibility.

In evaluating its exposure to variability of returns from other interests in the investee a decision-maker considers the following:

(a) the greater the magnitude of, and variability associated with, its economic interests, considering its remuneration and other interests in aggregate, the more likely the decision-maker is a principal,

(b) whether its exposure to variability of returns is different from that of the other investors and, if so, whether this might influence its actions. For example, this might be the case when a decision-maker holds subordinated interests in, or provides other forms of credit enhancement to, an investee.

The decision-maker evaluates its exposure relative to the total variability of returns of the investee. This evaluation is made primarily on the basis of returns expected from the activities of the investee but does not ignore the decision maker's maximum exposure to variability of returns of the investee through other interests that the decision-maker holds. *[IFRS 10.B72]*.

As indicated at (a) above, in evaluating its exposure to variability of returns from other interests, the investor considers its remuneration and other interests in aggregate. So, even if the initial assessment about remuneration is that the decision-maker is an agent (see 6.4 above), the remuneration needs to be considered in the assessment of exposure to variability of returns.

Since the magnitude and variability of exposure to returns are considered together with the other factors, there is no bright line as to what level of other direct interests, on their own, would cause a decision-maker to be a principal or an agent. That is, the scope of authority, removal rights, and remuneration also need to be considered. The examples in IFRS 10 (see 6.6 below) also do not specify the magnitude and variability of the remuneration.

6.5.1 Evaluating returns received via an indirect investment in another entity

In Example 6.25 above, the exposure of the investor (the parent of the fund manager) to variable returns was through a direct investment in the fund. However, what if the exposure to variable returns arises from an investor's indirect involvement with an investee, e.g. via a joint venture or an associate?

When assessing whether an investor has control of an investee, the investor determines whether it is exposed, or has rights, to variable returns from its involvement with the investee. IFRS 10 discusses 'returns' as a broad term, and the examples in paragraph B57 of the standard (see 5 above) suggest the exposure to variable returns encompasses both direct and indirect involvement with the investee.

The Basis for Conclusions accompanying IFRS 10 further clarifies that the IASB intended the term 'returns' as a broad term, stating that 'The Board confirmed its intention to have a broad definition of "returns" that would include synergistic returns as well as more direct returns, for example, dividends or changes in the value of an investment. In practice, an investor can benefit from controlling an investee in a variety of ways. The Board concluded that to narrow the definition of returns would artificially restrict those ways of benefiting.' [IFRS 10.BC63].

Therefore, in our view, when an investor evaluates the exposure to variable returns from its involvement with another entity, the returns received indirectly via another entity that is not under the control of that investor, are included in that assessment. This is regardless of the structure of the indirect involvement – that is, whether it is held through a joint venture, an associate, or neither influence nor joint control exists such that it is just an investment.

In the case of an indirect interest there are essentially two different ways of assessing the returns – the dividend flow and/or the change in fair value of the intermediate investment. While the dividend flow is not in the control of the investor, it still receives the returns via the change in value of its intermediate investment, and therefore these returns cannot be ignored.

Example 6.26: Illustration of exposure to variability of returns through indirect interests

Company A has a wholly-owned subsidiary, GP, which is the General Partner and fund manager of a Fund. A has a 50% interest in the shares of Company B and, as a result of the contractual arrangement with the other investors in B, has joint control of B. GP has a 1% interest in the Fund, with the remaining 99% of the Fund owned by B.

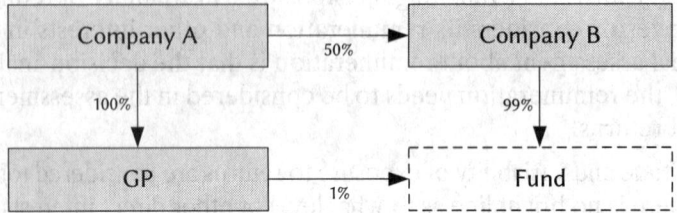

It has been assessed and concluded that GP, in its capacity as the fund manager, has power over the Fund. Therefore, by extension, A has power over the Fund. At the same time, GP also concluded that it is acting on behalf and for the benefit of another party or parties, i.e. as an agent for the investors, and therefore does not control the Fund.

B also evaluated its involvement with the Fund and determined it has no power over the Fund, and therefore does not control it.

A has joint control of B. It does not have control over B and therefore does not control how the returns from the Fund are ultimately distributed to the investors in B.

While A does not control how the returns from the Fund are ultimately distributed, its indirect entitlement to the returns of the Fund is considered with its direct investment through the GP when evaluating whether there is sufficient exposure to variable returns, when combined with power, to conclude that control exists.

6.6 Application examples in IFRS 10

IFRS 10 provides a number of application examples in relation to the determination of whether a decision-maker is a principal or an agent. These are reflected in Examples 6.27 to 6.33 below.

As with all of the examples included in the Application Guidance, the examples portray hypothetical situations. Although some aspects of the examples may be present in actual fact patterns, all relevant facts and circumstances of a particular fact pattern would need to be evaluated when applying IFRS 10. *[IFRS 10.B1]*. When reaching a conclusion on a particular fact pattern, each of the factors discussed above is weighted according to the facts and circumstances of each case, which will require judgement. *[IFRS 10.B60]*.

Example 6.27:   Determining whether a decision-maker is a principal or agent (1)

A decision-maker (fund manager) establishes, markets and manages a publicly traded, regulated fund according to narrowly defined parameters set out in the investment mandate as required by its local laws and regulations. The fund was marketed to investors as an investment in a diversified portfolio of equity securities of publicly traded entities. Within the defined parameters, the fund manager has discretion about the assets in which to invest. The fund manager has made a 10% *pro rata* investment in the fund and receives a market-based fee for its services equal to 1% of the net asset value of the fund. The fees are commensurate with the services provided. The fund manager does not have any obligation to fund losses beyond its 10% investment. The fund is not required to establish, and has not established, an independent board of directors. The investors do not hold any substantive rights that would affect the decision-making authority of the fund manager, but can redeem their interests within particular limits set by the fund.

Analysis

Although operating within the parameters set out in the investment mandate and in accordance with the regulatory requirements, the fund manager has decision-making rights that give it the current ability to direct the relevant activities of the fund – the investors do not hold substantive rights that could affect the fund manager's decision-making authority. The fund manager receives a market-based fee for its services that is commensurate with the services provided and has also made a *pro rata* investment in the fund. The remuneration and its investment expose the fund manager to variability of returns from the activities of the fund without creating exposure that is of such significance that it indicates that the fund manager is a principal.

In this example, consideration of the fund manager's exposure to variability of returns from the fund together with its decision-making authority within restricted parameters indicates that the fund manager is an agent. Thus, the fund manager concludes that it does not control the fund. *[IFRS 10.B72 Example 13]*.

Example 6.28:   Determining whether a decision-maker is a principal or agent (2)

A decision-maker establishes, markets and manages a fund that provides investment opportunities to a number of investors. The decision-maker (fund manager) must make decisions in the best interests of all investors and in accordance with the fund's governing agreements. Nonetheless, the fund manager has wide decision-making discretion and there are no other rights held by others that affect this discretion. The fund manager receives a market-based fee for its services equal to 1% of assets under management and 20% of all the fund's profits if a specified profit level is achieved. The fees are commensurate with the services provided. The fund manager does not hold a direct interest in the fund.

Analysis

Although it must make decisions in the best interests of all investors, the fund manager has extensive decision-making authority to direct the relevant activities of the fund. The fund manager is paid fixed and performance-related fees that are commensurate with the services provided. In addition, the remuneration aligns the interests of the fund manager with those of the other investors to increase the value of the fund, without creating exposure to variability of returns from the activities of the fund that is of such significance that the remuneration, when considered in isolation, indicates that the fund manager is a principal. Therefore, the fund manager is an agent. *[IFRS 10.B72 Example 14]*.

See Examples 6.29 to 6.31 below for an evaluation of other factors based on the same fact pattern and initial analysis.

Example 6.29:   Determining whether a decision-maker is a principal or agent (3)

Assume the fact pattern and initial analysis in Example 6.28 above.

However, in this example the fund manager also has a 2% investment in the fund that aligns its interests with those of the other investors. The fund manager does not have any obligation to fund losses beyond its 2% investment. The investors can remove the fund manager by a simple majority vote, but only for breach of contract.

Analysis

The fund manager's 2% investment increases its exposure to variability of returns from the activities of the fund without creating exposure that is of such significance that it indicates that the fund manager is a principal. The other investors' rights to remove the fund manager are considered to be protective rights because they are exercisable only for breach of contract. In this example, although the fund manager has extensive decision-making authority and is exposed to variability of returns from its interest and remuneration, the fund manager's exposure indicates that the fund manager is an agent. Thus, the fund manager concludes that it does not control the fund. *[IFRS 10.B72 Example 14A]*.

Example 6.30:   Determining whether a decision-maker is a principal or agent (4)

Assume the fact pattern and initial analysis in Example 6.28 above.

However, in this example, the fund manager has a more substantial *pro rata* investment in the fund (than the 2% in Example 6.29 above), but does not have any obligation to fund losses beyond that investment. The investors can remove the fund manager by a simple majority vote, but only for breach of contract.

Analysis

In this scenario, the other investors' rights to remove the fund manager are considered to be protective rights because they are exercisable only for breach of contract. Although the fund manager is paid fixed and performance-related fees that are commensurate with the services provided, the combination of the fund manager's investment together with its remuneration could create exposure to variability of returns from the activities of the fund that is of such significance that it indicates that the fund manager is a principal. The greater the magnitude of, and variability associated with, the fund manager's economic interests (considering its remuneration and other interests in aggregate), the more emphasis the fund manager would place on those economic interests in the analysis, and the more likely the fund manager is a principal.

For example, having considered its remuneration and the other factors, the fund manager might consider a 20% investment to be sufficient to conclude that it controls the fund. However, in different circumstances (i.e. if the remuneration or other factors are different), control may arise when the level of investment is different. *[IFRS 10.B72 Example 14B]*.

Example 6.31:   Determining whether a decision-maker is a principal or agent (5)

Assume the fact pattern and initial analysis in Example 6.28 above.

However, in this example, the fund manager has a 20% *pro rata* investment in the fund, but does not have any obligation to fund losses beyond its 20% investment. The fund has a board of directors, all of whose members are independent of the fund manager and are appointed by the other investors. The board appoints the fund manager annually. If the board decided not to renew the fund manager's contract, the services performed by the fund manager could be performed by other managers in the industry.

Analysis

Although the fund manager is paid fixed and performance-related fees that are commensurate with the services provided, the combination of the fund manager's 20% investment together with its remuneration creates exposure to variability of returns from the activities of the fund that is of such significance that it indicates that the fund manager is a principal. However, the investors have substantive rights to remove the fund manager – the board of directors provides a mechanism to ensure that the investors can remove the fund manager if they decide to do so.

In this scenario, the fund manager places greater emphasis on the substantive removal rights in the analysis. Thus, although the fund manager has extensive decision-making authority and is exposed to variability of returns of the fund from its remuneration and investment, the substantive rights held by the other investors indicate that the fund manager is an agent. Thus, the fund manager concludes that it does not control the fund. *[IFRS 10.B72 Example 14C]*.

Example 6.32:   Determining whether a decision-maker is a principal or agent (6)

An investee is created to purchase a portfolio of fixed rate asset-backed securities, funded by fixed rate debt instruments and equity instruments. The equity instruments are designed to provide first loss protection to the debt investors and receive any residual returns of the investee. The transaction was marketed to potential debt investors as an investment in a portfolio of asset-backed securities with exposure to the credit risk associated with the possible default of the issuers of the asset-backed securities in the portfolio and to the interest rate risk associated with the management of the portfolio. On formation, the equity instruments represent 10% of the value of the assets purchased. A decision-maker (the asset manager) manages the active asset portfolio by making investment decisions within the parameters set out in the investee's prospectus. For those services, the asset manager receives a market-based fixed fee (i.e. 1% of assets under management) and performance-related fees (i.e. 10% of profits) if the investee's profits exceed a specified level. The fees are commensurate with the services provided. The asset manager holds 35% of the equity in the investee.

The remaining 65% of the equity, and all the debt instruments, are held by a large number of widely dispersed unrelated third party investors. The asset manager can be removed, without cause, by a simple majority decision of the other investors.

Analysis

The asset manager is paid fixed and performance-related fees that are commensurate with the services provided. The remuneration aligns the interests of the fund manager with those of the other investors to increase the value of the fund. The asset manager has exposure to variability of returns from the activities of the fund because it holds 35% of the equity and from its remuneration.

Although operating within the parameters set out in the investee's prospectus, the asset manager has the current ability to make investment decisions that significantly affect the investee's returns – the removal rights held by the other investors receive little weighting in the analysis because those rights are held by a large number of widely dispersed investors. In this example, the asset manager places greater emphasis on its exposure to variability of returns of the fund from its equity interest, which is subordinate to the debt instruments. Holding 35% of the equity creates subordinated exposure to losses and rights to returns of the investee, which are of such significance that it indicates that the asset manager is a principal. Thus, the asset manager concludes that it controls the investee. *[IFRS 10.B72 Example 15]*.

The conclusions in Examples 6.27 to 6.32 above in respect of whether the fund manager is a principal (and therefore has control) or an agent (and therefore does not have control) can be summarised as follows:

Remuneration	Equity holding	Removal rights	Control?
1% of NAV	10%	None	No
1% of NAV plus 20% profits above a certain level	None	None	No
1% of NAV plus 20% profits above a certain level	2%	Only for breach of contract	No
1% of NAV plus 20% profits above a certain level	20% (illustrative)	Only for breach of contract	Yes
1% of NAV plus 20% profits above a certain level	20%	Yes – annually by board appointed by other investors	No
1% of NAV plus 10% profits above a certain level	35% of equity (0% of debt)	Yes – by simple majority of other widely diverse investors	Yes

Example 6.33 below illustrates a slightly different type of structure where there is an entitlement to a residual return rather than a *pro rata* return.

Example 6.33: Determining whether a decision-maker is a principal or agent (7)

A decision-maker (the sponsor) sponsors a multi-seller conduit, which issues short-term debt instruments to unrelated third party investors. The transaction was marketed to potential investors as an investment in a portfolio of highly rated medium-term assets with minimal exposure to the credit risk associated with the possible default by the issuers of the assets in the portfolio. Various transferors sell high quality medium-term asset portfolios to the conduit. Each transferor services the portfolio of assets that it sells to the conduit and manages receivables on default for a market-based servicing fee. Each transferor also provides first loss protection against credit losses from its asset portfolio through over-collateralisation of the assets transferred to the conduit. The sponsor establishes the terms of the conduit and manages the operations of the conduit for a market-based fee. The fee is commensurate with the services provided. The sponsor approves the sellers permitted to sell to the conduit, approves the assets to be purchased by the conduit and makes decisions about the funding of the conduit. The sponsor must act in the best interests of all investors.

The sponsor is entitled to any residual return of the conduit and also provides credit enhancement and liquidity facilities to the conduit. The credit enhancement provided by the sponsor absorbs losses of up to 5% of all of the conduit's assets, after losses are absorbed by the transferors. The liquidity facilities are not advanced against defaulted assets. The investors do not hold substantive rights that could affect the decision-making authority of the sponsor.

Analysis

Even though the sponsor is paid a market-based fee for its services that is commensurate with the services provided, the sponsor has exposure to variability of returns from the activities of the conduit because of its rights to any residual returns of the conduit and the provision of credit enhancement and liquidity facilities (i.e. the conduit is exposed to liquidity risk by using short-term debt instruments to fund medium-term assets). Even though each of the transferors has decision-making rights that affect the value of the assets of the conduit, the sponsor has extensive decision-making authority that gives it the current ability to direct the activities that most significantly affect the conduit's returns (i.e. the sponsor established the terms of the conduit, has the right to make decisions about the assets (approving the assets purchased and the transferors of those assets) and the funding of the conduit (for which new investment must be found on a regular basis)). The right to residual returns of the conduit and the provision of credit enhancement and liquidity facilities expose the sponsor to variability of returns from the activities of the conduit that is different from that of the other investors. Accordingly, that exposure indicates that the sponsor is a principal and thus the sponsor concludes that it controls the conduit. The sponsor's obligation to act in the best interest of all investors does not prevent the sponsor from being a principal. *[IFRS 10.B72 Example 16]*.

6.7 Other illustrative examples

Example 6.34 below illustrates the application of the guidance relating to the determination of a principal or an agent for a bank that establishes a structured entity to facilitate a securitisation.

Example 6.34: **Determining whether a bank is a principal or agent in relation to a securitisation**

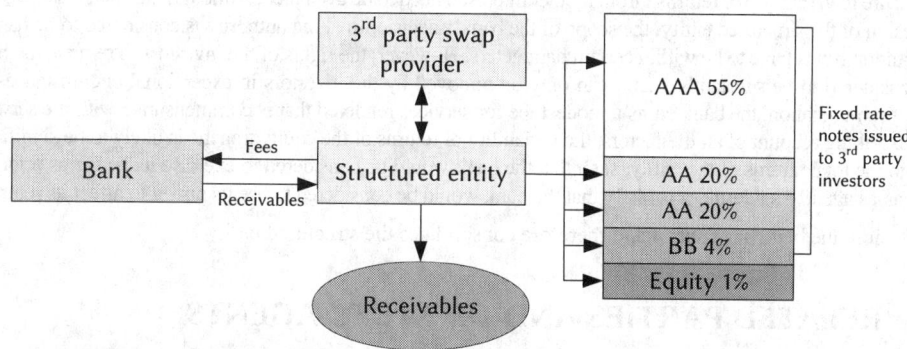

A bank establishes a structured entity to facilitate a securitisation. It transfers floating rate receivables to the structured entity. The structured entity issues fixed rate notes in tranches to investors (rated AAA, AA, A and BB) and an equity tranche to the bank. The AAA tranche is the most senior and the equity tranche is the most junior in the event that there is insufficient cash to meet the payments under the terms of the notes.

The bank services the receivables on behalf of the structured entity including the management of defaults (if any), and has substitution rights over the receivables within certain parameters (for example, asset quality).

The bank receives a fee for managing the receivables, that is 1% of the notional amount of the receivables and is commensurate with the level of work performed and only includes market terms. The investors are not able to remove the bank from performing this function, other than in exceptional circumstances, such as negligence by the bank.

A third party provides an interest rate swap to convert the cash flows of the receivables into the cash flows required to be paid to meet the terms of the notes.

As the bank retains only the equity tranche, it concludes that it is no longer exposed to substantially all the risks and rewards of ownership and can derecognise the receivables on transfer to the structured entity and recognises just the equity tranche as its continuing involvement in the receivables.

Analysis

The purpose and design of the structured entity was to:

(a) enable the bank to generate external funding through the securitisation structure; and

(b) provide investors with an attractive investment opportunity.

The activities of the structured entity that significantly affect its returns are:

- selection and transfer of assets at inception;
- determining which assets are held by the structured entity (i.e. asset substitution); and
- management of defaults on the receivables.

The bank has decision-making rights over all of these relevant activities in its capacity as sponsor and service provider, so it has power over the structured entity.

The bank has exposure to variable returns through its holding of the equity tranche of the notes, in addition to the 1% management fee.

However, the question arises as to whether the bank is using its power as principal or as agent. To make that determination, the four factors (scope of decision-making authority, rights held by other investors, remuneration and exposure to variability of returns through other interests) need to be evaluated. Although the bank was involved in the design of the structured entity, the scope of the bank's decision-making authority is considered to be narrow as substitution rights have to be within certain parameters. However, the rights of the investors to remove the bank is not considered to be substantive, as it can only be removed by the investors in exceptional circumstances. In respect of remuneration, the bank earns a modest fee for services rendered that is commensurate with the services provided. Taking account of all the factors, the variability of returns of the equity tranche is likely to be significant relative to the total returns of the entity, such that the bank would be considered to exercise its power as principal rather than as agent. As a result, it is likely that the bank would be considered to use its power to affect its returns.

In conclusion, the bank has control and therefore consolidates the structured entity.

7 RELATED PARTIES AND *DE FACTO* AGENTS

IFRS 10 also requires an investor to consider whether there are other parties who are acting on behalf of the investor by virtue of their relationship with it. That is, IFRS 10 requires consideration of whether the other parties are acting as *de facto* agents for the investor. The determination of whether other parties are acting as *de facto* agents requires judgement, considering not only the nature of the relationship but also how those parties interact with each other and the investor. *[IFRS 10.B73]*.

Such relationships need not be contractual. A party is a *de facto* agent when the investor has, or those that direct the activities of the investor have, the ability to direct that party to act on the investor's behalf. In these circumstances, the investor considers its *de facto* agent's decision-making rights and its indirect exposure, or rights, to variable returns through the *de facto* agent together with its own when assessing control of an investee. *[IFRS 10.B74]*.

IFRS 10 lists several examples of parties that might be *de facto* agents for an investor:

(a) the investor's related parties;

(b) a party that received its interest in the investee as a contribution or loan from the investor;

(c) a party that has agreed not to sell, transfer or encumber its interests in the investee without the investor's prior approval (except for situations in which the investor and the other party have the right of prior approval and the rights are based on mutually agreed terms by willing independent parties);

(d) a party that cannot finance its operations without subordinated financial support from the investor;

(e) an investee for which the majority of the members of its governing body or for which its key management personnel are the same as those of the investor; and

(f) a party that has a close business relationship with the investor, such as the relationship between a professional service provider and one of its significant clients. *[IFRS 10.B75]*.

However, just because a party falls within the examples above, that does not mean that it is necessarily a *de facto* agent for the investor, as shown in the diagram below. It simply means that management must carefully evaluate whether that party is a *de facto* agent for the investor. Parties that are actually *de facto* agents are only a sub-set of the list above. Therefore, management must determine whether the other party is acting on behalf of the investor because of its relationship to the investor. IFRS 10 does not provide much explanation on how this evaluation is to be made; IFRS 10 only states that the evaluation considers the nature of the relationship and how the parties interact with each other. *[IFRS 10.B73]*.

Figure 6.8: Identifying parties that might be de facto agents

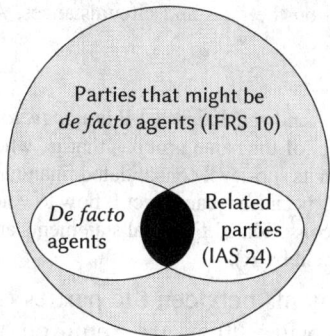

In our view, given the breadth of the parties that might be a *de facto* agent in IFRS 10, there are likely to be numerous parties that need to be evaluated to determine if they are actually *de facto* agents, which requires careful evaluation of the facts and circumstances, including the purpose and design of the investee.

If a party is determined to be a *de facto* agent, then its rights and exposures to variable returns are considered together with those of the investor when evaluating whether an investor has control of an investee. *[IFRS 10.B74]*. Just because one party is a *de facto* agent of the other party, that does not mean that the *de facto* agent is controlled by the investor. Consolidation procedures in situations when a *de facto* agent exists are discussed at 7.2 below.

7.1 Customer-supplier relationships

Normally, a typical supplier-customer relationship is not expected to result in one party being a *de facto* agent of the other. This is because in a typical supplier-customer relationship, one party cannot direct the other party to act on its behalf. Instead, the activities of each are directed by their respective shareholders (and Board of Directors and management).

However, a party with a 'close business relationship' is an example of a *de facto* agent. *[IFRS 10.B75(f)]*. Accordingly, where a close business relationship exists between a customer and a supplier, consideration needs to be given to whether the supplier is a *de facto* agent of the customer. For example, this might be the case if:

- an entity has only one significant customer;
- the customer and supplier have common management or common shareholders;
- the customer has the ability to direct product design, sales, etc.; or
- the supplier is a service provider (e.g. investment banker, attorney) that assists in structuring a transaction.

7.2 Non-controlling interests when there is a *de facto* agent

When consolidating a subsidiary, a parent only reflects its exposures to variable returns (including those held by its subsidiaries), in its consolidated financial statements. Any rights or exposures to variable returns held by a *de facto* agent that is not in the group would generally be shown as non-controlling interests. This is illustrated in Example 6.35 below.

Example 6.35: Control evaluation and consolidation with a de facto agent

A has a 40% interest in Z, whose relevant activities are directed by voting shares that entitle the holder to a *pro rata* share of returns of Z. Based on the facts and circumstances, A concludes that, by itself, its 40% interest does not give A control over Z.

B holds a 15% interest in Z.

A evaluates the facts and circumstances and concludes that B is a *de facto* agent of A. This might be concluded if, for example, A and B are members of the same group – that is, when A and B have the same ultimate parent, but B is not part of A's group in its sub-level consolidated financial statements. Based on the combined interest, A concludes that it controls Z, because it can direct B how to vote by virtue of being a *de facto* agent. Accordingly, A consolidates Z in its consolidated financial statements and reflects a non-controlling interest in Z of 60% (that is, all interests not held by A).

Careful evaluation of arrangements between the parties is needed to ensure that there are no other rights and exposures that are required to be accounted for in the consolidated financial statements.

8 CONTROL OF SPECIFIED ASSETS

IFRS 10 requires that an investor has to consider whether it treats a portion of an investee as a deemed separate entity and, if so, whether it controls the deemed separate entity (a 'silo'). *[IFRS 10.B76].*

It therefore clarifies that an investor can have control over specified assets of an investee (i.e. whether a 'silo' exists within a host entity). IFRS 10 gives a very strict rule as to when a portion of an entity is deemed to be a silo, and therefore, evaluated separately for consolidation from the remainder of the host entity.

Under IFRS 10, an investor treats a portion of an investee as a deemed separate entity if and only if specified assets of the investee (and related credit enhancements, if any) are the only source of payment for specified liabilities of, or specified other interests in, the investee. This means that parties other than those with the specified liability do not have rights or obligations related to the specified assets or to residual cash flows from those assets. In substance, none of the returns from the specified assets can be used by the remaining investee and none of the liabilities of the deemed separate entity are payable from the assets of the remaining investee. Thus, in substance, all the assets, liabilities and equity of that deemed separate entity ('silo') are ring-fenced from the overall investee. *[IFRS 10.B77].*

The description of a silo above includes the phrase 'in substance', but it is unclear how this should be interpreted. Some proponents take the view that this would allow a portion of an investee to be regarded as ring-fenced if the possibility of using the assets of the silo to meet liabilities of the rest of the investee (or *vice versa*) was remote. In our view, this means that the silo has to be 'legally ring-fenced', and if there is any possibility that the assets could be used to meet liabilities of the rest of the investee, it is not a silo. The phrase 'in substance' is used in the standard to ensure that any terms in the contract that might override a ring fence would need to have substance, not that a silo can be established through 'in substance' ring fencing.

In many cases, where a silo exists, it will be because a trust or similar legal structure exists to ring-fence the assets and liabilities from the host and other silos within the host entity.

Under IFRS 10, it is clear that an investor needs to identify and consolidate any silos that it controls. Accordingly, it is crucial to identify silos (as discussed at 8.1 below).

Identifying whether a silo exists, and whether an investor controls a silo, can be complex. However, the same process outlined in the diagram for assessing control included at 3.1 above can be used for silos, with the initial step of identifying a silo, as shown in the diagram below. Understanding the purpose and design of an investee is critical when identifying whether a silo exists, and if so which investor, if any, has control of that silo.

Figure 6.9:   Identifying and assessing control of a silo

Silos
Determine whether a deemed separate entity (a silo) exists. Consider:
- Are the specified assets of the investee (and related credit enhancements, if any) the only source of payment for specified liabilities of, or specified other interests in, the investee?
- Do parties other than those with the specified liability have rights or obligations related to the specified assets or to residual cash flows from those assets?
- In substance, can any of the returns from the specified assets be used by the remaining investee and are any of the liabilities of the deemed separate entity payable from the assets of the remaining investee?

Power (Identify power)
Determine which party, if any, has power, that is, the current ability to direct the relative activities. Power arises from the rights which may include:
- Voting rights
- Potential voting rights (e.g. options or convertible instruments)
- Rights to appoint key management personnel
- Decision making rights within a management contract
- Removal or 'kick-out' rights

However, power does not arise from protective rights.

Returns (Assess returns)
Assess whether the investor is exposed, or has rights, to variable returns from its involvement with the investee. Returns can be positive, negative, or both. Examples of returns include:
- Dividends
- Remuneration
- Economies of scale, cost savings, scarce products, proprietary knowledge, synergies, or other returns that are not available to other interest holders

Linkage (Evaluate linkage)
Evaluate whether the investor has the ability to use its power to affect the investor's returns from its involvement with the investee. If applicable, determine whether the investor is a principal or an agent, considering:
- Scope of its authority
- Rights held by other parties
- Remuneration
- Exposure to variability from other interests

Understand purpose and design of investee

8.1   Identifying a silo

When identifying a silo, it is important to meet the condition that IFRS 10 requires to be satisfied for there to be a silo (see 8 above). Silos occur most often in the following industries:
- insurance (see 8.1.1 below); and
- investment funds (see 8.1.2 below).

8.1.1   Identifying silos in the insurance industry

For insurers, silos may arise in a structure such as a multi-cell reinsurance vehicle, which is an entity comprised of a number of 'cells' where the assets and liabilities are ring-fenced.

Insurers should evaluate whether investments made on behalf of insurance contract holders (policyholders) would be considered silos under IFRS 10. The evaluation will depend on the facts and circumstances of the particular case, and may vary by jurisdiction and by policy, given the differences in regulatory environments and types of policies offered by insurance entities.

When determining whether policies held are ring-fenced (whether a silo exists) relevant facts and circumstances, including local laws and contractual arrangements with the contract holder, must be assessed.

Where a silo exists and the shares in the silo are held by the insurance company on behalf of policyholders and all returns from the sub-funds are passed to the policyholders, the following needs to be considered:

- Does the insurance company have a contractual obligation to hold investments in the sub-funds?
- Are the investments legally ring-fenced such that they may not be used to satisfy other liabilities of the insurance company in the event of liquidation?
- Do the policyholders select the investments?
- Will other funds beyond the value of the specified assets in the silo be necessary to fulfil the obligation to the policyholders?
- Is there an exact matching of the policy to the assets held?

All of the relevant facts and circumstances would need to be considered when determining if a silo exists. As discussed at 8.2 below, if a silo exists, control is evaluated for each silo. However, if a silo does not exist, this simply means that the control evaluation is made at the entity level.

8.1.2   Identifying silos in the investment funds industry

Silos may exist in the investment fund industry. Certain investment vehicles are set up as 'umbrella funds' with a number of sub-funds, each with its own investment goals and strategies e.g. a sub-fund may specialise in the shares of small companies, or in a particular country, or a particular industry. An assessment will need to be made as to whether a sub-fund should be considered a silo under IFRS 10. The evaluation will depend on the facts and circumstances of the particular case as to whether the sub-funds are legally ring-fenced from each other and the investment vehicle itself, and may vary by jurisdiction, given the differences in regulatory environments and types of such investment vehicles.

8.2   Evaluating control of a silo

If a silo exists, the next step is to identify the relevant activities (the activities that most significantly affect the silo's returns). Only the relevant activities of that silo would be considered, even if other activities affect the returns from other portions of the host.

The next step is then to identify which investor has the ability to direct the relevant activities, (i.e. who has the power over the silo). Only rights that affect the relevant activities of the silo would be considered. Rights that affect the relevant activities for other portions of the host entity would not be considered.

To conclude whether an investor has control over the silo, the investor also evaluates whether the investor has exposure to variable returns from that silo, and whether the investor can use its power over the silo to affect the amount of the investor's returns. Only exposure to variable returns from that silo would be considered; exposures to variable returns from other portions of the host would be excluded. *[IFRS 10.B78]*.

8.3 Consolidation of a silo

If an investor concludes that it controls a silo, it consolidates only the silo. That investor does not consolidate the remaining portions of the host entity.

Similarly, if an investor concludes that it controls a host entity, but not a silo within that entity, it would only consolidate the host entity, but exclude the silo. *[IFRS 10.B79]*.

9 CONTINUOUS ASSESSMENT

IFRS 10 clarifies that an investor is required to reassess whether it controls an investee if the facts and circumstances indicate that there are changes to one of the three elements of control, *[IFRS 10.8, B80]*, which are repeated below. For example, the following would be likely to be triggers:

- power over the investee:
  - an investor increases or decreases its holdings in the investee – see Example 6.36 below;
  - a potential voting right is granted, expires, or changes from being substantive to non-substantive (or *vice versa*) – see Example 6.37 at 9.1 below;
  - a change in how power over an investee can be exercised. For example, changes to decision making rights, which mean that the relevant activities of the investee are no longer governed through voting rights, but instead, are directed by contract (or *vice versa*); *[IFRS 10.B81]*
  - bankruptcy filings – see Example 6.40 at 9.2 below;
  - troubled debt restructurings – see Example 6.41 at 9.2 below;
  - changes in voting patterns;
  - action taken by others without the investor being involved in the event – see Example 6.42 at 9.3 below; *[IFRS 10.B82]*
- exposures, or rights, to variable returns from involvement with the investee – in many cases, these changes occur concurrent with a change in power, such as when acquiring an interest or selling an interest in an investee:
  - an investor can lose control of an investee if it ceases to be entitled to receive returns or to be exposed to obligations because, for example, a contract to receive performance related fees is terminated; *[IFRS 10.B83]* and
- ability of the investor to use its power over the investee to affect the amount of the investor's returns:
  - when the investor is a decision-maker (i.e. a principal or agent), changes in the overall relationship between the investor and other parties can mean that the investor no longer acts as agent, even though it has previously acted as agent or *vice versa*. *[IFRS 10.B84]*.

Therefore, it is possible that a previously unconsolidated investee would need to be consolidated (or *vice versa*) as facts and circumstances change. However, absent a change in facts and circumstances, control assessments are not expected to change.

Example 6.36:   Providing seed money for a fund

A fund manager provides all of the seed money for a new fund upon inception. Until such times as other investors invest in that fund, the fund manager would likely control that fund. This is because the fund manager has the power to direct the relevant activities of that fund, exposure to variable returns from its involvement with the fund, and the ability to use its power over the fund to affect the amount of its returns.

As third parties invest in the fund and dilute (or acquire) the fund manager's interest, this would likely result in a reassessment of whether the fund manager has control. As the third parties invest, they are likely to obtain rights to direct the relevant activities (that is, the third parties will gain power). In many cases, analysing the facts and circumstances may indicate that the fund manager is acting as an agent of those third parties (as discussed at 6 above). Accordingly, the fund manager would deconsolidate the fund upon its determination that it no longer had control.

9.1   Changes in market conditions

IFRS 10 discusses when a change in market conditions triggers a reassessment of control.

An investor's initial assessment of control or its status as a principal or an agent does not change simply because of a change in market conditions (e.g. a change in the investee's returns driven by market conditions), unless the change in market conditions changes one or more of the three elements of control listed in paragraph 7 of IFRS 10 (see 9 above) or changes the overall relationship between a principal and an agent (see 6 above). *[IFRS 10.B85]*.

In response to concerns, the IASB decided to add this guidance to address the reassessment of control when there are changes in market conditions. The IASB observed that a change in market conditions alone would not generally affect the consolidation conclusion, or the status as a principal or an agent, for two reasons. The first is that power arises from substantive rights, and assessing whether those rights are substantive includes the consideration of many factors, not only those that are affected by a change in market conditions. The second is that an investor is not required to have a particular specified level of exposure to variable returns in order to control an investee. If that were the case, fluctuations in an investor's expected returns might result in changes in the consolidation conclusion. *[IFRS 10.BC152]*.

Accordingly, only a market condition that causes a change in one of the three criteria would trigger a reassessment (see Example 6.42 below). Evaluating whether a change in a market condition triggers a reassessment of control should be considered in the context of the investee's purpose and design.

As discussed at 5 above, with respect to the second criterion, the focus is on the existence of an exposure to variable returns, not the amount of the variable returns. While a change in market conditions often affects the amount of the exposure to variable returns, it typically does not affect whether the exposure exists.

However, when power has been delegated to a decision-maker, a change in market conditions could change whether the magnitude and variability of exposures to variable returns from remuneration and/or other interests are such that they indicate that the decision-maker is a principal (as discussed at 6.4 and 6.5 above, respectively). That is, a change in market conditions could change the evaluation of whether a decision-maker has the ability to use its power over the investee to affect the amount of the decision-maker's returns (the linkage between power and returns). Accordingly, a change in market conditions may trigger a reassessment of control in principal-agency evaluations.

As discussed at 4.3.4.A above, when evaluating the exercise price of an option in the context of whether potential voting rights give control, the evaluation is not solely based on the nature of the option as of the end of the reporting period. During the development of IFRS 10, some constituents raised concerns as to whether frequent changes in the control assessment solely because of market conditions would mean that an investor consolidates and deconsolidates an investee if potential voting rights moved in and out of the money. In response, the IASB noted that determining whether a potential voting right is substantive is not based solely on a comparison of the strike or conversion price of the instrument and the then current market price of its underlying share. Although the strike or conversion price is one factor to consider, determining whether potential voting rights are substantive requires a holistic approach, considering a variety of factors. This includes assessing the purpose and design of the instrument, considering whether the investor can benefit for other reasons such as by realising synergies between the investor and the investee, and determining whether there are any barriers (financial or otherwise) that would prevent the holder of potential voting rights from exercising or converting those rights. Accordingly, a change in market conditions (i.e. the market price of the underlying shares) alone would not typically result in a change in the consolidation conclusion. *[IFRS 10.BC124]*.

Example 6.37:   Value of option changes from 'in-the-money' to 'out-of-the-money'

A holds 40% of the voting rights of B, and holds a currently exercisable in-the-money option to acquire a further 20% of the voting rights of B. Assuming that voting rights give power over B, the option is substantive and no other facts and circumstances are relevant, A would likely have power over B, because A could currently exercise its right to obtain a majority of B's voting shares.

Consider a situation in which the in-the-money option changed to being slightly (but not deeply) out-of-the-money, due to a change in market conditions (and this change was not previously expected to occur, as discussed at 4.3.4 above). This would probably not trigger reassessment, because the option is likely to remain substantive, and therefore there is no change in how power over B is evaluated.

Consider a second situation in which the option changed to being deeply-out-of-the-money due to a change in market conditions (and this change was not previously expected to occur and it was now expected to remain deeply-out-of-the-money for the remainder of the option period, as discussed at 4.3.4 above). This would likely trigger reassessment, since the option would no longer be substantive, and the fact that the option was previously a substantive right was a critical factor in assessing whether A had power over B.

Example 6.38:   Structured entity reassessments

There are two investors in a structured entity; one holds the debt, and the other holds the equity. In the initial assessment, the investors concluded that the equity holder had control because it had the power to direct the relevant activities, exposure to variable returns through its equity interests, and the ability to use its power over the structured entity to affect the equity holder's returns. Due to a change in market conditions, the value of the equity diminishes. This fact, by itself, would probably not trigger reassessment, because the equity holder continues to have exposure to variable returns (i.e. it continues to be exposed to further decreases in equity, and has potential upside if market conditions improve). Accordingly, the conclusion that the equity holder had control of the structured entity would probably not change.

However, if, concurrently with the deterioration of the equity, there are other changes in facts and circumstances (e.g. the equity holder loses its ability to direct the relevant activities), this might trigger a reassessment. In this case, the trigger is actually the other change in facts and circumstances, not the decrease in equity itself. In this case, whether the debt holder has control depends on whether it has rights that give it the current ability to direct the relevant activities, and the ability to affect its exposure to variable returns.

Example 6.39:   Investee loses money due to change in market conditions

C holds 100% of the voting rights of D, which is a profitable entity. In its initial assessment, C concludes that it controls D.

Due to a change in the market conditions, D begins to lose money and is no longer profitable (e.g. due to a decrease in demand for its products). This would probably *not* trigger reassessment, because the change in market conditions would likely not change the identification of the relevant activities, how those activities are directed, the investors' exposure to variable returns, or the linkage between power and returns.

However, at some point, D might become so unprofitable as to consider restructuring its debt or filing for bankruptcy. This situation is discussed at 9.2 below.

9.2   Bankruptcy filings and troubled debt restructurings

Filing for bankruptcy or restructuring a debt will usually trigger reassessment as to which investor, if any, controls the investee (see 4.3.2 above). While control should be reassessed at such triggering points, it does not necessarily mean the conclusion as to which entity consolidates will change. Examples 6.40 and 6.41 below illustrate situations when the control conclusion might change, and possibly result in a bank consolidating an entity that it had previously concluded it did not control.

Example 6.40:   Bankruptcy filing

A made a loan to B. Because of A's position as a senior creditor, if B defaults on the loan, A has the right to direct B to sell certain assets to repay the loan to A. In its initial assessment of control, A concluded that this right was a protective right, because it concluded that defaulting on the loan would be an exceptional circumstance. Consequently, this right did not give A power over B, and therefore, A did not control B. A concluded that the voting rights, which are held by the equity investors, give the equity investors power over B.

B later defaults on the loan and files for bankruptcy, giving A the right to direct B to sell certain assets to repay the loan to A. Upon B filing for bankruptcy, A would need to evaluate whether having this right, which was previously protective, gives A power.

Before concluding which investors, if any, control B once it files for bankruptcy, consideration would also be given to what rights the equity investors have, if any, to direct the relevant activities of B, and also to whether A and the equity investors have exposure to variable returns from B.

Example 6.41:   Troubled debt restructuring

Consider the same facts as Example 6.40 above, except that A and B agree to restructure the loan, rather than B filing for bankruptcy. During the restructuring, A determines which assets will be sold to repay the loan, with management and the equity investors agreeing to this plan. In addition, management agreed to an incentive scheme under which payments are based on asset sale and loan repayment targets.

Upon restructuring the loan, A would need to evaluate whether determining which assets should be sold to repay the loan gives A power. This might be the case if voting rights do not give power over B, because management is required to comply with the asset sale plan mandated by A.

Before concluding which investors, if any, control B, consideration would also be given to what rights the equity investors have, if any, to direct the relevant activities of B, and also to whether A and the equity investors have exposure to variable returns from B.

In some jurisdictions, it is possible that a trustee or court administrator may have power (and possibly control) over an investee that files for bankruptcy. In such situations, consideration needs to be given not only to whether the trustee has power, but also whether it has an exposure to variable returns from the investee, and if so, whether it has the ability to use that power to affect its exposure to variable returns. In many cases, a trustee or court administrator might have power, but this power is held as an agent (see 6 above). However, a determination will need to be made as to whether the trustee or court administrator is an agent for a specific lender, or for the creditors as a group. This will depend on individual facts and circumstances for the jurisdiction.

In the situations in Examples 6.40 and 6.41 above, it might be determined that the lender obtained control over the investee. In this case, judgement will also be needed to determine the date at which the lender obtained control over the investee. Is it the date that the investee filed for bankruptcy or restructured the debt? Or, did the lender obtain control over the investee before the actual filing, or restructuring, when it became evident that the investee would likely have to file for bankruptcy or restructure the debt?

9.3 Control reassessment as a result of action by others

An investor may gain or lose power over an investee as a result of action by others (i.e. without direct involvement in the change in circumstances). For example, an investor can gain power over an investee because decision-making rights held by another party or parties that previously prevented the investor from controlling an investee have elapsed. [IFRS 10.B82].

Alternatively, actions of others, such as a government, could cause an investor to lose the ability to make key operational decisions and therefore direct the relevant activities of the investee. However, IFRS 10 does not include any consolidation exception when the functional currency of an investee is subject to a long-term lack of exchangeability. As explained in the Basis for Conclusions, the Board decided to remove from the previous version the exclusion of a subsidiary from consolidation when there are severe long-term restrictions that impair a subsidiary's ability to transfer funds to the parent. It did so because such circumstances may not preclude control. The Board decided that a parent, when assessing its ability to control a subsidiary, should consider restrictions on the transfer of funds from the subsidiary to the parent. In themselves, such restrictions do not preclude control. [IFRS 10.BCZ21].

Another example would be where other investors acquire rights from other parties. In such cases, it might be more difficult to determine whether an event has happened that would cause an investor to reassess control, because the information might not be publicly available. Consider the situation in Example 6.42 below.

Example 6.42: Control reassessment without being involved

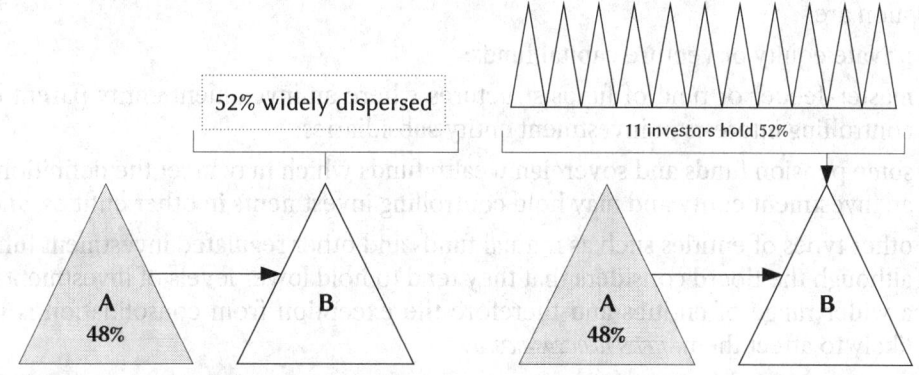

A holds 48% of the voting rights of B, with the remaining 52% being widely dispersed. In its initial assessment, A concludes that the absolute size of its holding, relative to the other shareholdings, gives it power over B.

Over time, some of the shareholders begin to consolidate their interests, such that eventually, the 52% is held by a much smaller group of shareholders. Depending on the regulatory environment, and rights held by A regarding the right to receive information when shareholders acquire other interests in B, it is possible, although perhaps unlikely, that A would not be aware of this occurrence. Nonetheless, it would seem that IFRS 10 would require A to re-evaluate whether it has control over B, because the other shareholders are no longer widely dispersed, and thus A may not have the current ability to direct the relevant activities of B.

While the situation in Example 6.42 above might be uncommon, management should consider what systems and processes are needed to monitor external events for changes that could trigger reassessment. Without knowledge of such events, and a process for gathering this information, it may be difficult to determine the date when the other voters became sufficiently concentrated to conclude that the investor no longer has control. The same might apply where an investor has determined that it does not have control due to there being a relatively small number of other shareholders, but the other voters become sufficiently dispersed or disorganised such that the investor now has control. Depending on the facts and circumstances, there could be a lag in the period between when the facts and circumstances actually change, and when management is able to conclude that the investor has control.

10 INVESTMENT ENTITIES

In October 2012, the IASB issued *Investment Entities (Amendments to IFRS 10, IFRS 12 and IAS 27)*. This introduces an exception to the principle that all subsidiaries shall be consolidated. The amendments define an investment entity and require a parent that is an investment entity to measure its investments in particular subsidiaries at fair value through profit or loss in accordance with IFRS 9, with limited exceptions. This amendment applied for annual periods beginning on or after 1 January 2014. *[IFRS 10.C1B]*.

This exception is intended to address what many in the asset management and private equity industries, and users of their financial statements, believe is a significant issue with the consolidation requirements in IFRS 10. As a part of the deliberations ultimately leading to the issuance of IFRS 10, the IASB received many letters noting that for 'investment entities', rather than enhancing decision-useful information, consolidating the controlled investment actually obscures such information. This feedback was persuasive and consequently the IASB decided to issue the investment entity exception.

The Board considers that the entities most likely to be affected by the investment entity exception are:

- private equity or venture capital funds;
- master-feeder or fund of funds structures where an investment entity parent has controlling interests in investment entity subsidiaries;
- some pension funds and sovereign wealth funds which may meet the definition of an investment entity and may hold controlling investments in other entities; and
- other types of entities such as mutual funds and other regulated investment funds, although the Board considers that they tend to hold lower levels of investments in a wider range of entities and therefore the exception from consolidation is less likely to affect them. *[IFRS 10.BC298-BC300]*.

In December 2014, the IASB issued *Investment Entities: Applying the Consolidation Exception (Amendments to IFRS 10, IFRS 12 and IAS 28)* which clarifies two aspects of the investment entity exception. This amendment applied for annual periods beginning on or after 1 January 2016 but could be adopted earlier. *[IFRS 10.C1D]*. This amendment is discussed at 10.2.1.A below.

10.1 Definition of an investment entity

IFRS 10 requires that a parent must determine whether it is an investment entity.

An investment entity is an entity that:

(a) obtains funds from one or more investors for the purpose of providing those investors with investment management services;

(b) commits to its investors that its business purpose is to invest funds solely for returns from capital appreciation, investment income, or both; and

(c) measures and evaluates the performance of substantially all of its investments on a fair value basis. *[IFRS 10.27]*.

An entity shall consider all facts and circumstances when assessing whether it is an investment entity, including its purpose and design. An entity that possesses (all of) the three elements (a) to (c) above is an investment entity. *[IFRS 10.B85A]*.

In addition, when considering the investment entity definition, an entity shall consider whether it has the following typical characteristics:

- it has more than one investment;
- it has more than one investor;
- it has investors that are not related parties of the entity; and
- it has ownership interests in the form of equity or similar interests. *[IFRS 10.28]*.

The absence of any of these typical characteristics does not necessarily disqualify an entity from being classified as an investment entity. However, it indicates that additional judgement is required in determining whether the entity is an investment entity and therefore, where any of these characteristics are absent, disclosure is required by IFRS 12 of the reasons for the entity concluding that it is nonetheless, an investment entity. *[IFRS 10.28, B85N, IFRS 12.9A]*.

In November 2016, the Interpretations Committee discussed a number of questions regarding the investment entity requirements in IFRS 10, including whether an entity qualifies as an investment entity if it does not have one or more of the typical characteristics of an investment entity listed in paragraph 28 of IFRS 10. In its March 2017 agenda decision not to add this question to its standard-setting agenda, the Committee concluded that an entity that possesses all three elements of the definition of an investment entity in paragraph 27 of IFRS 10 is an investment entity, even if that entity does not have one or more of the typical characteristics of an investment entity listed in paragraph 28 of IFRS 10.[9]

If facts and circumstances indicate that there are changes to one or more of the three elements (a) to (c) above, that make up the definition of an investment entity, or changes to the typical characteristics of an investment entity, a parent shall reassess whether it is an investment entity. *[IFRS 10.29]*.

A parent that either ceases to be an investment entity or becomes an investment entity shall account for the change in its status prospectively from the date at which the change in status occurred. *[IFRS 10.30]*.

10.2 Determining whether an entity is an investment entity

The first part of the definition of an investment entity in paragraph 27 of IFRS 10 is the requirement that an investment entity provide investors with investment management services. IFRS 10 does not specify how the investment entity must provide these services. In March 2017 (see 10.1 above), the Interpretations Committee noted that IFRS 10 does not preclude an investment entity from outsourcing the performance of these services to a third party and therefore concluded that an investment entity responsible for providing investment management services to its investors can engage another party to perform some or all of the services on its behalf.[10]

Application guidance is provided in respect of the definition (b) in 10.1 above, as follows:
- business purpose (see 10.2.1 below);
- exit strategies (see 10.2.2 below); and
- earnings from investments (see 10.2.3 below).

Application guidance is provided in respect of definition (c) in 10.1 above, as follows:
- Fair value measurement (see 10.2.4 below).

Application guidance is provided in respect of the four typical characteristics described in 10.1 above, as follows:
- more than one investment (see 10.2.5 below);
- more than one investor (see 10.2.6 below);
- unrelated investors (see 10.2.7 below); and
- ownership interests (see 10.2.8 below).

10.2.1 Business purpose

The definition of an investment entity requires that the purpose of the entity is to invest solely for capital appreciation, investment income (such as dividends, interest or rental income), or both. *[IFRS 10.B85B]*.

Documents that include a discussion of an entity's investment objectives, such as offering memoranda, publications distributed by the entity and other corporate or partnership documents, typically provide evidence of an entity's business purpose. Further evidence may include the manner in which an entity presents itself to other parties (such as potential investors or potential investees). *[IFRS 10.B85B]*.

However, an entity that presents itself as an investor whose objective is to jointly develop, produce or market products with its investees, has a business purpose that is inconsistent with the business purpose of an investment entity. This is because the entity will earn returns from the development, production and marketing activity as well as from its investments. *[IFRS 10.B85B]*.

10.2.1.A Entities that provide investment-related services

An investment entity may provide investment-related services (e.g. investment advisory services, investment management, investment support and administrative services), either directly or through a subsidiary, to third parties as well as its investors and not lose its investment entity status. This applies even if those activities are substantial to the entity, subject to the entity continuing to meet the definition of an investment entity. [IFRS 10.B85C]. In March 2017, the Interpretations Committee confirmed that an investment entity may provide investment-related services to third parties, either directly or through a subsidiary, as long as those services are ancillary to its core investment activities and thus do not change the business purpose of the investment entity (see 10.1 above).[11]

An investment entity may also participate in the following investment-related activities either directly or through a subsidiary, if these activities are undertaken to maximise the investment return (capital appreciation or investment income) from its investees and do not represent a separate substantial business activity or a separate substantial source of income to the investment entity:

- providing management services and strategic advice to an investee; and
- providing financial support to an investee such as a loan, capital commitment or guarantee. [IFRS 10.B85D].

The rationale for these provisions is that investment-related services to third parties are simply an extension of the investment entity's investing activities and should not prohibit an entity from qualifying as an investment entity. [IFRS 10.BC239].

An investment entity must consolidate a subsidiary that is itself not an investment entity and whose main purpose and activities are providing services that relate to the investment entity's investment activities. [IFRS 10.32]. If the subsidiary that provides the investment-related services or activities is itself an investment entity, the investment entity parent must measure that subsidiary at fair value through profit or loss. [IFRS 10.B85E].

This means that only those entities that are not investment entities that provide investment related services are consolidated. See 10.3 below for further discussion of the accounting consequences resulting from this requirement.

The requirement to consolidate particular subsidiaries of an investment entity is intended to be a limited exception, capturing only operating subsidiaries that support the investment entity's investing activities as an extension of the operations of the investment entity parent. [IFRS 10.BC240E]. When an entity assesses whether it qualifies as an investment entity, it considers whether providing services to third parties is ancillary to its core investing services. However, the definition of an investment entity requires that the purpose of the entity is to invest solely for capital appreciation, investment income or both (see 10.1 above). Consequently, an entity whose main purpose is to provide investment-related services in exchange for consideration from third parties has a business purpose that is different from the business purpose of an investment entity. This is because the entity's main activity is earning fee income in exchange for its services in contrast to an investment entity whose fee income will be derived from its core activities, which are designed for earning capital appreciation, investment income or both. [IFRS 10.BC240F].

If the subsidiary is not an investment entity, the investment entity parent must assess whether the main activities undertaken by the subsidiary support the core investment activities of the parent. If so, the subsidiary's activities are considered to be an extension of the parent's core investing activities and the subsidiary must be consolidated. These support services provided to the parent and other members of the group could include administration, treasury, payroll and accounting services. [IFRS 10.BC240H].

In November 2016, the Interpretations Committee received a question as to whether a subsidiary provides services that relate to its parent investment entity's investment activities by holding an investment portfolio as beneficial owner. In its agenda decision in March 2017, the Committee concluded that an investment entity does not consider the holding of investments by a subsidiary as beneficial owner (and recognised in the subsidiary's financial statements) to be a service that relates to the parent investment entity's investment activities (see 10.1 above), and observed that it had previously discussed a similar question in March 2014 (see 10.2.1.B below).[12]

The requirement that an investment entity measures at fair value through profit or loss all of its subsidiaries that are themselves investment entities is consistent with the decision not to distinguish between investment entity subsidiaries established for different reasons. [IFRS 10.BC240B]. See 10.2.1.B below.

10.2.1.B Entities that are intermediate holding companies established for tax optimisation purposes

It is explained in the Basis for Conclusion that some respondents to the original Investment Entities ED suggested that at least some investment entity subsidiaries should be consolidated (for example, wholly-owned investment entity subsidiaries that are created for legal, tax or regulatory purposes). However, the Board considers that fair value measurement of all of an investment entity's subsidiaries (except for subsidiaries providing investment-related services or activities) would provide the most useful information and therefore decided to require fair value management for all investment entity subsidiaries. [IFRS 10.BC272].

Some investment entities establish wholly-owned intermediate subsidiaries in some jurisdictions which own all or part of the portfolio of investments in the group structure. The sole purpose of the intermediate subsidiaries is to minimise the tax paid in the 'parent' investment entity. There is no activity within the subsidiaries and the tax advantage arises from returns being channelled through the jurisdiction of the intermediate subsidiary. In March 2014, the Interpretations Committee discussed a request to clarify whether the 'tax optimisation' described above should be considered investment-related services or activities. The Interpretations Committee noted that the IASB believes that fair value measurement of all of an investment entity's subsidiaries would provide the most useful information, except for subsidiaries providing investment-related services or activities and that the IASB had decided against requiring an investment entity to consolidate investment entity subsidiaries that are formed for tax purposes. The Interpretations Committee further noted that one of the characteristics of the 'tax optimisation' subsidiaries described is 'that there is no activity within the subsidiary'. Accordingly, the Interpretations Committee concluded that the parent should not consolidate such subsidiaries and should account for such intermediate subsidiaries at fair value because they do not provide investment-related services or activities and therefore do not meet the requirements for consolidation. Consequently, the Interpretations Committee considered that sufficient guidance already exists, and it decided not to add the issue to its agenda.[13]

10.2.2 Exit strategies

One feature that differentiates an investment entity from other entities is that an investment entity does not plan to hold its investments indefinitely; it holds them for a limited period. *[IFRS 10.B85F]*.

For investments that have the potential to be held indefinitely (typically equity investments and non-financial asset investments), the investment entity must have a documented exit strategy. This documented exit strategy must state how the entity plans to realise capital appreciation from substantially all of these potentially indefinite life investments. An investment entity should also have an exit strategy for any debt instruments that have the potential to be held indefinitely (e.g. perpetual debt instruments). *[IFRS 10.B85F]*.

The investment entity need not document specific exit strategies for each individual investment but should identify different potential strategies for different types or portfolios of investments, including a substantive time frame for exiting the investments. Exit mechanisms that are only put in place for default events, such as breach of contract or non-performance, are not considered exit strategies. *[IFRS 10.B85F]*.

Exit strategies can vary by type of investment. Examples of such strategies for investments in equity securities include an initial public offering, selling the investment in a public market, a private placement, a trade sale of a business, distributions (to investors) of ownership interests in investees and sales of assets (including the sale of an investee's assets followed by a liquidation of an investee). For real estate investments, an example of an exit strategy includes the sale of the real estate through specialised property dealers or the open market. *[IFRS 10.B85G]*.

An investment entity may have an investment in another investment entity that is formed in connection with the entity for legal, regulatory, tax or similar business reasons. In this case, the investment entity investor need not have an exit strategy for that investment, provided that the investment entity investee has appropriate exit strategies for its investments. *[IFRS 10.B85H]*. This is intended to prevent an entity that conducts most of its investing activities through a subsidiary that is a holding company from failing to qualify as an investment entity. *[IFRS 10.BC248]*.

10.2.3 Earnings from investments

An investment entity must commit to its investors that its business purpose is to invest funds solely for returns from capital appreciation, investment income or both.

An entity does not meet this condition when it, or another member of the group containing the entity (i.e. the group that is controlled by the entity's ultimate parent) obtains, or has the objective of obtaining, other benefits from the entity's investments

that are not available to other parties that are not related to the investee. 'Other benefits' means benefits in addition to capital appreciation or investment return and such benefits include:
- the acquisition, use, exchange or exploitation of the processes, assets or technology of an investee including the entity or another group member having disproportionate, or exclusive, rights to acquire assets, technology, products or services of any investee; for example, by holding an option to purchase an asset from an investee if the asset's development is deemed successful;
- joint arrangements or other agreements between the entity or another group member and an investee to develop, produce, market or provide products or services;
- financial guarantees or assets provided by an investee to serve as collateral for borrowing arrangements of the entity or another group member (however, an investment entity would still be able to use an investment in an investee as collateral for any of its borrowings);
- an option held by a related party of the entity to purchase, from that entity or another group member, an ownership interest in an investee of the entity; and
- except as described below, transactions between the entity or another group member and an investee that:
  - are on terms that are unavailable to entities that are not related parties of either the entity, another group member or the investee;
  - are not at fair value; or
  - represent a substantial portion of the investee's or the entity's business activity, including business activities of other group entities. *[IFRS 10.B85I]*.

These requirements in respect of 'other benefits' are anti-avoidance provisions. As explained in the Basis for Conclusions, the Board was concerned that an entity that meets the definition of an investment entity could be inserted into a larger corporate group in order to achieve a particular accounting outcome. This concern is illustrated by an example of a parent entity using an 'internal' investment entity subsidiary to invest in subsidiaries that may be making losses (e.g. research and development activities on behalf of the overall group) and therefore record its investments at fair value, rather than reflecting the underlying activities of the investee. Because of these concerns, the Board has included the requirement that the investment entity, or other members of the group containing the entity, should not obtain benefits from its investees that would be unavailable to other parties that are not related to the investee. *[IFRS 10.BC242]*.

It is also clarified that an entity should demonstrate that fair value is the primary measurement attribute used to evaluate the performance of its investments, both internally and externally. *[IFRS 10.BC252]*.

An entity is not disqualified from being classified as an investment entity because it has investees in the same industry, market or geographical area that trade with each other. This applies where the investment entity has a strategy to invest in more than one investee in that industry, market or geographical area in order to benefit from synergies that increase the capital appreciation and investment income from those investees. *[IFRS 10.B85J]*. The Board decided that trading transactions or synergies that arise between the investments of an investment entity should not be prohibited because their existence does not necessarily mean that the investment entity is receiving any returns beyond solely capital appreciation, investment return, or both. *[IFRS 10.BC243]*.

10.2.4 Fair value measurement

In order to qualify as an investment entity, a reporting entity must measure and evaluate the performance of substantially all of its investments on a fair value basis. This is because using fair value results in more relevant information than, for example, consolidation for subsidiaries or the use of the equity method for interests in associates or joint ventures. In order to demonstrate fair value measurement, an investment entity should:

(a) provide investors with fair value information and measure substantially all of its investments at fair value in its financial statements whenever fair value is permitted in accordance with IFRSs; and

(b) report fair value information to the entity's key management personnel who use fair value as the primary measurement attribute to evaluate the performance of substantially all of its investments and to make investment decisions. *[IFRS 10.B85K]*.

In order to meet the requirements in (a) above, an investment entity would:

- elect to account for any investment property using the fair value model in IAS 40 – *Investment Property;*
- elect the exemption from applying the equity method in IAS 28 for its investments in associates and joint ventures; and
- measure its financial assets at fair value using the requirements in IFRS 9. *[IFRS 10.B85L]*.

As described in the Basis for Conclusions, investments measured at fair value in the statement of financial position with fair value changes recognised in other comprehensive income rather than through profit or loss still satisfy the fair value measurement condition of the definition of an investment entity. *[IFRS 10.BC251]*. However, an investment entity should not account for more than an insignificant amount of financial assets at amortised cost under IFRS 9, nor fail to elect the fair value measurement options in IAS 28 or IAS 40. *[IFRS 10.BC250]*.

Fair value measurement applies only to an investment entity's investments. There is no requirement to measure non-investment assets such as property, plant and equipment or liabilities such as financial liabilities at fair value. *[IFRS 10.B85M]*.

10.2.5 Holding more than one investment

An investment entity would typically hold several investments to diversify its risk and maximise its returns. These may be held directly or indirectly, for example by holding a single investment in another investment entity that itself holds several investments. *[IFRS 10.B85O]*.

However, holding a single investment does not necessarily prevent an entity from meeting the definition of an investment entity. Examples where an investment entity may hold only a single investment are when the entity:

- is in its start-up period and has not yet identified suitable investments and, therefore, has not yet executed its investment plan to acquire several investments;
- has not yet made other investments to replace those it has disposed of;
- is established to pool investors' funds to invest in a single investment when that investment is unobtainable by individual investors (e.g. when the required minimum investment is too high for an individual investor); or
- is in the process of liquidation. *[IFRS 10.B85P]*.

As holding only one investment is not a typical characteristic of an investment entity, this would require disclosure as a significant judgement (see 10.1 above).

10.2.6 Having more than one investor

An investment entity would typically have several investors who pool their funds to gain access to investment management services and investment opportunities they might not have had access to individually. In the Board's opinion, having more than one investor makes it less likely that the entity, or other members of the group containing the entity, would obtain benefits other than capital appreciation or investment income (see 10.2.3 above). *[IFRS 10.B85Q]*.

Although the Board considers that an investment entity would typically have more than one investor, there is no conceptual reason why an investment fund with a single investor should be disqualified from being an investment entity. Therefore, the presence of more than one investor is a typical characteristic of an investment entity rather than as part of the definition of an investment entity. *[IFRS 10.BC260]*.

An investment entity may be formed by, or for, a single investor that represents or supports the interests of a wider group of investors such as a pension fund, a government investment fund or a family trust. *[IFRS 10.B85R]*.

The Board acknowledges that there may be times when the entity temporarily has a single investor. For example, an investment entity may have a single investor when it:

- is within its initial offering period and the entity is actively identifying suitable investors;
- has not yet identified suitable investors to replace ownership interests that have been redeemed; or
- is in the process of liquidation. *[IFRS 10.B85S]*.

These examples are not stated to be exhaustive and there could be other reasons why an investment entity might have only one investor. Having only one investor is not a typical characteristic of an investment entity. The fact that an entity is considered to be an investment entity despite having only one investor is a significant judgement requiring disclosure (see 10.1 above).

10.2.7 Unrelated investors

An investment entity would typically have several investors that are not related parties of the entity or other members of the group containing the entity. The existence of unrelated investors makes it less likely that the entity, or other members of the group containing the entity, would obtain benefits other than capital appreciation or investment income (see 10.2.3 above). *[IFRS 10.B85T]*.

As the definition of a related party includes an entity which has significant influence over a reporting entity, when read literally this means that, typically, an entity that is significantly influenced by one or more parties by, for example, having investors with a greater than twenty percent ownership interest (see Chapter 11 at 4), cannot be an investment entity.

However, an entity may still qualify as an investment entity even though its investors are related to the entity. To support this, an example is illustrated in which an investment entity sets up a separate 'parallel' fund for a group of its employees (such as key management personnel) or other related party investors, which mirrors the investment of the entity's main investment fund. It is stated that this 'parallel' fund may qualify as an investment entity even though all of its investors are related parties. *[IFRS 10.B85U]*. In this example, the key determinant in concluding that the parallel fund is an investment entity is that it is being managed for capital appreciation or investment income.

Although IFRS 10 provides only one example of a fund which qualifies as an investment entity with investors that are related parties, it is explained in the Basis for Conclusions that respondents to the Investment Entities ED provided 'examples of entities with related investors that they believed should qualify as investment entities'. *[IFRS 10.BC261]*.

10.2.8 Ownership interests

An investment entity is typically, but is not required to be, a separate legal entity. Ownership interests in an investment entity will usually be in the form of equity or similar interests (e.g. partnership interests), to which proportionate shares of the net assets of the investment entity are attributed. However, having different classes of investors, some of which have rights only to a specific investment or groups of investments or which have different proportionate shares of the net assets, does not preclude an entity from being an investment entity. *[IFRS 10.B85V]*.

It is rationalised in the Basis of Conclusions that holding a proportionate share of the net assets of an investment entity explains in part why fair value is more relevant to investors of an investment entity because the value of each ownership interest is linked directly to the fair value of the entity's investments. *[IFRS 10.BC263]*. However, whether there is this form of ownership interest in an entity should not be a deciding factor and would inappropriately exclude certain structures from investment entity status. One example illustrated by the Basis for Conclusions of entities that do not have units of ownership interest in the form of equity or similar interests is a pension fund or sovereign wealth fund with a single direct investor which may have beneficiaries that are entitled to the net assets of the investment fund, but do not have ownership units. Another example is funds with different share classes or funds in which investors have discretion to invest in individual assets. *[IFRS 10.BC264, BC266]*. In both of these examples, the investors are entitled to a proportionate share of at least part of the assets of the fund although not the entire fund.

An entity that has significant ownership interests in the form of debt that does not meet the definition of equity may still qualify as an investment entity, provided that the debt holders are exposed to variable returns from changes in the fair value of the entity's net assets. *[IFRS 10.B85W]*.

10.2.9 Investment entity illustrative examples

The following examples illustrate the application of the investment entity criteria and are based on illustrative examples contained in IFRS 10.

Example 6.43:   A limited partnership that is an investment entity

An entity, Limited Partnership (LP), is formed in 2019 with a 10-year life. The offering memorandum states that LP's purpose is to invest in entities with rapid growth potential, with the objective of realising capital appreciation over their life. Entity GP (the general partner of LP) provides 1% of the capital to LP and has responsibility for identifying suitable investments for the partnership. Approximately 75 limited partners, who are unrelated to Entity GP, provide 99% of the capital to the partnership. LP begins its investment activities in 2019 but no investments are identified until 2020 when LP acquires a controlling interest in ABC Corp.

The group structure at 31 December 2020 is illustrated as follows:

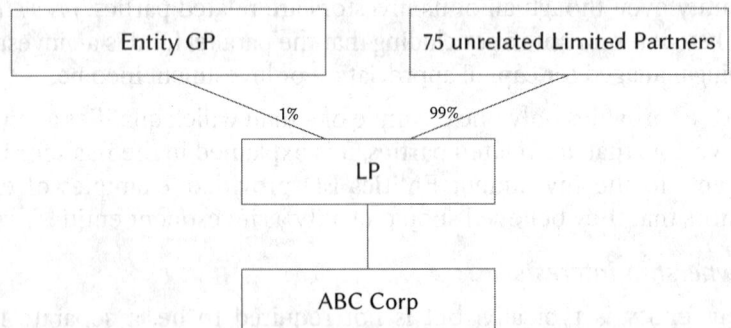

In 2021, LP acquires equity interests in five additional operating companies. Other than acquiring those equity interests, LP conducts no other activities. LP measures and evaluates its investments on a fair value basis and this information is provided to Entity GP and the external investors.

LP plans to dispose of its interests in each of its investees during the 10-year stated life of the partnership. Such disposals include the outright sale for cash, the distribution of marketable equity securities to investors following the successful public offering of the investees' securities and the disposal of investments to the public or other unrelated entities.

In this example, LP meets the definition of an investment entity from formation in 2019 to 31 December 2021 because:

- LP has obtained funds from limited partners and is providing them with investment management services;
- LP's only activity is acquiring equity interests in operating companies with the purpose of realising capital appreciation over the life of the investments. LP has identified and documented exit strategies for its investments, all of which are equity investments; and
- LP measures and evaluates its investments on a fair value basis and reports this financial information to its investors.

In addition, LP displays the following typical characteristics of an investment entity:
- LP is funded by many investors;
- its limited partners are unrelated to LP; and
- ownership in LP is represented by units of partnership interests acquired through a capital contribution.

LP does not hold more than one investment throughout the period. However, this is because it was still in its start-up period and had not identified suitable investment opportunities. *[IFRS 10.IE1-IE6]*.

Example 6.44: Start-up high technology fund that is not an investment entity

An entity, High Technology Fund, is formed by Technology Corp. to invest in start-up technology companies for capital appreciation. Technology Corp. holds a 70% interest in High Technology Fund and controls it; the other 30% ownership interest is held by 10 unrelated investors. Technology Corp. holds options to acquire investments held by High Technology Fund, at their fair value, which would be exercised if the technology developed by the investees would benefit the operations of Technology Corp.

The group structure is illustrated below:

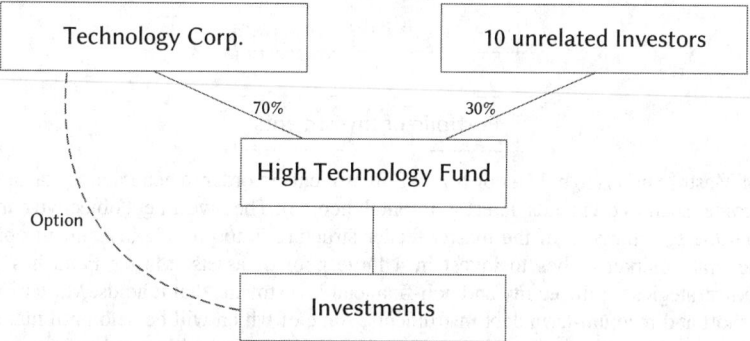

High Technology Fund has no plans for exiting the investments. High Technology Fund is managed by an investment advisor that acts as agent for the investors in High Technology Fund.

In this example, although High Technology Fund's business purpose is investing for capital appreciation and it provides investment management services to its investors, High Technology Fund is not an investment entity because:

- Technology Corp., the parent of High Technology Fund, holds options to acquire investments in investees held by High Technology Fund if assets developed by the investees would benefit the operations of Technology Corp. This provides a benefit in addition to capital appreciation and investment income; and
- the investment plans of High Technology Fund do not include exit strategies for its investments, which are equity instruments. The options held by Technology Corp. are not controlled by High Technology Fund and do not constitute an exit strategy. *[IFRS 10.IE7-IE8]*.

Example 6.45:   Master and feeder funds that are investment entities

An entity, Master Fund, is formed in 2021 with a 10-year life. The equity of Master Fund is held by two related feeder funds. The feeder funds are established in connection with each other to meet legal, regulatory, tax or similar requirements. The feeder funds are capitalised with a 1% investment from the general partner and 99% from equity investors that are unrelated to the general partner (with no party holding a controlling financial interest).

The group structure is illustrated below:

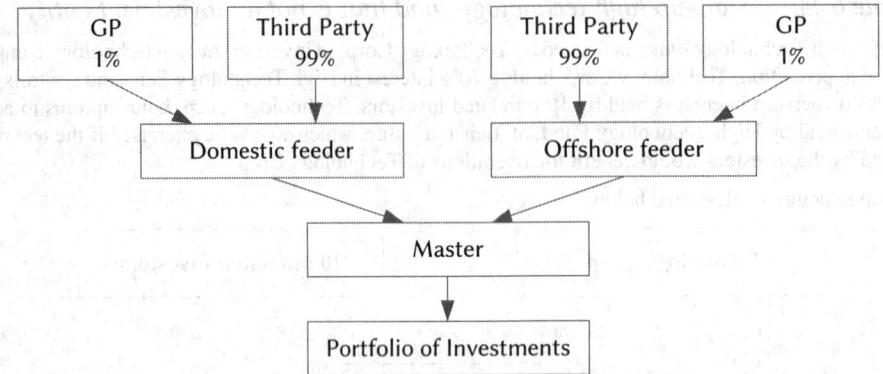

The purpose of Master Fund is to hold a portfolio of investments in order to generate capital appreciation and investment income (such as dividends, interest or rental income). The investment objective communicated to investors is that the sole purpose of the master-feeder structure is to provide investment opportunities for investors in separate market niches to invest in a large pool of assets. Master Fund has identified and documented exit strategies for the equity and non-financial investments that it holds. Master Fund also holds a portfolio of short and medium-term debt instruments, some of which will be held until maturity and some of which will be traded but Master Fund has not specifically identified which investments will be held and which will be traded. Master Fund measures and evaluates substantially all of its investments, including its debt investments, on a fair value basis. In addition, investors receive periodic financial information, on a fair value basis, from the feeder funds. Ownership in both Master Fund and the feeder funds is represented through units of equity.

In this example, Master Fund and the two feeder funds all meet the definition of an investment entity because:

- both Master Fund and the two feeder funds have obtained funds for the purpose of providing investors with investment management services;
- the business purpose of the master-feeder structure, which was communicated directly to investors of the feeder funds, is investing solely for capital appreciation and investment income and Master Fund has identified and documented potential exit strategies for its equity and non-equity financial instruments;
- although the feeder funds do not have an exit strategy for their interests in Master Fund, the feeder funds can nevertheless be considered to have an exit strategy for their investments because Master Fund was formed in connection with the feeder funds and holds investments on behalf of the feeder funds; and
- the investments held by Master Fund are measured and evaluated on a fair value basis and information about the investments made by Master Fund is provided to investors on a fair value basis through the feeder funds.

Master Fund and the feeder funds were formed in connection with each other for legal, regulatory, tax or similar requirements. When considered together, they display the following typical characteristics of an investment entity:
- the feeder fund indirectly holds more than one investment because Master Fund holds a portfolio of investments;
- although Master Fund is wholly capitalised by feeder funds, the feeder funds are funded by many investors who are unrelated to the feeder funds (and to the general partner); and
- ownership in the feeder funds is represented by units of equity interests through a capital contribution. *[IFRS 10.IE12-IE15].*

10.2.10 Multi-layered fund structures

Example 6.45 above illustrates a multi-layered fund structure. The reason and purpose of these is usually to accomplish one or more of the following:
- regulatory reasons to invest in certain jurisdictions; or
- risk mitigation reasons, that is, to ring fence particular investees; or
- investment-return enhancement, where the after-tax returns on an investment can be enhanced by using vehicles in certain jurisdictions.

When an investment entity has a subsidiary that is an intermediate parent that is formed in connection with the parent investment entity for legal, regulatory, tax or similar business reasons, the investment entity investor need not have an exit strategy for that subsidiary. This is on condition that the intermediate investment entity parent has appropriate exit strategies for its investments. *[IFRS 10.B85H].* In addition, an entity must consider all facts and circumstances in assessing whether it is an investment entity, including its purpose and design. *[IFRS 10.B85A].* Illustrative Example 4 of IFRS 10, represented by Example 6.45 above, indicates that funds formed in connection with each other for legal, regulatory, tax or similar requirements can be considered together to determine whether they display the characteristics of an investment entity. In Example 6.45 above, both Domestic Feeder and Offshore Feeder are considered to be investment entities.

10.3 Accounting by an investment entity

In its consolidated financial statements, an investment entity shall:
- consolidate any subsidiary that is not an investment entity and whose main purpose and activities are providing services that relate to the investment entity's investment activities and apply the requirements of IFRS 3 to the acquisition of any such subsidiary (see 10.2.1.A above); *[IFRS 10.32]* and
- measure all other investments in a subsidiary at fair value through profit or loss in accordance with IFRS 9. *[IFRS 10.31].*

In addition, as discussed at 10.2.4 above, the investment entity must elect to account for its own investments in investment property, associates, joint ventures and financial assets at fair value. However, where applicable, some of these investments could be measured at fair value through other comprehensive income. Other assets (e.g. property, plant and equipment) and financial liabilities need not be measured at fair value unless this is required by the relevant IFRS.

The following diagram illustrates the accounting in the consolidated financial statements of an investment entity in a simple group structure:

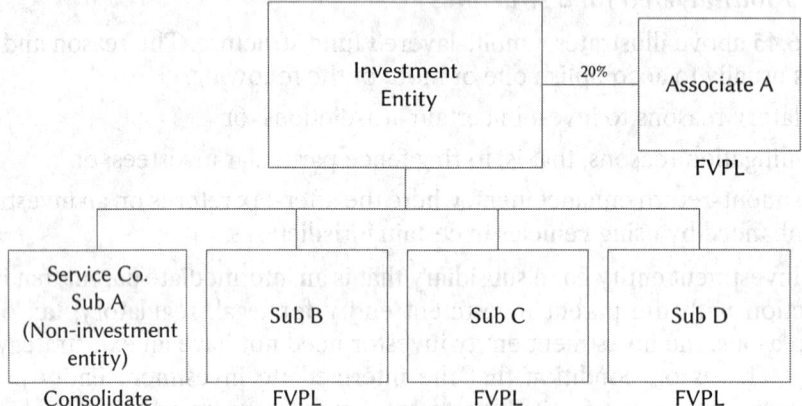

The accounting is less intuitive for investment entities with intermediate holding company subsidiaries. If the intermediate holding company does not meet the conditions for consolidation, then the intermediate holding company, including its investments in subsidiaries, is measured at fair value through profit or loss. The underlying subsidiaries are not measured separately.

The diagram below illustrates the accounting for an investment entity parent using the same group structure as above but with an intermediate parent established for tax optimisation purposes inserted between the investment entity parent and the subsidiaries. As discussed at 10.2.1.B above, the Interpretations Committee has clarified that intermediate holding companies established for tax optimisation purposes should be measured by a parent investment entity at fair value through profit or loss. Therefore, in this situation, the underlying subsidiaries are not separately measured at fair value through profit or loss (or consolidated in the case of the non-investment entity service company). Instead, the intermediate holding entity, including its investments in subsidiaries, is measured at fair value through profit or loss. Parent investment entities with this type of group structure may wish to provide further information in their financial reports to help explain their performance.

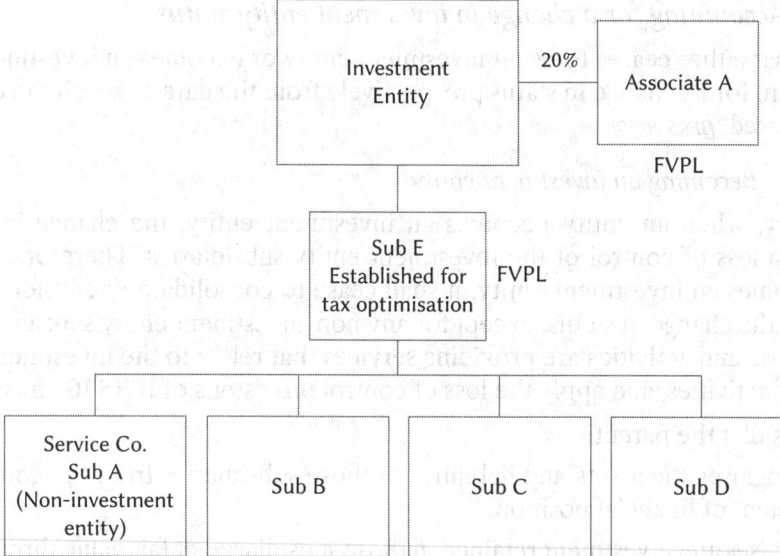

If Subsidiary A (the non-investment entity service company) was owned directly by the investment entity parent, rather than by Subsidiary E, it would be consolidated.

When an investment entity has no subsidiaries that are consolidated (i.e. all subsidiaries are measured at fair value through profit or loss as illustrated above), it presents separate financial statements as its only financial statements. *[IAS 27.8A]*.

When an investment entity parent prepares consolidated financial statements, any subsidiary measured at fair value through profit or loss in those consolidated financial statements must also be accounted for in the same way in its separate financial statements (i.e. at fair value through profit or loss). *[IAS 27.11A]*. When an investment entity parent has subsidiaries that are consolidated in its consolidated financial statements, the parent has a separate accounting policy choice to account for those subsidiaries either at cost, in accordance with IFRS 9 or using the equity method in its separate financial statements (see Chapter 8 at 2).

Fair value will be as determined by IFRS 13. US GAAP currently requires an investment entity to recognise its underlying investments at fair value at each reporting period and provides a practical expedient that permits an entity with an investment in an investment entity to use Net Asset Value (NAV), without adjustment, as fair value in specific circumstances. However, under IFRS 13, net asset value cannot be presumed to equal fair value as the asset being measured is the equity investment in an investment entity not the underlying assets and liabilities of the investment entity itself. Instead, the characteristics of the investment being measured need to be considered when determining its fair value. The use of net asset value in determining fair value is discussed in Chapter 14 at 2.5.1.A.

10.3.1 Accounting for a change in investment entity status

A parent that either ceases to be an investment entity or becomes an investment entity shall account for its change in status prospectively from the date at which the change in status occurred. *[IFRS 10.30]*.

10.3.1.A Becoming an investment entity

In summary, when an entity becomes an investment entity, the change in status is treated as a loss of control of the investment entity subsidiaries. Therefore, when an entity becomes an investment entity, it shall cease to consolidate its subsidiaries from the date of the change in status, except for any non-investment entity subsidiary whose main purpose and activities are providing services that relate to the investment entity's investment activities, and apply the loss of control provisions of IFRS 10. *[IFRS 10.B101]*.

This means that the parent:

- derecognises the assets and liabilities of those subsidiaries from the consolidated statement of financial position;
- recognises any investment retained in those subsidiaries at fair value through profit or loss in accordance with IFRS 9; and
- recognises a gain or loss associated with the loss of control attributed to the subsidiaries. *[IFRS 10.25]*.

Similarly, in the separate financial statements of the parent, when an entity becomes an investment entity, it shall account for an investment in a subsidiary at fair value through profit or loss in accordance with IFRS 9. The difference, if any, between the previous carrying amount of the subsidiary and its fair value at the date of the change in status of the investor shall be recognised as a gain or loss in profit or loss. If the parent has previously recorded its investment in accordance with IFRS 9 at fair value through other comprehensive income (OCI), the cumulative amount of any gain or loss recognised previously in OCI in respect of that subsidiary shall be treated as if the entity had disposed of it at the date of change in status. This gain or loss in OCI would not be recycled to profit or loss. *[IAS 27.11B(b)]*.

IFRS 10 is silent in respect of any accounting changes required when an entity becomes an investment entity in respect of its own investment property, associates, joint ventures and financial assets. However, it is a condition of being an investment entity that a reporting entity must measure and evaluate the performance of substantially all of its investments on a fair value basis. This implies that those assets should have been measured already on a fair value basis in order for the entity to meet the requirements of an investment entity.

10.3.1.B Ceasing to be an investment entity

In summary, when an entity ceases to be an investment entity, the event is treated similar to a business combination. Therefore, when an entity ceases to be an investment entity, it shall apply IFRS 3 to any subsidiary that was previously measured at fair value through profit or loss. This means that all of the individual assets and liabilities of the subsidiary are recognised at fair value (unless IFRS 3 requires otherwise) and the difference between the previous fair value and the value of the individual assets and liabilities is goodwill. The date of change of status is the deemed acquisition date. The fair value of the subsidiary at the deemed acquisition date shall represent the transferred deemed consideration when measuring any goodwill or gain from a bargain purchase that arises from the deemed acquisition. All subsidiaries shall be consolidated in accordance with IFRS 10 from the date of change in status. *[IFRS 10.B100]*.

In the separate financial statements of the parent, when the parent ceases to be an investment entity, it shall account for an investment in a subsidiary either at cost, in accordance with IFRS 9, or using the equity method as described in IAS 28. The date of the change in status shall be the deemed acquisition date. The fair value of the subsidiary at the deemed acquisition date when accounting for the investment, under any of the permitted methods, shall represent the transferred deemed consideration. *[IAS 27.11B(a)]*.

10.4 Accounting by a parent of an investment entity

A parent of an investment entity that is not itself an investment entity cannot use the investment entity exception. It must therefore consolidate all entities that it controls including those controlled through an investment entity subsidiary. *[IFRS 10.33]*.

As described in the Basis for Conclusions, the Board considered whether to permit the exception to consolidation to be 'rolled up' to a non-investment entity parent but rejected this approach. This was despite the fact that the majority of respondents to the *Investment Entities* Exposure Draft argued that if fair value information was more relevant than consolidation at an investment entity subsidiary level, it is also more relevant at the non-investment entity parent level. According to the Board, non-investment entities do not have the unique business models of investment entities; they have other substantial activities besides investing or do not manage substantially all of their investments on a fair value basis. Consequently, in the Board's view, the argument for a fair value measurement is weakened at non-investment entity level. *[IFRS 10.BC276-278]*.

The Board also noted the following in arriving at its conclusion:

- concern that a non-investment entity could achieve different accounting outcomes by holding subsidiaries directly or indirectly through an investment entity; *[IFRS 10.BC280]*
- practical difficulties when a non-investment entity parent and an investment entity invest in the same investment or when an investment entity subsidiary holds a subsidiary that invests in the equity of a non-investment entity parent; *[IFRS 10.BC281]*
- although US GAAP permits 'rolled up' accounting in certain circumstances, this is linked to industry-specific guidance that is not generally contained in IFRSs; *[IFRS 10.BC282]* and
- inconsistency with the roll-up of fair value accounting option permitted by IAS 28. However, the Board thought it was important to retain the fair value accounting that is currently allowed for venture capital organisations, mutual funds, unit trusts and similar entities and that the differences between using equity accounting and fair value accounting was considered to be smaller than between consolidation and fair value measurement for investments in subsidiaries. *[IFRS 10.BC283]*.

Ultimately, due to concerns about potential abuses, the Board considered that the investment entity exception is not retained by a non-investment entity parent in its consolidated financial statements.

11 FUTURE DEVELOPMENTS

11.1 Post-Implementation Review of IFRS 10

At the time of writing, the IASB is in the first phase of the Post-implementation Review of IFRS 10, which involves an initial identification and assessment of the matters to be examined. The publication of the *Request for Information* focusing on particular areas has been postponed until the fourth quarter of 2020.

References

1. Regulation (EC) No. 1606/2002 of the European Parliament and of the Council of 19 July 2002 on the application of international accounting standards, preamble para. (3).
2. Agenda paper for the meeting of the Accounting Regulatory Committee on 24th November 2006 (document ARC/19/2006), *Subject: Relationship between the IAS Regulation and the 4th and 7th Company Law Directives – Meaning of 'Annual Accounts'*, European Commission: Internal Market and Services DG: Free movement of capital, company law and corporate governance: Accounting/RC MX D(2006), 7 November 2006, para. 5.1.
3. Directive 2013/34/EU of the European Parliament and of the Council of 26 June 2013 on the annual financial statements, consolidated financial statements and related reports of certain types of undertakings, amending Directive 2006/43/EC of the European Parliament and of the Council and repealing Council Directives 78/660/EEC and 83/349/EEC, preamble para. (1).
4. *IFRIC Update*, January 2010, pp.2-3.
5. *Effect analysis IFRS 10 Consolidated Financial Statements and IFRS 12 Disclosure of Interests in Other Entities*, IASB, September 2011, pp.25-26.
6. *IFRIC Update*, May 2015, pp.7-8.
7. *IFRIC Update*, September 2013, p.3.
8. *IFRIC Update*, January 2015, p.10.
9. *IFRIC Update*, March 2017, pp.7-8.
10. *IFRIC Update*, March 2017, pp.7-8.
11. *IFRIC Update*, March 2017, pp.7-8.
12. *IFRIC Update*, March 2017, pp.7-8.
13. *IFRIC Update*, March 2014, p.4.

Chapter 7

Consolidation procedures and non-controlling interests

1	INTRODUCTION		497
2	CONSOLIDATION PROCEDURES		497
	2.1	Basic principles	497
	2.2	Proportion consolidated	498
		2.2.1 Attribution when non-controlling interests change in an accounting period	500
	2.3	Consolidating foreign operations	500
	2.4	Intragroup eliminations	501
	2.5	Non-coterminous accounting periods	502
	2.6	Consistent accounting policies	503
3	CHANGES IN CONTROL		503
	3.1	Commencement and cessation of consolidation	503
		3.1.1 Acquisition of a subsidiary that is not a business	504
		3.1.2 Acquisition in stages: associate or joint venture (equity accounted) that is not a business becomes a subsidiary	506
		3.1.2.A Measuring the previously held interest	506
		3.1.2.B Measuring the non-controlling interest	507
	3.2	Accounting for a loss of control	508
		3.2.1 Interpretations Committee and IASB discussions about the sale of a single asset entity containing real estate.	510
	3.3	Accounting for a loss of control where an interest is retained in the former subsidiary	512
		3.3.1 Interest retained in the former subsidiary – financial asset	512

	3.3.2	Interest retained in the former subsidiary – associate or joint venture	513
		3.3.2.A Conflict between IFRS 10 and IAS 28 (September 2014 amendments not applied)	515
		3.3.2.B Conflict between IFRS 10 and IAS 28 (September 2014 amendments applied)	518
		3.3.2.C Reclassification of items of other comprehensive income where the interest retained in the former subsidiary is an associate or joint venture accounted using the equity method	520
		3.3.2.D Application of partial gain recognition where the gain exceeds the carrying amount of the investment in the associate or joint venture accounted using the equity method	520
		3.3.2.E Examples of accounting for sales or contributions to an existing associate	521
		3.3.2.F Determination of the fair value of the retained interest in a former subsidiary which is an associate or joint venture	522
		3.3.2.G Presentation of comparative information for a former subsidiary that becomes an investee accounted for using the equity method	522
	3.3.3	Interest retained in the former subsidiary – joint operation	523
3.4	Loss of control in multiple arrangements		524
3.5	Other comprehensive income		526
3.6	Deemed disposal		530
3.7	Demergers and distributions of non-cash assets to owners		530
	3.7.1	Scope of IFRIC 17	531
	3.7.2	Recognition and measurement in IFRIC 17	531
	3.7.3	Presentation and disclosure	533

4 CHANGES IN OWNERSHIP INTEREST WITHOUT A LOSS OF CONTROL 533

4.1	Reattribution of other comprehensive income	534
4.2	Goodwill attributable to non-controlling interests	536
4.3	Non-cash acquisition of non-controlling interests	538
4.4	Transaction costs	538
4.5	Contingent consideration on purchase of a non-controlling interest	539

5 NON-CONTROLLING INTERESTS 540

5.1	The definition of non-controlling interests	540

Consolidation procedures and non-controlling interests 493

	5.2	Initial measurement of non-controlling interests	541
		5.2.1 Initial measurement of non-controlling interests in a business combination	541
		5.2.2 Initial measurement of non-controlling interests in a subsidiary that is not a business combination	544
	5.3	Measurement of non-controlling interests where an associate holds an interest in a subsidiary	544
	5.4	Presentation of non-controlling interests	545
	5.5	Non-controlling interests classified as financial liabilities	546
	5.6	Subsequent measurement of non-controlling interests	547
		5.6.1 Loss-making subsidiaries	548
6	CALL AND PUT OPTIONS OVER NON-CONTROLLING INTERESTS		548
	6.1	Call options only	549
		6.1.1 Options giving the acquirer present access to returns associated with that ownership interest	549
		6.1.2 Options not giving the acquirer present access to returns associated with that ownership interest	550
	6.2	Put options only	551
		6.2.1 The financial liability for the NCI put	552
		6.2.2 The NCI put provides a present ownership interest	553
		6.2.3 The NCI put does not provide a present ownership interest	554
		6.2.3.A Non-controlling interest is not recognised – financial liability recognised (Approach 1)	555
		6.2.3.B Full recognition of non-controlling interest (Approach 2)	556
		6.2.3.C Partial recognition of non-controlling interest (Approach 3)	556
		6.2.3.D Non-controlling interest is subsequently derecognised (Approach 4)	557
		6.2.4 Assessing whether multiple transactions should be accounted for as a single arrangement	558
		6.2.4.A Identifying a linked transaction	561
		6.2.4.B Accounting for the linked transaction (where a policy to account as a single business combination is followed)	561
	6.3	Combination of call and put options	563
	6.4	Call and put options entered into in relation to existing non-controlling interests	563
	6.5	Put and call options in separate financial statements	564
7	FUTURE DEVELOPMENTS		564

7.1 Sale or contribution of assets between an investor and its associate or joint venture (amendments to IFRS 10 and IAS 28) 564
7.2 Sale or contribution of assets to a joint operation (where the entity has joint control or is a party to the joint operation) 565
7.3 Accounting for put options written on non-controlling interests – *Financial Instruments* with Characteristics of Equity ('FICE') project 566
7.4 Mandatory purchase of non-controlling interests 567
7.5 Post-implementation Reviews of IFRS 10, IFRS 11 and IFRS 12 568

List of examples

Example 7.1:	Potential voting rights	499
Example 7.2:	Eliminating intragroup transactions	501
Example 7.3:	Acquisition of a subsidiary that is not a business	505
Example 7.4:	Acquisition of a subsidiary that is not a business where previously held interest is an equity-accounted joint venture	507
Example 7.5:	Disposal of a subsidiary	513
Example 7.6:	Loss of control of a subsidiary that does not contain a business as a result of a transaction involving an associate	519
Example 7.7:	Sale of a subsidiary to an existing associate	521
Example 7.8:	Step-disposal of a subsidiary (1)	524
Example 7.9:	Step-disposal of a subsidiary (2)	526
Example 7.10:	Reclassification of other comprehensive income	527
Example 7.11:	Deemed disposal through share issue by subsidiary	530
Example 7.12:	Reattribution of other comprehensive income upon a decrease in ownership interest that does not result in a loss of control	534
Example 7.13:	Reattribution of other comprehensive income upon an increase in ownership interest	535
Example 7.14:	Reclassification of reattributed exchange differences upon subsequent loss of control	535
Example 7.15:	Reallocation of goodwill to non-controlling interests	536
Example 7.16:	Initial measurement of non-controlling interests in a business combination (1)	542
Example 7.17:	Initial measurement of non-controlling interests in a business combination (2)	543
Example 7.18:	Initial measurement of non-controlling interests in a business combination by a partly owned subsidiary	543

Example 7.19:	Measurement of non-controlling interest where an associate accounted using the equity method holds an interest in a subsidiary 544
Example 7.20:	Put option and gaining control accounted for as a single transaction 562

Chapter 7

Consolidation procedures and non-controlling interests

1 INTRODUCTION

Chapter 6 discusses the requirements of IFRS 10 – *Consolidated Financial Statements* – relating to the concepts underlying control of an entity (a subsidiary), the requirement to prepare consolidated financial statements and what subsidiaries are to be consolidated within a set of consolidated financial statements. The development, objective and scope of IFRS 10 are dealt with in Chapter 6 at 1.2 and 2.

This chapter deals with the accounting requirements of IFRS 10 relating to the preparation of consolidated financial statements.

2 CONSOLIDATION PROCEDURES

2.1 Basic principles

Consolidated financial statements represent the financial statements of a group (i.e. the parent and its subsidiaries) in which the assets, liabilities, equity, income, expenses and cash flows of the parent and its subsidiaries are presented as those of a single economic entity. *[IFRS 10 Appendix A]*. This approach is referred to as 'the entity concept'. As noted in Chapter 6 at 10, an investment entity generally measures its investments in subsidiaries at fair value through profit or loss in accordance with IFRS 9 – *Financial Instruments* – with limited exceptions. *[IFRS 10.31-33]*.

When preparing consolidated financial statements, an entity first combines the financial statements of the parent and its consolidated subsidiaries on a 'line-by-line' basis by adding together like items of assets, liabilities, equity, income, expenses and cash flows. IFRS 10 requires a parent to prepare consolidated financial statements using uniform accounting policies for like transactions and other events in similar circumstances (see 2.6 below). *[IFRS 10.19, 21, B87]*. Consolidation of an investee begins from the date the investor obtains control of the investee and ceases when the investor loses control of the investee. *[IFRS 10.20, 21, B88]*.

In order to present financial information about the group as that of a single economic entity, the entity must: *[IFRS 10.21, B86]*

(a) combine like items of assets, liabilities, equity, income, expenses and cash flows of the parent with those of its subsidiaries;

(b) offset (eliminate) the carrying amount of the parent's investment in each subsidiary and the parent's portion of equity of each subsidiary (IFRS 3 – *Business Combinations* – explains how to account for any related goodwill, *[IFRS 3.B63(a)]*, – see Chapter 9 at 13); and

(c) eliminate in full intragroup assets and liabilities, equity, income, expenses and cash flows relating to transactions between entities of the group (profits or losses resulting from intragroup transactions that are recognised in assets, such as inventory and fixed assets, are eliminated in full). Intragroup losses may indicate an impairment that requires recognition in the consolidated financial statements. IAS 12 – *Income Taxes* – applies to temporary differences that arise from the elimination of profits and losses resulting from intragroup transactions. See 2.4 below.

Income and expenses of a subsidiary are based on the amounts of the assets and liabilities recognised in the consolidated financial statements at the acquisition date. IFRS 10 gives the example of depreciation expense, which will be based on the fair values of the related depreciable assets recognised in the consolidated financial statements at the acquisition date, *[IFRS 10.21, B88]*, but many items will have a fair value on acquisition that will affect subsequent recognition of income and expense.

Point (b) above refers to the elimination of the parent's investment and the parent's portion of equity. The equity in a subsidiary not attributable, directly or indirectly, to the parent, represents a non-controlling interest. *[IFRS 10 Appendix A]*. The profit or loss and each component of other comprehensive income of a subsidiary are attributed to the owners of the parent and to the non-controlling interests. *[IFRS 10.24, B94]*. Non-controlling interests in subsidiaries are presented within equity, separately from the equity of the owners of the parent. *[IFRS 10.22]*. Changes in a parent's ownership interest in a subsidiary that do not result in the parent losing control of the subsidiary are accounted for as equity transactions. *[IFRS 10.23]*. Accounting for non-controlling interests is discussed in more detail at 2.2, 4 and 5 below.

2.2 Proportion consolidated

The basic procedures described above effectively mean that 100% of the assets, liabilities, income, expenses and cash flows of a subsidiary are consolidated with those of the parent, irrespective of the parent's ownership interest in the subsidiary. However, the profit or loss and each component of other comprehensive income of the subsidiary, and the equity of the subsidiary, are attributed to the parent and the non-controlling interest (if the subsidiary is not wholly owned).

As discussed in Chapter 6 at 4.3.4, when assessing control, an investor considers any potential voting rights that it holds as well as those held by others. Common examples of potential voting rights include options, forward contracts, and conversion features of a convertible instrument.

If there are potential voting rights, or other derivatives containing potential voting rights, the proportion of profit or loss, other comprehensive income and changes in equity allocated to the parent and non-controlling interests (see 5.6 below) in preparing consolidated financial statements is generally determined solely on the basis of existing ownership interests. It does not reflect the possible exercise or conversion of potential voting rights and other derivatives. *[IFRS 10.21, 24, B89, B94].*

Usually, there is no difference between the existing ownership interests and the present legal ownership interests in the underlying shares. However, allocating the proportions of profit or loss, other comprehensive income, and changes in equity based on present legal ownership interests is not always appropriate. For example, there may be situations where the terms and conditions of the potential voting rights mean that the existing ownership interest does not correspond to the legal ownership of the shares. IFRS 10 recognises that, in some circumstances, an entity has, in substance, an existing ownership interest as a result of a transaction that currently gives it access to the returns associated with an ownership interest. In such circumstances, the proportion allocated to the parent and non-controlling interests is determined by taking into account the eventual exercise of those potential voting rights and other derivatives that currently give the entity access to the returns. *[IFRS 10.21, B90].*

Where this is the case, such instruments are not within the scope of IFRS 9 (since IFRS 9 does not apply to subsidiaries that are consolidated). *[IFRS 9.2.1(a)].* This scope exclusion prevents double counting of the changes in the fair value of such a derivative under IFRS 9, and of the effective interest created by the derivative in the underlying investment. In all other cases, instruments containing potential voting rights in a subsidiary are accounted for in accordance with IFRS 9. *[IFRS 10.21, B91].*

Example 7.1 below illustrates this principle.

Example 7.1: Potential voting rights

Entities A and B hold 40% and 60%, respectively, of the equity of Entity C. Entity A also holds a currently exercisable option over one third of Entity B's holding (of shares in Entity C) which, if exercised, would give Entity A a 60% interest in Entity C. The terms of the option are such that it leads to the conclusion that Entity C is controlled by and therefore is a subsidiary of Entity A, but do not give Entity A present access to the returns of the underlying shares. Therefore, in preparing its consolidated financial statements, Entity A attributes 60% of profit or loss, other comprehensive income and changes in equity of Entity C to the non-controlling interest.

Whether potential voting rights and other derivatives, in substance, already provide existing ownership interests in a subsidiary that currently give an entity access to the returns associated with that ownership interest will be a matter of judgement. Issues raised by put and call options over non-controlling interests, including whether or not such options give an entity present access to returns associated with an ownership interest (generally in connection with a business combination) are discussed further at 6 below. This chapter uses the term 'present ownership interest' to include existing legal ownership interests together with potential voting rights and other derivatives that, in substance, already provide existing ownership interests in a subsidiary.

The proportion allocated between the parent and a subsidiary might differ when a non-controlling interest holds cumulative preference shares (see 5.6 below).

2.2.1 Attribution when non-controlling interests change in an accounting period

Non-controlling interests may change during the accounting period. For example, a parent may purchase shares in a subsidiary held by non-controlling interests.

By acquiring some (or all) of the non-controlling interest, the parent will be allocated a greater proportion of the profits or losses of the subsidiary in periods after the additional interest is acquired. *[IFRS 10.BCZ175]*.

Therefore, the profit or loss and other comprehensive income of the subsidiary for the part of the reporting period prior to the transaction are attributed to the owners of the parent and the non-controlling interest based on their ownership interests prior to the transaction. Following the transaction, the profit or loss and other comprehensive income of the subsidiary are attributed to the owners of the parent and the non-controlling interest based on their new ownership interests after the transaction.

2.3 Consolidating foreign operations

IFRS 10 does not specifically address how to consolidate subsidiaries that are foreign operations. As explained in IAS 21 – *The Effects of Changes in Foreign Exchange Rates*, an entity may present its financial statements in any currency (or currencies). If the presentation currency differs from the entity's functional currency, it needs to translate its results and financial position into the presentation currency. Therefore, when a group contains individual entities with different functional currencies, the results and financial position of each entity are translated into the presentation currency of the consolidated financial statements. *[IAS 21.38]*. The requirements of IAS 21 in respect of this translation process are explained in Chapter 15 at 6.

A reporting entity comprising a group with intermediate holding companies may adopt either the direct method or the step-by-step method of consolidation. IFRIC 16 – *Hedges of a Net Investment in a Foreign Operation* – refers to these methods as follows: *[IFRIC 16.17]*

- *direct method* – The financial statements of the foreign operation are translated directly into the functional currency of the ultimate parent.
- *step-by-step method* – The financial statements of the foreign operation are first translated into the functional currency of any intermediate parent(s) and then translated into the functional currency of the ultimate parent (or the presentation currency, if different).

An entity has an accounting policy choice of which method to use, which it must apply consistently for all net investments in foreign operations. *[IFRIC 16.17]*. It is asserted that both methods produce the same amounts in the presentation currency. *[IAS 21.BC18]*. We agree that both methods will result in the same amounts in the presentation currency for the statement of financial position. However, this does not necessarily hold true for income and expense items particularly if an indirectly held foreign operation is disposed of (as acknowledged in IFRIC 16, and discussed below). Differences will also arise between the two methods if an average rate is used, although these are likely to be insignificant. See Chapter 15 at 6.1.1, 6.1.5 and 6.6.3.

IFRIC 16 explains:

> 'The difference becomes apparent in the determination of the amount of the foreign currency translation reserve that is subsequently reclassified to profit or loss. An ultimate parent entity using the direct method of consolidation would reclassify the cumulative foreign currency translation reserve that arose between its functional currency and that of the foreign operation. An ultimate parent entity using the step-by-step method of consolidation might reclassify the cumulative foreign currency translation reserve reflected in the financial statements of the intermediate parent, i.e. the amount that arose between the functional currency of the foreign operation and that of the intermediate parent, translated into the functional currency of the ultimate parent.' *[IFRIC 16.BC36]*.

IFRIC 16 also provides guidance on what does and does not constitute a valid hedge of a net investment in a foreign operation, and on how an entity should determine the amounts to be reclassified from equity to profit or loss for both the hedging instrument and the hedged item, where the foreign operation is disposed of. It notes that in a disposal of a subsidiary by an intermediate parent, the use of the step-by-step method of consolidation may result in the reclassification to profit or loss of a different amount from that used to determine hedge effectiveness. An entity can eliminate this difference by determining the amount relating to that foreign operation that would have arisen if the entity had used the direct method of consolidation. However, IAS 21 does not require an entity to make this adjustment. Instead, it is an accounting policy choice that should be followed consistently for all net investments. *[IFRIC 16.17]*.

IFRIC 16 is discussed in more detail in Chapter 15 at 6.1.5 and 6.6.3 and Chapter 53 at 5.3.

2.4 Intragroup eliminations

IFRS 10 requires intragroup assets and liabilities, equity, income, expenses and cash flows relating to transactions between entities of the group to be eliminated. Profits or losses resulting from intragroup transactions that are recognised in assets, such as inventory and fixed assets, are eliminated in full as shown in Example 7.2 below. *[IFRS 10.21, B86(c)]*.

Example 7.2: Eliminating intragroup transactions

Entity A holds a 75% interest in its subsidiary, Entity B. Entity A sold inventory costing €100,000 to Entity B for €200,000, giving rise to a profit in Entity A of €100,000. Entity B still held the inventory at the end of the reporting period. Tax effects are ignored in this example.

Under IFRS 10, as well as the intragroup sale between Entity A and Entity B, the unrealised profit is eliminated from the group's point of view in consolidation as follows:

	€'000 DR	€'000 CR
Revenue in Entity A	200	
Cost of sales in Entity A		100
Inventory in Entity B		100

The profit from the sale of inventory of €100,000 is reversed against group profit or loss. As the parent made the sale, no amount of the eliminated profit is attributed to the non-controlling interest.

If the fact pattern was reversed, such that Entity B sold inventory to Entity A, and Entity A still held the inventory at the end of the reporting period, the €100,000 of profit would still be reversed in the consolidated financial statements. However, in this instance, as the subsidiary made the sale, €25,000 of the eliminated profit (i.e. the non-controlling interest's 25% share of the €100,000 profit) would be allocated to the non-controlling interest. Therefore, the reduction in profit would be attributed to the owners of the parent and non-controlling interests, in their proportionate interests, 75% and 25%.

If the inventory held by Entity B had been sold to a third party for €300,000 before the end of the reporting period (resulting in a profit in Entity A of €100,000 for the sale to Entity B at €200,000 and a profit in Entity B of €100,000 for the sale to a third party at €300,000), no intragroup elimination of profit is required. The group has sold an asset with a cost of €100,000 for €300,000 creating a profit to the group of €200,000. In this case, the intragroup elimination is limited to the sale between Entities A and B as follows:

	€'000 DR	€'000 CR
Revenue in Entity A	200	
Cost of sales in Entity B		200

Even though losses on intragroup transactions are eliminated in full, they may still indicate an impairment that requires recognition in the consolidated financial statements. *[IFRS 10.21, B86(c)]*. For example, if a parent sells a property to a subsidiary at fair value and this is lower than the carrying amount of the asset, the transfer may indicate that the property (or the cash-generating unit to which that property belongs) is impaired in the consolidated financial statements. This will not always be the case as the value-in-use of the asset (or cash-generating unit) may be sufficient to support the higher carrying value. Transfers between companies under common control involving non-monetary assets are discussed in Chapter 8 at 4.4.1; impairment is discussed in Chapter 20.

Intragroup transactions may give rise to a current and/or deferred tax expense or benefit in the consolidated financial statements. IAS 12 applies to temporary differences that arise from the elimination of profits and losses resulting from intragroup transactions. *[IFRS 10.21, B86(c)]*. These issues are discussed in Chapter 33 at 7.2.5 and 8.7. The application of IAS 12 to intragroup dividends and unpaid intragroup interest, royalties or management charges is discussed in Chapter 33 at 7.5.4, 7.5.5 and 8.5.

Where an intragroup balance is denominated in a currency that differs to the functional currency of a transacting group entity, exchange differences will arise. See Chapter 15 at 6.3 for discussion of the accounting for exchange differences on intragroup balances in consolidated financial statements.

2.5 Non-coterminous accounting periods

The financial statements of the parent and its subsidiaries used in the preparation of the consolidated financial statements shall have the same reporting date. If the end of the reporting period of the parent is different from that of a subsidiary, the subsidiary must prepare, for consolidation purposes, additional financial information as of the same date as the financial statements of the parent, unless it is impracticable to do so. *[IFRS 10.21, B92]*. 'Impracticable' presumably means when the entity cannot apply the requirement after making every reasonable effort to do so. *[IAS 1.7]*.

If it is impracticable for the subsidiary to prepare such additional financial information, then the parent consolidates the financial information of the subsidiary using the most recent financial statements of the subsidiary. These must be adjusted for the effects of significant transactions or events that occur between the date of those financial statements and the date of the consolidated financial statements. The difference between the date of the subsidiary's financial statements and that of the consolidated financial statements must not be more than three months. The length of the reporting periods and any difference between the dates of the financial statements must be the same from period to period. *[IFRS 10.21, B93]*. It is not necessary, as in some national GAAPs, for the subsidiary's reporting period to end before that of its parent.

This requirement seems to imply that, where a subsidiary that was previously consolidated using non-coterminous financial statements is now consolidated using coterminous financial statements (i.e. the subsidiary changed the end of its reporting period), comparative information should be restated so that financial information of the subsidiary is included in the consolidated financial statements for an equivalent period in each period presented. However, it may be that other approaches not involving restatement of comparatives would be acceptable, particularly where the comparative information had already reflected the effects of significant transactions or events during the period between the date of the subsidiary's financial statements and the date of the consolidated financial statements. Where comparatives are not restated, additional disclosures might be needed about the treatment adopted and the impact on the current period of including information for the subsidiary for a period different from that of the parent.

IAS 21 addresses what exchange rate should be used in translating the assets and liabilities of a foreign operation that is consolidated on the basis of financial statements made up to a different date to the reporting date used for the reporting entity's financial statements. *[IAS 21.46]*. This issue is discussed further in Chapter 15 at 6.4.

2.6 Consistent accounting policies

If a member of the group uses accounting policies other than those adopted in the consolidated financial statements for like transactions and events in similar circumstances, appropriate adjustments are made to that group member's financial statements in preparing the consolidated financial statements to ensure conformity with the group's accounting policies. *[IFRS 10.21, B87]*.

IFRS 4 – *Insurance Contracts* – contains an exception to this general rule, as further discussed in Chapter 55 at 8.2.1.C. *[IFRS 4.25(c), BC132]*. However, there is no such exception in IFRS 17 – *Insurance Contracts*.

3 CHANGES IN CONTROL

3.1 Commencement and cessation of consolidation

A parent consolidates a subsidiary from the date on which the parent first obtains control, and ceases consolidating that subsidiary on the date on which the parent loses control. *[IFRS 10.20, 21, B88]*. IFRS 3 defines the acquisition date, which is the date on which the acquirer obtains control of the acquiree, *[IFRS 3.8, Appendix A]*, (see Chapter 9 at 4.2).

The requirement to continue consolidating (albeit in a modified form) also applies to a subsidiary held for sale accounted for under IFRS 5 – *Non-current Assets Held for Sale and Discontinued Operations* (see Chapter 4).

3.1.1 Acquisition of a subsidiary that is not a business

These basic principles also apply when a parent acquires a controlling interest in an entity that is not a business, as defined in IFRS 3 (see Chapter 9 at 3.2). *[IFRS 3.3, IFRS 3 Appendix A, IFRS 3.B7-B12D]*. Under IFRS 10, an entity must consolidate all investees that it controls, not just those that are businesses, and therefore the parent will recognise any non-controlling interest in the subsidiary (see 5 below). IFRS 3 states that when an entity acquires a group of assets or net assets that is not a business, the acquirer allocates the cost of the group between the individual identifiable assets acquired and liabilities assumed based on their relative fair values at the date of purchase. Such a transaction or event does not give rise to goodwill. *[IFRS 3.2(b)]*. The cost of the group of assets is the sum of all consideration given and any non-controlling interest recognised and also includes transaction costs incurred, if any. The allocation of the transaction price (or cost) to the identifiable assets acquired and liabilities assumed is discussed further in Chapter 9 at 2.2.2.

In our view, if the non-controlling interest has a present ownership interest and is entitled to a proportionate share of net assets upon liquidation, the acquirer has a choice to recognise the non-controlling interest on initial measurement at:

(a) its proportionate share in the recognised amounts (i.e. fair values at the date of acquisition) of the entity's identifiable net assets;

(b) its fair value (measured in accordance with IFRS 13 – *Fair Value Measurement*);

(c) its proportionate share of the consolidated book values of the net assets – including transaction costs. The basis for including transaction costs is that these are included in the consolidated book values of the subsidiary's net assets; or

(d) its proportionate share of the consolidated book values of the net assets – excluding transaction costs. The basis for excluding transaction costs is that these are borne by the parent and are not part of the net assets attributable to the non-controlling interest.

Approaches (a) and (b) above are consistent with the choices on the initial recognition of non-controlling interest required by IFRS 3. *[IFRS 3.19]*. However, it could be argued that an asset acquisition is an economically dissimilar transaction to a business combination, and therefore the guidance in IFRS 3 may not be a 'similar related issue' under the hierarchy in IAS 8 – *Accounting Policies, Changes in Accounting Estimates and Errors* – for selection and application of accounting policies. *[IAS 8.11(a)]*. Under this view, Approaches (c) and (d) above, which are based on the proportionate share of the consolidated book values of the entity's net assets, may also be supported. As explained in 3.1.2 below, there are different approaches to determining the cost of the group of the assets in situations where the entity acquired was an associate or joint venture accounted under the equity method prior to the acquisition. Consequently, the consolidated book values of the net assets (and the non-controlling interest under Approaches (c) and (d)) may differ from the amounts that would be recognised had the transaction been a business combination. See Examples 7.3 and 7.4 below.

In all other cases, non-controlling interest is recognised at fair value (measured in accordance with IFRS 13), unless another measurement basis is required in accordance with IFRS (e.g. any share-based payment transaction classified as equity is measured in accordance with IFRS 2 – *Share-based Payment*).

The acquisition of a subsidiary that is not a business (where there is no pre-existing interest) is illustrated in Example 7.3 below.

Example 7.3:   Acquisition of a subsidiary that is not a business

Entity A pays £160,000 to acquire an 80% controlling interest in the equity shares of Entity B, which holds a single building (measured using the cost model under IAS 16 –*Property, Plant and Equipment*) that is not a business. The fair value of the building is £200,000. An unrelated third party holds the remaining 20% interest in the equity shares. The fair value of the non-controlling interest (NCI) is £40,000. In this case, the fair value of the NCI (as an equity interest) is the same as the NCI's proportionate share of the fair values of the identifiable net assets of Entity B. Transaction costs are £4,000. Tax effects and transaction costs, if any, are ignored in this example. As noted at 3.1.1 above, there are four approaches to determining NCI which are illustrated below.

Approach (a) – measure NCI based on the proportionate share of the identifiable fair values of the net assets of Entity B

Entity A initially records the following accounting entry:

	£'000 DR	£'000 CR
Building	204	
NCI (20% × £200,000)		40
Cash		164

Approach (b) – measure NCI at its fair value

Entity A initially records the following accounting entry:

	£'000 DR	£'000 CR
Building	204	
NCI (at fair value)		40
Cash		164

Approach (c) – measure NCI based on the proportionate share of the consolidated book values of the net assets of Entity B (including transaction costs)

Entity A initially records the following accounting entry:

	£'000 DR	£'000 CR
Building	205	
NCI (at 20% / 80% × £164,000 or 20% × £205,000)		41
Cash		164

Approach (d) – measure NCI based on the proportionate share of the consolidated book values of the net assets of Entity B (excluding transaction costs)

Entity A initially records the following accounting entry:

	£'000 DR	£'000 CR
Building	204	
NCI (at 20% / 80% × £160,000 or 20% × £200,000)		40
Cash		164

3.1.2 Acquisition in stages: associate or joint venture (equity accounted) that is not a business becomes a subsidiary

An entity that has an interest in an associate or joint venture that does not constitute a business may obtain control and so become a parent of a subsidiary that does not constitute a business. Current accounting standards do not address the accounting treatment for an acquisition in stages from associate or joint venture to a subsidiary that is considered as an asset acquisition rather than a business combination. This raises questions as to how to measure the previously held interest and the non-controlling interests on acquisition.

3.1.2.A Measuring the previously held interest

As discussed at 3.1.1 above, the cost of the group of assets is the sum of all the consideration given (including transaction costs incurred, if any) and any non-controlling interest recognised. It is therefore necessary to determine the 'cost' of the previously held interest, being part of the consideration given for the group of assets acquired. In January 2019, the Interpretations Committee issued an agenda decision regarding a different, but relevant, example of the step acquisition of an investment in a subsidiary accounted for at cost in the separate financial statements of the parent. The Interpretations Committee concluded that a reasonable reading of the requirements in IFRSs could result in the application of either one of two approaches to determine 'cost': the 'fair value as deemed cost' approach or the 'accumulated cost' approach.[1] See Chapter 8 at 2.1.1.C. Therefore, in our view, the following approaches are acceptable methods of measuring the previously held interest in the associate or joint venture.

Approach 1 – Fair value as deemed cost

Where a fair value as deemed cost approach is applied, the fair value of the previously held interest at the date that control is obtained is deemed to be the cost for the purposes of accounting for the acquisition of the subsidiary. Under this approach, the transaction is viewed as if the entity is exchanging its initial interest (plus consideration for the additional interest) for a controlling interest in the investee (exchange view).

Approach 2 – Equity-accounted carrying amount as accumulated cost

Following an 'accumulated cost' method, the carrying amount of the associate or joint venture could be considered the relevant cost in accounting for the acquisition of the subsidiary. Although there is a change in status, it is not appropriate to remeasure the existing ownership interest as the subsidiary is not a business. Accordingly, no gain or loss is recorded on the acquisition of the subsidiary, assuming that the carrying amount of the new subsidiary is recoverable.

In certain circumstances, it may be acceptable to take a third approach and consider the cost of the previously held interest to be the accumulated historical cost consideration for the investment in the associate or joint venture. Given the agenda decision of the Interpretations Committee mentioned above, any difference arising between the previous carrying amount and the accumulated historical costs will be recognised in profit or loss. However, caution should be taken with using this approach as it may not always provide relevant information. If the accumulated historical cost consideration was lower than the equity-accounted carrying amount of the previous associate or joint venture, there would be a loss recognised, even though there is no economic loss arising from the transaction. Where the accumulated historical cost consideration exceeds the equity-accounted carrying amount of the previous associate or joint venture, care should be taken to ensure that the subsidiary is not carried at above its recoverable amount.

3.1.2.B Measuring the non-controlling interest

Example 7.4 illustrates the computation of the non-controlling interest and the cost of the building in the consolidated financial statements where a subsidiary (that does not meet the definition of a business) is acquired following the purchase of an additional interest in an equity-accounted joint venture.

Example 7.4: *Acquisition of a subsidiary that is not a business where previously held interest is an equity-accounted joint venture*

Entity A acquires a 50% interest in Entity C upon formation of a joint venture with Entity B in 2015. Each venturer contributed $5m which was used by Entity C to purchase a building accounted using the cost model in IAS 16. The functional currency of all entities is US dollars ($).

In 2020, cumulative earnings of the joint venture were $1.5 million and cumulative dividends declared were $0.5 million. Immediately prior to the following transaction, Entity A has an equity accounted joint venture with a carrying amount of $5.5 million ($5m initial investment + 50% × ($1.5m – $0.5m)).

Entity A and Entity B entered into an arrangement whereby Entity A acquired 30% of the shares of Entity C in exchange for $4.5 million cash paid to Entity B. Transaction costs incurred by Entity A are $0.2 million. Following the transaction, Entity A has an 80% controlling interest in the equity shares of Entity C, which holds a single building that is not a business. Assuming that there are no control premiums or other investment premiums or discounts, the fair value of the non-controlling interest (NCI) is $3 million. The fair value of 100% of Entity C at the acquisition date is $15 million. Tax effects, if any, are ignored in this example.

For an asset acquisition, the cost of the group of assets is the sum of all the consideration given (i.e. the cash paid of $4.5m plus the 'cost' of the previously held interest in Entity C) and any NCI recognised, together with transaction costs.

How should Entity A measure the previously held interest in Entity C?

As noted at 3.1.2.A above, there are two main approaches to determine the 'cost' of the previously held interest – Approach 1: cost equals the fair value of the previously held interest, and Approach 2: use the equity-accounted interest as cost of the previous interest.

Under Approach 1, Entity A records the previously held interest in Entity C at its fair value of $7.5 million (50% × $15m). Accordingly, on acquisition, Entity A records a gain of $2 million on remeasurement of the previously held interest.

Under Approach 2, Entity A measures its previously held interest in Entity C at its previous equity accounted value of $5.5 million. No gain or loss is recognised on the transaction.

How should Entity A measure the NCI in the step acquisition?

As noted at 3.1.1 above, there are four approaches:

- Approach (a) – measure NCI based on the proportionate share of the fair values of the identifiable net assets;
- Approach (b) – measure NCI at its fair value;
- Approach (c) – measure NCI based on the proportionate share of the consolidated book values of the net assets of Entity C (including transaction costs); and
- Approach (d) – measure NCI based on the proportionate share of the consolidated book values of the net assets of Entity C (excluding transaction costs).

Entity A records the following amounts for NCI:

	Previously held interest – deemed cost	
	Approach 1 (fair value) $m	Approach 2 (equity-accounted value) $m
Fair value of building (i)	15.0	15.0
Deemed cost of previous interest (ii)	7.5	5.5
Consideration paid for second tranche (iii)	4.5	4.5
Transaction costs (iv)	0.2	0.2
Fair value of NCI (v)	3.0	3.0
NCI – Approach (a): 20% of fair value of building (i)	3.0	3.0
NCI – Approach (b): fair value (v)	3.0	3.0
NCI – Approach (c): 20/80 of [(ii) + (iii)+(iv)]	3.1	2.6
NCI – Approach (d): 20/80 of [(ii) + (iii)]]	3.0	2.5

The cost of the building consolidated is as follows:

	Previously held interest – deemed cost	
	Approach 1 (fair value) $m	Approach 2 (equity-accounted value) $m
NCI – Approach (a)	15.2	13.2
NCI – Approach (b)	15.2	13.2
NCI – Approach (c)	15.3	12.8
NCI – Approach (d)	15.2	12.7

The cost of the building comprises the sum of:
- the deemed cost of the previously held interest (i.e. $7.5 million under Approach 1 and $5.5 million under Approach 2);
- the consideration paid for the second tranche of $4.5 million;
- transaction costs of $0.2 million; and
- NCI recognised as in the earlier table above.

3.2 Accounting for a loss of control

IFRS 10 clarifies that an investor is required to reassess whether it controls an investee if the facts and circumstances indicate that there are changes to one or more of the three elements of control. *[IFRS 10.8, B80]*. The elements of control are: power over the investee; exposure, or rights, to variable returns from the investor's involvement with the investee; and the investor's ability to use its power over the investee to affect the amount of the investor's returns. *[IFRS 10.7]*. See Chapter 6 at 9 for further discussion, including examples of situation where a change in control may arise.

A parent may lose control of a subsidiary because of a transaction that changes its absolute or relative ownership level. For example, a parent may lose control of a subsidiary if:
- it sells some or all of the ownership interests;
- it contributes or distributes some or all of the ownership interests; or
- a subsidiary issues new ownership interests to third parties (therefore a dilution in the parent's interests occurs).

Alternatively, a parent may lose control without a change in absolute or relative ownership levels. For example, a parent may lose control on expiry of a contractual agreement that previously allowed the parent to control the subsidiary, [IFRS 10.BCZ180], or on entry into a contractual arrangement which gives joint control with another party (or parties). A parent may also lose control if the subsidiary becomes subject to the control of a government, court, administrator, receiver, liquidator or regulator. This evaluation may require the exercise of judgement, based on the facts and circumstances, including the laws in the relevant jurisdiction (see Chapter 6 at 4.3.2 and 9.2).

If a parent loses control of a subsidiary, it is required to: [IFRS 10.25, 26, B98]

(a) derecognise the assets (including any goodwill) and liabilities of the former subsidiary at their carrying amounts at the date when control is lost;

(b) derecognise the carrying amount of any non-controlling interests in the former subsidiary at the date when control is lost. This includes any components of other comprehensive income attributable to them;

(c) recognise the fair value of the consideration received, if any, from the transaction, event or circumstances that resulted in the loss of control;

(d) recognise a distribution if the transaction, event or circumstances that resulted in the loss of control involves a distribution of shares in the subsidiary to owners in their capacity as owners (see 3.7 below);

(e) recognise any investment retained in the former subsidiary at its fair value at the date when control is lost (see 3.3 below);

(f) reclassify to profit or loss, or transfer directly to retained earnings if required by other IFRSs, the amounts recognised in other comprehensive income in relation to the subsidiary (see 3.5 below).

If a parent loses control of a subsidiary, the parent accounts for all amounts previously recognised in other comprehensive income in relation to that subsidiary on the same basis as would be required if the parent had directly disposed of the related assets or liabilities. [IFRS 10.26, B99]. This is discussed at 3.5 below; and

(g) recognise any resulting difference as a gain or loss in profit or loss attributable to the parent.

Any amounts owed to or by the former subsidiary (which cease to be eliminated on consolidation) should be accounted for in accordance with the relevant IFRSs. [IFRS 10.25]. Such balances are often financial assets or financial liabilities, which are initially recognised at fair value in accordance with IFRS 9 at the date of loss of control. [IFRS 9.5.1.1, 5.1.1A, 5.1.2, 5.1.3]. See Chapter 49 at 3.

Sometimes, the parent may receive contingent consideration on the sale of a subsidiary. In most cases, the parent will have a contractual right to receive cash or another financial asset from the purchaser and, therefore, such balances are often financial assets within the scope of IFRS 9, and consequently initially measured at fair value. [IFRS 9.5.1.1]. See also Chapter 45 at 3.7.1.B.

IFRS 5's requirements apply to a non-current asset (or disposal group) that is classified as held for sale. See Chapter 4 at 2. The presentation requirements when the subsidiary of which the parent loses control meets the definition of a discontinued operation are discussed in Chapter 4 at 3.

Chapter 20 at 8.5 addresses the allocation of goodwill when an operation is disposed of which forms part of a cash-generating unit to which goodwill has been allocated.

IFRS 10 refers only to loss of control of a subsidiary, without drawing a distinction between when the subsidiary is a business or not nor whether this happens as part of the ordinary activities of an entity or not. During 2019 and 2020, the Interpretations Committee and the IASB discussed whether IFRS 10 or IFRS 15 – *Revenue from Contracts with Customers* – applies when an entity loses control of a single asset entity containing real estate as part of its ordinary activities.[2] This is discussed further at 3.2.1 below.

Where a parent loses control over a subsidiary because it has sold or contributed its interest in a subsidiary to an associate or joint venture (accounted for using the equity method), there is a conflict between the requirements of IFRS 10 and those of IAS 28 – *Investments in Associates and Joint Ventures*. This is because IAS 28 restricts any gain arising on the sale of an asset to an associate or joint venture (or on the contribution of a non-monetary asset in exchange for an equity interest in an associate or a joint venture) to that attributable to the unrelated investors' interests in the associate or joint venture, whereas IFRS 10 does not. In order to resolve the conflict, in September 2014, the IASB had issued *Sale or Contribution of Assets between an Investor and its Associate or Joint Venture (Amendments to IFRS 10 and IAS 28)* – but subsequently deferred the effective date of application of the amendments. This issue is discussed further at 3.3.2 and 7.1 below.

The following parts of this section address further issues relating to accounting for the loss of control of a subsidiary including: where an interest is retained in the former subsidiary (see 3.3 below), loss of control in multiple arrangements (see 3.4 below), the treatment of other comprehensive income on loss of control (see 3.5 below), deemed disposals (see 3.6 below), and demergers and distributions (see 3.7 below).

3.2.1 Interpretations Committee and IASB discussions about the sale of a single asset entity containing real estate.

As noted at 3.2 above, in June 2019, the Interpretations Committee discussed a request about the accounting for a transaction in which an entity, as part of its ordinary activities, enters into a contract with a customer to sell real estate by selling its equity interest in a subsidiary.[3] The entity established the subsidiary some time before it enters into the contract with the customer; the subsidiary has one asset – real estate inventory – and a related tax asset or liability. The entity has applied IFRS 10 in consolidating the subsidiary before it loses control of the subsidiary as a result of the transaction with the customer.

The request and the Interpretations Committee's discussion focused only on situations where the entity had control over (and, therefore, consolidated) the subsidiary prior to entering into a contract with a customer.

The request asked the Interpretations Committee to consider the following questions:
- Whether the entity applies IFRS 10 or IFRS 15 to the transaction?
- If the entity applies IFRS 10 to the transaction, whether the entity can present the component parts of any gain or loss resulting from the transaction within separate line items in the statement of profit or loss or, instead, is required to present any gain or loss within one line item in that statement?
- If the conclusion is that IFRS 15 applies to the transaction, would this conclusion continue to apply if, in addition to the real estate and any related tax asset or liability, the subsidiary has other assets or liabilities (for example, a financing liability)?

This issue impacts whether the transaction gives rise to a gain or loss on sale of the subsidiary (if IFRS 10 applies) or revenue is recognised (if IFRS 15 applies). This is more than just a presentational issue as the outcome of these discussions may also impact the timing of recognition and measurement of the consideration received. For example, the amount and timing of revenue recognition would be determined by IFRS 15, if that standard applies.

The Interpretations Committee did not make any decisions in June 2019 and, at the time of writing, had not issued an agenda decision on this matter. Instead, the issue was referred to the IASB.

In October 2019, the IASB directed its Staff to research the feasibility of narrow-scope standard setting.[4] In June 2020, the IASB discussed a possible narrow-scope amendment to IFRSs that would have required an entity to apply IFRS 15, instead of IFRS 10, to sales of subsidiaries that have all of the following characteristics:
- the entity contracts with a customer for goods or services that are the output of its ordinary activities in exchange for consideration;
- the subsidiary contains only inventory and any related income tax asset or liability; and
- the entity retains no interest in the inventory transferred to the customer.

The IASB decided against proposing this amendment.[5]

During the discussions held at both the Interpretations Committee and the IASB, a number of members of the Committee and the Board considered that, absent an amendment, IFRS 10 (rather than IFRS 15) would apply to the transaction considered. During the June 2020 discussion, some Board members thought there was merit in a narrow-scope amendment. However, concerns were raised about potential unintended consequences of proposing a narrow-scope amendment without a more comprehensive discussion. Any narrow-scope amendment would affect the scope of both IFRS 10 and IFRS 15 and, as such, Board members wanted to learn more from stakeholders about the need for and consequences of such a project. However, these considerations were not noted in the relevant IFRIC Update and IASB Update that were issued as summaries of the meetings. At the time of writing, this matter was expected to be considered as part of Phase 2 of the Post-implementation Review (PIR) of IFRS 10,[6] which was scheduled to commence in Q4 2020.[7]

Until the deliberation process on this question is completed, there may continue to be some diversity in practice. However, in the meantime, entities may need to consider the discussions on this matter as they determine the appropriate standard to apply to transactions with customers involving the loss of control of a single asset entity. This issue is discussed further in Chapter 27 at 3.5.1.J.

A related issue has been submitted to the Interpretations Committee concerning the accounting for a sale and leaseback transaction.[8] In that fact pattern, the parent sells 100% of the shares in its wholly owned subsidiary established some time before which contains a real estate asset (which does not constitute a business under IFRS 3) to a third party and leases the real estate asset back. The sales price exceeds the carrying amount of the transferred asset, resulting in a gain. The parent loses control of the subsidiary at the point of transfer. The transfer of the real estate asset would meet the requirements to be accounted as a 'sale' and for the transaction to be a 'sale and leaseback' accounted under paragraph 100 of IFRS 16 – *Leases* – which would mean only a portion of the gain would be recognised (see Chapter 23 at 8). The question posed to the Interpretations Committee was whether the IFRS 16 sale and leaseback guidance applies or whether the transaction should be accounted as a loss of control of a subsidiary in accordance with IFRS 10. Under IFRS 10, a gain on loss of control would be recognised and then the parent would account for the lease entered into with the third party. This issue had not been considered by the Interpretations Committee at the time of writing.

3.3 Accounting for a loss of control where an interest is retained in the former subsidiary

According to IFRS 10, when a parent loses control of a subsidiary, it must recognise any investment retained in the former subsidiary at its fair value at the date when control is lost. Any gain or loss on the transaction will be recorded in profit or loss. The fair value of any investment that it retains at the date control is lost, including any amounts owed by or to the former subsidiary, will be accounted for, as applicable, as:

- the fair value on initial recognition of a financial asset (see Chapter 49 at 3); or
- the cost on initial recognition of an investment in an associate or joint venture (see Chapter 11 at 7.4.1).

The IASB's view is that the loss of control of a subsidiary is a significant economic event that marks the end of the previous parent-subsidiary relationship and the start of a new investor-investee relationship, which is recognised and measured initially at the date when control is lost. IFRS 10 is based on the premise that an investor-investee relationship differs significantly from a parent-subsidiary relationship. Therefore, the IASB decided that 'any investment the parent has in the former subsidiary after control is lost should be measured at fair value at the date that control is lost and that any resulting gain or loss should be recognised in profit or loss.' *[IFRS 10.BCZ182]*.

The following discussion addresses the accounting for the loss of control in certain situations – where the interest retained in the former subsidiary is a financial asset (see 3.3.1 below); where the interest retained in the former subsidiary is an associate or joint venture that is accounted for using the equity method (see 3.3.2 below); and where the interest retained in the former subsidiary is a joint operation (see 3.3.3 below).

3.3.1 Interest retained in the former subsidiary – financial asset

Example 7.5 below illustrates the above requirement where the interest retained in the former subsidiary is a financial asset.

Consolidation procedures and non-controlling interests

Example 7.5: Disposal of a subsidiary

A parent sells an 85% interest in a wholly owned subsidiary as follows:
- after the sale the parent elects to account for the interest at fair value through other comprehensive income under IFRS 9;
- the subsidiary did not recognise any amounts in other comprehensive income;
- net assets of the subsidiary before the disposal are $500 million;
- cash proceeds from the sale of the 85% interest are $750 million; and
- the fair value of the 15% interest retained by the parent is $130 million.

The parent accounts for the disposal of an 85% interest as follows:

	$m DR	$m CR
Financial asset	130	
Cash	750	
Net assets of the subsidiary derecognised (summarised)		500
Gain on loss of control of subsidiary		380

The gain recognised on the loss of control of the subsidiary is calculated as follows:

	$m	$m
Gain on interest disposed of		
Cash proceeds on disposal of 85% interest	750	
Carrying amount of 85% interest (85% × $500 million)	(425)	
		325
Gain on interest retained		
Carrying amount of 15% investment carried at fair value through other comprehensive income	130	
Carrying amount of 15% interest (15% × $500 million)	(75)	
		55
Gain recognised on loss of control of subsidiary		380

Although IFRS 10 requires that any investment retained in the former subsidiary is to be recognised at its fair value at the date when control is lost, no guidance is given in the standard as to how such fair value should be determined. However, IFRS 13 provides detailed guidance on how fair value should be determined for financial reporting purposes. IFRS 13 is discussed in detail in Chapter 14.

3.3.2 Interest retained in the former subsidiary – associate or joint venture

It can be seen that the requirements in IFRS 10 discussed above result in a gain or loss upon loss of control as if the parent had sold all of its interest in the subsidiary, not just that relating to the percentage interest that has been sold.

IFRS 10's requirements also apply where a parent loses control over a subsidiary that has become an associate or a joint venture. However, there is a conflict between these requirements and those of IAS 28 for transactions where a parent sells or contributes an interest in a subsidiary to an associate or a joint venture (accounted for using the equity method) and the sale or contribution results in a loss of control in the subsidiary by the parent. This is because IAS 28 restricts any gain arising on the sale of an asset to an associate or a joint venture, or on the contribution of a non-monetary asset in exchange for an equity interest in an associate or a joint venture, to that attributable to unrelated investors' interests in the associate or joint venture. *[IAS 28.28, 30]*. In order to resolve the conflict, in September 2014, the IASB had issued *Sale or Contribution of Assets between an Investor and its Associate or Joint Venture (Amendments to IFRS 10 and IAS 28)* ('the September 2014 amendments'). These amendments, where applied, would require the gain or loss resulting from the loss of control of a subsidiary that does not contain a business (as defined in IFRS 3 – see Chapter 9 at 3.2), *[IFRS 3.3, Appendix A, B7-B12D]*, as a result of a sale or contribution of a subsidiary to an existing associate or a joint venture (that is accounted for using the equity method) – to be recognised only to the extent of the unrelated investors' interests in the associate or joint venture. The same requirement applies to the remeasurement gain or loss relating to the former subsidiary if, following the transaction, a parent retains an investment in a former subsidiary and the former subsidiary is now an associate or a joint venture that is accounted for using the equity method. *[IFRS 10.25, 26, B99A]*. See Example 7.6 at 3.3.2.B below. However, a full gain or loss would be recognised on the loss of control of a subsidiary that constitutes a business, including cases in which the investor retains joint control of, or significant influence over, the investee. *[IFRS 10.25, 26, B98, B99]*.

IFRS 10, prior to the revisions resulting from the September 2014 amendments, does not draw a distinction in accounting for the loss of control of a subsidiary that is a business and one that is not.

The September 2014 amendments were to be applied prospectively to transactions occurring in annual periods beginning on or after 1 January 2016, with earlier application permitted. *[IFRS 10.C1C, IAS 28.45C]*. However, in December 2015, the IASB issued a further amendment – *Effective Date of Amendments to IFRS 10 and IAS 28*. This amendment deferred the effective date of the September 2014 amendment until the IASB has finalised any revisions that result from the IASB's research project on the equity method (although the IASB now plans no further work on this project until the Post-implementation Reviews (PIRs) of IFRS 10, IFRS 11 – *Joint Arrangements* – and IFRS 12 – *Disclosure of Interests in Other Entities* – are undertaken).[9] At the time of writing, work on Phase 2 of the PIRs of IFRS 10, IFRS 11 and IFRS 12 was scheduled to commence with a Request for Information in Q4 2020.[10] See 7.5 below. Nevertheless, the IASB has continued to allow early application of the September 2014 amendments as it did not wish to prohibit the application of better financial reporting. *[IFRS 10.BC190O, IAS 28.BC37J]*.

The accounting treatment where the September 2014 amendments are not applied is explained at 3.3.2.A below, whereas 3.3.2.B below addresses the accounting treatment where the September 2014 amendments are applied. In these sections, IFRS 10's approach is also referred to as 'full gain recognition' whereas IAS 28's approach is also referred to as 'partial gain recognition'.

Sections 3.3.2.C to 3.3.2.G below are relevant to loss of control transactions where the retained interest in the former subsidiary is an associate or joint venture accounted for using the equity method, whether or not the September 2014 amendments are applied (except where stated).

3.3.2.A   Conflict between IFRS 10 and IAS 28 (September 2014 amendments not applied)

Examples of situations that result in the loss of control of a subsidiary, where the interest retained in the former subsidiary is an associate or joint venture accounted for using the equity method, include:

- Scenario 1 – a 'downstream' sale or contribution of the investment in the subsidiary (which is a business) to an existing associate or joint venture;
- Scenario 2 – a 'downstream' sale or contribution of the investment in the subsidiary (which is not a business) to an existing associate or joint venture;
- Scenario 3 – a direct sale or dilution of the investment in the subsidiary (which is a business) for cash in a transaction involving a third party; and
- Scenario 4 – a direct sale or dilution of the investment in the subsidiary (which is not a business) for cash in a transaction involving a third party.

While the discussion below refers to these scenarios for simplicity, the same principles apply where the consideration received is not cash, for example, receipt of non-cash assets such as an interest in a subsidiary, or the assumption of liabilities.

Transactions involving the formation of an associate or joint venture, with contributions (which could include an investment in a subsidiary) from the investors or venturers, are discussed further in Chapter 11 at 7.6.5. *[IAS 28.28-31]*.

For the purposes of this discussion, the September 2014 amendments have not been early adopted. In determining the accounting under the scenarios listed above prior to applying the September 2014 amendments, it is important first to determine whether the transactions fall within scope of IFRS 10 or IAS 28.

According to IAS 28, gains and losses resulting from 'downstream' transactions between an entity (including its consolidated subsidiaries) and its associate or joint venture are recognised in the entity's financial statements only to the extent of unrelated investors' interests in the associate or joint venture. 'Downstream' transactions are, for example, sales or contributions of assets from the investor to its associate or its joint venture. The investor's share in the associate's or joint venture's gains or losses resulting from these transactions is eliminated. *[IAS 28.28]*. Where a 'downstream' transaction provides evidence of impairment, the losses shall be recognised in full. *[IAS 28.29]*. These requirements in IAS 28 only apply to 'downstream' transactions with an associate or joint venture accounted for using the equity method and not to all transactions where the retained interest in the former subsidiary is an associate or joint venture accounted for using the equity method. This means that paragraph 28 of IAS 28 only applies in Scenarios 1 and 2 above.

In our view, an entity is not precluded from applying paragraph 25 of IFRS 10, i.e. full gain recognition (see 3.2 above), in accounting for the loss of control of a subsidiary that is not a business. The September 2014 amendments (and indeed other pronouncements, such as *Accounting for Acquisitions of Interests in Joint Operations (Amendments to IFRS 11)* issued May 2014), however, do set out different accounting treatments depending on whether an entity is a business or not. Therefore, we believe that entities *not* applying the September 2014 amendments are entitled to make an accounting policy determination as to whether paragraph 25 of IFRS 10 applies to *all* transactions involving a loss of control of a subsidiary (or *only* to such transactions where the subsidiary is a business).

Therefore, in our view, the following accounting policy determinations should be made:

(a) Do the requirements of paragraph 25 of IFRS 10 apply to:
- a loss of control of a subsidiary that is a business ('narrow view'); or
- a loss of control of a subsidiary (whether a business or not) ('wide view')?

(b) Where there is a conflict between the requirements of paragraph 25 of IFRS 10 and paragraph 28 of IAS 28, which accounting standard should take precedence?

(c) Where the transaction falls within the scope of neither paragraph 25 of IFRS 10 nor paragraph 28 of IAS 28, what accounting policy should be applied?

Scenarios 1 and 3 fall within the scope of paragraph 25 of IFRS 10, whether a 'wide view' or 'narrow view' is taken for accounting policy determination (a) above. However, Scenarios 2 and 4 will only fall within the scope of IFRS 10 if a 'wide view' is taken. Only Scenarios 1 and 2 fall within the scope of paragraph 28 of IAS 28.

In June 2019, the Interpretations Committee discussed the accounting for a transaction in which an entity, as part of its ordinary activities, enters into a contract with a customer to sell real estate by selling its equity interest in a subsidiary which holds the respective real estate as its single asset. In particular, this included the question as to whether IFRS 10 or IFRS 15 should be applied to this transaction. The Interpretations Committee did not make any decisions and, at the time of writing, had not issued an agenda decision on this matter.[11] Instead, the issue was referred to the IASB. In June 2020, the IASB discussed a possible narrow-scope amendment to IFRSs to require an entity to apply IFRS 15 instead of IFRS 10 to sales of some types of subsidiary to a customer, but decided not to add the project to its workplan.[12] At the time of writing, this matter was expected to be considered as part of Phase 2 of the Post-implementation Review (PIR) of IFRS 10,[13] which was scheduled to commence in Q4 2020.[14]

A related issue concerning a sale and leaseback of real estate – where the parent sells the shares in a wholly owned subsidiary holding solely a real estate asset to a third party and leases back the real estate asset from the third party – has also been submitted to the Interpretations Committee, but had not been considered by the Committee at the time of writing.[15]

Until the deliberation process on these issues are completed, there may continue to be some diversity in practice. However, in the meantime, considering the discussions referred to above, entities may need to be mindful when applying a 'narrow view' mentioned above. See 3.2.1 above.

Figure 7.1 below summarises how the above policy determinations apply to the four scenarios where the September 2014 amendments are not applied. There is a more detailed discussion, including illustrative examples, of sales or contributions to an associate or joint venture (including on formation of an associate or joint venture) in Chapter 11 at 7.6.5.

Consolidation procedures and non-controlling interests 517

Figure 7.1   *Loss of control transactions where the retained interest in the former subsidiary is an associate or joint venture accounted for using the equity method*

	Subsidiary meets the definition of a business	*Subsidiary does not meet the definition of a business*
Sale or contribution of investment in former subsidiary in downstream transaction with existing associate or joint venture	*Scenario 1* • Both IFRS 10.25 (as the subsidiary is a business) and IAS 28.28 (as this is a 'downstream' transaction) apply to this scenario, so a conflict arises. • An entity would need to develop an accounting policy to resolve the conflict, which would result in either applying full gain recognition (IFRS 10 approach) or partial gain recognition (IAS 28 approach). • In our view, an entity must apply this accounting policy consistently to like transactions. This does not preclude a different choice of which standard takes precedence to the choice made for transactions in Scenario 2.	*Scenario 2* • IAS 28.28 (as this is a 'downstream' transaction) applies to this scenario. Therefore, partial recognition applies. • However, if a 'wide view' is taken on the scope of IFRS 10.25, a conflict arises. An entity would then need to develop an accounting policy to resolve the conflict, which would result in either applying full gain recognition (IFRS 10 approach) or partial gain recognition (IAS 28 approach). In our view, an entity must apply this accounting policy consistently to like transactions (see comments on Scenario 1).
Sale or dilution of investment in former subsidiary for cash in transaction with third party	*Scenario 3* • IAS 28.28 does not apply (as this is not a 'downstream' transaction). • IFRS 10.25 applies (as the subsidiary is a business). • Therefore, an entity applies full gain recognition (IFRS 10 approach) to the transaction.	*Scenario 4* • IAS 28.28 does not apply (as this is not a 'downstream transaction'). • IFRS 10.25 only applies if a 'wide view' is taken. • Therefore, if a 'wide view' over the scope of IFRS 10.25 applies, an entity applies full gain recognition (IFRS 10 approach) to the transaction. • If a 'narrow view' over the scope of IFRS 10.25 applies, an entity must develop and apply an appropriate accounting policy that provides relevant and reliable information in accordance with IAS 8.

Where it is determined that a transaction falls within the scope of neither paragraph 25 of IFRS 10 nor paragraph 28 of IAS 28 (which might be the case for Scenario 4 if a 'narrow view' is taken for accounting policy determination (a) above), management should use its judgement in developing and applying an appropriate accounting policy that results in relevant and reliable information. *[IAS 8.10-12]*.

It is possible that some transactions that fall within Scenarios 1 and 3, and in Scenarios 2 and 4 may be similar in substance. This may be a relevant consideration when developing an appropriate accounting policy. Nevertheless, different accounting outcomes may arise depending on the accounting policy determinations made by the entity. In our view, accounting policies should be applied consistently to like transactions.

An entity only needs to make a determination as to whether a 'wide view' or 'narrow view' of the scope of IFRS 10 applies, if it enters into a transaction that falls within Scenarios 2 or 4 (because Scenarios 1 and 3 always fall within the scope of IFRS 10). However, once that determination has been required to be made, the 'wide view' or 'narrow view' over the scope of paragraph 25 of IFRS 10 should be applied consistently.

However, a different accounting policy could be adopted for transactions that are businesses and transactions that are not businesses (even where a 'wide view' of the application of IFRS 10 is taken). For example, an entity taking a 'wide view' over application of IFRS 10 may consider it appropriate that IFRS 10 takes precedence in Scenario 1 (where the subsidiary is a business) but IAS 28 takes precedence in Scenario 2 (where the subsidiary is not a business). This is because transactions involving the loss of control of a subsidiary that is a business have a different nature to those involving a subsidiary that is not a business and an entity may feel that partial gain recognition is more appropriate for the loss of control of a subsidiary that is not a business.

Note that if the September 2014 amendments (discussed at 3.3.2.B and 7.1 below) were applied, full gain recognition would be required in Scenario 1, whereas partial gain recognition would be required in Scenario 2.

3.3.2.B Conflict between IFRS 10 and IAS 28 (September 2014 amendments applied)

As noted at 3.3.2 above, in September 2014, the IASB had issued *Sale or Contribution of Assets between an Investor and its Associate or Joint Venture (Amendments to IFRS 10 and IAS 28)*. Although the mandatory application of the September 2014 amendments was subsequently deferred, the amendments remain available for early application.

In the Basis for Conclusions, the IASB clarified that the amendments do not apply where a transaction with a third party leads to a loss of control (even if the retained interest in the former subsidiary becomes an associate or joint venture that is accounted for using the equity method), nor where the investor elects to measure its investments in associates or joint ventures at fair value in accordance with IFRS 9. *[IFRS 10.BC190I]*.

Consequently, the September 2014 amendments impact the accounting for Scenarios 1 and 2 (i.e. the situations where there was a conflict between IAS 28 and IFRS 10), as discussed at 3.3.2.A above. The amendments do not specifically address the accounting for Scenarios 3 and 4, and the analysis included in 3.3.2.A above remains relevant to such situations.

The September 2014 amendments added the guidance explained in the following paragraph in relation to the accounting for the loss of control of a subsidiary that does not contain a business. Consequently, on the loss of control of a subsidiary that constitutes a business, including cases in which the investor retains joint control of, or significant influence over, the investee, the guidance below is not to be applied. In such cases, the full gain or loss determined under the requirements of IFRS 10 (see 3.2 and 3.3 above) is to be recognised. *[IFRS 10.25, 26, B98, B99]*.

If a parent loses control of a subsidiary that does not contain a business, as defined in IFRS 3, as a result of a transaction involving an associate or a joint venture that is accounted for using the equity method, the parent is to determine the gain or loss in accordance with paragraphs B98-B99 (see 3.2 above). The gain or loss resulting from the transaction (including the amounts previously recognised in other comprehensive income that would be reclassified to profit or loss in accordance with paragraph B99) is to be recognised in the parent's profit or loss only to the extent of the unrelated investors' interests in that associate or joint venture. The remaining part of the gain is to be eliminated against the carrying amount of the investment in that associate or joint venture. In addition, if the parent retains an investment in the former subsidiary and the former subsidiary is now an associate or a joint venture that is accounted for using the equity method, the parent is to recognise the part of the gain or loss resulting from the remeasurement at fair value of the investment retained in that former subsidiary in its profit or loss only to the extent of the unrelated investors' interests in the new associate or joint venture. The remaining part of that gain is to be eliminated against the carrying amount of the investment retained in the former subsidiary. If the parent retains an investment in the former subsidiary that is now accounted for in accordance with IFRS 9, the part of the gain or loss resulting from the remeasurement at fair value of the investment retained in the former subsidiary is to be recognised in full in the parent's profit or loss. *[IFRS 10.25, 26, B99A]*.

An example, based on one provided by IFRS 10 illustrating the application of this guidance, is reflected in Example 7.6 below.[16]

Example 7.6: *Loss of control of a subsidiary that does not contain a business as a result of a transaction involving an associate*

A parent has a 100% interest in a subsidiary that does not contain a business. The parent sells 70% of its interest in the subsidiary to an associate in which it has a 20% interest. As a consequence of this transaction, the parent loses control of the subsidiary. The carrying amount of the net assets of the subsidiary is €100 and the carrying amount of the interest sold is €70 (€100 × 70%). The fair value of the consideration received is €210, which is also the fair value of the interest sold. The investment retained in the former subsidiary is an associate accounted for using the equity method and its fair value is €90. The gain determined in accordance with paragraphs B98-B99 of IFRS 10 is €200 and after the elimination required by paragraph B99A of IFRS 10 amounts to €146. This gain comprises two parts:

(a) a gain of €140 resulting from the sale of the 70% interest in the subsidiary to the associate. This gain is the difference between the fair value of the consideration received (€210) and the carrying amount of the interest sold (€70). In accordance with paragraph B99A, the parent recognises in its profit or loss the amount of the gain attributable to the unrelated investors' interests in the existing associate. This is 80% of this gain, that is €112 (€140 × 80%). The remaining 20% of the gain (€28 = €140 × 20%), is eliminated against the carrying amount of the investment in the existing associate.

(b) a gain of €60 resulting from the remeasurement at fair value of the investment directly retained in the former subsidiary. This gain is the difference between the fair value of the investment retained in the former subsidiary (€90) and 30% of the carrying amount of the net assets of the subsidiary (€30 = €100 × 30%). In accordance with paragraph B99A, the parent recognises in its profit or loss the amount of the gain attributable to the unrelated investors' interests in the new associate. This is 56% (70% × 80%) of the gain, that is €34 (€60 × 56%). The remaining 44% of the gain (€26 = €60 × 44%) is eliminated against the carrying amount of the investment retained in the former subsidiary.

This example would therefore give rise to the following journal, assuming cash consideration of €210:

	€ DR	€ CR
Cash	210	
Investment in new associate (former subsidiary) (see (1) below)	64	
Gain on disposal (see (2) below)		146
Net assets of former subsidiary (previously consolidated)		100
Investment in existing associate		28

(1) This represents the fair value of the investment in the former subsidiary (now an associate) of €90 less the eliminated gain of €26 (see (b) above).

(2) This represents the gain of €200 less the eliminated gains of €28 (eliminated against the investment in the associate – see (a) above) and €26 (eliminated against the investment in the new associate / former subsidiary – see (1) above).

3.3.2.C Reclassification of items of other comprehensive income where the interest retained in the former subsidiary is an associate or joint venture accounted using the equity method

As discussed at 3.2 above, on loss of control of a subsidiary, an entity must reclassify to profit or loss, or transfer directly to retained earnings if required by other IFRSs, the amounts recognised in other comprehensive income in relation to the subsidiary (see 3.5 below). Where the retained interest in the former subsidiary is an associate or joint venture accounted using the equity method, the question arises as to whether amounts recognised in other comprehensive income that are required to be reclassified to profit or loss are reclassified in full or in part.

In our view, where an IFRS 10 approach is applied, other comprehensive income reclassified is recognised in full on loss of control of the subsidiary, consistent with a full gain approach. While IAS 28 does not explicitly address this issue, we believe that where an IAS 28 approach is applied, partial gain reclassification of other comprehensive income applies such that only the proportion attributable to unrelated investors' interests in the associate or joint venture is reclassified. This treatment is consistent with the September 2014 amendments (see 3.3.2.B above).

[IFRS 10.25, 26, B99A, BC190J].

3.3.2.D Application of partial gain recognition where the gain exceeds the carrying amount of the investment in the associate or joint venture accounted using the equity method

Occasionally, upon sale or contribution of a subsidiary to an associate or joint venture (that is accounted for using the equity method), the investor's share of the gain exceeds the carrying value of the investment in the associate or joint venture. Where partial gain recognition is applied, the question arises as to what extent is any profit in excess of the carrying value of the investment eliminated. This is addressed in Chapter 11 at 7.6.1.A.

3.3.2.E Examples of accounting for sales or contributions to an existing associate

Scenario 1 is illustrated in Example 7.7 below, showing both an IFRS 10 and an IAS 28 approach (a choice between these approaches is permitted where the September 2014 amendments are not applied). As noted at 3.3.2.B above, an IFRS 10 approach is required for Scenario 1 where the September 2014 amendments are applied. Scenario 3 (where the IFRS 10 approach is required) is illustrated in Example 7.11 at 3.6 below (for a deemed disposal) and in Example 11.5 in Chapter 11 at 7.4.1 (a direct sale to a third party).

Example 7.7: *Sale of a subsidiary to an existing associate*

Parent P owns a 60% interest in its subsidiary S. The carrying value of S's net identifiable assets in the consolidated financial statements of P is £120 million. P measured the non-controlling interest using the proportionate share of net assets; therefore, the non-controlling interest is £48 million (40% of £120 million). In addition, goodwill of £15 million was recognised upon the original acquisition of S and has not subsequently been impaired. The goodwill is allocated to S for the purposes of impairment testing.

Subsequently, P sells its interest in S to its associate A, in which it has a 40% interest, for £96 million cash, being the fair value of its 60% interest in S. Therefore, P has a 40% interest in the enlarged associate A (which now holds the 60% interest in S).

If the September 2014 amendments to IFRS 10 and IAS 28 have not been early adopted, either a full gain is recognised (see Approach 1), or the gain is restricted to that attributable to the other investor in S (see Approach 2). See 3.3.2.A above. If the September 2014 amendments have been early adopted, the full gain is recognised (as S is a business). See 3.3.2.B above.

Approach 1 – IFRS 10 approach

This results in a gain of £9 million on disposal, recognised as follows:

	£m DR	£m CR
Cash	96.0	
Non-controlling interest	48.0	
Gain on disposal		9.0
Net assets of S (previously consolidated)		120.0
Goodwill (previously shown separately)		15.0

Approach 2 – IAS 28 approach

Where the September 2014 amendments are not early adopted and the gain recognised is restricted to the 60% attributable to the other investors in A, a gain of £5.4 million on disposal is recognised (with the remaining £3.6 million adjusted against the carrying amount of the investment in A), as follows:

	£m DR	£m CR
Cash	96.0	
Non-controlling interest	48.0	
Gain on disposal		5.4
Investment in A		3.6
Net assets of S (previously consolidated)		120.0
Goodwill (previously shown separately)		15.0

3.3.2.F   Determination of the fair value of the retained interest in a former subsidiary which is an associate or joint venture

As indicated at 3.3.1 above, no guidance is given in IFRS 10 as to how the fair value of the retained interest in the former subsidiary should be determined. However, IFRS 13 provides detailed guidance on how fair value should be determined for financial reporting purposes. IFRS 13 is discussed in detail in Chapter 14.

One particular issue that has been discussed by the IASB, which might be relevant in determining the fair value of a retained interest that is an associate or a joint venture, is the unit of account for investments in subsidiaries, joint ventures and associates. In September 2014, the IASB issued an Exposure Draft that proposed, *inter alia*, the following clarifications to the requirements for measuring fair value, in accordance with IFRS 13, for investments in subsidiaries, joint ventures and associates:

- the unit of account for investments in subsidiaries, joint ventures and associates would be the investment as whole; and
- when a quoted price in an active market is available for the individual financial instruments that comprise the entire investment, the fair value measurement would be the product of the quoted price of the financial instrument (P) multiplied by the quantity (Q) of instruments held (i.e. price × quantity, P × Q).[17]

During 2015, the IASB continued its deliberations on these proposals and decided that further research should be undertaken with respect to the fair value measurement of investments in subsidiaries, associates and joint ventures that are quoted in an active market.[18] In January 2016, the IASB decided not to consider this topic further until completion of the Post-implementation Review (PIR) of IFRS 13.[19] The IASB completed its review of the findings of the PIR in March 2018[20] and the Project Report and Feedback Statement was published in December 2018.[21]

The IASB concluded that IFRS 13 is working as intended and that the project was complete with no further work required. Although the Project Report and Feedback Statement noted that many stakeholders expressed a view that the IASB should clarify how IFRS 13 deals with the issue of prioritising the unit of account or Level 1 inputs, the IASB decided that it would conduct no other follow up activities in this area (because the costs of further work would exceed its benefits).

However, the IASB decided that it would consider the PIR's findings on the usefulness of disclosures in its work on *Better Communication in Financial Reporting*, continue liaison with the valuation profession, monitor new developments in practice and promote knowledge development and sharing.[22]

These issues are discussed further in Chapter 14 at 5.1.1.

3.3.2.G   Presentation of comparative information for a former subsidiary that becomes an investee accounted for using the equity method

Where a parent loses control of a subsidiary, so that the former subsidiary becomes an associate or a joint venture accounted for using the equity method, the effect is that the former parent/investor's interest in the investee is reported:

- using the equity method from the date on which control is lost in the current reporting period; and
- using full consolidation for any earlier part of the current reporting period, and of any earlier reporting period, during which the investee was controlled.

It is not acceptable for an entity to restate financial information for reporting periods prior to the loss of control using the equity method to provide comparability with the new presentation. Consolidation continues until control is lost, *[IFRS 10.21, B88]*, and equity accounting starts only from the date on which an entity becomes an associate or joint venture (see Chapter 11 at 7.3).

3.3.3 Interest retained in the former subsidiary – joint operation

In some transactions, it is possible that an entity would lose control of a subsidiary but retain an interest in a joint operation to be accounted for under IFRS 11. For example, a parent might contribute an existing business to a newly created joint operation and obtain joint control of the combined operation. Alternatively, it could be achieved by a parent with a 100% subsidiary selling a 50% interest to another party, with the transaction resulting in the formation of a joint operation, with each party having a 50% share of the assets and liabilities of the joint operation.

As set out at 3.2 above, in accounting for a loss of control of a subsidiary, a parent is required, *inter alia*, to:

(a) derecognise the assets and liabilities of the subsidiary;

(b) recognise any investment retained in the former subsidiary at fair value at the date when control is lost; and

(c) recognise any resulting gain or loss in profit or loss.

However, it is unclear how these requirements should be applied when the retained interest is in the assets and liabilities of a joint operation. One view is that the retained interest should be remeasured at fair value. Another view is that the retained interest should not be derecognised or remeasured at fair value, but should continue to be recognised and measured at its carrying amount. This is an issue that the Interpretations Committee has previously considered as part of a wider discussion of other transactions of changes of interests in a joint operation that is a business, for which there is a lack of guidance, or where there is diversity of views.

In July 2016, the Interpretations Committee discussed whether an entity should remeasure its retained interest in the assets and liabilities of a joint operation when the entity loses control of a business, or an asset or group of assets that is not a business. In the transaction discussed, the entity either retains joint control of a joint operation or is a party to a joint operation (with rights to assets and obligations for liabilities) after the transaction.

The Interpretations Committee noted that paragraphs B34–B35 of IFRS 11 specify that an entity recognises gains or losses on the sale or contribution of assets to a joint operation only to the extent of the other parties' interests in the joint operation. *[IFRS 11.22, B34, B35]*. The requirements in these paragraphs could be viewed as conflicting with the requirements in IFRS 10, which specify that an entity remeasures any retained interest when it loses control of a subsidiary.

The Interpretations Committee observed that the IASB had issued amendments to IFRS 10 and IAS 28 in September 2014 to address the accounting for the sale or contribution of assets to an associate or a joint venture. Those amendments (which are discussed at 3.3.2.B above and 7.1 below) address a similar conflict that exists between the requirements in IFRS 10 and IAS 28. The IASB decided to defer the effective date of the amendments to IFRS 10 and IAS 28 and further consider a number of related issues at a later date. The Interpretations Committee observed that the Post-implementation Reviews (PIRs) of IFRS 10 and IFRS 11 would provide the IASB with an opportunity to consider loss of control transactions and a sale or contribution of assets to an associate or a joint venture. At the time of writing, work on Phase 2 of the PIRs of IFRS 10 and IFRS 11 was scheduled to commence with a Request for Information in Q4 2020.[23] See 7.5 below.

Because of the similarity between the transaction discussed by the Interpretations Committee and a sale or contribution of assets to an associate or a joint venture (see 3.3.2 above), the Interpretations Committee concluded that the accounting for the two types of transactions should be considered concurrently by the IASB. Consequently, the Interpretations Committee decided not to add this issue to its agenda but, instead, to recommend that the IASB consider the issue at the same time that it further considers the accounting for the sale or contribution of assets to an associate or a joint venture.[24] In the meantime, we believe that, where a parent loses control over a subsidiary but retains an interest in a joint operation that is a business, entities have an accounting policy choice as to whether to remeasure the retained interest at fair value or not.

3.4 Loss of control in multiple arrangements

If a parent loses control of a subsidiary in two or more arrangements or transactions, sometimes they should be accounted for as a single transaction. *[IFRS 10.26, B97]*. IFRS 10 only allows a parent to recognise a gain or loss on disposal of a subsidiary when the parent loses control over it. This requirement could present opportunities to structure the disposal in a series of disposals, thereby potentially reducing the loss recognised. Example 7.8 below illustrates the issue in IFRS 10 as follows. *[IFRS 10.BCZ185]*.

Example 7.8:   Step-disposal of a subsidiary (1)

A parent controls 70% of a subsidiary. The parent intends to sell all of its 70% controlling interest in the subsidiary. The parent could structure the disposal in two different ways:

- the parent could initially sell 19% of its ownership interest without loss of control and then, soon afterwards, sell the remaining 51% and lose control; or
- the parent could sell its entire 70% interest in one transaction.

In the first case, any difference between the amount by which the non-controlling interests are adjusted and the fair value of the consideration received upon sale of the 19% interest would be recognised directly in equity (as it is a transaction with owners in their capacity as owners) while the gain or loss from the sale of the remaining 51% interest would be recognised in profit or loss (once control is lost). In the second case, however, a gain or loss on the sale of the whole 70% interest would be recognised in profit or loss.

However, even if an entity wanted to conceal losses on a disposal of a subsidiary, the opportunities are limited given the requirements of IAS 36 – *Impairment of Assets* – and IFRS 5, which usually require recognition of an impairment loss even before the completion of any sale, *[IFRS 10.BCZ186]*, (although they do not require reclassification of losses recognised in other comprehensive income).

In determining whether to account for the arrangements as a single transaction, a parent considers all the terms and conditions of the arrangements and their economic effects. One or more of the following circumstances indicate that it is appropriate for a parent to account for multiple arrangements as a single transaction: *[IFRS 10.26, B97]*

- they are entered into at the same time or in contemplation of each other;
- they form a single transaction designed to achieve an overall commercial effect;
- the occurrence of one arrangement is dependent on the occurrence of at least one other arrangement; or
- one arrangement considered on its own is not economically justified, but it is economically justified when considered together with other arrangements. An example is a disposal of shares priced below market that is compensated by a subsequent disposal priced above market.

These indicators clarify that arrangements that are part of a package are accounted for as a single transaction. However, there is a risk that by casting too wide a net, an entity might end up accounting for a transaction that is truly separate as part of transaction in which the loss of control occurred.

IFRS 10 is silent on how an entity accounts for multiple arrangements that are part of a single transaction. Depending on the facts and circumstances, the parent accounts for these transactions in one of the following ways:

- *Advance payment* – If the parent does not lose control over the subsidiary and access to the benefits associated with ownership until later steps in the transaction, then it accounts for the first step of the transaction as an advance receipt of consideration and continues to consolidate the subsidiary until the later date. In many cases, the assets and liabilities of the consolidated subsidiary would be a disposal group held for sale under IFRS 5 (see Chapter 4 at 2.1.3.A).
- *Immediate disposal* – If the parent loses control and access to benefits associated on the first step of the transaction, then it ceases to consolidate the former subsidiary immediately, recognises a gain or loss on disposal, and accounts for the consideration due in the second step as deferred consideration receivable.

Example 7.9 below illustrates a fact pattern where the entity would need to evaluate how to account for transactions that are linked.

Example 7.9: Step-disposal of a subsidiary (2)

A parent initially controls 70% of a subsidiary that has net assets of $1,000,000 and a foreign currency translation loss that was recognised in other comprehensive income and is accumulated within equity of $100,000. Of this amount, $30,000 was allocated to non-controlling interest, and is included within the non-controlling interest of $300,000. No goodwill was recognised in respect of this subsidiary and the subsidiary is not part of a CGU to which goodwill is allocated. In November 2019, the parent sells 19% of its ownership interest for $200,000. In February 2020, the parent sells the remaining 51% for $550,000 in an arrangement that is considered part of a single overall transaction. It is assumed that there are no gains or losses in the intervening period.

The net assets of the subsidiary are not impaired under IAS 36, which is confirmed by the fact that the total sales price exceeds the parent's share in the net assets by $50,000 ($750,000 less $700,000). The total loss on disposal can be calculated as follows:

	$'000 DR	$'000 CR
Proceeds from the sale ($200,000 + $550,000)	750	
Net assets of the subsidiary derecognised		1,000
Non-controlling interest derecognised	300	
Reclassification of parent's share of the loss in other comprehensive income		70
Loss on disposal of the subsidiary attributable to the parent	20	

If the parent is considered not to have lost control over the investment in the subsidiary until February 2020 then it accounts for the $200,000 received in the first step of the transaction as an advance receipt of consideration. The parent continues to consolidate the subsidiary until the later date, at which point the loss on disposal of $20,000 would be recognised.

If the parent is considered to have lost control over the investment in the subsidiary on the first step of the transaction, then it ceases to consolidate the former subsidiary immediately, recognises a loss on disposal of $20,000, and accounts for the consideration of $550,000 due in the second step as deferred consideration receivable.

3.5 Other comprehensive income

If a parent loses control of a subsidiary, all amounts previously recognised in other comprehensive income are accounted for on the same basis as would be required if the parent had directly disposed of the related assets or liabilities. If a gain or loss previously recognised in other comprehensive income would be reclassified to profit or loss on the disposal of the related assets or liabilities, the parent reclassifies the gain or loss from equity to profit or loss (as a reclassification adjustment) when it loses control of the subsidiary. Therefore:

(a) if a revaluation surplus previously recognised in other comprehensive income would be transferred directly to retained earnings on the disposal of the asset, the parent transfers the revaluation surplus directly to retained earnings when it loses control of the subsidiary; *[IFRS 10.26, B99]*

(b) remeasurement gains or losses on a defined benefit plan recognised in other comprehensive income would not be reclassified to profit or loss when the parent loses control of the subsidiary, but may be transferred within equity, *[IAS 19.122]*, and

(c) on disposal of a subsidiary that includes a foreign operation, the cumulative amount of the exchange differences relating to that foreign operation (that is recognised in other comprehensive income and accumulated in the separate component of equity) is reclassified from equity to profit or loss, except for the amounts that have been attributed to the non-controlling interests. Those amounts are derecognised, and not reclassified to profit or loss. *[IAS 21.48-48B]*. This would appear to mean that it is only the parent's share of the cumulative exchange differences that is reclassified; those attributable to the non-controlling interests are not reclassified as they have already been included within the carrying amount of the non-controlling interest that is derecognised as part of calculating the gain or loss attributable to the parent.

There are two different interpretations of how to treat other comprehensive income accumulated in equity that would be reclassified to profit or loss on the disposal of the related assets or liabilities, both of which are acceptable. Approach (1) below is more consistent with the treatment of exchange differences relating to foreign operations, as described at (c) above.

(1) *Reclassification of other comprehensive income related to parent interest only* – IFRS 10 requires derecognition of the non-controlling interests (including any components of other comprehensive income attributable to them) at the date when control is lost, which implies derecognition of the non-controlling interests without any need for reclassification. *[IFRS 10.26, B98(a)]*. In addition, IFRS 10 requires recognition of a gain or loss in profit or loss to be attributable to the parent, *[IFRS 10.26, B98(d)]*, which again implies that there should be no reclassification of other comprehensive income in respect of the non-controlling interests.

(2) *Reclassification of other comprehensive income related to parent and the non-controlling interest* – IFRS 10 specifically requires that 'if a gain or loss previously recognised in other comprehensive income would be reclassified to profit or loss on the disposal of the related assets or liabilities, the parent shall reclassify the gain or loss from equity to profit or loss (as a reclassification adjustment) when it loses control of the subsidiary.' *[IFRS 10.26, B99]*. That would clearly require reclassification of the entire balance of other comprehensive income accumulated within equity. However, where this is done, the portion of the reclassification adjustment attributable to the non-controlling interest should be included as part of the profit or loss attributable to the non-controlling interests, not as part of the profit or loss attributable to the parent.

Example 7.10 below illustrates the application of the above requirements.

Example 7.10:   Reclassification of other comprehensive income

A parent sells a 70% interest in a 90%-owned subsidiary to a third party for a cash consideration of €28 million. The fair value of the 20% interest retained by the parent is €8 million.

At the date of disposal, the net assets of the subsidiary were €30 million. Included within those net assets, the subsidiary had recognised, in its own financial statements, the following:

- property, plant and equipment of €5 million that has resulted in a revaluation reserve of €2 million;
- derivative financial assets of €3.2 million (designated in a cash flow hedge) that have resulted in a cash flow hedge reserve of €3 million;
- a net defined benefit liability of €3 million that has resulted in a reserve relating to net remeasurement losses of €1.5 million; and
- net assets of a foreign operation of €10 million that has resulted in a cumulative translation reserve in respect of net translation gains on the foreign operation of €4 million.

In the parent's consolidated financial statements, the parent has recognised 90% of these reserves in equivalent equity reserve balances, with the 10% attributable to the non-controlling interest included as part of the carrying amount of the non-controlling interest.

The impact of the subsidiary on the statement of financial position included in the parent's consolidated financial statements immediately prior to the disposal is as follows:

	€m	€m
Net assets of the subsidiary		30.00
Equity attributable to parent		
− PP&E revaluation reserve		1.80
− Cash flow hedge reserve		2.70
− IAS 19 net remeasurement loss reserve	1.35	
− Cumulative translation reserve		3.60
− Other equity/retained earnings		20.25
Non-controlling interest		3.00

If the parent follows Approach (1) for the cash flow hedge reserve and makes a reserve transfer for the IAS 19 – *Employee Benefits* – net remeasurement loss reserve, the impact of the disposal on the parent's consolidated financial statements is as follows:

	€m DR	€m CR
Cash proceeds from the disposal	28.00	
Retained 20% investment at fair value	8.00	
Derecognition of net assets of the subsidiary		30.00
Derecognition of non-controlling interest	3.00	
Reserves reclassified to profit or loss		
− Cash flow hedge reserve (a)	2.70	
− Cumulative translation reserve (b)	3.60	
Reserves transferred to retained earnings		
− PP&E revaluation reserve (c)	1.80	
− IAS 19 net remeasurement loss reserve (d)		1.35
Retained earnings resulting from above transfers		0.45
Gain on disposal (attributable to parent)		15.30

The parent:

(a) reclassifies its €2.7 million cash flow hedge reserve to profit or loss for the period. This is reflected in the gain on disposal. The remaining 10% (i.e. €0.3 million) is included as part of the carrying amount of the non-controlling interest that is derecognised as part of the gain or loss recognised on disposal of the subsidiary, but is not reclassified to profit or loss nor is it transferred within equity;

(b) reclassifies its cumulative translation reserve of €3.6 million (90% × €4 million) relating to the parent's interest to profit or loss. Again, this is reflected in the gain on disposal. The €0.4 million (10% × €4 million) relating to the non-controlling interest is included as part of the carrying amount of the non-controlling interest that is derecognised in calculating the gain or loss recognised on disposal of the subsidiary, but is not reclassified to profit or loss nor is it transferred within equity;

(c) transfers its revaluation reserve of €1.8 million relating to its 90% share of the revaluation surplus on property, plant and equipment within equity to retained earnings. It is not reclassified to profit or loss. The remaining 10% attributable to the non-controlling interest is included as part of the carrying amount of the non-controlling interest that is derecognised in calculating the gain or loss recognised on disposal of the subsidiary, but is not reclassified to profit or loss nor is it transferred within equity; and

(d) transfers its reserve of €1.35 million relating to its 90% share of the net remeasurement losses on the defined benefit liability within equity to retained earnings. It is not reclassified to profit or loss.

The remaining 10% attributable to the non-controlling interest is included as part of the carrying amount of the non-controlling interest that is derecognised in calculating the gain or loss recognised on disposal of the subsidiary, but is not reclassified to profit or loss nor is it transferred within equity. This results in the same position as if the parent had not recognised a separate reserve for the net remeasurement losses on the defined benefit liability, but had included them within retained earnings.

If, instead, the parent follows Approach (2) for the cash flow hedge reserve, the impact of the disposal on the parent's consolidated financial statements is as follows:

	€m DR	€m CR
Cash proceeds from the disposal	28.00	
Retained 20% investment at fair value	8.00	
Derecognition of net assets of the subsidiary		30.00
Derecognition of non-controlling interests	3.00	
Reserves reclassified to profit or loss		
– Cash flow hedge reserve (a)		2.70
– Cumulative translation reserve (b)		3.60
Non-controlling interest (reclassification of cash flow hedge reserve) (a)	0.30	
Reserves transferred to retained earnings		
– PP&E revaluation reserve (c)		1.80
– IAS 19 net remeasurement loss reserve (d)	1.35	
Retained earnings resulting from above transfers		0.45
Gain on reclassification of cash flow hedge reserve (attributable to non-controlling interests) (a)		0.30
Gain on disposal (attributable to parent)		15.30

The parent:
(a) reclassifies the entire €3 million surplus on the cash flow hedge reserve to profit or loss for the period. The 90% of the balance (i.e. €2.7 million) attributable to the parent is included within the gain on disposal that is attributable to the parent, while the remaining 10% (i.e. €0.3 million) attributable to the non-controlling interests is reclassified to profit or loss, and is included within the profit or loss attributable to the non-controlling interest;

(b) reclassifies its cumulative translation reserve of €3.6 million (90% × €4 million) relating to the parent's interest to profit or loss. Again, this is reflected in the gain on disposal. The €0.4 million (10% × €4 million) relating to the non-controlling interest is included as part of the carrying amount of the non-controlling interest that is derecognised in calculating the gain or loss recognised on disposal of the subsidiary, but is not reclassified to profit or loss nor is it transferred within equity;

(c) transfers its revaluation reserve of €1.8 million relating to its 90% share of the revaluation surplus on property, plant and equipment within equity to retained earnings. It is not reclassified to profit or loss. The remaining 10% attributable to the non-controlling interest is included as part of the carrying amount of the non-controlling interest that is derecognised in calculating the gain or loss recognised on disposal of the subsidiary, but is not reclassified to profit or loss nor is it transferred within equity; and

(d) transfers its reserve of €1.35 million relating to its 90% share of the net remeasurement losses on the defined benefit liability within equity to retained earnings. It is not reclassified to profit or loss. The remaining 10% attributable to the non-controlling interest is included as part of the carrying amount of the non-controlling interest that is derecognised in calculating the gain or loss recognised on disposal of the subsidiary, but is not reclassified to profit or loss nor is it transferred within equity. This results in the same position as if the parent had not recognised a separate reserve for the net remeasurement losses on the defined benefit liability, but had included them within retained earnings.

3.6 Deemed disposal

A subsidiary may cease to be a subsidiary, or a group may reduce its interest in a subsidiary, other than by actual disposal. This is commonly referred to as a 'deemed disposal'. Deemed disposals may arise for many reasons, including:

- a group does not take up its full allocation in a rights issue by a subsidiary in the group;
- a subsidiary declares scrip dividends that are not taken up by its parent, so that the parent's proportional interest is diminished;
- another party exercises its options or warrants issued by a subsidiary;
- a subsidiary issues shares to third parties; or
- a contractual agreement by which a group obtained control over a subsidiary is terminated or changed.

A deemed disposal that results in the loss of control of a subsidiary is accounted for as a regular disposal. This accounting is illustrated in Example 7.11 below.

Example 7.11: Deemed disposal through share issue by subsidiary

A parent entity P owns 600,000 of the 1,000,000 shares issued by its subsidiary S, giving it a 60% interest. The carrying value of S's net identifiable assets in the consolidated financial statements of P is £120 million. P measured the non-controlling interest using the proportionate share of net assets; therefore, the non-controlling interest is £48 million (40% of £120 million). In addition, goodwill of £15 million was recognised upon the original acquisition of S and has not subsequently been impaired. The goodwill is allocated to S for the purposes of impairment testing.

Subsequently, S issues 500,000 shares to a new investor for £80 million. As a result, P's 600,000 shares now represent 40% of the 1,500,000 shares issued by S in total and S becomes an associate of P.

IFRS 10 requires the remaining interest in the former subsidiary to be recognised at fair value. P considers that, based on the requirements of IFRS 13, the fair value of its 600,000 shares in S is £96 million.

This results in a gain of £9 million on disposal, recognised as follows:

	£m DR	£m CR
Interest in S	96	
Non-controlling interest	48	
Gain on disposal		9
Net assets of S (previously consolidated)		120
Goodwill (previously shown separately)		15

As indicated at 3.3.2.F above, the IASB has discussed issues relating to the unit of account for investments in subsidiaries, joint ventures and associates, and their fair value measurement under IFRS 13.

3.7 Demergers and distributions of non-cash assets to owners

Groups may dispose of subsidiaries by way of a demerger. This situation typically involves the transfer of the subsidiaries to be disposed of, either:

- directly to shareholders, by way of a dividend in kind; or
- to a newly formed entity in exchange for the issue of shares by that entity to the shareholders of the disposing entity.

IFRS 10 requires recognition of a distribution of shares of the subsidiary to owners in their capacity as owners, but does not describe how to account for such transactions. *[IFRS 10.26, B98(b)]*. Instead, IFRIC 17 – *Distributions of Non-cash Assets to Owners* –addresses distributions of subsidiary shares to shareholders. The application of IFRIC 17 in the context of demergers is discussed below. The application of IFRIC 17 to assets in general is discussed in Chapter 8 at 2.4.2.

3.7.1 Scope of IFRIC 17

IFRIC 17 applies to the following types of distribution (described by IFRIC 17 as 'non-reciprocal') by an entity to its owners in their capacity as owners: *[IFRIC 17.3]*

(a) distributions of non-cash assets such as items of property, plant and equipment, businesses as defined in IFRS 3 (see Chapter 9 at 3.2), ownership interests in another entity, or disposal groups as defined in IFRS 5 (see Chapter 4 at 2.1); and

(b) distributions that give owners a choice of receiving either non-cash assets or a cash alternative.

The scope of IFRIC 17 is limited in several respects:

- it only applies to distributions in which all owners of the same class of equity instruments are treated equally; *[IFRIC 17.4]*
- it does not apply to 'a distribution of a non-cash asset that is ultimately controlled by the same party or parties before and after the distribution', *[IFRIC 17.5]*, which means that IFRIC 17 does not apply when:
  - a group of individual shareholders receiving the distribution, as a result of contractual arrangements, collectively have the power to govern financial and operating policies of the entity making the distribution so as to obtain benefits from its activities; *[IFRIC 17.6]* or
  - an entity distributes some of its ownership interests in a subsidiary but retains control of the subsidiary. The entity making a distribution that results in the entity recognising a non-controlling interest in its subsidiary accounts for the distribution in accordance with IFRS 10. *[IFRIC 17.7]*. In this situation, the requirements of IFRS 10 discussed at 4 below would be applied.

  This exclusion applies to the separate, individual and consolidated financial statements of an entity that makes the distribution; *[IFRIC 17.5]* and
- it only addresses the accounting by an entity that makes a non-cash asset distribution. It does not address the accounting by shareholders who receive the distribution. *[IFRIC 17.8]*.

3.7.2 Recognition and measurement in IFRIC 17

An entity making a non-cash distribution to its owners recognises a liability to pay a dividend when the dividend is appropriately authorised and is no longer at the discretion of the entity. This is the date: *[IFRIC 17.10]*

(a) when declaration of the dividend (e.g. by management or the board of directors) is approved by the relevant authority (e.g. shareholders) if the jurisdiction requires such approval; or

(b) when the dividend is declared (e.g. by management or the board of directors) if the jurisdiction does not require further approval.

An entity measures the liability at the fair value of the assets to be distributed. *[IFRIC 17.11]*. If the owners have a choice between receiving a non-cash asset or cash, the entity estimates the dividend payable by considering both the fair value of each alternative and the associated probability of owners selecting each alternative. *[IFRIC 17.12]*. IFRIC 17 does not specify any method of assessing probability nor its effect on measurement. In a demerger involving the distribution of shares in a subsidiary, the fair value will be determined based on the guidance in IFRS 13. As indicated at 3.3.2.F above, the IASB has discussed issues relating to the unit of account for investments in subsidiaries, joint ventures and associates, and their fair value measurement under IFRS 13.

IFRS 5's requirements apply also to a non-current asset (or disposal group) that is classified as held for distribution to owners acting in their capacity as owners (held for distribution to owners). *[IFRS 5.5A, 12A]*. This means that a non-current asset (or disposal group) classified as held for distribution within scope of IFRS 5 will be carried at the lower of its carrying amount and fair value less costs to distribute (i.e. incremental costs directly attributable to the distribution, excluding finance costs and income tax expense). *[IFRS 5.15A]*. Assets not subject to the measurement provisions of IFRS 5 are measured in accordance with the relevant standard. *[IFRS 5.5]*. See further discussion in Chapter 4 at 2.2.

At the end of each reporting period and at the date of settlement, the carrying amount of the dividend payable is adjusted to reflect any changes in the fair value of the assets being distributed and changes are recognised in equity as adjustments to the amount of the distribution. *[IFRIC 17.11, 13]*.

When the dividend payable is settled, any difference between the carrying amount of the assets distributed and the carrying amount of the dividend payable is recognised as a separate line item in profit or loss. *[IFRIC 17.14-15]*. IFRIC 17 does not express any preference for particular line items or captions in the income statement.

The non-cash assets that are to be distributed are measured in accordance with other applicable IFRSs up to the time of settlement as IFRIC 17 does not override the recognition and measurement requirements of other IFRSs. While the Interpretations Committee recognised concerns about the potential 'accounting mismatch' in equity resulting from measuring the dividend payable and the related assets on a different basis, *[IFRIC 17.BC55]*, it concluded that:

> '... there was no support in IFRSs for requiring a remeasurement of the assets because of a decision to distribute them. The IFRIC noted that the mismatch concerned arises only with respect to assets that are not carried at fair value already. The IFRIC also noted that the accounting mismatch is the inevitable consequence of IFRSs using different measurement attributes at different times with different triggers for the remeasurement of different assets and liabilities.'
> *[IFRIC 17.BC56]*.

3.7.3 Presentation and disclosure

An entity discloses the following information in respect of distributions of non-cash assets within the scope of IFRIC 17:
- the carrying amount of the dividend payable at the beginning and end of the reporting period; [IFRIC 17.16]
- the increase or decrease in the carrying amount recognised in the reporting period as result of a change in the fair value of the assets to be distributed; [IFRIC 17.16] and
- if, after the end of a reporting period but before the financial statements are authorised for issue, an entity declares a dividend to distribute a non-cash asset, it discloses: [IFRIC 17.17]
    - the nature of the asset to be distributed;
    - the carrying amount of the asset to be distributed as of the end of the reporting period;
    - the fair value of the asset to be distributed as of the end of the reporting period, if it is different from its carrying amount; and
    - information about the method(s) used to determine that fair value required by paragraphs 93(b), (d), (g) and (i) and 99 of IFRS 13 (see Chapter 14 at 20.1 and 20.3). [IFRS 13.93, 99].

Chapter 4 at 3 discusses the presentation requirements of IFRS 5 where the demerger meets the definition of a discontinued operation. Chapter 4 at 2.2.4 discusses the presentation of non-current assets and disposal groups held for sale. The same requirements apply to non-current assets and disposal groups held for distribution. [IFRS 5.5A].

4 CHANGES IN OWNERSHIP INTEREST WITHOUT A LOSS OF CONTROL

An increase or decrease in a parent's ownership interest that does not result in a loss of control of a subsidiary is accounted for as an equity transaction, i.e. a transaction with owners in their capacity as owners. [IFRS 10.23]. A parent's ownership interest may change without a loss of control, e.g. when a parent buys shares from or sells shares to a non-controlling interest, a subsidiary redeems shares held by a non-controlling interest, or when a subsidiary issues new shares to a non-controlling interest.

The carrying amounts of the controlling and non-controlling interests are adjusted to reflect the changes in their relative interests in the subsidiary. IFRS 10 states that 'the entity shall recognise directly in equity any difference between the amount by which the non-controlling interests are adjusted and the fair value of the consideration paid or received, and attribute it to the owners of the parent.' [IFRS 10.24, B96]. In other words, no changes to a subsidiary's assets (including goodwill) and liabilities are recognised in a transaction in which a parent increases or decreases its ownership interest in a subsidiary but retains control. [IFRS 10.BCZ173]. Increases or decreases in the ownership interest in a subsidiary do not result in the recognition of a gain or loss.

4.1 Reattribution of other comprehensive income

If there has been a partial disposal of a subsidiary without a loss of control and the disposal includes a foreign operation, the proportionate share of the cumulative amount of exchange differences recognised in other comprehensive income is reattributed to the non-controlling interests in that foreign operation (see Chapter 15 at 6.6.2). *[IAS 21.48C]*. If the entity subsequently disposes of the remainder of its interest in the subsidiary, the exchange differences reattributed to the non-controlling interests are derecognised (i.e. along with the rest of the non-controlling interest balance) but are not separately reclassified to profit or loss (see Chapter 15 at 6.6.1). *[IAS 21.48B]*. In other words, on loss of control, only the exchange differences attributable to the controlling interest immediately before loss of control are reclassified to profit or loss. The accounting is illustrated in Example 7.14 below.

Although not explicitly addressed in IFRS 10 or IAS 21, the IASB has clarified that IFRS requires the reattribution of other amounts recognised in other comprehensive income. The May 2009 IASB Update noted that in the Board's view 'there is no need to clarify the following points, because the relevant requirements are clear: …

- When a change in ownership in a subsidiary occurs but does not result in the loss of control, the parent must reattribute other comprehensive income between the owners of the parent and the non-controlling interest.'[25]

Example 7.12 below illustrates accounting for reattribution of other comprehensive income.

Example 7.12: *Reattribution of other comprehensive income upon a decrease in ownership interest that does not result in a loss of control*

A parent has a wholly owned subsidiary that has net assets of ¥4,000,000, and total other comprehensive income accumulated within equity of ¥1,000,000 related to exchange differences on a foreign operation. No goodwill has been recognised in respect of this subsidiary. The parent sells a 10% interest in the subsidiary for ¥500,000 and does not lose control. The carrying amount of the non-controlling interest is ¥400,000 which includes ¥100,000 (i.e. 10%) of the total other comprehensive income of ¥1,000,000 related to exchange differences on a foreign operation reattributed to the non-controlling interest (as shown below).

The parent accounts for the transaction through equity as follows:

	¥'000 DR	¥'000 CR
Cash	500	
Parent's share of other comprehensive income (¥1,000,000 × 10%)	100	
Parent's other reserves		200
Non-controlling interest's share of other comprehensive income (¥1,000,000 × 10%)		100
Non-controlling interest (excluding share of other comprehensive income) (¥4,000,000 × 10% − (¥1,000,000 × 10%))		300

The IASB's views also clarify that the reattribution approach is required on an increase in ownership interest without gaining control. Again, neither IFRS 10 nor IAS 21 addresses this explicitly. Example 7.13 below illustrates the reattribution approach upon an increase in ownership interest.

Example 7.13: **Reattribution of other comprehensive income upon an increase in ownership interest**

A parent holds an 80% interest in a subsidiary that has net assets of ¥4,000,000. No goodwill has been recognised in respect of this subsidiary. The carrying amount of the 20% non-controlling interest is ¥800,000 which includes ¥200,000 that represents the non-controlling interest's share of total other comprehensive income of ¥1,000,000 related to exchange differences on a foreign operation. The parent acquires an additional 10% interest in the subsidiary for ¥500,000, which increases its total interest to 90%. The carrying amount of the non-controlling interest is now ¥400,000 which includes ¥100,000 (i.e. 10%) of the total other comprehensive income of ¥1,000,000 related to exchange differences on a foreign operation, after reattributing ¥100,000 to the parent (as shown below).

The parent accounts for the transaction through equity as follows:

	¥'000 DR	¥'000 CR
Non-controlling interest's share of other comprehensive income (¥1,000,000 × 10%)	100	
Non-controlling interest (excluding share of other comprehensive income) (¥800,000 × 10% / 20% − (¥1,000,000 × 10%))	300	
Parent's other reserves	200	
Parent's share of other comprehensive income (¥1,000,000 × 10%)		100
Cash		500

Example 7.14 below illustrates the reclassification of reattributed exchange differences upon subsequent loss of control. This shows that the reattribution of the exchange differences arising on the change in the parent's ownership of the subsidiary (as illustrated in Examples 7.12 and 7.13 above) affects the gain recognised on loss of control of the subsidiary.

Example 7.14: **Reclassification of reattributed exchange differences upon subsequent loss of control**

Assume the same facts as in Examples 7.12 or 7.13 above. Following those transactions, the parent now holds a 90% interest in a subsidiary that has net assets of ¥4,000,000. No goodwill has been recognised in respect of this subsidiary. The carrying amount of the 10% non-controlling interest is ¥400,000 which includes ¥100,000 of the total other comprehensive income of ¥1,000,000 related to exchange differences on a foreign operation, as reattributed to the non-controlling interest. The parent subsequently sells its 90% interest for ¥4,700,000. For the purposes of illustration, there have been no subsequent changes in net assets nor other comprehensive income up to the date of sale.

The parent accounts for the transaction as follows:

	¥'000 DR	¥'000 CR
Cash proceeds from sale	4,700	
Net assets of subsidiary derecognised		4,000
Non-controlling interest derecognised	400	
Parent's share of other comprehensive income reclassified (¥1,000,000 × 90%)		900
Gain recognised on disposal of subsidiary attributable to parent		2,000

4.2 Goodwill attributable to non-controlling interests

It is not clear under IFRS 10 what happens to the non-controlling interests' share of goodwill, when accounting for transactions with non-controlling interests.

However, we believe that the parent should reallocate a proportion of the goodwill between the controlling and non-controlling interests when their relative ownership interests change. Otherwise, the loss recognised upon loss of control (see 3.2 above) or goodwill impairment would not reflect the ownership interest applicable to that non-controlling interest. Chapter 20 at 9 discusses how an entity tests goodwill for impairment, where there is a non-controlling interest. The issues arising include:

- calculation of the 'gross up' of the carrying amount of goodwill (for the purposes of the impairment test) because the non-controlling interest is measured at its proportionate share of net identifiable assets and hence its share of goodwill is not recognised;
- the allocation of impairment losses between the parent and the non-controlling interest; and
- reallocation of goodwill between the non-controlling interest and controlling interest after a change in a parent's ownership interest in a subsidiary that does not result in loss of control.

Under IFRS 3, the proportion of goodwill that is attributable to the non-controlling interest is not necessarily equal to the ownership percentage. The most common situation where this occurs is when the parent recognised the non-controlling interest at its proportionate share of the acquiree's identifiable net assets and therefore does not recognise any goodwill for the non-controlling interest (see Chapter 9 at 5.1 and 8.2). This situation might also occur because goodwill has been recognised for both the parent and the non-controlling interest but the parent's goodwill reflects a control premium that was paid upon acquisition (see Chapter 9 at 8.1).

Example 7.15 below illustrates one approach to reallocating goodwill where there is a change in ownership of the subsidiary with no loss of control (for a situation where the non-controlling interest is recognised initially at its fair value).

Example 7.15: Reallocation of goodwill to non-controlling interests

A parent pays €920 million to acquire an 80% interest in a subsidiary that owns net assets with a fair value of €1,000 million. The fair value of the non-controlling interest at the acquisition date is €220 million.

	Share of net assets €m	Share of goodwill €m	Total €m
Parent	800	120	920
Non-controlling interest	200	20	220
	1,000	140	1,140

Decrease in ownership percentage

A year after the acquisition, the parent sells a 20% interest in the subsidiary to a third party for €265 million. There has been no change in the net assets of the subsidiary since acquisition.

The parent's interest decreases to 60% and its share of net assets decreases to €600 million. Correspondingly, the share of net assets attributable to the non-controlling interest increases from €200 million to €400 million.

The parent company sold a 20% interest in its subsidiary. Therefore, one approach for reallocating goodwill is to allocate €30 million (20% / 80% × €120 million) of the parent's goodwill to the non-controlling interest. After the transaction, the parent's share of goodwill is €90 million (€120 million – €30 million).

In its consolidated financial statements, the parent accounts for this transaction as follows:

	€m DR	€m CR
Cash	265	
Non-controlling interests ((€400m – €200m) + €30m)		230
Equity of the parent		35

Increase in ownership percentage

Taking the initial fact pattern as a starting point, the parent acquires an additional 10% interest in the subsidiary for €115 million. There has been no change in the net assets of the subsidiary since acquisition.

The parent's interest increases to 90% and its share of net assets increases to €900 million. Correspondingly, the share of net assets attributable to the non-controlling interest is reduced from €200 million to €100 million. The parent acquired half of the non-controlling interest. Using the proportionate allocation approach discussed above, the parent allocates €10 million (10% / 20% × €20 million) of the non-controlling interest's goodwill to the parent.

In its consolidated financial statements, the parent accounts for this transaction as follows:

	€m DR	€m CR
Non-controlling interest ((€200m – €100m) + €10m)	110	
Equity of the parent	5	
Cash		115

In Example 7.15 above, the non-controlling interest was recognised and measured at its fair value at the acquisition date. If the non-controlling interest had been measured based on its proportionate share of net assets, the proportionate allocation approach described in the example would have resulted in the same accounting for the transaction where the parent's ownership interest had decreased. However, where the parent increased its ownership interest, as the carrying amount of the non-controlling interest did not include any amount for goodwill, the adjustment to the non-controlling interest would only have been €100 million resulting in a debit to the parent's equity of €15 million.

The proportionate allocation approach described in Example 7.15 above is just one method that may result in relevant and reliable information. However, other approaches may also be appropriate depending on the circumstances. We consider that an entity is not precluded from attributing goodwill on a basis other than ownership percentages if to do so is reasonable, e.g. because the non-controlling interest is measured on a proportionate share (rather than fair value) and because of the existence of a control premium. In such circumstances, an allocation approach which takes into account the acquirer's control premium will result in a goodwill balance that most closely resembles the balance that would have been recorded had the non-controlling interest been recorded at fair value. An entity may also be able to allocate impairment losses on a basis that recognises the disproportionate sharing of the controlling and the non-controlling interest in the goodwill book value. This is discussed further in Chapter 20 at 9.

4.3 Non-cash acquisition of non-controlling interests

One issue considered by the Interpretations Committee is the accounting for the purchase of a non-controlling interest by the controlling shareholder when the consideration includes non-cash items, such as an item of property, plant and equipment. More specifically, the submitter asked the Interpretations Committee to clarify whether the difference between the fair value of the consideration given and the carrying amount of such consideration should be recognised in equity or in profit or loss. The submitter asserted that, according to the requirements of the then IAS 27 – *Consolidated and Separate Financial Statements* (now reflected in IFRS 10), the difference described should be recognised in equity, whereas applying IFRIC 17 by analogy, the difference should be recognised in profit or loss (see 3.7 above).

The Interpretations Committee noted that the requirements of the then IAS 27 (now reflected in IFRS 10), deal solely with the difference between the carrying amount of the non-controlling interest and the fair value of the consideration given; this difference is required to be recognised in equity. These requirements do not deal with the difference between the fair value of the consideration given and the carrying amount of such consideration. *[IFRS 10.24, B96]*. The difference between the fair value of the assets transferred and their carrying amount arises from the derecognition of those assets. IFRSs generally require an entity to recognise, in profit or loss, any gain or loss arising from the derecognition of an asset.[26]

4.4 Transaction costs

Although IFRS 10 is clear that changes in a parent's ownership interest in a subsidiary that do not result in the parent losing control of the subsidiary are equity transactions (i.e. transactions with owners in their capacity as owners), *[IFRS 10.23]*, it does not specifically address how to account for related transaction costs. Only incremental costs directly attributable to the equity transaction that otherwise would have been avoided qualify as transaction costs. *[IAS 32.37]*.

In our view, any directly attributable incremental transaction costs incurred to acquire an outstanding non-controlling interest in a subsidiary, or to sell a non-controlling interest in a subsidiary without loss of control, are deducted from equity. This is regardless of whether the consideration is in cash or shares. This is consistent with both guidance elsewhere in IFRS regarding the treatment of such costs, *[IAS 32.35, 37, IAS 1.109]*, and the view expressed by the Interpretations Committee.[27] Although where shares are given as consideration there is no change in total consolidated equity, there are in fact two transactions – an issue of new equity and a repurchase of existing equity. The entity accounts for the transaction costs on the two elements in the same manner as if they had occurred separately. The tax effects of transaction costs of equity instruments are discussed in Chapter 33 at 10.3.5.

IFRS does not specify where to allocate the costs in equity – in particular, whether to the parent (who incurred the costs) or to the non-controlling interest (whose equity was issued/repurchased). Therefore, the parent may choose where to allocate the costs within equity, based on the facts and circumstances surrounding the change in ownership, and any legal requirements of the jurisdiction.

Regardless of the account in equity to which the charge is allocated, the amount is not reclassified to profit or loss in future periods. Consequently, if the costs are allocated to the non-controlling interest, this amount must be separately tracked. If a subsidiary is later sold in a separate transaction (i.e. loss of control), the transaction costs previously recognised directly in equity to acquire or sell the non-controlling interest are not reclassified from equity to profit and loss, because they do not represent components of other comprehensive income.

4.5 Contingent consideration on purchase of a non-controlling interest

IFRS 10 does not provide guidance on accounting for remeasurement of contingent consideration relating to the purchase of a non-controlling interest. The question arises as to whether the remeasurement should be accounted for in profit or loss, or in equity (on the grounds that it is related to the purchase of the non-controlling interest – see 4 above). This discussion assumes that the purchase of the non-controlling interest is separate from the business combination. It is not uncommon for a written put and/or a purchased call option over a non-controlling interest to be put in place at the time of a business combination. The accounting for such transactions (including forward contracts to sell non-controlling interests) is discussed in 6 below.

IFRS 3 addresses the accounting for remeasurement of contingent consideration recognised by the acquirer in a business combination. Contingent consideration is initially recognised at its fair value. Contingent consideration classified as equity is not remeasured and its subsequent settlement is accounted for within equity. Other contingent consideration that is within the scope of IFRS 9 or is not within the scope of IFRS 9 is measured at fair value at each reporting date and changes in its fair value are recognised in profit or loss in accordance with IFRS 9. *[IFRS 3.39, 40, 58, IFRS 9.4.2.1(e)]*. See Chapter 9 at 7.1.

The purchase of a non-controlling interest is not a business combination and, consequently, IFRS 3 requirements do not apply. In practice, most contingent consideration meets the definition of a financial liability and would fall within the scope of IFRS 9.

In our view, a distinction should be drawn between the initial recognition of the contingent consideration classified as a financial liability, which is a transaction with the non-controlling interest, and its subsequent measurement. On initial recognition, contingent consideration is recognised at its fair value, the non-controlling interest purchased is derecognised (and any balancing adjustment is reflected in parent equity). Subsequent movements in contingent consideration classified as a financial liability are recognised in accordance with IFRS 9 (in profit or loss, as explained below) rather than regarded as relating to a transaction with the non-controlling interest (and recognised in equity). If the contingent consideration is classified as an equity instrument, it will not be remeasured. *[IFRS 3.58]*.

Depending on the terms and conditions, the contingent consideration may be classified as a financial liability at amortised cost, or at fair value through profit or loss. *[IFRS 9.4.2.1-4.2.2]*. In both cases, subsequent remeasurements for any changes in estimated contractual cash flows or fair value, or on final settlement of the financial liability are recognised in profit or loss (except for any fair value movements attributable to own credit risk required to be recognised in other comprehensive income, where the financial liability is designated at fair value through profit or loss). See Chapter 48 at 3, 4 and 7, and Chapter 50 at 2.2, 2.4 and 3.

5 NON-CONTROLLING INTERESTS

5.1 The definition of non-controlling interests

IFRS 10 defines a non-controlling interest as 'equity in a subsidiary not attributable, directly or indirectly, to a parent.' *[IFRS 10 Appendix A]*. The principle underlying accounting for non-controlling interests is that all residual economic interest holders of any part of the consolidated entity have an equity interest in that consolidated entity.

Consequently, non-controlling interests relate to consolidated subsidiaries, and not to those investments in subsidiaries accounted at fair value through profit or loss in accordance with IFRS 9 by an investment entity (see Chapter 6 at 10.3). *[IFRS 10.31-33]*. This principle applies regardless of the decision-making ability of that interest holder and where in the group that interest is held. Therefore, any equity instruments issued by a subsidiary that are not owned by the parent (apart from those that are required to be classified by IAS 32 – *Financial Instruments: Presentation* – as financial liabilities in the consolidated financial statements, as discussed at 5.5 below) are non-controlling interests, including:

- ordinary shares;
- convertible debt and other compound financial instruments;
- preference shares that are classified as equity (including both those with, and without, an entitlement to a *pro rata* share of net assets on liquidation);
- warrants;
- options over own shares; and
- options under share-based payment transactions.

Options and warrants are non-controlling interests, regardless of whether they are vested and regardless of the exercise price (e.g. whether they are 'in-the-money').

IAS 32 defines an equity instrument as 'any contract that evidences a residual interest in the assets of an entity after deducting all of its liabilities'. *[IAS 32.11]*. This is consistent with the definition of 'equity' in the IASB's *Conceptual Framework for Financial Reporting* published in 2018. *[CF 4.63-4.64]*. Hence, the reference to 'equity' in the definition of a non-controlling interest refers to those 'equity instruments' of a subsidiary that are not attributable, directly or indirectly, to its parent. This also means that financial instruments that are not classified within equity in accordance with IAS 32 (e.g. total return swaps) are not included within the definition of a non-controlling interest.

If a parent has an indirect ownership interest in the subsidiary, this is taken into account in computing the non-controlling interest. For example, if a parent has a 60% direct interest in Subsidiary A (which in turn owns 80% of Subsidiary B), there will be a 52% (i.e. 100% − (60% × 80%)) non-controlling interest in Subsidiary B's equity. Where Subsidiary A acquired Subsidiary B in a business combination, there will also be a 40%

non-controlling interest in the goodwill arising in the consolidated financial statements. This situation is illustrated in Example 7.18 at 5.2.1 below (note though that in the specific example the non-controlling interest in the goodwill arising on acquisition of the Target is not simply 40% of the goodwill amount, as the Target has also issued warrants).

5.2 Initial measurement of non-controlling interests

5.2.1 Initial measurement of non-controlling interests in a business combination

IFRS 3 requires any non-controlling interest in an acquiree to be recognised, *[IFRS 3.10]*, but there are differing measurement requirements depending on the type of equity instrument.

There is a choice of two measurement methods for those components of non-controlling interests that are both present ownership interests and entitle their holders to a proportionate share of the entity's net assets in the event of a liquidation ('qualifying non-controlling interests'). They can be measured at either:

(a) acquisition-date fair value (consistent with the measurement principle for other components of the business combination); or

(b) the present ownership instruments' proportionate share in the recognised amounts of the acquiree's identifiable net assets.

The choice of method is to be made for each business combination on a transaction-by-transaction basis, rather than being a policy choice. This choice of measurement is discussed in Chapter 9 at 8.

However, this choice is not available for all other components of non-controlling interests, which are required to be measured at their acquisition-date fair values, unless another measurement basis is required by IFRSs. *[IFRS 3.19]*.

Of the items listed in 5.1 above, entities are only given a choice of either proportionate share in the recognised amounts of the acquiree's identifiable net assets or acquisition-date fair value, for ordinary shares or preference shares classified as equity that are entitled to a *pro rata* share of net assets on liquidation.

Another measurement basis (referred to as a 'market-based measure') is required by IFRS 3 for share-based payment transactions classified as equity in accordance with IFRS 2 – these are measured in accordance with the method in IFRS 2. *[IFRS 3.30, B62A, B62B]*. The accounting for replaced and not replaced share-based payment transactions in a business combination is discussed in Chapter 9 at 7.2 and 8.4 and in Chapter 34 at 11.2 and 11.3.

The other items listed in 5.1 above, e.g. the equity component of convertible debt or other compound financial instruments, preference shares classified as equity without an entitlement to a *pro rata* share of net assets upon liquidation, warrants and options over own shares, must be measured at acquisition-date fair value.

These issues are discussed in more detail in Chapter 9 at 8.

The measurement of non-controlling interests in a business combination is illustrated in Example 7.16 below.

Example 7.16: Initial measurement of non-controlling interests in a business combination (1)

Parent acquires 80% of the ordinary shares of Target for €950,000 in cash. The total fair value of the equity instruments issued by Target is €1,165,000 and the fair value of its identifiable net assets is €850,000. The fair value of the 20% of the ordinary shares owned by non-controlling shareholders is €190,000. In addition, the subsidiary has also written gross settled call options over its own shares with a fair value of €25,000, which are considered equity instruments under IAS 32.

Option 1 – Non-controlling interests at fair value

The impact of the business combination and the measurement of non-controlling interests are as follows:

	€'000 DR	€'000 CR
Fair value of identifiable net assets	850	
Goodwill (€950,000 + €215,000 – €850,000)	315	
Cash		950
Non-controlling interests (€190,000 + €25,000)		215

The non-controlling interests are measured at the fair value of all equity instruments issued by Target that are not owned by the parent (i.e. ordinary shares and gross settled call options).

Option 2 – Qualifying non-controlling interests are measured at proportionate share of identifiable net assets

The impact of the business combination and the measurement of non-controlling interests are as follows:

	€'000 DR	€'000 CR
Fair value of identifiable net assets	850	
Goodwill (€950,000 – (80% × €850,000) + €25,000)	295	
Cash		950
Non-controlling interests (20% × €850,000 + €25,000)		195

The non-controlling interests that are present ownership interests and entitle their holders to a proportionate share of the Target's net assets in the event of liquidation (i.e. the ordinary shares) are measured at the non-controlling interests' proportionate share of the identifiable net assets of Target. The non-controlling interests that are not present ownership interests or do not entitle their holders to a proportionate share of the Target's net assets in the event of liquidation (i.e. the gross settled call options) are measured at their fair value.

Reconciliation of goodwill

Goodwill as determined under the two methods can be reconciled as follows:

	€'000
Option 2: Goodwill (€950,000 – (80% × €850,000) + €25,000)	295
Goodwill related to the non-controlling interest in ordinary shares (€190,000 – 20% × €850,000)	20
Option 1: Goodwill (€1,165,000 – €850,000)	315

This makes clear that Option 2 effectively ignores the goodwill related to ordinary shares that are held by non-controlling shareholders.

In Example 7.16 above, under Option 2, the computation of the non-controlling interests represented by the ordinary shares was based solely on the fair value of the identifiable net assets, i.e. no deduction was made in respect of the other component of non-controlling interests. IFRS 3 does not state whether this should be the case.

An alternative view would be that such other components of non-controlling interests should be deducted from the value of the net identifiable net assets acquired based on their acquisition-date fair value (or market-based measure) or based on their liquidation rights, as illustrated in Example 7.17 below.

Example 7.17: *Initial measurement of non-controlling interests in a business combination (2)*

Option 3 – Qualifying non-controlling interests are measured at proportionate share of identifiable net assets net of other components of non-controlling interests

The impact of the business combination and the measurement of non-controlling interests are as follows:

	€'000 DR	€'000 CR
Fair value of identifiable net assets	850	
Goodwill (€950,000 – 80% × (€850,000 – €25,000))	290	
Cash		950
Non-controlling interests ((20% × (€850,000 – €25,000)) + €25,000)		190

The difference between goodwill of €295,000 (Option 2 in Example 7.16 above) and €290,000 is 20% of €25,000, i.e. the amount attributable to the non-controlling interest in the call options.

In Example 7.16 above, Option 2 resulted in no goodwill being attributable to non-controlling interests. However, if the Target had been acquired, not by Parent, but by a 60%-owned subsidiary of Parent, we believe that the goodwill recognised remains the same, but that some of the goodwill is attributable to the non-controlling interests in the acquiring subsidiary as illustrated in Example 7.18 below.

Example 7.18: *Initial measurement of non-controlling interests in a business combination by a partly owned subsidiary*

Assume the same facts as in Example 7.16 above, except that a 60% Subsidiary of Parent acquires 80% of the ordinary shares of Target for €950,000 in cash.

Under Option 2, the impact of the business combination and the measurement of non-controlling interests in Parent's consolidated financial statements are as follows:

	€'000 DR	€'000 CR
Fair value of identifiable net assets	850	
Goodwill (€950,000 – (80% × €850,000) + €25,000)	295	
Cash		950
Non-controlling interests in Target (20% × €850,000 + €25,000)		195
Non-controlling interest in 60% Subsidiary		–

Although the overall impact on the non-controlling interest (NCI) in 60% Subsidiary is nil, this is represented by:

	€'000 DR	€'000 CR
NCI share of fair value of identifiable net assets (40% × 80% × €850,000)		272
NCI share of goodwill (40% × (€295,000 – €25,000))		108
NCI share of cash consideration (40% × €950,000)	380	

5.2.2 Initial measurement of non-controlling interests in a subsidiary that is not a business combination

The initial measurement of non-controlling interests in a subsidiary that is not a business combination is discussed at 3.1.1 and 3.1.2 above.

5.3 Measurement of non-controlling interests where an associate holds an interest in a subsidiary

Neither IFRS 10 nor IAS 28 explains how to account for non-controlling interests when the group owns an associate which has a holding in a subsidiary. A non-controlling interest is defined as 'the equity in a subsidiary not attributable, directly or indirectly to a parent'. *[IFRS 10 Appendix A]*. It is unclear whether this should be computed based on the ownership interests held by the group (i.e. by the parent and any consolidated subsidiary), or whether it should also take into account the indirect ownership of the subsidiary held by the associate.

The reciprocal interests can also give rise to a measure of double-counting of profits and net assets between the investor and its associate.

We believe that there are two possible approaches to determine the amount of non-controlling interests in the subsidiary:

(a) the non-controlling interests are determined after considering the associate's ownership of the subsidiary ('look through approach'); or

(b) the non-controlling interests are determined based on the holdings of the group in the subsidiary ('black box approach').

An entity should apply the chosen approach consistently.

In applying the 'look through approach', the parent must not recognise the share of the subsidiary's results recognised by the associate applying the equity method, in order to avoid double-counting. The 'black box approach' will often lead to reporting higher consolidated net assets and results than when using the 'look through approach' as this adjustment is not made, although the amounts attributed to owners of the parent should be the same under both approaches. The two approaches are illustrated in Example 7.19 below.

Example 7.19: Measurement of non-controlling interest where an associate accounted using the equity method holds an interest in a subsidiary

Parent P owns directly 60% of subsidiary S. P also directly owns 40% of associate A that in turn holds a 30% interest in S. S has earned profits of US$1,000,000 in the period and has net assets of US$3,000,000 (which are consolidated in both P's consolidated financial statements and equity accounted by A) at the reporting date. A has net assets of US$1,100,000 (excluding its share of the net assets of S). There are no transactions between A and S (which was not acquired in a business combination).

Approach 1 ('look through approach')

This approach involves determining the ownership attributable to the non-controlling interests (NCI) after considering A's ownership of S. This approach views the equity method as primarily a method of consolidation (albeit on a single line), as further discussed in Chapter 11 at 7.2.

Therefore, under the 'look through' approach, P's total ownership interest in S is 72% (and the NCI's interest is 28%). P's effective ownership interest of 72% in S represents 60% held directly and an additional effective interest of 12% (40% × 30%) via A.

Therefore, P consolidates the profits of S of US$1,000,000, with:

Profits of S attributable to owners of P	US$720,000 (US$1,000,000 × 72%)
Profits of S attributable to the NCI	US$280,000 (US$1,000,000 × 28%)

However, when equity accounting for A, P does not recognise its share of S's results recognised by the associate A of US$120,000 (US$1,000,000 × (40% × 30%)). This is to avoid double counting as S's results have already been consolidated and P's effective ownership of 12% of S that is indirectly held via A has been attributed to owners of the parent.

The assets and liabilities of S are consolidated, with:

Net assets of S attributable to owners of P	US$2,160,000 (72% × US$3,000,000)
Net assets of S attributable to the NCI	US$840,000 (28% × US$3,000,000)
Investment in A	US$440,000 (Note 1)

Note 1 – when equity accounting for A, P does not recognise its share of S's net assets recognised by A of US$360,000 (US$3,000,000 × (40% × 30%)) to avoid double-counting as the net assets of S owned by A have already been included in the amounts attributable to the owners of P. Therefore, the investment in A is reported at P's 40% share of A's net assets (excluding A's share of S), i.e. 40% × US$1,100,000.

Approach 2 ('black box approach')

Under this approach (the 'black box approach'), when determining NCI, P considers the ownership interests in S not held by the group (i.e. by P and its subsidiaries). This approach views the equity method as primarily a method of valuing an investment, as further discussed in Chapter 11 at 7.2.

Accordingly, P's ownership interest is 60% and the NCI's ownership interest is 40%.

Therefore, P consolidates the profits of S of US$1,000,000, with:

Profits of S attributable to owners of P	US$600,000 (60% × US$1,000,000)
Profits of S attributable to the NCI	US$400,000 (40% × US$1,000,000)

The assets and liabilities of S are consolidated, with:

Net assets of S attributable to owners of P	US$1,800,000 (60% × US$3,000,000)
Net assets of S attributable to the NCI	US$1,200,000 (40% × US$3,000,000)
Investment in A	US$800,000 (Note 2)

Note 2 – when equity accounting for A, P does not eliminate its share of S's results of US$120,000 and net assets of US$360,000. Therefore, the investment in A is reported at P's 40% share of A's net assets (including the associate's share of S), i.e. 40% × (US$1,100,000 + (30% × US$3,000,000)).

The results and net assets in respect of S (including the effect of equity accounting for A's holding in S) that are attributed to owners of P are the same as in Approach 1. However, the total consolidated results and net assets exceed those reported in Approach 1 by US$120,000 and US$360,000 respectively (being P's effective ownership interest of 12% in S's profits and net assets that are equity accounted in Approach 2). While this approach has the merit that the attribution of S's profits and net assets to NCI reflects the 40% ownership interests in S not held by the group, a downside is the double counting of 12% of S's profits and net assets that are equity accounted by A.

5.4 Presentation of non-controlling interests

IFRS 10 requires non-controlling interests to be presented in the consolidated statement of financial position within equity, separately from the equity of the owners of the parent. *[IFRS 10.22]*. Profit or loss and each component of other comprehensive income are attributed to the owners of the parent and to the non-controlling interests. Attribution of total comprehensive income to the non-controlling interests continues even if it results in a deficit balance. *[IFRS 10.24, B94]*. Deficit balances are considered further at 5.6.1 below.

The presentation of non-controlling interests in the primary financial statements is addressed in Chapter 3 at 3.1.5 (statement of financial position), *[IAS 1.54]*, 3.2.2 (statement of profit or loss), *[IAS 1.81B]*, 3.2.4 (statement of comprehensive income), *[IAS 1.81B]*, and 3.3 (statement of changes in equity). *[IAS 1.106]*.

5.5 Non-controlling interests classified as financial liabilities

In spite of the general requirement in IFRS 10 to treat non-controlling interests as equity, a non-controlling interest is classified by IAS 32 as a financial liability and payments to the non-controlling interest as interest expense if the group as a whole has an obligation to deliver cash or another financial asset in respect of the instrument, or to settle it in a manner that results in its classification as a financial liability. *[IAS 32.AG29]*. See Chapter 47 at 4.8.1.

One particular issue considered by the Interpretations Committee is the classification, in the consolidated financial statements of a group, of puttable instruments that are issued by a subsidiary but that are not held, directly or indirectly, by the parent. The question asked was whether these instruments, which are classified as equity instruments in the financial statements of the subsidiary in accordance with IAS 32, *[IAS 32.16A, 16B]*, should be classified as equity or liability in the parent's consolidated financial statements.

The Interpretations Committee noted that paragraphs 16A-16D of IAS 32 state that puttable instruments and instruments that impose on the entity an obligation to deliver to another party a *pro rata* share of the net assets of the entity only on liquidation meet the definition of a financial liability. These instruments are classified as equity in the financial statements of the subsidiary as an exception to the definition of a financial liability if all relevant requirements are met. *[IAS 32.16A, 16B, 16C, 16D]*. This exception applies only to the financial statements of the subsidiary and does not extend to the parent's consolidated financial statements. *[IAS 32.AG29A]*. Consequently, these financial instruments should be classified as financial liabilities in the parent's consolidated financial statements.[28]

In our view, where a non-controlling interest is classified as equity in consolidated financial statements, it is subject to all the requirements of IAS 32 relating to own equity. For example, put or call options over non-controlling interests accounted for as equity should be accounted for in consolidated financial statements as contracts over own equity instruments under IAS 32 (see Chapter 47 at 11).

In some cases, the effect of options over what are in law non-controlling interests may be such that no non-controlling interests are recognised in the financial statements, particularly when such options are issued as part of a business combination (see 6 below).

5.6 Subsequent measurement of non-controlling interests

A proportion of profit or loss, other comprehensive income and changes in equity is only attributed to those instruments included within non-controlling interests if they give rise to an existing ownership interest. Non-controlling interests, that are potential voting rights and other derivatives that require exercise or conversion (such as options, warrants, or share-based payment transactions), generally do not receive an allocation of profit or loss, other comprehensive income and changes in equity. *[IFRS 10.21, 24, B89, B94].* However, as discussed at 2.2 above, allocating the proportions of profit or loss, other comprehensive income and changes in equity based on present legal ownership interests is not always appropriate. An entity also considers the eventual exercise of potential rights and other derivatives if, in substance, they provide an existing ownership interest that currently gives it access to the returns associated with that ownership interest. In that case, the proportion allocated to the parent and non-controlling interests takes into account the eventual exercise of those potential voting rights and other derivatives. *[IFRS 10.21, B90].* As noted at 2.2 above, this chapter uses the term 'present ownership interest' to include existing legal ownership interests, together with potential voting rights and other derivatives that, in substance, already provide existing ownership interests in a subsidiary.

Where a gain or loss is recognised by a non-wholly-owned subsidiary in an upstream transaction with its parent, the gain or loss is eliminated on consolidation. Therefore, the profit or loss allocated to the non-controlling interest excludes the non-controlling interest's share of that eliminated gain or loss (see 2.4 above).

Where a subsidiary has granted options over its own shares under an equity-settled share-based payment transaction, the share-based payment expense recognised in profit or loss will be attributable to the parent and any other non-controlling interest that has a present ownership in the subsidiary. None of the expense is attributed to the non-controlling interest represented by the options under the share-based payment transaction. The corresponding entry taken to equity by the subsidiary in respect of the options under the share-based payment transaction will be recognised as non-controlling interest in the consolidated financial statements.

If a subsidiary has outstanding cumulative preference shares classified as equity that are held by non-controlling interests, the parent is required to compute its share of profits or losses after adjusting for the dividends on these shares, whether or not such dividends have been declared. *[IFRS 10.24, B95].* This effectively means that the non-controlling interests represented by the cumulative preference shares are being allocated a portion of the profit or loss equivalent to the dividends.

In addition, where an entity has a complicated equity structure with several classes of equity shares that have varying entitlements to net profits, equity or liquidation preferences, the parent needs to assess carefully the rights attaching to each class of equity share in determining the appropriate percentage of ownership interest.

When the proportion of equity held by the non-controlling interests changes, e.g. because a potential voting right is exercised, the carrying amount originally recognised in non-controlling interests is adjusted to reflect the change in the relative interests in the subsidiary. *[IFRS 10.24, B96]*. In our view, this requirement in IFRS 10 also means that if potential voting rights lapse unexercised, the amount originally recognised in non-controlling interests is reversed, so that the carrying amounts of the controlling and non-controlling interests reflect the relative interests in the subsidiary. Otherwise, amounts previously recognised related to lapsed potential voting rights would remain recognised as part of the non-controlling interests until the next remeasurement of non-controlling interests occurs, which may be an unrelated transaction, or which may never occur.

5.6.1 Loss-making subsidiaries

Total comprehensive income is attributed 'to the owners of the parent and to the non-controlling interests even if this results in the non-controlling interests having a deficit balance.' *[IFRS 10.24, B94]*. This approach is consistent with the fact that the controlling and the non-controlling interests participate proportionately in the risks and rewards of an investment in the subsidiary. The IASB observed that although it is true that non-controlling interests have no further obligation to contribute assets to the entity, neither does the parent. *[IFRS 10.BCZ165]*.

Guarantees or other support arrangements by the parent often protect the non-controlling interests from losses of the subsidiary in excess of their equity. The IASB believes that the parent ought to account for such arrangements separately, and that the accounting for these arrangements should not affect how an entity should attribute comprehensive income to the parent and the non-controlling interests. *[IFRS 10.BCZ162-164]*.

6 CALL AND PUT OPTIONS OVER NON-CONTROLLING INTERESTS

Some business combinations involve options over some or all of the outstanding shares. For example, the acquirer might have a call option, i.e. a right to acquire the outstanding shares at a future date for a particular price. Alternatively, the acquirer might have granted a put option to the other shareholders whereby they have the right to sell their shares to the acquirer at a future date for a particular price. In some cases, there may be a combination of such call and put options, the terms of which may be equivalent or may be different.

IFRS 3 gives no guidance as to how to account for such options in a business combination. Therefore, when determining the appropriate accounting in the consolidated financial statements in such situations, IFRS 10, IAS 32, and IFRS 9 need to be considered. The accounting for call and put options depends on whether or not the acquirer has obtained present access to returns associated with the ownership interest in the shares of the acquiree subject to the call and/or put option. Potential voting rights that represent a present ownership interest are discussed in general at 2.2 and 5.6 above but specific considerations for call and/or put options are discussed at 6.1 and 6.2.2 below.

While the discussion below deals with options, similar considerations to those discussed at 6.1 and 6.2 below apply where the acquirer entered into a forward purchase contract for the shares held by the other shareholders (see 6.3 below).

Although the discussion at 6.1 and 6.2 below focuses on call and put options entered into at the same time as control of the subsidiary is gained, an entity may enter into the options with non-controlling shareholders after gaining control. This situation is discussed at 6.4 below, although the appropriate accounting in the consolidated financial statements will still be based on the discussions in 6.1 and 6.2 below.

Sometimes, put and/or call options over non-controlling interests may be subject to employment conditions. The guidance in 6.1 to 6.5 below is intended to apply to put and/or call options over non-controlling interests as shareholders rather than when such arrangements constitute an employee benefit (accounted under IAS 19 – see Chapter 35 at 12 and 13) or share-based payment arrangement (accounted under IFRS 2 – see Chapter 34). See Chapter 34 at 2.2 and Chapter 35 at 2.2 for a discussion of when cash-settled awards may fall within the scope of IAS 19 or IFRS 2.

6.1 Call options only

Call options are considered when determining whether the entity has obtained control, as discussed at Chapter 6 at 4.3.4. Where it is determined that an entity has control over another entity, the proportions of profit or loss, other comprehensive income and changes in equity allocated to the parent and non-controlling interests are based on present ownership interests, and generally do not reflect the possible exercise or conversion of potential voting rights under call options. *[IFRS 10.21, 24, B89, B94]*. The eventual exercise of potential voting rights under the call option are reflected in the proportion of profit or loss, other comprehensive income and changes in equity only if in substance the entity already has access to the returns associated with that ownership interest. *[IFRS 10.21, 24, B90, B94]*. This assessment depends on the terms of the call option, and judgement is required.

6.1.1 Options giving the acquirer present access to returns associated with that ownership interest

A call option is likely to give the acquiring entity present access to returns associated with the ownership interest in the shares subject to the call in limited circumstances, for example:

- when the option price is fixed with a low exercise price and it is agreed between the parties that either no dividends will be paid to the other shareholders (or the acquiring entity can control that no dividends will be paid prior to exercise of the option) or the dividend payments lead to an adjustment of the option exercise price; or
- when the terms are set such that the other shareholders effectively receive only a lender's return.

This is because any accretion in the fair value of the underlying ownership interest under the option (for example, due to improved financial performance of the acquiree subsequent to the granting of the call option) is likely to be realised by the acquirer.

If a call option gives the acquiring entity present access to returns over all of the shares held by non-controlling shareholders, then there will be no non-controlling interest presented in equity. The acquirer accounts for the business combination as though it acquired a 100% interest. The acquirer also recognises a financial liability for the present value of the exercise price to be paid to the non-controlling shareholders under the call option. Changes in the carrying amount of the financial liability are recognised in profit or loss, in accordance with IFRS 9. If the call option expires unexercised, then the acquirer has effectively disposed of a partial interest in its subsidiary in return for the amount recognised as the 'liability' at the date of expiry and accounts for the transaction as a change in ownership interest without a loss of control, as discussed at 4 above.

6.1.2 Options not giving the acquirer present access to returns associated with that ownership interest

A call option may not give present access to the returns associated with the ownership interest in the shares subject to the call where the option's terms contain one or more of the following features:

- the option exercise price has not yet been determined or will be the fair value (or an amount that approximates fair value) of the shares at the date of exercise;
- the option exercise price is based on expected future results or net assets of the subsidiary at the date of exercise; or
- it has been agreed between the parties that, prior to the exercise of the option, all retained profits may be freely distributed to the existing shareholders according to their current shareholdings.

If a call option does not give present access to the returns associated with the ownership interest in the shares subject to the call, IFRS 10 requires that the instruments containing the potential voting rights be accounted for in accordance with IFRS 9. *[IFRS 10.21, B91]*. Derivatives on an interest in a subsidiary are accounted for as financial instruments unless the derivative meets the definition of an equity instrument of the entity in IAS 32. *[IFRS 9.2.1(a)]*. The accounting by the parent in its consolidated financial statements depends on whether the call option meets the definition of a financial asset or an equity instrument:

- *Financial asset* – A call option is initially recognised as a financial asset at its fair value, with any subsequent changes in its fair value recognised in profit or loss. If the call option is exercised, the fair value of the option at that date is included as part of the consideration paid for the acquisition of the non-controlling interest (see 4 above). If it lapses unexercised, any carrying amount is expensed in profit or loss.
- *Equity instrument* – A call option is accounted for in a similar way to a call option over an entity's own equity shares, as discussed in Chapter 47 at 11.2.1. This is because it is an option over the non-controlling interest in the

consolidated financial statements, and IFRS 10 regards the non-controlling interest as 'equity' in those financial statements. Because such a call option over the non-controlling interest's shares will be gross-settled, the initial fair value of the option is recognised as a debit to equity (and is not subsequently remeasured). If the call option is exercised, this initial fair value is included as part of the consideration paid for the acquisition of the non-controlling interest (see 4 above). If a call option lapses unexercised, there is no entry required within equity.

The above discussion addresses the initial debit entry on recognising the call option at fair value (as a financial asset, or within equity). However, the related initial credit entry will depend on the transactions giving rise to the call option. For example, the entity may have paid consideration for the option in a separate transaction or as part of a larger transaction (such as where a business combination involves an outright purchase of shares as well as the acquisition of a call option over the remaining shares).

6.2 Put options only

Under current IFRS, it is not clear how to account for put options that are granted to holders of non-controlling interests ('NCI puts') at the date of acquiring control of a subsidiary (or, indeed, after gaining control). There is a lack of explicit guidance in IFRS and potential contradictions between the requirements of IFRS 10 and IAS 32.

This issue has been the subject of much debate over the years. Although it is clear that, under current IFRS, the NCI put itself gives rise to a liability representing the exercise price (see 6.2.1 below for a discussion of the measurement of this liability), there are a number of decisions that must be made in order to account for the arrangements, including:

- whether or not the terms of the NCI put mean that it gives the parent a present ownership interest in the underlying securities (see 6.2.2 below); and
- where the parent does not have a present ownership interest, whether or not a non-controlling interest continues to be recognised, i.e. should the parent recognise both the non-controlling interest and the financial liability for the NCI put.

In the latter case, there are a number of additional decisions that must be made, in particular the basis on which the non-controlling interest is recognised.

Although the Interpretations Committee unequivocally confirmed as early as 2006 that an NCI put with an exercise price to be settled in cash is itself a financial liability,[29] the nature of the financial liability remains controversial and has been discussed by the Interpretations Committee and the IASB on a number of occasions. In June 2014, the IASB decided that this issue will be considered as part of the broader project looking at the distinction between liabilities and equity – the Financial Instruments with Characteristics of Equity ('FICE') project.[30] In June 2018, the IASB issued *Discussion Paper – Financial instruments with Characteristics of Equity* and intends to decide the direction of the project in Q4 2020.[31] The FICE project is discussed further at 7.3 below.

The previous deliberations have been in the context of an NCI put that is required to be settled for cash. The Interpretations Committee has also considered a request in 2016 regarding how an entity accounts for an NCI put in its consolidated financial statements where the NCI put has a strike price that will be settled by delivery of a variable number of the parent's own equity instruments. Specifically, the Interpretations Committee was asked to consider whether, in its consolidated financial statements, the parent recognises:

(a) a financial liability representing the present value of the option's strike price – in other words, a gross liability; or

(b) a derivative financial liability presented on a net basis measured at fair value.

The Interpretations Committee was also asked whether the parent applies the same accounting in its consolidated financial statements for NCI puts for which the parent has the choice to settle the exercise price either in cash or by way of delivery of a variable number of its own equity instruments to the same value.

However, on the basis of its previous discussions and the IASB's FICE project, the Interpretations Committee decided in November 2016 not to add this issue to its agenda.[32]

Given that the Interpretations Committee did not conclude on this matter, in our view, both approaches are acceptable.

Like the previous deliberations of the Interpretations Committee and the IASB, the discussion that follows relates to NCI puts that are required to be settled in cash.

6.2.1 The financial liability for the NCI put

As indicated at 5.1 above, IFRS 10 regards the non-controlling interest as 'equity' in the consolidated financial statements. Under current IFRS, any contractual obligation to purchase non-controlling interests – such as a put option granted to non-controlling interests – gives rise to a financial liability measured at the present value of the redemption amount (for example, for the present value of the forward repurchase price, option exercise price or other redemption amount). Subsequently, the financial liability is measured in accordance with IFRS 9 (see Chapter 47 at 5.3 and 11.3.2). *[IAS 32.23, AG27(b)].*

IAS 32 offers no guidance as to how the financial liability should be measured if the number of shares to be purchased and/or the date of purchase are not known. In our view, it would be consistent with the requirement of IFRS 13 that liabilities with a demand feature such as a demand bank deposit should be measured at not less than the amount payable on demand, *[IFRS 13.47]*, to adopt a 'worst case' approach (see Chapter 47 at 5.3 and Chapter 14 at 11.5). In other words, it should be assumed that the purchase will take place on the earliest possible date for the maximum number of shares.

The accounting for the remaining aspects of the put option is discussed below; this depends in part upon an assessment of the terms of the transaction and, in some areas, involves a choice of accounting policy which, once selected, must be applied consistently.

Figure 7.2 below summarises the analysis that we believe should be performed, the questions to be addressed and the approaches that apply.

Figure 7.2   Decision tree for accounting for put options over non-controlling interest

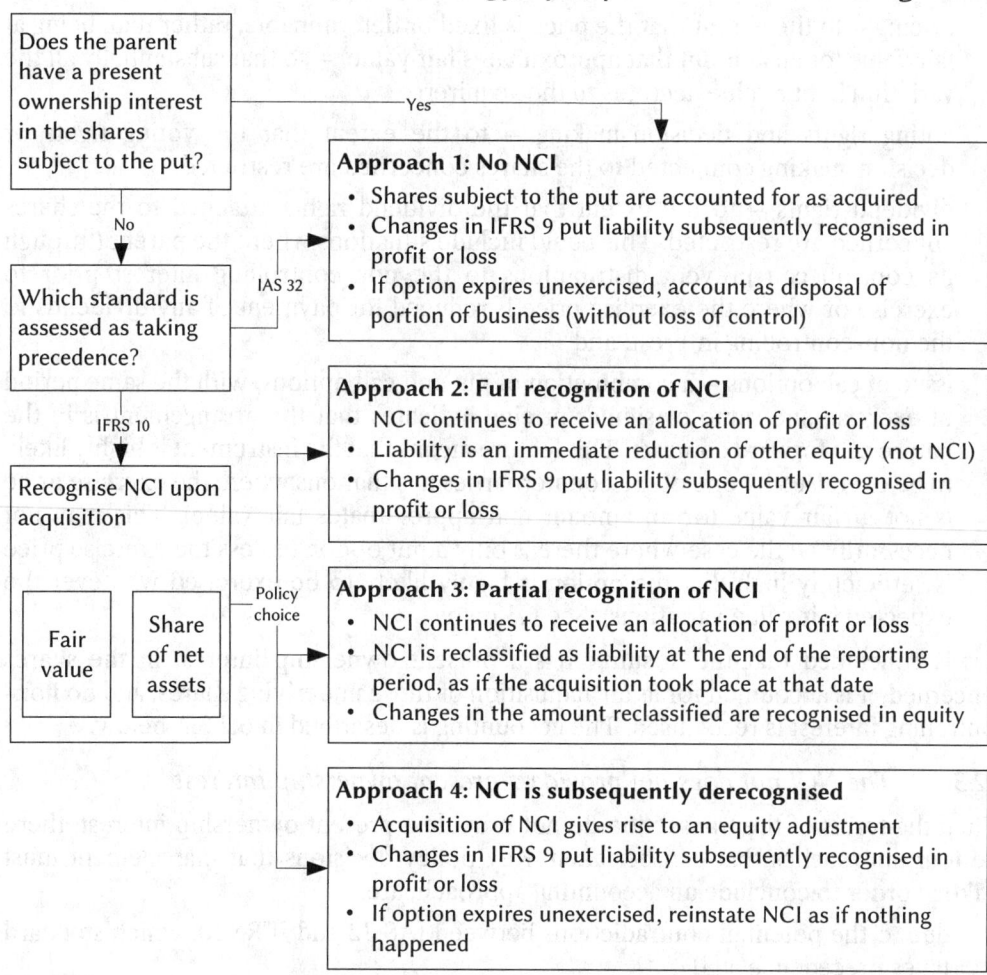

The diagram above (and 6.2.3.A to 6.2.3.D below) indicate that, under Approaches 1, 2 and 4, changes in the IFRS 9 financial liability subsequent to initial recognition are recognised in profit or loss. This would be the case regardless of whether the financial liability is subsequently remeasured at amortised cost or at fair value through profit or loss under IFRS 9. However, if the financial liability is designated at fair value under IFRS 9, the fair value changes attributable to changes in credit risk are normally recognised in other comprehensive income (see Chapter 50 at 2.4).

6.2.2   The NCI put provides a present ownership interest

In our view, in the same way as for call options, an entity has to consider whether the terms of the transaction give it present access to the returns associated with the ownership interest in the shares subject to the NCI put. If so, the shares are accounted for as if they had been acquired by the entity.

Factors that indicate that the NCI put might provide a present ownership interest include:
- pricing – to the extent that the price is fixed or determinable, rather than being at fair value (or an amount that approximates fair value) – so that substantially all the variation in fair value accretes to the acquirer;
- voting rights and decision-making – to the extent that the voting rights or decision-making connected to the shares concerned are restricted;
- dividend rights – to the extent that the dividend rights attached to the shares concerned are restricted. This could include situations where the parent (through its control) can prevent distributions to the non-controlling interest prior to exercise or where the exercise price is reduced for payment of any dividends to the non-controlling interest; and
- issue of call options – a combination of put and call options, with the same period of exercise and same or similar pricing indicates that the arrangement is in the nature of a forward contract. This feature means that the instrument is highly likely to be exercised by one of the counterparties in situations where the exercise price is not at fair value (or an amount that approximates fair value). This may not necessarily be the case where there is only a put option (unless the exercise price is sufficiently high that the option is highly likely to be exercised whatever the expected fair value variations). See 6.3 below.

If it is concluded that the acquirer has a present ownership interest in the shares concerned, it is accounted for as an acquisition of those underlying shares, and no non-controlling interest is recognised. The accounting is described in 6.2.3.A below.

6.2.3 The NCI put does not provide a present ownership interest

When the terms of the transaction do not provide a present ownership interest, there are four approaches that can be taken. Key policy decisions that management must make in order to conclude an accounting approach, are:
- due to the potential contradictions between IAS 32 and IFRS 10, which standard takes precedence; and
- if a non-controlling interest is recognised on initial acquisition, whether or not it continues to be recognised.

If the entity chooses to base its accounting policy on IAS 32, i.e. IAS 32 takes precedence, then it will only recognise a financial liability for the NCI put and not recognise a non-controlling interest. The approach is described at 6.2.3.A below.

If the accounting policy choice is that IFRS 10 takes precedence, the entity will initially recognise both the non-controlling interest and the financial liability under the NCI put. It initially measures any non-controlling interests, either at fair value or at the proportionate share of net assets, with this choice available for each transaction (as discussed at 5.2.1 above). *[IFRS 3.19]*. There is then a further accounting policy choice as to whether the non-controlling interest that was initially recognised continues to be recognised (as described at 6.2.3.B to 6.2.3.D below).

6.2.3.A Non-controlling interest is not recognised – financial liability recognised (Approach 1)

Approach 1 must be used when the entity has a present ownership interest in the shares concerned (see 6.2.2 above).

Approach 1 may also be used when the entity does not have a present ownership interest, but concludes that IAS 32 takes precedence over IFRS 10. By recognising a liability for the put option over the shares held by the non-controlling interest, no non-controlling interest is recognised. The business combination is accounted for on the basis that the underlying shares subject to the NCI put have been acquired. Thus, if the acquirer has granted a put option over all of the remaining shares, the business combination is accounted for as if the acquirer has obtained a 100% interest in the acquiree. No non-controlling interest is recognised when the acquirer completes the purchase price allocation and determines the amount of goodwill to recognise. The consideration transferred for the business combination includes the present value of the amount payable upon exercise of the NCI put to the non-controlling shareholders.

Approach 1 is based on the requirements and guidance within IAS 32.

IAS 32 requires the NCI put to be recognised as a liability, as discussed in 6.2.1 above. *[IAS 32.23]*. IAS 32 also states that when a subsidiary issues a financial instrument and a parent or another entity in the group agrees additional terms directly with the holders of the instrument (e.g. a guarantee), the group may not have discretion over distributions or redemption. Although the subsidiary may appropriately classify the instrument without regard to these additional terms in its financial statements, the effect of other agreements between members of the group and the holders of the instrument is taken into account in the consolidated financial statements. To the extent that there is such an obligation or settlement provision, the instrument (or the component of it that is subject to the obligation) is classified as a financial liability in the consolidated financial statements. *[IAS 32.AG29]*. The implication is that the underlying financial instruments (i.e. the shares in the subsidiary) are represented by the financial liability. Accordingly, since the shares held by those non-controlling shareholders are not treated as equity interests in the consolidated financial statements, there is no non-controlling interest to be accounted for under IFRS 10. This means that the profit or loss (and changes in other comprehensive income) with respect to the subsidiary are allocated to the parent and not to the non-controlling interest, as there is none.

Under this approach, any dividends paid to the other shareholders are recognised as an expense in the consolidated financial statements, except where they represent a repayment of the liability (e.g. where the exercise price is adjusted by the dividends paid).

The NCI put is accounted for as a financial liability under IFRS 9. *[IAS 32.23, IFRS 9.4.2.1, 4.2.2]*. Changes in the carrying amount of the financial liability are recognised in profit or loss.

If the NCI put is exercised, the financial liability is extinguished by the payment of the exercise price.

If the NCI put is not exercised, then the entity has effectively disposed of a partial interest in its subsidiary, without loss of control, in return for the amount recognised as the financial liability at the date of expiry. The entity accounts for the transaction as discussed at 4 above. The consideration received is the amount of the financial liability extinguished and any difference between this and the carrying amount of the non-controlling interest (as of the date that the NCI put expires) is recognised within equity.

6.2.3.B Full recognition of non-controlling interest (Approach 2)

Approach 2 is one of the alternatives that may be used when the entity does not have a present ownership interest in the shares concerned, and concludes that IFRS 10 takes precedence. The acquirer initially recognises the non-controlling interest, either at fair value or at the proportionate share of the acquiree's net assets.

Approach 2 takes the view that the non-controlling interest continues to be recognised within equity until the NCI put is exercised. The carrying amount of non-controlling interest changes due to allocations of profit or loss, allocations of changes in other comprehensive income and dividends declared for the reporting period (see 5.6 above).

The financial liability for the NCI put is recognised at the present value of the amount payable upon exercise of the NCI put, and is subsequently accounted for under IFRS 9 like any other written put option on equity instruments. On initial recognition, the corresponding debit is made to another component of equity attributable to the parent, not to the non-controlling interest.

All subsequent changes in the carrying amount of the financial liability that result from the remeasurement of the present value of the amount payable upon exercise of the NCI put are recognised in the profit or loss attributable to the parent, and not the non-controlling interest's share of the profit or loss of the subsidiary.

If the NCI put is exercised, the entity accounts for an increase in its ownership interest as an equity transaction (see 4 above). Consequently, the financial liability, as remeasured immediately before the transaction, is extinguished by payment of the exercise price and the non-controlling interest purchased is derecognised against equity attributable to owners of the parent.

If the NCI put expires unexercised, the financial liability is reclassified to the same component of equity that was previously reduced (on initial recognition).

6.2.3.C Partial recognition of non-controlling interest (Approach 3)

Approach 3 is one of the alternatives that may be used when the entity does not have a present ownership interest in the shares concerned but initially applies IFRS 10 and recognises a non-controlling interest, either at fair value or at the proportionate share of the acquiree's net assets.

Under Approach 3, while the NCI put remains unexercised, the accounting at the end of each reporting period is as follows:

(a) the entity determines the amount that would have been recognised for the non-controlling interest, including an update to reflect allocations of profit or loss, allocations of changes in other comprehensive income and dividends declared for the reporting period, as required by IFRS 10 (see 5.6 above);

(b) the entity derecognises the non-controlling interest as if it was acquired at that date;

(c) the entity recognises a financial liability at the present value of the amount payable on exercise of the NCI put in accordance with IFRS 9. There is no separate accounting for the unwinding of the discount due to the passage of time; and

(d) the entity accounts for the difference between (b) and (c) as an equity transaction.

If the NCI put is exercised, the same treatment is applied up to the date of exercise. The amount recognised as the financial liability at that date is extinguished by the payment of the exercise price.

If the NCI put expires unexercised, the position is unwound so that the non-controlling interest is recognised at the amount it would have been, as if the put option had never been granted (i.e. measured initially at the date of the business combination, and remeasured for subsequent allocations of profit or loss, other comprehensive income and changes in equity attributable to the non-controlling interest). The financial liability is derecognised, with a corresponding credit to the same component of equity.

6.2.3.D Non-controlling interest is subsequently derecognised (Approach 4)

Approach 4 may be used when the entity does not have a present ownership interest in the shares concerned, and concludes that IFRS 10 takes precedence. When the NCI put is granted in a business combination, the acquirer initially recognises the non-controlling interest, either at fair value or at the proportionate share of the acquiree's net assets.

When the parent recognises the financial liability for the NCI put, it derecognises the non-controlling interest. There are two ways of viewing this, but the accounting effect is the same:

- This transaction is an immediate acquisition of the non-controlling interest. The non-controlling interest is treated as having been acquired when the NCI put is granted, as in Approach 1. However, in accordance with IFRS 10, any difference between the liability recognised (at the present value of the amount payable upon exercise of the NCI put) and the amount of non-controlling interest derecognised is recognised directly in equity. (Under Approach 1, the difference is reflected in the measurement of goodwill).

- This transaction is viewed as a reclassification of an equity instrument to a financial liability. In accordance with IAS 32, when the financial liability is recognised, the present value of the amount payable upon exercise of the NCI put is reclassified from equity with the effect that the non-controlling interest is derecognised. Any difference between the carrying value of non-controlling interest and the liability is adjusted against another component of equity.

The financial liability for the NCI put is subsequently accounted for under IFRS 9, with all changes in the carrying amount recognised in profit or loss.

Dividends paid to the other shareholders are recognised as an expense of the group, unless they represent a repayment of the liability (e.g. where the exercise price is adjusted by the dividends paid). This means that the profit or loss (and changes in other comprehensive income) with respect to the subsidiary are allocated to the parent and not to the non-controlling interest, as there is none.

If the NCI put is exercised, the carrying amount of the financial liability at that date is extinguished by the payment of the exercise price.

If the NCI put expires unexercised, the liability is derecognised with the non-controlling interest being reinstated as if nothing happened. Any difference between the liability and non-controlling interest is recognised against another component of equity, generally the same component reduced when the liability was initially recognised.

6.2.4 Assessing whether multiple transactions should be accounted for as a single arrangement

As discussed at 3.4 above, IFRS 10 provides guidance on when to account for two or more arrangements as a single transaction when a parent loses control of a subsidiary. However, neither IFRS 10 nor IFRS 3 specifically addresses the accounting for a sequence of transactions that begins with an acquirer gaining control over another entity, followed by acquiring additional ownership interests shortly thereafter.

This frequently happens where public offers are made to a group of shareholders and there is a regulatory requirement for an acquirer to make an offer to the non-controlling shareholders of the acquiree.

The Interpretations Committee considered this issue and tentatively agreed that the initial acquisition of the controlling stake and the subsequent mandatory tender offer should be treated as a single transaction. However, there was no consensus among the Interpretations Committee members on whether a liability should be recognised for the mandatory tender offer at the date that the acquirer obtains control of the acquiree. A small majority expressed the view that a liability should be recognised in a manner that is consistent with IAS 32. Other Interpretations Committee members expressed the view that a mandatory tender offer to purchase non-controlling interests is not within the scope of IAS 32 or IAS 37 – *Provisions, Contingent Liabilities and Contingent Assets* – and that a liability should therefore not be recognised.[33] The issue was escalated to the IASB[34] which subsequently decided that the project on put options written on non-controlling interests should be incorporated into the broader project looking at the distinction between liabilities and equity – the Financial Instruments with Characteristics of Equity ('FICE') project (see 7.3 and 7.4 below).[35]

In our view, a simple distinction between a statutory obligation and a contractual obligation is not always clear. Statutory requirements (such as a mandatory tender offer or a statutory process that has the same effect) may have the effect of modifying the contractual terms of the equity instruments, thereby giving rise to a contractual obligation to purchase the equity instruments. The rules and regulations regarding tender offers differ by jurisdiction and careful analysis of the facts and circumstances is needed. In any event, even if it is established there is no contractual obligation, the effects of a mandatory tender offer are economically similar to a contractual NCI put and, in the absence of specific IFRS accounting guidance, it may be appropriate to account in the same way. We believe that this is an area where the IASB should provide further clarification.

Meanwhile, in the absence of any explicit guidance in IFRS for such transactions, we believe that entities generally have an accounting policy choice to:

(a) account for the transaction as a single linked transaction in which control is gained (a single business combination); or

(b) account for the transaction as a discrete transaction (a business combination, followed by an acquisition of non-controlling interests).

However, policy (a) can only be applied where the acquisition of non-controlling interest is assessed as linked to the same transaction as that by which control is gained (as explained in 6.2.4.A below). Entities would need to apply the policy consistently (for example, if policy (a) is applied, it should be applied for all transactions where the criteria for linked transactions are met). Entities applying policy (a) should refer to 6.2.4.B below for accounting for linked transactions.

Where an entity adopts policy (b) to account for the transaction as a discrete transaction, a further determination needs to be made as to whether (and at what point), based on the facts and circumstances, the mandatory tender offer gives rise to a contractual obligation. The accounting is as follows:

- Where a mandatory tender offer is considered to give rise to a contractual obligation to purchase the equity shares (or the transaction is accounted by analogy in the same way as a contractual put), an obligation for the NCI put is recognised in accordance with the guidance on Approaches 1 to 4 described in 6.2 above (and consistent with the guidance in 6.4 below). While the exact point at which a contractual obligation arises in the mandatory tender process will depend on the specific facts and circumstances in the relevant jurisdiction, we would generally expect that an irrevocable and enforceable offer made by the acquirer to purchase the non-controlling interests will constitute a contractual obligation.

- If no contractual obligation arises in advance of the purchase (and the transaction is not accounted by analogy in the same way as a contractual put), the purchase of the non-controlling interest is accounted for as a separate equity transaction when it occurs (see 4 above). An obligation is recognised for the statutory obligation for the mandatory tender offer, if onerous, in accordance with IAS 37.

560 *Chapter 7*

This is summarised in the following decision tree at Figure 7.3 below.

Figure 7.3   Accounting for a mandatory tender offer

This shows a simplified decision chart for accounting for a mandatory tender offer following the acquisition of a controlling stake in an investee. It is important that this is read in conjunction with the text in 6.2.4 above as well as the sections cross referenced from the boxes in the chart.

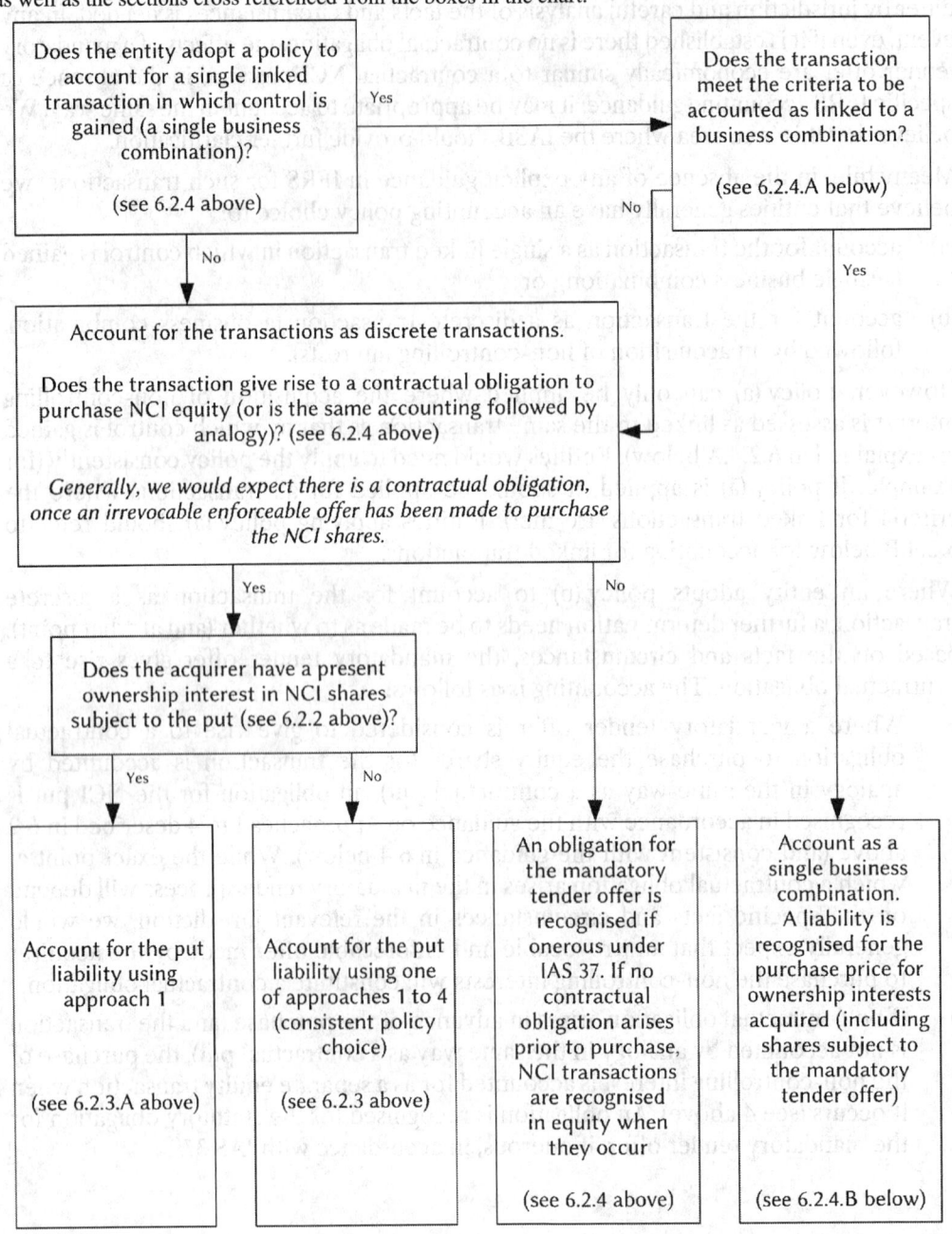

6.2.4.A Identifying a linked transaction

The acquisition of the non-controlling interest is a linked transaction when it arises from the same transaction as that by which control was gained. This will generally be the case where it arises as part of the same offer, including where legal or regulatory requirements lead to the offer being extended through the creation of a shareholder put, or acquirer compulsory acquisition rights.

In many cases, it will be clear where there is a single offer. Where it is not clear, the existence of all of the following factors indicate a linked transaction:

- the option over the remaining interest and subsequent acquisition is not negotiated separately by the non-controlling shareholders;
- the offer period is short; and
- the price per share offered for subsequent increases is fixed and consistent with the price paid for the controlling interest.

These factors are generally all present in the case of public offers to the entire group of shareholders. They may not all be present for private offers where, for example, some of the options may be for extended terms.

If a put option is granted over the non-controlling interest and the terms of the put option are such that the present ownership interest attached to the underlying shares is gained at the same time as gaining control, this will satisfy the second criterion above. Whilst the put may nominally extend over a long period, the effect is that ownership has already passed to the acquirer. See 6.2.2 above for the factors to be considered in assessing whether or not the acquirer gains present ownership interest over the underlying shares. Where the other criteria above are also met, this is a linked transaction.

6.2.4.B Accounting for the linked transaction (where a policy to account as a single business combination is followed)

A linked transaction is accounted for as if all ownership interests were acquired at the acquisition date as part of the transaction to gain control.

The consideration transferred is the sum of the amount paid for the controlling and non-controlling interest (that is acquired as part of the linked transaction) and the percentage acquired is the sum of the respective shareholdings. If, at the date of gaining control the non-controlling interest has not actually been acquired, a financial liability is recognised at the present value of the amount payable upon exercise of the option to acquire the non-controlling interest.

If at the date the non-controlling interest is actually acquired, the percentage acquired differs to that originally accounted for as being acquired, the purchase accounting is adjusted to reflect the actual percentage acquired. A 'true up' exercise is performed to adjust the total consideration paid and therefore the amount of goodwill recognised. It is not accounted for as a partial disposal of non-controlling interest (changes in ownership interest without loss of control are addressed at 4 above). The non-controlling interest is measured as of the date of acquisition, not as of the date that the offer expires.

When the transaction is linked because the arrangement provides a present ownership interest in the non-controlling interest, the entity will not recognise the non-controlling interest. Accounting for the transaction is as described in Approach 1 at 6.2.3.A above.

Example 7.20 below illustrates the accounting for a linked transaction.

Example 7.20:   Put option and gaining control accounted for as a single transaction

Entity A acquires a 60% controlling interest in listed Entity B. As Entity A has obtained a controlling interest in Entity B, the regulator requires Entity A to offer to purchase the remaining shares of Entity B from all other shareholders of Entity B, paying the same price per share as in the transaction in which Entity A obtained control of Entity B ('mandatory tender offer'). Entity A makes the mandatory tender offer immediately and the offer period lasts for 30 days.

At the end of 30 days, other shareholders of Entity B owning 30% accept the mandatory tender offer for their shares. The offer to acquire the remaining 10% of shares held in Entity B expires unexercised.

When considering whether the mandatory tender offer is linked to the acquisition of 60% of Entity B's shares, in which Entity A gained control, it is relevant that:

- the price per share is fixed and at the same price as paid by Entity A to acquire 60% of Entity B's shares;
- the shareholders of Entity B who own the 40% did not negotiate to receive the offer;
- the offer benefits the shareholders of Entity B (by providing the same opportunity to sell their shares that the shareholder(s) who sold the 60% received);
- although the offer was initiated by Entity A, it stemmed from a regulatory requirement triggered by the acquisition of Entity B (it was not at Entity A's discretion to make the offer); and
- the offer period is relatively short.

Entity A concludes that the mandatory tender offer is linked to the transaction when control was gained and is therefore part of the business combination. Therefore, Entity A records the following journal entries:

a) Acquisition of 60% and entering into the mandatory tender offer over the remaining 40% of Entity B's shares (granting the offer):

Dr Net assets (summarised, 100% of fair value of net assets of Entity B, as required by IFRS 3)

Dr Goodwill (as if Entity A acquired 100% of Entity B)

   Cr Cash transferred (on acquisition date)

   Cr Financial liability (present value of offer price to be paid at the expiry date of the option relating to the 40% of Entity B's shares subject to the mandatory tender offer)

b) Accounting for the liability in accordance with IFRS 9 (unwinding of the discount during the 30-day period):

Dr Finance expense

   Cr Financial liability

c) Actual acquisition of 30% offered at the end of the 30-day period is accounted for as a reduction of the financial liability:

Dr Financial liability

   Cr Cash

d) Reclassification of the financial liability to equity for the 10% outstanding at the end of the offer period – Entity A adjusts the initial purchase price allocation related to Entity B to recognise any non-controlling interest, with an offset to goodwill:

Dr Financial liability (offer price of 10% of shares)
      Cr Non-controlling interest (either (1) fair value of the non-controlling interest in Entity B or (2) the 10% shareholders' proportionate share of Entity B's identifiable net assets), measured as of the acquisition date (the date that control was gained, and not the date that the offer expires)

Dr/Cr Goodwill (difference, if applicable).

6.3 Combination of call and put options

In some business combinations, there might be a combination of call and put options, the terms of which may be equivalent or may be different.

The appropriate accounting for such options is determined based on the discussions in 6.1 and 6.2 above. However, where there is a call and put option with equivalent terms, particularly at a fixed price, the combination of the options is more likely to mean that they give the acquirer a present ownership interest. Where the exercise price is at fair value (or an amount that approximates fair value), however, the returns of ownership arising from fair value movements will accrete to the non-controlling interest and consequently, this situation is unlikely to give the acquirer a present ownership interest.

In cases where the combination of call and put options gives the acquirer a present ownership interest, where the options are over all of the shares not held by the parent, the acquirer has effectively acquired a 100% interest in the subsidiary at the date of the business combination. The entity may be in a similar position as if it had acquired a 100% interest in the subsidiary with either deferred consideration (where the exercise price is fixed) or contingent consideration (where the settlement amount is not fixed, but is dependent upon a future event). See Chapter 9 at 7.

As noted at 6 above, similar considerations also apply where the acquirer entered into a forward purchase contract for the shares held by the other shareholders.

6.4 Call and put options entered into in relation to existing non-controlling interests

The discussion in 6.1 and 6.2 above focused on call and put options entered into at the same time as control is gained of the subsidiary. However, an entity may enter into the options with non-controlling shareholders after gaining control. The appropriate accounting policy will still be based on the discussions in 6.1 and 6.2 above.

Where the entity already has a controlling interest and as a result of the options now has a present ownership interest in the remaining shares concerned, or concludes that IAS 32 takes precedence, the non-controlling interest is no longer recognised within equity. The transaction is accounted for as an acquisition of the non-controlling interest, i.e. it is accounted for as an equity transaction (see 4 above), because such acquisitions are not business combinations under IFRS 3.

6.5 Put and call options in separate financial statements

Purchased call options (and written put options) over shares in an acquired subsidiary are derivatives in the separate financial statements. Note that this treatment differs from that in the consolidated financial statements which is addressed generally at 6 above.

A purchased call option over shares in an acquired subsidiary is initially recognised as a financial asset at its fair value, with any subsequent changes in the fair value of the option recognised in profit or loss. Similarly, a written put option over shares in an acquired subsidiary is initially recognised as a financial liability at its fair value, with any subsequent changes in the fair value of the option recognised in profit or loss.

The initial credit entry for the call option (and the initial debit entry for the put option) will depend on the transactions giving rise to the options. For example, the entity may have paid (or received) consideration for the call (or put option) in a separate transaction or as part of a larger transaction.

Where a purchased call option (or written put) option lapses, the financial asset (or financial liability) is derecognised, with a debit (or credit) to profit or loss. Where a purchased call option (or written put option) is exercised, the financial asset (or financial liability) is derecognised with an adjustment to the cost of investment of purchasing the shares subject to the option.

The fair value of the purchased call option (or written put option) may not be significant if it is exercisable at the fair value (or at an amount that approximates fair value) of the underlying shares at the date of exercise. Where there is both a purchased call and a written put option, particularly where the options have the same fixed redemption price, it is likely that the fair values of the purchased call option and written put option will differ.

7 FUTURE DEVELOPMENTS

The IASB has been engaged in a number of implementation projects that have led or could lead to 'narrow-scope amendments' to IFRS 10 and other IFRSs and could change the consolidation procedures applied or the accounting for non-controlling interests. However, these have all been put 'on hold' until the finalisation, or are being reconsidered as part, of related research projects. These issues are discussed at 7.1 to 7.5 below.

In addition, during 2019 and 2020, the Interpretations Committee and the IASB have held discussions about the accounting for a transaction in which an entity, as part of its ordinary activities, enters into a contract with a customer to sell real estate by selling its equity interest in a subsidiary.[36] This issue, which impacts whether a gain or loss on sale of a subsidiary or revenue is recognised, is not resolved at the time of writing. It is discussed further at 3.2.1 above. At the time of writing, this issue was expected to be considered as part of Phase 2 of the Post-implementation Review of IFRS 10 (see 7.5 below).[37]

7.1 Sale or contribution of assets between an investor and its associate or joint venture (amendments to IFRS 10 and IAS 28)

One issue that the IASB has been trying to resolve was a conflict between the IFRS 10 requirements relating to loss of control over a subsidiary and those of IAS 28 for transactions where a parent sells or contributes an interest in a subsidiary to an associate or a joint venture. In order to resolve the conflict, in September 2014, the IASB had issued *Sale or Contribution of Assets between an Investor and its Associate or Joint Venture (Amendments to IFRS 10 and IAS 28)*.

These amendments, where applied, would require the gain or loss resulting from the loss of control of a subsidiary that does not contain a business (as defined in IFRS 3) – as a result of a sale or contribution of a subsidiary to an existing associate or a joint venture (that is accounted for using the equity method) – to be recognised only to the extent of the unrelated investors' interests in the associate or joint venture. The same requirement applies to the remeasurement gain or loss relating to the former subsidiary if, following the transaction, a parent retains an investment in a former subsidiary and the former subsidiary is now an associate or a joint venture that is accounted for using the equity method. *[IFRS 10.25, 26, B99A]*. However, a full gain or loss would be recognised on the loss of control of a subsidiary that constitutes a business, including cases in which the investor retains joint control of, or significant influence over, the investee. *[IFRS 10.25, 26, B98, B99]*.

In the Basis for Conclusions, the IASB clarifies that the amendments do not apply where a transaction with a third party leads to a loss of control (even if the retained interest in the former subsidiary becomes an associate or joint venture that is accounted for using the equity method), nor where the investor elects to measure its investments in associates or joint ventures at fair value in accordance with IFRS 9. *[IFRS 10.BC190I]*.

These amendments were to be applied prospectively to transactions occurring in annual periods beginning on or after 1 January 2016, with earlier application permitted. *[IFRS 10.C1C, IAS 28.45C]*. However, in December 2015, the IASB issued a further amendment – *Effective Date of Amendments to IFRS 10 and IAS 28*. This amendment deferred the effective date of the September 2014 amendments until the IASB has finalised any revisions that result from the IASB's research project on the equity method. *[IFRS 10.C1C, BC190M-190N]*. The IASB has decided to defer further work on the equity method project until the Post-implementation Reviews (PIRs) of IFRS 10, IFRS 11 and IFRS 12 are undertaken).[38] At the time of writing, work on Phase 2 of the PIRs of IFRS 10, IFRS 11 and IFRS 12 was scheduled to commence with a Request for Information in Q4 2020.[39] See 7.5 below.

Nevertheless, the IASB has continued to allow early application of the September 2014 amendments, which must be disclosed, as it did not wish to prohibit the application of better financial reporting. *[IFRS 10.C1C, BC190L-190O, IAS 28.45C, BC37J]*.

The amendments are discussed at 3.3.2 and 3.3.2.B above.

7.2 Sale or contribution of assets to a joint operation (where the entity has joint control or is a party to the joint operation)

In July 2016, the Interpretations Committee discussed whether an entity should remeasure its retained interest in the assets and liabilities of a joint operation when the entity loses control of a business, or an asset or group of assets that is not a business. In the transaction discussed, the entity either retains joint control of a joint operation or is a party to a joint operation (with rights to assets and obligations for liabilities) after the transaction.

Because of the similarity between the transaction being discussed by the Interpretations Committee and a sale or contribution of assets to an associate or joint venture (see 7.1 above), the Interpretations Committee decided not to add the issue to its agenda, but instead to recommend that the IASB consider the issue at the same time that it further considers the accounting for the sale or contribution of assets to an associate or a joint venture. The Interpretations Committee observed that the Post-implementation Reviews (PIRs) of IFRS 10 and IFRS 11 would provide the IASB with an opportunity to consider loss of control transactions and a sale or contribution of assets to an associate or joint venture.[40] At the time of writing, work on Phase 2 of the PIRs of IFRS 10 and IFRS 11 was scheduled to commence with a Request for Information in Q4 2020.[41] See 7.5 below.

The decision of the Interpretations Committee, and the accounting for such transactions are discussed further at 3.3.3 above.

7.3 Accounting for put options written on non-controlling interests – *Financial Instruments* with Characteristics of Equity ('FICE') project

The Interpretations Committee and the IASB have been debating the accounting for put options written on non-controlling interests ('NCI puts') over a number of years. Many of these issues have now been considered by the FICE project.

In June 2018, the IASB issued *Discussion Paper – Financial instruments with Characteristics of Equity*.[42] The Discussion Paper proposes an approach that articulates the principles for classification of financial instruments as either financial liabilities or equity (from the perspective of the issuer), without significantly altering most existing classification outcomes of IAS 32 (although there would be some changes). There are separate classification principles for derivative financial instruments (because of particular challenges arising from classification of derivatives on own equity).

The IASB's preferred approach would require consistent accounting for redemption obligation arrangements, including NCI puts and compound instruments. The requirement to identify a gross liability component would also apply to redemption obligation arrangements that require a transfer of a variable number of own shares, if the amount of the contractual obligation to transfer own shares is independent of the entity's available economic resources.

Applying the IASB's preferred approach (should the proposals ultimately lead to amendments to IFRSs) to the accounting for an NCI put in the consolidated financial statements would thus require:

- recognition of a liability component at the redemption amount (which will be subsequently measured in accordance with IFRS 9);
- derecognition of the non-controlling interest – the ordinary shares of the subsidiary that represent the non-controlling interest – on which put options are written, at the fair value of the ordinary shares of the subsidiary at the date the put options are issued; and
- recognition of an equity component for the (implicit) written call option on the subsidiary's shares. If the NCI put is a fair value put, the equity component would be nil.

Under the IASB's preferred approach, gains or losses, including those arising from subsequent measurement of the liability component, would be recognised as income and expense, while changes in the equity components would be recognised in the statement of changes in equity. If the NCI put is exercised and settled by delivering cash at the end of the option exercise period, the financial liability would be derecognised and the carrying amount of the equity component would be reclassified within equity. If the NCI put expires unexercised, the financial liability and the carrying amount of the equity component would be derecognised, and the non-controlling interest in the shares of the subsidiary would be recognised.[43]

Throughout 2019 and 2020, the IASB has continued to discuss the FICE project. From March 2019 to July 2019, the IASB discussed emerging themes from the feedback to the Discussion Paper through comment letters and outreach activities but no decisions were made.[44] In September 2019, the IASB tentatively decided on an approach that addresses practice issues by clarifying some principles in IAS 32 and directed the Staff to prepare a detailed project proposal.[45] In October 2019, the IASB discussed the project plan, including the practice issues in scope of the project and the indicative project timeline, but made no decisions.[46] In April 2020 (following an earlier discussion in December 2019), the IASB made tentative decisions clarifying when a derivative on own equity would meet the 'fixed-for-fixed condition' to be classified as equity in IAS 32. At the time of writing, the IASB was expected to continue its discussions on other topics included in the project plan discussed in October 2019 at a future meeting[47] and a decision on the project direction was expected to be made in Q4 2020.[48] See Chapter 47 at 12 for further discussion of the FICE project, including the Discussion Paper.

7.4 Mandatory purchase of non-controlling interests

As discussed more fully at 6.2.4 above, neither IFRS 10 nor IFRS 3 specifically addresses the accounting for a sequence of transactions that begins with an acquirer gaining control over another entity, followed by it acquiring additional ownership interests shortly thereafter. This frequently happens where public offers are made to a group of shareholders and there is a regulatory requirement for an acquirer to make an offer to the non-controlling shareholders of the acquiree. This issue had been considered by the Interpretations Committee and was escalated to the IASB. In February 2017, the IASB tentatively decided as part of its FICE project (see 7.3 above) to consider whether it should take any action to address the accounting for mandatory tender offers, including potential disclosure requirements.[49]

As noted at 7.3 above, in June 2018, the IASB issued *Discussion Paper – Financial instruments with Characteristics of Equity*. The Discussion Paper takes the view that classification based on an assessment of contractual terms consistent with IFRS 9 would result in, for example, the obligations that arise in mandatory tender offers, which have similar consequences to those that arise from written put options, not being considered for the purpose of classification because they are beyond the scope of IAS 32. Other IFRSs might have specific guidance for issues that arise when an entity accounts for rights and obligations arising from law (such as IAS 37). However, the IASB did not design other IFRSs to address the classification of liabilities and equity.

Alternatively, if the treatment of rights and obligations that arise from law were considered as equivalents of contractual terms under IAS 32 then mandatory tender offers might be accounted for consistently with written put options. However, the Discussion Paper considered that such a fundamental change to the scope of IAS 32 and IFRS 9 to include rights and obligations that arise from law could have consequences beyond the distinction between liabilities and equity.

In the IASB's preliminary view, an entity would apply the IASB's preferred approach to the contractual terms of a financial instrument consistently with IAS 32 and IFRS 9. The IASB will consider whether it should take any action to address the accounting for mandatory tender offers, including potential disclosure requirements, following its analysis of responses to this Discussion Paper.[50] As noted at 7.3 above, at the time of writing, a decision on the FICE project direction was expected to be made in Q4 2020.[51]

7.5 Post-implementation Reviews of IFRS 10, IFRS 11 and IFRS 12

In April 2020, the IASB discussed the findings from the first phase of the Post-implementation Reviews (PIRs) of IFRS 10, IFRS 11 and IFRS 12. The findings were presented in a Staff Paper[52] to help the IASB identify areas in the Standards on which further information is needed for the second phase of the PIRs. The IASB decided to proceed with Phase 2 of the PIRs and publish a Request for Information.

The PIR of IFRS 10 will focus on: power over an investee, the link between power and returns (with a focus on identifying agency relationships), accounting requirements (with a focus on changes in ownership interests) and the investment entity consolidation exception.[53]

In respect of changes in ownership interests (relevant to this chapter), the Staff Paper stated that 'Stakeholders said IFRS Standards do not provide comprehensive requirements on how to account for changes in ownership interest that modify the relationship between an investor and an investee, for example, a transaction in which a parent loses control of a subsidiary but retains an interest in a joint operation'.[54]

Other findings from the first phase of the PIRs included in the accompanying Staff Paper that are relevant to the topics discussed in this chapter concerned:

- the partial acquisition of an entity that does not constitute a business:

    The Staff Paper noted that this issue can be linked to a more general discussion on whether the existence of a legal entity should affect the accounting for a transaction. This was also an issue in respect of the accounting when an entity, as part of its ordinary activities, enters into a contract with a customer to sell real estate by selling its equity interest in a single asset entity that is a subsidiary, as discussed by the Interpretations Committee and the IASB during 2019 and 2020 (see 3.2.1 above). The IASB has stated that it will consider any feedback obtained as part of the PIR in any reconsideration of the topic;[55]

- options that give access to the returns associated with an ownership interest;
- the determination of non-controlling interest where a subsidiary is partially held by an associate; and
- the initial measurement of a retained interest after loss of control.[56]

Some stakeholders asked that the PIR should consider the interaction of IFRS 10 with other IFRSs including certain topics relevant to this chapter. However, the Staff recommended that the public consultation should not include questions on the equity method (which is the subject of a separate research project) and put options on non-controlling interests (covered by the FICE project – see 7.3 and 7.4 above).

At the time of writing, work on Phase 2 of the PIRs of IFRS 10, IFRS 11 and IFRS 12 was scheduled to commence with a Request for Information in Q4 2020.[57]

References

1 *IFRIC Update*, January 2019.
2 *IFRIC Update*, June 2019, *IASB Update*, October 2019, June 2020.
3 *IFRIC Update*, June 2019.
4 *IASB Update*, October 2019.
5 *IASB Update*, June 2020.
6 IFRS Foundation website, https://www.ifrs.org/projects/2020/sale-of-a-single-asset-entity-containing-real-estate-ifrs-10/ (accessed 2 September 2020).
7 IFRS Foundation website, IASB work-plan, https://www.ifrs.org/projects/work-plan/ (accessed 2 September 2020).
8 IFRS Foundation website, https://cdn.ifrs.org/-/media/feature/groups/ifric/requests-to-be-considered-at-a-future-committee-meeting/sale-and-leaseback-in-a-corporate-wrapper-ifrs-16.pdf (accessed 2 September 2020).
9 *IASB Update*, May 2016.
10 IFRS Foundation website, IASB work-plan, https://www.ifrs.org/projects/work-plan/ (accessed 2 September 2020).
11 *IFRIC Update*, June 2019.
12 IASB Update, October 2019, June 2020.
13 IFRS Foundation website, https://www.ifrs.org/projects/2020/sale-of-a-single-asset-entity-containing-real-estate-ifrs-10/ (accessed 2 September 2020).
14 IFRS Foundation website, IASB work-plan, https://www.ifrs.org/projects/work-plan/ (accessed 2 September 2020).
15 IFRS Foundation website, https://cdn.ifrs.org/-/media/feature/groups/ifric/requests-to-be-considered-at-a-future-committee-meeting/sale-and-leaseback-in-a-corporate-wrapper-ifrs-16.pdf (accessed 2 September 2020).
16 *Sale or Contribution of Assets between an Investor and its Associate or Joint Venture, (Amendments to IFRS 10 and IAS 28)*, IFRS 10, paras. 25, 26, B99A, Example 17.
17 Exposure Draft (ED/2014/4), *Measuring Quoted Investments in Subsidiaries, Joint Ventures and Associates at Fair Value (Proposed amendments to IFRS 10, IFRS 12, IAS 27, IAS 28 and IAS 36 and Illustrative Examples for IFRS 13)*, IASB, September 2014.
18 *IASB Update*, July 2015.
19 *IASB Update*, January 2016.
20 *IASB Update*, March 2018.
21 IFRS Project Report and Feedback Statement *Post-implementation Review of IFRS 13 – Fair Value Measurement*, December 2018.
22 *IASB Update*, March 2018.
23 IFRS Foundation website, IASB work-plan, https://www.ifrs.org/projects/work-plan/ (accessed 2 September 2020).
24 *IFRIC Update*, July 2016.
25 *IASB Update*, May 2009.
26 *IFRIC Update*, January 2013.
27 *IFRIC Update*, May 2009.
28 *IFRIC Update*, November 2013.
29 *IFRIC Update*, November 2006.
30 Archive IFRS Foundation website, http://archive.ifrs.org/Current-Projects/IASB-Projects/Proposed-amendments-IAS-32/Project-news/Pages/Project-update-June-2014.aspx (accessed 2 September 2020).
31 IFRS Foundation website, IASB work-plan, https://www.ifrs.org/projects/work-plan/ (accessed 2 September 2020).
32 *IFRIC Update*, November 2016.
33 *IFRIC Update*, March 2013.
34 *IASB Update*, May 2013.
35 Archive IFRS Foundation website, http://archive.ifrs.org/Current-Projects/IASB-Projects/Proposed-amendments-IAS-32/Project-news/Pages/Project-update-June-2014.aspx (accessed 2 September 2020).
36 *IFRIC Update*, June 2019, *IASB Update*, October 2019, June 2020.

37 IFRS Foundation website, https://www.ifrs.org/projects/2020/sale-of-a-single-asset-entity-containing-real-estate-ifrs-10/ (accessed 2 September 2020).
38 *IASB Update*, May 2016.
39 IFRS Foundation website, IASB work-plan, https://www.ifrs.org/projects/work-plan/ (accessed 2 September 2020).
40 *IFRIC Update*, July 2016.
41 IFRS Foundation website, IASB work-plan, https://www.ifrs.org/projects/work-plan/ (accessed 2 September 2020).
42 Discussion Paper (DP/2018/1), *Financial Instruments with Characteristics of Equity*, IASB, June 2018.
43 DP/2018/1, paras. 5.35-5.42.
44 *IASB Update*, March 2019, June 2019, July 2019.
45 *IASB Update*, September 2019.
46 *IASB Update*, October 2019.
47 *IASB Update*, December 2019, April 2020.
48 IFRS Foundation website, IASB work-plan, https://www.ifrs.org/projects/work-plan/ (accessed 2 September 2020).
49 *IASB Update*, February 2017.
50 DP/2018/1, paras. 8.27-8.36.
51 IFRS Foundation website, IASB work-plan, https://www.ifrs.org/projects/work-plan/ (accessed 2 September 2020).
52 IASB Staff Paper, Agenda ref. 7A, April 2020.
53 *IASB Update*, April 2020.
54 IASB Staff Paper, Agenda ref. 7A, para. 64, April 2020.
55 IFRS Foundation website, https://www.ifrs.org/projects/2020/sale-of-a-single-asset-entity-containing-real-estate-ifrs-10/ (accessed 2 September 2020).
56 IASB Staff Paper, Agenda ref. 7A, paras. 62-79, April 2020.
57 IFRS Foundation website, IASB work-plan (accessed 2 September 2020).

Chapter 8 Separate and individual financial statements

1 SEPARATE AND INDIVIDUAL FINANCIAL STATEMENTS 575
   1.1 Consolidated financial statements and separate financial statements 577
      1.1.1 Separate financial statements and interests in associates and joint ventures..579
      1.1.2 Separate financial statements and interests in joint operations 580
      1.1.3 Publishing separate financial statements without consolidated financial statements or financial statements in which investments in associates or joint ventures are equity accounted 581
   1.2 Entities incorporated in the EU and consolidated and separate financial statements 582
2 REQUIREMENTS OF SEPARATE FINANCIAL STATEMENTS 583
   2.1 Cost method..584
      2.1.1 Cost of investment 584
          2.1.1.A Investments acquired for own shares or other equity instruments 586
          2.1.1.B Investments acquired in common control transactions 587
          2.1.1.C Cost of investment in subsidiary, associate or joint venture acquired in stages 588
          2.1.1.D Investment in a subsidiary accounted for at cost: Partial disposal 590
          2.1.1.E Formation of a new parent.. 591
          2.1.1.F Formation of a new parent: calculating the cost and measuring equity 594
          2.1.1.G Reverse acquisitions in the separate financial statements 595

		2.1.2	Deemed cost on transition to IFRS 597
	2.2	IFRS 9 method 597
	2.3	Equity method 597
		2.3.1	First-time adoption of IFRS 598
	2.4	Dividends and other distributions 598
		2.4.1	Dividends from subsidiaries, joint ventures or associates 599
			2.4.1.A The dividend exceeds the total comprehensive income 599
			2.4.1.B The carrying amount exceeds the consolidated net assets 600
			2.4.1.C Returns of capital 601
		2.4.2	Distributions of non-cash assets to owners (IFRIC 17) 601
			2.4.2.A Scope 601
			2.4.2.B Recognition, measurement and presentation 602
3	DISCLOSURE 604
	3.1	Separate financial statements prepared by parent electing not to prepare consolidated financial statements 604
	3.2	Separate financial statements prepared by an investment entity 605
	3.3	Separate financial statements prepared by an entity other than a parent electing not to prepare consolidated financial statements 605
		3.3.1	Entities with no subsidiaries but exempt from applying IAS 28 606
4	COMMON CONTROL OR GROUP TRANSACTIONS IN INDIVIDUAL OR SEPARATE FINANCIAL STATEMENTS 606
	4.1	Introduction 606
	4.2	Recognition 609
	4.3	Measurement 610
		4.3.1	Fair value in intra-group transactions 610
	4.4	Application of the principles in practice 611
		4.4.1	Transactions involving non-monetary assets 611
			4.4.1.A Sale of PP&E from the parent to the subsidiary for an amount of cash not representative of the fair value of the asset. 612
			4.4.1.B The parent exchanges PP&E for a non-monetary asset of the subsidiary. 613
			4.4.1.C Acquisition and sale of assets for shares 615
			4.4.1.D Contribution and distribution of assets 617
			4.4.1.E Transfers between subsidiaries 617
		4.4.2	Acquiring and selling businesses – transfers between subsidiaries 618
			4.4.2.A Has a business been acquired? 619

		4.4.2.B	If a business has been acquired, how should it be accounted for?... 619
		4.4.2.C	Purchase and sale of a business for equity or cash not representative of the fair value of the business.. 619
		4.4.2.D	If the net assets are not a business, how should the transactions be accounted for? 620
	4.4.3	Transfers of businesses between parent and subsidiary 620	
		4.4.3.A	Distributions of businesses without consideration – subsidiary transferring business to the parent 621
		4.4.3.B	Legal merger of parent and subsidiary 623
	4.4.4	Incurring expenses and settling liabilities without recharges 626	
	4.4.5	Financial instruments within the scope of IFRS 9 627	
		4.4.5.A	Interest-free or non-market interest rate loans 627
		4.4.5.B	Financial guarantee contracts: parent guarantee issued on behalf of subsidiary 629
4.5	Disclosures 630		

List of examples

Example 8.1:	Cost of a subsidiary in separate financial statements when the pooling of interest method is applied in consolidated financial statements 587
Example 8.2:	Cost of a subsidiary acquired in stages 589
Example 8.3:	Partial disposal of a subsidiary accounted at cost when an investor retains an interest that is neither a subsidiary, associate nor joint venture 591
Example 8.4:	Formation of new parent that does not acquire all of original parent's ordinary shares 592
Example 8.5:	Formation of new parent, statutory share capital and adjustments to equity 595
Example 8.6:	Reverse acquisition – legal parent's statement of financial position in separate financial statements 596
Example 8.7:	Non-cash asset distributed to shareholders 603
Example 8.8:	Sale of PP&E at an undervalue 612
Example 8.9:	Exchange of assets with dissimilar values 614
Example 8.10:	Transactions between subsidiaries 618
Example 8.11:	Interest-free and below market rate loans within groups 628
Example 8.12:	Financial guarantee contracts 630

Chapter 8   Separate and individual financial statements

1   SEPARATE AND INDIVIDUAL FINANCIAL STATEMENTS

This chapter deals with two aspects of the preparation of financial statements by entities: their separate financial statements, which are defined by IFRS, and some of the consequences of intra-group transactions for their individual financial statements, where guidance in IFRS is limited and incomplete.

Under IFRS, 'separate financial statements' are defined in IAS 27 – *Separate Financial Statements* – as 'those presented by an entity in which the entity could elect, subject to the requirements in this standard, to account for its investments in subsidiaries, joint ventures and associates either at cost, in accordance with IFRS 9 – *Financial Instruments*, or using the equity method as described in IAS 28 – *Investments in Associates and Joint Ventures*.' *[IAS 27.4]*. In other words, they are the unconsolidated financial statements or financial statements in which the investments in subsidiaries are not consolidated in accordance with IFRS 10 – *Consolidated Financial Statements*.

The IASB takes the view that the needs of users of financial statements are fully met by requiring entities to consolidate subsidiaries and equity account for associates and joint ventures. It is recognised that entities with subsidiaries, associates or joint ventures may wish, or may be required by local law, to present financial statements in which their investments are accounted for on another basis, e.g. as equity investments or under the equity method. *[IAS 27.2]*.

Accordingly, IFRS does not require the preparation of separate financial statements. However, where an investor with subsidiaries, associates or joint ventures does prepare separate financial statements purporting to comply with IFRS, they must be prepared in accordance with IAS 27. *[IAS 27.3]*.

It follows from this definition that the financial statements of an entity that does not have a subsidiary, associate or joint venture are not 'separate financial statements'. *[IAS 27.7]*.

This chapter also addresses matters that are not exclusive to separate financial statements but relate to any stand-alone financial statements prepared by any entity within a group. We have called these 'individual financial statements', although they may also be referred to (amongst other names) as 'stand-alone', 'solus' or 'single-entity' financial statements.

576 *Chapter 8*

The term 'individual financial statements' for the purpose of this chapter is a term that covers (i) financial statements of entities that do not have investments in associates, joint ventures and subsidiaries, and (ii) financial statements of entities that have only investments in associates and/or joint ventures. When an entity has no investments in associates, joint ventures and subsidiaries in both current and comparative period effectively there is no difference between individual and separate financial statements of such an entity.

The diagram below summarises the interactions between consolidated, individual and separate financial statements. This is further discussed in 1.1 below.

Figure 8.1:   Interactions between consolidated, individual and separate financial statements

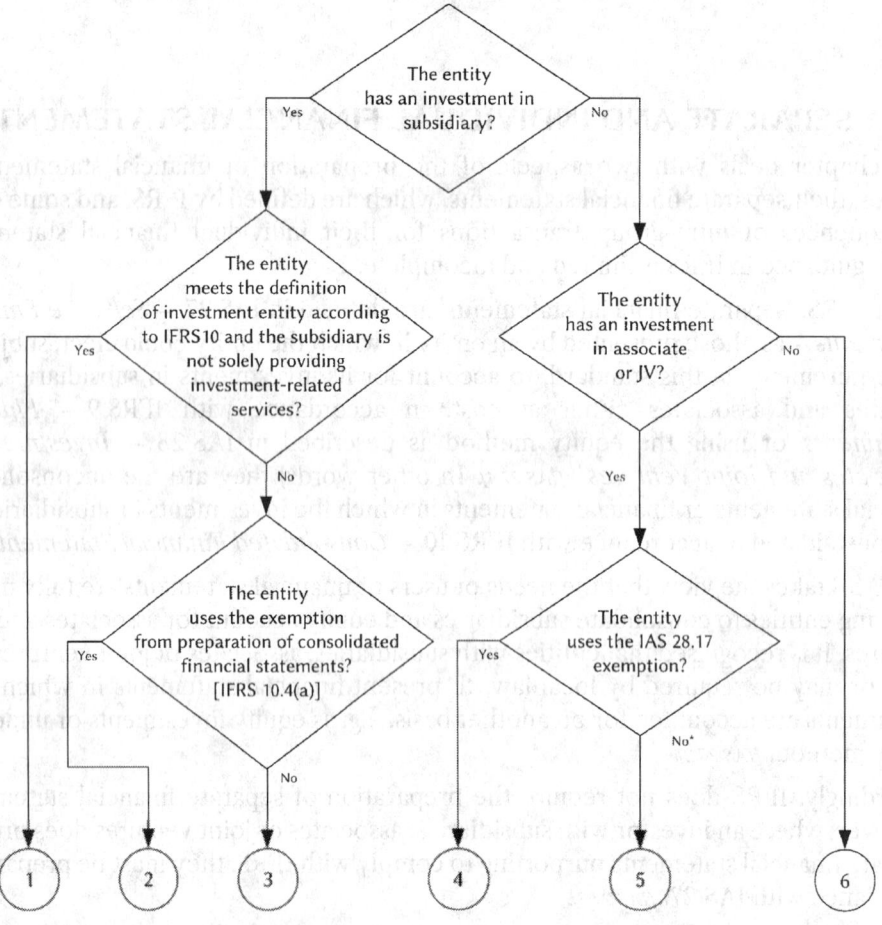

Notes:
1   The entity would prepare separate financial statements as its only financial statements. *[IAS 27.8A]*. In this situation IFRS 10 would require that investments in subsidiaries, associates and/or joint ventures are accounted for in accordance with IFRS 9. Hence, the cost or equity method would not be available as an accounting policy choice to account for investments in subsidiaries, associates and/or joint ventures in the separate financial statements.
2   If the entity is either not an investment entity, or it is an investment entity and has a subsidiary or subsidiaries that provide(s) investment-related services, the entity would need to prepare consolidated financial statements. If the entity then made use of the exemption from preparing consolidated financial statements, the entity may prepare separate financial statements as its only IFRS financial statements.

3   If the entity is not an investment entity, or it is an investment entity and has a subsidiary or subsidiaries that provide(s) investment-related services, and the entity has not made use of the exemption from preparing consolidated financial statements, the entity would need to prepare consolidated financial statements. In addition, the entity may prepare separate financial statements.

4   If the entity has an investment in an associate and/or a joint venture and the entity has made use of the exemption to apply the equity method to these investments, the entity may prepare separate financial statements as its only financial statements, in which investments in the associate /joint venture are accounted for at cost or in accordance with IFRS 9.

5   The entity prepares individual financial statements and applies the equity method to its investment in an associate and/or a joint venture. Separate financial statements may be prepared in addition wherein the company may elect a different accounting policy to account for its investment in an associate or a joint venture, such as at cost or in accordance with IFRS 9.

6   When an entity has no investments in subsidiaries, associates or joint ventures, the entity's individual financial statements are identical to the separate financial statements. In certain jurisdictions these individual financial statements may be referred to as separate financial statements due to local Companies Act, or similar, naming conventions. However, as they do not have an investment in either a subsidiary, associate or joint venture, they do not meet the definition of separate financial statements in IAS 27. *[IAS 27.7]*.

*   The entity may, in certain circumstances (e.g. where the investment is held by or indirectly through an entity that is a venture capital organisation or mutual fund), elect to measure an investment in an associate or a joint venture at fair value through profit or loss in accordance with IFRS 9. *[IAS 28.18]*. If the entity elects this policy for all such investments in joint ventures and associates, the financial statements may be referred to as separate financial statements. If the election is not made for one or more investments the financial statements are individual financial statements.

Transactions often take place between a parent entity and its subsidiaries or between subsidiaries within a group that may or may not be carried out at fair value. As a result there may be uncertainty and ambiguity about how these transactions should be accounted for. IAS 24 – *Related Party Disclosures* – requires only that these transactions are disclosed and provides no accounting requirements.

Whilst such transactions do not influence the consolidated financial statements of the ultimate parent (as they are eliminated in the course of consolidation), they can have a significant impact on the individual or separate financial statements of the entities concerned or on the consolidated financial statements prepared for a sub-group.

These issues are discussed at 4 below.

1.1   Consolidated financial statements and separate financial statements

A parent is an entity that controls one or more entities and any parent entity should present consolidated financial statements in which the assets, liabilities, equity, income, expenses and cash flows of the parent and its subsidiaries are presented as those of a single economic entity. *[IFRS 10.4, Appendix A]*.

A parent need not present consolidated financial statements if it meets all the following conditions:

(i)   it is a wholly-owned subsidiary or is a partially-owned subsidiary of another entity and all its other owners, including those not otherwise entitled to vote, have been informed about, and do not object to, the parent not presenting consolidated financial statements;

(ii) its debt or equity instruments are not traded in a public market (a domestic or foreign stock exchange or an over-the-counter market, including local and regional markets);

(iii) it did not file, nor is it in the process of filing, its financial statements with a securities commission or other regulatory organisation for the purpose of issuing any class of instruments in a public market; and

(iv) its ultimate or any intermediate parent produces financial statements that are available for public use and comply with IFRSs, in which subsidiaries are consolidated or are measured at fair value through profit or loss in accordance with this IFRS. *[IFRS 10.4(a)]*.

This exemption is discussed further in Chapter 6 at 2.2.1. It should be noted that if the entity chooses to prepare consolidated financial statements even if it is exempt from doing so it must comply with all IFRS requirements related to consolidated financial statements.

An entity that avails itself of the above exemption may prepare separate financial statements as its only financial statements. *[IAS 27.8]*. For example, most intermediate holding companies take advantage of this exemption. If such an entity prepares unconsolidated financial statements that are in accordance with IFRS, they must comply with the provisions of IAS 27 for such statements and they will then be separate financial statements as defined. The requirements for separate financial statements are dealt with in 2 below.

IFRS 10 includes an exception to the consolidation principle for a parent that meets the definition of an investment entity. An investment entity measures its investments in subsidiaries, other than those solely providing services that relate to its investment activities, at fair value through profit or loss in accordance with IFRS 9 instead of consolidating those subsidiaries. The investment entity exception is discussed in Chapter 6 at 10. Investment entities measure their investments in those subsidiaries in the same way in their separate financial statements as required in the consolidated financial statements. *[IAS 27.11A]*. As a result, IAS 27 clarifies that an investment entity that is required, throughout the current period and all comparative periods presented, to apply the exception to consolidation for all of its subsidiaries in accordance with paragraph 31 of IFRS 10 presents separate financial statements as its only financial statements. *[IAS 27.8A]*. An investment entity that prepares separate financial statements as its only financial statements, discloses that fact and presents the disclosures relating to investment entities required by IFRS 12 – *Disclosure of Interests in Other Entities* – about its interests in subsidiaries. *[IAS 27.16A]*. The exemption from preparing consolidated financial statements, in criterion (iv) above, is available to a parent entity that is a subsidiary of an investment entity, even when the investment entity does not prepare consolidated financial statements but measures its subsidiaries at fair value through profit or loss. *[IFRS 10.BC28A-28B]*.

The requirements to prepare consolidated and separate financial statements in accordance with IFRS are very often subject to local jurisdictional rules. For instance, for entities incorporated in the European Union, local law may exempt the entity from preparing consolidated financial statements under local GAAP if it applies 'IFRS as adopted by the European Union'. However, IFRS 10 provides specific IFRS requirements which need to be considered when financial statements are prepared on the basis of IFRS as issued by the IASB. For example, as discussed in Chapter 6 at 2.2.4, in our view, consolidated financial statements must be prepared by an entity that was a parent during the reporting period, even if that entity is no longer a parent at the end of the reporting period (e.g. because it disposed of all its subsidiaries). IFRS 10 requires a parent to consolidate a subsidiary until the date on which the parent ceases to control the subsidiary. *[IFRS 10.20]*. This means that if a parent does not prepare consolidated financial statements pursuant to a concession in local law, we believe, the parent may not present separate financial statements in compliance with IFRS. See 1.2 below regarding the interrelationship between IFRS and local European law in respect of consolidated and separate financial statements.

1.1.1 Separate financial statements and interests in associates and joint ventures

IAS 28 must be applied by 'all entities that are investors with joint control of, or significant influence over, an investee'. *[IAS 28.2]*. IAS 28 requires that an investment in an associate or a joint venture be accounted for in the entity's separate financial statements in accordance with paragraph 10 of IAS 27. *[IAS 28.44]*.

An entity that is an investor may present separate financial statements as its only financial statements if it is a parent that is exempt from preparing consolidated financial statements by the scope exemption in paragraph 4(a) of IFRS 10 (see above). If it does not have subsidiaries it may still present separate financial statements as its only financial statements if the same criteria as in (i)-(iv) above apply (they are replicated in paragraph 17 of IAS 28) and all its other owners, including those not otherwise entitled to vote, have been informed about, and do not object to, the entity not applying the equity method to its investees.

A parent cannot prepare financial statements in purported compliance with IFRS in which subsidiaries are consolidated, but associates and joint ventures are not accounted for under IAS 28 but on some other basis (e.g. at cost). Financial statements prepared on such a basis would be neither consolidated financial statements (because of the failure to apply IAS 28) nor separate financial statements (because of the failure to account for subsidiaries on the basis of the direct equity interest).

The conditions for exemption in paragraph 17 of IAS 28 mentioned above are the same as those in IFRS 10. This means that (as illustrated in the diagram at 1 above):

- An entity that has subsidiaries and is exempt under IFRS 10 from preparing consolidated accounts is automatically exempt in respect of its associates or joint ventures as well, i.e. it does not have to account for them under IAS 28.
- An entity that has associates or joint ventures but no subsidiaries, and does not meet all the exemption criteria in 1.1 above, is required to apply equity accounting for its associates in its own (non-consolidated) financial statements. Such non-consolidated financial statements include the investment in the associate or joint venture on the basis of the reported results and net assets of the investment. Unless the entity opts to account for all associates or joint ventures using the equity method in its separate financial statements (see 2.3 below) such non-consolidated financial statements are *not* 'separate financial statements' as defined in IAS 27 (see definition above) and therefore do not have to meet the additional measurement and disclosure requirements required by IAS 27 for separate financial statements that are described at 3 below in order to comply with IFRS. Most of these disclosures would not be relevant to accounts that include the results of the associate or joint venture as they are based on providing information that is not otherwise given.

For example, a wholly-owned subsidiary that has debt or equity instruments that are traded in a public market must account for its interests in associates and joint ventures in accordance with IAS 28 and the resulting financial statements are not 'separate financial statements' as defined in IAS 27. If such an investor also presents separate financial statements, the Board expects that the investor is likely to account for its investments in associates or joint ventures either at cost or in accordance with IFRS 9. *[IAS 27.BC10D]*.

Although IAS 27 also allows for a policy to use the equity method to account for investments in associates and joint ventures in the separate financial statements, this could be different to some national GAAPs, under which investors that have no subsidiaries (and therefore do not prepare consolidated financial statements) but have associates or joint ventures, are not permitted to account for their share of the profits and net assets of associates or joint ventures in their statutory financial statements.

As indicated above, we believe that, an entity that has held interests in subsidiaries and disposed of any remaining interest in the period, is required to prepare consolidated financial statements at the end of that period. In our view, this same principle applies to investments in associates and joint ventures when these constitute the only investments of the investor and these investments are sold during the period, i.e. such an entity is required to prepare individual financial statements at the end of period when such investments were sold or otherwise disposed of.

1.1.2 Separate financial statements and interests in joint operations

IFRS 11 – *Joint Arrangements* – differentiates between joint operations and joint ventures. In the separate financial statements, joint ventures are accounted for at cost, in accordance with IFRS 9, or using the equity method as required by paragraph 10 of IAS 27. A joint operator applies paragraphs 20 to 22 of IFRS 11 to account for a joint operation. *[IFRS 11.26]*. This means that regardless of the type of financial statements prepared, the joint operator in a joint operation recognises in relation to the joint operation its:

- assets, including its share of any assets held jointly;
- liabilities, including its share of any liabilities incurred jointly;
- revenue from the sale of its share of the output arising from the joint operation;
- share of the revenue from the sale of the output by the joint operation; and
- expenses, including its share of any expenses incurred jointly. *[IFRS 11.20]*.

Similarly, in its individual financial statements, a party that participates in, but does not have joint control of, a joint operation, accounts for its interest in the way outlined above provided it has rights to the assets and obligations for the liabilities, relating to the joint operation (see Chapter 12 at 6.4). *[IFRS 11.23]*.

In March 2015, the Interpretations Committee published a number of agenda decisions relating to IFRS 11. Two of those are relevant to separate financial statements.[1] The first issue is the accounting by a joint operator in its separate financial statements for its share of the assets and liabilities of a joint operation when it is structured through a separate vehicle. The Interpretations Committee noted that IFRS 11 requires the joint operator to account for its rights and obligations in relation to the joint operation. It also noted that those rights and obligations, in respect of that interest, are the same regardless of whether separate or consolidated financial statements are prepared, by referring to paragraph 26 of IFRS 11. Consequently, the same accounting is required in the consolidated financial statements and in the separate financial statements of the joint operator.

The Interpretations Committee also noted that IFRS 11 requires the joint operator to account for its rights and obligations, which are its share of the assets held by the entity and its share of the liabilities incurred by it. Accordingly, the Interpretations Committee observed that the joint operator would not additionally account in its separate or consolidated financial statements its shareholding in the separate vehicle, whether at cost or fair value.

The second issue relates to the accounting by a joint operation that is a separate vehicle in its financial statements. This issue has arisen because the recognition by joint operators in both consolidated and separate financial statements of their share of assets and liabilities held by the joint operation leads to the question of whether those same assets and liabilities should also be recognised in the financial statements of the joint operation itself. The Interpretations Committee decided not to add the issue to its agenda, because sufficient guidance exists:[2]

(a) IFRS 11 applies only to the accounting by the joint operators and not to the accounting by a separate vehicle that is a joint operation;

(b) the financial statements of the separate vehicle would therefore be prepared in accordance with applicable Standards; and

(c) company law often requires a legal entity/separate vehicle to prepare financial statements. Consequently, the reporting entity for the financial statements would include the assets, liabilities, revenues and expenses of that legal entity/separate vehicle. However, when identifying the assets and liabilities of the separate vehicle, it is necessary to understand the joint operators' rights and obligations relating to those assets and liabilities and how those rights and obligations affect those assets and liabilities.

1.1.3 Publishing separate financial statements without consolidated financial statements or financial statements in which investments in associates or joint ventures are equity accounted

IAS 27 does not directly address the publication requirements for separate financial statements. In some jurisdictions, an entity that prepares consolidated financial statements is prohibited from publishing its separate financial statements without also publishing its consolidated financial statements.

However, in our view, IAS 27 does not prohibit an entity that prepares consolidated financial statements from publishing its separate financial statements compliant with IAS 27 without also publishing its consolidated financial statements, provided that:

(a) the separate financial statements identify the consolidated financial statements prepared under IFRS 10 to which they relate. *[IAS 27.17]*. In other words, they must draw attention to the fact that the entity also prepares consolidated financial statements and disclose the address where the consolidated financial statements are available, for example, by providing contact details of a person or an e-mail address from which a hard copy of the document can be obtained or a website address where the consolidated financial statements can be found and downloaded; and

(b) the consolidated financial statements have been prepared and approved no later than the date on which the separate financial statements have been approved. Thus, it is not possible to publish the separate financial statements before the consolidated financial statements have been finalised.

The same conditions should be applied by an entity having no subsidiaries that prepares financial statements in which investments in associates or joint ventures are equity accounted, but publishes its separate financial statements (in which the investments in associates and joint ventures are not equity accounted) without also publishing its financial statements in which investments in associates or joint ventures are equity accounted.

Separate financial statements of a parent entity can also be considered compliant with IAS 27 when the exemption to present consolidated financial statements criteria in paragraph 4(a) of IFRS 10 are met.

IAS 27 requires a parent to identify the consolidated financial statements prepared by the parent. *[IAS 27.17]*. Therefore, if the parent has not issued consolidated financial statements prepared in accordance with IFRS at the date the separate financial statements are issued, this requirement cannot be met and therefore the separate financial statements cannot be considered to be in compliance with IAS 27. This will also be the case if the consolidated financial statements are prepared, but are not in accordance with IFRS (e.g. prepared in accordance with local GAAP).

The matter of whether separate financial statements could be issued before the respective consolidated financial statements was explicitly considered by the Interpretations Committee in March 2006. The Interpretations Committee concluded that separate financial statements issued before consolidated financial statements could not comply with IFRS as issued by the IASB, because 'separate financial statements should identify the financial statements prepared in accordance with paragraph 9 of IAS 27 to which they relate (the consolidated financial statements), unless one of the exemptions provided by paragraph 10 is applicable'.[3] Although IAS 27 has changed since the Interpretations Committee has considered that issue, the current version of IAS 27 still requires separate financial statements to identify financial statements prepared in accordance with IFRS 10, IFRS 11 or IAS 28. *[IAS 27.17]*. It therefore implies that consolidated financial statements should be available before or at the same date as separate financial statements. However, the situation may be different if local requirements set specific rules relating to the timing of publication of financial statements. This is for example, the case for an entity that is incorporated in the European Union (EU), as described in 1.2 below.

1.2 Entities incorporated in the EU and consolidated and separate financial statements

The EU Regulation on International Accounting Standards requires IFRS to be applied by certain entities in their consolidated financial statements. As a result of the EU endorsement mechanism, IFRS as adopted in the EU may differ in some respects from the body of Standards and Interpretations issued by the IASB (see Chapter 1 at 4.2.1). In some circumstances a difference between IFRS and IFRS as adopted by the European Union may affect separate financial statements.

The Interpretations Committee had concluded that separate financial statements issued before consolidated financial statements cannot comply with IFRS as issued by the IASB. However, in January 2007 the European Commission stated that 'the Commission Services are of the opinion that, if a company chooses or is required to prepare its annual accounts in accordance with IFRS as adopted by the EU, it can prepare and file them independently from the preparation and filing of its consolidated accounts – and thus in advance, where the national law transposing the Directives requires or permits separate publication'.[4] In other words, under 'IFRS as adopted by the EU' it might be possible to issue separate financial statements before the consolidated financial statements are issued. The details about differences between scope of consolidation under IFRS 10 and European Union national legislation are described in Chapter 6 at 2.2.5.

2 REQUIREMENTS OF SEPARATE FINANCIAL STATEMENTS

In separate financial statements investments in subsidiaries, associates and joint ventures are accounted for either:

- at cost (see 2.1 below);
- in accordance with IFRS 9 (see 2.2 below); or
- using the equity method as described in IAS 28 (see 2.3 below).

The above applies to all situations except when such investments are classified as held for sale (or included in a disposal group that is classified as held for sale) in accordance with IFRS 5 – *Non-current Assets Held for Sale and Discontinued Operations*. When this is the case, investments in subsidiaries, associates and joint ventures that are accounted for at cost, or using the equity method in the separate financial statements, are measured in accordance with IFRS 5, *[IAS 27.10]*, i.e. at the lower of carrying amount and fair value less cost to sell (see Chapter 4). Investments that are accounted for in accordance with IFRS 9 in the separate financial statements and which are classified as held for sale continue to be measured in accordance with IFRS 9 (see Chapter 4 at 2.2.1).

Each 'category' of investment must be accounted for consistently. *[IAS 27.10]*. While 'category' is not defined, we take this to mean, for example, that it would be permissible for a parent that is not an investment entity to account for all subsidiaries at cost and all associates under IFRS 9.

Where an investment in an associate or joint venture is accounted for in accordance with IFRS 9 in the consolidated financial statements, it must also be accounted for in the same way in the separate financial statements. *[IAS 27.11]*. The circumstances in which IFRS 9 is applied to account for investments in associates and joint ventures in consolidated financial statements are discussed in Chapter 11 at 5 and Chapter 12 at 2.2, respectively.

A parent that meets the definition of an investment entity is required to measure its investments in particular subsidiaries at fair value through profit or loss in accordance with IFRS 9 in its consolidated financial statements, *[IFRS 10.31]*, and is required to account for them in the same way in the separate financial statements. *[IAS 27.11A]*. When an investment entity parent has shares in subsidiaries that only provide investment related services (and therefore are not subject to obligatory fair value measurement), that parent effectively has shares in two categories of subsidiaries. It therefore has still an accounting policy choice to account for those subsidiaries that only provide investment related services at cost, in accordance with IFRS 9, or using the equity method in its separate financial statements.

When an entity becomes an investment entity the difference between the previous carrying value of the investments in a subsidiary and its fair value at the date of change in status of the parent is recognised as a gain or loss in profit or loss. When a parent ceases to be an investment entity, it should follow paragraph 10 of IAS 27 and account for the investments in a subsidiary either at cost (the then fair value of the subsidiary at the date of the change in the status becomes the deemed cost), continue to account for the investment in accordance with IFRS 9, or apply the equity method. *[IAS 27.11B]*.

IAS 27 contains specific requirements related to the treatment of dividends from investments in subsidiaries, joint ventures or associates that are recognised in profit or loss unless the entity elects to use equity method, in which case the dividend is recognised as a reduction of the carrying amount of the investment. *[IAS 27.12]*. IAS 36 – *Impairment of Assets* – includes specific triggers for impairment reviews on receipt of dividends. These are discussed at 2.4.1 below.

2.1 Cost method

There is no general definition or description of 'cost' in IAS 27. How the term applies in practice is described in 2.1.1 below.

IAS 27 addresses the cost of investment in a new holding company that becomes the parent of an existing parent in a one-for-one share exchange. This is discussed further in 2.1.1.E and 2.1.1.F below.

IAS 27 also indicates that when an entity ceases to be an investment entity and its accounting policy is to account for investments in subsidiaries, associates or joint ventures at cost, the fair value as at the date of the change in status shall be used as the deemed cost. *[IAS 27.11B]*.

IFRS 1 – *First-time Adoption of International Financial Reporting Standards* – allows a 'deemed cost' transitional amendment for those applying IFRS for the first time in separate financial statements (see 2.1.2 below).

2.1.1 Cost of investment

IAS 27 does not define what is meant by 'cost' except in the specific circumstances of certain types of group reorganisation, described below, and when an entity ceases to be an investment entity and accounts for investments in subsidiaries at cost as indicated above.

As discussed further in Chapter 3 at 4.3, IAS 8 – *Accounting Policies, Changes in Accounting Estimates and Errors* – states that, in the absence of specific requirements in IFRS, management should first refer to the requirements and guidance in IFRS that deal with similar and related issues.

The glossary to IFRS defines cost as 'the amount of cash or cash equivalents paid or the fair value of the other consideration given to acquire an asset at the time of its acquisition or construction'.

'Consideration given' is likewise not defined, and therefore we believe that the key sources of guidance in IFRSs are:

- 'consideration transferred' in the context of a business combination, as referred to in paragraph 37 of IFRS 3 – *Business Combinations; [IFRS 3.37]*
- 'cost' as applied in relation to acquisitions of property, plant and equipment in accordance with IAS 16 – *Property, Plant and Equipment*, intangible assets in accordance with IAS 38 – *Intangible Assets* – and investment property in accordance with IAS 40 – *Investment Property*, and

- 'cost' in the context of determination of the cost of an investment in an associate as discussed in the agenda decision issued by the Interpretations Committee in July 2009.

Applying the requirements of IFRS 3, the 'consideration transferred' in a business combination comprises the sum of the acquisition date fair values of assets transferred by the acquirer, liabilities incurred by the acquirer to the former owners of the acquiree, and equity interests issued by the acquirer. This includes any liability (or asset) for contingent consideration, which is measured and recognised at fair value at the acquisition date. Subsequent changes in the measurement of the changes in the liability (or asset) are recognised in profit or loss (see Chapter 9 at 7.1).

'Cost' as applied in relation to acquisitions of property, plant and equipment is the amount of cash or cash equivalents paid or the fair value of the other consideration given to acquire an asset at the time of its acquisition or construction or, where applicable, the amount attributed to that asset when initially recognised in accordance with the specific requirements of other IFRS, e.g. IFRS 2 – *Share-based Payment*. *[IAS 16.6]*.

The Interpretations Committee and IASB have discussed the topic *Variable payments for the separate acquisition of PPE and intangible assets* for a number of years, attempting to clarify how the initial recognition of the variable payments, such as contingent consideration, and subsequent changes in the value of those payments should be recognised. The scope of the past deliberations did not specifically include the cost of an investment in a subsidiary, associate or joint venture. However, as they consider general principles about the recognition of variable payments, we believe they can also be considered relevant in determining the cost of such investments.

There was diversity of views about whether the liability for contingent consideration relating to separate acquisition of property, plant and equipment and intangible assets falls within the scope of IAS 37 – *Provisions, Contingent Liabilities and Contingent Assets* – or within the scope of IAS 39 – *Financial Instruments: Recognition and Measurement* (this is still relevant after IFRS 9 adoption as well). This affects the initial recognition and also subsequent accounting for changes in the value of the contingent consideration. The issue was discussed by the Interpretations Committee in the past however it was considered too broad to be addressed and was referred to the IASB.[5]

Until the IASB issues further guidance, differing views remain about the circumstances in which, and to what extent, variable payments such as contingent consideration should be recognised when initially recognising the underlying asset. There are also differing views about the extent to which subsequent changes should be recognised through profit or loss or capitalised as part of the cost of the asset.

In practice, in the separate financial statements, the following approaches have developed in relation to the recognition of such contingent consideration: (i) recognition of the contingent consideration only when payments are made; or (ii) inclusion of a best estimate of the contingent consideration in the initial determination of the cost of the investment. Under both approaches, the recognition of the contingent consideration when actually paid or changes from initial measurement are recognised either in profit or loss, or as an increase or decrease to the cost of the investment in a subsidiary.

An entity should exercise judgement in developing and consistently applying an accounting policy that results in information that is relevant and reliable in its particular circumstances. [IAS 8.10].

Similar challenges to the above arise when the seller in a business combination contractually agrees to indemnify the acquirer for the outcome of a contingency or uncertainty related to all or part of a specific asset or liability (see Chapter 9 at 5.6.4 below). Such indemnification agreements often relate to uncertain tax positions or litigations. Whilst there is guidance about how to deal with the resulting indemnification assets in the consolidated financial statements of the acquirer there is no comparable guidance about the accounting of such indemnification agreements in the separate financial statements of the acquirer. As these indemnification assets have some similarities to contingent consideration an entity may apply the guidance explained above by analogy in developing its accounting policy for indemnification agreements.

Contingent consideration is discussed in relation to intangible assets, property, plant and equipment and investment property in Chapter 17 at 4.5, Chapter 18 at 4.1.9 and Chapter 19 at 4.10 respectively.

Another question that arises in relation to cost is the treatment of any transaction costs as, under IFRS 3, these costs are generally recognised as expenses.

The Interpretations Committee, at its meeting in July 2009, in discussing the determination of the initial carrying amount of an equity method investment, noted that IFRSs consistently require assets not measured at fair value through profit or loss to be measured on initial recognition at cost. Generally stated, cost includes the purchase price and other costs directly attributable to the acquisition or issuance of the asset such as professional fees for legal services, transfer taxes and other transaction costs.[6]

Given that IAS 27 does not separately define 'cost', we believe it is appropriate to apply this general meaning of 'cost' in determining the cost of investments in subsidiaries, associates or joint ventures in separate financial statements. Therefore, in our opinion, the cost of investment in a subsidiary in the separate financial statements includes any transaction costs incurred even if such costs are expensed in the consolidated financial statements.

2.1.1.A Investments acquired for own shares or other equity instruments

In some jurisdictions, local law may permit investments acquired for an issue of shares to be recorded at a notional value (for example, the nominal value of the shares issued). In our view, this is not an appropriate measure of cost under IFRS.

A transaction in which an investment in a subsidiary, associate or joint venture is acquired in exchange for an issue of shares or other equity instruments is not specifically addressed under IFRS, since it falls outside the scope of both IFRS 9 and also IFRS 2 (see Chapter 34 at 2.2.3).

However, we believe that it would be appropriate, by analogy with IFRS on related areas (like IFRS 3), to account for such a transaction at the fair value of the consideration given (being fair value of equity instruments issued) or the assets received, if that is more reliably measured, together with directly attributable transaction costs.

2.1.1.B Investments acquired in common control transactions

When an investment in a subsidiary, associate or joint venture is acquired in a common control transaction, in our view, the cost should generally be measured at the fair value of the consideration given (be it cash, other assets or additional shares) plus, where applicable any costs directly attributable to the acquisition. However, when the purchase consideration does not correspond to the fair value of the investment acquired, in our view, the acquirer has an accounting policy choice to account for the investment at fair value of consideration given or may impute an equity contribution or dividend distribution and in effect account for the investment at its fair value.

Example 8.1 below illustrates the determination of the cost of an investment in a subsidiary in separate financial statements as described above.

Example 8.1: **Cost of a subsidiary in separate financial statements when the pooling of interest method is applied in consolidated financial statements**

Parent has a 100% direct interest in Sub 1 and Sub 2. As part of a group reorganisation, the parent transfers its direct interest in Sub 2 to Sub 1 in exchange for consideration of:

Scenario 1 – €200 (equal to the fair value of Sub 2).

Scenario 2 – €150.

The carrying amount of the investment in Sub 2 in the separate financial statements of Parent is €50. The carrying amount of Sub 2's net assets in the separate financial statements of Sub 2 is €110.

Sub 1 accounts for the acquisition of Sub 2 using the pooling of interest method in its consolidated financial statements.

In Scenario 1, the cost of an investment in a subsidiary that is acquired as part of a group reorganisation is the fair value of the consideration given (be it cash, other assets or additional shares), plus, where applicable, any costs directly attributable to the acquisition. Therefore, the cost to Sub 1 is €200. The cost is not the carrying amount of the investment in Sub 2 in the separate financial statements of Parent (i.e. €50), nor the carrying amount of Sub 2's net assets in the separate financial statements of Sub 2 (i.e. €110).

In Scenario 2, the conclusion in Scenario 1 applies even if the fair value of the consideration given is more or less than the fair value of the acquiree. Therefore, the cost of investment is €150. However, the acquirer may choose to recognise an equity element (equity contribution or dividend distribution). In this case, the cost of investment is €200 with €50 recognised as an equity contribution.

In July and September 2011, the Interpretations Committee discussed group reorganisations in separate financial statements in response to a request asking for clarification on how entities that are established as new intermediate parents within a group determine the cost of their investments when they account for these investments at cost in accordance with paragraph 10(a) of IAS 27. In the agenda decision issued, the Interpretations Committee noted that the normal basis for determining the cost of an investment in a subsidiary under paragraph 10(a) of IAS 27 has to be applied to reorganisations that result in the new intermediate parent having more than one direct subsidiary.[7] This differs from the wording in the original proposed wording for the tentative decision which referred to 'the general principle of determining cost by the fair value of the consideration given'.[8]

Some have read this to mean that 'the normal basis for determining the cost of investment' in a common control transaction is not restricted to using the fair value of the consideration given, but that another basis for determining cost may be appropriate.

One situation where we believe that it would be acceptable not to use the fair value of the consideration given is for a common control transaction where an investment in a subsidiary constituting a business is acquired in a share-for-share exchange. In that circumstance, we believe that it is also acceptable to measure the cost based on the carrying amount of the investment in the subsidiary in the transferor entity's separate financial statements immediately prior to the transaction, rather than at the fair value of the shares given as consideration.

Common control transactions are discussed further at 4 below. There are specific measurement requirements applicable to certain arrangements involving the formation of a new parent or intermediate parent, which are described at 2.1.1.E and 2.1.1.F below.

2.1.1.C   Cost of investment in subsidiary, associate or joint venture acquired in stages

It may be that an investment in a subsidiary, associate or joint venture is acquired in stages so that, up to the date on which control, significant influence or joint control is first achieved, the initial investment was accounted for at fair value under IFRS 9. This raises the question of what the carrying amount should be in the separate financial statements when the cost method is applied.

The Interpretations Committee discussed this issue and concluded in January 2019 on how an entity should apply the requirements of paragraph 10 of IAS 27 for the following fact pattern: the entity holds an initial investment in another entity (investee) that is an investment in an equity instrument as defined in paragraph 11 of IAS 32 – *Financial Instruments: Presentation*; the investee is not an associate, joint venture or subsidiary of the entity and, accordingly, the entity applies IFRS 9 in accounting for its initial investment (initial interest); subsequently the entity acquires an additional interest in the investee (additional interest), which results in the entity obtaining control of the investee, i.e. the investee becomes a subsidiary of the entity.

The Interpretations Committee observed that IAS 27 does not define 'cost', nor does it specify how an entity determines the cost of an investment acquired in stages and concluded that a reasonable reading of the requirements in IFRSs could result in the application of either one of the following two approaches:

- Approach 1 *Fair value as deemed cost approach*

    Under this approach the transaction is viewed as if the entity is exchanging its initial interest (plus consideration paid for the additional interest) for a controlling interest in the investee (exchange view). As a result, the cost of investment will be determined as the fair value of the initial interest at the date of obtaining control of the subsidiary, plus any consideration paid for the additional interest.

- Approach 2 *Accumulated cost approach*

    Under this approach the transaction is viewed as if the entity is purchasing the additional interest while retaining the initial interest (non-exchange view). As a result, the cost of investment will be determined as the consideration paid for the initial interest (original consideration), plus any consideration paid for the additional interest.

Based on its analysis, the Committee concluded that a reasonable reading of the IFRS requirements could result in the application of either one of the two approaches.

In the exchange view the step acquisition transaction is considered a significant economic event – this is because an entity obtains control. The parallel can be drawn, for example, to a business combination achieved in stages *[IFRS 3.BC384]* or an entity that ceases to be an investment entity. *[IFRS 10.BC271]*. In these situations, the fair value of the existing investment is deemed to be the consideration paid at the date of the transaction or event.

Alternatively, the accumulated cost approach considers both the initial acquisition of an interest that is neither an interest in a subsidiary, an associate or a joint venture, and the acquisition of the controlling stake to be separate transactions.

The application of either one of the two approaches is an accounting policy choice and hence it should be applied consistently to all step acquisition transactions. The selected approach would also be disclosed in accordance with requirements of paragraphs 117-124 of IAS 1 – *Presentation of Financial Statements*.

Although both approaches are acceptable, the Committee decided to report to the Board that, in their view, the fair value as deemed cost approach would provide more useful information to users of financial statements than the accumulated cost approach.[9]

The Committee also considered how an entity should account for any difference between the fair value of the initial interest at the date of obtaining control and its original consideration when applying the accumulated cost approach. The Committee concluded that the difference meets the definitions of income or expenses in the *Conceptual Framework for Financial Reporting*. Accordingly, the Committee concluded that, the entity recognises this difference in profit or loss, regardless of whether, before obtaining control, the investment had been measured at fair value through profit and loss or fair value through other comprehensive income, in accordance with paragraph 88 of IAS 1.

The two approaches are further explained in the following Example 8.2:

Example 8.2:   Cost of a subsidiary acquired in stages

Entity A has a 10% interest in Entity B, which it acquired in January 2021 for €300. This investment is a financial asset measured at fair value in accordance with IFRS 9, in both the consolidated and separate financial statements of Entity A for the six months ended 30 June 2021. On 1 July 2021, Entity A acquires a further 45% interest in Entity B for €2,160 (its then fair value), giving Entity A control over Entity B. The original 10% interest has a fair value of €480 at that date. In addition, transaction costs were incurred amounting to €50.

Approach 1 – Fair value as deemed cost approach

The cost of investment after both transactions is the sum of the fair value of the initial interest at the date of obtaining control of the subsidiary plus any consideration paid for the additional interest plus transaction costs – €2,690 (€480 + €2,160 + €50).

Approach 2 – Accumulated cost approach

The cost of investment after both transactions is the sum of the consideration given for each tranche plus transaction costs – €2,510 (€300 + €2,160 + €50). The reversal of increase in the fair value of €180 (€480 – €300) relating to the initial 10% interest is recognised in profit or loss, regardless whether the entity accounted for the initial interest at fair value through other comprehensive income or at fair value through profit or loss.

If changes to the carrying amount of the investment had resulted from an impairment charge, this charge may not necessarily be reversed. This is because the investment must still be considered for impairment in the separate financial statements of the investor.

Although the January 2019 agenda decision does not deal with IAS 28, we believe that the above approach could also be applied by analogy to step acquisition transactions where an existing investment accounted for under IFRS 9 subsequently becomes an associate or a joint venture, to which the equity method is applied.

2.1.1.D Investment in a subsidiary accounted for at cost: Partial disposal

An entity that accounts for its investments in subsidiaries at cost in accordance with paragraph 10 of IAS 27 might dispose of parts of its investment in a subsidiary so that following the disposal the entity has neither control, joint control nor significant influence over the investee. This raises the question of how the carrying amount of the retained interests should be determined in the separate financial statements.

The Interpretations Committee, during its September 2018 and January 2019 meetings, discussed how an entity should account for a transaction whereby it disposes of part of its investment in a subsidiary that was previously accounted for at cost in accordance with paragraph 10 of IAS 27, so that following the disposal the entity has neither control, joint control nor significant influence over the investee.[10]

The Committee concluded that paragraph 9 of IAS 27 requires an entity to apply all applicable IFRS in preparing its separate financial statements, except when accounting for investments in subsidiaries, associates and joint ventures to which paragraph 10 of IAS 27 applies. After the partial disposal transaction, the investee is not a subsidiary, associate or joint venture of the entity. Accordingly, the entity applies IFRS 9 for the first time in accounting for its retained interest in the investee. The Committee observed that the presentation election in paragraph 4.1.4 of IFRS 9 applies at initial recognition of an investment in an equity instrument which permits the holder of particular investments in equity instruments to present subsequent changes in fair value in other comprehensive income. Therefore, an investment in an equity instrument within the scope of IFRS 9 is eligible for the election if it is neither held for trading (as defined in Appendix A of IFRS 9) nor contingent consideration recognised by an acquirer in a business combination to which IFRS 3 applies.

Assuming the retained interest is not held for trading in the fact pattern discussed by the Committee:

(a) the retained interest is eligible for the presentation election in paragraph 4.1.4 of IFRS 9; and

(b) the entity would make this presentation election when it first applies IFRS 9 to the retained interest (i.e. at the date of losing control of the investee).[11]

Any difference between the cost of the retained interest and its fair value on the date the entity loses control of the investee meets the definitions of income or expense in the *Conceptual Framework for Financial Reporting*. Accordingly, the Committee concluded that, applying paragraph 88 of IAS 1, the entity recognises this difference in profit or loss. This is the case regardless of whether the entity presents subsequent changes in fair value of the retained interest in profit or loss or other comprehensive income. The Committee also noted that its conclusion is consistent with the requirements in paragraph 22(b) of IAS 28 and paragraph 11B of IAS 27, which deal with similar and related issues.

Example 8.3: Partial disposal of a subsidiary accounted at cost when an investor retains an interest that is neither a subsidiary, associate nor joint venture

Entity A has a 60% interest in Entity B, which it acquired for €2,700 in 2019. This investment is measured at cost of €2,700 in the separate financial statements of Entity A at 30 June 2021. On 1 July 2021, Entity A sells a 50% interest in Entity B for €3,000 (its then fair value) and retains a 10% interest in Entity B. The fair value of 10% interest is €600 at that date. As the retained interest is not held for trading the entity elects to account for the retained interest at fair value through other comprehensive income. The total gain from the partial disposal to be recognised in profit or loss amounts to €900 (€3,000 + €600 − €2,700).

2.1.1.E Formation of a new parent

IAS 27 explains how to calculate the cost of the investment when a parent reorganises the structure of its group by establishing a new entity as its parent and meets the following criteria:

(a) the new parent obtains control of the original parent by issuing equity instruments in exchange for existing equity instruments of the original parent;

(b) the assets and liabilities of the new group and the original group are the same immediately before and after the reorganisation; and

(c) the owners of the original parent before the reorganisation have the same absolute and relative interests in the net assets of the original group and the new group immediately before and after the reorganisation.

The new parent measures cost at the carrying amount of its share of the equity items shown in the separate financial statements of the original parent at the date of the reorganisation (see 2.1.1.F below). *[IAS 27.13]*.

This approach also applies if the entity that puts a new parent between it and the shareholders is not itself a parent, i.e. it has no subsidiaries. In such cases, references in the three conditions to 'original parent' and 'original group' are to the 'original entity'. *[IAS 27.14]*.

The type of reorganisation to which these requirements apply involves an existing entity and its shareholders agreeing to create a new parent between them without changing either the composition of the group or their own absolute and relative interests. This is not a general rule that applies to all common control transactions. Transfers of subsidiaries from the ownership of one entity to another within a group are not within the scope. The IASB has deliberately excluded extending the amendment to other types of reorganisations or to common control transactions more generally because of its plans to address this in its project on common control transactions. *[IAS 27.BC27]*.

The IASB has identified business combinations under common control as a priority research project. In June 2014, the Board tentatively decided that the research project should consider business combinations under common control and group restructurings, and to give priority to considering transactions that involve third parties.[12] In October 2017, the Board tentatively decided to clarify that the scope of the business combinations under common control project includes transactions under common control in which a reporting entity obtains control of one or more businesses, regardless of whether IFRS 3 would identify the reporting entity as the acquirer if IFRS 3 were applied to the transaction.[13] The scope will not specify to which financial statements of that reporting entity – consolidated, separate or individual – any accounting requirements developed in this project will apply. This is because the financial statements affected by any accounting requirements developed in the business combinations under common control project will depend on specifics of the transaction. This is also consistent with how the scope is set out in IFRS 3.[14] The next step planned is the issuance of a Discussion Paper for public comment. At the time of writing the IASB intends to issue the Discussion Paper in November 2020.[15]

In the meantime, entities will continue to account for such common control transactions in accordance with their accounting policies (see Chapter 10 at 3 and 4.4 below).

As well as the establishment of a new ultimate parent of a group, arrangements that could meet the criteria in paragraph 13 of IAS 27 mentioned above include the following:

(a) Reorganisations in which the new parent does not acquire all classes of the equity instruments issued by the original parent.

For example, the original parent may have preference shares that are classified as equity in addition to ordinary shares; the new parent does not have to acquire the preference shares in order for the transaction to be within scope. *[IAS 27.BC24(a)].*

(b) A new parent obtains control of the original parent without acquiring all of the ordinary shares of the original parent. *[IAS 27.BC24(a)].* The absolute and relative holdings must be the same immediately before and after the transaction. *[IAS 27.13(c)].*

The requirements will apply, for example, if a controlling group of shareholders insert a new entity between themselves and the original parent that holds all of their original shares in the same ratio as before.

Example 8.4: Formation of new parent that does not acquire all of original parent's ordinary shares

Shareholders A and B each hold 35% of the equity instruments of Original Parent. A and B transfer their shares to New Parent in a share-for-share exchange so that both now hold 50% of the shares in New Parent. The absolute and relative interests of A and B and those of the other shareholders in Original Parent are unchanged, so the arrangement is a reorganisation to which the cost method for reorganisations applies.

(c) The establishment of an intermediate parent within a group. *[IAS 27.BC24(b)].*

The principle is exactly the same as inserting a new parent company over the top of a group. 'Original Parent' will be an intermediate company within a group, owned by another group company. If the transaction is within scope, the intermediate parent will acquire Original Parent from its parent (the Owner) in a share for share swap. The group structure before and after the transaction can be summarised as follows:

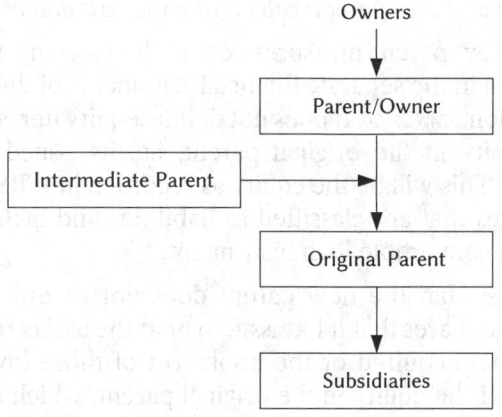

If the composition of the underlying group changes, perhaps because the intermediate parent acquires only part of that group or because it acquires another subsidiary as part of the reorganisation, then the arrangement will not be within scope as the assets and liabilities of the group immediately after the reorganisation would not be 'the same' as those immediately before the reorganisation. *[IAS 27.13(b)]*. However, there might be arrangements where to establish an intermediate parent, shares have to be issued for an amount of cash, the value of which is typically driven by various legal concerns. Consequently, the assets and liabilities of the new group differ from the assets and liabilities of the original group (or subgroup) by the amount of cash received on the initial issue of shares by intermediate parent. In those cases, the issuance of shares of the intermediate parent in exchange for cash was merely done to allow the entity to be incorporated under the local jurisdiction. We believe that such arrangements are within the scope of the exemption, provided that the amount of cash is truly '*de minimis*'; that is, not sufficient to form a substantive part of the group reorganisation transaction such that the assets and liabilities of the group immediately before and after the reorganisation might still be considered 'the same'.

The formation of a new parent was also considered by the Interpretation Committee in 2011. The Interpretations Committee noted 'that the normal basis for determining the cost of an investment in a subsidiary under [...] paragraph 10(a) of IAS 27 [...] has to be applied to reorganisations that result in the new intermediate parent having more than one direct subsidiary. [...] Paragraphs 13 and 14 of IAS 27 [...] apply only when the assets and liabilities of the new group and the original group (or original entity) are the same before and after the reorganisation'. The Interpretations Committee observed that the reorganisations that result in the new intermediate parent having more than one direct subsidiary do not meet the conditions in IAS 27 and therefore the exemptions for group reorganisations in IAS 27 do not apply. They also cannot be applied by analogy because this guidance is an exception to the normal basis for determining the cost of investment in a subsidiary.[16]

For example, if in the group structure as presented above, the Intermediate Parent had been inserted between the Original Parent and its subsidiaries, paragraphs 13 and 14 of IAS 27 would not apply as there are several subsidiaries acquired by the Intermediate Parent. In this case, there has been no 'parent' that has been established by the Intermediate Parent as its new parent.

2.1.1.F   Formation of a new parent: calculating the cost and measuring equity

IAS 27 states that the new parent measures cost at the carrying amount of its share of the 'equity items' shown in the separate financial statements of the original parent at the date of the reorganisation. *[IAS 27.13]*. It does not define 'equity items' but the term appears to mean the total equity in the original parent, i.e. its issued capital and reserves attributable to owners. This will be the equity as recorded in IFRS financial statements, so it will exclude shares that are classified as liabilities and include, for example, the equity component of a convertible loan instrument.

It is important to stress that the new parent does not record its investment at the consideration given (the shares that it has issued) or at the assets received (the fair value of the investments it has acquired or the book cost of those investments). Instead, it must look to the total of the equity in the original parent, which is the acquired entity. Even then, it does not record the investment at the amount of original parent's investments but at the amount of its equity; that is to say, its net assets.

The requirements do not apply to the measurement of any other assets or liabilities in the separate financial statements of either the original parent or the new parent, or in the consolidated financial statements. *[IAS 27.BC25]*.

It is possible for the original parent to have negative equity because its liabilities exceed its assets. IAS 27 does not discuss this but we consider that in these circumstances the investment should be recorded at zero. There is no basis for recording an investment as if it were a liability.

The above applies only when the new parent issues equity instruments but it does not address the measurement of the equity of the new parent. IFRS has no general requirements for accounting for the issue of own equity instruments. Rather, consistent with the position taken by the *Conceptual Framework* that equity is a residual rather than an item 'in its own right', the amount of an equity instrument is normally measured by reference to the item (expense or asset) in consideration for which the equity is issued, as determined in accordance with IFRS applicable to that other item. The new parent will record the increase in equity at the carrying amount of the investments it has acquired (i.e. at cost), regardless of the amount and face value of the equity instruments issued.

The amount at which the new parent's issued share capital is recorded will depend on the relevant law in the jurisdiction applicable to the new parent. The shares may be recorded at fair value, which is the fair value of the investments acquired, or at an amount calculated on some other basis. Local law may allow a company to record its issued share capital at a nominal amount, e.g. the nominal (face) value of the shares. In some jurisdictions, intermediate holding companies that acquire an asset from a parent (the 'transferor') for shares at a premium are required by law to record the share capital issued (its nominal value and share premium) at the carrying value in the transferor's books of the asset transferred; if the nominal value exceeds this book amount, the shares are recorded at their total nominal value.

Once the share capital has been recorded, there will usually need to be an adjustment to equity so that in total the equity is equal to the carrying amount (i.e. cost) of the investments acquired. This adjustment may increase or decrease the acquirer's equity (comparing to share capital value) as it depends on the relative carrying amounts of the investment in the owner, original parent's equity and the number and value of the shares issued as consideration, as shown in the following example.

Example 8.5:   Formation of new parent, statutory share capital and adjustments to equity

Intermediate Parent A acquires the investments in Original Parent from Parent; the structure after the arrangement is as illustrated above in 2.1.1.E. Parent carries its investment in Original Parent at €200 but it has a fair value of €750. Original Parent's equity in its separate financial statements is £650. Intermediate Parent A issues shares with a nominal value of €100 to Parent.

In accordance with IAS 27 paragraph 13, Intermediate Parent records its investment in Original Parent at €650. Depending on local law, it might record its share capital (including share premium where appropriate) at:

(i)   €750, being the fair value of the consideration received for the shares. It records a negative adjustment of €100 elsewhere in equity; or

(ii) €100, being the nominal value of the shares issued. It records a credit adjustment of €550 elsewhere in equity; or

(iii) €200, being the carrying value of the investment in Parent. It records a credit adjustment of €450 elsewhere in equity.

2.1.1.G   Reverse acquisitions in the separate financial statements

For the purposes of consolidated financial statements IFRS 3 takes the view that the acquirer is usually the entity that issues its equity interests to acquire other entity, but recognises that in some business combinations, so-called 'reverse acquisitions', the issuing entity is the acquiree (see Chapter 9 at 14).

Under IFRS 3, a reverse acquisition occurs when the entity that issues securities (the legal acquirer) is identified as the acquiree for accounting purposes based on the guidance in the IFRS 3 (see Chapter 9 at 4.1). Perhaps more accurately, the legal acquiree must be identified as the acquirer for accounting purposes.

Existing IFRSs do not contain any guidance on accounting for reverse acquisitions in the separate financial statements. The application guidance in IFRS 3 only deals with the reverse acquisition accounting in the consolidated financial statements (see Chapter 9 at 14.3); no mention is made as to what should happen in the separate financial statements, if any, of the legal parent/accounting acquiree. However, the previous version of IFRS 3 indicated that reverse acquisition accounting applies only in the consolidated financial statements, and that in the legal parent's separate financial statements, the investment in the legal subsidiary is accounted for in accordance with the requirements in IAS 27. *[IFRS 3(2007).B8]*.

Chapter 8

Example 8.6: *Reverse acquisition – legal parent's statement of financial position in separate financial statements*

Entity A, the entity issuing equity instruments and therefore the legal parent, is acquired in a reverse acquisition by Entity B, the legal subsidiary, on 30 September 2021. The accounting for any income tax effects is ignored.

Statements of financial position of Entity A and Entity B immediately before the business combination are:

	Entity A €	Entity B €
Current assets	500	700
Non-current assets	1,300	3,000
Total assets	1,800	3,700
Current liabilities	300	600
Non-current liabilities	400	1,100
Total liabilities	700	1,700
Owner's equity		
Issued equity		
100 ordinary shares	300	
60 Ordinary shares		600
Retained earnings	800	1,400
Total shareholders' equity	1,100	2,000

Other information

(a) On 30 September 2021, Entity A issues 2.5 shares in exchange for each ordinary share of Entity B. All of Entity B's shareholders exchange their shares in Entity B. Therefore, Entity A issues 150 ordinary shares in exchange for all 60 ordinary shares of Entity B.

(b) The fair value of each ordinary share of Entity B at 30 September 2021 is €40. The quoted market price of Entity A's ordinary shares at that date is €16.

(c) The fair values of Entity A's identifiable assets and liabilities at 30 September 2021 are the same as their carrying amounts, except that the fair value of Entity A's non-current assets at 30 September 2021 is €1,500.

Using the facts above, the statement of financial position of Entity A, the legal parent, in its separate financial statements immediately following the business combination will be as follows:

	Entity A €
Current assets	500
Non-current assets	1,300
Investment in subsidiary (Entity B)	2,400
Total assets	4,200
Current liabilities	300
Non-current liabilities	400
Total liabilities	700
Owner's equity	
Issued equity	
250 ordinary shares	2,700
Retained earnings	800
	3,500

The investment in the subsidiary is included at its cost of €2,400, being the fair value of the shares issued by Entity A (150 × €16). It can be seen that the issued equity is different from that in the consolidated financial statements and its non-current assets remain at their carrying amounts before the business combination (see Example 9.36 in Chapter 9 at 14.1).

2.1.2 Deemed cost on transition to IFRS

IFRS 1 allows a first-time adopter an exemption with regard to its investments in subsidiaries, joint ventures and associates in its separate financial statements. *[IFRS 1.D15]*. If it elects to apply the cost method, it can either measure the investment in its separate opening IFRS statement of financial position at cost determined in accordance with IAS 27 or at deemed cost. Deemed cost is either:

(i) fair value (determined in accordance with IFRS 13 – *Fair Value Measurement*) at the entity's date of transition to IFRSs in its separate financial statements; or

(ii) previous GAAP carrying amount as at the entity's date of transition to IFRSs in its separate financial statements.

As with the other asset measurement exemptions, the first-time adopter may choose either (i) or (ii) above to measure each individual investment in subsidiaries, joint ventures or associates that it elects to measure using a deemed cost. *[IFRS 1.D15]*.

2.2 IFRS 9 method

Under IFRS 9, the equity investments in subsidiaries, joint ventures or associates would likely be classified as financial assets measured at fair value through profit or loss or, as financial assets measured at fair value through other comprehensive income (OCI), if an entity elects at initial recognition to present subsequent changes in their fair value in OCI. In the former case, changes in the fair value of the investments will be recognised in profit or loss. In the latter case, gains or losses from changes in the fair value will be recognised in OCI and will never be reclassified to profit or loss. The classification requirements of IFRS 9 are discussed in Chapter 48, and the measurement principles of IFRS 9 on initial and subsequent measurement are discussed in detail in Chapters 49 and 50.

One issue that has been discussed by the IASB that is relevant in determining the fair value of investments in subsidiaries, joint ventures and associates is the unit of account for such investments. The Board, for the time being, have decided not to finalise these discussions.[17]

2.3 Equity method

IAS 27 allows entities to use the equity method as described in IAS 28 to account for investments in subsidiaries, joint ventures and associates in their separate financial statements.[18] Where the equity method is used, dividends from those investments are recognised as a reduction from the carrying value of the investment.[19] The application of the equity method under IAS 28 is discussed in Chapter 11 at 7. Some jurisdictions require the use of the equity method to account for investments in subsidiaries, associates and joint ventures in the separate financial statements. In many cases this was the only GAAP difference to IFRS and hence the IASB provided the option to use the equity method.

In the Basis for Conclusions to IAS 27, the IASB indicates that in general, the application of the equity method to investments in subsidiaries, joint ventures and associates in the separate financial statements of an entity is expected to result in the same net assets and profit or loss attributable to the owners as in the entity's consolidated financial statements. However, there may be situations where this might not be the case, including:[20]

- Impairment testing requirements in IAS 28.

    For an investment in a subsidiary accounted for in separate financial statements using the equity method, goodwill that forms part of the carrying amount of the investment in the subsidiary is not tested for impairment separately. Instead, the entire carrying amount of the investment in the subsidiary is tested for impairment in accordance with IAS 36 as a single asset. However, in the consolidated financial statements of the entity, because goodwill is recognised separately, it is tested for impairment by applying the requirements in IAS 36 for testing goodwill for impairment.

- Subsidiary that has a net liability position.

    IAS 28 requires an investor to discontinue recognising its share of further losses when its cumulative share of losses of the investee equals or exceeds its interest in the investee, unless the investor has incurred legal or constructive obligations or made payments on behalf of the investee, in which case a liability is recognised, whereas there is no such requirement in relation to the consolidated financial statements.

- Capitalisation of borrowing costs incurred by a parent in relation to the assets of a subsidiary.

    IAS 23 – *Borrowing Costs* – notes that, in some circumstances, it may be appropriate to include all borrowings of the parent and its subsidiaries when computing a weighted average of the borrowing costs. When a parent borrows funds and its subsidiary uses them for the purpose of obtaining a qualifying asset, in the consolidated financial statements of the parent the borrowing costs incurred by the parent are considered to be directly attributable to the acquisition of the subsidiary's qualifying asset. However, this would not be appropriate in the separate financial statements of the parent where the parent's investment in the subsidiary is a financial asset which is not a qualifying asset.

In the above situations, there will not be alignment of the net assets and profit or loss of an investment in a subsidiary between the consolidated and separate financial statements.

2.3.1 First-time adoption of IFRS

IFRS 1 allows a first-time adopter that accounts for an investment in a subsidiary, joint venture or associate using the equity method in the separate financial statements to apply the exemption for past business combinations to the acquisition of the investment. *[IFRS 1.D15A]*. The exemption for past business combinations is discussed in Chapter 5 at 5.2. The first-time adopter can also apply certain exemptions to the assets and liabilities of subsidiaries, associates and joint ventures when it becomes a first-time adopter for the separate financial statements later than its parent or subsidiary. *[IFRS 1.D15A]*. These exemptions are discussed in Chapter 5 at 5.9.

2.4 Dividends and other distributions

IAS 27 contains a general principle for dividends received from subsidiaries, joint ventures or associates. This is supplemented by specific indicators of impairment in

IAS 36 that apply when a parent entity receives the dividend. The general principle and the specific impairment indicators are discussed in 2.4.1 below.

IFRIC 17 – *Distributions of Non-cash Assets to Owners* – considers in particular the treatment by the entity making the distribution. Details about the requirements of that Interpretation are discussed in 2.4.2 below.

2.4.1 Dividends from subsidiaries, joint ventures or associates

IAS 27 states that an entity recognises dividends from subsidiaries, joint ventures or associates in its separate financial statements when its right to receive the dividend is established. The dividend is recognised in profit or loss unless the entity elects to use the equity method, in which case the dividend is recognised as a reduction from the carrying amount of the investment. *[IAS 27.12]*.

Dividends are recognised only when they are declared (i.e. the dividends are appropriately authorised and no longer at the discretion of the entity). IFRIC 17 expands on this point: the relevant authority may be the shareholders, if the jurisdiction requires such approval, or management or the board of directors, if the jurisdiction does not require further approval. *[IFRIC 17.10]*. If the declaration is made after the reporting period but before the financial statements are authorised for issue, the dividends are not recognised as a liability at the end of the reporting period because no obligation exists at that time. Such dividends are disclosed in the notes in accordance with IAS 1. *[IAS 10.13]*. A parent cannot record income or a reduction of the equity accounted investment and recognise an asset until the dividend is a liability of its subsidiary, joint venture or associate, the paying company.

Once dividends are taken to income the investor must determine whether or not the investment has been impaired as a result. IAS 36 requires the entity to assess at each reporting date whether there are any 'indications of impairment'. Only if indications of impairment are present will the impairment test itself have to be carried out. *[IAS 36.8-9]*.

The list of indicators in IAS 36 includes the receipt of a dividend from a subsidiary, joint venture or associate where there is evidence that:

(i) the dividend exceeds the total comprehensive income of the subsidiary, joint venture or associate in the period the dividend is declared; or

(ii) the carrying amount of the investment in the separate financial statements exceeds the carrying amounts in the consolidated financial statements of the investee's net assets, including associated goodwill. *[IAS 36.12(h)]*.

2.4.1.A The dividend exceeds the total comprehensive income

There are circumstances in which receipt of a dividend will trigger the first indicator, even if the dividend is payable entirely from the profit for the period.

First, the indicator states that the test is by reference to the income in the period in which the declaration is made. Dividends are usually declared after the end of the period to which they relate; an entity whose accounting period ends on 31 December 2021 will not normally declare a dividend in respect of its earnings in that period until its financial statements have been drawn up, i.e. some months into the next period ended 31 December 2022. We assume that it is expected that the impairment review itself will take place at the end of the period, in line with the general requirements of IAS 36 referred to above, in which case the dividends received in the period will be compared to the income of the subsidiary for that period. This means that there may be a mismatch, for example, dividends declared on the basis of 2021 profits will be compared to total comprehensive income in 2022.

Second, the test is by reference to total comprehensive income, not profit or loss for the period. Total comprehensive income reflects the change in equity during a period resulting from transactions and other events, other than those changes resulting from transactions with owners in their capacity as owners. Total comprehensive income takes into account the components of 'other comprehensive income' that are not reflected in profit or loss that include:

(a) changes in revaluation surpluses of property, plant and equipment or intangible assets (see Chapters 18 and 17, respectively);
(b) remeasurements of defined benefit plans (see Chapter 35);
(c) gains and losses arising from translating the financial statements of a foreign operation (see Chapter 15);
(d) fair value changes from financial instruments measured at fair value through other comprehensive income (see Chapter 49); and
(e) the effective portion of gains and losses on hedging instruments in a cash flow hedge (see Chapter 53). *[IAS 1.7]*.

This means that all losses on remeasurement that are allowed by IFRS to bypass profit or loss and be taken directly to other components of equity are taken into account in determining whether a dividend is an indicator of impairment. If a subsidiary, joint venture or associate pays a dividend from its profit for the year that exceeds its total comprehensive income because there have been actuarial losses on the pension scheme or a loss on remeasuring its hedging derivatives, then receipt of that dividend is an indicator of impairment to the parent.

The opposite should also be true – a dividend that exceeds profit for the period but does not exceed total comprehensive income (if, for example, the entity has a revaluation surplus on its property) is not an indicator of impairment. However, IAS 36 makes clear that its list of indicators is not exhaustive and if there are other indicators of impairment then the entity must carry out an impairment test in accordance with IAS 36. *[IAS 36.13]*.

It must be stressed that this test is solely to see whether a dividend triggers an impairment review. It has no effect on the amount of dividend that the subsidiary, joint venture or associate may pay, which is governed by local law.

2.4.1.B   The carrying amount exceeds the consolidated net assets

An indicator of impairment arises if, after paying the dividend, the carrying amount of the investment in the separate financial statements exceeds the carrying amount in the consolidated financial statements of the investee's net assets, including associated goodwill.

It will often be clear when dividends are paid out of profits for the period by subsidiaries, joint ventures or associates, whether the consolidated net assets of the investee in question have declined below the carrying amount of the investment. However, this might require the preparation of consolidated financial statements by an intermediate parent which is exempted from the preparation of consolidated financial statements.

Similar issues to those described above may arise, e.g. the subsidiary, joint venture or associate may have made losses or taken some sort of remeasurement to other comprehensive income in the period in which the dividend is paid. However, it is the net assets in the consolidated financial statements that are relevant, not those in the subsidiary's, joint venture's or associate's own financial statements, which may be different if the parent acquired the subsidiary.

Testing assets for impairment is described in Chapter 20. There are particular problems to consider in trying to assess the investments in subsidiaries, joint ventures and associates for impairment. These are discussed in Chapter 20 at 12.4.

2.4.1.C   Returns of capital

Returns of share capital are not usually considered to be dividends and hence they are not directly addressed by IAS 27. They are an example of a 'distribution', the broader term applied when an entity gives away its assets to its members.

At first glance, a return of capital appears to be an obvious example of something that ought to reduce the carrying value of the investment in the parent. We do not think that is necessarily the case. Returns of capital cannot easily be distinguished from dividends. For example, depending on local law, entities may be able to:

- make repayments that directly reduce their share capital; or
- create reserves by transferring amounts from share capital into retained earnings and, at the same time or later, pay dividends from that reserve.

Returns of capital can be accounted for in the same way as dividends, i.e. by applying the impairment testing process described above. However, the effect on an entity that makes an investment (whether on initial acquisition of a subsidiary or on a subsequent injection of capital) and immediately receives it back (whether as a dividend or return of capital) generally will be that of a return of capital that reduces the carrying value of the parent's investment. In these circumstances there will be an impairment that is equal to the dividend that has been received (provided that the consideration paid as investment was at fair value). If there is a delay between the investment and the dividend or return of capital then the impairment (if any) will be a matter of judgement based on the criteria discussed above.

2.4.2   Distributions of non-cash assets to owners (IFRIC 17)

Entities sometimes make distributions of assets other than cash, e.g. items of property, plant and equipment, businesses as defined in IFRS 3, ownership interests in another entity or disposal groups as defined in IFRS 5. IFRIC 17 has the effect that gains or losses relating to some non-cash distributions to shareholders will be accounted for in profit or loss. The Interpretation addresses only the accounting by the entity that makes a non-cash asset distribution, not the accounting by recipients.

2.4.2.A   Scope

IFRIC 17 applies to any distribution of a non-cash asset, including one that gives the shareholder a choice of receiving either non-cash assets or a cash alternative if it is within scope. [IFRIC 17.3].

The Interpretations Committee did not want the Interpretation to apply to exchange transactions with shareholders, which can include an element of distribution, e.g. a sale to one of the shareholders of an asset having a fair value that is higher than the sales price. [IFRIC 17.BC5]. Therefore, it applies only to non-reciprocal distributions in which all owners of the same class of equity instruments are treated equally. [IFRIC 17.4].

The Interpretation does not apply to distributions if the assets are ultimately controlled by the same party or parties before and after the distribution, whether in the separate, individual or consolidated financial statements of an entity that makes the distribution. [IFRIC 17.5]. This means that it will not apply to distributions made by subsidiaries but only to distributions made by parent entities or individual entities that are not themselves parents. In order to avoid ambiguity regarding 'common control' and to ensure that demergers achieved by way of distribution are dealt with, the Interpretation emphasises that 'common control' is used in the same sense as in IFRS 3. A distribution to a group of individual shareholders will only be out of scope if those shareholders have ultimate collective power over the entity making the distribution as a result of contractual arrangements. [IFRIC 17.6].

If the non-cash asset distributed is an interest in a subsidiary over which the entity retains control, this is accounted for by recognising a non-controlling interest in the subsidiary in equity in the consolidated financial statements of the entity, as required by IFRS 10 paragraph 23 (see Chapter 7 at 4). [IFRIC 17.7].

2.4.2.B   Recognition, measurement and presentation

A dividend is not a liability until the entity is obliged to pay it to the shareholders. [IFRIC 17.10]. The obligation arises when payment is no longer at the discretion of the entity, which will depend on the requirements of local law. In some jurisdictions, the UK for example, shareholder approval is required before there is a liability to pay. In other jurisdictions, declaration by management or the board of directors may suffice.

The liability is measured at the fair value of the assets to be distributed. [IFRIC 17.11]. If an entity gives its owners a choice of receiving either a non-cash asset or a cash alternative, the entity estimates the dividend payable by considering both the fair value of each alternative and the associated probability of owners selecting each alternative. [IFRIC 17.12]. IFRIC 17 does not specify any method of assessing probability nor its effect on measurement.

IFRS 5's requirements apply also to a non-current asset (or disposal group) that is classified as held for distribution to owners acting in their capacity as owners (held for distribution to owners). [IFRS 5.5A, 12A, 15A]. This means that assets or asset groups within scope of IFRS 5 will be carried at the lower of carrying amount and fair value less costs to distribute. [IFRS 5.15A]. Assets not subject to the measurement provisions of IFRS 5 are measured in accordance with the relevant standard. In practice, most non-cash distributions of assets out of scope of the measurement provisions of IFRS 5 will be of assets held at fair value in accordance with the relevant standard, e.g. financial instruments and investment property carried at fair value. [IFRS 5.5]. Accordingly, there should be little difference, if any, between their carrying value and the amount of the distribution.

The liability is adjusted as at the end of any reporting period at which it remains outstanding and at the date of settlement with any adjustment being taken to equity. [IFRIC 17.13]. When the liability is settled, the difference, if any, between its carrying amount and the carrying amount of the assets distributed is accounted for as a separate line item in profit or loss. *[IFRIC 17.14-15]*. IFRIC 17 does not express any preference for particular line items or captions in the statement of profit or loss.

It is rare for entities to distribute physical assets such as property, plant and equipment to shareholders, although these distributions are common within groups and hence out of scope of IFRIC 17. In practice, the Interpretation will have most effect on demergers by way of distribution, as illustrated in the following example.

Example 8.7:   Non-cash asset distributed to shareholders

Conglomerate Plc has two divisions, electronics and music, each of which is in a separate subsidiary. On 18 December 2020 the shareholders approve a non-cash dividend in the form of the electronics division, which means that the dividend is a liability when the annual financial statements are prepared as at 31 December 2020. The distribution is to be made on 17 January 2021.

In Conglomerate Plc's separate financial statements at 18 December and 31 December, the investment in Electronics Ltd, which holds the electronics division, is carried at €100 million; the division has consolidated net assets of €210 million. The fair value of the electronics division at 18 December and 31 December is €375 million, so is the amount at which the liability to pay the dividend is recorded in Conglomerate Plc's separate financial statements and in its consolidated financial statements, as follows:

Conglomerate Plc

Separate financial statements			Consolidated financial statements		
	€	€		€	€
Dr equity	375		Dr equity	375	
Cr liability		375	Cr liability		375

In Conglomerate's separate financial statements its investment in Electronics Ltd of €100 million is classified as held for distribution to owners. In the consolidated financial statements, the net assets of €210 million are so classified.

If the value of Electronics Ltd had declined between the date of declaration of the dividend and the period end, say to €360 million (more likely if there had been a longer period between declaration and the period end) then the decline would be reflected in equity and the liability recorded at €360 million. Exactly the same entry would be made if the value were €375 million at the period end and €360 million on the date of settlement (Dr liability €15 million, Cr equity €15 million).

The dividend is paid on 17 January 2021 at which point the fair value of the division is €360 million. There was no change in the carrying value of the investment in the separate financial statements and of the net assets in the consolidated financial statements between 31 December and distribution date. The difference between the assets distributed and the liability is recognised as a gain in profit or loss.

Conglomerate Plc

Separate financial statements			Consolidated financial statements		
	€	€		€	€
Dr liability	360		Dr liability	360	
Cr profit or loss		260	Cr profit or loss		150
Cr asset held for sale		100	Cr disposal group		210

The entity must disclose, if applicable:

(a) the carrying amount of the dividend payable at the beginning and end of the period; and

(b) the increase or decrease in the carrying amount recognised in the period as a result of a change in the fair value of the assets to be distributed. *[IFRIC 17.16]*.

If an entity declares a dividend that will take the form of a non-cash asset after the end of a reporting period but before the financial statements are authorised the following disclosure should be made:

(a) the nature of the asset to be distributed;

(b) the carrying amount of the asset to be distributed as of the end of the reporting period; and

(c) the estimated fair value of the asset to be distributed as of the end of the reporting period, if it is different from its carrying amount, and the information about the method used to determine that fair value required by IFRS 13 – paragraphs 93(b), (d), (g) and (i) and 99 (see Chapter 14 at 20.3). [IFRIC 17.17].

3 DISCLOSURE

An entity applies all applicable IFRSs when providing disclosures in the separate financial statements. [IAS 27.15]. In addition there are a number of specific disclosure requirements in IAS 27 which are discussed below.

3.1 Separate financial statements prepared by parent electing not to prepare consolidated financial statements

When separate financial statements are prepared for a parent that, in accordance with the exemption discussed at 1.1 above, elects not to prepare consolidated financial statements, those separate financial statements are to disclose: [IAS 27.16]

(a) the fact that the financial statements are separate financial statements; that the exemption from consolidation has been used; and the name and the principal place of business (and country of incorporation, if different) of the entity whose consolidated financial statements that comply with IFRS have been produced for public use and the address where those consolidated financial statements are obtainable;

(b) a list of significant investments in subsidiaries, joint ventures and associates, including:

   (i) the name of those investees;

   (ii) the principal place of business (and country of incorporation, if different) of those investees; and

   (iii) its proportion of the ownership interest and, if different, proportion of voting rights held in those investees; and

(c) a description of the method used to account for the investments listed under (b).

In addition to disclosures required by IAS 27, an entity also has to disclose in its separate financial statements qualitative and quantitative information about its interests in unconsolidated structured entities as required by IFRS 12. IFRS 12 does not generally apply to an entity's separate financial statements to which IAS 27 applies but if it has interests in unconsolidated structured entities and prepares separate financial statements as its only financial statements, it must apply the requirements in paragraphs 24 to 31 of IFRS 12 when preparing those separate financial statements (see Chapter 13 at 6). [IFRS 12.6(b)].

The disclosures in IFRS 12 are given only where the parent has taken advantage of the exemption from preparing consolidated financial statements. Where the parent has not taken advantage of the exemption, and also prepares separate financial statements, it gives the disclosures at 3.3 below in respect of those separate financial statements.

3.2 Separate financial statements prepared by an investment entity

When an investment entity that is a parent (other than a parent electing not to prepare consolidated financial statements) prepares separate financial statements as its only financial statements, it discloses that fact. The investment entity also presents disclosures relating to investment entities required by IFRS 12 (see Chapter 13 at 4.6). *[IAS 27.16A]*.

3.3 Separate financial statements prepared by an entity other than a parent electing not to prepare consolidated financial statements

As drafted, IAS 27 requires the disclosures at (a), (b) and (c) below to be given by:

- a parent preparing separate financial statements in addition to consolidated financial statements (i.e. whether or not it is required to prepare consolidated financial statements – the disclosures in 3.1 above apply only when the parent has actually taken advantage of the exemption, not merely when it is eligible to do so); and
- an entity (not being a parent) that is an investor in an associate or in a joint venture in respect of any separate financial statements that it prepares, i.e. whether:
  (i)   as its only financial statements (if permitted by IAS 28); or
  (ii) in addition to financial statements in which the results and net assets of associates or joint ventures are included.

The relevance of certain of these disclosures to financial statements falling within (i) above is not immediately obvious (see 3.3.1 below).

Where an entity is both a parent and either an investor in an associate or in a joint venture, it should follow the disclosure requirements governing parents – in other words, it complies with the disclosures in 3.1 above if electing not to prepare consolidated financial statements and otherwise with the disclosures below.

Separate financial statements prepared by an entity other than a parent electing not to prepare consolidated financial statements must disclose: *[IAS 27.17]*

(a) the fact that the statements are separate financial statements and the reasons why those statements are prepared if not required by law;

(b) a list of significant investments in subsidiaries, joint ventures and associates, including for each such investment its:
   (i)   name;
   (ii) principal place of business (and country of incorporation, if different); and
   (iii) proportion of ownership interest and, if different, proportion of voting power held; and

(c) a description of the method used to account for the investments listed under (b).

The separate financial statements must also identify the financial statements prepared in accordance with the requirements of IFRS 10 (requirement to prepare consolidated financial statements), IFRS 11 or IAS 28 to which they relate. *[IAS 27.17]*. In other words, they must draw attention to the fact that the entity also prepares consolidated financial statements or, as the case may be, financial statements in which the associates or joint ventures are accounted for using the equity method.

The implication of this disclosure requirement is that an entity which publishes both separate and consolidated financial statements under IFRS cannot issue the separate financial statements before the consolidated financial statements have been prepared and approved, since there would not be, at the date of issue of the separate financial statements, any consolidated financial statements 'to which they relate'. This is discussed at 1.1.3 above.

If the parent has issued consolidated financial statements prepared not in accordance with IFRS but with its local GAAP, the parent cannot make reference to the financial statements prepared in accordance with IFRS 10, IFRS 11 or IAS 28, therefore the separate financial statements cannot be considered in compliance with IAS 27.

3.3.1 Entities with no subsidiaries but exempt from applying IAS 28

Entities which have no subsidiaries, but which have investments in associates or joint ventures are permitted by IAS 28 to prepare separate financial statements as their only financial statements if they satisfy the conditions described at 1.1.1 above.

IAS 27 requires such entities to make the disclosures in (a) to (c) above in 3.3. In addition, the entity is supposed to identify the financial statements prepared in accordance with IAS 28, *[IAS 27.17]*, but in this situation, there are no such financial statements.

4 COMMON CONTROL OR GROUP TRANSACTIONS IN INDIVIDUAL OR SEPARATE FINANCIAL STATEMENTS

4.1 Introduction

Transactions often take place between a parent entity and its subsidiaries or between subsidiaries within a group that may or may not be carried out at fair value.

Whilst such transactions do not affect the consolidated financial statements of the parent as they are eliminated in the course of consolidation, they can have a significant impact on the separate financial statements of the parent and/or subsidiaries and/or a set of consolidated financial statements prepared for a sub-group. IAS 24 requires only that these transactions are disclosed and provides no accounting requirements.

The IASB generally considers that the needs of users of financial statements are fully met by requiring entities to consolidate subsidiaries and to equity account for associates and joint ventures. Accounting issues within individual or separate financial statements are not a priority and are usually only addressed in IFRS when a standard affects consolidated and individual or separate statements in different ways, e.g. accounting for pensions or employee benefits.

We consider that it is helpful to set out some general principles in accounting for these transactions that enhance the consistency of application of IFRS whether for the separate financial statements of a parent, the individual financial statements of an entity that is not a parent or the consolidated financial statements of a sub-group.

The considerations provided in this section in certain circumstances apply also to sub-group consolidated financial statements in relation to common control transactions with entities controlled by the ultimate parent or ultimate controlling party or parties, but that are outside the sub-group.

We have considered how to apply these principles to certain common types of arrangement between entities under common control, which are described in more detail at 4.4 below:

- sales, exchanges and contributions of non-monetary assets including sales and exchanges of investments not within the scope of IFRS 9, i.e. investments in subsidiaries, associates or joint ventures (see 4.4.1 below);
- transfers of businesses, including contributions and distribution of businesses (see 4.4.2 and 4.4.3 below);
- incurring costs and settling liabilities without recharge (see 4.4.4 below);
- loans that bear interest at non-market rates or are interest free (see 4.4.5.A below); and
- financial guarantee contracts given by a parent over a subsidiary's borrowings in the financial statements of a subsidiary (see 4.4.5.B below).

Other arrangements that are subject to specific requirements in particular standards are dealt with in the relevant chapters. These include:

- financial guarantee contracts over a subsidiary's borrowings in the accounts of the parent (see Chapter 49 at 3.3.3);
- share-based payment plans of a parent (see Chapter 34 at 12); and
- employee benefits (see Chapter 35 at 3.3.2).

In determining how to account for transactions between entities under common control, we believe that the following two aspects need to be considered:

(a) Is the transaction at fair value? Is the price in the transaction the one that would be received to sell an asset or paid to transfer a liability in an orderly transaction between market participants? It is necessary to consider whether the transaction is of a type that market participants could or would enter into. It is also important to remember that an arm's length transaction includes the repayment terms that would be expected of independent parties and this might not be the case in intra-group transactions.

(b) Is it a contractual arrangement and, if so, is the entity whose financial statements are being considered a party to the contract?

If the transaction is at fair value and the entity is a party to the contract, we believe that it should be accounted for in accordance with the terms of the contract and general requirements of IFRS related to this type of transaction.

The principles for accounting for transactions between group entities that are not transacted at fair value are presented in the following flowchart. Detailed comments of the principles are provided further in 4.2 and 4.3 below.

608 Chapter 8

Group entities represent entities under common control of the same parent or the same controlling party or parties. The flowchart therefore does not apply to transactions of group entities with joint ventures or associates of any of the group entities.

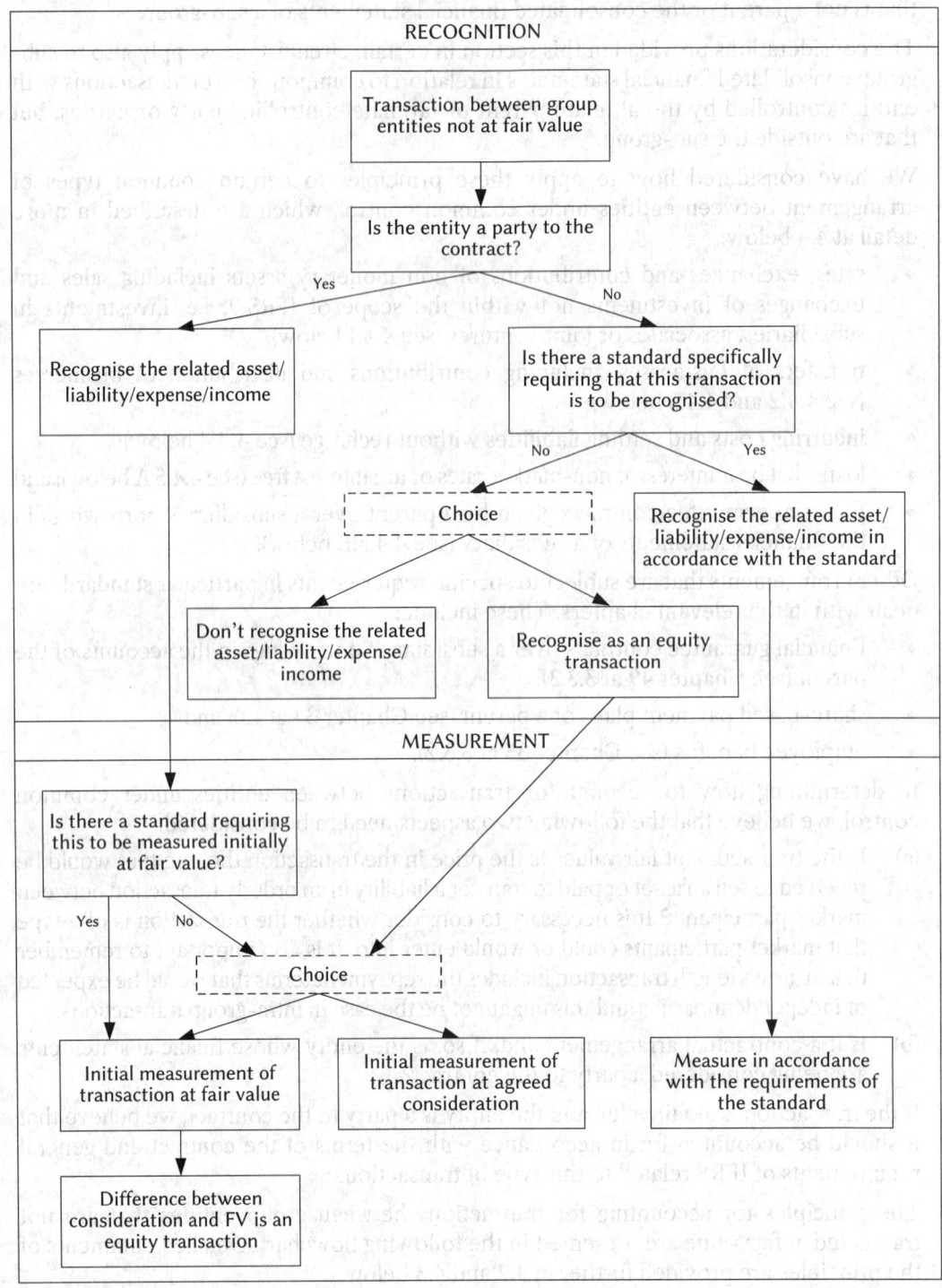

If there is more than one acceptable way of accounting for specific transactions and therefore a choice of accounting policies, the entity should apply its chosen policy consistently to similar arrangements and disclose it if it is material. However, not all group entities need adopt the same accounting policy in their individual, separate or sub-group consolidated financial statements. Nor is there a requirement for symmetrical accounting by the entities involved in the transaction.

4.2 Recognition

If an entity is a party to a contract under which it receives a right and incurs an obligation, then on the assumption that there is substance to the transaction, it will be recognised in the financial statements of the entity.

An entity may receive a right without incurring an obligation or *vice versa* without being a party to a contract. There are many different types of arrangement that contain this feature, either in whole or in part:

- Some arrangements are not contractual at all, such as capital contributions and distributions, that are in substance gifts made without consideration.
- Some standards require transactions to which the entity is not a party to be reflected in their financial statements. In effect, the accounting treatment is representing that the subsidiary has received a capital contribution from the parent, which the subsidiary has then spent on employee remuneration or *vice versa*. IFRS 2 has such requirements (see Chapter 34 at 12).
- Some are contractual arrangements for the other party, e.g. a parent enters into a contract to engage an auditor for the subsidiary, and pays the audit fees without any recharge.

If an entity is not a party to a contractual relationship and there is no IFRS requiring recognition then the entity may choose not to recognise the transaction at all.

If it chooses to recognise the transaction then recognition will depend on whether the entity is a parent or a subsidiary, as well as the specific nature of the transaction. In some circumstances a parent may treat a debit as either an addition to its investment in its subsidiary or as an expense and a credit as a gain to profit or loss. It is not generally possible for the parent to recognise gains in equity as these are usually transactions with subsidiaries, not shareholders. A subsidiary can only treat the transaction as a credit or debit to income (income or expense) or a debit to asset or credit to liability and an equal and opposite debit or credit to equity (distribution of or contribution to equity).

One example where a subsidiary is required by an IFRS to record an expense when it is not a party to a contractual arrangement is a share-based payment. If the employees of a subsidiary are granted options by the parent company over its shares in exchange for services to the subsidiary, the subsidiary must record a cost for that award within its own financial statements, even though it may not legally be a party to it. The parent must also record the share-based payment as an addition to the investment in the subsidiary (see Chapter 34 at 12.2.4).

Although the entity not party to the contract might have a choice to either record the transaction or not, the other entity within the group that might have entered into the contract on behalf of the entity is required to recognise the transaction. Where a group entity is incurring expenses on behalf of another entity this group entity might be able to capitalise the expenses as part of the cost of the investment (e.g. a parent is incurring expenses of the subsidiary without recharging them), treat them as a distribution (e.g. a sister company is incurring expenses of the entity without recharging them) or to expense them.

The principles apply equally to transactions between a parent and its subsidiaries and those between subsidiaries in a group. If the transaction is between two subsidiaries, and both of the entities are either required or choose to recognise an equity element in the transaction, one subsidiary recognises a capital contribution from the parent, while the other subsidiary recognises a distribution to the parent. The parent may choose whether or not to recognise the equity transfer in its stand-alone financial statements.

4.3 Measurement

If a standard requires the transaction to be recognised initially at fair value, it must be measured at that fair value regardless of the actual consideration. A difference between the fair value and the consideration may mean that other goods or services are being provided, e.g. the transaction includes a management fee. This will be accounted for separately on one of the bases described below. If there is still a difference having taken account of all goods or services, it is accounted for as an equity transaction, i.e. as either a contribution to or distribution of equity.

In all other cases, where there is a difference between the fair value and the consideration after having taken account of all goods or services being provided, there is a choice available to the entity to:

(a) recognise the transaction at fair value, irrespective of the actual consideration; any difference between fair value and agreed consideration will be a contribution to or a distribution of equity for a subsidiary, or an increase in the investment held or a distribution received by the parent; or

(b) recognise the transaction at the actual consideration stated in any agreement related to the transaction.

Except for accounting for the acquisition of businesses where the pooling of interest method can be considered (see 4.4.2 below), the transfer of businesses between a parent and its subsidiary (see 4.4.3 below), and the acquisition of an investment in a subsidiary constituting a business that is acquired in a share-for-share exchange (see 2.1.1.B above), there is no other basis for the measurement of the transactions between entities under common control other than those stated in (a) and (b) above. Therefore, predecessor values accounting (accounting based on the carrying amounts of the transferor) cannot be applied.

4.3.1 Fair value in intra-group transactions

The requirements for fair value measurement included in IFRS 13 should be applied to common control transactions. However, fair value can be difficult to establish in intra-group transactions.

If there is more than one element to the transaction, this means in principle identifying all of the goods and services being provided and accounting for each element at fair value. This is not necessarily straightforward: a bundle of goods and services in an arm's length arrangement will usually be priced at a discount to the price of each of the elements acquired separately and this is reflected in the fair value attributed to the transaction. It can be much harder to allocate fair values in intra-group arrangements where the transaction may not have a commercial equivalent.

As we have already noted, the transaction may be based on the fair value of an asset but the payment terms are not comparable to those in a transaction between independent parties. The purchase price often remains outstanding on intercompany account, whereas commercial arrangements always include agreed payment terms. Interest-free loans are common between group companies; these loans may have no formal settlement terms and, while this makes them technically repayable on demand, they too may remain outstanding for prolonged periods.

As a result, there can be a certain amount of estimation when applying fair values to group arrangements.

Some IFRSs are based on the assumption that one entity may not have the information available to the other party in a transaction, for example:

- a lessee may not know the lessor's internal rate of return, in which case IFRS 16 – *Leases* – allows to substitute it with the lessee's incremental borrowing rate (see Chapter 23 at 5.2.2); and
- in exchanges of assets, IAS 16 and IAS 38 note that one party may not have information about the fair value of the asset it is receiving, the fair value of the asset it is giving up or it may be able to determine one of these values more easily than the other (see Chapter 18 at 4.4 and 4.4.1.B below).

In an intra-group transaction it will be difficult to assume that one group company knows the fair value of the transaction but the other does not. The approximations allowed by these standards will probably not apply.

However, if a subsidiary is not wholly owned, such transactions are undertaken generally on arm's length terms as non-controlling shareholders are impacted. Therefore, in a situation where such a transaction is not done on arm's length terms the reasons for and implications of the transaction must be assessed and carefully analysed.

4.4 Application of the principles in practice

The following sections deal with common transactions that occur between entities under common control. While the scenarios depict transactions between a parent and its subsidiaries they apply similarly to transactions between subsidiaries. Most of the examples in these sections deal with transactions having a non-arm's length element. As for any other transactions undertaken at fair value (at arm's length), respective IFRSs that are applicable have to be taken into account.

Deferred tax has been ignored for the purposes of the examples.

4.4.1 Transactions involving non-monetary assets

The same principles apply when the asset that is acquired for a consideration different to its fair value is inventory (IAS 2 – *Inventories* – Chapter 22), property, plant and equipment ('PP&E') (IAS 16 – Chapter 18), an intangible asset (IAS 38 – Chapter 17) or investment property (IAS 40 – Chapter 19). These standards require assets to be initially recognised at cost.

The same principles generally also apply to the acquisition of an investment in a subsidiary, an associate or joint venture when the purchase consideration does not reflect the fair value of the investment, and such investments are accounted for initially at cost in the separate financial statements as discussed at 2.1 above. Investments acquired in common control transactions are discussed at 2.1.1.B above.

4.4.1.A Sale of PP&E from the parent to the subsidiary for an amount of cash not representative of the fair value of the asset.

The parent and subsidiary are both parties to the transaction and both must recognise it. As the asset is recognised by the acquiring entity at cost, and not necessarily at fair value, a choice exists as to how the cost is determined. Does the consideration comprise two elements, cash and equity, or cash alone?

In some jurisdictions, some entities are legally required to conduct such transactions at fair value.

Example 8.8: Sale of PP&E at an undervalue

A parent entity sells PP&E that has a carrying amount of 50 and a fair value of 100 to its subsidiary for cash of 80.

Method (a)			Method (b)		
Recognise the transaction at fair value, regardless of the values in any agreement, with any difference between that amount and fair value recognised as an equity transaction. (Note 1)			Recognise the transaction at the consideration agreed between the parties, being the amount of cash paid.		
Subsidiary					
	€	€		€	€
Dr PP&E	100		Dr PP&E	80	
Cr Cash		80	Cr Cash		80
Cr Equity		20			
Parent					
	€	€		€	€
Dr Cash	80		Dr Cash	80	
Dr Investment	20		Cr PP&E		50
Cr PP&E		50	Cr Gain (profit or loss)		30
Cr Gain (profit or loss)		50			

Note 1 This may only be applied where fair value can be measured reliably

However, what if the asset is sold for more than fair value? What are the implications if, in the above example, the PP&E sold for 80 has a carrying value of 80 but its fair value is 75? There are a number of explanations that may affect the way in which the transaction is accounted for:

- The excess reflects additional services or goods included in the transaction, e.g. future maintenance that will be accounted for separately.
- The excess reflects the fact that the asset's value in use ('VIU') is at least 80. There are instances when PP&E is carried at an amount in excess of fair value because its VIU, or the VIU of the cash-generating unit of which it is a part, is unaffected by falls in fair value. Plant and machinery often has a low resale value; vehicles lose much of their fair value soon after purchase; and falls in property values may not affect the VIU of the head office of a profitable entity (see Chapter 20). In such cases there is no reason why the subsidiary cannot record the asset it has acquired for the cash it has paid, which means that it effectively inherits the transferor's carrying value. An impairment test potentially would not reveal any requirement to write down the asset, assuming of course that other factors do not reduce the asset's VIU (e.g. the fact that the asset will after the sale be part of a different cash generating unit).
- The excess over fair value is a distribution by the subsidiary to the parent that will be accounted for in equity. This treatment is a legal requirement in some jurisdictions, which means that the overpayment must meet the legal requirements for dividends, principally that there be sufficient distributable profits to meet the cost.
- The asset is impaired before transfer, i.e. both its fair value and VIU are lower than its carrying amount, in which case it must be written down by the transferor before the exchange takes place. If it is still sold for more than its fair value, the excess will be accounted for as a distribution received (by the parent) and a distribution made by the subsidiary (as above).

4.4.1.B   The parent exchanges PP&E for a non-monetary asset of the subsidiary.

The parent and subsidiary are both parties to the transaction and both must recognise it. The exchange of an asset for another non-monetary asset is accounted for by recognising the received asset at fair value, unless the transaction lacks commercial substance (as defined by IAS 16) or the fair value of neither of the exchanged assets can be measured reliably. *[IAS 16.24]*. The requirements of IAS 16 are explained in Chapter 18 at 4.4; the treatment required by IAS 38 and IAS 40 is the same.

The mere fact that an exchange transaction takes place between entities under common control does not of itself indicate that the transaction lacks commercial substance. However, in an exchange transaction between unrelated parties the fair value of the assets is usually the same but this does not necessarily hold true of transactions between entities under common control.

If the fair value of both assets can be measured reliably there may be a difference between the two. IAS 16 suggests that, if an entity is able to determine reliably the fair value of either the asset received or the asset given up, then the fair value of the asset given up is used to measure the cost of the asset received. *[IAS 16.26]*. However, IAS 16 actually requires an entity to base its accounting for the exchange on the asset whose fair value is most clearly evident. *[IAS 16.26]*. If fair values are different it is possible that the group entities have entered into a non-reciprocal transaction. This means that the entity has the policy choice described at 4.3 above, which in this case means that there are three alternative treatments; it can recognise the transaction as follows:

- Method (a) – an exchange of assets at fair value of the asset received with an equity transaction. Any difference between the fair value of the asset received and the fair value of the asset given up is an equity transaction, while the difference between the carrying value of the asset given up and its fair value is recognised in profit or loss;
- Method (b) – an exchange of assets at fair value of the asset received without recognising an equity element. The asset received is recognised at its fair value with any resulting difference to the carrying value of the asset given up is recognised in profit or loss; or
- Method (c) – apply a 'cost' method based on IAS 16 (the fair value of the asset given up is used to measure the cost of the asset received) under which each entity records the asset at the fair value of the asset it has given up. This could result in one of the parties recording the asset it had received at an amount in excess of its fair value, in which case it may be an indicator for impairment of the asset. It would be consistent with the principles outlined at 4.3 above to treat the write down as an equity transaction, i.e. an addition to the carrying value of the subsidiary by the parent and a distribution by the subsidiary.

Example 8.9: Exchange of assets with dissimilar values

A parent entity transfers an item of PP&E to its subsidiary in exchange for an item of PP&E of the subsidiary, with the following values:

Subsidiary		Parent	
	€		€
Carrying Value	20	Carrying Value	50
Fair Value	80	Fair Value	100

The fair value of both assets can be measured reliably.

The accounting for the transaction by the parent and the subsidiary under each of the methods is as follows:

Method (a)					
Subsidiary			Parent		
	€	€		€	€
Dr PP&E	100		Dr PP&E	80	
Cr PP&E		20	Dr Investment	20	
Cr Gain (profit or loss)		60	Cr PP&E		50
Cr Equity		20	Cr Gain (profit or loss)		50

Method (b)				
Subsidiary		Parent		
	€ €		€	€
Dr PP&E	100	Dr PP&E	80	
Cr PP&E	20	Cr PP&E		50
Cr Gain (profit or loss)	80	Cr Gain (profit or loss)		30

Method (c)				
Subsidiary		Parent		
	€ €		€	€
Dr PP&E	80	Dr PP&E (100 – 20)	80	
Cr PP&E	20	Dr Investment	20	
Cr Gain (profit or loss)	60	Cr PP&E		50
		Cr Gain (profit or loss)		50

If the fair value of only one of the exchanged assets can be measured reliably, IAS 16 allows both parties to recognise the asset they have received at the fair value of the asset that can be measured reliably. *[IAS 16.26]*. Underlying this requirement is a presumption that the fair value of both assets is the same, but one cannot assume this about common control transactions.

If the fair value of neither of the exchanged assets can be measured reliably, or the transaction does not have commercial substance, both the parent and subsidiary recognise the received asset at the carrying amount of the asset they have given up.

4.4.1.C   Acquisition and sale of assets for shares

These transactions include the transfer of inventory, property plant and equipment, intangible assets, investment property and investments in subsidiaries, associates and joint ventures by one entity in return for shares of the other entity. These transactions are usually between a parent and subsidiary where the subsidiary is the transferee that issues shares to the parent in exchange for the assets received.

(a)   Accounting treatment by the subsidiary

Transactions that include the transfer of inventory, property plant and equipment, intangible assets, and investment property are within the scope of IFRS 2, as goods have been received in exchange for shares. The assets are recognised at fair value, unless the fair value cannot be estimated reliably, and an increase in equity of the same amount is recognised. If the fair value of the assets cannot be estimated reliably, the fair value of the shares is used instead. *[IFRS 2.10]*.

Transactions in which an investment in a subsidiary, associate or joint venture is acquired in exchange for shares is not specifically addressed under IFRS, since it falls outside the scope of both IFRS 9 and IFRS 2. However, we believe that it might be appropriate, by analogy with IFRS on related areas (like IFRS 3), to account for such a transaction at the fair value of the consideration given (being fair value of equity instruments issued) or the assets received, if that is more easily measured, together with directly attributable transaction costs. As discussed at 2.1.1.B above, when the purchase consideration does not correspond to the fair value of the investment acquired, in our view, the acquirer has an accounting policy choice to account for the investment at fair value of the consideration given or may impute an equity contribution or dividend distribution and in effect account for the investment at its fair value. Alternatively, if the investment in a subsidiary constitutes a business and is acquired in a share-for-share exchange, it is also acceptable to measure the cost based on the original carrying amount of the investment in the subsidiary in the transferor entity's separate financial statements, rather than at the fair value of the shares given as consideration.

(b) Accounting treatment by the parent

The parent has disposed of an asset in exchange for an increased investment in a subsidiary. Based on what has been said at 2.1.1 above, the cost of investment should be recorded at the fair value of the consideration given i.e. the fair value of the asset sold. Such a transaction has also the nature of an exchange of assets and by analogy to paragraph 24 of IAS 16, the investment should be measured at fair value unless the exchange transaction lacks commercial substance or the fair value of neither the investment received nor the asset given up is reliably measurable. If the investment cannot be measured at fair value, it is measured at the carrying value of the asset given up. *[IAS 16.24]*.

The asset's fair value may be lower than its carrying value but it is not impaired unless its VIU is insufficient to support that carrying value (see 4.4.1.A above). If there is no impairment, the parent is not prevented from treating the carrying value of the asset as an addition to the investment in the subsidiary solely because the fair value is lower. If the asset is impaired then this should be recognised before reclassification, unless the reorganisation affects, and increases, the VIU.

If the fair value is higher than the carrying value and the investment is accounted for at fair value as discussed above, the transferring entity recognises a gain. In certain circumstances it might not be appropriate to account for the transaction at fair value due to lack of commercial substance. For example, exchanging the asset for an investment in the shares of a subsidiary that holds nothing but the asset given as consideration may not give rise to a gain on transfer.

4.4.1.D Contribution and distribution of assets

These transactions include transfers of inventory, property plant and equipment, intangible assets, investment property and investments in subsidiaries, associates and joint ventures from one entity to another for no consideration. These arrangements are not contractual but are equity transactions: either specie capital contributions (an asset is gifted by a parent to a subsidiary) or non-cash distributions (an asset is given by a subsidiary to its parent). IFRIC 17 explicitly excludes intra-group non-cash distributions from its scope (see 2.4.2 above). *[IFRIC 17.5]*.

The relevant standards (IAS 2, IAS 16, IAS 38 and IAS 40) refer to assets being recognised at cost. Similarly, investments in subsidiaries, associates and joint ventures may be recognised at cost under IAS 27 as discussed at 2.1 above. Following the principles described at 4.3 above, the entity receiving the asset has a choice: recognise it at zero or at fair value. It is in practice more common for an entity that has received an asset in what is purely an equity transaction to recognise it at fair value.

The entity that gives away the asset must reflect the transaction. A parent that makes a specie capital contribution to its subsidiary will recognise an increased investment in that subsidiary (in principle at fair value, recognising a gain or loss based on the difference from the carrying amount of the asset) provided the increase does not result in the impairment of the investment, or an expense (based on the carrying amount of the asset given away). A subsidiary that makes a distribution in specie to its parent might account for the transaction by derecognising the distributed asset at its carrying value against retained earnings. However, the subsidiary could also account for the distribution at fair value, if the fair value could be established reliably. This would potentially result in recognising a gain in profit or loss for the difference between the fair value of the asset and its carrying value. There would also be a charge to equity for the distribution, recognised and measured at the fair value of the asset. This is consistent with IFRIC 17, although the distribution is not in scope.

4.4.1.E Transfers between subsidiaries

As noted at 4.2 above, similar principles apply when the arrangement is between two subsidiaries rather than a subsidiary and parent. To illustrate this, assume that the transaction in Example 8.8 above takes place between two subsidiaries rather than parent and subsidiary.

Example 8.10:   Transactions between subsidiaries

The facts are as in Example 8.8 above except that Subsidiary A sells PP&E that has a carrying amount of €50 and a fair value of €100 to its fellow-subsidiary B for cash of €80. As before, it is assumed that fair value can be measured reliably.

Method (a)	Method (b)
Recognise the transaction at fair value, regardless of the values in any agreement, with any difference between that amount and fair value recognised as an equity transaction.	Recognise the transaction at the consideration agreed between the parties, being the amount of cash paid.

Subsidiary A

	€	€		€	€
Dr Cash	80		Dr Cash	80	
Dr Equity (Note 1)	20		Cr PP&E		50
Cr PP&E		50	Cr Gain (profit or loss)		30
Cr Gain (profit or loss)		50			

Subsidiary B

	€	€		€	€
Dr PP&E	100		Dr PP&E	80	
Cr Cash		80	Cr Cash		80
Cr Equity (Note 1)		20			

Note 1   From subsidiary A's perspective there is an equity element to the transaction representing the difference between the fair value of the asset and the contractual consideration. This reflects the amount by which the transaction has reduced A's fair value and has been shown as a distribution by A to its parent. From subsidiary B's perspective, the equity element is a capital contribution from the parent.

Parent (Note 2)

	€	€		
Dr Investment in B	20		No entries made	
Cr Investment in A		20		

Note 2   Parent can choose to reallocate the equity element of the transaction between its two subsidiaries so as to reflect the changes in value.

In some circumstances the transfer of an asset from one subsidiary to another may affect the value of the transferor's assets to such an extent as to be an indicator of impairment in respect of the parent's investment in its shares. This can happen if the parent acquired the subsidiary for an amount that includes goodwill and the assets generating part or all of that goodwill have been transferred to another subsidiary. As a result, the carrying value of the shares in the parent may exceed the fair value or VIU of the remaining assets. This is discussed further in Chapter 20 at 12.3.

4.4.2   Acquiring and selling businesses – transfers between subsidiaries

One group entity may sell, and another may purchase, the net assets of a business rather than the shares in the entity. The acquisition may be for cash or shares and both entities must record the transaction in their individual or separate financial statements. There can also be transfers for no consideration. As this chapter only addresses transactions between entities under common control, any arrangement described in this section from the perspective of the transferee will be as common control transactions out of scope of IFRS 3. The common control exemption is discussed in Chapter 10 at 2.

If the arrangement is a business combination for the acquiring entity it will also not be within scope of IFRS 2. *[IFRS 2.5]*.

The transferor needs to recognise the transfer of a business under common control. If the consideration received does not represent fair value of the business transferred or there is the transfer without any consideration, the principles described in 4.4.2.C below should be applied to decide whether any equity element is recognised.

4.4.2.A   Has a business been acquired?

IFRS 3 defines a business as 'an integrated set of activities and assets that is capable of being conducted and managed for the purpose of providing a return in the form of dividends, lower costs or other economic benefits directly to investors or other owners, members or participants'. *[IFRS 3 Appendix A]*. See Chapter 9 at 3.2 for descriptions of the features of a business.

4.4.2.B   If a business has been acquired, how should it be accounted for?

As described in Chapter 10 at 3, we believe that until such time as the IASB finalises its conclusions under its project on common control transactions entities should apply either:

(a)   the pooling of interest method; or

(b)   the acquisition method (as in IFRS 3).

In our view, where the acquisition method of accounting is selected, the transaction must have substance from the perspective of the reporting entity. This is because the method results in a reassessment of the value of the net assets of one or more of the entities involved and/or the recognition of goodwill. Chapter 10 discusses the factors that will give substance to a transaction and although this is written primarily in the context of the acquisition of an entity by another entity, it applies equally to the acquisition of a business by an entity or a legal merger of two subsidiaries.

4.4.2.C   Purchase and sale of a business for equity or cash not representative of the fair value of the business

The principles are no different to those described at 4.4.1.A above. The entity may:

- recognise the transaction at fair value, regardless of the values in any agreement, with any difference between that amount and fair value recognised as an equity transaction; or
- recognise the transaction at the consideration agreed between the parties, being the amount of cash paid or fair value of shares issued.

From the perspective of the acquirer of the business, the above choice matters only when the acquisition method is applied in accounting for the business acquired. Depending on which approach is applied, goodwill on the acquisition may be different (or there can even be a gain on bargain purchase recognised). This is discussed further in Chapter 10 at 3.2. When the pooling of interest method is applied, the difference between the consideration paid and carrying value of net assets received is always recognised in equity no matter whether the consideration agreed between the parties represents the fair value of the business. If no consideration is payable for the transfer of the business, this could affect the assessment as to whether the transaction has substance to enable the acquisition method to be applied.

From the perspective of the seller of the business, the choice will impact any gain or loss recognised on the disposal. Recognising the transaction on the basis of the consideration agreed will result in a gain or loss based on the difference between the consideration received and the carrying value of the business disposed. Recognising the transaction at fair value including an equity element imputed will result in the gain or loss being the difference between the fair value of the business and its carrying value. If no consideration is received for the transfer of the business, the transaction may be considered to be more in the nature of a distribution in specie, the accounting for which is discussed at 4.4.1.D above.

4.4.2.D If the net assets are not a business, how should the transactions be accounted for?

Even though one entity acquires the net assets of another, this is not necessarily a business combination. IFRS 3 rules out of scope acquisitions of assets or net assets that are not businesses, noting that:

> 'This IFRS does not apply to [...] the acquisition of an asset or a group of assets that does not constitute a *business*. In such cases the acquirer shall identify and recognise the individual identifiable assets acquired (including those assets that meet the definition of, and recognition criteria for, *intangible assets* in IAS 38 – *Intangible Assets*) and liabilities assumed. The cost of the group shall be allocated to the individual identifiable assets and liabilities on the basis of their relative *fair values* at the date of purchase. Such a transaction or event does not give rise to goodwill.' *[IFRS 3.2(b)]*.

If the acquisition is not a business combination, it will be an acquisition of assets for cash or shares or for no consideration (see 4.4.1.A, 4.4.1.C and 4.4.1.D above).

4.4.3 Transfers of businesses between parent and subsidiary

As an acquisition of a business by a subsidiary from its parent in exchange for cash, other assets or equity instruments may meet the definition of a business combination, the guidance provided in 4.4.2 above is applicable. Therefore, this section mainly deals with the transfer of a business from a subsidiary to its parent.

A feature that all transfers of businesses to parent entities have in common, whatever the legal form that they take, is that it is difficult to categorise them as business combinations. There is no acquirer whose actions result in it obtaining control of an acquired business; the parent already controlled the business that has been transferred to it.

A transfer without any consideration is comparable to a distribution by a subsidiary to its parent. The transfer can be a dividend but there are other legal arrangements that have similar effect that include reorganisations sanctioned by a court process or transfers after liquidation of the transferor entity. Some jurisdictions allow a legal merger between a parent and subsidiary to form a single entity. The general issues related to distributions of business are addressed in 4.4.3.A below, while the special concerns raised by legal mergers are addressed in 4.4.3.B below.

4.4.3.A Distributions of businesses without consideration – subsidiary transferring business to the parent.

From one perspective the transfer is a distribution and the model on which to base the accounting is that of receiving a dividend. Another view is that the parent has exchanged the investment in shares for the underlying assets and this is essentially a change in perspective from an equity interest to a direct investment in the net assets and results. Neither analogy is perfect, although both have their supporters.

In all circumstances, the following two major features will impact the accounting of the transfer by the parent:

- whether the subsidiary transfers the entirety of its business or only part of it; and
- whether the transfer is accounted for at fair value or at 'book value'.

Book value in turn may depend on whether the subsidiary has been acquired by the parent, in which case the relevant book values would be those reflected in the consolidated financial statements of the parent, rather than those in the subsidiary's financial statements.

The two perspectives (dividend approach and exchange of investment for assets) translate into two approaches to accounting by the parent:

(i) Parent effectively has received a distribution that it accounts for in its statement of profit or loss at the fair value of the business received. It reflects the assets acquired and liabilities assumed at their fair value, including goodwill, which will be measured as at the date of the transfer. The existing investment is written off to the statement of profit or loss:

- this treatment can be applied in all circumstances;
- this is the only appropriate method when the parent carries its investment in shares at fair value applying IFRS 9; and
- when the subsidiary transfers one of its businesses but continues to exist, the investment is not immediately written off to the statement of profit or loss, but is subject to impairment testing.

(ii) Parent has exchanged its investment or part of its investment for the underlying assets and liabilities of the subsidiary and accounts for them at book values. The values that are reported in the consolidated financial statements become the cost of these assets for the parent:

- this method is not appropriate if the investment in the parent is carried at fair value, in which case method (i) must be applied; and
- when the subsidiary transfers one of its businesses but continues to exist, the investment is not immediately written off to the statement of profit or loss, but is subject to impairment testing.

The two linked questions when using this approach are how to categorise the difference between the carrying value of the investment and the assets transferred and whether or not to reflect goodwill or an 'excess' (negative goodwill) in the parent's financial statements. This will depend primarily on whether the subsidiary had been acquired by the parent (the only circumstances in which this approach allows goodwill in the parent's financial statements after the transfer) and how any remaining 'catch up' adjustment is classified.

These alternative treatments are summarised in the following table:

Subsidiary set up or acquired	Basis of accounting	Goodwill recognised	Effect on statement of profit or loss
Subsidiary set up by parent	Fair value.	Goodwill or negative goodwill at date of transfer.	Dividend recognised at fair value of the business. Investment written off or tested for impairment.
	Book value from consolidated accounts.	No goodwill or negative goodwill. (Note 1)	Catch up adjustment recognised fully in equity or as income, except that the element relating to a transaction recorded directly in equity may be recognised in equity. (Note 2) Investment written off or tested for impairment.
Subsidiary acquired by parent	Fair value.	Goodwill or negative goodwill at date of transfer.	Dividend recognised at fair value of the business. Investment written off or tested for impairment.
	Book value from consolidated accounts. (Note 3)	Goodwill as at date of original acquisition. (Note 3)	Catch up adjustment recognised fully in equity or as income, except that the element relating to a transaction recorded directly in equity may be recognised in equity. (Note 2) Investment written off or tested for impairment.

Notes

(1) If the parent established the subsidiary itself and its investment reflects only share capital it has injected, an excess of the carrying value over the net assets received will not be recognised as goodwill. This generally arises because of losses incurred by the transferred subsidiary.

If the subsidiary's net assets exceed the carrying value of the investment, then this will be due to profits or other comprehensive income retained in equity.

(2) The catch-up adjustment is not an equity transaction so all of it can be recognised in income. However, to the extent that it has arisen from a transaction that had occurred directly in equity, such as a revaluation, an entity can make a policy choice to recognise this element in equity. In this case the remaining amount is recognised in income. The entity can also take a view that as although the transfer of business is a current period transaction, the differences relate to prior period and hence should be recognised in equity.

(3) Because this was originally an acquisition, the values in the consolidated financial statements (and not the subsidiary's underlying records) become 'cost' for the parent. The assets and liabilities will reflect fair value adjustments made at the time of the business combination. Goodwill or negative goodwill will be the amount as at the date of the original acquisition.

If the business of the acquired subsidiary is transferred to the parent company as a distribution shortly after acquisition of that subsidiary, the accounting shall follow IAS 27 in relation to the dividend payment by the subsidiary. It might be accounted for effectively as a return of capital. The parent eliminates its investment in the subsidiary or part of its investment (based on the relative fair value of the business transferred compared to the value of the subsidiary), recognising instead the assets and liabilities of the business acquired at their fair value including the goodwill that has arisen on the business combination. The effect is to reflect the substance of the arrangement which is that the parent acquired a business. Comparative data is not restated in this case.

4.4.3.B Legal merger of parent and subsidiary

A legal merger can occur for numerous reasons, including facilitating a listing or structuring to transfer the borrowings obtained to acquire an entity to be repaid by the entity itself or to achieve tax benefits. Legal mergers are also referred to as 'hive up' or 'hive down' transactions. Legal mergers always affect the individual or separate financial statements of the entities involved. As legal mergers are not specifically discussed in IFRS, different views and approaches are encountered in practice.

In many jurisdictions it is possible to effect a 'legal merger' of a parent and its subsidiary whereby the two separate entities become a single entity without any issue of shares or other consideration. This is usually the case when there is a legal merger of a parent with its 100% owned subsidiary. Depending on the jurisdiction, different scenarios might take place.

It is not uncommon for a new entity to be formed as a vehicle used in the acquisition of an entity from a third party in a separate transaction. Subsequently both entities legally merge. Judgement is required to make an assessment as to whether a legal merger occurs 'close to' the date of acquisition, including considering the substance of the transaction and the reasons for structuring. If this is the case i.e. a new entity is formed concurrently with (or near the date of) the acquisition of a subsidiary, and there is a legal merger of the new entity and the subsidiary, these transactions are viewed as a single transaction in which a subsidiary is acquired and is discussed in Chapter 9.

Even though the substance of the legal merger may be the same, whether the survivor is the parent or subsidiary affects the accounting. The below discussion assumes that both the parent and subsidiary contain businesses.

a)   The parent is the surviving entity

The parent's consolidated financial statements

The legal merger of the parent and its subsidiary on its own does not affect the consolidated financial statements of the group. When non-controlling interests (NCI) are acquired in conjunction with the legal merger transaction, the transaction with the NCI holders is accounted for as a separate equity transaction (i.e. transactions with owners in their capacity as owners). [IFRS 10.23].

Even if there is no consolidated group after the legal merger, in our view, according to IFRS 10 consolidated financial statements are still required (including comparative financial statements) in the reporting period in which the legal merger occurs. Individual financial statements are the continuation of the consolidated group – in subsequent reporting periods, the amounts are carried forward from the consolidated financial statements (and shown as the comparatives in the individual financial statements).

In the reporting period in which the legal merger occurs the parent is also permitted, but not required, to present separate financial statements under IFRS.

Separate financial statements

In the parent's separate financial statements two approaches are available if the investment in the subsidiary was previously measured at cost. An entity chooses its policy and applies it consistently. Under both approaches, any amounts that were previously recognised in the parent's separate financial statements continue to be recognised at the same amount, except for the investment in the subsidiary that is merged into the parent.

The approaches to consider are as follows:

(i) The legal merger is in substance the distribution of the business from subsidiary to the parent.

The investment in the subsidiary is first re-measured to fair value as at the date of the legal merger, with any resulting gain or loss recognised in profit or loss. The investment in the subsidiary is then de-recognised. The acquired assets (including investments in subsidiaries, associates, or joint ventures held by the merged subsidiary) and assumed liabilities are recognised at fair value. Any difference gives rise to goodwill or income (bargain purchase, which is recognised in profit or loss).

(ii) The legal merger is in substance the redemption of shares in the subsidiary, in exchange for the underlying assets of the subsidiary.

Giving up the shares for the underlying assets is essentially a change in perspective of the parent of its investment, from a 'direct equity interest' to 'the reported results and net assets.' Hence, the values recognised in the consolidated financial statements become the cost of these assets for the parent. The acquired assets (including investments in subsidiaries, associates, or joint ventures held by the merged subsidiary) and assumed liabilities are recognised at the carrying amounts in the consolidated financial statements as of the date of the legal merger. This includes any associated goodwill, intangible assets, or other adjustments arising from measurement at fair value upon acquisition that were recognised when the subsidiary was originally acquired, less the subsequent related amortisation, depreciation, impairment losses, as applicable.

The difference between:

(1) the amounts assigned to the assets and liabilities in the parent's separate financial statements after the legal merger; and

(2) the carrying amount of the investment in the merged subsidiary before the legal merger;

is recognised in one of the following (accounting policy choice):

- profit or loss;
- directly in equity; or
- allocated to the appropriate component in the separate financial statements in the current period (e.g. current period profit or loss, current period other comprehensive income, or directly to equity) of the parent based on the component in which they were recognised in the financial statements of the merged subsidiary.

If the investment in the subsidiary was measured at fair value in the separate financial statements of the parent then only method (i) is applicable, because there is a direct swap of the investment with the underlying business. The parent would already have reflected the results of transactions that the subsidiary entered into since making its investment – depending on designation either in other comprehensive income or in profit or loss. Because the underlying investment in the subsidiary is de-recognised, this may trigger the reclassification within equity of any amounts previously recognised in other comprehensive income.

In the separate financial statements, regardless of which approaches or variety of approaches are used, comparative information should not be restated to include the merged subsidiary. The financial position and results of operations of the merged subsidiary are reflected in the separate financial statements only from the date on which the merger occurred.

b) The subsidiary is the surviving entity

Some argue that the legal form of a merger is more important in the context of the individual or separate financial statements of the subsidiary as these have a different purpose, being the financial statements of a legal entity. Others contend that as the legal mergers are not regulated in IFRS the accounting policy selected should reflect the economic substance of transactions, and not merely the legal form. This results in two possible approaches, the economic approach and the legal approach. The economic approach is on balance the approach that usually provides the more faithful representation of the transaction. The legal approach, may however be appropriate when facts and circumstances indicate that the needs of the users of the general-purpose financial statements after the legal merger are best served by using the financial statements of the surviving subsidiary as the predecessor financial statements. This need must outweigh the needs of users who previously relied upon the general-purpose financial statements of the parent (as such information might no longer be available e.g. where following the merger there is no group). Consideration is given as to whether either set of users can otherwise obtain the information needed using, for example, special-purpose financial statements.

(i) The economic approach

The legal merger between the parent and subsidiary is considered to have no substance. The amounts recognised after the legal merger are the amounts that were previously recognised in the consolidated financial statements, including goodwill and intangible assets recognised upon acquisition of that subsidiary. The consolidated financial statements after the legal merger also reflect any amounts in the consolidated financial statements (pre-merger) related to subsidiaries, associates, and joint ventures held by the surviving subsidiary. If the surviving subsidiary prepares separate financial statements after the legal merger, the subsidiary recognises the amounts that were previously recognised in the consolidated financial statements of the parent, as a contribution from the parent in equity.

(ii) The legal approach

The financial statements after the legal merger reflect the legal form of the transaction from the perspective of the subsidiary. There are two methods (as described below) with respect to recognising the identifiable assets acquired of the parent or liabilities assumed from the parent; regardless of which is used, amounts recognised previously in the consolidated financial statements with respect to the parent's acquisition of the surviving subsidiary (e.g. goodwill, intangible assets, fair value purchase price adjustments) are not recognised by the subsidiary. The surviving subsidiary does not recognise any change in the basis of subsidiaries, associates and joint ventures that it held before the legal merger unless its ownership following the merger increased.

Fair value method

If a merged parent meets a definition of business, the transaction is accounted for as an acquisition, with the consideration being a 'contribution' from the parent recognised in equity at fair value. Principles in IFRS 3 apply then by analogy.

The subsidiary recognises:

(1) the identifiable assets acquired and liabilities assumed from the parent at fair value;

(2) the fair value of the parent as a business as a contribution to equity; and

(3) the difference between (1) and (2) as goodwill or gain on a bargain purchase.

Book value method

Under this method the subsidiary accounts for the transaction as a contribution from the parent at book values. The subsidiary recognises the identifiable assets acquired or liabilities assumed from the parent at the historical carrying amounts and the difference is recognised in equity. The historical carrying amounts might be the carrying amounts previously recognised in the parent's separate financial statements, the amounts in the ultimate parent's consolidated financial statements, or in a sub-level consolidation (prior to the merger).

Whatever variation of the legal approach is applied, the subsidiary may not recognise amounts that were previously recognised in the consolidated financial statements that related to the operations of the subsidiary, because there is no basis in IFRS for the subsidiary to recognise fair value adjustments to its internally generated assets or goodwill that were recognised by its parent when it was first acquired. Therefore, the carrying amount of the assets (including investments in subsidiaries, associates, and joint ventures) and liabilities held by subsidiary are the same both before and after a legal merger (there is no revaluation to fair value). There is also no push-down accounting of any goodwill or fair value adjustments recognised in the consolidated financial statements related to the assets and liabilities of the subsidiary that were recognised when the parent acquired the subsidiary.

In the separate financial statements, regardless of which approaches, or variety of approaches are used, comparative information should not be restated to include the merged parent. The financial position and results of operations of the merged parent are reflected in the separate financial statements only from the date on which the merger occurred.

4.4.4 Incurring expenses and settling liabilities without recharges

Entities may incur costs that provide a benefit to fellow group entities, e.g. audit, management or advertising fees, and do not recharge the costs. The beneficiary is not party to the transaction and does not directly incur an obligation to settle a liability. It may elect to recognise the cost, in which case it will charge profit or loss and credit equity with equivalent amounts; there will be no change to its net assets. If the expense is incurred by the parent, it could elect to increase the investment in the subsidiary rather than expensing the amount. This could lead to a carrying value that might be impaired. Fellow subsidiaries may expense the cost or recognise a distribution to the parent directly in equity. There is no policy choice if the expense relates to a share-based payment, in which case IFRS 2 mandates that expenses incurred for a subsidiary be added to the carrying amount of the investment in the parent and be recognised by the subsidiary (see Chapter 34 at 12).

Many groups recharge expenses indirectly, by making management charges, or recoup the funds through intra-group dividends, and in these circumstances it would be inappropriate to recognise the transaction in any entity other than the one that makes the payment.

A parent or other group entity may settle a liability on behalf of a subsidiary. If this is not recharged, the liability will have been extinguished in the entity's accounts. This raises the question of whether the gain should be taken to profit or loss or to equity. IFRS 15 – *Revenue from Contracts with Customers* – defines income as increases in economic benefits during the accounting period in the form of inflows or enhancements of assets or decreases of liabilities that result in an increase in equity, other than those relating to contributions from equity participants. *[IFRS 15 Appendix A]*. Except in unusual circumstances, the forgiveness of debt will be a contribution from owners and therefore ought to be taken to equity.

It will usually be appropriate for a parent to add the payment to the investment in the subsidiary as a capital contribution, subject always to impairment of the investment but a parent may conclude that it is more appropriate to expense the cost. If one subsidiary settles a liability of its fellow subsidiary, both of the entities may choose to recognise an equity element in the transaction; one subsidiary recognises a capital contribution from the parent, while the other subsidiary recognises a distribution to the parent.

4.4.5 Financial instruments within the scope of IFRS 9

IFRS 9 (except for certain trade receivables) requires the initial recognition of financial assets and financial liabilities to be at fair value, *[IFRS 9.5.1.1]*, so management has no policy choice. Financial instruments arising from group transactions are initially recognised at their fair value, with any difference between the fair value and the terms of the agreement recognised as an equity transaction.

4.4.5.A Interest-free or non-market interest rate loans

Parents might lend money to subsidiaries on an interest-free or low-interest basis and *vice versa*. A feature of some intra-group payables is that they have no specified repayment terms and are therefore repayable on demand. The fair value of a financial liability with a demand feature is not less than the amount payable on demand, discounted from the first date that the amount could be required to be paid. This means that an intra-group loan payable on demand has a fair value that is the same as the cash consideration given.

Loans are recognised at fair value on initial recognition based on the market rate of interest for similar loans at the date of issue (see Chapter 49 at 3.3.1). *[IFRS 9.B5.1.1]*. The party making the loan has a receivable recorded at fair value and must on initial recognition account for the difference between the fair value and the loan amount.

If the party making the non-market loan is a parent, it adds this to the carrying value of its investment. The subsidiary will initially record a capital contribution in equity. Subsequently, the parent will recognise interest income and the subsidiary interest expense using the effective interest method so that the loan is stated at the amount receivable/repayable at the redemption date. When the loan is repaid, the overall effect in parent's financial statements is of a capital contribution made to the subsidiary as it has increased its investment and recognised income to the same extent (assuming, of course, no impairment). By contrast, the subsidiary has initially recognised a gain in equity that has been reversed as interest has been charged.

If the subsidiary makes the non-market loan to its parent, the difference between the loan amount and its fair value is treated as a distribution by the subsidiary to the parent, while the parent reflects a gain. Again, interest is recognised so that the loan is stated at the amount receivable and payable at the redemption date. This has the effect of reversing the initial gain or loss taken to equity. Note that the effects in the parent's financial statements are not symmetrical to those when it makes a loan at below market rates. The parent does not need to deduct the benefit it has received from the subsidiary from the carrying value of its investment.

The following example illustrates the accounting for a variety of intra-group loan arrangements.

Example 8.11: Interest-free and below market rate loans within groups

Entity S is a wholly owned subsidiary of Entity P. In each of the following scenarios one of the entities provides an interest free or below market rate loan to the other entity.

1. P provides an interest free loan in the amount of $100,000 to S. The loan is repayable on demand.

On initial recognition the receivable is measured at its fair value, which in this case is equal to the cash consideration given. The loan is classified as a current liability in the financial statements of the subsidiary. The classification in the financial statements of the parent depends upon management intention. If the parent had no intention of demanding repayment in the near term, the parent would classify the receivable as non-current in accordance with paragraph 66 of IAS 1.

If S makes an interest-free loan to parent, the accounting is the mirror image of that for the parent.

2. P provides an interest free loan in the amount of $100,000 to S. The loan is repayable when funds are available.

Generally, a loan that is repayable when funds are available will be classified as a liability. The classification of such a loan as current or non-current and the measurement at origination date will depend on the expectations of the parent and subsidiary of the availability of funds to repay the loan. If the loan is expected to be repaid in three years, measurement of the loan would be the same as in scenario 3.

If S makes an interest-free loan to parent, the accounting is the mirror image of that for the parent.

3. P provides an interest free loan in the amount of $100,000 to S. The loan is repayable in full after 3 years. The fair value of the loan (based on current market rates of 10%) is $75,131.

At origination, the difference between the loan amount and its fair value (present value using current market rates for similar instruments) is treated as an equity contribution to the subsidiary, which represents a further investment by the parent in the subsidiary.

Journal entries at origination:

		Parent	$	$
Dr		Loan receivable from subsidiary	75,131	
Dr		Investment in subsidiary	24,869	
	Cr	Cash		100,000

		Subsidiary	$	$
Dr		Cash	100,000	
	Cr	Loan payable to parent		75,131
	Cr	Equity – capital contribution		24,869

Journal entries during the periods to repayment:

	Parent	$	$
Dr	Loan receivable from subsidiary (Note 1)	7,513	
Cr	Profit or loss – notional interest		7,513

	Subsidiary	$	$
Dr	Profit or loss – notional interest	7,513	
Cr	Loan payable to parent		7,513

Note 1 Amounts represent year one assuming no payments before maturity. Year 2 and 3 amounts would be $8,264 and $9,092 respectively i.e. accreted at 10%. At the end of year 3, the recorded balance of the loan will be $100,000.

4. S provides a below market rate loan in the amount of $100,000 to P. The loan bears interest at 4% and is repayable in full after 3 years (i.e. $112,000 at the end of year 3). The fair value of the loan (based on current market rates of 10%) is $84,147.

At origination, the difference between the loan amount and its fair value is treated as a distribution from the subsidiary to the parent.

Journal entries at origination:

	Parent	$	$
Dr	Cash	100,000	
Cr	Loan payable to subsidiary		84,147
Cr	Profit or loss – distribution from subsidiary		15,853

	Subsidiary	$	$
Dr	Loan receivable from parent	84,147	
Dr	Retained earnings – distribution	15,853	
Cr	Cash		100,000

Journal entries during the periods to repayment:

	Parent	$	$
Dr	Profit or loss – notional interest	8,415	
Cr	Loan payable to subsidiary		8,415

	Subsidiary	$	$
Dr	Loan receivable from parent (Note 1)	8,415	
Cr	Profit or loss – notional interest		8,415

Note 1 Amounts represent year one assuming no payments before maturity. Year 2 and 3 amounts would be $9,256 and $10,182, respectively i.e. accreted at 10% such that at the end of year 3 the recorded balance of the loan will be $112,000 being the principal of the loan ($100,000) plus the interest payable in cash ($12,000).

4.4.5.B Financial guarantee contracts: parent guarantee issued on behalf of subsidiary

Financial guarantees given by an entity that are within the scope of IFRS 9 must be recognised initially at fair value. *[IFRS 9.5.1.1]*. If a parent or other group entity gives a guarantee on behalf of an entity, this must be recognised in its separate or individual financial statements. It is normally appropriate for a parent that gives a guarantee to treat the debit that arises on recognising the guarantee at fair value as an additional investment in its subsidiary. This is described in Chapter 49 at 3.4.

The situation is different for the subsidiary or fellow subsidiary that is the beneficiary of the guarantee. There will be no separate recognition of the financial guarantee unless it is provided to the lender separate and apart from the original borrowing, does not form part of the overall terms of the loan and would not transfer with the loan if it were assigned by the lender to a third party. This means that few guarantees will be reflected separately in the financial statements of the entities that benefit from the guarantees.

Example 8.12:   Financial guarantee contracts

A group consists of two entities, H plc (the parent) and S Ltd (H's wholly owned subsidiary). Entity H has a stronger credit rating than S Ltd. S Ltd is looking to borrow €100, repayable in five years. A bank has indicated it will charge interest of 7.5% per annum. However, the bank has offered to lend to S Ltd at a rate of 7.0% per annum if H plc provides a guarantee of S Ltd.'s debt to the bank and this is accepted by S Ltd. No charge was made by H plc to S Ltd in respect of the guarantee. The fair value of the guarantee is calculated at €2, which is the difference between the present value of the contractual payments discounted at 7.0% and 7.5%. If the bank were to assign the loan to S Ltd to a third party, the assignee would become party to both the contractual terms of the borrowing with S Ltd as well as the guarantee from H plc.

H plc will record the guarantee at its fair value of €2.

S Ltd will record its loan at fair value including the value of the guarantee provided by the parent. It will simply record the liability at €100 but will not recognise separately the guarantee provided by the parent.

If the guarantee was separate, S Ltd would record the liability at its fair value without the guarantee of €98 with the difference of €2 recorded as a capital contribution.

4.5   Disclosures

Where there have been significant transactions between entities under common control that are not on arm's length terms, it will be necessary for the entity to disclose its accounting policy for recognising and measuring such transactions.

IAS 24 applies whether or not a price has been charged so gifts of assets or services and asset swaps are within scope. Details and terms of the transactions must be disclosed (see Chapter 39 at 2.5).

References

1   *IFRIC Update*, March 2015, p.11.
2   *IFRIC Update*, March 2015, p.11.
3   *IFRIC Update*, March 2006, p.7.
4   Agenda paper for the meeting of the Accounting Regulatory Committee on 2nd February 2007 (document ARC/08/2007), *Subject: Relationship between the IAS Regulation and the 4th and 7th Company Law Directives – Can a company preparing both individual and consolidated accounts in accordance with adopted IFRS issue the individual accounts before the consolidated accounts?*, European Commission: Internal Market and Services DG: Free movement of capital, company law and corporate governance: Accounting/PB D(2006), 15 January 2007, para. 3.1.
5   *IFRIC Update*, March 2016, p.5.
6   *IFRIC Update*, July 2009, p.3.
7   *IFRIC Update*, September 2011, p.3.
8   Staff Paper, IFRS Interpretations Committee Meeting, July 2011, Agenda reference 7, *IAS 27 Consolidated and Separate Financial Statements – Group reorganisations in separate financial statements*, Appendix A.
9   *IFRIC Update*, January 2019, p.8.
10 *IFRIC Update*, January 2019, p.4.
11 *IFRIC Update*, January 2019, p.4.
12 *IASB Update*, June 2014, p.9.
13 *IASB Update*, October 2017, p.4.
14 Slide deck, ASAF Meeting, December 2017, Agenda ref 8A, *Business Combinations under Common Control, Scope of the project*, p.21.
15 IASB Work plan as at 21 September 2020.
16 *IFRIC Update*, September 2011, p.3.

17 IFRS Project report and Feedback Statement, December 2018, *Post-implementation Review of IFRS 13 Fair Value Measurement.*
18 *Equity Method in Separate Financial Statements* (Amendments to IAS 27), para. 4.
19 *Equity Method in Separate Financial Statements* (Amendments to IAS 27), para. 12.
20 *Equity Method in Separate Financial Statements* (Amendments to IAS 27), para. BC10G.

Chapter 9   Business combinations

1	INTRODUCTION 639	
	1.1 IFRS 3 (as revised in 2008) and subsequent amendments 640	
	1.1.1 Post-implementation review..642	
2	SCOPE OF IFRS 3 647	
	2.1 Mutual entities...647	
	2.2 Arrangements out of scope of IFRS 3...647	
	2.2.1 Formation of a joint arrangement..647	
	2.2.2 Acquisition of an asset or a group of assets that does not constitute a business 647	
	2.2.3 Business combinations under common control............................649	
3	IDENTIFYING A BUSINESS COMBINATION 650	
	3.1 Identifying a business combination..650	
	3.2 Definition of a business...650	
	3.2.1 Inputs, processes and outputs 650	
	3.2.2 Assessment whether acquired set of activities and assets constitutes a business 651	
	3.2.3 Concentration test..652	
	3.2.4 Assessing whether an acquired process is substantive 654	
	3.2.5 'Capable of' from the viewpoint of a market participant 655	
	3.2.6 Identifying business combinations 656	
	3.2.7 Development stage entities 658	
4	ACQUISITION METHOD OF ACCOUNTING.. 659	
	4.1 Identifying the acquirer 659	
	4.1.1 New entity formed to effect a business combination................. 660	
	4.1.2 Stapling arrangements 665	
	4.2 Determining the acquisition date 665	
5	RECOGNITION AND MEASUREMENT OF ASSETS ACQUIRED, LIABILITIES ASSUMED AND NON-CONTROLLING INTERESTS................... 666	

5.1	General principles		666
5.2	Recognising identifiable assets acquired and liabilities assumed		667
	5.2.1	Amendments to IFRS 3 – Reference to the Conceptual Framework (effective on or after 1 January 2022)	668
5.3	Acquisition-date fair values of identifiable assets acquired and liabilities assumed		669
5.4	Classifying or designating identifiable assets acquired and liabilities assumed		670
5.5	Recognising and measuring particular assets acquired and liabilities assumed		671
	5.5.1	Operating leases in which the acquiree is the lessor	671
	5.5.2	Intangible assets	672
		5.5.2.A Examples of identifiable intangible assets	673
		5.5.2.B Customer relationship intangible assets	675
		5.5.2.C Combining an intangible asset with a related contract, identifiable asset or liability	678
		5.5.2.D In-process research or development project expenditure	679
		5.5.2.E Emission rights	680
		5.5.2.F Determining the fair values of intangible assets	681
	5.5.3	Reacquired rights	684
	5.5.4	Assembled workforce and other items that are not identifiable	685
		5.5.4.A Assembled workforce	685
		5.5.4.B Items not qualifying as assets	685
	5.5.5	Assets with uncertain cash flows (valuation allowances)	686
	5.5.6	Assets that the acquirer does not intend to use or intends to use in a way that is different from other market participants	687
	5.5.7	Investments in equity-accounted entities	688
	5.5.8	Assets and liabilities related to contacts with customers	688
5.6	Exceptions to the recognition and/or measurement principles		690
	5.6.1	Contingent liabilities	690
		5.6.1.A Initial recognition and measurement	690
		5.6.1.B Subsequent measurement and accounting	691
	5.6.2	Income taxes	691
	5.6.3	Employee benefits	692
	5.6.4	Indemnification assets	693
		5.6.4.A Acquirer's obligation to transfer proceeds from realisation of acquired contingent asset ('Reverse indemnification liabilities')	694
	5.6.5	Reacquired rights	695

	5.6.6	Assets held for sale	695
	5.6.7	Share-based payment transactions	695
	5.6.8	Leases in which the acquiree is the lessee	696
	5.6.9	Insurance contracts within the scope of IFRS 17	696

6 RECOGNISING AND MEASURING GOODWILL OR A GAIN IN A BARGAIN PURCHASE 696

    6.1 Subsequent accounting for goodwill 697

7 CONSIDERATION TRANSFERRED 698

    7.1 Contingent consideration 699
        7.1.1 Initial recognition and measurement 700
            7.1.1.A Estimating an appropriate discount rate 703
        7.1.2 Classification of a contingent consideration obligation 704
        7.1.3 Subsequent measurement and accounting 706

    7.2 Replacement share-based payment awards 707
    7.3 Acquisition-related costs 707
    7.4 Business combinations achieved without the transfer of consideration 708
        7.4.1 Business combinations by contract alone 709
    7.5 Combinations involving mutual entities 709

8 RECOGNISING AND MEASURING NON-CONTROLLING INTERESTS 710

    8.1 Measuring qualifying non-controlling interests at acquisition-date fair value 711
    8.2 Measuring qualifying non-controlling interests at the proportionate share of the value of net identifiable assets acquired 711
    8.3 Implications of method chosen for measuring non-controlling interests 712
    8.4 Measuring share-based payment and other components of non-controlling interests 714
    8.5 Call and put options over non-controlling interests 715

9 BUSINESS COMBINATIONS ACHIEVED IN STAGES ('STEP ACQUISITIONS') 717

    9.1 Accounting for previously held interests in a joint operation 723

10 BARGAIN PURCHASE TRANSACTIONS 724

11 ASSESSING WHAT IS PART OF THE EXCHANGE FOR THE ACQUIREE 726

    11.1 Effective settlement of pre-existing relationships 728
    11.2 Remuneration for future services of employees or former owners of the acquiree 731
        11.2.1 Arrangements for contingent payments to employees or selling shareholders 731

	11.2.2	Share-based payment awards exchanged for awards held by the acquiree's employees	734
11.3		Reimbursement for paying the acquirer's acquisition-related costs	734
11.4		Restructuring plans	734
12 MEASUREMENT PERIOD			736
12.1		Adjustments made during measurement period to provisional amounts	737
12.2		Adjustments made after end of measurement period	738
13 SUBSEQUENT MEASUREMENT AND ACCOUNTING			739
14 REVERSE ACQUISITIONS			739
14.1		Measuring the consideration transferred	740
14.2		Measuring goodwill	742
14.3		Preparation and presentation of consolidated financial statements	742
14.4		Non-controlling interest	745
14.5		Earnings per share	746
14.6		Cash consideration	747
14.7		Share-based payments	749
14.8		Reverse acquisitions involving a non-trading shell company	749
14.9		Reverse acquisitions and acquirers that are not legal entities	751
15 PUSH DOWN ACCOUNTING			752
16 DISCLOSURES			753
16.1		Nature and financial effect of business combinations	753
	16.1.1	Business combinations during the current reporting period	753
	16.1.2	Business combinations effected after the end of the reporting period	755
16.2		Financial effects of adjustments recognised in the current reporting period	756
16.3		Other necessary information	757
16.4		Illustrative disclosures	757

List of examples

Example 9.1:	Acquisition of wind farm – concentration test (1)	653
Example 9.2:	Acquisition of wind and solar farms – concentration test (2)	653
Example 9.3:	Extractive industries – definition of a business (1)	656
Example 9.4:	Extractive industries – definition of a business (2)	656
Example 9.5:	Real estate – definition of a business (1)	657

Example 9.6:	Real estate – definition of a business (2)	657
Example 9.7:	Life sciences – definition of a business (1)	658
Example 9.8:	Life sciences – definition of a business (2)	659
Example 9.9:	Business combination effected by a Newco for cash consideration (1)	661
Example 9.10:	Business combination effected by a Newco for cash consideration: spin-off transaction (2)	662
Example 9.11:	Newco formed to facilitate a debt-to-equity swap transaction	663
Example 9.12:	Customer relationship intangible assets	675
Example 9.13:	Acquirer's intention not to use an intangible asset	687
Example 9.14:	Contract liability of an acquiree	689
Example 9.15:	Reverse indemnification liability	695
Example 9.16:	Contingent consideration – applying the probability-weighted payout approach to determine fair value	702
Example 9.17:	Share-settled contingent consideration – financial liability or equity?	706
Example 9.18:	Initial measurement of non-controlling interests in a business combination (1)	712
Example 9.19:	Initial measurement of non-controlling interests in a business combination (2)	713
Example 9.20:	Measurement of non-controlling interest represented by preference shares and employee share options	715
Example 9.21:	Business combination achieved in stages – original investment treated as FVOCI without recycling	718
Example 9.22:	Business combination achieved in stages – original investment treated as an associate under IAS 28	720
Example 9.23:	Business combination achieved in stages – loss arising on step-acquisition	723
Example 9.24:	Gain on a bargain purchase (1)	725
Example 9.25:	Gain on a bargain purchase (2)	726
Example 9.26:	Settlement of pre-existing non-contractual relationship	729
Example 9.27:	Settlement of pre-existing contractual relationship – Supply contract	729
Example 9.28:	Settlement of pre-existing contractual relationship – Loan agreement	730
Example 9.29:	Settlement of pre-existing contractual relationship – Reacquired technology licensing agreement	730
Example 9.30:	Contingent payments to employees	733
Example 9.31:	Recognition or otherwise of a restructuring liability as part of a business combination	735
Example 9.32:	Adjustments made during measurement period to provisional amounts	737
Example 9.33:	Identification of an asset during measurement period	738

Example 9.34:	Reverse acquisition – calculating the fair value of the consideration transferred 740
Example 9.35:	Reverse acquisition – measuring goodwill (1) 742
Example 9.36:	Reverse acquisition – measuring goodwill (2) 742
Example 9.37:	Reverse acquisition – consolidated statement of financial position immediately after the business combination 744
Example 9.38:	Reverse acquisition – non-controlling interest 745
Example 9.39:	Reverse acquisition – earnings per share 747
Example 9.40:	Reverse acquisition effected with cash consideration 748
Example 9.41:	Reverse acquisition of a non-trading shell company 751
Example 9.42:	Footnote X: Acquisitions 758

Chapter 9   Business combinations

1   INTRODUCTION

A business combination is defined by the IASB ('the Board') as a 'transaction or other event in which an acquirer obtains control of one or more businesses'. *[IFRS 3 Appendix A]*.

Over the years, business combinations have been defined in different ways. Whatever definition has been applied, it includes circumstances in which an entity obtains control of an integrated set of activities and assets that constitute a business.

In accounting terms there have traditionally been two distinctly different forms of reporting the effects of a business combination; the purchase method of accounting (or acquisition method of accounting) and the pooling of interests method (or merger accounting).

The two methods of accounting look at business combinations through quite different eyes. An acquisition was seen as the absorption of the target by the acquirer; there is continuity only of the acquiring entity, in the sense that only the post-acquisition results of the target are reported as earnings of the acquiring entity and the comparative figures remain those of the acquiring entity. In contrast, a pooling of interests or merger is seen as the pooling together of two formerly distinct shareholder groups; in order to present continuity of both entities there is retrospective restatement to show the enlarged entity as if the two entities had always been together, by combining the results of both entities pre- and post-combination and also by restatement of the comparatives. However, the pooling of interests method has fallen out of favour with standard setters, including the IASB, as they consider virtually all business combinations as being acquisitions. The purchase method has become the established method of accounting for business combinations. Nevertheless, the pooling of interests method is still sometimes used for business combinations involving entities under common control where the transactions have been scoped out of the relevant standard dealing with business combinations (see Chapter 10).

The other main issues facing accountants have been in relation to accounting for an acquisition. Broadly speaking, the acquiring entity has had to determine the fair values of the identifiable assets and liabilities of the target. Depending on what items are included within this allocation process and what values are placed on them, this will result in a difference to the consideration given that has to be accounted for. Where the amounts allocated to the assets and liabilities are less than the overall consideration given, the difference is accounted for as goodwill. Goodwill is an asset that is not amortised, but subjected to some form of impairment test, although some national standards still require amortisation. Where the consideration given is less than the values allocated to the identifiable assets and liabilities, the issue has then been whether and, if so, when, such a credit should be taken to the income statement.

1.1 IFRS 3 (as revised in 2008) and subsequent amendments

This chapter discusses IFRS 3 – *Business Combinations* – as revised in 2008 and amended subsequently and its associated Basis for Conclusions and Illustrative Examples.

The specific requirements of IAS 38 – *Intangible Assets* – relating to intangible assets acquired as part of a business combination accounted for under IFRS 3 are dealt with as part of the discussion of IFRS 3 in this chapter; the other requirements of IAS 38 are covered in Chapter 17. Impairment of goodwill is addressed in Chapter 20 at 8.

In May 2011, the IASB issued a series of IFRSs that deal broadly with consolidated financial statements. IFRS 10 – *Consolidated Financial Statements* – is a single standard addressing consolidation. The requirements of IFRS 10 are discussed in Chapters 6 and 7 which address, respectively, its consolidation requirements and consolidation procedures. Some consequential amendments were made to IFRS 3, principally to reflect that the guidance on 'control' within IFRS 10 is to be used to identify the acquirer in a business combination.

IFRS 13 – *Fair Value Measurement* – changed the definition of 'fair value' to an explicit exit value, but it did not change when fair value is required or permitted under IFRS. Its impact on IFRS 3 is considered at 5.3 below and reference should be made to Chapter 14 for a full discussion. Unless otherwise indicated, references to fair value in this chapter are to fair value as defined by IFRS 13.

In October 2012, the IASB amended IFRS 10 to provide an exception to the consolidation requirement for entities that meet the definition of an investment entity. As a result of this amendment, the scope of IFRS 3 was also amended. The investment entities exception is discussed in Chapter 6 at 10.

In December 2013, the IASB issued two cycles of Annual Improvements – *Cycles 2010-2012* and *2011-2013* – that had the following impact on IFRS 3:
- Contingent consideration in a business combination that is not classified as equity is subsequently measured at fair value through profit or loss whether or not it falls within the scope of IFRS 9 – *Financial Instruments* (see 7.1.2 and 7.1.3 below).
- The formation of joint arrangements, both joint operations and joint ventures, is outside the scope of IFRS 3. The amendment has also clarified that the scope exception applies only to the accounting in the financial statements of the joint arrangement itself (see 2.2.1 below).
- A clarification that the guidance on ancillary services in IAS 40 – *Investment Property*, [IAS 40.11-14], is intended to distinguish an investment property from an owner-occupied property, not whether a transaction is a business combination or an asset acquisition (see 3.2.6 below).

As a result of the issue of IFRS 15 – *Revenue from Contracts with Customers* – in May 2014, a consequential amendment has been made to the requirements for the subsequent measurement of a contingent liability recognised in a business combination (see 5.6.1.B below).

Some consequential amendments have been made to IFRS 3 as a result of the issue of IFRS 9. These relate principally to the requirements for:
- classifying or designating identifiable assets acquired and liabilities assumed (see 5.4 below);
- business combinations achieved in stages (see 9 below); and
- contingent consideration classified as an asset or liability (see 7.1 below).

In January 2016, the IASB issued IFRS 16 – *Leases* – which requires lessees to recognise assets and liabilities for most leases under a single accounting model (i.e. no classification of a lease contract as either operating or finance lease for lessees). For lessors there is little change to the existing accounting in IAS 17 – *Leases*. A number of consequential amendments have been made to IFRS 3 in respect of leases accounted for under IFRS 16. These relate to the requirements for:
- classifying or designating identifiable assets acquired and liabilities assumed (see 5.4 below);
- recognising and measuring particular assets acquired and liabilities assumed (see 5.5.1 below); and
- exceptions to the recognition and/or measurement principles (see 5.6.8 below).

In May 2017, the IASB issued IFRS 17 – *Insurance Contracts*. IFRS 17 replaces IFRS 4 – *Insurance Contracts* – and is effective for reporting periods beginning on or after 1 January 2023, with early application permitted. IFRS 17 introduced a new exception to measurement principles in IFRS 3 (see 5.6.9 below).

In December 2017, the IASB issued amendments to IFRS 3 and IFRS 11 – *Joint Arrangements* – as part of the *Annual Improvements to IFRS Standards 2015-2017 Cycle*. The amendments clarified how a party to a joint operation accounts for a transaction in which it obtains control of a joint operation that constitutes a business (see 9.1 below).

In October 2018, as a result of the *Post Implementation Review of IFRS 3*, the IASB issued narrow-scope amendments to IFRS 3 to address the challenges in applying the definition of a business. In particular, the amendments clarified the minimum requirements for a business (under the amended definition a business can exist without including all of the inputs and processes needed to create outputs), removed the assessment of whether market participants are capable of replacing any missing elements, narrowed the definitions of a business and outputs by excluding from the definition of outputs returns in the form of lower costs, introduced an optional fair value concentration test (see 3.2.3 below for details) and added guidance to help entities assess whether an acquired process is substantive. The amended requirements are further discussed in 3.2 below.

In May 2020, the IASB issued amendments to IFRS 3 to update the reference to the *Conceptual Framework for Financial Reporting* issued in March 2018 (*2018 Conceptual Framework*). Further, the amendments added an exception to the recognition principle of IFRS 3 to avoid the issue of potential 'day 2' gains or losses arising for liabilities and contingent liabilities that would be within the scope of IAS 37 – *Provisions, Contingent Liabilities and Contingent Assets* – or IFRIC 21 – *Levies*, if incurred separately. The amendments also clarified guidance for contingent assets. The amendments are effective for annual reporting periods beginning on or after 1 January 2022 and apply prospectively. Earlier application is permitted. The existing and amended requirements are further discussed in 5.2 and 5.6.1 below.

1.1.1 Post-implementation review

In June 2015, the IASB completed the post-implementation review (PIR) of IFRS 3. The PIR was conducted in two phases. The first phase, which consisted of an initial assessment of all the issues that arose on the implementation of IFRS 3 and a consultation with interested parties about those issues, identified the main questions to be addressed in the PIR of IFRS 3. In the second phase the IASB considered the comments received from a *Request for Information – Post-Implementation Review: IFRS 3 Business Combinations*, along with the information gathered through other consultative activities and a review of relevant academic studies.

In June 2015, the IASB issued its *Report and Feedback Statement – Post-implementation Review of IFRS 3 Business Combinations* (RFS), which summarised the PIR process, the feedback received and conclusions reached by the IASB. The review of academic literature provided evidence that generally supported the current requirement on business combinations accounting, particularly in relation to the usefulness of reported goodwill, other intangible assets and goodwill impairment. However, investors expressed mixed views on certain aspects of the current accounting, including subsequent accounting for goodwill, separate recognition of intangible assets, measurement of non-controlling interests and subsequent accounting for contingent consideration. Also, many investors do not support the current requirements on step acquisitions and loss of control, and are asking for additional information about the subsequent performance of an acquired business. Many preparers, auditors and regulators identified implementation challenges in the requirements. In particular, applying the definition of a business, measuring the fair value of contingent consideration, contingent liabilities and intangible assets, testing goodwill for impairment on an annual basis and accounting for contingent payments to selling shareholders who become employees.[1]

Taking into account all of the evidence collected, the IASB decided to add to its research agenda the following areas of focus, assessed as being of high significance:

- effectiveness and complexity of testing goodwill for impairment;
- subsequent accounting for goodwill (i.e. impairment-only approach compared with an amortisation and impairment approach);
- challenges in applying the definition of a business; and
- identification and fair value measurement of intangible assets such as customer relationships and brand names.[2]

The narrow scope amendments issued by the IASB in October 2018 help entities determine whether an acquired set of activities and assets is a business or not. The amendments clarified the minimum requirements to be a business, removed the assessment of a market participant's ability to replace missing elements, and narrowed the definition of outputs. They also added guidance to assess whether an acquired process is substantive and introduced an optional concentration test to permit a simplified assessment. New illustrative examples were also added to explain application of the amended requirements (see 3.2 below).

The other three areas of high significance listed above are being considered by the IASB within its *Goodwill and Impairment* research project. In July 2018, the IASB set three research objectives for the research project:

- to explore ways to improve disclosure requirements to enable investors to assess whether a business combination was a good investment decision and whether, after the acquisition, the acquired business is performing as was expected at the time of the acquisition;
- to improve the calculation of value in use in IAS 36 – *Impairment of Assets*; and
- to simplify the accounting for goodwill.[3]

In addition, at that meeting, the IASB tentatively decided to issue a discussion paper (DP) as the research project's next step.

In March 2020 the IASB published the DP *Business Combinations – Disclosures, Goodwill and Impairment*. The DP sets out the IASB's preliminary views on how companies can provide better information so that investors can hold management to account for acquisitions of other companies. The preliminary views focus on disclosure of information and on accounting for goodwill. These are summarised in the table below:[4]

Area for discussion	The IASB's preliminary views:
Better disclosures for business combinations	<ul><li>require entities to disclose management's objectives for acquisitions in the year of acquisition and how acquisitions have performed against those objectives in subsequent periods;</li><li>require entities to disclose information about acquisitions monitored by their chief operating decision maker, as described in IFRS 8 – Operating Segments. Information should not be created solely for external reporting;</li><li>an entity should continue to provide information about an acquisition for as long as its chief operating decision maker continues to monitor the acquisition against its objectives. If the chief operating decision maker does not monitor an acquisition or stops monitoring it shortly after the acquisition occurred, the entity would be required to disclose this fact and explain why;</li><li>require entities to describe synergies management expected from an acquisition and disclose the estimated amount of synergies, or range of amounts. This information would help investors to better understand the factors that contributed to the acquisition price;</li><li>require entities to disclose the amount of defined benefit pension and debt liabilities taken over in the acquired business, separately from other classes of liabilities. This information would help investors assess companies' return on capital employed.</li></ul>

Improving the effectiveness of the impairment test for goodwill	• is not feasible to improve significantly the effectiveness of the impairment test for goodwill at a reasonable cost to entities; • it is not possible to eliminate shielding from the impairment test because goodwill has to be tested for impairment together with other assets and these groups of assets could contain headroom. Goodwill is 'shielded' from impairment because the headroom of the business with which an acquired business is integrated absorbs the decline in the recoverable amount of the acquired business; • the impairment test cannot always signal how well the acquired business is performing. If the impairment test is performed well, the test can be expected to achieve its objective of ensuring that the carrying amount of a group of assets containing goodwill as a whole is not higher than its recoverable amount; • if estimates of future cash flows are too optimistic (point of criticism was raised by the stakeholders in relation to that), this is best addressed by auditors and regulators, not by changing IFRS Standards. Entities are required by IAS 36 to use reasonable and supportable estimates when performing an impairment test.
Re-introduction of amortisation of goodwill	• retain the existing impairment-only model for the subsequent accounting for goodwill. The IASB believes that there is no compelling evidence that amortising goodwill would result in a significant improvement in financial reporting. However, the majority for this decision was small, so the IASB is interested in stakeholders' views on this topic.

Area for discussion	The IASB's preliminary views:
Relief from the mandatory annual impairment test	• remove the requirement to carry out an annual quantitative impairment test for goodwill when no indicator of impairment exists; but • continue to require an entity to assess whether any such indication exists. The IASB believes the change would not make the test significantly less robust because when there is no indication of impairment it is unlikely that the quantitative test would identify large impairment losses and performing the test every year cannot remove shielding.
Value in use – cash flows from a future restructuring or a future enhancement	• remove the requirement in IAS 36, that excludes from the estimation of value in use of an asset (or a cash-generating unit), the cash flows that are expected to arise from a future restructuring or a future enhancement. The cash flow forecasts would still need to be reasonable and supportable.
Value in use – use of post-tax inputs	• allow the use of post-tax discount rates and post-tax cash flows.
Presentation of a total equity before goodwill	• require entities to present on the balance sheet the amount of total equity excluding goodwill. The amount of total equity excluding goodwill may not fit easily into all balance sheet formats as a subtotal. However, there could be other ways an entity could present the amount on the balance sheet. For example, the amount of total equity excluding goodwill could be presented on the balance sheet as a free-standing amount.
Recognising acquired intangible assets separately from goodwill	• the requirements in IFRS 3 and IAS 38 on separate recognition of acquired intangible assets should be retained. When it issued IFRS 3, the IASB broadened the range of acquired intangible assets recognised separately from goodwill. The IASB believes that it has no compelling evidence that it should change the range of intangible assets recognised in a business combination.

The IASB has asked for feedback on its preliminary views by 31 December 2020. Feedback will help the IASB decide whether and how to develop detailed proposals in the next stage of the project. At the time of writing, the IASB's work plan indicated that Discussion Paper Feedback is expected in the first half of 2021.[5]

2 SCOPE OF IFRS 3

Entities are required to apply the provisions of IFRS 3 to transactions or other events that meet the definition of a business combination (see 3.1 below). *[IFRS 3.2]*.

2.1 Mutual entities

The acquisition method of accounting applies to combinations involving only mutual entities (e.g. mutual insurance companies, credit unions and cooperatives) and combinations in which separate entities are brought together by contract alone (e.g. dual listed corporations and stapled entity structures). *[IFRS 3.BC58]*. The IASB considers that the attributes of mutual entities are not sufficiently different from those of investor-owned entities to justify a different method of accounting for business combinations between two mutual entities. It also considers that such combinations are economically similar to business combinations involving two investor-owned entities and should be similarly reported. *[IFRS 3.BC71-BC72]*. Similarly, the IASB has concluded that the acquisition method should be applied for combinations achieved by contract alone. *[IFRS 3.BC79]*. Additional guidance is given in IFRS 3 for applying the acquisition method to such business combinations (see 7.4 and 7.5 below).

2.2 Arrangements out of scope of IFRS 3

The standard does not apply to:

(a) the accounting for the formation of a joint arrangement in the financial statements of the joint arrangement itself (see Chapter 11 at 7.6.5.B and 2.2.1 below for details);

(b) the acquisition of an asset or a group of assets that does not constitute a business (see 2.2.2 below for details);

(c) a combination of entities or businesses under common control (see Chapter 10); or

(d) the acquisition by an investment entity, as defined in IFRS 10 (see Chapter 6 at 10.1), of an investment in subsidiary that is required to be measured at fair value through profit or loss. *[IFRS 3.2, 2A]*.

2.2.1 Formation of a joint arrangement

The scope exception of IFRS 3 for the formation of a joint arrangement relates only to the accounting in the financial statements of the joint arrangement, i.e. the joint venture or joint operation (see Chapter 11 at 7.6.5.B for details), and not to the accounting for the joint venturer's or joint operator's interest in the joint arrangement. *[IFRS 3.BC61B-BC61D]*.

By contrast, a particular type of arrangement in which the owners of multiple businesses agree to combine their businesses into a new entity (sometimes referred to as a roll-up transaction) does not include a contractual agreement requiring unanimous consent to decisions about the relevant activities. Majority consent on such decisions is not sufficient to create a joint arrangement. Therefore, such arrangements should be accounted for by the acquisition method. *[IFRS 3.BC60]*.

2.2.2 Acquisition of an asset or a group of assets that does not constitute a business

Although the acquisition of an asset or a group of assets is not within the scope of IFRS 3, in such cases the acquirer has to identify and recognise the individual identifiable assets acquired (including intangible assets) and liabilities assumed. The cost of the group is allocated to the individual identifiable assets and liabilities on the basis of their relative fair values at the date of purchase. These transactions or events do not give rise to goodwill. *[IFRS 3.2]*. Thus, existing book values or values in the acquisition agreement may not be appropriate.

The cost of the group of assets is the sum of all consideration given and any non-controlling interest recognised. If the non-controlling interest has a present ownership interest and is entitled to a proportionate share of net assets upon liquidation, the acquirer has a choice to recognise the non-controlling interest at its proportionate share of net assets, its proportionate share of the consolidated book values of the net assets including or excluding transaction costs or its fair value; in all other cases, non-controlling interest is recognised at fair value, unless another measurement basis is required in accordance with IFRS. An example could be the acquisition of an incorporated entity that holds a single property, where this is assessed not to be a business (see Chapter 7 at 3.1.1).

It may be difficult to determine whether or not an acquired asset or a group of assets constitutes a business (see 3.2 below), yet this decision can have a considerable impact on an entity's reported results and the presentation of its financial statements; accounting for a business combination under IFRS 3 differs from accounting for an asset(s) acquisition in a number of important respects:

- goodwill or a gain on bargain purchase only arise on business combinations;
- assets acquired and liabilities assumed are generally accounted for at fair value in a business combination, while they are generally assigned a carrying amount based on their relative fair values in an asset acquisition;
- directly attributable acquisition-related costs are expensed if they relate to a business combination, but are generally capitalised as part of the cost of the asset in an asset acquisition;
- while deferred tax assets and liabilities must be recognised if the transaction is a business combination, they are not recognised under IAS 12 – *Income Taxes* – if it is an asset acquisition (see Chapter 33 at 7.2);
- where the consideration is in the form of shares, IFRS 2 – *Share-based Payment* – does not apply in a business combination, but will apply in an asset acquisition;
- another difference may arise where the transaction involves contingent consideration. While IFRS 3 provides guidance on the accounting for contingent consideration in the acquisition of a business (see 7.1 below), IAS 16 – *Property, Plant and Equipment* – and IAS 38 provide no clear guidance on accounting for contingent consideration in an asset(s) acquisition (see Chapter 17 at 4.5 and Chapter 18 at 4.1.9); and
- disclosures are much more onerous for business combinations than for asset acquisitions.

The accounting differences above will not only affect the accounting as of the acquisition date, but will also have an impact on future depreciation, possible impairment and other costs.

In November 2017, the Interpretations Committee issued an agenda decision that clarified how an entity accounts for the acquisition of a group of assets that does not constitute a business. More specifically, the submitter of the request asked for clarity on how to allocate the transaction price to the identifiable assets acquired and liabilities assumed when:

(a) the sum of the individual fair values of the identifiable assets and liabilities is different from the transaction price; and

(b) the group includes identifiable assets and liabilities initially measured both at cost and at an amount other than cost.

The Interpretations Committee concluded that a reasonable reading of the requirements in paragraph 2(b) of IFRS 3 on the acquisition of a group of assets that does not constitute a business results in one of the following two approaches:

(a) Under the first approach, an entity accounts for the acquisition of the group as follows:
  (i) it identifies the individual identifiable assets acquired and liabilities assumed that it recognises at the date of the acquisition;
  (ii) it determines the individual transaction price for each identifiable asset and liability by allocating the cost of the group based on the relative fair values of those assets and liabilities at the date of the acquisition; and then
  (iii) it applies the initial measurement requirements in applicable IFRSs to each identifiable asset acquired and liability assumed. The entity accounts for any difference between the amount at which the asset or liability is initially measured and its individual transaction price applying the relevant requirements.

(b) Under the second approach, for any identifiable asset or liability initially measured at an amount other than cost, an entity initially measures that asset or liability at the amount specified in the applicable standard. The entity deducts from the transaction price of the group the amounts allocated to the assets and liabilities initially measured at an amount other than cost, and then allocates the residual transaction price to the remaining identifiable assets and liabilities based on their relative fair values at the date of the acquisition.

The Interpretations Committee also concluded that an entity should apply its reading of the requirements consistently to all such acquisitions and an entity would also disclose the selected approach applying paragraphs 117–124 of IAS 1 – *Presentation of Financial Statements* – if that disclosure would assist users of financial statements in understanding how those transactions are reflected in reported financial performance and financial position.[6]

2.2.3 Business combinations under common control

The application guidance in Appendix B to IFRS 3 gives some guidance on accounting for business combinations involving entities or businesses under common control and therefore excluded from the requirements of the standard. *[IFRS 3.B1-B4]*. These arrangements are discussed further in Chapter 10.

3 IDENTIFYING A BUSINESS COMBINATION

IFRS 3 requires an entity to determine whether a transaction or event is a *business combination;* the definition requires that the assets acquired and liabilities assumed constitute a *business*. If the assets acquired and liabilities assumed do not constitute a business, the transaction is to be accounted for as an asset acquisition (see 2.2.2 above). *[IFRS 3.3]*.

3.1 Identifying a business combination

IFRS 3 defines a business combination as a 'transaction or other event in which an acquirer obtains control of one or more businesses'. *[IFRS 3 Appendix A]*.

IFRS 3 notes that an acquirer might obtain control of an acquiree (i.e. the business or businesses over which the acquirer obtains control) in a variety of ways, for example:

(a) transferring cash, cash equivalents or other assets (including net assets that constitute a business);

(b) incurring liabilities;

(c) issuing equity interests;

(d) providing more than one type of consideration; or

(e) without transferring consideration – including by contract alone (see 7.4 below). *[IFRS 3.B5]*.

A business combination may be structured in a variety of ways for legal, taxation or other reasons, which include but are not limited to:

(a) one or more businesses become subsidiaries of an acquirer or the net assets of one or more businesses are legally merged into the acquirer;

(b) one combining entity transfers its net assets, or its owners transfer their equity interests, to another combining entity or its owners;

(c) all of the combining entities transfer their net assets, or the owners of those entities transfer their equity interests, to a newly formed entity (sometimes referred to as a roll-up or put-together transaction); or

(d) a group of former owners of one of the combining entities obtains control of the combined entity. *[IFRS 3.B6]*.

3.2 Definition of a business

IFRS 3 defines a business as 'an integrated set of activities and assets that is capable of being conducted and managed for the purpose of providing goods or services to customers, generating investment income (such as dividends or interest) or generating other income from ordinary activities'. *[IFRS 3 Appendix A]*.

3.2.1 Inputs, processes and outputs

The application guidance to IFRS 3 describes the components of a business as inputs and processes applied to those inputs that have the ability to contribute to the creation of outputs. The three elements are described as follows:

- *Input*

    Any economic resource that creates outputs or has the ability to contribute to the creation of outputs when one or more processes are applied to it. Examples include non-current assets (including intangible assets or rights to use non-current assets), intellectual property, the ability to obtain access to necessary materials or rights and employees.

- *Process*

    Any system, standard, protocol, convention or rule is a process if, when applied to an input or inputs, it either creates or has the ability to contribute to the creation of outputs. Examples include strategic management processes, operational processes and resource management processes. These processes typically are documented, but the intellectual capacity of an organised workforce having the necessary skills and experience following rules and conventions may provide the necessary processes that are capable of being applied to inputs to create outputs. Accounting, billing, payroll and other administrative systems typically are not processes used to create outputs so their presence or exclusion generally will not affect whether an acquired set of activities and assets is considered a business.

- *Output*

    The result of inputs and processes applied to those inputs that provide goods or services to customers, generate investment income (such as dividends or interest) or generate other income from ordinary activities. *[IFRS 3.B7]*.

Although businesses usually have outputs, outputs need not be present at the acquisition date for an integrated set of activities and assets to be identified as a business. *[IFRS 3.B8]*. The nature of the elements of a business varies by industry and by the structure of an entity's operations (activities), including the entity's stage of development. Established businesses often have many different types of inputs, processes and outputs, whereas new businesses often have few inputs and processes and sometimes only a single output (product). Nearly all businesses also have liabilities, but a business need not have liabilities. Furthermore, an acquired set of activities and assets that is not a business as defined, might have liabilities. *[IFRS 3.B9]*.

3.2.2 Assessment whether acquired set of activities and assets constitutes a business

To assess whether a transaction is the acquisition of a business, an entity may apply first a quantitative concentration test (also known as a screening test). The entity is not required to apply the test but may elect to do so separately for each transaction or other event.

If the concentration test is met, the set of activities and assets is determined not to be a business and no further assessment is required. Otherwise, or if the entity elects not to apply the test, the entity shall perform the qualitative analysis of whether an acquired set of assets and activities includes at a minimum, an input and a substantive process that together significantly contribute to the ability to create outputs. *[IFRS 3.B7A]*.

The concentration test is further discussed at 3.2.3 below and assessment of whether an acquired process is substantive is considered at 3.2.4 below.

3.2.3 Concentration test

IFRS 3 sets out an optional concentration test designed to simplify the evaluation of whether an acquired set of activities and assets is not a business. An acquired set of activities and assets is not a business if substantially all of the fair value of the gross assets acquired is concentrated in a single identifiable asset or group of similar identifiable assets. IFRS 3 notes that for the purposes of the concentration test:

(a) gross assets acquired exclude cash and cash equivalents, deferred tax assets, and goodwill resulting from the effects of deferred tax liabilities;

(b) the fair value of the gross assets acquired includes any consideration transferred (plus the fair value of any non-controlling interest and the fair value of any previously held interest) in excess of the fair value of net identifiable assets acquired. The fair value of the gross assets acquired may normally be determined as the total obtained by adding the fair value of the consideration transferred (plus the fair value of any non-controlling interest and the fair value of any previously held interest) to the fair value of the liabilities assumed (other than deferred tax liabilities), and then excluding the items identified in subparagraph (a) above. However, if the fair value of the gross assets acquired is more than that total, a more precise calculation may sometimes be needed;

(c) a single identifiable asset includes any asset or group of assets that would be recognised and measured as a single identifiable asset in a business combination;

(d) if a tangible asset is attached to, and cannot be physically removed and used separately from, another tangible asset (or from an underlying asset subject to a lease, as defined in IFRS 16), without incurring significant cost, or significant diminution in utility or fair value to either asset (for example, land and buildings), those assets are considered a single identifiable asset;

(e) when assessing whether assets are similar, an entity considers the nature of each single identifiable asset and the risks associated with managing and creating outputs from the assets (that is, the risk characteristics);

(f) the following are not considered similar assets:
   (i) a tangible asset and an intangible asset;
   (ii) tangible assets in different classes (for example, inventory, manufacturing equipment and automobiles) unless they are considered a single identifiable asset in accordance with the criterion in subparagraph (d) above;
   (iii) identifiable intangible assets in different classes (for example, brand names, licences and intangible assets under development);
   (iv) a financial asset and a non-financial asset;
   (v) financial assets in different classes (for example, accounts receivable and investments in equity instruments); and
   (vi) identifiable assets that are within the same class of asset but have significantly different risk characteristics. *[IFRS 3.B7B]*.

In addition, IFRS 3 clarifies that the requirements above do not modify the guidance on similar assets in IAS 38; or the meaning of the term 'class' in IAS 16, IAS 38 and IFRS 7 – *Financial Instruments: Disclosures*. [IFRS 3.B7C].

Examples 9.1 and 9.2 below illustrate application of the guidance on the concentration test to the specific scenarios.

Example 9.1:   Acquisition of wind farm – concentration test (1)

Greentech A acquires all outstanding shares of Greentech B, which owns 25 windmills of similar types and specifications that each have an in-place lease. The fair value of the consideration paid is equal to the aggregate fair value of the 25 windmills acquired. Each windmill includes the land leased from the local authority and a wind turbine. All windmills are in the same wind farm and leased out to the small local olive oil producers under the mid-term contracts. The local oil producers are from the same area and are similar in all other respects. No employees, other assets, processes or other activities are transferred.

Greentech A elects to apply the optional concentration test and concludes that:

(a) each windmill is considered a single identifiable asset for the following reasons:
   (i) the wind turbine is attached to and cannot be physically removed and used separately from the leased land plot on which it is located without incurring significant cost; and
   (ii) the windmill and the in-place lease are considered a single identifiable asset because they would be recognised and measured as a single identifiable asset in a business combination (see paragraph B42 of IFRS 3);
(b) the group of 25 windmills is a group of similar identifiable assets because the assets (all windmills) are similar in nature and the risks associated with managing and creating outputs are not significantly different. This is because the types and specifications of windmills and customers are not significantly different; and
(c) consequently, substantially all of the fair value of the gross assets acquired is concentrated in a group of similar identifiable assets.

Greentech A concludes that the optional concentration test is met and, therefore, the set of activities and assets is not a business and no further assessment is required.

Example 9.2:   Acquisition of wind and solar farms – concentration test (2)

Assume that in the Example 9.1 above in addition to the wind farm Greentech B also owns a solar farm located in the foreign country and the aggregate fair value associated with the solar farm is similar to the aggregate fair value associated with the 25 windmills acquired. The fair value of the consideration paid is approximately equal to the aggregate fair value of the wind and solar farms acquired. As in Example 9.1 no employees, other assets, other processes or other activities are transferred.

Greentech A elects to apply the optional concentration test set and concludes that the 25 windmills and the solar farm are not a group of similar identifiable assets because the windmills and the solar farm differ significantly in the risks associated with operating the assets and obtaining and managing customers. In particular, the technology employed in wind and solar energy operations are significantly different and the risks associated with the two classes of customers are also dissimilar because customers operate in different economic environments. In addition, the fair value of the windmills is similar to the aggregate fair value of the solar farm. Consequently, substantially all of the fair value of the gross assets acquired is not concentrated in a single identifiable asset or a group of similar identifiable assets.

Greentech A concludes that the optional concentration test is not met, and, therefore, further assessment is required.

The Illustrative Examples to IFRS 3 on application of definition of a business contain further illustrations of the application of the concentration test, including approach to the determination of the fair value of the gross assets acquired. [IFRS 3.IE73-123].

3.2.4 Assessing whether an acquired process is substantive

The existence of a process (or processes) is what distinguishes a business from a set of activities and assets that is not a business. Consequently, the Board decided that to be considered a business, an acquired set of activities and assets must include, at a minimum, an input and a substantive process that together significantly contribute to the ability to create outputs. [IFRS 3.B8].

IFRS 3 also clarifies that an acquired contract is an input and not a substantive process. Nevertheless, an acquired contract, for example, a contract for outsourced property management or outsourced asset management, may give access to an organised workforce. An entity assesses whether an organised workforce accessed through such a contract performs a substantive process that the entity controls, and thus has acquired. Factors to be considered in making that assessment include the duration of the contract and its renewal terms. [IFRS 3.B12D(a)].

In addition, the Basis for Conclusions on IFRS 3 clarifies that presence of more than an insignificant amount of goodwill is not a relevant indicator that the acquired process is substantive. [IFRS 3.B12D(a)].

IFRS 3 includes guidance to help entities to assess whether an acquired process is substantive. That guidance seeks more persuasive evidence when there are no outputs because the existence of outputs already provides some evidence that the acquired set of activities and assets is a business. [IFRS 3.BC21M]. However, if an acquired set of activities and assets has outputs, continuation of revenue does not on its own indicate that both an input and a substantive process have been acquired. [IFRS 3.B8A].

If a set of activities and assets does not have outputs at the acquisition date, an acquired process (or group of processes) shall be considered substantive only if:

(a) it is critical to the ability to develop or convert an acquired input or inputs into outputs; and

(b) the inputs acquired include both an organised workforce that has the necessary skills, knowledge, or experience to perform that process (or group of processes) and other inputs that the organised workforce could develop or convert into outputs. Those other inputs could include:

   (i) intellectual property that could be used to develop a good or service (e.g. technology);

   (ii) other economic resources that could be developed to create outputs (e.g. in-process research and development projects); or

   (iii) rights to obtain access to necessary materials or rights that enable the creation of future outputs (e.g. real estate and mineral interests). [IFRS 3.B12B].

If a set of activities and assets has outputs at the acquisition date, an acquired process (or group of processes) shall be considered substantive if, when applied to an acquired input or inputs, it:

(a) is critical to the ability to continue producing outputs, and the inputs acquired include an organised workforce with the necessary skills, knowledge, or experience to perform that process (or group of processes); or

(b) significantly contributes to the ability to continue producing outputs and:
   (i) is considered unique or scarce; or
   (ii) cannot be replaced without significant cost, effort, or delay in the ability to continue producing outputs. *[IFRS 3.B12C]*.

Difficulties in replacing an acquired organised workforce may indicate that the acquired organised workforce performs a process that is critical to the ability to create outputs. *[IFRS 3.B12D(b)]*.

IFRS 3 also clarifies that a process (or group of processes) is not critical if, for example, it is ancillary or minor within the context of all the processes required to create outputs. *[IFRS 3.B12D(c)]*.

3.2.5 'Capable of' from the viewpoint of a market participant

IFRS 3 clarifies that an acquired set of activities and assets does not need to include all of the inputs or processes necessary to operate that set of activities and assets as a business, i.e. it does not need to be self-sustaining. *[IFRS 3.B8]*. The definition of a business in IFRS 3 requires that inputs, and processes applied to those inputs, have the 'ability to contribute to the creation of outputs' rather than the 'ability to create outputs'. *[IFRS 3.BC21F]*. Determining whether a set of activities and assets is a business shall be based on whether the integrated set is capable of being conducted and managed as a business by a market participant. Therefore, it is not a relevant consideration whether a vendor operated a transferred set as a business or whether a buyer intends to operate it as a business. *[IFRS 3.B11]*. The acquired set would be a business, even if an acquirer stops all the operations of the acquiree and disposes of assets acquired as a scrap, if any other market participant would be able to operate the acquired set as a business. Under IFRS 3, a market participant would be able to operate an acquired set as a business, if it includes at a minimum, an input and a substantive process that together significantly contribute to the ability to create outputs. However, if an acquirer obtains control of an input or set of inputs without any processes, the acquired input(s) would not be considered a business, even if a market participant had all the processes necessary to operate the input(s) as a business. It is not a relevant consideration whether market participants would be capable of replacing any missing inputs or processes, for example by integrating the acquired activities and assets. *[IFRS 3.BC21H-21I]*.

3.2.6 Identifying business combinations

Significant judgement is required in determining whether an acquired set of activities and assets constitute a business. The following are examples from extractive industries and real estate that illustrate the issues.

Example 9.3: Extractive industries – definition of a business (1)

E&P Co A (an oil and gas exploration and production company) acquires a mineral interest from E&P Co B, on which it intends to perform exploration activities to determine if reserves exist. The mineral interest is an unproven property and there have been no exploration activities performed on the property. E&P Co A elects not to apply the optional concentration test.

Inputs – mineral interest

Processes – none

Output – none

Conclusion

In this scenario, we do not believe E&P Co A acquired a business. While E&P Co A acquired an input (mineral interest), it did not acquire any processes. Whether or not a market participant has the necessary processes in place to operate the input as a business is not relevant to the determination of whether the acquired set is a business because no processes, whether substantive or not, were acquired from E&P Co B.

E&P Co A elected not to apply the optional concentration test. However, we do not believe the conclusion would be different, if it had elected to do so. The transferred set includes only a mineral interest that would be recognised and measured as a single identifiable intangible asset in a business combination; consequently there are no other assets or processes to which significant portion of the fair value of the gross assets acquired would be assigned. Therefore, the fair value of the gross assets acquired is concentrated in a single identifiable asset acquired.

Example 9.4: Extractive industries – definition of a business (2)

E&P Co A acquires a property similar to that in Example 9.3 above, except that oil and gas production activities are in place and the acquired set also includes a SCADA system. The target's employees are not part of the transferred set. E&P Co A will take over the operations by using its own employees.

Inputs – oil and gas reserves and SCADA system

Processes – operational processes associated with oil and gas production embodied in the SCADA system

Output – revenues from oil and gas production

Conclusion

In this scenario, we believe that E&P Co A has acquired a business. The acquired set includes both inputs and processes, and has outputs. Although the employees are not being transferred to the acquirer, for a set that has outputs transfer of the organized workforce is not necessary to conclude that it constitutes a business. An acquired process is substantive if, when applied to an acquired input or inputs, it significantly contributes to the ability to continue producing outputs and cannot be replaced without significant cost, effort, or delay in the ability to continue producing outputs. We believe that the SCADA systems that consist of physical equipment, including pumps, meters and other assets used to facilitate gathering, processing, storing and transporting of oil and gas serve as a substantive process because they significantly contribute to the ability to continue producing outputs and cannot be replaced without significant cost, effort or delay in the ability to continue producing outputs.

E&P Co A elected not to apply the optional concentration test. However, we do not believe that conclusion would be different if it had elected to do so. This is because, while the acquired set includes only oil and gas reserves and the SCADA system, they generally would not be considered either as a single identifiable asset or group of similar identifiable assets, and we expect that a significant portion of the fair value of the consideration would be assigned to both the value of the transferred oil and gas reserves and the value of assets comprising the SCADA system, which would normally include the operational processes associated with oil and gas production embodied in the SCADA system.

In the real estate industry, IAS 40 notes that where ancillary services (i.e. processes) are provided and they are insignificant to the overall arrangement, this will not prevent the classification of the asset as investment property. *[IAS 40.11]*. (see Chapter 19 at 2.8). The guidance on ancillary services, *[IAS 40.11-14]*, is intended to distinguish an investment property from an owner-occupied property, not whether a transaction is a business combination or an asset acquisition. Entities acquiring investment properties must assess whether the property is a business applying the requirements of IFRS 3. *[IAS 40.14A]*. See Chapter 19 at 3.3.

Therefore, evaluating whether it is a real estate business where certain processes are transferred involves assessing those processes in the light of the guidance in IFRS 3.

Example 9.5:   Real estate – definition of a business (1)

Company A acquires land and a vacant building from Company B. No processes, other assets or employees (for example, leases and other contracts, maintenance or security personnel, or a leasing office) are acquired in the transaction. Company A elects not to apply the optional concentration test.

Inputs – land and vacant building constructed on that land

Processes – none

Output – none

Conclusion

In this scenario, we do not believe Company A has acquired a business. While Company A acquired inputs (land and a vacant building), it did not acquire any processes. Whether or not a market participant has the necessary processes in place to operate the inputs as a business is irrelevant to the determination of whether the acquired set is a business as no processes, whether substantive or not, were acquired from Company B.

Company A elected not to apply the optional concentration test. However, we do not believe the conclusion would be different if it elected to do so. The transferred set includes only land and a vacant building, and the vacant building is attached to and cannot be physically removed and used separately from the land without significant diminution in its utility and fair value. Thus, the land and the building are considered a single identifiable asset for the purposes of the concentration test. In addition, there are no other assets or processes to which a significant portion of the fair value of the gross assets acquired would be assigned. Therefore, the fair value of the gross assets acquired is concentrated in a single identifiable asset acquired.

However, irrespective of the determination whether a business is acquired or not, the classification of the acquired property as an investment property would depend on whether the property meets the definition of investment property in IAS 40. For example, if Company A intends to lease out the property without the provision of significant ancillary services, it would classify the property as an investment property. Otherwise, if Company A intends to operate the property as owner-managed hotel, it would classify the property as property, plant and equipment. Refer to Chapter 19 at 2.8 and 3.3 for further discussion.

Example 9.6:   Real estate – definition of a business (2)

Company A acquires an operating hotel, the hotel's employees, the franchise agreement, inventory, a reservations system and all 'back office' operations. Company A elects not to apply the optional concentration test.

Inputs – non-current assets, franchise agreement, inventory, a reservation system and employees

Processes – undocumented operational and resource management processes associated with operating the hotel

Output – revenues from operating the hotel

Conclusion

In this scenario, we believe Company A has acquired a business. The acquired set has outputs and includes both inputs and processes. In addition, the organised workforce has necessary skills, knowledge or experience to perform processes (i.e. operational and resource management processes associated with operating the acquired hotel) that are substantive because they are critical to the ability to continue producing outputs when applied to the acquired inputs (i.e. non-current assets and franchise agreement).

Company A elected not to apply the optional concentration test. However, we do not believe that, generally, the conclusion would be different, if it had elected to do so. The acquired set includes non-current assets, inventory, a reservation system and a franchise agreement that are not considered similar assets for the purposes of the concentration test and might have significant individual fair values. In addition, when an operating hotel is acquired in its entirety, it may be the case that a not insignificant portion of the fair value of consideration paid is attributed to the intellectual capacity of the organised workforce acquired, provided skills, knowledge and experience they have, are valued by market participants.

However, as indicated in the Example 9.6 above, the classification of the acquired property as an investment property would depend on whether the property meets the definition of investment property in IAS 40. For example, if Company A intends to close the hotel and lease out the property to the third party without the provision of significant ancillary services it would classify the property as an investment property, Otherwise, if Company A intends to continue operating the acquired hotel it would classify the property as property, plant and equipment. (Refer to Chapter 19 at 2.8 and 3.3 for further discussion).

The illustrative examples to IFRS 3 provide further illustrations of the application of principles of IFRS 3 to specific scenarios.

3.2.7 Development stage entities

Development stage entities may qualify as businesses, and their acquisitions accounted for as business combinations because outputs are not required at the acquisition date. The IASB concluded that if the set has no outputs, to qualify as a business the set should include not only a process that is critical to the ability to develop or convert the acquired input or inputs into outputs, but also both an organised workforce that has the necessary skills, knowledge or experience to perform that process, and other inputs that the acquired organised workforce could develop or convert into outputs. *[IFRS 3.B12B]*. The IASB observed that many entities in the development stage will meet this criterion because technology, intellectual property, or other assets are being developed into a good or service. *[IFRS 3.BC21Q]*.

The application of this guidance may be particularly relevant to transactions in the life sciences industry. This is illustrated in the following examples.

Example 9.7:   Life sciences – definition of a business (1)

Biotech A acquires all of the outstanding shares in Biotech B, which is a development stage company with a licence for a product candidate. Due to a loss of funding, Biotech B has no employees and no other assets. Neither clinical trials nor development are currently being performed. When additional funding is obtained, Biotech A plans to commence phase I clinical trials for the product candidate. Biotech A elects not to apply the optional concentration test.

Input – licence for a product candidate

Processes – none

Outputs – none

Conclusion

In this scenario, Biotech A has not acquired a business. While Biotech B has an input (licence), it lacks processes to apply to the licence in order to create outputs. Furthermore, Biotech B has no employees or any other inputs.

Biotech A elected not to apply the optional concentration test. However, we do not believe the conclusion would be different if it elected to do so. The transferred set includes only a licence for a product candidate that is a single identifiable asset because it would be recognised and measured as a single identifiable intangible asset in a business combination and there are no other assets or processes to which a significant portion of the fair value of the gross assets acquired would be assigned. Therefore, the fair value of the gross assets acquired is concentrated in a single identifiable asset acquired.

Example 9.8:   Life sciences – definition of a business (2)

Biotech C acquires all of the outstanding shares in Biotech D, a development stage company that has a licence for a product candidate. Phase III clinical trials are currently being performed by Biotech D employees (one of whom founded Biotech D and discovered the product candidate). Biotech D's administrative and accounting functions are performed by a contract employee. Biotech C elects not to apply the optional concentration test.

Inputs – licence for a product candidate and employees

Processes – operational and management processes associated with the performance and supervision of the clinical trials

Output – none

Conclusion

In this scenario, Biotech C has acquired a business because it has acquired not only a process that is critical to the ability to develop acquired inputs into outputs but also both an organised workforce that has the necessary skills, knowledge or experience to perform that process and other inputs that the acquired organised workforce could develop into output. Biotech D undertakes a Phase III clinical trials process that is critical to develop the acquired input into output (i.e. a commercially developed product that will be sold or licensed) and has both sufficiently qualified and experienced employees, including a scientist who discovered the product candidate and obtained a licence for the product candidate.

Biotech C elected not to apply the optional concentration test. However, we do not believe the conclusion would be different if it had elected to do so. This is because, while the acquired set includes only a single identifiable asset, a licence for a product candidate, we expect that a significant portion of the fair value of the consideration would have been assigned to the value of the intellectual capacity of the employees transferred in the acquisition.

4   ACQUISITION METHOD OF ACCOUNTING

IFRS 3 requires a business combination to be accounted for by applying the acquisition method. *[IFRS 3.4]*. Applying the acquisition method involves the following steps:

(a)   identifying an acquirer (see 4.1 below);

(b)   determining the acquisition date (see 4.2 below);

(c)   recognising and measuring the identifiable assets acquired, the liabilities assumed, and any non-controlling interest in the acquiree (see 5 below); and

(d)   recognising and measuring goodwill or a gain in a bargain purchase (see 6 below). *[IFRS 3.5]*.

4.1   Identifying the acquirer

The first step in applying the acquisition method is identifying the acquirer. IFRS 3 requires one of the combining entities to be identified as the acquirer. *[IFRS 3.6]*. For this purpose, the guidance in IFRS 10 is to be used, i.e. the acquirer is the entity that obtains control of the acquiree. *[IFRS 3.7, B13]*. An investor controls an investee when it is exposed, or has rights, to variable returns from its involvement with the investee and has the ability to affect those returns through its power over the investee. *[IFRS 10.6]*. This is discussed further in Chapter 6 at 3.

If IFRS 10 does not clearly indicate which of the combining entities is the acquirer, additional guidance in IFRS 3 includes various other factors to take into account. *[IFRS 3.7, B13]*.

The various other factors require significant judgement, particularly where the business combination may be a 'reverse acquisition' or where the combination occurred by contract alone.

In a business combination effected primarily by transferring cash or other assets or by incurring liabilities, the acquirer is usually the entity that transfers the cash or other assets or incurs the liabilities. *[IFRS 3.B14]*.

In a business combination effected primarily by exchanging equity interests, the acquirer is usually the entity that issues its equity interests, but in some business combinations, so-called 'reverse acquisitions', the issuing entity is the acquiree. Application guidance on the accounting for reverse acquisitions is provided in Appendix B to IFRS 3 (see 14 below). In identifying the acquirer, IFRS 3 requires that other facts and circumstances should also be considered, including:

- the relative voting rights in the combined entity after the business combination. The acquirer is usually the combining entity whose owners as a group retain or receive the largest portion of the voting rights in the combined entity, after taking due account of any unusual or special voting arrangements and options, warrants or convertible securities;
- the existence of a large minority voting interest in the combined entity if no other owner or organised group of owners has a significant voting interest. The acquirer is usually the combining entity whose single owner or organised group of owners holds the largest minority voting interest in the combined entity;
- the composition of the governing body of the combined entity. The acquirer is usually the combining entity whose owners have the ability to elect or appoint or to remove a majority of the members of the governing body of the combined entity;
- the composition of the senior management of the combined entity. The acquirer is usually the combining entity whose (former) management dominates the management of the combined entity; and
- the terms of the exchange of equity interests. The acquirer is usually the combining entity that pays a premium over the pre-combination fair value of the equity interests of the other combining entity or entities. *[IFRS 3.B15]*.

The acquirer is usually the combining entity whose relative size is significantly greater than that of the other combining entity or entities, whether this be measured by, for example, assets, revenues or profit. *[IFRS 3.B16]*.

If the business combination involves more than two entities, determining the acquirer includes considering, among other things, which of the combining entities initiated the combination, as well as the relative size of the combining entities. *[IFRS 3.B17]*.

The acquirer is not necessarily a legal entity. In September 2011, the Interpretations Committee concluded that an acquirer that is a reporting entity but not a legal entity, can be the acquirer in a reverse acquisition[7] (see 14.9 below). For normal acquisitions, this conclusion would also apply. Therefore, for example, a combined rather than consolidated group might be identified as the acquirer, provided that the combined financial statements are IFRS-compliant (see Chapter 6 at 2.2.6).

4.1.1 New entity formed to effect a business combination

A new entity formed to effect a business combination is not necessarily the acquirer. This will depend among others on whether it has issued equity interests or paid cash. If it has issued equity interests, one of the combining entities is to be identified as the acquirer by applying the guidance described above. [IFRS 3.B18].

If a new entity transfers cash or other assets or incurs liabilities as consideration, it may be the acquirer. IFRS 3 does not specify in what circumstances this may be the case but it is clear that 'control' is the fundamental concept when identifying an acquirer. Generally, a new entity that was formed to effect a business combination other than through the issue of shares will be identified as an acquirer if this new entity is an extension of the party (or parties) that ultimately gains control of the combining entities. The determination of whether such a new entity is an extension of the selling party (or parties) or the party (or parties) that ultimately gains control over the combining entities, requires a thorough analysis of all the facts and circumstances. This analysis requires an assessment of the purpose and design of the transaction. Sometimes, even if the transaction results in a change of control, the underlying substance of the transaction may be for a purpose other than a party or parties to gain control of an entity. In such a situation, even if a new entity transfers cash or other assets and/or incurs liabilities as consideration, it may be appropriate to conclude that this new entity is not an extension of the party (or parties) ultimately gaining control and, therefore cannot be identified as an acquirer (see Example 9.11 below). However, when the purpose and design of the transaction indicate that its underlying substance is to gain control over the business by the new ultimate controlling party (or parties), then this new entity is an extension of such party (or parties) and, therefore, would likely be identified as an acquirer. An example of the latter is a situation where the newly formed entity ('Newco') is used by a group of investors or another entity to acquire a controlling interest in a target entity in an arm's length transaction.

Example 9.9: Business combination effected by a Newco for cash consideration (1)

Entity A intends to acquire the voting shares (and therefore obtain control) of Target Entity. Entity A incorporates Newco and uses this entity to effect the business combination. Entity A provides a loan at commercial interest rates to Newco. The loan funds are used by Newco to acquire 100% of the voting shares of Target Entity in an arm's length transaction.

The group structure post-transaction is as follows:

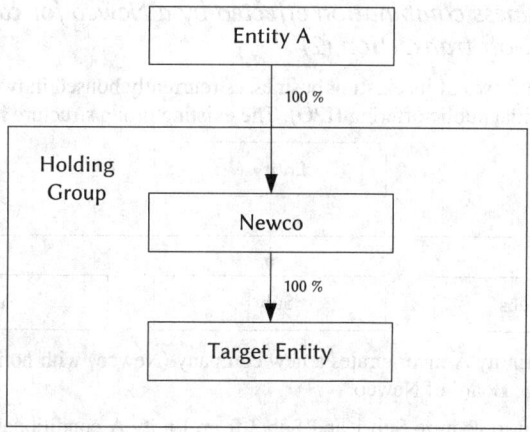

Under its local regulations, Newco is required to prepare IFRS-compliant consolidated financial statements for the Holding Group (the reporting entity). (In most situations like this, Newco would be exempt from preparing consolidated financial statements – see Chapter 6 at 2.2.1.)

The acquirer is the entity that obtains control of the acquiree. Whenever a new entity is formed to effect a business combination other than through the issue of shares, it is appropriate to consider whether Newco is an extension of one of the transacting parties. If it is an extension of the transacting party (or parties) that ultimately gain control of the other combining entities, Newco is the acquirer.

In this situation, Entity A has obtained control of Target Entity in an arm's length transaction, using Newco to effect the acquisition. The transaction has resulted in a change in control of Target Entity and Newco is in effect an extension of Entity A acting at its direction to obtain control for Entity A. Accordingly, Newco would be identified as the acquirer at the Holding Group level.

If, rather than Entity A establishing Newco, a group of investors had established it as the acquiring vehicle through which they obtained control of Target Entity then, we believe, Newco would also be regarded as the acquirer since it is an extension of the group of investors.

Another specific situation in which a Newco might be identified as the acquirer is illustrated in Example 9.10 below, where a parent uses a Newco to facilitate a public flotation of shares in a group of subsidiary companies. Although a Newco incorporated by the existing parent of the subsidiaries concerned would not generally be identified as the acquirer, in this particular situation the critical distinguishing factor is that the acquisition of the subsidiaries was conditional on an Initial Public Offering ('IPO') of Newco. This means that there has been a substantial change in the ownership of the subsidiaries by virtue of the IPO and indicates that the purpose and design of the transaction is to achieve a change in control over the transferred business. The Interpretations Committee discussed similar fact patterns[8] but has subsequently observed that accounting for arrangements involving the creation of a newly formed entity is too broad to be addressed through an interpretation or an annual improvement. The Interpretations Committee concluded that it would be better considered within the context of a broader project on accounting for common control transactions.[9] In December 2017, the IASB tentatively decided that the scope of its project on business combinations under common control would include transfers of businesses under common control that are conditional on a future IPO.[10] At the time of writing, the project is on the IASB's active agenda with the next step likely to be a discussion paper in the fourth quarter of 2020 (see Chapter 10 at 6).[11]

Example 9.10: *Business combination effected by a Newco for cash consideration: spin-off transaction (2)*

Entity A proposes to spin off two of its existing businesses (currently housed in two separate entities, Sub 1 and Sub 2) as part of an initial public offering (IPO). The existing group structure is as follows:

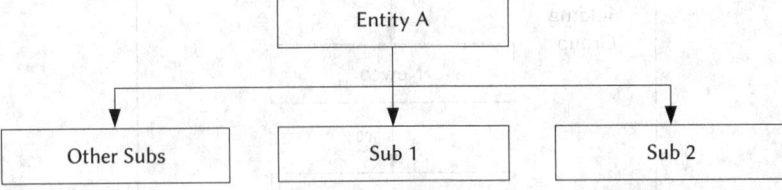

To facilitate the spin off, Entity A incorporates a new company (Newco) with nominal equity and appoints independent directors to the Board of Newco.

Newco signs an agreement to acquire Sub 1 and Sub 2 from Entity A conditional on the IPO proceeding. Newco issues a prospectus offering to issue shares for cash to provide Newco with funds to acquire Sub 1 and Sub 2. The IPO proceeds and Newco acquires Sub 1 and Sub 2 for cash. Entity A's nominal equity leaves virtually 100% ownership in Newco with the new investors.

Following the IPO, the respective group structures of Entity A and Newco appear as follows:

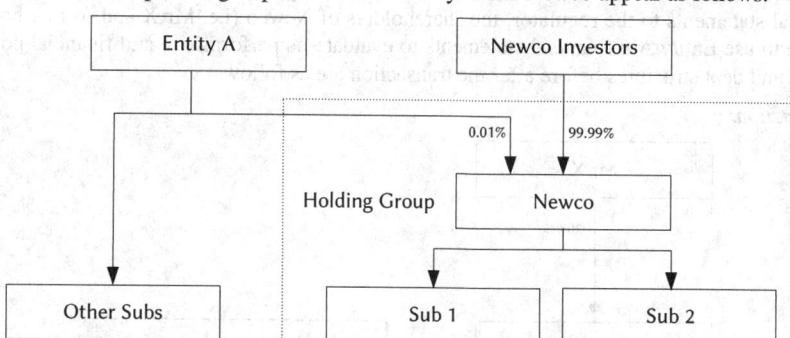

In this case, we believe it would likely be appropriate to identify Newco as the acquirer. The Newco investors have obtained control and virtually 100% ownership of Sub 1 and Sub 2 in an arm's length transaction, using Newco to effect the acquisition. The transaction has resulted in a change in control of Sub 1 and Sub 2 (i.e. Entity A losing control and Newco investors, via Newco, obtaining control). Newco could in effect be considered as an extension of the Newco investors since:

- the acquisition of Sub 1 and Sub 2 was conditional on the IPO proceeding so that the IPO is an integral part of the transaction as a whole evidencing that Newco is an extension of new investors to acquire control of Sub 1 and Sub 2; and

- there is a substantial change in the ownership of Sub1 and Sub 2 by virtue of the IPO (i.e. Entity A only retains a negligible ownership interest in Newco).

Accordingly, Newco might be identified as the acquirer at the Holding Group level.

Whether a Newco formed to facilitate an IPO is capable of being identified as an acquirer depends on the facts and circumstances and ultimately requires judgement. If, for example, Entity A incorporates Newco and arranges for it to acquire Sub 1 and Sub 2 prior to the IPO proceeding, Newco might be viewed as an extension of Entity A or possibly an extension of Sub 1 or Sub 2. This is because the IPO and the reorganisation may not be seen as being part of one integral transaction, and therefore the transaction would be a combination of entities under common control (see Chapter 10 at 4.4). In that situation, Newco would not be the acquirer.

Example 9.11 below illustrates a situation where, despite the fact that the transaction results in a change of control, the purpose and design indicate that the substance of the transaction was to achieve something other than gaining control. Assessing the purpose and design of a transaction is a judgement that requires careful consideration of all facts and circumstances.

Example 9.11: Newco formed to facilitate a debt-to-equity swap transaction

Entity A was wholly owned by a single shareholder Mr X and had issued bonds whose ownership is widely dispersed. Five years before the maturity of the bonds, Entity A initiated and negotiated with bondholders to swap their bonds for an equity interest in Entity A, in order to facilitate Entity A's future market expansion strategy. Mainly due to tax reasons, the transaction was structured as follows: Mr X formed Newco with *de minimis* share capital, appointed to its Board of Directors the same individuals that comprise the Board of Directors of Entity A, and contributed its interest in Entity A for nil consideration. The bondholders then swapped their bonds for new shares issued by Newco. As result of the transaction, Mr X owns indirectly through Newco 30% of Entity A's shares, and the former bondholders hold 70%. Neither Mr X, nor any individual former bondholder, nor any organised sub-group of former bondholders, controls Newco. No changes were made or are expected to be made to the Board of Directors of Entity A or Newco, on which the former bondholders are not represented. While under the local legislation, Newco is required to present its IFRS financial statements to the regulator, the shareholders of Newco (i.e. Mr X and former bondholders) will continue to use Entity A's financial statements to evaluate its performance and financial position. The shareholding and debt structures before after the transaction are as follows:

Before transaction:

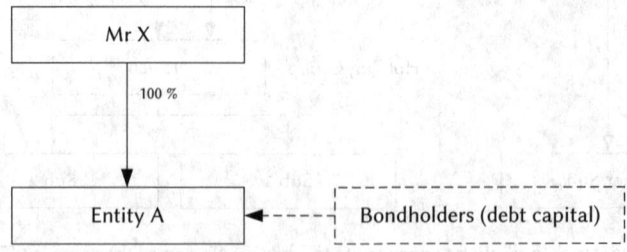

After transaction:

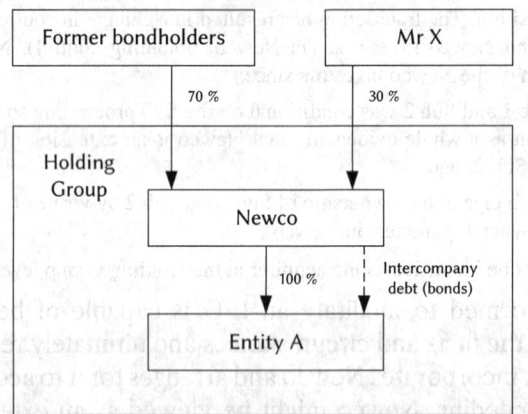

In this transaction, Mr X loses control over Entity A and the former bondholders as a group obtain the majority of shares in Newco and indirectly in Entity A. In order to assess whether the purpose and design of the transaction is to obtain ultimate control over Entity A by the former bondholders as a group, and hence whether it is appropriate to consider Newco as an extension of the former bondholders, the following facts and circumstances are identified:

- the debt-to-equity swap was initiated by Entity A to facilitate its future market expansion strategy;
- the Newco was formed mainly for tax reasons;
- there was no concerted effort by the bondholders to form Newco to acquire control over Entity A;
- there was no new cash involved in this transaction;
- there is no existing or planned Board representation of the former bondholders at Newco or Entity A level. This suggests that the intention of the bondholders was not to change control over Entity A through Newco;
- financial statements of Entity A will continue to be used to provide the shareholders of Newco (Mr X and former bondholders) with information about the financial performance and financial position of Entity A; and
- neither Mr X, nor any individual bondholder, or any organised sub-group of bondholders, controls Newco after the transaction.

When assessing all these facts and circumstances, the purpose and design of this transaction appears to reflect a facilitation of a debt-to-equity swap rather than an intended change in control over Entity A, even though the change of control happened as well. Therefore, in this specific example, it is appropriate to consider Newco as an extension of Entity A rather than as extension of the former bondholders and, therefore, not to identify Newco as the acquirer.

4.1.2 Stapling arrangements

In 2014, the Interpretations Committee considered whether an acquirer identified for the purpose of IFRS 3 is a parent for the purpose of IFRS 10 in circumstances in which a business combination is achieved by contract alone, such as a stapling arrangement, with no combining entity obtaining control of the other combining entities. When considering this issue, the Interpretations Committee thought that the guidance outlined in paragraph B15(a) of IFRS 3, i.e. that the acquirer is usually the combining entity whose owners as a group receive the largest portion of the voting rights in the combined entity, would be relevant to identifying which of the combining entities is the acquirer in the stapling transaction considered.[12]

4.2 Determining the acquisition date

The next step in applying the acquisition method is determining the acquisition date, 'the date on which the acquirer obtains control of the acquiree'. *[IFRS 3.8, Appendix A]*. This is generally the 'closing date', i.e. the date on which the acquirer legally transfers the consideration, acquires the assets and assumes the liabilities of the acquiree. *[IFRS 3.9]*. However, although the standard refers to the 'closing date', this does not necessarily mean that the transaction has to be closed or finalised at law before the acquirer obtains control over the acquiree.

The acquirer might obtain control on a date that is either earlier or later than the closing date. If a written agreement provides that the acquirer obtains control of the acquiree on a date before the closing date, the acquisition date might precede the closing date. *[IFRS 3.9]*. This does not mean that the acquisition date can be artificially backdated or otherwise altered, for example, by the inclusion of terms in the agreement indicating that the acquisition is to be effective as of an earlier date, with the acquirer being entitled to profits arising after that date, even if the purchase price is based on the net asset position of the acquiree at that date.

The Basis for Conclusions accepts that, for convenience, an entity might wish to designate an acquisition date at the beginning or end of a month, the date on which it closes its books, rather than the actual acquisition date during the month. Unless events between the 'convenience' date and the actual acquisition date result in material changes in the amounts recognised, that entity's practice would comply with the requirements of IFRS 3. *[IFRS 3.BC110]*.

The date control is obtained will be dependent on a number of factors, including whether the acquisition arises from a public offer or a private deal, is subject to approval by other parties, or is effected by the issue of shares.

However, in all cases, whether control has been obtained by a certain date is a matter of fact, and all pertinent facts and circumstances surrounding a business combination need to be considered in assessing when the acquirer has obtained control. To evaluate whether control has been obtained, the acquirer would need to apply the guidance in IFRS 10 (see Chapter 6 at 3).

For an acquisition by way of a public offer, the date of acquisition could be:
- when the offer has become unconditional because sufficient irrevocable acceptances have been received; or
- the date that the offer closes.

Since the nature of public offers can be different depending on the jurisdiction they are in, it is always necessary to consider the impact of the nature and terms of the offer and any other relevant laws or regulations in determining the date of acquisition.

In a private deal, the date would generally be when an unconditional offer has been accepted by the vendors, the acquirer obtains substantive voting rights in the investee and all other criteria of control in IFRS 10 are met.

Thus, where an offer is conditional on the approval of the acquiring entity's shareholders, until that approval has been received, it is unlikely that control will have been obtained. Where the offer is conditional upon receiving some form of regulatory approval, then it will depend on the nature of that approval. If it is a substantive hurdle, such as obtaining the approval of a competition authority, it is unlikely that control is obtained prior to that approval. However, where the approval is merely a formality, or 'rubber-stamping' exercise, then this would not preclude control having been obtained at an earlier date, provided that at that earlier date, the acquirer effectively obtains power to direct the relevant activities of the acquiree.

Where the acquisition is effected by the issue of shares, then the date of control will generally be when the exchange of shares takes place.

Application of the IFRS 10 criteria for control may also result in the determination of the acquisition date as the date when acquirer obtains substantive voting rights via options held over the acquiree's shares (see Chapter 6 at 4.3.4).

5 RECOGNITION AND MEASUREMENT OF ASSETS ACQUIRED, LIABILITIES ASSUMED AND NON-CONTROLLING INTERESTS

The next step in applying the acquisition method involves recognising and measuring the identifiable assets acquired, the liabilities assumed and any non-controlling interest in the acquiree.

5.1 General principles

The identifiable assets acquired and liabilities assumed of the acquiree are recognised as of the acquisition date and measured at fair value as at that date, with certain limited exceptions. *[IFRS 3.10, 14, 18, 20]*.

Any non-controlling interest in the acquiree is to be recognised at the acquisition date. Non-controlling interests that are present ownership interests and entitle their holders to a proportionate share of the entity's net assets in the event of liquidation can be measured on one of two bases:

- at fair value at that date; or
- at the non-controlling interest's proportionate share of the acquiree's net identifiable assets.

All other components of non-controlling interests are measured at their acquisition-date fair values, unless another measurement basis is required by IFRSs. *[IFRS 3.10, 19]*. See 8 below.

5.2 Recognising identifiable assets acquired and liabilities assumed

To qualify for recognition, an item acquired or assumed must be:
(a) an asset or liability at the acquisition date; and
(b) part of the business acquired (the acquiree) rather than the result of a separate transaction. *[IFRS 3.BC112]*.

For annual reporting periods beginning before 1 January 2022, the identifiable assets acquired and liabilities assumed must meet the definitions of assets and liabilities in the 1989 *Framework* (unless the entity early adopts the May 2020 amendments – see 5.2.1 below). *[IFRS 3.11, CF(2001) 4.4]*.

Applying the definitions in the 1989 *Framework* adopted in 2001 means that costs that the acquirer expects but is not obliged to incur in the future cannot be provided for. For example, the entity's plans to reorganise the acquiree's activities (e.g. plans to exit from an activity, or terminate the employment of or relocate employees) are not liabilities at the acquisition date. These costs will be recognised by the acquirer in its post-combination financial statements in accordance with other IFRSs. *[IFRS 3.11]*. Liabilities for restructuring or exit activities can only be recognised if they meet the definition of a liability at the acquisition date. *[IFRS 3.BC132]*. Although the standard no longer contains the explicit requirements relating to restructuring plans, the Basis for Conclusions clearly indicates that the requirements for recognising liabilities associated with restructuring or exit activities remain the same. *[IFRS 3.BC137]*. This is discussed further at 11.4 below.

The first condition for recognition makes no reference to reliability of measurement or probability as to the inflow or outflow of economic benefits. This is because the IASB considers them to be unnecessary. Reliability of measurement is a part of the overall recognition criteria in the 1989 *Framework*, which includes the concept of 'probability' to refer to the degree of uncertainty that the future economic benefits associated with an asset or liability will flow to or from the entity. *[IFRS 3.BC125-BC130]*. Thus, identifiable assets and liabilities are recognised regardless of the degree of probability that there will be inflows or outflows of economic benefits. However, in recognising a contingent liability, IFRS 3 requires that its fair value can be measured reliably (see 5.6.1.A below).

The second condition requires that the identifiable assets acquired and liabilities assumed must be part of the exchange for the acquiree, rather than the result of separate transactions. *[IFRS 3.12]*. Explicit guidance is given in the standard for making such an assessment as discussed at 11 below. An acquirer may recognise some assets and liabilities that had not previously been recognised in the acquiree's financial statements, e.g. intangible assets, such as internally-generated brand names, patents or customer relationships. *[IFRS 3.13]*.

Guidance on recognising intangible assets and operating leases, as well as items for which IFRS 3 provides limited exceptions to the recognition principles and conditions are discussed at 5.5 and 5.6 below.

5.2.1 Amendments to IFRS 3 – Reference to the Conceptual Framework (effective on or after 1 January 2022)

In May 2020, the IASB issued amendments to IFRS 3 to update the reference to the 2018 *Conceptual Framework*. The amendments are effective for annual reporting periods beginning on or after 1 January 2022 and apply prospectively. Earlier application is permitted.

For annual reporting periods beginning on or after 1 January 2022, the identifiable assets acquired and liabilities assumed must meet the definitions of assets and liabilities in the 2018 *Conceptual Framework*. [IFRS 3(2022).11].

The IASB issued the revised 2018 *Conceptual Framework* in March 2018. The revised version includes comprehensive changes to the previous *Framework*, issued in 1989 and partly revised in 2010 (the 1989 *Framework*). In particular, definitions of assets and liabilities in the 2018 *Conceptual Framework* are different from those in the 1989 *Framework*. The 2018 *Conceptual Framework* clarified the definition of an asset, removing the requirement for 'expected' future economic benefits. It instead defines an asset as a present economic resource controlled by the entity as a result of past events and defines an economic resource as a right that has the 'potential' to produce economic benefits. Similarly, the 2018 *Conceptual Framework* removes from the definition of a liability the requirement for 'expected' outflows of resources. It instead requires that an obligation has the 'potential' to require the entity to transfer an economic resource to another party.[13]

Therefore, at the time the 2018 *Conceptual Framework* was issued, IASB determined that replacing the reference from the 1989 *Framework* to the 2018 *Conceptual Framework* in IFRS 3 could increase the population of assets and liabilities qualifying for recognition in a business combination. The IASB noted that this would not create a problem if those assets and liabilities would continue to meet recognition criteria after the acquisition date. However, since after the acquisition date IFRS 3 requires an acquirer to account for most types of assets and liabilities recognised in a business combination in accordance with other applicable IFRSs, some assets or liabilities recognised in a business combination might not qualify for recognition subsequently, under those other IFRSs. In such cases, the acquirer would have to derecognise the asset or liability and recognise a resulting loss or gain immediately after the acquisition date (so-called day 2 gain or loss). That gain or loss would not represent an economic gain or loss and would not be a faithful representation of any aspect of the acquirer's financial performance.[14]

To avoid these unintended consequences, at the time of issuing the 2018 *Conceptual Framework*, the IASB made a consequential amendment to IFRS 3 that specified that acquirers are required to apply the definitions of an asset and a liability and supporting guidance in the 1989 *Framework* rather than the 2018 *Conceptual Framework* (see Chapter 2). However, this was deemed a temporary solution. The IASB then began assessing how IFRS 3 could be updated for the revised definitions without these unintended consequences. In May 2020, the Board issued amendments to update IFRS 3 to refer to the 2018 *Conceptual Framework*, and to provide an exception to the recognition principle of IFRS 3 to avoid the issue of potential day 2 gains or losses arising for liabilities and contingent liabilities that would be within the scope of IAS 37 or IFRIC 21, if incurred separately.

For such provisions and contingent liabilities within the scope of IAS 37, the exception requires an acquirer to apply IAS 37 (instead of the definitions in the 2018 *Conceptual Framework*) to determine whether a present obligation exists at the acquisition date, as a result of past events. For levies within the scope of IFRIC 21, the exception requires an acquirer to apply IFRIC 21 to determine whether the obligating event that gave rise to a liability to pay the levy had occurred by the acquisition date. *[IFRS 3(2000).21B]*.

A present obligation identified by applying the exception might meet the definition of a contingent liability. This would be the case if it were not probable that an outflow of resources embodying economic benefits would be required to settle the obligation, or if the amount of the obligation could not be measured with sufficient reliability.

The acquirer shall recognise at acquisition date a contingent liability assumed in a business combination if it is a present obligation that arises from past events and its fair value can be measured reliably. Therefore, contrary to the requirements of IAS 37, the acquirer recognises a contingent liability assumed in a business combination at the acquisition date even if it is not probable that an outflow of resources embodying economic benefits will be required to settle the obligation. [IFRS 3(2000).21B].

In the IASB's view, the obligations recognised as liabilities applying the amended IFRS 3 would be the same as those recognised applying IFRS 3 at present.[15]

The amendments also clarified guidance for contingent assets (see 5.5.4.B below for details).

5.3 Acquisition-date fair values of identifiable assets acquired and liabilities assumed

The general principle is that the identifiable assets acquired and liabilities assumed are measured at their acquisition-date fair values. In this chapter, reference to fair value means fair value as measured by IFRS 13.

IFRS 13 provides guidance on how to measure fair value, but it does not change when fair value is required or permitted under IFRS. IFRS 13 is discussed in detail in Chapter 14. IFRS 3 allows some assets and liabilities to be measured at other than fair value on initial recognition, as described at 5.6 below.

IFRS 13 defines 'fair value' as the price that would be received to sell an asset or paid to transfer a liability in an orderly transaction between market participants at the measurement date under current market conditions. It is explicitly an exit price. *[IFRS 13.2]*.

Where IFRS 3 requires an identifiable asset acquired or liability assumed to be measured at its fair value at the acquisition date, although an entity applies the IFRS 13 measurement requirements, it does not need to disclose information about those acquisition-date fair value measurements under IFRS 13. However, the IFRS 13 disclosure requirements would apply to any fair value measurement after initial recognition, for example the fair value measurement of contingent consideration classified as a financial liability (see Chapter 14 at 20). *[IFRS 13.91]*.

IFRS 3 specifies those assets and liabilities that are not measured at fair value, including income taxes and employee benefits. *[IFRS 3.20]*. These are discussed at 5.6 below.

5.4 Classifying or designating identifiable assets acquired and liabilities assumed

The acquirer must classify or designate the identifiable assets and liabilities assumed on the basis of its own contractual terms, economic conditions, operating and accounting policies and other relevant conditions as at the acquisition date. [IFRS 3.15].

The standard provides two exceptions: [IFRS 3.17]

- classification under IFRS 16 of leases in which the acquiree is the lessor, see discussion below); and
- classification of a contract as an insurance contract in accordance with IFRS 4 (however IFRS 17 will remove this classification exception for entities that apply that standard).[16]

In both of these cases, the contracts are classified on the basis of the contractual terms and other factors at the inception of the contract or at the date of modification. This could be the acquisition date if the terms of the contract have been modified in a manner that would change its classification. [IFRS 3.17].

Thus, if an acquiree is a lessor under a lease contract that has been classified appropriately as an operating lease under IFRS 16, the acquirer would continue to account for the lease as an operating lease in the absence of any modification to the terms of the contract. Only if, prior to or as at the acquisition date, the terms of the lease were modified in such a way that it would be reclassified as a finance lease under IFRS 16 (see Chapter 23 at 6.4), would the acquirer derecognise the underlying asset and recognise instead a financial asset (net investment in a lease).

Examples of classifications or designations made by the acquirer on the basis of conditions at the acquisition date include but are not limited to:

(a) classifying financial assets and liabilities as measured at fair value through profit or loss or at amortised cost, or as a financial asset measured at fair value through other comprehensive income, in accordance with IFRS 9;

(b) designating a derivative instrument as a hedging instrument in accordance with IFRS 9; and

(c) assessing whether an embedded derivative should be separated from the host contract in accordance with IFRS 9 (which is a matter of 'classification' as IFRS 3 uses that term). [IFRS 3.16].

The requirements for the classification of financial assets and liabilities under IFRS 9 are discussed in Chapter 48. Although, IFRS 9 prohibits reclassifications of financial liabilities and allows reclassifications of financial assets when, and only when, an entity changes its business model for managing financial assets as described in Chapter 48 at 9, these do not apply in the circumstances of a business combination. The acquirer has to make its own classification at the acquisition date. If it has not had to consider the classification of such assets or liabilities before, it could choose to adopt the classification applied by the acquiree or adopt a different classification if appropriate. However, if it already has an accounting policy for like transactions, the classification should be consistent with that existing policy.

As discussed in Chapter 53 at 6, there are a number of conditions that need to be met for hedge relationships to qualify for hedge accounting, in particular formal designation and documentation, and an ongoing assessment of the designated hedge. If an acquiree has derivative or other financial instruments that have been used as hedging instruments in a hedge relationship, IFRS 3 requires the acquirer to make its own designation about the hedging relationship that satisfy the conditions for hedge accounting, based on the conditions as they exist at the acquisition date. If the hedging relationship is being accounted for as a cash flow hedge by the acquiree, the acquirer does not inherit the acquiree's existing cash flow hedge reserve, as this clearly represents cumulative pre-acquisition gains and losses. This has implications for the assessment of hedge effectiveness and the measurement of ineffectiveness because, so far as the acquirer is concerned, it has started a new hedge relationship with a hedging instrument that is likely to have a non-zero fair value. This may mean that although the acquiree can continue to account for the relationship as a cash flow hedge, the acquirer is unable to account for it as a cash flow hedge in its financial statements.

In the situations discussed above, the effect of applying the principle in IFRS 3 only affects the post-business combination accounting for the financial instruments concerned. The financial instruments that are recognised as at the acquisition date, and their measurement at their fair value at that date, do not change.

However, the requirement for the acquirer to assess whether an embedded derivative should be separated from the host contract based on acquisition date conditions could result in additional assets or liabilities being recognised (and measured at their acquisition-date fair value) that differ from those recognised by the acquiree. Embedded derivatives are discussed in Chapter 46.

5.5 Recognising and measuring particular assets acquired and liabilities assumed

IFRS 3 gives some application guidance on recognising and measuring particular assets acquired and liabilities assumed in a business combination, discussed below.

5.5.1 Operating leases in which the acquiree is the lessor

If the acquiree is a lessor in an operating lease, i.e. it has an item of property, plant and equipment that is leased to another party, there is no requirement for the acquirer to recognise intangible assets or liabilities if the terms of the lease are favourable or unfavourable relative to market terms and prices. Instead, off-market terms are reflected in the acquisition-date fair value of the asset (such as a building or a patent) subject to the lease. *[IFRS 3.B42]*. The IASB sought to avoid any inconsistency with the fair value model in IAS 40, which requires the fair value of investment property to take into account rental income from current leases. *[IFRS 3.BC146]*.

The requirement to reflect the off-market terms in the fair value of the asset subject to an operating lease in which the acquiree is the lessor applies to any type of asset, to the extent market participants would take them into consideration when pricing the asset, and is not restricted to investment properties accounted for under the fair value model in IAS 40. Based on the requirements of IAS 16 and IAS 38, an entity would be required to adjust the depreciation or amortisation method for the leased asset so as to reflect the timing of the cash flows attributable to the underlying leases. *[IFRS 3.BC148]*.

5.5.2 Intangible assets

Identifiable intangible assets may have to be recognised by an acquirer although they have not previously been recognised by the acquiree. *[IFRS 3.B31]*. IFRS 3 and IAS 38 give guidance on the recognition of intangible assets acquired in a business combination.

IFRS 3 and IAS 38 both define an 'intangible asset' as 'an identifiable non-monetary asset without physical substance'. *[IFRS 3 Appendix A, IAS 38.8]*. The definition requires an intangible asset to be 'identifiable' to distinguish it from goodwill. *[IAS 38.11]*. Both standards regard an asset as identifiable if it:

(a) is separable, i.e. capable of being separated or divided from the entity and sold, transferred, licensed, rented or exchanged, either individually or together with a related contract, identifiable asset or liability, regardless of whether the entity intends to do so (the 'separability' criterion); or

(b) arises from contractual or other legal rights, regardless of whether those rights are transferable or separable from the entity or from other rights and obligations (the 'contractual-legal' criterion). *[IFRS 3 Appendix A, IAS 38.12]*.

IFRS 3 provides the following application guidance.

- *Separability*

An intangible asset is separable even if the acquirer has no intention of selling, licensing or otherwise exchanging it. An acquired intangible asset is separable if there is evidence of exchange transactions for that type of asset or an asset of a similar type, even if those transactions are infrequent and regardless of whether the acquirer is involved in them. For example, customer and subscriber lists are frequently licensed and thus separable. Even if an acquiree believes its customer lists have characteristics that distinguish them from others, this would not generally prevent the acquired customer list being considered separable. However, if confidentiality terms or other agreements prohibit an entity from selling, leasing or otherwise exchanging information about its customers, then the customer list would not be separable. *[IFRS 3.B33]*.

An intangible asset may be separable from goodwill in combination with a related contract, identifiable asset or liability. Two examples are given by IFRS 3:

(a) market participants exchange deposit liabilities and related depositor relationship intangible assets in observable exchange transactions. Therefore, the acquirer should recognise the depositor relationship intangible asset separately from goodwill; or

(b) an acquiree owns a registered trademark and documented but unpatented technical expertise used to manufacture the trademarked product. When it sells the trademark, the owner must also transfer everything else necessary for the new owner to produce a product or service indistinguishable from that produced by the former owner. Because the unpatented technical expertise must be separated from the acquiree or combined entity and sold if the related trademark is sold, it meets the separability criterion. *[IFRS 3.B34]*.

- *Contractual-legal*

An intangible asset that meets the contractual-legal criterion is identifiable, and hence accounted for separately from goodwill, even if the asset is not transferable or separable from the acquiree or from other rights and obligations. For example:

(a) an acquiree owns and operates a nuclear power plant. The licence to operate the power plant is a separate intangible asset, even if the acquirer cannot sell or transfer it separately from the power plant itself. IFRS 3 goes on to say that an acquirer may recognise the operating licence and the power plant as a single asset for financial reporting purposes if their useful lives are similar; or

(b) an acquiree owns a technology patent that it has licensed to others for their exclusive use outside the domestic market, for which it has received a specified percentage of future foreign revenue. Both the technology patent and the related licence agreement meet the contractual-legal criterion for separate recognition even if it would not be practical to sell or exchange them separately from one another. *[IFRS 3.B32]*.

Accordingly, under IFRS 3, intangible assets are recognised separately from goodwill if they are identifiable, i.e. they either are separable or arise from contractual or other legal rights. *[IFRS 3.B31]*. They must be assigned an acquisition-date fair value.

5.5.2.A   Examples of identifiable intangible assets

We have considered above a number of different types of identifiable intangible assets that are recognised separately from goodwill, such as customer and subscriber lists, depositor relationships, registered trademarks, unpatented technical expertise, licences and technology patents.

IAS 38 also explicitly requires an acquirer to recognise as a separate intangible asset in-process research and development of the acquiree, in accordance with IFRS 3, if the project meets the definition of an intangible asset. *[IAS 38.34]*. IFRS 3 itself only refers to this in its Basis for Conclusions. *[IFRS 3.BC149-BC156]*. This is discussed at 5.5.2.D below.

IFRS 3's Illustrative Examples list items acquired in a business combination that are identifiable intangible assets, noting that the examples are not intended to be all-inclusive. *[IFRS 3.IE16-IE44]*. The assets listed are designated as being 'contractual', or 'non-contractual', in which case they do not arise from contractual or other legal rights but are separable. It emphasises that assets do not have to be separable to meet the contractual-legal criterion.

The table below summarises the items included in the Illustrative Examples. See the Illustrative Examples for further explanations.

Intangible assets arising from contractual or other legal rights (regardless of being separable)	Other intangible assets that are separable
Marketing-related	
– Trademarks, trade names, service marks, collective marks and certification marks – Trade dress (unique colour, shape or package design) – Newspaper mastheads – Internet domain names – Non-competition agreements	
Customer-related	
– Order or production backlog – Customer contracts and the related customer relationships	– Customer lists – Non-contractual customer relationships
Artistic-related	
– Plays, operas and ballets – Books, magazines, newspapers and other literary works – Musical works such as compositions, song lyrics and advertising jingles – Pictures and photographs – Video and audio-visual material, including motion pictures or films, music videos and television programmes	
Contract-based	
– Licensing, royalty and standstill agreements – Advertising, construction, management, service or supply contracts – Construction permits – Franchise agreements – Operating and broadcast rights – Servicing contracts such as mortgage servicing contracts – Employment contracts – Use rights such as drilling, water, air, mineral, timber-cutting and route authorities	
Technology-based	
– Patented technology – Computer software and mask works – Trade secrets, such as secret formulas, processes or recipes	– Unpatented technology – Databases, including title plants

Some items have been designated as being 'contractual' due to legal protection, for example, trademarks and trade secrets. The guidance explains that even without that legal protection, they would still normally meet the separability criterion.

Customer relationships established through contracts are deemed identifiable as they meet the contractual-legal criterion. However, there need not be a current contract or any outstanding orders at the date of acquisition for customer relationships to meet the identifiability criteria. Customer relationships can also be recognised as intangible assets if they arise outside a contract but in this case, they must be separable to be recognised. This is discussed further in 5.5.2.B below.

IFRS 3's Illustrative Examples clarify that for contracts with terms that are favourable or unfavourable relative to the market terms, the acquirer recognises either a liability assumed or an asset acquired in a business combination. For example, if the terms of a customer contract are unfavourable in comparison to market terms, the acquirer should recognise a corresponding liability. *[IFRS 3.IE34]*. Conversely, for supply contracts acquired in a business combination that are beneficial from the perspective of the acquiree because the pricing of those contracts is favourable in comparison to market terms, the acquirer recognises a contract-based intangible asset. However, this guidance is not applicable to lease contracts within the scope of IFRS 16. For such contracts, off-market terms are either reflected in the acquisition-date fair value of the asset (such as a building or a patent) subject to the lease if the acquiree is the lessor (see 5.5.1 above) or captured in the acquisition-date carrying amount of the right-of-use asset if the acquiree is the lessee (see 5.6.8 below).

5.5.2.B Customer relationship intangible assets

Further guidance on customer relationships acquired in a business combination is provided in IFRS 3's Illustrative Examples, which form the basis of the example below. These demonstrate how an entity should interpret the contractual-legal and separability criteria in the context of acquired customer relationships. *[IFRS 3.IE30]*.

Example 9.12: Customer relationship intangible assets

(i) Supply agreement

Acquirer Company (AC) acquires Target Company (TC) in a business combination. TC has a five-year agreement to supply goods to Customer. Both TC and AC believe that Customer will renew the agreement at the end of the current contract. The agreement is not separable.

The agreement, whether cancellable or not, meets the contractual-legal criterion. Because TC establishes its relationship with Customer through a contract, both the agreement itself and also TC's customer relationship with Customer meet the contractual-legal criterion.

(ii) Sporting goods and electronics

AC acquires TC in a business combination. TC manufactures goods in two distinct lines of business: sporting goods and electronics. Customer purchases both sporting goods and electronics from TC. TC has a contract with Customer to be its exclusive provider of sporting goods but has no contract for the supply of electronics to Customer. Both TC and AC believe that only one overall customer relationship exists between TC and Customer.

The contract to be Customer's exclusive supplier of sporting goods, whether cancellable or not, meets the contractual-legal criterion. In addition, as TC establishes its relationship with Customer through a contract, the customer relationship with Customer meets the contractual-legal criterion. Because TC has only one customer relationship with Customer, the fair value of that relationship incorporates assumptions about TC's relationship with Customer related to both sporting goods and electronics. However, if AC determines that it has two separate customer relationships with Customer, for sporting goods and for electronics, AC would need to assess whether the customer relationship for electronics is separable before it could be recognised as an intangible asset.

(iii) Order backlog and recurring customers

AC acquires TC in a business combination. TC does business with its customers solely through purchase and sales orders. At the acquisition date, TC has a backlog of customer purchase orders from 60 per cent of its customers, all of whom are recurring customers. The other 40 per cent of TC's customers are also recurring customers. However, as at the acquisition date, TC has no open purchase orders or other contracts with those customers.

Regardless of whether they are cancellable or not, the purchase orders from 60 per cent of TC's customers meet the contractual-legal criterion. Additionally, because TC has established its relationship with 60 per cent of its customers through contracts, not only the purchase orders but also TC's customer relationships meet the contractual-legal criterion. Because TC has a practice of establishing contracts with the remaining 40 per cent of its customers, its relationship with those customers also arises through contractual rights and therefore meets the contractual-legal criterion even though TC does not have contracts with those customers at the acquisition date.

(iv) Motor insurance contracts

AC acquires TC, an insurer, in a business combination. TC has a portfolio of one-year motor insurance contracts that are cancellable by policyholders.

Because TC establishes its relationships with policyholders through insurance contracts, the customer relationship with policyholders meets the contractual-legal criterion.

Sometimes the acquirer may be a customer of the acquiree immediately before the business combination. While a separate customer relationship intangible asset would generally be recognised by the acquirer for the existing relationships between the acquiree and its third-party customers, no separate intangible asset should be recognised for the pre-existing relationship, either contractual or not, between the acquiree and the acquirer. Instead, this relationship will be implicitly considered in the determination of a gain or loss on effective settlement of the pre-existing relationship as illustrated in Example 9.27 at 11.1 below. This is different from any reacquired rights, for which the acquirer would recognise a separate asset (see 5.5.3 below).

One of the most difficult areas of interpretation is whether an arrangement is contractual or not. Contractual customer relationships are always recognised separately from goodwill, but non-contractual customer relationships are recognised only if they are separable. Consequently, determining whether a relationship is contractual is critical to identifying and measuring customer relationship intangible assets and different conclusions could result in substantially different accounting outcomes.

Paragraph IE28 in the Illustrative Examples explains that a customer relationship is deemed to exist if the entity has information about the customer and regular contact with it and the customer can make direct contact with the entity. A customer relationship 'may also arise through means other than contracts, such as through regular contact by sales or service representatives'. However, the argument is taken a stage further. Regardless of whether any contracts are in place at the acquisition date, 'customer relationships meet the contractual-legal criterion for recognition if an entity has a practice of establishing contracts with its customers'. *[IFRS 3.IE28]*. An example of what is meant by this is given in Example 9.12 above. In the third illustration, 'Order backlog and recurring customers', it states 'Because TC has a practice of establishing contracts with the remaining 40 per cent of its customers, its relationship with those customers also arises through contractual rights and therefore meets the contractual-legal criterion even though TC does not have contracts with those customers at the acquisition date'.

In 2008 the Interpretations Committee considered the circumstances in which non-contractual customer relationships arise. The staff's survey of Interpretations Committee members indicated that there were diverse practices regarding which customer relationships have a contractual basis and which do not. In addition, valuation experts seemed to be taking different views.[17]

The Interpretations Committee noted that the IFRS Glossary of Terms defined the term 'contract'. Whilst the manner in which a relationship is established is relevant to confirming the existence of a customer relationship, it should not be the primary basis for determining whether an intangible asset is recognised by the acquirer. What might be more relevant is whether the entity has a practice of establishing contracts with its customers or whether relationships arise through other means, such as through regular contact by sales and service representatives (i.e. the matters identified in paragraph IE28). The existence of contractual relationships and information about a customer's prior purchases would be important inputs in valuing a customer relationship intangible asset, but should not determine whether it is recognised.[18] Therefore, a customer base (e.g. customers of a fast food franchise or movie theatres) is an example of a non-contractual customer relationship that would not be recognised in a business combination.

The Interpretations Committee was unable to develop an Interpretation clarifying the distinction between contractual and non-contractual. Given the widespread confusion the matter was referred to the IASB and the FASB with a recommendation to review and amend IFRS 3 by:[19]

- removing the distinction between 'contractual' and 'non-contractual' customer-related intangible assets recognised in a business combination; and
- reviewing the indicators that identify the existence of a customer relationship in paragraph IE28 of IFRS 3 and including them in the standard.

However, the IASB deferred both recommendations of the Interpretations Committee to the PIR of IFRS 3, which was completed in June 2015. As a result of the PIR of IFRS 3 the issue of identification and fair value measurement of intangible assets such as customer relationships and brand names was added to the IASB's active agenda within its *Goodwill and Impairment* research project. In March 2020, the IASB published the DP *Business Combinations – Disclosures, Goodwill and Impairment*. The DP sets out the IASB's preliminary view that the requirements in IFRS 3 and IAS 38 for separate recognition of acquired intangible assets should be retained (see 1.1.1 above). Therefore, divergent treatments will remain in practice, depending on how entities interpret 'contractual' and 'non-contractual' customer-related intangible assets in a particular business combination, until further guidance is provided in this area.

5.5.2.C Combining an intangible asset with a related contract, identifiable asset or liability

IAS 38 states that an intangible asset acquired in a business combination might be separable, but only together with a related contract, identifiable asset, or liability. In such cases, the acquirer recognises the intangible assets separately from goodwill, but together with the related item. *[IAS 38.36]*.

Similarly, the acquirer may recognise a group of complementary intangible assets as a single asset provided the individual assets have similar useful lives. For example, 'the terms "brand" and "brand name" are often used as synonyms for trademarks and other marks. However, the former are general marketing terms that are typically used to refer to a group of complementary assets such as a trademark (or service mark) and its related trade name, formulas, recipes and technological expertise.' *[IAS 38.37]*.

It is not clear whether an intangible asset that is only separable in combination with a tangible asset should be recognised together as a single asset for financial reporting purposes in all circumstances. IFRS 3 gives an example of a licence to operate a nuclear power plant, and says that the fair value of the operating licence and the fair value of the power plant may be recognised as a single asset for financial reporting purposes, if the useful lives of those assets are similar (see 5.5.2 above), yet the requirements in IAS 38 only refer to similar useful lives in the context of a group of complementary intangible assets.

In practice entities account for intangible assets separately from the related tangible asset if the useful lives are different. The Rank Group Plc considers that its casino and gaming licences have indefinite useful lives and accounts for them separately from the buildings with which they are acquired, as disclosed in its accounting policy.

> *Extract 9.1: The Rank Group Plc (2019)*
>
> Notes to the financial statements [extract]
>
> 1   General information and accounting policies [extract]
>
> Summary of significant accounting policies [extract]
>
> 1.12   Intangible assets [extract]
>
> (b)   Casino and other gaming licences and concessions
>
> The Group capitalises acquired casino and other gaming licences and concessions. Management believes that casino and other gaming licences have indefinite lives as there is no foreseeable limit to the period over which the licences are expected to generate net cash inflows and each licence holds a value outside the property in which it resides. Each licence is reviewed annually for impairment.
>
> In respect of the concession in Belgium, the carrying value is amortised over the expected useful life of the concession.

Guidance on determining useful lives of intangible assets is discussed in Chapter 17 at 9.1.

5.5.2.D In-process research or development project expenditure

IFRS 3 itself only refers to in-process research and development in its Basis for Conclusions, where it is made clear that the acquirer recognises all tangible and intangible research and development assets acquired in a business combination. *[IFRS 3.BC149-BC156]*.

IAS 38's general recognition conditions require it to be probable that expected future economic benefits will flow to the entity and that the costs can be measured reliably before an intangible asset can be recognised. *[IAS 38.21]*.

IAS 38 states that 'an acquiree's in-process research and development project meets the definition of an intangible asset when it meets the definition of an asset, and is identifiable, i.e. is separable or arises from contractual or other legal rights.' *[IAS 38.34]*.

In-process research and development projects, whether or not recognised by the acquiree, are protected by legal rights and are clearly separable as on occasion they are bought and sold by entities without there being a business acquisition. Both of the standard's general recognition criteria, probability of benefits and reliable measurement, are always considered to be satisfied for in-process research and development projects acquired in a business combination. The fair value of an intangible asset reflects expectations about the probability of these benefits, despite uncertainty about the timing or the amount of the inflow. There will be sufficient information to measure the fair value of the asset reliably if it is separable or arises from contractual or other legal rights. If there is a range of possible outcomes with different probabilities, this uncertainty is taken into account in the measurement of the asset's fair value. *[IAS 38.33-35]*.

Therefore, recognising in-process research and development as an asset on acquisition applies different criteria to those that are required for internal projects. The research costs of internal projects may under no circumstances be capitalised. *[IAS 38.54]*. Before capitalising development expenditure, entities must meet a series of exacting requirements. They must demonstrate the technical feasibility of the intangible assets, their intention and ability to complete the assets and use them or sell them and must be able to measure reliably the attributable expenditure. *[IAS 38.57]*. The probable future economic benefits must be assessed using the principles in IAS 36 which means that they have to be calculated as the net present value of the cash flows generated by the asset or, if it can only generate cash flows in conjunction with other assets, of the cash-generating unit of which it is a part. *[IAS 38.60]*. This process is described further in Chapter 17 at 6.

What this means is that entities will be required to recognise on acquisition some research and development expenditure that they would not have been able to recognise if it had been an internal project. The IASB is aware of this inconsistency, but concluded that this did not provide a basis for subsuming in-process research and development within goodwill. *[IAS 38.BC82]*.

Although the amount attributed to the project is accounted for as an asset, IAS 38 goes on to require that any subsequent expenditure incurred after the acquisition of the project is to be accounted for in accordance with paragraphs 54 to 62 of IAS 38. *[IAS 38.42]*. These requirements are discussed in Chapter 17 at 6.2.

In summary, this means that the subsequent expenditure is:

(a) recognised as an expense when incurred if it is research expenditure;

(b) recognised as an expense when incurred if it is development expenditure that does not satisfy the criteria for recognition as an intangible asset in paragraph 57; and

(c) added to the carrying amount of the acquired in-process research or development project if it is development expenditure that satisfies the recognition criteria in paragraph 57. *[IAS 38.43]*.

The inference is that the in-process research and development expenditure recognised as an asset on acquisition that never progresses to the stage of satisfying the recognition criteria for an internal project will ultimately be impaired, although it may be that this impairment will not arise until the entity is satisfied that the project will not continue. However, since it is an intangible asset not yet available for use, such an evaluation cannot be significantly delayed as it will need to be tested for impairment annually by comparing its carrying amount with its recoverable amount, as discussed in Chapter 20 at 10. *[IAS 36.10]*.

5.5.2.E   Emission rights

Emission rights or allowances under a cap and trade emission rights scheme (see Chapter 17 at 11.2) meet the definition of an intangible asset and should therefore be recognised at the acquisition date at their fair value. Likewise, the acquirer is required to recognise a liability at fair value for the actual emissions made at the acquisition date.

One approach that is adopted in accounting for such rights is the 'net liability approach' whereby the emission rights are recorded at a nominal amount and the entity will only record a liability once the actual emissions exceed the emission rights granted and still held. As discussed in Chapter 17 at 11.2.5, the net liability approach is not permitted for purchased emission rights and therefore is also not permitted to be applied to emission rights of the acquiree in a business combination. Although the acquiree may not have recognised an asset or liability at the date of acquisition, the acquirer should recognise the emission rights as intangible assets at their fair value and a liability at fair value for the actual emissions made at the acquisition date.

One impact of this is that subsequent to the acquisition, the consolidated income statement will show an expense for the actual emissions made thereafter, as a provision will have to be recognised on an ongoing basis. As discussed in Chapter 17 at 11.2.2, there are different views of the impact that such 'purchased' emission rights have on the measurement of the provision and on accounting for the emissions.

Business combinations   681

The emission rights held by the acquiree will relate to specific items of property, plant and equipment. Therefore, when determining the fair value of these assets, care needs to be taken to ensure that there is no double counting of the rights held.

5.5.2.F   Determining the fair values of intangible assets

Little guidance relating to fair value remains in IFRS 3 as it is now included in IFRS 13 (discussed at 5.3 above and in Chapter 14). IAS 38 states that the fair value of an intangible asset will reflect market participants' expectations at the acquisition date about the probability that the expected future economic benefits embodied in the asset will flow to the entity. *[IAS 38.33]*. Like IFRS 3, IAS 38 incorporates IFRS 13's definition of fair value (see 5.3 above). *[IAS 38.8]*.

There are three broad approaches to valuing intangible assets that correspond to the valuation approaches referred to in IFRS 13. *[IFRS 13.62]*. These are the market, income and cost approaches. The diagram below shows these valuation approaches, together with some of the primary methods used to measure the fair value of intangible assets that fall under each approach, shown in the boxes on the right.

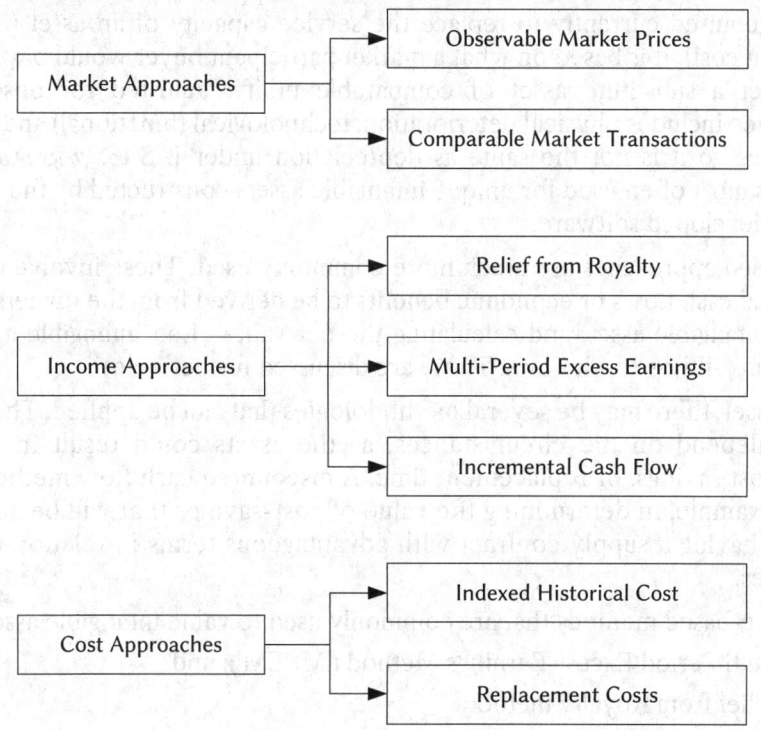

IFRS 13 does not limit the types of valuation techniques an entity might use to measure fair value. Instead the standard indicates that entities should use valuation techniques that are appropriate in the circumstances and for which sufficient data are available, which may result in the use of multiple valuation techniques. Regardless of the technique(s) used, a fair value measurement should maximise the use of relevant observable inputs and minimise the use of the unobservable inputs. *[IFRS 13.61]*. The resulting fair value measurement should also reflect an exit price, i.e. the price to sell an asset. *[IFRS 13.2]*.

In practice, the ability to use a market-based approach is very limited as intangible assets are generally unique and are not typically traded. For example, there are generally no observable transactions for unique rights such as brands, newspaper mastheads, music and film publishing rights, patents or trademarks noted in paragraph 78 of IAS 38, i.e. a number of the intangible assets that IFRS 3 and IAS 38 require an acquirer to recognise in a business combination.

The premise of the cost approach is that an investor would pay no more for an intangible asset than the cost to recreate it. The cost approach reflects the amount that would be required currently to replace the service capacity of an asset (i.e. current replacement cost). It is based on what a market participant buyer would pay to acquire or construct a substitute asset of comparable utility, adjusted for obsolescence. Obsolescence includes physical deterioration, technological (functional) and economic obsolescence so it is not the same as depreciation under IAS 16. *[IFRS 13.B8, B9]*. This approach is most often used for unique intangible assets constructed by the entity, e.g. internally-developed software.

Income-based approaches are much more commonly used. These involve identifying the expected cash flows or economic benefits to be derived from the ownership of the particular intangible asset, and calculating the fair value of an intangible asset at the present value of those cash flows. These are discussed further below.

For each asset, there may be several methodologies that can be applied. The methods used will depend on the circumstances, as the assets could result in additional revenue, cost savings, or replacement time. A discounted cash flow method may be used, for example, in determining the value of cost-savings that will be achieved as a result of having a supply contract with advantageous terms in relation to current market rates.

Two income-based methods that are commonly used to value intangible assets are:

- the Multi Period Excess Earnings Method ('MEEM'); and
- the Relief from Royalty method.

The MEEM is a residual cash flow methodology that is often used in valuing the primary intangible asset acquired. The key issue in using this method is how to isolate the income/cash flow that is related to the intangible asset being valued.

As its name suggests, the value of an intangible asset determined under the MEEM is estimated through the sum of the discounted future excess earnings attributable to the intangible asset. The excess earnings is the difference between the after-tax operating cash flow attributable to the intangible asset and the required cost of invested capital on all other assets used in order to generate those cash flows. These contributory assets include property, plant and equipment, other identifiable intangible assets and net working capital. The allowance made for the cost of such capital is based on the value of such assets and a required rate of return reflecting the risks of the particular assets. As noted at 5.5.4 below, although it cannot be recognised as a separate identifiable asset, an assembled workforce may have to be valued for the purpose of calculating a 'contributory asset charge' in determining the fair value of an intangible asset under the MEEM.

The Relief from Royalty method is often used to calculate the value of a trademark or trade name. This approach is based on the concept that if an entity owns a trademark, it does not have to pay for the use of it and therefore is relieved from paying a royalty. The amount of that theoretical payment is used as a surrogate for income attributable to the trademark. The valuation is arrived at by computing the present value of the after-tax royalty savings, calculated by applying an appropriate royalty rate to the projected revenue, using an appropriate discount rate. The legal protection expenses relating to the trademark and an allowance for tax at the appropriate rate are deducted. The Relief from Royalty method was applied by adidas AG in its 2015 financial statements.

> *Extract 9.2: adidas AG (2015)*
>
> **CONSOLIDATED FINANCIAL STATEMENTS** [extract]
> **Notes** [extract]
> **04   ACQUISITION OF SUBSIDIARIES AS WELL AS ASSETS AND LIABILITIES** [extract]
>
> The following valuation methods for the acquired assets were applied:
>
> - **Trademarks**: The 'relief-from-royalty method' was applied for the trademarks/brand names. The fair value was determined by discounting notional royalty savings after tax and adding a tax amortisation benefit, resulting from the amortisation of the acquired asset.

It may be that the value of an intangible asset will reflect not only the present value of the future post-tax cash flows as indicated above, but also the value of any tax benefits (sometimes called 'tax amortisation benefits') that might generally be available to the owner if the asset had been bought separately, i.e. not as part of a business combination. adidas AG discloses in the extract above that fair value of trademarks and similar rights includes a tax amortisation benefit. Whether such tax benefits are included will depend on the nature of the intangible asset and the relevant tax jurisdiction. If tax amortisation benefits are included, an asset that has been purchased as part of a business combination may not actually be tax-deductible by the entity, either wholly or in part. This therefore raises a potential impairment issue that is discussed in Chapter 20 at 8.3.1.

In the extract below, Allied Electronics Corporation discloses in its annual financial statements the use of the Relief from Royalty method for valuation of trade names and the Multi-Period Excess Earnings Method to value customer relationships acquired in business combinations.

> Extract 9.3: Allied Electronics Corporation (2018)
>
> ANNUAL FINANCIAL STATEMENTS [extract]
>
> Notes to the financial statements [extract]
>
> 29. JUDGEMENTS MADE BY MANAGEMENT [extract]
>
> • Purchase price allocation of acquisitions [extract]
>
> The following valuation techniques were used in measuring the fair value of material assets acquired:
>
> i) Relief-from-royalty method (trade names)
>
> ii) Multi-period excess earnings method (customer relationships)
>
> 39. ACQUISITION OF SUBSIDIARIES AND BUSINESSES [extract]
>
> MEASUREMENT OF FAIR VALUES
>
> The valuation techniques used for measuring the fair value of material assets acquired were as follows.
>
> *Intangible assets acquired*
>
> Valuation technique
>
> i) Relief-from-royalty method used to value Trade names.
>
> The relief-from-royalty method considers the discounted estimated royalty payments that are expected to be avoided as a result of the patents or trademarks being owned.
>
> This methodology requires significant judgements relating to the key inputs applied. Discount rates and Royalty rates were the key inputs used in valuation.
>
> ii) Multi-period excess earnings method used to value customer relationships.
>
> The multi-period excess earnings method considers the present value of net cash flows expected to be generated by the customer relationships, by excluding any cash flows related to contributory assets.
>
> This methodology requires significant judgements relating to the key inputs applied.
>
> Useful economic lives of customer relationships, contributory asset charges, discount and customer attrition rates were the key inputs used in valuation.

Because fair value is an exit price, the acquirer's intention in relation to intangible assets, e.g. where the acquirer does not intend to use an intangible asset of the acquiree is not taken into account in attributing a fair value. This is explicitly addressed in IFRS 3 and IFRS 13 and discussed at 5.5.6 below and in Chapter 14 at 10.1.

5.5.3 Reacquired rights

A reacquired right, that is a right previously granted to the acquiree to use one or more of the acquirer's recognised or unrecognised assets, must be recognised separately from goodwill. Reacquired rights include a right to use the acquirer's trade name under a franchise agreement or a right to use the acquirer's technology under a technology licensing agreement. *[IFRS 3.B35]*.

A reacquired right is not treated as the settlement of a pre-existing relationship. Reacquisition of, for example, a franchise right does not terminate the right. The difference is that the acquirer, rather than the acquiree by itself, now controls the franchise right. The IASB also rejected subsuming reacquired rights into goodwill, noting that they meet both contractual-legal and separability criteria and therefore qualify as identifiable intangible assets. *[IFRS 3.BC182-BC184]*.

Guidance on the valuation of such reacquired rights, and their subsequent accounting, is discussed at 5.6.5 below.

Although the reacquired right itself is not treated as a termination of a pre-existing relationship, contract terms that are favourable or unfavourable relative to current market transactions are accounted for as the settlement of a pre-existing relationship. The acquirer has to recognise a settlement gain or loss. *[IFRS 3.B36]*. Guidance on the measurement of any settlement gain or loss is discussed at 11.1 below.

5.5.4 Assembled workforce and other items that are not identifiable

The acquirer subsumes into goodwill the value of any acquired intangible asset that is not identifiable as at the acquisition date.

5.5.4.A Assembled workforce

A particular example of an intangible asset subsumed into goodwill is an assembled workforce. IFRS 3 regards this as being an existing collection of employees that permits the acquirer to continue to operate an acquired business from the acquisition date without having to hire and train a workforce. *[IFRS 3.B37]*.

Although individual employees might have employment contracts with the employer, the collection of employees, as a whole, does not have such a contract. In addition, an assembled workforce is not separable; it cannot be sold, transferred, licensed, rented or otherwise exchanged without causing disruption to the acquirer's business. Therefore, it is not an identifiable intangible asset to be recognised separately from goodwill. *[IFRS 3.BC178]*.

Nor does the assembled workforce represent the intellectual capital of the skilled workforce, which is the (often specialised) knowledge and experience that employees of an acquiree bring to their jobs. *[IFRS 3.B37]*. Prohibiting an acquirer from recognising an assembled workforce as an intangible asset does not apply to intellectual property and the value of intellectual capital may well be reflected in the fair value of other intangible assets. For example, a process or methodology such as a software program would be documented and generally would be the property of the entity; the employer usually 'owns' the intellectual capital of an employee. The ability of the entity to continue to operate is unlikely to be affected significantly by changing programmers, even replacing the particular programmer who created the program. The intellectual property is part of the fair value of that program and is an identifiable intangible asset if it is separable from the entity. *[IFRS 3.BC180]*.

5.5.4.B Items not qualifying as assets

The acquirer subsumes into goodwill any value attributed to items that do not qualify as assets at the acquisition date.

- *Potential contracts with new customers*

Potential contracts that the acquiree is negotiating with prospective new customers at the acquisition date might be valuable to the acquirer. The acquirer does not recognise them separately from goodwill because those potential contracts are not themselves assets at the acquisition date. Nor should the acquirer subsequently reclassify the value of those contracts from goodwill for events that occur after the acquisition date. The acquirer should, of course, assess the facts and circumstances surrounding events occurring shortly after the acquisition to determine whether there was a separately recognisable intangible asset at the acquisition date. *[IFRS 3.B38]*.

- *Contingent assets*

If the acquiree has a contingent asset, it should not be recognised unless it meets the definition of an asset in the 1989 *Framework* adopted in 2001, even if it is virtually certain that it will become unconditional or non-contingent. Therefore, an asset would only be recognised if the entity has an unconditional right at the acquisition date. This is because it is uncertain whether a contingent asset, as defined by IAS 37 actually exists at the acquisition date. Under IAS 37, it is expected that some future event will confirm whether the entity has an asset. *[IFRS 3.BC276]*. Contingent assets under IAS 37 are discussed in Chapter 26 at 3.2.2. *[IAS 37.33]*.

In May 2020, the IASB issued amendments to IFRS 3 to update the reference to the 2018 *Conceptual Framework*. The amendments are effective for annual reporting periods beginning on or after 1 January 2022 and apply prospectively. Earlier application is permitted. (see details at 5.2.1 above).

The amendments updated IFRS 3 so that it refers to the 2018 *Conceptual Framework* rather than the 1989 *Framework*. Thus, for annual reporting periods beginning on or after 1 January 2022 the identifiable assets acquired, and liabilities assumed must meet the definitions of assets and liabilities in the 2018 *Conceptual Framework*. *[IFRS 3(2022).11]*.

Notwithstanding the fact that the definitions of assets and liabilities in the 2018 *Conceptual Framework* are different from those in the 1989 *Framework*, the IASB concluded that this would not affect accounting for contingent assets acquired in a business combination. *[IFRS 3(2022).BC114D]*. However, to avoid any doubt about whether updating the references to the 2018 *Conceptual Framework* would change the guidance on contingent assets acquired in a business combination, the IASB added to IFRS 3 an explicit statement clarifying that contingent assets do not qualify for recognition at the acquisition date. *[IFRS 3(2022).23A]*.

- *Future contract renewals*

In measuring the fair value of an intangible asset, the acquirer would take into account assumptions that market participants would use when pricing the intangible asset, such as expectations of future contract renewals. It is not necessary for the renewals themselves to meet the identifiability criteria. *[IFRS 3.B40]*. Any value attributable to the expected future renewal of the contract is reflected in the value of, for example, the customer relationship, rather than being subsumed within goodwill.

However, any potential contract renewals that market participants would consider in determining the fair value of reacquired rights would be subsumed within goodwill. Refer to the discussion at 5.6.5 below.

5.5.5 Assets with uncertain cash flows (valuation allowances)

Under IFRS 3, the acquirer may not recognise a separate provision or valuation allowance for assets that are initially recognised at fair value. Because receivables, including loans, are to be recognised and measured at fair value at the acquisition date, any uncertainty about collections and future cash flows is included in the fair value measure (see Chapter 49 at 3.3.4). *[IFRS 3.B41].* Therefore, although an acquiree may have assets, typically financial assets such as receivables and loans, against which it has recognised a provision or valuation allowance for expected credit losses or uncollectible amounts, an acquirer cannot 'carry over' any such valuation allowances nor create its own allowances in respect of those financial assets.

Subsequent measurement of financial instruments under IFRS 9 is dealt with in Chapter 50. Chapter 51 at 7.4 deals specifically with the interaction between the initial measurement of debt instruments acquired in a business combination and the impairment model of IFRS 9.

5.5.6 Assets that the acquirer does not intend to use or intends to use in a way that is different from other market participants

An acquirer may intend not to use an acquired asset, for example, a brand name or research and development intangible asset or it may intend to use the asset in a way that is different from the way in which other market participants would use it. IFRS 3 requires the acquirer to recognise all such identifiable assets, and measure them at their fair value determined in accordance with their highest and best use by market participants (see 5.3 above and in Chapter 14 at 10.1). This requirement is applicable both on initial recognition and when measuring fair value less costs of disposal for subsequent impairment testing. *[IFRS 3.B43].* This means that no immediate impairment loss should be reflected if the acquirer does not intend to use the intangible asset to generate its own cash flows, but market participants would.

However, if the entity is not intending to use the intangible asset to generate cash flows, it is unlikely that it could be regarded as having an indefinite life for the purposes of IAS 38, and therefore it should be amortised over its expected useful life. This is likely to be relatively short.

Example 9.13:   Acquirer's intention not to use an intangible asset

Entity A acquires a competitor, Entity B. One of the identifiable intangible assets of Entity B is the trade name of one of Entity B's branded products. As Entity A has a similar product, it does not intend to use that trade name post-acquisition. Entity A will discontinue sales of Entity B's product, thereby eliminating competition and enhancing the value of its own branded product. The cash flows relating to the acquired trade name are therefore expected to be nil. Can Entity A attribute a fair value of nil to that trade name?

The fair value of the asset has to be determined in accordance with its use by market participants. Entity A's future intentions about the asset should only be reflected in determining the fair value if that is what other market participants would do.

- There are other market participants that would continue to sell the product;
- Entity A could probably have sold the trade name after acquisition but has chosen not to do so;
- Even if all other market participants would, like Entity A, not sell the product in order to enhance the value of their own products, the trade name is still likely to have some value.

Accordingly, a fair value is attributed to that trade name.

As Entity A is not intending to use the trade name to generate cash flows but to use it defensively by preventing others from using it, the trade name should be amortised over the period it is expected to contribute directly or indirectly to the entity's future cash flows.

5.5.7 Investments in equity-accounted entities

An acquiree may hold an investment in an associate, accounted for under the equity method (see Chapter 11 at 3). There are no recognition or measurement differences between an investment that is an associate or a trade investment because the acquirer has not acquired the underlying assets and liabilities of the associate. Accordingly, the fair value of the associate should be determined on the basis of the value of the investment, rather than the underlying fair values of the identifiable assets and liabilities of the associate. The impact of having listed prices for investments in associates when measuring fair value is discussed further in Chapter 14 at 5.1.1. Any goodwill relating to the associate is subsumed within the carrying amount for the associate rather than within the goodwill arising on the overall business combination. Nevertheless, although this fair value is effectively the 'cost' to the group to which equity accounting is applied, the underlying fair values of the various identifiable assets and liabilities also need to be determined to apply equity accounting (see Chapter 11 at 7).

This also applies if an acquiree holds an investment in a joint venture that under IFRS 11 is accounted for under the equity method (see Chapter 12 at 7).

5.5.8 Assets and liabilities related to contracts with customers

As part of a business combination, an acquirer may assume liabilities or acquire assets recognised by the acquiree in accordance with IFRS 15, for example, contract assets, receivables or contract liabilities.

Under IFRS 15, if a customer pays consideration, or an entity has a right to an amount of consideration that is unconditional (i.e. a receivable), before the entity transfers a good or service to the customer, the entity presents a contract liability. *[IFRS 15.106]*. An acquirer recognises a contract liability (e.g. deferred revenue) related to a contract with a customer that it has assumed if the acquiree has received consideration (or the amount is due) from the customer. To determine whether to recognise a contract liability, however, an acquirer may also need to consider the definition of a performance obligation in IFRS 15. That is, at the acquisition date, the acquirer would identify the remaining promised goods and services in a contract with a customer and evaluate whether the goods and services it must transfer to a customer in the future are an assumed performance obligation for which the acquired entity has received consideration (or the amount is due). This is important because the consideration received (or the amount due) may relate to a satisfied or partially satisfied performance obligation for which no (or not all) revenue was recognised pre-combination (e.g. due to variable consideration being constrained). Since it was not party to the acquiree's performance pre-combination, an acquirer may need to consider how that affects its financial statements. For example, whether any consideration received that relates to the acquiree's pre-combination performance should be presented as revenue or other income.

Chapter 28 at 3 provides additional guidance on identifying performance obligations in a contract with a customer. If a contract liability for an assumed performance obligation is recognised, the acquirer derecognises the contract liability and recognises revenue as it provides those goods or services after the acquisition date.

In accordance with the requirements in IFRS 3, at the date of acquisition, an assumed contract liability is measured at its fair value, which would reflect the acquiree's obligation to transfer some (if advance covers only a portion of consideration for the remaining promised goods and services) or all (if advance covers full consideration for the remaining promised goods and services) of the remaining promised goods and services in a contract with a customer, as at the acquisition date. The acquirer does not recognise a contract liability or a contract asset for the contract with customer that is an executory contract (see Chapter 26 at 1.3) at the acquisition date. However, for executory contracts with customers with terms that are favourable or unfavourable relative to the market terms, the acquirer recognises either a liability assumed or an asset acquired in a business combination (see 5.5.2.A above). The fair value is measured in accordance with the requirements in IFRS 13 and may require significant judgement. One method that might be used in practice to measure fair value of the contract liability is a cost build-up approach. That approach is based on a market participant's estimate of the costs that will be incurred to fulfil the obligation plus a 'normal' profit margin for the level of effort or assumption of risk by the acquirer after the acquisition date. The normal profit margin also should be from the perspective of a market participant and should not include any profit related to selling or other efforts completed prior to the acquisition date.

Example 9.14:   Contract liability of an acquiree

Target is an electronics company that sells contracts to service all types of electronics equipment for an annual fee of $120,000 that is paid in advance. Acquirer purchases Target in a business combination. At the acquisition date, Target has one service contract outstanding with 6 months remaining and for which a contract liability of $60,000 was recorded in Target's pre-acquisition financial statements.

To fulfil the contract over its remaining 6-month term, Acquirer estimates that a market participant would incur costs of $45,000, and expect a profit margin for that fulfilment effort of 20% (i.e. $9,000), and thus would expect to receive $54,000 for the fulfilment of the remaining performance obligation.

Accordingly, Acquirer will recognise a contract liability of $54,000 in respect of the acquired customer contract.

In addition to the contract liability, an acquirer may also assume refund liabilities of the acquiree. Under IFRS 15, an entity recognises a refund liability if the entity receives consideration from a customer and expects to refund some or all of that consideration to the customer, including refund liabilities relating to a sale with a right of return. *[IFRS 15.55]*. A refund liability, therefore, is different from a contract liability and might be recognised even if at the acquisition date no contract liability should be recognised. Under IFRS 3, refund liabilities are also measured at their fair value at the acquisition date with fair value determined in accordance with the requirements of IFRS 13. The requirements in IFRS 13 for measuring the fair value of liabilities are discussed in more detail in Chapter 14 at 11.

If an entity performs by transferring goods or services to a customer before the customer pays consideration or before payment is due, the entity presents a contract as a contract asset, excluding amounts presented as receivable. *[IFRS 15.107]*. Contract assets represent entity's rights to consideration in exchange for goods or services that the entity has transferred to a customer when that right is conditioned on something other than the passage of time (e.g. the entity's future performance). *[IFRS 15 Appendix A]*. A receivable is an unconditional right to receive consideration from the customer *[IFRS 15.105]* (see also Chapter 32 at 2.1.1).

The value of acquired contracts with customers may be recognized in multiple assets and liabilities (e.g. receivables, contract assets, right of return assets, intangible assets, contract liabilities, refund liabilities).

Under IFRS 3 at the date of acquisition, all acquired assets related to the contract with customers are measured at their fair value at that date determined under IFRS 13. The IFRS 13 requirements for measuring the fair value of assets are discussed in more detail in Chapter 14 at 5.

When measuring the fair value of acquired contracts with customers, an acquirer should verify that all of the components of value have been considered (i.e. an acquirer should verify that none of the components of value have been omitted or double counted). An acquirer also should verify that all of the components are appropriately reflected in the fair value measurement. After the date of acquisition, an acquirer applies IFRS 15 to account for any of the acquiree's assets, liabilities, income and expenses that fall within that standard's scope. *[IFRS 3.54]*. Because IFRS 15 does not measure revenue (or any assets or liabilities within its scope) on a fair value basis, so-called 'day 2' measurement differences may arise post-combination. Neither IFRS 3 nor IFRS 15 specify how to account for such differences and, therefore, the acquirer may need to develop an accounting policy in accordance with IAS 8 – *Accounting Policies, Changes in Accounting Estimates and Errors*.

5.6 Exceptions to the recognition and/or measurement principles

There are a number of exceptions to the principles in IFRS 3 that all assets acquired and liabilities assumed should be recognised and measured at fair value. For the particular items discussed below, this will result in some items being:

(a) recognised either by applying additional recognition conditions or by applying the requirements of other IFRSs, with results that differ from applying the recognition principle and conditions; and/or

(b) measured at an amount other than their acquisition-date fair values. *[IFRS 3.21]*.

5.6.1 Contingent liabilities

IAS 37 defines a contingent liability as:

(a) a possible obligation that arises from past events and whose existence will be confirmed only by the occurrence or non-occurrence of one or more uncertain future events not wholly within the control of the entity; or

(b) a present obligation that arises from past events but is not recognised because:

   (i) it is not probable that an outflow of resources embodying economic benefits will be required to settle the obligation; or

   (ii) the amount of the obligation cannot be measured with sufficient reliability.

[IFRS 3.22, IAS 37.10].

5.6.1.A Initial recognition and measurement

Under IAS 37, contingent liabilities are not recognised as liabilities; instead they are disclosed in financial statements. However, IFRS 3 does not apply the recognition rules of IAS 37. Instead, IFRS 3 requires the acquirer to recognise a liability at its fair value if there is a present obligation arising from a past event that can be reliably measured, even if it is not probable that an outflow of resources will be required to settle the obligation. *[IFRS 3.23]*. If a contingent liability only represents a possible obligation arising from a past event, whose existence will be confirmed only by the occurrence or non-occurrence of one or more uncertain future events not wholly within the control of the entity, no liability is to be recognised under IFRS 3. *[IFRS 3.BC275]*. No liability is recognised if the acquisition-date fair value of a contingent liability cannot be measured reliably.

5.6.1.B   Subsequent measurement and accounting

IFRS 3 requires that after initial recognition and until the liability is settled, cancelled or expires, the acquirer measures a contingent liability that is recognised in a business combination at the higher of:

(a) the amount that would be recognised in accordance with IAS 37; and
(b) the amount initially recognised less, if appropriate, the cumulative amount of income recognised in accordance with the principles of IFRS 15. *[IFRS 3.56]*.

The implications of part (a) of the requirement are clear. If the acquiree has to recognise a provision in respect of the former contingent liability, and the best estimate of this liability is higher than the original fair value attributed by the acquirer, then the greater liability should now be recognised by the acquirer with the difference taken to the income statement. It would now be a provision to be measured and recognised in accordance with IAS 37. What is less clear is part (b) of the requirement. The reference to 'the cumulative amount of income recognised in accordance with the principles of IFRS 15' might relate to the recognition of income in respect of those loan commitments that are contingent liabilities of the acquiree, but have been recognised at fair value at date of acquisition. The requirement would appear to mean that, unless the recognition of income in accordance with the principles of IFRS 15 is appropriate, the amount of the liability cannot be reduced below its originally attributed fair value until the liability is settled, cancelled or expires.

Despite the fact that the requirement for subsequent measurement discussed above was originally introduced for consistency with IAS 39 – *Financial Instruments: Recognition and Measurement*, which was replaced by IFRS 9, *[IFRS 3.BC245]*, IFRS 3 makes it clear that this requirement does not apply to contracts accounted for in accordance with IFRS 9. *[IFRS 3.56]*. This would appear to mean that contracts that are excluded from the scope of IFRS 9, but are accounted for by applying IAS 37, i.e. loan commitments other than those that are commitments to provide loans at below-market interest rates, will fall within the requirements of IFRS 3 outlined above.

5.6.2   Income taxes

In developing IFRIC 23 – *Uncertainty over Income Tax Treatments*, the Interpretation Committee considered whether the Interpretation should address the accounting for tax assets and liabilities acquired or assumed in a business combination when there is uncertainty over income tax treatments. It noted that IFRS 3 applies to all assets acquired and liabilities assumed in a business combination and concluded that on this basis the Interpretation should not explicitly address tax assets and liabilities acquired or assumed in a business combination. *[IFRIC 23.BC23]*.

Nonetheless, IFRS 3 requires an entity to account for deferred tax assets and liabilities that arise as part of a business combination by applying IAS 12. *[IFRS 3.24]*. Accordingly, the Interpretation applies to such assets and liabilities when there is uncertainty over income tax treatments that affect deferred tax. *[IFRIC 23.BC24]*.

IFRS 3 suggests that current tax should be measured at fair value, which differs from the subsequent measurement required by IFRIC 23. Entities must consider whether the application of IFRS 3 fair value requirements to current tax assets and liabilities (which may result in possible Day 2 gains and losses) takes precedence over the requirements of IFRIC 23 for the measurement of current tax assets and liabilities. We believe either approach is acceptable, provided that it is applied consistently (see also Chapter 33 at 9.1.1).

As mentioned above, IFRS 3 requires the acquirer to recognise and measure, in accordance with IAS 12, a deferred tax asset or liability, arising from the assets acquired and liabilities assumed in a business combination. *[IFRS 3.24]*. The acquirer is also required to account for the potential tax effects of temporary differences and carryforwards of an acquiree that exist at the acquisition date or arise as a result of the acquisition in accordance with IAS 12. *[IFRS 3.25]*.

IAS 12 requires that:

(a) acquired deferred tax benefits recognised within the measurement period (see 12 below) reduce the goodwill related to that acquisition if they result from new information obtained about facts and circumstances existing at the acquisition date. If the carrying amount of goodwill is zero, any remaining deferred tax benefits are to be recognised in profit or loss; and

(b) all other acquired tax benefits realised are to be recognised in profit or loss, unless IAS 12 requires recognition outside profit or loss. *[IAS 12.68]*.

It will therefore be necessary to assess carefully the reasons for changes in the assessment of deferred tax made during the measurement period to determine whether it relates to facts and circumstances at the acquisition date or if it is a change in facts and circumstances since acquisition date. As an anti-abuse clause, if the deferred tax benefits acquired in a business combination are not recognised at the acquisition date but are recognised after the acquisition date with a corresponding gain in profit or loss, paragraph 81(k) of IAS 12 requires a description of the event or change in circumstances that caused the deferred tax benefits to be recognised.

IAS 12 also requires that tax benefits arising from the excess of tax-deductible goodwill over goodwill for financial reporting purposes is accounted for at the acquisition date as a deferred tax asset in the same way as other temporary differences. *[IAS 12.32A]*.

The requirements of IAS 12 relating to the deferred tax consequences of business combinations are discussed further in Chapter 33 at 12.

5.6.3 Employee benefits

IFRS 3 requires the acquirer to recognise and measure a liability (or asset, if any) related to the acquiree's employee benefit arrangements in accordance with IAS 19 – *Employee Benefits* (see Chapter 35), rather than at their acquisition-date fair values. *[IFRS 3.26, BC296-BC300]*.

5.6.4 Indemnification assets

The seller in a business combination may contractually indemnify the acquirer for the outcome of the contingency or uncertainty related to all or part of a specific asset or liability. These usually relate to uncertainties as to the outcome of pre-acquisition contingencies, e.g. uncertain tax positions, environmental liabilities, or legal matters. The amount of the indemnity may be capped or the seller will guarantee that the acquirer's liability will not exceed a specified amount.

IFRS 3 considers that the acquirer has obtained an indemnification asset. *[IFRS 3.27]*.

From the acquirer's perspective, the indemnification is an acquired asset to be recognised at its acquisition-date fair value. However, IFRS 3 makes an exception to the general principles in order to avoid recognition or measurement anomalies for indemnifications related to items for which liabilities are either not recognised or are not required to be measured at fair value (e.g. uncertain tax positions related to recognised deferred tax assets and liabilities). *[IFRS 3.BC302-BC303]*. Accordingly, under IFRS 3 the acquirer measures an indemnification asset on the same basis as the indemnified item, subject to the need for a valuation allowance for uncollectible amounts, if necessary.

- If the indemnification relates to an asset or a liability that is measured at fair value, the acquirer will recognise the indemnification asset at its fair value. The effects of uncertainty about future cash flows (i.e. the collectability of the asset) are included in the fair value measure and a separate valuation allowance is not necessary (see 5.5.5 above). *[IFRS 3.27]*.
- The indemnification may relate to an asset or liability that is not measured at fair value. A common example is an indemnification pertaining to a deferred tax liability that is measured in accordance with IAS 12, rather than at its fair value (see 5.6.2 above). If the indemnified item is recognised as a liability but is measured on a basis other than fair value, the indemnification asset is recognised and measured using consistent assumptions, subject to management's assessment of collectability and any contractual limitations on the indemnified amount. *[IFRS 3.27-28]*.
- If the indemnified item is not recognised as a liability at the date of acquisition, the indemnification asset is not recognised. An indemnification could relate to a contingent liability that is not recognised at the acquisition date because its fair value is not reliably measurable, *[IFRS 3.28]*, or it is only a possible obligation at that date (see 5.6.1 above).

Thereafter, the indemnification asset continues to be measured using the same assumptions as the indemnified liability or asset. *[IFRS 3.57]*. Thus, where the change in the value of the related indemnified liability or asset has to be recognised in profit or loss, this will be offset by any corresponding change in the value recognised for the indemnification asset. The acquirer derecognises the indemnification asset only when it collects the asset, sells it or otherwise loses the right to it. *[IFRS 3.57]*.

5.6.4.A Acquirer's obligation to transfer proceeds from realisation of acquired contingent asset ('Reverse indemnification liabilities')

A business combination sometimes includes an agreement under which the acquirer is required to transfer to the seller all or part of the proceeds the acquirer subsequently receives from the realisation of a contingent asset of the acquiree that existed at acquisition date.

The acquirer should analyse whether it is acting as an agent for the seller in relation to that particular contingent asset. If so, the obligation, and the realisation of the contingent asset, must be accounted for separately from the business combination.

However, if the acquirer is not acting as an agent for the seller, the question arises as to how the acquirer should account for such an agreement. IFRS 3 does not provide specific guidance in that respect.

IFRS 3 defines a contingent consideration as 'an obligation of the acquirer to transfer additional assets ... to the former owners of an acquiree as part of the exchange for control of the acquiree if specified future events occur or conditions are met'. *[IFRS 3 Appendix A]*. Future realisation of the contingent asset therefore could be treated as a specified future event giving rise to the contingency. Under this 'contingent consideration liability' approach, at the acquisition date, an acquirer would recognise a contingent consideration liability measured at its fair value at that date (see 7.1 below).

However, since IFRS 3 prohibits the recognition of a contingent asset acquired in a business combination, there seems to be an accounting anomaly when the 'contingent consideration liability' approach is applied, as such application of IFRS 3 would lead to recognition of an obligation that economically does not exist at the acquisition date, because the respective future outflow of economic resources will only occur when the referenced contingent asset is realised, and a corresponding inflow of economic resources occurs. As result, the amount of goodwill would be initially overstated with subsequent recognition of the gain in a post-combination profit or loss, not containing any economic substance, since it was agreed by the seller and the acquirer in advance that all economic benefits or losses associated with the realization of the particular contingent asset would be transferred to the seller. It should be noted that such 'artificial' gain would be recognised subsequently irrespective of whether or not the related contingent asset is subsequently recognised, or it expires.

The alternative approach that allows elimination of such a recognition and measurement anomaly, assumes that the agreement effectively indemnifies the acquirer from transfer of economic resources if a particular contingent asset acquired in a business combination does not realise subsequently (hereinafter – 'reverse indemnification liability' approach). The 'reverse indemnification liability' approach is based on application by analogy of the indemnification asset guidance in IFRS 3, which was introduced by the IASB to avoid a similar anomaly when it revised IFRS 3 in 2008. In the Basis for Conclusions to IFRS 3, the IASB clarifies that under the indemnification asset guidance, the acquirer does not apply the recognition principle in determining whether or when to recognise an indemnification asset. Instead, the acquirer recognises the asset when it recognises the related liability. *[IFRS 3.BC 303]*. Accordingly, under the 'reverse indemnification liability' approach, no liability is recognised until the related asset is recognised, that is, when its realisation is virtually certain.

We believe, for the reasons explained above, the 'contingent consideration liability' approach may not represent the substance of the transaction. The application of the 'reverse indemnification liability approach' is illustrated in the Example 9.15 below.

Example 9.15: Reverse indemnification liability

Entity A acquires Entity B from Seller C for a cash consideration. The net assets of Entity B include a contingent asset related to a court case, which, per IFRS 3, is not recognised by the acquirer as part of the net assets acquired. Entity A and Seller C agreed that, in the event the contingent asset is subsequently realised, the related cash received should be transferred to Seller C. Assume that Entity A is not identified in this case as an agent that collects and transfers the contingent asset on behalf of Seller C.

Based on the fact that there is a direct link between the obligation of the entity to transfer certain amount of consideration to Seller C and realisation of the particular contingent asset not recognised at the acquisition date, Entity A treats that obligation as 'reverse indemnification liability'. Accordingly, no liability is recognised at the acquisition date. Entity A will recognise the liability in the post-combination periods, only if the related contingent asset is realised.

5.6.5 Reacquired rights

Reacquired rights (see 5.5.3 above) are valued on the basis of the remaining contractual term of the related contract, regardless of whether market participants would consider potential contractual renewals when measuring their fair value. *[IFRS 3.29]*.

If the terms of the contract giving rise to the reacquired right are favourable or unfavourable relative to current market transactions for the same or similar items, this is accounted for as the settlement of a pre-existing relationship and the acquirer has to recognise a settlement gain or loss. *[IFRS 3.B36]*. Guidance on the measurement of any settlement gain or loss is discussed at 11.1 below. An example of accounting for the settlement gain or loss on the acquisition of a reacquired rights is illustrated in Example 9.29 below.

After acquisition, the intangible asset is to be amortised over the remaining contractual period of the contract, without including any renewal periods. *[IFRS 3.55, BC308]*. As the reacquired right is no longer a contract with a third party it might be thought that the acquirer could assume indefinite renewals of its contractual term, effectively making the reacquired right an intangible asset with an indefinite life. However, the IASB considers that a right reacquired from an acquiree has, in substance, a finite life. *[IFRS 3.BC308]*.

If the acquirer subsequently sells a reacquired right to a third party, the carrying amount of the intangible asset is to be included in determining the gain or loss on the sale. *[IFRS 3.55, BC310]*.

5.6.6 Assets held for sale

Non-current assets or disposal groups classified as held for sale at the acquisition date in accordance with IFRS 5 – *Non-current Assets Held for Sale and Discontinued Operations* – are measured at fair value less costs to sell (see Chapter 4 at 2.2). *[IFRS 3.31]*. This avoids the need to recognise a loss for the selling costs immediately after a business combination (a so-called Day 2 loss).

5.6.7 Share-based payment transactions

Liabilities or equity instruments related to the acquiree's share-based payments are measured in accordance with IFRS 2 (referred to as the 'market-based measure'), rather than at fair value, as are replacement schemes where the acquirer replaces the acquiree's share-based payments with its own. *[IFRS 3.30, IFRS 13.6]*. The measurement rules of IFRS 2 are not based on the fair value of the award at a particular date; measuring share-based payment awards at their acquisition-date fair values would cause difficulties with the subsequent accounting in accordance with IFRS 2. *[IFRS 3.BC311]*.

Additional guidance given in IFRS 3 for accounting for the replacement of share-based payment awards (i.e. vested or unvested share-based payment transactions) in a business combination is discussed at 7.2 and 11.2 below. Any equity-settled share-based payment transactions of the acquiree that the acquirer does not exchange for its own share-based payment transactions will result in a non-controlling interest in the acquiree being recognised, as discussed at 8.4 below.

5.6.8 Leases in which the acquiree is the lessee

IFRS 3 requires the acquirer to measure the acquired lease liability as if the lease contract were a new lease at the acquisition date. That is, the acquirer applies IFRS 16's initial measurement provisions, using the present value of the remaining lease payments at the acquisition date. The acquirer follows the requirements for determining the lease term, lease payments and discount rate as discussed in Chapter 23 at 4.

IFRS 3 also requires the acquirer to measure the right-of-use asset at an amount equal to the recognised liability, adjusted to reflect the favourable or unfavourable terms of the lease, relative to market terms. Because the off-market nature of the lease is captured in the right-of-use asset, the acquirer does not separately recognise an intangible asset or liability for favourable or unfavourable lease terms relative to market terms.

Under IFRS 3, the acquirer is not required to recognise right-of-use assets and lease liabilities for leases with lease terms which end within 12 months of the acquisition date and leases for low-value assets acquired in a business combination. As indicated in the Basis for Conclusions for IFRS 16, the IASB considered whether to require an acquirer to recognise assets and liabilities relating to off-market terms for short-term leases and leases of low-value assets. However, the IASB observed that the effect of off-market terms would rarely be material for short-term leases and leases of low-value assets and so decided not to require this. *[IFRS 3.BC298]*.

5.6.9 Insurance contracts within the scope of IFRS 17

IFRS 17 replaces IFRS 4 and is effective for reporting periods beginning on or after 1 January 2023, with early application permitted. IFRS 17 introduces a new exception to measurement principles in IFRS 3. Under IFRS 3, as amended by IFRS 17, the acquirer in a business combination shall measure a group of contracts within the scope of IFRS 17 as a liability or asset in accordance with paragraphs 39 and B93-B95 of IFRS 17, at the acquisition date.[20]

6 RECOGNISING AND MEASURING GOODWILL OR A GAIN IN A BARGAIN PURCHASE

The final step in applying the acquisition method is recognising and measuring goodwill or a gain in a bargain purchase.

IFRS 3 defines 'goodwill' in terms of its nature, rather than in terms of its measurement. It is defined as 'an asset representing the future economic benefits arising from other assets acquired in a business combination that are not individually identified and separately recognised.' *[IFRS 3 Appendix A]*.

However, having concluded that the direct measurement of goodwill is not possible, the standard requires that goodwill is measured as a residual. *[IFRS 3.BC328]*.

Goodwill at the acquisition date is computed as the excess of (a) over (b) below:

(a) the aggregate of:
  (i) the consideration transferred (generally measured at acquisition-date fair value);
  (ii) the amount of any non-controlling interest in the acquiree; and
  (iii) the acquisition-date fair value of the acquirer's previously held equity interest in the acquiree.

(b) the net of the acquisition-date fair values (or other amounts recognised in accordance with the requirements of the standard) of the identifiable assets acquired and the liabilities assumed. *[IFRS 3.32]*.

Having concluded that goodwill should be measured as a residual, the IASB, in deliberating IFRS 3, considered the following two components to comprise 'core goodwill':

- The fair value of the going concern element of the acquiree's existing business. This represents the ability of the established business to earn a higher rate of return on an assembled collection of net assets than would be expected if those net assets had to be acquired separately. The value stems from the synergies of the net assets of the business, as well as from other benefits, such as factors related to market imperfections, including the ability to earn monopoly profits and barriers to market entry (by potential competitors, whether through legal restrictions or costs of entry).

- The fair value of the expected synergies and other benefits from combining the acquirer's and acquiree's net assets and businesses. These are unique to each combination, and different combinations would produce different synergies and, hence, different values. *[IFRS 3.BC313, BC316]*.

However, in practice the amount of goodwill recognised in a business combination will probably not be limited to 'core goodwill'. Items that do not qualify for separate recognition (see 5.5.4 above) and items that are not measured at fair value, e.g. deferred tax assets and liabilities, will also affect the amount of goodwill recognised.

Even though goodwill is measured as a residual, after identifying and measuring all the items in (a) and (b), the acquirer should have an understanding of the factors that make up the goodwill recognised. IFRS 3 requires the disclosure of qualitative description of those factors (see 16.1.1 below).

Where (b) exceeds (a), IFRS 3 regards this as giving rise to a gain on a bargain purchase. *[IFRS 3.34]*. Bargain purchase transactions are discussed further at 10 below.

The measurement of (b) has been discussed at 5 above. The items included within (a) are discussed at 7, 8 and 9 below.

6.1 Subsequent accounting for goodwill

The main issue relating to the goodwill acquired in a business combination is how it should be subsequently accounted for. The requirements of IFRS 3 in this respect are straightforward; the acquirer measures goodwill acquired in a business combination at the amount recognised at the acquisition date less any accumulated impairment losses. *[IFRS 3.B63]*.

Goodwill is not to be amortised. Instead, the acquirer has to test it for impairment annually, or more frequently if events or changes in circumstances indicate that it might be impaired, in accordance with IAS 36. The requirements of IAS 36 relating specifically to the impairment of goodwill are dealt with in Chapter 20 at 8. In June 2015, the IASB completed the post-implementation review of IFRS 3, as a result the *Goodwill and Impairment* research project has been initiated that discusses potential improvements to subsequent accounting of goodwill (please refer to 1.1.1 above).

7 CONSIDERATION TRANSFERRED

The consideration transferred in a business combination comprises the sum of the acquisition-date fair values of assets transferred by the acquirer, liabilities incurred by the acquirer to the former owners of the acquiree and equity interests issued by the acquirer. The consideration may take many forms, including cash, other assets, a business or subsidiary of the acquirer, and securities of the acquirer (e.g. ordinary shares, preferred shares, options, warrants, and debt instruments). The consideration transferred also includes the fair value of any contingent consideration and may also include some or all of any acquirer's share-based payment awards exchanged for awards held by the acquiree's employees measured in accordance with IFRS 2 rather than at fair value. These are discussed further at 7.1 and 7.2 below. *[IFRS 3.37]*.

The consideration transferred could include assets or liabilities whose carrying amounts differ from their fair values. These are remeasured to fair value at the acquisition date and any resulting gains or losses are recognised in profit or loss. If the transferred assets or liabilities remain within the combined entity after the acquisition date because they were transferred to the acquiree rather than to its former owners, the acquirer retains control of them. They are retained at their existing carrying amounts and no gain or loss is recognised. *[IFRS 3.38]*.

Where the assets given as consideration or the liabilities incurred by the acquirer are financial assets or financial liabilities as defined by IAS 32 – *Financial Instruments: Presentation* (see Chapter 47), the guidance in IFRS 13 on determining the fair values of such financial instruments should be followed (see Chapter 14).

These assets and liabilities might be denominated in a foreign currency, in which case the entity may have hedged the foreign exchange risk. IFRS 9 (or IAS 39, if an entity when it first applied IFRS 9 chose as its accounting policy to continue to apply the hedge requirements in IAS 39 instead of the hedge requirements in IFRS 9) allows an entity to apply hedge accounting when hedging the movements in foreign currency exchange rates for a firm commitment to acquire a business in a business combination. *[IFRS 9.B6.3.1, IAS 39.AG98]*. In January 2011, the Interpretations Committee considered the treatment of gains or losses arising from hedging this risk under IAS 39 and in particular whether they would result in an adjustment to the amount that is recognised for goodwill. When a basis adjustment is made to a hedged item, it is after other applicable

IFRSs have been applied. Accordingly, the Interpretations Committee noted that 'such a basis adjustment is made to goodwill (or the gain from a bargain purchase) after the application of the guidance in IFRS 3'.[21] That conclusion applies under IFRS 9 as well.

Where equity interests are issued by the acquirer as consideration, the guidance in IFRS 13 on determining the fair value of an entity's own equity should be followed (see Chapter 14 at 11). *[IFRS 13.34]*. IFRS 3 clarifies that they are to be measured at their fair values at the acquisition date, rather than at an earlier agreement date (or on the basis of the market price of the securities for a short period before or after that date). *[IFRS 3.BC337-342]*.

Although a valid conceptual argument could be made for the use of the agreement date, it was observed that the parties to a business combination are likely to take into account expected changes between the agreement date and the acquisition date in the fair value of the acquirer and the market price of the acquirer's securities issued as consideration. While an acquirer and a target entity both consider the fair value of the target on the agreement date in negotiating the amount of consideration to be paid, the distorting effects are mitigated if acquirers and targets generally consider their best estimates of the fair values on the acquisition dates. In addition, measuring the equity securities on the acquisition date avoids the complexities of dealing with situations in which the number of shares or other consideration transferred can change between the agreement date and the acquisition date. *[IFRS 3.BC342]*.

Measuring the fair value of an entity's own equity issued on or close to the agreement date would not result in a consistent measure of the consideration transferred. The fair values of all other forms of consideration transferred are measured at the acquisition date as are the fair values of the assets acquired and liabilities assumed. *[IFRS 3.BC338-BC342]*.

The acquisition-date fair value of the acquiree's equity interests may be more reliably measurable than that of the acquirer's equity interests. In that case, IFRS 3 requires goodwill to be calculated using the fair value of the acquiree's equity interests rather than the fair value of the equity interests transferred. *[IFRS 3.33]*.

IFRS 3 gives additional guidance if no consideration is transferred by the acquirer. This is discussed at 7.4 below.

7.1 Contingent consideration

Contingent consideration generally arises where the acquirer agrees to transfer additional consideration to the former owners of the acquired business after the acquisition date if certain specified events occur or conditions are met in the future, although it can also result in the return of previously transferred consideration. *[IFRS 3 Appendix A]*.

When entering into a business combination, the parties to the arrangement may not always agree on the exact value of the business, particularly if there are uncertainties as to the success or worth of particular assets or the outcome of uncertain events. They therefore often agree to an interim value for the purposes of completing the deal, with additional future payments to be made by the acquirer. That is, they share the economic risks relating to the uncertainties about the future of the business. These future payments may be in cash or shares or other assets and may be contingent upon the achievement of specified events, and/or may be linked to future financial performance over a specified period of time. Examples of such additional payments contingent on future events are:

- earnings above an agreed target over an agreed period;
- components of earnings (e.g. revenue) above an agreed target over an agreed period;
- approval of a patent/licence;
- successful completion of specified contract negotiations;
- cash flows arising from specified assets over an agreed period; and
- remaining an employee of the entity for an agreed period of time.

An arrangement can have a combination of any of the above factors.

A business combination may include an agreement under which the acquirer is required to transfer to the seller all or part of the proceeds the acquirer eventually receives from the realisation of a contingent asset that existed at acquisition date. We believe that accounting for such obligation as a part of the contingent consideration does not necessarily reflect the substance of the agreement; rather it would be better depicted by the 'reverse indemnification liability' accounting. (see 5.6.4.A above).

While these payments may be negotiated as part of gaining control of another entity, the accounting may not necessarily always reflect this, particularly if these payments are made to those who remain as employees of the business after it is acquired. In the latter case, depending on the exact terms of the arrangement, the payment made may be accounted for as remuneration for services provided subsequent to the acquisition, rather than as part of the consideration paid for the business.

These payments are also often referred to as 'earn-outs'. The guidance in IFRS 3 for determining whether the arrangements involving employees should be accounted for as contingent consideration or remuneration is discussed further at 11.2 below.

The IASB clarified in June 2009 that pre-existing contingent consideration from a prior business combination of an acquiree does not meet the definition of contingent consideration in the acquirer's business combination. It is one of the identifiable liabilities assumed in the subsequent acquisition. Usually it makes no difference whether the pre-existing contingent consideration is treated as contingent consideration or as an identifiable liability as they are both financial liabilities to be accounted for under IFRS 9.[22] As discussed further below, they are initially recognised and measured at fair value at the date of acquisition, with any subsequent remeasurements recognised in profit or loss in accordance with IFRS 9.

7.1.1 Initial recognition and measurement

Contingent consideration is recognised at its fair value as part of the consideration transferred in exchange for the acquiree. *[IFRS 3.39]*.

IFRS 13 has specific requirements with respect to measuring fair value for liabilities. An entity has to determine the price it would need to pay to transfer the liability to a market participant at the measurement date. An entity must assume that the market participant would fulfil the obligation (i.e. it would not be settled or extinguished). *[IFRS 13.34(a)]*. The specific requirements are discussed in detail in Chapter 14 at 11. In light of these requirements, it is likely that the fair value of contingent consideration will need to be measured 'from the perspective of a market participant that holds the identical item as an asset at the measurement date'. *[IFRS 13.37]*. That is, the entity measures the fair value of the liability by reference to the fair value of the corresponding asset held by the counterparty.

The initial measurement of the fair value of contingent consideration is based on an assessment of the facts and circumstances that exist at the acquisition date. Although the fair value of some contingent payments may be difficult to measure, it is argued that 'to delay recognition of, or otherwise ignore, assets or liabilities that are difficult to measure would cause financial reporting to be incomplete and thus diminish its usefulness in making economic decisions'. *[IFRS 3.BC347]*. Information used in negotiations between buyer and seller will often be helpful in estimating the fair value of the contingent consideration. *[IFRS 3.BC348]*.

An estimate of zero for the fair value of contingent consideration would not be reliable. *[IFRS 3.BC349]*. Equally, it would be inappropriate to assume an estimate of 100% for the acquisition-date fair value of the obligation to make the payments under the contingent consideration arrangement.

The fair value of contingent consideration will be measured in accordance with IFRS 13 which does not limit the valuation techniques an entity might use. However, there are two commonly used approaches to estimating the fair value of contingent consideration that an entity might consider:

- the probability-weighted average of payouts associated with each possible outcome ('probability-weighted payout approach'); or
- the payout associated with the probability-weighted average of outcomes ('deterministic approach').

Both approaches will produce the same results when the arrangement has a linear payout structure. However, as illustrated in the Example 9.16 below, the results of their application will be different when the payout structure is nonlinear.

Therefore, entities should consider the relationship between the underlying performance metric or outcome and the payout associated with that metric or outcome to determine whether a probability-weighted payout or deterministic approach should be used. A contingent consideration arrangement can be characterised as having either a linear or non-linear relationship between outcomes and payouts. With a linear payout, the relationship between the underlying outcomes and the associated payouts is constant whereas in a non-linear payout the relationship between the underlying outcomes and the associated payouts is not constant. In situations where the payout structure is non-linear, using the deterministic approach is unlikely to give a reliable result. Because of this, understanding the payout structure and selecting an appropriate approach to estimate an earn-out's fair value is important.

The method that arguably gives the most reliable result in all circumstances is the probability-weighted payout approach. This method requires taking into account the range of possible outcomes, the payouts associated with each possible outcome and the probability of each outcome arising. The probability-weighted payout is then discounted. This approach is illustrated in the following example.

Example 9.16: Contingent consideration – applying the probability-weighted payout approach to determine fair value

Entity G acquires Entity H and as part of the arrangement, Entity G agrees to pay an additional amount of consideration to the seller in the future, as follows:

- if the 12-months' earnings in two years' time (also referred to as the trailing 12 months) are €1 million or less – nothing will be paid;
- if the trailing 12 months' earnings in two years' time are between €1 million and €2 million – 2 × 12-months' earnings will be paid;
- if the trailing 12 months' earnings in two years' time are greater than €2 million – 3 × 12-months' earnings will be paid.

At the date of acquisition, the possible twelve-month earnings of Entity H in two years' time are determined to be, as follows:

- €0.8 million – 40%
- €1.5 million – 40%
- €2.5 million – 20%

The probability-weighted payout is:

(40% × €0) + (40% × €1.5 million × 2) + (20% × €2.5 million × 3) = €2.7 million

This €2.7 million is then discounted at the date of acquisition to determine its fair value.

If Entity G applied the deterministic approach, the estimated fair value of the contingent consideration would be different.

The payout associated with the probability-weighted average of outcomes is:

(40% × €0.8 million + 40% × €1.5 million + 20% × €2.5 million) × 2 = €2.84 million

This €2.84 million then should be discounted at the date of acquisition to determine its fair value. However, as noted above, applying a deterministic approach to an arrangement for which the payout structure is nonlinear could result in an incorrect expected payout. Thus, in the fact pattern above it would not be appropriate for Entity G to apply a deterministic approach.

Since the liability must be measured at fair value, selecting the discount rate to be applied also requires significant judgement to assess the underlying risks associated with the outcomes and the risks of payment (see 7.1.1.A below for further discussion). The entity's own credit risk will need to be taken into account when measuring fair value, which could include adjusting the discount rate. In addition, IFRS 13 indicates that in those situations where the identical item is held by another party as an asset, the fair value of the liability should be determined from the perspective of a market participant that holds this asset. This guidance applies even if the corresponding asset is not traded or recognised for financial reporting purposes. As such, when determining the fair value of a contingent consideration liability, one should consider market participants' assumptions related to the item when held as an asset. The IASB and the FASB indicated that 'in an efficient market, the price of a liability held by another party as an asset must equal the price for the corresponding asset. If those prices differed, the market participant transferee (i.e. the party taking on the obligation) would be able to earn a profit by financing the purchase of the asset with the proceeds received by taking on the liability. In such cases, the price for the liability and the price for the asset would adjust until the arbitrage opportunity was eliminated.' *[IFRS 13.BC89]*.

IFRS 3 also recognises that, in some situations, the agreement may give the acquirer the right to the return of previously transferred consideration if specified future events occur or conditions are met. Such a right falls within the definition of 'contingent consideration', and is to be accounted for as such by recognising an asset at its acquisition-date fair value. *[IFRS 3.39-40, Appendix A].*

7.1.1.A   Estimating an appropriate discount rate

As discussed at 7.1.1 above, determining the appropriate discount rate to be applied requires significant judgement and requires that an entity consider the risks and uncertainty related to the asset or liability being measured.

Market participants generally require compensation for taking on the uncertainty inherent in the cash flows of an asset or a liability. This compensation is known as a risk premium. IFRS 13 states that in order to faithfully represent fair value, a present value technique should include a risk premium. The standard acknowledges that determining the appropriate risk premium might be difficult. However, the degree of difficulty alone is not a sufficient reason to exclude a risk premium if market participants would demand one. *[IFRS 13.B16].*

Depending on the present value technique used, risk may be incorporated in the cash flows or in the discount rate. However, identical risks should not be captured in both the cash flows and the discount rate in the same valuation analysis. For example, if the probability of default and loss given default for a liability are already incorporated in the discount rate (i.e. a risk-adjusted discount rate), the projected cash flows should not be further adjusted for the expected losses (see Chapter 14 at 21.2 for further discussion).

When determining the discount rate to use in measuring the fair value of contingent consideration, an entity should consider the risks associated with:

- the underlying outcome;
- the nature of the payout structure (e.g. a constant, fixed payment on achievement of the contingency versus a variable payment based on a multiple of earnings); and
- the ability of the holder to collect the contingent consideration payment (i.e. credit risk).

The first risk, which is associated with the underlying outcome, is generally represented as the required rate of return on the capital necessary to produce the outcome. For example, if the outcome is based on a measure such as revenue or EBIT, the required rates of return on the debt and equity capital used to generate the outcome should provide the starting point for estimating the discount rate. In this case, a weighted-average cost of capital may be an appropriate rate of return. On the other hand, if the outcome is based on net income, the cost of equity may be a more appropriate rate of return because the debt capital has already received its return via the interest payment. Furthermore, since the contingent consideration will be based on the target's performance, the risk should reflect the uncertainty specific to the target, rather than to a hypothetical market participant.

The second risk is inherent in the nature of the payout structure. In some circumstances, the risk of the underlying outcome may be captured in a weighted-average cost of capital or cost of equity. However, they may understate the discount rate. In particular, when the payout structure is non-linear, there may be additional risks that need to be considered. In other words, the contractual features that define the structure of the earn-out could make it a riskier arrangement. For example, assume there is an earn-out with the following characteristics: the payout is three times EBIT if more than €1 million; there is a 50% probability of EBIT being €1 million; and a 50% probability of EBIT being €2 million. The risk of EBIT being €1,000,000 versus €1,000,001 is small. That is, it represents only a fraction of a percentage. However, for the earn-out, there is incremental risk associated with that last € of EBIT. If EBIT is €1,000,000, the earn-out is not triggered, but if it is €1,000,001, the payout is required.

The third risk is the ability of the holder to collect the contingent consideration payment (i.e. credit risk of the buyer). Contingent consideration arrangements generally do not represent a direct claim on the cash flows from the underlying outcome (such as a specified portion of the target's earnings), but rather a subordinate, unsecured claim on the buyer. The credit risk of the buyer should be considered, taking into account the seniority of the contingent consideration claim in the buyer's capital structure and the expected timing of the payout. The buyer's own credit risk is considered in determining fair value because IFRS 13 presumes the liability is transferred to a market participant of equal credit standing. *[IFRS 13.42]*.

As discussed at 7.1.1 above, the fair value of a contingent consideration liability will likely need to be measured from the perspective of a market participant that holds the identical instrument as an asset. If the risk premium of the contingent consideration arrangement were to increase, the fair value would decline (i.e. due to a higher discount rate) for the holder of the contingent consideration asset. This increase in the risk premium would have a symmetrical effect on the liability (i.e. the discount).

7.1.2 Classification of a contingent consideration obligation

Most contingent consideration obligations are financial instruments, and many are derivative instruments. Some arrangements oblige the acquirer to deliver equity securities if specified future events occur, rather than, say, making additional cash payments.

The classification of a contingent consideration obligation that meets the definition of a financial instrument as either a financial liability or equity is to be based on the definitions in IAS 32 (see Chapter 47). *[IFRS 3.40]*.

These requirements, and the impact of subsequent measurement and accounting (which is discussed further at 7.1.3 below), are summarised in the diagram below.

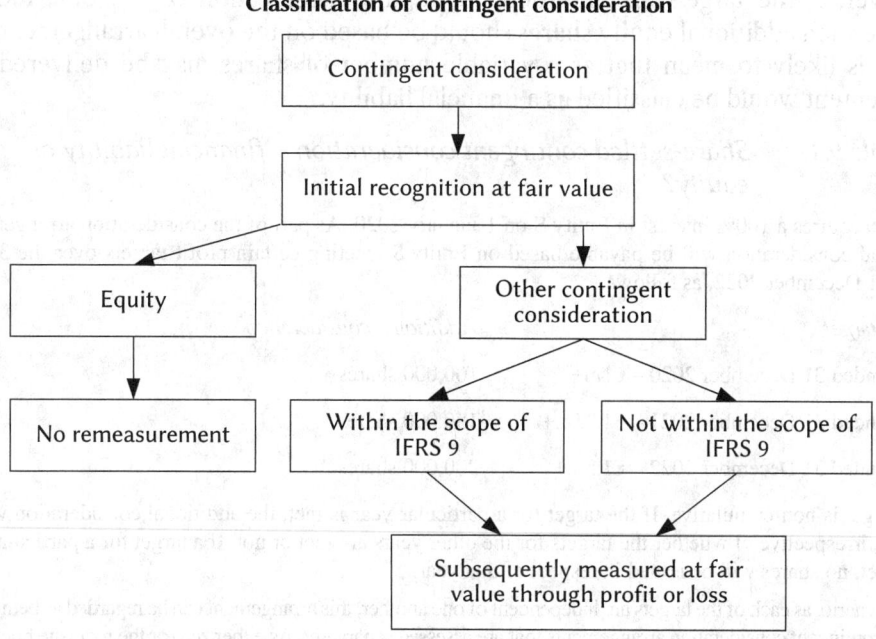

Classification of contingent consideration

Contingent consideration will often meet the definition of a financial liability. This includes those arrangements where the acquirer is obliged to deliver equity securities because IAS 32 defines a financial liability to include 'a contract that will or may be settled in the entity's own equity instruments' and is:

- 'a non-derivative for which the entity is or may be obliged to deliver a variable number of the entity's own equity instruments'; or
- 'a derivative that will or may be settled other than by the exchange of a fixed amount of cash or another financial asset for a fixed number of the entity's own equity instruments'. [IAS 32.11].

Most contingent consideration arrangements that are to be settled by delivering equity shares will involve a variable number of shares; e.g. an arrangement obliges the acquirer to issue between zero and 1 million additional equity shares on a sliding scale based on the acquiree's post-combination earnings. This arrangement will be classified as a financial liability. Only in situations where the arrangement involves issuing, say, zero or 1 million shares depending on a specified event or target being achieved would the arrangement be classified as equity. Where the arrangement involves a number of different discrete targets that are independent of one another, which if met will result in additional equity shares being issued as further consideration, we believe that the classification of the obligation to provide such financial instruments in respect of each target is assessed separately in determining whether equity classification is appropriate.

However, if the targets are interdependent, the classification of the obligation to provide such additional equity shares should be based on the overall arrangement, and as this is likely to mean that as a variable number of shares may be delivered, the arrangement would be classified as a financial liability.

Example 9.17: Share-settled contingent consideration – financial liability or equity?

Entity P acquires a 100% interest in Entity S on 1 January 2020. As part of the consideration arrangements, additional consideration will be payable based on Entity S meeting certain profit targets over the 3 years ended 31 December 2022, as follows:

Profit target	*Additional consideration*
Year ended 31 December 2020 – €1m+	100,000 shares
Year ended 31 December 2021 – €1.25m+	150,000 shares
Year ended 31 December 2022 – €1.5m+	200,000 shares

Each target is non-cumulative. If the target for a particular year is met, the additional consideration will be payable, irrespective of whether the targets for the other years are met or not. If a target for a particular year is not met, no shares will be issued in respect of that year.

In this scenario, as each of the targets are independent of one another, this arrangement can be regarded as being three distinct contingent consideration arrangements that are assessed separately. As either zero or the requisite number of shares will be issued if each target is met, the obligation in respect of each arrangement is classified as equity.

If the targets were dependent on each other, for example, if they were based on an average for the 3 year period, a specified percentage increase on the previous year's profits, or the later targets were forfeited if the earlier targets were not met, the classification would be assessed on the overall arrangement. As this would mean that a variable number of shares may be delivered, the obligation under such an arrangement would have to be classified as a financial liability.

For those contingent consideration arrangements where the agreement gives the acquirer the right to the return of previously transferred consideration if specified future events occur or conditions are met, IFRS 3 merely requires that such a right is classified as an asset. *[IFRS 3.40].*

7.1.3 Subsequent measurement and accounting

The IASB has concluded that subsequent changes in the fair value of a contingent consideration obligation generally do not affect the fair value of the consideration transferred for the acquiree. Subsequent changes in value relate to post-combination events and changes in circumstances of the combined entity and should not affect the measurement of the consideration transferred or goodwill. *[IFRS 3.BC357].*

Accordingly, IFRS 3 requires that changes in the fair value of contingent consideration resulting from events after the acquisition date such as meeting an earnings target, reaching a specified share price, or meeting a milestone on a research and development project are accounted for as follows:

- contingent consideration classified as equity is not subsequently remeasured (consistent with the accounting for equity instruments generally), and its subsequent settlement is accounted for within equity;

- other contingent consideration that either is within the scope of IFRS 9 or within the scope of other standards (e.g. a consideration payable is a non-financial liability) is remeasured at fair value at each reporting date and changes in fair value are recognised in profit or loss. *[IFRS 3.58]*.

The IASB also decided that any gain or loss resulting from changes in the fair value of a contingent consideration arrangement classified as a liability, that are recognised in profit or loss should include changes in own credit risk. *[IFRS 3.BC360I]*.

If the changes are the result of additional information about the facts and circumstances that existed at the acquisition date, they are measurement period adjustments and are to be accounted for as discussed at 12 below. *[IFRS 3.58]*.

7.2 Replacement share-based payment awards

Acquirers often exchange share-based payment awards (i.e. replacement awards) for awards held by employees of the acquiree. These exchanges frequently occur because the acquirer wants to avoid the effect of having non-controlling interests in the acquiree, the acquirer's shares are often more liquid than the shares of the acquired business after the acquisition, and/or to motivate former employees of the acquiree toward the overall performance of the combined, post-acquisition business.

If the acquirer replaces any acquiree awards, the consideration transferred will include some or all of any replacement share-based payment awards. However, arrangements that remunerate employees or former owners for future services are excluded from consideration transferred (see 11.2 below).

Replacement awards are modifications of share-based payment awards in accordance with IFRS 2. *[IFRS 3.B56-B62]*. Discussion of this guidance, including illustrative examples is dealt with in Chapter 34 at 11.2.

The acquirer is required to include some or all replacement awards (i.e. vested or unvested share-based payment transactions) as part of the consideration transferred, irrespective of whether it is obliged to replace acquiree's awards or does so voluntarily. There is only one situation in which none of the market-based measure of the awards is included in the consideration transferred: if acquiree awards would expire as a consequence of the business combination and the acquirer replaces those when it was not obliged to do so. In that case, all of the market-based measure of the awards is recognised as remuneration cost in the post-combination financial statements. *[IFRS 3.B56]*.

Any equity-settled share-based payment transactions of the acquiree that the acquirer does not exchange for its own share-based payment transactions will result in non-controlling interest in the acquiree being recognised and measured at their market-based measure as discussed at 8.4 below. *[IFRS 3.B62A, B62B]*.

7.3 Acquisition-related costs

IFRS 3 requires acquisition-related costs to be accounted for as expenses in the periods in which the costs are incurred and the related services are received with the exception of the costs of registering and issuing debt and equity securities that are recognised in accordance with IAS 32 and IFRS 9, i.e. as a reduction of the proceeds of the debt or equity securities issued. *[IFRS 3.53]*. In addition, IFRS 3 requires that a transaction that reimburses the acquiree or its former owners for paying the acquirer's acquisition-related costs is not to be included in applying the acquisition method (see 11.3 below). This is in order to mitigate concerns about potential abuse, e.g. a buyer might ask a seller to make payments to third parties on its behalf, but the consideration to be paid for the business is sufficient to reimburse the seller for making such payments. *[IFRS 3.51-53, BC370]*.

An acquirer's costs incurred in connection with a business combination include:

- direct costs of the transaction, such as costs for the services of lawyers, investment bankers, accountants, and other third parties and issuance costs of debt or equity instruments used to effect the business combination; and
- indirect costs of the transaction, such as recurring internal costs, e.g. the cost of maintaining an acquisition department.

Acquisition-related costs, whether for services performed by external parties or internal staff of the acquirer, are not part of the fair value exchange between the buyer and seller for the acquired business. Accordingly, they are not part of the consideration transferred for the acquiree. Rather, they are separate transactions in which the buyer makes payments in exchange for the services received, to be accounted for separately. It might be necessary to recognise expenses and a liability for such costs before the deal is closed, if recognition criteria for a liability is met at the earlier date, even if fees are payable only upon successful completion of the business combination.

7.4 Business combinations achieved without the transfer of consideration

An acquirer sometimes obtains control of an acquiree without transferring consideration. The standard emphasises that the acquisition method applies to a business combination achieved without the transfer of consideration. *[IFRS 3.43]*. IFRS 3 indicates that such circumstances include:

(a) the acquiree repurchases a sufficient number of its own shares for an existing investor (the acquirer) to obtain control;

(b) minority veto rights lapse that previously kept the acquirer from controlling an acquiree in which the acquirer held the majority voting rights; and

(c) the acquirer and the acquiree agree to combine their businesses by contract alone. In that case, the acquirer transfers no consideration in exchange for control of an acquiree and holds no equity interests in the acquiree, either on the acquisition date or previously. Examples of business combinations achieved by contract alone include bringing two businesses together in a stapling arrangement or forming a dual listed corporation. *[IFRS 3.43]*.

In computing the amount of goodwill in a business combination, IFRS 3 normally requires the acquirer to aggregate:

- the consideration transferred;
- the amount of any non-controlling interest in the acquiree; and
- the acquisition-date fair value of the acquirer's previously held equity interest in the acquiree. *[IFRS 3.32]*.

However, where the consideration transferred is nil, IFRS 3 requires the entity to use the acquisition-date fair value of the acquirer's interest in the acquiree instead. *[IFRS 3.33, B46]*.

In the first two circumstances described in (a) and (b) above, the acquirer has a previously-held equity interest in the acquiree. To include also the acquisition-date fair value of the previously-held interest would result in double-counting the value of the acquirer's interest in the acquiree. The acquisition-date fair value of the acquirer's interest in the acquiree should only be included once in the computation of goodwill. These two circumstances would also be examples of business combinations achieved in stages (see 9 below).

The fair value of the acquirer's interest in the acquiree is to be measured in accordance with IFRS 13.

7.4.1 Business combinations by contract alone

In a business combination achieved by contract alone ((c) above), IFRS 3 requires that the acquirer attributes to the owners of the acquiree the amount of the acquiree's net assets recognised under the standard (see 2.1 above). In other words, the equity interests in the acquiree held by parties other than the acquirer are a non-controlling interest in the acquirer's consolidated financial statements, even if it results in all of the equity interests in the acquiree being attributed to the non-controlling interest. *[IFRS 3.44]*.

This might suggest that no goodwill is to be recognised in a business combination achieved by contract alone as the second item in part (a) will be equal to part (b) of the goodwill computation set out at 6 above. However, we believe that this requirement to attribute the equity interests in the acquiree to the non-controlling interest is emphasising the presentation within equity in the consolidated financial statements. Thus, where the option of measuring non-controlling interests in an acquiree at its acquisition-date fair value is chosen, goodwill would be recognised. If the option of measuring the non-controlling interest at its proportionate share of the value of net identifiable assets acquired is chosen, no goodwill would be recognised (except to the extent any is recognised as a result of there being other equity instruments that are required to be measured at their acquisition-date fair value or other measurement basis required by IFRSs). These options are discussed at 8 below.

7.5 Combinations involving mutual entities

Combinations involving mutual entities are within the scope of IFRS 3. A mutual entity is defined by IFRS 3 as 'an entity, other than an investor-owned entity, that provides dividends, lower costs or other economic benefits directly to its owners, members or participants. For example, a mutual insurance company, a credit union and a co-operative entity are all mutual entities.' *[IFRS 3 Appendix A]*.

The standard notes that the fair value of the equity or member interests in the acquiree (or the fair value of the acquiree) may be more reliably measurable than the fair value of the member interests transferred by the acquirer. In that situation, the acquirer should determine the amount of goodwill by using the acquisition-date fair value of the acquiree's equity interests as the equivalent to the consideration transferred in the goodwill computation set out at 7.4 above, instead of the acquirer's equity interests transferred as consideration. *[IFRS 3.B47]*.

IFRS 3 clarifies that the acquirer in a combination of mutual entities recognises the acquiree's net assets as a direct addition to capital or equity, not as an addition to retained earnings, which is consistent with the way other types of entity apply the acquisition method. *[IFRS 3.B47]*.

IFRS 3 recognises that mutual entities, although similar in many ways to other businesses, have distinct characteristics that arise primarily because their members are both customers and owners. Members of mutual entities generally expect to receive benefits for their membership, often in the form of reduced fees charged for goods and services or patronage dividends. Patronage dividends are distributions paid to members (or investors) in mutual entities and the portion allocated to each member is often based on the amount of business the member did with the mutual entity during the year. *[IFRS 3.B48]*. The fair value of a mutual entity should include the assumptions that market participants would make about future member benefits. If, for example, a present value technique is used to measure the fair value of the mutual entity, the cash flow inputs should be based on the expected cash flows of the mutual entity, which are likely to reflect reductions for member benefits, such as reduced fees charged for goods and services. *[IFRS 3.B49]*.

8 RECOGNISING AND MEASURING NON-CONTROLLING INTERESTS

IFRS 3 requires any non-controlling interest in an acquiree to be recognised, *[IFRS 3.10]*, but provides a choice of two measurement methods. This choice only applies to those components of non-controlling interests that are present ownership interests and entitle their holders to a proportionate share of the entity's net assets in the event of a liquidation ('qualifying non-controlling interests').

These measurement methods are:

- Option 1, to measure such components of non-controlling interests at acquisition-date fair value (consistent with the measurement principle for other components of the business combination).
- Option 2, to measure such components of non-controlling interests at their proportionate share of the value of net identifiable assets acquired (described at 5 above).

This choice is not available for all other components of non-controlling interests. These are measured at their fair values, unless another measurement basis is required by IFRSs. *[IFRS 3.19]*.

IFRS 3 defines non-controlling interest as 'the equity in a subsidiary not attributable, directly or indirectly, to a parent'. *[IFRS 3 Appendix A]*. This is the same as that in IFRS 10. As discussed in Chapter 7 at 5.1, this definition includes not only equity shares in the subsidiary held by other parties, but also other elements of 'equity' in the subsidiary. These could relate to, say, other equity instruments such as options or warrants, the equity element of convertible debt instruments, and the 'equity' related to share-based payment awards held by parties other than the parent.

The application to particular instruments is set out in the table below.

Instruments issued by the acquiree	Measurement required by IFRS 3
Ordinary shares	Proportionate share of net assets OR fair value
Preference shares entitled to a *pro rata* share of net assets upon liquidation	Proportionate share of net assets OR fair value
Preference shares *not* entitled to a *pro rata* share of net assets upon liquidation	Fair value
Equity component of convertible debt and other compound financial instruments◊	Fair value
Share warrants◊	Fair value
Options over own shares◊	Fair value
Options under share-based payment transactions◊	IFRS 2 'market-based measure'

◊ In practice, because these instruments are generally not entitled to a share of net assets as of the acquisition date, their proportionate share of net assets is nil.

An illustration of the consequences of applying these requirements is given at 8.4 below.

The choice of method is to be made for each business combination on a transaction-by-transaction basis, rather than being a policy choice. Each option, combined with the accounting in IFRS 10 for changes in ownership interest of a subsidiary (see Chapter 7 at 4) could have a significant effect on the amount recognised for goodwill.

8.1 Measuring qualifying non-controlling interests at acquisition-date fair value

An acquirer will sometimes be able to measure the fair value of a non-controlling interest on the basis of a quoted price in an active market for the equity shares it does not hold. If a quoted price in an active market is unavailable, the acquirer will need to measure the fair value of the non-controlling interest by using other valuation techniques. *[IFRS 3.B44]*.

The fair value of the acquirer's interest in the acquiree and the non-controlling interest on a per-share basis might differ. This may happen because the consideration transferred by the acquirer may include a control premium, or conversely, the inclusion of a discount for lack of control (also referred to as a non-controlling interest discount) in the per-share value of the non-controlling interest if market participants would take into account such a premium or discount when pricing the non-controlling interest. *[IFRS 3.B45]*. In that case it would not be appropriate to extrapolate the fair value of an acquirer's interest (i.e. the amount that the acquirer paid per share) to determine the fair value of the non-controlling interests. In case if acquiree's shares are quoted on an active market, IFRS 13 requires the fair value of non-controlling interest to be determined using the quoted price of the shares at the acquisition date ('PxQ').

8.2 Measuring qualifying non-controlling interests at the proportionate share of the value of net identifiable assets acquired

Under this option, the non-controlling interest is measured at the share of the value of the net assets acquired and liabilities assumed of the acquiree (see 5 above). The result is that the amount recognised for goodwill is only the acquirer's share. However, if any part of the outstanding non-controlling interest is subsequently acquired, no additional goodwill is recorded as under IFRS 10 this is an equity transaction (see Chapter 7 at 4.2).

8.3 Implications of method chosen for measuring non-controlling interests

The following example illustrates the impact of the two measurement options on measuring those components of qualifying non-controlling interests.

Example 9.18:   Initial measurement of non-controlling interests in a business combination (1)

Entity B has 40% of its shares publicly traded on an exchange. Entity A purchases the 60% non-publicly traded shares in one transaction, paying €630. Based on the trading price of the shares of Entity B at the date of gaining control a value of €400 is assigned to the 40% non-controlling interest, indicating that Entity A has paid a control premium of €30. The fair value of Entity B's identifiable net assets is €700. For the purposes of the illustration, Entity B has no other instruments that would be regarded as non-controlling interests.

Option 1 – Non-controlling interest at fair value

Entity A accounts for the acquisition as follows:

	Dr €	Cr €
Fair value of identifiable net assets acquired	700	
Goodwill	330	
Cash		630
Non-controlling interest in entity B		400

Option 2 – Certain non-controlling interests are measured at proportionate share of identifiable net assets

Entity A accounts for the acquisition as follows:

	€	€
Fair value of identifiable net assets acquired	700	
Goodwill	210	
Cash		630
Non-controlling interest in entity B (€700 × 40%)		280

The IASB has noted that there are likely to be three main differences arising from measuring the non-controlling interest at its proportionate share of the acquiree's net identifiable assets, rather than at fair value. First, the amounts recognised in a business combination for the non-controlling interest and goodwill are likely to be lower (as illustrated in the above example).

Second, if a cash generating unit to which the goodwill has been allocated is subsequently impaired, any resulting impairment of goodwill recognised through income is likely to be lower than it would have been if the non-controlling interest had been measured at fair value. *[IFRS 3.BC217]*. Chapter 20 at 9 discusses testing goodwill for impairment in entities with non-controlling interests. This guidance includes, considerations when an entity applies an allocation methodology that recognises the disproportionate sharing of the controlling and non-controlling interests in the goodwill book value, i.e. taking into account the acquirer's control premium, if any.

The third difference noted by the IASB is that which arises if the acquirer subsequently purchases some or all of the shares held by the non-controlling shareholders. Under IFRS 10, such a transaction is to be accounted for as an equity transaction (see Chapter 7 at 4). By acquiring the non-controlling interest, usually at fair value (unless there are some special circumstances surrounding the acquisition), the equity of the group is reduced by the non-controlling interest's share of any unrecognised changes in fair value of the net assets of the business, including goodwill. Measuring the non-controlling interest initially as a proportionate share of the acquiree's net identifiable assets, rather than at fair value, means that the reduction in the reported equity attributable to the acquirer is likely to be larger. *[IFRS 3.BC218]*. If in Example 9.18 above, Entity A were subsequently to acquire all of the non-controlling interest for, say, €500, then assuming that there had been no changes in the carrying amounts for the net identifiable assets and the goodwill, the equity attributable to the parent, Entity A, would be reduced by €220 (€500 – €280) if Option 2 (proportionate share of fair value of identifiable net assets) had been adopted. If Option 1 (full fair value) had been adopted, the reduction would only be €100 (€500 – €400).

In Example 9.18 above, the acquiree had no other instruments that would be regarded as non-controlling interests. This will not always be the case. The impact of the measurement of such non-controlling interests on goodwill is illustrated in Example 9.19 below.

Example 9.19: Initial measurement of non-controlling interests in a business combination (2)

Parent acquires 80% of the ordinary shares of Target, a private entity, for €950 in cash. The total fair value of the equity instruments issued by Target is €1,165 and the fair value of its identifiable net assets is €850. The fair value of the 20% of the ordinary shares owned by non-controlling shareholders is €190. In addition, the subsidiary has also written gross settled call options over its own shares with a fair value of €25, which are considered equity instruments under IAS 32.

Option 1 – Non-controlling interest at fair value

The impact of the business combination, and the measurement of non-controlling interests, are as follows:

	Dr €	Cr €
Fair value of identifiable net assets	850	
Goodwill (€1,165 – €850)	315	
Cash		950
Non-controlling interest (€190 + €25)		215

Under this method, goodwill represents the difference between the fair value of Target and the fair value of its identifiable net assets. The non-controlling interests are measured as the fair value of all equity instruments issued by Target that are not owned by the parent (i.e. ordinary shares and gross settled call options).

Option 2 – Certain non-controlling interests are measured at proportionate share of identifiable net assets

The impact of the business combination, and the measurement of non-controlling interests, are as follows:

	€	€
Fair value of identifiable net assets	850	
Goodwill ((€950 + €195) – €850)	295	
Cash		950
Non-controlling interest (20% × €850 + €25)		195

Under this method, goodwill represents the difference between the total of the consideration transferred and the amount of the non-controlling interests less the fair value of the net assets acquired and liabilities assumed. The non-controlling interests that are present ownership interests and entitle their holders to a proportionate share of the Target's net assets in the event of liquidation (i.e. the ordinary shares) are measured at the non-controlling interest's proportionate share of the identifiable net assets of Target. The non-controlling interests that are not present ownership interests or do not entitle their holders to a proportionate share of the Target's net assets in the event of liquidation (i.e. the gross settled call options) are measured at their fair value.

Reconciliation of goodwill

Goodwill as determined under the two methods can be reconciled as follows:

Option 2: Goodwill (€950 – 80% × €850 + €25)	295
Goodwill related to the non-controlling interest in ordinary shares (€190 – 20% × €850)	20
Option 1: Goodwill (€1,165 – €850)	315

This makes clear that Option 2 effectively ignores the goodwill related to ordinary shares that are held by non-controlling shareholders.

In Example 9.19 above, under Option 2, the computation of the non-controlling interests represented by the ordinary shares was based solely on the fair value of the identifiable net assets; i.e. no deduction was made in respect of the other component of non-controlling interest. IFRS 3 does not explicitly state whether this should be the case or not. An alternative view would be that other components of non-controlling interests should be deducted from the value of the identifiable net assets based on their acquisition-date fair value (or market-based measure) or based on their liquidation rights (see Chapter 7 at 5.2.1). This alternative is illustrated in Chapter 7 in Example 7.17.

8.4 Measuring share-based payment and other components of non-controlling interests

These options in measuring the fair values of non-controlling interests only apply to present ownership interests that entitle their holders to a proportionate share of the entity's net assets in the event of a liquidation. All other components of non-controlling interests must be measured at their fair values, unless another measurement basis is required by IFRSs. *[IFRS 3.19]*. For example, a preference share that entitles the holders only to a preferred return of capital and accrued and unpaid dividends (or any other restricted right) in the event of a liquidation does not qualify for the measurement choice in paragraph 19 of IFRS 3 because it does not entitle its holder to a proportionate share of the entity's net assets in the event of liquidation.

The exception to fair values relates to outstanding share-based payment transactions that are not replaced by the acquirer:

- If vested, they are measured at their market-based measure.
- If unvested, they are measured at their market-based measure as if the acquisition date were the grant date. *[IFRS 3.B62A]*.

The market-based measure of unvested share-based payment transactions is allocated to the non-controlling interest on the basis of the ratio of the portion of the vesting period completed to the greater of the total vesting period or the original vesting period of the share-based payment transaction. The balance is allocated to post-combination service. *[IFRS 3.B62B]*.

The above requirements for equity-settled share-based payment transactions of the acquiree are discussed further in Chapter 34 at 11.

Example 9.20: Measurement of non-controlling interest represented by preference shares and employee share options

Preference shares

TC has issued 100 preference shares, which are classified as equity. The preference shares have a nominal value of £1 each. The preference shares give their holders a right to a preferential dividend in priority to the payment of any dividend to the holders of ordinary shares. On liquidation of TC, the holders of the preference shares are entitled to receive out of the assets available for distribution the amount of £1 per share in priority to the holders of ordinary shares but there are no further rights on liquidation.

AC acquires all ordinary shares of TC. The acquisition-date fair value of the preference shares is £120.

The non-controlling interests that relate to TC's preference shares do not entitle their holders to a proportionate share of the entity's net assets in the event of liquidation. They are measured at their fair value of £120.

If the preference shares have an equal right and ranking to the ordinary shares in the event of liquidation, they have a present ownership interest and could then be measured at their fair value or at or at their proportionate share in the acquiree's recognised amounts of the identifiable net assets. If the fair value of the preference shares is £160 and the proportionate share of TC's identifiable net assets attributable to the preference shares is £140, the acquirer can elect to measure the preference shares at either of these amounts.

Employee share options

TC has issued share options to its employees. The share options are classified as equity and are vested at the acquisition date. The share options do not expire on the acquisition date and AC does not replace them. They do not represent present ownership interest and do not entitle their holders to a proportionate share of TC's net assets in the event of liquidation. The market-based measure of the share options in accordance with IFRS 2 at the acquisition date is £200. The acquirer measures the non-controlling interests that are related to the share options at their market-based measure of £200.

8.5 Call and put options over non-controlling interests

In some business combinations where less than 100% of the equity shares are acquired, it may be that the transaction also involves options over some or all of the outstanding shares held by the non-controlling shareholders. The acquirer may have a call option, i.e. a right to acquire the outstanding shares at a future date for cash at a particular price. Alternatively, it may have granted a put option to the other shareholders whereby they have the right to sell their shares to the acquirer at a future date for cash at a particular price. In some cases, there may be a combination of call and put options, the terms of which may be equivalent or may be different.

IFRS 3 gives no guidance as to how such options should impact on the accounting for a business combination. This issue is discussed in Chapter 7 at 6.

Similarly, IFRS 3 does not explicitly address the accounting for a sequence of transactions that begin with an acquirer gaining control over another entity, followed by acquiring additional ownership interests shortly thereafter. This frequently happens where public offers are made to a group of shareholders and there is a regulatory requirement for an acquirer to make an offer to the non-controlling shareholders of the acquiree.

The Interpretations Committee considered this issue and tentatively decided that the guidance in IFRS 10 on how to determine whether the disposal of a subsidiary achieved in stages should be accounted for as one transaction, or as multiple transactions, *[IFRS 10.B97],* should also be applied to circumstances in which the acquisition of a business is followed by successive purchases of additional interests in the acquiree. The Interpretations Committee tentatively agreed that the initial acquisition of the controlling stake and the subsequent mandatory tender offer should be treated as a single transaction.

Meanwhile, in the absence of any explicit guidance in IFRS for such transactions, we believe that entities generally have an accounting policy choice as to whether the transactions should be treated as a single acquisition in which control is gained (a single business combination), or are to be treated as discrete transactions (a business combination, followed by an acquisition of non-controlling interests). However, the former policy can only be applied where the acquisition of non-controlling interest is assessed as linked to the same transaction as that by which control is gained. This issue is discussed in Chapter 7 at 6.2.4.

However, there was no consensus among the Interpretations Committee members on whether a liability should be recognised for the mandatory tender offer at the date that the acquirer obtains control of the acquiree. A small majority expressed the view that a liability should be recognised in a manner that is consistent with IAS 32. Other Interpretations Committee members expressed the view that a mandatory tender offer to purchase NCI is not within the scope of IAS 32 or IAS 37 and that a liability should therefore not be recognised. The issue was escalated to the IASB and at its May 2013 meeting the Board tentatively decided to discuss both issues when it discusses the measurement of put options written on NCI.[23] In June 2014, the IASB decided that the project on put options written on NCI should be incorporated into the broader project looking at the distinction between liabilities and equity – the *Financial Instruments with Characteristics of Equity* ('FICE') project.[24] In June 2018, the IASB issued for comment a Discussion Paper, *Financial Instruments with Characteristics of Equity* ('DP'). The IASB has used the example of mandatory tender offers in the DP to illustrate some of the challenges of the FICE project. Comments were requested by 7 January 2019. Based on the feedback received on the DP, the IASB tentatively decided to explore making clarifying amendments to IAS 32 to address common accounting challenges that arise in practice when applying IAS 32. In October 2019, staff presented to the Board an agenda paper that discussed the project plan to clarify amendments to IAS 32. This paper included a summary discussion of the objectives of the clarifying amendments to IAS 32, issues to be considered on classification, presentation and disclosure, as well as an indicative project timeline. The preliminary list of classification issues to be addressed by the project plan included accounting for obligations to redeem own equity instruments, e.g. accounting for written put options on non-controlling interests (NCI puts). The agenda paper stated that one area highlighted by respondents is the interaction of IAS 32 requirements on classification of such obligations with IFRS 3, in particular whether the NCI put is part of the business combination transaction and the resulting implication on the calculation of goodwill.[25] In the staff's view, the IASB would be able to address the issue efficiently and effectively without fundamentally rewriting IAS 32, for example by exploring the following:

- adding an explanation of the principle in IAS 32 for recognising an obligation to redeem own equity instruments for cash (or another financial asset) as a gross financial liability;
- clarifying the accounting within equity;
- clarifying the presentation of income and expenses related to the subsequent measurement of the financial liability especially if the NCI is puttable at fair value.[26]

According to the indicative project timeline included in the agenda paper, the analysis of obligations to redeem own equity instruments (including NCI puts) is expected to be submitted to the Board for its deliberations in the second half of 2020.[27] The FICE DP is also discussed in Chapter 47 at 12.

9 BUSINESS COMBINATIONS ACHIEVED IN STAGES ('STEP ACQUISITIONS')

The third item in part (a) of the goodwill computation set out at 6 above is the acquisition-date fair value of the acquirer's previously held equity interest in the acquiree.

An acquirer sometimes obtains control of an acquiree in which it held an equity interest immediately before the acquisition date. For example, on 31 January 2021, Entity A holds a 35 per cent non-controlling equity interest in Entity B. On that date, Entity A purchases an additional 40 per cent interest in Entity B, which gives it control of Entity B. IFRS 3 refers to such a transaction as a business combination achieved in stages, sometimes also referred to as a 'step acquisition'. *[IFRS 3.41]*.

If the acquirer holds a non-controlling equity investment in the acquiree immediately before obtaining control, the acquirer remeasures that previously held equity investment at its acquisition-date fair value and recognises any resulting gain or loss in profit or loss or other comprehensive income, as appropriate. *[IFRS 3.42]*.

In effect, the acquirer exchanges its status as an owner of an investment asset in an entity for a controlling financial interest in all of the underlying assets and liabilities of that entity (acquiree) and the right to direct how the acquiree and its management use those assets in its operations. *[IFRS 3.BC384]*.

In addition, any changes in the value of the acquirer's equity interest in the acquiree recognised in other comprehensive income (e.g. the investment was designated as measured at fair value through other comprehensive income without recycling to profit or loss upon derecognition) is recognised on the same basis that would be required if the acquirer had directly disposed of the previously held equity investment. *[IFRS 3.42]*.

The acquirer's non-controlling equity investment in the acquiree, after remeasurement to its acquisition-date fair value, is then included as the third item of part (a) of the goodwill computation set out at 6 above.

Under IFRS 9 investments in equity instruments that are not held for trading would likely be classified as either:
- financial assets designated as measured at fair value through profit or loss; or
- financial assets measured at fair value through other comprehensive income if an entity made an irrevocable election at initial recognition to present subsequent changes in their fair value in other comprehensive income.

In the former case no transfer would be necessary as gains or losses from changes in the fair value would be already included in profit or loss in the previous periods. In the latter case, as illustrated in the Example 9.21 below gains or losses from changes in the fair value accumulated in other comprehensive income would never be reclassified to profit or loss but may be transferred into the retained earnings on 'deemed disposal' of the investment, if an entity initially recognised these changes in a separate component of equity rather than directly within the retained earnings.

Example 9.21:   *Business combination achieved in stages – original investment treated as FVOCI without recycling*

Investor acquires a 20 per cent ownership interest in Investee (a service company) on 1 January 2020 for £3,500,000 cash, which is the fair value of the investment at that date. The Investor has concluded that despite of its 20% holding it does not have significant influence over the Investee. At that date, the fair value of Investee's identifiable assets is £10,000,000, and the carrying amount of those assets is £8,000,000. Investee has no liabilities or contingent liabilities at that date. The following shows Investee's statement of financial position at 1 January 2020 together with the fair values of the identifiable assets:

Investee's statement of financial position at 1 January 2020	Carrying amounts £'000	Fair values £'000
Cash and receivables	2,000	2,000
Land	6,000	8,000
	8,000	10,000
Issued equity: 1,000,000 ordinary shares	5,000	
Retained earnings	3,000	
	8,000	

During the year ended 31 December 2020, Investee reports a profit of £6,000,000 but does not pay any dividends. In addition, the fair value of Investee's land increases by £3,000,000 to £11,000,000. However, the amount recognised by Investee in respect of the land remains unchanged at £6,000,000. The following shows Investee's statement of financial position at 31 December 2020 together with the fair values of the identifiable assets:

Investee's statement of financial position at 31 December 2020	Carrying amounts £'000	Fair values £'000
Cash and receivables	8,000	8,000
Land	6,000	11,000
	14,000	19,000
Issued equity: 1,000,000 ordinary shares	5,000	
Retained earnings	9,000	
	14,000	

Accounting for the initial investment before obtaining control

Investor's initial 20 per cent investment in Investee is included in Investor's consolidated financial statements under the equity method. Accordingly, it is initially recognised at its cost of £3,500,000 and adjusted thereafter for its share of the profits of Investee after the date of acquisition of £1,200,000 (being 20% × £6,000,000). Investor's policy for property, plant and equipment is to use the cost model under IAS 16; therefore in applying the equity method it does not include its share of the increased value of the land held by Investee. IAS 28 requires that on the acquisition of an associate, any difference between the cost of the acquisition and its share of the fair values of the associate's identifiable assets and liabilities is accounted for as goodwill, but is included within the carrying amount of the investment in the associate. Accordingly, Investor has included goodwill of £1,500,000 arising on its original investment of 20%, being £3,500,000 less £2,000,000 (20% × £10,000,000). Therefore, Investor's consolidated statement of financial position at 31 December 2020, before the acquisition of the additional 60 per cent ownership interest, is as follows:

Investor's consolidated statement of financial position at 31 December 2020	£'000
Cash	26,500
Investment in associate	4,700
	31,200
Issued equity	30,000
Retained earnings	1,200
	31,200

In its separate financial statements, Investor includes its investment in the associate at its cost of £3,500,000.

Accounting for the business combination

Although Investor has previously equity accounted for its 20% interest in Investee (and calculated goodwill on that acquisition), the computation of goodwill in its consolidated financial statements as a result of obtaining control over Investee is the same as that in Example 9.21 above:

	£'000
Consideration transferred for 60% interest acquired on 1 January 2021	22,000
Non-controlling interest – share of fair values of identifiable net assets at that date (20% × £19,000,000)	3,800
Acquisition-date fair value of initial 20% interest	6,000
	31,800
Acquisition-date fair values of identifiable net assets acquired	19,000
Goodwill	12,800

Investor recognises a gain of £1,300,000 in profit or loss as a result of remeasuring its existing interest from its equity-accounted amount of £4,700,000 at the date of obtaining control to its acquisition-date fair value of £6,000,000.

The following shows Investor's consolidation worksheet immediately after the acquisition of the additional 60 per cent ownership interest in Investee, together with consolidation adjustments and associated explanations.

	Investor	Investee	Consolidation adjustments		Consolidated	
			Dr	Cr		
	£'000	£'000	£'000	£'000	£'000	
Cash and receivables	4,500	8,000			12,500	
Investment in investee	26,700	–		26,700	–	
Land		6,000	5,000		11,000	(a)
Goodwill			12,800		12,800	(b)
	31,200	14,000			36,300	
Issued equity	30,000	5,000	5,000		30,000	(c)
Retained earnings	1,200	9,000	9,000		1,200	(d)
Profit for 2020				1,300	1,300	(e)
Non-controlling interest				3,800	3,800	(a)
	31,200	14,000			36,300	

Notes

The above consolidation adjustments result in:

(a) Investee's identifiable net assets being stated at their full fair values at the date Investor obtains control of Investee, i.e. £19,000,000, including land of £11,000,000. The 20 per cent non-controlling interest in Investee is also stated at the non-controlling interest's 20 per cent share of the fair values of Investee's identifiable net assets, i.e. £3,800,000 (20% × £19,000,000).

(b) goodwill being recognised from the acquisition date based on the computation set out at 6 above, i.e. £12,800,000.

(c) issued equity of £30,000,000 comprising the issued equity of Investor of £30,000,000.

(d) a retained earnings balance of £1,200,000 being Investor's equity accounted share of Investee while it was an associate.

(e) profit of £1,300,000 being the amount of gain on remeasurement of the previously existing interest in Investee at its acquisition-date fair value (£6,000,000 – £4,700,000). As a result, total retained earnings in the statement of financial position are £2,500,000.

Although the examples above illustrate the requirements of IFRS 3 when the previously held investment has been accounted for as an equity investment designated as FVOCI (without recycling) or as an associate, the requirements in IFRS 3 for step acquisitions apply to all previously held non-controlling equity investments in the acquiree, including those that were accounted for as joint ventures or joint operations under IFRS 11. Accounting for step-acquisitions of former joint operations that are businesses is discussed at 9.1 below. IAS 28's requirements also apply to joint ventures. [IAS 28.2].

As a result of obtaining control over a former associate or joint venture, the acquirer accounts for the business combination by applying the other requirements under IFRS 3 as it would in any other business combination. Thus, it needs to recognise the net of the acquisition-date fair values (or other amounts recognised in accordance with the requirements of the standard) of the identifiable assets acquired and the liabilities assumed relating to the former associate or joint venture (see 5 above), i.e. perform a new purchase price allocation. This will include reassessing the classification and designation of assets and liabilities, including the classification of financial instruments, embedded derivatives and hedge accounting, based on the circumstances that exist at the acquisition date (see 5.4 above).

Obtaining control over a former associate or joint venture means that the investor 'loses' significant influence or 'joint control' over it. Therefore, any amounts recognised in other comprehensive income relating to the associate or joint venture should be recognised by the investor on the same basis that would be required if the associate or joint venture had directly disposed of the related assets or liabilities. For associates and joint ventures, this is discussed further in Chapter 11 at 7.12.1.

In Example 9.22 above, a gain was recognised as a result of the step-acquisition of the former associate. However, a loss may have to be recognised as a result of the step-acquisition.

Example 9.23:   Business combination achieved in stages – loss arising on step-acquisition

An investor has an equity-accounted interest in a listed associate comprising 1,000 shares with a carrying value of €1,000. The quoted price of the associate's shares is €0.90 per share, i.e. €900 in total. As there is an impairment indicator, the investment is tested for impairment in accordance with IAS 36. However, as the investor determines that the investment's value in use exceeds €1,000, no impairment loss is recognised.

In the following period, the investor acquires all of the other outstanding shares in the associate. Up to the date of obtaining control, the investor has recognised a further share of profits of the associate, such that the equity-accounted interest in the associate is now €1,050. At the date of obtaining control, the fair value of the shares has increased to €0.93. The existing shares are remeasured to fair value at that date and a loss of €120 (€1,050 less €930) is recognised in profit or loss.

9.1 Accounting for previously held interests in a joint operation

A party to a joint operation (i.e. either a joint operator or a party that does not share joint control) may obtain control of a joint operation that is a business (as defined in IFRS 3). The IASB views a transaction where control is gained as a significant change in the nature of, and the economic circumstances surrounding, the interest in the joint operation. Therefore, when a party to a joint operation obtains control of a joint operation that is a business, it must remeasure to fair value the entire interest it previously held in that joint operation. In other words, such a transaction must be accounted for as a business combination achieved in stages. *[IFRS 3.42A].*

Chapter 12 at 8.3.2 discusses how a party that participates in (but does not have joint control over) a joint operation, accounts for obtaining joint control over that joint operation that is a business (as defined in IFRS 3).

10 BARGAIN PURCHASE TRANSACTIONS

IFRS 3 regards a bargain purchase as being a business combination in which:
- the net of the acquisition-date fair values (or other amounts recognised in accordance with the requirements of the standard) of the identifiable assets acquired and the liabilities assumed, exceeds
- the aggregate of:
  - the consideration transferred (generally measured at acquisition-date fair value);
  - the amount of any non-controlling interest in the acquiree; and
  - the acquisition-date fair value of the acquirer's previously held equity interest in the acquiree. *[IFRS 3.34]*.

The IASB considers bargain purchases anomalous transactions – business entities and their owners generally do not knowingly and willingly sell assets or businesses at prices below their fair values. *[IFRS 3.BC371]*. Nevertheless, occasionally, an acquirer will make a bargain purchase, for example, in a forced sale in which the seller is acting under compulsion. *[IFRS 3.35]*. These may occur in a forced liquidation or distress sale (e.g. after the death of a founder or key manager) in which owners need to sell a business quickly. The IASB observed that an economic gain is inherent in a bargain purchase and concluded that, in concept, the acquirer should recognise that gain at the acquisition date. However, there may not be clear evidence that a bargain purchase has taken place, and because of this there remained the potential for inappropriate gain recognition resulting from measurement bias or undetected measurement errors. *[IFRS 3.BC372-BC375]*.

Therefore, before recognising a gain on a bargain purchase, the acquirer should reassess all components of the computation to ensure that the measurements are based on all available information as of the acquisition date. This means ensuring that it has correctly identified all of the assets acquired and all of the liabilities assumed and does not have to recognise any additional assets or liabilities. Having done so, the acquirer must review the procedures used to measure all of the following:

(a) the identifiable assets acquired and liabilities assumed;
(b) the non-controlling interest in the acquiree, if any;
(c) for a business combination achieved in stages, the acquirer's previously held equity interest in the acquiree; and
(d) the consideration transferred. *[IFRS 3.36]*.

If an excess remains, the acquirer recognises a gain in profit or loss on the acquisition date. All of the gain is attributed to the acquirer. *[IFRS 3.34]*.

The computation means that a gain on a bargain purchase and goodwill cannot both be recognised for the same business combination. *[IFRS 3.BC376-BC377]*.

IFRS 3 acknowledges that the requirements to measure particular assets acquired or liabilities assumed in accordance with other IFRSs, rather than their fair value, may result in recognising a gain (or change the amount of a recognised gain) on acquisition. *[IFRS 3.35, BC379]*.

The computation of a gain on a bargain purchase is illustrated in the following example, which is based on one included within the Illustrative Examples accompanying IFRS 3. *[IFRS 3.IE45-IE49].*

Example 9.24: Gain on a bargain purchase (1)

Entity A acquires 80% of the equity interests of Entity B, a private entity, in exchange for cash of €150m. Because the former owners of Entity B needed to dispose of their investments in Entity B by a specified date, they did not have sufficient time to market Entity B to multiple potential buyers. The management of Entity A initially measures the separately recognisable identifiable assets acquired and the liabilities assumed as of the acquisition date in accordance with the requirements of IFRS 3. The identifiable assets are measured at €250m and the liabilities assumed are measured at €50m. Entity A engages an independent consultant, who determines that the fair value of the 20% non-controlling interest in Entity B is €42m.

Entity B's identifiable net assets of €200m (being €250m – €50m) exceed the fair value of the consideration transferred plus the fair value of the non-controlling interest in Entity B. Therefore, Entity A reviews the procedures it used to identify and measure the assets acquired and liabilities assumed and to measure the fair value of both the non-controlling interest in Entity B and the consideration transferred. After that review, Entity A decides that the procedures and resulting measures were appropriate. Entity A measures the gain on its purchase of the 80% interest as follows:

	€m	€m
Fair value of the identifiable net assets acquired (€250m – €50m)		200
Less:		
Fair value of the consideration transferred for Entity A's 80% interest	150	
Fair value of non-controlling interest in Entity B	42	
		(192)
Gain on bargain purchase of 80% interest in Entity B		8

Entity A would record its acquisition of Entity B in its consolidated financial statements as follows:

	Dr €m	Cr €m
Identifiable net assets acquired	250	
Cash		150
Liabilities assumed		50
Gain on bargain purchase		8
Equity – non-controlling interest in Entity B		42

If Entity A chose to measure the non-controlling interest in Entity B on the basis of its proportionate interest in the identifiable net assets of the acquiree, the gain on the purchase of the 80% interest would have been as follows:

	€m	€m
Fair value of the identifiable net assets acquired (€250m – €50m)		200
Less:		
Fair value of the consideration transferred for Entity A's 80% interest	150	
Non-controlling interest in Entity B (20% × €200m)	40	
		(190)
Gain on bargain purchase of 80% interest in Entity B		10

On that basis, Entity A would record its acquisition of Entity B in its consolidated financial statements as follows:

	Dr €m	Cr €m
Identifiable net assets acquired	250	
Cash		150
Liabilities assumed		50
Gain on bargain purchase		10
Equity – non-controlling interest in Entity B		40

It can be seen from the above example that the amount of the gain recognised is affected by the way in which the non-controlling interest is measured. Indeed, it might be that if the non-controlling interest is measured at its acquisition-date fair value, goodwill is recognised rather than a gain as shown below.

Example 9.25:   Gain on a bargain purchase (2)

This example uses the same facts as in Example 9.23 above, except that the independent consultant, determines that the fair value of the 20% non-controlling interest in Entity B is €52m.

In this situation, the fair value of the consideration transferred plus the fair value of the non-controlling interest in Entity B exceeds the amount of the identifiable net assets acquired, giving rise to goodwill on the acquisition as follows:

	€m
Fair value of the consideration transferred for Entity A's 80% interest	150
Fair value of non-controlling interest in Entity B	52
	202
Less: Fair value of the identifiable net assets acquired (€250m – €50m)	(200)
Goodwill on acquisition of 80% interest in Entity B	2

Therefore, although Entity A in the above example might have made a 'bargain purchase', the requirements of IFRS 3 lead to no gain being recognised.

11   ASSESSING WHAT IS PART OF THE EXCHANGE FOR THE ACQUIREE

To be included in the accounting for the business combination, the identifiable assets acquired and liabilities assumed must be part of the exchange for the acquiree, rather than a result of separate transactions. *[IFRS 3.12]*.

IFRS 3 recognises that the acquirer and the acquiree may have a pre-existing relationship or other arrangement before the negotiations for the business combination, or they may enter into an arrangement during the negotiations that is separate from the business combination. In either situation, the acquirer is required to identify any amounts that are separate from the business combination and thus are not part of the exchange for the acquiree. *[IFRS 3.51]*. This requires the acquirer to evaluate the substance of transactions between the parties.

There are three types of transactions that IFRS 3 regards as separate transactions that should not be considered part of the exchange for the acquiree:

- a transaction that effectively settles pre-existing relationships between the acquirer and acquiree, e.g. a lawsuit, supply contract, franchising or licensing arrangement (see 11.1 below);
- a transaction that remunerates employees or former owners of the acquiree for future services (see 11.2 below); or
- a transaction that reimburses the acquiree or its former owners for paying the acquirer's acquisition-related costs (see 11.3 below). *[IFRS 3.52]*.

The acquirer should consider the following factors to determine whether a transaction is part of the exchange for the acquiree or whether it is separate. The standard stresses that these factors are neither mutually exclusive nor individually conclusive. *[IFRS 3.B50]*.

- *The reasons for the transaction*

  Understanding the reasons why the parties to the combination, the acquirer and the acquiree and their owners, directors and managers – and their agents – entered into a particular transaction or arrangement may provide insight into whether it is part of the consideration transferred and the assets acquired or liabilities assumed. If a transaction is arranged primarily for the benefit of the acquirer or the combined entity rather than for the benefit of the acquiree or its former owners before the combination, that portion of the transaction price paid (and any related assets or liabilities) is less likely to be part of the exchange for the acquiree. The acquirer would account for that portion separately from the business combination.

- *Who initiated the transaction*

  A transaction or other event that is initiated by the acquirer may be entered into for the purpose of providing future economic benefits to the acquirer or combined entity with little or no benefit received by the acquiree or its former owners before the combination. A transaction or arrangement initiated by the acquiree or its former owners is less likely to be for the benefit of the acquirer or the combined entity and more likely to be part of the business combination transaction.

- *The timing of the transaction*

  A transaction between the acquirer and the acquiree during the negotiations of the terms of a business combination may have been entered into in contemplation of the business combination to provide future economic benefits to the acquirer or the combined entity. If so, the acquiree or its former owners before the business combination are likely to receive little or no benefit from the transaction except for benefits they receive as part of the combined entity.

One particular area that may be negotiated between acquirer and acquiree could be a restructuring plan relating to the activities of the acquiree. This is discussed at 11.4 below.

11.1 Effective settlement of pre-existing relationships

The acquirer and acquiree may have a relationship that existed before they contemplated the business combination, referred to as a 'pre-existing relationship'. This may be contractual, e.g. vendor and customer or licensor and licensee, or non-contractual, e.g. plaintiff and defendant. *[IFRS 3.B51]*.

The purpose of this guidance is to ensure that a transaction that in effect settles a pre-existing relationship between the acquirer and the acquiree is excluded from the accounting for the business combination. If a potential acquiree has an asset, a receivable for an unresolved claim against the potential acquirer, the acquiree's owners could agree to settle that claim as part of an agreement to sell the acquiree to the acquirer. If the acquirer makes a lump sum payment to the seller-owner for the business, part of that payment is to settle the claim. In effect, the acquiree relinquished its claim against the acquirer by transferring its receivable as a dividend to the acquiree's owner. Thus, at the acquisition date the acquiree has no receivable to be acquired as part of the combination, and the acquirer should account separately for its settlement payment. *[IFRS 3.BC122]*.

The acquirer is to recognise a gain or a loss on effective settlement of a pre-existing relationship, measured on the following bases:

- for a pre-existing non-contractual relationship, such as a lawsuit, the gain or loss is measured at its fair value;
- for a pre-existing contractual relationship, such as a supply contract, the gain or loss is measured as the lesser of:

   (a) the amount by which the contract is favourable or unfavourable from the perspective of the acquirer when compared with terms for current market transactions for the same or similar terms. (A contract that is unfavourable in terms of current market terms is not necessarily an onerous contract in which the unavoidable costs of meeting the obligations under the contract exceed the economic benefits expected to be received under it); and

   (b) the amount of any settlement provisions in the contract available to the counterparty to whom the contract is unfavourable.

   If (b) is less than (a), the difference is included as part of the business combination accounting.

The amount of gain or loss will depend in part on whether the acquirer had previously recognised a related asset or liability, and the reported gain or loss therefore may differ from the amount calculated by applying the above requirements. *[IFRS 3.B52]*.

If there is an 'at market' component to the settlement (i.e. part of the payment reflects the price any market participant would pay to settle the relationship), this is to be accounted for as part of goodwill and may not be treated as a separate intangible asset.[28]

The requirements for non-contractual relationships are illustrated in the following example.

Example 9.26: **Settlement of pre-existing non-contractual relationship**

On 1 January 2021 Entity A acquires a 100% interest in Entity B for €250m in cash.

At the beginning of 2019 a dispute arose over the interpretation of a contract for the development and implementation by Entity A of an e-business platform for Entity C, which at the end of 2018 was merged with Entity B. The contract, signed in 2014 and for which work was completed in December 2017, provided for payment of part of the contract price by allocating to Entity A 5% of the profit from the platform for five years from the system's installation, i.e. from January 2018 to January 2023. At the end of 2018 the merged Entity ceased to use the platform developed by Entity A as Entity B had its own platform. Entity A, however, believes that 5% of certain profits should be payable by Entity B for the period January 2019 to January 2023 regardless of the system used by Entity B. Several legal hearings took place in 2019 and 2020. However, at the date of acquisition the dispute is still unresolved. Entity B recognised a provision amounting to €12m reflecting the best estimate of the expenditure required to settle the present obligation at 1 January 2021. No assets are recognised by Entity A with respect to the dispute prior to the date of acquisition.

The acquisition by Entity A of Entity B includes the effective settlement of the dispute between Entity A and Entity B which is accounted for as a separate transaction from the business combination. On 1 January 2021 Entity A recognises a gain on effective settlement of the dispute at its fair value, which is not necessarily equal to the amount of the provision reported by Entity B. The amount of consideration transferred for the acquisition of Entity B is increased accordingly. Assuming the fair value of the dispute at 1 January 2021 is assessed to be €15m, Entity A will recognise a gain on effective settlement of €15m, and the consideration transferred for the purposes of determining goodwill will total €265m (€250m + €15m).

The requirements for contractual relationships are illustrated in the following example relating to a supply contract. *[IFRS 3.IE54-IE57].*

Example 9.27: **Settlement of pre-existing contractual relationship – Supply contract**

Entity A purchases electronic components from Entity B under a five-year supply contract at fixed rates. Currently, the fixed rates are higher than the rates at which Entity A could purchase similar electronic components from another supplier. The supply contract allows Entity A to terminate the contract before the end of the initial five-year term but only by paying a €6m penalty. With three years remaining under the supply contract, Entity A pays €50m to acquire Entity B, which is the fair value of Entity B based on what other market participants would be willing to pay.

Included in the total fair value of Entity B is €8m related to the fair value of the supply contract with Entity A. The €8m represents a €3m component that is 'at market' because the pricing is comparable to pricing for current market transactions for the same or similar items (selling effort, customer relationships and so on) and a €5 million component for pricing that is unfavourable to Entity A because it exceeds the price of current market transactions for similar items. Entity B has no other identifiable assets or liabilities related to the supply contract, and Entity A has not recognised any assets or liabilities related to the supply contract before the business combination.

In this example, Entity A calculates a loss of €5m (the lesser of the €6m stated settlement amount and the amount by which the contract is unfavourable to the acquirer) separately from the business combination. The €3m 'at-market' component of the contract is part of goodwill. This means that in the business combination, the acquirer does not recognise any pre-existing relationship between the acquiree and the acquirer as a separate intangible asset acquired.

Whether Entity A had recognised previously an amount in its financial statements related to a pre-existing relationship will affect the amount recognised as a gain or loss for the effective settlement of the relationship. Suppose that Entity A had recognised a €6m liability for the supply contract before the business combination. In that situation, Entity A recognises a €1m settlement gain on the contract in profit or loss at the acquisition date (the €5m measured loss on the contract less the €6m loss previously recognised). In other words, Entity A has in effect settled a recognised liability of €6m for €5m, resulting in a gain of €1m. *[IFRS 3.IE57].*

Another example of settlement of a pre-existing contractual relationship, which should be recognised separately from the business combination, is where the acquirer has a loan payable to or receivable from the acquiree.

Example 9.28: Settlement of pre-existing contractual relationship – Loan agreement

Entity A acquires a 100% interest in Entity B for €500m in cash.

Before the acquisition, Entity B granted a fixed interest rate loan to Entity A and as at the date of acquisition Entity A has recognised a financial liability in respect of the loan amounting to €50m. Fair value of that financial liability is assessed to be €45m. The fair value of the net identifiable assets and liabilities of Entity B as at the date of acquisition is €460m, including €45m in respect of the fixed rate loan to Entity A.

The amount of consideration transferred for the acquisition of Entity B is decreased by the fair value of the financial liability and the financial liability is derecognised. As such, the consideration transferred for purposes of determining goodwill is €455m (€500m – €45m). The amount by which the loan agreement is favourable to the acquirer is recognised as a gain in the consolidated profit or loss. The net identifiable assets and liabilities of Entity B exclude the receivable due from Entity A.

Entity A accounts for the acquisition of Entity B and settlement of the financial liability as follows:

	€m	€m
Net identifiable assets and liabilities acquired (€460m – €45m)	415	
Loan due to Entity B	50	
Goodwill (€455m – €415m)	40	
Gain on derecognition of loan due to Entity B (€50m – €45m)		5
Cash – consideration for business combination (€500m – €45m)		455
Cash – effective settlement of loan due to Entity B		45

A pre-existing relationship may be a contract that the acquirer recognises as a reacquired right. As indicated at 5.6.5 above, if the contract includes terms that are favourable or unfavourable when compared with pricing for current market transactions for the same or similar items, the acquirer recognises, separately from the business combination, a gain or loss for the effective settlement of the contract, measured in accordance with the requirements described above. *[IFRS 3.B53].*

Example 9.29: Settlement of pre-existing contractual relationship – Reacquired technology licensing agreement

Entity A acquires a 100% interest in Entity B for €350m in cash.

Before the acquisition, Entity A sold to Entity B an exclusive right to use Entity A's technology in a specified territory. Entity B also pays a revenue-based royalty on a monthly basis. The terms of the technology licensing agreement state that if Entity A terminates the arrangement without cause, Entity A would be required to pay a penalty of €30m. Neither Entity A nor Entity B has recognised any assets or liabilities related to the licence agreement.

The fair value of the licence agreement is assessed to be €120m, which includes a value of €20m for the future royalties which are below current market rates. Therefore, the licence agreement is unfavourable to Entity A and favourable to Entity B. The fair value of the net identifiable assets and liabilities of Entity B as at the date of the business combination is €320m, including the fair value of the licence agreement of €120m.

The reacquired licence right is recognised at €100m, being the licence's fair value at current market rates (€120m – €20m). Entity A recognises a loss on settlement of the agreement at the lower of:

- €20m, which is the amount by which the royalty is unfavourable to Entity A compared to market terms;
- €30m, which is the amount that Entity A would have to pay to terminate the right at the date of acquisition.

A loss is therefore recognised of €20m. The amount of consideration transferred for the acquisition of Entity B is decreased accordingly to €330m (€350m – €20m).

Entity A accounts for the acquisition of Entity B and the reacquired technology licensing agreement as follows:

	€m	€m
Net identifiable assets and liabilities acquired (€320m – €20m)	300	
Goodwill (€330m – €300m)	30	
Loss on settlement of technology licensing agreement	20	
Cash – consideration for business combination (€350m – €20m)		330
Cash – effective settlement of technology licensing agreement		20

11.2 Remuneration for future services of employees or former owners of the acquiree

A transaction that remunerates employees or former owners of the acquiree for future services is excluded from the business combination accounting and accounted for separately. *[IFRS 3.52]*.

11.2.1 Arrangements for contingent payments to employees or selling shareholders

Whether arrangements for contingent payments to employees (or selling shareholders) are contingent consideration to be included in the measure of the consideration transferred (see 7.1 above) or are separate transactions to be accounted for as remuneration will depend on the nature of the arrangements.

Such payments are also often referred to as 'earn-outs'. The approach to accounting for earn-out arrangements is summarised in the diagram below:

Approach to accounting for earn-outs

```
                    Earn-out arrangement
                            |
                            v
                 Apply IFRS 3 to classify
                    /              \
                   v                v
             Remuneration      Contingent consideration
              /      \                  |
             v        v                 v
    Settled in or   Settled in cash or
    linked to own   in other assets in
    shares          a way not linked
                    to own shares
       |                |                |
       v                v                v
  Apply IFRS 2     Apply IAS 19     Apply IFRS 3
```

Understanding the reasons why the acquisition agreement includes a provision for contingent payments, who initiated the arrangement and when the parties entered into the arrangement may be helpful in assessing the nature of the arrangement. *[IFRS 3.B54]*.

If it is not clear whether the arrangement for payments to employees or selling shareholders is part of the exchange for the acquiree or is a transaction separate from the business combination, there are a number of indicators in IFRS 3. *[IFRS 3.B55]*. These are summarised in the table below:

Indicators to consider when classifying payments as remuneration or contingent consideration

Lead to conclusion as remuneration	Indicators to consider when assessing terms of additional payments to selling shareholders that remain employees	Lead to conclusion as contingent consideration
Payments forfeited on termination	Continuing employment	Payments are not affected by termination
Coincides with or exceeds payment period	Duration of required employment	Shorter than the payment period
Not reasonable compared to other key employees of the group	Level of other elements of remuneration	Reasonable compared to the other key employees of the group
Other non-employee selling shareholders receive lower additional payments (on a per share basis)	Incremental payments to other non-employee selling shareholders	Other non-employee selling shareholders receive similar additional payments (on a per share basis)
Selling shareholders remaining as employees owned substantially all shares (in substance profit-sharing)	Number of shares owned when all selling shareholders receive same level of additional consideration (on a per share basis)	Selling shareholders remaining as employees owned only a small portion of shares
Formula for additional payment consistent with other profit-sharing arrangements rather than the valuation approach	Linkage of payments to valuation of business	Initial consideration at lower end of range of business valuation, and formula for additional payment linked to the valuation approach
Formula is based on performance, such as percentage of earnings	Formula for additional payments	Formula is based on a valuation formula, such as multiple of earnings, indicating it is connected to a business valuation

Although these points are supposed to be indicators, continuing employment is an exception. It is categorically stated that 'a contingent consideration arrangement in which the payments are automatically forfeited if employment terminates is remuneration for post-combination services'. *[IFRS 3.B55(a)]*. In January 2013, the Interpretations Committee clarified that this conclusion assumes that the service condition is substantive.[29] With this exception, no other single indicator is likely to be enough to be conclusive as to the accounting treatment.

The guidance in IFRS 3 expands the points in the table above, but also notes that:

(i) The relevant terms of continuing employment may be included in an employment agreement, acquisition agreement or some other document. *[IFRS 3.B55(a)]*.

(ii) Other pre-acquisition ownership interests may be relevant, e.g. those held by parties related to selling shareholders such as family members, who continue as key employees. *[IFRS 3.B55(e)]*.

Where it is determined that some or all of the arrangement is to be accounted for as contingent consideration, the requirements in IFRS 3 discussed at 7.1 above should be applied. If some or all of the arrangement is post-combination remuneration, it will be accounted for under IFRS 2 if it represents a share-based payment transaction (see Chapter 34) or otherwise under IAS 19 (see Chapter 35).

The requirements for contingent payments to employees are illustrated in the following example. *[IFRS 3.IE58-IE60]*.

Example 9.30: Contingent payments to employees

Entity B appointed a candidate as its new CEO under a ten-year contract. The contract required Entity B to pay the candidate $5m if Entity B is acquired before the contract expires. Entity A acquires Entity B eight years later. The CEO was still employed at the acquisition date and will receive the additional payment under the existing contract.

In this example, Entity B entered into the employment agreement before the negotiations of the combination began, and the purpose of the agreement was to obtain the services of CEO. Thus, there is no evidence that the agreement was arranged primarily to provide benefits to Entity A or the combined entity. Therefore, the liability to pay $5m is accounted for as part of the acquisition of Entity B.

In other circumstances, Entity B might enter into a similar agreement with CEO at the suggestion of Entity A during the negotiations for the business combination. If so, the primary purpose of the agreement might be to provide severance pay to CEO, and the agreement may primarily benefit Entity A or the combined entity rather than Entity B or its former owners. In that situation, Entity A accounts for the liability to pay CEO in its post-combination financial statements separately from the acquisition of Entity B.

Not all arrangements relate to judgements about whether an arrangement is remuneration or contingent consideration and other agreements and relationships with selling shareholders may have to be considered. The terms of other arrangements and the income tax treatment of contingent payments may indicate that contingent payments are attributable to something other than consideration for the acquiree. These can include agreements not to compete, executory contracts, consulting contracts and property lease agreements. For example, the acquirer might enter into a property lease arrangement with a significant selling shareholder. If the lease payments specified in the lease contract are significantly below market, some or all of the contingent payments to the lessor (the selling shareholder) required by a separate arrangement for contingent payments might be, in substance, payments for the use of the leased property that the acquirer should recognise separately in its post-combination financial statements. In contrast, if the lease contract specifies lease payments that are consistent with market terms for the leased property, the arrangement for contingent payments to the selling shareholder may be contingent consideration in the business combination.

11.2.2 Share-based payment awards exchanged for awards held by the acquiree's employees

The acquirer may exchange share-based payment awards (i.e. replacement awards) for awards held by employees of the acquiree.

If the acquirer replaces any acquiree awards, the consideration transferred will include some or all of any replacement awards. Any amount not included in the consideration transferred is treated as a post-combination remuneration expense.

IFRS 3 includes application guidance dealing with replacement awards. *[IFRS 3.B56-B62]*. Replacement awards are modifications of share-based payment awards in accordance with IFRS 2. Discussion of this guidance, including illustrative examples that reflect the substance of the Illustrative Examples that accompany IFRS 3, *[IFRS 3.IE61-IE71]*, is dealt with in Chapter 34 at 11.2.

11.3 Reimbursement for paying the acquirer's acquisition-related costs

The third example of a separate transaction is included to mitigate concerns about potential abuse. IFRS 3 requires the acquirer to expense its acquisition-related costs – they are not included as part of the consideration transferred for the acquiree. This means that they are not reflected in the computation of goodwill. As a result, acquirers might modify transactions to avoid recognising those costs as expenses. They might disguise reimbursements, e.g. a buyer might ask a seller to make payments to third parties on its behalf; the seller might agree to make those payments if the total amount to be paid to it is sufficient to reimburse it for payments made on the buyer's behalf. *[IFRS 3.BC370]*.

The same would apply if the acquirer asks the acquiree to pay some or all of the acquisition-related costs on its behalf and the acquiree has paid those costs before the acquisition date, so that at the acquisition date the acquiree does not record a liability for them. *[IFRS 3.BC120]*. This transaction has been entered into on behalf of the acquirer, or primarily for the benefit of the acquirer.

11.4 Restructuring plans

One particular area that could be negotiated between the acquirer and the acquiree or its former owners is a restructuring plan relating to the acquiree's activities.

In our view, a restructuring plan that is implemented by or at the request of the acquirer is not a liability of the acquiree as at the date of acquisition and cannot be part of the accounting for the business combination under the acquisition method, regardless of whether the combination is contingent on the plan being implemented. IFRS 3 does not contain the same explicit requirements relating to restructuring plans that were in the previous version of IFRS 3, but the Basis for Conclusions accompanying IFRS 3 clearly indicate that the requirements for recognising liabilities associated with restructuring or exit activities remain the same. *[IFRS 3.BC137]*. Furthermore, as discussed at 5.2 above, an acquirer recognises liabilities for restructuring or exit activities acquired in a business combination only if they meet the definition of a liability at the acquisition date. *[IFRS 3.BC132]*.

A restructuring plan that is decided upon or put in place between the date the negotiations for the business combination started and the date the business combination is consummated is only likely to be accounted for as a pre-combination transaction of the acquiree if there is no evidence that the acquirer initiated the restructuring and the plan makes commercial sense even if the business combination does not proceed.

If a plan initiated by the acquirer is implemented without an explicit link to the combination this may indicate that control has already passed to the acquirer at this earlier date.

This is discussed further in the following example.

Example 9.31: Recognition or otherwise of a restructuring liability as part of a business combination

The acquirer and the acquiree (or the vendors of the acquiree) enter into an arrangement before the acquisition that requires the acquiree to restructure its workforce or activities. They intend to develop the main features of a plan that involve terminating or reducing its activities and to announce the plan's main features to those affected by it so as to raise a valid expectation that the plan will be implemented. The combination is contingent on the plan being implemented.

Does such a restructuring plan that the acquiree puts in place simultaneously with the business combination, i.e. the plan is effective upon the change in control, but was implemented by or at the request of the acquirer qualify for inclusion as part of the liabilities assumed in accounting for the business combination?

If these facts are analysed:

(a) *the reason:* a restructuring plan implemented at the request of the acquirer is presumably arranged primarily for the benefit of the acquirer or the combined entity because of the possible redundancy expected to arise from the combination of activities of the acquirer with activities of the acquiree, e.g. capacity redundancy leading to closure of the acquiree's facilities;

(b) *who initiated:* if such a plan is the result of a request of the acquirer, it means that the acquirer is expecting future economic benefits from the arrangement and the decision to restructure;

(c) *the timing:* the restructuring plan is usually discussed during the negotiations; therefore, it is contemplated in the perspective of the future combined entity.

Accordingly, a restructuring plan that is implemented as a result of an arrangement between the acquirer and the acquiree is not a liability of the acquiree as at the date of acquisition and cannot be part of the accounting for the business combination under the acquisition method.

Does the answer differ if the combination is not contingent on the plan being implemented?

The answer applies regardless of whether the combination is contingent on the plan being implemented. A plan initiated by the acquirer will most likely not make commercial sense from the acquiree's perspective absent the business combination. For example, there are retrenchments of staff whose position will only truly become redundant once the entities are combined. In that case, this is an arrangement to be accounted for separately rather than as part of the business combination exchange. This arrangement may also indicate that control of acquiree has already passed to the acquirer as otherwise there would be little reason for the acquiree to enter into an arrangement that makes little or no commercial sense to it.

12 MEASUREMENT PERIOD

IFRS 3 contains provisions in respect of a 'measurement period' which provides the acquirer with a reasonable period of time to obtain the information necessary to identify and measure all of the various components of the business combination as of the acquisition date in accordance with the standard, i.e.:

(a) the identifiable assets acquired, liabilities assumed and any non-controlling interest in the acquiree;

(b) the consideration transferred for the acquiree (or the other amount used in measuring goodwill);

(c) in a business combination achieved in stages, the equity interest in the acquiree previously held by the acquirer; and

(d) the resulting goodwill or gain on a bargain purchase. *[IFRS 3.46]*.

For most business combinations, the main area where information will need to be obtained is in relation to the acquiree, i.e. the identifiable assets acquired and the liabilities assumed, particularly as these may include items that the acquiree had not previously recognised as assets and liabilities in its financial statements and, in most cases, need to be measured at their acquisition-date fair value (see 5 above). Information may also need to be obtained in determining the fair value of any contingent consideration arrangements (see 7.1 above).

The measurement period ends as soon as the acquirer receives the information it was seeking about facts and circumstances that existed as of the acquisition date or learns that it cannot obtain more information. The measurement period cannot exceed one year from the acquisition date. *[IFRS 3.45]*. The Basis for Conclusions notes that in placing this constraint it was 'concluded that allowing a measurement period longer than one year would not be especially helpful; obtaining reliable information about circumstances and conditions that existed more than a year ago is likely to become more difficult as time passes. Of course, the outcome of some contingencies and similar matters may not be known within a year. But the objective of the measurement period is to provide time to obtain the information necessary to measure the fair value of the item as of the acquisition date. Determining the ultimate settlement amount of a contingency or other item is not necessary. Uncertainties about the timing and amount of future cash flows are part of the measure of the fair value of an asset or liability.' *[IFRS 3.BC392]*.

Under IFRS 3, if the initial accounting is incomplete at the end of the reporting period in which the combination occurs, the acquirer will include provisional amounts. *[IFRS 3.45]*. IFRS 3 specifies particular disclosures about those items (see 16.2 below). *[IFRS 3.BC393]*.

Although paragraph 45 refers to the initial accounting being 'incomplete by the end of the reporting period' and the acquirer reporting 'provisional amounts for the items for which the accounting is incomplete', *[IFRS 3.45]*, it is clear from the Illustrative Examples accompanying IFRS 3 that this means being incomplete at the date of authorising for issue the financial statements for that period (see Example 9.32 below). Thus, any items that are finalised up to that date should be reflected in the initial accounting.

12.1 Adjustments made during measurement period to provisional amounts

During the measurement period, the acquirer retrospectively adjusts the provisional amounts recognised at the acquisition date to reflect new information obtained about facts and circumstances at the acquisition date that, if known, would have affected the measurement of the amounts recognised.

Similarly, the acquirer recognises additional assets or liabilities if new information is obtained about facts and circumstances at the acquisition date and, if known, would have resulted in the recognition of those assets and liabilities as of that date. [IFRS 3.45].

IFRS 3 requires the acquirer to consider all pertinent factors to distinguish information that should result in an adjustment to the provisional amounts from that arising from events that occurred after the acquisition date. Factors to be considered include the date when additional information is obtained and whether the acquirer can identify a reason for a change to provisional amounts. Clearly, information obtained shortly after the acquisition date is more likely to reflect circumstances that existed at the acquisition date than information obtained several months later. If the acquirer sells an asset to a third party shortly after the acquisition date for an amount that is significantly different to its provisional fair value, this is likely to indicate an 'error' in the provisional amount unless there is an intervening event that changes its fair value. [IFRS 3.47].

Adjustments to provisional amounts that are made during the measurement period are recognised as if the accounting for the business combination had been completed at the acquisition date. This may be in a prior period, so the acquirer revises its comparative information as needed. This may mean making changes to depreciation, amortisation or other income effects. [IFRS 3.49]. These requirements are illustrated in the following example, which is based on one included within the Illustrative Examples accompanying IFRS 3. [IFRS 3.IE50-IE53]. The deferred tax implications are ignored.

Example 9.32:   *Adjustments made during measurement period to provisional amounts*

Entity A acquired Entity B on 30 September 2020. Entity A sought an independent valuation for an item of property, plant and equipment acquired in the combination. However, the valuation was not complete by the time Entity A authorised for issue its financial statements for the year ended 31 December 2020. In its 2020 annual financial statements, Entity A recognised a provisional fair value for the asset of €30,000. At the acquisition date, the item of property, plant and equipment had a remaining useful life of five years.

Five months after the acquisition date (and after the date on which the financial statements were issued), Entity A received the independent valuation, which estimated the asset's acquisition-date fair value at €40,000.

In its financial statements for the year ended 31 December 2021, Entity A retrospectively adjusts the 2020 prior year information as follows:

(a) The carrying amount of property, plant and equipment as of 31 December 2020 is increased by €9,500. That adjustment is measured as the fair value adjustment at the acquisition date of €10,000 less the additional depreciation that would have been recognised if the asset's fair value at the acquisition date had been recognised from that date (€500 for three months' depreciation).

(b) The carrying amount of goodwill as of 31 December 2020 is decreased by €10,000.

(c) Depreciation expense for 2020 is increased by €500.

Entity A disclosed in its 2020 financial statements that the initial accounting for the business combination has not been completed because the valuation of property, plant and equipment has not yet been received.

In its 2021 financial statements, Entity A will disclose the amounts and explanations of the adjustments to the provisional values recognised during the current reporting period. Therefore, Entity A will disclose that the 2020 comparative information is adjusted retrospectively to increase the fair value of the item of property, plant and equipment at the acquisition date by €10,000, resulting in an increase to property, plant and equipment of €9,500, offset by a decrease to goodwill of €10,000 and an increase in depreciation expense of €500.

The example below illustrates that adjustments during the measurement period are also made where information is received about the existence of an asset as at the acquisition date:

Example 9.33: Identification of an asset during measurement period

Entity C acquired Entity D on 30 November 2020. Entity C engaged an independent appraiser to assist with the identification and determination of fair values to be assigned to the acquiree's assets and liabilities. However, the appraisal was not finalised by the time Entity C authorised for issue its financial statements for the year ended 31 December 2020, and therefore the amounts recognised in its 2020 annual financial statements were on a provisional basis.

Six months after the acquisition date, Entity C received the independent appraiser's final report, in which it was identified by the independent appraiser that the acquiree had an intangible asset with a fair value at the date of acquisition of €20,000. As this had not been identified at the time when Entity C was preparing its 2020 annual financial statements, no value had been included for it.

In its financial statements for the year ended 31 December 2021, Entity C retrospectively adjusts the prior year information to reflect the recognition of this intangible asset.

Although a change in the provisional amount recognised for an identifiable asset will usually mean a corresponding decrease or increase in goodwill, new information obtained could affect another identifiable asset or liability. If the acquirer assumed a liability to pay damages relating to an accident in one of the acquiree's facilities, part or all of which was covered by the acquiree's liability insurance policy, new information during the measurement period about the fair value of the liability would affect goodwill. This adjustment to goodwill would be offset, in whole or in part, by a corresponding adjustment resulting from a change to the provisional amount recognised for the claim receivable from the insurer. *[IFRS 3.48]*. Similarly, if there is a non-controlling interest in the acquiree, and this is measured based on the proportionate share of the net identifiable assets of the acquiree (see 8 above), any adjustments to those assets that had initially been determined on a provisional basis will be offset by the proportionate share attributable to the non-controlling interest.

12.2 Adjustments made after end of measurement period

After the end of the measurement period, the acquirer can only revise the accounting for a business combination to correct an error in accordance with IAS 8. *[IFRS 3.50]*. This would probably be the case only if the original accounting was based on a misinterpretation of the facts which were available at the time; it would not apply simply because new information had come to light which changed the acquiring management's view of the value of the item in question.

Adjustments after the end of the measurement period are not made for the effect of changes in estimates. In accordance with IAS 8, the effect of a change in estimate is recognised in the current and future periods (see Chapter 3 at 4.5).

13 SUBSEQUENT MEASUREMENT AND ACCOUNTING

Assets acquired, liabilities assumed or incurred and equity instruments issued in a business combination are usually accounted for in accordance with the applicable IFRSs. However, there is specific guidance on subsequent measurement of and accounting for the following:

(a) reacquired rights (see 5.6.5 above);

(b) contingent liabilities recognised as of the acquisition date (see 5.6.1.B above);

(c) indemnification assets (see 5.6.4 above); and

(d) contingent consideration (see 7.1.3 above). [IFRS 3.54].

Other IFRSs provide guidance on subsequent measurement and accounting: [IFRS 3.B63]

(a) IAS 38 prescribes the accounting for identifiable intangible assets acquired in a business combination (see Chapter 17), although accounting for some intangible assets is not prescribed by IAS 38 but by other IFRSs (see Chapter 17 at 2). [IFRS 3.B39]. Goodwill is measured at the amount recognised at the acquisition date less any accumulated impairment losses, measured in accordance with IAS 36 (see Chapter 20 at 8);

(b) IFRS 4 provides guidance on the subsequent accounting for an insurance contract acquired in a business combination (see Chapter 55); IFRS 17, if adopted, provides guidance on the initial and subsequent measurement of a group of contracts within the scope of IFRS 17 acquired in a business combination (see Chapter 56);

(c) IAS 12 prescribes the subsequent accounting for deferred tax assets (including unrecognised deferred tax assets) and liabilities acquired in a business combination (see Chapter 33);

(d) IFRS 2 provides guidance on subsequent measurement and accounting for the portion of replacement share-based payment awards issued by an acquirer that is attributable to employees' future services (see Chapter 34 at 11); and

(e) IFRS 10 provides guidance on accounting for changes in a parent's ownership interest in a subsidiary after control is obtained (see Chapter 7).

14 REVERSE ACQUISITIONS

The standard takes the view that the acquirer is usually the entity that issues its equity interests, but recognises that in some business combinations, so-called 'reverse acquisitions', the issuing entity is the acquiree.

Under IFRS 3, a reverse acquisition occurs when the entity that issues securities (the legal acquirer) is identified as the acquiree for accounting purposes based on the guidance in the standard as discussed at 4.1 above. Perhaps more accurately, the legal acquiree must be identified as the acquirer for accounting purposes.

Reverse acquisitions sometimes occur when a private operating entity wants to become a public entity but does not want to register its equity shares. The private entity will arrange for a public entity to acquire its equity interests in exchange for the equity interests of the public entity. Although the public entity is the legal acquirer because it issued its equity interests, and the private entity is the legal acquiree because its equity interests were acquired, application of the guidance results in identifying: [IFRS 3.B19]

(a) the public entity as the acquiree for accounting purposes (the accounting acquiree); and

(b) the private entity as the acquirer for accounting purposes (the accounting acquirer).

If the transaction is accounted for as a reverse acquisition, all of the recognition and measurement principles in IFRS 3, including the requirement to recognise goodwill, apply. The standard also notes that the legal acquirer must meet the definition of a business (see 3.2 above) for the transaction to be accounted for as a reverse acquisition, [IFRS 3.B19], but does not say how the transaction should be accounted for where the accounting acquiree is not a business. It clearly cannot be accounted for as an acquisition of the legal acquiree by the legal acquirer under the standard either, if the legal acquirer has not been identified as the accounting acquirer based on the guidance in the standard. This is discussed further at 14.8 below.

14.1 Measuring the consideration transferred

The first item to be included in the computation of goodwill in a reverse acquisition is the consideration transferred by the accounting acquirer, i.e. the legal acquiree/subsidiary. In a reverse acquisition, the accounting acquirer usually issues no consideration for the acquiree; equity shares are issued to the owners of the accounting acquirer by the accounting acquiree. The fair value of the consideration transferred by the accounting acquirer is based on the number of equity interests the legal subsidiary would have had to issue to give the owners of the legal parent the same percentage equity interest in the combined entity that results from the reverse acquisition. The fair value of the number of equity interests calculated in that way is used as the fair value of consideration transferred. [IFRS 3.B20].

These requirements are illustrated in the following example, which is based on one included within the Illustrative Examples accompanying IFRS 3. [IFRS 3.IE1-IE5].

Example 9.34: Reverse acquisition – calculating the fair value of the consideration transferred

Entity A, the entity issuing equity instruments and therefore the legal parent, is acquired in a reverse acquisition by Entity B, the legal subsidiary, on 30 September 2021. The accounting for any income tax effects is ignored.

Statements of financial position of Entity A and Entity B immediately before the business combination are:

	Entity A €	Entity B €
Current assets	500	700
Non-current assets	1,300	3,000
Total assets	1,800	3,700
Current liabilities	300	600
Non-current liabilities	400	1,100
Total liabilities	700	1,700
Owner's equity		
Issued equity		
100 ordinary shares	300	–
60 Ordinary shares	–	600
Retained earnings	800	1,400
Total shareholders' equity	1,100	2,000

Other information

(a) On 30 September 2021, Entity A issues 2.5 shares in exchange for each ordinary share of Entity B. All of Entity B's shareholders exchange their shares in Entity B. Therefore, Entity A issues 150 ordinary shares in exchange for all 60 ordinary shares of Entity B.

(b) The fair value of each ordinary share of Entity B at 30 September 2021 is €40. The quoted market price of Entity A's ordinary shares at that date is €16.

(c) The fair values of Entity A's identifiable assets and liabilities at 30 September 2021 are the same as their carrying amounts, except that the fair value of Entity A's non-current assets at 30 September 2021 is €1,500.

Calculating the fair value of the consideration transferred

As a result of Entity A (legal parent/acquiree) issuing 150 ordinary shares, Entity B's shareholders own 60 per cent of the issued shares of the combined entity (i.e. 150 of 250 issued shares). The remaining 40 per cent are owned by Entity A's shareholders. If the business combination had taken the form of Entity B issuing additional ordinary shares to Entity A's shareholders in exchange for their ordinary shares in Entity A, Entity B would have had to issue 40 shares for the ratio of ownership interest in the combined entity to be the same. Entity B's shareholders would then own 60 out of the 100 issued shares of Entity B – 60 per cent of the combined entity.

As a result, the fair value of the consideration effectively transferred by Entity B and the group's interest in Entity A is €1,600 (i.e. 40 shares each with a fair value of €40).

The fair value of the consideration effectively transferred should be based on the most reliable measure. In this example, the quoted market price of Entity A's shares provides a more reliable basis for measuring the consideration effectively transferred than the estimated fair value of the shares in Entity B, and the consideration is measured using the market price of Entity A's shares – 100 shares with a fair value per share of €16, i.e. €1,600.

The final paragraph in the above example would appear to be based on the requirements of paragraph 33 of the standard, i.e. 'in a business combination in which the acquirer and the acquiree (or its former owners) exchange only equity interests, the acquisition-date fair value of the acquiree's equity interests may be more reliably measurable than the acquisition-date fair value of the acquirer's equity interests. If so, the acquirer shall determine the amount of goodwill by using the acquisition-date fair value of the acquiree's equity interests instead of the acquisition-date fair value of the equity interests transferred.' *[IFRS 3.33]*. In the above example, this did not result in a difference as the value of the consideration measured under both approaches was the same. However, the example above indicates that there is a quoted market price for Entity A's shares which is a more reliable basis than the fair value of Entity B's shares. Therefore, if the quoted market price of Entity A's shares had been, say, €14 per share, the fair value of the consideration effectively transferred would have been measured at €1,400.

14.2 Measuring goodwill

As there is no non-controlling interest in the accounting acquiree, and assuming that the accounting acquirer had no previously held equity interest in the accounting acquiree, goodwill is measured as the excess of (a) over (b) below:

(a) the consideration effectively transferred (generally measured at acquisition-date fair value) by the accounting acquirer, i.e. the legal subsidiary;

(b) the net of the acquisition-date fair values (or other amounts recognised in accordance with the requirements of the standard) of the identifiable assets acquired and the liabilities assumed of the accounting acquiree, i.e. the legal parent.

Example 9.35: Reverse acquisition – measuring goodwill (1)

Using the facts in Example 9.34 above, this results in goodwill of €300, measured as follows:

	€	€
Consideration effectively transferred by Entity B		1,600
Net recognised values of Entity A's identifiable assets and liabilities:		
Current assets	500	
Non-current assets	1,500	
Current liabilities	(300)	
Non-current liabilities	(400)	
		1,300
Goodwill		300

Example 9.36: Reverse acquisition – measuring goodwill (2)

If Example 9.35 had been based on the same facts as Example 9.34 except that the quoted market price of Entity A's shares had been €14 per share, the fair value of the consideration effectively transferred is €1,400, resulting in goodwill of €100.

14.3 Preparation and presentation of consolidated financial statements

Although the accounting for the reverse acquisition reflects the legal subsidiary as being the accounting acquirer, the consolidated financial statements are issued in the name of the legal parent/accounting acquiree. Consequently they have to be described in the notes as a continuation of the financial statements of the legal subsidiary/accounting acquirer, with one adjustment, which is to adjust retroactively the accounting acquirer's legal capital to reflect the legal capital of the accounting acquiree. Comparative information presented in those consolidated financial statements is therefore that of the legal subsidiary/accounting acquirer, not that originally presented in the previous financial statements of the legal parent/accounting acquiree as adjusted to reflect the legal capital of the legal parent/accounting acquiree. *[IFRS 3.B21]*.

The consolidated financial statements reflect:

(a) the assets and liabilities of the legal subsidiary/accounting acquirer recognised and measured at their pre-combination carrying amounts, i.e. not at their acquisition-date fair values;

(b) the assets and liabilities of the legal parent/accounting acquiree recognised and measured in accordance with IFRS 3, i.e. generally at their acquisition-date fair values;

(c) the retained earnings and other equity balances of the legal subsidiary/accounting acquirer before the business combination, i.e. not those of the legal parent/accounting acquiree;

(d) the amount recognised as issued equity instruments in the consolidated financial statements determined by adding the issued equity of the legal subsidiary/accounting acquirer outstanding immediately before the business combination to the fair value of the legal parent/accounting acquiree. However, the equity structure (i.e. the number and type of equity instruments issued) reflects the equity structure of the legal parent/accounting acquiree, including the equity instruments issued by the legal parent to effect the combination. Accordingly, the equity structure of the legal subsidiary/accounting acquirer is restated using the exchange ratio established in the acquisition agreement to reflect the number of shares of the legal parent/accounting acquiree issued in the reverse acquisition;

(e) the non-controlling interest's proportionate share of the legal subsidiary's/accounting acquirer's pre-combination carrying amounts of retained earnings and other equity interests (as discussed in 14.4 below);
[IFRS 3.B22]

(f) the income statement for the current period reflects that of the legal subsidiary/accounting acquirer for the full period together with the post-acquisition results of the legal parent/accounting acquiree based on the attributed fair values.

It is unclear why the application guidance in (d) above refers to using 'the fair value of the legal parent/accounting acquiree', when, as discussed previously at 14.1 above, the guidance for determining 'the fair value of the consideration effectively transferred' uses a different method of arriving at the value of the consideration given. We believe that the amount recognised as issued equity should reflect whichever value has been determined for the consideration effectively transferred.

Continuing with Example 9.34 above, the consolidated statement of financial position immediately after the business combination will be as follows:

Example 9.37: *Reverse acquisition – consolidated statement of financial position immediately after the business combination*

Using the facts in Example 9.34 above, the consolidated statement of financial position immediately after the date of the business combination is as follows (the intermediate columns for Entity B (legal subsidiary/accounting acquirer) and Entity A (legal parent/accounting acquiree) are included to show the workings):

	Entity B Book values €	Entity A Fair values €	Consolidated €
Current assets	700	500	1,200
Non-current assets	3,000	1,500	4,500
Goodwill	–	300	300
Total assets	3,700	2,300	6,000
Current liabilities	600	300	900
Non-current liabilities	1,100	400	1,500
Total liabilities	1,700	700	2,400
Owner's equity			
Issued equity			
250 ordinary shares	600	1,600	2,200
Retained earnings	1,400	–	1,400
Total shareholders' equity	2,000	1,600	3,600

The amount recognised as issued equity interests in the consolidated financial statements (€2,200) is determined by adding the issued equity of the legal subsidiary immediately before the business combination (€600) and the fair value of the consideration effectively transferred (€1,600). However, the equity structure appearing in the consolidated financial statements (i.e. the number and type of equity interests issued) must reflect the equity structure of the legal parent, including the equity interests issued by the legal parent to effect the combination. As noted above, we believe that the amount recognised as issued equity should reflect whichever value has been determined for the consideration effectively transferred.

The application guidance in IFRS 3 only deals with the reverse acquisition accounting in the consolidated financial statements; no mention is made as to what should happen in the separate financial statements, if any, of the legal parent/accounting acquiree. However, the previous version of IFRS 3 indicated that reverse acquisition accounting applies only in the consolidated financial statements, and that in the legal parent's separate financial statements, the investment in the legal subsidiary is accounted for in accordance with the requirements in IAS 27 – *Consolidated and Separate Financial Statements*. (see Chapter 8 at 2.1.1.G for further discussion). *[IFRS 3(2007).B8].*

14.4 Non-controlling interest

In a reverse acquisition, some of the owners of the legal subsidiary/accounting acquirer might not exchange their equity instruments for equity instruments of the legal parent/accounting acquiree. Those owners are required to be treated as a non-controlling interest in the consolidated financial statements after the reverse acquisition. This is because the owners of the legal subsidiary that do not exchange their equity instruments for equity instruments of the legal parent have an interest only in the results and net assets of the legal subsidiary, and not in the results and net assets of the combined entity. Conversely, even though the legal parent is the acquiree for accounting purposes, the owners of the legal parent have an interest in the results and net assets of the combined entity. *[IFRS 3.B23]*.

As indicated at 14.3 above, the assets and liabilities of the legal subsidiary/accounting acquirer are recognised and measured in the consolidated financial statements at their pre-combination carrying amounts. Therefore, in a reverse acquisition the non-controlling interest reflects the non-controlling shareholders' proportionate interest in the pre-combination carrying amounts of the legal subsidiary's net assets even if the non-controlling interests in other acquisitions are measured at fair value at the acquisition date. *[IFRS 3.B24]*.

These requirements are illustrated in the following example, which is based on one included within the Illustrative Examples accompanying IFRS 3. *[IFRS 3.IE11-IE15]*.

Example 9.38:   Reverse acquisition – non-controlling interest

This example uses the same facts as in Example 9.34 above, except that only 56 of Entity B's 60 ordinary shares are exchanged. Because Entity A issues 2.5 shares in exchange for each ordinary share of Entity B, Entity A issues only 140 (rather than 150) shares. As a result, Entity B's shareholders own 58.3 per cent of the issued shares of the combined entity (i.e. 140 shares out of 240 issued shares).

As in Example 9.34 above, the fair value of the consideration transferred for Entity A, the accounting acquiree) is calculated by assuming that the combination had been effected by Entity B issuing additional ordinary shares to the shareholders of Entity A in exchange for their ordinary shares in Entity A. That is because Entity B is the accounting acquirer, and IFRS 3 requires the acquirer to measure the consideration exchanged for the accounting acquiree (see 14.1 above).

In calculating the number of shares that Entity B would have had to issue, the non-controlling interest is excluded from the calculation. The majority shareholders own 56 shares of Entity B. For that to represent a 58.3 per cent ownership interest, Entity B would have had to issue an additional 40 shares. The majority shareholders would then own 56 out of the 96 issued shares of Entity B and therefore 58.3 per cent of the combined entity.

As a result, the fair value of the consideration transferred for Entity A, the accounting acquiree, is €1,600 (i.e. 40 shares, each with a fair value of €40). That is the same amount as when all 60 of Entity B's shareholders tender all 60 of its ordinary shares for exchange (see Example 9.34 above). The recognised amount of the group's interest in Entity A, the accounting acquiree, does not change if some of Entity B's shareholders do not participate in the exchange.

The non-controlling interest is represented by the 4 shares of the total 60 shares of Entity B that are not exchanged for shares of Entity A. Therefore, the non-controlling interest is 6.7 per cent. The non-controlling interest reflects the proportionate interest of the non-controlling shareholders in the pre-combination carrying amounts of the net assets of Entity B, the legal subsidiary. Therefore, the consolidated statement of financial position is adjusted to show a non-controlling interest of 6.7 per cent of the pre-combination carrying amounts of Entity B's net assets (i.e. €134 or 6.7 per cent of €2,000).

The consolidated statement of financial position at 30 September 2021(the date of the business combination) reflecting the non-controlling interest is as follows (the intermediate columns for Entity B (legal subsidiary/accounting acquirer), non-controlling interest and Entity A (legal parent/ accounting acquiree) are included to show the workings):

	Entity B Book values €	Non-controlling interest €	Entity A Fair values €	Consolidated €
Current assets	700	–	500	1,200
Non-current assets	3,000	–	1,500	4,500
Goodwill	–	–	300	300
Total assets	3,700	–	2,300	6,000
Current liabilities	600	–	300	900
Non-current liabilities	1,100	–	400	1,500
	1,700	–	700	2,400
Owner's equity				
Issued equity				
240 ordinary shares	600	(40)	1,600	2,160
Retained earnings	1,400	(94)	–	1,306
Non-controlling interest	–	134	–	134
	2,000	–	1,600	3,600

The non-controlling interest of €134 has two components. The first component is the reclassification of the non-controlling interest's share of the accounting acquirer's retained earnings immediately before the acquisition (€1,400 × 6.7 per cent or €93.80). The second component represents the reclassification of the non-controlling interest's share of the accounting acquirer's issued equity (€600 × 6.7 per cent or €40.20).

14.5 Earnings per share

The equity structure, i.e. the number and type of equity instruments issued, in the consolidated financial statements following a reverse acquisition reflects the equity structure of the legal parent/accounting acquiree, including the equity instruments issued by the legal parent to effect the business combination. *[IFRS 3.B25]*.

Where the legal parent is required by IAS 33 – *Earnings per Share* – to disclose earnings per share information (see Chapter 37), then for the purpose of calculating the weighted average number of ordinary shares outstanding (the denominator of the earnings per share calculation) during the period in which the reverse acquisition occurs:

(a) the number of ordinary shares outstanding from the beginning of that period to the acquisition date is computed on the basis of the weighted average number of ordinary shares of the legal subsidiary/accounting acquirer outstanding during the period multiplied by the exchange ratio established in the acquisition agreement; and

(b) the number of ordinary shares outstanding from the acquisition date to the end of that period is the actual number of ordinary shares of the legal parent/accounting acquiree outstanding during that period. *[IFRS 3.B26]*.

The basic earnings per share disclosed for each comparative period before the acquisition date is calculated by dividing:

(a) the profit or loss of the legal subsidiary/accounting acquirer attributable to ordinary shareholders in each of those periods; by

(b) the legal subsidiary's historical weighted average number of ordinary shares outstanding multiplied by the exchange ratio established in the acquisition agreement. *[IFRS 3.B27]*.

These requirements are illustrated in the following example, which is based on one included within the Illustrative Examples accompanying IFRS 3. *[IFRS 3.IE9, 10]*.

Example 9.39: Reverse acquisition – earnings per share

This example uses the same facts as in Example 9.34 above. Assume that Entity B's earnings for the annual period ended 31 December 2020 were €600, and that the consolidated earnings for the annual period ending 31 December 2021 were €800. Assume also that there was no change in the number of ordinary shares issued by Entity B (legal subsidiary, accounting acquirer) during the annual period ended 31 December 2020 and during the period from 1 January 2021 to the date of the reverse acquisition (30 September 2021), nor by Entity A (legal parent, accounting acquiree) after that date.

Earnings per share for the annual period ended 31 December 2021 is calculated as follows:

Number of shares deemed to be outstanding for the period from 1 January 2021 to the acquisition date (i.e. the number of ordinary shares issued by Entity A (legal parent, accounting acquiree) in the reverse acquisition, or more accurately, the weighted average number of ordinary shares of Entity B (legal subsidiary, accounting acquirer) outstanding during the period multiplied by the exchange ratio established in the acquisition agreement, i.e. 60 × 2.5)	150
Number of shares of Entity A (legal parent, accounting acquiree) outstanding from the acquisition date to 31 December 2021	250
Weighted average number of shares outstanding (150 × 9/12) + (250 × 3/12)	175
Earnings per share (€800 ÷ 175)	€4.57

The restated earnings per share for the annual period ending 31 December 2020 is €4.00 (being €600 ÷ 150, i.e. the earnings of Entity B (legal subsidiary, accounting acquirer) for that period divided by the number of ordinary shares Entity A issued in the reverse acquisition (or more accurately, by the weighted average number of ordinary shares of Entity B (legal subsidiary, accounting acquirer) outstanding during the period multiplied by the exchange ratio established in the acquisition agreement, i.e. 60 × 2.5). Any earnings per share information for that period previously disclosed by either Entity A or Entity B is irrelevant.

14.6 Cash consideration

In some circumstances the combination may be effected whereby some of the consideration given by the legal acquirer (Entity A) to acquire the shares in the legal acquiree (Entity B) is cash.

Normally, the entity transferring cash consideration would be considered to be the acquirer. [IFRS 3.B14]. However, despite the form of the consideration, the key determinant in identifying an acquirer is whether it has control over the other (see 4.1 above).

Therefore, if there is evidence demonstrating that the legal acquiree, Entity B, has obtained control over Entity A by being exposed, or having rights, to variable returns from its involvement with Entity A and having the ability to affect those returns through its power over Entity A, Entity B is then the acquirer and the combination should be accounted for as a reverse acquisition.

In that case, how should any cash paid be accounted for?

One approach might be to treat the payment as a pre-acquisition transaction with a resulting reduction in the consideration and in net assets acquired (with no net impact on goodwill). However, we do not believe this is appropriate. Any consideration, whether cash or shares, transferred by Entity A cannot form part of the consideration transferred by the acquirer as Entity A is the accounting acquiree. As discussed at 14.3 above, although the consolidated financial statements following a reverse acquisition are issued under the name of the legal parent (Entity A), they are to be described in the notes as a continuation of the financial statements of the legal subsidiary (Entity B). Therefore, since the consolidated financial statements are a continuation of Entity B's financial statements, in our view the cash consideration paid from Entity A (the accounting acquiree) should be accounted for as a distribution from the consolidated group to the accounting acquirer's (Entity B's) shareholders as at the combination date.

Where a cash payment is made to effect the combination, the requirements of IFRS 3 need to be applied with care as illustrated in the following example.

Example 9.40: *Reverse acquisition effected with cash consideration*

Entity A has 100,000 ordinary shares in issue, with a market price of £2.00 per share, giving a market capitalisation of £200,000. It acquires all of the shares in Entity B for a consideration of £500,000 satisfied by the issue of 200,000 shares (with a value of £400,000) and a cash payment of £100,000 to Entity B's shareholders. Entity B has 200,000 shares in issue, with an estimated fair value of £2.50 per share. After the combination Entity B's shareholders control the voting of Entity A and, as a result, have been able to appoint Entity B's directors and key executives to replace their Entity A counterparts. Accordingly, Entity B is considered to have obtained control over Entity A. Therefore, Entity B is identified as the accounting acquirer. The combination must be accounted for as a reverse acquisition, i.e. an acquisition of Entity A (legal parent/ accounting acquiree) by Entity B (legal subsidiary/ accounting acquirer).

How should the consideration transferred by the accounting acquirer (Entity B) for its interest in the accounting acquiree (Entity A) be determined?

Applying the requirements of paragraph B20 of IFRS 3 (discussed at 14.1 above) to the transaction might erroneously lead to the following conclusion. Entity A has had to issue 200,000 shares to Entity B's shareholders, resulting in Entity B's shareholders having 66.67% (200,000 ÷ 300,000) of the equity and Entity A's shareholders 33.33% (100,000 ÷ 300,000). If Entity B's share price is used to determine the fair value of the consideration transferred, then under paragraph B20, Entity B would have had to issue 100,000 shares to Entity A's shareholders to result in the same % shareholdings (200,000 ÷ 300,000 = 66.67%). This would apparently give a value of the consideration transferred of 100,000 @ £2.50 = £250,000. This does not seem correct, for the reasons discussed below.

If there had been no cash consideration at all, Entity A would have issued 250,000 shares to Entity B's shareholders, resulting in Entity B's shareholders having 71.43% (250,000 ÷ 350,000) of the equity and Entity A's shareholders 28.57% (100,000 ÷ 350,000). If Entity B's share price is used to determine the value of the consideration transferred, then under paragraph B20, Entity B would have had to issue 80,000 shares to Entity A's shareholders to result in the same % shareholdings (200,000 ÷ 280,000 = 71.43%). This would give a value for the consideration transferred of 80,000 @ £2.50 = £200,000. If it was thought that the fair value of Entity A's shares was more reliably measurable, paragraph 33 of IFRS 3 would require the consideration to be measured using the market price of Entity A's shares. As Entity B has effectively acquired 100% of Entity A, the value of the consideration transferred would be £200,000 (the same as under the revised paragraph B20 calculation above).

In our view, the proper analysis of the paragraph B20 calculation in this case is that of the 100,000 shares that Entity B is deemed to have issued, only 80,000 of them are to acquire Entity A's shares, resulting in consideration transferred of £200,000. The extra 20,000 shares are to compensate Entity A's shareholders for the fact that Entity B's shareholders have received a cash distribution of £100,000, and is effectively a stock distribution to Entity A's shareholders of £50,000 (20,000 @ £2.50), being their share (33.33%) of a total distribution of £150,000. However, since the equity structure (i.e. the number and type of shares) appearing in the consolidated financial statements reflects that of the legal parent, Entity A, this 'stock distribution' will not actually be apparent. The only distribution that will be shown as a movement in equity is the £100,000 cash paid to Entity B's shareholders.

14.7 Share-based payments

In a reverse acquisition, the legal acquirer (Entity A) may have an existing share-based payment plan at the date of acquisition. How does the entity account for awards held by the employees of the accounting acquiree?

Under IFRS 3, accounting for a reverse acquisition takes place from the perspective of the accounting acquirer, not the legal acquirer. Therefore, the accounting for the share-based payment plan of Entity A is based on what would have happened if Entity B rather than Entity A had issued such equity instruments. As indicated at 14.1 above, in a reverse acquisition, the acquisition-date fair value of the consideration transferred by the accounting acquirer for its interest in the accounting acquiree is based on the number of equity interests the legal subsidiary would have had to issue to give the owners of the legal parent the same percentage equity interest in the combined entity that results from the reverse acquisition. The fair value of the number of equity interests calculated in that way can be used as the fair value of consideration transferred in exchange for the acquiree. Therefore, although the legal form of awards made by the accounting acquiree (Entity A) does not change, from an accounting perspective, it is as if these awards have been exchanged for a share-based payment award of the accounting acquirer (Entity B).

As a result, absent any legal modification to the share-based payment awards in Entity A, the acquisition-date fair value of the legal parent/accounting acquiree's (Entity A's) share-based payments awards are included as part of the consideration transferred by the accounting acquirer (Entity B), based on the same principles as those described in paragraphs B56 to B62 of IFRS 3 – see 7.2 above and Chapter 34 at 11.2. *[IFRS 3.B56-B62]*. That is, the portion of the fair value attributed to the vesting period prior to the reverse acquisition is recognised as part of the consideration paid for the business combination and the portion that vests after the reverse acquisition is treated as post-combination expense.

14.8 Reverse acquisitions involving a non-trading shell company

The requirements for reverse acquisitions in IFRS 3, and the guidance provided by the standard, discussed above are based on the premise that the legal parent/accounting acquiree has a business which has been acquired by the legal subsidiary/accounting acquirer. In some situations, this may not be the case, for example where a private entity arranges to have itself 'acquired' by a non-trading public entity as a means of obtaining a stock exchange listing. As indicated at 14 above, the standard notes that the legal parent/accounting acquiree must meet the definition of a business (see 3.2 above) for the transaction to be accounted for as a reverse acquisition, *[IFRS 3.B19]*, but does not say how the transaction should be accounted for where the accounting acquiree is not a business. It clearly cannot be accounted for as an acquisition of the legal acquiree by the legal acquirer under the standard either, if the legal acquirer has not been identified as the accounting acquirer based on the guidance in the standard.

In our view, such a transaction should be accounted for in the consolidated financial statements of the legal parent as a continuation of the financial statements of the private entity (the legal subsidiary), together with a deemed issue of shares, equivalent to the shares held by the former shareholders of the legal parent, and a re-capitalisation of the equity of the private entity. This deemed issue of shares is, in effect, an equity-settled share-based payment transaction whereby the private entity has received the net assets of the legal parent, generally cash, together with the listing status of the legal parent.

Under IFRS 2, for equity-settled share-based payments, an entity measures the goods or services received, and the corresponding increase in equity, directly at the fair value of the goods or services received. If the entity cannot estimate reliably the fair value of the goods and services received, the entity measures the amounts, indirectly, by reference to the fair value of the equity instruments issued. *[IFRS 2.10]*. For transactions with non-employees, IFRS 2 presumes that the fair value of the goods and services received is more readily determinable. *[IFRS 2.13]*. This would suggest that the increase in equity should be based on the fair value of the cash and the fair value of the listing status. As it is unlikely that a fair value of the listing status can be reliably estimated, the increase in equity should be measured by reference to the fair value of the shares that are deemed to have been issued.

Indeed, even if a fair value could be attributed to the listing status, if the total identifiable consideration received is less than the fair value of the equity given as consideration, the transaction should be measured based on the fair value of the shares that are deemed to be issued. *[IFRS 2.13A]*.

This issue was considered by the Interpretations Committee between September 2012 and March 2013. The Interpretations Committee's conclusions, which accord with the analysis given above, are that for a transaction in which the former shareholders of a non-listed operating entity become the majority shareholders of the combined entity by exchanging their shares for new shares of a listed non-trading company, it is appropriate to apply the IFRS 3 guidance for reverse acquisitions by analogy. This results in the non-listed operating entity being identified as the accounting acquirer, and the listed non-trading entity being identified as the accounting acquiree. The accounting acquirer is deemed to have issued shares to obtain control of the acquiree. If the listed non-trading entity is not a business, the transaction is not a business combination, but a share-based payment transaction which should be accounted for in accordance with IFRS 2. Any difference in the fair value of the shares deemed to have been issued by the accounting acquirer and the fair value of the accounting acquiree's identifiable net assets represents a service received by the accounting acquirer. The Interpretations Committee concluded that regardless of the level of monetary or non-monetary assets owned by the non-listed operating entity the entire difference should be considered to be payment for the service of obtaining a stock exchange listing for its shares and no amount should be considered a cost of raising capital.[30]

Example 9.41: Reverse acquisition of a non-trading shell company

Entity A is a non-trading public company with 10,000 ordinary shares in issue. On 1 January 2021, Entity A issues 190,000 ordinary shares in exchange for all of the ordinary share capital of Entity B, a private trading company, with 9,500 ordinary shares in issue.

At the date of the transaction, Entity A has $85,000 of cash and the quoted market price of Entity A's ordinary shares is $12.

The fair value of Entity B has been determined by an independent professional valuer as being $2,185,000, giving a value per share of $230.

Following the transaction, apart from one non-executive director, all of the directors of Entity A resign and four new directors from Entity B are appointed to the Board of Entity A.

As a result of Entity A issuing 190,000 ordinary shares, Entity B's shareholders own 95 per cent of the issued share capital of the combined entity (i.e. 190,000 of the 200,000 issued shares), with the remaining 5 per cent held by Entity A's existing shareholders.

How should this transaction be accounted for in the consolidated financial statements of Entity A?

As the shareholders of Entity A only retain a 5 per cent interest in the combined entity after the transaction, and the Board is dominated by appointees from Entity B, this cannot be accounted for as an acquisition of Entity B by Entity A. Also, as Entity A is a non-trading cash shell company, and therefore not comprising a business (see 3.2 above), it cannot be accounted for as a reverse acquisition of Entity A by Entity B.

The consolidated financial statements should reflect the substance of the transaction which is that Entity B is the continuing entity. Entity B is deemed to have issued shares in exchange for the $85,000 cash held by Entity A together with the listing status of Entity A.

However, the listing status does not qualify for recognition as an intangible asset, and therefore needs to be expensed in profit or loss. As the existing shareholders of Entity A have a 5 per cent interest in the combined entity, Entity B would have had to issue 500 shares for the ratio of ownership interest in the combined entity to be the same. Based on the fair value of an Entity B share of $230, the accounting for the deemed share-based payment transaction is:

	Dr $	Cr $
Cash received	85,000	
Listing expense (income statement)	30,000	
Issued equity (500 × $230)		115,000

As Entity B is a private entity, it may be that a more reliable basis for determining the fair value of the deemed shares issued would have been to use the quoted market price of Entity A's shares at the date of the transaction. On this basis, the issued equity would have been $120,000 (10,000 × $12), giving rise to a listing expense of $35,000.

In summary, the accounting for this transaction is similar in many respects to that which would have been the case if the transaction had been accounted for as a reverse acquisition; the main difference being that no goodwill arises on the transaction, and that any amount that would have been so recognised is accounted for as a listing expense. Indeed, if the transaction had been accounted for as a reverse acquisition, the overall effect may have been the same if an impairment loss on the 'goodwill' had been recognised.

14.9 Reverse acquisitions and acquirers that are not legal entities

In September 2011, the Interpretations Committee considered whether a business that is not a legal entity could be the acquirer in a reverse acquisition. The Interpretations Committee concluded that an acquirer that is a reporting entity, but not a legal entity, can be considered to be the acquirer in a reverse acquisition. The Interpretations Committee observed that IFRSs and the 1989 *Conceptual Framework* do not require a 'reporting entity' to be a legal entity. Therefore, as long as the business that is not a legal entity obtains control of the acquiree and, in accordance with Appendix A of IFRS 3, the acquiree is 'the business or businesses that the acquirer obtains control of in a business combination' then '...the entity whose equity interests are acquired (the legal acquiree) must be the acquirer for accounting purposes for the transaction to be considered a reverse acquisition.' *[IFRS 3.7, Appendix A, B19]*. As this issue is not widespread, the Interpretations Committee did not add this issue to its agenda.[31] The 2018 *Conceptual Framework* (effective for annual periods beginning on or after 1 January 2020) does not alter that analysis, as it states explicitly that reporting entity is not necessarily a legal entity. *[CF 3.10]*.

15 PUSH DOWN ACCOUNTING

The term 'push down accounting' relates to the practice adopted in some jurisdictions of incorporating, or 'pushing down', the fair value adjustments which have been made by the acquirer into the financial statements of the acquiree, including the goodwill arising on the acquisition. It is argued that the acquisition, being an independently bargained transaction, provides better evidence of the values of the assets and liabilities of the acquiree than those previously contained within its financial statements, and therefore represents an improved basis of accounting. There are, however, contrary views, which hold that the transaction in question was one to which the reporting entity was not a party, and there is no reason why an adjustment should be made to the entity's own accounting records.

Whatever the theoretical arguments, it is certainly true that push down accounting could be an expedient practice, because it obviates the need to make extensive consolidation adjustments in each subsequent year, based on parallel accounting records. Nevertheless, if the acquiree is preparing its financial statements under IFRS, in our view it cannot apply push down accounting and reflect the fair value adjustments made by the acquirer and the goodwill that arose on its acquisition.

All of the requirements of IFRS must be applied when an entity prepares its financial statements. IFRS requires assets and liabilities to be recognised initially at cost or fair value, depending on the nature of the assets and liabilities. The acquisition of an entity by another party is not a transaction undertaken by that entity itself; hence it cannot be a transaction to determine cost.

Application of push down accounting would result in the recognition and measurement of assets and liabilities that are prohibited by some standards (such as internally generated intangibles and goodwill) and the recognition and measurement of assets and liabilities at amounts that are not permitted under IFRS. While some IFRS standards include an option or requirement to revalue particular assets, this is undertaken as part of a process of determining accounting policies rather than as one-off revaluations. For example:

- IAS 2 – *Inventories* – requires that inventories are measured at the lower of cost and net realisable value (see Chapter 22 at 3).
- IAS 16 requires that items of property, plant and equipment are initially measured at cost. Subsequently, property, plant and equipment can be measured at cost or at revalued amount. However, revaluations must be applied consistently and must be performed on a regular basis. Therefore a one-off revaluation is not permitted (see Chapter 18 at 6).

- IAS 38 requires that intangible assets are initially measured at cost. Subsequently, they can be revalued only in rare circumstances where there is an active market. In addition, IAS 38 specifically prohibits the recognition of internally generated goodwill. Therefore a one-off revaluation is not permitted (see Chapter 17 at 8.2).

16 DISCLOSURES

The disclosure requirements of IFRS 3 are set out below. Note that, although IFRS 13 provides guidance on how to measure fair value, IFRS 13 disclosures are not required for items that are recognised at fair value only at initial recognition. *[IFRS 13.91(a)]*. For example, the information about the fair value measurement of non-controlling interest in an acquiree if measured at fair value at the acquisition date is disclosed in accordance with the requirements of IFRS 3. *[IFRS 3.B64(o)(i)]*.

It should be noted that the disclosures to be made under IFRS 3 are explicitly required to be provided in the interim financial statements for business combinations occurring during the interim period, even if these interim financial statements are condensed. *[IAS 34.16A(i)]*.

16.1 Nature and financial effect of business combinations

The first disclosure objective is that the acquirer discloses information that enables users of its financial statements to evaluate the nature and financial effect of a business combination that occurs either:

(a) during the current reporting period; or

(b) after the end of the reporting period but before the financial statements are authorised for issue. *[IFRS 3.59]*.

Information that is required to be disclosed by the acquirer to meet the above objective is specified in the application guidance of the standard. *[IFRS 3.60]*.

16.1.1 Business combinations during the current reporting period

To meet the above objective, the acquirer is required to disclose the following information for each business combination that occurs during the reporting period: *[IFRS 3.B64]*

(a) the name and a description of the acquiree;

(b) the acquisition date;

(c) the percentage of voting equity interests acquired;

(d) the primary reasons for the business combination and a description of how the acquirer obtained control of the acquiree;

(e) a qualitative description of the factors that make up the goodwill recognised, such as expected synergies from combining operations of the acquiree and the acquirer, intangible assets that do not qualify for separate recognition or other factors;

(f) the acquisition-date fair value of the total consideration transferred and the acquisition-date fair value of each major class of consideration, such as:

(i) cash;
(ii) other tangible or intangible assets, including a business or subsidiary of the acquirer;
(iii) liabilities incurred, for example, a liability for contingent consideration; and
(iv) equity interests of the acquirer, including the number of instruments or interests issued or issuable and the method of measuring the fair value of those instruments or interests;

(g) for contingent consideration arrangements and indemnification assets:
  (i) the amount recognised as of the acquisition date;
  (ii) a description of the arrangement and the basis for determining the amount of the payment; and
  (iii) an estimate of the range of outcomes (undiscounted) or, if a range cannot be estimated, that fact and the reasons why a range cannot be estimated. If the maximum amount of the payment is unlimited, the acquirer discloses that fact;

(h) for acquired receivables:
  (i) the fair value of the receivables;
  (ii) the gross contractual amounts receivable; and
  (iii) the best estimate at the acquisition date of the contractual cash flows not expected to be collected;

  The disclosures are to be provided by major class of receivable, such as loans, direct finance leases and any other class of receivables;

(i) the amounts recognised as of the acquisition date for each major class of assets acquired and liabilities assumed;

(j) for each contingent liability recognised in accordance with paragraph 23 of the standard (see 5.6.1 above), the information required in paragraph 85 of IAS 37 (see Chapter 26 at 7.1). If a contingent liability is not recognised because its fair value cannot be measured reliably, the acquirer discloses:
  (i) the information required by paragraph 86 of IAS 37 (see Chapter 26 at 7.2); and
  (ii) the reasons why the liability cannot be measured reliably;

(k) the total amount of goodwill that is expected to be deductible for tax purposes;

(l) for transactions that are recognised separately from the acquisition of assets and assumption of liabilities in the business combination in accordance with paragraph 51 of the standard (see 11 above):
  (i) a description of each transaction;
  (ii) how the acquirer accounted for each transaction;
  (iii) the amounts recognised for each transaction and the line item in the financial statements in which each amount is recognised; and
  (iv) if the transaction is the effective settlement of a pre-existing relationship, the method used to determine the settlement amount;

(m) the disclosure of separately recognised transactions required by (l) above includes the amount of acquisition-related costs and, separately, the amount of those costs recognised as an expense and the line item or items in the statement of comprehensive income in which those expenses are recognised. The amount of any issue costs not recognised as an expense and how they were recognised are also to be disclosed;

(n) in a bargain purchase (see 10 above):
  (i) the amount of any gain recognised and the line item in the statement of comprehensive income in which the gain is recognised; and
  (ii) a description of the reasons why the transaction resulted in a gain;

(o) for each business combination in which the acquirer holds less than 100 per cent of the equity interests in the acquiree at the acquisition date (i.e. there is a non-controlling interest – see 8 above):
  (i) the amount of the non-controlling interest in the acquiree recognised at the acquisition date and the measurement basis for that amount; and
  (ii) for each non-controlling interest in an acquiree measured at fair value, the valuation techniques and significant inputs used to measure that value;

(p) in a business combination achieved in stages (see 9 above):
  (i) the acquisition-date fair value of the equity interest in the acquiree held by the acquirer immediately before the acquisition date; and
  (ii) the amount of any gain or loss recognised as a result of remeasuring to fair value the equity interest in the acquiree held by the acquirer before the business combination and the line item in the statement of comprehensive income in which that gain or loss is recognised;

(q) the following information:
  (i) the amounts of revenue and profit or loss of the acquiree since the acquisition date included in the consolidated statement of comprehensive income for the reporting period; and
  (ii) the revenue and profit or loss of the combined entity for the current reporting period as though the acquisition date for all business combinations that occurred during the year had been as of the beginning of the annual reporting period.

If disclosure of any of the information required by this subparagraph is impracticable, the acquirer shall disclose that fact and explain why the disclosure is impracticable. IFRS 3 uses the term 'impracticable' with the same meaning as in IAS 8 (see Chapter 3 at 4.7).

Although it is not explicitly stated in paragraph B64 of the standard, it is evident that the above information is required to be given for each material business combination. This is due to the fact that the standard states that for individually immaterial business combinations occurring during the reporting period that are material collectively, the acquirer has to disclose, in aggregate, the information required by items (e) to (q) above. *[IFRS 3.B65]*.

16.1.2 Business combinations effected after the end of the reporting period

If the acquisition date of a business combination is after the end of the reporting period but before the financial statements are authorised for issue, the acquirer is required to disclose the information set out in 16.1.1 above for that business combination, unless the initial accounting for the business combination is incomplete at the time the financial statements are authorised for issue. In that situation, the acquirer describes which disclosures could not be made and the reasons why they cannot be made. *[IFRS 3.B66]*.

16.2 Financial effects of adjustments recognised in the current reporting period

The second objective is that the acquirer discloses information that enables users of its financial statements to evaluate the financial effects of adjustments recognised in the current reporting period that relate to business combinations that occurred in the period or previous reporting periods. *[IFRS 3.61]*.

Information that is required to be disclosed by the acquirer to meet the above objective is specified in the application guidance of the standard. *[IFRS 3.62]*.

To meet the above objective, the acquirer is required to disclose the following information for each material business combination or in the aggregate for individually immaterial business combinations that are material collectively: *[IFRS 3.B67]*

(a) if the initial accounting for a business combination is incomplete (see 12 above) for particular assets, liabilities, non-controlling interests or items of consideration and the amounts recognised in the financial statements for the business combination thus have been determined only provisionally:

  (i) the reasons why the initial accounting for the business combination is incomplete;

  (ii) the assets, liabilities, equity interests or items of consideration for which the initial accounting is incomplete; and

  (iii) the nature and amount of any measurement period adjustments recognised during the reporting period in accordance with paragraph 49 of the standard (see 12.1 above);

(b) for each reporting period after the acquisition date until the entity collects, sells or otherwise loses the right to a contingent consideration asset, or until the entity settles a contingent consideration liability or the liability is cancelled or expires (see 7.1 above):

  (i) any changes in the recognised amounts, including any differences arising upon settlement;

  (ii) any changes in the range of outcomes (undiscounted) and the reasons for those changes; and

  (iii) the valuation techniques and key model inputs used to measure contingent consideration;

(c) for contingent liabilities recognised in a business combination, the acquirer shall disclose the information required by paragraphs 84 and 85 of IAS 37 for each class of provision (see Chapter 26 at 7.1);

(d) a reconciliation of the carrying amount of goodwill at the beginning and end of the reporting period showing separately:

  (i) the gross amount and accumulated impairment losses at the beginning of the reporting period;

(ii) additional goodwill recognised during the reporting period, except goodwill included in a disposal group that, on acquisition, meets the criteria to be classified as held for sale in accordance with IFRS 5 (see Chapter 4 at 2.1);

(iii) adjustments resulting from the subsequent recognition of deferred tax assets during the reporting period in accordance with paragraph 67 of the standard (there should in fact be no such adjustment to disclose as any adjustment is recognised in profit or loss (see 5.6.2 above));

(iv) goodwill included in a disposal group classified as held for sale in accordance with IFRS 5 and goodwill derecognised during the reporting period without having previously been included in a disposal group classified as held for sale;

(v) impairment losses recognised during the reporting period in accordance with IAS 36. (IAS 36 requires disclosure of information about the recoverable amount and impairment of goodwill in addition to this requirement (see Chapter 20 at 13.3));

(vi) net exchange rate differences arising during the reporting period in accordance with IAS 21 – *The Effects of Changes in Foreign Exchange Rates* (see Chapter 15 at 6.5);

(vii) any other changes in the carrying amount during the reporting period; and

(viii) the gross amount and accumulated impairment losses at the end of the reporting period;

(e) the amount and an explanation of any gain or loss recognised in the current reporting period that both:

(i) relates to the identifiable assets acquired or liabilities assumed in a business combination that was effected in the current or previous reporting period; and

(ii) is of such a size, nature or incidence that disclosure is relevant to understanding the combined entity's financial statements.

16.3 Other necessary information

IFRS 3 includes a catch-all disclosure requirement, that if in any situation the information required to be disclosed set out above, or by other IFRSs, does not satisfy the objectives of IFRS 3, the acquirer discloses whatever additional information is necessary to meet those objectives. *[IFRS 3.63]*.

In addition, IAS 7 – *Statement of Cash Flows* – requires disclosures in respect of obtaining control of subsidiaries and other businesses (see Chapter 40 at 6.3). *[IAS 7.39-42]*.

16.4 Illustrative disclosures

An illustration of some of the disclosure requirements of IFRS 3 is given by way of an example in the Illustrative Examples accompanying the standard. The example, which is reproduced below, assumes that the acquirer, AC, is a listed entity and that the acquiree, TC, is an unlisted entity. The illustration presents the disclosures in a tabular format that refers to the specific disclosure requirements illustrated. (The references to paragraph B64 correspond to the equivalent item at 16.1.1 above and those to paragraph B67 correspond to the equivalent item at 16.2 above.) It is also emphasised that an actual footnote might present many of the disclosures illustrated in a simple narrative format. *[IFRS 3.IE72]*.

Example 9.42: *Footnote X: Acquisitions*

Paragraph reference		
B64(a-d)	On 30 June 20X0 AC acquired 15 per cent of the outstanding ordinary shares of TC. On 30 June 20X2 AC acquired 60 per cent of the outstanding ordinary shares of TC and obtained control of TC. TC is a provider of data networking products and services in Canada and Mexico. As a result of the acquisition, AC is expected to be the leading provider of data networking products and services in those markets. It also expects to reduce costs through economies of scale.	
B64(e)	The goodwill of CU2,500 arising from the acquisition consists largely of the synergies and economies of scale expected from combining the operations of AC and TC.	
B64(k)	None of the goodwill recognised is expected to be deductible for income tax purposes. The following table summarises the consideration paid for TC and the amounts of the assets acquired and liabilities assumed recognised at the acquisition date, as well as the fair value at the acquisition date of the non-controlling interest in TC.	
	At 30 June 20X2	
	Consideration	CU
B64(f)(i)	Cash	5,000
B64(f)(iv)	Equity instruments (100,000 ordinary shares of AC)	4,000
B64(f)(iii); B64(g)(i)	Contingent consideration arrangement	1,000
B64(f)	Total consideration transferred	10,000
B64(p)(i)	Fair value of AC's equity interest in TC held before the business combination	2,000
		12,000
B64(m)	Acquisition-related costs (included in selling, general and administrative expenses in AC's statement of comprehensive income for the year ended 31 December 20X2)	1,250
B64(i)	Recognised amounts of identifiable assets acquired and liabilities assumed	
	Financial assets	3,500
	Inventory	1,000
	Property, plant and equipment	10,000
	Identifiable intangible assets	3,300
	Financial liabilities	(4,000)
	Contingent liability	(1,000)
	Total identifiable net assets	12,800
B64(o)(i)	Non-controlling interest in TC	(3,300)
	Goodwill	2,500
		12,000
B64(f)(iv)	The fair value of the 100,000 ordinary shares issued as part of the consideration paid for TC (CU4,000) was measured using the closing market price of AC's ordinary shares on the acquisition date.	

B64(f)(iii) B64(g) B67(b)	The contingent consideration arrangement requires AC to pay the former owners of TC 5 per cent of the revenues of XC, an unconsolidated equity investment owned by TC, in excess of CU7,500 for 20X3, up to a maximum amount of CU2,500 (undiscounted).
	The potential undiscounted amount of all future payments that AC could be required to make under the contingent consideration arrangement is between CU0 and CU2,500.
	The fair value of the contingent consideration arrangement of CU1,000 was estimated by applying the income approach. The fair value measurement is based on significant inputs that are not observable in the market, which IFRS 13 refers to as Level 3 inputs. Key assumptions include a discount rate range of 20-25 per cent and assumed probability-adjusted revenues in XC of CU10,000-20,000.
	As of 31 December 20X2, neither the amount recognised for the contingent consideration arrangement, nor the range of outcomes or the assumptions used to develop the estimates had changed.
B64(h)	The fair value of the financial assets acquired includes receivables under finance leases of data networking equipment with a fair value of CU2,375. The gross amount due under the contracts is CU3,100, of which CU450 is expected to be uncollectible.
B67(a)	The fair value of the acquired identifiable intangible assets of CU3,300 is provisional pending receipt of the final valuations for those assets.
B64(j) B67(c) IAS 37.84, 85	A contingent liability of CU1,000 has been recognised for expected warranty claims on products sold by TC during the last three years. We expect that the majority of this expenditure will be incurred in 20X3 and that all will be incurred by the end of 20X4. The potential undiscounted amount of all future payments that AC could be required to make under the warranty arrangements is estimated to be between CU500 and CU1,500. As of 31 December 20X2, there has been no change since 30 June 20X2 in the amount recognised for the liability or any change in the range of outcomes or assumptions used to develop the estimates.
B64(o)	The fair value of the non-controlling interest in TC, an unlisted company, was estimated by applying a market approach and an income approach. The fair value measurements are based on significant inputs that are not observable in the market and thus represent a fair value measurement categorised within Level 3 of the fair value hierarchy as described in IFRS 13. Key assumptions include the following: (a) a discount rate range of 20-25 per cent; (b) a terminal value based on a range of terminal EBITDA multiples between 3 and 5 times (or, if appropriate, based on long term sustainable growth rates ranging from 3 to 6 per cent); (c) financial multiples of companies deemed to be similar to TC; and (d) adjustments because of the lack of control or lack of marketability that market participants would consider when measuring the fair value of the non-controlling interest in TC.
B64(p)(ii)	AC recognised a gain of CU500 as a result of measuring at fair value its 15 per cent equity interest in TC held before the business combination. The gain is included in other income in AC's statement of comprehensive income for the year ending 31 December 20X2.
B64(q)(i)	The revenue included in the consolidated statement of comprehensive income since 30 June 20X2 contributed by TC was CU4,090. TC also contributed profit of CU1,710 over the same period.
B64(q)(ii)	Had TC been consolidated from 1 January 20X2 the consolidated statement of comprehensive income would have included revenue of CU27,670 and profit of CU12,870.

References

1. Report and Feedback Statement *Post-implementation Review of IFRS 3 Business Combinations*, pp.5-6.
2. Report and Feedback Statement *Post-implementation Review of IFRS 3 Business Combinations*, pp.7-10.
3. *IFRIC Update*, July 2018
4. Snapshot *Business Combinations—Disclosures, Goodwill and Impairment*, March 2020 and Discussion Paper DP/2020/1, *Business Combinations—Disclosures, Goodwill and Impairment*
5. *IASB Work Plan* as at 31 August 2020.
6. *IFRIC Update*, November 2017.
7. *IFRIC Update*, September 2011.
8. *IFRIC Update*, July 2011.
9. *IFRIC Update*, September 2011.
10. *IASB Update*, December 2017.
11. *IASB Work Plan* as at 31 August 2020.
12. *IFRIC Update*, May 2014.
13. Exposure Draft ED/2019/3, *Reference to the Conceptual Framework*. Proposed amendments to IFRS 3, Basis for Conclusions paragraph BC12, p.13.
14. ibid. para. BC6, p.12.
15. ibid. para. BC20, p.15
16. IFRS 17 – *Insurance contracts*, Appendix D Amendments to other IFRS Standards, IFRS 3 Business Combinations, May 2017.
17. *IFRIC Update*, September 2008.
18. *IFRIC Update*, March 2009.
19. *IFRIC Update*, March 2009.
20. IFRS 17 – *Insurance contracts*, Appendix D Amendments to other IFRS Standards, IFRS 3 Business Combinations, May 2017.
21. *IFRIC Update,* January 2011.
22. Staff Paper, IASB meeting, June 2009, Agenda reference 13C, *Annual Improvements Process, Contingent consideration of an Acquiree ("pre-existing contingent consideration")*, p.3.
23. *IASB Update*, May 2013.
24. *Put options written on non-controlling interests (Proposed amendments to IAS 32)*, Project news, IASB Website, 23 June 2014.
25. Staff Paper, IASB meeting, October 2019, Agenda Reference 5, *Financial Instruments with Characteristics of Equity (FICE), Clarifying amendments to IAS 32 Project plan*, para. 30, p.11-12.
26. ibid. para. 29, p.11.
27. ibid. para. 69, paras. 26-27.
28. *IFRIC Update*, November 2010.
29. *IFRIC Update*, January 2013.
30. *IFRIC Update*, March 2013.
31. *IFRIC Update*, September 2011.

Chapter 10　Business combinations under common control

1   INTRODUCTION 765
    1.1   Common control transactions 765
    1.2   Group reorganisations..766
    1.3   Scope of this chapter..767
2   THE IFRS 3 SCOPE EXCLUSION 768
    2.1   Business combinations under common control................................768
          2.1.1   Common control by an individual or group of individuals 769
          2.1.2   Transitory control 771
3   ACCOUNTING FOR BUSINESS COMBINATIONS INVOLVING ENTITIES OR
    BUSINESSES UNDER COMMON CONTROL 773
    3.1   Pooling of interests method or acquisition method 773
    3.2   Application of the acquisition method under IFRS 3.........................777
    3.3   Application of the pooling of interests method 779
          3.3.1   General requirements..780
          3.3.2   Carrying amounts of assets and liabilities 780
          3.3.3   Restatement of financial information for periods prior to
                  the date of the combination 783
          3.3.4   Equity reserves and history of assets and liabilities carried
                  over.. 785
          3.3.5   Acquisition of non-controlling interest as part of a
                  business combination under common control............................ 787
4   ACCOUNTING FOR TRANSACTIONS UNDER COMMON CONTROL (OR
    OWNERSHIP) INVOLVING A NEWCO 789
    4.1   Introduction.. 789
    4.2   Setting up a new top holding company...790

	4.2.1	Setting up a new top holding company: transactions effected through issuing equity interests 791

- 4.2.1 Setting up a new top holding company: transactions effected through issuing equity interests 791
- 4.2.2 Setting up a new top holding company: transactions involving consideration other than equity interests 793
- 4.3 Inserting a new intermediate parent within an existing group 794
- 4.4 Transferring businesses outside an existing group using a Newco 795

5 ACCOUNTING FOR TRANSFERS OF ASSOCIATES OR JOINT VENTURES UNDER COMMON CONTROL 797

6 FUTURE DEVELOPMENTS 800

- 6.1 BCUCC research project – background and scope 800
- 6.2 BCUCC research project – accounting methods and disclosures 801
  - 6.2.1 When to apply which measurement approach 802
  - 6.2.2 How to apply the acquisition method 803
  - 6.2.3 How to apply the predecessor approach 804
  - 6.2.4 Disclosures about transactions within the scope of the project 804
- 6.3 BCUCC research project – next steps 805

List of examples

Example 10.1:	Common control involving individuals	770
Example 10.2:	The meaning of 'transitory' common control	772
Example 10.3:	Accounting for business combinations under common control – use of acquisition method? (1)	775
Example 10.4:	Accounting for business combinations under common control – use of acquisition method? (2)	776
Example 10.5:	Acquisition method – cash consideration less than the fair value of acquired business	778
Example 10.6:	Pooling of interests method – carrying amounts of assets acquired and liabilities assumed	782
Example 10.7:	Pooling of interests method – restatement of financial information for periods prior to the date of the combination (1)	784
Example 10.8:	Pooling of interests method – restatement of financial information for periods prior to the date of the combination (2)	785
Example 10.9:	Pooling of interests method – no restatement of financial information for periods prior to the date of the combination – impact of carrying over equity reserves and history	786

Example 10.10:	Pooling of interests method – acquisition of non-controlling interest as part of a business combination under common control	788
Example 10.11:	Newco inserted at the top of an existing group	791
Example 10.12:	Newco inserted at the top of entities owned by the same shareholders thereby creating a new reporting group	792
Example 10.13:	Newco inserted as a new intermediate parent within an existing group	794
Example 10.14:	Newco created to take over a business of an existing group (spin-off)	796
Example 10.15:	Transfer of an associate within an existing group	799

Chapter 10 Business combinations under common control

1 INTRODUCTION

1.1 Common control transactions

Transactions between entities under common control (or common control transactions) occur frequently in business. For example, many entities conduct their business activities through subsidiaries and there are often transactions between the entities comprising the group. It is also common for entities under common control, which are not a group for financial reporting purposes, to transact with each other.

Examples of common control transactions include the sale of goods, property and other assets, the provision of services (including those of employees), leasing, transfers under licence agreements, financing transactions and the provision of guarantees.

It cannot always be assumed that common control transactions are undertaken on an arm's length basis or that equal values have been exchanged. Standard setters internationally have developed standards that require disclosures about related party transactions (which include common control transactions), rather than requiring the transactions to be recognised at an arm's length price. The IASB also adopted this approach in IAS 24 – *Related Party Disclosures* – which is a disclosure standard and does not establish recognition or measurement requirements. Entities would need to account for such transactions in accordance with the requirements of any IFRS specifically applicable to that transaction. *[IAS 8.7]*.

In January 2018, the IFRS Interpretations Committee (or Interpretations Committee) confirmed that IFRSs do not provide a general exception or exemption from applying the requirements in a particular standard to common control transactions. The Interpretations Committee observed that 'unless a Standard specifically excludes common control transactions from its scope, an entity applies the applicable requirements in the Standard to common control transactions'.[1]

Nonetheless, IFRSs do not provide a complete framework and particular common control transactions may not be covered in any IFRS. Specific requirements may also be absent when common control transactions are excluded from the scope of a standard that would otherwise apply. There is often more than one acceptable way of accounting for common control transactions which gives rise to an accounting policy choice. General guidance on accounting for transactions between a parent and its subsidiaries, or between subsidiaries within a group, is included in Chapter 8 at 4.

One specific area where there is a scope exclusion for common control transactions is IFRS 3 – *Business Combinations* (discussed in Chapter 9). That standard addresses business combinations but excludes 'a combination of entities or businesses under common control' from its scope. *[IFRS 3.2]*. The IASB noted that current IFRSs do not specify how to account for business combinations under common control and is carrying out a research project with proposals to address this gap, in order to improve the comparability and transparency of accounting for such transactions.[2] This research project, *Business Combinations under Common Control* (discussed at 6 below), is not limited to transactions that strictly satisfy the description of business combinations under common control currently excluded from the scope of IFRS 3. It also considers other types of group reorganisations where there is a lack of specific requirements.

This chapter discusses the implications of the scope exclusion in IFRS 3 for business combinations under common control and the absence of guidance in IFRSs for certain types of group reorganisations, as well as the accounting treatments which may currently be adopted for such transactions.

1.2 Group reorganisations

Group reorganisations involve restructuring the relationships between entities or businesses within a group (or under common control) and can take many forms. They may be undertaken for various reasons, for example to reorganise activities with an aim to achieve synergies, to simplify a group structure, or to obtain tax efficiency (e.g. by creating a tax grouping in a particular jurisdiction). In some cases, a group reorganisation takes place to split an existing group into two or more separate groups or to create a single new reporting group, possibly as a prelude to a subsequent sale or initial public offering (IPO).

Group reorganisations involve transferring entities or businesses between existing or newly formed entities under common control. From the perspective of the controlling party, the transfer does not affect the entities or businesses that party holds. In principle, such changes should have no impact on the consolidated financial statements of an existing group (except for any potential tax consequences), provided there are no non-controlling interests affected. This is because the effects of transactions within an existing group are generally eliminated in full (see Chapter 7 at 2.4). Alternatively, some reorganisations may involve transferring entities or businesses outside the existing group (e.g. demergers).

Transfers of entities or businesses between existing or newly formed entities under common control may be in exchange for cash or shares. Other transfers may be without any consideration, such as a distribution by a subsidiary to its parent or a contribution by a parent to its subsidiary. There can also be legal arrangements that have a similar effect, including reorganisations sanctioned by a court process or transfers after liquidation of the transferor (i.e. the transferring entity). In addition, some jurisdictions allow a legal merger between a parent and its subsidiary to form a single entity.

From the perspective of the transferee in the reorganisation (i.e. the receiving entity), there may well be a business combination that needs to be accounted for. This business combination would be excluded from the scope of IFRS 3 if it satisfies the description of a business combination under common control. Alternatively, the transaction may not represent a business combination as defined in IFRS 3 because the assets acquired and liabilities assumed do not constitute a business (i.e. an asset acquisition) or because neither of the combining entities can be identified as the acquirer (e.g. in some situations where a newly formed entity is involved). The accounting by the receiving entity in a group reorganisation is often not covered in existing IFRSs.

The transferor in the reorganisation will need to account for its part of the transaction in its own financial statements. The relevant requirements for transferors are discussed in other chapters, as set out at 1.3 below.

1.3 Scope of this chapter

This chapter deals with common control transactions that involve the transfer of control over one or more businesses (as defined in IFRS 3) and focuses on the perspective of the receiving entity. That receiving entity may or may not be identifiable as the acquirer if IFRS 3 were applied to the transaction (see Chapter 9 at 4.1). If the entity or net assets being transferred do not meet the definition of a business (see Chapter 9 at 3.2), the transaction represents an asset acquisition. The accounting for acquisitions of (net) assets under common control is discussed in Chapter 8 at 4.4.2.D.

This chapter consecutively addresses:

- the scope exclusion in IFRS 3 for business combinations under common control (see 2 below);
- the accounting for business combinations under common control excluded from the scope of IFRS 3 (see 3 below);
- the accounting for transactions under common control (or sometimes common ownership) involving a newly formed entity (see 4 below);
- the accounting for transfers of investments in associates or joint ventures from entities under common control (see 5 below); and
- the status of the IASB's research project on business combinations under common control (see 6 below).

Although the discussion at 3 and 4 below (particularly the examples contained therein) generally refers to 'consolidated financial statements' and transfers of 'entities', the accounting may be equally applicable to the separate or individual financial statements of an entity that receives the net assets of a business (rather than the shares in the entity holding that business) in a common control transaction. In contrast, if the receiving entity obtains control over a business housed in a separate legal entity, it would recognise an investment in a subsidiary in accordance with IAS 27 – *Separate Financial Statements* – in its separate financial statements (and individual financial statements are not applicable). This is consistent with business combinations that are in the scope of IFRS 3. That standard specifies only to which transactions it applies, but not to which financial statements (e.g. consolidated, separate, individual).

This chapter, however, does not specifically deal with the accounting for common control transactions in separate or individual financial statements, which is covered in Chapter 8 at 4. Chapter 8 also discusses the accounting for legal mergers between a parent and its subsidiary (at 4.4.3.B).

Although no control is obtained by the receiving entity, this chapter does address the transfer of an investment in an associate or joint venture from an entity under common control (at 5 below). The issue is whether the scope exclusion in IFRS 3 for business combinations under common control can be applied by analogy to this scenario.

The transferor that loses control over an entity or business in a common control transaction will also need to account for the transaction in its own financial statements. In doing so, it will need to consider the requirements of other relevant IFRSs, in particular, the requirements of IFRS 10 – *Consolidated Financial Statements* – relating to disposals of, or loss of control over, subsidiaries (see Chapter 7 at 3.2) and the requirements of IFRS 5 – *Non-current Assets Held for Sale and Discontinued Operations* – relating to disposal groups held for sale and discontinued operations (see Chapter 4). The discussion in Chapter 7 at 3.7 and in Chapter 8 at 2.4.2 relating to demergers (e.g. the spin-off of a subsidiary or business) may also be relevant.

Finally, any transaction between entities under common control is a related party transaction under IAS 24, the requirements of which are dealt with in Chapter 39.

2 THE IFRS 3 SCOPE EXCLUSION

IFRS 3 establishes principles and requirements for how the acquirer accounts for a business combination, which is defined as 'a transaction or other event in which an acquirer obtains control of one or more businesses'. *[IFRS 3.1, Appendix A]*. Identifying a business combination, including the definition of a business, is discussed generally in Chapter 9 at 3.

However, IFRS 3 excludes from its scope 'a combination of entities or businesses under common control'. *[IFRS 3.2(c)]*. The application guidance of the standard provides further guidance to determine when a business combination is regarded a business combination under common control. *[IFRS 3.B1-B4]*.

If the transaction is not a business combination in the first place, because the assets acquired and liabilities assumed do not constitute a business as defined, it is accounted for as an asset acquisition. *[IFRS 3.3]*. The accounting for acquisitions of (net) assets under common control is discussed in Chapter 8 at 4.4.2.D. In addition, a transaction may not be a business combination as defined in IFRS 3 because, applying that standard, no acquirer can be identified. This is considered in more detail at 4.1 below.

2.1 Business combinations under common control

For the purpose of the scope exclusion, a business combination involving entities or businesses under common control is 'a business combination in which all of the combining entities or businesses are ultimately controlled by the same party or parties both before and after the business combination, and that control is not transitory'. *[IFRS 3.B1]*. This will include transactions such as the transfer of subsidiaries or businesses between entities within a group, provided the transaction meets the definition of a business combination in IFRS 3.

The extent of non-controlling interests in each of the combining entities before and after the business combination is not relevant to determining whether the combination involves entities under common control. [IFRS 3.B4]. This is because a partially-owned subsidiary is nevertheless under the control of the parent entity. Therefore transactions involving partially-owned subsidiaries are also outside the scope of the standard. Similarly, the fact that one of the combining entities is a subsidiary that has been excluded from the consolidated financial statements of the group in accordance with IFRS 10 is not relevant to determining whether a combination involves entities under common control. [IFRS 3.B4]. This is because the parent entity controls the subsidiary regardless of that fact.

2.1.1 Common control by an individual or group of individuals

The scope exclusion is not restricted to transactions between entities within a group. An entity can be controlled by an individual or a group of individuals acting together under a contractual arrangement. That individual or group of individuals may not be subject to the financial reporting requirements of IFRSs. It is not necessary for combining entities to be included as part of the same consolidated financial statements for a business combination to be regarded as one involving entities under common control. [IFRS 3.B3]. Thus, if a transaction involves entities controlled by the same individual, even if it results in a new reporting group, the acquisition method would not always be applied.

A group of individuals controls an entity if, as a result of contractual arrangements, they collectively have the power to govern its financial and operating policies so as to obtain benefits from its activities. Therefore, a business combination is outside the scope of IFRS 3 if the same group of individuals has ultimate collective power to control each of the combining entities and that ultimate collective power is not transitory. [IFRS 3.B2].

The mere existence of common ownership is not sufficient. For the scope exclusion to apply to a group of individuals, there has to be a 'contractual arrangement' between them such that they have control over the entities involved in the transaction. IFRS 3 does not indicate what form such an arrangement should take. However, in describing a 'joint arrangement', IFRS 11 – *Joint Arrangements* – explains that 'contractual arrangements can be evidenced in several ways' and that 'an enforceable contractual arrangement is often, but not always, in writing, usually in the form of a contract or documented discussions between the parties'. [IFRS 11.B2]. This also implies that it is possible for a contractual arrangement to be in non-written form. If it is not written, great care needs to be taken with all of the facts and circumstances to determine whether it is appropriate to exclude a transaction from the scope of IFRS 3.

One particular situation where there might be such an unwritten arrangement, is where the individuals involved are members of the same family. In such situations, whether common control exists between family members very much depends on the specific facts and circumstances and requires judgement.

A starting point could be the definition in IAS 24 of 'close members of the family of a person' as 'those family members who may be expected to influence, or be influenced by, that person in their dealings with the entity and include:

(a) that person's children and spouse or domestic partner;
(b) children of that person's spouse or domestic partner; and
(c) dependants of that person or that person's spouse or domestic partner.' [IAS 24.9].

If the individuals concerned are 'close members of the family' as defined in IAS 24 (see Chapter 39 at 2.2.1), then it is possible that they will act collectively, and the scope exclusion in IFRS 3 may apply. This could be the case where one family member may effectively control the voting of a dependent family member (e.g. scenario (a) in Example 10.1 below). It is also possible that a highly influential parent may be able to ensure that adult family members act collectively (e.g. scenario (b) in Example 10.1 below). In this case there would need to be clear evidence that the family influence has resulted in a pattern of collective family decisions. However, common control is unlikely to exist where the family members are adult siblings (e.g. scenario (c) in Example 10.1 below), as such individuals are more likely to act independently. We believe that there should be a presumption that common control does not exist between non-close family members and sufficient evidence that they act collectively, rather than independently, would need to exist to overcome this conclusion.

In all such situations involving family members, whenever there is sufficient evidence that the family members (irrespective of the family relationship) have acted independently, then the scope exclusion in IFRS 3 for business combinations under common control does not apply.

Example 10.1: Common control involving individuals

Entity A has three shareholders, Mr X, Mr Y and Mr Z. Mr X and Mr Y are family members who each hold a 30% interest in Entity A. Mr X and Mr Y also each hold a 30% interest in Entity B. There is no written contractual arrangement between Mr X and Mr Y requiring them to act collectively as shareholders in Entity A and Entity B. Both Entity A and Entity B are businesses as defined in IFRS 3.

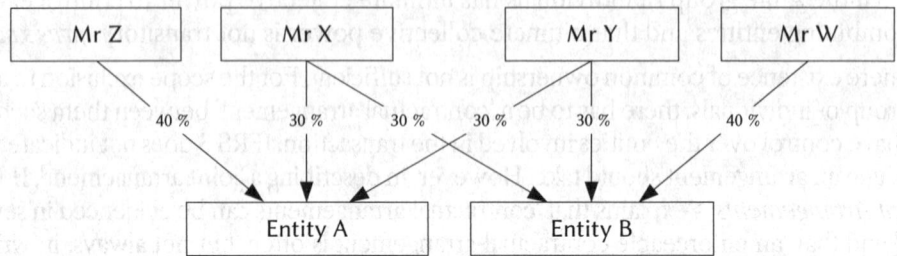

If Entity A acquires 100% of Entity B, is this a business combination under common control and therefore outside the scope of IFRS 3 when the nature of the family relationship is:

(a) Mr X is the father and Mr Y is his young dependent son; or
(b) Mr X is a patriarchal father and – because of his highly influential standing – his adult son Mr Y has traditionally followed his father's decisions; or
(c) Mr X and Mr Y are adult siblings?

Whether common control exists between family members very much depends on the facts and circumstances, as often there will not be any written agreement between family members. However, the influence that normally arises within relationships between 'close members of the family' as defined in IAS 24 means that it is possible that they will act collectively, such that there is common control. If so, the business combination would be outside the scope of IFRS 3.

Scenario (a)

The business combination may be outside the scope of IFRS 3. The father, Mr X, may effectively control the voting of his dependent son, Mr Y, by acting on his behalf and thus vote the entire 60% combined holding collectively. However, if there is evidence that Mr X and Mr Y are acting independently (e.g. by voting differently at shareholder or board meetings), the scope exclusion would not apply since these close family members have not been acting collectively to control the entities.

Scenario (b)

The business combination may be outside the scope of IFRS 3. A highly influential parent may be able to ensure that adult family members act collectively. However, there would need to be clear evidence that the family influence has resulted in a pattern of collective family decisions. If there is any evidence that Mr X and Mr Y are acting independently (e.g. by voting differently at shareholder or board meetings), the scope exclusion would not apply since the parent and adult family member have not been acting collectively to control the entities.

Scenario (c)

Common control is unlikely to exist, and therefore the business combination would be in scope of IFRS 3. In this scenario where Mr X and Mr Y are adult siblings (and not considered close family members otherwise), it is less likely that an unwritten arrangement will exist. Where family members are not 'close', they are less likely to have influence over each other and more likely to act independently. Accordingly, there is a presumption that common control does not exist between non-close family members and sufficient evidence that they act collectively, rather than independently, would be needed to overcome this conclusion.

If in Example 10.1 above, Mr X and Mr Y had been unrelated, then, in the absence of a written agreement, consideration would need to be given to all facts and circumstances to determine whether it is appropriate to exclude the transaction from the scope of IFRS 3. In our view, there would need to be very strong evidence of them acting together to control both entities in a collective manner, in order to demonstrate that an unwritten contractual arrangement really exists, and that such control is not transitory.

Prior to the acquisition of Entity B by Entity A in Example 10.1 above, another question is whether financial statements can be prepared under IFRS for a 'reporting entity' that does not comprise a group under IFRS 10 (i.e. combined financial statements comprised of such 'sister' companies). This issue is discussed in Chapter 6 at 2.2.6.

2.1.2 Transitory control

IFRS 3 requires that common control is 'not transitory' as a condition for the scope exclusion to apply. In contrast, if common control is only transitory, the business combination is still within the scope of the standard. The condition was included when IFRS 3 was first issued in 2004 to deal with concerns that business combinations between parties acting at arm's length could be structured through the use of 'grooming' transactions so that, for a brief period immediately before and after the combination, the combining entities or businesses are under common control. In this way, it might have been possible for combinations that would otherwise be accounted for in accordance with IFRS 3 using the purchase method (now called 'acquisition method') to be accounted for using some other method. *[IFRS 3(2007).BC28]*. Questions have been raised, however, on the meaning of 'transitory control'.

The Interpretations Committee was asked in 2006 whether a reorganisation involving the formation of a new entity (Newco) to facilitate the sale of part of an organisation is a business combination within the scope of IFRS 3. Some suggested that, because control of Newco is transitory (i.e. it is subsequently sold), a combination involving that Newco would be within the scope of the standard. The Interpretations Committee however observed that paragraph 22 of IFRS 3 (now paragraph B18) states that when an entity is formed to issue equity instruments to effect a business combination, one of the combining entities that existed before the combination must be identified as the acquirer. To be consistent, the Interpretations Committee noted that the question of whether the entities or businesses are under common control, applies to the combining entities that existed before the combination (i.e. excluding the newly formed entity that did not exist before). Accordingly, the Interpretations Committee decided not to add this topic to its agenda.[3] Although the issue was considered in the context of the original IFRS 3, the comments remain valid as the relevant requirements in the current version of the standard are substantially unchanged.

Therefore, whether or not a Newco is set up within an existing group to facilitate the disposal of businesses is irrelevant as to whether or not common control is transitory. However, does the fact that the reorganisation results in the parent of the existing group losing control over those businesses, mean that common control is transitory?

In our view, the answer is 'no'. An intention to sell the businesses or go to an IPO shortly after the reorganisation does not, by itself, preclude the scope exclusion in IFRS 3 from applying. The requirement 'that control is not transitory' is intended as an anti-avoidance mechanism to prevent business combinations between parties acting at arm's length from being structured through the use of 'grooming' transactions so that, for a brief period immediately before and after the combination, the combining entities or businesses are under common control. Whether or not common control is transitory should be assessed by looking at the duration of control of the combining businesses in the period both before and after the reorganisation – it is not limited to an assessment of the duration of control only after the reorganisation.

Example 10.2:   The meaning of 'transitory' common control

Entity A currently has two businesses (as defined in IFRS 3) operated through wholly-owned subsidiaries Entity X and Entity Y. The group structure (ignoring other entities within the group) is as follows:

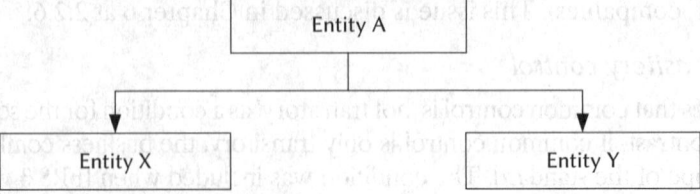

Entity A proposes to combine the two businesses (currently housed in two separate entities, Entity X and Entity Y) into one entity and then spin-off the combined entity as part of an IPO. Both businesses have been owned by Entity A for several years. The reorganisation will be structured such that Entity A will first establish a new entity (Newco) and transfer its interests in Entity X and Entity Y to Newco, resulting in the following group structure:

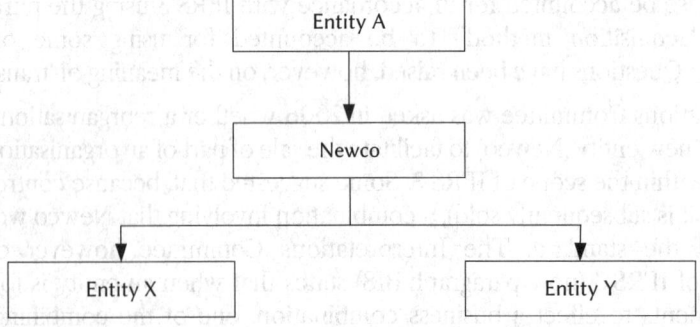

Newco will then be subject to an IPO, with the result that Entity A will lose control.

If Newco were to prepare consolidated financial statements, would the reorganisation undertaken to facilitate the disposal of Entity X and Entity Y be in the scope of IFRS 3? Or would the scope exclusion for business combinations under common control apply?

The question of whether the entities or businesses are under common control applies to the combining entities that existed before the combination, excluding the newly formed entity, i.e. Entity X and Entity Y. These are clearly entities that have been under the common control of Entity A, and remain so after the transfer.

If Newco prepares consolidated financial statements without there being an intended IPO, the scope exclusion would apply. However, as the purpose of the transaction was to facilitate the disposal of the businesses by way of an IPO, such that Entity A loses control over Entity X and Entity Y, does this mean that common control is 'transitory'?

In our view, the answer is 'no'. Common control is not considered to be transitory and therefore the reorganisation is excluded from the scope of IFRS 3. This is consistent with the ordinary meaning of 'transitory', i.e. something which is fleeting, brief or temporary. The common control of Entity X and Entity Y was not fleeting in the fact pattern as both entities had been controlled by Entity A for several years. In contrast, if Entity Y had only recently come into the group, this may well indicate that control is transitory.

Although Example 10.2 above involves a newly formed entity, the same considerations apply regardless of how the reorganisation may have been structured prior to the IPO. For example, Entity X may have acquired Entity Y or the net assets and trade of Entity Y, with Entity X then being subject to an IPO. In such a situation, Entity X would apply the scope exclusion for business combinations under common control.

3 ACCOUNTING FOR BUSINESS COMBINATIONS INVOLVING ENTITIES OR BUSINESSES UNDER COMMON CONTROL

IFRS 3 prescribes a single method of accounting for all business combinations that are within its scope, i.e. the acquisition method. No other methods are described and the standard does not address the appropriate accounting for business combinations under common control excluded from its scope. The 'pooling of interests' method and 'fresh start' method are only referred to in the Basis for Conclusions as possible methods of accounting, but were not deemed appropriate for all business combinations. *[IFRS 3.BC23]*.

The discussion at 3.1 to 3.3.5 below considers how entities should account for business combinations under common control outside the scope of IFRS 3 (described at 2 above). If the assets acquired and liabilities assumed do not constitute a business, the transaction is accounted for as an asset acquisition. The accounting for acquisitions of (net) assets under common control is discussed in Chapter 8 at 4.4.2.D. Transactions under common control involving a Newco, which may or may not be a business combination as defined in IFRS 3, are considered separately at 4 below.

Legal mergers between a parent and its subsidiary are discussed in Chapter 8 at 4.4.3.B.

3.1 Pooling of interests method or acquisition method

IFRS 3 scopes out business combinations under common control and is not prescriptive otherwise as to the method of accounting for such transactions. Entities should therefore develop an accounting policy that results in relevant and reliable information by applying the hierarchy in paragraphs 10-12 of IAS 8 – *Accounting Policies, Changes in Accounting Estimates and Errors* (discussed in Chapter 3 at 4.3).

Applying that hierarchy, entities may refer to IFRS 3 as a standard that deals with a similar and related issue, and apply the acquisition method by analogy. Entities may also consider the most recent pronouncements of other standard-setting bodies having a similar framework to IFRS, other accounting literature and accepted industry practices, to the extent that these do not conflict with any IFRS or the *Conceptual Framework for Financial Reporting (Conceptual Framework)*. Several standard-setting bodies have issued guidance and some allow or require a pooling of interests-type method (also referred to as 'predecessor accounting', 'merger accounting' or 'carry over accounting' in some jurisdictions) to account for business combinations under common control.

Accordingly, we believe that a receiving entity accounting for a business combination under common control should apply either:

(a) the acquisition method set out in IFRS 3 (see 3.2 below); or

(b) the pooling of interests method (see 3.3 below).

We do not consider that the 'fresh start' method, whereby all assets and liabilities of all combining businesses are restated to fair value, is an appropriate method of accounting for business combinations under common control.

However, in our view, this accounting policy choice is only available if the transaction has substance for the combining parties. This is because the acquisition method results in measuring the net identifiable assets of one or more of the businesses involved at their acquisition-date fair values (with some limited exceptions; see Chapter 9 at 5) and/or the recognition of goodwill (or gain on a bargain purchase). IFRS contains limited circumstances when net assets may be restated to fair value and prohibits the recognition of internally generated goodwill. A common control transaction should not be used to circumvent these limitations. Careful consideration is required of all facts and circumstances, before it is concluded that a transaction has substance. If there is no substance to the transaction, the pooling of interests method is the only method that may be applied to that transaction. If there is substance to the transaction, whichever accounting policy is adopted, should be applied consistently.

Evaluating whether the transaction has substance will involve consideration of multiple factors, including (but not necessarily limited to):

- the purpose of the transaction;
- the involvement of outside parties in the transaction, such as non-controlling interests or other third parties;
- whether or not the transaction is conducted at fair value;
- the existing activities of the entities involved in the transaction; and
- whether or not it is bringing entities together into a 'reporting entity' that did not exist before.

The concept of 'reporting entity' is clarified in the 2018 *Conceptual Framework*. A reporting entity is described as an entity that is required, or chooses, to prepare financial statements. This can be a single entity or a portion of an entity or comprise more than one entity. A reporting entity is not necessarily a legal entity. *[CF 3.10]*. Further discussion is included in Chapter 2 at 6.2.

Example 10.3: **Accounting for business combinations under common control – use of acquisition method? (1)**

Entity A currently has two businesses (as defined in IFRS 3) operated through wholly-owned subsidiaries Entity B and Entity C. The group structure (ignoring other entities within the group) is as follows:

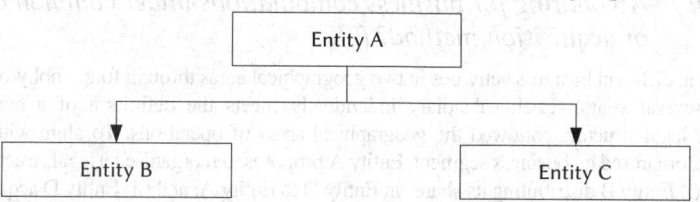

Entity A proposes to combine the two complementary businesses (currently housed in two separate entities, Entity B and Entity C) into one entity, in anticipation of spinning off the combined entity by way of an IPO. Both businesses have been owned by Entity A for several years. The reorganisation will be structured such that Entity C will acquire the shares of Entity B from Entity A for cash at their fair value of £1,000. The carrying amount of the net assets of Entity B is £200 (both in the individual financial statements of Entity B and in the consolidated financial statements of Entity A). The net of the acquisition-date fair values of the identifiable assets acquired and liabilities assumed of Entity B (measured in accordance with IFRS 3) is £600.

How should this transaction (to facilitate a subsequent spin-off) be accounted for in the consolidated financial statements of both Entity C and Entity A?

As far as Entity C is concerned, there is a business combination that needs to be accounted for. That business combination is however excluded from the scope of IFRS 3, as it is under common control and that control not transitory. In this fact pattern, there is substance to the transaction. There is a business purpose to the transaction; it has been conducted at fair value; both Entity B and Entity C have existing activities; and they have been brought together into a reporting entity that did not exist before (assuming no general purpose combined financial statements were prepared before; see Chapter 6 at 2.2.6). Accordingly, Entity C can apply either the acquisition method as set out in IFRS 3 or the pooling of interests method in its consolidated financial statements. The selected accounting policy should be applied consistently to similar transactions.

If Entity C selects the acquisition method, it will need to identify whether Entity C or Entity B is the acquirer (see 3.2 below). Assuming that Entity C is identified as the acquirer, in summary, this will mean that the net identifiable assets of Entity B will be initially reflected at their acquisition-date fair values (£600), together with goodwill of £400 (£1,000 less £600), in the consolidated statement of financial position. Only the post-acquisition results of Entity B will be reflected in the consolidated statement of comprehensive income.

As far as Entity A is concerned (i.e. from the perspective of the controlling party), there has been no change in the reporting entity – all that has happened is that Entity B, rather than being directly held and controlled by Entity A, is now indirectly held and controlled through Entity C (i.e. no change in control). Accordingly, there is no business combination and the effects resulting from the intragroup transaction are eliminated in full. Thus, the carrying amounts for Entity B's net assets included in the consolidated financial statements of Entity A do not change. There are also no non-controlling interests (NCI) affected. The transaction therefore has no impact on the consolidated financial statements of Entity A (except for any potential tax consequences).

In Example 10.3 above, Entity C had to account for its business combination with Entity B, as it was preparing consolidated financial statements. In some situations, Entity C would not need to account for the business combination at all, as it may be exempt as an intermediate parent company from preparing consolidated financial statements (see Chapter 6 at 2.2.1). If in Example 10.3 above, Entity C had acquired the business of Entity B, rather than the shares, then the same accounting policy choice would have to be made for the business combination in Entity C's financial statements, even if they are not consolidated financial statements.

However, in other types of reorganisations, careful consideration of the factors above may indicate that there is no substance to the transaction. This is illustrated in Example 10.4 below by transaction (ii).

Example 10.4: Accounting for business combinations under common control – use of acquisition method? (2)

Entity A engages in different business activities in two geographical areas through four wholly-owned subsidiaries (all owned for several years). Each subsidiary individually meets the definition of a business in IFRS 3. Traditionally, the legal structure followed the geographical areas of operations. To align with its management structure, which is organised by business segment, Entity A proposes to reorganise its legal structure. This two-step process involves (i) Entity B distributing its shares in Entity D to Entity A, and (ii) Entity D acquiring the shares in Entity E. The transaction price for (ii) reflects the carrying amount of Entity E's net assets as included in the consolidated financial statements of Entity A. The group structure before and after this reorganisation is as follows:

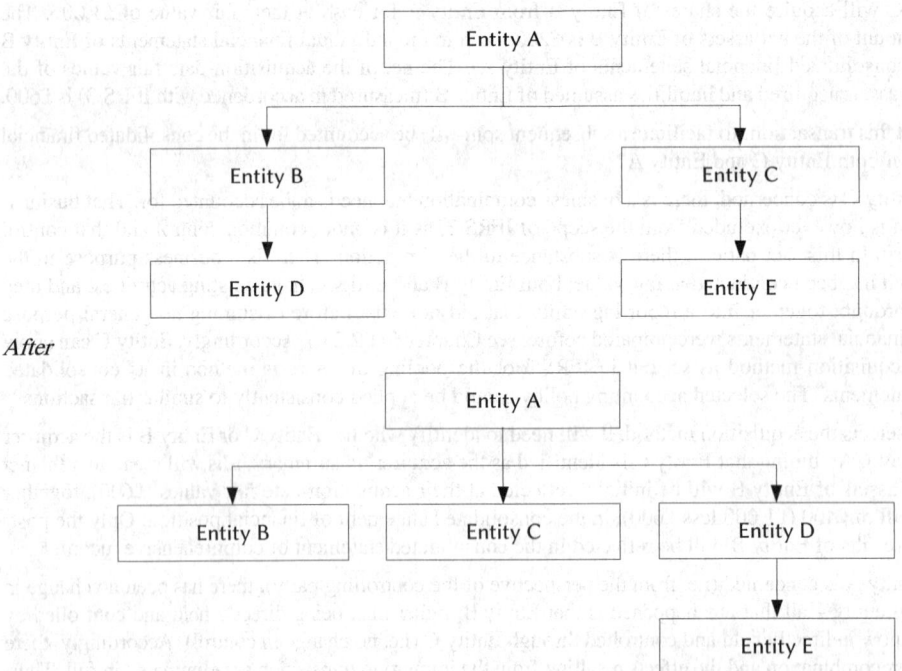

How should this transaction (to align the group's legal and management structure) be accounted for in the consolidated financial statements of both Entity A and Entity D?

As far as Entity A is concerned, neither its own acquisition of the shares in Entity D (by way of distribution from Entity B) nor the transfer of shares in Entity E from Entity C to Entity D represents a business combination. As described in Example 10.3 above, from the perspective of the controlling party, there is no change of control. Because there is also no NCI affected, the reorganisation has no impact on the consolidated financial statements of Entity A (except for any potential tax consequences).

In contrast, in the consolidated financial statements of Entity D, there is a business combination that needs to be accounted for. That business combination is however excluded from the scope of IFRS 3, as it is under common control and that control not transitory. In this fact pattern, the transaction is bringing entities together into a reporting entity that did not exist before (assuming no general purpose combined financial statements were prepared before; see Chapter 6 at 2.2.6) and both Entity D and Entity E have existing activities. Nevertheless, there is no substance to the transaction. There is no clear business purpose to the transaction; the restructuring is purely internal, with no external parties being involved; and the transaction is not conducted at fair value. Consequently, Entity D cannot apply the acquisition method in its consolidated financial statements. This reorganisation will be accounted for using the pooling of interests method.

In Example 10.4 above, Entity D had to account for its business combination with Entity E, as it was preparing consolidated financial statements. In some situations, Entity D would not need to account for the business combination at all, as it may be exempt as an intermediate parent company from preparing consolidated financial statements (see Chapter 6 at 2.2.1). If in Example 10.4 above, Entity D had acquired the business of Entity E, rather than the shares, then the business combination would similarly have to be accounted for using the pooling of interests method in Entity D's financial statements, even if they are not consolidated financial statements.

3.2 Application of the acquisition method under IFRS 3

The application of the acquisition method is set out in IFRS 3 and discussed generally in Chapter 9. This method involves the following steps:

(a) identifying the acquirer (see Chapter 9 at 4.1);
(b) determining the acquisition date (see Chapter 9 at 4.2);
(c) recognising and measuring the identifiable assets acquired, the liabilities assumed, and any non-controlling interest in the acquiree (see Chapter 9 at 5); and
(d) recognising and measuring goodwill or a gain on a bargain purchase (see Chapter 9 at 6). *[IFRS 3.5]*.

As far as (a) above is concerned, it may be that in some cases the identification of the acquirer means that the business combination needs to be accounted for as a reverse acquisition (see Chapter 9 at 14). Careful consideration is required where the business combination under common control involves a Newco, as it may be a high hurdle for a Newco to be identified as the acquirer under IFRS 3 (see 4 below).

As far as (d) above is concerned, goodwill at the acquisition date is computed as the excess of (a) over (b) below:

(a) The aggregate of:
   (i) the consideration transferred (generally measured at acquisition-date fair value);
   (ii) the amount of any non-controlling interest in the acquiree; and
   (iii) the acquisition-date fair value of the acquirer's previously held equity interest in the acquiree.
(b) The net of the acquisition-date fair values (or other amounts measured in accordance with IFRS 3) of the identifiable assets acquired and the liabilities assumed. *[IFRS 3.32]*.

Where (b) exceeds (a) above, IFRS 3 regards this as giving rise to a gain on a bargain purchase. *[IFRS 3.34]*.

The requirements of IFRS 3 in relation to the acquisition method have clearly been developed for dealing with business combinations between parties transacting on an arm's length basis. The consideration transferred in a business combination at arm's length will generally be measured at the acquisition-date fair values of the assets transferred, liabilities incurred and/or equity interests issued by the acquirer (see Chapter 9 at 7). The fair value of that consideration normally reflects the value of the acquired business. For business combinations under common control, however, this may not be the case. The transaction may not be at arm's length and the fair value of the consideration transferred may not reflect the value of the acquired business.

Where a higher value is given up than received, economically, the difference represents a distribution from the receiving entity's equity. Conversely, where a higher value is received than given up, the difference represents a contribution to the receiving entity's equity. Nevertheless, IFRS neither requires nor prohibits the acquirer to recognise a non-arm's length element in a business combination under common control. If such transaction is not at arm's length, this may suggest that there is no substance to the transaction and application of the acquisition method might not be appropriate (see 3.1 above). If, however, the acquisition method is appropriate, in our view, the receiving entity may either:

(a) recognise the transaction at the consideration transferred as agreed between the parties (measured at the acquisition-date fair value in accordance with IFRS 3); or

(b) recognise the transaction at the fair value of the acquired business (with the difference between the fair value of the consideration transferred and the fair value of the acquired business as a contribution to or distribution from equity).

Whichever accounting policy is adopted, it should be applied consistently.

This is considered in Example 10.5 below. As the example does not include any non-controlling interest in the acquiree, nor any previously held interest in the acquiree by the acquirer, the computation of goodwill or a gain on a bargain purchase only involves the comparison between (a)(i) and (b) above.

Example 10.5: Acquisition method – cash consideration less than the fair value of acquired business

Assume the same facts as in Example 10.3 above, except that Entity C, rather than acquiring Entity B from Entity A for cash at its fair value of £1,000, only pays cash of £700. Assuming there is still substance to the transaction, how should this be reflected by Entity C when applying the acquisition method for its acquisition of Entity B?

In our view, there are two acceptable ways of accounting:

(a) The transaction is recognised at the consideration transferred as agreed between Entity A and Entity C, being the acquisition-date fair value of the cash given as consideration, i.e. £700. Accordingly, goodwill of only £100 (£700 less £600) is recognised.

(b) The transaction is recognised at the fair value of the acquired business (£1,000), with a deemed capital contribution from Entity A for the excess over the acquisition-date fair value of the cash given as consideration, i.e. £300 (£1,000 less £700), reflected in Entity C's equity. Accordingly, goodwill of £400 (£1,000 less £600) is recognised.

Whichever method is adopted, it should be applied on a consistent basis.

If Entity C only paid cash of £500, assuming there is still substance to the transaction, then the impact under (a) and (b) above would be as follows:

(a) Since the consideration transferred is only £500, no goodwill is recognised. However, a gain on a bargain purchase of £100 (being the excess of the acquisition-date fair value of the net identifiable assets of Entity B of £600 over the consideration transferred of £500) is recognised immediately in profit or loss.

(b) As before, goodwill of £400 is recognised, but a capital contribution of £500 (£1,000 less £500) would be reflected in equity.

In Example 10.3 and Example 10.5 above, the consideration transferred by Entity C was in cash. However, what if Entity C issued shares to Entity A to effect this business combination under common control?

If an acquirer issues equity interests to effect a business combination, IFRS 3 requires the consideration transferred to be measured at the acquisition-date fair value of these equity interests issued. *[IFRS 3.37]*. As discussed in Chapter 9 at 7, in a business combination in which the acquirer and the acquiree (or its former owners) exchange only equity interests, the acquisition-date fair value of the acquiree's equity interests may be more reliably measurable than that of the acquirer's equity interests. In that case, IFRS 3 requires goodwill to be calculated using the fair value of the acquiree's equity interests rather than the fair value of the equity interests transferred. *[IFRS 3.33]*.

IFRS 3 does not include detailed guidance on measuring the fair value of equity interests issued as consideration. In such circumstances, IFRS 13 – *Fair Value Measurement* – is relevant as it applies when another IFRS requires or permits fair value measurements. *[IFRS 13.5]*. Fair value is defined as 'the price that would be received to sell an asset or paid to transfer a liability in an orderly transaction between market participants at the measurement date'. *[IFRS 13.9]*. IFRS 13 requires that entities maximise the use of relevant observable inputs and minimise the use of unobservable inputs to meet the objective of a fair value measurement. *[IFRS 13.36]*. If either the acquirer's or acquiree's shares are quoted, this would indicate which fair value is more reliably measurable. However, in arrangements between entities under common control, a quoted price for either the acquirer's or the acquiree's shares might not always be available. IFRS 13 is discussed in detail in Chapter 14.

In Example 10.5 above, if Entity C issued shares to Entity A to acquire Entity B, and there is no quoted price for either Entity B's or Entity C's shares, then the fair value of the consideration transferred would need to be based on whichever shares are considered to be more reliably measurable. If this were Entity C's shares and their fair value was only £700, then Entity C would similarly have an accounting policy choice between (a) and (b) above. This choice exists regardless of whether Entity C transfers cash or equity interests as consideration. However, if Entity B's shares are considered to be more reliably measurable, both approaches would result in a similar outcome. This is because the consideration transferred by Entity C would then be based on the fair value of Entity B, i.e. £1,000. Thus, goodwill of £400 would be recognised, with the £1,000 consideration transferred reflected in equity.

3.3 Application of the pooling of interests method

We believe that if an entity does not adopt an accounting policy of using the acquisition method under IFRS 3, or if the transaction has no substance, the pooling of interests method should be applied when accounting for business combinations under common control (see 3.1 above).

3.3.1 General requirements

IFRS 3 makes no reference to the pooling of interests method, except in the context of rejecting it as a method of accounting for business combinations generally. Various local standard-setters have issued guidance and some allow or require a pooling of interests-type method (sometimes known as 'predecessor accounting', 'merger accounting' or 'carry over accounting') to account for business combinations under common control. The pooling of interests method is generally considered to involve the following:[4]

- The assets and liabilities of the combining parties are reflected at their carrying amounts.

  No adjustments are made to reflect fair values, or recognise any new assets or liabilities, at the date of the combination that would otherwise be done under the acquisition method. The only adjustments made are to align accounting policies.

- No 'new' goodwill is recognised as a result of the combination.

  The only goodwill that is recognised is any existing goodwill relating to either of the combining parties. Any difference between the consideration transferred and the acquired net assets is reflected within equity.

- The income statement reflects the results of the combining parties.

Different practices exist as to where in equity any difference between the consideration transferred and acquired net assets is presented (e.g. in retained earnings or a separate merger reserve). IFRS generally does not prescribe presentation within equity. Also, this is often influenced by legal or regulatory requirements in an entity's jurisdiction.

Apart from the second bullet point above, the application of the pooling of interests method, in the context of accounting for business combinations under common control under IFRS, does raise particular issues as discussed at 3.3.2 to 3.3.5 below.

3.3.2 Carrying amounts of assets and liabilities

In general, no adjustments would be expected to be required to conform accounting policies of the entities involved in a business combination under common control. This is because in preparing the consolidated financial statements of the ultimate parent under IFRS, uniform accounting policies should have been adopted by all members of the group. *[IFRS 10.B87]*. However, it may be necessary to make adjustments where the combining entities or businesses used different accounting policies when preparing their own financial statements or were not part of the same group before.

The main issue relating to the use of predecessor carrying amounts, when the receiving entity applies the pooling of interests method for business combinations under common control, is whether the carrying amounts of the assets acquired and liabilities assumed should be based on:

(a) the carrying amounts recognised by the controlling party (e.g. those reported in the consolidated financial statements of the parent); or
(b) the carrying amounts recognised by the transferred business (e.g. those reported in the financial statements of the acquiree).

A difference between (a) and (b) above might result from fair value adjustments and/or goodwill that have/has arisen on the past acquisition of the transferred business by that controlling party.

The carrying amounts of the receiving entity's assets and liabilities remain the same as those in its existing financial statements prior to the business combination under common control.

In our view, the receiving entity applying the pooling of interests method should generally use the carrying amounts in (a) above for the transferred business. This is because the carrying amounts recognised by the controlling party may be more recent (and therefore relevant) and reflect the perspective of that party that effectively directs the transaction. Nevertheless, in certain circumstances, it may be acceptable to use the amounts in (b) above, but this may not always be appropriate. When evaluating if the carrying amounts in (b) above can be used, the following factors should be considered:

- The timing of the business combination under common control in comparison to when the transferred business was previously acquired by the controlling party, if applicable. Generally, the carrying amounts in (a) are deemed more relevant as they were reassessed more recently. However, the longer the period since the previous acquisition by the controlling party, the less relevant this factor may be.
- Whether the transaction is a 'grooming transaction' in preparation for a spin-off, sale or similar external transaction. Generally, the carrying amounts in (a) above will be more relevant in such a situation (for the reasons explained above).
- The identity and nature of the users of the financial statements. If a broad group of users of the financial statements of the receiving entity after the transaction are parties that previously relied upon the financial statements of, or including, the transferred business before the transaction (e.g. if there are significant non-controlling interests and/or creditors), using the amounts in (b) might provide more relevant information.
- Whether consistent accounting policies are used within the group for similar and related common control transactions (e.g. whether the accounting policy for this transaction is consistent with the accounting policy applied to legal mergers between a parent and a subsidiary – see Chapter 8 at 4.4.3.B).

The rationale for using the carrying amounts as recognised by the controlling party is explained further in Example 10.6 below.

Example 10.6: Pooling of interests method – carrying amounts of assets acquired and liabilities assumed

Entity A currently has two businesses (as defined in IFRS 3) operated through wholly-owned subsidiaries Entity B and Entity C. The group structure (ignoring other entities within the group) is as follows:

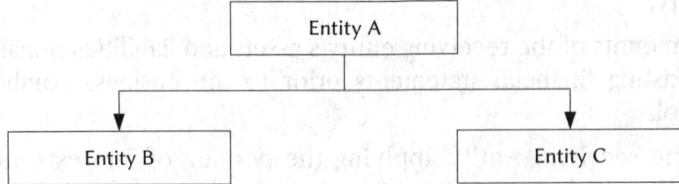

Both entities have been owned by Entity A for a number of years.

On 1 October 2021, Entity A restructures the group by transferring its investment in Entity C to Entity B, such that Entity C becomes a subsidiary of Entity B. The accounting policy adopted for business combinations under common control excluded from IFRS 3 is to apply the pooling of interests method.

In Entity B's consolidated financial statements for the year ended 31 December 2021, which carrying amounts should be reflected in respect of the assets and liabilities of Entity C?

Entity B generally should use the carrying amounts reported in Entity A's consolidated financial statements, rather than the carrying amounts reported in Entity C's own financial statements.

Accordingly, they will be based on their fair value as at the date Entity C became part of the Entity A group and adjusted for subsequently in accordance with the applicable IFRSs. Any goodwill relating to Entity C that was recognised in Entity A's consolidated financial statements, will also be recognised in Entity B's consolidated financial statements. Any difference between the equity of Entity C and those carrying amounts are adjusted against equity. The carrying amounts of the net assets of Entity B will remain as before.

The rationale for applying this approach is that the transaction is essentially a transfer of the assets and liabilities of Entity C from the consolidated financial statements of Entity A to the financial statements of Entity B. From a group perspective of Entity B's shareholder, nothing has changed except the location of those assets and liabilities. Entity B has effectively taken on the group's ownership. Therefore, the carrying amounts used in the consolidated financial statements are the appropriate and most relevant values to apply to the assets and liabilities of Entity C, as they represent the carrying amounts to the Entity A group.

In our view, when applying the pooling of interests method to business combinations under common control, the receiving entity should apply the approach outlined above regardless of the legal form of the transaction. Therefore if, in Example 10.6 above, Entity B had acquired the business of Entity C, rather than the shares, or the entities had been merged into one legal entity whereby Entity B was the continuing entity, then the same treatment would apply in Entity B's financial statements, even if they are not consolidated financial statements.

3.3.3 Restatement of financial information for periods prior to the date of the combination

Another issue is whether the receiving entity should restate financial information for periods prior to the date of the business combination when applying the pooling of interests method. That is, from which date should the transaction be accounted for and how should comparative information for the prior period(s) be presented?

The pooling of interests method is generally considered to involve the combining parties being presented as if they had always been combined. To this effect, the receiving entity accounts for the transaction from the beginning of the period in which the combination occurs (irrespective of its actual date) and restates comparatives to include all combining parties. However, in applying the IAS 8 hierarchy (see 3.1 above), an entity would need to consider whether the pooling of interests method is consistent with IFRS 10 specifically. That standard indicates that an entity only includes the income and expenses of a subsidiary in the consolidated financial statements from the date the entity gains control. *[IFRS 10.B88]*.

The Interpretations Committee discussed the presentation of comparatives when applying the pooling of interests method to business combinations under common control, prior to the issuance of IFRS 10, under the regime of IAS 27 – *Consolidated and Separate Financial Statements* (now superseded). However, as resolving the issue would require interpreting the interaction of multiple IFRSs and the IASB had added a project on business combinations under common control to its research agenda, the Interpretations Committee decided not to add the issue to its agenda.[5] There was no substantial change in IFRS 10 from superseded IAS 27 regarding the measurement of income and expenses of a subsidiary in the consolidated financial statements.[6]

One view is that the concept of pooling does not conflict with the requirements of IFRS 10, on the basis that the combined entity is considered a continuation from the perspective of the controlling party. In business combinations under common control, ultimately, there has been no change in control, because the controlling party already had control over the combined resources – it has merely changed the location of its resources. Accordingly, the receiving entity restates the periods prior to the combination to reflect that there has been no change in ultimate control. Paragraph B88 of IFRS 10 restricts when the pooling of interests method is applied (i.e. not until the combining parties have actually come under direct control), not how it is applied.

Another view is that the requirements of IFRS 10 are inconsistent with the concept of pooling, on the basis that the combined entity did not exist before, from the perspective of the combining parties. Therefore, the consolidated financial statements of the receiving entity cannot include financial information of a subsidiary prior to the date it obtains control, in accordance with paragraph B88 of IFRS 10. The fact that the business combination is outside of the scope of IFRS 3 is irrelevant when considering the requirements of IFRS 10. Accordingly, the pooling of interests method does not involve restatement of periods prior to the combination and affects only the values assigned to the assets and liabilities of the transferred business when the receiving entity obtains control (see 3.3.2 above).

Therefore, we believe that, in applying the pooling of interests method, the receiving entity has a choice of two views for its accounting policy:

- View 1 – Restatement of periods prior to the business combination under common control (retrospective approach)

  The financial information in the consolidated financial statements is restated for periods prior to the business combination under common control, to reflect the combination as if it had occurred from the beginning of the earliest period presented, regardless of the actual date of the combination.

  However, financial information for periods prior to the business combination is restated only for the period that the parties were under common control of the same controlling party (or parties).

- View 2 – No restatement of periods prior to the business combination under common control (prospective approach)

  The financial information in the consolidated financial statements is not restated for periods prior to the business combination under common control. The receiving entity accounts for the combination prospectively from the date on which it occurred.

An entity must consistently apply its chosen accounting policy.

These views are illustrated in Examples 10.7 and 10.8 below.

Example 10.7: Pooling of interests method – restatement of financial information for periods prior to the date of the combination (1)

Assume the same facts as in Example 10.6 above.

Entity B obtains control over Entity C on 1 October 2021. In preparing its consolidated financial statements for the year ended 31 December 2021 (including comparatives for one year), from which date should Entity B include financial information for Entity C when applying the pooling of interests method?

Entity B has a choice of two views for its accounting policy, which must be applied consistently:

View 1 – Restatement of periods prior to the business combination under common control

Entity B and C have been owned by Entity A for a number of years (i.e. common control already existed at the start of the first comparative period presented). Entity B therefore restates the financial information in its consolidated financial statements for 2021 (both the current year pre-combination results and the 2020 comparatives) to include financial information for Entity C as from 1 January 2020.

View 2 – No restatement of periods prior to the business combination under common control

Entity B does not restate the financial information in its consolidated financial statements for 2021 (neither the current year pre-combination results nor the 2020 comparatives). No financial information is included for Entity C prior to 1 October 2021.

In Example 10.7 above, Entity C had been part of the Entity A group for a number of years. What if this had not been the case? Entity B still has a choice of two views, to restate or not to restate. Should it choose restatement, then financial information in the consolidated financial statements for periods prior to the combination is restated only for the period that the entities were under common control of the same controlling party (or parties). If the controlling party has not always controlled these combined resources, then application of the pooling of interests method reflects that fact. That is, an entity cannot restate the comparative financial information for a period that common control by the same controlling party (or parties) did not exist.

Example 10.8: *Pooling of interests method – restatement of financial information for periods prior to the date of the combination (2)*

Assume the same facts as in Example 10.6 above, except that in this situation Entity A had acquired Entity C on 1 July 2020. That is, (non-transitory) common control exists at the time of Entity B's acquisition of Entity C, but Entity B and Entity C were not under common control during the entire comparative period.

In preparing its consolidated financial statements for the year ended 31 December 2021 (including comparatives for one year), from which date should Entity B include financial information for Entity C when applying the pooling of interests method?

View 1 – Restatement of periods prior to the business combination under common control

If Entity B applies View 1 as its accounting policy, it restates the financial information in its consolidated financial statements for 2021 (both the current year pre-combination results and the 2020 comparatives). However, Entity B includes financial information for Entity C only as from 1 July 2020 (i.e. when both entities were first under common control of Entity A).

View 2 – No restatement of periods prior to the business combination under common control

If Entity B applies View 2 as its accounting policy, the change in fact pattern has no impact as Entity B does not restate the financial information in its consolidated financial statements for 2021 (neither the current year pre-combination results nor the 2020 comparatives). No financial information is included for Entity C prior to 1 October 2021.

3.3.4 Equity reserves and history of assets and liabilities carried over

The concept of pooling generally is based on the premise of a continuation of the combining parties. Consistently, the pre-combination equity composition and history associated with the assets and liabilities would be carried forward upon the combination occurring and may affect the post-combination accounting. For instance, certain equity reserves may be transferred within equity or reclassified to profit or loss when specific conditions are met. Examples include fair value reserves of financial assets at FVOCI, hedging reserves, foreign currency translation reserves and other asset revaluation reserves. Similarly, previous impairment losses recognised for assets may possibly reverse post-combination.

If the receiving entity in a business combination under common control adopts View 1 at 3.3.3 above, pooling is applied in full and the history of the combining parties (since they were under common control of the same controlling party or parties) is continued as described above.

If the receiving entity adopts View 2 at 3.3.3 above, it would need to decide whether or not to retain the pre-combination equity reserves and history of assets and liabilities of the transferred business. We believe that the receiving entity has a further accounting policy choice here, between:

- View 2a – No restatement of periods prior to the business combination under common control, but retention of equity reserves and history

    This view considers the absence of restatement as only a presentation issue, but to all intents and purposes the concept of pooling is applied in full.

    While the financial information for periods prior to the business combination is not restated, the transferred business continues within the combined entity as if pooling had been applied since the combining parties were under common control of the same controlling party (or parties). The pre-combination equity reserves and history of assets and liabilities of the transferred business are carried over as at the date of transaction and are reflected in the post-combination financial statements of the receiving entity.

- View 2b – No restatement of periods prior to the business combination under common control, with reset of equity balances and history

    This view considers the absence of restatement as more than only a presentation issue. Rather, the business combination is viewed as an initial recognition event at that date, using the measurement principle of pooling.

    While the financial information for periods prior to the business combination is not restated, the transaction gives rise to an initial recognition of the assets and liabilities of the transferred business at their predecessor carrying amounts. This means that they essentially have a new deemed cost and their history is not retained. Equally, the equity reserves of the transferred business are not carried over but adjusted to another component of equity (e.g. retained earnings). The post-combination financial statements of the receiving entity do not reflect any pre-combination history of the transferred business.

    Since any cash flow hedge reserves are not retained, this view may have consequences for hedge effectiveness going forward.

An entity must consistently apply the chosen accounting policy.

Overall, View 2a and View 2b above result in the same net asset position at the date of the combination. This is because under both views the assets and liabilities of the transferred business are carried over at their predecessor carrying amounts. However, they will have a different effect on the composition of equity at the date of the combination and the treatment of certain transactions post-combination.

This is illustrated in Example 10.9 below.

Example 10.9: Pooling of interests method – no restatement of financial information for periods prior to the date of the combination – impact of carrying over equity reserves and history

Assume the same facts as in Example 10.7 above, with Entity B adopting View 2 – No restatement of periods prior to the business combination under common control.

Entity B then has an accounting policy choice as to whether or not retain the pre-combination equity reserves and history of assets and liabilities of Entity C. How does this choice affect the accounting for the post-combination disposal of a foreign operation described below, in Entity B's consolidated financial statements for the year ending 31 December 2021?

On 1 October 2021, the date of the combination occurring, Entity C had a foreign currency translation reserve of €100 (credit) relating to a foreign operation – for example, an equity-accounted associate. On 31 October 2021, Entity C sold the associate carried at €500 for €700. Assume that the foreign exchange rate had remained unchanged during October 2021.

View 2a – No restatement of periods prior to the business combination under common control, but retention of equity reserves and history

Entity B recognises the foreign currency translation reserve of €100 at the date of the combination. When the associate (i.e. the underlying foreign operation) is subsequently sold, that €100 is reclassified from equity to profit or loss for the year. Therefore, a net gain on disposal of €300 is recognised in the statement of profit or loss (€700 less €500 plus €100), with a €100 debit entry to OCI.

View 2b – No restatement of periods prior to the business combination under common control, with reset of equity reserves and history

Entity B does not recognise the foreign currency translation reserve at the date of the combination. When the associate is subsequently sold, a net gain on disposal of €200 is recognised (€700 less €500) and no additional amount is reclassified from equity to the profit or loss for the year.

3.3.5 Acquisition of non-controlling interest as part of a business combination under common control

As discussed at 2.1 above, the extent of non-controlling interests in each of the combining entities before and after the business combination is not relevant to determining whether the combination involves entities under common control for the purposes of the scope exclusion in IFRS 3. *[IFRS 3.B4]*. Accordingly, the accounting for business combinations under common control is not restricted to combinations involving wholly-owned entities.

It may be that in a business combination under common control involving a partially-owned subsidiary, any non-controlling interest in that subsidiary is acquired at the same time as the common control transaction.

Where the receiving entity applies the pooling of interests method, the question arises as to what date the acquisition of the non-controlling interest should be reflected in its consolidated financial statements. This is particularly pertinent where the receiving entity restates financial information for periods prior to the date of the combination under View 1 as set out at 3.3.3 above.

In our view, there are two separate transactions to be accounted for:

(a) the reorganisation of entities under common control; and

(b) the acquisition of the non-controlling interest.

The basic principle of accounting for business combinations under common control using the pooling of interests method is that the structure of ownership is discretionary and any reorganisation thereof is without economic substance from the perspective of the controlling party. The receiving entity may reflect that perspective and present the combining parties as if they had always been combined, regardless of the actual date of the combination (see 3.3.3 above). However, it is inconsistent with the principles of pooling to reflect ownership of a portion or all of a business prior to the date the controlling party (either directly or indirectly) obtained that ownership interest.

The acquisition of the non-controlling interest is a transaction with economic substance from the perspective of the controlling party. IFRS 10 states that the change in ownership interest resulting from such a transaction is accounted for as an equity transaction at that date. *[IFRS 10.23, B96]*. Also, IFRS does not include a principle that transactions with a third party (such as the acquisition of non-controlling interest) may be accounted for as of a date earlier than when the transaction is actually consummated.

Accordingly, the receiving entity accounts for the acquisition of non-controlling interest at the actual date of acquisition. It is not appropriate to reflect the acquisition of non-controlling interest as if it occurred as of any prior date (as may be done for the controlling interest transferred), even if the acquisition occurs simultaneously with a common control transaction. This is consistent with requirements in IFRS to present separately income attributable to the owners of the parent (see Chapter 3 at 3.2) and to calculate earnings per share based on profit or loss attributable to ordinary shareholders of the parent (see Chapter 37 at 3 and at 6.2).

The discussion above is illustrated in Example 10.10 below.

Example 10.10: Pooling of interests method – acquisition of non-controlling interest as part of a business combination under common control

Parent A controls Entity B and Entity C. Both subsidiaries are businesses as defined in IFRS 3. From the group's perspective, there is a 40% non-controlling interest in Entity C that is held by an unrelated party, Entity Z. Entity B obtains control of Entity C by issuing additional shares on the same date to:

- acquire Parent A's 60% interest in Entity C; and
- acquire Entity Z's 40% interest in Entity C.

The group structure before and after these transactions is as follows:

Before

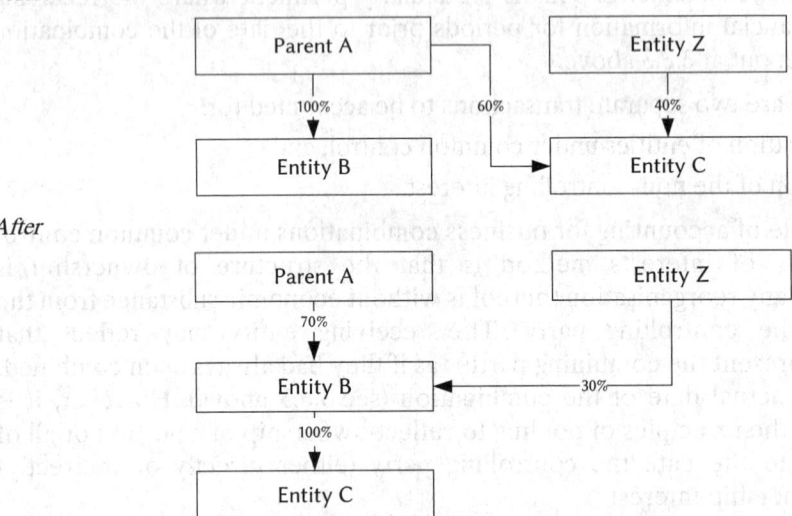

After

How should Entity B account for the acquisition of Entity Z's 40% interest in Entity C when applying the pooling of interests method in its consolidated financial statements?

Entity B should account for the acquisition of Entity Z's 40% interest in Entity C at the actual date of the transaction, regardless of whether financial information for periods prior to the business combination under common control is restated (see 3.3.3 above). Thus, if Entity B restates its consolidated financial statements to reflect comparative information for Entity C for the period before the combination, it will include the 40% non-controlling interest in Entity C within equity until the actual date of the transaction. The change in ownership interest resulting from the acquisition of Entity Z's 40% interest will be accounted for as an equity transaction at that date.

4 ACCOUNTING FOR TRANSACTIONS UNDER COMMON CONTROL (OR OWNERSHIP) INVOLVING A NEWCO

4.1 Introduction

The receiving entity in a common control transaction involving the transfer of control over one or more businesses is not always an existing entity, but could also be a newly formed entity (or Newco). This raises particular questions since IFRS 3 indicates that a new entity formed to effect a business combination is not necessarily the acquirer. If a new entity issues equity interests to effect a business combination, one of the combining entities that existed before the transaction shall be identified as the acquirer by applying the guidance in paragraphs B13-B17. In contrast, a new entity that transfers cash or other assets or incurs liabilities as consideration may be the acquirer. *[IFRS 3.B18]*.

Whether a Newco can be identified as the acquirer may be relevant to determine if a transaction is a business combination and thus within the scope of IFRS 3 (unless otherwise excluded). The standard defines a business combination as 'a transaction or other event in which an acquirer obtains control of one or more businesses'. *[IFRS 3 Appendix A]*. This requires one of the combining entities to be identified as the acquirer. IFRS 3 also states that 'the accounting acquiree must meet the definition of a business for the transaction to be accounted for as a reverse acquisition'. *[IFRS 3.B19]*. Since a Newco does not have its own operations, it would not be a business as defined. Accordingly, if a Newco combines with only one business, neither party might be capable of being identified as the acquirer under IFRS 3 and the transaction would not be a business combination.

Whether a Newco can be identified as the acquirer is also relevant in case the acquisition method is applied. When, for example, a Newco combines with two businesses and is identified as the acquirer, acquisition-date fair values would be attributed to the assets acquired and liabilities assumed of both existing businesses, and any goodwill or gain on a bargain purchase relating to those businesses would be recognised. In contrast, if Newco itself is not the acquirer under IFRS 3, one of the existing businesses must be identified as the acquirer and the acquisition method of accounting would be applied only to the other business.

IFRS 3 does not specify in which circumstances a Newco that effects a business combination other than through the issue of shares may be the acquirer, but it is clear that 'control' is the fundamental concept when identifying an acquirer. This is discussed further in Chapter 9 at 4.1.1. The analysis requires careful consideration of all facts and circumstances, and ultimately depends on whether a Newco can be considered as an extension of the party (or parties) that ultimately gains control over the combining entities. In common control transactions, however, there is typically no change of ultimate control over the transferred business or businesses. In that situation, a Newco would not be identified as an acquirer under IFRS 3.

That conclusion might be different when a reorganisation involving a Newco is used to facilitate an external sale or IPO. That is, if the transfer under common control is an integral part of another transaction that ultimately results in a change of control over the transferred business or businesses, the facts and circumstances may be such that a Newco could be regarded as the acquirer under IFRS 3. This situation is illustrated in Example 9.10 in Chapter 9 at 4.1.1, where the transfer of two businesses from a parent to a newly incorporated entity for cash (i.e. under common control) is contingent on the completion of an IPO of that Newco. In this scenario, the parent loses ultimate control over the two businesses and Newco could in effect be considered as an extension of its new shareholders after the IPO. However, if the change of control is only planned, but not an integral part of the transaction, Newco would be viewed as an extension of the parent (or possibly the transferred businesses) and would not be the acquirer.

While the Interpretations Committee discussed a few similar fact patterns in 2011, it ultimately observed that the accounting for arrangements involving the creation of a newly formed entity and for common control transactions is too broad to be addressed through an interpretation or an annual improvement. The Interpretations Committee concluded that these matters would be better considered in the context of a broader project on accounting for common control transactions.[7] In December 2017, the IASB tentatively decided that transactions followed by or conditional on a future sale or IPO are included within the scope of its research project on business combinations under common control (see 6.1 below).

The discussion at 4.2, 4.3 and 4.4 below addresses different scenarios involving a Newco. While this chapter mainly deals with transactions under common control, Examples 10.11, 10.12 and 10.14 below also discuss the accounting treatment where the same group of shareholders owns the combining entities before and after the transaction, but without a single shareholder, or sub-group of the shareholders by virtue of a contractual arrangement (see 2.1.1 above), having control. All of the examples at 4.2, 4.3 and 4.4 below assume that all entities are owned 100% by the party or parties at the top of the particular structure.

4.2 Setting up a new top holding company

In Examples 10.11 and 10.12 below, a new holding company has been inserted between shareholders and either an existing group or a series of entities with common ownership (but not necessarily common control). At 4.2.1 below, Newco issues shares to effect the transaction and is not identified as the acquirer in either case. However, the accounting consequences may differ depending on whether or not the transaction represents a business combination according to IFRS 3. Transactions such as this may also be effected for consideration other than shares or a combination of shares and other consideration. Arrangements in which Newco transfers cash or other assets or incurs liabilities are discussed at 4.2.2 below.

4.2.1 Setting up a new top holding company: transactions effected through issuing equity interests

Example 10.11: *Newco inserted at the top of an existing group*

A Newco is incorporated and inserted at the top of an existing group, which is a business as defined in IFRS 3. Newco issues shares to the existing shareholders of Entity A in exchange for the shares already held in that entity. There are no changes to the shareholder group. The group structure before and after this transaction is as follows:

Before

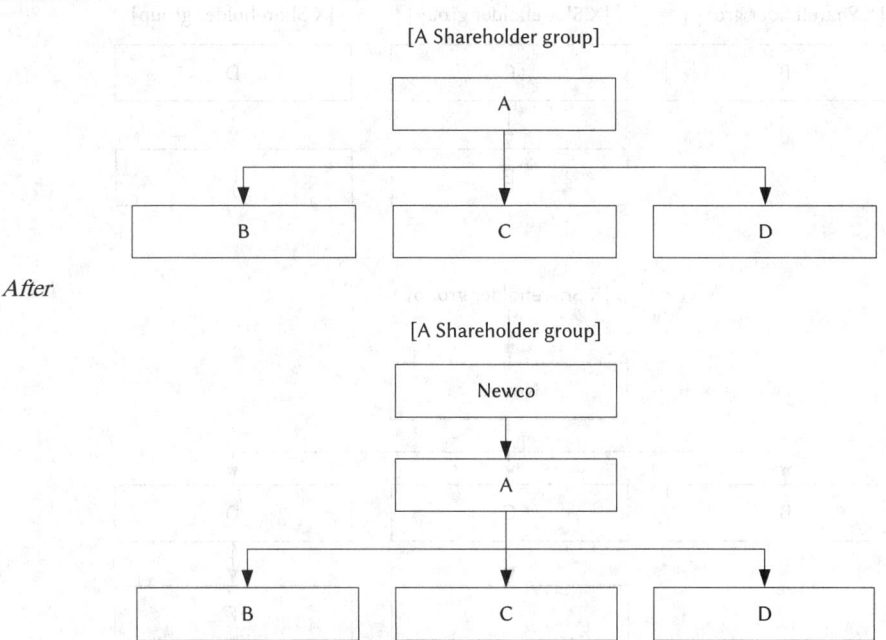

After

How should this reorganisation be accounted for in Newco's consolidated financial statements?

In many situations, this type of transaction will not be 'under common control' since there will be no contractual arrangement between the shareholders (see 2.1.1 above). However, whether there is common ownership or common control by one individual, or a sub-group of the shareholders, over the combining parties is irrelevant in this specific scenario.

The transaction does not meet the definition of a business combination under IFRS 3, because neither Newco nor Entity A can be identified as the acquirer. Newco cannot be identified as the acquirer as it issues shares to effect the combination. Entity A cannot be identified as the acquirer (in a reverse acquisition) as Newco is not a business as defined. On that basis, the transaction is outside the scope of IFRS 3.

Applying the IAS 8 hierarchy, Newco cannot elect to apply the acquisition method as set out in IFRS 3 since the transaction does not result in any change of economic substance (e.g. in terms of any real alteration to the composition or ownership of the group). Accordingly, the consolidated financial statements of Newco reflect that the arrangement is in substance a continuation of the existing group. Any difference in share capital is reflected as an adjustment to equity.

In Example 10.11 above, the transaction does not represent a business combination as none of the combining parties can be identified as the acquirer according to IFRS 3. This is because Newco issues equity interests to obtain control of only one business. In Example 10.12 below, whilst Newco still issues shares to effect the transaction, the combination involves more than one business.

792 Chapter 10

Example 10.12: Newco inserted at the top of entities owned by the same shareholders thereby creating a new reporting group

A Newco is incorporated and inserted at the top of a number of entities owned by the same shareholders. Newco issues shares to the existing shareholders of Entities B, C and D in exchange for the shares already held in those entities. Entities B, C and D are businesses as defined in IFRS 3. The group structure before and after this transaction is as follows:

Before

After

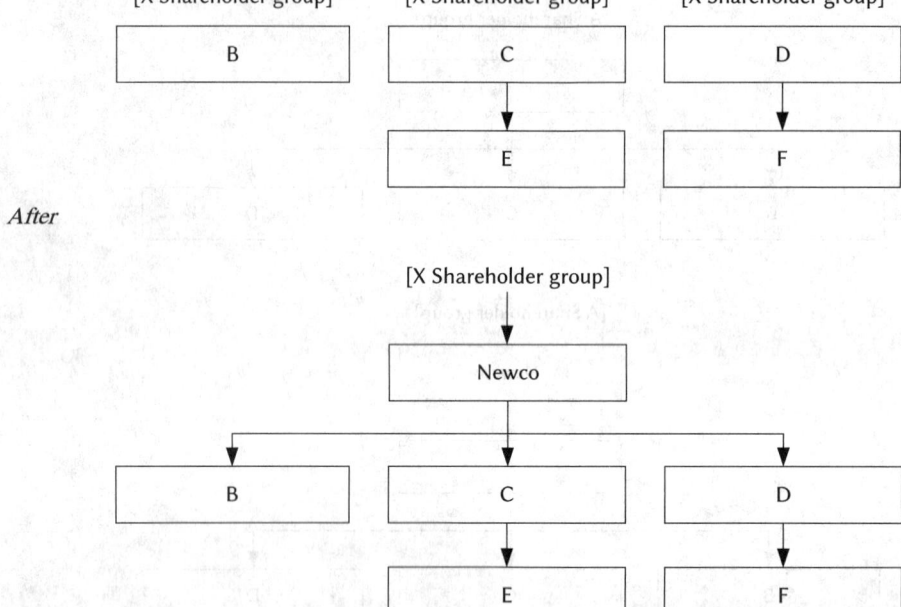

How should this reorganisation be accounted for in Newco's consolidated financial statements?

Unlike the situation in Example 10.11 above, this transaction meets the definition of a business combination under IFRS 3. Entity B and sub-groups C and D (each a business as defined) have been brought together to form a new reporting entity under a new parent entity (Newco). Accordingly, the transaction is within the scope of IFRS 3 unless otherwise excluded. In this context it is relevant whether Entities B, C and D are under common control (that is not 'transitory' – see 2.1.2 above) or just under common ownership.

If the transaction satisfies the description of a business combination under common control, it is outside the scope of IFRS 3. In practice, this type of transaction may be under common control since the number of shareholders will generally be relatively few. Accordingly, there may well be one individual, or a sub-group of the shareholders with a contractual arrangement (see 2.1.1 above), who controls Entities B, C and D. The scope exclusion applies as long as that common control is not transitory. In that case, subject to certain conditions (see 3.1 above), there is an accounting policy choice between the pooling of interests method and acquisition method.

If Entities B, C and D are not under common control (or if common control is transitory), then the business combination is within the scope of IFRS 3 and the acquisition method must be applied.

Pooling of interests method

If the pooling of interests method is used, the assets and liabilities of all combining parties will be reflected at their predecessor carrying amounts. The application of this method is discussed at 3.3 above.

Acquisition method

If the acquisition method set out in IFRS 3 is used, Newco cannot be the acquirer as it issues shares to effect the combination (and there is no change in control arising). Accordingly, one of the pre-existing entities (Entity B, C or D) will need to be identified as the acquirer (see Chapter 9 at 4.1). If, for example, Entity B is identified as the acquirer, the consolidated financial statements of Newco are effectively a continuation of Entity B, and will reflect pre-combination carrying amounts for Entity B and acquisition-date fair values of the assets acquired and liabilities assumed, together with any resulting goodwill, for sub-groups C and D. The financial information presented in those financial statements for periods prior to the acquisition date is that of Entity B. Newco cannot be accounted for as acquiree in a reverse acquisition, because it is not a business as defined. The application of the acquisition method is discussed generally in Chapter 9 and for business combinations under common control specifically at 3.2 above.

4.2.2 Setting up a new top holding company: transactions involving consideration other than equity interests

In Examples 10.11 and 10.12 above, a Newco has been inserted between shareholders and either an existing group or a series of entities with common ownership (but not necessarily common control). In neither case could Newco itself be identified as the acquirer under IFRS 3, since it issued equity interests to effect the combination. Even if a Newco transferred cash or other assets or incurred liabilities as consideration, Newco is generally not the acquirer and the way in which the transaction is accounted for would not change.

Only in limited circumstances would it be possible to identify Newco as the acquirer under IFRS 3, as discussed at 4.1 above. This might happen, for example, if the transaction was contingent on completion of an IPO that resulted in a change of control over Newco. In that case, the application of the acquisition method would result in fair values being attributed to the assets acquired and liabilities assumed of the existing businesses, and the recognition of goodwill or a gain on a bargain purchase relating to those businesses.

Unless the acquisition method is applied, any cash (or other form of consideration) paid to the shareholders is effectively a distribution and should be accounted for as such. If the acquisition method can be applied, any cash paid to the shareholders in their capacity as owners of the identified acquirer is accounted for as a distribution. Any cash paid to the shareholders as owners of the acquirees forms part of the consideration transferred for the entities acquired. Determining whether cash is paid to shareholders in their capacity as owners of the identified acquirer or as owners of the acquirees may require judgement.

4.3 Inserting a new intermediate parent within an existing group

In Example 10.13 below, a new intermediate holding company has been inserted within an existing group, so as to form a new sub-group.

Example 10.13: **Newco inserted as a new intermediate parent within an existing group**

A Newco is incorporated and inserted above a number of entities within an existing group so as to form a new sub-group. Newco issues shares to Parent A in return for the shares in Entities C and D, both businesses as defined in IFRS 3. The group structure before and after this transaction is as follows:

Before

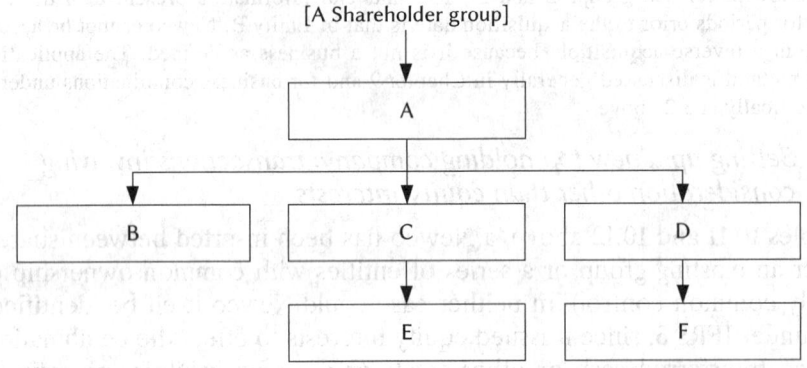

After

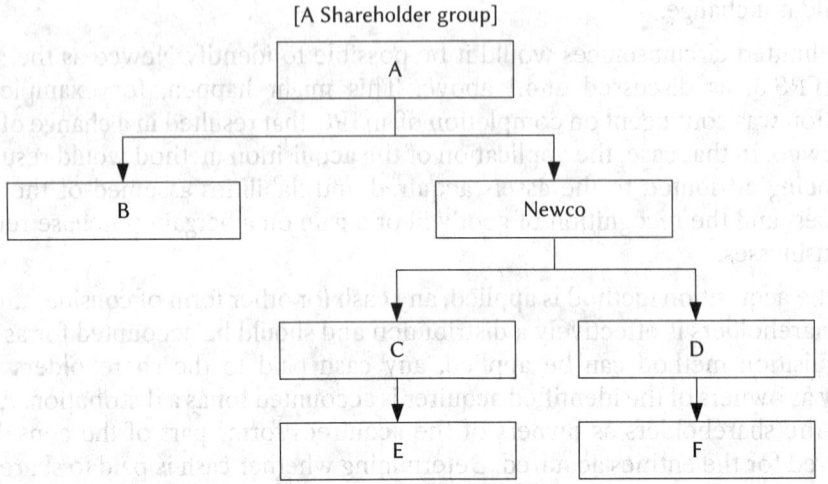

In most situations, Newco will be exempt from preparing consolidated financial statements (see Chapter 6 at 2.2.1). However, if it does prepare consolidated financial statements, how should this reorganisation be accounted for in Newco's consolidated financial statements?

This type of reorganisation will generally satisfy the description of a business combination under common control in IFRS 3. The transaction is a business combination (Entities C and D are businesses as defined) and all combining parties are under common control of Parent A. Accordingly, the transaction is excluded from the scope of IFRS 3 as long as that common control is not 'transitory', and in making that assessment Newco is excluded (see 2.1.2 above). Assuming that the scope exclusion applies, subject to certain restrictions (see 3.1 above), there is an accounting policy choice between the pooling of interests method and acquisition method. If common control is transitory, then the business combination is within the scope of IFRS 3 and the acquisition method must be applied.

Pooling of interests method

If the pooling of interests method is used, the assets and liabilities of all combining parties will be reflected at their predecessor carrying amounts. The application of this method is discussed at 3.3 above.

Acquisition method

If the acquisition method as set out in IFRS 3 is used, Newco cannot be the acquirer as it issues shares to effect the combination (and there is no change in control arising). Accordingly, one of the pre-existing entities (Entity C or D) will need to be identified as the acquirer (see Chapter 9 at 4.1). If, for example, Entity C is identified as the acquirer, the consolidated financial statements of Newco are effectively a continuation of Entity C, and will reflect pre-combination carrying amounts for sub-group C and acquisition-date fair values of the assets acquired and liabilities assumed, together with any resulting goodwill, for sub-group D. The financial information presented in those financial statements for periods prior to the acquisition date is that of Entity C. Newco cannot be accounted for as acquiree in a reverse acquisition, because it is not a business as defined. The application of the acquisition method is discussed generally in Chapter 9 and for business combinations under common control specifically at 3.2 above.

In Example 10.13 above, the reorganisation was effected by Newco issuing shares. If Newco gave cash or other consideration as part of the transaction, then in most situations this will not affect the analysis above and the further consequences would be the same as those described at 4.2.2 above.

Only in limited circumstances would it be possible to identify Newco as the acquirer under IFRS 3, as discussed at 4.1 above. This accounting may be appropriate when, for example, the transaction was contingent on completion of an IPO that resulted in a change of control over Newco. In that case, the application of the acquisition method would result in fair values being attributed to the assets acquired and liabilities assumed of both sub-groups C and D, and the recognition of goodwill or a gain on a bargain purchase relating to those businesses.

4.4 Transferring businesses outside an existing group using a Newco

Example 10.14 below illustrates a scenario where a business is transferred outside an existing group to a Newco owned by the same shareholders.

Example 10.14: Newco created to take over a business of an existing group (spin-off)

Entity C, a subsidiary of Parent A, transfers the shares held in its subsidiary, Entity E, to a newly formed entity, Newco. In return, Newco issues shares to the existing shareholders of Parent A. Entity E is a business as defined in IFRS 3. The group structure before and after this transaction is as follows:

Before

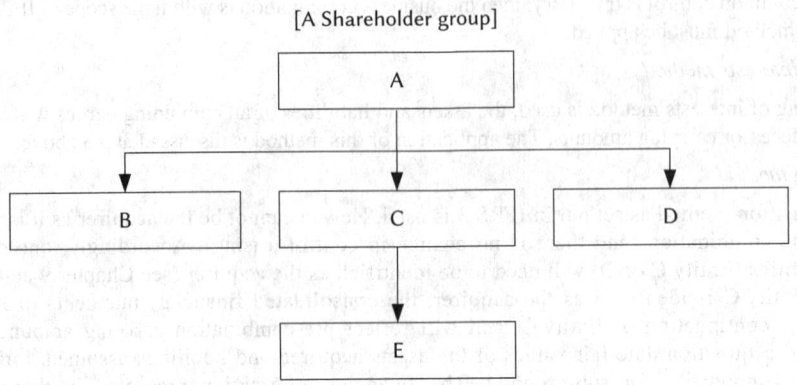

After

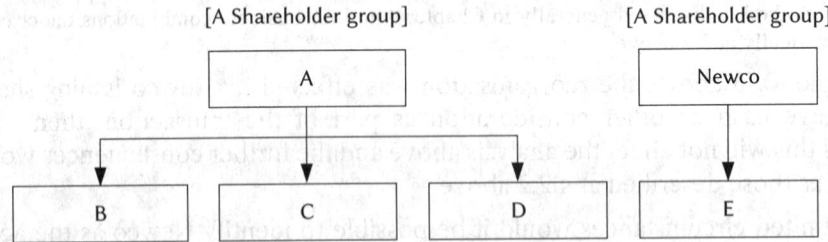

How should this reorganisation be accounted for in Newco's consolidated financial statements?

In many situations, this type of transaction will not be 'under common control' since there will be no contractual arrangement between the shareholders (see 2.1.1 above). However, whether there is common ownership or common control by one individual, or a sub-group of the shareholders, over the combining parties is irrelevant in this specific scenario.

The transaction does not meet the definition of a business combination under IFRS 3, because neither Newco nor Entity E can be identified as the acquirer. Newco cannot be identified as the acquirer as it issues shares to effect the combination. Entity E cannot be identified as the acquirer (in a reverse acquisition) as Newco is not a business as defined. On that basis, the transaction is outside the scope of IFRS 3.

Applying the IAS 8 hierarchy, Newco cannot elect to apply the acquisition method as set out in IFRS 3 since the transaction does not result in any change of economic substance for Newco and Entity E (e.g. in terms of any real alteration to the composition or ownership of Entity E). Accordingly, the consolidated financial statements of Newco reflect that the arrangement is in substance a continuation of Entity E. Any difference in share capital is reflected as an adjustment to equity.

Apart from any necessary change in share capital, the accounting treatment set out in Example 10.14 above is the same as would have been applied if the business was transferred by distributing the shares in Entity E directly to Parent A's shareholders, without the use of a Newco. In that case, there would be no question that there had been a business combination at all. Entity E would not reflect any changes in its financial statements. The only impact for Entity E would be that, rather than only having one shareholder (Entity C), it now has a number of shareholders.

In Example 10.14 above, the reorganisation was effected by Newco issuing shares. If Newco gave cash or other consideration as part of the transaction, then in most situations this will not affect the analysis above. The only difference is that any consideration transferred to the shareholders is effectively a distribution and should be accounted for as such (see 4.2.2 above).

Only in limited circumstances would it be possible to identify Newco as the acquirer under IFRS 3, as discussed at 4.1 above. This accounting may be appropriate when, for example, the transaction was contingent on completion of an IPO that resulted in a change of control over Newco. In that case, the application of the acquisition method would result in fair values being attributed to the assets acquired and liabilities assumed of Entity E, and the recognition of goodwill or a gain on a bargain purchase relating to that business.

For Entity A, this transaction is a spin-off (or demerger) of Entity E, and therefore the discussion in Chapter 7 at 3.7 and in Chapter 8 at 2.4.2 would be relevant.

5 ACCOUNTING FOR TRANSFERS OF ASSOCIATES OR JOINT VENTURES UNDER COMMON CONTROL

Although this chapter principally addresses common control transactions in which the receiving entity obtains control over a business, a reorganisation may also involve the transfer of an associate or joint venture between entities under common control (e.g. within an existing group). Investments in associates and joint ventures are generally accounted for using the equity method as set out in IAS 28 – *Investments in Associates and Joint Ventures* (see Chapter 11). That standard states that 'the concepts underlying the procedures used in accounting for the acquisition of a subsidiary are also adopted in accounting for the acquisition of an investment in an associate or a joint venture'. *[IAS 28.26]*. Consequently, the question arises whether the scope exclusion for business combinations under common control in IFRS 3 can be extended to the acquisition of an investment in an associate or joint venture from an entity under common control (i.e. where significant influence or joint control is obtained, rather than control).

This question is relevant when the investment in an associate or joint venture is acquired in a separate common control transaction, rather than as part of a larger business combination under common control. That is, if an associate or joint venture is being transferred as part of a business combination under common control (i.e. where the investment is one of the identifiable assets of the acquired business), the entire transaction is excluded from the scope of IFRS 3 and the receiving entity would need to develop an accounting policy as discussed at 3.1 above.

In October 2012, the Interpretations Committee was asked whether it is appropriate to apply the scope exclusion for business combinations under common control in IFRS 3 by analogy to the acquisition of an interest in an associate or joint venture from an entity under common control. On the one hand, it was noted that paragraph 32 of IAS 28 has guidance on such acquisitions and does not distinguish between acquisitions under common control and acquisitions not under common control. Paragraph 10 of IAS 8 requires management to use its judgement in developing and applying an accounting policy only in the absence of an IFRS that specifically applies to a transaction. On the other hand, it was noted that paragraph 26 of IAS 28 refers to adopting 'the concepts underlying the procedures used in accounting for the acquisition of a subsidiary' and that paragraph 2(c) of IFRS 3 excludes business combinations under common control from its scope. The Interpretations Committee 'observed that some might read these paragraphs as contradicting the guidance in paragraph 32 of IAS 28, and so potentially leading to a lack of clarity'. Ultimately, the Interpretations Committee noted that accounting for the acquisition of an interest in an associate or joint venture under common control would be better considered within the context of broader projects on accounting for business combinations under common control and the equity method. Consequently, it decided in May 2013 not to take the issue onto its agenda.[8]

In June 2017, the Interpretations Committee reconsidered this topic and *tentatively* decided that the requirements in IFRSs provide an adequate basis to account for the acquisition of an interest in an associate or joint venture from an entity under common control. The Interpretations Committee observed that IAS 28 does not include a scope exception for acquisitions under common control and, accordingly, applies to the transaction. Paragraph 26 of IAS 28 should not be used as a basis to apply the scope exclusion for business combinations under common control in paragraph 2(c) of IFRS 3 by analogy. The Interpretations Committee also observed that in accounting for the acquisition of the interest, an entity would assess whether the transaction includes a transaction with owners in their capacity as owners – if so, the entity determines the cost of the investment taking into account that transaction with owners.[9] However, the tentative agenda decision was eventually not finalised, as that might have been premature pending developments in the IASB's research project on business combinations under common control (see 6 below). Although the acquisition of an interest in an associate or joint venture under common control is itself outside the scope of the project, the IASB acknowledged that there is an interaction with transactions within the scope. This interaction would be considered in the course of the project, but had not been discussed publicly at the time of writing.[10]

Based on the discussions of the Interpretations Committee described above, we believe there are two possible approaches to account for the acquisition of an investment in an associate or joint venture from an entity under common control, when applying the equity method. As IAS 28 is not clear, in our view, the receiving entity has an accounting policy choice between:

- Approach 1 – acquisition accounting

    The requirements in IAS 28 are applied as there is no scope exclusion for the acquisition of an interest in an associate or joint venture from an entity under common control. The receiving entity/investor compares the cost of the investment against its share of the net fair value of the investee's assets and liabilities on the date of acquisition, to identify any goodwill or gain on a bargain purchase. Goodwill is included in the carrying amount of the investment. Any gain on a bargain purchase is recognised in profit or loss. *[IAS 28.32]*. If the common control transaction is not at arm's length, we believe that the receiving entity has an accounting policy choice to impute an equity contribution or distribution when it determines the cost of the investment.

- Approach 2 – pooling of interests

The scope exclusion for business combinations under common control in IFRS 3 is applied by analogy to the acquisition of an interest in an associate or joint venture from an entity under common control. This is on the basis that IAS 28 indicates that the concepts applied to accounting for acquisitions of investments in associates or joint ventures are similar to those applied to acquisitions of subsidiaries. As such, the receiving entity/investor may recognise the investment in the associate or joint venture at its predecessor equity-accounted carrying amount on the date of acquisition. Any difference between this amount and the consideration given is accounted for as an equity contribution or distribution.

An entity must consistently apply the chosen accounting policy. The two approaches are illustrated in Example 10.15 below.

Example 10.15: Transfer of an associate within an existing group

Entity B and Entity C are under common control of Entity A. Entity C holds an investment in Associate D, which it sells to Entity B for cash. The transaction can be illustrated as follows:

Before

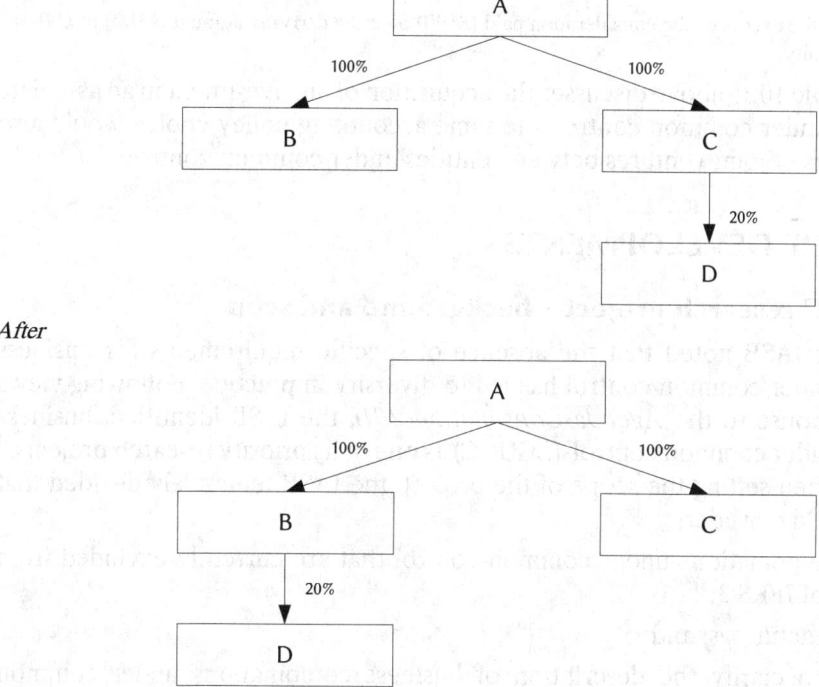

After

In Entity C's financial statements, the equity-accounted carrying amount of its 20% interest in Associate D is £100. The net fair value of the identifiable assets and liabilities of Associate D is £800 (based on 100%). Entity B gives consideration of £190 to Entity C for the 20% interest in Associate D, which is the fair value of the 20% interest.

The consolidated financial statements of Entity A will not be impacted (except for any potential tax consequences), because from the group's perspective there has been no change. How should Entity B account for this transaction in its own financial statements when applying the equity method to investments in associates?

In our view, there are two approaches that Entity B can apply in accounting for this common control transaction, but whichever approach is adopted, it should be applied consistently.

Approach 1 – acquisition accounting

Under this approach, IAS 28 applies as it does to any other acquisition of an investment in an associate (see Chapter 11 at 7). Accordingly, the receiving entity calculates its share of the net fair value of the investee's identifiable assets and liabilities applying paragraph 32 of IAS 28.

Entity B recognises an investment in an associate with a cost of £190 (fair value of consideration given). This amount comprises Entity B's share of the net fair value of Associate D's identifiable assets and liabilities of £160 (20% × £800) and goodwill of £30 (£190 less £160).

Approach 2 – pooling of interests

Under this approach, the scope exclusion in paragraph 2(c) of IFRS 3 is applied by analogy to the acquisition of an interest in an associate from an entity under common control. This is because paragraph 26 of IAS 28 indicates that the concepts underlying the procedures used in accounting for the acquisition of a subsidiary are also adopted in accounting for the acquisition of an investment in an associate. Similarly, the receiving entity may elect to account for such transactions on a carry-over basis as its accounting policy.

Entity B recognises an investment in an associate based on the equity-accounted carrying amount in Entity C's financial statements as at the acquisition date, which is £100. Entity B does not reassess the fair values of Associate D's identifiable assets and liabilities. Rather, Entity B continues to recognise any adjustments that Entity C recognised in accordance with paragraph 32 of IAS 28 due to differences in fair values at the date Entity C acquired its interest in Associate D.

Entity B recognises the excess of the consideration paid (£190) over the carrying amount (£100) of £90 as a distribution from equity.

Although Example 10.15 above discusses the acquisition of an investment in an associate from an entity under common control, the same accounting policy choice would also apply to transfers of joint ventures between entities under common control.

6 FUTURE DEVELOPMENTS

6.1 BCUCC research project – background and scope

Historically, the IASB noted that the absence of specific requirements for business combinations under common control has led to diversity in practice. Following views received in response to the *Agenda Consultation 2011*, the IASB identified 'business combinations under common control' (BCUCC) as one of its priority research projects.[11] In June 2014, when setting the scope of the project, the IASB tentatively decided that the project should consider:

- business combinations under common control that are currently excluded from the scope of IFRS 3;
- group restructurings; and
- the need to clarify the description of business combinations under common control, including the meaning of 'common control'.

The IASB also tentatively decided that the project should give priority to considering transactions that involve third parties, for example, those undertaken in preparation for an IPO.[12] At that time, the IASB did not discuss which reporting entity (e.g. acquirer, acquiree, transferor, ultimate parent) and which financial statements of that reporting entity (e.g. consolidated, separate, individual) the project would focus on.

The *2015 Agenda Consultation* confirmed the importance and urgency of providing guidance on business combinations under common control. Accordingly, as discussed in the November 2016 Feedback Statement on the 2015 Agenda Consultation, the IASB decided to retain BCUCC as one of the eight projects on its research programme. It was noted that the topic is highly ranked by comment letter respondents from a wide range of countries and in emerging market outreach, and is important to regulators and members of the Advisory Council.[13]

During the second half of 2017, the IASB continued its discussions on the scope of the BCUCC research project. Although 'business combinations under common control' are described in IFRS 3, there are application questions as to whether particular transactions satisfy that description. Specifically, interested parties had raised questions on the meaning of 'transitory control' and whether particular business combinations satisfy the description of 'under common control'. In addition, the staff had noticed that 'group restructuring' is not a defined term and is understood differently by different parties. Hence, the question arose what transactions, other than business combinations under common control, are included in the scope of the project.[14]

In October and December 2017, the IASB tentatively decided to clarify that the scope of the project (which focuses on the perspective of the receiving entity) includes transactions under common control in which a reporting entity obtains control of one or more businesses, regardless of whether:

- the reporting entity can be identified as the acquirer if IFRS 3 were applied to the transaction (e.g. when a Newco issues shares to acquire one business under common control);[15]
- the transaction is preceded by an external acquisition and/or followed by an external sale of one or more of the combining parties; or
- the transaction is conditional on a future sale, such as in an IPO.[16]

This means that the project will address both business combinations under common control and other common control transactions involving the transfer of control over one or more businesses. Consistent with IFRS 3, the scope of the project specifies only which transactions it applies to. Therefore, depending on whether the receiving entity acquires the shares or net assets of a business and whether it has other subsidiaries, any guidance developed in the project may affect the consolidated, individual and/or separate financial statements. The interaction with other common control transactions that are outside the scope of the project (e.g. transfers of investments in associates or joint ventures under common control) would also be considered in the course of the project, but had not been discussed publicly at the time of writing.[17]

6.2 BCUCC research project – accounting methods and disclosures

Previous research and outreach activities had shown that, in practice, BCUCC are sometimes accounted for using the acquisition method, but variations of the predecessor method are more typically used.[18] Throughout 2018 and 2019, the IASB discussed possible methods of accounting for transactions within the scope of the project, focusing on the information needs of non-controlling shareholders, potential shareholders, lenders and other creditors of the receiving entity.[19] In the deliberations, broadly speaking, three alternative measurement approaches were explored as to how the receiving entity could reflect the acquired assets and liabilities in a BCUCC:

- 'Historical cost' approach – where the receiving entity allocates the consideration transferred across the acquired assets and liabilities (e.g. based on their relative fair values; consistent with the accounting required for asset acquisitions).
- 'Current value' approach – where the receiving entity reflects the acquired assets and liabilities at their current values (e.g. at their fair values; consistent with the acquisition method required by IFRS 3 for business combinations).
- 'Predecessor' approach – where the receiving entity reflects the acquired assets and liabilities at their historical carrying amounts.[20]

In September 2019, the IASB tentatively decided that the forthcoming consultation document should not propose a single measurement approach for all transactions within the scope of the project. Instead, it reached the preliminary view that a current value approach based on the acquisition method should be required for some BCUCC and a predecessor approach for all other BCUCC.[21]

6.2.1 When to apply which measurement approach

In September 2019, the IASB tentatively decided that a current value approach based on the acquisition method should be required for BCUCC that affect non-controlling shareholders of a receiving entity, unless equity instruments of the receiving entity are not traded in a public market and one of the following conditions applies:

- all non-controlling shareholders are the receiving entity's related parties as defined in IAS 24 (i.e. an exception); or
- the receiving entity chooses to apply a predecessor approach and all its non-controlling shareholders have been informed about, and not objected to, the receiving entity applying that approach (i.e. an exemption).

IFRSs describe a public market as a domestic or foreign stock exchange or an over-the-counter market, including local and regional markets (e.g. paragraph 4(a)(ii) of IFRS 10).

The IASB tentatively decided that a predecessor approach should be required for all other transactions within the scope of the project.[22]

Figure 10.1 below summarises the IASB's preliminary views on when each measurement approach would apply to BCUCC.

Figure 10.1   Illustration of the IASB's tentative decisions on when the acquisition method and the predecessor approach would apply[23]

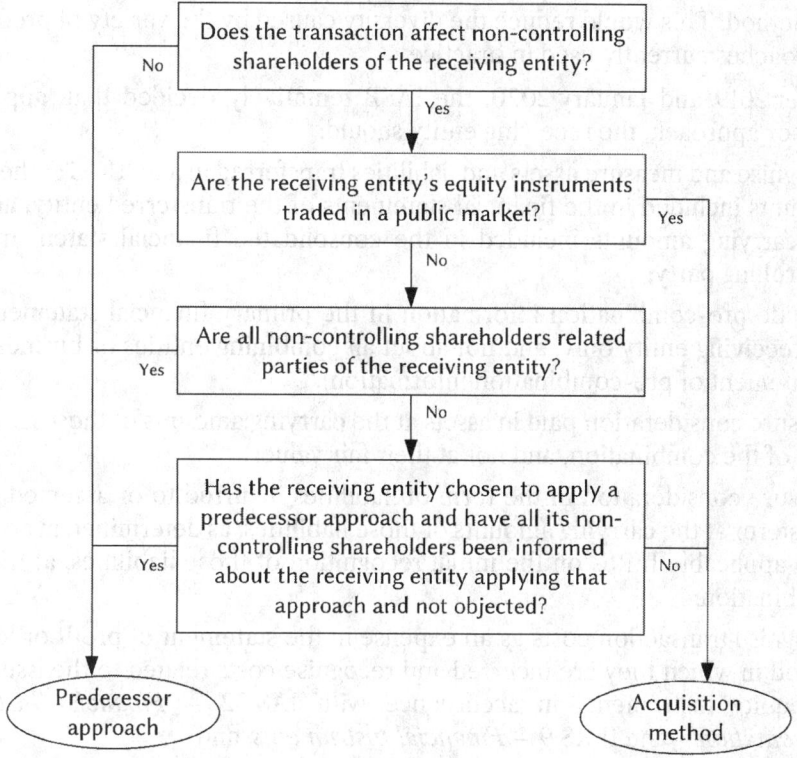

6.2.2   How to apply the acquisition method

In December 2019, the IASB discussed whether and how the acquisition method set out in IFRS 3 should be modified for BCUCC to address a feature that is not present in business combinations *not* under common control. That is, the potential for an equity transaction in addition to the acquisition of a business.

The IASB tentatively decided that the receiving entity should recognise any excess fair value of the acquired identifiable net assets over the fair value of the consideration transferred as an increase in the receiving entity's equity (i.e. a contribution to equity), and not as a gain on a bargain purchase in the statement of profit or loss.

In contrast, the IASB tentatively decided not to require the receiving entity to identify, measure and recognise any overpayment as a distribution from equity.[24]

6.2.3 How to apply the predecessor approach

The IASB also discussed how a predecessor approach should be applied, so as to specify a single method. This would reduce the diversity caused by the variety of predecessor-type approaches currently used in practice.

In October 2019 and January 2020, the IASB tentatively decided that, applying the predecessor approach, the receiving entity should:

- recognise and measure assets and liabilities transferred in a BCUCC at the carrying amounts included in the financial statements of the transferred entity, and not at the carrying amounts included in the consolidated financial statements of the controlling party;
- provide pre-combination information in the primary financial statements about the receiving entity only, and not about all combining entities or business (i.e. no restatement of pre-combination information);[25]
- measure consideration paid in assets at the carrying amounts of those assets at the date of the combination, and not at their fair value;
- measure consideration in the form of liabilities incurred to or assumed from the transferor at the carrying amounts of those liabilities, as determined in accordance with applicable IFRSs on the initial recognition of those liabilities, at the date of combination;
- recognise transaction costs as an expense in the statement of profit or loss in the period in which they are incurred and recognise costs related to the issue of debt or equity instruments in accordance with IAS 32 – *Financial Instruments: Presentation* – and IFRS 9 – *Financial Instruments*; and
- recognise as a change in equity any difference between the consideration paid and the carrying amounts of assets and liabilities received.

Further, the IASB tentatively decided not to prescribe:

- how the receiving entity would measure consideration paid in its own shares; and
- in which component or components of its equity the receiving entity would present any difference between the consideration paid and the carrying amounts of assets and liabilities received.[26]

6.2.4 Disclosures about transactions within the scope of the project

As a final step, in February 2020, the IASB discussed what information the receiving entity should disclose about BCUCC. It tentatively decided that when the acquisition method is used, the receiving entity should apply all disclosure requirements in IFRS 3 and all preliminary views on disclosure published in the Discussion Paper *Business Combinations – Disclosures, Goodwill and Impairment* (see Chapter 9 at 1.1.1 for more details on this Discussion Paper). The IASB also tentatively decided that it should provide guidance on applying the disclosure requirements of IFRS 3 and IAS 24 to BCUCC.

In addition, the IASB reached the preliminary view that when the predecessor approach is used, the receiving entity should:

- apply particular disclosure requirements in IFRS 3 and particular preliminary views on disclosure published in the Discussion Paper *Business Combinations – Disclosures, Goodwill and Impairment*; and
- disclose the amount recognised in equity for the difference between the consideration paid and the carrying amounts of assets and liabilities received, and the component of equity in which that difference is recognised.

The IASB tentatively decided not to require disclosure of pre-combination information for BCUCC reported applying the predecessor approach.[27]

6.3 BCUCC research project – next steps

In February 2020, the IASB completed its discussion about reporting BCUCC and decided that the consultation document for this project should be a Discussion Paper.[28] The Discussion Paper will set out the IASB's preliminary views and, at the time of writing, is expected during the fourth quarter of 2020.[29]

References

1. *IFRIC Update*, January 2018, Committee's agenda decisions, Agenda Paper 2.
2. www.ifrs.org, Projects, Current work plan, Business Combinations under Common Control, About, accessed on 24 July 2020.
3. *IFRIC Update*, March 2006, p.6.
4. For example, see FASB ASC 805-50, *Business Combinations – Related Issues*; and FRC FRS 102 Section 19, *Business Combinations and Goodwill*, paras. 29-32.
5. *IFRIC Update*, January 2010, p.3.
6. Paragraph B88 of IFRS 10 essentially retains the wording of paragraph 26 of superseded IAS 27, which was as follows: "The income and expenses of a subsidiary are included in the consolidated financial statements from the acquisition date as defined in IFRS 3. Income and expenses of the subsidiary shall be based on the values of the assets and liabilities recognised in the parent's consolidated financial statements at the acquisition date...".
7. *IFRIC Update*, September 2011, pp.2-3.
8. *IFRIC Update*, May 2013, pp.3-4.
9. *IFRIC Update*, June 2017, Committee's tentative agenda decisions, Agenda Paper 8.
10. Staff Paper, IASB Meeting, December 2017, Agenda Paper 23A, *Business Combinations under Common Control – Review of related projects*, paras. 30-32.
11. *Feedback Statement: Agenda Consultation 2011*, December 2012, p.11.
12. *IASB Update*, June 2014, p.8.
13. *IASB Work plan 2017-2021 (Feedback Statement on the 2015 Agenda Consultation)*, November 2016, p.27.
14. Staff Paper, IASB Meeting, October 2017, Agenda Paper 23, *Business Combinations under Common Control – Scope of the project*, paras. 9-17.
15. *IASB Update*, October 2017, *Agenda Paper 23*.
16. *IASB Update*, December 2017, *Agenda Paper 23B*.
17. Live webinar by IASB staff, January 2018, *Business Combinations under Common Control – Scope of the project*.
18. Staff Paper, IASB Meeting, September 2017, Agenda Paper 23, *Business Combinations under Common Control – Education session*, pp.19-35.
19. Project update by Gary Kabureck (IASB member), June 2020, *In brief: Combinations of businesses under common control – one size does not fit all*.
20. Staff Paper, IASB Meeting, June 2018, Agenda Paper 23, *Business Combinations under Common Control – Way forward for transactions affecting NCI*, p.11.

21 *IASB Update*, September 2019, *Agenda Paper 23*.
22 *IASB Update*, September 2019, *Agenda Paper 23*.
23 Staff Paper, IASB Meeting, February 2020, Agenda Paper 23, *Business Combinations under Common Control – Cover paper*, p.3.
24 *IASB Update,* December 2019, *Agenda Papers 23 and 23A*.
25 *IASB Update*, October 2019, *Agenda Paper 23*.
26 *IASB Update*, January 2020, *Agenda Paper 23B*.
27 *IASB Update*, February 2020, *Agenda Paper 23A*.
28 *IASB Update,* February 2020, *Agenda Papers 23A and 23B*.
29 www.ifrs.org, Projects, Current work plan, Business Combinations under Common Control, Project history, Next milestone, accessed on 28 August 2020.

Chapter 11 Investments in associates and joint ventures

1	INTRODUCTION	813
2	OBJECTIVE AND SCOPE OF IAS 28	813
	2.1 Objective	813
	2.2 Scope	814
3	DEFINITIONS	814
4	SIGNIFICANT INFLUENCE	814
	4.1 Severe long-term restrictions impairing ability to transfer funds to the investor	815
	4.2 Lack of significant influence	815
	4.3 Holdings of less than 20% of the voting power	816
	4.4 Potential voting rights	816
	4.5 Voting rights held in a fiduciary capacity	817
	4.6 Fund managers	817
5	EXEMPTIONS FROM APPLYING THE EQUITY METHOD	818
	5.1 Parents exempt from preparing consolidated financial statements	818
	5.2 Subsidiaries meeting certain criteria	818
	5.3 Investments in associates or joint ventures held by venture capital organisations and similar organisations	819
	5.3.1 Investment entities exception	820
	5.3.2 Application of IFRS 9 to exempt investments in associates or joint ventures	820
	5.3.2.A Entities with a mixture of activities	821
	5.4 Partial use of fair value measurement of associates	821
6	CLASSIFICATION AS HELD FOR SALE (IFRS 5)	824

7	APPLICATION OF THE EQUITY METHOD	824
	7.1 Overview	825
	7.2 Comparison between equity accounting and consolidation	827
	7.3 Date of commencement of equity accounting	828
	7.4 Initial carrying amount of an associate or joint venture	828
	7.4.1 Initial carrying amount of an associate or joint venture following loss of control of an entity	829
	7.4.2 Piecemeal acquisition of an associate or joint venture	830
	7.4.2.A Financial instrument becoming an associate or joint venture	830
	I Applying an accumulated cost approach	832
	II Applying a fair value as deemed cost approach	835
	7.4.2.B Step increase in an existing associate or joint venture without a change in status of the investee	835
	7.4.2.C Existing associate that becomes a joint venture, or vice versa	837
	7.4.2.D Common control transactions involving sales of associates	838
	7.5 Share of the investee	838
	7.5.1 Accounting for potential voting rights	838
	7.5.2 Cumulative preference shares held by parties other than the investor	838
	7.5.3 Several classes of equity	839
	7.5.4 Where the reporting entity is a group	839
	7.5.5 Where the investee is a group: non-controlling interests in an associate's or joint venture's consolidated financial statements	840
	7.6 Transactions between the reporting entity and its associates or joint ventures	841
	7.6.1 Elimination of 'upstream' and 'downstream' transactions	841
	7.6.1.A Elimination of 'downstream' unrealised profits in excess of the investment	845
	7.6.1.B Transactions between associates and/or joint ventures	846
	7.6.2 Reciprocal interests	847
	7.6.2.A Reciprocal interests in reporting entity accounted for under the equity method by the associate	847
	7.6.2.B Reciprocal interests in reporting entity not accounted for under the equity method by the associate	849

	7.6.3	Loans and borrowings between the reporting entity and its associates or joint ventures	850
	7.6.4	Statement of cash flows	850
	7.6.5	Contributions of non-monetary assets to an associate or a joint venture	850
		7.6.5.A 'Commercial substance'	852
		7.6.5.B Contributions of non-monetary assets – practical application	853
		I 'Artificial' transactions	855
		II Accounting for the acquisition of a business on formation of a joint venture	856
		7.6.5.C Conflict between IAS 28 and IFRS 10	857
7.7	Non-coterminous accounting periods		859
7.8	Consistent accounting policies		860
	7.8.1	Exemption for associates or joint ventures that are investment entities	861
	7.8.2	Temporary exemption from IFRS 9 applied by an insurer	861
7.9	Loss-making associates or joint ventures		862
7.10	Distributions received in excess of the carrying amount		863
7.11	Equity transactions in an associate's or joint venture's financial statements		863
	7.11.1	Dividends or other forms of distributions	864
	7.11.2	Issues of equity instruments	864
	7.11.3	Equity-settled share-based payment transactions	864
	7.11.4	Effects of changes in parent/non-controlling interests in subsidiaries	867
7.12	Discontinuing the use of the equity method		870
	7.12.1	Investment in associate or joint venture that is a business becoming a subsidiary	870
	7.12.2	Investment in associate or joint venture that is not a business becoming a subsidiary	871
	7.12.3	Retained investment in the former associate or joint venture is a financial asset	871
	7.12.4	Investment in associate becomes a joint venture (or vice versa)	872
	7.12.5	Partial disposals of interests in associate or joint venture where the equity method continues to be applied	872
	7.12.6	Deemed disposals	873
8	IMPAIRMENT LOSSES		876
	8.1	General	876
	8.2	Investment in the associate or joint venture	877

	8.3	Other interests that are not part of the net investment in the associate or joint venture	878
9	SEPARATE FINANCIAL STATEMENTS		881
	9.1	Impairment of investments in associates or joint ventures in separate financial statements	882
10	PRESENTATION AND DISCLOSURES		882
	10.1	Presentation	882
		10.1.1 Statement of financial position	882
		10.1.2 Profit or loss	883
		10.1.2.A Impairment of associates or joint ventures	884
		10.1.3 Other items of comprehensive income	884
		10.1.4 Statement of cash flows	884
	10.2	Disclosures	885
11	FUTURE DEVELOPMENTS		885

List of examples

Example 11.1:	Entity owning a discrete venture capital organisation	821
Example 11.2:	Entity with a venture capital organisation segment	821
Example 11.3:	Venture capital consolidations and partial use of fair value through profit or loss	822
Example 11.4:	Application of the equity method	826
Example 11.5:	Accounting for retained interest in an associate or joint venture following loss of control of a subsidiary that is a business due to sale of shares to third party	829
Example 11.6:	Accounting for existing financial instruments on the step-acquisition of an associate (cost-based approach)	834
Example 11.7:	Accounting for existing financial instruments on the step-acquisition of an associate (fair value (IFRS 3) approach)	835
Example 11.8:	Accounting for an increase in the ownership of an associate	836
Example 11.9:	Cumulative preference shares issued by an associate	839
Example 11.10:	Share in an associate or a joint venture where the reporting entity is a group	840
Example 11.11:	Elimination of profit on sale by investor to associate ('downstream transaction')	842
Example 11.12:	Elimination of profit on sale by associate to reporting entity ('upstream transaction')	843
Example 11.13:	Sale of asset from venturer to joint venture at a loss	844
Example 11.14:	Sale of asset from joint venture to venturer at a loss	844

Example 11.15:	Elimination of downstream unrealised profits in excess of the investment	845
Example 11.16:	Elimination of profits and losses resulting from transactions between associates and/or joint ventures	847
Example 11.17:	Elimination of equity-accounted reciprocal interests	848
Example 11.18:	Elimination of reciprocal interests not accounted for under the equity method	849
Example 11.19:	Contribution of non-monetary assets to form a joint venture	853
Example 11.20:	Contribution of non-monetary assets to form a joint venture with cash equalisation payment between venturers/investors	855
Example 11.21:	Contribution of subsidiary to form a joint venture – applying IFRS 10	858
Example 11.22:	Accounting for a loss-making associate	863
Example 11.23:	Equity-settled share-based payment transactions of associate	865
Example 11.24:	Accounting for the effect of transactions with non-controlling interests recognised through equity by an associate	869
Example 11.25:	Deemed disposal of an associate	874
Example 11.26:	Long-term interests in associates and joint ventures	879

Chapter 11 Investments in associates and joint ventures

1 INTRODUCTION

An entity may conduct its business directly or through strategic investments in other entities. IFRS broadly distinguishes three types of strategic investment:
- entities controlled by the reporting entity (subsidiaries);
- entities jointly controlled by the reporting entity and one or more third parties (joint arrangements classified as either joint operations or joint ventures); and
- entities that, while not controlled or jointly controlled by the reporting entity, are subject to significant influence by it (associates).

The equity method of accounting is generally used to account for investments in associates and joint ventures. It involves a modified form of consolidation of the results and assets of investees in the investor's financial statements. The essence of the equity method of accounting is that, rather than full scale consolidation on a line-by-line basis, it requires incorporation of the investor's share of the investee's:
- net assets, in one line in the investor's consolidated statement of financial position;
- profit or loss, in one line in the investor's consolidated statement of profit or loss; and
- other comprehensive income (OCI), in one line in the investor's consolidated statement of other comprehensive income.

2 OBJECTIVE AND SCOPE OF IAS 28

2.1 Objective

The objective of the standard is to prescribe the accounting for investments in associates and to set out the requirements for the application of the equity method when accounting for investments in associates and joint ventures. *[IAS 28.1]*.

IAS 27 – *Separate Financial Statements* – allows an entity, in its separate financial statements, to account for its investments in subsidiaries, joint ventures and associates using the equity method of accounting as described in IAS 28 – *Investments in Associates and Joint Ventures*. *[IAS 27.10]*. This is discussed further in Chapter 8 at 2.3.

2.2 Scope

The standard is applied by all entities that are investors with joint control of a joint venture, or significant influence over an associate. *[IAS 28.2]*. Although there are no exemptions from the standard itself, there are exemptions from applying the equity method by certain types of entities as discussed at 5 below.

3 DEFINITIONS

The following terms are used in IAS 28 with the meanings specified: *[IAS 28.3]*

An *associate* is an entity over which the investor has significant influence.

Consolidated financial statements are the financial statements of a group in which assets, liabilities, equity, income, expenses and cash flows of the parent and its subsidiaries are presented as those of a single economic entity.

The *equity method* is a method of accounting whereby the investment is initially recognised at cost and adjusted thereafter for the post-acquisition change in the investor's share of the investee's net assets. The investor's profit or loss includes its share of the investee's profit or loss and the investor's OCI includes its share of the investee's OCI.

A *joint arrangement* is an arrangement of which two or more parties have joint control.

Joint control is the contractually agreed sharing of control of an arrangement, which exists only when decisions about the relevant activities require the unanimous consent of the parties sharing control.

A *joint venture* is a joint arrangement whereby the parties that have joint control of the arrangement have rights to the net assets of the arrangement.

A *joint venturer* is a party to a joint venture that has joint control of that joint venture.

Significant influence is the power to participate in the financial and operating policy decisions of the investee but is not control or joint control of those policies. *[IAS 28.3]*.

IAS 28 also notes that the following terms are defined in paragraph 4 of IAS 27 and in Appendix A of IFRS 10 – *Consolidated Financial Statements* – and are used in IAS 28, with the meanings specified in the IFRS in which they are defined:

- control of an investee;
- group;
- parent;
- separate financial statements; and
- subsidiary. *[IAS 28.4]*.

4 SIGNIFICANT INFLUENCE

Under IAS 28, a holding of 20% or more of the voting power of the investee (held directly or indirectly, through subsidiaries) is presumed to give rise to significant influence, unless it can be clearly demonstrated that this is not the case. Conversely, a holding of less than 20% of the voting power is presumed not to give rise to significant influence, unless it can be clearly demonstrated that there is in fact significant influence. The existence of a substantial or majority interest of another investor in the investee does not necessarily preclude the investor from having significant influence. *[IAS 28.5]*. An entity should consider both ordinary shares and other categories of shares in determining its voting rights.

IAS 28 states that the existence of significant influence will usually be evidenced in one or more of the following ways:

(a) representation on the board of directors or equivalent governing body of the investee;
(b) participation in policy-making processes, including participation in decisions about dividends and other distributions;
(c) material transactions between the investor and the investee;
(d) interchange of managerial personnel; or
(e) provision of essential technical information. *[IAS 28.6]*.

Significant influence may also exist over another entity through potential voting rights (see 4.4 below).

An entity loses significant influence over an investee when it loses the power to participate in the financial and operating policy decisions of that investee. The loss of significant influence can occur with or without a change in absolute or relative ownership levels. It could occur because of a contractual arrangement. It could also occur, for example, when an associate becomes subject to the control of a government, court, administrator or regulator. *[IAS 28.9]*. The accounting for loss of significant influence over an associate is discussed at 7.12 below.

In some jurisdictions, an entity can seek protection from creditors to reorganise its business (e.g. under Chapter 11 of the Bankruptcy Code in the United States). In such situations, an investor (which is not under bankruptcy protection itself) with an interest in such an associate will need to evaluate the facts and circumstances to assess whether it is still able to exercise significant influence over the financial and operating policies of the investee.

4.1 Severe long-term restrictions impairing ability to transfer funds to the investor

An investor should, when assessing its ability to exercise significant influence over an entity, consider the effect of severe long-term restrictions on the transfer of funds from the associate to the investor or other restrictions in exercising significant influence. However, such restrictions do not, in isolation, preclude the exercise of significant influence. *[IAS 28.BCZ18]*.

4.2 Lack of significant influence

The presumption of significant influence may sometimes be overcome in the following circumstances:

- the investor has failed to obtain representation on the investee's board of directors;
- the investee or other shareholders are opposing the investor's attempts to exercise significant influence;
- the investor is unable to obtain timely or adequate financial information required to apply the equity method; or
- a group of shareholders that holds the majority ownership of the investee operates without regard to the views of the investor.

Determining whether the presumption of significant influence has been overcome requires considerable judgement. IFRS 12 – *Disclosure of Interests in Other Entities* – requires that an entity must disclose significant judgements and assumptions made in determining that it does not have significant influence even though it holds 20% or more of the voting rights of another entity. *[IFRS 12.9(d)]*. This is discussed further in Chapter 13 at 3. In our experience, many regulators take a keen interest in these decisions.

4.3 Holdings of less than 20% of the voting power

Although there is a presumption that an investor that holds less than 20% of the voting power in an investee cannot exercise significant influence, *[IAS 28.5]*, careful judgement is needed to assess whether significant influence may still exist if one of the indicators in paragraphs 6(a)-(e) of IAS 28 (discussed at 4 above) are present.

For example, an investor may still be able to exercise significant influence in the following circumstances:

- the investor's voting power is much larger than that of any other shareholder of the investee;
- the corporate governance arrangements may be such that the investor is able to appoint members to the board, supervisory board or significant committees of the investee. The investor will need to apply judgement to the facts and circumstances to determine whether representation on the respective boards or committees is enough to provide significant influence; or
- the investor has the power to *veto* significant financial and operating decisions.

Determining which policies are significant requires considerable judgement. IFRS 12 requires that an entity must disclose significant judgements and assumptions made in determining that it does have significant influence where it holds less than 20% of the voting rights of another entity. *[IFRS 12.9(e)]*. This is discussed further in Chapter 13 at 3. Extract 11.1 below shows Aveng Limited's disclosure of significant influence when it has voting rights of less than 20%.

Extract 11.1: Aveng Limited (2019)

Accounting policies [extract]

3. SIGNIFICANT ACCOUNTING JUDGEMENTS AND ESTIMATES [extract]

3.1 Judgements and estimation assumptions [extract]

3.1.3 Equity-accounted investments [extract]

Equity-accounted entities are entities in which the Group holds less than 20% of the voting power, but the Group has determined that it has significant influence in entities where it holds less than 20% of the voting power. This includes Specialised Road Technologies Proprietary Limited and RPP Developments Proprietary Limited. The Group's significant influence is due to the Group having a representation on the Board of directors in each of these entities and the Group's participation in decisions over the relevant activities of the entities.

4.4 Potential voting rights

An entity may own share warrants, share call options, debt or equity instruments that are convertible into ordinary shares, or other similar instruments that have the potential, if exercised or converted, to give the entity voting power or reduce another party's voting power over the financial and operating policies of another entity (potential voting rights). *[IAS 28.7].*

When assessing whether an entity has significant influence over the financial and operating policies of another entity, IAS 28 requires consideration of the existence and effect of potential voting rights that are currently exercisable or convertible, including potential voting rights held by another entity.

Potential voting rights are not currently exercisable or convertible when they cannot be exercised or converted until a future date or until the occurrence of a future event. *[IAS 28.7].*

IAS 28 adds some further points of clarification. In assessing whether potential voting rights contribute to significant influence, an entity must examine facts and circumstances that affect potential voting rights, including their terms of exercise and any other contractual arrangements, whether considered individually or in combination. However, an entity does not include in the assessment the intention of management and the financial ability to exercise or convert those potential voting rights. *[IAS 28.8].*

IAS 28 does not include guidance on potential voting rights comparable to that included in IFRS 10 (see Chapter 6 at 4.3.4). In the amendments introduced to IAS 28 when IFRS 10, 11 and 12 were issued, the IASB did not reconsider the definition of significant influence and concluded that it would not be appropriate to address one element of the definition in isolation. Any such consideration would be done as part of a wider review of accounting for associates. *[IAS 28.BC16].* Therefore, potential voting rights that are currently exercisable are included in the assessment of significant influence even if they are not 'substantive' in terms of IFRS 10. An example is a currently exercisable call option that is out of the money.

4.5 Voting rights held in a fiduciary capacity

Voting rights on shares held as security remain the rights of the provider of the security and are generally not considered in the assessment of significant influence if the rights are exercisable only in accordance with instructions from the provider of the security or in its interest. Furthermore, voting rights that are held in a fiduciary capacity might not be those of the entity itself and therefore, similarly, are not considered in the assessment of significant influence. By contrast, if voting rights are held by a nominee on behalf of the entity, they should be considered in the assessment.

4.6 Fund managers

At its November 2016 meeting, the IFRS Interpretations Committee (the Interpretations Committee) discussed a request to clarify whether, and how, a fund manager assesses if it has significant influence over a fund that it manages and in which it has a direct investment. In the scenario described in the submission, the fund manager applies IFRS 10 and determines that it is an agent, and thus does not control the fund. The fund manager has also concluded that it does not have joint control of the fund.

This issue was previously discussed in 2014 and 2015 but at that time the Interpretations Committee decided not to finalise the agenda decision, but instead to place this issue on hold and monitor how any research project on equity accounting progresses. However, in November 2016, the Interpretations Committee did not see any benefit in keeping this issue on hold until further progress is made on the research project, which is now part of the IASB's research pipeline (see 11 below).

The Interpretations Committee observed that a fund manager assesses whether it has control, joint control or significant influence over a fund that it manages by applying the relevant IFRS standard, which in the case of significant influence, is IAS 28. Unlike IFRS 10, IAS 28 does not contemplate whether and how decision-making authority held in the capacity of an agent affects the assessment of significant influence. The Committee believes that developing any such requirements could not be undertaken in isolation of a comprehensive review of the definition of significant influence in IAS 28. Additionally, paragraph 7(b) of IFRS 12 requires an entity to disclose information about significant judgements and assumptions it has made in determining that it has significant influence over another entity. The Interpretations Committee concluded that it would be unable to resolve the question efficiently within the confines of existing IFRS standards. Consequently, it decided not to add the issue to its agenda.[1]

5 EXEMPTIONS FROM APPLYING THE EQUITY METHOD

Under IAS 28, an entity with joint control of, or significant influence over, an investee accounts for its investment in an associate or a joint venture using the equity method, except when that investment qualifies for exemption in accordance with paragraphs 17 to 19 of the standard. *[IAS 28.16]*. These exemptions are discussed at 5.1 to 5.4 below.

5.1 Parents exempt from preparing consolidated financial statements

An entity need not apply the equity method to its investment in an associate or a joint venture if the entity is a parent that is exempt from preparing consolidated financial statements by the scope exception in paragraph 4(a) of IFRS 10 (see Chapter 6 at 2.2.1). *[IAS 28.17]*.

5.2 Subsidiaries meeting certain criteria

An entity need not apply the equity method to its investment in an associate or a joint venture if all the following apply:

(a) the entity is a wholly-owned subsidiary, or is a partially-owned subsidiary of another entity and its other owners, including those not otherwise entitled to vote, have been informed about, and do not object to, the entity not applying the equity method; and

(b) the entity's debt or equity instruments are not traded in a public market (a domestic or foreign stock exchange or an over-the-counter market, including local and regional markets); and

(c) the entity did not file, nor is it in the process of filing, its financial statements with a securities commission or other regulatory organisation, for issuing any class of instruments in a public market; and

(d) the ultimate or any intermediate parent of the entity produces financial statements available for public use that comply with IFRSs, in which subsidiaries are consolidated or are measured at fair value through profit or loss in accordance with IFRS 10. *[IAS 28.17]*.

This exemption will apply only where the investor in an associate or a joint venture is not also a parent. If it is a parent, it must look to the similar exemption from preparation of consolidated financial statements in IFRS 10, which also contains the conditions (a) to (d) above for a parent to be exempt from preparing consolidated financial statements under IFRS 10.

This exemption is available only to entities that are themselves either wholly-owned subsidiaries or partially-owned subsidiaries whose non-controlling shareholders do not object to the presentation of financial statements that do not include associates or joint ventures using the equity method. Some of these 'intermediate' entities will not be exempt, for example if none of their parent companies prepares consolidated financial statements in accordance with IFRS. A typical example is that of an entity that is a subsidiary of a US group that prepares consolidated financial statements in accordance with US GAAP only. In addition, any entity that has publicly traded debt or equity, or is in the process of obtaining a listing for such instruments, will not satisfy the criteria for exemption.

Many jurisdictions apply a national GAAP that is based on IFRS but requires some form of endorsement process. The question then arises as to whether the exemption in (d) above can be applied when the ultimate or intermediate parent entity produces financial statements available for public use that comply with a national GAAP that is based on IFRS. In our view, the exemption in (d) can be applied if certain criteria are met. These are discussed in Chapter 6 at 2.2.1.D.

The effect of the above requirements is that a reporting entity that has associates or joint ventures, but no subsidiaries, and does not meet all the criteria in (a)-(d) above, is required to apply equity accounting for its associates or joint ventures in its own (non-consolidated) financial statements (not to be confused with its 'separate financial statements' – see 9 below).

5.3 Investments in associates or joint ventures held by venture capital organisations and similar organisations

When an investment in an associate or a joint venture is held by, or is held indirectly through, an entity that is a venture capital organisation, a mutual fund, unit trust or similar entity including an investment-linked insurance fund, the entity may elect to measure investments in those associates and joint ventures at fair value through profit or loss in accordance with IFRS 9 – *Financial Instruments*. An entity shall make this election separately for each associate or joint venture, at initial recognition of the associate or joint venture. *[IAS 28.18]*.

IFRS 17 – *Insurance Contracts* – amends paragraph 18 of IAS 28 to explain that an investment-linked insurance fund could be, for example, a fund held by an entity as the underlying items for a group of insurance contracts with direct participation features. For the purposes of the fair value election, insurance contracts include investment contracts with discretionary participation features. An entity shall apply that amendment when it applies IFRS 17 (see Chapter 56).

This exemption is related to the fact that fair value measurement provides more useful information for users of the financial statements than application of the equity method. In the Basis for Conclusions to IAS 28, the IASB clarified that this is an exemption from the requirement to measure interests in joint ventures and associates using the equity method, rather than an exception to the scope of IAS 28 for the accounting for joint ventures and associates held by these entities. *[IAS 28.BC12, BC13]*.

This exemption raises the question of exactly which entities comprise 'venture capital organisations, or mutual funds, unit trusts and similar entities including investment-linked insurance funds', since they are not defined in IAS 28.

Although IFRS 10 does not have an exemption from consolidation for 'venture capital organisations, or mutual funds, unit trusts and similar entities including investment-linked insurance funds', it does have a scope exclusion for entities that meet the definition of an investment entity as discussed at 5.3.1 below.

5.3.1 Investment entities exception

IFRS 10 requires entities that meet the definition of an investment entity to measure investments in subsidiaries at fair value through profit or loss in accordance with IFRS 9. The investment entities exception is discussed further in Chapter 6 at 10.

The application of the investment entity exception is not an accounting policy choice. If an entity meets the definition of an investment entity, it is required to measure its subsidiaries at fair value through profit or loss. To meet this definition, an investment entity must, as well as meeting other criteria, elect the exemption from applying the equity method in IAS 28 for its investments in associates and joint ventures. *[IFRS 10.B85L(b)]*.

As discussed further at 7.8.1 below, if an entity that is not itself an investment entity has an interest in an associate or joint venture that is an investment entity, the investor may retain the fair value measurement applied by that investment entity associate or joint venture to the investment entity associate's or joint venture's interests in subsidiaries. *[IAS 28.36A]*.

5.3.2 Application of IFRS 9 to exempt investments in associates or joint ventures

The reason that IAS 28 allows venture capital organisations, mutual funds, unit trusts and similar entities to measure investments in associates and joint ventures at fair value is because such entities often manage their investments based on fair values and so the application of IFRS 9 produces more relevant information. Furthermore, the financial statements would be less useful if changes in the level of ownership in an investment resulted in frequent changes in the method of accounting for the investment. Where investments are measured at fair value, the fair value is determined in accordance with IFRS 13 – *Fair Value Measurement* (see Chapter 14).

5.3.2.A   Entities with a mixture of activities

The exemption clearly applies to venture capital organisations and other similar financial institutions whose main activities consist of managing an investment portfolio comprising investments unrelated to the investor's business. Although the exemption is not intended to apply to other entities that hold investments in several associates, there are cases in which entities have significant venture capital activities as well as significant other activities. It is clear from paragraph 18 of IAS 28 that the exemption applies to investments that are indirectly held through a venture capital or similar organisation (as well as to those held by the organisations themselves). Therefore, where an entity has a mixture of activities, if it can demonstrate that it runs a venture capital activity rather than merely undertaking, on an *ad hoc* basis, transactions that a venture capital activity would undertake, the exemption applies. *[IAS 28.18].*

Example 11.1:   Entity owning a discrete venture capital organisation

Parent P operates a construction business and owns a venture capital organisation (Subsidiary V) that invests in the telecommunications industry. Even though P itself is not a venture capital organisation, V would be able to apply the exemption and account for its investments at fair value under IFRS 9. In the consolidated financial statements of P, the investments held by V could also be accounted for at fair value under IFRS 9, with changes in fair value recognised in profit or loss in the period of change.

Example 11.2:   Entity with a venture capital organisation segment

Bank A has several separate activities. One segment's business is that of a venture capital organisation. A's share of investees held by the venture capital organisation segment provides it with significant influence, but not control.

Even though A is itself not a venture capital organisation, it would be able to apply the exemption and account for its investments at fair value under IFRS 9, with changes in fair value recognised in profit or loss in the period of change.

5.4   Partial use of fair value measurement of associates

IAS 28 explains that an entity may elect to measure a portion of an investment in an associate held indirectly through a venture capital organisation (or a mutual fund, unit trust and similar entities, including investment-linked insurance funds at fair value through profit or loss) in accordance with IFRS 9 regardless of whether the venture capital organisation (or the mutual fund, unit trust and similar entities, including investment-linked insurance funds) has significant influence over that portion of the investment. If the entity makes that election, it applies the equity method to any remaining portion of its investment in an associate that is not held through a venture capital or similar organisation. *[IAS 28.19].*

In the Basis for Conclusions to IAS 28, the IASB noted a discussion of whether the partial use of fair value should be allowed only in the case of venture capital organisations (or mutual funds, unit trusts and similar entities including investment-linked insurance funds) that have designated their portion of the investment in the associate at fair value through profit or loss in their own financial statements. The IASB noted that several situations might arise in which those entities do not measure their portion of the investment in the associate at fair value through profit or loss. In those situations, however, from the group's perspective, the appropriate determination of the business purpose would lead to the measurement of this portion of the investment in the associate at fair value through profit or loss in the consolidated financial statements. Consequently, the IASB decided that an entity should be able to measure a portion of an investment in an associate held by a venture capital organisation (or a mutual fund, unit trust and similar entities including investment-linked insurance funds) at fair value through profit or loss regardless of whether this portion of the investment is measured at fair value through profit or loss in those entities' financial statements. [IAS 28.BC22].

Example 11.3 below (which is based on four scenarios considered by the Interpretations Committee at its meeting in May 2009[2]) illustrates this partial use exemption.

Example 11.3: Venture capital consolidations and partial use of fair value through profit or loss

A parent entity has two wholly-owned subsidiaries (A and B), each of which has an ownership interest in the same associate, Entity C. A is a venture capital business that holds its interest via an investment-linked fund. B is a holding company. Neither of the investments held by A and B is held for trading.

Scenario 1: both investments in the associate result in significant influence on a stand-alone basis

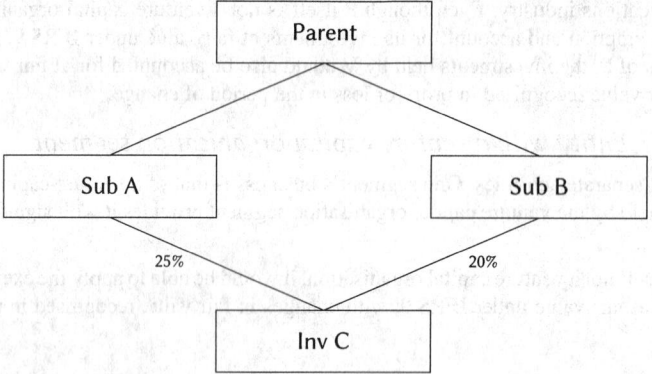

A accounts for its 25% share in the associate at fair value through profit or loss in accordance with IFRS 9 (see Chapter 50 at 2.4).

B accounts for its 20% share in the associate using the equity method in accordance with IAS 28 (see 7 below).

The parent entity must equity account for its 20% interest held by B. Under the partial use of fair value exemption, the parent entity may elect to measure the 25% interest held by A at fair value through profit or loss.

Scenario 2: neither of the investments in the associate results in significant influence on a stand-alone basis but do provide the parent with significant influence on a combined basis.

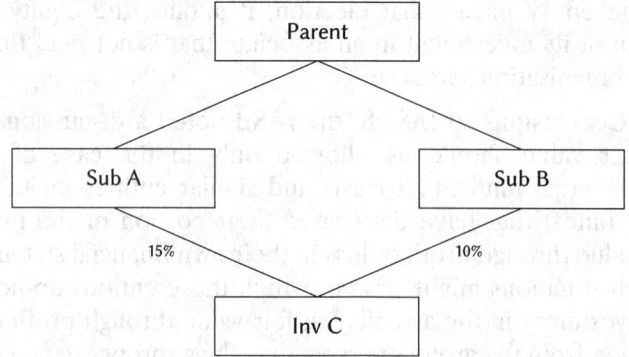

A accounts for its 15% share in the associate at fair value through profit or loss in accordance with IFRS 9 (see Chapter 50 at 2.4).

B designated its 10% share in the associate as at fair value through OCI in accordance with IFRS 9 (see Chapter 50 at 2.5).

The parent entity must equity account for its 10% interest held by B, even though B would not have significant influence on a stand-alone basis. Under the partial use of fair value exemption, the parent entity may elect to measure the 15% interest held by A at fair value through profit or loss.

Scenario 3: one of the investments in the associate results in significant influence on a stand-alone basis and the other investment in the associate does not result in significant influence on a stand-alone basis

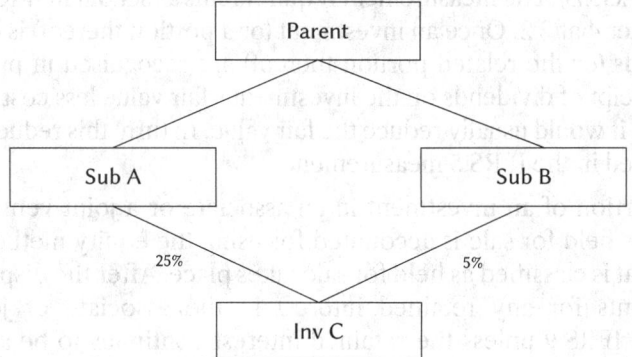

A accounts for its 25% share in the associate at fair value through profit or loss in accordance with IFRS 9 (see Chapter 50 at 2.4).

B designated its 5% share in the associate as at fair value through OCI in accordance with IFRS 9 (see Chapter 50 at 2.5).

The parent entity must equity account for its 5% interest held by B, even though B would not have significant influence on a stand-alone basis. Under the partial use of fair value exemption, the parent entity may elect to measure the 25% interest held by A at fair value through profit or loss.

Scenario 4: same as scenario 3, but with the ownership interests switched between the subsidiaries

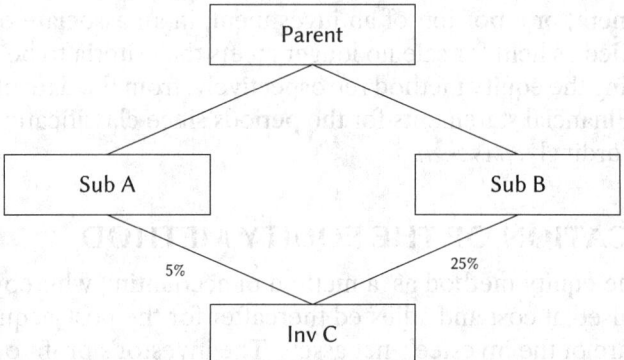

A accounts for its 5% share in the associate at fair value through profit or loss in accordance with IFRS 9 (see Chapter 50 at 2.4).

B accounts for its 25% share in the associate using the equity method in accordance with IAS 28 (see 7 below).

The parent entity must equity account for its 25% interest held by B. Under the partial use of fair value exemption, the parent entity may elect to measure the 5% interest held by A at fair value through profit or loss.

6 CLASSIFICATION AS HELD FOR SALE (IFRS 5)

IAS 28 requires that an entity applies IFRS 5 – *Non-current Assets Held for Sale and Discontinued Operations* – to an investment, or a portion of an investment, in an associate or a joint venture that meets the criteria to be classified as held for sale. *[IAS 28.20]*. The detailed IFRS requirements for classification as held for sale are discussed in Chapter 4 at 2.1.2. In this situation, the investor discontinues the use of the equity method from the date that the investment (or the portion of it) is classified as held for sale. Instead, the associate or joint venture is measured at the lower of its carrying amount and fair value less cost to sell. *[IFRS 5.15]*. The measurement requirements as set out in IFRS 5 are discussed in detail in Chapter 4 at 2.2. Once an investment (or a portion thereof) is classified as held for sale, dividends (or the related portion thereof) are recognised in profit or loss. The impact of the receipt of dividends on the investment's fair value less cost to sell should be assessed because it would usually reduce the fair value. In turn, this reduction could result in a loss recognised in the IFRS 5 measurement.

Any retained portion of an investment in an associate or a joint venture that has not been classified as held for sale is accounted for using the equity method until disposal of the portion that is classified as held for sale takes place. After the disposal takes place, an entity accounts for any retained interest in the associate or joint venture in accordance with IFRS 9 unless the retained interest continues to be an associate or a joint venture, in which case the entity uses the equity method. *[IAS 28.20]*.

As explained in the Basis for Conclusions to IAS 28, the IASB concluded that if a portion of an interest in an associate or joint venture fulfilled the criteria for classification as held for sale, it is only that portion that should be accounted for under IFRS 5. An entity should maintain the use of the equity method for the retained interest until the portion classified as held for sale is finally sold. The reason being that even if the entity has the intention of selling a portion of an interest in an associate or joint venture, until it does so, it still has significant influence over, or joint control of, that investee. *[IAS 28.BC23-27]*.

When an investment, or a portion of an investment, in an associate or a joint venture previously classified as held for sale no longer meets the criteria to be so classified, it is accounted for using the equity method retrospectively, from the date of its classification as held for sale. Financial statements for the periods since classification as held for sale are amended accordingly. *[IAS 28.21]*.

7 APPLICATION OF THE EQUITY METHOD

IAS 28 defines the equity method as 'a method of accounting whereby the investment is initially recognised at cost and adjusted thereafter for the post-acquisition change in the investor's share of the investee's net assets. The investor's profit or loss includes its share of the investee's profit or loss and the investor's other comprehensive income includes its share of the investee's other comprehensive income.' *[IAS 28.3]*.

7.1 Overview

IAS 28 states that 'Under the equity method, on initial recognition the investment in an associate or a joint venture is recognised at cost, and the carrying amount is increased or decreased to recognise the investor's share of the profit or loss of the investee after the date of acquisition. The investor's share of the investee's profit or loss is recognised in the investor's profit or loss. Distributions received from an investee reduce the carrying amount of the investment. Adjustments to the carrying amount may also be necessary for changes in the investor's proportionate interest in the investee arising from changes in the investee's other comprehensive income. Such changes include those arising from the revaluation of property, plant and equipment and from foreign exchange translation differences. The investor's share of those changes is recognised in the investor's other comprehensive income [...]'. *[IAS 28.10]*. On acquisition of the investment, any difference between the cost of the investment and the entity's share of the net fair value of the investee's identifiable assets and liabilities is accounted for as follows:

- Goodwill relating to an associate or a joint venture is included in the carrying amount of the investment. Amortisation of that goodwill is not permitted.
- Any excess of the entity's share of the net fair value of the investee's identifiable assets and liabilities over the cost of the investment is included as income in the determination of the entity's share of the associate or joint venture's profit or loss in the period in which the investment is acquired.

Appropriate adjustments to the entity's share of the associate's or joint venture's profit or loss after acquisition are made to account, for example, for depreciation of the depreciable assets based on their fair values at the acquisition date. Similarly, appropriate adjustments to the entity's share of the associate's or joint venture's profit or loss after acquisition are made for impairment losses, such as for goodwill or property, plant and equipment (PP&E). *[IAS 28.32]*.

IAS 28 does not provide guidance where the accounting as required by paragraph 32 of IAS 28 is incomplete by the end of the reporting period in which the acquisition of the investment occurs. According to paragraph 26 of IAS 28, the concepts underlying the procedures used in accounting for the acquisition of a subsidiary are also adopted in accounting for the acquisition of an investment in an associate or a joint venture. On this basis we believe that, in such a situation, an entity could use by analogy the guidance in IFRS 3 – *Business Combinations* – regarding provisional accounting in the measurement period (see Chapter 9 at 12). Hence, the entity estimates and discloses provisional amounts for the items for which the accounting is incomplete. Those provisional amounts are adjusted retrospectively in the following reporting period to reflect new information obtained about facts and circumstances that existed at the acquisition date that, if known, would have affected the amounts recognised at that date.

These requirements are illustrated in Example 11.4 below.

Example 11.4:   Application of the equity method

On the first day of its financial year, Entity A acquires a 35% interest in Entity B, over which it can exercise significant influence. A paid €475,000 for its interest in B. The book value of B's net identifiable assets at acquisition date was €900,000, and the fair value €1,100,000. The difference of €200,000 relates to an item of PP&E with a remaining useful life of 10 years. During the year, B made a profit of €80,000 and paid a dividend of €120,000. B also owned an investment in securities classified as at fair value through OCI that increased in value by €20,000 during the year. For the purposes of the example, any deferred tax implications have been ignored.

A accounts for its investment in B under the equity method as follows:

	€	€
Acquisition date of investment in B		
Share in book value of B's net identifiable assets: 35% of €900,000	315,000	
Share in fair valuation of B's net identifiable assets: 35% of (€1,100,000 – €900,000) *	70,000	
Goodwill on investment in B: €475,000 – €315,000 – €70,000 *	90,000	
Cost of investment		475,000

	€	€
Profit during the year		
Share in the profit reported by B: 35% of €80,000	28,000	
Adjustment to reflect effect of fair valuation * 35% of ((€1,100,000 – €900,000) ÷ 10 years)	(7,000)	
Share of profit in B recognised in income by A		21,000
Revaluation of asset at fair value through OCI		
Share in revaluation recognised in OCI by A: 35% of €20,000		7,000
Dividend received by A during the year		
35% of €120,000		(42,000)
End of the financial year		
Share in book value of B's net assets:		
€315,000 + 35% (€80,000 – €120,000 + €20,000)	308,000	
Share in fair valuation of B's net identifiable assets: €70,000 – €7,000 *	63,000	
Goodwill on investment in B *	90,000	
Closing balance of A's investment in B		461,000

* These line items are normally not presented separately but are combined with the ones immediately above.

IAS 28 explains that equity accounting is necessary because recognising income simply based on distributions received may not be an adequate measure of the income earned by an investor on an investment in an associate or a joint venture, since distributions received may bear little relation to the performance of the associate or joint venture. Through its significant influence over the associate, or joint control of the joint venture, the investor has an interest in the associate's or joint venture's performance and, as a result, the return on its investment. The investor accounts for this interest by extending the scope of its financial statements to include its share of profits or losses of such an investee. As a result, application of the equity method provides more informative reporting of the net assets and profit or loss of the investor. *[IAS 28.11]*.

7.2 Comparison between equity accounting and consolidation

For some time there has been a debate about whether the equity method of accounting is primarily a method of consolidation or a method of valuing an investment, as IAS 28 does not provide specific guidance either way.

An investor that controls a subsidiary has control over the assets and liabilities of that subsidiary. While an investor that has significant influence over an associate or joint control of a joint venture controls its holding in the shares of the associate or joint venture, it does not control the assets and liabilities of that associate or joint venture. Therefore, the investor does not account for the assets and the liabilities of the associate or joint venture, but accounts only for its investment in the associate or joint venture as a whole.

Although the equity method, in accordance with IAS 28, generally adopts consolidation principles, it also has features of a valuation methodology as discussed below.

IAS 28 notes that many procedures appropriate for the application of the equity method and described in more detail at 7.3 to 7.12 below, are similar to the consolidation procedures described in IFRS 10 (see Chapter 7). Furthermore, IAS 28 explains that the concepts underlying the procedures used in accounting for the acquisition of a subsidiary are also adopted in accounting for the acquisition of an investment in an associate or a joint venture. *[IAS 28.26]*. However, it is unclear precisely what these concepts are, as no further explanation is given. The position has been confused even further because in the context of an amendment to IAS 39 – *Financial Instruments: Recognition and Measurement* [now IFRS 9] regarding the application of the exemption in paragraph 2(g) [now paragraph 2.1(f)], it is stated that 'The Board noted that paragraph 20 of IAS 28 [now paragraph 26 of IAS 28] explains only the methodology used to account for investments in associates. This should not be taken to imply that the principles for business combinations and consolidations can be applied by analogy to accounting for investments in associates and joint ventures.' *[IFRS 9.BCZ2.42]*.

The similarities between equity accounting and consolidation include:

- appropriate adjustments to the entity's share of the associate's or joint venture's profits or losses after acquisition are made to account, for example, for depreciation of the depreciable assets based on their fair values at the acquisition date;
- recognising goodwill relating to an associate or a joint venture in the carrying amount of the investment;
- non-amortisation of the goodwill;
- any excess of the investor's share of the net fair value of the associate's identifiable assets and liabilities over the cost of the investment is included as income in the determination of the entity's share of the associate or joint venture's profit or loss in the period in which the investment is acquired;
- the elimination of unrealised profits on 'upstream' and 'downstream' transactions (see 7.6.1 below); and
- application of uniform accounting policies for like transactions.

However, there are also several differences between equity accounting and consolidation, including:

- the investor ceases to recognise its share of losses of an associate or joint venture once the investment has been reduced to zero;
- the treatment of loans and borrowings (including preference shares classified as debt by the investee) between the reporting entity and its associates or joint ventures (see 7.6.3 below);
- the investor cannot capitalise its own borrowing costs in respect of an associate's or joint venture's assets under construction (an equity accounted investment is not a qualifying asset under IAS 23 – *Borrowing Costs* – regardless of the associate's or joint venture's activities or assets); *[IAS 23.BC22]* and
- the investor considers whether there is any additional impairment loss with respect to its net investment.

As there is no clear principle underlying the application of the equity method, different views on how to account for certain transactions for which the standard has no clear guidance might be taken, depending on which principle (i.e. consolidation or valuation of an investment) is deemed to take precedence. We address these issues in the following sections.

7.3 Date of commencement of equity accounting

An investor will begin equity accounting for an associate or a joint venture from the date on which it has obtained significant influence over the associate or joint control over the joint venture (and is not otherwise exempt from equity accounting for it). In most situations, this is when the investor acquires the investment in the associate or joint venture. Determining whether an entity has significant influence is discussed at 4 above.

7.4 Initial carrying amount of an associate or joint venture

Under the equity method, an investment is initially recognised at cost. *[IAS 28.3, 10]*. However, 'cost' for this purpose is not defined.

In July 2009, the Interpretations Committee discussed the lack of definition and issued an agenda decision, clarifying that the cost of an investment in an associate at initial recognition comprises its purchase price and any directly attributable expenditures necessary to obtain it.[3] Therefore, any acquisition-related costs are not expensed (as is the case in a business combination under IFRS 3) but are included as part of the cost of the associate.

The glossary to IFRS defines cost as being the 'amount of cash or cash equivalents paid or the fair value of the other consideration given to acquire an asset at the time of its acquisition or construction ...'.

'Consideration given' is likewise not defined, and therefore we believe that the key sources of guidance in IFRS are:

- 'consideration transferred' in the context of a business combination, as referred to in paragraph 37 of IFRS 3; *[IFRS 3.37]* and
- 'cost' as applied in relation to acquisitions of PP&E in accordance with IAS 16 – *Property, Plant and Equipment*, intangible assets in accordance with IAS 38 – *Intangible Assets* – and investment property in accordance with IAS 40 – *Investment Property*.

Applying the requirements of IFRS 3, the 'consideration transferred' in a business combination comprises the sum of the acquisition-date fair values of assets transferred by the acquirer, liabilities incurred by the acquirer to the former owners of the acquiree, and equity interests issued by the acquirer. This includes any liability (or asset) for contingent consideration, which is measured and recognised at fair value at the acquisition date. Subsequent changes in the measurement of the liability (or asset) are recognised in profit or loss (see Chapter 9 at 7.1).

Consequently, in our view, the same treatment may be applied to contingent consideration arrangements in relation to the purchase of an associate or a joint venture, i.e. the initial carrying amount of an associate or joint venture includes the fair value of any contingent consideration arrangement. In this case, subsequent changes in the contingent consideration would be accounted for under IFRS 9. Further guidance on accounting for contingent consideration when determining the cost of an asset can be found in Chapter 17 at 4.5 and Chapter 18 at 4.1.9.

The considerations regarding applying the cost requirements of other standards have previously been discussed by the Interpretations Committee, and the discussions are summarised in Chapter 8 at 2.1.1.

The Interpretations Committee agenda decision did not provide any specific guidance in relation to a piecemeal acquisition of an associate or a joint venture. This is discussed further at 7.4.2 below.

7.4.1 Initial carrying amount of an associate or joint venture following loss of control of an entity

If a parent entity loses control of a subsidiary that constitutes a business in a transaction that is not a downstream transaction (see 7.6.5 below) and the retained interest is an investment in an associate or joint venture, then the entity must apply paragraph 25 of IFRS 10. The retained interest must be remeasured at its fair value, and this fair value becomes the cost on initial recognition of the investment in an associate or joint venture.

If the subsidiary does not constitute a business, it is not clear whether paragraph 25 of IFRS 10 applies to such a loss of control transaction. Therefore, we believe that an entity can develop an accounting policy either to apply paragraph 25 of IFRS 10 to the loss of control over only those subsidiaries that constitute a business, or to the loss of control over all subsidiaries (i.e. those that constitute a business and those that do not).

Where an entity does not apply paragraph 25 of IFRS 10 to subsidiaries that do not constitute a business, it can apply the guidance in IAS 28 if the loss of control occurs through a downstream transaction discussed at 7.6.5 below. For all other types of transactions, an entity develops an accounting policy in accordance with IAS 8 – *Accounting Policies, Changes in Accounting Estimates and Errors* – on how to account for the retained interest.

Example 11.5: Accounting for retained interest in an associate or joint venture following loss of control of a subsidiary that is a business due to sale of shares to third party

Entity A owns 100% of the shares of Entity B. B meets the definition of a business. The interest was originally purchased for £500,000 and £40,000 of directly attributable costs relating to the acquisition were incurred.

Upon its reporting date, A sells 60% of the shares in B to Entity C for £1,300,000. As a result of the sale, C obtains control over B, but by retaining a 40% interest, A determines that it has significant influence over B.

At the date of disposal, the carrying amount of the net identifiable assets of B in A's consolidated financial statements is £1,200,000 and there is also goodwill of £200,000 relating to the acquisition of B. The fair value of the identifiable assets and liabilities of B is £1,600,000. The fair value of A's retained interest of 40% of the shares of B is £800,000, which includes goodwill.

Upon A's sale of 60% of the shares of B, it deconsolidates B and accounts for its investment in B as an associate using the equity method of accounting.

A's initial carrying amount of the associate must be based on the fair value of the retained interest, i.e. £800,000. It is not based on 40% of the original cost of £540,000 (purchase price plus directly attributable costs) as might be suggested by the Interpretations Committee statement discussed at 7.4 above, nor is it based on 40% of the carrying amount of the net identifiable assets plus goodwill, totalling £1,400,000.

Although it is clear that the initial carrying amount of the associate in the above example is the fair value of the retained interest, i.e. £800,000, does this mean that Entity A in applying the equity method under IAS 28 needs to remeasure the underlying assets and liabilities in Entity B at their fair values at the date Entity B becomes an associate i.e. effectively perform a new purchase price allocation?

In our view, under paragraph 25 of IFRS 10, Entity A effectively accounts for the investment in Entity B as if it had acquired the retained investment at fair value as at the date control is lost and hence should be treated the same as the initial acquisition of an investment in an associate in terms of paragraph 32 of IAS 28 (see 7.4 above). Therefore, the answer to the above question is 'yes'. Accordingly, to apply the equity method from the date control is lost, Entity A must remeasure all the identifiable assets and liabilities underlying the investment at their fair values (or other measurement basis required by IFRS 3 at that date).

This is because IAS 28 indicates that on initial recognition of an investment in an associate, the concepts underlying the procedures used in accounting for the acquisition of a subsidiary are also adopted in accounting for the acquisition of an investment in an associate, and that fair values are applied to measure all the identifiable assets and liabilities in calculating any goodwill or bargain purchase that exists. *[IAS 28.26, 32]*.

Accordingly, in Example 11.5 above, based on the fair value of the identifiable assets and liabilities of Entity B of £1,600,000, Entity A's initial carrying amount of £800,000 will include goodwill of £160,000, being £800,000 – £640,000 (40% of £1,600,000).

The Post-Implementation Review (PIR) of IFRS 13 considered whether the unit of account for investments in subsidiaries, joint ventures and associates was the investment as a whole and not the individual financial instruments that constitute the investment. The PIR has been completed and at its March 2018 meeting, the IASB considered the findings of the PIR and concluded that IFRS 13 is working as intended. Hence no clarification in this regard was made. These issues are discussed further in Chapter 14 at 5.1.1.

7.4.2 Piecemeal acquisition of an associate or joint venture

7.4.2.A Financial instrument becoming an associate or joint venture

An entity may gain significant influence or joint control over an existing investment upon acquisition of a further interest or due to a change in circumstances. IAS 28 is unclear on how an investor should account for an existing investment, accounted for under IFRS 9, that subsequently becomes an associate or a joint venture, to be accounted for under the equity method. In our view there are various approaches available. These are discussed in more detail below.

As discussed at 7.4 above, the Interpretations Committee, in July 2009, clarified that the initial cost of an equity accounted investment comprises the purchase price and directly attributable expenditures necessary to obtain it. Although the implications for the piecemeal acquisition of an associate are not explicitly addressed, it appeared that, since the Interpretations Committee considered that the initial recognition of the associate is to be based on its cost, the accounting should reflect an 'accumulated cost' approach.

However, in July 2010, the Interpretations Committee received a request to address the accounting for an investment in an associate when the investment was purchased in stages and classified as available-for-sale (AFS) in terms of IAS 39 until it became an associate.[4] Interestingly, despite the earlier decision in 2009, the Staff Paper produced for the meeting recommended that 'the fair value of an investment classified as AFS prior to the investor obtaining significant influence over that investment should be the deemed cost of that pre-existing interest at the date the investor obtains significant influence over the associate. The accumulated changes in fair value accounted for in OCI should be reclassified to profit or loss at that date.' The Staff Paper further recommended that such a clarification of IAS 28 be included within the Annual Improvements project.[5] Thus, the Staff was recommending that a 'fair value as deemed cost' approach should be applied.

Although the Staff made these recommendations, it is not entirely clear what the Interpretations Committee made of them. The IFRIC Update following the meeting merely states that the Interpretations Committee discussed at what amount the investment in an associate should be initially measured and the accounting for any accumulated changes in fair value relating to the investment recognised in OCI, at the date significant influence is obtained and the investment is no longer categorised as AFS. However, due to the acknowledged diversity in practice in accounting for associates purchased in stages, the Interpretations Committee recommended that the issue be referred to the IASB for consideration.[6] To date this has not yet been considered by the IASB.

In January 2019, the Interpretations Committee issued an agenda decision regarding the step acquisition of an investment in a subsidiary accounted for at cost in the separate financial statements of the parent. In the request, the initial interest is an equity instrument of another entity and is measured at fair value in accordance with IFRS 9. The Committee concluded that a reasonable reading of the requirements in IFRS Standards could result in the application of either one of the two approaches to determine 'cost': the 'fair value as deemed cost' approach or the 'accumulated cost' approach. These approaches are discussed in more detail below. The Interpretations Committee concluded that, when the accumulated cost approach is applied, any difference between the fair value of the initial interest at the date of obtaining control of the subsidiary and its original consideration meets the definitions of income or expenses in the *Conceptual Framework for Financial Reporting*. Accordingly, applying paragraph 88 of IAS 1 – *Presentation of Financial Statements*, the entity recognises this difference in profit or loss, regardless of whether, before obtaining control, the entity had presented subsequent changes in fair value of the initial interest in profit or loss or in OCI. Even though this agenda decision related specifically to investments in subsidiaries in the separate financial statements of the parent, we believe it is also relevant to step acquisitions of equity accounted associates and joint ventures because paragraph 3 of IAS 28 also requires investments in associates and joint ventures to be measured at cost.[7]

In the light of these statements by the Interpretations Committee, we believe that an entity should account for the step acquisition of an associate or a joint venture by applying either:

(a) an 'accumulated cost' approach; or
(b) a 'fair value as deemed cost' approach.

Once selected, the investor must apply the selected policy consistently.

I   Applying an accumulated cost approach

Where an accumulated cost approach is applied to account for a step acquisition of an associate or a joint venture, this involves the determination of:

(a) the cost of the investment;
(b) whether or not any catch-up adjustment is required when first applying equity accounting (i.e. an adjustment for the share of investee's profits and other equity movements as if the previously held interest were equity accounted); and
(c) the goodwill implicit in the investment (or gain on bargain purchase).

Not all these aspects of the accounting for a piecemeal acquisition of an associate or a joint venture were addressed by the Interpretations Committee agenda decisions in 2009 and 2019. Accordingly, in our view, the combination of answers to these questions results in four possible accumulated cost approaches that may be applied to account for a step acquisition of an associate or a joint venture where a cost-based approach is adopted. Once selected, the investor must apply the selected policy consistently.

In all accumulated cost approaches, cost is the sum of the consideration given for each tranche together with any directly attributable costs. However, because of the answers to (b) and (c) above, the four accumulated cost approaches are as follows:

	Catch-up equity accounting adjustment for previously held interest	Determination of goodwill/gain on bargain purchase
Approach 1	None	Difference between sum of the consideration and share of fair value of net identifiable assets at date investment becomes an associate or joint venture
Approach 2	None	
Approach 3	For profits (less dividends), and changes in OCI	Difference between the cost of each tranche and the share of fair value of net identifiable assets acquired in each tranche
Approach 4	For profits (less dividends), changes in OCI and changes in fair value of net assets	

The basis for using the above accumulated cost approaches can be set out as follows. The explanations below assume that the piecemeal acquisition has occurred in two tranches; the second resulting in the entity obtaining significant influence. Where an entity purchases multiple tranches prior to obtaining significant influence, references below to the 'first tranche' should be read as applying to all tranches prior to obtaining significant influence.

Approach 1

Paragraph 32 of IAS 28 states that an investment is accounted for using the equity method 'from the date on which it becomes an associate or a joint venture.' Recognising any catch-up adjustments may be interpreted as a form of equity accounting for a period prior to gaining significant influence, which contradicts this principle of IAS 28.

Paragraph 32 of IAS 28 (see 7.1 above) also goes on to state that any notional goodwill or gain on a bargain purchase is determined 'on acquisition of the investment'. However, paragraph 32 of IAS 28 does not specify on which date the fair values of the net identifiable assets are to be determined. It may be interpreted to mean only at the date that the investment becomes an associate or a joint venture. This is also consistent with the approach in IFRS 3, whereby the underlying fair values of net identifiable assets are only determined at one time, rather than determining them several times for individual transactions leading to the change in the economic event.

Approach 2

No catch-up adjustment is recognised, similarly to the reasons noted in Approach 1.

Paragraph 32 of IAS 28 is interpreted to mean that the fair values of the associate's or joint venture's net identifiable assets are determined at a date that corresponds to the date at which consideration was given. Therefore, the fair values are determined for each tranche. This may require the fair values to be determined for previous periods when no such exercise was performed at the date of the original purchase.

Approach 3

A catch-up adjustment is recognised to reflect the application of the equity method as described in paragraph 10 of IAS 28 (see 7.1 above), with respect to the first tranche. However, the application of that paragraph restricts the adjustment to only the share of profits (less dividends) and OCI relating to the first tranche. That is, there is no catch-up adjustment made for changes in the fair value of the net identifiable assets not recognised by the investee (except for any adjustments necessary to give effect to uniform accounting policies).

The reading of paragraph 32 is the same as for Approach 2.

Approach 4

This approach is based on the underlying philosophy of equity accounting, which is to reflect the investor's share of the underlying net identifiable assets plus goodwill inherent in the purchase price. Therefore, where the investment was acquired in tranches, a catch-up adjustment is necessary to apply equity accounting from the date the investment becomes an associate or a joint venture as required by paragraph 32 of IAS 28. The catch-up adjustment reflects not only the post-acquisition share of profits and OCI relating to the first tranche, but also the share of the unrecognised fair value adjustments based on the fair values at the date of becoming an associate or a joint venture.

The reading of paragraph 32 is the same as for Approach 2.

The above four accumulated cost approaches are illustrated in Example 11.6. Although the example illustrates the step-acquisition of an associate, the accounting would be the same if the transaction had resulted in the step-acquisition of a joint venture.

Chapter 11

Example 11.6: *Accounting for existing financial instruments on the step-acquisition of an associate (cost-based approach)*

An investor acquired a 10% interest in an investee for $100 on 1 January 2018. Three years later, on 1 January 2021, the investor acquired a further 15% interest in the investee for $225. The investor now holds a 25% interest and can exercise significant influence. For the purposes of the example, directly attributable costs have been ignored. Also, any deferred tax implications have been ignored.

The investor had been accounting for its initial 10% interest at fair value in accordance with IFRS 9. The financial information relating to the investee can be summarised as follows:

	2018		2021	
	100%	10%	100%	15%
	$	$	$	$
Purchase consideration		100		225
Change in fair value		50		
Fair value of shares at 31 December 2018		150		
At 1 January:				
Book value of net identifiable assets of investee	600		900	
Fair value of net identifiable assets of investee *)	800	80	1,200	180
From 1 January 2018 to 1 January 2021:				
Profit	500	50		
Dividends declared	(200)	(20)		
Increase in fair value of net identifiable assets of investee	400	40		
Cost plus post-acquisition changes in net identifiable assets		130		
Other changes in fair value of the investee		10		

*) The fair value uplift from $600 to $800 relates entirely to non-depreciable assets.

The accounting for this step-acquisition under each of the accumulated cost approaches is as follows (all amounts in $):

	Catch-up equity accounting adjustment	Initial equity accounted amount	Goodwill in initial amount of associate
Approach 1	0	100 + 225 = 325	Consideration less share of fair value of net identifiable assets at time investment becomes an associate 325 − (25% × 1200) = 25
Approach 2	0	100 + 225 = 325	Cost less share of fair value of net identifiable assets at each tranche 100 − (10% × 800) = 20 + 225 − (15% × 1200) = 45 Total = 65
Approach 3	10% of profits (less dividends) 10% × (500 − 200) = 30	325 + 30 = 355	
Approach 4	10% of profits (less dividends) and changes in fair value of assets 10% × (500 − 200 + 400) = 70	325 + 70 = 395	

The result in both the separate and consolidated financial statements is as follows:

Cost of investment

In all four accumulated cost approaches, the difference between the fair value of the original 10% of $150 and the cost of the first tranche of $100 is adjusted against profit or loss to bring the asset back to its original cost.

The investor continues to recognise dividend income in the statement of comprehensive income (in profit or loss) up to the date the entity becomes an associate, irrespective of whether the investor measures the investment at fair value through profit or loss or at fair value through OCI.

Catch-up adjustment

For the accumulated cost approaches 3 and 4, the 'catch-up' equity accounting adjustment relating to the first tranche is recognised against the appropriate balance within equity – that is, retained earnings, or other equity reserve. To the extent that they are recognised, these will be reflected in OCI in the statement of comprehensive income.

II   Applying a fair value as deemed cost approach

Where a fair value as deemed cost approach is applied to accounting for a step acquisition of an associate or a joint venture, the fair value of the previously held interest at the date that significant influence or joint control is obtained is deemed to be the cost for the initial application of equity accounting. Since the investment would already be measured at fair value under IFRS 9, there is no further change to its carrying value. If the investment had been accounted for at fair value through OCI under IFRS 9, amounts accumulated in equity are not reclassified to profit or loss at the date that significant influence is gained, although the cumulative gain or loss may be transferred within equity. [IFRS 9.5.2.1, 5.7.5, B5.7.1, B5.7.3]. If the investment had been accounted for at fair value through profit or loss, any changes from original cost would already be reflected in profit or loss.

Consistent with the guidance in IFRS 3 for acquisitions achieved in stages, the calculation of goodwill at the date the investor obtains significant influence or joint control is made only at that date, using information available at that date.

This fair value as deemed cost approach is illustrated in Example 11.7 below. Although the example illustrates the step-acquisition of an associate, the accounting would be the same if the transaction had resulted in the step-acquisition of a joint venture.

Example 11.7:   Accounting for existing financial instruments on the step-acquisition of an associate (fair value (IFRS 3) approach)

Using the same information as in Example 11.6 above, under a fair value as deemed cost approach to acquisitions in stages, in the consolidated financial statements of the investor, the fair value of the 10% existing interest would be deemed to be part of the cost for the initial application of equity accounting. The 10% existing interest was effectively revalued through profit or loss to $150 if the investor measured the original investment at fair value through profit or loss. If the investor measured the original investment at fair value through OCI, any amount in OCI relating to this interest may be reclassified within equity. Goodwill is calculated as the difference between $375 (the fair value of the existing 10% interest and the cost of the additional 15% interest) and $300 (25% of the fair value of net identifiable assets at the date significant influence is attained of $1,200).

It should be noted that the methodology illustrated in Example 11.7 above is, in fact, consistent with the accounting that is required by IAS 28 in the reverse situation i.e. when there is a loss of significant influence in an associate (or loss of joint control in a joint venture), resulting in the discontinuance of the equity method (see 7.12.3 below).

7.4.2.B   Step increase in an existing associate or joint venture without a change in status of the investee

An entity may acquire an additional interest in an existing associate that continues to be an associate accounted for under the equity method. Similarly, an entity may acquire an additional interest in an existing joint venture that continues to be a joint venture accounted for under the equity method. IAS 28 does not explicitly deal with such transactions.

In these situations, we believe that the purchase price paid for the additional interest is added to the existing carrying amount of the associate or the joint venture and the existing interest in the associate or joint venture is not remeasured.

This increase in the investment must still be split notionally between goodwill and the additional interest in the fair value of the net identifiable assets of the associate or joint venture. This split is based on the fair value of the net identifiable assets at the date of the increase in the associate or joint venture. However, no remeasurement is made for previously unrecognised changes in the fair values of net identifiable assets.

The reasons for using the above treatment are discussed further below and the treatment is illustrated in Example 11.8. This differs from the treatment required by IFRS 3 when an increased investment in an associate or joint venture results in the investor obtaining control over the investee.

IFRS 3 is clear that when an entity acquires an additional interest in an existing associate or joint venture that gives it control, the entity is required to revalue the previously held interest in that investment and any gain or loss is recognised in profit or loss. *[IFRS 3.41-42]*. This treatment reflects the significant change in the nature of, and economic circumstances surrounding, that investment, which therefore warrants a change in the classification and measurement of that investment. *[IFRS 3.BC384]*.

By contrast. when an investor increases its ownership interest in an existing associate or joint venture and that investment's classification remains unchanged, there is no significant change in the nature and economic circumstances of the investment. Hence, there is no justification for remeasurement of the existing ownership interest at the time of the increase. Rather the investor applies an accumulated cost approach equivalent to Approach 2 discussed at 7.4.2.A above, i.e. the purchase price paid for the additional interest is added to the existing carrying amount of the associate or joint venture and the existing interest in the associate or joint venture is not remeasured.

Paragraph 32 of IAS 28 establishes the requirement that the cost of an investment in an associate or joint venture is allocated between the share of the fair value of net identifiable assets and the goodwill. This requirement is not limited to the initial application of equity accounting but applies to each acquisition of an investment. However, this does not result in any revaluation of the existing share of net assets.

Rather, the existing ownership interests are accounted for under paragraphs 10 and 32 of IAS 28, whereby the carrying value is adjusted only for the investor's share of the associate or joint venture's profits or losses and other recognised equity transactions. No entry is recognised to reflect changes in the fair value of assets and liabilities that are not recognised under the accounting policies applied for the associate or joint venture.

Although Example 11.8 below illustrates an increase in ownership of an associate that continues to be an associate, the accounting would be the same if the transaction had been an increase in ownership of a joint venture.

Example 11.8:   Accounting for an increase in the ownership of an associate

Entity A obtains significant influence over Entity B by acquiring an investment of 25% at a cost of £3,000. At the date of the acquisition, the fair value of the associate's net identifiable assets is £10,000. The investment is accounted for under the equity method in the consolidated financial statements of A.

Two years later, A acquires an additional investment of 20% in B at a cost of £4,000, increasing its total investment in B to 45%. The investment is, however, still an associate and still accounted for using the equity method of accounting.

For the purposes of the example, directly attributable costs have been ignored and it is assumed that no profit or loss arose during the period since the acquisition of the first 25%. Therefore, the carrying amount of the investment immediately prior to the additional investment is £3,000. However, an asset held by the associate has increased in value by £5,000 so that the fair value of the associate's net identifiable assets is now £15,000.

To summarise, amounts are as follows:

	£
Fair value of net identifiable assets of Entity B at acquisition	10,000
Increase in fair value	5,000
Fair value of net identifiable assets of Entity B two years later	15,000

Because of the additional investment, the equity-accounted amount for the associate increases by £4,000. The notional goodwill applicable to the second tranche of the acquisition is £1,000 [£4,000 − (20% × £15,000)].

The impact of the additional investment on A's equity-accounted amount for B is summarised as follows:

	% held	Carrying amount	Share of net identifiable assets	Goodwill included in investment
		£	£	£
Existing investment	25	3,000	2,500	500
Additional investment	20	4,000	3,000	1,000
Total investment	45	7,000	5,500	1,500

The accounting described above applies when the additional interest in an existing associate (or joint venture) continues to be accounted for as an associate (or joint venture) under the equity method. The accounting for an increase in an associate or a joint venture that becomes a subsidiary is discussed in Chapter 9 at 9.

7.4.2.C Existing associate that becomes a joint venture, or vice versa

In the situations discussed at 7.4.2.B above, the acquisition of the additional interests did not result in a change in status of the investee, i.e. the associate remained an associate or the joint venture remained a joint venture. However, an associate may become a joint venture, either by the acquisition of an additional interest, or through a contractual agreement that gives the investor joint control. Equally, in some situations, a contractual agreement may end, or part of an interest may be disposed of and a joint venture becomes an associate. In all these situations, IAS 28 requires that the entity continues to apply the equity method and does not remeasure the retained interest. *[IAS 28.24]*. Therefore, the accounting described in Example 11.8 above would apply.

7.4.2.D Common control transactions involving sales of associates

We believe there are two possible approaches for the accounting by an acquirer/investor applying the equity method when it acquires an investment in an associate from an entity that is under common control. This is because IFRS 3 and IAS 28 are not clear. Therefore, there is an interpretation of whether, and how, to apply IFRS 3 principles to investments in associates. An entity accounts for such transactions using a consistent accounting policy. This is discussed further in Chapter 10 at 5.

7.5 Share of the investee

7.5.1 Accounting for potential voting rights

In applying the equity method to a single investment of a specified number of ordinary shares of the investee, the proportionate share of the associate or joint venture to be accounted for will be based on the investor's ownership interest in the ordinary shares.

This will also generally be the case when potential voting rights or other derivatives containing potential voting rights exist in addition to the single investment in the ordinary shares, since IAS 28 states that an entity's interest in an associate or a joint venture is determined solely based on existing ownership interests and does not reflect the possible exercise or conversion of potential voting rights and other derivative instruments. *[IAS 28.12]*.

However, as an exception to this, IAS 28 recognises that in some circumstances, an entity has, in substance, an existing ownership interest because of a transaction that currently gives it access to the returns associated with an ownership interest. In such circumstances, the proportion allocated to the entity is determined by considering the eventual exercise of those potential voting rights and other derivative instruments that currently give the entity access to the returns. *[IAS 28.13]*. The standard does not provide any example of such circumstances, but an example might be a presently exercisable option over shares in the investee at a fixed price combined with the right to veto any distribution by the investee before the option is exercised or combined with features that adjust the exercise price with respect to dividends paid.

IFRS 9 does not apply to interests in associates and joint ventures that are accounted for using the equity method. When instruments containing potential voting rights in substance currently give access to the returns associated with an ownership interest in an associate or a joint venture, the instruments are not subject to IFRS 9. In all other cases, instruments containing potential voting rights in an associate or a joint venture are accounted for in accordance with IFRS 9. *[IAS 28.14]*. Once the potential voting rights are exercised and the share in the investee increases, the fair value of such instruments at the exercise date is part of the cost to be recognised in accounting for the step increase (see 7.4.2 above).

7.5.2 Cumulative preference shares held by parties other than the investor

If an associate or joint venture has outstanding cumulative preference shares that are held by parties other than the investor and that are classified as equity, the investor computes its share of profits or losses after adjusting for the dividends on such shares, whether or not the dividends have been declared. *[IAS 28.37]*.

Although Example 11.9 below illustrates cumulative preference shares issued by an associate, the accounting would be the same if the shares were issued by a joint venture.

Example 11.9: Cumulative preference shares issued by an associate

An entity holds an investment of 30% in the ordinary shares of an associate that has net assets of £200,000 and net profit for the year of £24,500. The associate has issued 5,000 cumulative preference shares with a nominal value of £10 which entitle its holders to a 9% cumulative preference dividend. The cumulative preference shares are classified by the associate as equity in accordance with the requirements of IAS 32 – *Financial Instruments: Presentation.* The associate has not declared dividends on the cumulative preference shares in the past two years.

The investor calculates its share of the associate's net assets and net profit as follows:

	£
Net assets	200,000
9% Cumulative preference shares	(50,000)
Undeclared dividend on cumulative preference shares	
2 years × 9% × £50,000 =	(9,000)
Net assets value attributable to ordinary shareholders	141,000
Investor's 30% share of the net assets	42,300
Net profit for the year	24,500
Share of profit of holders of cumulative preference shares	
9% of £50,000 =	(4,500)
Net profit attributable to ordinary shareholders	20,000
Investor's 30% share of the net profit	6,000

If the investor also owned all the cumulative preference shares, then it would assess whether those preference shares are accounted for under IFRS 9 or IAS 28 (see 7.5.1 above). Assuming that the preference shares are accounted for under IAS 28, the investor's share in the net assets of the associate would be £42,300 + £50,000 + £9,000 = £101,300. Its share in the net profit would be £6,000 + £4,500 = £10,500.

7.5.3 Several classes of equity

When an associate or joint venture has a complicated equity structure with several classes of equity shares that have varying entitlements to net profits, equity or liquidation preferences, the investor needs to assess carefully the rights attaching to each class of equity share in determining the appropriate percentage of ownership interest.

7.5.4 Where the reporting entity is a group

A group's share in an associate or joint venture is the aggregate of the holdings in that associate or joint venture by the parent and its subsidiaries. The holdings of the group's other associates or joint ventures are ignored for this purpose. *[IAS 28.27]*. Example 11.10 below illustrates the group's share in an associate where investments are also held by other entities in the group.

Example 11.10: **Share in an associate or a joint venture where the reporting entity is a group**

Parent A holds a 100% investment in Subsidiary B, which in turn holds a 25% investment in Associate Z. In addition, A also holds a 30% investment in Associate C and a 50% investment in Joint Venture D, each of which holds a 10% investment in Z.

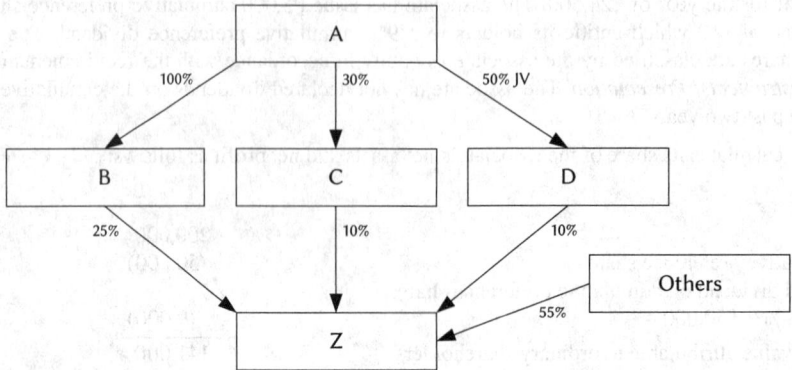

In its consolidated financial statements, A accounts for a 25% investment in Z under the equity method because:

- the investments in Z held by C and D should not be considered; and
- A consolidates the assets of B, which include a 25% investment in Z.

7.5.5 Where the investee is a group: non-controlling interests in an associate's or joint venture's consolidated financial statements

When an associate or joint venture itself has subsidiaries, the profits or losses, OCI and net assets considered in applying the equity method are those recognised in the associate's or joint venture's consolidated financial statements, but after any adjustments necessary to give effect to uniform accounting policies (see 7.8 below). *[IAS 28.27]*.

It may be that the associate or joint venture does not own all the shares in some of its subsidiaries, in which case its consolidated financial statements will include non-controlling interests (NCI). Under IFRS 10, any NCI are presented in the consolidated statement of financial position within equity, separately from the equity of the owners of the parent. Profit or loss and each component of OCI are attributed to the owners of the parent and to the NCI. *[IFRS 10.22, B94]*. The profit or loss and OCI reported in the associate or joint venture's consolidated financial statements will include 100% of the amounts relating to the subsidiaries, but the overall profit or loss and total comprehensive income will be split between the amounts attributable to the owners of the parent (i.e. the associate or joint venture) and those attributable to the NCI. The net assets in the consolidated statement of financial position will also include 100% of the amounts relating to the subsidiaries, with any NCI in the net assets presented in the consolidated statement of financial position within equity, separately from the equity of the owners of the parent.

IAS 28 does not explicitly say whether the investor should base the accounting for its share of the associate's or joint venture's profits, OCI and net assets under the equity method on the amounts before or after any NCI in the associate's or joint venture's consolidated accounts. However, as the investor's interest in the associate or joint venture is as an owner of the parent, the share is based on the profit or loss, comprehensive income and equity (net assets) that are reported as being attributable to the owners of the parent in the associate's or joint venture's consolidated financial statements, i.e. after any amounts attributable to the NCI. This is consistent with the implementation guidance to IAS 1, where it is indicated that the amounts disclosed for 'share of profits of associates' and 'share of other comprehensive income of associates' represent the amounts 'attributable to owners of the associates, i.e. it is after tax and non-controlling interests in the associates'.[8]

7.6 Transactions between the reporting entity and its associates or joint ventures

7.6.1 Elimination of 'upstream' and 'downstream' transactions

IAS 28 requires gains and losses resulting from what it refers to as 'upstream' and 'downstream' transactions between an entity (including its consolidated subsidiaries) and its associate or joint venture to be recognised in the entity's financial statements only to the extent of unrelated investors' interests in the associate or joint venture. 'Upstream' transactions are, for example, sales of assets from an associate or a joint venture to the investor. 'Downstream' transactions are, for example, sales or contributions of assets from the investor to its associate or its joint venture. The investor's share in the associate's or joint venture's gains or losses resulting from these transactions is eliminated. *[IAS 28.28]*.

IAS 28 is not entirely clear as to how this very generally expressed requirement translates into accounting entries, but we suggest that an appropriate approach is as follows:

- in the income statement, the adjustment is taken against either the investor's profit or the share of the associate's or joint venture's profit, whichever is the entity that recorded the profit on the transaction; and
- in the statement of financial position, the adjustment should be made against the asset which was the subject of the transaction if it is held by the investor or against the carrying amount of the associate or joint venture if the asset is held by the associate or joint venture.

This is consistent with the approach required by IAS 28 in dealing with the elimination of unrealised gains and losses arising on contributions of non-monetary assets to an associate or joint venture in exchange for an equity interest in the associate or joint venture (see 7.6.5 below).

Examples 11.11 and 11.12 below illustrate our suggested approach to this requirement of IAS 28. Both examples deal with the reporting entity H and its 40% associate A. The journal entries are based on the premise that H's financial statements are initially prepared as a simple aggregation of H and the relevant share of its associates. It is further assumed that prior period equity accounting journal entries are not carried forward to the next reporting period. The entries below would then be applied to the numbers at that stage of the process. Although these examples illustrate transactions between the reporting entity and an associate, the accounting would be the same if the transactions occurred between the reporting entity and a joint venture.

Example 11.11: Elimination of profit on sale by investor to associate ('downstream transaction')

One month before its reporting date, Entity H sells inventory costing £750,000 to Associate A for £1 million. Within the first month after the reporting date, A sells the inventory to a third party for £1.2 million. What adjustments are made in the group financial statements of H before and after the reporting date?

Before the reporting date, H has recorded revenue of £1 million and cost of sales of £750,000. However since, at the reporting date, the inventory is still held by A, only 60% of this transaction is regarded by IAS 28 as having taken place (in effect with the other shareholders of A). This is reflected by the equity accounting entry:

	£	£
Revenue	400,000	
Cost of sales		300,000
Investment in A		100,000

This effectively defers recognition of 40% of the profit on sale (£250,000 × 40%) and offsets the deferred profit against the carrying amount of H's investment in A.

After the reporting date, when the inventory is sold on by A, this deferred profit can be released by H, reflected by the following equity accounting entry:

	£	£
Opening reserves	100,000	
Cost of sales	300,000	
Revenue		400,000

Opening reserves are adjusted because the financial statement working papers (if prepared as assumed that no equity accounting journal entries are carried forward) will already include this profit in opening reserves, since it forms part of H's opening reserves.

An alternative approach would be to eliminate the profit on 40% of the sale against the cost of sales. Before the reporting date, this is reflected by the equity accounting entry:

	£	£
Cost of sales	100,000	
Investment in A		100,000

After the reporting date, when the inventory is sold on by A, this deferred profit can be released by H, reflected by the following equity accounting entry:

	£	£
Opening reserves	100,000	
Cost of sales		100,000

An argument in favour of the alternative approach is that the revenue figures should not be adjusted because the sales to associates or joint ventures need to be disclosed as related party transactions. However, this may be outweighed by the drawback of the approach, namely that it causes volatility in H's reported gross margin as revenue and the related net margin are not necessarily recognised in the same accounting period.

Example 11.12: Elimination of profit on sale by associate to reporting entity ('upstream transaction')

This is the mirror image of the transaction in Example 11.11 above. Before H's reporting date, A sells inventory costing £750,000 to H for £1,000,000. After the reporting date, H sells the inventory to a third party for £1.2 million. What adjustments are made in the group financial statements of H before and after the reporting date?

H's share of the profit of A as included on the financial statement working papers before the reporting date will include a profit of £250,000 (£1,000,000 – £750,000), 40% of which (£100,000) is regarded under IAS 28 as unrealised by H, and is therefore deferred and offset against closing inventory:

	£	£
Share of profit of A	100,000	
Inventory		100,000

In the following period when the inventory is sold H's separate financial statements will record a profit of £200,000, which must be increased by the £100,000 deferred from the previous period. The entry is:

	£	£
Opening reserves	100,000	
Share of profit of A		100,000

Again, opening reserves are adjusted because the financial statement working papers (if prepared as assumed above) will already include this profit in opening reserves, this time, however, as part of H's share of the opening reserves of A.

A slightly counter-intuitive consequence of this treatment is that, at the reporting date, the investment in A in H's consolidated statement of financial position will have increased by £100,000 more than the share of profit of associates as reported in group profit or loss (and in the following period by £100,000 less). This is because the statement of financial position adjustment at the reporting date is made against inventory rather than the carrying value of the investment in A, which could be reflecting the fact that A has, indeed, made a profit. It might therefore be necessary to indicate in the notes to the financial statements that part of the profit made by A is regarded as unrealised by the group and has therefore been deferred to the following reporting period by offsetting it against inventory.

It may be that a transaction between an investor and its associate or joint venture indicates a reduction in the net realisable value or an impairment loss of the asset that is the subject of the transaction. IAS 28 requires that when downstream transactions provide evidence of a reduction in the net realisable value of the assets to be sold or contributed, or of an impairment loss of those assets, those losses shall be recognised in full by the investor. When upstream transactions provide evidence of a reduction in the net realisable value of the assets to be purchased or of an impairment loss of those assets, the investor shall recognise its share in those losses. *[IAS 28.29]*.

The effect of these requirements is illustrated in Examples 11.13 and 11.14 below. Although these examples illustrate transactions between the reporting entity and a joint venture, the accounting would be the same if the transactions occurred between the reporting entity and an associate.

Example 11.13: Sale of asset from venturer to joint venture at a loss

Two entities A and B establish Joint Venture C in which A and B each hold 50%. A and B each contribute €5 million in cash to C in exchange for equity shares. C then uses €8 million of its €10 million cash to acquire from A a property recorded in the financial statements of A at €10 million. €8 million is agreed to be the fair market value of the property. How should A account for these transactions?

The required accounting entry by A is as follows:

	€m	€m
Cash (1)	3	
Investment in C (2)	5	
Loss on sale (3)	2	
Property (4)		10

(1) €8 million received from C less €5 million contributed to C.

(2) Represented by 50% of C's cash €2 million (€10 million from A and B minus €8 million to A), plus 50% of €8 million (carrying value of the property in books of C).

(3) Loss on sale of property €2 million (€8 million received from C less €10 million carrying value = €2 million) not adjusted since the transaction indicated an impairment of the property. In effect, it is the result that would have been obtained if A had recognised an impairment charge immediately prior to the sale and then recognised no gain or loss on the sale.

(4) Derecognition of A's original property.

Example 11.14: Sale of asset from joint venture to venturer at a loss

On 1 January 2021, two entities A and B establish Joint Venture C in which A and B each hold 50%. A and B each contribute €5 million in cash to C in exchange for equity shares. C then uses €8 million of its €10 million cash to acquire a property from an independent third-party D. Property prices fall during 2021 and on 31 December 2021, the property is sold to A for €7 million settled in cash, which is agreed to be its market value. How should A account for these transactions in its financial statements for the year ended 31 December 2021?

The required accounting entry by A is as follows:

	€m	€m
Property (1)	7.0	
Investment in C (2)	4.5	
Share of loss of C (3)	0.5	
Cash (4)		12.0

(1) €7 million paid to C.

(2) Represented by 50% of C's cash €9 million (€10 million from A and B minus €8 million to D plus €7 million received from A).

(3) Loss in C's books is €1 million (€8 million cost of property less €7 million proceeds of sale). A recognises its 50% share because the transaction indicates an impairment of the asset. In effect, it is the result that would have been obtained if C had recognised an impairment charge immediately prior to the sale and then recognised no gain or loss on the sale.

(4) €5 million cash contributed to C plus €7 million consideration for property.

7.6.1.A   Elimination of 'downstream' unrealised profits in excess of the investment

Occasionally an investor's share of the unrealised profit on the sale of an asset to an associate or a joint venture exceeds the carrying value of the investment held. In that case, to what extent is any profit in excess of the carrying value of the investment eliminated?

IAS 28 is unclear about the elimination of 'downstream' unrealised gains in excess of the investment. Consequently, the Interpretations Committee received a request asking for clarification of the accounting treatment when the amount of gains to eliminate in a 'downstream' transaction in accordance with paragraph 28 of IAS 28 exceeds the amount of the entity's interest in the joint venture. The request specifically asked whether:

- the gain from the transaction should be eliminated only to the extent that it does not exceed the carrying amount of the entity's interest in the joint venture; or
- the remaining gain in excess of the carrying amount of the entity's interest in the joint venture should also be eliminated and if so, what it should be eliminated against.

The Interpretations Committee determined that the entity should eliminate the gain from a 'downstream' transaction to the extent of the related investor's interest in the joint venture, even if the gain to be eliminated exceeds the carrying amount of the entity's interest in the joint venture, as required by paragraph 28 of IAS 28. Any eliminated gain that is in excess of the carrying amount of the entity's interest in the joint venture should be recognised as deferred income.[9] In July 2013, the IASB tentatively agreed with the views of the Interpretations Committee and directed the staff to draft amendments to IAS 28.[10] However, in June 2015, the IASB tentatively decided to defer further work on this topic to the equity accounting research project. This is discussed further at 11 below.

Considering the absence of guidance in IAS 28, we believe that, until the IASB issues an amendment to IAS 28, the investor can either recognise the excess as 'deferred income' or restrict the elimination to the amount required to reduce the investment to zero. The treatment chosen is based on the investor's accounting policy choice for dealing with other situations where IAS 28 is unclear, reflecting whether the investor considers the equity method of accounting to be primarily a method of consolidation (which would be consistent with recognition of the excess as deferred income) or a method of valuing an investment (which would be consistent with restricting the elimination to the amount that reduces the investment to zero). The investor should apply a consistent accounting policy to such situations.

Example 11.15:   Elimination of downstream unrealised profits in excess of the investment

An investor has a 40% investment in an associate, which it carries in its statement of financial position at €800,000. The investor sells a property to the associate in exchange for cash, which results in a profit of €3 million. After the sale, 40% of that profit (i.e. €1.2 million) is unrealised from the investor's perspective. It is assumed that the requirements for determining when a performance obligation is satisfied in IFRS 15 – *Revenue from Contracts with Customers* – have been met.

The two approaches for determining to what extent a profit in excess of the carrying value of the investment should be eliminated are as follows:

Method of consolidation approach – excess of the unrealised profit over the carrying value of the investment recognised as 'deferred income'

This approach gives precedence to the requirements in paragraph 26 of IAS 28, which is also consistent with the general requirement to apply IFRS 10 consolidation elimination principles. *[IAS 28.26]*. Although paragraph 38 of IAS 28 requires an investor to discontinue application of the equity method when an investor's share of losses equals or exceeds its interest in the associate (see 7.9 below), *[IAS 28.38]*, the elimination does not represent a real 'loss' to the investor but is simply the non-recognition of a gain because of normal consolidation principles. Therefore, paragraph 38 of IAS 28 is subordinate to the requirement to eliminate unrealised profits.

Accordingly, the investor eliminates the investor's total share of the unrealised profit against the carrying amount of the investment in the associate until reaching zero, recognising the excess as a 'deferred income' or similar balance, as follows:

	€	€
Profit on sale of property	1,200,000	
Investment in associate		800,000
'Deferred income'		400,000

This leaves a net profit of €1.8 million recognised in the consolidated financial statements. The investor recognises deferred income as the asset or the investment in the associate is realised (e.g. upon disposal of the investor's investment in the associate, or upon the disposal or depreciation of the asset by the associate).

Method of valuing investment approach – restricts the elimination to the amount required to reduce the investment to zero

This approach views the requirements of paragraph 38 of IAS 28 as taking precedence over the requirements of paragraph 28 of IAS 28 to eliminate unrealised profits from a transaction between the investor and the associate. The elimination of the full amount of the share of unrealised profit effectively results in the recognition of a 'loss' to the investor. Furthermore, by deferring the 'loss', the investor is effectively recognising a negative investment balance, which is not permitted or required under IAS 28 when the investor does not have any further legal or constructive obligations in relation to the asset or the associate.

Accordingly, if the investor does not have any further legal or constructive obligations in relation to the asset or the associate, no liability exists, and no further profit is deferred. The investor eliminates the unrealised profit to the extent that it reduces the carrying value of the investment to zero, as follows:

	€	€
Profit on sale of property	800,000	
Investment in associate		800,000

This leaves a net profit of €2.2 million recognised in the consolidated financial statements. The investor does not recognise further profits in the associate until they exceed the unrecognised unrealised profits of €400,000.

7.6.1.B Transactions between associates and/or joint ventures

When transactions take place between associates and/or joint ventures, which are accounted for under the equity method, we believe the investor should apply the requirements of IAS 28 and IFRS 10 by analogy and eliminate its share of any unrealised profits or losses. *[IAS 28.26, 29, IFRS 10.B86]*.

Example 11.16: **Elimination of profits and losses resulting from transactions between associates and/or joint ventures**

Entity H has a 25% interest in Associate A and a 30% interest in Joint Venture B.

During the reporting period, A sold inventory costing £1.0 million to B for £1.2 million. All of the inventory remains on B's statement of financial position at the end of the reporting period.

H eliminates £15,000 (i.e. 30% × 25% × £200,000) as its share of the profits that is unrealised.

Although paragraph 28 of IAS 28 refers only to upstream and downstream transactions between an investor and its associate or its joint venture, we consider this to be an illustration of the typical transactions to be eliminated as a result of the requirements of paragraph 26 of IAS 28 which says that 'Many of the procedures that are appropriate for the application of the equity method are similar to the consolidation procedures described in IFRS 10', and are not the only situations to be eliminated by this principle. Therefore, applying the same principles in paragraph 28 of IAS 28 and paragraph B86 of IFRS 10, the unrealised profit in the investor's financial statements arising from any transaction between the associates (and/or joint ventures) is eliminated to the extent of the related investor's interests in the associates (and/or joint ventures) as appropriate.

In practice, however, it may be difficult to determine whether such transactions have taken place.

7.6.2 Reciprocal interests

Reciprocal interests (or 'cross-holdings') arise when an associate itself holds an investment in the reporting entity. It is unlikely that a joint venture would hold an investment in the reporting entity but, if it did, the discussion below would apply equally to that situation.

7.6.2.A Reciprocal interests in reporting entity accounted for under the equity method by the associate

Where the associate's investment in the reporting entity is such that the associate in turn has significant influence over the reporting entity and accounts for that investment under the equity method, a literal interpretation of paragraph 27 of IAS 28 is that an investor records its share of an associate's profits and net assets, including the associate's equity accounted profits and net assets of its investment in the investor. The reciprocal interests can therefore give rise to a measure of double counting of profits and net assets between the investor and its associate. Paragraph 26 of IAS 28 states that many of the procedures appropriate for the application of the equity method are similar to the consolidation procedures described in IFRS 10. Therefore, the requirement in paragraph B86 of IFRS 10 to eliminate intragroup balances, transactions, income and expenses should be applied by analogy. *[IAS 28.26, IFRS 10.B86]*.

Neither IFRS 10 nor IAS 28 explains how an entity should go about eliminating the double counting that arises from reciprocal holdings. We believe that a direct holding only (or net approach) is applicable, whereby the profit of the investor is calculated by adding its direct investment in the associate to its trading profits, as shown in Example 11.17.

Example 11.17: Elimination of equity-accounted reciprocal interests

Entity A has a 40% equity interest in Entity B and conversely, B has a 30% interest in A. How should A and B account for their reciprocal investment?

The structure of the reciprocal holdings is shown in the diagram below:

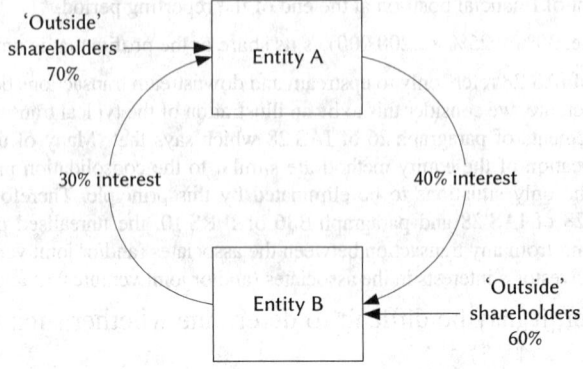

Entity A
Share in equity of B	40%
Shares in A held by 'outside' shareholders	70%
Trading profit of A (before share in profit of B)	€60,000
Net assets of A (before share in net assets of B)	€600,000
Number of shares in issue	100,000

Entity B
Share in equity of A	30%
Shares in B held by 'outside' shareholders	60%
Trading profit of B (before share in profit of A)	€110,000
Net assets of B (before share in net assets of A)	€1,100,000
Number of shares in issue	40,000

Income

The profit for the period is calculated by adding the direct interest in the associate's profit:

Profit of A = Trading profit of A + 40% × trading profit of B = €60,000 + 40% × €110,000 = €104,000
Profit of B = Trading profit of B + 30% × trading profit of A = €110,000 + 30% × €60,000 = €128,000

Statement of financial position

A similar approach can be applied to calculate the net assets of A and B:

Net assets of A including share in B without eliminations = €600,000 + 40% × €1,100,000 = €1,040,000
Net assets of B including share in A without eliminations = €1,100,000 + 30% × €600,000 = €1,280,000

Earnings per share

The profits related to the reciprocal interests have been ignored. Therefore, in calculating the earnings per share it is necessary to adjust the number of shares to eliminate the reciprocal holdings: For A it can be argued that it indirectly owns 40% of B's 30% interest, i.e. A indirectly owns 12% (= 40% × 30%) of its own shares. Those shares should therefore be treated as being equivalent to 'treasury shares' and be ignored for the purposes of the EPS calculation.

Number of A shares after elimination of 'treasury shares' = 100,000 × (100% − 12%) = 88,000 shares

Similarly, B indirectly owns 30% of A's 40% interest, i.e. B indirectly owns 12% (= 30% × 40%) of its own shares.

Number of B shares after elimination of 'treasury shares' = 40,000 × (100% − 12%) = 35,200 shares

The earnings per share for the shareholders of A and B should be calculated as follows:

Earnings per share A = €104,000 ÷ 88,000 = €1.18
Earnings per share B = €128,000 ÷ 35,200 = €3.64

The earnings per share is equivalent to the hypothetical dividend per share in the case of full distribution of all profits.

Conclusion

This method takes up the investor's share of the associate's profits excluding the equity income arising on the reciprocal shareholdings and eliminates only the effects of an entity's indirect investment in its own shares. The financial statements therefore reflect both the interests of the 'outside' shareholders and the interests that B shareholders have in A. It is worthwhile noting that the combined underlying trading profit of A and B is only €170,000 (i.e. €60,000 + €110,000), whereas their combined reported profit is €232,000 (i.e. €104,000 + €128,000). Similarly, the combined underlying net assets of A and B are only €1,700,000, whereas the combined reported net assets are €2,320,000.

The elimination of reciprocal interests was discussed by the Interpretations Committee in August 2002. The Interpretations Committee agreed not to require publication of an Interpretation on this issue but did state that 'like the consolidation procedures applied when a subsidiary is consolidated, the equity method requires reciprocal interests to be eliminated.'[11]

7.6.2.B Reciprocal interests in reporting entity not accounted for under the equity method by the associate

In some situations, the associate's investment in the reporting entity is such that the associate does not have significant influence over the reporting entity and accounts for that investment under IFRS 9, either as at fair value through OCI or at fair value through profit or loss. Although the associate is not applying the equity method, the reciprocal interest can still give rise to a measure of double counting of profits and net assets between the investor and its associate when the investor accounts for its share of the profits and net assets of the associate. Again, paragraph 26 of IAS 28 states that many of the procedures appropriate for the application of the equity method are similar to the consolidation procedures described in IFRS 10. Therefore, the requirement in paragraph B86 of IFRS 10 to eliminate intragroup balances, transactions, income and expenses should be applied by analogy. Accordingly, in our view, the investor eliminates income from the associate's investment in the investor, in the investor's equity accounting. This elimination includes dividends and changes in fair value recognised either in profit or loss or OCI.

Example 11.18: **Elimination of reciprocal interests not accounted for under the equity method**

Investor A has a 20% interest in an Associate B. B has a 10% interest in A, which does not give rise to significant influence.

Scenario 1

B recognises a profit of $1,300 for the year, which includes a dividend of $100 received from A and a gain of $200 from measuring its investment in A at fair value through profit or loss.

In this scenario, A's equity method share of B's profit is $200, being 20% of B's profit of $1,000 after excluding income (dividend of $100 plus fair value gain of $200) on its investment in A.

Scenario 2

B recognises a profit of $1,100 for the year, which includes a dividend of $100 received from A and recognises $200 in OCI from measuring its investment in A as a financial asset at fair value through OCI.

In this scenario, A's equity method share of B's profit is $200, being 20% of B's profit of $1,000 after excluding income (dividend of $100) on its investment in A. A's share of B's OCI also excludes the gain of $200 recognised in OCI arising from its investment in A.

In both scenarios, A also reduces its equity balance and its investment in B by its effective 2% interest in its own shares and uses the reduced number of shares in determining earnings per share.

7.6.3 Loans and borrowings between the reporting entity and its associates or joint ventures

The requirement in paragraph 28 of IAS 28 to eliminate partially unrealised profits or losses on transactions with associates or joint ventures is expressed in terms of transactions involving the transfer of assets. The requirement for partial elimination of profits could be read to not apply to items such as interest paid on loans and borrowings between the reporting entity and its associates or joint ventures, since such loans and borrowings do not involve the transfer of assets giving rise to gains or losses. Moreover, they are not normally regarded as part of the investor's share of the net assets of the associate or joint venture, but as separate transactions, except in the case of loss-making associates or joint ventures, where interests in long-term loans and borrowings are considered part of the reporting entity's equity investment for the purpose of determining the carrying value of the associate or joint venture against which losses may be offset (see 7.9 below). If this reading of IAS 28 is followed, loans and borrowings between the reporting entity and its associates or joint ventures would not be eliminated in the reporting entity's consolidated accounts because the respective assets and liabilities of associates and joint ventures are not recognised by the group.

However, if the associate or joint venture has capitalised the borrowing costs then the investor would need to eliminate a relevant share of its interest income and realise it as the associate depreciates the qualifying asset. The same principle applies to eliminate a share of the capitalised management or advisory fees charged to an associate or joint venture.

7.6.4 Statement of cash flows

In the statement of cash flows (whether in the consolidated or separate financial statements) no adjustment is made in respect of the cash flows relating to transactions with associates or joint ventures. This contrasts with the requirement in any consolidated statement of cash flows to eliminate the cash flows between members of the group in the same way that intragroup transactions are eliminated in the profit and loss account and statement of financial position.

7.6.5 Contributions of non-monetary assets to an associate or a joint venture

It is fairly common for an entity to create or change its interest in an associate or a joint venture by contributing some of the entity's existing non-monetary assets to that associate or joint venture. This raises several questions as to how such transactions should be accounted for, in particular whether they should be accounted for at book value or fair value.

IAS 28 requires the contribution of a non-monetary asset to an associate or a joint venture in exchange for an equity interest in the associate or joint venture to be accounted for in accordance with paragraph 28, except when the contribution lacks commercial substance, as described in IAS 16 (see 7.6.5.A below and Chapter 18 at 4.4). *[IAS 28.30]*. Paragraph 28 requires gains and losses resulting from transactions between an entity and its associate or joint venture to be recognised only to the extent of unrelated interests in the associate or joint venture. The investor's share in the associate's or joint venture's gains or losses resulting from those transactions is eliminated (see 7.6.1 above for a discussion of the requirements relating to such transactions). However, there is a conflict between the requirements of IAS 28 and the requirements in IFRS 10 relating to accounting for the loss of control of a subsidiary, when a subsidiary is contributed by the investor to an associate or joint venture, and control over the subsidiary is consequently lost. This is discussed below at 7.6.5.C.

If a contribution lacks commercial substance, the gain or loss is regarded as unrealised and is not recognised unless paragraph 31 of IAS 28 (see below) also applies. Such unrealised gains and losses are to be eliminated against the investment accounted for using the equity method and are not to be presented as deferred gains or losses in the entity's consolidated statement of financial position or in the entity's statement of financial position in which investments are accounted for using the equity method. *[IAS 28.30]*. Where 'unrealised' losses are eliminated in this way, the effect will be to apply what is sometimes referred to as 'asset swap' accounting. In other words, the carrying value of the investment in the associate or joint venture will be the same as the carrying value of the non-monetary assets transferred in exchange for it, subject of course to any necessary provision for impairment uncovered by the transaction.

If, in addition to receiving an equity interest in an associate or a joint venture, an entity receives monetary or non-monetary assets, the entity recognises in full in profit or loss the portion of the gain or loss on the non-monetary contribution relating to the monetary or non-monetary assets received. *[IAS 28.31]*.

In January 2018, the Interpretations Committee was asked how an entity should account for a transaction in which it contributes PP&E to a newly formed associate in exchange for shares in the associate. In the fact pattern described in the request, the entity and the fellow investors in the associate are entities under common control. The investors each contribute items of PP&E to the new entity in exchange for shares in that entity. The Interpretations Committee firstly observed that unless a standard specifically excludes common control transactions from its scope, an entity applies the applicable requirements in the standard to common control transactions. In terms of paragraph 28 of IAS 28, the entity should recognise gains and losses resulting from the downstream transactions only to the extent of unrelated investors' interests in the associate. The word 'unrelated' does not mean the opposite of 'related' as it is used in the definition of a related party in IAS 24 – *Related Party Disclosures*. Finally, the Interpretations Committee observed that if there is initially any indication that the fair value of the PP&E contributed might differ from the fair value of the acquired equity interest, the entity first assesses the reasons for this difference and reviews the procedures and assumptions it has used to determine fair value. The entity should recognise a gain or loss on contributing the PP&E and a carrying amount for the investment in the associate that reflects the determination of those amounts based on the fair value of the assets contributed, unless the transaction provides objective evidence that the entity's interest in the associate might be impaired. If this is the case, the entity also considers the impairment requirements in IAS 36 – *Impairment of Assets*. If, having reviewed the procedures and assumptions used to determine fair value, the fair value of the PP&E is more than the fair value of the acquired interest in the associate, this would provide objective evidence that the entity's interest in the associate might be impaired. The Interpretations Committee concluded that the principles and requirements in IFRS standards provide an adequate basis for an entity to account for the contribution of non-monetary assets to an associate in the fact pattern described in the request and did not add any items to its agenda.[12]

7.6.5.A 'Commercial substance'

As noted above, IAS 28 requires that a transaction should not be treated as realised when it lacks commercial substance as described in IAS 16. That standard states that an exchange of assets has 'commercial substance' if:

(a) the configuration (risk, timing and amount) of the cash flows of the asset received differs from the configuration of the cash flows of the asset transferred; or

(b) the entity-specific value of the portion of the entity's operations affected by the transaction changes because of the exchange; and

(c) the difference in (a) or (b) above is significant relative to the fair value of the assets exchanged. *[IAS 16.25]*.

IAS 16's 'commercial substance' test is designed to enable an entity to measure, with reasonable objectivity, whether the asset that it has acquired in a non-monetary exchange is different to the asset it has given up.

The first stage is to determine the cash flows both of the asset given up and of the asset acquired (the latter being the interest in the associate or joint venture). This determination may be sufficient by itself to satisfy (a) above, as it may be obvious that there are significant differences in the configuration of the cash flows. The type of income may have changed. For example, if the entity contributed a non-monetary asset such as a property or intangible asset to the associate or joint venture, the reporting entity may now be receiving a rental or royalty stream from the associate or joint venture, whereas previously the asset contributed to the cash flows of the cash-generating unit of which it was a part.

However, determining the cash flows may not result in a clear-cut conclusion, in which case the entity-specific value will have to be calculated. This is not the same as a value in use calculation under IAS 36, in that the entity can use a discount rate based on its own assessment of the risks specific to the operations, not those that reflect current market assessments, *[IAS 16.BC22]*, and post-tax cash flows. *[IAS 16.25]*. The transaction will have commercial substance if these entity-specific values are not only different to one another but also significant compared to the fair values of the assets exchanged.

The calculation may not be highly sensitive to the discount rate as the same rate is used to calculate the entity-specific value of both the asset surrendered and the entity's interest in the associate or joint venture. However, if the entity considers that a high discount rate is appropriate, this will have an impact on whether or not the difference is significant relative to the fair value of the assets exchanged. It is also necessary to consider the significance of:

(a) the requirement discussed above that the entity should recognise in its income statement the portion of any gain or loss arising on the transfer attributable to the other investors;

(b) the general requirements of IAS 28 in respect of transactions between investors and their associates or joint ventures; and

(c) the general requirement of IFRS 3 to recognise assets acquired in a business combination at fair value (see Chapter 9 at 5).

As a result, we consider that it is likely that transactions entered into with genuine commercial purposes in mind are likely to pass the 'commercial substance' tests outlined above.

7.6.5.B Contributions of non-monetary assets – practical application

IAS 28 does not give an example of the accounting treatment that it envisages when a gain is treated as 'realised'. We believe that the intended approach is that set out in Example 11.19 below. In essence, this approach reflects the fact that the reporting entity has:

(a) acquired an interest in an associate or joint venture and therefore the entity's share of the fair value of the net identifiable assets must be accounted for at fair value (see 7.1 above); but

(b) is required by IAS 28 to restrict any gain arising because of the exchange relating to its own assets to the extent that the gain is attributable to the other investor in the associate or joint venture. This leads to an adjustment of the carrying amount of the investment in the associate or joint venture.

In Example 11.19 below, we consider the accounting by Entity A to the transaction where the non-monetary assets it has contributed are intangible assets. On the other hand, Entity B has contributed an interest in a subsidiary. In some transactions, particularly the formation of joint ventures, both parties may contribute interests in subsidiaries. The requirements in IFRS 10 relating to the accounting for loss of control of a subsidiary are inconsistent with the accounting required by IAS 28, as discussed at 7.6.5.C below. Although Example 11.19 below is based on a transaction resulting in the formation of a joint venture, the accounting treatment by Entity A would be the same if it had obtained an interest in an associate.

Example 11.19: Contribution of non-monetary assets to form a joint venture

A and B are two major pharmaceutical companies, which agree to form a joint venture (JV Co). A will own 40% of the joint venture, and B, 60%. The total fair value of the new business of JV Co is £250 million.

A's contribution to the venture is several intangible assets, in respect of which A's consolidated statement of financial position reflects a carrying amount of £60 million. The fair value of the intangible assets contributed by A is considered to be £100 million, i.e. equivalent to 40% of the total fair value of JV Co of £250 million.

B contributes a subsidiary, in respect of which B's consolidated statement of financial position reflects separable net identifiable assets of £85 million and goodwill of £15 million. The fair value of the separable net identifiable assets is £120 million. The fair value of the business contributed is £150 million (60% of total fair value of JV Co of £250 million).

The book and fair values of the assets/businesses contributed by A and B can therefore be summarised as follows:

(in £m)	A Book value	A Fair value	B Book value	B Fair value
Intangible assets	60	100		
Separable net identifiable assets			85	120
Goodwill			15	30
Total	60	100	100	150

How should A apply IAS 28 in accounting for the set-up of the joint venture?

The requirements of paragraph 32 of IAS 28 require that A should recognise the identifiable assets at fair value upon the acquisition of its 40% interest in the new venture. However, as noted above, any gain or loss recognised by A must reflect only the extent to which it has disposed of the assets to the other partners in the venture (i.e. in this case, 60% – the extent to which A's intangible assets are effectively transferred to B through B's 60% interest in the new venture). *[IAS 28.30, 32].*

This gives rise to the following accounting entry.

	£m	£m
Investment in JV Co		
– Share of net identifiable assets of JV Co (1)	72	
– Goodwill (2)	12	
Intangible assets contributed to JV Co (3)		60
Gain on disposal (4)		24

(1) 40% of fair value of separable net identifiable assets (including A's intangible assets) of new entity £88 million (40% of [£100 million + £120 million] as in table above) less elimination of 40% of gain on disposal £16 million (40% of £40 million, being the difference between the book value [£60 million] and fair value [£100 million] of A's intangible assets, as in table above, contributed to JV Co) = £72 million.

This is equivalent to, and perhaps more easily calculated as, 40% of [book value of A's intangible assets + fair value of B's separable net identifiable assets], i.e. 40% × [£60 million + £120 million] = £72 million.

Under the equity method, this £72 million together with the £12 million of goodwill (see (2) below) would be included as the equity accounted amount of JV Co.

(2) Fair value of consideration given £100 million (as in table above) less fair value of 40% share of separable net identifiable assets of JV Co acquired £88 million (see (1) above) = £12 million.

This is equivalent to, and perhaps more easily calculated as, 40% of the fair value of B's goodwill, i.e. 40% × £30 million = £12 million.

Under the equity method, as noted at (1) above, this £12 million together with the £72 million relating to the separable net identifiable assets would be included as the equity accounted amount of JV Co.

(3) Previous carrying amount of intangible assets contributed by A, now deconsolidated.

(4) Fair value of business acquired £100 million (40% of £250 million) less book value of intangible assets disposed of £60 million (as in table above) = £40 million, less 40% of gain eliminated (£16 million) = £24 million. The £16 million eliminated reduces A's share of JV Co's separable net identifiable assets by £16 million (see (1) above).

It is common when joint ventures are set up in this way for the fair value of the assets contributed not to be exactly in proportion to the fair values of the venturers' agreed relative shares. Cash 'equalisation' payments are then made between the venturers so that the overall financial position of the venturer does correspond to the agreed relative shares in the venture. Our suggested treatment of such payments in the context of a transaction within the scope of IAS 28 is illustrated in Example 11.20 below. Although the example is based on a transaction resulting in the formation of a joint venture, the accounting treatment by party A would be the same if it had obtained an interest in an associate.

Example 11.20: Contribution of non-monetary assets to form a joint venture with cash equalisation payment between venturers/investors

Suppose that the transaction in Example 11.19 above was varied so that A is to have only a 36% interest in JV Co. However, as shown by the introductory table in Example 11.19 above, A is contributing intangible assets worth 40% of the total fair value of JV Co. Accordingly, B makes good the shortfall by making a cash payment to A equivalent to 4% of the fair value of JV Co, i.e. £10 million (4% of £250 million).

This would require A to make the following accounting entries.

	£m	£m
Investment in JV Co:		
– Share of net identifiable assets of JV Co (1)	64.8	
– Goodwill (2)	10.8	
Cash (equalisation payment from B)	10.0	
Intangible assets contributed to JV Co (3)		60.0
Gain on disposal (4)		25.6

(1) 36% of fair value of separable net identifiable assets of new entity £79.2 million (36% of [£100 million + £120 million] as in table in Example 11.19 above) less elimination of 36% of gain on disposal £14.4 million (36% of £40 million, being the difference between the book value [£60 million] and fair value [£100 million] of A's intangible assets, as in table in Example 11.19 above, contributed to JV Co) = £64.8 million.

This is equivalent to, and perhaps more easily calculated as, 36% of [book value of A's intangible assets + fair value of B's separable net identifiable assets], i.e. 36% × [£60 million + £120 million] = £64.8 million.

Under the equity method, this £64.8 million together with the £10.8 million of goodwill (see (2) below) would be included as the equity accounted amount of JV Co.

(2) Fair value of consideration given £100 million (as in table in Example 11.19 above), less cash equalisation payment received £10 million = £90 million less fair value of 36% share of separable net identifiable assets of JV Co acquired £79.2 million (see (1) above) = £10.8 million.

This is equivalent to, and perhaps more easily calculated as, 36% of the fair value of B's goodwill], i.e. 36% × £30 million = £10.8 million.

Under the equity method, as noted at (1) above, this £10.8 million together with the £64.8 million relating to the separable net identifiable assets would be included as the equity accounted amount of JV Co.

(3) Previous carrying amount of intangible assets contributed by A, now deconsolidated.

(4) Fair value of business acquired £90 million (36% of £250 million) plus cash equalisation payment £10 million = £100 million, less book value of intangible assets disposed of £60 million (as in table in Example 11.19 above) = £40 million, less 36% of gain eliminated (£14.4 million) = £25.6 million. The £14.4 million eliminated reduces A's share of JV Co's separable net identifiable assets by £14.4 million (see (1) above).

I   *'Artificial' transactions*

A concern with transactions such as this is that it is the relative, rather than the absolute, value of the transaction that is of concern to the parties. In other words, in Example 11.19 above, it could be argued that the only clear inference that can be drawn is that A and B have agreed that the ratio of the fair values of the assets/businesses they have each contributed is 40:60, rather than that the business as a whole is worth £250 million. Thus, it might be open to A and B, without altering the substance of the transaction, to assert that the value of the combined operations is £500 million (with a view to enlarging their net assets) or £200 million (with a view to increasing future profitability).

Another way in which the valuation of the transaction might be distorted is through disaggregation of the consideration. Suppose that the £60 million net assets contributed by A in Example 11.19 above comprised:

	£m
Cash	12
Intangible assets	48
	60

Further suppose that, for tax reasons, the transaction was structured such that A was issued with 4% of the shares of JV Co in exchange for the cash and 36% in exchange for the intangible assets. This could lead to the suggestion that, as there can be no doubt as to the fair value of the cash, A's entire investment must be worth £120 million (i.e. £12 million × 40 / 4). Testing transactions for their commercial substance will require entities to focus on the fair value of the transaction as a whole and not to follow the strict legal form.

Of course, once cash equalisation payments are introduced, as in Example 11.20 above, the transaction terms may provide evidence as to both the relative and absolute fair values of the assets contributed by each party.

11   Accounting for the acquisition of a business on formation of a joint venture

IFRS 3 does not apply to business combinations that arise on the formation of a joint venture. *[IFRS 3.2(a)]*. Therefore, it is not clear under IFRS how the acquisition by JV Co of the former business of B in Example 11.20 above should be accounted for. Indeed, it could have been the case that A had also contributed a subsidiary, and JV Co would have to account for the former businesses of both A and B. We consider that under the GAAP hierarchy in IAS 8 the pooling of interest method is still available when accounting for the businesses acquired on the formation of a joint venture and there may be other approaches (including the acquisition method) that will be considered to give a fair presentation in particular circumstances.

Where a new company is formed to create a joint venture and both venturers contribute a business, we believe that it would also be acceptable under the GAAP hierarchy in paragraph 11 of IAS 8 (see Chapter 3 at 4.3) to apply the acquisition method to both businesses, as IFRS does not prevent entities from doing this and it provides useful information to investors. However, in this case, the entity should ensure the disclosures made are sufficient for users of the financial statements to understand the transaction fully.

If JV Co were to apply the acquisition method, it could mean that the equity-accounted amounts included in the financial statements of B may bear little relation to its share of the net assets of the joint venture as reported in the underlying financial statements of the investee. This would be the case if B accounted for the transaction by applying IAS 28 rather than IFRS 10 (see 7.6.5.C below). For example, B's share of any amortisation charge recorded by JV Co must be based on the carrying amount of B's share of JV Co's intangible assets, not as recorded in JV Co's books (i.e. at fair value) but as recorded in B's books, which will be based on book value for intangible assets contributed by B and at fair value for intangible assets contributed by A. Accordingly it may be necessary for B to keep a 'memorandum' set of books for equity accounting purposes reflecting its share of assets that were originally its own at book value and those originally of A at fair value. The same would apply to A if it had also contributed a subsidiary. In any event, in Example 11.20 above, JV Co will have to account for the intangibles contributed by A at fair value because the transaction represents a share-based payment transaction in terms of IFRS 2 – *Share-based Payment*. Therefore, A will need to keep a 'memorandum' record relating to these intangibles, so that it can make the necessary adjustments in its equity accounting to reflect amortisation charges based on its original book values.

Alternatively, if JV Co were to apply the pooling of interest method and therefore reflect assets contributed from both A and B at their book values, A would need to keep a 'memorandum' set of books for equity accounting purposes because its share of assets that were originally those of B should be carried at fair value rather than carry-over cost.

7.6.5.C Conflict between IAS 28 and IFRS 10

In Example 11.19 above, we considered the accounting by Entity A to the transaction where the non-monetary assets it has contributed are intangible assets. On the other hand, Entity B has contributed an interest in a subsidiary. The requirements in IFRS 10 relating to the accounting for the loss of control of a subsidiary are inconsistent with the accounting required by IAS 28. Under IAS 28, the contributing investor is required to restrict any gain arising because of the exchange relating to its own assets to the extent that the gain is attributable to the other party to the associate or joint venture. This results in an adjustment to the carrying amount of the investment in the associate or joint venture. However, under IFRS 10, where an entity loses control of an entity, but retains an interest that is to be accounted for as an associate or joint venture, the retained interest must be remeasured at its fair value and is included in calculating the gain or loss on disposal of the subsidiary. This fair value becomes the cost on initial recognition of the associate or joint venture. *[IFRS 10.25]*. Consequently, under IFRS 10, the gain is not restricted to the extent attributable to the other party to the associate or joint venture and there is no adjustment to reduce the investor's share of the fair values of the net identifiable assets contributed to the associate or joint venture (i.e. no adjustment to the carrying amount of the investment in the associate or joint venture).

In September 2014, the IASB issued *Sale or Contribution of Assets between an Investor and its Associate or Joint Venture* (amendments to IFRS 10 and IAS 28) to address the conflict between IFRS 10 and IAS 28.[13] The amendments require that:

- the partial gain or loss recognition for transactions between an investor and its associate or joint venture applies only to the gain or loss resulting from the sale or contribution of assets that do not constitute a business as defined in IFRS 3; and
- the gain or loss resulting from the sale or contribution of assets that constitute a business as defined in IFRS 3 to an associate or joint venture be recognised in full. *[IAS 28.31A]*.

In addition, the amendments address where an entity might sell or contribute assets in two or more arrangements (transactions). When determining whether assets that are sold or contributed constitute a business as defined in IFRS 3, an entity considers whether the sale or contribution of those assets is part of multiple arrangements that should be accounted for as a single transaction in accordance with the requirements in paragraph B97 of IFRS 10. *[IAS 28.31B].*

In December 2015, the IASB deferred the effective date of these amendments indefinitely due to feedback that the recognition of a partial gain or loss when a transaction involves assets that do not constitute a business, even if these assets are housed in a subsidiary, is inconsistent with the initial measurement requirements of paragraph 32(b) of IAS 28 (see 7.1 above). This issue will be reconsidered as part of the equity method research project (see 11 below). However, entities may apply the amendments before the effective date.

Until the amendments become mandatorily effective, we believe that entities have an accounting policy choice to apply IFRS 10 or IAS 28 to the contribution of an interest in a subsidiary that constitutes a business. In determining a policy, entities may take into consideration the fact that the requirements of IFRS 10 deal with the specific issue of loss of control, whereas the requirements of IAS 28 are more generic. Once selected, the entity must apply the policy consistently.

Even when the selected policy is to apply IFRS 10 to contributions of an interest in a subsidiary that constitutes a business, IAS 28 would generally apply to other forms of non-monetary assets contributed, such as items of PP&E, intangible assets and an interest in a subsidiary that does not constitute a business. However, an entity may elect to apply paragraph 25 of IFRS 10 to the loss of control of investments in all subsidiaries (i.e. those that constitute a business and those that do not) (see 7.4.1 above), and as a result, not apply IAS 28 to those contributions.

In Example 11.21 below, we illustrate how Entity B, which has contributed a subsidiary that constitutes a business in return for its interest in the joint venture in the transaction set out in Example 11.19 above, would account for the transaction by applying the requirements of IFRS 10, i.e. Entity B has elected to apply IFRS 10 to the loss of control transaction even though it is a downstream transaction. Although the example is based on a transaction resulting in the formation of a joint venture, the accounting treatment by Entity B would be the same if it had obtained an interest in an associate.

Example 11.21: Contribution of subsidiary to form a joint venture – applying IFRS 10

A and B are two major pharmaceutical companies, which agree to form a joint venture (JV Co). A will own 40% of the joint venture, and B 60%. The parties agree that the total value of the new business of JV Co is £250 million.

A's contribution to the venture is several intangible assets, in respect of which A's consolidated statement of financial position reflects a carrying amount of £60 million. The fair value of the intangible assets contributed by A is considered to be £100 million, i.e. equivalent to 40% of the total fair value of JV Co of £250 million.

B contributes a subsidiary that is a business, in respect of which B's consolidated statement of financial position reflects separable net identifiable assets of £85 million and goodwill of £15 million. The fair value of the separable net identifiable assets is considered to be £120 million. The implicit fair value of the business contributed is £150 million (60% of total fair value of JV Co of £250 million).

The book and fair values of the assets/businesses contributed by A and B can therefore be summarised as follows:

(in £m)	A Book value	A Fair value	B Book value	B Fair value
Intangible assets	60	100		
Separable net identifiable assets			85	120
Goodwill			15	30
Total	60	100	100	150

The application of IFRS 10 to the transaction would result in B reflecting the following accounting entry.

	£m	£m
Investment in JV Co:		
– Share of net identifiable assets of JV Co (1)	132	
– Goodwill (2)	18	
Separable net identifiable assets and goodwill contributed to JV Co (3)		100
Gain on disposal (4)		50

(1) 60% of fair value of separable net identifiable assets of new entity £132 million (60% of [£100 million + £120 million] as in table above). There is no elimination of 60% of the gain on disposal.

Under the equity method, this £132 million together with the £18 million of goodwill (see (2) below) would be included as the equity accounted amount of JV Co.

(2) Fair value of consideration given of £60 million (being 40% of £150 million as in table above) plus fair value of retained interest of £90 million (being 60% of £150 million) less fair value of 60% share of separable net identifiable assets of JV Co acquired £132 million (see (1) above).

Under the equity method, as noted at (1) above, this £18 million together with the £132 million relating to the separable net identifiable assets would be included as the equity accounted amount of JV Co.

(3) Previous carrying amount of net identifiable assets contributed by B as in table above, now deconsolidated. In reality there would be a number of entries to deconsolidate these on a line-by-line basis.

(4) Fair value of consideration received of £60 million (being 60% of £100 million as in table above) plus fair value of retained interest of £90 million (being 60% of £150 million) less book value of assets disposed of £100 million (see (3) above) = £50 million.

7.7 Non-coterminous accounting periods

In applying the equity method, the investor should use the most recent financial statements of the associate or joint venture. Where the reporting dates of the investor and the associate or joint venture are different, IAS 28 requires the associate or joint venture to prepare, for the use of the investor, financial statements as of the same date as those of the investor unless it is impracticable to do so. *[IAS 28.33]*.

When the financial statements of an associate or joint venture used in applying the equity method are prepared as of a different reporting date from that of the investor, adjustments must be made for the effects of significant transactions or events, for example a sale of a significant asset or a major loss on a contract, that occurred between that date and the date of the investor's financial statements. In no circumstances can the difference between the reporting date of the associate or the joint venture and that of the investor be more than three months. *[IAS 28.34, BCZ19]*. There are no exemptions from this requirement despite the fact that it may be quite onerous in practice, for example, because:

- the associate or joint venture might need to produce interim financial statements so that the investor can comply with this requirement; or
- the associate or joint venture may be a listed company in its own right whose financial information is considered price-sensitive, which means that the associate or joint venture may not be able to provide detailed financial information to one investor without providing equivalent information to all other investors at the same time.

The length of the reporting periods and any difference in the reporting dates must be the same from period to period. *[IAS 28.34]*. This implies that where an associate or joint venture was previously equity accounted for based on non-coterminous financial statements and is now equity accounted for using coterminous financial statements, it is necessary to restate comparative information so that financial information in respect of the associate or joint venture is included in the investor's financial statements for an equivalent period in each period presented. However, it may be that other approaches not involving restatement of comparatives would be acceptable, particularly where the comparative information had already reflected the effects of significant transactions or events during the period between the date of the associate's or joint venture's financial statements and the date of the investor's financial statements. Where comparatives are not restated, additional disclosures might be needed about the treatment adopted and the impact on the current period of including information for the associate or joint venture for a period different from that of the investor.

IAS 28 requires merely that a non-coterminous accounting period of an associate or a joint venture used for equity accounting purposes ends within three months of that of the investor. It is not necessary for such a non-coterminous period to end before that of the investor.

7.8 Consistent accounting policies

IAS 28 requires the investor's financial statements to be prepared using uniform accounting policies for like transactions and events in similar circumstances. *[IAS 28.35]*. If an associate or joint venture uses different accounting policies from those of the investor for like transactions and events in similar circumstances, adjustments must be made to conform the associate's or joint venture's accounting policies to those of the investor when the associate's or joint venture's financial statements are used by the investor in applying the equity method. *[IAS 28.36]*.

In practice, this may be easier said than done, since the investor has only significant influence, and not control, over the associate, and therefore may not have access to the relevant underlying information in sufficient detail to make such adjustments with certainty. Restating the financial statements of an associate to IFRS may require extensive detailed information that may simply not be required under the associate's local GAAP (for example, in respect of business combinations, share-based payments, financial instruments and revenue recognition). Although there may be some practical difficulties where the entity has joint control over a joint venture, we would expect this to arise less often, as joint control is likely to give the investor more access to the information required.

7.8.1 Exemption for associates or joint ventures that are investment entities

If an entity that is not itself an investment entity has an interest in an associate or joint venture that is an investment entity, the entity may, when applying the equity method, elect to retain the fair value measurement applied by that investment entity associate or joint venture to the investment entity associate's or joint venture's interests in subsidiaries. This election is made separately for each investment entity associate or joint venture, at the later of the date on which:

(a) the investment entity associate or joint venture is initially recognised;

(b) the associate or joint venture becomes an investment entity; and

(c) the investment entity associate or joint venture first becomes a parent. *[IAS 28.36A]*.

7.8.2 Temporary exemption from IFRS 9 applied by an insurer

For an insurer that meets specified criteria, IFRS 4 – *Insurance Contracts* – provides a temporary exemption that permits, but does not require, the insurer to apply IAS 39 rather than IFRS 9 until IFRS 17 becomes effective. An entity is permitted, but not required, to retain the relevant accounting policies applied by the associate or joint venture as follows:

(a) the entity applies IFRS 9 but the associate or joint venture applies the temporary exemption from IFRS 9; or

(b) the entity applies the temporary exemption from IFRS 9 but the associate or joint venture applies IFRS 9. *[IFRS 4.20O]*.

When an entity uses the equity method to account for its investment in an associate or joint venture:

(a) if IFRS 9 was previously applied in the financial statements used to apply the equity method to that associate or joint venture (after reflecting any adjustments made by the entity), then IFRS 9 shall continue to be applied; or

(b) if the temporary exemption from IFRS 9 was previously applied in the financial statements used to apply the equity method to that associate or joint venture (after reflecting any adjustments made by the entity), then IFRS 9 may be subsequently applied. *[IFRS 4.20P]*.

An entity may apply the above exemptions separately for each associate or joint venture. *[IFRS 4.20Q]*.

7.9 Loss-making associates or joint ventures

An investor in an associate or joint venture should recognise its share of the losses of the associate or joint venture until its share of losses equals or exceeds its interest in the associate or joint venture, at which point the investor discontinues recognising its share of further losses. For this purpose, the investor's interest in an associate or joint venture is the carrying amount of the investment in the associate or joint venture under the equity method together with any long-term interests that, in substance, form part of the investor's net investment in the associate or joint venture. For example, an item for which settlement is neither planned nor likely to occur in the foreseeable future is, in substance, an extension of the entity's investment in that associate or joint venture. *[IAS 28.38]*. The items that form part of the net investment are discussed further in Chapter 15 at 6.3.1. The IASB argued that this requirement ensures that investors are not able to avoid recognising the loss of an associate or joint venture by restructuring their investment to provide the majority of funding through non-equity investments. *[IAS 28.BCZ39-40]*.

Such items include:

- preference shares; or
- long-term receivables or loans (unless supported by adequate collateral),

but do not include:

- trade receivables;
- trade payables; or
- any long-term receivables for which adequate collateral exists, such as secured loans. *[IAS 28.38]*.

Once the investor's share of losses recognised under the equity method has reduced the investor's investment in ordinary shares to zero, its share of any further losses is applied to reduce the other components of the investor's interest in an associate or joint venture in the reverse order of their seniority (i.e. priority in liquidation). *[IAS 28.38]*.

Once the investor's interest is reduced to zero, additional losses are provided for, and a liability is recognised, only to the extent that the investor has incurred legal or constructive obligations or made payments on behalf of the associate or joint venture. If the associate or joint venture subsequently reports profits, the investor resumes recognising its share of those profits only after its share of the profits equals the share of losses not recognised. *[IAS 28.39]*. Whilst IAS 28 does not say so explicitly, it is presumably envisaged that, when profits begin to be recognised again, they are applied to write back the various components of the investor's interest in the associate or joint venture (see previous paragraph) in the reverse order to that in which they were written down (i.e. in order of their priority in a liquidation).

IAS 28 is not explicit about the allocation of losses recognised in the income statement and losses incurred in OCI. Therefore, management will need to develop an appropriate policy. The policy chosen should be disclosed and consistently applied.

In addition to the recognition of losses arising from application of the equity method, an investor in an associate or joint venture must consider the additional requirements of IAS 28 in respect of impairment losses (see 8 below).

Example 11.22: Accounting for a loss-making associate

At the beginning of the year Entity H invests €5 million to acquire a 30% equity interest in Associate A. In addition, H lends €9 million to A, but does not provide any guarantees or commit itself to provide further funding. How should H account for the €20 million loss that A made during the year?

H's share in A's loss is €20 million × 30% = €6 million. If H's loan to A is considered part of the net investment in A then the carrying amount of the associate is reduced by €6 million, from €14 million (= €5 million + €9 million) to €8 million. That is, the equity interest is reduced to nil and the loan is reduced to €8 million. However, if the loan is not part of the net investment in A then H accounts for the loss as follows:

- the equity interest in the associate is reduced from €5 million to zero;
- a loss of €1 million remains unrecognised because H did not provide any guarantees and has no commitments to provide further funding. If in the second year, however, A were to make a profit of €10 million then H would recognise a profit of only €2 million (= €10 million × 30% – €1 million). However, if in the second year H were to provide a €1.5 million guarantee to A and A's net profit were nil, then H would need to recognise an immediate loss of €1 million (i.e. the lower of the unrecognised loss of €1 million and the guarantee of €1.5 million) because it now has a legal obligation pay A's debts; and
- as there are several indicators of impairment, the loan from H to A should be tested for impairment in accordance with IFRS 9.

7.10 Distributions received in excess of the carrying amount

When an associate or joint venture makes dividend distributions to the investor in excess of the investor's carrying amount it is not immediately clear how the excess should be accounted for. A liability under IAS 37 – *Provisions, Contingent Liabilities and Contingent Assets* – should be recognised only if the investor is obliged to refund the dividend, has incurred a legal or constructive obligation or made payments on behalf of the associate. In the absence of such obligations, it is appropriate that the investor recognises the excess in net profit for the period. When the associate or joint venture subsequently makes profits, the investor starts recognising profits only when they exceed the excess cash distributions recognised in net profit plus any previously unrecognised losses (see 7.9 above).

7.11 Equity transactions in an associate's or joint venture's financial statements

The financial statements of an associate or joint venture that are used for the purposes of equity accounting by the investor may include items within its statement of changes in equity that are not reflected in the profit or loss or other components of comprehensive income, for example, dividends or other forms of distributions, issues of equity instruments and equity-settled share-based payment transactions. Where the associate or joint venture has subsidiaries and consolidated financial statements are prepared, those financial statements may include the effects of changes in the parent's (i.e. the associate's or joint venture's) ownership interest and NCI in a subsidiary that did not arise from a transaction that resulted in loss of control of that subsidiary.

Although the description of the equity method in IAS 28 requires that the investor's share of the profit or loss of the associate or joint venture is recognised in the investor's profit or loss, and the investor's share of changes in items of OCI of the associate or joint venture is recognised in OCI of the investor, *[IAS 28.10]*, no explicit reference is made to other items that the associate or joint venture may have in its statement of changes in equity.

Therefore, the guidance in the sections that follow may be considered in determining an appropriate accounting treatment.

7.11.1 Dividends or other forms of distributions

Although paragraph 10 of IAS 28 does not explicitly refer to dividends or other forms of distribution that are reflected in the associate's statement of changes in equity, it does state that distributions received from an investee reduce the carrying amount of the investment. Generally, the distributions received will be the equivalent of the investor's share of the distributions made to the owners of the associate reflected in the associate's statement of changes in equity. Thus, they are effectively eliminated as part of applying the equity method.

However, this may not always be the case. For example, when an associate declares scrip dividends which are not taken up by the investor, the investor's proportionate interest in the associate is reduced. In this situation, the investor should account for this as a deemed disposal (see 7.12.6 below).

7.11.2 Issues of equity instruments

Where an associate or joint venture has issued equity instruments, the effect on its net assets will be reflected in the associate's or joint venture's statement of changes in equity. Where the investor has participated in the issue of these equity instruments, it will account for its cost of doing so by increasing its carrying amount of the associate or joint venture. If, as a consequence of the investor's participation in such a transaction, the investee has become an associate or joint venture of the investor, or the investor has increased its percentage ownership interest in an existing associate or joint venture (but without obtaining control), the investor should account for this as an acquisition of an associate or joint venture or a piecemeal acquisition of an associate or joint venture (see 7.4.2 above). Thus, the amounts reflected in the associate's or joint venture's statement of changes in equity are effectively eliminated as part of applying the equity method.

If, on the other hand, the investor has not participated in the issue of equity instruments reflected in the associate's or joint venture's statement of changes in equity, e.g. shares have been issued to third parties or the investor has not taken up its full allocation of a rights issue by the associate or joint venture, the investor's proportionate interest in the associate or joint venture is reduced. In such situations, it should account for the transaction as a deemed disposal (see 7.12.6 below).

7.11.3 Equity-settled share-based payment transactions

Another item that may feature in an associate's or joint venture's statement of changes in equity is the credit entry relating to any equity-settled share-based payment transactions of the associate or joint venture; the debit entry of such transactions is recognised by the associate or joint venture as an expense within its profit or loss.

How should such a transaction be reflected by the investor in equity accounting for the associate or joint venture, particularly the impact of the credit to equity recognised by the associate or joint venture?

As the share-based payment expense is included within the profit or loss of the associate or joint venture, this will be reflected in the share of the associate's or joint venture's profit or loss recognised in the investor's profit or loss. *[IAS 28.10]*. As far as the credit to equity that is included in the associate's or joint venture's statement of changes in equity is concerned, there are two possible approaches:

(a) ignore the credit entry; or
(b) reflect the investor's share of the credit entry as a 'share of other changes in equity of associates or joint ventures' in the investor's statement of changes in equity.

We believe that approach (a) should be followed, rather than approach (b). The description of the equity method in IAS 28 states that 'the carrying amount [of the investment in an associate or a joint venture] is increased or decreased to recognise the investor's share of the profit or loss of the investee after the date of acquisition. ... Adjustments to the carrying amount may also be necessary for changes in the investor's proportionate interest in the investee arising from changes in the investee's other comprehensive income.' *[IAS 28.10]*.

As far as the credit to shareholders' equity recognised by the associate or joint venture is concerned, this is not part of comprehensive income and given that paragraph 10 of IAS 28 implies that the investor recognises only its share of the elements of profit or loss and of OCI, the investor should not recognise any portion of the credit to shareholders' equity recognised by the associate or joint venture. If and when the options are exercised, the investor will account for its reduction in its proportionate interest as a deemed disposal (see 7.12.6 below).

This approach results in the carrying amount of the equity investment no longer corresponding to the proportionate share of the net assets of the investee (as reported by the investee). However, this is consistent with the requirement in IAS 28 for dealing with undeclared dividends on cumulative preference shares held by parties other than the investor (see 7.5.2 above). *[IAS 28.37]*. In that situation, the undeclared dividends have not yet been recognised by the investee at all, but the investor still reduces its share of the profit or loss (and therefore its share of net assets). The impact of applying this approach is illustrated in Example 11.23 below. Although the example is based on an equity-settled share-based payment transaction of an associate, the accounting treatment would be the same if it been a transaction undertaken by a joint venture.

Example 11.23: Equity-settled share-based payment transactions of associate

Entity A holds a 30% interest in Entity B and accounts for its interest in B as an associate using the equity method. This interest arose on incorporation of B. Accordingly, there are no fair value adjustments required related to the assets of B in A's consolidated financial statements and its equity-accounted amount represents an original cost of £1,500 (30% of B's issued equity of £5,000) together with A's 30% share of B's retained profits of £5,000.

B issues share options to its employees which are to be accounted for by B as an equity-settled share-based payment transaction. The options entitle the employees to subscribe for shares of B, representing an additional 20% interest in the shares of B. If the options are exercised, the employees will pay £2,400 for the shares. The grant date fair value of the options issued is £900 and, for the purposes of the example, it is assumed that the options are immediately vested. Accordingly, B has recognised a share-based payment expense of £900 in profit or loss and a credit to equity of the same amount.

The impact of accounting for this equity-settled share-based payment transaction on B's financial statements and on A's consolidated financial statements is summarised below.

Immediately before the granting of the options

B's financial statements

	£		£
Net assets	10,000	Issued equity	5,000
		Retained earnings	5,000
Total	10,000	Total	10,000

A's consolidated financial statements

	£		£
Investment in B	3,000	Issued equity	10,000
Other net assets	21,000	Retained earnings	14,000
Total	24,000	Total	24,000

Immediately after the granting of the options*

B's financial statements

	£		£
Net assets	10,000	Issued equity	5,000
		Retained earnings	5,000
		Loss for period	(900)
		Share-based payment reserve	900
Total	10,000	Total	10,000

A's consolidated financial statements

	£		£
Investment in B	2,730	Issued equity	10,000
Other net assets	21,000	Retained earnings	14,000
		Loss for period	(270)
Total	23,730	Total	23,730

* For the purposes of illustration, B's expense and the corresponding credit to equity have been shown separately within equity as 'loss for period' and 'share-based payment reserve' respectively. A's 30% share of the expense has similarly been shown separately within equity.

Immediately after exercise of the options*

B's financial statements

	£		£
Net assets	10,000	Issued equity	5,000
Cash on exercise of options	2,400	Additional equity on exercise of options	2,400
		Retained earnings	5,000
		Loss for period	(900)
		Share-based payment reserve	900
Total	12,400	Total	12,400

A's consolidated financial statements

	£		£
Investment in B	3,100	Issued equity	10,000
Other net assets	21,000	Retained earnings	14,000
		Loss for period	(270)
		Gain on deemed disposal	370
Total	24,100	Total	24,100

* As a result of the employees exercising the options for £2,400, assume that A's proportionate interest in B has reduced from 30% to 25%. A is considered still to have significant influence over B, which remains an associate of A. This deemed disposal results in A recognising a gain on deemed disposal in its profit or loss for the period. This gain is computed by comparing A's proportionate share of net assets of B before and after the exercise of the options as follows:

	£	
Net assets attributable to A's 30% interest	2,730	(30% of £9,100)
Net assets attributable to A's 25% interest	3,100	(25% of £12,400)
Gain on deemed disposal	370	

As indicated in Example 11.23 above, when the options are exercised, the investor will account for the reduction in its proportionate interest in the associate or joint venture as a deemed disposal (see 7.12.6 below). On the other hand, if the options had lapsed unexercised, having already vested, the associate or joint venture would make no further accounting entries to reverse the expense already recognised, but may make a transfer between different components of equity (see Chapter 34 at 6.1.3). In that situation, because the investor's share of the net assets of the associate or joint venture is increased as a result (effectively, the impact of the original expense on the share of net assets is reversed), we believe the investor can account for the increase as a debit to the investment in associate and the credit as either a gain in profit or loss or as a credit within equity. Once selected, the investor must apply the selected policy consistently.

7.11.4 Effects of changes in parent/non-controlling interests in subsidiaries

It may be that the associate or joint venture does not own all the shares in some of its subsidiaries, in which case its consolidated financial statements will include NCI. Under IFRS 10, any NCI are presented in the consolidated statement of financial position within equity, separately from the equity of the owners of the parent. Profit or loss and each component of OCI are attributed to the owners of the parent and to the NCI. *[IFRS 10.22, B94]*. The profit or loss and OCI reported in the associate's or joint venture's consolidated financial statements will include 100% of the amounts relating to the subsidiaries, but the overall profit or loss and total comprehensive income will be split between the amounts attributable to the owners of the parent (i.e. the associate or joint venture) and those attributable to the NCI. The net assets in the consolidated statement of financial position will also include 100% of the amounts relating to the subsidiaries, with any NCI in the net assets presented in the consolidated statement of financial position within equity, separately from the equity of the owners of the parent.

The issue of whether the investor's share of the associate's or joint venture's profits, OCI and net assets under the equity method should be based on the amounts before or after any NCI in the associate's or joint venture's consolidated accounts is discussed at 7.5.5 above. As the investor's interest in the associate or joint venture is as an owner of the parent, it is appropriate that the share is based on the profit or loss, comprehensive income and equity (net assets) that are reported as being attributable to the owners of the parent in the associate's or joint venture's consolidated financial statements, i.e. after any amounts attributable to the NCI.

Under IFRS 10, changes in a parent's ownership interest in a subsidiary that do not result in a loss of control are accounted for as equity transactions. *[IFRS 10.23]*. In such circumstances the carrying amounts of the controlling and non-controlling interests are adjusted to reflect the changes in their relative interests in the subsidiary. Any difference between the amount by which the NCI are adjusted and the fair value of the consideration paid or received is recognised directly in equity and attributed to the owners of the parent. *[IFRS 10.B96]*.

How should such an amount attributed to the owners of the parent that is recognised in the associate's or joint venture's statement of changes in equity be reflected by the investor in equity accounting for the associate or joint venture?

In our view, the investor may account for its share of the change of interest in the net assets/equity of the associate or joint venture because of the associate's or joint venture's equity transaction by applying either of the approaches set out below:

(a) reflect it as part of the share of other changes in equity of associates or joint ventures' in the investor's statement of changes in equity; or

(b) reflect it as a gain or loss within the share of associate's or joint venture's profit or loss included in the investor's profit or loss.

Once selected, the investor must apply the selected policy consistently.

Approach (a) reflects the view that although paragraph 10 of IAS 28 refers to the investor accounting for its share of the investee's profit or loss and other items of comprehensive income only, this approach is consistent with the equity method as described in paragraph 10 of IAS 28 because it:

(a) reflects the post-acquisition change in the net assets of the investee; *[IAS 28.3]* and

(b) faithfully reflects the investor's share of the associate's transaction as presented in the associate's consolidated financial statements. *[IAS 28.27]*.

Since, the transaction does not change the investor's ownership interest in the associate it is not a deemed disposal (see 7.12.6 below) and, therefore, there is no question of a gain or loss on disposal arising.

By contrast, Approach (b) reflects the view that:

(a) the investor should reflect the post-acquisition change in the net assets of the investee; *[IAS 28.3]*

(b) from the investor's perspective the transaction is not 'a transaction with owners in their capacity as owners' – the investor does not equity account for the NCI (see 7.5.5 above). So, whilst the investee must reflect the transaction as an equity transaction, from the investor's point of view the increase in the investment is a 'gain'. This is consistent with the treatment of unrealised profits between a reporting entity and an associate (see 7.6.1 above). The NCI's ownership is treated as an 'external' ownership interest to the investor's group. Therefore, consistent with this approach, any transaction which is, from the investor's perspective a transaction with an 'external' ownership interest can give rise to a gain or loss;

(c) the increase in the investee's equity is also not an item of OCI as referred to in paragraph 10 of IAS 28;

(d) any increase in the amount of an asset should go to profit or loss if not otherwise stated in IFRS. Paragraph 88 of IAS 1 states that an 'entity shall recognise all items of income and expense in a period in profit or loss unless an IFRS requires or permits otherwise.'

We believe it is appropriate for the investor to recognise the change in net assets/equity relating to the transaction with NCI since this approach does not ignore the principle in paragraph 3 of IAS 28 of recognising post–acquisition changes in the investee's net assets.

These approaches are illustrated in Example 11.24 below. Although the example is based on a transaction by an associate, the accounting would be the same if it had been undertaken by a joint venture.

Example 11.24: Accounting for the effect of transactions with non-controlling interests recognised through equity by an associate

Entity A holds a 20% interest in Entity B (an associate) that in turn has a 100% ownership interest in Subsidiary C. The net assets of C included in B's consolidated financial statements are €1,000. For the purposes of the example all other assets and liabilities in B's financial statements and in A's consolidated financial statements are ignored.

B sells 20% of its interest in C to a third party for €300. B accounts for this transaction as an equity transaction in accordance with IFRS 10, giving rise to a credit in equity of €100 that is attributable to the owners of B. The credit is the difference between the proceeds of €300 and the share of net assets of C that are now attributable to the NCI of €200 (20% of €1,000).

The financial statements of A and B before the transaction are summarised below:

Before

A's consolidated financial statements

	€		€
Investment in B	200	Equity	200
Total	200	Total	200

B's consolidated financial statements

	€		€
Assets (from C)	1,000	Equity	1,000
Total	1,000	Total	1,000

The financial statements of B after the transaction are summarised below:

After

B's consolidated financial statements

	€		€
Assets (from C)	1,000	Equity	1,000
Cash	300	Equity transaction with NCI	100
		Equity attributable to owners	1,100
		NCI	200
Total	1,300	Total	1,300

As a result of the sale of B's 20% interest in C, B's net assets attributable to the owners of B have increased from €1,000 to €1,100. Although A has not participated in the transaction, the investor's share of net assets in B has increased from €200 to €220.

A should account for this increase in net assets arising from this equity transaction using either of the following approaches:

Approach (a) – 'share of other changes in equity' in investor's statement of changes in equity

The change of interest in the net assets/equity of B resulting from B's equity transaction should be reflected in A's financial statements as 'share of other changes in equity of associates' in its statement of changes in equity.

Therefore, A reflects its €20 share of the change in equity and maintains the same classification as the associate i.e. a direct credit to equity.

Approach (b) – gain or loss within share of associate's profit or loss included in investor's profit or loss

The change of interest in the net assets/equity of B resulting from B's equity transaction should be reflected in A's financial statements as a 'gain' in profit or loss.

Therefore, A reflects its €20 share of the change in equity in profit or loss.

7.12 Discontinuing the use of the equity method

An investor discontinues the use of the equity method on the date that its investment ceases to be either an associate or a joint venture. The subsequent accounting depends upon the nature of the retained investment. If the investment becomes a subsidiary, it will be accounted for in accordance with IFRS 10 and IFRS 3 as discussed at 7.12.1 below. If the retained investment is a financial asset, it will be accounted for in accordance with IFRS 9 as discussed at 7.12.3 below. *[IAS 28.22]*. If an investment in an associate becomes an investment in a joint venture, or an investment in a joint venture becomes an investment in an associate, the entity continues to apply the equity method, as discussed at 7.12.4 below. *[IAS 28.24]*.

Where an investment in an associate or a joint venture (or a portion thereof) meets the criteria to be classified as held for sale, the entity applies IFRS 5 as discussed at 6 above. *[IAS 28.20]*.

7.12.1 Investment in associate or joint venture that is a business becoming a subsidiary

If an increased investment in an associate or joint venture that is a business, or a change in circumstances, leads to an investor obtaining control over the investee, the investment becomes a subsidiary. The entity discontinues the use of the equity method and accounts for its investment in accordance with IFRS 3 and IFRS 10. *[IAS 28.22]*. In this situation, IFRS 3 requires revaluation of the previously held interest in the equity accounted investment at its acquisition-date fair value, with recognition of any gain or loss in profit or loss. *[IFRS 3.41-42]*. The accounting for an increase in an associate or joint venture that becomes a subsidiary is discussed further in Chapter 9 at 9.

In addition, the entity accounts for all amounts previously recognised in OCI in relation to that investment on the same basis as would have been required if the investee had directly disposed of the related assets or liabilities. *[IAS 28.22]*.

Therefore, if a gain or loss previously recognised in OCI by the investee would be reclassified to profit or loss on the disposal of the related assets or liabilities, the entity reclassifies the gain or loss from equity to profit or loss (as a reclassification adjustment) when the equity method is discontinued. For example, if an associate or a joint venture has cumulative exchange differences relating to a foreign operation and the entity discontinues the use of the equity method, the entity shall reclassify to profit or loss the gain or loss that had previously been recognised in OCI in relation to the foreign operation. *[IAS 28.23]*.

7.12.2 Investment in associate or joint venture that is not a business becoming a subsidiary

Current accounting standards do not address the accounting treatment for an acquisition in stages from associate or joint venture to subsidiary that is considered an asset acquisition rather than a business combination. This raises questions as to how to measure the previously held interest and the non-controlling interests on acquisition. There is more than one acceptable approach for the measurement of both the previously held interest and the non-controlling interests on acquisition. These are discussed in detail in Chapter 7 at 3.1.2.

7.12.3 Retained investment in the former associate or joint venture is a financial asset

If an investor disposes of a portion of its investment, such that it no longer has significant influence or joint control over the investee, it will discontinue the use of the equity method. If the retained interest is a financial asset, the entity measures the retained interest at fair value. The fair value of the retained interest is to be regarded as its fair value on initial recognition as a financial asset in accordance with IFRS 9.

In such situations, the entity recognises in profit or loss any difference between:

(a) the fair value of any retained interest and any proceeds from disposing of a part interest in the associate or joint venture; and

(b) the carrying amount of the investment at the date the equity method was discontinued.

Furthermore, the entity accounts for all amounts previously recognised in OCI in relation to that investment on the same basis as would have been required if the investee had directly disposed of the related assets or liabilities. *[IAS 28.22]*.

Therefore, if a gain or loss previously recognised in OCI by the investee would be reclassified to profit or loss on the disposal of the related assets or liabilities, the entity reclassifies the gain or loss from equity to profit or loss (as a reclassification adjustment) when the equity method is discontinued. For example, if an associate or a joint venture has cumulative exchange differences relating to a foreign operation and the entity discontinues the use of the equity method, the entity reclassifies to profit or loss the gain or loss that had previously been recognised in OCI in relation to the foreign operation. *[IAS 28.23]*.

After the partial disposal of an interest in a joint venture (or in an associate) that includes a foreign operation, if the retained interest is a financial asset that itself includes a foreign operation, IAS 21 – *The Effects of Changes in Foreign Exchange Rates* – requires it to be accounted for as a disposal. *[IAS 21.48A]*. As a result, the reclassification adjustment from equity to profit or loss is for the full amount that is in OCI and not just a proportionate amount based upon the interest disposed of. The Basis for Conclusions to IAS 21 explains that the loss of significant influence or joint control is a significant economic event that warrants accounting for the transaction as a disposal under IAS 21, *[IAS 21.BC33-34]*, and hence the transfer of the full exchange difference rather than just the proportionate share that would be required if this was accounted for as a partial disposal under IAS 21.

The accounting described above applies not only when an investor disposes of an interest in an associate or joint venture, but also where it ceases to have significant influence due to a change in circumstances. For example, when an associate issues shares to third parties, changes to the board of directors may result in the investor no longer having significant influence over the associate. Therefore, the investor will discontinue the use of the equity method.

7.12.4 Investment in associate becomes a joint venture (or vice versa)

If an investment in an associate becomes an investment in a joint venture or an investment in a joint venture becomes an investment in an associate, the entity does not discontinue the use of the equity method. In such circumstances, the entity continues to apply the equity method and does not remeasure the retained interest. *[IAS 28.24]*.

When the change in status of the investment results from the acquisition of an additional interest in the investee, the increase in the investment is accounted for as discussed at 7.4.2.C above. When the change in status results from the disposal of an interest in the investee, this is accounted for as explained at 7.12.5 below.

As discussed at 6 and at 7.12 above, if a portion of an interest in an associate or joint venture fulfils the criteria for classification as held for sale, it is only that portion that is accounted for under IFRS 5. An entity maintains the use of the equity method for the retained interest until the portion classified as held for sale is finally sold.

7.12.5 Partial disposals of interests in associate or joint venture where the equity method continues to be applied

IAS 28 does not explicitly state that an entity should recognise a gain or loss when it disposes of a part of its interest in an associate or a joint venture, but the entity continues to apply the equity method. However, as explained below, it is evident that a gain or loss should be recognised on the partial disposal.

The standard requires that when an entity's ownership interest in an associate or a joint venture is reduced, but the entity continues to apply the equity method, the entity reclassifies to profit or loss the proportion of the gain or loss that had previously been recognised in OCI relating to that reduction in ownership interest if that gain or loss would be required to be reclassified to profit or loss on the disposal of the related assets or liabilities. *[IAS 28.25]*.

In addition, IAS 21 requires for such partial disposals that the investor should 'reclassify to profit or loss only the proportionate share of the cumulative amount of the exchange differences recognised in other comprehensive income'. *[IAS 21.48C]*.

That means that the investor recognises in profit or loss a proportion of:
- foreign exchange differences recognised in OCI under IAS 21;
- accumulated hedging gains and losses recognised in OCI under IFRS 9 (see Chapter 53) (or IAS 39); and
- any other amounts previously recognised in OCI that would have been recognised in profit or loss if the associate had directly disposed of the assets to which they relate,

in each case proportionate to the interest disposed of.

IAS 21 requires that the proportion of the foreign exchange differences are reclassified 'when the gain or loss on disposal is recognised'. *[IAS 21.48]*. In addition, the Interpretations Committee in the context of deemed disposals (see 7.12.6 below), noted that reclassification of amounts to profit or loss from OCI is generally required as part of determining the gain or loss on a disposal.

Although IFRS 10 requires that partial disposals of subsidiaries, where control is retained, are accounted for as equity transactions (see Chapter 7 at 4) and no profit or loss is recognised, we do not believe that this has an impact on the accounting for a partial disposal of an associate or a joint venture (which continues to be accounted for under the equity method). Under equity accounting an investor accounts only for its own interest. Given that the other investors' ownership in the associate is not reflected in the accounts of an investor there is no basis for concluding that partial disposals can be treated as equity transactions.

7.12.6 Deemed disposals

An investor's interest in an associate or a joint venture may be reduced other than by an actual disposal. Such a reduction in interest, which is commonly referred to as a deemed disposal, gives rise to a 'dilution' gain or loss. Deemed disposals may arise for a number of reasons, including:
- the investor does not take up its full allocation in a rights issue by the associate or joint venture;
- the associate or joint venture declares scrip dividends which are not taken up by the investor so that its proportional interest is reduced;
- another party exercises its options or warrants issued by the associate or joint venture; or
- the associate or joint venture issues shares to third parties.

In some situations, the circumstances giving rise to the dilution in the investor's interest may be such that the investor no longer has significant influence over the investee. In that case, the investor will account for the transaction as a disposal, with a retained interest in a financial asset measured at fair value. This is described at 7.12.3 above. However, in other situations, the deemed disposal will give rise to only a partial disposal, such that the investor will continue to equity account for the investee.

As discussed in more detail at 7.12.5 above, although IAS 28 does not explicitly state that an entity should recognise a gain or loss on partial disposal of its interest in an associate or a joint venture when the entity continues to apply the equity method, it is evident that a gain or loss should be recognised on partial disposals.

In the absence of further guidance, we believe that gains or losses on deemed disposals should be recognised in profit or loss, and this will include amounts reclassified from OCI.

However, what is not clear is whether any of the notional goodwill component of the carrying amount of the associate or joint venture should be considered in the calculation of the gain or loss on the deemed disposal. We believe that it is appropriate to consider the entire carrying amount of the associate or joint venture, i.e. including the notional goodwill, as shown in Example 11.25 below. Although the example is based on a deemed disposal of an associate, the accounting would be the same if it had been a deemed disposal of a joint venture.

IAS 28 defines the equity method as 'a method of accounting whereby the investment is initially recognised at cost and adjusted thereafter for the post acquisition change in the investor's share of the investee's net assets. ...' *[IAS 28.3]*. A literal reading of this definition suggests that in calculating the loss on dilution, the investor should take account of only the change in its share of the associate's or joint venture's net assets and not account for a change in the notional goodwill component.

However, paragraph 42 of IAS 28 specifically states that goodwill included in the carrying amount of an investment in an associate or a joint venture is not separately recognised. *[IAS 28.42]*. Hence, we believe that it should not be excluded from the cost of a deemed disposal either.

Although the IASB did not explicitly consider accounting for deemed disposals of associates or joint ventures, paragraph 26 of IAS 28 refers to the concepts underlying the procedures used in accounting for the acquisition of a subsidiary in accounting for acquisitions of an investment in an associate or joint venture. Therefore, it is appropriate to consider the notional goodwill component when accounting for deemed disposals of associates or joint ventures in the same way as for deemed disposals of subsidiaries.

Example 11.25: Deemed disposal of an associate

At the start of the reporting period, Investor A acquired a 30% interest in Entity B at a cost of £500,000. A has significant influence over B and accounts for its investment in B under the equity method. B has net identifiable assets of £1,000,000 at the date of acquisition, which have a fair value of £1,200,000. During the year, B recognised a post-tax profit of £200,000 and paid a dividend of £18,000. B also recognised foreign exchange losses of £40,000 in OCI.

B's net assets at the end of the reporting period can be determined as follows:

	£
Net identifiable assets – opening balance	1,000,000
Profit for year	200,000
Dividends paid	(18,000)
Foreign exchange losses	(40,000)
B's net assets – closing balance	1,142,000

A's interest in B at the end of the reporting period is calculated as follows:

	£
On acquisition (including goodwill of £500,000 – (30% × £1,200,000) = £140,000):	500,000
Share of profit after tax (30% × £200,000)	60,000
Elimination of dividend (30% of £18,000)	(5,400)
A's share of exchange differences (30% × £40,000)	(12,000)
A's interest in B at the end of the reporting period under the equity method	542,600

which can also be determined as follows:

	£
A's share of B's net identifiable assets (30% × £1,142,000)	342,600
Goodwill	140,000
A's share of fair value uplift (30% × £200,000) †	60,000
A's interest in B at the end of the reporting period	542,600

† This assumes that none of the uplift related to depreciable assets, such that the £200,000 did not diminish after the acquisition.

At the start of the next reporting period, B has a rights issue that A does not participate in. The rights issue brings in an additional £150,000 in cash and dilutes A's interest in B to 25%.

Consequently, B's net assets at this date are:

	£
B's net assets before the rights issue	1,142,000
Additional cash	150,000
B's net assets after the rights issue	1,292,000

The loss on the deemed disposal, considering the entire carrying amount of the associate, including the notional goodwill is calculated as follows:

	£	£
Carrying amount of the investment before the deemed disposal		542,600
Cost of deemed disposal (£542,600 × (30% – 25%) / 30%)	(90,433)	
Share of the contribution (£150,000 × 25%)	37,500	
Reduction in carrying amount of associate	(52,933)	(52,933)
Reclassification of share in currency translation: (£40,000 × 30% × (25% – 30%) / 30%)	(2,000)	
Loss deemed disposal	(54,933)	
Carrying amount of the investment after the deemed disposal		489,667

8 IMPAIRMENT LOSSES

8.1 General

Determining whether an investment in an associate or joint venture is impaired may be more complicated than it initially appears, as it involves carrying out several separate impairment assessments:

- Assets of the associate or joint venture

  It is generally not appropriate for the investor simply to multiply the amount of the impairment recognised in the investee's own books by the investor's percentage of ownership, because the investor should measure its interest in an associate's or joint venture's identifiable net assets at fair value at the date of acquisition of an associate or a joint venture. Therefore, if the value that the investor attributes to the associate's or joint venture's net assets differs from the carrying amount of those net assets in the associate's or joint venture's own books, the investor should restate any impairment losses recognised by the associate or joint venture and it also needs to consider whether it needs to recognise any impairments that the associate or joint venture itself did not recognise in its own books.

  Any goodwill recognised on the statement of financial position of an associate or joint venture needs to be separated into two elements:

  - goodwill that existed at the date the investor acquired its interest in the associate or joint venture, and
  - goodwill that arises on subsequent acquisitions by the associate or joint venture.

  Goodwill that existed at the date the investor acquired its interest is not an identifiable asset of the associate or joint venture from the perspective of the investor. It should be combined with the investor's goodwill on the acquisition of its interest in the associate or joint venture.

  Goodwill that arises on subsequent acquisitions by the associate or joint venture should be accounted for in the books of the associate or joint venture, including being tested for impairment in accordance with IAS 36. The investor should not make any adjustments to the associate's or joint venture's accounting for that goodwill.

- Investment in the associate or joint venture

  After application of the equity method, including recognising the associate's or joint venture's losses (see 7.9 above), the entity applies the requirements discussed at 8.2 below to determine whether there is any objective evidence that its net investment in the associate or joint venture is impaired. *[IAS 28.40]*.

- Other interests that are not part of the net investment in the associate or joint venture

  The entity applies the impairment requirements in IFRS 9 (see Chapter 51) to its other interests in the associate or joint venture that are in the scope of IFRS 9 and that do not constitute part of the net investment (see 8.3 below). *[IFRS 9.2.1(a)]*.

This has the effect of it being extremely unlikely that any impairment charge recognised in respect of an associate or joint venture will simply be the investor's share of any impairment charge recognised by the associate or joint venture itself, even when the associate or joint venture complies with IFRS.

IAS 28 requires the recoverable amount of an investment in an associate or a joint venture to be assessed individually, unless the associate or joint venture does not generate cash inflows from continuing use that are largely independent of those from other assets of the entity. *[IAS 28.43]*.

8.2 Investment in the associate or joint venture

After application of the equity method, including recognising the associate's or joint venture's losses (see 7.9 above), the entity applies the following requirements to determine whether there is any objective evidence that its net investment in the associate or joint venture is impaired. *[IAS 28.40]*. The entity applies the impairment requirements in IFRS 9 (see Chapter 51) to its other interests in the associate or joint venture that are in the scope of IFRS 9 and that do not constitute part of the net investment. *[IFRS 9.2.1(a)]*.

- The net investment in an associate or joint venture is impaired and impairment losses are incurred if, and only if, there is objective evidence of impairment as a result of one or more events that occurred after the initial recognition of the net investment (a 'loss event') and that loss event (or events) has an impact on the estimated future cash flows from the net investment that can be reliably estimated. It may not be possible to identify a single, discrete event that caused the impairment. Rather, the combined effect of several events may have caused the impairment. Losses expected because of future events, no matter how likely, are not recognised. Objective evidence that the net investment is impaired includes observable data that comes to the attention of the entity about the following loss events:
    - significant financial difficulty of the associate or joint venture;
    - a breach of contract, such as a default or delinquency in payments by the associate or joint venture;
    - the entity, for economic or legal reasons relating to its associate's or joint venture's financial difficulty, granting to the associate or joint venture a concession that the entity would not otherwise consider;
    - it becomes probable that the associate or joint venture will enter bankruptcy or another financial reorganisation; or
    - the disappearance of an active market for the net investment because of financial difficulties of the associate or joint venture. *[IAS 28.41A]*.
- The disappearance of an active market because the associate's or joint venture's equity or financial instruments are no longer publicly traded is not evidence of impairment. A downgrade of an associate's or joint venture's credit rating or a decline in the fair value of the associate or joint venture is not, of itself, evidence of impairment, although it may be evidence of impairment when considered with other available information. *[IAS 28.41B]*.
- In addition to the types of events mentioned above, objective evidence of impairment of the net investment in the equity instruments of the associate or joint venture includes information about significant changes with an adverse effect that have taken place in the technological, market, economic or legal environment in which the associate or joint venture operates, and indicates that the cost of the

investment in the equity instrument may not be recovered. A significant or prolonged decline in the fair value of an investment in an equity instrument below its cost is also objective evidence of impairment. *[IAS 28.41C]*.

Goodwill that forms part of the carrying amount of the net investment in an associate or a joint venture is not separately recognised and therefore is not tested for impairment separately. Instead, the entire carrying amount of the investment is tested for impairment in accordance with IAS 36 as a single asset, by comparing its recoverable amount (the higher of value in use and fair value less costs to sell) with its carrying amount whenever indicators of impairment exist, as described in the bullets above. Any impairment loss is not allocated to any asset, including goodwill, that forms part of the carrying amount of the net investment in the associate or joint venture. Accordingly, any reversal of that impairment loss is recognised in accordance with IAS 36 to the extent that the recoverable amount of the net investment subsequently increases. In determining the value in use of the net investment, an entity estimates:

- its share of the present value of the estimated future cash flows expected to be generated by the associate or joint venture, including the cash flows from the operations of the associate or joint venture and the proceeds from the ultimate disposal of the investment; or
- the present value of the estimated future cash flows expected to arise from dividends to be received from the investment and from its ultimate disposal.

Using appropriate assumptions, both methods give the same result. *[IAS 28.42]*. In effect, IAS 28 requires the investor to regard its investment in an associate or joint venture as a single cash-generating unit, rather than 'drilling down' into the separate cash-generating units determined by the associate or joint venture. The IASB does not explain why it adopted this approach, although we imagine that it may have been for the very practical reason that although an investor has significant influence over an associate, it does not have control and therefore may not have access to the relevant underlying information. Furthermore, IAS 28 requires the investment as a whole to be reviewed for impairment as if it were a financial asset.

8.3 Other interests that are not part of the net investment in the associate or joint venture

The IASB issued an amendment to IAS 28 clarifying that an entity applies IFRS 9 to long-term interests in an associate or joint venture to which the equity method is not applied but that, in substance, form part of the net investment in the associate or joint venture (long-term interests). This clarification is relevant because it implies that the expected credit loss model in IFRS 9 applies to such long-term interests. The IASB also clarified that, in applying IFRS 9, an entity does not take account of any losses of the associate or joint venture, or any impairment losses on the net investment, recognised as adjustments to the net investment in the associate or joint venture that arise from applying IAS 28. *[IAS 28.14A]*. The amendment is effective for annual periods beginning on or after 1 January 2019. Early application of the amendments is permitted and must be disclosed. *[IAS 28.45G]*. Entities must apply the amendments retrospectively, with the following exceptions:

- An entity that first applies the amendments at the same time it first applies IFRS 9 shall apply the transition requirements in IFRS 9 to the long-term interests.
- An entity that first applies the amendments after it first applies IFRS 9 shall apply the transition requirements in IFRS 9 necessary for applying the amendments to long-term interests. For that purpose, references to the date of initial application in IFRS 9 shall be read as referring to the beginning of the annual reporting period in which the entity first applies the amendments (the date of initial application of the amendments). The entity is not required to restate prior periods to reflect the application of the amendments. The entity may restate prior periods only if it is possible without the use of hindsight.
- When first applying the amendments, an entity that applies the temporary exemption from IFRS 9 in accordance with IFRS 4 is not required to restate prior periods to reflect the application of the amendments. The entity may restate prior periods only if it is possible without the use of hindsight.
- If an entity does not restate prior periods, at the date of initial application of the amendments it shall recognise in the opening retained earnings (or other component of equity, as appropriate) any difference between the previous carrying amount of long-term interests at that date; and the carrying amount of those long-term interests at that date.

To illustrate how entities apply the requirements in IAS 28 and IFRS 9 with respect to long-term interests, the Board published an illustrative example, on which Example 11.26, below, is based.

Example 11.26: Long-term interests in associates and joint ventures

An investor has the following three types of interests in an associate:

(a) O Shares – ordinary shares representing a 40% ownership interest to which the investor applies the equity method. This interest is the least senior of the three interests, based on their relative priority in liquidation.

(b) P Shares – non-cumulative preference shares that form part of the net investment in the associate and that the investor measures at fair value through profit or loss applying IFRS 9.

(c) LT Loan – a long-term loan that forms part of the net investment in the associate and that the investor measures at amortised cost applying IFRS 9, with a stated interest rate and an effective interest rate of 5% a year. The associate makes interest-only payments to the investor each year. The LT Loan is the most senior of the three interests.

The LT Loan is not an originated credit-impaired loan. Throughout the years illustrated, there has not been any objective evidence that the net investment in the associate is impaired applying IAS 28, nor does the LT Loan become credit-impaired applying IFRS 9.

The associate does not have any outstanding cumulative preference shares classified as equity, as described in paragraph 37 of IAS 28. Throughout the years illustrated, the associate neither declares nor pays dividends on O Shares or P Shares.

The investor has not incurred any legal or constructive obligations, nor made payments on behalf of the associate, as described in paragraph 39 of IAS 28. Accordingly, the investor does not recognise its share of the associate's losses once the carrying amount of its net investment in the associate is reduced to zero.

The amount of the investor's initial investment in O Shares is €200, in P Shares is €100 and in the LT Loan is €100. On acquisition of the investment, the cost of the investment equals the investor's share of the net fair value of the associate's identifiable assets and liabilities.

This table summarises the carrying amount at the end of each year for P Shares and the LT Loan applying IFRS 9 but before applying IAS 28, and the associate's profit (loss) for each year. The amounts for the LT Loan are shown net of the loss allowance.

At the end of year	P Shares applying IFRS 9 (fair value) (€)	LT Loan applying IFRS 9 (amortised cost) (€)	Profit (Loss) of the Associate (€)
1	110	90	50
2	90	70	(200)
3	50	50	(500)
4	40	50	(150)
5	60	60	–
6	80	70	500
7	110	90	500

The table below summarises the amounts recognised in the investor's profit or loss. When recognising interest revenue on the LT Loan in each year, the investor does not take account of any adjustments to the carrying amount of the LT Loan that arose from applying IAS 28 (paragraph 14A of IAS 28). Accordingly, the investor recognises interest revenue on the LT Loan based on the effective interest rate of 5% each year.

	Items recognised			
During year	Impairment (losses), including reversals, applying IFRS 9 (€)	Gains (losses) of P Shares applying IFRS 9 (€)	Share of profit (loss) of the associate recognised applying the equity method (€)	Interest revenue applying IFRS 9 (€)
1	(10)	10	20	5
2	(20)	(20)	(80)	5
3	(20)	(40)	(200)	5
4	–	(10)	(30)	5
5	10	20	(30)	5
6	10	20	200	5
7	20	30	200	5

(1) In Year 1, the increase in fair value of the P Shares of €10 is the difference between the €110 and €100; the increase in the loss allowance of the LT Loan of (€10) is the difference between €90 and €100; and the investor's share of profit of €20 is €50 × 40%. At the end of Year 1, the carrying amount of the O Shares is €220, P Shares is €110 and the LT Loan (net of loss allowance) is €90.

(2) In Year 2, the decrease in fair value of the P Shares of (€20) is the difference between the €90 and €110; the increase in the loss allowance of the LT Loan of (€20) is the difference between €70 and €90; and the investor's share of losses of €80 is €200 × 40%. At the end of Year 2, the carrying amount of the O Shares is €140, P Shares is €90 and the LT Loan (net of loss allowance) is €70.

(3) Applying paragraph 14A of IAS 28, the investor applies IFRS 9 to the P Shares and the LT Loan before it applies paragraph 38 of IAS 28. Accordingly, in Year 3 the decrease in fair value of the P Shares of (€40) is the difference between the €50 and €90; the increase in the loss allowance of the LT Loan of (€20) is the difference between €50 and €70; and the investor's share of losses of €200 is €500 × 40%. The investor recognises its share of the associate's loss in reverse order of seniority as specified in paragraph 38 of IAS 28 and allocates €140 to the O Shares, €50 to the P Shares and €10 to the LT Loan. At the end of Year 3, the carrying amount of the O Shares is zero, P Shares is zero and the LT Loan (net of loss allowance) is CU40.

(4) In Year 4, the decrease in fair value of the P Shares of (€10) is the difference between the €40 and €50. Recognition of the change in fair value of €10 in Year 4 results in the carrying amount of P Shares being negative €10. Consequently, the investor reverses a portion of €10 of the associate's losses previously allocated to P Shares. Applying paragraph 38 of IAS 28, the investor limits the recognition of the associate's losses to €40 because the carrying amount of its net investment in the associate is then zero.

At the end of Year 4, the carrying amount of the O Shares is zero, P Shares is zero and the LT Loan (net of loss allowance) is zero. There is also an unrecognised share of the associate's losses of €30 (the investor's share of the associate's cumulative losses of €340 – €320 losses recognised cumulatively + €10 losses reversed).

(5) In Year 5, the increase in fair value of the P Shares of €20 is the difference between the €60 and €40; the decrease in the loss allowance of €10 is the difference between €60 and €50. After applying IFRS 9 to the P Shares and the LT Loan, these interests have a positive carrying amount. Consequently, the investor allocates the previously unrecognised share of the associate's losses of €30 to these interests, being €20 to the P Shares and €10 to the LT Loan. At the end of Year 5, the carrying amount of the O Shares is zero, P Shares is zero and the LT Loan (net of loss allowance) is zero.

(6) In Year 6, the increase in fair value of the P Shares of €20 is the difference between the €80 and €60; the decrease in the loss allowance of €10 is the difference between €70 and €60; and the investor's share of the associate's profit of €200 is €500 × 40%. The investor allocates the associate's profit to each interest in the order of seniority. The investor limits the amount of the associate's profit it allocates to the P Shares and the LT Loan to the amount of equity method losses previously allocated to those interests, which in this example is €60 for both interests. The balancing €60 is allocated to the investment in the O Shares. At the end of Year 6, the carrying amount of the O Shares is €80, P Shares is €80 and the LT Loan (net of loss allowance) is €70.

(7) In Year 7, the increase in fair value of the P Shares of €30 is the difference between the €110 and €80; the decrease in the loss allowance of €20 is the difference between €90 and €70; and the investor's share of the associate's profit of €200 is €500 × 40%, allocated in full to the investment in the O Shares. At the end of Year 7, the carrying amount of the O Shares is €280, P Shares is €110 and the LT Loan (net of loss allowance) is €90.

9 SEPARATE FINANCIAL STATEMENTS

IAS 27 was amended in August 2014 to allow entities the option to account for investments in subsidiaries, associates and joint ventures using the equity method of accounting.

For the purposes of IAS 28, *separate financial statements* are as defined in IAS 27, [IAS 28.4], as those presented by an entity, in which the entity could elect to account for its investments in subsidiaries, joint ventures and associates either at cost, in accordance with IFRS 9 or using the equity method as described in IAS 28.

An investment in an associate or joint venture is accounted for in the entity's separate financial statements in accordance with paragraph 10 of IAS 27. [IAS 28.44]. IAS 27 requires that, in separate financial statements, investments in subsidiaries, associates or joint ventures are accounted for either:

- at cost;
- in accordance with IFRS 9; or
- using the equity method as described in IAS 28.

The entity applies the same accounting for each category of investments. Investments accounted for at cost or using the equity method are accounted for in accordance with IFRS 5 when they are classified as held for sale (or included in a disposal group that is classified as held for sale). [IAS 27.10].

If an entity elects, in accordance with paragraph 18 of IAS 28, to measure its investments in associates or joint ventures at fair value through profit or loss in accordance with IFRS 9 (see 5.3 above) it also accounts for those investments in the same way in its separate financial statements. [IAS 27.11].

IAS 27 requires the investor to recognise all dividends, whether relating to pre-acquisition or post-acquisition profits of the investee, in profit or loss within its separate financial statements once the right to receive payment has been established. *[IAS 27.12]*. The investor then needs to consider whether there are indicators of impairment as set out in paragraph 12(h) of IAS 36 (see Chapter 8 at 2.4.1).

The detailed IFRS requirements for separate financial statements as set out in IAS 27 are discussed more fully in Chapter 8.

9.1 Impairment of investments in associates or joint ventures in separate financial statements

An issue considered by the Interpretations Committee and the IASB is how impairments of investments in associates should be determined in the separate financial statements of the investor. In January 2013, the Interpretations Committee issued an agenda decision[14] stating that according to paragraphs 4 and 5 of IAS 36 and paragraph 2(a) of IAS 39 (now paragraph 2.1(a) of IFRS 9), investments in subsidiaries, joint ventures, and associates that are not accounted for in accordance with IFRS 9 are within the scope of IAS 36 for impairment purposes. Consequently, in its separate financial statements, an entity should apply the provisions of IAS 36 to test for impairment its investments in subsidiaries, joint ventures, and associates that are carried at cost or using the equity method.

10 PRESENTATION AND DISCLOSURES

10.1 Presentation

10.1.1 Statement of financial position

Unless an investment, or a portion of an investment, in an associate or a joint venture is classified as held for sale in accordance with IFRS 5 (see 6 above), the investment, or any retained interest in the investment not classified as held for sale, is classified as a non-current asset. *[IAS 28.15]*. The aggregate of investments in associates and joint ventures accounted for using the equity method are presented as a discrete line item in the statement of financial position. *[IAS 1.54(e)]*.

IAS 28 does not explicitly define what is meant by 'investment ... in an associate or a joint venture'. However, paragraph 38 states that 'the interest in an associate or a joint venture is the carrying amount of the investment in the associate or joint venture determined under the equity method together with any long-term interests that, in substance, form part of the investor's net investment in the associate or joint venture... Such items may include preference shares and long-term receivables or loans but do not include trade receivables, trade payables or any long-term receivables for which adequate collateral exists, such as secured loans.' *[IAS 28.38]*. Some have interpreted this as a requirement to present the investment in ordinary shares and other long-term interests in associates within the same line item.

Yet, when associates are profitable, long-term interests such as loans are normally accounted for under IFRS 9 rather than under the equity method. Therefore, it is generally considered acceptable to present the investment in ordinary shares in associates and joint ventures and other long-term interests in associates and joint ventures in separate line items.

Goodwill relating to an associate or joint venture is included in the carrying amount of the investment, *[IAS 28.32]*, as is illustrated in Extract 11.2 below.

> **Extract 11.2: RWE Aktiengesellschaft (2019)**
>
> **03 Consolidated financial statements** [extract]
>
> **3.6 Notes** [extract]
>
> **Consolidation principles** [extract]
>
> For investments accounted for using the equity method, goodwill is not reported separately, but rather included in the value recognised for the investment. In other respects, the consolidation principles described above apply analogously. If impairment losses on the equity value become necessary, we report such under income from investments accounted for using the equity method. The financial statements of investments accounted for using the equity method are prepared using uniform accounting policies.

10.1.2 Profit or loss

In the statement of comprehensive income or separate income statement, the aggregate of the investor's share of the profit or loss of associates and joint ventures accounted for using the equity method must be shown. *[IAS 1.82(c)]*. 'Profit or loss' in this context is interpreted in the implementation guidance to IAS 1 as meaning the 'profit attributable to owners' of the associates and joint ventures, i.e. it is after tax and non-controlling interests in the associates or joint ventures.[15] There is no requirement as to where in the statement of comprehensive income or separate income statement the investor's share of the profit or loss of associates and joint ventures accounted for using the equity method should be shown, and different approaches are therefore seen in practice. As discussed in Chapter 3 at 3.2.2.A, some entities present operating income on the face of the income statement. In this case, equity accounted investments may form part of operating activities with their results included in that measure and with non-operating investments excluded from it. Another acceptable alternative is to exclude the results of all associates and joint ventures from operating profit.

Nokia Corporation for example includes its share of the (post-tax) results of associates after operating profit, but before pre-tax profit:

> **Extract 11.3: Nokia Corporation (2019)**
>
> **Financial statements** [extract]
>
> **Consolidated income statement** [extract]
>
> | For the year ended December 31 | Notes | 2019 EURm | 2018 EURm | 2017 EURm |
> |---|---|---|---|---|
> | Operating profit/(loss) | | 485 | (59) | 16 |
> | Share of results of associated companies and joint ventures | 34 | 12 | 12 | 11 |
> | Financial income and expenses | 11 | (341) | (313) | (537) |
> | **Profit/(loss) before tax** | | **156** | **(360)** | **(510)** |

In contrast, Nestlé S.A. includes its share of the post-tax results of associates below tax expense:

Extract 11.4: Nestlé S.A. (2019)

Consolidated income statement for the year ended 31 December 2019 [extract]

In millions of CHF	Notes	2019	2018
Profit before taxes, associates and joint ventures		15 062	12 991
Taxes	13	(3 159)	(3 439)
Income from associates and joint ventures	14	1 001	916
Profit for the year		12 904	10 468

10.1.2.A Impairment of associates or joint ventures

It is unclear where impairments of associates or joint ventures should be presented in the statement of comprehensive income or separate income statement. IAS 28 requires an impairment test to be performed 'after application of the equity method', *[IAS 28.40]*, which could be read as implying that impairment of an associate or joint venture is not part of the investor's share of the profit or loss of an associate or joint venture accounted for using the equity method. On the other hand, the guidance on accounting for impairment losses on associates is presented under the heading 'Application of the equity method' in IAS 28, which suggests that accounting for impairments of associates is part of the equity method. In practice, both interpretations appear to have gained a degree of acceptance.

RWE Aktiengesellschaft, for example, reports impairment losses on associates within income from investments accounted for using the equity method (see Extract 11.2 at 10.1.1 above).

10.1.3 Other items of comprehensive income

The investor's share of items recognised in OCI by the associate or joint venture is recognised in the investor's OCI. *[IAS 28.10]*.

Paragraph 82A of IAS 1 clarifies that entities must present the share of OCI of associates and joint ventures accounted for using the equity method, separated into the share of items that, in accordance with other IFRSs:

- will not be subsequently reclassified to profit or loss; and
- will be reclassified subsequently to profit or loss when specific conditions are met. *[IAS 1.82A]*.

'Other comprehensive income' in this context is interpreted in the implementation guidance to IAS 1 as meaning the 'other comprehensive income attributable to owners' of the associates and joint ventures, i.e. it is after tax and non-controlling interests in the associates or joint ventures.[16]

10.1.4 Statement of cash flows

IAS 7 – *Statement of Cash Flows* – notes that for an equity accounted investment, reporting in the cash flow statement is limited to cash flows between the investor and the investee, such as dividends received. The question arises as to whether dividends received should be recognised as operating or investing cash flows. As discussed in Chapter 40 at 4.4.1, IAS 7 is not prescriptive; however, entities should select an accounting policy and apply it consistently.

10.2 Disclosures

The disclosure requirements for associates and joint ventures are dealt with in IFRS 12, together with the disclosure requirements for subsidiaries and unconsolidated structured entities. The disclosure requirements in relation to associates and joint ventures are discussed in Chapter 13 at 5.

11 FUTURE DEVELOPMENTS

As discussed in 7.2 above, many procedures appropriate for the application of the equity method are similar to the consolidation procedures described in IFRS 10 (see Chapter 7). Furthermore, IAS 28 explains that the concepts underlying the procedures used in accounting for the acquisition of a subsidiary are also adopted in accounting for the acquisition of an investment in an associate or a joint venture. *[IAS 28.26]*. This does raise several practical difficulties, and there has been an ongoing debate about whether the equity method of accounting is a consolidation method or a measurement method. Although IAS 28 generally adopts consolidation principles it nevertheless retains features of a valuation methodology.

In 2015, the IASB tentatively decided to undertake a research project on the equity method. However, in May 2016 the IASB[17] deferred this project until the Post-Implementation Review (PIR) of IFRS 10, IFRS 11 – *Joint Arrangements* – and IFRS 12 are complete which will include seeking feedback on investors' information needs regarding equity method investments. In its meeting in May 2020, the IASB received an update on its research programme. It is noted that 'The staff aim to start work on the pipeline research project on the Equity Method in the next few months because there may be synergies with analysis of responses the Board may receive to the Request for Information on the PIR of IFRS 11 and IFRS 12.'[18]

In addition, in December 2019 the IASB issued ED/2019/7 *General Presentation and Disclosures.* This exposure draft proposes amended requirements for the presentation of the results of equity-accounted investees. See Chapter 3 at 6.1.2 for discussion of this exposure draft.

References

1 *IFRIC Update*, November 2016.
2 Staff Paper, Interpretations Committee meeting, May 2009, Agenda reference 3, *Venture capital consolidations and partial use of fair value through profit or loss.*
3 *IFRIC Update*, July 2009.
4 *IFRIC Update*, July 2010.
5 Staff paper, Interpretations Committee meeting, July 2010, Agenda reference 16, *IAS 28 – Investments in Associates – Purchase in stages – fair value as deemed cost*, paras. 24 and 29.
6 *IFRIC Update*, July 2010.
7 *IFRIC Update*, January 2019.
8 IAS 1 IG6 'XYZ Group – Statement of comprehensive income for the year ended 31 December 20X7 (illustrating the presentation of profit and loss and other comprehensive income in one statement and the classification of expenses within profit by function)'.
9 *IFRIC Update*, May 2013.
10 *IASB Update*, July 2013.
11 *IFRIC Update*, August 2002, p.3.
12 *IFRIC Update*, January 2018.
13 *Sale or Contribution of Assets between an Investor and its Associate or Joint Venture (amendments to IFRS 10 and IAS 28)*, September 2014.
14 *IFRIC Update*, January 2013.
15 IAS 1 IG6 'XYZ Group – Statement of comprehensive income for the year ended 31 December 20X7 (illustrating the presentation of profit and loss and other comprehensive income in one statement and the classification of expenses within profit by function)'.
16 IAS 1 IG6 'XYZ Group – Statement of comprehensive income for the year ended 31 December 20X7 (illustrating the presentation of profit and loss and other comprehensive income in one statement and the classification of expenses within profit by function)'.
17 *IASB Update*, May 2016.
18 Staff paper, IASB meeting, May 2020, Agenda reference 8, *Research Update*.

Chapter 12 Joint arrangements

1 INTRODUCTION 891
   1.1 The nature of joint arrangements.. 891
2 OBJECTIVE AND SCOPE OF IFRS 11 892
   2.1 Objective 892
   2.2 Scope...892
       2.2.1 Application by venture capital organisations and similar entities..892
       2.2.2 Application to joint arrangements held for sale 892
       2.2.3 Accounting by a joint operation 893
3 JOINT ARRANGEMENT...893
   3.1 Unit of account 894
4 JOINT CONTROL 895
   4.1 Assessing control...897
       4.1.1 Sequential activities 897
   4.2 Rights to control collectively 898
       4.2.1 Protective rights, including some veto rights............................898
       4.2.2 Potential voting rights and joint control 899
       4.2.3 Other evidence of joint control 899
       4.2.4 Delegated decision-making 900
       4.2.5 Related parties and de facto agents..900
       4.2.6 Role of a government 901
   4.3 Unanimous consent 901
       4.3.1 Arrangements involving parties that participate in a joint arrangement but who do not have joint control 902
       4.3.2 Ultimate voting authority..902
       4.3.3 Arbitration 903
       4.3.4 Statutory mechanisms 903
   4.4 Other practical issues with assessing joint control 903

| | | 4.4.1 | Undivided share, lease or a joint arrangement | 903 |
| | | 4.4.2 | Evaluate multiple agreements together | 904 |

5 CLASSIFICATION OF A JOINT ARRANGEMENT: JOINT OPERATIONS AND JOINT VENTURES 904
   5.1 Separate vehicle or not 906
   5.2 Legal form of the separate vehicle 907
   5.3 Contractual terms 908
      5.3.1 Guarantees 910
      5.3.2 Contractual terms upon liquidation or dissolution of joint arrangement 910
   5.4 Other facts and circumstances 911
      5.4.1 Facts and circumstances indicating rights to assets 911
          5.4.1.A Output not taken in proportion to ownership 911
          5.4.1.B Consideration of derecognition requirements for financial instruments 912
      5.4.2 Facts and circumstances indicating obligations for liabilities 912
          5.4.2.A Assessing the obligation related to cash calls or capital contributions 913
      5.4.3 Interpretations Committee agenda decisions 913
          5.4.3.A How and why particular facts and circumstances create rights and obligations 914
          5.4.3.B Implication of 'economic substance' 915
          5.4.3.C Application of 'other facts and circumstances' to specific fact patterns 916
      5.4.4 Comprehensive example illustrating evaluation of facts and circumstances 916
   5.5 Illustrative examples accompanying IFRS 11 917

6 ACCOUNTING FOR JOINT OPERATIONS 923
   6.1 Joint arrangements not structured through a separate vehicle 923
   6.2 Accounting for rights and obligations 923
   6.3 Determining the relevant IFRS 924
   6.4 Interest in a joint operation without joint control 927
   6.5 Joint operations with a party that participates in a joint arrangement but does not have joint control 927
   6.6 Transactions between a joint operator and a joint operation 928
   6.7 Accounting for a joint operation in separate financial statements ... 928

7 ACCOUNTING FOR JOINT VENTURES 929
   7.1 Interest in a joint venture without joint control 929
   7.2 Contributions of non-monetary assets to a joint venture 930

	7.3	Accounting for a joint venture in separate financial statements	930
8	**CONTINUOUS ASSESSMENT**		930
	8.1	When to reassess under IFRS 11	931
		8.1.1 Changes in ownership	931
	8.2	Changes in ownership of a joint venture that constitutes a business	932
		8.2.1 Acquisition of an interest in a joint venture	932
		8.2.2 Gaining control over a former joint venture	933
		8.2.3 Former subsidiary becomes a joint venture	933
		8.2.4 Joint venture becomes an associate (or vice versa)	934
		8.2.5 Joint venture becomes a financial asset (or vice versa)	934
		8.2.6 Disposal of an interest in a joint venture	935
		8.2.7 Interest in a joint venture held for sale	935
	8.3	Changes in ownership of a joint operation that is a business	936
		8.3.1 Acquisition of an interest in a joint operation	936
		8.3.2 Obtaining control or joint control over a joint operation that is a business	937
		8.3.3 Former subsidiary becomes a joint operation	937
		8.3.4 Other changes in ownership of a joint operation	938
		8.3.5 Disposal of interest in a joint operation	938
	8.4	Changes in ownership of a joint arrangement that does not constitute a business	938
		8.4.1 Joint operator obtains control or parties that participate in a joint arrangement but do not have joint control obtain joint control	938
9	**DISCLOSURES**		939
10	**FUTURE DEVELOPMENTS**		939

List of examples

Example 12.1:	Master agreement for manufacturing and distribution	894
Example 12.2:	Agreements with control and joint control	895
Example 12.3:	Directing sequential activities separately	898
Example 12.4:	Directing sequential activities jointly	898
Example 12.5:	Protective rights and joint control	899
Example 12.6:	De facto agents in joint control	901
Example 12.7:	Role of a government	901
Example 12.8:	Ultimate decision-making authority – no joint control (1)	902
Example 12.9:	Ultimate decision-making authority – no joint control (2)	903
Example 12.10:	An undivided share, a lease or a joint arrangement?	903
Example 12.11:	Layered agreements	904

Example 12.12:	Modification of legal form by contractual terms	909
Example 12.13:	Construction and real estate sales	913
Example 12.14:	Modification of legal form and contractual arrangement by facts and circumstances	916
Example 12.15:	Construction services	917
Example 12.16:	Shopping centre operated jointly	918
Example 12.17:	Joint manufacturing and distribution of a product	918
Example 12.18:	Bank operated jointly	920
Example 12.19:	Oil and gas exploration, development and production activities	921
Example 12.20:	Liquefied natural gas arrangement	922
Example 12.21:	Accounting for rights to assets and obligations for liabilities	923
Example 12.22:	Joint operation with a party that participates in a joint arrangement but does not have joint control	928

Chapter 12   Joint arrangements

1 INTRODUCTION

1.1 The nature of joint arrangements

An entity may pursue an economic activity with one or more third parties and share decision-making relating to those activities. IFRS 11 – *Joint Arrangements* – is applicable when the arrangement establishes joint control over an activity between two or more of the parties involved. *[IFRS 11.4]*.

A joint arrangement is an arrangement that has the following characteristics:

(a) the parties are bound by a contractual arrangement; and

(b) the contractual arrangement gives two or more of those parties joint control of the arrangement. *[IFRS 11.5]*.

The terms 'joint arrangement,' 'joint control' 'joint operation' and 'joint venture' are specifically defined by IFRS 11 and have important accounting consequences. However, these terms also may be used loosely in practice and may appear in legal documents and public statements by management.

IFRS 11 classifies joint arrangements into one of two types: joint operations and joint ventures. *[IFRS 11.6]*. Parties to a joint operation have rights to the assets, and obligations for the liabilities, whereas parties to a joint venture have rights to the net assets of the arrangement. *[IFRS 11 Appendix A, BC24]*. A joint operation results in the recognition of assets and liabilities and revenues and expenses. *[IFRS 11.BC25]*. Whether a separate legal entity is involved is not the definitive issue in classification (see 5.1 below).

An entity must apply judgement to classify an existing jointly controlled entity either as a joint operation or a joint venture based on an assessment of the parties' rights and obligations that arise from the arrangement. *[IFRS 11.BC28]*.

No matter the terminology used to describe the arrangement, or its purpose, management needs to evaluate the terms of the arrangement, and the relevant facts and circumstances, to determine if it is a joint arrangement as defined in IFRS 11.

2 OBJECTIVE AND SCOPE OF IFRS 11

2.1 Objective

The objective of IFRS 11 is to establish principles for financial reporting by entities that have an interest in a joint arrangement. *[IFRS 11.1]*. As a result, the standard defines and provides guidance on:

- what a joint arrangement is and when joint control is present (see 3 and 4 below);
- the two types of joint arrangements and how to classify an arrangement (see 5 below); and
- how to account for each type of joint arrangement in the financial statements of a party to a joint arrangement (see 6, 7 and 8 below). *[IFRS 11.2]*.

2.2 Scope

IFRS 11 applies to all entities that are a party to a joint arrangement. *[IFRS 11.3]*. A 'party to a joint arrangement' is defined as 'an entity that participates in a joint arrangement, regardless of whether that entity has joint control of the arrangement'. *[IFRS 11 Appendix A]*. Therefore, an entity could be required to apply IFRS 11 to an arrangement even though it does not have joint control of it (see 6.4 below).

2.2.1 Application by venture capital organisations and similar entities

IFRS 11 applies to all entities that are party to a joint arrangement, including venture capital organisations, mutual funds, unit trusts, investment-linked insurance funds and similar entities (referred to hereafter as 'venture capital organisations'). However, venture capital organisations can choose to measure investments in joint ventures at fair value under the measurement exemption in IAS 28 – *Investments in Associates and Joint Ventures* – (see Chapter 11 at 5.3), but remain subject to the disclosure requirements of IFRS 12 – *Disclosure of Interests in Other Entities* (see Chapter 13 at 5). *[IFRS 11.BC15-18]*.

It should be noted that a venture capital organisation with investments in subsidiaries and associates and/or joint ventures could qualify as an 'investment entity' under IFRS 10 – *Consolidated Financial Statements*, and measure its investments in subsidiaries at fair value, only if it elected also to measure its investments in associates and/or joint ventures at fair value through profit or loss. *[IFRS 10.B85L]*.

2.2.2 Application to joint arrangements held for sale

As discussed at 8.2.7 below, an investment in a joint venture (or portion thereof) that is classified as held for sale under IFRS 5 – *Non-current Assets Held for Sale and Discontinued Operations* – is accounted for under IFRS 5 and is effectively scoped out of IFRS 11 and IAS 28. *[IAS 28.20]*. Similarly, a joint operation that is held for sale under IFRS 5 would be effectively scoped out of IFRS 11 and accounted for under IFRS 5.

2.2.3 Accounting by a joint operation

The scope of IFRS 11 does not address the accounting by the joint operation itself.

In March 2015, the IFRS Interpretations Committee (the Interpretations Committee) published its agenda decision on the issue of the accounting by a joint operation that is a separate vehicle in its financial statements. This issue arises because the joint operators recognise their share of assets and liabilities held by the joint operation, which leads to the question of whether those same assets and liabilities should also be recognised in the financial statements of the joint operation itself. The Interpretations Committee decided not to add the issue to its agenda, because the following guidance exists:

- IFRS 11 applies only to the accounting by the joint operators and not to the accounting by a separate vehicle that is a joint operation;
- the financial statements of the separate vehicle would therefore be prepared in accordance with applicable IFRSs. Note that IFRS 3 – *Business Combinations* – does not apply to 'the accounting for the formation of a joint arrangement in the financial statements of the joint arrangement itself' (see Chapter 9 at 2.2.1); *[IFRS 3.2(a)]* and
- company law often requires a legal entity or separate vehicle to prepare financial statements. Consequently, the financial statements would include the assets, liabilities, revenues and expenses of that legal entity or separate vehicle. The determination of which assets and liabilities to recognise and their measurement will depend on rights and obligations of the separate vehicle and specific facts and circumstances.

3 JOINT ARRANGEMENT

IFRS 11 defines a joint arrangement as 'an arrangement of which two or more parties have joint control'. *[IFRS 11 Appendix A].*

IFRS 11 notes that the contractual arrangement that binds the parties together is often, but not always, in writing. Unwritten agreements are rare in practice. Laws can also create enforceable arrangements, with or without a contract. *[IFRS 11.B2].* A joint arrangement can be structured through a separate vehicle (see 5.1 below). That entity's articles, charter or by-laws also may include aspects of the contractual arrangement. *[IFRS 11.B3].*

Contractual arrangements generally specify the following:

- purpose, activity and duration of the joint arrangement;
- appointment of members of the board of directors (or equivalent governing body);
- decision-making processes:
  - matters requiring decisions from the parties;
  - voting rights of the parties; and
  - required level of agreement for those matters;
- capital or other contribution requirements; and
- sharing of assets, liabilities, revenues, expenses or profit or loss relating to the joint arrangement. *[IFRS 11.B4].*

Understanding the terms of the contractual arrangement is crucial in determining whether joint control exists (see 4 below) and, if so, in deciding whether the joint arrangement is a joint operation or joint venture (see 5 below). In addition, a contract to receive goods or services may be entered into by a joint arrangement or on behalf of a joint arrangement. The terms and conditions of the joint arrangement could impact how the contract to receive goods or services is accounted for. (See Chapter 23 at 3.1.1).

3.1 Unit of account

The unit of account of a joint arrangement is the activity that two or more parties have agreed to control jointly. A party should assess its rights to the assets and obligations for the liabilities relating to that activity, regardless of whether the activity is conducted in a separate vehicle. *[IFRS 11.BC20, BC35]*. IFRS 11 does not define 'activity'. Therefore, the determination of the unit of account may require judgement in arrangements that are complex.

The purpose and design of an arrangement may provide insight into how to identify the unit of account (see 4.4.2 below). For example, a framework agreement can establish multiple joint arrangements of different types. *[IFRS 11.18]*. The possibility also exists that, within the same separate vehicle, parties to the arrangement may undertake different activities in which they have different rights to the assets, and obligations for the liabilities, resulting in different types of joint arrangements conducted within the same separate vehicle. The IASB believes such situations would be rare in practice. *[IFRS 11.BC36]*. We are aware of scenarios where the activity is larger than a single entity or separate vehicle. We refer to these as 'layered agreements', which are discussed in Example 12.11 at 4.4.2 below.

Example 12.1 below illustrates a case where a master agreement may be accounted for as several distinct joint arrangements, each of which is classified as either a joint operation or a joint venture.

Example 12.1: Master agreement for manufacturing and distribution

A single contract between two parties specifies the terms and conditions related to manufacturing and distribution activities and dictates how these activities are carried out in various jurisdictions through several entities. The activities are carried out concurrently and not sequentially (see 4.1.1 below). In each entity, the parties jointly control the relevant activities.

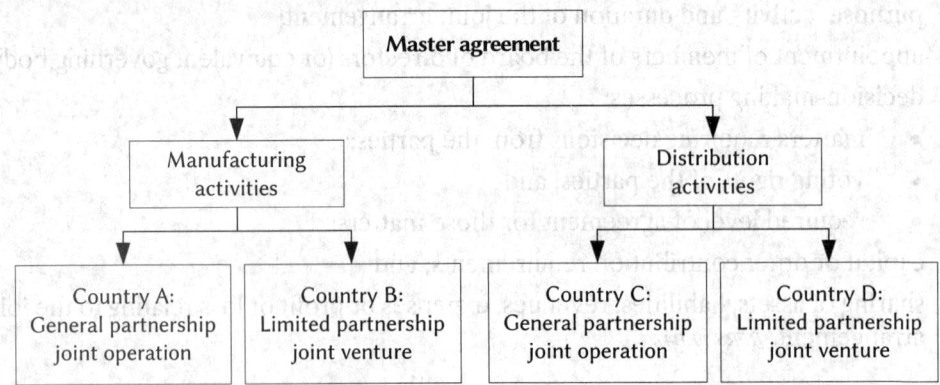

The parties may determine that this agreement contains several discrete joint arrangements (one for each activity in each jurisdiction, which corresponds to an entity). In this case, it is likely that each entity would be classified as a joint venture *or* a joint operation. This would be the case if the terms and conditions relating to each activity were distinct for each separate vehicle. Although in this example, it is concluded that the general partnerships are joint operations and the limited partnerships are joint ventures, this may not always be the case depending on the legal form, contractual terms, and facts and circumstances.

In some cases, there will be multiple contractual agreements between parties that relate to the same activities, which may need to be analysed together to determine whether a joint arrangement exists and, if so, the type of joint arrangement.

In other cases, there may be a single master agreement between two parties that covers several different activities. Some of these activities may be controlled solely by one of the two parties, while the parties may jointly control other activities. Careful analysis is required to determine the unit of account and to assess whether any of the arrangements are jointly controlled. Example 12.2 below illustrates a case where a contract contains multiple agreements, only one of which is a joint arrangement.

Example 12.2:   Agreements with control and joint control

Assume the same information as in Example 12.1 with the following variation: One party has the ability to direct the manufacturing activities of the entity in Country A and the other party has the ability to direct the manufacturing activities of the entity in Country B. As in Example 12.1, in Countries C and D the parties jointly control the relevant activities.

In this case, there would not be joint control between the two parties in the entities in Countries A and B. Rather, each party controls its respective entities, and therefore these entities would not be joint arrangements. The distribution activities conducted in the entities in Countries C and D would still be joint arrangements and each would be classified as either a joint operation or a joint venture. See Example 12.17, at 5.5 below, for a case where two parties have two joint arrangements and each joint arrangement relates to a specific activity.

4   JOINT CONTROL

As noted above, the crucial element in having a joint arrangement is joint control, and, therefore, it is important to understand this concept.

Joint control is 'the contractually agreed sharing of control of an arrangement, which exists only when decisions about the relevant activities require the unanimous consent of the parties sharing control.' *[IFRS 11.7, Appendix A]*.

As discussed at 2.2 above, not all the parties to the joint arrangement need to have joint control of the relevant activities for the arrangement to be classified as a joint arrangement. Therefore, IFRS 11 distinguishes between parties that have joint control of a joint arrangement and those that do not. *[IFRS 11.11]*. A joint operator and a joint venturer refer to parties that have joint control of a joint operation and joint venture respectively. *[IFRS 11 Appendix A]*. IFRS 11 does not explicitly define a party that participates in, but does not have joint control of, a joint arrangement. We refer to these parties as 'parties that participate in a joint arrangement but do not have joint control'. IFRS 11 specifies the accounting for parties that participate in a joint arrangement but do not have joint control (see 6.4 and 7.1 below).

The following flowchart provided in IFRS 11 illustrates how a party to a joint arrangement should evaluate whether joint control exists. [IFRS 11.B10].

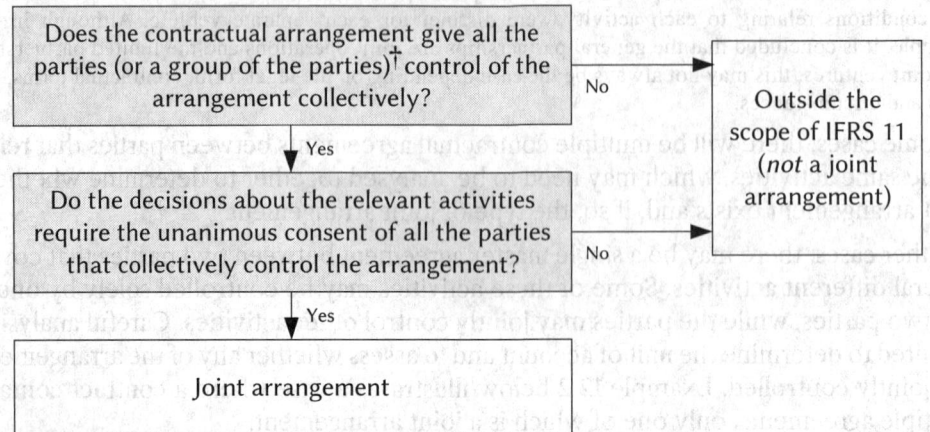

† The reference to 'a group of the parties' refers to a situation in which there is joint control between two or more parties, but there are other parties to the joint arrangement that do not participate in joint control.

We discuss key aspects of joint control within this chapter, as follows:

- contractual arrangement – See 3 above;
- assessing control – See 4.1 below;
- rights to control collectively – See 4.2 below;
- unanimous consent – See 4.3 below; and
- other practical issues with assessing joint control – See 4.4 below.

All facts and circumstances are considered when assessing whether all the parties, or a group of the parties, have joint control of an arrangement and judgement is required. [IFRS 11.12].

In some cases, it will be clear that there is no collective control (see 4.2 below), or no unanimous consent (see 4.3 below). If neither one of the two criteria is met, the activity is not a joint arrangement. For example, an advertising cost-sharing agreement between a retailer and a wholesaler that does not establish joint control over the advertising activities would not meet the definition of a joint arrangement. Similarly, we believe that it would be rare for a publicly listed entity to be subject to joint control, since it would be unusual to have a contractual agreement among all the shareholders to direct the activities of such an entity.

When it is not clear whether joint control exists, a party to a joint arrangement needs to exercise significant judgement to determine whether there is joint control. In such cases, IFRS 12 requires an entity to disclose information about the significant judgements and assumptions made (see Chapter 13 at 3). [IFRS 12.7].

When an arrangement is outside the scope of IFRS 11, an entity accounts for its interest in the arrangement in accordance with relevant IFRSs, such as IFRS 10, IAS 28 or IFRS 9 – *Financial Instruments*. [IFRS 11.B11, C14].

4.1 Assessing control

The first step in evaluating joint control is to assess whether the contractual arrangement gives a single party control of the arrangement. [IFRS 11.10]. The IASB believes that the definition of control and the application requirements to assess control in IFRS 10 will assist an entity in determining whether it unilaterally controls an arrangement or whether it jointly controls an arrangement along with other parties. [IFRS 11.BC14]. Therefore, if one of the parties to the arrangement is exposed, or has rights, to variable returns from its involvement in the arrangement and has the ability to affect those returns through its power, it would have control over the arrangement and joint control will not be possible. [IFRS 11.B5].

To perform this assessment, it is therefore necessary first to consider the following factors within IFRS 10 as they relate to the activities of the arrangement:

- the purpose and design of the arrangement (see Chapter 6 at 3.2);
- what the relevant activities of the arrangement are and how decisions about those activities are made (see Chapter 6 at 4.1);
- whether the rights of the party give it the current ability to direct the relevant activities (see Chapter 6 at 4.2 to 4.6);
- whether the party is exposed, or has rights, to variable returns from its involvement with the arrangement (see Chapter 6 at 5); and
- whether the party has the ability to use its power over the investee to affect the amount of its returns (see Chapter 6 at 6). [IFRS 10.B3].

4.1.1 Sequential activities

The determination of the relevant activities of an arrangement might be complicated when the arrangement includes different activities that occur at different times. For example, some joint arrangements operate in sequential production phases, such as those in the mining, construction, real estate, and life-sciences industries. These arrangements generally fall into two types of situations:

- parties have rights to direct different activities; or
- parties collectively direct all of the activities.

In the first situation, each party would assess whether it has the rights to direct the activities that most significantly affect returns, and therefore whether they control the arrangement (see Chapter 6 at 4.1.1). The parties to the arrangement should reconsider this assessment over time if relevant facts or circumstances change. [IFRS 11.13].

Example 12.3 and 12.4 illustrate the above principles. They are based on an example taken from IFRS 10. *[IFRS 10.B13 Example 1].*

Example 12.3:   Directing sequential activities separately

Companies A and B enter into an arrangement, structured through a separate vehicle, to develop and market a medical product. A is responsible for developing and obtaining regulatory approval for the medical product. This includes having the unilateral ability to make all decisions relating to the development of the product and to obtain regulatory approval. Once the regulator has approved the product, B will manufacture and market it and has the unilateral ability to make all decisions about the manufacturing and marketing of the project. All of the activities – developing and obtaining regulatory approval as well as manufacturing and marketing of the medical product – are relevant activities. The most relevant activity is the developing and obtaining regulatory approval of the medical product.

In Example 12.3 above, there is no joint control because the parties to the arrangement do not collectively direct the most relevant activity of the arrangement. Rather, one party directs each activity. However, if the fact pattern were different such that they collectively directed the most relevant activity of the arrangement, then there would be joint control. This is described in Example 12.4 below.

Example 12.4:   Directing sequential activities jointly

Companies A and B enter into an arrangement, structured through a separate vehicle, to develop and market a medical product. A and B are responsible for developing and obtaining regulatory approval for the medical product. The arrangement establishes joint control over the decisions relating to the development of the product and to obtain regulatory approval. Once the regulator has approved the product, B will manufacture and market it and have the unilateral ability to make all decisions about the manufacturing and marketing of the project. All of the activities – developing and obtaining regulatory approval as well as manufacturing and marketing of the medical product – are relevant activities. The most relevant activity is the developing and obtaining regulatory approval of the medical product.

4.2   Rights to control collectively

Joint control can exist only when the parties collectively control the arrangement. *[IFRS 11.B5].* In other words, all the parties, or a group of the parties, must act together to direct the activities that significantly affect the returns of the arrangement, *[IFRS 11.8],* which is referred to as 'collective control'. Factors to consider when determining whether a group of parties have collective control are addressed in the following sections.

4.2.1   Protective rights, including some veto rights

IFRS 10 defines protective rights as 'rights designed to protect the interest of the party holding those rights without giving that party power over the entity to which those rights relate'. *[IFRS 10 Appendix A].*

Protective rights relate to fundamental changes to the activities of the arrangement or apply in exceptional circumstances. Since power is an essential element of control, protective rights do not give a party control over the arrangement. Holding protective rights cannot prevent another party from having power over an arrangement (see Chapter 6 at 4.2.2). *[IFRS 10.B26-27].*

Accordingly, when assessing whether a group of the parties collectively control an arrangement, consideration must be given to whether rights held by any of the parties are:
- protective – in which case, the other parties might collectively control the arrangement, and those parties might have joint control; or
- substantive – in which case, such rights could prevent the other parties from having joint control, and possibly give the holder of those rights control.

Example 12.5 below illustrates this point with veto rights, which are often protective rights.

Example 12.5: Protective rights and joint control

Companies A, B and C enter into a joint arrangement to conduct an activity in Entity Z. The contractual agreement between A and B states that they must agree to direct all the activities of Z. The agreement of C is not required, except that C has the right to veto the issuance of debt or equity instruments by Z. The ability to veto the issuance of equity and debt instruments is considered a protective right because the right is designed to protect C's interest without giving C the ability to direct the activities that most significantly affect Z's returns.

In this fact pattern, A and B have joint control over Z because they collectively have the ability to direct Z and the contractual agreement requires their unanimous consent. Although C is a party to the joint arrangement, C does not have joint control because C holds only a protective right with respect to Z.

An arrangement may be structured such that, rather than giving some parties protective rights, one party has the deciding vote in case of a tie or disagreement (see 4.3.2 below).

4.2.2 Potential voting rights and joint control

Common examples of potential voting rights include options, forward contracts, and conversion features of a convertible instrument that, if exercised, would change the decision-making rights of the parties to the arrangement.

IFRS 11 does not explicitly address how to deal with potential voting rights when assessing whether there is joint control. However, since joint control requires the parties collectively to have 'control' as defined in IFRS 10, a party to a joint arrangement must consider the requirements of IFRS 10 regarding potential voting rights. To evaluate whether a potential voting right is substantive, and whether joint control exists, it is necessary to understand the purpose and design of the potential voting right and the context in which it was issued or granted. Guidance on how to assess whether a potential voting right is substantive is discussed further in Chapter 6 at 4.3.4.

If the potential voting right is substantive, then the holder could have joint control together with the other parties, if the terms of the contractual arrangement confer joint control.

4.2.3 Other evidence of joint control

In some cases, it may be difficult to determine whether the rights of a group of the parties give them collective power over an arrangement. In such cases, the parties consider other evidence to indicate whether they have the current ability to direct the relevant activities collectively. IFRS 10 lists several examples of this evidence (see Chapter 6 at 4.5).

Another fact that may indicate that a group of the parties have collective control, is whether the parties can obtain the financial information needed to account for the arrangement (e.g. to apply the equity method in the case of a joint venture) and to provide the required disclosures. If the group of the parties cannot obtain information regarding an arrangement (e.g. because management of that arrangement refuses to provide it), this might indicate that the parties do not have collective control (and therefore, no joint control) over that arrangement.

4.2.4 Delegated decision-making

In some cases, one of the parties may be appointed as the operational manager of the arrangement. This commonly occurs in the extractive and real estate industries, for example, when one of the parties has extensive experience in the type of activities conducted. The operational manager is frequently referred to as the 'operator', but since IFRS 11 uses the terms 'joint operation' and 'joint operator' with specific meaning, to avoid confusion we refer to such a party as the 'manager'. The other parties to the arrangement may delegate some or all the decision-making rights to this manager.

To evaluate joint control, a party to the arrangement would need to assess whether the contractual arrangement gives the manager control of the arrangement (see 4.1 above). IFRS 10 also describes how to assess whether the manager is acting as a principal or an agent on behalf of all, or a group of, the parties to the arrangement. Careful consideration of the following is required (see Chapter 6 at 6):

- The scope of the manager's decision-making authority.
- The rights held by others (e.g. protective rights and removal rights).
- The manager's exposure to the variable returns of the arrangement through management fees earned.
- The manager's exposure to the variable returns of the arrangement through other interests, for example, a direct investment held by the manager in the joint arrangement.

See Chapter 43 at 7.1 for discussion of the application of IFRS 11 to entities in the extractive industries where this situation is more common.

Therefore, depending on the facts and circumstances, it is possible that joint control exists even when a manager is appointed if the arrangement requires contractually agreed unanimous consent for decisions about the relevant activities. Accordingly, arrangements where the manager appears to have power over the relevant activities should be analysed carefully to determine whether joint control exists and, if so, which parties share in the joint control.

4.2.5 Related parties and de facto agents

One party to an arrangement may act as a *de facto* agent for another party (see Chapter 6 at 7). *De facto* agents may include related parties (as defined in IAS 24 – *Related Party Disclosures*). Determining whether joint control is established includes assessing whether any of the parties to the arrangement is acting as a *de facto* agent of another party. Example 12.6 illustrates this point.

Example 12.6:   De facto agents in joint control

A contractual arrangement has three parties: A has 50% of the voting rights and B and C each have 25%. The contractual arrangement between A, B and C specifies that at least 75% of the voting rights are required to make decisions about the relevant activities of the arrangement.

Analysis

A, B and C collectively control the relevant activities of the arrangement. However, there is neither control nor joint control, because more than one combination of parties can reach 75% and therefore direct the relevant activities.

Variation – If the facts and circumstances changed, such that C is a *de facto* agent of B, then A and B would have joint control, because effectively B would direct 50% (in combination with C's 25%) and A would need B to agree to direct the relevant activities.

Identifying *de facto* agents can be complex and requires judgement and a careful evaluation of all the facts and circumstances.

4.2.6 Role of a government

In some countries, the government may retain a substantial interest in certain arrangements. When a government entity is party to an arrangement, the arrangement needs to be evaluated carefully to determine whether joint control or control exists. This is illustrated in Example 12.7 below.

Example 12.7:   Role of a government

A government owns land, which is believed to contain oil reserves. The government enters into a contractual arrangement with an oil company to drill for oil and sell the product, which the oil company does through a separate vehicle. The oil company evaluates the contractual terms of the arrangement closely to determine whether it has joint control, control, or some other type of interest. The ownership percentages in the separate vehicle do not necessarily determine whether there is control by one party or joint control.

In some cases, the contractual terms may give all final decision-making authority over the relevant activities to the government, in which case, the government would have control.

However, in other cases, the decision-making authority may require unanimous consent by the government and the oil company to direct the activities, in which case, they would have joint control.

4.3 Unanimous consent

If all the parties, or a group of the parties, control the arrangement collectively, joint control exists only when decisions about the relevant activities require the unanimous consent of the parties that control the arrangement collectively. *[IFRS 11.9, B6]*. Accordingly, it is not necessary for every party to the arrangement to have joint control. Only those parties that collectively control the arrangement must agree.

In a joint arrangement, no single party controls the arrangement. A party with joint control of an arrangement can prevent any of the other parties, or a group of the parties, from controlling the arrangement. *[IFRS 11.10]*. In other words, the requirement for unanimous consent means that any party with joint control of the arrangement can prevent any of the other parties, or a group of the parties, from making unilateral decisions (about the relevant activities) without its consent. *[IFRS 11.B9]*.

IFRS 11 provides additional guidance on when unanimous consent exists. For example, a contractual arrangement can establish unanimous consent implicitly where the proportion of the voting rights needed to make decisions about the relevant activities effectively requires a specified combination of the parties to agree. *[IFRS 11.B7]*. When that minimum proportion voting rights can be achieved by more than one combination of the parties agreeing, the arrangement is not a joint arrangement unless it specifies which parties (or combination of parties) are required to agree unanimously to decisions about the relevant activities of the arrangement. *[IFRS 11.B8]*. IFRS 11 provides some examples to illustrate this point. Examples 1 and 2 are summarised in the following table. *[IFRS 11.B8 Example 1, 2]*.

Example 1	Example 2
Minimum voting requirement	**Minimum voting requirement**
75% vote to direct relevant activities	75% vote to direct relevant activities
Party A – 50%	Party A – 50%
Party B – 30%	Party B – 25%
Party C – 20%	Party C – 25%
Conclusion	**Conclusion**
Joint control – A and B collectively control the arrangement (since their votes, and only their votes, together meet the requirement). Since there is only one combination of parties that collectively control the arrangement, it is clear that A and B must unanimously agree. C is a 'party that participates in a joint arrangement but does not have joint control' (see 4 above).	*No joint control* – multiple combinations of parties could collectively control the arrangement (i.e. A and B or A and C could vote together to meet the requirement). Since there are multiple combinations, and the contractual agreement does not specify which parties must agree, there is no unanimous consent.

4.3.1 Arrangements involving parties that participate in a joint arrangement but who do not have joint control

Unanimous consent needs to be explicitly or implicitly established by contract. For example, two parties, A and B, each have 35% of the voting rights in an arrangement with the remaining 30% being widely dispersed and decisions about the relevant activities require approval by a majority of the voting rights. In this situation, A and B have joint control of the arrangement only if the contractual arrangement specifies that decisions about the relevant activities of the arrangement require agreement of both A and B. *[IFRS 11.B8 Example 3]*. The fact that the remaining 30% of the voting rights are widely dispersed does not implicitly create joint control.

4.3.2 Ultimate voting authority

Sometimes an arrangement provides all parties with a voting right, but in the case of a deadlock, or disagreement, one party has the deciding vote (i.e. the final decision or override powers). If any single party could direct the relevant activities unilaterally, there would not be joint control. Example 12.8 below illustrates this point.

Example 12.8: Ultimate decision-making authority – no joint control (1)

Companies G and H enter into an agreement and set up a joint steering committee. H has ultimate decision-making authority in cases where the joint steering committee cannot reach an agreement. In this case, there would not be joint control because the agreement of G is not needed.

To evaluate whether H has control, it would also need to assess whether it has exposure to variable returns, and the ability to affect those returns through its power, as required by IFRS 10 (see Chapter 6).

Just because one party has a deciding vote does not necessarily mean that it has control, particularly if other parties can act without the agreement of that party. This is illustrated in Example 12.9 below.

Example 12.9:   Ultimate decision-making authority – no joint control (2)

Companies I, J and K enter into an agreement and set up a joint steering committee. Each party has one vote and two votes are needed to carry a motion. K has ultimate decision-making authority in cases where the joint steering committee cannot reach an agreement. For example, if no combination of I, J and K can agree with each other, K would have the ultimate decision-making authority.

There is no joint control, since there are multiple combinations of parties that could vote together, and the contractual agreement does not specify which parties must agree. For example, I and J could agree together, without the agreement of K.

4.3.3   Arbitration

Contractual arrangements often include terms and conditions relating to the resolution of disputes and may provide for arbitration. The existence of such terms and conditions does not prevent the arrangement from being jointly controlled and, consequently, from being a joint arrangement. *[IFRS 11.B10]*. Rather, a party to a joint arrangement evaluates the facts and circumstances related to the arbitration procedures. For example, whether the arbitration process is neutral to both parties, which might be achieved by using a mutually agreed upon arbitrator, in which case, there might be joint control. Alternatively, arbitration procedures that favour one party might indicate that there is no joint control.

4.3.4   Statutory mechanisms

Statutory mechanisms can create legally enforceable rights and obligations (see 3 above). Accordingly, when evaluating whether an arrangement implicitly results in joint control, an entity should consider the statutory requirements in the relevant jurisdiction under which the contractual arrangement was established.

4.4   Other practical issues with assessing joint control

4.4.1   Undivided share, lease or a joint arrangement

In some cases, it is necessary to consider whether a party owns an undivided share in a commonly-owned asset, has a right to use an asset in return for a payment or series of payments (i.e. a lease), or whether the parties have a joint arrangement. Example 12.10 illustrates this point.

Example 12.10:   An undivided share, a lease or a joint arrangement?

Five parties jointly buy an aircraft. By contractual agreement, each party has the right to use the aircraft for a certain number of days each year and shares proportionately in the maintenance costs. They share decision-making regarding the maintenance and disposal of the aircraft, which are the relevant activities for that aircraft. Those decisions require the unanimous agreement of all the parties. The contractual agreement covers the expected life of the aircraft and can be changed only by unanimous agreement.

Analysis

The agreement is a joint arrangement. Through the contractual agreement, the five parties agreed to share the use and costs of maintaining the aircraft, and decisions require unanimous consent.

Variation – The contractual agreement covers the expected life of the aircraft and can be changed only by agreement of parties holding 75% of the voting rights. There are multiple combinations of how the 75% threshold can be achieved and the contractual agreement does not specify which parties must agree. Therefore, there is no unanimous consent.

Analysis

The agreement is not a joint arrangement, as the contractual agreement does not establish joint control.

4.4.2 Evaluate multiple agreements together

Sometimes it is necessary to evaluate multiple agreements together, to understand the purpose and design of an arrangement, and to determine whether there is joint control. A party may appear to have joint control of a joint arrangement when considering one agreement in isolation, but that party may not have joint control when considered in the full context of its purpose and design. Example 12.11 below illustrates this point.

Example 12.11: Layered agreements

Companies A, B, C and D enter into Agreement No.1 to undertake oil and gas exploration. Committee No.1 is formed to direct all related activities, including review and approval of annual budgets and operating policies. Committee No.1 consists of six members, of whom D nominates three members. A, B, and C each nominate one of the remaining three members. The decisions of Committee No.1 require the unanimous vote of the members.

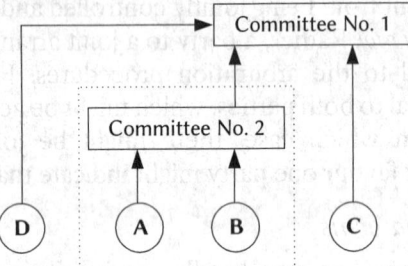

A and B enter into Agreement No.2, which establishes Committee No.2 to coordinate cooperation between A and B, with respect to the same oil and gas exploration activity. A and B each appoint one representative to Committee No.2. Committee No.2 has the power to make decisions to be submitted for approval to Committee No.1. Any matter to be decided by Committee No.2 requires the consent of both parties. However, if agreement cannot be reached between A and B, B has the deciding vote. The decisions made in Committee No.2 are binding on A and B and they must vote accordingly in Committee No.1.

In this fact pattern, there are two separate contractual agreements. However, they are evaluated together to determine if there is a joint arrangement, because they relate to the same oil and gas exploration activity. For example, if Agreement No.1 were considered in isolation, it would appear that A, B, C and D all have joint control over the arrangement because its decisions require the unanimous vote of the members.

However, Agreement No.1 should be evaluated together with Agreement No.2. Accordingly, only B, C and D would have joint control over the joint arrangement. Since B can effectively direct A how to vote (by virtue of Agreement No.2) in Committee No.2, A does not have joint control with the other parties, since it is effectively a *de facto* agent of B and will represent a 'party that participates in a joint arrangement but does not have joint control' (see 4.2.5 above).

5 CLASSIFICATION OF A JOINT ARRANGEMENT: JOINT OPERATIONS AND JOINT VENTURES

IFRS 11 requires an entity to determine the type of joint arrangement in which it is involved. *[IFRS 11.14]*. A joint arrangement is classified as either a joint operation or a joint venture. *[IFRS 11.6]*. The classification of a joint arrangement as a joint operation or a joint venture depends upon the rights and obligations of the parties to the arrangement. *[IFRS 11.14]*.

The table below compares the two types of joint arrangements and provides an overview of the accounting for each under IFRS 11. *[IFRS 11.15, 16]*.

Type of arrangement	Joint operation	Joint venture
Definition	The parties with *joint control* have rights to the assets and obligations for the liabilities of the arrangement.	The parties with *joint control* have rights to the net assets of the arrangement.
Parties with joint control	*Joint operator* is a party with joint control in a joint operation.	*Joint venturer* is a party with joint control in a joint venture.
Accounting overview	A *joint operator* (and parties that participate in a joint arrangement but who do not have joint control) accounts for the following in accordance with the applicable IFRS: Its assets, including its share of any assets held jointly Its liabilities, including its share of any liabilities incurred jointly Its revenue from the sale of its share of the output arising from the joint operation Its share of revenue from the sale of the output by the joint operation Its expenses, including its share of any expenses incurred jointly.	A *joint venturer* accounts for its investment in the joint venture using the equity method. Parties that participate in a joint arrangement but who do not have joint control account for the investment in accordance with IFRS 9, unless the parties have significant influence, in which case the parties shall apply the equity method.

This process to classify a joint arrangement is illustrated in the following flowchart, which is based on the guidance included in paragraphs B21 and B33 of IFRS 11. The flowchart includes several criteria to be met for the joint arrangement to be a joint venture. The first step is to assess whether there is a separate vehicle. If not, the joint arrangement is automatically a joint operation. However, when there is a separate vehicle, if just one of the additional criteria indicates that the parties have the rights to the assets and obligations for the liabilities, the joint arrangement would be a joint operation. In all other cases it would be classified as a joint venture. IFRS 11 also includes examples illustrating this evaluation, some within the application guidance and others as illustrative examples accompanying the standard (see 5.5 below).

Classifying a joint arrangement

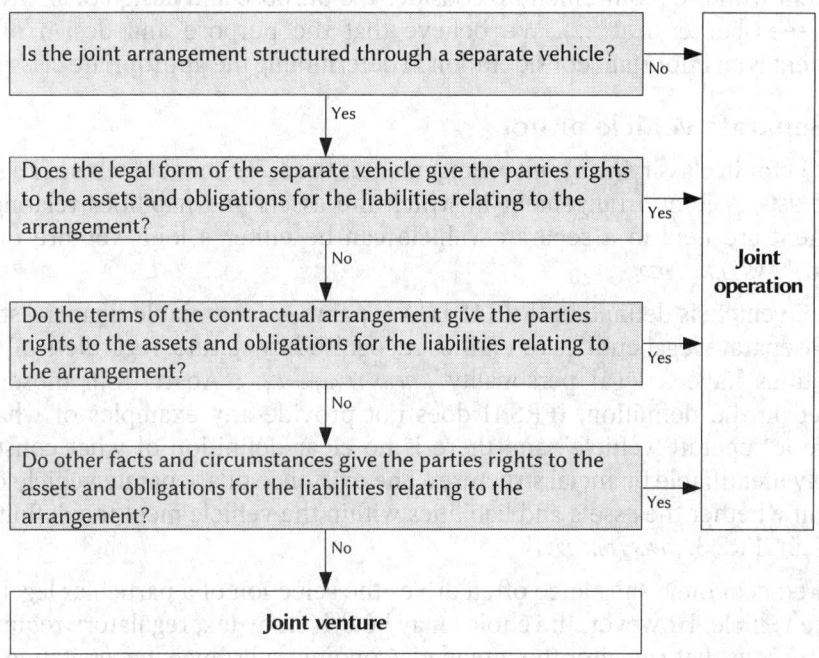

We discuss key aspects of the classification process within this chapter as follows:
- separate vehicle – see 5.1 below;
- legal form of the separate vehicle – see 5.2 below;
- contractual terms – see 5.3 below; and
- other facts and circumstances – see 5.4 below. *[IFRS 11.17, B15]*.

Judgement is required in assessing whether a joint arrangement is a joint operation or a joint venture. An entity evaluates its rights and obligations arising from a joint arrangement in order to classify it. *[IFRS 11.17]*. IFRS 12 requires an entity to disclose information when it has to make significant judgements and assumptions to classify the type of joint arrangement, specifically when the arrangement has been structured through a separate vehicle (see Chapter 13 at 3). *[IFRS 12.7]*.

When classifying a joint arrangement, parties to the joint arrangement would normally reach the same conclusion regarding classification. To reach different conclusions regarding the classification of a joint arrangement would mean that the parties have different rights to assets and obligations for the liabilities within the same separate vehicle.

When classifying a joint arrangement as either a joint operation or a joint venture, it may be necessary to analyse two (or more) agreements separately, such as when there is a framework or master agreement (see 3.1 above).

The classification of joint arrangements depends upon the parties' rights and obligations arising from the arrangement in the normal course of business. *[IFRS 11.B14]*. These concepts are discussed in more detail in the context of analysing the contractual terms of the arrangement, and the other facts and circumstances at 5.3 and 5.4 below, respectively.

The requirement to classify a joint arrangement based on the normal course of business is consistent with the requirement to consider the purpose and design of an investee in IFRS 10 (see Chapter 6 at 3.2). We believe that the purpose and design of a joint arrangement is an important consideration in determining the appropriate classification.

5.1 Separate vehicle or not

The first factor in classifying a joint arrangement is the assessment of whether a separate vehicle exists. A joint arrangement in which the assets and liabilities relating to the arrangement are held in a separate vehicle can be either a joint venture or a joint operation. *[IFRS 11.B19, B20]*.

A separate vehicle is defined in IFRS 11 as 'A separately identifiable financial structure, including separate legal entities or entities recognised by statute, regardless of whether those entities have a legal personality.' *[IFRS 11 Appendix A]*. Apart from those entities mentioned in the definition, IFRS 11 does not provide any examples of what might constitute a 'separate vehicle', and there is no clear definition of what constitutes a 'separately identifiable financial structure'. The existence of a separate vehicle does not depend on whether the assets and liabilities within the vehicle meet the definition of a 'business' in IFRS 3. *[IFRS 11.BC29]*.

The desired economic substance often drives the selection of a particular legal form of a separate vehicle. However, the choice may be driven by tax, regulatory requirements or other reasons that can alter the intended economic substance, necessitating that the parties use contractual arrangements to modify the effects that the legal form would otherwise have on their rights and obligations. *[IFRS 11.BC32]*.

Many common arrangements, such as partnerships, corporations, trusts and syndicates, are likely to be considered separate vehicles, although local laws should be considered. In some jurisdictions, an oral agreement is considered sufficient to create a contractual partnership, and thus, the hurdle for having a separate vehicle could be quite low.

A contract alone may create a separate vehicle, such as when it creates a deemed separate entity (referred to as a 'silo' in IFRS 10), or creates a partnership. A silo exists when specified assets of an arrangement are the only source of payment for specified liabilities of an arrangement, and parties other than those with the specified liability do not have rights or obligations related to the specified assets or to residual cash flows from those assets. That is, a silo exists when, in substance, all the assets, liabilities and equity of that deemed separate entity are ring-fenced from the 'host' arrangement. The identification of silos is discussed further in Chapter 6 at 8.1.

The term 'separate vehicle' is broader than an 'entity' as illustrated in the diagram below. We understand that this was done primarily to address concerns that, in some jurisdictions, separate vehicles created to establish a joint arrangement are not necessarily legal reporting entities or juristic persons.

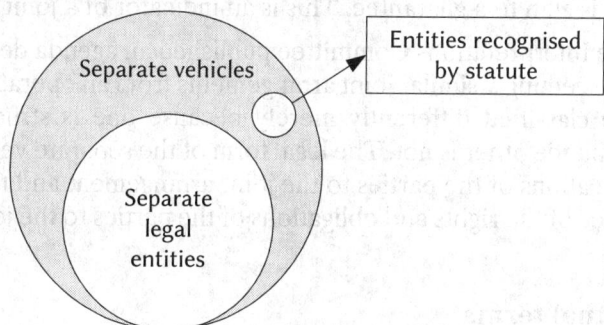

The IASB concluded that it would be rare that a joint arrangement would give the parties rights to the net assets without having a separate vehicle. *[IFRS 11.BC27]*.

5.2 Legal form of the separate vehicle

Once it is determined that a separate vehicle exists, the second step is to analyse the legal form of the separate vehicle to determine whether it gives the parties rights to the net assets, or rights to the assets and obligations for the liabilities of the arrangement. *[IFRS 11.B21]*. In other words, does the separate vehicle confer separation between the parties and the separate vehicle?

The legal form of the separate vehicle is relevant as an initial indicator of the parties' rights to the assets, and obligations for the liabilities, relating to the arrangement. The exception is when the legal form of the separate vehicle does not confer separation between the parties and the vehicle, in which case the conclusion is reached that the arrangement is a joint operation. *[IFRS 11.B24, BC31]*.

If the legal form of the separate vehicle does confer separation between the parties and the separate vehicle, the classification is not yet conclusive. The terms agreed by the parties in their contractual arrangement (see 5.3 below) and other facts and circumstances (see 5.4 below) can override the assessment of the rights and obligations conferred upon the parties by the legal form of the separate vehicle and the arrangement can still be classified as a joint operation. *[IFRS 11.B23]*.

Local laws may affect the form of the separate vehicle. For example, in many countries, a corporation confers separation between the parties and the separate vehicle and provides the parties with rights to net assets. These are indicators that the corporation is a joint venture. That is, the liabilities of the corporation are limited to the corporation. Creditors do not have recourse to the investors in the corporation for those liabilities. However, this may not be true in all countries.

Similarly, partnerships that have unlimited liability, which are common in many countries, often do not confer separation between the parties and the separate vehicle. That is, they provide the partners with rights to the assets and obligations for the liabilities, indicating that the arrangement is a joint operation. When creditors of the partnership have direct recourse to the joint arrangement partners, the partners are the primary obligors, which is indicative of a joint operation. However, in a partnership where creditors have recourse to the partners only after the partnership has defaulted, there is separation between the partners and the vehicle. The liability of the partners as secondary obligor is akin to a guarantee. This is an indicator of a joint venture.

In March 2015, the Interpretations Committee published an agenda decision in which it observed that two seemingly similar joint arrangements from an operational perspective might need to be classified differently merely because one is structured through a separate vehicle and the other is not. The legal form of the separate vehicle could affect the rights and obligations of the parties to the joint arrangement and thereby affect the economic substance of the rights and obligations of the parties to the joint arrangement. *[IFRS 11.B22, BC43]*.

5.3 Contractual terms

The next step in classifying a joint arrangement structured through a separate vehicle is to examine the contractual terms of the arrangement. While the legal form of the separate vehicle gives certain rights and obligations to each of the parties, the contractual terms of the joint arrangement may unwind the effects of the legal form and give the parties different rights and obligations.

IFRS 11 includes examples (which are not exhaustive) of common contractual terms found in joint arrangements and indicates whether these are examples of joint operations or joint ventures. These are included in the table below. *[IFRS 11.B27]*.

Joint operation	Joint venture
Terms of the contractual arrangement	
The parties are provided with rights to the assets, obligations for the liabilities, relating to the arrangement.	The parties are provided with rights to the net assets of the arrangement (i.e. it is the separate vehicle, not the parties, that has rights to the assets and obligations for the liabilities relating to the arrangement).

Joint arrangements

Joint operation	Joint venture
Rights to assets	
The parties share all interests (e.g. rights, title or ownership) in the assets relating to the arrangement in a specified proportion (e.g. in proportion to the parties' ownership interest in the arrangement or in proportion to the activity carried out through the arrangement that is directly attributed to them).	The assets brought into the arrangement or subsequently acquired by the joint arrangement are the arrangement's assets. The parties have no interests (i.e. no rights, title or ownership) in the assets of the arrangement.
Obligations for liabilities	
The parties share all liabilities, obligations, costs and expenses in a specified proportion (e.g. in proportion to the parties' ownership interest in the arrangement or in proportion to the activity carried out through the arrangement that is directly attributed to them).	The joint arrangement is liable for the debts and obligations of the arrangement.
	The parties are liable under the arrangement only to the extent of their respective investments in the arrangement, or to their respective obligations to contribute any unpaid or additional capital to the arrangement, or both.
The parties are liable for claims raised by third parties	Creditors of the joint arrangement do not have rights of recourse against any party with respect to debts or obligations of the arrangement.
Revenues and expenses and profits or losses	
Each party receives an allocation of revenues and expenses based on the relative performance of each party to the joint arrangement. For example, the contractual arrangement might establish that revenues and expenses are allocated based on the capacity that each party uses in a plant operated jointly, which could differ from their ownership interest in the joint arrangement. In other instances, the parties might have agreed to share the profit or loss relating to the arrangement based on a specified proportion such as the parties' ownership interest in the arrangement. This would not prevent the arrangement from being a joint operation if the parties have rights to the assets, and obligations for the liabilities, relating to the arrangement.	Each party has a share in the profit or loss relating to the activities of the arrangement.
Guarantees	
The parties to joint arrangements are often required to provide guarantees to third parties that, for example, receive a service from, or provide financing to, the joint arrangement. The provision of such guarantees, or the commitment by the parties to provide them, does not determine, by itself, that the joint arrangement is a joint operation. The feature that determines whether the joint arrangement is a joint operation or a joint venture is whether the parties have obligations for the liabilities relating to the arrangement (for some of which the parties might or might not have provided a guarantee). See 5.3.1 below.	

In many cases, the rights and obligations agreed to by the parties in their contractual arrangements are consistent, or do not conflict, with the rights and obligations conferred on the parties by the legal form of the separate vehicle. *[IFRS 11.B25]*. However, as discussed at 5.2 above, this is not always the case, *[IFRS 11.B26]*, as illustrated in Example 12.12 below. *[IFRS 11 Example 4]*.

Example 12.12: Modification of legal form by contractual terms

Companies A and B jointly start a Corporation C over which they have joint control. The legal form of the separate vehicle (a corporation) preliminarily indicates that C is a joint venture.

However, the contractual arrangement states that A and B have rights to the assets of C and are obligated for the liabilities of C in a specified proportion. Effectively, this contractual term unwinds the effects of the legal form (corporation). Therefore, C is a joint operation.

When the contractual arrangement specifies that the parties have rights to the assets, and obligations for the liabilities, relating to the joint arrangement, they are parties to a joint operation, and do not further consider other facts and circumstances when classifying the joint arrangement. *[IFRS 11.B28]*.

5.3.1 Guarantees

Parties to joint arrangements may provide guarantees to third parties. For example, a party to a joint arrangement may provide a guarantee or commitment that:

- services provided by the joint arrangement to the third party will be of a certain quality or nature;
- it will support the joint arrangement in the event of distress; or
- it will repay funding received from the third party.

One might think that providing a guarantee (or commitment to provide a guarantee) gives a party an obligation for a liability, which would indicate that the joint arrangement should be classified as a joint operation. However, IFRS 11 states this is not the case. The issuance of guarantees, or a commitment by the parties to provide guarantees, does not determine, by itself, that the joint arrangement is a joint operation. *[IFRS 11.B27]*. Although perhaps counter-intuitive, the fact that a guarantee is not determinative of the classification of a joint operation is consistent with the principles in IFRS 11. This is because the guarantee does not give the guarantor a present obligation for the underlying liabilities. Accordingly, a guarantee is not determinative of having an obligation for a liability.

Similarly, an obligation to contribute unpaid or additional capital to a joint arrangement is not an indicator that the arrangement is a joint operation; it could be a joint venture. *[IFRS 11.B27]*. Cash calls and obligations to contribute unpaid or additional capital are discussed in more detail at 5.4.2.A below.

If the issuer of the guarantee must pay or perform under that guarantee, this may indicate that facts and circumstances have changed, or this event may be accompanied by a change in the contractual terms of the arrangement. These changes would trigger a reassessment of whether the arrangement is still subject to joint control and, if so, whether the joint arrangement is a joint operation or a joint venture, as discussed at 8 below.

When a guarantee meets the definition of a 'financial guarantee' (see Chapter 45 at 3.4), the party issuing the guarantee must account for the guarantee in accordance with IFRS 9, irrespective of the classification of the joint arrangement.

5.3.2 Contractual terms upon liquidation or dissolution of joint arrangement

In some joint arrangements, the parties contribute assets to the joint arrangement to use in the activity while it continues to operate. However, if the joint arrangement is liquidated or dissolved, the contributed assets revert to the contributing party. The question is whether this contractual term gives the parties rights to the assets. If so, the joint arrangement is classified as a joint operation.

In our view, a contractual agreement whereby assets contributed to a joint arrangement revert to the contributing party upon liquidation or dissolution of the joint arrangement, does not necessarily mean that the arrangement is a joint operation. In such a case, the contributing party does not expect to receive the contributed assets in the normal course of business (see 5 above). That is, the purpose and design of the joint arrangement is not intended to give rights to assets, or obligations for liabilities to the contributing party, at least while the joint arrangement continues as a going concern. The joint arrangement should be analysed in the context of its purpose and design.

All relevant facts and circumstances should be considered in reaching a conclusion. If the party contributing the asset has a currently exercisable call option on that asset, it should consider this in evaluating whether it has rights to the assets and obligations for the liabilities of the joint arrangement (i.e. whether it is a joint operation). The call option is accounted for in accordance with the relevant IFRS.

5.4 Other facts and circumstances

When the legal form of the separate vehicle and the terms of the contractual arrangement do not specify that the parties have rights to the assets, and obligations for the liabilities, relating to the arrangement, then the parties must consider all other facts and circumstances to assess whether the arrangement is a joint operation or a joint venture. *[IFRS 11.B29, B30]*. The 'other facts and circumstances' should be substantive and infer rights to the assets and obligations for the liabilities of the separate vehicle to classify the joint arrangement as a joint operation.

In March 2015, the Interpretations Committee published agenda decisions, discussed at 5.4.3 below, that provide a helpful overview of the issues that require judgement and the guidance that should be considered. The assessment of 'other facts and circumstances' can be challenging in practice.

5.4.1 Facts and circumstances indicating rights to assets

When the activities of an arrangement are primarily designed for the provision of output to the parties, this indicates that the parties have rights to substantially all the economic benefits of the assets of the arrangement. The parties to such arrangements often ensure their access to the outputs provided by the arrangement by preventing the arrangement from selling output to third parties. *[IFRS 11.B31]*.

5.4.1.A Output not taken in proportion to ownership

In March 2015, the Interpretations Committee published an agenda decision that addressed the accounting treatment when the joint operator's share of output purchased differs from its share of ownership interest in the joint operation. The Interpretations Committee specifically considered a variation to Example 5 of the application guidance to IFRS 11. *[IFRS 11.B32 Example 5]*. Example 5 considers a joint arrangement structured through a separate vehicle from which the parties to the joint arrangement have committed to purchase substantially all the output produced at a price designed to achieve a break-even result. In that example, the parties to the joint arrangement are considered to have rights to the assets and obligations for the liabilities and the arrangement is classified as a joint operation. In the variation considered, the parties' percentage ownership interest in the separate vehicle differs from the percentage share of the output produced, which each party is obliged to purchase.

The Interpretations Committee identified several issues:
- When the joint arrangement agreement does not specify the allocation of assets, liabilities, revenues or expenses, should the share of assets, liabilities, revenue and expenses recognised reflect the percentage of ownership of the legal entity, or should it reflect the percentage of output purchased by each joint operator?
- When the share of output purchased by each party varies over the life of the joint arrangement, over what time horizon should the share of output be considered?
- If the joint operators made a substantial investment in the joint operation that differed from their ownership interest, it would be necessary to determine the other elements of the arrangements that could explain why there is a difference between the percentage of ownership interest and the percentage share of the output produced that each party is obliged to purchase.

The Interpretations Committee noted that it is important to understand why the share of the output purchased differs from the ownership interests in the joint operation and that judgement would be needed to determine the appropriate classification and accounting for the joint arrangement. However, the Interpretations Committee decided not to add the issue to its agenda because it would require the development of additional guidance.[1]

5.4.1.B Consideration of derecognition requirements for financial instruments

When classifying a joint arrangement, one must be mindful of the derecognition requirements with respect to financial instruments. This is particularly important where the activities of the joint arrangement relate to transferred receivables and securitisation arrangements (see Chapter 52 at 3.2).

Therefore, when determining whether the facts and circumstances indicate that a party has rights to net assets (a joint venture), or rights to assets and obligations for liabilities (a joint operation), an entity considers whether the assets that have been transferred to the joint arrangement meet the criteria for derecognition by the transferor. The conclusions reached with respect to derecognition are likely to affect the amounts recognised when applying the equity method (if the joint arrangement is a joint venture), or accounting for the rights to the assets (if the joint arrangement is a joint operation).

5.4.2 Facts and circumstances indicating obligations for liabilities

When the parties to a joint arrangement are substantially the only source of cash flows contributing to the continuity of the operations of the arrangement, this indicates that the parties have an obligation for the liabilities relating to the arrangement. *[IFRS 11.B32]*.

Many situations may result in the parties to a joint arrangement being substantially the only source of cash flows; for example, when the parties:
- make payments to third parties under previously issued guarantees on behalf of the joint arrangement;
- are obligated to provide loan financing or working capital funding in the normal course of business;
- commit to provide cash calls in the future (see 5.4.2.A below); or
- are obligated to purchase all the output produced by the joint arrangement, which they may or may not resell to third parties.

5.4.2.A Assessing the obligation related to cash calls or capital contributions

Questions have arisen as to whether parties would be considered 'substantially the only source of cash flows' if they provide cash flows at inception of a joint arrangement, but are not expected to do so thereafter, and no other parties are expected to provide cash flows until the end of an activity. Alternatively, parties might provide cash flows through a series of 'cash calls' throughout the arrangement. IFRS 11 is clear that an obligation to contribute unpaid or additional capital to a joint arrangement, by itself, is not an indicator that the arrangement is a joint operation; it could be a joint venture. *[IFRS 11.B27].*

In our view, the provision of cash flows at the inception of a joint arrangement, and/or the expectation that no other parties will provide cash flows until the end of an activity, are not conclusive in determining whether there is an obligation for a liability. That is, it is not conclusive whether the joint arrangement is a joint operation or a joint venture (see Example 12.13 below).

Example 12.13: Construction and real estate sales

Two parties established a separate vehicle over which they have joint control. Neither the legal form nor the contractual terms of the joint arrangement give the parties rights to the assets or obligations for the liabilities of the arrangement. Other facts and circumstances are as follows:

- the purpose of the joint arrangement is to construct a residential complex for selling residential units to the public;
- contributed equity by the parties is sufficient to purchase land and raise debt finance from third parties to fund construction; and
- sales proceeds will be used as follows (in this priority):
  - repayment of external debt; and
  - remaining profit distributed to parties.

Analysis

Since there is a separate vehicle, and because neither the legal form nor the contractual terms of the joint arrangement give the parties rights to the assets or obligations for the liabilities of the vehicle, the preliminary analysis indicates that this is a joint venture. The fact that the parties are the only source of cash flows at inception does not necessarily indicate that the parties have rights to the assets or obligations for the liabilities. That is, more information is needed and judgement will be required in determining whether this is a joint venture or a joint operation.

Variation – The contributed equity is not sufficient to purchase the land and raise debt financing. There is an expectation, or requirement, that the parties will have to contribute cash to the joint arrangement through a series of cash calls. The fact that the parties are expected to be a source of cash flows is not sufficiently conclusive to indicate that the parties have rights to the assets, and/or obligations for the liabilities. That is, more information is needed before concluding whether this is a joint venture or a joint operation.

The above example refers to the fact that there was third party financing available to fund construction. In March 2015, the Interpretations Committee published an agenda decision confirming that the availability of third-party financing does not preclude the classification as a joint operation (see 5.4.3.C below).

5.4.3 Interpretations Committee agenda decisions

In January 2013, the Interpretations Committee received several requests to clarify the application of the 'other facts and circumstances' criterion in IFRS 11, which it discussed during its meetings in 2013 and 2014. In March 2015, the Interpretations Committee issued an agenda decision dealing with the following issues:

- how and why particular facts and circumstances create rights and obligations (see 5.4.3.A below);
- implication of 'economic substance' (see 5.4.3.B below); and
- application of 'other facts and circumstances' to specific fact patterns (see 5.4.3.C below):
  - output sold at a market price;
  - financing from a third party;
  - nature of output (i.e. fungible or bespoke output); and
  - determining the basis for 'substantially all of the output'.

5.4.3.A How and why particular facts and circumstances create rights and obligations

The Interpretations Committee noted the following regarding a joint arrangement that is structured through a separate vehicle, whose legal form causes the separate vehicle to be considered in its own right:[2]

(a) the assessment of other facts and circumstances is performed when there is no contractual arrangement to reverse or modify the rights and obligations conferred by the legal form of the separate vehicle through which the arrangement has been structured;

(b) the assessment focuses on whether the other facts and circumstances establish, for each party to the joint arrangement, rights to the assets and obligations for the liabilities relating to the joint arrangement;

(c) parties to the joint arrangement have rights to the assets of the joint arrangement through other facts and circumstances when they: *[IFRS 11.B31-B32]*

  (i) have rights to substantially all of the economic benefits (for example, 'output') of assets of the arrangement; and

  (ii) have obligations to acquire those economic benefits and thus assume the risks relating to those economic benefits (for example, the risks relating to the output); and

(d) parties to the joint arrangement have obligations for liabilities of the joint arrangement through other facts and circumstances when: *[IFRS 11.B14, B32-B33]*

  (i) because of their rights to, and obligations for, the assets of the joint arrangement, they provide cash flows that are used to settle liabilities of the joint arrangement; and

  (ii) settlement of the liabilities of the joint arrangement occurs on a continuous basis.

A joint arrangement structured through a separate vehicle is classified as a joint operation only when each party to the joint arrangement meets the above criteria and therefore has both rights to the assets of the joint arrangement and obligations for the liabilities of the joint arrangement through other facts and circumstances.

Although the Interpretations Committee decided not to add this issue to its agenda, it observed that a joint arrangement could be classified as a joint operation based on other facts and circumstances, only if an entity is able to demonstrate that:

(a) each party to the joint arrangement has rights and obligations relating to economic benefits of the assets of the arrangement; and

(b) each party is obliged to provide cash to the arrangement through enforceable obligations, which is used to settle the liabilities of the joint arrangement on a continuous basis.

It is therefore irrelevant whether the activities of the separate vehicle are closely related to the activities of the parties on their own, or whether the parties are closely involved in the operations of the arrangements. *[IFRS 11.BC43]*.

In July 2014, the Interpretations Committee discussed the classification of a specific type of joint arrangement structure established for a bespoke construction project to deliver a construction service to a single customer. In this specific example, it examined common features of 'project entities' with regard to assessing 'other facts and circumstances.' The staff analysis listed several common features of 'project entities' that would not, by themselves, indicate that the parties have rights to the assets and obligations for the liabilities, i.e. that the joint arrangement is a joint operation.[3]

- The separate vehicle has no workforce of its own.
- The separate vehicle is a limited-life entity that has been set up for a single project.
- The parties are responsible for delivering the goods or services to the customers.
- The parties are jointly or severally liable for all the debts of the separate vehicle.
- The customers of the separate vehicle are obtained through the commercial resources of the parties (for example, their personnel, websites, classified ads, trade name).
- The parties finance any loss or cash needs of the separate vehicle, for example, when there are budget overruns or delivery delays.
- Litigation arising from the operations of the separate vehicle is managed by the parties or is accompanied by legal actions directly against the parties.

5.4.3.B Implication of 'economic substance'

The assessment of other facts and circumstances should focus on whether each party to the joint arrangement has rights to the assets and obligations for the liabilities of the joint arrangement. This raises questions about the role of the concept of 'economic substance' in the assessment of other facts and circumstances.

The Interpretations Committee determined that the assessment of other facts and circumstances should be undertaken with a view towards whether those facts and circumstances create enforceable rights to assets and obligations for liabilities (see 4.3.4 above). These obligations may be legal or constructive. Therefore, this evaluation should include consideration of the design and purpose of the joint arrangement, its business needs and its past practices to identify all obligations, whether legal or constructive.[4]

5.4.3.C Application of 'other facts and circumstances' to specific fact patterns

The Interpretations Committee also explored the following four fact patterns and considered how 'other facts and circumstances' should be applied in each of these cases:[5]

- Output sold at a market price – The sale of output from the joint arrangement to the parties at market price, on its own, is not a determinative factor for the classification of the joint arrangement. Instead, parties would need to exercise judgement and consider whether the cash flows provided to the joint arrangement through the parties' purchase of the output from the joint arrangement at market price, along with any other funding that the parties are obliged to provide, would be sufficient to enable the joint arrangement to settle its liabilities on a continuous basis.

- Financing from a third party – If the cash flows to the joint arrangement from the sale of output to the parties, along with any other funding that the parties are obliged to provide, satisfy the joint arrangement's liabilities, then third-party financing alone would not affect the classification of the joint arrangement. This conclusion is appropriate irrespective of whether the financing occurs at inception or during the course of the joint arrangement's operations. In this situation, the joint arrangement will, or may, settle some of its liabilities using cash flows from third-party financing, but the resulting obligation to the third-party finance provider will, in due course, be settled using cash flows that the parties are obliged to provide.

- Nature of output (i.e. fungible or bespoke output) – Whether the output that is produced by the joint arrangement and purchased by the parties is fungible or bespoke, is not a determinative factor for the classification of the joint arrangement. IFRS 11's focus is on the existence of cash flows flowing from the parties to satisfy the joint arrangement's liabilities.

- Determining the basis for 'substantially all of the output' – The Interpretations Committee noted that the economic benefits of the assets of the joint arrangement would relate to the cash flows arising from the parties' rights to, and obligations for, the assets. *[IFRS 11.B31-B32]*. Therefore, the term 'substantially all of the output' is based on the monetary value of the output, instead of physical quantities.

5.4.4 Comprehensive example illustrating evaluation of facts and circumstances

Example 12.14 below (summarised from Example 5 of IFRS 11) illustrates how the facts and circumstances might indicate that the joint arrangement is a joint operation, even if the legal form and contractual terms point towards the joint arrangement being a joint venture. *[IFRS 11.B32, Example 5]*.

Example 12.14: Modification of legal form and contractual arrangement by facts and circumstances

Companies A and B jointly establish a Corporation C over which they have joint control. The legal form of C, an incorporated entity, initially indicates that the assets and liabilities held in C are the assets and liabilities of C. The contractual arrangement between the parties does not specify that the parties have rights to the assets or obligations for the liabilities of C. Accordingly, the legal form of C and the terms of the contractual arrangement indicate that the arrangement is a joint venture.

However, A and B agree to the following:

- A and B will purchase all the output produced by C in a ratio of 50:50.
- C cannot sell any of the output to third parties, unless A and B approve this. The purpose of the arrangement is to provide A and B with the output they require, so sales to third parties are expected to be uncommon and not material.
- The price of the output sold to A and B is set by the parties at a level that is designed to cover the costs of production and administrative expenses incurred by C. The arrangement is intended to operate at a break-even level.

Analysis

- The obligation of A and B to purchase all the output produced by C reflects the exclusive dependence of C upon A and B for the generation of cash flows and, thus, implicitly that A and B have an obligation for the liabilities of C.
- The fact that A and B have rights to all the output produced by C means that they are consuming, and therefore have rights to, all the economic benefits of the assets of C.

These facts and circumstances indicate that the arrangement is a joint operation.

Variation 1 – If, instead of A and B using their share of the output themselves, they sold their share of the output to third parties, C would still be a joint operation because C remains exclusively dependent on A and B for generation of cash flows.

Variation 2 – If A and B changed the terms of the contractual arrangement so that the arrangement was able to sell output to third parties, this would result in C assuming demand, inventory and credit risks, such that A and B would not have substantially all of the economic benefits of C's assets. In this case, it is likely that the joint arrangement would be a joint venture.

5.5 Illustrative examples accompanying IFRS 11

IFRS 11 provides several examples that illustrate aspects of IFRS 11, but are not intended to provide interpretative guidance. The examples portray hypothetical situations illustrating the judgements that might be used when applying IFRS 11 in different situations. *[IFRS 11.IE1]*. Examples 12.15 to 12.20 are based on these illustrative examples accompanying IFRS 11. *[IFRS 11.IE2-IE52, Examples 1-6]*.

Example 12.15: Construction services

Companies A and B (the parties) provide many types of public and private construction services. They set up a contractual arrangement to design and construct a road between two cities for a government. The contractual arrangement determines the participation shares of A and B and establishes joint control of the arrangement, the purpose of which is the delivery of the road.

The parties set up a separate vehicle (Entity Z) through which to conduct the arrangement. On behalf of A and B, Z enters into the contract with the government. In addition, the assets and liabilities relating to the arrangement are held in Z. The main feature of Z's legal form is that the parties, not Z, have rights to the assets, and obligations for the liabilities, of Z.

The contractual arrangement between A and B also establishes that:

(a) the rights to all the assets needed to undertake the activities of the arrangement are shared by the parties based on their participation shares in the arrangement;

(b) the parties have several and joint responsibility for all operating and financial obligations relating to the activities of the arrangement based on their participation shares in the arrangement; and

(c) the profit or loss resulting from the activities of the arrangement is shared by A and B based on their participation shares in the arrangement.

For the purposes of coordinating and overseeing the activities, A and B appoint an operator, who will be an employee of one of the parties. After a specified time, the role of the operator will rotate to an employee of the other party. A and B agree that the activities will be executed by the operator's employees on a 'no gain or loss' basis.

In accordance with the terms specified in the contract with the government, Z invoices the construction services to the government on behalf of the parties.

Analysis

The joint arrangement is carried out through a separate vehicle whose legal form does not confer separation between the parties and the separate vehicle (i.e. the assets and liabilities held in Z are the parties' assets and liabilities). This is reinforced by the terms agreed by the parties in their contractual arrangement, which state that A and B have rights to the assets, and obligations for the liabilities, relating to the arrangement that is conducted through Z.

The joint arrangement is a joint operation.

A and B each recognise in their financial statements their share of the assets (e.g. property, plant and equipment (PP&E), accounts receivable) and their share of any liabilities resulting from the arrangement (e.g. accounts payable to third parties) based on their agreed participation share.

Each also recognises its share of the revenue and expenses resulting from the construction services provided to the government through Z.

Example 12.16: Shopping centre operated jointly

Two real estate companies (the parties) set up a separate vehicle (Entity X) for acquiring and operating a shopping centre. The contractual arrangement between the parties establishes joint control of the activities that are conducted in X. The main feature of X's legal form is that the entity, not the parties, has rights to the assets, and obligations for the liabilities, relating to the arrangement. The activities include the rental of the retail units, managing the car park, maintaining the centre and its equipment, such as lifts, and building the reputation and customer base for the centre as a whole.

The terms of the contractual arrangement are such that:

(a) X owns the shopping centre. The contractual arrangement does not specify that the parties have rights to the shopping centre;

(b) the parties are not liable in respect of the debts, liabilities or obligations of X. If X is unable to pay any of its debts or other liabilities or to discharge its obligations to third parties, the liability of each party to any third party will be limited to the unpaid amount of that party's capital contribution;

(c) the parties have the right to sell or pledge their interests in X; and

(d) each party receives a share of the income from operating the shopping centre (which is the rental income net of the operating costs) in accordance with its interest in X.

Analysis

The joint arrangement is carried out through a separate vehicle whose legal form causes the separate vehicle to be considered in its own right (i.e. the assets and liabilities held in the separate vehicle are the assets and liabilities of the separate vehicle and not the assets and liabilities of the parties). In addition, the terms of the contractual arrangement do not specify that the parties have rights to the assets, or obligations for the liabilities, relating to the arrangement. Instead, the terms of the contractual arrangement establish that the parties have rights to the net assets of X.

Based on the description above, there are no other facts and circumstances that indicate that the parties have rights to substantially all the economic benefits of the assets relating to the arrangement, and that the parties have an obligation for the liabilities relating to the arrangement.

The joint arrangement is a joint venture.

The parties recognise their rights to the net assets of X as investments and account for them using the equity method.

Example 12.17: Joint manufacturing and distribution of a product

Companies A and B (the parties) have set up a strategic and operating agreement (the framework agreement) in which they have agreed the terms according to which they will conduct the manufacturing and distribution of a product (product P) in different markets.

The parties have agreed to conduct manufacturing and distribution activities by establishing joint arrangements, as described below:

(a) Manufacturing activity: the parties have agreed to undertake the manufacturing activity through a joint arrangement (the manufacturing arrangement). The manufacturing arrangement is structured in a separate vehicle (Entity M) whose legal form causes it to be considered in its own right (i.e. the assets and liabilities held in M are the assets and liabilities of M and not the assets and liabilities of the parties). In accordance with the framework agreement, the parties have committed themselves to purchasing the whole production of product P manufactured by the manufacturing arrangement in accordance with their ownership interests in M. The parties subsequently sell product P to another arrangement, jointly controlled by the two parties themselves, that has been established exclusively for the distribution of product P as described below. Neither the framework agreement nor the contractual arrangement between A and B dealing with the manufacturing activity specifies that the parties have rights to the assets, and obligations for the liabilities, relating to the manufacturing activity.

(b) Distribution activity: the parties have agreed to undertake the distribution activity through a joint arrangement (the distribution arrangement). The parties have structured the distribution arrangement in a separate vehicle (Entity D) whose legal form causes it to be considered in its own right (i.e. the assets and liabilities held in D are the assets and liabilities of D and not the assets and liabilities of the parties). In accordance with the framework agreement, the distribution arrangement orders its requirements for product P from the parties according to the needs of the different markets where the distribution arrangement sells the product. Neither the framework agreement nor the contractual arrangement between A and B dealing with the distribution activity specifies that the parties have rights to the assets, and obligations for the liabilities, relating to the distribution activity.

In addition, the framework agreement establishes:

(a) that the manufacturing arrangement will produce product P to meet the requirements for product P that the distribution arrangement places on the parties;

(b) the commercial terms relating to the sale of product P by the manufacturing arrangement to the parties. The manufacturing arrangement will sell product P to the parties at a price agreed by A and B that covers all production costs incurred. Subsequently, the parties sell the product to the distribution arrangement at a price agreed by A and B; and

(c) that any cash shortages that the manufacturing arrangement may incur will be financed by the parties in accordance with their ownership interests in M.

Analysis

The framework agreement sets up the terms under which parties A and B conduct the manufacturing and distribution of product P. These activities are undertaken through joint arrangements whose purpose is either the manufacturing or the distribution of product P.

The parties carry out the manufacturing arrangement through M whose legal form confers separation between the parties and the entity. In addition, neither the framework agreement nor the contractual arrangement dealing with the manufacturing activity specifies that the parties have rights to the assets, and obligations for the liabilities, relating to the manufacturing activity. However, when considering the following facts and circumstances the parties have concluded that the manufacturing arrangement is a joint operation:

(a) The parties have committed themselves to purchasing the whole production of product P manufactured by the manufacturing arrangement. Consequently, A and B have rights to substantially all the economic benefits of the assets of the manufacturing arrangement.

(b) The manufacturing arrangement manufactures product P to meet the quantity and quality needs of the parties so that they can fulfil the demand for product P of the distribution arrangement. The exclusive dependence of the manufacturing arrangement upon the parties for the generation of cash flows and the parties' commitments to provide funds when the manufacturing arrangement incurs any cash shortages indicate that the parties have an obligation for the liabilities of the manufacturing arrangement, because those liabilities will be settled through the parties' purchases of product P or by the parties' direct provision of funds.

The parties carry out the distribution activities through D, whose legal form confers separation between the parties and the entity. In addition, neither the framework agreement nor the contractual arrangement dealing with the distribution activity specifies that the parties have rights to the assets, and obligations for the liabilities, relating to the distribution activity.

There are no other facts and circumstances that indicate that the parties have rights to substantially all the economic benefits of the assets relating to the distribution arrangement or that the parties have an obligation for the liabilities relating to that arrangement.

The distribution arrangement is a joint venture.

A and B each recognise in their financial statements their share of the assets (e.g. PP&E, cash) and their share of any liabilities resulting from the manufacturing arrangement (e.g. accounts payable to third parties) based on their ownership interest in M. Each party also recognises its share of the expenses resulting from the manufacture of product P incurred by the manufacturing arrangement and its share of the revenues relating to the sales of product P to the distribution arrangement.

The parties recognise their rights to the net assets of the distribution arrangement as investments and account for them using the equity method.

Variation

Assume that the parties agree that the manufacturing arrangement described above is responsible not only for manufacturing product P, but also for its distribution to third-party customers.

The parties also agree to set up a distribution arrangement, like the one described above, to distribute product P exclusively to assist in widening the distribution of product P in additional specific markets.

The manufacturing arrangement also sells product P directly to the distribution arrangement. No fixed proportion of the production of the manufacturing arrangement is committed to be purchased by, or to be reserved to, the distribution arrangement.

Analysis

The variation has affected neither the legal form of the separate vehicle in which the manufacturing activity is conducted nor the contractual terms relating to the parties' rights to the assets, and obligations for the liabilities, relating to the manufacturing activity. However, it causes the manufacturing arrangement to be a self-financed arrangement because it can undertake trade on its own behalf, distributing product P to third-party customers and, consequently, assuming demand, inventory and credit risks. Even though the manufacturing arrangement might also sell product P to the distribution arrangement, in this scenario the manufacturing arrangement is not dependent on the parties to be able to carry out its activities on a continuous basis.

In this case, the manufacturing arrangement is a joint venture.

The variation has no effect on the classification of the distribution arrangement as a joint venture.

The parties recognise their rights to the net assets of the manufacturing arrangement and their rights to the net assets of the distribution arrangement as investments and account for them using the equity method.

Example 12.18: Bank operated jointly

Banks A and B (the parties) agreed to combine their corporate, investment banking, asset management and services activities by establishing a separate vehicle (Bank C). Both parties expect the arrangement to benefit them in different ways. A believes that the arrangement could enable it to achieve its strategic plans to increase its size, offering an opportunity to exploit its full potential for organic growth through an enlarged offering of products and services. B expects the arrangement to reinforce its offering in financial savings and market products.

The main feature of C's legal form is that it causes the separate vehicle to be considered in its own right (i.e. the assets and liabilities held in the separate vehicle are the assets and liabilities of the separate vehicle and not the assets and liabilities of the parties). A and B each have a 40 per cent ownership interest in C, with the remaining 20 per cent being listed and widely held. The shareholders' agreement between A and B establishes joint control of the activities of C. In addition, A and B entered into an irrevocable agreement under which, even in the event of a dispute, both banks agree to provide the necessary funds in equal amount and, if required, jointly and severally, to ensure that C complies with the applicable legislation and banking regulations, and honours any commitments made to the banking authorities. This commitment represents the assumption by each party of 50 per cent of any funds needed to ensure that C complies with legislation and banking regulations.

Analysis

The joint arrangement is carried out through a separate vehicle whose legal form confers separation between the parties and the separate vehicle. The terms of the contractual arrangement do not specify that the parties have rights to the assets, or obligations for the liabilities, of C, but it establishes that the parties have rights to the net assets of C. The commitment by the parties to provide support if C is not able to comply with the applicable legislation and banking regulations is not by itself a determinant that the parties have an obligation for the liabilities of C. There are no other facts and circumstances that indicate that the parties have rights to substantially all the economic benefits of the assets of C and that the parties have an obligation for the liabilities of C.

The joint arrangement is a joint venture.

Both A and B recognise their rights to the net assets of C as investments and account for them using the equity method.

Example 12.19: Oil and gas exploration, development and production activities

Companies A and B (the parties) set up a separate vehicle (Entity H) and a Joint Operating Agreement (JOA) to undertake oil and gas exploration, development and production activities in country O. The main feature of H's legal form is that it causes the separate vehicle to be considered in its own right (i.e. the assets and liabilities held in the separate vehicle are the assets and liabilities of the separate vehicle and not the assets and liabilities of the parties).

Country O has granted H permits for the oil and gas exploration, development and production activities to be undertaken in a specific assigned block of land (fields).

The shareholders' agreement and JOA agreed by the parties establish their rights and obligations relating to those activities. The main terms of those agreements are summarised below.

Shareholders' agreement

The board of H consists of a director from each party. Each party has a 50 per cent shareholding in H. The unanimous consent of the directors is required for any resolution to be passed.

Joint Operating Agreement (JOA)

The JOA establishes an Operating Committee. This Committee consists of one representative from each party. Each party has a 50 per cent participating interest in the Operating Committee.

The Operating Committee approves the budgets and work programmes relating to the activities, which also require the unanimous consent of the representatives of each party. One of the parties is appointed as operator and is responsible for managing and conducting the approved work programmes.

The JOA specifies that the rights and obligations arising from the exploration, development and production activities are shared among the parties in proportion to each party's shareholding in H. In particular, the JOA establishes that the parties share:

(a) the rights and the obligations arising from the exploration and development permits granted to H (e.g. the permits, rehabilitation liabilities, any royalties and taxes payable);

(b) the production obtained; and

(c) all costs associated with all work programmes.

The costs incurred in relation to all the work programmes are covered by cash calls on the parties. If either party fails to satisfy its monetary obligations, the other is required to contribute to H the amount in default. The amount in default is regarded as a debt owed by the defaulting party to the other party.

Analysis

The parties carry out the joint arrangement through a separate vehicle whose legal form confers separation between the parties and the separate vehicle. The parties reversed the initial assessment of their rights and obligations arising from the legal form of the separate vehicle in which the arrangement is conducted. They have done this by agreeing terms in the JOA that entitle them to rights to the assets (e.g. exploration and development permits, production, and any other assets arising from the activities) and obligations for the liabilities (e.g. all costs and obligations arising from the work programmes) that are held in H.

The joint arrangement is a joint operation.

Both A and B recognise in their financial statements their own share of the assets and of any liabilities resulting from the arrangement based on their agreed participating interest. On that basis, each party also recognises its share of the revenue (from the sale of their share of the production) and its share of the expenses.

Example 12.20: Liquefied natural gas arrangement

Company A owns an undeveloped gas field that contains substantial gas resources. Company A determines that the gas field will be economically viable only if the gas is sold to customers in overseas markets. To do so, a liquefied natural gas (LNG) facility must be built to liquefy the gas so that it can be transported by ship to the overseas markets.

A enters into a joint arrangement with Company B to develop and operate the gas field and the LNG facility. Under that arrangement, A and B (the parties) agree to contribute the gas field and cash, respectively, to a new separate vehicle, C. In exchange for those contributions, the parties each take a 50 per cent ownership interest in C. The main feature of C's legal form is that it causes the separate vehicle to be considered in its own right (i.e. the assets and liabilities held in the separate vehicle are the assets and liabilities of the separate vehicle and not the assets and liabilities of the parties).

The contractual arrangement between the parties specifies that:

(a) A and B must each appoint two members to the board of C. The board of directors must unanimously agree the strategy and investments made by C;

(b) day-to-day management of the gas field and LNG facility, including development and construction activities, will be undertaken by the staff of B in accordance with the directions jointly agreed by the parties. C will reimburse B for the costs it incurs in managing the gas field and LNG facility;

(c) C is liable for taxes and royalties on the production and sale of LNG as well as for other liabilities incurred in the ordinary course of business, such as accounts payable, site restoration and decommissioning liabilities; and

(d) A and B have equal shares in the profit from the activities carried out in the arrangement and, are entitled to equal shares of any dividends distributed by C.

The contractual arrangement does not specify that either party has rights to the assets, or obligations for the liabilities, of C.

The board of C decides to enter into a financing arrangement with a syndicate of lenders to help fund the development of the gas field and construction of the LNG facility. The estimated total cost of the development and construction is CU1,000 million.

The lending syndicate provides C with a CU700 million loan. The arrangement specifies that the syndicate has recourse to A and B only if C defaults on the loan arrangement during the development of the field and construction of the LNG facility. The lending syndicate agrees that it will not have recourse to A and B once the LNG facility is in production because it has assessed that the cash inflows that C should generate from LNG sales will be sufficient to meet the loan repayments. Although at this time the lenders have no recourse to A and B, the syndicate maintains protection against default by C by taking a lien on the LNG facility.

Analysis

The joint arrangement is carried out through a separate vehicle whose legal form confers separation between the parties and the separate vehicle. The terms of the contractual arrangement do not specify that the parties have rights to the assets, or obligations for the liabilities, of C, but they establish that the parties have rights to the net assets of C. The recourse nature of the financing arrangement during the development of the gas field and construction of the LNG facility (i.e. A and B providing separate guarantees during this phase) does not, by itself, impose on the parties an obligation for the liabilities of C (i.e. the loan is a liability of C). A and B have separate liabilities, which are their guarantees to repay that loan if C defaults during the development and construction phase.

There are no other facts and circumstances that indicate that the parties have rights to substantially all the economic benefits of the assets of C and that the parties have an obligation for the liabilities of C.

The joint arrangement is a joint venture. The parties recognise their rights to the net assets of entity C as investments and account for them using the equity method.

6 ACCOUNTING FOR JOINT OPERATIONS

For a joint operation, the joint operator recognises its:

- assets, including its share of any assets held jointly;
- liabilities, including its share of any liabilities incurred jointly;
- revenue from the sale of its share of the output arising from the joint operation;
- share of the revenue from the sale of the output by the joint operation; and
- expenses, including its share of any expenses incurred jointly. *[IFRS 11.20]*.

IFRS 11 requires each of these items to be accounted for in accordance with the applicable IFRS. *[IFRS 11.21]*. Careful consideration should be given to the nature of the rights to the assets, and the obligations for the liabilities (or the share of assets, liabilities, revenues, and expenses) if any, of the joint operation (see 6.3 below).

6.1 Joint arrangements not structured through a separate vehicle

For joint arrangements not structured through a separate vehicle, the contractual arrangement establishes the parties' rights to the assets, and obligations for the liabilities, relating to the arrangement, and the parties' rights to the corresponding revenues and obligations for the corresponding expenses. *[IFRS 11.B16]*.

A contractual arrangement often describes the nature of the activities that are the subject of the arrangement and how the parties intend to undertake those activities together. For example, the parties could conduct an activity together, with each party being responsible for a specific task and each using its own assets and incurring its own liabilities and the parties share revenues and expenses. In such a case, each joint operator recognises in its financial statements the assets and liabilities used for the specific task, and recognises its share of the revenues and expenses in accordance with the contractual arrangement. *[IFRS 11.B17]*. When the parties agree, for example, to share and operate an asset together and share the output or revenue from the asset and operating costs, each joint operator accounts for its share of the joint asset, its agreed share of any liabilities, and of the output, revenues and expenses. *[IFRS 11.B18]*.

6.2 Accounting for rights and obligations

An entity's rights and obligations for the assets, liabilities, revenues and expenses relating to a joint operation as specified in the contractual arrangement, are the basis for accounting for a joint operation under IFRS 11. This may differ from its ownership interest in the joint operation. *[IFRS 11.BC38]*.

When the joint operator has differing rights (and percentages) to various assets, and/or differing obligations for various liabilities, these are reflected in its financial statements even when those rights and obligations differ from the joint operator's proportion of equity ownership. Example 12.21 below illustrates joint operation accounting in this case.

Example 12.21: Accounting for rights to assets and obligations for liabilities

Entities D and E establish Joint Arrangement F, using a separate vehicle, classified as a joint operation. Accordingly, D and E account for their rights to assets and their obligations for liabilities relating to F in accordance with the relevant IFRS.

D and E each own 50% of the equity (e.g. shares) in F. However, the contractual terms of the joint arrangement state that D has the rights to all of Building No. 1 and the obligation to pay all the third-party debt in F. D and E have rights to all other assets in F, and obligations for all other liabilities in F in proportion to their equity interests (i.e. 50%). F's balance sheet is as follows (in CUs):

Assets		Liabilities and equity	
Cash	20	Debt	120
Building No. 1	120	Employee benefit plan obligation	50
Building No. 2	100	Equity	70
Total assets	240	Total liabilities and equity	240

Under IFRS 11, D would record the following in its financial statements, to account for its rights to the assets in F and its obligations for the liabilities in F. This differs from consolidating a blended percentage of all assets and liabilities.

Assets		Liabilities and equity	
Cash	10	Debt [2]	120
Building No. 1 [1]	120	Employee benefit plan obligation	25
Building No. 2	50	Equity	35
Total assets	180	Total liabilities and equity	180

(1) Since D has the rights to all of Building No. 1, it records that amount in its entirety.
(2) D's obligations are for the third-party debt in its entirety.

6.3 Determining the relevant IFRS

As noted at 6 above, joint operators are required to recognise their rights to assets and their obligations for liabilities in accordance with the relevant IFRSs. In some cases, the relevant IFRS is clear, but questions have arisen in other cases.

- Right of use – The illustrative examples of joint operations in IFRS 11 refer to recognising the joint operator's share of assets, such as PP&E, accounts receivable and cash (see, for example, paragraphs IE8 and IE21 of IFRS 11), rather than recognising a 'right of use'. Therefore, a joint operator would recognise its share of an asset in accordance with IAS 16 – *Property, Plant and Equipment*, or IAS 38 – *Intangible Assets*, as applicable. When the contractual terms of the joint operation provide a joint operator with a right to use an asset, not a share of the asset itself, the joint operator would apply IFRS 16 – *Leases* (see Chapter 23).

- Liability for entire balance of certain liabilities – One of the joint operators may have a direct legal liability for the entire balance of certain liabilities of the joint operation. It may also have a right to reimbursement by the other parties for their share of that liability of the joint operation. The joint operator would recognise 100 per cent of the joint operation's liabilities and a receivable for the reimbursement due from the other parties for their share of such liability. IFRS prohibits the offsetting of the liability against the receivable. If the other parties were unable to pay, the joint operator would not be able to recognise a receivable for the full amount due. Accordingly, the receivable would be impaired, which would result in a reduction in profit in the joint operator's financial statements.

This principle was emphasised in March 2019 when the Interpretations Committee finalised an agenda decision dealing with liabilities in relation to a joint operator's interest in a joint operation. In the fact pattern described in the request, the joint operation is not structured through a separate vehicle. One of the joint operators, as the sole signatory, enters into a lease contract with a third-party lessor for an item of PP&E that will be operated jointly as part of the joint operation's activities. The joint operator that signed the lease contract has the right to recover a share of the lease costs from the other joint operators in accordance with the contractual arrangement to the joint operation. The request asked about the recognition of liabilities by the joint operator that signed the lease agreement. In relation to its interest in a joint operation, paragraph 20(b) of IFRS 11 (see 6 above) requires a joint operator to recognise its liabilities, including its share of any liabilities incurred jointly. Accordingly, a joint operator identifies and recognises both:

(a) liabilities it incurs in relation to its interest in the joint operation; and

(b) its share of any liabilities incurred jointly with other parties to the joint arrangement.

Identifying the liabilities that a joint operator incurs and those incurred jointly requires an assessment of the terms and conditions in all contractual agreements that relate to the joint operation, including consideration of the laws pertaining to those agreements. The Interpretations Committee observed that the liabilities a joint operator recognises include those for which it has primary responsibility. Based on this agenda decision, the joint operator that is the sole signatory of the lease agreement would recognise the full lease liability and corresponding right of use asset in its financial statements. The agenda decision did not address how the joint operator should account for its right to recover a share of the lease costs from the other joint operators in accordance with the contractual arrangement to the joint operation. The joint operator would need to assess the relevant IFRS to apply to this right, for example, whether it represents a sub-lease of the right of use asset to the other joint operators.

The Interpretations Committee also highlighted the importance of disclosing information about joint operations that is sufficient for a user of financial statements to understand the activities of the joint operation and a joint operator's interest in that operation. The Interpretations Committee concluded that the principles and requirements in IFRSs provide an adequate basis for the operator to identify and recognise its liabilities in relation to its interest in a joint operation. Consequently, the Interpretations Committee decided not to add this matter to its standard-setting agenda. Respondents to the tentative agenda decision suggested that the Board consider more broadly the accounting for this type of joint operation as part of its Post-implementation Review of IFRS 11.[6]

- Jointly and severally liable – In some cases, the joint arrangement (or legal form of the separate vehicle, if applicable) gives joint and several liability for the obligations of the arrangement. This may result in the joint operator recognising the entire obligation due, not just its share. The facts and circumstances need to be assessed in each case, and the liability accounted for in accordance with IAS 37 – *Provisions, Contingent Liabilities and Contingent Assets.*

- Obligation to reimburse other parties – A party to the joint arrangement who has an obligation to reimburse another party would recognise a financial liability for the amount related to the reimbursement.

- Service fee income – In some joint operations, one joint operator receives fees from the other joint operators for providing management services in respect of the joint operation. IFRS 11 does not specifically require that such parties account for any fees received in accordance with IFRS 15 – *Revenue from Contracts with Customers.* Paragraph BC55 of IFRS 15 explains that a contract with a collaborator or a partner in a joint arrangement could also be within the scope of IFRS 15 if that collaborator or partner meets the definition of a customer for some or all of the terms of the arrangement.

- Inter-company sales – In March 2015, the Interpretations Committee published an agenda decision that addressed the issue of revenue recognition by a joint operator. If a joint arrangement is structured through a separate vehicle, classified as a joint operation, the joint operators' purchase of all the output from the joint operation, is in effect a sale to itself. The Interpretations Committee interpreted paragraph 20(d) of IFRS 11 (see 6 above) to mean that a joint operator would recognise its share of the joint operation's revenue only when the joint operation sells its output to third parties (i.e. other parties who have rights to the assets and obligations for the liabilities relating to the joint operation).

- Sale of output by a joint operator – In March 2019, the Interpretations Committee finalised an agenda decision dealing with another matter of revenue recognition by a joint operator. The request dealt with the recognition of revenue by a joint operator for output arising from a joint operation when the output it receives in a reporting period is different from the output to which it is entitled. This is commonly known in the oil and gas industry as an overlift or underlift (see Chapter 43 at 12.4). In the fact pattern described in the request, the joint operator has the right to receive a fixed proportion of the output arising from the joint operation and is obliged to pay for a fixed proportion of the production costs incurred. For operational reasons, the output received by the joint operator and transferred to its customers in a particular reporting period is different from the output to which it is entitled. That difference will be settled through future deliveries of output arising from the joint operation – it cannot be settled in cash. Applying IFRS 15, the joint operator recognises revenue as a principal for the transfer of all the output to its customers. The request asked whether, in the fact pattern described, the joint operator recognises revenue to depict the transfer of output to its customers in the reporting period or, instead, to depict its entitlement to a fixed proportion of the output produced from the joint operation's activities in that period. In relation to its interest in a joint operation, paragraph 20(c) of IFRS 11 (see 6 above) requires a joint operator to recognise its revenue from the sale of its share of the output arising from the joint operation. Accordingly, the revenue recognised by a joint operator depicts the output it has received from the joint operation and sold, rather than, for example, the production of output.

The Interpretations Committee concluded that, in the fact pattern described in the request, the joint operator recognises revenue that depicts only the transfer of output to its customers in each reporting period, i.e. revenue recognised applying IFRS 15. This means, for example, that the joint operator does not recognise revenue for the output to which it is entitled but which it has not received from the joint operation and sold. The Interpretations Committee concluded that the principles and requirements in IFRS Standards provide an adequate basis for a joint operator to determine its revenue from the sale of its share of output arising from a joint operation as described in the request. Consequently, the Interpretations Committee decided not to add this matter to its standard-setting agenda.

The agenda decision did not address the cost of goods sold and hence diversity in practice will continue in this respect. See Chapter 43 at 12.4.2 for more detail.[7]

6.4 Interest in a joint operation without joint control

A party that participates in a joint arrangement but does not have joint control (see 4 above) is not a joint operator. However, if that party has rights to assets and obligations for liabilities, the accounting is the same as that for a joint operator, as discussed above. *[IFRS 11.23]*.

If the party that participates in a joint arrangement but does not have joint control does not have rights to the assets and obligations for the liabilities relating to the joint operation, it accounts for its interest in the joint operation in accordance with other applicable IFRS. *[IFRS 11.23]*. For example, if it has:

(a) an interest in a separate vehicle over which it has significant influence, it should apply IAS 28;

(b) an interest in a separate vehicle over which it does not have significant influence, it should account for that interest as a financial asset under IFRS 9; or

(c) an interest in an arrangement without a separate vehicle, it should apply other applicable IFRS (see 4.4.1 above).

Effectively, if the joint arrangement is a joint operation, and the party has rights to the assets and obligations for the liabilities relating to that joint operation, it does not matter whether the parties to that joint arrangement have joint control or not – the accounting is the same. The disclosure requirements of IFRS 12 that may apply are discussed in Chapter 13 at 5.

6.5 Joint operations with a party that participates in a joint arrangement but does not have joint control

A joint operation conducted through a separate vehicle may involve a party that participates in the joint arrangement but does not have joint control (see 4 and 6.4 above). In such cases, a joint operator does not recognise the rights to assets and obligations for the liabilities attributable to such party or recognise a higher percentage with a 'non-controlling interest'. Rather, a joint operator only recognises its share of any assets held jointly and its obligations for its share of any liabilities incurred jointly. Example 12.22 illustrates this point.

Example 12.22: *Joint operation with a party that participates in a joint arrangement but does not have joint control*

Entities A and B enter into a joint operation that is structured through a separate vehicle Z. Each of the two entities owns 40% of the shares of the separate vehicle. The remaining 20% of Z is owned by C, which participates in the joint arrangement but does not have joint control. C does have rights to the assets and obligations for the liabilities of Z.

Accordingly, A, B and C (see 6.4 above) recognise their assets, including their share of any assets held jointly, and their liabilities, including their share of any liabilities incurred jointly, in accordance with relevant IFRS.

In A's financial statements, it recognises its assets, liabilities, revenues and expenses in Z, which would be 40% of Z's assets, liabilities, revenues and expenses, in accordance with the relevant IFRS. A does not recognise a 'non-controlling interest' related to C's interest in Z.

6.6 Transactions between a joint operator and a joint operation

IFRS 11 addresses transactions such as the sale, contribution or purchase of assets between a joint operator and a joint operation. *[IFRS 11.22].*

When a joint operator enters into a transaction with its joint operation, such as a sale or contribution of assets to the joint operation, the joint operator is conducting the transaction with the other parties to the joint operation. The joint operator recognises gains and losses resulting from such a transaction only to the extent of the other parties' interests in the joint operation. *[IFRS 11.B34].*

However, when these transactions provide evidence of a reduction in the net realisable value of the assets to sold or contributed to the joint operation, or of an impairment loss of those assets, those losses are recognised fully by the joint operator. *[IFRS 11.B35].*

When a joint operator enters into a transaction with its joint operation, such as a purchase of assets from the joint operation, it does not recognise its share of the gains and losses until the joint operator resells those assets to a third party. *[IFRS 11.B36].*

However, when these transactions provide evidence of a reduction in the net realisable value of the assets to be purchased, or of an impairment loss of those assets, a joint operator recognises its share of those losses. *[IFRS 11.B37].*

When there is a transaction between a joint operator and a joint operation, consideration should be given to whether the transaction changes the nature of the joint operator's rights to assets, or obligations for liabilities. Any such changes should be reflected in the joint operator's financial statements, and the new assets and liabilities should be accounted for in accordance with the relevant IFRS.

6.7 Accounting for a joint operation in separate financial statements

In the separate financial statements, both a joint operator and a party that participates in a joint arrangement but does not have joint control (see 6.4 above) account for their interests in the same manner as accounting for a joint operation in consolidated financial statements. That is, regardless of whether or not the joint operation is structured through a separate vehicle, such a party would recognise in its separate financial statements:

- assets, including its share of any assets held jointly;
- liabilities, including its share of any liabilities incurred jointly;
- revenue from the sale of its share of the output arising from the joint operation;
- share of the revenue from the sale of the output by the joint operation; and
- expenses, including its share of any expenses incurred jointly. *[IFRS 11.20-23, 26(a), 27(a)]*.

Accordingly, the guidance at 6 to 6.6 above also applies to accounting for joint operations in separate financial statements.

7 ACCOUNTING FOR JOINT VENTURES

Joint ventures are accounted for using the equity method. IFRS 11 does not describe how to apply the equity method. Rather, if an entity has joint control over a joint venture, it recognises its interest in the joint venture as an investment and accounts for it by applying the equity method in accordance with IAS 28, unless it is exempted from doing so by IAS 28. *[IFRS 11.24]*. The requirements of IAS 28, including the accounting for transactions between a joint venturer and the joint venture, are discussed in Chapter 11.

As discussed at 2.2.1 above, venture capital organisations, mutual funds, unit trusts and similar entities, including investment-linked insurance funds, can choose to measure investments in joint ventures at fair value or apply the equity method under IAS 28. This is considered a measurement exemption under IFRS 11 and IAS 28 (see Chapter 11 at 5.3).

This means, however, that such entities are subject to the disclosure requirements for joint ventures set out in IFRS 12 (see Chapter 13 at 5).

Although this option included in IAS 28 is available to venture capital organisations and similar entities, IFRS 10 states that an 'investment entity' for the purposes of that standard would elect the exemption from applying the equity method in IAS 28 for its investments in associates and joint ventures. *[IFRS 10.B85L]*.

7.1 Interest in a joint venture without joint control

IAS 28 also applies if a party that participates in a joint arrangement but does not have joint control (see 6.4 above) in a joint venture has significant influence over the entity. *[IFRS 11.25]*. However, the disclosure requirements differ (see Chapter 13 at 5). If the party that participates in a joint arrangement does not have joint control but does have significant influence in a joint venture, but the joint venture is not an entity (i.e. but is in a separate vehicle) (see 5.1 above), IAS 28 would not apply, and the investor would apply the relevant IFRS.

If the party participates in a joint arrangement but does not have joint control and does not have significant influence, its interest in the joint venture would be accounted for as a financial asset under IFRS 9. *[IFRS 11.25, C14]*.

7.2 Contributions of non-monetary assets to a joint venture

When an entity contributes a non-monetary asset or liability to a joint venture in exchange for an equity interest in the joint venture, it recognises the portion of the gain or loss attributable to the other parties to the joint venture except when the contribution lacks commercial substance.

The measurement of the non-monetary asset in the financial statements of the joint venture (i.e. not the joint venturer) can differ, depending on the method of settlement. When the consideration given by the joint venture is its own shares, the transaction is an equity-settled share-based payment transaction in the scope of IFRS 2 – *Share-based Payment*. As a result, the joint venture measures the non-monetary asset received at its fair value. When the consideration given by the joint venture is not its own shares, the transaction is outside the scope of IFRS 2; we believe the joint venture should measure the non-monetary asset received at its cost, which is the fair value of the consideration given.

However, when the contributed non-monetary asset is a subsidiary of an entity, a conflict arises between the requirements of IAS 28 and IFRS 10. This is discussed in Chapter 11 at 7.6.5.C and at 8.2.3 below.

7.3 Accounting for a joint venture in separate financial statements

In its separate financial statements, a joint venturer accounts for its interest in the joint venture at cost, as a financial asset under IFRS 9, or under the equity method. *[IFRS 11.26(b)]*. These separate financial statements are prepared in addition to those prepared using the equity method. The requirements for separate financial statements are discussed in Chapter 8 at 2.

In its separate financial statements, a party that participates in, but does not have joint control of a joint venture (see 6.4 above) accounts for its interest as a financial asset under IFRS 9, unless it has significant influence over the joint venture. *[IFRS 11.27(b)]*. In this case, it may choose whether to account for its interest in the joint venture at cost, as a financial asset under IFRS 9, or the equity method. *[IAS 27.10]*.

However, if an entity elects, in accordance with IAS 28, to measure its investments in associates or joint ventures at fair value through profit or loss in accordance with IFRS 9, it also accounts for those investments in the same way in its separate financial statements. *[IAS 27.11]*.

8 CONTINUOUS ASSESSMENT

IFRS 11 incorporates the notion of continuous assessment, consistent with the requirements in IFRS 10.

If facts and circumstances change, an entity that is a party in a joint arrangement reassesses whether:

- it still has joint control of the arrangement; and *[IFRS 11.13]*
- the classification of the joint arrangement has changed. *[IFRS 11.19]*.

8.1 When to reassess under IFRS 11

A party reassesses upon any change in facts and circumstances whether it has joint control, and whether the classification of the joint arrangement has changed.

Reassessment of a joint arrangement occurs upon a change in:

- How activities are directed – For example, Company A sets up Company Z to develop a new product or technology. Initially, Z had a Board of Directors elected by shareholders, separate management and the relevant activities were directed by voting rights held exclusively by A. If A enters into an agreement with Company B so that A and B must agree on all decisions (e.g. they replace the Board and make decisions for management), reassessment would be required to evaluate whether A and B have joint control of Z.
- Legal form – For example, a separate vehicle that initially did not confer separation between the parties and the vehicle (e.g. a general partnership) and was considered a joint operation, is converted into a separate vehicle that now does confer separation between the parties and the vehicle (e.g. a corporation). Reassessment would be required to evaluate whether this indicates a change in classification from a joint operation to a joint venture.
- Contractual terms – For example, the terms of a joint arrangement are renegotiated, such that the parties have rights to the assets or obligations for the liabilities. Reassessment would be required to evaluate whether this indicates a change in classification to a joint operation.
- Other facts and circumstances – For example, the terms and conditions of a joint operation are renegotiated. Initially, a joint arrangement could sell output only to the parties of the joint arrangement. Thereafter, the joint arrangement may also sell output to third-party customers. Reassessment would be required to evaluate whether this indicates a change in classification from a joint operation to a joint venture.

As discussed at 5.3.1 above, another event that might trigger reassessment would be an event that leads a guarantor to have to pay (or perform) under a guarantee.

8.1.1 Changes in ownership

The accounting for changes in ownership of a joint arrangement depends firstly on whether the underlying assets and liabilities constitute a 'business' as defined in IFRS 3. Secondly, it depends on the type of interest held before and after the change in ownership occurred.

The diagram below provides a reference for additional guidance when the assets and liabilities meet the definition of a business. The key questions that arise on these transactions are:
- Should a cost-based approach or a fair value (IFRS 3) approach be used?
- Should any previously held (retained) interest be remeasured?
- Should a profit on sale be recognised and, if so, how should it be measured?

Matrix of transactions involving changes of interest in a business

To: \ From:	Holder of financial asset	Investor in associate	Joint Venturer	Joint Operator	Parent
Holder of financial asset	IFRS 9 See Chapter 48	IFRS not clear See Chapter 11 at 7.4.2.A		See 8.3.1 below	IFRS 3 See Chapter 9 at 9
Investor in associate or Joint Venturer	IAS 28 and IFRS 9 See Chapter 11 at 7.12.3	IAS 28 See Chapter 11 at 7.4.2.B, 7.4.2.C, 7.12.4 and 7.12.5		See 8.3.1 below	IFRS 3 and IAS 28 See Chapter 11 at 7.12.1 and Chapter 9 at 9
Joint Operator	IFRS not clear See 8.3.4 below	IFRS not clear See 8.3.4 below		See 8.3.2 and 8.3.4 below	See 8.3.2 below
Parent	IFRS 10 See Chapter 7 at 3.3	IFRS 10 See Chapter 11 at 7.4.1 and 8.2.3 below		IFRS is not clear See 8.3.3 below	IFRS 10 See Chapter 7 at 4

The rights and obligations of the parties that participate in a joint arrangement but who do not have joint control (see 6.4 above) should determine the appropriate category according to the table above.[8]

At 8.2 and 8.3 below, we discuss changes in accounting that result from changes in ownership in joint ventures and joint operations that constitute a business, respectively.

The accounting for a change in an interest in a joint arrangement that does not meet the definition of a business is discussed at 8.4 below.

8.2 Changes in ownership of a joint venture that constitutes a business

8.2.1 Acquisition of an interest in a joint venture

The accounting for the acquisition of an interest in a joint venture that meets the definition of a business is accounted for under IAS 28 (see Chapter 11 at 7.4) and the procedures are similar to those applied to the acquisition of a business in IFRS 3.

However, it is clear from the scope of IFRS 3 that the formation of a joint venture that constitutes a business, in the financial statements of the joint venture itself, is not covered by IFRS 3. *[IFRS 3.2]*.

8.2.2 Gaining control over a former joint venture

If an entity gains control over a former joint venture, and the acquiree meets the definition of a business, the entity applies IFRS 3 (see Chapter 9 at 9).

8.2.3 Former subsidiary becomes a joint venture

Under IFRS 10, if a parent entity loses control of a subsidiary that constitutes a business in a transaction that is not a downstream transaction (see 7.2 above), the retained interest must be remeasured at its fair value, and this fair value becomes the cost on initial recognition of an investment in an associate or joint venture. [IFRS 10.25]. If the subsidiary does not constitute a business, we believe that an entity can develop an accounting policy to apply paragraph 25 of IFRS 10 to:

- the loss of control of only subsidiaries that constitute a business; or
- to the loss of control of all subsidiaries, i.e. those that constitute a business and those that do not.

Where an entity does not apply paragraph 25 of IFRS 10 to subsidiaries that do not constitute a business, it can apply the guidance in IAS 28 if the loss of control occurs through a downstream transaction (see Chapter 11 at 7.6.5). For all other types of transactions, an entity develops an accounting policy in accordance with IAS 8 – *Accounting Policies, Changes in Accounting Estimates and Errors* – on how to account for the retained interest.

Where the loss of control occurs through a downstream transaction, the requirements in IFRS 10 relating to the accounting for the loss of control of a subsidiary are inconsistent with the accounting required by IAS 28. Under IAS 28, the contributing investor is required to restrict any gain arising on disposal of its own assets to the amount attributable to the other party to the joint venture (see 7.2 above). However, under IFRS 10, the gain is not restricted in this manner and there is no adjustment to reduce the fair values of the net assets contributed to the associate or joint venture. In September 2014, the IASB issued *Sale or Contribution of Assets between an Investor and its Associate or Joint Venture* (amendments to IFRS 10 and IAS 28) to address the conflict between IFRS 10 and IAS 28.[9] The amendments require that:

- the partial gain or loss recognition for transactions between an investor and its associate or joint venture applies only to the gain or loss resulting from the sale or contribution of assets that do not constitute a business as defined in IFRS 3; and
- the gain or loss resulting from the sale or contribution of assets that constitute a business as defined in IFRS 3, between an investor and its associate or joint venture be recognised in full.

In December 2015, the IASB deferred the effective date of these amendments indefinitely due to feedback that the recognition of a partial gain or loss when a transaction involves assets that do not constitute a business, even if these assets are housed in a subsidiary, is inconsistent with the initial measurement requirements of paragraph 32(b) of IAS 28. This issue will be reconsidered as part of the equity method research project (see Chapter 11 at 11). However, entities may early apply the amendments before the effective date.

We believe that until the amendments become mandatorily effective, and where the non-monetary asset contributed is an interest in a subsidiary that constitutes a business, entities have an accounting policy choice as to whether to apply IFRS 10 or IAS 28. This policy choice arises because of the conflict between the requirements of IFRS 10, which deal with the specific issue of loss of control, and the requirements of IAS 28, which are more generic. Once selected, the entity must apply the selected policy consistently. Where the requirements of IFRS 10 are followed for transactions involving a contribution of an interest in a subsidiary that constitutes a business, IAS 28 would generally apply to other forms of non-monetary assets contributed, such as items of PP&E or intangible assets and an interest in a subsidiary that does not constitute a business. However, disposal of a former subsidiary that does not constitute a business could be accounted for under paragraph 25 of IFRS 10 if the entity has a policy of applying that paragraph to the loss of control of all subsidiaries (as discussed above).

8.2.4 Joint venture becomes an associate (or vice versa)

If a joint venturer loses joint control but retains an interest in an associate, it would continue to apply the equity method. An entity does not remeasure its retained interest in an associate when it loses joint control over a joint venture. The same applies where an entity gains joint control over an associate that becomes an investment in a joint venture. *[IAS 28.24]*. In the Basis for Conclusions to IAS 28, the IASB acknowledged that the nature of the investor-investee relationship changes upon changing from joint venture to associate (or *vice versa*). However, since the investment continues to be accounted for using the equity method (i.e. there is no change in the measurement requirements) and there is no change in the group, it is not an event that warrants remeasurement of the retained interest at fair value. *[IAS 28.BC30]*.

If an entity's ownership interest in an associate or a joint venture is reduced, but the investment continues to be classified either as an associate or a joint venture respectively, the entity shall reclassify to profit or loss the proportion of the gain or loss that had previously been recognised in other comprehensive income (OCI) relating to that reduction in ownership interest if that gain or loss would be required to be reclassified to profit or loss on the disposal of the related assets or liabilities. *[IAS 28.25]*.

The above requirements of IAS 28 also are discussed in Chapter 11 at 7.4.2.C and 7.12.4.

8.2.5 Joint venture becomes a financial asset (or vice versa)

If a joint venture becomes a financial asset, the measurement method changes. An entity measures its retained interest in the financial asset at fair value, which becomes its fair value on initial recognition as a financial asset.

The entity recognises in profit or loss any difference between:

(a) the fair value of any retained interest and any proceeds from disposing of a part interest in the joint venture; and

(b) the carrying amount of the interest in the joint venture at the date the equity method was discontinued.

If a gain or loss previously recognised by the entity in OCI would be reclassified to profit or loss on the disposal of the related assets or liabilities, IAS 28 requires the entity to reclassify the gain or loss from equity to profit or loss when the equity method is discontinued. For example, gains and losses related to foreign currency translation adjustments accumulated in equity would be reclassified to profit or loss. *[IAS 28.22, 23]*.

The above requirements of IAS 28 also are discussed in Chapter 11 at 7.12.3.

An entity may gain joint control over an existing investment (accounted for as a financial asset). IAS 28 is unclear on how piecemeal acquisitions of a joint venture should be treated. This issue is discussed in Chapter 11 at 7.4.2.A.

8.2.6 Disposal of an interest in a joint venture

When an entity disposes of its interest in a joint venture and loses joint control, it ceases to apply the equity method as of that date. It also derecognises its interest and recognises any gain or loss upon sale, as discussed at 8.2.5 above. *[IAS 28.22, 23]*. In such cases, an entity cannot restate its financial statements for the period (or the comparative period) as if it did not have joint control during the reporting period. IAS 28 requires that the entity use the equity method up to the date that the joint venturer disposes of its interest in the joint venture. This assumes that the entity is not exempt from preparing financial statements by IFRS 10, IAS 27 – *Separate Financial Statements* – or IAS 28 and that it is not using the fair value measurement exemption (see 2.2.1 above).

8.2.7 Interest in a joint venture held for sale

When a joint venturer plans to dispose of part of its interest in a joint venture, it applies IFRS 5 (see Chapter 4) and only reclassifies the interest to be disposed of as held for sale when that portion meets the criteria for classification as held for sale. The joint venturer continues to account for the retained interest in the joint venture using the equity method until the disposal of the interest classified as held for sale occurs. This is because an entity continues to have joint control over its entire interest in the joint venture until it disposes of that interest. Upon disposal, it reassesses the nature of its retained interest and accounts for that interest accordingly (e.g. as a financial asset if joint control is lost). *[IAS 28.20]*.

If an interest (or a portion of an interest) in a joint venture no longer meets the criteria to be classified as held for sale, the interest is accounted for using the equity method retrospectively from the date of its classification as held for sale. *[IAS 28.21]*.

The above requirements of IAS 28 also are discussed in Chapter 11 at 6.

8.3 Changes in ownership of a joint operation that is a business

8.3.1 Acquisition of an interest in a joint operation

An entity that acquires an interest in a joint operation that is a business as defined in IFRS 3 is required to apply, to the extent of its share, all of the principles of IFRS 3 and other IFRSs that do not conflict with IFRS 11, which include:

(a) measuring identifiable assets and liabilities at fair value, other than items for which exceptions are given in IFRS 3 and other IFRSs;

(b) recognising acquisition-related costs as expenses in the periods in which the costs are incurred and the services are received, with the exception that the costs to issue debt or equity securities are recognised in accordance with IAS 32 – *Financial Instruments: Presentation* – and IFRS 9;

(c) recognising deferred tax assets and deferred tax liabilities that arise from the initial recognition of assets or liabilities, except for deferred tax liabilities that arise from the initial recognition of goodwill;

(d) recognising as goodwill any excess of the consideration transferred over the net amount of identifiable assets acquired and the liabilities assumed; and

(e) testing for impairment a cash-generating unit to which goodwill has been allocated at least annually, and whenever there is an indication that the unit may be impaired, as required by IAS 36 – *Impairment of Assets*. [IFRS 11.B33A].

In addition, the entity should disclose the information that is required in those IFRSs in relation to business combinations.

The IASB recognised that the acquisition of an interest in a joint operation did not meet the definition of a business combination in IFRS 3, but it concluded that it was the most appropriate approach to account for an acquisition of an interest in a joint operation whose activity meets the definition of a business, as defined in IFRS 3. [IFRS 11.BC45E, BC45F].

The above approach also applies to the formation of a joint operation, but only if an existing business (as defined in IFRS 3) is contributed by one of the parties that participates in the joint operation. In other words, the above approach should not be applied if the parties that participate in the joint operation contribute only (groups of) assets that do not constitute businesses to the joint operation on its formation. [IFRS 11.B33B]. The requirements apply to the acquisition of both the initial interest and additional interests in a joint operation (while still maintaining joint control) in which the activity of the joint operation constitutes a business. [IFRS 11.21A].

If a joint operator increases its interest in a joint operation that is a business (as defined in IFRS 3) by acquiring an additional interest while still retaining joint control, it should not remeasure its previously held interest in that joint operation. [IFRS 11.B33C].

This requirement does not apply to 'the acquisition of an interest in a joint operation when the parties sharing joint control, including the entity acquiring the interest in the joint operation, are under the common control of the same ultimate controlling party or parties both before and after the acquisition, and that control is not transitory'. [IFRS 11.B33D].

8.3.2 Obtaining control or joint control over a joint operation that is a business

In December 2017, the IASB issued an amendment to IFRS 3 and IFRS 11: *Previously Held Interests in a Joint Operation*, as part of the *Annual Improvements to IFRS Standards 2015-2017 Cycle*. The amendments clarify that, when a party to a joint operation obtains control over the joint operation that meets the definition of a business, it applies the requirements for a business combination achieved in stages. This includes remeasuring previously held interests in the assets and liabilities of the joint operation at fair value. In doing so, the acquirer remeasures its entire previously held interest in the joint operation. *[IFRS 3.42A].*

By contrast, when a party that participates in, but does not have joint control of, a joint operation that is a business, and then obtains joint control, the previously held interest in that joint operation is not remeasured. An entity applies those amendments to transactions in which it obtains joint control on or after the beginning of the first annual reporting period beginning on or after 1 January 2019. Earlier application is permitted. *[IFRS 11.B33CA].*

8.3.3 Former subsidiary becomes a joint operation

It is possible that an entity loses control of a subsidiary and retains an interest in a joint operation. To account for the loss of control of a subsidiary, paragraph 25 of IFRS 10 requires a parent to:

(a) derecognise the assets and liabilities of the subsidiary;

(b) recognise any investment retained in the former subsidiary at fair value at the date when control is lost; and

(c) recognise any resulting gain or loss in profit or loss.

However, it is unclear how these requirements should be applied when the retained interest is in the assets and liabilities of a joint operation. One view is that the retained interest should be remeasured at fair value. Another view is that the retained interest should not be derecognised or remeasured at fair value, but should continue to be recognised and measured at its carrying amount.

In July 2016, the Interpretations Committee discussed this issue and noted that paragraphs B34 to B35 of IFRS 11 (see 6.6 above) could be viewed as conflicting with the requirements in IFRS 10, which specify that an entity should remeasure any retained interest when it loses control of a subsidiary. The IASB decided not to add this issue to its agenda but, instead, to recommend that the Board consider the issue at the same time the Board further considers the accounting for the sale or contribution of assets to an associate or a joint venture.

In the meantime, we believe that, when a parent loses control over a subsidiary but retains an interest in a joint operation that is a business, entities have an accounting policy choice as to whether to remeasure the retained interest at fair value.

8.3.4 Other changes in ownership of a joint operation

IFRS 11 does not explicitly address the accounting for a former joint operation, and the situations in which:

- it becomes an associate or a financial instrument – when a former joint operation becomes an associate or financial instrument, it would generally be appropriate to derecognise the assets and liabilities previously recognised in accordance with IFRS 11 and account for the new interest based on the applicable IFRS at that date. This approach may also be appropriate when the rights to assets or obligations for liabilities that the entity held when it was a joint operation differ from its rights or obligations when it ceases to be a party to a joint operation;
- the rights to assets or obligations with respect to that joint operation change – when a joint operator's rights to assets or obligations for liabilities change (e.g. other operators obtain rights to the assets or assume obligations for those liabilities), the joint operator would generally:
  - derecognise the relevant portion of the assets and liabilities;
  - recognise the fair value of any consideration received;
  - recognise the resulting gain or loss; and
  - recognise any rights to assets it acquires from other joint operators, and obligations it assumes from other joint operators, or from the joint arrangement itself.

If an interest in a joint operation (or portion thereof) no longer meets the criteria to be classified as held for sale, an entity restates the financial statements for the periods since classification as held for sale. [IFRS 5.28].

8.3.5 Disposal of interest in a joint operation

When an entity disposes of its interest in a joint operation, it ceases to account for the rights to assets and obligations for liabilities and recognises any gain or loss as of the disposal date, in accordance with the relevant IFRS. The only exception would be if the same rights to assets or obligations for liabilities replaced that interest directly. In this case, there would be no change in accounting, because, in both cases, the assets and liabilities are recognised in accordance with the relevant IFRS (see 6 and 8.3.4 above).

Consistent with the treatment of joint ventures (see 8.2.6 above) an entity continues to reflect its interest in a joint operation for the reporting period (and comparative period) in which it held that interest. An entity does not restate its financial statements as if it never held the interest in the disposed joint operation.

8.4 Changes in ownership of a joint arrangement that does not constitute a business

8.4.1 Joint operator obtains control or parties that participate in a joint arrangement but do not have joint control obtain joint control

At its January 2016 meeting, the Interpretations Committee discussed whether previously held interests in the assets and liabilities of a joint operation, which does not constitute a business, should be remeasured when:

- a joint operator or a party that participates in a joint arrangement but do not have joint control obtains control of a joint operation; and
- a change of interests resulting in a party that participates in a joint arrangement but does not have joint control obtains joint control over the joint operation.

The Interpretations Committee noted that paragraph 2(b) of IFRS 3 explains the requirements for accounting for an asset acquisition in which the asset or group of assets do not meet the definition of a business. The Interpretations Committee noted that paragraph 2(b) of IFRS 3 specifies that a cost-based approach should be used in accounting for an asset acquisition, and that in a cost-based approach the existing assets generally are not remeasured (see Chapter 9 at 2.2.2). The Interpretations Committee also observed that it was not aware of significant diversity in practice and, therefore, decided not to add this issue to its agenda.[10]

9 DISCLOSURES

The disclosure requirements regarding joint arrangements accounted for under IFRS 11 are included in IFRS 12 and are discussed in Chapter 13 at 5. IFRS 12 combines the disclosure requirements for an entity's interests in subsidiaries, joint arrangements, associates and structured entities into one comprehensive disclosure standard.

10 FUTURE DEVELOPMENTS

At its meeting in April 2020, the IASB decided to proceed with the Post-implementation Review of IFRSs 10, IFRS 11 and IFRS 12. In relation to IFRS 11, the review will focus on a) collaboration arrangements outside the scope of IFRS 11; b) the classification of joint arrangements as joint operations based on other facts and circumstances; and c) accounting requirements, with a focus on joint operations. The Board also decided that the review would not cover the interaction of IFRS 10, IFRS 11 and IFRS 12 with other IFRS Standards.

References

1 *IFRIC Update*, March 2015.
2 *IFRIC Update*, March 2015.
3 Staff Paper (March 2014 Interpretations Committee Meeting), IFRS 11 *Joint Arrangements* – Consideration of some common joint arrangement structures (Agenda reference 5B).
4 Staff Paper (March 2015 Interpretations Committee Meeting), IFRS 11 *Joint Arrangements* – Tentative agenda decision comment letter analysis (Agenda reference 4).
5 *IFRIC Update*, March 2015.
6 *IFRIC Update*, March 2019.
7 *IFRIC Update*, March 2019.
8 Staff Paper (July 2015 Interpretations Committee Meeting), IFRS 11 *Joint Arrangements* – Remeasurement of previously held interests (Agenda reference 6).
9 *Sale or Contribution of Assets between an Investor and its Associate or Joint Venture (amendments to IFRS 10 and IAS 28)*, September 2014.
10 *IFRIC Update*, January 2016.

Chapter 13 Disclosure of interests in other entities

1	INTRODUCTION			945
2	OBJECTIVE AND SCOPE OF IFRS 12			945
	2.1	Objective		945
	2.2	Scope		946
		2.2.1	Definitions	946
			2.2.1.A Interests in other entities	947
			2.2.1.B Structured entities	948
			2.2.1.C Interaction of IFRS 12 and IFRS 5	950
		2.2.2	Interests disclosed under IFRS 12	950
			2.2.2.A Subsidiaries	951
			2.2.2.B Joint arrangements	951
			2.2.2.C Associates	952
			2.2.2.D Unconsolidated structured entities	952
		2.2.3	Interests not within the scope of IFRS 12	952
			2.2.3.A Employee benefit plans	953
			2.2.3.B Separate financial statements	953
			2.2.3.C Interests in joint arrangements that result in neither joint control nor significant influence and are not interests in structured entities	953
			2.2.3.D Interests in other entities accounted for in accordance with IFRS 9	954
3	DISCLOSURE OF SIGNIFICANT ESTIMATES AND JUDGEMENTS			954
4	DISCLOSURE OF INTERESTS IN SUBSIDIARIES			957
	4.1	Disclosure about the composition of the group		957
	4.2	Disclosure of interests of non-controlling interests		958
	4.3	Disclosure of the nature and extent of significant restrictions		962

	4.4	Disclosure of the nature of the risks associated with interests in consolidated structured entities	963
		4.4.1 Terms of contractual arrangements to provide financial support to consolidated structured entities	964
		4.4.2 Financial or other support to consolidated structured entities with no contractual obligation	965
		4.4.3 Financial or other support to unconsolidated structured entities which resulted in consolidation of those entities	966
		4.4.4 Current intentions to provide financial or other support	966
	4.5	Disclosure of changes in ownership interests in subsidiaries	966
		4.5.1 Changes that do not result in loss of control	966
		4.5.2 Changes that do result in loss of control	967
	4.6	Disclosures required by investment entities	968
		4.6.1 Disclosures about the composition of the group	968
		4.6.2 Disclosures required when investment entity status changes	968
		4.6.3 Disclosures required in respect of significant restrictions, commitments and financial and other support	969
		4.6.4 Valuation methodologies and nature of investing activities	969
5	DISCLOSURE OF INTERESTS IN JOINT ARRANGEMENTS AND ASSOCIATES		970
	5.1	Disclosure of the nature, extent and financial effects of interests in joint arrangements and associates	970
		5.1.1 Summarised financial information of individually material joint ventures and associates	972
		5.1.2 Financial information of individually immaterial joint ventures and associates	975
	5.2	Risks associated with interests in joint ventures and associates	976
		5.2.1 Disclosure of commitments relating to joint ventures	977
		5.2.2 Disclosure of contingent liabilities relating to joint ventures and associates	978
6	DISCLOSURE OF INTERESTS IN UNCONSOLIDATED STRUCTURED ENTITIES		978
	6.1	Disclosure of the nature of interests in unconsolidated structured entities	979
		6.1.1 Disclosure of the nature, purpose, size, activities and financing of structured entities	979
		6.1.1.A Nature and purpose	979
		6.1.1.B Size	980
		6.1.1.C Activities	980
		6.1.1.D Financing	980

	6.1.2	Disclosures of sponsored structured entities for which no interest is held at the reporting date 982
6.2	Disclosure of the nature of risks of unconsolidated structured entities 986	
	6.2.1	Disclosures of interests in structured entities and of the maximum exposure to loss from those interests 986
	6.2.2	Disclosures of actual and intended financial and other support to structured entities 989
6.3	Additional disclosures regarding the nature of risks from interests in unconsolidated structured entities 989	
	6.3.1	Disclosure of support 991
	6.3.2	Disclosure of losses 991
	6.3.3	Disclosure of types of income received 992
	6.3.4	Disclosure of ranking and amounts of potential losses 992
	6.3.5	Disclosure of liquidity arrangements 993
	6.3.6	Disclosure of funding difficulties 993
	6.3.7	Disclosure of the forms of funding of an unconsolidated structured entity 993

7 FUTURE DEVELOPMENTS 993
    7.1   Post-implementation Review of IFRSs 10, 11 and 12 993

List of examples

Example 13.1:	Variability of returns arising from issue of credit default swap (1) 948
Example 13.2:	Variability of returns arising from issue of credit default swap (2) 948
Example 13.3:	Disclosure of significant judgements and assumptions made in determining the type of joint arrangement 955
Example 13.4:	Illustrative example of disclosure of a contractual arrangement that could require parental support to a consolidated structured entity 964
Example 13.5:	Illustrative example of disclosure of financial or other support provided to a consolidated structured entity 966
Example 13.6:	Illustrative example of disclosure of changes in ownership interest in subsidiary that does not result in loss of control 967
Example 13.7:	Illustrative example of disclosures for sponsored structured entities where no interest exists at the reporting date 984
Example 13.8:	Losses incurred from investments in unconsolidated structured entities 991

Example 13.9: Maximum exposure to and ranking of loss exposure by
type of structured entity..992

Chapter 13 Disclosure of interests in other entities

1 INTRODUCTION

IFRS 12 – *Disclosure of Interests in Other Entities* – is a disclosure standard. IFRS 12 was issued in May 2011. It includes all of the disclosure requirements related to interests in subsidiaries, joint arrangements, associates and consolidated and unconsolidated structured entities.

The recognition and measurement of subsidiaries, joint arrangements and associates are dealt with in IFRS 10 – *Consolidated Financial Statements*, IFRS 11 – *Joint Arrangements*, IAS 27 – *Separate Financial Statements* – and IAS 28 – *Investments in Associates and Joint Ventures*.

2 OBJECTIVE AND SCOPE OF IFRS 12

2.1 Objective

The stated objective of IFRS 12 is 'to require an entity to disclose information that enables users of its financial statements to evaluate:

(a) the nature of, and risks associated with, its *interest in other entities*; and

(b) the effects of those interests on its financial position, financial performance and cash flows'. *[IFRS 12.1]*.

To meet the objective of the standard, an entity must disclose:

(a) the significant judgements and assumptions it has made in determining:
   (i) the nature of its interest in another entity or arrangement;
   (ii) the type of joint arrangement in which it has an interest;
   (iii) that it meets the definition of an investment entity if applicable; and

(b) information about its interests in:
   (i) subsidiaries;
   (ii) joint arrangements and associates; and
   (iii) structured entities that are not controlled by the entity (unconsolidated structured entities). *[IFRS 12.2]*.

If the disclosures required by the standard, together with the disclosures required by other IFRSs, do not meet the objective of IFRS 12, an entity must disclose whatever additional information is necessary to meet that objective. [IFRS 12.3].

IFRS 12 provides no illustrative examples to support any of its disclosure requirements. In addition, several of the terms used in the standard are undefined. This may lead to diversity in practice where the wording of a disclosure requirement is unclear.

IAS 34 – *Interim Financial Reporting* – requires entities becoming or ceasing to be investment entities, as defined in IFRS 10, to disclose the information required in paragraph 9B (see 4.6.2 below). [IAS 34.16A(k)]. IAS 34 also requires an entity to include certain disclosures about the effect of changes in the composition of the entity during the interim period and obtaining or losing control of subsidiaries and long-term investments. [IAS 34.16A(i)].

2.2 Scope

IFRS 12 applies to any entity that has an interest in any of the following:

(a) subsidiaries;
(b) joint arrangements (i.e. joint operations or joint ventures);
(c) associates; and
(d) unconsolidated structured entities. [IFRS 12.5].

2.2.1 Definitions

The following definitions from Appendix A to IFRS 12 are relevant to the scope of IFRS 12.

Income from a structured entity 'includes, but is not limited to, recurring and non-recurring fees, interest, dividends, gains or losses on the remeasurement or derecognition of interests in structured entities and gains or losses from the transfer of assets and liabilities to the structured entity'.

Interest in another entity refers to 'contractual and non-contractual involvement that exposes an entity to variability of returns from the performance of the other entity. An interest in another entity can be evidenced by, but is not limited to, the holding of equity or debt instruments as well as other forms of involvement such as the provision of funding, liquidity support, credit enhancement and guarantees. It includes the means by which an entity has control, or joint control of, or significant influence over, another entity. An entity does not necessarily have an interest in another entity solely because of a typical customer supplier relationship'.

A structured entity is an entity 'that has been designed so that voting or similar rights are not the dominant factor in deciding who controls the entity, such as when any voting rights relate to administrative tasks only and the relevant activities are directed by means of contractual arrangements'.

Appendix A to IFRS 12 provides a list of terms defined in IAS 27, IAS 28, IFRS 10 and IFRS 11, which are used in IFRS 12 with the meanings specified in those IFRSs. The terms include the following:

- associate;
- consolidated financial statements;
- control of an entity;
- equity method;
- group;
- investment entity; and
- joint arrangement.

2.2.1.A Interests in other entities

An interest in another entity refers to contractual and non-contractual involvement that exposes the reporting entity to variability of returns from the performance of the other entity. Consideration of the purpose and design of the other entity may help the reporting entity when assessing whether it has an interest in that entity and, therefore, whether it is required to provide the disclosures in IFRS 12. That assessment must include consideration of the risks that the other entity was designed to create and the risks that the other entity was designed to pass on to the reporting entity and other parties. *[IFRS 12.B7]*.

IFRS 10 defines 'variability of returns'. As discussed in more detail in Chapter 6 at 5, IFRS 10 explains that variable returns are returns that are not fixed and have the potential to vary as a result of the performance of an investee. Variable returns can be only positive, only negative or both positive and negative. An investor assesses whether returns from an interest are variable and how variable these returns are, on the basis of the substance of the arrangement and regardless of the legal form of the returns. For example, an investor can hold a bond with fixed interest payments. The fixed interest payments are variable returns for the purpose of IFRS 10 because they are subject to default risk and they expose the investor to the credit risk of the issuer of the bond. The amount of variability (i.e. how variable those returns are) depends on the credit risk of the bond. Similarly, fixed performance fees for managing an investee's assets are variable returns because they expose the investor to the performance risk of the investee. The amount of variability depends on the investee's ability to generate sufficient income to pay the fee. *[IFRS 10.B56]*.

Thus, the definition of an 'interest' in IFRS 12 is much wider than equity instruments in an entity. As IFRS 12 requires disclosures of interests that a reporting entity holds in other entities, preparers will need to ensure that their reporting systems and processes are sufficient to identify those 'interests'.

IFRS 12 clarifies that a reporting entity is typically exposed to variability of returns from the performance of another entity by holding instruments (such as equity or debt instruments issued by the other entity) or having another involvement that absorbs variability. *[IFRS 12.B8]*. This is illustrated in Example 13.1 below.

Example 13.1: Variability of returns arising from issue of credit default swap (1)

A reporting entity issues a credit default swap to a structured entity. The credit default swap protects the structured entity from the default of interest and principal payments on its loan portfolio.

The reporting entity has an involvement in the structured entity that exposes it to variability of returns from the performance of the structured entity because the credit default swap absorbs variability of returns of the structured entity. *[IFRS 12.B8]*.

Some instruments are designed to transfer risk from the reporting entity to another entity. Such instruments create variability of returns for the other entity but do not typically expose the reporting entity to variability of returns from the performance of the other entity. *[IFRS 12.B9]*. This is illustrated in Example 13.2 below.

Example 13.2: Variability of returns arising from issue of credit default swap (2)

A reporting entity enters into a credit default swap with a structured entity. The credit default swap gives the structured entity exposure to Entity Z's credit risk. The purpose of the arrangement is to give the investors in the structured entity exposure to Entity Z's credit risk (Entity Z is unrelated to any other party involved in the arrangement).

The reporting entity does not have any involvement with the structured entity that exposes it to variable returns from the structured entity because the credit default swap transfers variability to the structured entity rather than absorbing variability of returns of the structured entity.

Purchased call options and written put options (in each case unless the exercise price is at fair value) would also be interests in other entities, because these instruments typically absorb variability created by assets held in the entity. In contrast, some derivative instruments such as interest rate swaps, can both create and absorb variability and judgement will need to be exercised in determining whether these derivatives are interests in other entities.

We believe that plain vanilla swaps and other derivatives that both create and absorb variability, based on market rates or indices and which rank senior to the issued notes, do not absorb the risks the entity was designed to pass on, and are not an exposure to variable returns. They are therefore unlikely to be interests in other entities that would require disclosure under IFRS 12. See Chapter 6 at 5.3.1.

An entity does not necessarily have an interest in another entity because of a typical customer supplier relationship. However, as explained above, IFRS 10 states that fixed performance fees for managing an investee's assets create variable returns for the investor. The fixed performance fees are 'variable' because they expose the investor to the performance risk of the investee. *[IFRS 10.B56]*. Therefore, investment management fees and other fees based on assets under management are treated as variable interests.

2.2.1.B Structured entities

Whether an entity is a structured entity or not is important because additional disclosures are required by IFRS 12 for interests in structured entities. These disclosures are discussed at 4.4 and 6 below.

As defined at 2.2.1 above, a structured entity is an entity that has been designed so that voting or similar rights are not the dominant factor in deciding who controls the entity, such as when any voting rights relate to administrative tasks only and the relevant activities are directed by means of contractual arrangements.

IFRS 12 states that a structured entity often has some or all of the following features or attributes:
(a) restricted activities;
(b) a narrow and well-defined objective, such as:
    (i) to effect a tax-efficient lease;
    (ii) to carry out research and development activities;
    (iii) to provide a source of capital or funding to an entity; or
    (iv) to provide investment opportunities for investors by passing on risks and rewards associated with the assets of the structured entity to investors.
(c) insufficient equity to permit the structured entity to finance its activities without subordinated financial support; and
(d) financing in the form of multiple contractually linked instruments to investors that create concentrations of credit or other risks (tranches). *[IFRS 12.B22].*

The following examples of entities that are regarded as structured entities are illustrated:
- securitisation vehicles;
- asset-backed financings; and
- some investment funds. *[IFRS 12.B23].*

The IASB's rationale for including specific disclosures of investments in structured entities is that users have requested such disclosures because they believed involvement with these entities posed more risk than involvement with traditional operating entities. The increased risk exposure arises because, for example, the structured entity may have been created to pass risks and returns arising from specified assets to investors, or may have insufficient equity to fund losses on its assets, if they arise.

The Basis for Conclusions explains that the type of entity the Board envisages being characterised as a structured entity is an entity created to accomplish a narrow and well-defined objective, listing as examples entities established to effect a lease, entities established for research and development activities or entities established for the securitisation of financial assets. *[IFRS 12.BC82].* IFRS 12 definition of a structured entity implies that any entity which is not controlled by voting or similar rights is a structured entity. Conversely, any entity controlled by voting or similar rights cannot be a structured entity.

It is not clear what the IASB means by 'similar' (to voting) rights in the definition of a structured entity. No illustrative examples are provided. This will require the exercise of judgement by reporting entities; therefore, there may be diversity in practice about what constitutes a 'similar' right and therefore whether an entity is a structured entity. One example of 'similar' rights is an investment fund for which investors can vote to remove the manager of the fund without cause as long as a certain proportion of investors demand such a vote. The assessment of whether this right (to remove the fund manager) could be considered substantive, and therefore whether the investment fund is a structured entity, would depend on the number of investors who would need to collaborate in order to force the vote and other facts and circumstances. See Chapter 6 at 4 for additional guidance on identifying the significant activities of an entity, the rights to make decisions about those activities, and evaluating whether those rights are substantive.

IFRS 12 does not state whether the 'features or attributes' of structured entities discussed above are determinative as to whether an entity is a structured entity or whether the features or attributes should always be subordinate to the definition (i.e. if the entity was controlled by voting or similar rights then the features or attributes would be irrelevant). Our view is that the features and attributes are subordinated to the definition. However, the features or attributes are often present in a structured entity.

The IASB considered, but rejected, defining a structured entity in a way similar to a variable interest entity (VIE) in US GAAP. That approach, in the IASB's opinion, would have introduced complicated guidance solely for disclosure purposes that was not previously in IFRSs. [IFRS 12.BC83]. US GAAP defines a VIE, in essence, as an entity whose activities are not directed through voting or similar rights, whose total equity is not sufficient to permit the entity to finance its activities without additional subordinated financial support, or whose equity is structured with non-substantive voting rights. The IASB had two reasons for not making the definition of a structured entity dependant on total equity at risk (as in US GAAP). First, including insufficient equity at risk in the definition of a structured entity would require extensive application guidance to help determine the sufficiency of the equity, to which the IASB was opposed. Second, the IASB feared that some traditional operating entities might be caught by this definition when it had no intention of catching such entities. [IFRS 12.BC83-85].

IFRS 12 clarifies that an entity that is controlled by voting rights is not a structured entity simply, because, for example, it receives funding from third parties following a restructuring. [IFRS 12.B24]. However, such funding is likely to give the investee a variable interest in the restructured entity that may still be a subsidiary as defined by IFRS 10.

2.2.1.C   Interaction of IFRS 12 and IFRS 5

The requirements in IFRS 12, except as described in paragraph B17, apply to an entity's interests listed in paragraph 5 (see 2.2 above) that are classified (or included in a disposal group that is classified) as held for sale or discontinued operations in accordance with IFRS 5 – *Non-current Assets Held for Sale and Discontinued Operations*. [IFRS 12.5A].

An entity is not required to disclose summarised financial information, for its interests in a subsidiary, a joint venture or an associate in accordance with paragraphs B10-B16 of IFRS 12 when the entity's interests in that subsidiary, joint venture or associate (or a portion of its interest in a joint venture or an associate) is classified or included in a disposal group that is classified as held for sale in accordance with IFRS 5. [IFRS 12.B17].

2.2.2   Interests disclosed under IFRS 12

IFRS 12 requires that an entity must present information separately for interests in:
(a) subsidiaries;
(b) joint ventures;
(c) joint operations;
(d) associates; and
(e) unconsolidated structured entities. [IFRS 12.B4].

A reporting entity should consider the level of detail necessary to satisfy the disclosure objective and how much emphasis to place on each of the requirements of IFRS 12. Disclosures can be aggregated or disaggregated so that useful information is not obscured by either the inclusion of a large amount of insignificant detail or the aggregation of items that have different characteristics. *[IFRS 12.4]*. However, a reporting entity must disclose how it has aggregated its interests in similar entities. *[IFRS 12.B3]*.

In determining whether to aggregate information, an entity shall consider qualitative and quantitative information about the different risk and return characteristics of each entity to the reporting entity. The entity must present the disclosures in a manner that clearly explains to users of the financial statements the nature and extent of its interests in those other entities. *[IFRS 12.B5]*.

Examples of aggregation levels within classes of entities that the standard considers appropriate are:

- nature of activities (e.g. a research and development entity, a revolving credit card securitisation entity);
- industry classification; and
- geography (e.g. country or region). *[IFRS 12.B6]*.

This guidance on aggregation implies latitude for entities to exercise their judgement in determining the appropriate level of disclosure. However, summarised financial information is required separately for each material partly owned subsidiary, each material joint venture and associate and requires minimum disclosures in respect of unconsolidated structured entities.

2.2.2.A   Subsidiaries

IFRS 10 defines a subsidiary as 'an entity that is controlled by another entity'. *[IFRS 10 Appendix A]*. IFRS 10 provides guidance as to the circumstances in which an entity is controlled by another entity. See Chapter 6.

2.2.2.B   Joint arrangements

IFRS 11 defines a joint arrangement as 'an arrangement in which two or more parties have joint control'. Joint control is 'the contractually agreed sharing of control of an arrangement, which exists only when decisions about the relevant activities require the unanimous consent of the parties sharing control'. A joint operation is 'a joint arrangement whereby the parties that have joint control of the arrangement have rights to the assets, and obligations for the liabilities, relating to the arrangement'. A joint venture is 'a joint arrangement whereby the parties that have joint control of the arrangement have rights to the net assets of the arrangement'. *[IFRS 11 Appendix A]*. IFRS 11 provides guidance as to the circumstances in which joint control exists and on the characteristics of joint operations and joint ventures. See Chapter 12.

Interests in joint arrangements which are not structured entities and which do not result in the reporting entity obtaining joint control or significant influence over the joint arrangement are outside the scope of IFRS 12. See 2.2.3.C below.

2.2.2.C Associates

IAS 28 defines an associate as 'an entity over which the investor has significant influence'. *[IAS 28.3]*. IAS 28 provides guidance on the circumstances in which significant influence is exercised. See Chapter 11.

2.2.2.D Unconsolidated structured entities

'Unconsolidated structured entities' refers to all structured entities which are not consolidated by a reporting entity. Therefore, the definition of 'unconsolidated structured entity' includes structured entities that are joint arrangements and associates (unless specially excluded from the scope of the standard under 2.2.3 below), structured entities that are subsidiaries of parents that prepare separate financial statements (unless consolidated financial statements are also prepared – see 2.2.3.B below), and structured entities over which the reporting entity does not have significant influence.

Where an unconsolidated structured entity is a joint venture or associate then the disclosures required for unconsolidated structured entities at 6 below apply in addition to the separate disclosures at 5 below for interests in joint ventures and associates. The IASB concluded that an entity should capture most, and in some cases all, of the disclosures required for interests in unconsolidated structured entities by providing the disclosures for interests in joint ventures and associates. Accordingly, the IASB considers that the requirement to make both sets of disclosures where applicable should not result in a significant incremental increase in the amount of information that an entity would be required to provide. *[IFRS 12.BC77]*.

As discussed at 2.2.1.A above, the definition of a variable interest is widely drawn so that a derivative issued to a structured entity may result in an interest in an unconsolidated structured entity, depending on the purpose and design of the entity. This interest would require disclosures under IFRS 12 that would not apply to an identical instrument issued to an entity which is not a structured entity. The disclosures focus on an entity's exposure to risk from interests in structured entities that the entity rightly does not consolidate because it does not control them. *[IFRS 12.BC69]*.

In determining disclosures in respect of structured entities over which a reporting entity does not have significant influence, the reporting entity should apply the general concept of materiality. Materiality is defined by both IAS 1 – *Presentation of Financial Statements* – and IAS 8 – *Accounting Policies, Changes in Accounting Estimates and Errors* – and is discussed in Chapter 3 at 4.1.5.A.

2.2.3 Interests not within the scope of IFRS 12

IFRS 12 clarifies that certain interests are not within its scope.

2.2.3.A Employee benefit plans

Post-employment benefit plans or other long-term employee benefit plans to which IAS 19 – *Employee Benefits* – applies are not within the scope of IFRS 12. *[IFRS 12.6(a)]*. Without this exemption, some employee benefit plans might meet the definition of a structured entity.

2.2.3.B Separate financial statements

An entity's separate financial statements to which IAS 27 applies are not within the scope of IFRS 12. The purpose of this exemption is to prevent a parent duplicating IFRS 12 disclosures in both its consolidated and separate financial statements. See Chapter 8 for guidance on separate financial statements.

However, an entity that has interests in unconsolidated structured entities and prepares separate financial statements as its only financial statements is required to make the disclosures required by paragraphs 24-31 of IFRS 12 in respect of the unconsolidated structured entities (see 6 below). In addition, an investment entity that prepares financial statements in which all of its subsidiaries are measured at fair value through profit or loss (i.e. an investment entity which has subsidiaries but does not prepare consolidated financial statements) shall make the disclosures relating to investment entities discussed at 4.6 below. *[IFRS 12.6(b)]*. As discussed at 2.2.2.D above, unconsolidated structured entities include subsidiaries, joint ventures and associates that are structured entities.

The financial statements of an entity that does not have an interest in a subsidiary, associate or a joint venturer's interest in a joint venture are not separate financial statements. *[IAS 27.7]*. These financial statements are within the scope of IFRS 12.

2.2.3.C Interests in joint arrangements that result in neither joint control nor significant influence and are not interests in structured entities

An interest held by an entity that participates in, but does not have joint control of, a joint arrangement is outside the scope of IFRS 12 unless that interest results in significant influence in that arrangement or is an interest in a structured entity. *[IFRS 12.6(c)]*.

IFRS 11 states that an arrangement can be a joint arrangement even though not all of the parties have joint control of the arrangement. It distinguishes between parties that have joint control of a joint arrangement (joint operators or joint ventures) and parties that participate in, but do not have joint control of, a joint arrangement. *[IFRS 11.11]*.

Determining whether an interest in a joint arrangement (which is not a structured entity) results in neither joint control nor significant influence will be a matter of judgement based on the facts and circumstances as explained in IFRS 11. See Chapter 12 for guidance on assessing joint control and Chapter 11 for guidance on assessing significant influence.

2.2.3.D   Interests in other entities accounted for in accordance with IFRS 9

An interest in another entity that is accounted for under IFRS 9 – *Financial Instruments* – is outside the scope of IFRS 12. However, IFRS 12 applies to the following interests:

(i)   interests in associates or joint ventures measured at fair value through profit or loss in accordance with IAS 28; or

(ii) interests in unconsolidated structured entities. *[IFRS 12.6(d)]*.

In addition, IFRS 12 requires specific disclosures for unconsolidated subsidiaries of an investment entity measured at fair value through profit and loss. See 4.6 below.

Interests in unconsolidated structured entities which are not subsidiaries, joint arrangements or associates would normally be accounted for in accordance with IFRS 9. See Chapter 49 for guidance on recognition and initial measurement of financial instruments in accordance with IFRS 9.

3   DISCLOSURE OF SIGNIFICANT ESTIMATES AND JUDGEMENTS

IFRS 12 requires that an entity disclose information about significant judgements and assumptions it has made (and changes to those judgements and assumptions) in determining:

(a) that it has control of another entity, i.e. an investee as described in paragraphs 5 and 6 of IFRS 10;

(b) that it has joint control of an arrangement or significant influence over another entity; and

(c) the type of joint arrangement (i.e. joint operation or joint venture) when the arrangement has been structured through a separate vehicle. *[IFRS 12.7]*.

The significant judgements and assumptions disclosed in accordance with the requirements above include those made by an entity when changes in facts and circumstances are such that the conclusion about whether it has control, joint control or significant influence changes during the reporting period. *[IFRS 12.8]*.

In order to comply with the requirements above, an entity must disclose, for example, significant judgements and assumptions made in determining that:

- it does not control another entity even though it holds more than half of the voting rights of the other entity;
- it controls another entity even though it holds less than half of the voting rights of the other entity;
- it is an agent or principal as defined by IFRS 10 (see Chapter 6 at 6);
- it does not have significant influence even though it holds 20 per cent or more of the voting rights of another entity;
- it has significant influence even though it holds less than 20 per cent of the voting rights of another entity. *[IFRS 12.9]*.

The following extract from BP plc's financial statements illustrates disclosure of the significant judgements and assumptions used in determining significant influence with a less than 20 per cent holding of voting rights.

> Extract 13.1: BP p.l.c. (2019)
>
> Notes on financial statements [extract]
> 1. Significant accounting policies, judgements, estimates and assumptions [extract]
>   Interests in other entities [extract]
>   Interests in associates [extract]
>   Significant judgement: investment in Rosneft
>
> Judgement is required in assessing the level of control or influence over another entity in which the group holds an interest. For BP, the judgement that the group has significant influence over Rosneft Oil Company (Rosneft), a Russian oil and gas company is significant. As a consequence of this judgement, BP uses the equity method of accounting for its investment and BP's share of Rosneft's oil and natural gas reserves is included in the group's estimated net proved reserves of equity-accounted entities. If significant influence was not present, the investment would be accounted for as an investment in an equity instrument measured at fair value as described under 'Financial assets' below and no share of Rosneft's oil and natural gas reserves would be reported
>
> Significant influence is defined in IFRS as the power to participate in the financial and operating policy decisions of the investee but is not control or joint control of those policies. Significant influence is presumed when an entity owns 20% or more of the voting power of the investee. Significant influence is presumed not to be present when an entity owns less than 20% of the voting power of the investee.
>
> BP owns 19.75% of the voting shares of Rosneft. The Russian federal government, through its investment company JSC Rosneftegaz, owned 50% plus one share of the voting shares of Rosneft at 31 December 2019. IFRS identifies several indicators that may provide evidence of significant influence, including representation on the board of directors of the investee and participation in policy-making processes. BP's group chief executive, as at 31 December 2019, Bob Dudley, has been a member of the board of directors of Rosneft since 2013 and remains one of BP's nominated directors following his resignation as BP's group chief executive. He is also chairman of the Rosneft board's Strategic Planning Committee. A second BP-nominated director, Guillermo Quintero, has been a member of the Rosneft board and its HR and Remuneration Committee since 2015. BP also holds the voting rights at general meetings of shareholders conferred by its 19.75% stake in Rosneft. BP's management consider, therefore, that the group has significant influence over Rosneft, as defined by IFRS.

The following example illustrates disclosure of significant judgements and assumptions made by an entity in determining whether a joint arrangement is a joint operation or a joint venture.

Example 13.3: *Disclosure of significant judgements and assumptions made in determining the type of joint arrangement*

The directors have determined that the Group's investment in ABC Inc. should be accounted for as a joint operation rather than a joint venture. Although the legal form of ABC Inc. and the contractual terms of the joint arrangement indicate that the arrangement is a joint venture, sales to third parties by ABC Inc. are expected to be uncommon and not material. In addition, the price of the output sold to the venturers is set by all parties at a level that is designed to cover only the costs of production and administrative expenses incurred by ABC Inc. On this basis, the directors consider that, in substance, the arrangement gives the venturers rights to the assets, and obligations for the liabilities, relating to the arrangement and not rights to the net assets of the arrangements and therefore is a joint operation.

When a parent determines that it is an investment entity in accordance with IFRS 10, the investment entity must disclose information about significant judgements and assumptions it has made in determining that it is an investment entity. If the investment entity does not have one or more of the typical characteristics of an investment entity (as per IFRS 10), it must disclose the reasons for concluding that it is nevertheless an investment entity. *[IFRS 12.9A]*. The definition of an investment entity is discussed in Chapter 6 at 10.1. The following extract from 3i Group plc's financial statements illustrates disclosure of these significant judgements and assumptions.

> Extract 13.2: 3i Group plc (2020)
>
> Significant accounting policies [extract]
>
> C Critical accounting judgements and estimates [extract]
>
> (a) Critical judgements [extract]
>
> I. Assessment as an investment entity [extract]
>
> The Board has concluded that the Company continues to meet the definition of an investment entity, as its strategic objective of investing in portfolio investments and providing investment management services to investors for the purpose of generating returns in the form of investment income and capital appreciation remains unchanged.

IAS 1 requires an entity to disclose the judgements that management has made in the process of applying the entity's accounting policies and that have the most significant effect on the amounts recognised in the financial statements. *[IAS 1.122]*. IFRS 12 adds to those general requirements by specifically requiring an entity to disclose all significant judgements and estimates made in determining the nature of its interest in another entity or arrangement, and in determining the type of joint arrangement in which it has an interest. The IASB's intention is that disclosure should be required for all situations in which an entity exercises significant judgement in assessing the nature of its interest in another entity. *[IFRS 12.BC16]*.

There is no requirement for a reporting entity to disclose significant judgements and assumptions made in determining whether an entity in which it has an interest is a structured entity. Such a judgement or assumption affects disclosure only and not the determination of control, joint control or significant influence. However, where such judgements or assumptions have a significant impact on the volume of disclosures in the financial statements we believe that it would be useful for a reader of the financial statements for such judgements or assumptions to be disclosed, consistent with the requirements of IAS 1.

There is no requirement to disclose quantitative information to help assess the accounting consequences of an entity's decision to consolidate (or not consolidate) another entity. IFRS 3 – *Business Combinations* – already requires disclosures about the nature and effect of a business combination when an entity obtains control of another entity. Where an entity requires significant judgement to conclude that it does not control another entity, the IASB observed that the entity will often conclude that it has either joint control or significant influence over that other entity. IFRS 12 already requires disclosures of quantitative information about an entity's interests in joint ventures and associates and information about risk exposures to unconsolidated structured entities. Therefore, based on this, the IASB concluded that there was no need for a separate disclosure requirement. *[IFRS 12.BC19]*.

4 DISCLOSURE OF INTERESTS IN SUBSIDIARIES

An entity must disclose information that enables users of its consolidated financial statements

(a) to understand:
   (i) the composition of the group; and
   (ii) the interest that non-controlling interests have in the group's activities and cash flows; and

(b) to evaluate:
   (i) the nature and extent of significant restrictions on its ability to access or use assets, and settle liabilities, of the group;
   (ii) the nature of, and changes in, the risks associated with its interests in consolidated structured entities;
   (iii) the consequences of changes in its ownership interest in a subsidiary that do not result in loss of control; and
   (iv) the consequences of losing control of a subsidiary during the reporting period. [IFRS 12.10].

4.1 Disclosure about the composition of the group

IFRS 12 does not elaborate on what is meant by information that enables users 'to understand' the composition of the group. Judgement will therefore be required as to the extent of the disclosures made.

It may be helpful to users of the financial statements to illustrate the composition of the group via a diagram or group organisation chart.

In interpreting the requirement to disclose information that enables users to understand the composition of the group for subsidiaries with immaterial or no non-controlling interests, preparers might wish to refer to the non-financial disclosures required for subsidiaries with non-controlling interests that are material to the entity (see 4.2 below). Applying these disclosures to other material subsidiaries would mean disclosing:

- the names of those entities;
- the principal place of business (and country of incorporation, if different) of those entities; and
- the proportion of ownership interest (and the proportion of the voting rights, if different) held in those entities.

Users of the financial statements might also benefit from a description of the nature of the operations and principal activities of each material subsidiary and an indication of the operating segment(s) to which each material subsidiary has been allocated. A description of the nature of the group's operations and its principal activities is required by IAS 1. [IAS 1.138(b)].

Where the financial statements of a subsidiary used in the preparation of the consolidated financial statements are as of a date or for a period that is different from that of the consolidated financial statements, an entity must disclose:

- the date of the reporting period of the financial statements of that subsidiary; and
- the reason for using a different date or period. [IFRS 12.11].

The following extract shows UBS AG's disclosure of individually significant subsidiaries.

Extract 13.3: UBS Group AG (2019)

Notes to the UBS Group AG consolidated financial statements [extract]

Note 31   **Interests in subsidiaries and other entities** [extract]

a)   **Interests in subsidiaries** [extract]

UBS defines its significant subsidiaries as those entities that, either individually or in aggregate, contribute significantly to the Group's financial position or results of operations, based on a number of criteria, including the subsidiaries' equity and their contribution to the Group's total assets and profit or loss before tax, in accordance with the requirements set by IFRS 12, Swiss regulations and the rules of the US Securities and Exchange Commission (SEC).

Individually significant subsidiaries

The two tables below list the Group's individually significant subsidiaries as of 31 December 2019. Unless otherwise stated, the subsidiaries listed below have share capital consisting solely of ordinary shares that are held entirely by the Group, and the proportion of ownership interest held is equal to the voting rights held by the Group.

The country where the respective registered office is located is also the principal place of business.

[...]

Individually significant subsidiaries of UBS AG as of 31 December 2019[1]

Company	Registered office	Primary business	Share capital in million		Equity interest accumulated in %
UBS Americas Holding LLC	Wilmington, Delaware, USA	Corporate Center	USD	3,150.0 [2]	100.0
UBS Americas Inc.	Wilmington, Delaware, USA	Corporate Center	USD	0.0	100.0
UBS Asset Management AG	Zurich, Switzerland	Asset Management	CHF	43.2	100.0
UBS Bank USA	Salt Lake City, Utah, USA	Global Wealth Management	USD	0.0	100.0
UBS Europe SE	Frankfurt, Germany	Global Wealth Management	EUR	446.0	100.0
UBS Financial Services Inc.	Wilmington, Delaware, USA	Global Wealth Management	USD	0.0	100.0
UBS Securities LLC	Wilmington, Delaware, USA	Investment Bank	USD	1,283.1 [3]	100.0
UBS Switzerland AG	Zurich, Switzerland	Personal & Corporate Banking	CHF	10.0	100.0

1   Includes direct and indirect subsidiaries of UBS AG.
2   Comprised of common share capital of USD 1,000 and non-voting preferred share capital of USD 3,150,000,000.
3   Comprised of common share capital of USD 100,000 and non-voting preferred share capital of USD 1,283,000,000.

4.2 Disclosure of interests of non-controlling interests

A reporting entity must disclose, for each of its subsidiaries that have non-controlling interests that are material:

(a)   the name of the subsidiary;

(b)   the principal place of business (and country of incorporation if different from the principal place of business) of the subsidiary;

(c)   the proportion of ownership interests held by non-controlling interests;

(d) the proportion of voting rights held by non-controlling interests, if different to the proportion of ownership interests held;

(e) the profit or loss allocated to the non-controlling interests of the subsidiary during the reporting period;

(f) accumulated non-controlling interests of the subsidiary at the end of the reporting period; and

(g) summarised financial information about the subsidiary (see below). *[IFRS 12.12]*.

The summarised financial information required to be disclosed is as follows:

(a) dividends paid to non-controlling interests; and

(b) summarised financial information about the assets, liabilities, profit or loss and cash flows of the subsidiary that enables users to understand the interest that non-controlling interests have in the group's activities and cash flows. The information might include but is not limited to, for example, current assets, non-current assets, current liabilities, non-current liabilities, revenue, profit or loss and total comprehensive income. *[IFRS 12.B10]*. The summarised financial information must be presented before inter-company eliminations. *[IFRS 12.B11]*.

The IASB believes that these disclosures will help users when estimating future profit or loss and cash flows by identifying, for example, the assets and liabilities that are held by subsidiaries, the risk exposures of particular group entities (e.g. by identifying which subsidiaries hold debt) and those subsidiaries that generate significant cash flows. *[IFRS 12.BC27]*. From this, one could infer that the summarised financial information should disclose significant amounts of bank loans separately from other liabilities.

The IASB does not believe the requirement to provide information about subsidiaries with material non-controlling interests is particularly onerous on the grounds that an entity should have the information available in preparing its consolidated financial statements. *[IFRS 12.BC29]*. However, IASB believes a requirement to disclose information about subsidiaries with immaterial or no non-controlling interests might prove to be onerous to prepare without any significant benefit for users, who are expected to benefit most from having financial information about subsidiaries with material non-controlling interests. *[IFRS 12.BC28]*.

Non-controlling interest is equity in a subsidiary not attributable, directly or indirectly, to a parent. *[IFRS 10 Appendix A]*. This means that these disclosures do not apply to instruments that might have the legal characteristics of equity, but which are classified as financial liabilities under IFRS. This would also apply to instruments that are classified as equity in the separate financial statements of a subsidiary but classified as financial liabilities in the consolidated financial statements. Similarly, when a parent has concluded that it already has a present ownership interest in shares held by a non-controlling interest by virtue of call or put options in respect of those shares (see Chapter 7 at 6), then IFRS 12 disclosures in respect of those shares are not required by the parent because there is no non-controlling interest in the financial statements.

IFRS 12 is clear that this information is required only in respect of non-controlling interests that are material to the reporting entity (i.e. the group). A subsidiary may have a significant non-controlling interest in a lower tier subsidiary, but disclosure is not required if that interest is not material at group level. Similarly, these disclosures do not apply to non-controlling interests that are material in aggregate but not individually.

In January 2015, the Interpretations Committee discussed a request to clarify the level at which the financial information required by (e) to (g) above should be provided where a subsidiary has non-controlling interests that are material to the group. The issue was whether the information provided should be either:

- at the subsidiary (i.e. entity) level based on the separate financial statements of the subsidiary; or
- at a subgroup level for the subgroup of the subsidiary and based on either (i) the amounts of the subgroup included in the consolidated financial statements of the parent or, (ii) the amounts included in the consolidated financial statements of the subgroup. In both (i) and (ii), transactions and balances between the subgroup and other subsidiaries of the reporting entity outside the subgroup would not be eliminated.

The Interpretations Committee noted that the decision on which approach is used to present the disclosures required by (e) to (g) above should reflect the one that best meets the disclosure objective (see (a) at 4 above) in the circumstances.

In respect of (e) and (f), the Interpretations Committee observed that a reporting entity should apply judgement in determining the level of disaggregation of information about subsidiaries that have material non-controlling interest. That is, whether:

- the entity presents this information about the subgroup of the subsidiary; or
- whether it is necessary in achieving the disclosure objective to disaggregate the information further to present information about the individual subsidiaries that have material non-controlling interest within that subgroup.

In respect of (g) above, the Interpretations Committee observed that, in order to meet the overall disclosure requirement, information would need to be prepared on a basis that was consistent with the information included in the consolidated financial statements from the perspective of the reporting entity. This would mean, for example, that if the subsidiary was acquired in a business combination, the amounts disclosed should reflect the effects of the acquisition accounting (e.g. goodwill and fair value adjustments). The Interpretations Committee further observed that in providing the information, an entity would apply judgement in determining whether this information was presented at a subgroup level or whether further disaggregation was necessary about individual subsidiaries that have material non-controlling interest within that subgroup. However, the Interpretations Committee noted that the information supplied would include transactions between the subgroup/subsidiary and other members of the reporting entity's group without elimination, but that transactions within the subgroup would be eliminated.

On the basis of the above analysis, the Interpretations Committee concluded that neither an Interpretation nor an amendment to IFRS 12 was necessary and decided not to add the issue to its agenda.[1]

Robert Bosch Gesellschaft mit beschränkter Haftung's financial statements illustrate disclosure of summarised financial information in respect of subsidiaries that have material non-controlling interests. Similar information is also disclosed for 2018 that is not reproduced in the extract.

Extract 13.4: Robert Bosch Gesellschaft mit beschränkter Haftung (2019)

Notes [extract]
Consolidation [extract]
Consolidated group [extract]

Condensed financial information on fully consolidated subsidiaries with material non-controlling interests [extract]

Figures in millions euros	Bosch Automotive Diesel Systems Co., Ltd., Wuxi, China 2019	United Automotive Electronic Systems Co., Ltd., Shanghai, China 2019	Bosch HUAYU Steering Systems Group, Shanghai, China 2019	Bosch Ltd., Bengaluru, India 2019
Current assets	1,408	1,580	1,336	860
Non-current assets	400	1,439	569	946
Current liabilities	568	1,074	1,204	454
Non-current liabilities	46	189	11	51
Sales revenue	1,897	2,834	1,707	1,281
Profit after tax	413	336	243	130
Comprehensive income	420	347	247	143
Cash flows from operating activities	390	505	244	–17
Cash flows from investing activities	–62	–339	–92	304
Cash flows from financing activities	–327	–148	–87	–317
Share of capital attributable to non-controlling interests	34.0%	49.0%	49.0%	29.5%
Profit/loss attributable to non-controlling interests	140	165	119	38
Equity attributable to non-controlling interests	406	860	338	384
Dividends paid to non-controlling interests	111	68	42	14

The condensed financial information of the respective entities corresponds to the figures before consolidation entries.

IFRS 12 does not address disclosure of non-controlling interests in the primary statements. IAS 1 requires disclosure of total non-controlling interests within equity in the statement of financial position, profit or loss and total comprehensive income for the period attributable to non-controlling interests and a reconciliation of the opening and closing carrying amount of each component of equity (which would include non-controlling interests) in the statement of changes in equity. *[IAS 1.54, 81B, 106]*.

4.3 Disclosure of the nature and extent of significant restrictions

An entity must disclose:

(a) significant restrictions (e.g. statutory, contractual and regulatory restrictions) on its ability to access or use assets and settle the liabilities of the group, such as:

  (i) those that restrict the ability of a parent or its subsidiaries to transfer cash or other assets to (or from) other entities within the group;

  (ii) guarantees or other requirements that may restrict dividends and other capital distributions being paid, or loans and advances being made or repaid, to (or from) other entities within the group;

(b) the nature and extent to which protective rights of non-controlling interests can significantly restrict the entity's ability to access or use the assets and settle the liabilities of the group (such as when a parent is obliged to settle liabilities of a subsidiary before settling its own liabilities, or approval of non-controlling interests is required either to settle the assets or settle the liabilities of a subsidiary); and

(c) the carrying amounts in the consolidated financial statements of the assets and liabilities to which the restrictions apply. *[IFRS 12.13]*.

These requirements were included in IFRS 12 to clarify that information disclosed in respect of significant restrictions of subsidiaries to transfer funds should include the nature and extent to which protective rights of non-controlling interests can restrict an entity's ability to access and use the assets and settle the liabilities of a subsidiary. *[IFRS 12.BC31]*.

The Basis for Conclusions clarifies that these disclosures are intended to be limited to information about the nature and effect of significant restrictions on an entity's ability to access and use assets or settle liabilities of the group. They are not intended, in the IASB's opinion, to require an entity to disclose, for example, a list of all the protective rights held by non-controlling interests that are embedded in law and regulation. *[IFRS 12.BC32]*.

The IASB also considers that the restrictions required to be disclosed by IFRS 12 are those that exist because of legal boundaries within the group, such as restrictions on transferring cash between group entities. They are not, in the IASB's opinion, intended to replicate those in other IFRSs relating to restrictions such as those in IAS 16 – *Property, Plant and Equipment* – or IAS 40 – *Investment Property*. *[IFRS 12.BC33]*.

Deutsche Bank AG makes the following disclosures about significant restrictions to access or use the group's assets:

> **Extract 13.5: Deutsche Bank Aktiengesellschaft (2019)**
> Notes to the consolidated financial statements [extract]
> Additional Notes [extract]
> 37 – Information on Subsidiaries [extract]
> Significant restrictions to access or use the Group's assets
>
> Statutory, contractual or regulatory requirements as well as protective rights of noncontrolling interests might restrict the ability of the Group to access and transfer assets freely to or from other entities within the Group and to settle liabilities of the Group.
>
> Since the Group did not have any material noncontrolling interests at the balance sheet date, any protective rights associated with these did not give rise to significant restrictions.

The following restrictions impact the Group's ability to use assets:

- The Group has pledged assets to collateralize its obligations under repurchase agreements, securities financing transactions, collateralized loan obligations and for margining purposes for OTC derivative liabilities.
- The assets of consolidated structured entities are held for the benefit of the parties that have bought the notes issued by these entities.
- Regulatory and central bank requirements or local corporate laws may restrict the Group's ability to transfer assets to or from other entities within the Group in certain jurisdictions.

Restricted assets

	Dec 31, 2019		Dec 31, 2018	
in € m.	Total assets	Restricted assets	Total assets	Restricted assets
Interest-earning deposits with banks	104,327	159	176.022	188
Financial assets at fair value through profit or loss	530,713	43,190	573,344	48,320
Financial assets at fair value through other comprehensive income	45,503	2,943	51,182	4,375
Loans at amortized cost	429,841	71,369	400,297	76,573
Other	187,290	3,017	147,293	1,991
Total	1,297,674	120,678	1,348,137	131,447

The table above excludes assets that are not encumbered at an individual entity level but which may be subject to restrictions in terms of their transferability within the Group. Such restrictions may be based on local connected lending requirements or similar regulatory restrictions. In this situation, it is not feasible to identify individual balance sheet items that cannot be transferred. This is also the case for regulatory minimum liquidity requirements. The Group identifies the volume of liquidity reserves in excess of local stress liquidity outflows. The aggregate amount of such liquidity reserves that are considered restricted for this purpose is €31.2 billion as of December 31, 2019 (as of December 31, 2018: €34.9 billion).

4.4 Disclosure of the nature of the risks associated with interests in consolidated structured entities

IFRS 12 requires a number of disclosures in respect of financial or other support provided to consolidated structured entities. In short, the standard requires disclosure of certain intra-group transactions that are eliminated in consolidation and details of certain commitments by a group to itself. For groups with a number of structured entities, it is important that consolidation reporting packages capture the necessary information, as these transactions may have already been eliminated on consolidation.

The IASB concluded that it would help users of financial statements in understanding an entity's exposure to risks if the entity disclosed the terms of contractual arrangements that could require it to provide financial support to a consolidated structured entity, including events or circumstances that could expose the entity to a loss. *[IFRS 12.BC34]*. In determining how to meet this disclosure objective, we believe that an entity should consider all of the non-controlling interests held in the subsidiaries including the differing shares held in those subsidiaries.

For the same reason, the IASB concluded that an entity should disclose its risk exposure from non-contractual obligations to provide support to both consolidated and unconsolidated structured entities. *[IFRS 12.BC35]*.

The detailed disclosures that are required in respect of interests in consolidated structured entities are discussed at 4.4.1 to 4.4.4 below.

4.4.1 Terms of contractual arrangements to provide financial support to consolidated structured entities

An entity must disclose the terms of any contractual arrangements that could require the parent or its subsidiaries to provide financial support to a consolidated structured entity, including events or circumstances that expose the reporting entity to a loss (e.g. liquidity arrangements or credit rating triggers associated with obligations to purchase assets of the structured entity or provide financial support). *[IFRS 12.14].*

As discussed at 4.4 above, the IASB's intent seems to be to address circumstances in which differing shares held by non-controlling interests affect the profit and comprehensive income attributable to non-controlling interests.

Example 13.4: Illustrative example of disclosure of a contractual arrangement that could require parental support to a consolidated structured entity

The parent company has given a contractual commitment to its subsidiary, SE Limited, whereby if the assets held as collateral by SE Limited for its issued loan notes fall below a credit rating of 'AAA' then the parent will substitute assets of an equivalent fair value with an 'AAA' rating. The maximum fair value of assets to be substituted is €10,000,000.

The following extract from HSBC Holdings plc's financial statements illustrates disclosure of financial support to consolidated structured entities.

Extract 13.6: HSBC Holdings plc (2019)

Notes on the financial statements [extract]
20 Structured entities [extract]

HSBC is mainly involved with both consolidated and unconsolidated structured entities through the securitisation of financial assets, conduits and investment funds, established either by HSBC or a third party.

Consolidated structured entities [extracts]

Total assets of HSBC's consolidated structured entities, split by entity type [extract]

	Conduits $bn	Securitisations $bn
At 31 Dec 2019	8.6	9.6
At 31 Dec 2018	9.2	5.7

Conduits [extracts]

HSBC has established and manages two types of conduits: securities investment conduits ('SICs') and multi-seller conduits.

Securities investment conduits

The SICs purchase highly rated ABSs to facilitate tailored investment opportunities.

- At 31 December 2019, Solitaire, HSBC's principal SIC, held $2.1bn of ABSs (2018: $2.3bn). It is currently funded entirely by commercial paper ('CP') issued to HSBC. Although HSBC continues to provide a liquidity facility, Solitaire has no need to draw on it as long as HSBC purchases its issued CP, which HSBC intends to do for the foreseeable future. At 31 December 2019, HSBC held $3.2bn of CP (2018: $3.4bn).
- [...]

Multi-seller conduit

HSBC's multi-seller conduit was established to provide access to flexible market-based sources of finance for its clients. Currently, HSBC bears risk equal to the transaction-specific facility offered to the multi-seller conduit, amounting to $12.4bn at 31 December 2019 (2018: $16.1bn). First loss protection is provided by the originator of the assets, and not by HSBC, through transaction-specific credit enhancements. A layer of secondary loss protection is provided by HSBC in the form of programme-wide enhancement facilities.

4.4.2 Financial or other support to consolidated structured entities with no contractual obligation

If, during the reporting period a parent or any of its subsidiaries has, without having any contractual obligation to do so, provided financial or other support to a consolidated structured entity (e.g. purchasing assets of or instruments issued by the structured entity), the entity must disclose:

(a) the type and amount of support provided, including situations in which the parent or its subsidiaries assisted the structured entity in obtaining financial support; and

(b) the reasons for providing the support. *[IFRS 12.15]*.

The transactions requiring disclosure are intra-group transactions eliminated on consolidation.

'Support' is not defined in IFRS. A literal reading of 'purchasing assets of or instruments issued' is that any transfer of consideration to a structured entity in exchange for an asset is the provision of support requiring disclosure by the standard. The Basis for Conclusions explains that the IASB did not define 'support' because a definition of support would either be so broad that it would be an ineffective definition or invite structuring so as to avoid the disclosure. The IASB believes that support is widely understood as a provision of resources to another entity, either directly or indirectly. In the case of implicit agreements, the support is provided without having the contractual obligation to do so. However, in order to address respondents' concerns about distinguishing the provision of financial support from any other commercial transaction, the IASB clarified that disclosure is required when an entity has provided non-contractual support to a consolidated or unconsolidated structured entity in which it previously had or currently has an interest. *[IFRS 12.BC105-106]*.

Examples of the type of support that the IASB envisages being disclosed for unconsolidated structured entities (see 6.3 below) are liquidity arrangements or credit rating triggers associated with obligations to purchase assets of the structured entity or provide financial support. These examples imply that the IASB does not intend transactions in the ordinary course of business to be caught by the requirement to disclose support provided to consolidated structured entities. By 'asset purchase', it is implied that they are referring to a 'forced' purchase caused by, for example, liquidity or credit rating triggers.

Interpreting financial or other support is therefore likely to involve judgement. One possible interpretation is that 'support' includes:

- any transaction involving the gifting of funds;
- an equity investment;
- a long-term loan;
- forgiveness of debt;
- a transaction carried out on non-market terms resulting in a net outflow of resources from the reporting entity;
- a transaction not made in the ordinary course of business; or
- implicit or explicit guarantees of a structured entity's performance.

IFRS 12 does not explain what is meant by 'other support' and whether this extends to such non-financial support as the provision of human resources or management services outside of the ordinary course of business.

Example 13.5:   Illustrative example of disclosure of financial or other support provided to a consolidated structured entity

During the reporting period the parent provided financial support in the form of assets with a fair value of €12,000,000 (2020: €0) and a credit rating of 'AAA' to its subsidiary, SE 2 Limited, in exchange for assets with an equivalent fair value. There was no contractual obligation to exchange these assets. The transaction was initiated because the assets held by SE 2 Limited had a credit rating of less than 'AA' and a further ratings downgrade could potentially trigger calls on loan notes issued by SE 2 Limited. The parent did not suffer a loss on the transaction.

These disclosures are also required in respect of unconsolidated structured entities. See 6.2.2 and 6.3 below.

4.4.3   Financial or other support to unconsolidated structured entities which resulted in consolidation of those entities

If, during the reporting period, a parent or any of its subsidiaries has, without having a contractual obligation to do so, provided financial or other support to a previously unconsolidated structured entity and that provision of support resulted in the entity controlling the structured entity, the entity (i.e. the reporting entity) must disclose an explanation of the relevant factors in making that decision. *[IFRS 12.16]*.

The comments at 4.4.2 above regarding the definition of 'support' apply here also.

4.4.4   Current intentions to provide financial or other support

An entity must disclose any current intentions to provide financial or other support to a consolidated structured entity, including intentions to assist the structured entity in obtaining financial support. *[IFRS 12.17]*.

IFRS 12 does not define 'intentions'. The Basis for Conclusions states that it means 'the entity has decided' to provide financial support (i.e. it has current intentions to do this). *[IFRS 12.BC104]*. This implies that a decision to provide support has been approved at an appropriately senior level at the entity. Judgement will be required by entities in interpreting this requirement and defining the meaning of 'intention' in this context. The wording in the Basis of Conclusions does not require any such 'intention' to have been communicated to the structured entity that will receive the support or that there has been established a constructive obligation as defined in IAS 37 – *Provisions, Contingent Liabilities and Contingent Assets*.

The comments at 4.4.2 above in respect of the definition of 'support' apply here also.

These disclosures are also required in respect of unconsolidated structured entities. See 6.2.2 below.

4.5   Disclosure of changes in ownership interests in subsidiaries

4.5.1   Changes that do not result in loss of control

An entity must present a schedule that shows the effects on the equity attributable to owners of the parent of any changes in its ownership interests in a subsidiary that do not result in loss of control. *[IFRS 12.18]*. This schedule must be presented in addition to the information required by IAS 1 in the statement of changes in equity.

IAS 1 requires an entity to present, for each component of equity, a reconciliation between the carrying amount at the beginning and the end of the period, separately disclosing transactions with owners in their capacity as owners, showing separately contributions by and distributions to owners and changes in ownership interests with subsidiaries that do not result in a loss of control. *[IAS 1.106(d)]*.

Despite this existing disclosure requirement, the IASB decided to require that if a parent has equity transactions with non-controlling interests, it should disclose in a separate schedule the effects of those transactions on the equity of the owners of the parent. See Chapter 7 for guidance on the accounting for equity transactions with non-controlling interests.

The IASB's rationale for this duplication is that many respondents to a 2005 exposure draft, which proposed amendments to a previous version of IAS 27, requested more prominent disclosure of the effects of transactions with non-controlling interests on the equity of the owners of the parent. In addition, a schedule showing the effects on the controlling interest's equity of changes in a parent's ownership interests in a subsidiary that do not result in loss of control is required by US GAAP. *[IFRS 12.BC38-39]*.

IFRS 12 does not prescribe a format for this additional schedule. An example of the type of disclosure required is illustrated below.

Example 13.6: *Illustrative example of disclosure of changes in ownership interest in subsidiary that does not result in loss of control*

On 5 October 2021 the Group disposed of 25% of the ownership interests of Subsidiary Limited. Following the disposal, the Group still controls Subsidiary Limited and retains 70% of the ownership interests.

The transaction has been accounted for as an equity transaction with non-controlling interests (NCI), resulting in the following:

	€'000
Proceeds from sale of 25% ownership interest	550
Net assets attributable to NCI	(500)
Increase in equity attributable to parent	50
Represented by:	
Decrease in currency revaluation reserve	(250)
Decrease in available for sale reserve	(100)
Increase in retained earnings	400
	50

4.5.2 Changes that do result in loss of control

An entity must disclose the gain or loss, if any, resulting from the loss of control of a subsidiary calculated in accordance with paragraph 25 of IFRS 10, and:

(a) the portion of that gain or loss attributable to measuring any investment in the retained subsidiary at its fair value at the date that control is lost; and

(b) the line item(s) in profit or loss in which the gain or loss is recognised (if not presented separately). *[IFRS 12.19]*.

See Chapter 7 at 3 for more guidance on accounting for a loss of control of a subsidiary under IFRS 10.

4.6 Disclosures required by investment entities

An investment entity that is required by IFRS 10 to apply the exception from consolidation and instead account for its investment in a subsidiary at fair value through profit or loss must disclose that fact. *[IFRS 12.19A].*

If an investment entity has a subsidiary that it consolidates because that subsidiary is not an investment entity and whose main purpose and activities are providing services to the investment entity's investment activities, the disclosure requirements in IFRS 12 apply to the financial statements in which the investment entity consolidates that subsidiary. *[IFRS 12.BC61I].*

4.6.1 Disclosures about the composition of the group

For each unconsolidated subsidiary, an investment entity must disclose:

(a) the subsidiary's name;
(b) the principal place of business (and country of incorporation if different from the principal place of business) of the subsidiary; and
(c) the proportion of ownership interest held by the investment entity and, if different, the proportion of voting rights held. *[IFRS 12.19B].*

If an investment entity is the parent of another investment entity, the parent must also provide the disclosures (a) to (c) above for investments that are controlled by its investment entity subsidiary. The disclosures may be provided by including, in the financial statements of the parent, the financial statements of the subsidiary that contain this information. *[IFRS 12.19C].*

We would expect preparers to apply judgement where the list of subsidiaries is extensive. There is no explicit requirement in IFRS 12 to disclose this information in respect of consolidated subsidiaries (see 4.1 above).

4.6.2 Disclosures required when investment entity status changes

When an entity becomes, or ceases to be, an investment entity it must disclose:

- the change of investment entity status; and
- the reasons for the change.

In addition, an entity that becomes an investment entity must disclose the effect of the change of status on the financial statements for the period presented, including:

- the total fair value, as of the date of change of status, of the subsidiaries that cease to be consolidated;
- the total gain or loss, if any, calculated in accordance with paragraph B101 of IFRS 10; and
- the line item(s) in profit or loss in which the gain or loss is recognised (if not presented separately). *[IFRS 12.9B].*

The accounting effect of becoming or ceasing to become an investment entity is discussed in Chapter 6 at 10.3.1.

4.6.3 Disclosures required in respect of significant restrictions, commitments and financial and other support

An investment entity must disclose:

- the nature and extent of any significant restrictions (e.g. resulting from borrowing arrangements, regulatory requirements or contractual arrangements) on the ability of an unconsolidated subsidiary to transfer funds to the investment entity in the form of cash dividends or to repay loans or advances made to the unconsolidated subsidiary by the investment entity; and
- any current commitments or intentions to provide financial or other support to an unconsolidated subsidiary, including commitments or intentions to assist the subsidiary in obtaining financial support. *[IFRS 12.19D]*.

If, during the reporting period, an investment entity or any of its subsidiaries has, without having a contractual obligation to do so, provided financial or other support to an unconsolidated subsidiary (e.g. purchasing assets of, or instruments issued by, the subsidiary or assisting the subsidiary in obtaining financial support), the entity must disclose:

- the type and amount of support provided to each unconsolidated subsidiary; and
- the reasons for providing the support. *[IFRS 12.19E]*.

In addition, an investment entity must disclose the terms of any contractual arrangements that require the entity or its unconsolidated subsidiaries to provide financial support to an unconsolidated, controlled, structured entity, including events and circumstances that could expose the reporting entity to a loss (e.g. liquidity arrangements or credit rating triggers associated with obligations to purchase assets of the structured entity or to provide financial support). *[IFRS 12.19F]*.

During a reporting period an investment entity or any of its unconsolidated subsidiaries may have, without having a contractual obligation to do so, provided financial or other support to an unconsolidated structured entity that the investment entity did not control. In such a situation, if that provision of financial support resulted in the investment entity controlling the structured entity, the investment entity must provide an explanation of the relevant factors considered in reaching the decision to provide that support. *[IFRS 12.19G]*.

These disclosures are similar to those required for consolidated subsidiaries including consolidated structured entities discussed at 4.3, 4.4.1, 4.4.2 and 4.4.4 above – see the comments in these sections.

4.6.4 Valuation methodologies and nature of investing activities

IFRS 12 does not require any disclosure of fair value measurements made by investment entities. This information is already required by IFRS 7 – *Financial Instruments: Disclosures* – and by IFRS 13 – *Fair Value Measurement* – when reporting investments at fair value through profit or loss or other comprehensive income in accordance with IFRS 9. *[IFRS 12.BC61C]*.

5 DISCLOSURE OF INTERESTS IN JOINT ARRANGEMENTS AND ASSOCIATES

An entity must disclose information that enables users of its financial statements to evaluate:

(a) the nature, extent and financial effects of its interests in joint arrangements and associates, including the nature and effects of its contractual relationship with other investors with joint control of, or significant influence over, joint arrangements and associates; and

(b) the nature of, and changes in, the risks associated with its interests in joint ventures and associates. *[IFRS 12.20]*.

These requirements, explained in detail at 5.1 and 5.2 below, apply in full to both consolidated financial statements and individual financial statements of entities with joint arrangements and associates.

IFRS 12 does not address the presentation of joint ventures and associates in the primary statements. IAS 1 requires separate presentation of investments accounted for using the equity method on the face of the statement of financial position, although it does not require a split of those investments between joint ventures and associates. *[IAS 1.54]*. IAS 1 also requires a reporting entity's post tax share of the profit or loss of associates and joint ventures accounted for using the equity method to be disclosed on the face of the statement of comprehensive income. *[IAS 1.82]*.

5.1 Disclosure of the nature, extent and financial effects of interests in joint arrangements and associates

An entity must disclose:

(a) for each joint arrangement and associate that is material to the reporting entity:
 (i) the name of the joint arrangement or associate;
 (ii) the nature of the entity's relationship with the joint venture or associate (by, for example, describing the nature of the activities of the joint arrangement or associate and whether they are strategic to the entity's activities);
 (iii) the principal place of business (and country of incorporation, if applicable and different from the principal place of business) of the joint arrangement or associate; and
 (iv) the proportion of ownership interest held by the entity and, if different, the proportion of voting rights held (if applicable).

(b) for each joint venture (but not a joint operation) and associate that is material to the reporting entity:
 (i) whether the investment in the joint venture or associate is measured using the equity method or at fair value;
 (ii) summarised financial information about the joint venture or associate (see 5.1.1 below); and
 (iii) if the joint venture or associate is accounted for using the equity method, the fair value of the investment in the joint venture or associate, if there is a quoted market price for the investment.

(c) financial information (see 5.1.2 below) about the entity's investments in joint ventures and associates that are not individually material:
  (i) in aggregate for all individually immaterial joint ventures and, separately;
  (ii) in aggregate for all individually immaterial associates. *[IFRS 12.21]*.

Disclosures (b) and (c) are not required by an investment entity. *[IFRS 12.21A]*.

In January 2015, the Interpretations Committee discussed a request to clarify the requirement described above to disclose summary financial information about material joint ventures and associates and its interaction with the aggregation principle of IFRS 12 (see 2.2.2 above). The issue was whether the summary financial information can be disclosed in aggregate for all material joint ventures and associates, or whether such information should be disclosed individually for each material joint venture or associate. The Interpretations Committee also discussed a request to clarify whether an investor should be excused from disclosing information related to a listed joint venture or associate if the local regulatory requirements prevented the investor from disclosing such information until the joint venture or associate has released its own financial statements. The Interpretations Committee noted that it expected the requirement to prepare summarised financial information about a joint venture or associate in IFRS 12 to lead to the disclosure of summarised information on an individual basis for each joint venture or associate that is material to the reporting entity. The Interpretations Committee observed that this reflects the IASB's intentions as described in the Basis for Conclusions to IFRS 12. The Interpretations Committee also noted that there is no provision in IFRS 12 that permits non-disclosure of this information (on the grounds of confidentially or local regulatory requirements) and that outreach performed indicated that there was no significant diversity observed in practice on this issue. Consequently, the Interpretations Committee determined that neither an Interpretation nor an amendment to a standard was necessary and decided not to add this issue to its agenda.[2]

An entity must also disclose:
(a) the nature and extent of any significant restrictions (e.g. resulting from borrowing arrangements, regulatory requirements or contractual arrangements between investors with joint control of or significant influence over a joint venture or associate) on the ability of the joint ventures or associates to transfer funds to the entity in the form of cash dividends or to repay loans or advances made by the entity;
(b) when the financial statements of a joint venture or associate used in applying the equity method are as of a date or for a period that is different from that of the entity:
  (i) the date of the end of the reporting period of the financial statements of that joint venture or associate; and
  (ii) the reason for using a different date or period.
(c) the unrecognised share of losses of a joint venture or associate, both for the reporting period and cumulatively, if the entity has stopped recognising its share of losses of the joint venture or associate when applying the equity method. *[IFRS 12.22]*.

The implication from this wording is that these disclosures in respect of significant restrictions, reporting dates and unrecognised losses are required separately for each material joint venture or associate.

A summary of the disclosures required for individually material and, collectively for immaterial joint ventures and associates is shown in the table below.

Topic	Material joint ventures and associates	Individually immaterial joint ventures and associates
Accounting policy	✓	✗
Summarised financial information	✓	✓ (in aggregate)
Fair value, if quoted market price is available	✓	✗
Restrictions on ability to transfer funds	✓	✓ (in aggregate)
Date of financial statements, if different from entity	✓	✓ (in aggregate)
Unrecognised share of losses	✓	✓ (in aggregate)

5.1.1 Summarised financial information of individually material joint ventures and associates

The summarised financial information specified by (b)(ii) at 5.1 above for each material joint venture and associate is as follows:

(a) dividends received;

(b) summarised financial information for the joint venture or associate including, but not necessarily limited to:

    (i) current assets;

    (ii) non-current assets;

    (iii) current liabilities;

    (iv) non-current liabilities;

    (v) revenue;

    (vi) profit or loss from continuing operations;

    (vii) post-tax profit or loss from discontinued operations;

    (viii) other comprehensive income; and

    (ix) total comprehensive income. *[IFRS 12.B12]*.

Additionally, for material joint ventures (but not associates) the following information must be disclosed:

(a) cash and cash equivalents included in current assets;

(b) current financial liabilities (excluding trade and other payables and provisions);

(c) non-current financial liabilities (excluding trade and other payables and provisions);

(d) depreciation and amortisation;
(e) interest income;
(f) interest expense; and
(g) income tax expense or income. *[IFRS 12.B13]*.

The summarised financial information presented must be the 100 per cent amounts included in the IFRS financial statements of the joint venture or associate (and not the entity's share of those amounts). However, if the entity accounts for the joint venture or associate using the equity method:

(a) the amounts included in the IFRS financial statements of the joint venture or associate must be adjusted to reflect adjustments made by the entity when using the equity method, such as the fair value adjustments made at the time of acquisition and adjustments for differences in accounting policies (see Chapter 11 at 7); and

(b) the entity must provide a reconciliation of the summarised financial information presented to the carrying amount of its interest in the joint venture or associate. *[IFRS 12.B14]*.

In January 2015, the Interpretations Committee discussed the basis on which an entity should prepare the required summarised financial information for joint ventures and associates. The Interpretations Committee observed that a reporting entity that has subsidiaries should present the summarised financial information required about a joint venture or associate that is material to the reporting entity based on the consolidated financial statements for the joint venture or associate. If it does not have subsidiaries, the presentation should be based on the financial statements of the joint venture or associate in which its own joint ventures or associates are equity-accounted. The Interpretations Committee noted that these views are consistent with paragraph 14 of IFRS 12, which requires that the amounts included in the financial statements of the joint venture or associate must be adjusted to reflect adjustments made by the reporting entity using the equity method (see (a) above). Consequently, the Interpretations Committee decided that neither an interpretation nor an amendment to a standard was necessary and decided not to add this issue to its agenda.[3]

The standard does not specify what components should be included in the reconciliation required by (b) above. As clarified by the Interpretations Committee, the amounts included in the IFRS financial statements of the joint venture or associate should be adjusted to reflect fair value and accounting policy adjustments per (a) above. The implication is that this should also include the reporting entity's goodwill attributable to the joint venture or associate. However, this is only the goodwill attributable to the reporting entity's share of the joint venture or associate. The goodwill attributable to the rest of the joint venture or associate is presumably not known. Care will therefore be needed in presenting any such goodwill and in adequately explaining how the summarised IFRS financial information reconciles to the carrying amount of the reporting entity's interest in the joint venture or associate. Any pre-existing goodwill in the books of the joint venture or associate at the time it became a joint venture or associate of the reporting entity should be eliminated from the amounts in (a) as a fair value adjustment.

An entity may present the summarised financial information required on the basis of the joint venture's or associate's financial statements if:

(a) the entity measures its interest in the joint venture or associate at fair value in accordance with IAS 28; and

(b) the joint venture or associate does not prepare IFRS financial statements and preparation on that basis would be impracticable or cause undue cost. In that case, the entity must disclose the basis on which the summarised financial information has been prepared. *[IFRS 12.B15]*.

This implies that the summarised financial information of the joint venture or associate can be prepared on a non-IFRS basis in those circumstances where both conditions (a) and (b) are satisfied.

Where a joint venture or associate measured at fair value in accordance with IAS 28 does prepare IFRS financial statements, or where the preparation of IFRS financial information would not be impracticable or cause undue cost, the summarised financial information disclosed should be the unadjusted IFRS numbers of the joint venture or associate (as compared to the adjusted basis used where the equity method is applied).

In principle, the IASB concluded that the disclosure requirements for joint ventures and associates should be the same for all entities regardless of whether those entities are venture capital organisations, mutual funds, unit trusts or similar entities which are permitted by IAS 28 to hold investments in joint ventures and associates at fair value. *[IFRS 12.BC60]*.

Nevertheless, the minimum line item disclosures required for material associates are less than those required for material joint ventures on the grounds that, in the IASB's opinion, an entity is generally more involved with joint ventures than with associates because joint control means that an entity has a veto over decisions relating to the relevant activities of the joint venture. Accordingly, the IASB considers that the different nature of the relationship between a joint venturer and its joint ventures from that between an investor and its associates warrants a different level of detail in the disclosures of summarised financial information. *[IFRS 12.BC50-51]*.

IFRS 12 requires that an entity should present the summarised financial information for each material joint venture on a '100 per cent' basis and reconcile that to the carrying amount of its investment in the joint venture or associate. An alternative would be to present summarised financial information for each material joint venture on the basis of the reporting entity's proportionate interest in the joint venture. However, the IASB rejected that alternative approach on the grounds that it would be confusing to present the assets, liabilities and revenue of a joint venture or associate when the entity has neither rights to, nor obligations for, the assets and liabilities of the joint ventures or associates. *[IFRS 12.BC49]*.

Summarised financial information is not required for material joint operations since assets and liabilities arising from joint operations are the reporting entity's own assets and liabilities and consequently are recognised separately in the entity's financial statements. They are accounted for in accordance with the requirements of applicable IFRSs, and are therefore subject to the disclosure requirements of those IFRSs. *[IFRS 12.BC52]*. See Chapter 12 at 6 for guidance on accounting for joint operations.

In the below extract, TOTAL S.A. disclose summarised financial information for the year 2019 for significant associates. Similar information is also provided for previous years 2018 and 2017 that is not reproduced in the extract.

> Extract 13.7: TOTAL S.A. (2019)
> 8 Consolidated Financial Statements [extract]
> 8.7 Notes to the Consolidated Financial Statements [extract]
> NOTE 8 Equity affiliates, other investments and related parties [extract]
> 8.1 Equity affiliates: investments and loans [extract]
> A) Information related to associates [extract]
>
> Information (100% gross) related to significant associates is as follows:
>
> | Exploration and production activities (M$) | Novatek[a] 2019 | Liquefaction entities 2019 | PetroCedeño 2019 |
> |---|---|---|---|
> | Non current assets | 24,081 | 30,578 | 3,994 |
> | Current assets | 6,898 | 9,994 | 7,457 |
> | TOTAL ASSETS | 30,979 | 40,572 | 11,451 |
> | Shareholder's equity | 24,884 | 23,640 | 4,548 |
> | Non current liabilities | 3,727 | 11,445 | 76 |
> | Current liabilities | 2,368 | 5,487 | 6,827 |
> | TOTAL LIABILITIES | 30,979 | 40,572 | 11,451 |
> | Revenue from sales | 13,227 | 22,684 | 356 |
> | NET INCOME | 8,260 | 5,692 | (33) |
> | OTHER COMPREHENSIVE INCOME | 1,807 | – | – |
> | % owned | 19.40% | | 30.32% |
> | Revaluation identifiable assets on equity affiliates | 1,641 | 1,714 | – |
> | Equity value | 6,469 | 5,493 | 1,379 |
> | Profit/(loss) | 1,508 | 637 | (10) |
> | Share of Other Comprehensive Income, net amount | 634 | 23 | – |
> | Dividends paid to the Group | 266 | 752 | – |
>
> (a) Information includes the best Group's estimates of results at the date of TOTAL's financial statements.
>
> Novatek, listed in Moscow and London, is the 2nd largest producer of natural gas in Russia. The Group share of Novatek's market value amounted to $11,938 million as at December 31, 2019. Novatek is consolidated by the equity method. TOTAL, in fact, exercises significant influence particularly via its representation on the Board of Directors of Novatek and its interest in Yamal LNG and the project Arctic LNG 2.
>
> The Group is not aware of significant restrictions limiting the ability of OAO Novatek to transfer funds to its shareholder, be it under the form of dividends, repayment of advances or loans made.
>
> The Group's interests in associates operating liquefaction plants are combined. The amounts include investments in: Nigeria LNG (15.00%), Angola LNG (13.60%), Yemen LNG (39.62%), Qatar Liquefied Gas Company Limited (Qatargas) (10.00%), Qatar Liquefied Gas Company Limited II (16.70%), Oman LNG (5.54%), and Abu Dhabi Gas Liquefaction Company Limited (5.00%), Arctic LNG 2 (10.00%)
>
> PetroCedeño produces and upgrades extra-heavy crude oil in Venezuela.

5.1.2 Financial information of individually immaterial joint ventures and associates

An entity must disclose, in aggregate, the carrying amount of its interests in all individually immaterial joint ventures or associates that are accounted for using the equity method. An entity must also disclose separately the aggregate amount of its share of those joint ventures' or associates':

(a) profit or loss from continuing operations;
(b) post-tax profit or loss from discontinued operations;
(c) other comprehensive income; and
(d) total comprehensive income.

Separate disclosures are required for joint ventures and associates. *[IFRS 12.B16].*

IFRS 12 does not specifically require a reporting entity's share of (a) to (d) to be disclosed for material joint ventures or associates.

IFRS 12 clarifies that this financial information is not required when a joint venture or associate is held for sale in accordance with IFRS 5. *[IFRS 12.B17].*

In the below extract Bayer Aktiengesellschaft has provided a summary of aggregated information related to associates and joint ventures:

Extract 13.8: Bayer Aktiengesellschaft (2019)

B Consolidated Financial Statements [extract]
Notes to the Consolidated Financial Statements of the Bayer Group [extract]
Notes to the Statements of Financial Position [extract]
16. Investments accounted for using the equity method [extract]

Twelve (2018: five) associates and five (2018: ten) joint ventures were accounted for in the consolidated financial statements using the equity method. A list of these companies is available at www.bayer.com/shareownership2019.

The following table contains a summary of the aggregated income statement data and aggregated carrying amounts of the associates and joint ventures accounted for using the equity method (excluding the Covestro Group):

B 16/1

Earnings Data and Carrying Amounts of Companies Accounted for Using the Equity Method

€ million	Associates 2018	Associates 2019	Joint Ventures 2018	Joint Ventures 2019
Income after income taxes	(2)	(24)	(75)	(136)
Other comprehensive income after income taxes	30	32	–	–
Total comprehensive income after income taxes	28	8	(75)	(136)
Share of income after income taxes	(1)	(6)	(34)	166
Share of total comprehensive income after income taxes	17	21	(34)	166
Carrying amount as of December 31	95	356	420	166

5.2 Risks associated with interests in joint ventures and associates

An entity must disclose:

(a) commitments that it has relating to its joint ventures separately from the amount of other commitments; and
(b) contingent liabilities (as defined in IAS 37) relating to its interests in joint ventures or associates (including its share of contingent liabilities incurred jointly with other investors with joint control of, or significant influence over, the joint ventures and associates) separately from the amount of other contingent liabilities.

5.2.1 Disclosure of commitments relating to joint ventures

IAS 24 – *Related Party Disclosures* – already requires aggregate commitments relating to joint ventures to be disclosed separately from other commitments. [IAS 24.18-19]. IFRS 12 clarifies that the commitments required to be disclosed under IAS 24 include an entity's share of commitments made jointly with other investors with joint control of a joint venture. Commitments are those that may give rise to a future outflow of cash or other resources. [IFRS 12.B18].

IFRS 12 provides the following examples of unrecognised commitments that should be disclosed under IAS 24:

(a) unrecognised commitments to contribute funding or resources as a result of, for example:
  (i) the constitution or acquisition agreements of a joint venture (that, for example, require an entity to contribute funds over a specific period);
  (ii) capital intensive projects undertaken by a joint venture;
  (iii) unconditional purchase obligations, comprising procurement of equipment, inventory or services that an entity is committed to purchasing from, or on behalf of, a joint venture;
  (iv) unrecognised commitments to provide loans or other financial support to a joint venture;
  (v) unrecognised commitments to contribute resources to a joint venture, such as assets or services;
  (vi) other non-cancellable unrecognised commitments relating to a joint venture; and
(b) unrecognised commitments to acquire another party's ownership interest (or a portion of that ownership interest) in a joint venture if a particular event occurs or does not occur in the future. [IFRS 12.B19].

There is no requirement to disclose these commitments for individual joint ventures. However, IAS 24 requires disclosure of information about those transactions and outstanding balances, including commitments, necessary for users to understand the potential effect of the relationship on the financial statements. [IAS 24.18]. This implies that there should be separate disclosure of different types of significant commitments. IAS 24 does not require the names of any joint ventures to be disclosed.

In the below extract, BP plc has provided information about commitments made to joint ventures and associates:

Extract 13.9: BP p.l.c. (2019)

Notes on financial statements [extract]

13. Capital commitments

Authorized future capital expenditure for property, plant and equipment (excluding right-of-use assets) by group companies for which contracts had been signed at 31 December 2019 amounted to $11,382 million (2018 $8,319 million, 2017 $11,340 million). BP has contracted capital commitments amounting to $787 million (2018 $1,227 million, 2017 $1,451 million) in relation to associates. BP's share of contracted capital commitments of joint ventures amounted to $1,024 million (2018 $619 million, 2017 $483 million).

5.2.2 Disclosure of contingent liabilities relating to joint ventures and associates

IFRS 12 requires separate disclosure of contingent liabilities relating to an entity's interests in joint ventures and associates from the amount of other contingent liabilities.

IAS 37 defines a contingent liability as an obligation that derives from an entity's actions where:

(a) by an established pattern of past practice, published policies or a sufficiently specific current statement, the entity has indicated to other parties that it will accept certain responsibilities; and

(b) as a result, the entity has created a valid expectation on the part of those other parties that it will discharge those responsibilities. *[IAS 37.10]*.

IAS 37 requires disclosure, for each class of contingent liability at the end of a reporting period, a brief description of the nature of the contingent liability and, where practicable:

(a) an estimate of its financial effect, measured under the requirements of the standard;

(b) an indication of the uncertainties relating to the amount or timing of any outflow; and

(c) the possibility of any reimbursement. *[IAS 37.86]*.

IAS 37 further defines what is intended by 'class' and the circumstances in which aggregation of disclosures of contingent liabilities is appropriate.

Further detail on contingent liabilities is contained in Chapter 26 at 7.2.

6 DISCLOSURE OF INTERESTS IN UNCONSOLIDATED STRUCTURED ENTITIES

An entity must disclose information that enables users of its financial statements:

(a) to understand the nature and extent of its interests in unconsolidated structured entities; and

(b) to evaluate the nature of, and changes to, the risks associated with its interests in unconsolidated structured entities. *[IFRS 12.24]*.

These disclosures are not required by an investment entity for an unconsolidated structured entity that it controls and for which it presents the disclosures required at 4.6 above. *[IFRS 12.25A]*.

Disclosure requirements in respect of risks associated with interests in consolidated structured entities are discussed at 4.4 above.

As discussed at 2.2.2.D above, these disclosures also apply to interests in joint ventures and associates that are also structured entities, in addition to the disclosures required at 5 above for joint ventures and associates.

The information required by (a) and (b) above includes information about an entity's exposure to risk from involvement that it had with unconsolidated structured entities in previous periods (e.g. sponsoring the structured entity) even if the entity no longer has any contractual involvement with the structured entity at the reporting date. *[IFRS 12.25]*.

Some of the disclosure requirements for unconsolidated structured entities overlap with those of IFRS 7, since many interests in unconsolidated structured entities are financial assets within the scope of IFRS 7. However, IFRS 12 disclosures describe an entity's risk exposures, but IFRS 7 requires disclosures about risks associated with financial instruments. IFRS 12 adopts a different perspective and requires an entity to disclose its exposure to risks from its interest in a structured entity. *[IFRS 12.BC72]*.

6.1 Disclosure of the nature of interests in unconsolidated structured entities

6.1.1 Disclosure of the nature, purpose, size, activities and financing of structured entities

An entity must disclose qualitative and quantitative information about its interests in unconsolidated structured entities, including, but not limited to, the nature, purpose, size and activities of the structured entity and how the structured entity is financed. *[IFRS 12.26]*.

The IASB concluded that this requirement should provide users with sufficient information about the assets held by structured entities and the funding of those assets without requiring specific disclosures of the assets of unconsolidated structured entities in which the entity has an interest in all circumstances. If relevant to an assessment of its exposure to risk, an entity would be required to provide additional information about the assets and funding of structured entities. *[IFRS 12.BC96]*.

6.1.1.A Nature and purpose

Examples of the nature and purpose of a structured entity might include:

- to manage balance sheet exposure and risk, including securitisation of assets;
- to provide investors with a synthetic exposure to debt and equity instruments such as credit linked notes and equity linked notes;
- to provide investors with a variety of investment opportunities through managed investment strategies; and
- to obtain and facilitate funding.

Quilter plc discloses the nature, purpose and type of interest in unconsolidated structured entities in a narrative format as follows:

> **Extract 13.10: Quilter plc (2019)**
> Notes to the consolidated financial statements [extract]
> 20: Structured entities [extract]
> 20(a): Group's involvement in structured entities [extract]
>
> Some investment vehicles are classified as structured entities because they have a narrow and well defined purpose. In structured entities, voting rights are not the predominant factor in deciding who controls the entity but rather it is the Group's exposure to the variability of returns from these entities.
>
> The Group invests in collective investment vehicles, including OEICs and unit trusts, in order to match unit-linked investment contract liabilities. Shareholder funds are also invested in collective investment vehicles, principally in respect of money market funds as an alternative to bank deposits. These structured entities are not consolidated where the Group determines that it does not have control.
>
> The Group's holdings in collective investment vehicles are subject to the terms and conditions of the respective investment vehicle's offering documentation and are susceptible to market price risk arising from uncertainties about future values of those investment vehicles. All of the investment vehicles in the investment portfolios are managed by portfolio managers who are compensated by the respective investment vehicles for their services. Such compensation generally consists of an asset-based fee and a performance based incentive fee, and is reflected in the valuation of the investment vehicles.

6.1.1.B Size

The requirement to disclose the size of a structured entity is often met by providing information about the total value of the assets of the entity. However, the Basis for Conclusions states that IFRS 12 does not require specific disclosure of the reported assets of unconsolidated structured entities in which the entity has an interest. *[IFRS 12.BC96]*. This suggests that other measures of size would be acceptable, including the notional value of securities issued by structured entities.

6.1.1.C Activities

When disclosing the activities of a structured entity, these activities should include the primary activities for which the entity was designed, which are the activities that significantly affect the entity's returns. See Chapter 6 at 3 and 4 for guidance on purpose and design of an investee and relevant activities, respectively, as described in IFRS 10.

For example, the activities that could significantly affect the entity's returns, include:

- providing a source of long-term capital to an entity or funding to support a reporting entity's ongoing major or central operations through issuing notes; or
- providing a supply of goods and services that is consistent with a reporting entity's ongoing major or central operations which, without the existence of the structured entity, would have to be provided by the reporting entity itself.

6.1.1.D Financing

This disclosure requirement is not limited to financing provided by the reporting entity to the structured entity and would include financing received by the structured entity from unrelated third parties. It is also not limited to equity financing and includes all forms of financing that allow the structured entity to conduct its business activities.

Barclays Bank PLC's financial statements illustrate disclosures of financing of structured entities.

> **Extract 13.11: Barclays PLC (2019)**
>
> Notes to the financial statements for the year ended 31 December 2019 [extract]
> Scope of consolidation [extract]
> 35 Structured entities [extract]
> Unconsolidated structured entities in which the Group has an interest [extract]
> Other interests in unconsolidated structured entities [extract]
>
> The Group's interests in structured entities not held for the purposes of short-term trading activities are set out below, summarised by the purpose of the entities and limited to significant categories, based on maximum exposure to loss.
>
> Nature of interest [extract]
>
> | | Multi-seller conduit programmes £m | Lending £m |
> |---|---|---|
> | **As at 31 December 2019** | | |
> | Trading portfolio assets | – | – |
> | Financial assets at fair value through the income statement | | |
> | [...] | | |
> | – Loans and advances | – | 159 |
> | [...] | | |
> | Loans and advances at amortised cost | 5,930 | 8,132 |
> | Other assets | 17 | 4 |
> | Total on-balance sheet exposures | 5,947 | 8,295 |
> | Total off-balance sheet notional amounts | 8,649 | 3,751 |
> | Maximum exposure to loss | 14,596 | 12,046 |
> | Total assets of the entity | 78,716 | 145,181 |
>
> [...]
>
> *Multi-seller conduit programme*
>
> The multi-seller conduit engages in providing financing to various clients and holds whole or partial interests in pools of receivables or similar obligations. These instruments are protected from loss through overcollateralisation, seller guarantees, or other credit enhancements provided to the conduit. The Group's off-balance sheet exposure included in the table above represents liquidity facilities that are provided to the conduit for the benefit of the holders of the commercial paper issued by the conduit and will only be drawn where the conduit is unable to access the commercial paper market. If these liquidity facilities are drawn, the Group is protected from loss through overcollateralisation, seller guarantees, or other credit enhancements provided to the conduit.
>
> *Lending*
>
> The portfolio includes lending provided by the Group to unconsolidated structured entities in the normal course of its lending business to earn income in the form of interest and lending fees and includes loans to structured entities that are generally collateralised by property, equipment or other assets. All loans are subject to the Group's credit sanctioning process. Collateral arrangements are specific to the circumstances of each loan with additional guarantees and collateral sought from the sponsor of the structured entity for certain arrangements. During the period the Group incurred an impairment of £7m (2018: £67m) against such facilities.

6.1.2 Disclosures of sponsored structured entities for which no interest is held at the reporting date

If an entity has sponsored an unconsolidated structured entity for which it does not disclose the risk information required by 6.2 below (e.g. because it does not have an interest in the entity at the reporting date), the entity must disclose:

(a) how it has determined which structured entities it has sponsored;

(b) income from those structured entities during the reporting period, including a description of the types of income presented; and

(c) the carrying amount (at the time of transfer) of all assets transferred to those structured entities during the reporting period. *[IFRS 12.27]*.

The rationale for this disclosure requirement is that sponsoring a structured entity can create risks for a reporting entity, even though the entity may not retain an interest in the structured entity. The Basis for Conclusions states that 'if the structured entity encounters difficulties, it is possible that the sponsor could be challenged on its advice or actions, or might choose to act to protect its reputation.' *[IFRS 12.BC87]*.

IFRS 12 does not define 'sponsored'. However, an illustrative example in IFRS 10 uses the word 'sponsors' in a similar context when it states that 'a decision maker (the sponsor) sponsors a multi-seller conduit'. In the IFRS 10 example, the sponsor establishes the terms of the conduit and manages the operations of the conduit for a market-based fee. *[IFRS 10.B72 Example 16]*.

Determining whether the reporting entity is the sponsor of a structured entity will be a matter of individual facts and circumstances and may require judgement to be exercised. For example, a structured entity may have been created to achieve two possible objectives that could satisfy both the reporting entity and third party investors in the structured entity. Factors that may indicate that a reporting entity has sponsored a structured entity include:

- the reporting entity established and set up the entity; and
- the reporting entity was involved in the creation and design of the structured entity; or
- the reporting entity is the majority user of the structured entity; or
- the reporting entity's name appears in the name of the structured entity or on the products issued by the structured entity.

The information required by (b) and (c) above must be presented in a tabular format unless some other format is more appropriate and the sponsoring activities must be classified into relevant categories. *[IFRS 12.28]*.

Many financial institutions define 'sponsor' for the purpose of their IFRS 12 disclosures as illustrated by this disclosure from HSBC Holdings plc's financial statements.

> *Extract 13.12: HSBC Holdings plc (2019)*
>
> Notes on the financial statements [extract]
> 1. Basis of preparation and significant accounting policies [extract]
> 1.2 Summary of significant accounting policies [extract]
> (a) Consolidation and related policies [extract]
> HSBC sponsored structured entities
>
> HSBC is considered to sponsor another entity if, in addition to ongoing involvement with the entity, it had a key role in establishing that entity or in bringing together relevant counterparties so the transaction that is the purpose of the entity could occur. HSBC is generally not considered a sponsor if the only involvement with the entity is merely administrative.

The information required by (a) and (b) above must be disclosed whether or not any assets were transferred to the structured entity during the reporting period. There is no time limit set for these disclosures so, in theory, they could continue indefinitely after the cessation of any interest in the structured entity. IFRS 12 does not specify whether (c) above refers to assets transferred to the structured entity by the reporting entity or to the total assets transferred to the structured entity irrespective of who the transferor may be. However, the Basis for Conclusions states that the IASB concluded that the asset information disclosed should refer not only to assets transferred by the sponsor but to all assets transferred to the structured entity during the reporting period. *[IFRS 12.BC90]*.

Income received from structured entities would not be confined to the income derived from the reporting entity's 'interest(s)' as defined by IFRS 12, but would cover all types of income received and reported by the entity. IFRS 12 states that 'income from a structured entity' includes, but is not limited to:

- recurring and non-recurring fees (structuring fees, management fees, placing agent fees, etc.);
- interest;
- dividends;
- gains or losses on the remeasurement or derecognition of interests in structured entities; and
- gains or losses from the transfer of assets or liabilities to the structured entity.
[IFRS 12 Appendix A].

There is no requirement for a quantitative split of the fee income by type although it may be useful for users of the financial statements.

An illustrative example of the disclosures required by (a) to (c) above is shown below.

Example 13.7: *Illustrative example of disclosures for sponsored structured entities where no interest exists at the reporting date*

The Group considers itself the sponsor of a number of structured entities. The Group designed and established these entities. In some cases, it also transferred assets to them, in others it markets products associated with the entities in its own name and/or provides guarantees regarding the performance of the entities.

For some structured entities, the Group has no interest at the reporting date. However, it has sold assets to those entities during the reporting period in such a way that it has no continuing involvement in those assets and has earned fees for selling those assets and for other transactions carried out for the entities. The table below presents the Group's income recognised during the reporting period and the fair value of any assets transferred to those structured entities during the reporting period as follows:

Income from unconsolidated structured entities in which no interest is held at 31 December 2021	Income 2021 €'000	Income 2020 €'000
Commissions and fees	69	50
Interest income	48	47
Gains and losses on sale of assets	66	–
	183	97
Split by:		
Mortgage-backed securitisations	75	41
CDOs and CLOs	50	20
Asset-backed commercial paper	25	30
Property, credit-related and other investing	33	6
	183	97

Carrying amounts of assets transferred to unconsolidated structured entities in reporting period	Transferred in year 2021 €'000	Transferred in year 2020 €'000
Mortgage-backed securitisations	3,065	–
CDOs and CLOs	2,536	–
Asset-backed commercial paper	1,325	3,000
Property, credit-related and other investing	178	–
	7,104	3,000

UBS AG makes the following disclosures in respect of sponsored unconsolidated structured entities in which UBS did not have an interest at the year-end.

> **Extract 13.13: UBS Group AG (2019)**
>
> Notes to the UBS Group AG consolidated financial statements [extract]
> Note 31   Interests in subsidiaries and other entities [extract]
> c)   Interests in unconsolidated structured entities [extract]
>
> **Sponsored unconsolidated structured entities in which UBS did not have an interest**
>
> For several sponsored SEs, no interest was held by the Group at year-end. However, during the respective reporting period the Group transferred assets, provided services and held instruments that did not qualify as an interest in these sponsored SEs, and accordingly earned income or incurred expenses from these entities. The table below presents the income earned and expenses incurred directly from these entities during the year as well as corresponding asset information. The table does not include income earned and expenses incurred from risk management activities, including income and expenses from financial instruments used to economically hedge instruments transacted with the unconsolidated SEs.
>
> The majority of the fee income arose from investment funds that are sponsored and administrated by the Group, but managed by third parties. As the Group does not provide any active management services, UBS was not exposed to risk from the performance of these entities and was therefore deemed not to have an interest in them. In certain structures, the fees receivable may be collected directly from the investors and have therefore not been included in the table below.
>
> The Group also recorded other net income from financial instruments measured at fair value through profit or loss from mark-to-market movements arising primarily from derivatives, such as interest rate and currency swaps as well as credit derivatives, through which the Group purchases protection, and financial liabilities designated at fair value, which do not qualify as interests because the Group does not absorb variability from the performance of the entity. Total income reported does not reflect economic hedges or other mitigating effects from the Group's risk management activities.
>
> During 2019, UBS and third parties transferred assets of USD 1 billion and USD 1 billion, respectively, into sponsored securitization vehicles created in the year (2018: USD 1 billion and USD 1 billion, respectively). UBS and third parties also transferred assets of USD 0 billion and USD 1 billion, respectively, into sponsored client vehicles created in the year (2018: USD 2 billion and USD 0 billion, respectively). For sponsored investment funds, transfers arose during the period as investors invested and redeemed positions, thereby changing the overall size of the funds, which, when combined with market movements, resulted in a total closing net asset value of USD 42 billion (31 December 2018: USD 18 billion).
>
> **Sponsored unconsolidated structured entities in which UBS did not have an interest at year-end**
>
> | | As of or for the year ended | | | |
> |---|---|---|---|---|
> | | 31.12.19 | | | |
> | USD million, except where indicated | Securitization vehicles | Client vehicles | Investment funds | Total |
> | Net interest income | (1) | 0 | (1) | (2) |
> | Net fee and commission income | | 13 | 50 | 63 |
> | Other net income from financial instruments measured at fair value through profit or loss | 19 | (18) | 9 | 11 |
> | **Total income** | 19 | (5) | 58 | 72 |
> | **Asset information (USD billion)** | 2[1] | 1[2] | 42[3] | |
>
> 1   Represents the amount of assets transferred to the respective securitization vehicles.
> 2   Represents the amount of assets transferred to the respective client vehicles.
> 3   Represents the total net asset value of the respective investment funds.

Aviva plc made the following disclosures in respect of investment management fees earned in respect of its asset management business. Similar information is also disclosed for 2018 that is not reproduced in the extract.

> *Extract 13.14: Aviva plc (2019)*
>
> Notes to the consolidated financial statements [extract]
>
> 27 – Interests in structured entities [extract]
>
> (c) Other interests in unconsolidated structured entities [extract]
>
> The Group receives management fees and other fees in respect of its asset management businesses. The Group does not sponsor any of the funds or investment vehicles from which it receives fees. Management fees received for investments that the Group manages but does not have a holding in also represent an interest in unconsolidated structured entities. As these investments are not held by the Group, the investment risk is borne by the external investors and therefore the Group's maximum exposure to loss relates to future management fees. The table below shows the assets under management of entities that the Group manages but does not have a holding in and the fees earned from those entities.
>
> | | 2019 Assets Under Management £m | 2019 Investment Management Fees £m |
> |---|---:|---:|
> | Investment funds[1] | 6,885 | 32 |
> | Specialised investment vehicles: | 3,108 | 10 |
> | Analysed as: | | |
> | OEICs | 33 | – |
> | PLPs | 3,075 | 10 |
> | **Total** | **9,993** | **42** |
>
> 1 Investment funds relate primarily to the Group's Polish pension funds.

6.2 Disclosure of the nature of risks of unconsolidated structured entities

The IASB decided that, although it agreed with the concept that an entity should generally be allowed to tailor its disclosures to meet the specific information needs of its users, disclosure requirements should contain a minimum set of requirements that should be applied by all entities. In making this decision, the IASB was convinced by comments from users who pointed out that without any specific disclosure requirements, comparability would be impaired and an entity might not disclose information that users find important. *[IFRS 12.BC94]*.

These minimum disclosures are discussed at 6.2.1 and 6.2.2 below.

6.2.1 Disclosures of interests in structured entities and of the maximum exposure to loss from those interests

An entity must disclose, in a tabular form, unless another format is more appropriate, a summary of:

(a) the carrying amounts of the assets and liabilities recognised in its financial statements relating to its interests in unconsolidated structured entities;

(b) the line items in the statement of financial position in which those assets and liabilities are recognised;

(c) the amount that best represents the entity's maximum exposure to loss from its interests in unconsolidated structured entities, including how the maximum exposure to loss is determined. If an entity cannot quantify its maximum exposure to loss from its interests in consolidated structured entities it must disclose that fact and the reasons; and

(d) a comparison of the carrying amounts of the assets and liabilities of the entity that relate to its interests in unconsolidated structured entities and the entity's maximum exposure to loss from those entities. [IFRS 12.29].

Disclosure of an entity's maximum exposure to loss was considered necessary by the IASB as it was concerned that, if only information about expected losses was required, an entity might often identify a positive expected value of returns from its interests in unconsolidated structured entities and, as a consequence, would not disclose any loss exposure. [IFRS 12.BC97].

IFRS 12 does not define maximum exposure to loss. The IASB decided not to provide such a definition of 'loss' but to leave it to the entity to identify what constitutes a loss in the particular context of that reporting entity. The entity should then disclose how it has determined maximum loss exposure. The IASB acknowledged that an entity might not always be able to calculate the maximum exposure to loss, such as when a financial instrument exposes an entity to theoretically unlimited losses. The IASB decided that when this is the case an entity should disclose the reasons why it is not possible to calculate the maximum exposure to loss. [IFRS 12.BC98-99].

We believe that 'maximum exposure to loss' refers to the maximum loss that an entity could be required to record in its statement of comprehensive income as a result of its involvement with a structured entity. Further, this maximum possible loss must be disclosed regardless of the probability of such losses actually being incurred. IFRS 12 is silent on whether the maximum exposure is gross or net of collateral or hedging instruments held that would mitigate any loss. Consistent with the equivalent disclosures required by IFRS 7, we believe that the maximum exposure to loss should be disclosed gross of any collateral or hedging instruments and that separate disclosure should be made in respect of instruments held that would mitigate the loss on a net basis. [IFRS 7.36].

The IASB also decided to require an entity to disclose a comparison of the carrying amounts of the assets and liabilities in its statement of financial position and its maximum exposure to loss. This is because the information will provide users with a better understanding of the differences between the expected loss exposure and the expectation of whether it is likely that an entity will bear all or only some of the losses. The IASB reasoned that this information would help an entity explain why the maximum exposure to loss is unrepresentative of its actual exposure if that is the case. [IFRS 12.BC100].

UBS AG makes the following disclosures in respect of its interests in unconsolidated structured entities. Similar information is also disclosed for 2018 that is not reproduced in the extract.

Extract 13.15: UBS Group AG (2019)

Notes to the UBS Group AG consolidated financial statements [extract]
Note 31   Interests in subsidiaries and other entities [extract]
c)   Interests in unconsolidated structured entities [extract]

During 2019, the Group sponsored the creation of various SEs and interacted with a number of non-sponsored SEs, including securitization vehicles, client vehicles as well as certain investment funds, that UBS did not consolidate as of 31 December 2019 because it did not control these entities.

The table below presents the Group's interests in and maximum exposure to loss from unconsolidated SEs as well as the total assets held by the SEs in which UBS had an interest as of year-end, except for investment funds sponsored by third parties, for which the carrying amount of UBS's interest as of year-end has been disclosed.

Interests in unconsolidated structured entities

	31.12.19				
USD million, except where indicated	Securitization vehicles	Client vehicles	Investment funds	Total	Maximum exposure to loss[1]
Financial assets at fair value held for trading	462	130	5,874	6,466	6,466
Derivative financial instruments	9	9	36	55	53
Loans and advances to customers			174	174	174
Financial assets at fair value not held for trading	81	8[2]	157	245	997
Financial assets measured at fair value through other comprehensive income		3,955		3,955	3,955
Other financial assets measured at amortized cost	335	16[2]		351	1,372
Total assets	888[3]	4,118	6,242	11,247	
Derivative financial instruments	2[4]	225	324	552	1
Total liabilities	2	225	324	552	
Assets held by the unconsolidated structured entities in which UBS had an interest (USD billion)	55[5]	73[6]	413[7]		

[...]

1   For the purpose of this disclosure, maximum exposure to loss amounts do not consider the risk-reducing effects of collateral or other credit enhancements.
2   Represents the carrying amount of loan commitments. The maximum exposure to loss for these instruments is equal to the notional amount.
3   As of 31 December 2019, USD 0.6 billion of the USD 0.9 billion (31 December 2018: USD 0.6 billion of the USD 0.8 billion) was held in Corporate Center – Non-core and Legacy Portfolio.
4   Comprised of credit default swap liabilities and other swap liabilities. The maximum exposure to loss for credit default swap liabilities is equal to the sum of the negative carrying value and the notional amount. For other swap liabilities, no maximum exposure to loss is reported.
5   Represents the principal amount outstanding.
6   Represents the market value of total assets.
7   Represents the net asset value of the investment funds sponsored by UBS and the carrying amount of UBS's interests in the investment funds not sponsored by UBS.

> The Group retains or purchases interests in unconsolidated SEs in the form of direct investments, financing, guarantees, letters of credit, derivatives and through management contracts.
>
> The Group's maximum exposure to loss is generally equal to the carrying amount of the Group's interest in the SE, with the exception of guarantees, letters of credit and credit derivatives, for which the contract's notional amount, adjusted for losses already incurred, represents the maximum loss that the Group is exposed to. In addition, the current fair value of derivative swap instruments with a positive replacement value only, such as total return swaps, is presented as the maximum exposure to loss. Risk exposure for these swap instruments could change over time with market movements.
>
> The maximum exposure to loss disclosed in the table on the previous page does not reflect the Group's risk management activities, including effects from financial instruments that may be used to economically hedge the risks inherent in the unconsolidated SE or the risk-reducing effects of collateral or other credit enhancements.
>
> In 2019 and 2018, the Group did not provide support, financial or otherwise, to an unconsolidated SE when not contractually obligated to do so, nor has the Group an intention to do so in the future.
>
> In 2019 and 2018, income and expenses from interests in unconsolidated SEs primarily resulted from mark-to-market movements recognized in *Other net income from financial instruments measured at fair value through profit of loss*, which have generally been hedged with other financial instruments, as well as fee and commission income received from UBS-sponsored funds.

6.2.2 Disclosures of actual and intended financial and other support to structured entities

If during the reporting period an entity has, without having a contractual obligation to do so, provided financial or other support to an unconsolidated structured entity in which it previously had or currently has an interest (for example, purchasing assets of or instruments issued by the structured entity), the entity must disclose:

(a) the type and amount of support provided, including situations in which the entity assisted the structured entity in obtaining financial support; and

(b) the reasons for providing the support. *[IFRS 12.30]*.

An entity must also disclose any current intentions to provide financial or other support to an unconsolidated structured entity, including intentions to assist the structured entity in obtaining financial support. *[IFRS 12.31]*.

See 4.4.2 and 4.4.4 above for discussion of these disclosure requirements.

Example 13.5 at 4.4.2 above is an illustrative disclosure of the provision of financial support to a structured entity.

6.3 Additional disclosures regarding the nature of risks from interests in unconsolidated structured entities

In addition to the requirements at 6.2 above, IFRS 12 also requires an entity to disclose additional information that is necessary to meet the disclosure objective to disclose information that allows users of a reporting entity's financial statements to evaluate the nature of, and changes to, the risks associated with its interests in unconsolidated structured entities. Examples of additional information that, depending on the circumstances, might be relevant to an assessment of the risks to which a reporting entity is exposed where it has an interest in an unconsolidated structured entity are:

(a) the terms of an arrangement that could require the entity to provide support to a unconsolidated structured entity (e.g. liquidity arrangements or credit rating triggers associated with obligations to purchase assets of the structured entity or provide financial support) including:
   (i) a description of the events or circumstances that could expose the reporting entity to a loss;
   (ii) whether there are any terms that would limit the obligation;
   (iii) whether there are any other parties that provide financial support and, if so, how the reporting entity's obligation ranks with those of other parties;

(b) losses incurred by the entity during the reporting period relating to its interests in unconsolidated structured entities;

(c) the types of income the entity received during the reporting period from its interests in unconsolidated structured entities;

(d) whether an entity is required to absorb losses of an unconsolidated structured entity before other parties, the maximum limit of such losses for the entity and (if relevant) the ranking and amounts of potential losses borne by parties whose interests rank lower than the entity's interest in the unconsolidated structured entity;

(e) information about any liquidity requirements, guarantees or other commitments with third parties that may affect the fair value or risk of the entity's interests in unconsolidated structured entities;

(f) any difficulties an unconsolidated structured entity has experienced in financing its activities during the reporting period; and

(g) in relation to the funding of an unconsolidated structured entity, the forms of funding (e.g. commercial paper or medium term notes) and their weighted-average life. That information might include maturity analyses of the assets and funding of an unconsolidated structured entity if the structured entity has longer-term assets funded by shorter-term funding. *[IFRS 12.B25-26]*.

No prescriptive format is required for these disclosures. Therefore, a reporting entity will have to decide whether a tabular or narrative format is suitable depending on its individual circumstances. The examples above are not exhaustive.

The IASB does not intend each item in the list of examples above to apply in all circumstances. The IASB's intention regarding the disclosure of risk is that each entity should disclose information that is important when assessing that exposure but not to cloud the information with unnecessary detail that would be considered irrelevant. If an entity has a large exposure to risk because of transactions with a particular unconsolidated structured entity, then the Board would expect extensive disclosure about that exposure. In contrast, if the entity has very little exposure to risk, little disclosure would be required. Therefore, the list of additional information above is a list of examples of information that might be relevant and not a list of requirements that should be applied regardless of the circumstances. *[IFRS 12.BC113-114]*.

Given that this information is required in respect of structured entities that the reporting entity does not control, and over which it may not exercise significant influence, some of the disclosures suggested in respect of (d), (f) and (g) above may be difficult to provide. This is because they require current information about the activities of the structured entity, rather than information about the interests held by the reporting entity.

Comments on some of the suggested disclosures are at 6.3.1 to 6.3.7 below.

6.3.1 Disclosure of support

Example 13.5 above illustrates disclosure of a contractual arrangement that could require support to a structured entity.

Example 13.6 above illustrates disclosure of support provided to a structured entity where there is no contractual obligation to provide such support.

The meaning of 'support' is discussed at 4.4.2 above.

6.3.2 Disclosure of losses

IFRS 12 does not elaborate on 'losses incurred' but we believe that it refers to both realised and unrealised losses and losses recognised in both profit and loss and other comprehensive income. It may be informative to explain to users of the financial statements the line items in the primary statements in which the losses have been recognised. It would also be informative to disclose the aggregate losses incurred in respect of investments held at the reporting date as well as the losses incurred in the reporting period for those interests disposed of during the period.

Example 13.8: Losses incurred from investments in unconsolidated structured entities

The Group has incurred the following realised and unrealised losses in respect of its investments in unconsolidated structured entities:

	2021 €'000	2020 €'000
Realised losses	200	200
Unrealised losses (profit and loss)	400	300
Unrealised losses (other comprehensive income)	500	400
	1,100	900
Split by:		
Collateralised debt obligations	800	700
Credit card receivables	300	200
	1,100	900

Aggregate losses incurred	Transferred in year 2021 €'000	Transferred in year 2020 €'000
Collateralised debt obligations	2,300	1,500
Credit card receivables	1,700	1,400
	4,000	2,900

6.3.3 Disclosure of types of income received

This disclosure is similar to the disclosure required at 6.1.2 above in respect of unconsolidated structured entities for which the reporting entity does not have an interest at the reporting date. However, (c) above refers only to the types of income received and does not refer to the need for a specific quantification of the income received.

'Income from a structured entity' includes, but is not limited to:

- recurring and non-recurring fees (structuring fees, management fees, placing agent fees, etc.);
- interest;
- dividends;
- gains or losses on the remeasurement or derecognition of interests in structured entities; and
- gains or losses from the transfer of assets or liabilities to the structured entity.

[IFRS 12 Appendix A].

6.3.4 Disclosure of ranking and amounts of potential losses

Disclosure is required of the maximum limit of losses for a reporting entity where a reporting entity is required to absorb losses of a structured entity before other parties. This requirement is likely to be relevant for reporting entities which hold notes in securitised structured entities or where the interests in the structured entity are held are in the form of multiple contractually linked or 'tranched' notes.

An example of the type of disclosure that could be made is shown below.

Example 13.9: *Maximum exposure to and ranking of loss exposure by type of structured entity*

The following table shows the maximum exposure to loss for ABC Bank by type of structured entity and by seniority of interest, where ABC Bank's interest ranks lower than those of other investors and so ABC Bank absorbs losses before other parties.

€'000	Seniority of interests				
	Subordinated interests	Mezzanine interests	Senior interests	Most senior interests	Total
Mortgage backed securitisations					
i) ABC Bank's maximum exposure to loss	150	592	850	346	1,938
ii) Potential losses borne by more junior interests	–	897	7,875	10,332	19,104
CDOs and CLOs					
i) ABC Bank's maximum exposure to loss	60	167	243	32	502
ii) Potential losses borne by more junior interests	27	456	4,787	5,311	10,581
Asset backed commercial paper					
i) ABC Bank's maximum exposure to loss	–	–	–	379	379
ii) Potential losses borne by more junior interests	–	–	–	25	25

6.3.5 Disclosure of liquidity arrangements

This disclosure might include:

- liquidity arrangements, guarantees or other commitments provided by third parties to the structured entity which affect the fair value or risk of the reporting entity's interests in the structured entity; and
- liquidity arrangements, guarantees or other commitments provided by third parties to the reporting entity which affect the risks of the reporting entity's interests in the structured entity.

We do not believe that this disclosure is intended to include liquidity arrangements, guarantees or other commitments made by the structured entity to third parties as while an arrangement provided to a third party may itself qualify as an interest in a structured entity, it would not normally affect the fair value of an entity's interests in an unconsolidated structured entity.

6.3.6 Disclosure of funding difficulties

Disclosure of 'any difficulties' that a structured entity has experienced in financing its activities during a reporting period could potentially be wide-ranging. In practice, we believe that such a disclosure is likely to focus on issues of debt (including short-term commercial paper) and equity securities that have failed either in whole or in part.

6.3.7 Disclosure of the forms of funding of an unconsolidated structured entity

This disclosure appears to refer to the overall funding of the structured entity including forms of funding in which the reporting entity has not participated. A tabular presentation may be the most appropriate way of making this disclosure.

7 FUTURE DEVELOPMENTS

7.1 Post-implementation Review of IFRSs 10, 11 and 12

At its meeting in April 2020,[4] the IASB decided to proceed with the Post-implementation Review and publish a Request for Information. In relation to IFRS 12, the Board decided the Request for Information will focus on the quality of information an entity provides and whether and how well the disclosure objectives are met by an entity applying the requirements. The Board also decided that the Post-implementation Review would not cover the interaction of IFRS 10, IFRS 11 and IFRS 12 with other IFRS Standards. At the time of writing the chapter, the Board has indicated that the Request for Information will be published in the fourth quarter of 2020.

References

1 *IFRIC Update*, January 2015, p.6.
2 *IFRIC Update*, January 2015, p.7.
3 *IFRIC Update*, January 2015, p.7.
4 *IASB Update*, April 2020.

Chapter 14 Fair value measurement

1	INTRODUCTION AND BACKGROUND		1003
	1.1	Introduction	1003
		1.1.1 Post-implementation review	1004
	1.2	Overview of IFRS 13	1004
	1.3	Objective of IFRS 13	1006
2	SCOPE		1007
	2.1	Items in the scope of IFRS 13	1008
		2.1.1 Fair value disclosures	1008
		2.1.2 Measurements based on fair value	1009
		2.1.3 Short-term receivables and payables	1009
	2.2	Scope exclusions	1010
		2.2.1 Share-based payments	1010
		2.2.2 Lease transactions	1010
		2.2.3 Measurements similar to fair value	1011
		2.2.4 Exemptions from the disclosure requirements of IFRS 13	1011
	2.3	Present value techniques	1011
	2.4	Fair value measurement exceptions and practical expedients in other standards	1011
		2.4.1 Fair value measurement exceptions	1011
		2.4.2 Practical expedient for impaired financial assets carried at amortised cost	1012
	2.5	Practical expedients and measurement exceptions within IFRS 13	1012
		2.5.1 Practical expedients in IFRS 13	1012
		2.5.1.A Use of net asset value to measure fair value	1012
		2.5.2 Measurement exception to the fair value principles for financial instruments	1014
3	DEFINITIONS		1014
4	THE FAIR VALUE FRAMEWORK		1016

	4.1		Definition of fair value	1016
	4.2		The fair value measurement framework	1017
5	THE ASSET OR LIABILITY		1019
	5.1	The unit of account	1019
		5.1.1	Unit of account and P×Q	1020
		5.1.2	Unit of account and the portfolio exception	1022
		5.1.3	Unit of account versus the valuation premise	1024
		5.1.4	Does IFRS 13 allow fair value to be measured by reference to an asset's (or liability's) components?	1024
	5.2	Characteristics of the asset or liability	1025
		5.2.1	Condition and location	1025
		5.2.2	Restrictions on assets or liabilities	1026
			5.2.2.A In determining the fair value of a restricted security, is it appropriate to apply a constant discount percentage over the entire life of the restriction?	1028
			5.2.2.B Considerations when a restriction is present on a call option for its entire contractual life	1028
6	THE PRINCIPAL (OR MOST ADVANTAGEOUS) MARKET	1029
	6.1	The principal market	1030
		6.1.1	Can an entity have more than one principal market for the same asset or liability?	1031
		6.1.2	In situations where an entity has access to multiple markets, should the determination of the principal market be based on entity-specific volume and activity or market-based volume and activity?	1032
	6.2	The most advantageous market	1033
7	MARKET PARTICIPANTS	1034
	7.1	Characteristics of market participants	1034
	7.2	Market participant assumptions	1035
8	THE TRANSACTION	1038
	8.1	Evaluating whether there has been a significant decrease in the volume and level of activity for an asset or liability	1039
		8.1.1	Can a market exhibit a significant decrease in volume or level of activity and still be considered active?	1041
	8.2	Identifying transactions that are not orderly	1043
		8.2.1	Are all transactions entered into to meet regulatory requirements or transactions initiated during bankruptcy assumed to be not orderly?	1044
		8.2.2	Is it possible for orderly transactions to take place in a 'distressed' market?	1044

	8.3	Estimating fair value when there has been a significant decrease in the volume and level of activity	1045
		8.3.1 Assessing the relevance of observable data	1046
		8.3.2 Selection and use of valuation techniques when there has been a significant decrease in volume or level of activity	1047
9	THE PRICE		1050
	9.1	Transaction costs	1050
		9.1.1 Are transaction costs in IFRS 13 the same as 'costs to sell' in other IFRSs?	1051
		9.1.2 Transaction costs in IFRS 13 versus acquisition-related transaction costs in other IFRSs	1051
	9.2	Transportation costs	1052
10	APPLICATION TO NON-FINANCIAL ASSETS		1052
	10.1	Highest and best use	1053
		10.1.1 Highest and best use: determining what is legally permissible	1055
		10.1.2 Highest and best use versus current use	1056
		10.1.3 Highest and best use versus intended use (including defensive value)	1057
	10.2	Valuation premise for non-financial assets	1058
		10.2.1 Valuation premise – stand-alone basis	1059
		10.2.2 Valuation premise – in combination with other assets and/or liabilities	1059
		10.2.3 How should associated liabilities be considered when measuring the fair value of a non-financial asset?	1061
		10.2.4 Unit of account versus the valuation premise	1062
11	APPLICATION TO LIABILITIES AND AN ENTITY'S OWN EQUITY		1063
	11.1	General principles	1064
		11.1.1 Fair value of a liability	1064
		11.1.2 Fair value of an entity's own equity	1064
		11.1.3 Settlement value versus transfer value	1064
	11.2	Measuring the fair value of a liability or an entity's own equity when quoted prices for the liability or equity instruments are not available	1065
		11.2.1 Liabilities or an entity's own equity that are held by other parties as assets	1066
		11.2.2 Liabilities or an entity's own equity not held by other parties as assets	1069
		11.2.2.A Use of present value techniques to measure fair value for liabilities and an entity's own equity instruments not held by other parties as assets	1070

		11.2.2.B	Consideration of an entry price in measuring a liability or entity's own equity not held as an asset	1072
	11.3	Non-performance risk		1073
		11.3.1	Liabilities issued with third-party credit enhancements	1076
			11.3.1.A Do the requirements of IFRS 13 regarding third-party credit enhancements in a fair value measurement apply to liabilities other than debt?	1077
		11.3.2	Does IFRS 13 require an entity to consider the effects of both counterparty credit risk and its own credit risk when valuing its derivative transactions?	1078
		11.3.3	How should an entity incorporate credit risk into the valuation of its derivative contracts?	1078
			11.3.3.A How do credit adjustments work?	1079
			11.3.3.B Valuation methods	1080
			11.3.3.C Data challenges	1083
		11.3.4	Does the existence of master netting agreements and/or CSAs eliminate the need to consider an entity's own credit risk when measuring the fair value of derivative liabilities?	1085
			11.3.4.A Portfolio approaches and credit mitigation arrangements	1085
			11.3.4.B Portfolio-level credit adjustments	1086
	11.4	Restrictions preventing the transfer of a liability or an entity's own equity		1087
	11.5	Financial liability with a demand feature		1088
12	FINANCIAL ASSETS AND LIABILITIES WITH OFFSETTING POSITIONS			1088
	12.1	Criteria for using the portfolio approach for offsetting positions		1088
		12.1.1	Accounting policy considerations	1089
		12.1.2	Presentation considerations	1090
		12.1.3	Is there a minimum level of offset required to use the portfolio approach?	1090
		12.1.4	Can Level 1 instruments be included in a portfolio of financial instruments with offsetting risks when calculating the net exposure to a particular market risk?	1091
	12.2	Measuring fair value for offsetting positions		1092
		12.2.1	Exposure to market risks	1095
		12.2.2	Exposure to the credit risk of a particular counterparty	1096
13	FAIR VALUE AT INITIAL RECOGNITION			1096
	13.1	Exit price versus entry price		1096

	13.1.1	Assessing whether the transaction price equals fair value at initial recognition 1096
13.2	Day one gains and losses 1097	
	13.2.1	Day one losses for over-the-counter derivative transactions 1098
	13.2.2	Day one gains and losses when entry and exit markets for the transaction are deemed to be the same 1099
13.3	Related party transactions 1099	

14 VALUATION TECHNIQUES 1099

14.1	Selecting appropriate valuation techniques 1100	
	14.1.1	Single versus multiple valuation techniques 1101
	14.1.2	Using multiple valuation techniques to measure fair value 1101
	14.1.3	Valuation adjustments 1104
		14.1.3.A Adjustments to valuation techniques that use unobservable inputs 1105
	14.1.4	Making changes to valuation techniques 1105
14.2	Market approach 1106	
14.3	Cost approach 1107	
	14.3.1	Use of depreciated replacement cost to measure fair value 1107
14.4	Income approach 1108	

15 INPUTS TO VALUATION TECHNIQUES 1108

15.1	General principles 1108	
15.2	Premiums and discounts 1111	
	15.2.1	Blockage factors (or block discounts) 1112
15.3	Pricing within the bid-ask spread 1114	
	15.3.1	Mid-market pricing 1114
	15.3.2	What does the bid-ask spread include? 1114
15.4	Risk premiums 1115	
15.5	Broker quotes and pricing services 1116	
	15.5.1	How should values provided by central clearing organisations for margin purposes be evaluated when determining the fair value of centrally cleared derivatives for financial reporting? 1117

16 THE FAIR VALUE HIERARCHY 1117

16.1	The fair value hierarchy 1118	
16.2	Categorisation within the fair value hierarchy 1118	
	16.2.1	Assessing the significance of inputs 1120
	16.2.2	Transfers between levels within the fair value hierarchy 1122
	16.2.3	Information provided by third-party pricing services or brokers 1122

			16.2.4	Categorisation of over-the-counter derivative instruments......1124

17 LEVEL 1 INPUTS 1125
- 17.1 Use of Level 1 inputs...1125
  - 17.1.1 Level 1 liabilities and instruments classified in an entity's own equity...1126
- 17.2 Alternative pricing methods...1126
- 17.3 Quoted prices in active markets that are not representative of fair value...1126
- 17.4 Unit of account...1127

18 LEVEL 2 INPUTS 1127
- 18.1 Use of Level 2 inputs 1127
- 18.2 Examples of Level 2 inputs 1128
- 18.3 Market corroborated inputs...1129
- 18.4 Making adjustments to a Level 2 input..1130
- 18.5 Recently observed prices in an inactive market....................................1130

19 LEVEL 3 INPUTS 1131
- 19.1 Use of Level 3 inputs 1131
- 19.2 Examples of Level 3 inputs..1132

20 DISCLOSURES 1133
- 20.1 Disclosure objectives..1133
  - 20.1.1 Format of disclosures 1135
  - 20.1.2 Level of disaggregation..1135
    - 20.1.2.A Determining appropriate classes of assets and liabilities for disclosure 1135
  - 20.1.3 Differentiating between 'recurring' and 'non-recurring' 1136
- 20.2 Accounting policy disclosures 1137
- 20.3 Disclosures for recognised fair value measurements...........................1138
  - 20.3.1 Disclosures for recognised recurring fair value measurements..1139
    - 20.3.1.A Recurring fair value measurements categorised as Level 1 or Level 2 1139
    - 20.3.1.B Recurring fair value measurements categorised as Level 3 1139
  - 20.3.2 Disclosures for recognised non-recurring fair value measurements..1140
  - 20.3.3 Fair value hierarchy categorisation... 1141
  - 20.3.4 Transfers between hierarchy levels for recurring fair value measurements..1144
  - 20.3.5 Disclosure of valuation techniques and inputs........................1146

		20.3.5.A	Significant unobservable inputs for Level 3 fair value measurements 1146
	20.3.6		Level 3 reconciliation 1149
	20.3.7		Disclosure of valuation processes for Level 3 measurements 1151
	20.3.8		Sensitivity of Level 3 measurements to changes in significant unobservable inputs 1152
		20.3.8.A	Quantitative sensitivity of Level 3 measurements of financial instruments to changes in significant unobservable inputs 1153
	20.3.9		Highest and best use 1156
20.4	Disclosures for unrecognised fair value measurements 1156
20.5	Disclosures regarding liabilities issued with an inseparable third-party credit enhancement 1156
20.6	Proposed amendments resulting from the Targeted Standards-level Review of Disclosures project 1157

21 APPLICATION GUIDANCE – PRESENT VALUE TECHNIQUES 1159

21.1	General principles for use of present value techniques 1159
21.2	The components of a present value measurement 1161
	21.2.1 Time value of money 1162
	21.2.2 Risk and uncertainty in a present value technique 1162
21.3	Discount rate adjustment technique 1163
	21.3.1 Illustrative example of the discount rate adjustment technique 1165
21.4	Expected present value technique 1165
	21.4.1 Expected present value technique – method 1 and method 2 1167

22 CONVERGENCE WITH US GAAP 1170

22.1	The development of IFRS 13 1170
22.2	US GAAP differences 1171
	22.2.1 Practical expedient for alternative investments 1171
	22.2.2 Fair value of liabilities with a demand feature 1172
	22.2.3 Recognition of day-one gains and losses 1172
	22.2.4 Disclosures 1172

List of examples

Example 14.1:	Adjusting fair value for condition and location 1026
Example 14.2:	Restrictions on assets 1026
Example 14.3:	Entity-specific restrictions on assets 1027
Example 14.4:	The effect of determining the principal market 1029

Example 14.5:	Determining the principal market – consistent principal market	1032
Example 14.6:	Determining the principal market – market-based versus entity-specific	1032
Example 14.7:	Determining the most advantageous market	1033
Example 14.8:	Considering different market participants when determining the highest and best use of an asset group	1036
Example 14.9:	Estimating a market rate of return when there is a significant decrease in volume or level of activity	1047
Example 14.10:	Transportation costs	1052
Example 14.11:	Highest and best use versus current use	1056
Example 14.12:	Highest and best use versus intended use	1058
Example 14.13:	Consistent assumptions about highest and best use in an asset group	1060
Example 14.14:	Debt obligation: quoted price	1068
Example 14.15:	Debt obligation: present value technique	1068
Example 14.16:	Decommissioning liability	1071
Example 14.17:	Non-performance risk	1074
Example 14.18:	Structured note	1074
Example 14.19:	Applying the portfolio approach to a group of financial assets and financial liabilities whose market risks are substantially the same and whose fair value measurement is categorised within Level 1 of the fair value hierarchy	1093
Example 14.20:	Calculating net exposure	1094
Example 14.21:	Interest rate swap at initial recognition	1098
Example 14.22:	Multiple valuation techniques – software asset	1102
Example 14.23:	Multiple valuation techniques – machine held and used	1103
Example 14.24:	Blockage factors	1113
Example 14.25:	Disclosure of assets measured at fair value and their categorisation in the fair value hierarchy	1142
Example 14.26:	Comparison of policies for recognising transfers	1145
Example 14.27:	Significant unobservable inputs (Level 3)	1148
Example 14.28:	Reconciliation of fair value measurements categorised within Level 3 of the fair value hierarchy	1150
Example 14.29:	Disclosure of gains and losses included in profit or loss for fair value measurements categorised within Level 3 of the fair value hierarchy	1151
Example 14.30:	Narrative description of sensitivity to significant unobservable inputs	1153
Example 14.31:	Discount rate adjustment technique	1165
Example 14.32:	Expected present value techniques	1168
Example 14.33:	Comparison of present value techniques	1169

Chapter 14 Fair value measurement

1 INTRODUCTION AND BACKGROUND

1.1 Introduction

Many IFRSs permit or require entities to measure or disclose the fair value of assets, liabilities or equity instruments. However, until 2011 there was limited guidance in IFRS on how to measure fair value and, in some cases, the guidance was conflicting. To remedy this, the International Accounting Standards Board (IASB or the Board) issued IFRS 13 – *Fair Value Measurement* – in May 2011. The standard was the result of a convergence project between the IASB and the US Financial Accounting Standards Board (FASB) (collectively, the Boards). The standard first applied to annual periods beginning on or after 1 January 2013. *[IFRS 13.C1]*.

IFRS 13 defines fair value, provides principles-based guidance on how to measure fair value under IFRS and requires information about those fair value measurements to be disclosed. *[IFRS 13.1]*. IFRS 13 does not attempt to remove the judgement that is involved in estimating fair value, however, it provides a framework that is intended to reduce inconsistency and increase comparability in the fair value measurements used in financial reporting.

IFRS 13 does not address which assets or liabilities to measure at fair value or when those measurements must be performed. An entity must look to the other standards in that regard. The standard applies to all fair value measurements, when fair value is required or permitted by IFRS, with some limited exceptions, which are discussed later in this chapter (see 2 below). The standard also applies to measurements, such as fair value less costs to sell, that are based on fair value. However, it does not apply to similar measurement bases, such as value in use.

This chapter outlines the requirements of IFRS 13, its definitions, measurement framework and disclosure requirements. It addresses some of the key questions that are being asked about how to apply IFRS 13, recognising that some aspects of the standard are still unclear and different views may exist. Further issues and questions may be raised in the future as entities continue to apply the standard and practices evolve.

1.1.1 Post-implementation review

During 2018, the IASB concluded its post-implementation review (PIR) of IFRS 13, which was intended to assess the effect of the standard on financial reporting. In particular, the Board's aim was to assess 'whether:

- the information required by IFRS 13 is useful to users of financial statements;
- areas of IFRS 13 present implementation challenges and might result in inconsistent application of the requirements; and
- unexpected costs have arisen when preparing, auditing or enforcing the requirements of IFRS 13 or when obtaining the information that the Standard requires entities to provide.'[1]

Areas of focus in the PIR included: the usefulness of disclosures about fair value measurements; whether to prioritise unit of account or the use of Level 1 inputs; applying the requirements for highest and best use in fair value measurements of non-financial assets; and the use of judgement in relation to specific areas of IFRS 13 (e.g. assessing whether a market is active (see 8.1.1 below), determining whether an unobservable input is significant when categorising a fair value measurement within the hierarchy (see 16.2.1 below).[2]

In December 2018, the IASB released its Report and Feedback Statement on the PIR of IFRS 13, in which it stated its conclusion that IFRS 13 is working as it intended. As a result of the PIR, the Board decided to:

a. feed the PIR findings regarding the usefulness of disclosures into the Board's work on Better Communication in Financial Reporting, in particular, into the Targeted Standards-level Review of Disclosures and the Primary Financial Statements projects;

b. continue liaising with the valuation profession, monitor new developments in practice and promote knowledge development and sharing; and

c. conduct no other follow-up activities as a result of findings from the PIR.[3]

In 2018, the Board selected IFRS 13 as one of the two Standards (the other was IAS 19 – *Employee Benefits*) on which to test the draft guidance for the Board to use when developing and drafting disclosure objectives and requirements in future. During 2019 and 2020, the Board decided to propose amendments to the disclosure objective of IFRS 13 and items of information that could be used to meet those objectives. At the time of writing, the Board was expected to publish its exposure draft in March 2021 and allow 180 days for comment.[4] The proposed amendments are discussed further at 20.6 below.

1.2 Overview of IFRS 13

The framework of IFRS 13 is based on a number of key concepts including unit of account, exit price, valuation premise, highest and best use, principal market, market participant assumptions and the fair value hierarchy. The requirements incorporate financial theory and valuation techniques, but are solely focused on how these concepts are to be applied when determining fair value for financial reporting purposes.

IFRS 13 does not address the issue of what to measure at fair value or when to measure fair value. The IASB separately considers these issues on a project-by-project basis. Other IFRSs determine which items must be measured at fair value and when. IFRS 13 addresses how to measure fair value. The principles in IFRS 13 provide the IASB with a consistent definition that, together with the *Conceptual Framework for Financial Reporting* (see Chapter 2 at 9), will assist in determining whether fair value is the appropriate measurement basis to be used in any given future project.

The definition of fair value in IFRS 13 is based on an exit price notion, which incorporates the following key concepts:

- Fair value is the price to sell an asset or transfer a liability and, therefore, represents an exit price, not an entry price.
- The exit price for an asset or liability is conceptually different from its transaction price (an entry price). While exit and entry price may be identical in many situations, the transaction price is not presumed to represent the fair value of an asset or liability on its initial recognition.
- Fair value is an exit price in the principal market, i.e. the market with the highest volume and level of activity. In the absence of a principal market, it is assumed that the transaction to sell the asset or transfer the liability would occur in the most advantageous market. This is the market that would maximise the amount that would be received to sell an asset or minimise the amount that would be paid to transfer a liability, taking into account transport and transaction costs. In either case, the entity must have access to the market on the measurement date.

  While transaction costs are considered in determining the most advantageous market, they do not form part of a fair value measurement (i.e. they are not added to or deducted from the price used to measure fair value). However, an exit price would be adjusted for transportation costs if location is a characteristic of the asset or liability being measured. This is discussed further at 9 below.
- Fair value is a market-based measurement, not an entity-specific measurement. When determining fair value, management uses the assumptions that market participants would use when pricing the asset or liability. However, an entity need not identify specific market participants.

These key concepts and the following aspects of the guidance in IFRS 13 require particular focus when applying the standard.

- If another standard provides a fair value measurement exemption that applies when fair value cannot be measured reliably, an entity may need to consider the measurement framework in IFRS 13 in order to determine whether fair value can be reliably measured (see 2 below).
- If there is a principal market for the asset or liability, a fair value measurement represents the price in that market at the measurement date (regardless of whether that price is directly observable or estimated using another valuation technique), even if the price in a different market is potentially more advantageous (see 6 below).
- Fair value measurements should take into consideration the characteristics of the asset or liability being measured, but not characteristics of the transaction to sell the asset or transfer a liability. Transportation costs, for example, must be deducted from the price used to measure fair value when location is a characteristic of the item being measured at fair value (see 5 and 9 below). This principle also clarifies when a restriction on the sale or use of an asset or transfer of a liability affects the measurement of fair value (see 5 below) and when premiums and discounts can be included.

- In particular, an entity is prohibited from making adjustments for the size of an entity's holding in comparison to current trading volumes (i.e. blockage factors, see 15 below).
- The fair value measurement of non-financial assets must reflect the highest and best use of the asset from a market participant's perspective, which might be its current use or some alternative use. This establishes whether to assume a market participant would derive value from using the non-financial asset on its own or in combination with other assets or with other assets and liabilities (see 10 below).
- The standard clarifies that a fair value measurement of a liability must consider non-performance risk (which includes, but is not limited to, an entity's own credit risk, see 11 below).
- IFRS 13 provides guidance on how to measure the fair value of an entity's own equity instruments (see 11 below) and aligns it with the fair value measurement of liabilities. If there are no quoted prices available for the transfer of an identical or a similar liability or entity's own equity instrument, but the identical item is held by another party as an asset, an entity uses the fair value of the corresponding asset (from the perspective of the market participant that holds that asset) to measure the fair value of the liability or equity instrument. When no corresponding asset exists, the fair value of the liability is measured from the perspective of a market participant that owes the liability (see 11 below).
- A measurement exception in IFRS 13 allows entities to measure financial instruments with offsetting risks on a portfolio basis, provided certain criteria are met both initially and on an ongoing basis (see 12 below).
- The requirements of IFRS 13 in relation to valuation techniques apply to all methods of measuring fair value. Traditionally, references to valuation techniques in IFRS have indicated a lack of market-based information with which to value an asset or liability. Valuation techniques as discussed in IFRS 13 are broader and, importantly, include market-based approaches (see 14 below). When selecting inputs to use, an entity must prioritise observable inputs over unobservable inputs (see 16 below).
- IFRS 13 provides application guidance to assist entities measuring fair value in situations where there has been a decrease in the volume or level of activity (see 8 below).
- Categorisation within the fair value hierarchy is required for all fair value measurements. Disclosures required by IFRS 13 are substantially greater for those fair value measurements that are categorised within Level 3 (see 16 and 20 below).

1.3 Objective of IFRS 13

A primary goal of IFRS 13 is to increase the consistency and comparability of fair value measurements used in financial reporting under IFRS. It provides a common objective whenever IFRS permits or requires a fair value measurement, irrespective of the type of asset or liability being measured or the entity that holds it.

The objective of a fair value measurement is to estimate the price at which an orderly transaction would take place between market participants under the market conditions that exist at the measurement date. *[IFRS 13.2]*.

By highlighting that fair value considers market conditions that exist at the measurement date, the IASB is emphasising that the intent of the measurement is to convey the current value of the asset or liability at the measurement date and not its potential value at some future date. In addition, a fair value measurement does not consider management's intent to sell the asset or transfer the liability at the measurement date. Instead, it represents a market-based measurement that contemplates a hypothetical transaction between market participants at the measurement date (these concepts are discussed further at 6 to 9 below). *[IFRS 13.3]*.

IFRS 13 makes it clear that the objective of a fair value measurement remains the same, regardless of the reason for the fair value measurement (e.g. impairment testing or a recurring measurement) or the extent of observable information available to support the measurement. While the standard requires that the inputs used to measure fair value be prioritised based on their relative observability (see 16 below), the nature of the inputs does not affect the objective of the measurement. That is, the requirement to determine an exit price under current market conditions is not relaxed because the reporting entity cannot observe similar assets or liabilities being transacted at the measurement date. *[IFRS 13.2]*.

Even when fair value is estimated using significant unobservable inputs (because observable inputs do not exist), the goal is to determine an exit price based on the assumptions that market participants would consider when transacting for the asset or liability on the measurement date, including assumptions about risk. This might require the inclusion of a risk premium in the measurement to compensate market participants for the uncertainty inherent in the expected cash flows of the asset or liability being measured. *[IFRS 13.3]*.

IFRS 13 generally does not provide specific rules or detailed 'how-to' guidance. Given the broad use of fair value measurements in accounting for various kinds of assets and liabilities (both financial and non-financial), providing detailed valuation guidance was not deemed practical. As such, the application of IFRS 13 requires significant judgement; but this judgement is applied using the core concepts of the standard's principles-based framework for fair value measurements.

2 SCOPE

IFRS 13 applies whenever another IFRS requires or permits the measurement or disclosure of fair value, or a measure that is based on fair value (such as fair value less costs to sell), *[IFRS 13.5]*, with the following exceptions:

(a) The measurement and disclosure requirements do not apply to:
- share-based payment transactions within the scope of IFRS 2 – *Share-based Payment;*
- leasing transactions accounted for in accordance with IFRS 16 – *Leases* (see 2.2.2 below); and
- measurements that are similar to fair value, but are not fair value, such as net realisable value in IAS 2 – *Inventories* – or value in use in IAS 36 – *Impairment of Assets* (see 2.2.3 below). *[IFRS 13.6]*.

(b) The measurement requirements in IFRS 13 apply, but the disclosure requirements do not apply to:
- plan assets measured at fair value in accordance with IAS 19;
- retirement benefit plan investments measured at fair value in accordance with IAS 26 – *Accounting and Reporting by Retirement Benefit Plans*; and
- assets for which recoverable amount is fair value less costs of disposal in accordance with IAS 36 (see 2.2.4 below). *[IFRS 13.7]*.

2.1 Items in the scope of IFRS 13

The measurement framework in IFRS 13 applies to both fair value measurements on initial recognition and subsequent fair value measurements, if permitted or required by another IFRS. *[IFRS 13.8]*. This includes both assets and liabilities, as well as an entity's own equity instruments measured at fair value. *[IFRS 13.4]*. Fair value measurement at initial recognition is discussed further at 13 below.

IFRS 13 establishes how to measure fair value. It does not prescribe:
- what should be measured at fair value;
- when to measure fair value (i.e. the measurement date); or
- how (or whether) to account for any subsequent changes in fair value (e.g. in profit or loss or in other comprehensive income). However, the standard does partly address day one gains or losses on initial recognition at fair value, requiring that they be recognised in profit or loss immediately unless the IFRS that permits or requires initial measurement at fair value specifies otherwise.

An entity must consider the relevant IFRSs (e.g. IFRS 3 – *Business Combinations*, IFRS 9 – *Financial Instruments*, IAS 40 – *Investment Property*) for each of these requirements.

Note that IFRS 9 became effective for annual periods beginning on or after 1 January 2018, superseding IAS 39 – *Financial Instruments: Recognition and Measurement*. However, entities that are applying IFRS 4 – *Insurance Contracts*, have an optional temporary exemption that permits an insurance company whose activities are predominantly connected with insurance to defer adoption of IFRS 9. If an entity uses this optional exemption, it continues to apply IAS 39 until it first applies IFRS 17 – *Insurance Contracts*. IFRS 17 is effective for annual periods beginning on or after 1 January 2023. All entities are also allowed to continue applying IAS 39 hedge accounting requirements. References to IFRS 9 in this chapter are also relevant for IAS 39.

2.1.1 Fair value disclosures

The scope of IFRS 13 includes disclosures of fair value. This refers to situations where an entity is permitted, or may be required, by a standard or interpretation to disclose the fair value of an item whose carrying amount in the financial statements is not fair value. Examples include:
- IAS 40, which requires the fair value to be disclosed for investment properties measured using the cost model; *[IAS 40.79(e)]* and

- IFRS 7 – *Financial Instruments: Disclosures*, which requires the fair value of financial instruments that are subsequently measured at amortised cost in accordance with IFRS 9 to be disclosed. *[IFRS 7.25]*.

In such situations, the disclosed fair value must be measured in accordance with IFRS 13 and an entity would also need to make certain disclosures about that fair value measurement in accordance with IFRS 13 (see 20 below).

In certain circumstances, IFRS 7 provides relief from the requirement to disclose the fair value of a financial instrument that is not measured subsequently at fair value. An example is when the carrying amount is considered a reasonable approximation of fair value. *[IFRS 7.29]*. In these situations, an entity would not need to measure the fair value of the financial asset or financial liability for disclosure purposes. However, it would need to consider the requirements of IFRS 13 in order to determine whether the carrying amount is a reasonable approximation of fair value.

2.1.2 Measurements based on fair value

The measurement of amounts (whether recognised or only disclosed) that are based on fair value, such as fair value less costs to sell, are within the scope of IFRS 13. This includes the following:

- a non-current asset (or disposal group) held for sale measured at fair value less costs to sell in accordance with IFRS 5 – *Non-current Assets Held for Sale and Discontinued Operations*, where the fair value less costs to sell is lower than its carrying amount (see Chapter 4);
- commodity inventories that are held by commodity broker-traders and measured at fair value less costs to sell, as discussed in IAS 2 (see Chapter 22);
- where the recoverable amount for an asset or cash-generating unit(s), determined in accordance with IAS 36, is its fair value less costs of disposal. This includes impairment testing of investments in associates accounted for in accordance with IAS 28 – *Investments in Associates and Joint Ventures*, where that standard requires the test to be performed in accordance with IAS 36 (see Chapter 20); and
- biological assets (including produce growing on a bearer plant), agricultural produce measured at fair value less costs to sell in accordance with IAS 41 – *Agriculture* (see Chapter 42).

In each of these situations, the fair value component is measured in accordance with IFRS 13. Costs to sell or costs of disposal are determined in accordance with the applicable standard, for example, IFRS 5.

2.1.3 Short-term receivables and payables

Prior to the issuance of IFRS 13, paragraph B5.4.12 of the then extant IFRS 9 allowed entities to measure short-term receivables and payables with no stated interest rate at invoice amounts without discounting, when the effect of not discounting was immaterial. *[IFRS 9(2012).B5.4.12]*. That paragraph was deleted as a consequence of the IASB issuing IFRS 13.

In the absence of that paragraph, some questioned whether discounting would be required for such short-term receivables and payables. The IASB amended IFRS 13, as part of its 2010-2012 cycle of *Improvements to IFRSs*, to clarify that, when making those amendments to IFRS 9, it did not intend to remove the ability to measure such short-term receivables and payables at their invoice amount. The Board also noted that, when the effects of applying them are immaterial, paragraph 8 of IAS 8 – *Accounting Policies, Changes in Accounting Estimates and Errors* – permits entities not to apply accounting policies set out in IFRSs. *[IFRS 13.BC138A, IAS 8.8].*

2.2 Scope exclusions

2.2.1 Share-based payments

IFRS 2 requires certain share-based payments to be measured at grant date fair value (see Chapter 34). However, the objective of an IFRS 2 fair value measurement is not entirely consistent with IFRS 13. Rather than trying to distinguish between these two measures, the IASB decided to exclude share-based payment transactions that are accounted for in accordance with IFRS 2 from the scope of IFRS 13. The grant date fair value of such share-based payments is, therefore, measured and disclosed in accordance with IFRS 2, not IFRS 13. *[IFRS 13.BC21].*

2.2.2 Lease transactions

As noted at 2 above, the standard does not apply to any leasing transactions accounted for in accordance with IFRS 16. The fair value measurement and disclosures requirements in IFRS 16 apply instead (see Chapter 23 for further discussion on IFRS 16). This scope exception does not extend to lease assets acquired or liabilities assumed in a business combination in accordance with IFRS 3. IFRS 13 would apply to that measurement of fair value. In addition, after adoption of IFRS 16, an entity may need to apply IFRS 13 to sale and leaseback transactions.

At the time of issuing IFRS 13, the IASB noted that applying IFRS 13's requirements might have significantly changed the classification of leases and the timing of recognising gains or losses for sale and leaseback transactions. In addition, at the time that the IASB was undertaking its leases project (which resulted in the issuance of IFRS 16) and the IASB was concerned that such a requirement may have required entities to make potentially burdensome significant changes to their accounting systems for IFRS 13 and the new leases standard. *[IFRS 13.BC22].*

While it is clear that leasing transactions that were within the scope of IFRS 16 are excluded from IFRS 13, lease liabilities (for lessees) and finance lease receivables (for lessors) are financial instruments, per paragraph AG9 of IAS 32 – *Financial Instruments: Presentation*, and are, therefore, within the scope of IFRS 7. *[IFRS 7.3, IAS 32.AG9].* As discussed at 2.1.1 above, paragraph 25 of IFRS 7 requires an entity to disclose, for each class of financial asset and financial liability, a comparison of fair value to carrying amount (except where the carrying amount is a reasonable approximation of fair value). *[IFRS 7.25, 29(a)].* Lease liabilities are explicitly excluded from this disclosure requirements. *[IFRS 7.29(d)].* However, finance lease receivables are not. Therefore, since IFRS 7 is not excluded from the scope of IFRS 13, lessors will need to measure the fair value of finance lease receivables in accordance with IFRS 13, in order to provide that IFRS 7 disclosure (unless the carrying amount is a reasonable approximation for fair value).

2.2.3 Measurements similar to fair value

Some IFRSs permit or require measurements that are similar to fair value, but are not fair value. These measures are excluded from the scope of IFRS 13. Such measures may be derived using techniques that are similar to those permitted in IFRS 13. IAS 36, for example, requires value in use to be determined using discounted cash flows (see Chapter 20). An entity may also consider the selling price of an asset, for example, in determining net realisable value for inventories in accordance with IAS 2 (see Chapter 22). Despite these similarities, the objective is not to measure fair value. Therefore, IFRS 13 does not apply to these measurements.

2.2.4 Exemptions from the disclosure requirements of IFRS 13

As noted at 2 above, IFRS 13's disclosure requirements do not apply to plan assets measured at fair value in accordance with IAS 19, retirement benefit plan investments measured at fair value in accordance with IAS 26 and assets for which recoverable amount is fair value less costs of disposal in accordance with IAS 36.

In addition, the disclosure requirements in IFRS 13 do not apply to any fair value measurements at initial recognition. That is, the disclosure requirements of IFRS 13 apply to fair value measurements after initial recognition (this is discussed further at 20 below).

The fair value measurement requirements of IFRS 13 still apply to each of these items above, even though the disclosure requirements do not. Therefore, an entity would measure the item in accordance with IFRS 13 and then make the required disclosures in accordance with the applicable standard (i.e. IAS 19, IAS 26, IAS 36) or the standard that requires fair value at initial recognition. For example, an entity that acquires a brand as part of a business combination would be required by IFRS 3 to measure the intangible asset at fair value at initial recognition. The acquirer would measure the asset's fair value in accordance with IFRS 13, but would disclose information about that fair value measurement in accordance with IFRS 3 (since those fair values are measured at initial recognition), not IFRS 13.

2.3 Present value techniques

IFRS 13 provides guidance for using present value techniques, such as a discounted cash flow analysis, to measure fair value (see 21 below for additional discussion on the application of present value techniques). However, the use of present value techniques does not always result in a fair value measurement. As discussed in 2.2.3 above, some IFRSs use present value techniques to measure assets and liabilities at amounts that are not intended to represent a fair value measurement. Unless the objective is to measure fair value, IFRS 13 does not apply.

2.4 Fair value measurement exceptions and practical expedients in other standards

2.4.1 Fair value measurement exceptions

Some standards provide an exception to a requirement to measure an asset or liability at fair value. IFRS 13 does not eliminate these exceptions. *[IFRS 13.BC8]*.

IFRS typically limits fair value measurement exceptions to circumstances where fair value is not reliably measurable and, where applied, requires the application of a cost model. For example, IAS 41 permits the use of a cost model if, on initial recognition of a biological asset, an entity is able to rebut the presumption that fair value can be reliably measured. In addition, it requires an entity to revert to the fair value model if fair value subsequently becomes reliably measurable. *[IAS 41.30].* Additional disclosures are often required to explain why fair value cannot be reliably measured and, if possible, the range of estimates within which fair value is highly likely to lie, as is required in IAS 40 for investment properties, for example. *[IAS 40.79(e)(iii)].*

In these situations, an entity would need to consider the requirements of IFRS 13 in order to determine whether fair value can be reliably measured. If the entity concludes that it could reliably measure fair value based on the requirements of IFRS 13, even in situations where observable information is not available, it would not be able to apply these exceptions.

2.4.2 Practical expedient for impaired financial assets carried at amortised cost

Prior to the issuance of IFRS 9, IAS 39 allowed, as a practical expedient, creditors to measure the impairment of a financial asset carried at amortised cost based on an instrument's fair value using an observable market price. *[IAS 39(2017).AG84].* If the practical expedient was used, IFRS 13 applied to the measurement of fair value. When the practical expedient was not used, the measurement objective was not intended to be fair value (and IFRS 13 did not apply). Instead, IAS 39's requirements for measuring the impairment of the financial asset carried at amortised cost applied.

Under IFRS 9, entities are allowed to use observable market information to estimate the credit risk of a particular or similar financial instrument and as a consequence the fair value can no longer be used. Instead, IFRS 9's requirements for measuring the impairment of the financial asset carried at amortised cost would apply.

2.5 Practical expedients and measurement exceptions within IFRS 13

2.5.1 Practical expedients in IFRS 13

In addition to the various practicability exceptions discussed at 2.4 above, IFRS 13 provides two practical expedients to assist with applying the fair value framework in certain instances. These practical expedients, each of which is discussed separately in this chapter, are the use of mid-market pricing within a bid-ask spread (see 15.3.1 below) and the use of alternative pricing methods (e.g. matrix pricing) when an entity holds a large number of similar assets and liabilities for which quoted prices exist, but are not easily accessible (see 17.2 below).

2.5.1.A Use of net asset value to measure fair value

Under US GAAP, the equivalent standard, Topic 820 – *Fair Value Measurement* – in the FASB Accounting Standards Codification (ASC 820), provides a practical expedient to measure the fair value of certain investments in investment companies using net asset value (NAV) or its equivalent if certain criteria are met. However, IFRS 13 does not explicitly permit the use of NAV to estimate the fair value of certain alternative investments. Therefore, under IFRS, NAV cannot be presumed to equal fair value, as the asset that is being measured is the equity investment in an investment entity, not the underlying assets (and liabilities) of the investment entity itself. While NAV may represent the fair value of the equity interest in certain situations (for example, in situations where an open-ended fund provides a source of liquidity through ongoing subscriptions and redemptions at NAV), one cannot presume this to be the case. Instead, the characteristics of the investment being measured need be considered when determining its fair value (differences from US GAAP are discussed further at 22 below).

If a quoted price in an active market for an identical instrument is available (i.e. a Level 1 input), the fair value of the equity instrument would need to be measured using that price, even if this deviates from NAV. An example where the Level 1 input may differ from NAV is shares in certain closed-end funds that trade on exchanges at prices that differ from the reported NAV of the funds.

In situations where there is no quoted price for an identical instrument, reported NAV may represent a starting point in estimating fair value. However, adjustments may be required to reflect the specific characteristics that market participants would consider in pricing the equity investment in an investment entity. It may be helpful to understand the factors that would reconcile a reported NAV of the investment entity to the fair value used by the reporting entity in order to provide explanations to investors, if necessary, and to support disclosures required by IFRS 13 and other IFRSs. Factors to consider include, but are not limited to, the following:

(a) Is the reported NAV an appropriate input for use in measuring fair value?

Before concluding that the reported NAV is an appropriate input when measuring fair value, a reporting entity should evaluate the effectiveness of the investment entity's valuation practices, by considering the valuation techniques and inputs used by the investment entity when estimating NAV. This assists in determining whether the investment entity's valuation practices and inputs are aligned with those that would need to be used by a market participant in respect of the equity instruments of the investment entity.

(b) Are adjustments to reported NAV needed to reflect characteristics that market participants would consider in pricing an equity investment?

A reporting entity should consider the characteristics of the equity investment that are not reflected in reported NAV. The fair value of the underlying assets within an investment entity would, for example, ignore any restrictions or possible obligations imposed on the holder of an equity investment in an investment entity. Obligations may take the form of commitments to contribute further capital, as and when called for by the investment entity. If market participants would be expected to place a discount or premium on the reported NAV because of features, risk or other factors relating to the equity investment, then the fair value measurement of the investment would need to be adjusted for those factors.

However, in some cases adjustments to NAV may not be required. For example, if a fund is open to new investors, presumably the fair value of the fund investment would not be expected to exceed the amount that a new investor would be required to invest directly with the fund to obtain a similar interest. Similarly, the hypothetical seller of a fund investment would not be expected to accept lower proceeds than it would receive by redeeming its investment directly with the fund (if possible). As such, the willingness and ability of an investment entity to provide a source of liquidity for the investment through subscriptions and redemptions are important considerations in assessing whether adjustments to NAV would be required in determining the exit price of an investment.

Information related to relevant secondary market transactions should be considered unless they are determined to be disorderly. Limited Partners in such funds may seek to sell their investments for a variety of reasons, including mergers or acquisitions, the need for liquidity or a change in strategy, among others. While premiums have been observed in practice, discounts on sales of investments in investment entities are also common. Likewise, sales of an investment in an investment entity to independent third parties at the reported NAV without a premium or discount, may suggest that no adjustment is needed.

2.5.2 Measurement exception to the fair value principles for financial instruments

IFRS 13 makes it clear that the concepts of 'highest and best use' and 'valuation premise' only apply to the measurement of non-financial assets. Such concepts could have significantly changed the valuation of some over-the-counter (OTC) derivatives, many of which are measured on a portfolio basis. That is, reporting entities typically determine valuation adjustments related to bid-ask spreads and credit risk for OTC derivative contracts considering the net exposure of a portfolio of contracts to a particular market risk or credit risk. To address this concern, IFRS 13 provides an exception to the principles of fair value when measuring financial instruments with offsetting risks, if certain criteria are met.

The exception allows an entity to estimate the fair value of a portfolio of financial instruments based on the sale or transfer of its net position for a particular market risk exposure (rather than to the individual instruments in the portfolio). The exception also enables an entity to consider its credit exposure to a particular counterparty on a net basis, provided there is an arrangement in place that mitigates credit risk upon default (e.g. a master netting agreement).

See 12 below for additional discussion on measuring the fair value of financial assets and financial liabilities with offsetting risks.

3 DEFINITIONS

The following table summarises the terms that are defined in IFRS 13. *[IFRS 13 Appendix A]*.

Figure 14.1: IFRS 13 Definitions

Term	Definition
Active market	A market in which transactions for the asset or liability take place with sufficient frequency and volume to provide pricing information on an ongoing basis.
Cost approach	A valuation technique that reflects the amount that would be required currently to replace the service capacity of an asset (often referred to as current replacement cost).
Entry price	The price paid to acquire an asset or received to assume a liability in an exchange transaction.
Exit price	The price that would be received to sell an asset or paid to transfer a liability.
Expected cash flow	The probability-weighted average (i.e. mean of the distribution) of possible future cash flows.
Fair value	The price that would be received to sell an asset or paid to transfer a liability in an orderly transaction between market participants at the measurement date.

Highest and best use	The use of a non-financial asset by market participants that would maximise the value of the asset or the group of assets and liabilities (e.g. a business) within which the asset would be used.
Income approach	Valuation techniques that convert future amounts (e.g. cash flows or income and expenses) to a single current (i.e. discounted) amount. The fair value measurement is determined on the basis of the value indicated by current market expectations about those future amounts.
Inputs	The assumptions that market participants would use when pricing the asset or liability, including assumptions about risk, such as the following: (a) the risk inherent in a particular valuation technique used to measure fair value (such as a pricing model); and (b) the risk inherent in the inputs to the valuation technique. Inputs may be observable or unobservable.
Level 1 inputs	Quoted prices (unadjusted) in active markets for identical assets or liabilities that the entity can access at the measurement date.
Level 2 inputs	Inputs other than quoted prices included within Level 1 that are observable for the asset or liability, either directly or indirectly.
Level 3 inputs	Unobservable inputs for the asset or liability.
Market approach	A valuation technique that uses prices and other relevant information generated by market transactions involving identical or comparable (i.e. similar) assets, liabilities or a group of assets and liabilities, such as a business.
Market-corroborated inputs	Inputs that are derived principally from or corroborated by observable market data by correlation or other means.
Market participant	Buyers and sellers in the principal (or most advantageous) market for the asset or liability that have all of the following characteristics: (a) They are independent of each other, i.e. they are not related parties as defined in IAS 24 – *Related Party Disclosures* (see Chapter 39), although the price in a related party transaction may be used as an input to a fair value measurement if the entity has evidence that the transaction was entered into at market terms. (b) They are knowledgeable, having a reasonable understanding about the asset or liability and the transaction using all available information, including information that might be obtained through due diligence efforts that are usual and customary. (c) They are able to enter into a transaction for the asset or liability. (d) They are willing to enter into a transaction for the asset or liability, i.e. they are motivated but not forced or otherwise compelled to do so.
Most advantageous market	The market that maximises the amount that would be received to sell the asset or minimises the amount that would be paid to transfer the liability, after taking into account transaction costs and transport costs.
Non-performance risk	The risk that an entity will not fulfil an obligation. Non-performance risk includes, but may not be limited to, the entity's own credit risk.
Observable inputs	Inputs that are developed using market data, such as publicly available information about actual events or transactions, and that reflect the assumptions that market participants would use when pricing the asset or liability.

Term	Definition
Orderly transaction	A transaction that assumes exposure to the market for a period before the measurement date to allow for marketing activities that are usual and customary for transactions involving such assets or liabilities; it is not a forced transaction (e.g. a forced liquidation or distress sale).
Principal market	The market with the greatest volume and level of activity for the asset or liability.
Risk premium	Compensation sought by risk-averse market participants for bearing the uncertainty inherent in the cash flows of an asset or a liability. Also referred to as a 'risk adjustment'.
Transaction costs	The costs to sell an asset or transfer a liability in the principal (or most advantageous) market for the asset or liability that are directly attributable to the disposal of the asset or the transfer of the liability and meet both of the following criteria: (a) They result directly from and are essential to that transaction. (b) They would not have been incurred by the entity had the decision to sell the asset or transfer the liability not been made (similar to costs to sell, as defined in IFRS 5).
Transport costs	The costs that would be incurred to transport an asset from its current location to its principal (or most advantageous) market.
Unit of account	The level at which an asset or a liability is aggregated or disaggregated in an IFRS for recognition purposes.
Unobservable inputs	Inputs for which market data are not available and that are developed using the best information available about the assumptions that market participants would use when pricing the asset or liability.

Credit risk and *market risk* are defined in IFRS 7 (see Chapter 54).

Key management personnel is defined in IAS 24 (see Chapter 39).

4 THE FAIR VALUE FRAMEWORK

4.1 Definition of fair value

Fair value is defined as 'the price that would be received to sell an asset or paid to transfer a liability in an orderly transaction between market participants at the measurement date'. *[IFRS 13.9]*.

The definition of fair value in IFRS 13 is not significantly different from the previous definition in IFRS, which was 'the amount for which an asset could be exchanged, or a liability settled, between knowledgeable, willing parties in an arm's length transaction'. *[IFRS 13.BC29]*. However, the definition in IFRS 13 and its guidance in the fair value framework clarify the following:

- The definition of fair value in IFRS 13 is a current exit price, not an entry price. *[IFRS 13.BC36]*.

  The exit price for an asset or liability is conceptually different from its transaction price (an entry price). While exit and entry prices may be identical in many situations, the transaction price is not presumed to represent the fair value of an asset or liability on its initial recognition as measured in accordance with IFRS 13.

- The exit price objective of a fair value measurement applies regardless of the reporting entity's intent and/or ability to sell the asset or transfer the liability at the measurement date. *[IFRS 13.BC39, BC40].* Fair value is the exit price in the principal market (or in the absence of a principal market, the most advantageous market – see 6 below – in which the reporting entity would transact). However, the price in the exit market should not be adjusted for transaction costs – i.e. transaction costs incurred to acquire an item are not added to the price used to measure fair value and transaction costs incurred to sell an item are not deducted from the price used to measure fair value. *[IFRS 13.25].*

  In addition, fair value is a market-based measurement, not an entity-specific measurement, and, as such, is determined based on the assumptions that market participants would use when pricing the asset or liability. *[IFRS 13.BC31].*

- A fair value measurement contemplates the sale of an asset or transfer of a liability, not a transaction to offset the risks associated with an asset or liability (see 8 below for further discussion).

- The transaction to sell the asset or transfer the liability is a hypothetical transaction as at the measurement date that is assumed to be orderly and considers an appropriate period of exposure to the market (see 8 below for further discussion). *[IFRS 13.15].*

- The objective of a fair value measurement does not change based on the level of activity in the exit market or the valuation technique(s) used. That is, fair value remains a market-based exit price that considers the current market conditions as at the measurement date, even if there has been a significant decrease in the volume and level of activity for the asset or liability. *[IFRS 13.2, B41].*

4.2 The fair value measurement framework

In addition to providing a single definition of fair value, IFRS 13 includes a framework for applying this definition to financial reporting. Many of the key concepts used in the fair value framework are interrelated and their interaction should be considered in the context of the entire approach.

As discussed at 1.3 above, the objective of a fair value measurement is 'to estimate the price at which an orderly transaction to sell the asset or to transfer the liability would take place between market participants at the measurement date under current market conditions'. *[IFRS 13.B2].*

In light of this objective, when measuring fair value, an entity must determine all of the following:

(a) the particular asset or liability that is the subject of the measurement (consistent with its unit of account – see 5 below);

(b) for a non-financial asset, the valuation premise that is appropriate for the measurement (consistent with its highest and best use – see 10 below);

(c) the principal (or most advantageous) market for the asset or liability (see 6 below); and

(d) the valuation technique(s) appropriate for the measurement (see 14 below), considering the availability of data with which to develop inputs (see 15 below) that represent the assumptions that market participants would use when pricing the asset or liability (see 7 below) and the level of the fair value hierarchy within which the inputs are categorised (see 16 below). *[IFRS 13.B2].*

The following diagram illustrates our view of the interdependence of the various components of the fair value measurement framework in IFRS 13.

Figure 14.2:   The fair value measurement framework

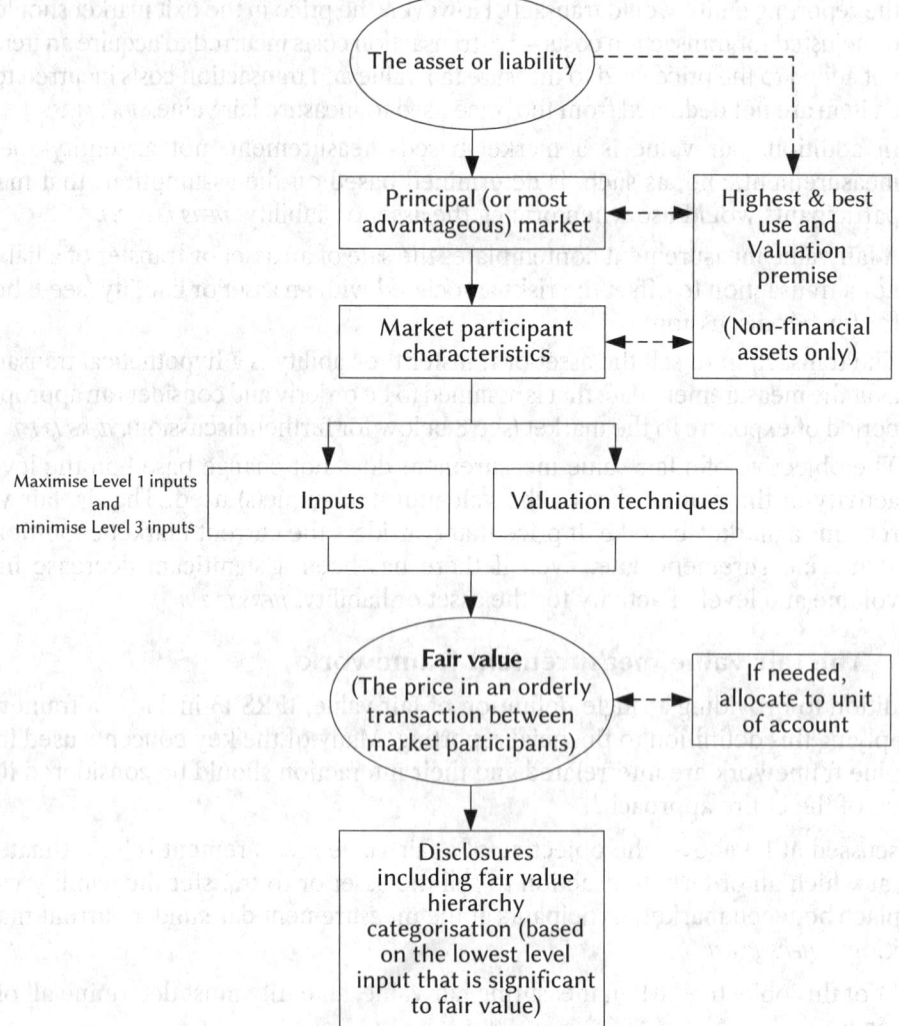

In practice, navigating the fair value framework may be more straightforward for certain types of assets (e.g. assets that trade in a formalised market) than for others (e.g. intangible assets). For non-financial assets that derive value when used in combination with other assets or for which a developed market does not exist, resolving the circular nature of the relationship between valuation premise, highest and best use and exit market is important in applying the fair value framework (refer to 10 below for additional discussion on the fair value measurement of non-financial assets).

IFRS 13 clarifies that the concepts of 'highest and best use' and 'valuation premise' are only applicable when determining the fair value of non-financial assets. Therefore, the fair value framework is applied differently to non-financial assets versus other items, such as financial instruments, non-financial liabilities and instruments classified in a reporting entity's shareholders' equity (refer to 12 below for additional discussion on the fair value of financial instruments with offsetting positions and to 11 below for the fair value measurement of liabilities and instruments classified in an entity's shareholders' equity). Although there are differences in the application of the fair value framework for non-financial assets, the objective of the fair value measurement remains the same, that is, an exit price in the principal (or most advantageous) market.

As discussed in more detail at 12 below, IFRS 13 provides an exception to the principles of fair value, allowing entities to measure a group of financial instruments based on the price to sell (or transfer) its net position for a particular risk exposure, if certain criteria are met. The use of this exception may require a reporting entity to allocate portfolio-level valuation adjustments to the appropriate unit of account.

5 THE ASSET OR LIABILITY

IFRS 13 states that a fair value measurement is for a particular asset or liability, which is different from the price to offset certain of the risks associated with that particular asset or liability.

This is an important distinction, particularly in the valuation of certain financial instruments that are typically not 'exited' through a sale or transfer, but whose risks are hedged through other transactions (e.g. derivatives). However, IFRS 13 does allow for financial instruments with offsetting risks to be measured based on their net risk exposure to a particular risk, in contrast to the assets or liabilities that give rise to this exposure (see 12 below for additional discussion on the criteria to qualify for this measurement exception and application considerations).

5.1 The unit of account

The identification of exactly what asset or liability is being measured is fundamental to determining its fair value. Fair value may need to be measured for either:

- a stand-alone asset or liability (e.g. a financial instrument or an operating asset); or
- a group of assets, a group of liabilities, or a group of assets and liabilities (e.g. a cash-generating unit or a business).

The unit of account defines what is being measured for financial reporting purposes. It is an accounting concept that determines the level at which an asset or liability is aggregated or disaggregated for the purpose of applying IFRS 13, as well as other standards.

Unless specifically addressed in IFRS 13 (see 5.1.1 and 5.1.2 below), the appropriate unit of account is determined by the applicable IFRS (i.e. the standard that permits or requires the fair value measurement or disclosure). *[IFRS 13.13, 14]*. Assume, for example, that an investment property is valued at CU100. Further assume that the investment property is owned by a single asset entity (or corporate wrapper) and the shares in the entity are only valued at CU90. If another entity were to acquire the shares of the single asset entity for CU90, at acquisition, the entity would allocate the purchase price to the property inside it. The property would, therefore, initially be recognised at CU90. Assume that, at year-end, the fair value of the property is CU110 and that the entity measures the property at fair value in accordance with IAS 40. Assume that the fair value of the shares in the single asset entity are CU99. IAS 40 requires that an entity measure an investment property, not the shares of a single entity that owns it. *[IAS 40.33]*. As such, the property would be measured at its fair value of CU110.

5.1.1 Unit of account and P×Q

IFRS 13 does specify the unit of account to be used when measuring fair value in relation to a reporting entity that holds a position in a single asset or liability that is traded in an active market (including a position comprising a large number of identical assets or liabilities, such as a holding of financial instruments). In this situation, IFRS 13 requires an entity to measure the asset or liability based on the product of the quoted price for the individual asset or liability and the quantity held (P×Q).

This requirement is generally accepted when the asset or liability being measured is a financial instrument in the scope of IFRS 9. However, when an entity holds an investment in a listed subsidiary, joint venture or associate, some believe the unit of account is the entire holding and the fair value should include an adjustment (e.g. a control premium) to reflect the value of the investor's control, joint control or significant influence over their investment as a whole.

Questions have also arisen on to how this requirement applies to cash-generating units that are equivalent to listed investments. Some argue that, because IAS 36 requires certain assets and liabilities to be excluded from a cash-generating unit (CGU), the unit of account is not identical to a listed subsidiary, joint venture or associate and an entity can include adjustments that are consistent with the CGU as a whole. Similarly, some argue that approach is appropriate because in group financial statements an entity is accounting for the assets and liabilities of consolidated entities, rather than the investment. However, others argue that if the CGU is effectively the same as an entity's investment in a listed subsidiary, joint venture or associate, the requirement to use P×Q should apply.

IFRS 13 requires entities to select inputs that are consistent with the characteristics of the asset or liability being measured and would be considered by market participants when pricing the asset or liability (see 7.2 below). Apart from block discounts (which are specifically prohibited), determining whether a premium or discount applies to a particular fair value measurement requires judgement and depends on specific facts and circumstances.

As discussed at 15.2 below, the standard indicates that premiums or discounts should not be incorporated into fair value measurements unless all of the following conditions are met:

- the application of the premium or discount reflects the characteristics of the asset or liability being measured;
- market participants, acting in their economic best interest, would consider these premiums or discounts when pricing the asset or liability; and
- the inclusion of the premium or discount is not inconsistent with the unit of account in the IFRS that requires (or permits) the fair value measurement.

Therefore, when an entity holds an investment in a listed subsidiary, joint venture or associate, if the unit of account is deemed to be the entire holding, it would be appropriate to include, for example, a control premium when determining fair value, provided that market participants would take this into consideration when pricing the asset. If, however, the unit of account is deemed to be the individual share of the listed subsidiary, joint venture or associate, the requirement to use P×Q (without adjustment) to measure the fair value would override the requirements in IFRS 13 that permit premiums or discounts to be included in certain circumstances.

In September 2014, in response to these questions regarding the unit of account for an investment in a listed subsidiary, joint venture or associate, the IASB proposed amendments to clarify that:[5]

- The unit of account for investments in subsidiaries, joint ventures and associates should be the investment as a whole and not the individual financial instruments that constitute the investment.
- For investments that are comprised of financial instruments for which a quoted price in an active market is available, the requirement to use P×Q would take precedence, irrespective of the unit of account. Therefore, for all such investments, the fair value measurement would be the product of P×Q, even when the reporting entity has an interest that gives it control, joint control or significant influence over the investee.
- When testing CGUs for impairment, if those CGUs correspond to an entity whose financial instruments are quoted in an active market, the fair value measurement would be the product of P×Q.

    When testing for impairment in accordance with IAS 36, the recoverable amount of a CGU is the higher of its value in use or fair value less costs of disposal. The fair value component of fair value less costs of disposal is required to be measured in accordance with IFRS 13.

    When a CGU effectively corresponds to a listed entity, the same issue arises regarding whether the requirement to use P×Q, without adjustment, to measure fair value applies.

    Consistent with its proposal in relation to listed investments in subsidiaries, joint ventures and associates, the IASB proposed that, if the CGU corresponds to an entity whose financial instruments are quoted in an active market, the requirement to use P×Q would apply.

The exposure draft also included proposed clarifications for the portfolio exception, discussed at 5.1.2 below.

The IASB proposed the following transition requirements:

- For quoted investments in subsidiaries, joint ventures and associates, an entity would recognise a cumulative catch-up adjustment to opening retained earnings for the period in which the proposed amendments are first applied. The entity would then recognise the change in measurement of the quoted investments during that period in profit or loss (i.e. retrospective application).
- For impairment testing in accordance with IAS 36, an entity would apply the requirements on a prospective basis. If an entity incurs an impairment loss or reversal during the period of initial application, it would provide quantitative information about the likely effect on the impairment loss, or reversal amount, had the amendments been applied in the immediately preceding period presented.

The exposure draft did not include a proposed effective date. However, permitting early adoption was proposed. Furthermore, the Board proposed that a first-time adopter of IFRS be able to apply the amendments at the beginning of the earliest period for which it presents full comparative information under IFRS in its first IFRS financial statements (i.e. prospectively from the date of the first-time adopter's transition to IFRS). The comment period for this exposure draft ended on 16 January 2015 and the Board began redeliberations in March 2015. During redeliberations, additional research was undertaken on fair value measurements of investments in subsidiaries, associates and joint ventures that are quoted in an active market and on the measurement of the recoverable amount of cash-generating units on the basis of fair value less costs of disposal when the cash-generating unit is an entity that is quoted in an active market.

Following the redeliberations, in its January 2016 meeting, the IASB concluded that the research would be fed into the PIR of IFRS 13.[6] As part of its PIR of IFRS 13, the IASB specifically asked about prioritising Level 1 inputs in relation to the unit of account. The feedback was discussed at the IASB's March 2018 meeting. In respect of the valuation of quoted subsidiaries, associates and joint ventures, the PIR found that there were continuing differences in views between users and preparers over whether to prioritise Level 1 inputs or the unit of account. The issue is not pervasive in practice according to the PIR findings. However, respondents noted it can have a material effect when it does occur. Some stakeholders said that there are material differences between measuring an investment using the P×Q and a valuation using a method such as discounted cash flows. Respondents indicated the reasons for such differences include:

- share prices do not reflect market liquidity for the shares or;
- that they do not reflect the value of control and/or synergies.

A few respondents also noted that markets may lack depth and are, therefore, susceptible to speculative trading, asymmetrical information and other factors.[7]

As noted at 1.1.1 above, the IASB released its Report and Feedback Statement on the PIR in December 2018. The Board decided not to conduct any follow-up activities as a result of findings from the PIR and stated, as an example, that it will not do any further work on the issue of unit of account versus P×Q because the costs of such work would outweigh the benefits for the following reasons:

- the Board's previous significant work on the topic and the PIR suggest the issue is narrow and affects only a limited population of entities;
- users have not expressed major concerns with reporting in practice, although they would like better transparency; and
- there are differences in views between preparers and users, meaning any follow-up work would be likely to require significant resource. Thus, this project may be possible only as part of a major amendment to IFRS 13 or other IFRS Standards.[8]

5.1.2 Unit of account and the portfolio exception

There is some debate about whether IFRS 13 prescribes the unit of account in relation to the portfolio exception. Under IFRS 13, a reporting entity that manages a group of financial assets and financial liabilities with offsetting risks on the basis of its net exposure to market or credit risks is allowed to measure the group based on the price that would be received to sell its net long position, or paid to transfer its net short position, for a particular risk (if certain criteria are met).

Some believe the portfolio exception in IFRS 13 specifies the unit of measurement for any financial instruments within the portfolio(s), i.e. that the net exposure of the identified group to a particular risk, and not the individual instruments within the group, represents the new unit of measurement. This may have a number of consequences. For example, the entity may be able to include premiums or discounts in the fair value measurement of the portfolio that are consistent with that unit of account, but not the individual instruments that make up the portfolio. In addition, because the net exposure for the identified group may not be actively traded (even though some financial instruments within the portfolio may be) P×Q may not be applied to the actively traded instruments within the portfolio.

Others believe that the portfolio exception does not override the unit of account as provided in IFRS 9. Therefore, any premiums or discounts that are inconsistent with this unit of account, i.e. the individual financial instruments within the portfolio, would be excluded from the fair value measurement under the portfolio exception, including any premiums or discounts related to the size of the portfolio.

Regardless of which view is taken, it is clear in the standard that the portfolio exception does not change the financial statement presentation requirements (see 12 below for further discussion on the portfolio exception and 15.2 below for further discussion on premiums and discounts).

In the US, ASC 820 has been interpreted by many as prescribing the unit of measurement when the portfolio exception is used. That is, when the portfolio approach is used to measure an entity's net exposure to a particular market risk, the net position becomes the unit of measurement. This view is consistent with how many US financial institutions determined the fair value of their over-the-counter derivative portfolios prior to the amendments to ASC 820 (ASU 2011-04)[9] (see 22 below). We understand that the IASB did not intend application of the portfolio exception to override the requirements in IFRS 13 regarding the use of P×Q to measure instruments traded in active markets and the prohibition on block discounts which raises questions as to how the portfolio exception would be applied to Level 1 instruments.

In 2013, the IFRS Interpretations Committee referred a request to the Board on the interaction between the use of Level 1 inputs and the portfolio exception. The IASB noted that this issue had similarities with the issues of the interaction between the use of Level 1 inputs and the unit of account that arises when measuring the fair value of investments in listed subsidiaries, joint ventures and associates (see 5.1.1 above). The IASB discussed this issue in December 2013, but only in relation to portfolios that comprise only Level 1 financial instruments whose market risks are substantially the same. For that specific circumstance, the Board tentatively decided that the measurement of such portfolios should be the one that results from multiplying the net position by the Level 1 prices (e.g. multiplying the net long or short position by the Level 1 price for either a gross long or short position). Given this tentative decision, in September 2014 the IASB proposed adding a non-authoritative example to illustrate the application of the portfolio exception in this specific circumstance.[10] However, after reviewing the comments received on the proposal, the Board concluded that it was not necessary to add the proposed non-authoritative illustrative example to IFRS 13 (see 12.2 below for further discussion) because the example would have been non-authoritative and the comments received did not reveal significant diversity in practice for the specific circumstance of portfolios that comprise only Level 1 financial instruments whose market risks are substantially the same.[11]

5.1.3 Unit of account versus the valuation premise

In valuing non-financial assets, the concepts of 'unit of account' and 'valuation premise' are distinct, even though both concepts deal with determining the appropriate level of aggregation (or disaggregation) for assets and liabilities. The unit of account identifies what is being measured for financial reporting and drives the level of aggregation (or disaggregation) for presentation and disclosure purposes (e.g. whether categorisation in the fair value hierarchy is determined at the individual asset level or for a group of assets). Valuation premise is a valuation concept that addresses how a non-financial asset derives its maximum value to market participants, either on a stand-alone basis or through its use in combination with other assets and liabilities.

Since financial instruments do not have alternative uses and their fair values typically do not depend on their use within a group of other assets or liabilities, the concepts of highest and best use and valuation premise are not relevant for financial instruments. As a result, the fair value for financial instruments should be largely based on the unit of account prescribed by the standard that requires (or permits) the fair value measurement.

The distinction between these two concepts becomes clear when the unit of account of a non-financial asset differs from its valuation premise. Consider an asset (e.g. customised machinery) that was acquired other than by way of a business combination, along with other assets as part of an operating line. Although the unit of account for the customised machinery may be as a stand-alone asset (i.e. it is presented for financial reporting purposes at the individual asset level in accordance with IAS 16 – *Property, Plant and Equipment*), the determination of the fair value of the machinery may be derived from its use with other assets in the operating line (see 10.2 below for additional discussion on the concept of valuation premise).

5.1.4 Does IFRS 13 allow fair value to be measured by reference to an asset's (or liability's) components?

IFRS 13 states that the objective of a fair value measurement is to determine the price that would be received for an asset or paid to transfer a liability at the measurement date. That is, a fair value measurement is to be determined for a particular asset or liability. The unit of account determines what is being measured by reference to the level at which the asset or liability is aggregated (or disaggregated) for accounting purposes.

Unless separation of an asset (or liability) into its component parts is required or allowed under IFRS (e.g. a requirement to separate under IFRS 9), we generally do not believe it is appropriate to consider the unit of account at a level below that of the legal form of the asset or liability being measured. A valuation methodology that uses a 'sum-of-the-parts' approach may still be appropriate under IFRS 13; for example, when measuring complex financial instruments, entities often use valuation methodologies that attempt to determine the value of the entire instrument based on its component parts.

However, in situations where fair value can be determined for an asset or liability as a whole, we would generally not expect that an entity would use a higher amount to measure fair value because the sum of the parts exceeds the whole. Using a higher value inherently suggests that the asset would be broken down and the various components, or risk attributes, transferred to different market participants who would pay more for the pieces than a market participant would for the asset or liability as a whole. Such an approach is not consistent with IFRS 13's principles, which contemplate the sale of an asset or transfer of a liability (consistent with its unit of account) in a single transaction.

5.2 Characteristics of the asset or liability

When measuring fair value, IFRS 13 requires an entity to consider the characteristics of the asset or liability. For example, age and miles flown are attributes to be considered in determining a fair value measure for an aircraft. Examples of such characteristics could include:

- the condition and location of an asset; and
- restrictions, if any, on the sale or use of an asset or transfer of a liability (see 5.2.2, 10.1 and 11.4 below).

The fair value of the asset or liability must take into account those characteristics that market participants would take into consideration when pricing the asset or liability at the measurement date. *[IFRS 13.11, 12]*. For example, when valuing individual shares in an unlisted company, market participants might consider factors such as the nature of the company's operations; its performance to date and forecast future performance; and how the business is funded, including whether it is highly leveraged.

The requirement to consider the characteristics of the asset or liability being measured is not new to fair value measurement under IFRS. For example, prior to the issuance of IFRS 13, IAS 41 referred to measuring the fair value of a biological asset or agricultural produce in its present location and condition and IAS 40 stated that an entity should identify any differences between the investment property being measured at fair value and similar properties for which observable market prices are available and make the appropriate adjustments for those differences. *[IFRS 13.BC46]*.

5.2.1 Condition and location

An asset may not be in the condition or location that market participants would require for its sale at an observable market price. In order to determine the fair value of the asset as it currently exists, the market price needs to be adjusted to the price market participants would be prepared to pay for the asset in its current condition and location. This includes deducting the cost of transporting the asset to the market, if location is a characteristic of the asset being measured, and may include deducting the costs of converting or transforming the asset, as well as a normal profit margin.

For non-financial assets, condition and location considerations may influence, or be dependent on, the highest and best use of an asset (see 10 below). That is, an asset's highest and best use may require an asset to be in a different condition. However, the objective of a fair value measurement is to determine the price for the asset in its current form. Therefore, if no market exists for an asset in its current form, but there is a market for the converted or transformed asset, an entity could adjust this market price for the costs a market participant would incur to re-condition the asset (after acquiring the asset in its current condition) and the compensation they would expect for the effort. Example 14.1 below illustrates how costs to convert or transform an asset might be considered in determining fair value based on the current use of the asset.

Example 14.1: Adjusting fair value for condition and location

An entity owns a pine forest. The pine trees take approximately 25 years to mature, after which they can be cut down and sold. The average age of the trees in the forest is 14 years at the end of the reporting period. The current use of the forest is presumed to be its highest and best use.

There is no market for the trees in their current form. However, there is a market for the harvested timber from trees aged 25 years or older. To measure the fair value of the forest, the entity uses an income approach and uses the price for 25-year-old harvested timber in the market today as an input. However, since the trees are not yet ready for harvest, the cash flows must be adjusted for the costs a market participant would incur. Therefore, the estimated cash flows include costs to manage the forest (including silviculture activities, such as fertilising and pruning the trees) until the trees reach maturity; costs to harvest the trees; and costs to transport the harvested logs to the market. The entity estimates these costs using market participant assumptions. The entity also adjusts the value for a normal profit margin because a market participant acquiring the forest today would expect to be compensated for the cost and effort of managing the forest for the period (i.e. 11 years) before the trees will be harvested and the timber is sold (i.e. this would include compensation for costs incurred and a normal profit margin for the effort of managing the forest).

5.2.2 Restrictions on assets or liabilities

IFRS 13 indicates that the effect on fair value of a restriction on the sale or use of an asset will differ depending on whether the restriction is deemed to be a characteristic of the asset or the entity holding the asset. A restriction that would transfer with the asset in an assumed sale would generally be deemed a characteristic of the asset and, therefore, would likely be considered by market participants when pricing the asset. Conversely, a restriction that is specific to the entity holding the asset would not transfer with the asset in an assumed sale and, therefore, would not be considered when measuring fair value. Determining whether a restriction is a characteristic of the asset or of the entity holding the asset may be contractual in some cases. In other cases, this determination may require judgement based on the specific facts and circumstances.

The following illustrative examples highlight the distinction between restrictions that are characteristics of the asset and those of the entity holding the asset, including how this determination affects the fair value measurement. *[IFRS 13.IE28-IE29]*. Restrictions on non-financial assets are discussed further at 10 below.

Example 14.2: Restrictions on assets

An entity holds an equity instrument for which sale is legally restricted for a specified period. The restriction is a characteristic of the instrument that would transfer to market participants. As such, the fair value of the instrument would be measured based on the quoted price for an otherwise identical unrestricted equity instrument that trades in a public market, adjusted for the effect of the restriction. The adjustment would reflect the discount market participants would demand for the risk relating to the inability to access a public market for the instrument for the specified period. The adjustment would vary depending on:

- the nature and duration of the restriction;
- the extent to which buyers are limited by the restriction; and
- qualitative and quantitative factors specific to both the instrument and the issuer.

Example 14.3:   Entity-specific restrictions on assets

A donor of land specifies that the land must be used by a sporting association as a playground in perpetuity. Upon review of relevant documentation, the association determines that the donor's restriction would not transfer to market participants if the association sold the asset (i.e. the restriction on the use of the land is specific to the association). Furthermore, the association is not restricted from selling the land. Without the restriction on the use of the land, the land could be used as a site for residential development. In addition, the land is subject to an easement (a legal right that enables a utility to run power lines across the land).

Under these circumstances, the effect of the restriction and the easement on the fair value measurement of the land is as follows:

(a) Donor restriction on use of land – The donor restriction on the use of the land is specific to the association and thus would not transfer to market participants. Therefore, regardless of the restriction on the use of the land by the association, the fair value of the land would be measured based on the higher of its indicated value:

   (i) as a playground (i.e. the maximum value of the land is through its use in combination with other assets or with other assets and liabilities); or

   (ii) as a residential development (i.e. the fair value of the asset would be maximised through its use by market participants on a stand-alone basis).

(b) Easement for utility lines – Because the easement for utility lines is a characteristic of the land, this easement would be transferred to market participants with the land. The fair value of the land would include the effect of the easement, regardless of whether the land's valuation premise is as a playground or as a site for residential development.

In contrast to Example 14.2 above, Example 14.3 illustrates a restriction on the use of donated land that applies to a specific entity, but not to other market participants.

The calculation of the fair value should take account of any restrictions on the sale or use of an asset, if those restrictions relate to the asset rather than to the holder of the asset and the market participant would take those restrictions into account in his determination of the price that he is prepared to pay.

A liability or an entity's own equity instrument may be subject to restrictions that prevent the transfer of the item. When measuring the fair value of a liability or equity instrument, IFRS 13 does not allow an entity to include a separate input (or an adjustment to other inputs) for such restrictions. This is because the effect of the restriction is either implicitly or explicitly included in other inputs to the fair value measurement. Restrictions on liabilities and an entity's own equity are discussed further at 11.4 below.

IFRS 13 has different treatments for restrictions on assets and those over liabilities. The IASB believes this is appropriate because restrictions on the transfer of a liability relate to the performance of the obligation (i.e. the entity is legally obliged to satisfy the obligation and needs to do something to be relieved of the obligation), whereas restrictions on the transfer of an asset generally relate to the marketability of the asset. In addition, nearly all liabilities include a restriction preventing the transfer of the liability. In contrast, most assets do not include a similar restriction. As a result, the effect of a restriction preventing the transfer of a liability, theoretically, would be consistent for all liabilities and, therefore, would require no additional adjustment beyond the factors considered in determining the original transaction price. If an entity is aware that a restriction on the transfer of a liability is not already reflected in the price (or in the other inputs used in the measurement), it would adjust the price or inputs to reflect the existence of the restriction. *[IFRS 13.BC99, BC100]*. However, this would be rare because nearly all liabilities include a restriction and, when measuring fair value, market participants are assumed by IFRS 13 to be sufficiently knowledgeable about the liability to be transferred.

5.2.2.A In determining the fair value of a restricted security, is it appropriate to apply a constant discount percentage over the entire life of the restriction?

We generally do not believe a constant discount percentage should be used to measure the fair value of a restricted security because market participants would consider the remaining time on the security's restriction and that time period changes from period to period. Market participants, for example, would generally not assign the same discount for a restriction that terminates in one month, as they would for a two-year restriction.

One approach to value the restriction may be through an option pricing model that explicitly incorporates the duration of the restriction and the characteristics of the underlying security. The principal economic factor underlying a discount for lack of marketability is the increased risk resulting from the inability to quickly and efficiently return the investment to a cash position (i.e. the risk of a price decline during the restriction period). One way in which the price of this risk may be determined is by using an option pricing model that estimates the value of a protective put option. For example, restricted or non-marketable securities are acquired along with a separate option that provides the holder with the right to sell those shares at the current market price for unrestricted securities. The holder of such an option has, in effect, purchased marketability for the shares. The value of the put option may be considered an estimate of the discount for the lack of marketability associated with the restricted security. Other techniques or approaches may also be appropriate in measuring the discount associated with restricted securities.

5.2.2.B Considerations when a restriction is present on a call option for its entire contractual life

In certain instances, there may be a legal restriction preventing sale for an asset's entire life. Consider the following example where an entity holds a call option to acquire a controlling stake in its associate. The call option is an integral part of the shareholders' agreement to acquire the associate and, therefore, cannot be sold or transferred to a third party. The call option is not currently exercisable and is, therefore, accounted for under IFRS 9 and measured at fair value. The call option is assumed to have a positive fair value because the strike price per share of the option is significantly lower than the fair value per share of the associate. The entity needs to consider whether and, if so, how the effect of this restriction should be incorporated into the measurement of fair value for the call option.

This restriction is contractually specified and is, therefore, considered a characteristic of the asset and would be considered by market participants when pricing the call option. Therefore, it must be considered when measuring the fair value of the call option.

To understand how the restriction should be incorporated into the fair value measurement, the entity needs to consider how market participants would view it. Unlike the situation in Example 14.2 above, the restriction is not for a portion of the instrument's life, but instead for the entire contractual life (i.e. until the option expires). In contrast to an investment in shares, market participant holders of a call option can realise the value of the option both through its sale and by exercising it. In this example, although there is a restriction on sale, there is no restriction on exercise. That is, the entity could assume that market participants would realise value from exercising the option. Therefore, in this example, no adjustment related to the sale restriction would be made to the fair value of the call option.

When considering what market participants would assume, an entity should not consider its own intentions. For example, the entity determines that in this case, the strategic risks or costs involved are too great to justify the decision to exercise the option to realise its value. As discussed at 7.2 below, fair value must be determined from the perspective of a market participant. Therefore, the fair value would not be nil solely because the entity does not intend to exercise the option.

6 THE PRINCIPAL (OR MOST ADVANTAGEOUS) MARKET

A fair value measurement contemplates an orderly transaction to sell the asset or transfer the liability in either:

(a) the principal market for the asset or liability; or

(b) in the absence of a principal market, the most advantageous market for the asset or liability. *[IFRS 13.16]*.

IFRS 13 is clear that, if there is a principal market for the asset or liability, the fair value measurement represents the price in that market at the measurement date (regardless of whether that price is directly observable or estimated using another valuation technique). The price in the principal market must be used even if the price in a different market is potentially more advantageous. *[IFRS 13.18]*. This is illustrated in Example 14.4. *[IFRS 13.IE19-IE20]*.

Example 14.4: The effect of determining the principal market

An asset is sold in two different active markets at different prices. An entity enters into transactions in both markets and can access the price in those markets for the asset at the measurement date.

	Market A $	Market B $
Price that would be received	26	25
Transaction costs in that market	(3)	(1)
Costs to transport the asset to the market	(2)	(2)
Net amount that would be received	21	22

If Market A is the principal market for the asset (i.e. the market with the greatest volume and level of activity for the asset), the fair value of the asset would be measured using the price that would be received in that market, even though the net proceeds in Market B are more advantageous. In this case, the fair value would be $24, after taking into account transport costs excluding transactions costs.

The identification of a principal (or most advantageous) market could be impacted by whether there are observable markets for the item being measured. However, even where there is no observable market, fair value measurement assumes a transaction takes place at the measurement date. The assumed transaction establishes a basis for estimating the price to sell the asset or to transfer the liability. *[IFRS 13.21].*

6.1 The principal market

The principal market is the market for the asset or liability that has the greatest volume or level of activity for the asset or liability. *[IFRS 13 Appendix A].* There is a general presumption that the principal market is the one in which the entity would normally enter into a transaction to sell the asset or transfer the liability, unless there is evidence to the contrary. In practice, an entity would first consider the markets it can access. Then it would determine which of those markets has the greatest volume and liquidity in relation to the particular asset or liability. *[IFRS 13.17].* Management is not required to perform an exhaustive search to identify the principal market; however, it cannot ignore evidence that is reasonably available when considering which market has the greatest volume and level of activity. *[IFRS 13.17].* For example, it may be appropriate to take into account information available in trade journals, if reliable market information about volumes transacted is available in such journals. Absent evidence to the contrary, the principal market is presumed to be the market in which an entity normally enters into transactions for the asset and liability.

The principal market is considered from the perspective of the reporting entity, which means that the principal market could be different for different entities (this is discussed further at 6.1.1 below). For example, a securities dealer may exit a financial instrument by selling it in the inter-dealer market, while a manufacturing company would sell a financial instrument in the retail market. The entity must be able to access the principal market as at the measurement date. Therefore, continuing with our example, it would not be appropriate for a manufacturing company to assume that it would transact in the inter-dealer market (even when considering a hypothetical transaction) because the company does not have access to this market.

Because IFRS 13 indicates that the principal market is determined from the perspective of the reporting entity, some have questioned whether the principal market should be determined on the basis of: (a) entity-specific volume (i.e. the market where the reporting entity has historically sold, or intends to sell, the asset with the greatest frequency and volume); or (b) market-based volume and activity. However, IFRS 13 is clear that the principal market for an asset or liability should be determined based on the market with the greatest volume and level of activity that the reporting entity can access. It is not determined based on the volume or level of activity of the reporting entity's transactions in a particular market. That is, the determination as to which market(s) a particular entity can access is entity-specific, but once the accessible markets are identified, market-based volume and activity determine the principal market. *[IFRS 13.BC52].*

The recognition in IFRS 13 that different entities may sell identical instruments in different markets (and therefore at different exit prices) has important implications, particularly with respect to the initial recognition of certain financial instruments, such as derivatives. For example, a derivative contract between a dealer and a retail customer would likely be initially recorded at different fair values by the two entities, as they would exit the derivative in different markets and, therefore, at different exit prices. Day one gains and losses are discussed further at 13.2 below.

Although an entity must be able to access the market at the measurement date, IFRS 13 does not require an entity to be able to sell the particular asset or transfer the particular liability on that date. *[IFRS 13.20]*. For example, if there is a restriction on the sale of the asset, IFRS 13 simply requires that the entity be able to access the market for that asset when that restriction ceases to exist. It is important to note that the existence of the restriction may still affect the price a market participant would pay (see 5.2.2 above for discussion on restrictions on assets and liabilities).

In general, the market with the greatest volume and deepest liquidity will probably be the market in which the entity most frequently transacts. In these instances, the principal market would likely be the same as the most advantageous market (see 6.2 below).

Prior to the adoption of IFRS 13, some entities determined fair value based solely on the market where they transact with the greatest frequency (without considering other markets with greater volume and deeper liquidity). As noted above, IFRS 13 requires an entity to consider the market with the greatest volume and deepest liquidity for the asset. Therefore, an entity cannot presume a commonly used market is the principal market. For example, if an entity previously measured the fair value of agricultural produce based on its local market, but there is a deeper and more liquid market for the same agricultural produce (for which transportation costs are not prohibitive), the latter market would be deemed the principal market and would be used when measuring fair value.

6.1.1 Can an entity have more than one principal market for the same asset or liability?

IFRS 13 states that 'because different entities (and businesses within those entities) with different activities may have access to different markets, the principal (or most advantageous) market for the same asset or liability might be different for different entities (and businesses within those entities). Therefore, the principal (or most advantageous) market (and thus, market participants) shall be considered from the perspective of the entity, thereby allowing for differences between and among entities with different activities.' *[IFRS 13.19]*.

Therefore, in certain instances it may be appropriate for a reporting entity to determine that it has different principal markets for the same asset or liability. However, such a determination would need to be based on the reporting entity's business units engaging in different activities to ensure they were accessing different markets.

Determining the principal market is not based on management's intent. Therefore, we would not expect a reporting entity to have different principal markets for identical assets held within a business unit solely because management has different exit strategies for those assets.

Consider Example 14.5 below, in which multiple exit markets exist for an asset and the reporting entity has access to all of the various exit markets. The fact that a reporting entity (or business unit within a reporting entity) has historically exited virtually identical assets in different markets does not justify the entity utilising different exit markets in determining the fair value of these assets, unless the entity has different business units engaging in different activities. Instead, the concept of a principal market (and most advantageous market) implies that one consistent market should generally be considered in determining the fair value of these identical assets.

Example 14.5: *Determining the principal market – consistent principal market*

The following three markets exist for a particular asset. The company has the ability to transact in all three markets (and has historically done so).

Market	Price
A	€30,000
B	€25,000
C	€22,000

Under the principal market concept, it would not be appropriate to value identical assets at different prices solely because management intends to the sell the assets in different markets. Likewise, a consistent fair value measurement for each asset utilising a blended price that is determined based on the proportion of assets that management intends to sell in each market would not be appropriate. Instead, each of the assets would be measured at the price in the market determined to be the company's principal market.

If Market B were determined to represent the principal market for the asset being measured, each asset would be valued at €25,000. Selling the assets in either Market A or Market C would result in a gain or loss for the company. We believe this result is consistent with one of the fundamental concepts in the fair value framework. That is, the consequences of management's decisions (or a company's comparative advantages or disadvantages) should be recognised when those decisions are executed (or those advantages or disadvantages are achieved).

6.1.2 In situations where an entity has access to multiple markets, should the determination of the principal market be based on entity-specific volume and activity or market-based volume and activity?

In most instances, the market in which a reporting entity would sell an asset (or transfer a liability) with the greatest frequency will also represent the market with the greatest volume and deepest liquidity for all market participants. In these instances, the principal market would be the same regardless of whether it is determined based on entity-specific volume and activity or market-based volume and activity. However, when this is not the case, a reporting entity's principal market is determined using market-based volume.

Different entities engage in different activities. Therefore, some entities have access to certain markets that other entities do not. For example, an entity that does not function as a wholesaler would not have access to the wholesale market and, therefore, would need to look to the retail market as its principal market. Once the markets to which a particular entity has access have been identified, the determination of the principal market should not be based on management's intent or entity-specific volume, but rather should be based on the market with the greatest volume and level of activity for the asset or liability.

Example 14.6: *Determining the principal market – market-based versus entity-specific*

The following three markets exist for Entity A's fleet of vehicles. Entity A has the ability to transact in all three markets (and has historically done so). As at the measurement date, the entity has 100 vehicles (same make, model and mileage) that it needs to measure at fair value. Volumes and prices in the respective markets are as follows:

Market	Price	The entity's volume for the asset in the market (based on history and/or intent)	Total market-based volume for the asset
A	£30,000	60%	15%
B	£25,000	25%	75%
C	£20,000	15%	10%

Based on this information, Market B would be the principal market as this is the market in which the majority of transactions for the asset occur. As such, the fair value of the 100 cars as at the measurement date would be £2.5 million (i.e. £25,000 per car). Actual sales of the assets in either Market A or C would result in a gain or loss to the entity, i.e. when compared to the fair value of £25,000.

6.2 The most advantageous market

As noted above, if there is a principal market for the asset or liability being measured, fair value should be determined using the price in that market, even if the price in a different market is more advantageous at the measurement date.

Only in situations where there is no principal market for the asset or liability being measured, can an entity consider the most advantageous market. *[IFRS 13.16]*.

The most advantageous market is the one that maximises the amount that would be received to sell the asset or minimises the amount that would be paid to transfer the liability, after considering transaction costs and transport costs. *[IFRS 13 Appendix A]*.

This definition reasonably assumes that most entities transact with an intention to maximise profits or net assets. Assuming economically rational behaviour, the IASB observed that the principal market would generally represent the most advantageous market. However, when this is not the case, the IASB decided to prioritise the price in the most liquid market (i.e. the principal market) as this market provides the most representative input to determine fair value and also serves to increase consistency among reporting entities. *[IFRS 13.BC52]*.

When determining the most advantageous market, an entity must take into consideration the transaction costs and transportation costs it would incur to sell the asset or transfer the liability. The market that would yield the highest price after deducting these costs is the most advantageous market. This is illustrated in Example 14.7. *[IFRS 13.IE19.21-IE22]*.

Example 14.7: *Determining the most advantageous market*

Consider the same facts as in Example 14.4. If neither market is the principal market for the asset, the fair value of the asset would be measured using the price in the most advantageous market.

The most advantageous market is the market that maximises the amount that would be received to sell the asset, after taking into account transaction costs and transport costs (i.e. the net amount that would be received in the respective markets).

	Market A $	Market B $
Price that would be received	26	25
Transaction costs in that market	(3)	(1)
Costs to transport the asset to the market	(2)	(2)
Net amount that would be received	21	22

Because the entity would maximise the net amount that *would be received* for the asset in Market B ($22), that is the most advantageous market. Market B is the most advantageous market even though the fair value that would be recognised in that market ($23 = $25 – $2) is lower than in Market A ($24 = $26 – $2).

It is important to note that, while transaction costs and transportation costs are considered in determining the most advantageous market, the treatment of these costs in relation to measuring fair value differs (transaction costs and transportation costs are discussed further at 9 below).

7 MARKET PARTICIPANTS

When measuring fair value, an entity is required to use the assumptions that market participants would use when pricing the asset or liability. However, IFRS 13 does not require an entity to identify specific market participants. Instead, an entity must identify the characteristics of market participants that would generally transact for the asset or liability being measured. Determining these characteristics takes into consideration factors that are specific to the asset or liability; the principal (or most advantageous) market; and the market participants in that market. *[IFRS 13.22, 23]*. This determination, and how these characteristics affect a fair value measurement, may require significant judgement.

The principal (or most advantageous) market is determined from the perspective of the reporting entity (or business units within a reporting entity). As a result, other entities within the same industry as the reporting entity will most likely be considered market participants. However, market participants may come from outside of the reporting entity's industry, especially when considering the fair value of assets on a stand-alone basis. For example, a residential real estate development entity may be considered a market participant when measuring the fair value of land held by a manufacturing company if the highest and best use of the land is deemed to be residential real estate development.

7.1 Characteristics of market participants

IFRS 13 defines market participants as 'buyers and sellers in the principal (or most advantageous) market for the asset or liability'. *[IFRS 13 Appendix A]*.

IFRS 13 assumes that market participants have all of the following characteristics:
- they are independent of each other, that is, they are not related parties, as defined in IAS 24 (see Chapter 39);
- they are knowledgeable, having a reasonable understanding about the asset or liability using all available information, including information obtained through usual and customary due diligence efforts;
- they are able to enter into a transaction for the asset or liability; and
- they are willing to enter into a transaction for the asset or liability, that is, they are motivated but not forced or otherwise compelled to do so. *[IFRS 13 Appendix A, BC55-BC59]*.

Since market participants are independent of each other, the hypothetical transaction is assumed to take place between market participants at the measurement date, not between the reporting entity and another market participant. While market participants are not related parties, the standard does allow the price in a related party transaction to be used as an input in a fair value measurement provided the entity has evidence the transaction was entered into at market terms. *[IFRS 13.BC57]*.

Market participants in the principal (or most advantageous) market should have sufficient knowledge about the asset or liability for which they are transacting. The appropriate level of knowledge does not necessarily need to come from publicly available information, but could be obtained in the course of a normal due diligence process.

When determining potential market participants, certain characteristics should be considered. These include the legal capability and the operating and financial capacity to purchase the asset or assume the liability. Market participants must have both the willingness and the ability to transact for the item being measured. For example, when measuring the fair value less costs of disposal of a cash-generating unit (CGU), as part of testing the CGU for impairment in accordance with IAS 36, the market participants considered in the analysis should be in both a financial and operating position to purchase the CGU.

7.2 Market participant assumptions

IFRS 13 specifies that fair value is not the value specific to one entity, but rather is meant to be a market-based measurement. If market participants would consider adjustments for the inherent risk of the asset or liability, or consider the risk in the valuation technique used to measure fair value, then such risk adjustments should be considered in the fair value assumptions. For example, when measuring the fair value of certain financial instruments, market participants may include adjustments for liquidity, uncertainty and/or non-performance risk.

Fair value is not the value specific to the reporting entity and it is not the specific value to one market participant whose risk assessment or specific synergies may differ from other market participants. The reporting entity should consider those factors that market participants, in general, would consider. Fair value should not be measured based on a single market participant's assumptions or their specific intent or use of the asset or liability. To illustrate, assume a single market participant, Market Participant A, is willing to pay a higher price for an asset than the remaining market participants, due to specific synergies that only Market Participant A could achieve. In such a situation, fair value would not be the price that Market Participant A would be willing to pay for the asset. Instead, fair value would be the price that typical market participants would pay for the asset.

The underlying assumptions used in a fair value measurement are driven by the characteristics of the market participants who would transact for the item being measured and the factors those market participants would consider when pricing the asset or liability. Importantly, IFRS 13 notes that fair value should be based on assumptions that market participants acting in their 'economic best interest' would use when pricing an asset or liability. *[IFRS 13.22]*. That is, market participants are assumed to transact in a manner that is consistent with the objective of maximising the value of their business, their net assets or profits. In certain instances, this may result in market participants considering premiums or discounts (e.g. control premiums or discounts for lack of marketability) when determining the price at which they would transact for a particular asset or liability (see 15.2 below for additional discussion on the consideration of premiums and discounts in a fair value measurement).

In situations where market observable data is not available, the reporting entity can use its own data as a basis for its assumptions. However, adjustments should be made to the entity's own data if readily available market data indicates that market participant assumptions would differ from the assumptions specific to that reporting entity (see 19 below for further discussion regarding Level 3 inputs).

The intended use and risk assumptions for an asset or asset group may differ among market participants transacting in the principal market for the asset. For example, the principal market in which the reporting entity would transact may contain both strategic and financial buyers. Both types of buyers would be considered in determining the characteristics of market participants; however, the fair value measurement of an asset may differ among these two types of market participants. The following example from the standard illustrates this point. [IFRS 13.IE3-IE6].

Example 14.8: Considering different market participants when determining the highest and best use of an asset group

An entity acquires assets and assumes liabilities in a business combination. One of the groups of assets acquired comprises Assets A, B and C. Asset C is billing software integral to the business developed by the acquired entity for its own use in conjunction with Assets A and B (i.e. the related assets). The entity measures the fair value of each of the assets individually, consistently with the specified unit of account for the assets. The entity determines that the highest and best use of the assets is their current use and that each asset would provide maximum value to market participants principally through its use in combination with other assets or with other assets and liabilities (i.e. its complementary assets and the associated liabilities). There is no evidence to suggest that the current use of the assets is not their highest and best use.

In this situation, the entity would sell the assets in the market in which it initially acquired the assets (i.e. the entry and exit markets from the perspective of the entity are the same). Market participant buyers with whom the entity would enter into a transaction in that market have characteristics that are generally representative of both strategic buyers (such as competitors) and financial buyers (such as private equity or venture capital firms that do not have complementary investments) and include those buyers that initially bid for the assets. Although market participant buyers might be broadly classified as strategic or financial buyers, in many cases there will be differences among the market participant buyers within each of those groups, reflecting, for example, different uses for an asset and different operating strategies.

As discussed below, differences between the indicated fair values of the individual assets relate principally to the use of the assets by those market participants within different asset groups:

(a) Strategic buyer asset group – The entity determines that strategic buyers have related assets that would enhance the value of the group within which the assets would be used (i.e. market participant synergies). Those assets include a substitute asset for Asset C (the billing software), which would be used for only a limited transition period and could not be sold on its own at the end of that period. Because strategic buyers have substitute assets, Asset C would not be used for its full remaining economic life. The indicated fair values of Assets A, B and C within the strategic buyer asset group (reflecting the synergies resulting from the use of the assets within that group) are €360, €260 and €30, respectively. The indicated fair value of the assets as a group within the strategic buyer asset group is €650.

(b) Financial buyer asset group – The entity determines that financial buyers do not have related or substitute assets that would enhance the value of the group within which the assets would be used. Because financial buyers do not have substitute assets, Asset C (i.e. the billing software) would be used for its full remaining economic life. The indicated fair values of Assets A, B and C within the financial buyer asset group are €300, €200 and €100, respectively. The indicated fair value of the assets as a group within the financial buyer asset group is €600.

The fair values of Assets A, B and C would be determined on the basis of the use of the assets as a group within the strategic buyer group (€360, €260 and €30). Although the use of the assets within the strategic buyer group does not maximise the fair value of each of the assets individually, it maximises the fair value of the assets as a group (€650).

The example above illustrates that the principal (or most advantageous) market for an asset group may include different types of market participants (e.g. strategic and financial buyers), who would make different assumptions in pricing the assets.

When there are two or more different types of market participants that would transact for the asset, or the asset group, separate fair value estimates of the assets should generally be performed for each type of market participant in order to identify which type of market participant (and the appropriate related assumptions) should be considered in the fair value measurement.

In each of these analyses, the intended use of the asset and any resulting market participant synergies are considered. These include synergies among the assets in the asset grouping and synergies in combination with other assets held by (or available to) market participants generally. The selection of the appropriate market participants is based on the type of market participants that generate the maximum value for the asset group, in aggregate.

This is illustrated in Example 14.8 above. Fair value would be measured by reference to assumptions made by the Strategic Buyer because the fair value of the group of assets (€650) exceeds that of the Financial Buyer (€600). Consequently, the fair value of the individual assets within the asset grouping would be estimated based on the indicated values related to the market participants with the highest overall value for the asset grouping. In other words, once the assets are appropriately grouped based on their valuation premise, they should be valued using a consistent set of assumptions (i.e. the assumptions for the same type of market participants and the same related use). As shown in the example, this is true even though the fair value measurement of a specific asset, Asset C in the example, is deemed to be higher for the Financial Buyer.

Example 14.8 above also highlights the interdependence between the key concepts within the IFRS 13 fair value framework. Understanding the interrelationships between market participants, exit market and the concepts of valuation premise and highest and best use is important when measuring the fair value of non-financial assets (the concepts of 'valuation premise' and 'highest and best use' are discussed at 10 below).

In the example, the indicated value for the assets as a group is determined based on the valuation premise (i.e. their use in combination with other assets) and market participant assumptions that would maximise the value of the asset group as a whole (i.e. assumptions consistent with strategic buyers). The valuation premise for Assets A, B and C is based on their use in combination with each other (or with other related assets and liabilities held by or available to market participants), consistent with the highest and best use of these assets.

The example also highlights the distinction between the unit of account (i.e. what is being measured and presented for financial reporting purposes) and the valuation premise, which forms the basis of how assets are grouped for valuation purposes (i.e. as a group or on a stand-alone basis). The unit of account may be the individual assets (i.e. Asset A, separate from Asset B and Asset C), but the valuation premise is the asset group comprised of Assets A, B and C. Therefore, the indicated value of the assets in combination (€650) must be attributed to the assets based on their unit of account, resulting in the fair value measurement to be used for financial reporting purposes.

8 THE TRANSACTION

As at the measurement date, the transaction to sell an asset or transfer a liability is, by definition, a hypothetical transaction for the particular asset or liability being measured at fair value. If the asset had actually been sold or the liability actually transferred as at the measurement date, there would be no asset or liability for the reporting entity to measure at fair value.

IFRS 13 assumes this hypothetical transaction will take place in the principal (or most advantageous) market (see 6 above) and will:

- be orderly in nature;
- take place between market participants that are independent of each other, but knowledgeable about the asset or liability (see 7 above for additional discussion on market participants);
- take place under current market conditions; and
- occur on the measurement date. *[IFRS 13.15]*.

These assumptions are critical in ensuring that the estimated exit price in the hypothetical transaction is consistent with the objective of a fair value measurement. For example, the concept of an orderly transaction is intended to distinguish a fair value measurement from the exit price in a distressed sale or forced liquidation. Unlike a forced liquidation, an orderly transaction assumes that the asset or liability is exposed to the market prior to the measurement date for a period that is usual and customary to allow for information dissemination and marketing. That is, the hypothetical transaction assumes that market participants have sufficient knowledge and awareness of the asset or liability, including that which would be obtained through customary due diligence even if, in actuality, this process may not have begun yet (or may never occur at all, if the entity does not sell the asset or transfer the liability).

The hypothetical transaction between market participants does not consider whether management actually intends to sell the asset or transfer the liability at the measurement date; nor does it consider the reporting entity's ability to enter into the transaction on the measurement date. *[IFRS 13.20]*. To illustrate, consider a hypothetical transaction to sell a security that, due to a restriction, cannot be sold as at the measurement date. Although the restriction may affect the measurement of fair value, it does not preclude the entity from assuming a hypothetical transaction to sell the security (see 5.2.2 above for further discussion on restrictions).

An orderly transaction assumes there will be adequate market exposure, so that market participants would be sufficiently knowledgeable about the asset or liability. This does not mean the hypothetical exchange takes place at some point in the future. A fair value measurement considers market conditions as they exist at the measurement date and is intended to represent the current value of the asset or liability, not the potential value of the asset or liability at some future date. The transaction is therefore assumed to take place on the measurement date and the entity assumes that the marketing activities and due diligence activities have already been performed. For example, assume an entity is required to re-measure an asset to fair value at its reporting date of 31 December 2021. The customary marketing activities and due diligence procedures required for the asset to be sold take six months. The asset's fair value should not be based on the price the entity expects to receive for the asset in June 2022. Instead, it must be determined based on the price that would be received if the asset were sold on 31 December 2021, assuming adequate market exposure had already taken place.

Although a fair value measurement contemplates a price in an assumed transaction, pricing information from actual transactions for identical or similar assets and liabilities is considered in measuring fair value. IFRS 13 establishes a fair value hierarchy (discussed at 16 below) to prioritise the inputs used to measure fair value, based on the relative observability of those inputs. The standard requires that valuation techniques maximise the use of observable inputs and minimise the use of unobservable inputs. As such, even in situations where the market for a particular asset is deemed to be inactive (e.g. due to liquidity issues), relevant prices or inputs from this market should still be considered in the measurement of fair value. It would not be appropriate for an entity to default solely to a model's value based on unobservable inputs (a Level 3 measurement), when Level 2 information is available. Judgement is required in assessing the relevance of observable market data to determine the priority of inputs under the fair value hierarchy, particularly in situations where there has been a significant decrease in market activity for an asset or liability, as discussed at 8.1 below.

Assessing whether a transaction is orderly can require significant judgement. The Boards believe this determination can be more difficult if there has been a significant decrease in the volume or level of activity for the asset or liability in relation to normal market activity. As such, IFRS 13 provides various factors to consider when assessing whether there has been a significant decrease in the volume or level of activity in the market (see 8.1 below) as well as circumstances that may indicate that a transaction is not orderly (see 8.2 below). Making these determinations is based on the weight of all available evidence. *[IFRS 13.B43]*.

8.1 Evaluating whether there has been a significant decrease in the volume and level of activity for an asset or liability

There are many reasons why the trading volume or level of activity for a particular asset or liability may decrease significantly. For example, shifts in supply and demand dynamics, changing levels of investors' risk appetites and liquidity constraints of key market participants could all result in a significant reduction in the level of activity for certain items or class of items. While determining fair value for any asset or liability that does not trade in an active market often requires judgement, the application guidance in IFRS 13 is primarily focused on assets and liabilities in markets that have experienced a significant reduction in volume or activity. Prior to a decrease in activity, a market approach is often the primary valuation approach used to estimate fair value for these items, given the availability and relevance of observable data. Under a market approach, fair value is based on prices and other relevant information generated by market transactions involving assets and liabilities that are identical or comparable to the item being measured. As transaction volume or activity for the asset decreases significantly, application of the market approach can prove more challenging and the use of additional valuation techniques may be warranted.

The objective of a fair value measurement remains the same even when there has been a significant decrease in the volume or level of activity for the asset or liability.

Paragraph B37 of IFRS 13 provides a number of factors that should be considered when evaluating whether there has been a significant decrease in the volume or level of activity for the asset or liability. The entity must 'evaluate the significance and relevance of factors such as the following:

(a) there are few recent transactions;

(b) price quotations are not developed using current information;

(c) price quotations vary substantially either over time or among market-makers (e.g. some brokered markets);

(d) indices that previously were highly correlated with the fair values of the asset or liability are demonstrably uncorrelated with recent indications of fair value for that asset or liability;

(e) there is a significant increase in implied liquidity risk premiums, yields or performance indicators (such as delinquency rates or loss severities) for observed transactions or quoted prices when compared with the entity's estimate of expected cash flows, taking into account all available market data about credit and other non-performance risk for the asset or liability;

(f) there is a wide bid-ask spread or significant increase in the bid-ask spread;

(g) there is a significant decline in the activity of, or there is an absence of, a market for new issues (i.e. a primary market) for the asset or liability or similar assets or liabilities;

(h) little information is publicly available (e.g. for transactions that take place in a principal-to-principal market)'. *[IFRS 13.B37].*

These factors are not intended to be all-inclusive and should be considered along with any additional factors that are relevant based on the individual facts and circumstances. Determining whether the asset or liability has experienced a significant decrease in activity is based on the weight of the available evidence.

IFRS 13 is clear that a decrease in the volume or level of activity, on its own, does not necessarily indicate that a transaction price or quoted price does not represent fair value or that a transaction in that market is not orderly. Additional analysis is required in these instances to assess the relevance of observed transactions or quoted prices in these markets. When market volumes decrease, adjustments to observable prices (which could be significant) may be necessary (see 8.3 below). As discussed at 16 below, an adjustment based on unobservable inputs that is significant to the fair value measurement in its entirety would result in a Level 3 measurement. Observed prices associated with transactions that are not orderly would not be deemed to be representative of fair value. As part of the PIR feedback some respondents highlighted this as an issue where additional guidance is required, however as noted in 1.1.1 above the IASB has decided that no follow-up actions will be undertaken. In their view the requirements are principle-based, and there will always be a need for exercise of judgement, the challenges raised are detailed valuation assessments and an accounting standard-setter may not be best placed to provide guidance in this area. Lastly, there is evidence of practice having developed guidance to aid these assessments. Those aids are used by some and promote consistent application.

8.1.1 Can a market exhibit a significant decrease in volume or level of activity and still be considered active?

A significant decrease in the volume of transactions does not automatically imply that a market is no longer active. IFRS 13 defines a market as active if transactions for the asset or liability occur with sufficient frequency and volume to provide pricing information on an ongoing basis. While the same factors may be used to assess whether a market has experienced a significant decrease in activity and to determine whether a market is active or inactive, these are separate and distinct determinations.

The determination that a market has experienced a significant decrease in volume does not change the requirements of IFRS 13 related to the use of relevant observable data from active markets. That is, despite a decrease from recent (or historical) levels of activity, transactions for an asset or liability in a particular market may still occur with sufficient frequency and volume to provide pricing information on an ongoing basis, thereby qualifying as an active market. If there has been a significant decrease in activity, but a market is still deemed to be active, entities would continue to measure the fair value of identical instruments that trade in this market using P×Q (Level 1 measurement).

An example of this is related to 2011 trading activity for Greek sovereign bonds. During that calendar year, the economic situation in Greece had deteriorated and some had questioned whether the Greek sovereign bonds were still being actively traded. In a public statement, ESMA indicated that, '[b]ased on trading data obtained from the Bank of Greece, it [was their] opinion that, as of 30 June 2011, the market was active for some Greek sovereign bonds but could be judged inactive for some others.'[12] While ESMA provided no predictions about the level of trading activity as at 31 December 2011, ESMA clearly stated their expectation that a fair value measurement of Greek sovereign bonds, in interim and annual financial statements during 2011 should be a Level 1 measurement in situations where there was still an active market. Furthermore, ESMA expected entities to use a Level 2 measurement method that maximises the use of observable market data to measure the fair value of those bonds that were traded in inactive markets.

Determining whether a particular market is considered liquid or active versus illiquid or inactive may require significant judgement and consider a variety of factors (e.g. what the bid-ask spread represents, how deep the bid-ask spread has to be to signal an inactive market, what is the sufficient level of trade volume to signify an active market, etc.). This can be particularly challenging in emerging markets.

While traditionally, the focus of such assessments has been public markets and listed securities, we have observed that sometimes trading in unlisted securities may be more active than in some listed securities.[13] In its 2008 report, the IASB Expert Advisory Panel noted 'There is no bright line between active markets and inactive markets. However, the biggest distinction between prices observed in active markets and prices observed in inactive markets is typically that, for inactive markets, an entity needs to put more work into the valuation process to gain assurance that the transaction price provides evidence of fair value or to determine the adjustments to transaction prices that are necessary to measure the fair value of the instrument.

'The issue to be addressed, therefore, is not about market activity per se, but about whether the transaction price observed represents fair value. Characteristics of an inactive market include a significant decline in the volume and level of trading activity, the available prices vary significantly over time or among market participants or the prices are not current. However, these factors alone do not necessarily mean that a market is no longer active. An active market is one in which transactions are taking place regularly on an arm's length basis. What is "regularly" is a matter of judgement and depends upon the facts and circumstances of the market for the instrument being measured at fair value'.[14]

Similar challenges exist for entities assessing whether a market is active for thinly traded investments. While trading volumes may be low, it may be challenging to conclude a market is not active when it regularly provides pricing information. This may be particularly difficult in some emerging markets. Therefore, significant judgement will be needed to assess whether a market is active, based on the weight of evidence available.

Determining whether a market is active may be more challenging if regulators challenge an entity's judgement. For example, in its July 2015 enforcement report, ESMA noted that, in order to assess the existence of an active market, the entity had 'calculated a number of ratios and compared them against the following benchmarks:

- daily % of average value of trades / capitalisation lower than 0.05%;
- daily equivalent value of trades lower than CU50,000;
- daily bid-ask spread higher or equal to 3%;
- maximum number of consecutive days with unvaried prices higher than 3;
- % of trading days lower than 100%.'[15]

After performing this analysis and considering the limited trading volume, the issuer concluded that shares held in three of its listed available-for-sale investments were not traded in active markets. As a result, it measured fair value using a valuation technique based on Level 3 inputs. The enforcer disagreed with the issuer's assessment of whether the markets were active and thought that the quoted prices for these investments should have been used to measure fair value. In reaching this decision, the enforcer specifically noted that 'the indicators used by the issuer were insufficient to conclude that the transaction price did not represent fair value or that transactions occurred with insufficient frequency and volume. ... [T]he issuer did not gather sufficient information to determine whether transactions were orderly or took place with sufficient frequency and volume to provide pricing information. Therefore, based on available data, it was not possible to conclude that the markets, where the investments were listed, were not active and further analysis should have been performed to measure fair value.'[16] The enforcer also raised concerns that the valuations based on Level 3 inputs were much higher than the quoted prices. Care will be needed when reaching a conclusion that a market is not active as this is a high hurdle.

During the PIR on IFRS 13, many respondents indicated they found the assessment of whether a market is active to be challenging and asked for additional guidance. The IASB decided not to provide additional guidance, noting in particular that the requirements are principles-based and, as such, judgement will always be needed in their application.[17]

8.2 Identifying transactions that are not orderly

IFRS 13 defines an orderly transaction as 'a transaction that assumes exposure to the market for a period before the measurement date to allow for marketing activities that are usual and customary for transactions involving such assets or liabilities; it is not a forced transaction (e.g. a forced liquidation or distress sale)'. *[IFRS 13 Appendix A]*. This definition includes two key components:

(i) adequate market exposure is required in order to provide market participants the ability to obtain an awareness and knowledge of the asset or liability necessary for a market-based exchange; and

(ii) the transaction should involve market participants that, while being motivated to transact for the asset or liability, are not compelled to do so.

According to IFRS 13, 'circumstances that may indicate that a transaction is not orderly include the following:

(a) There was not adequate exposure to the market for a period before the measurement date to allow for marketing activities that are usual and customary for transactions involving such assets or liabilities under current market conditions;

(b) There was a usual and customary marketing period, but the seller marketed the asset or liability to a single market participant;

(c) The seller is in or near bankruptcy or receivership (i.e. the seller is distressed);

(d) The seller was required to sell to meet regulatory or legal requirements (i.e. the seller was forced);

(e) The transaction price is an outlier when compared with other recent transactions for the same or a similar asset or liability'. *[IFRS 13.B43]*.

These factors are not intended to be all-inclusive and should be considered along with any additional factors that may be pertinent to the individual facts and circumstances.

An entity must consider the following when measuring fair value or estimating market risk premiums:

- if the evidence indicates that a transaction is not orderly, the entity places little, if any, weight (compared with other indications of fair value) on that transaction price;

- if the evidence indicates that a transaction is orderly, the entity must take that transaction price into account. The amount of weight placed on that transaction price (compared with other indications of fair value) will depend on facts and circumstances, such as:
    (i) the volume of the transaction;
    (ii) the comparability of the transaction to the asset or liability being measured; and
    (iii) the proximity of the transaction to the measurement date; and

- if an entity does not have sufficient information to determine whether a transaction is orderly, it must take that transaction price into account. However, it may not be representative of fair value, particularly where it is not the only or primary measure of fair value or market risk premium. Therefore, the entity must place less weight on those transactions (i.e. transactions the entity cannot conclude are orderly) and more weight on transactions that are known to be orderly. *[IFRS 13.B44]*.

IFRS 13 acknowledges that the determination of whether a transaction is orderly may be more difficult if there has been a significant decrease in the volume or level of activity. However, the standard is clear that, even when there has been a significant decrease in the volume or level of activity for an asset or liability, it is not appropriate to conclude that all transactions in that market are not orderly (i.e. distressed or forced). *[IFRS 13.B43]*. Instead, further assessment as to whether an observed transaction is not orderly generally needs to be made at the individual transaction level.

IFRS 13 does not require an entity to undertake all possible efforts in assessing whether a transaction is orderly. However, information that is available without undue cost and effort cannot be ignored. For instance, when an entity is party to a transaction, the standard presumes it would have sufficient information to conclude whether the transaction is orderly. *[IFRS 13.B44]*. Conversely, the lack of transparency into the details of individual transactions occurring in the market, to which the entity is not a party, can pose practical challenges for many entities in making this assessment. Recognising this difficulty, the IASB provided additional guidance in paragraph B44(c) of IFRS 13, which indicates that while observable data should not be ignored when the reporting entity does not have sufficient information to conclude on whether the transaction is orderly, the entity should place less weight on those transactions in comparison to other transactions that the reporting entity has concluded are orderly (see 8.3 below for further discussion). *[IFRS 13.B44(c)]*.

8.2.1 Are all transactions entered into to meet regulatory requirements or transactions initiated during bankruptcy assumed to be not orderly?

Although an entity may be viewed as being compelled to sell assets to comply with regulatory requirements, such transfers are not necessarily disorderly. If the entity was provided with the usual and customary period of time to market the asset to multiple potential buyers, the transaction price may be representative of the asset's fair value. Similarly, transactions initiated during bankruptcy are not automatically assumed to be disorderly. The determination of whether a transaction is not orderly requires a thorough evaluation of the specific facts and circumstances, including the exposure period and the number of potential buyers.

8.2.2 Is it possible for orderly transactions to take place in a 'distressed' market?

Yes. While there may be increased instances of transactions that are not orderly when a market has undergone a significant decrease in volume, it is not appropriate to assume that all transactions that occur in a market during a period of dislocation are distressed or forced. This determination is made at the individual transaction level and requires the use of judgement based on the specific facts and circumstances. While market factors such as an imbalance in supply and demand can affect the prices at which transactions occur in a given market, such an imbalance, in and of itself, does not indicate that the parties to a transaction were not knowledgeable and willing market participants or that a transaction was not orderly. For example, a transaction in a dislocated market is less likely to be considered a 'distressed sale' when multiple buyers have bid on the asset.

In addition, while a fair value measurement incorporates the assumptions that sellers, as well as buyers, would consider in pricing the asset or liability, an entity's conclusion that it would not sell its own asset (or transfer its own liability) at prices currently observed in the market does not mean these transactions should be presumed to be distressed. IFRS 13 makes clear that fair value is a market-based measurement, not an entity-specific measurement, and notes that the entity's intention to hold an asset or liability is not relevant in estimating its fair value. The objective of a fair value measurement is to estimate the exit price in an orderly transaction between willing market participants at the measurement date under current market conditions. This price should include a risk premium that reflects the amount market participants would require as compensation for bearing any uncertainty inherent in the cash flows, and this uncertainty (as well as the compensation demanded to assume it) may be affected by current marketplace conditions. The objective of a fair value measurement does not change when markets are inactive or in a period of dislocation.

An example of the application of this principle relates to 2020 trading activity in many public markets during the coronavirus pandemic. The pandemic resulted in downturns and significant volatility in the financial and commodities markets worldwide. Despite the downturns seen in many public markets, this did not generally translate into significant decreases in volume in those markets. Therefore, even if a financial instrument's value declined, since the markets remained active, entities had to continue using a Level 1 measurement as they could not presume the transactions were distressed. While volatility in the financial markets may suggest that the prices are aberrations and do not reflect fair value, it would not be appropriate for an entity to disregard market prices at the measurement date. IFRS 13 makes it clear that fair value is a market-based measurement, not an entity-specific measurement, and notes that the reporting entity's intention to hold an asset or liability in a market downturn is not relevant. *[IFRS 13.3]*.

8.3 Estimating fair value when there has been a significant decrease in the volume and level of activity

Estimating the price at which market participants would be willing to enter into a transaction if there has been a significant decrease in the volume or level of activity for the asset or liability will depend on the specific facts and circumstances and will require judgement. However, the core concepts of the fair value framework continue to apply. For example, an entity's intentions regarding the asset or liability (e.g. to sell an asset or settle a liability), are not relevant when measuring fair value because that would result in an entity-specific measurement. *[IFRS 13.B42]*.

If there has been a significant decrease in the volume or level of activity for the asset or liability, it may be appropriate to reconsider the valuation technique being used or to use multiple valuation techniques, for example, the use of both a market approach and a present value technique (see 8.3.2 below for further discussion). *[IFRS 13.B40]*.

If quoted prices provided by third parties are used, an entity must evaluate whether those quoted prices have been developed using current information that reflects orderly transactions or a valuation technique that reflects market participant assumptions, including assumptions about risk. This evaluation must take into consideration the nature of a quote (e.g. whether the quote is an indicative price or a binding offer). In weighting a quoted price as an input to a fair value measurement, more weight is given to quotes that reflect the result of actual transactions or those that represent binding offers. Less weight is given to quotes that are not binding, reflect indicative pricing or do not reflect the result of transactions.

In some instances, an entity may determine that a transaction or quoted price requires an adjustment, such as when the price is stale or when the price for a similar asset requires significant adjustment to make it comparable to the asset being measured. *[IFRS 13.B38]*. The impact of these adjustments may be significant to the fair value measure and, if so, would affect its categorisation in the fair value hierarchy (see 16.2 below for further discussion on categorisation within the fair value hierarchy).

8.3.1 Assessing the relevance of observable data

While observable prices from inactive markets may not be representative of fair value in all cases, this data should not be ignored. Instead, paragraphs B38 and B44 of IFRS 13 clarify that additional analysis is required to assess the relevance of the observable data. *[IFRS 13.B38, B44]*. The relevance of a quoted price from an inactive market is dependent on whether the transaction is determined to be orderly. If the observed price is based on a transaction that is determined to be forced or disorderly, little, if any, weight should be placed on it compared with other indications of value.

If the quoted price is based on a transaction that is determined to be orderly, this data point should be considered in the estimation of fair value. However, the relevance of quoted prices associated with orderly transactions can vary based on factors specific to the asset or liability being measured and the facts and circumstances surrounding the price. Some of the factors to be considered include:

- the condition and(or) location of the asset or liability;
- the similarity of the transactions to the asset or liability being measured (e.g. the extent to which the inputs relate to items that are comparable to the asset or liability);
- the size of the transactions;
- the volume or level of activity in the markets within which the transactions are observed;
- the proximity of the transactions to the measurement date; and
- whether the market participants involved in the transaction had access to information about the asset or liability that is usual and customary.

If the adjustments made to the observable price are significant and based on unobservable data, the resulting measurement would represent a Level 3 measurement.

Figure 14.3: Orderly transactions: measuring fair value and estimating market risk premiums

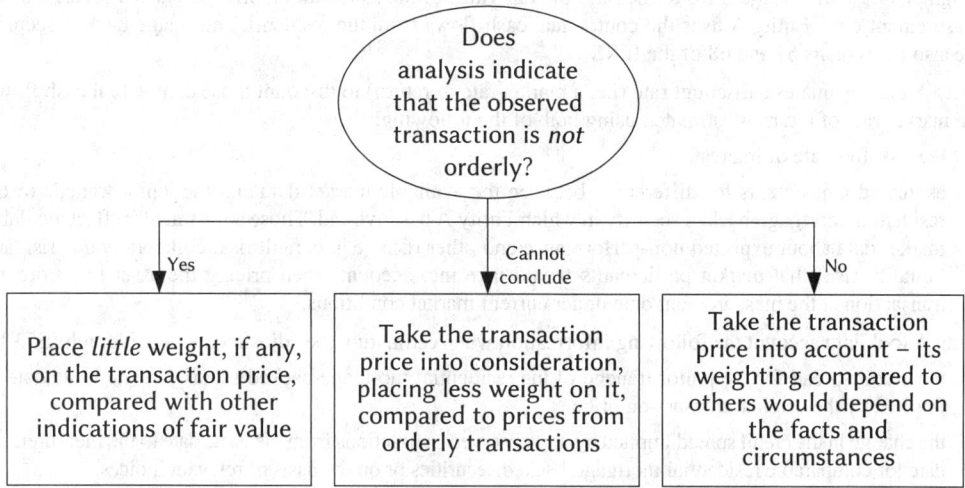

8.3.2 Selection and use of valuation techniques when there has been a significant decrease in volume or level of activity

As discussed above, when activity has significantly decreased for an asset or liability, an assessment of the relevance of observable market data will be required and adjustments to observable market data may be warranted. A significant decrease in volume or activity can also influence which valuation technique(s) are used and how those techniques are applied.

The following example from IFRS 13 highlights some key valuation considerations for assets that trade in markets that have experienced a significant decrease in volume and level of activity. *[IFRS 13.IE49-IE58]*.

Example 14.9: Estimating a market rate of return when there is a significant decrease in volume or level of activity

Entity A invests in a junior AAA-rated tranche of a residential mortgage-backed security on 1 January 20X8 (the issue date of the security). The junior tranche is the third most senior of a total of seven tranches. The underlying collateral for the residential mortgage-backed security is unguaranteed non-conforming residential mortgage loans that were issued in the second half of 20X6.

At 31 March 20X9 (the measurement date) the junior tranche is now A-rated. This tranche of the residential mortgage-backed security was previously traded through a brokered market. However, trading volume in that market was infrequent, with only a few transactions taking place per month from 1 January 20X8 to 30 June 20X8 and little, if any, trading activity during the nine months before 31 March 20X9.

Entity A takes into account the factors in paragraph B37 of the IFRS to determine whether there has been a significant decrease in the volume or level of activity for the junior tranche of the residential mortgage-backed security in which it has invested. After evaluating the significance and relevance of the factors, Entity A concludes that the volume and level of activity of the junior tranche of the residential mortgage-backed security have significantly decreased. Entity A supported its judgement primarily on the basis that there was little, if any, trading activity for an extended period before the measurement date.

Because there is little, if any, trading activity to support a valuation technique using a market approach, Entity A decides to use an income approach using the discount rate adjustment technique described in paragraphs B18-B22 of the IFRS to measure the fair value of the residential mortgage-backed security at the measurement date. Entity A uses the contractual cash flows from the residential mortgage-backed security (see also paragraphs 67 and 68 of the IFRS).

Entity A then estimates a discount rate (i.e. a market rate of return) to discount those contractual cash flows. The market rate of return is estimated using both of the following:

(a) the risk-free rate of interest.

(b) estimated adjustments for differences between the available market data and the junior tranche of the residential mortgage-backed security in which Entity A has invested. Those adjustments reflect available market data about expected non-performance and other risks (e.g. default risk, collateral value risk and liquidity risk) that market participants would take into account when pricing the asset in an orderly transaction at the measurement date under current market conditions.

Entity A took into account the following information when estimating the adjustments in paragraph IE53(b):

(a) the credit spread for the junior tranche of the residential mortgage-backed security at the issue date as implied by the original transaction price.

(b) the change in the credit spread implied by any observed transactions from the issue date to the measurement date for comparable residential mortgage-backed securities or on the basis of relevant indices.

(c) the characteristics of the junior tranche of the residential mortgage-backed security compared with comparable residential mortgage-backed securities or indices, including all the following:

   (i) the quality of the underlying assets, i.e. information about the performance of the underlying mortgage loans such as delinquency and foreclosure rates, loss experience and prepayment rates;

   (ii) the seniority or subordination of the residential mortgage-backed security tranche held; and

   (iii) other relevant factors.

(d) relevant reports issued by analysts and rating agencies.

(e) quoted prices from third parties such as brokers or pricing services.

Entity A estimates that one indication of the market rate of return that market participants would use when pricing the junior tranche of the residential mortgage-backed security is 12 per cent (1,200 basis points). This market rate of return was estimated as follows:

(a) Begin with 300 basis points for the relevant risk-free rate of interest at 31 March 20X9.

(b) Add 250 basis points for the credit spread over the risk-free rate when the junior tranche was issued in January 20X8.

(c) Add 700 basis points for the estimated change in the credit spread over the risk-free rate of the junior tranche between 1 January 20X8 and 31 March 20X9. This estimate was developed on the basis of the change in the most comparable index available for that time period.

(d) Subtract 50 basis points (net) to adjust for differences between the index used to estimate the change in credit spreads and the junior tranche. The referenced index consists of subprime mortgage loans, whereas Entity A's residential mortgage-backed security consists of similar mortgage loans with a more favourable credit profile (making it more attractive to market participants). However, the index does not reflect an appropriate liquidity risk premium for the junior tranche under current market conditions. Thus, the 50 basis point adjustment is the net of two adjustments:

   (i) the first adjustment is a 350 basis point subtraction, which was estimated by comparing the implied yield from the most recent transactions for the residential mortgage-backed security in June 20X8 with the implied yield in the index price on those same dates. There was no information available that indicated that the relationship between Entity A's security and the index has changed.

   (ii) the second adjustment is a 300 basis point addition, which is Entity A's best estimate of the additional liquidity risk inherent in its security (a cash position) when compared with the index (a synthetic position). This estimate was derived after taking into account liquidity risk premiums implied in recent cash transactions for a range of similar securities.

As an additional indication of the market rate of return, Entity A takes into account two recent indicative quotes (i.e. non-binding quotes) provided by reputable brokers for the junior tranche of the residential mortgage-backed security that imply yields of 15-17 per cent. Entity A is unable to evaluate the valuation technique(s) or inputs used to develop the quotes. However, Entity A is able to confirm that the quotes do not reflect the results of transactions.

Because Entity A has multiple indications of the market rate of return that market participants would take into account when measuring fair value, it evaluates and weights the respective indications of the rate of return, considering the reasonableness of the range indicated by the results.

Entity A concludes that 13 per cent is the point within the range of indications that is most representative of fair value under current market conditions. Entity A places more weight on the 12 per cent indication (i.e. its own estimate of the market rate of return) for the following reasons:

(a) Entity A concluded that its own estimate appropriately incorporated the risks (e.g. default risk, collateral value risk and liquidity risk) that market participants would use when pricing the asset in an orderly transaction under current market conditions.

(b) The broker quotes were non-binding and did not reflect the results of transactions, and Entity A was unable to evaluate the valuation technique(s) or inputs used to develop the quotes.

In Example 14.9 above, Entity A uses an income approach (i.e. discount rate adjustment technique, see 21 below for further discussion regarding present value techniques) to estimate the fair value of its residential mortgage-backed security (RMBS), because limited trading activity precluded a market approach as at the measurement date.

Example 14.9 illustrates that the entity's use of an income approach does not change the objective of the fair value measurement, which is a current exit price. Valuation models should take into account all the factors that market participants would consider when pricing an asset or liability. The discount rate used by Entity A, for example, tries to incorporate all of the risks (e.g. liquidity risk, non-performance risk) market participants would consider in pricing the RMBS under current market conditions. Liquidity, credit or any other risk factors market participants would consider in pricing the asset or liability may require adjustments to model values if such factors are not sufficiently captured in the model.

Entity A prioritises observable inputs (to the extent available) over unobservable inputs in its application of the income approach. Entity A assesses market-based data from various sources to estimate the discount rate. For example, the entity estimates the change in the credit spread of the RMBS since its issuance based on spread changes observed from the most comparable index, for which trades continue to occur. Using the best available market information, the entity adjusts this input to account for differences between the observed index and the RMBS. These adjustments include the entity's assessment of the additional liquidity risk inherent in the RMBS compared to the index.

Paragraph 89 of IFRS 13 indicates that an entity may use its own internal assumptions when relevant observable market data does not exist. *[IFRS 13.89]*. However, if reasonably available data indicates that market participant assumptions would differ, the entity should adjust its assumptions to incorporate that information. Relevant market data is not limited to transactions for the identical asset or liability being measured.

In the above example, Entity A is unable to use a market approach because of limited trading activity for the RMBS. Therefore, Entity A considers implied liquidity risk premiums from recent transactions for a range of similar securities to estimate the incremental premium market participants would demand for its RMBS in the current market (as compared to the benchmark spread). In addition, Entity A considers two indicative broker quotes to estimate an appropriate discount rate for its RMBS. Although these quotes are specific to the RMBS being valued, Entity A puts less weight on these quotes since they are not binding and are not based on actual transactions. Furthermore, Entity A was unable to evaluate the valuation techniques and underlying data used by the brokers.

Importantly, the illustrative example is not intended to imply that an entity's own assumptions carry more weight than non-binding broker quotes. Rather, the example illustrates that each indication of value needs to be assessed based on the extent these indications rely on observable versus unobservable inputs.

Even though the market approach could not be used because of limited trading activity for the RMBS, Entity A was able to corroborate many of the assumptions used in developing the discount rate with relevant observable market data. As a result, the decision by the entity to place additional weight on its own market-corroborated assumptions (and less on the broker quotes) was warranted. When differences between broker quotes or pricing service data and an entity's own determination of value are significant, management should seek to understand the reasons behind these differences, if possible.

9 THE PRICE

'Fair value is the price that would be received to sell an asset or paid to transfer a liability in an orderly transaction in the principal (or most advantageous) market at the measurement date under current market conditions (i.e. an exit price) regardless of whether that price is directly observable or estimated using another valuation technique'. *[IFRS 13.24].*

IFRS 13 requires the entity to estimate fair value based on the price that would be received to sell the asset or transfer the liability being measured (i.e. an exit price). While the determination of this price may be straightforward in some cases (e.g. when the identical instrument trades in an active market), in others it will require significant judgement. However, IFRS 13 makes it clear that the price used to measure fair value shall not be adjusted for transaction costs, but would consider transportation costs. *[IFRS 13.25, 26].*

The standard's guidance on the valuation techniques and inputs to these techniques used in determining the exit price (including the prohibition on block discounts) is discussed at 14 and 15 below.

9.1 Transaction costs

Transaction costs are defined as the costs to sell an asset or transfer a liability in the principal (or most advantageous) market for the asset or liability that are directly attributable to the disposal of an asset or the transfer of the liability. In addition, these costs must be incremental, i.e. they would not have been incurred by the entity had the decision to sell the asset or transfer the liability not been made. *[IFRS 13 Appendix A].* Examples of transaction costs include commissions or certain due diligence costs. As noted above, transaction costs do not include transportation costs.

Fair value is not adjusted for transaction costs. This is because transaction costs are not a characteristic of an asset or a liability; they are a characteristic of the transaction. While not deducted from fair value, an entity considers transaction costs in the context of determining the most advantageous market in the absence of a principal market (see 6.2 above) because in this instance the entity is seeking to determine the market that would maximise the net amount that would be received for the asset.

9.1.1 Are transaction costs in IFRS 13 the same as 'costs to sell' in other IFRSs?

As discussed at 2.1.2 above, some IFRSs permit or require measurements based on fair value, where costs to sell or costs of disposal are deducted from the fair value measurement. IFRS 13 does not change the measurement objective for assets accounted for at fair value less cost to sell. The 'fair value less cost to sell' measurement objective includes: (1) fair value; and (2) cost to sell. The fair value component is measured in accordance with the IFRS 13.

Consistent with the definition of transaction costs in IFRS 13, IAS 36 describes costs of disposal as 'the direct incremental costs attributable to the disposal of the asset or cash-generating unit, excluding finance costs and income tax expense'. *[IAS 36.6]*. IAS 41 and IFRS 5 similarly define costs to sell.

As such, transaction costs excluded from the determination of fair value in accordance with IFRS 13 will generally be consistent with costs to sell or costs of disposal, determined in other IFRSs (listed at 2.1.2 above), provided they exclude transportation costs.

Since the fair value component is measured in accordance with IFRS 13, the standard's disclosure requirements apply in situations where the fair value less cost to sell measurement is required subsequent to the initial recognition, unless specifically exempt from the disclosure requirements (see 20 below). In addition, IFRS 13 clarifies that adjustments used to arrive at measurements based on fair value (e.g. the cost to sell when estimating fair value less cost to sell) should not be considered when determining where to categorise the measurement in the fair value hierarchy (see 16 below).

9.1.2 Transaction costs in IFRS 13 versus acquisition-related transaction costs in other IFRSs

The term 'transaction costs' is used in many IFRSs, but sometimes it refers to transaction costs actually incurred when acquiring an item and sometimes to transaction costs expected to be incurred when selling an item. While the same term might be used, it is important to differentiate between these types of transaction costs.

IAS 36, IAS 41 and IFRS 5 discuss costs to sell or dispose of an item (as discussed at 9.1.1 above). In contrast, other standards refer to capitalising or expensing transaction costs incurred in the context of acquiring an asset, assuming a liability or issuing an entity's own equity (a buyer's perspective). IFRS 3, for example, requires acquisition-related costs to be expensed in the period incurred. *[IFRS 3.53]*.

IFRS 13 indicates that transaction costs are not included in a fair value measurement. As such, actual transaction costs (e.g. commissions paid) that are incurred by an entity when acquiring an asset would not be included at initial recognition when fair value is the measurement objective. Likewise, transaction costs that would be incurred in a hypothetical sales transaction would also not be included in a fair value measurement.

Some standards permit acquisition-related transaction costs to be capitalised at initial recognition, then permit or require the item, to which those costs relate, to be subsequently measured at fair value. In those situations, some or all of the acquisition-related transaction costs that were capitalised will effectively be expensed as part of the resulting fair value gain or loss. This is consistent with current practice. For example, IAS 40 permits transaction costs to be capitalised as part of an investment property's cost on initial recognition. *[IAS 40.20]*. However, if the fair value model is applied to the subsequent measurement of the investment property, transaction costs would be excluded from the fair value measurement.

Similarly, at initial recognition, financial assets or liabilities in the scope of IFRS 9 are generally measured at their 'fair value plus or minus, in the case of a financial asset or liability not at fair value through profit or loss, transaction costs that are directly attributable to the acquisition or issue of the financial asset or liability'. *[IFRS 9.5.1.1]*. For those items subsequently measured at amortised cost, these transaction costs will be captured as part of the instrument's effective interest rate.

9.2 Transportation costs

Transportation costs represent those that would be incurred to transport an asset or liability to (or from) the principal (or most advantageous) market. If location is a characteristic of the asset or liability being measured (e.g. as might be the case with a commodity), the price in the principal (or most advantageous) market should be adjusted for transportation costs. The following simplified example illustrates this concept.

Example 14.10: Transportation costs

Entity A holds a physical commodity measured at fair value in its warehouse in Europe. For this commodity, the London exchange is determined to be the principal market as it represents the market with the greatest volume and level of activity for the asset that the entity can reasonably access.

The exchange price for the asset is £25. However, the contracts traded on the exchange for this commodity require physical delivery to London. Entity A determines that it would cost £5 to transport the physical commodity to London and the broker's commission would be £3 to transact on the London exchange.

Since location is a characteristic of the asset and transportation to the principal market is required, the fair value of the physical commodity would be £20 – the price in the principal market for the asset £25, less transportation costs of £5. The £3 broker commission represents a transaction cost that would not adjust the price in the principal market.

10 APPLICATION TO NON-FINANCIAL ASSETS

Many non-financial assets, either through the initial or subsequent measurement requirements of an IFRS or, the requirements of IAS 36 for impairment testing (if recoverable amount is based on fair value less costs of disposal), are either permitted or required to be measured at fair value (or a measure based on fair value). For example, management may need to measure the fair value of non-financial assets and liabilities when completing the purchase price allocation for a business combination in accordance with IFRS 3. First-time adopters of IFRS might need to measure fair value of assets and liabilities if they use a 'fair value as deemed cost' approach in accordance with IFRS 1 – *First-time Adoption of International Financial Reporting Standards*.

In addition to the principles described in the sections above, the fair value measurement of non-financial assets must reflect the highest and best use of the asset from a market participant's perspective.

The highest and best use of an asset establishes the valuation premise used to measure the fair value of the asset. In other words, whether to assume market participants would derive value from using the non-financial asset (based on its highest and best use) on its own or in combination with other assets or with other assets and liabilities. As discussed below, this might be its current use or some alternative use.

As discussed at 4.2 above, the concepts of highest and best use and valuation premise in IFRS 13 are only relevant for non-financial assets (and not financial assets and liabilities). This is because:

- financial assets have specific contractual terms; they do not have alternative uses. Changing the characteristics of the financial asset (i.e. changing the contractual terms) causes the item to become a different asset and the objective of a fair value measurement is to measure the asset as it exists as at the measurement date;
- the different ways by which an entity may relieve itself of a liability are not alternative uses. In addition, entity-specific advantages (or disadvantages) that enable an entity to fulfil a liability more or less efficiently than other market participants are not considered in a fair value measurement; and
- the concepts of highest and best use and valuation premise were developed within the valuation profession to value non-financial assets, such as land. *[IFRS 13.BC63]*.

10.1 Highest and best use

Fair value measurements of non-financial assets take into account 'a market participant's ability to generate economic benefits by using the asset in its *highest and best use* or by selling it to another market participant that would use the asset in its highest and best use'. *[IFRS 13.27]*.

Highest and best use refers to 'the use of a non-financial asset by market participants that would maximise the value of the asset or the group of assets and liabilities (e.g. a business) within which the asset would be used'. *[IFRS 13 Appendix A]*.

The highest and best use of an asset considers uses of the asset that are:

(a) physically possible: the physical characteristics of the asset that market participants would take into account when pricing the asset (e.g. the location or size of a property);

(b) legally permissible: any legal restrictions on the use of the asset that market participants would take into account when pricing the asset (e.g. the zoning regulations applicable to a property); and

(c) financially feasible: whether a use of the asset that is physically possible and legally permissible generates adequate income or cash flows (taking into account the costs of converting the asset to that use) to produce an investment return that market participants would require from an investment in that asset put to that use. *[IFRS 13.28]*.

Highest and best use is a valuation concept that considers how market participants would use a non-financial asset to maximise its benefit or value. The maximum value of a non-financial asset to market participants may come from its use: (a) in combination with other assets or with other assets and liabilities; or (b) on a stand-alone basis.

In determining the highest and best use of a non-financial asset, paragraph 28 of IFRS 13 indicates uses that are physically possible, legally permissible (see 10.1.1 below for further discussion) and financially feasible should be considered. As such, when assessing alternative uses, entities should consider the physical characteristics of the asset, any legal restrictions on its use and whether the value generated provides an adequate investment return for market participants.

Provided there is sufficient evidence to support these assertions, alternative uses that would enable market participants to maximise value should be considered, but a search for potential alternative uses need not be exhaustive. In addition, any costs to transform the non-financial asset (e.g. obtaining a new zoning permit or converting the asset to the alternative use) and profit expectations from a market participant's perspective are also considered in the fair value measurement.

If there are multiple types of market participants who would use the asset differently, these alternative scenarios must be considered before concluding on the asset's highest and best use. While applying the fair value framework may be straightforward in many situations, in other instances, an iterative process may be needed to consistently apply the various components. This may be required due to the interdependence among several key concepts in IFRS 13's fair value framework (see Figure 14.2 at 4.2 above). For example, the highest and best use of a non-financial asset determines its valuation premise and affects the identification of the appropriate market participants. Likewise, the determination of the principal (or most advantageous) market can be important in determining the highest and best use of a non-financial asset.

Determining whether the maximum value to market participants would be achieved either by using an asset in combination with other assets and liabilities as a group, or by using the asset on a stand-alone basis, requires judgement and an assessment of the specific facts and circumstances.

A careful assessment is particularly important when the highest and best use of a non-financial asset is in combination with one or more non-financial assets.

As discussed at 10.2 below, assets in an asset group should all be valued using the same valuation premise. For example, if the fair value of a piece of machinery on a manufacturing line is measured assuming its highest and best use is in conjunction with other equipment in the manufacturing line, those other non-financial assets in the asset group (i.e. the other equipment on the manufacturing line) would also be valued using the same premise. As highlighted by Example 14.13 at 10.2.2 below, once it is determined that the value for a set of assets is maximised when considered as a group, all of the assets in that group would be valued using the same premise, regardless of whether any individual asset within the group would have a higher value on a stand-alone basis. During the PIR some respondents noted application of this concept as challenging and requested further guidance on for example what is meant by legally permissible however the Board concluded that there was insufficient evidence of inconsistent application of requirements and that it is doubtful whether supporting material would be helpful in the situations when the application of the highest and best use is challenging.[18]

10.1.1 Highest and best use: determining what is legally permissible

To be legally permissible, the standard indicates a use of a non-financial asset need not be legal (or have legal approval) at the measurement date, but it must not be legally prohibited in the jurisdiction. *[IFRS 13.BC69]*.

What is legally permissible is a matter of law. However, the IASB seems to be distinguishing between a use that is explicitly prohibited and a use that would be permitted if the jurisdiction's specific legal requirements were met. However, in some situations it may be difficult to determine whether a use is capable of being legally permitted when, at the measurement date, it is subject to legal restrictions that are not easily overcome.

The standard gives the example of a land development. Assume the government has prohibited building on or developing certain land (i.e. the land is a protected area). For the entity to develop the land, a change of law would be required. Since development of this land would be illegal, it cannot be the highest and best use of the land. Alternatively, assume the land has been zoned for commercial use, but nearby areas have recently been developed for residential use and, as such, market participants would consider residential development as a potential use of the land. Since re-zoning the land for residential development would only require approval from an authority and that approval is usually given, this alternative use could be deemed to be legally permissible.

It is assumed that market participants would consider all relevant factors, as they exist at the measurement date, in determining whether the legally permissible use of the non-financial asset may be something other than its current use. That is, market participants would consider the probability, extent and timing of different types of approvals that may be required in assessing whether a change in the legal use of the non-financial asset could be obtained.

The scenarios, of protected land and re-zoning of land, considered above illustrate either end of the spectrum; uses that are unlikely and likely to be legally permissible, respectively. However, consider the protected land example above. Assume the government were expected to change the law in the near future to permit residential development, but there had not been any similar changes in law to date. An entity would need to consider the weight of evidence available and whether market participants would have similar expectations. This may be more difficult without past history of similar changes in law. However, an entity might consider factors such as whether expectations are based on verbal assurances or written evidence; whether the process to change the law has begun; and the risk that the change in law will not be approved. It may also help to determine whether market participants would pay for this potential. However, this fact, on its own, is unlikely to be sufficient to support a use being legally permissible.

In our view, an entity would need to have sufficient evidence to support its assumption about the potential for an alternative use, particularly in light of IFRS 13's presumption that the highest and best use is an asset's current use. In the example above of re-zoning land for residential development, the entity's belief that re-zoning was possible (or even likely) is unlikely to be sufficient evidence that the re-zoning is legally permissible. However, the fact that nearby areas had recently been re-zoned for residential use may provide additional evidence as to the likelihood that the land being measured could similarly be re-zoned. If obtaining re-zoning permission is not merely perfunctory, there may be a significant burden on the entity to prove that market participants would consider commercial use of the land 'legally permissible'.

10.1.2 Highest and best use versus current use

Although IFRS 13 presumes that an entity's current use of an asset is its highest and best use, market or other factors may suggest that a different use by market participants would maximise the value of that asset. *[IFRS 13.29]*. Because the highest and best use of an asset is determined based on market participants' expectations, reporting entities may need to consider alternative uses of an asset (e.g. land) in their analysis of fair value. An entity's current or intended use of a non-financial asset might not be the highest and best use of the asset, and thus would not determine its premise of value. Instead, the highest and best use of the asset (or asset group) should be determined based on how market participants would maximise the asset's value. For example, market participants may maximise the value of land, currently used as a site for a manufacturing facility, for residential housing instead.

The consideration of alternative uses is not intended to be exhaustive. It is not necessary that all possible alternatives be considered. Instead, judgement is required in assessing those alternative uses that market participants would consider in pricing the asset. As noted above, consideration of what is physically possible, legally permissible and financially feasible would be part of this assessment. Example 14.11, based on an example in IFRS 13, illustrates this further. If an entity determines that the highest and best use of an asset is different from its current use, IFRS 13 requires that fact to be disclosed as well as the reason why the non-financial asset is being used in a manner that differs from its highest and best use (disclosures are discussed further at 20 below). *[IFRS 13.93(i)]*.

It is important to note that even if the current use of a non-financial asset is the same as its highest and best use, the underlying assumptions used to value the asset should not be entity-specific, but instead should be based on the assumptions that market participants would use when transacting for the asset in its current condition. Entity-specific synergies, if they would differ from market participant synergies, would not be considered in the determination of the highest and best use of the asset. This is illustrated in Example 14.11. *[IFRS 13.IE7-IE8]*.

Example 14.11: Highest and best use versus current use

An entity acquires land in a business combination. The land is currently developed for industrial use as a site for a factory. The current use of the land is presumed to be its highest and best use unless market or other factors suggest a different use. Nearby sites have recently been developed for residential use as sites for high-rise apartment buildings. On the basis of that development and recent zoning and other changes to facilitate that development, the entity determines that the land currently used as a site for a factory could be developed as a site for residential use (i.e. for high-rise apartment buildings) because market participants would take into account the potential to develop the site for residential use when pricing the land.

The highest and best use of the land would be determined by comparing both of the following:

(a) the value of the land as currently developed for industrial use (i.e. the land would be used in combination with other assets, such as the factory, or with other assets and liabilities);

(b) the value of the land as a vacant site for residential use, taking into account the costs of demolishing the factory and other costs (including the uncertainty about whether the entity would be able to convert the asset to the alternative use) necessary to convert the land to a vacant site (i.e. the land is to be used by market participants on a stand-alone basis).

The highest and best use of the land would be determined on the basis of the higher of those values. In situations involving real estate appraisal, the determination of highest and best use might take into account factors relating to the factory operations, including its assets and liabilities.

Assume that the fair value of the land in-use as a manufacturing operation is determined to be $4,000,000 and that the fair value for the land as a vacant site that can be used for residential purposes is $5,000,000. In order to convert the land from a manufacturing operation to a vacant site for residential use, the manufacturing facility must be removed. Assuming demolition and other costs of $500,000.* In order to determine the fair value of the land, the price of the land as a residential development site ($5,000,000) would need to be adjusted for the transformation costs ($500,000) necessary to prepare the land for residential use. Therefore, the amount of $4,500,000 must be used as the fair value of the land.

* For simplicity purposes, this example does not specifically discuss other types of costs that may need to be considered in determining the fair value of the land for residential use (such as the effect of intangible or other assets related to the manufacturing facility).

10.1.3 Highest and best use versus intended use (including defensive value)

An entity's intended use of an asset, at the time it is acquired, may not be the same as how market participants would use the asset. If the highest and best use and the entity's intended use of an asset are not the same, it could result in differences between the price to acquire the asset and fair value measured in accordance with IFRS 13 (see 13 below). IFRS 13 requires that the highest and best use of an asset be determined from the perspective of market participants, even if management intends a different use, *[IFRS 13.29, 30]*, as is illustrated in Example 14.12.

In certain instances, the highest and best use of an asset may be to not actively use it, but instead to lock it up or 'shelve it' (commonly referred to as a defensive asset). That is, the maximum value provided by an asset may be its defensive value. IFRS 13 clarifies that the fair value of an asset used defensively is not assumed to be zero or a nominal amount. Instead, an entity should consider the incremental value such a use provides to the assets being protected, such as the incremental value provided to an entity's existing brand name by acquiring and shelving a competing brand. Generally speaking, a nominal fair value is appropriate only when an asset is abandoned (i.e. when an entity would be willing to give the asset away for no consideration).

Importantly, an entity's decision to use an asset defensively does not mean that market participants would necessarily maximise the asset's value in a similar manner. Likewise, an entity's decision to actively use an asset does not preclude its highest and best use to market participants as being defensive in nature. The following example in IFRS 13 illustrates these points. *[IFRS 13.IE9]*.

Example 14.12: Highest and best use versus intended use

An entity acquires a research and development (R&D) project in a business combination. The entity does not intend to complete the project. If completed, the project would compete with one of its own projects (to provide the next generation of the entity's commercialised technology). Instead, the entity intends to hold (i.e. lock up) the project to prevent its competitors from obtaining access to the technology. In doing this the project is expected to provide defensive value, principally by improving the prospects for the entity's own competing technology. To measure the fair value of the project at initial recognition, the highest and best use of the project would be determined on the basis of its use by market participants. For example:

(a) The highest and best use of the R&D project would be to continue development if market participants would continue to develop the project and that use would maximise the value of the group of assets or of assets and liabilities in which the project would be used (i.e. the asset would be used in combination with other assets or with other assets and liabilities). That might be the case if market participants do not have similar technology, either in development or commercialised. The fair value of the project would be measured on the basis of the price that would be received in a current transaction to sell the project, assuming that the R&D would be used with its complementary assets and the associated liabilities and that those assets and liabilities would be available to market participants.

(b) The highest and best use of the R&D project would be to cease development if, for competitive reasons, market participants would lock up the project and that use would maximise the value of the group of assets or of assets and liabilities in which the project would be used. That might be the case if market participants have technology in a more advanced stage of development that would compete with the project if completed and the project would be expected to improve the prospects for their own competing technology if locked up. The fair value of the project would be measured on the basis of the price that would be received in a current transaction to sell the project, assuming that the R&D would be used (i.e. locked up) with its complementary assets and the associated liabilities and that those assets and liabilities would be available to market participants.

(c) The highest and best use of the R&D project would be to cease development if market participants would discontinue its development. That might be the case if the project is not expected to provide a market rate of return if completed and would not otherwise provide defensive value if locked up. The fair value of the project would be measured on the basis of the price that would be received in a current transaction to sell the project on its own (which might be zero).

If the highest and best use in this example was (a), then that is the value that the entity must ascribe to the R&D project, even though its intended use is to lock-up the project.

The fair value of the in-process research and development project in Example 14.12 above depends on whether market participants would use the asset offensively, defensively or abandon it (as illustrated by points (a), (b) and (c) in the example, respectively). As discussed at 10.1 above, if there are multiple types of market participants who would use the asset differently, these alternative scenarios must be considered before concluding on the asset's highest and best use.

10.2 Valuation premise for non-financial assets

Dependent on its highest and best use, the fair value of the non-financial asset will either be measured based on the value it would derive on a stand-alone basis or in combination with other assets or other assets and liabilities – i.e. the asset's valuation premise.

10.2.1 Valuation premise – stand-alone basis

If the highest and best use of the asset is to use it on a stand-alone basis, an entity measures the fair value of the asset individually. In other words, the asset is assumed to be sold to market participants for use on its own. Fair value is the price that would be received in a current transaction under those circumstances. *[IFRS 13.31(b)]*. For instance, alternative (c) of Example 14.12 above suggests the highest and best use of the research and development project could be to cease development. Since its highest and best use is on a stand-alone basis, the fair value of the project would be the price that would be received in a current transaction to sell the project on its own and assuming a market participant would cease development of the project. In addition, the asset should be measured based only on its current characteristics, potentially requiring an adjustment for transformation costs. For example, if land that is used as a factory site is to be valued on a stand-alone basis, transformation costs (e.g. the cost of removing the factory) should be considered in the fair value measurement.

When the valuation premise of one non-financial asset in an asset group is valued on a stand-alone basis, all of the other assets in the group should also be valued using a consistent valuation premise. For example, based on Example 14.11 at 10.1.2 above, if the highest and best use of the land is determined to be on a stand-alone basis (i.e. as vacant land), the fair value of the equipment in the factory could be determined under two alternative valuation premises: (a) stand-alone (i.e. the value of the equipment sold on a stand-alone basis); or (b) in conjunction with other equipment on the operating line, but in a different factory (i.e. not in combination with the land, since the land would be valued on a stand-alone basis). Regardless of the valuation premise used to measure the equipment, market participant assumptions regarding the cost of redeployment, such as costs for disassembling, transporting and reinstalling the equipment should be considered in the fair value measurement.

10.2.2 Valuation premise – in combination with other assets and/or liabilities

If the highest and best use of a non-financial asset is in combination with other assets as a group or in combination with other assets and liabilities, the fair value of the asset is the price that would be received in a current transaction to sell the asset and would assume that:

(i) market participants would use the asset together with other assets or with other assets and liabilities; and

(ii) those assets and liabilities (i.e. its complementary assets and the associated liabilities) would be available to market participants. *[IFRS 13.31(a)(i)]*. That is, the fair value of the asset would be measured from the perspective of market participants who are presumed to hold the complementary assets and liabilities (see 10.2.3 below for further discussion regarding associated liabilities).

Once an entity determines that the valuation premise for a non-financial asset is its use in combination with a set of assets (or assets and liabilities), all of the complementary non-financial assets in that group should be valued using the same valuation premise (i.e. assuming the same highest and best use), regardless of whether any individual asset within the group would have a higher value under another premise. *[IFRS 13.31(a)(iii)].* Example 14.13 illustrates this further.

Example 14.13:   Consistent assumptions about highest and best use in an asset group

A wine producer owns and manages a vineyard and produces its own wine onsite. The grapes growing on the vines are measured at fair value less costs to sell in accordance with IAS 41 at the end of each reporting period. At the point of harvest, the grapes are measured at the point of harvest at fair value less costs to sell in accordance with IAS 41 (being the grapes' 'cost' when transferred to IAS 2). The wine producer elects to measure its land and vines using IAS 16's revaluation model (fair value less any subsequent accumulated depreciation and accumulated impairment). All other non-financial assets are measured at cost.

At the end of the reporting period, the entity assesses the highest and best use of the grapes growing on the vines, the vines and the land from the perspective of market participants. The grapes growing on the vines, vines and land could continue to be used, in combination with the entity's other assets and liabilities, to produce and sell its wine (i.e. its current use). Alternatively, the land could be converted into residential property. Conversion would include removing the grapes growing on the vines, vines and plant and equipment from the land.

Scenario A

The entity determines that the highest and best use of these assets in combination as a vineyard (i.e. its current use). The entity must make consistent assumptions for assets in the group (for which highest and best use is relevant, i.e. non-financial assets). Therefore, the highest and best use of all non-financial assets in the group is to produce and sell wine, even if conversion into residential property might yield a higher value for the land on its own.

Scenario B

The entity determines that the highest and best use of these assets is to convert the land into residential property, even if the current use might yield a higher value for the grapes growing on the vines and/or the vines. The entity would need to consider what a market participant would do to convert the land, which could include the cost of rezoning, selling cuttings from the vines or simply removing the vines and the grapes growing thereon, and the sale of the buildings and equipment, either individually or as an asset group.

Since the highest and best use of these assets is not their current use in this scenario, the entity would disclose that fact, as well as the reason why those assets are being used in a manner that differs from their highest and best use.

When the asset's highest and best use is in combination with other items, the effect of the valuation premise on the measurement of fair value will depend on the specific circumstances. IFRS 13 gives the following examples.

(a)   The fair value of the asset might be the same whether it is on a stand-alone basis or in an asset group.

This may occur if the asset is a business that market participants would continue to operate, for example, when a business is measured at fair value at initial recognition in accordance with IFRS 3. The transaction would involve valuing the business in its entirety. The use of the assets as a group in an ongoing business would generate synergies that would be available to market participants (i.e. market participant synergies that, therefore, should affect the fair value of the asset on either a stand-alone basis or in combination with other assets or with other assets and liabilities).

(b) An asset's use in an asset group might be incorporated into the fair value measurement through adjustments to the value of the asset used on a stand-alone basis.

For example, assume the asset to be measured at fair value is a machine that is installed and configured for use. If the fair value measurement is determined using an observed price for a similar machine that is not installed or otherwise configured for use, it would need to be adjusted for transport and installation costs so that the fair value measurement reflects the current condition and location of the machine.

(c) An asset's use in an asset group might be incorporated into the fair value measurement through the market participant assumptions used to measure the fair value of the asset.

For example, the asset might be work in progress inventory that is unique and market participants would convert the inventory into finished goods. In that situation, the fair value of the inventory would assume that market participants have acquired or would acquire any specialised machinery necessary to convert the inventory into finished goods.

(d) An asset's use in combination with other assets or with other assets and liabilities might be incorporated into the valuation technique used to measure the fair value of the asset.

That might be the case when using the multi-period excess earnings method to measure the fair value of an intangible asset because that valuation technique specifically takes into account the contribution of any complementary assets and the associated liabilities in the group in which such an intangible asset would be used.

(e) In more limited situations, when an entity uses an asset within a group of assets, the entity might measure the asset at an amount that approximates its fair value when allocating the fair value of the asset group to the individual assets of the group.

For example, this might be the case if the valuation involves real property and the fair value of improved property (i.e. an asset group) is allocated to its component assets (such as land and improvements). *[IFRS 13.B3]*.

Although the approach used to incorporate the valuation premise into a fair value measurement may differ based on the facts and circumstances, the determination of a non-financial asset's valuation premise (based on its highest and best use) and the inputs applied in the valuation technique used to estimate fair value should always be considered from the perspective of market participants, not the reporting entity.

10.2.3 How should associated liabilities be considered when measuring the fair value of a non-financial asset?

As discussed at 10.2.2 above, an asset's highest and best use might be in combination with associated liabilities and complementary assets in an asset group. IFRS 13.B3(d), for example, notes that an asset's use in combination with other assets and liabilities might be incorporated when using the multi-period excess earnings method to measure the fair value of an intangible asset that has been acquired in a business acquisition. *[IFRS 13.B3]*. The multi-period excess earnings method specifically takes into account the contribution of any complementary assets and the associated liabilities in the group in which such an intangible asset would be used.

'Associated liabilities' is not defined and IFRS 13 provides limited guidance on the types of liabilities that could be considered associated to a non-financial asset. IFRS 13 provides some guidance, stating that associated liabilities can include those that fund working capital, but must exclude liabilities used to fund assets other than those within the group of assets. *[IFRS 13.31(a)(ii)]*.

Management will need to exercise judgement in determining which liabilities to include or exclude from the group, based on the specific facts and circumstances. This assessment must reflect what market participants would consider when determining the non-financial asset's highest and best use. Entities will need to be careful to exclude entity-specific assumptions when valuing liabilities, particularly if valuation techniques are used that are based on their own data (valuation techniques are discussed further at 14 below).

The clarification on considering associated liabilities when measuring the fair value of non-financial assets was generally intended to align the guidance in IFRS 13 with current practice for measuring the fair value of certain non-financial assets (e.g. intangible assets). We generally would not expect this clarification to result in significant changes to the valuation of most non-financial assets. For example, real estate should generally be valued independently from any debt used to finance the property.

10.2.4 Unit of account versus the valuation premise

Fair value measurement of a non-financial asset assumes the asset is sold consistently with its unit of account (as specified in other IFRSs), irrespective of its valuation premise. This assumption applies even if the highest and best use of the asset is in combination with other assets and/or liabilities. This is because the fair value measurement contemplates the sale of the individual asset to market participants that already hold, or are able to obtain, the complementary assets and liabilities. *[IFRS 13.32]*. Only when the unit of account of the item being measured at fair value is an asset group (which may be the case when measuring non-financial assets for impairment as part of a cash-generating unit), can one consider the sale of an asset group. That is, the valuation premise for a non-financial asset does not override the unit of account as defined by the applicable IFRS. However, this can be confusing in practice as both concepts deal with determining the appropriate level of aggregation or disaggregation for assets and liabilities.

Unit of account is an accounting concept. It identifies what is being measured for financial reporting purposes. When applying IFRS 13, this drives the level of aggregation (or disaggregation) for presentation and disclosure purposes, for example, whether the information presented and disclosed in the financial statements is for an individual asset or for a group of assets.

The valuation premise is a valuation concept (sometimes referred to as the 'unit of valuation'). It determines how the asset or liability is measured, i.e. based on the value it derives on a stand-alone basis or the value it derives in conjunction with other assets and liabilities. As discussed above, the unit of account established by an IFRS may be an individual item. However, that item may need to be grouped with others for the purpose of measuring fair value, i.e. the valuation premise may differ from the unit of account.

For example, an entity may own an investment property that is attached to land and contains other assets, such as fixtures and fittings. The unit of account for the investment property would likely be the stand-alone asset in accordance with IAS 40. However, the value of this asset on a stand-alone basis may have little meaning since it is physically attached to the land and derives its benefit in combination with the fixtures and fittings in the building. Therefore, when determining fair value, the valuation premise would likely reflect its use in combination with other assets.

It is important to note that when the valuation premise for measuring the fair value of a non-financial asset (or group of assets and corresponding liabilities) differs from its unit of account, categorisation within IFRS 13's fair value hierarchy (for disclosure purposes) must be determined at a level consistent with the unit of account for the asset or liability (see 16.2 below).

11 APPLICATION TO LIABILITIES AND AN ENTITY'S OWN EQUITY

IFRS 13 applies to liabilities, both financial and non-financial, and an entity's own equity whenever an IFRS requires those instruments to be measured at fair value. For example, in accordance with IFRS 3, in a business combination management might need to determine the fair value of liabilities assumed, when completing the purchase price allocation, and the fair value of its own equity instruments to measure the consideration given.

For financial liabilities and an entity's own equity that are within the scope of IAS 32 or IFRS 9, it is important to note that IFRS 13 would apply to any initial and subsequent fair value measurements that are recognised in the statement of financial position. In addition, if those instruments are not subsequently measured at fair value in the statement of financial position, for example financial liabilities may be subsequently measured at amortised cost, an entity may still need to disclose their fair value in the notes to the financial statements. At a minimum, this would be a requirement for financial liabilities. In these situations, IFRS 13 would also need to be applied to measure the instruments' fair value for disclosure.

The classification of an instrument as either a liability or equity instrument by other IFRSs may depend on the specific facts and circumstances, such as the characteristics of the transaction and the characteristics of the instrument. Examples of these instruments include contingent consideration issued in a business combination in accordance with IFRS 3 or equity warrants issued by an entity in accordance with IFRS 9. In developing the requirements in IFRS 13 for measuring the fair value of liabilities and an entity's own equity, the Boards concluded the requirements should generally be consistent between these instruments. That is, the accounting classification of an instrument, as either a liability or own equity, should not affect that instrument's fair value measurement. *[IFRS 13.BC106]*.

Prior to the issuance of IFRS 13, IFRS did not provide guidance on how to measure the fair value of an entity's own equity instruments. While IFRS 13 may be consistent with how many entities valued their own equity prior to adoption of IFRS 13, it changed practice for entities that concluded the principal market for their own equity (and therefore the assumption of market participants in that market) would be different when valuing the instrument as an asset. For example, this might have been the case if an entity measuring the fair value of a warrant previously assumed a volatility that differs from the volatility assumptions market participants would use in pricing the warrant as an asset.

11.1 General principles

Under IFRS 13, a fair value measurement assumes that a liability or an entity's own equity instrument is transferred to a market participant at the measurement date and that:

- for liabilities – the liability continues and the market participant transferee would be required to fulfil the obligation. That is, the liability is not settled with the counterparty or otherwise extinguished; and
- for an entity's own equity – the equity instrument would remain outstanding and the market participant transferee would take on the rights and responsibilities associated with the instrument. The instrument would not be cancelled or otherwise extinguished on the measurement date. *[IFRS 13.34]*.

11.1.1 Fair value of a liability

IFRS 13 states that the fair value measurement of a liability contemplates the transfer of the liability to a market participant at the measurement date. The liability is assumed to continue (i.e. it is not settled or extinguished), and the market participant to whom the liability is transferred would be required to fulfil the obligation.

The fair value of a liability also reflects the effect of non-performance risk. Non-performance risk is the risk that an obligation will not be fulfilled. This risk includes, but may not be limited to, the entity's own credit risk (see 11.3 below). The requirement that non-performance risk remains unchanged before and after the transfer implies that the liability is hypothetically transferred to a market participant of equal credit standing.

The clarification in IFRS 13 that fair value is not based on the price to settle a liability with the existing counterparty, but rather to transfer it to a market participant of equal credit standing, affects the assumptions about the principal (or most advantageous) market and the market participants in the exit market for the liability (see 11.1.3 below for further detail on the distinction between the settlement notion for liabilities and the transfer notion in IFRS 13).

11.1.2 Fair value of an entity's own equity

For an entity's own equity, IFRS 13 states that the fair value measurement would contemplate a transfer of the equity instrument. The equity instrument would remain outstanding and the market participant transferee would take on the rights and responsibilities associated with the instrument. The instrument would not be cancelled or otherwise extinguished on the measurement date.

The requirements for measuring the fair value of an entity's own equity are generally consistent with the requirements for measuring liabilities, except for the requirement to incorporate non-performance risk, which does not apply directly to an entity's own equity.

11.1.3 Settlement value versus transfer value

While IFRS 13 requires the use of an exit price to measure fair value, an entity might not intend (or be able) to transfer its liability to a third party. For example, it might be more beneficial for the entity to fulfil or settle a liability or the counterparty might not permit the liability to be transferred to another party. The issuer of an equity instrument may only be able to exit from that instrument if it ceases to exist or if the entity repurchases the instrument from the holder. Even if an entity is unable to transfer a liability, the IASB believes the transfer notion is necessary for measuring fair value, because 'it captures market participants' expectations about the liquidity, uncertainty and other associated factors whereas, a settlement notion may not because it may consider entity-specific factors'. *[IFRS 13.BC82]*.

Under a transfer notion, the fair value of a liability is based on the price that would be paid to market participants to assume the obligation. The guidance is clear that an entity's intention to settle or otherwise fulfil the liability or exit the equity instrument is not relevant when measuring its fair value. Because the fair value of the liability is considered from the perspective of market participants, and not the entity itself, any relative efficiencies (or inefficiencies) of the reporting entity in settling the liability would not be considered in the fair value measurement.

Unlike a transfer notion, a settlement notion may allow for the consideration of a reporting entity's specific advantages (or disadvantages) in settling (or performing) the obligation. However, the Boards concluded that 'when a liability is measured at fair value, the relative efficiency of an entity in settling the liability using its own internal resources appears in profit or loss over the course of its settlement, and not before'. *[IFRS 13.BC81]*.

While similar thought processes are needed to estimate both the amount to settle a liability and the amount to transfer that liability, *[IFRS 13.BC82]*, IFRS 13 requires the fair value of a liability to be measured on the assumption that the liability is transferred to a market participant. Therefore, an entity cannot presume that the fair value of a liability is the same as its settlement value. In particular, the requirement to reflect the effect of non-performance risk in the fair value measurement of a liability could result in a difference between the fair value of a liability and the settlement value because it is unlikely that the counterparty would accept a different amount as settlement of the obligation if the entity's credit standing changed (i.e. the settlement value would not necessarily consider changes in credit risk). The IASB was expected to address this issue in its project on non-financial liabilities (see Chapter 26), but further development on this research project had been on hold pending developments in the *Conceptual Framework* project. The IASB issued the new conceptual framework in March 2018 and, following this, the Board, at its January 2020 meeting, decided to add a project to its work plan to amend aspects of IAS 37 – *Provisions, Contingent Liabilities and Contingent Assets* – to specify whether the rate at which an entity discounts a provision should reflect the entity's own credit risk, among other objectives.[19]

11.2 Measuring the fair value of a liability or an entity's own equity when quoted prices for the liability or equity instruments are not available

In many cases, there may be no quoted prices available for the transfer of an instrument that is identical or similar to an entity's own equity or a liability, particularly as liabilities are generally not transferred. For example, this might be the case for debt obligations that are legally restricted from being transferred, or for decommissioning liabilities that the entity does not intend to transfer. In such situations, an entity must determine whether the identical item is held by another party as an asset:

- if the identical item is held by another party as an asset – an entity is required to measure the fair value of a liability or its own equity from the perspective of a market participant that holds the asset (see 11.2.1 below); *[IFRS 13.37]* and
- if the identical item is not held by another party as an asset – an entity measures the fair value of the liability or equity instrument using a valuation technique from the perspective of a market participant that owes the liability or has issued the claim on equity (see 11.2.2 below). *[IFRS 13.40]*.

Regardless of how an entity measures the fair value of a liability or its own equity, the entity is required to maximise the use of relevant observable inputs and minimise the use of unobservable inputs to meet the objective of a fair value measurement. That is, it must estimate the price at which an orderly transaction to transfer the liability or its own equity would take place between market participants at the measurement date under current market conditions. *[IFRS 13.36]*.

11.2.1 Liabilities or an entity's own equity that are held by other parties as assets

If there are no quoted prices available for the transfer of an identical or a similar liability or the entity's own equity instrument and the identical item is held by another party as an asset, an entity uses the fair value of the corresponding asset to measure the fair value of the liability or equity instrument. *[IFRS 13.37]*. The fair value of the asset should be measured from the perspective of the market participant that holds that asset at the measurement date. This approach applies even when the identical item held as an asset is not traded (i.e. when the fair value of the corresponding asset is a Level 3 measurement). For example, under the guidance in IFRS 13, the fair value of a contingent consideration liability should equal its fair value when held as an asset despite the fact that the asset would likely be a Level 3 measurement.

In these situations, the entity measures the fair value of the liability or its own equity by:

(a) using the quoted price in an active market for the identical item held by another party as an asset, if that price is available. This is illustrated in Example 14.14 below;

(b) if that price is not available, using other observable inputs, such as the quoted price in a market that is not active for the identical item held by another party as an asset; or

(c) if the observable prices in (a) and (b) are not available, using another valuation technique (see 14 below for further discussion), such as:

   (i) an income approach, as is illustrated in Example 14.15 below; or

   (ii) a market approach. *[IFRS 13.38]*.

As with all fair value measurements, inputs used to determine the fair value of a liability or an entity's own equity from the perspective of a market participant that holds the identical instrument as an asset must be prioritised in accordance with the fair value hierarchy. Accordingly, IFRS 13 indicates that the fair value of a liability or equity instrument held by another party as an asset should be determined based on the quoted price of the corresponding asset in an active market, if available. This is illustrated in Example 14.14 below. If such a price is not available, other observable inputs for the identical asset would be used, such as a quoted price in an inactive market. In the absence of quoted prices for the identical instrument held as an asset, other valuation techniques, including an income approach (as is illustrated in Example 14.15 below) or a market approach, would be used to determine the liability's or equity's fair value. In these instances, the objective is still to determine the fair value of the liability or equity from the perspective of a market participant that holds the identical instrument as an asset.

In some cases, the corresponding asset price may need to be adjusted for factors specific to the identical item held as an asset but not applicable to the liability, such as the following:

- the quoted price for the asset relates to a similar (but not identical) liability or equity instrument held by another party as an asset. IFRS 13 gives the example of a liability or equity instrument where the credit quality of the issuer is different from that reflected in the fair value of the similar liability or equity instrument held as an asset; and
- the unit of account for the asset is not the same as for the liability or equity instrument. For instance, assume the price for an asset reflected a combined price for a package that comprised both the amounts due from the issuer and a third-party credit enhancement. If the unit of account for the liability is only its own liability, not the combined package, the entity would adjust the observed price for the asset to exclude the effect of the third-party credit enhancement. *[IFRS 13.39]*.

In addition, IFRS 13 states that when using the price of a corresponding asset to determine the fair value of a liability or entity's own equity, the fair value of the liability or equity should not incorporate the effect of any restriction preventing the sale of that asset. *[IFRS 13.39]*. If the quoted price did reflect the effect of a restriction, it would need to be adjusted. That is, all else being equal, the liability's or equity's fair value would be the same as the fair value of an otherwise unrestricted corresponding asset.

The fair value of a liability may also differ from the price of its corresponding asset when the instrument is priced within a bid-ask spread. In these instances, the liability should be valued based on the price within the bid-ask spread that is most representative of where the liability would be exited, not the corresponding asset (see 15.3 below for discussion on pricing within the bid-ask spread).

The Boards believe the fair value of a liability or equity instrument will equal the fair value of a properly defined corresponding asset (i.e. an asset whose features mirror those of the liability), assuming an exit from both positions in the same market. This assumes markets are efficient and arbitrage free. For example, if the prices differed for a liability and the corresponding asset, the market participant taking on the liability would be able to earn a profit by financing the purchase of the asset with the proceeds received by taking on the liability. In an efficient market, the price for the liability and the price for the asset would adjust until the arbitrage opportunity was eliminated. In the Boards' view, the price for the liability or equity instrument and the corresponding asset would generally only differ if the entity was measuring an asset relating to a similar (not identical) instrument or the unit of account was different. The Boards did consider whether the effects of illiquidity could create a difference but noted that they are difficult to differentiate from credit-related effects. *[IFRS 13.BC88, BC89]*.

The following two examples extracted from IFRS 13 include factors to consider when measuring the fair value of a liability or entity's own equity by estimating the fair value of the corresponding asset held by another party. *[IFRS 13.IE40-IE42]*. The first example highlights how entities need to assess whether the quoted price for a corresponding asset includes the effects of factors not applicable to the liability. However, for the sake of simplicity, the example does not consider bid-ask spread considerations.

Example 14.14: Debt obligation: quoted price

On 1 January 20X1 Entity B issues at par a €2 million BBB-rated exchange-traded five-year fixed rate debt instrument with an annual 10% coupon. Entity B designated this financial liability as at fair value through profit or loss.

On 31 December 20X1 the instrument is trading as an asset in an active market at €929 per €1,000 of par value after payment of accrued interest. Entity B uses the quoted price of the asset in an active market as its initial input into the fair value measurement of its liability (€929 × [€2,000,000 ÷ €1,000] = €1,858,000).

In determining whether the quoted price of the asset in an active market represents the fair value of the liability, Entity B evaluates whether the quoted price of the asset includes the effect of factors not applicable to the fair value measurement of a liability, for example, whether the quoted price of the asset includes the effect of a third-party credit enhancement if that credit enhancement would be separately accounted for from the perspective of the issuer. Entity B determines that no adjustments are required to the quoted price of the asset. Accordingly, Entity B concludes that the fair value of its debt instrument at 31 December 20X1 is €1,858,000. Entity B categorises and discloses the fair value measurement of its debt instrument within Level 1 of the fair value hierarchy.

The second example provides factors that would be incorporated when using a present value technique to estimate the fair value of a financial liability (e.g. changes in credit spreads for the liability), as well as factors that would be excluded (e.g. adjustments related to transferability restrictions or profit margin). *[IFRS 13.IE43-IE47]*.

Example 14.15: Debt obligation: present value technique

On 1 January 20X1 Entity C issues at par in a private placement a $2,000,000 BBB-rated five-year fixed rate debt instrument with an annual 10% coupon. Entity C designated this financial liability as at fair value through profit or loss.

At 31 December 20X1 Entity C still carries a BBB credit rating. Market conditions, including available interest rates, credit spreads for a BBB-quality credit rating and liquidity, remain unchanged from the date the debt instrument was issued. However, Entity C's credit spread has deteriorated by 50 basis points because of a change in its risk of non-performance. After taking into account all market conditions, Entity C concludes that if it was to issue the instrument at the measurement date, the instrument would bear a rate of interest of 10.5% or Entity C would receive less than par in proceeds from the issue of the instrument.

For the purpose of this example, the fair value of Entity C's liability is calculated using a present value technique. Entity C concludes that a market participant would use all the following inputs when estimating the price the market participant would expect to receive to assume Entity C's obligation:

(a) the terms of the debt instrument, including all the following:
  (i) coupon of 10%;
  (ii) principal amount of $2,000,000; and
  (iii) term of four years.
(b) the market rate of interest of 10.5% (which includes a change of 50 basis points in the risk of non-performance from the date of issue).

On the basis of its present value technique, Entity C concludes that the fair value of its liability at 31 December 20X1 is $1,968,641.

Entity C does not include any additional input into its present value technique for risk or profit that a market participant might require for compensation for assuming the liability. Because Entity C's obligation is a financial liability, Entity C concludes that the interest rate already captures the risk or profit that a market participant would require as compensation for assuming the liability. Furthermore, Entity C does not adjust its present value technique for the existence of a restriction preventing it from transferring the liability.

While the example above assumes that relevant market data on the non-performance risk of the debt obligation is readily available, estimating the appropriate credit spreads is often the most challenging aspect of using a present value technique to value a debt instrument. Credit spreads on identical or similar liabilities issued by the same obligor represent high quality market data. But even when issued by the same obligor, credit spreads on liabilities with significantly different features or characteristics may not appropriately capture the credit risk of the liability being measured. When spreads on identical instruments do not exist and data from comparable debt instruments (e.g. option adjusted spreads (OAS)) is used, the specific characteristics of these comparable liabilities (e.g. tenor, seniority, collateral, coupon, principal amortisation, covenant strength, etc.) should be analysed carefully. In addition, credit default swap (CDS) spreads, which represent the compensation required by the CDS issuer to accept the default risk of a debt issuer (i.e. the reference obligor), may also provide useful market data.

In some instances, observable market data is not available for a specific debt issuer, but the issuer has a reported credit rating. In these circumstances, credit spreads or CDS spreads of similarly rated entities or debt instruments may be used as a proxy to evaluate the credit risk of the liability being measured. Once again, the specific characteristics of these similar debt instruments and the subject liability should be compared.

Other situations may involve a liability with no observable credit quality measures (e.g. credit spreads) issued by an entity that is not rated. In these circumstances, techniques such as a regression or other quantitative analysis may be performed to determine the credit quality of the issuer. Comparing financial metrics such as profit margins, leverage ratios, and asset sizes between the non-rated issuer of the liability being measured to rated entities may allow a credit rating to be estimated. Once a credit rating has been determined, an appropriate credit spread could be quantified from other comparable (i.e. similarly rated) debt instruments.

11.2.2 Liabilities or an entity's own equity not held by other parties as assets

While many liabilities are held by market participants as corresponding assets, some are not. For example, there is typically no corresponding asset holder for a decommissioning liability. When no observable price is available for a liability and no corresponding asset exists, the fair value of the liability is measured from the perspective of a market participant that owes the liability, using an appropriate valuation technique (e.g. a present value technique). *[IFRS 13.40]*.

Generally, an instrument classified as an entity's own equity would have a corresponding asset. However, if no corresponding asset exists and no observable price is available for an entity's own equity, fair value is measured from the perspective of a market participant that has issued the claim on equity, using an appropriate valuation technique.

IFRS 13 gives two examples of what an entity might take into account in measuring fair value in this situation:

(a) the future cash outflows that a market participant would expect to incur in fulfilling the obligation (i.e. a present value technique). This includes any compensation a market participant would require for taking on the obligation. This approach is discussed further at 11.2.2.A below; and

(b) the amount that a market participant would receive to enter into an identical liability, or issue an identical equity instrument. This approach is discussed further at 11.2.2.B below. *[IFRS 13.41]*.

11.2.2.A Use of present value techniques to measure fair value for liabilities and an entity's own equity instruments not held by other parties as assets

If an entity uses a present value technique to measure the fair value of a liability or its own equity not held by other parties as assets, IFRS 13 requires the entity to estimate the future cash outflows that a market participant would expect to incur in fulfilling the obligation, among other things. The estimated cash flows include:

- market participants' expectations about the costs of fulfilling the obligation; and
- compensation that a market participant would require for taking on the obligation. This compensation includes the return that a market participant would require for the following:
    (i) undertaking the activity (i.e. the value of fulfilling the obligation) – for example, by using resources that could be used for other activities; and
    (ii) assuming the risk associated with the obligation (i.e. a *risk premium* that reflects the risk that the actual cash outflows might differ from the expected cash outflows). *[IFRS 13.B31]*.

In some cases, the components of the return a market participant would require will be indistinguishable from one another. In other cases, an entity will need to estimate those components separately. For example, assume an entity uses the price a third-party contractor would charge as part of the discounted cash flows. If the contract is priced on a fixed fee basis, both the return for undertaking the activity and the risk premium would be indistinguishable. However, as is shown in Example 14.16 below, if the contractor would charge on a cost-plus basis, an entity would need to estimate the components separately, because the contractor in that case would not bear the risk of future changes in costs. *[IFRS 13.B32]*.

A risk premium can be included in such fair value measurements, either by:

(a) adjusting the cash flows (i.e. as an increase in the amount of cash outflows); or

(b) adjusting the rate used to discount the future cash flows to their present values (i.e. as a reduction in the discount rate).

However, an entity must ensure adjustments for risk are not double-counted or omitted. *[IFRS 13.B33]*.

IFRS 13 provides the following example, which illustrates how these considerations would be captured when using a valuation technique to measure the fair value of a liability not held by another party as an asset. *[IFRS 13.IE35-IE39]*.

Example 14.16: Decommissioning liability

On 1 January 20X1 Entity A assumes a decommissioning liability in a business combination. The entity is legally required to dismantle and remove an offshore oil platform at the end of its useful life, which is estimated to be 10 years. Entity A uses the expected present value technique to measure the fair value of the decommissioning liability.

If Entity A were contractually allowed to transfer its decommissioning liability to a market participant, Entity A would conclude that a market participant would use all the following inputs, probability-weighted as appropriate, when estimating the price it would expect to receive:

(a) labour costs;
(b) allocation of overhead costs;
(c) the compensation that a market participant would require for undertaking the activity and for assuming the risk associated with the obligation to dismantle and remove the asset. Such compensation includes both of the following:
   (i) profit on labour and overhead costs; and
   (ii) the risk that the actual cash outflows might differ from those expected, excluding inflation;
(d) effect of inflation on estimated costs and profits;
(e) time value of money, represented by the risk-free rate; and
(f) non-performance risk relating to the risk that Entity A will not fulfil the obligation, including Entity A's own credit risk.

The significant assumptions used by Entity A to measure fair value are as follows:

(a) Labour costs are developed on the basis of current marketplace wages, adjusted for expectations of future wage increases and a requirement to hire contractors to dismantle and remove offshore oil platforms. Entity A assigns probability assessments to a range of cash flow estimates as follows:

Cash flow estimate £	Probability assessment	Expected cash flows £
100,000	25%	25,000
125,000	50%	62,500
175,000	25%	43,750
		131,250

The probability assessments are developed on the basis of Entity A's experience with fulfilling obligations of this type and its knowledge of the market.

(b) Entity A estimates allocated overhead and equipment operating costs using the rate it applies to labour costs (80% of expected labour costs). This is consistent with the cost structure of market participants.

(c) Entity A estimates the compensation that a market participant would require for undertaking the activity and for assuming the risk associated with the obligation to dismantle and remove the asset as follows:

   (i) A third-party contractor typically adds a mark-up on labour and allocated internal costs to provide a profit margin on the job. The profit margin used (20%) represents Entity A's understanding of the operating profit that contractors in the industry generally earn to dismantle and remove offshore oil platforms. Entity A concludes that this rate is consistent with the rate that a market participant would require as compensation for undertaking the activity.

   (ii) A contractor would typically require compensation for the risk that the actual cash outflows might differ from those expected because of the uncertainty inherent in locking in today's price for a project that will not occur for 10 years. Entity A estimates the amount of that premium to be 5% of the expected cash flows, including the effect of inflation.

(d) Entity A assumes a rate of inflation of 4% over the 10-year period on the basis of available market data.

(e) The risk-free rate of interest for a 10-year maturity on 1 January 20X1 is 5%. Entity A adjusts that rate by 3.5% to reflect its risk of non-performance (i.e. the risk that it will not fulfil the obligation), including its credit risk. Therefore, the discount rate used to compute the present value of the cash flows is 8.5%.

Entity A concludes that its assumptions would be used by market participants. In addition, Entity A does not adjust its fair value measurement for the existence of a restriction preventing it from transferring the liability even if such a restriction exists. As illustrated in the following table, Entity A measures the fair value of its decommissioning liability as £194,879.

	Expected cash flows £
Expected labour costs	131,250
Allocated overhead and equipment costs (0.80 × £131,250)	105,000
Contractor's profit mark-up [0.20 × (£131,250 + £105,000)]	47,250
Expected cash flows before inflation adjustment	283,500
Inflation factor (4% for 10 years)	1.4802
Expected cash flows adjusted for inflation	419,637
Market risk premium (0.05 × £419,637)	20,982
Expected cash flows adjusted for market risk	440,619
Expected present value using discount rate of 8.5% for 10 years	194,879

In practice, estimating the risk premium for a decommissioning liability, such as in the example above, requires significant judgement, particularly in circumstances where the decommissioning activities will be performed many years in the future. Information about the compensation market participants would demand to assume decommissioning liability may be limited, because very few decommissioning liabilities are transferred in the manner contemplated by IFRS 13.

Because of these data limitations, entities might look to risk premiums observed from business combinations where decommissioning liabilities are assumed, including their own business combination transactions. IFRS 13 indicates that when market information is not reasonably available, an entity may consider its own data in developing assumptions related to the market risk premium (see 19 below for additional discussion on the use of an entity's own data to determine unobservable inputs).

Alternatively, as noted above, the market risk premium might be estimated by considering the difference between a fixed-price arrangement and a cost-plus arrangement with a third party to complete the remediation and monitor the site. The difference between the fixed-price arrangement and the cost-plus arrangement may provide insight into the risk premium market participants would demand to fulfil the obligation.

While all available evidence about market participant assumptions regarding the market risk premium should be considered, circumstances may exist when an explicit assumption cannot be determined. In such cases, based on the specific guidance in IFRS 13 – which acknowledges that explicit assumptions in some cases may not be able to be incorporated into the measurement of decommissioning liability – we believe the market risk premium may be incorporated into the fair value measurement on an implicit basis.

11.2.2.B Consideration of an entry price in measuring a liability or entity's own equity not held as an asset

Although fair value represents an exit price, IFRS 13 indicates that in certain situations an entry price may be considered in estimating the fair value of a liability or an entity's own equity instrument. This approach uses assumptions that market participants would use when pricing the identical item (e.g. having the same credit characteristics) in the principal (or most advantageous) market – that is, the principal (or most advantageous) market for issuing a liability or equity instrument with the same contractual terms.

The standard allows for entry prices to be considered in estimating the fair value of a liability because the IASB believes that a liability's entry and exit prices will be identical in many instances. As a result, the price at which a market participant could enter into the identical liability on the measurement date (e.g. an obligation having the same credit characteristics) may be indicative of its fair value.

However, an entry price may differ from the exit price for a liability for a number of reasons. For example, an entity may transfer the liability in a different market from that in which the obligation was incurred. When entry and exit prices differ, IFRS 13 is clear that the objective of the measurement remains an exit price.

11.3 Non-performance risk

IFRS 13 requires a fair value measurement of a liability to incorporate non-performance risk (i.e. the risk that an obligation will not be fulfilled). Conceptually, non-performance risk encompasses more than just an entity's credit risk. It may also include other risks, such as settlement risk. In the case of non-financial instruments, such as commodity contracts, non-performance risk could represent the risk associated with physically extracting and transferring an asset to the point of delivery. When measuring the fair value of a liability, an entity must:

- Take into account the effect of its credit risk (credit standing) and any other factors that could influence the likelihood whether or not the obligation will be fulfilled.
- Assume that non-performance risk will be the same before and after the transfer of a liability.
- Ensure the effect of non-performance risk on the fair value of the liability is consistent with its unit of account for financial reporting purposes.

    If a liability is issued with a third-party credit enhancement that the issuer accounts for separately from the liability, the fair value of the liability does not include the effect of the credit enhancement (e.g. a third-party guarantee of debt). That is, the issuer would take into account its own credit standing and not that of the third-party guarantor when measuring the fair value of the liability (see 11.3.1 below).
    [IFRS 13.42-44].

An entity takes into account the effect of its credit risk (credit standing) on the fair value of the liability in all periods in which the liability is measured at fair value because market participants valuing the entity's obligations as assets would take into account the effect of the entity's credit standing when estimating the prices at which they would transact. *[IFRS 13.IE31].* Valuation techniques continue to evolve and new concepts are developing in relation to considering non-performance risk. Whether an entity should incorporate them into an IFRS 13 fair value measurement depends on whether market participants would take them into account.

Incorporating non-performance risk into subsequent fair value measurements of a liability is also consistent with the notion that credit risk affects the initial measurement of a liability. Since the terms of a liability are determined based on an entity's credit standing at the time of issuance (and since IFRS 13 assumes the liability is transferred to another party with the same credit standing at the measurement date), subsequent changes in an entity's credit standing will result in the obligation's terms being favourable or unfavourable relative to current market requirements. The standard gives the following example illustrating how the fair value of the same instrument could be different depending on the credit risk of the issuer. *[IFRS 13.IE32]*.

Example 14.17: Non-performance risk

Assume that Entity X and Entity Y each enter into a contractual obligation to pay cash (¥500,000) to Entity Z in five years. Entity X has an AA credit rating and can borrow at 6%, and Entity Y has a BBB credit rating and can borrow at 12%. Entity X will receive about ¥374,000 in exchange for its promise (the present value of ¥500,000 in five years at 6%). Entity Y will receive about ¥284,000 in exchange for its promise (the present value of ¥500,000 in five years at 12%). The fair value of the liability to each entity (i.e. the proceeds) incorporates that entity's credit standing.

The effect of non-performance risk on the fair value measurement of the liability will depend on factors, such as the terms of any related credit enhancement or the nature of the liability – that is, whether the liability is an obligation to deliver cash (a financial liability) or an obligation to deliver goods or services (a non-financial liability). The following example, from the standard, illustrates changes in fair value measurement due to changes in non-performance risk. As indicated in this example, changes to an entity's non-performance risk does not require there to be a change in credit rating. Instead, such changes are often based on changes in credit spreads. *[IFRS 13.IE34]*.

Example 14.18: Structured note

On 1 January 20X9 Entity A, an investment bank with an AA credit rating, issues a five-year fixed rate note to Entity B. The contractual principal amount to be paid by Entity A at maturity is linked to an equity index. No credit enhancements are issued in conjunction with or otherwise related to the contract (i.e. no collateral is posted and there is no third-party guarantee). Entity A designated this note as at fair value through profit or loss. The fair value of the note (i.e. the obligation of Entity A) during 20X9 is measured using an expected present value technique. Changes in fair value are as follows:

(a) *Fair value at 1 January 20X9* – The expected cash flows used in the expected present value technique are discounted at the risk-free rate using the government bond curve at 1 January 20X9, plus the current market observable AA corporate bond spread to government bonds, if non-performance risk is not already reflected in the cash flows, adjusted (either up or down) for Entity A's specific credit risk (i.e. resulting in a credit-adjusted risk-free rate). Therefore, the fair value of Entity A's obligation at initial recognition takes into account non-performance risk, including that entity's credit risk, which presumably is reflected in the proceeds.

(b) *Fair value at 31 March 20X9* – During March 20X9 the credit spread for AA corporate bonds widens, with no changes to the specific credit risk of Entity A. The expected cash flows used in the expected present value technique are discounted at the risk-free rate using the government bond curve at 31 March 20X9, plus the current market observable AA corporate bond spread to government bonds, if non-performance risk is not already reflected in the cash flows, adjusted for Entity A's specific credit risk (i.e. resulting in a credit-adjusted risk-free rate). Entity A's specific credit risk is unchanged from initial recognition. Therefore, the fair value of Entity A's obligation changes as a result of changes in credit spreads generally. Changes in credit spreads reflect current market participant assumptions about changes in non-performance risk generally, changes in liquidity risk and the compensation required for assuming those risks.

(c) *Fair value at 30 June 20X9* – As at 30 June 20X9 there have been no changes to the AA corporate bond spreads. However, on the basis of structured note issues corroborated with other qualitative information, Entity A determines that its own specific creditworthiness has strengthened within the AA credit spread. The expected cash flows used in the expected present value technique are discounted at the risk-free rate using the government bond yield curve at 30 June 20X9, plus the current market observable AA corporate bond spread to government bonds (unchanged from 31 March 20X9), if non-performance risk is not already reflected in the cash flows, adjusted for Entity A's specific credit risk (i.e. resulting in a credit-adjusted risk-free rate). Therefore, the fair value of the obligation of Entity A changes as a result of the change in its own specific credit risk within the AA corporate bond spread.

The standard's assumption that the non-performance risk related to a liability is the same before and after its transfer is not intended to reflect reality. In most cases, the reporting entity and the market participant transferee will have different credit standings. However, this assumption is important when measuring fair value under IFRS 13 for the following reasons:

- if the transaction results in changes to the non-performance risk associated with the liability, the market participant taking on the obligation would not enter into the transaction without reflecting that change in the price.

    IFRS 13 gives the following examples; a creditor would not generally permit a debtor to transfer its obligation to another party of lower credit standing, nor would a transferee of higher credit standing be willing to assume the obligation using the same terms negotiated by the transferor if those terms reflect the transferor's lower credit standing;

- if IFRS 13 did not specify the credit standing of the entity taking on the obligation, there could be fundamentally different fair values for a liability depending on an entity's assumptions about the characteristics of the market participant transferee; and

- those who might hold the entity's liability as an asset would consider the effect of the entity's credit risk and other risk factors when pricing those assets (see 11.2.1 above). *[IFRS 13.BC94].*

The requirements of IFRS 13 regarding non-performance risk, when measuring fair value for liabilities, are consistent with the fair value measurement guidance in IFRSs prior to the issuance of IFRS 13. Specifically, IFRS 9 refers to making adjustments for credit risk if market participants would reflect that risk when pricing a financial instrument. However, the IASB acknowledged that there was inconsistent application of that principle for two reasons. Firstly, IFRS 9 referred to credit risk generally and did not specifically refer to the reporting entity's own credit risk. Secondly, there were different interpretations about how an entity's own credit risk should be reflected in the fair value of a liability using the settlement notion, under the previous definition of fair value, because it was unlikely that the counterparty would accept a different amount as settlement of the obligation if the entity's credit standing changed. *[IFRS 13.BC92, BC93].* As such, adoption of IFRS 13 may have resulted in a change for some entities in this regard.

In developing IFRS 13, there was some debate among constituents about the usefulness of including non-performance risk after initial recognition because this might lead to counter-intuitive and potentially confusing reporting (i.e. gains for credit deterioration and losses for credit improvements). However, in the IASB's view, this does not affect how to measure fair value, but rather whether an IFRS should require fair value measurement subsequent to initial recognition, which is outside the scope of IFRS 13. The standard is clear that a measurement that does not consider the effect of an entity's non-performance risk is not a fair value measurement. *[IFRS 13.BC95]*. The adoption of IFRS 9 may have resolved some of these concerns. For financial liabilities designated at fair value through profit or loss (using the fair value option), IFRS 9 requires fair value changes that are the result of changes in an entity's own credit risk to be presented in other comprehensive income, unless doing so would introduce an accounting mismatch. If it would introduce an accounting mismatch, the whole fair value change is presented in profit or loss (see Chapter 50 for further discussion). *[IFRS 9.5.7.7]*.

11.3.1 Liabilities issued with third-party credit enhancements

As discussed at 11.3 above, IFRS 13 requires entities to measure the fair value of a liability issued with an inseparable third-party credit enhancement from the issuer's perspective, i.e. considering the issuer's credit risk rather than that of the third-party providing the credit enhancement. This would apply in situations where a credit enhancement (or guarantee) is purchased by an issuer, then combined with a liability and issued as a combined security to an investor. IFRS 13's requirements are based on the fact that the third-party credit enhancement does not relieve the issuer of its ultimate obligation under the liability. Generally, if the issuer fails to meet its payment obligations to the investor, the guarantor has an obligation to make the payments on the issuer's behalf and the issuer has an obligation to the guarantor. By issuing debt combined with a credit enhancement, the issuer is able to market its debt more easily and can either reduce the interest rate paid to the investor or receive higher proceeds when the debt is issued.

IFRS 13 requires the fair value measurement of a liability to follow the unit of account of the liability for financial reporting purposes. The standard anticipates that there may be instances where, even though it may be inseparable, the credit enhancement may need to be separated (i.e. separately recognised) for financial reporting purposes. However, this assumes that: (i) the unit of account is clear in other standards, which may not be the case; and (ii) that standards, such as IFRS 9, may permit or require separation when a credit enhancement is inseparable.

As discussed in Figure 14.4 below, if the unit of account excludes the credit enhancement, the fair value of the liability measured from the issuer's perspective in accordance with IFRS 13, will not equal its fair value as a guaranteed liability held by another party as an asset. The fair value of the asset held by the investor considers the credit standing of the guarantor. However, under the guarantee, any payments made by the guarantor result in a transfer of the issuer's debt obligation from the investor to the guarantor. That is, the amount owed by the issuer does not change; the issuer must now pay the guarantor instead of the investor. Therefore, as discussed at 11.2.1 above, if the fair value of a third-party guaranteed liability is measured based on the fair value of the corresponding asset, it would need to be adjusted. *[IFRS 13.BC96-BC98]*.

Figure 14.4: Liabilities with credit enhancements

	Issuer's perspective (i.e. the obligor)	Perspective of the entity that holds the corresponding asset
Credit enhancement provided by the issuer (e.g. collateral or master netting agreement)		
Separate unit of account?	Dependent on the relevant IFRS (e.g. IFRS 9). Depending on the nature of the credit enhancement, it may be recognised (e.g. collateral recognised as an asset in the financial statements of the issuer) or unrecognised (e.g. a master netting agreement).	Dependent on the relevant IFRS (e.g. IFRS 9) and the nature of the credit enhancement.
Considered in the fair value measurement?	Generally, yes. The fair value measurement of a liability takes into consideration the credit standing of the issuer. The effect may differ depending on the terms of the related credit enhancement.	Possibly. If the credit enhancement is not accounted for separately, the fair value of the corresponding asset would take into consideration the effect of the related credit enhancement.
Credit enhancement provided by a third-party (e.g. financial guarantee)		
Separate unit of account?	Dependent on the relevant IFRS (e.g. IFRS 9). Likely to be a separate unit of account and remain unrecognised, unless the issuer fails to meet its obligations under the liability.	Dependent on the relevant IFRS (e.g. IFRS 9) and the nature of the credit enhancement.
Considered in the fair value measurement?	Generally, no. If the credit enhancement is accounted for separately from the liability, the issuer would take into account its own credit standing and not that of the third-party guarantor when measuring the fair value of the liability.	Possibly. If the credit enhancement is not accounted for separately, the fair value of the corresponding asset would take into consideration the effect of the related third-party credit enhancement.

11.3.1.A   Do the requirements of IFRS 13 regarding third-party credit enhancements in a fair value measurement apply to liabilities other than debt?

The requirements of IFRS 13 for liabilities issued with third-party credit enhancements apply to all liabilities that are measured or disclosed at fair value on a recurring basis. Although the requirements would not affect financial liabilities after their initial recognition if they are subsequently measured at amortised cost in accordance with IFRS 9, it would apply to the disclosure of the fair value of those liabilities, as required by IFRS 7.

While an issuer's accounting for guaranteed debt may be the most common application of this guidance, the clarification with respect to the unit of account for certain types of credit enhancements could affect other liabilities, including derivative instruments measured at fair value in accordance with IFRS 9. Many OTC derivative contracts are subject to credit support requirements under an International Swaps and Derivatives Association[20] (ISDA) Master Agreement between the derivative counterparties. The application of this guidance to OTC derivatives will depend on the nature of the credit support provided. For example, while credit support is typically provided through the posting of collateral, in certain industries posting a letter of credit (LOC) for the benefit of a derivative counterparty is not uncommon.

In those instances where a LOC is posted for the benefit of a derivative counterparty, we believe the requirement in paragraph 44 of IFRS 13, to consider the issuer's credit risk rather than that of the third party providing the LOC, would generally apply. *[IFRS 13.44]*. If an entity defaults on its derivative contracts, the bank issuing the LOC will pay the counterparty and the entity's obligation merely transfers from the original counterparty to the issuing bank. In other words, the entity will have a continuing obligation, even in the event it defaults on the derivative. As such, the entity's non-performance risk (not that of the bank providing the LOC) would be considered in determining the fair value of the derivative liability. We believe this generally would apply even if the LOC were deemed separable from the derivative contract. In our view, including the effect of separable credit enhancements while excluding the effect of inseparable credit enhancements would contradict the principles of IFRS 13.

11.3.2 Does IFRS 13 require an entity to consider the effects of both counterparty credit risk and its own credit risk when valuing its derivative transactions?

IFRS 13 addresses the issue of credit risk both explicitly and implicitly. As discussed at 11.3 above, in relation to an entity's own credit risk in the valuation of liabilities, the guidance is explicit; the fair value of a liability should reflect the effect of non-performance risk, which includes own credit risk.

The standard's requirements are less explicit regarding counterparty credit risk. IFRS 13 requires the fair value of an asset or liability to be measured based on market participant assumptions. Because market participants consider counterparty credit risk in pricing a derivative contract, an entity's valuation methodology should incorporate counterparty credit risk in its measurement of fair value.

11.3.3 How should an entity incorporate credit risk into the valuation of its derivative contracts?

As discussed at 11.3.2 above, IFRS 13 requires entities to consider the effects of credit risk when determining a fair value measurement, e.g. by calculating a debit valuation adjustment (DVA) or a credit valuation adjustment (CVA) on their derivatives.

As no specific method is prescribed in IFRS 13, various approaches are used in practice by derivatives dealers and end-users to estimate the effect of credit risk on the fair value of OTC derivatives.

The degree of sophistication in the credit adjustment valuation method used by a reporting entity is influenced by the qualitative factors noted below. Estimation can be complex and requires the use of significant judgement, which is often influenced by various qualitative factors, including:

- the materiality of the entity's derivative's carrying value to its financial statements;
- the number and type of contracts for derivatives in the entity's portfolio;

- the extent to which derivative instruments are either deeply in or out of the money;
- the existence and terms of credit mitigation arrangements (e.g. collateral arrangements in place);
- the cost and availability of technology to model complex credit exposures;
- the cost and consistent availability of suitable input data to calculate an accurate credit adjustment; and
- the creditworthiness of the entity and its counterparties.

While the degree of sophistication and complexity may differ by entity and by the size and nature of the derivative portfolio, any inputs used under any methodology should be consistent with assumptions market participants would use. The complexity and judgement involved in selecting and consistently applying a method may require entities to provide additional disclosures to assist users of financial statements (see 20 below). 11.3.3.A to 11.3.3.B below provide further insights into some of the considerations for determining valuation adjustments for credit risk on derivatives measured at fair value, except for which a quoted price in an active market is available (i.e. over-the-counter derivatives).

In situations where an entity has a master netting agreement or credit support annex[21] (CSA) with a counterparty, the entity may consider the credit risk of its derivative instruments with that counterparty on a net basis if it qualifies to use the measurement exception noted at 2.5.2 above (see 12 below for more detail on applying the measurement exception for financial instruments with offsetting credit risks).

11.3.3.A How do credit adjustments work?

In simple terms, the requirement for a credit adjustment as a component of fair value measurement can be analogised to the need for a provision on a trade receivable or an impairment charge on an item of property, plant and equipment. Whilst this analogy helps conceptualise the requirement, the characteristics of derivatives mean that the calculation itself can be significantly more complex than for assets measured at amortised cost.

Consistent with the fact that credit risk affects the initial measurement of a derivative asset or liability, IFRS 13 requires that changes in counterparty credit risk or an entity's own credit standing be considered in subsequent fair value measurements. It cannot be assumed that the parties to the derivative contract will perform.

The terms of the asset or liability were determined based on the counterparty's or entity's credit standing at the time of entering into the contract. In addition, IFRS 13 assumes a liability is transferred to another party with the same credit standing at the measurement date. As a result, subsequent changes in a counterparty's or entity's credit standing will result in the derivative's terms being favourable or unfavourable relative to current market conditions.

Unlike the credit exposure of a 'vanilla' receivable, which generally remains constant over time (typically at the principal amount of the receivable), the bilateral nature of the credit exposure in many derivatives varies, whereby both parties to the contract may face potential exposure in the future. As such, many instruments may possibly have a value that is either positive (a derivative asset) or negative (a derivative liability) at different points in time based on changes in the underlying variables of the contract.

Figure 14.5 below illustrates the effect on the income statement and on the statement of financial position of CVA and DVA adjustments as a component of fair value measurement on a single derivative asset or liability.

Figure 14.5:   Accounting for CVA and DVA

	Derivative asset example – CVA	$		Derivative liability example – DVA	$
Derivative position valued using the risk-free curve (1)	Risk-free derivative asset	100,000		Risk-free derivative liability	(100,000)
Credit adjustment required (2)	Counterparty credit adjustment	(10,000)		Debit adjustment based on own credit	5,000
Credit-adjusted derivative position	Derivative asset	90,000		Derivative liability	(95,000)

Subsequent credit movements

Counterparty credit improves	A gain arises in the income statement and is reflected by a larger derivative asset in the statement of financial position	Own credit improves	A loss arises in the income statement and is reflected by a larger derivative liability in the statement of financial position
Counterparty credit deteriorates	A further CVA charge is required in the income statement and is reflected by a reduced derivative asset in the statement of financial position	Own credit deteriorates	A further DVA credit is required to the income statement and is reflected by a reduced derivative liability in the statement of financial position

Notes:
(1)   The table represents a point-in-time during the life of a derivative asset or liability
(2)   For illustrative purposes, we have assumed the counterparty credit valuation adjustment is $10,000 and the debit valuation adjustment is $5,000. These credit adjustments are not intended to reflect reality

11.3.3.B   Valuation methods

The determination of a credit adjustment can be complex. Part of the complexity stems from the particular nature of credit risk in many OTC derivative contracts. Credit risk associated with a derivative contract is similar to other forms of credit risk in that the cause of economic loss is an obligor's default on its contractual obligation. However, for many derivative products, two features set credit risk in OTC derivative contracts apart from traditional forms of credit risk in instruments such as debt:

- the uncertainty of the future exposure associated with the instrument – this is due to the uncertainty of future changes in value of the derivative, as the cash flows required under the instrument stem from: (a) movements in underlying variables that drive the value of the contract; and (b) the progression of time towards the contract's expiry; and
- the bilateral nature of credit exposure in many derivatives, whereby both parties to the contract may face potential exposure in the future – this can occur in instruments, such as swaps and forwards, given the potential for these derivatives to 'flip' from an asset to a liability (or *vice versa*), based on changes in the underlying variables to the contract (e.g. interest rates or foreign exchange rates).

As previously noted at 11.3.3 above, IFRS does not prescribe any specific valuation methods to quantify the impact of non-performance risk on derivatives' fair value. IFRS 13 is a principles-based standard intended to provide a general framework for measuring fair value. It was not intended to provide detailed application guidance for calculating the fair value of various types of assets and liabilities. Likewise, IFRS 9 does not provide specific valuation guidance related to derivatives. As a result, extensive judgement needs to be applied, potentially resulting in diversity in the methods and approaches used to quantify credit risk, particularly as it pertains to derivatives. As discussed at 11.3.3 above, a variety of factors may influence the method an entity chooses for estimating credit adjustments. In addition, the cost and availability of technology and input data to model complex credit exposures will also be a contributing factor.

In recent years, some derivative dealers have started to include a funding valuation adjustment (FVA) in the valuation of their uncollateralised derivative positions, as is illustrated in in the extract from the financial statements of ING Groep N.V. below. FVA is included in order to capture the funding cost (or benefit) that results from posting (or receiving) collateral on inter-bank transactions that are used to economically hedge the market risk associated with these uncollateralised trades. The methods for determining FVA can vary. As such, determining whether these methods comply with IFRS 13 requires judgement based on the specific facts and circumstances.

A number of valuation adjustments have also emerged in addition to CVA, DVA and FVA. Examples include self-default potential hedging (LVA), collateral (CollVA) and market hedging positions (HVA), as well as tail risk (KVA), collectively these are now referred to as X-Value Adjustments (XVA). It is important to note that some of these valuation adjustments may be useful for internal reporting, but may not be appropriate to use when measuring fair value in accordance with IFRS 13. As noted above, the inputs used in measuring fair value must reflect the assumptions of market participants transacting for the asset or liability in the principal (or most advantageous) market at the measurement date.

Extract 14.1: ING Groep N.V. (2019)

Notes to the Consolidated financial statements [Extract]

1 Basis of preparation and accounting policies [Extract]

1.6 Financial instruments [Extract]

1.6.3 Fair values of financial assets and liabilities

All financial assets and liabilities are recognised initially at fair value. Subsequently, except for financial assets and financial liabilities measured at amortised cost, all the other financial assets and liabilities are measured at fair value.

Fair value is defined as the price that would be received to sell an asset or paid to transfer a liability in an orderly transaction between market participants at the measurement date. It assumes that market participants would use and take into account the characteristics of the asset or liability when pricing the asset or liability. Fair values of financial assets and liabilities are based on unadjusted quoted market prices where available. Such quoted market prices are primarily obtained from exchange prices for listed financial instruments. Where an exchange price is not available, quoted prices in an active market may be obtained from independent market vendors, brokers, or market makers. In general, positions are valued at the bid price for a long position and at the offer price for a short position or are valued at the price within the bid-offer spread that is most representative of fair value in the circumstances. In some cases where positions are marked at mid-market prices, a fair value adjustment is calculated.

For certain financial assets and liabilities, quoted market prices are not available. For such instruments, fair value is determined using valuation techniques. These range from discounting of cash flows to various valuation models, where relevant pricing factors including the market price of underlying reference instruments, market parameters (volatilities, correlations and credit ratings), and customer behaviour are taken into account. ING maximises the use of market observable inputs and minimises the use of unobservable inputs in determining the fair value. It can be subjective dependent on the significance of the unobservable input to the overall valuation. All valuation techniques used are subject to internal review and approval. Most data used in these valuation techniques are validated on a daily basis when possible.

When a group of financial assets and liabilities are managed on the basis of their net risk exposures, the fair value of a group of financial assets and liabilities are measured on a net portfolio level.

To include credit risk in fair value, ING applies both Credit and Debit Valuation Adjustments (CVA, DVA). Own issued debt and structured notes that are designated as measured at FVPL are adjusted for credit risk by means of a DVA. Additionally, derivatives valued at fair value are adjusted for credit risk by a CVA. The CVA is of a bilateral nature as both the credit risk on the counterparty as well as the credit risk on ING are included in the adjustment. All input data that is used in the determination of the CVA is based on market implied data. Additionally, wrong-way risk (when exposure to a counterparty is increasing and the credit quality of that counterparty deteriorates) and right-way risk (when exposure to a counterparty is increasing and the credit quality of that counterparty improves) are taken into account in the measurement of the valuation adjustment. ING applies an additional 'Funding Valuation Adjustment' (FVA) to the uncollateralised derivatives based on the market price of funding liquidity.

Significant judgements and critical accounting estimates and assumptions:

Even if market prices are available, when markets are less liquid there may be a range of prices for the same security from different price sources. Selecting the most appropriate price requires judgement and could result in different estimates of fair value.

Valuation techniques are subjective in nature and significant judgement is involved in establishing fair values for certain financial assets and liabilities. Valuation techniques involve various assumptions regarding pricing factors. The use of different valuation techniques and assumptions could produce significantly different estimates of fair value.

Price testing is performed to assess whether the process of valuation has led to an appropriate fair value of the position and to an appropriate reflection of these valuations in the statement of profit or loss. Price testing is performed to minimise the potential risks for economic losses due to incorrect or misused models.

Reference is made to Note 38 'Fair value of assets and liabilities' and Market risk paragraph in the 'Risk management' section of the Annual Report for the basis of the determination of the fair value of financial instruments and related sensitivities.

11.3.3.C   Data challenges

In addition to the method employed to determine a credit adjustment, the inputs used in the various approaches can often require significant judgement. Regardless of the method used, probability of default, loss given default (i.e. the amount that one party expects not to recover if the other party defaults) or credit spread assumptions are important inputs. While the sources of information may vary, the objective remains unchanged – that is, to incorporate inputs that reflect the assumptions of market participants in the current market.

Where available, IFRS 13 requires entities to make maximum use of market-observable credit information. For example, credit default swap (CDS) spreads may provide a good indication of the market's current perception of a particular reporting entity's or counterparty's creditworthiness. However, CDS spreads will likely not be available for smaller public companies or private entities. In these instances, reporting entities may need to consider other available indicators of creditworthiness, such as publicly traded debt or loans.

In the absence of any observable indicator of creditworthiness, a reporting entity may be required to combine a number of factors to arrive at an appropriate credit valuation adjustment. For example, it may be necessary to determine an appropriate credit spread using a combination of own issuance credit spread data, publicly available information on competitors' debt pricing, sector specific CDS spreads or relevant indices, or historical company or sector-specific probabilities of default.

In all cases, identifying the basis for selecting the proxy, benchmark or input, including any analysis performed and assumptions made, should be documented. Such an analysis may include calculating financial ratios to evaluate the reporting entity's financial position relative to its peer group and their credit spreads. These metrics may consider liquidity, leverage and general financial strength, as well as comparable attributes such as credit ratings, similarities in business mix and level of regulation or geographic footprint.

The use of historical default rates would seem to be inconsistent with the exit price notion in IFRS 13, particularly when credit spread levels in the current environment differ significantly from historical averages. Therefore, when current observable information is unavailable, management should adjust historical data to arrive at its best estimate of the assumptions that market participants would use to price the instrument in an orderly transaction in the current market.

Figure 14.6 below highlights some of the common sources of credit information and the advantages and disadvantages of using each input for the credit adjustment calculation.

Figure 14.6:   Credit data requirements

Data requirements	Advantages	Disadvantages
CDS curve (own or counterparty)	• Market observable • Information is current (for counterparties with adequate CDS trading volume) • Easy to source from third party data providers • Exposure specific data available for most banking counterparties	• Not available for many entities • May not be representative of all the assets of the entity • May have liquidity issues due to low trading volumes, resulting in higher-than-expected spreads and additional volatility in calculations • CDS quotes may be indicative quotes, not necessarily reflective of actual trades
Current debt credit spread	• Market observable • Available for some publicly traded debt instruments • Easy to source from third party data providers	• May require an adjustment for illiquidity • May require a judgemental adjustment due to maturity mismatch and amount of security of debt issuance and derivative to be valued
Sector-specific CDS Index or competitor CDS Curve	• Market-observable • Information is current • Easy to source from third party data providers • Proxy CDS curve mapping is possible for almost all entities	• Not exposure-specific; may require judgemental adjustments to reflect differences between proxy and entity (e.g. size, credit rating, etc.) • Index CDS curves can be influenced by macro-economic factors, which do not affect entity or affect entity to a lesser or greater extent
Debt issuance credit spread	• Market observable • Information can be current, in case a recent issuance can be referenced (or where pricing terms are available ahead of debt issuance) • Easy to source from third party data providers and/or from treasurer, through communications with the banks	• Information can be outdated and may require an adjustment for illiquidity • As it is not always possible to reference a recent issuance, a judgemental adjustment may be required to bridge gap between debt issue date and derivative valuation date (i.e. financial reporting date) • May require a judgemental adjustment due to maturity mismatch of debt issuance and derivative to be valued
Credit rating/ historical default information (e.g. Moody's publication of Historic Probability of Default)	• Rating agency data available for most entities • Easy to source from third party data providers	• Information can be outdated • Conversion to probability of default may be based on historical information • May require an adjustment from long-term average measure to a 'point-in-time' measure • Not associated with a specific maturity; ratings are generally long-term average estimates of creditworthiness, which may not be appropriate for short term derivatives
Internal credit risk analysis	• May be applied by most entities • Ability to customise internal models	• Based on unobservable information • Information can be outdated • May not be consistent with what other market participants would use

11.3.4 Does the existence of master netting agreements and/or CSAs eliminate the need to consider an entity's own credit risk when measuring the fair value of derivative liabilities?

IFRS 13 is clear that non-performance risk should be considered from the perspective of the liability being measured, not the entity obligated under the liability. As such, non-performance risk may differ for various liabilities of the same entity. This difference may result from the specific terms of the liability (e.g. seniority or priority in the event of liquidation) or from specific credit enhancements related to the liability (e.g. collateral).

Bilateral collateral arrangements, master netting agreements and other credit enhancement or risk mitigation tools will reduce the credit exposure associated with a liability (or asset) and should be considered in determining the fair value of the liability. Although these agreements reduce credit exposure, they typically do not eliminate the exposure completely. For example, most CSAs do not require collateral to be posted until a certain threshold has been reached, and once reached require collateral only for the exposure in excess of the threshold. Therefore, while the existence of master netting agreements or CSAs mitigates the effect of own credit risk on the fair value of a liability, their presence alone would not enable an entity to ignore its own credit risk. Entities should assess their credit exposure to a specific liability when determining how their own credit risk would affect its fair value.

11.3.4.A Portfolio approaches and credit mitigation arrangements

When calculating derivative credit adjustments, reporting entities may factor in their ability to reduce their counterparty exposures through any existing netting or collateral arrangements. The measurement exception in IFRS 13 (see 12 below) allows a reporting entity to measure the net credit risk of a portfolio of derivatives to a single counterparty, assuming there is an enforceable arrangement in place that mitigates credit risk upon default (e.g. a master netting agreement). *[IFRS 13.48]*.

- *Netting arrangements*

    A master netting agreement is a legally binding contract between two counterparties to net exposures under other agreements or contracts (e.g. relevant ISDA agreements, CSAs and any other credit enhancements or risk mitigation arrangements in place) between the same two parties. Such netting may be effected with periodic payments (payment netting), settlement payments following the occurrence of an event of default (close-out netting) or both. In cases of default, such an agreement serves to protect the parties from paying out on the gross amount of their payable positions, while receiving less than the full amount on their gross receivable positions with the same counterparty.

    IFRS 7 requires disclosure of the effects of set-off and related netting on an entity's financial position (see Chapter 54 for further discussion).

    In situations where an entity meets the criteria to apply the measurement exception in IFRS 13 (discussed at 12 below), it will still need to assess whether it has the practical ability to implement a credit valuation method which reflects the net counterparty exposure. This can be challenging, particularly for those entities that do not have systems in place to capture the relevant net positions by debtor/counterparty.

Also, an allocation of the portfolio level adjustments is required, as discussed at 11.3.4.B below.

A further complication arises if the net exposure represents the position across different classes of derivatives (e.g. interest rate swaps and foreign exchange forwards). Basic valuation methods can attempt to approximate a net position through the creation of an appropriate 'modelled net position' representing the net risk.

- *Collateral arrangements*

    In many instances, counterparty credit exposure in derivative transactions can be further reduced through collateral requirements. Such arrangements serve to limit the potential exposure of one counterparty to the other by requiring the out-of-the-money counterparty to post collateral (e.g. cash or liquid securities) to the in-the-money counterparty. While these and other credit mitigation arrangements often serve to reduce credit exposure, they typically do not eliminate the exposure completely.

    Many collateral agreements, for example, do not require collateral to be posted until a certain threshold has been reached, and then, collateral is required only for the exposure in excess of the threshold. In addition, even when transactions with a counterparty are subject to collateral requirements, entities remain exposed to what is commonly referred to as 'gap risk' (i.e. the exposure arising from fluctuations in the value of the derivatives before the collateral is called and between the time it is called and the time it is actually posted).

    Finally, collateral arrangements may be either unilateral or bilateral. Unilateral arrangements require only one party to the contract to post collateral. Under bilateral agreements, both counterparties are subject to collateral requirements, although potentially at different threshold levels.

Given their ability to reduce credit exposure, netting and collateral arrangements are typically considered in determining the CVA for a portfolio of derivatives. This can add to the complexity of the calculation as total expected credit exposure should be determined not just for a single derivative contract (whose value changes over time), but for a portfolio of derivative contracts (which can include both derivative assets and derivative liabilities). Simply taking the sum of the CVA of individual trades could dramatically overstate the potential credit exposure, as it would not take into account positions in the portfolio with offsetting exposures. Consequently, when netting agreements and collateral arrangements are in place, and a company has elected to measure its derivative positions with offsetting credit risk using the measurement exception in IFRS 13, the expected exposure is generally analysed at the portfolio level (i.e. on a net basis).

11.3.4.B   Portfolio-level credit adjustments

The measurement exception (the portfolio approach) permits measuring non-performance risk of derivatives with the same counterparty on a portfolio basis (see 12 below), allowing the mitigating effect of CSAs and master netting agreements to have their full effect in the financial statements taken as a whole. The use of the measurement exception does not change the fact that the unit of account is the individual derivative contract, a concept particularly important when an individual derivative is designated as a hedging instrument in a hedging relationship.

There is no specific guidance under IFRS on how portfolio level credit adjustments should be allocated to individual derivatives. A number of quantitative allocation methods have been observed in practice and have been accepted as long as a reporting entity is able to support that the method is: (a) appropriate for its facts and circumstances; and (b) applied consistently. Given the renewed focus on credit adjustments, it is likely that valuation methods will become more sophisticated and new techniques and refinements to the above portfolio allocation techniques will arise.

11.4 Restrictions preventing the transfer of a liability or an entity's own equity

A liability or an entity's own equity may be subject to restrictions that prevent the transfer of the item. When measuring the fair value of a liability or equity instrument, IFRS 13 does not allow an entity to include a separate input (or an adjustment to other inputs) for such restrictions. This is because the effect of the restriction is either implicitly or explicitly included in other inputs to the fair value measurement. The standard gives the example of both a creditor and an obligor accepting a transaction price for a liability with full knowledge that the obligation includes a restriction that prevents its transfer. In this case, the restriction is implicitly included in the price. Therefore, further adjustment would be inappropriate. *[IFRS 13.45, 46]*. In Example 14.16 above, the fair value of the decommissioning liability was not adjusted for the existence of a restriction because that restriction was contemplated in developing the inputs to the valuation techniques used to measure fair value.

Paragraph 46 of IFRS 13 states that a separate adjustment for lack of transferability is not necessary for either the initial or subsequent fair value measurement of a liability. This differs from the treatment of asset restrictions. *[IFRS 13.46]*. IFRS 13 considers liability restrictions and asset restrictions differently because:

- restrictions on the transfer of a liability relate to the performance of the obligation (i.e. the entity is legally obliged to satisfy the obligation and needs to do something to be relieved of the obligation), whereas restrictions on the transfer of an asset relate to the marketability of the asset; and
- unlike assets, virtually all liabilities include a restriction preventing their transfer. As a result, the effect of a restriction preventing the transfer of a liability would, in theory, be consistent for all liabilities.

The standard also appears to assume that the effect of a restriction on the fair value of a liability remains constant over the life of the liability. Therefore, no additional adjustments are required in subsequent measurements if the effect of the restriction was already captured in the initial pricing of the liability. Unlike restrictions on assets, which typically expire and whose effect on fair value changes over time, restrictions on liabilities usually remain throughout the life of the obligation.

The Basis for Conclusions to IFRS 13 states that if an entity is aware that a restriction on transfer is not already reflected in the price (or in the other inputs used in the measurement), it would adjust the price or inputs to reflect the existence of the restriction. *[IFRS 13.BC99, BC100]*.

However, in our view this would be rare because nearly all liabilities include a restriction and, when measuring fair value, market participants are assumed by IFRS 13 to be sufficiently knowledgeable about the liability to be transferred.

11.5 Financial liability with a demand feature

IFRS 13 states that the 'fair value of a financial liability with a demand feature (e.g. a demand deposit) is not less than the amount payable on demand, discounted from the first date that the amount could be required to be paid'. *[IFRS 13.47]*. This is consistent with the requirements in IFRS 9. In many cases, the observed market price for these financial liabilities would be the demand amount, i.e. the price at which they are originated between the customer and the deposit-taker. Recognising such a financial liability at less than the demand amount may give rise to an immediate gain on the origination of the deposit, which the IASB believes is inappropriate. *[IFRS 13.BCZ102-BCZ103]*.

12 FINANCIAL ASSETS AND LIABILITIES WITH OFFSETTING POSITIONS

IFRS 13 specifies that the concepts of 'highest and best use' and 'valuation premise' are not relevant when measuring the fair value of financial instruments. Therefore, the fair value of financial assets and financial liabilities is based on the unit of account prescribed by the IFRS that requires (or permits) the fair value measurement, which is generally the individual financial instrument. However, IFRS 13 provides a measurement exception that allows an entity to determine the fair value of a group of financial assets and liabilities with offsetting risks based on the sale or transfer of its *net* exposure to a particular risk (or risks), if certain criteria are met. *[IFRS 13.48]*. This measurement approach is an exception to the principles of fair value because it represents an entity-specific measure (i.e. an entity's net risk exposure is a function of the other financial instruments specifically held by that entity and its unique risk preferences).

It may be possible for entities to offset multiple risks (e.g. both market and credit risks) within the same portfolio. In addition, since the focus is on offsetting risks, entities may offset credit and market risks stemming from a group of financial instruments at different levels of aggregation. For example, under IFRS 13, management could continue its existing practice of offsetting credit risk at the counterparty level (e.g. based on its portfolio of interest rate swaps with a particular counterparty) while offsetting market risks on a more aggregated portfolio basis (e.g. based on its portfolio of interest rate swaps with all counterparties), provided all of the criteria in 12.1 below are met.

This guidance is largely consistent with practice under IFRS prior to adoption of IFRS 13 when determining valuation adjustments for derivative instruments related to bid-ask spreads and credit risk.

12.1 Criteria for using the portfolio approach for offsetting positions

Entities that hold a group of financial assets and liabilities are generally exposed to market risks (e.g. interest rate risk, currency risk or other price risk) and to the credit risk of each of its counterparties. IFRS 13 allows entities to make an accounting policy choice (see 12.1.1 below) to measure the fair value of a group of financial assets and

liabilities based on the price that would be received to sell a net long position or transfer a net short position for a particular risk exposure (that is, a portfolio approach). In order to use the portfolio approach, entities are required to meet all of the following criteria, both initially and on an ongoing basis:
- the entity manages the group of financial assets and financial liabilities on the basis of the entity's net exposure to a particular market risk(s) or credit risk, in accordance with the entity's documented risk management or investment strategy;
- the entity provides information based on the group of financial assets and financial liabilities to the entity's key management personnel; and
- the entity measures (either by requirement or by choice) the financial assets and financial liabilities at fair value in the statement of financial position at each reporting date. *[IFRS 13.49]*.

The measurement exception for offsetting positions only applies to financial assets and financial liabilities within the scope of IFRS 9. *[IFRS 13.52]*. Also, as indicated by these criteria, the portfolio approach only applies to financial instruments with offsetting risks. As such, a group of financial instruments comprised of only financial assets (e.g. a portfolio of loans) would not qualify for the exception and would need to be valued in a manner consistent with the appropriate unit of account. However, an entity need not maintain a static portfolio to use the measurement exception, i.e. the entity could have assets and liabilities within the portfolio that are traded.

When IFRS 13 was issued, paragraph 52 stated that the measurement exception only applied to financial assets and financial liabilities within the scope of IFRS 9. However, it was not the Boards' intention to exclude contracts to buy or sell a non-financial item (e.g. physically settled commodity derivative contracts) that are within the scope of IFRS 9 (and that are measured at fair value) from the scope of the measurement exception. *[IFRS 13.BC119A, BC119B]*. If a contract to buy or sell a non-financial item is within the scope of IFRS 9, those standards treat that contract as if it were a financial instrument. Therefore, the IASB amended paragraph 52 to clarify that all contracts within the scope of IFRS 9 are eligible for the measurement exception, regardless of whether they meet the definitions of financial assets or financial liabilities in IAS 32. *[IFRS 13.52]*.

12.1.1 Accounting policy considerations

As noted above, the use of the portfolio approach is an accounting policy decision, to be made in accordance with IAS 8 (see Chapter 3), which must include an entity's policy regarding measurement assumptions – i.e. for both allocating bid-ask adjustments and credit adjustments (see 12.2 below).

An entity can choose to use the portfolio approach on a portfolio-by-portfolio basis. In addition, if entities choose this policy for a particular portfolio, they are not required to apply the portfolio approach to all of the risks of the financial assets and liabilities that make up the particular group. For example, an entity could choose to measure only the credit risk associated with a group of financial instruments on a net basis, but not the group's exposure to market risk.

An entity may also decide to apply the portfolio approach to only certain market risks related to the group. For example, an entity that is exposed to both interest rate and foreign currency risk in a portfolio of financial assets and liabilities could choose to measure only its interest rate risk exposure on a net basis.

The accounting policy decision can be changed if an entity's risk exposure preferences change, for example, a change in strategy to have fewer offsetting positions. In that case, the entity can decide not to use the exception but instead to measure the fair value of its financial instruments on an individual instrument basis. We generally expect that an entity's use of the portfolio approach would be consistent from period to period as changes in risk management policies are typically not common. *[IFRS 13.51, BC121]*.

12.1.2 Presentation considerations

IFRS 13 is clear that applying the portfolio approach for measurement purposes does not affect financial statement presentation. For example, an entity might manage a group of financial assets and liabilities based on the net exposure(s) for internal risk management or investment strategy purposes, but be unable to present those instruments on a net basis in the statement of financial position because the entity does not have a positive intention and ability to settle those instruments on a net basis, as is required by IAS 32. *[IAS 32.42]*.

If the requirements for presentation of financial instruments in the statement of financial position differ from the basis for the measurement, an entity may need to allocate the portfolio-level adjustments (see 12.2 below) to the individual assets or liabilities that make up the portfolio. Entities may also need to allocate portfolio-level adjustments for disclosure purposes when items in the group would be categorised within different levels of the fair value hierarchy (see 16 below for additional discussion on the allocation of portfolio-level adjustments related to the fair value hierarchy disclosures).

IFRS 13 does not prescribe any methodologies for allocating portfolio-level adjustments; instead, it states that the allocation should be performed in a reasonable and consistent manner that is appropriate in the circumstances. *[IFRS 13.50]*.

12.1.3 Is there a minimum level of offset required to use the portfolio approach?

While there are explicit criteria that an entity must meet in order to use the portfolio approach, IFRS 13 does not specify any minimum level of offset within the group of financial instruments. For example, if an entity has positions with offsetting credit risk to a particular counterparty, we believe use of the portfolio approach is appropriate even if the extent of offset is minimal (provided that the entity has in place a legally enforceable agreement, as discussed at 12.2.2 below, that provides for offsetting upon default and all the other required criteria are met). To illustrate, even if the gross credit exposure was CU 100,000 (long) and CU 5,000 (short), upon counterparty default the entity would be exposed to a credit loss of only CU 95,000 under the terms of its master netting agreement.

With respect to market risk, considering the degree of offset may require additional judgement. Entities should assess the appropriateness of using the portfolio approach based on the nature of the portfolio being managed (e.g. derivative versus cash instruments) and its documented risk management policies (or investment strategies).

An entity should use the portfolio approach in a manner consistent with the IASB's basis for providing the measurement exception and not in a manner to circumvent other principles within the standard.

12.1.4 Can Level 1 instruments be included in a portfolio of financial instruments with offsetting risks when calculating the net exposure to a particular market risk?

It is our understanding that Level 1 instruments can be included when using the exception to value financial instruments with offsetting risks. An entity is allowed to consider the effect of holding futures contracts when evaluating its net exposure to a particular market risk, such as interest rate risk. Paragraph 54 of IFRS 13 gives an example stating that 'an entity would not combine the interest rate risk associated with a financial asset with the commodity price risk associated with a financial liability because doing so would not mitigate the entity's exposure to interest rate risk or commodity price risk'. *[IFRS 13.54]*.

We understand that some constituents believe that the requirement in IFRS 13 to measure instruments that trade in active markets based on P×Q does not apply to the measurement of the net exposure when the portfolio exception is used, since the net exposure does not trade in an active market. As such, these constituents argue that the measurement of the net exposure and the allocation of this value back to the instruments that comprise the group are not constrained by the price at which the individual instruments trade in active markets. Others believe that although Level 1 instruments, such as futures contracts, may be considered when calculating an entity's net exposure to a particular market risk, the quoted price (unadjusted) for these Level 1 instruments should be used when allocating the fair value to the individual units of account for presentation and disclosure purposes, to comply with the requirement in IFRS 13 to measure Level 1 instruments at P×Q. However, depending on the extent of Level 1 instruments in the group, it may not always be possible to allocate the fair value determined for the net exposure back to the individual instruments in a manner that results in each of these instruments being recorded at P×Q. For this reason, there are constituents who believe that the use of the portfolio exception should never result in the measurement of Level 1 instruments at an amount other than P×Q. That is, the determination of the fair value of the net exposure is constrained by the requirement that all Level 1 instruments within the group are recorded at a value based on P×Q.

As discussed at 5.1.2 above, we understand that the IASB did not intend the portfolio exception to change existing practice under IFRS or override the requirement in IFRS 13 to measure Level 1 instruments at P×Q or the prohibition on block discounts. However, given the lack of clarity, some have asked questions about how these requirements would apply in practice. In 2013, the IFRS Interpretations Committee referred a request to the Board on the interaction between the use of Level 1 inputs and the portfolio exception. The IASB discussed this issue in December 2013, but only in relation to portfolios that comprise only Level 1 financial instruments whose market risks are substantially the same. The Board tentatively decided that the measurement of such portfolios should be the one that results from multiplying the net position by the Level 1 prices. Therefore, in September 2014, the IASB proposed adding a non-authoritative example to illustrate the application of the portfolio exception in these circumstances.

As discussed at 5.1.2 above and 12.2 below, in April 2015, after considering responses to this proposal from constituents, the IASB concluded it was not necessary to add the proposed illustrative example to IFRS 13.

12.2 Measuring fair value for offsetting positions

If the portfolio approach is used to measure an entity's net exposure to a particular market risk, the net risk exposure becomes the unit of measurement. That is, the entity's net exposure to a particular market risk (e.g. the net long or short Euro interest rate exposure within a specified maturity bucket) represents the asset or liability being measured.

In applying the portfolio approach, an entity must assume an orderly transaction between market participants to sell or transfer the net risk exposure at the measurement date under current market conditions. The fair value of the portfolio is measured on the basis of the price that would be received to sell a net long position (i.e. an asset) for a particular risk exposure or transfer a net short position (i.e. a liability) for a particular risk exposure. *[IFRS 13.48]*. That is, the objective of the valuation is to determine the price that market participants would pay (or receive) in a single transaction for the entire net risk exposure, as defined.

Some argue that, as a result, an adjustment based on the size of the net exposure could be considered in the valuation if market participants would incorporate such an adjustment when transacting for the net exposure. Since the unit of measurement is the net exposure, size is considered a characteristic of the asset (net long position) or liability (net short position) being measured, not a characteristic of the entity's specific holdings. Many have interpreted the equivalent requirements in US GAAP in this way.

Others believe that the portfolio exception does not override the unit of account guidance provided in IFRS 9 and, therefore, any premiums or discounts that are inconsistent with that unit of account, i.e. the individual financial instruments within the portfolio, must be excluded. This would include any premiums or discounts related to the size of the portfolio. As discussed at 5.1.2 above, we understand the IASB did not intend the portfolio exception to override the requirement in IFRS 13 to measure Level 1 instruments at P×Q or the prohibition on block discounts which raises questions as to how the portfolio exception would be applied to Level 1 instruments.

In 2013, the IFRS Interpretations Committee referred a request to the Board on the interaction between the use of Level 1 inputs and the portfolio exception. The IASB discussed this issue in December 2013, but only in relation to portfolios that comprise only Level 1 financial instruments whose market risks are substantially the same. The Board tentatively decided that the measurement of such portfolios should be the one that results from multiplying the net position by the Level 1 prices. In September 2014, the IASB proposed adding the following non-authoritative example to illustrate the application of the portfolio exception in these circumstances.

Example 14.19: Applying the portfolio approach to a group of financial assets and financial liabilities whose market risks are substantially the same and whose fair value measurement is categorised within Level 1 of the fair value hierarchy[22]

Entity A holds a group of financial assets and financial liabilities consisting of a long position of 10,000 financial assets and a short position of 9,500 financial liabilities whose market risks are substantially the same. Entity A manages that group of financial assets and financial liabilities on the basis of its net exposure to market risks. The fair value measurement of all the financial instruments in the group is categorised within Level 1 of the fair value hierarchy.

The mid-price and the most representative bid and ask prices are as follows:

	Bid	Mid	Ask
Most representative exit price	£99	£100	£101

Entity A applies the exception in paragraph 48 of the IFRS that permits Entity A to measure the fair value of the group of financial assets and financial liabilities on the basis of the price that would be received to sell, in this particular case, a net long position (i.e. an asset) in an orderly transaction between market participants at the measurement date under current market conditions.

Accordingly, Entity A measures the net long position (500 financial assets) in accordance with the corresponding Level 1 prices. Because the market risks arising from the financial instruments are substantially the same, the measurement of the net position coincides with the measurement of the exposure arising from the group of financial assets and financial liabilities. Consequently, Entity A measures the group of financial assets and financial liabilities on the basis of the price that it would receive if it would exit or close out its outstanding exposure as follows:

	Quantity held (Q)	Level 1 price (P)	P×Q
Net long position	500	£99	£49,500

Entity A would have also achieved the same measurement of £49,500 by measuring the net long position at the mid-price (i.e. £100 × 500 = £50,000) adjusted by a bid-offer reserve (£1 × 500 = £500).

Entity A allocates the resulting measurement (i.e. £49,500) to the individual (10,000) financial assets and (9,500) financial liabilities. In accordance with paragraph 50 of IFRS 13, Entity A performs this allocation on a reasonable basis that is consistent with previous allocations of that nature using a methodology appropriate to the circumstances.

In response to this proposal, some respondents raised concerns because they believed there was a risk that constituents may infer principles from this simple example that could lead to unintended consequences. Respondents noted that the illustrative example did not address:

- other scenarios and circumstances to which the portfolio approach would apply. For example, situations where the instruments in the portfolio are categorised within Level 2 or Level 3 of the fair value hierarchy or for which different Level 1 prices are available; and
- allocation of the resulting measurement to each instrument in the portfolio for disclosure purposes.

The proposed illustrative example also raised questions about the interaction between the portfolio exception and the use of mid-market pricing as a practical expedient in accordance with paragraph 71 of IFRS 13 and may have required clarification of the term 'bid-offer reserve adjustment' used in the example. Despite these concerns, the majority of the respondents agreed that the proposed additional illustrative example appropriately illustrated application of the portfolio approach.[23]

As discussed at 5.1.2 above, in April 2015, after considering responses to this proposal from constituents, the IASB concluded that it was not necessary to add the proposed illustrative example to IFRS 13. However, in reaching this decision, the Board noted that the proposed illustrative example appropriately illustrated the application of the portfolio approach. 'That is, if an entity elects to use the exception in paragraph 48 of IFRS 13, the appropriate fair value measurement of the net risk exposure arising from a group of financial assets and financial liabilities whose market risks are substantially the same, and whose fair value measurement is categorised within Level 1 of the fair value hierarchy, would be determined by multiplying the financial instruments included in the resulting net position by the corresponding unadjusted Level 1 price'.[24] *[IFRS 13.48]*.

While the proposed non-authoritative example provides one approach to consider, in light of the above discussion, entities will need to use judgement to determine the most appropriate approach to employ when applying the portfolio exception.

When measuring fair value using the portfolio approach, IFRS 13 also requires that the market risks be substantially the same (see 12.2.1 below) and that the fair value measurement must take into consideration any exposure to the credit risk of a particular counterparty (see 12.2.2 below).

It is also important to note that when applying the portfolio approach, entities may offset credit and market risks at different levels of aggregation. This approach is consistent with risk management practices employed by many entities. Such an approach may be required because it is unlikely that all of the financial assets and liabilities giving rise to the net exposure for a particular market risk will be with the same counterparty. The example below illustrates this concept.

Example 14.20: Calculating net exposure

Entity XYZ holds a portfolio of long and short derivative positions (USD interest rate swaps and USD/JPY foreign currency forwards) with various counterparties as follows:

- Counterparties A, B and C: only interest rate swaps.
- Counterparty D: interest rate swaps and foreign currency forwards.
- Counterparties E, F and G: only foreign currency forwards.

Entity XYZ has executed master netting agreements in respect of credit risk with each of its counterparties except counterparty G. In addition, the agreement in place with counterparty D can be applied across products.

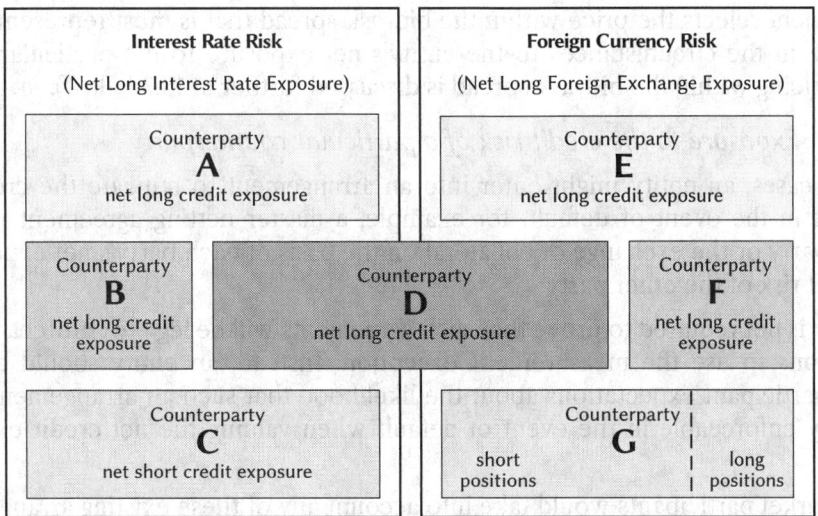

Using the measurement exception, Entity XYZ may consider its credit risk exposure to each individual counterparty except counterparty G on a net basis (i.e. net long credit exposure to Counterparty A, net short credit exposure to Counterparty C, etc.).

At the same time, the entity may consider its net long exposure to USD interest rate risk from its portfolio of derivatives with counterparties A, B, C and D. The entity may also consider its net long exposure to foreign currency risk (Japanese yen risk) from its portfolio of derivatives with counterparties D, E, F and G.

12.2.1 Exposure to market risks

When measuring fair value using the measurement exception for offsetting positions, the entity is required to ensure the following in relation to market risks:

- Market risk (or risks), to which the entity is exposed within that portfolio, is substantially the same. For example, combining the interest rate risk associated with a financial asset with the commodity price risk associated with a financial liability would not be appropriate because it would not mitigate the entity's exposure to interest rate risk or commodity price risk.

  The standard requires any basis risk resulting from the market risk parameters not being identical to be taken into account in the fair value measurement of the financial assets and financial liabilities within the group. *[IFRS 13.54]*

- The duration of the entity's exposure to a particular market risk (or risks) must be substantially the same. *[IFRS 13.55]*.

  The standard gives the example of an entity that uses a 12-month futures contract against the cash flows associated with 12 months' worth of interest rate risk exposure on a five-year financial instrument. The futures and five-year financial instruments are within a group that is made up of only those financial assets and financial liabilities. The entity measures the fair value of the exposure to 12-month interest rate risk on a net basis and the remaining interest rate risk exposure (i.e. years 2-5) on a gross basis.

Management selects the price within the bid-ask spread that is most representative of fair value in the circumstances to the entity's net exposure to the particular market risk(s) (pricing within the bid-ask spread is discussed further at 15.3 below). *[IFRS 13.53]*.

12.2.2 Exposure to the credit risk of a particular counterparty

In some cases, an entity might enter into an arrangement to mitigate the credit risk exposure in the event of default, for example, a master netting agreement with the counterparty or the exchange of collateral on the basis of each party's net exposure to the credit risk of the other party.

An entity is not required to prove that such agreements will be legally enforceable in all jurisdictions to use the measurement exception. Instead, an entity should consider market participant expectations about the likelihood that such an arrangement would be legally enforceable in the event of default when valuing the net credit exposure. *[IFRS 13.56]*.

When market participants would take into account any of these existing arrangements, the fair value measurement (using the measurement exception for offsetting positions) must include the effect of the entity's net exposure to the credit risk of that counterparty and/or the counterparty's net exposure to the credit risk of the entity.

13 FAIR VALUE AT INITIAL RECOGNITION

13.1 Exit price versus entry price

IFRS 13 defines fair value as the price that would be received to sell the asset or paid to transfer the liability; this is an exit price notion. When an entity acquires an asset, or assumes a liability, the price paid (or the transaction price) is an entry price. Conceptually, entry prices and exit prices are different. Entities do not necessarily sell assets at the prices paid to acquire them. Similarly, entities do not necessarily transfer liabilities at the prices received to assume them. This distinction is significant and can have important implications on the initial recognition of assets and liabilities at fair value. However, IFRS 13 acknowledges that, in many cases, an entry price may equal an exit price (e.g. when the transaction takes place in the entity's principal market); since one party is selling an asset, that transaction is also an exit transaction. *[IFRS 13.57, 58]*.

13.1.1 Assessing whether the transaction price equals fair value at initial recognition

Prior to the issuance of IFRS 13, it was common for entities to use the transaction price as fair value of an asset or liability on its initial recognition. While IFRS 13 acknowledges that in many situations, an entry price may equal an exit price, it does not presume that these prices are equal. Therefore, an entity must determine whether the transaction price represents the fair value of an asset or liability at initial recognition. *[IFRS 13.59]*.

Paragraph B4 of IFRS 13 provides certain factors that an entity should consider in making this determination. For example, a transaction price may not represent fair value if the unit of account represented by the transaction price is different from the unit of account for the asset or liability measured at fair value. *[IFRS 13.B4(c)]*. This may be the case with a complex financial instrument where the transaction price includes a fee for structuring the transaction or when an entity acquires a block and the transaction price includes a block discount.

Another factor to consider is whether the market in which an entity acquired the asset (or assumed the liability) is different from the principal (or most advantageous) market in which the entity will sell the asset (or transfer the liability). *[IFRS 13.B4(d)]*. For example, a securities dealer may acquire an asset in the retail market but sell it in the inter-dealer market. However, the fair value measurement should consider the fact that, while the inter-dealer price (i.e. the exit price in a hypothetical transaction) may differ from the retail price (i.e. transaction price), another dealer would also expect to earn a profit on the transaction. Accordingly, a pricing model's value should incorporate assumptions regarding the appropriate profit margin that market participants (i.e. other dealers) would demand when estimating the instrument's fair value at inception.

Other examples identified by paragraph B4 of IFRS 13 include:
- the transaction is between related parties – although IFRS 13 does allow the price in a related party transaction to be used as an input into a fair value measurement if the entity has evidence that the transaction was entered into at market terms; and
- the transaction takes place under duress or the seller is forced to accept the price in the transaction – for example, if the seller is experiencing financial difficulty. *[IFRS 13.B4(a)-(b)]*.

In addition, the measurement of fair value in accordance with IFRS 13 should take into consideration market participant assumptions about risk. Adjustments for uncertainty associated with a valuation technique or certain inputs used to measure fair value are required if market participants would incorporate such risk adjustments when pricing the asset or liability. A measurement (e.g. a 'mark-to-model' measurement) that ignores these market participant adjustments for risk is not representative of fair value.

While helpful in identifying the factors entities should consider in assessing whether a transaction price would equal fair value, the examples provided in the standard are not intended to be exhaustive.

13.2 Day one gains and losses

IFRS 13's measurement framework applies to initial fair value measurements, if permitted or required by another IFRS. At initial recognition, if the measurement of fair value in accordance with IFRS 13 and the transaction price differ, the entity recognises the resulting gain or loss in profit or loss unless the related IFRS (i.e. the IFRS that permits or requires the initial measurement at fair value) specifies otherwise. *[IFRS 13.60]*.

As noted in Example 14.21 below, IFRS 9 has specific requirements with regard to the recognition of inception (or 'day one') gains and losses for financial instruments within the scope of the standard (see Chapter 49). In developing IFRS 13, the IASB did not change the recognition threshold in those standards in relation to day one gains or losses. However, IFRS 9 was amended to clarify that an entity: (i) measures the fair value of financial instruments at initial recognition in accordance with IFRS 13, then; (ii) considers the requirements of IFRS 9 in determining whether (and when) the resulting difference (if any) between fair value at initial recognition and the transaction price is recognised. *[IFRS 13.BC138]*.

13.2.1 Day one losses for over-the-counter derivative transactions

The definition of fair value as an exit price affects the accounting by retail customers as much as financial institutions (i.e. dealers). For example, retail customers whose entry and exit market for a financial asset (or financial liability) measured at fair value is with a wholesaler (e.g. a dealer) could experience a day one loss, because the price at which a wholesaler would sell a financial asset to a retail customer would generally exceed the price a wholesaler would pay to acquire that financial asset from a retail customer (this difference in price is commonly referred to as the bid-ask spread in many financial markets).

The following example from IFRS 13 discusses how an interest rate swap at initial recognition may be measured differently by a retail counterparty (i.e. an end-user) and a dealer. [IFRS 13.IE24-IE26].

Example 14.21: Interest rate swap at initial recognition

Entity A (a retail counterparty) enters into an interest rate swap in a retail market with Entity B (a dealer) for no initial consideration (i.e. the transaction price is zero). Entity A can access only the retail market. Entity B can access both the retail market (i.e. with retail counterparties) and the dealer market (i.e. with dealer counterparties).

From the perspective of Entity A, the retail market in which it initially entered into the swap is the principal market for the swap. If Entity A were to transfer its rights and obligations under the swap, it would do so with a dealer counterparty in that retail market. In that case the transaction price (zero) would represent the fair value of the swap to Entity A at initial recognition, i.e. the price that Entity A would receive to sell or pay to transfer the swap in a transaction with a dealer counterparty in the retail market (i.e. an exit price). That price would not be adjusted for any incremental (transaction) costs that would be charged by that dealer counterparty.

From the perspective of Entity B, the dealer market (not the retail market) is the principal market for the swap. If Entity B were to transfer its rights and obligations under the swap, it would do so with a dealer in that market. Because the market in which Entity B initially entered into the swap is different from the principal market for the swap, the transaction price (zero) would not necessarily represent the fair value of the swap to Entity B at initial recognition. If the fair value differs from the transaction price (zero), Entity B applies IFRS 9 to determine whether it recognises that difference as a gain or loss at initial recognition.

This example seems to indicate that a retail counterparty may not have any gain or loss at initial recognition because the retail counterparty would likely be presumed to transact both at inception and on disposal (i.e. a hypothetical exit) in the same principal market (i.e. the retail market with securities dealers). However, this example does not address the bid-ask spread.

The bid-ask spread is the difference between the price a prospective dealer is willing to pay for an instrument (the 'bid' price) and the price at which the dealer would sell that same instrument (the 'ask' price), allowing the dealer to earn a profit for its role as a 'market maker' in the over-the-counter marketplace. The bid-ask spread may differ by dealer, as well as by the market and type of instrument that is being transacted.

IFRS 13 requires that instruments that trade in markets with bid-ask spreads (e.g. a dealer market) be measured at the price within the bid-ask spread that is most representative of fair value in the circumstances (pricing within the bid-ask spread is discussed further at 15.3 below). Therefore, an inception loss could be experienced by the retail counterparty due to a difference in the price within the bid-ask spread that the retail counterparty could hypothetically exit the instrument and the price within the bid-ask spread that the retail counterparty actually transacted.

The IASB has acknowledged that the fair value of an interest rate swap may differ from its transaction price because of the bid-ask spread, even when the entry and exit markets for the swap are identical. *[IFRS 13.BC165]*. In addition to the bid-ask spread, retail counterparties may recognise additional losses or expenses at the inception of derivative contracts. For example, if the transaction price for a complex derivative includes a structuring fee, the retail counterparty would likely recognise a loss when measuring the fair value of the derivative. Because the transaction price includes the price for the derivative instrument, as well as the fee paid by the retail counterparty to the dealer for structuring the transaction, the unit of account represented by the transaction price differs from the unit of account for the instrument being measured, as discussed in paragraph B4(c) of IFRS 13. *[IFRS 13.B4(c)]*.

13.2.2 Day one gains and losses when entry and exit markets for the transaction are deemed to be the same

IFRS 13 contains no explicit prohibitions on the recognition of day one gains or losses, even in situations where the entry and exit markets are the same. For example, it may be acceptable in certain situations for a dealer to recognise a day one gain or loss on a transaction where the entry and exit markets are deemed to be the same (e.g. inter-dealer market). A difference in the price within the bid-ask spread at which a dealer could exit a transaction versus where it entered the transaction could be one reason to record an inception gain or loss. IFRS 13 clarifies that the exit price within the bid-ask spread that is most representative of fair value in the circumstances should be used to measure fair value, regardless of where in the fair value hierarchy the input falls (pricing within the bid-ask spread is discussed further at 15.3 below).

Notwithstanding the guidance in IFRS 13, IFRS 9 provide specific requirements in relation to the recognition of any day one gains or losses. For example, where fair value is not measured using a quoted price in an active market (without adjustment), recognition of day one gains or losses is generally prohibited (see Chapter 49).

13.3 Related party transactions

As discussed at 7 above, the definition of market participants makes it clear that buyers and sellers for the item being measured are not related parties (as defined in IAS 24). That is, the hypothetical transaction used to determine fair value in IFRS 13 is assumed to take place between market participants that are independent from one another. However, IFRS 13 indicates that the price in a related party transaction may be used as an input into a fair value measurement if there is evidence the transaction was entered into at market terms. The Boards believe such an approach is consistent with the requirements of IAS 24. As with disclosures made in accordance with IAS 24, evidence to support that a related party transaction was executed at market terms may be difficult to substantiate absent corroborating market data from transactions between independent parties.

14 VALUATION TECHNIQUES

There are two key distinctions between the way previous IFRSs considered valuation techniques and the approach in IFRS 13. On adoption of the standard, these distinctions, in and of themselves, may not have changed practice. However, they may have required management to reconsider their methods of measuring fair value.

Firstly, IFRS 13's requirements in relation to valuation techniques apply to all methods of measuring fair value. Traditionally, references to valuation techniques in IFRS have indicated a lack of market-based information with which to value an asset or liability. Valuation techniques as discussed in IFRS 13 are broader and, importantly, include market-based approaches.

Secondly, IFRS 13 does not prioritise the use of one valuation technique over another, unlike existing IFRSs, or require the use of only one technique (with the exception of the requirement to measure identical financial instruments that trade in active markets at price multiplied by quantity (P×Q)). Instead, the standard establishes a hierarchy for the inputs used in those valuation techniques, requiring an entity to maximise observable inputs and minimise the use of unobservable inputs (the fair value hierarchy is discussed further at 16 below). *[IFRS 13.74]*. In some instances, the approach in IFRS 13 may be consistent with previous requirements in IFRS. For example, the best indication of fair value continues to be a quoted price in an active market. However, since IFRS 13 indicates that multiple techniques should be used when appropriate and sufficient data is available, judgement will be needed to select the techniques that are appropriate in the circumstances. *[IFRS 13.61]*.

14.1 Selecting appropriate valuation techniques

IFRS 13 recognises the following three valuation approaches to measure fair value.

- *Market approach:* based on market transactions involving identical or similar assets or liabilities;
- *Income approach:* based on future amounts (e.g. cash flows or income and expenses) that are converted (discounted) to a single present amount; and
- *Cost approach:* based on the amount required to replace the service capacity of an asset (frequently referred to as current replacement cost).

IFRS 13 requires that an entity use valuation techniques that are consistent with one or more of the above valuation approaches (these valuation approaches are discussed in more detail at 14.2 to 14.4 below). *[IFRS 13.62]*. These approaches are consistent with generally accepted valuation methodologies used outside financial reporting. Not all of the approaches will be applicable to all types of assets or liabilities. However, when measuring the fair value of an asset or liability, IFRS 13 requires an entity to use valuation techniques that are appropriate in the circumstances and for which sufficient data is available. As a result, the use of multiple valuation techniques may be required. *[IFRS 13.61, 62]*.

The determination of the appropriate technique(s) to be applied requires significant judgement, sufficient knowledge of the asset or liability and an adequate level of expertise regarding the valuation techniques. Within the application of a given approach, there may be a number of possible valuation techniques. For instance, there are a number of different techniques used to value intangible assets under the income approach (such as the multi-period excess earnings method and the relief-from-royalty method) depending on the nature of the asset.

As noted above, the fair value hierarchy does not prioritise the valuation techniques to be used; instead, it prioritises the inputs used in the application of these techniques. As such, the selection of the valuation technique(s) to apply should consider the exit market (i.e. the principal (or most advantageous) market) for the asset or liability and use valuation inputs that are consistent with the nature of the item being measured. Regardless of the technique(s) used, the objective of a fair value measurement remains the same – i.e. an exit price under current market conditions from the perspective of market participants.

Selection, application, and evaluation of the valuation techniques can be complex. As such, reporting entities may need assistance from valuation professionals.

14.1.1 Single versus multiple valuation techniques

The standard does not contain a hierarchy of valuation techniques because particular valuation techniques might be more appropriate in some circumstances than in others.

Selecting a single valuation technique may be appropriate in some circumstances, for example, when measuring a financial asset or liability using a quoted price in an active market. However, in other situations, more than one valuation technique may be deemed appropriate and multiple approaches should be applied. For example, it may be appropriate to use multiple valuation techniques when measuring fair value less costs of disposal for a cash-generating unit to test for impairment. *[IFRS 13.63]*.

The nature of the characteristics of the asset or liability being measured and the availability of observable market prices may contribute to the number of valuation techniques used in a fair value analysis. For example, the fair value of a business is often estimated by giving consideration to multiple valuation approaches; such as an income approach that derives value from the present value of the expected future cash flows specific to the business and a market approach that derives value from market data (such as EBITDA or revenue multiples) based on observed transactions for comparable assets. On the other hand, financial assets that frequently trade in active markets are often valued using only a market approach given the availability and relevance of observable data.

Even when the use of a single approach is deemed appropriate, entities should be aware of changing circumstances that could indicate using multiple approaches may be more appropriate. For example, this might be the case if there is a significant decrease in the volume and level of activity for an asset or liability in relation to normal market activity. Observable transactions that once formed the basis for the fair value estimate may cease to exist altogether or may not be determinative of fair value and, therefore, require an adjustment to the fair value measurement (this is discussed further at 8.3 above). As such, the use of multiple valuation techniques may be more appropriate.

14.1.2 Using multiple valuation techniques to measure fair value

When the use of multiple valuation techniques is considered appropriate, their application is likely to result in a range of possible values. IFRS 13 requires that management evaluate the reasonableness of the range and select the point within the range that is most representative of fair value in the circumstances. *[IFRS 13.63]*.

As with the selection of the valuation techniques, the evaluation of the results of multiple techniques requires significant judgement. The merits of each valuation technique applied, and the underlying assumptions embedded in each of the techniques, will need to be considered. Evaluation of the range does not necessarily require the approaches to be calibrated to one another (i.e. the results from different approaches do not have to be equal). The objective is to find the point in the range that most reflects the price to sell an asset or transfer a liability between market participants.

If the results from different valuation techniques are similar, the issue of weighting multiple value indications becomes less important since the assigned weights will not significantly alter the fair value estimate. However, when indications of value are disparate, entities should seek to understand why significant differences exist and what assumptions might contribute to the variance. Paragraph B40 of IFRS 13 indicates that when evaluating results from multiple valuation approaches, a wide range of fair value measurements may be an indication that further analysis is needed. *[IFRS 13.B40]*. For example, divergent results between a market approach and income approach may indicate a misapplication of one or both of the techniques and would likely necessitate additional analysis.

The standard gives two examples that illustrate situations where the use of multiple valuation techniques is appropriate and, when used, how different indications of value are assessed.

Firstly, an entity might determine that a technique uses assumptions that are not consistent with market participant assumptions (and, therefore, is not representative of fair value). This is illustrated in Example 14.22 below, where the entity eliminates use of the cost approach because it determines a market participant would not be able to construct the asset itself. *[IFRS 13.IE15-IE17]*.

Example 14.22: Multiple valuation techniques – software asset

An entity acquires a group of assets. The asset group includes an income-producing software asset internally developed for licensing to customers and its complementary assets (including a related database with which the software asset is used) and the associated liabilities. To allocate the cost of the group to the individual assets acquired, the entity measures the fair value of the software asset. The entity determines that the software asset would provide maximum value to market participants through its use in combination with other assets or with other assets and liabilities (i.e. its complementary assets and the associated liabilities). There is no evidence to suggest that the current use of the software asset is not its highest and best use. Therefore, the highest and best use of the software asset is its current use. (In this case the licensing of the software asset, in and of itself, does not indicate that the fair value of the asset would be maximised through its use by market participants on a stand-alone basis.)

The entity determines that, in addition to the income approach, sufficient data might be available to apply the cost approach but not the market approach. Information about market transactions for comparable software assets is not available. The income and cost approaches are applied as follows:

(a) The income approach is applied using a present value technique. The cash flows used in that technique reflect the income stream expected to result from the software asset (licence fees from customers) over its economic life. The fair value indicated by that approach is ¥15 billion.

(b) The cost approach is applied by estimating the amount that currently would be required to construct a substitute software asset of comparable utility (i.e. taking into account functional and economic obsolescence). The fair value indicated by that approach is ¥10 billion.

Through its application of the cost approach, the entity determines that market participants would not be able to construct a substitute software asset of comparable utility. Some characteristics of the software asset are unique, having been developed using proprietary information, and cannot be readily replicated. The entity determines that the fair value of the software asset is ¥15 billion, as indicated by the income approach.

Secondly, as is illustrated in Example 14.23 below, *[IFRS 13.IE11-IE14]*, an entity considers the possible range of fair value measures and considers what is most representative of fair value by taking into consideration that:

- one valuation technique may be more representative of fair value than others;
- inputs used in one valuation technique may be more readily observable in the marketplace or require fewer adjustments (inputs are discussed further at 15 below);
- the resulting range in estimates using one valuation technique may be narrower than the resulting range from other valuation techniques; and
- divergent results from the application of the market and income approaches would indicate that additional analysis is required, as one technique may have been misapplied, or the quality of inputs used in one technique may be less reliable.

Example 14.23: Multiple valuation techniques – machine held and used

An entity acquires a machine in a business combination. The machine will be held and used in its operations. The machine was originally purchased by the acquired entity from an outside vendor and, before the business combination, was customised by the acquired entity for use in its operations. However, the customisation of the machine was not extensive. The acquiring entity determines that the asset would provide maximum value to market participants through its use in combination with other assets or with other assets and liabilities (as installed or otherwise configured for use). There is no evidence to suggest that the current use of the machine is not its highest and best use. Therefore, the highest and best use of the machine is its current use in combination with other assets or with other assets and liabilities.

The entity determines that sufficient data are available to apply the cost approach and, because the customisation of the machine was not extensive, the market approach. The income approach is not used because the machine does not have a separately identifiable income stream from which to develop reliable estimates of future cash flows. Furthermore, information about short-term and intermediate-term lease rates for similar used machinery that otherwise could be used to project an income stream (i.e. lease payments over remaining service lives) is not available. The market and cost approaches are applied as follows:

(a) The market approach is applied using quoted prices for similar machines adjusted for differences between the machine (as customised) and the similar machines. The measurement reflects the price that would be received for the machine in its current condition (used) and location (installed and configured for use). The fair value indicated by that approach ranges from $40,000 to $48,000.

(b) The cost approach is applied by estimating the amount that would be required currently to construct a substitute (customised) machine of comparable utility. The estimate takes into account the condition of the machine and the environment in which it operates, including physical wear and tear (i.e. physical deterioration), improvements in technology (i.e. functional obsolescence), conditions external to the condition of the machine such as a decline in the market demand for similar machines (i.e. economic obsolescence) and installation costs. The fair value indicated by that approach ranges from $40,000 to $52,000.

The entity determines that the higher end of the range indicated by the market approach is most representative of fair value and, therefore, ascribes more weight to the results of the market approach. That determination is made on the basis of the relative subjectivity of the inputs, taking into account the degree of comparability between the machine and the similar machines. In particular:

(a) The inputs used in the market approach (quoted prices for similar machines) require fewer and less subjective adjustments than the inputs used in the cost approach.

(b) The range indicated by the market approach overlaps with, but is narrower than, the range indicated by the cost approach.

(c) There are no known unexplained differences (between the machine and the similar machines) within that range.

Accordingly, the entity determines that the fair value of the machine is $48,000.

If customisation of the machine was extensive or if there were not sufficient data available to apply the market approach (e.g. because market data reflect transactions for machines used on a stand-alone basis, such as a scrap value for specialised assets, rather than machines used in combination with other assets or with other assets and liabilities), the entity would apply the cost approach. When an asset is used in combination with other assets or with other assets and liabilities, the cost approach assumes the sale of the machine to a market participant buyer with the complementary assets and the associated liabilities. The price received for the sale of the machine (i.e. an exit price) would not be more than either of the following:

(a) the cost that a market participant buyer would incur to acquire or construct a substitute machine of comparable utility; or

(b) the economic benefit that a market participant buyer would derive from the use of the machine.

Both Examples 14.22 and 14.23 highlight situations where it was appropriate to use more than one valuation approach to estimate fair value. Although the indication of value from the cost approach was ultimately not given much weight in either example, performing this valuation technique was an important part of the estimation process. Even when a particular valuation technique is given little weight, its application can highlight specific characteristics of the item being measured and may help in assessing the value indications from other techniques.

Determining the point in a range of values that is 'most representative of fair value' can be subjective and requires the use of judgement by management. In addition, although Example 14.23 refers to 'weighting' the results of the valuation techniques used, in our view, this is not meant to imply that an entity must explicitly apply a percentage weighting to the results of each technique to determine fair value. However, this may be appropriate in certain circumstances.

The standard does not prescribe a specific weighting methodology (e.g. explicit assignment of percentages versus qualitative assessment of value indications). As such, evaluating the techniques applied in an analysis will require judgement based on the merits of each methodology and their respective assumptions.

Identifying a single point within a range is not the same as finding the point within the range that is most representative of fair value. As such, simply assigning arbitrary weights to different indications of value is not appropriate. The weighting of multiple value indications is a process that requires significant judgement and a working knowledge of the different valuation techniques and inputs. Such knowledge is necessary to properly assess the relevance of these methodologies and inputs to the asset or liability being measured. For example, in certain instances it may be more appropriate to rely primarily on the fair value indicated by the technique that maximises the use of observable inputs and minimises the use of unobservable inputs. In all cases, entities should document how they considered the various indications of value, including how they evaluated qualitative and quantitative factors, in determining fair value.

14.1.3 Valuation adjustments

In certain instances, adjustments to the output from a valuation technique may be required to appropriately determine a fair value measurement in accordance with IFRS 13. An entity makes valuation adjustments if market participants would make those adjustments when pricing an asset or liability (under the market conditions at the measurement date). This includes any adjustments for measurement uncertainty (e.g. a risk premium).

Valuation adjustments may include the following:

(a) an adjustment to a valuation technique to take into account a characteristic of an asset or a liability that is not captured by the valuation technique. The need for such an adjustment is typically identified during calibration of the value calculated using the valuation technique with observable market information (see 14.1.3.A below);

(b) applying the point within the bid-ask spread that is most representative of fair value in the circumstances (see 15.3 below);

(c) an adjustment to take into account credit risk (e.g. an entity's non-performance risk or the credit risk of the counterparty to a transaction) (see 11.3 above); and

(d) an adjustment to take into account measurement uncertainty (e.g. when there has been a significant decrease in the volume or level of activity when compared with normal market activity for the asset or liability, or similar assets or liabilities, and the entity has determined that the transaction price or quoted price does not represent fair value). *[IFRS 13.BC145]*.

14.1.3.A Adjustments to valuation techniques that use unobservable inputs

Regardless of the valuation technique(s) used, the objective of a fair value measurement remains the same – i.e. an exit price under current market conditions from the perspective of market participants. As such, if the transaction price is determined to represent fair value at initial recognition (see 13 above) and a valuation technique that uses unobservable inputs will be used to measure the fair value of an item in subsequent periods, the valuation technique must be calibrated to ensure the valuation technique reflects current market conditions. *[IFRS 13.64]*.

Calibration ensures that a valuation technique incorporates current market conditions. The calibration also helps an entity to determine whether an adjustment to the valuation technique is necessary by identifying potential deficiencies in the valuation model. For example, there might be a characteristic of the asset or liability that is not captured by the valuation technique.

If an entity measures fair value after initial recognition using a valuation technique (or techniques) that uses unobservable inputs, an entity must ensure the valuation technique(s) reflect observable market data (e.g. the price for a similar asset or liability) at the measurement date. *[IFRS 13.64]*. That is, it should be calibrated to observable market data, when available.

14.1.4 Making changes to valuation techniques

The standard requires that valuation techniques used to measure fair value be applied on a consistent basis among similar assets or liabilities and across reporting periods. *[IFRS 13.65]*. This is not meant to preclude subsequent changes, such as a change in its weighting when multiple valuation techniques are used or a change in an adjustment applied to a valuation technique.

An entity can make a change to a valuation technique or its application (or a change in the relative importance of one technique over another), provided that change results in a measurement that is equally representative (or more representative) of fair value in the circumstances.

IFRS 13 provides the following examples of circumstances that may trigger a change in valuation technique or relative weights assigned to valuation techniques:

(a) new markets develop;
(b) new information becomes available;
(c) information previously used is no longer available;
(d) valuation techniques improve; or
(e) market conditions change. *[IFRS 13.65]*.

In addition, a change in the exit market, characteristics of market participants that would transact for the asset or liability, or the highest and best use of an asset by market participants could also warrant a change in valuation techniques in certain circumstances.

Changes to fair value resulting from a change in the valuation technique or its application are accounted for as a change in accounting estimate in accordance with IAS 8. However, IFRS 13 states that the disclosures in IAS 8 for a change in accounting estimate are not required for such changes. *[IFRS 13.66]*. Instead, information would be disclosed in accordance with IFRS 13 (see 20.3.5 below for further discussion). If a valuation technique is applied in error, the correction of the technique would be accounted as a correction of an error in accordance with IAS 8.

14.2 Market approach

IFRS 13 describes the market approach as a widely used valuation technique. As defined in the standard, the market approach 'uses prices and other relevant information generated by market transactions involving identical or comparable (i.e. similar) assets, liabilities or a group of assets and liabilities, such as a business'. *[IFRS 13.B5]*. Hence, the market approach uses prices that market participants would pay or receive for the transaction, for example, a quoted market price. The market price may be adjusted to reflect the characteristics of the item being measured, such as its current condition and location, and could result in a range of possible fair values.

Valuation techniques consistent with the market approach use prices and other market data derived from observed transactions for the same or similar assets, for example, revenue, or EBITDA multiples. Multiples might be in ranges with a different multiple for each comparable asset or liability. The selection of the appropriate multiple within the range requires judgement, considering qualitative and quantitative factors specific to the measurement. *[IFRS 13.B6]*.

Another example of a market approach is matrix pricing. Matrix pricing is a mathematical technique used principally to value certain types of financial instruments, such as debt securities, where specific instruments (e.g. cusips) may not trade frequently. The method derives an estimated price of an instrument using transaction prices and other relevant market information for benchmark instruments with similar features (e.g. coupon, maturity or credit rating). *[IFRS 13.B7]*.

14.3 Cost approach

'The cost approach reflects the amount that would be required currently to replace the service capacity of an asset'. This approach is often referred to as current replacement cost. *[IFRS 13.B8]*. The cost approach (or current replacement cost) is typically used to measure the fair value of tangible assets, such as plant or equipment.

From the perspective of a market participant seller, the price that would be received for the asset is based on the cost to a market participant buyer to acquire or construct a substitute asset of comparable utility, adjusted for obsolescence.

Obsolescence is broader than depreciation, whether for financial reporting or tax purposes. According to the standard, obsolescence encompasses:

- physical deterioration;
- functional (technological) obsolescence; and
- economic (external) obsolescence. *[IFRS 13.B9]*.

Physical deterioration and functional obsolescence are factors specific to the asset. Physical deterioration refers to wear, tear or abuse. For example, machines in a factory might deteriorate physically due to high production volumes or a lack of maintenance. Something is functionally obsolete when it does not function in the manner originally intended (excluding any physical deterioration). For example, layout of the machines in the factory may make their use, in combination, more labour intensive, increasing the cost of those machines to the entity. Functional obsolescence also includes the impact of technological change, for example, if newer, more efficient and less labour-intensive models were available, demand for the existing machines might decline, along with the price for the existing machines in the market.

Economic obsolescence arises from factors external to the asset. An asset may be less desirable or its economic life may reduce due to factors such as regulatory changes or excess supply. Consider the machines in the factory; assume that, after the entity had purchased its machines, the supplier had flooded the market with identical machines. If demand was not as high as the supplier had anticipated, it could result in an oversupply and the supplier would be likely to reduce the price in order to clear the excess stock.

14.3.1 Use of depreciated replacement cost to measure fair value

As discussed at 14.3 above, IFRS 13 permits the use of a cost approach for measuring fair value. However, care is needed in using depreciated replacement cost to ensure the resulting measurement is consistent with the requirements of IFRS 13 for measuring fair value.

Before using depreciated replacement cost as a method to measure fair value, an entity should ensure that both:

- the highest and best use of the asset is its current use (see 10 above); and
- the exit market for the asset (i.e. the principal market or in its absence, the most advantageous market, see 6 above) is the same as the entry market (i.e. the market in which the asset was/will be purchased).

In addition, an entity should ensure that both:
- the inputs used to determine replacement cost are consistent with what market participant buyers would pay to acquire or construct a substitute asset of comparable utility; and
- the replacement cost has been adjusted for obsolescence that market participant buyers would consider – i.e. that the depreciation adjustment reflects all forms of obsolescence (i.e. physical deterioration, technological (functional) and economic obsolescence), which is broader than depreciation calculated in accordance with IAS 16.

Even after considering these factors, the resulting depreciated replacement cost must be assessed to ensure market participants would actually transact for the asset, in its current condition and location, at this price. The Illustrative Examples to IFRS 13 reflect this stating that 'the price received for the sale of the machine (i.e. an exit price) would not be more than either of the following:

(a) the cost that a market participant buyer would incur to acquire or construct a substitute machine of comparable utility; or

(b) the economic benefit that a market participant buyer would derive from the use of the machine.' *[IFRS 13.IE11-IE14]*.

14.4 Income approach

The income approach converts future cash flows or income and expenses to a single current (i.e. discounted) amount. A fair value measurement using the income approach will reflect current market expectations about those future cash flows or income and expenses. *[IFRS 13.B10]*.

The income approach includes valuation techniques such as:

(a) present value techniques (see 21 below);

(b) option pricing models – examples include the Black-Scholes-Merton formula or a binomial model (i.e. a lattice model) – that incorporate present value techniques and reflect both the time value and the intrinsic value of an option; and

(c) the multi-period excess earnings method. This method is used to measure the fair value of some intangible assets. *[IFRS 13.B11]*.

The standard does not limit the valuation techniques that are consistent with the income approach to these examples; an entity may consider other valuation techniques.

The standard provides some application guidance, but only in relation to present value techniques (see 21 below for further discussion regarding this application guidance).

15 INPUTS TO VALUATION TECHNIQUES

15.1 General principles

When selecting the inputs to use in a valuation technique, IFRS 13 requires that they:
- be consistent with the characteristics of the asset or liability that market participants would take into account (see 5.2 above);

- exclude premiums or discounts that reflect size as a characteristic of the entity's holding, rather than a characteristic of the item being measured (for example, blockage factors); and
- exclude other premiums or discounts if they are inconsistent with the unit of account (see 5.1 above for discussions regarding unit of account). *[IFRS 13.69]*.

Premiums, discounts and blockage factors are discussed further at 15.2 below.

In all cases, if there is a quoted price in an active market (i.e. a Level 1 input) for the identical asset or a liability, an entity shall use that price without adjustment when measuring fair value. Adjustments to this price are only permitted in certain circumstances, which are discussed at 17.1 below.

Regardless of the valuation techniques used to estimate fair value, IFRS 13 requires that these techniques maximise the use of relevant observable inputs and minimise the use of unobservable inputs. *[IFRS 13.67]*. This requirement is consistent with the idea that fair value is a market-based measurement and, therefore, is determined using market-based observable data, to the extent available and relevant.

The standard provides some examples of markets in which inputs might be observable.

(a) *Exchange markets* – where closing prices are both readily available and generally representative of fair value, e.g. the Hong Kong Stock Exchange;

(b) *Dealer markets* – where dealers stand ready to trade for their own account. Typically, in these markets, bid and ask prices (see 15.3 below) are more readily available than closing prices. Dealer markets include over-the-counter markets, for which prices are publicly reported;

(c) *Brokered markets* – where brokers attempt to match buyers with sellers but do not stand ready to trade for their own account. The broker knows the prices bid and asked by the respective parties, but each party is typically unaware of another party's price requirements. In such markets, prices for completed transactions may be available. Examples of brokered markets include electronic communication networks in which buy and sell orders are matched, and commercial and residential real estate markets;

(d) *Principal-to-principal markets* – where transactions, both new and re-sales, are negotiated independently with no intermediary. Little, if any, information about these transactions in these markets may be publicly available. *[IFRS 13.68, B34]*.

The standard clarifies that the relevance of market data must be considered when assessing the priority of inputs in the fair value hierarchy. When evaluating the relevance of market data, the number and range of data points should be considered, as well as whether this data is directionally consistent with pricing trends and indications from other more general market information.

Relevant market data reflects the assumptions that market participants would use in pricing the asset or liability being measured. Recent transaction prices for the reference asset or liability (or similar assets and liabilities) are typically considered to represent relevant market data, unless the transaction is determined not to be orderly (see 8 above for a discussion of factors to consider when determining if a transaction is orderly). However, even in situations where a transaction is considered to be orderly, observable transaction prices from inactive markets may require adjustment to address factors, such as timing differences between the transaction date and the measurement date or differences between the asset being measured and a similar asset that was the subject of the transaction. In those instances where the adjustments to observable data are significant and are determined using unobservable data, the resulting measurement would be considered a Level 3 measurement.

Whether observable or unobservable, all inputs used in determining fair value should be consistent with a market-based measurement. As such, the use of unobservable inputs is not intended to allow for the inclusion of entity-specific assumptions in a fair value measurement. While IFRS 13 acknowledges that unobservable inputs may sometimes be developed using an entity's own data, the guidance is clear that these inputs should reflect market participant assumptions. When valuing an intangible asset using unobservable inputs, for example, an entity should take into account the intended use of the asset by market participants, even though this may differ from the entity's intended use. The entity may use its own data, without adjustment, if it determines that market participant assumptions are consistent with its own assumptions (see 19.1 below for additional discussion on how an entity's own assumptions may be applied in a fair value measurement).

The term 'input' is used in IFRS 13 to refer broadly to the assumptions that market participants would use when pricing an asset or liability, rather than to the data entered into a pricing model. This important distinction implies that an adjustment to a pricing model's value (e.g. an adjustment for the risk that a pricing model might not replicate a market price due to the complexity of the instrument being measured) represents an input, which should be evaluated when determining the measurement's category in the fair value hierarchy. For example, when measuring a financial instrument, an adjustment for model risk would be considered an input (most likely a Level 3 input) that, if deemed significant (see 16.2.1 below for further discussion on assessing the significance of inputs) may render the entire fair value estimate a Level 3 measurement.

It is also important to note that an input is distinct from a characteristic. IFRS 13 requires an entity to consider the characteristics of the asset or liability (if market participants would take those characteristics into account when pricing the asset or liability at the measurement date). *[IFRS 13.11]*. As discussed at 5.1 above, examples of such characteristics could include:

- the condition and location of an asset; and
- restrictions, if any, on the sale or use of an asset or transfer of a liability.

To draw out the distinction between an input and a characteristic, consider the example of a restricted security that has the following characteristics, which would be considered by a market participant:

- the issuer is a listed entity; and
- the fact that the security is restricted.

An entity is required to select inputs in pricing the asset or liability that are consistent with its characteristics. In some cases, those characteristics result in the application of an adjustment, such as a premium or discount. In our example, the inputs could be:

- a quoted price for an unrestricted security; and
- a discount adjustment (to reflect the restriction).

The quoted price for the unrestricted security may be an observable and a Level 1 input. However, given the restriction and the standard's requirement that inputs be consistent with the characteristics of the asset or liability being measured, the second input in measuring fair value is an adjustment to the quoted price to reflect the restriction. If this input is unobservable, it would be a Level 3 input and, if it is considered to be significant to the entire measurement, the fair value measurement of the asset would also be categorised within Level 3 of the fair value hierarchy.

15.2 Premiums and discounts

IFRS 13 indicates that when measuring fair value, entities should select inputs that: (i) are consistent with the characteristics of the asset or liability being measured; and (ii) would be considered by market participants when pricing the asset or liability. In certain instances, these characteristics could result in a premium or discount being incorporated into the fair value measurement.

Determining whether a premium or discount applies to a particular fair value measurement requires judgement and depends on specific facts and circumstances.

IFRS 13 distinguishes between premiums or discounts that reflect size as a characteristic of the entity's holding (specifically, a blockage factor) and control premiums, discounts for non-controlling interests and discounts for lack of marketability that are related to characteristics of the asset or liability being measured.

Control premiums, discounts for non-controlling interests and discounts for lack of marketability reflect characteristics of the asset or liability being measured at fair value. Provided these adjustments are consistent with the unit of account (see 5.1 above) of the asset or liability being measured they can be taken into consideration when measuring fair value. *[IFRS 13.69]*.

Apart from block discounts (discussed at 15.2.1 below), IFRS 13 does not provide explicit guidance on the types of premiums or discounts that may be considered, or when they should be applied to a fair value measurement. Instead, the guidance indicates that premiums and discounts (e.g. control premiums or discounts for lack of marketability) should be incorporated into non-Level 1 fair value measurements if all of the following conditions are met:

- the application of the premium or discount reflects the characteristics of the asset or liability being measured;
- market participants, acting in their 'economic best interest' (see 7.2 above), would consider these premiums or discounts when pricing the asset or liability; and
- the inclusion of the premium or discount is not inconsistent with the unit of account in the IFRS that requires (or permits) the fair value measurement (see 5.1 above).

IFRS 13 emphasises that prices of instruments that trade in active markets (i.e. Level 1 measurements) should generally not be adjusted and should be measured based on the quoted price of the individual instrument multiplied by the quantity held (P×Q).

Figure 14.7: **Differentiating between blockage factors and other premiums and discounts**

Examples of premiums and discounts	Blockage factor (or block discount)	Control premium	Discount for lack of marketability
Can fair value be adjusted for the premium or discount?	No	Yes, in certain circumstances.	Yes, in certain circumstances.
In what situations would these arise?	When an entity sells a large holding of instruments such that the market's normal daily trading volume is not sufficient to absorb the entire quantity (i.e. flooding the market). IFRS 13 does not permit an entity to take block discounts into consideration in the measurement of fair value.	When an entity transacts for a controlling interest in another entity (and the unit of account is deemed to be the controlling interest and not the individual shares).	When an asset or liability is not readily marketable, for example, where there is no established market of readily available buyers and sellers or as a result of restrictions.
Example	An entity holds a 20% investment in a listed company. The normal daily trading for those shares on the exchange is 1-2%. If the entity were to sell its entire holding, the price per share would be expected to decrease by 30%.	An entity transacts for a controlling interest in a private business and determines that the fair value of the business is greater than the aggregate value of the individual shares due to its ability to control the acquired entity.	The shares of a private company for which no liquid market exists.
What does the premium or discount represent?	The difference between the price to sell: • the individual asset or liability; and • an entity's entire holding. IFRS 13 does not permit an entity to include such a difference in the measurement of fair value.	The difference between the price to sell: • the individual shares in the controlled entity; and • the entire controlling interest.	The difference between the price to sell: • an asset or liability does not trade in a liquid market; and • an identical asset or liability for which a liquid market exists.

15.2.1 Blockage factors (or block discounts)

IFRS 13 explicitly prohibits the consideration of blockage factors (or block discounts) in a fair value measurement. *[IFRS 13.69, 80].* While the term blockage factor may be subject to different interpretations, during their deliberations the Boards indicated that they view a blockage factor as an adjustment to the quoted price of an asset or liability because the market's normal trading volume is not sufficient to absorb the quantity held by a reporting entity.

Regardless of the hierarchy level in which a measurement is categorised, blockage factors are excluded from a fair value measurement because such an adjustment is specific to the size of an entity's holding and its decision to transact in a block. That is, the Boards believe such an adjustment is entity-specific in nature. *[IFRS 13.BC157].* However, the standard clarifies that there is a difference between size being a characteristic of the asset or liability being measured (based on its unit of account) and size being a characteristic of the reporting entity's holding. While any adjustment for the latter is not permitted, the former should be considered if it is consistent with how market participants would price the asset or liability. *[IFRS 13.69].*

The following example illustrates how IFRS 13 distinguishes between size as a characteristic of the item being measured and size as a characteristic of an entity's holding.

Example 14.24: Blockage factors

Bank X has one outstanding OTC derivative contract with Dealer A.

The notional amount of this contract is $1 billion, which is significantly larger than the market norm for these types of contracts.

Bank Y has 100 identical OTC derivative contracts outstanding with various dealers (whose risks are not offsetting because all the contracts are assets and therefore are not measured using the measurement exception).

Each of the 100 contracts has a notional amount of $10 million, which is consistent with the market norm for these types of contracts.

Although Bank X and Bank Y have virtually identical market exposures (ignoring credit risk for simplicity), IFRS 13 would allow Bank X to consider a discount for lack of marketability but would preclude Bank Y from applying a similar discount.

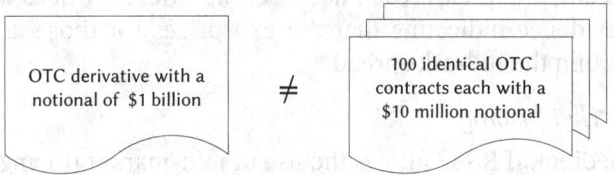

For Bank X, the large notional amount (CU 1 billion) is a characteristic of the instrument being measured and would likely be considered by market participants when transacting for the derivative based on its unit of account (the derivative contract). As such, the fair value of the individual derivative should incorporate an adjustment for size if market participants would consider one in pricing the instrument.

In contrast, the unit of account for Bank Y's 100 derivative contracts is the individual OTC contracts, not the aggregate gross exposure stemming from the 100 contracts (i.e. the block). In pricing the individual contracts, market participants would likely not consider a discount associated with the size of the contracts, since the notional amount for each contract is consistent with the market norm. In accordance with IFRS 13, Bank Y would be prohibited from applying a discount based on the size of its entire holding (i.e. the 100 contracts) as this would represent a block discount that cannot be considered in a fair value measurement.

As discussed at 5.1 above, the unit of account is determined by the relevant IFRS that permits or requires an asset or liability to be measured at fair value, unless IFRS 13 states otherwise. In some cases, the unit of account may be clear, for example, the unit of account for financial instruments in the scope of IFRS 9 is typically the individual instrument. However, it may be less clear in other standards, for example, the unit of account for a cash-generating unit when testing non-financial assets for impairment in accordance with IAS 36. In December 2018, the IASB concluded its PIR of IFRS 13, in which it had considered issues relating to prioritising Level 1 inputs or the unit of account. This is discussed further at 5.1.1 above.

15.3 Pricing within the bid-ask spread

The 'bid price' represents the price at which a dealer or market maker is willing to buy an asset (or dispose of a liability). The 'ask price' (or offer price) represents the price at which a dealer or market maker is willing to sell an asset (or assume a liability). The spread between these two prices represents the profit a dealer requires for making a market in a particular security (i.e. providing two-way liquidity).

The use of bid prices to measure assets and ask prices to measure liabilities is permitted, but not required. Instead, for assets and liabilities that are bought and sold in markets where prices are quoted using a bid-ask spread (e.g. over-the-counter markets), the entity must use the price within the bid-ask spread that is most representative of fair value in the circumstances to measure fair value. In making this assessment, entities should evaluate their recent transaction history to support where in the bid-ask spread they are able to exit their positions. For some entities this could result in valuing assets at the bid price and liabilities at the ask price, but in other instances judgement is required to determine the point in the bid-ask spread that is most indicative of fair value. The use of the price within the bid-ask spread that is most representative of fair value applies regardless of whether the input (i.e. the bid or ask price) is observable or not (i.e. regardless of its categorisation in the fair value hierarchy – see 16 below for further discussion). *[IFRS 13.70]*.

Entities need to be consistent in their application of this concept. It would not be appropriate for an entity to measure similar assets at different prices within the bid-ask spread, without evidence indicating that the exit prices for those assets would be at different points within the bid-ask spread.

15.3.1 Mid-market pricing

As a practical expedient, IFRS 13 allows the use of mid-market pricing, or other pricing conventions that are used by market participants, when measuring fair value within the bid-ask spread. *[IFRS 13.71]*. Use of a mid-market pricing convention results in a valuation of an asset or liability at the mid-point of the bid-ask spread. Extract 14.1 at 11.3.3.B above illustrates use of mid-market pricing.

The guidance does not limit or restrict the use of mid-market pricing to specific types of instruments or entities. However, as discussed at 14 above, valuation techniques used to measure fair value should be consistently applied. *[IFRS 13.65]*.

15.3.2 What does the bid-ask spread include?

The commentary in the Basis for Conclusions acknowledges that the previous guidance in IAS 39 only includes transaction costs in the bid-ask spread. The Boards chose not to specify what is included in the bid-ask spread, except for transaction costs. However, they did make it clear that, in their view, the bid-ask spread does not include adjustments for counterparty credit risk. *[IFRS 13.BC164, IAS 39(2010).AG70]*.

The IASB has not provided any clarity regarding the interaction between the guidance in IFRS 13 on transaction costs (i.e. transaction costs are not considered an attribute of the asset or liability and, accordingly, are excluded from fair value measurements) and the guidance on the use of prices within the bid-ask spread. If transaction costs are included in the bid-ask spread, measuring an asset at the bid price would include certain future transaction costs in the fair value measurement for the asset.

Given the lack of any specific guidance on this issue, there may be some diversity in practice between entities with respect to how transaction costs are considered. However, we would expect an entity to apply a consistent approach to all of its own fair value measurements.

15.4 Risk premiums

IFRS 13 defines a risk premium as 'compensation sought by risk-averse market participants for bearing the uncertainty inherent in the cash flows of an asset or a liability'. *[IFRS 13 Appendix A]*. Regardless of the valuation technique(s) used, a fair value measurement is intended to represent an exit price and, as such, should include a risk premium that reflects the compensation market participants would demand for bearing the uncertainty inherent in the cash flows of an asset or liability. *[IFRS 13.B16, B39]*. While this risk premium should reflect compensation required in an orderly transaction (not a forced or distressed sale), it should also capture market participant assumptions regarding risk under current market conditions. Example 14.9 discussed at 8.3.2 above illustrates that this risk adjustment may include assumptions about liquidity and uncertainty based on relevant market data.

IFRS 13 explicitly states that '[a] fair value measurement should include a risk premium reflecting the amount market participants would demand as compensation for the uncertainty inherent in the cash flows. Otherwise, the measurement would not faithfully represent fair value. In some cases, determining the appropriate risk premium might be difficult. However, the degree of difficulty alone is not a sufficient reason to exclude a risk premium'. *[IFRS 13.B16]*.

The objective of a risk premium is often misunderstood. Many incorrectly assume that a risk premium is unnecessary when fair value is determined using probability-weighted cash flows. That is, they believe it is appropriate to discount probability-weighted cash flows using a risk-free rate under the assumption that all uncertainty is captured by probability-weighting the cash flows. While expected cash flows (i.e. the probability-weighted average of possible future cash flows) incorporate the uncertainty in the instrument's cash flows, they do not incorporate the compensation that market participants demand for bearing that uncertainty. *[IFRS 13.B25-B29]*. In order to capture this required compensation in the measurement, a market risk premium must be added (either as an adjustment to the discount rate or to the expected cash flows). IFRS 13's application guidance addresses this point when discussing systematic and unsystematic risk and certainty-equivalent cash flows (see 21 below for additional discussion on how risk premiums are applied in a present value technique).

It is important to note that increased risk associated with an asset generally decreases the fair value of that asset, whereas increased risk associated with a liability generally increases the fair value of that liability (with the exception of non-performance risk).

Uncertainty associated with an asset reduces the amount a market participant would pay for the asset. In contrast, all else being equal, compensation for an uncertainty related to a liability results in an increase to the amount that the market participant would expect to receive for assuming the obligation. If that compensation is accounted for in the discount rate, rather than in the cash flows, it would result in an increase in the discount rate used to measure the fair value of an asset. However, it would result in a reduction of the discount rate used in the fair value measurement of the liability (i.e. the discount rate must be lower so that the resulting fair value of the liability is higher). [IFRS 13.BC91]. This concept only applies when measuring the fair value of a liability that does not have a corresponding asset using an income approach. As discussed at 11.2.1 above, when a quoted price for the transfer of an identical or similar liability or entity's own equity instrument is held by another party as an asset, the fair value of this liability or own equity instrument should be determined from the perspective of the market participant that holds the identical item as an asset.

15.5 Broker quotes and pricing services

When quoted prices from brokers or pricing services are used to measure fair value, it is the entity's responsibility to understand the source and nature of this information to accurately assess its relevance. When there has been a significant decrease in the volume or level of activity for the asset or liability, management should evaluate whether the prices received from brokers or pricing services are based on current information from orderly transactions or valuation techniques that appropriately reflect market participant assumptions regarding risk. IFRS 13 states that entities should place less reliance on third-party quotes that are not based on transactions, compared to other value indications that are based on market transactions. [IFRS 13.B46].

When information from brokers and pricing services is based on transaction data, entities should assess whether, and to what extent, the observed prices are a result of orderly transactions when determining the weight to place on these data points, compared to other value indications (see 8.2 above for additional information on the factors an entity may consider when assessing whether transactions are orderly). Facts and circumstances will determine the weight that an entity should place on a transaction price, including:

- the comparability of the transaction to the asset or liability being measured at fair value;
- the proximity of the transaction to the measurement date;
- the size of the transaction; and
- the nature of the quote (e.g. binding versus indicative quote) and the number of quotes received.

See 16.2.3 below for additional discussion on fair value hierarchy considerations when using quoted prices from brokers and pricing services.

15.5.1 How should values provided by central clearing organisations for margin purposes be evaluated when determining the fair value of centrally cleared derivatives for financial reporting?

For OTC derivatives that are centrally cleared, counterparties are typically required on an ongoing basis to post collateral based on the change in value of the derivative (sometimes referred to as 'variation margin'). As a result, entities with centrally cleared OTC derivatives will periodically receive a 'value mark' from a clearing organisation that states the amount of variation margin to be posted or received.

However, this value should not be presumed to represent fair value (an exit price) in accordance with IFRS 13. Different clearing organisations may have different approaches for calculating variation margin requirements and while practice may continue to evolve, it is our understanding that the 'value marks' provided generally do not represent an actual transaction price (i.e. a price at which the reporting entity could execute a trade to buy or sell the contract). Instead, this value may be based on a clearing organisation's analysis of information provided by clearing members and certain of its own assumptions. While this value may potentially be an appropriate estimate of fair value in certain instances, the reporting entity should understand how this value is determined and evaluate whether it includes only those factors that would be considered by market participants in an orderly transaction to sell or transfer the derivative. For example, to provide themselves with additional protection, some clearing organisations may include an incremental amount in their variation margin requirement in excess of the 'true' change in the value of the derivative.

As with pricing information provided by brokers or third-party pricing services, reporting entities are responsible for understanding the source and nature of information provided by central clearing organisations. An entity should assess whether the value indication represents fair value in accordance with IFRS 13 or whether an adjustment may be needed. See 16.2.4 below for a discussion of the categorisation of centrally cleared OTC derivatives in the fair value hierarchy.

16 THE FAIR VALUE HIERARCHY

The fair value hierarchy is intended to increase consistency and comparability in fair value measurements and the related disclosures. *[IFRS 13.72]*. Application of the hierarchy requires an entity to prioritise observable inputs over those that are unobservable when measuring fair value. In addition, for disclosures, it provides a framework for users to consider the relative subjectivity of the fair value measurements made by the reporting entity.

16.1 The fair value hierarchy

The fair value hierarchy classifies the inputs used to measure fair value into three levels, which are described in Figure 14.8.

Figure 14.8: Fair value hierarchy

	Level 1	Level 2	Level 3
Definition [IFRS 13 Appendix A]	Quoted prices (unadjusted) in active markets for identical assets or liabilities that the entity can access at the measurement date.	Inputs other than quoted prices included within level 1 that are observable for the asset or liability, either directly or indirectly.	Unobservable inputs for the asset or liability.
Example	The price for a financial asset or financial liability for the identical asset is traded on an active market (e.g. Tokyo Stock Exchange).	Interest rates and yield curves observable at commonly quoted intervals, implied volatilities, and credit spreads.	Projected cash flows used in a discounted cash flow calculation.

Valuation techniques used to measure fair value must maximise the use of relevant observable inputs and minimise the use of unobservable inputs. The best indication of fair value is a quoted price in an active market (i.e. 'a market in which transactions for the asset or liability take place with sufficient frequency and volume to provide pricing information on an ongoing basis' [IFRS 13 Appendix A]).

The fair value hierarchy focuses on prioritising the inputs used in valuation techniques, not the techniques themselves. [IFRS 13.74]. While the availability of inputs might affect the valuation technique(s) selected to measure fair value, as discussed at 14 above, IFRS 13 does not prioritise the use of one technique over another (with the exception of the requirement to measure identical financial instruments that trade in active markets at P×Q). The determination of the valuation technique(s) to be used requires significant judgement and will be dependent on the specific characteristics of the asset or liability being measured and the principal (or most advantageous) market in which market participants would transact for the asset or liability.

Although the valuation techniques themselves are not subject to the fair value hierarchy, a risk adjustment that market participants would demand to compensate for a risk inherent in a particular valuation technique (e.g. a model adjustment) is considered an input that must be assessed within the fair value hierarchy. As discussed at 16.2 below, if this type of risk adjustment is included, it should be considered when categorising the fair value measurement within the fair value hierarchy.

16.2 Categorisation within the fair value hierarchy

IFRS 13 distinguishes between where in the fair value hierarchy an individual input to a valuation technique may fall and where the entire measurement is categorised for disclosure purposes.

Inputs used in a valuation technique may fall into different levels of the fair value hierarchy. However, for disclosure purposes, the fair value measurement must be categorised in its entirety (i.e. the fair value measure for the asset or liability or the group of assets and/or liability, depending on the unit of account) within the hierarchy. Categorising the entire measurement (and the required disclosure of this information, see 20.3.3 below) provides users of financial statements with an indication of the overall observability or subjectivity of a fair value measurement.

Categorisation of a fair value measurement (as a whole) within the hierarchy, therefore, is dependent on what constitutes an 'observable' input and a 'significant' input. Observability affects all levels of the hierarchy and is important for classifying each input (discussed at 17-19 below). The significance of an unobservable input affects categorisation of the measurement (as a whole) with Level 2 and Level 3 of the hierarchy (see 16.2.1 below).

It is important to note that the categorisation of fair value measurement within the fair value hierarchy does not provide information about asset quality. Rather, it provides information about the observability of the significant inputs used in a fair value measurement.

The appropriate categorisation may be obvious when only a single input is used, for example, when measuring fair value using a quoted price in an active market, without adjustment. However, an asset or liability that is not traded in an active market with a quoted price will often require more than one input to determine its fair value. For example, an over-the-counter option on a traded equity security measured at fair value using an option pricing model requires the following market-based inputs: (i) expected volatility; (ii) expected dividend yield; and (iii) the risk-free rate of interest.

IFRS 13 clarifies that the hierarchy categorisation of a fair value measurement, in its entirety, is determined based on the lowest level input that is significant to the entire measurement. The standard also makes it clear that adjustments to arrive at measurements based on fair value (e.g. 'costs to sell' when measuring fair value less costs to sell) are not be taken into account in this determination. *[IFRS 13.73]*. In the over-the-counter equity option example, assume that the risk-free interest rate and the dividend yield were determined to be Level 2 inputs, but the expected volatility was determined to be a Level 3 input. If expected volatility was determined to be significant to the overall value of the option, the entire measurement would be categorised within Level 3 of the fair value hierarchy.

If an observable input requires an adjustment using an unobservable input and that adjustment actually results in a significantly higher or lower fair value measurement, the standard is clear that the resulting fair value measurement would be categorised within Level 3 of the fair value hierarchy. *[IFRS 13.75]*. Consider our example of a restricted security discussed at 15.1 above. While the quoted price for the unrestricted security may be observable, if Level 3 inputs are needed to determine the effect of the restriction on the instrument's fair value, and this effect is significant to the measurement, the asset would be categorised within Level 3 of the fair value hierarchy. In addition, as discussed at 8 above, in certain situations adjustments to a transaction price in an inactive market may be required. If these adjustments are based on unobservable inputs and significant to the measurement, the item would be categorised within Level 3 of the fair value hierarchy.

It is important to understand that the determination of the hierarchy level in which the fair value measure falls (and, therefore, the category in which it will be disclosed – see 20.3.3 below) is based on the fair value measurement for the specific item being measured, which will be dependent on the unit of account for the asset or liability. This may create practical challenges in relation to fair value measurements for non-financial assets and financial assets and liabilities with offsetting risk measured using the measurement exception discussed at 12 above. For example, in situations where the unit of account for a non-financial asset is the individual item, but the valuation premise is in combination with other assets (or other assets and liabilities), the value of the asset group would need to be attributed to the individual assets or liabilities or to the various instruments within each level of the fair value hierarchy. For example, consider Example 14.13 at 10.2.2 above. The unit of account for the grapes growing on the vines was that specified by IAS 41 and the vines and the land was that specified by IAS 16. However, their highest and best use was in combination, together and with other assets. The value of that group would need to be attributed to each of the assets, including the grapes growing on the vines, the vines and land, as the fair value of these individual assets should be categorised within the fair value hierarchy.

In its final report on the PIR on IFRS 13, the IASB noted that 'some respondents reported a perception that the fair value hierarchy implies that information about items on Level 1 or Level 2 is always more relevant to users than information about items on Level 3. They indicated that this perception puts pressure on classification. They also said that this perception can be mistaken, as evidenced by academic research.' Furthermore, respondents noted that categorisation within the hierarchy may be affected by some negative perceptions associated with categorisation within Level 3 of the fair value hierarchy (e.g. including the volume of disclosure required).[25] There are measurement uncertainties for both Level 2 and Level 3 fair value measurements, as both may include unobservable inputs. Therefore, significant judgement is often needed to determine whether a particular asset or liability should be categorised within Level 2 or Level 3 of the fair value hierarchy. It may be particularly challenging for entities to determine the level of evidence required to support a Level 2 classification, especially when the measurement is determined using information received from third parties (see 16.2.3 below).

16.2.1 Assessing the significance of inputs

Assessing the significance of a particular input to the entire measurement requires judgement and consideration of factors specific to the asset or liability (or group of assets and/or liabilities) being measured. *[IFRS 13.73]*.

IFRS 13 does not provide specific guidance on how entities should evaluate the significance of individual inputs. This determination will require judgement and consideration of factors specific to the asset or liability (or group of assets and liabilities) being measured. In the absence of any 'bright lines' for determining significance, there may be a lack of comparability between different entities with fair value measurements that use the same inputs.

The standard is clear that it considers significance in relation to 'the entire measurement'. In our view, this requires the assessment to consider the fair value measure itself, rather than any resulting change in fair value, regardless of whether that change is recognised (i.e. in profit or loss or other comprehensive income) or unrecognised. For example, assume an investment property is measured at fair value at the end of each reporting period. In the current reporting period, the fair value of the investment property reduces by CU 200,000 to CU 500,000. The significance of any inputs to the fair value measurement would be assessed by reference to the CU 500,000, even though CU 200,000 is the amount that will be recognised in profit or loss. However, a reporting entity may deem it appropriate to also consider significance in relation to the change in fair value from prior periods, in addition to considering the significance of an input in relation to the entire fair value measurement. Such an approach may be helpful in relation to cash-based instruments (e.g. loans or structured notes with embedded derivatives) whose carrying amounts, based on fair value, are heavily affected by their principal or face amount.

As noted in 16.2 above, if an observable input requires an adjustment using an unobservable input and that adjustment actually results in a significantly higher or lower fair value measurement, the standard is clear that the resulting fair value measurement would be categorised within Level 3 of the hierarchy. *[IFRS 13.75]*. What is not clear, however, is the appropriate categorisation when an observable input requires an adjustment using an unobservable input and: (a) that adjustment does not actually result in a significantly higher or lower fair value in the current period; but (b) the potential adjustment from using a different unobservable input would result in a significantly higher or lower fair value measurement. As noted in 16.2 above, the categorisation of a fair value measurement indicates the overall observability or subjectivity of a measurement, in its entirety. To this end, in some cases, the use of sensitivity analysis or stress testing (i.e. using a range of reasonably possible alternative input values as of the measurement date) might be appropriate to assess the effects of unobservable inputs on a fair value measure. In situations where more than one unobservable input is used in a fair value measure, the assessment of significance should be considered based on the aggregate effect of all the unobservable inputs.

During the PIR on IFRS 13, many respondents indicated they found the assessment of whether an unobservable input is significant to the measurement as a whole challenging and asked for additional guidance. Some indicated that this assessment may be affected by negative perceptions associated with categorisation within Level 3 of the fair value hierarchy (e.g. including the volume of disclosure required). The IASB decided not to provide additional guidance, noting in particular that the requirements are principles-based and, as such, judgement will always be needed in their application.[26]

Entities should have a documented policy with respect to their approach to determining the significance of unobservable inputs on its fair value measurements and apply that policy consistently. This is important in light of the disclosure requirements in IFRS 13, particularly for fair value measurements categorised within Level 3 of the fair value hierarchy (see 20.3 below).

16.2.2 Transfers between levels within the fair value hierarchy

For assets or liabilities that are measured at fair value (or measurements based on fair value) at the end of each reporting period, their categorisation within the fair value hierarchy may change over time. This might be the case if the market for a particular asset or liability that was previously considered active (Level 1) becomes inactive (Level 2 or Level 3) or if significant inputs used in a valuation technique that were previously unobservable (Level 3) become observable (Level 2) given transactions that were observed around the measurement date. Such changes in categorisation within the hierarchy are referred to in IFRS 13 as transfers between levels within the fair value hierarchy.

An entity is required to select, and consistently apply, a policy for determining when transfers between levels of the fair value hierarchy are deemed to have occurred, that is, the timing of recognising transfers. This policy must be the same for transfers into and out of the levels. Examples of policies for determining the timing of transfers include:

- the date of the event or change in circumstances that caused the transfer;
- the beginning of the reporting period; or
- the end of the reporting period. *[IFRS 13.95]*.

The standard requires an entity to disclose this policy (see 20.2 below). In addition, the selected timing (i.e. when transfers are deemed to have occurred) has a direct impact on the information an entity needs to collate in order to meet the disclosure requirements in IFRS 13 – specifically those required by IFRS 13.93(c) and (e)(iv) – for both transfers between Levels 1 and 2 and transfers into and out of Level 3 (these disclosure requirements are discussed at 20.3.2 below). *[IFRS 13.93(c), 93(e)(iv)]*.

16.2.3 Information provided by third-party pricing services or brokers

IFRS 13 does not preclude the use of quoted prices provided by third parties, such as pricing services or brokers, provided those quoted prices are developed in accordance with the standard. Quoted prices provided by third parties represent an important source of information in estimating fair value for many entities. While not precluded, the standard makes it clear that the use of broker quotes, third-party pricing services, or a third-party valuation specialist does not alleviate management's responsibility for the fair value measurements (and the related disclosures) that will be included in its financial statements. *[IFRS 13.B45]*.

It is important for entities to understand the source of information received from brokers and pricing services, particularly when there has been a significant decrease in the volume or level of activity for the asset or liability, as management needs to assess the relevance of these quotes. This is discussed further at 8.3 above.

As discussed at 15.5 above, an entity should evaluate whether quotes from brokers and pricing services are based on current information that reflects orderly transactions or were determined using valuation techniques that appropriately reflect market participant assumptions regarding risk. Entities should place less weight on third-party quotes that are not based on transactions compared to fair value indications that are based on market transactions.

Determining the level in which assets and liabilities are categorised within the fair value hierarchy for disclosure purposes often requires judgement. Information provided by third-party pricing services or brokers could represent Level 1, Level 2, or Level 3 inputs depending on the source of the information and the type of instrument being measured. For example, pricing services may provide quoted market prices (e.g. closing price) for financial instruments traded in active markets. These prices are Level 1 measurements.

Alternatively, a pricing service may provide an entity with consensus pricing information (e.g. information obtained by polling dealers for indications of mid-market prices for a particular asset class). The non-binding nature of consensus pricing would generally result in its categorisation as Level 3 information, assuming no additional corroborating evidence.

Pricing services may also use valuation models to estimate values for certain instruments. For example, pricing services may use matrix pricing to determine the value of many fixed-income securities. The hierarchy level in which these instruments would be categorised depends on the observability of the valuation model's inputs. Therefore, entities that use pricing services should understand the data sources and valuation methods used to derive those third-party quotes. This information will determine where the entity's instruments would be categorised within the fair value hierarchy.

Similarly, the level within the hierarchy in which a broker quote is categorised depends on the nature of the quote. *[IFRS 13.B47]*. In certain brokered markets, firm quotes are disclosed and an entity has the ability to 'hit' or execute a transaction at the quoted price. Depending on the level of activity in these markets, those quotes may be categorised as Level 1 or Level 2. However, when an entity has to solicit a quote from a broker, the quotes are often non-binding and may include a disclaimer that releases the broker from being held to that price in an actual transaction. On their own, non-binding quotes would generally represent a Level 3 input. In addition, when the quote includes explanatory language or a disclaimer, the entity should assess whether the quote represents fair value (exit price) or whether an adjustment is needed.

If an entity uses multiple quotes within a narrow range when measuring fair value, it will likely provide stronger evidence of fair value than a single quote or quotes that are widely dispersed. However, the number of quotes should not, in and of itself, affect the categorisation within the fair value hierarchy. An entity would still need to consider the nature of those quotes. For example, multiple Level 3 inputs, within a reasonable range, would not result in a Level 2 measurement without additional observable corroborating evidence.

In August 2014, the IFRS Interpretations Committee received a request to clarify the circumstances in which a fair value measurement, in its entirety, that uses prices that are provided by third parties (e.g. consensus prices) could be categorised within Level 1 of the fair value hierarchy, particularly in relation to debt securities that are actively traded. The submitter highlighted that categorisation within the fair value hierarchy for debt securities is not straightforward and that there were divergent views on the appropriate level within the hierarchy such fair value measurements should be categorised.

After considering the analyses and outreach performed by its staff, the Interpretations Committee decided not to add this issue to its agenda, noting the following:[27]

- the guidance in IFRS 13 relating to the categorisation within the fair value hierarchy was sufficient to draw an appropriate conclusion on this issue;
- the fair value hierarchy prioritises the inputs to valuation techniques, not the valuation techniques used to measure fair value. When the fair value of assets or liabilities is measured based on prices provided by third parties, the categorisation of those measurements within the fair value hierarchy depends on the evaluation of the inputs used by the third party to derive those prices; not on the pricing methodology the third party has used; and
- only unadjusted quoted prices in active markets for identical assets or liabilities that the entity can access at the measurement date qualify as Level 1 measurement. Therefore, a fair value measurement that is based on prices provided by third parties can only be categorised within Level 1 of the fair value hierarchy if that measurement relies solely on unadjusted quoted prices in an active market for an identical instrument that the entity can access at the measurement date (i.e. P×Q, without adjustment).

16.2.4 Categorisation of over-the-counter derivative instruments

Depending on the observability of the inputs used, fair value measurements of over-the-counter derivatives that are not centrally cleared would likely be within either Level 2 or Level 3 of the fair value hierarchy.

Although these instruments may initially be executed in active markets, quoted prices for the identical asset or liability will often not be available when measuring fair value subsequently. For example, consider a 10-year plain vanilla interest-rate swap entered into on 1 January 20X1 that is not centrally cleared. While there may be quoted prices for 10-year swaps, when measuring the fair value of the swap on 31 March 20X1, the subject instrument would represent a 9.75-year swap for which quoted prices are generally not available. As a result, most over-the-counter derivative contracts that are not centrally cleared are valued based on inputs used in pricing models.

In addition, centrally cleared derivatives would not be categorised within Level 1 unless their fair value was determined based on an unadjusted quoted price in active markets for an identical instrument. Some constituents have questioned whether a 'value mark', periodically provided by a central clearing organisation for variation margin purposes, represents a Level 1 measurement. As discussed at 15.5.1 above, a reporting entity should not presume that the value provided by a central clearing organisation for margin purposes represents fair value in accordance with IFRS 13. Instead, entities need to understand the source and nature of the information provided by the central clearing organisation and assess whether the value indication represents fair value in accordance with IFRS 13 or whether an adjustment may be needed.

Even in those circumstances where an entity determines that the information received from the central clearing organisation is representative of fair value and does not require adjustment, it is our understanding that the 'value marks' provided typically do not represent actual trades of the identical instrument and therefore would not be a Level 1 measurement.

See 15.5.1 above for additional discussion on the consideration of values provided by central clearing organisations when determining the fair value.

17 LEVEL 1 INPUTS

'Level 1 inputs are quoted prices (unadjusted) in active markets for identical assets or liabilities that the entity can access at the measurement date'. *[IFRS 13.76]*. According to IFRS 13, this price represents the most reliable evidence of fair value. If a quoted price in an active market is available, an entity must use this price to measure fair value without adjustment; although adjustments are permitted in limited circumstances (see 17.3 below). *[IFRS 13.77]*.

17.1 Use of Level 1 inputs

As a general principle, IFRS 13 mandates the use of quoted prices in active markets for identical assets and liabilities whenever available. With limited exceptions, quoted prices in active markets should not be adjusted when determining the fair value of identical assets and liabilities, as the IASB believes these prices provide the most reliable evidence of fair value.

Adjustments can only be made to a quoted price in an active market (a Level 1 input) in the following circumstances:

(a) when an entity holds a large number of similar (but not identical) assets or liabilities (e.g. debt securities) that are measured at fair value and a quoted price in an active market is available but is not readily accessible for each of those assets or liabilities individually. That is, since the assets or liabilities are not identical and given the large number of similar assets or liabilities held by the entity, it would be difficult to obtain pricing information for each individual asset or liability at the measurement date.

In this situation, IFRS 13 provides a practical expedient; an entity may measure fair value using an alternative pricing method that does not rely exclusively on quoted prices (e.g. matrix pricing);

(b) when a quoted price in an active market does not represent fair value at the measurement date.

This may be the case, for example, if significant events, such as transactions in a principal-to-principal market, trades in a brokered market or announcements, take place after the close of a market but before the measurement date. An entity must establish and consistently apply a policy for identifying those events that might affect fair value measurements; or

(c) when measuring the fair value of a liability or an entity's own equity instrument using the quoted price for the identical item traded as an asset in an active market and that price needs to be adjusted for factors specific to the item or the asset. *[IFRS 13.79]*.

These exceptions are discussed further at 17.1.1, 17.2 and 17.3 below. Level 1 inputs are most commonly associated with financial instruments, for example, shares that are actively traded on a stock exchange. It may be that an asset or liability is traded in multiple active markets, for example, shares that are listed on more than one stock exchange. In light of this, the standard emphasises the need within Level 1 to determine both, the principal (or most advantageous) market (see 6 above) and whether the entity can enter into a transaction for the asset or liability at the price in that market at the measurement date (see 8 above). *[IFRS 13.78]*.

As discussed at 16.2 above, if no adjustment is made to a Level 1 input, the result is the entire fair value measurement being categorised within Level 1 of the fair value hierarchy. However, any adjustment made to a Level 1 input or use of the practical expedient in (a) above would result in categorisation within a lower level of the fair value hierarchy. If the adjustment uses significant unobservable inputs, it would need to be categorised within Level 3. *[IFRS 13.75]*.

17.1.1 Level 1 liabilities and instruments classified in an entity's own equity

Quoted prices in active markets for identical liabilities and instruments classified as an entity's own equity are Level 1 measurements. These instruments would likewise be categorised within Level 1 when a quoted price exists for the identical instrument traded as an asset in an active market, provided no adjustment to the quoted price is required.

The fair value of corporate debt issued by a reporting entity, for example, would be a Level 1 measurement if the asset corresponding to the issuer's liability (i.e. the corporate bond) trades in an active market and no adjustment is made to the quoted price. While the liability itself is not transferred in an active market, the IASB concluded that Level 1 categorisation is appropriate when the identical instrument trades as an asset in an active market.

If an adjustment to the corresponding asset's price is required to address differences between the asset and the liability or equity instrument (as discussed at 11 above), *[IFRS 13.79(c)]*, the adjusted price would not be a Level 1 measurement. For example, an adjustment to the quoted price of an asset that includes the effect of a third-party credit enhancement would be warranted when measuring the fair value of the liability. In this case, the corresponding asset and the liability would have different units of account (as discussed at 11.3.1 above).

17.2 Alternative pricing methods

When an entity holds a large number of similar assets and liabilities for which quoted prices exist, but are not easily accessible, IFRS 13 allows for the use of alternative pricing methods (e.g. matrix pricing) as a practical expedient. *[IFRS 13.79(a)]*. The IASB provided this practical expedient to ease the administrative burden associated with obtaining quoted prices for each individual instrument. However, if the practical expedient is used, the resulting fair value measurement would not be considered a Level 1 measurement.

17.3 Quoted prices in active markets that are not representative of fair value

IFRS 13 recognises that in certain situations a quoted price in an active market might not represent the fair value of an asset or liability, such as when significant events occur on the measurement date, but after the close of trading. In these situations, entities would adjust the quoted price to incorporate this new information into the fair value measurement. *[IFRS 13.79(b)]*. However, if the quoted price is adjusted, the resulting fair value measurement would no longer be considered a Level 1 measurement.

An entity's valuation policies and procedures should address how these 'after-hour' events will be identified and assessed. Controls should be put in place to ensure that any adjustments made to quoted prices are appropriate under IFRS 13 and are applied in a consistent manner.

17.4 Unit of account

Although the unit of account is generally determined in accordance with other IFRSs, IFRS 13 addresses the unit of account for Level 1 assets and liabilities. Paragraph 80 of IFRS 13 states that 'if an entity holds a position in a single asset or liability (including a position comprising a large number of identical assets or liabilities, such as a holding of financial instruments) and the asset or liability is traded in an active market, the fair value of the asset or liability shall be measured within Level 1 as the product of the quoted price for the individual asset or liability and the quantity held by the entity'. *[IFRS 13.80]*. By dictating that fair value be determined based on P×Q, IFRS 13 effectively prescribes the unit of account as the individual asset or liability in these situations.

This requirement is generally accepted when the asset or liability being measured is a financial instrument in the scope of IFRS 9. However, when an entity holds an investment in a listed subsidiary, joint venture or associate, some believe the fair value should include an adjustment (e.g. a control premium) to reflect the value of the investor's control, joint control or significant influence over their investment as a whole. In September 2014, the IASB issued an exposure draft that proposed clarifying that the requirement in IFRS 13 to use P×Q, without adjustment, to measure fair value would apply even in situations where the unit of account is the entire investment. After considering the responses from constituents, the IASB had directed its staff to perform additional research before they deliberated further. That research was fed into the PIR of IFRS 13. In December 2018, the IASB concluded its PIR and decided to do no further work on this topic. This is discussed further at 5.1.1 above.

18 LEVEL 2 INPUTS

18.1 Use of Level 2 inputs

Level 2 inputs include quoted prices (in non-active markets or in active markets for similar assets or liabilities), observable inputs other than quoted prices and inputs that are not directly observable, but are corroborated by observable market data. *[IFRS 13.82]*.

The inclusion of market-corroborated inputs is significant because it expands the scope of Level 2 inputs beyond those directly observable for the asset or liability. Inputs determined through mathematical or statistical techniques, such as correlation or regression, may be categorised as Level 2 if the inputs into, and/or the results from, these techniques can be corroborated with observable market data.

IFRS 13 requires that a Level 2 input be observable (either directly or indirectly through corroboration with market data) for substantially the full contractual term of the asset or liability being measured. *[IFRS 13.81]*. Therefore, a long-term input extrapolated from short-term observable market data (e.g. a 30-year yield extrapolated from the observable 5-, 10- and 15-year points on the yield curve) would generally not be considered a Level 2 input.

18.2 Examples of Level 2 inputs

IFRS 13's application guidance provides a number of examples of Level 2 inputs for specific assets or liabilities. These examples are included in Figure 14.9 below, which is adapted from IFRS 13. *[IFRS 13.B35]*.

Figure 14.9:   Examples of Level 2 inputs

Asset or Liability	Example of a Level 2 Input
Receive-fixed, pay-variable interest rate swap based on the Interbank Offered Rate (IBOR) swap rate	The IBOR swap rate if that rate is observable at commonly quoted intervals for substantially the full term of the swap.
Receive-fixed, pay-variable interest rate swap based on a yield curve denominated in a foreign currency	The swap rate based on a yield curve denominated in a foreign currency that is observable at commonly quoted intervals for substantially the full term of the swap. This would be a Level 2 input if the term of the swap is 10 years and that rate is observable at commonly quoted intervals for 9 years, provided that any reasonable extrapolation of the yield curve for year 10 would not be significant to the fair value measurement of the swap in its entirety.
Receive-fixed, pay-variable interest rate swap based on a specific bank's prime rate	The bank's prime rate derived through extrapolation if the extrapolated values are corroborated by observable market data, for example, by correlation with an interest rate that is observable over substantially the full term of the swap.
Three-year option on exchange-traded shares	The implied volatility for the shares derived through extrapolation to year 3 if both of the following conditions exist: (i) Prices for one-year and two-year options on the shares are observable. (ii) The extrapolated implied volatility of a three-year option is corroborated by observable market data for substantially the full term of the option. In this situation, the implied volatility could be derived by extrapolating from the implied volatility of the one-year and two-year options on the shares and corroborated by the implied volatility for three-year options on comparable entities' shares, provided that correlation with the one-year and two-year implied volatilities is established.
Licensing arrangement	For a licensing arrangement that is acquired in a business combination and was recently negotiated with an unrelated party by the acquired entity (the party to the licensing arrangement), a Level 2 input would be the royalty rate in the contract with the unrelated party at inception of the arrangement.
Cash-generating unit	A valuation multiple (e.g. a multiple of earnings or revenue or a similar performance measure) derived from observable market data, e.g. multiples derived from prices in observed transactions involving comparable (i.e. similar) businesses, taking into account operational, market, financial and non-financial factors.

Finished goods inventory at a retail outlet	For finished goods inventory that is acquired in a business combination, a Level 2 input would be either a price to customers in a retail market or a price to retailers in a wholesale market, adjusted for differences between the condition and location of the inventory item and the comparable (i.e. similar) inventory items so that the fair value measurement reflects the price that would be received in a transaction to sell the inventory to another retailer that would complete the requisite selling efforts. Conceptually, the fair value measurement will be the same, whether adjustments are made to a retail price (downward) or to a wholesale price (upward). Generally, the price that requires the least amount of subjective adjustments should be used for the fair value measurement.
Building held and used	The price per square metre for the building (a valuation multiple) derived from observable market data, e.g. multiples derived from prices in observed transactions involving comparable (i.e. similar) buildings in similar locations.

18.3 Market corroborated inputs

Level 2 inputs, as discussed at 18.1 above, include market-corroborated inputs. That is, inputs that are not directly observable for the asset or liability, but, instead, are corroborated by observable market data through correlation or other statistical techniques.

IFRS 13 does not provide any detailed guidance regarding to the application of statistical techniques, such as regression or correlation, when attempting to corroborate inputs to observable market data (Level 2) inputs. However, the lack of any specific guidance or 'bright lines' for evaluating the validity of a statistical inference by the IASB should not be construed to imply that the mere use of a statistical analysis (such as linear regression) would be deemed valid and appropriate to support Level 2 categorisation (or a fair value measurement for that matter). Any statistical analysis that is relied on for financial reporting purposes should be evaluated for its predictive validity. That is, the statistical technique should support the hypothesis that the observable input has predictive value with respect to the unobservable input.

In Figure 14.9 at 18.2 above, for the three-year option on exchange-traded shares, the implied volatility derived through extrapolation has been categorised as a Level 2 input because the input was corroborated (through correlation) to an implied volatility based on an observable option price of a comparable entity. In this example, the determination of an appropriate proxy (i.e. a comparable entity) is a critical component in supporting that the implied volatility of the actual option being measured is a market-corroborated input.

In practice, identifying an appropriate benchmark or proxy requires judgement that should appropriately incorporate both qualitative and quantitative factors. For example, when valuing equity-based instruments (e.g. equity options), an entity should consider the industry, nature of the business, size, leverage and other factors that would qualitatively support the expectation that the benchmarks are sufficiently comparable to the subject entity. Qualitative considerations may differ depending on the type of input being analysed or the type of instrument being measured (e.g. a foreign exchange option versus an equity option).

In addition to the qualitative considerations discussed above, quantitative measures are used to validate a statistical analysis. For example, if a regression analysis is used as a means of corroborating non-observable market data, the results of the analysis can be assessed based on statistical measures.

18.4 Making adjustments to a Level 2 input

The standard acknowledges that, unlike a Level 1 input, adjustments to Level 2 inputs may be more common, but will vary depending on the factors specific to the asset or liability. [IFRS 13.83].

There are a number of reasons why an entity may need to make adjustments to Level 2 inputs. Adjustments to observable data from inactive markets (see 8 above), for example, might be required for timing differences between the transaction date and the measurement date, or differences between the asset being measured and a similar asset that was the subject of the transaction. In addition, factors such as the condition or location of an asset should also be considered when determining if adjustments to Level 2 inputs are warranted.

If the Level 2 input relates to an asset or liability that is similar, but not identical to the asset or liability being measured, the entity would need to consider what adjustments may be required to capture differences between the item being measured and the reference asset or liability. For example, do they have different characteristics, such as credit quality of the issuer in the case of a bond? Adjustments may be needed for differences between the two. [IFRS 13.83].

If an adjustment to a Level 2 input is significant to the entire fair value measurement, it may affect the fair value measurement's categorisation within the fair value hierarchy for disclosure purposes. If the adjustment uses significant unobservable inputs, it would need to be categorised within Level 3 of the hierarchy. [IFRS 13.84].

18.5 Recently observed prices in an inactive market

Valuation technique(s) used to measure fair value must maximise the use of *relevant* observable inputs and minimise the use of unobservable inputs. While recently observed transactions for the same (or similar) items often provide useful information for measuring fair value, transactions or quoted prices in inactive markets are not necessarily indicative of fair value. A significant decrease in the volume or level of activity for the asset or liability may increase the chances of this. However, transaction data should not be ignored, unless the transaction is determined to be disorderly (see 8 above).

The relevance of observable data, including last transaction prices, must be considered when assessing the weight this information should be given when estimating fair value and whether adjustments are needed (as discussed at 18.4 above). Adjustments to observed transaction prices may be warranted in some situations, particularly when the observed transaction is for a similar, but not identical, instrument. Therefore, it is important to understand the characteristics of the item being measured compared with an item being used as a benchmark.

When few, if any, transactions can be observed for an asset or liability, an index may provide relevant pricing information if the underlying risks of the index are similar to the item being measured. While the index price may provide general information about market participant assumptions regarding certain risk features of the asset or liability, adjustments are often required to account for specific characteristics of the instrument being measured or the market in which the instrument would trade (e.g. liquidity considerations). While this information may not be determinative for the particular instrument being measured, it can serve to either support or contest an entity's determination regarding the relevance of observable data in markets that are not active.

IFRS 13 does not prescribe a methodology for applying adjustments to observable transactions or quoted prices when estimating fair value. Judgement is needed when evaluating the relevance of observable market data and determining what (if any) adjustments should be made to this information. However, the application of this judgement must be within the confines of the stated objective of a fair value measurement within the IFRS 13 framework. Since fair value is intended to represent the exit price in a transaction between market participants in the current market, an entity's intent to hold the asset due to current market conditions, or any entity-specific needs, is not relevant to a fair value measurement and is not a valid reason to adjust observable market data.

19 LEVEL 3 INPUTS

All unobservable inputs for an asset or liability are Level 3 inputs. The standard requires an entity to minimise the use of Level 3 inputs when measuring fair value. As such, they should only be used to the extent that relevant observable inputs are not available, for example, in situations where there is limited market activity for an asset or liability. *[IFRS 13.86, 87]*.

19.1 Use of Level 3 inputs

A number of IFRSs permit or require the use of fair value measurements regardless of the level of market activity for the asset or liability as at the measurement date (e.g. the initial measurement of intangible assets acquired in a business combination). As such, IFRS 13 allows for the use of unobservable inputs to measure fair value in situations where observable inputs are not available. In these cases, the IASB recognises that the best information available with which to develop unobservable inputs may be an entity's own data. However, IFRS 13 is clear that while an entity may begin with its own data, this data should be adjusted if:

- reasonably available information indicates that other market participants would use different data; or
- there is something particular to the entity that is not available to other market participants (e.g. an entity-specific synergy). *[IFRS 13.89]*.

For example, when measuring the fair value of an investment property, we would expect that a reporting entity with a unique tax position would consider the typical market participant tax rate in its analysis. While this example is simplistic and is meant only to illustrate a concept, in practice significant judgement will be required when evaluating what information about unobservable inputs or market data may be reasonably available.

It is important to note that an entity is not required to undertake exhaustive efforts to obtain information about market participant assumptions when pricing an asset or liability. Nor is an entity required to establish the absence of contrary data. As a result, in those situations where information about market participant assumptions does not exist or is not reasonably available, a fair value measurement may be based primarily on the reporting entity's own data. *[IFRS 13.89]*.

Even in situations where an entity's own data is used, the objective of the fair value measurement remains the same – i.e. an exit price from the perspective of a market participant that holds the asset or owes the liability. As such, unobservable inputs should reflect the assumptions that market participants would use, which includes the risk inherent in a particular valuation technique (such as a pricing model) and the risk inherent in the inputs. As discussed at 7.2 above, if a market participant would consider those risks in pricing an asset or liability, an entity must include that risk adjustment; otherwise the result would not be a fair value measurement. When categorising the entire fair value measurement within the fair value hierarchy, an entity would need to consider the significance of the model adjustment as well as the observability of the data supporting the adjustment. *[IFRS 13.87, 88]*.

19.2 Examples of Level 3 inputs

IFRS 13's application guidance provides a number of examples of Level 3 inputs for specific assets or liabilities, as outlined in Figure 14.10 below. *[IFRS 13.B36]*.

Figure 14.10: Examples of Level 3 inputs

Asset or Liability	Example of a Level 3 Input
Long-dated currency swap	An interest rate in a specified currency that is not observable and cannot be corroborated by observable market data at commonly quoted intervals or otherwise for substantially the full term of the currency swap. The interest rates in a currency swap are the swap rates calculated from the respective countries' yield curves.
Three-year option on exchange-traded shares	Historical volatility, i.e. the volatility for the shares derived from the shares' historical prices. Historical volatility typically does not represent current market participants' expectations about future volatility, even if it is the only information available to price an option.
Interest rate swap	An adjustment to a mid-market consensus (non-binding) price for the swap developed using data that are not directly observable and cannot otherwise be corroborated by observable market data.
Decommissioning liability assumed in a business combination	A current estimate using the entity's own data about the future cash outflows to be paid to fulfil the obligation (including market participants' expectations about the costs of fulfilling the obligation and the compensation that a market participant would require for taking on the obligation to dismantle the asset) if there is no reasonably available information that indicates that market participants would use different assumptions. That Level 3 input would be used in a present value technique together with other inputs, e.g. a current risk-free interest rate or a credit-adjusted risk-free rate if the effect of the entity's credit standing on the fair value of the liability is reflected in the discount rate rather than in the estimate of future cash outflows.
Cash-generating unit	A financial forecast (e.g. of cash flows or profit or loss) developed using the entity's own data if there is no reasonably available information that indicates that market participants would use different assumptions.

20 DISCLOSURES

The disclosure requirements in IFRS 13 apply to fair value measurements recognised in the statement of financial position, after initial recognition, and disclosures of fair value (i.e. those items that are not measured at fair value in the statement of financial position, but whose fair value is required to be disclosed). However, as discussed at 2.2.4 above, IFRS 13 provides a scope exception in relation to disclosures for:

- plan assets measured at fair value in accordance with IAS 19;
- retirement benefit plan investments measured at fair value in accordance with IAS 26; and
- assets for which recoverable amount is fair value less costs of disposal in accordance with IAS 36.

In addition to these scope exceptions, the IASB decided not to require the IFRS 13 disclosures for items that are recognised at fair value only at initial recognition. Disclosure requirements in relation to fair value measurements at initial recognition are covered by the standard that is applicable to that asset or liability. For example, IFRS 3 requires disclosure of the fair value measurement of assets acquired and liabilities assumed in a business combination. *[IFRS 13.BC184]*.

However, it should be noted that, unlike IAS 19, IAS 26 and IAS 36, there is no scope exemption for IFRS 3 or other standards that require fair value measurements (or measures based on fair value) at initial recognition. Therefore, if those standards require fair value measurements (or measures based on fair value) after initial recognition, IFRS 13's disclosure requirements would apply.

From the IASB discussions of respondents input on the PIR, the IASB decided to feed the PIR findings regarding the usefulness of disclosures into the work on Better Communications in Financial Reporting, in particular, the projects on Primary Financial Statements and the Targeted Standards-level Review of Disclosures.[28] The Primary Financial Statements project considered challenges in determining the appropriate level of disaggregation identified in the PIR (see 5.1.3 and 10.2.4 above, as well as 20.1.2 below), which resulted in an exposure draft – *ED/2019/7 General Presentation and Disclosures* – issued in December 2019, with a comment period ending 30 September 2020 (see Chapter 3). The Targeted Standards-level Review of Disclosures project reviewed the disclosure requirements in IFRS 13 (see 20.6 below).

20.1 Disclosure objectives

IFRS 13 requires a number of disclosures designed to provide users of financial statements with additional transparency regarding:

- the extent to which fair value is used to measure assets and liabilities;
- the valuation techniques, inputs and assumptions used in measuring fair value; and
- the effect of Level 3 fair value measurements on profit or loss (or other comprehensive income).

The standard establishes a set of broad disclosure objectives and provides the minimum disclosures an entity must make (see 20.2 to 20.5 below for discussion regarding the minimum disclosure requirements in IFRS 13).

The objectives of IFRS 13's disclosure requirements are to:

(a) enable users of financial statements to understand the valuation techniques and inputs used to develop fair value measurements; and

(b) help users to understand the effect of fair value measurements on profit or loss and other comprehensive income for the period when fair value is based on unobservable inputs (Level 3 inputs). *[IFRS 13.91]*.

After providing the minimum disclosures required by IFRS 13 and other standards, such as IAS 1 – *Presentation of Financial Statements* – or IAS 34 – *Interim Financial Reporting*, an entity must assess whether its disclosures are sufficient to meet the disclosure objectives in IFRS 13. If not, additional information must be disclosed in order to meet those objectives. *[IFRS 13.92]*. This assessment requires judgement and will depend on the specific facts and circumstances of the entity and the needs of the users of its financial statements.

An entity must consider all the following:

- the level of detail needed to satisfy the disclosure requirements;
- how much emphasis to place on each of the various requirements;
- the level of aggregation or disaggregation (see 20.1.2 below); and
- whether users of financial statements need additional information to evaluate the quantitative information disclosed. *[IFRS 13.92]*.

An entity might, for example, disclose the nature of the item being measured at fair value, including the characteristics of the item being measured that are taken into account in the determination of relevant inputs. In addition, when describing the valuation techniques and inputs used for fair value measurements categorised within Levels 2 and 3, the entity might disclose how third-party information (such as broker quotes, pricing services, net asset values and relevant market data) was taken into account when measuring fair value. For example, for residential mortgage-backed securities, an entity might disclose the following:

(i) the types of underlying loans (e.g. prime loans or sub-prime loans);

(ii) collateral;

(iii) guarantees or other credit enhancements;

(iv) seniority level of the tranches of securities;

(v) the year of issue;

(vi) the weighted-average coupon rate of the underlying loans and the securities;

(vii) the weighted-average maturity of the underlying loans and the securities;

(viii) the geographical concentration of the underlying loans; and

(ix) information about the credit ratings of the securities. *[IFRS 13.IE64(a)]*.

IFRS 13 includes the above example to illustrate the type of additional information an entity might disclose based on the considerations outlined in paragraph 92 of IFRS 13. These additional disclosures are intended to help financial statement users better understand and evaluate the quantitative information provided by the entity (e.g. the quantitative information the entity disclosed regarding the valuation of its residential mortgage-backed securities holdings).

20.1.1 Format of disclosures

IFRS 13's requirements, with regard to the format of disclosures, are limited to the presentation of quantitative information. An entity is required to use a tabular format to present the quantitative disclosures required by IFRS 13, unless another format is more appropriate. *[IFRS 13.99]*.

20.1.2 Level of disaggregation

IFRS 13 requires disclosures to be presented by class of asset or liability (the definition of a class of asset or liability is discussed at 20.1.2.A below). Unlike certain other IFRSs, IFRS 13 does not specify the level of aggregation or disaggregation an entity must use when complying with its disclosure requirements. Instead, as discussed below, it simply provides the basis for making this determination. As such, the appropriate class of assets and liabilities may depend on the entity's specific facts and circumstances and the needs of users of its financial statements.

According to the standard, a class of assets and liabilities will often require greater disaggregation than the line items presented in the statement of financial position. Therefore, an entity must present information in sufficient detail to permit reconciliation back to the statement of financial position. *[IFRS 13.94]*. Such a reconciliation could be presented through the use of subtotals that correspond to line items disclosed in the statement of financial position; however, other approaches may be acceptable.

During the PIR of IFRS 13, respondents indicated that the level of aggregation or disaggregation was a challenge. In particular, respondents said that the information was less useful if aggregated too much and suggested more guidance and examples would be helpful to promote more appropriate levels of aggregation. This was considered as part of the Board's Primary Financial Statements project (see 20 above).

20.1.2.A Determining appropriate classes of assets and liabilities for disclosure

Determining appropriate classes of assets and liabilities requires judgement. An entity bases this determination on the nature, characteristics and risks of the asset or liability and the level of the fair value hierarchy within which the fair value measurement is categorised (see 16.2 above for further discussion). *[IFRS 13.94]*. In addition, the standard specifies that the number of classes may need to be greater for fair value measurements categorised within Level 3 of the fair value hierarchy because they have a greater degree of uncertainty and subjectivity.

Other IFRSs may specify classes for asset or liability. For example, IAS 16 and IAS 38 – *Intangible Assets* – require disclosures by class of property, plant and equipment or intangible respectively. If another IFRS specifies the class for an asset or a liability and that class meets the requirements for determining a class in accordance with IFRS 13, an entity may use that class in providing IFRS 13's required disclosures. *[IFRS 13.94]*.

The determination of a class includes considering the fair value measurement's categorisation within the fair value hierarchy as noted above with respect to Level 3 measurements. IFRS 13 requires disclosure of this categorisation for each class of asset or liability (see 20.3 to 20.4 below). While an entity takes the fair value categorisation into consideration when determining a class, this does not mean assets or liabilities within a single class cannot be categorised within different levels of the hierarchy. For example, assume an entity has grouped all its buildings within one class in accordance with IAS 16 and measures all those buildings using the revaluation approach in that standard. Further assume that the fair value measurements of some buildings are categorised within Level 2, while others are categorised within Level 3, based on the availability of observable inputs used in the fair value measurement. In and of itself, the assets' categorisation within two levels of the hierarchy does not necessarily mean the entity would need to further disaggregate the IAS 16 class of buildings into two classes for disclosure in accordance with IFRS 13. However, it may be appropriate to do that if the differing categorisation indicated the buildings categorised within Level 2 were different in their nature, characteristics or risks compared to those categorised within Level 3.

20.1.3 Differentiating between 'recurring' and 'non-recurring'

IFRS 13 has different disclosure requirements for those fair value measurements that are recognised (rather than just disclosed), depending on whether those measurements are recurring or non-recurring in nature (see 20.3 below). Therefore, it is important to understand the distinction.

- *Recurring* fair value measurements are those that another IFRS requires or permits to be recognised in the statement of financial position at the end of each reporting period. For example, the fair value of a financial asset classified as fair value through profit or loss in accordance with IFRS 9 would need to be measured at the end each reporting period. Other examples include a liability to distribute non-cash assets to shareholders, measured at fair value in accordance with IFRIC 17 – *Distributions of Non-cash Assets to Owners.*

  In our view, revaluations of property, plant and equipment in accordance with IAS 16 represent a recurring fair value measurement. The revaluation model in IAS 16 requires that revaluations be made 'with sufficient regularity to ensure that the carrying amount does not differ materially from that which would be determined using fair value at the end of the reporting period'. *[IAS 16.31].* Furthermore, 'the frequency of revaluations depends upon the changes in fair values of the items of property, plant and equipment being revalued. When the fair value of a revalued asset differs materially from its carrying amount, a further revaluation is required'. *[IAS 16.34].* Therefore, while an entity might not revalue an asset each year, the objective is to ensure the carrying amount approximates fair value, subject to materiality.

- *Non-recurring* fair value measurements are those that another IFRS requires or permits to be recognised in the statement of financial position in particular circumstances. For example, IFRS 5 requires an entity to measure an asset held for sale at the lower of its carrying amount and fair value less costs to sell. Since the asset's fair value less costs to sell is only recognised in the statement of financial position when it is lower than its carrying amount, that fair value measurement is non-recurring. However, it should be noted that in a disposal group, not all assets and liabilities are subject to the measurement requirements of IFRS 5. If financial assets categorised as fair value through other comprehensive income in accordance of IFRS 9 were included in a disposal group, an entity would continue to measure these assets in accordance with IFRS 9 at fair value. These fair value measurements would continue to be recurring. *[IFRS 13.93(a)].*

20.2 Accounting policy disclosures

In general, the requirements to disclose an entity's accounting policies will be addressed by the standard that requires or permits an item to be measured at fair value. The disclosure requirements of IAS 8 would address any changes to an entity's accounting policies (see Chapter 3). In addition to these, IFRS 13 requires the disclosure of two policies. [IFRS 13.95, 96].

Firstly, if an entity makes an accounting policy decision to use the exception in relation to the measurement of fair value for financial assets and financial liabilities with offsetting positions, it must disclose that fact (see 12 above for further discussion regarding the measurement exception and criteria for selecting this accounting policy choice). [IFRS 13.96].

Secondly, an entity must disclose its policy for determining when transfers between levels of the fair value hierarchy are deemed to have occurred (see 16.2.2 above for further discussion regarding this policy choice). [IFRS 13.95].

As discussed at 14.1.4 above, changes to fair value resulting from a change in the valuation technique or its application are accounted for as a change in accounting estimate in accordance with IAS 8 (unless the valuation technique is applied in error, which would be accounted for as a correction of an error in accordance with IAS 8). However, information would be disclosed in accordance with IFRS 13, not IAS 8; specifically, that there has been a change in valuation technique and the reasons for the change (see 20.3.5 below for further discussion). [IFRS 13.93(d)]. This is illustrated in the extract from the financial statements of ING Groep N.V below.

Extract 14.2: ING Groep N.V. (2014)

Notes to the consolidated annual accounts [Extract]

1 Accounting policies [Extract]

Critical accounting policies [Extract]

Fair values of real estate

Real estate investments are reported at fair value. The fair value of real estate investments is based on regular appraisals by independent qualified valuers. The fair values are established using valuation methods such as: comparable market transactions, capitalisation of income methods or discounted cash flow calculations. The underlying assumption used in the valuation is that the properties are let or sold to third parties based on the actual letting status. The discounted cash flow analyses and capitalisation of income method are based on calculations of the future rental income in accordance with the terms in existing leases and estimations of the rental values for new leases when leases expire and incentives like rental free periods. The cash flows are discounted using market based interest rates that reflect appropriately the risk characteristics of real estate.

Market conditions in recent years have led to a reduced level of real estate transactions. Transaction values were significantly impacted by low volumes of actual transactions. As a result comparable market transactions have been used less in valuing ING's real estate investments by independent qualified valuers. More emphasis has been placed on discounted cash flow analysis and capitalisation of income method.

Reference is made to Note 43 'Fair value of assets and liabilities' for more disclosure on fair values of real estate investments.

The valuation of real estate involves various assumptions and techniques. The use of different assumptions and techniques could produce significantly different valuations. Consequently, the fair values presented may not be indicative of the net realisable value. In addition, the calculation of the estimated fair value is based on market conditions at a specific point in time and may not be indicative of future fair values. To illustrate the uncertainty of our real estate investments valuation, a sensitivity analysis on the changes in fair value of real estate is provided in the 'Risk management' section.

20.3 Disclosures for recognised fair value measurements

Paragraph 93 of IFRS 13 establishes the minimum disclosure requirements for fair value measurements (and those based on fair value) that are recognised in the statement of financial position after initial recognition. The requirements vary depending on whether the fair value measurements are recurring or non-recurring and their categorisation within the fair value hierarchy (i.e. Level 1, 2, or 3 – see 16 above for further discussion regarding the fair value hierarchy).

Irrespective of the frequency with which the fair value is measured, the disclosures under IFRS 13 are intended to provide financial statement users with additional insight into the relative subjectivity of various fair value measurements and enhance their ability to broadly assess an entity's quality of earnings.

In order to meet the disclosure objectives, the following information, at a minimum, must be disclosed for all fair value measurements. Disclosures are required for each class of asset and liability, whether recurring or non-recurring, that are recognised in the statement of financial position after initial recognition: *[IFRS 13.93]*

(a) the fair value measurement at the end of the reporting period (see Example 14.25 at 20.3.3 below);

(b) for non-financial assets, if the highest and best use differs from its current use, an entity must disclose that fact and why the non-financial asset is being used in a manner that differs from its highest and best use;

(c) the fair value measurement's categorisation within the fair value hierarchy (Level 1, 2 or 3 – see Example 14.25 at 20.3.3 below);

(d) if categorised within Level 2 or Level 3 of the fair value hierarchy:

    (i) a description of the valuation technique(s) used in the fair value measurement;

    (ii) the inputs used in the fair value measurement;

    (iii) if there has been a change in valuation technique (e.g. changing from a market approach to an income approach or the use of an additional valuation technique):

- the change; and
- the reason(s) for making it;

(e) quantitative information about the significant unobservable inputs used in the fair value measurement for those categorised within Level 3 of the fair value hierarchy. Example 14.27 at 20.3.5.A below illustrates how this information might be disclosed;

(f) if categorised within Level 3 of the fair value hierarchy, a description of the valuation processes used by the entity (including, for example, how an entity decides its valuation policies and procedures and analyses changes in fair value measurements from period to period).

This requirement focuses on valuation processes rather than the specific valuation techniques, which are covered by the requirements in (d) above.

In addition to these requirements, an entity must provide the disclosures discussed at 20.3.1 and 20.3.2 below depending on whether the measurement is recurring or non-recurring.

20.3.1 Disclosures for recognised recurring fair value measurements

The disclosure requirements in paragraph 93 of IFRS 13 (see 20.3 above and 20.3.1.A and 20.3.1.B below) apply to all fair value measurements that are recognised in the financial statements on a recurring basis. Given the increased subjectivity, IFRS 13 requires additional disclosures for fair value measurements categorised within Level 3 of the fair value hierarchy than for those categorised within Levels 1 or 2 (see 20.3.1.B below).

20.3.1.A Recurring fair value measurements categorised as Level 1 or Level 2

For recurring fair value measurements that are categorised within either Level 1 or Level 2 of the fair value hierarchy, an entity must disclose both:

- information required to comply with the disclosure requirements discussed at 20.3 above; and
- for any transfers between Level 1 and Level 2 of the fair value hierarchy:
  (i) the amounts of any transfers between Level 1 and Level 2 of the fair value hierarchy;
  (ii) the reasons for those transfers; and
  (iii) the entity's policy for determining when transfers between levels are deemed to have occurred (see 16.2.2 and 20.2 above for further discussion).

  The standard requires transfers into each level to be disclosed and discussed separately from transfers out of each level. *[IFRS 13.93]*.

20.3.1.B Recurring fair value measurements categorised as Level 3

In addition to the disclosure requirements listed at 20.3 above, recurring fair value measurements that are categorised within Level 3 of the fair value hierarchy are subject to additional disclosure requirements:

(a) a reconciliation from the opening balances to the closing balances, disclosing separately changes during the period (also referred to as the Level 3 roll-forward);

(b) a narrative description of the sensitivity of Level 3 fair value measurements to changes in unobservable inputs; and

(c) for financial assets and financial liabilities only, quantitative sensitivity analysis for Level 3 fair value measurements. *[IFRS 13.93]*.

These additional disclosure requirements for Level 3 fair value measurements are discussed further at 20.3.5 to 20.3.8 below.

20.3.2 Disclosures for recognised non-recurring fair value measurements

Certain disclosure requirements in IFRS 13 do not apply to fair value measurements that are non-recurring in nature (e.g. a non-current asset (or disposal group) held for sale measured at fair value less costs to sell in accordance with IFRS 5 where the fair value less costs to sell is lower than its carrying amount). Specifically, the following disclosures are *not* required for non-recurring recognised fair value measurements:

- information about any transfers between Level 1 and Level 2 of the fair value hierarchy;
- a reconciliation of the opening balances to the closing balances for Level 3 measurements (also referred to as the Level 3 roll-forward);
- a narrative description of the sensitivity of Level 3 fair value measurements to changes in unobservable inputs; and
- for financial assets and financial liabilities, quantitative sensitivity analysis for Level 3 fair value measurements. *[IFRS 13.93].*

Information regarding transfers between hierarchy levels and the Level 3 reconciliation do not lend themselves to non-recurring measurements and, therefore, are not required. While discussing the sensitivity of Level 3 measurements to changes in unobservable inputs might provide financial statement users with some information about how the selection of these inputs affects non-recurring valuations, the Boards ultimately decided that this information is most relevant for recurring measurements.

However, entities are required to disclose the reason for any non-recurring fair value measurements made subsequent to the initial recognition of an asset or liability. *[IFRS 13.93].* For example, the entity may intend to sell or otherwise dispose of it, thereby resulting in the need for its measurement at fair value less costs to sell based on the requirements of IFRS 5, if lower than the asset's carrying amount.

While obvious for recurring measurements, determining the periods in which the fair value disclosures should be made for non-recurring measurements is less clear. For example, assume a listed entity classifies a building as held for sale in accordance with IFRS 5 at the end of its second quarter and appropriately decreases the carrying value of the asset to its then fair value less costs to sell. In its interim financial statements, the entity would make all of the disclosures required by IFRS 13 for non-recurring fair value measurements. During the second half of the financial year, the sale falls through and the asset is no longer held for sale. In accordance with IFRS 5, the asset is measured at its carrying amount before the asset (or disposal group) was classified as held for sale, adjusted for any depreciation, as this is lower than its recoverable amount. The entity continues to account for the asset in accordance with IAS 16. While the carrying value of the asset at the end of the financial year is no longer *at* fair value less costs to sell, the asset was adjusted to fair value less costs to sell during the year. Therefore, in its annual financial statements, the entity would again disclose the information required by IFRS 13 for non-recurring fair value measurements. While not explicit in IFRS 13, we believe this approach is consistent with the interim and annual disclosure requirements for assets subsequently measured under the revaluation model in IAS 34 and IFRS 5.

In these situations, we recommend that the disclosures clearly indicate that the fair value information presented is not current, but rather as at the date fair value was measured. Entities should also indicate if the carrying amount of the asset no longer equals its fair value.

20.3.3 Fair value hierarchy categorisation

IFRS 13 requires entities to disclose the fair value hierarchy level in which each fair value measurement is categorised. As noted at 16.2 above, the categorisation of a fair value measurement of an asset or liability in the fair value hierarchy is based on the lowest level input that is significant to the fair value measurement in its entirety. Although the hierarchy disclosure is presented by class of asset or liability, it is important to understand that the determination of the hierarchy level in which a fair value measurement falls (and therefore the category in which it will be disclosed) is based on the fair value measurement for the specific item being measured and is, therefore, driven by the unit of account for the asset or liability.

For example, in situations where the unit of account for a financial instrument is the individual item, but the measurement exception for financial instruments is used (as discussed at 12 above), entities may need to allocate portfolio-level adjustments to the various instruments that make up the net exposure for purposes of hierarchy categorisation.

This may seem inconsistent to certain constituents given the discussion at 12 above about the consideration of size as a characteristic of the net risk exposure when the measurement exception for financial instruments is used. However, the IASB and FASB staffs have indicated that the determination of the net risk exposure as the unit of measurement applies only for measurement considerations and was not intended to change current practice with respect to disclosures. As such, the entire net exposure would not be categorised within a single level of the fair value hierarchy (e.g. Level 2), unless all of the individual items that make up the net exposure fell within that level.

To illustrate, consider an individual derivative that is valued using the measurement exception as part of a group of derivative instruments with offsetting credit risk (due to the existence of a legally enforceable netting agreement). Assuming the portfolio included instruments that on their own must be categorised within different levels of the fair value hierarchy (i.e. Level 2 and Level 3), for disclosure purposes, the portfolio-level adjustment for credit risk (considering the effect of master netting agreements) may need to be attributed to the individual derivative transactions within the portfolio or to the group of transactions that fall within each of the levels of the hierarchy. This example assumes that the portfolio-level adjustment for credit risk is based on observable market data. If the portfolio-level adjustment was determined using unobservable inputs, the significance of the adjustment to the measurement of the individual derivative instruments would need to be considered in order to determine if categorisation in Level 2 or Level 3 was appropriate.

The following example from IFRS 13 illustrates how an entity might disclose, in tabular format, the fair value hierarchy category for each class of assets and liabilities measured at fair value at the end of each reporting period. [IFRS 13.IE60].

Example 14.25: Disclosure of assets measured at fair value and their categorisation in the fair value hierarchy

(£ in millions)		Fair value measurements at the end of the reporting period using:			
Description	31/12/X1	Quoted prices in active markets for identical assets (Level 1)	Significant other observable inputs (Level 2)	Significant unobservable inputs (Level 3)	Total gains (losses)
Recurring fair value measurements					
Trading equity securities[a]:					
Real estate industry	93	70	23		
Oil and gas industry	45	45			
Other	15	15			
Total trading equity securities	153	130	23		
Other equity securities[a]:					
Financial services industry	150	150			
Healthcare industry	163	110		53	
Energy industry	32			32	
Private equity fund investments[b]	25			25	
Other	15		15		
Total other equity securities	385	275		110	

(£ in millions)		Fair value measurements at the end of the reporting period using:			
Description	31/12/X1	Quoted prices in active markets for identical assets (Level 1)	Significant other observable inputs (Level 2)	Significant unobservable inputs (Level 3)	Total gains (losses)
Debt securities:					
Residential mortgage-backed securities	149		24	125	
Commercial mortgage-backed securities	50			50	
Collateralised debt obligations	35			35	
Risk-free government securities	85	85			
Corporate bonds	93	9	84		
Total debt securities	412	94	108	210	

Hedge fund investments:					
Equity long/short	55		55		
Global opportunities	35		35		
High-yield debt securities	90			90	
Total hedge fund investments	180		90	90	
Derivatives:					
Interest rate contracts	57		57		
Foreign exchange contracts	43		43		
Credit contracts	38			38	
Commodity futures contracts	78	78			
Commodity forward contracts	20		20		
Total derivatives	236	78	120	38	
Investment properties:					
Commercial – Asia	31			31	
Commercial – Europe	27			27	
Total investment properties	58			58	
Total recurring fair value measurements	1,424	577	341	506	
Non-recurring fair value measurements					
Assets held for sale[(c)]	26		26		(15)
Total non-recurring fair value measurements	26		26		(15)

(a) On the basis of its analysis of the nature, characteristics and risks of the securities, the entity has determined that presenting them by industry is appropriate.

(b) On the basis of its analysis of the nature, characteristics and risks of the investments, the entity has determined that presenting them as a single class is appropriate.

(c) In accordance with IFRS 5, assets held for sale with a carrying amount of £35 million were written down to their fair value of £26 million, less costs to sell of £6 million (or £20 million), resulting in a loss of £15 million, which was included in profit or loss for the period.

(Note: A similar table would be presented for liabilities unless another format is deemed more appropriate by the entity.)

In the above example, the gain or loss recognised during the period for assets and liabilities measured at fair value on a non-recurring basis is separately disclosed and discussed in the notes to the financial statements.

20.3.4 Transfers between hierarchy levels for recurring fair value measurements

IFRS 13 requires entities to disclose information regarding all transfers between fair value hierarchy levels (i.e. situations where an asset or liability was categorised within a different level in the fair value hierarchy in the previous reporting period). *[IFRS 13.93(c), 93(e)(iv)]*. However, this disclosure requirement only applies to assets and liabilities held at the end of the reporting period which are measured at fair value on a recurring basis. Information regarding transfers into or out of Level 3 is captured in the Level 3 reconciliation (discussed at 20.3.6 below) as these amounts are needed to roll forward Level 3 balances from the beginning to the end of the period being disclosed. The amounts of any transfers between Level 1 and Level 2 of the fair value hierarchy are also required to be disclosed. Regardless of the hierarchy levels involved, transfers into each level of the hierarchy are disclosed separately from transfers out of each level. That is, all transfers are required to be presented on a gross basis by hierarchy level, whether included in the Level 3 reconciliation or disclosed separately.

For all transfer amounts disclosed, an entity is required to discuss the reasons why the categorisation within the fair value hierarchy has changed (i.e. transferred between hierarchy levels). *[IFRS 13.93(c), 93(e)(iv)]*. Reasons might include the market for a particular asset or liability previously considered active (Level 1) becoming inactive (Level 2 or Level 3), or significant inputs used in a valuation technique that were previously unobservable (Level 3) becoming observable (Level 2) given transactions that were observed around the measurement date.

As discussed at 16.2.2 and 20.2 above, IFRS 13 also requires that entities disclose and consistently follow their policy for determining when transfers between fair value hierarchy levels are deemed to have occurred. That is, an entity's policy about the timing of recognising transfers into the hierarchy levels should be the same as the policy for recognising transfers out, and this policy should be used consistently from period to period. Paragraph 95 of IFRS 13 includes the following examples of potential policies: the actual date of the event or change in circumstances that caused the transfer, the beginning of the reporting period or the end of the reporting period. In practice, some variation of these approaches may also be used by entities. For example, some entities may use an intra-period approach using a transfer amount based on the fair value as at the month-end in which the transfer occurred, as opposed to the actual date within the month. *[IFRS 13.95]*. The following illustrative example demonstrates the differences between the three methods noted above.

Example 14.26: Comparison of policies for recognising transfers

Assume an entity acquires an asset at 31 December 20X1 for €1,000 that was categorised within Level 2 of the fair value hierarchy at year end 20X1 and throughout Q1 20X2. At the end of Q1 20X2, the fair value of the asset based on market observable information was €950, and, as such, the asset was excluded from the Level 3 reconciliation. During Q2 20X2, observable market information was no longer available, so the entity categorised the asset in Level 3 at the end of Q2 20X2. During Q2 20X2, the fair value of the asset decreased from €950 to €750, with €50 of the change in fair value arising subsequent to the time when market observable information was no longer available.

Under the three approaches described above, the Level 3 reconciliation for Q2 20X2 would be as follows.

	Transferred to Level 3 at:		
	Beginning of the period	Actual date	End of the period
Beginning fair value	–	–	–
Purchases, issuances and settlements	–	–	–
Transfers in	€950	€800	€750
Total losses	(€200)	(€50)	–
Ending fair value	€750	€750	€750

As previously noted, the disclosures under IFRS 13 are intended to provide information that enables users to identify the effects of fair value measurements that are more subjective in nature on reported earnings, and, thereby, enhance financial statement users' ability to make their own assessment regarding earnings quality. We believe that this objective is best met by considering the level of observability associated with the fair value measurement made at the end of the reporting period (i.e. the observability of the inputs used to determine fair value on the last day in the period). As such, while no specific approach is required under IFRS, we believe a beginning-of-period approach for recognising transfers provides greater transparency on the effect that unobservable inputs have on fair value measurements and reported earnings. Under this view, all changes in fair value that arise during the reporting period of the transfer are disclosed as a component of the Level 3 reconciliation.

While the 'actual date' approach more precisely captures the date on which a change in the observability of inputs occurred, its application can be more operationally complex. In addition, in our view, it does not necessarily provide more decision-useful information than the beginning-of-period approach. This is because, for a given period, the intra-period approach results in an allocation of the fair value changes between hierarchy levels that is inconsistent with the actual categorisation of the item as at the end of the reporting period. As such, the intra-period approach implies that a portion of the earnings recognised during the period is of a higher (or lower) quality solely because there was observable information regarding the value of the instrument at some point during the period.

To further illustrate this point, assume an entity acquires an investment in a private company in Q1 for €1,000. In the middle of Q2, the company completes an initial public offering that values the investment at €1,500. At the end of Q2, the fair value of the investment is €2,200 based on a quoted market price. Under the intra-period approach for the six-month period ended Q2, €500 would be included as an unrealised gain in the Level 3 reconciliation, despite the fact that the entire €1,200 unrealised gain recognised during the six-month period is supported by observable market information (i.e. a quoted price less cash paid).

Of the three alternatives, we believe the end-of-period approach is the least effective in achieving IFRS 13's disclosure objectives. Under this approach, the Level 3 reconciliation would not reflect any unrealised gains or losses for items that move from Level 2 to Level 3 during the reporting period.

20.3.5 Disclosure of valuation techniques and inputs

Entities are required to describe the valuation techniques and inputs used to measure the fair value of items categorised within Level 2 or Level 3 of the fair value hierarchy. In addition, entities are required to disclose instances where there has been a change in the valuation technique(s) used during the period, and the reason for making the change. As discussed at 20.3.5.A below, the standard also requires quantitative information about the significant unobservable inputs to be disclosed for Level 3 fair value measurements. *[IFRS 13.93(d)]*.

Importantly, the disclosures related to valuation techniques and inputs (including the requirement to disclose quantitative information about unobservable inputs) apply to both recurring and non-recurring fair value measurements. *[IFRS 13.93(d)]*.

20.3.5.A Significant unobservable inputs for Level 3 fair value measurements

For Level 3 measurements, IFRS 13 specifically requires that entities provide quantitative information about the significant unobservable inputs used in the fair value measurement. *[IFRS 13.93(d)]*. For example, an entity with asset-backed securities categorised within Level 3 would be required to quantitatively disclose the inputs used in its valuation models related to prepayment speed, probability of default, loss given default and discount rate (assuming these inputs were all unobservable and deemed to be significant to the valuation).

Consistent with all of the disclosures in IFRS 13, entities are required to present this information separately for each class of assets or liabilities based on the nature, characteristics and risks of their Level 3 measurements. *[IFRS 13.93]*. As such, we expect that entities will likely disclose both the range and weighted average of the unobservable inputs used across a particular class of Level 3 assets or liabilities. In addition, entities should assess whether the level of disaggregation at which this information is provided results in meaningful information to users, consistent with the objectives of IFRS 13.

In some situations, significant unobservable inputs may not be developed by the reporting entity itself, such as when an entity uses third-party pricing information without adjustment. In these instances, IFRS 13 states that an entity is not required to create quantitative information to comply with its disclosure requirements. However, when making these disclosures, entities cannot ignore information about significant unobservable inputs that is 'reasonably available'.

Determining whether information is 'reasonably available' will require judgement, and there may be some diversity in practice stemming from differences in entities' access to information and information vendors may be willing or able to provide. If the valuation has been developed, either by the entity or an external valuation expert at the direction of the entity, quantitative information about the significant unobservable inputs would be expected to be reasonably available and therefore should be disclosed. As a result, entities need to ensure any valuers they use provide them with sufficient information to make the required disclosures.

In contrast, when an entity receives price quotes or other valuation information from a third-party pricing service or broker, the specific unobservable inputs underlying this information may not always be reasonably available to the entity. While determining whether information is reasonably available in these instances will require judgement, we would expect entities to make good-faith efforts to obtain the information needed to meet the disclosure requirements in IFRS 13. In addition, some diversity in practice may stem from differences in entities' access to information and the nature of information that various vendors may be willing or able to provide. However, in all cases, any adjustments made by an entity to the pricing data received from a third party should be disclosed if these adjustments are not based on observable market data and are deemed to be significant to the overall measurement.

The following example from IFRS 13 illustrates the type of information an entity might provide to comply with the requirement to disclose quantitative information about Level 3 fair value measurements. *[IFRS 13.IE63]*. Extract 14.4 from BP p.l.c. and Extract 14.5 from Rio Tinto plc at 20.3.8.A below also illustrates this disclosure in relation to derivatives categorised within Level 3.

Example 14.27: Significant unobservable inputs (Level 3)

Quantitative information about fair value measurements using significant unobservable inputs (Level 3)				
(£ in millions) Description	Fair value at 31/12/X9	Valuation technique(s)	Unobservable input	Range (weighted average)
Other equity securities:				
Healthcare industry	53	Discounted cash flow	weighted average cost of capital	7%-16% (12.1%)
			long-term revenue growth rate	2%-5% (4.2%)
			long-term pre-tax operating margin	3%-20% (10.3%)
			discount for lack of marketability[a]	5%-20% (17%)
			control premium[a]	10%-30% (20%)
		Market comparable companies	EBITDA multiple[b]	10-13 (11.3)
			revenue multiple[b]	1.5-2.0 (1.7)
			discount for lack of marketability[a]	5%-20% (17%)
			control premium[a]	10%-30% (20%)
Energy industry	32	Discounted cash flow	weighted average cost of capital	8%-12% (11.1%)
			long-term revenue growth rate	3%-5.5% (4.2%)
			long-term pre-tax operating margin	7.5%-13% (9.2%)
			discount for lack of marketability[a]	5%-20% (10%)
			control premium[a]	10%-20% (12%)
		Market comparable companies	EBITDA multiple[b]	6.5-12 (9.5)
			revenue multiple[b]	1.0-3.0 (2.0)
			discount for lack of marketability[a]	5%-20% (10%)
			control premium[a]	10%-20% (12%)
Private equity fund investments(b)	25	Net asset value[c]	n/a	n/a
Debt securities:				
Residential mortgage-backed securities	125	Discounted cash flow	constant prepayment rate	3.5%-5.5% (4.5%)
			probability of default	5%-50% (10%)
			loss severity	40%-100% (60%)
Commercial mortgage-backed securities	50	Discounted cash flow	constant prepayment rate	3%-5% (4.1%)
			probability of default	2%-25% (5%)
			loss severity	10%-50% (20%)
Collateralised debt obligations	35	Consensus pricing	offered quotes	20-45
			comparability adjustments (%)	−10%-+15% (+5%)
Hedge fund investments:				
High-yield debt securities	90	Net asset value[c]	n/a	n/a
Derivatives:				
Credit contracts	38	Option model	annualised volatility of credit[d]	10%-20%
			counterparty credit risk[e]	0.5%-3.5%
			own credit risk[e]	0.3%-2.0%

(£ in millions) Description	Fair value at 31/12/X9	Valuation technique(s)	Unobservable input	Range (weighted average)
Investment properties:				
Commercial – Asia	31	Discounted cash flow	long-term net operating income margin	18%-32% (20%)
			cap rate	0.08-0.12 (0.10)
		Market comparable companies	price per square metre ($)	$3,000-$7,000 ($4,500)
Commercial – Europe	27	Discounted cash flow	long-term net operating income margin	15%-25% (18%)
			cap rate	0.06-0.10 (0.08)
		Market comparable companies	price per square metre (€)	€4,000-€12,000 (€8,500)

(a) Represents amounts used when the entity has determined that market participants would take into account these premiums and discounts when pricing the investments.
(b) Represents amounts used when the entity has determined that market participants would use such multiples when pricing the investments.
(c) The entity has determined that the reported net asset value represents fair value at the end of the reporting period.
(d) Represents the range of volatility curves used in the valuation analysis that the entity has determined market participants would use when pricing the contracts.
(e) Represents the range of the credit default swap curves used in the valuation analysis that the entity has determined market participants would use when pricing the contracts.

(Note: A similar table would be presented for liabilities unless another format is deemed more appropriate by the entity.)

20.3.6 Level 3 reconciliation

IFRS 13 requires a reconciliation (also referred to as the Level 3 roll-forward) of the beginning and ending balances for any recurring fair value measurements that utilise significant unobservable inputs (i.e. Level 3 inputs). Therefore, any asset or liability (measured at fair value on a recurring basis) that was determined to be a Level 3 measurement at either the beginning or the end of a reporting period would need to be considered in the Level 3 reconciliation.

To reconcile Level 3 balances for the period presented, entities must present the following information for each class of assets and liabilities:
- balance of Level 3 assets or liabilities (as at the beginning of the period);
- total gains or losses;
- purchases, sales, issues and settlements (presented separately);
- transfers in and/or out of Level 3 (presented separately); and
- balance of Level 3 assets or liabilities (as at the end of the period).

In addition, entities are required to separately present gains or losses included in earnings from those gains or losses recognised in other comprehensive income, and to describe in which line items these gains or losses are reported in profit or loss, or in other comprehensive income. To enhance the ability of financial statement users to assess an entity's quality of earnings, IFRS 13 also requires entities to separately disclose the amount of total gains and losses reported in profit or loss (for the period) that are attributable to changes in unrealised gains and losses for assets and liabilities categorised within Level 3 and are still held at the end of the reporting period. Effectively, this requires an entity to distinguish its unrealised gains and losses from its realised gains and losses for Level 3 measurements.

The following example from IFRS 13 illustrates how an entity could comply with the Level 3 reconciliation requirements. *[IFRS 13.IE61]*. Extract 14.4 from BP p.l.c. and Extract 14.5 from Rio Tinto plc at 20.3.8.A below also illustrates these disclosure requirements in relation to derivatives categorised within Level 3.

Example 14.28: **Reconciliation of fair value measurements categorised within Level 3 of the fair value hierarchy**

($ in millions)	Fair value measurements using significant unobservable inputs (Level 3)											
	Other equity securities			Debt securities			Hedge fund investments	Derivatives	Investment properties			
	Healthcare industry	Energy industry	Private equity fund	Residential mortgage-backed securities	Commercial mortgage-backed securities	Collateralised debt obligations	High-yield debt securities	Credit contracts	Asia	Europe	Total
Opening balance	49	28	20	105	39	25	145	30	28	26	495
Transfers into Level 3				(a)(b)60							60
Transfers out of Level 3				(b)(c)(5)							(5)
Total gains or losses for the period											
Included in profit or loss			5	(23)	(5)	(7)	7	5	3	1	(14)
Included in other comprehensive income	3	1									4
Purchases, issues, sales and settlements											
Purchases	1	3		16	17			18			55
Issues											
Sales				(12)			(62)				(74)
Settlements								(15)			(15)
Closing balance	53	32	25	125	50	35	90	38	31	27	506
Change in unrealised gains or losses for the period included in profit or loss for assets held at the end of the reporting period			5	(3)	(5)	(7)	(5)	2	3	1	(9)

(a) Transferred from Level 2 to Level 3 because of a lack of observable market data, resulting from a decrease in market activity for the securities.
(b) The entity's policy is to recognise transfers into and transfers out of Level 3 as at the date of the event or change in circumstances that caused the transfer.
(c) Transferred from Level 3 to Level 2 because observable market data became available for the securities.
(Note: A similar table would be presented for liabilities unless another format is deemed more appropriate by the entity.)

IFRS 13 also provides the following example to illustrate how an entity could comply with the requirements to separately disclose the amount of total gains and losses reported in profit or loss that are attributable to changes in unrealised gains and losses for assets and liabilities categorised within Level 3 and are still held at the end of the reporting period. [IFRS 13.IE62].

Example 14.29: Disclosure of gains and losses included in profit or loss for fair value measurements categorised within Level 3 of the fair value hierarchy

($ in millions)	Financial income	Non-financial income
Total gains or losses for the period included in profit or loss	(18)	4
Change in unrealised gains or losses for the period included in profit or loss for assets held at the end of the reporting period	(13)	4

(Note: A similar table would be presented for liabilities unless another format is deemed more appropriate by the entity.)

20.3.7 Disclosure of valuation processes for Level 3 measurements

Entities are required to describe the valuation processes used for fair value measurements categorised within Level 3 of the fair value hierarchy, whether on a recurring or non-recurring basis. This is illustrated in the extract from the financial statements of UBS Group AG below. The Boards decided to require these disclosures for Level 3 measurements because they believe this information, in conjunction with the other Level 3 disclosures, will help users assess the relative subjectivity of these measurements.

Extract 14.3: UBS Group AG (2019)

Notes to the UBS Group AG consolidated financial statements [Extract]

Note 24 Fair value measurement [Extract]

b) Valuation governance

UBS's fair value measurement and model governance framework includes numerous controls and other procedural safeguards that are intended to maximize the quality of fair value measurements reported in the financial statements. New products and valuation techniques must be reviewed and approved by key stakeholders from risk and finance control functions. Responsibility for the ongoing measurement of financial and non-financial instruments at fair value resides with the business divisions. In carrying out their valuation responsibilities, the businesses are required to consider the availability and quality of external market data and to provide justification and rationale for their fair value estimates.

Fair value estimates are validated by risk and finance control functions, which are independent of the business divisions. Independent price verification is performed by Finance through benchmarking the business divisions' fair value estimates with observable market prices and other independent sources. Controls and a governance framework are in place and are intended to ensure the quality of third-party pricing sources where used. For instruments where valuation models are used to determine fair value, independent valuation and model control groups within Finance and Risk Control evaluate UBS's models on a regular basis, including valuation and model input parameters as well as pricing. As a result of the valuation controls employed, valuation adjustments may be made to the business divisions' estimates of fair value to align with independent market data and the relevant accounting standard.

IFRS 13 provides an example of how an entity could comply with the requirements to disclose the valuation processes for its Level 3 fair value measurements, suggesting this disclosure might include the following:

(i) for the group within the entity that decides the entity's valuation policies and procedures:
- its description;
- to whom that group reports; and
- the internal reporting procedures in place (e.g. whether and, if so, how pricing, risk management or audit committees discuss and assess the fair value measurements);

(ii) the frequency and methods for calibration, back testing and other testing procedures of pricing models;

(iii) the process for analysing changes in fair value measurements from period to period;

(iv) how the entity determined that third-party information, such as broker quotes or pricing services, used in the fair value measurement was developed in accordance with the IFRS; and

(v) the methods used to develop and substantiate the unobservable inputs used in a fair value measurement. *[IFRS 13.IE65]*.

20.3.8 Sensitivity of Level 3 measurements to changes in significant unobservable inputs

IFRS 13 requires entities to provide a narrative description of the sensitivity of recurring Level 3 fair value measurements to changes in the unobservable inputs used, if changing those inputs would significantly affect the fair value measurement. However, except in relation to financial instruments (see 20.3.8.A below) there is no requirement to quantify the extent of the change to the unobservable input, or the quantitative effect of this change on the measurement (i.e. only discuss directional change).

At a minimum, the unobservable inputs quantitatively disclosed based on the requirements described at 20.3.5 above must be addressed in the narrative description. In addition, entities are required to describe any interrelationships between the unobservable inputs and discuss how they might magnify or mitigate the effect of changes on the fair value measurement.

This disclosure, combined with the quantitative disclosure of significant unobservable inputs, is designed to enable financial statement users to understand the directional effect of certain inputs on an item's fair value and to evaluate whether the entity's views about individual unobservable inputs differ from their own. The Boards believe these disclosures can provide meaningful information to users who are not familiar with the pricing models and valuation techniques used to measure a particular class of assets or liabilities (e.g. complex structured instruments).

The following example from IFRS 13 illustrates how an entity could comply with the disclosure requirements related to the sensitivity of Level 3 measurements to changes in significant unobservable inputs. *[IFRS 13.IE66].*

Example 14.30: Narrative description of sensitivity to significant unobservable inputs

The significant unobservable inputs used in the fair value measurement of the entity's residential mortgage-backed securities are prepayment rates, probability of default and loss severity in the event of default. Significant increases (decreases) in any of those inputs in isolation would result in a significantly lower (higher) fair value measurement. Generally, a change in the assumption used for the probability of default is accompanied by a directionally similar change in the assumption used for the loss severity and a directionally opposite change in the assumption used for prepayment rates.

We note that the above example is fairly general in nature, because no numbers relating to how the unobservable inputs might be changed, or how such a change would affect fair value, are required to be disclosed. However, in making this disclosure we would encourage entities to avoid over-generalisations that may not hold true in all cases.

20.3.8.A Quantitative sensitivity of Level 3 measurements of financial instruments to changes in significant unobservable inputs

In addition to the qualitative sensitivity analysis, IFRS 13 requires quantitative sensitivity analysis for Level 3 fair value measurements of financial assets and financial liabilities (as noted at 20.3.1.B above, this is only for recurring fair value measurements), which is generally consistent with the existing disclosure requirement in IFRS 7 (see Chapter 54). If changing one or more of the unobservable inputs to reflect reasonably possible alternative assumptions would change fair value significantly, an entity must disclose the fact and the effect of those changes.

The entity must also disclose how the effect of a change to reflect a reasonably possible alternative assumption was calculated. For the purpose of this disclosure requirement, significance is judged with respect to profit or loss, and total assets or total liabilities, or, when changes in fair value are recognised in other comprehensive income and total equity.

The following extracts from BP p.l.c. and Rio Tinto plc illustrates the disclosures required for Level 3 measurements.

Extract 14.4: BP p.l.c. (2014)

Notes on financial statements [Extract]

28. Derivative financial instruments [Extract]

Level 3 derivatives

The following table shows the changes during the year in the net fair value of derivatives held for trading purposes within level 3 of the fair value hierarchy.

					$ million
	Oil price	Natural gas price	Power price	Other	Total
Net fair value of contracts at 1 January 2014	(18)	313	86	475	856
Gains recognized in the income statement	350	152	141	94	737
Settlements	(86)	(56)	(13)	(180)	(335)
Transfers out of level 3	–	(228)	–	–	(228)
Net fair value of contracts at 31 December 2014	246	181	214	389	1,030

					$ million
	Oil price	Natural gas price	Power price	Other	Total
Net fair value of contracts at 1 January 2013	105	304	(43)	71	437
Gains (losses) recognized in the income statement	(47)	62	81	–	96
Purchases	110	1	–	–	111
New contracts	–	–	–	475	475
Settlements	(143)	(52)	10	(71)	(256)
Transfers out of level 3	(43)	(1)	36	–	(8)
Exchange adjustments	–	(1)	2	–	1
Net fair value of contracts at 31 December 2013	(18)	313	86	475	856

The amount recognized in the income statement for the year relating to level 3 held for trading derivatives still held at 31 December 2014 was a $456 million gain (2013 $110 million gain related to derivatives still held at 31 December 2013).

The most significant gross assets and liabilities categorized in level 3 of the fair value hierarchy are US natural gas contracts. At 31 December 2014, the gross US natural gas price instruments dependent on inputs at level 3 of the fair value hierarchy were an asset of $586 million and liability of $526 million (net fair value of $60 million), with $126 million, net, valued using level 2 inputs. US natural gas price derivatives are valued using observable market data for maturities up to 60 months in basis locations that trade at a premium or discount to the NYMEX Henry Hub price, and using internally developed price curves based on economic forecasts for periods beyond that time. The significant unobservable inputs for fair value measurements categorized within level 3 of the fair value hierarchy for the year ended 31 December 2014 are presented below.

	Unobservable inputs	Range $/mmBtu	Weighted average $/mmBtu
Natural gas price contracts	Long-dated market price	3.44-6.39	4.64

If the natural gas prices after 2019 were 10% higher (lower), this would result in a decrease (increase) in derivative assets of $85 million, and decrease (increase) in derivative liabilities of $64 million, and a net decrease (increase) in profit before tax of $21 million.

Extract 14.5: Rio Tinto plc (2019)

Notes to the 2019 financial statements [Extract]

30 Financial instruments and risk management [Extract]

C (b) Level 3 financial assets and financial liabilities

The table below shows the reconciliation of our level 3 financial assets and financial liabilities.

	2019 Level 3 financial assets and financial liabilities US$m	2018 Level 3 financial assets and financial liabilities US$m
Opening balance	637	(7)
Adjustment from transition to IFRS 9	–	19
Currency translation adjustments	(1)	(23)
Total realised (losses)/gains included in:		
– net operating costs	(7)	9
Total unrealised (losses)/gains included in:		
– net operating costs	(254)	375
Total unrealised gains transferred into other comprehensive income through cash flow hedges	28	181
Additions	1	67
Disposals/maturity of financial instruments	(21)	(6)
Transfers	–	22
Closing balance	**383**	**637**
Total (losses)/gains for the year included in the income statement for assets and liabilities held at year end	(263)	346

Sensitivity analysis in respect of level 3 derivatives

To value the long-term aluminium embedded derivatives, which had a fair value of US$120 million at 31 December 2019 (2018: US$338 million), we use unobservable inputs when the term of the derivative extends beyond observable market prices. In 2019, changing the level 3 inputs to reasonably possible alternative assumptions does not change the fair value significantly, taking into account the expected remaining term of contracts. In 2018 our most significant assumption involved flat lining aluminium prices beyond the market forward curve and increasing the price by expected inflation up to the date of expiry of each contract (market prices used in 2018:US$2,426 per metric tonne in 2029 to US$2,507 in 2030). The effect of a 10% increase in this pricing assumption was a US$22 million decrease in carrying value. A 10% decrease in long-term metal pricing assumptions resulted in a US$14 million increase in carrying value.

We also have royalty receivables, with a carrying value of US$124 million (2018: US$158 million), arising from the sale of our coal assets in prior periods. These are classified as 'Other investments, including loans' within the balance sheet. The fair values are determined using level 3 unobservable inputs.

The main unobservable input is the long-term coal price used over the life of the royalty receivable. A 15% increase in the coal spot price would result in a US$214 million increase (2018: US$181 million increase) in the carrying value. A 15% decrease in the coal spot price would result in a US$57 million decrease (2018: US$95 million decrease) in the carrying value. We have used a 15% assumption to calculate our exposure as it represents the annual coal price movement that we deem to be reasonably probable (on an annual basis over the long run).

20.3.9 Highest and best use

As discussed at 10 above, if the highest and best use of a non-financial asset differs from its current use, entities are required to disclose this fact and why the non-financial asset is being used in a manner that differs from its highest and best use. *[IFRS 13.93(i)]*. The Boards believe this information is useful to financial statement users who project expected cash flows based on how an asset is actually being used.

20.4 Disclosures for unrecognised fair value measurements

For each class of assets and liabilities not measured at fair value in the statement of financial position, but for which the fair value is disclosed (e.g. financial assets carried at amortised cost whose fair values are required to be disclosed in accordance with IFRS 7), entities are required to disclose the following:

(a) the level of the fair value hierarchy within which the fair value measurements are categorised in their entirety (Level 1, 2 or 3);

(b) if categorised within Level 2 or Level 3 of the fair value hierarchy:
 (i) a description of the valuation technique(s) used in the fair value measurement;
 (ii) a description of the inputs used in the fair value measurement;
 (iii) if there has been a change in valuation technique (e.g. changing from a market approach to an income approach or the use of an additional valuation technique):
  - the change; and
  - the reason(s) for making it; and

(c) for non-financial assets, if the highest and best use differs from its current use, an entity must disclose that fact and why the non-financial asset is being used in a manner that differs from its highest and best use. *[IFRS 13.97]*.

None of the other IFRS 13 disclosures are required for assets and liabilities whose fair value is only disclosed. For example, even though certain fair value disclosures are categorised within Level 3, entities are not required to provide quantitative information about the unobservable inputs used in their valuation because these items are not measured at fair value in the statement of financial position.

20.5 Disclosures regarding liabilities issued with an inseparable third-party credit enhancement

IFRS 13 includes an additional disclosure requirement for liabilities measured at fair value that have been issued with an inseparable third-party credit enhancement (see 11.3.1 above for further discussion regarding these instruments). The standard requires that an issuer disclose the existence of the third-party credit enhancement and whether it is reflected in the fair value measurement of the liability. *[IFRS 13.98]*.

20.6 Proposed amendments resulting from the Targeted Standards-level Review of Disclosures project

The Targeted Standards-level Review of Disclosures project is being conducted by the IASB as a specific response to certain problems that users had identified with IFRS disclosures, namely: not enough relevant information; too much irrelevant information; and ineffective communication of the information provided. At its July 2018 meeting, the Board selected IFRS 13 as one of the two standards (the other was IAS 19) on which to test the draft guidance for the Board to use when developing and drafting disclosure objectives and requirements in future.

The Board, at their September 2019 meeting, decided to propose amendments to the disclosure objective of IFRS 13. This included 'a high-level, catch-all disclosure objective requiring an entity to:

a. disclose information that enables users of financial statements to evaluate an entity's exposure to uncertainties associated with its fair value measurements. The disclosed information should, in particular, enable users to understand: the significance of assets, liabilities and of an entity's own equity instruments measured at fair value; how the fair value measurements have been determined; and how changes in those measurements affect the entity's financial statements

b. consider the level of detail necessary to satisfy the specific disclosure objectives ... and ensure that any useful information about the entity's fair value measurements is not obscured by a large amount of insignificant detail'.[29]

The proposal is also expected to include specific disclosure objectives that would require an entity to disclose information that enables users of financial statements to:

- understand the amount, nature and other characteristics of the classes of assets, liabilities and an entity's own equity instruments within each level of the fair value hierarchy;
- understand the significant techniques and inputs used in deriving its fair value measurements;
- understand the significant drivers of changes in the fair value measurements from the beginning of a reporting period to the end of that period; and
- understand the range of reasonably possible fair values at the reporting date for the assets, liabilities and an entity's own equity instruments measured at fair value.[30]

The Board, at their November 2019 and February 2020 meetings, decided to propose amendments to the items of information that could be used to meet those objectives. The Board's tentative conclusions are outlined in Figure 14.11 below.[31]

The Board, at their June 2020 meeting, decided to allow 180 days for comment on an exposure draft of its proposed amendments and is expected to publish its exposure draft in March 2021.[32] The exposure draft is expected to include proposed amendments to disclosures in IFRS 13 and IAS 19, as well as a request for stakeholder feedback on the Board's overall process.

Figure 14.11: *IASB's tentative decisions on potential items of information that entities might use to meet the soon-to-be proposed disclosure objectives*

Disclosure objectives expected to be proposed	Items of information expected to be proposed
An entity shall disclose information that enables users of financial statements to understand the amount, nature and other characteristics of the classes of assets, liabilities and an entity's own equity instruments within each level of the fair value hierarchy	*For assets, liabilities and own equity instruments measured at fair value in the statement of financial position* 1. An entity shall disclose the fair value measurements at the end of the reporting period for recurring and non-recurring measurements by the level of the fair value hierarchy within which those measurements are categorised in their entirety. 2. While not mandatory, the following may enable an entity to meet the objective for recurring and non-recurring fair value measurements: (a) a description of the nature, characteristics and risks of the assets, liabilities and own equity instruments in each level of the fair value hierarchy (or a cross-reference to where that information is disclosed). (b) a description of any inseparable third-party credit enhancement and whether such enhancement is reflected in the fair value measurement. *For assets and liabilities not measured at fair value but for which fair value is disclosed* 1. An entity shall disclose the fair value measurements at the end of the reporting period by level of the fair value hierarchy within which those measurements are categorised in their entirety. 2. While not mandatory, a description of the nature, characteristics and risks of the assets, liabilities and own equity instruments (or a cross-reference to where that information is disclosed) may enable an entity to meet the objective.
An entity shall disclose information that enables users of financial statements to understand the significant techniques and inputs used in deriving its fair value measurements	1. An entity shall disclose the fact if it makes an accounting policy decision to use the valuation exception in paragraph 48 of IFRS 13 for financial assets and financial liabilities. 2. While not mandatory, the following may enable an entity to meet the objective for recurring and non-recurring fair value measurements: (a) a description of the significant valuation techniques used in the fair value measurement. (b) a description of any change in valuation technique and the reason(s) for making it. (c) a description of the significant inputs used in the fair value measurement, for example, quantitative information or narrative information. (d) a description of the fact that and reasons why the highest and best use of a non-financial asset differs from its current use.

| An entity shall disclose information that enables users of financial statements to understand the drivers of change in the fair value measurements from the beginning of a reporting period to the end of that period | 1. An entity shall disclose a reconciliation from the opening to the closing balances of recurring fair value measurements classified in Level 3 of the fair value hierarchy.
2. While not mandatory, the following may enable an entity to meet the objective for recurring fair value measurements:
  (a) any explanation of significant drivers of change in fair value measurements – other than those classified in Level 3 of the fair value hierarchy
  (b) the reasons for any transfers between levels of the fair value hierarchy during the period and the entity's policy for determining when transfers are deemed to have occurred.

Examples of drivers of changes include but are not limited to:
  (a) the amounts of any transfers between levels of the fair value hierarchy.
  (b) total gains or losses for the period recognised in profit or loss, and the line item(s) in profit or loss in which those gains or losses are recognised.
  (c) total gains or losses for the period in (b) above included in profit or loss that is attributable to the change in unrealised gains or losses, and the line item(s) in profit or loss in which those unrealised gains or losses are recognised.
  (d) total gains or losses for the period recognised in other comprehensive income, and the line item(s) in profit or loss in which those gains or losses are recognised.
  (e) purchases, sales, issues and settlements.
  (f) effect of foreign exchange rate differences. |
| An entity shall disclose information that enables users of financial statements to understand the reasonably possible fair values at the reporting date for the assets, liabilities and an entity's own equity instruments measured at fair value | While not mandatory, the following may enable an entity to meet the objective for recurring fair value measurements:
1. a description of the uncertainty caused by the use of significant inputs if those inputs could have reasonably been different at the reporting date and resulted in a significantly higher or lower fair value measurement.
2. the range of possible fair values reflecting the higher and lower fair value measurement using the reasonably possible alternative inputs at the reporting date.
3. a description of interrelationships between inputs used in fair value measurement and how they magnify or mitigate the effect of changes in inputs on fair value measurement.
4. how the effect of a change to reflect reasonably possible alternative inputs was calculated. |

21 APPLICATION GUIDANCE – PRESENT VALUE TECHNIQUES

This section focuses on the application guidance in IFRS 13 regarding the use of present value techniques to estimate fair value.

21.1 General principles for use of present value techniques

A present value technique is an application of the income approach, which is one of the three valuation approaches prescribed by IFRS 13. Valuation techniques under the income approach, such as present value techniques or option pricing models, convert expected future amounts to a single present amount. That is, a present value technique uses the projected future cash flows of an asset or liability and discounts those cash flows at a rate of return commensurate with the risk(s) associated with those cash flows. Present value techniques, such as discounted cash flow analyses, are frequently used to estimate the fair value of business entities, non-financial assets and non-financial liabilities, but are also useful for valuing financial instruments that do not trade in active markets.

The standard does not prescribe the use of a single specific present value technique, nor does it limit the use of present value techniques to those discussed. The selection of a present value technique will depend on facts and circumstances specific to the asset or liability being measured at fair value and the availability of sufficient data. *[IFRS 13.B12]*.

The application guidance in IFRS 13 regarding the use of present value techniques specifically focuses on three techniques: a discount rate adjustment technique and two methods of the expected cash flow (expected present value) technique. These approaches are summarised in the following table.

Figure 14.12:   Comparison of present value techniques described in IFRS 13

	Discount rate adjustment technique (see 21.3 below)	Expected present value technique	
		Method 1 (see 21.4 below)	Method 2 (see 21.4 below)
Nature of cash flows	Conditional cash flows – may be contractual or promised or the most likely cash flows	Expected cash flows	Expected cash flows
Cash flows based on probability weighting?	No	Yes	Yes
Cash flows adjusted for certainty?	No	Yes – cash risk premium is deducted. Cash flows represent a certainty-equivalent cash flow	No
Cash flows adjusted for other market risk?	No	Yes	Yes – to the extent not already captured in the discount rate
Discount rate adjusted for the uncertainty inherent in the cash flows?	Yes – uses an observed or estimated market rate of return, which includes adjustment for the possible variation in cash flows.	No – already captured in the cash flows	No – already captured in the cash flows
Discount rate adjusted for the premium a market participant would require to accept the uncertainty?	Yes	No – represents time value of money only (i.e. the risk-free rate is used)	Yes – represents the expected rate of return (i.e. the risk-free rate is adjusted to include the risk premium)

Additional considerations when applying present value techniques to measuring the fair value of a liability and an entity's own equity instrument not held by other parties as assets are discussed at 11 above. The Board conducted a research project on discount rates used in IFRS Standards and published their findings in February 2019. In that summary they noted that the output from the research would be used as an input for the Targeted Standard-level Review of Disclosures project for present values measures which includes IFRS 13 (see 20.6 above).[33]

21.2 The components of a present value measurement

Present value measurements use future cash flows or values to estimate amounts in the present, using a discount rate. Present value techniques can vary in complexity depending on the facts and circumstances of the item being measured. Nevertheless, for the purpose of measuring fair value in accordance with IFRS 13, the standard requires a present value technique to capture all the following elements from the perspective of market participants at the measurement date:

- an estimate of future cash flows for the asset or liability being measured;
- expectations about the uncertainty inherent in the future cash flows (i.e. the possible variations in the amount and timing of the cash flows);
- the time value of money – represented by a risk-free interest rate. That is, the rate on risk-free monetary assets that have maturity dates (or durations) that coincide with the period covered by the cash flows and pose neither uncertainty in timing nor risk of default to the holder;
- a risk premium (i.e. the price for bearing the uncertainty inherent in the cash flows);
- other factors that market participants would take into account in the circumstances; and
- for a liability, the non-performance risk relating to that liability, including the entity's (i.e. the obligor's) own credit risk. *[IFRS 13.B13]*.

Since present value techniques may differ in how they capture these elements, IFRS 13 sets out the following general principles that govern the application of any present value technique used to measure fair value:

(a) both cash flows and discount rates should:
- reflect assumptions that market participants would use when pricing the asset or liability;
- take into account only the factors attributable to the asset or liability being measured; and
- have internally consistent assumptions.

    For example, if the cash flows include the effect of inflation (i.e. nominal cash flows), they would be discounted at a rate that includes the effect of inflation, for example, a rate built off the nominal risk-free interest rate. If cash flows exclude the effect of inflation (i.e. real cash flows), they should be discounted at a rate that excludes the effect of inflation. Similarly, post-tax and pre-tax cash flows should be discounted at a rate consistent with those cash flows; and

(b) discount rates should also:

- be consistent with the underlying economic factors of the currency in which the cash flows are denominated; and
- reflect assumptions that are consistent with those assumptions inherent in the cash flows.

This principle is intended to avoid double-counting or omitting the effects of risk factors. For example, a discount rate that reflects non-performance (credit) risk is appropriate if using contractual cash flows of a loan (i.e. a discount rate adjustment technique – see 21.3 below). The same rate would not be appropriate when using probability-weighted cash flows (i.e. an expected present value technique – see 21.4 below) because the expected cash flows already reflect assumptions about the uncertainty in future defaults. *[IFRS 13.B14]*.

21.2.1 Time value of money

The objective of a present value technique is to convert future cash flows into a present amount (i.e. a value as at the measurement date). Therefore, time value of money is a fundamental element of any present value technique. *[IFRS 13.B13(c)]*. A basic principle in finance theory, time value of money holds that 'a dollar today is worth more than a dollar tomorrow', because the dollar today can be invested and earn interest immediately. Therefore, the discount rate in a present value technique must capture, at a minimum, the time value of money. For example, a discount rate equal to the risk-free rate of interest encompasses only the time value element of a present value technique. If the risk-free rate is used as a discount rate, the expected cash flows must be adjusted into certainty-equivalent cash flows to capture any uncertainty associated with the item being measured and the compensation market participants would require for this uncertainty.

21.2.2 Risk and uncertainty in a present value technique

At its core, the concept of value measures expected rewards against the risks of realising those rewards. Present value techniques implicitly contain uncertainty as they generally deal with estimates rather than known amounts. In many cases, both the amount and timing of the cash flows are uncertain. The standard notes that even contractually fixed amounts are uncertain if there is risk of default. *[IFRS 13.B15]*.

Market participants generally require compensation for taking on the uncertainty inherent in the cash flows of an asset or a liability. This compensation is known as a risk premium. IFRS 13 states that in order to faithfully represent fair value, a present value technique should include a risk premium. The standard acknowledges that determining the appropriate risk premium might be difficult. However, the degree of difficulty alone is not a sufficient reason to exclude a risk premium if market participants would demand one. *[IFRS 13.B16]*.

Depending on the present value technique used, risk may be incorporated in the cash flows or in the discount rate. However, identical risks should not be captured in both the cash flows and the discount rate in the same valuation analysis. For example, if the probability of default and loss given default for a liability are already incorporated in the discount rate (i.e. a risk-adjusted discount rate), the projected cash flows should not be further adjusted for the expected losses.

The present value techniques discussed in the application guidance to IFRS 13 differ in how they adjust for risk and in the type of cash flows they use.

- The discount rate adjustment technique uses a risk-adjusted discount rate and contractual, promised or most likely cash flows (see 21.3 below).
- Method 1 of the expected present value technique uses cash certain equivalent cash flows and a risk-free rate (see 21.4 below).
- Method 2 of the expected present value technique uses expected cash flows that are not risk-adjusted and a discount rate adjusted to include the risk premium that market participants require. That rate is different from the rate used in the discount rate adjustment technique (see 21.4 below). *[IFRS 13.B17]*.

If the risks are accounted for fully and appropriately, the three present value techniques noted above should all produce an identical fair value measurement, regardless of whether risk is captured in the cash flows or the discount rate (see 21.4.1 below for a numerical example illustrating this point).

21.3 Discount rate adjustment technique

The discount rate adjustment technique attempts to capture all of the risk associated with the item being measured in the discount rate and is most commonly used to value assets and liabilities with contractual payments, such as debt instruments. This technique uses a single set of cash flows from the range of possible estimated amounts and discounts those cash flows using a rate that reflects all of the risk related to the cash flows.

According to the standard, the cash flows may be contractual or promised or the most likely cash flows. In all cases, those cash flows are conditional upon the occurrence of specified events. For example, contractual or promised cash flows for a bond are conditional on the event of no default by the debtor. *[IFRS 13.B18]*.

The discount rate is derived from observable rates of return for comparable assets and liabilities that are traded in the market and incorporates the following:

- the risk-free interest rate;
- market participants' expectations about possible variations in the amount or timing of the cash flows;
- the price for bearing the uncertainty inherent in these cash flows (or risk premium); and
- other risk factors specific to the asset or liability.

As such, under this technique the cash flows are discounted at an observed or estimated market rate appropriate for such conditional cash flows (that is, a market rate of return).

The discount rate adjustment technique requires an analysis of market data for comparable assets or liabilities. Comparability is established by considering:

- the nature of the cash flows – for example, whether the cash flows are contractual or non-contractual and whether the cash flows are likely to respond similarly to changes in economic conditions; and
- other factors, such as credit standing, collateral, duration, restrictive covenants and liquidity. *[IFRS 13.B19]*.

Alternatively, if a single comparable asset or liability does not fairly reflect the risk inherent in the cash flows of the asset or liability being measured, it may be possible to derive a discount rate using a 'build-up' approach. That is, the entity should use data for several comparable assets or liabilities in conjunction with the risk-free yield curve. Example 14.31 at 21.3.1 below illustrates this further.

If the discount rate adjustment technique is applied to fixed receipts or payments, the adjustment for any risk inherent in the cash flows is included in the discount rate. In some applications of the discount rate adjustment technique to cash flows that are not fixed receipts or payments, an entity may need to make an adjustment to the cash flows to achieve comparability with the observed asset or liability from which the discount rate is derived. *[IFRS 13.B22]*.

Although IFRS 13 does not prescribe when a particular present value technique should be used, the extent of market data available for a particular type of asset or liability will influence when use of the discount rate adjustment technique is appropriate. Paragraph B19 of IFRS 13 states that the 'discount rate adjustment technique requires an analysis of market data for comparable assets or liabilities'. *[IFRS 13.B19]*. Therefore, certain assets and liabilities may not lend themselves to the use of the discount rate adjustment technique, even though it may be possible to derive discount rates using market data from several comparable items when no single observable rate of return reflects the risk inherent in the item being measured.

The most challenging aspect of applying this technique is the identification of market observable rates of return that appropriately capture the risk inherent in the asset or liability being measured. Understanding the various risk factors associated with certain types of assets and liabilities is not always easy and quantifying the effect of these factors is even more difficult. However, it may be helpful to deconstruct a discount rate into its component parts to understand what risks are being considered; beginning with the risk-free rate, which represents the time value of money. In addition to the risk-free rate, entities should consider credit or non-performance risk if the subject asset or liability requires performance in the future (including, but not limited to, a cash payment). For example, in the case of a financial asset, the discount rate would include compensation required by market participants to assume the risk that the counterparty will be unable to fulfil its obligation. Not all discount rates require an explicit adjustment for credit (or non-performance) risk. Equity interests, for example, may assume perpetual residual cash flows from the operations of a business, rather than a contractual future payment. In this case, an additional component of risk is captured through an equity risk premium, instead of a credit risk adjustment. The long-term incremental rate of return of equity interests over long-term risk-free interest rates may generally represent an identifiable component of risk.

When applying the discount rate adjustment technique, the credit spread (above the risk-free rate) will implicitly include assumptions about probabilities of default and losses given default without requiring an adjustment to the projected cash flows used in the analysis. However, a credit adjusted risk-free rate may not sufficiently capture all the risk related to the subject asset or liability. Depending on facts and circumstances of the item being measured, the observable rate of return should also capture other potential variability with respect to the timing and amount of the cash flows (e.g. potential variability due to prepayment risk for financial instruments such as mortgage backed securities) and the price for bearing such uncertainty (risk premium).

In addition, when assessing discount rates, it is important to keep in mind the exit price objective of a fair value measurement in IFRS 13. Because the discount rate represents the rate of return required by market participants in the current market, it should also incorporate factors such as illiquidity and the current risk appetite of market participants.

21.3.1 Illustrative example of the discount rate adjustment technique

The following example from IFRS 13 illustrates how a build-up approach is applied when using the discount rate adjustment technique. *[IFRS 13.B20-21].*

Example 14.31: Discount rate adjustment technique

Assume that Asset A is a contractual right to receive CU 800 in one year (i.e. there is no timing uncertainty). There is an established market for comparable assets, and information about those assets, including price information, is available. Of those comparable assets:

Asset B is a contractual right to receive CU 1,200 in one year and has a market price of CU 1,083. Therefore, the implied annual rate of return (i.e. a one-year market rate of return) is 10.8% [(CU 1,200 ÷ CU1,083) – 1].

Asset C is a contractual right to receive CU 700 in two years and has a market price of CU 566. Therefore, the implied annual rate of return (i.e. a two-year market rate of return) is 11.2% [(CU 700 ÷ CU 566)$^{0.5}$ – 1].

All three assets are comparable with respect to risk (i.e. dispersion of possible payoffs and credit).

(i) *Comparability based nature of the cash flows and other factors*

On the basis of the timing of the contractual payments to be received for Asset A relative to the timing for Asset B and Asset C (i.e. one year for Asset B versus two years for Asset C), Asset B is deemed more comparable to Asset A. Using the contractual payment to be received for Asset A (CU 800) and the one-year market rate derived from Asset B (10.8%), the fair value of Asset A is CU 722 (CU 800 ÷ 1.108).

(ii) *Using the build-up approach*

In the absence of available market information for Asset B, the one-year market rate could be derived from Asset C using the build-up approach. In that case the two-year market rate indicated by Asset C (11.2%) would be adjusted to a one-year market rate using the term structure of the risk-free yield curve. Additional information and analysis might be required to determine whether the risk premiums for one-year and two-year assets are the same. If it is determined that the risk premiums for one-year and two-year assets are not the same, the two-year market rate of return would be further adjusted for that effect.

As evidenced in the example above, using a build-up approach requires that market data for comparable assets be available. In addition, when applying the build-up approach, significant judgement may be required in determining comparability between the item being measured and the available benchmarks, as well as quantifying the appropriate adjustments necessary to account for any differences that may exist between the item being measured and the applicable benchmark (e.g. differences in credit risks, nature and timing of the cash flows, etc.).

21.4 Expected present value technique

The expected present value technique is typically used in the valuation of business entities, assets and liabilities with contingent or conditional payouts and items for which discount rates cannot be readily implied from observable transactions.

This technique uses, as a starting point, a set of cash flows that represent the probability-weighted average of all possible future cash flows (i.e. the expected cash flows). Unlike the cash flows used in the discount rate adjustment technique (i.e. contractual, promised or most likely amounts), expectations about possible variations in the amount and/or timing of the cash flows are explicitly incorporated in the projection of the expected cash flows themselves, rather than solely in the discount rate. *[IFRS 13.B23].*

The application guidance in IFRS 13 identifies two types of risk, based on portfolio theory:

(a) *unsystematic (diversifiable) risk* – the risk specific to a particular asset or liability; and

(b) *systematic (non-diversifiable) risk* – the common risk shared by an asset or a liability with the other items in a diversified portfolio (i.e. market risk). *[IFRS 13.B24].*

According to portfolio theory, in a market in equilibrium, market participants will be compensated only for bearing the systematic risk inherent in the cash flows. If the market is inefficient or is out of equilibrium, other forms of return or compensation might be available.

While, in theory, all possible future cash flows are meant to be considered, in practice, a discrete number of scenarios are often used to capture the probability distribution of potential cash flows.

- The number of possible outcomes to be considered will generally depend on the characteristics of the specific asset or liability being measured. For example, the outcome of a contingency may be binary, therefore, only two possible outcomes need be considered. In contrast, certain complex financial instruments are valued using option pricing models, such as Monte Carlo simulations, that generate thousands of possible outcomes.
- Estimating the probability distribution of potential outcomes requires judgement and will depend on the nature of the item being measured.

Assuming the entity's use of the asset is consistent with that of market participants, an entity might look to its own historical performance, current and expected market environments (including expectations of volatility) and budgetary considerations to develop expectations about future cash flows and appropriate weightings. However, as discussed at 19.1 above, the use of an entity's own data can only be a starting point when measuring fair value. Adjustments may be needed to ensure that the measurement is consistent with market participant assumptions. For example, synergies that can be realised by the entity should not be considered unless they would similarly be realised by market participants.

The concept of a risk premium is just as important under an expected present value technique as it is under the discount rate adjustment technique. The use of probability-weighted cash flows under an expected present value technique does not remove the need to consider a market risk premium when estimating fair value. While 'expected cash flows' capture the uncertainty in the amount and timing of the future cash flows, the probability weighting does not include the compensation market participants would demand for bearing this uncertainty. For example, assume Asset A is a contractual right to receive CU 10,000. Asset B has a payout that is conditional upon the toss of a coin: if 'heads', Asset B pays CU 20,000; and if 'tails' it pays nothing. Assuming no risk of default, both assets have an expected value of CU 10,000 (i.e. CU 10,000 × 100% for Asset A, and CU 20,000 × 50% + CU 0 × 50% for Asset B). However, risk-averse market participants would find Asset A more valuable than Asset B, as the cash-certain payout of CU 10,000 for Asset A is less risky than the expected cash flow of CU 10,000 for Asset B.

Although the variability in the cash flows of Asset B has been appropriately captured by probability-weighting all the possible cash flows (i.e. there is no subjectivity involved in the determination of the probability weighting in the simplified example since the payout is based on a coin toss), Asset B's expected value does not capture the compensation market participants would require for bearing the uncertainty in the cash flows. As such, all else being equal, the price for Asset B would be lower than the price for Asset A. That is, the required rate of return for Asset B would be higher than that for Asset A, in order to compensate the holder for the incremental risk in Asset B's cash flows (relative to Asset A).

21.4.1 Expected present value technique – method 1 and method 2

The standard describes two methods of the expected present value technique. The key difference between Method 1 and Method 2 is where the market risk premium is captured. However, either method should provide the same fair value measurement, i.e. where the risk premium is treated should have no effect on relative fair values.

- *Method 1* – the expected cash flows are adjusted for the systematic (market) risk by subtracting a cash risk premium. This results in risk-adjusted expected cash flows that represent a certainty-equivalent cash flow. The cash flows are then discounted at a risk-free interest rate. *[IFRS 13.B25]*.

  Because all of the risk factors have been incorporated into the cash flows under Method 1, the discount rate used would only capture the time value of money. That is, use of a risk-free discount rate is appropriate when using this technique, provided that credit risk considerations are not applicable or have already been considered in the cash flows.

  A certainty-equivalent cash flow is an expected cash flow adjusted for risk so that a market participant is indifferent to trading a certain cash flow for an expected cash flow. For example, if a market participant was willing to trade an expected cash flow of CU 1,200 for a cash flow that the market participant is certain to receive of CU 1,000, the CU 1,000 is the certainty-equivalent of the CU 1,200 (i.e. the CU 200 would represent the cash risk premium). *[IFRS 13.B25]*.

- *Method 2* – adjusts for systematic (market) risk by applying a risk premium to the risk-free interest rate (i.e. the risk premium is captured in the discount rate). As such, the discount rate represents an expected rate of return (i.e. the expected rate associated with probability-weighted cash flows). In Method 2, the expected cash flows are discounted using this rate. *[IFRS 13.B26]*.

  The use of a risk-free discount rate is not appropriate under Method 2, because the expected cash flows, while probability weighted, do not represent a certainty-equivalent cash flow. The standard suggests that models used for pricing risky assets, such as the capital asset pricing model, could be used to estimate the expected rate of return. As discussed at 21.3 above, the discount rate used in the discount rate adjustment technique also uses a rate of return, but it is related to conditional cash flows. A discount rate determined in accordance with the discount rate adjustment technique is likely to be higher than the discount rate used in Method 2, which is an *expected* rate of return relating to expected or probability-weighted cash flows. *[IFRS 13.B26]*.

Capturing the risk premium in the cash flows versus the discount rate has no effect on relative fair values under each method. That is, Method 1 and Method 2 should result in the same fair value measurement, all else being equal.

Example 14.32 below illustrates the application of Method 1 and Method 2 when measuring fair value. *[IFRS 13.B27-B29]*. The selection of Method 1 or Method 2 will depend on facts and circumstances specific to the asset or liability being measured, the extent to which sufficient data are available and the judgements applied. *[IFRS 13.B30]*. However, in practice, Method 1 is rarely used because in most cases, to mathematically estimate the cash certainty adjustment, one must already know the market risk premium that would be applied to the discount rate under Method 2.

Example 14.32: Expected present value techniques

An asset has expected cash flows of £780 in one year determined on the basis of the possible cash flows and probabilities shown below. The applicable risk-free interest rate for cash flows with a one-year horizon is 5% and the systematic risk premium for an asset with the same risk profile is 3%.

Possible cash flows £	Probability	Probability-weighted cash flows £
500	15%	75
800	60%	480
900	25%	225
Expected cash flows		780

In this simple example, the expected cash flows of £780 represent the probability-weighted average of the three possible outcomes. In more realistic situations, there could be many possible outcomes. However, to apply the expected present value technique, it is not always necessary to take into account distributions of all possible cash flows using complex models and techniques. Rather, it might be possible to develop a limited number of discrete scenarios and probabilities that capture the array of possible cash flows. For example, an entity might use realised cash flows for some relevant past period, adjusted for changes in circumstances occurring subsequently (e.g. changes in external factors, including economic or market conditions, industry trends and competition as well as changes in internal factors affecting the entity more specifically), taking into account the assumptions of market participants.

In theory, the present value (i.e. the fair value) of the asset's cash flows is the same whether determined using Method 1 or Method 2, as follows:

(a) Using Method 1, the expected cash flows are adjusted for systematic (i.e. market) risk. In the absence of market data directly indicating the amount of the risk adjustment, such adjustment could be derived from an asset pricing model using the concept of certainty equivalents. For example, the risk adjustment (i.e. the cash risk premium of £22) could be determined using the systematic risk premium of 3% (£780 – [£780 × (1.05/1.08)]), which results in risk-adjusted expected cash flows of £758 (£780 – £22). The £758 is the certainty equivalent of £780 and is discounted at the risk-free interest rate (5%). The present value (i.e. the fair value) of the asset is £722 (£758/1.05).

(b) Using Method 2, the expected cash flows are not adjusted for systematic (i.e. market) risk. Rather, the adjustment for that risk is included in the discount rate. Thus, the expected cash flows are discounted at an expected rate of return of 8% (i.e. the 5% risk-free interest rate plus the 3% systematic risk premium). The present value (i.e. the fair value) of the asset is £722 (£780/1.08).

In Example 14.33 below, we have expanded the example from IFRS 13 to include the discount rate adjustment technique (described at 21.3 above). Example 14.33 shows how all three techniques converge to the same fair value measurement, while highlighting the difference in the discount rates applied under each approach.

Example 14.33: Comparison of present value techniques

An entity is estimating the fair value of an asset that will expire in one year and has determined that the probability distribution of the future cash flows is as follows.

Possible cash flows £	Probability	Probability-weighted cash flows £
500	15%	75
800	60%	480
900	25%	225
	Expected cash flows	780

Assume that the risk-free interest rate is 5% and the risk premium is 3%. The table below shows that all three present value techniques yield identical results:

Method	Contractual cash flows	Most likely cash flows	Expected cash flows	Certainty-equivalent adjustment	Certainty-equivalent cash flows	Discount rate	Present value
Discount rate adjustment technique	N/A	£800	N/A	N/A	N/A	10.8%	£722
EPV Method 1 – Adjust expected cash flows for risk premium	N/A	N/A	£780	£ (22)	£758	5.0%	£722
EPV Method 2 – Adjust discount rate for risk premium	N/A	N/A	£780	N/A	N/A	8.0%	£722

Method	Fair value	Calculation
Discount rate adjustment technique	£722	= Most likely cash flow / (1 + risk-free rate + adjustment for cash flow uncertainty + risk premium)
EPV Method 1	£722	= (Expected cash flow – certainty-equivalent adjustment[a]) / (1 + risk-free rate)
EPV Method 2	£722	= Expected cash flow / (1 + risk-free rate + risk premium)

(a) Certainty-equivalent adjustment = Expected cash flow – [Expected cash flow × (1 + risk-free rate) / (1 + risk-free rate + risk premium)]

The three techniques differ in the manner in which the risks in the cash flows are captured, but not the level of the risk inherent in those cash flows. In the discount rate adjustment technique, the most likely cash flow (£800) is discounted at a rate that reflects all the risk inherent in the investment (i.e. time value of money, possible variations in the amount of cash flows, risk premium).

Method 1 of the expected present value technique incorporates asset-specific and systematic uncertainty directly into the cash flows (certainty-equivalent cash flow of £758) and therefore uses the risk-free rate for discounting, as all the risks associated with the investment are incorporated in the cash flows. The adjustment to the cash flows for systematic risk is based on the 3% risk premium.

Instead of using the risk premium to estimate a certainty-equivalent cash flow, Method 2 of the expected present value technique incorporates the risk premium in the discount rate. The difference between the discount rate in Method 1 and Method 2 is the market risk premium.

22 CONVERGENCE WITH US GAAP

22.1 The development of IFRS 13

IFRS 13 was the result of a convergence project between the IASB and the US Financial Accounting Standards Board (FASB). However, the Boards began developing their fair value measurement standards separately. The FASB issued Statement of Financial Accounting Standards No. 157 – *Fair Value Measurements* (SFAS 157, now ASC 820) in 2006. The IASB's initial discussion paper issued in 2006 and subsequent exposure draft issued in 2009, were developed using the requirements of SFAS 157. However, the proposed requirements were not wholly consistent with that guidance and responses from constituents emphasised the need for a common set of requirements regarding the determination of fair value measurements under both IFRS and US GAAP. As a result, the Boards began joint discussions in 2010. From the IASB's perspective, the project had four main objectives:

- 'to establish a single set of requirements for all fair value measurements required or permitted by IFRSs to reduce complexity and improve consistency in their application, thereby enhancing the comparability of information reported in financial statements;
- to clarify the definition of fair value and related guidance to communicate the measurement objective more clearly;
- to enhance disclosures about fair value measurements that will help users of financial statements assess the valuation techniques and inputs used to develop fair value measurements; and
- to increase the convergence' of IFRSs and US GAAP. *[IFRS 13.BC6]*.

The Boards' joint discussions resulted in the issuance of IFRS 13 and Accounting Standards Update (ASU) 2011-04 and created a generally uniform framework for applying fair value measurement in both IFRS and US GAAP (refer to 22.2 below for further discussion of the differences).

IFRS 13 was also part of the IASB's response to G20 requests in relation to the financial crisis. Therefore, the disclosures required by the standard are intended to help users assess the valuation techniques and inputs used to measure fair value. The IASB had originally proposed to require entities to disclose a quantitative sensitivity analysis for non-financial assets and liabilities measured at fair value. While the proposed disclosures were favoured by users and were consistent with the recommendations from the IASB's Expert Advisory Panel, the proposals were heavily criticised by preparers. Their concerns included the additional cost involved. Therefore, the Boards decided not to include this requirement until additional outreach could be completed. Until such time that this project is completed, sensitivity disclosures are only required for financial assets and liabilities (this continues the current disclosure requirements in IFRS 7). *[IFRS 13.BC208]*. As part of the PIR of IFRS 13, the board received feedback that maintaining convergence with US GAAP was important in that it leads to increased comparability for financial statements globally. This increased comparability is facilitating efficient capital markets, increased user confidence and reduced compliance costs. It was also indicated that the convergence has led to more material to be available for stakeholders around fair value measurements.[34]

22.2 US GAAP differences

As noted above, the Boards' joint fair value measurement project resulted in both the issuance of IFRS 13 and amendments to particular aspects of ASC 820. These standards now have a consistent definition of fair value and represent converged guidance in relation to how to measure fair value. However, some differences still remain. The main differences are discussed at 22.2.1 to 22.2.4 below.

It is also worth noting that there continue to be differences between IFRS and US GAAP as to what is measured at fair value, but those differences were outside the scope of the joint project, which focused on how to measure fair value.

In 2014, the Financial Accounting Foundation issued its post-implementation review of SFAS 157, concluding that the standard met its intended objectives.[35] While agreeing that a comprehensive review of the fair value guidance was not needed, the FASB noted that it plans to potentially address more challenging aspects of the standard in the years ahead.[36] The FASB issued an amendment *Fair Value Measurement (Topic 820) Disclosure Framework* (ASU 2018-13) in August 2018 that eliminates, adds and modifies certain disclosure requirements for fair value measurements as part of its disclosure framework project.

The amendments are effective for all entities for fiscal years beginning after 15 December 2019 and for interim periods within those fiscal years. An entity is permitted to early adopt either the entire standard or only the provisions that eliminate or modify requirements.[37] The IASB has not made similar amendments to IFRS 13, as the discussions confirmed through the PIR, the Board is aware of all the issues the FASB identified. As discussed at 20 above, the IASB has fed the PIR findings regarding the usefulness of disclosures into the work on Better Communications in Financial Reporting.

22.2.1 Practical expedient for alternative investments

ASC 820 provides a practical expedient to measure the fair value of certain investments in investment companies (e.g. investments in hedge funds or private equity funds that do not have readily determinable fair values) using net asset value (NAV), without adjustment.[38] Furthermore, in May 2015, the FASB issued ASU 2015-07 – *Fair Value Measurement (Topic 820): Disclosures for Investments in Certain Entities That Calculate Net Asset Value per Share (or Its Equivalent)*, which eliminates the requirement to categorise in the fair value hierarchy investments measured using the NAV practical expedient.[39] While this exemption provides some relief for entities, they now have additional disclosure requirements specific to investments that are measured using the NAV practical expedient. These requirements are intended to help financial statement users reconcile amounts reported to the face of the financial statements and better understand the nature and risk of these investments, including whether the investments, if sold, are likely to be sold at amounts different from their NAV.

IFRS 13 does not have a similar practical expedient. Nor does it provide a similar disclosure exemption or requirements specific to such investments. Therefore, IFRS preparers cannot presume that NAV, or an equivalent measure, will be the same as fair value as measured in accordance with IFRS 13 (this is discussed further at 2.5.1.A above). In addition, entities will need to categorise such investments within the fair value hierarchy and comply with the general disclosure requirements in IFRS 13.

At the time IFRS 13 was issued, the IASB believed it would be difficult to identify when such a practical expedient would be applied, given the different practices entities across the world use to calculate NAV. This difference was expected to be addressed as part of the IASB's project on Investment Entities. However, when the IASB issued *Investment Entities (Amendments to IFRS 10, IFRS 12 and IAS 27)* in October 2012, a footnote was added to paragraph 238(a) of the Basis for Conclusions to IFRS 13 which confirmed it had reconsidered providing a net asset value practical expedient, but decided against providing one for the reason outlined above and because it was outside the scope of the Investment Entities project to provide fair value measurement guidance for investments in investment entities. *[IFRS 13.BC238(a)]*.

22.2.2 Fair value of liabilities with a demand feature

The guidance in IFRS on measuring the fair value of a financial liability with a demand feature differs slightly from US GAAP. IFRS 13 states that the fair value of a liability with a demand feature cannot be less than the present value of the amount payable on demand, which is consistent with the existing requirements in IFRS. US GAAP has specific industry guidance for banks and depository institutions.[40] The industry specific guidance states that the fair value of deposit liabilities with no defined maturities is the amount payable on demand at the reporting date. Since deposit liabilities, withdrawable on demand, of banks and depository institutions are excluded from the scope of the fair value option guidance in ASC 825, the industry guidance in US GAAP around how to fair value these liabilities is applicable to disclosure, only. *[IFRS 13.BC238(b)]*.

22.2.3 Recognition of day-one gains and losses

While fair value is defined in IFRS 13 as an exit price (which can differ from an entry price), the standard defers to other IFRSs on whether to recognise any difference between fair value and transaction price at initial recognition, that is, day-one gains or losses. IFRS 9 restricts the recognition of day-one gains and losses when fair value is determined using unobservable inputs.

US GAAP contains no specific threshold regarding the observability of fair value inputs. As such, US GAAP does not specifically prohibit the recognition of day-one gains or losses even when the fair value measurement is based on significant unobservable inputs (i.e. a Level 3 measurement – see 16.2 above for further discussion regarding categorisation within the fair value hierarchy).

22.2.4 Disclosures

IFRS 13 and ASC 820 have some differences in the disclosure requirements for fair value measurements. For example, IFRS 13 does not provide exceptions to its disclosure requirements for non-public entities, whereas ASC 820 does. The IASB believes that *IFRS for Small and Medium-Sized Entities* addresses the accounting for entities that do not have public accountability, and the disclosures about their fair value measurements. *[IFRS 13.BC238(c)]*.

References

1. IFRS Project Report and Feedback Statement: *Post-implementation Review of IFRS 13 Fair Value Measurement*, December 2018, p.6.
2. IFRS Project Report and Feedback Statement: *Post-implementation Review of IFRS 13 Fair Value Measurement*, December 2018, p.6.
3. IFRS Project Report and Feedback Statement: *Post-implementation Review of IFRS 13 Fair Value Measurement*, December 2018, p.3.
4. *IASB Update*, June 2020 and website of the IFRS foundation and IASB, https://www.ifrs.org/projects/work-plan/standards-level-review-of-disclosures/#current-stage (accessed 19 August 2020)
5. Exposure Draft ED/2014/4 *Measuring Quoted Investments in Subsidiaries, Joint Ventures and Associates at Fair Value (Proposed amendments to IFRS 10, IFRS 12, IAS 27, IAS 28, IAS 36 and Illustrative Examples for IFRS 13)*, IASB, September 2014.
6. *IASB Update*, January 2016.
7. Agenda Paper 7B, *Post-implementation Review of IFRS 13 Fair Value Measurement: Background-Detailed analysis of feedback received* and Agenda Paper 7D, *Post-implementation Review of IFRS 13 Fair Value Measurement: Background – Prioritising Level 1 inputs or the unit of account*, IASB meeting, March 2018.
8. IFRS Project Report and Feedback Statement: *Post-implementation Review of IFRS 13 Fair Value Measurement*, December 2018, p.14.
9. FASB Accounting Standards Update 2011-04, *Amendments to Achieve Common Fair Value Measurement and Disclosure Requirements in U.S. GAAP and IFRSs*.
10. Exposure Draft ED/2014/4 *Measuring Quoted Investments in Subsidiaries, Joint Ventures and Associates at Fair Value (Proposed amendments to IFRS 10, IFRS 12, IAS 27, IAS 28, IAS 36 and Illustrative Examples for IFRS 13)*, IASB, September 2014.
11. *IASB Update*, April 2015.
12. European Securities and Markets Authority public statement *Sovereign Debt in IFRS Financial Statements* issued in November 2011.
13. Financial Times article, *Value of private companies hits high of $490bn as tech start-ups shun markets*, 29 May 2017: '…said Peter Christiansen, a former Blackrock director who now heads research at Scenic. "We expect the trend will be towards private markets looking more and more like the public markets." '.
14. Report of the IASB Expert Advisory Panel: *Measuring and disclosing the fair value of financial instruments in markets that are no longer active*, October 2008, paragraphs 17-18.
15. Decision ref EECS/0115-03, European Securities and Markets Authority report *17th Extract from the EECS's Database of Enforcement*, July 2015, pp.7-8.
16. Decision ref EECS/0115-03, European Securities and Markets Authority report *17th Extract from the EECS's Database of Enforcement*, July 2015, pp.7-8.
17. IFRS Project Report and Feedback Statement: *Post-implementation Review of IFRS 13 Fair Value Measurement*, December 2018, p.16.
18. IFRS Project Report and Feedback Statement: *Post-implementation Review of IFRS 13 Fair Value Measurement*, December 2018, p.15.
19. *IASB Update*, January 2020.
20. The International Swaps and Derivatives Association (ISDA) agreement is part of a framework of documents designed to enable OTC derivatives to be documented fully and flexibly. The ISDA master agreement sets out the standard terms that apply to all transactions and is published by the International Swaps and Derivatives Association.
21. A credit support annex (CSA) is a legal document that regulates the credit support (collateral) for derivative transactions and forms part of an ISDA Master Agreement.
22. Proposed illustrative example 13A, paragraphs IE47A-IE47G, Exposure Draft ED/2014/4 *Measuring Quoted Investments in Subsidiaries, Joint Ventures and Associates at Fair Value (Proposed amendments to IFRS 10, IFRS 12, IAS 27, IAS 28, IAS 36 and Illustrative Examples for IFRS 13)*, IASB, September 2014.
23. IASB Staff Paper, Agenda Paper reference 6 for the April 2015 IASB meeting – *Measuring Quoted Investments in Subsidiaries, Joint Ventures and Associates at Fair Value (Proposed amendments to IFRS 10, IFRS 12, IAS 27, IAS 28 and IAS 36 and Illustrative Examples for IFRS 13) – Illustrative Example for IFRS 13 – Portfolios*.
24. *IASB Update*, April 2015.
25. IFRS Project Report and Feedback Statement: *Post-implementation Review of IFRS 13 Fair Value Measurement*, December 2018, pp.16, 18.
26. IFRS Project Report and Feedback Statement: *Post-implementation Review of IFRS 13 Fair Value Measurement*, December 2018, p.16.
27. *IFRIC Update*, January 2015.

28 IFRS Project Reporting and Feedback Statement: *Post-implementation Review of IFRS 13 Fair Value Measurement*, December 2018, pp.12-13.
29 *IASB Update*, September 2019.
30 *IASB Update*, September 2019.
31 *IASB Update*, November 2019 and *IASB Update*, February 2020.
32 *IASB Update*, June 2020 and website of the IFRS foundation and IASB, https://www.ifrs.org/projects/work-plan/standards-level-review-of-disclosures/#current-stage (accessed 19 August 2020).
33 IFRS Standards Project summary: *Discount Rates in IFRS Standards*.
34 *IASB Update*, Paper 7B, March 2018; IFRS Project Reporting and Feedback Statement: *Post-implementation Review of IFRS 13 Fair Value Measurement*, December 2018, p.17.
35 Financial Accounting Foundation, *Post-Implementation Review Report – FASB Statement No. 157, Fair Value Measurements (Codified in Accounting Standards Codification Topic 820, Fair Value Measurements and Disclosures)*, February 2014.
36 FASB, Response to FAF Post-implementation Review Report of FAS 157 on *Fair Value Measurement*, dated 10 March 2014.
37 Website of the FASB, https://www.fasb.org/jsp/FASB/Document_C/DocumentPage?cid=1176171116516&acceptedDisclaimer=true (accessed 18 August 2020).
38 FASB Accounting Standards Codification Topic 820 – *Fair Value Measurements and Disclosures* – sections 10-35-59 – 10-35-62.
39 FASB Accounting Standards Codification Topic 820 – *Fair Value Measurements and Disclosures* – section 10-35-54B, which is added by ASU 2015-07 – *Fair Value Measurement (Topic 820): Disclosures for Investments in Certain Entities That Calculate Net Asset Value per Share (or Its Equivalent)*.
40 FASB Accounting Standards Codification Topic 825 – *Financial Instruments* and Topic 942 – *Financial Services – Depository and Lending*.

Chapter 15   Foreign exchange

1 INTRODUCTION 1179
    1.1 Background 1179
    1.2 Relevant pronouncements 1180
2 IAS 21: OBJECTIVE, SCOPE AND DEFINITIONS 1180
    2.1 Objective of the standard 1180
    2.2 Scope 1180
    2.3 Definitions of terms 1181
3 SUMMARY OF THE APPROACH REQUIRED BY IAS 21 1182
4 DETERMINATION OF AN ENTITY'S FUNCTIONAL CURRENCY 1182
    4.1 General 1182
    4.2 Intermediate holding companies or finance subsidiaries 1184
    4.3 Investment holding companies 1186
    4.4 Branches and divisions 1186
    4.5 Documentation of judgements made 1187
5 REPORTING FOREIGN CURRENCY TRANSACTIONS IN THE
   FUNCTIONAL CURRENCY OF AN ENTITY 1187
    5.1 Initial recognition 1187
         5.1.1 Identifying the date of transaction 1188
         5.1.2 Deposits and other consideration received or paid in
               advance 1189
         5.1.3 Using average rates 1190
         5.1.4 Practical difficulties in determining exchange rates 1191
               5.1.4.A Dual rates 1191
               5.1.4.B Suspension of rates: temporary lack of
                         exchangeability 1192
               5.1.4.C Suspension of rates: longer term lack of
                         exchangeability 1192

	5.2	Reporting at the ends of subsequent reporting periods		1193
	5.3	Treatment of exchange differences		1194
		5.3.1	Monetary items	1194
		5.3.2	Non-monetary items	1195
	5.4	Determining whether an item is monetary or non-monetary		1196
		5.4.1	Deposits or progress payments	1197
		5.4.2	Deposits and advance payments for actively traded commodities	1198
		5.4.3	Investments in preference shares	1198
		5.4.4	Foreign currency share capital	1199
		5.4.5	Deferred tax	1199
		5.4.6	Post-employment benefit plans – foreign currency assets	1200
		5.4.7	Post-employment benefit plans – foreign currency plans	1200
	5.5	Change in functional currency		1201
	5.6	Books and records not kept in functional currency		1203
6	USE OF A PRESENTATION CURRENCY OTHER THAN THE FUNCTIONAL CURRENCY			1204
	6.1	Translation to the presentation currency		1204
		6.1.1	Functional currency is not that of a hyperinflationary economy	1205
		6.1.2	Functional currency is that of a hyperinflationary economy	1209
		6.1.3	Dual rates, suspension of rates and lack of exchangeability	1212
		6.1.4	Calculation of average rate	1212
		6.1.5	Accounting for foreign operations where sub-groups exist	1214
	6.2	Translation of equity items		1215
		6.2.1	Share capital	1215
		6.2.2	Other equity balances resulting from transactions with equity holders	1215
		6.2.3	Other equity balances resulting from income and expenses being recognised in other comprehensive income	1216
	6.3	Exchange differences on intragroup balances		1216
		6.3.1	Monetary items included as part of the net investment in a foreign operation	1217
			6.3.1.A Trade receivables or payables included as part of the net investment in a foreign operation	1217
			6.3.1.B Manner of settlement of monetary items included as part of the net investment in a foreign operation	1218
			6.3.1.C Currency of monetary items included as part of the net investment in a foreign operation	1219

		6.3.1.D	Treatment in the individual financial statements of monetary items included as part of the net investment in a foreign operation 1220
		6.3.1.E	Monetary items transacted by other members of the group 1220
		6.3.1.F	Monetary items becoming part of the net investment in a foreign operation 1221
		6.3.1.G	Monetary items ceasing to be part of the net investment in a foreign operation 1223
	6.3.2	Dividends 1223	
	6.3.3	Unrealised profits on intragroup transactions 1224	
6.4	Non-coterminous period ends 1224		
6.5	Goodwill and fair value adjustments 1225		
6.6	Disposal or partial disposal of a foreign operation 1227		
	6.6.1	Disposals and transactions treated as disposals 1227	
		6.6.1.A	Disposals of a foreign operation 1227
		6.6.1.B	Transactions treated as disposals 1229
	6.6.2	Partial disposals 1230	
		6.6.2.A	What constitutes a partial disposal? 1230
		6.6.2.B	Partial disposal of a proportionate interest in a subsidiary 1230
		6.6.2.C	Repayment of a permanent as equity loan by a subsidiary 1230
		6.6.2.D	Partial disposal of interest in an associate or joint arrangement 1231
	6.6.3	Comparison of the effect of step-by-step and direct methods of consolidation on accounting for disposals 1231	

7 CHANGE OF PRESENTATION CURRENCY 1234

8 INTRODUCTION OF THE EURO 1241

9 TAX EFFECTS OF ALL EXCHANGE DIFFERENCES 1242

10 DISCLOSURE REQUIREMENTS 1242

    10.1 Exchange differences 1242

    10.2 Presentation and functional currency 1243

    10.3 Convenience translations of financial statements or other financial information 1243

    10.4 Judgements made in applying IAS 21 and related disclosures 1244

11 FUTURE DEVELOPMENTS 1244

List of examples

Example 15.1:	Factors to be considered when determining the functional currency	1184
Example 15.2:	Functional currency of intermediate holding companies or finance subsidiaries	1185
Example 15.3:	Establishing the transaction date (1)	1188
Example 15.4:	Establishing the transaction date (2)	1189
Example 15.5:	Reporting an unsettled foreign currency transaction in the functional currency	1194
Example 15.6:	Reporting a settled foreign currency transaction in the functional currency	1194
Example 15.7:	Deposits or progress payments	1197
Example 15.8:	Deposit paid for future delivery of gold	1198
Example 15.9:	Change in functional currency	1202
Example 15.10:	Translation of a non-hyperinflationary functional currency to a non-hyperinflationary presentation currency	1207
Example 15.11:	Translation of a hyperinflationary functional currency to a non-hyperinflationary presentation currency	1210
Example 15.12:	Calculation of average rate	1213
Example 15.13:	Receivables/payables included as part of net investment in a foreign operation	1217
Example 15.14:	Monetary item in functional currency of either the reporting entity or the foreign operation	1219
Example 15.15:	Monetary item becoming part of the net investment in a foreign operation	1221
Example 15.16:	Unrealised profits on an intragroup transaction	1224
Example 15.17:	Translation of goodwill	1225
Example 15.18:	Disposal of a foreign operation	1227
Example 15.19:	Disposal of a partially owned foreign subsidiary	1229
Example 15.20:	Disposal of an indirectly held foreign operation	1232
Example 15.21	Change of presentation currency	1235

Chapter 15   Foreign exchange

1   INTRODUCTION

1.1   Background

An entity can engage in foreign currency activities in two ways. It may enter directly into transactions which are denominated in foreign currencies, the results of which need to be translated into the currency in which the company measures its results and financial position. Alternatively, it may conduct foreign operations through a foreign entity, such as a subsidiary, associate, joint arrangement or branch which keeps its accounting records in terms of its own currency. In this case it will need to translate the financial statements of the foreign entity for the purposes of inclusion in the consolidated financial statements.

Before an international standard was developed, there were four distinct methods which could be used in the translation process:

(a) *current rate method* – all assets and liabilities are translated at the current rate of exchange, i.e. the exchange rate at the end of the reporting period;

(b) *temporal method* – assets and liabilities carried at current prices (e.g. cash, receivables, payables, and investments at market value) are translated at the current rate of exchange. Assets and liabilities carried at past prices (e.g. property, investments at cost, prepayments) are translated at the rate of exchange in effect at the dates to which the prices pertain;

(c) *current/non-current method* – all current assets and current liabilities are translated at the current rate of exchange. Non-current assets and liabilities are translated at historical rates, i.e. the exchange rate in effect at the time the asset was acquired or the liability incurred; and

(d) *monetary/non-monetary method* – monetary assets and liabilities, i.e. items which represent the right to receive or the obligation to pay a fixed amount of money, are translated at the current rate of exchange. Non-monetary assets and liabilities are translated at the historical rate.

There was no consensus internationally on the best theoretical approach to adopt. In essence, the arguments surround the choice of exchange rates to be used in the translation process and the subsequent treatment of the exchange differences which arise.

1.2 Relevant pronouncements

The principal international standard dealing with this topic is IAS 21 – *The Effects of Changes in Foreign Exchange Rates,* the original version of which dates back to 1983. In December 2003, the IASB issued a revised version of IAS 21 as part of a wide ranging project to improve its standards and this forms the core of the current standard, although it has been subject to a number of subsequent amendments.

One interpretation of the earlier version of IAS 21 issued by the SIC remains applicable. SIC-7 – *Introduction of the Euro* – deals with the application of IAS 21 to the changeover from the national currencies of participating Member States of the European Union to the euro and is covered at 8 below. IFRIC 16 – *Hedges of a Net Investment in a Foreign Operation* – is not actually an interpretation of IAS 21, but provides guidance on applying certain aspects of the standard and is discussed at 6.1.5 and 6.6.3 below.

IFRIC 22 – *Foreign Currency Transactions and Advance Consideration* – provides guidance on determining the date of a transaction for the purposes of applying IAS 21 when consideration is paid or received in advance. This interpretation is primarily discussed at 5.1.2 below.

2 IAS 21: OBJECTIVE, SCOPE AND DEFINITIONS

2.1 Objective of the standard

An entity may carry on foreign activities in two ways. It may have transactions in foreign currencies or it may have foreign operations. In addition, an entity may present its financial statements in a foreign currency. IAS 21 does not set out what the objective of foreign currency translation should be, but just states that the objective of the standard is 'to prescribe how to include foreign currency transactions and foreign operations in the financial statements of an entity and how to translate financial statements into a presentation currency'. *[IAS 21.1]*.

It also indicates that the principal issues to be addressed are 'which exchange rate(s) to use and how to report the effects of changes in exchange rates in the financial statements'. *[IAS 21.2]*.

2.2 Scope

IAS 21 should be applied: *[IAS 21.3]*

(a) in accounting for transactions and balances in foreign currencies, except for those derivative transactions and balances that are within the scope of IFRS 9 – *Financial Instruments;*

(b) in translating the results and financial position of foreign operations that are included in the financial statements of the entity by consolidation or the equity method; and

(c) in translating an entity's results and financial position into a presentation currency.

IFRS 9 applies to many foreign currency derivatives and, accordingly, these are excluded from the scope of IAS 21. However, those foreign currency derivatives that are not within the scope of IFRS 9 (e.g. some foreign currency derivatives that are embedded in other contracts) are within the scope of IAS 21. In addition, IAS 21 applies when an entity translates amounts relating to derivatives from its functional currency to its presentation currency. *[IAS 21.4]*.

IAS 21 also does not apply to hedge accounting for foreign currency items, including the hedging of a net investment in a foreign operation. *[IAS 21.5]*. This is dealt with in IFRS 9 (or IAS 39 – *Financial Instruments: Recognition and Measurement*[1]) which has detailed rules on hedge accounting that are different from the requirements of IAS 21 (see Chapter 53). *[IAS 21.27]*.

The requirements of IAS 21 are applicable to financial statements that are described as complying with International Financial Reporting Standards. They do not apply to translations of financial information into a foreign currency that do not meet these requirements, although the standard does specify information to be disclosed in respect of such 'convenience translations' (see 10.3 below). *[IAS 21.6]*.

IAS 21 does not apply to the presentation in a statement of cash flows of the cash flows arising from transactions in a foreign currency, or to the translation of cash flows of a foreign operation. *[IAS 21.7]*. These are dealt with in IAS 7 – *Statement of Cash Flows* (see Chapter 40 at 5.3).

2.3 Definitions of terms

The definitions of terms which are contained in IAS 21 are as follows: *[IAS 21.8]*

Closing rate is the spot exchange rate at the end of the reporting period.

Exchange difference is the difference resulting from translating a given number of units of one currency into another currency at different exchange rates.

Exchange rate is the ratio of exchange for two currencies.

Fair value is the price that would be received to sell an asset or paid to transfer a liability in an orderly transaction between market participants at the measurement date.

Foreign currency is a currency other than the functional currency of the entity.

Foreign operation is an entity that is a subsidiary, associate, joint arrangement or branch of a reporting entity, the activities of which are based or conducted in a country or currency other than those of the reporting entity.

Functional currency is the currency of the primary economic environment in which the entity operates.

A *group* is a parent and all its subsidiaries.

Monetary items are units of currency held and assets and liabilities to be received or paid in a fixed or determinable number of units of currency.

Net investment in a foreign operation is the amount of the reporting entity's interest in the net assets of that operation.

Presentation currency is the currency in which the financial statements are presented.

Spot exchange rate is the exchange rate for immediate delivery.

The terms 'functional currency', 'monetary items' and 'net investment in a foreign operation' are elaborated on further within the standard. These are discussed at 4, 5.4 and 6.3.1 below.

3 SUMMARY OF THE APPROACH REQUIRED BY IAS 21

Many reporting entities comprise a number of individual entities (e.g. a group is made up of a parent and one or more subsidiaries). Various types of entities, whether members of a group or otherwise, may have investments in associates or joint arrangements. They may also have branches or divisions (see 4.4 below). It is necessary for the results and financial position of each individual entity included in the reporting entity to be translated into the currency in which the reporting entity presents its financial statements (if this presentation currency is different from the individual entity's functional currency). *[IAS 21.18]*.

In preparing financial statements, the following approach should be followed:

- Each entity – whether a stand-alone entity, an entity with foreign operations (such as a parent) or a foreign operation (such as a subsidiary or branch) – determines its functional currency. *[IAS 21.17]*. This is discussed at 4 below.

  In the case of group financial statements, it should be emphasised that there is not a 'group' functional currency; each entity included within the group financial statements, be it the parent, or a subsidiary, associate, joint arrangement or branch, has its own functional currency.

- Where an entity enters into a transaction denominated in a currency other than its functional currency, it translates those foreign currency items into its functional currency and reports the effects of such translation in accordance with the provisions of IAS 21 discussed at 5 below. *[IAS 21.17]*.

- The results and financial position of any individual entity within the reporting entity whose functional currency differs from the presentation currency are translated in accordance with the provisions of IAS 21 discussed at 6 below. *[IAS 21.18]*.

  IAS 21 permits the presentation currency of a reporting entity to be any currency (or currencies), although relevant laws or regulations might restrict that choice. Therefore, this translation process will also apply to the parent's figures if its functional currency is different from the presentation currency.

  The standard also permits a stand-alone entity preparing financial statements or an entity preparing separate financial statements in accordance with IAS 27 – *Separate Financial Statements* – to present its financial statements in any currency (or currencies). If the entity's presentation currency differs from its functional currency, its results and financial position are also translated into the presentation currency in accordance with this process. *[IAS 21.19]*.

4 DETERMINATION OF AN ENTITY'S FUNCTIONAL CURRENCY

4.1 General

Functional currency is defined as the currency of 'the primary economic environment in which the entity operates' (see 2.3 above). This will normally be the one in which it primarily generates and expends cash. *[IAS 21.9]*.

IAS 21 sets out a number of factors or indicators that any entity should or may need to consider in determining its functional currency. When the factors or indicators are mixed and the functional currency is not obvious, management should use its judgement to determine the functional currency that most faithfully represents the economic effects of the underlying transactions, events and conditions. As part of this approach, management should give priority to the primary indicators before considering the other indicators, which are designed to provide additional supporting evidence to determine an entity's functional currency. *[IAS 21.12]*.

The primary factors that IAS 21 requires an entity to consider in determining its functional currency are as follows: *[IAS 21.9]*

(a) the currency:
   (i) that mainly influences sales prices for goods and services (this will often be the currency in which sales prices for its goods and services are denominated and settled); and
   (ii) of the country whose competitive forces and regulations mainly determine the sales prices of its goods and services.
(b) the currency that mainly influences labour, material and other costs of providing goods or services (this will often be the currency in which such costs are denominated and settled).

Where the functional currency of the entity is not obvious from the above, the following factors may also provide evidence of an entity's functional currency: *[IAS 21.10]*

(a) the currency in which funds from financing activities (i.e. issuing debt and equity instruments) are generated; and
(b) the currency in which receipts from operating activities are usually retained.

An operation that is 'integral' to its parent, i.e. it carries on business as if it were an extension of the parent's operations, will always have the same functional currency as the parent. (In this context, the term parent is drawn broadly and is the entity that has the foreign operation as its subsidiary, branch, associate or joint arrangement). *[IAS 21.BC6]*. Therefore the following additional factors are also considered in determining the functional currency of a foreign operation, particularly whether its functional currency is the same as that of the reporting entity: *[IAS 21.11]*

(a) whether the activities of the foreign operation are carried out as an extension of the reporting entity, rather than being carried out with a significant degree of autonomy. An example of the former is when the foreign operation only sells goods imported from the reporting entity and remits the proceeds to it. An example of the latter is when the operation accumulates cash and other monetary items, incurs expenses, generates income and arranges borrowings, all substantially in its local currency;
(b) whether transactions with the reporting entity are a high or a low proportion of the foreign operation's activities;
(c) whether cash flows from the activities of the foreign operation directly affect the cash flows of the reporting entity and are readily available for remittance to it; and
(d) whether cash flows from the activities of the foreign operation are sufficient to service existing and normally expected debt obligations without funds being made available by the reporting entity.

Although the standard says that these factors 'are' considered in determining the functional currency of a foreign operation, this contradicts the requirement in the standard that management gives priority to the primary indicators before considering the other indicators. If it is obvious from the primary indicators what the entity's functional currency is, then there is no need to consider any of the other factors.

Example 15.1: Factors to be considered when determining the functional currency

A French entity (Parent A) has a US subsidiary (Subsidiary B) that produces and sells knitwear in the United States.

It is clear from the primary factors in IAS 21 that Subsidiary B's functional currency is the US dollar, because the US dollar mainly influences sales prices for goods, labour, material and other costs of providing goods, and the competitive forces and regulations that mainly determine the sales prices of the goods are located in the United States.

However, suppose Subsidiary B is financed by an inter-company loan denominated in euros granted from Parent A and the cash flows generated by Subsidiary B are transferred to Parent A on a regular basis. Should these additional factors be taken into account in determining the functional currency of Subsidiary B?

In our view, they should not. These additional factors only have to be considered when it is not obvious from the primary factors what Subsidiary B's functional currency is.

However, in practice, there are occasions when the functional currency is not completely clear from the primary factors and it will often be necessary to consider the other indicators. For example, if Subsidiary B was not producing the knitwear itself, but purchasing it from sources outside of the US (such that its operating costs were not predominantly in US dollars) this would mean that it was no longer obvious based on the primary factors that its functional currency was the US dollar and the additional factors would be taken into account in determining Subsidiary B's functional currency.

Since an entity's functional currency reflects the underlying transactions, events and conditions that are relevant to it, once it is determined, IAS 21 requires that the functional currency is not changed unless there is a change in those underlying transactions, events and conditions. *[IAS 21.13]*. The implication of this is that management of an entity cannot decree what the functional currency is – it is a matter of fact, albeit subjectively determined fact based on management's judgement of all the circumstances.

4.2 Intermediate holding companies or finance subsidiaries

For many entities the determination of functional currency may be relatively straightforward. However, for some entities, particularly entities within a group, this may not be the case. One particular difficulty is the determination of the functional currency of an intermediate holding company or finance subsidiary within an international group.

Example 15.2:   Functional currency of intermediate holding companies or finance subsidiaries

An international group is headquartered in the UK. The UK parent entity has a functional currency of pound sterling, which is also the group's presentation currency. The group has three international sub-operations, structured as follows:

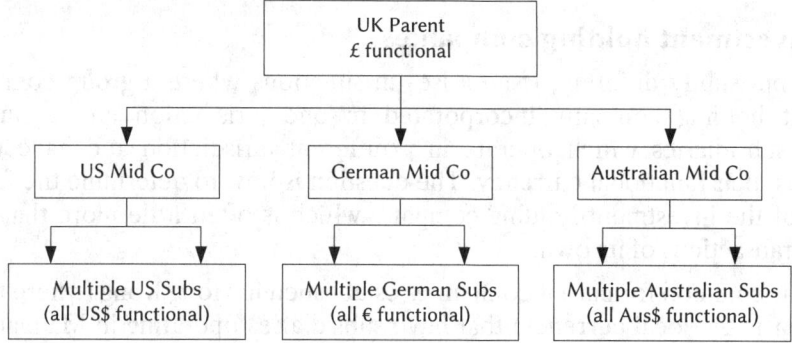

What is the functional currency of the three Mid Cos?

There are a variety of factors to be considered for intermediate holding companies or finance subsidiaries when deciding on the appropriate functional currency. Therefore, there will not be a single analysis applicable to all such entities.

IAS 21 defines a 'foreign operation' as 'an entity that is a subsidiary…the activities of which are based or conducted in a country or currency other than those of the reporting entity' (see 2.3 above). This definition would seem to suggest that a foreign operation must have its own 'activities'.

Also, paragraph 9 of the standard states that the functional currency is 'the currency of the primary economic environment in which the entity operates'. However, under paragraph 9 this is determined by reference to the currency that mainly influences sales prices and the operation's costs, and is therefore not directly relevant to intermediate holding companies or finance subsidiaries (see 4.1 above). Paragraphs 10 and 11 set out a number of factors to consider in determining the functional currency of a foreign operation. The theme running through these factors is the extent to which the activities and cash flows of the foreign operation are independent of those of the reporting entity.

In the case of an intermediate holding company or finance subsidiary, the acid-test question to consider is whether it is an extension of the parent and performing the functions of the parent – i.e. whether its role is simply to hold the investment in, or provide finance to, the foreign operation on behalf of the parent company or whether its functions are essentially an extension of a local operation (e.g. performing selling, payroll or similar activities for that operation) or indeed it is undertaking activities on its own account.

This means that subsidiaries that do nothing but hold investments or borrow money on behalf of the parent will normally have the functional currency of the parent. The borrowings of such companies are frequently guaranteed by the parent, which is itself likely to be a relevant factor. In other words, on whose credit is the lender relying? If the lender is looking to the ultimate parent, then the functional currency is likely to be that of the ultimate parent. However, if the lender is looking to the sub-group, then the functional currency of the companies in the sub-group will be relevant. Accordingly, any analysis that such a company has a functional currency other than that of the parent will require careful consideration of the features of the entity which give rise to that conclusion. Complex situations are likely to require the application of careful management judgement as indicated by the standard.

As for other entities within a group, each entity should be reviewed for its particular circumstances against the indicators and factors set out in the standard. This review requires management to use its judgement in determining the functional currency that most faithfully represents the economic effects of the underlying transactions, events and conditions applicable to that entity.

4.3 Investment holding companies

A similar, but subtly different, issue arises in situations where a group comprises an investment holding company incorporated in one jurisdiction and a number of operating subsidiaries which operate in a different jurisdiction and have the local currency as their functional currency. The question is how to determine the functional currency of the investment holding company which is often little more than a 'shell' with few transactions of its own.

This issue is common for parent companies established in Hong Kong (where the Hong Kong dollar is the local currency) that have subsidiaries operating in Mainland China (where Renminbi is the local currency), although very similar situations arise in other jurisdictions. Often the investment holding company will be listed in Hong Kong, incur some expenses, e.g. directors' remuneration, limited staff costs and office rental payments, in Hong Kong dollars and raise capital (shares and borrowings) in Hong Kong dollars. Furthermore, dividends from subsidiaries will either be received in Hong Kong dollars or be converted into Hong Kong dollars on receipt.

In 2010, the IFRS Interpretations Committee was asked to consider this issue and the staff identified two broad approaches being used in practice, namely:

- the parent uses the currency of its local environment, i.e. the one in which its operating expenses are denominated, it receives dividends from its subsidiaries and it raises funding; and
- the parent uses the currency of the local environment of its subsidiaries as its functional currency as this is the environment which drives the dividend income it receives, which is its primary source of revenue, i.e. the parent is seen as an extension of its subsidiaries.

The Interpretations Committee chose not to take the issue onto its agenda because any guidance it could provide would be in the nature of application guidance and simply emphasised that judgement needed to be applied.[2] In practice the judgement will often be based on whether the holding company's operations are considered sufficiently substantive to enable it to have a different functional currency from its subsidiaries.

4.4 Branches and divisions

IAS 21 uses the term 'branch' to describe an operation within a legal entity that may have a different functional currency from the entity itself. However, it contains no definition of that term, nor any further guidance on what arrangements should be regarded as a branch.

Many countries' governments have established legal and regulatory regimes that apply when a foreign entity establishes a place of business (often called a branch) in that country. Where an entity has operations that are subject to such a regime, it will normally be appropriate to regard them as a branch and evaluate whether those operations have their own functional currency. In this context, the indicators in paragraph 11 of the standard used to assess whether an entity has a functional currency that is different from its parent (see 4.1 above) will be particularly relevant.

An entity may also have an operation, e.g. a division, that operates in a different currency environment to the rest of the entity but which is not subject to an overseas branch regime. If that operation represents a sufficiently autonomous business unit it may be appropriate to view it as a branch and evaluate whether it has a functional currency that is different to the rest of the legal entity. However, in our experience, this situation will not be a common occurrence.

4.5 Documentation of judgements made

Since the determination of an entity's functional currency is critical to the translation process under IAS 21, we believe that an entity should clearly document its decision about its functional currency, setting out the factors taken into account in making that determination, particularly where it is not obvious from the primary factors set out in paragraph 9 of the standard. We recommend that the ultimate parent entity of a group should do this for each entity within the group and agree that determination with the local management of those entities, particularly where those entities are presenting financial statements in accordance with IFRS. Although the determination of functional currency is a judgemental issue, it would be expected that within the group the same determination would be made as to the functional currency of a particular entity. If local management has come up with a different analysis of the facts from that of the parent, it should be discussed to ensure that both parties have considered all the relevant facts and circumstances and a final determination made.

By documenting the decision about the functional currency of each entity, and the factors taken into account in making that determination, the reporting entity will be better placed in the future to determine whether a change in the underlying transactions, events and conditions relating to that entity warrant a change in its functional currency.

5 REPORTING FOREIGN CURRENCY TRANSACTIONS IN THE FUNCTIONAL CURRENCY OF AN ENTITY

Where an entity enters into a transaction denominated in a currency other than its functional currency then it will have to translate those foreign currency items into its functional currency and report the effects of such translation. The general requirements of IAS 21 are as follows.

5.1 Initial recognition

A foreign currency transaction is a transaction that is denominated or requires settlement in a foreign currency, including transactions arising when an entity: *[IAS 21.20]*

(a) buys or sells goods or services whose price is denominated in a foreign currency;

(b) borrows or lends funds when the amounts payable or receivable are denominated in a foreign currency; or

(c) otherwise acquires or disposes of assets, or incurs or settles liabilities, denominated in a foreign currency.

On initial recognition, foreign currency transactions should be translated into the functional currency using the spot exchange rate between the foreign currency and the functional currency on the date of the transaction. *[IAS 21.21]*. The date of a transaction is the date on which it first qualifies for recognition in accordance with IFRS. For convenience, an average rate for a week or month may be used for all foreign currency transactions occurring during that period, if the exchange rate does not fluctuate significantly. *[IAS 21.22]*.

5.1.1 Identifying the date of transaction

The date of a transaction is the date on which it first qualifies for recognition in accordance with IFRS. Although this sounds relatively straightforward, the following example illustrates the difficulty that can sometimes arise in determining the transaction date:

Example 15.3:   Establishing the transaction date (1)

A Belgian entity buys an item of inventory from a Canadian supplier. The dates relating to the transaction, and the relevant exchange rates, are as follows:

Date	Event	€1=C$
14 April 2021	Goods are ordered	1.50
5 May 2021	Goods are shipped from Canada and invoice dated that day	1.53
7 May 2021	Invoice is received	1.51
10 May 2021	Goods are received	1.54
14 May 2021	Invoice is recorded	1.56
7 June 2021	Invoice is paid	1.60

IAS 2 – *Inventories* – does not make any reference to the date of initial recognition of inventory. However, IFRS 9 deals with the initial recognition of financial liabilities. It requires the financial liability to be recognised when, and only when, the entity becomes a party to the contractual provisions of the instrument. *[IFRS 9.3.1.1]*. In discussing firm commitments to purchase goods, it indicates that an entity placing the order does not recognise the liability at the time of the commitment, but delays recognition until the ordered goods have been shipped or delivered, *[IFRS 9.B3.1.2(b)]*, normally on the date that the risks and rewards of ownership are considered to have passed.

Accordingly, it is unlikely that the date the goods are ordered should be used as the date of the transaction.

If the goods are shipped free on board (f.o.b.) then the risks and rewards of ownership are normally considered to pass on shipment (5 May) and this date should be used. If, however, the goods are not shipped f.o.b. then the risks and rewards of ownership will often be considered to pass on delivery (10 May) and therefore the date the goods are received should be treated as the date of the transaction. In practice, the transaction date will depend on the precise terms of the agreement (which are often based on standardised agreements such as the Incoterms rules).

The dates on which the invoice is received and is recorded are irrelevant to when the risks and rewards of ownership pass and therefore should not in principle be considered to be the date of the transaction. In practice, it may be acceptable that as a matter of administrative convenience that the exchange rate at the date the invoice is recorded is used, particularly if there is no undue delay in processing the invoice. If this is done then care should be taken to ensure that the exchange rate used is not significantly different from that ruling on the 'true' date of the transaction.

It is clear from IAS 21 that the date the invoice is paid is not the date of the transaction because if it were then no exchange differences would arise on unsettled transactions.

In the example above, one of the difficulties in identifying the date of transaction is the fact that IAS 2 contains little guidance on determining when purchased inventory should be recognised as an asset. Some standards, particularly those published more recently such as IFRS 15 – *Revenue from Contracts with Customers* – contain more detailed guidance in this respect. Nevertheless, determining the date of transaction may still require the application of judgement and the date that a transaction is recorded in an entity's books and records will not necessarily be the same as the date at which it qualifies for recognition under IFRS. Other situations where this issue is likely to arise is where an entity is recording a transaction that relates to a period, rather than one being recognised at a single point in time, as illustrated below:

Example 15.4: Establishing the transaction date (2)

On 30 September 2021 Company A, whose functional currency is the euro, acquires a US dollar bond for US$8,000 which is measured at amortised cost. The bond carries fixed interest of 5% per annum paid quarterly, i.e. US$100 per quarter. The exchange rate on acquisition is US$1 to €1.50.

On 31 December 2021, the US dollar has appreciated and the exchange rate is US$1 to €2.00. Interest received on the bond on 31 December 2021 is US$100 (= €200).

Although the interest might only be recorded on 31 December 2021, the rate on that date is not the spot rate ruling at the date of the transaction. Since the interest has accrued over the 3 month period, it should be translated at the spot rates applicable to the accrual of interest during the 3 month period. Accordingly, a weighted average rate for the 3 month period should be used. Assuming that the appropriate average rate is US$1 to €1.75 the interest income is €175 (= US$100 × 1.75).

Accordingly, there is also an exchange gain on the interest receivable of €25 (= US$100 × [2.00 – 1.75]) to be reflected in profit or loss. The journal entry for recording the receipt of the interest on 31 December 2021 is therefore as follows:

	€	€
Dr. Cash	200	
Cr. Interest income (profit or loss)		175
Cr. Exchange gain (profit or loss)		25

5.1.2 Deposits and other consideration received or paid in advance

An entity might receive (or pay) a deposit in a foreign currency in advance of delivering (or receiving) goods or services in circumstances where the resulting liability (or asset) is considered a non-monetary item – see 5.4.1 below. IFRIC 22 explains that, in general, the appropriate application of IAS 21 in these circumstances is to use the exchange rate at the date the advance payment is recognised, normally the payment date, rather than a subsequent date (or dates) when the goods or services are actually delivered. *[IFRIC 22.8]*. If there are multiple payments or receipts in advance, an entity should determine a date of transaction for each payment or receipt of advance consideration. *[IFRIC 22.9]*.

IFRIC 22 applies to a foreign currency transaction (or part of it) when an entity recognises a non-monetary asset or non-monetary liability arising from the payment or receipt of advance consideration before the related asset, expense or income (or part of it) is recognised. *[IFRIC 22.4]*. It does not apply when an entity measures the asset, income or expense arising from the advance payment at fair value or at the fair value of the consideration paid or received at a date other than the date of initial recognition of the non-monetary asset or non-monetary liability, for example the measurement of goodwill when applying IFRS 3 – *Business Combinations*. *[IFRIC 22.5]*.

The interpretation need not be applied to income taxes or insurance contracts (including reinsurance contracts) issued or reinsurance contracts held. *[IFRIC 22.6]*. In fact, once IFRS 17 – *Insurance Contracts* – is applied, a group of insurance contracts is treated as a monetary item (see Chapter 56 at 7.3) and therefore the interpretation is unlikely to be relevant. *[IFRIC 22.BC8, IFRS 17.30]*.

5.1.3 Using average rates

Rather than using the actual rate ruling at the date of the transaction 'an average rate for a week or month may be used for all foreign currency transactions occurring during that period', if the exchange rate does not fluctuate significantly (see 5.1 above). *[IAS 21.22]*. For entities which engage in a large number of foreign currency transactions it will be more convenient for them to use an average rate rather than using the exact rate for each transaction. If an average rate is to be used, what guidance can be given in choosing and using such a rate?

(a) Length of period

As an average rate should only be used as an approximation of actual rates then care has to be taken that significant fluctuations in the day-to-day exchange rates do not arise in the period selected. For this reason the period chosen should not be too long. We believe that the period should be no longer than one month and where there is volatility of exchange rates it will be better to set rates on a more frequent basis, say, a weekly basis, especially where the value of transactions is significant.

(b) Estimate of average rate relevant to date of transaction

The estimation of the appropriate average rate will depend on whether the rate is to be applied to transactions which have already occurred or to transactions which will occur after setting the rate. Obviously, if the transactions have already occurred then the average rate used should relate to the period during which those transactions occurred; e.g. purchase transactions for the previous week should be translated using the average rate for that week, not an average rate for the week the invoices are being recorded.

If the rate is being set for the following period the rate selected should be a reasonable estimate of the expected exchange rate during that period. This could be done by using the closing rate at the end of the previous period or by using the actual average rate for the previous period. We would suggest that the former be used. Whatever means is used to estimate the average rate, the actual rates during the period should be monitored and if there is a significant move in the exchange rate away from the average rate then the rate being applied should be revised.

(c) Application of average rate to type of item

We believe that average rates should be used only as a matter of convenience where there are a large number of transactions. Even where an average rate is used, we recommend that the actual rate should be used for large one-off transactions such as the purchase of a fixed asset or an overseas investment or taking out a foreign loan. Where the number of foreign currency transactions is small it will probably not be worthwhile setting and monitoring average rates and therefore actual rates should be used.

5.1.4 Practical difficulties in determining exchange rates

In most cases determining an exchange rate will be a relatively straightforward exercise, but this will not always be the case, particularly where there are restrictions on entities wishing to exchange one currency for another, typically a local currency for a foreign currency. For example:

- legal restrictions might permit sales of local currency only at an official rate rather than a rate that reflects more fully market participants' views of the currency's relative value or its underlying economics. Those official rates may or may not be pegged to another country's currency, for example the US dollar;
- exchange rates set by governments might vary according to the nature of the underlying transaction; and
- the volume of currency that can be exchanged through official mechanisms may be limited by formal or informal restrictions imposed by government, often designed to help manage the government's sometimes scarce foreign exchange reserves.

These situations are often encountered in countries that have more of a closed economy and which may be experiencing a degree of economic strain. High inflation or even hyperinflation and devaluations can be symptomatic of these situations as can the development of a 'black market' in foreign currencies, the use of which could to some extent be unlawful. Determining an appropriate exchange rate to use in these circumstances can be difficult as discussed at 5.1.4.A to 5.1.4.C below.

In more extreme cases of economic strain or hyperinflation a country may eventually replace its local currency completely or even adopt a third country's currency as its own. Examples of the latter include Ecuador and Zimbabwe which have both in recent times effectively adopted the US dollar as their official currency. In addition to the underlying economic problems these actions are designed to address they may also go some way towards addressing some of the associated financial reporting issues.

It is also important to recognise that economic characteristics such as those mentioned above are not always associated with difficult economic conditions, e.g. many successful economies have a currency that to some extent is, or has been, pegged to another currency or is otherwise linked to a different currency,

5.1.4.A Dual rates

One of the practical difficulties in translating foreign currency amounts that was noted above is where there is more than one exchange rate for that particular currency depending on the nature of the transaction. In some cases the difference between the exchange rates can be small and therefore it probably does not matter which rate is actually used. However, in other situations the difference can be quite significant.

In these circumstances, what rate should be used? IAS 21 states that 'when several exchange rates are available, the rate used is that at which the future cash flows represented by the transaction or balance could have been settled if those cash flows had occurred at the measurement date'. *[IAS 21.26]*. Companies should therefore look at the nature of the transaction and apply the appropriate exchange rate.

5.1.4.B Suspension of rates: temporary lack of exchangeability

Another practical difficulty which could arise is where for some reason exchangeability between two currencies is temporarily lacking at the transaction date or subsequently at the end of the reporting period. In this case, IAS 21 requires that the rate to be used is 'the first subsequent rate at which exchanges could be made'. *[IAS 21.26]*.

5.1.4.C Suspension of rates: longer term lack of exchangeability

The standard does not address the situation where there is a longer-term lack of exchangeability and the rate has not been restored. The Interpretations Committee considered this in the context of a number of issues associated with the Venezuelan currency, the Bolivar.

A number of official exchange mechanisms have been operating in the country, each with different exchange rates and each theoretically available for specified types of transaction. In practice, however, there have for a number of years been significant restrictions on entities' ability to make more than limited remittances out of the country using these mechanisms.

When the committee considered the issue in 2018 it described the circumstances in Venezuela in the following terms:

- the exchangeability of the foreign operation's functional currency with other currencies is administered by jurisdictional authorities and this exchange mechanism incorporates the use of (an) exchange rate(s) set by the authorities, i.e. (an) official exchange rate(s);
- the foreign operation's functional currency is subject to a long-term lack of exchangeability with other currencies, i.e. the exchangeability is not temporarily lacking; it has not been restored after the end of the reporting period;
- the lack of exchangeability with other currencies has resulted in the foreign operation being unable to access foreign currencies using the exchange mechanism described above.

In order to comply with IAS 21, the committee decided the rate to be used in these circumstances is the one which an entity would have access to through a legal exchange mechanism at the end of the reporting period (or at the date of a transaction). Consequently an entity should assess whether (any of) the official exchange rate(s) represents such a rate and use that rate if it does.[3]

The committee did not say what rate should be used if using the official exchange rate(s) did not comply with IAS 21. However, some entities have used an estimated exchange rate, an approach that is not precluded in the circumstances described above and which has been accepted by at least one European regulator.[4]

The committee noted that in general economic conditions are constantly evolving and highlighted the importance of reassessing at each reporting date whether (any of) the official exchange rate(s) should be used. It also drew attention to disclosure requirements in IFRS that might be relevant in these circumstances and these are covered at 10.4 below.[5]

The extreme circumstances in Venezuela which has led some entities to estimate an exchange rate rather than use an official or otherwise observable rate could in theory arise elsewhere. However, such situations would occur only rarely.[6]

The committee later decided to recommend that the IASB propose narrow-scope amendments to IAS 21 which would specify how an entity should determine the spot exchange rate and the disclosures it should provide when exchangeability between two currencies is lacking. They would also define exchangeability and thus a lack of exchangeability.[7] The progress of this project is covered in further detail at 11 below.

5.2 Reporting at the ends of subsequent reporting periods

At the end of each reporting period: *[IAS 21.23]*

(a) foreign currency monetary items should be translated using the closing rate;

(b) non-monetary items that are measured in terms of historical cost in a foreign currency should be translated using the exchange rate at the date of the transaction; and

(c) non-monetary items that are measured at fair value in a foreign currency should be translated using the exchange rate at the date when the fair value was determined.

The carrying amount of an item should be determined in conjunction with the relevant requirements of other standards. For example, property, plant and equipment may be measured in terms of fair value or historical cost in accordance with IAS 16 – *Property, Plant and Equipment*. Irrespective of whether the carrying amount is determined on the basis of historical cost or fair value, if the amount is determined in a foreign currency, IAS 21 requires that amount to be translated into the entity's functional currency. *[IAS 21.24]*.

The carrying amount of some items is determined by comparing two or more amounts. For example, IAS 2 requires the carrying amount of inventories to be determined as the lower of cost and net realisable value. Similarly, in accordance with IAS 36 – *Impairment of Assets* – the carrying amount of an asset for which there is an indication of impairment should be the lower of its carrying amount before considering possible impairment losses and its recoverable amount. When such an asset is non-monetary and is measured in a foreign currency, the carrying amount is determined by comparing:

- the cost or carrying amount, as appropriate, translated at the exchange rate at the date when that amount was determined (i.e. the rate at the date of the transaction for an item measured in terms of historical cost); and

- the net realisable value or recoverable amount, as appropriate, translated at the exchange rate at the date when that value was determined (e.g. the closing rate at the end of the reporting period).

The effect of this comparison may be that an impairment loss is recognised in the functional currency but would not be recognised in the foreign currency, or *vice versa*. *[IAS 21.25]*.

5.3 Treatment of exchange differences

5.3.1 Monetary items

The general rule in IAS 21 is that exchange differences on the settlement or retranslation of monetary items should be recognised in profit or loss in the period in which they arise. *[IAS 21.28]*.

When monetary items arise from a foreign currency transaction and there is a change in the exchange rate between the transaction date and the date of settlement, an exchange difference results. When the transaction is settled within the same accounting period as that in which it occurred, all the exchange difference is recognised in that period. However, when the transaction is settled in a subsequent accounting period, the exchange difference recognised in each period up to the date of settlement is determined by the change in exchange rates during each period. *[IAS 21.29]*.

These requirements can be illustrated in the following examples:

Example 15.5: Reporting an unsettled foreign currency transaction in the functional currency

A French entity purchases plant and equipment on credit from a Canadian supplier for C$328,000 in January 2021 when the exchange rate is €1=C$1.64. The entity records the asset at a cost of €200,000. At the French entity's year end at 31 March 2021 the account has not yet been settled. The closing rate is €1=C$1.61. The amount payable would be retranslated at €203,727 in the statement of financial position and an exchange loss of €3,727 would be reported as part of the profit or loss for the period. The cost of the asset would remain as €200,000.

Example 15.6: Reporting a settled foreign currency transaction in the functional currency

A UK entity sells goods to a German entity for €87,000 on 28 February 2021 when the exchange rate is £1=€1.45. It receives payment on 31 March 2021 when the exchange rate is £1=€1.50. On 28 February the UK entity will record a sale and corresponding receivable of £60,000. When payment is received on 31 March the actual amount received is only £58,000. The loss on exchange of £2,000 would be reported as part of the profit or loss for the period.

There are situations where the general rule above will not be applied. The first exception relates to exchange differences arising on a monetary item that, in substance, forms part of an entity's net investment in a foreign operation (see 6.3.1 below). In this situation the exchange differences should be recognised initially in other comprehensive income until the disposal of the investment (see 6.6 below). However, this treatment only applies in the financial statements that include the foreign operation and the reporting entity (e.g. consolidated financial statements when the foreign operation is a consolidated subsidiary or equity method investment). It does not apply to the reporting entity's separate financial statements or the financial statements of the foreign operation. Rather, the exchange differences will be recognised in profit or loss in the period in which they arise in the financial statements of the entity that has the foreign currency exposure. *[IAS 21.32]*. This is discussed further at 6.3.1 below.

The next exception relates to hedge accounting for foreign currency items, to which IFRS 9 applies. The application of hedge accounting requires an entity to account for some exchange differences differently from the treatment required by IAS 21. For example, IFRS 9 requires that exchange differences on monetary items that qualify as hedging instruments in a cash flow hedge or a hedge of a net investment in a foreign operation are recognised initially in other comprehensive income to the extent the hedge is effective. Hedge accounting is discussed in more detail in Chapter 53.

Another situation where exchange differences on monetary items are not recognised in profit or loss in the period they arise would be where an entity capitalises borrowing costs under IAS 23 – *Borrowing Costs* – since that standard requires exchange differences arising from foreign currency borrowings to be capitalised to the extent that they are regarded as an adjustment to interest costs (see Chapter 21 at 5.4). *[IAS 23.6]*.

One example of a monetary item given by IAS 21 is 'provisions that are to be settled in cash'. In most cases it will be appropriate for the exchange differences arising on provisions to be recognised in profit or loss in the period they arise. However, it may be that an entity has recognised a decommissioning provision under IAS 37 – *Provisions, Contingent Liabilities and Contingent Assets*. One practical difficulty with such a provision is that due to the long timescale of when the actual cash outflows will arise, an entity may not be able to say with any certainty the currency in which the transaction will actually be settled. Nevertheless if it is determined that it is expected to be settled in a foreign currency it will be a monetary item. The main issue then is what should happen to any exchange differences. IFRIC 1 – *Changes in Existing Decommissioning, Restoration and Similar Liabilities* – applies to any decommissioning or similar liability that has been both included as part of the cost of an asset and measured as a liability in accordance with IAS 37 (see Chapter 26 at 6.3.1). IFRIC 1 requires, *inter alia*, that any adjustment to such a provision resulting from changes in the estimated outflow of resources embodying economic benefits (e.g. cash flows) required to settle the obligation should not be recognised in profit or loss as it occurs, but should be added to or deducted from the cost of the asset to which it relates. The requirement of IAS 21 to recognise the exchange differences arising on the provision in profit or loss in the period in which they arise conflicts with this requirement in IFRIC 1. Accordingly, we believe that either approach could be applied as an accounting policy choice. However, in our experience, such exchange differences are most commonly dealt with in accordance with IFRIC 1, particularly by entities with material long-term provisions.

5.3.2 Non-monetary items

When non-monetary items are measured at fair value in a foreign currency they should be translated using the exchange rate as at the date when the fair value was determined. Therefore, any re-measurement gain or loss will include an element relating to the change in exchange rates. In this situation, the exchange differences are recognised as part of the gain or loss arising on the fair value re-measurement.

When a gain or loss on a non-monetary item is recognised in other comprehensive income, any exchange component of that gain or loss should also be recognised in other comprehensive income. *[IAS 21.30]*. For example, IAS 16 requires some gains and losses arising on a revaluation of property, plant and equipment to be recognised in other comprehensive income (see Chapter 18 at 6.2). When such an asset is measured in a foreign currency, the revalued amount should be translated using the rate at the date the value is determined, resulting in an exchange difference that is also recognised in other comprehensive income. *[IAS 21.31]*.

Conversely, when a gain or loss on a non-monetary item is recognised in profit or loss, e.g. financial instruments that are measured at fair value through profit or loss in accordance with IFRS 9 (see Chapter 50 at 2.4) or an investment property accounted for using the fair value model (see Chapter 19 at 6), any exchange component of that gain or loss should be recognised in profit or loss. [IAS 21.30].

An example of an accounting policy dealing with the reporting of foreign currency transactions in the functional currency of an entity is illustrated below.

Extract 15.1: ING Groep N.V. (2018)

Notes to the Consolidated annual accounts [extract]

1 Accounting policies [extract]

Foreign currency translation [extract]

Functional and presentation currency

Items included in the annual accounts of each of the Group's entities are measured using the currency of the primary economic environment in which the entity operates (the functional currency). The Consolidated annual accounts are presented in euros, which is Group's presentation currency.

Transactions and balances [extract]

Foreign currency transactions are translated into the functional currency using the exchange rate prevailing at the date of the transactions. Exchange rate differences resulting from the settlement of such transactions and from the translation at year-end exchange rates of monetary assets and liabilities denominated in foreign currencies are recognised in the statement of profit or loss, except when deferred in equity as part of qualifying cash flow hedges or qualifying net investment hedges.

Non-monetary items that are measured in terms of historical cost in a foreign currency are translated using the exchange rate at the date of the transaction.

Exchange rate differences on non-monetary items, measured at fair value through profit or loss, are reported as part of the fair value gain or loss. Non-monetary items are retranslated at the date fair value is determined. Exchange rate differences on non-monetary items measured at fair value through the revaluation reserve are included in the revaluation reserve in equity.

5.4 Determining whether an item is monetary or non-monetary

IAS 21 generally requires that monetary items denominated in foreign currencies be retranslated using closing rates at the end of the reporting period and non-monetary items should not be retranslated (see 5.2 above). Monetary items are defined as 'units of currency held and assets and liabilities to be received or paid in a fixed or determinable number of units of currency'. [IAS 21.8]. The standard elaborates further on this by stating that 'the essential feature of a monetary item is a right to receive (or an obligation to deliver) a fixed or determinable number of units of currency'. Examples given by IAS 21 are pensions and other employee benefits to be paid in cash; provisions that are to be settled in cash; cash dividends that are recognised as a liability; and lease liabilities. [IAS 21.16]. More obvious examples are cash and bank balances; trade receivables and payables; and loan receivables and payables.

IFRS 9 also indicates that where a foreign currency bond is held as a debt instrument measured at fair value through other comprehensive income, it should first be accounted for at amortised cost in the underlying currency, thus effectively treating that amount as if it was a monetary item. This guidance is discussed further in Chapter 50 at 4.1.

IAS 21 also states that 'a contract to receive (or deliver) a variable number of the entity's own equity instruments or a variable amount of assets in which the fair value to be received (or delivered) equals a fixed or determinable number of units of currency is a monetary item'. *[IAS 21.16]*. No examples of such contracts are given in IAS 21. However, it would seem to embrace those contracts settled in the entity's own equity shares that under IAS 32 – *Financial Instruments: Presentation* – would be presented as financial assets or liabilities (see Chapter 47 at 5.2).

Conversely, the essential feature of a non-monetary item is the absence of a right to receive (or an obligation to deliver) a fixed or determinable number of units of currency. Examples given by the standard are amounts prepaid for goods and services; goodwill; intangible assets; inventories; property, plant and equipment; provisions that are to be settled by the delivery of a non-monetary asset; and right-of-use assets. *[IAS 21.16]*. IFRS 9 states that investments in equity instruments are non-monetary items. *[IFRS 9.B5.7.3]*. It follows that equity investments in subsidiaries, associates or joint ventures are non-monetary items.

Even with this guidance there will clearly be a number of situations where the distinction may not be altogether clear.

5.4.1 Deposits or progress payments

Entities may be required to pay deposits or progress payments when acquiring certain assets, such as property, plant and equipment or inventories, from foreign suppliers. The question then arises as to whether such payments should be retranslated as monetary items or not.

Example 15.7: Deposits or progress payments

A Dutch entity contracts to purchase an item of plant and machinery for US$10,000 on the following terms:

Payable on signing contract (1 August 2021)	– 10%
Payable on delivery (19 December 2021)	– 40%
Payable on installation (7 January 2022)	– 50%

At 31 December 2021 the entity has paid the first two amounts on the due dates when the respective exchange rates were €1=US$1.25 and €1=US$1.20. The closing rate at the end of its reporting period, 31 December 2021, is €1=US$1.15.

		(i) €	(ii) €
First payment	– US$1,000	800	870
Second payment	– US$4,000	3,333	3,478
		4,133	4,348

(i) If the payments made are regarded as prepayments or as progress payments then the amounts should be treated as non-monetary items and included in the statement of financial position at €4,133. This would appear to be consistent with US GAAP which in defining 'transaction date' states: 'A long-term commitment may have more than one transaction date (for example, the due date of each progress payment under a construction contract is an anticipated transaction date).'

(ii) If the payments made are regarded as deposits, and are refundable, then the amounts could possibly be treated as monetary items and included in the statement of financial position at €4,348 and an exchange gain of €215 recognised in profit or loss. A variant of this would be to only treat the first payment as a deposit until the second payment is made, since once delivery is made it is less likely that the asset will be returned and a refund sought from the supplier.

In practice, it will often be necessary to consider the terms of the contract to ascertain the nature of the payments made in order to determine the appropriate accounting treatment and this may well require the application of judgement, something acknowledged in IFRIC 22 (see 5.1.2 above). *[IFRIC 22.BC17]*.

5.4.2 Deposits and advance payments for actively traded commodities

In most cases the analysis at 5.4.1 above will be equally relevant for deposits or payments made in advance for commodities that are actively traded and have an observable market price. However, the fact that a market price for a commodity is available means it is easier for entities to enter into contracts to purchase or sell such items that give rise to monetary items as illustrated in the following example.

Example 15.8: Deposit paid for future delivery of gold

Company X is a German entity which has the euro as its functional currency. It manufactures and sells jewellery using various metals including gold. On 1 October 2021, when the quoted price of gold is US$100,000/kg, Company X enters into two contracts, each involving the purchase of 2kg of gold to be delivered on 31 January 2022. The gold will be used to make jewellery so the contracts will be treated as normal purchases rather than derivatives within the scope of IFRS 9 (see Chapter 45 at 4.2). Each contract requires Company X to pay a deposit of US$40,000 to the supplier immediately and this amount will be deducted from the total price which is due to be paid on 28 February 2022.

Fixed price contract

The first contract specifies that the total amount to be paid for the gold is US$200,000 with the remaining US$160,000 becoming payable in February.

The nature of this contract is no different to that of the one illustrated in Example 15.7 above. The deposit represents a prepayment of 20% of the cost of gold and will consequently be accounted for as a non-monetary asset. Therefore, Company X will not retranslate the balance between payment in October 2020 and delivery in January 2021. At the point of delivery Company X will recognise a payable of US$160,000, which will be a monetary liability.

Variable price contract

The second contract, which secures supply rather than price, specifies that the total price to be paid for the gold is determined by the US dollar denominated spot price on 31 January 2022. If the spot price on delivery is below US$20,000/kg, the total amount due for the gold will be less than the US$40,000 deposit and the supplier will either repay Company X any excess or apply the excess against a future order.

Although this second contract may seem very similar to the first, the analysis is somewhat different. The cost of the gold can only be determined on 31 January 2022 and, regardless of the market price of gold, the remaining amount Company X has to settle is the 'market value of the gold on 31 January 2022' minus US$40,000. Therefore, as the deposit does not expose Company X to the price of gold and it merely reduces the future payable by US$40,000, it is considered to be a monetary item.

If the market price of gold is below US$20,000/kg at the point of delivery, Company X will receive gold and cash or credit that together are worth US$40,000.

In other words, Company X should always receive US$40,000 of value for its US$40,000 deposit at the date of delivery. Therefore, the deposit paid in respect of the second contract represents a US dollar denominated monetary asset.

5.4.3 Investments in preference shares

Entities may invest in preference shares of other entities. Whether such shares are monetary items or not will depend on the rights attaching to the shares. IFRS 9 states that investments in equity instruments are non-monetary items (see 5.4 above). *[IFRS 9.B5.7.3]*. Thus, if the terms of the preference shares are such that they are classified by the issuer as equity, rather than as a financial liability, then they are non-monetary items. However, if the terms of the preference shares are such that they are classified by the issuer as a financial liability (e.g. a preference share that provides for mandatory redemption by the issuer for a fixed or determinable amount at a fixed or determinable future date) and by the holder as a financial asset measured at amortised cost or at fair value through other comprehensive income (see Chapter 50 at 4.1), they should be treated as monetary items.

5.4.4 Foreign currency share capital

An entity may issue share capital denominated in a currency that is not its functional currency or, due to changes in circumstances that result in a re-determination of its functional currency, may find that its share capital is no longer denominated in its functional currency. Neither IAS 21, IAS 32 nor IFRS 9 address the treatment of translation of share capital denominated in a currency other than the functional currency. In theory two treatments are possible: the foreign currency share capital (and any related share premium or additional paid-in capital) could be maintained at a fixed amount by being translated at a historical rate of exchange, or it could be retranslated annually at the closing rate as if it were a monetary amount. In the latter case a second question would arise: whether to recognise the difference arising on translation in profit or loss or in other comprehensive income or to deal with it within equity.

Where the shares denominated in a foreign currency are ordinary shares, or are otherwise irredeemable and classified as equity instruments, in our experience the most commonly applied view is that the shares should be translated at historical rates and not remeasured. This view reflects the fact that the effect of rate changes is not expected to have an impact on the entity's cash flows associated with those shares. Such capital items are included within the examples of non-monetary items listed in US GAAP (FASB ASC 830 – *Foreign Currency Matters*) as accounts to be remeasured using historical exchange rates when the temporal method is being applied. IAS 21 requires non-monetary items that are measured at historical cost in a foreign currency to be translated using the historical rate (see 5.2 above).

Where such share capital is retranslated at the closing rate, we do not believe that it is appropriate for the exchange differences to be recognised in profit or loss, since they do not affect the cash flows of the entity. Further, because the retranslation of such items has no effect on assets or liabilities it is not an item of income or expense to be recognised in other comprehensive income. Instead, the exchange differences should be taken to equity. Consequently, whether such share capital is maintained at a historical rate, or is dealt with in this way, the treatment has no impact on the overall equity of the entity.

Where the shares are not classified as equity instruments, but as financial liabilities, under IAS 32, e.g. preference shares that provide for mandatory redemption by the issuer for a fixed or determinable amount at a fixed or determinable future date, then, as with investments in such shares (see 5.4.3 above), they should be treated as monetary items and translated at the closing rate. Any exchange differences will be recognised in profit or loss, unless the shares form part of a hedging relationship and IFRS 9 would require the exchange differences to be accounted for differently (see Chapter 53).

5.4.5 Deferred tax

One of the examples of a monetary item included within the exposure draft that preceded IAS 21 was deferred tax.[8] However, this was dropped from the list of examples in the final standard. No explanation is given in IAS 21 as to why this is the case. Until 2007, IAS 12 – *Income Taxes* – suggested that any deferred foreign tax assets or liabilities are monetary items since it stated that 'where exchange differences on deferred foreign tax liabilities or assets are recognised in the income statement, such differences may be classified as deferred tax expense (income) if that presentation is considered to be the most useful to financial statement users'.[9] The reference to 'income statement' has now been changed to 'statement of comprehensive income', although the suggestion remains the same.

5.4.6 Post-employment benefit plans – foreign currency assets

For most entities, benefits payable under a defined benefit post-employment plan will be payable in the functional currency of the entity. However, such a plan may have monetary assets that are denominated in a foreign currency and/or non-monetary assets, the fair value of which are determined in a foreign currency. (Where benefits are payable in a currency that is different to the entity's functional currency, the considerations at 5.4.7 below will be relevant.)

Consider, for example, a UK company with the pound sterling as its functional currency which has a funded pension scheme in which benefit payments are based on the employees' sterling denominated salaries and are paid in sterling. The majority of plan assets comprise a mix of sterling denominated bonds, UK equities and UK properties. However, those assets also include a number of US dollar denominated bonds and equities issued by US companies that are listed on a US stock exchange. IAS 19 – *Employee Benefits* – requires all these assets to be measured at their fair value at the end of the reporting period, but how should the entity deal with any exchange differences or changes in fair value attributable to changes in exchange rates arising on the US assets?

IAS 21 gives as an example of a monetary item 'pensions and other employee benefits to be paid in cash'. Further, the accounting for defined benefit schemes under IAS 19 requires an entity to reflect net interest on the net defined benefit asset or liability in profit or loss and any difference between this amount and the actual return on plan assets in other comprehensive income (see Chapter 35 at 10.3 and 10.4.2). *[IAS 19.120, 127(b)]*. Consequently, it would seem appropriate to view the net pension asset or liability as a single unit of account measured in sterling. Therefore the gains and losses on all the US plan assets attributable to changes in foreign exchange rates would be dealt with as remeasurements in accordance with IAS 19 and recognised in other comprehensive income.

5.4.7 Post-employment benefit plans – foreign currency plans

For some entities the pension benefits payable under a post-employment benefit plan will not be payable in the functional currency of the entity. For example, a UK entity in the oil and gas industry may determine that its functional currency is the US dollar, but its employee costs including the pension benefits are payable in sterling. How should such an entity account for its post-employment benefit plan?

One of the examples of a monetary item given by IAS 21 is 'pensions and other employee benefits to be paid in cash'. However, the standard does not expand on this, and does not appear to make any distinction between pensions provided by defined contribution plans or defined benefit plans. Nor does it distinguish between funded or unfunded defined benefit plans.

Clearly for pensions that are payable under a defined contribution plan (or one that is accounted for as such) this is straightforward. Any liability for outstanding contributions at the end of the reporting period is a monetary item that should be translated at the closing rate, with any resulting exchange differences recognised in profit or loss. For an unfunded defined benefit plan in which the benefit payments are denominated in a foreign currency, applying IAS 21 would also seem to be straightforward. The defined benefit obligation is regarded as a monetary liability and exchange differences on the entire balance are recognised in profit or loss.

A funded defined benefit plan is a more a complex arrangement to assess under IAS 21, particularly if the plan assets include items that considered in their own right would be non-monetary and/or foreign currency monetary items. However, in the light of the guidance in IAS 21 noted above, our preferred view is to consider such arrangements as a single monetary item denominated in the currency in which the benefit payments are made. Therefore the requirements of IAS 19 will be applied in the currency in which the benefit payments are denominated and foreign currency gains or losses on the net asset or liability would be recognised in profit or loss.

Another approach would be to argue that a funded scheme is more akin to a non-monetary item and the exchange differences relating to the defined benefit obligation are similar to actuarial gains and losses. The calculation of the obligation under IAS 19 will be based on actuarial assumptions that reflect the currency of the obligation to the employee (for example, the discount rate used 'shall be consistent with the currency and estimated term' of the obligation *[IAS 19.83]*). Any variations from those assumptions on both the obligation and the assets are dealt with in the same way under IAS 19. Actuarial assumptions are 'an entity's best estimates of the variables that will determine the ultimate cost of providing post-employment benefits' and include financial assumptions. *[IAS 19.76]*. Although IAS 19 does not refer to exchange rates, it is clearly a variable that will determine the ultimate cost to the entity of providing the post-employment benefits. On that basis, the exchange differences relating to the defined benefit obligation would be accounted for in a similar manner to actuarial gains and losses. Although not our preferred accounting treatment, we consider this to be an acceptable approach.

Some might argue that the plan should be regarded as a 'foreign operation' under IAS 21 (see 2.3 above). However, in this situation it is very difficult to say that its 'functional currency' can be regarded as being different from that of the reporting entity given the relationship between the plan and the reporting entity (see 4 above). Thus, it would appear that the entity cannot treat the plan as a foreign operation with a different functional currency from its own.

5.5 Change in functional currency

IAS 21 requires management to use its judgement to determine the entity's functional currency such that it most faithfully represents the economic effects of the underlying transactions, events and conditions that are relevant to the entity (see 4 above).

Accordingly, once the functional currency is determined, it may be changed only if there is a change to those underlying transactions, events and conditions. For example, a change in the currency that mainly influences the sales prices of goods and services may lead to a change in an entity's functional currency. *[IAS 21.36]*.

When there is a change in an entity's functional currency, the entity should apply the translation procedures applicable to the new functional currency prospectively from the date of the change. *[IAS 21.35]*.

In other words, an entity translates all items into the new functional currency using the exchange rate at the date of the change. The resulting translated amounts for non-monetary items are treated as their historical cost. Exchange differences arising from the translation of a foreign operation recognised in other comprehensive income are not reclassified from equity to profit or loss until the disposal of the operation (see 6.6 below). *[IAS 21.37]*.

Example 15.9: Change in functional currency

The management of Entity A has considered the functional currency of the entity to be the euro. However, as a result of a change in circumstances affecting the operations of the entity, management determines that on 1 January 2021 the functional currency of the entity is now the US dollar. The exchange rate at that date is €1=US$1.20. Entity A's statement of financial position at 1 January 2021 in its old functional currency is as follows:

	€
Property, plant and equipment	200,000
Current assets	
Inventories	10,000
Receivables	20,000
Cash	5,000
	35,000
Current liabilities	
Payables	15,000
Taxation	3,000
	18,000
Net current assets	17,000
	217,000
Long-term loans	120,000
	97,000

Included within the statement of financial position at 1 January 2021 are the following items:

- Equipment with a cost of €33,000 and a net book value of €16,500. This equipment was originally purchased for £20,000 in 2015 and has been translated at the rate ruling at the date of purchase of £1=€1.65.
- Inventories with a cost of €6,000. These were purchased for US$6,000 and have been translated at the rate ruling at the date of purchase of €1=US$1.00.
- Payables of €5,000 representing the US$6,000 due in respect of the above inventories, translated at the rate ruling at 1 January 2021.
- Long-term loans of €15,000 representing the outstanding balance of £10,000 on a loan originally taken out to finance the acquisition of the above equipment, translated at £1=€1.50, the rate ruling at 1 January 2021.

Entity A applies the translational procedures applicable to its new functional currency prospectively from the date of change. Accordingly, all items in its statement of financial position at 1 January 2021 are translated at the rate of €1=US$1.20 giving rise to the following amounts:

	$
Property, plant and equipment	240,000
Current assets	
Inventories	12,000
Receivables	24,000
Cash	6,000
	42,000
Current liabilities	
Payables	18,000
Taxation	3,600
	21,600
Net current assets	20,400
	260,400
Long-term loans	144,000
	116,400

As far as the equipment that was originally purchased for £20,000 is concerned, the cost and net book value in terms of Entity A's new functional currency are US$39,600 and US$19,800 respectively, being €33,000 and €16,500 translated at €1=US$1.20. Entity A does not go back and translate the £20,000 cost at whatever the £ sterling/US dollar exchange rate was at the date of purchase and calculate a revised net book value on that basis.

Similarly, the inventories purchased in US dollars are included at $7,200, being €6,000 translated at €1=US$1.20. This is despite the fact that Entity A knows that the original cost was $6,000.

As far as the payables in respect of the inventories are concerned, these are included at $6,000, being €5,000 translated at €1=US$1.20. This represents the original amount payable in US dollars. However, this is as it should be since the original payable had been translated into euros at the rate ruling at 1 January 2021 and has just been translated back into US dollars at the same rate. The impact of the change in functional currency is that whereas Entity A had recognised an exchange gain of €1,000 while the functional currency was the euro, no further exchange difference will be recognised in respect of this amount payable. Exchange differences will now arise from 1 January 2021 on those payables denominated in euros, whereas no such differences would have arisen on such items prior to that date.

Similarly, the £10,000 amount outstanding on the loan will be included at $18,000, being €15,000 translated at €1=US$1.20. This is equivalent to the translation of the £10,000 at a rate of £1=US$1.80, being the direct exchange rate between the two currencies at 1 January 2021. In this case, whereas previously exchange gains and losses would have been recognised on this loan balance based on movements of the £/€ exchange rate, as from 1 January 2021 the exchange gains and losses will be recognised based on the £/$ exchange rate.

Often an entity's circumstances change gradually over time and it may not be possible to determine a precise date on which the functional currency changes. In these circumstances an entity will need to apply judgement to determine an appropriate date from which to apply the change, which might coincide with the beginning or end of an interim or annual accounting period.

Where an entity's functional currency changes, its management will often choose to align the entity's presentation currency with the new functional currency. The approach to be adopted when changing presentation currency is covered at 7 below.

5.6 Books and records not kept in functional currency

Occasionally, an entity may keep its underlying books and records in a currency that is not its functional currency under IAS 21. For example, it could record its transactions in terms of the local currency of the country in which it is located, possibly as a result of local requirements. In these circumstances, at the time the entity prepares its financial statements all amounts should be converted into the functional currency in accordance with the requirements of the standard discussed at 5.1 to 5.3 above.[10] This process is intended to produce the same amounts in the functional currency as would have occurred had the items been recorded initially in the functional currency. For example, monetary items should be translated into the functional currency using the closing rate, and non-monetary items that are measured on a historical cost basis should be translated using the exchange rate at the date of the transaction that resulted in their recognition which will result in local currency denominated transactions giving rise to exchange differences. *[IAS 21.34]*.

6 USE OF A PRESENTATION CURRENCY OTHER THAN THE FUNCTIONAL CURRENCY

An entity may, subject the requirement of relevant laws and regulations, present its financial statements in any currency (or currencies) (see 3 above). If the presentation currency differs from the entity's functional currency, it needs to translate its results and financial position into the presentation currency. For example, when a group contains individual entities with different functional currencies, the results and financial position of each entity are expressed in a common currency so that consolidated financial statements may be presented. *[IAS 21.38]*. There is no concept of a 'group' functional currency. Each entity within the group has its own functional currency, and the results and financial position of each entity have to be translated into the presentation currency that is used for the consolidated financial statements. *[IAS 21.18]*.

The requirements of IAS 21 in respect of this translation process are discussed below. The procedures to be adopted apply not only to the inclusion of foreign subsidiaries in consolidated financial statements but also to the incorporation of the results of associates and joint arrangements. *[IAS 21.44]*. They also apply when the results of a foreign branch are to be incorporated into the financial statements of an individual entity or a stand-alone entity preparing financial statements or when an entity preparing separate financial statements in accordance with IAS 27 presents its financial statements in a currency other than its functional currency.

In addition to these procedures, IAS 21 has additional provisions that apply when the results and financial position of a foreign operation are translated into a presentation currency so that the foreign operation can be included in the financial statements of the reporting entity by consolidation or the equity method. *[IAS 21.44]*. These additional provisions are covered at 6.3 to 6.5 below.

6.1 Translation to the presentation currency

Under IAS 21, the method of translation depends on whether the entity's functional currency is that of a hyperinflationary economy or not, and if it is, whether it is being translated into a presentation currency which is that of a hyperinflationary economy or not. A hyperinflationary economy is defined in IAS 29 – *Financial Reporting in Hyperinflationary Economies* (see Chapter 16 at 2.3). The requirements of IAS 21 discussed below can be summarised as follows:

	Presentation currency	
	Non-hyperinflationary	Hyperinflationary
Non-hyperinflationary functional currency		
Assets/liabilities		
– current period	Closing rate (current B/S date)	Closing rate (current B/S date)
– comparative period	Closing rate (comparative B/S date)	Closing rate (comparative B/S date)
Equity items		
– current period	Not specified	Not specified
– comparative period	Not specified	Not specified
Income/expenses (including those recognised in other comprehensive income)		
– current period	Actual rates (or appropriate average for current period)	Actual rates (or appropriate average for current period)
– comparative period	Actual rates (or appropriate average for comparative period)	Actual rates (or appropriate average for comparative period)
Exchange differences	Separate component of equity	Separate component of equity
Hyperinflationary functional currency		
Assets/liabilities		
– current period	Closing rate (current B/S date)	Closing rate (current B/S date)
– comparative period	Closing rate (comparative B/S date)	Closing rate (current B/S date)
Equity items		
– current period	Closing rate (current B/S date)	Closing rate (current B/S date)
– comparative period	Closing rate (comparative B/S date)	Closing rate (current B/S date)
Income/expenses (including those recognised in other comprehensive income)		
– current period	Closing rate (current B/S date)	Closing rate (current B/S date)
– comparative period	Closing rate (comparative B/S date)	Closing rate (current B/S date)
Exchange differences	Not specified	Not applicable

6.1.1 Functional currency is not that of a hyperinflationary economy

The results and financial position of an entity whose functional currency is not the currency of a hyperinflationary economy should be translated into a different presentation currency using the following procedures: *[IAS 21.39]*

(a) assets and liabilities for each statement of financial position presented (i.e. including comparatives) are translated at the closing rate at the reporting date;

(b) income and expenses for each statement of comprehensive income or separate income statement presented (i.e. including comparatives) are translated at exchange rates at the dates of the transactions; and

(c) all resulting exchange differences are recognised in other comprehensive income.

For practical reasons, the reporting entity may use a rate that approximates the actual exchange rate, e.g. an average rate for the period, to translate income and expense items.

However, if exchange rates fluctuate significantly, the use of the average rate for a period is inappropriate. *[IAS 21.40]*.

As discussed at 5.1.2 above, IFRIC 22 explains how to determine the 'date of transaction' for the purposes of an entity recording a foreign currency transaction in its functional currency, particularly when payments are made or received in advance of the associated transaction occurring. However, in our view, this guidance does not apply to the translation of an entity's results into a presentation currency; instead the date of transaction for this purpose is the date on which income or expense is recorded in profit or loss or other comprehensive income of the foreign operation.

A foreign operation may have reclassification adjustments to profit or loss of gains or losses previously recognised in other comprehensive income, for example as a result of the application of cash flow hedge accounting. However, IAS 21 does not explicitly address how these adjustments should be translated into the presentation currency. In our experience the most commonly applied approach is to regard them as income or expenses of the foreign operation to be translated at the exchange rate at the date of reclassification in accordance with paragraph 39(b). For cash flow hedges, this better reflects the hedge accounting reported in the foreign operation's own financial statements. Nevertheless, some would argue that reclassification adjustments do not represent income or expenses. Consequently, paragraph 39(b) would not apply and the reclassification is translated using the historical exchange rates at the dates the original gains or losses arose. In our view, each of these approaches represents an acceptable accounting policy choice.

The translational process above makes only limited reference to the translation of equity items, although the selection of accounting policy for translating reclassification adjustments is likely to influence whether an entity translates the associated equity balance in order to prevent a residual amount being left within the reserve. The treatment of such items is discussed at 6.2 below.

IAS 21 indicates that the exchange differences referred to in item (c) above result from: *[IAS 21.41]*

- translating income and expenses at the exchange rates at the dates of the transactions and assets and liabilities at the closing rate. Such exchange differences arise both on income and expense items recognised in profit or loss and on those recognised in other comprehensive income; and
- translating the opening net assets at a closing rate that differs from the previous closing rate.

This is not in fact completely accurate since if the entity has had any transactions with equity holders that have resulted in a change in the net assets during the period there are likely to be further exchange differences that need to be recognised to the extent that the closing rate differs from the rate used to translate the transaction. This will particularly be the case where a parent has subscribed for further equity shares in a subsidiary.

The reason why these exchange differences are not recognised in profit or loss is because the changes in exchange rates have little or no direct effect on the present and future cash flows from operations. *[IAS 21.41]*.

The application of these procedures is illustrated in the following example.

Foreign exchange

Example 15.10: *Translation of a non-hyperinflationary functional currency to a non-hyperinflationary presentation currency*

An Australian entity owns 100% of the share capital of a foreign entity which was set up a number of years ago when the exchange rate was A$1=FC2. It is consolidating the financial statements of the subsidiary in its consolidated financial statements for the year ended 31 December 2021. The exchange rate at the year-end is A$1=FC4 (2020: A$1=FC3). For the purposes of illustration, it is assumed that exchange rates have not fluctuated significantly and the appropriate weighted average rate for the year was A$1=FC3.5, and that the currency of the foreign entity is not that of a hyperinflationary economy. The income statement of the subsidiary for that year and its statement of financial position at the beginning and end of the year in its functional currency and translated into Australian dollars are as follows:

Income statement

	FC	A$
Sales	35,000	10,000
Cost of sales	(33,190)	(9,483)
Depreciation	(500)	(143)
Interest	(350)	(100)
Profit before taxation	960	274
Taxation	(460)	(131)
Profit after taxation	500	143

Statements of financial position	2020 FC	2021 FC	2020 A$	2021 A$
Property, plant and equipment	6,000	5,500	2,000	1,375
Current assets				
Inventories	2,700	3,000	900	750
Receivables	4,800	4,000	1,600	1,000
Cash	200	600	67	150
	7,700	7,600	2,567	1,900
Current liabilities				
Payables	4,530	3,840	1,510	960
Taxation	870	460	290	115
	5,400	4,300	1,800	1,075
Net current assets	2,300	3,300	767	825
	8,300	8,800	2,767	2,200
Long-term loans	3,600	3,600	1,200	900
	4,700	5,200	1,567	1,300
Share capital	1,000	1,000	500	500
Retained profits*	3,700	4,200	1,500	1,643
Exchange reserve*			(433)	(843)
	4,700	5,200	1,567	1,300

* The opening balances for 2020 in A$ have been assumed and represent cumulative amounts since the foreign entity was set up.

The movement of A$(410) in the exchange reserve included as a separate component of equity is made up as follows:

(i) the exchange loss of A$392 on the opening net investment in the subsidiary, calculated as follows:

Opening net assets at opening rate	– FC4,700 at FC3 = A$1 =	A$1,567
Opening net assets at closing rate	– FC4,700 at FC4 = A$1 =	A$1,175
Exchange loss on net assets		A$392

(ii) the exchange loss of A$18, being the difference between the income account translated at an average rate, i.e. A$143, and at the closing rate, i.e. A$125.

When the exchange differences relate to a foreign operation that is consolidated but not wholly-owned, accumulated exchange differences arising from translation and attributable to non-controlling interests are allocated to, and recognised as part of, non-controlling interests in the consolidated statement of financial position. *[IAS 21.41]*.

An example of an accounting policy dealing with the translation of entities whose functional currency is not that of a hyperinflationary economy is illustrated in the following extract.

> **Extract 15.2: Lloyds Banking Group plc (2018)**
> Notes to the consolidated financial statements [extract]
> Note 2: Accounting policies [extract]
> (N) Foreign currency translation
>
> Items included in the financial statements of each of the Group's entities are measured using the currency of the primary economic environment in which the entity operates (the functional currency). Foreign currency transactions are translated into the appropriate functional currency using the exchange rates prevailing at the dates of the transactions. Foreign exchange gains and losses resulting from the settlement of such transactions and from the translation at year end exchange rates of monetary assets and liabilities denominated in foreign currencies are recognised in the income statement, except when recognised in other comprehensive income as qualifying cash flow or net investment hedges. Non-monetary assets that are measured at fair value are translated using the exchange rate at the date that the fair value was determined. Translation differences on equities and similar non-monetary items held at fair value through profit and loss are recognised in profit or loss as part of the fair value gain or loss. Translation differences on non-monetary financial assets measured at fair value through other comprehensive income, such as equity shares, are included in the fair value reserve in equity unless the asset is a hedged item in a fair value hedge.
>
> The results and financial position of all group entities that have a functional currency different from the presentation currency are translated into the presentation currency as follows: the assets and liabilities of foreign operations, including goodwill and fair value adjustments arising on the acquisition of a foreign entity, are translated into sterling at foreign exchange rates ruling at the balance sheet date; and the income and expenses of foreign operations are translated into sterling at average exchange rates unless these do not approximate to the foreign exchange rates ruling at the dates of the transactions in which case income and expenses are translated at the dates of the transactions.
>
> Foreign exchange differences arising on the translation of a foreign operation are recognised in other comprehensive income and accumulated in a separate component of equity together with exchange differences arising from the translation of borrowings and other currency instruments designated as hedges of such investments (see (F)(3) above). On disposal or liquidation of a foreign operation, the cumulative amount of exchange differences relating to that foreign operation are reclassified from equity and included in determining the profit or loss arising on disposal or liquidation.

The IASB had considered an alternative translation method, which would have been to translate all amounts (including comparatives) at the most recent closing rate. This was considered to have several advantages: it is simple to apply; it does not generate any new gains and losses; and it does not change ratios such as return on assets. Supporters of this method believed that the process of merely expressing amounts in a different currency should preserve the same relationships among amounts as measured in the functional currency. *[IAS 21.BC17]*. These views were probably based more on the IASB's proposals for allowing an entity to present its financial statements in a currency other than its functional currency, rather than the translation of foreign operations for inclusion in consolidated financial statements. Such an approach does have theoretical appeal. However, the major drawback is that it would require the comparatives to be restated from those previously reported.

The IASB rejected this alternative and decided to require the method that the previous version of IAS 21 required for translating the financial statements of a foreign operation. *[IAS 21.BC20]*. It is asserted that this method results in the same amounts in the presentation currency regardless of whether the financial statements of a foreign operation are first translated into the functional currency of another group entity and then into the presentation currency or translated directly into the presentation currency. *[IAS 21.BC18]*. We agree that it will result in the same amounts for the statement of financial position, regardless of whether the translation process is a single or two-stage process. However, it does not necessarily hold true for income and expense items particularly if an indirectly held foreign operation is disposed of – this is discussed further at 6.1.5 and 6.6.3 below. Differences will also arise between the two methods if an average rate is used, although these are likely to be insignificant.

The IASB states that the method chosen avoids the need to decide the currency in which to express the financial statements of a multinational group before they are translated into the presentation currency. In addition, it produces the same amounts in the presentation currency for a stand-alone entity as for an identical subsidiary of a parent whose functional currency is the presentation currency. *[IAS 21.BC19]*. For example, if a Swiss entity with the Swiss franc as its functional currency wishes to present its financial statements in euros, the translated amounts in euros should be the same as those for an identical entity with the Swiss franc as its functional currency that are included within the consolidated financial statements of its parent that presents its financial statements in euros.

6.1.2 Functional currency is that of a hyperinflationary economy

The results and financial position of an entity whose functional currency is the currency of a hyperinflationary economy should be translated into a different presentation currency using the following procedures: *[IAS 21.42]*

(a) all amounts (i.e. assets, liabilities, equity items, income and expenses, including comparatives) are translated at the closing rate at the date of the most recent statement of financial position; except that

(b) when amounts are translated into the currency of a non-hyperinflationary economy, comparative amounts are those that were presented as current year amounts in the relevant prior year financial statements (i.e. not adjusted for subsequent changes in the price level or subsequent changes in exchange rates).

Similarly, in the period during which the functional currency of a foreign operation such as a subsidiary becomes hyperinflationary and applies IAS 29 for the first time, the parent's consolidated financial statements for the comparative period should not be restated for the effects of hyperinflation. Nor should any exchange differences associated with such a foreign operation that were accumulated in a separate component of equity be reclassified within equity. Instead they will be reclassified to profit or loss on disposal or partial disposal of the foreign operation as set out at 6.6 below.[11]

When an entity's functional currency is the currency of a hyperinflationary economy, the entity should restate its financial statements in accordance with IAS 29 before applying the translation method set out above, except for comparative amounts that are translated into a currency of a non-hyperinflationary economy (see (b) above). *[IAS 21.43]*.

When the economy ceases to be hyperinflationary and the entity no longer restates its financial statements in accordance with IAS 29, it should use as the historical costs for translation into the presentation currency the amounts restated to the price level at the date the entity ceased restating its financial statements. *[IAS 21.43]*.

Example 15.11: Translation of a hyperinflationary functional currency to a non-hyperinflationary presentation currency

Using the same basic facts as Example 15.10 above, but assuming that the functional currency of the subsidiary is that of a hyperinflationary economy, the income statement of the subsidiary for that year and its statement of financial position at the beginning and end of the year in its functional currency and translated into Australian dollars are as shown below. The IAS 29 hyperinflation adjustments have not been illustrated below. For a discussion of these adjustments, see Chapter 16, particularly at 11 which explains how they may be presented in a situation such as this.

Income statement	FC	A$		
Sales	35,000	8,750		
Cost of sales	(33,190)	(8,298)		
Depreciation	(500)	(125)		
Interest	(350)	(87)		
Profit before taxation	960	240		
Taxation	(460)	(115)		
Profit after taxation	500	125		
Statements of financial position	2020 FC	2021 FC	2020 A$	2021 A$
Property, plant and equipment	6,000	5,500	2,000	1,375
Current assets				
Inventories	2,700	3,000	900	750
Receivables	4,800	4,000	1,600	1,000
Cash	200	600	67	150
	7,700	7,600	2,567	1,900
Current liabilities				
Payables	4,530	3,840	1,510	960
Taxation	870	460	290	115
	5,400	4,300	1,800	1,075
Net current assets	2,300	3,300	767	825
	8,300	8,800	2,767	2,200
Long-term loans	3,600	3,600	1,200	900
	4,700	5,200	1,567	1,300
Share capital	1,000	1,000	333	250
Consolidation adjustment*			167	250
Retained profits**	3,700	4,200	1,500	1,625
Exchange reserve**			(433)	(825)
	4,700	5,200	1,567	1,300

*   The consolidation adjustment plus the restated A$ amount of share capital eliminates against the parent's investment in subsidiary recorded at the historical exchange rate of A$1=FC2, i.e. A$500. If the example incorporated the IAS 29 hyperinflation adjustments, this difference would include both translation and hyperinflation effects.

**   The opening balances for 2020 in A$ have been assumed and represent cumulative amounts since the foreign entity was set up.

The movement in retained profits is represented by the A$125 profit for the year and the movement in the exchange reserve is an exchange loss of A$392 which represents the reduction in opening net assets due to the movements in exchange, calculated as follows:

Opening balance at opening rate	– FC4,700 at FC3 = A$1 =	A$1,567
Opening balance at closing rate	– FC4,700 at FC4 = A$1 =	A$1,175
Exchange loss		A$(392)

Historically it was considered unclear what should happen to such an exchange difference (and also the movement in share capital caused by the change in exchange rates) since paragraph 42 of IAS 21 makes no reference to any possible exchange differences arising from this process. Typically, they were recognised, in aggregate with the related adjustment arising from applying IAS 29 (which in the example above are ignored), in other comprehensive income or directly in equity.[12]

However, in March 2020 the IFRS Interpretations Committee clarified that the exchange differences above should be recognised in other comprehensive income. The agenda decision also addressed how the adjustments from applying IAS 29 should be presented and a more extensive discussion of this issue is included in Chapter 16 at 11, although in summary they would be recognised in other comprehensive income if considered exchange differences and directly in equity otherwise.[13]

An example of an accounting policy dealing with the translation of entities whose functional currency is that of a hyperinflationary economy is illustrated in the following extract.

Extract 15.3: Sberbank of Russia (2018)

Notes to the Consolidated Financial Statements – 31 December 2018 [extract]

42   Basis of Preparation and Significant Accounting Policies [extract]

Foreign currency translation. The functional currency of each of the Group's consolidated entities is the currency of the primary economic environment in which the entity operates. The Bank's functional currency and the Group's presentation currency is the national currency of the Russian Federation, Russian Rouble ("RR").

Monetary assets and liabilities are translated into each entity's functional currency at the applicable exchange rate at the respective reporting dates. Foreign exchange gains and losses resulting from the settlement of the transactions performed by the companies of the Group and from the translation of monetary assets and liabilities into each entity's functional currency are recognized in profit or loss. Effects of exchange rate changes on the fair value of equity instruments are recorded as part of the fair value gain or loss.

The results and financial position of each group entity (except for the subsidiary bank in Belarus the economy of which was considered hyperinflationary before 2015) are translated into the presentation currency as follows:

(I)   assets and liabilities for each statement of financial position presented are translated at the applicable closing rate at the respective reporting date;

(II)   income and expenses for each statement of profit or loss and statement of other comprehensive income are translated either at the rates prevailing at the dates of the transactions or at average exchange rates (in case this average is a reasonable approximation of the cumulative effect of the rates prevailing on the transaction dates).

The results and financial position of an entity whose functional currency is the currency of a hyperinflationary economy shall be translated into a different presentation currency using the following procedure: all amounts (i.e. assets, liabilities, equity items, income and expenses, including comparatives) shall be translated at the closing rate at the date of the most recent statement of financial position.

When amounts are translated into the currency of a non-hyperinflationary economy, comparative amounts shall be those that were presented as current year amounts in the relevant prior year financial statements (i.e. not adjusted for subsequent changes in the price level or subsequent changes in exchange rates).

Exchange differences arising on the translation of results and financial position of each of the Group's consolidated entities are included in Exchange differences on translating foreign operations in other comprehensive income and taken to a separate component of equity – Foreign currency translation reserve.

6.1.3 Dual rates, suspension of rates and lack of exchangeability

The problems of dual rates, suspensions of rates and lack of exchangeability in relation to the translation of foreign currency transactions and balances into an entity's functional currency and the related requirements of IAS 21 dealing with such issues have already been discussed in 5.1.4 above. However, the standard makes no reference to them in the context of translating the results and financial position of an entity into a different presentation currency, particularly where the results and financial position of a foreign operation are being translated for inclusion in the financial statements of the reporting entity by consolidation or the equity method.

Where the problem is one of a temporary suspension of rates, the predominant practice noted by the Interpretations Committee is for the requirement in IAS 21 relating to transactions and balances to be followed; i.e. by using 'the first subsequent rate at which exchanges could be made'. In this context the rate will be the one at which future cash flows could be settled when viewing the net investment as a whole.[14] This approach is broadly consistent with US GAAP which states that the rate to be used to translate foreign financial statements should be, in the absence of unusual circumstances, the rate applicable to dividend remittance.

The standard does not address the situation where there is a longer-term lack of exchangeability. In these circumstances the discussion at 5.1.4.C above, including the Interpretations Committee's consideration of this issue in the context of the Venezuelan currency, will be relevant. Determining the appropriate exchange rate(s) to use will require the application of judgement. The rate(s) selected will depend on the entity's individual facts and circumstances, particularly its legal ability to convert currency or to settle transactions using a specific rate and its intent to use a particular mechanism, including whether the rate available through that mechanism is published or readily determinable. The disclosure requirements highlighted by the committee and covered at 10.4 below will also be relevant in these circumstances.

6.1.4 Calculation of average rate

When translating the results of an entity whose functional currency is not that of a hyperinflationary economy, for practical reasons, the reporting entity may use a rate that approximates the actual exchange rate, e.g. an average rate for the period, to translate income and expense items. *[IAS 21.40]*.

The standard does not give any guidance on the factors that should be taken into account in determining what may be an appropriate average rate for the period – it merely says that 'if exchange rates fluctuate significantly, the use of the average rate for the period is inappropriate'. *[IAS 21.40]*. What methods are, therefore, available to entities to use in calculating an appropriate average rate? Possible methods might be:

(a) mid-year rate;
(b) average of opening and closing rates;
(c) average of month end/quarter end rates;
(d) average of monthly average rates;
(e) monthly/quarterly results at month end/quarter end rates; or
(f) monthly/quarterly results at monthly/quarterly averages.

Example 15.12: Calculation of average rate

A Spanish entity has a foreign subsidiary and is preparing its consolidated financial statements for the year ended 30 April 2021. It intends to use an average rate for translating the results of the subsidiary. The relevant exchange rates for €1=FC are as follows:

Month	Month end	Average for month	Average for quarter	Average for year
April 2020	1.67			
May 2020	1.63	1.67		
June 2020	1.67	1.64		
July 2020	1.64	1.65	1.65	
August 2020	1.67	1.64		
September 2020	1.70	1.63		
October 2020	1.67	1.68	1.65	
November 2020	1.65	1.70		
December 2020	1.66	1.66		
January 2021	1.64	1.67	1.68	
February 2021	1.60	1.65		
March 2021	1.61	1.63		
April 2021	1.61	1.62	1.63	1.65

Average of month end rates – 1.65

Average of quarter end rates – 1.64

The results of the subsidiary for each of the 12 months to 30 April 2021 and the translation thereof under each of the above methods (using monthly figures where appropriate) are shown below:

Method (a)   FC31,050 @ 1.67 = €18,593
Method (b)   FC31,050 @ 1.64 = €18,933
Method (c) – monthly   FC31,050 @ 1.65 = €18,818
Method (c) – quarterly FC31,050 @ 1.64 = €18,933
Method (d)   FC31,050 @ 1.65 = €18,818

Month	FC	(e) quarterly €	(e) monthly €	(f) quarterly €	(f) monthly €
May 2020	1,000		613		599
June 2020	1,100		659		671
July 2020	1,200	2,012	732	2,000	727
August 2020	1,300		778		793
September 2020	1,300		765		798
October 2020	1,350	2,365	808	2,394	804
November 2020	1,400		848		824
December 2020	1,400		843		843
January 2021	2,000	2,927	1,220	2,857	1,198
February 2021	5,000		3,125		3,030
March 2021	10,000		6,211		6,135
April 2021	4,000	11,801	2,484	11,656	2,469
Total	31,050	19,105	19,086	18,907	18,891

It can be seen that by far the simplest methods to use are the methods (a) to (d).

In our view methods (a) and (b) should not normally be used as it is unlikely in times of volatile exchange rates that they will give appropriate weighting to the exchange rates which have been in existence throughout the period in question. They are only likely to give an acceptable answer if the exchange rate has been static or steadily increasing or decreasing throughout the period.

Method (c) based on quarter end rates has similar drawbacks and therefore should not normally be used.

Method (c) based on month end rates and method (d) are better than the previous methods as they do take into account more exchange rates which have applied throughout the year, with method (d) being more precise, as this will have taken account of daily exchange rates. Average monthly rates for most major currencies are likely to be given in publications issued by the government, banks and other sources and therefore it is unnecessary for entities to calculate their own. The work involved in calculating an average for the year, therefore, is not very onerous. Method (d) will normally give reasonable and acceptable results when there are no seasonal variations in items of income and expenditure.

Where there are seasonal variations in items of income and expenditure, using a single average rate for the entire reporting period is unlikely to result in a reasonable approximation of applying actual rates. In these situations appropriate exchange rates should be applied to the appropriate items. This can be done by using either of methods (e) or (f) preferably using figures and rates for each month. Where such a method is being used care should be taken to ensure that the periodic accounts are accurate and that cut-off procedures have been adequate, otherwise significant items may be translated at the wrong average rate.

Where there are significant one-off items of income and expenses then it is likely that actual rates at the date of the transaction will need to be used to translate such items.

6.1.5 Accounting for foreign operations where sub-groups exist

A reporting entity comprising a group with intermediate holding companies may adopt either the direct or the step-by-step method of consolidation. The direct method involves the financial statements of foreign operations being translated directly into the presentation currency of the ultimate parent. The step-by-step method involves the financial statements of the foreign operation first being translated into the functional currency of any intermediate parent(s) and then into the presentation currency of the ultimate parent. [IFRIC 16.17].

It is asserted that both methods will result in the same amounts being reported in the presentation currency. [IAS 21.BC18]. However, as set out at 6.6.3 below, particularly in Example 15.20, and as acknowledged by the Interpretations Committee,[15] this assertion is demonstrably untrue in certain situations.

Whilst the various requirements of the standard appear to indicate that the direct method should be used and the Interpretations Committee has indicated it is the conceptually correct method,[16] IAS 21 does not require an entity to use the direct method or to make adjustments to produce the same result. Rather, an entity has an accounting policy choice as to which of the two methods it should use and the method selected should be used consistently for all net investments. [IFRIC 16.17].

6.2 Translation of equity items

The method of translation of the results and financial position of an entity whose functional currency is not the currency of a hyperinflationary economy is discussed at 6.1.1 above. The translation process makes only limited reference to the translation of equity items. The exposure draft that preceded the standard had proposed that '... equity items other than those resulting from income and expense recognised in the period ... shall be translated at the closing rate'. However, the IASB decided not to specify in the standard the translation rate for equity items,[17] but no explanation has been given in the Basis for Conclusions about this matter.

So how should entities deal with the translation of equity items?

6.2.1 Share capital

Where an entity presents its financial statements in a currency other than its functional currency, it would seem more appropriate that its share capital (whether they are ordinary shares, or are otherwise irredeemable and classified as equity instruments) should be translated at historical rates of exchange. Such capital items are included within the examples of non-monetary items listed in US GAAP as accounts to be remeasured using historical exchange rates when the temporal method is being applied (see 5.4.4 above). IAS 21 requires non-monetary items that are measured at historical cost in a foreign currency to be translated using the historical rate (see 5.2 above). Translation at an historical rate would imply using the rate ruling at the date of the issue of the shares. However, where a subsidiary is presenting its financial statements in the currency of its parent, it may be that the more appropriate historical rate for share capital that was in issue at the date it became a subsidiary would be that ruling at the date it became a subsidiary of the parent, rather than at earlier dates of issue.

Where such share capital is retranslated at the closing rate, we do not believe that it is appropriate for the exchange differences to be recognised in other comprehensive income nor for them to be taken to the separate component of equity required by IAS 21 (since to do so could result in them being reclassified from equity to profit or loss upon disposal of part of the entity's operations in the future), but should either be taken to retained earnings or some other reserve. Consequently, whether such share capital is maintained at a historical rate, or is dealt with in this way, the treatment has no impact on the overall equity of the entity.

6.2.2 Other equity balances resulting from transactions with equity holders

In addition to share capital, an entity may have other equity balances resulting from the issue of shares, such as a share premium account (additional paid-in capital). Like share capital, the translation of such balances could be done at either historical rates or at the closing rate. However, we believe that whichever method is adopted it should be consistent with the treatment used for share capital. Again, where exchange differences arise through using the closing rate, we believe that it is not appropriate for them to be recognised in other comprehensive income or taken to the separate component of equity required by IAS 21.

A similar approach should be adopted where an entity has acquired its own equity shares and has deducted those 'treasury shares' from equity as required by IAS 32 (see Chapter 47 at 9).

6.2.3 Other equity balances resulting from income and expenses being recognised in other comprehensive income

Under IAS 21, income and expenses recognised in other comprehensive income are translated at the exchange rates ruling at the dates of the transaction. *[IAS 21.39(b), 41].* Examples of such items include certain gains and losses on:

- revalued property, plant and equipment under IAS 16 (see Chapter 18 at 6.2) and revalued intangible assets under IAS 38 – *Intangible Assets* (see Chapter 17 at 8.2);
- debt instruments measured at fair value through other comprehensive income, investments in equity instruments designated at fair value through other comprehensive income and financial liabilities designated at fair value through profit or loss under IFRS 9 (see Chapter 50 at 2.3, 2.5 and 2.4 respectively);
- gains and losses on cash flow hedges under IFRS 9 (see Chapter 53); and
- any amounts of current and deferred tax recognised in other comprehensive income under IAS 12 (see Chapter 33 at 10).

This would suggest that where these gains and losses are accumulated within a separate reserve or component of equity, then any period-end balance should represent the cumulative translated amounts of such gains and losses. However, as IAS 21 is silent on the matter it would seem that it would be acceptable to translate these equity balances at the closing rate.

The treatment of equity balances that are subsequently reclassified to profit or loss, for example cash flow hedge reserves of a foreign operation, typically depends on the exchange rate used to translate the reclassification adjustments (a topic which is discussed at 6.1.1 above). Where reclassification adjustments are translated using the exchange rate at the date of reclassification, translating the equity balance at closing rate should mean no residual balance is left in the reserve once the hedge accounting is completely accounted for. Conversely, where reclassification adjustments are translated using exchange rates at the dates the original gains or losses arose, an entity would avoid a residual balance remaining in the reserve by not retranslating the equity balance. However, whether such balances are maintained at the original translated rates, or are translated at closing rates, the treatment has no impact on the overall equity of the entity.

6.3 Exchange differences on intragroup balances

The incorporation of the results and financial position of a foreign operation with those of the reporting entity should follow normal consolidation procedures, such as the elimination of intragroup balances and intragroup transactions of a subsidiary. *[IAS 21.45].* On this basis, there is a tendency sometimes to assume that exchange differences on intragroup balances should not impact on the reported profit or loss for the group in the consolidated financial statements. However, an intragroup monetary asset (or liability), whether short-term or long-term, cannot be eliminated against the corresponding intragroup liability (or asset) without the entity with the currency exposure recognising an exchange difference on the intragroup balance.

This exchange difference will be reflected in that entity's profit or loss for the period (see 5.3.1 above) and, except as indicated below, IAS 21 requires this exchange difference to continue to be included in profit or loss in the consolidated financial statements. This is because the monetary item represents a commitment to convert one currency into another and exposes the reporting entity to a gain or loss through currency fluctuations.

6.3.1 Monetary items included as part of the net investment in a foreign operation

An exception to the general rule at 6.3 above applies where an exchange difference arises on a balance that, in substance, forms part of an entity's net investment in a foreign operation, for example an intragroup balance with a subsidiary. Instead the exchange difference is not recognised in profit or loss in the consolidated financial statements, but is recognised in other comprehensive income and accumulated in a separate component of equity until the disposal of the foreign operation (see 6.6 below). *[IAS 21.32, 45]*.

The 'net investment in a foreign operation' is defined as being 'the amount of the reporting entity's interest in the net assets of that operation'. *[IAS 21.8]*. This will include a monetary item that is receivable from or payable to a foreign operation for which settlement is neither planned nor likely to occur in the foreseeable future (often referred to as a 'permanent as equity' loan) because it is, in substance, a part of the entity's net investment in that foreign operation. Such monetary items may include long-term receivables or loans. They do not include trade receivables or trade payables. *[IAS 21.15]*.

6.3.1.A Trade receivables or payables included as part of the net investment in a foreign operation

In spite of what IAS 21 says about trade receivables and payables, in our view they can be included as part of the net investment in the foreign operation, but only if cash settlement is not made or planned to be made in the foreseeable future. However, if a subsidiary makes payment for purchases from its parent, but is continually indebted to the parent as a result of new purchases, then in these circumstances, since individual transactions are settled, no part of the inter-company balance should be regarded as part of the net investment in the subsidiary. Accordingly, exchange differences on such balances should be recognised in profit or loss.

These requirements are illustrated in the following example.

Example 15.13: Receivables/payables included as part of net investment in a foreign operation

A UK entity, A, has a Belgian subsidiary, B. A has a receivable due from B amounting to £1,000,000.

In each of the following scenarios, could the receivable be included as part of A's net investment in B?

Scenario 1

The receivable arises from the sale of goods, together with interest payments and dividend payments which have not been paid in cash but have been accumulated in the inter-company account. A and B agree that A can claim at any time the repayment of this receivable. It is likely that there will be a settlement of the receivable in the foreseeable future.

Although the standard states that trade receivables and payables are not included, we do not believe that it necessarily precludes deferred trading balances from being included. In our view, such balances can be included as part of the net investment in the foreign operation, but only if cash settlement is not made or planned to be made in the foreseeable future.

In this scenario, the settlement of A's receivable due from B is not planned; however, it is likely that a settlement will occur in the foreseeable future. Accordingly, the receivable does not qualify to be treated as part of A's net investment in B. The term 'foreseeable future' is not defined and no specific time period is implied. It could be argued that the receivable should only be considered as part of the net investment if it will be repaid only when the reporting entity disinvests from the foreign operation. However, it is recognised that in most circumstances this would be unrealistic and therefore a shorter time span should be considered in determining the foreseeable future.

Scenario 2

The receivable represents a loan made by A to B and it is agreed that the receivable will be repaid in 20 years.

In this scenario, A's receivable due from B has a specified term for repayment. This suggests that settlement is planned. Accordingly, the receivable does not qualify to be treated as part of A's investment in B.

Scenario 3

A and B have previously agreed that the receivable under scenario 2 will be repaid in 20 years but A now decides that it will replace the loan on maturity either with a further inter-company loan or with an injection of equity. This approach is consistent with A's intention to maintain the strategic long-term investment in B.

In this scenario, the words from paragraph 15 of IAS 21 '... settlement is neither planned nor likely to occur in the foreseeable future ...' are potentially problematic, since a loan with a fixed maturity must, *prima facie*, have a planned settlement. However, from the date A decides that it will re-finance the inter-company debt upon maturity with a further long-term instrument, or replace it with equity, the substance of the inter-company loan is that it is part of the entity's net investment in the foreign operation, and there is no actual 'intent' to settle the investment without replacement. On this basis, loans with a stated maturity may qualify to be treated in accordance with paragraph 32 of IAS 21, with foreign currency gains and losses recognised in other comprehensive income and accumulated in a separate component of equity in the consolidated financial statements. However, in our view, management's intention to refinance the loan must be documented appropriately, for example in the form of a minute of a meeting of the management board or board of directors. In addition, there should not be any established historical pattern of the entity demanding repayment of such inter-company debt without replacement.

Consequently, when the purpose of the loan is to fund a long-term strategic investment then it is the entity's overall intention with regard to the investment and ultimate funding thereof, rather than the specific terms of the inter-company loan funding the investment, that should be considered.

Scenario 4

The receivable arises from the sale of goods, together with interest payments and dividend payments which have not been paid in cash but have been accumulated in the inter-company account. However, in this scenario, A and B agree that A can claim the repayment of this receivable only in the event that the subsidiary is disposed of. A has no plans to dispose of entity B.

In this scenario, the settlement of A's receivable due from B is not planned nor is it likely to occur in the foreseeable future. Although the term 'foreseeable future' is not defined, it will not go beyond a point of time after the disposal of a foreign operation. Accordingly, the receivable does qualify for being treated as part of a net investment in a foreign operation.

The question of whether or not a monetary item is as permanent as equity can, in certain circumstances, require the application of significant judgement.

6.3.1.B Manner of settlement of monetary items included as part of the net investment in a foreign operation

The meaning of the term 'settlement' is set out in certain standards for specific purposes. For instance, IAS 1 – *Presentation of Financial Statements* – now refers to the meaning of settlement for the purpose of classifying a liability as current or non-current (see Chapter 3 at 3.1.4.B) and this would include extinguishment of a liability by the entity issuing its own equity instrument. *[IAS 1(2023).76A]*. In addition, until 2018, the IASB's conceptual framework suggested that settlement may occur when one liability is replaced with another. However, IFRS contains no general definition and we believe it can be appropriate to use a different meaning when applying IAS 21 if it is clear the substance of a monetary item is that it forms part of an entity's net investment in a foreign operation. This will be the case if an entity expects a monetary item to be settled in a manner that does not actually change the substance of its net investment in a foreign operation.

For example, consider a parent that makes a three-year loan to a subsidiary that is a foreign operation. If it is both planned and likely that (a) the original loan will be settled at maturity but immediately replaced with another three-year loan from the parent for the same amount and (b) any such replacement loan will be similarly rolled over for the foreseeable future, the original and replacement loans would, in substance, represent part of the parent's net investment in the subsidiary. Likewise, if the loan is expected (or even contractually required) to be settled by the subsidiary issuing equity shares to the parent, the loan would still represent part of the parent's net investment in the subsidiary.

6.3.1.C Currency of monetary items included as part of the net investment in a foreign operation

When a monetary item is considered to form part of a reporting entity's net investment in a foreign operation and is denominated in the functional currency of the reporting entity, an exchange difference will be recognised in profit or loss for the period when it arises in the foreign operation's individual financial statements. If the item is denominated in the functional currency of the foreign operation, an exchange difference will be recognised in profit or loss for the period when it arises in the reporting entity's separate financial statements. Such exchange differences are only recognised in other comprehensive income and accumulated in a separate component of equity in the financial statements that include the foreign operation and the reporting entity (i.e. financial statements in which the foreign operation is consolidated or accounted for using the equity method). *[IAS 21.32, 33]*.

Example 15.14: Monetary item in functional currency of either the reporting entity or the foreign operation

A UK entity has a Belgian subsidiary. On the last day of its financial year, 31 March 2020, the UK entity lends the subsidiary £1,000,000. Settlement of the loan is neither planned nor likely to occur in the foreseeable future, so the UK entity regards the loan as part of its net investment in the Belgian subsidiary. The exchange rate at 31 March 2020 was £1=€1.40. Since the loan was made on the last day of the year there are no exchange differences to recognise for that year. At 31 March 2021, the loan has not been repaid and is still regarded as part of the net investment in the Belgian subsidiary. The relevant exchange rate at that date was £1=€1.50. The average exchange rate for the year ended 31 March 2021 was £1=€1.45.

In the UK entity's separate financial statements no exchange difference is recognised since the loan is denominated in its functional currency of pound sterling. In the Belgian subsidiary's financial statements, the liability to the parent is translated into the subsidiary's functional currency of euros at the closing rate at €1,500,000, giving rise to an exchange loss of €100,000, i.e. €1,500,000 less €1,400,000 (£1,000,000 @ £1=€1.40). This exchange loss is reflected in the Belgian subsidiary's profit or loss for that year. In the UK entity's consolidated financial statements, this exchange loss included in the subsidiary's profit or loss for the year will be translated at the average rate for the year, giving rise to a loss of £68,966 (€100,000@ £1=€1.45). This will be recognised in other comprehensive income and accumulated in the separate component of equity together with an exchange gain of £2,299, being the difference between the amount included in the Belgian subsidiary's income statement translated at average rate, i.e. £68,966, and at the closing rate, i.e. £66,667 (€100,000 @ £1=€1.50). The overall exchange loss recognised in other comprehensive income is £66,667. This represents the exchange loss on the increased net investment of €1,400,000 in the subsidiary made at 31 March 2020, i.e. £1,000,000 (€1,400,000 @ £1=€1.40) less £933,333 (€1,400,000 @ £1=€1.50).

If, on the other hand, the loan made to the Belgian subsidiary had been denominated in the equivalent amount of euros at 31 March 2020, i.e. €1,400,000, the treatment would have been as follows:

In the UK entity's separate financial statements, the amount receivable from the Belgian subsidiary would be translated at the closing rate at £933,333 (€1,400,000 @ £1=€1.50), giving rise to an exchange loss of £66,667, i.e. £1,000,000 (€1,400,000 @ £1=€1.40) less £933,333, which is included in its profit or loss for the year. In the Belgian subsidiary's financial statements, no exchange difference is recognised since the loan is denominated in its functional currency of euros. In the UK entity's consolidated financial statements, the exchange loss included in its profit or loss for the year in its separate financial statements will be recognised in other comprehensive income and accumulated in the separate component of equity. As before, this represents the exchange loss on the increased net investment of €1,400,000 in the subsidiary made at 31 March 2020, i.e. £1,000,000 (€1,400,000 @ £1=€1.40) less £933,333 (€1,400,000 @ £1=€1.40).

In most situations, intragroup balances for which settlement is neither planned nor likely to occur in the foreseeable future will be denominated in the functional currency of either the reporting entity or the foreign operation. However, this will not always be the case. If a monetary item is denominated in a currency other than the functional currency of either the reporting entity or the foreign operation, the exchange difference arising in the reporting entity's separate financial statements and in the foreign operation's individual financial statements are also recognised in other comprehensive income and accumulated in the separate component of equity in the financial statements that include the foreign operation and the reporting entity (i.e. financial statements in which the foreign operation is consolidated or accounted for using the equity method). *[IAS 21.33]*.

6.3.1.D Treatment in the individual financial statements of monetary items included as part of the net investment in a foreign operation

The exception for exchange differences on monetary items forming part of the net investment in a foreign operation applies only in the financial statements that include the foreign operation (for example consolidated financial statements when the foreign operation is a subsidiary). In the individual financial statements of the entity (or entities) with the currency exposure the exchange differences have to be reflected in that entity's profit or loss for the period.

6.3.1.E Monetary items transacted by other members of the group

As illustrated in the examples above, the requirements of IAS 21 whereby exchange differences on a monetary item that forms part of the net investment in a foreign operation are recognised in other comprehensive income clearly apply where the monetary item is transacted between the parent preparing the consolidated financial statements and the subsidiary that is the foreign operation. However, loans from any entity (and in any currency) qualify for net investment treatment, so long as the conditions of paragraph 15 are met. *[IAS 21.15A]*.

6.3.1.F Monetary items becoming part of the net investment in a foreign operation

An entity's plans and expectations in respect of an intragroup monetary item may change over time and the status of such items should be assessed each period. For example, a parent may decide that its subsidiary requires refinancing and instead of investing more equity capital in the subsidiary decides that an existing inter-company account, which has previously been regarded as a normal monetary item, should become a long-term deferred trading balance and no repayment of such amount will be requested within the foreseeable future. In our view, such a 'capital injection' should be regarded as having occurred at the time it is decided to redesignate the inter-company account. Consequently, the exchange differences arising on the account up to that date should be recognised in profit or loss and the exchange differences arising thereafter would be recognised in other comprehensive income on consolidation. This is discussed further in the following example.

Example 15.15: Monetary item becoming part of the net investment in a foreign operation

A UK entity has a wholly owned Canadian subsidiary whose net assets at 31 December 2020 were C$2,000,000. These net assets were arrived at after taking account of a liability to the UK parent of £250,000. Using the closing exchange rate of £1=C$2.35 this liability was included in the Canadian company's statement of financial position at that date at C$587,500. On 30 June 2021, when the exchange rate was £1=C$2.45, the parent decided that in order to refinance the Canadian subsidiary it would regard the liability of £250,000 as a long-term liability which would not be called for repayment in the foreseeable future. Consequently, the parent thereafter regarded the loan as being part of its net investment in the subsidiary. In the year ended 31 December 2021 the Canadian company made no profit or loss other than any exchange difference to be recognised on its liability to its parent. The relevant exchange rate at that date was £1=C$2.56. The average exchange rate for the year ended 31 December 2021 was £1=C$2.50.

The financial statements of the subsidiary in C$ and translated using the closing rate are as follows:

Statement of financial position	31 December 2021		31 December 2020	
	C$	£	C$	£
Assets	2,587,500	1,010,742	2,587,500	1,101,064
Amount due to parent	640,000	250,000	587,500	250,000
Net assets	1,947,500	760,742	2,000,000	851,064
Income statement				
Exchange difference		(52,500)		

If the amount due to the parent is not part of the parent's net investment in the foreign operation, this exchange loss would be translated at the average rate and included in the consolidated profit and loss account as £21,000. As the net investment was C$2,000,000 then there would have been an exchange loss recognised in other comprehensive income of £69,814, i.e. £851,064 less £781,250 (C$2,000,000 @ £1=C$2.56), together with an exchange gain of £492, being the difference between profit or loss translated at average rate, i.e. £21,000, and at the closing rate, i.e. £20,508.

However, the parent now regards the amount due as being part of the net investment in the subsidiary. The question then arises as to when this should be regarded as having happened and how the exchange difference on it should be calculated. No guidance is given in IAS 21.

In our view, the 'capital injection' should be regarded as having occurred at the time it is decided to redesignate the inter-company account. The exchange differences arising on the account up to that date should be recognised in profit or loss. Only the exchange difference arising thereafter would be recognised in other comprehensive income on consolidation. The inter-company account that was converted into a long-term loan becomes part of the entity's (UK parent's) net investment in the foreign operation (Canadian subsidiary) at the moment in time when the entity decides that settlement is neither planned nor likely to occur in the foreseeable future, i.e. 30 June 2021. Accordingly, exchange differences arising on the long-term loan are recognised in other comprehensive income and accumulated in a separate component of equity from that date. The same accounting treatment would have been applied if a capital injection had taken place at the date of redesignation.

At 30 June 2021 the subsidiary would have translated the inter-company account as C$612,500 (£250,000 @ £1=C$2.45) and therefore the exchange loss up to that date was C$25,000. Translated at the average rate this amount would be included in consolidated profit or loss as £10,000, with only an exchange gain of £234 recognised in other comprehensive income, being the difference between profit or loss translated at average rate, i.e. £10,000, and at the closing rate, i.e. £9,766. Accordingly, £11,000 (£21,000 less £10,000) offset by a reduction in the exchange gain on the translation of profit or loss of £258 (£492 less £234) would be recognised in other comprehensive income. This amount represents the exchange loss on the 'capital injection' of C$612,500. Translated at the closing rate this amounts to £239,258 which is £10,742 less than the original £250,000.

Some might argue that an approach of regarding the 'capital injection' as having occurred at the beginning of the accounting period would have the merit of treating all of the exchange differences for this year in the same way. However, for the reasons provided above we do not regard such an approach as being acceptable.

Suppose, instead of the inter-company account being £250,000, it was denominated in dollars at C$587,500. In this case the parent would be exposed to the exchange risk; what would be the position?

The subsidiary's net assets at both 31 December 2020 and 2021 would be:

Assets	C$2,587,500
Amount due to parent	C$587,500
Net assets	C$2,000,000

As the inter-company account is expressed in Canadian dollars, there will be no exchange difference thereon in the subsidiary's profit or loss.

There will, however, be an exchange loss in the parent as follows:

C$587,500	@ 2.35 =	£250,000
	@ 2.56 =	£229,492
		£20,508

Again, in the consolidated financial statements as the inter-company account is now regarded as part of the equity investment some of this amount should be recognised in other comprehensive income. For the reasons stated above, in our view it is only the exchange differences that have arisen after the date of redesignation, i.e. 30 June 2021, that should be recognised in other comprehensive income.

On this basis, the exchange loss would be split as follows:

C$587,500	@ 2.35 =	£250,000	
	@ 2.45 =	£239,796	
			£10,204
	@ 2.45 =	£239,796	
	@ 2.56 =	£229,492	
			£10,304

The exchange loss up to 30 June 2021 of £10,204 would be recognised in consolidated profit or loss and the exchange loss thereafter of £10,304 would be recognised in other comprehensive income. This is different from when the account was expressed in sterling because the 'capital injection' in this case is C$587,500 whereas before it was effectively C$612,500.

6.3.1.G Monetary items ceasing to be part of the net investment in a foreign operation

The previous section dealt with the situation where a pre-existing monetary item was subsequently considered to form part of the net investment in a foreign operation. However, what happens where a monetary item ceases to be considered part of the net investment in a foreign operation, either because the circumstances have changed such that it is now planned or is likely to be settled in the foreseeable future or indeed that the monetary item is in fact settled?

Where the circumstances have changed such that the monetary item is now planned or is likely to be settled in the foreseeable future, then similar issues to those discussed at 6.3.1.F above apply; i.e. are the exchange differences on the intragroup balance to be recognised in profit or loss only from the date of change or from the beginning of the financial year? For the same reasons set out in Example 15.15 above, in our view, the monetary item ceases to form part of the net investment in the foreign operation at the moment in time when the entity decides that settlement is planned or is likely to occur in the foreseeable future. Accordingly, exchange differences arising on the monetary item up to that date are recognised in other comprehensive income and accumulated in a separate component of equity. The exchange differences that arise after that date are recognised in profit or loss.

Consideration also needs to be given as to the treatment of the cumulative exchange differences on the monetary item that have been recognised in other comprehensive income, including those that had been recognised in other comprehensive income in prior years. The treatment of these exchange differences is to recognise them in other comprehensive income and accumulate them in a separate component of equity until the disposal of the foreign operation. *[IAS 21.45]*. The principle question is whether the change in circumstances or actual settlement in cash of the intragroup balance represents a disposal or partial disposal of the foreign operation and this is considered in more detail at 6.6 below.

6.3.2 Dividends

If a subsidiary pays a dividend to the parent during the year the parent should record the dividend at the rate ruling when the dividend was declared. An exchange difference will arise in the parent's own financial statements if the exchange rate moves between the declaration date and the date the dividend is actually received. This exchange difference is required to be recognised in profit or loss and will remain there on consolidation.

The same will apply if the subsidiary declares a dividend to its parent on the last day of its financial year and this is recorded at the year-end in both entities' financial statements. There is no problem in that year as both the intragroup balances and the dividends will eliminate on consolidation with no exchange differences arising. However, as the dividend will not be received until the following year an exchange difference will arise in the parent's financial statements in that year if exchange rates have moved in the meantime. Again, this exchange difference should remain in consolidated profit or loss as it is no different from any other exchange difference arising on intragroup balances resulting from other types of intragroup transactions. It should not be recognised in other comprehensive income.

It may seem odd that the consolidated results can be affected by exchange differences on inter-company dividends. However, once the dividend has been declared, the parent now effectively has a functional currency exposure to assets that were previously regarded as part of the net investment. In order to minimise the effect of exchange rate movements entities should, therefore, arrange for inter-company dividends to be paid on the same day the dividend is declared, or as soon after the dividend is declared as possible.

6.3.3 Unrealised profits on intragroup transactions

The other problem area is the elimination of unrealised profits resulting from intragroup transactions when one of the parties to the transaction is a foreign subsidiary.

Example 15.16: Unrealised profits on an intragroup transaction

An Italian parent has a wholly owned Swiss subsidiary. On 30 November 2021 the subsidiary sold goods to the parent for CHF1,000. The cost of the goods to the subsidiary was CHF700. The goods were recorded by the parent at €685 based on the exchange rate ruling on 30 November 2021 of €1=CHF1.46. All of the goods are unsold by the year-end, 31 December 2021. The exchange rate at that date was €1=CHF1.52. How should the intragroup profit be eliminated?

IAS 21 contains no specific guidance on this matter. However, US GAAP requires the rate ruling at the date of the transaction to be used.

The profit shown by the subsidiary is CHF300 which translated at the rate ruling on the transaction of €1=CHF1.46 equals €205. Consequently, the goods will be included in the statement of financial position at:

Per parent company statement of financial position	€685
Less unrealised profit eliminated	€205
	€480

It can be seen that the resulting figure for inventory is equivalent to the original euro cost translated at the rate ruling on the date of the transaction. Whereas if the subsidiary still held the inventory it would be included at €461 (CHF700 @ €1=CHF1.52).

If in the above example the goods had been sold by the Italian parent to the Swiss subsidiary then the approach in US GAAP would say the amount to be eliminated is the amount of profit shown in the Italian entity's financial statements. Again, this will not necessarily result in the goods being carried in the consolidated financial statements at their original cost to the group.

6.4 Non-coterminous period ends

IAS 21 recognises that in preparing consolidated financial statements it may be that a foreign operation is consolidated on the basis of financial statements made up to a different date from that of the reporting entity (see Chapter 7 at 2.5). In such a case, the standard initially states that the assets and liabilities of the foreign operation are to be translated at the exchange rate at the end of the reporting period of the foreign operation rather than at the date of the consolidated financial statements. However, it then goes on to say that adjustments are made for significant changes in exchange rates up to the end of the reporting period of the reporting entity in accordance with IFRS 10 – *Consolidated Financial Statements*. The same approach is used in applying the equity method to associates and joint ventures in accordance with IAS 28 – *Investments in Associates and Joint Ventures* (see Chapters 11 and 12). *[IAS 21.46]*.

The rationale for this approach is not explained in IAS 21. The initial treatment is that required by US GAAP and the reason given in that standard is that this presents the functional currency performance of the subsidiary during the subsidiary's financial year and its position at the end of that period in terms of the parent company's reporting (presentation) currency. The subsidiary may have entered into transactions in other currencies, including the functional currency of the parent, and monetary items in these currencies will have been translated using rates ruling at the end of the subsidiary's reporting period. The income statement of the subsidiary will reflect the economic consequences of carrying out these transactions during the period ended on that date. In order that the effects of these transactions in the subsidiary's financial statements are not distorted, the financial statements should be translated using the closing rate at the end of the subsidiary's reporting period.

However, an alternative argument could have been advanced for using the closing rate ruling at the end of the parent's reporting period. All subsidiaries within a group should normally prepare financial statements up to the same date as the parent entity so that the parent can prepare consolidated financial statements that present fairly the financial performance and financial position about the group as that of a single entity. The use of financial statements of a subsidiary made up to a date earlier than that of the parent is only an administrative convenience and a surrogate for financial statements made up to the proper date. Arguably, therefore the closing rate that should have been used is that which would have been used if the financial statements were made up to the proper date, i.e. that ruling at the end of the reporting period of the parent. Another reason for using this rate is that there may be subsidiaries that have the same functional currency as the subsidiary with the non-coterminous year end that do make up their financial statements to the same date as the parent company and therefore in order to be consistent with them the same rate should be used.

6.5 Goodwill and fair value adjustments

The treatment of goodwill and fair value adjustments arising on the acquisition of a foreign operation should depend on whether they are part of: *[IAS 21.BC27]*

(a) the assets and liabilities of the acquired entity (which would imply translating them at the closing rate); or

(b) the assets and liabilities of the parent (which would imply translating them at the historical rate).

In the case of fair value adjustments these clearly relate to the acquired entity. However, in the case of goodwill, historically different views have been held as set out in the following example.

Example 15.17:   Translation of goodwill

A UK company acquires all of the share capital of an Australian company on 30 June 2021 at a cost of A$3m. The fair value of the net assets of the Australian company at that date was A$2.1m. In the consolidated financial statements at 31 December 2021 the goodwill is recognised as an asset in accordance with IFRS 3. The relevant exchange rates at 30 June 2021 and 31 December 2021 are

£1=A$2.61 and £1=A$2.43 respectively. At what amount should the goodwill on consolidation be included in the statement of financial position?

	A$	(i) £	(ii) £
Goodwill	900,000	344,828	370,370

(i) This method regards goodwill as being an asset of the parent and therefore translated at the historical rate. Supporters of this view believe that, in economic terms, the goodwill is an asset of the parent because it is part of the acquisition price paid by the parent, particularly in situations where the parent acquires a multinational operation comprising businesses with many different functional currencies. *[IAS 21.BC30]*.

(ii) This method regards goodwill as being part of the parent's net investment in the acquired entity and therefore translated at the closing rate. Supporters of this view believe that goodwill should be treated no differently from other assets of the acquired entity, in particular intangible assets, because a significant part of the goodwill is likely to comprise intangible assets that do not qualify for separate recognition; the goodwill arises only because of the investment in the foreign entity and has no existence apart from that entity; and the cash flows that support the continued recognition of the goodwill are generated in the entity's functional currency. *[IAS 21.BC31]*.

The IASB was persuaded by the arguments set out in (ii) above. *[IAS 21.BC32]*. Accordingly, IAS 21 requires that any goodwill arising on the acquisition of a foreign operation and any fair value adjustments to the carrying amounts of assets and liabilities arising on the acquisition of that foreign operation should be treated as assets and liabilities of the foreign operation. Thus they are expressed in the functional currency of the foreign operation and are translated at the closing rate in accordance with the requirements discussed at 6.1 above. *[IAS 21.47]*.

Clearly, if an entity acquires a single foreign entity this will be a straightforward exercise. Where, however, the acquisition is of a multinational operation comprising a number of businesses with different functional currencies this will not be the case. The goodwill needs to be allocated to the level of each functional currency of the acquired operation. However, the standard gives no guidance on how this should be done.

In our experience, the most commonly applied way of allocating goodwill to different functional currencies is an economic value approach. This approach effectively calculates the goodwill relating to each different functional currency operation by allocating the cost of the acquisition to the different functional currency operations on the basis of the relative economic values of those businesses and then deducting the fair values that have been attributed to the net assets of those businesses as part of the fair value exercise in accounting for the business combination (see Chapter 9 at 5). We consider that any other basis for allocating goodwill to different functional currencies would need to be substantiated.

The level to which goodwill is allocated for the purpose of foreign currency translation may be different from the level at which the goodwill is tested for impairment under IAS 36 (see Chapter 20 at 8.1). *[IAS 21.BC32]*. In many cases the allocation under IAS 21 will be at a lower level. This will apply not only on the acquisition of a multinational operation but could also apply on the acquisition of a single operation where the goodwill is allocated to a larger cash generating unit under IAS 36 that is made up of businesses with different functional currencies.

As a consequence of this different level of allocation one particular difficulty that entities are likely to face is how to deal with an impairment loss that is recognised in respect of goodwill under IAS 36. If the impairment loss relates to a larger cash generating unit made up of businesses with different functional currencies, again some allocation of this impairment loss will be required to determine the amount of the remaining carrying amount of goodwill in each of the functional currencies for the purposes of translation under IAS 21.

6.6 Disposal or partial disposal of a foreign operation

The requirements relating to disposals and partial disposals of foreign operations have been amended a number of times in recent years and the current requirements are considered at 6.6.1 and 6.6.2 below. However, these amendments have given rise to a number of application issues, some of which were considered by the Interpretations Committee in 2010, although their deliberations were ultimately inconclusive.

6.6.1 Disposals and transactions treated as disposals

6.6.1.A Disposals of a foreign operation

Exchange differences resulting from the translation of a foreign operation to a different presentation currency are to be recognised in other comprehensive income and accumulated within a separate component of equity (see 6.1 above).

On the disposal of a foreign operation, the exchange differences relating to that foreign operation that have been recognised in other comprehensive income and accumulated in the separate component of equity should be recognised in profit or loss when the gain or loss on disposal is recognised. *[IAS 21.48]*. This will include exchange differences arising on an intragroup balance that, in substance, forms part of an entity's net investment in a foreign operation (see 6.3 above).

Example 15.18: Disposal of a foreign operation

A German entity has a Swiss subsidiary which was set up on 1 January 2018 with a share capital of CHF200,000 when the exchange rate was €1=CHF1.55. The subsidiary is included in the parent's separate financial statements at its original cost of €129,032. The profits of the subsidiary, all of which have been retained by the subsidiary, for each of the three years ended 31 December 2020 were CHF40,000, CHF50,000 and CHF60,000 respectively, so that the net assets at 31 December 2020 are CHF350,000. In the consolidated financial statements the results of the subsidiary have been translated at the respective average rates of €1=CHF1.60, €1=CHF1.68 and €1=CHF1.70 and the net assets at the respective closing rates of €1=CHF1.71, €1=CHF1.65 and €1=CHF1.66. All exchange differences have been recognised in other comprehensive income and accumulated in a separate exchange reserve. The consolidated reserves have therefore included the following amounts in respect of the subsidiary:

	Retained profit €	Exchange reserve €
1 January 2018	–	–
Movement during 2018	25,000	(13,681)
31 December 2018	25,000	(13,681)
Movement during 2019	29,762	5,645
31 December 2019	54,762	(8,036)
Movement during 2020	35,294	(209)
31 December 2020	90,056	(8,245)

The net assets at 31 December 2020 of CHF350,000 are included in the consolidated financial statements at €210,843.

On 1 January 2021 the subsidiary is sold for CHF400,000 (€240,964), thus resulting in a gain on disposal in the parent entity's books of €111,932, i.e. €240,964 less €129,032.

In the consolidated financial statements for 2021, IAS 21 requires the cumulative exchange losses of €8,245 to be recognised in profit or loss for that year. Assuming they were included as part of the gain on disposal (which was explicitly required by earlier versions of IAS 27)[18] this gain would be reduced to €21,876, being €30,121 (the difference between the proceeds of €240,964 and net asset value of €210,843 at the date of disposal) together with the cumulative exchange losses of €8,245.

In this example, this gain on disposal of €21,876 represents the parent's profit of €111,932 less the cumulative profits already recognised in group profit or loss of €90,056.

The following accounting policies of Pearson reflect these requirements as shown below.

> **Extract 15.4: Pearson plc (2018)**
>
> Notes to the consolidated financial statements [extract]
>
> 1a   Accounting policies [extract]
>
>   Foreign currency translation [extract]
>
> 3. *Group companies* The results and financial position of all Group companies that have a functional currency different from the presentation currency are translated into the presentation currency as follows:
>
> i)   Assets and liabilities are translated at the closing rate at the date of the balance sheet
>
> ii) Income and expenses are translated at average exchange rates
>
> iii) All resulting exchange differences are recognised as a separate component of equity.
>
> On consolidation, exchange differences arising from the translation of the net investment in foreign entities, and of borrowings and other currency instruments designated as hedges of such investments, are taken to shareholders' equity. The Group treats specific inter-company loan balances, which are not intended to be repaid in the foreseeable future, as part of its net investment. When a foreign operation is sold, such exchange differences are recognised in the income statement as part of the gain or loss on sale.
>
> The principal overseas currency for the Group is the US dollar. The average rate for the year against sterling was $1.34 (2017: $1.30) and the year-end rate was $1.27 (2017: $1.35).

This treatment is to be adopted not only when an entity sells an interest in a foreign entity, but also when it disposes of its interest through liquidation, repayment of share capital, or abandonment of that entity. *[IAS 21.49]*.

The requirement to reclassify the cumulative exchange differences to profit or loss cannot be avoided, for example, by an entity merely disposing of the net assets and business of the foreign operation, rather than disposing of its interest in the legal entity that is the foreign operation. This is because paragraph 49 refers to the disposal of a foreign operation, and a foreign operation as defined by IAS 21 must have 'activities' (see 2.3 above). Following the disposal of the net assets and business, there no longer are 'activities'. Furthermore, a foreign operation need not be an incorporated entity but may be a branch, the disposal of which would necessarily take the form of an asset sale. The legal form of the entity should make no difference to the accounting treatment of exchange differences, including the reclassification of cumulative exchange differences from equity to profit or loss. It also follows that reclassification of exchange differences could potentially be required on the disposal of a branch or similar operation within a legal entity if it represents a separate foreign operation (see 4.4 above).

Where it is a subsidiary that is disposed of, the related exchange differences that have been attributed to the non-controlling interests should be derecognised and therefore included in the calculation of the gain or loss on disposal, but should not be reclassified to profit or loss. *[IAS 21.48B]*. This is illustrated in the following example.

Example 15.19: Disposal of a partially owned foreign subsidiary

Entity P, which is incorporated in France and has the euro as its functional currency, owns 80% of Entity S which has US dollars as its functional currency. In P's consolidated financial statements, the following amounts have been recognised in relation to its investment in S:

- net assets of €1,000 and associated non-controlling interests of €200;
- foreign exchange gains of €100 were recognised in other comprehensive income, of which €20 was attributable to non-controlling interests and is therefore included in the €200 non-controlling interests;
- €80 of foreign exchange gains have therefore been accumulated in a separate component of equity relating to P's 80% share in S.

P sells its 80% interest in S for €1,300 and records the following amounts:

Dr Cash	1,300	
Dr NCI	200	
Dr OCI	80	
Cr Net assets		1,000
Cr Profit on disposal		580

It can be seen that €80 of the foreign currency gains previously recognised in OCI, i.e. the amount attributed to P, is reclassified to profit or loss (profit on disposal) and reported as a loss in OCI. However, the €20 of such gains attributed to the non-controlling interests is not reclassified in this way and is simply derecognised along with the rest of the NCI balance.

6.6.1.B Transactions treated as disposals

In addition to the disposal of an entity's entire interest in a foreign operation, the following partial disposals are accounted for as disposals: *[IAS 21.48A]*

(a) when the partial disposal involves the loss of control of a subsidiary that includes a foreign operation, regardless of whether the entity retains a non-controlling interest in its former subsidiary after the partial disposal; and

(b) when the retained interest after the partial disposal of an interest in a joint arrangement or a partial disposal of an interest in an associate that includes a foreign operation is a financial asset that includes a foreign operation.

Therefore all exchange differences accumulated in the separate component of equity relating to that foreign operation are reclassified on its disposal even if the disposal results from a sale of only part of the entity's interest in the operation, for example if a parent sold 60% of its shares in a wholly owned subsidiary which as a result became an associate.

The treatment of exchange differences relating to an investment in an associate or joint venture that becomes a subsidiary in a business combination is not clearly specified in IAS 21. However, in these circumstances, IAS 28 clearly requires the reclassification of equity accounted exchange differences of the associate or joint venture that were recognised in other comprehensive income (see Chapter 9 at 9 and Chapter 11 at 7.12.1 and at 7.12.2) and, in our view, the same treatment should apply to the exchange differences arising on the associate or joint venture itself.

6.6.2 Partial disposals

6.6.2.A What constitutes a partial disposal?

A partial disposal of an entity's interest in a foreign operation is any reduction in its ownership interest, except for those that are accounted for as disposals (see 6.6.1 above). *[IAS 21.48D]*.

A write-down of the carrying amount of a foreign operation, either because of its own losses or because of an impairment recognised by the investor, does not constitute a partial disposal, therefore no deferred exchange difference should be reclassified from equity to profit or loss at the time of the write-down. *[IAS 21.49]*. Similarly, it is implicit in the requirement of IFRS 5 – *Non-current Assets Held for Sale and Discontinued Operations* – for separate disclosure of cumulative gains and losses recognised in equity relating to a disposal group (see Chapter 4 at 2.2.4) that the classification of a foreign operation as held for sale under IFRS 5 does not give rise to a reclassification of foreign exchange differences to profit or loss at that time.

Also, a dividend made by a foreign operation that is accounted for as revenue by its parent, investor or venturer in its separate financial statements (see Chapter 8 at 2.4.1) should not be treated as a disposal or partial disposal of a net investment. *[IAS 21.BC35]*.

The term 'ownership interest' is not defined within IFRS, although it is used in a number of standards,[19] normally to indicate an investor's proportionate interest in an entity. This might seem to indicate that a partial disposal arises only when an investor reduces its proportionate interest in the foreign operation. However, the Interpretations Committee has indicated that a partial disposal may also be interpreted to mean an absolute reduction in ownership interest[20] (other than those indicated above), for example the repayment by a foreign operation of a permanent as equity loan made to it by the reporting entity. Accordingly, in our view, entities will need to apply judgement and select an appropriate accounting policy for determining what constitutes a partial disposal.

6.6.2.B Partial disposal of a proportionate interest in a subsidiary

On the partial disposal of a proportionate interest in a subsidiary that includes a foreign operation, the proportionate share of the cumulative amount of exchange differences recognised in other comprehensive income should be reattributed to the non-controlling interests in that foreign operation. *[IAS 21.48C]*. In other words, these exchange differences will not be reclassified to profit or loss. Further, if the entity subsequently disposes of the remainder of its interest in the subsidiary, the exchange differences reattributed will not be reclassified to profit or loss at that point either (see 6.6.1 above).

6.6.2.C Repayment of a permanent as equity loan by a subsidiary

Where an entity considers the repayment by a subsidiary of a permanent as equity loan a partial disposal (see 6.6.2.A above), IAS 21 is unclear whether related foreign currency differences should be reclassified from equity to profit and loss. Consequently, in our opinion, entities should select an appropriate accounting policy and apply that policy consistently.

In our experience the most commonly applied policy is for entities not to reclassify exchange differences in these circumstances. This is consistent with the explicit requirements of IAS 21 which require only that an entity reattribute to the non-controlling interests any exchange differences in that foreign operation. *[IAS 21.48C]*.

However, in analysing the issue for the Interpretations Committee in 2010, the IFRIC staff indicated, albeit without any technical analysis, that in their opinion exchange differences should be reclassified to profit or loss on settlement of such a monetary item.[21] The Interpretations Committee, which did not take the issue onto its agenda, noted that diversity may exist in practice[22] and, consequently, we also consider this treatment to be an acceptable policy choice. A logical extension of this accounting policy choice would involve reclassifying exchange differences as a result of similar transactions, for example the repayment of share capital by a foreign subsidiary.

6.6.2.D   Partial disposal of interest in an associate or joint arrangement

In a partial disposal of an associate or joint arrangement where the retained interest remains or becomes an associate or joint arrangement, the proportionate share of the cumulative amount of exchange differences recognised in other comprehensive income should be reclassified from equity to profit or loss. *[IAS 21.48C]*. There is an equivalent requirement in IAS 28 applying to all gains and losses recognised in other comprehensive income that would be reclassified to profit or loss on disposal of the related assets or liabilities. *[IAS 28.25]*. In this context, the Interpretations Committee has concluded that this treatment applies however an investor's ownership interest is reduced, for example if an associate that is a foreign operation issues shares to third parties.[23]

Whether the repayment by an associate or joint arrangement of a permanent as equity loan made to it by the reporting entity results in reclassification of exchange differences to profit or loss depends on whether the reporting entity considers such a transaction to represent a partial disposal (see 6.6.2.A above). In other words, it will be an entity's accounting policy choice.

6.6.3   Comparison of the effect of step-by-step and direct methods of consolidation on accounting for disposals

We illustrated the basic requirement to reclassify cumulative exchange differences from equity to profit or loss on the disposal of a foreign operation in Example 15.18 at 6.6.1.A above where a parent sold a direct interest in a subsidiary. This requirement also applies on the sale of an indirect subsidiary. However, where the intermediate holding company and the subsidiary each have different functional currencies, the method of consolidation can have an impact on the amount of exchange differences reclassified from equity to profit or loss on the disposal of the subsidiary.

If the step-by-step method is used, this amount will have been measured based on the functional currencies of the intermediate holding company and the subsidiary. The translation of that amount into the presentation currency of the ultimate parent will not be the same as if the ultimate parent had consolidated the subsidiary individually. In this second case (the direct method), the exchange differences on translation of the subsidiary would have been measured based on the functional currency of the subsidiary and the presentation currency used by the ultimate parent. This is illustrated in the following example.

Example 15.20: Disposal of an indirectly held foreign operation

On 1 January 2020, Entity A is incorporated in the UK with share capital of £300m. It sets up a wholly-owned Swiss subsidiary, Entity B, on the same day with share capital of CHF200m. Entity B in turn sets up a wholly-owned German subsidiary, Entity C, with share capital of €45m. All of the capital subscribed in each of the entities, to the extent that it has not been invested in a subsidiary, is used to acquire operating assets in their country of incorporation. The functional currency of each of the entities is therefore pound sterling, the Swiss franc and the euro respectively. The relevant exchange rates at 1 January 2020 are £1=CHF2.50=€1.50.

For the purposes of the example, it is assumed that in the year ended 31 December 2020 each of the entities made no profit or loss. The relevant exchange rates at that date were £1=CHF3.00=€1.25.

On 1 January 2021, the German subsidiary, Entity C, is sold by Entity B for €45m.

The exchange differences relating to Entity C that will be reclassified from equity to profit or loss in the consolidated financial statements of the Entity A group for the year ended 31 December 2021 on the basis that each of the subsidiaries are consolidated individually (the direct method) will be as follows:

Consolidating each subsidiary individually (the direct method)

The opening consolidated statement of financial position of the Entity A group at 1 January 2020 is as follows:

Millions	Entity A £	Entity B CHF	Entity B £	Entity C €	Entity C £	Adjustments £	Consolidated £
Investment in B	80.0					(80.0)	
Investment in C		75.0	30.0			(30.0)	
Other net assets	220.0	125.0	50.0	45.0	30.0		300.0
	300.0	200.0	80.0	45.0	30.0		300.0
Share capital	300.0						300.0
Share capital		200.0	80.0			(80.0)	
Share capital				45.0	30.0	(30.0)	

The consolidated statement of financial position of the Entity A group at 31 December 2020 is as follows:

Millions	Entity A £	Entity B CHF	Entity B £	Entity C €	Entity C £	Adjustments £	Consolidated £
Investment in B	80.0					(80.0)	
Investment in C		75.0	25.0			(25.0)	
Other net assets	220.0	125.0	41.7	45.0	36.0		297.7
	300.0	200.0	66.7	45.0	36.0		297.7
Share capital	300.0						300.0
Share capital		200.0	80.0			(80.0)	
Share capital				45.0	30.0	(30.0)	
Exchange – B			(13.3)			5.0	(8.3)
Exchange – C					6.0		6.0
	300.0	200.0	66.7	45.0	36.0		297.7

The exchange differences in respect of Entity B and Entity C are only shown for illustration purposes; the consolidated statement of financial position would only show the net amount of £(2.3)m as a separate component of equity. The exchange difference of £6.0m in respect of Entity C is that arising on the translation of its opening net assets of €45m into the presentation currency of pound sterling based on the opening and closing exchange rates of £1=€1.50 and £1=€1.25 respectively, as required by paragraph 39 of IAS 21. Accordingly, it is this amount of £6.0m that will be reclassified from equity to profit or loss for the year ended 31 December 2021 upon the disposal of Entity C as required by paragraph 48 of IAS 21.

If the consolidated statement of financial position for the Entity A group at 31 December 2020 had been prepared on the basis of a sub-consolidation of the Entity B sub-group incorporating Entity C, the position would have been as follows:

Consolidating using a sub-group consolidation (the step-by-step method)

The exchange rates at 1 January 2020 and 31 December 2020 are the equivalent of €1=CHF1.667 and €1=CHF2.400.

The sub-consolidation of Entity B and Entity C at 31 December 2020 is as follows:

Millions	Entity B CHF	Entity C €	Entity C CHF	Adjustments CHF	Consolidated CHF
Investment in C	75.0			(75.0)	
Other net assets	125.0	45.0	108.0		233.0
	200.0	45.0	108.0		233.0
Share capital	200.0				200.0
Share capital		45.0	75.0	(75.0)	
Exchange – C			33.0		33.0
	200.0	45.0	108.0		233.0

The exchange difference of CHF33.0m in respect of Entity C is that arising on the translation of its opening net assets of €45m into the functional currency of that of Entity B, the Swiss franc, based on the opening and closing exchange rates of €1=CHF1.667 and €1=CHF2.400 respectively.

In the consolidated financial statements of the Entity B sub-group for the year ended 31 December 2021, it is this amount of CHF33.0m that would be reclassified from equity to profit or loss upon the disposal of Entity C.

The consolidated statement of financial position of the Entity A group at 31 December 2020 prepared using this sub-consolidation would be as follows:

Millions	Entity A £	Entity B sub-group CHF	Entity B sub-group £	Adjustments £	Consolidated £
Investment in B	80.0			(80.0)	
Other net assets	220.0	233.0	77.7		297.7
	300.0	233.0	77.7		297.7
Share capital	300.0				200.0
Share capital		200.0	80.0	(80.0)	
Exchange – C		33.0	11.0		11.0
Exchange – B group			(13.3)		(13.3)
	300.0	233.0	77.7		297.7

The exchange differences in respect of Entity C and those for the Entity B sub-group are only shown for illustration purposes; the consolidated statement of financial position would only show the net amount of £(2.3)m as a separate component of equity. As can be seen, the consolidated position for the Entity A group is the same as that using the direct method. However, using the step-by-step method, the exchange difference of £11.0m in respect of Entity C is the exchange difference of CHF33.0 included in the Entity B sub-consolidation translated into the presentation currency used in the Entity A consolidated financial statements.

As indicated above, it is this amount of CHF33.0m that would be reclassified from equity to profit or loss upon the disposal of Entity C in the consolidated financial statements of the Entity B sub-group for the year ended 31 December 2021. In the consolidated financial statements of the Entity A group for the year ended 31 December 2021, it would be the translated amount of exchange differences of £11.0m that would be reclassified from equity to profit or loss on the disposal of Entity C.

Although the Interpretations Committee has indicated that the direct method is conceptually correct, IFRIC 16 permits the use of either approach as an accounting policy choice (see 6.1.5 above).

In certain situations, the methods of consolidation seem to result in more extreme differences. For example, consider the disposal of a US subsidiary by a US intermediate holding company (both of which have the US dollar as their functional currency) within a group headed by a UK parent (which has sterling as its functional and presentation currency). The US subsidiary that is disposed of is a foreign operation so exchange differences accumulated in the separate component of equity relating to it should be reclassified from equity to profit or loss on its disposal. Under the direct method of consolidation, this amount will represent exchange differences arising from translating the results and net assets of the US subsidiary directly into sterling. However, under the step-by-step method, these exchange differences will be entirely attributable to the intermediate parent undertaking and so there would be no reclassification from equity to profit or loss.

7 CHANGE OF PRESENTATION CURRENCY

IAS 21 does not address how an entity should approach presenting its financial statements if it changes its presentation currency. This is a situation that is commonly faced when the reporting entity determines that its functional currency has changed (the accounting implications of which are set out in IAS 21 and discussed at 5.5 above). However, it can occur in other situations too.

Changing presentation currency is, in our view, similar to a change in accounting policy, the requirements for which are set out in IAS 8 – *Accounting Policies, Changes in Accounting Estimates and Errors*. Therefore, when an entity chooses to change its presentation currency, we consider it appropriate to follow the approach in IAS 8 which requires retrospective application except to the extent that this is impracticable (see Chapter 3 at 4.4 and 4.7). It will also require the presentation of a statement of financial position at the beginning of the comparative period (see Chapter 3 at 2.3 and 2.4). However, the fact that IAS 21 allows a free choice of presentation currency means an entity need not demonstrate that using a different presentation currency provides reliable and more relevant information as it would for a voluntary change of accounting policy (see Chapter 3 at 4.4).

It almost goes without saying that the comparatives should be restated and presented in the new presentation currency. Further, applying the change retrospectively in line with IAS 8 means they should be determined as if this had always been the entity's presentation currency (at least to the extent practicable). The SEC, the US regulator, also requires a change in presentation currency to be approached in this way.[24]

The main issue arising in practice is determining the amount of the different components of equity, particularly the exchange differences that IAS 21 requires to be accumulated in a separate component of equity, and how much of those differences relate to each operation within the group. The following example illustrates the impact of a change in presentation currency of a relatively simple group.

Example 15.21: Change of presentation currency

A Canadian parent, P, was established on 1 January 2019 and issued new shares for C$20 million. On the same date it established two wholly owned subsidiaries, S1 and S2 incorporated in Canada and the UK respectively and subscribed C$10 million and £4.5 million for their entire share capital. The functional currency of each group company was determined to be its local currency, i.e. Canadian dollars for P and S1 and the pound sterling for S2.

During 2019, S1 made a profit of C$800,000, S2 made a profit of £350,000 and P made a loss of C$25,000. On 30 September 2019, P issued new shares for C$10 million of which £4 million was used immediately to subscribe for additional shares in S2.

During 2020, S1 made a profit of C$700,000, S2 made a profit of £750,000 and P made a loss of C$30,000 before dividends received from S2. On 30 June 2020, S2 paid dividends (out of profits then made) of £700,000 to P and on 30 September 2020 P paid dividends of C$1,000,000 to its shareholders.

The relevant exchange rates for C$1=£ were as follows:

1 January 2019	2.10
30 September 2019	2.28
31 December 2019	2.35
Average for 2019	2.24
30 June 2020	2.55
30 September 2020	2.63
31 December 2020	2.40
Average for 2020	2.52

Consequently, the statement of changes in equity in P's consolidated financial statements for 2019 and 2020 can be summarised as follows:

	Paid-in capital C$	Retained earnings C$	Foreign exchange C$	Total C$
1 January 2019	–	–	–	–
Issue of shares	30,000,000	–	–	30,000,000
Comprehensive income	–	1,559,000	1,443,500	3,002,500
31 December 2019	30,000,000	1,559,000	1,443,500	33,002,500
Comprehensive income	–	2,560,000	457,500	3,017,500
Dividends	–	(1,000,000)	–	(1,000,000)
31 December 2020	30,000,000	3,119,000	1,901,000	35,020,000

The comprehensive income reflected within retained earnings represents the profit for each year, calculated as follows:

2019: C$800,000 + (£350,000 × 2.24) – C$25,000 = C$1,559,000

2020: C$700,000 + (£750,000 × 2.52) – C$30,000 = C$2,560,000

The foreign exchange differences recognised in other comprehensive income, which are entirely attributable to S2, can be calculated as follows:

	2019			2020		
	£	Rate	C$	£	Rate	C$
Opening net assets*	4,500,000	2.10	9,450,000	8,850,000	2.35	20,797,500
		2.35	10,575,000		2.40	21,240,000
Exchange gain			1,125,000			442,500
Additional capital	4,000,000	2.28	9,120,000	–	–	–
		2.35	9,400,000	–	–	–
Exchange gain			280,000			–
Dividend	–	–	–	(700,000)	2.55	(1,785,000)
	–	–	–		2.40	(1,680,000)
Exchange gain			–			105,000
Profit	350,000	2.24	784,000	750,000	2.52	1,890,000
		2.35	822,500		2.40	1,800,000
Exchange gain/(loss)			38,500			(90,000)
	8,850,000		1,443,500	8,900,000		457,500

*for 2019, includes the proceeds received for issuing shares on 1 January.

For the year ended 31 December 2021, P decided to change its presentation currency to sterling. (This may or may not have coincided with a change of P's functional currency.) In P's consolidated financial statements for the year ended 31 December 2021, what amounts should be included in respect of the comparative period?

Direct method

If P's accounting policy was to use the direct method of consolidation (see 6.1.5 above), its financial statements for 2019 and 2020 would have been prepared by translating the financial statements of each entity within the group directly into sterling (where necessary). The revised statement of changes in equity in P's consolidated financial statements can be summarised as follows and these are the amounts that will be reflected as comparative amounts in P's consolidated financial statements for the year ended 31 December 2021:

	Paid-in capital £	Retained earnings £	Foreign exchange £	Total £
1 January 2019	–	–	–	–
Issue of shares	13,909,775	–	–	13,909,775
Comprehensive income	–	695,982	(562,140)	133,842
31 December 2019	13,909,775	695,982	(562,140)	14,043,617
Comprehensive income	–	1,015,873	(87,595)	928,278
Dividends	–	(380,228)	–	(380,228)
31 December 2020	13,909,775	1,331,627	(649,735)	14,591,667

The table above assumes that P will record its paid-in capital at historical exchange rates (£13,909,775 = C$20,000,000 ÷ 2.10 + C$10,000,000 ÷ 2.28). Alternatively, P could retranslate those amounts at year end rates although any difference arising would simply be recorded in another component of equity (but not the foreign exchange reserve) and this difference would not affect profit or loss or other comprehensive income in any period (see 6.2.1 and 6.2.2 above).

The calculations showing how these amounts have been determined are shown below.

The comprehensive income reflected within retained earnings represents the profit for each year, calculated as follows:

2019: (C$800,000 ÷ 2.24) + £350,000 – (C$25,000 ÷ 2.24) = £695,982

2020: (C$700,000 ÷ 2.52) + £750,000 – (C$30,000 ÷ 2.52) = £1,015,873

In this case, the profit calculated in this way results in the same amount as translating the consolidated profit of C$1,559,000 and C$2,560,000 presented in Canadian dollars at the average rate for the period of C$2.24=£1 and C$2.52=£1 respectively. In practice minor differences can arise as a result of imperfections in the average rates used.

Similarly, the net assets presented above are the same as the amounts obtained by translating consolidated net assets of C$33,002,500 and C$35,020,000 at the closing rates at the end of the relevant period, C$2.35=£1 and C$2.40=£1 respectively. This should always be the case.

However, the foreign exchange reserve is fundamentally different to that in the financial statements presented in Canadian dollars. In this case it represents exchange differences arising from the translation of both P's and S1's financial statements into sterling whereas previously it represented exchange differences arising from the translation of S2's financial statements into Canadian dollars.

The foreign exchange differences recognised in other comprehensive income that are attributable to P can be calculated as follows:

	2019			2020		
	C$	Rate	£	C$	Rate	£
Opening net assets*	550,000	2.10	261,905	1,405,000	2.35	597,872
		2.35	234,042		2.40	585,417
Exchange loss			(27,863)			(12,455)
Additional capital**	880,000	2.28	385,965	–	–	–
		2.35	374,468	–	–	–
Exchange loss			(11,497)			–
Dividend received	–	–	–	1,785,000	2.55	700,000
					2.40	743,750
Exchange gain			–			43,750
Dividend paid	–	–	–	(1,000,000)	2.63	(380,228)
					2.40	(416,667)
Exchange loss			–			(36,439)
Loss	(25,000)	2.24	(11,161)	(30,000)	2.52	(11,905)
		2.35	(10,638)		2.40	(12,500)
Exchange gain/(loss)			523			(595)
	1,405,000		(38,837)	2,160,000		(5,739)

*for 2019, includes the proceeds received for issuing shares on 1 January (C$20,000,000) less amounts invested in S1 (C$10,000,000) and S2 (C$9,450,000 = £4,500,000 × 2.10) on the same date.

**reduced by the amounts invested in S2 on the same date.

The foreign exchange differences recognised in other comprehensive income that are attributable to S1 can be calculated as follows:

	2019			2020		
	C$	Rate	£	C$	Rate	£
Opening net assets*	10,000,000	2.10	4,761,905	10,800,000	2.35	4,595,745
		2.35	4,255,319		2.40	4,500,000
Exchange loss			(506,586)			(95,745)
Profit	800,000	2.24	357,143	700,000	2.52	277,778
		2.35	340,426		2.40	291,667
Exchange (loss)/gain			(16,717)			13,889
	10,800,000		(523,303)	11,500,000		(81,856)

* for 2019, includes the proceeds received for issuing shares on 1 January.

Therefore the total foreign exchange loss arising in 2019 is £562,140 (£38,837 + £523,303) and in 2020 is £87,595 (£5,739 + £81,856).

Under this method amounts in the foreign exchange reserve would be reclassified to profit or loss on the subsequent disposal of S1, but not on the subsequent disposal of S2.

Step-by-step method

If P's accounting policy was to use the step-by-step method of consolidation (see 6.1.5 above), the first step in producing its consolidated financial statements for 2019 and 2020 would have been to translate the financial statements of S2 into Canadian dollars, the functional currency of P, to produce consolidated financial statements in Canadian dollars (effectively those that P had prepared historically). The second step involves translating these consolidated financial statements into sterling.

These financial statements (and hence the comparative amounts included in the financial statements for the year ended 31 December 2021) will appear to be the same as those produced under the direct method (assuming equity items are dealt with similarly, i.e. paid-in capital is translated at the relevant rate at the date of issue and that retained earnings represent each element translated at the relevant rates, being 2019 and 2020 profit at the average rate for the year, and dividends at the date of payment). However, the balance on the foreign exchange reserve will be attributable to different entities within the group (see 6.6.3 above). The calculations showing how these amounts have been determined are shown below.

The foreign exchange differences recognised in other comprehensive income in the financial statements presented in Canadian dollars that are attributable to S2 will remain attributable to S2, albeit that they are translated into sterling at the average rate:

2019: C$1,443,500 ÷ 2.24 = £644,420

2020: C$457,500 ÷ 2.52 = £181,548

The remaining exchange differences recognised in other comprehensive income, which arise from retranslating P's consolidated financial statements presented in Canadian dollars into sterling, are attributable to P. They can be calculated as follows:

		2019				2020		
	C$	Rate		£	C$	Rate		£
Opening net assets*	20,000,000	2.10		9,523,809	33,002,500	2.35		14,043,617
		2.35		8,510,638		2.40		13,751,042
Exchange loss				(1,013,171)				(292,575)
Additional capital	10,000,000	2.28		4,385,965	–			–
		2.35		4,255,319	–			–
Exchange loss				(130,646)				–
Dividend paid	–	2.24		–	(1,000,000)	2.63		(380,228)
		2.35		–		2.40		(416,667)
Exchange loss				–				(36,439)
Comprehensive income	3,002,500	2.24		1,340,402	3,017,500	2.52		1,197,421
		2.35		1,277,660		2.40		1,257,292
Exchange (loss)/gain				(62,742)				59,871
	33,002,500			(1,206,559)	35,020,000			(269,143)

* for 2019, includes the proceeds received for issuing shares on 1 January.

In contrast to the direct method, under this method amounts in the foreign exchange reserve would be reclassified to profit or loss on the subsequent disposal of S2, but not on the subsequent disposal of S1.

In the example above, it was reasonably straightforward to recreate the consolidated equity balances and identify the amounts of accumulated exchange differences related to each entity within the group using the new presentation currency. This is because the group had a very simple structure with operations having only two functional currencies, a short history and few (external and internal) equity transactions. Whilst entities should strive for a theoretically perfect restatement, in practice it is unlikely to be such an easy exercise.

As noted above, where an accounting policy is changed, IAS 8 requires retrospective application except to the extent that this is impracticable, in which case an entity should adjust the comparative information to apply the new accounting policy prospectively from the earliest practicable date. A similar approach is, in our view, appropriate when an entity changes its presentation currency. In this context the most important component of equity to determine correctly (or as near correctly as possible) is normally the foreign exchange reserve because that balance, or parts of it, has to be reclassified from equity to profit or loss in the event of any future disposal of the relevant foreign operation, and could therefore affect future earnings.

Where an entity applies the direct method of consolidation, it could be impracticable to determine precisely the amount of exchange differences accumulated within the separate component of equity relating to each individual entity within the group. In these circumstances, approximations will be necessary to determine the amounts at the beginning of the earliest comparative period presented, although all subsequent exchange differences should be accumulated in accordance with the requirements of IAS 21. For an entity that set its foreign exchange reserve to zero on transition to IFRS (see Chapter 5 at 5.7) it may be able to go back to that date and recompute the necessary components of equity. This should be less of an issue for entities applying the step-by-step method.

UBS and BBA Aviation changed their presentation currency in 2018 and 2011 respectively and included the following explanations in their accounting policies.

> Extract 15.5: UBS Group AG (2018)
> Notes to the UBS Group AG consolidated financial statements [extract]
> Note 1   Summary of significant accounting policies [extract]
> 1)   Changes in functional and presentation currency [extract]
>
> Change in functional currencies
>
> As a consequence of legal entity structural changes over recent years – notably the transfer of the Personal & Corporate Banking and Global Wealth Management businesses booked in Switzerland from UBS AG to UBS Switzerland AG, and the creation of UBS Business Solutions AG, which houses a significant portion of the employees and associated costs that were previously held in UBS AG's Head Office in Switzerland and UBS AG's London Branch – a concentration of US dollar-influenced and –managed business activities now exist in UBS AG's Head Office in Switzerland and UBS AG's London Branch. In addition, from the fourth quarter of 2018, for risk management purposes UBS adopted the US dollar as the risk-neutral currency and has adjusted its structural risk positions accordingly. As a result of these changes, effective from 1 October 2018, the functional currency of UBS Group AG and UBS AG's Head Office in Switzerland changed prospectively from Swiss francs to US dollars and that of UBS AG's London Branch changed from British pounds to US dollars, in compliance with the requirements of IAS 21, *The Effects of Changes in Foreign Exchange Rates*.
>
> Change in presentation currency
>
> In 2018, the presentation currency of UBS Group AG's consolidated financial statements has changed from Swiss francs to US dollars to align with the functional currency changes of significant Group entities. UBS has restated prior periods for this voluntary presentational change in line with IAS 8, *Accounting Policies, Changes in Accounting Estimates and Errors*, from 1 January 2004. This point in time represented the earliest date from which it was practicable to perform a restatement, given the lack of sufficiently reliable data for earlier periods. As a consequence, foreign currency translation (FCT) gains or losses prior to 2004 have been disregarded, with FCT effects first calculated from 1 January 2004 onward. In addition, UBS has included a second comparative balance sheet as of 1 January 2017 in line with IAS 1, *Presentation of Financial Statements*.
>
> Income and expenses as well as *Other comprehensive income* (OCI) were translated to US dollars at the respective average exchange rates prevailing for the relevant periods. Additionally, *Other income* was restated to reflect releases of FCT gains or losses from OCI to the income statement when calculated under the new US dollar presentation currency. The effect of such restatements for 2018, 2017 and 2016 was not material to the income statements of these periods.
>
> Assets, liabilities and total equity were translated at closing exchange rates prevailing on the respective balance sheet dates, after reflection of deferred tax effects relating to the restatement. Share capital issued, share premium and treasury shares held were translated at historic average rates, whereby differences between historic average rate and closing exchange rate realized upon repayment of share capital or disposal of treasury shares were reported as *Share premium*. Cumulative amounts recognized in OCI in respect of cash flow hedges and financial assets measured at FVOCI (prior to 1 January 2018: financial assets classified as available for sale) were translated at closing exchange rate as of respective balance sheet dates, with any translation effects adjusted through *Retained earnings*.
>
> The restated FCT balance as of 1 October 2018 included a cumulative gain of USD 767 million related to previously applied net investment hedges entered into by UBS Group AG or UBS AG's Head Office to hedge investments in foreign operations against their former Swiss franc functional currency.
>
> The restated basic and diluted earnings per share (EPS) were USD 0.26 and USD 0.25 for the year ended 31 December 2017, which compares to CHF 0.28 and CHF 0.27 basic and diluted EPS under the previous Swiss franc presentation currency. For the year ended 31 December 2016, restated basic and diluted EPS were USD 0.90 and USD 0.88, which compares to CHF 0.86 and CHF 0.84 basic and diluted EPS under the previous Swiss franc presentation currency.

> **Extract 15.6: BBA Aviation plc (2011)**
> Accounting policies [extract]
> Presentation currency
>
> The Group's revenues, profits and cash flows are primarily generated in US dollars, and are expected to remain principally denominated in US dollars in the future. During the year, the Group changed the currency in which it presents its consolidated financial statements from pounds sterling to US dollars, in order to better reflect the underlying performance of the Group.
>
> A change in presentation currency is a change in accounting policy which is accounted for retrospectively. Statutory financial information included in the Group's Annual Report and Accounts for the year ended 31 December 2010 previously reported in sterling has been restated into US dollars using the procedures outlined below:
>
> - assets and liabilities denominated in non-US dollar currencies were translated into US dollars at the closing rates of exchange on the relevant balance sheet date;
> - non-US dollar income and expenditure were translated at the average rates of exchange prevailing for the relevant period;
> - the cumulative hedging and translation reserves were set to nil at 1 January 2004, the date of transition to IFRS, and these reserves have been restated on the basis that the Group has reported in US dollars since that date. Share capital, share premium and the other reserves were translated at the historic rates prevailing at 1 January 2004, and subsequent rates prevailing on the date of each transaction;
> - all exchange rates were extracted from the Group's underlying financial records.

8 INTRODUCTION OF THE EURO

From 1 January 1999, the effective start of Economic and Monetary Union (EMU), the euro became a currency in its own right and the conversion rates between the euro and the national currencies of those countries who were going to participate in the first phase were irrevocably fixed, such that the risk of subsequent exchange differences related to these currencies was eliminated from that date on.

In October 1997, the SIC issued SIC-7 which deals with the application of IAS 21 to the changeover from the national currencies of participating Member States of the European Union to the euro. Consequential amendments have been made to this interpretation as a result of the IASB's revised version of IAS 21.

Although the Interpretation is no longer relevant with respect to the national currencies of those countries that participated in the first phase, SIC-7 makes it clear that the same rationale applies to the fixing of exchange rates when countries join EMU at later stages. *[SIC-7.3]*.

Under SIC-7, the requirements of IAS 21 regarding the translation of foreign currency transactions and financial statements of foreign operations should be strictly applied to the changeover. *[SIC-7.3]*.

This means that, in particular:

(a) Foreign currency monetary assets and liabilities resulting from transactions should continue to be translated into the functional currency at the closing rate. Any resultant exchange differences should be recognised as income or expense immediately, except that an entity should continue to apply its existing accounting policy for exchange gains and losses related to hedges of the currency risk of a forecast transaction. *[SIC-7.4]*.

The effective start of the EMU after the reporting period does not change the application of these requirements at the end of the reporting period; in accordance with IAS 10 – *Events after the Reporting Period* – it is not relevant whether or not the closing rate can fluctuate after the reporting period. *[SIC-7.5]*.

Like IAS 21, the Interpretation does not address how foreign currency hedges should be accounted for. The effective start of EMU, of itself, does not justify a change to an entity's established accounting policy related to hedges of forecast transactions because the changeover does not affect the economic rationale of such hedges. Therefore, the changeover should not alter the accounting policy where gains and losses on financial instruments used as hedges of forecast transactions are initially recognised in other comprehensive income and reclassified from equity to profit or loss to match with the related income or expense in a future period; *[SIC-7.6]*

(b) Cumulative exchange differences relating to the translation of financial statements of foreign operations recognised in other comprehensive income should remain accumulated in a separate component of equity and be reclassified from equity to profit or loss only on the disposal (or partial disposal) of the net investment in the foreign operation. *[SIC-7.4]*.

The fact that the cumulative amount of exchange differences will be fixed under EMU does not justify immediate recognition as income or expenses since the wording and the rationale of IAS 21 clearly preclude such a treatment. *[SIC-7.7]*.

9 TAX EFFECTS OF ALL EXCHANGE DIFFERENCES

Gains and losses on foreign currency transactions and exchange differences arising on translating the results and financial position of an entity (including a foreign operation) into a different currency may have tax effects to which IAS 12 applies. *[IAS 21.50]*. The requirements of IAS 12 are discussed in Chapter 33. In broad terms the tax effects of exchange differences will follow the reporting of the exchange differences, i.e. they will be recognised in profit or loss except to the extent they relate to exchange differences recognised in other comprehensive income, in which case they will also be recognised in other comprehensive income. *[IAS 12.58]*.

The tax base of a non-monetary asset such as property, plant or equipment, will sometimes be determined in a currency other than the entity's functional currency. Consequently, changes in the exchange rate will give rise to temporary differences that result in a recognised deferred tax liability or asset (subject to recoverability). The resulting deferred tax should be recognised in profit or loss, *[IAS 12.41]*, and presented with other deferred taxes rather than with foreign exchange gains or losses (see Chapter 33 at 10.1.1).[25]

10 DISCLOSURE REQUIREMENTS

10.1 Exchange differences

IAS 21 requires the amount of exchange differences recognised in profit or loss (except for those arising on financial instruments measured at fair value through profit or loss in accordance with IFRS 9) to be disclosed. *[IAS 21.52]*. Since IAS 21 does not specify where such exchange differences should be presented in the income statement entities should apply judgement in the light of the requirements of IAS 1 to determine the appropriate line item(s) in which exchange differences are included. For example, an entity which has an operating and a financing section within its income statement might include exchange differences arising on operating items (such as trade payables and receivables) in other operating income or expense and exchange differences on financing items (such as loans and borrowings) in the financing section. In the light of this, we recommend that entities in disclosing the amount of such exchange differences indicate the line item(s) in which they are included. Further, the classification of exchange differences (both gains and losses) arising from transactions of a similar nature should be classified consistently throughout the periods presented.

The standard also requires disclosure of the net exchange differences recognised in other comprehensive income and accumulated in a separate component of equity, and a reconciliation of such amounts at the beginning and end of the period. *[IAS 21.52]*.

10.2 Presentation and functional currency

When the presentation currency is different from the functional currency, that fact should be stated, together with disclosure of the functional currency and the reason for using a different presentation currency. *[IAS 21.53]*. For this purpose, in the case of a group, the references to 'functional currency' are to that of the parent. *[IAS 21.51]*.

When there is a change in the functional currency of either the reporting entity or a significant foreign operation, that fact and the reason for the change in functional currency should be disclosed. *[IAS 21.54]*.

10.3 Convenience translations of financial statements or other financial information

Paragraph 55 of IAS 21 indicates that when an entity presents its financial statements in a currency that is different from its functional currency, it should describe the financial statements as complying with IFRS only if they comply with all the requirements of each applicable standard and interpretation of those standards, including the translation method set out in IAS 21 (see 6.1 above). *[IAS 21.55]*.

However, the standard recognises that an entity sometimes presents its financial statements or other financial information in a currency that is not its functional currency without meeting the above requirements. Examples noted by IAS 21 are where an entity converts into another currency only selected items from its financial statements or where an entity whose functional currency is not the currency of a hyperinflationary economy converts the financial statements into another currency by translating all items at the most recent closing rate. Such conversions are not in accordance with IFRS; nevertheless IAS 21 requires disclosures to be made. *[IAS 21.56]*.

The standard requires that when an entity displays its financial statements or other financial information in a currency that is different from either its functional currency or its presentation currency and the requirements of paragraph 55 are not met, it should: *[IAS 21.57]*

(a) clearly identify the information as supplementary information to distinguish it from the information that complies with IFRS;

(b) disclose the currency in which the supplementary information is displayed; and

(c) disclose the entity's functional currency and the method of translation used to determine the supplementary information.

For the purpose of these requirements, in the case of a group, the references to 'functional currency' are to that of the parent. *[IAS 21.51]*.

10.4 Judgements made in applying IAS 21 and related disclosures

IAS 1 requires disclosure of the significant judgements that management has made in the process of applying the entity's accounting policies and that have the most significant effect on the amounts recognised in the financial statements (see Chapter 3 at 5.1.1.B). *[IAS 1.122]*. The application of IAS 21 can, in certain circumstances, require the exercise of significant judgement, particularly the determination of functional currency (see 4 above) and assessing whether intragroup monetary items are permanent as equity (see 6.3.1 above). Where relevant, information about these particular judgements should be disclosed.

Whilst considering a number of issues associated with the Venezuelan currency (see 5.1.4.C and 6.1.3 above), the Interpretations Committee drew attention to a number of disclosure requirements in IFRS that might be relevant when an entity has material foreign operations subject to extensive currency controls, multiple exchange rates and/or a long-term lack of exchangeability. In particular, the committee highlighted the importance of providing information that is relevant to an understanding of the entity's financial statements. *[IAS 1.122]*.

In addition to disclosing the significant judgements in applying an entity's accounting policies, the committee also considered the following disclosures to be important:[26]

- significant accounting policies applied; *[IAS 1.117-121]*
- sources of estimation uncertainty that have a significant risk of resulting in a material adjustment to the carrying amounts of assets and liabilities within the next financial year, which may include a sensitivity analysis; *[IAS 1.125-133]* and
- the nature and extent of significant restrictions on an entity's ability to access or use assets and settle the liabilities of the group, or in relation to its joint ventures or associates. *[IFRS 12.10, 13, 20, 22]*.

Finally, the following may also be relevant:[27]

- the nature and extent of risks (including foreign exchange risk) arising from financial instruments (from a qualitative and quantitative perspective and including sensitivity analyses); *[IFRS 7.31-42, B6-B24]*
- significant cash held by the entity that is not available for use by the group, including due to exchange controls; *[IAS 7.48, 49]* and
- the amount of foreign exchange differences recognised in profit or loss and other comprehensive income. *[IAS 21.52]*.

11 FUTURE DEVELOPMENTS

The IASB has tentatively decided to amend IAS 21 to address the spot exchange rate an entity should use when a currency lacks exchangeability and the disclosures it would provide. As noted at 5.1.4.C and at 6.1.3 above, this is in response to specific issues experienced when applying the standard to in Venezuela. At the time of writing, the IASB had made a number of tentative decisions about these proposals as set out below and intended to publish an exposure draft of proposed amendments in due course, although they had not specified an expected publication date.

When an entity assesses exchangeability, and thus whether a currency is experiencing a lack of exchangeability, it is expected the proposals will require an entity to:

- consider whether it could obtain the foreign currency within a time frame that includes a normal administrative delay;
- consider its ability to obtain foreign currency, not its intention (or decision) to do so;
- consider only markets or exchange mechanisms that create enforceable rights and obligations;
- assume that the purpose of obtaining foreign currency is to:
  - settle individual foreign currency transactions, or assets or liabilities related to those transactions, when it reports foreign currency transactions in the functional currency; or
  - realise the entity's net assets when it uses a presentation currency other than the functional currency (or to realise its net investment in a foreign operation when it translates the results and financial position of that foreign operation);
- conclude that a currency lacks exchangeability in circumstances in which it is able to obtain only some amounts of foreign currency, when, for a particular purpose, it is able to obtain no more than an insignificant amount of foreign currency;

Additionally, when an entity (i) reports foreign currency transactions in its functional currency, and (ii) can obtain less than the amount of foreign currency it needs to settle all balances and transactions in that currency, the entity would be required to assess exchangeability on an aggregated basis for all the related foreign currency balances and transactions.

When a currency lacks exchangeability, the estimated spot rate would be a rate that:

- the entity would have been able to access at the reporting date had the currency been exchangeable;
- would have arisen in an orderly transaction between market participants; and
- would faithfully reflect the economic conditions prevailing at that date.

An observable rate (that does not meet the definition of a spot rate) could be used if that rate approximates the spot rate in the following circumstances:

- when the observable rate meets the definition of a spot rate for particular transactions or balances but not those for which the entity assesses exchangeability; or
- when the observable rate is the first subsequent rate at which exchanges could be made if exchangeability is restored before financial statements are authorised for issue.

The estimated exchange rate should be applied to:

- the entire transaction or balance of an asset or liability (when the entity reports foreign currency transactions in the functional currency); or
- the financial statements as a whole (when the entity uses a presentation currency other than the functional currency).

Disclosure of the following should be given:

- details of the currency that lacks exchangeability and a description of the restrictions that result in that lack of exchangeability;
- a description of the transactions affected by the lack of exchangeability;

- the carrying amount of assets and liabilities denominated in the currency that lacks exchangeability;
- the spot rate(s) used and whether such a rate is an observable rate that approximates the spot rate or one that has been estimated;
- a description of the estimation technique applied, and qualitative and quantitative information about the inputs used in that estimation technique; and
- qualitative information about each type of risk to which the entity is exposed because of a currency's lack of exchangeability, and the nature and carrying amount of assets and liabilities exposed to each type of risk.

Additionally, when a foreign operation's functional currency lacks exchangeability, an entity would be required to disclose:

- the name of the foreign operation, its nature (whether it is a subsidiary, joint operation, joint venture, associate or branch) and its principal place of business;
- summarised financial information about the foreign operation; and
- the nature and terms of any contractual arrangements that could require the entity to provide financial support to that foreign operation, including events or circumstances that could expose the reporting entity to a loss.

The entity would also be required to disclose the balance of assets to which such arrangements give rise.[28]

The amendments are expected to apply prospectively from the beginning of the annual reporting period in which they are first applied (the date of initial application) without restatement of comparative information. For foreign currency transactions accounted for in an entity's functional currency the entity would translate foreign currency monetary items, and non-monetary items measured at fair value in a foreign currency, at the date of initial application using the estimated spot exchange rate at that date and recognise any effect of initially applying the amendment in opening retained earnings. An entity that uses a presentation currency other than its functional currency (or translates a foreign operation) would translate all assets and liabilities at the date of initial application using the estimated spot exchange rate at that date, translate equity items at the date of initial application using the estimated spot exchange rate at that date if the entity's functional currency is hyperinflationary and recognise any effect of initially applying the amendment as an adjustment to the cumulative amount of translation differences in equity. No decisions about the effective date had been taken although early adoption would be permitted.[29]

Aside from this, IAS 21 has caused a more general degree of concern in recent years, especially in certain emerging economies. In particular, some have criticised IAS 21 as designed for companies that operate in a reserve currency, e.g. the US dollar or euro; and volatility in exchange rates, including during the financial crisis, led some to ask the IASB to reconsider IAS 21. However, after performing research and outreach as part of its periodic agenda consultations, the IASB decided not to include in its work plan any further work on the topic.[30] Therefore it seems unlikely there will be any significant changes to the standard in the foreseeable future, although it is possible that further narrow-scope amendments or interpretative guidance will be considered.

References

1 After applying IFRS 9 an entity can actually continue applying some or all of the hedge accounting requirements of IAS 39. These options are considered further in Chapter 44 at 5 and in Chapter 53 at 11.2 but are not dealt with any further in this chapter.
2 *IFRIC Update*, March 2010, Staff Paper (Agenda reference 13), *Determining the functional currency of an investment holding company*, IASB, January 2010 and Staff Paper (Agenda reference 4A), *Determining the functional currency of an investment holding company*, IASB, March 2010.
3 *IFRIC Update*, September 2018.
4 Staff Paper (Agenda reference 2), *IAS 21 – Extreme long-term lack of exchangeability*, IASB, June 2018, Staff Paper (Agenda reference 10), *IAS 21 – Determination of the exchange rate when there is a long-term lack of exchangeability*, IASB, September 2018 and *22nd Extract from EECS's database of enforcement decisions*, ESMA, April 2018, Decision Ref. EECS/0118-09.
5 *IFRIC Update*, September 2018.
6 Staff Paper (Agenda reference 10), *IAS 21 – Determination of the exchange rate when there is a long-term lack of exchangeability*, IASB, September 2018.
7 *IFRIC Update*, June 2019.
8 *Exposure Draft of Revised IAS 21*, IASB, May 2002, para. 14.
9 IAS 12 (2007), *Income Taxes*, 2007 Bound Volume, IASB, para. 78.
10 In this context, IAS 21 does not actually refer to those requirements relating to the treatment of exchange differences arising from the translation process. However, we believe that any resulting exchange differences should be recognised as discussed at 5.3 above.
11 *IFRIC Update*, March 2020.
12 Staff Paper (Agenda reference 4A), *Translating a Hyperinflationary Foreign Operation (IAS 21 and IAS 29)*, IASB, September 2019.
13 *IFRIC Update*, March 2020.
14 *IFRIC Update*, November 2014 and Staff Paper (Agenda reference 16), *Foreign exchange restrictions and hyperinflation*, IASB, July 2014.
15 *IFRIC Update*, March 2008, p.2.
16 *IFRIC Update*, March 2008, p.2.
17 *IASB Update*, February 2003, p.5.
18 IAS 27 (2007), *Consolidated and Separate Financial Statements*, IASB, 2007 Bound Volume, para. 30.
19 For example, IAS 27, *Separate Financial Statements*, IASB, paras. 16(b)(iii) and 17(b)(iii), IFRS 3, *Business Combinations*, IASB, para. B63(e) and IFRS 10, *Consolidated Financial Statements*, IASB, para. 23.
20 *IFRIC Update*, September 2010, p.2.
21 Staff Paper (Agenda reference 7D), *CTA Recycling in IAS 27R Transactions*, IASB, March 2010 and Staff Paper (Agenda reference 11), *Repayment of investment/CTA*, IASB, July 2010, paras. 10(a) and 11.
22 *IFRIC Update*, September 2010, p.2.
23 *IFRIC Update*, July 2009.
24 *Financial Reporting Manual*, SEC, July 2019, para. 6630.1.
25 *IFRIC Update*, January 2016.
26 *IFRIC Update*, November 2014 and *IFRIC Update*, September 2018.
27 Staff Paper (Agenda reference 16), *Foreign exchange restrictions and hyperinflation*, IASB, July 2014.
28 *IASB Update*, April 2020.
29 *IASB Update*, July 2020.
30 *IASB Update*, May 2016.

Chapter 16 Hyperinflation

1 INTRODUCTION 1251
   1.1 Background 1251
   1.2 Hyperinflationary economies 1252
   1.3 Restatement approach 1252
2 THE REQUIREMENTS OF IAS 29 1253
   2.1 The context of IAS 29 1253
   2.2 Scope 1254
   2.3 Definition of hyperinflation 1254
   2.4 The IAS 29 restatement process 1255
3 SELECTION OF A GENERAL PRICE INDEX 1256
   3.1 Selecting a general price index 1256
   3.2 General price index not available for all periods 1256
4 ANALYSIS AND RESTATEMENT OF THE STATEMENT OF FINANCIAL POSITION 1257
   4.1 Monetary and non-monetary items 1258
      4.1.1 Monetary or non-monetary distinction 1258
      4.1.2 Monetary items 1259
      4.1.3 Non-monetary items carried at current cost 1260
      4.1.4 Non-monetary items carried at historical cost 1260
   4.2 Inventories 1263
   4.3 Restatement of associates, joint ventures and subsidiaries 1263
   4.4 Calculation of deferred taxation 1264
5 RESTATEMENT OF THE STATEMENT OF CHANGES IN EQUITY 1266
6 RESTATEMENT OF THE STATEMENT OF PROFIT AND LOSS AND OTHER COMPREHENSIVE INCOME 1268
   6.1 Restatement of interest and exchange differences 1269

	6.2	Calculation of the gain or loss on the net monetary position 1270
	6.3	Measurement of reclassification adjustments within equity 1270
7	RESTATEMENT OF THE STATEMENT OF CASH FLOWS	 1272
8	RESTATEMENT OF COMPARATIVE FIGURES	 1273
9	INTERIM REPORTING	 1273
10	TRANSITION	 1274
	10.1	Economies becoming hyperinflationary 1274
	10.2	Economies ceasing to be hyperinflationary 1275
	10.3	Economies exiting severe hyperinflation 1276
11	TRANSLATION TO A DIFFERENT PRESENTATION CURRENCY	 1277
	11.1	Translation on initial application and ceasing application of IAS 29 1279
	11.2	Presentation currency considerations for comparative information 1280
12	DISCLOSURES	 1281

List of examples

Example 16.1:	Accounting for hyperinflation under IAS 29 1253
Example 16.2:	Restatement of property, plant and equipment 1261
Example 16.3:	Borrowing costs and net realisable value adjustments 1262
Example 16.4:	Restatement of deferred taxation 1265
Example 16.5:	Restatement of equity 1267
Example 16.6:	Restatement of historical cost statement of profit and loss and other comprehensive income 1269
Example 16.7:	Measurement of reclassification adjustments 1271
Example 16.8:	Economies ceasing to be hyperinflationary in an interim period 1275

Chapter 16 Hyperinflation

1 INTRODUCTION

1.1 Background

Accounting standards are applied on the assumption that the value of money (the unit of measurement) is constant over time, which normally is an acceptable practical assumption. However, when the effect of inflation on the value of money is no longer negligible, the usefulness of historical cost based financial reporting is often significantly reduced. High rates of inflation give rise to a number of problems for entities that prepare their financial statements on a historical cost basis, for example:

- historical cost figures expressed in terms of monetary units do not show the 'value to the business' of assets;
- holding gains on non-monetary assets that are reported as operating profits do not represent real economic gains;
- financial information presented for the current period is not comparable with that presented for the prior periods; and
- 'real' capital can be reduced because profits reported do not take account of the higher replacement costs of resources used in the period. Therefore, if calculating a nominal 'return on capital' based on profit, and not distinguishing this properly from a real 'return of capital', the erosion of capital may go unnoticed in the financial statements. This is the underlying point in the concept of capital maintenance.

The IASB's *The Conceptual Framework for Financial Reporting* discusses the concept of capital maintenance, which raises the issue of how an entity defines capital. In general terms, an entity maintains its capital if it has as much capital at the end of the period as it had at the beginning, the issue being how this evaluation is measured. Whilst there are different concepts of capital maintenance, IFRS is ultimately based on the financial capital maintenance concept.

Under the financial capital maintenance concept, the capital of the entity will be maintained if the financial amount of net assets at the end of a period is at least equal to the financial amount of net assets at the beginning of that period, excluding contributions from and distributions to owners during the period. *[CF(2010) 4.59(a)]*. To facilitate the evaluation of capital maintenance in a hyperinflationary environment, IAS 29 – *Financial Reporting in Hyperinflationary Economies* – was adopted in April 2001.

The IASB and IFRS Interpretations Committee (Interpretations Committee) subsequently addressed the subject of hyperinflation only to clarify the provisions of the standard. In 2005, IFRIC 7 – *Applying the Restatement Approach under IAS 29 Financial Reporting in Hyperinflationary Economies* – was issued to provide guidance on applying IAS 29 in the reporting period in which an entity's functional currency first becomes hyperinflationary (see 10.1 below). In 2010 the IASB issued an amendment to IFRS 1 – *First-time Adoption of International Financial Reporting Standards* – for countries that exit severe hyperinflation (see 10.3 below).

1.2 Hyperinflationary economies

For entities used to working in economies with low inflation it is easy to overlook that there are countries where inflation is a major economic concern. In some of these countries, inflation has reached such levels that (1) the local currency is no longer a useful measure of value in the economy and (2) the general population may prefer not to hold its wealth in the local currency. Instead, they hold their wealth in a stable foreign currency or non-monetary assets. Such a condition is often referred to as hyperinflation.

There are several characteristics that need to be considered under IFRS to determine whether hyperinflation exists. The IASB does not monitor inflation rates in specific jurisdictions, nor does it conclude on the applicability of the characteristics to these jurisdictions. Conversely, under US GAAP hyperinflation is clearly defined and deemed to exist when the cumulative rate of inflation over a three-year period exceeds 100%. For the purposes of reporting under US accounting standards, the International Practices Task Force (IPTF), a task force of the SEC Regulations Committee, monitors the inflation status of different countries.

As the IPTF's criteria are similar to those used under IFRS, this provides a useful guide for entities reporting under IFRS. However, it should be noted that hyperinflation accounting may need to be applied earlier under IFRS than US accounting standards as IAS 29 applies from the beginning of the reporting period in which hyperinflation is identified and the IPTF usually only meet in May and November each year. Minutes of these meetings are publicly available.[1]

In practice, few countries are considered hyperinflationary by the IPTF. For the purposes of IAS 29, the same countries are usually considered hyperinflationary, but where the assessment of the characteristics is unclear, consensus is at times facilitated by local regulators and professional bodies.

1.3 Restatement approach

The problems of historical cost based financial reporting may reach such a magnitude under hyperinflationary circumstances that financial reporting in the hyperinflationary currency is no longer useful. Therefore, a solution is needed to allow meaningful financial reporting by entities that operate in these hyperinflationary economies.

IAS 29 requires a restatement approach, whereby financial information recorded in the hyperinflationary currency is adjusted by applying a general price index and expressed in the measuring unit current at the end of the reporting period (i.e. the accounting value is adjusted for a factor of current purchasing power). This process aims to improve comparability between periods by restating financial information for changes in the purchasing power of money.

2 THE REQUIREMENTS OF IAS 29

2.1 The context of IAS 29

The underlying premise of IAS 29 is that 'reporting of operating results and financial position in the local [hyperinflationary] currency without restatement is not useful'. *[IAS 29.2]*. The standard's approach is therefore to require that:

(a) the financial statements of an entity whose functional currency is the currency of a hyperinflationary economy shall be stated in terms of the measuring unit current at the end of the reporting period;

(b) the corresponding figures for the previous period required by IAS 1 – *Presentation of Financial Statements* – and any information in respect of earlier periods shall also be stated in terms of the measuring unit current at the end of the reporting period; and

(c) the gain or loss on the net monetary position shall be included in profit or loss and separately disclosed. *[IAS 29.8-9]*.

IAS 29 requires amounts recorded in the statement of financial position, not already expressed in terms of the measuring unit current at the end of the reporting period, to be restated in terms of the current measuring unit at the end of the reporting period, by applying a general price index. *[IAS 29.11]*. The example below illustrates how this would apply to the statement of financial position of an entity:

Example 16.1: Accounting for hyperinflation under IAS 29

An entity that operates in a hyperinflationary economy is required under IAS 29 to restate all non-monetary items in its statement of financial position to the measuring unit current at the end of the reporting period by applying a general price index as follows:

	Before restatement (HC)	Historical general price index*	Year-end general price index	After restatement (HC)
Plant and equipment	225	150	600	900
Inventory	250	500	600	300
Cash	100			100
Total assets	575			1,300
Accounts payable	180			180
Long-term debt	250			250
Equity **	145			870
	575			1,300

*   General price index at the date of purchase
** The restatement of equity is not illustrated here, but discussed at 5 below.

The simplified example above already raises a number of questions, such as:
- Which items are monetary and which are non-monetary?
- How does the entity select the appropriate general price index?
- What was the general price index when the assets were acquired?

The standard provides guidance on the restatement to the measuring unit current at the end of the reporting period, but concedes that the consistent application of these inflation accounting procedures and judgements from period to period is more important than the precise accuracy of the resulting amounts included in the restated financial statements. *[IAS 29.10]*. The requirements of the standard look deceptively straightforward but their application may represent a considerable challenge. These difficulties and other aspects of the practical application of the IAS 29 method of accounting for hyperinflation are discussed below.

2.2 Scope

IAS 29 shall be applied by all entities whose functional currency is the currency of a hyperinflationary economy. *[IAS 29.1]*.

The standard should be applied in an entity's separate financial statements (if prepared) and its consolidated financial statements, as well as by parents that include such an entity in their consolidated financial statements.

If an entity whose functional currency is that of a hyperinflationary economy wishes to present the financial statements in a different presentation currency, or if their parent has a different presentation currency, the financial statements of the entity first have to be restated under IAS 29. Only then, can the financial statements be translated under IAS 21 – *The Effects of Changes in Foreign Exchange Rates* (see 11 below).

Almost all entities operating in hyperinflationary economies will be subject to the accounting regime of IAS 29, unless they can legitimately argue that the local hyperinflationary currency is not their functional currency as defined by IAS 21 (see Chapter 15 at 4). *[IAS 21.14]*.

2.3 Definition of hyperinflation

Determining whether an economy is hyperinflationary in accordance with IAS 29 requires judgement. The standard does not establish an absolute inflation rate at which hyperinflation is deemed to arise. Instead, it considers the following characteristics of the economic environment of a country to be strong indicators of the existence of hyperinflation:

(a) the general population prefers to keep its wealth in non-monetary assets or in a relatively stable foreign currency. Amounts of local currency held are immediately invested to maintain purchasing power;

(b) the general population regards monetary amounts not in terms of the local currency but in terms of a relatively stable foreign currency. Prices may be quoted in that currency;

(c) sales and purchases on credit take place at prices that compensate for the expected loss of purchasing power during the credit period, even if the period is short;

(d) interest rates, wages and prices are linked to a price index; and

(e) the cumulative inflation rate over three years is approaching, or exceeds, 100%. *[IAS 29.3]*.

The above list is not exhaustive and there may be other indicators that an economy is hyperinflationary, such as the existence of price controls and restrictive exchange controls. In determining whether an economy is hyperinflationary, condition (e) is quantitatively measurable while the other indicators require reliance on more qualitative evidence.

IAS 29 expresses a preference that all entities that report in the currency of the same hyperinflationary economy apply this Standard from the same date. Nevertheless, once an entity has identified the existence of hyperinflation, it should apply IAS 29 from the beginning of the reporting period in which it identified the existence of hyperinflation. *[IAS 29.4]*.

Identifying when a currency becomes hyperinflationary, and, just as importantly, when it ceases to be so, is not easy in practice and is frequently hampered by a lack of reliable statistics. The consideration of trends and the application of common sense is important in this judgement, as are consistency of measurement and of presentation. As discussed at 1.2 above, the IPTF monitors hyperinflationary countries for US GAAP and this may be useful for IFRS reporters. Transition into and out of hyperinflationary economies are discussed further at 10 below.

2.4 The IAS 29 restatement process

Restatement of financial statements in accordance with IAS 29 can be seen as a process comprising the following steps:

(a) selection of a general price index (see 3 below);

(b) analysis and restatement of the statement of financial position (see 4 below);

(c) restatement of the statement of changes in equity (see 5 below);

(d) restatement of the statement of profit and loss and other comprehensive income (see 6 below);

(e) calculation of the gain or loss on the net monetary position (see 6.2 below);

(f) restatement of the statement of cash flows (see 7 below); and

(g) restatement of comparative figures (see 8 below).

3 SELECTION OF A GENERAL PRICE INDEX

The standard requires entities to use a general price index that reflects changes in general purchasing power. Ideally all entities that report in the same hyperinflationary currency should use the same price index. *[IAS 29.37]*.

3.1 Selecting a general price index

It is generally accepted practice to use a Consumer Price Index (CPI) for this purpose, unless that index is clearly flawed. National statistical offices in most countries issue several price indices that potentially could be used for the purposes of IAS 29. *[IAS 29.37]*. Important characteristics of a good general price index include the following:

- a wide range of goods and services has been included in the price index;
- reflective of currency-wide, rather than regional, purchasing power;
- continuity and consistency of measurement techniques and underlying assumptions;
- free from bias;
- frequently updated; and
- available for a long period.

The entity should use the above criteria to choose the most reliable and most readily available general price index and use that index consistently. It is important that the index selected is representative of the real position of the hyperinflationary currency concerned.

3.2 General price index not available for all periods

IAS 29 requires an entity to make an estimate of the price index if the general price index is not available for all periods for which the restatement of long-lived assets is required. The entity could base the estimate, for example, on the movements in the exchange rate between the functional currency and a relatively stable foreign currency. *[IAS 29.17]*. It should be noted that this method is only appropriate if the currency of the hyperinflationary economy is freely exchangeable, i.e. not subject to currency controls and 'official' exchange rates. Entities should also be mindful that, especially in the short term, the exchange rate may fluctuate significantly in response to factors other than changes in the domestic price level.

Entities could use a similar approach when they cannot find a general price index that meets the minimum criteria for reliability (e.g. because the national statistical office in the hyperinflationary economy may be subject to significant political bias). However, this would only be acceptable if there was a widespread consensus that all available general price indices are fatally flawed.

4 ANALYSIS AND RESTATEMENT OF THE STATEMENT OF FINANCIAL POSITION

A broad outline of the process to restate assets and liabilities in the statement of financial position in accordance with the requirements of IAS 29 is shown in the diagram below:

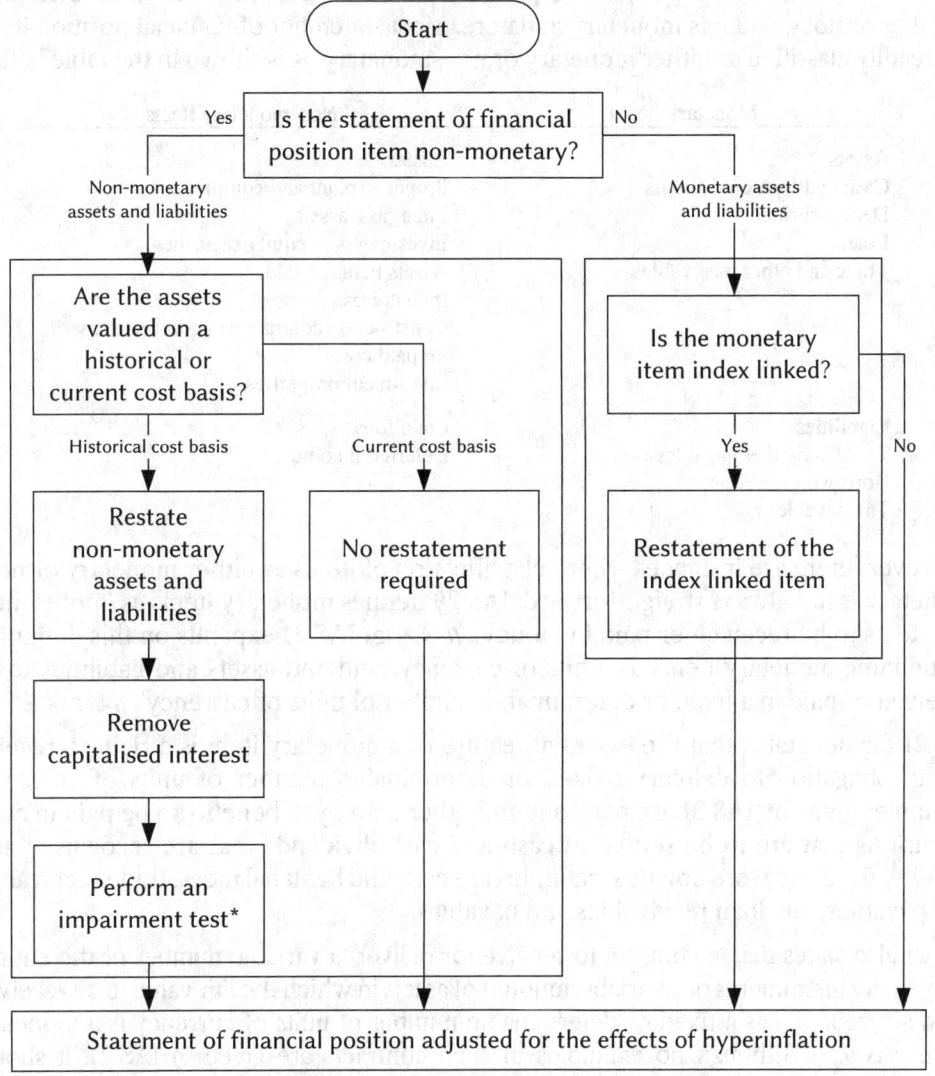

* IAS 29 requires the restated amount of a non-monetary item to be reduced in accordance with the appropriate IFRS when the restated amount exceeds its recoverable amount. [IAS 29.19].

The above flowchart does not illustrate the restatement of investees and subsidiaries (see 4.3 below), deferred taxation (see 4.4 below) and equity (see 5 below).

4.1 Monetary and non-monetary items

4.1.1 Monetary or non-monetary distinction

Monetary items are not restated as they are already expressed in the measurement unit current at the end of the reporting period. Therefore an entity needs to determine whether or not an item is monetary in nature. Most statement of financial position items are readily classified as either monetary or non-monetary as is shown in the table below:

Monetary items	Non-monetary items
Assets	**Assets**
Cash and cash equivalents	Property, plant and equipment
Debt securities	Intangible assets
Loans	Investments in equity securities
Trade and other receivables	Assets held for sale
	Inventories
	Construction contract work-in-progress
	Prepaid costs
	Investment properties
Liabilities	**Liabilities**
Trade and other payables	Deferred income
Borrowings	
Tax payable	

However, there are instances where classification of items as either monetary or non-monetary is not always straightforward. IAS 29 defines monetary items as 'money held and items to be received or paid in money'. [IAS 29.12]. IAS 21 expands on this definition by defining monetary items as 'units of currency held and assets and liabilities to be received or paid in a fixed or determinable number of units of currency'. [IAS 21.8].

IAS 21 further states that the essential feature of a monetary item is a right to receive (or an obligation to deliver) a fixed or determinable number of units of currency. Examples given by IAS 21 are pensions and other employee benefits to be paid in cash, provisions that are to be settled in cash and cash dividends that are recognised as a liability. [IAS 21.16]. More obvious examples are cash and bank balances, trade receivables and payables, and loan receivables and payables.

IAS 21 also states that 'a contract to receive (or deliver) a variable number of the entity's own equity instruments or a variable amount of assets in which the fair value to be received (or delivered) equals a fixed or determinable number of units of currency is a monetary item.' [IAS 21.16]. Although no examples of such contracts are given in IAS 21, it should include those contracts settled in the entity's own equity shares that would be presented as financial assets or liabilities under IAS 32 – *Financial Instruments: Presentation*.

Conversely, the essential feature of a non-monetary item is the absence of a right to receive (or an obligation to deliver) a fixed or determinable number of units of currency. Examples given by IAS 21 are amounts prepaid for goods and services (e.g. prepaid rent); goodwill; intangible assets; inventories; property, plant and equipment; right-of-use assets; and provisions that are to be settled by the delivery of a non-monetary asset. [IAS 21.16]. IFRS 9 – *Financial Instruments* – states that all equity instruments are non-monetary. [IFRS 9.B5.7.3]. Therefore, equity investments in subsidiaries, associates or joint ventures would also be considered non-monetary items. IAS 29 provides separate rules on restatement of such investees (see 4.3 below).

Even with this guidance there may be situations where the distinction is not clear. Certain assets and liabilities may require careful analysis before they can be classified. Examples of items that are not easily classified as either monetary or non-monetary include:

(a) *provisions:* these can be monetary, non-monetary or partly monetary. For example, a warranty provision would be:

   (i) entirely monetary when customers only have a right to return the product and obtain a cash refund equal to the amount they originally paid;

   (ii) non-monetary when customers have the right to have any defective product replaced; and

   (iii) partly monetary if customers can choose between a refund and a replacement of the defective product.

   Classification as either a monetary or a non-monetary item is not acceptable in (iii) above. To meet the requirements of IAS 29, part of the provision should be treated as a non-monetary item and the remainder as a monetary item;

(b) *deferred tax assets and liabilities:* characterising these as monetary or non-monetary can be difficult as explained at 4.4 below;

(c) *associates and joint ventures:* IAS 29 provides separate rules on restatement of investees that do not rely on the distinction between monetary and non-monetary items (see 4.3 below);

(d) *deposits or progress payments paid or received:* if the payments made are regarded as prepayments or as progress payments then the amounts should be treated as non-monetary items. However, if the payments made are in effect refundable deposits then the amounts should probably be treated as monetary items; and

(e) *index-linked assets and liabilities:* classification is particularly difficult when interest rates, lease payments or prices are linked to a price index.

In summary, the practical application of the monetary/non-monetary distinction can be complex and will require judgement on the part of preparers of financial statements. Further examples of problem areas in the application of the monetary/non-monetary distinction are discussed in Chapter 15 at 5.4.

4.1.2 Monetary items

Generally, monetary items are not restated to reflect the effect of inflation because they already reflect their purchasing power at the end of the reporting period. However, monetary assets and liabilities linked by agreement to changes in prices, such as index-linked bonds and loans, should be adjusted in accordance with the terms of the underlying agreement to show the repayment obligation at the end of the reporting period. *[IAS 29.13]*. This adjustment should be offset against the gain or loss on the net monetary position (see 6.2 below). *[IAS 29.28]*.

This type of restatement is not a hyperinflation accounting adjustment, but rather a gain or loss on a financial instrument. Accounting for inflation-linked bonds and loans under IFRS 9 may well lead to complexity in financial reporting. Depending on the specific wording of the inflation adjustment clause, such contracts may give rise to embedded derivatives and gains or losses will have to be recorded either in profit or loss or other comprehensive income depending on how the instrument is classified under IFRS 9 (see Chapter 46 at 5.1.6 and Chapter 48 at 6.3.5).

4.1.3 Non-monetary items carried at current cost

Non-monetary items carried at current cost are not restated because they are already expressed in terms of the measuring unit current at the end of the reporting period. *[IAS 29.29]*. Current cost is not defined by the standard, but the IASB's *Conceptual Framework* provides the following definition: 'Assets are carried at the amount of cash or cash equivalents that would have to be paid if the same or an equivalent asset was acquired currently. Liabilities are carried at the undiscounted amount of cash or cash equivalents that would be required to settle the obligation currently'. *[CF(2010) 4.55(b)]*. IAS 29 expands this definition by including net realisable value and fair value into the concept of 'amounts current at the end of the reporting period'. *[IAS 29.14]*. In summary, this would include items carried at a value that reflects purchasing power at the balance sheet date.

It is important to note that non-monetary items that were revalued at some earlier date are not necessarily carried at current cost, and need to be restated from the date of their latest revaluation. *[IAS 29.18]*.

In many hyperinflationary economies, national legislation may require entities to adjust historical cost based financial information in a way that is not in accordance with IAS 29 (for example, national legislation may require entities to adjust the carrying amount of tangible fixed assets by applying a multiplier). Though financial information adjusted in accordance with national legislation is sometimes described as 'current cost' information, it will seldom meet the definition of current cost in accordance with the *Conceptual Framework*. *[CF(2010) 4.55(b)]*. Where this is the case, entities must first determine the carrying value on the historical cost basis for these assets and liabilities before applying the requirements of IAS 29.

4.1.4 Non-monetary items carried at historical cost

Non-monetary items carried at historical cost, or cost less depreciation, are stated at amounts that were current at the date of their acquisition. The restated cost, or cost less depreciation, of those items is calculated as follows:

$$\text{net book value restated for hyperinflation} = \text{historical cost} \times \frac{\text{general price index at the end of the reporting period}}{\text{general price index at the date of acquisition}}$$

Application of this formula to property, plant and equipment, inventories of raw materials and merchandise, goodwill, patents, trademarks and similar assets appears to be straightforward, but does require detailed records of their acquisition dates and accurate price indices at those dates. *[IAS 29.15]*. It should be noted though that IAS 29 permits certain approximations as long as the procedures and judgements are consistent from period to period. *[IAS 29.10]*. Where sufficiently detailed records are not available or capable of estimation, IAS 29 suggests that it may be necessary to obtain an 'independent professional assessment' of the value of the items as the basis for their restatement in the first period of application of the standard, but also notes that this will only be in rare circumstances. *[IAS 29.16]*.

Example 16.2: Restatement of property, plant and equipment

The table below illustrates how the restatement of a non-monetary item (for example, property, plant and equipment) would be calculated in accordance with the requirements of IAS 29. When IAS 29 is first applied, the item is restated from the date of acquisition. In subsequent periods it is restated from the previous reporting period as shown below.

Net book value of property, plant and equipment	Historical restatements	Conversion factor	Restated for hyperinflation	
Opening balance, 1 January	510	2.40	1,224	(a)
– Additions (May)	360	1.80	648	(b)
– Disposals (March)	(105)	2.40	(252)	(c)
– Depreciation	(200)		(448)	(d)
Closing balance, 31 December	565		1,172	(e)

(a) The opening balance is restated by adjusting the historical balance for the increase in the price index between the beginning and the end of the reporting period.

(b) The additions are restated for the increase in the price index from May to December.

(c) The disposals are restated for the increase in the price index between the beginning and the end of the reporting period, assuming all disposals were acquired in a previous reporting period.

(d) Depreciation has been recalculated using the cost balance restated for hyperinflation on an asset by asset basis as a starting point. The alternative approach, to restate the depreciation charge by applying the appropriate conversion factor, could be easier to apply but may not be accurate enough when there is a significant level of additions and disposals during the reporting period.

(e) The closing balance is in practice determined by adding up items (a)-(d). Alternatively, the entity could calculate the closing balance by restating the acquisition cost and related accumulated depreciation of the individual assets for the change in the price index during the period of ownership.

The calculations described under (a)-(e) all require estimates regarding the general price index at given dates and are sometimes based on averages or best estimates of the actual date of the transaction.

When an entity purchases an asset and payment is deferred beyond normal credit terms, it would normally recognise the present value of the cash payment as its cost. *[IAS 16.23]*. When it is impracticable to determine the amount of interest, IAS 29 provides relief by allowing such assets to be restated from the payment date rather than the date of purchase. *[IAS 29.22]*.

Once the calculation discussed above has been completed, additional adjustments may need to be made. In order to arrive at the final restated cost of the non-monetary items, the provisional restated cost needs to be adjusted for borrowing costs and impairment, if applicable, as follows: *[IAS 29.19, 21]*

| restated costs | = | net book value restated for hyperinflation | – | borrowing costs that compensate for inflation capitalised under IAS 23 | – | adjustment to recoverable amount |

IAS 29 only permits partial capitalisation of borrowing costs, unlike the full capitalisation that is ordinarily required by IAS 23 – *Borrowing Costs* (see Chapter 21), because of the risk of double counting as the entity would both restate the capital expenditure financed by borrowing and capitalise that part of the borrowing costs that compensates for the inflation during the same period. *[IAS 29.21]*. The difficulty when borrowing costs are capitalised is that IAS 29 only permits capitalisation of borrowing costs to the extent that those costs do not compensate for inflation. The standard does not provide any guidance on how an entity should go about determining the component of borrowing costs that compensates for the effects of inflation. Therefore, entities will need to develop an appropriate methodology.

It is possible that an IAS 29 inflation adjustment based on the general price index leads to non-monetary assets being stated above their recoverable amount. Therefore, IAS 29 requires that the restated amount of a non-monetary item is reduced, in accordance with the appropriate standard, when it exceeds its recoverable amount from the item's future use (including sale or other disposal). *[IAS 29.19]*. This requirement should be taken to mean that any overstatement of non-monetary assets not within the scope of IFRS 9 should be calculated and accounted for in accordance with IAS 36 – *Impairment of Assets* – or the measurement provisions of IAS 2 – *Inventories* (see 4.2 below). That is, the asset is written down to its recoverable amount or net realisable value and the loss is recognised in profit or loss.

The example below illustrates how, after it has restated the historical cost based carrying amount of property, plant and equipment by applying the general price index, an entity adjusts the net book value restated for hyperinflation for these considerations:

Example 16.3:   Borrowing costs and net realisable value adjustments

After the entity has restated the historical cost based carrying amount of property, plant and equipment by applying the general price index, it needs to adjust the net book value restated for hyperinflation to take account of borrowing costs capitalised since the acquisition of the asset as follows:

Net book value restated for hyperinflation (inclusive of borrowing costs)	1,725	
Borrowing costs capitalised at historical cost under IAS 23	42	
Borrowing costs that compensated for inflation	(30)	
Borrowing costs permitted to be capitalised under IAS 29	12	
Borrowing costs that compensated for inflation	(30)	
Relevant conversion factor for the borrowing costs	2.10 ×	
	(63)	(a)
Net book value restated for hyperinflation and after adjustment of capitalised borrowing costs	1,662	
Net book value restated for hyperinflation and after adjustment of capitalised borrowing costs	1,662	
Amount recoverable from the item's future use	1,550	
	112	
Adjustment to lower recoverable amount	(112)	(b)
Carrying amount restated under IAS 29	1,550	

(a) The borrowing costs capitalised in the original historical cost financial statements are reversed, as they are not permitted under IAS 29.

(b) To the extent that the 'net book value restated for hyperinflation and after adjustment of capitalised borrowing costs' exceeds the 'amount recoverable from the item's future use', the restated amount should be reduced to the lower 'amount recoverable from the item's future use'.

Where an entity's functional currency becomes hyperinflationary and it applies IAS 29 for the first time, IFRIC 7 requires the application of IAS 29 as if the economy had always been hyperinflationary. *[IFRIC 7.3]*. Therefore, such an entity should consider whether an impairment trigger is present at the beginning of the current period and, if any impairment is identified, determine whether it relates to the current period or whether it should have been recognised earlier. In making such a determination in practice there are likely to be a number of complexities including the degree of hindsight that might be involved.

4.2 Inventories

Inventories of finished and partly finished goods should be restated from the dates on which the costs of purchase and of conversion were incurred. *[IAS 29.15]*. This means that the individual components of finished goods should be restated from their respective purchase dates. Similarly, if production takes place in several distinct phases, the costs associated with each of those phases should be restated from the date that the cost was incurred.

Given the large number of transactions affecting an entity's inventory position, it may be difficult to determine the date of acquisition of individual items of inventory. Therefore, entities commonly approximate the ageing of inventories based on inventory turnover. Similarly, the level of the general price index at the date of acquisition is often determined at the average level for the month because an up-to-date price index is not available for each day of the month. Determining the appropriate level of the general price index can be difficult when the price index is updated relatively infrequently and the entity's business is highly seasonal.

IAS 29 requires restatement of inventory by applying a general price index, which could result in an overvaluation when the price of inventory items increases at a different rate from the general price index. At the end of each period it is therefore essential to ensure that items of inventory are not valued in excess of their net realisable value. Any overstated inventories should be written down to net realisable value under IAS 2. *[IAS 29.19]*.

4.3 Restatement of associates, joint ventures and subsidiaries

IAS 29 provides separate rules for the restatement of associates and joint ventures that are accounted for under the equity method. If the investee itself operates in a hyperinflationary currency, the entity should restate the statement of financial position, statement of profit and loss and other comprehensive income of the investee in accordance with the requirements of IAS 29 in order to calculate its share of the investee's net assets and results of operations. *[IAS 29.20]*. The standard does not permit the investment in the investee to be treated as a single indivisible item for the purposes of the IAS 29 restatement. Restating the financial statements of an associate before application of the equity method will often be difficult because the investor may not have access to the detailed information required. The fact that the investor can exercise significant influence or has joint control over an investee often does not mean that the investor has unrestricted access to the investee's books and records at all times.

When the investor does not operate in the hyperinflationary currency, but the investee does, the same processes described above are still required to be completed prior to the equity accounting process.

Once restated, the results of a foreign currency investee are translated into the investor's presentation currency at the closing rate. *[IAS 29.20]*. IAS 21 contains a similar provision that requires that all current year amounts related to an entity (i.e. investee), whose functional currency is the currency of a hyperinflationary economy, to be translated at the closing rate at the date of the most recent statement of financial position (see Chapter 15 at 6.1). *[IAS 21.42]*.

If a parent that reports in the currency of a hyperinflationary economy has a subsidiary that also reports in the currency of a hyperinflationary economy, then the financial statements of that subsidiary must first be restated by applying a general price index of the country in whose currency it reports before they are included in the consolidated financial statements issued by its parent. *[IAS 29.35]*. When an investor has a subsidiary whose functional currency is the currency of a hyperinflationary economy, IAS 21 further clarifies that all current year amounts related to the subsidiary should be translated at the closing rate at the date of the most recent statement of financial position (see Chapter 15 at 6.1). *[IAS 21.42]*. The restatement of related comparative amounts is discussed at 11.2 below.

If a parent that reports in the currency of a hyperinflationary economy has a subsidiary that reports in a currency that is not hyperinflationary, the financial statements of that subsidiary should be translated in accordance with paragraph 39 of IAS 21 (see Chapter 15 at 6.1). *[IAS 21.39]*.

In addition, IAS 29 requires that when financial statements with different reporting dates are consolidated, all items, whether non-monetary or monetary are restated into the measuring unit current at the date of the consolidated financial statements. *[IAS 29.36]*.

4.4 Calculation of deferred taxation

Determining whether deferred tax assets and liabilities are monetary or non-monetary is difficult because:

- deferred taxation could be seen as a valuation adjustment that is either monetary or non-monetary depending on the asset or liability it relates to, or
- it could also be argued that any deferred taxation payable or receivable in the very near future is almost identical to current tax payable and receivable. Therefore, at least the short-term portion of deferred taxation, if payable or receivable, should be treated as if it were monetary.

IFRIC 7 provides guidance to facilitate the first-time application of IAS 29. Although the interpretation notes that there continues to be a difference of opinion as to whether deferred taxation is monetary or non-monetary, *[IFRIC 7.BC21-BC22]*, the debate has been settled for practical purposes because:

- IAS 12 – *Income Taxes* – requires deferred taxation in the closing statement of financial position for the year to be calculated based on the difference between the carrying amount and the tax base of assets and liabilities, without making a distinction between monetary and non-monetary items; and
- IFRIC 7 requires an entity to remeasure the deferred tax items in any comparative period in accordance with IAS 12 after it has restated the nominal carrying amounts of its non-monetary items at the date of the opening statement of

financial position of the reporting period by applying the measuring unit at that date. These remeasured deferred tax items are then restated for the change in the measuring unit between the beginning and the end of reporting period. *[IFRIC 7.4]*.

The following example, which is based on the illustrative example in IFRIC 7, shows how an entity should restate its deferred taxation in the comparative period. *[IFRIC 7.IE1-IE6]*.

Example 16.4: Restatement of deferred taxation

Entity A owns a building that it acquired in December 2019. The carrying amount and tax base of the building, and the deferred tax liability are as follows:

Before IAS 29 restatement	2021	2020
Building (not restated)	300	400
Tax base	200	333
Tax rate	30%	30%
Deferred tax liability:		
$(300 - 200) \times 30\%$ =	30	
$(400 - 333) \times 30\%$ =		20

Entity A has identified the existence of hyperinflation in 2021 and therefore applies IAS 29 from the beginning of 2021. Entity A will use the following general price index and conversion factors to restate its financial statements:

	General price index
December 2019	95
December 2020	135
December 2021	223

The table below shows the method required by IFRIC 7:

	2021	2020
Building (not restated)	300	400
Building (restated in 2021 financial statements):		
$300 \times (223 \div 95)$ =	704	
$400 \times (223 \div 95)$ =		939
Building (restated in 2020 financial statements):		
$400 \times (135 \div 95)$ =		568 (a)
Tax base	200	333 (b)
Deferred tax liability (restated in 2021 financial statements):		
$(704 - 200) \times 30\%$ =	151	
$(568 - 333) \times 30\% = 71; 71 \times (223 \div 135)$ =		117

Entity A measures the temporary difference at the end of 2020 by comparing (a) the restated carrying amount of the building in 2020 accounts to (b) its tax base at that date. The temporary difference calculated in that manner is then multiplied by the applicable tax rate and the resulting amount is then adjusted for the hyperinflation during 2021, resulting in a deferred tax liability of 117.

After Entity A has restated its financial statements for a given year, all corresponding figures in the financial statements for a subsequent reporting period, including deferred tax items, are restated by applying the change in the measuring unit for that subsequent reporting period only to the restated financial statements for the previous reporting period. *[IFRIC 7.5]*.

IAS 29 refers to IAS 12 for guidance on the calculation of deferred taxation by entities operating in hyperinflationary economies. *[IAS 29.32]*. IAS 12 recognises that IAS 29 restatements of assets and liabilities may give rise to temporary differences when equivalent adjustments are not allowed for tax purposes. *[IAS 12.IE.A18]*. Where IAS 29 adjustments give rise to temporary differences, IAS 12 requires the following accounting treatment:

(1) the deferred tax income or expense is recognised in profit or loss; and

(2) if, in addition to the restatement, non-monetary assets are also revalued, the deferred tax movement relating to the revaluation is recognised in other comprehensive income and the deferred tax relating to the restatement is recognised in profit or loss. *[IAS 12.IE.A18]*.

For example, deferred taxation arising on revaluation of property, plant and equipment is recognised in other comprehensive income, just as it would be if the entity were not operating in a hyperinflationary economy. On the other hand, restatement in accordance with IAS 29 of property, plant and equipment that is measured at historical cost is recognised in profit or loss. Thus the treatment of deferred taxation related to non-monetary assets valued at historical cost and those that are revalued, is consistent with the general requirements of IAS 12.

5 RESTATEMENT OF THE STATEMENT OF CHANGES IN EQUITY

When an entity first applies IAS 29, it restates the components of owners' equity at the beginning of the earliest period presented as follows:

- the components of owners' equity, except retained earnings and any revaluation surplus, are restated by applying a general price index from the dates the components were contributed or otherwise arose;
- any revaluation surplus that arose in previous periods is eliminated; and
- restated retained earnings are derived from all the other amounts in the restated statement of financial position. *[IAS 29.24]*.

At the end of the first period and in subsequent periods, all components of owners' equity are restated by applying a general price index from the beginning of the period or the date of contribution, if later. *[IAS 29.25]*. Subsequent revaluations may give rise to a revaluation surplus within equity.

IFRS does not define retained earnings and many jurisdictions require entities to appropriate part of the balance into specific (often non-distributable) reserves. In such cases, entities will need to apply judgement to determine whether these reserves are essentially part of retained earnings (and so are not restated by applying the general price index as described in paragraph 24 of IAS 29). If they are considered a separate component of equity, then they are restated by applying the general price index as explained above, both at the beginning of the first period when an entity applies IAS 29 and at the end of the first period and subsequent periods. Where entities have made such judgements concerning the types of reserves held and these judgements have a significant effect on the amounts recognised in the financial statements, IAS 1 requires disclosure to users of the financial statements. *[IAS 1.122]*.

Though IAS 29 provides guidance on the restatement of assets, liabilities and individual components of shareholders' equity, national laws and regulations with which the entity needs to comply might not permit such revaluations. This can mean that IAS 29 may require restatement of distributable reserves, but that from the legal point of view in the jurisdiction concerned, those same reserves remain unchanged. That is, it is possible that 'restated retained earnings' under IAS 29 will not all be legally distributable.

It may therefore be unclear to users of financial statements restated under IAS 29 to what extent components of equity are distributable. Because of its global constituents, the IASB's standards cannot deal with specific national legal requirements relating to a legal entity's equity. Entities reporting under IAS 29 should therefore disclose the extent to which components of equity are distributable where this is not obvious from the financial statements. In our view it is important for entities to give supplementary information in the circumstances where the IAS 29 adjustments have produced large apparently distributable reserves that are in fact not distributable.

Example 16.5:   Restatement of equity

The table below shows the effect of a hypothetical IAS 29 restatement on individual components of equity. Issued share capital and share premium increase by applying the general price index, the revaluation reserve is eliminated as required, and retained earnings is the balancing figure derived from all other amounts in the restated statement of financial position.

	Amounts before restatement	Amounts after IAS 29 restatement	Components of equity under national law
Issued capital and share premium	1,500	3,150	1,500
Revaluation reserve	800	–	800
Retained earnings	350	1,600	350
Total equity	2,650	4,750	2,650

A user of the financial statements of the entity might get the impression, based on the information restated in accordance with IAS 29, that distributable reserves have increased from 350 to 1,600. However, if national law does not permit revaluation of assets, liabilities and components of equity, then distributable reserves remain unchanged.

It is unclear how an entity should deal with other reserves that could potentially be reclassified to profit or loss, for example those arising from debt instruments measured at fair value through other comprehensive income in accordance with IFRS 9. In our view an entity should develop an accounting policy under which it either reclassifies the amount initially recognised in other comprehensive income or an amount adjusted for hyperinflation (see 6.3 below).

6 RESTATEMENT OF THE STATEMENT OF PROFIT AND LOSS AND OTHER COMPREHENSIVE INCOME

IAS 29 requires that all items in historical cost based statements of profit and loss and other comprehensive income be expressed in terms of the measuring unit current at the end of the reporting period. *[IAS 29.26]*. The standard contains a similar requirement for current cost based statements of profit and loss and other comprehensive income, because the underlying transactions or events are recorded at current cost at the time they occurred rather than in the measuring unit current at the end of the reporting period. *[IAS 29.30]*. Therefore, all amounts in the statement of profit and loss and other comprehensive income need to be restated as follows:

$$\text{restated amount} = \text{amount before restatement} \times \frac{\text{general price index at the end of the reporting period}}{\text{general price index when the underlying income or expenses were initially recorded}}$$

Actually performing the above calculation on a real set of financial statements is often difficult because an entity would need to keep a very detailed record of when it entered into transactions and when it incurred expenses. Instead of using the exact price index for a transaction it may be more practical to use an average price index that approximates the actual rate at the date of the transaction. For example, an average rate for a week or a month might be used for all transactions occurring during that period. However, it must be stressed that if price indices fluctuate significantly, the use of an average for the period may be inappropriate.

There may be items in statements of profit and loss and other comprehensive income, e.g. interest income and expense that comprise an element that is intended to compensate for the effect of hyperinflation. However, even those items need to be restated as IAS 29 specifically requires that 'all amounts need to be restated' (see 6.1 below). *[IAS 29.26, 30]*.

Example 16.6 below illustrates how an entity might, for example, restate its revenue to the measuring unit current at the end of the reporting period. A similar calculation would work well for other items in statements of profit and loss and other comprehensive income, with the exception of:

(a) depreciation and amortisation charges which are often easier to restate by using the cost balance restated for hyperinflation as a starting point;

(b) deferred taxation which should be based on the temporary differences between the carrying amount and tax base of assets and liabilities, the restated opening balance carrying amount of statement of financial position items, and the underlying tax base of those items (see 4.4 above); and

(c) the net monetary gain or loss which results from the IAS 29 restatements (see 6.2 below).

Example 16.6: **Restatement of historical cost statement of profit and loss and other comprehensive income**

An entity would restate its revenue for the period ending 31 December 2021, when the general price index was 2,880, as shown in the table below.

	General price index	Conversion factor	Revenue before restatement	Restated revenue
31 January 2021	1,315	(2,880 ÷ 1,315) = 2.19	40	87.6
28 February 2021	1,345	(2,880 ÷ 1,345) = 2.14	35	74.9
31 March 2021	1,371	etc. = 2.10	45	94.5
30 April 2021	1,490	1.93	45	87.0
31 May 2021	1,600	1.80	65	117.0
30 June 2021	1,846	1.56	70	109.2
31 July 2021	1,923	1.50	70	104.8
31 August 2021	2,071	1.39	65	90.4
30 September 2021	2,163	1.33	75	99.9
31 October 2021	2,511	1.15	75	86.0
30 November 2021	2,599	1.11	80	88.6
31 December 2021	2,880	1.00	80	80.0
			745	1,119.9

Inevitably, in practice there is some approximation in this process because of the assumptions that the entity is required to make, for example the use of weighted averages rather than more detailed calculations and assumptions as to the timing of the underlying transactions (e.g. the calculation above assumes the revenues for the month are earned on the final day of the month, which is not realistic).

6.1 Restatement of interest and exchange differences

A common question is whether an entity should restate exchange differences under IAS 29, because the standard considers that 'foreign exchange differences related to invested or borrowed funds, are also associated with the net monetary position'. *[IAS 29.28]*. Nevertheless, the standard requires that all items in the statement of profit and loss and other comprehensive income are expressed in terms of the measuring unit current at the end of the reporting period. 'Therefore all amounts need to be restated by applying the change in the general price index from the dates when the items of income and expenses were initially recorded in the financial statements'. *[IAS 29.26]*.

Interest and exchange differences should therefore be restated for the effect of inflation, as are all other items in the statement of profit and loss and other comprehensive income, and be presented on a gross basis. However, it may be helpful if they are presented together with the gain or loss on net monetary position in the statement of profit and loss and other comprehensive income. *[IAS 29.28]*.

6.2 Calculation of the gain or loss on the net monetary position

In theory, hyperinflation only affects the value of money and monetary items and does not affect the value, as distinct from the price, of non-monetary items. Therefore, any gain or loss because of hyperinflation will be the gain or loss on the net monetary position of the entity. By arranging the items in an ordinary statement of financial position, it can be shown that the monetary position minus the non-monetary position is always equal to zero:

	Total	Monetary items	Non-monetary items
Monetary assets	280	280	
Non-monetary assets	170		170
Monetary liabilities	(200)	(200)	
Non-monetary liabilities	(110)		(110)
Assets minus liabilities	140		
Shareholders' equity	(140)		(140)
Net position	0	80	(80)

Theoretically, the gain or loss on the net monetary position can be calculated by applying the general price index to the entity's monetary assets and liabilities. This would require the entity to determine its net monetary position on a daily basis, which would be entirely impracticable given the resources required to prepare daily IFRS compliant accounts as well as the difficulties in making the monetary/non-monetary distinction (see 4.1 above). The standard therefore allows the gain or loss on the net monetary position to be estimated by applying the change in a general price index to the weighted average for the period of the difference between monetary assets and monetary liabilities. *[IAS 29.27, 31]*. Due care should be exercised in estimating the gain or loss on the net monetary position, as a calculation based on averages for the period (or monthly averages) can be unreliable if addressed without accurate consideration of the pattern of hyperinflation and the volatility of the net monetary position.

However, as shown in the above table, any restatement of the non-monetary items must be met by an equal restatement of the monetary items. Therefore, in preparing financial statements it is more practical to assume that the gain or loss on the net monetary position is exactly the reverse of the restatement of the non-monetary items. A stand-alone calculation of the net gain or loss can be used to verify the reasonableness of the restatement of the non-monetary items.

The gain or loss on the net monetary position as calculated above, as well as any adjustments on inflation-linked instruments (see 4.1.2 above), should be included in profit or loss and disclosed separately. It may be helpful to present it together with items that are also associated with the net monetary position such as interest income and expense, and foreign exchange differences related to invested or borrowed funds. *[IAS 29.28]*.

6.3 Measurement of reclassification adjustments within equity

IAS 29 does not provide guidance on the measurement basis of reclassifications from other comprehensive income. For example, it is not clear when a debt instrument at fair value through other comprehensive income is sold, whether the amount reclassified into profit and loss is based on the amounts historically recorded in other comprehensive income, or alternatively based on an inflation adjusted amount. Another example is the case of cash flow hedges where gains or losses in an earlier reporting period are recycled to profit and loss to offset against the gains or losses of the hedged item at a later date.

The conflict arises due to the manner in which the statement of profit and loss and other comprehensive income is constructed, including the need to classify items in other comprehensive income as amounts to be recycled, or not. The need to classify items in other comprehensive income into items that are recycled to profit or loss, or not, would indicate that amounts initially recorded in other comprehensive income should be recycled at the amounts originally recorded. While this may satisfy the requirements for other comprehensive income, this leads to a loss of relevant information in the statement of profit and loss and other comprehensive income. Using the examples cited above, the gain or loss on disposal of a debt instrument at fair value through other comprehensive income would no longer be presented in terms of the index being used for purposes of restating amounts in profit or loss. In the case of a cash flow hedge, the offset that would also be expected in profit or loss is also lost. The alternative view would be to recycle amounts that have been restated in terms of the current index that is being applied. This is illustrated in the example below.

Example 16.7:   Measurement of reclassification adjustments

An entity issued a three-year CU 100,000 fixed (15%) rate bond on 31 December 2019. Before the bond was issued, the entity entered into a fully effective cash flow hedge of changes in three-year interest rates that resulted in a gain of CU 6,000 being recognised in other comprehensive income. The entity would reclassify this gain from equity to profit or loss as a reclassification adjustment in the same period or periods during which the bond affects profit or loss, i.e. over three years assuming it is repaid at maturity. Therefore, in a non-hyperinflationary environment, for each of these three years, CU 2,000 would be reclassified from other comprehensive income to profit or loss as an adjustment to interest expense (assuming a straight-line approach was considered appropriate).

IAS 29 is not explicit on whether the reclassification from other comprehensive income should be adjusted for the effects of hyperinflation. The following example illustrates the difference between adjusting and not adjusting the reclassification of the cash flow hedge gains for the effect of hyperinflation. For the purpose of this example, assume the general price index was 100 at 31 December 2020 and 150 at 31 December 2021.

	2021 Hyperinflationary Adjusted CU	2021 Hyperinflationary Non-Adjusted CU	2021 Non-hyperinflationary CU
Net profit:			
Interest expense	...	...	...
Reclassification of cash flow hedge gains	(a) 3,000	2,000	2,000
Other comprehensive income:			
Reclassification of cash flow hedge gains	(3,000)	(2,000)	(2,000)

(a) 6,000 × (150/100) / 3

While the approach of adjusting for hyperinflation would ensure relevant information in the statement of profit and loss and other comprehensive income, it would lead to different amounts being originally recorded and subsequently recycled in other comprehensive income.

As no direct guidance is given in IAS 29, the development of an accounting policy in terms of the IAS 8 – *Accounting Policies, Changes in Accounting Estimates and Errors* – hierarchy would be required. In developing such an accounting policy an entity would need to apply judgement and consider the objective of the standard that gives rise to the amounts that are recycled to profit or loss. The basic accounting requirements before the application of IAS 29 for the hedge accounting example cited above is currently contained in IFRS 9 (or IAS 39 – *Financial Instruments: Recognition and Measurement* – if the hedge accounting requirements of IFRS 9 have not yet been adopted). Understanding the objective of hedge accounting and what risks have been hedged in the designated relationship would be relevant inputs in developing an appropriate accounting policy. Once developed, the general recommendation of IFRS to apply procedures and judgements consistently should be followed for a particular class of equity reclassification. As there are numerous different types of reclassifications within equity, an entity may need to determine a relevant policy for each class of adjustment that could occur.

7 RESTATEMENT OF THE STATEMENT OF CASH FLOWS

The standard requires that all items in the statement of cash flows be expressed in terms of the measuring unit current at the end of the reporting period. *[IAS 29.33]*. This is a difficult requirement to fulfil in practice.

IAS 7 – *Statement of Cash Flows* – requires the following information to be presented:

(a) cash flows from operating activities, which are the principal revenue-producing activities of the entity and other activities that are not investing or financing activities;

(b) cash flows from investing activities, which are the acquisition and disposal of long-term assets and other investments not included in cash equivalents; and

(c) cash flows from financing activities, which are activities that result in changes in the size and composition of the equity capital and borrowings of the entity.
[IAS 7.6, 10].

In effect IAS 29 requires restatement of most items in a statement of cash flows, therefore implying that the actual cash flows at the time of the transactions will be different from the numbers presented in the statement of cash flows itself. However, not all items are restated using the same method and many of the restatements are based on estimates. For example, items in the statement of profit and loss and other comprehensive income are restated using an estimate of the general price index at the time that the revenues were earned and the costs incurred. Unavoidably this will give rise to some inconsistencies. Similarly, the restatement of statement of financial position items will give rise to discrepancies because some items are not easily classified as either monetary or non-monetary. This raises the question of how an entity should classify the monetary gain or loss relating to a statement of financial position item in its statement of cash flows.

It is not clear from IAS 29 how a monetary gain or loss should be presented in the statement of cash flows. In practice different approaches have been adopted, such as:

(a) presenting the effect of inflation on operating, investing and financing cash flows separately for each of these activities and presenting the net monetary gain or loss as a reconciling item in the cash and cash equivalents reconciliation;

(b) presenting the monetary gain or loss on cash and cash equivalents and the effect of inflation on operating, investing and financing cash flows as one number; and

(c) attributing the effect of inflation on operating, investing and financing cash flows to the underlying item and presenting the monetary gain or loss on cash and cash equivalents separately.

Irrespective of the method chosen, users of statements of cash flows prepared in the currency of a hyperinflationary economy should be mindful of the fact that figures presented in the statement of cash flows may have been restated in accordance with IAS 29 and may differ from the actual underlying cash flows. In our view it is important for entities that have a significant proportion of their activities in hyperinflationary economies to consider whether the entity should provide sufficient additional disclosures to ensure that the financial statements are fully understood. Whether this is limited to a general explanation of the mismatch between reported and actual amounts, or specific information on major transactions is provided, would depend on the nature and materiality of transactions affected.

8 RESTATEMENT OF COMPARATIVE FIGURES

The standard requires that all financial information be presented in terms of the measurement unit current at the end of the current reporting period, therefore:

- corresponding figures for the previous reporting period, whether they were based on a historical cost approach or a current cost approach, are restated by applying a general price index; and
- information that is disclosed in respect of earlier periods is also expressed in terms of the measuring unit current at the end of the reporting period. *[IAS 29.34].*

Where IAS 29 was applied in the previous reporting period, this will be a straightforward mathematical computation to apply the measuring unit current at the end of the reporting period to the prior year comparative figures. An example of this can be seen in the restatement of the opening balance of property, plant and equipment in Example 16.2 above. When IAS 29 is applied for the first time, this is a more complex process, as discussed at 10.1 below.

9 INTERIM REPORTING

The illustrative examples to IAS 34 – *Interim Financial Reporting* – state that interim financial reports in hyperinflationary economies are prepared using the same principles as at financial year end. *[IAS 34.B32].* This means that the financial statements must be stated in terms of the measuring unit current at the end of the interim period and that the gain or loss on the net monetary position is included in net income (profit or loss). The comparative financial information reported for prior periods must also be restated to the current measuring unit. *[IAS 34.B33].* Hence, an entity that reports quarterly information must restate the comparative statements of financial position, statement of profit and loss and other comprehensive income, and other primary financial statements each quarter.

In restating its financial information an entity may not 'annualise' the recognition of the gain or loss on the net monetary position or use an estimated annual inflation rate in preparing an interim financial report in a hyperinflationary economy. *[IAS 34.B34]*.

Interim reporting of a group containing a subsidiary that reports in a hyperinflationary currency results in particular issues in the year that the subsidiary's functional currency becomes hyperinflationary. These are discussed further at 11.2 below.

10 TRANSITION

10.1 Economies becoming hyperinflationary

When the functional currency of an entity becomes hyperinflationary it must start applying IAS 29. The standard requires that the financial statements and any information in respect of earlier periods should be stated in terms of the measuring unit current at the end of the reporting period. *[IAS 29.8]*. IFRIC 7 clarifies that items should be restated fully retrospectively. In the first year in which the entity identifies the existence of hyperinflation, the requirements of IAS 29 should be applied as if the economy had always been hyperinflationary. The opening statement of financial position at the beginning of the earliest period presented in the financial statements should be restated as follows:

- non-monetary items measured at historical cost should be restated to reflect the effect of inflation from the date the assets were acquired and the liabilities were incurred or assumed; and
- non-monetary items carried at amounts current at dates other than those of acquisition or incurrence should be restated to reflect the effect of inflation from the dates those carrying amounts were determined. *[IFRIC 7.3]*.

In practice, the process of applying IAS 29 fully retrospectively requires a number of steps to determine the appropriate comparative values, and specifically the opening equity reserves, to ensure the correct balances at the reporting date. Supposing an entity, with a 31 December reporting date, became hyperinflationary in its 2021 reporting period, the statement of financial position at 1 January 2020 (i.e. the beginning of the earliest comparative period), restated to the monetary unit present at that date, would need to be calculated, as well as the components of equity restated to derive the restated retained earnings position at that date (as discussed at 5 above).

To calculate the gain or loss on net monetary position for the 2020 comparative reporting period:

- all items in the opening statement of financial position, including items carried at amounts current at that date, are adjusted for the inflation during the year to the monetary unit present at 31 December 2020;
- the 2020 financial statements are restated to the monetary unit at 31 December 2020; and
- the gain or loss on the net monetary position is calculated as discussed at 6.2 above.

The financial information determined in this way would then be adjusted for hyperinflation during 2021 to the monetary unit present at 31 December 2021, including items carried at amounts current at the previous reporting dates, to correctly establish the comparatives to be reported.

10.2 Economies ceasing to be hyperinflationary

Determining when a currency stops being hyperinflationary is not easy in practice. It is important to review trends, not just at the end of the reporting period but also subsequently. In addition, consistency demands that the financial statements do not unnecessarily fall in and out of a hyperinflationary presentation, where a more careful judgement would have avoided it.

When an economy ceases to be hyperinflationary, entities should discontinue preparation and presentation of financial statements in accordance with IAS 29. The amounts expressed in the measuring unit current at the end of the previous reporting period will be treated as the basis of the carrying amounts of items in its subsequent statement of financial position. *[IAS 29.38]*.

The previous reporting period used as the basis for the carrying amounts going forward may be the last annual reporting period or it may be an interim period depending on whether the entity prepares interim reports. Therefore, for interim reporters, it should be noted that, an amalgamation of interim periods during which IAS 29 was applied with those where it was not, may result in financial statements that are difficult to interpret. This is shown in Example 16.8 below.

Example 16.8: *Economies ceasing to be hyperinflationary in an interim period*

An entity has a financial year end of 31 December and prepares interim financial statements on a quarterly basis. The last annual financial statements were prepared for the period ending 31 December 2020 when the economy was hyperinflationary. In August 2021 the economy ceased to be hyperinflationary. The table below shows the impact on the financial statements.

Period	Impact on financial statements
Annual 31 December 2020	Hyperinflationary accounting.
Interim 31 March 2021	Hyperinflationary accounting.
Interim 30 June 2021	Hyperinflationary accounting.
Interim 30 September 2021	No longer in the scope of IAS 29. Balances at 30 June 2021 used as the basis for carrying amounts going forward. Comparatives will include adjustments for hyperinflation up to 30 June 2021.
Annual 31 December 2021	No longer in the scope of IAS 29. Balances at 31 December 2021 will use 30 June 2021 as the basis for carrying amounts going forward. Comparatives will include adjustments for hyperinflation up to 30 June 2021.

The following extract illustrates the effect of ceasing to be hyperinflationary on financial results.

Extract 16.1: Belarusian National Reinsurance Organisation (2015)

Statement of profit or loss and other comprehensive income for the year ended 31 December 2015 [extract]
All amounts in millions of BYR

	Notes	2015	2014
Loss on net monetary position due to hyperinflation effect		–	(210 592)
Profit before tax		230 687	(68 498)
Income tax expense	19	(73 600)	(30 413)
Profit /(loss) for the year		157 087	(98 911)

Notes to the financial statements [extract]

(2) BASIS OF PREPARATION [extract]

The accompanying financial statements have been prepared in accordance with International Financial Reporting Standards ("IFRS").

[…]

Hyperinflation

In 2014 and earlier the economy of the Republic of Belarus was classified as a hyperinflationary economy under the criteria included in IAS 29, and IAS 29. Starting from 1 January 2015 the economy of the Republic of Belarus ceased to be classified as a hyperinflationary economy. Therefore, all non-monetary items (assets, liabilities and equity) are presented in units of measure as of 31 December 2014 as the opening balances as at 1 January 2015. In the statement of profit or loss and other comprehensive income for the period ended 31 December 2015, non-monetary items have been presented as the opening balances as at 1 January 2015 units of measure as at 31 December 2014.

10.3 Economies exiting severe hyperinflation

IFRS 1 includes an exemption for entities that have been subject to severe hyperinflation before the date of transition to IFRS, or on reapplication into IFRS after being unable to prepare IFRS compliant financial statements. Severe hyperinflation has both of the following characteristics:

(a) a reliable general price index is not available to all entities with transactions and balances in the currency; and

(b) exchangeability between the currency and a relatively stable foreign currency does not exist. *[IFRS 1.D27]*.

This exemption was included in response to a specific issue that occurred in Zimbabwe in 2008. In Zimbabwe the ability to produce financial statements had been completely undermined by severe hyperinflation. In response to this situation, an exemption was created in IFRS 1 which would be available to any entity that is either adopting IFRS for the first time, or is reapplying IFRS due to severe hyperinflation. In practice, the existence of severe hyperinflation (as described by the standard) is a rare economic occurrence (see Chapter 5 at 5.17).

11 TRANSLATION TO A DIFFERENT PRESENTATION CURRENCY

IAS 21 requires an entity to determine its functional currency as the currency of the primary economic environment in which it operates. If the functional currency is that of a hyperinflationary economy, the entity's financial statements are restated in accordance with IAS 29. An entity cannot avoid restatement by adopting as its functional currency, a currency other than the functional currency as determined in accordance with IAS 21. *[IAS 21.14]*.

However, an entity is permitted to present its financial statements in any presentation currency it chooses. Likewise, when a group contains individual entities with different functional currencies, the results and financial position of each entity are expressed in a common currency so that consolidated financial statements may be presented. *[IAS 21.38]*. A different presentation currency will not alter the entity's functional currency or the requirement to apply IAS 29.

It is noted that jurisdictions considered to be hyperinflationary are frequently subject to severe exchange controls and therefore determining an appropriate exchange rate for translation to a presentation currency may be difficult. Where judgement has been used to determine an appropriate rate, this should be disclosed. In 2014, the Interpretations Committee noted that predominant practice is to apply by extension the principle in paragraph 26 of IAS 21 (see Chapter 15 at 6.1.3), which gives guidance on which exchange rate to use when reporting foreign currency transactions in the functional currency when several exchange rates are available.[2]

If an entity, whose functional currency is hyperinflationary, wants to translate its financial statements into a different presentation currency it must first restate its financial statements in accordance with IAS 29, *[IAS 21.43]*, and then apply the following procedures under IAS 21:

'(a) all amounts (i.e. assets, liabilities, equity items, income and expenses, including comparatives) shall be translated at the closing rate at the date of the most recent statement of financial position, except that

(b) when amounts are translated into the currency of a non-hyperinflationary economy, comparative amounts shall be those that were presented as current year amounts in the relevant prior year financial statements (i.e. not adjusted for subsequent changes in the price level or subsequent changes in exchange rates).' *[IAS 21.42]*.

In other words, when an entity that applies IAS 29 translates its financial statements into a non-hyperinflationary presentation currency, the comparative information should not be restated under IAS 29. Instead IAS 21 should be applied and the comparative amounts should be those that were presented as current year amounts in the prior period. The following table summarises the impact of hyperinflation on various scenarios of translation into an alternative presentation currency.

	Translation to non-hyperinflationary presentation currency	Consolidation into non-hyperinflationary group	Consolidation into hyperinflationary group
Example	Argentinian entity* presenting its financial statements in euros	Argentinian subsidiary consolidated by parent presenting its financial statements in euros	Argentinian subsidiary consolidated by a Venezuelan parent*
Restate comparatives for hyperinflation	No	No	Yes
Exchange rate to use for comparative period	Closing rate at comparative balance sheet date	Closing rate at comparative balance sheet date	Closing rate at current balance sheet date
Restatement upon initial application of IAS 29 recognised in	Opening balance sheet of current period	Opening balance sheet of current period	Opening balance sheet of earliest comparative period

* At the time of writing both the Argentinian Peso and Venezuelan Bolivar were considered to be hyperinflationary.

All exchange differences that arise on the translation of an entity whose functional currency is not the currency of a hyperinflationary economy should be recognised in other comprehensive income (see Chapter 15 at 6.1). *[IAS 21.39]*. IAS 21 does not however stipulate the same treatment for exchange differences arising on translation of an entity whose functional currency is hyperinflationary. *[IAS 21.42]*.

In March 2020, the IFRS Interpretations Committee issued an agenda decision on the appropriate treatment of such exchange differences. They noted that the translation of a hyperinflationary entity into a non-hyperinflationary currency may result in a change in the entity's net investment in the hyperinflationary foreign operation. This change would include two effects:

- a restatement effect resulting from restating the entity's interest in the equity of the hyperinflationary foreign operation as required by IAS 29; and
- a translation effect resulting from translating the entity's interest in the equity of the hyperinflationary foreign operation (excluding the effect of any restatement required by IAS 29) at a closing rate that differs from the previous closing rate.

They noted that IAS 1 states that components of other comprehensive income include gains and losses arising from translating the financial statements of a foreign operation. *[IAS 1.7]*. IAS 21 explains that exchange differences arising from translating the financial statements of a non-hyperinflationary foreign operation are recognised in other comprehensive income and not in profit or loss because the changes in exchange rates have little or no direct effect on the present and future cash flows from operations. *[IAS 21.41]*. The Committee observed that this explanation is also relevant if the foreign operation's functional currency is hyperinflationary. Accordingly, the Committee concluded that an entity presents in other comprehensive income any exchange difference resulting from the translation of a hyperinflationary foreign operation, and that an entity should present:

- the IAS 29 restatement effect and the IAS 21 translation effect in other comprehensive income, if the entity considers that the combination of those two effects meets the definition of an exchange difference in IAS 21; or

- the IAS 21 translation effect in other comprehensive income if the entity considers that only the translation effect meets the definition of an exchange difference in IAS 21. In this case, consistent with the requirements in paragraph 25 of IAS 29, the entity presents the IAS 29 restatement effect in equity. *[IAS 29.25]*.[3]

In practice, clearly differentiating between an exchange difference and equity adjustment can be difficult, particularly as hyperinflation and exchange rate effects are inversely correlated and that the split may differ depending on the timing and frequency of reporting.

11.1 Translation on initial application and ceasing application of IAS 29

Related questions arise in the year an entity first becomes hyperinflationary, as the retrospective application of IAS 29 gives rise to an adjustment for the initial application of the standard. As discussed at 5 above, retained earnings are restated to an amount derived from all the other amounts in the statement of financial position. It could be argued that the impact of initial adoption of IAS 29 should be recognised directly in equity similar to a change in accounting policy. However, as the adjustment is normally closely related to (past) changes in exchange rates, an argument could also be made that this adjustment could be presented in other comprehensive income.

It is also unclear how to deal with the accumulated foreign currency translation reserve that relates to the now hyperinflationary foreign operation. The agenda decision issued in March 2020 by the Interpretations Committee also addresses the question whether an entity reclassifies within equity the cumulative pre-hyperinflation exchange differences when a foreign operation becomes hyperinflationary. That is, whether the entity transfers the cumulative pre-hyperinflation exchange differences to a component of equity that is not subsequently reclassified to profit or loss.

Paragraph 41 of IAS 21 requires an entity to present the cumulative amount of exchange differences recognised in other comprehensive income in a separate component of equity until disposal of the foreign operation. Furthermore, paragraphs 48 and 48C of IAS 21 require an entity to reclassify the cumulative amount of those exchange differences from equity to profit or loss on disposal or partial disposal of a foreign operation in certain circumstances. *[IAS 21.41]*.

Accordingly, the Committee concluded that an entity presents the cumulative amount of the exchange differences as a separate component of equity until disposal or partial disposal of the foreign operation and does not reclassify within equity the cumulative pre-hyperinflation exchange differences once the foreign operation becomes hyperinflationary.[4] If an entity considers that the combination of the IAS 29 restatement effect and the IAS 21 translation effects meet the definition of an exchange difference in IAS 21 (as discussed at 11 above) then – upon initial application of IAS 29 – both those effects should be accounted as part of the cumulative amount of the exchange differences.

When the economy ceases to be hyperinflationary, and restatement in accordance with IAS 29 is no longer required, an entity uses the amounts restated to the price level at the date it ceased restating its financial statements as the historical costs for translation into the presentation currency. *[IAS 21.43]*.

11.2 Presentation currency considerations for comparative information

Given that IAS 29 requires a hyperinflationary entity to restate its comparative figures, the question arises as to how an entity (a parent), which does not operate in a hyperinflationary economy, should account for the restatement of an entity (a subsidiary) that operates in an economy that became hyperinflationary in the current reporting period when incorporating it within its consolidated financial statements. This issue has been clarified by IAS 21 which specifically prohibits restatement of comparative figures when the presentation currency is not hyperinflationary. *[IAS 21.42(b)]*. This means that when the financial statements of a hyperinflationary subsidiary are translated into the non-hyperinflationary presentation currency for consolidation into the financial statements of the parent, the comparative amounts are not adjusted.

However, the impact on interim financial statements of such a parent may be more difficult to resolve. For example, a non-hyperinflationary parent (with a December year-end) may own a subsidiary whose functional currency is considered hyperinflationary from, say, 1 July 2021 onwards. The subsidiary's second quarter results would not have been adjusted for the impact of hyperinflation, while its third quarter results would reflect the effects of hyperinflation for the period from the beginning of the year to the reporting date. This results in the parent needing to reflect a 'catch up effect' in its third quarter or full year reporting. As the prior year comparative figures cannot be restated under IAS 21, the full effect would be included in the current period. *[IAS 21.42(b)]*. However, paragraph 4 of IAS 29 specifically states that the standard '...applies to the financial statements of any entity from the beginning of the reporting period in which it identifies the existence of hyperinflation in the country in whose currency it reports'.

If separate information is presented for each quarter, it is not clear how this effect should be taken into consideration in preparing the parent's third quarter results, specifically whether the year-to-date results are adjusted as though the subsidiary was hyperinflationary from the beginning of the year or only from the beginning of the third quarter. Possible approaches would include:

- reporting the difference between the year-to-date profit for the third quarter and the year-to-date profit for the second quarter in which the subsidiary is restated under IAS 29 (i.e. with purchasing power adjustments to 30 June); or
- reporting the third quarter profits as the difference between the year-to-date profit in which the subsidiary is restated under IAS 29, less the year-to-date second quarter profits as they were actually reported (i.e. non-hyperinflation based results).

As there is no clear guidance on the appropriate method of quantification, entities should adopt a consistent approach and disclose this judgement and the impact thereof on the financials if it has a significant impact, as required by IAS 1. The first approach is consistent with the requirement that the year-end accounts will be prepared as if the economy had been hyperinflationary from the beginning of 2021, will provide a better basis for comparison in 2021 and result in individual quarters in 2020 being more comparable. Nevertheless, IAS 34 does not specifically address the issue of restating previous interim periods upon first application of IAS 29 and we consider the second approach to also be acceptable. In particular, if the hyperinflationary subsidiary is relatively small within the overall consolidated accounts of the parent, then the benefit of restating previous interim periods will often be limited.

Additional questions arising in respect of the preparation of quarterly interim financial statements in the scenario described above would include:

- Would the parent entity need to re-issue interim reports that had been issued earlier in the current year?
- In the period that the subsidiary's economy becomes hyperinflationary, would the parent entity adjust the comparative interim information for hyperinflation (and year to date interim information) for the same interim period in the prior year?
- In the first quarter of the following financial period (2022), would the parent entity adjust the comparative information for hyperinflation (and year to date interim information) for the same interim period in the prior year (2021)?

Although the subsidiary will apply the requirements of IAS 29 on a retrospective basis, the parent will incorporate the results of the subsidiary into the group financial statements as required by IAS 21. Hyperinflation only commenced after the end of the interim reports, which is a non-adjusting event in accordance with IAS 10 – *Events after the Reporting Period*. Hence in response to the first question, the interim financial statements were compliant with the requirements of the standards, and the parent would not be required to re-issue prior interim financial statements in the year that the subsidiary's functional currency becomes hyperinflationary, although we believe re-issue is permissible.

Hyperinflationary adjustments would only occur in the interim financial statements of the parent from the date that the subsidiary became hyperinflationary onwards. Further, IAS 21 would preclude the restatement of comparative interim financial statements as contemplated in the second question above. *[IAS 21.42(b)]*.

The issue addressed in the third question is not specifically addressed by IAS 21 or IAS 34. We consider that the parent entity is allowed but not required to restate its comparative (2021) interim statements in its 2022 reporting. The Interpretations Committee discussed a request on this issue, noting little diversity in practice with the majority of respondents not restating comparative information, and therefore declined to add the matter to its standard setting agenda.[5] These specific requirements of IAS 34 are considered in Chapter 41 at 9.6.2.

12 DISCLOSURES

IAS 29 requires that entities should disclose the following information when they apply the provisions of the standard:

(a) the fact that the financial statements and the corresponding figures for previous periods have been restated for the changes in the general purchasing power of the functional currency and, as a result, are stated in terms of the measuring unit current at the end of the reporting period;

(b) whether the financial statements are based on a historical cost approach or a current cost approach; and

(c) the identity and level of the price index at the end of the reporting period and the movement in the index during the current and the previous reporting period. *[IAS 29.39]*.

It should be noted that disclosure of financial information that is restated under IAS 29 as a supplement to unrestated financial information is not permitted. This is to prevent entities from giving the historical cost based financial information greater prominence than the information that is restated under IAS 29. The standard also discourages separate presentation of unrestated financial information, but does not explicitly prohibit it. *[IAS 29.7]*. However, such unrestated financial statements would not be in accordance with IFRS and should be clearly identified as such. An entity that is required (for example by local tax authorities or stock exchange regulators) to present unrestated financial statements needs to ensure that the IFRS financial statements are perceived to be the main financial statements rather than mere supplemental information.

The following excerpt illustrates the disclosure of the loss on net monetary position, the basis of preparation and the required disclosures in respect of the relevant price index.

Extract 16.2: Priorbank JSC (2014)

Consolidated income statement for the year ended 31 December 2014 [extract]
(in millions of Belarusian rubles in terms of purchasing power of the Belarusian ruble as at 31 December 2014)

	Notes	2014	2013
Loss on net monetary position		(414,573)	(336,754)
Income before income tax expense		1,141,881	1,251,055
Income tax expense	14	(373,037)	(310,069)
Profit for the year		768,844	940,986
Attributable to:			
– shareholders of the Bank		746,437	923,141
– non-controlling interests		22,407	17,845
		768,844	940,986

Notes to 2014 IFRS Consolidated financial statements [extract]

2. Basis of preparation [extract]

General [extract]

These consolidated financial statements have been prepared in accordance with International Financial Reporting Standards ("IFRS").

Inflation accounting

With the effect from 1 January 2011, the Belarusian economy is considered to be hyperinflationary in accordance with the criteria in IAS 29 "*Financial Reporting in Hyperinflationary Economies*" ("IAS 29"). Accordingly, adjustments and reclassifications for the purposes of presentation of IFRS financial statements include restatement, in accordance with IAS 29, for changes in the general purchasing power of the Belorussian ruble. The standard requires that the financial statements prepared in the currency of a hyperinflationary economy be stated in terms of the measuring unit current at the reporting date.

On the application of IAS 29 the Bank used the conversion coefficient derived from the consumer price index in the Republic of Belarus ("CPI") published by the National Statistics Committee. The CPIs for the nine-year period and corresponding conversion coefficient since the time when the Republic of Belarus previously ceased to be considered hyperinflationary, i.e. since 1 January 2006, were as follows:

Year	Index, %	Conversion coefficient
2006	106.6	528.9
2007	112.1	471.8
2008	113.3	416.4
2009	110.1	378.2
2010	109.9	344.2
2011	208.7	164.9
2012	121.7	135.4
2013	116.6	116.2
2014	116.2	100

Monetary assets and liabilities are not restated because they are already expressed in terms of the monetary unit current as at 31 December 2014. Non-monetary assets and liabilities (items which are not already expressed in terms of the monetary unit as at 31 December 2014) are restated by applying the relevant index. The effect of inflation on the Bank's net monetary position is included in the consolidated income statement as loss on net monetary position.

The application of IAS 29 results in an adjustment for the loss of purchasing power of the Belarusian ruble recorded in the income statement. In a period of inflation, an entity holding an excess of monetary assets over monetary liabilities loses purchasing power, which results in a loss on the net monetary position. This loss/gain is derived as the difference resulting from the restatement of non-monetary assets and liabilities, equity and items in the statement of comprehensive income. Corresponding figures for the year ended 31 December 2013 have also been restated so that they are presented in terms of the purchasing power of the Belarusian Ruble as at 31 December 2014.

Telefónica, S.A. is an example of a parent entity that has subsidiaries that operate in an economy subject to hyperinflation. As a parent entity, Telefónica, S.A. would not restate the comparative amounts and, therefore, has reported a reconciling item for the effect of hyperinflation adjustments.

Extract 16.3: Telefónica, S.A. (2019)

Notes to the consolidated financial statements (consolidated annual accounts) for the year ended December 31, 2019 [extract]

Note 25. Income tax matters [extract]

Deferred taxes movement

The movements in deferred taxes in the Telefónica Group in 2019 and 2018 are as follows:

Millions of euros	Deferred tax assets	Deferred tax liabilities
Balance at December 31, 2018	7,631	2,674
Reclassification entry into force IFRIC 23	–	313
Additions	1,070	586
Disposals	(1,123)	(323)
Transfers	(882)	(250)
Translation differences and hyperinflation adjustments	(33)	(87)
Company movements and others	19	(5)
Balance at December 31, 2019	6,682	2,908

References

1 Minutes of the meetings of the International Practices Task Force are available at www.thecaq.org/about-us/our-committees/international-practices-task-force/ (accessed on 7 Sep 2020)

2 *IFRIC Update*, November 2014, p.8.
3 *IFRIC Update*, March 2020.
4 *IFRIC Update*, March 2020.
5 *IFRIC Update*, March 2020.

Chapter 17 — Intangible assets

1 INTRODUCTION 1291
   1.1   Background 1291
   1.2   Terms used in IAS 38 1292
2 OBJECTIVE AND SCOPE OF IAS 38 1294
   2.1   What is an intangible asset? 1295
        2.1.1   Identifiability 1295
        2.1.2   Control 1296
        2.1.3   Future economic benefits 1298
   2.2   Is IAS 38 the appropriate IFRS? 1298
        2.2.1   Whether to record a tangible or intangible asset 1298
        2.2.2   Classification of programme and other broadcast rights as inventory or intangible assets 1299
3 RECOGNITION AND MEASUREMENT 1301
   3.1   Recognition 1301
        3.1.1   When to recognise programme and other broadcast rights 1302
   3.2   Measurement 1304
   3.3   Subsequent expenditure 1305
4 SEPARATE ACQUISITION 1305
   4.1   Recognition 1305
   4.2   Components of cost 1306
   4.3   Costs to be expensed 1306
   4.4   Income from incidental operations while an asset is being developed 1307
   4.5   Measurement of intangible assets acquired for contingent consideration 1308
   4.6   Acquisition by way of government grant 1310
   4.7   Exchanges of assets 1310

			4.7.1	Measurement of assets exchanged	1311
			4.7.2	Commercial substance	1311
5	ACQUISITION AS PART OF A BUSINESS COMBINATION				1312
	5.1	Recognition of intangible assets acquired in a business combination			1313
		5.1.1	Probable inflow of benefits		1313
		5.1.2	Reliability of measurement		1313
		5.1.3	Identifiability in relation to an intangible asset acquired in a business combination		1313
			5.1.3.A	Contractual-legal rights	1314
			5.1.3.B	Separability	1315
	5.2	Examples of intangible assets acquired in a business combination			1315
	5.3	Measuring the fair value of intangible assets acquired in a business combination			1316
	5.4	Customer relationship intangible assets acquired in a business combination			1317
	5.5	In-process research and development			1318
6	INTERNALLY GENERATED INTANGIBLE ASSETS				1319
	6.1	Internally generated goodwill			1319
	6.2	Internally generated intangible assets			1319
		6.2.1	Research phase		1321
		6.2.2	Development phase		1321
		6.2.3	Research and development in the pharmaceutical industry		1325
		6.2.4	Internally generated brands, mastheads, publishing titles and customer lists		1326
		6.2.5	Website costs (SIC-32)		1326
		6.2.6	Agile software development		1328
	6.3	Cost of an internally generated intangible asset			1329
		6.3.1	Establishing the time from which costs can be capitalised		1329
		6.3.2	Determining the costs eligible for capitalisation		1330
7	RECOGNITION OF AN EXPENSE				1330
	7.1	Catalogues and other advertising costs			1331
8	MEASUREMENT AFTER INITIAL RECOGNITION				1333
	8.1	Cost model for measurement of intangible assets			1333
	8.2	Revaluation model for measurement of intangible assets			1334
		8.2.1	Revaluation is only allowed if there is an active market		1334
		8.2.2	Frequency of revaluations		1335
		8.2.3	Accounting for revaluations		1335
9	AMORTISATION OF INTANGIBLE ASSETS				1338

9.1	Assessing the useful life of an intangible asset as finite or indefinite		1338
	9.1.1	Factors affecting the useful life	1338
	9.1.2	Useful life of contractual or other legal rights	1340
9.2	Intangible assets with a finite useful life		1341
	9.2.1	Amortisation period and method	1341
		9.2.1.A Amortising customer relationships and similar intangible assets	1343
		9.2.1.B Amortisation of programme and other broadcast rights	1344
	9.2.2	Revenue-based amortisation	1345
	9.2.3	Review of amortisation period and amortisation method	1347
	9.2.4	Residual value	1347
9.3	Intangible assets with an indefinite useful life		1349
9.4	Impairment losses		1350
9.5	Retirements and disposals		1350
	9.5.1	Derecognition of parts of intangible assets	1352

10 DISCLOSURE 1352

10.1	General disclosures	1353
10.2	Statement of financial position presentation	1356
10.3	Profit or loss presentation	1357
10.4	Additional disclosures when the revaluation model is applied	1357
10.5	Disclosure of research and development expenditure	1358

11 SPECIFIC ISSUES REGARDING INTANGIBLE ASSETS 1358

11.1	Rate-regulated activities		1358
11.2	Emissions trading schemes		1359
	11.2.1	Emissions trading schemes – IFRIC 3	1360
	11.2.2	Emissions trading schemes – Net liability approaches	1361
	11.2.3	Emissions trading schemes – Government grant approach	1364
	11.2.4	Amortisation and impairment testing of emission rights	1365
	11.2.5	Emission rights acquired in a business combination	1365
	11.2.6	Sale of emission rights	1365
	11.2.7	Accounting for emission rights by brokers and traders	1366
11.3	Accounting for green certificates or renewable energy certificates		1366
	11.3.1	Accounting by producers using renewable energy sources	1367
	11.3.2	Accounting by distributors of renewable energy	1367
	11.3.3	Accounting by brokers and traders	1367
11.4	Accounting for REACH costs		1368
	11.4.1	Costs of registering a new substance performed by the entity itself	1369

	11.4.2	Costs of acquiring test data from an existing registrant	1369
	11.4.3	Costs of registering an existing substance performed by the entity itself	1369
11.5	Crypto-assets		1370
	11.5.1	Crypto-assets – Recognition and initial measurement	1370
	11.5.2	Crypto-assets – Subsequent measurement	1371
		11.5.2.A Crypto-assets – Cost model	1371
		11.5.2.B Crypto-assets – Revaluation model	1371
	11.5.3	Crypto-assets – Standard setter activity	1372
11.6	Cloud computing		1372
	11.6.1	Types of cloud computing arrangement and determination of applicable IFRSs	1372
	11.6.2	Evaluating whether a cloud computing arrangement contains a lease	1373
	11.6.3	Evaluating whether a cloud computing arrangement contains an intangible asset	1374
	11.6.4	Accounting for a cloud computing arrangement that includes an intangible asset	1376
		11.6.4.A Fees in the arrangement	1376
		11.6.4.B Implementation costs	1377
	11.6.5	Accounting for a cloud computing arrangement that does not include an intangible asset	1378
		11.6.5.A Fees in the arrangement	1378
		11.6.5.B Internal and third-party implementation costs	1379

List of examples

Example 17.1:	Demonstrating control over the future services of employees	1297
Example 17.2:	Determining when to recognise a broadcast right	1303
Example 17.3:	Incidental operations	1307
Example 17.4:	Contingent consideration relating to a football player's registration	1309
Example 17.5:	Customer relationship intangible assets acquired in a business combination	1317
Example 17.6:	Research phase and development phase under IAS 38	1323
Example 17.7:	Recognition of internally generated intangible assets	1329
Example 17.8:	Application of revaluation model to intangible assets that are partially recognised or received by way of government grant	1334
Example 17.9:	Accounting for upward and downward revaluations	1336

Example 17.10:	Restatement of accumulated amortisation after a revaluation	1337
Example 17.11:	Assessing the useful life of an intangible asset	1339
Example 17.12:	Legal rights and useful life	1340
Example 17.13:	Amortisation method and useful life for customer relationships	1343
Example 17.14:	Output-based versus revenue-based amortisation	1345
Example 17.15:	Amortisation of an intangible asset with a residual value	1348
Example 17.16:	Review of indefinite useful lives	1349
Example 17.17:	Impairment of an intangible asset with an indefinite useful life	1350
Example 17.18:	Application of 'net liability' approach	1362
Example 17.19:	Impact of purchased emission rights on the application of 'net liability' approach	1362

Chapter 17　　　　　　　　Intangible assets

1　INTRODUCTION

1.1　Background

IAS 38 – *Intangible Assets* – is structured along similar lines as IAS 16 – *Property, Plant and Equipment*.

Prior to IAS 38 accounting practice for intangible assets had largely developed on an issue-by-issue basis, with the result being a variety of treatments for particular types of intangible assets. There have been many topical issues over the years: research and development (as long ago as the 1970s), brands and similar assets (particularly those arising in business combinations), and assets and costs that are directly and indirectly related to the internet and personal communications. In time, it became apparent that two different types of intangible rights shared characteristics that made a single standard meaningful.

Firstly, there are internal costs incurred by entities from which they expect to benefit in the future. The critical issue is identifying whether, when and how much of these costs should be recognised as assets, and how much should be recognised immediately as expenses. For example, there are many types of expenditure from which an entity may expect to benefit in future, but it is not possible to identify an asset or the relationship between the cost and future benefits is too tenuous to allow capitalisation.

Secondly, there are intangible rights acquired separately or as part of business combinations. For intangible rights acquired in a business combination, a key issue is whether the intangible rights are distinguishable from goodwill and should be recognised separately. This has become more important as a consequence of goodwill not being amortised, which means that entities must identify as separate intangible assets certain rights, e.g. customer relationships that had historically been subsumed within goodwill.

Unlike IAS 16 whose scope is defined by its title (it applies to property, plant and equipment), IAS 38 includes a definition of the assets to which it applies. However, this is so general (an intangible asset is an identifiable non-monetary asset without physical substance) that the standard must exclude certain assets and items of expenditure that would otherwise fall within it. The definition could include assets generated by other standards, which are therefore excluded from scope. Incidentally, this shows just how broad the definition could be as the list of scope exemptions includes deferred tax assets, leases and assets arising from employee benefits which are within scope of, respectively, IAS 12 – *Income Taxes*, IFRS 16 – *Leases* – and IAS 19 – *Employee Benefits*. *[IAS 38.3]*. Additional clarification comes from the prohibition on recognising internally-generated goodwill. This means that expenditure on brands and similar assets cannot be recognised as an intangible asset as it is not possible to distinguish these costs from the costs of developing the business as a whole. *[IAS 38.63, 64]*. However, arguably the opposite approach is taken with the intangible assets identified in a business combination where the standard encourages separate recognition through a broad approach given to concepts such as separability. This remains a difficult and controversial area, discussed at 5 below. The requirements of IFRS 3 – *Business Combinations* – are discussed in Chapter 9.

This chapter addresses the specific provisions of IAS 38, with the requirements relating to intangible assets acquired as part of a business combination being covered both at 5 below and in Chapter 9. IFRS 13 – *Fair Value Measurement* – includes the guidance relating to the determination of fair values (see Chapter 14). Impairment of intangible assets is addressed in IAS 36 – *Impairment of Assets*, covered in Chapter 20.

Other intangible assets are dealt with by specific accounting pronouncements. The amount spent on the operation and development of websites led to the issue of SIC-32 – *Intangible Assets – Web Site Costs* – that is discussed at 6.2.5 below. Although IAS 38 addresses acquisition by way of government grant, this has not proved sufficient to address accounting for various schemes designed to influence business behaviour, especially in environmental areas. Emissions trading schemes give rise to intangible rights and the attempts to devise a satisfactory accounting model for these and similar schemes are considered at 11.2 below.

Recent years have seen an increase in the use and trading of crypto-assets such as Bitcoin and Ether. These may meet the relatively wide definition of intangible assets and can be accounted for under IAS 38. Crypto-assets are discussed at 11.5 below.

Cloud computing arrangements, which are becoming increasingly common as an alternative to on-site software and computing infrastructure, are discussed at 11.6 below.

1.2   Terms used in IAS 38

The following terms are used in IAS 38 with the meanings specified:

Term	Definition
Intangible asset	An identifiable non-monetary asset without physical substance. *[IAS 38.8]*.
Asset	An asset is a resource: *[IAS 38.8]* (a) controlled by an entity as a result of past events; and (b) from which future economic benefits are expected to flow to the entity.
Monetary assets	Money held and assets to be received in fixed or determinable amounts of money. *[IAS 38.8]*.

Identifiable	An asset is identifiable if it either: *[IAS 38.12]* (a) is separable, i.e. capable of being separated or divided from the entity and sold, transferred, licensed, rented or exchanged, either individually or together with a related contract, identifiable asset or liability, regardless of whether the entity intends to do so; or (b) arises from contractual or other legal rights, regardless of whether those rights are transferable or separable from the entity or from other rights and obligations.
Control	The power to obtain the future economic benefits flowing from the underlying resource and to restrict the access of others to those benefits. *[IAS 38.13]*.
Cost	The amount of cash or cash equivalents paid or the fair value of other consideration given to acquire an asset at the time of its acquisition or construction, or, when applicable, the amount attributed to that asset when initially recognised in accordance with the specific requirements of other IFRSs, e.g. IFRS 2 – *Share-based Payment*. *[IAS 38.8]*.
Carrying amount	The amount at which the asset is recognised in the statement of financial position after deducting any accumulated amortisation and accumulated impairment losses thereon. *[IAS 38.8]*.
Amortisation	The systematic allocation of the depreciable amount of an intangible asset over its useful life. *[IAS 38.8]*.
Depreciable amount	The cost of an asset, or other amount substituted for cost, less its residual value. *[IAS 38.8]*.
Residual value	The estimated amount that the entity would currently obtain from disposal of the intangible asset, after deducting the estimated costs of disposal, if the intangible asset were already of the age and in the condition expected at the end of its useful life. *[IAS 38.8]*.
Useful life	(a) the period over which an asset is expected to be available for use by an entity; or (b) the number of production or similar units expected to be obtained from the asset by an entity. *[IAS 38.8]*.
Impairment loss	The amount by which the carrying amount of the asset exceeds its recoverable amount. *[IAS 38.8]*.
Research	Original and planned investigation undertaken with the prospect of gaining new scientific or technical knowledge and understanding. *[IAS 38.8]*.
Development	The application of research findings or other knowledge to a plan or design for the production of new or substantially improved materials, devices, products, processes, systems or services before the start of commercial production or use. *[IAS 38.8]*.
Entity-specific value	The present value of the cash flows an entity expects to arise from the continuing use of an asset and from its disposal at the end of its useful life or expects to incur when settling a liability. *[IAS 38.8]*.
Fair value	The price that would be received to sell an asset or paid to transfer a liability in an orderly transaction between market participants at the measurement date. (See Chapter 14). *[IAS 38.8]*.
Active market	A market in which transactions for the asset or liability take place with sufficient frequency and volume to provide pricing information on an ongoing basis. *[IFRS 13 Appendix A]*.

2 OBJECTIVE AND SCOPE OF IAS 38

The objective of IAS 38 is to prescribe the accounting treatment for intangible assets that are not specifically dealt with in another standard. *[IAS 38.1]*.

IAS 38 does not apply to accounting for:

(a) intangible assets that are within the scope of another standard;

(b) financial assets, as defined in IAS 32 – *Financial Instruments: Presentation*;

(c) the recognition and measurement of exploration and evaluation assets within the scope of IFRS 6 – *Exploration for and Evaluation of Mineral Resources*; and

(d) expenditure on the development and extraction of, minerals, oil, natural gas and similar non-regenerative resources. *[IAS 38.2]*.

Examples of specific types of intangible asset that fall within the scope of another standard include: *[IAS 38.3]*

(a) intangible assets held by an entity for sale in the ordinary course of business, to which IAS 2 – *Inventories* – applies (see Chapter 22);

(b) deferred tax assets, which are governed by IAS 12 (see Chapter 33);

(c) leases of intangible assets accounted for in accordance with IFRS 16 (see Chapter 23). Rights under licensing agreements for such items as motion picture films, video recordings, plays, manuscripts, patents and copyrights that are outside the scope of IFRS 16 *[IFRS 16.3]* are within the scope of IAS 38; *[IAS 38.6]*

(d) assets arising from employee benefits, for which IAS 19 is relevant (see Chapter 35);

(e) financial assets as defined in IAS 32. The recognition and measurement of some financial assets are covered by IFRS 10 – *Consolidated Financial Statements*, IAS 27 – *Separate Financial Statements* – and IAS 28 – *Investments in Associates and Joint Ventures* (see Chapters 6, 8, 11 and 44 to 54);

(f) goodwill acquired in a business combination, which is determined under IFRS 3 (see Chapter 9);

(g) deferred acquisition costs, and intangible assets, arising from an insurer's contractual rights under insurance contracts within the scope of IFRS 4 – *Insurance Contracts*, or IFRS 17 – *Insurance Contracts* – if applied. IFRS 4 sets out specific disclosure requirements for those deferred acquisition costs but not for those intangible assets. Therefore, the disclosure requirements in this standard apply to those intangible assets (see Chapter 55);

(h) non-current intangible assets classified as held for sale, or included in a disposal group that is classified as held for sale, in accordance with IFRS 5 – *Non-current Assets Held for Sale and Discontinued Operations* (see Chapter 4); and

(i) assets arising from contracts with customers that are recognised in accordance with IFRS 15 – *Revenue from Contracts with Customers*.

IAS 38 excludes insurance contracts and expenditure on the exploration for, or development and extraction of oil, gas and mineral deposits in extractive industries from its scope because activities or transactions in these areas are so specialised that they give rise to accounting issues that need to be dealt with in a different way.

However, the standard does apply to other intangible assets used in extractive industries or by insurers (such as computer software), and other expenditure incurred by them (such as start-up costs). *[IAS 38.7]*.

Finally, the standard makes it clear that it applies to expenditures on advertising, training, start-up and research and development activities. *[IAS 38.5]*.

2.1 What is an intangible asset?

IAS 38 defines an asset as 'a resource controlled by an entity as a result of past events; and from which future economic benefits are expected to flow to the entity'. *[IAS 38.8]*. Intangible assets form a sub-section of this group and are further defined as 'an identifiable non-monetary asset without physical substance'. *[IAS 38.8]*. The IASB considers that the essential characteristics of intangible assets are that they are:

- controlled by the entity;
- will give rise to future economic benefits for the entity;
- lack physical substance; and
- are identifiable.

An item with these characteristics is classified as an intangible asset regardless of the reason why an entity might hold that asset. *[IAS 38.BC5]*. There is one exception: intangible assets held for sale (either in the ordinary course of business or as part of a disposal group) and accounted for under IAS 2 or IFRS 5 are specifically excluded from the scope of IAS 38. *[IAS 38.3]*.

Businesses frequently incur expenditure on all sorts of intangible resources such as scientific or technical knowledge, design and implementation of new processes or systems, licences, intellectual property, market knowledge, trademarks, brand names and publishing titles. Examples that fall under these headings include computer software, patents, copyrights, motion picture films, customer lists, mortgage servicing rights, fishing licences, import quotas, franchises, customer or supplier relationships, customer loyalty, market share and marketing rights. *[IAS 38.9]*.

Although these items are mentioned by the standard, not all of them will meet the standard's eligibility criteria for recognition as an intangible asset, which requires identifiability, control over a resource and the existence of future economic benefits. Expenditure on items that do not meet all three criteria will be expensed when incurred, unless they have arisen in the context of a business combination as discussed at 5 below. *[IAS 38.10]*.

2.1.1 Identifiability

IAS 38's requirement that an intangible asset must be 'identifiable' was introduced to try to distinguish it from internally generated goodwill (which, outside a business combination, should not be recognised as an asset *[IAS 38.48]*), but also to emphasise that, especially in the context of a business combination, there will be previously unrecorded items that should be recognised in the financial statements as intangible assets separately from goodwill. *[IAS 38.BC7, BC8]*.

IFRS 3 defines goodwill as 'representing the future economic benefits arising from other assets acquired in a business combination that are not individually identified and separately recognised.' *[IFRS 3 Appendix A]*. For example, future economic benefits may result from synergy between the identifiable assets acquired or from assets that, individually, do not qualify for recognition in the financial statements. *[IAS 38.11]*.

IAS 38 states that an intangible asset is identifiable when it either: *[IAS 38.12]*

(a) is separable, meaning that it is capable of being separated or divided from the entity and sold, transferred, licensed, rented or exchanged, either individually or together with a related contract, identifiable asset or liability, regardless of whether the entity intends to do so; or

(b) arises from contractual or other legal rights, regardless of whether those rights are transferable or separable from the entity or from other rights and obligations.

The explicit requirement to recognise assets arising from contractual rights alone confirms the IASB's position that the existence of contractual or legal rights is a characteristic that distinguishes an intangible asset from goodwill, even if those rights are not readily separable from the entity as a whole. The Board cites as an example of such an intangible asset a licence that, under local law, is not transferable except by sale of the entity as a whole. *[IAS 38.BC10]*. Therefore, the search for intangible assets is not restricted to rights that are separable.

However, preparers should not restrict their search for intangible assets to those embodied in contractual or other legal rights, since the definition of identifiability merely requires such rights to be capable of separation. Non-contractual rights are required to be recognised as an intangible asset if the right could be sold, transferred, licensed, rented or exchanged. In considering the responses to ED 3 – *Business Combinations* – the Board observed that the existence of an exchange transaction for a non-contractual relationship provides evidence both that the item is separable, and that the entity is able to control the expected future economic benefits flowing from it, meaning that the relationship should be recognised as an intangible asset. Only in the absence of exchange transactions for the same or similar non-contractual customer relationships would an entity be unable to demonstrate that such relationships are separable or that it can control the expected future economic benefits flowing from those relationships. *[IAS 38.BC13]*.

2.1.2 Control

IAS 38 defines control as the power to obtain the future economic benefits generated by the resource and the ability to restrict the access of others to those benefits. Control normally results from legal rights, in the way that copyright, a restraint of trade agreement or a legal duty on employees to maintain confidentiality protects the economic benefits arising from market and technical knowledge. *[IAS 38.13-14]*. While it will be more difficult to demonstrate control in the absence of legal rights, the standard is clear that legal enforceability of a right is not a necessary condition for control, because an entity may be able to control the future economic benefits in some other way. *[IAS 38.13]*. The existence of exchange transactions for similar non-contractual rights can provide sufficient evidence of control to require separate recognition as an asset. *[IAS 38.16]*. Obviously, determining that this is the case in the absence of observable contractual or other legal rights requires the exercise of judgement based on an understanding of the specific facts and circumstances involved.

For example, the standard acknowledges that an entity usually has insufficient control over the future economic benefits arising from an assembled workforce (i.e. a team of skilled workers, or specific management or technical talent) or from training for these items to meet the definition of an intangible asset. *[IAS 38.15]*. There would have to be other legal rights before control could be demonstrated.

Example 17.1:   Demonstrating control over the future services of employees

Entity A acquires a pharmaceutical company. A critical factor in the entity's decision to acquire the company was the reputation of its team of research chemists, who are renowned in their field of expertise. However, in the absence of any other legal rights it would not be possible to show that the entity can control the economic benefits embodied in that team and its skills because any or all of those chemists could leave. Therefore, it is most unlikely that Entity A could recognise an intangible asset in relation to the acquiree's team of research chemists.

Entity B acquires a football club. A critical factor in the entity's decision to acquire the club was the reputation of its players, many of whom are regularly selected to play for their country. A footballer cannot play for a club unless he is registered with the relevant football authority. It is customary to see exchange transactions involving players' registrations. The payment to a player's previous club in connection with the transfer of the player's registration enables the acquiring club to negotiate a playing contract with the footballer that covers a number of seasons and prevents other clubs from using that player's services. In these circumstances Entity B would be able to demonstrate sufficient control to recognise the cost of obtaining the players' registrations as an intangible asset.

In neither of the above examples is an asset being recognised for the assembled workforce. In the case of the football team, the asset being recognised comprises the economic benefits embodied in the players' registrations, arising from contractual rights. In particular, it is the ability to prevent other entities from using that player's services (i.e. restricting the access of others to those benefits), *[IAS 38.13]*, combined with the existence of exchange transactions involving similar players' registrations, *[IAS 38.16]*, that distinguishes this type of arrangement from a normal contract of employment. In cases when the transfer fee is a stand-alone payment and not part of a business combination, i.e. when an entity separately acquires the intangible resource, it is much more likely that it can demonstrate that its purchase meets the definition of an asset (see 4 below).

Similarly, an entity would not usually be able to recognise an asset for an assembled portfolio of customers or a market share. In the absence of legal rights to protect or other ways to control the relationships with customers or the loyalty of its customers, the entity usually has insufficient control over the expected economic benefits from these items to meet the definition of an intangible asset. However, exchange transactions, other than as part of a business combination, involving the same or similar non-contractual customer relationships may provide evidence of control over the expected future economic benefits in the absence of legal rights. In that case, those customer relationships could meet the definition of an intangible asset. *[IAS 38.16]*. IFRS 3 includes a number of examples of customer-related intangible assets acquired in business combinations that meet the definition of an intangible asset, which are discussed in more detail at 5 below. *[IFRS 3.IE23-31]*.

It is worth emphasising that intangible assets should only be recognised when they meet both the definition of an intangible asset and the applicable recognition criteria in IAS 38, *[IAS 38.18]*, which are discussed at 3.1 below. All that is established in the discussion above is whether the intangible right meets the definition of an asset.

The extract below illustrates the range of intangible assets that require recognition under IAS 38.

> **Extract 17.1: RELX PLC (2019)**
> Notes to the consolidated financial statements
> for the year ended 31 December 2019 [extract]
> 15 Intangible assets [extract]
> **Accounting policy** [extract]
>
> Intangible assets acquired as part of business combinations comprise: market-related assets (e.g. trademarks, imprints, brands); customer-related assets (e.g. subscription bases, customer lists, customer relationships); editorial content; software and systems (e.g. application infrastructure, product delivery platforms, in-process research and development); contract-based assets (e.g. publishing rights, exhibition rights, supply contracts); and other intangible assets. Internally generated intangible assets typically comprise software and systems development where an identifiable asset is created that is probable to generate future economic benefits.

2.1.3 Future economic benefits

Future economic benefits include not only future revenues from the sale of products or services but also cost savings or other benefits resulting from the use of the asset by the entity. For example, the use of intellectual property in a production process may reduce future production costs rather than increase future revenues. *[IAS 38.17]*.

2.2 Is IAS 38 the appropriate IFRS?

An asset is defined generally and in IAS 38 as 'a resource controlled by an entity as a result of past events; and from which future economic benefits are expected to flow to the entity'. *[IAS 38.8]*. Intangible assets form a sub-section of this group and are further defined as 'an identifiable non-monetary asset without physical substance'. *[IAS 38.8]*. As we have discussed earlier, this definition could include assets covered by another standard which are therefore excluded from its scope (see 2 above). However, in some circumstances it is not clear whether IAS 38 or another standard applies.

2.2.1 Whether to record a tangible or intangible asset

Before the advent of IAS 38 many entities used to account for assets without physical substance in the same way as property, plant and equipment. Indeed, the standard notes that intangible assets can be contained in or on a physical medium such as a compact disc (in the case of computer software), legal documentation (in the case of a licence or patent) or film, requiring an entity to exercise judgement in determining whether to apply IAS 16 or IAS 38. *[IAS 38.4]*. For example:

- software that is embedded in computer-controlled equipment that cannot operate without it is an integral part of the related hardware and is treated as property, plant and equipment; *[IAS 38.4]*
- application software that is being used on a computer is treated as an intangible asset because it is generally easily replaced and is not an integral part of the related hardware, whereas the operating system normally is integral to the computer and is included in property, plant and equipment; *[IAS 38.4]*

- a database that is stored digitally is considered to be an intangible asset where the value of the physical medium is wholly insignificant compared to that of the data collection; and
- research and development expenditure may result in an asset with physical substance (e.g. a prototype), but as the physical element is secondary to its intangible component, the related knowledge, it is treated as an intangible asset. *[IAS 38.5]*.

It is worthwhile noting that the 'parts approach' in IAS 16 requires an entity to account for significant parts of an asset separately because they have a different economic life or are often replaced, *[IAS 16.44]*, (see Chapter 18). This raises 'boundary' problems between IAS 16 and IAS 38 when software and similar expenditure is involved. We believe that where IAS 16 requires an entity to identify parts of an asset and account for them separately, the entity needs to evaluate whether any intangible-type part is actually integral to the larger asset or whether it is really a separate asset in its own right. The intangible part is more likely to be an asset in its own right if it was developed separately or if it can be used independently of the item of property, plant and equipment of which it apparently forms part.

This view is consistent with that taken in IFRS 3, when it asserts that related tangible and intangible components of an asset with similar useful lives (meaning that IAS 16 would not require separate accounting of parts of an asset) can be combined into a single asset for financial reporting purposes. *[IFRS 3.B32(b)]*.

2.2.2 Classification of programme and other broadcast rights as inventory or intangible assets

The appropriate classification of broadcast rights depends on the particular facts and circumstances as they apply to an entity. However, it is possible for an entity to conclude that some of its broadcast rights are intangible assets while others should be treated as inventory.

Programme and other broadcast rights meet the definition of intangible assets because they are identifiable non-monetary assets without physical substance. IAS 38 specifically includes within its scope rights under licensing agreements for items such as motion picture films and video recordings. *[IAS 38.6]*. In addition, a broadcast right meets the other criteria for recognition as an intangible asset, being identifiable, as it arises from contractual rights *[IAS 38.12(b)]* and controlled by the entity. *[IAS 38.13]*.

Rights to programmes held exclusively for sale to other parties also meet the definition of inventory and are therefore within the scope of IAS 2. *[IAS 38.3]*. It is possible to argue that programmes held with a view to broadcasting them to an audience are comparable to 'materials or supplies to be consumed in the production process or in the rendering of services', *[IAS 2.6]*, which would mean that they could also be treated as inventory. Equally, it can be argued that such programme rights are intangible assets as they are used in the production or supply of services but not necessarily consumed because they can be used again.

Therefore, it is possible for entities to choose whether programme or other broadcast rights are classified as intangible assets or as inventory. However, the classification of income, expenses and cash flows in respect of those rights should be consistent with the manner of their classification in the statement of financial position.

Accordingly, where a broadcast right is classified as an intangible asset:

- it is classified in the statement of financial position as current or non-current according to the entity's operating cycle (see 10.2 below);
- the intangible asset is amortised, with amortisation included in the statement of profit or loss within the depreciation and amortisation expense, or within a functional expense category (such as cost of sales);
- in the cash flow statement, payments for the acquisition of intangible broadcast rights are classified as an investing activity (if the asset is classified as non-current on acquisition) or as an operating activity if the asset is classified as current; and
- rights are measured at a revalued amount only if the criteria in IAS 38 are met (see 8.2 below). Otherwise the asset is carried at cost less accumulated amortisation and impairments. Any impairment of the asset is determined in accordance with IAS 36.

Where a broadcast right is classified as inventory:

- it is classified in the statement of financial position as a current asset either as part of inventory or as a separate category;
- the entity recognises an expense in cost of sales as the right is consumed;
- payments for the acquisition of inventory are classified as operating activities in the statement of cash flows; and
- rights are carried at the lower of cost and net realisable value.

Both of these classifications are found in practice. Vivendi accounts for its film and television rights catalogues as intangible assets (see Extract 17.3 at 3.1.1 below). ITV on the other hand, presents its programme rights as current assets under the caption 'Programme rights and other inventory'.

Extract 17.2: ITV plc (2019)

Notes to the Financial Statements [extract]
Section 3: Operating Assets and Liabilities [extract]
3.1. **Working capital** [extract]
3.1.1 **Programme rights and commitments** [extract]

Broadcast programme rights [extract]

Acquired programme rights (which include films) and sports rights are purchased for the primary purpose of broadcasting on the ITV family of channels, including VOD and SVOD platforms. These are recognised within current assets as payments are made or when the rights are ready for broadcast. The Group generally expenses these rights through operating costs over a number of transmissions reflecting the pattern and value in which the right is consumed.

Commissions, which primarily comprise programmes purchased, based on editorial specification and over which the Group has some control, are recognised in current assets as payments are made and are generally expensed to operating costs in full on first transmission. Where a commission is repeated on any platform, incremental costs associated with the broadcast are included in operating costs.

[...]

The Broadcast programme rights and other inventory at the year end are shown in the table below:

	2019 £m	2018 £m
Acquired programme rights	173	154
Commissions	106	99
Sports rights	44	45
	323	298

3 RECOGNITION AND MEASUREMENT

3.1 Recognition

An item that meets the definition of an intangible asset (see 2.1 above) should only be recognised if, at the time of initial recognition of the expenditure:

(a) it is probable that the expected future economic benefits that are attributable to the asset will flow to the entity; and

(b) the cost of the asset can be measured reliably. *[IAS 38.21]*.

Although IAS 38 does not define 'probable', it is defined in other standards as 'more likely than not'. *[IAS 37.23, IFRS 5 Appendix A]*. In assessing whether expected future economic benefits are probable, the entity should use reasonable and supportable assumptions that represent management's best estimate of the set of economic conditions that will exist over the useful life of the asset. *[IAS 38.22]*. In making this judgement the entity considers the evidence available at the time of initial recognition, giving greater weight to external evidence. *[IAS 38.23]*.

This test (that the item meets both the definition of an intangible asset and the criteria for recognition) is performed each time an entity incurs potentially eligible expenditures, whether to acquire or internally generate an intangible asset or to add to, replace part of, or service it subsequent to initial recognition. *[IAS 38.18]*. If these criteria are not met at the time the expenditure is incurred, an expense is recognised and it is never reinstated as an asset. *[IAS 38.68, 71]*.

The guidance in IAS 38 on the recognition and initial measurement of intangible assets takes account of the way in which an entity obtained the asset. Separate rules for recognition and initial measurement apply for intangible assets depending on whether they were:

- acquired separately (see 4 below);
- acquired by way of government grant (see 4.6 below);
- obtained in an exchange of assets (see 4.7 below);
- acquired as part of a business combination (see 5 below); and
- generated internally (see 6 below). *[IAS 38.19]*.

The difficulties that may arise in applying these criteria when an entity enters into a contract to buy an intangible asset for delivery in some future period are discussed in detail (in the context of programme broadcast rights) at 3.1.1 below.

For recognition purposes IAS 38 does not distinguish between an internally and an externally developed intangible asset other than when considering the treatment of goodwill. When the definition of an intangible asset and the relevant recognition criteria are met, all such assets should be recognised. *[IAS 38.BCZ40]*. Preparers do not have the option to decide, as a matter of policy, that costs relating to internally generated intangible assets are expensed if the recognition criteria in the standard are met. *[IAS 38.BCZ41]*.

3.1.1 When to recognise programme and other broadcast rights

Television stations frequently enter into contracts to buy programme rights related to long-running televisions series or future sports events that are not yet available for broadcast, sometimes over a specified period or for a certain number of showings or viewings. Payments might be made at the beginning of or during the broadcast period, which raises the question of when those programme rights and the related obligations for payment should be recognised in the statement of financial position.

The IASB's *Conceptual Framework* discusses the concept of executory contracts. An executory contract is a contract, or a portion of a contract, that is equally unperformed – neither party has fulfilled any of its obligations, or both parties have partially fulfilled their obligations to an equal extent. *[CF 4.56]*. An executory contract establishes a combined right and obligation to exchange economic resources. This combined right and obligation are interdependent and cannot be separated, hence they constitute a single asset or liability. *[CF 4.57]*. To the extent that either party fulfils its obligations under the contract, the contract is no longer executory. If the reporting entity performs first under the contract, that performance is the event that changes the reporting entity's right and obligation to exchange economic resources into a right to receive an economic resource. That right is an asset. If the other party performs first, that performance is the event that changes the reporting entity's right and obligation to exchange economic resources into an obligation to transfer an economic resource. That obligation is a liability. *[CF 4.58]*. Therefore, obligations under contracts that are equally proportionately unperformed are generally not recognised as liabilities in the financial statements. For example, liabilities in connection with non-cancellable orders of inventory or items of property, plant and equipment are generally not recognised in an entity's statement of financial position until the goods have been delivered. The same approach can also be applied to broadcast rights.

Accordingly, an entity recognises a broadcast right at the first date that it controls an asset. The meaning of control is discussed at 2.1.2 above.

Determining the date at which control is obtained is a complex matter that depends on the specific facts and circumstances of each case. Factors that may be relevant include whether:

(a) the underlying resource is sufficiently developed to be identifiable. For example, a right to broadcast a film or play might not be sufficiently developed until a manuscript or screenplay is written or a director and actors are hired. For a right to broadcast a sporting event to be identifiable it might be appropriate to establish the existence of a venue, participants or the number or timing of events subject to the right;

(b) the entity has legal, exclusive rights to broadcast (with exclusivity potentially defined in terms of a defined period or geographical area);

(c) there is a penalty payable for non-delivery of the content (e.g. the film or sporting event subject to the broadcast right);

(d) it is probable that the event will occur or the content will be delivered (e.g. completion of a film or a lack of history of cancellations, strikes or rain-outs); and

(e) it is probable that economic benefits will flow to the entity.

Example 17.2: Determining when to recognise a broadcast right

A sporting competition – rights secured over a number of seasons

Entity A (the licensee) signs a contract with a licensor for the exclusive rights to broadcast matches in a long-established sporting competition covering the whole season for a number of years. The entity is required to pay agreed amounts at the start of each season, with the rights to that season and future seasons reverting to the licensor if payment is not made on time. Entity A concludes that an obligation does not exist until the beginning of each season for the amount payable to secure rights for that season.

Based on an evaluation of the factors above, the entity concludes that it has an asset for the rights to broadcast matches in each season and recognises that asset at the start of each season. The entity discloses a commitment for amounts payable in future years without recognising any asset or liability at that time.

Rights to broadcast the future output of a film production company

Entity B (the licensee) signs a contract with a film production company (the licensor) whereby the entity agrees to pay amounts in the future for a specified number of films that the licensor will release in that year, but neither the licensee not the licensor knows which films will be released when they sign the contract.

Based on an evaluation of the facts and circumstances, Entity B concludes that the underlying resource (the films) is not sufficiently developed to be identifiable at the time of signing the contract. Instead, the entity concludes that the criteria for recognising an intangible asset are not met until delivery of the films by the licensor.

This approach is illustrated in the extract from Vivendi below, which distinguishes between contracts requiring recognition and commitments to pay amounts in future periods when content is delivered.

Extract 17.3: Vivendi SE (2019)

Notes to the Consolidated Financial Statements [extract]
NOTE 10. CONTENT ASSETS AND COMMITMENTS [extract]
10.2. CONTRACTUAL CONTENT COMMITMENTS [extract]
Commitments given recorded in the Statement of Financial Position: content liabilities [extract]

		Minimum future payments as of December 31, 2019			Total minimum future payments as of December 31, 2018
			Due in		
(in millions of euros)	Total	2020	2021-2024	After 2024	
Music royalties to artists and repertoire owners	2,264	2,251	13	–	2,049
Film and television rights (a)	198	198	–	–	169
Sports rights	394	394	–	–	434
Creative talent, employment agreements and others	362	270	87	5	297
Content liabilities	**3,218**	**3,113**	**100**	**5**	**2,949**

Off-balance sheet commitments given/(received) [extract]

		Minimum future payments as of December 31, 2019			Total minimum future payments as of December 31, 2018
			Due in		
(in millions of euros)	Total	2020	2021-2024	After 2024	
Film and television rights (a)	3,136	1,093	2,013	30	2,630
Sport rights	(b)1,998	425	1,556	17	1,735
Creative talent, employment agreements and others (c)	1,362	693	635	34	1,172
Given commitments	**6,496**	**2,211**	**4,204**	**81**	**5,537**
Film and television rights (a)	(159)	(100)	(58)	(1)	(188)
Sports rights	(104)	(52)	(52)	–	(7)
Creative talent, employment agreements and others (c)			not available		
Other	(6)	(2)	(4)	–	(3)
Received commitments	**(269)**	**(154)**	**(114)**	**(1)**	**(198)**
Total net	**6,227**	**2,057**	**4,090**	**80**	**5,339**

As illustrated in Extract 17.2 at 2.2.2 above, ITV follows a similar type of approach for acquired programme rights under which an asset is recognised as payments are made and is recognised in full when the acquired programming is available for transmission.

3.2 Measurement

On initial recognition an intangible asset should be measured at cost. *[IAS 38.24]*. The standard defines this as the amount of cash or cash equivalents paid or the fair value of other consideration given to acquire an asset at the time of its acquisition or construction. When the nature of the consideration given is governed by other IFRSs, the cost of the asset is the amount initially recognised in accordance with the specific requirements of that standard, e.g. IFRS 2. *[IAS 38.8]*.

IAS 38's initial measurement depends, in part, on the manner in which the asset is acquired and these are discussed in more detail at 4 to 7 below. The components of the cost of an internally generated intangible asset are discussed in more detail at 6.3 below.

3.3 Subsequent expenditure

Although IAS 38 is based on a general recognition principle that applies to both initial acquisition and subsequent expenditures, the hurdle for the recognition of subsequent expenditure as an addition to an intangible asset is set higher, because it must first be confirmed that the expenditure is not associated with the replacement of an existing asset (see 9.5.1 below) or the creation of an internally generated intangible that would not be eligible for recognition under the standard (see 6 below). The standard presumes that only rarely will subsequent expenditure, i.e. expenditure incurred after the initial recognition of an acquired intangible asset or after completion of an internally generated intangible asset, be recognised in the carrying amount of an asset. In most cases, subsequent expenditures are likely to maintain the expected future economic benefits embodied in an existing intangible asset rather than meet the definition of an intangible asset and the recognition criteria in IAS 38. The standard also notes that it is often difficult to attribute subsequent expenditure directly to a particular intangible asset rather than to the business as a whole. *[IAS 38.20]*.

Capitalisation of subsequent expenditure on brands, mastheads, publishing titles, customer lists and similar items is expressly forbidden even if they were initially acquired externally, which is consistent with the general prohibition on recognising them if internally generated. This is because the standard argues that such expenditure cannot be distinguished from the cost of developing the business of which they are a part. *[IAS 38.20, 63]*. Thus, at best such expenditure creates unrecognised internally generated goodwill that might be crystallised only in a business combination.

4 SEPARATE ACQUISITION

4.1 Recognition

Separately acquired intangible rights will normally be recognised as assets. IAS 38 assumes that the price paid to acquire an intangible asset usually reflects expectations about the probability that the future economic benefits embodied in it will flow to the entity. In other words, the entity always expects there to be a flow of economic benefits, even if it is uncertain about the timing or amount. *[IAS 38.25]*. Therefore, the standard assumes that the cost of a separately acquired intangible asset can usually be measured reliably, especially in the case of cash or other monetary purchase considerations. *[IAS 38.26]*.

Not all external costs incurred to secure intangible rights automatically qualify for capitalisation as separately acquired assets, because they do not meet the definition of an intangible asset in the first place. An entity that subcontracts the development of intangible assets (e.g. development-and-supply contracts or R&D contracts) to other parties (its suppliers) must exercise judgement in determining whether it is acquiring an intangible asset or whether it is obtaining goods and services that are being used in the development of an intangible asset by the entity itself. In the latter case, the entity will only be able to recognise an intangible asset if the expenditure meets IAS 38's requirements for internally-generated assets (see 6 below).

In determining whether a supplier is providing services to develop an internally generated intangible asset, the terms of the supply agreement should be examined to see whether the supplier is bearing a significant proportion of the risks associated with a failure of the project. For example, if the supplier is always compensated under a development-and-supply contract for development services and tool costs irrespective of the project's outcome, the entity on whose behalf the development is undertaken should account for those activities as its own.

If the entity pays the supplier upfront or by milestone payments during the course of a project, it will not necessarily recognise an intangible asset on the basis of those payments. Only costs incurred after it becomes probable that economic benefits are expected to flow to the entity will be part of the cost of an intangible asset (see 6.2 below).

4.2 Components of cost

The cost of a separately acquired intangible asset comprises:

- its purchase price, including import duties and non-refundable purchase taxes, after deducting trade discounts and rebates; and
- any directly attributable cost of preparing the asset for its intended use, *[IAS 38.27]*, for example:
  - costs of employee benefits arising directly from bringing the asset to its working condition;
  - professional fees arising directly from bringing the asset to its working condition; and
  - costs of testing whether the asset is functioning properly. *[IAS 38.28]*.

Capitalisation of expenditure ceases when the asset is in the condition necessary for it to be capable of operating in the manner intended by management. *[IAS 38.30]*. This may well be before the date on which it is brought into use.

If payment for an intangible asset is deferred beyond normal credit terms, its cost is the cash price equivalent. The difference between this amount and the total payments is recognised as interest expense over the period of credit unless it is capitalised in accordance with IAS 23 – *Borrowing Costs* (see Chapter 21). *[IAS 38.32]*.

4.3 Costs to be expensed

The following types of expenditure are not considered to be part of the cost of a separately acquired intangible asset:

- costs of introducing a new product or service, including costs of advertising and promotional activities;
- costs of conducting business in a new location or with a new class of customer, including costs of staff training;

- administration and other general overhead costs;
- costs incurred in using or redeploying an intangible asset;
- costs incurred while an asset capable of operating in the manner intended by management has yet to be brought into use; and
- initial operating losses, such as those incurred while demand for the asset's output builds up. *[IAS 38.29-30]*.

Accordingly, start-up costs, training costs, advertising and promotional activities, and relocation or reorganisation costs should be expensed (see 7 below).

4.4 Income from incidental operations while an asset is being developed

When an entity generates income while it is developing or constructing an asset, the question arises as to whether this income should reduce the initial carrying value of the asset being developed or be recognised in profit or loss. IAS 38 requires an entity to consider whether the activity giving rise to income is necessary to bring the asset to the condition necessary for it to be capable of operating in the manner intended by management, or not. The income and related expenses of incidental operations (being those not necessary to develop the asset for its intended use) should be recognised immediately in profit or loss and included in their respective classifications of income and expense. *[IAS 38.31]*. Such incidental operations can occur before or during the development activities. The example below illustrates these requirements.

Example 17.3: Incidental operations

Entity A is pioneering a new process for the production of a certain type of chemical. Entity A will be able to patent the new production process. During the development phase, A is selling quantities of the chemical that are produced as a by-product of the development activities that are taking place. The expenditure incurred comprises labour, raw materials, assembly costs, costs of equipment and professional fees.

The revenues and costs associated with the production and sale of the chemical are accounted for in profit or loss for the period, while the development costs that meet the strict recognition criteria of IAS 38 are recognised as an intangible asset. Development costs that fail the IAS 38 recognition test are also expensed.

As the above example suggests, identifying the revenue from incidental operations will often be much easier than allocating costs to incidental operations. Furthermore, it will often be challenging to determine when exactly a project moves from the development phase into its start-up phase.

IAS 38 is not explicit on how to account for income earned in relation to activity that is determined necessary to bring the intangible asset into its intended use. IAS 16 however does provide guidance in relation to this for items of PP&E that are under construction (see Chapter 18 at 4.2.1). In May 2020, the IASB issued an amendment to IAS 16 – *Property, Plant and Equipment: Proceeds before Intended Use*, which prescribes new accounting and disclosure requirements. These amendments remove the requirement to deduct any proceeds from selling items produced from the cost of an item of PP&E, while bringing that asset to the location and condition necessary for it to be capable of operating in the manner intended by management. Instead, the amendments require the proceeds from selling any such items, together with the cost of those items measured in accordance with IAS 2, to be recognised in profit or loss in accordance with applicable standards. *[IAS 16.20A]*. In the absence of specific guidance in IAS 38, an entity should refer to the hierarchy in IAS 8 – *Accounting Policies, Changes in Accounting Estimates and Errors* – to develop an appropriate accounting policy (see Chapter 3 at 4.3). The hierarchy requires an entity to firstly consider the requirements in IFRSs dealing with similar and related issues. *[IAS 8.11]*. Therefore, an entity should consider the extent to which it could apply the guidance in IAS 16, discussed above, to income earned in relation to activity that is determined necessary to bring the intangible asset into its intended use.

An example of such income would be where income is generated from the sale of samples produced during the testing of a new process or from the sale of a production prototype. However, care must be taken to confirm whether the incidence of income indicates that the intangible asset is ready for its intended use, in which case capitalisation of costs would cease, revenue would be recognised in profit or loss and the related costs of the activity would include a measure of amortisation of the asset.

4.5 Measurement of intangible assets acquired for contingent consideration

Transactions involving contingent consideration are often very complex and payment is dependent on a number of factors. In the absence of specific guidance in IAS 38, entities trying to determine an appropriate accounting treatment are required not only to understand the commercial complexities of the transaction itself, but also to negotiate a variety of accounting principles and requirements.

Consider a relatively simple example where an entity acquires an intangible asset for consideration comprising a combination of up-front payment, guaranteed instalments for a number of years and additional amounts that vary according to future activity (revenue, profit or number of units output).

Where the goods and services in question have been delivered, there is no doubt that there is a financial liability under IFRS 9 – *Financial Instruments*. A contingent obligation to deliver cash meets the definition of a financial liability (see Chapter 47). Therefore, if the obligation to make the variable payment does not depend on the acquiring entity's future activity and the event that gives rise to the payment is outside its control then a financial liability would be recognised. *[IAS 32.25]*.

However, where the purchaser can influence or control the crystallisation of the contingent payments or they are wholly dependent on its future activities, the circumstances are more difficult to interpret. In these cases, the determination of whether the payment should be capitalised or expensed is usually based on the reason for the contingent payment. For example, if the contingent payment is based on period volumes sold or produced it will generally be expensed. Conversely, when the reason for the payment is more clearly linked to the initial value of the asset, rather than its use over time, the entity may elect a policy to either:

- include the fair value of all contingent payments in the initial measurement of the asset; or
- recognise a liability only when the contingent payment crystallises.

Under both approaches, subsequent changes in the contingent consideration liability or subsequent payments are either capitalised when incurred, or expensed as incurred.

When it discussed accounting for contingent consideration between July 2013 and March 2016, the Interpretations Committee ultimately concluded that the issue was too broad for the Committee to address and referred it back to the Board. In May 2016, the IASB tentatively agreed that this issue would be included in the research pipeline between 2017 and 2021.[1] In February 2018, the Board decided that the IASB staff should carry out work to determine how broad the research project should be.[2] At the time of writing this is not listed as an active research project on the IASB's work plan.[3]

Until this matter is resolved, an entity should adopt and apply a consistent accounting policy to initial recognition and subsequent payments, in accordance with the hierarchy in IAS 8. An entity should exercise judgement in developing and consistently applying an accounting policy that results in information that is relevant and reliable in its particular circumstances. *[IAS 8.10]*. For intangible assets, these approaches are illustrated in the following example. Note that this example does not include a number of common contingent payments, e.g. those related to usage or revenue, or non-floating rate changes in finance costs.

Example 17.4:   Contingent consideration relating to a football player's registration

Entity A is a football club which signs a new player on a 4 year contract. In securing the registration of the new player, Entity A agrees to make the following payments to the player's former club:

- €5.5 million on completion of the transfer;
- €2.8 million on the first anniversary of the transfer;
- €1 million as soon as the player has made 25 appearances for the club;
- €0.2 million when the player is first selected to play for his country; and
- 25% of the gross proceeds from any onward sale of the player before the expiry of the initial contract term.

It is determined that the expenditure meets the definition of an intangible asset because it allows Entity A to negotiate a playing contract with the footballer that covers 4 seasons and prevents other clubs from using that player's services over that time. How does Entity A determine the cost of the player registration?

View 1 – All of the above payments are contractual and a financial liability arises under IFRS 9 as soon as that player signs for the club. Accordingly, the cost of the intangible asset comprises the initial payment of €5.5 million, plus an amount representing the present value of the €2.8 million payable in one year and an amount to reflect the fair value of the other contingent payments (for example, determined using some kind of probability-weighted estimation technique).

View 2 – The contractual terms requiring a payment of €1 million on the player achieving 25 appearances for the club and another payment of 25% of the gross proceeds from any onward sale of the player are not liabilities of Entity A at the inception of the contract, as there is no obligation on the part of Entity A to use the player in more than 24 fixtures or to sell the player before the end of the 4 year contract term. Accordingly, these elements of the contract are excluded from the initial cost of the intangible asset and are not recognised until the obligating event occurs. However, the element that is contingent on the player being selected to play for his country is not within the entity's control and is included in the initial measurement of cost.

An entity taking view 2 would not include the appearance payment or the share of sale proceeds within the cost of the intangible asset, even when the related obligation is eventually recognised. The entity would most likely regard the €1 million appearance payment as an expense on the grounds that this is subsequent expenditure that does not qualify for recognition as an intangible asset (see 3.3 above).

Merck has developed an accounting policy for contingent consideration in relation to the acquisition of assets. In this case, whether or not the payment of the contingent consideration is within the entity's control, is the determining factor as to whether it is recognised as part of the cost on acquisition.

> *Extract 17.4: MERCK Kommanditgesellschaft auf Aktien (2018)*
>
> **Notes to the Consolidated Financial Statements** [extract]
>
> **(63) Contingent consideration** [extract]
>
> Contingent consideration in connection with the purchase of individual assets outside of business combinations is recognized as a financial liability only when the consideration is contingent upon future events that are beyond Merck's control. In cases where the payment of contingent consideration is within Merck's control, the liability is recognized only as from the date when a non-contingent obligation arises. Contingent consideration linked to the purchase of individual assets primarily relates to future milestone payments in connection with in-licensed intellectual property in the Healthcare business sector.
>
> Changes in the fair value of financial assets and financial liabilities from contingent consideration are recognized as other operating income or other operating expenses, except for changes due to interest rate fluctuations and the effect from unwinding discounts. Interest rate effects from unwinding of discounts as well as changes due to interest rate fluctuations are recognized in financial income or financial expenses.

4.6 Acquisition by way of government grant

An intangible asset may sometimes be acquired free of charge, or for nominal consideration, by way of a government grant. Governments frequently allocate airport-landing rights, licences to operate radio or television stations, emission rights (see 11.2 below), import licences or quotas, or rights to access other restricted resources. *[IAS 38.44]*.

Government grants should be accounted for under IAS 20 – *Accounting for Government Grants and Disclosure of Government Assistance* – which permits initial recognition of intangible assets received either at fair value or a nominal amount. *[IAS 20.23]*.

This represents an accounting policy choice for an entity that should be applied consistently to all intangible assets acquired by way of a government grant.

It may not be possible to measure reliably the fair value of all of the permits allocated by governments because they may have been allocated for no consideration, may not be transferable and may only be bought and sold as part of a business. Some of the issues surrounding the determination of fair value in the absence of an active market are considered in Chapter 14. Other allocated permits such as milk quotas are freely traded and therefore do have a readily ascertainable fair value.

4.7 Exchanges of assets

Asset exchanges are transactions that have challenged standard-setters for many years. An entity might swap certain intangible assets that it does not require or is no longer allowed to use for those of a counterparty that has other surplus assets. For example, it is not uncommon for airlines and media groups to exchange landing slots and newspaper titles, respectively, to meet demands of competition authorities. The question arises whether such transactions should be recorded at cost or fair value, which would give rise to a gain in the circumstances where the fair value of the incoming asset exceeds the carrying amount of the outgoing one. Equally, it is possible that a transaction could be arranged with no real commercial substance, solely to boost apparent profits.

Three separate International Accounting Standards contain virtually identical guidance on accounting for exchanges of assets: IAS 16 (see Chapter 18), IAS 40 – *Investment Property* (see Chapter 19) and IAS 38.

4.7.1 Measurement of assets exchanged

In the context of asset exchanges, the standard contains guidance on the reliable determination of fair values in the circumstances where market values do not exist. Note that while fair value is defined by reference to IFRS 13 (see Chapter 14), the requirements in this section are specific to asset exchanges in IAS 38.

IAS 38 requires all acquisitions of intangible assets in exchange for non-monetary assets, or a combination of monetary and non-monetary assets, to be measured at fair value. The acquired intangible asset is measured at fair value unless: *[IAS 38.45]*

(a) the exchange transaction lacks commercial substance; or

(b) the fair value of neither the asset received nor the asset given up is reliably measurable.

The acquired asset is measured in this way even if an entity cannot immediately derecognise the asset given up. If an entity is able to reliably determine the fair value of either the asset received or the asset given up, then it uses the fair value of the asset given up to measure cost unless the fair value of the asset received is more clearly evident. *[IAS 38.47]*. If the fair value of neither the asset given up, nor the asset received can be measured reliably the acquired intangible asset is measured at the carrying amount of the asset given up. *[IAS 38.45]*.

In this context the fair value of an intangible asset is reliably measurable if the variability in the range of reasonable fair value measurements is not significant for that asset or the probabilities of the various estimates within the range can be reasonably assessed and used when measuring fair value. *[IAS 38.47]*.

4.7.2 Commercial substance

A gain or loss is only recognised on an exchange of non-monetary assets if the transaction is determined to have commercial substance. Otherwise, the acquired asset is measured at the cost of the asset given up. *[IAS 38.45]*.

The commercial substance test for asset exchanges was put in place to prevent gains being recognised in income when the transaction had no discernible effect on the entity's economics. *[IAS 16.BC21]*. The commercial substance of an exchange is determined by forecasting and comparing the future cash flows expected to be generated by the incoming and outgoing assets. Commercial substance means that there must be a significant difference between the two forecasts. An exchange transaction has commercial substance if: *[IAS 38.46]*

(a) the configuration (i.e. risk, timing and amount) of the cash flows of the asset received differs from the configuration of the cash flows of the asset transferred; or

(b) the entity-specific value of the portion of the entity's operations affected by the transaction changes as a result of the exchange; and

(c) the difference in (a) or (b) is significant relative to the fair value of the assets exchanged.

IAS 38 defines the entity-specific value of an intangible asset as the present value of the cash flows an entity expects to arise from its continuing use and from its disposal at the end of its useful life. *[IAS 38.8]*. In determining whether an exchange transaction has commercial substance, the entity-specific value of the portion of the entity's operations affected by the transaction should reflect post-tax cash flows. *[IAS 38.46]*. This is different to the calculation of an asset's value in use under IAS 36 (see Chapter 20), as it uses a post-tax discount rate based on the entity's own risks rather than IAS 36, which requires use of the pre-tax rate that the market would apply to a similar asset.

The standard acknowledges that the result of this analysis might be clear without having to perform detailed calculations. *[IAS 38.46]*.

5 ACQUISITION AS PART OF A BUSINESS COMBINATION

The requirements of IFRS 3 apply to intangible assets acquired in a business combination. The recognition and initial measurement requirements are discussed in detail in Chapter 9 and a summary is given below. The emphasis in IFRS 3 is that, in effect, it does not matter whether assets meeting the definition of an intangible asset have to be combined with other intangible assets, incorporated into the carrying value of a complementary item of property, plant and equipment with a similar useful life or included in the assessment of the fair value of a related liability. The important requirement is that the intangible asset is recognised separately from goodwill.

The process of identifying intangible assets in a business combination might involve, for example:

- reviewing the list of items that meet the definition of an intangible asset in IFRS 3 (see 5.2 below);
- a review of documents such as those related to the acquisition, other internal documents produced by the entity, public filings, press releases, analysts' reports, and other externally available documents; and
- comparing the acquired business to similar businesses and their intangible assets.

Intangible assets that are used differ considerably between industries and between individual entities. Therefore, considerable expertise and careful judgement is required in determining whether there are intangible assets that need to be recognised and valued separately.

IFRS 3 provides a long list of items that should be recognised separately from goodwill (see 5.2 below). The list is not intended to be exhaustive.

5.1 Recognition of intangible assets acquired in a business combination

As noted at 3.1 above, an intangible asset should only be recognised if: *[IAS 38.21]*

(a) it is probable that the expected future economic benefits that are attributable to the asset will flow to the entity; and

(b) the cost of the asset can be measured reliably.

5.1.1 Probable inflow of benefits

In the case of a business combination, the probability recognition criterion is always considered to be satisfied. The cost of the intangible asset is its fair value at the acquisition date. The standard indicates that the fair value reflects expectations about the probability that the future economic benefits embodied in the asset will flow to the entity. *[IAS 38.33]*. In other words, the existence of a fair value means that an inflow of economic benefits is considered to be probable, in spite of any uncertainties about timing or amount.

5.1.2 Reliability of measurement

Under IFRS 3, the cost of the intangible asset acquired in a business combination can always be measured reliably. *[IAS 38.BC19A]*.

In developing IFRS 3, the Board concluded that the needs of users were better served by recognising intangible assets, on the basis of an estimate of fair value, rather than subsuming them in goodwill, even if a significant degree of judgement is required to estimate fair value. *[IAS 38.BC19B]*. Accordingly, if an asset acquired in a business combination is separable or arises from contractual or other legal rights, there is sufficient information to measure reliably the fair value of the asset. Thus, the requirement at 3.1 above for reliable measurement of cost is always considered to be satisfied for intangible assets acquired in business combinations. *[IAS 38.33]*.

5.1.3 Identifiability in relation to an intangible asset acquired in a business combination

Intangible assets need to be identifiable to distinguish them from goodwill and the two elements of identifiability are the existence of contractual or other legal rights and separability. Separability means that the asset is capable of being sold, transferred, licensed, rented or exchanged without having to dispose of the whole business. An intangible asset is considered to be separable regardless of whether the entity intends to sell or otherwise transfer it. *[IAS 38.12]*.

If an intangible asset acquired in a business combination is separable or arises from contractual or other legal rights, sufficient information exists to measure reliably the fair value of the asset. Where there are a range of possible outcomes with different probabilities in estimating an intangible asset's fair value, this uncertainty should be factored into the measurement of the asset's fair value. *[IAS 38.35]*.

The IASB recognised that an intangible asset acquired in a business combination might be separable, but only together with a related contract, identifiable asset or liability. In such cases, IAS 38 requires the acquirer to recognise the intangible asset separately from goodwill, but together with the related contract, asset or liability. *[IAS 38.36]*.

Acquirers are permitted to recognise a group of complementary intangible assets as a single asset provided the individual assets in the group have similar useful lives. For example, the terms 'brand' and 'brand name' are often used as synonyms for trademarks and other marks. However, 'brands' are regarded as general marketing terms that are typically used to refer to a group of complementary assets such as a trademark or service mark and its related trade name, formulas, recipes and technological expertise. *[IAS 38.37]*. Anheuser-Busch InBev, for example, acknowledges the relationship between trademarks and other complementary assets such as formulas, recipes or technological expertise acquired in business combinations.

> Extract 17.5: Anheuser-Busch InBev NV/SA (2019)
>
> Notes to the consolidated financial statements [extract]
> 3. Summary of significant accounting policies [extract]
> (G) INTANGIBLE ASSETS [extract]
> Brands [extract]
>
> If part of the consideration paid in a business combination relates to trademarks, trade names, formulas, recipes or technological expertise these intangible assets are considered as a group of complementary assets that is referred to as a brand for which one fair value is determined.

IFRS 3 contains additional guidance on the application of the contractual-legal and separability criteria that indicate how far the IASB expects entities to go to ensure that intangible assets acquired in a business combination are recognised separately from goodwill.

5.1.3.A Contractual-legal rights

An intangible asset that arises from contractual or other legal rights is recognised separately from goodwill even if it is not transferable or separable from the acquiree or from other rights and obligations. For example:

(a) an acquiree owns and operates a nuclear power plant. The licence to operate that power plant is an intangible asset that meets the contractual-legal criterion for recognition separately from goodwill, even if the acquirer cannot sell or transfer it separately from the acquired power plant. However, IFRS 3 goes on to say that an acquirer may recognise the fair value of the operating licence and the fair value of the power plant as a single asset for financial reporting purposes if the useful lives of those assets are similar;

(b) an acquiree owns a technology patent. It has licensed that patent to others for their exclusive use outside the domestic market, receiving a specified percentage of future foreign revenue in exchange. Both the technology patent and the related licence agreement meet the contractual-legal criterion for recognition separately from goodwill even if selling or exchanging the patent and the related licence agreement separately from one another would not be practical. *[IFRS 3.B32]*.

5.1.3.B Separability

IFRS 3 emphasises that the separability criterion means that an acquired intangible asset is capable of being separated or divided from the acquiree, regardless of the intentions of the acquirer. It adds that an acquired intangible asset is recognised separately from goodwill if there is evidence of exchange transactions for that type of asset or an asset of a similar type, even if those transactions are infrequent and regardless of whether the acquirer is involved in them. For example, customer and subscriber lists are frequently licensed and thus merit recognition as intangible assets. The standard acknowledges that an acquiree might try to distinguish its customer lists from those that are frequently licensed generally, in order to justify no recognition. However, in the absence of a truly distinguishing feature, such as confidentiality or other agreements that prohibit an entity from selling, leasing or otherwise exchanging information about its customers, these non-contractual rights should be recognised separately from goodwill. *[IFRS 3.B33]*.

An intangible asset that is not individually separable from the acquiree or combined entity should still be recognised separately from goodwill if it could be separable in combination with a related contract, identifiable asset or liability. For example, an acquiree owns a registered trademark and documented but unpatented technical expertise used to manufacture the trademarked product. The entity could not transfer ownership of the trademark without everything else necessary for the new owner to produce an identical product or service. Because the unpatented technical expertise must be transferred if the related trademark is sold, it is separable and not included in the carrying value of goodwill. *[IFRS 3.B34]*.

The requirements described above demonstrate how IFRS 3 and IAS 38 define intangible assets in a way that eliminates as much as possible any barrier to recognising them separately from goodwill.

5.2 Examples of intangible assets acquired in a business combination

IFRS 3 provides a long list of examples of items acquired in a business combination that meet the definition of an intangible asset and should therefore be recognised separately from goodwill. *[IFRS 3.IE16-44]*. The list is not intended to be exhaustive and other items acquired in a business combination might still meet the definition of an intangible asset. *[IFRS 3.IE16]*.

The table below summarises the items included in the IASB's Illustrative Example. Reference should be made to the Illustrative Example itself for any further explanation about some of these items.

Intangible assets arising from contractual or other legal rights (regardless of being separable)	Other intangible assets that are separable
Marketing-related	
– Trademarks, trade names, service marks, collective marks and certification marks	
– Internet domain names	
– Trade dress (unique colour, shape or package design)	
– Newspaper mastheads	
– Non-competition agreements	
Customer-related	
– Order or production backlog	– Customer lists
– Customer contracts and the related customer relationships	– Non-contractual customer relationships
Artistic-related	
– Plays, operas and ballets	
– Books, magazines, newspapers and other literary works	
– Musical works such as compositions, song lyrics and advertising jingles	
– Pictures and photographs	
– Video and audio-visual material, including films, music videos and television programmes	
Contract-based	
– Licensing, royalty and standstill agreements	
– Advertising, construction, management, service or supply contracts	
– Construction permits	
– Franchise agreements	
– Operating and broadcast rights	
– Servicing contracts such as mortgage servicing contracts	
– Employment contracts that are beneficial contracts from the perspective of the employer because the pricing of those contracts is below their current market value	
– Use rights such as drilling, water, air, mineral, timber-cutting and route authorities	
Technology-based	
– Patented technology	– Unpatented technology
– Computer software and mask works	– Databases, including title plants
– Trade secrets such as secret formulas, processes and recipes	

Further details on the requirements relating to intangible assets acquired as part of a business combination are covered in Chapter 9.

5.3 Measuring the fair value of intangible assets acquired in a business combination

IFRS 3 assumes that there will always be sufficient information to measure reliably the fair value of an intangible asset acquired in a business combination if it is separable or arises from contractual or other legal rights.

The issues underlying the initial measurement of these intangible assets are discussed further in Chapter 9. The requirements of IFRS 13 are discussed in Chapter 14, which also addresses the challenges of applying IFRS 13 at initial recognition since fair value is defined as an exit price. In particular, the selection of appropriate valuation techniques, inputs to those valuation techniques and the application of the fair value hierarchy are discussed in Chapter 14.

5.4 Customer relationship intangible assets acquired in a business combination

Further guidance on customer relationships acquired in a business combination is provided by IFRS 3 in the Illustrative Examples, which form the basis of the example below. These demonstrate how the contractual-legal and separability criteria, discussed at 2.1.1 above, interact in the recognition of acquired customer relationships. *[IFRS 3.IE30]*.

Example 17.5: Customer relationship intangible assets acquired in a business combination

Supply agreement

Acquirer Company (A) acquires Target Company (T) in a business combination. T has a five-year agreement to supply goods to Customer (C). Both T and A believe that C will renew the supply agreement at the end of the current contract. The supply agreement is not separable.

Because T establishes its relationship with C through a contract, not only the supply agreement (whether cancellable or not) but also T's customer relationship with C meet the contractual-legal criterion for identification as an intangible asset. Therefore, both the supply agreement and the customer relationship intangible asset are recognised separately from goodwill.

Sporting goods and electronics

A acquires T in a business combination. T manufactures goods in two distinct lines of business: sporting goods and electronics. Customer (C) purchases both sporting goods and electronics from T. T has a contract with C to be its exclusive provider of sporting goods, but has no contract for the supply of electronics to C. Both T and A believe that there is only one overall customer relationship between T and C.

As in the previous example, both the contract for the exclusive supply of sporting goods (whether cancellable or not) and the related customer relationship qualify for identification as an intangible asset because the contractual-legal criterion is met. Because T and A believe that there is only one customer relationship, the fair value of the intangible asset incorporates assumptions regarding T's relationship with C for both sporting goods and electronics.

However, if A determined that there were two customer relationships with C – one for sporting goods and another for electronics – the customer relationship for electronics would only be recognised if it meets the separability criterion for identification as an intangible asset (because there is not a current or past contract it can be linked to).

Order backlog and recurring customers

A acquires T in a business combination on 31 December 2020. T does business with its customers solely through purchase and sales orders. At 31 December 2020, T has a backlog of customer purchase orders from 60 per cent of its customers, all of whom are recurring customers. The other 40 per cent of T's customers are also recurring customers. However, as of 31 December 2020, T has no open purchase orders or other contracts with those customers.

The purchase orders from 60 per cent of T's customers (whether cancellable or not) meet the contractual-legal criterion, so the order backlog is recognised as an intangible asset separate from goodwill. Additionally, because T has a practice of establishing contracts (purchase and sales orders) with all of its customers, its relationship with all of its customers (not just the 60 per cent in respect of which there is a backlog of purchase orders) also arises through contractual rights, and therefore meets the contractual-legal criterion for identification as an intangible asset, even though T does not have contracts with 40% of those customers at 31 December 2020.

Motor insurance contracts

A acquires T, an Insurer, in a business combination. T has a portfolio of one-year motor insurance contracts that are cancellable by policyholders.

Because T establishes its relationships with policyholders through insurance contracts, the customer relationship with policyholders meets the contractual-legal criterion for identification as an intangible asset.

One of the most difficult areas of interpretation is whether an arrangement is contractual or not. Contractual customer relationships are always recognised separately from goodwill but non-contractual customer relationships are recognised only if they are separable. Consequently, determining whether a relationship is contractual is critical to identifying and measuring customer relationship intangible assets and different conclusions could result in substantially different accounting outcomes. This is discussed in more detail in Chapter 9 at 5.5.2.B.

Given the widespread confusion the matter was referred to the IASB and the FASB with a recommendation to review and amend IFRS 3 by:

- removing the distinction between 'contractual' and 'non-contractual' customer-related intangible assets recognised in a business combination; and
- reviewing the indicators that identify the existence of a customer relationship in paragraph IE28 of IFRS 3 and including them in the standard.

When it considered the issue in March 2009, the Interpretations Committee was unable to develop an Interpretation clarifying the distinction between contractual and non-contractual.

The IASB deferred both recommendations of the Interpretations Committee to the post-implementation review (PIR) of IFRS 3, which was completed in June 2015. As a result of the PIR of IFRS 3 the issue of the identification and fair value measurement of intangible assets such as customer relationships and brand names was added to the IASB's active agenda within its *Goodwill and Impairment* research project. In April 2018, the IASB decided not to consider allowing any identifiable intangible assets acquired in a business combination to be included within goodwill.[4] The research project is covered in further detail in Chapter 9 at 1.1.1 and 5.5.2.B.

Despite the IASB's decision there will be divergent treatments in practice, depending on how entities interpret 'contractual' and 'non-contractual' customer-related intangible assets in a particular business combination.

5.5 In-process research and development

The term 'in-process research and development' (IPR&D) refers to those identifiable intangible assets resulting from research and development activities that are acquired in a business combination. An acquirer should recognise IPR&D separately from goodwill if the project meets the definition of an intangible asset. This is the case when the IPR&D project meets the definition of an asset and is identifiable, i.e. it is separable or arises from contractual or other legal rights. *[IAS 38.34]*.

IPR&D projects, whether or not recognised by the acquiree, are protected by legal rights and are clearly separable, as they can be bought and sold by entities in the normal course of business.

Any subsequent expenditure incurred on the project after its acquisition should be accounted for in accordance with the general rules in IAS 38 on internally generated intangible assets which are discussed at 6.2 below. *[IAS 38.42]*. In summary, this means that the subsequent expenditure is accounted for as follows: *[IAS 38.43]*

- research expenditure is recognised as an expense when incurred;
- development expenditure that does not satisfy the criteria for recognition as an intangible asset is recognised as an expense when incurred; and
- development expenditure that satisfies the recognition criteria is added to the carrying value of the acquired in-process research or development project.

This approach results in some IPR&D projects acquired in business combinations being treated differently from similar projects started internally because there are different criteria for recognition. The IASB acknowledged this point but decided that it could not support a treatment that allowed acquired IPR&D to be subsumed within goodwill. *[IAS 38.BC82]*. Until the Board finds time to address this issue, users of financial statements will have to live with the problem that an asset can be recognised for acquired research and development projects despite the fact that the entity might recognise as an expense the costs of internal projects at a similar stage of development.

The implication is that if an acquired project is ultimately successful, the asset recognised will have a higher carrying amount and related amortisation charged to profit and loss over its useful life than an equivalent internal project.

If the carrying value cannot be justified, the acquired asset will be impaired. An impairment test will be performed before the end of the period of acquisition and annually thereafter in accordance with the requirements of IAS 36 for intangible assets not yet available for use (see Chapter 20). *[IAS 36.10]*. Any impairment loss will be reflected in the entity's statement of profit or loss as a post-acquisition event.

6 INTERNALLY GENERATED INTANGIBLE ASSETS

6.1 Internally generated goodwill

IAS 38 explicitly prohibits the recognition of internally generated goodwill as an asset because internally generated goodwill is neither separable nor does it arise from contractual or legal rights. *[IAS 38.48]*. As such, it is not an identifiable resource controlled by the entity that can be measured reliably at cost. *[IAS 38.49]*. It therefore does not meet the definition of an intangible asset under the standard or that of an asset under the IASB's *Conceptual Framework*. The standard maintains that the difference between the fair value of an entity and the carrying amount of its identifiable net assets at any time may capture a range of factors that affect the fair value of the entity, but that such differences do not represent the cost of intangible assets controlled by the entity. *[IAS 38.50]*.

6.2 Internally generated intangible assets

The IASB recognises that it may be difficult to decide whether an internally generated intangible asset qualifies for recognition because of problems in:

(a) confirming whether and when there is an identifiable asset that will generate expected future economic benefits; and

(b) determining the cost of the asset reliably, especially in cases where the cost of generating an intangible asset internally cannot be distinguished from the cost of maintaining or enhancing the entity's internally generated goodwill or of running day-to-day operations. *[IAS 38.51]*.

To avoid the inappropriate recognition of an asset, IAS 38 requires that internally generated intangible assets are not only tested against the general requirements for recognition and initial measurement (discussed at 3 above), but also meet criteria which confirm that the related activity is at a sufficiently advanced stage of development, is both technically and commercially viable and includes only directly attributable costs. *[IAS 38.51]*. Those criteria comprise detailed guidance on accounting for intangible assets in the research phase (see 6.2.1 below), the development phase (see 6.2.2 below) and on components of cost of an internally generated intangible asset (see 6.3 below).

If the general recognition and initial measurement requirements are met, the entity classifies the generation of the internally developed asset into a research phase and a development phase. *[IAS 38.52]*. Only expenditure arising from the development phase can be considered for capitalisation, with all expenditure on research being recognised as an expense when it is incurred. *[IAS 38.54]*. If it is too difficult to distinguish an activity between a research phase and a development phase, all expenditure is treated as research. *[IAS 38.53]*.

The standard distinguishes between research and development activities as follows:

Research is original and planned investigation undertaken with the prospect of gaining new scientific or technical knowledge and understanding. *[IAS 38.8]*.

The standard gives the following examples of research activities: *[IAS 38.56]*

(a) activities aimed at obtaining new knowledge;

(b) the search for, evaluation and final selection of, applications of research findings or other knowledge;

(c) the search for alternatives for materials, devices, products, processes, systems or services; and

(d) the formulation, design, evaluation and final selection of possible alternatives for new or improved materials, devices, products, processes, systems or services.

Development is the application of research findings or other knowledge to a plan or design for the production of new or substantially improved materials, devices, products, processes, systems or services before the start of commercial production or use. *[IAS 38.8]*.

The standard gives the following examples of development activities:

(a) the design, construction and testing of pre-production or pre-use prototypes and models;

(b) the design of tools, jigs, moulds and dies involving new technology;

(c) the design, construction and operation of a pilot plant that is not of a scale economically feasible for commercial production; and

(d) the design, construction and testing of a chosen alternative for new or improved materials, devices, products, processes, systems or services. *[IAS 38.59]*.

6.2.1 Research phase

An entity cannot recognise an intangible asset arising from research or from the research phase of an internal project. Instead, any expenditure on research or the research phase of an internal project should be expensed as incurred because the entity cannot demonstrate that there is an intangible asset that will generate probable future economic benefits. *[IAS 38.54-55]*.

If an entity cannot distinguish the research phase from the development phase, it should treat the expenditure on that project as if it were incurred in the research phase only and recognise an expense accordingly. *[IAS 38.53]*.

6.2.2 Development phase

The standard requires recognition of an intangible asset arising from development (or the development phase of an internal project) while it imposes stringent conditions that restrict recognition. These tests create a balance, ensuring that the entity does not recognise unrecoverable costs as an asset.

An intangible asset arising from development or from the development phase of an internal project should be recognised if, and only if, an entity can demonstrate all of the following:

(a) the technical feasibility of completing the intangible asset so that it will be available for use or sale;

(b) its intention to complete the intangible asset and use or sell it;

(c) its ability to use or sell the intangible asset;

(d) how the intangible asset will generate probable future economic benefits. Among other things, the entity can demonstrate the existence of a market for the output of the intangible asset or the intangible asset itself or, if it is to be used internally, the usefulness of the intangible asset;

(e) the availability of adequate technical, financial and other resources to complete the development and to use or sell the intangible asset; and

(f) its ability to measure reliably the expenditure attributable to the intangible asset during its development. *[IAS 38.57]*.

The fact that an entity can demonstrate that the asset will generate probable future economic benefits distinguishes development activity from the research phase, where it is unlikely that such a demonstration would be possible. *[IAS 38.58]*.

It may be challenging to obtain objective evidence on each of the above conditions because:

- condition (b) relies on management intent;
- conditions (c), (e) and (f) are entity-specific (i.e. whether development expenditure meets any of these conditions depends both on the nature of the development activity itself and the financial position of the entity); and
- condition (d) above is more restrictive than is immediately apparent because the entity needs to assess the probable future economic benefits using the principles in IAS 36, i.e. using discounted cash flows. If the asset will generate economic benefits only in conjunction with other assets, the entity should apply the concept of cash-generating units. *[IAS 38.60]*. The application of IAS 36 is discussed in Chapter 20.

IAS 38 indicates that evidence may be available in the form of:
- a business plan showing the technical, financial and other resources needed and the entity's ability to secure those resources;
- a lender's indication of its willingness to fund the plan confirming the availability of external finance; *[IAS 38.61]* and
- detailed project information demonstrating that an entity's costing systems can measure reliably the cost of generating an intangible asset internally, such as salary and other expenditure incurred in securing copyrights or licences or developing computer software. *[IAS 38.62]*.

In any case, an entity should maintain books and records in sufficient detail that allow it to prove whether it meets the conditions set out by IAS 38.

Certain types of product (e.g. pharmaceuticals, aircraft and electrical equipment) require regulatory approval before they can be sold. Regulatory approval is not one of the criteria for recognition under IAS 38 and the standard does not prohibit an entity from capitalising its development costs in advance of approval. However, in some industries regulatory approval is vital to commercial success and its absence indicates significant uncertainty around the possible future economic benefits. This is the case in the pharmaceuticals industry, where it is rarely possible to determine whether a new drug will secure regulatory approval until it is actually granted. Accordingly, it is common practice in this industry for costs to be expensed until such approval is obtained. See Extract 17.7 and the discussion at 6.2.3 below.

The standard does not define the terms 'research phase' and 'development phase' but explains that they should be interpreted more broadly than 'research' and 'development' which it does define. *[IAS 38.52]*. The features characterising the research phase have less to do with what activities are performed, but relate more to an inability to demonstrate at that time that there is an intangible asset that will generate probable future benefits. *[IAS 38.55]*. This means that the research phase may include activities that do not necessarily meet the definition of 'research'. For example, the research phase for IAS 38 purposes may extend to the whole period preceding a product launch, regardless of the fact that activities that would otherwise characterise development are taking place at the same time, because certain features that would mean the project has entered its development phase are still absent (such as confirming an ability to use or sell the asset; demonstrating sufficient market demand for a product; or uncertainty regarding the source of funds to complete the project). As a result, an entity might not be able to distinguish the research phase from the development phase of an internal project to create an intangible asset, in which case it should treat the expenditure on that project as if it were incurred in the research phase only and recognise an expense accordingly. *[IAS 38.53]*. It also means that the development phase may include activities that do not necessarily meet the definition of 'development'. The example below illustrates how an entity would apply these rules in practice.

Example 17.6: Research phase and development phase under IAS 38

Entity K is working on a project to create a database containing images and articles from newspapers around the world, which it intends to sell to customers over the internet. K has identified the following stages in its project:

(a) Research stage – gaining the technical knowledge necessary to transfer images to customers and assessing whether the project is feasible from a technological point of view;

(b) Development stage – performing market analysis to identify potential demand and customer requirements; developing the ability to exploit the image capture technology including configuration of the required database software and acquiring the required data to populate the database, designing the customer interface and testing a prototype of the system; and

(c) Production stage – before and after the commercial launch of the service, debugging the system and improving functionality to service higher user volumes; updating and managing the database to ensure its currency.

The above can be summarised as follows:

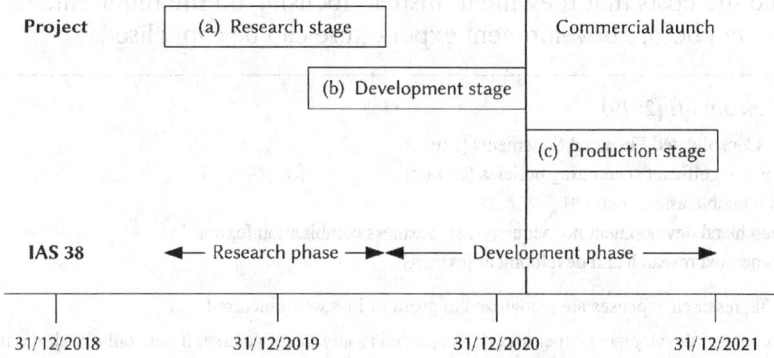

The activities in the research stage included under (a) meet the definition of research under IAS 38 and would be accounted for as part of the research phase of the project, as an expense.

The activities in the development stage included under (b) meet the definition of development under IAS 38. However, whilst K has started to plan the commercial exploitation of its image and data capture technology, it will not be immediately apparent that the project is economically viable. Until this point is reached, for example when the entity has established there is demand for the database and it is likely that a working prototype of the system will be available, the development activities cannot be distinguished from the research activities taking place at the same time. Accordingly, the initial development activities are accounted for as if they were incurred in the research phase. Only once it becomes possible to demonstrate the existence of an intangible asset that will generate future income streams, can project expenditure be accounted for under IAS 38 as part of the development phase.

There may be a period after the commercial launch of the service that would still be accounted for as part of the development phase. For example, activities to improve functionality to deal with higher actual customer volumes could constitute development. This does not necessarily mean that K can capitalise all this expenditure because it needs to pass the double hurdle of:

- the presumption in IAS 38.20 that 'there are no additions to such an asset or replacements of part of it'; and
- the six criteria in IAS 38.57 for recognition of development costs as an asset (see above).

Activity to ensure that the database is up-to-date is a routine process that does not involve major innovations or new technologies. Therefore, these activities in the production stage do not meet the definition of 'research' or 'development' and the related costs are recognised as an expense.

As the above example illustrates, the guidance in IAS 38 seems to take a somewhat restricted view as to how internally generated intangible assets are created and managed in practice, as well as the types of internally generated intangible assets. It requires activity to be classified into research and development phases, but this analysis does not easily fit with intangible assets that are created for use by the entity itself. The standard therefore does not address the everyday reality for software companies, television production companies, newspapers and data vendors that produce intangible assets in industrial-scale routine processes.

Many of the intangible assets produced in routine processes (e.g. software, television programmes, newspaper content and databases) meet the recognition criteria in the standard, but no specific guidance is available that could help an entity in dealing with the practical problems that arise when accounting for them.

Generally, entities disclose little detail of the nature of their research and development activities and the costs that they incur, instead focusing on the requirements of IAS 38 that must be met before development expenditure can be capitalised.

> Extract 17.6: Sanofi (2019)
> Notes to the Consolidated Financial Statements [extract]
> B/ Summary of significant accounting policies [extract]
> B.4. Other intangible assets [extract]
> B.4.1. Research and development not acquired in a business combination [extract]
> Internally generated research and development [extract]
>
> Under IAS 38, research expenses are recognized in profit or loss when incurred.
>
> Internally generated development expenses are recognized as an intangible asset if, and only if, all the following six criteria can be demonstrated: (a) the technical feasibility of completing the development project; (b) Sanofi's intention to complete the project; (c) Sanofi's ability to use the project; (d) the probability that the project will generate future economic benefits; (e) the availability of adequate technical, financial and other resources to complete the project; and (f) the ability to measure the development expenditure reliably.

The difficulty in applying the IAS 38 recognition criteria for development costs in the pharmaceutical industry are discussed further at 6.2.3 below. Technical and economic feasibility are typically established very late in the process of developing a new product, which means that usually only a small proportion of the development costs is capitalised.

When the development phase ends will also influence how the entity recognises revenue from the project. As noted at 4.4 above, during the development phase an entity can only recognise income from incidental operations, being those not necessary to develop the asset for its intended use, as revenue in profit or loss. [IAS 38.31]. During the phase in which the activity is necessary to bring the intangible asset into its intended use, any income should be deducted from the cost of the development asset. Examples include income from the sale of samples produced during the testing of a new process or from the sale of a production prototype. Only once it is determined that the intangible asset is ready for its intended use would revenue be recognised from such activities. At the same time capitalisation of costs would cease and the related costs of the revenue generating activity would include a measure of amortisation of the asset.

6.2.3 Research and development in the pharmaceutical industry

Entities in the pharmaceutical industry consider research and development to be of primary importance to their business. Consequently, these entities spend a considerable amount on research and development every year and one might expect them to carry significant internally generated development intangible assets on their statement of financial position. However, their financial statements reveal that they often consider the uncertainties in the development of pharmaceuticals to be too great to permit capitalisation of development costs.

One of the problems is that, in the case of true 'development' activities in the pharmaceutical industry, the final outcome can be uncertain and the technical and economic feasibility of new products or processes is typically established very late in the development phase, which means that only a small proportion of the total development costs can ever be capitalised. In particular, many products and processes require approval by a regulator such as the US Food and Drug Administration (FDA) before they can be applied commercially and until that time the entity may be uncertain of their success. After approval, of course, there is often relatively little in the way of further development expenditure.

In the pharmaceutical sector, the capitalisation of development costs for new products or processes usually begins at the date on which the product or process receives regulatory approval. In most cases that is the point when the IAS 38 criteria for recognition of intangible assets are met. It is unlikely that these criteria will have been met before approval is granted by the regulator.

Extracts 17.7 and 17.8 below illustrate some of the difficulty in applying the IAS 38 recognition criteria for development costs in the pharmaceutical industry.

Extract 17.7: MERCK Kommanditgesellschaft auf Aktien (2018)

Notes to the Consolidated Financial Statements [extract]

(55) Research and development costs

Research and development costs comprise the costs of research and development departments, the expenses incurred as a result of research and development collaborations as well as the costs of clinical trials in the Healthcare business sector (both before and after approval is granted).

The costs of research cannot be capitalized and are expensed in full in the period in which they are incurred. As internally generated intangible assets, it is necessary to capitalize development expenses if the cost of the internally generated intangible asset can be reliably determined and the asset can be expected to lead to future economic benefits. The condition for this is that the necessary resources are available for the development of the asset, technical feasibility of the asset is given, its completion and use are intended, and marketability is given. Owing to the high risks up to the time that pharmaceutical products are approved, these criteria are not met in the Healthcare business sector regarding the development of drug candidates. Costs incurred after regulatory approval were insignificant and were therefore not recognized as intangible assets. In the Life Science and Performance Materials business sectors, development expenses are capitalized as soon as the aforementioned criteria have been met. Provided the relevant criteria set forth in IAS 38 are fulfilled, software development costs are capitalized.

Reimbursements for R&D are offset against research and development costs.

> *Extract 17.8: Bayer Aktiengesellschaft (2018)*
>
> **B Consolidated Financial Statements** [extract]
>
> Notes to the Consolidated Financial Statements of the Bayer Group [extract]
>
> 3 Basic principles, methods and critical accounting estimates [extract]
>
> **Research and development expenses**
>
> For accounting purposes, research expenses are defined as costs incurred for current or planned investigations undertaken with the prospect of gaining new scientific or technical knowledge and understanding. Development expenses are defined as costs incurred for the application of research findings or specialist knowledge to plans or designs for the production, provision or development of new or substantially improved products, services or processes, respectively, prior to the commencement of commercial production or use. Research and development (R&D) expenses are incurred in the Bayer Group for in-house R&D activities as well as numerous research and development collaborations and alliances with third parties. R&D expenses mainly comprise the costs for active ingredient discovery, clinical studies, research and development activities in the areas of application technology and engineering, field trials, regulatory approvals and approval extensions.
>
> Research costs cannot be capitalized. The conditions for capitalization of development costs are closely defined: a key precondition for recognition of an intangible asset is that it is sufficiently certain that the development activity will generate future cash flows that will cover the associated development costs. Since our own development projects are often subject to regulatory approval procedures and other uncertainties, the conditions for the capitalization of costs incurred before receipt of approvals are not normally satisfied. In the case of R&D collaborations, a distinction is generally made between payments on contract signature, upfront payments, milestone payments and cost reimbursements for work performed. If an intangible asset (such as the right to the use of an active ingredient) is acquired in connection with any of these payment obligations, the respective payment is capitalized even if it is uncertain whether further development work will ultimately lead to the production of a saleable product. Reimbursements of the cost of R&D work are recognized in profit or loss, except where they are required to be capitalized.

6.2.4 Internally generated brands, mastheads, publishing titles and customer lists

IAS 38 considers internally generated brands, mastheads, publishing titles, customer lists and items similar in substance to be indistinguishable from the cost of developing a business as a whole so it prohibits their recognition. *[IAS 38.63-64]*. As discussed at 3.3 above, the same applies to subsequent expenditures incurred in connection with such intangible assets even when originally acquired externally. *[IAS 38.20]*. For example, expenditure incurred in redesigning the layout of newspapers or magazines, which represent subsequent expenditure on publishing titles and mastheads, should not be capitalised.

6.2.5 Website costs (SIC-32)

SIC-32 clarifies how IAS 38 applies to costs in relation to websites designed for use by the entity in its business. An entity's own website that arises from development and is for internal or external access is an internally generated intangible asset under the standard. *[SIC-32.7]*. A website designed for external access may be used for various purposes such as to promote and advertise an entity's own products and services, provide electronic services to customers, and sell products and services. A website may be used within the entity to give staff access to company policies and customer details, and allow them to search relevant information. *[SIC-32.1]*.

SIC-32 does not apply to items that are accounted for under another standard, such as the development or operation of a website (or website software) for sale to another entity

(IAS 2 and IFRS 15); acquiring or developing hardware supporting a website (IAS 16); or a website (or website software) subject to a leasing arrangement (IFRS 16). *[SIC-32.5-6]*.

Under SIC-32, an intangible asset should be recognised for website development costs if and only if, it meets the general recognition requirements in IAS 38 (see 3.1 above) and the six conditions for recognition as development costs (see 6.2.2 above). Most important of these is the requirement to demonstrate how the website will generate probable future economic benefits. *[SIC-32.8]*. The Interpretation deems an entity unable to demonstrate this for a website developed solely or primarily for promoting and advertising its own products and services. All expenditure on developing such a website should be recognised as an expense when incurred. Accordingly, it is unlikely that costs will be eligible for capitalisation unless an entity can demonstrate that the website is used directly in the income-generating process, for example where customers can place orders on the entity's website. *[SIC-32.8]*.

The following stages of a website's development are identified by the interpretation: *[SIC-32.2, 9]*

(a) *planning* includes undertaking feasibility studies, defining objectives and specifications, evaluating alternatives and selecting preferences. Expenditures incurred in this stage are similar in nature to the research phase and should be recognised as an expense when they are incurred;

(b) *application and infrastructure development* includes obtaining a domain name, purchasing and developing hardware and operating software, installing developed applications and stress testing. The requirements of IAS 16 are applied to expenditure on physical assets. Other costs are recognised as an expense, unless they can be directly attributed, or allocated on a reasonable and consistent basis, to preparing the website for its intended use and the project to develop the website meets the SIC-32 criteria for recognition as an intangible asset;

(c) *graphical design development* includes designing the appearance of web pages. Costs incurred at this stage should be accounted for in the same way as expenditure incurred in the 'application and infrastructure development' stage described under (b) above;

(d) *content development* includes creating, purchasing, preparing and uploading information, either textual or graphical in nature, on the website before the completion of the website's development. The costs of content developed to advertise and promote an entity's own products and services are always expensed as incurred. Other costs incurred in this stage should be recognised as an expense unless the criteria for recognition as an asset described in (b) above are satisfied; and

(e) the *operating stage*, which starts after completion of the development of a website, when an entity maintains and enhances the applications, infrastructure, graphical design and content of the website. *[SIC-32.3]*. Expenditure incurred in this stage should be expensed as incurred unless it meets the asset recognition criteria in IAS 38.

In making these assessments, the entity should evaluate the nature of each activity for which expenditure is incurred, independently of its consideration of the website's stage of development. *[SIC-32.9]*. This means that even where a project has been determined to qualify for recognition as an intangible asset, not all costs incurred in relation to a qualifying stage of development are eligible for capitalisation. For example, whilst the direct costs of developing an online ordering system might qualify for recognition as an asset, the costs of training staff to operate that system should be expensed because training costs are deemed not necessary to creating, producing or preparing the website for it to be capable of operating (see 6.3 above). *[IAS 38.67]*. Examples of other costs that would be recognised as an expense regardless of the stage of the project are given in the Illustrative Example to SIC-32, including:

(a) selling, administrative and other general overhead expenditure unless it can be directly attributed to preparing the web site for use to operate in the manner intended by management;

(b) clearly identified inefficiencies in the project, such as those relating to alternative solutions explored and rejected; and

(c) initial operating losses incurred before the web site achieves planned performance.

A website qualifying for recognition as an intangible asset should be measured after initial recognition by applying the cost model or the revaluation model in IAS 38 as discussed at 8.1 and 8.2 below. In respect of the useful life of website assets, the expectation is that it should be short. *[SIC-32.10]*.

The criteria for recognition as an asset are restrictive. On-line fashion retailer, ASOS, does not capitalise website development costs, as demonstrated in the extract below.

Extract 17.9: ASOS Plc (2019)

Notes to the Financial Statements

For the year to 31 August 2019 [extract]

24 ACCOUNTING POLICIES [extract]

Additional accounting policy information [extract]

j) Other intangible assets [extract]

The cost of acquiring and developing software that is not integral to the related hardware is capitalised separately as an intangible asset. This does not include internal website development and maintenance costs, which are expensed as incurred unless representing a technological advance leading to future economic benefit. Capitalised software costs include external direct costs of material and services and the payroll and payroll-related costs for employees who are directly associated with the project.

6.2.6 Agile software development

A similar assessment process to that discussed in 6.2.5 above needs to be undertaken in accounting for agile software development, where there are similar challenges in determining whether expenditures should be recognised as an intangible asset or be expensed as incurred. Agile software development also has further complexities that must be carefully considered, for example;

- it is difficult to determine a relevant unit of account (i.e. is the unit of account the entire suite of software applications, individual applications, functional elements, or lines of code);

- an entity may not have clear budgets for its agile software development, so there is an increased risk of incorrectly recognising inefficiencies and cost overruns as part of the resulting intangible asset;

- it can be difficult to maintain the appropriate balance between capitalising new development costs, derecognising past development costs, and determining the amortisation period of the asset; and
- some of the steps in the continuous update process applied in agile software development are more akin to maintenance and should therefore be expensed as incurred.

6.3 Cost of an internally generated intangible asset

On initial recognition, an intangible asset should be measured at cost, *[IAS 38.24]*, which the standard defines as the amount of cash or cash equivalents paid or the fair value of other consideration given to acquire an asset at the time of its acquisition or construction. When applicable, cost is the amount attributed to that asset when initially recognised in accordance with the specific requirements of other IFRSs, e.g. IFRS 2. *[IAS 38.8]*. It is important to ensure that cost includes only the expenditure incurred after the recognition criteria are met and to confirm that only costs directly related to the creation of the asset are capitalised.

6.3.1 Establishing the time from which costs can be capitalised

The cost of an internally generated intangible asset is the sum of the expenditure incurred from the date when the intangible asset first meets the recognition criteria of the standard, *[IAS 38.65]*, and meets the detailed conditions for recognition of development phase costs as an asset (see 6.2.2 above).

Costs incurred before these criteria are met are expensed, *[IAS 38.68]*, and cannot be reinstated retrospectively, *[IAS 38.65]*, because IAS 38 does not permit recognition of past expenses as an intangible asset at a later date. *[IAS 38.71]*.

The following example, which is taken from IAS 38, illustrates how these above rules should be applied in practice.

Example 17.7: Recognition of internally generated intangible assets

An entity is developing a new production process. During 2020, expenditure incurred was €1,000, of which €900 was incurred before 1 December 2020 and €100 was incurred between 1 December 2020 and 31 December 2020. The entity is able to demonstrate that, at 1 December 2020, the production process met the criteria for recognition as an intangible asset. The recoverable amount of the know-how embodied in the process (including future cash outflows to complete the process before it is available for use) is estimated to be €500.

At the end of 2020, the production process is recognised as an intangible asset at a cost of €100 (expenditure incurred since the date when the recognition criteria were met, that is, 1 December 2020). The €900 expenditure incurred before 1 December 2020 is recognised as an expense because the recognition criteria were not met until 1 December 2020. This expenditure does not form part of the cost of the production process recognised in the statement of financial position.

During 2021, expenditure incurred is €2,000. At the end of 2021, the recoverable amount of the know-how embodied in the process (including future cash outflows to complete the process before it is available for use) is estimated to be €1,900.

At the end of 2021, the cost of the production process is €2,100 (€100 expenditure recognised at the end of 2020 plus €2,000 expenditure recognised in 2021). The entity recognises an impairment loss of €200 to adjust the carrying amount of the process before impairment loss (€2,100) to its recoverable amount (€1,900). This impairment loss will be reversed in a subsequent period if the requirements for the reversal of an impairment loss in IAS 36 are met.

6.3.2 Determining the costs eligible for capitalisation

The cost of an internally generated intangible asset comprises all directly attributable costs necessary to create, produce, and prepare the asset to be capable of operating in the manner intended by management. Examples of directly attributable costs are:

(a) costs of materials and services used or consumed in generating the intangible asset;

(b) costs of employee benefits arising from the generation of the intangible asset;

(c) fees to register a legal right;

(d) amortisation of patents and licences that are used to generate the intangible asset; and

(e) borrowing costs that meet the criteria under IAS 23 for recognition as an element of cost. *[IAS 38.66]*.

Indirect costs and general overheads, even if they can be allocated on a reasonable and consistent basis to the development project, cannot be recognised as part of the cost of any intangible asset. The standard also specifically prohibits recognition of the following items as a component of cost:

(a) selling, administrative and other general overhead expenditure unless this expenditure can be directly attributed to preparing the asset for use;

(b) identified inefficiencies and initial operating losses incurred before the asset achieves planned performance; and

(c) expenditure on training staff to operate the asset. *[IAS 38.67]*.

For these purposes it does not make any difference whether the costs are incurred directly by the entity or relate to services provided by third parties.

7 RECOGNITION OF AN EXPENSE

Unless expenditure is incurred in connection with an item that meets the criteria for recognition as an intangible asset, and is an eligible component of cost, it should be expensed. The only exception is in connection with a business combination, where the cost of an item that cannot be recognised as an intangible asset will form part of the carrying amount of goodwill at the acquisition date. *[IAS 38.68]*.

Some of the ineligible components of cost are identified at 4.3 and 6.3 above and include costs that are not directly related to the creation of the asset, such as costs of introducing a new product or costs incurred to redeploy an asset. IAS 38 provides other examples of expenditure that is recognised as an expense when incurred:

(a) start-up costs, unless they qualify for recognition as part of the cost of property, plant and equipment under IAS 16 (see Chapter 18). Start-up costs recognised as an expense may consist of establishment costs such as legal and secretarial costs incurred in setting up a legal entity, expenditure to open a new facility or business or expenditures for starting new operations or launching new products or processes;

(b) training costs;

(c) advertising and promotional activities (including mail order catalogues); and

(d) relocation or reorganisation costs. *[IAS 38.69]*.

For these purposes no distinction is made between costs that are incurred directly by the entity and those that relate to services provided by third parties. However, the standard does not prevent an entity from recording a prepayment if it pays for the delivery of goods before obtaining a right to access those goods. Similarly, a prepayment can be recognised when payment is made before the services are received. *[IAS 38.70]*.

In March 2020 the Interpretations Committee considered whether training costs to fulfil a contract should be recognised as an asset or expensed. The costs in the fact pattern submitted to the Committee were those incurred to train an entity's employees so that they understand the customer's equipment and processes. The Committee noted that paragraph 69(b) of IAS 38 includes expenditure on training activities as an example of expenditure that is incurred to provide future economic benefits to an entity, but no intangible asset or other asset is acquired or created that can be recognised. Consequently, paragraph 69 states that such expenditure on training activities is recognised as an expense when incurred. Paragraph 15 of IAS 38 explains that an entity usually has insufficient control over the expected future economic benefits arising from a team of skilled staff and from training for these items to meet the definition of an intangible asset. In addition, in explaining the requirements in IFRS 15 regarding costs to fulfil a contract, paragraph BC307 of IFRS 15 states that 'if the other Standards preclude the recognition of any asset arising from a particular cost, an asset cannot then be recognised under IFRS 15'. Accordingly, the Committee concluded that, in the fact pattern submitted, the entity recognises the training costs to fulfil the contract with the customer as an expense when incurred. The Committee noted that the entity's ability to charge to the customer the costs of training does not affect that conclusion.[5] This issue is discussed in more detail in Chapter 31 at 5.2.

7.1 Catalogues and other advertising costs

The Board considers that advertising and promotional activities do not qualify for recognition as an intangible asset because their purpose is to enhance or create internally generated brands or customer relationships, which themselves cannot be recognised as intangible assets. *[IAS 38.BC46B]*. An entity has a different asset, a prepayment, if it has paid for goods or services before they are provided, as described above. However, the Board did not believe this justified an asset being recognised beyond the point at which the entity gained the right to access the related goods or received the related services. *[IAS 38.BC46D]*. Entities cannot, therefore maintain a prepayment asset and defer recognising an expense in the period between receiving the material from a supplier and delivery to its customers or potential customers. *[IAS 38.BC46E]*.

Accordingly, the IASB is deliberate in using the phrase 'obtaining the right to access those goods' when it defines the point that an expense is recognised. This is because the date of physical delivery could be altered without affecting the substance of the commercial arrangement with the supplier. *[IAS 38.BC46E]*. Recognition is determined by the point when the goods have been constructed by the supplier in accordance with the terms of the customer contract and the entity could demand delivery in return for payment. *[IAS 38.69A]*. Therefore an entity must recognise an expense for customer catalogues once they are ready for delivery from the printer, even if the entity has arranged for the printer to send catalogues directly to customers when advised by the entity's sales department. Similarly in the case of services, an expense is recognised when those services are received by the entity, and not deferred until the entity uses them in the delivery of another service, for example, to deliver an advertisement to its customers. *[IAS 38.69A].*

The Board rejected calls to make a special case for mail order catalogues, where it was argued that they created a distribution network, on the grounds that their primary objective was to advertise goods to customers. *[IAS 38.BC46G].* For this reason the wording in the standard cites mail order catalogues as an example of expenditure on advertising and promotional activities that is recognised as an expense. *[IAS 38.69].*

Standard marketing activities may consist of mailings, advertisements in print media, TV and a continuous internet presence. The respective contractual agreements usually include a clearly identifiable service or asset and include only advertising and promotional costs. As discussed above, the costs must be expensed when the goods or services are received. However, the timing of the receipt of the goods and services may be unclear, particularly in situations where multiple suppliers are used to deliver the marketing activity. For example, where an entity engages an advertising agency to conceptualise a television, radio or print media advertisement, but also engages other parties to produce the material. An entity will need to carefully examine such arrangements to determine when it obtains the right to access to the goods and services provided by the respective party(ies) to determine when the cost should be expensed.

Advertising and promotional activities can take a number of different forms, encompassing multiple rights and obligations. For example, some sponsorship arrangements may include separable rights that are not advertising and promotional costs, such as exclusive distribution rights of products at an event or in a location, or the right to use the logo of the event. Providing the recognition criteria in IAS 38 are met, these rights may be eligible to be recognised as an intangible asset. Entities need to consider in each case what service or right is being received, together with when the payments are made and, in some circumstances, it may be appropriate to recognise a prepayment or intangible asset for those expenditures.

Some companies use celebrities (e.g. athletes, models and actors) to promote their brands and products. Contracts often cover a term of several years and may contain multiple performance obligations for the celebrity and several different payment obligations for the company. Entities will need to apply judgement and consider the facts and circumstances of each contract to determine whether it has received the services at a point in time or whether there is an ongoing performance for which an intangible asset should be recognised.

Some companies, especially in the food and beverages and personal care sector, provide their customers with marketing and promotional materials ranging from samples (e.g. small perfume bottles that are distributed for free to the end customers) to long-lived assets (e.g. large umbrellas with the logo of the beverage brand used in garden restaurants or large advertising signs). These costs are usually expensed when the company has a right to access those goods (not when they are distributed to customers), as it does not get any benefit from them other than marketing and brand promotion.

8 MEASUREMENT AFTER INITIAL RECOGNITION

IAS 38, in common with a number of other standards, provides an entity the option to choose between two alternative treatments: *[IAS 38.72]*

- the *cost model*, which requires measurement at cost less any accumulated amortisation and any accumulated impairment losses; *[IAS 38.74]* or
- the *revaluation model*, which requires measurement at a revalued amount, being its fair value at the date of the revaluation, less any subsequent accumulated amortisation and any subsequent accumulated impairment losses. *[IAS 38.75]*.

The revaluation option is only available if there is an active market for the intangible asset. *[IAS 38.75, 81-82]*. Active market is defined by IFRS 13; see Chapter 14 at 3. There are no provisions in IAS 38 that allow fair value to be determined indirectly, for example by using the techniques and financial models applied to estimate the fair value of intangible assets acquired in a business combination. Therefore, in accordance with IFRS 13, an entity must measure the fair value of an intangible under the revaluation model using the price in an active market for an identical asset, i.e. a Level 1 price. For further guidance on the price in an active market, see Chapter 14 at 17. If an entity chooses an accounting policy to measure an intangible asset at revalued amount, it must apply the revaluation model to all the assets in that class, unless there is no active market for those other assets. *[IAS 38.72]*. A class of intangible assets is a grouping of assets of a similar nature and use in an entity's operations. *[IAS 38.73]*. Examples of separate classes of intangible asset include:

(a) brand names;
(b) mastheads and publishing titles;
(c) computer software;
(d) licences and franchises;
(e) copyrights, patents and other industrial property rights, service and operating rights;
(f) recipes, formulae, models, designs and prototypes; and
(g) intangible assets under development. *[IAS 38.119]*.

The standard requires assets in the same class to be revalued at the same time, as to do otherwise would allow selective revaluation of assets and the reporting of a mixture of costs and values as at different dates within the same asset class. *[IAS 38.73]*.

8.1 Cost model for measurement of intangible assets

Under the cost model, after initial recognition, the carrying amount of an intangible asset is its cost less any accumulated amortisation and accumulated impairment losses. *[IAS 38.74]*. The rules on amortisation of intangible assets are discussed at 9.2 and 9.3 below; and impairment is discussed at 9.4 below.

8.2 Revaluation model for measurement of intangible assets

An entity can only apply the revaluation model if the fair value can be determined by reference to an active market. *[IAS 38.75, 81-82]*. An active market will rarely exist for intangible assets (see 8.2.1 below). *[IAS 38.78]*.

After initial recognition an intangible asset should be carried at a revalued amount, which is its fair value at the date of the revaluation less any subsequent accumulated amortisation and any subsequent accumulated impairment losses. *[IAS 38.75]*. To prevent an entity from circumventing the recognition rules of the standard, the revaluation model does not allow:

- the revaluation of intangible assets that have not previously been recognised as assets; or
- the initial recognition of intangible assets at amounts other than cost. *[IAS 38.76]*.

These rules are designed to prevent an entity from recognising at a 'revalued' amount an intangible asset that was never recorded because its costs were expensed as they did not at the time meet the recognition rules. As noted at 6.3.1 above, IAS 38 does not permit recognition of past expenses as an intangible asset at a later date. *[IAS 38.71]*.

However, it is permitted to apply the revaluation model to the whole of an intangible asset even if only part of its cost was originally recognised as an asset because it did not meet the criteria for recognition until part of the way through the process. *[IAS 38.77]*. Since the prohibition on initial recognition of intangible assets at amounts other than cost would also prevent the revaluation of quotas and permits allocated by governments and similar bodies – which are amongst the few intangible assets that do have an active market – the standard specifically makes an exception and allows the revaluation model to be applied to 'an intangible asset that was received by way of a government grant and recognised at a nominal amount'. *[IAS 38.77]*.

The example below illustrates how this would work in practice.

Example 17.8: Application of revaluation model to intangible assets that are partially recognised or received by way of government grant

Entity C spent €12,000,000 in preparing its application for a number of taxi licences, which it expensed because of the uncertain outcome of the process. The application was successful and C was granted a number of freely transferable taxi licences and paid a nominal registration fee of €50,000, which it recognised as an asset. There is an active and liquid market in these taxi licences.

C can apply the revaluation model under IAS 38 to these taxi licences, because it previously recognised the licence (even if it only recognised part of the costs as an asset) and there is an active market in these licences.

Entity D obtained a number of freely transferable fishing quotas free of charge, which it recognised at a nominal amount as permitted under IAS 20. There is an active and liquid market in these quotas.

D can apply the revaluation model under IAS 38 to these fishing quotas, because it previously recognised the quota (even if it only recognised it at a nominal amount) and there is an active market in these quotas.

8.2.1 Revaluation is only allowed if there is an active market

An entity can only elect to apply the revaluation model if the fair value can be determined by reference to an active market for the intangible asset. *[IAS 38.81-82]*. An active market is defined in IFRS 13 as one in which transactions for the item take place with sufficient frequency and volume to provide pricing information on an ongoing basis. *[IFRS 13 Appendix A]*.

Few intangible assets will be eligible for revaluation and indeed the standard concedes that such an active market would be uncommon. Nevertheless, in some jurisdictions, an active market may exist for freely transferable taxi licences, fishing licences or production quotas. *[IAS 38.78]*. However, by their very nature most intangible assets are unique or entity-specific. The standard lists brands, newspaper mastheads, music and film publishing rights, patents or trademarks as items that are ineligible for revaluation because each such asset is unique. *[IAS 38.78]*. The existence of a previous sale and purchase transaction is not sufficient evidence for the market to be regarded as active because of the requirement in the definition for a sufficient frequency and volume of transactions to allow the provision of ongoing pricing information. The standard notes that where contracts are negotiated between individual buyers and sellers or when transactions are relatively infrequent, the price of a previous transaction for one intangible asset may not provide sufficient evidence of the fair value of another. In addition, if prices are not available to the public, this is taken as evidence that an active market does not exist. *[IAS 38.78]*.

An entity should stop revaluing an asset if the market used to determine its fair value ceases to meet the criteria for an active market. The valuation is 'frozen' from that date, and reduced thereafter by subsequent amortisation and any subsequent impairment losses. *[IAS 38.82]*. The IASB believes that the disappearance of a previously active market may indicate that the asset needs to be tested for impairment in accordance with IAS 36. *[IAS 38.83]*.

If an active market for the previously revalued asset emerges at a later date, the entity is required to apply the revaluation model from that date. *[IAS 38.84]*.

8.2.2 Frequency of revaluations

IAS 38 requires revaluations to be performed 'with such regularity that at the end of the reporting period the carrying amount of the asset does not differ materially from its fair value'. *[IAS 38.75]*. The standard lets entities judge for themselves the frequency of revaluations depending on the volatility of the fair values of the underlying intangible assets. Significant and volatile movements in fair value would necessitate annual revaluation, whereas a less frequent update would be required for intangibles whose price is subject only to insignificant movements. *[IAS 38.79]*. Nevertheless, since an entity can only revalue assets for which a price is quoted in an active market, there should be no impediment to updating that valuation at each reporting date. As noted above, when an entity has a number of items in the same class of intangible assets, the standard requires that they are all valued at the same time. *[IAS 38.73]*.

8.2.3 Accounting for revaluations

Increases in an intangible asset's carrying amount as a result of a revaluation should be credited to other comprehensive income under the heading of revaluation surplus, except to the extent that the revaluation reverses a revaluation decrease of the same asset that was previously recognised in profit or loss. *[IAS 38.85]*. Conversely, decreases in an intangible asset's carrying amount as a result of a revaluation should be recognised in profit or loss, unless the decrease reverses an earlier upward revaluation, in which case the decrease should first be recognised in other comprehensive income to extinguish

1336 Chapter 17

the revaluation surplus in respect of the asset. *[IAS 38.86]*. The example below illustrates how this works.

Example 17.9:   Accounting for upward and downward revaluations

Entity E acquired an intangible asset that it accounts for under the revaluation model. The fair value of the asset changes as follows:

	£	£ Change
Acquisition	530	–
Date A	550	+20
Date B	520	–30
Date C	510	–10
Date D	555	+45

The table below shows how entity E should account for the upward and downward revaluations.

	Value of asset	Cumulative revaluation reserve	Revaluation recognised in other comprehensive income	Revaluation recognised in profit or loss
	£	£	£	£
Acquisition	530	–	–	–
Date A	550	20	20	–
Date B	520	–	(20)	(10)
Date C	510	–	–	(10)
Date D	555	25	25	20

The diagram below summarises this information (the impact of amortisation on the carrying amount and revaluation surplus has been ignored in this example for the sake of simplicity).

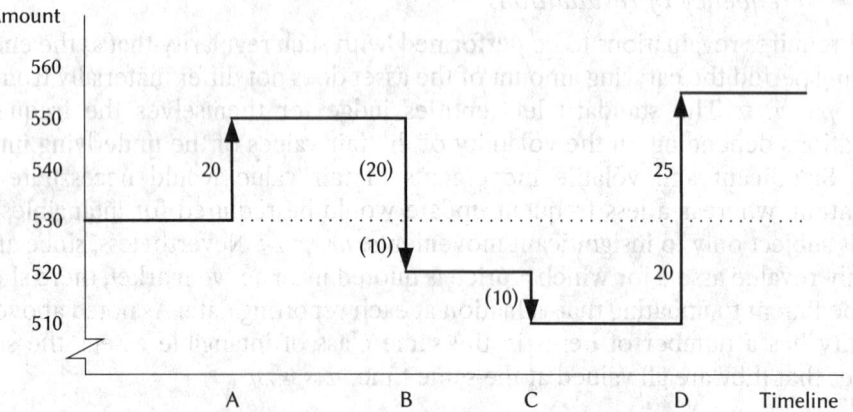

The upward revaluation at Date A is accounted for in other comprehensive income. The downward revaluation at Date B first reduces the revaluation reserve for that asset to nil and the excess of £10 is recognised as a loss in profit or loss. The second downward revaluation at Date C is recognised as a loss in profit or loss. The upward revaluation at Date D first reverses the cumulative loss recognised in profit or loss and the excess is accounted for in other comprehensive income.

In the example above, the impact of amortisation on the carrying amount of the assets and the revaluation surplus was ignored for the sake of simplicity. However, the cumulative revaluation surplus included in other comprehensive income may be transferred directly to retained earnings when the surplus is realised, which happens either on the retirement or disposal of the asset, or as the asset is used by the entity. *[IAS 38.87]*. In the latter case, the amount of the surplus regarded as realised is the amount of amortisation in excess of what would have been charged based on the asset's historical cost. *[IAS 38.87]*. See Chapter 18 at 6.2 for an example. In practice this means two things:

- an entity applying the revaluation model would need to track both the historical cost and revalued amount of an asset to determine how much of the revaluation surplus has been realised; and
- any revaluation surplus is amortised over the life of the related asset. Therefore, in the case of a significant downward revaluation there is a smaller revaluation surplus available against which the downward revaluation can be offset before recognition in the statement of profit or loss.

The transfer from revaluation surplus to retained earnings is not made through profit or loss. *[IAS 38.87]*. It is not the same as recycling a gain or loss previously recognised in other comprehensive income. Accordingly, the transfer will appear as a line item in the Statement of Changes in Equity rather than in other comprehensive income.

When an intangible asset is revalued, the carrying amount of that asset is adjusted to the revalued amount. At the date of the revaluation, the asset is treated in one of the following ways:

(a) the gross carrying amount is adjusted in a manner that is consistent with the revaluation of the carrying amount of the asset. For example, the gross carrying amount may be restated by reference to observable market data or it may be restated proportionately to the change in the carrying amount. The accumulated amortisation at the date of the revaluation is adjusted to equal the difference between the gross carrying amount and the carrying amount of the asset after taking into account accumulated impairment losses; or

(b) the accumulated amortisation is eliminated against the gross carrying amount of the asset. *[IAS 38.80]*.

The example below illustrates how the adjustments are calculated.

Example 17.10: Restatement of accumulated amortisation after a revaluation

Entity F revalued an intangible asset from its carrying amount of £120 to its fair value of £150. The gross carrying amount is adjusted to £345 by reference to the observable market data. The adjustment is in a manner consistent with the revaluation of the intangible asset. Under the observable market data approach (in the column, approach (a)), the accumulated depreciation is adjusted to £195, which is the difference between the gross revalued amount of £345 and the net revalued amount of £150. The proportionate restatement approach (in the column, approach (b)) leads to grossing up of both gross carrying amount and the accumulated amortisation. The elimination approach (in the column, approach (c)) results in elimination of the accumulated amortisation.

	Before revaluation	After revaluation		
		Observable market data (a)	Proportionate restatement (b)	Eliminating amortisation (c)
	£	£	£	£
Gross carrying amount	300	345	375	150
Accumulated amortisation	(180)	(195)	(225)	–
Net carrying amount	120	150	150	150

9 AMORTISATION OF INTANGIBLE ASSETS

9.1 Assessing the useful life of an intangible asset as finite or indefinite

IAS 38 defines the useful life of an intangible asset as:

(a) the period over which an asset is expected to be available for use by an entity; or

(b) the number of production or similar units expected to be obtained from the asset by an entity. *[IAS 38.8]*.

The standard requires an entity to assess whether the useful life of an intangible asset is finite or indefinite. *[IAS 38.88]*. An intangible asset with a finite useful life is amortised over its useful life or the number of production units (or similar units) constituting that useful life, whereas an intangible asset with an indefinite useful life is not amortised. *[IAS 38.89]*.

The standard requires an intangible asset to be classified as having an indefinite useful life 'when, based on an analysis of all of the relevant factors, there is no foreseeable limit to the period over which the asset is expected to generate net cash inflows for the entity'. *[IAS 38.88]*. Therefore, for this purpose the term 'indefinite' does not mean 'infinite'. *[IAS 38.91]*.

Entities should not confuse the absence of a foreseeable limit to an asset's life with an ability to renew, refresh or upgrade an asset to ensure it continues to generate future cash flows. Some intangible assets are based on legal rights that are conveyed in perpetuity rather than for finite terms, whether or not those terms are renewable. If the cash flows are expected to continue indefinitely, the useful life is indefinite. *[IAS 38.BC62]*.

An important underlying assumption in making the assessment of the useful life of an intangible asset is that it 'reflects only that level of future maintenance expenditure required to maintain the asset at its standard of performance assessed at the time of estimating the asset's useful life, and the entity's ability and intention to reach such a level. A conclusion that the useful life of an intangible asset is indefinite should not depend on planned future expenditure in excess of that required to maintain the asset at that standard of performance.' *[IAS 38.91]*. Determining exactly what constitutes the level of expenditure 'required to maintain the asset at that standard of performance' is a matter of judgement. However, a clear distinction exists between this type of expenditure and costs that might be incurred to renew, refresh or upgrade an asset to ensure it continues to generate future cash flows. Expenditure to ensure that an intangible asset does not become obsolete is not the type of maintenance expenditure that, though very necessary to ensure continuing future cash flows, would be indicative of an indefinite life. Indeed, the standard asserts that assets subject to technological change would be expected to have a short useful life. *[IAS 38.92]*.

9.1.1 Factors affecting the useful life

The standard identifies a number of factors that may affect the useful life of an intangible asset:

(a) the expected usage of the asset by the entity and whether the asset could be managed efficiently by another management team;

(b) typical product life cycles for the asset and public information on estimates of useful lives of similar assets that are used in a similar way;

(c) technical, technological, commercial or other types of obsolescence;

(d) the stability of the industry in which the asset operates and changes in the market demand for the products or services output from the asset;
(e) expected actions by competitors or potential competitors;
(f) the level of maintenance expenditure required to obtain the expected future economic benefits from the asset and the entity's ability and intention to reach such a level;
(g) the period of control over the asset and legal or similar limits on the use of the asset, such as the expiry dates of related leases, discussed further at 9.1.2 below; and
(h) whether the useful life of the asset is dependent on the useful life of other assets of the entity. *[IAS 38.90]*.

The standard explicitly warns against both:

- overestimating the useful life of an intangible asset. For example, a history of rapid changes in technology means that the useful lives of computer software and many other intangible assets that are susceptible to technological obsolescence will be short; *[IAS 38.92]* and
- underestimating the useful life. Whilst uncertainty justifies estimating the useful life of an intangible asset on a prudent basis, it does not justify choosing a life that is unrealistically short. *[IAS 38.93]*.

Where an intangible asset is acquired in a business combination, but the acquiring entity does not intend to use it to generate future cash flows, it is unlikely that it could have anything other than a finite useful life. Indeed, whilst in our view an entity would not recognise an immediate impairment loss on acquisition, the estimated useful life of the asset is likely to be relatively short (see Chapter 9 at 5.5.6).

The following examples, based on those in IAS 38's Illustrative Examples, show how some of the features that affect the useful life are taken into account in assessing that life.

Example 17.11: Assessing the useful life of an intangible asset

Acquired customer list

A direct-mail marketing company acquires a customer list and expects that it will be able to derive benefit from the information on the list for at least one year, but no more than three years.

The customer list would be amortised over management's best estimate of its useful life, say 18 months. Although the direct-mail marketing company may intend to add customer names and other information to the list in the future, the expected benefits of the acquired customer list relate only to the customers on that list at the date it was acquired. The customer list also would be reviewed for indicators of impairment in accordance with IAS 36 at the end of each reporting period. *[IAS 36.9]*.

An acquired trademark used to identify and distinguish a leading consumer product that has been a market-share leader for the past eight years

The trademark has a remaining legal life of five years but is renewable every 10 years at little cost. The acquiring entity intends to renew the trademark continuously and evidence supports its ability to do so. An analysis of product life cycle studies, market, competitive and environmental trends, and brand extension opportunities provides evidence that the trademarked product will generate net cash inflows for the acquiring entity for an indefinite period.

The trademark would be treated as having an indefinite useful life because it is expected to contribute to net cash inflows indefinitely. Therefore, the trademark would not be amortised until its useful life is determined to be finite. It would be tested for impairment in accordance with IAS 36 annually and whenever there is an indication that it may be impaired. *[IAS 36.10]*.

It is clear from the above discussion that despite the fairly detailed guidance in the standard an entity will need to exercise judgement in estimating the useful life of intangible assets.

9.1.2 Useful life of contractual or other legal rights

Where an intangible asset arises from contractual or other legal rights, the standard requires an entity to take account of both economic and legal factors influencing its useful life and determine the useful life as the shorter of:

- the period of the contractual or other legal rights; and
- the period (determined by economic factors) over which the entity expects to obtain economic benefits from the asset. *[IAS 38.94-95]*.

If the contractual or other legal rights can be renewed, the useful life of the intangible asset should include the renewal period only if there is evidence to support renewal by the entity without significant cost.

However, renewal periods must be ignored if the intangible asset is a reacquired right that was recognised in a business combination. *[IAS 38.94]*. The existence of the following factors may indicate that an entity is able to renew the contractual or other legal rights without significant cost:

(a) there is evidence, possibly based on experience, that the contractual or other legal rights will be renewed. If renewal is contingent upon the consent of a third party, this includes evidence that the third party will give its consent;

(b) there is evidence that any conditions necessary to obtain renewal will be satisfied; and

(c) the cost to the entity of renewal is not significant when compared with the future economic benefits expected to flow to the entity from renewal. *[IAS 38.96]*.

A renewal period is only added to the estimate of useful life if its cost is insignificant when compared with the future economic benefits expected to flow to the entity from renewal. *[IAS 38.94]*. If this is not the case, then the original asset's useful life ends at the contracted renewal date and the renewal cost is treated as the cost to acquire a new intangible asset. *[IAS 38.96]*. An entity needs to exercise judgement in assessing what it regards as a significant cost.

In the case of a reacquired contractual right, recognised as an intangible asset in a business combination accounted for under IFRS 3, its useful life is the remaining contractual period of the contract in which the right was granted. Renewal periods may not be taken into account. *[IAS 38.94]*.

The following examples are derived from those in IAS 38's Illustrative Examples and show the effect of contractual or other legal rights on the useful life of an intangible asset, when assessed together with other factors. The useful life may be shorter than the legal rights or, if supported by facts and circumstances, renewal rights could mean that the intangible asset's life is indefinite.

Example 17.12: Legal rights and useful life

An acquired copyright that has a useful life that is shorter than its remaining legal life of 50 years

An analysis of consumer habits and market trends provides evidence that the copyrighted material will generate net cash inflows for only 30 more years.

The copyright would be amortised over its 30-year estimated useful life and not over the term of the legal rights of 50 years. The copyright also would be reviewed for impairment in accordance with IAS 36 by assessing at the end of each reporting period whether there is any indication that it may be impaired.

An acquired broadcasting licence that expires in five years but is assessed as having an indefinite useful life

The broadcasting licence is renewable every 10 years if the entity provides at least an average level of service to its customers and complies with the relevant legislative requirements. The licence may be renewed indefinitely at little cost and has been renewed twice before the most recent acquisition. The acquiring entity intends to renew the licence indefinitely and evidence supports its ability to do so. Historically, there has been no compelling challenge to the licence renewal. The technology used in broadcasting is not expected to be replaced by another technology at any time in the foreseeable future. Therefore, the licence is expected to contribute to the entity's net cash inflows indefinitely.

The broadcasting licence would be treated as having an indefinite useful life because it is expected to contribute to the entity's net cash inflows indefinitely. Therefore, the licence would not be amortised until its useful life is determined to be finite. The licence would be tested for impairment in accordance with IAS 36 annually (as part of a cash-generating unit) and whenever there is an indication that it may be impaired.

An acquired airline route authority between two European cities that expires in three years but is assessed as having an indefinite useful life

The route authority may be renewed every five years, and the acquiring entity intends to comply with the applicable rules and regulations surrounding renewal. Route authority renewals are routinely granted at a minimal cost and historically have been renewed when the airline has complied with the applicable rules and regulations. The acquiring entity expects to provide service indefinitely between the two cities from its hub airports and expects that the related supporting infrastructure (airport gates, slots, and terminal facility leases) will remain in place at those airports for as long as it has the route authority. An analysis of demand and cash flows supports those assumptions.

Because the facts and circumstances support the acquiring entity's ability to continue providing air service indefinitely between the two cities, the intangible asset related to the route authority is treated as having an indefinite useful life. Therefore, the route authority would not be amortised until its useful life is determined to be finite. It would be tested for impairment in accordance with IAS 36 annually (as part of a cash-generating unit) and whenever there is an indication that it may be impaired.

9.2 Intangible assets with a finite useful life

9.2.1 Amortisation period and method

Amortisation is the systematic allocation of the depreciable amount of an intangible asset over its useful life. The depreciable amount is the cost of an asset, or other amount substituted for cost (e.g. revaluation), less its residual value. *[IAS 38.8]*. The depreciable amount of an intangible asset with a finite useful life should be allocated on a systematic basis over its useful life in the following manner: *[IAS 38.97]*

- amortisation should begin when the asset is available for use, i.e. when it is in the location and condition necessary for it to be capable of operating in the manner intended by management. Therefore, even if an entity is not using the asset, it should still be amortised because it is available for use, although there may be exceptions from this general rule (see 9.2.3 below);
- amortisation should cease at the earlier of:
  - the date that the asset is classified as held for sale, or included in a disposal group that is classified as held for sale, in accordance with IFRS 5; and
  - the date that the asset is derecognised.
- the amortisation method should reflect the pattern of consumption of the economic benefits that the intangible asset provides. If that pattern cannot be reliably determined, a straight-line basis should be used.

Amortisation of an intangible asset with a finite useful life continues until the asset has been fully depreciated or is classified as held for sale, as noted above, or derecognised. Amortisation does not cease simply because an asset is not being used, *[IAS 38.117]*, although this fact might give rise to an indicator of impairment.

The standard allows a variety of amortisation methods to be used to depreciate the asset on a systematic basis over its useful life, such as the straight-line method, the diminishing balance method and the unit of production method. *[IAS 38.98]*. The factors to consider in determining the most appropriate amortisation method are similar to those that are relevant for the depreciation of property, plant and equipment in accordance with IAS 16 (see Chapter 18). For example, entities can adopt a 'sum of the digits' methodology, where amortisation reflects higher consumption of benefits in the earlier part of the asset's useful life, as this is a variant of the diminishing balance method (see Chapter 18).

In selecting an appropriate amortisation method for intangible assets acquired in a business combination, entities should ensure consistency with any assumptions that were used in determining the fair value of the asset. For example, a customer relationship asset may be valued by taking into account an assumed churn-rate that implies a higher level of customer relationships ending in the earlier periods following the business combination. These factors may indicate that a straight-line method of amortisation is not the most appropriate method to reflect the pattern of consumption of the economic benefits that the intangible asset provides, as the valuation assumed that benefit to be frontloaded.

The amortisation charge for each period should be recognised in profit or loss unless IFRS specifically permits or requires it to be capitalised as part of the carrying amount of another asset (e.g. inventory or work in progress). *[IAS 38.97, 99]*.

There is a rebuttable presumption that an amortisation method based on the pattern of expected revenues is not appropriate. This is because a revenue-based method reflects a pattern of generation of economic benefits from operating the business (of which the asset is a part), rather than the consumption of the economic benefits embodied in the asset itself (see 9.2.2 below). By contrast, an amortisation method based on estimated total output (a unit of production method) is appropriate.

The future economic benefits of some intangible assets are clearly consumed on a declining balance basis. This often applies to customer relationships and similar assets acquired as part of a business combination. Both the fair value and the future economic benefits from the customer relationship or similar asset decline over time as the consumption of the economic benefits embodied in the asset declines. Therefore amortising the customer relationship on a declining balance method would be appropriate.

It is important to distinguish this from an asset whose fair value shows a declining balance profile over its life but where the future economic benefits are consumed on a time basis, e.g. a motor vehicle where the entity will obtain as much benefit in year 4 as in year 1. A straight-line method of amortisation properly reflects the consumption of benefits from the motor vehicle.

9.2.1.A Amortising customer relationships and similar intangible assets

As discussed above, in selecting an appropriate amortisation method for intangible assets acquired in a business combination, entities should ensure consistency with any assumptions used in determining the fair value of the asset.

In practice entities rarely use declining balance methods for amortisation. One reason for customer relationships and similar intangible assets is the uncertainty about the future economic benefits that might arise several years in the future and the difficulty in distinguishing them from cash flows that have been generated by internally-generated assets of the business. As a pragmatic solution, supported by valuations experts, entities often use a straight-line method over a shorter period so that at all points the amortised carrying amount of the asset is below the curve for the expected benefits. This is illustrated in the following example and chart. As long as the benefits expected to arise in the period after the intangible asset is fully amortised are not expected to be significant and the entity applies the requirements of IAS 38 to review the useful life and amortisation method (see 9.2.3 below), this method will give a reasonable approximation of the consumption of economic benefits.

Example 17.13: Amortisation method and useful life for customer relationships

An entity identifies a customer relationship on acquiring another business. The entity completes its initial accounting at the end of 20X0 and the customer relationship is valued at €4 million. The valuations expert consulted by the entity assesses the total period from which benefits will be derived from the customer relationship is 9 years but that the benefits will show a declining balance over this period. After discussions with the valuer, the entity concludes that the best estimate of the useful life of the customer relationship for accounting purposes is 5 years and a straight-line method over this period will adequately reflect the consumption of future economic benefits from the customer relationship, given that the amount and timing of benefits after 5 years is inherently uncertain as to timing or amount. The entity notes that a straight-line method over 9 years would not adequately reflect the consumption of future economic benefits.

The relationship between the total economic life, useful life and amortisation method is illustrated in the following chart.

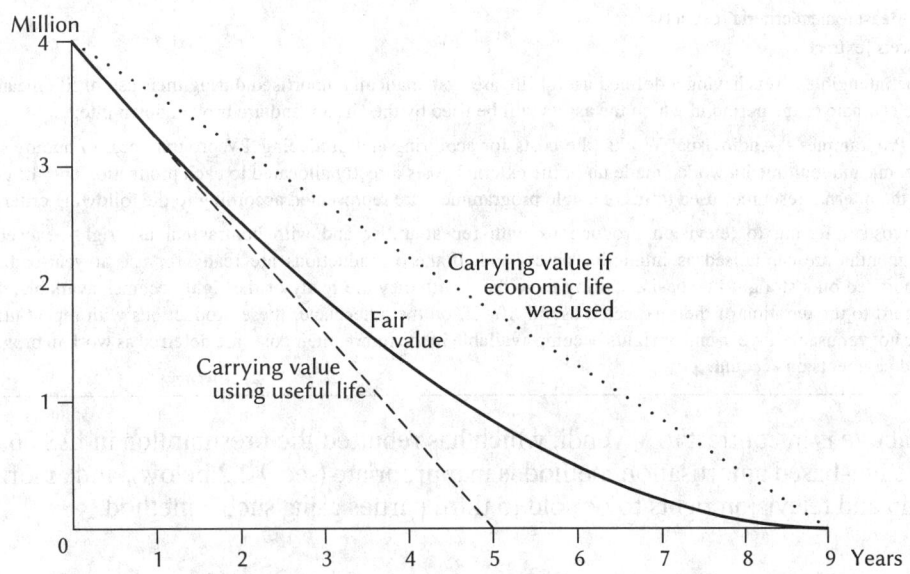

9.2.1.B Amortisation of programme and other broadcast rights

The value of programme and other broadcast rights diminishes because the programmes or events have been broadcast to the same audience before and as result of the passage of time, e.g. audiences lose interest in old programmes or repeats of events for which the result is known or the right is for a limited period. In accounting for this diminution in value, in practice, entities usually take into account how often a programme has been broadcast and, less frequently, the passage of time as such.

When an entity accounts for broadcast rights as inventory, the problem arises that IAS 2 requires valuation 'at the lower of cost and net realisable value' and does not appear to recognise the concept of amortisation of inventories. *[IAS 2.9]*. However, it has been argued that a programme right embodies a series of identifiable components, i.e. first transmission, second transmission, etc., which an entity should account for separately. This appears to be the approach that ITV applies in writing off its programme rights (see Extract 17.2 at 2.2.2 above).

An entity that accounts for programme and other broadcast rights as intangible assets would need to comply with the requirements of IAS 38, which requires that the amortisation method reflects the pattern in which the asset's future economic benefits are expected to be consumed by the entity. *[IAS 38.97]*. As discussed at 9.2.1 above, the standard permits a range of amortisation methods (e.g. the straight-line method, the diminishing balance method and the unit of production method), provided that the chosen method reflects the pattern in which the asset's future economic benefits are expected to be consumed. *[IAS 38.97-98]*.

RAI is an example of a company that amortises some of its programme rights on a straight-line basis.

Extract 17.10: RAI – Radiotelevisione italiana SpA. (2018)

Notes to the Consolidated Financial Statements as at 31 December 2018 [extract]

3) Measurement criteria [extract]

Assets [extract]

The intangible assets having a defined useful life are systematically amortised during their useful life meant as the estimate of the period in which the assets will be used by the Group, and are broken down into:

a) Programmes – Audiovisual Works: the costs for acquiring and producing TV programmes, of audiovisual, cinema and multimedia works, made up of the external costs directly allocated to each production and the costs of the internal resources used to make single programmes, are represented according to the following criteria:

1) costs referring to television productions with repeat utility and with contractual use rights exceeding 12 months are capitalised as intangible assets and, if these productions are ready for use at year-end, are amortised on a straight-line basis, starting from the month they are ready or the right becomes available, with regard to the duration of their expected useful life. If, on the other hand, these productions with repeat utility are not yet usable at year-end or rights become available in the future, their costs are deferred as work in progress and payments on account.

The above is in contrast to Vivendi, which has rebutted the presumption in IAS 36 that a revenue-based amortisation method is inappropriate (see 9.2.2 below), and amortises its film and television rights to be sold to third parties using such a method.

Intangible assets 1345

> Extract 17.11: Vivendi SE (2019)
>
> Notes to the Consolidated Financial Statements [extract]
> NOTE 1. ACCOUNTING POLICIES AND VALUATION METHODS [extract]
> 1.3. PRINCIPLES GOVERNING THE PREPARATION OF THE CONSOLIDATED FINANCIAL STATEMENTS [extract]
> 1.3.5. Assets [extract]
> 1.3.5.3. Content assets [extract]
> Canal+ Group [extract]
>
> *Theatrical films and television rights produced or acquired to be sold to third parties* [extract]
>
> Theatrical films and television rights produced or acquired before their initial exhibition to be sold to third parties, are recorded as a content asset at capitalized cost (mainly direct production and overhead costs) or at their acquisition cost. The cost of theatrical films and television rights are amortized, and other related costs are expensed, pursuant to the estimated revenue method (i.e., based on the ratio of the current period's gross revenues to estimated total gross revenues from all sources on an individual production basis). Vivendi considers that amortization pursuant to the estimated revenue method reflects the rate at which the entity plans to consume the future economic benefits related to the asset, and there is a high correlation between revenue and the consumption of the economic benefits embodied in the intangible assets.

Only in specific circumstances will it be appropriate to use a revenue-based method of amortisation. These circumstances are discussed at 9.2.2 below.

9.2.2 Revenue-based amortisation

Consumption of the future economic benefits of an asset is the principle on which amortisation is based. Whether this completely precluded revenue-based methods of amortisation had become a matter of debate, particularly in the context of service concession arrangements that are accounted for using the intangible asset model (see Chapter 25 at 4.3.1).

In May 2014, the IASB clarified IAS 38 by introducing a rebuttable presumption that a revenue-based approach is not appropriate. Revenue reflects the output of the intangible asset but it also measures the impact of other factors, such as changes in sales volumes and selling prices, the effects of selling activities and changes to inputs and processes. The price component of revenue may be affected by inflation. *[IAS 38.98A]*.

The following example illustrates how a revenue-based method of amortisation diverges from the units-of-production method when the price per unit is not fixed.

Example 17.14: Output-based versus revenue-based amortisation

Entity Z acquires a five-year licence to manufacture a product for a cost of £1,220,000. It is expected that the production line used for making the product has a capacity of 100,000 units per year. The entity plans to produce at full capacity each year and to sell all of its output. However, it expects the price per unit to be £10 in year 1 and increase by 10% each year thereafter. On this basis, the profile of amortisation on a unit of production basis (UoP) and on a revenue basis would be as follows:

	Units	UoP charge	Revenue	Charge
Year 1	100,000	244,000	1,000,000	200,000
Year 2	100,000	244,000	1,100,000	220,000
Year 3	100,000	244,000	1,210,000	242,000
Year 4	100,000	244,000	1,330,000	266,000
Year 5	100,000	244,000	1,460,000	292,000
Total	500,000	1,220,000	6,100,000	1,220,000

The IASB acknowledged certain 'limited circumstances' that would allow revenue-based amortisation. Therefore, the presumption that they are not acceptable is rebuttable only:

(a) when the rights embodied in that intangible asset are expressed as a measure of revenue; or

(b) when it can be demonstrated that revenue and the consumption of the economic benefits embodied in the intangible asset are highly correlated. [IAS 38.98A].

A 'highly correlated' outcome would only be achieved where a revenue-based method of amortisation is expected to give a similar answer as one of the other methods permitted by IAS 38. For example, if revenue is earned evenly over the expected life of the asset, the pattern of amortisation would be similar to a straight-line basis. In situations where unit prices are fixed and all production is sold, the pattern of amortisation would replicate the use of the units-of-production method. However, when unit prices are not fixed, revenue would not provide the same answer and its use would therefore be inappropriate (as in the example above). [IAS 38.98B]. The revised standard notes that revenue is the predominant limiting factor that is inherent in the intangible asset in circumstances in which it is appropriate to use it as the basis of amortisation. In other words, in these circumstances, revenue determines the useful life of the asset, rather than, for example, a number of years or the number of units produced.

The amended standard includes two examples in which revenue earned can be regarded as a measure of consumption of an intangible asset.

- A contract may allow the extraction of gold from a mine until total cumulative revenue from the sale of gold reaches $2 billion; or
- The right to operate a toll road could be based on a fixed total amount of revenue to be generated from cumulative tolls, i.e. the operator can collect up to €100 million from the tolls collected. [IAS 38.98C].

Some respondents had argued that a units of production method did not seem practicable when the units of production were not homogeneous. For example, a producer of a motion picture generates revenue through showing the picture in theatres, selling DVDs, licensing the rights to characters to toy manufacturers and licensing the broadcast rights to television. The IASB acknowledges that such situations require the exercise of judgement. The Board did consider whether an intangible asset should be divided into components for amortisation purposes 'but refrained from developing guidance in this respect for intangible assets'. [IAS 38.BC72H-72I].

9.2.3 Review of amortisation period and amortisation method

An entity should review the amortisation period and the amortisation method for an intangible asset with a finite useful life at least at each financial year-end. If the expected useful life of the asset has changed, the amortisation period should be changed accordingly. *[IAS 38.104]*. An entity may, for example, consider its previous estimate of the useful life of an intangible asset inappropriate upon recognition of an impairment loss on the asset. *[IAS 38.105]*.

If the expected pattern of consumption of the future economic benefits embodied in the asset has changed, the amortisation method should be changed to reflect the new pattern. *[IAS 38.104]*. The standard provides two examples of when this might happen:

- if it becomes apparent that a diminishing balance method of amortisation is appropriate rather than a straight-line method; *[IAS 38.106]* and
- if use of the rights represented by a licence is deferred pending action on other components of the business plan. In this case, economic benefits that flow from the asset may not be received until later periods. *[IAS 38.106]*. This implies that circumstances may exist in which it is appropriate not to recognise an amortisation charge in relation to an intangible asset, because the entity may not yet be ready to use it. For example, telecommunication companies acquired UMTS (3G) licences, before constructing the physical network necessary to use the licence. Note that an entity must perform an impairment test at least annually for any intangible asset that has not yet been brought into use. *[IAS 36.10]*.

Both changes in the amortisation period and the amortisation method should be accounted for as changes in accounting estimates in accordance with IAS 8 which requires such changes to be recognised prospectively by revising the amortisation charge in the current period and for each future period during the asset's remaining useful life. *[IAS 8.36, 38, IAS 38.104]*.

9.2.4 Residual value

The residual value of an intangible asset is the estimated amount that an entity would currently obtain from disposal of the asset, after deducting the estimated costs of disposal, if the asset were already of the age and in the condition expected at the end of its useful life. *[IAS 38.8]*.

IAS 38 requires entities to assume a residual value of zero for an intangible asset with a finite useful life, unless there is a commitment by a third party to purchase the asset at the end of its useful life or there is an active market (as defined by IFRS 13) for the asset from which to determine its residual value and it is probable that such a market will exist at the end of the asset's useful life. *[IAS 38.100]*. This presumption has been retained from the previous version of IAS 38 as an anti-abuse measure to prevent entities from circumventing the requirement to amortise all intangible assets. *[IAS 38.BC59]*.

Given the definition of 'active market' (see 8.2.1 above) it seems highly unlikely that, in the absence of a commitment by a third party to buy the asset, an entity will ever be able to prove that the residual value is other than zero. A residual value other than zero implies that the entity intends to dispose of the asset before the end of its economic life. *[IAS 38.101]*. Third party commitments can be found in contracts in the scope of IFRIC 12 – *Service Concession Arrangements* (see Chapter 25) and one of IAS 38's Illustrative examples includes a residual value; see Example 17.15 below.

If an entity can demonstrate a case for estimating a residual value other than zero, its estimate should be based on current prices for the sale of a similar asset that has reached the end of its useful life and has operated under conditions similar to those in which the asset will be used. *[IAS 38.102]*. The standard requires a review of the residual value at each financial year end. This review can result in an upward or downward revision of the estimated residual value and thereby affect the depreciable amount of the asset; that change to depreciation should be accounted for prospectively as a change in an accounting estimate in accordance with IAS 8. *[IAS 38.102]*.

The following example is based on one of IAS 38's Illustrative Examples. The intangible asset being considered has a residual value at the end of its useful life.

Example 17.15: Amortisation of an intangible asset with a residual value

An acquired patent that expires in 15 years

A product protected by patented technology is expected to be a source of net cash inflows for at least 15 years. The entity has a commitment from a third party to purchase that patent in five years for 60 per cent of the fair value of the patent at the date it was acquired, and the entity intends to sell the patent in five years.

The patent will be amortised over its five-year useful life to the entity, with a residual value equal to 60 per cent of the patent's fair value at the date it was acquired. The patent will also be reviewed for impairment in accordance with IAS 36 by assessing at the end of each reporting period whether there is any indication that it may be impaired.

The standard does not permit negative amortisation in the event that the residual value of an intangible asset increases to an amount greater than the asset's carrying amount. Instead, the asset's amortisation charge will be zero until its residual value decreases to an amount below the asset's carrying amount. *[IAS 38.103]*.

9.3 Intangible assets with an indefinite useful life

IAS 38 prohibits amortisation of an intangible asset with an indefinite useful life. *[IAS 38.107]*. Instead, IAS 36 requires such an asset to be tested for impairment annually and whenever there is an indication that the intangible asset may be impaired. *[IAS 38.108]*.

An entity should review and validate at the end of each reporting period its decision to classify the useful life of an intangible asset as indefinite. *[IAS 38.109]*. If events and circumstances no longer support an indefinite useful life, the change from indefinite to finite life should be accounted for as a change in accounting estimate under IAS 8, *[IAS 38.109]*, which requires such changes to be recognised prospectively (i.e. in the current and future periods). *[IAS 8.36]*. Furthermore, reassessing the useful life of an intangible asset as finite rather than indefinite is an indicator that the asset may be impaired. *[IAS 38.110]*. See Chapter 20 for a discussion on impairment.

The following examples from IAS 38's Illustrative Examples illustrate circumstances in which an entity considers whether the useful life of an intangible asset is still indefinite.

Example 17.16: Review of indefinite useful lives

A broadcasting licence is no longer to be renewed

The facts are as in Example 17.12 above. A licensing authority has allowed broadcast licences to be renewed indefinitely at little cost and an entity, having renewed the licence twice, had concluded that it had an indefinite useful life. However, the licensing authority subsequently decides that it will no longer renew broadcasting licences, but rather will auction the licences. At the time the licensing authority's decision is made, the entity's broadcasting licence has three years until it expires. The entity expects that the licence will continue to contribute to net cash inflows until the licence expires.

Because the broadcasting licence can no longer be renewed, its useful life is no longer indefinite. Thus, the acquired licence would be amortised over its remaining three-year useful life and immediately tested for impairment in accordance with IAS 36.

A trademark for a line of products acquired several years ago in a business combination

At the time of the business combination the acquiree had been producing the line of products for 35 years with many new models developed under the trademark. At the acquisition date the acquirer expected to continue producing the line, and an analysis of various economic factors indicated there was no limit to the period the trademark would contribute to net cash inflows, so the trademark was not amortised by the acquirer. However, management has recently decided that production of the product line will be discontinued over the next four years.

Because the useful life of the acquired trademark is no longer regarded as indefinite, the carrying amount of the trademark would be tested for impairment in accordance with IAS 36, written down to recoverable amount as appropriate and the carrying amount amortised over its remaining four-year useful life.

9.4 Impairment losses

An impairment loss is the amount by which the carrying amount of an asset exceeds its recoverable amount. *[IAS 38.8]*. An entity applies IAS 36 in determining whether an intangible asset is impaired (see Chapter 20). *[IAS 38.111]*.

IAS 36 requires an entity to perform an annual impairment test on every intangible asset that has an indefinite useful life and every intangible asset that is not yet available for use. Many intangible assets with indefinite lives do not generate independent cash inflows as individual assets and so are tested for impairment with other assets of the cash-generating unit of which they are part (see Chapter 20). *[IAS 36.10, 22]*. This means that impairment losses, if any, will be allocated in accordance with IAS 36 and, if any goodwill allocated to the cash-generating unit has been written off, the other assets of the cash-generating unit, including the intangible asset, will be reduced *pro rata* to their carrying amount (see Chapter 20 at 11.2). *[IAS 36.104]*.

Example 17.17:   Impairment of an intangible asset with an indefinite useful life

A trademark acquired 10 years ago that distinguishes a leading consumer product

The trademark was regarded as having an indefinite useful life when it was acquired because the trademarked product was expected to generate cash inflows indefinitely. However, unexpected competition has recently entered the market and will reduce future sales of the product. Management estimates that cash inflows generated by the product will be 20 per cent less for the foreseeable future. However, management expects that the product will continue to generate cash inflows indefinitely at those reduced amounts.

As a result of the projected decrease in future cash inflows, the entity determines that the estimated recoverable amount of the trademark and the assets that comprise the cash-generating unit is less than its carrying amount. An impairment loss is recognised for the cash-generating unit of which it is a part. Because it is still regarded as having an indefinite useful life, the trademark would continue not to be amortised but would be tested for impairment in accordance with IAS 36 annually, i.e. as part of the cash-generating unit, and whenever there is an indication that it may be impaired.

Note that a trademark may generate independent cash inflows if, for example, it is licenced to another party; otherwise, as in Example 17.17 above, it will be part of a cash-generating unit.

9.5 Retirements and disposals

An intangible asset should be derecognised on disposal (e.g. by sale, by entering into a finance lease, or by donation) or when no future economic benefits are expected from its use or disposal. *[IAS 38.112, 114]*.

The date of disposal of an intangible asset is the date the recipient obtains control of that asset in accordance with the requirements for determining when a performance obligation is satisfied in IFRS 15. *[IAS 38.114]*. In the case of a disposal by a sale and leaseback, an entity should apply IFRS 16 (see Chapter 23).

The gain or loss on derecognition, which is determined as the difference between the net disposal proceeds and the carrying amount of the asset, should be accounted for in profit or loss unless IFRS 16 requires otherwise on a sale and leaseback. Gains on disposal should not be presented as revenue. [IAS 38.113].

In June 2020, the IFRS Interpretations Committee issued an agenda decision on the recognition of player transfer payments received by a football club. In the fact pattern considered by Committee, the entity recognised the player registration right as an intangible asset applying IAS 38. Accordingly, the Committee concluded that the entity should apply the requirements of paragraph 113 of IAS 38 and recognise the transfer payment received as part of the gain or loss arising from the derecognition of the registration right. The agenda decision stated that the entity should not recognise the transfer payment received, or any gain arising, as revenue applying IFRS 15.[6]

Although the agenda decision only addressed the accounting for intangible assets in connection with player registration rights, the same accounting would also apply to other types of intangible assets that are sold.

For an entity whose ordinary activities include the development and transfer of players, it is conceivable that circumstances exist in which registration rights associated with some players meet the definition of inventories. In applying that definition, on initial recognition such an entity would consider whether the registration right is acquired for development and sale in the ordinary course of business (and therefore would be recognised as inventory under IAS 2, rather than an intangible asset under IAS 38). Whether a registration right meets the definition of inventories requires an assessment of the facts and circumstances.[7]

The consideration to be included in the calculation of the gain or loss is determined in accordance with the requirements for determining the transaction price in paragraphs 47 to 72 of IFRS 15 (see Chapter 29 at 2). [IAS 38.116]. If the transaction price includes variable consideration, subsequent changes to the estimated amount of the consideration included in the gain or loss on disposal are accounted for in accordance with the requirements for changes in the transaction price in IFRS 15 (see Chapter 29 at 2.9). [IAS 38.116].

If the receipt of the consideration does not match the timing of the transfer of the asset (e.g. the consideration is prepaid or paid after the date of disposal), then the arrangement may also contain a financing component for which the transaction price will need to be adjusted, if significant (see Chapter 29 at 2.5).

In the case of a reacquired contractual right, recognised as an intangible asset in a business combination accounted for under IFRS 3, if the right is subsequently reissued or sold to a third party, any gain or loss is determined using the remaining carrying amount of the reacquired right. [IAS 38.115A].

9.5.1 Derecognition of parts of intangible assets

The standard requires an entity to recognise the cost of replacing a part of an intangible asset as a component of the asset's carrying amount and to derecognise that component when the part is replaced. 'If it is not practicable for an entity to determine the carrying amount of the replaced part, it may use the cost of the replacement as an indication of what the cost of the replaced part was at the time it was acquired or internally generated.' *[IAS 38.115]*. As noted by the standard, the nature of intangible assets is such that, in many cases, there are no additions or replacements that would meet its recognition criteria, so this should be an unlikely event (see 3.3 above). *[IAS 38.20]*.

However, this requirement raises the question of how to account for the disposal of a part of a larger intangible item, acquired in a single transaction but capable of being subdivided for separate disposal. An example would be the division of the global rights to sell a particular product into a number of agreements providing exclusive rights over a particular continent or other geographic territory. In this case, the part disposed of is an identifiable and separable part of the original intangible asset. Because the rights are exclusive, the part still meets the definition of an intangible asset because it is embodied in legal rights that allow the acquirer to control the benefits arising from the asset, either by providing access to earn revenues in that geographic market or by restricting the access of others to that market. *[IAS 38.13]*. In that case, an entity would apply the requirements above for the derecognition of a replacement part of an asset, by determining the carrying amount of the separate part or, if to do so is impracticable, deducting the proceeds of disposal from the depreciated replacement cost of the original asset (in effect treating the value of the newly separated part as an indicator of original cost).

Where the subdivision of rights is not established on an exclusive basis, it would be more difficult to regard a separable component of the original intangible as having been disposed of. For example, rights might be assigned to a third party over a geographic area, but the entity retains the ability to sell goods in that market as well. In such circumstances it may not be appropriate to derecognise a portion of the original intangible asset. Instead the entity may have transferred a right of use (or lease) over the asset to the third party, or entered into a form of joint arrangement. The issues raised by the partial disposal of previously undivided interests in property, plant and equipment are discussed in Chapter 18.

Accounting for the partial derecognition of goodwill on the disposal of an operation that forms part of a cash-generating unit is discussed in Chapter 20 at 8.5.

10 DISCLOSURE

The main requirements in IAS 38 are set out below, but it may be necessary to refer to the disclosure requirements of IFRS 5 in Chapter 4, the disclosure requirements of IAS 36 in Chapter 20 in the event of a disposal or impairment, and the fair value disclosures in IFRS 13 in Chapter 14 when fair value is used or disclosed.

10.1 General disclosures

IAS 38 requires certain disclosures to be presented by class of intangible assets. A class of intangible assets is defined as a grouping of assets of a similar nature and use in an entity's operations. The standard provides examples of classes of assets, which may be disaggregated (or aggregated) into smaller (or larger) groups if this results in more relevant information for the users of the financial statements (see 8 above for examples of classes of intangible assets). *[IAS 38.119].* Although separate information is required for internally generated intangible assets and other intangible assets, these categories are not considered to be separate classes when they relate to intangible assets of a similar nature and use in an entity's operations. Hence the standard requires the following disclosures to be given for each class of intangible assets, distinguishing between internally generated intangible assets and other intangible assets:

(a) whether the useful lives are indefinite or finite and, if finite, the useful lives or the amortisation rates used;

(b) the amortisation methods used for intangible assets with finite useful lives;

(c) the gross carrying amount and any accumulated amortisation (aggregated with accumulated impairment losses) at the beginning and end of the period;

(d) the line item(s) of the statement of comprehensive income in which any amortisation of intangible assets is included; and

(e) a reconciliation of the carrying amount at the beginning and end of the period showing:

　(i) additions, indicating separately those from internal development, those acquired separately, and those acquired through business combinations;

　(ii) assets classified as held for sale or included in a disposal group classified as held for sale in accordance with IFRS 5 and other disposals;

　(iii) increases or decreases during the period resulting from revaluations and from impairment losses recognised or reversed in other comprehensive income in accordance with IAS 36 (if any);

　(iv) impairment losses recognised in profit or loss during the period in accordance with IAS 36 (if any);

　(v) impairment losses reversed in profit or loss during the period in accordance with IAS 36 (if any);

　(vi) any amortisation recognised during the period;

　(vii) net exchange differences arising on the translation of the financial statements into the presentation currency, and on the translation of a foreign operation into the presentation currency of the entity; and

　(viii) other changes in the carrying amount during the period. *[IAS 38.118].*

The standard permits an entity to present the reconciliation required under (e) above either for the net carrying amount or separately for the gross carrying amount and the accumulated amortisation and impairments.

Paragraph 38 of IAS 1 – *Presentation of Financial Statements* – requires comparative information for the reconciliation in (e) above.

An entity may want to consider separate disclosure of intangible assets acquired by way of government grant or obtained in an exchange of assets, even though disclosure is not specifically required under (e)(i) above.

An example of these general disclosures is given by International Consolidated Airlines Group, S.A.

Extract 17.12: International Consolidated Airlines Group, S.A. (2019)

NOTES TO THE CONSOLIDATED FINANCIAL STATEMENTS [extract]

2. Significant accounting policies [extract]

Intangible assets

a Goodwill

Goodwill arises on the acquisition of subsidiaries, associates and joint ventures and represents the excess of the consideration paid over the net fair value of the identifiable assets and liabilities of the acquiree. Where the net fair value of the identifiable assets and liabilities of the acquiree is in excess of the consideration paid, a gain on bargain purchase is recognised immediately in the Income statement.

For the purpose of assessing impairment, goodwill is grouped at the lowest levels for which there are separately identifiable cash flows (cash generating units). Goodwill is tested for impairment annually and whenever indicators exist that the carrying value may not be recoverable.

b Brands

Brands arising on the acquisition of subsidiaries are initially recognised at fair value at the acquisition date. Long established brands that are expected to be used indefinitely are not amortised but assessed annually for impairment.

c Customer loyalty programmes

Customer loyalty programmes arising on the acquisition of subsidiaries are initially recognised at fair value at the acquisition date. A customer loyalty programme with an expected useful life is amortised over the expected remaining useful life. Established customer loyalty programmes that are expected to be used indefinitely are not amortised but assessed annually for impairment.

d Landing rights

Landing rights acquired in a business combination are recognised at fair value at the acquisition date. Landing rights acquired from other airlines are capitalised at cost.

Capitalised landing rights based outside the EU are amortised on a straight-line basis over a period not exceeding 20 years. Capitalised landing rights based within the EU are not amortised, as regulations provide that these landing rights are perpetual.

e Contract based intangibles

Contract based intangibles acquired in a business combination are recognised initially at fair value at the acquisition date and amortised over the remaining life of the contract.

f Software

The cost to purchase or develop computer software that is separable from an item of related hardware is capitalised separately and amortised on a straight-line basis generally over a period not exceeding five years, with certain specific software developments amortised over a period of up to 10 years.

g Emissions allowances

Purchased emissions allowances are recognised at cost. Emissions allowances are not revalued or amortised but are tested for impairment whenever indicators exist that the carrying value may not be recoverable.

15. **Intangible assets and impairment review** [extract]
a   Intangible assets

€ million	Goodwill	Brand	Customer loyalty programmes	Landing rights[1]	Software	Other	Total
Cost							
Balance at January 1, 2018	596	451	253	1,519	948	128	3,895
Additions	–	–	–	55	195	105	355
Disposals	–	–	–	–	(14)	(20)	(34)
Exchange movements	(1)	–	–	(15)	(13)	(2)	(31)
Balance at December 31, 2018	595	451	253	1,559	1,116	211	4,185
Additions	–	–	–	5	232	120	357
Disposals	–	–	–	–	(28)	(55)	(83)
Exchange movements	3	–	–	52	56	6	117
December 31, 2019	598	451	253	1,616	1,376	282	4,576
Amortisation and impairment							
Balance at January 1, 2018	249	–	–	101	475	52	877
Charge for the year	–	–	–	6	123	3	132
Disposals	–	–	–	–	(13)	–	(13)
Exchange movements	–	–	–	(1)	(8)	–	(9)
Balance at December 31, 2018	249	–	–	106	577	55	987
Charge for the year	–	–	–	6	131	5	142
Disposals	–	–	–	–	(28)	–	(28)
Exchange movements	–	–	–	3	30	–	33
December 31, 2019	249	–	–	115	710	60	1,134
Net book values							
December 31, 2019	349	451	253	1,501	666	222	3,442
December 31, 2018	346	451	253	1,453	539	156	3,198

1   The net book value includes non-EU based landing rights of €94 million (2018: €100 million) that have a definite life. The remaining life of these landing rights is 15 years.

In addition to the disclosures required above, any impairment of intangible assets is to be disclosed in accordance with IAS 36, which is discussed in Chapter 20 at 13, *[IAS 38.120]*, while the nature and amount of any change in useful life, amortisation method or residual value estimates should be disclosed in accordance with the provisions of IAS 8. *[IAS 38.121]*.

There are a number of additional disclosure requirements, some of which only apply in certain circumstances:

(a) for an intangible asset assessed as having an indefinite useful life, the carrying amount of that asset and the reasons supporting the assessment of an indefinite useful life. In giving these reasons, the entity should describe the factor(s) that played a significant role in determining that the asset has an indefinite useful life;

(b) a description, the carrying amount and remaining amortisation period of any individual intangible asset that is material to the entity's financial statements;

(c) for intangible assets acquired by way of a government grant and initially recognised at fair value (see 4.6 above):

(i) the fair value initially recognised for these assets;
(ii) their carrying amount; and
(iii) whether they are measured after recognition under the cost model or the revaluation model.
(d) the existence and carrying amounts of intangible assets whose title is restricted and the carrying amounts of intangible assets pledged as security for liabilities;
(e) the amount of contractual commitments for the acquisition of intangible assets. *[IAS 38.122]*.

In describing the factors (as required under (a) above) that played a significant role in determining that the useful life of an intangible asset is indefinite, an entity considers the list of factors in IAS 38.90 (see 9.1.1 above). *[IAS 38.123]*.

Finally, an entity is encouraged, but not required, to disclose the following information:
(a) a description of any fully amortised intangible asset that is still in use; and
(b) a brief description of significant intangible assets controlled by the entity but not recognised as assets because they did not meet the recognition criteria in this Standard or because they were acquired or generated before the version of IAS 38 issued in 1998 was effective. *[IAS 38.128]*.

10.2 Statement of financial position presentation

IAS 1 uses the term 'non-current' to include tangible, intangible and financial assets of a long-term nature, although it does not prohibit the use of alternative descriptions as long as the meaning is clear. *[IAS 1.67]*. Although most intangible assets are non-current, an intangible asset may meet the definition of a current asset (i.e. it has an economic life of less than 12 months) when it is acquired and should be classified accordingly.

IAS 1 requires intangible assets to be shown as a separate category of asset on the face of the statement of financial position. *[IAS 1.54]*. Intangible assets will, therefore, normally appear as a separate category of asset in the statement of financial position at a suitable point within non-current assets, or at a point in an undifferentiated statement of financial position that reflects their relative liquidity, *[IAS 1.60]*, that is, the time over which they are to be amortised or sold. An entity that holds a wide variety of different intangible assets may need to present these in separate line items on the face of the statement of financial position if such presentation is relevant to an understanding of the entity's financial position. *[IAS 1.55]*.

While the figure for intangible assets may include goodwill, the relevant standards require more detailed disclosures of the constituent elements to be included in the notes to the financial statements. In many cases though, entities will be able to aggregate the intangible assets into slightly broader categories in order to reduce the number of lines items on the face of their statement of financial position.

Nestlé is an example of an entity that chooses to present goodwill separately from other intangible assets on the face of the statement of financial position.

Extract 17.13: Nestlé S.A. (2019)
Consolidated balance sheet
as at December 31, 2019 [extract]

In millions of CHF	Notes	2019	2018
Assets [extract]			
Non-current assets			
Property, plant and equipment	8	28 762	29 956
Goodwill	9	28 896	31 702
Intangible assets	9	17 824	18 634
Investments in associates and joint ventures	14	11 505	10 792
Financial assets	12	2 611	2 567
Employee benefits assets	10	510	487
Current income tax assets		55	58
Deferred tax assets	13	2 114	1 816
Total non-current assets		92 277	96 012

10.3 Profit or loss presentation

No specific guidance is provided within IAS 1, and only limited guidance is available within IAS 38, on the presentation of amortisation, impairment, and gains or losses related to intangible assets in the statement of profit or loss.

- Gains on the sale of intangible assets should not be presented within revenue. *[IAS 38.113]*.
- An entity should disclose the line item(s) of the statement of comprehensive income in which any amortisation of intangible assets is included. *[IAS 38.118(d)]*.

In the absence of detailed guidance on how to present such items in the statement of profit or loss, it will, in practice, usually be appropriate to present them in a similar way as those related to property, plant and equipment.

10.4 Additional disclosures when the revaluation model is applied

IAS 38 requires an entity, which accounts for intangible assets at revalued amounts, to disclose the following additional information:

(a) by class of intangible assets:
   (i) the effective date of the revaluation;
   (ii) the carrying amount of revalued intangible assets; and
   (iii) the carrying amount that would have been recognised had the revalued class of intangible assets been measured after recognition using the cost model; and
(b) the amount of the revaluation surplus that relates to intangible assets at the beginning and end of the period, indicating the changes during the period and any restrictions on the distribution of the balance to shareholders. *[IAS 38.124]*.

Classes of revalued assets can be aggregated for disclosure purposes. However, an entity cannot combine classes of intangible asset measured under the revaluation model with other classes measured at cost. *[IAS 38.125]*. Where assets are carried at fair value, an entity will also have to comply with the disclosure requirements of IFRS 13, as appropriate. These requirements are discussed in Chapter 14.

10.5 Disclosure of research and development expenditure

An entity should disclose the aggregate total amount of research or development expenditure (see 6.2 above) that is recognised in profit or loss as an expense during the period. *[IAS 38.126-127]*.

11 SPECIFIC ISSUES REGARDING INTANGIBLE ASSETS

11.1 Rate-regulated activities

In many countries the provision of utilities (e.g. water, natural gas or electricity) to consumers is regulated by the national government. Regulations differ between countries but often regulators operate a cost-plus system under which a utility is allowed to make a fixed return on investment. A regulator may allow a utility to recoup its investment by increasing the prices over a defined period. Consequently, the future price that a utility is allowed to charge its customers may be influenced by past cost levels and investment levels.

Under a number of national GAAPs accounting practices have developed whereby an entity accounts for the effects of regulation by recognising a 'regulatory' asset or liability that reflects the increase or decrease in future prices approved by the regulator. Such 'regulatory assets' may have been classified as intangible assets under those national GAAPs.

This issue has been a matter of significant interest for entities in those countries adopting IFRS, because the recognition of these regulatory assets and liabilities is prohibited under IFRS. Just as the requirement to charge a lower price for the delivery of goods and services in the future does not meet the definition of a past obligating event, or a liability, in IAS 37 – *Provisions, Contingent Liabilities and Contingent Assets* (see Chapter 26), the ability to charge higher prices for goods services to be rendered in the future does not meet the definition of an intangible asset in IAS 38. In particular, the right obtained from the regulator to set higher prices is not accompanied by a legal requirement for a customer to buy those goods and services in future, meaning that the entity cannot demonstrate sufficient control over the related benefits to meet the definition of an intangible asset.

IFRS 14 – *Regulatory Deferral Accounts* – permits certain assets and liabilities to be recognised under very limited circumstances and to ease the adoption of IFRS for rate-regulated entities. It allows rate-regulated entities to continue recognising regulatory deferral accounts in connection with their first-time adoption of IFRS, e.g. Canadian utility entities. First-time adopters do not need to make major changes in accounting policy for regulatory deferral accounts on transition to IFRS until a comprehensive IASB project is completed, but existing IFRS preparers are prohibited from adopting the standard. Entities that adopt IFRS 14 must present the regulatory deferral accounts as separate line items on the statement of financial position and present movements in these account balances as separate line items in the statement of profit or loss and other comprehensive income. The standard requires disclosures on the nature of, and risks associated with, the entity's rate regulation and the effects of that rate regulation on its financial statements. The further application of IFRS 14 is discussed in Chapter 5.

The IASB is continuing its comprehensive rate-regulated activities project and continues to discuss aspects of the model.

The Board continued its discussions on the model in late 2019 and early 2020, with the publication of an Exposure Draft expected in the second half of 2020.[8] For further discussion of the IASB's rate-regulated activities project see Chapter 27 at 4.4.

11.2 Emissions trading schemes

Governments around the world have introduced or are in the process of developing schemes to encourage corporations and individuals to reduce emissions of pollutants. These schemes comprise tradable emissions allowances or permits, an example of which is a 'cap and trade' model whereby participants are allocated emission rights or allowances equal to a cap (i.e. a maximum level of allowable emissions, usually less than the entity's current quantity) and are permitted to trade those allowances.

While there are variants to these arrangements, a cap and trade emission rights scheme typically has the following features:

- an entity participating in the scheme (participant) sets a target to reduce its emissions to a specified level (the cap). The participant is issued allowances equal in number to its cap by a government or government agency. Allowances may be issued free of charge, or participants may have to pay the government for them (see below);
- the scheme operates for defined compliance periods;
- participants are free to buy and sell allowances at any time;
- if at the end of the compliance period a participant's actual emissions exceed its emission rights, the participant will have to buy additional rights in the market or it will incur a penalty;
- in some schemes emission rights surpluses and deficits may be carried forward to future periods; and
- the scheme may provide for brokers – who are not themselves participants – to buy and sell emission rights.

The EU Emissions Trading Scheme, still by far the biggest international scheme for trading greenhouse gas emission allowances, now allocates many allowances by auction, not free allocation.[9]

A number of attempts have been made by the Interpretations Committee and the IASB to formulate guidance on how these schemes might be accounted for, but without reaching a definitive conclusion. IFRIC 3 – *Emission Rights* – was issued in 2004 (see 11.2.1 below). However, the interpretation met with significant resistance and was withdrawn in 2005, despite the IASB considering it to be an appropriate interpretation of existing IFRSs.[10]

Until the IASB completes a new project on emissions trading schemes, an entity has the option either:
(a) to apply IFRIC 3, which despite having been withdrawn, is considered to be an appropriate interpretation of existing IFRS; or
(b) to develop its own accounting policy for cap and trade schemes based on the hierarchy of authoritative guidance in IAS 8.

In April 2016, the IASB provided an update on its Pollutant Pricing Mechanisms (formerly referred to as Emissions Trading Schemes) Project in which it noted the diversity in how Pollutant Pricing Mechanisms (which include emissions trading schemes) are accounted for and that some of the issues identified related to possible gaps and inconsistencies in IFRSs.[11] At the time of writing no further work on the project had been performed by the IASB and this was not an active research project.[12]

11.2.1 Emissions trading schemes – IFRIC 3

IFRIC 3 dealt with accounting for cap and trade schemes by entities that participated in them.[13] The provisions of the interpretation were also considered to be relevant to other schemes designed to encourage reduced levels of emissions and share some of the features outlined above.[14]

IFRIC 3 took the view that a cap and trade scheme did not give rise to a net asset or liability, but that it gave rise to various items that were to be accounted for separately:[15]

(a) *an asset for allowances held* – Allowances, whether allocated by government or purchased, were to be regarded as intangible assets and accounted for under IAS 38. Allowances issued for less than fair value were to be measured initially at their fair value;[16]

(b) *a government grant* – When allowances are issued for less than fair value, the difference between the amount paid and fair value was a government grant that should be accounted for under IAS 20. Initially the grant was to be recognised as deferred income in the statement of financial position and subsequently recognised as income on a systematic basis over the compliance period for which the allowances were issued, regardless of whether the allowances were held or sold;[17]

(c) *a liability for the obligation to deliver allowances equal to emissions that have been made* – As emissions are made, a liability was to be recognised as a provision that falls within the scope of IAS 37. The liability was to be measured at the best estimate of the expenditure required to settle the present obligation at the reporting date. This would usually be the present market price of the number of allowances required to cover emissions made up to the reporting date.[18]

The interpretation also noted that the existence of an emission rights scheme could represent an indicator of impairment of the related assets, requiring an IAS 36 impairment test to be performed, because the additional costs of compliance could reduce the cash flows expected to be generated by those assets.[19]

Those who called for the withdrawal of IFRIC 3 identified a number of accounting mismatches arising from its application:[20]

- a measurement mismatch between the assets and liabilities recognised in accordance with IFRIC 3;
- a mismatch in the location in which the gains and losses on those assets are reported; and
- a possible timing mismatch because allowances would be recognised when they are obtained – typically at the start of the year – whereas the emission liability would be recognised during the year as it is incurred.

In light of these accounting mismatches, it is perhaps no surprise that in practice very few companies have applied IFRIC 3 on a voluntary basis. Instead companies have developed a range of different approaches in accounting for cap and trade emission rights schemes, which are discussed below:

- 'net liability' approaches;
- 'government grants' approach.

Whatever approach is used, companies should disclose their accounting policies regarding grants of emission rights, the emission rights themselves, the liability for the obligation to deliver allowances equal to emissions that have been made and the presentation in the statement of profit or loss. *[IAS 1.117, 121]*.

11.2.2 Emissions trading schemes – Net liability approaches

Under the 'net liability' approach emission allowances received by way of grant are recorded at a nominal amount and the entity will only recognise a liability once the actual emissions exceed the emission rights granted and still held, thereby requiring the entity to purchase additional allowances in the market or incur a regulatory penalty. Purchased grants are initially recognised at cost.

We believe that an entity can apply such a 'net liability' approach, because in the absence of specific guidance on the accounting for emission rights, IAS 20 allows non-monetary government grants and the related asset (in this case the emission rights) received to be measured at a nominal amount (i.e. nil). *[IAS 20.23]*.

Under IAS 37, a provision can only be recorded if the recognition criteria in the standard are met, including that the entity has a present obligation as a result of a past event, it is probable that an outflow of economic resources will be required to settle the obligation and a reliable estimate can be made, *[IAS 37.14]*, (see Chapter 26). As far as emissions are concerned, the 'obligating event' is the emission itself, therefore a provision is considered for recognition as emissions are made, but an outflow of resources is not probable until the reporting entity has made emissions in excess of any rights held. This means that an entity should not recognise a provision for any anticipated future shortfall of emission rights, nor should it accrete a provision over the period of the expected shortfall.

Under IAS 37 the entire obligation to deliver allowances should be measured on the basis of the best estimate of the expenditure required to settle the present obligation at the end of the reporting period (see Chapter 26). *[IAS 37.36]*. Accordingly any provision is based on the lower of the expected cost to purchase additional allowances in the market or the amount of any regulatory penalty.

Although it has been criticised for using a nominal value for the rights and a net approach for measuring the liability, the 'net liability' approach appears to have gained acceptance in practice.

Example 17.18: Application of 'net liability' approach

Company A received allowances representing the right to produce 10,000 tonnes of CO_2 for the year to 31 December 2020. The expected emissions for the full year are 12,000 tonnes of CO_2. At the end of the third quarter, it has emitted 9,000 tonnes of CO_2. The market price of the allowances at the end of each quarter is €10/tonne, €12/tonne, €14/tonne and €16/tonne respectively.

Under the 'net liability' approach, the provision at the end of the first, second and third quarters would be nil, because the company has not yet exceeded its emissions target. Only in the fourth quarter is a provision recognised, for the excess tonnage emitted, at 2,000 tonnes × €16/tonne = €32,000.

In the above example, the company cannot anticipate the future shortfall of 2,000 tonnes before the fourth quarter by accreting the provision over the year, nor can it recognise on day one the full provision for the 2,000 tonnes expected shortfall. This is because there is no past obligating event to be recognised until the emissions target has actually been exceeded.

Some schemes operate over a period of more than one year, such that the entity is unconditionally entitled to receive allowances for, say, a 3-year period, and it is possible to carry over unused emission rights from one year to the next. In our view, these circumstances would justify application of the net liability approach for the entire period concerned, not just the reporting period for which emission rights have been transferred to the entity. When applying the net liability approach, an entity may choose an accounting policy that measures deficits on the basis of:

- an annual allocation of emission rights; or
- an allocation that covers the entire first period of the scheme (e.g. 3 years) provided that the entity is unconditionally entitled to all the allowances for the first period concerned.

For such schemes, the entity must apply the chosen method consistently at every reporting date. If the entity chooses the annual allocation basis, a deficit is measured on that basis and there can be no carrying over of rights from one year to the next or back to the previous year.

In Example 17.18 above, the entity had an expected shortfall of 2,000 tonnes. Suppose that during the year it had purchased emission rights to cover some or all of the expected shortfall. How should these be accounted for?

Example 17.19: Impact of purchased emission rights on the application of 'net liability' approach

In Example 17.18 above, Company A had an expected shortfall of 2,000 tonnes. The same facts apply, except that at the end of the second quarter, it purchases emission rights for 1,000 tonnes at €12/tonne, i.e. a cost of €12,000. It records these rights as an intangible asset at cost. No impairment has been necessary.

In recognising the provision for its excess emissions of 2,000 tonnes at the end of the year, can the entity apply a method whereby the provision is based on the carrying amount of the emission rights it already owns (the 'carrying value method'), with the balance based on the market price at the year end? That is, can the entity recognise a provision of €28,000, being €12,000 (1,000 tonnes at €12/tonne) plus €16,000 (1,000 tonnes at €16/tonne)?

Because the cost of emissions can only be settled by delivering allowances and the liability to the government cannot be transferred, it is argued that the cost to the entity of settling the obligation is represented by the current carrying value of the emission rights held.

Another view is that measurement of the obligation should be determined independently of considerations as to how settlement may be funded by the entity. Accordingly, the provision would be measured, as in Example 17.18, at €32,000 (based on the market value of emission rights at the year-end). However, the entity may consider the emission rights it holds as a reimbursement right under IAS 37, which is recognised at an amount not exceeding the related provision (see Chapter 26). *[IAS 37.53]*.

Under this alternative 'net liability / reimbursement rights' approach, the entity would re-measure (to fair value) the emission rights that it holds. Therefore although Company A has recognised a provision (and an expense) of €32,000, at the same time it would revalue its purchased emission rights, as a reimbursement right, from €12/tonne to €16/tonne. It would thus recognise a gain of €4,000 (1,000 tonnes × €4/tonne), resulting in a net expense of €28,000 in the statement of profit or loss. This is the same as the profit or loss effect of applying the 'net liability / carrying value' approach.

In practice both the 'net liability' approach and the 'net liability / reimbursement rights' approach have gained acceptance.

In the extract below, MOL Hungarian Oil and Gas Plc applies a 'net liability' approach, i.e. emission rights granted free of charge are accounted for at their nominal value of zero and no government grant is recognised. A liability for the obligation to deliver allowances is only recognised when the level of emissions exceed the level of allowances granted. MOL Hungarian Oil and Gas Plc measures the liability at the cost of purchased allowances up to the level of purchased allowances held, and then at the market price of allowances ruling at the reporting date, with movements in the liability recognised in operating profit.

Extract 17.14: MOL Hungarian Oil and Gas Plc. (2019)

NOTES TO THE FINANCIAL STATEMENTS [extract]

NON-FINANCIAL ASSETS AND LIABILITIES [extract]

9. Property, plant and equipment and intangible assets [extract]

b) Intangible assets [extract]

Accounting policies [extract]

Free granted quotas are not recorded in the financial statements, while purchased quotas are initially recognised as intangible assets at cost at the emitting segments subsequently remeasured to fair value through profit or loss.

15. Provisions [extract]

Accounting policies [extract]

Provision for Emission quotas

The Group recognises provision for the estimated CO_2 emissions costs when actual emission exceeds the emission rights granted and still held. When actual emission exceeds the amount of emission rights granted, provision is recognised for the exceeding emission rights based on the purchase price of allowance concluded in forward contracts or market quotations at the reporting date.

11.2.3 Emissions trading schemes – Government grant approach

Another approach which has gained acceptance in practice is to recognise the emission rights granted by the government initially at their fair value and record a corresponding government grant in the statement of financial position. The government grant element is subsequently recognised as income in accordance with the requirements of IAS 20. To that extent, the approach follows that required by IFRIC 3. However, rather than measuring the liability for the obligation to deliver allowances at the present market price of those allowances, the liability is measured instead by reference to the amounts recorded when those rights were first granted.

As with the 'net liability' approach, critics have argued that the government grant approach would not be in line with the 'best estimate' determined under IAS 37 as the amount that an entity would rationally pay to settle the obligation at the reporting date or to transfer it to a third party at that time. *[IAS 37.37]*.

Repsol initially recognises the emission rights at fair value as a government grant under IAS 20 and illustrates clearly that the measurement of the liability follows that of the related emission rights. To the extent that emissions are not covered by emission rights, the liability is recognised at the fair value of such allowances at the reporting date.

> **Extract 17.15: Repsol, S.A. (2019)**
> NOTES TO THE 2019 FINANCIAL STATEMENTS [extract]
> OTHER DISCLOSURES [extract]
> (31) CLIMATE CHANGE AND ENVIRONMENTAL INFORMATION [extract]
> 31.1) CO_2 emission allowances [extract]
> *Accounting policies — CO_2 emission allowances*
>
> Emission allowances are recognized as an intangible asset and are initially recognized at acquisition cost. Those allowances free of charge under the emissions trading system for the 2013-2020 period, are initially recognized at the market price prevailing at the beginning of the year in which they are issued, against deferred income as a grant. As the corresponding tons of CO_2 are issued, the deferred income is reclassified to profit or loss.
>
> They are not amortized as their carrying amount matches their residual value and are subject to an impairment test based on their recoverable amount, (measured with reference to the price of the benchmark contract in the futures market provided by the ECX – European Climate Exchange).
>
> The Group records an expense under "*Other operating expenses*" in the income statement for the CO_2 emissions released during the year, recognizing a provision calculated based on the tons of CO_2 emitted, measured at: (i) their carrying amount in the case of the allowances that the Group has at year end; and (ii) the closing list price in the case of allowances that it does not yet have at year end.
>
> When the emissions allowances for the tons of CO_2 emitted are delivered to the authorities, the intangible assets as well as their corresponding provision are derecognized from the balance sheet without any effect on the income statement.
>
> When carbon emission allowances are actively managed to take advantage of market trading opportunities, the trading allowances portfolio is classified as trading inventories (see Note 17).

The fair value on initial recognition of emission rights that are accounted as intangible assets will be based on the requirements of IFRS 13 which are discussed in Chapter 14. If there is no active market for emission rights, the selection of appropriate valuation techniques, inputs to those valuation techniques and the application of the fair value hierarchy are discussed in Chapter 14.

11.2.4 Amortisation and impairment testing of emission rights

In the case of cap and trade schemes, emission rights that are accounted for as intangible assets are unlikely to be amortised as their depreciable amount is usually nil. Their expected residual value at inception will be equal to their fair value. Thereafter, although their residual value is equal to their market value, there is no consumption of economic benefit while the emission right is held. The economic benefits are realised instead by surrendering the rights to settle obligations under the scheme for emissions made, or by selling rights to another party. It is necessary to perform an IAS 36 impairment test whenever there is an indication of impairment (see Chapter 20). If the market value of an emission right drops below its carrying amount, this does not automatically result in an impairment charge because emission rights are likely to be tested for impairment as part of a larger cash generating unit.

11.2.5 Emission rights acquired in a business combination

At the date of acquisition of a business, an acquirer is required to recognise the acquiree's identifiable intangible assets, in this case emission rights, at their fair values. [IFRS 3.18].

However, an acquirer should only recognise a provision for actual emissions that have occurred up to that date. This means that an acquirer cannot apply the 'net liability' approach to emission rights acquired in a business combination. Instead, an acquirer should treat acquired emission rights in the same way as purchased emission rights (see 11.2.2 above). An acquirer that applies IFRIC 3 or the 'government grant' approach would recognise acquired emission rights at their fair value, but cannot recognise a deferred credit for a 'government grant' as it acquired the emission rights by way of a business combination.

Consequently, an acquirer may report a higher emission expense in its statement of profit or loss in the compliance period in which it acquires a business.

11.2.6 Sale of emission rights

The sale of emission rights that are accounted for as intangible assets should be recognised in accordance with IAS 38. This means that they should be derecognised on disposal or when no future economic benefits are expected from their use or disposal. [IAS 38.112]. The gain or loss arising from derecognition of the emission rights should be determined as the difference between the net disposal proceeds and the carrying amount of emission rights. [IAS 38.113].

Prior to the sale the entity may not have recognised the obligation, to deliver allowances equal to the emissions caused, at its fair value at the date of derecognition. If that were the case then the entity would need to ensure that the liability in excess of the emission rights held by the company after the sale is recognised at the present fair value of the emission rights.

Both the gain or loss on the derecognition of the emission rights and the adjustment of the liability should be recognised when the emission rights are derecognised. Any gain should not be classified as revenue. [IAS 38.113].

If an entity that applies the 'net liability' approach were to sell all its emission rights at the start of the compliance period, it would not be permitted to defer the gain on that sale even if it was certain that the entity would need to repurchase emission rights later in the year to cover actual emissions. A gain is recognised immediately on the sale and a provision is recognised as gases are emitted.

If an entity enters into a forward contract to sell an emission right, it may be acting effectively as a broker-trader. The entity should determine whether the contract is a derivative within the scope of IFRS 9 by applying the requirements in that Standard (see Chapter 46).

11.2.7 Accounting for emission rights by brokers and traders

IFRIC 3 did not address accounting by brokers and traders that are not themselves participants in a cap and trade scheme. However, they hold emission rights as assets held for sale in the ordinary course of business, which means that they meet the definition of inventories in IAS 2. *[IAS 2.6]*. Under that standard a broker-trader may choose between measuring emission rights at the lower of cost and net realisable value or at fair value less costs to sell. Commodity broker-traders who measure their inventories at fair value less costs to sell may recognise changes in fair value less costs to sell in profit or loss in the period of the change. *[IAS 2.3]*.

When a company trades derivatives based on the emission rights, they fall within the scope of IFRS 9 and are accounted for at fair value through profit or loss unless they hedge the fair value of the emission rights granted to the company or qualify for the 'own use exemption'. *[IFRS 9.2.4]*.

When an entity holds emission rights for own use and also has a trading department trading in emission rights, the company should split the books between emission rights held for own use and those held for trading. The emission rights should be treated as intangible assets and inventory respectively. This is illustrated in Extract 17.15 above.

11.3 Accounting for green certificates or renewable energy certificates

Some governments have launched schemes to promote power production from renewable sources, based on green certificates, renewable energy certificates, green tags or tradable renewable certificates. There are similarities between green certificates and emission rights, except that whilst emission rights are granted to reflect a future limit on emissions, green certificates are awarded on the basis of the amount of green energy already produced.

In a typical scheme, producers of electricity are granted certificates by the government based on the power output (kWh) derived from renewable sources. Entities distributing electricity (produced from both renewable and traditional sources) are required to hand over to the government a number of certificates based on the total kWh of electricity sold to consumers during the year, or pay a penalty to the extent that an insufficient number of certificates is rendered. It is this requirement that creates a valuable market for the certificates, allowing producers to sell their certificates to distributors, using the income to subsidise in effect the higher cost of generation from renewable sources.

11.3.1 Accounting by producers using renewable energy sources

As in the case of emission rights, the award of green certificates is treated as a government grant by a producer. An intangible asset representing an entitlement to that grant is recognised at the point in time when the green electricity is produced. As with any government grant, the entitlement is initially measured at either fair value or a nominal amount, depending on the entity's chosen policy. *[IAS 20.23]*.

Where the entitlement asset is initially recognised at fair value, a credit entry is recorded in the statement of profit or loss as either a reduction in production costs for the period (on the basis that the purpose of the grant is to compensate the producer for the higher cost of using renewable energy sources) or as other income, but not as revenue. *[IAS 20.29]*. Subsequent revaluation of the intangible asset is only allowed if an active market exists for the green certificates, and the other requirements of IAS 38 are applied (see 8.2 above). The intangible is derecognised when the certificate is sold by the producer.

11.3.2 Accounting by distributors of renewable energy

When the distributor is also a producer of renewable energy, it has the option to use certificates granted to it or to sell them in the market. Accordingly, the permissible accounting treatments of green certificates are in principle the same as those for emission rights discussed at 11.2 above. The distributor is obliged to remit certificates and therefore recognises a provision as sales are recorded (in the same way that a provision for emission rights is recognised as emissions are made). The distributor might apply a 'net liability' approach, discussed at 11.2.2 above, and only start to recognise a provision once it has achieved a level of sales exceeding that covered by certificates granted to the entity in its capacity as a producer.

If a distributor is not also a producer of renewable energy, it recognises a provision as sales are made, measured at the fair value of green certificates to be remitted. A corresponding cost is included in cost of sales. The provision is remeasured to fair value at each reporting date. If the entity purchases certificates in the market, they are recognised as an intangible asset and initially measured at cost. Subsequent revaluation is only allowed if an active market exists for the green certificates, and the other requirements of IAS 38 are applied (see 8.2 above).

Alternatively, as discussed in Example 17.19 at 11.2.2 above, the asset held may be designated by management as a reimbursement right in respect of the associated liability, allowing remeasurement to fair value. Similarly, the entity could apply a carrying value method, measuring the provision based on the value and extent of certificates already held and applying fair value only to the extent that it has an obligation to make further purchases in the market or to incur a penalty if it fails to do so.

11.3.3 Accounting by brokers and traders

As discussed at 11.2.7 above, brokers and traders should apply IAS 2 where green certificates are held for sale in the ordinary course of business; account for derivatives based on green certificates in accordance with IFRS 9; and properly distinguish those held for own use (carried within intangible assets) from certificates held for trading (included in inventory).

11.4 Accounting for REACH costs

The European Regulation[21] concerning the Registration, Evaluation, Authorisation and Restriction of Chemicals (REACH) came into force on 1 June 2007. The regulation requires manufacturers or importers of substances to register them with a central European Chemicals Agency (ECHA). An entity will not be able to manufacture or supply unregistered substances. As a consequence, entities will incur different types of costs, such as:

- costs of identifying the substances that need to be registered;
- testing and other data collection costs, including outsourcing services from external laboratories, costs of tests in own laboratories – testing materials, labour costs and related overheads;
- registration fees payable to ECHA; and
- legal fees.

These costs may be part of the development of a new manufacturing process or product, or in the use of a new chemical in an existing manufacturing process or product. They might be incurred solely by an entity or shared with other entities (clients, partners or even competitors). Under the REACH legislation, cost sharing might be achieved by the submission of a joint registration (whereby testing and other data collection costs are shared before the registration is filed) or by reimbursement (whereby an entity pays an existing registrant for access to the registration and testing data used in its earlier application for registration). Accordingly, questions arise as to whether such costs should be capitalised or recognised as an expense and, if capitalised, on what basis the related intangible asset should be amortised.

In our view, a registration under the REACH regulation is an intangible asset as defined by IAS 38. *[IAS 38.8]*. As it gives rise to a legal right, the registration is identifiable. *[IAS 38.12(b)]*. Because a registration cannot be arbitrarily withdrawn and also establishes intellectual property rights over the data used in the application for registration, a resource is controlled. *[IAS 38.13]*. The future economic benefits relating to the registration arise from either the right to reimbursement for the use by others of data supporting the entity's earlier application; or from the revenues to be earned and cost savings to be achieved by the entity from the use of registered substances in its business activities. *[IAS 38.17]*.

The appropriate accounting treatment under IAS 38 depends upon whether the required data is collected by the entity or acquired from an existing registrant and on whether the registration being completed is for a substance already used in an existing process or product (an existing substance) or intended to be used for the first time or in a new process or product (a new substance). The flow chart below demonstrates how these different features interact with the requirements of IAS 38.

Intangible assets 1369

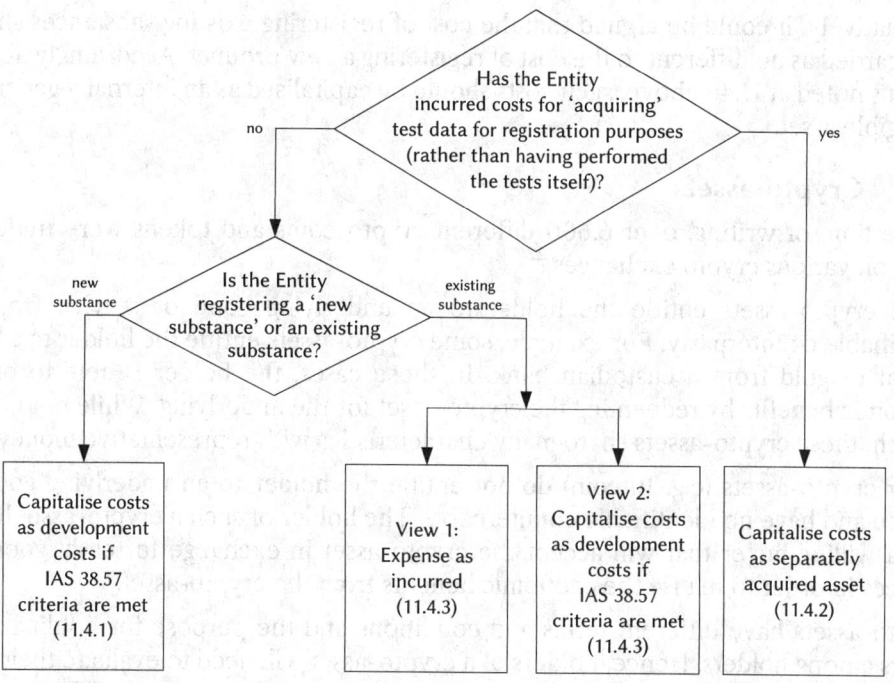

11.4.1 Costs of registering a new substance performed by the entity itself

If the entity itself incurs REACH costs, these activities meet the definition of development in IAS 38. [IAS 38.8]. Accordingly, the entity must also meet the rigorous rules in the standard described at 6.2.2 above which confirm that the related development project is at a sufficiently advanced stage, is economically viable and includes only directly attributable costs. [IAS 38.57].

Costs of identifying the substances that need to be registered would have to be recognised as an expense when incurred, as this activity is regarded as research. [IAS 38.56].

11.4.2 Costs of acquiring test data from an existing registrant

An entity may acquire test data from an existing registrant that has already been used by it in its earlier application for registration. These costs should be capitalised as a separately acquired intangible asset (see 4 above).

11.4.3 Costs of registering an existing substance performed by the entity itself

In this case two alternative treatments are acceptable. If the costs of obtaining a REACH registration for existing substances used in existing processes are regarded as subsequent expenditure on an existing intangible asset, the related costs should be recognised as an expense as incurred, [IAS 38.20], (see 3.3 above). As unregistered substances will no longer be available for use, this might indicate that the registration maintains the economic benefits associated with the related production process or product and does not improve it.

Alternatively, it could be argued that the cost of registering existing substances should be regarded as no different to the cost of registering a new product. Accordingly, for the reasons noted at 11.4.1 above, such costs should be capitalised as an internally generated intangible asset.

11.5 Crypto-assets

At the time of writing, over 6,600 different crypto-coins and tokens were traded or listed on various crypto exchanges.[22]

Some crypto-assets entitle the holder to an underlying good or service from an identifiable counterparty. For example, some crypto-assets entitle the holder to a fixed weight of gold from a custodian bank. In those cases, the holder is able to obtain economic benefits by redeeming the crypto-asset for the underlying. While not money as such, these crypto-assets share many characteristics with representative money.

Other crypto-assets (e.g. Bitcoin) do not entitle the holder to an underlying good or service and have no identifiable counterparty. The holder of such a crypto-asset has to find a willing buyer that will accept the crypto-asset in exchange for cash, goods or services in order to realise the economic benefits from the crypto-asset.

Crypto-assets have different terms and conditions and the purpose for holding them differs among holders. Hence, holders of a crypto-asset will need to evaluate their own facts and circumstances in order to determine which accounting classification and measurement under current IFRS should be applied. Depending on the standard, the holder may also need to assess its business model in order to determine the appropriate classification and measurement.

Crypto-assets generally meet the relatively wide definition of an intangible asset, as they are identifiable, lack physical substance, are controlled by the holder and give rise to future economic benefits for the holder.

11.5.1 Crypto-assets – Recognition and initial measurement

Crypto-assets that meet the definition of an intangible asset and are being accounted for under IAS 38 are only recognised if it is probable that future economic benefits will flow to the entity and its cost can be measured reliably (see 3.1 above). Separately acquired intangible assets will normally be recognised, as IAS 38 assumes that the acquisition price reflects the expectation about future economic benefits. Thus, an entity always expects future economic benefits, for these intangibles, even if there is uncertainty about the timing or amount (See 4.1 above).

Crypto-assets that meet the definition of an intangible asset and are being accounted for under IAS 38 are initially measured at cost (see 3.2 above).

The cost of acquiring crypto-assets would typically include the purchase price (after deducting trade discounts and rebates if any) and the related transaction costs, which could include blockchain processing fees. Where an intangible asset is acquired in exchange for another non-monetary asset, the cost is measured at fair value, unless the transaction lacks commercial substance or the fair value of neither the asset acquired nor the asset given up can be measured reliably. In such instances, the cost of the intangible asset is measured as the carrying amount of the asset given up.

11.5.2 Crypto-assets – Subsequent measurement

As discussed at 8 above, there are two subsequent measurement approaches under IAS 38 that can be applied as an accounting policy choice to each class of intangible asset, namely:

- Cost model.
- Revaluation model (subject to criteria as discussed below).

An entity that holds different types of crypto-assets would need to assess whether they constitute different classes of intangible assets as the rights and underlying economics of different crypto-assets vary widely.

11.5.2.A Crypto-assets – Cost model

The cost method under IAS 38 entails subsequent measurement at cost less any amortisation and impairment (see 8.1 above).

Many crypto-assets such as Bitcoin do not have an expiry date, and there appears to be no foreseeable limit to the period over which they could be exchanged with a willing counterparty for cash or other goods or services.

A holder will therefore need to consider if there is a foreseeable limit to the period over which such a crypto-asset is expected to generate net cash inflows for the entity. If there is no foreseeable limit, such a crypto-asset could be considered to have an indefinite useful life and, as a result, no amortisation is required. However, intangible assets with an indefinite useful life need to be tested for impairment at least annually and whenever there is an indication of impairment (see 9.3 above).

Where there is a foreseeable limit to the period over which a crypto-asset is expected to generate net cash inflows for the holder, a useful life should be estimated and the cost of the crypto-asset, less any residual value, should be amortised on a systematic basis over this useful life (see 9.2 above). In addition, such a crypto-asset is also subject to IAS 36 impairment testing whenever there is an indication of impairment.

11.5.2.B Crypto-assets – Revaluation model

An entity can only apply the revaluation model if the fair value can be determined by reference to an active market (see 8.2 above), which IFRS 13 defines as 'a market in which transactions for the asset or liability take place with sufficient frequency and volume to provide pricing information on an ongoing basis'.

There are no provisions in IAS 38 that allow for the fair value of an intangible asset to be determined indirectly, for example by using valuation techniques and financial models applied to estimate the fair value of intangible assets acquired in a business combination. Consequently, if no observable price in an active market for an identical asset exists (i.e. a Level 1 price under IFRS 13), the holder will need to apply the cost method to crypto-assets held.

In assessing whether an active market exists for a crypto-asset, the holder will need to consider whether there is economic substance to the observable transactions, as many trades on crypto-exchanges are non-cash transactions in which one crypto-asset is exchanged for another.

Under the revaluation model, intangible assets are measured at their fair value on the date of revaluation less any subsequent amortisation and impairment losses.

The net increase in fair value over the initial cost of the intangible asset is recorded in the revaluation reserve via other comprehensive income. A net decrease below cost is recorded in profit or loss. The cumulative revaluation reserve may be transferred directly to retained earnings upon derecognition, and possibly by transferring the additional amortisation on the revalued amount to retained earnings as the asset is used, but IAS 38 does not allow the revaluation reserve to be transferred via profit or loss.

11.5.3 Crypto-assets – Standard setter activity

Accounting standard setters are monitoring the development of crypto-assets and the related accounting practices by holders. Some standard setters have undertaken research into the accounting for crypto-assets, while some have expressed a view on what they consider to be appropriate accounting under IFRS. For example, in Japan the standard setter has issued authoritative guidance for the accounting of crypto-assets under local GAAP.

In November 2018, the IASB decided not to add to its work plan a project on holdings of cryptocurrencies or initial coin offerings, but instead would monitor the development of crypto-assets. The IASB asked the Interpretations Committee to consider publishing an agenda decision on how entities apply existing IFRS Standards to holdings of cryptocurrencies, a subset of crypto assets.[23]

In June 2019, the Committee published an agenda decision on this matter. The Committee observed that a holding of cryptocurrency meets the definition of an intangible asset under IAS 38 because it is capable of being separated from the holder and sold or transferred individually, and does not give the holder a right to receive a fixed or determinable number of units of currency. The Committee concluded that where cryptocurrencies are held for sale in the ordinary course of business, then IAS 2 applies, otherwise they should be accounted for under IAS 38.

The Committee determined that cryptocurrencies are not financial assets as they are not cash or equity instruments of another entity. They also do not give rise to a contractual right for the holder, and they are not a contract that will or may be settled in the holder's own equity instruments.[24]

11.6 Cloud computing

11.6.1 Types of cloud computing arrangement and determination of applicable IFRSs

As the use of technology, data and connectivity expands, cloud computing arrangements are becoming more common. Cloud computing arrangements are arrangements in which the customer does not currently have possession of the underlying software used in the arrangement. Rather, the customer accesses and uses the software on an as-needed basis (e.g. through the internet, or via a dedicated line). Examples of cloud computing arrangements include software as a service, platform as a service, infrastructure as a service and other hosting arrangements. IFRS standards do not contain explicit guidance on a customer's accounting for cloud computing arrangements or the costs to implement them. A customer in a cloud computing arrangement will need to carefully evaluate which

IFRS standards to apply when accounting for the costs of a cloud computing arrangement, and may need to apply various IFRS standards, including IAS 38, IFRS 16, and IAS 16. The following diagram summarises the accounting for cloud computing arrangements.

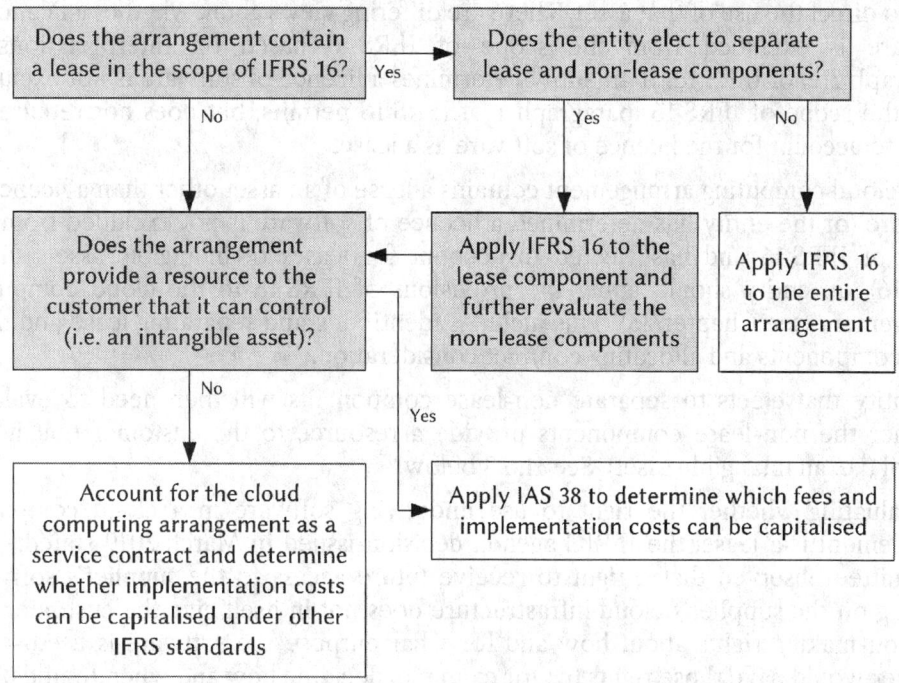

The IFRS Interpretations Committee received a submission about the customer's accounting for a 'Software as a service' cloud computing arrangement, which was discussed at Committee meetings in September 2018, November 2018, and March 2019. In the IASB staff's analysis of the submission, it noted that an entity should first evaluate whether the rights granted in the cloud computing arrangement are within the scope of IAS 38 or IFRS 16. Otherwise, the arrangement is generally a service contract.[25]

11.6.2 Evaluating whether a cloud computing arrangement contains a lease

IFRS 16 defines a lease as 'a contract, or part of a contract, that conveys the right to use an asset (the underlying asset) for a period of time in exchange for consideration'. *[IFRS 16 Appendix A]*. A contract conveys the right to use an asset if, throughout the period of use, the customer has both:

(a) the right to obtain substantially all the economic benefits from use of the asset (an identified asset); and

(b) the right to direct the use of that asset. *[IFRS 16.9, B9]*.

Paragraphs B9 to B31 of IFRS 16 provide application guidance on the definition of a lease. Among other requirements, that application guidance specifies that a customer generally has the right to direct the use of an asset by having decision-making rights to change how and for what purpose the asset is used throughout the period of use. Accordingly, in a contract that contains a lease the supplier has given up those decision-making rights and transferred them to the customer at the lease commencement date.

Therefore, an entity should evaluate whether a cloud computing arrangement includes the right to use an asset (e.g. underlying servers or other tangible assets) for which it has the right to obtain substantially all the economic benefits from use of the asset and the right to direct the use of that asset. There are differing views about whether a licence of software is excluded from the scope of IFRS 16 based on interpretations of paragraph 3(e) of IFRS 16. If an entity determines a licence of software is not excluded from the scope of IFRS 16, paragraph 4 of IFRS 16 permits, but does not require, an entity to account for the licence of software as a lease.

If the cloud computing arrangement contains a lease of an asset other than a licence of software (or the entity has determined a licence of software is not excluded from the scope of IFRS 16 and has elected to account for leases of intangible assets under IFRS 16), an entity should apply the provisions of IFRS 16 to the cloud computing arrangement (see Chapter 23). This includes identifying and separating lease and non-lease components and allocating contract consideration.

An entity that elects to separate non-lease components will then need to evaluate whether the non-lease components provide a resource to the customer that it can control (i.e. an intangible asset). See 11.6.3 below.

In evaluating whether the right to use underlying software in a cloud computing arrangement is a lease, the IFRIC agenda decision issued in March 2019 stated, 'The Committee observed that a right to receive future access to the supplier's software running on the supplier's cloud infrastructure does not in itself give the customer any decision-making rights about how and for what purpose the software is used – the supplier would have those rights by, for example, deciding how and when to update or reconfigure the software, or deciding on which hardware (or infrastructure) the software will run. Accordingly, if a contract conveys to the customer only the right to receive access to the supplier's application software over the contract term, the contract does not contain a software lease.'[26]

11.6.3 Evaluating whether a cloud computing arrangement contains an intangible asset

IAS 38 defines an intangible asset as 'an identifiable non-monetary asset without physical substance'. *[IAS 38.8]*. An asset is a resource controlled by the entity, and an entity controls an intangible asset if it has the power to obtain the future economic benefits flowing from the underlying resource and to restrict the access of others to those benefits. *[IAS 38.13]*.

Therefore, an entity should evaluate whether a cloud computing arrangement provides the customer a resource that it can control (i.e. if the customer has the power to obtain the future economic benefits flowing from the underlying resource and to restrict the access of others to those benefits). If the customer receives a resource that it can control, then it should apply the guidance in IAS 38 to that resource (assuming it is not accounting for the intangible asset as a lease – see 11.6.1 above).

IFRS standards do not provide specific guidance on whether a cloud computing arrangement provides the customer a resource that it can control (i.e. an intangible asset). One situation in which an intangible asset for a software licence exists in a cloud

computing arrangement (and is therefore substantive) is when both of the following are met at the inception of the arrangement:
- the customer has the contractual right to take possession of the software during the hosting period without significant penalty; and
- it is feasible for the customer to run the software on its own hardware or contract with another party unrelated to the supplier to host the software.

These facts indicate that the customer controls the underlying licence even if it is hosted by the supplier. There may be other possible situations in which a customer concludes that a cloud computing arrangement provides the customer with a resource that it can control. However, the fact that an arrangement conveys to the customer a licence of software hosted by the supplier is not, in and of itself, a sufficient basis to conclude that the arrangement contains an intangible asset. The licence must be substantive.

The evaluation of the facts listed above is performed at the inception of the arrangement (or upon a modification of the arrangement) because the evaluation of whether an arrangement includes an intangible asset should be based on the facts and circumstances when the arrangement is entered into.

In evaluating whether the customer has the right to take possession of the software during the hosting period without a significant penalty, and the right is therefore substantive, an entity may consider whether it has both of the following:
- the ability to take delivery of the software without incurring significant costs; and
- the ability to use the software separately without a significant diminution in utility or value

To support the view that a customer has the ability to take delivery of software included in a cloud computing arrangement without incurring significant costs, an entity may consider the following factors:
- whether financial penalties or operational barriers act as a significant disincentive to the customer taking possession of the software. An example of such a barrier is a contractual requirement that significant fees or penalties must be paid to the supplier in connection with taking possession of the software. Another form of penalty may be a requirement to pay or forfeit a significant amount of 'unused' hosting fees on cancellation of the cloud computing contract. Accordingly, a cloud computing arrangement should be evaluated carefully to determine if the amount of fees that the customer must either 1) pay on cancellation, or 2) forfeit if fees are prepaid represents a 'significant cost';
- the evaluation of whether a penalty is significant should be based on whether the amount of the penalty creates a sufficiently large disincentive such that the customer would not incur the penalty to take possession of the software. In evaluating whether any fees or penalties are significant, an entity may evaluate the amount of the fees or penalties in the context of the overall arrangement economics;
- whether there is an explicit, reasonable mechanism in the contractual arrangement by which the customer can exercise a right to take possession of the software;

- whether other economic barriers or costs exist that act as a significant disincentive to the customer taking possession of the software. For example, new hardware may be required to run the software, but the cost of obtaining that hardware is so high that a significant disincentive exists. Furthermore, if specialised technicians are needed to run the software, the cost to hire the technicians also may be a significant disincentive; and
- whether there is an absence of an adequate number of qualified replacement service providers. A lack of service providers that could host the licenced software due to: (i) unique features, functionality or operating system requirements of the software; (ii) the need to hire specialised technicians to run the software at a significant cost; or (iii) other factors that may be significant disincentives.

To support the view that a customer has the ability to use the software separately without a significant diminution in utility or value, an entity may consider the following factors:

- whether the customer can utilise all of the functionality of the software if the software is not hosted by the supplier. For example, if the software would not be able to process substantially the same number of transactions in approximately the same period if not hosted by the supplier, this may indicate that the customer cannot use the software separately from the supplier's hosting services without a significant diminution in utility or value; and
- whether software upgrades are only available to customers for whom the supplier hosts the software. If the functionality provided by upgrades to the software is important to customers, and such upgrades would not be made available if the software is not hosted by the supplier, the utility of the software to a customer is likely significantly diminished if the supplier's hosting services are discontinued.

If the cloud computing arrangement does not provide the customer with an intangible asset for the software (and does not contain a lease), then the right to access the underlying software in the cloud computing arrangement is generally a service contract. However, when an arrangement conveys to the customer only a right to access and the customer pays the supplier before it receives the service, that prepayment gives the customer a right to future service and would be recognised as a prepaid asset by the customer.

11.6.4   Accounting for a cloud computing arrangement that includes an intangible asset

11.6.4.A   Fees in the arrangement

Under IAS 38, an item that meets the definition of an intangible asset should only be recognised if, at the time of initial recognition of the expenditure:

- it is probable that the expected future economic benefits that are attributable to the asset will flow to the entity; and
- the cost of the asset can be measured reliably. *[IAS 38.21]*.

This test (that the item meets both the definition of an intangible asset and the criteria for recognition) is performed when an entity incurs potentially eligible expenditures, whether to acquire or internally generate an intangible asset or to add to, replace part of, or service it subsequent to initial recognition.

Separately acquired intangible rights (i.e. software licences in cloud computing arrangements) will normally be recognised as assets. IAS 38 assumes that the price paid to acquire an intangible asset usually reflects expectations about the probability that the future economic benefits embodied in it will flow to the entity. That is, the entity always expects there to be a flow of economic benefits, even if it is uncertain about the timing or amount. Therefore, the standard assumes that the cost of a separately acquired intangible asset can usually be measured reliably, especially where the purchase consideration is in the form of cash or other monetary assets.

In some cases, entities enter into a cloud computing arrangement that requires them to pay the cloud computing supplier or other third party to provide implementation activities and other services such as training employees to use the software, maintenance work to be performed by the third party, rights to future upgrades and enhancements, data conversion, and hardware.

An entity should allocate the fee in a cloud computing arrangement to these implementation activities and other services. One way an entity could allocate the fees in a cloud computing arrangement to each element in the contract (e.g. software licence, hosting, implementation activities) is based on the relative standalone price or relative fair value of each element in the contract. The statement of work for the implementation activities can often be complicated, so an entity will need to apply judgement to determine the components of implementation costs to which the purchase consideration should be allocated, which will determine the amounts that should be capitalised and the amounts that should be expensed as incurred.

Elements that meet both the definition of an intangible asset and the criteria for recognition should be accounted for in accordance with IAS 38. Elements outside the scope of IAS 38 (e.g. hosting) should be accounted for based on other IFRS standards. In addition, IAS 38 specifically states that certain expenditures should be expensed as incurred (i.e. training costs, start-up costs), see 7 above.

The asset recognised for the software licence should be the present value of the licence obligation if the cloud computing arrangement is to be paid for over time. An entity should record a liability to the extent that all or a portion of the amount allocated to the software licence is not paid on or before the recognition of the licence.

11.6.4.B Implementation costs

Customers often incur implementation costs to get a cloud computing arrangement ready for use. Implementation costs can include the following:

- research costs (e.g. needs assessment and software evaluation);
- hardware costs;
- costs to configure or customise the underlying software;
- changes to other entity systems;
- training costs;
- data conversion; and
- testing.

Costs incurred by customers to implement a cloud computing arrangement that includes a software licence are accounted for based on the nature of the costs. The guidance in IAS 38 should be applied by customers that obtain software licences to evaluate whether to capitalise or expense certain costs.

Costs that are recognised as an asset for developing software or obtaining a software licence included in a cloud computing arrangement include external direct costs of materials and services incurred in developing or obtaining the software and payroll and payroll related costs (benefits) for employees who are directly involved with and who devote time to developing the cloud computing system, to the extent the time is spent directly on the project's development activities. External direct costs include, among others, fees paid to develop the software or supplemental software (e.g. to write program code), cost to purchase the cloud computing software licence from third parties and travel expenses incurred by employees in their duties directly associated with developing the cloud computing system. Examples of employee activities include program coding and testing during development.

11.6.5 Accounting for a cloud computing arrangement that does not include an intangible asset

11.6.5.A Fees in the arrangement

If a cloud computing arrangement does not contain a lease in the scope of IFRS 16 and does not contain an intangible asset in the scope of IAS 38, then the right to access the underlying software in the cloud computing arrangement is generally a service contract. Therefore, an entity should expense the fees paid for the cloud computing arrangement as the service is provided.

Entities generally recognise an asset for costs they prepay that relate to a service they will receive over time, which may be the case for cloud computing arrangements. For example, a customer that makes payments to a supplier of cloud computing services in advance of the related service period may determine that it is appropriate to recognise a prepaid asset (e.g. prepaid service contract) for those costs. Importantly, these costs are considered a prepaid asset that should be subsequently recognised as operating expense (and not presented as amortisation that is used to calculate EBITDA) as the services are provided.

Up-front payments the customer makes to the cloud computing supplier that relate to enhancing the functionality of the cloud computing service to be received over time should also generally be treated as a prepaid asset that is expensed over the term of the arrangement.

Careful consideration of the services provided under a long-term cloud computing service or other arrangement is required to determine the appropriate accounting for the related costs. This includes gaining an understanding of what the services are (e.g. the long-term service versus component implementation services rendered at the start of the arrangement) and when they are provided so that the costs of the service arrangement are recognised in the appropriate period.

In situations where the cloud computing supplier provides component implementation services, it may be difficult to identify and allocate consideration to the component implementation services.

11.6.5.B Internal and third-party implementation costs

In a cloud computing service arrangement (i.e. an arrangement without a software licence), a customer may incur implementation and other up-front costs to get the cloud computing arrangement ready for use and directly or indirectly relate to the software service received over time. These costs may relate to activities performed by the customer's internal personnel or third parties.

Implementation costs can include the following:
- Research costs (e.g. needs assessment and software evaluation).
- Hardware costs.
- Costs to configure the underlying software.
- Customisation of software.
- Changes to other entity systems.
- Training costs.
- Data conversion.
- Testing.

The guidance in IAS 38 addresses how customers that obtain software licences evaluate whether to capitalise or expense certain costs, but it does not apply when software is accounted for as a service (i.e. service arrangements that do not include a software licence). Entities incur implementation and other up-front costs for a variety of service arrangements. As a result, entities will need to carefully review both the services they will receive and the implementation costs they will incur.

Careful consideration will be required if a customer contracts with a third-party supplier (unrelated to the software service supplier), or incurs internal costs to perform certain activities that are directly or indirectly related to a software service arrangement. Customers should carefully evaluate these types of costs to determine whether the costs should be expensed, recognised as a prepaid asset, or capitalised, depending on the specific services that are provided.

References

1. *IASB Update*, May 2016.
2. *IASB Update*, February 2018.
3. *IASB Work plan – research projects, IASB website*, https://www.ifrs.org/projects/work-plan/ (accessed on 31 August 2020).
4. *IASB Update*, April 2018.
5. *IFRIC Update*, March 2020.
6. *IFRIC Update*, June 2020.
7. *IFRIC Update*, November 2019.
8. *IASB Update*, March 2020.
9. European Commission website, http://ec.europa.eu/clima/policies/ets/index_en.htm (accessed on 31 August 2020).
10. *IASB Update*, June 2005.
11. IASB Staff Paper, *Pollutant Pricing Mechanisms, Project update and response to the Agenda Consultation*, April 2016.
12. *IASB Work plan – research projects, IASB website*, https://www.ifrs.org/projects/work-plan/ (accessed on 31 August 2020).

13 IFRIC 3, *Emission Rights*, 2005 Bound Volume, IASB, para. 2.
14 IFRIC 3.3.
15 IFRIC 3.5.
16 IFRIC 3.6.
17 IFRIC 3.7.
18 IFRIC 3.8.
19 IFRIC 3.9.
20 *IASB Update*, June 2005.
21 Regulation (EC) No. 1907/2006 of the European Parliament and of the Council of 18 December 2006 concerning the Registration, Evaluation, Authorisation and Restriction of Chemicals (REACH), establishing a European Chemicals Agency, amending Directive 1999/45/EC and repealing Council Regulation (EEC) No. 793/93 and Commission Regulation (EC) No. 1488/94 as well as Council Directive 76/769/EEC and Commission Directives 91/155/EEC, 93/67/EEC, 93/105/EC and 2000/21/EC.
22 CoinMarketCap website, http://www.coinmarketcap.com (accessed on 31 August 2020).
23 *IASB Update*, November 2018.
24 *IFRIC Update*, June 2019.
25 IASB Staff Paper, *Cloud computing arrangements, Initial consideration*, September 2018, *IFRIC Update*, September 2018.
26 *IFRIC Update*, March 2019

Chapter 18   Property, plant and equipment

1 INTRODUCTION 1385
2 THE REQUIREMENTS OF IAS 16 1386
    2.1 Scope 1386
    2.2 Definitions used in IAS 16 1387
    2.3 IFRS 16 and the presentation of right-of-use assets 1388
3 RECOGNITION 1388
    3.1 Aspects of recognition 1389
        3.1.1 Spare parts and minor items 1389
        3.1.2 Environmental and safety equipment 1389
        3.1.3 Property economic benefits and property developments 1390
        3.1.4 Classification as PP&E or intangible asset 1390
        3.1.5 Classification of items as inventory or PP&E when minimum levels are maintained 1391
        3.1.6 Production stripping costs of surface mines 1392
        3.1.7 Bearer plants 1393
    3.2 Accounting for parts ('components') of assets 1393
    3.3 Initial and subsequent expenditure 1394
        3.3.1 Types of parts 1395
        3.3.2 Major inspections 1396
4 MEASUREMENT AT RECOGNITION 1397
    4.1 Elements of cost and cost measurement 1397
        4.1.1 'Directly attributable' costs 1399
        4.1.2 Borrowing costs 1399
        4.1.3 Administration and other general overheads 1400
        4.1.4 Cessation of capitalisation 1400
        4.1.5 Self-built assets 1400

	4.1.6	Deferred payment	1401
	4.1.7	Land and buildings to be redeveloped	1401
	4.1.8	Transfers of assets from customers	1402
	4.1.9	Variable and contingent consideration	1402
4.2	Incidental and non-incidental income		1403
	4.2.1	Income earned while bringing the asset to the intended location and condition	1404
	4.2.2	Income received during the construction of property	1405
	4.2.3	Liquidated damages during construction	1405
4.3	Accounting for changes in decommissioning and restoration costs		1405
4.4	Exchanges of assets		1406
	4.4.1	Commercial substance	1407
	4.4.2	Reliably measurable	1407
4.5	Assets held under leases		1408
4.6	Assets acquired with the assistance of government grants		1408

5 MEASUREMENT AFTER RECOGNITION: COST MODEL 1408

5.1	Significant parts of assets		1409
5.2	Depreciable amount and residual values		1410
5.3	Depreciation charge		1411
5.4	Useful lives		1411
	5.4.1	Repairs and maintenance	1413
	5.4.2	Land	1413
	5.4.3	Technological change	1414
5.5	When depreciation starts		1414
5.6	Depreciation methods		1415
	5.6.1	Diminishing balance methods	1416
	5.6.2	Unit-of-production method	1416
5.7	Impairment		1417

6 MEASUREMENT AFTER RECOGNITION: REVALUATION MODEL 1417

6.1	The meaning of fair value			1419
	6.1.1	Revaluing assets under IFRS 13		1419
		6.1.1.A	Highest and best use	1419
		6.1.1.B	Valuation approaches	1420
		6.1.1.C	The cost approach – current replacement cost	1421
6.2	Accounting for valuation surpluses and deficits			1422
6.3	Reversals of downward valuations			1424
6.4	Adopting a policy of revaluation			1425
6.5	Assets held under leases			1426

7 DERECOGNITION AND DISPOSAL 1426
7.1 IFRS 5 – *Non-current Assets Held for Sale and Discontinued Operations* 1427
7.2 Sale of assets held for rental 1427
7.3 Partial disposals and undivided interests 1428
7.3.1 Joint control 1428
7.3.2 Vendor retains control 1429
7.3.3 Partial disposal 1430
7.4 Derecognition and replacement of insured assets 1430

8 IAS 16 DISCLOSURE REQUIREMENTS 1431
8.1 General disclosures 1431
8.2 Additional disclosures for revalued assets 1434
8.3 Other disclosures 1436

List of examples
Example 18.1:	Recognition and derecognition of parts	1394
Example 18.2:	Diminishing balance depreciation	1416
Example 18.3:	Sum of the digits depreciation	1416
Example 18.4:	Highest and best use	1420
Example 18.5:	Effect of depreciation on the revaluation reserve	1422
Example 18.6:	Revaluation by eliminating accumulated depreciation	1423
Example 18.7:	Reversal of a downward valuation	1424

Chapter 18   Property, plant and equipment

1 INTRODUCTION

One fundamental topic in financial reporting is how to account periodically for performance when many of the expenditures an entity incurs in the current period also contribute to future accounting periods. Expenditure on property, plant and equipment ('PP&E') is the best example of this issue.

The accounting conventions permitted by the IASB are the subject of this chapter, although the underlying broad principles involved are among the first that accountants and business people learn in their professional life. The cost of an item of PP&E is capitalised when acquired (i.e. recorded in the statement of financial position as an asset); then subsequently a proportion of the cost is charged each year to profit or loss (i.e. the cost is spread over the future accounting periods expected to benefit from the item). Ideally, at the end of the item's working life the cost remaining on the statement of financial position should be equal to the disposal proceeds of the item, or be zero if there are none.

The principal standard is IAS 16 – *Property, Plant and Equipment*. The objective of this standard is to prescribe the accounting treatment for PP&E so that users of the financial statements can discern information about an entity's investment in its PP&E and the changes in such investment. The principal issues in accounting for PP&E are the recognition of the assets, the determination of their carrying amounts and the depreciation charges and impairment losses to be recognised in relation to them. *[IAS 16.1]*. Impairment is a major consideration in accounting for PP&E, as this procedure is intended to ensure PP&E costs that are not fully recoverable are immediately written down to a level that is fully recoverable. Impairment is covered by IAS 36 – *Impairment of Assets* – and dealt with as a separate topic in Chapter 20. In addition, there is a separate standard, IAS 40 – *Investment Property* – that deals with that particular category of PP&E which is discussed in Chapter 19.

IFRS 5 – *Non-current Assets Held for Sale and Discontinued Operations* – deals with the accounting required when items of PP&E are held for sale and is discussed in Chapter 4.

This chapter discusses the most recent version of IAS 16, which was published in March 2004 and became effective for periods beginning on or after 1 January 2005, as subsequently updated by various narrow-scope amendments, including minor consequential amendments arising from other standards.

In May 2020, the IASB issued an amendment to IAS 16 – *Property, Plant and Equipment: Proceeds before Intended Use*, which prescribes new accounting and disclosure requirements where an entity produces and then sells items (such as test production) prior to an asset being brought into use. This amendment is discussed at 4.2.1 below. The new accounting and disclosure requirements are effective for annual periods beginning on or after 1 January 2022.

In May 2017, the IASB issued IFRS 17 – *Insurance Contracts*, a comprehensive new accounting standard for insurance contracts covering recognition and measurement, presentation and disclosure. Once effective, IFRS 17 will replace IFRS 4 – *Insurance Contracts* – that was issued in 2005. As part of the consequential amendments arising from IFRS 17, the subsequent measurement requirements in IAS 16 will be amended (see 5 below). IFRS 17 and its consequential amendments to other standards are effective for annual periods beginning on or after 1 January 2023, with adjusted comparative figures required. Early application is permitted provided that IFRS 9 – *Financial Instruments* – has already been applied, or is applied for the first time, at the date on which IFRS 17 is first applied. The requirements of IFRS 17 are discussed in Chapter 56.

2 THE REQUIREMENTS OF IAS 16

2.1 Scope

All PP&E is within the scope of IAS 16 except as follows:
- when another standard requires or permits a different accounting treatment, for example, IAS 40 for investment properties held at fair value (but investment properties held using the cost model under IAS 40 should use the cost model in IAS 16 which is discussed at 5 below);
- PP&E classified as held for sale in accordance with IFRS 5;
- biological assets related to agricultural activity (covered by IAS 41 – *Agriculture*) other than bearer plants (see 3.1.7 below);
- the recognition and measurement of exploration and evaluation assets (covered by IFRS 6 – *Exploration for and Evaluation of Mineral Resources*); and
- mineral rights and mineral reserves such as oil, natural gas, and similar 'non-regenerative' resources. *[IAS 16.2-3, 5]*.

Although the standard scopes out non-bearer plant biological assets and mineral rights and reserves, it includes any PP&E used in developing or maintaining such resources. *[IAS 16.3]*. Therefore, exploration PP&E is included in the scope of the standard (see Chapter 43), as is agricultural PP&E (see Chapter 42).

Other standards may require an item of PP&E to be recognised on a basis different from that required by IAS 16. For example, under IFRS 16 – *Leases*, lessees will recognise most leases in their statement of financial position as lease liabilities with corresponding right-of-use assets (see 2.3 below). Consequently, accounting for right-of-use assets should be in accordance with IFRS 16 (see Chapter 23).

2.2 Definitions used in IAS 16

IAS 16 defines the main terms it uses throughout the standard as follows: *[IAS 16.6]*

Bearer plant is a living plant that:
- is used in the production or supply of agricultural produce;
- is expected to bear produce for more than one period; and
- has a remote likelihood of being sold as agricultural produce, except for incidental scrap sales (see 3.1.7 below).

Carrying amount is the amount at which an asset is recognised after deducting any accumulated depreciation and accumulated impairment losses.

Cost is the amount of cash or cash equivalents paid or the fair value of other consideration given to acquire an asset at the time of its acquisition or construction or, where applicable, the amount attributed to that asset when initially recognised in accordance with the specific requirements of other IFRSs, e.g. IFRS 2 – *Share-based Payment*.

Depreciable amount is the cost of an asset, or other amount substituted for cost, less its residual value.

Depreciation is the systematic allocation of the depreciable amount of an asset over its useful life.

Entity-specific value is the present value of the cash flows an entity expects to arise from the continuing use of an asset and from its disposal at the end of its useful life or expects to incur when settling a liability.

Fair value is the price that would be received to sell an asset or paid to transfer a liability in an orderly transaction between market participants at the measurement date. (See IFRS 13 – *Fair Value Measurement* – discussed in Chapter 14).

An *impairment loss* is the amount by which the carrying amount of an asset exceeds its recoverable amount.

Property, plant and equipment are tangible items that:
(a) are held for use in the production or supply of goods or services, for rental to others, or for administrative purposes; and
(b) are expected to be used during more than one period.

Recoverable amount is the higher of an asset's fair value less costs to sell and its value in use.

The *residual value* of an asset is the estimated amount that an entity would currently obtain from disposal of the asset, after deducting the estimated costs of disposal, if the asset were already of the age and in the condition expected at the end of its useful life.

Useful life is:
(a) the period over which an asset is expected to be available for use by an entity; or
(b) the number of production or similar units expected to be obtained from the asset by an entity.

These definitions are discussed in the relevant sections below.

2.3 IFRS 16 and the presentation of right-of-use assets

Lessees can present right-of-use assets in the statement of financial position either;
(a) separately from other assets; or
(b) include them within the same line item as that within which the corresponding assets would be presented if they were owned. *[IFRS 16.47]*.

Lessees can, therefore, include the leased right-of-use assets within PP&E on the face of the statement of financial position.

If right-of-use assets are not presented separately from other assets in the statement of financial position, an entity must disclose which line items include the right-of-use assets. *[IFRS 16.47]*.

The requirements above do not apply to right-of-use assets that meet the definition of investment property, which is presented in the statement of financial position as investment property. *[IFRS 16.48]*.

Presentation of right-of-use assets are discussed further in Chapter 23 at 5.7.

3 RECOGNITION

An item of PP&E should be recognised (i.e. its cost included as an asset in the statement of financial position) only if it is probable that future economic benefits associated with the item will flow to the entity and its cost can be measured reliably. *[IAS 16.7]*.

Extract 18.1 below describes Skanska's criteria for the recognition of PP&E.

> *Extract 18.1: Skanska AB (2019)*
> Notes including accounting and valuation principles [extract]
> Note 1.   Consolidated accounting and valuation principles [extract]
> **IAS 16 Property, Plant and Equipment** [extract]
>
> Property, plant and equipment are recognized as assets if it is probable that future economic benefits from them will flow to the Group and the cost of the assets can be reliably calculated. Property, plant and equipment are recognized at cost minus accumulated depreciation and any impairment losses. Cost includes the purchase price plus expenses directly attributable to the asset in order to bring it to the location and condition to be used in the intended manner. Examples of directly attributable expenses are delivery and handling costs, installation, ownership documents, consultant fees and legal services. Borrowing costs are included in the cost of property, plant and equipment produced by the Group. Impairment losses are applied in accordance with IAS 36.
>
> The cost of property, plant and equipment produced by the Group includes expenditures for materials and remuneration to employees, plus other applicable manufacturing costs that are considered attributable to the asset.
>
> Further expenditures are added to cost only if it is probable that the Group will derive future economic benefits from the asset and the cost can be reliably calculated. All other further expenditures are recognized as expenses in the period when they arise.
>
> The decisive factor in determining when a further expenditure is added to cost is whether the expenditure is related to replacement of identified components, or parts thereof, at which time such expenditures are capitalized. In cases where a new component is created, this expenditure is also added to cost. Any undepreciated carrying amounts for replaced components, or parts thereof, are disposed of and recognized as an expense at the time of replacement. If the cost of the removed component cannot be determined directly, its cost may be estimated as the cost of the new component adjusted by a suitable price index to take into account inflation. Repairs are recognized as expenses on a continuous basis.

3.1 Aspects of recognition

3.1.1 Spare parts and minor items

Items such as spare parts, stand-by equipment and servicing equipment are inventory unless they meet the definition of PP&E (see 2.2 above). *[IAS 16.8]*. This treatment is illustrated in Extract 18.2 below.

> **Extract 18.2: Heineken N.V. (2019)**
> Notes to the Consolidated Financial Statements [extract]
> 8 Non-current assets [extract]
> 8.2 Property, plant and equipment [extract]
> Accounting policies [extract]
> Owned assets [extract]
>
> Spare parts that meet the definition of P,P&E are capitalised and accounted for accordingly. If spare parts do not meet the recognition criteria of P,P&E, they are either carried in inventory or consumed and recorded in profit or loss.

Materiality judgements are considered when deciding how an item of PP&E should be accounted for. Major spare parts, for example, qualify as PP&E, while smaller spares would be carried as inventory and as a practical matter many companies have a minimum value for capitalising assets.

Some types of business may have a very large number of minor items of PP&E such as spare parts, tools, pallets and returnable containers, which nevertheless are used in more than one accounting period. There are practical problems in recording them on an asset-by-asset basis in an asset register; they are difficult to control and frequently lost. The main consequence is that it becomes very difficult to depreciate them. Generally, entities write off such immaterial assets as expenses in the period of addition. Skanska in Extract 18.7 below immediately depreciates such minor equipment, achieving the same result. The standard notes that there are issues concerning what actually constitutes a single item of PP&E. The 'unit of measure' for recognition is not prescribed and entities have to apply judgement in defining PP&E in their specific circumstances. The standard suggests that it may be appropriate to aggregate individually insignificant items (such as tools, moulds and dies) and to apply the standard to the aggregate amount (presumably without having to identify the individual assets). *[IAS 16.9]*.

3.1.2 Environmental and safety equipment

The standard acknowledges that there may be expenditures forced upon an entity by legislation that requires it to buy 'assets' that do not meet the recognition criteria because the expenditure does not directly increase the future economic benefits expected to flow from the asset. Examples would be safety or environmental protection equipment. IAS 16 explains that these expenditures qualify for recognition as they allow an entity to derive future economic benefits from related assets in excess of those that would flow if such expenditure had not been made. For example, a chemical manufacturer may install new chemical handling processes to comply with environmental requirements for the production and storage of dangerous chemicals; related plant enhancements are recognised as an asset because without them the entity is unable to manufacture and sell the chemicals or a plant might have to be closed down if these safety or environmental expenditures were not made. *[IAS 16.11]*.

An entity may voluntarily invest in environmental equipment even though it is not required by law to do so. The entity can capitalise those investments in environmental and safety equipment in the absence of a legal requirement as long as:

- the expenditure meets the definition of an asset; or
- there is a constructive obligation to invest in the equipment.

If the entity can demonstrate that the equipment is likely to increase the economic life of the related asset, the expenditure meets the definition of an asset. Otherwise, the expenditure can be capitalised when the entity can demonstrate all of the following:

- the entity can prove that a constructive obligation exists to invest in environmental and safety equipment (e.g. it is standard practice in the industry, environmental groups are likely to raise issues or employees demand certain equipment to be present);
- the expenditure is directly related to improvement of the asset's environmental and safety standards; and
- the expenditure is not related to repairs and maintenance or forms part of period costs or operational costs.

Whenever safety and environmental assets are capitalised, the standard requires the resulting carrying amount of the asset, and any related asset, to be reviewed for impairment in accordance with IAS 36 (see 5.7 below). *[IAS 16.11]*.

3.1.3 Property economic benefits and property developments

The standard requires that PP&E only be recognised when it is probable that future economic benefits associated with the item will flow to the entity.

For example, in relation to property development, many jurisdictions require permissions prior to development whilst developers, including entities developing property for their own use, typically incur significant costs prior to such permissions being granted.

In assessing whether such pre-permission expenditures can be capitalised – assuming they otherwise meet the criteria – a judgement must be made at the date the expenditure is incurred of whether it is sufficiently probable that the relevant permission will be granted. Such expenditure does not become part of the cost of the land; to the extent that it can be recognised it is part of the costs of a separate building. Furthermore, if during the application and approval process of such permits it is no longer expected that necessary permits will be granted, capitalisation of pre-permission expenditure should cease, any related amounts that were previously capitalised should be written off in accordance with IAS 36 and accordingly, the carrying amount of any related item of PP&E subject to development or redevelopment (or, if appropriate, the cash generating unit where such an asset belongs) should be tested for impairment, where applicable (see 5.7 below).

3.1.4 Classification as PP&E or intangible asset

The restrictions in IAS 38 – *Intangible Assets* – in respect of capitalising certain internally-generated intangible assets focus attention on the treatment of many internal costs. In practice, items such as computer software purchased by entities are frequently capitalised as part of a tangible asset, for example as part of an accounting or communications infrastructure. Equally, internally written software may be capitalised as part of a tangible production facility, and so on. Judgement must be exercised in deciding whether such items are to be accounted for under IAS 16 or IAS 38 and this distinction becomes increasingly important if the two standards prescribe differing treatments in any particular case. IAS 16, unlike IAS 38, does not refer to this type of asset. IAS 38 states that an entity needs to exercise judgement in determining whether an asset that incorporates both intangible and tangible elements should be treated under IAS 16 or as an intangible asset under IAS 38, for example:

- computer software that is embedded in computer-controlled equipment that cannot operate without that specific software is an integral part of the related hardware and is treated as PP&E;
- application software that is being used on a computer is generally easily replaced and is not an integral part of the related hardware, whereas the operating system normally is integral to the computer and is included in PP&E; and
- a database that is stored on a compact disc is considered to be an intangible asset because the value of the physical medium is wholly insignificant compared to that of the data collection. *[IAS 38.4]*.

It is worthwhile noting that as the 'parts approach' in IAS 16 requires an entity to account for significant parts of an asset separately, this raises 'boundary' problems between IAS 16 and IAS 38 when software and similar expenditure are involved. We believe that where IAS 16 requires an entity to identify significant parts of an asset and account for them separately, the entity needs to evaluate whether any software-type intangible part is actually integral to the larger asset or whether it is really a separate asset in its own right. The intangible part is more likely to be an asset in its own right if it was developed separately or if it can be used independently of the item of PP&E.

3.1.5 Classification of items as inventory or PP&E when minimum levels are maintained

Entities may acquire items of inventory on a continuing basis, either for sale in the ordinary course of business or to be consumed in a production process or when rendering services.

This means there will always be a core stock of that item (i.e. a minimum level of inventory is maintained). This does not in itself turn that inventory into an item of PP&E, since each individual item will be consumed within a single operating cycle. However, there may be cases where it is difficult to judge whether an item is part of inventory or is an item of PP&E. This may have implications on measurement because, for example, PP&E has a revaluation option (see 6 below) that is not available for inventory.

In our view, an item of inventory is accounted for as an item of PP&E if it:

- is not held for sale or consumed in a production process or during the process of rendering services;
- is necessary to operate or benefit from an asset during more than one operating cycle; and
- cannot be recouped through sale (or is significantly impaired after it has been used to operate the asset or benefit from that asset).

This applies even if the part of inventory that is an item of PP&E cannot be physically separated from the rest of inventories.

Consider the following examples:
- An entity acquires the right to use an underground cave for gas storage purposes for a period of 50 years. The cave is filled with gas, but a substantial part of that gas will only be used to keep the cave under pressure in order to be able to get gas out of the cave. It is not possible to distinguish the gas that will be used to keep the cave under pressure and the rest of the gas.
- An entity operates an oil refining plant. In order for the refining process to take place, the plant must contain a certain minimum quantity of oil. This can only be taken out once the plant is abandoned and would then be polluted to such an extent that the oil's value is significantly reduced.
- An entity sells gas and has at any one time a certain quantity of gas in its gas distribution network.

In the first example, therefore, the total volume of gas must be virtually split into (i) gas held for sale and (ii) gas held to keep the cave under pressure. The former must be accounted for under IAS 2 – *Inventories*. The latter must be accounted for as PP&E and depreciated over the period the cave is expected to be used.

In the second example the part of the crude that is necessary to operate (in technical terms) the plant and cannot be recouped (or can be recouped but would then be significantly impaired), even when the plant is abandoned, should be considered as an item of PP&E and amortised over the life of the plant.

In the third example the gas in the pipeline is not necessary to operate the pipeline. It is held for sale or to be consumed in the production process or process of rendering services. Therefore, this gas is accounted for as inventory.

3.1.6 *Production stripping costs of surface mines*

IFRIC 20 – *Stripping Costs in the Production Phase of a Surface Mine* – states that costs associated with a 'stripping activity asset' (i.e. the costs associated with gaining access to a specific section of the ore body) are accounted for as an additional component of an existing asset. Other routine stripping costs are accounted for as current costs of production (i.e. inventory).

The Interpretations Committee's intention was to maintain the principle of IAS 16 by requiring identification of the component of the ore body for which access had been improved, as part of the criteria for recognising stripping costs as an asset. An entity will have to allocate the stripping costs between the amount capitalised (as it reflects the future access benefit) and the amount that relates to the current-period production of inventory. This allocation should be based on a relevant production measure.

This component approach follows the principle of separating out parts of an asset that have costs that are significant in relation to the entire asset and when the useful lives of those parts are different. *[IAS 16.45]*.

This interpretation is discussed in more detail in Chapter 43 at 15.5.

3.1.7 Bearer plants

Bearer plants, defined as living plants that are used in the production or supply of agricultural produce, are expected to bear produce for more than one period and have a remote likelihood of being sold as a plant or harvested as agricultural produce, (except for incidental scrap sales such as for use as firewood). *[IAS 16.6, IAS 41.5B]*.

Bearer plants are within the scope of IAS 16 and subject to all of the requirements therein. This includes the ability to choose between the cost model and revaluation model for subsequent measurement. Agricultural produce growing on bearer plants, e.g. the fruit growing on a tree, remains within the scope of IAS 41 (see Chapter 42). *[IAS 16.3(b), IAS 41.5C]*.

The following are not included within the definition of bearer plants:

- plants cultivated to be harvested as agricultural produce, e.g. trees grown for use as lumber;
- plants cultivated to produce agricultural produce when there is more than a remote likelihood that the entity will also harvest and sell the plant as agricultural produce, other than as incidental scrap sales, e.g. trees that are cultivated both for their fruit and their lumber; and
- annual crops such as maize and wheat. *[IAS 41.5A]*.

Bearer plants are accounted for in the same way as self-constructed items of PP&E before they are brought to the location and condition necessary to be capable of operating in the manner intended by management. Consequently, references to 'construction' in IAS 16, with respect to bearer plants, cover the activities that are necessary to cultivate such plants before they are brought to the location and condition necessary to be capable of operating in the manner intended by management. *[IAS 16.22A]*.

Bearer plants are subject to the requirements of IAS 16, and so entities will need to consider the correct unit of account, analyse which costs can be capitalised prior to maturity, set useful lives for depreciation purposes and consider the possibility of impairment.

For a more detailed discussion of the requirements, including some of the measurement challenges for bearer plants under IAS 16, see Chapter 42 at 1, 2.2.1.A, 2.3.3, and 3.2.3.A.

3.2 Accounting for parts ('components') of assets

IAS 16 has a single set of recognition criteria, which means that subsequent expenditure must also meet these criteria before it is recognised.

Parts of an asset are to be identified so that the cost of replacing a part may be recognised (i.e. capitalised as part of the asset) and the previous part derecognised. These parts are often referred to as 'components'. 'Parts' are distinguished from day-to-day servicing but they are not otherwise identified and defined; moreover, the unit of measurement to which the standard applies (i.e. what comprises an item of PP&E) is not itself defined.

IAS 16 requires 'significant parts' of an asset to be depreciated separately. These are parts that have a cost that is significant in relation to the total cost of the asset. An entity will have to identify the significant parts of the asset on initial recognition in order for it to depreciate each such part of the asset properly. [IAS 16.43, 44]. There is no requirement to identify all parts. IAS 16 requires entities to derecognise an existing part when it is replaced, regardless of whether it has been depreciated separately, and allows the carrying value of the part that has been replaced to be estimated, if necessary:

'If it is not practicable for an entity to determine the carrying amount of the replaced part, it may use the cost of the replacement as an indication of what the cost of the replaced part was at the time it was acquired or constructed.' [IAS 16.70].

As a consequence, an entity may not actually identify the parts of an asset until it incurs the replacement expenditure, as in the following example.

Example 18.1: Recognition and derecognition of parts

An entity buys a piece of machinery with an estimated useful life of ten years for €10 million. The asset contains two identical pumps, which are assumed to have the same useful life as the machine of which they are a part. After seven years one of the pumps fails and is replaced at a cost of €200,000. The entity had not identified the pumps as separate parts and does not know the original cost. It uses the cost of the replacement part to estimate the carrying value of the original pump. With the help of the supplier, it estimates that the cost would have been approximately €170,000 and that this would have a remaining carrying value after seven year's depreciation of €51,000. Accordingly, it derecognises €51,000 and capitalises the cost of the replacement.

If the entity has no better information than the cost of the replacement part, it appears that it is permitted to use a depreciated replacement cost basis to calculate the amount derecognised in respect of the original asset.

3.3   Initial and subsequent expenditure

IAS 16 makes no distinction in principle between the initial costs of acquiring an asset and any subsequent expenditure upon it. In both cases any and all expenditure has to meet the recognition rules, and be expensed in profit or loss if it does not. IAS 16 states:

'An entity evaluates under this recognition principle all its property, plant and equipment costs at the time they are incurred. These costs include costs incurred initially to acquire or construct an item of property, plant and equipment and costs incurred subsequently to add to, replace part of, or service it.' [IAS 16.10].

The standard draws a distinction between servicing and more major expenditures. Day-to-day servicing, by which is meant the repair and maintenance of PP&E that largely comprises labour costs, consumables and other minor parts, should be recognised in profit or loss as incurred. *[IAS 16.12]*. However, if the expenditure involves replacing a significant part of the asset, this part should be capitalised as part of the PP&E, if the recognition criteria are met. The carrying amount of the part that has been replaced should be derecognised (see 7 below). *[IAS 16.13]*. Examples of this treatment of major maintenance expenditure are shown in Extract 18.1 above and in Extract 18.3 and Extract 18.4 below.

> Extract 18.3: Akzo Nobel N.V. (2019)
> NOTES TO THE CONSOLIDATED FINANCIAL STATEMENTS [extract]
> Note 1   Summary of significant accounting policies [extract]
> PROPERTY, PLANT AND EQUIPTMENT (NOTE 11) [extract]
>
> Costs of major maintenance activities are capitalized and depreciated over the estimated useful life. Maintenance costs which cannot be separately defined as a component of property, plant and equipment are expensed in the period in which they occur.

Under IFRS 16 lessees are required to recognise most leases in their statement of financial position as lease liabilities with corresponding right-of-use assets. Paragraph 10 of IAS 16 (described above) clarifies that the cost of an item of PP&E may include costs incurred relating to leases of assets that are used to construct, add to, replace part of or service an item of PP&E, such as depreciation of right-of-use assets.

3.3.1   Types of parts

IAS 16 identifies two particular types of parts of assets. The first is an item that requires replacement at regular intervals during the life of the asset such as relining a furnace after a specified number of hours of use, or replacing the interiors of an aircraft (e.g. seats and galleys) several times during the life of the airframe. The second type involves less frequently recurring replacements, such as replacing the interior walls of a building, or to make a nonrecurring replacement. The standard requires that under the recognition principle described at 3 above, an entity recognises in the carrying amount of an item of PP&E the cost of replacing part of such an item when that cost is incurred and the recognition criteria are met while derecognising the carrying amount of the parts that have been replaced (see 7 below). *[IAS 16.13]*.

IAS 16 does not state that these replacement expenditures necessarily qualify for recognition. Some of its examples, such as aircraft interiors, are clearly best treated as separate assets as they have a useful life different from that of the asset of which they are part. With the other examples, such as interior walls, it is less clear why they meet the recognition criteria. However, replacing internal walls or similar expenditures may extend the useful life of a building while upgrading machinery may increase its capacity, improve the quality of its output or reduce operating costs. Hence, this type of expenditure may give rise to future economic benefits.

This parts approach is illustrated by British Airways Plc in Extract 18.4 below and by Skanska in Extract 18.7 below.

> **Extract 18.4: British Airways Plc (2018)**
>
> Notes to the financial statements [extract]
>
> 2   Significant accounting policies [extract]
>
> Property, plant and equipment [extract]
>
> b   Fleet
>
> All aircraft are stated at the fair value of the consideration given after taking account of manufacturers' credits. Fleet assets owned, or held on finance leases, are depreciated at rates calculated to write down the cost to the estimated residual value at the end of their planned operational lives (which is the shorter of their useful life or lease term) on a straight-line basis. Depreciation rates are specific to aircraft type, based on the Group's fleet plans, within overall parameters of 6 and 29 years. For engines maintained under 'pay-as-you-go' contracts, the depreciation lives and residual values are the same as the aircraft to which the engines relate. For all other engines, the engine core is depreciated to its residual value over the average remaining life of the related fleet.
>
> Cabin interior modifications, including those required for brand changes and relaunches, are depreciated over the lower of five years and the remaining economic life of the aircraft.
>
> Aircraft and engine spares acquired on the introduction or expansion of a fleet, as well as rotable spares purchased separately, are carried as property, plant and equipment and generally depreciated in line with the fleet to which they relate.
>
> Major overhaul expenditure, including replacement spares and labour costs, is capitalised and amortised over the average expected life between major overhauls. All other replacement spares and other costs relating to maintenance of fleet assets (including maintenance provided under 'pay-as-you-go' contracts) are charged to the income statement on consumption or as incurred respectively.

Note that 'Pay-as-you-go' contracts are not described in the financial statements above. These are comprehensive turbine engine maintenance and overhaul contracts, usually based on a fixed hourly fee for each hour flown and including loan engines when required.

3.3.2   Major inspections

The standard also allows a separate part to be recognised if an entity is required to perform regular major inspections for faults, regardless of whether any physical parts of the asset are replaced. *[IAS 16.14]*.

The reason for this approach is to maintain a degree of consistency with IAS 37 – *Provisions, Contingent Liabilities and Contingent Assets* – which forbids an entity to make provisions if there are no obligations. Therefore an entity is prohibited by IAS 37 from making, for example, a provision to overhaul an owned aircraft engine by annually providing for a quarter of the cost for four years and then utilising the provision when the engine is overhauled in the fourth year. *[IAS 37 IE Example 11A, 11B]*. This had been a common practice in the airline and oil refining industries, although it had never been universally applied in either sector; some companies accounted for the expenditure when incurred, others capitalised the cost and depreciated it over the period until the next major overhaul – as illustrated in Extract 18.4 above.

IAS 16 applies the same recognition criteria to the cost of major inspections. Inspection costs are not provided for in advance, rather they are added to the asset's cost if the recognition criteria are satisfied and any amount remaining from the previous inspection (as distinct from physical parts) is derecognised. This process of recognition and derecognition should take place regardless of whether the cost of the previous inspection was identified (and considered a separate part) when the asset was originally acquired or constructed. Therefore, if the element relating to the inspection had previously been identified, it would have been depreciated between that time and the current overhaul. However, if it had not previously been identified, the recognition and derecognition rules still apply, but the standard allows the estimated cost of a future similar inspection to be used as an indication of what the cost of the existing inspection component was when the item was acquired or constructed that must be derecognised. *[IAS 16.14]*. This appears to allow the entity to reconstruct the carrying amount of the previous inspection (i.e. to estimate the net depreciated carrying value of the previous inspection that will be derecognised) rather than simply using a depreciated replacement cost approach.

4 MEASUREMENT AT RECOGNITION

IAS 16 draws a distinction between measurement at recognition (i.e. the initial recognition of an item of PP&E on acquisition) and measurement after recognition (i.e. the subsequent treatment of the item). Measurement after recognition is discussed at 5 and 6 below.

The standard states that 'an item of property, plant and equipment that qualifies for recognition as an asset shall be measured at its cost'. *[IAS 16.15]*. What may be included in the cost of an item is discussed below.

4.1 Elements of cost and cost measurement

IAS 16 sets out what constitutes the cost of an item of PP&E on its initial recognition, as follows:

'The cost of an item of property, plant and equipment comprises:

(a) its purchase price, including import duties and non-refundable purchase taxes, after deducting trade discounts and rebates.

(b) any costs directly attributable to bringing the asset to the location and condition necessary for it to be capable of operating in the manner intended by management.

(c) the initial estimate of the costs of dismantling and removing the item and restoring the site on which it is located, the obligation for which an entity incurs either when the item is acquired or as a consequence of having used the item during a particular period for purposes other than to produce inventories during that period.' *[IAS 16.16]*.

The purchase price of an individual item of PP&E may be an allocation of the price paid for a group of assets. If an entity acquires a group of assets that do not comprise a business ('the group'), the principles in IFRS 3 – *Business Combinations* – are applied to allocate the entire cost to individual items (see Chapter 9 at 2.2.2). In such cases the acquirer should identify and recognise the individual identifiable assets acquired (including those assets that meet the definition of, and recognition criteria for, intangible assets in IAS 38) and liabilities assumed. The cost of the group should be allocated to the individual identifiable assets and liabilities on the basis of their relative fair values at the date of purchase. Such a transaction or event does not give rise to goodwill. *[IFRS 3.2(b)]*. In its June 2017 meeting, the Interpretations Committee considered two possible ways of applying the requirements in paragraph 2(b) of IFRS 3 (as described above) on the acquisition of the group particularly when the sum of individual fair values of the identifiable assets and liabilities is different from the transaction price and the group includes identifiable assets and liabilities initially measured both at cost and at an amount other than cost.[1] These two approaches are discussed in detail in Chapter 9 at 2.2.2. See also similar discussion relating to investment property in Chapter 19 at 4.1.1.

If an asset is used to produce inventories during a particular period, the costs of obligations that are incurred during that period to dismantle, remove or restore the site on which such asset has been located are dealt with in accordance with IAS 2, as a consequence of having used the asset to produce inventories during that period (see Chapter 22). *[IAS 16.18]*.

Note that all site restoration costs and other environmental restoration and similar costs must be estimated and capitalised at initial recognition, in order that such costs can be recovered over the life of the item of PP&E, even if the expenditure will only be incurred at the end of the item's life. The obligations are calculated in accordance with IAS 37 and IFRIC 1 – *Changes in Existing Decommissioning, Restoration and Similar Liabilities* (see 4.3 below and Chapter 26 at 4 and 6.3). *[IAS 16.18]*. This is illustrated in Extract 18.5 below.

Extract 18.5: E.ON SE (2019)

Consolidated Financial Statements [extract]

Notes [extract]

(1)   Summary of Significant Accounting Policies [extract]

Property, Plant and Equipment [extract]

Property, plant and equipment are initially measured at acquisition or production cost, including decommissioning or restoration cost that must be capitalized, and are depreciated over the expected useful lives of the components, generally using the straight-line method, unless a different method of depreciation is deemed more suitable in certain exceptional cases.

Provisions for Asset Retirement Obligations and Other Miscellaneous Provisions [extract]

Obligations arising from the decommissioning or dismantling of property, plant and equipment are recognized during the period of their occurrence at their discounted settlement amounts, provided that the obligation can be reliably estimated. The carrying amounts of the respective property, plant and equipment are increased by the same amounts. In subsequent periods, capitalized asset retirement costs are amortized over the expected remaining useful lives of the assets, and the provision is accreted to its present value on an annual basis.

A common instance of (c) above is dilapidation obligations in lease agreements, under which a lessee is obliged to return premises to the landlord in an agreed condition. Arguably, a provision is required whenever the 'damage' is incurred. Therefore, if a retailer rents two adjoining premises and knocks down the dividing wall to convert the premises into one and has an obligation to make good at the end of the lease term, the tenant should immediately provide for the costs of so doing. The 'other side' of the provision entry is an asset that will be amortised over the lease term, notwithstanding the fact that some of the costs of modifying the premises may also have been capitalised as leasehold improvement assets. This is discussed in more detail in Chapter 26 at 6.9.

4.1.1 'Directly attributable' costs

This is the key issue in the measurement of cost. The standard gives examples of types of expenditure that are, and are not, considered to be directly attributable. The following are examples of those types of expenditure that are considered to be directly attributable and hence may be included in cost at initial recognition: *[IAS 16.17]*

(a) costs of employee benefits (as defined in IAS 19 – *Employee Benefits*) arising directly from the construction or acquisition of the item of PP&E. This means that the labour costs of an entity's own employees (e.g. site workers, in-house architects and surveyors) arising directly from the construction, or acquisition, of the specific item of PP&E may be recognised;

(b) costs of site preparation;

(c) initial delivery and handling costs;

(d) installation and assembly costs;

(e) costs of testing whether the asset is functioning properly, after deducting the net proceeds from selling any items produced while bringing the asset to that location and condition such as samples produced when testing equipment. This requirement has been amended, with an effective date of 1 January 2022. This amendment is discussed at 4.2.1 below; and

(f) professional fees.

Income received during the period of construction of PP&E is considered further at 4.2.2 below.

The cost of an item of PP&E may include costs incurred relating to leases of assets that are used to construct, add to, replace part of or service an item of PP&E, such as depreciation of right-of-use assets (see 3.3 above), if those lease costs are 'directly attributable to bringing the asset to the location and condition necessary for it to be capable of operating in the manner intended by management'. *[IAS 16.16]*.

Also, under IFRS 16, lessees are required to recognise all leases in their statement of financial position as lease liabilities with corresponding right-of-use assets, except for short-term leases and low-value assets if they choose to apply such exemptions.

4.1.2 Borrowing costs

Borrowing costs must be capitalised in respect of certain qualifying assets, if those assets are measured at cost. Therefore, an entity will capitalise borrowing costs on a self-constructed item of PP&E if it meets the criteria in IAS 23 – *Borrowing Costs*, as discussed at 4.1.5 below. *[IAS 16.22]*.

Entities are not required to capitalise borrowing costs in respect of assets that are measured at fair value. This includes revalued PP&E which is measured at fair value through Other Comprehensive Income ('OCI'). Generally, an item of PP&E within scope of IAS 16 will only be carried at revalued amount once construction is completed, so capitalisation of borrowing costs will have ceased (see 4.1.4 below). This is not necessarily the case with investment property in the course of construction (see Chapter 19 at 2.5). The cost of the asset, before adopting a policy of revaluation, will include capitalised borrowing costs. However, to the extent that entities choose to capitalise borrowing costs in respect of assets still in the course of construction that are carried at fair value, the methods allowed by IAS 23 should be followed. The treatment of borrowing costs is discussed separately in Chapter 21.

For disclosure purposes, an entity will still need to monitor the carrying amount of PP&E measured under revaluation model, including those borrowing costs that would have been recognised had such an asset been carried under the cost model (see 8.2 below).

4.1.3 Administration and other general overheads

Administration and other general overhead costs are not costs of an item of PP&E. This means that employee costs not related to a specific asset, such as site selection activities and general management time do not qualify for capitalisation. Entities are also not allowed to recognise so-called 'start up costs' as part of the item of PP&E. These include costs related to opening a new facility, introducing a new product or service (including costs of advertising and promotional activities), conducting business in a new territory or with a new class of customer (including costs of staff training) and similar items. *[IAS 16.19]*. These costs should be accounted for (in general, expensed as incurred) in the same way as similar costs incurred as part of the entity's on-going activities.

4.1.4 Cessation of capitalisation

Cost recognition ceases once an item of PP&E is in the location and condition necessary for it to be capable of operating in the manner intended by management. This will usually be the date of practical completion of the physical asset. IAS 16 therefore prohibits the recognition of relocation and reorganisation costs, costs incurred in using the asset or during the run up to full use once the asset is ready to be used, and any initial operating losses. *[IAS 16.20]*. An entity is not precluded from continuing to capitalise costs during an initial commissioning period that is necessary for running in machinery or testing equipment. By contrast no new costs should be capitalised if the asset is fully operational but is not yet achieving its targeted profitability because demand is still building up, for example in a new hotel that initially has high room vacancies or a partially let investment property. In these cases, the asset is clearly in the location and condition necessary for it to be capable of operating in the manner intended by management.

4.1.5 Self-built assets

If an asset is self-built by the entity, the same general principles apply as for an acquired asset. If the same type of asset is made for resale by the business, the cost of such asset is usually the same as the cost of constructing of an asset for sale, i.e. without including any internal profit element but including attributable overheads in accordance with IAS 2 (see Chapter 22). The costs of abnormal amounts of wasted resources, whether labour, materials or other resources, are not included in the cost of such self-built assets. IAS 23, discussed in Chapter 21, contains criteria relating to the recognition of any interest as a component of the carrying amount of a self-built item of PP&E. *[IAS 16.22]*.

Kendrion N.V. provides an example of an accounting policy for self-built assets.

> Extract 18.6: Kendrion N.V. (2019)
> NOTES TO THE CONSOLIDATED FINANCIAL STATEMENTS [extract]
> Significant accounting policies [extract]
> (c)   Property, plant and equipment [extract]
> (i)   Owned assets [extract]
>
> The cost of self-constructed assets includes the cost of materials, direct labour, the initial estimate, where relevant, of the costs of dismantling and removing the items and reinstating the site on which they are located, a reasonable proportion of production overheads, and capitalised borrowing costs.

4.1.6   Deferred payment

IAS 16 specifically precludes the capitalisation of hidden credit charges as part of the cost of an item of PP&E, so the cost of an item of PP&E is its cash price equivalent at the recognition date. This means that if payment is made in some other manner, the cost to be capitalised is the normal cash price. Thus, if the payment terms are extended beyond 'normal' credit terms, the cost to be recognised must be the cash price equivalent and any difference between the cash price equivalent and the total payment must be treated and recognised as an interest expense over the period of credit unless such interest is capitalised in accordance with IAS 23 (see 4.1.2 above). *[IAS 16.23]*. Right-of-use assets under IFRS 16 are discussed in Chapter 23. Assets partly paid for by government grants are discussed in Chapter 24.

4.1.7   Land and buildings to be redeveloped

It is common for property developers to acquire land with an existing building where the planned redevelopment necessitates the demolition of that building and its replacement with a new building that is to be held to earn rentals or will be owner occupied. Whilst IAS 16 requires that the building and land be classified as two separate items (see 5.4.2 below), in our view it is appropriate, if the existing building is unusable or likely to be demolished by any party acquiring it, that the entire or a large part of the purchase price be allocated to the land. Similarly, subsequent demolition costs should be treated as being attributable to the cost of the land.

Owner-occupiers may also replace existing buildings with new facilities for their own use or to rent to others. Here the consequences are different and the carrying amount of the existing building cannot be rolled into the costs of the new development. The existing building must be depreciated over its remaining useful life to reduce the carrying amount of the asset to its residual value (presumably nil) at the point at which it is demolished. Consideration will have to be given as to whether the asset is impaired in accordance with IAS 36 (see 5.7 below). Many properties do not directly generate independent cash inflows (i.e. they are part of a cash-generating unit) and reducing the useful life will not necessarily lead to an impairment of the cash-generating unit, although by the time the asset has been designated for demolition it may no longer be part of a cash-generating unit (see Chapter 20 at 2.1.3 and 3).

Developers or owner-occupiers replacing an existing building with a building to be sold in the ordinary course of their business will deal with the land and buildings under IAS 2 (see Chapter 22 at 4.2.2).

4.1.8 Transfers of assets from customers

An entity may be entitled to consideration in the form of goods, services or other non-cash consideration (e.g. PP&E), in exchange for transferring goods or services to a customer. Examples include:

- a supplier who receives a contribution to the development costs of specific tooling equipment from another manufacturer to whom the supplier will sell parts, using that specific tooling equipment under a supply agreement;
- suppliers of utilities who receive items of PP&E from customers that are used to connect them to a network through which they will receive ongoing services (e.g. electricity, gas, water or telephone services). A typical arrangement is one in which a builder or individual householder must pay for power cables, pipes, or other connections; and
- in outsourcing arrangements, the existing assets are often contributed to the service provider, or the customer must pay for assets, or both.

This raises questions about recognising assets for which the entity has not paid. In what circumstances should the entity recognise these assets, at what carrying amount and how is the 'other side' of the accounting entry dealt with? Is it revenue and if so, how and over what period is it recognised? There are a number of potential answers to this and, unsurprisingly, practice has differed.

When an entity (i.e. the seller or vendor) receives, or expects to receive, non-cash consideration in relation to a revenue contract that is within the scope of IFRS 15 – *Revenue from Contracts with Customers*, the fair value of the non-cash consideration is included in the transaction price. *[IFRS 15.66]*. The IFRS 15 requirements regarding non-cash consideration are discussed in detail in Chapter 29 at 2.6. Paragraph BC253 of IFRS 15 states that 'once recognised, any asset arising from the non-cash consideration would be measured and accounted for in accordance with other relevant requirements' (e.g. IAS 16). As such, the fair value measured in accordance with IFRS 15 would be the deemed cost of the item of PP&E on initial recognition.

4.1.9 Variable and contingent consideration

Transactions involving contingent consideration are often very complex and payment is dependent on a number of factors. In the absence of specific guidance in IAS 16, entities trying to determine an appropriate accounting treatment are required not only to understand the commercial complexities of the transaction itself, but also to navigate a variety of accounting principles and requirements.

Consider a relatively simple example where an entity acquires an item of PP&E for consideration comprising a combination of up-front payment, guaranteed instalments for a number of years and additional amounts that vary according to future activity (revenue, profit or number of units output).

Where the goods and services in question have been delivered, there is no doubt that there is a financial liability under IFRS 9. A contingent obligation to deliver cash meets the definition of a financial liability (see Chapter 47). Therefore, if the obligation to make the variable payment does not depend on the acquiring entity's future activity and the event that gives rise to the payment is outside its control, then a financial liability would be recognised. *[IAS 32.25]*.

However, where the purchaser can influence or control the crystallisation of the contingent payments, or they are wholly dependent on its future activities, the circumstances are more difficult to interpret. In these cases, the determination of whether the payment should be capitalised or expensed is usually based on the reason for the contingent payment. For example, if the contingent payment is based on period volumes sold or produced it will generally be expensed. Conversely, when the reason for the payment is more clearly linked to the initial value of the asset, rather than its use over time, the entity may elect a policy to either:

- include the fair value of all contingent payments in the initial measurement of the asset; or
- recognise a liability only when the contingent payment crystallises.

Under both approaches, subsequent changes in the contingent consideration liability or subsequent payments are either capitalised when incurred, or expensed as incurred.

When it discussed accounting for contingent consideration between July 2013 and March 2016, the Interpretations Committee ultimately concluded that the issue was too broad for the Committee to address and referred it back to the Board. In May 2016, the IASB tentatively agreed that this issue would be included in the research pipeline between 2017 and 2021. In February 2018, the Board decided that the IASB staff should carry out work to determine how broad the research project should be. At the time of writing this is not listed as an active research project on the IASB's work plan.

Until this matter is resolved, an entity should adopt and apply a consistent accounting policy to initial recognition and subsequent payments, in accordance with the hierarchy in IAS 8 – *Accounting Policies, Changes in Accounting Estimates and Errors*. An entity should exercise judgement in developing and consistently applying an accounting policy that results in information that is relevant and reliable in its particular circumstances. *[IAS 8.10]*. These approaches are illustrated in Chapter 17 at Example 17.4. Note that example 17.4 does not include a number of common contingent payments, e.g. those related to usage or revenue, or non-floating rate changes in finance costs.

4.2 Incidental and non-incidental income

Under IAS 16, the cost of an item of PP&E includes any costs directly attributable to bringing the asset to the location and condition necessary for it to be capable of operating in the manner intended by management. *[IAS 16.16(b)]*. However, before or during the construction of an asset, an entity may enter into incidental operations that are not, in themselves, necessary to meet this objective. *[IAS 16.21]*.

The standard gives the example of income earned by using a building site as a car park prior to starting construction. Because incidental operations are not required in order to bring an asset to the location or condition necessary for it to be capable of operating in the manner intended by management, the income and related expenses of incidental operations are recognised in profit or loss and included in their respective classifications of income and expense. *[IAS 16.21]*. Such incidental income and related expenses are not included in determining the cost of the asset.

If, however, some income is generated wholly and necessarily as a result of the process of bringing the asset into the location and condition for its intended use, for example from the sale of samples produced when testing the equipment concerned, then the income should be credited to the cost of the asset (see 4.2.1 below). *[IAS 16.17]*.

On the other hand, if the asset is already in the location and condition necessary for it to be capable of being used in the manner intended by management then IAS 16 requires capitalisation to cease and depreciation to start. *[IAS 16.20]*. In these circumstances all income earned from using the asset must be recognised as revenue in profit or loss and the related costs should include an element of depreciation of the asset.

4.2.1 Income earned while bringing the asset to the intended location and condition

As noted above, the directly attributable costs of an item of PP&E include the costs of testing whether the asset is functioning properly, after deducting the net proceeds from selling any items produced while bringing the asset to that location and condition. *[IAS 16.17]*. The standard gives the example of samples produced when testing equipment.

There are other situations in which income may be earned whilst bringing the asset to the intended location and condition. This issue is common in the mining and oil and gas sectors, where test production may be sold during the commission stage of a mine or oil well (see Chapter 43 at 12). In these and other examples, it is possible that the net proceeds from selling items produced while testing the plant under construction may exceed the cost of related testing. IAS 16 is not clear as to whether such excess proceeds should be recognised in profit or loss or as a deduction from the cost of the asset.

The Interpretations Committee received a request to clarify two specific aspects of IAS 16, including:

(a) whether the proceeds referred to in IAS 16 relate only to items produced from testing; and

(b) whether an entity deducts from the cost of an item of PP&E any proceeds that exceed the cost of testing.

After exploring different approaches to the issue, the Interpretations Committee recommended, and the IASB agreed, to propose an amendment to IAS 16.

In May 2020, the IASB issued an amendment to IAS 16 – *Property, Plant and Equipment: Proceeds before Intended Use*, which prescribes new accounting and disclosure requirements. These amendments remove the requirement to deduct from the cost of an item of PP&E any proceeds from selling items produced, while bringing that asset to the location and condition necessary for it to be capable of operating in the manner intended by management. Instead, the amendments require the proceeds from selling any such items, together with the cost of those items measured in accordance with IAS 2, to be recognised in profit or loss in accordance with applicable standards. *[IAS 16.20A]*.

The amendment does not provide additional guidance on determining when an item of property, plant and equipment is available for use. So even after the amendment, IAS 16 still requires the costs of testing to be added to the carrying value of the asset, but it now clarifies that testing costs are incurred when assessing whether the technical and physical performance of the asset is such that it is capable of being used in the production or supply of goods or services, for rental to others, or for administrative purposes. *[IAS 16(2022).17(e)]*.

These requirements are effective for annual periods beginning on or after 1 January 2022. Earlier application is permitted, but that fact should be disclosed. *[IAS 16.81N]*. The amendments also introduce additional disclosure requirements, which are discussed at 8.1 below. An entity should apply the amendments retrospectively, but only to items of property, plant and equipment that are brought to the location and condition necessary for them to be capable of operating in the manner intended by management on or after the beginning of the earliest period presented in the financial statements in which the entity first applies the amendments. The cumulative effect of initially applying the amendments should be recognised as an adjustment to the opening balance of retained earnings (or other component of equity, as appropriate) at the beginning of that earliest period presented. *[IAS 16.80D]*.

4.2.2 Income received during the construction of property

One issue that commonly arises is whether rental and similar income generated by existing tenants in a property development may be capitalised and offset against the cost of developing that property.

The relevant question is whether the leasing arrangements with the existing tenants are a necessary activity to bring the development property to the location and condition necessary for it to be capable of operating in the manner intended by management. Whilst the existence of the tenant may be a fact, it is not a necessary condition for the building to be developed to the condition intended by management; the building could have been developed in the absence of any existing tenants.

Therefore, rental and similar income from existing tenants are incidental to the development and should not be capitalised. Rather rental and similar income should be recognised in profit or loss in accordance with the requirements of IFRS 16 together with related expenses.

4.2.3 Liquidated damages during construction

Income may arise in other ways, for example, liquidated damages received as a result of delays by a contractor constructing an asset. Normally such damages received should be set off against the asset cost – the purchase price of the asset is reduced to compensate for delays in delivery.

4.3 Accounting for changes in decommissioning and restoration costs

IAS 16 requires the initial estimate of the costs of dismantling and removing an item of PP&E and restoring the site on which it is located to be included as part of the item's cost. This applies whether the obligation is incurred either when the item is acquired or as a consequence of having used the item during a particular period for purposes other than to produce inventories during that period. *[IAS 16.16]*. See 4.1 above. However, IAS 16 does not address the extent to which an item's carrying amount should be affected by changes in the estimated amount of dismantling and site restoration costs that occur after the estimate made upon initial measurement. This issue is the subject of IFRIC 1, which applies to any decommissioning, restoration or similar liability that has been both included as part of the cost of an asset measured in accordance with IAS 16 and recognised as a liability in accordance with IAS 37. *[IFRIC 1.2]*. It deals with the impact of events that change the measurement of an existing decommissioning, restoration or similar liability. Events include a change in the estimated cash flows, a change in the discount rate and the unwinding of the discount. *[IFRIC 1.3]*. This is discussed in detail in Chapter 26 at 6.3.

4.4 Exchanges of assets

An entity might swap an asset it does not require in a particular area, for one it does in another – the opposite being the case for the counterparty. Such exchanges are not uncommon in the telecommunications, media and leisure businesses, particularly after an acquisition. Governmental competition rules sometimes require such exchanges. The question arises whether such transactions give rise to a gain in circumstances where the carrying value of the outgoing facility is less than the fair value of the incoming one. This can occur when carrying values are less than market values, although it is possible that a transaction with no real commercial substance could be arranged solely to boost apparent profits.

IAS 16 requires all acquisitions of PP&E in exchange for non-monetary assets, or a combination of monetary and non-monetary assets, to be measured at fair value, subject to conditions:

'The cost of such an item of property, plant and equipment is measured at fair value unless (a) the exchange transaction lacks commercial substance or (b) the fair value of neither the asset received nor the asset given up is reliably measurable. The acquired item is measured in this way even if an entity cannot immediately derecognise the asset given up.' *[IAS 16.24]*.

The IASB concluded that the recognition of income from an exchange of assets does not depend on whether the assets exchanged are dissimilar. *[IAS 16.BC19]*.

If at least one of the two fair values can be measured reliably, that value is used for measuring the exchange transaction; if not, then the exchange is measured at the carrying value of the asset the entity no longer owns. *[IAS 16.24]*. For example, if the new asset's fair value is higher than the carrying amount of the old asset, a gain may be recognised.

This requirement is qualified by a 'commercial substance' test. If it is not possible to demonstrate that the transaction has commercial substance as defined by the standard (see 4.4.1 below), assets received in exchange transactions will be recorded at the carrying value of the asset given up. *[IAS 16.24]*.

If the transaction passes the 'commercial substance' test, then IAS 16 requires the exchanged asset to be recorded at its fair value. As discussed at 7 below, the standard requires gains or losses on items that have been derecognised to be included in profit or loss in the period of derecognition but does not allow gains on derecognition to be classified as revenue, except for certain assets previously held for rental. *[IAS 16.68, 68A]*. It gives no further indication regarding their classification in profit or loss. Such exchanges of goods and services are also excluded from the scope of IFRS 15 if the non-monetary exchange is between entities in the same line of business to facilitate sales to customers or potential customers (see Chapter 27 at 3). *[IFRS 15.5(d)]*.

4.4.1 Commercial substance

The commercial substance test was put in place as an anti-abuse provision to prevent gains from being recognised in income when the transaction had no discernible effect on the entity's economics. *[IAS 16.BC21]*. The commercial substance of an exchange is to be determined by forecasting and comparing the future cash flows budgeted to be generated by the incoming and outgoing assets. For there to be commercial substance, there must be a significant difference between the two forecasts. The standard sets out this requirement as follows:

'An entity determines whether an exchange transaction has commercial substance by considering the extent to which its future cash flows are expected to change as a result of the transaction. An exchange transaction has commercial substance if:

(a) the configuration (risk, timing and amount) of the cash flows of the asset received differs from the configuration of the cash flows of the asset transferred; or

(b) the entity-specific value of the portion of the entity's operations affected by the transaction changes as a result of the exchange; and

(c) the difference in (a) or (b) is significant relative to the fair value of the assets exchanged.' *[IAS 16.25]*.

As set out in the definitions of the standard, entity-specific value in item (b) above is the net present value of the future predicted cash flows from continuing use and disposal of the asset (see 2.2 above). Post-tax cash flows should be used for this calculation. The standard contains no guidance on the discount rate to be used for this exercise, nor on any of the other parameters involved, but it does suggest that the result of these analyses might be clear without having to perform detailed calculations. *[IAS 16.25]*. Care will have to be taken to ensure that the transaction has commercial substance as defined in the standard if an entity receives a similar item of PP&E in exchange for a similar asset of its own. Commercial substance may be difficult to demonstrate if the entity is exchanging an asset for a similar one in a similar location. However, in the latter case, the risk, timing and amount of cash flows could differ if one asset were available for sale and the entity intended to sell it whereas the previous asset could not be realised by sale or only sold over a much longer timescale. It is feasible that such a transaction could meet conditions (a) and (c) above. Similarly, it would be unusual if the entity-specific values of similar assets differed enough in any arm's length exchange transaction to meet condition (c).

Other types of exchange are more likely to pass the 'commercial substance' test, for example exchanging an interest in an investment property for one that the entity uses for its own purposes. The entity has exchanged a rental stream and instead has an asset that contributes to the cash flows of the cash-generating unit of which it is a part. In this case it is probable that the risk, timing and amount of the cash flows of the asset received would differ from the configuration of the cash flows of the asset transferred.

4.4.2 Reliably measurable

In the context of asset exchanges, the standard contains guidance on the reliable determination of fair values in the circumstances where market values do not exist. The 'reliable measurement' test for using fair value was included to measure these exchanges to minimise the risk that entities could 'manufacture' gains by attributing inflated values to the assets exchanged. *[IAS 16.BC23]*. Note that fair value is defined by reference to IFRS 13 and that the requirements below are specific to asset exchanges in IAS 16.

'The fair value of an asset is reliably measurable if (a) the variability in the range of reasonable fair value measurements is not significant for that asset or (b) the probabilities of the various estimates within the range can be reasonably assessed and used when measuring fair value. If an entity is able to measure reliably the fair value of either the asset received or the asset given up, then the fair value of the asset given up is used to measure the cost of the asset received unless the fair value of the asset received is more clearly evident.' *[IAS 16.26]*. If the fair value of neither the asset given up nor the asset received can be measured reliably (i.e. neither (a) nor (b) above are met), the cost of the asset is measured at the carrying amount of the asset given up; this means there is no gain on the transaction. *[IAS 16.24]*.

No further guidance is given in IAS 16 on how to assemble a 'range of reasonable fair value measurements' and the guidance in IFRS 13 should be followed (see Chapter 14).

4.5 Assets held under leases

IFRS 16 requires lessees to initially measure the right-of-use asset at the amount of lease liability, adjusted for lease prepayments, lease incentives received, initial direct costs and an estimate of restoration, removal and dismantling costs. IFRS 16 is discussed in detail in Chapter 23.

4.6 Assets acquired with the assistance of government grants

The carrying amount of an item of PP&E may be reduced by government grants in accordance with IAS 20 – *Accounting for Government Grants and Disclosure of Government Assistance.* *[IAS 16.28]*. This is one of the accounting treatments available which are discussed further in Chapter 24.

5 MEASUREMENT AFTER RECOGNITION: COST MODEL

IAS 16 allows one of two alternatives to be chosen as the accounting policy for measurement of PP&E after initial recognition. The choice made must be applied to an entire class of PP&E, which means that not all classes are required to have the same policy. *[IAS 16.29]*.

The first alternative is the cost model whereby the item, after recognition as an asset, is carried at cost less any accumulated depreciation and less any accumulated impairment losses. *[IAS 16.30]*. The alternative, the revaluation model, is discussed at 6 below.

Some entities operate, either internally or externally, an investment fund that provides investors with benefits determined by units in the fund. Similarly, some entities issue groups of insurance contracts with direct participation features and hold the underlying items. Some such funds or underlying items include owner-occupied property. For many contracts that specify a link to returns on underlying items, those underlying items include a mix of assets that are almost all measured at fair value through profit or loss. Accordingly, the IASB decided that measurement of owner-occupied property at fair value through profit or loss would be consistent with the measurement of the majority of the underlying assets and would prevent accounting mismatches. *[IFRS 17.BC65(c)]*.

Consequently, when IFRS 17 is adopted (see 1 above), the subsequent measurement requirements in IAS 16 will be amended by adding paragraphs 29A and 29B to permit entities to elect to measure owner-occupied properties in such specified circumstances as if they were investment properties measured at fair value through profit or loss in accordance with IAS 40, despite paragraph 29 (as described above). For the purposes of this election, insurance contracts include investment contracts with discretionary participation features. An entity shall treat owner-occupied property measured using the investment property fair value model as a separate class of PP&E. *[IAS 16.29A-29B]*.

5.1 Significant parts of assets

IAS 16 links its recognition concept of a 'part' of an asset, discussed at 3.2 above, with the analysis of assets for the purpose of depreciation. Each part of an asset with a cost that is significant in relation to the total cost of the item must be depreciated separately, which means that the initial cost must be allocated between the significant parts by the entity. *[IAS 16.43, 44]*. The standard once again refers to the airframe and engines of an aircraft but also sets out that if an entity acquires PP&E subject to an operating lease in which it is the lessor, it may be appropriate to depreciate separately amounts reflected in the cost of that item that are attributable to favourable or unfavourable lease terms relative to market terms. *[IAS 16.44]*.

A determination of the significant parts of office buildings can be seen in Extract 18.7 below from Skanska. This policy may have been based on the construction methods used for the particular buildings as it is unusual to see a separation between foundation and frame for office buildings. In addition, Extract 19.1 in Chapter 19 shows an example of the allocation for investment property, although favourable or unfavourable lease terms are not identified as a separate part.

Extract 18.7: Skanska AB (2019)

Notes including accounting and valuation principles [extract]

Note 1.   Consolidated accounting and valuation principles [extract]

IAS 16 Property, Plant and Equipment [extract]

Property, plant and equipment that consist of parts with different useful lives are treated as separate components of property, plant and equipment. Depreciation occurs on a straight-line basis during the estimated useful life, or based on degree of use, taking into account any residual value at the end of the period. Office buildings are divided into foundation and frame, with a depreciation period of 50 years, installations of 35 years, and non-weight-bearing parts of 15 years. In general, industrial buildings are depreciated over a 20-year period without allocation into different parts. Stone crushing and asphalt plants as well as concrete mixing plants are depreciated over 10 to 25 years depending on their condition when acquired and without being divided into different parts. For other buildings and equipment, division into different components occurs only if major components with different useful lives can be identified. For other machinery and equipment, the depreciation period is normally between five and 10 years. Minor equipment is recognized as an expense immediately. Gravel pits and stone quarries are depreciated as materials are removed. Land is not depreciated. Assessments of an asset's residual value and period of service are performed annually.

Because parts of an item of PP&E are identified by their significant cost rather than their effect on depreciation, they may have the same useful lives and depreciation method and the standard allows them to be grouped for depreciation purposes. *[IAS 16.45]*.

It also identifies other circumstances in which the significant parts do not correspond to the depreciable components within the asset. To the extent that an entity depreciates separately some parts of an item of PP&E, it also depreciates separately the remainder of the item. The remainder of such asset that has not separately been identified into parts may consist of other parts that are individually not significant and if the entity has varying expectations for these parts, it may need to use approximation techniques to calculate an appropriate depreciation method for all of these parts in a manner that faithfully represents the consumption pattern and/or useful life of such parts. *[IAS 16.46]*. The standard also allows an entity to depreciate separately such parts that are not significant in relation to the total cost of the whole asset. *[IAS 16.47]*.

The depreciation charge for each period is recognised in profit or loss unless it forms part of the cost of another asset and included in its carrying amount. *[IAS 16.48]*. Sometimes, the future economic benefits embodied in an asset are absorbed in producing other assets, for example, the depreciation of manufacturing plant and equipment is included as part of the cost of conversion of finished manufactured goods held in inventory in accordance with IAS 2, and similarly, depreciation of PP&E used for development activities may be included as part of the cost of an intangible asset recognised in accordance with IAS 38. *[IAS 16.49]*.

5.2 Depreciable amount and residual values

The depreciable amount of an item of PP&E is its cost, or other amount substituted for cost (e.g. valuation), less its estimated residual value. *[IAS 16.6]*. The standard states that an entity should review the residual value of an item of PP&E, and therefore all parts of it, at least at each financial year-end. If the estimated residual value differs from the previous estimate, the change should be accounted for prospectively as a change in accounting estimate in accordance with IAS 8 (see Chapter 3 at 4.5). *[IAS 16.51]*.

The residual value of an item of PP&E is the estimated amount that an entity would currently obtain from disposal of the asset, after deducting the estimated costs of disposal, if the asset were already of the age and assuming that it was already in the condition it will be in at the end of its useful life. *[IAS 16.6]*. Therefore, IAS 16 contains an element of continuous updating of one component of an asset's carrying value because it is the current disposal amount (e.g. value at financial reporting date) of an asset's future state (i.e. asset's condition in the future when the entity expects to dispose of it). This means that only the changes up to the financial reporting date are taken into account and that expected future changes in residual value other than the effects of expected wear and tear are not taken into account. *[IAS 16.BC29]*.

As any change in the residual value directly affects the depreciable amount, it may also affect the depreciation charge. This is because the depreciable amount (i.e. the amount actually charged to profit or loss over the life of the asset) is calculated by deducting the residual value from the cost (or other amount substituted for cost, such as valuation) of the asset. Sometimes, the residual value of an asset may increase to an amount equal to or greater than the asset's carrying amount. If it does, the residual value is capped at the asset's carrying amount. This means that in such a case, the asset's depreciation charge is zero unless and until its residual value subsequently decreases to an amount below the asset's carrying amount. *[IAS 16.53, 54]*.

In practice, many items of PP&E have a negligible residual value. This is usually because they are kept for significantly all of their useful lives. Residual values are of no relevance if the entity intends to keep the asset for significantly all of its useful life. If an entity uses residual values based on prices fetched in the market for a type of asset that it holds, it must also demonstrate an intention to dispose of that asset before the end of its economic life.

The requirement concerning the residual values of assets highlights how important it is that residual values are considered and reviewed in conjunction with the review of useful lives. The useful life is the period over which the entity expects to use the asset, not the asset's economic life.

5.3 Depreciation charge

The standard requires the depreciable amount of an asset to be allocated on a systematic basis over its useful life. *[IAS 16.50]*.

The standard makes it clear that depreciation must be charged on all items of PP&E, including those carried under the revaluation model, even if the fair value of an asset is higher than its carrying amount, as long as the residual value of the asset is lower than its carrying amount. *[IAS 16.52]*. If the residual value exceeds the carrying amount, no depreciation is charged until the residual value once again decreases to less than the carrying amount (see 5.2 above). *[IAS 16.54]*. IAS 16 makes it clear that the repair and maintenance of an asset do not, of themselves, negate the need to depreciate it. *[IAS 16.52]*.

There is no requirement in IAS 16 for an automatic impairment review if no depreciation is charged.

5.4 Useful lives

One of the critical assumptions on which the depreciation charge depends is the useful life of the asset. The standard requires the useful life of an asset to be estimated on a realistic basis and reviewed at least at the end of each financial year. The effects of changes in useful life are to be recognised prospectively as changes in accounting estimates in accordance with IAS 8 (see Chapter 3 at 4.5), over the remaining useful life of the asset. *[IAS 16.51]*.

As described at 2.2 above, the useful life of an asset is defined in terms of the asset's expected utility to the entity. *[IAS 16.57]*. It is the period over which the present owner will benefit from using the asset and not the total potential life of the asset; the two will often not be the same.

It is quite possible for an asset's useful life to be shorter than its economic life. The estimation of the useful life of the asset is a matter of judgement based on the experience of the entity with similar assets. Many entities have an asset management policy that may involve disposal of assets after a specified time or after consumption of a specified proportion of the future economic benefits embodied in the assets. *[IAS 16.57]*. This often occurs when disposing of assets when they still have a residual value, which means that another user can benefit from the asset. This is particularly common with property and motor vehicles, where there are effective second-hand markets, but less usual for plant and machinery. For example, an entity may have a policy of replacing all of its motor vehicles after three years, so this will be their estimated useful life for depreciation purposes. The entity will depreciate them over this period down to the estimated residual value. The residual values of motor vehicles are often easy to obtain and the entity will be able to reassess these residuals in line with the requirements of the standard. Thus, the estimation of the useful life of the asset is a matter of judgement based on the experience of the entity with similar assets. *[IAS 16.57].*

The future economic benefits embodied in an asset are consumed principally through usage. Other factors, however, should be taken into account such as technical or commercial obsolescence and wear and tear while an asset remains idle because they often result in the diminution of the economic benefits expected to be obtained from the asset. Consequently, IAS 16 provides guidance that all the following factors are to be considered when estimating the useful life of an asset:

(a) expected usage of the asset. Usage is assessed by reference to the asset's expected capacity or physical output;

(b) expected physical wear and tear, which depends on operational factors such as the number of shifts for which the asset is to be used and the repair and maintenance programme, and the care and maintenance of the asset while idle (see 5.4.1 below);

(c) technical or commercial obsolescence arising from changes or improvements in production, or from a change in the market demand for the product or service output of the asset. Expected future reductions in the selling price of an item that was produced using an asset could indicate the expectation of technical or commercial obsolescence of the asset, which, in turn, might reflect a reduction of the future economic benefits embodied in the asset (see 5.4.3 below); and

(d) legal or similar limits on the use of the asset, such as the expiry dates of related leases. *[IAS 16.56].*

Factor (d), above, states that the 'expiry dates of related leases' is considered when determining the asset's useful life. Generally, the useful life of the leasehold improvement is the same or less than the lease term. The interaction between the useful life of leasehold improvements and the term of the associated lease was discussed by the Interpretations Committee. In November 2019, the Committee concluded that an entity applies paragraphs 56 and 57 of IAS 16 in determining the useful life of non-removable leasehold improvements. If the lease term of the related lease is shorter than the economic life of those leasehold improvements, the entity considers whether it expects to use the leasehold improvements beyond that lease term. If the leasehold improvements are not expected to be used beyond the lease term, then an entity should conclude that the useful life of the non-removable leasehold improvements is the same as the lease term.[2] This issue is discussed in Chapter 23 at 4.4.1 in the context of cancellable leases. 'Lease term' under IFRS 16 is discussed in Chapter 23.

ArcelorMittal is an example of an entity depreciating an asset over its expected usage by reference to the production period.

> Extract 18.8: ArcelorMittal (2019)
> Consolidated Financial Statements [extract]
> Notes to consolidated financial statements [extract]
> NOTE 5: GOODWILL, INTANGIBLE AND TANGIBLE ASSETS [extract]
> 5.2 Property, plant and equipment and biological assets [extract]
>
> Property, plant and equipment used in mining activities is depreciated over its useful life or over the remaining life of the mine, if shorter, and if there is no alternative use. For the majority of assets used in mining activities, the economic benefits from the asset are consumed in a pattern which is linked to the production level and accordingly, assets used in mining activities are primarily depreciated on a units-of-production basis. A unit-of-production is based on the available estimate of proven and probable reserves.

5.4.1 Repairs and maintenance

The initial assessment of the useful life of the asset will take into account the expected routine spending on repairs and expenditure necessary for it to achieve that life. Although IAS 16 implies that this refers to an item of plant and machinery, care and maintenance programmes are relevant to assessing the useful lives of many other types of asset. For example, an entity may assess the useful life of a railway engine at thirty-five years on the assumption that it has a major overhaul every seven years. Without this expenditure, the life of the engine would be much less certain and could be much shorter. Maintenance necessary to support the fabric of a building and its service potential will also be taken into account in assessing its useful life. Eventually, it will always become uneconomic for the entity to continue to maintain the asset so, while the expenditure may lengthen the useful life, it is unlikely to make it indefinite.

Note that this applies whether the expenditure is capitalised because it meets the definition of a 'major inspection' (see 3.3.2 above) or if it is repairs and maintenance that is expensed as incurred.

5.4.2 Land

The standard requires the land and the building elements of property to be accounted for as separate components, even when they are acquired together. Land, which usually has an unlimited life, is not usually depreciated, while buildings are depreciable assets because they have limited useful life. IAS 16 states that the determination of the depreciable amount and useful life of a building is not affected by an increase in the value of the land on which it stands. *[IAS 16.58]*.

There are circumstances in which depreciation may be applied to land. In those instances in which land has a finite life (e.g. land that is used either for extractive purposes such as a quarry or mine, or for some purpose such as landfill), it will be depreciated in an appropriate manner that reflects the benefits to be derived from it, but it is highly unlikely that there will be any issue regarding separating the interest in land from any building element. *[IAS 16.58, 59]*. Further, the cost of such land may include an element for site dismantlement, removal or restoration, e.g. the initial estimate of the costs of dismantling and removing the item and restoring the site on which it is located, and any subsequent changes thereto (described in 4.3 above). *[IAS 16.16]*. This element will have to be separated from the land element and depreciated over an appropriate period. The standard describes this as 'the period of benefits obtained by incurring these costs' which will often be the estimated useful life of the site for its purpose and function. *[IAS 16.59]*. An entity engaged in landfill on a new site may make a provision for restoring it as soon as it starts preparation by removing the overburden. It will separate the land from the 'restoration asset' and depreciate the restoration asset over the landfill site's estimated useful life. If the land has an infinite useful life, an appropriate depreciation basis will have to be chosen that reflects the period of benefits obtained from the restoration asset.

If the estimated costs are revised in accordance with IFRIC 1, the adjusted depreciable amount of the asset is depreciated over its useful life. Therefore, once the related asset has reached the end of its useful life, all subsequent changes in the liability will be recognised in profit or loss as they occur, irrespective of whether the entity applies the cost or revaluation model. *[IFRIC 1.7]*.

5.4.3 Technological change

A current or expected future reduction in the market demand for the product or service output of an asset may be evidence of technical or commercial obsolescence, which, in turn, might reflect a reduction of the future economic benefits embodied in the asset. If an entity anticipates such technical or commercial obsolescence, it should reassess both the useful life of an asset and the pattern of consumption of future economic benefits. *[IAS 16.56(c), 61]*. In such cases, it might be more appropriate to use a diminishing balance method of depreciation to reflect the pattern of consumption (see 5.6.1 below).

The effects of technological change are often underestimated. It affects many assets, not only high technology plant and equipment such as computer systems. For example, many offices that have been purpose-built can become obsolete long before their fabric has physically deteriorated, for reasons such as the difficulty of introducing computer network infrastructures or air conditioning, poor environmental performance or an inability to meet new legislative requirements such as access for people with disabilities. Therefore, the estimation of an asset's useful life is a matter of judgement and the possibility of technological change must be taken into account. *[IAS 16.56, 57]*.

5.5 When depreciation starts

The standard is clear on when depreciation should start and finish, and sets out the requirements succinctly as follows:

- Depreciation of an asset begins when it is available for use, which is defined by the standard as occurring when the asset is in the location and condition necessary for it to be capable of operating in the manner intended by management. This is usually the point at which capitalisation of costs relating to the asset ceases as the physical asset is operational or ready for intended use (see 4.1.4 above).
- Depreciation of an asset ceases at the earlier of the date that the asset is classified as held for sale (or included in a disposal group that is classified as held for sale) in accordance with IFRS 5 and the date that the asset is derecognised (see 7 below). *[IAS 16.55]*.

Therefore, an entity does not stop depreciating an asset merely because it has become idle or has been retired from active use unless the asset is fully depreciated. However, if the entity is using a usage method of depreciation (e.g. the units-of-production method), the charge can be zero while there is no production. *[IAS 16.55]*. Of course, a prolonged period in which there is no production may raise questions as to whether the asset is impaired because an asset becoming idle is a specific example of an indication of impairment in IAS 36 (see Chapter 20 at 2.1). *[IAS 36.12(f)]*.

Assets held for sale under IFRS 5 are discussed at 7.1 below.

5.6 Depreciation methods

There is a variety of depreciation methods that can be used to allocate the depreciable amount of an asset on a systematic basis over its useful life. The standard is not prescriptive about what methods of depreciation should be used. It simply says that 'the depreciation method used shall reflect the pattern in which the asset's future economic benefits are expected to be consumed by the entity', mentioning the possible methods that can be used such as the straight-line method (which is the most common method where the depreciation results in a constant charge over the useful life if the asset's residual value does not change), the diminishing balance method (see 5.6.1 below) and the units of production method (see 5.6.2 below). The overriding requirement is to select the depreciation method that most closely reflects the expected pattern of consumption of the future economic benefits the asset brings over its useful life; and that the selected method is applied consistently from period to period unless there is a change in the expected pattern of consumption of those future economic benefits. *[IAS 16.60-62]*.

IAS 16 contains an explicit requirement that the depreciation method be reviewed at least at each financial year-end to determine if there has been a significant change in the pattern of consumption of an asset's future economic benefits. If there has been such a change, the depreciation method should be changed to reflect it. *[IAS 16.61]*. However, under IAS 8, this change is a change in accounting estimate and not a change in accounting policy. *[IAS 8.32(d), IAS 16.61]*. This means that the consequent depreciation adjustment should be made prospectively, i.e. the asset's depreciable amount should be written off over current and future periods using the new and more appropriate method of depreciation. *[IAS 8.36]*.

A revenue-based approach, e.g. using the ratio of revenue generated to total revenue expected to be generated, is not a suitable basis for depreciation. Depreciation is an estimate of the economic benefits of the asset consumed in the period. The revenue generated by an activity that requires the use of an asset generally reflects factors other than the consumption of the economic benefits of the asset. Revenue reflects the output of the asset, but it also reflects other factors that do not affect depreciation, such as changes in sales volumes and selling prices, the effects of selling activities and other inputs and processes. The price component of revenue may be affected by inflation or foreign currency exchange rates. This means that revenue does not, as a matter of principle, reflect how an asset is used or consumed. *[IAS 16.62A]*. While revenue-based methods of depreciation are considered inappropriate under IAS 16, the standard does permit other methods of depreciation that reflect the level of activity, such as the units of production method (see 5.6.2 below).

5.6.1 Diminishing balance methods

The diminishing balance method involves determining a percentage depreciation that will write off the asset's depreciable amount over its useful life. This involves solving for a rate that will reduce the asset's net book value to its residual value at the end of the useful life. The diminishing balance method results in a decreasing depreciation charge over the useful life of the asset. *[IAS 16.62]*.

Example 18.2: Diminishing balance depreciation

An asset costs €6,000 and has a life of four years and a residual value of €1,500. It calculates that the appropriate depreciation rate on the declining balance is 29% and that the depreciation charge in years 1-4 will be as follows:

		€
Year 1	Cost	6,000
	Depreciation at 29% of €6,000	(1,757)
	Net book value	4,243
Year 2	Depreciation at 29% of €4,243	(1,243)
	Net book value	3,000
Year 3	Depreciation at 29% of €3,000	(879)
	Net book value	2,121
Year 4	Depreciation at 29% of €2,121	(621)
	Net book value	1,500

The sum of digits method is another form of the reducing balance method, but one that is based on the estimated life of the asset and which can easily be applied if the asset has a residual value. If an asset has an estimated useful life of four years then the digits 1, 2, 3, and 4 are added together, giving a total of 10. Depreciation of four-tenths, three-tenths and so on, of the cost of the asset, less any residual value, will be charged in the respective years. The method is sometimes called the 'rule of 78', 78 being the sum of the digits 1 to 12.

Example 18.3: Sum of the digits depreciation

An asset costs €10,000 and is expected to be sold for €2,000 after four years. The depreciable amount is €8,000 (€10,000 – €2,000). Depreciation is to be provided over four years using the sum of the digits method.

		€
Year 1	Cost	10,000
	Depreciation at 4/10 of €8,000	(3,200)
	Net book value	6,800
Year 2	Depreciation at 3/10 of €8,000	(2,400)
	Net book value	4,400
Year 3	Depreciation at 2/10 of €8,000	(1,600)
	Net book value	2,800
Year 4	Depreciation at 1/10 of €8,000	(800)
	Net book value	2,000

5.6.2 Unit-of-production method

Under this method, the asset is written off in line with its expected use or estimated total output. *[IAS 16.62]*. By relating depreciation to the proportion of productive capacity utilised to date, it reflects the fact that the useful economic life of certain assets, principally machinery, is more closely linked to its usage and output than to time.

This method is normally used in extractive industries, for example, to amortise the costs of development of productive oil and gas facilities.

The essence of choosing a fair depreciation method is to reflect the consumption of economic benefits provided by the asset concerned. In most cases the straight-line basis will give perfectly acceptable results, and the vast majority of entities use this method. Where there are instances, such as the extraction of a known proportion of a mineral resource, or the use of a certain amount of the total available number of working hours of a machine, it may be that a unit of production method will give fairer results.

5.7 Impairment

All items of PP&E accounted for under IAS 16 are subject to the impairment requirements of IAS 36. Impairment is discussed in Chapter 20. *[IAS 16.63]*.

The question has arisen about the treatment of any compensation an entity may be due to receive as a result of an asset being impaired. For example an asset that is insured might be destroyed in a fire, so repayment from an insurance company might be expected. IAS 16 states that these events – the impairments or losses of items of PP&E, the related claims for or payments of compensation from third parties and any subsequent purchase or construction of replacement assets – are 'separate economic events' and should be accounted for separately as follows:

- impairments of PP&E are recognised in accordance with IAS 36 (see Chapter 20);
- derecognition of items of PP&E retired or disposed of should be determined in accordance with IAS 16 (see 7 below);
- compensation from third parties for items of PP&E that were impaired, lost or given up is included in determining profit and loss when it becomes receivable; and
- the cost of items of PP&E restored, purchased or constructed as replacements is determined in accordance with IAS 16 (see 3 and 4 above). *[IAS 16.65, 66]*.

6 MEASUREMENT AFTER RECOGNITION: REVALUATION MODEL

If the revaluation model is adopted, PP&E is initially recognised at cost and subsequently carried at a revalued amount, being its fair value (if it can be measured reliably) at the date of the revaluation, less subsequent accumulated depreciation and impairment losses. *[IAS 16.29, 31]*. In practice, 'fair value' will usually be the market value of the asset. There is no requirement for a professional external valuation or even for a professionally qualified valuer to perform the appraisal, although in practice professional advice is often sought.

Valuation frequency is not prescribed by IAS 16. Instead it states that revaluations are to be made with sufficient regularity to ensure that the carrying amount does not differ materially from that which would be determined using fair value at the end of the reporting period. *[IAS 16.31]*. Therefore, the frequency of revaluations depends upon the changes in fair values of the items of PP&E being revalued. When the fair value of a revalued asset differs materially from its carrying amount, a further revaluation is necessary. The standard suggests that some items of PP&E have frequent and volatile changes in fair value and these should be revalued annually. This is true for property assets in many jurisdictions, but even in such cases there may be quieter periods in which there is little movement in values. If there are only insignificant changes in fair value, frequent revaluations are unnecessary and it may only be necessary to perform revaluations at three or five-year intervals. *[IAS 16.34]*.

If the revaluation model is adopted, IAS 16 specifies that all items within a class of PP&E are to be revalued simultaneously to prevent selective revaluation of assets and the reporting of amounts in the financial statements that are a mixture of costs and values as at different dates. *[IAS 16.29, 36, 38]*. A class of PP&E is a grouping of assets of a similar nature and use in an entity's operations. This is not a precise definition. IAS 16 suggests that the following are examples of separate classes of PP&E:

(i) land;

(ii) land and buildings;

(iii) machinery;

(iv) ships;

(v) aircraft;

(vi) motor vehicles;

(vii) furniture and fixtures;

(viii) office equipment; and

(ix) bearer plants. *[IAS 16.37]*.

These are very broad categories of PP&E and it is possible for them to be classified further into groupings of assets of a similar nature and use. Office buildings and factories or hotels and fitness centres, could be separate classes of asset. If the entity used the same type of asset in two different geographical locations, e.g. clothing manufacturing facilities for similar products or products with similar markets, say in Sri Lanka and Guatemala, it is likely that these would be seen as part of the same class of asset. However, if the entity manufactured pharmaceuticals and clothing, both in European facilities, then few would argue that these could be assets with a sufficiently different nature and use to be a separate class. Ultimately it must be a matter of judgement in the context of the specific operations of individual entities.

IAS 16 permits a rolling valuation of a class of assets provided the revaluation of such class of assets is completed within a short period of time and 'provided the revaluations are kept up to date'. *[IAS 16.38]*. This final condition makes it difficult to see how rolling valuations can be performed unless the value of the assets changes very little (in which case the standard states that valuations need only be performed every three to five years) because if a large change is revealed, then presumably a wholesale revaluation is required.

An entity that uses the cost model for its investment property, as allowed by IAS 40, should apply the cost model in IAS 16 (see 5 above) for owned investment property. *[IAS 16.5]*. Investment property held by a lessee as a right-of-use asset will be measured in accordance with IFRS 16 (see Chapter 23 at 5.3.1).

6.1 The meaning of fair value

Fair value is defined in IFRS 13. IFRS 13 does not prescribe when to measure fair value but provides guidance on how to measure it under IFRS when fair value is required or permitted by IFRS.

IFRS 13 clarifies that fair value is an exit price from the perspective of market participants. 'Fair value' is defined as 'the price that would be received to sell an asset or paid to transfer a liability in an orderly transaction between market participants at the measurement date'. *[IAS 16.6, IFRS 13 Appendix A]*.

6.1.1 Revaluing assets under IFRS 13

IFRS 13 specifies that 'fair value is a market-based measurement, not an entity-specific measurement'. *[IFRS 13.2]*. Some of the principles that affect the revaluation of PP&E are the concept of highest and best use and the change in focus of the fair value hierarchy from valuation techniques to inputs. IFRS 13 also requires a significant number of disclosures, including the categorisation of a fair value measurement with the fair value measurement hierarchy.

The requirements of IFRS 13 are discussed in Chapter 14.

The following sections consider some of the key considerations when measuring the fair value of an item of PP&E.

6.1.1.A Highest and best use

IFRS 13 states that 'a fair value measurement of a non-financial asset takes into account a market participant's ability to generate economic benefits by using the asset in its highest and best use or by selling it to another market participant that would use the asset in its highest and best use'. *[IFRS 13.27]*. This evaluation will include uses that are 'physically possible, legally permissible and financially feasible'. *[IFRS 13.28]*.

The highest and best use is determined from the perspective of market participants that would be acquiring the asset, but the starting point is the asset's current use. It is presumed that an entity's current use of the asset is the asset's highest and best use, unless market or other factors suggest that a different use of the asset by market participants would maximise its value. *[IFRS 13.29]*.

Prior to the adoption of IFRS 13, IAS 16 did not imply that fair value and market value were synonymous, which allowed a broader meaning of the term 'fair value'. The term could certainly have been interpreted as encompassing the following two commonly used, market derived, valuation bases:

- market value in existing use, an entry value for property in continuing use in the business which is based on the concept of net current replacement cost; and
- open market value, which is an exit value and based on the amount that a property that is surplus to requirements could reach when sold.

Both of these bases are market-derived, yet they can differ for a variety of reasons. A property may have a higher value on the open market if it could be redeployed to a more valuable use. On the other hand, the present owner may enjoy some benefits that could not be passed on in a sale, such as planning consents that are personal to the present occupier. Market value in existing use will be presumed to be fair value under IFRS 13 for many types of business property unless market or other factors suggest that open market value is higher (i.e. open market value represents highest and best use). For most retail sites market value in existing use will be fair value; if there is market evidence that certain types of property have an alternative use with a higher value, e.g. pubs or warehouses that can be converted to residential use, this will have to be taken into account.

The fair value of an item of PP&E will either be measured based on the value it would derive on a standalone basis or in combination with other assets or other assets and liabilities, i.e. the asset's 'valuation premise'. 'Valuation premise' is a valuation concept that addresses how a non-financial asset derives its maximum value to market participants. The highest and best use of an item of PP&E 'might provide maximum value to market participants through its use in combination with other assets as a group or in combination with other assets and liabilities (e.g. a business)' or it 'might have maximum value to market participants on a stand-alone basis'. *[IFRS 13.31(a)-(b)]*.

The following example is derived from IFRS 13 and illustrates highest and best use in establishing fair value. *[IFRS 13.IE7-IE8]*.

Example 18.4: Highest and best use

An entity acquires land in a business combination. The land is currently developed for industrial use as a site for a factory. The current use of land is presumed to be its highest and best use unless market or other factors suggest evidence for a different use.

Scenario (1): In the particular jurisdiction, it can be difficult to obtain consents to change use from industrial to residential use for the land and there is no evidence that the area is becoming desirable for residential development. The fair value is based on the current industrial use of the land.

Scenario (2): Nearby sites have recently been developed for residential use as sites for high-rise apartment buildings. On the basis of that development and recent zoning and other changes that facilitated the residential development, the entity determines that the land currently used as a site for a factory could also be developed as a site for residential use because market participants would take into account the potential to develop the site for residential use when pricing the land.

This determination can be highly judgemental. For further discussion on highest and best use and valuation premise see Chapter 14 at 10.

6.1.1.B Valuation approaches

IFRS 13 does not limit the types of valuation techniques an entity might use to measure fair value but instead focuses on the types of inputs that will be used. The standard requires the entity to use the valuation technique that maximises the use of relevant observable inputs and minimises the use of unobservable inputs. *[IFRS 13.61]*. The objective is that the best available inputs should be used in valuing the assets. These inputs could be used in any valuation technique provided they are consistent with the three valuation approaches in the standard: the market approach, the cost approach and the income approach. *[IFRS 13.62]*.

The *market approach* uses prices and other relevant information generated by market transactions involving identical or comparable (i.e. similar) assets, liabilities or a group of assets and liabilities, such as a business. *[IFRS 13.B5]*. For PP&E, market techniques will usually involve market transactions in comparable assets or, for certain assets valued as businesses, market multiples derived from comparable transactions. *[IFRS 13.B5, B6]*.

The *cost approach* reflects the amount that would be required currently to replace the service capacity of an asset (i.e. current replacement cost). It is based on what a market participant buyer would pay to acquire or construct a substitute asset of comparable utility, adjusted for obsolescence. Obsolescence includes physical deterioration, functional (technological) and economic (external) obsolescence so it is broader than and not the same as depreciation under IAS 16. *[IFRS 13.B8, B9]*.

The *income approach* converts future amounts (e.g. cash flows or income and expenses) to a single discounted amount. The fair value reflects current market expectations about those future amounts. In the case of PP&E, this will usually mean using a present value (i.e. discounted cash flow) technique. *[IFRS 13.B10, B11]*.

See Chapter 14 at 14 for a further discussion of these valuation techniques.

IFRS 13 does not place any preference on the techniques. An entity can use any valuation technique, or use multiple techniques, as long as it applies the valuation technique consistently. A change in a valuation technique is considered a change in an accounting estimate in accordance with IAS 8. *[IFRS 13.66]*.

Instead, the inputs used to measure the fair value of an asset have a hierarchy. Level 1 inputs are those that are quoted prices in active markets (i.e. markets in which transactions take place with sufficient frequency and volume to provide pricing information on an ongoing basis) for identical assets that the entity can access at the measurement date. *[IFRS 13.76]*. Level 1 inputs have the highest priority, followed by inputs, other than quoted prices, that are observable for the asset either directly or indirectly (Level 2). The lowest priority inputs are those based on unobservable inputs (Level 3). *[IFRS 13.72]*. The valuation techniques, referred to above, will use a combination of inputs to determine the fair value of the asset.

As stated above, land and buildings are the most commonly revalued items of PP&E. These types of assets use a variety of inputs such as other sales, multiples or discounted cash flows. While some of these maybe Level 1 inputs, we generally expect the fair value measurement as a whole to be categorised within Level 2 or Level 3 of the fair value hierarchy for disclosure purposes (see 8.2 below).

IFRS 13 also requires additional disclosure in the financial statements that are discussed at 8.2 below of this chapter and in Chapter 14 at 20.

6.1.1.C   The cost approach – current replacement cost

IFRS 13 permits the use of a cost approach for measuring fair value, for example current replacement costs. Before using current replacement cost as a method to measure fair value, an entity should ensure that both:

- the highest and best use of the assets is consistent with their current use; and
- the principal market (or in its absence, the most advantageous market) is the same as the entry market.

The resulting current replacement cost should also be assessed to ensure market participants would actually transact for the asset in its current condition and location at this price. In particular, an entity should ensure that both:

- the inputs used to determine replacement cost are consistent with what market participant buyers would pay to acquire or construct a substitute asset of comparable utility; and
- the replacement cost has been adjusted for obsolescence that market participant buyers would consider so that the depreciation adjustment reflects all forms of obsolescence (i.e. physical deterioration, technological (functional) and economic obsolescence and environmental factors), which is broader than depreciation calculated in accordance with IAS 16.

For further discussion see Chapter 14 at 14.3.

6.2 Accounting for valuation surpluses and deficits

Increases in the carrying amount of PP&E as a result of revaluations should be credited to OCI and accumulated in a revaluation surplus account in equity. To the extent that a revaluation increase of an asset reverses a revaluation decrease of the same asset that was previously recognised as an expense in profit or loss, such increase should be credited to income in profit or loss. Decreases in valuation should be charged to profit or loss, except to the extent that they reverse the existing accumulated revaluation surplus on the same asset and therefore such decrease is recognised in OCI. The decrease recognised in OCI reduces the amount accumulated in equity under revaluation surplus account. *[IAS 16.39, 40]*. This means that it is not permissible under the standard to carry a negative revaluation reserve in respect of any item of PP&E.

The same rules apply to impairment losses. An impairment loss on a revalued asset is first used to reduce the revaluation surplus for that asset. Only when the impairment loss exceeds the amount in the revaluation surplus for that same asset is any further impairment loss recognised in profit or loss (see Chapter 20 at 11.1). *[IAS 36.61]*.

IAS 16 generally retains a model in which the revalued amount substitutes for cost in both statement of financial position and statement of profit or loss and on derecognition there is no recycling to profit and loss of amounts taken directly to OCI. The revaluation surplus included within equity in respect of an item of PP&E may be transferred directly to retained earnings when the asset is derecognised (i.e. transferring the whole of the surplus when the asset is retired or disposed of). *[IAS 16.41]*.

IAS 16 also allows some of the revaluation surplus to be transferred to retained earnings as the asset is used by an entity. In such a case, the difference between depreciation based on the revalued carrying amount of the asset and depreciation based on its original cost may be transferred from revaluation surplus to retained earnings in equity. This is illustrated in the Example 18.5 below. This recognises that any depreciation on the revalued part of an asset's carrying value has been realised by being charged to profit or loss. Thus, a transfer should be made of an equivalent amount from the revaluation surplus to retained earnings. Any remaining balance may also be transferred when the asset is disposed of. These transfers should be made directly from revaluation surplus to retained earnings and not through the statement of profit or loss. *[IAS 16.41]*.

Example 18.5: Effect of depreciation on the revaluation reserve

On 1 January 2018 an entity acquired an asset for €1,000. The asset has an economic life of ten years and is depreciated on a straight-line basis. The residual value is assumed to be €nil. At 31 December 2021 (when the cost net of accumulated depreciation is €600) the asset is valued at €900. The entity accounts for the revaluation by debiting the carrying value of the asset (using either of the methods discussed below) €300 and crediting €300 to the revaluation reserve. At 31 December 2021 the useful life of the asset is considered to be the remainder of its original life (i.e. six years) and its residual value is still considered to be €nil. In the year ended 31 December 2022 and in later years, the depreciation charged to profit or loss is €150 (€900/6 years remaining).

The usual treatment thereafter for each of the remaining 6 years of the asset's life, is to transfer €50 (€300/6 years) each year from the revaluation reserve to retained earnings (not through profit or loss). This avoids the revaluation reserve being maintained indefinitely even after the asset ceases to exist, which does not seem sensible.

Any effect on taxation, both current and deferred, resulting from the revaluation of PP&E is recognised and disclosed in accordance with IAS 12 – *Income Taxes*. *[IAS 16.42]*. This is dealt with in Chapter 33.

When an item of PP&E is revalued, the carrying amount of that asset is adjusted to the revalued amount. As alluded to in Example 18.5 above, there are two methods of accounting for accumulated depreciation when an item of PP&E is revalued. At the date of revaluation, the asset is treated in one of the following ways:

- the accumulated depreciation is eliminated against gross carrying amount of the asset; or
- the gross carrying amount is adjusted in a manner that is consistent with the revaluation of the carrying amount of the asset. For example, the gross carrying amount may be restated by reference to observable market data or it may be restated proportionately to the change in the carrying amount. The accumulated depreciation at the date of the revaluation is adjusted to equal the difference between the gross carrying amount and the carrying amount of the asset after taking into account accumulated impairment losses. *[IAS 16.35]*.

The first method available eliminates the accumulated depreciation against the gross carrying amount of the asset. After the revaluation, the gross carrying amount and the net carrying amount are same (i.e. reflecting the revalued amount). This is illustrated in Example 18.6 below.

Example 18.6: Revaluation by eliminating accumulated depreciation

On 31 December, a building has a carrying amount of €40,000, being the original cost of €70,000 less accumulated depreciation of €30,000. A revaluation is performed and the fair value of the asset is €50,000. The entity would record the following journal entries:

	Dr €	Cr €
Accumulated depreciation	30,000	
Building		20,000
Asset revaluation reserve		10,000

	Before €	After €
Building at cost	70,000	
Building at valuation		50,000
Accumulated depreciation	30,000	–
Net book value	40,000	50,000

Under the observable market data approach, the gross carrying amount will be restated and the difference compared to the revalued amount of the asset will be absorbed by the accumulated depreciation. Using the example above, assuming the gross carrying amount is restated to €75,000 by reference to the observable market data, the accumulated depreciation will be adjusted to €25,000 (i.e. the gross carrying amount of €75,000 less the carrying amount adjusted to its revalued amount of €50,000). The revaluation gain recognised is the same as the first method above at €10,000.

Alternatively, the gross carrying amount is restated proportionately to the change in carrying amount (i.e. a 25% uplift) resulting in the same revaluation gain as the methods above but the cost and accumulated depreciation carried forward reflect the gross cost of the asset of €87,500 and accumulated depreciation of €37,500. This method may be used if an asset is revalued using an index to determine its depreciated replacement cost (see 6.1.1.C above).

Notice that the revaluation gain recognised remained at €10,000 whichever method described above is used.

6.3 Reversals of downward valuations

IAS 16 requires that, if an asset's carrying amount is increased as a result of a revaluation, the increase should be credited directly to OCI and accumulated in equity under the heading of revaluation surplus. However, the increase should be recognised in profit or loss to the extent that it reverses a revaluation decrease of the same asset previously recognised in profit or loss (see 6.2 above). *[IAS 16.39]*.

The same rules apply to a reversal of an impairment loss – see discussion in Chapter 20 at 11.4.2.

If the revalued asset is being depreciated, we consider that the full amount of any reversal should not be taken to profit or loss. Rather, the reversal should take account of the depreciation that would have been charged on the previously higher book value. The text of IAS 16 does not specify this treatment but other interpretations would be inconsistent with IAS 36, which states:

> 'The increased carrying amount of an asset other than goodwill attributable to a reversal of an impairment loss shall not exceed the carrying amount that would have been determined (net of amortisation or depreciation) had no impairment loss been recognised for the asset in prior years.' *[IAS 36.117]*.

The following example demonstrates a way in which this could be applied.

Example 18.7: Reversal of a downward valuation

An asset has a cost of £1,000,000, a life of 10 years and a residual value of £nil. At the end of year 3, when the asset's NBV is £700,000, it is revalued to £350,000. This write down below cost of £350,000 is taken through profit or loss.

The entity then depreciated its asset by £50,000 per annum, so as to write off the carrying value of £350,000 over the remaining 7 years.

At the end of year 6, the asset's depreciated cost is £200,000 but it is now revalued to £500,000. The effect on the entity's asset is as follows:

	£000
Valuation	
At the beginning of year 6	350
Surplus on revaluation	150
At the end of the year	500
Accumulated depreciation	
At beginning of year 6 *	100
Charge for the year	50
Accumulated depreciation written back on revaluation	(150)
At the end of the year	–
Net book value at the end of year 6	500
Net book value at the beginning of year 6	250

* Two years' depreciation (years 4 and 5) at £50,000 per annum.

The total credit for the uplift in value is £300,000 on the revaluation in year 6 (i.e. £500,000 less £200,000). However, only £200,000 is taken through profit or loss. £100,000 represents depreciation that would otherwise have been charged to profit or loss in years 4 and 5. This will be taken directly to the revaluation surplus in OCI.

From the beginning of year 7, the asset at revalued amount of £500,000 will be written off over the remaining four years at £125,000 per annum.

In the example the amount of the revaluation that is credited to the revaluation surplus in OCI represents the difference between the net book value that would have resulted had the asset been held on a cost basis (£400,000) and the net book value on a revalued basis (£500,000).

Of course, this is an extreme example. Most assets that are subject to a policy of revaluation would not show such marked changes in value and it would be expected that there would be valuation movements in the intervening years rather than dramatic losses and gains in years 3 and 6. However, we consider that in principle this is the way in which downward valuations should be recognised.

There may be major practical difficulties for any entity that finds itself in the position of reversing revaluation deficits on depreciating assets, although whether in practice this eventuality often occurs is open to doubt. If there is any chance that it is likely to occur, the business would need to continue to maintain asset registers on the original, pre-write down basis.

6.4 Adopting a policy of revaluation

Although the initial adoption of a policy of revaluation by an entity that has previously used the cost model is a change in accounting policy, it is not dealt with as a prior period adjustment in accordance with IAS 8. Instead, the change is treated as a revaluation during the current period as set out at 6.2 above. *[IAS 8.17]*. This means that the entity is not required to obtain valuation information about comparative periods.

6.5 Assets held under leases

Under IFRS 16 lessees are required to recognise most leases in their statement of financial position as lease liabilities with corresponding right-of-use assets. A lessee subsequently measures the right-of-use asset using a cost model under IFRS 16 (applying the depreciation requirements in IAS 16, but subject to the specific requirements in paragraph 32 of IFRS 16), unless it applies one of the following measurement models allowed by IFRS 16 (see Chapter 23):

- the fair value model in IAS 40, but only if the lessee applies this to its investment property and the right-of-use asset meets the definition of investment property in IAS 40; or
- if the lessee applies the revaluation model in IAS 16 to a class of PP&E, the lessee would also have the option to revalue all of the right-of-use assets that relate to that class of PP&E. [IFRS 16.29-35].

7 DERECOGNITION AND DISPOSAL

Derecognition, i.e. removal of the carrying amount of an item of PP&E from the financial statements of the entity, occurs when an item of PP&E is either disposed of, or when no further economic benefits are expected to flow from its use or disposal. [IAS 16.67]. The disposal of an item of PP&E may occur in a variety of ways (e.g. by sale, by entering into a finance lease or by donation). IFRS 15 requires that revenue (and a gain or loss on disposal of a non-current asset not in the ordinary course of business) be recognised upon satisfaction of performance obligation by transferring control. Accordingly, the actual date of disposal of an item of PP&E is the date the recipient obtains control of that item in accordance with the requirements for determining when a performance obligation is satisfied in IFRS 15 (see Chapter 30). IFRS 16 applies to a disposal by way of a sale and leaseback. [IAS 16.69].

All gains and losses on derecognition must be included in profit and loss for the period when the item is derecognised, unless another standard applies; e.g. under IFRS 16 a sale and leaseback transaction might not give rise to a gain (see Chapter 23). [IAS 16.68].

Gains are not to be classified as revenue, although in some limited circumstances presenting gross revenue on the sale of certain assets may be appropriate (see 7.2 below). [IAS 16.68]. Gains and losses are to be calculated as the difference between any net disposal proceeds and the carrying value of the item of PP&E. [IAS 16.71]. This means that any revaluation surplus in equity relating to the asset disposed of is transferred directly to retained earnings when the asset is derecognised and not reflected in profit or loss (see 6.2 above). [IAS 16.41].

Replacement of 'parts' of an asset requires derecognition of the carrying value of the replaced part, even if that part had not been depreciated separately. In these circumstances, the standard allows the cost of the replacement part to be a guide in estimating the original cost of the replaced part at the time it was acquired or constructed, if that cannot be determined. [IAS 16.70].

The amount of consideration to be included in the gain or loss arising from the derecognition of an item of PP&E is determined in accordance with the requirements for determining the transaction price in paragraphs 47–72 of IFRS 15 (see Chapter 29 at 2). Any subsequent changes to the estimated amount of the consideration included in the gain or loss should be accounted for in accordance with the requirements for changes in the transaction price in IFRS 15 (see Chapter 29 at 2.9). *[IAS 16.72]*.

7.1 IFRS 5 – *Non-current Assets Held for Sale and Discontinued Operations*

IFRS 5 introduced a category of asset, 'held for sale', and PP&E within this category is outside the scope of IAS 16, although IAS 16 requires certain disclosures about assets held for sale to be made, as set out at 8.1 below.

IFRS 5 requires that an item of PP&E should be classified as held for sale if its carrying amount will be recovered principally through a sale transaction rather than continuing use, though continuing use is not in itself precluded for assets classified as held for sale. *[IFRS 5.6]*. An asset can also be part of a 'disposal group' (that is a group of assets that are to be disposed of together), in which case such group can be treated as a whole. Once this classification has been made, depreciation ceases, even if the asset is still being used, but the assets must be carried at the lower of their previous carrying amount and fair value less costs to sell. For assets (or disposal group) to be classified as held for sale, they must be available for immediate sale in their present condition, and the sale must be highly probable. *[IFRS 5.7]*.

Additionally, the sale should be completed within one year from the date of classification as held for sale, management at an 'appropriate level' must be committed to the plan, and an active programme of marketing the assets at current fair value must have been started. *[IFRS 5.8]*.

The requirements of IFRS 5 are dealt with in Chapter 4. IFRS 5 does not apply when assets that are held for sale in the ordinary course of business are transferred to inventories (see 7.2 below). *[IAS 16.68A]*.

7.2 Sale of assets held for rental

If an entity, in the course of its ordinary activities, routinely sells PP&E that it has held for rental to others, it should transfer such assets to inventories at their carrying amount when they cease to be rented and are then held for sale. The proceeds from the sale of such assets should be recognised as revenue in accordance with IFRS 15. *[IAS 16.68A]*. In contrast, the sale of investment property is generally not recognised as revenue. The rationale and possible treatment of investment property in such cases is discussed in detail in Chapter 19 at 9 and 10.

A number of entities sell assets that have previously been held for rental, for example, car rental companies that may acquire vehicles with the intention of holding them as rental cars for a limited period and then selling them. An issue was whether the sale of such assets, which arguably have a dual purpose of being rented out and then sold, should be presented gross (revenue and cost of sales) or net (gain or loss) in profit or loss.

The IASB concluded that the presentation of gross revenue, rather than a net gain or loss, would better reflect the ordinary activities of such entities.

IAS 7 – *Statement of Cash Flows* – further requires that both (i) the cash payments to manufacture or acquire assets held for rental and subsequently held for sale; and (ii) the cash receipts from rentals and sales of such assets are presented as cash flows from operating activities. *[IAS 7.14]*. The intention behind this requirement is to avoid initial expenditure on purchases of assets being classified as investing activities while inflows from sales are recorded within operating activities.

7.3 Partial disposals and undivided interests

IAS 16 requires an entity to derecognise 'an item' of PP&E on disposal or when it expects no future economic benefits from its use or disposal. *[IAS 16.67]*.

Items of PP&E are recognised when their costs can be measured reliably and it is probable that future benefits associated with the asset will flow to the entity. *[IAS 16.7]*. The standard 'does not prescribe the unit of measure for recognition, i.e. what constitutes an item of property, plant and equipment'. *[IAS 16.9]*.

However, items that are derecognised were not necessarily items on initial recognition. The item that is being disposed of may be part of a larger 'item' bought in a single transaction that can be subdivided into parts (i.e. separate items) for separate disposal; an obvious example is land or many types of property. The principle is the same as for the replacement of parts, which may only be identified and derecognised so that the cost of the replacement part may be recognised (see 3.2 above). The entity needs to identify the cost of the part disposed of by allocating the carrying value on a systematic and appropriate basis.

In these cases, the part disposed of is a physical part of the original asset. The standard assumes that disposal will be of a physical part (except in the specific case of major inspections and overhauls – see 3.3.2 above). However, some entities enter into arrangements in which they dispose of part of the benefits that will be derived from the assets.

Although IAS 16 defines an asset by reference to the future economic benefits that will be controlled by the entity as a result of the acquisition, it does not address disposals of a proportion of these benefits. An entity may dispose of an undivided interest in the whole asset (sometimes called an ownership 'in common' of the asset). This means that all owners have a proportionate share of the entire asset (e.g. the purchaser of a 25% undivided interest in 100 acres of land owns 25% of the whole 100 acres). These arrangements are common in, but are not restricted to, the extractive and property sectors. Vendors have to determine how to account for the consideration they have received from the purchaser. This will depend on the details of the arrangement and, in particular, whether the entity continues to control the asset or there is joint control.

7.3.1 Joint control

In some cases there may be joint control over the asset, in which case the arrangement will be within scope of IFRS 11 – *Joint Arrangements* – which will determine how to account for the disposal and the subsequent accounting. Joint control is discussed in detail in Chapter 12.

The accounting treatment may depend on whether the disposing entity holds an asset directly or holds it within a single-asset subsidiary. If the entity is disposing of an interest in an asset that is not held within a single-asset subsidiary and if the retained interest represents an investment in an entity a gain or loss is recognised as if 100% of asset had been sold because control has been lost. If the transaction is with other parties to a joint operation, the vendor will only recognise gains and losses to the extent of the other parties' interests. *[IFRS 11.B34].* In other words, it will recognise a part disposal. The retained interest will be analysed as a joint operation or a joint venture.

In the former case, the entity will account for its own assets, liabilities, revenue etc. while in the latter case it will apply the equity method to account for its interests in the joint venture (see Chapter 12 at 6 and 7, respectively). Undivided interests cannot be accounted for as joint arrangements in the absence of joint control.

In many jurisdictions it is common for certain assets, particularly properties, to be bought and sold by transferring ownership of a separate legal entity formed to hold the asset (a 'single-asset' entity) rather than the asset itself. If the asset is held in a single-asset subsidiary entity that becomes a joint venture, there is a conflict between the requirements of IFRS 10 – *Consolidated Financial Statements* – and IAS 28 – *Investments in Associates and Joint Ventures*. In September 2014, the IASB issued amendments to IFRS 10 and IAS 28, in dealing with the sale or contribution of assets between an investor and its associate or joint venture. The main consequence of the amendments is that a full gain or loss is recognised when a transaction involves a business (whether it is housed in a subsidiary or not). A partial gain or loss is recognised when a transaction involves assets that do not constitute a business, even if these assets are housed in a subsidiary. The amendments were to be applied prospectively for transactions occurring in annual periods commencing on or after 1 January 2016, with earlier application permitted.[3] However, in December 2015, the IASB issued a further amendment *Effective Date of Amendments to IFRS 10 and IAS 28*. This amendment defers the effective date of the September 2014 amendment until the IASB has finalised any revisions that result from the IASB's research project on the equity method (although the IASB now plans no further work on this project until the Post-implementation Review of IFRS 11 is undertaken).[4] *[IFRS 10.BC190N].* Nevertheless, the IASB has continued to allow early application of the September 2014 amendment as it did not wish to prohibit the application of better financial reporting.[5] *[IFRS 10.BC190O].* This issue is discussed further in Chapter 7 at 3.3.2, Chapter 11 at 7.6.5.C and in Chapter 12 at 8.2.3.

7.3.2 Vendor retains control

If the asset is not jointly controlled in the subsequent arrangement, the vendor might retain control over the asset. The vendor will recognise revenue or it will be a financing arrangement. If it is the former, then the issue is the period and pattern over which revenue is recognised.

If the vendor retains control, then it will not meet the requirements in IFRS 15 for treating the transaction as a sale, i.e. recognising revenue on entering into the arrangement. IFRS 15 requires that revenue (and a gain or loss on disposal of a non-current asset not in the ordinary course of business) be recognised upon satisfaction of a performance obligation by transferring control (see Chapter 30 at 1).

The arrangement could be akin to a lease, especially if the disposal is for a period of time. However, arrangements are only within the scope of IFRS 16 if they relate to a specified asset. Generally, a portion of a larger asset that is not physically distinct is not considered to be a specified asset. The related detailed requirements of IFRS 16 are discussed in Chapter 23 at 3.1.2.

If it is not a lease and the vendor continues to control the asset, the arrangement might be best characterised as a performance obligation for services to be spread over the term of the arrangement. That is, the initial receipt would be a liability and recognised in profit and loss over time.

Alternatively, it could be a financing-type arrangement, in which case the proceeds would be classified as a financial liability. In effect, the vendor is trading a share of any revenue to which it is entitled in exchange for funding by the purchaser of one or more activities relating to the asset. The purchaser receives a return that is comparable to a lender's rate of return out of the proceeds of production. This could be by receiving a disproportionate share of output until it has recovered its costs (the financing it has provided) as well as the agreed rate of return for the funding. These arrangements are found in the extractive sector, e.g. carried interests and farm-outs (see Chapter 43 at 6). In the development stage of a project, the asset in question will be classified as PP&E or as an intangible asset under IAS 38. Under a carried interest arrangement the carried party transfers a portion of the risks and rewards of a property, in exchange for a funding commitment from the carrying party.

7.3.3 Partial disposal

In some circumstances it is argued that the rights transferred by the vendor are such that it neither controls nor jointly controls the whole of the original asset and the question arises as to whether there is a part disposal of the asset. The arrangement cannot be accounted for as a joint operation as there is no joint control. Classification as a joint operation would allow a part disposal of an item of PP&E. It is noted that a party that participates in a joint operation but does not have joint control records its interests in the same way as a participant in a joint operation, accounting for its own assets and liabilities. *[IFRS 11.23]*. This is unaffected by the fact that the asset in question may be an interest in an undivided asset; it will still classify its interest in the asset as an item of PP&E. In those sectors where these arrangements are common and where an entity will be simultaneously vendor and acquirer in different arrangements, it is argued that the transactions should be treated symmetrically, i.e. as a part disposal of the undivided asset and an acquisition of an interest in PP&E. However, this interpretation depends entirely on the vendor ceding control of part of its rights and applying IAS 16 principles to obtain symmetry of accounting between acquisitions and disposals.

7.4 Derecognition and replacement of insured assets

Situations may arise where insured assets are destroyed in a fire, or similar destructive incident, and compensation (either in the form of cash or a replacement asset) from an insurance company is expected.

IAS 16 states that these events – the losses of items of PP&E, the related claims for or payments of compensation from third parties and any subsequent purchase or construction of replacement assets – are 'separate economic events' and should be accounted for separately as follows:

- derecognition of the items of PP&E that are destroyed with a corresponding loss recognised in profit and loss;

- compensation from the insurer or other third parties for the items of PP&E that are destroyed is recognised as an asset when it becomes receivable with a corresponding gain recognised in profit and loss; and
- the cost of items of PP&E restored, purchased or constructed as replacements are recognised in accordance with the requirements of IAS 16 (see 3 and 4 above). *[IAS 16.65, 66]*.

The items of PP&E that are destroyed will be reflected in the financial statements as a write-off rather than an impairment. Extract 18.9 below illustrates these requirements.

> *Extract 18.9: Eni S.p.A. (2016)*
> **Notes on Consolidated Financial Statements** [extract]
> **16 Property, plant and equipment** [extract]
>
> Write-off of €289 million (€678 million in 2015) related for €193 million to the EST conversion plant units at the Sannazzaro refinery, damaged in an accident occurred in December 2016.
>
> **39 Revenues** [extract]
> **Other income and revenues** [extract]
>
> Compensations of €122 million related to a loss in property value following an accident occurred at the EST conversion plant at the Sannazzaro refinery, which resulted in a write-off of the damaged units for €193 million and the recognition of a provision for removal and cleanup of €24 million. The portion of losses not covered by the insurance compensation (€95million) corresponds to the risk retained by Eni.

8 IAS 16 DISCLOSURE REQUIREMENTS

The main disclosure requirements of IAS 16 are set out below, but it should be noted that the related disclosure requirements in other standards such as IFRS 13, IAS 1 – *Presentation of Financial Statements* – and IAS 36 may also be relevant. See Chapters 14, 3 and 20, respectively.

8.1 General disclosures

For each class of PP&E the following should be disclosed in the financial statements:

(a) the measurement bases used for determining the gross carrying amount (e.g. cost or revaluation). *[IAS 16.73(a)]*. When more than one basis has been used, the gross carrying amount for that basis in each category may have to be disclosed (however the standard requires that if revaluation is adopted the entire class of PP&E must be revalued);

(b) the depreciation methods used. Selection of the depreciation method adopted is a matter of judgement and its disclosure provides information that allows users of financial statements to review the policies selected by management and enables them to compare with other entities. For similar reasons, it is necessary to disclose depreciation (in item (e)(vii) below), whether recognised in profit or loss or as a part of the cost of other assets, during a period; and accumulated depreciation at the end of the period (in item (d) below); *[IAS 16.73(b), 75]*

(c) the useful lives or the depreciation rates used. Selection of the useful lives or depreciation rates used is a matter of judgement and its disclosure provides information that allows users of financial statements to review the policies selected by management and enables them to compare with other entities; *[IAS 16.73(c), 75]*

(d) the gross carrying amount and the accumulated depreciation (aggregated with accumulated impairment losses) at the beginning and end of the period; *[IAS 16.73(d)]* and

(e) a reconciliation of the carrying amount at the beginning and end of the period showing:
   (i) additions;
   (ii) disposals, and assets classified as held for sale or included in a disposal group held for sale in accordance with IFRS 5;
   (iii) acquisitions through business combinations;
   (iv) increases or decreases resulting from revaluations and from impairment losses recognised or reversed directly in other comprehensive income under IAS 36;
   (v) impairment losses recognised in profit or loss during the period under IAS 36;
   (vi) impairment losses reversed in profit or loss during the period under IAS 36;
   (vii) depreciation;
   (viii) the net exchange differences arising on the translation of the financial statements from the functional currency into a different presentation currency, including the translation of a foreign operation into the presentation currency of the reporting entity; and
   (ix) other changes. *[IAS 16.73(e)]*.

Extract 18.10 below illustrates an accounting policy on PP&E together with the movement and reconciliation note (a comparative is provided in the financial statements but is not reproduced here).

Extract 18.10: Lucas Bols N.V. (2020)

CONSOLIDATED FINANCIAL STATEMENTS [extract]

NOTES TO THE CONSOLIDATED FINANCIAL STATEMENTS [extract]

3. SIGNIFICANT ACCOUNTING POLICIES [extract]

(i) Property, plant and equipment

(I) Recognition and measurement

Items of property, plant and equipment are measured at cost less accumulated depreciation and accumulated impairment losses.

(II) Subsequent costs

The cost of replacing part of an item of property, plant and equipment is recognised in the carrying amount of the item if it is probable that the future economic benefits embodied within the part will flow to the Group and its cost can be measured reliably. The costs of the day-to-day servicing of property, plant and equipment are recognised in the profit or loss as incurred.

Any gain or loss on disposal of an item of property, plant and equipment is recognised in profit or loss.

(III) Depreciation

Depreciation is recognised in the profit or loss on a straight-line basis over the estimated useful life of each part of an item of property, plant and equipment.

The estimated useful life is as follows:
- Fixtures and leasehold improvements   10 years
- Furniture   10 years
- Equipment   5 years
- Computers   3 years

The depreciation methods, residual value and useful life are reviewed annually and adjusted if appropriate.

15. PROPERTY, PLANT AND EQUIPMENT [extract]

AMOUNTS IN EUR '000	RIGHT OF USE ASSETS	EQUIPMENT	FIXTURES AND FITTINGS	FURNITURE	TOTAL
Cost					
Balance at 1 April 2019	7,778	1,764	5,562	319	15,422
Additions	95	1,030	350	7	1,482
Disposals	–	(632)	(1,966)	(218)	(2,816)
Reclassification	–	4	(5)	–	(1)
Effect of movement in exchange rates	19	–	–	–	19
Balance at 31 March 2020	7,892	2,166	3,941	108	14,106
Accumulated depreciation					
Balance at 1 April 2019	(727)	(1,118)	(2,949)	(259)	(5,053)
Depreciation for the year	(728)	(358)	(446)	(15)	(1,547)
Disposals	–	632	1,966	218	2,816
Reclassification	(13)	(5)	6	3	(9)
Effect of movement in exchange rates	(6)	–	–	–	(6)
Balance at 31 March 2020	(1,474)	(849)	(1,423)	(53)	(3,798)
Carrying amounts					
At 1 April 2019	7,051	646	2,613	61	10,371
At 31 March 2020	6,418	1,317	2,518	55	10,308

[…]

In the carrying value of right-of-use assets, which is mainly consists of building, an amount of EUR 74 thousand relates to office equipment (31 March 2019: nil) and EUR 14 thousand relates to lease cars (31 March 2019: 38 thousand). Included as part of Operating expenses, are short term lease expenses and low value lease expenses of EUR 75 thousand (31 March 2019: 75 thousand) Refer to note 24 for the lease liability.

IAS 16 also requires the disclosure of the following information, which is useful to gain a fuller understanding of the entire position of the entity's holdings of and its commitments to purchase property plant and equipment:

(a) the existence and amounts of restrictions on title, and PP&E pledged as security for liabilities;

(b) the amount of expenditures recognised in the carrying amount of an item of PP&E in the course of construction;

(c) the amount of contractual commitments for the acquisition of PP&E; and

(d) if it is not disclosed separately in the statement of comprehensive income, the amount of compensation from third parties for items of PP&E that were impaired, lost or given up that is included in profit or loss. *[IAS 16.74]*.

As noted at 4.2.1 above, in May 2020, the IASB issued amendments to IAS 16 dealing with the accounting for proceeds from selling items produced before an asset is capable of operating in the manner intended by management. Those amendments, which are effective for annual periods beginning on or after 1 January 2022, remove the disclosure requirements described in (d) above. Instead, the amendments introduce the requirement that, if not presented separately in the statement of comprehensive income, the financial statements, an entity should also disclose:

(a) the amount of compensation from third parties for items of property, plant and equipment that were impaired, lost or given up that is included in profit or loss; and

(b) the amounts of proceeds and cost included in profit or loss in accordance with paragraph 20A of IAS 16 that relate to items produced that are not an output of the entity's ordinary activities, and which line item(s) in the statement of comprehensive income include(s) such proceeds and cost. *[IAS 16.74A]*.

The standard also requires that, in accordance with IAS 8, an entity discloses the nature and effect of any change in an accounting estimate (e.g. depreciation methods, useful lives, residual values, and the estimated cost of dismantling, removing or restoring items of PP&E) that has an effect on the current period or is expected to have an effect in future periods. *[IAS 16.76]*.

8.2 Additional disclosures for revalued assets

In addition to the disclosures required by IFRS 13, the disclosure requirements in IAS 16 if the revaluation method is adopted are:

(a) the effective date of the revaluation;

(b) whether an independent valuer was involved;

(c) for each revalued class of PP&E, the carrying amount that would have been recognised had the assets been carried under the cost model; and

(d) the revaluation surplus, indicating the change for the period and any restrictions on the distribution of the balance to shareholders. *[IAS 16.77]*.

In particular the requirement under (c) is quite onerous for entities, as it entails their keeping asset register information in some detail in order to meet it.

In May 2014, the Interpretations Committee received a request to clarify whether an entity is required to reflect the capitalisation of borrowing costs to meet the disclosure requirement of IAS 16 for assets stated at revalued amounts and for which borrowing costs are not capitalised. Since the capitalisation of borrowing costs for such assets is not required (see Chapter 21 at 3.2), the determination of the amount of borrowing costs that would have been capitalised under a cost model – solely to meet a disclosure requirement – might be considered burdensome.

The Interpretations Committee noted that the requirements in paragraph 77(e) of IAS 16 (i.e. item (c) above) are clear. This paragraph requires an entity to disclose the amount at which assets stated at revalued amounts would have been stated had those assets been carried under the cost model. The amount to be disclosed includes borrowing costs capitalised in accordance with IAS 23 (see Chapter 21).[6]

IFRS 13 has a number of disclosure requirements for assets measured at fair value. Some of the significant disclosures under IFRS 13 which would apply to revalued PP&E are: *[IFRS 13.93]*

- if the highest and best use differs from its current use, an entity must disclose that fact and why the asset is being used in a manner different from its highest and best use;
- the fair value measurement's categorisation within the fair value measurement hierarchy (i.e. Level 1, 2 or 3);
- if categorised within Level 2 or 3 of the fair value hierarchy (which most revalued PP&E is likely to be):
  (i) a description of the valuation technique(s) used in the fair value measurement;
  (ii) the inputs used in the fair value measurement;
  (iii) if there has been a change in the valuation technique (e.g. changing from a market approach to an income approach or use of an additional technique):
    - the change; and
    - the reason(s) for making it;
- quantitative information about the significant unobservable inputs used in the fair value measurement for those categorised within Level 3 of the fair value measurement hierarchy;
- if categorised within Level 3 of the fair value measurement hierarchy, a description of the valuation processes used by the entity (including, for example, how an entity decides its valuation policies and procedures and analyses changes in fair value measurements from period to period).

In addition to these requirements, an entity must also provide the disclosures depending on whether the fair value measurement is recurring or non-recurring. Revalued PP&E are considered recurring fair value measurements and are subject to additional disclosure requirements, which include a qualitative sensitivity analysis. The disclosures for revalued PP&E categorised under Level 3 include a reconciliation from the opening balance to the closing balance, disclosing separately changes during the period to the following:

(i) total gains and losses for the period recognised in profit or loss, and the line item(s) in profit or loss in which these gains or losses are recognised;

(ii) total gains and losses for the period recognised in other comprehensive income, and the line item(s) in other comprehensive income in which those gains or losses are recognised;

(iii) purchases, sales, issues and settlements (separately disclosing each of those types of changes); and

(iv) transfers into or out of Level 3 of the fair value hierarchy (separately disclosing and discussing transfers into Level 3 from those out of Level 3) including:
  - the amounts of any transfers into or out of Level 3;
  - the reasons for those transfers; and
  - the entity's policy for determining when transfers between levels are deemed to have occurred. *[IFRS 13.93]*.

These requirements and examples of the requirements are discussed in more detail in Chapter 14 at 20.

8.3 Other disclosures

In addition to the disclosures required by IAS 1, IAS 16 (i.e. those discussed at 8.1 and 8.2 above) and IFRS 13, the standard emphasises that entities are also required to disclose information on impaired PP&E in accordance with IAS 36 (see Chapter 20 at 13.2.1 and 13.2.2). [IAS 16.78].

As users of financial statements may find other information relevant to their needs, the standard encourages, but does not require, entities to disclose other additional information such as the carrying amount of any temporarily idle PP&E, the gross carrying amount of any fully depreciated PP&E that is still in use and the carrying amount of any PP&E retired from active use but not classified as held for disposal in accordance with IFRS 5. For any PP&E measured using the cost model, the disclosure of its fair value is also encouraged when this is materially different from the carrying amount. [IAS 16.79].

References

1. *IFRIC Update*, June 2017.
2. *IFRIC Update*, November 2019.
3. *Sale or Contribution of Assets between an Investor and its Associate or Joint Venture, (Amendments to IFRS 10 and IAS 28)*, IASB, September 2014, IFRS 10, para. C1C and IAS 28, para. 45C.
4. *Research Programme – The research pipeline – Equity Method*, IASB website (accessed 22 September 2020).
5. *Effective Date of Amendments to IFRS 10 and IAS 28*, IASB, December 2015.
6. *IFRIC Update*, May 2014.

Chapter 19   Investment property

1	INTRODUCTION	1441
2	DEFINITIONS AND SCOPE	1442
	2.1 Property interest held under a lease	1444
	2.2 Land	1445
	2.3 Property leased to others	1445
	2.4 Property held for own use ('owner-occupied')	1445
	2.5 Investment property under construction	1446
	2.6 Property held or under construction for sale in the ordinary course of business	1446
	2.7 Property with dual uses	1447
	2.8 Property with the provision of ancillary services	1448
	2.9 Property where rentals are determined by reference to the operations in the property	1449
	2.10 Group of assets leased out under a single operating lease	1449
3	RECOGNITION	1451
	3.1 Expenditure prior to planning permissions/zoning consents	1451
	3.2 Other aspects of cost recognition	1452
	3.2.1 Repairs and maintenance	1452
	3.2.2 Allocation into parts	1452
	3.3 Acquisition of investment property or a business combination?	1452
	3.3.1 Definition of a business	1454
4	INITIAL MEASUREMENT	1457
	4.1 Attributable costs	1457
	4.1.1 Acquisition of a group of assets that does not constitute a business ('the group')	1457
	4.1.2 Deferred taxes when acquiring a 'single asset' entity that is not a business	1459

	4.2	Start-up costs and self-built property	1459
		4.2.1 Cost of a building to be demolished in connection with the construction of a new building	1459
	4.3	Deferred payments	1460
	4.4	Reclassifications from property, plant and equipment or from inventory	1461
	4.5	Initial measurement of property held under a lease	1461
	4.6	Initial measurement of assets acquired in exchange transactions	1461
	4.7	Initial recognition of tenanted investment property subsequently measured using the cost model	1461
	4.8	Borrowing costs	1462
	4.9	Lease incentives and initial direct costs of leasing a property	1462
		4.9.1 Lease incentives	1462
		4.9.2 Initial direct costs of obtaining a lease	1463
	4.10	Contingent costs	1464
	4.11	Income from tenanted property during development	1466
	4.12	Payments by the vendor to the purchaser	1466
5	MEASUREMENT AFTER INITIAL RECOGNITION		1467
	5.1	Measurement by insurers and similar entities	1467
6	THE FAIR VALUE MODEL		1468
	6.1	Estimating fair value	1469
		6.1.1 Methods of estimation	1471
		6.1.2 Observable data	1472
		6.1.3 Comparison with value in use	1472
		6.1.4 'Double counting'	1473
	6.2	Inability to determine fair value of completed investment property	1473
	6.3	The fair value of investment property under construction	1474
	6.4	Transaction costs incurred by the reporting entity on acquisition	1475
	6.5	Fixtures and fittings subsumed within fair value	1477
	6.6	Prepaid and accrued operating lease income	1477
		6.6.1 Accrued rental income and lease incentives	1477
		6.6.2 Prepaid rental income	1478
	6.7	Valuation adjustment to the fair value of properties held under a lease	1479
	6.8	Future capital expenditure and development value ('highest and best use')	1481
	6.9	Negative present value	1482
	6.10	Deferred taxation for property held by a 'single asset' entity	1483

7	THE COST MODEL		1483
	7.1	Initial recognition	1484
		7.1.1 Identification of physical parts	1484
		7.1.2 Identification of non-physical parts	1485
	7.2	Incidence of use of the cost model	1485
	7.3	Impairment	1486
8	IFRS 5 AND INVESTMENT PROPERTY		1486
9	TRANSFER OF ASSETS TO OR FROM INVESTMENT PROPERTY		1488
	9.1	Transfers from investment property to inventory	1490
	9.2	Accounting treatment of transfers	1490
10	DISPOSAL OF INVESTMENT PROPERTY		1492
	10.1	Calculation of gain or loss on disposal	1493
	10.2	Sale prior to completion of construction	1494
	10.3	Replacement of parts of investment property	1494
	10.4	Compensation from third parties	1494
11	INTERIM REPORTING AND IAS 40		1495
12	THE DISCLOSURE REQUIREMENTS OF IAS 40		1496
	12.1	Disclosures under both fair value and cost models	1496
		12.1.1 Methods and assumptions in fair value estimates	1497
		12.1.2 Level of aggregation for IFRS 13 disclosures	1504
		12.1.3 Disclosure of direct operating expenses	1505
	12.2	Additional disclosures for the fair value model	1505
		12.2.1 Presentation of changes in fair value	1506
		12.2.2 Extra disclosures where fair value cannot be determined reliably	1508
	12.3	Additional disclosures for the cost model	1508
	12.4	Presentation of sales proceeds	1509

List of examples

Example 19.1:	Definition of an investment property: a group of assets leased out under a single operating lease	1450
Example 19.2:	The fair value model and transaction costs incurred at acquisition	1476
Example 19.3:	Investment property and rent received in advance	1478
Example 19.4:	Valuation of a property held under a lease	1480
Example 19.5:	Transfers from inventory	1489

Chapter 19   Investment property

1   INTRODUCTION

IAS 40 – *Investment Property* – is an example of the particular commercial characteristics of an industry resulting in the special accounting treatment of a certain category of asset, i.e. investment property. However, it is not only investment property companies that hold investment property; any property that meets the investment property definition in IAS 40 is so classified, irrespective of the nature of the business of the reporting entity. This standard should be applied in the recognition, measurement and disclosure of investment property. *[IAS 40.1, 2]*.

The original standard, which was approved in 2000, was the first international standard to introduce the possibility of applying a fair value model for non-financial assets where all valuation changes from one period to the next are reported in profit or loss. This contrasts with the revaluation approach allowed under IAS 16 – *Property, Plant and Equipment* (see Chapter 18 at 6) where increases above cost, and their reversals, are recognised directly in Other Comprehensive Income ('OCI').

The exposure draft that preceded IAS 40 proposed that fair value should be the sole measurement model for investment property. However, some respondents were concerned that, in certain parts of the world, property markets were not sufficiently liquid to support fair value measurement for financial reporting purposes. Consequently, the cost option was introduced into the standard, as the Board believed, at that stage, that it was impracticable to require a fair value model for all investment property.

Despite the free choice of model available, IAS 40 has a rebuttable presumption that, other than in exceptional cases, an entity can measure the fair value of a completed investment property reliably on a continuing basis.

The question of the reliability of valuations was given greater focus following the change in scope of the standard in 2009 to include investment property under construction (see 2.5 below) because, following that change, the standard allows investment property under construction to be measured at cost if the fair value cannot be measured reliably. However, in this case, the standard is not explicit on whether this should be confined to 'exceptional cases' or not.

This chapter discusses the revised version of IAS 40, which was published in December 2003, as subsequently updated by various narrow-scope amendments and minor consequential amendments arising from other standards.

IFRS 17 – *Insurance Contracts* – will result in further changes to IAS 40 in later accounting periods (see 5.1 below).

2 DEFINITIONS AND SCOPE

An investment property is defined in IAS 40 as property (land or a building – or part of a building – or both) held by the owner or by the lessee as a right-of-use asset to earn rentals or for capital appreciation or both, rather than for:

(a) use in the production or supply of goods or services or for administrative purposes; or

(b) sale in the ordinary course of business. *[IAS 40.5]*.

This means that any entity, whatever the underlying nature of its business, can hold investment property assets if its intention on initial recognition (either by acquisition or change in use – see 9 below) is to hold them for rent or for capital appreciation or both. Subsequent to initial recognition, assets might be reclassified into and from investment property (see 9 below). It is also of note that property interest held by a lessee as right-of-use asset under an operating lease can be an investment property (see 2.1 below).

In contrast, 'owner-occupied' property is defined as property held by the owner or by the lessee as a right-of-use asset for use in the production or supply of goods or services or for administrative purposes. *[IAS 40.5]*. Such property falls outside the scope of IAS 40 and is accounted for under IAS 16 (see 2.4 below and Chapter 18), together with IFRS 16 – *Leases* (see Chapter 23), if relevant. Property held, or being constructed, with the intention of sale in the ordinary course of business also falls outside the scope of IAS 40 and is accounted for under IAS 2 – *Inventories* (see 2.6 below and Chapter 22).

IAS 40 applies to the measurement in a lessor's financial statements of investment property provided to a lessee under an operating lease (see 2.3 below). IAS 40 also applies to the subsequent measurement in a lessee's financial statements of investment property interests held under a lease if the lessee applies the fair value model in IAS 40 to its investment property (see 2.1 below). However, it does not deal with other accounting matters that are dealt with in IFRS 16 (see Chapter 23), including:

- classification of leases as finance or operating leases by a lessor;
- recognition of lease income arising from the leasing of investment property;
- initial measurement in a lessee's financial statements of property interests held under a lease;
- measurement in a lessor's financial statements of its net investment in a finance lease;
- accounting for sale and leaseback transactions; and
- disclosure of information about leases by lessors and lessees.

IAS 40 does not apply to:
- biological assets related to agricultural activity (see IAS 41 – *Agriculture* – and IAS 16); and
- mineral rights and mineral reserves such as oil, natural gas and similar non-regenerative resources. *[IAS 40.4]*.

Biological assets that are physically attached to land (for example, trees in a plantation forest) are measured at their fair value less estimated point-of-sale costs separately from the land. *[IAS 41.12]*. However, the land related to the agricultural activity is accounted for either as property under IAS 16 or investment property under IAS 40. *[IAS 41.2]*.

What primarily distinguishes investment property from other types of property interest is that its cash flows (from rental or sale) are largely independent of those from other assets held by the entity. By contrast, owner-occupied property used by an entity for administrative purposes or for the production or supply of goods or services does not generate cash flows itself but does so only in conjunction with other assets used in the production or supply process. IAS 16 applies to owned owner-occupied property and IFRS 16 applies to owner-occupied property held by a lessee as a right-of-use asset. *[IAS 40.7]*.

Even with the distinction described above, it may not be easy to distinguish investment property from owner-occupied property. The standard therefore gives guidance to help determine whether or not an asset is an investment property (see 2.1 to 2.10 below).

Circumstances may not be straightforward particularly if at initial recognition the intention of holding a property is mixed or undetermined (except for land – see 2.2 below). For example, entities that are not in the property industry may not be within the scope of IAS 40 if they sublease a property under an operating lease with the intention of subsequently using the property within their own business. Such a property would not meet the definition of an investment property in IAS 40 because it would not be held solely for rentals, capital appreciation or both. *[IFRS 16.BC179(b)]*. In this example, the intended use of the property as an owner-occupied property would even be clearer if the sublease of the property would only be for a short period of time. Consequently, considering how an entity's principal activities and its business strategy for the property, including the length of the lease to a tenant, impact the determination of the intended use of the property (and therefore, whether the property meets the definition of an investment property under IAS 40) may require the exercise of judgement based on specific facts and circumstances. An entity should develop criteria so that it can exercise that judgement consistently in accordance with the definition of investment property and the related guidance in IAS 40. Such criteria are required to be disclosed when classification is difficult (see 12.1 below). *[IAS 40.14]*.

It is also worthy of note that the Interpretations Committee has discussed the accounting for a structure that 'lacks the physical characteristics of a building', i.e. whether it should be accounted for as investment property in accordance with IAS 40. This primarily related to an emerging business model in which an entity owns telecommunication towers and leases spaces in the towers to telecommunication operators to which the operators attach their own devices. The entity may also provide some basic services to the telecommunication operators such as maintenance services.[1]

The request specifically sought clarification on whether a telecommunication tower should be viewed as a 'building' and thus 'property', as described in paragraph 5 of IAS 40 and how any service element in the leasing agreement and business model of the entity should be taken into consideration when analysing the issue.

The Interpretations Committee observed that the tower has some of the characteristics of investment property, in that spaces in the tower were let to tenants to earn rentals (e.g. leasing of spaces for telecommunication operators to which operators attach their own devices) but questioned whether the tower qualifies as a 'building' because it lacks features usually associated with a building such as walls, floors and a roof. They also observed that the same question could arise about other structures, such as gas storage tanks and advertising billboards.[2]

The Interpretations Committee observed that there would be merit in exploring approaches to amending IAS 40 to include structures that lack the physical characteristics associated with a building.[3] However, following research on this issue, the IASB decided not to pursue this issue because there appeared to be limited demand for fair value accounting for these types of structures and limited diversity in practice.[4]

2.1 Property interest held under a lease

Leases of property are included in the scope of IFRS 16 (see Chapter 23). Under IFRS 16, lessees apply a single model for most leases, i.e. unlike lessors, lessees do not need to classify leases as finance leases or as operating leases. IFRS 16 requires lessees to recognise most leases in their statement of financial position as lease liabilities with corresponding right-of-use assets.

Properties held by lessees as right-of-use assets that meet the definition of investment property, as described at 2 above, are included in the scope of IAS 40. This results in lessees using either the cost model and disclosing fair value, or using the fair value model, depending on whether the lessee accounts for the remainder of its investment property under the cost model or the fair value model. In the IASB's view, this approach will provide useful information to users of financial statements about the fair value of investment property held by a lessee as a right-of-use asset, which is consistent with information provided about owned investment property. *[IFRS 16.BC178]*.

An investment property held by a lessee as a right-of-use asset is recognised in accordance with IFRS 16. *[IAS 40.19A]*. IFRS 16 requires a lessee to measure right-of-use assets arising from leased property (whether the lessor provided finance leases or operating leases to the lessee) in accordance with the fair value model of IAS 40 if the leased property meets the definition of investment property and the lessee elects the fair value model in IAS 40 as an accounting policy (see 6 and 6.7 below). *[IFRS 16.34]*.

When a lessee uses the fair value model to measure an investment property that is held as a right-of-use asset, it will measure the right-of-use asset, and not the underlying property, at fair value. *[IAS 40.40A]*.

If the lessee elects to use the cost model to measure its investment property, the lessee should measure its right-of-use assets that meet the definition of investment property in IAS 40 using the cost model in IFRS 16 (see 7 below) unless such assets are held for sale in accordance with IFRS 5 – *Non-current Assets Held for Sale and Discontinued Operations* (see 8 below). *[IAS 40.56]*.

If the right-of-use assets meet the definition of investment property, these are presented in the statement of financial position as investment property (see Chapter 23 at 5.7). *[IFRS 16.48]*. In addition to the relevant disclosure requirements in IFRS 16 (see Chapter 23 at 5.8), a lessee also applies the disclosure requirements in IAS 40 for such right-of-use assets (see 12 below). *[IFRS 16.56]*.

Subsequent to initial recognition, the IASB indicated that a lease liability should be accounted for in a manner similar to other financial liabilities (i.e. on amortised cost basis). *[IFRS 16.BC182]*.

For further discussion on subsequent measurements of lease liabilities and right-of-use assets, see Chapter 23 at 5.3.

2.2 Land

Land is investment property if it is held to earn rentals or for capital appreciation or for both; or for a currently undetermined future use. This is in contrast to land that is held for sale in the ordinary course of business (typically in the shorter term) or held for the production or supply of goods and services or for administrative purposes. *[IAS 40.7, 8]*.

If, on initial recognition, land is held for a currently undetermined future use, i.e. if an entity has not determined whether it will use the land as owner-occupied property or for sale in the ordinary course of business, it is deemed to be held for capital appreciation and must be classified as investment property. *[IAS 40.8]*.

2.3 Property leased to others

Properties leased to third parties under one or more operating lease are generally investment properties, whether they are owned freehold by the reporting entity or are right-of-use assets relating to properties held by the reporting entity (see 2 and 2.1 above). This will also apply if the property is currently vacant while tenants are being sought. *[IAS 40.8]*.

However, in our opinion, an exception should be made in those cases where, despite being leased out, properties have been held for sale in the ordinary course of business since their initial recognition (either by acquisition or change in use – see 9 below). Leasing of property prior to sale is a common practice in the real estate industry in order to minimise cash outflows whilst the entity seeks a buyer and because prospective buyers may view the existence of such lease contracts positively, especially those that wish to acquire property for investment purposes.

In those circumstances – and notwithstanding that they are leased to tenants under operating leases – they should be accounted for as inventory under IAS 2 as long as it remains the intention to hold such properties for short-term sale in the ordinary course of business. The rent received would be recorded in profit or loss and would not be treated as a reduction in the cost of inventory. See Chapter 22 at 4.1 for further discussion.

Property that is leased to a third party under a finance lease is not an investment property but is accounted for under IFRS 16 (see Chapter 23). *[IAS 40.9]*.

2.4 Property held for own use ('owner-occupied')

As noted above, owner-occupied property, that is property held for use in the production or supply of goods or services or for administrative purposes, is specifically excluded from being treated as investment property and is subject to the provisions of IAS 16 and IFRS 16. Owner-occupied property includes:

- property that is going to be owner-occupied in the future (whether or not it has first to be redeveloped);
- property occupied by employees (whether or not they pay rent at market rates); and
- owner-occupied property awaiting disposal. *[IAS 40.9]*.

Note that the treatment in the consolidated accounts can be different from the treatment by individual group entities. For example, it may be the case that a property owned by one group company is held for occupation by another group company. This will be owner-occupied from the perspective of the group as a whole but can be classified as an investment property in the accounts of the individual entity that owns it, provided it meets the definition of an investment property. *[IAS 40.15]*. This classification in the individual entity's financial statements will apply even if the rental is not at arm's length and the individual entity is not in a position to benefit from capital appreciation. The IASB concluded that the more significant factor is that the property itself will generate cash flows that are largely independent from other assets held by the entity. *[IAS 40.7]*.

Associates and joint ventures are not part of the group. Therefore, a property owned by the group but occupied by an associate or a joint venture would be accounted for as investment property in the consolidated financial statements (provided, of course, it meets the investment property definition).

2.5 Investment property under construction

Property that is being constructed or developed for future use as investment property ('investment property under construction') is in the scope of IAS 40. *[IAS 40.8]*.

The fair value of investment property under construction is further discussed in 6.3 below.

2.6 Property held or under construction for sale in the ordinary course of business

Property held, or being constructed, with the intention of sale in the ordinary course of business is not an investment property. This includes property acquired exclusively for sale in the near future or for development and resale (such property is accounted for as inventory under IAS 2 (see Chapter 22)). *[IAS 40.9]*.

In practice, the classification between investment property and property intended for sale in the ordinary course of business is often a difficult judgement. There is only a fine line between:

- a property held for capital appreciation, and therefore classified as investment property; and
- a property intended for sale in the ordinary course of business, which would be classified as inventory.

For example, the owner will undertake activities to increase the property's value prior to sale or where there is uncertainty in obtaining permits required from relevant authorities prior to commencing construction activities. In the latter case, the property, e.g. land, may continue to appreciate in value during the period where there are no development activities – see 3.1 below.

Another example is where an entity acquires a tenanted property with a view to redevelop the property and to resell it in the future, but active development will only commence after the existing lease reaches the end of its term, i.e. the entity receives rent payments during the intervening period. As set out in 2.3 above, the receipt of rental income from a property would not necessarily be the deciding factor. Certainly, other than for land (see 2.2 above), IAS 40 provides no explicit 'default' classification when the future use of a property has not yet been determined (see also discussion in 2 above).

However, this judgement is important because whilst IAS 40 allows property held as inventory to be reclassified as investment property when there is a change in use and an operating lease with a third party is entered into, it is more difficult to reclassify investment property as inventory (see 8, 9 and 9.1 below). Accordingly, an entity should develop criteria so that it can exercise that judgement consistently in accordance with the definition of investment property and the related guidance in IAS 40. Such criteria are required to be disclosed when classification is difficult (see 12.1 below). *[IAS 40.14]*.

2.7 Property with dual uses

A property may be used partly to derive rental income and partly as owner-occupied property. For example, an office could be sub-divided by the owner with some floors being rented to tenants whilst retaining others for own use.

IAS 40 states that if a property has both investment property and non-investment property uses, providing the parts of the property could be sold or leased out under a finance lease separately, they should be accounted for separately. *[IAS 40.10]*.

However, to meet these requirements we consider that a property must actually be in a state and condition to enable it to be disposed of or leased out separately at the end of the reporting period. The fact that a property could be divided in future periods if the owner so chose is insufficient to conclude that the portions can be accounted for separately. Consequently, if a property requires sub-division before the portions could be disposed of separately, then those parts should not, in our view, be accounted for as separate portions and the entire property should be accounted for as either an investment property or as a non-investment property (e.g. as an owner-occupied property or as an inventory) until such sub-division occurs or unless sub-division is a non-substantive legal requirement.

In our view, an intention to lease out, or the action of leasing out a portion of a property under an operating lease is *prima facie* evidence that, if it so wished, the entity could also lease out the property under a finance lease – the difference between the two commonly being just the length of the lease. If, however, there is evidence that the property could not be leased out under a finance lease then IAS 40 could not be applied to that portion.

It also seems clear that 'separately' needs to be assessed both in terms of the physical separation (for example, mezzanine floors and partitioning walls) of the property and legal separation such as legally defined boundaries.

In many jurisdictions, properties that are physically sub-divided into different portions (for example, different floors) are registered in a land or property registry as one single property and need to be legally sub-divided before a portion can be leased out to a third party or disposed of. Often, these legal proceedings are undertaken only at or near the point of sale or the assignment of a lease on that portion of the property concerned. At the end of the reporting period the legal sub-division may not have occurred.

Accordingly, judgement is required to determine whether legal separation is a substantive requirement that will restrict the property being considered currently separable or whether it is a non-substantive requirement where the property is currently separable. For example:

- If the entity owning the property could not be prevented from legally sub-dividing the property, then it is already in a condition to be sold separately and this would not prevent the portion of the property concerned being accounted for as investment property. This would be the case where, for example: the process of sub-dividing the property was entirely within the control of the entity and did not require permission from a third party (which would include the relevant authorities); or if permission from a third party was required, but this was no more than a formality.
- Conversely, if the entity was required to obtain the permission of third parties before legally sub-dividing the property, and such permission could realistically be withheld, the portions of the property concerned are not accounted for separately until such legal sub-division occurs.

Therefore, if the portion of the property concerned otherwise meets the definition of investment property at the end of the reporting period, judgement is required to assess the legal position of the property in determining whether it is appropriate to account for a portion separately under IAS 40. Criteria used in the assessment should be disclosed and applied consistently (see 12.1 below). *[IAS 40.14]*.

In the event that no separation is possible, the property is an investment property only if an insignificant proportion is used for non-investment property purposes. *[IAS 40.10]*.

The setting of a threshold to evaluate whether or not something is significant or insignificant depends on judgement and circumstances. In the extract below, PSP Swiss Property discloses its judgement about dealing with property that it partially uses, but other entities will need to make their own assessment.

> *Extract 19.1: PSP Swiss Property Ltd (2019)*
>
> Notes to the consolidated 2019 financial statements [extract]
> 2   Summary of significant accounting policies[extract]
> 2.6   Accounting and valuation principles [extract]
>
> **Own-used properties**
>
> In accordance with IAS 16, own-used properties are carried at historical cost and depreciated over their useful economic life, broken down into significant components. The depreciation period (straight-line method) is 40 years for buildings and 20 years for operating equipment (such as air conditioning, elevators, ventilation, etc.). Associated land is not depreciated. In the case of partial own-use of a property, an area share of less than 25% is considered insignificant, with the result that the entire property is reported in the balance sheet as an investment property at fair value.

2.8 Property with the provision of ancillary services

If the owner supplies ancillary services to the user of the investment property, the property will not qualify as an investment property unless these services are an insignificant component of the arrangement as a whole. For example, security and maintenance services are described by the standard as being insignificant. *[IAS 40.11]*.

The crucial issue is the extent to which the owner retains significant exposure to the risks of running a business. The standard uses the example of a hotel. An owner-managed hotel, for example, would be precluded from being an investment property as the services provided to guests are a significant component of the commercial arrangements. *[IAS 40.12-13]*.

However, the nature of the asset in question is not the key factor; rather it is the nature of the owner's interest in the asset. If the owner's position is, in substance, that of a passive investor, any property may be treated as investment property. If, in contrast, the owner has outsourced day-to-day functions while retaining significant exposure to variation in the cash flows generated by the operations that are being executed in the building, a property should rather be treated as owner-occupied property. *[IAS 40.13]*.

The standard refers to owner-managed hotels as being precluded from being investment property. Hotel properties that are leased on arm's length terms to hotel operators may, however, fall to be accounted for as investment property. This is more likely to be the case when:

- the payments under the lease are not significantly determined by the results of the hotel operator (see 2.9 below), rather they reflect the general market for such properties; and
- the nature of the owner's rights in the arrangements with the operator is not divergent from those usually expected under a property lease.

The standard acknowledges that this question of significance can require judgements to be made. It specifies that an entity should develop consistent criteria for use in such instances that reflect the provisions described above. These criteria must be disclosed in those cases where classification is difficult. *[IAS 40.14]*.

See also 3.3 below where the question of classification of a property as a business or as an asset is considered.

2.9 Property where rentals are determined by reference to the operations in the property

It may also be inappropriate to consider a property as investment property if the owner is significantly exposed to the operation of the business in the property through a linkage between the rentals charged and the performance of the business.

A common example is the incidence of turnover- or profit-related rents in retail leases. If the turnover- or profit-related element is a very significant proportion of total rental, then consideration should be given to whether the landlord is so involved with the underlying business as to make classification of the property as investment property inappropriate. This will be a matter of judgement based on any other specific facts and circumstances (for example, the length of the lease, the level of exposure to the performance of the underlying business or the degree of involvement in the management of the underlying business).

2.10 Group of assets leased out under a single operating lease

It is sometimes the case in practice that a group of assets comprising land, buildings and 'other assets' is leased out by a lessor under a single lease contract in order to earn rentals. In such a case, the 'other assets' would generally comprise assets that relate to the manner in which the land and buildings are used under the lease. The issue that arises is under what circumstances the 'other assets' should be regarded by the lessor as part of an investment property rather than as a separate item of property, plant and equipment. This is illustrated in the following example:

Example 19.1: Definition of an investment property: a group of assets leased out under a single operating lease

A lessor enters into the following two single contract leases in order to earn rentals. All the individual assets subject to the leases meet the test of being classified as an operating lease. The lessor applies the fair value measurement model for subsequent measurement of investment property.

Lease 1: Vineyard and winery

A vineyard including a winery is leased out under an operating lease. The vineyard comprises the following assets:
- land;
- vineyard infrastructure (e.g. trellises);
- winery building structures;
- winery plant and machinery (crushing equipment, distilling equipment); and
- vines (grapes are excluded, as they belong to the lessee).

Lease 2: Port

A port is leased out under an operating lease. The port comprises the following assets:
- land;
- warehouses;
- transport infrastructure to and from the port (roads, rail tracks, bridges);
- wharves;
- light towers (that enable the 24-hour operation of the port); and
- specialised container cranes (to be able to move containers around).

To what extent can the 'other assets' included in the leases (but which are not considered to constitute a piece of land or a building) be included in the investment property definition under IAS 40?

The consequence of including plant and equipment in the definition of investment property is that if the investment property is accounted for at fair value, changes in the fair value of that plant and equipment will, like changes in the fair value of the land and buildings, be recognised in profit or loss.

From a literal reading of the definition of an investment property in paragraph 5 of IAS 40, it could be argued that an investment property can consist only of a building (or part of a building), a piece of land, or both and cannot include 'other assets'. However, such an interpretation is inconsistent with paragraph 50 of IAS 40, which implies that a broader interpretation is more appropriate. Paragraphs 50(a) and (b) of IAS 40 read as follows:

'In determining the carrying amount of investment property under the fair value model, an entity does not double-count assets or liabilities that are recognised as separate assets or liabilities. For example:

(a) equipment such as lifts or air-conditioning is often an integral part of a building and is generally included in the fair value of the investment property, rather than recognised separately as property, plant and equipment.

(b) if an office is leased on a furnished basis, the fair value of the office generally includes the fair value of the furniture, because the rental income relates to the furnished office. When furniture is included in the fair value of investment property, an entity does not recognise that furniture as a separate asset.' [IAS 40.50(a), 50(b)].

Although paragraph 50 addresses the fair valuation of investment property, it nevertheless implies that other assets that are integral to the land and buildings or are otherwise required to be included in the lease in order to generate rental income under the lease concerned should also be regarded as being part of the investment property.

Consequently, in our view, an item other than a piece of land or a building should be regarded by a lessor as being part of an investment property if this item is an integral part of it, that is, it is necessary for the land and buildings to be used by a lessee in the manner intended and is leased to the lessee on the same basis (e.g. as a package with the same lease term) as the land and buildings. The determination as to whether or not an item

constitutes an integral part of an investment property requires judgement and will depend on the particular facts and circumstances. However, it is our view that in order for all the assets to be classified as investment property, the following conditions should be present:
- the land and buildings should be the 'dominant assets' that form the investment property;
- the 'other assets' are leased to the lessee together with the land and building as a whole; and
- the entire group of assets is generating the income stream from the lease contract.

This means that, in the case of Lease 1, the investment property comprises the land, the vineyard infrastructure, the winery building structures and the winery plant and machinery. Vines, which meet the definition of biological assets, are subject to the requirements of IAS 41. They are excluded because 'biological assets related to agricultural activity' are outside the scope of IAS 40. *[IAS 40.4(a)].*

In the case of Lease 2, the investment property comprises all of the assets, i.e. the land, the warehouses, the transport infrastructure, the wharves, the light towers, and the specialised container cranes.

3 RECOGNITION

An owned investment property should be recognised as an asset when, and only when, it is probable that the future economic benefits that are associated with the investment property will flow to the entity and its cost can be measured reliably. *[IAS 40.16].*

These recognition criteria apply for any costs incurred, whether initially or subsequently. This means that all costs related to investment property, whether on initial recognition or thereafter (for example, to add to, or replace part of, or service a property) must meet the recognition criteria at the point at which the expenditure is incurred if they are to be capitalised. *[IAS 40.17].*

An investment property held by a lessee as a right-of-use asset is recognised in accordance with IFRS 16. *[IAS 40.19A].*

3.1 Expenditure prior to planning permissions/zoning consents

In many jurisdictions, permissions from relevant authorities are required prior to development of new or existing property, and the ability to start physical construction of the development depends on these permissions.

Application for such permissions supports the entity's intention as to the use of the property and may be considered as a factor in classifying the asset. However, unless an entity is considering a number of possible uses of the asset at its initial recognition, the uncertainty in obtaining relevant permission would usually not affect the classification of the property which, as set out in 2 above, is mainly based on the entity's intention when the property is first acquired. Subsequent to initial recognition, assets might be reclassified into and from investment property (see 9 below).

The likelihood of obtaining such permissions, however, is relevant in recognition and measurement of any additional costs to the property. Developers typically incur significant costs prior to such permissions being granted and such permissions are rarely guaranteed. Therefore, in assessing whether such pre-permission expenditure can be capitalised – assuming it otherwise meets the criteria – a judgement must be made, at the date the expenditure is incurred, of whether there is sufficient probability that the relevant permissions will be granted. Conversely, if during the application and approval process of such permits it is no longer expected that necessary permits will be granted, capitalisation of pre-permission expenditure should cease and any related amounts that were previously capitalised should be written off (either under the fair value model in IAS 40 (see 6 below) or in accordance with IAS 36 – *Impairment of Assets*, if the cost model is applied (see 7.3 below)). Further, if the cost model is used, the carrying amount of any related property subject to development or redevelopment (or, if appropriate, the cash generating unit where such an asset belongs) should be tested for impairment, where applicable, in accordance with IAS 36 (see 7.3 below).

3.2 Other aspects of cost recognition

3.2.1 Repairs and maintenance

Day-to-day servicing, by which is meant the repairs and maintenance of the property which largely comprises labour costs, consumables and minor parts, should be recognised in profit or loss as incurred. *[IAS 40.18]*. However, the treatment is different if large parts of the properties have been replaced – the standard cites the example of interior walls that are replacements of the original walls. In this case, the cost of replacing the part will be recognised at the time that cost is incurred if the recognition criteria are met, while the carrying amount of the original part is derecognised (see 10.3 below). *[IAS 40.19]*.

The inference is that by restoring the asset to its originally assessed standard of performance, the new part will meet the recognition criteria and future economic benefits will flow to the entity once the old part is replaced. The inference is also that replacement is needed for the total asset to be operative. This being the case, the new walls will therefore meet the recognition criteria and the cost will therefore be capitalised.

Other than interior walls, large parts that might have to be replaced include elements such as lifts, escalators and air conditioning equipment.

3.2.2 Allocation into parts

IAS 40 does not explicitly require an analysis of investment properties into components or parts. However, this analysis is needed for the purposes of recognition and derecognition of all expenditure after the asset has initially been recognised and (if the parts are significant) for depreciation of those parts (see Chapter 18 at 3.2 and 5.1). Some of this is not relevant to assets held under the fair value model that are not depreciated because the standard expects the necessary adjustments to the carrying value of the asset as a whole to be made via the fair value mechanism (see 6 below). However, entities that adopt the cost model are obliged to account for assets after initial recognition in accordance with the requirements of IAS 16. The cost model is discussed further at 7 below.

3.3 Acquisition of investment property or a business combination?

In its July 2011 meeting, the Interpretations Committee discussed a request seeking clarification on whether the acquisition of a single investment property, with lease agreements with multiple tenants over varying periods and associated processes, such as cleaning, maintenance and administrative services such as rent collection, constitutes a business as defined in IFRS 3 – *Business Combinations*.

The Interpretations Committee noted that the issue raises the question of whether there is any interaction between IAS 40 and IFRS 3. It discussed services that are 'ancillary services' (as discussed in paragraphs 11-14 of IAS 40 – see 2.8 above) that are not so significant as to disqualify a property from being an investment property but could nonetheless be considered 'processes' (as discussed in paragraphs B7-B12 of IFRS 3) that could result in the acquired set of activities constituting a business.[5]

IAS 40 notes, in relation to the need to distinguish investment property from owner-occupied property, that where certain ancillary processes exist in connection with an investment property they are often insignificant to the overall arrangement (see 2.8 above). Consequently, it may be appropriate to conclude that, where such acquired processes are considered by IAS 40 to be insignificant, an investment property acquisition is within the scope of IAS 40 rather than IFRS 3. However, it should be noted that IAS 40 and IFRS 3 are not mutually exclusive and this determination is not the specific purpose of the standard's observation about ancillary services. *[IAS 40.BC19-20]*.

Consequently, the IASB issued the *Annual Improvements to IFRSs 2011-2013 Cycle* on 12 December 2013 which amended IAS 40 to state explicitly that the judgement required to determine whether the acquisition of investment property is the acquisition of an asset or a group of assets – or a business combination within the scope of IFRS 3 – should only be made with reference to IFRS 3. *[IAS 40.14A]*.

This clarified that the discussion about 'ancillary services' in paragraphs 7-14 of IAS 40 (see 2.8 above) relates to whether or not property is owner-occupied property or investment property and not to determining whether or not a property is a business as defined in IFRS 3. Determining whether a specific transaction meets the definition of a business combination as defined in IFRS 3 and includes an investment property as defined in IAS 40 requires the separate application of both standards. *[IAS 40.14A]*.

IFRS 3 establishes different accounting requirements for a business combination as opposed to the acquisition of an asset or a group of assets that does not constitute a business (see 4.1.1 below). Therefore, determining whether an acquired investment property is a business or not, could result in significantly different accounting outcomes, both at the date of acquisition (i.e. at initial recognition) and subsequently. If dealt with as an acquisition of a business, then the initial accounting for investment property is considerably more complex. For example, amongst other requirements:

- initial direct costs are expensed (IAS 40 requires these to be capitalised – see 4.1 below);
- the initial recognition exception for deferred taxation does not apply (IAS 12 – *Income Taxes* – does not allow deferred taxation to be provided on existing temporary differences for acquisitions that are not business combinations); and
- goodwill is recognised (often itself 'created' by the provision of deferred taxation).

Judging whether an acquisition is a business combination or not is therefore of considerable importance. *[IAS 40.14A]*.

It will be a matter of judgement for preparers, but it may still be appropriate to conclude that, when applying the guidance in IFRS 3, if acquired processes are considered to be insignificant (whether by reference to guidance in IAS 40 or otherwise) an investment property acquisition is within the scope of IAS 40 rather than IFRS 3. This judgement will rest upon the facts and circumstances of each acquisition. If significant, disclosure of this judgement would be required by IAS 1 – *Presentation of Financial Statements*. *[IAS 1.122]*.

The definition of a business (see 3.3.1 below) is applied regardless of whether the entity purchases a property directly or, in the case of consolidated financial statements, via the shares in another entity.

3.3.1 Definition of a business

The IASB recognises the difficulties in determining whether an acquisition meets the definition of a business – which are not just limited to investment property – and explored this issue in its post-implementation review of IFRS 3 which was completed in June 2015. As a result, in October 2018 the IASB issued amendments to clarify the definition of a business in IFRS 3. The amendments are intended to assist entities to determine whether a transaction should be accounted for as a business combination or as an asset acquisition.

IFRS 3 continues to adopt a market participant's perspective to determine whether an acquired set of activities and assets is a business. This means that it is irrelevant whether the seller operated the set as a business or whether the acquirer intends to operate the set as a business. Some respondents to the post-implementation review of IFRS 3 noted that such a fact driven assessment may not provide the most useful information, as it does not consider the business rationale, strategic considerations and objectives of the acquirer. However, the IASB decided not to make any changes in this respect, because an assessment made from a market participant's perspective and driven by facts (rather than the acquirer's intentions) helps to prevent similar transactions being accounted for differently. Also, the IASB noted that bringing more subjective elements into the determination would likely have increased diversity in practice. *[IFRS 3.B11, BC21G]*.

The amendments to IFRS 3:

- clarified the minimum requirements for a business; clarify that to be considered a business, an acquired set of activities and assets must include, at a minimum, an input and a substantive process that together significantly contribute to the ability to create outputs;
- removed the assessment of whether market participants are capable of replacing any missing inputs or processes and continuing to produce outputs;
- added guidance and illustrative examples to help entities assess whether a substantive process has been acquired;
- narrowed the definitions of a business and of outputs by focusing on goods and services provided to customers and by removing the reference to an ability to reduce costs; and
- added an optional fair value concentration test that permits a simplified assessment of whether an acquired set of activities and assets is not a business.[6]

The IASB introduced an optional fair value concentration test (the 'concentration test') designed to simplify the evaluation of whether an acquired integrated set of activities and assets is not a business. Entities may elect whether or not to apply the concentration test on a transaction-by-transaction basis. *[IFRS 3.B7A]*.

The concentration test is met if substantially all of the fair value of the gross assets acquired is concentrated in a single identifiable asset or group of similar identifiable assets. The concentration test is based on gross assets, not on net assets, as the IASB concluded that whether a set of activities and assets includes a substantive process does not depend on how the set is financed. In addition, certain assets are excluded from the gross assets considered in the test. *[IFRS 3.B7B, BC21W]*.

The fair value of the gross assets acquired includes any consideration transferred (plus the fair value of any non-controlling interest and the fair value of any previously held interest) in excess of the fair value of net identifiable assets acquired. The fair value of the gross assets acquired may normally be determined as the total obtained by adding the fair value of the consideration transferred (plus the fair value of any non-controlling interest and the fair value of any previously held interest) to the fair value of the liabilities assumed (other than deferred tax liabilities), and then excluding cash and cash equivalents, deferred tax assets and goodwill resulting from the effects of deferred tax liabilities. These exclusions are made because cash acquired, and the tax base of the assets and liabilities acquired, are independent of whether the acquired set of activities and assets includes a substantive process. The IASB does not expect detailed calculations, however, if the fair value of the gross assets acquired is more than the total obtained using the calculation described above, a more precise calculation may sometimes be needed. *[IFRS 3.B7B, BC21V, BC21W]*.

For the concentration test, a single identifiable asset is any asset or group of assets that would be recognised and measured as a single identifiable asset in a business combination. If a tangible asset is attached to, and cannot be physically removed and used separately from, another tangible asset (or from an underlying asset subject to a lease, as defined in IFRS 16) without incurring significant cost or significant diminution in utility or fair value to either asset (for example, land and buildings), those assets are considered a single identifiable asset. When assessing whether assets are similar, an entity should consider the nature of each single identifiable asset and the risks associated with managing and creating outputs from the assets (that is, the risk characteristics). *[IFRS 3.B7B]*.

The following are not considered similar assets:
- a tangible asset and an intangible asset;
- tangible assets in different classes (e.g. inventory, manufacturing equipment and automobiles) unless they are considered a single identifiable asset in circumstances described above;
- identifiable intangible assets in different classes (e.g. brand names, licences and intangible assets under development);
- a financial asset and a non-financial asset;
- financial assets in different classes (e.g. accounts receivable and investments in equity instruments); and
- identifiable assets that are within the same class of asset but have significantly different risk characteristics. *[IFRS 3.B7B]*.

If the concentration test is met, the set of activities and assets is determined not to be a business and no further assessment is needed. If the concentration test is not met, or if an entity elects not to apply the concentration test, a detailed assessment must be performed applying the normal requirements in IFRS 3. As such, the concentration test never determines that a transaction is a business combination. *[IFRS 3.B7A, BC21Y]*.

The IASB also provided a series of illustrative examples to assist in applying the guidance in IFRS 3 on the definition of business. These illustrative examples accompany the standard and address, among other things, the application of the optional concentration test and the assessment whether an acquired process is substantive.

One of the illustrative examples demonstrates the application of optional concentration test in the acquisition of real estate. It describes an entity that purchases a portfolio of 10 single-family homes that each have an in-place lease. The fair value of the consideration paid is equal to the aggregate fair value of the 10 single-family homes acquired. Each single-family home includes the land, building and property improvements. Each home has a different floor area and interior design. The 10 single-family homes are located in the same area and the classes of customers (e.g. tenants) are similar. The risks associated with operating in the real estate market of the homes acquired are not significantly different. No employees, other assets, processes or other activities are transferred. *[IFRS 3.IE74]*.

After electing and applying the optional concentration test (as described above), the entity concludes that each single-family home is considered a single identifiable asset because the building and property improvements are attached to the land and cannot be removed without incurring significant cost. Also, the building and the in-place lease are considered a single identifiable asset because they would be recognised and measured as a single identifiable asset in a business combination. The entity also concludes that the group of 10 single-family homes is a group of similar identifiable assets because the assets (all single-family homes) are similar in nature and the risks associated with managing and creating outputs are not significantly different. This is because the types of homes and classes of customers are not significantly different.

Consequently, substantially all of the fair value of the gross assets acquired is concentrated in a group of similar identifiable assets. Therefore, the entity concludes that the acquired set of activities and assets is not a business. *[IFRS 3.IE75-76]*.

A second example assumes the same facts described above except that the entity also purchases a multi-tenant corporate office park with six 10-storey office buildings that are fully leased. The additional set of activities and assets acquired includes the land, buildings, leases and contracts for outsourced cleaning, security and maintenance. No employees, other assets, other processes or other activities are transferred. The aggregate fair value associated with the office park is similar to the aggregate fair value associated with the 10 single-family homes. The processes performed through the contracts for outsourced cleaning and security are ancillary or minor within the context of all the processes required to create outputs. *[IFRS 3.IE77]*.

After electing and applying the optional concentration test, the entity concludes that the single-family homes and the office park are not similar identifiable assets because they differ significantly in the risks associated with operating the assets, obtaining tenants and managing tenants. In particular, the scale of operations and risks associated with the two classes of customers are significantly different. Consequently, the fair value of the gross assets acquired is not substantially all concentrated in a group of similar identifiable assets, because the fair value of the office park is similar to the aggregate fair value of the 10 single-family homes. In this case, the entity must perform a detailed assessment applying the normal requirements in paragraphs B8–B12D of IFRS 3 and assess whether the acquired set of activities and assets meets the minimum requirements to be considered a business. *[IFRS 3.IE78]*.

See Chapter 9 at 3.2 for the detailed guidance in determining whether an acquisition meets the definition of a business.

4 INITIAL MEASUREMENT

4.1 Attributable costs

IAS 40 requires an owned investment property to be measured initially at cost, which includes transaction costs. *[IAS 40.20]*. If a property is purchased, cost means purchase price and any directly attributable expenditure such as professional fees, property transfer taxes and other transaction costs. *[IAS 40.21]*.

For investment property under construction (see 2.5 above), although there is no specific reference to IAS 16, we consider that the principles in IAS 16 must still be applied to the recognition of costs in IAS 40. This means that only those elements of cost that were allowed by IAS 16 could be capitalised and that capitalisation ceased when the asset has reached the condition necessary for it to be capable of operating in the manner intended by management. *[IAS 16.16(b)]*. These principles are set out in detail in Chapter 18 at 4.

For investment property held by a lessee as a right-of-use asset, see 4.5 below.

4.1.1 Acquisition of a group of assets that does not constitute a business ('the group')

The purchase price of an investment property may result from an allocation of the price paid for a group of assets. If an entity acquires a group of assets that do not comprise a business, the principles in IFRS 3 are applied to allocate the entire cost to individual items (see Chapter 9 at 2.2.2). In such cases the acquirer should identify and recognise the individual identifiable assets acquired and liabilities assumed and allocate the cost of the group to the individual identifiable assets and liabilities on the basis of their relative fair values at the date of purchase. Such a transaction or event does not give rise to goodwill. *[IFRS 3.2(b)]*.

In its June 2017 meeting, the Interpretations Committee considered a request for clarification on how to allocate the transaction price to the identifiable assets acquired and liabilities assumed when:

(a) the sum of individual fair values of the identifiable assets and liabilities is different from the transaction price; and

(b) the group includes identifiable assets and liabilities initially measured both at cost and at an amount other than cost.

The Interpretations Committee noted the requirement of paragraph 2(b) of IFRS 3 as described above and also noted that other IFRSs include initial measurement requirements for particular assets and liabilities, including IAS 40 for investment property. It observed that if an entity initially considers that there might be a difference as described in (a) above, the entity should first review the procedures it has used to determine those individual fair values to assess whether such a difference truly exists before allocating the transaction price.

The Interpretations Committee considered two possible ways of accounting for the acquisition of the group. These two approaches are discussed in detail in Chapter 9 at 2.2.2.

Under the first approach an entity:
- identifies the individual identifiable assets acquired and liabilities assumed that it recognises at the date of the acquisition;
- determines the individual transaction price for each identifiable asset and liability by allocating the cost of the group based on the relative fair values of those assets and liabilities at the date of the acquisition; and then
- applies the initial measurement requirements in applicable standards to each identifiable asset acquired and liability assumed. The entity accounts for any difference between the amount at which the asset or liability is initially measured and its individual transaction price applying the relevant requirements.

Applying the second approach, for any identifiable asset or liability initially measured at an amount other than cost, an entity initially measures that asset or liability at the amount specified by the applicable standard. The entity deducts from the transaction price of the group the amounts allocated to the assets and liabilities initially measured at an amount other than cost, and then allocates the residual transaction price to the remaining identifiable assets and liabilities based on their relative fair values at the date of acquisition.[7]

In its November 2017 meeting, the Interpretations Committee concluded that a reasonable reading of the requirements in paragraph 2(b) of IFRS 3 on the acquisition of the group results in one of the two approaches outlined above (i.e. a policy choice) and that an entity should apply its reading of the requirements consistently to all acquisitions of a group of assets that does not constitute a business. An entity would also disclose the selected approach applying paragraphs 117 to 124 of IAS 1 if that disclosure would assist users of financial statements in understanding how those transactions are reflected in reported financial performance and financial position.

In the light of its analysis, the Interpretations Committee decided not to add this matter to its standard-setting agenda. However, the Interpretations Committee observed that the amendment to the definition of a business in IFRS 3 (see 3.3.1 above) is likely to increase the population of transactions that constitute the acquisition of a group of assets so this matter will be monitored.[8]

For investment properties acquired as part of the group, the first approach could mean that a revaluation gain or loss may need to be recognised in profit or loss at the date of acquisition of the group to account for the difference between the allocated individual transaction price and the fair value of the investment property acquired. Using the second approach, investment properties are recorded at fair value as at acquisition date with no immediate impact on profit or loss at the date of the acquisition.

4.1.2 Deferred taxes when acquiring a 'single asset' entity that is not a business

In many jurisdictions, it is usual for investment property to be bought and sold by transferring ownership of a separate legal entity formed to hold the asset (a 'single asset' entity) rather than the asset itself.

When an entity acquires all of the shares of another entity that has an investment property as its only asset (i.e. the acquisition of a 'single asset' entity that is not a business) and the acquiree had recognised in its statement of financial position a deferred tax liability arising from measuring the investment property at fair value as allowed by IAS 40, a specific issue arises as to whether or not the acquiring entity should recognise a deferred tax liability on initial recognition of the transaction.

This specific situation was considered by the Interpretations Committee and, in its March 2017 meeting, it was concluded that the initial recognition exception in paragraph 15(b) of IAS 12 applies because the transaction is not a business combination. Accordingly, on acquisition, the acquiring entity recognises only the investment property and not a deferred tax liability in its consolidated financial statements. The acquiring entity therefore allocates the entire purchase price to the investment property.[9]

For an example and further discussions on the application of the initial recognition exception to assets acquired in the circumstances described above, see Chapter 33 at 7.2.9.

4.2 Start-up costs and self-built property

IAS 40 specifies that start-up costs (unless necessary to bring the property into working condition) and operating losses incurred before the investment property achieves the planned occupancy level, are not to be capitalised. *[IAS 40.23(a), 23(b)]*.

IAS 40 therefore prohibits a practice of capitalising costs until a particular level of occupation or rental income is achieved because at the date of physical completion the asset would be capable of operating in the manner intended by management. This forestalls an argument, sometimes advanced in the past, that the asset being constructed was not simply the physical structure of the building but a fully tenanted investment property, and its cost correspondingly included not simply the construction period but also the letting period.

If a property is self-built by an entity, the same general principles apply as for an acquired property (see 4.1 above). However, IAS 40 prohibits capitalisation of abnormal amounts of wasted material, labour or other resources incurred in constructing or developing the property. *[IAS 40.23(c)]*.

4.2.1 Cost of a building to be demolished in connection with the construction of a new building

It is not uncommon for property companies to acquire land with an existing building where the planned redevelopment requires the demolition of that building and its replacement with a new building that is to be held as investment property. Whether the acquired land and building will be accounted for as a single asset or two separate assets will depend on the subsequent accounting model applied by the entity.

If the entity measures the investment property under the fair value model (see 6 below), the entity classifies the land and building on initial recognition as one item of investment property under IAS 40 and measures the investment property based on its cost. *[IAS 40.20]*. Subsequently, the land and building are measured as one item at fair value at each reporting date. If the entity measures the investment property under the cost model (see 5 below), it will account for the land and building separately (see Chapter 18 at 5.4.2). When, depending on the facts and circumstances, the existing building is unusable or likely to be demolished by any party acquiring it, then it would be appropriate, in our view, to allocate the entire or a large part of the purchase price to the land. This is because the fair value of the existing building will likely be minimal or the fair value of the combined investment properties, comprising both land and building, may be close to that of the land. Similarly, subsequent demolition costs should be treated as being attributable to the cost of the land as part of site preparation costs (see Chapter 18 at 4.1.1).

Entities holding investment properties may also decide to replace existing buildings with new ones and continue to hold these as investment properties. If an entity uses the cost model to measure its investment properties, the carrying amount of the existing building cannot be rolled into the costs of the new building. The existing building must be depreciated over its remaining useful life to reduce the carrying amount of the asset to its residual value (presumably nil) at the point at which it is demolished. Consideration will have to be given as to whether the asset is impaired in accordance with IAS 36 (see 7.3 below and Chapter 18 at 5.7).

In contrast, if an entity that uses the fair model to measure its investment properties decides to replace an existing building with a new one but will continue to hold it as investment property, then the highest and best use of the land may not match the current use of the land. The value of the land may increase by constructing a different property (for example with more floors or with a different purpose). When determining the fair value of the investment property, the entity should take into account a market participant's ability to generate economic benefits by using the asset in its highest and best use or by selling it to another market participant that would use the asset in its highest and best use (see 6.8 below). *[IFRS 13.27]*. Therefore, the existing building and land will be measured as one based on its fair value. As the new building is constructed, the property (land and building) will continue to be measured as one based on fair value from a market participant's perspective.

Entities replacing an existing building with a building for their own use or a building to be sold in the ordinary course of their business will deal with the land and buildings under IAS 16 (see Chapter 18 at 4.1.7) or IAS 2 (see Chapter 22 at 4.2.2), respectively.

4.3   Deferred payments

If payment for a property is deferred, the cost to be recognised is the cash price equivalent (which in practice means the present value of the deferred payments due) at the recognition date. Any difference between the cash price and the total payments to be made is recognised as interest expense over the credit period. *[IAS 40.24]*.

4.4 Reclassifications from property, plant and equipment or from inventory

When an entity uses the cost model, transfers between investment property, owner-occupied property and inventories do not change the carrying amount of the property transferred and they do not change the cost of that property for measurement or disclosure purposes. *[IAS 40.59]*.

The treatment of transfers of properties measured using the revaluation option in IAS 16 to investment property is set out in 9.2 below.

4.5 Initial measurement of property held under a lease

An investment property held by a lessee as a right-of-use asset should be measured initially at its cost in accordance with IFRS 16 (see Chapter 23 at 5.2.1). *[IAS 40.29A]*. The treatment of initial direct costs by a lessee applying IFRS 16 is discussed at 4.9.2 below.

4.6 Initial measurement of assets acquired in exchange transactions

The requirements of IAS 40 for investment properties acquired in exchange for non-monetary assets, or a combination of monetary and non-monetary assets, are the same as those of IAS 16. *[IAS 40.27-29]*. These provisions are discussed in detail in Chapter 18 at 4.4.

4.7 Initial recognition of tenanted investment property subsequently measured using the cost model

During the development of the current IFRS 3 the IASB considered whether it would be appropriate for any favourable or unfavourable lease aspect of an investment property to be recognised separately.

The IASB concluded that this was not necessary for investment property that will be measured at fair value because the fair value of investment property takes into account rental income from leases and therefore the contractual terms of leases and other contracts in place.

However, a different position has been taken for investment property measured using the cost model. In this case the IASB observed that the cost model requires:

- the use of a depreciation or amortisation method that reflects the pattern in which the entity expects to consume the asset's future economic benefits; and
- each part of an item of property, plant and equipment that has a cost that is significant in relation to the total cost of the item to be depreciated separately.

Therefore, an acquirer of investment property in a business combination that is subsequently measured using the cost model will need to adjust the depreciation method for the investment property to reflect the timing of cash flows attributable to the underlying leases. *[IFRS 3.BC148]*.

In effect, therefore, this requires that the favourable or unfavourable lease aspect of the investment property – measured with reference to market conditions at the date of the business combination – be separately identified in order that it may be subsequently depreciated or amortised, usually over the remaining lease term. Any such amount is not presented separately in the financial statements.

This approach has also been extended to acquisition of all property, i.e. including those acquired outside a business combination (see 7.1.2 below).

4.8 Borrowing costs

IAS 23 – *Borrowing Costs* – generally mandates capitalisation of borrowing costs in respect of qualifying assets. However, application of IAS 23 to borrowing costs directly attributable to the acquisition, construction or production of qualifying assets that are measured at fair value, such as investment property, is not required because it would not affect the measurement of the investment property in the statement of financial position; it would only affect presentation of interest expense and fair value gains and losses in the income statement. Nevertheless, IAS 23 does not prohibit capitalisation of eligible borrowing costs to such assets as a matter of accounting policy.

To the extent that entities choose to capitalise eligible borrowing costs in respect of such assets, in our view, the methods allowed by IAS 23 should be followed.

The treatment of borrowing costs is discussed further in Chapter 21.

4.9 Lease incentives and initial direct costs of leasing a property

In negotiating a new or renewed operating lease, the lessor may provide incentives for the lessee to enter into the agreement. The lessor or the lessee (or both) may also incur costs that are directly attributable to negotiating and arranging a lease. However, IAS 40 provides no specific guidance on accounting for lease incentives and initial costs of obtaining a lease.

4.9.1 Lease incentives

Lease incentives are defined as 'payments made by a lessor to a lessee associated with a lease, or the reimbursement or assumption by a lessor of costs of a lessee'. *[IFRS 16 Appendix A]*. In practice, examples of such incentives are an up-front cash payment to the lessee or the reimbursement or assumption by the lessor of costs of the lessee (such as relocation costs, leasehold improvements and costs associated with a pre-existing lease commitment of the lessee). Alternatively, initial periods of the lease term may be agreed to be rent-free or at a reduced rent.

Under IFRS 16, lease incentives are deducted from 'lease payments' made by a lessee to a lessor relating to right-of-use asset during the lease term. *[IFRS 16 Appendix A]*. Accordingly, for lessees, lease incentives that are received by the lessee at or before the lease commencement date reduce the initial measurement of a lessee's right-of-use asset. *[IFRS 16.24(b)]*. Lease incentives that are receivable by the lessee at lease commencement date reduce a lessee's lease liability (and therefore the right-of-use asset as well). *[IFRS 16.27(a)]*.

For lessors, lease incentives that are paid or payable to the lessee are also deducted from lease payments. Lease payments under operating leases are recognised by lessors as income on either a straight-line basis or another systematic basis. *[IFRS 16.81]*. Accordingly, for operating leases, lessors should defer any lease incentives paid or payable to the lessee and recognise the resulting accrual as a reduction to lease income over the lease term in order to recognise the lease payments as income at an amount that is net of lease incentives. This means that such accrued rental income will be recovered as part of the cash payments to be received from the lessee over the remaining lease term.

Consequently, many lessors usually present any accrued rental income (i.e. outstanding unamortised deferred lease incentives) as a separate asset, but other lessors present these together with (or as part of) the related investment property. However, lease incentives do not form part of the cost of the investment property (see also 6.6.1 below for the requirement to adjust the fair value of an investment property to avoid 'double counting' in circumstances where a lease incentive exists and is recognised separately). It is therefore relevant to distinguish between lease incentives and other capital expenditure.

There is no additional guidance in IFRS 16 to assist in the identification of incentives, but a similar requirement existed in previous United Kingdom GAAP (in UITF abstract 28 – *Operating lease incentives*) and provides helpful additional detail:

'A payment (or other transfer of value) from a lessor to (or for the benefit of) a lessee should be regarded as a lease incentive when that fairly reflects its substance. A payment to reimburse a lessee for fitting-out costs should be regarded as a lease incentive where the fittings are suitable only for the lessee and accordingly do not add to the value of the property to the lessor. On the other hand, insofar as a reimbursement of expenditure enhances a property generally and causes commensurate benefit to flow to the lessor, it should be treated as reimbursement of expenditure on the property. For example, where the lifts in a building are to be renewed and a lease has only five years to run, a payment made by the lessor may not be an inducement to enter into a lease but payment for an improvement to the lessor's property.'[10]

The distinction between costs that enhance the value of the property, and those that are of value to the tenant, can be seen in Extract 19.2 below.

For further discussions on lease incentives, see Chapter 23 at 4.5.2, 5.2.1 and 5.2.2.

4.9.2 Initial direct costs of obtaining a lease

Lessors and lessees apply the same definition of initial direct costs.

Under IFRS 16, the requirement on initial direct costs is consistent with the concept of incremental costs of obtaining a contract in IFRS 15 – *Revenue from Contracts with Customers* (see Chapter 31 at 5.1). IFRS 16 defines initial direct costs as 'incremental costs of obtaining a lease that would not have been incurred if the lease had not been obtained ...'. *[IFRS 16 Appendix A]*. Examples of such costs are commissions and contingent fees that would not have been incurred if the lease had not been obtained. Accordingly, in addition to excluding allocated costs (e.g. salaries), initial direct costs exclude costs incurred regardless of whether the lease is successfully finalised (e.g. fees for certain legal advice, estate agent fees not contingent upon success). Example 13 of the Illustrative Examples to IFRS 16 also indicates that certain payments made to an existing lessee to incentivise that lessee to terminate its lease could also be regarded as initial direct costs.

Under IFRS 16, lessors are required to add initial direct costs incurred in obtaining an operating lease to the carrying amount of the underlying asset. These initial direct costs are recognised as an expense over the lease term on the same basis as lease income. *[IFRS 16.83]*. For lessees, IFRS 16 requires initial direct costs to be included in the initial measurement of the right-of-use asset. *[IFRS 16.24]*.

While IAS 40 does not contain specific guidance on the accounting treatment of initial direct costs of arranging leases over a property, such as legal and agency fees, such costs should be recognised as an expense over the term of the resultant lease. This treatment can also be seen in Extract 19.2 below. In practice, this means, if the cost model is used, such costs are presented as part of the cost of the investment property, even if they do not strictly form part of it and are then amortised separately over the lease term.

An entity using the fair value model should also initially include these costs as part of the carrying value of the investment property. However, in our view, at the next reporting date such initial costs could be recognised in profit and loss in the reported fair value gain or loss, as they would otherwise exceed the fair value of the related investment property. This is consistent with the treatment of transaction costs incurred on acquisition of a property discussed in 6.4 below.

Alternatively, for an entity using the fair value model, we also believe that the initial direct costs included in the carrying amount of the investment property could be recognised subsequently as an expense over the lease term on the same basis as the lease income. Accordingly, the amortisation of the initial direct costs is presented separately from the gain or loss from fair value adjustments on investment property. In addition, the gain or loss on fair value adjustments is credited by the same amount as the amortisation charge in each period to ensure that the carrying amount of the investment property (including the unamortised initial direct costs) is equal to its fair value at each reporting date.

> *Extract 19.2: The British Land Company PLC (2015)*
> NOTES TO THE ACCOUNTS [extract]
> 1   Basis of preparation, significant accounting policies and accounting judgements [extract]
> Net rental income [extract]
>
> Initial direct costs incurred in negotiating and arranging a new lease are amortised on a straight-line basis over the period from the date of lease commencement to the earliest termination date.
>
> Where a lease incentive payment, including surrender premia paid, does not enhance the value of a property, it is amortised on a straight-line basis over the period from the date of lease commencement to the earliest termination date.

For further discussions on initial direct costs of obtaining a lease, see Chapter 23 at 4.7, 5.2.1 and 6.3.

4.10 Contingent costs

The terms of purchase of investment property may sometimes include a variable or contingent amount that cannot be determined at the date of acquisition. For example, the vendor may have the right to additional consideration from the purchaser in the event that a certain level of income is generated from the property; or its value reaches a certain level; or if certain legislative hurdles, such as the receipt of zoning or planning permission, are achieved.

A common issue is whether these liabilities should be accounted for as a financial liability or as a provision. This is important because remeasurement of a financial liability is taken to profit or loss, whilst changes in a provision could, by analogy to IFRIC 1 – *Changes in Existing Decommissioning, Restoration and Similar Liabilities* – be recorded as an adjustment to the cost of the asset.

The Interpretations Committee took this question onto its agenda in January 2011,[11] but in May 2011 chose to defer further work on it until the IASB concluded on its discussions on the accounting for the liability for variable payments as part of the leases project.[12]

At its July 2013 meeting, the IASB considered this issue again and noted that the initial accounting for variable payments affects their subsequent accounting. Some IASB members expressed the view that the initial and subsequent accounting for variable payments for the purchase of assets are linked and should be addressed comprehensively. The IASB noted that accounting for variable payments is a topic that was discussed as part of the Leases and Conceptual Framework projects and decided that it would reconsider this issue after the proposals in the Exposure Draft – *Leases* (published in May 2013) had been redeliberated.[13]

The Interpretations Committee revisited this issue at its meetings in September 2015, November 2015 and March 2016. It determined that this issue is too broad for it to address within the confines of existing IFRSs. Consequently, the Interpretations Committee decided not to add this issue to its agenda and concluded that the IASB should address the accounting for variable payments comprehensively.[14]

As a result, in May 2016 the IASB tentatively decided to include '*Variable and Contingent Consideration*' in its pipeline of future research projects and noted that it expected to begin work on projects in its research pipeline between 2017 and 2021.[15] In February 2018, the IASB decided that the IASB staff should carry out work to determine how broad the research project should be.[16] At the time of writing this is not listed as an active research project on the IASB's work plan.[17]

For more related discussions of key accounting considerations, including general approaches applied in practice, see Chapter 17 at 4.5 and Chapter 18 at 4.1.9.

Until this matter is resolved, an entity should adopt and apply a consistent accounting policy to initial recognition and subsequent remeasurements of any liability recognised for the variable or contingent consideration for the purchase of an investment property in accordance with the hierarchy in IAS 8 – *Accounting Policies, Changes in Accounting Estimates and Errors*. An entity should exercise judgement in developing and consistently applying an accounting policy that results in information that is relevant and reliable in its particular circumstances. *[IAS 8.10]*. Of course, for investment property held at fair value, capitalising or expensing the remeasurements of any liability recognised for the variable or contingent consideration primarily affects classification within the income statement.

It is important to note that developing a policy (as described above) is not available for the contingent costs of acquiring investment property as part of a business combination. The treatment of contingent costs in these circumstances is described in Chapter 9 at 7.1.

4.11 Income from tenanted property during development

An issue that can arise is whether rental and similar income generated by existing tenants in a property development may be capitalised and offset against the cost of developing that property.

IAS 16 requires that the income and related expenses of incidental operations are recognised in profit or loss and included in their respective classifications of income and expense (see Chapter 18 at 4.2). *[IAS 16.21]*. We consider that rental and similar income from existing tenants are incidental operations to the development.

In our view there should not be a measurement difference between the cost of a property development dealt with under IAS 40 and the cost of development dealt with under IAS 16. Therefore, rental and similar income generated by existing tenants in a property dealt with under IAS 40 and now intended for redevelopment should not be capitalised against the costs of the development. Rather rental and similar income should be recognised in profit or loss in accordance with the requirements of IFRS 16 (see Chapter 23), together with related expenses. For these purposes it is irrelevant whether the investment property is held at cost or fair value.

4.12 Payments by the vendor to the purchaser

On occasion, a transaction for the purchase of an investment property may include an additional element where the vendor repays fixed or variable amounts to the purchaser – perhaps described as representing a rental equivalent for a period of time.

The question then arises whether, in the accounts of the purchaser, these payments should be recorded as income (albeit perhaps recognised over a period of time) or as a deduction from the acquisition cost of the investment property on initial recognition.

In our view such amounts are an integral part of the acquisition transaction and should invariably be treated as a deduction from the acquisition cost of the investment property because the payment is an element of a transaction between a vendor and purchaser of the property, rather than a landlord and tenant. In the event that the repayments by the vendor are spread over time, the fair value of the right to receive those payments should be deducted from the cost of the investment property and an equivalent financial asset recognised. The financial asset would be accounted for in accordance with IFRS 9 – *Financial Instruments* – which may lead to it being classified as financial asset at amortised cost or at fair value through profit or loss (see Chapter 48 at 2.1).

5 MEASUREMENT AFTER INITIAL RECOGNITION

Once recognised, IAS 40 allows an entity to choose one of the two methods of accounting for investment property as its accounting policy:

- fair value model (see 6 below); or
- cost model (see 7 below).

An entity has to choose one model or the other, and apply it to all its investment property (unless the entity is an insurer or similar entity, in which case there are exemptions that are described briefly at 5.1 below). *[IAS 40.30]*. This is because measuring all investment properties on the same basis provides more useful information than allowing an entity to choose the measurement basis for each property. *[IFRS 16.BC178]*.

The standard does not identify a preferred alternative; although the fair value model currently seems to be the more widely adopted model among entities in the real estate sector (see 7.2 below).

The standard discourages changes from the fair value model to the cost model, stating that it is highly unlikely that this will result in a more relevant presentation, which is a requirement of IAS 8 for any voluntary change in accounting policy. *[IAS 40.31]*.

All entities, regardless of which measurement option is chosen, are required to determine the fair value of their investment property, because even those entities that use the cost model are required to disclose the fair value of their investment property (see 12.3 below). *[IAS 40.32, 79(e)]*.

5.1 Measurement by insurers and similar entities

There is an exception to the requirement that an entity must apply its chosen measurement policy to all of its investment properties. This is applicable to insurance companies and other entities that hold specified assets, including investment properties, whose fair value or return is directly linked to the return paid on specific liabilities (i.e. liabilities that are secured by such investment properties).

These entities are permitted to choose either the fair value or the cost model for all such properties without it affecting the choice available for all other investment properties that they may hold. *[IAS 40.32A]*. However, for an insurer or other entity that operates an internal property fund that issues notional units, with some units held by investors in linked contracts and others held by the entity, all properties within such a fund must be held on the same basis because the standard does not permit the entity to measure the property held by such a fund partly at cost and partly at fair value. *[IAS 40.32B]*.

If an entity elected a model for those properties described above that is different from the model used for the rest of its investment properties, sales of investment properties between these pools of assets are to be recognised at fair value with any applicable cumulative change in fair value recognised in profit or loss. Consequently, if an investment property is sold from a pool in which the fair value model is used into a pool in which the cost model is used, the fair value of the property sold at the date of the sale becomes its deemed cost. *[IAS 40.32C]*.

When IFRS 17 is adopted, paragraph 32B of IAS 40 (as discussed above) will be amended. The previous reference to 'insurers and other entities [operating] an internal property fund that issues notional units' will be replaced by '[s]ome entities operate, either internally or externally, an investment fund that provides investors with benefits determined by units in the fund.' The revised paragraph will also refer to entities that issue insurance contracts with direct participation features, for which the underlying items include investment property, and will specify that for the purposes of applying paragraph 32A (as discussed above) and the amended paragraph 32B of IAS 40 only, insurance contracts include investment contracts with discretionary participation features.

The amended paragraph 32B of IAS 40 will clarify that an entity is not permitted to measure property held by the fund (as described above) or property that is an underlying item partly at cost and partly at fair value.

An entity will apply the above consequential amendment when it applies IFRS 17, which is effective for annual reporting periods beginning on or after 1 January 2023. Early application is permitted provided that IFRS 9 has already been applied, or is applied for the first time, at the date on which IFRS 17 is first applied.[18] For those entities early adopting IFRS 17 and for the detailed discussions and requirements of this new standard, see Chapter 56.

6 THE FAIR VALUE MODEL

Under this model all investment property is measured at its fair value at the end of the reporting period (except in the cases described in 6.2 and 6.3 below) and a gain or loss arising from changes in the fair value in the reporting period is recognised in profit or loss for that period. *[IAS 40.33, 35]*.

IFRS 13 – *Fair Value Measurement* – provides a fair value measurement framework that applies whenever fair value measurement is permitted or required (see Chapter 14). IFRS 13 does not specify when an entity is required to use fair value, but rather, provides guidance on how to measure fair value under IFRS when fair value is required or permitted by IFRS.

IFRS 13 defines fair value as 'the price that would be received to sell an asset or paid to transfer a liability in an orderly transaction between market participants at the measurement date.' *[IFRS 13.9, IAS 40.5]*.

While entities cannot presume this to be the case, in practice, the fair value estimate arrived at under IFRS 13 may be similar to that estimated for 'market value' as defined by the Royal Institution of Chartered Surveyors ('RICS') and the International Valuation Standards Council ('IVSC'). Their definition of 'market value' being 'the estimated amount for which an asset or liability should exchange on the valuation date between a willing buyer and a willing seller in an arm's length transaction, after proper marketing and where the parties had each acted knowledgeably, prudently and without compulsion.'[19]

Many entities use an external valuer to estimate fair value based on the RICS and/or IVSC Valuation Standards. Indeed, the use of an independent valuer with a recognised and relevant professional qualification and with recent experience in the location and category of the investment property being valued is encouraged by IAS 40, albeit not required. *[IAS 40.32]*.

The price in the principal (or most advantageous) market used to measure fair value shall not be adjusted for transaction costs. This is because transaction costs are not a characteristic of an asset or a liability; rather, they are specific to a transaction and will differ depending on how an entity enters into a transaction for the asset or liability. *[IFRS 13.25]*.

Transaction costs incurred by a purchaser on acquisition are dealt with at 6.4 below and in Chapter 14 at 9.1.2.

6.1 Estimating fair value

When estimating the fair value of the property in accordance with IFRS 13, the objective is to estimate the price that would be received to sell an investment property in an orderly transaction between market participants at the measurement date under current market conditions. *[IFRS 13.2]*. This objective applies regardless of the techniques and inputs used to measure fair value.

IAS 40 has certain requirements in addition to those in IFRS 13. In particular, IAS 40 requires that the fair value reflects, among other things, rental income from current leases and other assumptions that market participants would use when pricing investment property under current market conditions. *[IAS 40.40]*. For example, in a transaction to sell an investment property, it is likely that market participants would consider the existing lease agreements in place.

This is consistent with the general requirement in IFRS 13 that an entity should measure the fair value using the assumptions that market participants would use when pricing the asset or liability, assuming that market participants act in their economic best interest. *[IFRS 13.22]*.

Extract 19.3 below describes Unibail-Rodamco-Westfield's approach to valuations:

> Extract 19.3: Unibail-Rodamco-Westfield SE (2019)
>
> 5.2 NOTES TO THE CONSOLIDATED FINANCIAL STATEMENTS [extract]
> NOTE 5. INVESTMENT PROPERTIES, TANGIBLE AND INTANGIBLE ASSETS, GOODWILL [extract]
> 5.1 INVESTMENT PROPERTIES [extract]
> 5.1.1 ACCOUNTING PRINCIPLES [extract]
>
> **INVESTMENT PROPERTIES (IAS 40 & IFRS 13)**
>
> Under the accounting treatment recommended by IAS 40, investment properties are shown at their market value. According to IFRS 13, the fair value is defined as the price that would be received to sell an asset or paid to transfer a liability in an orderly transaction between market participants at the measurement date (i.e. an exit price). Expectations about future improvements or modifications to be made to the property interest to reflect its highest and best use have to be considered in the appraisal, such as the renovation of or an extension to the property interest.
>
> URW complies with the IFRS 13 fair value measurement rule and the position paper[1] on IFRS 13 established by EPRA, the representative body of the publicly listed real estate industry in Europe.
>
> Transaction costs incurred for an asset deal are capitalised in the value of the investment property. Capitalised expenses include capital expenditures, evictions costs, capitalised financial interests, letting fees and other internal costs related to development projects.
>
> In accordance with IFRS 16 and IAS 40, the right-of-use assets arising from leased property which meet the definition of an investment property are measured at fair value.
>
> Investment Properties Under Construction (IPUC) are covered by IAS 40 and are eligible to be measured at fair value. In accordance with the Group's investment properties valuation method, they are measured at fair value by an external appraiser twice a year. Projects for which the fair value is not reliably determinable are measured at cost until such time that a fair value measurement becomes reliable, or until one year before the construction completion.
>
> According to the Group, a development project is eligible for a fair value measurement once all three of the following criteria are fulfilled:
>
> - all administrative authorisations needed to complete the project are obtained;
> - the construction has started and costs are committed toward the contractor; and
> - substantial uncertainty in future rental income has been eliminated.
>
> If the time to delivery is less than one year, the project is accounted for at fair value.
>
> For properties measured at fair value, the market value adopted by URW is determined on the basis of appraisals by independent external experts, who value the Group's portfolio as at June 30 and December 31 of each year. The gross value is reduced by disposal costs and transfer taxes[2], depending on the country and on the tax situation of the property, in order to arrive at a net market value.
>
> For the Shopping Centres and Offices & Others portfolios, the independent appraisers – determine the fair market value based on the results of two methods: the discounted cash flow methodology as well as the yield methodology. Furthermore, the resulting valuations are cross-checked against the initial yield, value per sqm and the fair market values established through actual market transactions.
>
> Appraisers have been given access to all information relevant for valuations, such as the Group's confidential rent rolls, including information on vacancy, break options, expiry dates and lease incentives, performance indicators (e.g., footfall and sales where available), letting evidence and the Group's cash flow forecasts from annually updated detailed asset business plans. Appraisers make their independent assessments of current and forward looking cash flow profiles and usually reflect risk either in the cash flow forecasts (e.g. future rental levels, growth, investment requirements, void periods and incentives), in the applied required returns or discount rates and in the yield applied to capitalise the exit rent to determine an exit value.
>
> The sites of the Convention & Exhibition portfolio are qualified as Investment property.

> For the Convention & Exhibition portfolio, the valuation methodology adopted is mainly based on a discounted cash flow model applied to total net income projected over the life of the concession, or over the life of the long-term lease (notably the Porte de Versailles long-term lease) or leasehold, if it exists or otherwise over a ten-year period, with an estimation of the asset's value at the end of the given time period, based either on the residual contractual value for concessions or on capitalised cash flows over the last year. The valuations carried out by the appraisers took into account total net income, which comprised net rents and ancillary services, as well as net income from car parks. The cost of maintenance works, major repairs, refurbishments, redevelopments and extensions, as well as concession or leasehold fees, are included in projected cash flow figures.
>
> The income statement for a given year (Y) records the change in value for each property, which is determined as follows: market value Y – [market value Y-1 + amount of works and other costs capitalised in year Y].
>
> Capital gains on disposals of investment properties are calculated by comparison with their latest market value recorded in the closing statement of financial position for the previous financial year.
>
> Properties under construction carried at cost are subject to impairment tests, determined on the basis of the estimated recoverable value of the project. The recoverable value of a project is assessed by the Development & Investment teams through the expected delivery date, expected development costs, and considering a market exit capitalisation rate and the expected net rents. When the estimated recoverable value is lower than net book value, an impairment provision is booked.
>
> Properties held for sale are identified separately in the statement of financial position.
>
> *(1) EPRA position paper on IFRS 13 – Fair value measurement and illustrative disclosures, February 2013.*
> *(2) Transfer taxes are valued on the assumption that the property is sold directly, even though the cost of these taxes can, in certain cases, be reduced by selling the property's holding company.*

As discussed in 2.1 above, the fair value of right-of-use assets that meet the definition of investment property will need to be determined (whether for disclosure or measurement purposes). The IASB acknowledged that there might be costs involved with determining the fair value of right-of-use assets, particularly for entities that are not in the property industry but sublease property, for example, because that property is not needed for use within their business. *[IFRS 16.BC179]*. However, the IASB views the determination of the fair value of right-of-use assets as relatively straightforward, even for an entity that is not in the property industry, if the sublease does not contain any options or variable lease payments. Determining the fair value would involve projecting the cash flows that the entity expects to receive from subleasing the asset. The IASB concluded that, determining these cash flows would normally be relatively straightforward because it is likely that a sublease would already be in place. *[IFRS 16.BC180]*.

Further, if leases have variable and optional payments, or if there is no active market for the right-of-use asset, the IASB views that the principles in IFRS 13 and IAS 40 are sufficient to help lessees to measure the fair value of those right-of-use assets. In particular, the IASB noted that paragraph 50(d) of IAS 40 explains when to include in the measurement of the right-of-use asset options and variable lease payments that are not included in the measurement of the lease liability. *[IFRS 16.BC181]*.

6.1.1 Methods of estimation

IFRS 13 does not specify or rank the techniques an entity must use to measure fair value. However, it requires them to be consistent with one or more of the three broad approaches: the market approach; the income approach; and the cost approach. *[IFRS 13.62]*. As discussed at 6.1.2 below, IFRS 13 does require an entity to prioritise observable inputs over unobservable inputs. See Chapter 14 at 14 for further discussion on selecting appropriate techniques and inputs.

IFRS 16 specifies the basis for initial recognition of the cost of an investment property held by a lessee as a right-of-use asset (see 4.5 above). In line with the discussion in 6 above, paragraph 33 of IAS 40 requires the investment property held by a lessee as a right-of-use asset to be remeasured, if necessary, to fair value if the entity chooses the fair value model. *[IAS 40.41]*. When a lessee uses the fair value model to measure an investment property that is held as a right-of-use asset, it will measure the right-of-use asset, and not the underlying property, at fair value. *[IAS 40.40A]*. When lease payments are at market rates, the fair value of an investment property held by a lessee as a right-of-use asset at acquisition, net of all expected lease payments (including those relating to recognised lease liabilities), should be zero. Thus, remeasuring a right-of-use asset from cost in accordance with IFRS 16 to fair value (taking into account the requirements in paragraph 50 of IAS 40 – see 6.1.4 below) should not give rise to any initial gain or loss, unless fair value is measured at different times. This could occur when an election to apply the fair value model is made after initial recognition. *[IAS 40.41]*.

When an entity first acquires an investment property (or when an existing property first becomes investment property after a change in use – see 9 below) there could be an indication that its fair value will not be reliably measurable on a continuing basis. For example, there might be clear evidence that the variability in the range of reasonable fair value measurements will be so great, and the probabilities of the various outcomes so difficult to assess, that the usefulness of a single measure of fair value will be negated. However, it cannot be over-emphasised that IAS 40 describes such circumstances as 'exceptional cases'. *[IAS 40.48]*. This is discussed further at 6.2 below.

6.1.2 Observable data

When selecting the most appropriate inputs to a fair value measurement from multiple available inputs, those that maximise the use of observable data, rather than unobservable data, should be selected. *[IFRS 13.67]*. Just because the volume or level of activity in a market has significantly decreased, it does not mean that transactions in that market are not orderly or do not represent fair value. *[IFRS 13.B43]*.

Entities will need to consider the individual facts and circumstances in making this assessment. Notwithstanding the need for judgement, an entity must have a reasonable basis for concluding that a current observable market price can be ignored based on a view that it represents a liquidation or distressed sale value. *[IFRS 13.B43]*. This is discussed further in Chapter 14 at 8.

6.1.3 Comparison with value in use

Fair value is not the same as 'value in use' as defined in IAS 36. In particular, it does not take account of the entity specific factors of the holder that would not generally be available to knowledgeable willing buyers such as additional value derived from holding a portfolio of investment property assets, synergies between the properties and other assets or legal rights or tax benefits or burdens pertaining to the current owner.

Fair value is also not the same as net realisable value as, for example, net realisable value does not have to take account of market required returns but would have to take into account cost to sell. *[IFRS 13.6(c), BC24]*. See also Chapter 14 at 2.2.3.

However, in most cases, it is unlikely that the 'value in use' of an individual property will exceed the fair value of that property – see 7.3 below.

6.1.4 'Double counting'

An entity must take care, when determining the carrying amount of investment property under the fair value model, not to double count assets or liabilities that are recognised separately. IAS 40 describes a number of situations where this might otherwise happen as follows:

- equipment such as lifts or air-conditioning is often an integral part of a building and is generally included in the fair value of the investment property, rather than recognised separately as property, plant and equipment (see 6.5 below);
- if an office is leased on a furnished basis, the fair value of the office generally includes the fair value of the furniture, because the rental income relates to the furnished office. When furniture is included in the fair value of investment property, an entity does not recognise that furniture as a separate asset (see 6.5 below);
- the fair value of investment property excludes prepaid or accrued operating lease income, because the entity recognises it as a separate liability or asset (see 6.6 below); and
- the fair value of investment property held by a lessee as a right-of-use asset reflects expected cash flows, including variable lease payments that are expected to become payable. Accordingly, if a valuation obtained for a property is net of all payments expected to be made, it will be necessary to add back any recognised lease liability, to arrive at the carrying amount of the investment property using the fair value model (see 6.7 below). *[IAS 40.50]*.

6.2 Inability to determine fair value of completed investment property

It is a rebuttable presumption that an entity can determine the fair value of a property reliably on a continuing basis, that is, on each subsequent occasion in which it records the investment property in its financial statements. *[IAS 40.53]*.

The standard emphasises that it is only in exceptional cases and only on initial recognition (either by acquisition or change in use – see 9 below) that the entity will be able to conclude that it will not be able to reliably measure the investment property's fair value on a continuing basis. *[IAS 40.53]*.

Additionally, entities are strongly discouraged from arguing that fair value cannot be reliably measured. It may be a possible argument when, and only when, the market for comparable properties is inactive (e.g. there are few recent transactions, price quotations are not current or observed transaction prices indicate that the seller was forced to sell) and alternative reliable measurements of fair value (for example, based on discounted cash flow projections) are not available. In such exceptional cases, the property should be measured using the cost model in IAS 16 for owned investment property, or cost model in accordance with IFRS 16 for investment property held by a lessee as a right-of-use asset (see Chapter 23 at 5.3.1.A), until its disposal and assumed to have a nil residual value. *[IAS 40.53]*. This means that an owned investment property has to be carried at cost and the building and its component parts depreciated over their useful lives (see 7 below). In these circumstances, IAS 16's revaluation model, under which assets may be revalued to fair value, is specifically ruled out. If this exceptional situation occurs, the cost model in IAS 16 or in IFRS 16 should continue to be applied until disposal of such property. *[IAS 40.54]*. This also means that if this exceptional situation occurs, investment property should continue to be measured at cost even if a reliable measure of fair value subsequently becomes available (such treatment is different for investment property under construction – see 6.3 below). Although an entity measures an individual property at cost for this reason, all other investment property must continue to be carried at fair value. *[IAS 40.54]*.

The above exception is not permitted for investment property that has been previously measured using the fair value model. Once a property is initially recognised at its fair value, it must always be so recognised until disposed of or reclassified for owner-occupation or development for subsequent sale in the ordinary course of the business, even if comparable market transactions become less frequent or market prices become less easily available. *[IAS 40.55]*.

6.3 The fair value of investment property under construction

Entities who wish to measure their completed investment property at fair value will also need to measure their investment property under construction at fair value (subject to fair value being reliably determinable). *[IAS 40.33, 53]*.

Determining the fair value of investment property under construction will often be more judgemental than for completed property because:

- there are generally no observable transactions for investment property under construction. Where such assets are transacted, this is typically when they are in the very early stages of development or when they are nearly complete and substantially let; and
- additional assumptions must be made about the risks and costs of any incomplete construction.

In January 2009, the International Valuation Standards Board ('IVSB') released an Interim Position Statement – *The Valuation of Investment Property under Construction under IAS 40*. This Position Statement acknowledged that few investment properties under construction are transferred between market participants except as part of a sale of the owning entity or where the seller is either insolvent or facing insolvency and therefore unable to complete the project.

Despite this, the Position Statement set out that since the property is being developed for either income or capital appreciation, the cash flows associated with its construction and completion should normally be readily identifiable and capable of reliable estimation. Consequently, the IVSB considered that it would be rare for the fair value of an investment property under construction not to be capable of reliable determination.

However, this latter comment was excluded from the final *Guidance Note – The Valuation of Investment Property under Construction* which was issued by the IVSB in February 2010. The IVSB seems to have concluded that it was not its role to comment on this area, thus, no comment about the reliability of estimation was included.

It is worth noting that, in light of the requirements of IFRS 13, an entity will have to determine whether fair value can be reliably measured or not under the requirements in that standard. This is discussed in Chapter 14 at 2.4.1.

In any event, some entities do consider that not all of their investment property under construction can be reliably measured and have developed criteria to make that assessment, see Extract 19.3 above for an example.

There were persistent concerns that, in some situations, the fair value of investment property under construction could not be measured reliably. Where an entity that chooses the fair value model for its investment property determines that the fair value of an investment property under construction is not reliably measurable but it expects the fair value to be reliably measurable when construction is complete, the IASB decided to allow such investment property under construction to be measured at cost until such time as the fair value becomes reliably measurable or construction is completed (whichever comes earlier). *[IAS 40.53]*.

IAS 40 also sets out the following:

- Once an entity becomes able to measure reliably the fair value of an investment property under construction that it has previously measured at cost (see 7 below), it should measure that property at its fair value. *[IAS 40.53A]*.

- Once construction of such property is complete, it is presumed that fair value can be measured reliably. If this is not the case, and this will be only in exceptional situations, the property should be accounted for using the cost model in accordance with IAS 16 for owned investment property (see 7 below) or cost model in accordance with IFRS 16 for investment property held by a lessee as a right-of-use asset (see Chapter 23 at 5.3.1.A), together with the other requirements discussed in 6.2 above, i.e. use the cost model until disposal of the property (even if subsequently its fair value becomes reliably determinable) and assume that it has a nil residual value. *[IAS 40.53A]*.

- The presumption that the fair value of investment property under construction can be measured reliably can be rebutted only on initial recognition. Therefore, an entity that has measured an item of investment property under construction at fair value may not subsequently conclude that the fair value of the completed investment property cannot be measured reliably. *[IAS 40.53B]*.

6.4 Transaction costs incurred by the reporting entity on acquisition

An issue that arises in practice is whether transaction costs that have been incurred by the reporting entity on purchase of an investment property should be taken into account in determining the subsequent fair value of the property when applying the fair value model. This is illustrated in the following example:

Example 19.2:   *The fair value model and transaction costs incurred at acquisition*

On 1 January 20X1 Entity A acquired an investment property for a purchase price of €10,000. In addition, Entity A incurred legal costs of €200 in connection with the purchase and paid property transfer tax of €400. Accordingly, the investment property was initially recorded at €10,600. Entity A applies the fair value model for subsequent measurement of investment property:

	Development of prices in property market	Appraised market value of property €	Cost of property initially recognised €	Difference €
Scenario 1	Unchanged	10,000	10,600	(600)
Scenario 2	Slightly increased	10,250	10,600	(350)
Scenario 3	Significantly increased	11,000	10,600	400
Scenario 4	Decreased	9,500	10,600	(1,100)

The issue that arises in practice is whether or not the acquisition-related transaction costs that were incurred by Entity A on 1 January 20X1 can be considered in determining the fair value of the investment property at the next reporting date.

In our view, the acquisition-related transaction costs incurred by Entity A may not be considered separately in determining the fair value of an investment property. In the example above, on the next reporting date the carrying value to be recorded in the statement of financial position is its fair value. Changes from the initial carrying amount to the appraised market value at the subsequent reporting date (reflected in the 'Difference' column in the table) are recognised in profit or loss.

Although IAS 40 states that transaction costs incurred by a purchaser on the acquisition of an investment property are included in the cost of the investment property at initial recognition, *[IAS 40.21]*, if an entity applies the fair value model, the same investment property that was recorded at cost on initial recognition is subsequently measured at fair value in accordance with IFRS 13. The fact that the cost of the investment property recorded on initial recognition included legal and other transaction costs is irrelevant to the subsequent fair valuation of the asset.

IFRS 13 clarifies that '[t]he price in the principal (or most advantageous) market used to measure the fair value of the asset or liability shall not be adjusted for transaction costs. Transaction costs shall be accounted for in accordance with other IFRSs. Transaction costs are not a characteristic of an asset or a liability; rather, they are specific to a transaction and will differ depending on how an entity enters into a transaction for the asset or liability.' *[IFRS 13.25]*. See Chapter 14 at 9.1.2 for further discussion.

Likewise, when measuring the fair value of an investment property, it is not appropriate to add the acquisition-related transaction costs incurred by the purchaser to fair value, as these have no relevance to the fair value of the property. Therefore, some or all of the transaction costs incurred when acquiring the investment property that were capitalised in accordance with IAS 40 will effectively be expensed as part of the subsequent fair value gain or loss.

6.5 Fixtures and fittings subsumed within fair value

Fixtures and fittings such as lifts or air conditioning units are usually reflected within the fair value of the investment property rather than being accounted for separately. *[IAS 40.50(a)]*. In other cases, additional assets may be necessary in order that the property can be used for its specific purposes. The standard refers to furniture within a property that is being let as furnished offices, and argues that this should not be recognised as a separate asset if it has been included in the fair value of the investment property. *[IAS 40.50(b)]*.

The entity may have other assets that have not been included within the valuation, in which case these will be recognised separately and accounted for in accordance with IAS 16.

6.6 Prepaid and accrued operating lease income

6.6.1 Accrued rental income and lease incentives

The requirement in IAS 40 not to double-count assets or liabilities recognised separately is most commonly encountered when the carrying value of an investment property is reduced below its fair value to the extent that a separate asset arises under IFRS 16. For example, when an entity offers an initial rent-free period to a lessee, it will recognise an asset in the rent-free period and then amortise it over the remaining lease term, thereby spreading the reduction in rental income over the term of the lease. The amount of the separate asset should therefore be deducted from the carrying value of the investment property in order to avoid double counting and therefore ensure the carrying value does not exceed fair value (see 4.9.1 above). *[IAS 40.50(c)]*.

The British Land Company PLC explains the treatment in its accounting policies:

> **Extract 19.4: The British Land Company PLC (2015)**
> NOTES TO THE ACCOUNTS [extract]
> 1   Basis of preparation, significant accounting policies and accounting judgements [extract]
> **Net rental income** [extract]
>
> Where a rent-free period is included in a lease, the rental income foregone is allocated evenly over the period from the date of lease commencement to the earliest termination date.
>
> Rental income from fixed and minimum guaranteed rent reviews is recognised on a straight-line basis to the earliest termination date. Where such rental income is recognised ahead of the related cash flow, an adjustment is made to ensure that the carrying value of the related property including the accrued rent does not exceed the external valuation.

This treatment can also be seen in Extracts 19.5 and 19.6 below.

6.6.2 Prepaid rental income

The same principles are applied when rental income arising from an operating lease is received in advance. This is demonstrated in the example below:

Example 19.3: Investment property and rent received in advance

A company owns land with an estimated value of £10m as at 1 January 20X1 that is accounted for as investment property. The company applies the fair value option in IAS 40 and has a reporting period ending on 31 December each year.

The land was not let until, on 30 December 20X1, a lease of 50 years was granted for consideration of £9.5m received in advance. The lease is considered to be an operating lease. No rental income was recognised in 20X1 as it was considered immaterial. An external valuer estimated that, after the grant of the 50-year lease, the fair value of the company's interest in the land as at 31 December 20X1 was £1m. As at 31 December 20X2 the external valuer estimated the fair value of the interest in the property was £1.2m.

The resultant accounting entries are summarised below.

Extracts from the ledgers for the year ended 31 December 20X1

	As at 1 January 20X1	Journal (1)	Journal (2)	Journal (3)	As at 31 December 20X1
Investment property	10.0	–	(9.0)	9.5	10.5
Cash	–	9.5	–	–	9.5
Deferred income	–	(9.5)	–	–	(9.5)
Net Assets	10.0	–	(9.0)	9.5	10.5
Share capital	10.0	–	–	–	10.0
Retained profit	–	–	(9.0)	9.5	0.5
Total Equity	10.0	–	(9.0)	9.5	10.5

Journals:
(1) Issue of lease (£9.5m received on issue of lease).
(2) Write down investment property to £1m external valuation.
(3) Write up book value of property by the amount of unamortised deferred revenue in the statement of financial position.

Extracts from the ledgers for the year ended 31 December 20X2

	As at 1 January 20X2	Journal (1)	Journal (2)	Journal (3)	As at 31 December 20X2
Investment property	10.5	–	(9.3)	9.31	10.51
Cash	9.5	–	–	–	9.5
Deferred income	(9.5)	0.19	–	–	(9.31)
Net Assets	10.5	0.19	(9.3)	9.31	10.7
Share capital	10.0	–	–	–	10.0
Retained profit	0.5	0.19	(9.3)	9.31	0.7
Total Equity	10.5	0.19	(9.3)	9.31	10.7

Journals:
(1) Amortise rent (one year of the £9.5m received for 50 years).

(2) Write down investment property to £1.2m external valuation.
(3) Write up the book value of property by the amount of unamortised deferred revenue in the statement of financial position (£9.31m).

An example of an entity dealing with this in practice can be seen in Extract 19.5 below:

Extract 19.5: The Crown Estate (2018)

Notes to the Group and Parent consolidated financial statements [extract]
18. Investment properties [extract]

		2018	
Group	Investment property £m	Properties under development £m	Total £m
At opening valuation (before lease incentives)	10,939.7	175.6	11,115.3
Acquisitions	129.5	–	129.5
Capital expenditure	69.1	72.1	141.2
Capital receipts	(8.1)	–	(8.1)
Transfer to other categories	134.3	(134.3)	–
Transfer from owner occupied properties	47.0	–	47.0
Disposals	(290.3)	–	(290.3)
Revaluation	774.5	(6.1)	768.4
Impairment of discontinued operation	–	–	–
At closing valuation (before lease incentives)	11,795.7	107.3	11,903.0
Deferred income from lease premia received	1,633.1	–	1,633.1
Net finance lease payable	2.5	–	2.5
Closing fair value – as reported	13,431.3	107.3	13,538.6
Reconciliation to valuation			
At closing valuation (before lease incentives)	11,795.7	107.3	11,903.0
Lease incentives	17.0	–	17.0
Market value	11,812.7	107.3	11,920.0

6.7 Valuation adjustment to the fair value of properties held under a lease

IAS 40 states that the fair value of investment property held by a lessee as a right-of-use asset will reflect expected cash flows, including variable lease payments that are expected to become payable. Accordingly, if a valuation obtained for a property is net of all payments expected to be made, it will be necessary to add back any recognised lease liability, to arrive at the carrying amount of the investment property using the fair value model. *[IAS 40.50(d)]*.

Therefore, if the entity obtains a property valuation net of the valuer's estimate of the present value of future lease obligations (which is usual practice), to the extent that the lease obligations have already been accounted for in the statement of financial position as a lease obligation, an amount is to be added back to arrive at the fair value of the investment property for the purposes of the financial statements.

Where an entity subsequently measures its investment properties using the fair value model, there is no difference in accounting for investment property held by a lessee as right-of-use assets, i.e. whether the lessor provided a finance lease or an operating lease to the lessee (see also 2.1 above).

The valuation adjustment referred to above is achieved by adjusting for the lease liability recognised in the financial statements.

This is illustrated using the information in the following example:

Example 19.4: Valuation of a property held under a lease

Entity A pays €991,000 for a 50-year leasehold interest in a property which is classified as an investment property using the fair value model. In addition, a ground rent of €10,000 is payable annually during the lease term, the present value of which is calculated at €99,000 using a discount rate of 10% which reflects the rate implicit in the lease at that time. The company has initially recognised the investment property at the following amount:

	€'000
Amount paid	991
Present value of the ground rent obligation on acquisition	99
Cost recorded for financial reporting purposes	1,090

Assume at the next reporting date the leasehold interest in the property has a fair value of €1,006,000 measured (based on market participant assumptions) as follows:

	€'000
Present value of estimated future lease income	1,089
Less: Present value of the ground rent obligation at the reporting date *	(83)
Fair value	1,006

* The market required yield has changed to 12%. Therefore, the present value of the ground rent obligations of €10,000 per annum for the remaining 49 years is now €83,000.

At the same time the ground rent lease liability has reduced to €98,000 as payments are made.

This would give the following results:

	€'000
Fair value	1,006
Add recognised lease liability	98
Carrying value for financial reporting purposes	1,104

The statement of financial position of Entity A would therefore contain the following items:

	Investment property €'000	Lease liability €'000
On acquisition	1,090	99
End of year 1	1,104	98

An example of this in practice can be seen in Extract 19.5 above and in Extract 19.6 below:

> *Extract 19.6: Land Securities Group PLC (2020)*
>
> Notes to the financial statements [extract]
> Section 3 – Properties [extract]
> 14.   Investment properties [extract]
>
> The market value of the Group's investment properties, as determined by the Group's external valuer, differs from the net book value presented in the balance sheet due to the Group presenting tenant finance leases, capitalised head leases and lease incentives separately. The following table reconciles the net book value of the investment properties to the market value.
>
> | | 2020
Group (excl.
joint ventures)
£m |
> |---|---:|
> | Market value | 11,802 |
> | Less: properties treated as finance leases | (249) |
> | Plus: head leases capitalised | 60 |
> | Less: tenant lease incentives | (316) |
> | Net book value | 11,297 |
> | Net deficit on revaluation of investment properties | (1,000) |

6.8 Future capital expenditure and development value ('highest and best use')

It is common for the value of land to reflect its potential future use and the value of land may increase in the event that the owner obtains any required permissions for a change in the use of that land.

It may be, for example, that a permission to change from an industrial to residential use will increase the value of the property as a whole, notwithstanding that the existing industrial buildings are still in place. This increase in value is typically attributable to the land, rather than the buildings.

It is therefore important to note that IFRS 13 requires consideration of all relevant factors in determining whether the highest and best use of a property can be something other than its current use at the measurement date. IFRS 13 presumes that an entity's current use of an asset is generally its highest and best use unless market or other factors suggest that a different use of that asset by market participants would maximise its value. *[IFRS 13.29]*. IFRS 13 states:

'A fair value measurement of a non-financial asset takes into account a market participant's ability to generate economic benefits by using the asset in its highest and best use or by selling it to another market participant that would use the asset in its highest and best use. The highest and best use of a non-financial asset takes into account the use of the asset that is physically possible, legally permissible and financially feasible, as follows:

(a) A use that is physically possible takes into account the physical characteristics of the asset that market participants would take into account when pricing the asset (e.g. the location or size of a property).

(b) A use that is legally permissible takes into account any legal restrictions on the use of the asset that market participants would take into account when pricing the asset (e.g. the zoning regulations applicable to a property).

(c) A use that is financially feasible takes into account whether a use of the asset that is physically possible and legally permissible generates adequate income or cash flows (taking into account the costs of converting the asset to that use) to produce an investment return that market participants would require from an investment in that asset put to that use.' *[IFRS 13.27-28]*.

Considerable judgement may then have to be applied in determining when an anticipated change is legally permissible. For example, if approval is required for rezoning land or for an alternative use of existing property interests, it may be necessary to assess whether such approval is a substantive legal requirement or not. See Chapter 14 at 10.1 for further discussion on determining highest and best use and the assessment of 'legally permissible'.

If management determines that the highest and best use of an asset is something other than its current use, certain valuation matters must be considered. Appraisals that reflect the effect of a reasonably anticipated change in what is legally permissible should be carefully evaluated. If the appraised value assumes that a change in use can be obtained, the valuation must also reflect the cost associated with obtaining approval for the change in use and transforming the asset, as well as capture the risk that the approval might not be granted (that is, uncertainty regarding the probability and timing of the approval).

Expectations about future improvements or modifications to be made to the property to reflect its highest and best use may be considered in the appraisal, such as the renovation of the property or the conversion of an office into condominiums, but only if and when other market participants would also consider making these investments and reflect only the cash flows that market participants would take into account when assessing fair value.

See Chapter 14 at 10 for further discussion on application of IFRS 13 requirements to non-financial assets which includes determining highest and best use.

6.9 Negative present value

In some cases, an entity expects that the present value of its payments relating to an investment property (other than payments relating to recognised liabilities) will exceed the present value of the related cash receipts. An entity should apply IAS 37 – *Provisions, Contingent Liabilities and Contingent Assets* – to determine whether a liability should be recognised and, if so, how that liability should be measured. *[IAS 40.52]*.

6.10 Deferred taxation for property held by a 'single asset' entity

It is common in many jurisdictions for investment property to be bought and sold by transferring ownership of a separate legal entity formed to hold the asset (a 'single asset' entity) rather than the asset itself. In addition to the issue on initial recognition discussed in 4.1.2 above, this matter created diversity in practice when determining the expected manner of recovery of the asset for the purposes of IAS 12, i.e. whether or not the parent entity should reflect the fact that an asset held by a single asset entity is likely to be disposed of by selling the shares of the entity rather than the asset itself, and if so, whether the deferred taxation would be recognised with reference to the shares rather than the underlying property.

The Interpretations Committee clarified in its July 2014 meeting that IAS 12 requires the parent to recognise in its consolidated financial statements both the deferred tax related to the property inside the single asset entity and the deferred tax related to the shares of that single asset entity (the outside), if:

- tax law attributes separate tax bases to the asset inside and to the shares;
- in the case of deferred tax assets, the related deductible temporary differences can be utilised; and
- no specific exceptions in IAS 12 apply.[20]

Accordingly, in determining the expected manner of recovery of a property held by a single asset entity for the purposes of IAS 12, the parent entity should have regard to the asset itself. In line with this, it would not be appropriate to measure deferred taxation with reference to selling the shares of the single asset entity or include the related effects of tax in the valuation of the underlying property.

For further discussions on recognition of deferred taxes for investment property and for single asset entities, see Chapter 33 at 8.4.7 and 8.4.10, respectively.

7 THE COST MODEL

Except in the cases described in 8 below, the cost model requires that investment property held by a lessee as a right-of-use asset be measured after initial recognition in accordance with IFRS 16 and under the cost model set out in IAS 16 for owned investment property. *[IAS 40.56]*.

For further discussion on subsequent measurement of a right-of-use asset applying the cost model under IFRS 16, see Chapter 23 at 5.3.1.A.

Applying the cost model under IAS 16, this means that the owned asset must be recognised at cost, depreciated systematically over its useful life and impaired when appropriate. *[IAS 16.30]*. The residual value and useful life of each owned investment property must be reviewed at least at each financial year-end and, if expectations differ from previous estimates, the changes must be accounted for as a change in accounting estimate in accordance with IAS 8. *[IAS 16.51]*.

If an entity adopts the cost model, the fair value of its investment property must be disclosed (see 12.3 below).

7.1 Initial recognition

7.1.1 Identification of physical parts

The cost of the property must be analysed into appropriate significant components, each of which will have to be depreciated separately (see also Chapter 18 at 3.2 and 5.1).

The analysis into significant components is rarely a straightforward exercise since properties typically contain a large number of components with varying useful lives. Klépierre, which adopted the cost model for investment property prior to 2016 (see 7.2 below), disclosed its approach to this exercise – see Extract 19.7 below.

> Extract 19.7: Klépierre (2015)
> 6. Consolidated financial statements as of December 31, 2015
> 6.5. Appendices [extract]
> Note 2. Accounting principles and methods [extract]
> 2.10. Investment property [extract]
> 2.10.2 The component method
>
> The component method is applied based on the recommendations of the Fédération des Sociétés Immobilières et Foncières (French Federation of Property Companies) for components and useful life:
> - for properties developed by the companies themselves, assets are classified by component type and recognized at cost;
> - for other properties, components are broken down into four categories: business premises, shopping centers, offices and residential properties.
>
> Four components have been identified for each of these asset types (in addition to land):
> - structures;
> - facades, cladding and roofing;
> - general and technical installations (GTI);
> - fittings.
>
> Components are broken down based on the history and technical characteristics of each building.
>
> Klépierre uses the following matrix to determine components:
>
> | | Shopping centers | | Retail stores | |
> |---|---|---|---|---|
> | | Period | QP | Period | QP |
> | Structures | 30 to 50 years | 50% | 30 to 40 years | 50% |
> | Facades | 25 years | 15% | 15 to 25 years | 15% |
> | GTI | 20 years | 25% | 10 to 20 years | 25% |
> | Fitting | 10 to 15 years | 10% | 5 to 15 years | 10% |
>
> A wear and tear ratio is applied when the acquired property is not new. Purchase costs are split between land and buildings. The proportion allocated to buildings is amortized over the useful life of the structures. The residual value is equivalent to the current estimate of the amount the Company would achieve if the asset concerned were already of an age and condition commensurate with the end of its useful life, less disposal expenses.
>
> Given the useful life periods applied, the residual value of components is zero.

An entity is also required to recognise replacement parts and derecognise the replaced part as described in Chapter 18 at 7.

7.1.2 Identification of non-physical parts

IAS 16 sets out that if an entity acquires property, plant and equipment subject to an operating lease in which it is the lessor, it may be appropriate to depreciate separately amounts reflected in the cost of that item that are attributable to favourable or unfavourable lease terms relative to market terms. *[IAS 16.44]*. This will therefore apply to investment property accounted for under the cost model (see 4.7 above).

7.2 Incidence of use of the cost model

It appears less common for entities to measure investment property using the cost model than the fair value model.

In previous years, EY real estate financial statement surveys have consistently found that over 90% of the companies in those surveys used the fair value model (e.g. about 98% based on the recent survey published in 2019). There also seems to be a general, although not universal, market consensus among existing IFRS reporters that the fair value model is the more appropriate. For example, in its latest *Best Practices Recommendations Guidelines* issued in October 2019, the European Public Real Estate Association ('EPRA') recommends to its members that 'Real estate companies should account for their property investments based upon the fair value model.'[21]

Some IFRS reporters have moved from the cost model. For example, Klépierre adopted the cost model until the middle of 2016 when the fair value model was adopted. It made the following statement in its 2016 financial statements:

Extract 19.8: Klépierre (2016)

3   FINANCIAL STATEMENTS
3.1   Consolidated financial statements as of December 31, 2016
3.1.5   Appendices [extract]
NOTE 2 Significant accounting policies [extract]
2.4   Change in accounting policies (IAS 8) – Fair value option according to IAS 40

In the second half of 2016, Klépierre decided to choose the fair value method of IAS 40 for the accounting of its investment properties. Therefore the group presents comparative financial statements for 2015 (Consolidated statements of comprehensive income and Consolidated statements of financial position) showing the items affected by this change in accounting method. The fair value method is the preferential method under the provisions of IAS 40 and also the one recommended by the EPRA (European Public Real Estate Association). The fair value option facilitates comparisons with the financial statements of other property companies of which the majority applies this model. The change of accounting method was motivated by these elements.

The use of the cost model (rather than the fair value model) removes the need to recognise gains from increases in the fair value of property within profit or loss. However, it is unlikely to insulate an entity from reporting falls in the fair value of investment property below the depreciated cost of the property – see 7.3 below.

7.3 Impairment

Investment property measured at cost is subject to the requirements of IAS 36 in respect of impairment. As set out in Chapter 20 at 5, IAS 36 requires a recoverable amount to be determined as the higher of (i) value in use and (ii) fair value less costs of disposal. *[IAS 36.18]*.

Both value in use calculation and fair value calculation (where there is no price quoted for identical assets on an active market) are typically based on discounted cash flow models. The former will typically use entity specific cash flows, whilst the latter would generally use market expected cash flows. Both would use a market determined discount rate.

For a rental generating asset such as an investment property, the future cash flows to be taken into account in any projection would, in simple terms, be (i) the rental stream under the existing lease arrangements and (ii) an estimate of any rental stream thereafter.

The cash flows expected to be generated from the existing lease would be the same whether the basis was entity specific or market expected cash flows.

The estimate of any rental stream thereafter would also be the same unless the entity forecast it would outperform the market and achieve superior cash flows. This is unlikely to be an acceptable basis for a forecast as no entity can realistically expect to outperform the market for its whole portfolio or do so for more than the short term. Therefore, a forecast that cash flows from individual properties will outperform the market would have to be considered with scepticism.

Consequently, we would regard it as being a rare circumstance where the value in use of an individual investment property could be said to be higher than the fair value of that property. Indeed, in some circumstances – for example, where a fair value is partly dependent on a gain from planned future development (see 6.8 above) but where that expenditure is not to be allowed to be considered in a value in use calculation – value in use may be lower than fair value.

8 IFRS 5 AND INVESTMENT PROPERTY

Investment property measured using the cost model (under IAS 16 or IFRS 16 – see 7 above) which meets the criteria to be classified as held for sale, or is included within a disposal group classified as held for sale, is measured in accordance with IFRS 5. *[IAS 40.56]*. This means that such property will be held at the lower of carrying amount and fair value less costs to sell, and depreciation of the asset will cease. *[IFRS 5.15, 25]*.

As set out in Chapter 4 at 2.2.1, investment property measured at fair value is not subject to the measurement requirements of IFRS 5. However, such property is subject to the presentation requirements of that standard. Consequently, investment property that meets the definition of held for sale is required to be presented separately from other assets in the statement of financial position (see Chapter 4 at 2.2.4).

An example of an entity applying the presentation requirements of IFRS 5 to investment property measured at fair value is Accelerate Property Fund Ltd in its 2019 financial statements – see Extract 19.9 below.

Extract 19.9: Accelerate Property Fund Ltd (2019)
ANNUAL FINANCIAL STATEMENTS [extract]
CONSOLIDATED STATEMENT OF FINANCIAL POSITION [extract]

	Note(s)	2019 R'000
ASSETS		
Non-current assets		
Property, plant and equipment	12	688
Investment property	10	12 203 592
Derivatives	24	1 598
		12 205 878
Current assets		
Trade and other receivables	13	589 559
Current tax receivable	27	5 534
Derivatives	24	–
Cash and cash equivalents	14	84 131
		679 224
Non-current assets held for sale	26	789 707
Total assets		13 674 809

NOTES TO THE CONSOLIDATED AUDITED ANNUAL FINANCIAL STATEMENTS [extract]
26. NON-CURRENT ASSETS HELD FOR SALE [extract]

The following non-core office property are held for sale at 31 March 2019:
- Mr Price
- The Pines
- Glen Gables
- East Lynn
- Wanooka Place
- Flora Park
- 89 Hertzog Boulevard
- 99 - 101 Hertzog Boulevard
- 73 Hertzog Boulevard

Assets and liabilities
Non-current assets held for sale

	2019 R'000
Investment property	789 707

Investment property measured using the cost model is subject to both the measurement and presentation requirements of IFRS 5. Icade, which uses the cost model for its investment property, provides an accounting policy for such property held for sale in its 2017 financial statements – see Extract 19.10 below.

> *Extract 19.10: Icade (2017)*
>
> 2.   Notes to the consolidated financial statements [extract]
> Note 1. Accounting principles [extract]
> 1.10.   Assets held for sale and discontinued operations [extract]
>
> In accordance with IFRS 5, if the Group decides to dispose of an asset or group of assets, it should be classified as held for sale if:
>
> - the asset or group of assets is available for immediate sale in its present condition subject only to terms that are usual and customary for sales of such assets;
> - it is highly likely to be sold within one year.
>
> Consequently, this asset or group of assets is shown separately as "Assets held for sale" on the balance sheet. The liabilities related to this asset or group of assets are also shown separately on the liabilities side of the balance sheet.
>
> For the Group, only assets meeting the above criteria and subject to a formal disposal decision at the appropriate management level are classified as assets held for sale. The accounting consequences are as follows:
>
> - the asset (or group of assets) held for sale is measured at the lower of carrying amount and fair value less costs to sell;
> - the asset stops being depreciated with effect from the date of transfer.

9 TRANSFER OF ASSETS TO OR FROM INVESTMENT PROPERTY

IAS 40 specifies the circumstances in which a property, including property under construction or development, becomes, or ceases to be, an investment property. An entity should 'transfer a property to, or from, investment property when, and only when, there is a change in use. A change in use occurs when the property meets, or ceases to meet, the definition of investment property and there is evidence of the change in use. In isolation, a change in management's intentions for the use of a property does not provide evidence of a change in use. Examples of evidence of a change in use include:

(a) commencement of owner-occupation, or of development with a view to owner-occupation, for a transfer from investment property to owner-occupied property;

(b) commencement of development with a view to sale, for a transfer from investment property to inventories;

(c) end of owner-occupation, for a transfer from owner-occupied property to investment property; and

(d) inception of an operating lease to another party, for a transfer from inventories to investment property' (but see 2.3 above). *[IAS 40.57]*.

Extract 19.11 below describes how Land Securities Group PLC dealt with the requirements of (b) above.

> **Extract 19.11: Land Securities Group PLC (2020)**
> Notes to the financial statements [extract]
> Section 3 – Properties [extract]
> Accounting policy [extract]
>
> **Transfers between investment properties and trading properties**
>
> When the Group begins to redevelop an existing investment property for continued future use as an investment property, the property continues to be held as an investment property. When the Group begins to redevelop an existing investment property with a view to sell, the property is transferred to trading properties and held as a current asset. The property is re-measured to fair value as at the date of the transfer with any gain or loss being taken to the income statement. The re-measured amount becomes the deemed cost at which the property is then carried in trading properties.

Paragraph 57 of IAS 40, as described above, establishes a guiding principle regarding transfers to or from investment property based on whether there is evidence of a change in use and provides a non-exhaustive list of examples of such evidence. It reflects the principle that a change in use would involve:

(a) an assessment of whether a property meets, or has ceased to meet, the definition of investment property; and

(b) supporting evidence that a change in use has occurred.

Applying this principle, an entity transfers property under construction or development to, or from, investment property when, and only when, there is a change in the use of such property, supported by evidence. *[IAS 40.BC25, BC26]*.

Accordingly, a change in management's intentions, in isolation, would not be enough to support a transfer of property. This is because management's intentions, alone, do not provide evidence of a change in use. Observable actions toward effecting a change in use must have been taken by the entity during the reporting period to provide evidence that such a change has occurred. *[IAS 40.BC27]*.

The assessment of whether a change in use has occurred is based on an assessment of all the facts and circumstances and that judgement is needed to determine whether a property qualifies as investment property. *[IAS 40.BC28]*.

We illustrate the application of this principle with an example below:

Example 19.5: Transfers from inventory

In 20X1, an entity purchased land with the intention of constructing an apartment building on the land and selling the apartments to private customers. Accordingly, the land was classified as inventory. During 20X1, the prices for residential properties decreased and the entity decided to change its original business plans at the beginning of 20X2. Instead of constructing an apartment building and selling the apartments, the entity decided to construct an office building that it would lease out to tenants. The entity holds and manages other investment property as well.

During the first half of 20X2, the entity obtained permission from the relevant authorities to commence the construction and hired an architect to design the office building. The physical construction of the office building began in August 20X2. No operating leases had been agreed with other parties for the lease of office space. However, negotiations had been held with potential tenants.

The inception of an operating lease is generally evidence of a change in use for a transfer from inventories to investment property. *[IAS 40.57(d)]*. However, even in the absence of the inception of an operating lease, there may be other circumstances that provide evidence of a change in use. We would generally conclude that there is sufficient evidence for a change in use from inventory to investment property if all of the following criteria are met:

- the entity has prepared a business plan that reflects the future rental income generated by the property and this is supported with evidence that there is demand for rental space;
- the entity can demonstrate that it has the resources, including the necessary financing or capital, to hold and manage an investment property (which requires different skills than developing a property). If the entity also owns other investment property, this could be more easily demonstrated. However, if this property would be the entity's only investment property, it may be harder to demonstrate this;
- the change in use is legally permissible. That is, the entity has obtained permission from relevant authorities for the change in use. In cases where the approval of the change in use is merely a routine or a non-substantive legal requirement (i.e. not at the discretion of the authorities), the entity's request for permission may be sufficient evidence; and
- if the property must be further developed for the change in use, development has commenced.

For the scenario described in the fact pattern above, the entity met the above criteria at the point in time when it obtained permission from the relevant authorities to change the use of the property and commenced development of the property by hiring an architect. At that time, the land would be transferred from inventory to investment property.

9.1 Transfers from investment property to inventory

Transfers to inventory are more difficult to deal with by way of the application of a general principle since IFRS 5 explicitly deals with investment property held for sale. IAS 40 allows a transfer to inventory only when there is a change in use as evidenced, for example, by the start of development with a view to subsequent sale. *[IAS 40.57]*.

If an entity decides to dispose of an investment property without development with a view to sale, it is unlikely to be transferred to inventory as IFRS 5 is applied to property held for sale to the extent that the requirements therein are met (see 8 above).

The IASB is aware of this inconsistency in the application of IFRS 5 and IAS 2 to investment property and in 2010 it asked the Interpretations Committee to consider any necessary interpretation to resolve it. However, the Interpretations Committee decided to recommend proposals that indicated no change to existing practice.

Consequently, this means that, unless there is development with a view to sale, it may not be possible to reclassify investment property as inventory even if the entity holding that property changes its intentions and is no longer holding that property for rental or capital appreciation. Accordingly, when an entity decides to dispose of an investment property without development, it should continue to classify the property as an investment property until it is derecognised (see 10 below) and should not reclassify it as inventory. Similarly, if an entity begins to redevelop an existing investment property for continued future use as investment property, the property remains an investment property and is not reclassified as owner-occupied property during the redevelopment. *[IAS 40.58]*.

9.2 Accounting treatment of transfers

When an entity uses the cost model for investment property, transfers between investment property, owner-occupied property and inventories do not change the carrying amount of the property transferred and they do not change the cost of that property for measurement or disclosure purposes. *[IAS 40.59]*.

Transfers to and from investment property under the fair value model are accounted for as follows:

- *Transfers from inventory:* any difference between the fair value of the property at date of change in use and its previous carrying amount should be recognised in profit or loss. *[IAS 40.63]*. This treatment is consistent with the treatment of sales of inventories. *[IAS 40.64]*. However, this does not mean that revenue should be recognised upon transfer of an inventory to investment property because control of the property is not transferred to a customer (i.e. the same property remains with the entity) and it is not a transaction that has commercial substance.

- *Transfers to inventory or owner-occupation:* the cost for subsequent accounting for inventories under IAS 2, or for owner-occupied property under IAS 16 or IFRS 16, should be the property's fair value at the date of change in use. *[IAS 40.60]*.

- *Transfers from owner-occupation:* IAS 16 will be applied for owned property and IFRS 16 for property held by a lessee as a right-of-use asset up to the date of change in use. At that date, any difference between the carrying amount under IAS 16 or IFRS 16 and the fair value should be treated in the same way as a revaluation under IAS 16. *[IAS 40.61]*.

If the owner-occupied property had not previously been revalued, the transfer does not imply that the entity has now chosen a policy of revaluation for other property accounted for under IAS 16 in the same class. The treatment depends on whether it is a decrease or increase in value and whether the asset had previously been revalued or impaired in value.

The treatment required by IAS 40 is as follows. Up to the date when an owner-occupied property becomes an investment property carried at fair value, an entity depreciates the property (or the right-of use asset) and recognises any impairment losses that have occurred. The entity treats any difference at that date between the carrying amount of the property in accordance with IAS 16 or IFRS 16 and its fair value in the same way as a revaluation in accordance with IAS 16.

'In other words:

(a) any resulting decrease in the carrying amount of the property is recognised in profit or loss. However, to the extent that an amount is included in revaluation surplus for that property, the decrease is recognised in other comprehensive income and reduces the revaluation surplus within equity.

(b) any resulting increase in the carrying amount is treated as follows:

   (i) to the extent that the increase reverses a previous impairment loss for that property, the increase is recognised in profit or loss. The amount recognised in profit or loss does not exceed the amount needed to restore the carrying amount to the carrying amount that would have been determined (net of depreciation) had no impairment loss been recognised.

   (ii) any remaining part of the increase is recognised in other comprehensive income and increases the revaluation surplus within equity. On subsequent disposal of the investment property, the revaluation surplus included in equity may be transferred to retained earnings. The transfer from revaluation surplus to retained earnings is not made through profit or loss.' *[IAS 40.62]*.

IAS 40 also reconfirms that when an entity completes the construction or development of a self-constructed investment property that will be carried at fair value (i.e. no actual reclassification to investment property), any difference between the fair value of the property at that date and its previous carrying amount shall be recognised in profit or loss. *[IAS 40.65]*.

10 DISPOSAL OF INVESTMENT PROPERTY

IAS 40 requires that an investment property should be removed from the statement of financial position ('derecognised') on disposal or when it is permanently withdrawn from use and no future economic benefits are expected from its disposal. *[IAS 40.66]*.

A disposal of an investment property may be achieved by:
- its sale;
- when it becomes the subject of a finance lease (the owner becoming the lessor); or
- when it becomes the subject of a sale and leaseback deal resulting in an operating lease (the original owner becoming the lessee). *[IAS 40.67]*.

These derecognition rules also apply to a part of the investment property that has been replaced (see 10.3 below).

IFRS 16 applies if a property is disposed of by the owner becoming a lessor in a finance lease (see Chapter 23 at 6.2), or if a property is the subject of a sale and leaseback transaction (see Chapter 23 at 8). *[IAS 40.67]*.

If disposal of investment property is achieved by sale, the determination of the timing of recognition of any gain or loss should be in accordance with IFRS 15. Consequently, the date of disposal for investment property that is sold is the date the recipient obtains control of the investment property in accordance with the requirements for determining when a performance obligation is satisfied in IFRS 15. *[IAS 40.67]*. IFRS 15 requires revenue (and a gain or loss on disposal of a non-current asset not in the ordinary course of business) to be recognised when a performance obligation is satisfied, which will be when control of the asset is transferred to the customer. Control may be transferred at a point in time or over time. *[IFRS 15.31, 32]*. Accordingly, entities that dispose of an investment property through sale should recognise a gain or loss on disposal when control of the property transfers, which may be at a point in time. In many cases, control will transfer when the buyer obtains legal title and physical possession of the asset. However, this may occur prior to legal settlement if it can be demonstrated that control has passed to the buyer before that date.

Extract 19.12 below describes how Land Securities Group PLC dealt with the requirements described above.

> *Extract 19.12: Land Securities Group PLC (2020)*
> Notes to the financial statements [extract]
> Section 3 – Properties [extract]
> Accounting policy [extract]
>
> Disposal of properties [extract]
>
> Properties are treated as disposed when control of the property is transferred to the buyer. Typically, this will either occur on unconditional exchange or on completion. Where completion is expected to occur significantly after exchange, or where the Group continues to have significant outstanding obligations after exchange, the control will not usually transfer to the buyer until completion.

For the detailed discussion and requirements of IFRS 15 on satisfaction of performance obligations, see Chapter 30.

10.1 Calculation of gain or loss on disposal

Gains and losses on retirement or disposal of investment property are calculated based on the difference between the net disposal proceeds (after deducting direct costs of disposal) and the carrying amount of the asset. *[IAS 40.69]*. IAS 40 does not give guidance on how to determine the carrying amount of the asset. Possible alternatives would include the use of (i) the carrying amount in the financial statements of the last full period of account, or (ii) the carrying amount in the latest interim financial statements, or (iii) the updated carrying amount at the date of disposal. In our view, this is a policy choice for an entity to make and is primarily a matter of income statement presentation to the extent that an entity presents gains and losses on disposal separately from gains and losses on revaluation. This choice is illustrated in Extract 19.3 above where Unibail-Rodamco-Westfield uses the 'full period of account' approach.

Gains and losses on retirement or disposal of investment property are recognised in profit or loss, unless it is a sale and leaseback and IFRS 16 requires a different treatment, in the period of retirement or disposal (see also 12.4 below). *[IAS 40.69]*. Refer to Chapter 23 at 8 for a discussion of sale and leaseback under IFRS 16.

The amount of consideration to be included in the gain or loss arising from the derecognition of an investment property is determined in accordance with the requirements for determining the transaction price in paragraphs 47-72 of IFRS 15. *[IAS 40.70]*. Under IFRS 15, an entity is required to consider the terms of the contract and its customary business practices in determining the transaction price. Transaction price is defined as the amount of consideration to which an entity expects to be entitled in exchange for transferring the property to a buyer, excluding amounts collected on behalf of third parties (e.g. sales taxes). The consideration in a contract may include fixed amounts, variable amounts, or both. *[IFRS 15.47]*.

In many cases, the transaction price may be readily determined if the entity receives payment when it transfers the property and the price is fixed. In other situations, it could be more challenging as it may be affected by the nature, timing and amounts of consideration.

Determining the transaction price is discussed in detail in Chapter 29 at 2.

Subsequent changes to the estimated amount of the consideration included in the gain or loss should be accounted for in accordance with the requirements for changes in the transaction price in IFRS 15. *[IAS 40.70]*. This is further discussed in Chapter 29 at 3.5.

If an entity retains any liabilities after disposing of an investment property these are measured and accounted for in accordance with IAS 37 or other relevant standards. *[IAS 40.71]*. Accounting for such liabilities depends on specific facts and circumstances as such a liability may represent a provision or a contingent liability under IAS 37, or a financial liability under IFRS 9, or a separate performance obligation or variable consideration under IFRS 15.

Retention of liabilities on sale of goods may indicate that the seller has continuing involvement to the extent usually associated with ownership. Under IFRS 15, retention of liabilities or the existence of continuing managerial involvement might indicate that control of goods has not passed to a buyer, but on their own do not affect whether an entity can recognise a sale and the associated profit from the transfer of the property. Instead, an entity might need to consider whether it represents an assurance-type or service-type warranty or consideration payable to a customer and whether variable consideration requirements would apply. See also related discussions in Chapter 29 at 2.2.1.B.

10.2 Sale prior to completion of construction

It should be noted that property that is subject to sale prior to completion of construction, if not previously classified as investment property, is likely to be property intended for sale in the ordinary course of business (see 2.6 above) and is therefore not likely to be investment property. Accordingly, the requirements in IFRS 15 should be followed.

If, however, the property subject to sale prior to completion of construction is previously classified as investment property, guidance in IAS 40 would be followed – see discussions in 10 and 10.1 above. Any consequent construction services to be provided by the seller would likely be subjected to the requirements of IFRS 15.

For further discussion of IFRS 15, see Chapters 27 to 32.

10.3 Replacement of parts of investment property

When an entity that applies the fair value model wishes to capitalise a replacement part (provided it meets the criteria at 3 above), the question arises of how to deal with the cost of the new part and the carrying value of the original. The basic principle in IAS 40 is that the entity derecognises the carrying value of the replaced part. However, the problem frequently encountered is that even if the cost of the old part is known, its carrying value – at fair value – is usually by no means clear. It is possible also that the fair value may already reflect the loss in value of the part to be replaced, because the valuation reflected the fact that an acquirer would reduce the price accordingly. *[IAS 40.68]*.

As all fair value changes are taken to profit or loss, the standard concludes that it is not necessary to identify separately the elements that relate to replacements from other fair value movements. Therefore, if it is not practical to identify the amount by which fair value should be reduced for the part replaced, the cost of the replacement is added to the carrying amount of the asset and the fair value of the investment property as a whole is reassessed. The standard notes that this is the treatment that would be applied to additions that did not involve replacing any existing part of the property. *[IAS 40.68]*.

If the investment property is carried under the cost model, then the entity should derecognise the carrying amount of the original part. A replaced part may not have been depreciated separately, in which case, if it is not practicable to determine the carrying amount of the replaced part, the standard allows the entity to use the cost of the replacement as an indication of an appropriate carrying value. This does not mean that the entity has to apply depreciated replacement cost, rather that it can use the cost of the replacement as an indication of the original cost of the replaced part in order to reconstruct a suitable carrying amount for the replaced part. *[IAS 40.68]*.

10.4 Compensation from third parties

IAS 40 applies the same rules as IAS 16 to the treatment of compensation from third parties if property has been impaired, lost or given up (see Chapter 18 at 5.7). It stresses that impairments or losses of investment property, related claims for or payments of compensation from third parties and any subsequent purchase or construction of replacement assets are separate economic events that have to be accounted for separately. *[IAS 40.73]*.

Impairment of investment property will be recorded automatically if the fair value model is used; but if the property is accounted for using the cost model, it is to be calculated in accordance with IAS 36 (see 7.3 above and Chapter 20). If the entity no longer owns the asset, for example because it has been destroyed or subject to a compulsory purchase order, it will be derecognised (see 10 above). Compensation from third parties (for example, from an insurance company) for property that was impaired, lost or given up is recognised in profit or loss when it becomes receivable. The cost of assets restored, purchased or constructed as replacements is accounted for wholly on its own merits according to the recognition and measurement rules covered in 3 and 4 above. *[IAS 40.72, 73]*.

11 INTERIM REPORTING AND IAS 40

IAS 34 – *Interim Financial Reporting* – requires the use of the same principles for the recognition and the definitions of assets, liabilities, income and expenses for interim periods as will be used in annual financial statements.

IAS 40 requires, for those entities using the fair value model, investment property to be presented at fair value at the end of the reporting period. Accordingly, investment property measured using the fair value model should also be measured at fair value in any interim financial reports. IAS 34 expects this as it includes the following guidance in Part C of the illustrative examples accompanying the standard:

'IAS 16 *Property, Plant and Equipment* allows an entity to choose as its accounting policy the revaluation model whereby items of property, plant and equipment are revalued to fair value. Similarly, IAS 40 requires an entity to measure the fair value of investment property. For those measurements, an entity may rely on professionally qualified valuers at annual reporting dates though not at interim reporting date.' *[IAS 34 IE Example C7]*.

The United Kingdom regulator made a similar point in its 2009 report on its activities. It stated that:

'A key principle of IAS 34, "Interim Financial Reporting", is that interim accounts should be prepared applying the same accounting policies as those applied to the annual accounts. IAS 40, "Investment Property" requires companies applying the fair value model to carry their properties at fair value with changes reported in the income statement. Properties are therefore required to be carried at fair value at the half-year stage.'[22]

For those entities using the cost model in annual financial statements, IAS 40 requires the disclosure of the fair value of investment property (see 12.3 below). For interim financial statements prepared under IAS 34, there is no such explicit disclosure requirement. Preparers of the financial statements should therefore consider the principle of IAS 34 which is that:

'Timely and reliable interim financial reporting improves the ability of investors, creditors, and others to understand an entity's capacity to generate earnings and cash flows and its financial condition and liquidity.' *[IAS 34 Objective]*.

It is likely that an understanding of the fair value of investment property at the end of an interim reporting period would help this purpose.

In addition, Part C of the illustrative examples to IAS 34 sets out that IAS 40 requires an entity to estimate the fair value of investment property. It does not distinguish between those entities that measure investment property at fair value and those entities that use the cost model and disclose fair value.

Consequently, it is our view that the fair value of investment property at the end of the interim period should usually be disclosed in interim financial reports for those entities using the cost model in IAS 40.

IAS 34 is discussed in more detail in Chapter 41.

12 THE DISCLOSURE REQUIREMENTS OF IAS 40

For entities that adopt the fair value option in IAS 40, attention will focus on the judgemental and subjective aspects of property valuations, because they will be reported in profit or loss. IAS 40 requires significant amounts of information to be disclosed about these judgements and the cash-related performance of the investment property, as set out below.

Note also that the disclosures below apply in addition to those in IFRS 16 which require the owner of an investment property to provide lessors' disclosures about leases into which it has entered. IAS 40 also requires a lessee that holds an investment property as a right-of-use asset to provide lessees' disclosures as required by IFRS 16 and lessors' disclosures as required by IFRS 16 for any operating leases into which it has entered. *[IAS 40.74]*. Accordingly, see Chapter 23 at 5.8 and 6.7 for the required disclosures of lessees and lessors, respectively.

12.1 Disclosures under both fair value and cost models

Whichever model is chosen, fair value or cost, IAS 40 requires all entities to disclose the fair value of their investment property. Therefore, the following disclosures are required in both instances:

- whether the entity applies the cost model or the fair value model;
- when classification is difficult, the criteria it uses to distinguish investment property from owner-occupied property and from property held for sale in the ordinary course of business;
- the extent to which the fair value of investment property (as measured or disclosed in the financial statements) is based on a valuation by an independent valuer who holds a recognised and relevant professional qualification and has recent experience in the location and category of the investment property being valued. If there has been no such valuation, that fact shall be disclosed (e.g. a statement that the fair value of investment property is based on internal appraisals rather than on a valuation by an independent valuer as described above);
- the amounts recognised in profit or loss for:
  - rental income from investment property;

- direct operating expenses (including repairs and maintenance) arising from investment property that generated rental income during the period (see 12.1.3 below);
- direct operating expenses (including repairs and maintenance) arising from investment property that did not generate rental income during the period (see 12.1.3 below); and
- the cumulative change in fair value recognised in profit or loss on sale of an investment property from a pool of assets in which the cost model is used into a pool in which the fair value model is used (see 5.1 above);
- the existence and amounts of restrictions on the realisability of investment property or the remittance of income and proceeds of disposal; and
- contractual obligations to purchase, construct or develop investment property or for repairs, maintenance or enhancements. *[IAS 40.75]*.

12.1.1 Methods and assumptions in fair value estimates

IFRS 13 includes a fair value hierarchy which prioritises the inputs used in a fair value measurement. The hierarchy is defined as follows:

- Level 1 inputs – Quoted prices (unadjusted) in active markets for identical assets or liabilities that the entity can access at the measurement date;
- Level 2 inputs – Inputs other than quoted prices included with Level 1 that are observable for the asset or liability, either directly or indirectly; and
- Level 3 inputs – Unobservable inputs for the asset or liability. *[IFRS 13 Appendix A]*.

IFRS 13 also uses its fair value hierarchy to categorise each fair value measurement in its entirety for disclosure purposes. Categorisation within the hierarchy is based on the lowest level input that is significant to the fair value measurement as a whole. This is discussed further in Chapter 14 at 16.2.

Significant differences in disclosure requirements apply to fair value measurements categorised within each level of the hierarchy to provide users with insight into the observability of the fair value measurement (the full disclosure requirements of IFRS 13 are discussed further in Chapter 14 at 20).

In our view, due to the lack of an active market for identical assets, it would be rare for real estate to be categorised within Level 1 of the fair value hierarchy.

In market conditions where similar real estate is actively purchased and sold, and the transactions are observable, the fair value measurement might be categorised within Level 2. This categorisation will be unusual for real estate, but that determination will depend on the facts and circumstances, including the significance of adjustments to observable data.

In this regard, IFRS 13 provides a real estate specific example stating that a Level 2 input would be the price per square metre for the property interest derived from observable market data, e.g. multiples derived from prices in observed transactions involving comparable (i.e. similar) property interests in similar locations. *[IFRS 13.B35(g)]*. Accordingly, in active and transparent markets for similar assets (perhaps those that exist in some of the capital cities of developed economies), real estate valuations might be able to be categorised within Level 2, provided that no significant adjustments have been made to the observable data.

However, and likely to be much more common for real estate, if an adjustment to an observed transaction is based on unobservable data and that adjustment is significant to the fair value measurement as a whole, the fair value measurement would be categorised within Level 3 of the fair value hierarchy for disclosure purposes.

A Level 3 categorisation is likely to be the most common. For example, in February 2013, EPRA published its position paper on IFRS 13 – *EPRA Position Paper on IFRS 13, Fair Value Measurement & Illustrative Disclosures*. In this publication it is stated that:

'Estimating the fair value of an investment property inevitably requires a significant range of methodologies, inputs, and adjustments to reflect the wide range of factors which contribute towards the value of a property e.g. state and condition, location, in-place leases, development potential, infrastructure, etc. Consequently, even in the most transparent and liquid markets – and depending on the valuation technique – it is very likely that valuers will use one or more significant unobservable inputs or make at least one significant adjustment to an observable input. Accordingly, it is likely that the vast majority of property valuations will fall within the level 3 category.'[23]

IFRS 13 expands the disclosures related to fair value to enable users of financial statements to understand the valuation techniques and inputs used to develop fair value measurements.

In summary, it requires the following additional disclosures for all entities regardless of the model of measurement or the valuation technique used in measuring investment property:

- the level of the fair value hierarchy within which the fair value measurement in its entirety is categorised; *[IFRS 13.93(b)]*
- for Level 2 and Level 3 measurements, valuation technique and the inputs used, and changes in the valuation technique, if applicable, and the reasons for those changes; *[IFRS 13.93(d)]* and
- if the highest and best use of a non-financial asset differs from its current use, disclose that fact and the reason for it. *[IFRS 13.93(i)]*.

For entities applying the fair value model in measuring investment property, the following additional disclosure should be made:

- for Level 3 measurements, quantitative information regarding the significant unobservable inputs; *[IFRS 13.93(d)]*
- amount of transfers between Level 1 and Level 2, the reasons and related accounting policies; *[IFRS 13.93(c)]*
- for Level 3 measurements, a reconciliation from the opening balances to the closing balances (including gains and losses, purchases, sales, issues, settlements, transfers in and out of Level 3 and reasons and policies for transfer and where all such amounts are recognised); *[IFRS 13.93(e)]*

- for Level 3 measurements, the total gains or losses included in profit or loss that are attributable to the change in unrealised gains or losses relating to those assets and liabilities held at the reporting date, and a description of where such amounts are recognised; *[IFRS 13.93(f)]*
- for Level 3 measurements, a description of the valuation process used by the entity; *[IFRS 13.93(g)]* and
- for Level 3 measurements, a narrative description of the sensitivity of the fair value measurement to changes in unobservable inputs if a change in those inputs might result in a significantly different amount and, if applicable, a description of interrelationships between those inputs and other unobservable inputs and of how they might magnify or mitigate the effect of changes in the unobservable inputs. *[IFRS 13.93(h)]*.

Unibail-Rodamco-Westfield included the following disclosures in its 2019 financial statements, in addition to those disclosed in Extract 19.3 above.

Extract 19.13: Unibail-Rodamco-Westfield SE (2019)

5.2 NOTES TO THE CONSOLIDATED FINANCIAL STATEMENTS [extract]
NOTE 5. INVESTMENT PROPERTIES, TANGIBLE AND INTANGIBLE ASSETS, GOODWILL [extract]
5.1 INVESTMENT PROPERTIES [extract]
5.1.2 INVESTMENT PROPERTIES AT FAIR VALUE: IFRS BASIS [extracts]

(€Mn)	Dec. 31, 2019
Shopping Centres	38,971.4
France	12,991.9
United States	6,437.1
Central Europe	4,413.5
Spain	3,562.4
United Kingdom & Italy	2,407.8
Nordics	3,114.6
Austria	2,433.9
Germany	2,021.0
The Netherlands	1,589.3
Offices & Others	2,977.3
France	2,255.3
Other countries	722.1
Convention & Exhibition	2,641.2
TOTAL	44,589.9

(€Mn)	Shopping Centres	Offices & Others	Convention & Exhibition	Total investment properties	Properties held for sale	Total
Dec. 31, 2018[1]	40,142.2	3,295.1	2,631.5	46,068.8	16.5	46,085.3
Right-of-use assets	462.6	–	10.8	473.4	–	473.4
Acquisitions	(5.4)	3.3	–	(2.1)	–	(2.1)
Capitalised expenses[2]	679.5	226.7	161.4	1,067.6	–	1,067.6
Disposals/exits from the scope of consolidation	(253.8)	(798.4)	–	(1,052.2)	–	(1,052.2)
Reclassification and transfer of category[3]	(1,382.2)	63.6	(0.1)	(1,318.7)	2,050.1	731.4
Discounting impact	4.2	–	–	4.2	–	4.2
Valuation movements	(870.7)	170.9	(162.3)	(862.1)	–	(862.1)
Currency translation	194.9	16.2	–	211.1	–	211.1
Dec. 31, 2019	38,971.4	2,977.3	2,641.2	44,589.9	2,066.6	46,656.5

(1) December 31, 2017, and December 31, 2018, have been restated as follows:
  – hotel assets were transferred from the Convention & Exhibition segment to the Offices & Others segment and one asset was reclassified from the Shopping Centres segment to the Convention & Exhibition segment;
  – reclassification of Los Angeles Airport (LAX) and Chicago Airport from Intangible assets to Investment properties at fair value.

(2) Capitalised expenses mainly include:
  – Shopping Centres in France and the Netherlands;
  – Offices in France;
  – Convention & Exhibition sites such as Parc des Expositions de la Porte de Versailles.

(3) Includes the transfer from IPUC at cost to investment property under construction at fair value, mainly Westfield Mall of the Netherlands, La Part-Dieu extension project, Gaîté office project and Les Ateliers Gaîté retail project and the reclassification into Properties held for sale for –€2,050.1 Mn mainly related to the transaction regarding five French shopping centres described in notes 1.3 "Assets held for sale" and 14 "Subsequent events".

VALUATION ASSUMPTIONS AND SENSITIVITY

Considering the limited public data available, the complexity of real estate asset valuations, as well as the fact that appraisers use in their valuations the non-public rent rolls of the Group's assets, URW believes it is appropriate to classify its assets under Level 3 as per IFRS 13. In addition, unobservable inputs, including appraisers' assumption on growth rates and exit capitalisation rates, are used by appraisers to determine the fair value of URW's assets.

As at December 31, 2019, 98% of URW's portfolio was appraised by independent appraisers.

The outstanding balances of deferred lease incentives and key monies amortised over the firm term of the lease, which corrected the appraisal value, represented –€69.1 Mn (–€100.2 Mn as at December 31, 2018).

The following tables provide a number of quantitative elements used by the appraisers to assess the fair valuation of the Group's assets.

SHOPPING CENTRES

All shopping centres are valued using the discounted cash flow and/or yield methodologies.

Shopping Centres – Dec. 31, 2019		Net Initial Yield	Rent in € per sqm[a]	Discount Rate[b]	Exit Capitalisation Rate[c]	CAGR of NRI[d]
France	Max	7.7%	851	8.5%	7.5%	12.9%
	Min	2.0%	163	5.3%	3.6%	2.0%
	Weighted average	4.2%	527	5.8%	4.1%	3.7%
Central Europe	Max	6.8%	611	8.4%	7.8%	2.9%
	Min	4.4%	138	6.3%	4.7%	2.2%
	Weighted average	4.9%	393	6.8%	5.0%	2.5%
Spain	Max	8.0%	572	9.2%	6.8%	3.4%
	Min	4.1%	133	6.8%	4.3%	1.1%
	Weighted average	4.4%	355	7.0%	4.5%	3.1%
Nordics	Max	5.3%	449	8.3%	5.2%	3.8%
	Min	3.7%	187	6.1%	3.9%	2.5%
	Weighted average	4.1%	375	6.5%	4.1%	3.4%
Germany	Max	7.3%	473	8.0%	6.9%	3.8%
	Min	3.9%	161	5.9%	3.9%	2.3%
	Weighted average	4.6%	304	6.2%	4.5%	2.8%
Austria	Max	4.5%	407	6.1%	4.2%	2.8%
	Min	4.2%	362	6.1%	4.2%	2.3%
	Weighted average	4.4%	383	6.1%	4.2%	2.5%
The Netherlands	Max	7.2%	371	7.9%	7.1%	3.9%
	Min	4.2%	154	5.9%	4.3%	2.6%
	Weighted average	4.9%	252	6.6%	5.2%	3.2%
US	Max	11.0%	2,380	12.0%	10.5%	16.0%
	Min	3.1%	107	5.5%	4.3%	0.5%
	Weighted average	4.1%	584	6.3%	5.1%	4.1%
UK & Italy	Max	4.6%	703	6.1%	4.9%	3.6%
	Min	4.1%	661	6.1%	4.7%	2.3%
	Weighted average	4.3%	680	6.1%	4.9%	3.0%

Net Initial Yield, Discount Rate and Exit Capitalisation Rate weighted by Gross Market Value (GMV). Vacant assets, assets considered at bid value and assets under restructuring are not included in Min and Max calculation. Assets under development or not controlled, the trademark and the airport activities are not included in this table. Assets fully consolidated and in joint-control are included.

(a) Average annual rent (Minimum Guaranteed Rent + Sales Based Rent) per asset per sqm.
(b) Rate used to calculate the net present value of future cash flows.
(c) Rate used to capitalise the exit rent to determine the exit value of an asset.
(d) Compound Annual Growth Rate of Net Rental Income determined by the appraiser (between six and ten years depending on duration of DCF model used).

For the US, the split between Flagship and Regional shopping centres is as follows:

Shopping Centres – Dec. 31, 2019		Net Initial Yield	Rent in € per sqm[a]	Discount Rate[b]	Exit Capitalisation Rate[c]	CAGR of NRI[d]
US Flagships	Max	5.1%	2,380	7.0%	6.0%	5.5%
	Min	3.1%	415	5.5%	4.3%	2.8%
	Weighted average	3.8%	808	6.0%	4.8%	4.2%
US Regionals	Max	11.0%	494	12.0%	10.5%	16.0%
	Min	4.1%	107	6.5%	5.8%	0.5%
	Weighted average	6.0%	305	8.1%	6.9%	3.6%

Net Initial Yield, Discount Rate and Exit Capitalisation Rate weighted by GMV. Vacant assets, assets considered at bid value and assets under restructuring are not included in Min and Max calculation. Assets under development or not controlled, the trademark and the airport activities are not included in this table. Assets fully consolidated and in joint-control are included.

(a) Average annual rent (Minimum Guaranteed Rent + Sales Based Rent) per asset per sqm.
(b) Rate used to calculate the net present value of future cash flows.
(c) Rate used to capitalise the exit rent to determine the exit value of an asset.
(d) Compound Annual Growth Rate of Net Rental Income determined by the appraiser (ten years).

Based on an asset value excluding estimated transfer taxes and transaction costs, the Shopping Centres division's net initial yield (NIY) is stable at 4.3% as at December 31, 2019 compared to December 31, 2018.

A change of +25 basis points in NIY, the main output of the appraisal models, would result in a downward adjustment of −€2,871 Mn (or −5.5%) of URW's Shopping Centres portfolio value (excluding assets under development, the trademark and the airport activities).

OFFICES & OTHERS

Appraisers value the Group's offices using the discounted cash flow and yield methodologies.

Offices & Others – Dec. 31, 2019		Net Initial Yield on occupied space	Rent in € per sqm [a]	Discount Rate[b]	Exit Capitalisation Rate[c]	CAGR of NRI[d]
France	Max	9.6%	511	8.5%	8.0%	12.5%
	Min	4.6%	106	5.7%	3.8%	(0.2%)
	Weighted average	5.1%	400	5.9%	4.5%	2.8%
Nordics	Max	9.7%	227	9.4%	7.8%	3.1%
	Min	6.2%	175	7.0%	5.2%	2.3%
	Weighted average	7.6%	196	8.0%	6.4%	2.6%
Other countries	Max	12.2%	182	8.8%	8.9%	24.1%
	Min	4.6%	40	5.5%	3.8%	0.5%
	Weighted average	6.5%	129	7.4%	5.9%	3.4%
US	Max	8.9%	689	9.3%	8.5%	6.4%
	Min	4.5%	280	6.9%	5.9%	2.9%
	Weighted average	6.5%	446	7.5%	6.3%	5.2%

Net Initial Yield, Discount Rate and Exit Capitalisation Rate weighted by GMV. Vacant assets and assets under restructuring are not included in Min and Max calculation. Assets under development are not included in this table, as well as the United Kingdom asset. Assets fully consolidated and in joint-control are included.
(a) Average annual rent (Minimum Guaranteed Rent) per asset per sqm. The computation takes into account the areas allocated to company restaurants.
(b) Rate used to calculate the net present value of future cash flows.
(c) Rate used to capitalise the exit rent to determine the exit value of an asset.
(d) Compound Annual Growth Rate of Net Rental Income determined by the appraiser (between three and ten years, depending on duration of DCF model used).

For occupied offices and based on an asset value excluding estimated transfer taxes and transaction costs, the Offices & Others division's NIY decreased by – 27 basis points to 5.5% as at December 31, 2019.

A change of +25 basis points in NIY, the main output of the appraisal models, would result in a downward adjustment of –€118 Mn (–4.9%) of URW's Offices & Others portfolio value (occupied and vacant spaces, excluding assets under development).

CONVENTION & EXHIBITION

Based on these valuations, the average EBITDA yield (recurring earnings before interest, tax, depreciation and amortisation divided by the value of assets, excluding estimated transfer taxes and transaction costs) of Viparis consolidated venues is stable at 5.3% as at December 31, 2019, compared to December 31, 2018.

A change of +25 basis points in the weighted average cost of capital (WACC) as determined at December 31, 2019, would result in a downward adjustment of –€111.7 Mn (–4.7%) of the Convention & Exhibition portfolio value.

5.1.3   INVESTMENT PROPERTIES UNDER CONSTRUCTION AT COST [extracts]

(€Mn)	Dec. 31, 2019
Shopping Centres	**755.6**
France	262.8
United States	18.7
Central Europe	39.9
Spain	179.7
United Kingdom & Italy	21.7
Nordics	10.2
Austria	–
Germany	222.7
The Netherlands	–
Offices & Others	**387.8**
France	122.7
Other countries	265.1
Convention & Exhibition	–
TOTAL	**1,143.3**

As at December 31, 2019, assets under construction valued at cost are notably:
- shopping centres extension and renovation projects such as Garbera extension;
- shopping centres development such as Altamar;
- office developments such as Sisters in La Défense;
- mixed-used projects such as Westfield Hamburg.

Assets still stated at cost were subject to impairment tests as at December 31, 2019. Allowances were booked for a total amount of €72.8 Mn.

(€Mn)	Gross value	Impairment	Total investment properties at cost	Properties held for sale	Total
Dec. 31, 2018	1,663.3	(105.5)	1,557.8	49.7	1,607.5
Acquisitions	1.9	–	1.9	–	1.9
Capitalised expenses[(1)]	395.9	–	395.9	–	395.9
Disposals/exits from the scope of consolidation	(1.6)	–	(1.6)	–	(1.6)
Reclassification and transfer of category[(2)]	(742.5)	–	(742.5)	11.8	(730.7)
Impairment/reversal	–	(72.8)	(72.8)	–	(72.8)
Currency translation	5.1	(0.4)	4.7	–	4.7
Dec. 31, 2019	1,322.1	(178.7)	1,143.3	61.5	1,204.8

(1) Capitalised expenses mainly refer to investments in Westfield Hamburg development project as well as Westfield Mall of The Netherlands and La Part-Dieu extension project.

(2) Includes the reclassification into the category of the properties held for sale (–€11.8 Mn) and the transfer to investment property under construction at fair value, mainly Westfield Mall of the Netherlands, La Part-Dieu extension project, Gaîté office project and Les Ateliers Gaîté retail project.

12.1.2 Level of aggregation for IFRS 13 disclosures

IFRS 13 disclosures are required for each class of assets (and liabilities). These classes are determined based on:

- the nature, characteristics and risks of the asset or liability; and
- the level of the fair value hierarchy within which the fair value measurement is categorised. *[IFRS 13.94]*.

The determination of the appropriate class of assets will require significant judgement. See Chapter 14 at 20.1.2 for further discussion on this determination.

At one end of the spectrum, the properties in an operating segment (as defined by IFRS 8 – *Operating Segments*) may be a class of assets for the purpose of the disclosures required by IFRS 13. This may be the case if the properties have the same risk profile (for example, the segment comprises residential properties in countries with property markets of similar characteristics) even if there are a large number of properties in the segment.

At the other end of the spectrum, IFRS 13 disclosures may be required for individual properties or small groups of properties if the individual properties or groups of properties have different risk profiles (for example, a real estate entity with two properties – an office building in a developed country and a shopping centre in a developing country).

The number of classes may need to be greater for fair value measurements categorised within Level 3 of the fair value hierarchy because those measurements have a greater degree of uncertainty and subjectivity.

A class of assets and liabilities will often require greater disaggregation than the line items presented in the statement of financial position. However, sufficient information must be provided to permit reconciliation to the line items presented in the statement of financial position.

When determining the appropriate classes, entities should also consider all of the following:
- the level of detail necessary to satisfy the disclosure requirements;
- how much emphasis to place on each of the various requirements;
- how much aggregation or disaggregation to undertake; and
- whether users of financial statements need additional information to evaluate the quantitative information disclosed. *[IFRS 13.92]*.

Determining appropriate classes of assets and liabilities for which disclosures about fair value measurements should be provided requires considerable judgement. *[IFRS 13.94]*.

12.1.3 Disclosure of direct operating expenses

As set out in 12.1 above, entities are required to disclose both the direct operating expenses arising from investment property that generated rental income during the period and the amounts arising from investment property that did not generate rental income during the period.

In practice, this requirement can be interpreted in different ways and the outcome will depend upon a number of judgements, for example, the unit of account for the investment property. In the instance of a multi-tenanted property, the relevant unit may be considered either the entire building or a separately let floor.

It will therefore be necessary for an entity to interpret this requirement and apply that interpretation, as an accounting policy and judgement, consistently.

12.2 Additional disclosures for the fair value model

A reconciliation between the carrying amounts of investment property at the start and end of the period must be given showing the following:
- additions, disclosing separately those additions resulting from acquisitions and those resulting from subsequent expenditure recognised in the carrying amount of an asset;
- additions resulting from acquisitions through business combinations;
- assets classified as held for sale or included in a disposal group classified as held for sale in accordance with IFRS 5 and other disposals;
- net gains or losses from fair value adjustments;
- the net exchange differences arising on the translation of the financial statements into a different presentation currency, and on translation of a foreign operation into the presentation currency of the reporting entity;
- transfers to and from inventories and owner-occupied property; and
- other changes. *[IAS 40.76]*.

When a valuation obtained for investment property is adjusted significantly for the purpose of the financial statements, for example to avoid double-counting of assets or liabilities that are recognised separately (see 6.1.4 above), the entity must disclose a reconciliation between the valuation obtained and the adjusted valuation included in the financial statements, showing separately the aggregate amount of any recognised lease liabilities that have been added back, and any other significant adjustments. *[IAS 40.77]*. Extracts 19.5 and 19.6 above provide examples of such disclosure.

12.2.1 Presentation of changes in fair value

Neither IAS 1 nor IAS 40 specifies how changes in the fair value of investment property should be presented. The Extracts below show two different approaches. In Extract 19.14 below the change in fair value (here referred to as a '(Loss)/gain on revaluation of investment and development property') is presented together with the profit or loss on disposal of properties with an analysis of the components included in the notes to the accounts. By contrast, in Extract 19.15 below, the change in fair value is analysed and presented separately from the profit or loss on disposal of properties.

Extract 19.14: Capital & Counties Properties PLC (2019)
CONSOLIDATED INCOME STATEMENT [extract]
FOR THE YEAR ENDED 31 DECEMBER 2019

	Note	2019 £m	Re-presented[1] 2018 £m
Continuing operations			
Revenue	2	79.4	74.7
Rental income		77.6	71.3
Rental expenses		(16.5)	(13.9)
Net rental income	2	61.1	57.4
Other income		1.8	3.4
(Loss)/gain on revaluation and sale of investment and development property	3	(43.3)	39.2
Impairment of other receivables	4	(21.0)	(19.4)
		(1.4)	80.6
Administration expenses		(43.4)	(34.2)
Operating (loss)/profit		(44.8)	46.4

NOTES TO THE ACCOUNTS [extract]
3 (LOSS)/GAIN ON REVALUATION AND SALE OF INVESTMENT AND DEVELOPMENT PROPERTY

Continuing operations	2019 £m	Re-presented[1] 2018 £m
(Loss)/gain on revaluation of investment and development property	(41.1)	37.2
(Loss)/gain on sale of investment and development property	(2.2)	2.0
(Loss)/gain on revaluation and sale of investment and development property	(43.3)	39.2

Extract 19.15: Unibail-Rodamco-Westfield SE (2019)

5.1 CONSOLIDATED FINANCIAL STATEMENTS [extract]

5.1.1 CONSOLIDATED STATEMENT OF COMPREHENSIVE INCOME [extract]

(€Mn)	Notes	2019	2018
Net rental income		1,985.2	1,840.3
Property development and project management revenue		276.6	215.5
Property development and project management costs		(235.2)	(178.5)
Net property development and project management income	4.4.4	41.3	37.0
Property services and other activities revenues		310.1	307.2
Property services and other activities expenses		(211.4)	(198.9)
Net property services and other activities income	4.2.1/4.4.3	98.7	108.2
Share of the result of companies accounted for using the equity method		(77.9)	233.9
Income on financial assets		32.2	32.1
Contribution of companies accounted for using the equity method	6	(45.7)	266.0
Corporate expenses		(191.5)	(141.4)
Development expenses		(17.4)	(2.1)
Depreciation of other tangible assets		(2.0)	(1.9)
Administrative expenses	4.4.5	(210.9)	(145.5)
Acquisition and related costs	4.4.6	(45.8)	(268.7)
Proceeds from disposal of investment properties		957.2	985.4
Carrying value of investment properties sold		(908.3)	(905.3)
Result on disposal of investment properties	5.6	48.9	80.1
Proceeds from disposal of shares		223.0	463.4
Carrying value of disposed shares		(203.4)	(460.5)
Result on disposal of shares	3.4.2/5.6	19.7	3.0
Valuation gains on assets		924.0	885.1
Valuation losses on assets		(2,026.4)	(822.9)
Valuation movements on assets	5.5	(1,102.4)	62.2
Impairment of goodwill	5.4	(7.1)	(4.9)
NET OPERATING RESULT		781.8	1,977.8

Some companies include the change in fair value within their definition of operating profit. This approach appears to be just one of the available accounting policy choices but it is worth noting that at least one European regulator has concluded that fair value changes arising from investment property must be taken into account when determining operating results. This decision was reported in the European Securities and Markets Authority's ('ESMA') *Report – 11th Extract from the EECS's Database of Enforcement (ESMA/2011/265)*.

The regulator's rationale for this decision was that fair value changes in investment property are a normal part of the activities of a real estate company and feature in the description of the business model of that real estate business.[24]

12.2.2 Extra disclosures where fair value cannot be determined reliably

If an entity chooses the fair value model, but in an exceptional case cannot measure the fair value of the property reliably and accounts for the property under the cost model in IAS 16 or in accordance with IFRS 16, the reconciliation described in 12.2 above should disclose the amounts for such investment property separately from amounts relating to other investment property. In addition to this, the following should be disclosed:

- a description of the investment property;
- an explanation of why fair value cannot be measured reliably;
- if possible, the range of estimates within which fair value is highly likely to lie; and
- on disposal of investment property not carried at fair value:
  - the fact that the entity has disposed of investment property not carried at fair value;
  - the carrying amount of that investment property at the time of sale; and
  - the amount of gain or loss recognised. *[IAS 40.78]*.

The standard makes it clear that this situation, at least for completed investment property, would be exceptional (see 6.2 above). The situation for investment property under construction is discussed at 6.3 above.

12.3 Additional disclosures for the cost model

If investment property is measured using the cost model, the following disclosures are required by IAS 40 in addition to those at 12.1 above:

- the depreciation methods used;
- the useful lives or the depreciation rates used;
- the gross carrying amount and the accumulated depreciation (aggregated with accumulated impairment losses) at the beginning and end of the period;
- a reconciliation of the carrying amount of investment property at the beginning and end of the period, showing the following:
  - additions, disclosing separately those additions resulting from acquisitions and those resulting from subsequent expenditure recognised as an asset;
  - additions resulting from acquisitions through business combinations;
  - assets classified as held for sale or included in a disposal group classified as held for sale in accordance with IFRS 5 and other disposals;
  - depreciation;
  - the amount of impairment losses recognised, and the amount of impairment losses reversed, during the period in accordance with IAS 36 (see Chapter 20 at 13);
  - the net exchange differences arising on the translation of the financial statements into a different presentation currency, and on translation of a foreign operation into the presentation currency of the reporting entity;
  - transfers to and from inventories and owner-occupied property; and
  - other changes;

- the fair value of investment property. In the exceptional cases when an entity cannot measure the fair value of the investment property reliably (see 6.2 above), it shall disclose:
  - a description of the investment property;
  - an explanation of why fair value cannot be measured reliably; and
  - if possible, the range of estimates within which fair value is highly likely to lie. [IAS 40.79].

12.4 Presentation of sales proceeds

IAS 16 requires an entity that, in the course of its ordinary activities, routinely sells items of property, plant and equipment that it has held for rental to transfer such assets to inventories at their carrying amount when they cease to be rented and become held for sale. The proceeds from the sale of such assets are then recognised as revenue in accordance with IFRS 15 (see Chapter 18 at 7.2). [IAS 16.68A].

However, investment property, by definition, is held to earn rentals or for capital appreciation rather than for sale in the ordinary course of business. Consequently, we consider that this IAS 16 accounting treatment may not be applied by analogy to IAS 40 and proceeds from the sale of investment property may not be presented as revenue.

Despite this, however, it may be appropriate to present separately the material gains or losses on retirement or disposal of investment property elsewhere in the financial statements, either as part of the income statement or in the notes. [IAS 1.97]. For example, Unibail-Rodamco-Westfield has chosen to present proceeds from disposal of investment properties, together with the carrying amount derecognised and the net gain/loss on disposal on the face of its statement of comprehensive income (see Extract 19.15 above).

References

1. *IFRIC Update*, September 2012.
2. *IFRIC Update*, September 2012.
3. *IFRIC Update*, January 2013.
4. *IASB Update*, December 2014.
5. *IFRIC Update*, July 2011.
6. *Definition of a Business – Amendments to IFRS 3*, IASB, October 2018, p.4.
7. *IFRIC Update*, June 2017.
8. *IFRIC Update*, November 2017.
9. *IFRIC Update*, March 2017.
10. *UITF abstract 28 – Operating lease incentives*, UK Accounting Standards Board, February 2001, para. 3.
11. *IFRIC Update*, January 2011.
12. *IFRIC Update*, May 2011.
13. *IASB Update*, July 2013.
14. *IFRIC Update*, March 2016.
15. *IASB Update*, May 2016.
16. *IASB Update*, February 2018.
17. *IASB Work plan – research projects*, IASB website, https://www.ifrs.org/projects/work-plan/ (accessed on 16 July 2020).
18. *Amendments to IFRS 17*, IASB, June 2020, para. C1, p.40.
19. *IVS 104 Bases of Value*, International Valuation Standards, IVSC, effective 31 January 2020, para. 30.1.
20. *IFRIC Update*, July 2014.
21. *Best Practices Recommendations Guidelines*, EPRA, October 2019, section 4.1, p.26.

22 *Review Findings and Recommendations – 2009*, Financial Reporting Review Panel, July 2009, p.11.
23 *EPRA Position Paper on IFRS 13, Fair Value Measurement & Illustrative Disclosures*, EPRA, February 2013, p.4.
24 *Report – 11th Extract from the EECS's Database of Enforcement (ESMA/2011/265)*, European Securities and Markets Authority (ESMA), August 2011, paras. 76-81.

Chapter 20 Impairment of fixed assets and goodwill

1 INTRODUCTION 1517
   1.1 The theory behind the impairment review 1517
   1.2 Key features of the impairment review..1518
   1.3 Scope...1521
2 WHEN AN IMPAIRMENT TEST IS REQUIRED..1522
   2.1 Indicators of impairment 1522
      2.1.1 Market capitalisation 1523
      2.1.2 (Future) performance.. 1524
      2.1.3 Individual assets or part of CGU? 1524
      2.1.4 Interest rates 1524
3 DIVIDING THE ENTITY INTO CASH-GENERATING UNITS (CGUs)............1525
   3.1 CGUs and intangible assets...1531
      3.1.1 Intangible assets as corporate assets 1532
   3.2 Leased assets and CGUs... 1532
   3.3 Active markets and identifying CGUs 1534
4 IDENTIFYING THE CARRYING AMOUNT OF CGU ASSETS........................1535
   4.1 Consistency and the impairment test 1536
      4.1.1 Environmental provisions and similar provisions and liabilities...1537
      4.1.2 Lease liabilities under IFRS 16 1538
      4.1.3 Trade debtors and creditors 1538
      4.1.4 Pensions.. 1540
      4.1.5 Cash flow hedges... 1540
   4.2 Corporate assets.. 1542
      4.2.1 Leased corporate assets 1543

5	RECOVERABLE AMOUNT		1544
	5.1	Impairment of assets held for sale	1544
6	FAIR VALUE LESS COSTS OF DISPOSAL		1546
	6.1	Estimating FVLCD	1546
		6.1.1 FVLCD and the unit of account	1548
		6.1.2 Depreciated replacement cost or current replacement cost as FVLCD	1550
7	DETERMINING VALUE IN USE (VIU)		1551
	7.1	Estimating the future pre-tax cash flows of the CGU under review	1552
		7.1.1 Budgets and cash flows	1552
		7.1.2 Cash inflows and outflows from improvements and enhancements	1554
		7.1.3 Restructuring	1556
		7.1.4 Terminal values	1556
		7.1.5 Foreign currency cash flows	1557
		7.1.6 Internal transfer pricing	1558
		7.1.7 Overheads and share-based payments	1558
		7.1.8 Lease payments	1561
		7.1.8.A Lease payments during the lease term	1561
		7.1.8.B Lease payments beyond the current lease term	1561
		7.1.9 Events after the reporting period	1562
		7.1.10 'Traditional' and 'expected cash flow' approach to present value	1563
	7.2	Identifying an appropriate discount rate and discounting the future cash flows	1564
		7.2.1 Discount rates and the weighted average cost of capital	1567
		7.2.2 Calculating a pre-tax discount rate	1568
		7.2.3 Calculating VIU using post-tax cash flows	1570
		7.2.4 Approximations and short cuts	1574
		7.2.5 Disclosing pre-tax discount rates when using a post-tax methodology	1575
		7.2.6 Determining pre-tax rates taking account of tax losses	1577
		7.2.7 Entity-specific WACCs and different project risks within the entity	1578
		7.2.8 Entity-specific WACCs and capital structure	1578
		7.2.9 Use of discount rates other than the WACC	1580
		7.2.10 Impact of IFRS 16 adoption on the discount rate	1580
	7.3	Differences between fair value and value in use	1581
8	IMPAIRMENT OF GOODWILL		1582
	8.1	Goodwill and its allocation to cash-generating units	1582

Impairment of fixed assets and goodwill 1513

	8.1.1	The composition of goodwill	1583
	8.1.2	Identifying synergies and identifying CGUs or CGU groups for allocating goodwill	1585
	8.1.3	Measuring the goodwill allocated to CGUs or CGU groups	1586
	8.1.4	The effect of IFRS 8 – Operating Segments – on impairment tests	1587
		8.1.4.A Changes to operating segments	1588
		8.1.4.B Aggregation of operating segments for disclosure purposes	1588
	8.1.5	Goodwill initially unallocated to cash-generating units	1588
8.2	When to test cash-generating units with goodwill for impairment		1590
	8.2.1	Timing of impairment tests	1591
	8.2.2	Sequence of impairment tests for goodwill and other assets	1592
	8.2.3	Carry forward of a previous impairment test calculation	1592
	8.2.4	Reversal of impairment loss for goodwill prohibited	1593
8.3	Impairment of assets and goodwill recognised on acquisition		1593
	8.3.1	Testing goodwill 'created' by deferred tax for impairment	1593
	8.3.2	Deferred tax assets and losses of acquired businesses	1597
8.4	Impairment testing when a CGU crosses more than one operating segment		1597
8.5	Disposal of operation within a cash-generating unit to which goodwill has been allocated		1598
	8.5.1	Changes in composition of cash-generating units	1599
9	NON-CONTROLLING INTERESTS – THE IMPACT ON GOODWILL IMPAIRMENT TESTING		1602
	9.1	Testing for impairment in entities with non-controlling interests measured at the proportionate share of net identifiable assets	1604
		9.1.1 Acquisitions or sale of non-controlling interests measured at the proportionate share of net identifiable assets	1605
	9.2	Testing for impairment in entities with non-controlling interests initially measured at fair value	1606
	9.3	Testing for impairment in entities with non-controlling interests: alternative allocation methodologies	1607
10	IMPAIRMENT OF INTANGIBLE ASSETS WITH AN INDEFINITE USEFUL LIFE		1610
11	RECOGNISING AND REVERSING IMPAIRMENT LOSSES		1612
	11.1	Impairment losses on individual assets	1612
	11.2	Impairment losses and CGUs	1613
	11.3	Reversal of impairment loss relating to goodwill prohibited	1615
	11.4	Reversal of impairment losses relating to assets other than goodwill	1615

Chapter 20

Chapter 20

- 11.4.1 Reversals of impairments – cash-generating units 1618
- 11.4.2 Reversals of impairments – revalued assets 1618

12 GROUP AND SEPARATE FINANCIAL STATEMENT ISSUES 1619
- 12.1 VIU: relevant cash flows and non-arm's length prices (transfer pricing) 1619
- 12.2 Goodwill in individual (or subgroup) financial statements and the interaction with the group financial statements 1621
  - 12.2.1 Goodwill synergies arising outside of the reporting entity/subgroup 1621
  - 12.2.2 The effect of IFRS 8 – Operating segments – when allocating goodwill to CGU's in individual (or subgroup) financial statements 1621
  - 12.2.3 Acquisitions by subsidiaries and determining the level at which the group tests goodwill for impairment 1622
- 12.3 Group reorganisations and the carrying value of investments in subsidiaries 1623
- 12.4 Investments in subsidiaries, associates and joint ventures 1625
  - 12.4.1 Fair value less costs of disposal (FVLCD) for investments in subsidiaries, associates and joint ventures 1625
  - 12.4.2 VIU for investments in subsidiaries, associates and joint ventures 1626
    - 12.4.2.A VIU of investments in subsidiaries, associates and joint ventures using dividend discount models 1626
    - 12.4.2.B VIU of investments in subsidiaries, associates and joint ventures based on cash flows generated by underlying assets 1627
  - 12.4.3 Equity accounted investment and indicators of impairment 1627
  - 12.4.4 Equity accounted investments and long term loans 1628
  - 12.4.5 Equity accounted investments and CGUs 1628
  - 12.4.6 Equity accounted investments and testing goodwill for impairment 1629

13 DISCLOSURES REQUIRED BY IAS 36 1630
- 13.1 Introduction 1630
- 13.2 IAS 36 disclosures 1630
  - 13.2.1 Disclosures required for impairment losses or reversals 1630
  - 13.2.2 Material impairments 1631
- 13.3 Annual impairment disclosures required for goodwill and intangible assets with an indefinite useful life 1632

14 DEVELOPMENTS 1640

List of examples

Example 20.1:	Identification of cash-generating units and largely independent cash inflows	1525
Example 20.2:	Identification of cash-generating units	1526
Example 20.3:	Omni-channel business model	1527
Example 20.4:	Identification of cash-generating units – grouping of assets	1529
Example 20.5:	Identification of cash-generating units – single product entity	1530
Example 20.6:	Identification of cash-generating units – leased assets	1533
Example 20.7:	Identification of cash-generating units – internally-used products	1534
Example 20.8:	The effects of working capital on impairment tests	1539
Example 20.9:	Cash flow hedges and testing for impairment	1541
Example 20.10:	Allocation of corporate assets	1543
Example 20.11:	Impairment of assets held for sale	1545
Example 20.12:	Distinguishing enhancement and maintenance expenditure	1555
Example 20.13:	Transfer prices	1558
Example 20.14:	Calculating a discount rate	1565
Example 20.15:	Impairment calculations using pre- and post-tax cash flows and discount rates	1571
Example 20.16:	Calculating pre-tax discount rates from post-tax VIUs	1576
Example 20.17:	Different project risks and CGUs	1578
Example 20.18:	Effect of entity default risk on its WACC	1579
Example 20.19:	Identifying synergies	1585
Example 20.20:	Allocating goodwill and identifying CGUs	1586
Example 20.21:	Allocating goodwill to more than one CGU	1586
Example 20.22:	Impact of shortened accounting period	1590
Example 20.23:	Testing for impairment of goodwill allocated in the period after acquisition after the annual impairment testing date	1591
Example 20.24:	Apparent 'day one' impairment arising from recognition of deferred tax in a business combination	1593
Example 20.25:	Impairment testing assets whose fair value reflects tax amortisation benefits	1595
Example 20.26:	Impairment testing assets whose fair value reflects tax amortisation benefits (continued)	1596
Example 20.27:	Goodwill attributable to the disposal of an operation based on relative values	1598
Example 20.28:	Reallocation of goodwill to CGUs based on relative values	1599
Example 20.29:	Reallocation of goodwill to CGUs based on relative current values of notional goodwill	1600
Example 20.30:	A CGU with goodwill and non-controlling interest	1604
Example 20.31:	Non-controlling interests measured initially at fair value	1607

Example 20.32:	Measurement and allocation of goodwill impairment losses when there are non-controlling interests	1609
Example 20.33:	Recognition of an impairment loss creates a deferred tax asset	1613
Example 20.34:	Individually impaired assets within CGUs	1614
Example 20.35:	Impairment of goodwill	1615
Example 20.36:	Double counted losses	1617
Example 20.37:	Reversal of impairment losses	1617
Example 20.38:	A subgroup with goodwill that is not an operating segment for the group	1622
Example 20.39:	Monitoring goodwill arising from acquisitions by subsidiaries	1622
Example 20.40:	Group reorganisations and impairment	1624
Example 20.41:	Joint ventures are part of larger CGU	1629

Chapter 20 Impairment of fixed assets and goodwill

1 INTRODUCTION

In principle an asset is impaired when an entity will not be able to recover that asset's carrying value, either through using it or selling it. If circumstances arise which indicate assets might be impaired, a review should be undertaken of their cash generating abilities either through use or sale. This review will produce an amount which should be compared with the assets' carrying value, and if the carrying value is higher, the difference must be written off as an impairment in the statement of comprehensive income. The provisions within IAS 36 – *Impairment of Assets* – that set out exactly how this is to be done, and how the figures involved are to be calculated, are detailed and quite complex.

1.1 The theory behind the impairment review

The purpose of the impairment review is to ensure that intangible assets, including goodwill, and tangible assets are not carried at a figure greater than their recoverable amount (RA). This recoverable amount is compared with the carrying value (or carrying amount (CA)) of the asset to determine if the asset is impaired.

Recoverable amount is defined as the higher of fair value less costs of disposal (FVLCD) and value in use (VIU); the underlying concept being that an asset should not be carried at more than the amount it could raise, either from selling it now or from using it.

Fair value less costs of disposal essentially means what the asset could be sold for, having deducted costs of disposal (incrementally incurred direct selling costs). Value in use is defined in terms of discounted future cash flows, as the present value of the cash flows expected from the future use and eventual sale of the asset at the end of its useful life. As the recoverable amount is to be expressed as a present value, not in nominal terms, discounting is a central feature of the impairment test.

Diagrammatically, this comparison between carrying value and recoverable amount, and the definition of recoverable amount, can be portrayed as follows:

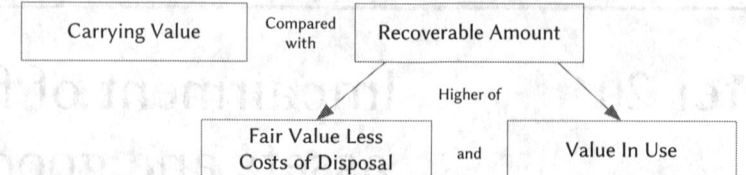

It may not always be necessary to identify both VIU and FVLCD, as if either of VIU or FVLCD is higher than the carrying amount then there is no impairment and no write-down is necessary. Thus, if FVLCD is greater than the carrying amount then no further consideration need be given to VIU, or to the need for an impairment write down. The more complex issues arise when the FVLCD is not greater than the carrying value, and so a VIU calculation is necessary.

1.2 Key features of the impairment review

Although an impairment review might theoretically be conducted by looking at individual assets, this will not always be possible. Goodwill does not have a separate FVLCD at all. Even if FVLCDs can be obtained for individual items of property, plant and equipment, estimates of VIUs usually cannot be. This is because the cash flows necessary for the VIU calculation are not usually generated by single assets, but by groups of assets being used together.

Often, therefore, the impairment review cannot be done at the level of the individual asset and it must be applied to a group of assets. IAS 36 uses the term cash generating unit (CGU) for the smallest identifiable group of assets that together have cash inflows that are largely independent of the cash inflows from other assets and that therefore can be the subject of a VIU calculation. This focus on the CGU is fundamental, as it has the effect of making the review essentially a business-value test. Goodwill cannot always be allocated to a CGU and may therefore be allocated to a group of CGUs. IAS 36 has detailed guidance in respect of the level at which goodwill is tested for impairment which is discussed at 8 below.

Most assets and CGUs need only be tested for impairment if there are indicators of impairment. The 'indications' of impairment may relate to either the assets themselves or to the economic environment in which they are operated. IAS 36 gives examples of indications of impairment, but makes it clear this is not an exhaustive list, and states explicitly that the entity may identify other indications that an asset is impaired, that would equally trigger an impairment review. *[IAS 36.13]*. There are more onerous requirements for goodwill, intangible assets with an indefinite useful life and intangible assets that are not available for use on the reporting date. These must be tested for impairment at least on an annual basis, irrespective of whether there are any impairment indicators. This is because the first two, goodwill and indefinite-lived intangible assets, are not subject to annual amortisation while it is argued that intangible assets are intrinsically subject to greater uncertainty before they are brought into use. Impairment losses are recognised as expenses in profit or loss except in the case of an asset carried at a revalued amount where the impairment loss is recorded first against any previously recognised revaluation gains in respect of that asset in other comprehensive income.

Figure 20.1 below illustrates the key stages in the process of measuring and recognising impairment losses under IAS 36. The key components of the diagram are discussed in detail in the remainder of this chapter.

Figure 20.1: Determining and accounting for impairment

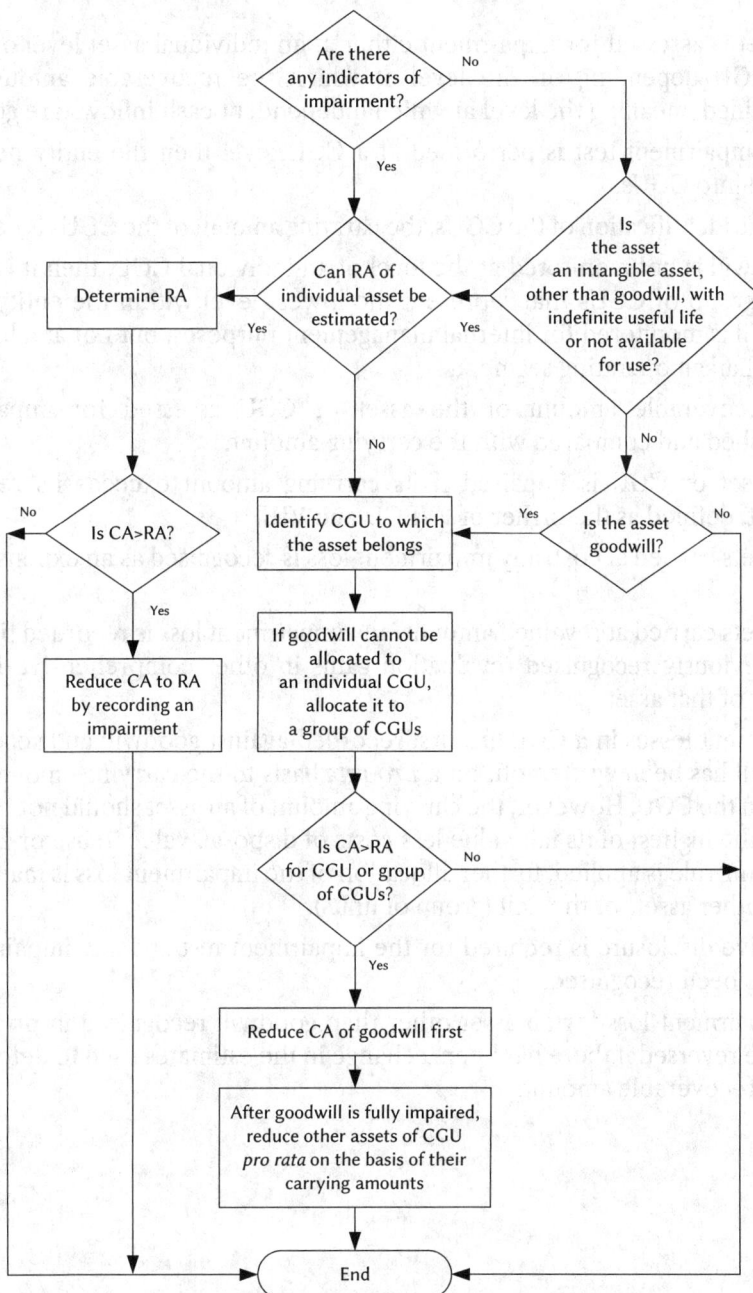

The entity assesses, at each reporting date, whether an impairment assessment is required and acts accordingly:
- If there is an indication that an asset may be impaired, an impairment test is required.
- For goodwill, intangible assets with an indefinite useful life and intangible assets that are not available for use on the reporting date an annual impairment test is required.
- An asset is assessed for impairment either at an individual asset level or the level of a CGU depending on the level at which the recoverable amount can be determined, meaning the level at which independent cash inflows are generated.
- If the impairment test is performed at a CGU level then the entity needs to be divided into CGUs.
- After the identification of the CGUs, the carrying amount of the CGUs is determined.
- If goodwill is not monitored at the level of an individual CGU, then it is allocated to the group of CGUs that represent the lowest level within the entity at which goodwill is monitored for internal management purposes, but not at a level that is larger than an operating segment.
- The recoverable amount of the asset or CGU assessed for impairment is established and compared with the carrying amount.
- The asset or CGU is impaired if its carrying amount exceeds its recoverable amount, defined as the higher of FVLCD and VIU.
- For assets carried at cost, any impairment loss is recognised as an expense in profit or loss.
- For assets carried at revalued amount, any impairment loss is recorded first against any previously recognised revaluation gains in other comprehensive income in respect of that asset.
- Impairment losses in a CGU are first recorded against goodwill and second, if the goodwill has been written off, on a *pro rata* basis to the carrying amount of other assets in the CGU. However, the carrying amount of an asset should not be reduced below the highest of its fair value less costs of disposal, value in use or zero. If the preceding rule is applied, further allocation of the impairment loss is made *pro rata* to the other assets of the unit (group of units).
- Extensive disclosure is required for the impairment test and any impairment loss that has been recognised.
- An impairment loss for an asset other than goodwill recognised in prior periods must be reversed if there has been a change in the estimates used to determine the asset's recoverable amount.

1.3 Scope

The standard is a general impairment standard and its provisions are referred to in other standards, for example IAS 16 – *Property, Plant and Equipment*, IAS 38 – *Intangible Assets*, IFRS 16 – *Leases* – and IFRS 3 – *Business Combinations* – where impairment is to be considered.

The standard has a general application to all assets, but the following are outside its scope:
- inventories (IAS 2 – *Inventories*);
- contract assets and assets arising from costs to obtain or fulfil a contract that are recognised in accordance with IFRS 15 – *Revenue from Contracts with Customers*;
- deferred tax assets (IAS 12 – *Income Taxes*);
- assets arising from employee benefits under IAS 19 – *Employee Benefits*;
- financial assets that are included in the scope of IFRS 9 – *Financial Instruments*;
- investment property that is measured at fair value under IAS 40 – *Investment Property*;
- biological assets under IAS 41 – *Agriculture*, except bearer plants, e.g. apple trees, which are in the scope of IAS 16 and therefore fall under the IAS 36 impairment guidance;
- deferred acquisition costs and intangible assets arising from an insurer's contractual rights under insurance contracts within the scope of IFRS 4 – *Insurance Contracts*; and
- non-current assets (or disposal groups) classified as held for sale in accordance with IFRS 5 – *Non-current Assets Held for Sale and Discontinued Operations*. *[IAS 36.2]*.

This, the standard states, is because these assets are subject to specific recognition and measurement requirements. *[IAS 36.3]*. The effect of these exclusions is to reduce the scope of IAS 36. While investment properties measured at fair value are exempt, investment properties not carried at fair value are in the scope of IAS 36. If a company has recorded oil and mineral exploration and evaluation assets and has chosen to carry them at cost, then these assets are to be tested under IAS 36 for impairment, once they have been assessed for impairment indicators in accordance with IFRS 6 – *Exploration for and Evaluation of Mineral Resources*. *[IFRS 6.2(b)]*. Financial assets classified as subsidiaries as defined in IFRS 10 – *Consolidated Financial Statements*, joint ventures as defined in IFRS 11 – *Joint Arrangements* – and associates as defined in IAS 28 – *Investments in Associates and Joint Ventures* – are within its scope. *[IAS 36.4]*. This will generally mean only those investments in the separate financial statements of the parent. However, interests in joint ventures and associates included in the consolidated accounts by way of the equity method are brought into scope by IAS 28. *[IAS 28.42]*.

The standard applies to assets carried at revalued amounts, e.g. under IAS 16 (or rarely IAS 38). *[IAS 36.4]*.

A lessee shall apply IAS 36 to determine whether the right-of-use asset is impaired and to account for any impairment loss identified. *[IFRS 16.33]*.

2 WHEN AN IMPAIRMENT TEST IS REQUIRED

There is an important distinction in IAS 36 between assessing whether there are indications of impairment and actually carrying out an impairment test. The standard has two different general requirements governing when an impairment test should be carried out:

- For goodwill and all intangible assets with an indefinite useful life the standard requires an annual impairment test. The impairment test may be performed at any time in the annual reporting period, but it must be performed at the same time every year. Different intangible assets may be tested for impairment at different times. *[IAS 36.10]*.

  In addition, the carrying amount of an intangible asset that has not yet been brought into use must be tested at least annually. This, the standard argues, is because intangible assets are intrinsically subject to greater uncertainty before they are brought into use. *[IAS 36.11]*.

- For all other classes of assets within the scope of IAS 36, the entity is required to assess at each reporting date (year-end or any interim period end) whether there are any indications of impairment. The impairment test itself only has to be carried out if there are such indications. *[IAS 36.8-9]*.

The particular requirements of IAS 36 concerning the impairment testing of goodwill and of intangible assets with an indefinite life are discussed separately at 8 (goodwill) and 10 (intangible assets with indefinite useful life) below, however the methodology used is identical for all types of assets.

For all other assets, an impairment test, i.e. a formal estimate of the asset's recoverable amount as set out in the standard, must be performed if indications of impairment exist. *[IAS 36.9]*. The only exception is where there was sufficient headroom in a previous impairment calculation that would not have been eroded by subsequent events or the asset or CGU is not sensitive to a particular indicator; the indicators and these exceptions are discussed further in the following section. *[IAS 36.15]*.

2.1 Indicators of impairment

Identifying indicators of impairment is a crucial stage in the impairment assessment process. IAS 36 lists examples of indicators but stresses that they represent the minimum indicators that should be considered by the entity and that the list is not exhaustive. *[IAS 36.12-13]*. They are divided into external and internal indicators.

External sources of information:

(a) A decline in an asset's value during the period that is significantly more than would be expected from the passage of time or normal use.

(b) Significant adverse changes that have taken place during the period, or will take place in the near future, in the technological, market, economic or legal environment in which the entity operates or in the market to which an asset is dedicated.

(c) An increase in the period in market interest rates or other market rates of return on investments if these increases are likely to affect the discount rate used in calculating an asset's value in use and decrease the asset's recoverable amount materially.

(d) The carrying amount of the net assets of the entity exceeds its market capitalisation.

Internal sources of information:

(e) Evidence of obsolescence or physical damage of an asset.

(f) Significant changes in the extent to which, or manner in which, an asset is used or is expected to be used, that have taken place in the period or soon thereafter and that will have an adverse effect on it. These changes include the asset becoming idle, plans to dispose of an asset sooner than expected, reassessing its useful life as finite rather than indefinite or plans to restructure the operation to which the asset belongs.

(g) Internal reports that indicate that the economic performance of an asset is, or will be, worse than expected. [IAS 36.12].

The standard amplifies and explains relevant evidence from internal reporting that indicates that an asset may be impaired:

(a) cash flows for acquiring the asset, or subsequent cash needs for operating or maintaining it, are significantly higher than originally budgeted;

(b) operating profit or loss or actual net cash flows are significantly worse than those budgeted;

(c) a significant decline in budgeted net cash flows or operating profit, or a significant increase in budgeted loss; or

(d) operating losses or net cash outflows for the asset, if current period amounts are aggregated with budgeted amounts for the future. [IAS 36.14].

The presence of indicators of impairment will not necessarily mean that the entity has to calculate the recoverable amount of the asset in accordance with IAS 36. A previous calculation may have shown that an asset's recoverable amount was significantly greater than its carrying amount and it may be clear that subsequent events have been insufficient to eliminate this headroom. Similarly, previous analysis may show that an asset's recoverable amount is not sensitive to one or more of these indicators. [IAS 36.15].

If there are indications that the asset is impaired, it may also be necessary to examine the remaining useful life of the asset, its residual value and the depreciation method used, as these may also need to be adjusted even if no impairment loss is recognised. [IAS 36.17].

2.1.1 Market capitalisation

If market capitalisation is lower than the carrying value of equity, this is a powerful indicator of impairment as it suggests that the market considers that the business value is less than the carrying value. However, the market may have taken account of factors other than the return that the entity is generating on its assets. For example, an individual entity may have a high level of debt that it is unable to service fully. A market capitalisation below equity will not necessarily be reflected in an equivalent impairment loss. An entity's response to this indicator depends very much on facts and circumstances. Most entities cannot avoid examining their CGUs in these circumstances unless there was sufficient headroom in a previous impairment calculation that would not have been eroded by subsequent events or none of the assets or CGUs is sensitive to market capitalisation as an indicator. If a formal impairment review is required when the market capitalisation is below equity, great care must be taken to ensure that the discount rate used to calculate VIU is consistent with current market assessments.

IAS 36 does not require a formal reconciliation between market capitalisation of the entity, FVLCD and VIU. However, entities need to be able to understand the reason for the shortfall and consider whether they have made sufficient disclosures describing those factors that could result in an impairment in the next periods. *[IAS 36.134(f)]*.

2.1.2 (Future) performance

Another significant element is an explicit reference in (b), (c) and (d) above to internal evidence that future performance will be worse than expected. Thus IAS 36 requires an impairment review to be undertaken if performance is or will be significantly below that previously budgeted. In particular, there may be indicators of impairment even if the asset is profitable in the current period if budgeted results for the future indicate that there will be losses or net cash outflows when these are aggregated with the current period results.

2.1.3 Individual assets or part of CGU?

Some of the indicators are aimed at individual fixed assets rather than the CGU of which they are a part, for example a decline in the value of an asset or evidence that it is obsolete or damaged. Such indicators may also imply that a wider review of the business or CGU is required. However, this is not always the case. For example, if there is a slump in property prices and the market value of the entity's new head office falls below its carrying value this would constitute an indicator of impairment and trigger a review. At the level of the individual asset, as FVLCD is below carrying amount, this might indicate that a write-down is necessary. However, the building's recoverable amount may have to be considered in the context of a CGU of which it is a part. This is an example of a situation where it may not be necessary to re-estimate an asset's recoverable amount because it may be obvious that the CGU has suffered no impairment. In short, it may be irrelevant to the recoverable amount of the CGU that it contains a head office whose market value has fallen.

2.1.4 Interest rates

Including interest rates as indicators of impairment could imply that assets are judged to be impaired if they are no longer expected to earn a market rate of return, even though they may generate the same cash flows as before. However, it may well be that an upward movement in general interest rates will not give rise to a write-down in assets because they may not affect the rate of return expected from the asset or CGU itself. The standard indicates that this may be an example where the asset's recoverable amount is not sensitive to a particular indicator.

The discount rate used in a VIU calculation should be based on the rate specific for the asset. An entity is not required to make a formal estimate of an asset's recoverable amount if the discount rate used in calculating the asset's VIU is unlikely to be affected by the increase in market rates. For example the recoverable amount for an asset that has a long remaining useful life may not be materially affected by increases in short-term rates. Further an entity is not required to make a formal estimate of an asset's recoverable amount if previous sensitivity analyses of the recoverable amount showed that it is unlikely that there will be a material decrease in the recoverable amount because future cash flows are also likely to increase to compensate for the increase in market rates. Consequently, the potential decrease in the recoverable amount may simply be unlikely to result in a material impairment loss. *[IAS 36.16]*.

Events in the financial crisis of 2008/2009 demonstrated that this may also be true for a decline in market interest rates. A substantial decline in short-term market interest rates did not lead to an equivalent decline in the (long term) market rates specific to assets.

3 DIVIDING THE ENTITY INTO CASH-GENERATING UNITS (CGUS)

If an impairment assessment is required, one of the first tasks will be to identify the individual assets affected and if those assets do not have individually identifiable and independent cash inflows, to divide the entity into CGUs. The group of assets that is considered together should be as small as is reasonably practicable, i.e. the entity should be divided into as many CGUs as possible and an entity must identify the lowest aggregation of assets that generate largely independent cash inflows. *[IAS 36.6, 68]*.

It must be stressed that CGUs are identified from cash inflows, not from net cash flows or indeed from any basis on which costs might be allocated (this is discussed further below).

The existence of a degree of flexibility over what constitutes a CGU is obvious. Indeed, the standard acknowledges that the identification of CGUs involves judgement. *[IAS 36.68]*. The key guidance offered by the standard is that CGU selection will be influenced by 'how management monitors the entity's operations (such as by product lines, businesses, individual locations, districts or regional areas) or how management makes decisions about continuing or disposing of the entity's assets and operations'. *[IAS 36.69]*. While monitoring by management may help identify CGUs, it does not override the requirement that the identification of CGUs is based on the lowest level at which largely independent cash inflows can be identified.

Example 20.1: Identification of cash-generating units and largely independent cash inflows

An entity obtains a contract to deliver mail to all users within a country, for a price that depends solely on the weight of the item, regardless of the distance between sender and recipient. It makes a significant loss in deliveries to outlying regions. Because of the entity's contractual service obligations, the CGU is the whole region covered by its mail services.

The division should not go beyond the level at which each income stream is capable of being separately monitored. For example, it may be difficult to identify a level below an individual factory as a CGU but of course an individual factory may or may not be a CGU.

An entity may be able to identify independent cash inflows for individual factories or other assets or groups of assets such as offices, retail outlets or assets that directly generate revenue such as those held for rental or hire.

Intangible assets such as brands, customer relationships and trademarks used by an entity for its own activities are unlikely to generate largely independent cash inflows and will therefore be tested together with other assets at a CGU level. This is also the case with intangible assets with indefinite useful lives and those that have not yet been brought into use, even though the carrying amount must be tested at least annually for impairment (see 2 above).

Focusing on cash inflows avoids a common misconception in identifying CGUs. Management may argue that the costs for each of their retail outlets are not largely independent because of purchasing synergies and therefore these outlets cannot be separate CGUs. In fact, this will not be the deciding feature. IAS 36 explicitly refers to the allocation of cash outflows that are necessarily incurred to generate the cash inflows. If they are not directly attributed, cash outflows can be 'allocated on a reasonable and consistent basis'. *[IAS 36.39(b)]*. Goodwill and corporate assets may also have to be allocated to CGUs as described in 8.1 and 4.2 below.

Management may consider that the primary way in which they monitor their business is for the entity as a whole or on a regional or segmental basis, which could also result in CGUs being set at too high a level. It is undoubtedly true, in one sense, that management monitors the business as a whole but in most cases they also monitor at a lower level that can be identified from the lowest level of independent cash inflows. For example, while management of a chain of cinemas will make decisions that affect all the cinemas such as the selection of films and catering arrangements, it will also monitor individual cinemas. Management of a chain of branded restaurants will monitor both the brand and the individual restaurants. In both cases, management may also monitor at an intermediate level, e.g. a level based on regions. In most cases, each restaurant or cinema will be a CGU, as illustrated in Example 20.2 – Example B below, because each will generate largely independent cash inflows, but brands and goodwill may be tested at a higher level.

In Example 20.2 below, Example A illustrates a practical approach which involves working down to the smallest group of assets for which a stream of cash inflows can be identified. These groups of assets will be CGUs unless the performance of their cash inflow-generating assets is dependent on those generated by other assets, or their cash inflows are affected by those of other assets. If the cash inflows generated by the group of assets are not largely independent of those generated by other assets, other assets should be added to the group to form the smallest collection of assets that generates largely independent cash inflows.

Example 20.2: Identification of cash-generating units

Example A – newspapers

An entity publishes 10 suburban newspapers, each with a different mast-head, across 4 distinct regions within a city centre. The price paid for a purchased mast-head is recognised as an intangible asset. The newspapers are distributed to residents free of charge. No newspaper is distributed outside its region. All of the revenue generated by each newspaper comes from advertising sales. An analysis of advertising sales shows that for each mast-head:

- approximately 90% of sales come from advertisers purchasing 'bundled' advertisements that appear in all those newspapers published in one particular region of the city;
- approximately 6% of sales come from advertisers purchasing 'bundled' advertisements that appear in all 10 newspapers in the city centre; and
- approximately 4% of sales come from advertisers purchasing advertisements that appear in one newspaper only.

What is the cash-generating unit for an individual mast-head?

Identify the smallest aggregation of assets for which a stream of cash inflows can be identified.

The fact that it is possible to use a *pro rata* allocation basis to determine the cash inflows attributable to each newspaper means that each mast-head is likely to represent the smallest aggregation of assets for which a stream of cash inflows can be identified.

Are the cash inflows generated by an individual mast-head largely independent of those of other mast-heads and, conversely, is that individual mast-head affecting the cash inflows generated by other mast-heads?

As approximately 96% of cash inflows for each mast-head arise from 'bundled' advertising sales across multiple mast-heads, the cash inflows generated by an individual mast-head are not largely independent.

Therefore, the individual mast-heads would most likely need to be aggregated to form the smallest collection of assets that generates largely independent cash inflows. On the basis that approximately 90% of cash inflows for each mast-head arise from 'bundled' advertising sales across all of the newspapers published in a particular region, it is likely that those mast-heads published in one region will together form a cash-generating unit.

Example B – retail outlets

An entity has a chain of retail outlets located in the same country. The business model of the entity is highly integrated and the majority of the entity's revenue generating decisions, such as decisions about investments and monitoring of performance, are carried out at an entity level by the executive committee, with some decisions (such as product range and marketing) delegated to the regional or store levels. The majority of the operations, such as purchasing, are centralised. Management operates its business on a regional basis; but sales are monitored at the individual store level.

The outlets are usually bought and sold in packages of outlets that are subject to common economic characteristics, e.g. outlets of similar size or location such as a shopping centre or city or region. Only in rare situations has the entity sold or closed down an individual outlet.

The determining factor for CGUs is the level at which largely independent cash inflows are generated, and not the manner in which the entity's operations are organised and monitored. The fact that operations and costs are managed centrally does not in itself affect the source and independence of the cash inflows. The interdependence of cash outflows is unlikely to be relevant to the identification of CGUs.

The key issue in deciding whether CGUs should be identified at the level of the individual store as opposed to a group of stores is whether, if a store is closed down, all the customers of that store would seek out another of the entity's stores such that there is no significant 'leakage' of customers from the store closure. Unless the customers transfer their business to another of the entity's stores, the individual stores are separate CGUs.

Management in Example B may consider that the primary way in which they monitor their business is on a regional or segmental basis, but cash inflows are monitored at the level of an individual store. Individual stores generate independent cash inflows in most circumstances and the overriding requirement under IAS 36 is that the identification of CGUs is based on largely independent cash inflows.

However, the business models of some retailers have significantly changed over the last years and with the increased importance of internet sales will probably further change in the years ahead. The following example illustrates a new evolving omni-channel business model and its potential impact on the identification of CGUs in the retail sector.

Example 20.3: Omni-channel business model

Retailer A sells a wide range of general household merchandise online and through its retail stores which are located in most large and medium-sized cities in the same country. In order to cater to the changing habits of consumers and significant growth of online shoppers, A established an online platform. Retailer A offers the same products in each of its stores and on the online platform.

A uses the 'click and collect' business model. With 'click and collect' a customer is able to place an order online for items and then choose from which store to collect. If the preferred store runs out of an item, the customer might choose another store in the same city instead of waiting until the item arrives in its preferred store. This is the case for both customers buying online for store collection and for customers wanting to purchase the product directly in the store. The customer could either choose to pay online for the goods or make payment in store at the point of pick up. The customer could also purchase an item online and wait for it to be delivered in 3 working days. Sales generated online account for a significant portion of total sales, ranging from 20% to 25% depending on the city, and are projected to grow steadily in the coming years. The stores also serve as a point of return for products that customers ordered online. A product purchased online or in a store can be returned in any store and experience shows that customers make use of this option by returning products to stores in the same city where the product was originally purchased, picked up or delivered. The customers may exchange the products returned with products from the store shelves or they may purchase other products within the store when picking up or returning products. Hence, the activity of picking up and returning products also triggers sales in the stores. Retailer A considers the stores as well as showrooms for the online business whereby customers get professional buying advice and are able to experience the look and feel of the products, but then acquire the products only later through the online platform. For supply chain optimisation purposes Retailer A through its store personnel also encourages its customers to order online.

The performance of the stores together with the relevant online sales is assessed by city and not on an individual store-level. The employees of the stores are paid on an hourly basis and have performance-based compensation which is based on sales in all stores in one city together with online sales generated by customers located in the same city.

In assessing the CGU level for impairment purposes the key question is at which level of the retailer's organisation are independent cash inflows generated? In the specific fact pattern above, customers treat stores in the same city as an alternative means of making purchases and transacting returns which seems to indicate that all stores in one city might be one CGU. In addition, in the above described integrated omni-channel business model, the cash-inflows generated by stores and the cash-inflows generated by the online channel may not be largely independent from each other as the online revenues influence the store revenues and *vice versa*. Online customers treat stores as a collection and return point for online sales and as showrooms to experience the products. All of this together, as well as the fact that the performance of the stores and of the employees is assessed by city including online sales for the city, suggests that independent cash inflows are generated at the city level. Therefore, in the specific fact pattern above, it would be reasonable to treat the stores in a city together with the allocated assets of the online sales channel as one CGU for impairment testing purposes. The recoverable amount would consider the sales in the stores in a city plus the online sales to customers in the city.

Alternatively, if the sales generated online are an insignificant component of total sales and stores are not treated to a large extent as substitutes for each other by customers, then each single store may be considered a CGU for impairment testing purposes, even if the performance of the stores are monitored together at a higher level.

As explained above, IAS 36 states that the identification of CGUs involves judgment and that in identifying CGUs an entity should consider various factors including how management monitors the entity's operations (such as by product line, business, individual location, district or regional area) or how management makes decisions about continuing or disposing of the entity's assets and operations. *[IAS 36.68-69]*.

Applying this guidance, the following quantitative and qualitative criteria might be considered in determining the appropriate CGUs in an omni-channel business model for impairment testing purposes:

- Whether the interdependency of the revenues from different sales channels (online, stores) is evidenced in the business model.
- Whether the retailer is able to measure the interdependencies of the revenues (i.e. online and stores).
- Whether the business model provides evidence that the sales channels are monitored together (e.g. on the level of customers allocated based on ZIP-Codes to stores in an area).

- Whether the profitability as well as the remuneration system are monitored/assessed on the combined basis of online and store revenues on a regional level (e.g. cities in Example 20.3 above).
- Whether in deciding about store openings and closures, the revenues of the online-business in the region (city in the example above) are considered.
- Whether online revenues are reaching a significant quantitative proportion of the overall revenues of the retailer's CGUs. It is important to note that IAS 36 does not give any specific guidance on when cash inflows are largely independent and therefore judgement is required. The level of interdependent online sales in Example 20.3 above is not meant to be a bright line but rather part of the specific fact pattern in the example and in practice the determination of CGUs will have to be made in the context of the overall facts and circumstances.

As illustrated in Example 20.4 below, it may be that the entity is capable of identifying individual cash inflows from assets but this is not conclusive. It may not be the most relevant feature in determining the composition of its CGUs which also depends on whether cash inflows are independent from cash inflows of other assets and on how cash inflows are monitored. If, however, the entity were able to allocate VIU on a reasonable basis, this might indicate that the assets are separate CGUs.

Example 20.4:   Identification of cash-generating units – grouping of assets

Example A – A tour operator's hotels

A tour operator owns three hotels of a similar class near the beach at a large holiday resort. These hotels are advertised as alternatives in the operator's brochure, at the same price. Holidaymakers are frequently transferred from one to another and there is a central booking system for independent travellers. In this case, it may be that the hotels can be regarded as offering genuinely substitutable products by a sufficiently high proportion of potential guests and can be grouped together as a single cash-generating unit. Effectively, the hotels are being run as a single hotel on three sites. The entity will have to bear in mind that disposal decisions may still be made on a hotel-by-hotel basis and have to weight this appropriately in its determination of its CGUs.

Example B – Flagship stores

Store Z is a flagship store located in a prime site location in a capital city. Although store Z is loss making, its commercial performance is in line with expectations and with budgets. How should the impairment issues of the flagship store Z be considered?

It is difficult to conclude that a flagship store is a corporate asset as it does generate separate cash inflows (corporate assets are discussed at 4.2 below). It may be possible to argue for the aggregation of a flagship store with other stores in the vicinity into a single CGU as flagship stores are usually designed to enhance the image of the brand and hence other stores as well. They may be budgeted to run with negative cash flows; perhaps in substance the losses are not an impairment. However, this argument for not recognising an impairment would generally only be acceptable during a start-up phase and it must be borne in mind that the added function of the flagship store is largely marketing. As marketing expenditures are expensed, it would not necessarily be inconsistent to take an impairment loss and the entity may have to consider whether it should capitalise these costs in the first place.

Example C – Container ships

A shipping company operates a series of container vessels of similar size in a specific region that it considers to be a single CGU. As well as this shipping business, it has other types and regions of shipping operations where CGUs are established on an appropriate basis.

Management can identify the actual cash inflows from the individual vessels but it determines that the following are the principal features that indicate that these container ships comprise a single CGU:
- the vessels are interchangeable within the contracts and none is on a long-term hire to any individual client, meaning that the allocation of the estimated cash inflows to individual vessels becomes arbitrary;
- the pricing of the contract is not vessel specific;
- a reasonable portion of the contracts require the operator to have a certain level of capacity available, comprising multiple vessels;
- the investment, continuance and disposal decisions are made by class of vessel and not linked to the actual revenue generated by that vessel;
- the class of vessels has a clear and distinctive market and management views and makes decisions by reference to the CGU, not individual assets.

The fact that one or more of the assets could be used individually, i.e. taken out of the 'pool', would not in itself prevent the assets being considered part of a single CGU.

Example C is illustrated in Extract 20.1 below.

> **Extract 20.1: A.P. Møller – Mærsk A/S (2019)**
> Consolidated financial statements –Notes
> Note 25 Significant accounting estimates and judgements [extract]
> Intangible assets and property, plant and equipment [extract]
>
> The determination of cash-generating units differs for the various businesses. Ocean operates its fleet of container vessels, containers and hub terminals in an integrated network, for which reason the Ocean activities are tested for impairment as a single cash-generating unit. In addition, the intermodal activities reported under Logistics & Services are included in the Ocean cash-generating unit for impairment testing to apply consistency between the asset base and related cash flows. In Logistics & Services, apart from intermodal, each entity is defined as a cash-generating unit. In gateway terminals, each terminal is considered individually in impairment tests, except when the capacity is managed as a portfolio, which is the case for certain terminals in Northern Europe and Global Ports Investments, Russia.

In Example C above, an analogy can be made to the conclusion in illustrative example IE11-IE16 of IAS 36 that plants B and C of entity M are part of one CGU which is illustrated in the following Example 20.5:

Example 20.5: *Identification of cash-generating units – single product entity*

Entity M produces a single product and owns plants A, B, C. Each plant is located in a different continent. A produces a component that is assembled in either B or C. The combined capacity of B and C is not fully utilised. M's products are sold worldwide from either plant B or C. For example, B's product can be sold in C's continent if the products can be delivered faster from B than from C. Utilisation levels from B and C depend on the allocation of sales between the two sites. There is no active market for A's products.

Most likely A, B and C together, therefore M as a whole, are the smallest identifiable group of assets that generates cash inflows that are largely independent. This is due to:
(a) A's cash inflows depending on sales of the final product by B and C; and
(b) cash inflows for B and C depend on the allocation of the production across the two sites.

As explained at 3.3 below, the conclusion would be different if an active market for A's product existed, resulting in A being one CGU and B and C together another CGU.

As a result of applying the methodology illustrated in Example 20.2 above, an entity could identify a large number of CGUs. However, the standard allows reasonable approximations and one way in which entities may apply this in practice is to group together assets that are separate CGUs, but which if considered individually for impairment would not be material. Retail outlets, usually separate CGUs, may be grouped if they are in close proximity to one another, e.g. all of the retail outlets in a city centre owned by a branded clothes retailer, if they are all subject to the same economic circumstances and grouping them together rather than examining them individually will have an immaterial effect. However, the entity will still have to scrutinise the individual CGUs to ensure that those that it intends to sell or that have significantly underperformed are not supported by the others with which they are grouped. They would need to be identified and dealt with individually.

In practice, different entities will inevitably have varying approaches when determining their CGUs. There is judgement to be exercised in determining an income stream and in determining whether it is largely independent of other streams. Given this, entities may tend towards larger rather than smaller CGUs, to keep the complexity of the process within reasonable bounds.

IAS 36 also requires that identification of cash generating units be consistent from period to period unless the change is justified; if changes are made and the entity records or reverses an impairment, disclosures are required. *[IAS 36.72, 73].*

Assets held for sale cannot remain part of a CGU. They generate independent cash inflows being the proceeds expected to be generated by sale. Once they are classified as held for sale they will be accounted for in accordance with IFRS 5 and carried at an amount that may not exceed their FVLCD (see 5.1 below and Chapter 4 for a further discussion of IFRS 5's requirements).

3.1 CGUs and intangible assets

IAS 36 requires certain intangible assets to be tested at least annually for impairment (see 2 above). These are intangible assets with an indefinite life and intangible assets that have not yet been brought into use. *[IAS 36.10-11].*

Although these assets must be tested for impairment at least once a year, this does not mean that they have to be tested by themselves. The same requirements apply as for all other assets. The recoverable amount is the higher of the FVLCD or VIU of the individual asset or of the CGU to which the asset belongs (see 3 above). If the individual intangible asset's FVLCD is lower than the carrying amount and it does not generate largely independent cash flows then the CGU to which it belongs must be reviewed for impairment.

Many intangible assets do not generate independent cash inflows as individual assets and so they are tested for impairment with other assets of the CGU of which they are part. A trade mark, for example, will generate largely independent cash flows if it is licensed to a third party but more commonly it will be part of a CGU.

If impairment is tested by reference to the FVLCD or VIU of the CGU, impairment losses, if any, will be allocated in accordance with IAS 36. Any goodwill allocated to the CGU has to be written off first. After that, the other assets of the CGU, including the intangible asset, will be, reduced *pro rata* based on their carrying amount (see 11.2 below). *[IAS 36.104].* However, the carrying amount of an asset should not be reduced below the highest of its fair value less costs of disposal, value in use or zero. If the preceding rule is applied, further allocation of the impairment loss is made *pro rata* to the other assets of the unit (group of units).

If the intangible asset is no longer useable then it must be written off, e.g. an in-process research and development project that has been abandoned, so it is no longer part of the larger CGU and its own recoverable amount is nil. Intangible assets held for sale are treated in the same way as all other assets held for sale – see 5.1 below.

3.1.1 Intangible assets as corporate assets

As discussed in 3.1 above, many intangible assets do not generate independent cash inflows as individual assets and should therefore be tested for impairment with other assets of the CGU of which they are part. However, one question an entity would need to assess beforehand, is whether the intangible assets in question meet the corporate assets definition '...assets other than goodwill that contribute to the future cash flows of both the cash-generating unit under review and other cash-generating units' or whether the intangible assets should be considered in determining cash-generating units? The judgement made in this respect can have a significant impact on the level at which cash-generating units are identified and therefore at which level assets are assessed for impairment. A careful consideration of all facts and circumstances is required to avoid carrying out impairment tests at a level that is too high with the result of masking potential impairments.

Assume a scenario where entity A acquires entity B. Entity B operates in a different industry to A. The reason for the acquisition was diversification with no expected cross synergies between A's and B's operations. Entity B sells product X under a European wide well-known brand and operates across Europe. Each country has its own manufacturing site from which mainly small local companies in the same country are served. Before the acquisition, entity B concluded that every manufacturing site in each country is a separate CGU. On acquisition of entity B an intangible asset for the brand is recorded in entity's A group financial statements. No goodwill was recorded. At which level should entity A set the cash-generating units for the acquired business? In our view in this specific example, the single brand would not result in a determination that the cash-generating unit(s) of entity B's business are at the overall level of B. There are individual production sites in each European country from which customers in the same country are served and there is no cross selling of products to customers in other European countries, therefore independent cash inflows can be identified on a country level resulting in the identification of cash-generating units on a country level. The treatment of the brand would follow the guidance as set out in 4.2 below for corporate assets, either because the brand is considered to be a corporate asset or by analogy.

On the other hand, if in the example above B was a professional services company operating European wide and entity B's brand identifies entity B as one integrated pan-European service provider and markets itself to customers as such, the determination of cash-generating unit(s) of entity B's business at an overall level of B including the brand may be appropriate, particularly where a majority of the customers have a presence in multiple European countries and are looking for one supplier that can serve each local presence.

As explained above, the identification of CGUs involves judgement and a careful consideration of all facts and circumstances is required.

3.2 Leased assets and CGUs

Many right-of-use assets recorded under IFRS 16 will be assessed for impairment on a CGU level rather than on individual asset level. While there might be instances where leased assets generate largely independent cash inflows, many leased assets will be used by an entity as an input in its main operating activities whether these are service providing or production of goods related. If a right-of-use asset is tested on a stand-alone basis and is fully impaired, the entity would need to assess the need to recognise an additional onerous lease provision for amounts not already recognised in the lease liability (see Chapter 26 at 6.2.1).

One question that might arise, particularly in relation to real estate leases, is what the unit of account for impairment purposes is. In other words, whether the right-of-use asset(s) resulting from a lease governed by one lease contract needs to be assessed and treated consistently on the overall contract level or whether for example the usage of different areas or floors of a leased building for different purposes could result in separate right-of-use assets for impairment assessments. Next to the general principle in IAS 36 on how assets contribute to the generation of independent cash inflows (individual asset, part of a CGU or as corporate asset), the answer to this question depends in our view on whether the lease contract is over identifiable asset(s) portions that are physically distinct and therefore could effectively be separate unit of accounts. In making this assessment, the guidance in B20 and B32 to IFRS 16 and IAS 40.10 could be considered. For leased assets/buildings that are used in parts for different purposes and where these portions are physically distinct, the usage and therefore the generation of independent cash inflows will drive the considerations under IAS 36. Judgement might be needed to determine the units of accounts of the right-of-use asset(s), and their allocation to different CGUs. This is illustrated in the following example:

Example 20.6: Identification of cash-generating units – leased assets

Retail store chain M leases 5 floors in a 10-storey building. The floors are used as follows by M:

- Ground floor: used for M's store X, leasehold improvements were made at the beginning of the lease;
- Second floor and third floor: used for M's HR and marketing department;
- Fourth floor: originally it was planned that the space would be utilised together with the fifth floor for the payroll department, but then floor four was sub-let to a law firm;
- Fifth floor: currently unoccupied. While M tried to lease this floor, it has been difficult to find a tenant and M now expects that the floor will be empty through the end of the lease.

Entity M signed one lease contract with the lessor for the five floors. The lease specifies the rent per floor, which equals the stand-alone price per floor. The building is configured in a way that every floor could be closed off, leased and used separately from the rest of the building.

As the five leased floors are used by entity M for different purposes and each floor is a physically distinguishable unit, M concluded that it needs to asses them separately in its CGU determination exercise.

In identifying cash-generating units for the stores, M considers whether, for example:

(a) Internal management reporting is organised to measure performance on a store-by-store basis;

(b) The business is run on a store-by-store profit basis or on a region/city basis.

The leased ground floor is used for retail store X. The ground floor does not generate largely independent cash inflows from the store and is therefore assessed for impairment together with the store. All M's stores are in different neighbourhoods and were determined to have different customer bases. Although store X is managed at a corporate level, X generates cash inflows that are largely independent of those of M's other stores. M therefore concluded that store X is a separate cash-generating unit.

The leased second and third floor are used for marketing and human resources corporate functions. The part of the right-of-use-asset in relation to these floors is a corporate asset and is allocated on a reasonable and consistent basis to the CGUs to which it relates (see 4.2.1 below).

The leased fourth floor is sub-let to a law firm. M assessed under the guidance of IFRS 16 whether the sublease is classified as a finance lease, resulting in de-recognition of the right-of-use asset and recording of a lease receivable equal to the amount of the net investment in the lease, or an operating lease, with continuing recognition of the right-of-use asset (see Chapter 23 at 7.3). M's assessment classified the sub-lease as an operating lease. M elects to account for the investment property in relation to fourth floor under the cost model (see Chapter 19 at 2.1 and 7). Due to the sub-lease, this part of the right-of-use-asset generates largely independent cash inflows and must be assessed for impairment on a stand-alone basis. Floor five is unoccupied and not used for M's operating activities. M therefore determines that this part of the right-of-use asset needs to be assessed for impairment on a stand-alone basis by comparing the carrying amount with the recoverable amount (higher of VIU and FVLCD). As the floor is expected to be unoccupied through the end of the lease the VIU will be zero. The fact that M expects not to use the fifth floor or is no longer looking for a tenant does not necessarily mean the FVLCD is zero. M would need to determine the fair value under consideration of IFRS 13 – *Fair Value Measurement* (see Chapter 14) and consider the need for any accelerated depreciation.

3.3 Active markets and identifying CGUs

The standard stresses the significance of an active market for the output of an asset or group of assets in identifying a CGU. An active market is a market in which transactions take place with sufficient frequency and volume to provide pricing information on an ongoing basis. *[IFRS 13 Appendix A]*. If there is an active market for the output produced by an asset or group of assets, the assets concerned are identified as a cash-generating unit, even if some or all of the output is used internally. *[IAS 36.70]*. The reason given for this rule is that the existence of an active market means that the assets or CGU could generate cash inflows independently from the rest of the business by selling on the active market. *[IAS 36.71]*. There are active markets for many metals, energy products (various grades of oil product, natural gas) and other commodities that are freely traded. When estimating cash inflows for the selling CGU or cash outflows for the buying CGU, the entity will replace internal transfer prices with management's best estimate of the price in a future arm's length transaction. Note that this is a general requirement for all assets and CGUs subject to internal transfer pricing (see 7.1.6 below).

Example A below, based on Example 1B in IAS 36's accompanying section of illustrative examples, illustrates the point. Example B describes circumstances in which the existence of an active market does not necessarily lead to the identification of a separate CGU.

Example 20.7:   Identification of cash-generating units – internally-used products

Example A – Plant for an Intermediate Step in a Production Process

A significant raw material used for plant Y's final production is an intermediate product bought from plant X of the same entity. X's products are sold to Y at an internal price that passes all margins to X. 60 per cent of X's final production is sold to Y and the remaining 40 per cent is sold to customers outside of the entity. Y sells 80 per cent of its products to customers outside of the entity. Transfer pricing is discussed at 7.1.6 below.

If X can sell its products in an active market and generate cash inflows that are largely independent of the cash inflows from Y, it is likely that X is a CGU even though part of its production is used by Y. Therefore, its cash inflows can be regarded as being largely independent. It is likely that Y is also a separate CGU. However, internal transfer prices do not reflect market prices for X's output. Therefore, in determining value in use of both X and Y, the entity adjusts financial budgets/forecasts to reflect management's best estimate of future prices that could be achieved in arm's length transactions for those of X's products that are used internally.

If, on the other hand, there is no active market, it is likely that the recoverable amount of each plant cannot be assessed independently of the recoverable amount of the other plant. The majority of X's production is used internally and could not be sold in an active market. Cash inflows of X depend on demand for Y's products. Therefore, X cannot be considered to generate cash inflows that are largely independent of those of Y. In addition, the two plants are managed together. As a consequence, it is likely that X and Y together are the smallest group of assets that generates cash inflows that are largely independent. *[IAS 36.IE5-10]*.

Example B – 'Market' for intermediate product not relevant to identification of a separate CGU

A vertically integrated operation located in Australia produces an intermediate product that is fully used internally to manufacture the end product. The Australian market is the principal market for the intermediate product and there is no active market as defined by IFRS 13 (see Chapter 14) for it in Australia. The entity has only one other competitor in Australia, which is also vertically integrated and, likewise, uses the intermediate product internally. Both entities are, and have always been, very profitable when looking at their vertically integrated manufacturing processes to the end-stage product.

There is an active market for the intermediate product in China, but the prices at which the product can be sold are so low that a company based in Australia whose sole activity is to sell the intermediate product into China would never be profitable and a company would never set up manufacturing operations in Australia in order to sell into China.

Each of the Australian companies will occasionally sell small surpluses of their intermediate products into the active market in China, rather than make that product available to their competitor in Australia.

The existence of an active market for the intermediate product in China might suggest that the operations involved should be treated as a separate CGU. However, the mere existence of an active market somewhere in the world does not mean that the asset or CGU could realistically generate cash inflows independently from the rest of the business by selling on that active market. If such sales are a genuine incidental activity (i.e. if it is genuinely a case of obtaining some proceeds from excess product that would otherwise be scrapped), it may be appropriate not to regard that market as an active market for the intermediate product for IAS 36 purposes.

If the market is not regarded as an active market for IAS 36 purposes, the assets/operations involved in producing the intermediate product will not be treated as a separate CGU.

4   IDENTIFYING THE CARRYING AMOUNT OF CGU ASSETS

After an entity has established its CGU(s) for the impairment assessment, it needs to determine the carrying amount of the CGU(s). The carrying amount must be determined on a basis that is consistent with the way in which the recoverable amount is determined. *[IAS 36.75]*.

The carrying amount of a CGU includes only those assets that can be attributed directly or allocated on a reasonable and consistent basis. These must be the assets that will generate the future cash inflows used in determining the CGU's recoverable amount. It does not include the carrying amount of any recognised liability, unless the recoverable amount of the cash-generating unit cannot be determined without taking it into account. Both FVLCD and VIU of a CGU are determined excluding cash flows that relate to assets that are not part of the cash-generating unit and liabilities that have been recognised. *[IAS 36.76]*.

The standard emphasises the importance of completeness in the allocation of assets to CGUs. Every asset used in generating the cash flows of the CGU being tested must be included in the CGU; otherwise an impaired CGU might appear to be unimpaired, as its carrying value would be understated by having missed out assets. *[IAS 36.77]*.

There are exceptions to the rule that recognised liabilities are not included in arriving at the CGU's carrying value or VIU. If the buyer would have to assume a liability if it acquired an asset or group of assets, then the fair value less costs of disposal would be the price to sell the assets or group of assets and the liability together. The liability would then need to be deducted from the CGU's carrying amount and VIU. This will enable a meaningful comparison between carrying amount and recoverable amount, whether the latter is based on FVLCD or VIU. *[IAS 36.78]*. See 4.1.1 below.

For practical reasons the entity may determine the recoverable amount of a CGU after taking into account assets and liabilities such as receivables or other financial assets, trade payables, pensions and other provisions that are outside the scope of IAS 36 and therefore not part of the CGU. *[IAS 36.79]*. If the value in use calculation for a CGU or its FVLCD are determined taking into account these sorts of items, then it is essential that the carrying amount of the CGU is determined on a consistent basis. However, this frequently causes confusion in practice, as described at 4.1 below.

Other assets such as goodwill and corporate assets may not be able to be attributed on a reasonable and consistent basis and the standard has separate rules regarding their treatment. The allocation of goodwill is dealt with separately at 8.1 below and corporate assets at 4.2 below.

4.1 Consistency and the impairment test

Consistency is a very important principle underlying IAS 36. In testing for impairment entities must ensure that the carrying amount of the CGU is consistent for VIU and FVLCD calculations. In calculating VIU, or using a discounted cash flow methodology for FVLCD, entities must ensure that there is consistency between the assets and liabilities of the CGU and the cash flows taken into account, as there must also be between the cash flows and discount rate.

The exceptions to the rule that recognised liabilities are not included in arriving at the CGU's carrying value. If the buyer would have to assume a liability if it acquired an asset or group of assets (CGU), then the fair value less costs of disposal of the CGU would be the price to sell the assets of the CGU and the liability together, less the costs of disposal. *[IAS 36.78]*. To provide a meaningful comparison this liability should then be deducted as well from the VIU and the carrying amount of the asset or group of assets (CGU).

The standards requirement to deduct the liability from both the CGU's carrying amount and from its VIU avoids the danger of distortion that can arise when cash flows that will be paid to settle the contractual obligation are included in the VIU discounted cash flow calculation. If the liability cash flows are included in the VIU discounted cash flow calculation, they would potentially be discounted using a different discount rate to the rate used to calculate the carrying value of the liability causing distortion. See 4.1.1 below for further discussion.

From a practical point of view an entity could simply calculate the VIU of a CGU excluding the liability cash outflows and compare that to the CGU carrying amount excluding the liability. While this would mean that the VIU is not comparable to the FVLCD, this would not cause an issue as long as the calculated VIU is above the CGU's carrying amount, therefore providing evidence that the CGU is not impaired.

It is also accepted in IAS 36 that an entity might for practical reasons determine the recoverable amount of a CGU after taking into account assets and liabilities such as receivables or other financial assets, trade payables, pensions and other provisions that are outside the scope of IAS 36.

In all cases:
- the carrying amount of the CGU must be calculated on the same basis for VIU and FVLCD, i.e. including the same assets and liabilities; and
- it is essential that cash flows are prepared on a consistent basis to the assets and liabilities within CGUs.

In addition, some of these assets and liabilities have themselves been calculated using discounting techniques. Therefore a danger of distortion arises resulting from differing discount rates, as discussed above.

4.1.1 Environmental provisions and similar provisions and liabilities

Paragraph 78 of IAS 36 illustrates liabilities that should be deducted from the carrying amount of the assets of a CGU because a buyer would assume the liability using an example of a mine in a country in which there is a legal obligation to restore the site by replacing the overburden. The restoration provision, which is the present value of the restoration costs, has been provided for and deducted from the carrying value of the assets of the CGU. It will be taken into account in the estimation of FVLCD but must also be deducted in arriving at VIU so that both methods of estimating recoverable amount are calculated on a comparable basis that aligns with the carrying amount of the CGU.

There are other provisions for liabilities that would be taken over by the purchaser of a CGU, e.g. property dilapidations or similar contractual restoration provisions. The provision will be accrued as the 'damage' is incurred and hence expensed over time rather than capitalised. If the provision is deducted from the assets of the CGU then it must also be deducted in arriving at VIU and it has to be taken into account in the estimation of FVLCD.

Indeed, many provisions made in accordance with IAS 37 – *Provisions, Contingent Liabilities and Contingent Assets* – may be reflected in the CGU's carrying amount as long as they will be treated appropriately in arriving at the recoverable amount of the CGU.

Including the cash outflows that will be paid to settle the contractual obligation in the VIU discounted cash flow calculation bears the danger of distortion as the cash flows for impairment purposes will be discounted using a different rate to the rate used to calculate the provision itself. The carrying amount of this class of liability will reflect a discount rate suitable for provisions, based on the time value of money and the risks relating to the provisions. This is likely to be considerably lower than a suitable discount rate for an asset and the distortion caused by this would have to be considered and adjusted if the effect is significant. A simple illustration is that the present value of a cash outflow of €100 in 10 years' time is €39 discounted at 10% but €68 if a discount rate of 4% is used. Deducting the respective cash flows discounted at the asset discount rate could result in an overstatement of the CGU's recoverable amount.

Therefore, to avoid the danger of distortion and to allow for a meaningful comparison between the carrying amount of the CGU and the recoverable amount, IAS 36 requires the carrying amount of the provision to be deducted in determining both the CGU's carrying amount and its VIU. *[IAS 36.78]*.

In 2015 the Interpretations Committee received a request to clarify the application of paragraph 78 of IAS 36. The submitter observed that the approach of deducting the liability from both the VIU and the CGU's carrying amount would produce a null result and therefore asked whether this was really the intention or whether an alternative approach was required.

In its November 2015 meeting the Interpretations Committee observed that when the CGU's fair value less costs of disposal (FVLCD) considers a recognised liability then paragraph 78 of IAS 36 requires both the CGU's carrying amount and its VIU to be adjusted by the carrying amount of the liability. In the Interpretations Committee's view this approach provides a straightforward and cost-effective method to perform a meaningful comparison of the recoverable amount and the carrying amount of the CGU. Moreover, it observed that this approach is consistent with the requirement in IAS 36 to reflect the risks specific to the asset in the present value measurement of the assets in the CGU and the requirements in IAS 37 to reflect the risk specific to the liability in the present value calculation of the liability.

The Interpretations Committee therefore decided that neither an interpretation nor an amendment to a Standard was necessary and did not add this issue to its agenda.

As mentioned at 4.1 above from a practical point of view an entity could calculate the VIU of a CGU without deducting the liability cash outflow and compare that to the CGU excluding the liability. As long as the calculated VIU is above the CGU's carrying amount no impairment would be required and the lack of comparability to the FVLCD would not cause an issue.

4.1.2 Lease liabilities under IFRS 16

A CGU may include a right-of-use asset recorded under IFRS 16. Right-of-use assets are assessed for impairment by applying IAS 36.

When it comes to lease arrangements, in most cases a CGU would be disposed of together with the associated lease arrangements. FVLCD for the CGU would consider the associated lease arrangements and therefore the need to make the contractual lease payments. This would require deducting the carrying amount of the lease liabilities when determining the carrying amount of the CGU.

It is important to note that lease payments reflected in the lease liability recorded in the statement of financial position will have to be excluded from the VIU calculation. If the carrying amount of the lease liabilities is deducted to arrive at the carrying amount of the CGU, the same carrying amount of the lease liabilities would need to be deducted from the VIU. IAS 36 does not allow the calculation of the VIU on a net basis directly, through reducing the future cash flows by the lease payments as this bears the risk of distortion that will arise due to the difference in the discount rate used for the VIU calculation and the discount rate used to calculate the carrying amount of the lease liability. *[IAS 36.78]*. See 7.1.8 below for further discussion around VIU and lease payments.

4.1.3 Trade debtors and creditors

Whether an entity includes or excludes trade debtors and creditors in the assets of the CGU, it must avoid double counting the cash flows that will repay the receivable or pay those liabilities. This may be tricky because cash flows do not normally distinguish between cash flows that relate to working capital and other items. A practical solution often applied is to include working capital items in the carrying amount of the CGU and include the effect of changes in the working capital balances in the cash flow forecast.

The following simplified example is based on a finite life CGU and illustrates the effects of including and excluding initial working capital items.

Example 20.8:   The effects of working capital on impairment tests

At the end of the year, Entity A's net assets comprise:

	€
Carrying value of assets in CGU	100,000
Working capital: net liability	(800)

Its budgeted cash flows before interest and tax for the following five years, including and excluding changes in working capital, and their net present value using a 10% discount rate are as follows:

Year	1	2	3	4	5	6
	€	€	€	€	€	€
Pre-tax cash flow [1]	10,000	20,000	30,000	40,000	50,000	
Opening working capital	(800)	(1,500)	(3,000)	(4,500)	(6,000)	(7,500)
Closing working capital	(1,500)	(3,000)	(4,500)	(6,000)	(7,500)	
Change in working capital	700	1,500	1,500	1,500	1,500	(7,500)

Notes

(1) cash flow before interest, excluding working capital changes

Year 5's closing working capital is treated as a cash outflow in year 6.

Cash flow including opening working capital	10,700	21,500	31,500	41,500	51,500	(7,500)
NPV at 10% discount rate	107,251					
Cash flow excluding opening working capital	11,500	21,500	31,500	41,500	51,500	(7,500)
NPV at 10% discount rate	107,979					

Including opening working capital:

	€
Carrying value of CGU net of working capital	99,200
NPV of cash flow including opening working capital	107,251
Headroom	8,051

Excluding working capital:

	€
Carrying value of CGU	100,000
NPV of cash flow excluding opening changes in working capital	107,979
Headroom	7,979

Note that the headroom is not exactly the same in both cases, due to the discounting effect of differences in the periods in which cash flows are incurred. Typically, the distortion caused by discounting will not be significant in relation to short term working capital items. However, in our view, if significant, such distortion should be adjusted.

Any other combination will not treat assets and cash flows consistently and will either overstate or understate headroom, e.g. it would be incorrect to compare the carrying value of the CGU net of the working capital (99,200) and the cash flows excluding the opening changes in working capital (107,979).

Example 20.8 above is based on a limited life CGU and therefore considers a cash outflow in the last year to settle the negative working capital balance. For a CGU with an indefinite life for which the value in use calculation includes a terminal value a sustainable level of working capital investment in the terminal year of the cash flow forecast would need to be assumed.

In some industries it is common for companies to operate on a negative working capital basis. Negative working capital provides a cash flow benefit in earlier years that reverses in later years, and at the latest at the end of its life for a limited life CGU. This increases the value of the CGU in question. For a CGU for which the value in use calculation includes a terminal value, effectively assuming a perpetual life, careful consideration is required in determining the extent to which negative working capital balances are expected to continue into perpetuity and in determining a sustainable level of negative working capital balances to avoid overstating the value in use for the CGU in question.

4.1.4 Pensions

As mentioned at 4 above, recognised liabilities are in general not included in arriving at the recoverable amount or carrying amount of a CGU.

Paragraph 79 of IAS 36 mentions pension obligations as items that might for practical reasons be included in calculating the recoverable amount of a CGU. In such a case, the carrying amount of the CGU is decreased by the carrying amount of those liabilities. *[IAS 36.79]*.

In practice, including cash flows for a pension obligation in the recoverable amount could be fraught with difficulty, especially if it is a defined benefit scheme, as there can be so many differences between the measurement basis of the pension liability and the cash flows that relate to pensions. Deducting the carrying amount of the pension obligation from both the value in use and the carrying amount of the CGU avoids this issue. If the pension liability is excluded from the carrying amount of the CGU, then any cash flows in relation to it should not be considered in the value in use calculation and the pension liability should not be deducted from the VIU.

Cash flows in relation to future services on the other hand, whether for defined contribution or defined benefit arrangements, should always be included in calculating the recoverable amount as these are part of the CGU's ongoing employee costs. In practice, it can be difficult to distinguish between cash flows reflecting repayment of the pension liability and cash flows that are future employee costs of the CGU.

4.1.5 Cash flow hedges

In the case of a cash flow hedge in relation to highly probable forecasted transactions, it often makes no significant difference for short term hedging arrangements if the hedging asset or liability and the hedging cash flows are included in the calculation of recoverable amount. The result is to gross up or net down the assets of the CGU and the relevant cash flows by an equivalent amount, after taking account of the distorting effects of differing discount rates. However, some entities argue that they ought to be able to take into account cash flows from instruments hedging their sales or purchases that are designated as cash flow hedges under IFRS 9 because not to do so misrepresents their economic position. In order to do this, they may wish to include the cash flows and either exclude the derivative asset or liability from the CGU or, alternatively, include the derivative asset or liability and reflect the related cash flow hedge reserve in the CGU as well (this latter treatment would not be a perfect offset to the extent of ineffectiveness). They argue that the cash flow hedges protect the fair value of assets through their effect on price risk. They also note that not taking cash flows from instruments hedging their sales or purchases introduces a profit or loss mismatch by comparison with instruments that meet the 'normal purchase/normal sale' exemption under which the derivative remains off balance sheet until exercised.

Although logical from an income perspective, IAS 36 does not support these arguments. The derivative asset or liability can only be included in the CGU as a practical expediency and the hedge reserve is neither an asset nor liability to be reflected in the CGU. As the carrying amount of the hedge instrument is a net present value, any impairment loss might be similar to that calculated by excluding the derivative financial instrument and its cash flows. However, there may be a difference between the two due to different discount rates being applied in the determination of the derivative's fair value and the determination of the VIU. IFRS 9 would not permit an entity to mitigate the effects of impairment by recycling the appropriate amount from the hedging reserve. Finally, entities must be aware that cash flow hedges may have negative values as well as positive ones.

Example 20.9: Cash flow hedges and testing for impairment

Entity A, which only has one CGU, enters into derivative contracts to hedge its commodity sales. These derivatives are accounted for as cash flow hedges and there is no ineffectiveness.

The entity is required to perform an impairment test.

Entity A's statement of financial position as at the impairment testing date is as follows:

	€
Asset/CGU	3,000
Derivatives fair value	1,125
Equity – other reserves	(3,000)
Equity – cash flow hedge reserve	(1,125)

As at the impairment testing date, the entity's cash flow forecasts are as follows:

Year	20X0	20X1	20X2	20X3
Forecast sales cash inflows		750	750	750
Forecast hedge cash inflows		450	450	450
Total cash inflows		1,200	1,200	1,200
NPV sales cash inflows	1,875	1,307	684	0
NPV total cash inflows	3,000	2,091	1,094	0
Fair value of hedge	1,125	784	410	0

IAS 36 requires the entity to exclude the cash flows from hedge transactions when calculating VIU. The carrying amount of the derivative is therefore excluded from the carrying amount of the cash-generating unit. The entity recognises an impairment loss of €1,125 as follows:

	€
Asset carrying amount	3,000
Recoverable amount (VIU)	1,875
Impairment loss	(1,125)

The entity is not prohibited from including within the VIU calculation the cash flows from a hedge instrument, provided the instrument's carrying amount is included within the carrying amount of the cash-generating unit and the effects of discounting are taken into account, thereby ensuring that the cash flows and carrying amount are consistently discounted. This approach would result in the same impairment of €1,125.

4.2 Corporate assets

An entity may have assets that are inherently incapable of generating cash inflows independently, such as headquarters buildings or central IT facilities that contribute to more than one CGU. IAS 36 calls such assets corporate assets. Corporate assets are defined as '...assets other than goodwill that contribute to the future cash flows of both the cash-generating unit under review and other cash-generating units'. In our view corporate assets can include intangible assets like brands and trademarks (see 3.1 above).

The characteristics that distinguish corporate assets are that they do not generate cash inflows independently of other assets or groups of assets and their carrying amount cannot be fully attributed to the CGU under review. *[IAS 36.100]*. Nevertheless, in order to test properly for impairment, the corporate asset's carrying value has to be tested for impairment along with the CGUs. Corporate assets therefore have to be allocated to the CGUs to which they belong and then tested for impairment along with those CGUs. *[IAS 36.101]*.

This presents a problem in the event of those assets themselves showing indications of impairment. It also raises a question of what those indications might actually be, in the absence of cash inflows directly relating to this type of asset. Some, but not all, of these assets may have relatively easily determinable fair values but while this is usually true of a headquarters building, it could not be said for a central IT facility. We have already noted at 2.1.3 above that a decline in value of the asset itself may not trigger a need for an impairment review and it may be obvious that the CGUs of which corporate assets are a part are not showing any indications of impairment – unless, of course, management has decided to dispose of the asset. It is most likely that a corporate asset will show indications of impairment if the CGU or group of CGUs to which it relates are showing indications and this is reflected in the methodology by which corporate assets are tested.

If possible, the corporate assets are to be allocated to individual CGUs on a 'reasonable and consistent basis'. *[IAS 36.102]*. This is not expanded upon and affords some flexibility, although consistency is vital; the same criteria must be applied at all times. If the carrying value of a corporate asset can be allocated on a reasonable and consistent basis between individual CGUs, each CGU has its impairment test done separately and its carrying value includes its share of the corporate asset. If the corporate asset's carrying value cannot be allocated to an individual CGU, there are three steps to consider. As noted above, indicators of impairment for corporate assets that cannot be allocated to individual CGUs are likely to relate to the CGUs that use the corporate asset as well. First the CGU is tested for impairment and any impairment is recognised. Then the group of CGUs is identified to which, as a group, all or part of the carrying value of the corporate asset can be allocated. This group must include the CGU that was the subject of the first test. Finally, all CGUs in this group have to be tested to determine if the group's carrying value (including the allocation of the corporate asset's carrying value) is in excess of the group's recoverable amount. *[IAS 36.102]*. If it is not sufficient, the impairment loss will be allocated *pro rata*, subject to the limitations of paragraph 105 of IAS 36, to all assets in the group of CGUs and the allocated portion of the corporate asset, as described at 11.2 below.

Some entities include a charge for the use of corporate assets rather than allocating the assets to CGUs and CGU groups. This is an acceptable approximation as long as entities ensure that the allocation is reasonable and that the total charge has the same NPV as the carrying amount of those assets and there is no impairment. Otherwise, there could be double counting or the omission of assets or cash outflows from CGUs or the misallocation of impairment to the assets of the CGU. Overheads are discussed further at 7.1.7 below.

In IAS 36's accompanying section of illustrative examples, Example 8 has a fully worked example of the allocation of corporate assets and calculation of a VIU. [IAS 36.IE69-IE79]. The table below is included in the example, and serves to illustrate the allocation of the corporate asset to CGUs:

Example 20.10: Allocation of corporate assets

An entity comprises three CGUs and a headquarters building. The carrying amount of the headquarters building of 150 is allocated to the carrying amount of each individual cash-generating unit. A weighted allocation basis is used because the estimated remaining useful life of A's cash-generating unit is 10 years, whereas the estimated remaining useful lives of B and C's cash-generating units are 20 years.

Schedule 1. Calculation of a weighted allocation of the carrying amount of the headquarters building

End of 20X0	A	B	C	Total
Carrying amount	100	150	200	450
Remaining useful life	10 years	20 years	20 years	
Weighting based on useful life	1	2	2	
Carrying amount after weighting	100	300	400	800
Pro rata allocation of the building	(100/800)= 12%	(300/800)= 38%	(400/800)= 50%	100%
Allocation of the carrying amount of the building (based on *pro rata* above)	19	56	75	150
Carrying amount (after allocation of the building)	119	206	275	600

The allocation need not be made on carrying value or financial measures such as revenue, employee numbers or a time basis might be a valid basis in certain circumstances.

One effect of this *pro rata* allocation process is that the amount of the head office allocated to each CGU will change as the useful lives and carrying values change. In the above example, the allocation of the head office to CGU A will be redistributed to CGUs B and C as A's remaining life shortens. Similar effects will be observed if the sizes of any other factor on which the allocation to the CGUs is made change relative to one another.

4.2.1 Leased corporate assets

Companies frequently enter into lease arrangements on a corporate level, such as a leased corporate headquarters or leased IT equipment. Under IFRS 16 these lease arrangements will result in the recognition of right-of-use assets. Similar to other corporate assets, the right-of-use assets carrying values have to be tested for impairment along with the CGUs they serve. An entity will frequently need to allocate the carrying amount of corporate right-of-use assets to (groups of) CGUs when performing the impairment test. As discussed under 4.2 above, some entities include a charge for the use of corporate assets rather than allocating the assets to CGUs and CGU groups. This is an acceptable approximation as long as entities ensure that the allocation is reasonable and that the total charge has the same NPV as the carrying amount of those assets and there is no impairment. Otherwise, there could be double counting or the omission of assets or cash outflows from CGUs or the misallocation of impairment to the assets of the CGU.

5 RECOVERABLE AMOUNT

The standard requires the carrying amount of the asset or CGU to be compared with the recoverable amount, which is the higher of VIU and FVLCD. *[IAS 36.18]*. If either the FVLCD or the VIU is higher than the carrying amount, no further action is necessary as the asset is not impaired. *[IAS 36.19]*. Recoverable amount is calculated for an individual asset, unless that asset does not generate cash inflows that are largely independent of those from other assets or groups of assets, in which case the recoverable amount is determined for the CGU to which the asset belongs. *[IAS 36.22]*.

Recoverable amount is the higher of FVLCD and VIU. IAS 36 defines VIU as the present value of the future cash flows expected to be derived from an asset or CGU. FVLCD is the fair value as defined in IFRS 13, being the price that would be received to sell an asset or paid to transfer a liability in an orderly transaction between market participants at the measurement date, less the costs of disposal. *[IAS 36.6]*.

Estimating the VIU of an asset involves estimating the future cash inflows and outflows that will be derived from the use of the asset and from its ultimate disposal, and discounting them at an appropriate rate. *[IAS 36.31]*. There are complex issues involved in determining the cash flows and choosing a discount rate and often there is no agreed methodology to follow (see 7.1 and 7.2 below for a discussion of some of these difficulties).

It may be possible to estimate FVLCD even in the absence of quoted prices in an active market for an identical asset but if there is no basis for making a reliable estimate then the value of an asset must be based on its VIU. *[IAS 36.20]*.

There are two practical points to emphasise. First, IAS 36 allows the use of estimates, averages and computational shortcuts to provide a reasonable approximation of FVLCD or VIU. *[IAS 36.23]*. Second, if the FVLCD is greater than the asset's carrying value, no VIU calculation is necessary. It is not uncommon for the FVLCD of an asset to be readily obtainable while the asset itself does not generate largely independent cash inflows, as is the case with many property assets held by entities. If the FVLCD of the asset is lower than its carrying value then the recoverable amount will have to be calculated by reference to the CGU of which the asset is a part. However, as explained at 2.1.3 above, it may be obvious that the CGU to which the property belongs has not suffered an impairment. In such a case it would not be necessary to assess the recoverable amount of the CGU.

5.1 Impairment of assets held for sale

The standard describes circumstances in which it may be appropriate to use an asset or CGU's FVLCD without calculating its VIU, as the measure of its recoverable amount. There may be no significant difference between FVLCD and VIU, in which case the asset's FVLCD may be used as its recoverable amount. This is the case, for example, if management is intending to dispose of the asset or CGU, as apart from its disposal proceeds there will be few if any cash flows from further use. *[IAS 36.21]*.

The asset may also be held for sale as defined by IFRS 5, by which stage it will be outside the scope of IAS 36, although IFRS 5 requires such assets to be measured immediately before their initial classification as held for sale 'in accordance with applicable IFRSs'. *[IFRS 5.18]*. A decision to sell is a triggering event for an impairment review, which means that any existing impairment will be recognised at the point of classification and not be rolled into the gain or loss on disposal of the asset. See Chapter 4 for a description of the subsequent measurement of the carrying amounts of the assets.

Clearly IFRS 5's requirement to test for impairment prior to reclassification is intended to avoid impairment losses being recognised as losses on disposal. However, one effect is that this rule may require the recognition of impairment losses on individual assets that form part of a single disposal group subsequently sold at a profit, as in the following example.

Example 20.11: Impairment of assets held for sale

Entity A decided to sell three assets in one transaction to the same acquirer. Each asset had been part of a different CGU. The decision to sell was made on 20 December 20X0, just prior to Entity A's year end of 31 December. The assets met IFRS 5's requirements for classification as a disposal group on 10 January 20X1.

The information about the carrying amounts and fair values less cost of disposal of individual assets at 20 December 20X0 and the disposal group on 10 January 20X1 is summarised below. There was no change in the fair values of these assets between the two dates.

Asset	Carrying amount	FVLCD of separate assets	Aggregate of the lower of the carrying amount and FVLCD	Fair value of the group
	€	€	€	€
X	4,600	4,300	4,300	n/a
Y	5,700	5,800	5,700	n/a
Z	2,400	2,500	2,400	n/a
Total	12,700	12,600	12,400	12,600

Although these assets were classified as held for sale subsequent to the year end, the decision to sell them was an indicator of impairment. Accordingly, it is necessary to determine whether the three assets together comprise a new CGU. If so, impairment would be assessed on the three assets together, prior to reclassification and remeasurement under IFRS 5.

If the three assets together do not comprise a CGU, they would have to be tested for impairment individually at the year end, which would result in an impairment loss on Asset X of €300. As there is no change in the recoverable amount between the year end and immediately before the classification under IFRS 5, the aggregate value of these assets prior to classification under IFRS 5 would be €12,400 (4,300 + 5,700 + 2,400). The FVLCD of the disposal group at the date of the first application of IFRS 5 (10 January 20X1) is €12,600. Therefore, according to the measurement criteria under IFRS 5 the carrying amount of the disposal group remains at €12,400. The impairment loss previously recognised on Asset X would only be reversed, should the FVLCD of the disposal group exceed €12,600.

IAS 36 does not allow an asset to be written down below the higher of its VIU or FVLCD. *[IAS 36.105]*. An entity might, however, expect to sell a CGU for less than the apparent aggregate FVLCD of individual assets, e.g. because the potential buyer expects further losses. If this happens, the carrying amount of the disposal group under IFRS 5 is capped at the FVLCD of the disposal group as a whole so the impairment loss is allocated to all non-current assets, even if their carrying amounts are reduced below their individual FVLCD. See Chapter 4.

6 FAIR VALUE LESS COSTS OF DISPOSAL

IFRS 13 specifies how to measure fair value, but does not change when fair value is required or permitted under IFRS. IFRS 13 is discussed in detail in Chapter 14.

The standard defines fair value as the price that would be received to sell an asset or paid to transfer a liability in an orderly transaction between market participants at the measurement date. It is explicitly an exit price. *[IFRS 13.2]*. When measuring FVLCD, fair value is measured in accordance with IFRS 13. Costs of disposal are calculated in accordance with IAS 36.

IFRS 13 specifically excludes VIU from its scope. *[IFRS 13.6]*.

Fair value, like FVLCD, is not an entity-specific measurement but is focused on market participants' assumptions for a particular asset or liability. *[IFRS 13.11]*. For non-financial assets, fair value has to take account of the highest and best use by a market participant to which the asset could be put. *[IFRS 13.27]*. An entity's current use of a non-financial asset is presumed to be its highest and best use unless market or other factors suggest that a different use by market participants would maximise the value of the asset. *[IFRS 13.29]*.

Entities are exempt from the disclosures required by IFRS 13 when the recoverable amount is FVLCD. *[IFRS 13.7(c)]*. IAS 36's disclosure requirements are broadly aligned with those of IFRS 13. See IAS 36's disclosure requirements at 13 below.

While IFRS 13 makes it clear that transaction costs are not part of a fair value measurement, in all cases, FVLCD should take account of estimated disposal costs. These include legal costs, stamp duty and other transaction taxes, costs of removing the asset and other direct incremental costs. Business reorganisation costs and employee termination costs (as defined in IAS 19, see Chapter 35) may not be treated as costs of disposal. *[IAS 36.28]*.

If the disposal of an asset would entail the buyer assuming a liability and there is only a single FVLCD for both taken together, then, to enable a meaningful comparison, the obligation must also be taken into account in calculating VIU and the carrying value of the asset. This is discussed at 4.1 above. *[IAS 36.29, 78]*.

6.1 Estimating FVLCD

IFRS 13 does not limit the types of valuation techniques an entity might use to measure fair value but instead focuses on the types of inputs that will be used. The standard requires the entity to use the valuation technique that 'maximis[es] the use of relevant observable inputs and minimis[es] the use of unobservable inputs'. *[IFRS 13.61]*. The objective is that the best available inputs should be used in valuing the assets. These inputs could be used in any valuation technique provided they are consistent with one of the three valuation approaches in the standard: the market approach, the cost approach and the income approach. *[IFRS 13.62]*. IFRS 13 does not place any preference on the techniques that are used as long as the entity achieves the objective of a fair value measurement, which means it must use the best available inputs. In some cases, a single valuation technique will be appropriate, while in other cases, multiple valuation techniques will need to be used to meet this objective. An entity must apply the valuation technique(s) consistently. A change in a valuation technique is considered a change in an accounting estimate in accordance with IAS 8 – *Accounting Policies, Changes in Accounting Estimates and Errors*. [IFRS 13.66].

The market approach uses prices and other relevant information generated by market transactions involving identical or comparable (i.e. similar) assets, liabilities or a group of assets and liabilities, such as a business. [IFRS 13.B5]. For items within scope of IAS 36, market techniques will usually involve market transactions in comparable assets or, for certain assets valued as businesses, market multiples derived from comparable transactions. [IFRS 13.B5, B6].

The cost approach reflects the amount that would be required currently to replace the service capacity of an asset (i.e. current replacement cost). It is based on what a market participant buyer would pay to acquire or construct a substitute asset of comparable utility, adjusted for obsolescence. Obsolescence includes physical deterioration, technological (functional) and economic obsolescence so it is not the same as depreciation under IAS 16. [IFRS 13.B8, B9]. See also 6.1.2 below.

The income approach converts future amounts (e.g. cash flows or income and expenses) to a single discounted amount. The fair value reflects current market expectations about those future amounts. This will usually mean using a discounted cash flow technique or one of the other techniques that fall into this classification (e.g. option pricing and multi-period excess earnings methods). [IFRS 13.B10, B11].

See Chapter 14 for a further discussion of these valuation approaches.

The inputs used in these valuation techniques to measure the fair value of an asset have a hierarchy. Those that are quoted prices in an active market for identical assets (Level 1) have the highest priority, followed by inputs, other than quoted prices, that are observable (Level 2). The lowest priority inputs are those based on unobservable inputs (Level 3). [IFRS 13.72]. The valuation techniques, referred to above, will use a combination of inputs to determine the fair value of the asset.

An active market is a market in which transactions take place with sufficient frequency and volume to provide pricing information on an ongoing basis. [IFRS 13 Appendix A].

Using the IFRS's approach, most estimates of fair value for IAS 36 purposes will use Level 2 inputs that are directly or indirectly observable and Level 3 inputs that are not based on observable market data but reflect assumptions used by market participants, including risk.

If Level 2 information is available then entities must take it into account in calculating FVLCD because this is a relevant observable input. Entities cannot base their valuation on Level 3 information only if Level 2 information is available.

IFRS 13 allows entities to use unobservable inputs, which can include the entity's own data, to calculate fair value, as long as the objectives (an exit price from the perspective of a market participant) and assumptions about risk are met. [IFRS 13.87-89]. This means that a discounted cash flow technique may be used if this is commonly used in that industry to estimate fair value. Cash flows used when applying the model may only reflect cash flows that market participants would take into account when assessing fair value. This includes the type, e.g. future capital expenditure, as well as the estimated amount of such cash flows. For example, an entity may wish to take into account cash flows relating to future capital expenditure, which would not be permitted for a VIU calculation (see 7.1.2 below). These cash flows can be included if, and only if, other market participants would consider them when evaluating the asset. It is not permissible to include assumptions about cash flows or benefits from the asset that would not be available to or considered by a typical market participant.

The entity cannot ignore external evidence. It must use the best information that is available to it and adjust its own data if 'reasonably available information indicates that other market participants would use different data or there is something particular to the entity that is not available to other market participants such as an entity-specific synergy'. An entity need not undertake exhaustive efforts to obtain information about market participant assumptions. 'However, an entity shall take into account all information about market participant assumptions that is reasonably available.' *[IFRS 13.89]*. This means using a relevant model, which requires consideration of industry practice, for example, multiples based on occupancy, revenue and EBITDA might be inputs in estimating the fair value of a hotel but the value of an oilfield would depend on its reserves. The fair value of an oil field would include the costs that would be incurred in accessing those reserves based on the costs a market participant expects to incur instead of the entity's own specific cost structure.

IAS 36 notes that sometimes it is not possible to obtain reliable evidence regarding the assumptions and techniques that market participants would use (IAS 36 uses the phrase 'no basis for making a reliable estimate'); if so, the recoverable amount of the asset must be based on its VIU. *[IAS 36.20]*. Therefore, the IASB accepts that there are some circumstances in which market conditions are such that it will not be possible to calculate a reliable estimate of the price at which an orderly transaction to sell the asset would take place under current market conditions. *[IAS 36.20]*. IFRS 13 includes guidance for identifying transactions that are not orderly. *[IFRS 13.B43]*. These are discussed in Chapter 14 at 8.2.

6.1.1 FVLCD and the unit of account

In determining FVLCD it is critical to determine the relevant unit of account appropriately.

IFRS 13 does specify the unit of account to be used when measuring fair value in relation to a reporting entity that holds a position in a single asset or liability that is traded in an active market (including a position comprising a large number of identical assets or liabilities, such as a holding of financial instruments). In this situation, IFRS 13 requires an entity to measure the asset or liability based on the product of the quoted price for the individual asset or liability and the quantity held (P×Q).

This requirement is generally accepted when the asset or liability being measured is a financial instrument in the scope of IFRS 9. However, when an entity holds an investment in a listed subsidiary, joint venture or associate, some believe the unit of account is the entire holding and the fair value should include an adjustment (e.g. a control premium) to reflect the value of the investor's control, joint control or significant influence over their investment as a whole.

Questions have also arisen as to how this requirement applies to cash-generating units that are equivalent to listed investments. Some argue that, because IAS 36 requires certain assets and liabilities to be excluded from a CGU, the unit of account is not identical to a listed subsidiary, joint venture or associate and an entity can include adjustments that are consistent with the CGU as a whole. Some similarly argue that approach is appropriate because, in group financial statements, an entity is accounting for the assets and liabilities of consolidated entities, rather than the investment. However, others argue that if the CGU is effectively the same as an entity's investment in a listed subsidiary, joint venture or associate, the requirement to use P×Q should apply.

IFRS 13 requires entities to select inputs that are consistent with the characteristics of the asset or liability being measured and would be considered by market participants when pricing the asset or liability. Apart from block discounts (which are specifically prohibited), determining whether a premium or discount applies to a particular fair value measurement requires judgement and depends on specific facts and circumstances.

The standard indicates that premiums or discounts should not be incorporated into fair value measurements unless all of the following conditions are met:

- the application of the premium or discount reflects the characteristics of the asset or liability being measured;
- market participants, acting in their economic best interest, would consider these premiums or discounts when pricing the asset or liability; and
- the inclusion of the premium or discount is not inconsistent with the unit of account in the IFRS that requires (or permits) the fair value measurement.

Therefore, when an entity holds an investment in a listed subsidiary, joint venture or associate and if the unit of account is deemed to be the entire holding, it seems to be appropriate to include, for example, a control premium when determining fair value, provided that market participants would take this into consideration when pricing the asset. If, however, the unit of account is deemed to be the individual share of the listed subsidiary, joint venture or associate, the requirement to use P×Q (without adjustment) to measure the fair value would override the requirements in IFRS 13 that permit premiums or discounts to be included in certain circumstances. In September 2014, in response to these questions regarding the unit of account for an investment in a listed subsidiary, joint venture or associate, the IASB proposed amendments to clarify that:

- The unit of account for investments in subsidiaries, joint ventures and associates be the investment as a whole and not the individual financial instruments that constitute the investment.
- For investments that are comprised of financial instruments for which a quoted price in an active market is available, the requirement to use P×Q would take precedence, irrespective of the unit of account. Therefore, for all such investments, the fair value measurement would be the product of P×Q, even when the reporting entity has an interest that gives it control, joint control or significant influence over the investee.
- When testing CGUs for impairment, if those CGUs correspond to an entity whose financial instruments are quoted in an active market, the fair value measurement would be the product of P×Q.

The comment period for this exposure draft ended on 16 January 2015 and the Board began redeliberations in March 2015. During redeliberations, additional research was undertaken on fair value measurements of investments in subsidiaries, associates and joint ventures that are quoted in an active market and on the measurement of the recoverable amount of cash-generating units on the basis of fair value less costs of disposal when the cash-generating unit is an entity that is quoted in an active market.

Following the redeliberations, in its January 2016 meeting, the IASB concluded that the research would be fed into the Post-implementation Review (PIR) of IFRS 13. As part of its PIR of IFRS 13, the IASB issued a Request for Information (RFI) and specifically asked about prioritising Level 1 inputs in relation to the unit of account. The feedback was discussed at the IASB's March 2018 meeting. In respect of the valuation of quoted subsidiaries, associates and joint ventures, the PIR found that there were continued differences in views between users and preparers over whether to prioritise Level 1 inputs or the unit of account. The issue is not pervasive in practice according to the PIR findings. However, respondents noted it can have a material effect when it does occur. Some stakeholders said that there are material differences between measuring an investment using the P×Q and a valuation using a method such as discounted cash flows. Respondents indicated the reasons for such differences include that share prices do not reflect market liquidity for the shares or that they do not reflect the value of control and/or synergies. A few respondents also noted that markets may lack depth and are, therefore, susceptible to speculative trading, asymmetrical information and other factors.

The IASB has decided not to conduct any follow-up activities as a result of findings from the PIR and stated, as an example, that it will not do any further work on the issue of unit of account versus P×Q because the costs of such work would outweigh the benefits.

The IASB has released its Report and Feedback Statement on the PIR in the last quarter of the 2018 calendar year.

This issue is discussed in more detail in Chapter 14 at 5.1.1.

6.1.2 Depreciated replacement cost or current replacement cost as FVLCD

Cost approaches, e.g. depreciated replacement cost (DRC) or current replacement cost, are one of the three valuation approaches that IFRS 13 considers to be appropriate for establishing FVLCD. Yet, the Basis for Conclusions of IAS 36 indicates that DRC is not suitable:

> 'Some argue that the replacement cost of an asset should be adopted as a ceiling for its recoverable amount. They argue that the value of an asset to the business would not exceed the amount that the enterprise would be willing to pay for the asset at the balance sheet date.
>
> 'IASC believed that replacement cost techniques are not appropriate to measuring the recoverable amount of an asset. This is because replacement cost measures the cost of an asset and not the future economic benefits recoverable from its use and/or disposal.' *[IAS 36.BCZ28-BCZ29]*.

We do not consider that this means that FVLCD cannot be based on DRC. Rather, this means that DRC can only be used if it meets the objective of IFRS 13 by being a current exit price and not the cost of an asset. If the entity can demonstrate that the price that would be received for the asset is based on the cost to a market participant buyer to acquire or construct a substitute asset of comparable utility, adjusted for obsolescence, then (and only then) is DRC an appropriate basis for FVLCD. See Chapter 14 at 14.3.

7 DETERMINING VALUE IN USE (VIU)

IAS 36 defines VIU as the present value of the future cash flows expected to be derived from an asset or CGU. IAS 36 requires the following elements to be reflected in the VIU calculation:

(a) an estimate of the future cash flows the entity expects to derive from the asset;
(b) expectations about possible variations in the amount or timing of those future cash flows;
(c) the time value of money, represented by the current risk free market rate of interest;
(d) the price for bearing the uncertainty inherent in the asset; and
(e) other factors, such as illiquidity that market participants would reflect in pricing the future cash flows the entity expects to derive from the asset. *[IAS 36.30]*.

The calculation requires the entity to estimate the future cash flows and discount them at an appropriate rate. *[IAS 36.31]*. It also requires uncertainty as to the timing of cash flows or the market's assessment of risk in those assets ((b), (d) and (e) above) to be taken into account either by adjusting the cash flows or the discount rate. *[IAS 36.32]*. The intention is that the VIU should be the expected present value of those future cash flows.

If possible, recoverable amount is calculated for the individual asset. However, it will frequently be necessary to calculate the VIU of the CGU of which the asset is a part. *[IAS 36.66]*. This is because the single asset may not generate sufficiently independent cash inflows. *[IAS 36.67]*.

Goodwill cannot be tested by itself so it always has to be tested as part of a CGU or group of CGUs (see 8 below).

Where a CGU is being reviewed for impairment, this will involve calculation of the VIU of the CGU as a whole unless a reliable estimate of the CGU's FVLCD can be made and the resulting FVLCD is above the total carrying amount of the CGU's net assets.

VIU calculations at the level of the CGU will thus be required when no satisfactory FVLCD is available or FVLCD is below the CGU's carrying amount and:

- the CGU includes goodwill, indefinite lived intangibles or intangibles not yet brought into use which must be tested annually for impairment;
- a CGU itself is suspected of being impaired; or
- intangible assets or other fixed assets are suspected of being impaired and individual future cash flows cannot be identified for them.

The standard contains detailed requirements concerning the data to be assembled to calculate VIU that can best be explained and set out as a series of steps. The steps also contain a discussion of the practicalities and difficulties in determining the VIU of an asset. The steps in the process are:

1: Dividing the entity into CGUs (see 3 above).
2: Allocating goodwill to CGUs or CGU groups (see 8.1 below).
3: Identifying the carrying amount of CGU assets (see 4 above).
4: Estimating the future pre-tax cash flows of the CGU under review (see 7.1 below).
5: Identifying an appropriate discount rate and discounting the future cash flows (see 7.2 below).
6: Comparing carrying value with VIU (assuming FVLCD is lower than carrying value) and recognising impairment losses (if any) (see 11.1 and 11.2 below).

Although this process describes the determination of the VIU of a CGU, steps 3 to 6 are the same as those that would be applied to an individual asset if it generated cash inflows independently of other assets. Impairment of goodwill is discussed at 8 below.

7.1 Estimating the future pre-tax cash flows of the CGU under review

In order to calculate the VIU the entity needs to estimate the future cash flows that it will derive from its use and consider possible variations in their amount or timing. *[IAS 36.30]*. In estimating future cash flows the entity must:

(a) Base its cash flow projections on reasonable and supportable assumptions that represent management's best estimate of the range of economic conditions that will exist over the remaining useful life of the asset. Greater weight must be given to external evidence.

(b) Base cash flow projections on the most recent financial budgets/forecasts approved by management, excluding any estimated future cash inflows or outflows expected to arise from future restructurings or from improving or enhancing the asset's performance. These projections can only cover a maximum period of five years, unless a longer period can be justified.

(c) Estimate cash flow projections beyond the period covered by the most recent budgets/forecasts by extrapolating them using a steady or declining growth rate for subsequent years, unless an increasing rate can be justified. This growth rate must not exceed the long-term average growth rate for the products, industries, or country or countries in which the entity operates, or for the market in which the asset is used, unless a higher rate can be justified. *[IAS 36.33]*.

7.1.1 Budgets and cash flows

The standard describes in some detail the responsibilities of management towards the estimation of cash flows. Management is required to ensure that the assumptions on which its current cash flow projections are based are consistent with past actual outcomes by examining the causes of differences between past cash flow projections and actual cash flows. If actual cash flows have been consistently below projected cash flows then management has to investigate the reason for it and assess whether the current cash flow projections are realistic or require adjustment. *[IAS 36.34]*.

IAS 36 states that the cash flows should be based on the most recent budgets and forecasts for a maximum of five years because reliable forecasts are rarely available for a longer period. If management is confident that its projections are reliable and can demonstrate this from past experience, it may use a longer period. *[IAS 36.35]*. In using budgets and forecasts, management is required to consider whether these really are the best estimate of economic conditions that will exist over the remaining useful life of the asset. *[IAS 36.38]*. It may be appropriate to revise forecasts where the economic environment or conditions have changed since the most recent financial budgets and forecasts were approved by management.

Cash flows for the period beyond that covered by the forecasts or budgets assume a steady, declining or even negative rate of growth. An increase in the rate may be used if it is supported by objective information. *[IAS 36.36]*.

Therefore, only in exceptional circumstances should an increasing growth rate be used, or should the period before a steady or declining growth rate be assumed to extend to more than five years. This five year rule is based on general economic theory that postulates above-average growth rates will only be achievable in the short-term, because such above-average growth will lead to competitors entering the market. This increased competition will, over a period of time, lead to a reduction of the growth rate, towards the average for the economy as a whole. IAS 36 suggests that entities will find it difficult to exceed the average historical growth rate for the products, countries or markets over the long term, say twenty years. *[IAS 36.37]*.

This stage of the impairment review illustrates the point that it is not only fixed assets that are being assessed. The future cash flows to be forecast are all cash flows – receipts from sales, purchases, administrative expenses, etc. It is akin to a free cash flow valuation of a business with the resulting valuation then being compared to the carrying value of the assets in the CGU.

The cash flow forecast should include three elements:
- cash inflows from the continuing use of the asset;
- the cash outflows necessary to generate these cash inflows, including cash outflows to prepare the asset for use, that can either be directly attributed, or allocated on a reasonable and consistent basis; and
- the net cash flows, if any, that the entity may receive or pay for the disposal of the asset at the end of its useful life. *[IAS 36.39]*.

Cash flows can be estimated by taking into account general price changes caused by inflation, or on the basis of stable prices. If inflation is excluded from the cash flow then the discount rate selected must also be adjusted to remove the inflationary effect. *[IAS 36.40]*. Generally, entities will use whichever method is most convenient to them that is consistent with the method they use in their budgets and forecasts. It is, of course, fundamental that cash flows and discount rate are both estimated on a consistent basis.

To avoid the danger of double counting, the future cash flows exclude those relating to financial assets, including receivables and liabilities such as payables, pensions and provisions. *[IAS 36.43]*. However, 4 above notes that paragraph 79 allows the inclusion of such assets and liabilities for practical reasons, in which case the cash flows must be reflected as well, and includes a discussion of some of the assets and liabilities that may or may not be reflected together with the implications of so doing. *[IAS 36.79]*.

The expected future cash flows of the CGU being assessed for impairment should not include cash inflows or outflows from financing activities or tax receipts or payments. This is because the discount rate used represents the financing costs and the future cash flows are themselves determined on a pre-tax basis. *[IAS 36.50, 51]*.

7.1.2 Cash inflows and outflows from improvements and enhancements

Whilst a part-completed asset must have the costs to complete it included in the cash flows, *[IAS 36.42]*, the general rule is that future cash flows should be forecast for CGUs or assets in their current condition. Forecasts should not include estimated future cash inflows or outflows that are expected to arise from improving or enhancing the asset's performance. *[IAS 36.44]*. Projections in the cash flow should include costs of day-to-day servicing that can be reasonably attributed to the use of the asset (for overheads see 7.1.7 below). *[IAS 36.41]*.

While the restriction on enhanced performance may be understandable, it adds an element of unreality that is hard to reconcile with other assumptions made in the VIU process. For example, the underlying forecast cash flows that the standard requires management to use will obviously be based on the business as it is actually expected to develop in the future, growth, improvements and all. Producing a special forecast based on unrealistic assumptions, even for this limited purpose, may be difficult.

Nevertheless, paragraph 48 explicitly states that improvements to the current performance of an asset may not be included in the estimates of future cash flows until the entity incurs the expenditure that provides those improvements. The treatment of such expenditure is illustrated in Example 6 in the standard's accompanying section of illustrative examples. *[IAS 36.48]*. The implication of this requirement is that if an asset is impaired, and even if the entity is going to make the future expenditure to reverse that impairment, the asset will still have to be written down. Subsequently, the asset's impairment can be reversed, to the degree appropriate, after the expenditure has taken place. Reversal of asset impairment is discussed at 11.4 below.

IAS 36 makes it clear that for a part-completed asset, all expected cash outflows required to make the asset ready for use or sale should be considered in the estimate of future cash flows, and mentions a building under construction or a development project as examples. *[IAS 36.42]*. The standard is also clear that the estimate of future cash flows should not include the estimated future cash inflows that are expected to arise from the increase in economic benefits associated with cash outflows to improve or enhance an asset's performance until an entity incurs these cash outflows. *[IAS 36.48]*. This raises the question of what to do once a project to enhance or improve the performance of an asset or a CGU has commenced and it has started to incur cash outflows. In our view, once a project has been committed to and has substantively commenced, an entity should consider future cash inflows that are expected to arise from the increase in economic benefits associated with the cash outflows to improve or enhance the asset. Important to note is that it must take into consideration all future cash outflows required to complete the project and any risks in relation with the project, reflected either in the cash flows or the discount rate.

An assumption of new capital investment is in practice intrinsic to the VIU test. What has to be assessed are the future cash flows of a productive unit such as a factory or hotel.

The cash flows, out into the far future, will include the sales of product, cost of sales, administrative expenses, etc. They must necessarily include capital expenditure as well, at least to the extent required to keep the CGU functioning as forecast. This is explicitly acknowledged as follows:

> 'Estimates of future cash flows include future cash outflows necessary to maintain the level of economic benefits expected to arise from the asset in its current condition. When a cash-generating unit consists of assets with different estimated useful lives, all of which are essential to the ongoing operation of the unit, the replacement of assets with shorter lives is considered to be part of the day-to-day servicing of the unit when estimating the future cash flows associated with the unit. Similarly, when a single asset consists of components with different estimated useful lives, the replacement of components with shorter lives is considered to be part of the day-to-day servicing of the asset when estimating the future cash flows generated by the asset.' *[IAS 36.49]*.

Accordingly, some capital expenditure cash flows must be built into the forecast cash flows. Whilst improving capital expenditure may not be recognised, routine or replacement capital expenditure necessary to maintain the function of the asset or assets in the CGU has to be included. Entities must therefore distinguish between maintenance, replacement and enhancement expenditure. This distinction may not be easy to draw in practice, as shown in the following example.

Example 20.12:   Distinguishing enhancement and maintenance expenditure

A telecommunications company provides fixed line, telephone, television and internet services. It must develop its basic transmission infrastructure (by overhead wires or cables along streets or railway lines, etc.) and in order to service a new customer it will have to connect the customer's home via cable and other equipment. It will extend its network to adjoining areas and perhaps acquire an entity with its own network. It will also reflect changes in technology, e.g. fibre optic cables replacing copper ones.

Obviously, when preparing the budgets which form the basis for testing the network for impairment, it will make assumptions regarding future revenue growth and will include the costs of connecting those customers. However, its infrastructure maintenance spend will inevitably include replacing equipment with the current technology. There is no option of continuing to replace equipment with something that has been technologically superseded. Once this technology exists, it will be reflected in the entity's budgets and taken into account in its cash flows when carrying out impairment tests, even though this new equipment will enhance the performance of the transmission infrastructure.

Further examples indicate another problem area – the effects of future expenditure that the entity has identified but which the entity has not yet incurred. An entity may have acquired an asset with the intention of enhancing it in future and may, therefore, have paid for future synergies which will be reflected in the calculation of goodwill. Another entity may have plans for an asset that involve expenditure that will enhance its future performance and without which the asset may be impaired.

Examples could include:

- a TV transmission company that, in acquiring another, would expect to pay for the future right to migrate customers from analogue to digital services; or
- an aircraft manufacturer that expects to be able to use one of the acquired plants for a new model at a future point, a process that will involve replacing much of the current equipment.

In both cases the long-term plans reflect both the capital spent and the cash flows that will flow from it. There is no obvious alternative to recognising an impairment when calculating the CGU or CGU group's VIU as IAS 36 insists that the impairment test has to be performed for the asset in its current condition. This means that it is not permitted to include the benefit of improving or enhancing the asset's performance in calculating its VIU.

In the TV example above, it does not appear to matter whether the entity recognises goodwill or has a separable intangible right that it has not yet brought into use.

An entity in this situation may attempt to avoid or reduce an impairment write down by calculating the appropriate FVLCD, as this is not constrained by rules regarding future capital expenditure. As discussed above, these cash flows can be included only to the extent that other market participants would consider them when evaluating the asset. It is not permissible to include assumptions about cash flows or benefits from the asset that would not be available to or considered by a typical market participant.

7.1.3 Restructuring

The standard contains similar rules with regard to any future restructuring that may affect the VIU of the asset or CGU. The prohibition on including the results of restructuring applies only to those plans to which the entity is not committed. Again, this is because of the general rule that the cash flows must be based on the asset in its current condition so future events that may change that condition are not to be taken into account. *[IAS 36.44, 45]*. When an entity becomes committed to a restructuring (as set out in IAS 37 – see Chapter 26), IAS 36 then allows an entity's estimates of future cash inflows and outflows to reflect the cost savings and other benefits from the restructuring, based on the most recent financial budgets/forecasts approved by management. *[IAS 36.46, 47]*. Treatment of such a future restructuring is illustrated by Example 5 in the standard's accompanying section of illustrative examples. The standard specifically points out that the increase in cash inflows as a result of such a restructuring may not be taken into account until after the entity is committed to the restructuring. *[IAS 36.47]*.

Entities will sometimes be required to recognise impairment losses that will be reversed once the expenditure has been incurred and the restructuring completed.

7.1.4 Terminal values

In the case of non-current assets, a large component of value attributable to an asset or CGU arises from its terminal value, which is the net present value of all of the forecast free cash flows that are expected to be generated by the asset or CGU after the explicit forecast period. IAS 36 includes specific requirements if the asset is to be sold at the end of its useful life. The disposal proceeds and costs should be based on current prices and costs for similar assets, adjusted if necessary for price level changes if the entity has chosen to include this factor in its forecasts and selection of a discount rate. The entity must take care that its estimate is based on a proper assessment of the amount that would be received in an arm's length transaction. *[IAS 36.52, 53]*.

Whether the life of an asset or CGU is considered to be finite or indefinite will have a material impact on the terminal value. It is therefore of the utmost importance for management to assess carefully the cash generating ability of the asset or CGU and whether the period over which this asset or CGU is capable of generating cash flows is defined or not. While many CGUs containing goodwill will have an indefinite life, the same is not necessarily true for CGUs without allocated goodwill. For example, if a CGU has one main operating asset with a finite life, as in the case of a mine, the cash flow period may need to be limited to the life of the mine. Whether it would be reasonable to assume that an entity would replace the principal assets of a CGU and therefore whether it would be appropriate to calculate the terminal value under consideration of cash flows into perpetuity will depend on the specific facts and circumstances.

In the case of assets or CGUs with indefinite useful lives, the terminal value is calculated by having regard to the forecast maintainable cash flows that are expected to be generated by the assets or CGUs in the final year of the explicit forecast period ('the terminal year'). It is essential that the terminal year cash flows reflect maintainable cash flows as otherwise any material one-off or abnormal cash flows that are forecast for the terminal year will inappropriately increase or decrease the valuation.

The maintainable cash flow expected to be generated by the asset or CGU is then capitalised by a perpetuity factor based on either:

- the discount rate if cash flows are forecast to remain relatively constant; or
- the discount rate less the long term growth rate if cash flows are forecast to grow.

Care is required in assessing the growth rate to ensure consistency between the long term growth rate used and the assumptions used by the entity generally in its business planning. IAS 36 requires an entity to use in the VIU calculation a steady or declining growth rate for subsequent years, unless an increasing rate can be justified. This growth rate must not exceed the long-term average growth rate for the products, industries, or country or countries in which the entity operates, or for the market in which the asset is used, unless a higher rate can be justified. *[IAS 36.33]*.

7.1.5 Foreign currency cash flows

Foreign currency cash flows should first be estimated in the currency in which they will be generated and then discounted using a discount rate appropriate for that currency. An entity should translate the present value calculated in the foreign currency using the spot exchange rate at the date of the value in use calculation. *[IAS 36.54]*. This is to avoid the problems inherent in using forward exchange rates, which are based on differential interest rates. Using such a rate would result in double-counting the time value of money, first in the discount rate and then in the forward rate. *[IAS 36.BCZ49]*. However, the method requires an entity to perform, in effect, separate impairment tests for cash flows generated in different currencies but make them consistent with one another so that the combined effect is meaningful. This is an extremely difficult exercise. Many different factors need to be taken into account including relative inflation rates and relative interest rates as well as appropriate discount rates for the currencies in question. Because of this, the possibility for error is great and the greatest danger is understating the present value of cash outflows by using too high a discount rate. In practice, valuers may assist entities to obtain a sufficiently accurate result by assuming that cash flows are generated in a single currency even though they may be received or paid in another. Significantly, the rate used to translate the cash flows could well be different from that used to translate the foreign currency assets, goodwill and liabilities of a subsidiary at the period end. For example, a non-monetary asset such as an item of property, plant and equipment may be carried at an amount based on exchange rates on the date on which it was acquired but generates foreign currency cash flows. In order to determine its recoverable amount if there are indicators of impairment, IAS 21 – *The Effects of Changes in Foreign Exchange Rates* – states that the recoverable amount will be calculated in accordance with IAS 36 and the present value of the cash flows translated at the exchange rate at the date when that value was determined. *[IAS 21.25]*. IAS 21 notes that this may be the rate at the reporting date. The VIU is then compared to the carrying value and the item is then carried forward at the lower of these two values.

7.1.6 Internal transfer pricing

If the cash inflows generated by the asset or CGU are based on internal transfer pricing, the best estimate of an external arm's length transaction price should be used in estimating the future cash flows to determine the asset's or CGU's VIU. *[IAS 36.70]*. Note that this applies to any cash inflow once a CGU has been identified; it is not restricted to CGUs that have been identified because there is an active market for their outputs, which are described at 3.3 above.

In practice, transfer pricing may be based on estimated market values, perhaps with a discount or other adjustment, be a cost-based price or be based on specific negotiation between the group companies. Transfer prices will reflect the taxation consequences to the transferring and acquiring companies and the prices may be agreed with the relevant taxation authorities. This is especially important to multinational companies but may affect transfer prices within a single jurisdiction.

Transfer pricing is extremely widespread. The following example describes a small number of bases for the pricing and the ways in which it might be possible to verify whether they approximate to an arm's length transaction price (and, of course, even where the methodology is appropriate, it is still necessary to ensure that the inputs into the calculation are reasonable). An arm's length price may not be a particular price point but rather a range of prices.

Example 20.13: Transfer prices

A vehicle manufacturer, Entity A has a CGU that manufactures parts, transferring them to the vehicle assembly division. The parts are specific to the manufacturer's vehicles and the manufacturer cannot immediately source them on the open market. However, Entity A and other manufacturers in the sector do enter into parts supply arrangements with third parties, which set up the specific tooling necessary to manufacture the parts and could provide an external comparable transaction to help validate that the parts' internal transfer price is equivalent to an arm's length transaction. If not, the forecasts should be adjusted.

Entity B is an oil company that transfers crude oil from the drilling division to the refinery, to be used in the production of gasoline. There are market prices for crude oil that can be used to estimate cash inflows in the drilling division CGU and cash outflows for the refinery CGU.

7.1.7 Overheads and share-based payments

When calculating the VIU, entities should include projections of cash outflows that are:

(i) necessarily incurred to generate the cash inflow from continuing use of the asset (or CGU); and

(ii) can be directly attributed, or allocated on a reasonable and consistent basis to the asset (or CGU). *[IAS 36.39(b)]*.

Projections of cash outflows include those for the day-to-day servicing of the asset/CGU as well as future overheads that can be attributed directly, or allocated on a reasonable and consistent basis, to the use of the asset/CGU. *[IAS 36.41]*.

In principle, all overhead costs should be considered and most should be allocated to CGUs when testing for impairment, subject to materiality.

Judgements might however be required to determine how far down to allocate some overhead costs and in determining an appropriate allocation basis, in particular when it comes to stewardship costs and overhead costs incurred at a far higher level in a group to the CGU/asset assessed for impairment. Careful consideration of the entity's specific relevant facts and circumstances and cost structure is needed.

Generally, overhead costs that provide identifiable services to a CGU (e.g. IT costs from a centralised function) as well as those that would be incurred by a CGU if it needed to perform the related tasks when operating on a 'stand-alone basis' (e.g. financial reporting function) should be allocated to the CGU being tested for impairment.

Conversely, overhead costs that are incurred with a view to acquire and develop a new business (e.g. costs for corporate development such as M&A activities) would generally not be allocated. These costs are similar in nature to future cash inflows and outflows that are expected to arise from improving or enhancing a CGU's performance which are not considered in the VIU according to paragraph 44 of IAS 36. *[IAS 36.44]*.

The selection of a reasonable and consistent allocation basis of overhead costs will require analysis of various factors including the nature of the CGU itself. A reasonable allocation basis for identifiable services may be readily apparent, for example in some cases volume of transaction processing for IT services or headcount for human resource services may be appropriate. However, a reasonable allocation basis for stewardship costs that are determined to be necessarily incurred by the CGU to generate cash inflows may require more analysis. For example, an allocation basis for stewardship costs such as revenue or headcount may not necessarily be reasonable when CGUs have different regulatory environments, (i.e. more regulated CGUs may require more governance time and effort) or maturity stages (i.e. CGUs in mature industries may require less governance effort). The allocation basis may need to differ by type of cost and in some cases may need to reflect an average metric over a period of time rather than a metric for a single period or may need to reflect future expected, rather than historic, metrics.

Overheads not fully pushed down to the lowest level of CGUs might need to be included in an impairment test at a higher level group of CGUs if it can be demonstrated that the overhead costs are necessarily incurred and can be attributed directly or allocated on a reasonable and consistent basis at that higher level. After a careful analysis, there could be instances when certain overhead costs are excluded from cash flow projections on the basis that they do not meet the criteria under paragraph 39(b) of IAS 36.

Many entities make internal charges, often called 'management charges', which purport to transfer overhead charges to other group entities. Care must be taken before using these charges as a surrogate for actual overheads as they are often based on what is permitted, (e.g. by the taxation authorities), rather than actual overhead costs. There is also the danger of double counting if a management charge includes an element for the use of corporate assets that have already been allocated to the CGU being tested, e.g. an internal rent charge.

In certain situations it may be argued that some stewardship costs are already included in the impairment test through the discount rate used. This would among other factors depend on the way the discount rate has been determined, and whether the relevant stewardship cost should be regarded more as a shareholder cost covered in the shareholders' expected return rather than a cost necessarily incurred by the CGU to generate the relevant cash flows. Due to the complexity of such an approach it would need to be applied with appropriate care.

In many jurisdictions employees' remuneration packages include share-based payments. Share-based payments may be cash-settled, equity-settled or give the entity or the counterparty the choice of settlement in equity or in cash. In practice, many share-based payment transactions undertaken by entities are awards of equity-settled shares and options. This gives the entity the possibility of rewarding employees without incurring any cash outflows and instead the cash costs are ultimately borne by the shareholders through dilution of their holdings.

When it comes to impairment assessment, a question that often faces entities is whether and how to consider share-based payments in the recoverable amount, in particular the VIU calculation. IAS 36 itself does not provide any specific guidance as to whether or how share-based payments should be considered in determining the recoverable amount.

As IAS 36 focuses on cash flows in determining VIU, it seems that expected cash outflows in relation to cash-settled share-based payments would need to be reflected in the VIU calculation. The future expected cash outflow could, for example, be reflected by the fair value of the award at the balance sheet date, through including the amount of that fair value expected to vest and be paid out in excess of the liability already recognised at that date in the VIU calculation. In such a case the liability already recognised at the date of the VIU determination would not form part of the carrying value of the CGU.

While theoretically this seems to be straight forward, in practice it can be quite a challenging and judgemental task, in particular when the entity consists of a large number of CGUs. Share-based payments are in general awarded by the parent to employees within the group. There may be no correlation between any change in the value of share-based payments after the grant date and the performance of the employing CGU. This may be relevant in assessing whether and how such changes in value and the ultimate expected cash flows are allocated to a specific CGU.

What is even less clear is whether an entity should reflect in the VIU calculation equity-settled share-based payments. Such share-based payment transactions will never result in any cash outflows for the entity, and therefore a literal reading of IAS 36 may indicate that they can be ignored in determining the recoverable amount. However, some might argue an entity should appropriately reflect all share-based payments in the VIU calculation, whether or not these result in a real cash outflow to the entity. Such share-based payments are part of an employee's remuneration package and therefore costs (in line with the treatment under IFRS 2 – *Share-based Payment*) incurred by the entity for services from the employee are necessary as part of the overall cash flow generating capacity of the entity. Others may argue that they need to be considered through adjusting the discount rate in order to reflect a higher return to equity holders to counter the dilutive effects of equity settled share-based payment awards.

The time span over which the recoverable amount is calculated is often much longer than the time period for which share-based payments have been awarded. Companies and their employees would often expect that further share-based payment awards will be made in the future during the time period used for the recoverable amount calculation. Depending on the respective facts and circumstances an entity would need to consider whether to include the effect of share-based payments over a longer period, considering the discussion above.

7.1.8 Lease payments

7.1.8.A Lease payments during the lease term

As mentioned under 4.1.2 above, the VIU calculation should not consider any cash flows for lease liabilities recorded in the statement of financial position. If the carrying amount of the lease liability is deducted to arrive at the carrying value of the CGU, the same carrying amount of the lease liability would need to be deducted from the VIU. *[IAS 36.78]*.

It is important to note that, while under IFRS 16 many payments in connection with lease arrangements are reflected in the lease liability, not all lease payments are reflected in the recognised lease liability. Variable lease payments that do not depend on an index or a rate and are not in-substance fixed, such as those based on performance or usage of the underlying asset, are not reflected in the recognised lease liability. These contractual payments therefore would still need to be reflected in the cash flow forecast used for the VIU calculation.

An entity accounts for each non-lease component within a contract separately from the lease component of the contract, unless the lessee applies the practical expedient in paragraph 15 of IFRS 16. Therefore, unless the practical expedient is applied, the non-lease components would need to be considered in the VIU calculation. If the practical expedient in paragraph 15 of IFRS 16 is applied, then the same guidance as discussed above for variable lease payments would apply to variable payments in relation to non-lease components.

In addition, IFRS 16 has certain exemptions for low-value assets and short-term leases. If a lessee elects to use these exemptions and therefore not to record a right-of-use asset and a lease liability on the balance sheet for these leases, then the cash flows in relation to these leases would still need to be included in the VIU cash flow forecast.

7.1.8.B Lease payments beyond the current lease term

When testing (groups) of CGUs it will frequently occur that cash flow forecasts in a VIU model are for a longer period than the lease term of the right-of-use assets included in the carrying amount of the CGU.

An assumption of new capital investments is in practice intrinsic to the VIU test. What has to be assessed are the future cash flows of the CGU. The cash flows, out into the future, will include sales of products or services, the cost of sales or services and all other cash flows necessary to generate independent cash inflows. They must necessarily include capital expenditure as well, at least to the extent required to keep the CGU functioning as forecasted.

In cases where the cash flows of the CGU are dependent on the underlying right-of-use assets, but the lease term will end during the cash flow forecast period, replacement of the underlying right-of-use asset will have to be assumed. This can be done either by assuming a new lease will be entered into and therefore considering lease payments for this replacement lease in the cash flow forecast or terminal value or by assuming a replacement asset will be purchased. This will depend on the entity's planned course of action. It would be inappropriate not to reflect such replacement needs in the CGU's cash flows if the CGU's future cash inflows depend thereon.

Special attention is required when a terminal value calculation is used, where the terminal value is calculated before the end of the lease term. For example, the terminal value may be based on the extrapolation of the cash flow expected for year 5, while the lease term ends at the end of year 8. This means that the cash flow at the end of year 5 does not represent a sustainable cash flow going forward. This may be addressed by including replacement leases or capital expenditures in the terminal year, and separately calculating an adjustment to reflect that some of these expenditures will only start after year 8 (if material).

7.1.9 Events after the reporting period

Events after the reporting period and information received after the end of the reporting period should be considered in the impairment assessment only if changes in assumptions provide additional evidence of conditions that existed at the end of the reporting period. Judgement of all facts and circumstances is required to make this assessment.

Information available after the year end might provide evidence that conditions were much worse than assumed. Whether an adjustment to the impairment assessment would be required or not would depend on whether the information casts doubts on the assumptions made in the estimated cash flows for the impairment assessment.

Competitive pressures resulting in price reductions after the year end do not generally arise overnight but normally occur over a period of time and may be more a reaction to conditions that already existed at the year-end in which case management would reflect this in the year end impairment assessment.

IAS 10 – *Events after the Reporting Period* – distinguishes events after the reporting period between adjusting and non-adjusting events (see Chapter 38). IAS 10 mentions abnormally large changes after the reporting period in asset prices or foreign exchange rates as examples of non-adjusting events and therefore these changes would in general not be a reason to update year end impairment calculations. The standard implies that abnormally large changes must be due to an event that occurred after the period end and therefore more or less assumes that the cause of such abnormally large changes are not conditions that already existed at the year-end. However, management would need to carefully assess the reason for the abnormally large change and consider whether it is due to conditions which already existed at the period end.

As stated under 7.1 above, cash flow projections used for the impairment test should be based on recent financial budgets/forecasts approved by management. This begs the question what should an entity do if a new budget/forecast is approved by management after the reporting period end but before the accounts are authorised for issue? A similar question arises in group scenarios where subsidiaries' accounts might be authorised for issue a significant time after the group accounts were authorised for issue. In both scenarios the same general considerations as explained above would apply. An entity would need to assess whether the revised budget/forecast is due to conditions that already existed at the reporting period end and therefore would need to be considered in the impairment assessment, or whether the change in budget/forecast is due to circumstances that arose after the end of the reporting period and therefore would only be considered in subsequent impairment tests. In a group scenario, this could lead to a situation where the revised budget/forecast would need to be considered on a subsidiary level when the subsidiaries' accounts are authorised for issue after the revised budget was approved, despite the fact that the group accounts were already authorised for issue based on the previous budget.

7.1.10 'Traditional' and 'expected cash flow' approach to present value

The elements that must be taken into account in calculating VIU are described at 7 above. IAS 36 requires an estimate of the future cash flows the entity expects to derive from the asset and the time value of money, represented by the current market risk-free rate of interest, to be reflected in the VIU calculation. However, the other elements that must be taken into account, all of which measure various aspects of risk, may be dealt with either as adjustments to the discount rate or to the cash flows. These elements are:

- expectations about possible variations in the amount or timing of those future cash flows;
- the price for bearing the uncertainty inherent in the asset; and
- other factors, such as illiquidity that market participants would reflect in pricing the future cash flows the entity expects to derive from the asset. *[IAS 36.30]*.

Adjusting for these factors in the discount rate is termed the 'traditional approach' in Appendix A to IAS 36. Alternatively, under the 'expected cash flow' approach these adjustments are made in arriving at the risk-adjusted cash flows. Either method may be used to compute the VIU of an asset or CGU. *[IAS 36.A2]*.

The traditional approach uses a single set of estimated cash flows and a single discount rate, often described as 'the rate commensurate with the risk'. This approach assumes that a single discount rate convention can incorporate all expectations about the future cash flows and the appropriate risk premium and therefore places most emphasis on the selection of the discount rate. *[IAS 36.A4]*.

Due to the problems and difficulties around capturing and reflecting all of the variables into a single discount rate, IAS 36 notes that the expected cash flow approach may be the more effective measurement tool. *[IAS 36.A6, A7]*.

The expected cash flow approach is a probability weighted net present value approach. This approach uses all expectations about possible cash flows instead of a single most likely cash flow and assigns probabilities to each cash flow scenario to arrive at a probability weighted net present value. The use of probabilities is an essential element of the expected cash flow approach. *[IAS 36.A10]*. The discount rate then considers the risks and variability for which the cash flows have not been adjusted. Appendix A notes some of the downsides of this approach, e.g. that the probabilities are highly subjective and that it might be inappropriate for measuring a single item or one with a limited number of outcomes. Nonetheless, it considers the most valid objection to the method to be the costs of obtaining additional information when weighed against its 'greater reliability'. [IAS 36.A10-13].

Whichever method is used, an entity needs to ensure that consistent assumptions are used for the estimation of cash flows and the selection of an appropriate discount rate in order to avoid any double-counting or omissions.

7.2 Identifying an appropriate discount rate and discounting the future cash flows

Finally, although probably inherent in their identification, the forecast cash flows of the CGU have to be allocated to different periods for the purpose of the discounting step. The present value of these cash flows should then be calculated by discounting them. The discount rate is to be a pre-tax rate that reflects current market assessments of the time value of money and the risks specific to the asset for which the future cash flow estimates have not been adjusted. [IAS 36.55].

This means the discount rate to be applied should be an estimate of the rate that the market would expect on an equally risky investment. The standard states:

> 'A rate that reflects current market assessments of the time value of money and the risks specific to the asset is the return that investors would require if they were to choose an investment that would generate cash flows of amounts, timing and risk profile equivalent to those that the entity expects to derive from the asset.' [IAS 36.56].

Therefore, if at all possible, the rate is to be obtained from market transactions or market rates, which means the rate implicit in current market transactions for similar assets or the weighted average cost of capital (WACC) of a listed entity that has a single asset (or a portfolio of assets) with similar service potential and risks to the asset under review. [IAS 36.56]. If such a listed entity could be found, care would have to be taken in using its WACC as the standard specifies for the VIU the use of a pre-tax discount rate that is independent of the entity's capital structure and the way it financed the purchase of the asset (see below). The effect of gearing and its effect on calculating an appropriate WACC is illustrated in Example 20.14.

Only in rare cases (e.g. property assets) can such market rates be obtained. If an asset-specific rate is not available from the market, surrogates should be used. [IAS 36.A16]. The discount rate that investors would require if they were to choose an investment that would generate cash flows of amounts, timing and risk profile equivalent to those that the entity expects to derive from the asset will not be easy to determine. IAS 36 suggests that, as a starting point, the entity may take into account the following rates:

(a) the entity's weighted average cost of capital determined using techniques such as the Capital Asset Pricing Model;

(b) the entity's incremental borrowing rate; and

(c) other market borrowing rates. [IAS 36.A17].

Appendix A also gives the following guidelines for selecting the appropriate discount rate:
- it should be adjusted to reflect the specific risks associated with the projected cash flows (such as country, currency, price and cash flow risks) and to exclude risks that are not relevant; *[IAS 36.A18]*
- to avoid double counting, the discount rate does not reflect risks for which future cash flow estimates have been adjusted; *[IAS 36.A18]*
- the discount rate is independent of the entity's capital structure and the way it financed the purchase of the asset; *[IAS 36.A19]*
- if the basis for the rate is post-tax (such as a weighted average cost of capital), it is adjusted for the VIU calculation to reflect a pre-tax rate; *[IAS 36.A20]* and
- normally the entity uses a single discount rate but it should use separate discount rates for different future periods if the VIU is sensitive to different risks for different periods or to the term structure of interest rates. *[IAS 36.A21]*.

The discount rate specific for the asset or CGU will take account of the period over which the asset or CGU is expected to generate cash inflows and it may not be sensitive to changes in short-term rates – this is discussed at 2.1.4 above. *[IAS 36.16]*.

It is suggested that the incremental borrowing rate of the business is relevant to the selection of a discount rate. This could only be a starting point as the appropriate discount rate should be independent of the entity's capital structure or the way in which it financed the purchase of the asset. In addition, the incremental borrowing rate may include an element of default risk for the entity as a whole, which is not relevant in assessing the return expected from the assets.

In practice, many entities use the WACC to estimate the appropriate discount rate. The appropriate way to calculate the WACC is an extremely technical subject, and one about which there is much academic literature and no general agreement. The selection of the rate is obviously a crucial part of the impairment testing process and in practice it will probably not be possible to obtain a theoretically perfect rate. The objective, therefore, must be to obtain a rate which is sensible and justifiable. There are probably a number of acceptable methods of arriving at the appropriate rate and one method is set out below. While this illustration may appear to be quite complex, it has been written at a fairly general level as the calculation of the appropriate discount rate may be difficult and specialist advice may be needed.

Example 20.14: Calculating a discount rate

This example illustrates how to estimate a discount rate (WACC) for a CGU. As it is highly unlikely that a listed company with a similar risk profile to the CGU in questions exists, the WACC has to be simulated by looking at a hypothetical company with a similar risk profile.

When estimating the WACC for the CGU, the following three elements needs to be estimated:
- gearing, i.e. the ratio of market value of debt to market value of equity;
- cost of debt; and
- cost of equity.

Gearing can best be obtained by reviewing quoted companies operating predominantly in the same industry as the CGU and identifying an average level of gearing for such companies. The companies need to be quoted so that the market value of equity can be readily determined.

Where companies in the sector typically have quoted debt, the cost of such debt can be determined directly. In order to calculate the cost of debt for bank loans and borrowings more generally, one method is to take the rate implicit in fixed interest government bonds – with a period to maturity similar to the expected life of the assets being reviewed for impairment – and to add to this rate a bank's margin, i.e. the commercial premium that would be added to the bond rate by a bank lending to the hypothetical company in this sector. In some cases, the margin being charged on existing borrowings to the company in question will provide evidence to help with establishing the bank's margin. Obviously, the appropriateness of this will depend upon the extent to which the risks facing the CGU being tested are similar to the risks facing the company or group as a whole.

If goodwill or intangible assets with an indefinite life were being included in a CGU reviewed for impairment (see 8 and 10 below) the appropriate Government bond rate to use might have to be adjusted towards that for irredeemable bonds. The additional bank's margin to add would be a matter for judgement but would vary according to the ease with which the sector under review was generally able to obtain bank finance and, as noted above, there might be evidence from the borrowings actually in place of the likely margin that would be chargeable. Sectors that invest significantly in tangible assets such as properties that are readily available as security for borrowings, would require a lower margin than other sectors where such security could not be found so easily.

Cost of equity is the hardest component of the cost of capital to determine. One technique referred to in the standard, frequently used in practice and written up in numerous textbooks is the 'Capital Asset Pricing Model' (CAPM). The theory underlying this model is that the cost of equity is equal to the risk-free rate plus a multiple, known as the beta, of the market risk premium. The risk-free rate is the same as that used to determine the nominal cost of debt and described above as being obtainable from government bond yields with an appropriate period to redemption. The market risk premium is the premium that investors require for investing in equities rather than government bonds. There are also reasons why this rate may be loaded in certain cases, for instance to take account of specific risks in the CGU in question that are not reflected in its market sector generally. Loadings are typically made when determining the cost of equity for a small company. The beta for a quoted company is a number that is greater or less than one according to whether market movements generally are reflected in a proportionately greater (beta more than one) or smaller (beta less than one) movement in the particular stock in question. Most betas fall into the range 0.4 to 1.5.

Various bodies, such as The London Business School, publish betas on a regular basis both for individual stocks and for industry sectors in general. Published betas are in general levered, i.e. they reflect the level of gearing in the company or sector concerned (although unlevered betas (based on risk as if financed with 100% equity) are also available and care must be taken not to confuse the two).

In addition to the volatility expressed in the beta, investors also reflect the exposure of the stock to a limited niche sector or exposure to a limited customer base. As a result, size premium could be required when the CGU is smaller size compared to its direct competitors.

The cost of equity for the hypothetical company having a similar risk profile to the CGU is:

Cost of equity = risk-free rate + (levered beta × market risk premium) + size premium (if deemed required)

Having determined the component costs of debt and equity and the appropriate level of gearing, the WACC for the hypothetical company having a similar risk profile to the CGU in question is:

$$\text{WACC} = (1-t) \times D \times \frac{g}{1+g} + E \times \left[1 - \frac{g}{1+g}\right]$$

where:

D is the cost of debt;
E is the cost of equity;
g is the gearing level (i.e. the ratio of debt to equity) for the sector; and
t is the rate of tax relief available on the debt servicing payments.

IAS 36 requires that the forecast cash flows are before tax and finance costs, though it is more common in discounted cash flow valuations to use cash flows after tax. However, as pre-tax cash flows are being used, the standard requires a pre-tax discount rate to be used. *[IAS 36.55]*. This will theoretically involve discounting higher future cash flows (before deduction of tax) with a higher discount rate. This higher discount rate is the post-tax rate adjusted to reflect the specific amount and timing of the future tax flows. In other words, the pre-tax discount rate is the rate that gives the same present value when discounting the pre-tax cash flows as the post-tax cash flows discounted at the post-tax rate of return. *[IAS 36.BCZ85]*.

Once the WACC has been calculated, the pre-tax WACC can be calculated. If a simple gross up is appropriate, it can be calculated by applying the fraction $1/(1-t)$. Thus, if the WACC comes out at, say, 10% the pre-tax WACC will be 10% divided by 0.7, if the relevant tax rate for the reporting entity is 30%, which will give a pre-tax rate of 14.3%. However, the standard warns that in many circumstances a gross up will not give a good enough answer as the pre-tax discount rate also depends on the timing of future tax cash flows and the useful life of the asset; these tax flows can be scheduled and an iterative process used to calculate the pre-tax discount rate. *[IAS 36.BCZ85]*. The relationship between pre- and post-tax rates is discussed further at 7.2.2 below.

The selection of discount rates leaves considerable room for judgement in the absence of more specific guidance, and it is likely that many very different approaches will be applied in practice, even though this may not always be evident from the financial statements. However, once the discount rate has been chosen, the future cash flows are discounted in order to produce a present value figure representing the VIU of the CGU or individual asset that is the subject of the impairment test.

7.2.1 Discount rates and the weighted average cost of capital

The WACC is often used in practice. It is usually acceptable to auditors as it is supported by valuation experts and is an accepted methodology based on a well-known formula and widely available information. In addition, many entities already know their own WACC. However, it can only be used as a starting point for determining an appropriate discount rate and some of the issues that must be taken into account are as follows:

a) the WACC is a post-tax rate and IAS 36 requires VIU to be calculated using pre-tax cash flows and a pre-tax rate. In the majority of cases, converting the former into the latter is not simply a question of grossing up the post-tax rate by the effective tax rate;

b) an entity's own WACC may not be suitable as a discount rate if there is anything atypical about the entity's capital structure compared with 'typical' market participants;

c) the WACC must reflect the risks specific to the asset and not the risks relating to the entity as a whole, such as default risk; and

d) the entity's WACC is an average rate derived from its existing business, yet entities frequently operate in more than one sector. Within a sector, different types of projects may have different levels of risk (e.g. a start-up as against an established product).

These issues are discussed further below.

One of the most difficult areas in practice is the effect of taxation on the WACC. In order to determine an appropriate pre-tax discount rate it is likely to be necessary to adjust the entity's actual tax cash flows.

Ultimately, the appropriate discount rate to select is one that reflects current market assessments of the time value of money and the risks specific to the asset in question, including taxation. Such a rate is one that reflects 'the return that investors would require if they were to choose an investment that would generate cash flows of amounts, timing and risk profile equivalent to those that the entity expects to derive from the asset'. [IAS 36.56].

7.2.2 Calculating a pre-tax discount rate

VIU is primarily an accounting concept rather than a business valuation of the asset or CGU. One fundamental difference is that IAS 36 requires pre-tax cash flows to be discounted using a pre-tax discount rate. Why not calculate VIU on a post-tax basis? The reason is the complexities created by tax losses carried forward, temporary tax differences and deferred taxes.

The standard explains in the Basis for Conclusions that, future income tax cash flows may affect recoverable amount. It is convenient to analyse future tax cash flows into two components:

(a) the future tax cash flows that would result from any difference between the tax base of an asset (the amount attributed to it for tax purposes) and its carrying amount, after recognition of any impairment loss. Such differences are described in IAS 12 as 'temporary differences'; and

(b) the future tax cash flows that would result if the tax base of the asset were equal to its recoverable amount. [IAS 36.BCZ81].

The concept is complex but refers to the following issues.

An impairment test, say at the end of 2016, takes account of estimated future cash flows. The tax that an entity will pay in future years that will be reflected in the actual tax cash flows that it expects may depend on tax depreciation that the entity has already taken (or is yet to take) in respect of the asset or CGU being tested for impairment. The value of the asset to the business on a post-tax basis must take account of all tax effects including those relating to the past and not only those that will only arise in future.

Although these 'temporary differences' are accounted for as deferred taxation, IAS 12:

(i) does not allow entities to recognise all deferred tax liabilities or deferred tax assets;

(ii) does not recognise deferred tax assets using the same criteria as deferred tax liabilities; and

(iii) deferred tax is not recognised on a discounted basis.

Therefore, deferred taxation as provided in the income statement and statement of financial position is not sufficient to take account of the actual temporary differences relating to the asset or CGU.

At the same time, an asset valuation implicitly assumes that the carrying amount of the asset is deductible for tax. For example, if the tax rate is 25%, an entity must receive pre-tax cash flows with a present value of 400 in order to recover a carrying amount of 300. [IAS 36.BCZ88]. In principle, therefore, VIU on a post-tax basis would include the present value of the future tax cash flows that would result if the tax base of the asset were equal to its value in use. Hence, IAS 36 indicates that the appropriate tax base to calculate VIU in a post-tax setting, is the VIU itself. *[IAS 36.BCZ84]*. Therefore, the calculated VIU should also be used to derive the pre-tax discount rate. It follows from this that the 'tax cash flows' to be taken into account will be those reflected in the post-tax VIU, so they will be neither the tax cash flows available in relation to the asset (based on its cost) nor the actual tax cash flows payable by the entity.

For these reasons, the (then) IASC decided to require an enterprise to determine value in use by using pre-tax future cash flows and a pre-tax discount rate.

This means that there is a different problem, calculating an appropriate pre-tax discount rate because there are no observable pre-tax discount rates. Two important points must be taken into account:

- The pre-tax discount rate is not always the post-tax discount rate grossed up by a standard rate of tax. There are some circumstances in which a gross-up will give a reasonable approximation, discussed further at 7.2.4 below.
- The pre-tax discount rate is not the post-tax rate grossed up by the effects of the entity's actual tax cash flows. As discussed above, a post-tax discount rate such as the WACC is based on certain assumptions about the tax-deductibility of the asset and not the actual tax cash flows experienced by the entity.

Recognising this, paragraph BCZ85 of IAS 36 states that 'in theory, discounting post-tax cash flows at a post-tax discount rate and discounting pre-tax cash flows at a pre-tax discount rate should give the same result, as long as the pre-tax discount rate is the post-tax discount rate adjusted to reflect the specific amount and timing of the future tax cash flows'. *[IAS 36.BCZ85]*.

Therefore, the only accurate way to calculate a pre-tax WACC is to calculate the VIU by applying a post-tax rate to post-tax cash flows, tax cash flows being based on the allowances and charges available to the asset and to which the revenue is subject (see discussion at 7.2.3 below). The effective pre-tax rate is calculated by removing the tax cash flows and, by iteration, one can identify the pre-tax rate that makes the present value of the adjusted cash flows equal the VIU calculated using post tax cash flows.

Paragraph BCZ85 includes an example of how to calculate a pre-tax discount rate where the tax cash flows are irregular because of the availability of tax deductions for the asset's capital cost. See also the calculations in Example 20.15 below – (a) illustrates a calculation of a pre-tax discount rate. This is a relatively straightforward calculation for a single asset at the inception of the relevant project.

It may be far more complex at a later date. This is because entities may be attempting to calculate a discount rate starting with post-tax cash flows and a post-tax discount rate at a point in time when there are already temporary differences relating to the asset. A discount rate based on an entity's prospective tax cash flows may under- or overstate IAS 36's impairment charge unless it reflects these previous allowances or disallowances. This is the same problem that will be encountered if an entity attempts to test VIU using post-tax cash flows as described at 7.2.3 below.

A notional adjustment will have to be made if the entity is not paying tax because it is making, or has made, tax losses. It is unwarranted to assume that the post- and pre-tax discount rates will be the same if the entity pays no tax because of its own tax losses as this will be double counting. It is taking advantage of the losses in the cash flows but excluding that value from the assets of the CGU.

Entities may attempt to deal with the complexity of determining a pre-tax rate by trying to calculate VIU on a post-tax basis but this approach means addressing the many difficulties that have been identified by the IASB and the reasons why it mandated a pre-tax approach in testing for impairment in the first place.

Some approximations and short cuts that may give an acceptable answer in practice are dealt with at 7.2.4 below.

7.2.3 Calculating VIU using post-tax cash flows

Because of the challenges in calculating an appropriate pre-tax discount rate and because it aligns more closely with their normal business valuation approach, some entities attempt to perform a VIU calculation based on a post-tax discount rate and post-tax cash flows.

In support of the post-tax approach, the example in paragraph BCZ85 of IAS 36, which explains how to calculate a pre-tax discount rate, is mistakenly understood as a methodology for a post-tax VIU calculation using an entity's actual tax cash flows.

Entities that try a post-tax approach generally use the year-end WACC and estimated post-tax cash flows for future years that reflect the actual tax that they expect to pay in those years. A calculation on this basis will only by chance correspond to an impairment test in accordance with IAS 36 because it is based on inappropriate assumptions, i.e. it does not take account of the temporary differences that affect the entity's future tax charges and will not be based on the assumption that the VIU is tax deductible. Some include in the post-tax calculation the benefit of tax deductions or tax losses by bringing them into the cash flows in the years in which the tax benefit is expected to be received. In these cases the calculation will not correctly take account of the timing differences reflected in the tax cash flows and may not accurately reflect the differences created by the assumption that the VIU is tax deductible.

In order to calculate a post-tax VIU that is the equivalent to the VIU required by IAS 36, an entity will usually have to make adjustments to the actual tax cash flows or otherwise adjust its actual post-tax cash flows.

There are two approaches that can give a post-tax VIU that is equivalent to IAS 36's pre-tax calculation:

(1) Post-tax cash flows based on notional tax cash flows. The assumptions that need to be made are the same as those used in calculating a pre-tax discount rate as described in paragraph BCZ85. Therefore, there must be no temporary differences associated with the asset which means including only the future cash flows that would result if the tax base of the asset were equal to its VIU. In addition, no account is taken of the existing tax losses of the entity. Both of these assumptions will probably mean making appropriate notional adjustments.

(2) Post-tax cash flows reflecting actual tax cash flows. The relevant deferred tax asset or liability, discounted as appropriate, should be treated as part of the net assets of the relevant CGU.

Impairment of fixed assets and goodwill 1571

It is very important to note that these are methodologies to determine IAS 36's required VIU and they will only be acceptable if the result can be shown to be materially the same as a pre-tax impairment calculation as required by IAS 36.

Note that for illustrative purposes all of the following examples assume that there is no headroom, i.e. the NPV of the relevant cash flows is exactly equal to the carrying value of the asset. This is to make it easier to observe the relationship between pre- and post-tax calculations. See 7.2.5 below for worked examples including headroom.

Example 20.15: *Impairment calculations using pre- and post-tax cash flows and discount rates*

The following examples illustrate impairment calculations using pre- and post-tax cash flows and discount rates.

(a)   Comparing pre- and post-tax rates

An entity has invested €2,139 in a facility with a 10 year life. Revenue and operating costs are expected to grow by 5% annually. The net present value of the post-tax future cash flows, discounted at the WACC of 8.1%, is equal to the cost of the plant.

The budgeted pre-tax cash flows are as follows:

Year	1	2	3	4	5	6	7	8	9	10
	€	€	€	€	€	€	€	€	€	€
Revenues	500	525	551	579	608	638	670	703	739	776
Operating expenses	(200)	(210)	(220)	(232)	(243)	(255)	(268)	(281)	(296)	(310)
Pre-tax cash flow	300	315	331	347	365	383	402	422	443	466

The following tax amortisation and tax rate apply to the business:

Tax and accounting depreciation	straight line
Tax rate	30%

These apply to the budgeted cash flows as follows:

Year	1	2	3	4	5	6	7	8	9	10
	€	€	€	€	€	€	€	€	€	€
Tax amortisation	214	214	214	214	214	214	214	214	214	214
Taxation	(26)	(30)	(35)	(40)	(45)	(51)	(56)	(62)	(69)	(75)
Post-tax cash flow	274	285	296	307	320	332	346	360	374	391

The pre-tax rate can be calculated using an iterative calculation and this can be compared to a gross up using the standard rate of tax. The NPV using these two rates is as follows:

Pre-tax rate (day 1) – iterative calculation	10.92%
Cost of investment at NPV future cash flows	€2,139
Standard gross up (day 1) (8.1% ÷ 70%).	11.57%
NPV at standard gross up	€2,077

The NPV of the pre-tax cash flows at 11.57% is €2,077. This is only 2.9% lower than the number calculated using the true pre-tax rate. In many circumstances, this difference would not have a material effect.

If the tax and accounting depreciation are straight line then the distortion introduced by a standard gross-up can be relatively small and could be of less significance to an impairment test than, for example, the potential variability in cash flows. See also 7.2.4 below.

(b) Comparing pre- and post-tax rates when the asset is impaired

Assume that the facility is much less successful than had previously been assumed and that the revenues are 20% lower than the original estimates. The pre- and post-tax cash flows are as follows.

Year	1	2	3	4	5	6	7	8	9	10
	€	€	€	€	€	€	€	€	€	€
Revenues	400	420	441	463	486	511	536	563	591	621
Operating expenses	(200)	(210)	(220)	(232)	(243)	(255)	(268)	(281)	(296)	(310)
Pre-tax cash flow	200	210	221	232	243	255	268	281	295	310
Tax amortisation	214	214	214	214	214	214	214	214	214	214
Taxation	4	1	(2)	(5)	(9)	(12)	(16)	(20)	(24)	(29)
Post-tax cash flow	204	211	219	227	234	243	252	261	271	281

The asset is clearly impaired as the previous cash flows were just sufficient to recover the carrying amount of the investment. If these revised cash flows are discounted using the pre- and post-tax discount rates discussed above, the resulting impairment is as follows:

		NPV	Impairment	Deferred tax	Net loss
Original investment		2,139			
Pre-tax cash flows, discounted at pre-tax discount rate	10.92%	1,426	713	214	499
Post-tax cash flows discounted at post-tax discount rate	8.1%	1,569	570	171	399

Unless adjustments are made to the post-tax calculation, it will understate the impairment loss by 143 (pre-tax) and 100 (post-tax, assuming full provision for the deferred tax asset). This difference is the present value of the deferred tax on the actual impairment loss, a point explored in more detail in (d) below.

(c) Impairment and variable tax cash flows

The assumption of straight-line amortisation for taxation and accounting purposes does not reflect the circumstances of certain sectors, particularly where there are significant deductions for tax for the cost of the asset being tested for impairment, e.g. in the extractive sector. Impairment tests have to be calculated on finite life assets and variable tax cash flows. In many jurisdictions there are, or have been, substantial tax allowances for the construction of the asset but high rates of tax in the production phase.

The following example assumes that the entity gets a tax deduction for the cost of the asset in year 1. Once again, this assumes that in year 1 the cost of the investment is equal to the NPV of the cash flows.

Year	1	2	3	4	5	6	7	8	9	10
	€	€	€	€	€	€	€	€	€	€
Revenues	500	525	551	579	608	638	670	704	739	776
Operating expenses	(200)	(210)	(220)	(232)	(243)	(255)	(268)	(281)	(296)	(310)
Pre-tax cash flow	300	315	331	347	365	383	402	422	443	465
Tax amortisation	2,367									
Taxation	620	(95)	(99)	(104)	(109)	(115)	(121)	(127)	(133)	(140)
Post-tax cash flow	920	220	232	243	256	268	281	295	310	325

Assuming the same post-tax WACC of 8.1%, the pre-tax WACC is now considerably lower owing to the effect of the tax deduction in the first year. It can be calculated using an iterative process at 8.76%, rather than 10.92%, which is the pre-tax rate in (a) and (b) above. Therefore, the NPV of the pre- and post-tax cash inflows is €2,367 rather than €2,139 – the first year tax allowances enhance the VIU of the project. If the entity discounted the pre-tax cash flows at 11.57%, the post-tax rate grossed up at the standard rate of taxation, these cash flows would have a NPV of €2,077, which is approximately 12% lower than the actual NPV. It is clear that a standardised gross up will not give a reasonable approximation in these circumstances.

(d) *Correctly measuring impairment using post-tax information*

If an entity applies a post-tax rate to post-tax cash flows, what can it do to ensure that impairment is correctly measured in accordance with IAS 36?

Assume, in example (c) above, that cash inflows decline by 20% commencing at the beginning of year 2. The net present value of the pre-tax cash flows at 8.76% is €1,516.

Year	2	3	4	5	6	7	8	9	10
	€	€	€	€	€	€	€	€	€
Pre-tax cash flow	210	221	232	243	255	268	281	295	310
Taxation	(63)	(66)	(69)	(73)	(77)	(80)	(84)	(89)	(93)
Post-tax cash flows	147	155	163	170	178	188	197	206	217

The asset's book value at the end of year 1, assuming straight line depreciation over 10 years, is €2,130. Impairment calculated using pre-tax cash flows and discount rates is as follows:

		€
Original investment		2,367
Net book value (end of year 1)		2,130
Pre-tax cash flows, discounted at pre-tax discount rate	8.76%	1,516
Impairment		614
Deferred tax asset (reduction in deferred tax liability)		(184)
Net impairment loss		430

A post-tax calculation overstates the impairment, as follows:

		€
Original investment		2,367
Net book value (end of year 1)		2,130
Post-tax cash flows, discounted at post-tax discount rate	8.1%	1,092
Impairment – overstated by 424		1,038
Deferred tax asset (reduction in deferred tax liability)		(311)
Net impairment loss – overstated by 297		727

It can be seen that unless adjustments are made to the post-tax calculation, it will overstate the impairment loss. There are two ways in which the post-tax calculation can be adjusted so as to give the right impairment charge.

Method (1): Post-tax cash flows based on notional tax cash flows. The assumptions that need to be made are the same as those used in calculating a pre-tax discount rate. Therefore, there must be no temporary differences associated with the asset which means including only the future cash flows that would result if the tax base of the asset were equal to its VIU.

This means assuming that the VIU of the asset (1,516) is deductible for tax purposes in year 2. This would usually be calculated iteratively

Year	2	3	4	5	6	7	8	9	10
	€	€	€	€	€	€	€	€	€
Pre-tax cash flow	210	221	232	243	255	268	281	295	310
Deemed tax amortisation	1,516								
Taxation	392	(66)	(69)	(73)	(77)	(80)	(84)	(89)	(93)
Post-tax cash flows	602	155	163	170	178	188	197	206	217

The present value of the notional post-tax cash flows at the post-tax discount rate of 8.1% is now €1,516, i.e. the VIU of the asset is fully deductible for tax purposes, so the impairment charge, before taxation, is €614, which is the same impairment as calculated above under the pre-tax cash flow model.

Method (2): Post-tax cash flows reflecting actual tax cash flows as adjusted for deferred tax. Again, this is an iterative calculation.

Year	2	3	4	5	6	7	8	9	10
	€	€	€	€	€	€	€	€	€
Pre-tax cash flow	210	221	232	243	255	268	281	295	310
Deferred tax	(455)								
Taxation	(63)	(66)	(69)	(73)	(77)	(80)	(84)	(89)	(93)
Post-tax cash flows	147	155	163	170	178	188	197	206	217
Post-tax cash flows as adjusted for deferred tax	602	155	163	170	178	188	197	206	217

The net present value of the post-tax cash flows at the post-tax discount rate is €1,092. The NPV of the post-tax cash flows as adjusted for deferred tax (see bottom line in the table), which is the VIU of the asset being tested for impairment, is €1,516 and the gross deferred tax liability relating to the asset is 1,516 at 30%, i.e. €455. The NPV of €455, discounted for one year at the post-tax discount rate of 8.1%, is €424. The deferred tax liability is discounted for one year due to the assumption used that all tax cash flows take place at the end of the year. Revised, the post-tax calculation is as follows:

		€
Original investment		2,367
Net book value (end of year 1)		2,130
Post-tax cash flows, discounted at post-tax discount rate	8.1%	1,092
Discounted deferred tax		424
Impairment (2,130 – (1,092 + 424))		614

The impairment loss will impact the deferred tax calculation in the usual way, i.e. 614 at 30% = €184.

It will rarely be practicable to apply this methodology to calculate a discount rate for a CGU, as so many factors need to be taken into account. Even if all assets within the CGU are individually acquired or self-constructed, they may have a range of lives for depreciation and tax amortisation purposes, up to and including indefinite lives.

If goodwill is being tested it has an indefinite life whilst the underlying assets in the CGU or CGU group to which it has been allocated will usually have finite lives. It is likely that a reasonable approximation to the 'true' discount rate is the best that can be achieved and this is discussed further below.

7.2.4 Approximations and short cuts

The illustrations in Example 20.15 at 7.2.3 above are of course simplified, and in reality it is unlikely that entities will need to schedule all of the tax cash flows and tax consequences in order to calculate a pre-tax discount rate every time they perform an impairment review. In practice, it will probably not be possible to obtain a rate that is theoretically perfect – the task is just too intractable for that. The objective, therefore, must be to obtain a rate which is sensible and justifiable. Some of the following may make the exercise a bit easier.

An entity may calculate a pre-tax rate using adjusted tax cash flows based on the methods and assumptions described above and then apply that rate to discount pre-tax cash flows for the VIU calculation. This pre-tax rate will only need to be reassessed in following years when there is an external factor that affects risks, relevant market rates or the taxation basis of the asset or CGU.

The market may conclude that the risks relating to a particular asset are higher or lower than had previously been assumed. The market might consider risks to have reduced if, for example, a new project, process or product proves to be successful; the converse would also be true if there were previously unforeseen problems with an activity. Relevant changes in market rates are those for instruments with a period to maturity similar to the expected life of the assets being reviewed for impairment, so these will not necessarily need to be recalculated every time an impairment review is carried out. Short-term market rates may increase or decrease without affecting the rate of return that the market would require on long-term assets. Significant changes in the basis of taxation could also affect the discount rate, e.g. if tax deductions are applied or removed for all of a class of asset or activity. The discount rate will not necessarily be affected if the entity ceases to make taxable profits.

Valuation practitioners often use approximations when computing tax cash flows that may also make the task more straightforward. It may often be a valid approximation to assume that the tax amortisation of assets equals their accounting depreciation. Tax cash flows will be based on the relevant corporate tax rate and the forecast earnings before interest and taxation to give post-tax 'cash flows' that can then be discounted using a post-tax discount rate. The circumstances in which this could lead to a material distortion (perhaps in the case of an impairment test for an individual asset) will probably be obvious. This approach is consistent with the overall requirement of IAS 36, which is that the appropriate discount rate to select is one that reflects current market assessments of the risks specific to the asset in question.

The circumstances in which a standardised gross up at the corporation tax rate will give the relevant discount rate are:

- no growth in cash flows;
- a perpetuity calculation; and
- tax cash flows that are a constant percentage of total cash flows.

As long as these conditions remain unchanged, it will be straightforward to determine the discount rate for an impairment review at either the pre- or post-tax level.

There may be a close approximation to these criteria for some CGUs, particularly if accounting and tax amortisation of assets is similar. This is illustrated in Example 20.16 below – see the comparison of discount rates at the end of the example. A simple gross up may be materially correct. The criteria are unlikely to apply to the VIU of individual assets because these are rarely perpetuity calculations and the deductibility for tax purposes may not resemble accounting depreciation. If it is inappropriate to make such a gross up, an iterative calculation may be necessary to compute the appropriate pre-tax discount rate.

7.2.5 Disclosing pre-tax discount rates when using a post-tax methodology

If an entity calculates impairment using a post-tax methodology, it must still disclose the appropriate pre-tax discount rate. *[IAS 36.134(d)(v)]*. There is a widely-held view that the relevant pre-tax discount rate is the rate that will discount the pre-tax cash flows to the same VIU as the post-tax cash flows discounted using the post-tax discount rate. This will not necessarily give an answer that is consistent with IAS 36, which makes it clear that pre- and post-tax discount rates will only give the same answer if 'the pre-tax discount rate is the post-tax discount rate adjusted to reflect the specific amount and timing of the future tax cash flows'. *[IAS 36.BCZ85]*. It is no different in principle whether grossing up for a pre-tax rate or grossing up for disclosure purposes.

IAS 36 indicates that the appropriate tax base to calculate VIU in a post-tax setting, is the VIU itself. Therefore, the calculated (post-tax) VIU should also be used to derive the pre-tax discount rate. Depreciation for tax purposes must also be based on the calculated VIU.

Assuming that there is no impairment, the post-tax VIU will be higher than the carrying value of the asset. To calculate the pre-tax rate, the tax amortisation must be based on this figure. If tax amortisation is based on the cost of the asset, the apparent pre-tax discount rate will show a rising trend over the life of the asset as the ratio of pre- to post-tax cash flows changes and the effect of discounting becomes smaller. These effects can be very marked.

Example 20.16:   Calculating pre-tax discount rates from post-tax VIUs

The assumptions underlying these calculations are as follows:

	€
Tax rate	25%
Post-tax discount rate	10%
Carrying amount beginning of year 1	1,500
Remaining useful life (years)	5
Straight line tax amortisation	

If the tax amortisation is based on the cost of the asset, the apparent pre-tax discount rate in each of the five years is as follows:

Year	1	2	3	4	5
	€	€	€	€	€
Revenue	1,000	1,020	1,040	1,061	1,082
Pre-tax cash flow	500	510	520	531	541
Tax amortisation	(300)	(300)	(300)	(300)	(300)
Taxation	50	53	55	58	60
Post-tax cash flows	450	457	465	473	481
NPV of post-tax cash flows using a 10% discount rate	1,756	1,484	1,175	827	437

The apparent pre-tax discount rate in any year will be the rate that discounts the pre-tax cash flows to the same NPV as the post-tax cash flows using the post-tax discount rate.

| Apparent pre-tax discount rate | 14.4% | 15.4% | 16.7% | 19.1% | 23.8% |

It is quite clear that these apparent pre-tax discount rates are incorrect. Although pre-tax rates are not observable in the market, they are derived from market rates and would not increase in a mechanical fashion over the life of the asset.

The correct way to calculate the tax amortisation is based on the VIU. Years 1 and 2 are illustrated in the following table:

Year	1	2	3	4	5
	€	€	€	€	€
Revenue	1,000	1,020	1,040	1,061	1,082
Pre-tax cash flow	500	510	520	531	541
Year 1					
Notional tax amortisation (VIU 1,819/5)	(364)	(364)	(364)	(364)	(364)
Taxation	34	37	39	42	44
Post-tax cash flows	466	473	481	489	497
Year 2					
Notional tax amortisation (VIU 1,554/4)		(389)	(389)	(389)	(389)
Taxation		30	33	36	38
		480	487	495	503

The NPV of the post-tax cash flows, which is the VIU of the asset being tested for impairment, is €1,819 in year 1 and €1,554 in year 2, and the tax base allowing for a tax amortisation is based on these VIUs as well, both solved iteratively. Years 3, 4 and 5 are calculated in the same way, with tax amortisation based on the VIUs in the following table:

Year	1	2	3	4	5
	€	€	€	€	€
VIU (NPV of post-tax cash flows)	1,819	1,554	1,247	890	478
Annual depreciation for remaining term	364	389	416	445	478
	(1,819/5)	(1,554/4)	(1,247/3)	(890/2)	478
Pre-tax discount rate	13.1%	13.1%	13.2%	13.3%	13.3%

We can now compare the correct and incorrectly computed pre-tax discount rates. A rate based on grossing up the post-tax rate at the standard rate of tax is included for comparison.

Year	1	2	3	4	5
Post-tax discount rate	10%	10%	10%	10%	10%
Pre-tax discount rate – correct	13.1%	13.1%	13.2%	13.3%	13.3%
Pre-tax discount rate – incorrect, based on cost	14.4%	15.4%	16.7%	19.1%	23.8%
Pre-tax rate – approximation based on gross-up	13.3%	13.3%	13.3%	13.3%	13.3%

Note that in circumstances where tax amortisation is equal to accounting depreciation, a straightforward gross-up at the tax rate may give a satisfactory discount rate.

A rate based on actual post-tax cash flows will also vary from year to year depending on the tax situation.

Neither of these distortions is consistent with the principle that the pre-tax discount rate is the rate that reflects current market assessments of the time value of money and the risks specific to the asset. *[IAS 36.55]*.

7.2.6 Determining pre-tax rates taking account of tax losses

A common problem relates to the effect of tax losses on the impairment calculation, as they may reduce the total tax paid in the period under review or even eliminate it altogether. As noted above, however, a post-tax discount rate is based on certain assumptions about the tax-deductibility of the asset and not the actual tax cash flows. It is therefore unwarranted to assume that the post- and pre-tax discount rates will be the same if the entity pays no tax because of its own tax losses. The pre-tax rate should not include the benefit of available tax benefits and any deferred tax asset arising from tax losses carried forward at the reporting date must be excluded from the assets of the CGU if the impairment review is based on VIU. Similarly, if the entity calculates a post-tax VIU (see 7.2.3 above), it will also make assumptions about taxation and not base the calculation on the actual tax cash flows.

In many circumstances, the past history of tax losses affects the level of risk in the cash flows in the period under review, but one must take care not to increase the discount rate to reflect risks for which the estimated cash flows have been adjusted. *[IAS 36.A15]*. To do so would be to double count.

7.2.7 Entity-specific WACCs and different project risks within the entity

The entity's WACC is an average rate derived from its existing business, yet entities frequently operate in more than one sector. Within a sector, different types of projects may have different levels of risk, e.g. a start-up against an established product. Therefore, entities must ensure that the different business risks of different CGUs are properly taken into account when determining the appropriate discount rates.

It must be noted that these areas of different risk will not always coincide with the assets or CGUs that are being tested for impairment as this is a test for impairment and not necessarily a determination of business value.

Example 20.17: Different project risks and CGUs

An aircraft manufacturer makes both civilian and military aircraft. The risks for both sectors are markedly different as they are much lower for defence contractors than for the civilian market. The assembly plants for civilian and military aircraft are separate CGUs. In this sector there are entities that are based solely in one or other of these markets, i.e. they are purely defence or civilian contractors, so there will be a basis for identifying the different discount rates for the different activities. If the entity makes its own components then the defence CGU or CGUs could include the manufacturing activity if defence is vertically integrated and components are made solely for military aircraft. Manufacturing could be a separate CGU if components are used for both activities and there is an external market for the products.

A manufacturer of soft drinks uses the same plant to produce various flavours of carbonated and uncarbonated drinks. Because the market for traditional carbonated drinks is declining, it develops and markets a new uncarbonated 'health' drink, which is still produced using the same plant. The risks of the product are higher than those of the existing products but it is not a separate CGU.

Many sectors generate many new products but have a high attrition rate as most of their new products fail (pharmaceuticals and biotechnology, for example) and this is likely built into industry WACCs. If the risk of failure is not reflected in the industry WACC because the entity is not typical of the industry then either the WACC or the cash flows ought to be adjusted to reflect the risk (but not so as to double count).

7.2.8 Entity-specific WACCs and capital structure

The discount rate is a pre-tax rate that reflects current market assessments of the time value of money and the risks specific to the asset for which the future cash flow estimates have not been adjusted. *[IAS 36.55]*. An entity's own WACC may not be suitable as a discount rate if there is anything atypical about the entity's capital structure compared with 'typical' market participants. In other words, would the market assess the cash flows from the asset or unit as being riskier or less risky than the entity-wide

Impairment of fixed assets and goodwill 1579

risks reflected in the entity-wide WACC? Some of the risks that need to be thought about are country risk, currency risks and price risk.

Country risk will reflect the area in which the assets are located. In some areas assets are frequently nationalised by governments or the area may be politically unstable and prone to violence. In addition, the potential impact of physical instability such as weather or earthquakes, and the effects of currency volatility on the expected return from the asset, must be considered.

Two elements of price risk are the gearing ratio of the entity in question (if, for example, it is much more or less geared than average) and any default risk built into its cost of debt. However, IAS 36 explicitly notes that the discount rate is independent of the entity's capital structure and the way the entity financed the purchase of the asset, because the future cash flows expected to arise from an asset do not depend on these features. [IAS 36.A19].

Example 20.18: Effect of entity default risk on its WACC

The formula for calculating the (post tax) WACC, as given in Example 20.14 at 7.2 above, is

$$WACC = (1-t) \times D \times \frac{g}{1+g} + E \times \left[1 - \frac{g}{1+g}\right]$$

where:

t is the rate of tax relief available on the debt servicing payments;

D is the pre-tax cost of debt;

E is the cost of equity;

g is the gearing level (i.e. the ratio of debt to equity) for the sector.

The cost of equity is calculated as follows:

Cost of equity = risk-free rate + (levered beta (β^*) × market risk premium) + size premium (if deemed required)

Assume that the WACC of a typical sector participant is as follows:

Cost of equity	
Risk free rate	4%
Levered beta (β)	1.1
Market risk premium	6%
Cost of equity after tax (market risk premium × β + risk-free rate)	10.6%
Cost of debt	
Risk free rate	4%
Credit spread	3%
Tax rate	25%
Cost of debt (pre-tax)	7%
Cost of debt (post-tax)	5.25%
Capital structure	
Debt / (debt + equity)	25%
Equity / (debt + equity)	75%
Post-tax cost of equity (10.6 × 75%)	8%
Post-tax cost of debt (5.25 × 25%)	1.3%
WACC (Post tax, nominal)	**9.3%**

* The beta is explained in Example 20.14 at 7.2 above.

However, the company has borrowed heavily and is in some financial difficulties. Its gearing ratio is 75% and its actual cost of debt, based on the market price of its listed bonds, is 18% (13.5% after taking account of tax at 25%). This makes its individual post-tax WACC 12.8% (10.6 × 25% + 13.5 × 75%). As a matter of fact the entity's individual post-tax WACC might actually be even higher than 12.8% as this rate is based on a levered beta for a typical sector participant, while the entity's own beta will probably be higher. Having said this, the entity's WACC is not an appropriate WACC for impairment purposes because it does not represent a market rate of return *on the assets*. Its entity WACC has been increased by default risk.

Ultimately, it might be acceptable to use the entity's own WACC, but an entity cannot conclude on this without going through the exercise of assessing for risk each of the assets or units and concluding on whether or not they contain additional risks that are not reflected in the WACC.

7.2.9 Use of discount rates other than the WACC

IAS 36 allows an entity to use rates other than the WACC as a starting point in calculating the discount rate. These include:

(a) the entity's incremental borrowing rate; and

(b) other market borrowing rates. *[IAS 36.A17]*.

If borrowing rates (which are, of course, pre-tax) were used as a starting point, could this avoid some of the problems associated with adjusting the WACC for the effects of taxation? Unfortunately, this is unlikely. Debt rates reflect the entity's capital structure and do not reflect the risk inherent in the asset. A pure asset/business risk would be obtained from an entity funded solely by equity and equity risk premiums are always observed on a post-tax basis. Therefore, the risk premium that must be added to reflect the required (increased) return over and above a risk free rate by an investor will always have to be adjusted for the effects of taxation.

It must be stressed that the appropriate discount rate, which is the one that reflects current market assessments of the time value of money and the risks specific to the asset in question, ought to be the same whatever the starting point for the calculation of the rate.

Vodafone in its description of its pre-tax discount rate starts from the relevant bond (i.e. debt) rate (Extract 20.2 at 13.3 below). However, this note also describes many of the elements of the WACC calculation and how Vodafone has obtained these; it does not suggest that Vodafone has used anything other than an adjusted WACC as a discount rate for the purposes of the impairment test.

7.2.10 Impact of IFRS 16 adoption on the discount rate

With adoption of IFRS 16, the carrying amount of many CGUs increased, reflecting the right-of-use assets added to the carrying value of the CGUs. On the other hand, the VIU of the CGUs increased by the net present value of the future lease payments discounted at the discount rate used under IAS 36 due to the removal of lease payments reflected in the lease liabilities from the VIU calculation. The transition method selected on the adoption of IFRS 16, impacted the amount of the right-of-use assets recorded. If under the modified retrospective approach an entity selected to record the right-of-use assets at an amount equal to the lease liabilities, then the addition of the right-of-use assets in the carrying amount of the CGU and the removal of the lease payments from the VIU calculation had usually an offsetting effect. As a result, generally, there was a limited effect on the impairment test on adoption of IFRS 16, i.e. the amount of headroom or impairment calculated was not substantially different. However, if the IAS 36 discount rate (for example, a discount rate based on the WACC) exceeded the IFRS 16 discount rate (for example, the lessees' incremental borrowing rate), this had a net negative impact on the results of the impairment test as the carrying amount of the CGU increased by more than the increase in the VIU of the CGU. This effect resulted in what appeared to be an impairment, or an increase in a previous impairment charge. However, from an economic perspective, the underlying business and cash flows had not changed, thus, it is difficult to justify why there would be an effect on the impairment test as a result of the discounting.

As a result of the adoption of IFRS 16, the composition of the asset base being tested for impairment (see 3 above), and the associated cash flows included in the VIU calculation (see 7.1.8 above) changed. Therefore, the discount rate used in determining VIU should, in our view, be recalculated to ensure consistency. In theory, we would expect that such discount rate would generally be somewhat lower than the IAS 36 discount rate used when operating leases were off-balance sheet under IAS 17 – *Leases*. Such a decrease does not result from any future anticipated change in behaviour or risk perception of market participants, but, instead, remains based on market conditions at the measurement date and results from the change in composition of the assets (recognition of right-of-use assets with lower inherent risks) and change in cash flows (lease payments as financing cash flows instead of operating cash flows which reduces the relative volatility of cash flows in the VIU calculation).

From a practical point of view, generally an entity might in early years of IFRS 16 adoption, use an alternative approach where, instead of adjusting the discount rate and excluding the lease cash flows reflected in the recognised lease liability from the VIU calculation as discussed in 7.1.8.A above, it continues to include the cash outflows in the VIU calculation, includes the right-of-use assets together with the lease liability in the carrying amount of the CGU and uses the unadjusted pre-IFRS 16 discount rate. As always, it will be of upmost importance to ensure that the discount rate used for the VIU calculation is reflective of the approach used, the cash flows included in the VIU calculation and the composition of the carrying amount of the CGU. We expect that observable debt/equity ratios in the market will, over time, reflect the move from a pre-IFRS 16 to a post-IFRS 16 basis. This might make it difficult to obtain appropriate discount rates on a pre-IFRS 16 basis for later years and this alternative approach might then no longer be appropriate.

7.3 Differences between fair value and value in use

IFRS 13 is explicit that it does not apply to value in use, noting that its measurement and disclosure requirements do not apply to 'measurements that have some similarities to fair value, such as [...] value in use ...'. *[IFRS 13.6(c)]*. IAS 36 includes an explanation of the ways in which fair value is different to value in use. Fair value, it notes, 'reflects the assumptions market participants would use when pricing the asset. In contrast, value in use reflects the effects of factors that may be specific to the entity and not applicable to entities in general.' *[IAS 36.53A]*. It gives a number of specific examples of factors that are excluded from fair value to the extent that they would not be generally available to market participants: *[IAS 36.53A]*

- the additional value derived from the grouping of assets. IAS 36's example is of the creation of a portfolio of investment properties in different locations;
- synergies between the asset being measured and other assets;
- legal rights or legal restrictions that are specific only to the current owner of the asset; and
- tax benefits or tax burdens that are specific to the current owner of the asset.

By contrast, an entity calculating FVLCD may include cash flows that are not permitted in a VIU calculation but only to the extent that other market participants would consider them when evaluating the asset. For example, cash inflows and outflows relating to future capital expenditure could be included if they would be taken into account by market participants (see 7.1.2 above).

8 IMPAIRMENT OF GOODWILL

8.1 Goodwill and its allocation to cash-generating units

By definition, goodwill can only generate cash inflows in combination with other assets which means that an impairment test cannot be carried out on goodwill alone. Testing goodwill for impairment requires it to be allocated to a CGU or to a group of CGUs of the acquirer. This is quite different to the process by which CGUs themselves are identified as that depends on identifying the smallest group of assets generating largely independent cash inflows. The cash flows of the CGU, or those of a CGU group if appropriate, must be sufficient to support the carrying value both of the assets and any allocated goodwill.

IFRS 3 states that the acquirer measures goodwill acquired in a business combination at the amount recognised at the acquisition date less any accumulated impairment losses and refers to IAS 36. *[IFRS 3.B63(a)]*. Initial recognition and measurement of goodwill acquired in a business combination is discussed in Chapter 9 at 6.

From the acquisition date, acquired goodwill is to be allocated to each of the acquirer's CGUs, or to a group of CGUs, that are expected to benefit from the synergies of the combination. This is irrespective of whether other assets or liabilities of the acquiree are assigned to those CGUs or group of CGUs. *[IAS 36.80]*.

The standard recognises that goodwill sometimes cannot be allocated on a non-arbitrary basis to an individual CGU, so permits it to be allocated to a group of CGUs. However, each CGU or group of CGUs to which the goodwill is so allocated must:

(a) represent the lowest level within the entity at which the goodwill is monitored for internal management purposes; and

(b) not be larger than an operating segment determined in accordance with IFRS 8 – *Operating Segments* – before aggregation. *[IAS 36.80, 81]*.

All CGUs or groups of CGUs to which goodwill has been allocated have to be tested for impairment on an annual basis.

The standard takes the view that applying these requirements results in goodwill being tested for impairment at a level that reflects the way an entity manages its operations and with which the goodwill would naturally be associated. Therefore, the development of additional reporting systems is typically not necessary. *[IAS 36.82]*.

This is, of course, consistent with the fact that entities do not monitor goodwill directly. Rather, they monitor the business activities, which means that goodwill allocated to the CGUs or CGU groups that comprise those activities will be 'monitored' indirectly. This also means, because goodwill is measured as a residual, that the goodwill balance in the statement of financial position may include elements other than goodwill relating to synergies. Some of these issues and their implications are discussed at 8.1.1 below. It also means that internally-generated goodwill will be taken into account when calculating the recoverable amount because the impairment test itself does not distinguish between purchased and internally-generated goodwill.

However, the difficulties with the concept of monitoring goodwill do not mean that entities can default to testing at an arbitrarily high level, e.g. at the operating segment level or for the entire entity by arguing that goodwill is not monitored.

IAS 36 emphasises that a CGU to which goodwill is allocated for the purpose of impairment testing may not coincide with the level at which goodwill is allocated in accordance with IAS 21 for the purpose of measuring foreign currency gains and losses (see Chapter 15). *[IAS 36.83]*. In many cases, the allocation under IAS 21 will be at a lower level. This will apply not only on the acquisition of a multinational operation but could also apply on the acquisition of a single operation where the goodwill is allocated to a larger cash generating unit under IAS 36 that is made up of businesses with different functional currencies. However, IAS 36 clarifies that the entity is not required to test the goodwill for impairment at that same level unless it also monitors the goodwill at that level for internal management purposes. *[IAS 36.83]*.

Groups that do not have publicly traded equity or debt instruments are not required to apply IFRS 8. In our view, these entities are still obliged to allocate goodwill to CGUs and CGU groups in the same way as entities that have to apply IFRS 8 as the restriction in IAS 36 refers to the definition of operating segment in IFRS 8, not to entities within scope of that standard.

IAS 36 does not provide any methods for allocating goodwill. This means that once the acquirer's CGUs or CGU groups that benefit from the synergies have been identified, discussed at 8.1.2 below, the entity must use an appropriate methodology to allocate that goodwill between them. Some approaches are described at 8.1.3 below.

8.1.1 The composition of goodwill

IAS 36 requires an entity to allocate goodwill to the CGUs that are expected to benefit from the synergies of the business combination, a challenging task because, in accounting terms, goodwill is measured as a residual (see Chapter 9). This means that in most cases goodwill includes elements other than the synergies on which the allocation to CGUs is based.

The IASB and FASB argue that what it refers to as 'core goodwill' is an asset. *[IFRS 3.BC323]*.

Core goodwill, conceptually, comprises two components: *[IFRS 3.BC313]*

(a) the fair value of the going concern element of the acquiree's existing business. 'The going concern element represents the ability of the established business to earn a higher rate of return on an assembled collection of net assets than would be expected if those net assets had to be acquired separately. That value stems from the synergies of the net assets of the business, as well as from other benefits (such as factors related to market imperfections, including the ability to earn monopoly profits and barriers to market entry – either legal or because of transaction costs – by potential competitors)'; and

(b) the fair value of the expected synergies and other benefits from combining the acquirer's and acquiree's net assets and businesses. Those synergies and other benefits are unique to each combination, and different combinations would produce different synergies and, hence, different values.

The problem for the allocation process is, firstly, that (a) relates to the acquired business taken as a whole and any attempt to allocate it to individual CGUs or CGU groups in the combined entity may well be futile. IFRS 3 refers to part of element (a) above, the value of an assembled workforce, which may not be recognised as a separate intangible asset. This is the existing collection of employees that permits the acquirer to continue to operate an acquired business from the acquisition date without having to hire and train a workforce. *[IFRS 3.B37]*. This has to be allocated to all the CGUs and CGU groups that benefit from the synergies.

Secondly, synergies themselves fall into two broad categories, operating synergies, which allow businesses to increase their operating income, e.g. through economies of scale or higher growth, or financial synergies that may result in a higher cash flow or lower cost of capital and includes tax benefits. Some financial synergies are quite likely to relate to the combined business rather than individual CGUs or CGU groups. Even though the expected future cash flows of the CGU being assessed for impairment should not include cash inflows or outflows from financing activities or tax receipts, *[IAS 36.50, 51]*, there is no suggestion in IAS 36 that these synergies cannot be taken into account in allocating goodwill.

In addition, goodwill measured as a residual may include amounts that do not represent core goodwill. IFRS 3 attempts to minimise these amounts by requiring an acquirer:

- to measure the consideration accurately, thus reducing any overvaluation of the consideration paid;
- to recognise the identifiable net assets acquired at their fair values rather than their carrying amounts; and
- to recognise all acquired intangible assets meeting the relevant criteria so that they are not subsumed into the amount initially recognised as goodwill. *[IFRS 3.BC317]*.

However, this process is not perfect. The acquirer might for example attribute value to potential contracts the acquiree is negotiating with prospective customers at the acquisition date but these are not recognised under IFRS 3 and neither are contingent assets, so their fair value is subsumed into goodwill. *[IFRS 3.B38, IFRS 3.BC276]*. Employee benefits and share-based payments are not recognised at their fair value. *[IFRS 3.26, 30]*. In practice, the most significant mismatch arises from deferred taxation, which is not recognised at fair value and can lead to the immediate recognition of goodwill. This is discussed at 8.3.1 below.

In summary, this means that the goodwill that is allocated to a CGU or CGU group may well include an element that relates to the whole of the acquired business or to an inconsistency in the measurement process as well as the synergies that follow from the acquisition itself. This point has been acknowledged by the IASB during the development of the standard:

> 'However, the Board was concerned that in the absence of any guidance on the precise meaning of "allocated on a reasonable and consistent basis", some might conclude that when a business combination enhances the value of all of the acquirer's pre-existing cash-generating units, any goodwill acquired in that business combination should be tested for impairment only at the level of the entity itself. The Board concluded that this should not be the case.' *[IAS 36.BC139]*.

In spite of the guidance in the standard, the meaning of the monitoring of goodwill as well as the allocation process remains somewhat elusive. Nevertheless, all goodwill arising in a business combination must be allocated to CGUs or CGU groups that benefit from the synergies, none may be allocated to CGUs or CGU groups that do not benefit and entities are not permitted to test at the level of the entity as a whole as a default. This means that identifying CGUs and CGU groups that benefit from the synergies is a crucial step in the process of testing goodwill for impairment.

8.1.2 Identifying synergies and identifying CGUs or CGU groups for allocating goodwill

IAS 36 requires goodwill to be allocated to CGUs or CGU groups that are expected to benefit from the synergies of the combination and only to those CGUs and CGU groups. This is irrespective of whether other assets or liabilities of the acquiree are assigned to those CGUs or group of CGUs. *[IAS 36.80]*.

Operating synergies fall into two broad groups, those that improve margin (e.g. through cost savings and economies of scale) and those that give an opportunity for future growth (e.g. through the benefits of the combined talent and technology).

Example 20.19: Identifying synergies

In all of the following cases, the acquiring entity can identify the synergies and the CGU or CGU group that benefits from them. Goodwill will be allocated to the relevant CGU or CGU group.

- A mining entity (group) extracts a metal ore that does not have an active market until it has been through a smelting and refining process. The entity considers the CGU to comprise the smelter together with the individual mines. When the entity acquires a mine, the synergies relate to cost savings as the mine's fixed costs are already covered by the existing refining operations. Goodwill is therefore allocated to the CGU comprising the smelter, the existing mines and the newly acquired mine.
- An airline is subject to cost pressures common in the sector. It acquires another operation with similar international operations on the basis that it can reduce its workforce and asset base. It will combine its operational management, including its sales, reporting and human resources functions, into one head office and consolidate all aircraft maintenance in a single site that currently has capacity. These cost savings are the synergies of the business combination and goodwill would therefore be allocated to the CGU or group of CGUs that benefit from these cost savings.
- A global consumer products company, which allocates goodwill at the operating segment level, purchases a company best-known for razors and razor blades. It has not previously manufactured razors although its 'grooming products' operating segment does manufacture other shaving products. The acquirer expects that it will be able to increase sales of its shaving products through association with the target company's razors and through branding. No assets of the acquired business are allocated to the grooming products operating segment but this segment will benefit from the synergies of the business combination and therefore goodwill from the acquisition will be allocated to it.

The process is further illustrated in the following example which shows the differences for the purposes of testing impairment between the CGU/CGU groups to which goodwill is allocated and the identification of CGUs.

Example 20.20: Allocating goodwill and identifying CGUs

Entity A operates three different types of fish restaurant: fifteen restaurants, twenty five pubs that contain restaurants serving fish and forty fish bars. Each is separately branded, although the brand is clearly identified with the Entity A identity, e.g. the restaurant range is branded 'Fish by A'. Each brand is identified as a separate operating segment: restaurants, pubs and fish bars.

Entity A acquired Entity B, which had a similar range of restaurants and bars (thirty in total) although that entity had not applied any branding to the types of restaurant.

Entity A recognised goodwill on acquisition and determined that ten of Entity B's outlets were to be allocated to each of its brands where they would be rebranded and included in the relevant operating segment.

Each restaurant, pub or fish bar is a separate CGU because it has separately identifiable largely independent cash inflows.

Management notes that it manages the 'A' brand at group (entity) level. This is not appropriate for testing goodwill as IAS 36 states that CGUs or CGU groups to which goodwill is allocated cannot be larger than an operating segment determined in accordance with IFRS 8. Also, management monitors operating segments that correspond to the three individual brands to which it has allocated the acquired outlets.

There are costs that cannot be clearly identified as relating to an individual restaurant, including marketing costs, sourcing of fish for the different brands and bulk purchasing. However, these costs are related to the brands which underlie Entity A's operating segments and the branding is evidence that there are synergies at this level. It is appropriate to allocate goodwill to the operating segments in order to test it for impairment. This does not prevent the separate outlets being identified as CGUs as IAS 36 allows an apportionment of costs. The independence of cash inflows is decisive.

8.1.3 Measuring the goodwill allocated to CGUs or CGU groups

Although goodwill has to be allocated IAS 36 does not provide any allocation methodologies. One allocation method is a 'direct' method, which is based on the difference between the fair value of the net assets and the fair value of the acquired business (or portion thereof) to be assigned to the CGUs, thereby calculating goodwill directly by reference to the allocated net assets. However, this method will not allocate any goodwill to a CGU if no assets or liabilities are assigned to the CGU and, arguably, it will allocate too little goodwill to CGUs that may benefit disproportionately because of synergies with the acquired business. A method that does not have these shortcomings is a 'with and without' method that requires the entity to calculate the fair value of the CGU or CGU groups that are expected to benefit before and after the acquisition; the difference represents the amount of goodwill to be allocated to that reporting unit. This will take account of buyer-specific synergies that relate to a CGU or CGU group. These methods are illustrated in the following example.

Example 20.21: Allocating goodwill to more than one CGU

Entity A acquires Entity B for $50 million, of which $35 million is the fair value of the identifiable assets acquired and liabilities assumed. The acquisition is to be integrated into two of Entity A's CGUs with the net assets being allocated as follows.

	CGU 1 $m	CGU 2 $m	Total $m
Acquired identifiable tangible and intangible assets	25	10	35

In addition to the net assets acquired that are assigned to CGU 2, the acquiring entity expects CGU 2 to benefit significantly from certain synergies related to the acquisition (e.g. CGU 2 is expected to realise higher sales of its products because of access to the acquired entity's distribution channels), while CGU 1 is expected to benefit from synergies to a lesser extent. There is no synergistic goodwill attributable to other CGUs.

Entity A calculates that the fair value of the acquired businesses allocated to CGU 1 and CGU 2 is $33 million and $17 million respectively. If goodwill is allocated to the CGUs based on the difference between the fair value of the net assets and the fair value of the acquired business, i.e. the direct method, the allocation would be as follows:

	CGU 1 $m	CGU 2 $m	Total $m
Acquired identifiable tangible and intangible assets	25	10	35
Fair value of acquired business allocated based on direct method	33	17	50
Goodwill assigned to CGUs	8	7	15

Alternatively, Entity A assigns goodwill to the CGUs based on the difference between the fair value of the net assets to be assigned and the fair value of the acquired business (or portion thereof), including the significant beneficial synergies that CGU 2 is expected to achieve. In this case, the fair value of the acquired business (or portion thereof) is determined using a 'with and without' method.

	CGU 1 $m	CGU 2 $m	Total $m
Fair value of CGU after acquisition	90	85	175
Fair value of CGU prior to acquisition	(62)	(63)	(125)
Fair value of acquired business allocated based on the 'with and without' method	28	22	50
Acquired identifiable tangible and intangible assets	(25)	(10)	(35)
Goodwill assigned to CGUs	3	12	15

In this case, the 'with and without' method may be more appropriate but this would depend on the availability and reliability of inputs. The 'direct' method may in other circumstances give a reasonable allocation of goodwill.

8.1.4 The effect of IFRS 8 – Operating Segments – on impairment tests

Goodwill to be tested for impairment cannot be allocated to a CGU or CGU group larger than an operating segment as defined by IFRS 8. *[IAS 36.80, 81, IFRS 8.11-12]*. IFRS 8 is discussed in Chapter 36.

Organisations managed on a matrix basis cannot test goodwill for impairment at the level of internal reporting, if this level crosses more than one operating segment as defined in IFRS 8. *[IFRS 8.5]*. In addition, the operating segments selected by the entities may not correspond with their CGUs.

These are entities that manage their businesses simultaneously on two different bases; for example, some managers may be responsible for different product and service lines while others are responsible for specific geographical areas. IFRS 8 notes that the characteristics that define an operating segment may apply to two or more overlapping sets of components for which managers are held responsible. Financial information is available for both and the chief operating decision maker may regularly review both sets of operating results of components. In spite of this, IFRS 8 requires the entity to characterise one of these bases as determining its operating segments. *[IFRS 8.10]*. Similarly, the entity will have to allocate its goodwill to CGUs or groups of CGUs no larger than operating segments even if this means an allocation of goodwill between segments on a basis that does not correspond with the way it is monitored for internal management purposes.

8.1.4.A Changes to operating segments

Changes to the way in which an entity manages its activities may result in changes to its operating segments. An entity may have to reallocate goodwill if it changes its operating segments, particularly if the entity has previously allocated goodwill at or close to segment level. Such a reallocation of goodwill is due to a change in circumstances and therefore will not be a change in accounting policy under IAS 8. *[IAS 8.34]*. This means that the previous impairment test will not need to be re-performed retrospectively.

In two situations, the disposal of an operation within a CGU and a change in the composition of CGUs due to a reorganisation, which are described at 8.5 below, IAS 36 proposes a reallocation based on relative values, unless another basis is more appropriate. A reallocation of goodwill driven by the identification of new operating segments is another form of reorganisation of the reporting structure, so the same methodology is appropriate. The entity should use a relative value approach, unless it can demonstrate that some other method better reflects the goodwill associated with the reorganised units (see 8.5.1 below). *[IAS 36.87]*.

This means a method based on the activities in their current state; e.g. an entity should not attempt to revert to the historical goodwill as it arose on the various acquisitions.

Generally an impairment review would be performed prior to the reallocation of goodwill.

An important issue in practice is the date from which the revised goodwill allocation applies. The goodwill allocation must be based on the way in which management is actually monitoring activities and cannot be based on management intentions. Under IFRS 8, operating segments are identified on the basis of internal reports that are regularly reviewed by the entity's chief operating decision maker in order to allocate resources to the segment and assess its performance. *[IFRS 8.5]*. Therefore, goodwill cannot be allocated to the revised operating segments until it can be demonstrated that the chief operating decision maker is receiving the relevant internal reports for the revised segments.

8.1.4.B Aggregation of operating segments for disclosure purposes

IFRS 8 allows an entity to aggregate two or more operating segments into a single reporting segment if this is 'consistent with the core principles' and, in particular, if the segments have similar economic characteristics. *[IFRS 8.12]*. Whilst this is specifically in the context of segmental reporting, it might also, in isolation, have suggested that individual operating segments could also be aggregated to form one operating segment that would also apply for impairment purposes. However, the 'unit of accounting' for goodwill impairment is before any aggregation. *[IAS 36.80(b)]*.

8.1.5 Goodwill initially unallocated to cash-generating units

IFRS 3 allows a 'measurement period' after a business combination to provide the acquirer with a reasonable time to obtain the information necessary to identify and measure all of the various components of the business combination as of the acquisition date in accordance with the standard. *[IFRS 3.46]*. The measurement period ends as soon as the acquirer receives the information it is seeking and cannot exceed one year from the acquisition date. *[IFRS 3.45]*.

IAS 36 recognises that in such circumstances, it might also not be possible to complete the initial allocation of the goodwill to a CGU or group of CGUs for impairment purposes before the end of the annual period in which the combination is effected. *[IAS 36.85]*. Where this is the case the goodwill (or part of it) is left unallocated for that period. Goodwill must then be allocated before the end of the first annual period beginning after the acquisition date. *[IAS 36.84]*. The standard requires disclosure of the amount of the unallocated goodwill together with an explanation as to why that is the case (see 13.3 below).

The question arises as to whether the entity ought to test, in such circumstances, the goodwill acquired during the current annual period before the end of the current annual period or in the following year if the annual impairment testing date is before the allocation of goodwill is completed.

In our view, it will depend on whether an entity is able during the 'measurement period' and until the initial allocation of goodwill is completed to quantify goodwill with sufficient accuracy and allocate goodwill on a provisional basis to CGUs or group of CGUs.

If the entity is able to quantify goodwill with sufficient accuracy, a provisional allocation of goodwill could be made in the following circumstances:

(a) the entity might know that all goodwill relates to a single CGU or to a group of CGUs no larger than a single operating segment; or

(b) the entity may know that the initial accounting for the combination is complete in all material respects, although some details remain to be finalised.

In circumstances where a provisional allocation of goodwill could be made, an entity should, in our view, tests this provisional goodwill for impairment in accordance with IAS 36 during the annual period in which the acquisition occurred and in the following years annual impairment test, even if this is before the allocation of goodwill is completed.

In addition, we believe an entity should carry out an impairment test where there are indicators of impairment. This is the case even if the fair values have not been finalised and the goodwill amount is only provisional or goodwill has not necessarily been allocated to the relevant CGUs or CGU groups and the test therefore has to be carried out at a higher, potentially even at the reporting entity level.

In our view, an entity would not need to test the goodwill for impairment until the allocation of goodwill has been finalised, if a provisional allocation of goodwill could not be made and there are no indications of impairment.

When the allocation of goodwill is finalised, in the first annual period after the acquisition date, the entity must consider appropriate actions.

In our view, the acquirer should test in some circumstances the final allocated goodwill for impairment retrospectively, on the basis that the test on provisional goodwill was in fact the first impairment test applying IAS 36. In the following cases an entity should update the prior year's impairment test retrospectively:

- if the entity allocated provisional goodwill to CGUs, although it had not completed its fair value exercise, and tested provisional goodwill of impairment in accordance with IAS 36 (see above); or
- if the entity did not allocate provisional goodwill to the related CGUs but there were indicators of impairment and the entity tested the provisional goodwill potentially at a different level to the ultimate allocation and the impairment test resulted in an impairment (see above).

If the entity did not allocate provisional goodwill to CGUs, there were indicators that the provisional goodwill may have been impaired and the impairment test at a higher, potentially entity level, did not result in an impairment, the entity can choose whether to update the prior year's impairment test retrospectively, but is not required to do so.

In all other scenarios, the acquirer performs only a current year impairment test (i.e. after the allocation has been completed) on a prospective basis.

If the acquirer updates the prior year's impairment test as outlined above, this update could decrease the original goodwill impairment recognised. Such a decrease is an adjustment to the original goodwill impairment. This will not qualify as a reversal and does not violate the prohibition on reversing any goodwill impairments in paragraph 124 of IAS 36. See 11.3 below.

If an entity were to change its annual reporting date, it could mean that it has a shorter period in which to allocate goodwill as IAS 36 requires that allocation of goodwill for impairment purposes is completed by the end of the first annual period after the acquisition and not within 12 months as required by IFRS 3. *[IAS 36.84]*.

Example 20.22: Impact of shortened accounting period

Entity A prepares its financial statements for annual periods ending on 31 December. It acquired Entity B on 30 September 20X0. In accounting for this business combination in its financial statements for the year ended 31 December 20X0, Entity A has only been able to determine the fair values to be assigned to Entity B's assets, liabilities and contingent liabilities on a provisional basis and has not allocated the resulting provisional amount of goodwill arising on the acquisition to any CGU (or group of CGUs). During 20X1, Entity A changes its annual reporting date to June and is preparing its financial statements as at its new period end of 30 June 20X1. IFRS 3 does not require the fair values assigned to Entity B's net assets (and therefore the initial amount of goodwill) to be finalised by that period end, since Entity A has until 30 September 20X1 to finalise the values. However, IAS 36 would appear to require the allocation of the goodwill to CGUs for impairment purposes be completed by the date of the 30 June 20X1 financial statements since these are for the first annual period beginning after the acquisition date, despite the fact that the initial accounting under IFRS 3 is not yet complete. The entity would therefore need to test goodwill for impairment for the financial reporting period ending 30 June 20X1.

8.2 When to test cash-generating units with goodwill for impairment

IAS 36 requires a CGU or group of CGUs to which goodwill has been allocated to be tested for impairment annually by comparing the carrying amount of the CGU or group of CGUs, including the goodwill, with its recoverable amount. *[IAS 36.90]*. The requirements of the standard in relation to the timing of such an annual impairment test (which need not be at the period end) are discussed below. This annual impairment test is not a substitute for management being aware of events occurring or circumstances changing between annual tests that might suggest that goodwill is impaired. *[IAS 36.BC162]*. IAS 36 requires an entity to assess at each reporting date whether there is an indication that a CGU may be impaired. *[IAS 36.9]*. So, whenever there is an indication that a CGU or group of CGUs may be impaired it is to be tested for impairment by comparing the carrying amount, including the goodwill, with its recoverable amount. *[IAS 36.90]*.

If the carrying amount of the CGU (or group of CGUs), including the goodwill, exceeds the recoverable amount of the CGU (or group of CGUs), then an impairment loss has to be recognised in accordance with paragraph 104 of the standard (see 11.2 below). *[IAS 36.90]*.

8.2.1 Timing of impairment tests

IAS 36 requires an annual impairment test of CGUs or groups of CGUs to which goodwill has been allocated. The impairment test does not have to be carried out at the end of the reporting period. The standard permits the annual impairment test to be performed at any time during an annual period, provided the test is performed at the same time every year. Different CGUs may be tested for impairment at different times.

However, if some or all of the goodwill allocated to a CGU or group of CGUs was acquired in a business combination during the current annual period, that unit must be tested for impairment before the end of the current annual period. *[IAS 36.96]*.

The IASB observed that acquirers can sometimes 'overpay' for an acquiree, so that the amount initially recognised for the business combination and the resulting goodwill exceeds the recoverable amount of the investment. The Board was concerned that without this requirement it might be possible for entities to delay recognising such an impairment loss until the annual period after the business combination. *[IAS 36.BC173]*.

It has to be said that the wording of the requirement may not achieve that result, as the goodwill may not have been allocated to a CGU in the period in which the business combination occurs. The time allowed for entities to allocate goodwill may mean that this is not completed until the period following the business combination. *[IAS 36.84]*. The potential consequences of this are discussed at 8.1.5 above.

Consider also the following example.

Example 20.23: *Testing for impairment of goodwill allocated in the period after acquisition after the annual impairment testing date*

Entity A prepares its financial statements for annual reporting periods ending on 31 December. It performs its annual impairment test for all cash-generating units (CGUs) to which it has allocated goodwill at 30 September.

On 31 October 20X0, Entity A acquires Entity B. Entity A completes the initial allocation of goodwill to CGUs at 31 October 20X1, before the end of the annual reporting period on 31 December 20X1. Therefore, Entity A does not allocate the goodwill until after its annual date for testing goodwill, 30 September 20X1.

There are no indicators of impairment of goodwill at 31 December 20X0. If there is any such indicator, Entity A is required to test goodwill for impairment at that date, regardless of the date of its annual impairment test. At 31 December 20X0, the entity had not yet allocated its goodwill and did not test it for impairment, because there were no impairment indications at that time. During 20X1, Entity A receives the information it was seeking about facts and circumstances that existed as of the acquisition date, but it does not finalise the fair values assigned to Entity B's net assets (and therefore the initial amount of goodwill) until 31 October 20X1. IAS 36 requires Entity A to allocate the goodwill to CGUs by the end of the financial year. It does this by December 20X1.

In this case, at the time of carrying out its annual impairment tests at 30 September 20X1, Entity A has not yet allocated the goodwill relating to Entity B; therefore no impairment test of that goodwill needs to be carried out at that time, provided there are no indicators of impairment. When it does allocate the goodwill by December 20X1, the requirement to perform an impairment test for the CGUs to which this goodwill is allocated does not seem to be applicable since the goodwill does not relate to a business combination during the current annual period. It actually relates to a business combination in the previous period; it is just that it has only been allocated for impairment purposes in the current period. Nevertheless, Entity A should perform an updated impairment test for the CGUs to which this goodwill is allocated for the purposes of its financial statements for the year ended 31 December 20X1 since this would seem to be the intention of the IASB. Not to do so, would mean that the goodwill would not be tested for impairment until September 20X2, nearly 2 years after the business combination.

IAS 36 requires the annual impairment test for a CGU to which goodwill has been allocated to be performed at the same time every year but is silent on whether an entity can change the timing of the impairment test. We believe a change in timing of the annual impairment test is acceptable if there are valid reasons for the change, the period between impairment tests does not exceed 12 months and the change is not made to avoid an impairment charge. The requirement that the period between impairment tests should not exceed 12 months could mean that an entity would need to test a CGU twice in a year if, for example, it wanted to change the date of the test from October to December. In our view it would in general not be appropriate to change the date of the impairment test again in consecutive years.

8.2.2 Sequence of impairment tests for goodwill and other assets

When a CGU to which goodwill has been allocated is tested for impairment, there may also be an indication of impairment of an asset within the unit. IAS 36 requires the entity to test the asset for impairment first and recognise any impairment loss on it before carrying out the impairment test for the goodwill, although this is unlikely to have any practical impact as the assets within the CGU by definition will not generate separate cash flows. An entity will have to go through the same process if there is an indication of an impairment of a CGU within a group of CGUs containing the goodwill. The entity must test the CGU for impairment first, and recognise any impairment loss for that CGU, before testing the group of CGUs to which the goodwill is allocated. *[IAS 36.97-98]*.

8.2.3 Carry forward of a previous impairment test calculation

IAS 36 permits the most recent detailed calculation of the recoverable amount of a CGU or group of CGUs to which goodwill has been allocated to be carried forward from a preceding period provided all of the following criteria are met:

(a) the assets and liabilities making up the CGU or group of CGUs have not changed significantly since the most recent recoverable amount calculation;

(b) the most recent recoverable amount calculation resulted in an amount that exceeded the carrying amount of the CGU or group of CGUs by a substantial margin; and

(c) based on an analysis of events that have occurred and circumstances that have changed since the most recent recoverable amount calculation, the likelihood that a current recoverable amount determination would be less than the current carrying amount of the CGU or group of CGUs is remote. *[IAS 36.99]*.

The Basis for Conclusions indicates that the reason for this dispensation is to reduce the costs of applying the impairment test, without compromising its integrity. *[IAS 36.BC177]*. However, clearly it is a matter of judgement as to whether each of the criteria is actually met.

8.2.4 Reversal of impairment loss for goodwill prohibited

Once an impairment loss has been recognised for goodwill, IAS 36 prohibits its reversal in a subsequent period. *[IAS 36.124]*. The standard justifies this on the grounds that any reversal 'is likely to be an increase in internally generated goodwill, rather than a reversal of the impairment loss recognised for the acquired goodwill', and IAS 38 prohibits the recognition of internally generated goodwill. *[IAS 36.125]*. The impairment test itself though does not distinguish between purchased and internally generated goodwill.

8.3 Impairment of assets and goodwill recognised on acquisition

There are a number of circumstances in which the fair value of assets or goodwill acquired as part of a business combination may be measured at a higher amount through recognition of deferred tax or notional tax benefits. This raises the question of how to test for impairment and even whether there is, in fact, a 'day one' impairment in value. In other circumstances, deferred tax assets may or may not be recognised as part of the fair value exercise and this, too, may affect subsequent impairment tests of the assets and goodwill acquired as part of the business combination.

8.3.1 Testing goodwill 'created' by deferred tax for impairment

As described in Chapter 33 at 12, the requirement of IAS 12 to recognise deferred tax on all temporary differences arising on net assets acquired in a business combination may have an impact on the amount of goodwill recognised. In a business combination, there is no initial recognition exemption for deferred tax and the corresponding accounting entry for a deferred tax asset or liability forms part of the goodwill arising or the bargain purchase gain recognised. *[IAS 12.22(a)]*. Where an intangible asset, which was not recognised in the acquiree's financial statements, is acquired in a business combination and the intangible's tax base is zero, a deferred tax liability based on the fair value of the intangible and the prevailing tax rate will be recognised. The corresponding debit entry will increase goodwill. This then begs the question of how to consider this in the VIU when performing an impairment test on that goodwill and whether there is indeed an immediate impairment that would need to be recognised. We explore the issues in the following examples.

Example 20.24: Apparent 'day one' impairment arising from recognition of deferred tax in a business combination

Entity A, which is taxed at 40%, acquires Entity B for €100m in a transaction that is a business combination. For simplicity assume the only asset of the entity is an intangible asset with a fair value of €60m.

It is assumed that the entity cannot get a deduction for tax purposes for the goodwill and the intangible asset, as is often the case for assets that arise only on consolidation. It is also assumed that the fair value of the intangible asset does not reflect the benefits of any tax deductions had the asset been tax deductible, which may not be an appropriate assumption and is discussed further below.

The fair value and tax base of the intangible are as follows:

	Fair value	Tax base
	€m	€m
Intangible asset	60	nil

This will give rise to the following initial entries on consolidation:

	€m	€m
Goodwill (balance)	64	
Intangible asset	60	
Deferred tax liability[1]		24
Cost of investment		100

[1] 40% of €60m
Of the goodwill of €64m, €24m is created through deferred tax on the intangible asset.

The carrying value of the consolidated assets of the subsidiary (excluding deferred tax) is now €124m consisting of goodwill of €64m and the intangible asset of €60m. However the fair value of the subsidiary is only €100m. Clearly €24m of the goodwill arises solely from the recognition of deferred tax. However, IAS 36.50, explicitly requires tax to be excluded from the estimate of future cash flows used to calculate any impairment. This raises the question of whether there should be an immediate impairment write-down of the assets to €100m.

We think that an immediate write down of goodwill created by deferred tax is unlikely to have been the intention of IAS 36 because certain assumptions about taxation have been incorporated into the carrying amount of goodwill that are represented by the deferred tax liability recorded in relation of the intangible asset recognised on consolidation. In order to remove all tax effects from the CGU, the carrying amount of goodwill that relates to taxation and the deferred tax liability should be removed for impairment testing purposes; otherwise it might not be possible to determine the appropriate pre-tax discount rate. This means, in effect, that as at the point of acquisition, the goodwill can be reduced by the deferred tax liability recorded on consolidation in order to test that goodwill for impairment. As a result, the entity does not have to recognise an immediate impairment loss.

Not recognising an immediate impairment loss is consistent with the fact that the goodwill due to deferred tax that is being recognised as part of this acquisition is not part of 'core goodwill' (see 8.1.1 above), but is a consequence of the exceptions in IFRS 3 to the basic principle that assets and liabilities be measured at fair value, deferred tax being one of these exceptions (see 8.1.1 above and Chapter 9 at 5.6.2).

Another way of describing this is the lack of tax basis inherent in the asset has already been reflected in the fair value assigned to the asset. As a result, the incremental fair value of the deferred tax liability is nil. Goodwill is reduced by the nominal versus fair value difference of the deferred tax liability which in this case is the full amount of the deferred tax liability related to the intangible.

Continuing with this simplified example, if it is assumed that the intangible asset is amortised over a finite useful life then the deferred tax relating to that asset (€24m in this example) will be released over that life with the effect that the net amount charged to the income statement of €36m (total amortisation less deferred tax, €60m – €24m) will be the same as if the amortisation charge were tax deductible.

At future impairment testing dates, one would adjust for any remaining deferred tax liability at the impairment testing date that resulted in an increase in goodwill at the acquisition date.

In many jurisdictions the amortisation of intangible assets is deductible for tax purposes. This generates additional benefits, called tax amortisation benefit (TAB), impacting the fair value of the intangible. Therefore, the fair value as part of a business acquisition for many intangible assets includes assumptions about the tax amortisation benefit that would be available if the asset were acquired separately. For example, the value of a trademark using the 'relief from royalty' method would be assumed to be the net present value of post-tax future royalty savings, under consideration of TAB, in the consolidated financial statements, based on the hypothetical case of not owning the trademark. In order to reach the fair value of the asset, its value before amortisation would be adjusted by a tax amortisation factor reflecting the corporate tax rate, a discount rate and a tax amortisation period (this is the period allowed for tax purposes, which is not necessarily the useful life for amortisation purposes of the asset). In a market approach, fair value is estimated from market prices paid for comparable assets and the prices will contain all benefits of owning the assets, including any tax amortisation benefit.

This means that the difference between the tax amortisation benefit and the gross amount of the deferred tax liability remains part of goodwill.

This is demonstrated in the following example:

Example 20.25: Impairment testing assets whose fair value reflects tax amortisation benefits

Assume that the entity in Example 20.24 above has acquired an intangible asset that would be tax deductible if separately acquired but that has a tax base of zero.

The entity concludes that the fair value of the intangible will reflect the tax benefit, whose gross amount is €40m (€60m × 40% / 60%) but in calculating the fair value this will be discounted to its present value – say €30m. The initial entry is now as follows:

	€m	€m
Goodwill (balance)	46	
Intangible asset (€(60m + 30m))	90	
Deferred tax liability[1]		36
Cost of investment		100

[1] 40% of €90m

Overall, the assets that cost €100m will now be recorded at €136m, as against the total of €124m in Example 20.24. This increase has come about because of recognition of deferred tax of €12m, which is 40% of €30m, the assumed tax amortisation benefit.

In this example, only €6m goodwill results from the recognition of deferred tax [€46m – (€100m – €60m)] and its treatment is discussed above. The €6m represents the difference between the nominal amount of deferred tax of €36m and the fair value of the tax amortisation benefit included in the intangible asset of €30m.

Unlike goodwill, the intangible asset will only have to be tested for impairment if there are indicators of impairment, if it has an indefinite useful life or if it has not yet been brought into use. *[IAS 36.10]*. If the intangible asset is being tested by itself for impairment, i.e. not as part of a CGU, its FVLCD would need to be determined on the same basis as for the purposes of the business combination, making the same assumptions about taxation. If FVLCD exceeds the carrying amount, there is no impairment.

However, as mentioned at 3.1 above, many intangible assets do not generate independent cash inflows as individual assets and so they are tested as part of a CGU. Assuming there is no goodwill in the CGU being tested, then the VIU of the CGU might be calculated on an after-tax basis using notional tax cash flows assuming the asset's tax basis is equal to its VIU as discussed at 7.2.3 above.

When goodwill is included in the CGU, the carrying amount of goodwill that results from the recognition of deferred tax (e.g. the €6m in Example 20.25 above) should be removed for impairment testing purposes. At future impairment testing dates, one should adjust for any remaining difference between the nominal deferred tax liability at the impairment testing date and the original fair value of the assumed tax basis embedded in the intangible asset carrying value that remains at the impairment testing date. This is consistent with the assumption that it could not have been the IASB's intention to have an immediate impairment at the time of acquisition and the same logic and approach is being carried forward from day 1 to future impairment tests.

Another way of describing this is that the fair value of the deferred tax liability in the above example is equal to 30, being the tax amortisation benefit embedded in the fair value of the intangible asset. This tax amortisation benefit does not actually exist given the intangible asset's tax basis is in fact nil. Goodwill is reduced by the nominal versus fair value difference of the deferred tax liability which in this case is 6. If one tests the CGU (including both the intangible asset and goodwill) for impairment, when calculating the VIU following the approach at 7.2.3 above on an after-tax basis (using notional tax cash flows assuming a tax basis equal to VIU) this should not lead to day 1 impairment, given the VIU calculation assumes a full tax basis similar to that assumed in the intangible carrying value, as goodwill has been reduced by the nominal versus fair value difference of the deferred tax liability of 6.

An entity might not continue to make this adjustment if it becomes impracticable to identify reliably the amount of the adjustment, in which case the entity would use VIU without this adjustment or use FVLCD of the CGU as the recoverable amount.

This is illustrated in the following example:

Example 20.26: Impairment testing assets whose fair value reflects tax amortisation benefits (continued)

Assume that the entity in Example 20.25 above amortises the intangible asset on a straight line basis over 10 years. When the entity performs its impairment test at the end of year one the carrying amount of the deferred tax liability and remaining fair value of the tax benefits embedded in the carrying amount of the intangible are as follow:

	acquisition date €m	amortisation year 1 €m	end of year 1 €m
Intangible asset	60	6	54
Tax amortisation benefit (TAB)	30	3	27
Carrying value of intangible asset incl. TAB	90	9	81
Deferred tax[1]	36	3.6	32.4

1 year 1: 40% of €90m and end of year 1 40% of €81m

In the impairment test at the end of year 1, goodwill would be adjusted for the difference between the remaining nominal deferred tax liability of €32.4m and the remaining tax benefit reflected in the carrying value of the intangible asset of €27m resulting in an adjustment of €5.4m to goodwill. The impairment test would therefore incorporate goodwill of €40.6m (€46m – €5.4m).

The standard's disclosure requirements including the pre-tax discount rate, principally described at 13.3 below, will apply.

8.3.2 Deferred tax assets and losses of acquired businesses

Deferred tax assets arising from tax losses carried forward at the reporting date must be excluded from the assets of the CGU for the purpose of calculating its VIU. However, tax losses may not meet the criteria for recognition as deferred tax assets in a business combination, which means that their value is initially subsumed within goodwill. Under IFRS 3 and IAS 12, only acquired deferred tax assets that are recognised within the measurement period (through new information about circumstances at the acquisition date) are to reduce goodwill, with any excess once goodwill has been reduced to zero being taken to profit or loss. After the end of the measurement period, all other acquired deferred tax assets are taken to profit or loss. *[IFRS 3.67, IAS 12.68]*.

Unless and until the deferred tax asset is recognised, this raises the same problems as at 8.3.1 above. Certain assumptions regarding future taxation are built into the carrying value of goodwill and one should consider excluding these amounts from the carrying amount of the CGU when testing for impairment. However, if at a later date it transpires that any tax losses carry forwards subsumed in goodwill cannot be utilised, then excluding these amounts from the carrying amount of the CGU for impairment testing is not appropriate and might lead to an impairment.

8.4 Impairment testing when a CGU crosses more than one operating segment

While IAS 36 is clear that goodwill cannot be tested at a level that is larger than an operating segment determined in accordance with IFRS 8, it does not contain similar guidance for other assets. Therefore, in our view, the basic principle of IAS 36 applies, meaning assets or a group of assets are tested at the lowest level at which largely independent cash inflows can be identified. In practice a CGU determined based on the lowest level of independent cash inflows could be larger than an operating segment and therefore could cross more than one operating segment. For example, in the telecom industry, the entire telecom fixed line network may be one CGU, while at the same time an entity may identify its operating segments based on types of clients (e.g. individual clients, business clients, other operators, etc.). The general guidance in IAS 36 would require an entity to assess at each reporting date whether there are impairment indicators for the CGU and if such impairment indicators exist, perform a formal impairment assessment at CGU level. Regardless of whether a CGU crosses more than one operating segment, goodwill would need to be tested at a lower operating segment level. For this operating segment level impairment test, the assets of the larger CGU, in particular the cross operating segment assets e.g. the fixed line network in the example above, would need to be allocated to the operating segments. The application of these principles in practice can be complex and may require judgement.

8.5 Disposal of operation within a cash-generating unit to which goodwill has been allocated

If goodwill has been allocated to a CGU (or a group of CGUs) and the entity disposes of an operation within that CGU, IAS 36 requires that the goodwill associated with the operation disposed of is included in the carrying amount of the operation when determining the gain or loss on disposal. For that purpose, the standard requires that the amount to be included is measured on the basis of the relative values of the operation disposed of and the portion of the CGU retained, unless the entity can demonstrate that some other method better reflects the goodwill associated with the operation disposed of. *[IAS 36.86]*.

The standard refers to the 'relative values' of the parts without specifying how these are to be calculated. The recoverable amount of the part that it has retained will be based on the principles of IAS 36, i.e. at the higher of FVLCD and VIU. This means that the VIU or FVLCD of the part retained may have to be calculated as part of the allocation exercise on disposal.

In addition, the VIU and FVLCD of the part disposed of will be materially the same. This is because the VIU will consist mainly of the net disposal proceeds; it cannot be based on the assumption that the sale would not take place.

Example 20.27: Goodwill attributable to the disposal of an operation based on relative values

An entity sells for €100 an operation that was part of a CGU to which goodwill of €60 has been allocated. The goodwill allocated to the CGU cannot be identified or associated with an asset group at a level lower than that CGU, except arbitrarily. The recoverable amount of the portion of the CGU retained is €300. Because the goodwill allocated to the CGU cannot be non-arbitrarily identified or associated with an asset group at a level lower than that CGU, the goodwill associated with the operation disposed of is measured on the basis of the relative values of the operation disposed of and the portion of the CGU retained. Therefore, 25 per cent of the goodwill allocated to the CGU, i.e. €15 is included in the carrying amount of the operation that is sold.

It will not necessarily follow, for example, that the business disposed of generated 25% of the net cash flows of the combined CGU. Therefore, the relative value method suggested by the standard to be applied in most circumstances may be based on a mismatch in the valuation bases used on the different parts of the business, reflecting the purchaser's assessment of the value of the part disposed of at the point of sale rather than that of the vendor at purchase.

The standard allows the use of some other method if it better reflects the goodwill associated with the part disposed of. The IASB had in mind a scenario in which an entity buys a business, integrates it with an existing CGU that does not include any goodwill in its carrying amount and immediately sells a loss-making part of the combined CGU. It is accepted that in these circumstances it may be reasonable to conclude that no part of the carrying amount of the goodwill has been disposed of. *[IAS 36.BC156]*. The loss-making business being disposed of could, of course, have been owned by the entity before the acquisition or it could be part of the acquired business. However, the standard is not clear in what other circumstances a base other than relative values would better reflect the goodwill associated with the part disposed of. Any other method must take account of the basic principle, which is that this is an allocation of the carrying amount of goodwill and not an impairment test. It is not relevant, for example, that the part retained may have sufficient headroom for all of the goodwill without any impairment. One has to bear in mind that any basis of allocation of goodwill on disposal other than that recommended by the standard could be an indication that goodwill should have been allocated on a different basis on acquisition. It could suggest that there may have been some reasonable basis of allocating goodwill to the CGUs within a CGU group.

However, as demonstrated in Example 20.29 below, in some circumstances the allocation based on relative values might lead to an immediate impairment which is not intuitive and therefore an alternative method may, depending on facts and circumstances, therefore better reflect the goodwill associated with the operation disposed of. In our view, an approach that is based on current relative values of notional goodwill in the part disposed of and the part retained could, depending on facts and circumstances, be seen as an acceptable alternative for the goodwill allocation as illustrated in 8.5.1 below.

8.5.1 Changes in composition of cash-generating units

If an entity reorganises the structure of its operations in a way that changes the composition of one or more CGUs to which goodwill has been allocated, IAS 36 requires that the goodwill be reallocated to the units affected. For this purpose, the standard requires the reallocation to be performed using a relative value approach similar to that discussed above when an entity disposes of an operation within a CGU, unless the entity can demonstrate that some other method better reflects the goodwill associated with the reorganised units. *[IAS 36.87]*. Generally an impairment review would need to be performed prior to the reallocation of goodwill. As a result, if the reorganisation is triggered by underperformance in any of the affected operations, it cannot mask any impairment.

Example 20.28: Reallocation of goodwill to CGUs based on relative values

Goodwill of €160 had previously been allocated to CGU A. A is to be divided and integrated into three other CGUs, B, C and D. Because the goodwill allocated to A cannot be non-arbitrarily identified or associated with an asset group at a level lower than A, it is reallocated to CGUs B, C and D on the basis of the relative values of the three portions of A before those portions are integrated with B, C and D. The recoverable amounts of these portions of A before integration with the other CGUs are €200, €300 and €500 respectively. Accordingly, the amounts of goodwill reallocated to CGUs B, C and D are €32, €48 and €80 respectively.

When goodwill is reallocated based on relative values, it may be necessary to assess impairment immediately following the reallocation, as the recoverable amount of the CGUs will be based on the principles of IAS 36 and the reallocation could lead to an immediate impairment.

Again, the standard gives no indication as to what other methods might better reflect the goodwill associated with the reorganised units.

As illustrated in Example 20.29 below, the reallocation based on relative values could lead to an immediate impairment after the reallocation. This is not intuitive given that an impairment review would have been performed immediately before the goodwill reallocation and the restructuring of a business would not be expected to result in an impairment of goodwill.

In our view an allocation based on the relative current value of notional goodwill could, depending on facts and circumstances, be seen as an acceptable alternative to the IAS 36 suggested approach of relative values. This method calculates the current value of notional goodwill in each of the components to be allocated to new CGUs by performing a notional purchase price allocation for each affected CGU. To do this the components fair value is compared with the fair value of the net identifiable assets to obtain the current value of notional goodwill. The carrying amount of the goodwill to be reallocated is then allocated to the new CGUs based on the relative current values of notional goodwill. This approach together with an example of circumstances under which the approach may be acceptable is illustrated in Example 20.29:

Example 20.29: Reallocation of goodwill to CGUs based on relative current values of notional goodwill

A US company acquired a European sub-group in 20X0 and recorded goodwill of €30 million. At the time Europe was a new market for the company and goodwill was fully allocated to one CGU A based on the geographic location Europe. Two years later the group fundamentally restructured its business in Europe. The restructuring resulted in the split of the existing CGU into three new CGUs B, C and D based on products. The goodwill of €30 million was assessed for impairment immediately prior to the restructuring and no impairment was identified. When the recoverable amount of each component of A allocated to B, C and D was assessed, FVLCD was higher than VIU for each component allocated and is therefore used as basis for the recoverable amount based in the relative value approach. For simplicity purposes the examples assume that there are no material disposal costs and therefore the fair value of the components equals the fair value less costs of disposal.

The fair value of the net identifiable assets and the fair value of each new CGU are given in the following table:

CGU	B €m	C €m	D €m	Total
Fair value of net identifiable assets	20	40	40	100
Book value of net identifiable assets	10	35	35	80
Fair value/FVLCD	40	80	40	160

The allocation based on the relative values of the three components of A allocated to B, C and D, as the required default method by the standard, would result in the following allocation of goodwill:

CGU	B €m	C €m	D €m	Total
Goodwill allocation	7.5	15	7.5	30
Book value of net identifiable assets	10	35	35	80
Total	17.5	50	42.5	110
Recoverable amount of CGU (FVLCD)	40	80	40	160
Immediate impairment	–	–	2.5	2.5

Goodwill of €7.5m (goodwill of €30m × recoverable amount €40m/overall recoverable amount €160m) is allocated to CGU B and D and €15m (goodwill of €30m × recoverable amount €80m/overall recoverable amount €160m) to CGU C. As can be seen, the relative value approach would result in an immediate impairment of €2.5m in CGU D. This is not intuitive, given that no impairment existed immediately prior to the restructuring and the restructuring of the business would not be expected to result in an immediate impairment. Another method of allocation might therefore better reflect the goodwill associated with the reorganised units. In our view, an allocation based on relative current values of notional goodwill could be an acceptable alternative method in this case. This would lead to the following allocation:

CGU	B €m	C €m	D €m	Total
CGU's fair value	40	80	40	160
Fair value net identifiable assets	20	40	40	100
Current value of notional goodwill	20	40	–	60
Historic goodwill allocated	10	20	–	30

This would allocate goodwill of €10m (goodwill of €30m × relative current value of notional goodwill €20 / overall current value of notional goodwill €60m) to CGU B, €20m (goodwill of €30m × relative current value of notional goodwill €40 / overall current value of notional goodwill €60m) to CGU C and €0m (goodwill of €30m × relative current value of notional goodwill €0 / overall current value of notional goodwill €60m) to CGU D. This allocation would not cause an immediate impairment directly after the reallocation as the following table shows.

CGU	B €m	C €m	D €m	Total
Goodwill allocation	10	20	–	30
Book value of net identifiable assets	10	35	35	80
Total	20	55	35	110
Recoverable amount (based on FVLCD)	40	80	40	160
Immediate impairment	–	–	–	–

The above example is based on a fact pattern where an existing CGU is split into three new CGUs. However, the method could be applied as well in circumstances where components of an existing CGU are allocated to other existing CGUs. The current values of notional goodwill used for reallocation purposes in such a case would need to be based only on the goodwill in the components being reallocated ignoring any goodwill in the existing CGUs to which the components are being allocated.

While the method illustrated above might be seen as an alternative method for goodwill reallocation it requires an entity to perform notional purchase price allocations for the components of each affected CGU and therefore potentially involves a significant time, effort and cost commitment. It is important to note that IAS 36 is not entirely clear whether an entity would need to use an alternative method that might better reflect the goodwill associated with the reorganised units, if the entity is aware of it, or whether an entity could always just default to the IAS 36.87 stated relative value method.

In practice, situations may be considerably more complex than Examples 20.27, 20.28 and 20.29 above. For example, after an acquisition, a combination of disposal of acquired businesses together with a reorganisation and integration may arise. The entity may sell some parts of its acquired business immediately but may also use the acquisition in order to replace part of its existing capacity, disposing of existing elements. In addition, groups frequently undertake reorganisations of their statutory entities. It is often the case that CGUs do not correspond to these individual entities and the reorganisations may be undertaken for taxation reasons so the ownership structure within a group may not correspond to its CGUs. This makes it clear how important it is that entities identify their CGUs and the allocation of goodwill to them, so that they already have a basis for making any necessary allocations when an impairment issue arises or there is a disposal.

9 NON-CONTROLLING INTERESTS – THE IMPACT ON GOODWILL IMPAIRMENT TESTING

The amount of goodwill recorded by an entity when it acquires a controlling stake in a subsidiary that is less than 100% of its equity depends on which of the two following methods have been used to calculate it. Under IFRS 3 an entity has a choice between two methods:

(i) Goodwill attributable to the non-controlling interests is not recognised in the parent's consolidated financial statements as the non-controlling interest is stated at its proportion of the net fair value of the net identifiable assets of the acquiree.

(ii) The non-controlling interest is measured at its acquisition-date fair value, which means that its share of goodwill will also be recognised.

Under method (i) above the carrying amount of that CGU comprises:

(a) both the parent's interest and the non-controlling interest in the identifiable net assets of the CGU; and

(b) the parent's interest in goodwill.

But part of the recoverable amount of the CGU determined in accordance with IAS 36 is attributable to the non-controlling interest in goodwill.

IFRS 3 allows both measurement methods. The choice of method is to be made for each business combination, rather than being a policy choice, and could have a significant effect on the amount recognised for goodwill. *[IFRS 3.19, IAS 36.C1].*

Previous acquisitions under IFRS 3 (2007) were required to be accounted for using method (i) and were not restated on transition to the revised standard. *[IFRS 3.64].*

These methods are described in more detail in Chapter 9 at 8.

The IASB itself has noted that there are likely to be differences arising from measuring the non-controlling interest at its proportionate share of the acquiree's net identifiable assets, rather than at fair value. First, the amounts recognised in a business combination for the non-controlling interest and goodwill are likely to be lower (as illustrated in the example given in Chapter 9 at 8.3). Second, if a CGU to which the goodwill has been allocated is subsequently impaired, any impairment of goodwill recognised through income is likely to be lower than it would have been if the non-controlling interest had been measured at fair value.

The Standard is clear that not all of the goodwill arising will necessarily be allocated to a CGU or group of CGUs which includes the subsidiary with the non-controlling interest. *[IAS 36.C2].*

Guidance is given on the allocation of impairment losses:

(a) If a subsidiary, or part of a subsidiary, with a non-controlling interest is itself a CGU, the impairment loss is allocated between the parent and the non-controlling interest on the same basis as that on which profit or loss is allocated. *[IAS 36.C6].*

(b) If it is part of a larger CGU, goodwill impairment losses are allocated to the parts of the CGU that have a non-controlling interest and the parts that do not on the following basis: *[IAS 36.C7]*

(i) to the extent that the impairment relates to goodwill in the CGU, the relative carrying values of the goodwill of the parts before the impairment; and

(ii) to the extent that the impairment relates to identifiable assets in the CGU, the relative carrying values of these assets before the impairment. Any such impairment is allocated to the assets of the parts of each unit *pro rata* on the basis of the carrying amount of each asset in the part.

In those parts that have a non-controlling interest the impairment loss is allocated between the parent and the non-controlling interest on the same basis as that on which profit or loss is allocated.

However, it is not always clear how an entity should test for impairment when there is NCI. The issues include:

- calculating the 'gross up' of the carrying amount of goodwill because NCI is measured at its proportionate share of net identifiable assets and hence its share of goodwill is not recognised (see 9.1 below);
- allocation of impairment losses between the parent and NCI; and
- reallocation of goodwill between NCI and controlling interests after a change in a parent's ownership interest in a subsidiary that does not result in a loss of control.

Each of these issues arises in one or more of the following situations:

(a) NCI is measured on a proportionate share, rather than fair value;

(b) because of the existence of a control premium there are indications that it would be appropriate to allocate goodwill between the parent and NCI on a basis that is disproportionate to the percentage of equity owned by the parent and the NCI shareholders; and

(c) there are subsequent changes in ownership between the parent and NCI shareholders, but the parent maintains control.

Increases in the parent's share are discussed at 9.1.1 below, as is the sale of an interest without the loss of control.

The Interpretations Committee considered these issues in 2010 but declined to propose an amendment to IAS 36 as part of the Annual Improvements. They were concerned that there could be possible unintended consequences of making any changes, and recommended that the Board should consider the implication of these issues as part of the IFRS 3 post-implementation review.[1] While these issues were not specifically addressed in the IFRS 3 post-implementation review, participants informed the Board that in their view the required impairment test is complex, time-consuming and expensive and involves significant judgements. The Board therefore decided to undertake research to consider improvements, in particular on whether there is scope for simplification when it comes to impairment testing. At the time of writing, this research is still ongoing.

In the absence of any guidance, we consider that an entity is not precluded from grossing up goodwill on a basis other than ownership percentages if to do so is reasonable. A rational gross up will result in a goodwill balance that most closely resembles the balance that would have been recorded had non-controlling interest been recorded at fair value. This is explored further at 9.3 below.

9.1 Testing for impairment in entities with non-controlling interests measured at the proportionate share of net identifiable assets

If an entity measures NCI at its proportionate interest in the net identifiable assets of a subsidiary at the acquisition date, rather than at the fair value, goodwill attributable to the NCI is included in the recoverable amount of the CGU but is not recognised in the consolidated financial statements. To enable a like-for-like comparison, IAS 36 requires the carrying amount of a non-wholly-owned CGU to be notionally adjusted by grossing up the carrying amount of goodwill allocated to the CGU to include the amount attributable to the non-controlling interest. This notionally adjusted carrying amount is then compared with the recoverable amount. [IAS 36.C3, C4]. If there is an impairment, the entity allocates the impairment loss as usual, first reducing the carrying amount of goodwill allocated to the CGU (see 11.2 below). However, because only the parent's goodwill is recognised, the impairment loss is apportioned between that attributable to the parent and that attributable to the non-controlling interest, with only the former being recognised. [IAS 36.C8].

If any impairment loss remains, it is allocated in the usual way to the other assets of the CGU *pro rata* on the basis of the carrying amount of each asset in the CGU (the allocation of impairment losses to CGUs is discussed at 11.2 below). [IAS 36.104].

These requirements are illustrated in the following example. [IAS 36.IE62-68]. Note that in these examples goodwill allocation and impairment is based on the ownership interests. At 9.3 below we discuss alternative allocation methodologies when there is a control premium.

Example 20.30: A CGU with goodwill and non-controlling interest

Entity X acquires an 80 per cent ownership interest in Entity Y for €1,600 on 1 January 20X0. At that date, Entity Y's identifiable net assets have a fair value of €1,500. Entity X recognises in its consolidated financial statements:

(a) goodwill of €400, being the difference between the cost of the business combination of €1,600 and the non-controlling interest of €300 (20% of €1,500) and the identifiable net assets of Entity Y of €1,500;

(b) Entity Y's identifiable net assets at their fair value of €1,500; and

(c) a non-controlling interest of €300.

At the end of 20X0 the carrying amount of Entity Y's identifiable assets has reduced to €1,350 (excluding goodwill) and Entity X determines that the recoverable amount of CGU Y is €1,000.

The carrying amount of CGU Y must be notionally adjusted to include goodwill attributable to the non-controlling interest, before being compared with the recoverable amount of €1,000. Goodwill attributable to Entity X's 80% interest in Entity Y at the acquisition date is €400. Therefore, goodwill notionally attributable to the 20% non-controlling interest in Entity Y at the acquisition date is €100, being (€400 ÷ 80% × 20%).

Testing CGU Y for impairment at the end of 20X0 gives rise to an impairment loss of €850 calculated as follows:

	Goodwill €	Identifiable net assets €	Total €
Carrying amount	400	1,350	1,750
Unrecognised non-controlling interest	100	–	100
Notionally adjusted carrying amount	500	1,350	1,850
Recoverable amount			1,000
Impairment loss			850

The impairment loss of €850 is allocated to the assets in the CGU by first reducing the carrying amount of goodwill to zero. Therefore, €500 of the €850 impairment loss for the CGU is allocated to the goodwill. However, because Entity X only holds a 80% ownership interest in Entity Y, it recognises only 80 per cent of that goodwill impairment loss (i.e. €400). The remaining impairment loss of €350 is recognised by reducing the carrying amounts of Entity Y's identifiable assets, as follows:

	Goodwill €	Identifiable net assets €	Total €
Carrying amount	400	1,350	1,750
Impairment loss	(400)	(350)	(750)
Carrying amount after impairment loss	–	1,000	1,000

Of the impairment loss of €350 relating to Entity Y's identifiable assets, €70 (i.e. 20% thereof) would be attributed to the non-controlling interest.

In this example the same result would have been achieved by just comparing the recoverable amount of €1,000 with the carrying amount of €1,750. However, what if the recoverable amount of the CGU had been greater than the carrying amount of the identifiable net assets prior to recognising the impairment loss?

Assume the same facts as above, except that at the end of 20X0, Entity X determines that the recoverable amount of CGU Y is €1,400. In this case, testing CGU Y for impairment at the end of 20X0 gives rise to an impairment loss of €450 calculated as follows:

	Goodwill €	Identifiable net assets €	Total €
Carrying amount	400	1,350	1,750
Unrecognised non-controlling interest	100	–	100
Notionally adjusted carrying amount	500	1,350	1,850
Recoverable amount			1,400
Impairment loss			450

All of the impairment loss of €450 is allocated to the goodwill. However, Entity X recognises only 80 per cent of that goodwill impairment loss, i.e. €360. This allocation of the impairment loss results in the following carrying amounts for CGU Y in the financial statements of Entity X at the end of 20X0:

	Goodwill €	Identifiable net assets €	Total €
Carrying amount	400	1,350	1,750
Impairment loss	(360)	–	(360)
Carrying amount after impairment loss	40	1,350	1,390

Of the impairment loss of €360, none of it is attributable to the non-controlling interest since it all relates to the majority shareholder's goodwill.

In this case the total carrying amount of the identifiable net assets and the goodwill has not been reduced to the recoverable amount of €1,400, but is actually less than the recoverable amount. This is because the recoverable amount of goodwill relating to the non-controlling interest (20% of [€500 – €450]) is not recognised in the consolidated financial statements.

9.1.1 Acquisitions or sale of non-controlling interests measured at the proportionate share of net identifiable assets

As described above, in order to enable a like-for-like comparison, IAS 36 requires the carrying amount of a non-wholly-owned CGU to be notionally adjusted by grossing up the carrying amount of goodwill allocated to the CGU to include the amount attributable to the non-controlling interest.

What happens if the non-controlling interest is acquired by the entity so that it is now wholly owned? IFRS 10 requires these purchases to be reflected as equity transactions, which means that there is no change to goodwill. *[IFRS 10.23]*. Other methods may have been used in the past that may still be reflected in the carrying amounts of goodwill. These methods could have partially or wholly reflected the fair value of the additional interest acquired.

No notional adjustment to goodwill is required when the remaining non-controlling interest is acquired. The carrying amount of the unit, including the recognised goodwill, i.e. the goodwill arising in the acquisition when control was obtained, should be tested against 100% of the recoverable amount of the unit.

In situations where only a portion but not the full outstanding non-controlling interest is acquired or where a portion of an existing holding is sold without loss of control, the question is whether goodwill should be grossed up based on the new non-controlling interest percentage after the transaction or the original percentage. In our view, the answer to this question depends on whether a purchase of an additional non-controlling interest or a sale of a portion of an existing holding occurred.

Assume a situation where entity A owns 80% of entity B, goodwill was recorded at 80 and the non-controlling interest was measured at the proportionate interest in the net identifiable assets. In previous impairment tests goodwill would have been grossed up to 100 (80 × 100% ÷ 80%). When entity A later acquires 10% of the remaining ownership interest in Entity B, leaving a non-controlling interest of 10%, should goodwill for future impairment assessments be grossed up using the current 10% or the previous 20% non-controlling interest? Using the current non-controlling interest holding of 10% would lead to grossed up goodwill of 88.9 (80 × 100% ÷ 90%). This would make an impairment less likely. The alternative is to gross up goodwill with the original non-controlling interest percentage of 20% meaning goodwill could continue to be grossed up to 100. We believe both approaches are acceptable in practice in situations where an additional non-controlling interest is acquired.

However, in our view, if instead entity A sold 20% of the ownership in entity B, resulting in a non-controlling interest of 40% the answer is different. The original non-controlling interest percentage of 20% should be used leading to grossed up goodwill of 100. Using an approach where goodwill is grossed up with the new non-controlling interest percentage, would lead to a goodwill of 133.3 (80 × 100% ÷ 60%). We do not believe it would be appropriate to use this grossed up amount, as no additional goodwill was created through the transaction.

Grossing up of goodwill may be complex in situations where subsequent transactions occur which might entail a combination of non-controlling interests measured initially at fair value and at proportionate interest of net identifiable assets or where there are multiple subsequent transactions involving non-controlling interests. Careful consideration of all facts and circumstances are required to come to an appropriate solution in such cases.

9.2 Testing for impairment in entities with non-controlling interests initially measured at fair value

The following examples in which the non-controlling interest is initially measured at fair value, are based on the Examples 7B and 7C in IAS 36's Illustrative Examples and illustrate the requirements for testing for impairment when non-controlling interest is initially measured at fair value. Note that in these examples goodwill impairment is allocated on the basis of the ownership interests. At 9.3 below we discuss alternative allocation methodologies when there is a control premium.

Example 20.31: Non-controlling interests measured initially at fair value

Entity X acquires an 80 per cent ownership interest in Entity Y for €2,100 on 1 January 20X0. At that date, Entity Y's identifiable net assets have a fair value of €1,500. Entity X chooses to measure the non-controlling interests at its fair value of €350. Goodwill is €950, which is the aggregate of the consideration transferred and the amount of the non-controlling interests (€2,100 + €350) less the net identifiable assets (€1,500).

(a)   The acquired subsidiary is a stand-alone CGU

Entity Y is a CGU but part of the goodwill is allocated to other CGUs of Entity X that are expected to benefit from the synergies of the combination. Goodwill of €450 is allocated to the Entity Y CGU and €500 to the other CGUs.

At the end of 20X0, the carrying amount of Entity Y's identifiable assets excluding goodwill has reduced to €1,350 and Entity X determines that the recoverable amount of CGU Y is €1,650.

	Goodwill €	Identifiable net assets €	Total €
Carrying amount	450	1,350	1,800
Recoverable amount			1,650
Impairment loss			150

Of the goodwill impairment loss of €150, €30 (20%) will be allocated to the non-controlling interest because the goodwill is allocated to the controlling interest and non-controlling interest on the same basis as profit or loss.

(b)   The acquired subsidiary is part of a larger CGU

Entity Y becomes part of a larger CGU, Z. As before, €500 of the goodwill is allocated to other CGUs of Entity X that are expected to benefit from the synergies of the combination. Goodwill of €450 is allocated to Z. Z's goodwill related to previous business combinations is €800.

At the end of 20X0, Parent determines that the recoverable amount of the Z CGU is €3,300. The carrying amount of its net assets excluding goodwill is €2,250.

	Goodwill €	Identifiable net assets €	Total €
Carrying amount	1,250	2,250	3,500
Recoverable amount			3,300
Impairment loss			200

All of the impairment loss of €200 is allocated to the goodwill. As the partially-owned subsidiary forms part of a larger CGU, the goodwill impairment loss must be allocated first to the parts of the cash-generating unit Z, and then to the controlling and non-controlling interests of Entity Y.

The impairment loss is allocated on the basis of the relative carrying values of the goodwill of the parts before the impairment. Entity Y is allocated 36% of the impairment (450 ÷ 1,250), in this case €72, of which €14.40 (20%) will be allocated to the non-controlling interest.

9.3   Testing for impairment in entities with non-controlling interests: alternative allocation methodologies

At 9 above we noted that in the absence of any guidance, we consider that an entity is not precluded from grossing up goodwill on a basis other than ownership percentages if to do so is reasonable. A rational gross up will result in a goodwill balance that most closely resembles the balance that would have been recorded had non-controlling interest been recorded at fair value.

There are therefore two broad methods of grossing up goodwill for impairment testing purposes when non-controlling interest is measured at its proportionate interest in the net identifiable assets of the subsidiary at the acquisition date:

(a) a 'mechanical' gross up of the controlling interest's goodwill on the basis of ownership interests; and

(b) a 'rational' gross up of the controlling interest's goodwill that takes into account the acquirer's control premium, if any.

Similarly, there are two broad methods of allocating goodwill impairment:

(a) a 'mechanical' allocation in which the impairment loss is allocated on the basis of ownership interests; and

(b) a 'rational' allocation, in which the entity applies an allocation methodology that recognises the disproportionate sharing of the controlling and non-controlling interests in the goodwill book value. The rational allocation takes into account the acquirer's control premium, if any.

When non-controlling interest is measured at its proportionate interest in the net identifiable assets of the subsidiary, there are alternatives for both the gross up and allocation methods. The following are all acceptable:

- rational gross up and rational allocation;
- rational gross up and mechanical allocation; and
- mechanical gross up and mechanical allocation.

A mechanical gross up and a rational allocation is not appropriate because a mechanical gross up results in the controlling and non-controlling interests having goodwill carrying values which are proportionate to their ownership interests.

Although the above methods of allocating goodwill and grossing up the NCI are acceptable, entities would be expected to be consistent year on year in the approach that they apply in testing any particular CGU or CGU group. This does not prevent an entity from applying different approaches to different CGUs or CGU groups, should that be appropriate in the circumstances. Both Examples 20.30 and 20.31 in 9.1 and 9.2 above are examples of mechanical allocation of impairment losses. In Example 20.31 the NCI is recorded initially at fair value, so there is no gross up methodology for goodwill but in Example 20.30, goodwill is grossed up mechanically.

The examples below illustrate the various methods. Depending on the circumstances, the gross up and allocation process could be much more complex than in the examples below. For example, where goodwill is being tested for impairment for a group of CGUs with multiple non-controlling interests measured at both fair value and proportionate interest in net identifiable assets, other (practical) approaches, not illustrated below may result in a reasonable measurement and allocation of goodwill impairment. Also, detailed records may need to be maintained to facilitate the gross up and allocation process.

Example 20.32: **Measurement and allocation of goodwill impairment losses when there are non-controlling interests**

An entity purchases 80% of a business for €160. The controlling and non-controlling interests share in profits on the basis of their ownership interests. The fair value of the net identifiable assets is €140 and the fair value of the non-controlling interest is €36. Goodwill is fully allocated to the business acquired.

Subsequent to the acquisition, the entity performs an impairment test and determines that the recoverable amount of the CGU is €160.

Scenario 1 – Non-controlling interest recorded at fair value

The entity elects to record the non-controlling interest at fair value, rather than the non-controlling interest's proportionate share of the recognised amounts of the acquiree's identifiable net assets. Accordingly, goodwill of €56 is recorded (= €160 + €36 – €140).

The initial carrying amount of the CGU is €196 (= €140 + €56). Assuming for simplicity that at the time of the impairment test the carrying amounts are unchanged, there is impairment of €36 (= €196 – €160). The entire impairment loss is applied against the goodwill balance of €56, reducing recorded goodwill to €20. The entity is required to allocate the impairment loss between the controlling and non-controlling interests.

Rational allocation: the goodwill impairment loss is allocated on a rational basis using a methodology that recognises the disproportionate sharing of the controlling and non-controlling interests in the goodwill book value. The rational allocation takes into account the acquirer's control premium, if any. Goodwill of €48 (= €160 – (€140 × 80%)) relates to the controlling interest and goodwill of €8 (= €36 – (€140 × 20%)) relates to the non-controlling interest. Therefore, a rational allocation method would result in impairment of €48 / €56 × €36 = €31 being allocated to the controlling interest and impairment of €8 / €56 × €36 = €5 being allocated to the non-controlling interest.

Mechanical allocation: the goodwill impairment loss is allocated on the basis of ownership interests. Therefore, impairment of €29 (= €36 × 80%) is allocated to the controlling interest while impairment of €7 (= €36 × 20%) is allocated to the non-controlling interest [Note 1].

Scenario 2 – Non-controlling interest recorded at its proportionate share of fair value of identifiable assets

The entity elects to record non-controlling interest at its proportionate share of the fair value of the acquiree's identifiable net assets, i.e. €28 (= €140 × 20%). Therefore, goodwill of €48 is recorded (= €160 + €28 – €140). In this case, the carrying amount of the CGU is €188 (= €140 + €48). The entity is required to gross up the carrying amount of the CGU for the purposes of determining whether the CGU is impaired.

Rational gross up and rational allocation: goodwill attributable to the non-controlling interest is calculated by grossing up the recognised goodwill using a factor which takes into account the premium, if any, relating to the fact that the entity has a controlling 80% interest. Assume the relevant gross up factor results in goodwill attributable to the non-controlling interest of €8 [Note 2]. Therefore, the adjusted carrying value of the reporting unit is €196 (= €188 + €8). There is impairment of €36 (= €196 – €160). The total impairment of €36 is then allocated between the controlling and non-controlling interest on a rational basis. Using the same rational allocation methodology as in Scenario 1 results in impairment of €31 being allocated to the controlling interest and impairment of €5 being allocated to the non-controlling interest. The impairment of €5 associated with the non-controlling interest is not recognised because no goodwill is recorded in the financial statements relating to the non-controlling interest.

Rational gross up and mechanical allocation: as above, assume the relevant gross up factor results in goodwill attributable to the non-controlling interest of €8 and the adjusted carrying value of the reporting unit is €196 (= €188 + €8). The total impairment of €36 is then allocated between the controlling and non-controlling interest based on their ownership interests, resulting in impairment of €29 (= €36 × 80%) being allocated to the controlling interest and impairment of €7 (= €36 × 20%) being allocated to the non-controlling interest. The impairment of €7 associated with the non-controlling interest is not recognised because no goodwill is recorded in the financial statements relating to the non-controlling interest.

Mechanical gross up and mechanical allocation: goodwill attributable to the non-controlling interest is €12 (= €48 ÷ (80/20)). Therefore, the adjusted carrying value of the reporting unit is €200 (= €188 + €12). There is impairment of €40 (= €200 (adjusted carrying value) less €160 (= recoverable amount). Impairment of €32 (= 80% × €40) is allocated to the controlling interest and impairment of €8 (= 20% × €40) is allocated to the non-controlling interest. The impairment of €8 associated with the non-controlling interest is not recognised because no goodwill is recorded in the financial statements relating to the non-controlling interest.

Note [1]: As a further illustration of the difference between the two methods, suppose that the entity determined that the recoverable amount was nil. In this case, under the rational allocation in Scenario 1, the non-controlling interest of €36 would be reduced to zero, as an impairment of €8 to goodwill and an impairment of €28 (= 20% of €140) to other identifiable assets would be each allocated to non-controlling interest. However, under mechanical allocation in Scenario 1, the non-controlling interest would be reduced by €39 (= 20% of the carrying value of €196) with the result being a non-controlling interest debit balance of €3.

Note [2]: Note that this results in total adjusted goodwill of €56, which is the same goodwill figure that is recorded in Scenario 1 when non-controlling interest is recorded at fair value.

10 IMPAIRMENT OF INTANGIBLE ASSETS WITH AN INDEFINITE USEFUL LIFE

IAS 38 makes the point that 'indefinite' does not mean 'infinite', and unforeseeable factors may affect the entity's ability and intention to maintain the asset at its standard of performance assessed at the time of estimating the asset's useful life. *[IAS 38.91]*. The requirements of IAS 36 for this type of asset can be summarised as follows:

1. all intangible assets with indefinite useful lives must be tested for impairment at least once per year and at the same time each year; *[IAS 36.10]*
2. any intangible asset with an indefinite useful life recognised during the reporting period must be tested for impairment before the end of the period; *[IAS 36.10]*
3. any intangible asset (regardless of whether it has an indefinite useful life or not) that is not yet available for use recognised during the reporting period must be tested for impairment before the end of the period; *[IAS 36.10-11]*
4. if an intangible asset that has an indefinite useful life or is not yet available for use can only be tested for impairment as part of a CGU, then that CGU must be tested for impairment at least annually; *[IAS 36.89]*
5. if there are indicators of impairment a period end test must also be performed; *[IAS 36.9]* and
6. for an intangible asset that has an indefinite useful life that is part of a CGU, there are specific concessions, discussed below, allowing an impairment test in a previous period to be used if that test showed sufficient headroom. *[IAS 36.24]*.

Any intangible asset not yet ready for use must be tested annually because its ability to generate sufficient future economic benefits to recover its carrying amount is usually subject to greater uncertainty before the asset is available for use than after it is available for use. *[IAS 36.11]*.

This will obviously affect any entity that capitalises development expenditure in accordance with IAS 38 where the period of development may straddle more than one accounting period. The requirement will also apply to in-process research and development costs recognised in a business combination (see Chapter 9 at 5.5.2.D).

An intangible asset with an indefinite useful life may generate independent cash inflows as an individual asset, in which case the impairment testing procedure for a single asset as set out at 7 above applies. Most intangible assets form part of the assets within a CGU, in which case the procedures relevant to testing a CGU as set out above apply. In particular IAS 36 makes it clear that if an intangible asset with an indefinite useful life, or any intangible asset not yet ready for use, is included in the assets of a CGU, then that CGU has to be tested for impairment annually. *[IAS 36.89]*. As with other assets, it may be that the FVLCD of the intangible asset with an indefinite useful life can be ascertained but the asset itself does not generate largely independent cash flows. If its individual FVLCD is lower than the carrying amount, this does not necessarily mean that the asset is impaired. The impairment test is still based on the CGU of which the asset is a part, and if the recoverable amount of the CGU is higher than the carrying amount of the CGU, there is no impairment loss.

IAS 36 allows a concession that applies to those intangible assets with an indefinite useful life that form part of a CGU, which is similar to the concession for goodwill. It allows the most recent detailed calculation of such an asset's recoverable amount made in a preceding period to be used in the impairment test in the current period if all of the following criteria are met:

(a) if the intangible asset is part of a CGU, the assets and liabilities making up that unit have not changed significantly since the most recent recoverable amount calculation;

(b) that calculation of the asset's recoverable amount exceeded its carrying amount by a substantial margin; and

(c) the likelihood that an updated calculation of the recoverable amount would be less than the asset's carrying amount is remote, based on an analysis of events and circumstances since the most recent calculation of the recoverable amount. *[IAS 36.24]*.

Thus if there was sufficient headroom on the last calculation and little has changed in the CGU to which the asset belongs, it can be revisited and re-used rather than having to start entirely from scratch, which considerably reduces the work involved in the annual test. The impairment test cannot be rolled forward forever, of course, and an entity will have to take a cautious approach to estimating when circumstances have changed sufficiently to require a new test.

Impairment losses experienced on intangible assets with an indefinite useful life are recognised exactly as set out at 11 below, either as an individual asset or as part of a CGU, depending upon whether the intangible concerned is part of a CGU or not. Note that there is an important distinction concerning the allocation of losses in a CGU between the treatment of goodwill and that of intangible assets with an indefinite useful life. If goodwill forms part of the assets of a CGU, any impairment loss first reduces the goodwill and thereafter the remaining assets are reduced *pro rata*. However, if an intangible asset is part of a CGU that is impaired, there is no requirement to write down the intangible before the other assets in the CGU, rather all assets are written down *pro rata*. For the *pro rata* allocation it is important to keep in mind that the carrying amount of an asset should not be reduced below the highest of its fair value less costs of disposal, value in use or zero. If the preceding rule is applied, further allocation of the impairment loss is made *pro rata* to the other assets of the unit (group of units).

11 RECOGNISING AND REVERSING IMPAIRMENT LOSSES

If the carrying value of an individual asset or of a CGU is equal to or less than its calculated VIU, there is no impairment. On the other hand, if the carrying value of the CGU is greater than its recoverable amount, an impairment write-down should be recognised.

There are three scenarios: an impairment loss on an individual asset, an impairment loss on an individual CGU and an impairment loss on a group of CGUs. The last of these may occur where there are corporate assets (see 4.2 above) or goodwill (see 11.2 below) that have been allocated to a group of CGUs rather than to individual ones.

11.1 Impairment losses on individual assets

For individual assets IAS 36 states:

> 'If, and only if, the recoverable amount of an asset is less than its carrying amount, the carrying amount of the asset shall be reduced to its recoverable amount. That reduction is an impairment loss.' *[IAS 36.59]*.

> 'An impairment loss shall be recognised immediately in profit or loss, unless the asset is carried at revalued amount in accordance with another Standard (for example, in accordance with the revaluation model in IAS 16). Any impairment loss of a revalued asset shall be treated as a revaluation decrease in accordance with that other Standard'. *[IAS 36.60]*.

If there is an impairment loss on an asset that has not been revalued, it is recognised in profit or loss. An impairment loss on a revalued asset is first used to reduce the revaluation surplus in other comprehensive income for that asset. Only when the impairment loss exceeds the amount in the revaluation surplus for that same asset is any further impairment loss recognised in profit or loss.

IAS 36 does not require impairment losses to be shown in any particular position in the income statement, although the requirements of IAS 1 – *Presentation of Financial Statements* – should always be considered. It may be necessary to add an appropriate line item in profit or loss if it is relevant for an understanding of the entity's financial performance. *[IAS 1.85]*.

Any amounts written off a fixed asset should be shown as part of the accumulated depreciation when an entity discloses the gross carrying amount and the accumulated depreciation at the beginning and the end of the period. *[IAS 16.73(d)]*. In the reconciliation required by IAS 16.73(e) any impairment recognised or reversed through profit and loss should be shown in a separate line item. If the asset is held at revalued amount then any impairment losses recognised or reversed should be shown in the reconciliation in one line item together with the revaluations. *[IAS 16.73(e)(iv)]*.

An impairment loss greater than the carrying value of the asset does not give rise to a liability unless another standard requires it, presumably as this would be equivalent to providing for future losses. *[IAS 36.62]*. An impairment loss will reduce the depreciable amount of an asset and the revised amount will be depreciated or amortised prospectively over the remaining life. *[IAS 36.63]*. However, an entity ought also to review the useful life and residual value of its impaired asset, as both of these may need to be revised. The circumstances that give rise to impairments frequently affect these as well.

Finally, an impairment loss will have implications for any deferred tax calculation involving the asset. The standard makes clear that if an impairment loss is recognised then any related deferred tax assets or liabilities are determined in accordance with IAS 12, by comparing the revised carrying amount of the asset with its tax base. *[IAS 36.64]*. Example 3 in the standard's accompanying section of illustrative examples, on which the following is based, illustrates the possible effects.

Example 20.33: Recognition of an impairment loss creates a deferred tax asset

An entity has an asset with a carrying amount of €2,000 whose recoverable amount is €1,300. The tax rate is 30% and the tax base of the asset is €1,500. Impairment losses are not deductible for tax purposes. The effect of the impairment loss is as follows:

	Before impairment €	Effect of impairment €	After impairment €
Carrying amount	2,000	(700)	1,300
Tax base	1,500	–	1,500
Taxable (deductible) temporary difference	500	(700)	(200)
Deferred tax liability (asset) at 30%	150	(210)	(60)

The entity will recognise the deferred tax asset to the extent that the respective recognition criteria of IAS 12 are met.

11.2 Impairment losses and CGUs

Impairment losses in a CGU can occur in two ways:

(i) an impairment loss is incurred in a CGU on its own, and that CGU may or may not have corporate assets or goodwill included in its carrying value; and

(ii) an impairment loss is identified that must be allocated across a group of CGUs because a corporate asset or goodwill is involved whose carrying value could only be allocated to a group of CGUs as a whole, rather than to individual CGUs (the allocation of corporate assets to CGUs is discussed at 4.2 above, and goodwill is discussed at 8 above). Note that if there are indicators of impairment in connection with a CGU with which goodwill is associated, i.e. the CGU is part of a CGU group to which the goodwill is allocated, this CGU should be tested and any necessary impairment loss taken, before goodwill is tested for impairment (see 8.2.2 above). *[IAS 36.88]*.

The relevant paragraphs from the standard deal with both instances but are readily understandable only if the above distinction is appreciated. The standard lays down that impairment losses in CGUs should be recognised to reduce the carrying amount of the assets of the unit (group of units) in the following order:

(a) first, to reduce the carrying amount of any goodwill allocated to the CGU or group of units; and

(b) second, if the goodwill has been written off, to reduce the other assets of the CGU (or group of CGUs) *pro rata* to their carrying amount, subject to the limitation that the carrying amount of an asset should not be reduced to the highest of fair value less costs of disposal, value in use or zero. *[IAS 36.104, 105]*.

The important point is to be clear about the order set out above. Goodwill must be written down first, and if an impairment loss remains, the other assets in the CGU or group of CGUs are written down *pro rata* to their carrying values subject to the limitation stated at (b) above.

This pro-rating is in two stages if a group of CGUs is involved:

(i) the loss reduces goodwill (which by definition in this instance is unallocated to individual CGUs in the group); and

(ii) any remaining loss is pro-rated between the carrying values of the individual CGUs in the group and within each individual CGU the loss is again pro-rated between the individual assets' carrying values.

Unless it is possible to estimate the recoverable amount of each individual asset within a CGU, it is necessary to allocate impairment losses to individual assets in such a way that the revised carrying amounts of these assets correspond with the requirements of the standard. Therefore, the entity does not reduce the carrying amount of an individual asset below the highest of its FVLCD or VIU (if these can be established), or zero. The amount of the impairment loss that would otherwise have been allocated to the asset is then allocated *pro rata* to the other assets of the CGU or CGU group. *[IAS 36.105]*. The standard argues that this arbitrary allocation to individual assets when their recoverable amount cannot be individually assessed is appropriate because all assets of a CGU 'work together'. *[IAS 36.106]*.

If corporate assets are allocated to a CGU or group of CGUs, then any remaining loss at (ii) above (i.e. after allocation to goodwill) is pro-rated against the allocated share of the corporate asset and the other assets in the CGU.

This process, then, writes down the carrying value attributed or allocated to a CGU until the carrying value of the net assets is equal to the computed recoverable amount. Due to the restriction of not reducing the carrying amount of an asset below its FVLCD or VIU, it is logically possible, after all assets and goodwill are either written off or down to their FVLCD or VIU, for the carrying value of the CGU to be higher than the computed recoverable amount. There is no suggestion that the net assets should be reduced any further because at this point the FVLCD would be the relevant impairment figure. The remaining amount will only be recognised as a liability if that is a requirement of another standard. *[IAS 36.108]*.

IAS 36 includes in the standard's accompanying section of illustrative examples Example 2 which illustrates the calculation, recognition and allocation of an impairment loss across CGUs.

However, the standard stresses that no impairment loss should be reflected against an individual asset if the CGU to which it belongs has not been impaired, even if its carrying value exceeds its FVLCD. This is expanded in the following example, based on that in paragraph 107 of the standard:

Example 20.34: Individually impaired assets within CGUs

A machine has suffered physical damage but is still working, although not as well as before it was damaged. The machine's FVLCD is less than its carrying amount. The machine does not generate independent cash inflows. The smallest identifiable group of assets that includes the machine and generates cash inflows that are largely independent of the cash inflows from other assets is the production line to which the machine belongs. The recoverable amount of the production line shows that the production line taken as a whole is not impaired.

Assumption 1: budgets/forecasts approved by management reflect no commitment of management to replace the machine.

The recoverable amount of the machine alone cannot be estimated because its VIU may be different from its FVLCD (because the entity is going to continue to use it) and can be determined only for the CGU to which it belongs (the production line).

As the production line is not impaired, no impairment loss is recognised for the machine. Nevertheless, the entity may need to reassess the depreciation period or the depreciation method for the machine. Perhaps a shorter depreciation period or a faster depreciation method is required to reflect the expected remaining useful life of the machine or the pattern in which economic benefits are expected to be consumed by the entity.

Assumption 2: budgets/forecasts approved by management reflect a commitment of management to replace the machine and sell it in the near future.

Cash flows from continuing use of the machine until its disposal are estimated to be negligible. The machine's VIU can be estimated to be close to its FVLCD. Therefore, the recoverable amount of the machine can be determined and no consideration is given to the CGU (the production line) to which it belongs. As the machine's carrying amount exceeds its FVLCD, an impairment loss is recognised to write it down to FVLCD. *[IAS 36.107].*

Note that it is assumed that the asset is still useable (otherwise it would not be contributing to the cash flows of the CGU and would have to be written off) and that it is not held for sale as defined by IFRS 5. If the asset is no longer part of the CGU, it will have to be tested for impairment on a stand-alone basis. For IFRS 5's requirements when an asset is held for sale, see 5.1 above.

11.3 Reversal of impairment loss relating to goodwill prohibited

As mentioned at 8.2.4 above, IAS 36 does not permit an impairment loss on goodwill to be reversed under any circumstances. *[IAS 36.124].* The standard justifies this on the grounds that such a reversal would probably be an increase in internally generated goodwill, rather than a reversal of the impairment loss recognised for the acquired goodwill, and that recognition of internally generated goodwill is prohibited by IAS 38. *[IAS 36.125].*

Example 20.35: Impairment of goodwill

Company A has a CGU that has a carrying value of $2,000,000 at 31 December 20X0. This carrying value comprises $500,000 relating to goodwill and $1,500,000 relating to net tangible assets.

In 20X1, as a result of losses, net tangible assets have decreased to $1,400,000 reducing the total carrying value of the unit to $1,900,000. Changes in the regulatory framework surrounding its business mean that the cash-generating unit has a recoverable amount of $1,600,000 and has thus suffered an impairment loss of $300,000. This is charged to profit or loss. The carrying value of goodwill is reduced to $200,000.

In 20X2 the company develops a new product with the result that the recoverable amount of the cash-generating unit rises to $1,700,000. Net tangible assets have remained at $1,400,000. Despite the recoverable amount of the business unit now being $1,700,000 compared to its carrying value of $1,600,000, it is not possible to reverse $100,000 of the prior year's impairment loss of $300,000.

11.4 Reversal of impairment losses relating to assets other than goodwill

For all other assets, including intangible assets with an indefinite life, IAS 36 requires entities to assess at each reporting date whether there is any indication that an impairment loss may no longer exist or may have decreased. If there is any such indication, the entity has to recalculate the recoverable amount of the asset. *[IAS 36.110].*

Therefore if there are indications that a previously recognised impairment loss has disappeared or reduced, it is necessary to determine again the recoverable amount (i.e. the higher of FVLCD or VIU) so that the reversal can be quantified. The standard sets out examples of what it notes are in effect 'reverse indications' of impairment. *[IAS 36.111].* These are the reverse of those set out in paragraph 12 of the standard as indications of impairment (see 2.1 above). *[IAS 36.112].* They are arranged, as in paragraph 12, into two categories: *[IAS 36.111]*

External sources of information:

(a) A significant increase in the asset's value.

(b) Significant changes during the period or expected in the near future in the entity's technological, market, economic or legal environment that will have a favourable effect.

(c) Decreases in market interest rates or other market rates of return on investments and those decreases are likely to affect the discount rate used in calculating the asset's value in use and increase the asset's recoverable amount materially.

Internal sources of information:

(d) Significant changes during the period or expected in the near future that will affect the extent to which, or manner in which, the asset is used. These changes include costs incurred during the period to improve or enhance the asset's performance or restructure the operation to which the asset belongs.

(e) Evidence from internal reporting that the economic performance of the asset is, or will be, better than expected.

Compared with paragraph 12, there are two notable omissions from this list of 'reverse indicators', one external and one internal.

The external indicator not included is the mirror of the impairment indicator 'the carrying amount of the net assets of the reporting entity is more than its market capitalisation'. No explanation is provided as to why, if a market capitalisation below shareholders' funds is an indication of impairment, its reversal should not automatically be an indication of a reversal. However, the most likely reason is that all of the facts and circumstances need to be considered before assuming that an impairment has reversed. In any event, deficits below market capitalisation may affect goodwill so the impairment charge cannot be reversed.

The internal indicator omitted from the list of 'reverse indicators' is that evidence of obsolescence or physical deterioration has been reversed. Once again no reason is given. It may be that the standard-setters have assumed that no such reversal could take place without the entity incurring costs to improve or enhance the performance of the asset or the CGU so that this is, in effect, covered by indicator (d) above.

The standard also reminds preparers that a reversal, like an impairment, is evidence that the depreciation method or residual value of the asset should be reviewed and may need to be adjusted, whether or not the impairment loss is reversed. *[IAS 36.113].*

A further restriction is that impairment losses should be reversed only if there has been a change in the estimates used to determine the impairment loss, e.g. a change in cash flows or discount rate (for VIU) or a change in FVLCD. The 'unwinding' of the discount will increase the present value of future cash flows as they become closer but IAS 36 does not allow the mere passage of time to trigger the reversal of an impairment. In other words the 'service potential' of the asset must genuinely improve if a reversal is to be recognised. *[IAS 36.114-116]*. However, this inability to recognise the rise in value can give rise to what is in effect a double recognition of losses, which may seem illogical, as demonstrated by the following example:

Example 20.36: Double counted losses

At the end of 20X0, an entity with a single CGU is carrying out an impairment review. The discounted forecast cash flows for years 20X2 and onwards would be just enough to support the carrying value of the entity's assets. However, 20X1 is forecasted to produce a loss and net cash outflow. The discounted value of this amount is accordingly written off the carrying value of the fixed assets in 20X0 as an impairment loss. It is then suffered again in 20X1 (at a slightly higher amount being now undiscounted) as the actual loss. Once that loss is past, the future cash flows are sufficient to support the original unimpaired value of the fixed assets. Nevertheless, the assets cannot be written back up through profit or loss to counter the double counting effect as the increase in value does not derive from a change in economic conditions or in the expected use of an asset.

In this type of scenario, which is common in practice, the entity will only 'benefit' as the assets are depreciated or amortised at a lower amount.

If, on the other hand, the revival in cash flows is the result of expenditure by the entity to improve or enhance the performance of the asset or the CGU or on a restructuring of the CGU, there may be an obvious improvement in the service potential and the entity may be able to reverse some or all of the impairment write down.

In the event of an individual asset's impairment being reversed, the reversal may not raise the carrying value above the figure it would have stood at taking into account depreciation, if no impairment had originally been recognised. *[IAS 36.117]*. Any increase above this figure would really be a revaluation, which would have to be accounted for in accordance with the standard relevant to the asset concerned. *[IAS 36.118]*.

Example 20.37: Reversal of impairment losses

At the beginning of year 1 an entity acquires an asset with a useful life of 10 years for $1,000. The asset generates net cash inflows that are largely independent of the cash inflows of other assets or groups of assets. At the end of year 3, when the carrying amount after depreciation is $700, the entity recognises that there has been an impairment loss of $210. The entity writes the asset down to $490. As the useful life is not affected, the entity commences amortisation at $70 per annum which, if applied in each of the years 4-10, would amortise the carrying value over the remaining useful life, as follows:

Table 1					Year					
	1	2	3	4	5	6	7	8	9	10
	$	$	$	$	$	$	$	$	$	$
NBV – beginning of the year	1,000	900	800	490	420	350	280	210	140	70
Depreciation	100	100	100	70	70	70	70	70	70	70
Impairment			210							
NBV – end of the year	900	800	490	420	350	280	210	140	70	–
NBV without impairment	900	800	700	600	500	400	300	200	100	–

At the beginning of year 5, before depreciation for the year, the asset's carrying value is $420. Thanks to improvements in technology, the entity is able to increase the asset's VIU to $550 by spending $120 on parts that improve and enhance its performance.

At the end of year 5, the asset can therefore be written up to the *lower* of:

- $600, which is the net book value of the asset after the additional expenditure, assuming that there had never been any impairment. This is the balance brought forward at the beginning of year 5 of $600 (Table 1 bottom row) plus expenditure of $120 less depreciation for the year of (720/6) = $120; and
- $550, which is the VIU at the end of year 5.

Therefore it can write the asset's net book value back up to $550. The entity can reverse $100 of the impairment write down and amortise the remaining net book value of the asset of $550 to zero over the remaining five years, year 6 to year 10, at $110 per annum (see Table 2 below).

Table 2

	Year					
	5	6	7	8	9	10
	$	$	$	$	$	$
Cost	1,000	1,120	1,120	1,120	1,120	1,120
Expenditure in the year	120					
Cost carried forward	1,120	1,120	1,120	1,120	1,120	1,120
Accumulated depreciation brought forward	580	570	680	790	900	1,010
Charge for the year (70 + 20 (120/6))	90	110	110	110	110	110
Reversal of impairment	(100)					
Accumulated depreciation carried forward	570	680	790	900	1,010	1,120
NBV	550	440	330	220	110	–

The standard includes an illustration of the reversal of an impairment loss in Example 4 of the standard's accompanying section of illustrative examples.

All reversals are to be recognised in the income statement immediately, except for revalued assets which are dealt with at 11.4.2 below. *[IAS 36.119]*.

If an impairment loss is reversed against an asset, its depreciation or amortisation is adjusted to allocate its revised carrying amount less residual value over its remaining useful life. *[IAS 36.121]*.

11.4.1 Reversals of impairments – cash-generating units

Where an entity recognises a reversal of an impairment loss on a CGU, the increase in the carrying amount of the assets of the unit should be allocated by increasing the carrying amount of the assets, other than goodwill, in the unit on a *pro rata* basis. However, the carrying amount of an individual asset should not be increased above the lower of its recoverable amount (if determinable) and the carrying amount that would have resulted had no impairment loss been recognised in prior years. Any 'surplus' reversal is to be allocated to the remaining assets *pro rata*, always remembering that goodwill, if allocated to an individual CGU, may not be increased under any circumstances. *[IAS 36.122, 123]*.

11.4.2 Reversals of impairments – revalued assets

If an asset is recognised at a revalued amount under another standard any reversal of an impairment loss should be treated as a revaluation increase under that other standard. Thus a reversal of an impairment loss on a revalued asset is credited to other comprehensive income. However, to the extent that an impairment loss on the same revalued asset was previously recognised as an expense in the income statement, a reversal of that impairment loss is recognised as income in the income statement. *[IAS 36.119, 120]*.

As with assets carried at cost, after a reversal of an impairment loss is recognised on a revalued asset, the depreciation charge should be adjusted in future periods to allocate the asset's revised carrying amount, less any residual value, on a systematic basis over its remaining useful life. *[IAS 36.121]*.

12 GROUP AND SEPARATE FINANCIAL STATEMENT ISSUES

The application of IAS 36 in group situations is not always straight forward and can give rise to a number of challenging questions. We explore some of these questions in the following sections, including:

- how to identify CGUs and relevant cash flows in the financial statements of an individual entity within a group, the consolidated financial statements of a subgroup, or when impairment testing equity accounted investments or those carried at cost; and
- whether the cash flows mentioned above need to be on an arm's length basis, i.e. at fair value, and the extent the restrictions imposed by IAS 36 need to be applied.

Note that we have used the term 'individual financial statements' for any stand-alone financial statements that apply IFRS, prepared by any entity within a group, whether or not those financial statements are within scope of IAS 27 – *Separate Financial Statements*. The term 'individual financial statements' includes separate financial statements, individual financial statements for subsidiary companies with no investments and, where the context requires, consolidated financial statements for a subgroup or, for a subgroup that does not have any subsidiaries, unconsolidated financial statements whose associates and joint ventures are accounted for using the equity method.

The distinction between individual financial statements and 'separate financial statements', a term that applies only to financial statements prepared in accordance with the provisions of IAS 27, is explained in Chapter 8 at 1.

12.1 VIU: relevant cash flows and non-arm's length prices (transfer pricing)

When it comes to impairment testing of:

- equity accounted investments;
- investments in subsidiaries, associates or joint ventures carried at cost in the separate financial statements of the parent; or
- assets/CGUs in individual group companies or subgroups financial statements,

the key questions are how to determine the cash flows for intra-group transactions and whether those cash flows need to be on an arm's length basis.

Many individual group companies or subgroups do not have truly independent cash flows because of the way in which groups allocate activities between group entities. Transactions between a parent entity and its subsidiaries, between subsidiaries within a group or between subsidiaries/parents and investments in associates and joint ventures may not be carried out on an arm's length basis. Entities may benefit from transactions entered into by others that are not reflected in their financial statements, e.g. management and other facilities provided by another group company, or may incur those expenses on their behalf without recharge.

In the context of impairment testing, this means that an entity needs to consider whether the relevant cash flows should be those actually generated by the asset (investment in subsidiary, joint venture, associate or individual asset or CGU) or those that it could generate on an arm's length basis. IAS 36 gives no clear answer to this question. There are two broad approaches, and preference for one from the other will often depend on local jurisdictions. Either:

- the VIU must be based on the cash flows directly generated under current arrangements, e.g. those received and receivable; or
- the cash flows must take into consideration the manner in which the group has organised its activities and make notional adjustments to reflect arm's length amounts.

Those arguing that notional adjustments are required, refer to the IAS 36 requirement to replace transfer prices with arm's length prices for CGUs within the same reporting entity/group once a CGU has been identified (see 7.1.6 above). *[IAS 36.70]*. The argument is that the same principle should apply in intra-group arrangements and therefore the internal transfer prices of the group entities in question should be substituted with arm's length prices. This may not be straightforward in practice, as it can be difficult to allocate arm's length prices in intra-group arrangements where there is often a 'bundle' of goods and services and where transactions may not have commercial equivalents.

A method that may work in practice, (and that should give broadly the same answer) as it reflects the arm's length prices of inputs and outputs, and therefore the substitution of transfer prices, is to start from the VIU of the CGU in the consolidated financial statements of which the subsidiary being tested for impairment is a part. This VIU could be apportioned between the various subsidiaries.

This approach rests, at least notionally, on the assumption that the group has allocated its activities between its various subsidiaries for its own benefit. Group companies may make transactions at off-market values at the request of the parent but at least in principle there would be a basis for charging arm's length prices.

It is necessary to avoid two potential pitfalls:

- taking account of a notional increase in income or VIU to one subsidiary but neglecting to reflect the notional increase in costs or loss of VIU to another; and
- including benefits or costs that cannot be converted into cash flows to the entity. This can be particularly problematic when testing goodwill, including the carrying value of investments when the purchase price reflects goodwill on acquisition. Most would consider this a constraint on the cash flows reflected in this impairment test. This may be revealed if there is a major difference between the subsidiary-based and CGU-based recoverable amount as there could be cash flows or synergies elsewhere in the group that cannot be reasonably attributed to the subsidiary or subgroup in question.

Those arguing notional adjustments are not required refer to the lack of guidance in IAS 36. The argument is that it is not clear that the same principle should apply, particularly in circumstances when using the contractual agreed cash flows would lead to an impairment which would be avoided by substitution of contractual agreed cash flows with arm's length prices.

12.2 Goodwill in individual (or subgroup) financial statements and the interaction with the group financial statements

In many jurisdictions, subsidiary entities are not exempt from preparing financial statements and these may be required to comply with IFRSs. These may be consolidated accounts for the subgroup that it heads. Such individual or subgroup financial statements might include goodwill for which an annual impairment test is required. Along with the question of whether intra-group cash flows need to be on an arm's length basis for impairment testing purposes, as discussed at 12.1 above, other principal questions are:

- how to treat synergies arising outside of the reporting entity/subgroup (see 12.2.1 below);
- whether the guidance in IFRS 8 applies in determining the level at which goodwill has to be tested for impairment in the consolidated financial statements of the subgroup or in individual financial statements (see 12.2.2 below); and
- how to deal with goodwill, arising at a subgroup level, in the group financial statements (see 12.2.3 below)?

12.2.1 Goodwill synergies arising outside of the reporting entity/subgroup

If goodwill is being tested in the consolidated subgroup or individual financial statements, it may be that the synergies that gave rise to the goodwill are in another part of the larger group because the subgroup is part of a CGU containing other subsidiary companies. It may not be possible to translate some synergies such as economies of scale into cash flows to the entity or subgroup in question. Although there is no impairment at the level of the CGU in the group consolidated financial statements, the entity may not be able to avoid writing down the goodwill in the individual or subgroup statements at the time the first impairment test is performed in the year of the acquisition. In our view, it would not be appropriate to consider synergies arising outside the individual or subgroup financial statements when testing impairment in the individual or subgroup financial statements unless these synergies would be available to market participants and therefore could be built into the FVLCD. Whether this write down needs to be recorded in the statement of profit or loss or whether it is appropriate to treat it as an equity transaction in the form of a distribution to the parent is a matter of judgement.

12.2.2 The effect of IFRS 8 – Operating segments – *when allocating goodwill to CGU's in individual (or subgroup) financial statements*

As discussed at 8.1 above, goodwill is not necessarily tested at the lowest level of CGUs (however defined in the context of these group entities or subgroups), but at the level of a CGU group at which goodwill is monitored. However, that CGU group cannot be larger than an operating segment before aggregation (see 8.1.4 above). *[IAS 36.80]*.

We believe that for the purposes of testing goodwill in the individual or subgroup's financial statements, companies must apply the guidance in IFRS 8 to determine its operating segments even if IFRS 8 is not applicable because the subsidiary (subgroup) is not public. Therefore, if the application of IFRS 8 would result in the identification of separate operating segments in the individual or subgroup's financial statements, goodwill cannot be tested for impairment at a level above the operating segments in those financial statements (i.e. the operating segments would serve as a ceiling). It would not be appropriate to apply paragraph 80 of IAS 36 in these circumstances based on the operating segments as determined by the ultimate parent entity for its consolidated financial statements.

However, the CGU/CGU group for the purposes of goodwill impairment testing could be at a level lower than the subgroup's operating segments.

Example 20.38:   A subgroup with goodwill that is not an operating segment for the group

A mining entity (group) extracts a metal ore that does not have an active market until it has been through a smelting and refining process. Each mine is held in a separate subsidiary, as is the refinery, and in two joint ventures. The refinery, subsidiaries and joint ventures are located in several different countries. The entity considers the CGU to comprise the subsidiary that holds the smelter together with the subsidiaries that hold the individual mines and the interests in the joint ventures.

The entity acquires a group of mine-holding subsidiaries in a country where there is a requirement to prepare consolidated financial statements at the highest level within that country. These consolidated financial statements, which are prepared using the acquisition method by the relevant intermediate parent, include goodwill. The entity does not consider the subgroup to be an operating segment. However, in the subgroup's financial statements, first of all the relevant operating segments would need to be determined from the subgroup's perspective. If it was concluded that from the subgroup's perspective there was only one operating segment, this would be the maximum level at which goodwill is tested for impairment in the subgroup's consolidated financial statements.

12.2.3   Acquisitions by subsidiaries and determining the level at which the group tests goodwill for impairment

IAS 36 requires goodwill to be allocated to the lowest level within the entity at which the goodwill is monitored for internal management purposes. If a subsidiary undertakes acquisitions and recognises goodwill in its own financial statements, the level at which the subsidiary's management monitors the goodwill may differ from the level at which the parent's or group's management monitors goodwill from the group's perspective.

If a subsidiary's management monitors its goodwill at a lower level than the level at which the parent's or group's management monitors its goodwill, a key issue is whether that lower level should, from the group's perspective, be regarded as the 'lowest level within the entity at which the goodwill is monitored for internal management purposes'? The answer is not necessarily, as is demonstrated in the following example.

Example 20.39:   Monitoring goodwill arising from acquisitions by subsidiaries

A parent acquired 100% of the issued shares of a company that operates autonomously and is required to prepare IFRS-compliant financial statements. The subsidiary has acquired various businesses both before and after becoming part of the group. Those business combinations have included significant amounts of goodwill.

The subsidiary's management monitors its acquired goodwill at the level of the subsidiary's operating segments identified in accordance with IFRS 8. However, management of the parent/group monitors its acquired goodwill at the level of the group's operating segments, which is a higher level than the subsidiary's operating segments. The subsidiary's operations form part of two of the group's six operating segments.

The subsidiary's goodwill comprises goodwill arising on its acquisitions, some of which took place *before*, and some *after*, the subsidiary became part of the group.

In contrast, the goodwill recognised by the group comprises:

- Goodwill acquired by the parent in the acquisition of the subsidiary;
- Goodwill acquired by the subsidiary since becoming part of the group;
- Goodwill acquired by the parent in other operating combinations (i.e. goodwill that relates to other subsidiaries and businesses that make up the group).

The goodwill acquired in the acquisition of the subsidiary that is recognised by the parent in its consolidated financial statements is therefore different from the goodwill recognised by the subsidiary (which relates only to the acquisitions made by the subsidiary itself and was measured at the date of the acquisition concerned, as any other goodwill would be internally generated goodwill from the subsidiary's perspective and therefore not recognised by the subsidiary).

In such circumstances the actions of the subsidiary's management in deciding the level at which it tests its goodwill for impairment will *not* cause the group to be 'locked in' to testing goodwill at the same level in the consolidated financial statements.

Rather, the group should test its goodwill for impairment at the level at which management of the group (i.e. of the parent) monitors its various investments in goodwill, namely, in this example, at the group's operating segment level.

12.3 Group reorganisations and the carrying value of investments in subsidiaries

A common form of group reorganisation involves the transfer of the entire business of a subsidiary to another subsidiary of the same parent. These transactions often take place at the book value of the transferor's assets rather than at fair value. If the original carrying value was a purchase price that included an element of goodwill, the remaining 'shell', i.e. an entity that no longer has any trade or activities, may have a carrying value in the parent company's statement of financial position in excess of its net worth/recoverable amount. It could be argued that as the subsidiary is now a shell with no possibility in its current state of generating sufficient profits to support its value, a loss should be recognised by the parent in its separate financial statements to reduce its investment in the shell company to its net worth/recoverable amount. However, the transfer of part of the group's business from one controlled entity to another has no substance from the perspective of the group and will have no effect in the consolidated accounts. There has also been no loss overall to the parent as a result of this reorganisation as the loss in net worth/recoverable amount in one subsidiary results in an increase in the net worth/recoverable amount in the other subsidiary.

This is, of course, a transaction between companies under common control as all of the combining entities or businesses are ultimately controlled by the same party or parties both before and after the business combination, and that control is not transitory. *[IFRS 3.B1]*. This means that the treatment by the acquirer is scoped out of IFRS 3.

From the transferor entity's perspective, the transaction combines a sale of its assets at an undervalue to the acquirer, by reference to the fair value of the transferred assets, and a distribution of the shortfall in value to its parent. The fair value of those assets to the parent may well not be reflected in the transferor's own statement of financial position because there is no push-down accounting under IFRS. The transferor is not obliged to record the 'distribution' to its parent at fair value. IFRIC 17 – *Distributions of Non-cash Assets to Owners* – issued in November 2008, requires gains or losses measured by reference to fair value of the assets distributed to be taken to profit or loss but, amongst other restrictions, excludes from its scope non-cash distributions made by wholly-owned group companies (see Chapter 8 at 2.4.2).

This interpretation of the transferor's transaction (as a sale at an undervalue and a deemed distribution to the parent) is wholly consistent with a legal analysis in some jurisdictions, for example the United Kingdom, where a company that does not have zero or positive distributable reserves is unable to sell its assets at an undervalue because it cannot make any sort of distribution.

The parent, in turn, could be seen as having made a capital contribution of the shortfall in value to the acquirer. The parent may choose to record the distribution from the transferor (and consequent impairment in its carrying value) and the contribution to the acquirer (and consequent increase in its carrying value). This is consistent with our analysis in Chapter 8 at 4.2 regarding intra-group transactions.

The acquirer will not necessarily record the capital contribution even if this is an option available to it.

However, the underlying principles are not affected by whether or not the acquirer makes this choice – there has been a transfer of value from one subsidiary to another. This demonstrates why the business transfer alone does not necessarily result in an impairment charge in the parent entity.

If the above analysis is not supportable in a particular jurisdiction then an impairment write down may have to be taken.

Actual circumstances may be less straightforward. In particular, the transferor and the acquirer may not be held directly by the same parent. This may make it necessary to record an impairment against the carrying value of the transferor ('shell') company in its intermediate parent to reflect its loss in value, which will be treated as an expense or as a distribution, depending on the policy adopted by the entity and the relevant facts and circumstances. See Chapter 8 at 4.1 for a discussion of the policy choices available to the entity. There may be another, higher level within the group at which the above arguments against impairment will apply.

Example 20.40: Group reorganisations and impairment

Topco has two directly held subsidiaries, Tradeco and Shellco. It acquired Shellco for £30 million and immediately thereafter transferred all of its trade and assets to its fellow subsidiary Tradeco for book value of £10 million with the proceeds being left outstanding on intercompany account. Shellco now has net assets of £10 million (its intercompany receivable) but a carrying value in Topco of £30 million. On the other hand, the value of Tradeco has been enhanced by its purchase of the business at an undervalue.

In our view, there are two acceptable ways in which Tradeco may account for this. The cost of the investment in Tradeco's individual financial statements may be the fair value of the cash given as consideration, i.e. £10 million. Alternatively, it is the fair value of the cash given as consideration (£10 million), together with a deemed capital contribution received from Topco for the difference up to the fair value of the business of Shellco of £20 million, which will be recognised in equity, giving a total consideration of £30 million.

The capital contribution measured under the second method represents the value distributed by Shellco to its parent Topco and thence to Tradeco. Meanwhile Topco could record a transfer of £20 million from the carrying value of Shellco to the carrying value of Tradeco.

If there is an intermediate holding company between Topco and Shellco but all other facts remain the same, then it would appear that an impairment ought to be made against the carrying value of Shellco in its immediate parent, which will be treated as an expense or as a distribution, depending on the policy adopted by the entity and the relevant facts and circumstances. The argument against impairment would still apply in Topco.

12.4 Investments in subsidiaries, associates and joint ventures

Investments in subsidiaries, associates and joint ventures carried at cost in separate financial statements of the parent and equity accounted investments are within the scope of IAS 36.

While a parent entity could elect to account for investments in subsidiaries, associates and joint ventures under IFRS 9, most parent entities choose to carry these investments at cost as permitted by IAS 27. *[IAS 36.4, IAS 27.10]*. IAS 27 was amended in 2014 to give parent entities the option to use the equity method to account for these investments in an entity's separate financial statements.

The recoverable amount for investments carried at cost or under the use of the equity method is the higher of FVLCD and VIU. Specific questions around FVLCD are dealt with at 12.4.1 below. Challenges in respect of VIU for investments carried at cost or under the equity method are dealt with at 12.4.2 below.

It is important to note that testing an investment in an associate or joint venture carried under the equity method using IAS 28 in group financial statements cannot always provide assurance about the recoverability of the cost of shares in the investor's separate financial statements, if they are carried at cost. *[IAS 27.10(a)]*. Accounting for the group's share of losses may take the equity interest below cost and an impairment test could reveal no need for an impairment loss in the consolidated financial statements. This might not necessarily provide any assurance about the (higher) carrying value of the shares in the separate financial statements.

12.4.1 Fair value less costs of disposal (FVLCD) for investments in subsidiaries, associates and joint ventures

In order to establish FVLCD an entity must apply IFRS 13's requirements as outlined at 6 above and described in detail in Chapter 14.

If an entity holds a position in a single asset or liability that is traded in an active market, IFRS 13 requires an entity to measure fair value using that price, without adjustment. This requirement is accepted when the asset or liability being measured is a financial instrument in the scope of IFRS 9. However, when an entity holds an investment in a subsidiary, joint venture or associate the question is what the unit of account is, the individual shares or the investment as a whole, and whether it would be appropriate to include a control premium when determining fair value provided that market participants take this into consideration when pricing the asset. See 6.1.1 above and Chapter 14 at 5.1.1 for considerations and recent developments in respect of this.

Unlike investments with quoted prices, discussed above, there are less issues if FVLCD is used to determine the recoverable amount of an asset that does not have a quoted price in an active market and is either:

- an investment in a subsidiary, joint venture or associate; or
- a CGU comprising the investment's underlying assets.

Using FVLCD may avoid some of the complexities of determining appropriate cash flows because of transfer pricing and other intra-group transaction issues, described in 12.1 above and 12.4.2 below.

12.4.2 VIU for investments in subsidiaries, associates and joint ventures

Unlike most other assets, an investment in a subsidiary, joint venture or associate can be viewed as either:

- an individual asset that can generate income, e.g. in the form of dividends; or
- as an asset that represents the underlying assets and liabilities that are under the control of the subsidiary, joint venture or the associate.

IAS 28 acknowledges this by stating:

'In determining the value in use of the investment, an entity estimates:

(a) its share of the present value of the estimated future cash flows expected to be generated by the associate or joint venture, including the cash flows from the operations of the associate or joint venture and the proceeds on the ultimate disposal of the investment; or

(b) the present value of the estimated future cash flows expected to arise from dividends to be received from the investment and from its ultimate disposal.

Under appropriate assumptions, both methods give the same result.' *[IAS 28.42]*.

This means that there are broadly two approaches in testing for impairment: one focuses on the investment and the cash flows the parent receives (dividends and ultimate disposal proceeds) and the other considers the recoverable amount of the underlying assets of the investment and the cash flows generated by these assets. These two approaches are considered at 12.4.2.A and 12.4.2.B below respectively. Whichever view is taken, the entity needs to ensure that the cash flows are appropriate (see 12.1 above in respect of considerations around intra-group transfer pricing).

It is important to note that, whether an entity calculates VIU using its share of the present value of estimated cash flows of the underlying assets or the dividends expected to be received, it is necessary to adjust them to reflect IAS 36 restrictions, e.g. those in respect of improvements and enhancements (see 7.1.2 above), restructuring (see 7.1.3 above), growth (see 7.1 and 7.1.1 above) and discount rates (see 7.2 above). A practical challenge may be to obtain sufficiently detailed information to make such adjustments for investments in entities that are not controlled by the parent, in which case the entity may have to use FVLCD to establish the recoverable amount.

12.4.2.A VIU of investments in subsidiaries, associates and joint ventures using dividend discount models

IAS 28 allows the VIU of the equity accounted interest to be based on the present value of the estimated future cash flows expected to arise from dividends to be received from the investment. *[IAS 28.42]*. This describes in broad terms what is also known as a dividend discount model (DDM). DDMs are financial models frequently used by financial institutions to value shares at the discounted value of future dividend payments. These models value a company on the basis of future cash flows that may be distributed to the shareholders in compliance with the capital requirements provided by law, discounted at a rate expressing the cost and risk of capital. By analogy this approach can be used to calculate the VIU for investments in subsidiaries, associates and joint ventures carried at cost in the separate financial statements of a parent and for equity accounted investments.

The Interpretations Committee considered the use of DDMs in testing for impairment under IAS 36. The Interpretations Committee rejected 'in general' the use of DDMs as an appropriate basis for calculating the VIU of a CGU in consolidated financial statements.[2] It was of the view that calculations using DDMs may be appropriate when calculating the VIU of a single asset, for example when determining whether an investment is impaired in the separate financial statements of an entity. It did not consider whether the cash flows used in the DDMs should be adjusted to reflect IAS 36 assumptions and restrictions, as discussed more fully under 12.4.2 above. However, in order to use a DDM for calculating VIU, IAS 36's requirements should be reflected in the future dividends calculated for use in the model.

12.4.2.B VIU of investments in subsidiaries, associates and joint ventures based on cash flows generated by underlying assets

When testing investments in subsidiaries, associates and joint ventures based on cash flows generated by underlying assets entities need to ensure that the cash flows are appropriate (see 12.1 above in respect of intra-group transfer pricing) and that the restrictions of IAS 36 are appropriately applied (see 12.4.2 above).

If an entity is testing its investments in subsidiaries, associates and joint ventures for impairment and it can demonstrate that the investment contains one or more CGUs in their entirety then it may in some circumstances be able to use the results of the group impairment tests of the underlying CGUs to test the investment for impairment. If the aggregate VIU (or FVLCD) of the CGU or CGUs is not less than the carrying value of the investment, then the investment may not be impaired. Note that the entity's investment reflects the net assets of the subsidiary, associates or joint venture while the CGU reflects the assets and liabilities on a gross basis, so appropriate adjustments will have to be made. In addition, when it comes to investments in associates and joint ventures, an investor with a minority holding will need to assess the impact of holding a minority stake without control.

It may not be so straightforward in practice. There are particular problems if the asset (the investment) and the underlying CGU are not the same. CGUs may overlap individual subsidiaries so, for example, a single CGU may contain more than one such subsidiary. Even if the CGU and investment coincide, the shares may have been acquired in a business combination. It is quite possible that the synergies that gave rise to goodwill on acquisition are in another part of the group not controlled by the intermediate parent in question. In such a case an entity might not be able to use the result of the group impairment test and so would have to calculate the recoverable amount of the investment.

12.4.3 Equity accounted investment and indicators of impairment

In connection with issuing IFRS 9, the IASB amended IAS 28 to include the impairment indicators an entity needs to use to determine whether it is necessary to recognise any additional impairment loss once it has accounted for losses, if any, under IAS 28. *[IAS 28.40-41A]*. These impairment indicators are the same indicators as previously stated in IAS 39 – *Financial Instruments: Recognition and Measurement* – for financial assets.

The indicators of impairment require 'objective evidence of impairment as a result of one or more events that have occurred after the initial recognition'. *[IAS 28.41A]*. However, one would not expect any significant difference in the impairment indicators under IAS 36 and IAS 28 because both look for objective evidence, sometimes in virtually identical terms and neither claims that its list of indicators is exclusive. *[IAS 36.13, IAS 28.41A]*. This means that an impairment test should not be avoided because an impairment indicator is not mentioned specifically in IAS 28.

If an entity has reason to believe that the carrying amount of an investment in an associate or joint venture is higher than the recoverable amount, this is most likely a sufficient indicator on its own to require an impairment test.

12.4.4 Equity accounted investments and long term loans

Investors frequently make long-term loans to associates or joint ventures that, from their perspective, form part of the net investment in the associate or joint venture. Under previous IFRS guidance, it was not clear whether these should be accounted for, and in particular tested for impairment, as part of the net investment under IAS 28 and IAS 36, or as stand-alone investments by applying the requirements of IFRS 9.

After receiving a request related to the interaction between IFRS 9 and IAS 28 and whether the measurement of long-term interests that form part of the net investment in associates and joint ventures should be governed by IFRS 9, IAS 28 or a combination of both, the IASB, in its October 2016 meeting, tentatively decided to propose amendments to IAS 28 to clarify that an entity applies IFRS 9, in addition to IAS 28, to long-term interests that form part of the net investment and to include the proposed amendments in the next cycle of annual improvements (2015–2017). However, in May 2017 the Board decided to finalise the amendments as a narrow scope amendment in its own right.

The amendments clarify that an entity applies IFRS 9 to long-term interests in an associate or joint venture to which the equity method is not applied but that, in substance, form part of the net investment in the associate or joint venture. This clarification is relevant because it implies that the expected credit loss model in IFRS 9 applies to such long-term interests.

The Board also clarified that, in applying IFRS 9, an entity does not take account of any losses of the associate or joint venture, or any impairment losses on the net investment, recognised as adjustments to the net investment in the associate or joint venture that arise from applying IAS 28.

To illustrate how entities apply the requirements in IAS 28 and IFRS 9 with respect to long-term interests, the Board also published an illustrative example when it issued the amendments.

The amendments were effective for periods beginning on or after 1 January 2019. Earlier application was permitted.

The amendments are to be applied retrospectively but they provide transition requirements similar to those in IFRS 9 for entities that apply the amendments after they first apply IFRS 9.

12.4.5 Equity accounted investments and CGUs

IAS 28 states that the recoverable amount of an investment in an associate or a joint venture should be assessed for each associate or joint venture, unless it does not generate cash inflows from continuing use that are largely independent of those from other assets of the entity. *[IAS 28.43]*. This means that each associate or joint venture is a separate CGU unless it is part of a larger CGU including other assets, which could include other associates or joint ventures.

Example 20.41: Joint ventures are part of larger CGU

A mining entity (group) extracts a metal ore that does not have an active market until it has been through a smelting and refining process. Each mine is held in a separate subsidiary, as is the refinery, and in two joint ventures. The refinery, subsidiaries and joint ventures are located in several different countries. The entity considers the CGU to comprise the subsidiary that holds the smelter together with the subsidiaries that hold the individual mines and the interests in the joint ventures.

If there is goodwill in the carrying amount of an associate or joint venture, this is not tested separately. *[IAS 28.42]*. However, there may be additional goodwill in the group that will be allocated to a CGU that includes an associate or joint venture, that will be tested for impairment by reference to the combined cash flows of assets and associates and joint ventures.

12.4.6 Equity accounted investments and testing goodwill for impairment

When calculating its share of an equity accounted investee's results, an investor makes adjustments to the investee's profit or loss to reflect depreciation and impairments of the investee's identifiable assets based on their fair values at the date the investor acquired its investment. This is covered in IAS 28 which states that:

> 'Appropriate adjustments to the investor's share of the associate's or joint venture's profits or losses after acquisition are also made to account, for example, for depreciation of the depreciable assets, based on their fair values at the acquisition date. Similarly, appropriate adjustments to the investor's share of the associate's or joint venture's profits or losses after acquisition are made for impairment losses recognised by the associate, such as for goodwill or property, plant and equipment.' *[IAS 28.32]*.

Although this refers to 'appropriate adjustments' for goodwill impairment losses, this should not be interpreted as requiring the investor to recalculate the goodwill impairment on a similar basis to depreciation and impairment of tangible and intangible assets. The 'appropriate adjustment' is to reverse that goodwill impairment that relates to pre-acquisition goodwill in the investee before calculating the investor's share of the investee's profit. After application of the equity method the entire equity-accounted carrying amount of the investor's investment, including the goodwill included in that carrying amount, is tested for impairment in accordance with IAS 28. *[IAS 28.40-43]*. Note that there is no requirement to test investments in associates or joint ventures for impairment annually but only when there are indicators that the amount may not be recoverable. These requirements are described in detail in Chapter 11 at 9.

Impairment write-offs made against investments accounted for under the equity method may be reversed if an impairment loss no longer exists or has decreased (see 11.4 above). Although IAS 36 does not allow impairments of goodwill to be reversed, *[IAS 36.124]*, this impairment is not a write-off against goodwill, but a write-off against the equity investment, so this prohibition does not apply. IAS 28 states that 'an impairment loss recognised in those circumstances is not allocated to any asset, including goodwill, that forms part of the carrying amount of the investment in the associate or joint venture. Accordingly, any reversal of that impairment loss is recognised in accordance with IAS 36 to the extent that the recoverable amount of the investment subsequently increases'. *[IAS 28.42]*.

13 DISCLOSURES REQUIRED BY IAS 36

13.1 Introduction

This section sets out the principal disclosures for impairment required in financial statements as set out in IAS 36. Any disclosures required relating to impairment by other standards are dealt with in the chapters concerned. Disclosures that may be required by other authorities such as national statutes or listing authorities are not included.

13.2 IAS 36 disclosures

The disclosures required fall into two broad categories:

(i) disclosures concerning any actual impairment losses or reversals made in the period, that are obviously only required if such a loss or reversal has occurred, regardless of the type of asset involved; and

(ii) yearly disclosures concerning the annual impairment tests required for goodwill and intangible assets with an indefinite useful life, that are required regardless of whether an impairment adjustment to these types of assets has occurred or not.

13.2.1 Disclosures required for impairment losses or reversals

For each class of assets the entity must disclose:

'(a) the amount of impairment losses recognised in profit or loss during the period and the line item(s) of the statement of comprehensive income in which those impairment losses are included.

(b) the amount of reversals of impairment losses recognised in profit or loss during the period and the line item(s) of the statement of comprehensive income in which those impairment losses are reversed.

(c) the amount of impairment losses on revalued assets recognised directly in other comprehensive income during the period.

(d) the amount of reversals of impairment losses on revalued assets recognised directly in other comprehensive income during the period.' *[IAS 36.126]*.

A class of assets is a grouping of assets of similar nature and use in an entity's operations. *[IAS 36.127]*.

These disclosures can be made as an integral part of the other disclosures, for example the property, plant and equipment note reconciling the opening and closing values (as set out in Chapter 18 at 8) may contain the required information. *[IAS 36.128]*.

Additionally, IAS 36 links disclosure of impairments with segment disclosures. Thus, if an entity reports segment information in accordance with IFRS 8 then any impairments or reversals must be disclosed by reportable segment as follows:

(a) the amount of impairment losses recognised in profit or loss and directly in other comprehensive income during the period; and

(b) the amount of reversals of impairment losses recognised in profit or loss and directly in other comprehensive income during the period. *[IAS 36.129]*.

13.2.2 Material impairments

If an impairment loss for an individual asset or a cash-generating unit is recognised or reversed during the period and is material to the financial statements of the reporting entity as a whole, the following disclosures are required:

(a) the events and circumstances that led to the recognition or reversal of the impairment loss;

(b) the amount of the impairment loss recognised or reversed;

(c) for an individual asset:
  (i) the nature of the asset; and
  (ii) if the entity reports segmental information in accordance with IFRS 8, the reportable segment to which the asset belongs.

(d) for a cash-generating unit:
  (i) a description of the cash-generating unit (such as whether it is a product line, a plant, a business operation, a geographical area, or a reportable segment as defined in IFRS 8);
  (ii) the amount of the impairment loss recognised or reversed by class of assets and if the entity reports segment information in accordance with IFRS 8, by reportable segment; and
  (iii) if the aggregation of assets for identifying the cash-generating unit has changed since the previous estimate of the cash-generating unit's recoverable amount (if any), a description of the current and former way of aggregating assets and the reasons for changing the way the cash-generating unit is identified.

(e) the recoverable amount of the asset or CGU and whether the recoverable amount of the asset or cash-generating unit is its fair value less costs of disposal (FVLCD) or its value in use (VIU);

(f) if the recoverable amount is FVLCD:
  (i) the level of the fair value hierarchy (as defined by IFRS 13, see 6.1 above) within which the fair value measurement of the asset or CGU is classified, without taking into account whether the costs of disposal are observable;
  (ii) if the fair value measurement is classified as Level 2 or Level 3 of the fair value hierarchy, a description of the valuation technique(s) used to measure FVLCD. The entity must disclose any change in valuation technique and the reason(s) for making such a change; and
  (iii) if the fair value measurement is classified as Level 2 or Level 3 of the fair value hierarchy, each key assumption on which management has based its determination of fair value less costs of disposal. Key assumptions are those to which the asset's or CGU's recoverable amount is most sensitive.

  The entity must also disclose the discount rate(s) used in the current measurement and previous measurement if FVLCD is measured using a present value technique; and

(g) if the recoverable amount is VIU, the discount rate used in the current estimate and previous estimate (if any) of VIU. *[IAS 36.130]*.

It is logically possible for impairment adjustments in aggregate to be material, yet no single one material in itself, in which case the previous requirement that relates to individual assets or CGUs could theoretically be circumvented. Therefore, the following 'catch all' requirement is added:

> 'An entity shall disclose the following information for the aggregate impairment losses and the aggregate reversals of impairment losses recognised during the period for which no information is disclosed in accordance with paragraph 130:
>
> (a) the main classes of assets affected by impairment losses and the main classes of assets affected by reversals of impairment losses.
>
> (b) the main events and circumstances that led to the recognition of these impairment losses and reversals of impairment losses.' *[IAS 36.131]*.

In addition, in these circumstances, if there are any cases of impairment adjustments where intangible assets with indefinite useful life and goodwill are not involved, IAS 36 encourages the disclosure of key assumptions made in the recoverable amount calculations used to determine any impairments recognised in the period. *[IAS 36.132]*. However, as set out below, an entity is required to give this type of disclosure when goodwill or intangible assets with an indefinite useful life are tested for impairment.

13.3 Annual impairment disclosures required for goodwill and intangible assets with an indefinite useful life

Paragraph 84 of IAS 36 accepts that following a business combination it may not have been possible to allocate all the goodwill to individual CGUs or groups of CGUs by the end of the period in which the acquisition has been made (see 8.1.5 above). In these circumstances the standard requires that the amount of any such unallocated goodwill be disclosed, together with the reasons why it has not been allocated. *[IAS 36.133]*.

The annual disclosures are intended to provide the user with information about the types of estimates that have been used in arriving at the recoverable amounts of goodwill and intangible assets with an indefinite useful life, that are included in the assets of the entity at the period end. They are divided into two broad categories:

(i) those concerning individual CGUs or group of CGUs in which the carrying amount of goodwill or of intangible assets with an indefinite useful life is 'significant' in comparison with the entity's total carrying amount of these items. In this category disclosures are to be made separately for each significant CGU or group of CGUs; and

(ii) those concerning CGUs or groups of CGUs in which the carrying amount of goodwill or of intangible assets with an indefinite useful life is not 'significant' individually in comparison with the entity's total carrying amount of these items. In this case the disclosures can be made in aggregate.

For each cash-generating unit or group of units for which the carrying amount of goodwill or intangible assets with indefinite useful lives allocated to that unit or group of units is significant, the following disclosures are required every year:

(a) the carrying amount of goodwill allocated to the CGU (group of CGUs);
(b) the carrying amount of intangible assets with indefinite useful lives allocated to the CGU (group of CGUs);
(c) the basis on which the CGU's or group of CGUs' recoverable amount has been determined (i.e. VIU or FVLCD):
(d) if the CGU's or group of CGUs' recoverable amount is based on VIU:
   (i) a description of each key assumption on which management has based its cash flow projections for the period covered by the most recent budgets/forecasts. Key assumptions are those to which the unit's (group of units') recoverable amount is most sensitive;
   (ii) a description of management's approach to determining the value(s) assigned to each key assumption, whether those value(s) reflect past experience or, if appropriate, are consistent with external sources of information, and, if not, how and why they differ from past experience or external sources of information;
   (iii) the period over which management has projected cash flows based on financial budgets/forecasts approved by management and, when a period greater than five years is used for a cash-generating unit (group of units), an explanation of why that longer period is justified;
   (iv) the growth rate used to extrapolate cash flow projections beyond the period covered by the most recent budgets/forecasts, and the justification for using any growth rate that exceeds the long-term average growth rate for the products, industries, or country or countries in which the entity operates, or for the market to which the unit (group of units) is dedicated;
   (v) the discount rate(s) applied to the cash flow projections.
(e) if the CGU's or group of CGUs' recoverable amount is based on FVLCD, the valuation technique(s) used to measure FVLCD. An entity is not required to provide the disclosures required by IFRS 13. If fair value less costs of disposal is not measured using a quoted price for an identical CGU or CGU group, an entity must disclose the following information:
   (i) a description of each key assumption on which management has based its determination of FVLCD. Key assumptions are those to which the unit's (group of units') recoverable amount is most sensitive;
   (ii) a description of management's approach to determining the value(s) assigned to each key assumption, whether those value(s) reflect past experience or, if appropriate, are consistent with external sources of information, and, if not, how and why they differ from past experience or external sources of information;
      (iiA) the level of the fair value hierarchy (see IFRS 13) within which the fair value measurement is categorised in its entirety (without giving regard to the observability of 'costs of disposal');
      (iiB) if there has been a change in valuation technique, the change and the reason(s) for making it;

If FVLCD is determined using discounted cash flow projections, the following information shall also be disclosed:

(iii) the period over which management has projected cash flows;

(iv) the growth rate used to extrapolate cash flow projections;

(v) the discount rate(s) applied to the cash flow projections.

(f) if a reasonably possible change in a key assumption on which management has based its determination of the CGU's or group of CGUs' recoverable amount would cause the CGU's or group of CGUs' carrying amount to exceed its recoverable amount:

(i) the amount by which the CGU's or group of CGUs' recoverable amount exceeds its carrying amount;

(ii) the value assigned to the key assumption;

(iii) the amount by which the value assigned to the key assumption must change, after incorporating any consequential effects of that change on the other variables used to measure recoverable amount, in order for the CGU's or group of CGUs' recoverable amount to be equal to its carrying amount. *[IAS 36.134]*.

As set out above, there are separate disclosure requirements for those CGUs or groups of CGUs that taken individually do not have significant amounts of goodwill in comparison with the total carrying value of goodwill or of intangible assets with an indefinite useful life. *[IAS 36.135]*.

First, an aggregate disclosure has to be made of the 'not significant' amounts of goodwill or of intangible assets with an indefinite useful life. If some or all of the carrying amount of goodwill or intangible assets with indefinite useful lives is allocated across multiple CGUs or group of CGUs, and the amount so allocated to each CGU or group of CGUs is not significant in comparison with the entity's total carrying amount of goodwill or intangible assets with indefinite useful lives, that fact shall be disclosed, together with the aggregate carrying amount of goodwill or intangible assets with indefinite useful lives allocated to those CGUs or group of CGUs.

In addition, if the recoverable amounts of any of those CGUs or group of CGUs are based on the same key assumption(s) and the aggregate carrying amount of goodwill or intangible assets with indefinite useful lives allocated to them is significant in comparison with the entity's total carrying amount of goodwill or intangible assets with indefinite useful lives, an entity shall disclose that fact, together with:

(a) the aggregate carrying amount of goodwill allocated to those CGUs or group of CGUs);
(b) the aggregate carrying amount of intangible assets with indefinite useful lives allocated to those CGUs or group of CGUs;
(c) a description of the key assumption(s);
(d) a description of management's approach to determining the value(s) assigned to the key assumption(s), whether those value(s) reflect past experience or, if appropriate, are consistent with external sources of information, and, if not, how and why they differ from past experience or external sources of information;
(e) if a reasonably possible change in the key assumption(s) would cause the aggregate of the CGU's or group of CGUs' carrying amounts to exceed the aggregate of their recoverable amounts:
   (i) the amount by which the aggregate of the CGU's or group of CGUs' recoverable amounts exceeds the aggregate of their carrying amounts;
   (ii) the value(s) assigned to the key assumption(s);
   (iii) the amount by which the value(s) assigned to the key assumption(s) must change, after incorporating any consequential effects of the change on the other variables used to measure recoverable amount, in order for the aggregate of the CGU's or group of CGUs' recoverable amounts to be equal to the aggregate of their carrying amounts. *[IAS 36.135]*.

Example 9 in IAS 36's Illustrative Examples gives an indication of the types of assumptions and other relevant information the IASB envisages being disclosed under this requirement. The IASB expects disclosure of: budgeted gross margins, average gross margins, expected efficiency improvements, whether values assigned to key assumptions reflect past experience, what improvements management believes are reasonably achievable each year, forecast exchange rates during the budget period, forecast consumer price indices during the budget period for raw materials, market share and anticipated growth in market share. If a reasonable possible change in a key assumption would cause the CGU's carrying amount to exceed its recoverable amount then the standard would require an entity to give disclose the value assigned to this key assumption and the amount by which the value assigned to the key assumption must change in order to cause an impairment. *[IAS 36.134(f)(ii)]*.

An example of disclosures including key assumptions and sensitivities is given by Vodafone Group Plc. The following extract from the annual report of Vodafone plc focuses on the current period disclosures. While disclosures for comparative years are required, and given by Vodafone in the annual report, these were for simplicity purposes not included in the following extract.

Extract 20.2: Vodafone Group Plc (2020)

Notes to the consolidated financial statements [extract]

4. Impairment losses [extract]

Impairment losses

Following our annual impairment review, the impairment charges recognised in the consolidated income statement within operating profit are stated below. Further detail on the events and circumstances that led to the recognition of the impairment charges is included later in this note.

Cash-generating unit	Reportable segment	2020 €m	2019 €m	2018 €m
Spain	Spain	840	2,930	–
Ireland	Other Europe	630	–	–
Romania	Other Europe	110	310	–
Vodafone Automotive	Common Functions	105	30	–
Vodafone Idea	Other Markets		255	–
		1,685	3,525	–

For the year ended 31 March 2019, the Group recorded a loss on disposal of Vodafone India of €3,420 million, including a loss on disposal of €1,276 million and a foreign exchange loss of €2,079 million which is included in discontinued operations. See note 27 "Acquisitions and disposals" for further details.

For the year ended 31 March 2018, the Group recorded a non-cash charge of €3,170 million (€2,245 million net of tax), included in discontinued operations, as a result of the re-measurement of Vodafone India's fair value less costs of disposal.

Goodwill

The remaining carrying value of goodwill at 31 March was as follows:

	2020 €m	2019 €m
Germany	22,900	12,479
Italy	2,480	3,654
	25,380	16,133
Other	5,891	7,220
	31,271	23,353

Key assumptions used in the value in use calculations

The key assumptions used in determining the value in use are:

Assumption	How determined
Projected adjusted EBITDA	Projected adjusted EBITDA has been based on past experience adjusted for the following: – In Europe, mobile revenue is expected to benefit from increased usage as customers transition to higher data bundles, and new products and services are introduced. Fixed revenue is expected to continue to grow as penetration is increased and more products and services are sold to customers; – In the Rest of the World, revenue is expected to continue to grow as the penetration of faster data-enabled devices rises along with higher data bundle attachment rates, and new products and services are introduced. The segment is also expected to benefit from increased usage and penetration of M-Pesa in Africa; and – Margins are expected to be impacted by negative factors such as the cost of acquiring and retaining customers in increasingly competitive markets and by positive factors such as the efficiencies expected from the implementation of Group initiatives.

Projected capital expenditure	The cash flow forecasts for capital expenditure are based on past experience and include the ongoing capital expenditure required to increase capacity, meet the population coverage requirements of certain of the Group's licences and facilitate the continued growth in revenue and EBITDA discussed above. In Europe, capital expenditure is required to roll out capacity-building next generation 5G and gigabit networks. In the Rest of the World, capital expenditure will be required for the continued rollout of current and next generation mobile networks in emerging markets. Capital expenditure includes cash outflows for the purchase of property, plant and equipment and computer software.
Projected licence and spectrum payments	To enable the continued provision of products and services, the cash flow forecasts for licence and spectrum payments for each relevant cash-generating unit include amounts for expected renewals and newly available spectrum. Beyond the five year forecast period, a long-run cost of spectrum is assumed.
Long-term growth rate	For the purposes of the Group's value in use calculations, a long-term growth rate into perpetuity is applied immediately at the end of the five year forecast period and is based on the lower of: – the nominal GDP growth rate forecasts for the country of operation; and – the long-term compound annual growth rate in adjusted EBITDA as estimated by management. Long-term compound annual growth rates determined by management may be lower than forecast nominal GDP growth rates due to the following market-specific factors: competitive intensity levels, maturity of business, regulatory environment or sector-specific inflation expectations.
Pre-tax risk adjusted discount rate	The discount rate applied to the cash flows of each of the Group's cash-generating units is generally based on the risk free rate for ten year bonds issued by the government in the respective market. Where government bond rates contain a material component of credit risk, high-quality local corporate bond rates may be used. These rates are adjusted for a risk premium to reflect both the increased risk of investing in equities and the systematic risk of the specific cash-generating unit. In making this adjustment, inputs required are the equity market risk premium (that is the required return over and above a risk free rate by an investor who is investing in the market as a whole) and the risk adjustment, beta, applied to reflect the risk of the specific cash-generating unit relative to the market as a whole. In determining the risk adjusted discount rate, management has applied an adjustment for the systematic risk to each of the Group's cash-generating companies determined using an average of the betas of comparable listed telecommunications companies and, where available and appropriate, across a specific territory. Management has used a forward-looking equity market risk premium that takes into consideration both studies by independent economists, the long-term average equity market risk premium and the market risk premiums typically used by valuations practitioners. The risk adjusted discount rate is also based on typical leverage ratios of telecommunications companies in each cash-generating unit's respective market or region.

Year ended 31 March 2020

For the year ended 31 March 2020, the Group recorded impairment charges of €0.8 billion, €0.6 billion, €0.1 billion and €0.1 billion with respect to the Group's investments in Spain, Ireland, Romania and Vodafone Automotive respectively. The impairment charges relate solely to goodwill and are recognised in the consolidated income statement within operating profit/(loss). The recoverable amounts for Spain, Ireland, Romania and Vodafone Automotive are €5.6 billion, €1.2 billion, €0.9 billion and €0.0 billion respectively, and based on value in use calculations.

The COVID-19 outbreak has developed rapidly in early 2020. Many countries have required businesses to limit or suspend operations and implemented travel restrictions and quarantine measures. The measures taken to contain the virus have adversely affected economic activity and disrupted many businesses. As the outbreak continues to progress and evolve, it is extremely challenging to predict the full extent and duration of its impact on Vodafone's businesses and the countries where Vodafone operates. Based on information available as at 31 March 2020, management has made additional adjustments to the five year business plans used in the Group's impairment testing in order to reflect the estimated impact. The impairment charges recognised and discussed immediately below, are based on expected cash flows after applying these adjustments.

Challenging trading and economic conditions in Spain materialised in the prior financial year and management recognised an impairment charge following a reduction in projected cash flows. During the year ended 31 March 2020 there has been an observable repositioning towards low-cost brands and competitive intensity within the multi-branded market is expected to remain elevated in the medium term. These factors have led to management projecting lower cash flows and recognising an impairment charge with respect to the Group's investment in Spain.

The impairment charge recognised with respect to Ireland is attributable to increased competition and the aforementioned increased economic uncertainty. As a consequence, growth and ARPUs are expected to be lower. Management has reflected these assumptions in expected cash flows.

The impairment charges recognised with respect to Romania and Vodafone Automotive reflect management's latest assessment of likely trading and economic conditions in the five year business plan. Management's view of the long-term potential in these markets remains unchanged.

The European Liberty Global assets acquired in July 2019 (see note 27) have been subsumed within existing cash-generating units in Germany, Czech Republic, Hungary and Romania. The primary reason for acquiring the businesses was to create a converged national provider of digital infrastructure in Germany, together with creating converged communications operators in the Czech Republic, Hungary and Romania. Following the integration of the acquired businesses, management considers the cash flows within these cash-generating units to be largely interdependent and monitors performance on a country-level basis.

On 31 March 2020, the Group merged its passive tower infrastructure in Italy with INWIT (see note 27). On the date of the merger, management monitored performance of its operations in Italy on a country-wide basis and considered Vodafone Italy, including its passive tower infrastructure, to be one cash-generating unit for the purpose of impairment testing as at 31 March 2020. No impairment in relation to Vodafone Italy would be necessary if impairment testing was performed on a post-merger basis at 31 March 2020.

Value in use assumptions

The table below shows key assumptions used in the value in use calculations.

	Assumptions used in value in use calculation					
	Germany %	Italy %	Spain %	Ireland %	Romania %	Vodafone Automotive %
Pre-tax risk adjusted discount rate	7.5	10.3	9.2	7.6	10.2	9.1
Long-term growth rate	0.5	0.5	0.5	0.5	1.0	1.9
Projected adjusted EBITDA[1]	3.8	0.2	8.2	3.0	8.0	31.3
Projected capital expenditure[2]	20.1-20.7	12.5-13.4	16.2-18.1	10.7-15.2	13.7-18.5	14.1-23.4

Sensitivity analysis

The estimated recoverable amount of the Group's operations in Germany and Italy exceed their carrying values by €6.6 billion and €1.8 billion respectively. If the assumptions used in the impairment review were changed to a greater extent than as presented in the following table, the changes would, in isolation, lead to an impairment loss being recognised for the year ended 31 March 2020.

	Change required for carrying value to equal recoverable amount	
	Germany pps	Italy pps
Pre-tax risk adjusted discount rate	1.1	1.7
Long-term growth rate	(1.0)	(2.0)
Projected adjusted EBITDA[1]	(3.2)	(3.1)
Projected capital expenditure[2]	11.4	7.9

Management considered the following reasonably possible changes in the key adjusted EBITDA[1] and long-term growth rate assumptions, leaving all other assumptions unchanged. Due to increased uncertainty following the COVID-19 outbreak, management has widened the range of reasonably possible changes in the key adjusted EBITDA growth rate assumption to plus or minus 5 percentage points (2019: 2 percentage points). The sensitivity analysis presented is prepared on the basis that the reasonably possible change in each key assumption would not have a consequential impact on other assumptions used in the impairment review. The associated impact on the impairment assessment is presented in the table below, with the exception of Vodafone Automotive, where no reasonably possible change in the key assumptions would materially change the impairment charge recognised.

Management believes that no reasonably possible or foreseeable change in the pre-tax adjusted discount rate or projected capital expenditure[2] would cause the difference between the carrying value and recoverable amount for any cash-generating unit to be materially different to the base case disclosed below.

	Recoverable amount less carrying value (prior to recognition of impairment charges)				
	Germany €bn	Italy €bn	Spain €bn	Ireland €bn	Romania €bn
Base case as at 31 March 2020	6.6	1.8	(0.8)	(0.6)	(0.1)
Change in projected adjusted EBITDA[1]					
Decrease by 5pps	(3.3)	(1.0)	(2.3)	(1.1)	(0.3)
Increase by 5pps	18.4	5.1	0.9	–	0.1
Change in long-term growth rate					
Decrease by 1pps	0.2	0.8	(1.5)	(0.8)	(0.2)
Increase by 1pps	15.8	3.0	–	(0.4)	–

The carrying values for Vodafone UK, Portugal, Czech Republic and Hungary include goodwill arising from acquisitions and/or the purchase of operating licences or spectrum rights. While the recoverable amounts for these operating companies are not materially greater than their carrying value, each has a lower risk of giving rise to an impairment that would be material to the Group given their relative size or the composition of their carrying value.

If the assumptions used in the impairment review were changed to a greater extent than as presented in the following table, the changes would, in isolation, lead to an impairment loss being recognised in the year ended 31 March 2020.

	Change required for carrying value to equal recoverable amount			
	UK pps	Portugal pps	Czech Republic pps	Hungary pps
Pre-tax risk adjusted discount rate	1.1	1.5	1.7	1.9
Long-term growth rate	(1.3)	(1.6)	(1.8)	(2.2)
Projected adjusted EBITDA[1]	(2.3)	(3.4)	(4.0)	(3.9)
Projected capital expenditure[2]	4.5	7.1	12.5	9.1

Notes:

1. Projected adjusted EBITDA is expressed as the compound annual growth rates in the initial five years for all cash-generating units of the plans used for impairment testing.
2. Projected capital expenditure, which excludes licences and spectrum, is expressed as capital expenditure as a percentage of revenue in the initial five years for all cash-generating units of the plans used for impairment testing.

VodafoneZiggo

The recoverable amount for VodafoneZiggo is not materially greater than its carrying value. If adverse impacts of economic, competitive, regulatory or other factors were to cause significant deterioration in the operations of VodafoneZiggo and the entity's expected future cash flows, this may lead to an impairment loss being recognised.

14 DEVELOPMENTS

The IASB is working on a goodwill and impairment research project after feedback received from the Post-Implementation Review of IFRS 3. In accordance with the project's objectives set by the Board in July 2018, the discussions to date were focused on the following areas:

- better disclosures for business combinations;
- reintroduction of amortisation of goodwill;
- presentation of total equity before goodwill subtotal;
- relief from mandatory annual impairment test;
- considering cash flows from a future restructuring or a future enhancement in value in use calculations; and
- removal of the explicit requirement to use pre-tax inputs and pre-tax discount rates in the value in use calculation.

In March 2020 the IASB published the Discussion Paper Business Combinations – Disclosures, Goodwill and Impairment. The Discussion Paper sets out the IASB's preliminary views on how companies can provide better information so that investors can hold companies to account for acquisitions of other companies. The preliminary views focus on disclosure of information and on accounting for goodwill. These are summarised in the table below:[3]

Area for discussion	The IASB's preliminary views:
Better disclosures for business combinations	• require entities to disclose management's objectives for acquisitions in the year of acquisition and how acquisitions have performed against those objectives in subsequent periods; • require entities to disclose information about acquisitions used by their chief operating decision maker, as described in IFRS 8. Information should not be created solely for external reporting; • an entity should continue to provide information about an acquisition for as long as its chief operating decision maker continues to monitor the acquisition against its objectives. If the chief operating decision maker does not monitor an acquisition or stops monitoring it shortly after the acquisition occurred, the entity would be required to disclose this fact and explain why;

	• require entities to describe synergies management expected from an acquisition and disclose the estimated amount of synergies, or range of amounts. This information would help investors to better understand the factors that contributed to the acquisition price; and • require entities to disclose the amount of defined benefit pension and debt liabilities taken over in the acquired business, separately from other classes of liabilities. This information would help investors assess companies' return on capital employed.
Improving the effectiveness of the impairment test for goodwill	• is not feasible to improve significantly the effectiveness of the impairment test for goodwill at a reasonable cost to entities; • it is not possible to eliminate shielding from the impairment test because goodwill has to be tested for impairment together with other assets and these groups of assets could contain headroom. Goodwill is 'shielded' from impairment because the headroom of the business with which an acquired business is integrated absorbs the decline in the recoverable amount of the acquired business; • the impairment test cannot always signal how well the acquired business is performing. If the impairment test is performed well, the test can be expected to achieve its objective of ensuring that the carrying amount of a group of assets containing goodwill as a whole is not higher than its recoverable amount; and • if estimates of future cash flows are too optimistic (point of criticism was raised by the stakeholders in relation to that), this is best addressed by auditors and regulators, not by changing IFRS Standards. Entities are required by IAS 36 to use reasonable and supportable estimates when performing an impairment test.
Re-introduction of amortisation of goodwill	• retain the existing impairment-only model for the subsequent accounting for goodwill. The IASB believes that there is no compelling evidence that amortising goodwill would result in a significant improvement in financial reporting. However, the majority for this decision was small, so the IASB is interested in stakeholders' views on this topic.

Area for discussion	The IASB's preliminary views:
Relief from the mandatory annual impairment test	• remove the requirement to carry out an annual quantitative impairment test for goodwill when no indicator of impairment exists; but • continue to require an entity to assess whether any such indication exists; • the IASB believes the change would not make the test significantly less robust because when there is no indication of impairment it is unlikely that the quantitative test would identify large impairment losses and performing the test every year cannot remove shielding; and • the change would reduce the cost of performing the impairment test.
Value in use – cash flows from a future restructuring or a future enhancement	• remove the requirement to exclude from the estimation of value in use, the cash flows that are expected to arise from a future restructuring or a future enhancement. The cash flow forecasts would still need to be reasonable and supportable.
Value in use – use of post-tax inputs	• allow the use of post-tax discount rates and post-tax cash flows.
Presentation of a total equity before goodwill	• require entities to present on the balance sheet the amount of total equity excluding goodwill.
Recognising acquired intangible assets separately from goodwill	• the requirements in IFRS 3 and IAS 38 on separate recognition of acquired intangible assets should be retained.

The IASB has asked for feedback on its preliminary views by 31 December 2020. Feedback will help the IASB decide whether and how to develop detailed proposals in the next stage of the project. At the time of writing, the IASB's work plan indicated that Discussion Paper Feedback is expected in the first half of 2021.[4]

References

1 *IFRIC Update*, September 2010.
2 *IFRIC Update*, September 2010.
3 IASB Snapshot Business Combinations – Disclosures, Goodwill and Impairment, March 2020 and Discussion Paper DP/2020/1, Business Combinations – Disclosures, Goodwill and Impairment.
4 IASB Work Plan as at 23 June 2020.

Chapter 21

Capitalisation of borrowing costs

1 INTRODUCTION 1645
2 THE REQUIREMENTS OF IAS 23 1645
   2.1 Core principle... 1645
   2.2 Scope..1646
3 QUALIFYING ASSETS 1646
   3.1 Inventories 1646
   3.2 Assets measured at fair value 1647
   3.3 Financial assets..1648
   3.4 Over time transfer of constructed good 1648
4 DEFINITION OF BORROWING COSTS 1649
   4.1 The definition of borrowing costs in IAS 23 1649
   4.2 Other finance costs...1650
5 BORROWING COSTS ELIGIBLE FOR CAPITALISATION 1650
   5.1 Directly attributable borrowing costs..1650
   5.2 Specific borrowings 1651
   5.3 General borrowings 1651
      5.3.1 Definition of general borrowings..1652
         5.3.1.A Borrowing costs on borrowings related to completed qualifying assets.. 1652
         5.3.1.B General borrowings related to specific non-qualifying assets.. 1653
      5.3.2 Calculation of capitalisation rate 1654
      5.3.3 Accrued costs and trade payables 1656
      5.3.4 Assets carried below cost in the statement of financial position 1657

	5.4		Exchange differences as a borrowing cost	1657
	5.5		Other finance costs as a borrowing cost	1659
		5.5.1	Derivative financial instruments	1659
		5.5.2	Gains and losses on derecognition of borrowings	1661
		5.5.3	Gains or losses on termination of derivative financial instruments	1662
		5.5.4	Dividends payable on shares classified as financial liabilities	1662
	5.6		Capitalisation of borrowing costs in hyperinflationary economies	1663
	5.7		Group considerations	1663
		5.7.1	Borrowings in one company and development in another	1663
		5.7.2	Qualifying assets held by joint arrangements	1664
6	COMMENCEMENT, SUSPENSION AND CESSATION OF CAPITALISATION			1664
	6.1		Commencement of capitalisation	1664
		6.1.1	Expenditures on a qualifying asset	1666
	6.2		Suspension of capitalisation	1668
		6.2.1	Impairment considerations	1669
	6.3		Cessation of capitalisation	1669
		6.3.1	Borrowing costs on 'land expenditures'	1670
7	DISCLOSURE REQUIREMENTS			1671
	7.1		The requirements of IAS 23	1671
	7.2		Disclosure requirements in other IFRSs	1671

List of examples

Example 21.1:	Calculation of capitalisation rate (no investment income)	1654
Example 21.2:	Calculation of amount to be capitalised – specific borrowings with investment income	1656
Example 21.3:	Foreign exchange differences in more than one period	1658
Example 21.4:	Floating to fixed interest rate swaps	1659
Example 21.5:	Cash flow hedge of variable-rate debt using an interest rate swap	1659
Example 21.6:	Expenditures on a qualifying asset before general borrowings are obtained	1667

Chapter 21 Capitalisation of borrowing costs

1 INTRODUCTION

A common question when determining the initial measurement of an asset is whether or not finance costs incurred on its acquisition or during the period of its construction should be capitalised. There have always been a number of strong arguments in favour of the capitalisation of directly attributable finance costs. For example, it is argued that they are just as much a cost as any other directly attributable cost; that expensing finance costs distorts the choice between purchasing and constructing an asset; that capitalising the costs leads to a carrying value that is far more akin to the market value of the asset; and that the financial statements are more likely to represent the true results of the project.

In accounting periods commencing prior to 1 January 2009, entities were permitted to capitalise borrowing costs as an alternative to expensing them in the period they were incurred. However, in March 2007, the IASB issued a revised version of IAS 23 – *Borrowing Costs* – mandating capitalisation of borrowing costs directly attributable to the acquisition, construction or production of a qualifying asset. This was done to achieve convergence in principle with US GAAP. *[IAS 23.BC2]*. It thereby eliminated some (but not all) of the differences with SFAS 34 – *Capitalization of Interest Cost*.[1]

The revised standard applied for the first time to accounting periods commencing on or after 1 January 2009, although early implementation was permitted. *[IAS 23.29]*. In this chapter we consider the requirements of this revised standard.

2 THE REQUIREMENTS OF IAS 23

2.1 Core principle

IAS 23 requires borrowing costs to be capitalised if they are directly attributable to the acquisition, construction or production of a qualifying asset (whether or not the funds have been borrowed specifically). These borrowing costs are included in the cost of the qualifying asset; all other borrowing costs are recognised as an expense in the period in which they are incurred. *[IAS 23.1, 8]*.

2.2 Scope

An entity should apply IAS 23 in accounting for borrowing costs. *[IAS 23.2]*. IAS 23 deals with the treatment of borrowing costs in general, rather than solely focusing on capitalising borrowing costs as part of the carrying value of assets.

The standard does not deal with the actual or imputed costs of equity, including preferred capital and other financial instruments not classified as a liability, used to fund the acquisition or construction of an asset. *[IAS 23.3]*. This means that any distributions or other payments made in respect of equity instruments, as defined by IAS 32 – *Financial Instruments: Presentation*, are not within the scope of IAS 23. Conversely, interest and dividends payable on instruments that are legally equity but classified as financial liabilities under IAS 32 appear to be within the scope of the standard (see 5.5.4 below).

An entity is not required to apply the standard (i.e. application is optional) to borrowing costs directly attributable to the acquisition, construction or production of:

- a qualifying asset measured at fair value (see 3.2 below); or
- inventories that are manufactured, or otherwise produced, in large quantities on a repetitive basis (see 3.1 below). *[IAS 23.4]*.

3 QUALIFYING ASSETS

IAS 23 defines a qualifying asset as 'an asset that necessarily takes a substantial period of time to get ready for its intended use or sale'. *[IAS 23.5]*.

Assets that are ready for their intended use or sale when acquired are not qualifying assets. *[IAS 23.7]*.

IAS 23 does not define 'substantial period of time' and this will therefore require the exercise of judgement after considering the specific facts and circumstances. In practice, an asset that normally takes twelve months or more to be ready for its intended use or sale will usually be a qualifying asset.

The standard indicates that, depending on the circumstances, the following may be qualifying assets: manufacturing plants, power generation facilities, investment properties, inventories, intangible assets and bearer plants. *[IAS 23.7]*.

3.1 Inventories

Inventories are within the scope of IAS 23 as long as they meet the definition of a qualifying asset and require a substantial period of time to bring them to a saleable condition. This means inventories that are manufactured, or otherwise produced, over a short period of time are not qualifying assets and are out of scope of IAS 23. *[IAS 23.7]*. However, even if inventories meet the definition of a qualifying asset and take a substantial period of time to get ready for sale, an entity is not required to apply the standard to borrowing costs directly attributable to the acquisition, construction or production of inventories if these are routinely manufactured or otherwise produced in large quantities on a repetitive basis. *[IAS 23.4(b), BC6]*.

Therefore, an entity may choose whether to apply the requirements of IAS 23 to such inventories as a matter of accounting policy. This optional scope exemption has been allowed because of the difficulty of calculating and monitoring the amount to be capitalised, i.e. the costs of capitalisation are likely to exceed the potential benefits. *[IAS 23.BC6]*. There are many examples of such inventories, including large manufactured or constructed items that take some time to complete but are routinely sold as standard items, such as aircraft and large items of equipment, or food and drink that take a long time to mature, such as cheese or alcohol that matures in bottle or cask.

Conversely, IAS 23 is required to be applied to bespoke inventories (i.e. those made according to the unique specifications of a particular customer) that are occasionally manufactured or produced on a single item by item basis and take a substantial period of time to get ready for sale.

See also further discussion in Chapter 29 at 2.5.2.G.

3.2 Assets measured at fair value

IAS 23 does not require entities to capitalise borrowing costs directly attributable to the acquisition, construction or production of assets measured at fair value that would otherwise be qualifying assets, for example, biological assets within the scope of IAS 41 – *Agriculture*. *[IAS 23.4(a)]*. If the assets are held under a fair value model (or a fair value less costs to sell model) with all changes going to profit or loss, then capitalisation would not affect measurement in the statement of financial position and would involve no more than a reallocation between finance costs and the fair value movement in profit or loss. However, this scope exemption is optional and would still allow an entity to choose whether to apply the requirements of IAS 23 to such assets as a matter of accounting policy.

IAS 23 does not restrict the exemption to assets where the fair value movement is taken to profit or loss. Assets measured at fair value that fall under the revaluation model of IAS 16 – *Property, Plant and Equipment* – are also eligible for this scope exemption even though the revaluation gain or loss goes to other comprehensive income, not profit or loss (see Chapter 18 at 4.1.2). While such assets may be subject to the scope exemption, the revaluation model in IAS 16 is only applied subsequent to initial recognition. *[IAS 16.31]*. Therefore, such assets might be qualifying assets at initial recognition, but subject to the scope exemption subsequently.

For example, assume that an entity borrows specific funds to construct a building, that the building is a qualifying asset and that the entity has a policy of revaluing all its land and buildings. When the constructed building is initially recognised, it will be measured at cost, which would include the directly attributable borrowing costs. *[IAS 16.15, 16(b)]*. Assume that the entity subsequently renovates the building, that the renovation takes a substantial amount of time to complete and that those costs qualify for capitalisation under IAS 16. Since the asset is being revalued it would fall under the scope exemption in IAS 23. Therefore, the entity would not be required to capitalise any directly attributable borrowing costs relating to this subsequent renovation even if it takes a substantial amount of time to complete.

However, for disclosure purposes, an entity will still need to monitor the carrying amount of such an asset, including those borrowing costs that would have been recognised had such an asset been carried under the cost model.

In May 2014 the Interpretations Committee received a request for clarification as to whether an entity is required to reflect the capitalisation of borrowing costs to meet the disclosure requirement of IAS 16 for assets stated at revalued amounts (see Chapter 18 at 8.2) and for which borrowing costs are not capitalised. Since, as discussed above, the capitalisation of borrowing costs for such assets is not required, the determination of the amount of borrowing costs that would have been capitalised under a cost model – solely to meet a disclosure requirement – might be considered burdensome.

The Interpretations Committee noted that the requirements in paragraph 77(e) of IAS 16 are clear. This paragraph requires an entity to disclose the amount at which assets stated at revalued amounts would have been stated had those assets been carried under the cost model. The amount to be disclosed includes borrowing costs capitalised in accordance with IAS 23.

The Interpretations Committee determined that, in the light of the existing IFRS requirements, neither an interpretation nor an amendment to a standard was necessary and consequently decided not to add this issue to its agenda.[2]

3.3 Financial assets

IAS 23 excludes all financial assets (which we consider include equity accounted investments) from the definition of qualifying assets. *[IAS 23.7]*.

3.4 Over time transfer of constructed good

In its November 2018 meeting, the Interpretations Committee discussed a request it received about the capitalisation of borrowing costs in relation to the construction of a residential multi-unit real estate development (building). In the fact pattern described in the request:

- A real estate developer (entity) constructs the building and sells the individual units in the building to customers.
- The entity borrows funds specifically for the purpose of constructing the building and incurs borrowing costs in connection with that borrowing.
- Before construction begins, the entity signs contracts with customers for the sale of some of the units in the building (sold units).
- The entity intends to enter into contracts with customers for the remaining part-constructed units (unsold units) as soon as it finds suitable customers.
- The terms of, and relevant facts and circumstances relating to, the entity's contracts with customers (for both the sold and unsold units) are such that, applying paragraph 35(c) of IFRS 15 – *Revenue from Contracts with Customers*, the entity transfers control of each unit over time and, therefore, recognises revenue over time (see Chapter 30 at 2.3). The consideration promised by the customer in the contract is in the form of cash or another financial asset.

The request asked whether the entity has a qualifying asset as defined in IAS 23 and, therefore, capitalises any directly attributable borrowing costs.

Applying paragraph 8 of IAS 23, an entity capitalises borrowing costs that are directly attributable to the acquisition, construction or production of a qualifying asset as part of the cost of that asset (see 5.1 below). Paragraph 5 of IAS 23 defines a qualifying asset as 'an asset that necessarily takes a substantial period of time to get ready for its intended use or sale' (see 3 above).

Accordingly, the entity assesses whether, in the fact pattern described in the request, it recognises an asset that necessarily takes a substantial period of time to get ready for its intended use or sale. Depending on the particular facts and circumstances, the entity might recognise a receivable, a contract asset and/or inventory.[3]

The Interpretations Committee concluded that, in the fact pattern described in the request:

- A receivable that the entity recognises is not a qualifying asset. Paragraph 7 of IAS 23 specifies that financial assets are not qualifying assets (see 3.3 above).
- A contract asset that the entity recognises is not a qualifying asset. The contract asset (as defined in Appendix A to IFRS 15 – see Chapter 27 at 2.2) would represent the entity's right to consideration that is conditional on something other than the passage of time in exchange for transferring control of a unit. The intended use of the contract asset – to collect cash or another financial asset – is not a use for which it necessarily takes a substantial period of time to get ready.
- Inventory (work-in-progress) for unsold units under construction that the entity recognises is not a qualifying asset. In the fact pattern described in the request, this asset is ready for its intended sale in its current condition (such an asset is not a qualifying asset, see 3 and 3.1 above) – i.e. the entity intends to sell the part-constructed units as soon as it finds suitable customers and, on signing a contract with a customer, will transfer control of any work-in-progress relating to that unit to the customer.

The Interpretations Committee concluded that the principles and requirements in IAS 23 provide an adequate basis for an entity to determine whether to capitalise borrowing costs in the fact pattern described in the request. Consequently, in its March 2019 meeting, the Interpretations Committee decided not to add this matter to its standard-setting agenda.[4]

See also further discussion in Chapter 29 at 2.5.2.G.

4 DEFINITION OF BORROWING COSTS

4.1 The definition of borrowing costs in IAS 23

Borrowing costs are interest and other costs that an entity incurs in connection with the borrowing of funds. *[IAS 23.5]*. Borrowing costs are defined in the standard to include:

- interest expense calculated using the effective interest method as described in IFRS 9 – *Financial Instruments*;
- interest in respect of lease liabilities recognised in accordance with IFRS 16 – *Leases*; and
- exchange differences arising from foreign currency borrowings to the extent that they are regarded as an adjustment to interest costs (see 5.4 below). *[IAS 23.6]*.

The standard addresses whether or not to capitalise borrowing costs as part of the cost of the asset. *[IAS 23.8, 9]*. The identification and measurement of finance costs are not dealt with in IAS 23 (see 4.2 below).

In determining whether interest expense arising from a customer contract (i.e. a contract within the scope of IFRS 15) with a significant financing component can be considered as borrowing costs eligible for capitalisation, see the discussion in Chapter 29 at 2.5.2.G.

Treatment of borrowing costs incurred by an operator in a service concession arrangement will depend on the accounting model used by the operator in accordance with IFRIC 12 – *Service Concession Arrangements*, see the discussions in Chapter 25 at 4.2 and 4.3.

4.2 Other finance costs

IAS 23 does not address many of the ways in which an entity may finance its operations or other finance costs that it may incur. For example, the standard does not address any of the following:

- the many derivative financial instruments such as interest rate swaps, floors, caps and collars that are commonly used to manage interest rate risk on borrowings;
- gains and losses on derecognition of borrowings, for example early settlement of directly attributable borrowings that have been renegotiated prior to completion of an asset in the course of construction; and
- dividends payable on shares classified as financial liabilities (such as certain redeemable preference shares).

The eligibility of these other finance costs for capitalisation under IAS 23 is discussed at 5.5 below.

IAS 23 does not preclude the classification of costs, other than those it identifies, as borrowing costs. However, they must meet the basic criterion in the standard, i.e. that they are costs that are directly attributable to the acquisition, construction or production of a qualifying asset, which would, therefore, preclude treating the unwinding of discounts as borrowing costs. Many unwinding discounts are treated as finance costs in profit or loss. These include discounts relating to various provisions such as those for onerous contracts and decommissioning costs. These finance costs will not be borrowing costs under IAS 23 because they do not arise in respect of funds borrowed by the entity that can be attributed to a qualifying asset. Therefore, they cannot be capitalised. In addition, as in the case of exchange differences, capitalisation of such costs should be permitted only 'to the extent that they are regarded as an adjustment to interest costs' (see 5.4 below). *[IAS 23.6(e)]*.

5 BORROWING COSTS ELIGIBLE FOR CAPITALISATION

5.1 Directly attributable borrowing costs

Borrowing costs are eligible for capitalisation as part of the cost of an asset if they are directly attributable to the acquisition, construction or production of a qualifying asset, when it is probable that such costs will result in future economic benefits to the entity and the costs can be measured reliably. *[IAS 23.8, 9]*.

IAS 23 starts from the premise that borrowing costs that are directly attributable to the acquisition, construction or production of a qualifying asset are those that would have been avoided if the expenditure on the qualifying asset had not been made. *[IAS 23.10]*. Recognising that it may not always be easy to identify a direct relationship between particular borrowings and a qualifying asset and to determine the borrowings that could otherwise have been avoided, the standard includes separate requirements for specific borrowings and general borrowings (see 5.2 and 5.3, respectively, below).

5.2 Specific borrowings

When an entity borrows funds specifically to obtain a particular qualifying asset, the borrowing costs that are directly related to that qualifying asset can be readily identified. *[IAS 23.10]*. The borrowing costs eligible for capitalisation would be the actual borrowing costs incurred on that specific borrowing during the period. *[IAS 23.12]*.

Entities frequently borrow funds in advance of expenditure on qualifying assets and may temporarily invest the borrowings. The standard makes it clear that any investment income earned on the temporary investment of those borrowings needs to be deducted from the borrowing costs incurred and only the net amount capitalised (see Example 21.2 below). *[IAS 23.12, 13]*.

There is no restriction in IAS 23 on the type of investment in which the funds can be invested but, in our view, to maintain the conclusion that the funds are specific borrowings, the investment must be of a nature that does not expose the principal amount to the risk of not being recovered. The riskier the investment, the greater is the likelihood that the borrowing is not specific to the qualifying asset. If the investment returns a loss rather than income, such losses are not added to the borrowing costs to be capitalised.

5.3 General borrowings

IAS 23 concedes that there may be practical difficulties in identifying a direct relationship between particular borrowings and a qualifying asset and in determining the borrowings that could otherwise have been avoided. *[IAS 23.11]*. This could be the case if the financing activity of an entity is co-ordinated centrally, for example, if an entity borrows to meet its funding requirements as a whole and the construction of the qualifying asset is financed out of general borrowings. Other circumstances that may cause difficulties are identified by the standard as follows:

- a group has a treasury function that uses a range of debt instruments to borrow funds at varying rates of interest and lends those funds on various bases to other entities in the group; or
- loans are denominated in or linked to foreign currencies and the group operates in highly inflationary economies or there are fluctuations in exchange rates. *[IAS 23.11]*.

In these circumstances, determining the amount of borrowing costs that are directly attributable to the acquisition of a qualifying asset may be difficult and require judgement. *[IAS 23.11]*.

When general borrowings are used in part to obtain a qualifying asset, IAS 23 requires the application of a capitalisation rate to the expenditure on that asset in determining the amount of borrowing costs eligible for capitalisation. However, the amount of borrowing costs capitalised during a period cannot exceed the amount of borrowing costs incurred during that period. [IAS 23.14].

The capitalisation rate applied should be the weighted average of the borrowing costs applicable to all borrowings of the entity that are outstanding during the period, excluding borrowing costs applicable to borrowings made specifically for the purpose of obtaining a qualifying asset until substantially all the activities necessary to prepare that asset for its intended use or sale are complete (see 5.3.1.A below). [IAS 23.14]. The capitalisation rate is then applied to the expenditure on the qualifying asset.

Expenditure on a qualifying asset includes only that expenditure resulting in the payment of cash, the transfer of other assets or the assumption of interest-bearing liabilities. Such expenditure must be reduced by any progress payments and grants received in connection with the asset (see IAS 20 – *Accounting for Government Grants and Disclosure of Government Assistance* – and Chapter 24). The standard accepts that, when funds are borrowed generally, the average carrying amount of the asset during a period, including borrowing costs previously capitalised, is normally a reasonable approximation of the expenditure to which the capitalisation rate is applied in that period. [IAS 23.18].

The standard does not provide specific guidance regarding interest income earned from temporarily investing excess general funds. However, any interest income earned is unlikely to be directly attributable to the acquisition or construction of a qualifying asset. In addition, the capitalisation rate required by IAS 23 focuses on the borrowings of the entity outstanding during the period of construction or acquisition and does not include temporary investments. As such, borrowing costs capitalised should not be reduced by interest income earned from the investment of general borrowings nor should such income be included in determining the appropriate capitalisation rate.

In some circumstances, it is appropriate for all borrowings made by the group (i.e. borrowings of the parent and its subsidiaries) to be taken into account in determining the weighted average of the borrowing costs. In other circumstances, it is appropriate for each subsidiary to use a weighted average of the borrowing costs applicable to its own borrowings. [IAS 23.15]. It is likely that this will largely be determined by the extent to which borrowings are made centrally (and, perhaps, interest expenses met in the same way) and passed through to individual group companies via intercompany accounts and intra-group loans. The capitalisation rate is discussed further at 5.3.2 below.

5.3.1 Definition of general borrowings

5.3.1.A Borrowing costs on borrowings related to completed qualifying assets

As noted at 5.3 above, determining general borrowings will not always be straightforward and, as a result, the determination of the amount of borrowing costs that are directly attributable to the acquisition of a qualifying asset is difficult and judgement is required.

The question has arisen as to whether a specific borrowing undertaken to obtain a qualifying asset ever changes its nature into a general borrowing. Differing views existed as to whether or not borrowings change their nature throughout the period they are outstanding. Some considered that once the asset for which the borrowing was incurred has been completed, and the entity chooses to use its funds on constructing other assets rather than repaying the loan, this changes the nature of the loan into a general borrowing. However, to the extent that the contract links the repayment of the loan to specific proceeds generated by the entity, its nature as a specific borrowing would be preserved. Others took the view that once the borrowing has been classified as specific, its nature does not change while it remains outstanding.

To address this diversity in practice, the IASB issued *Annual Improvements to IFRSs 2015-2017 Cycle* in December 2017 to amend the relevant part of paragraph 14 of IAS 23 to read as follows (emphasis added):

'The capitalisation rate shall be the weighted average of the borrowing costs applicable to *all* borrowings of the entity that are outstanding during the period. *However, an entity shall exclude from this calculation borrowing costs applicable to borrowings* made specifically for the purpose of obtaining a qualifying asset *until substantially all the activities necessary to prepare that asset for its intended use or sale are complete.*'[5]

The IASB concluded that the reference to 'borrowings made specifically for the purpose of obtaining a qualifying asset' in paragraph 14 of IAS 23 prior to the amendment should not apply to a borrowing originally made specifically to obtain a qualifying asset if that qualifying asset is now ready for its intended use or sale. *[IAS 23.BC14B]*.

The IASB observed that paragraph 8 of IAS 23 requires an entity to capitalise borrowing costs directly attributable to the acquisition, construction or production of a qualifying asset as part of the cost of that asset. Paragraph 10 of IAS 23 states that borrowing costs are directly attributable to a qualifying asset if those borrowing costs would have been avoided had the expenditure of the qualifying asset not been made. In other words, an entity could have repaid that borrowing if the expenditure on the qualifying asset had not been made. Accordingly, paragraph 14 of IAS 23 requires an entity to use all outstanding borrowings in determining the capitalisation rate, except those made specifically to obtain a qualifying asset not yet ready for its intended use or sale. *[IAS 23.BC14C]*.

The IASB concluded that if a specific borrowing remains outstanding after the related qualifying asset is ready for its intended use or sale, it becomes part of the funds an entity borrows generally. Accordingly, the IASB amended paragraph 14 of IAS 23, as described above, to clarify this requirement. *[IAS 23.BC14D]*.

Refer also to further discussion in 6.3 below to determine when all the activities necessary to prepare the qualifying asset for its intended use or sale are 'substantially' complete.

5.3.1.B   General borrowings related to specific non-qualifying assets

Prior to amendments referred to in 5.3.1.A above, another question arose regarding the treatment of general borrowings used to purchase a specific asset other than a qualifying asset for the purpose of capitalising borrowing costs in accordance with IAS 23.

In July 2009, the Interpretations Committee noted that because paragraph 14 of IAS 23 prior to the amendment refers only to qualifying assets:

- some conclude that borrowings related to specific assets other than qualifying assets cannot be excluded from determining the capitalisation rate for general borrowings; and
- others note the general principle in paragraph 10 that the borrowing costs that are directly attributable to the acquisition, construction or production of a qualifying asset are borrowing costs that would have been avoided if the expenditure on the qualifying asset had not been made.[6]

The IASB subsequently considered the issue of whether debt incurred specifically to acquire a non-qualifying asset could be excluded from general borrowings and noted that IAS 23 excludes only debt used to acquire qualifying assets from the determination of the capitalisation rate.[7]

Consequently, in June 2017, the Interpretations Committee recommended, and the IASB subsequently agreed, to clarify this issue when finalising the amendments to paragraph 14 of IAS 23 discussed in 5.3.1.A above.[8] As a result, the IASB clarified that an entity includes funds borrowed specifically to obtain an asset other than a qualifying asset as part of general borrowings. As described in 5.3.1.A above, the amendments to paragraph 14 of IAS 23 referring to 'all' borrowings clarify the requirements in this respect. *[IAS 23.BC14E].*

5.3.2 Calculation of capitalisation rate

As the standard acknowledges that determining general borrowings will not always be straightforward, it will be necessary to exercise judgement to meet the main objective – a reasonable measure of the directly attributable finance costs.

The following example illustrates the practical application of the method of calculating the amount of finance costs to be capitalised:

Example 21.1: Calculation of capitalisation rate (no investment income)

On 1 April 20X2 a company engages in the development of a property, which is expected to take five years to complete, at a cost of £6,000,000. The statements of financial position at 31 December 20X1 and 31 December 20X2, prior to capitalisation of interest, are as follows:

	31 December 20X1 £	31 December 20X2 £
Development property	–	1,200,000
Other assets	6,000,000	6,000,000
	6,000,000	7,200,000
Loans		
5.5% debenture stock	2,500,000	2,500,000
Bank loan at 6% p.a.	–	1,200,000
Bank loan at 7% p.a.	1,000,000	1,000,000
	3,500,000	4,700,000
Shareholders' equity	2,500,000	2,500,000

The bank loan with an effective interest rate of 6% was drawn down to match the development expenditure on 1 April 20X2, 1 July 20X2 and 1 October 20X2.

Expenditure was incurred on the development as follows:

	£
1 April 20X2	600,000
1 July 20X2	400,000
1 October 20X2	200,000
	1,200,000

As the bank loan at 6% p.a. is a new borrowing specifically to finance the development, the amount of interest to be capitalised for the year ended 31 December 20X2 would be the amount of interest charged by the bank of £42,000 ((£600,000 × 6% × 9/12) + (£400,000 × 6% × 6/12) + (£200,000 × 6% × 3/12)).

However, if all the borrowings were general (i.e. the bank loan at 6% was not specific to the development) and would have been avoided but for the development, then the amount of interest to be capitalised would be:

$$\frac{\text{Total interest expense for period}}{\text{Weighted average total borrowings}} \times \text{Development expenditure}$$

Total interest expense for the period:

	£
£2,500,000 × 5.5%	137,500
£1,200,000 (as above)	42,000
£1,000,000 × 7%	70,000
	249,500

Therefore, the capitalisation rate would be calculated as:

$$\frac{249,500}{3,500,000 + 700,000^*} = 5.94\%$$

* Weighted average amount of total borrowings is computed as the sum of £3,500,000 (or £3,500,000 × 12/12) and £700,000 (or (£600,000 × 9/12) + (£400,000 × 6/12) + (£200,000 × 3/12)).

The capitalisation rate would then be applied to the expenditure on the qualifying asset, resulting in an amount to be capitalised of £41,580 as follows:

	£
£600,000 × 5.94% × 9/12	26,730
£400,000 × 5.94% × 6/12	11,880
£200,000 × 5.94% × 3/12	2,970
	41,580

In this example, all borrowings are at fixed rates of interest and the period of construction extends at least until the end of the period, and the general borrowings have remained unchanged during the year, simplifying the calculation. The same principle is applied if borrowings are at floating rates i.e. only the interest costs incurred during that period, and the weighted average borrowings for that period, will be taken into account.

Note that the company's shareholders' equity (i.e. equity instruments – see further discussion in 5.5.4 below) cannot be taken into account. All of the outstanding borrowings are presumed to be general borrowings – unless they are specific borrowings used to obtain the same or another qualifying asset not yet ready for its intended use or sale (see discussions in 5.3.1.A and 5.3.1.B above).

The above example also assumes that loans are drawn down to match expenditure on the qualifying asset. If, however, a loan is drawn down immediately and investment income is received on the unapplied funds, then the calculation differs from that in Example 21.1 above. This is illustrated in Example 21.2 below.

Example 21.2: Calculation of amount to be capitalised – specific borrowings with investment income

On 1 April 20X2 a company engages in the development of a property, which is expected to take five years to complete, at a cost of £6,000,000. In this example, a bank loan of £6,000,000 with an effective interest rate of 6% was taken out on 31 March 20X2 and fully drawn. The total interest charge for the year ended 31 December 20X2 was consequently £270,000.

However, investment income was also earned at 3% on the unapplied funds during the period as follows (assume the same timings and expenditures incurred as in Example 21.1 above):

	£
£5,400,000 × 3% × 3/12	40,500
£5,000,000 × 3% × 3/12	37,500
£4,800,000 × 3% × 3/12	36,000
	114,000

Consequently, the amount of interest to be capitalised for the year ended 31 December 20X2 is:

	£
Total interest charge	270,000
Less: investment income	(114,000)
	156,000

5.3.3 Accrued costs and trade payables

As noted in 5.3 above, IAS 23 states that expenditure on qualifying assets includes only that expenditure resulting in the payment of cash, the transfer of other assets or the assumption of interest-bearing liabilities. *[IAS 23.18]*. Therefore, in principle, costs of a qualifying asset that have only been accrued but have not yet been paid in cash should be excluded from the amount on which interest is capitalised, as by definition no interest can have been incurred on an accrued payment. The same principle can be applied to non-interest-bearing liabilities e.g. non-interest-bearing trade payables or retention money that is not payable until the asset is completed.

The effect of applying this principle is often merely to delay the commencement of the capitalisation of interest since the capital expenditure will be included in the calculation once it has been paid in cash. If the time between incurring the cost and cash payment is not that large, the impact of this may not be material.

5.3.4 Assets carried below cost in the statement of financial position

An asset may be recognised in the financial statements during the period of production on a basis other than cost, i.e. it may have been written down below cost as a result of being impaired. An asset may be impaired when its carrying amount or expected ultimate cost, including costs to complete and the estimated capitalised interest thereon, exceeds its estimated recoverable amount or net realisable value (see 6.2.1 below).

The question then arises as to whether the calculation of interest to be capitalised should be based on the cost or carrying amount of the impaired asset. In this case, cost should be used, as this is the amount that the entity or group has had to finance. In the case of an impaired asset, the continued capitalisation based on the cost of the asset may well necessitate a further impairment. Accordingly, although the amount capitalised will be different, this should not affect net profit or loss as this is simply an allocation of costs between finance costs and impairment expense.

5.4 Exchange differences as a borrowing cost

An entity may borrow funds in a currency that is not its functional currency e.g. a US dollar loan financing a development in a company which has the Russian rouble as its functional currency. This may have been done on the basis that, over the period of the development, the borrowing costs, even after allowing for exchange differences, were expected to be less than the interest cost of an equivalent rouble loan.

IAS 23 defines borrowing costs as including exchange differences arising from foreign currency borrowings to the extent that they are regarded as an adjustment to interest costs. *[IAS 23.6(e)]*. The standard does not expand on this point. In January 2008, the Interpretations Committee considered a request for guidance on the treatment of foreign exchange gains and losses and on the treatment of any derivatives used to hedge such foreign exchange exposures. The Interpretations Committee decided not to add the issue to its agenda because:

- the standard acknowledges that judgement will be required in its application and appropriate disclosure of accounting policies and judgements would provide users with the information they need to understand the financial statements; and
- the IASB had considered this issue when developing the new IAS 23 and had decided not to provide any guidance.[9]

In our view, as exchange rate movements are partly a function of differential interest rates, in many circumstances the foreign exchange differences on directly attributable borrowings will be an adjustment to interest costs that can meet the definition of borrowing costs. However, care is needed if there are fluctuations in exchange rates that cannot be attributed to interest rate differentials. In such cases, we believe that a practical approach is to limit exchange losses taken as borrowing costs such that the total borrowing costs capitalised do not exceed the amount of borrowing costs that would be incurred on functional currency equivalent borrowings, taking into consideration the corresponding market interest rates and other conditions that existed at inception of the borrowings.

If this approach is used and the construction of the qualifying asset takes more than one accounting period, there could be situations where in one period only a portion of foreign exchange differences could be capitalised. However, in subsequent years, if the borrowings are assessed on a cumulative basis, foreign exchange losses previously expensed may now meet the recognition criteria. The two methods of dealing with this are illustrated in Example 21.3 below.

In our view, whether foreign exchange gains and losses are assessed on a discrete period basis or cumulatively over the construction period is a matter of accounting policy, which must be consistently applied. As alluded to above, IAS 1 – *Presentation of Financial Statements* – requires clear disclosure of significant accounting policies and judgements that are relevant to an understanding of the financial statements (see 7.2 below).

Example 21.3:   Foreign exchange differences in more than one period

Method A – The discrete period approach

The amount of foreign exchange differences eligible for capitalisation is determined for each period separately. Foreign exchange losses that did not meet the criteria for capitalisation in previous years are not capitalised in subsequent years.

Method B – The cumulative approach

The borrowing costs to be capitalised are assessed on a cumulative basis based on the cumulative amount of interest expense that would have been incurred had the entity borrowed in its functional currency. The amount of foreign exchange differences capitalised cannot exceed the amount of foreign exchange losses incurred on a cumulative basis at the end of the reporting period. The cumulative approach looks at the construction project as a whole as the unit of account ignoring the occurrence of reporting dates. Consequently, the amount of the foreign exchange differences eligible for capitalisation as an adjustment to the borrowing cost in the period is an estimate, which can change as the exchange rates vary over the construction period.

As discussed above, care is needed if there are fluctuations in exchange rates that cannot be attributed to interest rate differentials. In such cases, a practical approach is to limit exchange losses taken as borrowing costs such that the total borrowing costs capitalised do not exceed the amount of borrowing costs that would be incurred on functional currency equivalent borrowings, taking into consideration the corresponding market interest rates and other conditions that existed at inception of the borrowings. Applying this approach, an illustrative calculation of the amount of foreign exchange differences that may be capitalised under Method A and Method B is set out below.

	Year 1 $	Year 2 $	Total $
Interest expense in foreign currency (A)	25,000	25,000	50,000
Hypothetical interest expense in functional currency (B)	30,000	30,000	60,000
Foreign exchange loss (C)	6,000	3,000	9,000
Method A – Discrete Approach			
Foreign exchange loss capitalised – lower of C and (B minus A)	5,000	3,000	8,000
Foreign exchange loss expensed	1,000	–	1,000
Method B – Cumulative Approach			
Foreign exchange loss capitalised	5,000 *	4,000 **	9,000
Foreign exchange loss expensed	1,000	(1,000)	–

*   Lower of C and (B minus A) in Year 1.

**   Lower of C and (B minus A) in total across the two years. In this example this represents the sum of the foreign exchange loss of $3,000 capitalised using the discrete approach plus the $1,000 not capitalised in year 1.

5.5 Other finance costs as a borrowing cost

5.5.1 Derivative financial instruments

The most straightforward and commonly encountered derivative financial instrument used to manage interest rate risk is a floating to fixed interest rate swap, as in the following example.

Example 21.4: Floating to fixed interest rate swaps

Entity A has borrowed €4 million for five years at a floating interest rate to fund the construction of a building. In order to hedge the cash flow interest rate risk arising from these borrowings, Entity A has entered into a matching pay-fixed receive-floating interest rate swap, based on the same underlying nominal sum and duration as the original borrowing, that effectively converts the interest on the borrowings to fixed rate. The net effect of the periodic cash settlements resulting from the hedged item and hedging instruments is as if Entity A had borrowed €4 million at a fixed rate of interest.

These instruments are not addressed in IAS 23. IFRS 9 sets out the basis on which such instruments are recognised and measured. See Chapter 53 regarding how to account for effective hedges and the conditions that these instruments must meet.

An entity may consider that a specific derivative financial instrument, such as an interest rate swap, is directly attributable to the acquisition, construction or production of a qualifying asset. If the instrument does not meet the conditions for hedge accounting then the effects on profit or loss will be different from those if it does, and they will also be dissimilar from year to year. What is the impact of the derivative on borrowing costs eligible for capitalisation? In particular, does the accounting treatment of the derivative financial instrument affect the amount available for capitalisation? If hedge accounting is not adopted, does this affect the amount available for capitalisation?

The following examples illustrate the potential differences.

Example 21.5: Cash flow hedge of variable-rate debt using an interest rate swap

Entity A is constructing a building and expects it to take 18 months to complete. To finance the construction, on 1 January 20X1 the entity issues an eighteen-month, €20,000,000 variable-rate note payable, due on 30 June 20X2 at a floating rate of interest plus a margin of 1%. At that date the market rate of interest is 8%. Interest payment dates and interest rate reset dates occur on 1 January and 1 July until maturity. The principal is due at maturity. On 1 January 20X1, the entity also enters into an eighteen-month interest rate swap with a notional amount of €10,000,000 from which it will receive periodic payments at the floating rate and make periodic payments at a fixed rate of 9%, with settlement and rate reset dates every 30 June and 31 December. The fair value of the swap is zero at inception.

On 1 January 20X1, the debt is recorded at €20,000,000. No entry is required for the swap on that date because its fair value was zero at inception.

During the eighteen-month period, floating interest rates change as follows:

	Floating rate	Rate paid by Entity A on note payable
Period to 30 June 20X1	8%	9%
Period to 31 Dec 20X1	8.5%	9.5%
Period to 30 June 20X2	9.75%	10.75%

Under the interest rate swap, Entity A receives interest at the market floating rate as above and pays interest at 9% on the nominal amount of €10,000,000 throughout the period. Note that this example excludes the effect of issue costs and discounting. In addition, it is assumed that, if Entity A is entitled to, and applies, hedge accounting, there will be no ineffectiveness.

At 31 December 20X1, the swap has a fair value of €37,500, reflecting the fact that it is now in the money as Entity A is expected to receive a net cash inflow of this amount in the period until the instrument is terminated. There are no further changes in interest rates prior to the maturity of the swap and the fair value of the swap declines to zero at 30 June 20X2.

The cash flows incurred by the entity on its borrowing and interest rate swap are as follows:

	Cash payments		
	Interest on principal	Interest rate swap (net)	Total
	€	€	€
30 June 20X1	900,000	50,000	950,000
31 Dec 20X1	950,000	25,000	975,000
30 June 20X2	1,075,000	(37,500)	1,037,500
Total	2,925,000	37,500	2,962,500

There are a number of different ways in which Entity A could calculate the borrowing costs eligible for capitalisation, including the following:

(i) The interest rate swap meets the conditions for, and entity A applies, hedge accounting. The finance costs eligible for capitalisation as borrowing costs will be €1,925,000 in the year to 31 December 20X1 and €1,037,500 in the period ended 30 June 20X2.

(ii) Entity A does not apply hedge accounting. Therefore, it will reflect the fair value of the swap in profit or loss in the year ended 31 December 20X1, reducing the net finance costs by €37,500 to €1,887,500 and increasing the finance costs by an equivalent amount for the 6 months to 30 June 20X2 to €1,075,000. Under this method, it will not be appropriate to reflect the cash payments received in 20X2 for the settlement of the fair value of the swap in the borrowing costs eligible for capitalisation in the period ended 30 June 20X2 because the fair value of the swap is recognised in the income statement and already reflected in the amount of borrowing costs capitalised in 20X1.

However, if Entity A considers that it is inappropriate to reflect the fair value of the swap in borrowing costs eligible for capitalisation, it capitalises costs based on the net cash cost on an accrual accounting basis. In this case this will give the same result as in (i) above.

(iii) Entity A does not apply hedge accounting and considers only the costs incurred on the borrowing, not the interest rate swap, as eligible for capitalisation. The borrowing costs eligible for capitalisation would be €1,850,000 in 20X1 and €1,075,000 in 20X2.

In our view, all these methods are valid interpretations of IAS 23; however, the preparer will need to consider the most appropriate method in the particular circumstances after taking into consideration the discussion below.

In particular, if using method (ii), it is necessary to demonstrate that the gains or losses on the derivative financial instrument are directly attributable to the construction of a qualifying asset. In making this assessment it is necessary to consider the term of the derivative and this method may not be appropriate if the derivative has a different term to the underlying directly attributable borrowing. If the entity is not hedge accounting for the derivative financial instrument but considers its fair value movement to be directly attributable to the construction of a qualifying asset, then it will have to consider whether part of such fair value movement of the derivative relates to a period after the construction is completed and, therefore, excludes this part of the fair value movement when determining the borrowing costs eligible for capitalisation.

Based on the facts in this example, and assuming that entering into the derivative financial instrument is considered to be related to the borrowing activities of the entity, method (iii) may not be an appropriate method to use because it appears to be inconsistent with the underlying principle of IAS 23 – that the costs eligible for capitalisation are those costs that would have been avoided if the expenditure on the qualifying asset had not been made. *[IAS 23.10]*. However, method (iii) may be an appropriate method to use in certain circumstances where it is not possible to demonstrate that the gains or losses on a specific derivative financial instrument are directly attributable to a particular qualifying asset, rather than being used by the entity to manage its interest rate exposure on a more general basis.

Note that the discussions above mainly relate to derivative financial instruments entered into to manage the interest rate risk on specific borrowings. In our view, the same methods and considerations can be applied when determining the borrowing costs eligible for capitalisation when derivative financial instruments were entered into to manage the interest rate risk in relation to general borrowings.

Note also that method (i) appears to be permitted under US GAAP for fair value hedges. IAS 23 makes reference in its basis of conclusion that under US GAAP, derivative gains and losses (arising from the effective portion of a derivative instrument that qualifies as a fair value hedge) are considered to be part of the capitalised interest cost. IAS 23 does not address such derivative gains and losses. *[IAS 23.BC21]*.

Whichever policy is chosen by an entity, it needs to be consistently applied in similar situations.

5.5.2 Gains and losses on derecognition of borrowings

If an entity repays borrowings early, in whole or in part, then it may recognise a gain or loss on the early settlement. Such gains or losses include amounts attributable to expected future interest rates; in other words, the settlement includes an estimated prepayment of the future cash flows under the instrument. The gain or loss is a function of relative interest rates and how the interest rate of the instrument differs from current and anticipated future interest rates. There may be circumstances in which a loan is repaid while the qualifying asset is still under construction. IAS 23 does not address this issue.

IFRS 9 requires that gains and losses on extinguishment of debt should be recognised in profit or loss (see Chapter 52 at 6.3). Accordingly, in our view, gains and losses on derecognition of borrowings are not eligible for capitalisation. It would be extremely difficult to determine an appropriate amount to capitalise and it would be inappropriate thereafter to capitalise any interest amounts (on specific or general borrowings) if doing so would amount to double counting. Decisions to repay borrowings early are not usually directly attributable to the qualifying asset but are attributable to other circumstances of the entity.

The same approach would be applied to gains and losses arising from a refinancing when there is a substantial modification of the terms of borrowings as this is accounted for as an extinguishment of the original financial liability and the recognition of a new financial liability (see Chapter 52 at 6.2 to 6.3).

5.5.3 Gains or losses on termination of derivative financial instruments

If an entity terminates a derivative financial instrument, for example, an interest rate swap, before the end of the term of the instrument, it will usually have to either make or receive a payment, depending on the fair value of the instrument at that time. This fair value is typically based on expected future interest rates; in other words, it is an estimated prepayment of the future cash flows under the instrument.

The treatment of the gain or loss for the purposes of capitalisation will depend on the following:

- the basis on which the entity capitalises the gains and losses associated with derivative financial instruments attributable to qualifying assets (see 5.5.1 above); and
- whether the derivative is associated with a borrowing that has also been terminated.

Entities must adopt a treatment that is consistent with their policy for capitalising the gains and losses from derivative financial instruments that are attributable to qualifying investments (see 5.5.1 above).

The accounting under IFRS 9 will differ depending on whether the instrument has been designated as a hedge or not. Assuming the instrument has been designated as a cash flow hedge and that the borrowing has not also been repaid, the entity will usually maintain the cumulative gain or loss on the hedging instrument, subject to reclassification to profit or loss during the same period that the hedged cash flows affect profit or loss. In such a case, the amounts that are reclassified from other comprehensive income will be eligible for capitalisation for the remainder of the period of construction. On the other hand, if the borrowing has been repaid, the cumulative gain or loss in the cash flow hedge equity reserve will be reclassified immediately to profit or loss but will not be eligible for capitalisation.

Similarly, assuming the instrument has been designated as a fair value hedge and that the borrowing has not also been repaid, entities would continue to recognise the cumulative gain or loss on the hedging instrument in the carrying amount of the hedged item and this amount would form part of the ongoing determination of amortised cost of the financial liability using the effective interest rate method. Interest expense calculated using the effective interest method is eligible for capitalisation for the remainder of the period of construction (see 4.1 above).

If the entity has not applied hedge accounting for the derivative financial instrument and the borrowing has not also been repaid, but considers it to be directly attributable to the construction of the qualifying asset then it will have to consider whether part of the gain or loss relates to a period after construction is complete.

If the underlying borrowing is also terminated then the gain or loss will not be capitalised and the treatment will mirror that applied on derecognition of the borrowing, as described in 5.5.2 above.

5.5.4 Dividends payable on shares classified as financial liabilities

An entity might finance its operations in whole or in part by the issue of preference or other types of shares and in some circumstances, these will be classified as financial liabilities (see Chapter 47 at 4.5). In some circumstances, the dividends payable on these instruments would meet the definition of borrowing costs. For example, an entity might have funded the development of a qualifying asset by issuing preference shares that are classified as financial liabilities under IAS 32 (see Chapter 47 at 4.5). In this case, the 'dividends' would be treated as interest and meet the definition of borrowing costs and so should be capitalised following the principles on specific borrowings discussed in 5.2 above.

Companies with outstanding preference shares which are treated as liabilities under IAS 32 might subsequently obtain a qualifying asset. In such cases, these preference share liabilities would be considered to be part of the company's general borrowings. The related 'dividends' would meet the definition of borrowing costs and could be capitalised following the principles on general borrowings discussed in 5.3 above – i.e. that they are directly attributable to a qualifying asset.

Capitalisation of dividends or other payments made in respect of any instruments that are classified as equity in accordance with IAS 32 is not appropriate as these instruments would not meet the definition of financial liabilities. In addition, as discussed in 2.2 above, IAS 23 does not deal with the actual or imputed cost of equity, including preferred capital not classified as a liability. *[IAS 23.3]*.

5.6 Capitalisation of borrowing costs in hyperinflationary economies

In situations where IAS 29 – *Financial Reporting in Hyperinflationary Economies* – applies, an entity needs to distinguish between borrowing costs that compensate for inflation and those incurred in order to acquire or construct a qualifying asset.

IAS 29 states that '[t]he impact of inflation is usually recognised in borrowing costs. It is not appropriate both to restate the capital expenditure financed by borrowing and to capitalise that part of the borrowing costs that compensates for the inflation during the same period. This part of the borrowing costs is recognised as an expense in the period in which the costs are incurred.' *[IAS 29.21]*.

Accordingly, IAS 23 specifies that when an entity applies IAS 29, the borrowing costs that can be capitalised should be restricted and the entity must expense the part of borrowing costs that compensates for inflation during the same period in accordance with paragraph 21 of IAS 29 (as described above). *[IAS 23.9]*.

For detailed discussion and requirements of IAS 29, see Chapter 16.

5.7 Group considerations

5.7.1 Borrowings in one company and development in another

A question that can arise in practice is whether it is appropriate to capitalise interest in the group financial statements on borrowings that appear in the financial statements of a different group entity from that carrying out the development. Based on the underlying principle of IAS 23, capitalisation in such circumstances would only be appropriate if the amount capitalised fairly reflected the interest cost of the group on borrowings from third parties that could have been avoided if the expenditure on the qualifying asset were not made.

Although it may be appropriate to capitalise interest in the group financial statements, the entity carrying out the development should not capitalise any interest in its own financial statements as it has no borrowings. If, however, the entity has intra-group borrowings then interest on such borrowings may be capitalised in its own financial statements.

5.7.2 Qualifying assets held by joint arrangements

A number of sectors carry out developments through the medium of joint arrangements (see Chapter 12) – this is particularly common with property developments. In such cases, the joint arrangement may be financed principally by equity and the joint operators or joint venturers may have financed their participation in this equity through borrowings.

In situations where the joint arrangement is classified as a joint venture in accordance with IFRS 11 – *Joint Arrangements*, it is not appropriate to capitalise interest in the joint venture on the borrowings of the venturers as the interest charge is not a cost of the joint venture. Neither would it be appropriate to capitalise interest in the financial statements of the venturers, whether separate or consolidated financial statements, because the qualifying asset does not belong to them. The investing entities have an investment in a financial asset (i.e. an equity accounted investment), which is excluded by IAS 23 from being a qualifying asset (see 3.3 above).

In situations where the joint arrangement is classified as a joint operation in accordance with IFRS 11 and the operators are accounting for their own share of the assets, liabilities, revenue and expenses of the joint operation, then the operators should capitalise borrowing costs incurred that relate to their share of any qualifying asset. Borrowing costs eligible for capitalisation would be based on the operator's obligation for the loans of the joint operation together with any direct borrowings of the operator itself if the operator funds part of the acquisition of the joint operation's qualifying asset.

In situations where loans and borrowings exist between the reporting entity and a joint venture, see discussion in Chapter 11 at 7.6.3.

6 COMMENCEMENT, SUSPENSION AND CESSATION OF CAPITALISATION

6.1 Commencement of capitalisation

IAS 23 requires that capitalisation of borrowing costs as part of the cost of a qualifying asset commences when the entity first meets all of the following conditions:

(a) it incurs expenditures for the asset;

(b) it incurs borrowing costs; and

(c) it undertakes activities that are necessary to prepare the asset for its intended use or sale. *[IAS 23.17]*.

The standard is explicit that only the expenditure on a qualifying asset that has resulted in payments of cash, transfers of other assets or the assumption of interest-bearing liabilities, may be included in determining borrowing costs (see 5.3.3 above). Such expenditure must be reduced by any progress payments and grants received in connection with the asset (see 5.3 above). *[IAS 23.18]*.

The activities necessary to prepare an asset for its intended use or sale can include more than the physical construction of the asset. Necessary activities can start before the commencement of physical construction and include, for example, technical and administrative work such as the activities associated with obtaining permits prior to the commencement of the physical construction. *[IAS 23.19]*. However, this does not mean that borrowing costs can be capitalised if the permits that are necessary for the construction are not expected to be obtained. Consistent with the general principle in capitalisation and recognition of an asset, borrowing costs are capitalised as part of the cost of an asset when it is probable that they will result in future economic benefits to the entity and the costs can be measured reliably. *[IAS 23.9]*. Therefore, in assessing whether borrowing costs can be capitalised in advance of obtaining permits – assuming the borrowing costs otherwise meet the criteria – a judgement must be made, at the date the expenditure is incurred, as to whether it is sufficiently probable that the relevant permits will be granted. Conversely, if during the application and approval process of such permits it is no longer expected that the necessary permits will be granted, capitalisation of borrowing costs should cease, and accordingly, the carrying amount of any related qualifying asset subject to development or redevelopment, including any related borrowing costs that were previously capitalised, (or, if appropriate, the cash generating unit where such an asset belongs) should be tested for impairment, where applicable (see 6.2.1 below).

Borrowing costs may not be capitalised during a period in which there are no activities that change the condition of the asset. For example, a house-builder or property developer may not capitalise borrowing costs on its 'land bank' i.e. that land which is held for future development. Borrowing costs incurred while land is under development are capitalised during the period in which activities related to the development are being undertaken. However, borrowing costs incurred while land acquired for building purposes is held without any associated development activity represent a holding cost of the land. Such costs do not qualify for capitalisation and hence would be considered a period cost (i.e. expensed as incurred). *[IAS 23.19]*.

An entity may make a payment to a third-party contractor before that contractor commences construction activities. It is unlikely to be appropriate to capitalise borrowing costs in such a situation until the contractor commences activities that are necessary to prepare the asset for its intended use or sale. However, that would not preclude the payment being classified as a prepayment until such time as construction activities commence.

In its accounting policy, KAZ Minerals describes the period during which borrowing costs are capitalised, as well as noting that it uses either an actual rate or a weighted average cost of borrowings.

> **Extract 21.1: KAZ Minerals PLC (2019)**
> NOTES TO THE CONSOLIDATED FINANCIAL STATEMENTS [extract]
> 38. Summary of significant accounting policies [extract]
> (p)   Borrowing costs
>
> Borrowing costs directly relating to the acquisition, construction or production of a qualifying capital project under construction are capitalised and added to the project cost during construction until such time as the assets are considered substantially ready for their intended use, i.e. when they are capable of commercial production. Where funds are borrowed specifically to finance a project, the amount capitalised represents the actual borrowing costs incurred. Where surplus funds are available for a short period of time from money borrowed specifically to finance a project, the income generated from the temporary investment of such amounts is also capitalised and deducted from the total capitalised borrowing costs. Where the funds used to finance a project form part of general borrowings, the amount capitalised is calculated using a weighted average of rates applicable to relevant general borrowings of the Group during the year. All other borrowing costs are recognised in the income statement in the period in which they are incurred using the effective interest rate method.
>
> Borrowing costs that represent avoidable costs not related to the financing arrangements of the development projects and are therefore not directly attributable to the construction of these respective assets are expensed in the period as incurred. These borrowing costs generally arise where the funds are drawn down under the Group's financing facilities, whether specific or general, which are in excess of the near term cash flow requirements of the development projects for which the financing is intended, and the funds are drawn down ahead of any contractual obligation to do so.

6.1.1 Expenditures on a qualifying asset

In its June 2018 meeting, the Interpretations Committee discussed a request it received about the amount of borrowing costs eligible for capitalisation when an entity uses general borrowings to obtain a qualifying asset. In the fact pattern described in the request:

- an entity constructs a qualifying asset;
- the entity has no borrowings at the start of the construction of the qualifying asset;
- partway through construction, it borrows funds generally and uses them to finance the construction of the qualifying asset; and
- the entity incurs expenditures on the qualifying asset both before and after it incurs borrowing costs on the general borrowings.

The request asked whether an entity includes expenditures on a qualifying asset incurred before obtaining general borrowings in determining the amount of borrowing costs eligible for capitalisation.

The Interpretations Committee observed that an entity applies paragraph 17 of IAS 23 to determine the commencement date for capitalising borrowing costs. This paragraph requires an entity to begin capitalising borrowing costs when it meets all of the following conditions:

- it incurs expenditures for the asset;
- it incurs borrowing costs; and
- it undertakes activities that are necessary to prepare the asset for its intended use or sale (see also 6.1 above).

Applying paragraph 17 of IAS 23 to the fact pattern described in the request, the entity would not begin capitalising borrowing costs until it incurs borrowing costs.[10]

Once the entity incurs borrowing costs and therefore satisfies all the three conditions in paragraph 17 of IAS 23, as described above, it then applies paragraph 14 of IAS 23 (see 5.3 above) to determine the expenditures on the qualifying asset to which it applies the capitalisation rate. The Interpretations Committee observed that in doing so the entity does not disregard expenditures on the qualifying asset incurred before it obtains the general borrowings.

In its September 2018 meeting, the Interpretations Committee concluded that the principles and requirements in IFRS Standards provide an adequate basis for an entity to determine the amount of borrowing costs eligible for capitalisation in the fact pattern described in the request. Consequently, the Interpretations Committee decided not to add this matter to its standard-setting agenda.[11]

The following example illustrates the application of the principles described above.

Example 21.6: **Expenditures on a qualifying asset before general borrowings are obtained**

Construction on Entity A's building begins on 1 January 20X1 and ends on 30 June 20X2. The building meets the definition of a qualifying asset. Entity A incurs the following expenditures on constructing the building:

	£
1 January 20X1	250,000
30 June 20X1	450,000
31 December 20X1	480,000
	1,180,000
31 May 20X2	120,000
	1,300,000

On 1 July 20X1, Entity A issues three-years corporate bonds of £1,500,000 with interest payable annually at 3.5% every 30 June. The bonds form part of Entity A's general borrowings. A portion of the proceeds is used to finance the construction of the qualifying asset. Entity A had no general or specific borrowings before 1 July 20X1 and did not incur any borrowing costs before that date.

Using the information above, Entity A incurred £700,000 of expenditure before obtaining general borrowings on 1 July 20X1 and another £600,000 of expenditure after that date.

Applying paragraph 17 of IAS 23, Entity A begins to capitalise borrowing costs only after it has obtained the general borrowings, i.e. only when it starts incurring borrowing costs (see 6.1 above). Entity A does not capitalise borrowing costs before 1 July 20X1 (the day it issues the bonds) even though it has undertaken activities necessary to prepare the asset for its intended use or sale and has incurred expenditures for the asset before that date. This is because it did not incur any borrowing costs before 1 July 20X1.

Since Entity A has no other borrowings, the capitalisation rate is 3.5%. The capitalisation rate is applied to the expenditure on the qualifying asset, resulting in an amount eligible for capitalisation of £12,250 for the year ending 31 December 20X1. This is computed as follows:

	£
£250,000 × 3.5% × 6/12	4,375
£450,000 × 3.5% × 6/12	7,875
£480,000 × 3.5% × 0/12	–
	12,250

In the table above, Entity A does not disregard expenditures on the qualifying asset incurred before it obtained the general borrowings. However, since Entity A cannot capitalise borrowing costs before 1 July 20X1 (the day it started incurring borrowing costs), the eligible capitalisation period runs from 1 July 20X1 to 31 December 20X1 for the £700,000 of expenditure incurred before 1 July 20X1.

The accumulated expenditure as at beginning of 20X2 is £1,180,000 and the building construction is completed on 30 June 20X2. Accordingly, the amount eligible for capitalisation for the year ending 31 December 20X2 is computed as follows:

	£
£1,180,000 × 3.5% × 6/12	20,650
£120,000 × 3.5% × 1/12	350
	21,000

6.2 Suspension of capitalisation

An entity may incur borrowing costs during an extended period in which it suspends the activities necessary to prepare an asset for its intended use or sale. In such a case, IAS 23 states that capitalisation of borrowing costs should be suspended during extended periods in which active development is interrupted. *[IAS 23.20, 21]*. Such costs are costs of holding partially completed assets and do not qualify for capitalisation. However, the standard distinguishes between extended periods of interruption (when capitalisation would be suspended) and periods of temporary delay that are a necessary part of preparing the asset for its intended purpose (when capitalisation is not normally suspended). *[IAS 23.21]*.

An entity does not normally suspend capitalising borrowing costs during a period when it carries out substantial technical and administrative work. Also, capitalising borrowing costs would not be suspended when a temporary delay is a necessary part of the process of getting an asset ready for its intended use or sale. For example, capitalisation would continue during the extended period in a situation where construction of a bridge is delayed by temporary adverse weather conditions or high water levels, if such conditions are common during the construction period in the geographical region involved. *[IAS 23.21]*. Similarly, capitalisation continues during periods when inventory is undergoing slow transformation – the example is given of inventories taking an extended time to mature (presumably such products as Scotch whisky or Cognac, although the relevance of this may be limited as these products are likely to meet the optional exemption for 'routinely manufactured' products – see 3.1 above).

Borrowing costs incurred during extended periods of interruption caused, for example, by a lack of funding or a strategic decision to hold back project developments during a period of economic downturn are not considered a necessary part of preparing the asset for its intended purpose and should not be capitalised.

Other circumstances may not be straightforward. Therefore considering how the nature of the interruption, its length of duration, and the level of development activities during such period impact the determination as to whether the delay is a necessary part of the process of bringing the qualifying asset ready for its intended use or sale (and therefore, whether continuous capitalisation of eligible borrowing costs during such period is appropriate) may require the exercise of judgement based on particular facts and circumstances. Disclosure of this judgement is required if it is significant to the understanding of the financial statements (see 7.2 below).

6.2.1 Impairment considerations

When it is determined that capitalisation is appropriate, an entity continues to capitalise borrowing costs that are directly attributable to the acquisition, construction or production of a qualifying asset as part of the cost of the asset even if the capitalisation causes the expected ultimate cost of the asset to exceed its recoverable amount or net realisable value.

When the carrying amount of the qualifying asset exceeds its recoverable amount or net realisable value (depending on the type of asset), the carrying amount of the asset must be written down or written off in accordance with the relevant IFRSs. In certain circumstances, the amount of the write-down or write-off is written back in accordance with those relevant IFRSs. If the asset is incomplete, this assessment is performed by considering the expected ultimate cost of the asset. *[IAS 23.16]*. The expected ultimate cost, which will be compared to recoverable amount or net realisable value, must include costs to complete and the estimated capitalised interest thereon.

IAS 36 – *Impairment of Assets* – will apply if the qualifying asset is property, plant and equipment accounted for in accordance with IAS 16 or if the asset is otherwise within the scope of IAS 36 (see Chapter 20). For inventories that are qualifying assets, the requirements of IAS 2 – *Inventories* – on net realisable value will apply (see Chapter 22).

6.3 Cessation of capitalisation

The standard requires capitalisation of borrowing costs to cease when substantially all the activities necessary to prepare the qualifying asset for its intended use or sale are complete. *[IAS 23.22]*.

An asset is normally ready for its intended use or sale when the physical construction of the asset is complete, even though routine administrative work might still continue. If minor modifications, such as the decoration of a property to the purchaser's or user's specification, are all that are outstanding, this indicates that substantially all the activities are complete. *[IAS 23.23]*. In some cases, there may be a requirement for inspection (e.g. to ensure that the asset meets safety requirements) before the asset can be used. Usually 'substantially all the activities' would have been completed before this point in order to be ready for inspection. In such a situation, capitalisation would cease prior to the inspection.

When the construction of a qualifying asset is completed in parts and each part is capable of being used while construction continues on other parts, capitalisation should cease for the borrowing costs on the portion of borrowings attributable to that part when substantially all the activities necessary to prepare that part for its intended use or sale are completed. *[IAS 23.24]*. An example of this might be a business park comprising several buildings, each of which is capable of being fully utilised individually while construction continues on other parts. *[IAS 23.25]*. This principle also applies to single buildings where one part is capable of being fully utilised even if the building as a whole is incomplete (for example, individual floors of a high-rise office building).

For a qualifying asset that needs to be complete in its entirety before any part can be used as intended, it would be appropriate to capitalise related borrowing costs until all the activities necessary to prepare the entire asset for its intended use or sale are substantially complete. An example of this is an industrial plant, such as a steel mill, involving several processes which are carried out in sequence at different parts of the plant within the same site. [IAS 23.25].

However, other circumstances may not be as straightforward. As neither IAS 23 nor IAS 16 provide guidance on what constitutes a 'part', it will therefore depend on particular facts and circumstances and may require the exercise of judgement as to what constitutes a 'part'. Disclosure of this judgement is required if it is significant to the understanding of the financial statements (see 7.2 below).

6.3.1 Borrowing costs on 'land expenditures'

In its June 2018 meeting, the Interpretations Committee discussed a request it received about when an entity ceases capitalising borrowing costs on land. In the fact pattern described in the request:

- an entity acquires and develops land and thereafter constructs a building on that land – the land represents the area on which the building will be constructed;
- both the land and the building meet the definition of a qualifying asset; and
- the entity uses general borrowings to fund the expenditures on the land and construction of the building.

The request asked whether the entity ceases capitalising borrowing costs incurred in respect of expenditures on the land ('land expenditures') once it starts constructing the building or whether it continues to capitalise borrowing costs incurred in respect of land expenditures while it constructs the building.

The Interpretations Committee observed that in applying IAS 23 to determine when to cease capitalising borrowing costs incurred on land expenditures an entity considers:

- the intended use of the land; and
- in applying paragraph 24 of IAS 23, whether the land is capable of being used for its intended purpose while the construction continues on the building.

Land and buildings are used for owner-occupation (and therefore recognised as property, plant and equipment applying IAS 16); rent or capital appreciation (and therefore recognised as investment property applying IAS 40 – *Investment Property*); or for sale (and therefore recognised as inventory applying IAS 2). The intended use of the land is not simply for the construction of a building on the land, but rather to use it for one of these three purposes.

If the land is not capable of being used for its intended purpose while construction continues on the building, the entity considers the land and the building together to assess when to cease capitalising borrowing costs on the land expenditures. In this situation, the land would not be ready for its intended use or sale until substantially all the activities necessary to prepare both the land and building for that intended use or sale are complete (see 6.3 above).[12]

In its September 2018 meeting, the Interpretations Committee concluded that the principles and requirements in IFRS Standards provide an adequate basis for an entity to determine when to cease capitalising borrowing costs on land expenditures. Consequently, the Interpretations Committee decided not to add this matter to its standard-setting agenda.[13]

7 DISCLOSURE REQUIREMENTS

7.1 The requirements of IAS 23

An entity shall disclose:

- the amount of borrowing costs capitalised during the period; and
- the capitalisation rate used to determine the amount of borrowing costs eligible for capitalisation. *[IAS 23.26]*.

KAZ Minerals discloses in its 'finance costs' note its capitalisation rates used to determine its borrowing costs. The amount of borrowing costs capitalised during the period is also disclosed within the table that precedes this narrative disclosure and within the table of movements in the property, plant and equipment and mining assets notes.

> **Extract 21.2: KAZ Minerals PLC (2019)**
> NOTES TO THE CONSOLIDATED FINANCIAL STATEMENTS [extract]
> 12. Finance costs [extract]
> 1 In 2019, the Group capitalised to the cost of the Aktogay expansion project $6 million of borrowing costs from the DBK-Aktogay expansion facility at an average rate of interest of 5.98%. The Group also capitalised to the cost of the Aktogay expansion and the Baimskaya copper project and other qualifying assets $31 million of borrowing costs at an average rate of interest of 6.97% from all other borrowings outstanding during the year, which are regarded as general borrowings for Group reporting purposes. This follows the adoption on 1 January 2019 of '*Borrowing Costs Eligible for Capitalisation (Amendments to IAS 23)*', whereby project specific borrowings are included as general borrowings once those assets are operating as intended and therefore the associated interest will become available for capitalisation on other qualifying assets (see note 2(e)). In 2018, the Group capitalised to the cost of the Aktogay expansion project $4 million of general borrowing costs from the PXF facility only, at an average rate of interest of 4.97%. The interest cost on borrowings capitalised to qualifying assets is deductible for tax purposes against income in the current year.
>
> 2. Basis of preparation [extract]
> (e) Adoption of new standards and interpretations [extract]
>
> '*Borrowing Costs Eligible for Capitalisation (Amendments to IAS 23)*' was adopted on 1 January 2019. The amendment requires that project specific borrowings are included as general borrowings once those assets are operating as intended and therefore the associated interest will become available for capitalisation on other 'qualifying assets', being assets that necessarily take a substantial period of time to get ready for their intended use or sale. In the year ended 31 December 2019, this amendment brought the CDB-Bozshakol and Bozymchak, the CDB-Aktogay, and the first DBK-Aktogay loan borrowed specifically for the construction of the respective capital projects into general borrowings. The interest on these loans is therefore included in the capitalisation rate applied to expenditures on qualifying capital projects, such as the expansion of Aktogay (see note 12).

7.2 Disclosure requirements in other IFRSs

In addition to the disclosure requirements in IAS 23, an entity may need to disclose additional information in relation to its borrowing costs in order to comply with requirements in other IFRSs. For example, disclosures required by IAS 1 include:

- the nature and amount of material items included in profit or loss; *[IAS 1.97]*
- the measurement bases used in preparing the financial statements and other accounting policies used that are relevant to an understanding of the financial statements (see an example at Extract 21.1 above); *[IAS 1.117]* and

- the significant judgements made in the process of applying an entity's accounting policies that have the most significant effect on the recognised amounts (e.g. criteria in determining a qualifying asset or a 'part' of a qualifying asset, including definition of 'substantial period of time'). *[IAS 1.122]*.

As noted in 5.4 above, the Interpretations Committee considered a request for guidance on the treatment of foreign exchange gains and losses and on the treatment of any derivatives used to hedge such foreign exchange exposures.

The Interpretations Committee decided not to add the issue to its agenda but concluded both that (i) how an entity applies IAS 23 to foreign currency borrowings is a matter of accounting policy requiring an entity to exercise judgement and (ii) IAS 1 requires disclosure of significant accounting policies and judgements that are relevant to an understanding of the financial statements.[14] The requirements of IAS 1 are discussed in Chapter 3.

References

1 Effective from 15 September 2009, FASB Statement No. 34 (SFAS 34) – *Capitalization of Interest Cost* – was superseded by FASB Accounting Standards Codification (ASC) Topic 835-20 – *Capitalization of Interest*, a subtopic to FASB ASC Topic 835 – *Interest*.
2 *IFRIC Update*, May 2014.
3 *IFRIC Update*, November 2018.
4 *IFRIC Update*, March 2019.
5 *Annual Improvements to IFRS Standards 2015-2017 Cycle*, IASB, December 2017, p.15.
6 *IFRIC Update*, July 2009.
7 *IASB Update*, July 2009.
8 *IFRIC Update*, June 2017.
9 *IFRIC Update*, January 2008.
10 *IFRIC Update*, June 2018.
11 *IFRIC Update*, September 2018.
12 *IFRIC Update*, June 2018.
13 *IFRIC Update*, September 2018.
14 *IFRIC Update*, January 2008.

Chapter 22 Inventories

1 INTRODUCTION 1675
2 OBJECTIVE, SCOPE AND DEFINITIONS 1675
  2.1 Objective 1675
  2.2 Definitions 1676
  2.3 Scope 1676
       2.3.1 Practical application of the scope and recognition
              requirements of IAS 2 1677
              2.3.1.A Core inventories and spare parts 1677
              2.3.1.B Broadcast rights 1678
              2.3.1.C Emission rights 1679
              2.3.1.D Crypto-assets 1680
              2.3.1.E Transfers of rental assets to inventory 1681
              2.3.1.F Consignment stock and sale and repurchase
                         agreements 1681
              2.3.1.G Sales with a right of return 1682
3 MEASUREMENT 1682
  3.1 What may be included in cost? 1683
       3.1.1 Costs of purchase 1683
       3.1.2 Costs of conversion 1683
       3.1.3 Other costs 1685
              3.1.3.A Storage and distribution costs 1685
              3.1.3.B General and administrative overheads 1686
              3.1.3.C Borrowing costs and purchases on deferred
                         terms 1686
              3.1.3.D Service providers 1687
              3.1.3.E Forward contracts to purchase inventory 1688
              3.1.3.F Drug production costs within the
                         pharmaceutical industry 1688
  3.2 Measurement of cost 1689

	3.2.1	Techniques for the measurement of cost	1689
		3.2.1.A Standard cost	1689
		3.2.1.B Retail method	1689
	3.2.2	Cost formulas	1690
		3.2.2.A First-in, first-out (FIFO)	1691
		3.2.2.B Weighted average cost	1691
		3.2.2.C Last-in, first-out (LIFO)	1691
3.3	Net realisable value		1691
3.4	Measurement of crypto-assets in scope of IAS 2		1693
	3.4.1	Cost or lower net realisable value	1694
	3.4.2	Fair value less costs to sell	1694

4 REAL ESTATE INVENTORY 1695
  4.1 Classification of real estate as inventory 1695
  4.2 Costs of real estate inventory 1695
       4.2.1 Allocation of costs to individual units in multi-unit developments 1695
       4.2.2 Property demolition and lease costs 1696

5 RECOGNITION IN PROFIT OR LOSS 1697

6 DISCLOSURE REQUIREMENTS OF IAS 2 1697
  6.1 General requirements 1697
  6.2 Additional disclosure requirements for crypto-assets 1700

Chapter 22 — Inventories

1 INTRODUCTION

Under IFRS the relevant standard for inventories is IAS 2 – *Inventories*. The term 'inventories' includes raw materials, work-in-progress, finished goods and goods for resale in the ordinary course of business. Biological assets related to agricultural activity and agricultural produce at the point of harvest are however dealt with in IAS 41 – *Agriculture* (see Chapter 42). This chapter only deals with inventories within the scope of IAS 2.

Costs of inventories comprise expenditure which has been incurred in bringing the inventory to its present location and condition. All costs incurred in respect of inventories are charged as period costs, except for those which relate to those unconsumed inventories which are expected to be of future benefit to the entity. These are carried forward as an asset, until the entity transfers control to a third party, at which point revenue is recognised in accordance with IFRS 15 – *Revenue from Contracts with Customers* (see Chapter 30).

IAS 2 was last revised in 2003 primarily to clarify its scope and prohibit the use of the last-in, first-out (LIFO) formula to measure the cost of inventories. When IAS 2 was revised, all references to matching and to the historical cost system were deleted, even though historical cost was retained as the primary measurement approach for IAS 2 inventories.

2 OBJECTIVE, SCOPE AND DEFINITIONS

2.1 Objective

The objective of IAS 2 is to prescribe the accounting treatment for inventories. The standard notes that a primary issue in accounting for inventories is the cost to be recognised as an asset and carried forward until the related revenues are recognised. The standard provides guidance on the determination of cost and its subsequent recognition as an expense, including any write-down to net realisable value. Further to this, it provides guidance on the cost formulas that are used to assign costs to inventories. *[IAS 2.1]*.

2.2 Definitions

IAS 2 uses the following terms with the meanings specified below. *[IAS 2.6]*.

Inventories are assets:

(a) held for sale in the ordinary course of business;
(b) in the process of production for such sale; or
(c) in the form of materials or supplies to be consumed in the production process or in the rendering of services.

Net realisable value is the estimated selling price in the ordinary course of business less the estimated costs of completion and the estimated costs necessary to make the sale.

Fair value is the price that would be received to sell an asset or paid to transfer a liability in an orderly transaction between market participants at the measurement date (see Chapter 14).

2.3 Scope

IAS 2 applies to all inventories in financial statements except:

- financial instruments (see Chapters 44 to 54); and
- biological assets related to agricultural activity and agricultural produce at the point of harvest (see Chapter 42). *[IAS 2.2]*.

Agricultural produce that has been harvested by the entity from its biological assets is in scope; it is initially recognised at its fair value less costs to sell at the point of harvest, as set out in IAS 41 (see Chapter 42). This value becomes the cost of inventories at that date for the purposes of IAS 2. *[IAS 2.20]*.

The measurement provisions of IAS 2 do not apply to the measurement of inventories held by:

(a) producers of agricultural and forest products, agricultural produce after harvest, and minerals and mineral products, to the extent that they are measured at net realisable value in accordance with well-established practices in those industries. When such inventories are measured at net realisable value, changes in that value are recognised in profit or loss in the period of the change. *[IAS 2.3]*. This occurs, for example, when agricultural crops have been harvested or minerals have been extracted and sale is assured under a forward contract or a government guarantee, or when an active market exists and there is a negligible risk of failure to sell. *[IAS 2.4]*. However, in practice this approach is not common; and

(b) commodity broker-traders who measure their inventories at fair value less costs to sell. If these inventories are measured at fair value less costs to sell, the changes in fair value less costs to sell are recognised in profit or loss in the period of the change. *[IAS 2.3]*. Broker-traders are those who buy or sell commodities for others or on their own account and these inventories are principally acquired with the purpose of selling in the near future and generating a profit from fluctuations in price or broker-traders' margin. *[IAS 2.5]*.

In both cases, the standard stresses that these inventories are only scoped out from the measurement requirements of IAS 2; the standard's other requirements, such as disclosures, continue to apply. Fair value and net realisable value (NRV) are discussed at 3 below.

Inventories can include all types of goods purchased and held for resale including, for example, merchandise purchased by a retailer and other tangible assets such as land and other property held for resale, although investment property accounted for under IAS 40 – *Investment Property* – is not treated as an inventory item. The term also encompasses finished goods produced, or work in progress being produced, by the entity and includes materials and supplies awaiting use in the production process. Costs incurred to fulfil a contract with a customer that do not give rise to inventories (or assets within the scope of another standard) are accounted for in accordance with IFRS 15. *[IAS 2.8]*. Inventories may also include items of property, plant and equipment initially held for rental and subsequently transferred to inventories when they cease to be rented, *[IAS 16.68A]*, and intangible assets held by an entity for sale in the ordinary course of business. *[IAS 38.3(a)]*.

Collectibles, for example paintings or sculptures acquired for short-term investment purposes and traded in the ordinary course of business, could be within the scope of IAS 2. Depending on the facts and circumstances, these could be either:

- inventories measured at the lower of cost and net realisable value; or
- commodities, measured at fair value less costs to sell.

There is a separate standard, IFRS 5 – *Non-current Assets Held for Sale and Discontinued Operations* – that governs the accounting treatment of non-current assets held for sale, for example a group of assets held for sale such as a business being disposed of. An entity would apply IFRS 5 to any inventories that form part of a disposal group. IFRS 5 is discussed in Chapter 4.

2.3.1 Practical application of the scope and recognition requirements of IAS 2

2.3.1.A Core inventories and spare parts

In certain industries, for example the non-ferrous metals, gas extraction and petrochemical sectors, certain processes or storage arrangements always require a minimum amount of material to be present in the system during the production process in order to permit plants to operate or for production to be maintained. For example, cushion gas is required to maintain minimum storage pressure in gas cavern storage facilities and, in order for a crude oil refining process to take place, the plant must contain a certain minimum quantity of oil which can only be taken out if the pipeline is interrupted. Such materials have been referred to as 'core inventories' or 'minimum fill'. The issue with such minimum amounts of material is whether they should be accounted for as inventory in accordance with IAS 2 or as property, plant and equipment (PP&E) in accordance with IAS 16 – *Property, Plant and Equipment*.

The Interpretations Committee discussed the issue of 'core inventories' or 'minimum fill' at its March 2014 meeting and tentatively decided to develop an interpretation. The Interpretations Committee further directed the staff to define the scope of what is considered to be core inventories and to analyse the applicability of the concept to a range of industries.[1] At its July 2014 meeting, the Interpretations Committee discussed the feedback received from informal consultations with IASB members, the proposed scope of core inventories and the staff analysis of the applicability of the issue to a range of industries. In its redeliberations, the Interpretations Committee observed that what might constitute core inventories, and how they are accounted for, can vary between industries and that significant judgement might be needed in determining the appropriate accounting. The Interpretations Committee noted that it did not have clear evidence that the differences in accounting were caused by differences in how IAS 2 and IAS 16 were being applied and, in the absence of such evidence, the Interpretations Committee decided not to continue with the development of an interpretation and to remove this item from its agenda.[2]

It is our view that an item that is not held for sale or to be consumed in a production process should be accounted for as an item of PP&E under IAS 16 if it is necessary to operate or benefit from an asset during more than one operating cycle and its cost cannot be recouped through sale (or it is significantly impaired after it has been used to operate the asset or obtain benefit from the asset). This applies even if the part of inventory that is deemed to be an item of PP&E cannot physically be separated from other inventory. This topic is discussed further in Chapter 43 at 14.3 in the context of extractive industries.

By contrast, spare parts are classified as inventory unless they meet the definition of PP&E. The recognition of spare parts as PP&E and the accounting treatment of core inventories are discussed further in Chapter 18 at 3.1.1 and 3.1.5 respectively.

2.3.1.B Broadcast rights

Broadcasters purchase programmes under a variety of different arrangements. Often they commit to purchasing programmes that are at a very early stage of development, perhaps merely being concepts. The broadcaster may have exclusive rights over the programme or perhaps only have the rights to broadcast for a set period of time or on a set number of occasions. IFRSs are not clear on how these rights should be classified and when they should be recognised. The appropriate classification of broadcast rights depends on the particular facts and circumstances applicable to each case.

We believe that an entity may either treat these rights as intangible assets and classify them under IAS 38 – *Intangible Assets* (see Chapter 17 at 2.2.2) or classify them as inventory under IAS 2. Such rights would certainly seem to meet the definition of inventory under IAS 2. Given that the acquisition of these rights forms part of the cost of the broadcaster's programming schedule, they meet the general IAS 2 definition in that they are:

(a) held for sale in the ordinary course of business;

(b) in the process of production for such sale; or

(c) in the form of materials or supplies to be consumed in the production process or in the rendering of services. *[IAS 2.6]*.

When classified as inventory, the rights would usually be presented within current assets, even if the intention is not to consume them within 12 months. *[IAS 1.68]*. As with costs of other inventory the cash outflow from acquisition will be classified as an operating cash flow and the expense will be presented within cost of sales when the right is consumed.

Presenting these assets as a separate line item in the statement of financial position is also an alternative presentation observed in practice.

There is also the issue of the timing of recognition of these rights. In accordance with paragraph 4.3 of the 2018 revised *Conceptual Framework for Financial Reporting* an asset is a present economic resource controlled by an entity as a result of past events.

Hence it is necessary to determine when control is obtained. Under IFRS, executory contracts where both parties are still to perform (such as purchase orders where neither payment nor delivery has taken place) do not generally result in the recognition of assets and liabilities. When a broadcaster initially contracts to purchase a programme, it will not usually result in immediate recognition of an asset relating to that programme. At this point there will not normally be an asset under the control of the broadcaster. Factors that may be relevant in determining when the entity controls an asset include whether:

- the underlying resource is sufficiently developed to be identifiable (e.g. whether the manuscript or screenplay has been written, and whether directors and actors have been hired);
- the entity has legal, rights to broadcast, which may be in respect of a defined period or geographic area;
- there is a penalty to the licensor for non-delivery of the content;
- it is probable that content will be delivered; and
- it is probable that economic benefits will flow to the entity.

Where there is difficulty in determining when control of the asset is obtained it may be helpful to assess at what point any liability arises, since a liability will generally indicate that an asset has been acquired. In practice an entity might recognise an asset and a liability for a specific broadcast right on the following trigger dates:

- when a screening certificate is obtained;
- when programming is available for exhibition;
- the beginning of the season;
- the beginning of the license period; or
- the date the event occurs (e.g. game-by-game basis).

The issue of when a licensor recognises revenue under IFRS 15 on the sale of such broadcast rights is covered in Chapter 31 at 2.

2.3.1.C   Emission rights

In order to encourage entities to reduce emissions of pollutants, governments around the world have introduced schemes that comprise tradeable emissions allowances or permits. Entities using emission rights for their own purposes may elect to record the rights as intangible assets, whether at cost, revalued amount or, under the so-called 'net liability' approach, as rights that are re-measured to fair value. See Chapter 17 at 11.2.

It may also be appropriate to recognise emission rights, whether granted by the government or purchased by an entity, as inventory in accordance with IAS 2 if they are held for sale in the ordinary course of business or to settle an emissions liability in the ordinary course of business. If the purchased emission rights are recognised as inventories, they are subsequently measured at the lower of cost or net realisable value in accordance with IAS 2, unless they are held by commodity broker-traders.

Broker-traders account for emission rights as inventory. A broker-trader may recognise emission rights either at the lower of cost and net realisable value, or at fair value less costs to sell as permitted by IAS 2. An integrated entity may hold emission rights both for own-use and for trading. An entity accounts for these emission rights separately.

2.3.1.D   Crypto-assets

Crypto-assets have diverse terms and conditions, and the purpose for holding them differs among holders. As a result, the holders of a crypto-asset will need to evaluate their own facts and circumstances in determining which IFRS classification and measurement requirements should be applied. Depending on the relevant accounting standard, the holder may also need to assess its business model in order to determine the appropriate classification and measurement. Cryptocurrencies represent a subset of crypto-assets. In recent years, numerous cryptocurrencies (for example Bitcoin) and crypto-tokens have been launched. In June 2019, the IFRS Interpretations Committee discussed how IFRS standards apply to holdings of a subset of crypto-assets with the following characteristics:

- a digital or virtual currency recorded on a distributed ledger that uses cryptography for security;
- not issued by a jurisdictional authority or other party; and
- does not give rise to a contract between the holder and another party.

For the purpose of their discussion, the Committee referred to crypto-assets with these characteristics as 'cryptocurrency'. The Committee concluded that IAS 2 applies to cryptocurrencies when they are held for sale in the ordinary course of business. If IAS 2 is not applicable, an entity applies IAS 38 to holdings of cryptocurrencies.[3]

The Committee observed that a holding of cryptocurrency would meet the definition of an intangible asset in IAS 38 on the grounds that: a) it is capable of being separated from the holder and sold or transferred individually; and b) it does not give the holder a right to receive a fixed or determinable number of units of currency.

Other crypto-assets that do not have the characteristics of cryptocurrency considered by the Committee (and therefore not in scope of the agenda decision) may also meet the relatively wide definition of an intangible asset. The accounting for crypto-assets as intangible assets is discussed in Chapter 17 at 11.5.

However not all intangible assets are within the scope of IAS 38 as the standard is clear that it does not apply to items that are in the scope of another standard. For example, IAS 38 excludes from its scope intangible assets held by an entity for sale in the ordinary course of business, which are within scope of IAS 2, [IAS 38.3(a)], and financial assets as defined in IAS 32 – *Financial Instruments: Presentation*. [IAS 38.3(e)].

The Committee considered the definition of a financial asset in accordance with IAS 32 and concluded that a holding of cryptocurrency is not a financial asset. This is because a cryptocurrency is not cash. Nor is it an equity instrument of another entity. It does not give rise to a contractual right for the holder and it is not a contract that will or may be settled in the holder's own equity instruments. The definition of a financial asset in accordance with IAS 32 is discussed in Chapter 45 at 2.

Although this is often assumed, IAS 2 does not require inventory to be tangible. The Committee observed that cryptocurrencies could be held for sale in the ordinary course of business, for example, by a commodity broker-trader. In that circumstance, a holding of cryptocurrency is inventory for the entity, and IAS 2 applies to that holding.

Whether cryptocurrencies and other crypto-assets are held for sale in the ordinary course of business would depend on the specific facts and circumstances of the holder.

In practice, cryptocurrencies and other crypto-assets are generally not used in the production of inventory and, thus, would not be considered materials and supplies to be consumed in the production process. However, in limited circumstances, we believe that a crypto-asset could be held for consumption in the rendering of a service. For example, a crypto-asset, not readily convertible to cash, that only entitles the holder to a specific service (e.g. server capacity) could be considered inventory if the holder uses the underlying service to deliver its own services in the ordinary course of its business.

The measurement of cryptocurrencies and other crypto-assets that meet the definition of inventory is addressed at 3.4 below.

If an entity has made judgements regarding its accounting for holdings of cryptocurrencies, and those judgements have a significant effect on the amounts recognised in the financial statements, those judgements should be disclosed in accordance with the requirements of paragraph 122 of IAS 1 – *Presentation of Financial Statements*.[4] Such judgements may relate to the classification of cryptocurrency as inventory or intangible assets, and may also be relevant to holdings of other crypto-assets outside the scope of the Interpretations Committee's discussions.

2.3.1.E   Transfers of rental assets to inventory

An entity may, in the course of its ordinary activities, routinely sell items that had previously been held for rental and classified as property, plant and equipment. For example, car rental companies may acquire vehicles with the intention of holding them as rental cars for a limited period and then selling them. IAS 16 requires that when such items become held for sale in the ordinary course of business rather than for rental, they should be transferred to inventory at their carrying value. *[IAS 16.68A]*. Revenue from the subsequent sale is then recognised gross rather than net, as discussed in Chapter 18 at 7.2.

2.3.1.F   Consignment stock and sale and repurchase agreements

A manufacturer may enter into an arrangement with a distributor where the distributor sells inventory on behalf of the manufacturer. Under such arrangements, a manufacturer (consignor) may deliver inventory on a consignment basis to a distributor or dealer (consignee). The consignor retains the legal title to the inventory and consignee acts as a selling agent. Such consignment arrangements are common in certain industries, such as the automotive industry. Under IFRS 15, revenue will not be recognised for stock delivered to the consignee because control has not yet transferred (see Chapter 30 at 6), and the consignor would continue to account for the consignment inventory until control has passed.

Similarly, an entity may enter into sale and repurchase agreements with a customer where the entity agrees to repurchase inventory under particular circumstances. For example, the entity may agree to repurchase any inventory that the customer has not sold to a third party after six months. IFRS 15 contains complex guidance, explained in Chapter 30 at 5, which can result in the entity accounting for such arrangements as financing arrangements, as leases, or as a sale with a right of return.

Where an arrangement is accounted for as a financing arrangement, the seller will continue to recognise the inventory on its balance sheet and will also recognise a financial liability for the consideration received. If IFRS 15 requires the arrangement to be accounted for as a lease, the arrangement must be accounted for in accordance with IFRS 16 – *Leases*. In this case, if the seller is considered to be acting as lessor in an operating lease, the seller will continue to recognise the inventory on balance sheet. For arrangements that are considered to be a sale with a right of return, inventory will be derecognised and the seller will instead recognise a right of return asset. Sales with a right of return are considered further at 2.3.1.G below.

The entity will also have to consider appropriate disclosure for material amounts of inventory that is held on consignment or sale and return at a third party's premises.

2.3.1.G Sales with a right of return

An entity may provide its customers with a right to return goods that it has sold to them. The right may be contractual, or an implicit right that exists due to the entity's customary business practice, or a combination of both. Offering a right of return in a sales agreement obliges the selling entity to stand ready to accept any returned product. Under IFRS 15, the potential for customer returns needs to be considered when an entity estimates the transaction price because potential returns are a component of variable consideration. IFRS 15 also requires that the selling entity recognise the amount received or receivable that is expected to be returned to the customer as a refund liability and recognise a return asset for its right to recover goods returned by the customer. The carrying value of the return asset is presented separately from inventory. Sales with a right of return are discussed further in Chapter 28 at 3.7, Chapter 29 at 2.4 and Chapter 30 at 9.

3 MEASUREMENT

The standard's basic rule is that inventories are measured at the lower of cost and net realisable value, except those inventories scoped out of its measurement requirements as explained at 2.3 above. *[IAS 2.9]*. Net realisable value is 'the estimated selling price in the ordinary course of business less the estimated costs of completion and the estimated costs necessary to make the sale'. *[IAS 2.6]*. This is different to fair value, which IAS 2 defines in accordance with IFRS 13 – *Fair Value Measurement* – as 'the price that would be received to sell an asset or paid to transfer a liability in an orderly transaction between market participants at the measurement date'. *[IAS 2.6]*.

The standard points out that net realisable value is an entity-specific value, the amount that the entity actually expects to realise from selling that particular inventory in the ordinary course of business, while fair value is not. Fair value reflects the price at which an orderly transaction to sell the same inventory in the principal (or most advantageous) market for that inventory would take place between market participants at the measurement date. Therefore, net realisable value may not equal fair value less costs to sell. *[IAS 2.7]*. This is illustrated in the following extract in which AngloGold Ashanti discloses that net realisable value is based on estimated future sales prices of the product.

> Extract 22.1: AngloGold Ashanti Limited (2019)
> GROUP – NOTES TO THE FINANCIAL STATEMENTS [extract]
>
> 1   ACCOUNTING POLICIES [extract]
> 1.2   SIGNIFICANT ACCOUNTING JUDGEMENTS AND ESTIMATES [extract]
> USE OF ESTIMATES [extract]
> Stockpiles and metals in process [extract]
>
> Costs that are incurred in or benefit the production process are accumulated in stockpiles and metals in process values. Net realisable value tests are performed at least annually and represent the estimated future sales price of the product, based on prevailing and long-term metals prices, less estimated costs to complete production and bring the product to sale.

If there has been a downturn in a cyclical business such as real estate, an entity may argue that net realisable value is higher than fair value because the entity intends to hold the asset until prices recover. This is rarely supportable as the decline in fair value usually indicates that the price that will be achieved in the ordinary course of business has declined and time taken to dispose of assets has increased. Net realisable value is discussed at 3.3 below.

This basic measurement rule inevitably raises the question of what may be included in the cost of inventory.

3.1 What may be included in cost?

The costs attributed to inventories under IAS 2 comprise all costs of purchase, costs of conversion and other costs incurred in bringing the inventories to their present location and condition. *[IAS 2.10]*. This definition allows for significant judgement of the costs to be included in inventory.

3.1.1 Costs of purchase

Costs of purchase include import duties and unrecoverable taxes, transport, handling and other costs directly attributable to the acquisition of inventories. *[IAS 2.11]*.

All trade discounts and similar rebates should be deducted from the costs attributed to inventories. *[IAS 2.11]*. For example, a supplier may pay to its customer an upfront cash incentive when entering into a contract. This is a form of rebate and the incentive should be accounted for as a liability by the customer until it receives the related inventory, which is then shown at cost net of this incentive. Similarly, discounts for prompt settlement of invoices should be accounted for as a reduction of the cost of purchase and deducted from the costs of any unsold inventories.

3.1.2 Costs of conversion

Costs of conversion include direct costs such as direct labour and materials, as well as an allocation of fixed and variable production overheads. It must be remembered that the inclusion of overheads is not optional. Overheads may comprise indirect labour and materials or other indirect costs of production. For the most part there are few problems over the inclusion of direct costs in inventories, although difficulties may arise over the inclusion of certain types of overheads and over the allocation of overheads into the inventory valuation. Overhead costs must be apportioned using a 'systematic allocation of fixed and variable production overheads that are incurred in converting materials into finished goods'. [IAS 2.12]. Overheads should be allocated to the cost of inventory on a consistent basis from year to year, regardless of whether this will result in a net realisable value problem.

Variable production overheads are indirect costs of production that vary directly, or nearly directly, with the volume of production such as indirect material and indirect labour. [IAS 2.12]. Variable production overheads are allocated to each unit of production on the basis of the actual use of the production facilities. [IAS 2.13].

Fixed production overheads are indirect costs that remain relatively constant regardless of the volume of production, such as depreciation and maintenance of buildings, equipment and right-of-use assets used in the production process, and factory management expenses. [IAS 2.12].

The allocation of fixed production overheads is based on the normal capacity of the facilities. Normal capacity is defined as 'the production expected to be achieved on average over a number of periods or seasons under normal circumstances, taking into account the loss of capacity resulting from planned maintenance'. [IAS 2.13]. While actual capacity may be used if it approximates to normal capacity, overheads may not be fully allocated to production as a result of low output or idle capacity. In these cases, the unallocated overheads must be expensed. Similarly, in periods of abnormally high production, the fixed overhead absorption must be reduced, as otherwise inventories would be recorded at an amount in excess of cost. [IAS 2.13].

The occurrence of a natural disaster may often result in changes to an entity's operations, for example, by interrupting supply chains, restricting operations or increasing operating costs. If production volumes are lower than normal because of a natural disaster, the entity must not increase the amount of fixed overhead costs allocated to each unit of production. Rather, any unallocated overheads are recognised as an expense in the period in which they are incurred. Conversely, entities may have abnormally high production for certain products, for example due to panic-buying. In these circumstances, an entity needs to decrease the amount of fixed overhead allocated to each unit of production so that inventories are not measured above cost.

Entities need to assess whether wasted materials, labour, or other production costs are abnormal and, if so, they must be expensed as incurred. Entities may incur wasted materials, for example, to repackage goods that were originally destined for the wholesale market now redirected for retail sale to consumers (see 3.1.3.A below).

In computing the costs to be allocated via the overhead recovery rate, costs such as distribution and selling must be excluded, together with the cost of storing raw materials and work in progress, unless it is necessary that storage costs be incurred prior to further processing, which may occasionally be the case (see 3.1.3.A below).

Although not specifically referred to in IAS 2, when the revaluation model in IAS 16 is applied, depreciation of property, plant and equipment is based on the revalued amount, less the residual value of the asset and it is the revalued depreciation that, in our view, should be utilised in inventory valuation.

IAS 2 mentions the treatment to be adopted when a production process results in the simultaneous production of more than one product, for example, when joint products are produced or when there is a main product and a by-product. If the costs of converting each product are not separately identifiable, they should be allocated between the products on a rational and consistent basis. For example, this might be the relative sales value of each of the products either at the stage in the production process when the products become separately identifiable, or at the completion of production. If the value of the by-product is immaterial, it may be measured at net realisable value and this value deducted from the cost of the main product. *[IAS 2.14]*. In the extractive industries, it is common for more than one product to be extracted from the same reserves therefore joint and by-products are further discussed in Chapter 43 at 14.2 in the context of such industries.

3.1.3 Other costs

Other costs are to be included in inventories only to the extent that they are incurred to bring them into their present location and condition. Often judgement will be necessary to make this assessment. An example is given in IAS 2 of design costs for a special order for a particular customer and the standard notes that it may be appropriate to include such costs or other non-production overheads. *[IAS 2.15]*. However, a number of examples are given of costs that are specifically disallowed. These are:

(a) abnormal amounts of wasted materials, labour, or other production costs;

(b) storage costs, unless those costs are necessary in the production process prior to a further production stage;

(c) administrative overheads that do not contribute to bringing inventories to their present location and condition; and

(d) selling costs. *[IAS 2.16]*.

The amount of inventories recognised as an expense during the period, which is often referred to as cost-of-sales, consists of those costs previously included in the measurement of inventory that has been sold as well as unallocated production overheads and abnormal amounts of production costs of inventories. *[IAS 2.38]*.

3.1.3.A Storage and distribution costs

Storage costs are excluded from the cost of inventory unless they are necessary in the production process. *[IAS 2.16(b)]*. This prohibits, for example, including the overheads of a retail outlet as part of inventory.

However, where it is necessary to store raw materials or work in progress prior to a further processing or manufacturing stage (e.g. maturing stocks, such as cheese, wine or whisky), the costs of such storage should be included in production overheads.

Distribution costs are a cost of bringing an item to its present location, however, judgement may need to be applied in identifying which costs are necessarily incurred to bring the inventories to their present location and condition. For example, in the context of large retailers with distribution centres (e.g. supermarkets), the transport and logistics involved are essential to their ability to put goods on sale at a particular location in an appropriate condition. In these circumstances, warehousing costs and transportation from central or regional warehouses to retail outlets are considered a cost of bringing the asset to the point of sale and hence capitalised in the cost of inventories. [IAS 2.15]. Conversely:

- the cost of moving inventories from one retail outlet to another cannot be included in the carrying value of inventory; and
- entities may incur additional costs to store inventories due to lower than expected demand. Such costs need to be expensed when incurred as storage costs can only be capitalised when they are necessary to the production process, before further processing.

3.1.3.B General and administrative overheads

IAS 2 specifically disallows administrative overheads that do not contribute to bringing inventories to their present location and condition. [IAS 2.16(c)]. Other costs and overheads that do contribute are allowable as costs of production. There is a judgement to be made about such matters, as under a very broad interpretation any department could be considered to make a contribution. For example, the accounts department will normally support the following functions:

(a) production – by paying direct and indirect production wages and salaries, by controlling purchases and related payments, and by preparing periodic financial statements for the production units;

(b) marketing and distribution – by analysing sales and by controlling the sales ledger; and

(c) general administration – by preparing management accounts and annual financial statements and budgets, by controlling cash resources and by planning investments.

Only those costs of the accounts department that can be allocated to the production function can be included in the cost of conversion. Part of the management and overhead costs of a large retailer's logistical department may be included in cost if it can be related to bringing the inventory to its present location and condition. These types of cost are unlikely to be material in the context of the inventory total held by organisations. An entity determining that it needs to include a material amount of overhead of a borderline nature must ensure it can sensibly justify its inclusion under the provisions of IAS 2 by presenting an analysis of the function and its contribution to the production process similar to the above.

3.1.3.C Borrowing costs and purchases on deferred terms

IAS 2 states that IAS 23 – *Borrowing Costs* – identifies limited circumstances where borrowing costs are to be included in the cost of inventories. [IAS 2.17]. IAS 23 requires that borrowing costs be capitalised on qualifying assets but the scope of that standard exempts inventories that are manufactured in large quantities on a repetitive basis. [IAS 23.4, 8]. In addition, IAS 23 clarifies that inventories manufactured over a short period of time are not qualifying assets. [IAS 23.7]. However, any manufacturer that is producing small quantities over a long time period (e.g. maturing stocks of wine or whisky) has to capitalise borrowing costs. This is further discussed in Chapter 21 at 3.1.

IAS 2 also states that, on some occasions, an entity might purchase inventories on deferred settlement terms, accompanied by a price increase that effectively makes the arrangement a combined purchase and financing arrangement. Under these circumstances the price difference is recognised as an interest expense over the period of the financing. *[IAS 2.18]*.

Entities might also make prepayments for inventory, particularly raw materials in long-term supply contracts, raising the question of whether there is a financing component that should be accounted for separately.

If a purchaser accretes interest on long-term prepayments by recognising interest income, this will result in an increase in the cost of inventories and, ultimately, the cost of sales. The Interpretations Committee considered this in July 2015, noting that IAS 16 and IAS 38 include similar requirements to IAS 2 when payment for an asset is deferred (see Chapter 18 at 4.1.6 and Chapter 17 at 4.2).

Historically there has been no explicit requirement in IFRS to accrete interest income but the Interpretations Committee noted that IFRS 15 includes the requirement that the financing component of a transaction should be recognised separately in circumstances of both prepayment and deferral of payment (see Chapter 29 at 2.5). They concluded, therefore, that when a financing component is identified in a long-term supply contract of raw materials, that financing component should be accounted for separately. They acknowledged that judgement is required to identify when individual arrangements contain a financing component.[5]

As stated at 3.1.1 above, discounts for prompt settlement of suppliers' invoices should be deducted from the cost attributed to inventories.

3.1.3.D Service providers

Before IFRS 15 became effective, IAS 2 included the notion of work in progress (or 'inventory') of a service provider. However, this was consequentially removed from IAS 2 and replaced with the relevant requirements in IFRS 15. Costs to fulfil a contract, as defined in IFRS 15, are divided into two categories: (a) costs that give rise to an asset; and (b) costs that are expensed as incurred (see Chapter 31 at 5.2). *[IFRS 15.95-96]*. When determining the appropriate accounting treatment for such costs, IAS 2 (or any other more specific IFRS) is considered first and if costs incurred in fulfilling the contract are within the scope of this standard, those costs should be accounted for in accordance with IAS 2 (or other IFRS). If costs incurred to fulfil a contract are not within the scope of IAS 2 or any other applicable standard, an entity would need to consider the criteria in IFRS 15 for capitalisation of such costs (see Chapter 31 at 5.2).

IFRS 15 does not specifically deal with the classification and presentation of contract costs. In the absence of a standard that specifically deals with the classification and presentation of these costs, entities would need to apply the requirements in IAS 8 – *Accounting Policies, Changes in Accounting Estimates and Errors* – to select an appropriate classification. As discussed in Chapter 31 at 5.3.6, we believe that costs to fulfil a contract should be presented as a separate asset in the statement of financial position.

3.1.3.E Forward contracts to purchase inventory

The standard scopes out commodity broker-traders that measure inventory at fair value less costs to sell from its measurement requirements (see 2.3 above). If a broker-trader had a forward contract for purchase of inventory this contract would be accounted for as a derivative under IFRS 9 – *Financial Instruments* – since it would not meet the normal purchase or sale exemption (see Chapter 45 at 4.2) and when the contract was physically settled, the inventory would likewise be shown at fair value less costs to sell. *[IAS 2.3(b)]*. However, if such an entity were not measuring inventory at fair value less costs to sell it would be subject to the measurement requirements of IAS 2 and would therefore have to record the inventory at the lower of cost and net realisable value. This raises a question as to what cost is when such an entity takes delivery of inventory that has been purchased with a forward contract?

On delivery, the cash paid (i.e. the fixed price agreed in the forward contract) is in substance made up of two elements:

(i) an amount that settles the forward contract; and

(ii) an amount that represents the 'cost of purchase', being the market price at the date of purchase.

This 'cost of purchase' represents the forward contract price adjusted for the derivative asset or liability. For example, assume that the broker-trader was purchasing oil and the forward contracted price was $40 per barrel of oil, but at the time of delivery the spot price of oil was $50 and the forward contract had a fair value of $10 at that date. The oil would be recorded at the fair value on what is deemed to be the purchase date of $50. The $40 cash payment would in substance consist of $50 payment for the inventory offset by a $10 receipt on settlement of the derivative contract, which would be separately accounted for. This is exactly the same result as if the entity had been required to settle the derivative immediately prior to, and separate from, the physical delivery of the oil. The requirement to recognise inventory at the amount of cash paid ($40) plus the fair value of the derivative at the settlement date ($10), when the normal sale and purchase exemption does not apply and the derivative is not designated as part of a hedge relationship, was confirmed by the Interpretations Committee in the March 2019 agenda decision addressing physical settlement of contracts to buy or sell a non-financial item.[6]

If the entity purchasing the oil in the example above is not a broker-trader, and the acquisition meets the normal purchase or sale exemption given in IAS 32, the purchase of oil would be recognised at the entity's cost thereof; in terms of IAS 2, that is $40 per barrel of oil.

3.1.3.F Drug production costs within the pharmaceutical industry

After the development stage, pharmaceutical companies often commence production of drugs prior to obtaining the necessary regulatory approval to sell them (so called 'pre-launch inventories'). These drugs are produced in advance so that the sales of the newly authorised drug may commence as soon as regulatory approval is obtained. As long as the regulatory approval has been applied for and it is believed highly likely that this will be successfully obtained then it is appropriate to be recognising an asset and classifying this as inventory. If the likelihood of obtaining the approval declines, these inventories are written-down in 'cost of sales'. If regulatory approval is subsequently obtained, the write-down is reversed (to the extent that the original cost is realisable). Prior to this application for regulatory approval being made, any costs would need to be classified as research and development costs rather than inventory and the criteria within IAS 38 assessed to determine if capitalisation was appropriate (see Chapter 17 at 6.2.3).

3.2 Measurement of cost

3.2.1 Techniques for the measurement of cost

IAS 2 specifically allows the use of techniques for the measurement of cost of inventories such as the standard cost method or of the retail method, provided that the result approximates cost.

These techniques require an entity to use judgements or assumptions in developing an accounting estimate that meets the measurement objective, i.e. cost. The effects of a change in an input or in a measurement technique used to develop an accounting estimate is accounted for as a change in accounting estimate provided the change is not arising as a result of a correction of prior period errors. In this respect, a change in accounting estimate that results from new information or more experience is not the correction of an error.

3.2.1.A Standard cost

Standard costs should take into account normal levels of materials and supplies, labour, efficiency and capacity utilisation. They must be regularly reviewed and revised where necessary. *[IAS 2.21]*. Normal levels of activity are discussed in 3.1.2 above.

3.2.1.B Retail method

The retail method is often used in the retail industry for measuring inventories with high volumes of rapidly changing items with similar margins for which it is impracticable to use other measurement techniques. *[IAS 2.22]*. In these circumstances, the cost of inventory is determined by converting selling prices to cost by adjusting for a normal margin.

This technique involves applying judgement regarding the granularity of inputs required in determining the appropriate margin rate adjustments which would result in an acceptable approximation of cost. Paragraph 22 of IAS 2 states that an average percentage for each retail department is often used when applying this technique. *[IAS 2.22]*.

Inputs used in this technique must be consistent with how the entity determines appropriate write downs. Using average margin rates and selling prices that are determined inconsistently may result in anomalies such as items of inventory being measured above their cost. For example, in the garment industry, any remaining items from a past seasonal collection will often be sold through alternative distribution channels (i.e. other than in the entity's retail outlets or distributors) such as discounters. In this case, applying an average margin rate from sales in the main distribution channels to the selling price in these points of sale would require the entity to also determine any required write downs in a second step. Therefore, using average margin rates from all sales including sales to discounters and applying these rates to catalogue selling prices would result in measuring items above their cost because the margin rates used to convert selling prices to cost are inappropriately reduced.

3.2.2 Cost formulas

Items that are not ordinarily interchangeable and goods or services produced for specific projects should have their costs specifically identified and these costs will be matched with the goods physically sold. *[IAS 2.23]*. In practice this is a relatively unusual method of valuation, as the clerical effort required does not make it feasible unless there are relatively few high value items being bought or produced. Consequently, it would normally be used where the inventory comprised items such as antiques, jewellery and automobiles in the hands of dealers. This measurement technique is inappropriate where there are large numbers of items that are ordinarily interchangeable, as specific identification of costs could distort the profit or loss arising from these inventories through the method applied to selecting items that remain in inventories. *[IAS 2.24]*.

Where it is necessary to use a cost-flow assumption (i.e. when there are large numbers of ordinarily interchangeable items), IAS 2 allows either a FIFO (first-in, first-out) or a weighted average cost formula to be used. *[IAS 2.25]*.

The standard makes it clear that the same cost formula should be used for all inventories having a similar nature and use to the entity, although items with a different nature and use may justify the use of a different cost formula. *[IAS 2.25]*. For example, the standard acknowledges that inventories used in one operating segment may have a use to the entity different from the same type of inventories used in another operating segment. However, a difference in geographical location of inventories (or in their respective tax rules) is not sufficient, by itself, to justify the use of different cost formulas. *[IAS 2.26]*.

An entity may choose, as a result of particular facts and circumstances, to change its cost formula, for instance, from a FIFO-based cost formula to a weighted average cost formula. The change in a cost formula represents a change in the basis on which the value of the inventory has been determined, rather than a change in valuation of the inputs used to determine the cost of the inventory. An accounting policy is defined in IAS 8 as including specific bases applied by an entity in preparing and presenting financial statements. Therefore, a change in the cost formula represents a change in accounting policy which should only be made if it results in the financial statements providing reliable and more relevant information. *[IAS 8.14]*. If material, a change in accounting policy should be applied retrospectively, that is applied to transactions, other events and conditions as if it had always been applied in accordance with IAS 8 (see Chapter 3 at 4.4).

As part of its project on Exposure Draft ED/2017/5 – *Accounting Policies and Accounting Estimates – Proposed amendments to IAS 8*, the IASB proposed to confirm that selecting a cost formula does not constitute making an accounting estimate, it constitutes selecting an accounting policy.[7] When it last redeliberated this proposal in October 2019 as part of finalising the amendment, the Board decided that such clarification was in fact not needed because paragraph 36(a) of IAS 2 already states that selecting a cost formula constitutes selecting an accounting policy.

3.2.2.A   First-in, first-out (FIFO)

In the vast majority of businesses, it will not be practicable to keep track of the cost of identical items of inventory on an individual unit basis; nevertheless, it is desirable to approximate to the actual physical flows as far as possible. The FIFO method probably gives the closest approximation to actual cost flows, since it is assumed that when inventories are sold or used in a production process, the oldest are sold or used first. Consequently, the balance of inventory on hand at any point represents the most recent purchases or production. *[IAS 2.27]*. This can best be illustrated in the context of a business which deals in perishable goods (e.g. food retailers) since clearly such a business will use the first goods received earliest. The FIFO method, by allocating the earliest costs incurred against revenue, matches actual cost flows with the physical flow of goods reasonably accurately. In any event, even in the case of businesses which do not deal in perishable goods, this would reflect what would probably be a sound management policy. In practice, the FIFO method is generally used where it is not possible to value inventory on an actual cost basis.

3.2.2.B   Weighted average cost

The weighted average method, which like FIFO is suitable where inventory units are identical or nearly identical, involves the computation of an average unit cost by dividing the total cost of units by the number of units. The average unit cost then has to be revised with every receipt of inventory, or alternatively at the end of predetermined periods. *[IAS 2.27]*. In practice, weighted average systems are widely used in packaged inventory systems that are computer controlled, although its results are not very different from FIFO in times of relatively low inflation, or where inventory turnover is relatively quick.

3.2.2.C   Last-in, first-out (LIFO)

LIFO, as its name suggests, is the opposite of FIFO and assumes that the most recent purchases or production are used first. In certain cases, this could represent the physical flow of inventory (e.g. if a store is filled and emptied from the top). However IAS 2 prohibits the use of the LIFO method. *[IAS 2.BC9]*. LIFO is an attempt to match current costs with current revenues so that profit or loss excludes the effects of holding gains or losses. Essentially, therefore, LIFO is an attempt to achieve something closer to replacement cost accounting for the statement of profit or loss, whilst disregarding the statement of financial position. Consequently, the period-end balance of inventory on hand represents the earliest purchases of the item, resulting in inventories being stated in the statement of financial position at amounts which may bear little relationship to recent cost levels. Unlike IFRS, US GAAP allows LIFO and it is popular in the US as the Internal Revenue Service officially recognises LIFO as an acceptable method for the computation of tax provided that it is used consistently for tax and financial reporting purposes.

3.3   Net realisable value

IAS 2 contains substantial guidance on the estimation of net realisable value. When this is below cost, inventory must be written down.

The cost of inventory may have to be reduced to its net realisable value if the inventory has become damaged, is wholly or partly obsolete, or if its selling price has declined. The costs of inventory may not be recovered from sale because of increases in the costs to complete, or the estimated selling costs. *[IAS 2.28]*. However, the costs to consider in making this assessment should only comprise direct costs to complete and sell the inventory.

Writing inventory down to net realisable value should normally be done on an item-by-item basis. IAS 2 specifically states that it may be appropriate to group similar or related items but it is not appropriate to write down an entire class of inventory, such as finished goods, or all the inventory of a particular segment. However, it may be necessary to write down an entire product line or group of inventories in a given geographical area if the items cannot be practicably evaluated separately. *[IAS 2.29]*.

Estimates of net realisable value must be based on the most reliable evidence available and take into account fluctuations of price or cost after the end of the period only to the extent they confirm conditions existing at the end of the period. *[IAS 2.30, IAS 10.9(b)(ii)]*. A loss realised on a sale of a product after the end of the period may provide evidence of the net realisable value of that product at the end of the period. However if the selling price of this product is, for example, correlated to an exchange-traded commodity, and the loss realised can be attributed to a fall in prices of that commodity after the period end date, then this loss would not provide evidence of the net realisable value at the period end date. The impact of post balance sheet events in determining the net realisable value of inventories is discussed further in Chapter 38 at 3.1.

Natural disasters may affect consumer behaviour, for example, some entities may encounter periods of high demand as customers panic-buy whilst other entities may have to offer discounts to attract customers. As a result of a natural disaster, estimates of net realisable value may be subject to increased estimation uncertainty, and determining the appropriate assumptions may require significant judgement. Entities with perishable goods, for example, may have to dispose of goods they are unable to store or sell during this period. Other entities may have to determine whether to write-down their inventories to net realisable value if they become wholly or partially obsolete, or if their selling prices have declined. Also, estimates of net realisable value should take into account costs to complete or selling costs, for example, additional future storage costs, which may reduce the net realisable value of inventories.

Estimates of net realisable value must also take into account the purpose for which the inventory is held. Therefore, inventory held for a particular contract has its net realisable value based on the contract price, and only the NRV of any excess inventory held would be based on current market prices. If there is a firm contract to sell quantities in excess of inventory quantities that the entity holds or is able to obtain under a firm purchase contract, this may give rise to an onerous contract liability that should be provided for in accordance with IAS 37 – *Provisions, Contingent Liabilities and Contingent Assets* (see Chapter 26 at 6.2). *[IAS 2.31]*. For inventory such as unused office supplies that are held for internal use and not sale to third parties, the replacement cost is the best available measure of their net realisable value.

IAS 2 explains that materials and other supplies held for use in the production of inventories are not written down below cost if the final product in which they are to be used is expected to be sold at or above cost. *[IAS 2.32]*. This is the case even if these materials in their present condition have a net realisable value that is below cost and would therefore otherwise require write down. Thus, a whisky distiller would not write down an inventory of grain because of a fall in the grain price, so long as it expected to sell the whisky at a price which is sufficient to recover cost. If a decline in the price of materials indicates that the cost of the final product will exceed net realisable value, then a write down is necessary and the replacement cost of those materials may be the best measure of their net realisable value. *[IAS 2.32]*. If an entity writes down any of its finished goods, the carrying value of any related raw materials should also be reviewed to see if they too need to be written down.

Often raw materials are used to make a number of different products. In these cases, it is normally not possible to arrive at a particular net realisable value for each item of raw material based on the selling price of any one type of finished item. If the current replacement cost of those raw materials is less than their historical cost, a provision is only required to be made if the finished goods into which they will be made are expected to be sold at a loss. No provision should be made just because the anticipated profit will be less than normal.

When the circumstances that previously caused inventories to be written down below cost no longer exist, or when there is clear evidence of an increase in net realisable value because of changed economic circumstances, the amount of the write-down is reversed. The reversal cannot be greater than the amount of the original write-down, so that the new carrying amount will always be the lower of the cost and the revised net realisable value. *[IAS 2.33]*.

Extract 22.2 below shows how CRH plc describes its inventory valuation policies, including estimation of net realisable value.

> *Extract 22.2: CRH plc (2019)*
>
> Accounting Policies (including key accounting estimates and assumptions) [extract]
> Other Significant Accounting Policies [extract]
> Inventories – Note 18
>
> Inventories are stated at the lower of cost and net realisable value. Cost is based on the first-in/first-out principle (and weighted average, where appropriate) and includes all expenditure incurred in acquiring the inventories and bringing them to their present location and condition. Raw materials are valued on the basis of purchase cost on a first-in/first-out basis. In the case of finished goods and work-in-progress, cost includes direct materials, direct labour and attributable overheads based on normal operating capacity and excludes borrowing costs.
>
> Net realisable value is the estimated proceeds of sale less all further costs to completion, and less all costs to be incurred in marketing, selling and distribution. Estimates of net realisable value are based on the most reliable evidence available at the time the estimates are made, taking into consideration fluctuations of price or cost directly relating to events occurring after the end of the period, the likelihood of shortterm changes in buyer preferences, product obsolescence or perishability (all of which are generally low given the nature of the Group's products) and the purpose for which the inventory is held. Materials and other supplies held for use in the production of inventories are not written down below cost if the finished goods, in which they will be incorporated, are expected to be sold at or above cost.

3.4 Measurement of crypto-assets in scope of IAS 2

As discussed at 2.3.1.D above, crypto-assets each have their own terms and conditions and, as a result, the holders of a crypto-asset will need to evaluate these terms and conditions to determine which IFRS recognition and measurement requirements should be applied. In some cases, crypto-assets may meet the definition of inventory.

The value of holdings of cryptocurrencies and other crypto-assets can fluctuate significantly. Where the fair value of a cryptocurrency or other crypto-asset holding has changed significantly after the end of the reporting period, the holder should consider whether the changes in fair value are of such significance that non-disclosure could influence the economic decisions of users of the financial statement. If so, the holder should consider whether the change in fair value should be disclosed as a non-adjusting post-balance sheet event, in accordance with IAS 10 – *Events after the Reporting Period*.[8] IAS 10 is discussed in Chapter 38.

3.4.1 Cost or lower net realisable value

The costs of purchased crypto-asset inventories would typically comprise the purchase price, irrecoverable taxes and other costs directly attributable to the acquisition of the inventory (e.g. blockchain processing fees). The cost of inventory excludes anticipated selling costs as well as storage expenses *[IAS 2.16]* (e.g. costs of holding a wallet or other crypto-account).

The cost of crypto-assets recorded as inventory may not be recoverable if those crypto-assets have become wholly or partially obsolete (declining interest in the crypto-asset or its application) or if their selling prices have declined. Similarly, the cost of crypto-asset inventory may not be fully recoverable if the estimated costs to sell them have increased.

An entity holding crypto-asset inventory will need to estimate the net realisable value at each reporting period. For crypto-assets quoted on a crypto-asset exchange, the net realisable value would typically comprise the current quoted price less the estimated selling costs. These selling costs can fluctuate significantly depending on the current demand for processing on the particular blockchain.

3.4.2 Fair value less costs to sell

In June 2019, the IFRS Interpretations Committee observed that an entity may act as a broker-trader of cryptocurrencies.[9]

While there is no definition of a commodity under IFRS, crypto-assets that are fungible and immediately marketable at quoted prices could potentially be considered commodities if they were held by broker-traders. However, judgement should be exercised in determining whether a particular crypto-asset can be regarded as a commodity.

The quoted prices of crypto-assets may vary considerably between exchanges. A broker-trader measuring crypto-assets at fair value less costs to sell will need to determine the principal (or most advantageous) market for those assets, and whether they could enter into a transaction for the crypto-asset at the price in that market at the measurement date. The determination of the principal (or most advantageous) market is discussed in Chapter 14 at 6.

When a broker-trader measures its inventory at fair value less costs to sell, any changes in the recognised amount should be included in profit or loss for the period. *[IAS 2.3(b)]*. A broker-trader holder of a crypto-asset will need to estimate the costs to sell the crypto-asset at each reporting date, taking into consideration the transaction cost on the relevant blockchain and other fees required in order to convert the crypto-asset into cash. These fees could fluctuate significantly from period to period depending on the current demand for processing on the relevant blockchain.

4 REAL ESTATE INVENTORY

4.1 Classification of real estate as inventory

Many real estate businesses develop and construct residential properties for sale, and these developments often consist of several units. The strategy is to make a profit from the development and construction of the property rather than to make a profit in the long term from general price increases in the property market. The intention is to sell the property units as soon as possible following their construction and the sale is therefore in the ordinary course of the entity's business. When construction is complete it is not uncommon for individual property units to be leased at market rates to earn revenues to partly cover expenses such as interest, management fees, and real estate taxes. Large-scale buyers of commercial property, such as insurance companies, are often reluctant to buy unless a property has been let, as this assures immediate cash flows from the investment.

It is our view that if it is in the entity's ordinary course of business (supported by its strategy) to hold property for short-term sale rather than for long-term capital appreciation or rental income, the entire property (including the leased units) should be accounted for and presented as inventory. This will continue to be the case as long as it remains the intention to sell the property in the short term. Rent received should be included in other income as it does not represent a reduction in the cost of inventory.

Investment property is defined in IAS 40 as 'property ... held ... to earn rentals or for capital appreciation or both, rather than for ... use in the production or supply of goods or services or for administrative purposes; or ... sale in the ordinary course of business'. *[IAS 40.5]*. Therefore, in the case outlined above, the property does not meet the definition of investment property. Properties intended for sale in the ordinary course of business, no matter whether leased out or not, are outside the scope of IAS 40. However, if a property is not intended for sale, IAS 40 requires it to be transferred from inventory to investment property when there is a change in use. The change can be evidenced by the commencement of an operating lease to another party (see Chapter 19 at 9).

4.2 Costs of real estate inventory

4.2.1 Allocation of costs to individual units in multi-unit developments

A real estate developer of a multi-unit complex will be able to track and record various costs that are specific to individual units, such as individual fit out costs. However, there will also be various costs that are incurred which are not specific to any individual unit, such as the costs of land and any shared facilities, and a methodology will be required to allocate these costs to the individual units. This will of course impact the profit that is recognised on the sale of each individual unit.

There are two general approaches to this allocation, both of which we believe are acceptable under IAS 2. The first approach is to allocate these non-unit specific costs based on some relative cost basis. A reasonable proxy of relative cost is likely to be the size of each unit and hence an appropriate methodology would be to allocate the non-unit specific cost per square metre to the individual units based upon the floor area of each unit. Another proxy of (total) relative cost may be the use of the specific cost of each unit. Marking up the specific cost that is attributable to each unit by a fixed percentage so as to cover and account for the non-unit specific costs would also seem reasonable. This relative cost approach is consistent with the guidance under IAS 2 in respect of allocation of overheads which requires a 'systematic allocation of fixed and variable production overheads'. [IAS 2.12].

The second approach would be to allocate these non-unit specific costs based on the relative sales value of each unit. This methodology is specifically referred to by the standard in the context of a production process that results in more than one product being produced simultaneously. [IAS 2.14]. Whichever approach is adopted it must be used consistently. In addition, the developer should initially, as far as is practicable, segregate the non-unit specific costs between any commercial, retail and residential components before applying these methodologies.

4.2.2 Property demolition and lease costs

During the course of a property redevelopment project, an existing building may need to be demolished in order for the new development to take place. Should the cost of the building to be demolished be capitalised as part of the construction cost for the new building or should the cost be charged to profit or loss?

In all such cases an entity will need to exercise judgement in assessing the facts and circumstances. There are three distinct scenarios to consider:

(a) the entity is the owner-occupier, in which case the matter falls under IAS 16;

(b) the entity holds the property to earn rentals, in which case the matter falls under IAS 40; or

(c) the entity sells such properties in its normal course of business.

If it is the strategy of the developer to sell the developed property after construction, the new development falls within the scope of IAS 2, as it would be considered held for sale in the normal course of business by the developer. If the entity purchased the property in question consisting of land and an old building, the cost of the old building as well as demolition costs and costs of developing the new one would be treated as inventory if:

- at the time of purchase, it is the entity's intention to demolish the existing building; and
- the building will not be used or leased out prior to its demolition.

The cost of the new development will still be subject to the normal 'lower of cost and net realisable value' requirements.

If the property in question was purchased in a prior reporting period and subsequently occupied, the land and building would have been separately recognised under IAS 16 in that period. Depending on the facts and circumstances, if the existing building was unusable, or likely to be demolished by any party acquiring it, the entity might however have concluded that a large part of the purchase price related to the land. In such cases, the carrying amount of the existing building will likely be minimal. If the existing building is demolished in subsequent periods in order for the new development to take place, the building will be derecognised in accordance with IAS 16 (see Chapter 18 at 4.1.7) and, in our view, the entity cannot capitalise the carrying amount of the old building as part of the cost of the new building.

If a new development within the scope of IAS 2 is being constructed on land that is leased, the entity needs to determine whether the depreciation charge relating to the right-of-use asset represents a cost of conversion in bringing the inventories to their present location and condition as specified in paragraph 12 of IAS 2. If the entity concludes that this is the case, a systematic allocation of the depreciation of the right-of-use asset relating to that leased land used in the development process is included in the cost of the inventories. *[IAS 2.12]*.

5 RECOGNITION IN PROFIT OR LOSS

IAS 2 specifies that when inventory is sold, the carrying amount of the inventory must be recognised as an expense in the period in which the revenue is recognised. *[IAS 2.34]*.

Judging when to recognise revenue, and therefore when to recognise the related cost of sales, is one of the more complex accounting issues that can arise (see Chapters 27 to 32 for further discussions).

Consignment stock and sales with a right of return are discussed at 2.3.1.F above, and sales with a right of return are discussed at 2.3.1.G above. In addition, revenue recognition in accordance with IFRS 15 is dealt with in Chapters 27 to 32, to which reference should be made in considering such issues.

Inventory used to create another asset, for instance into a self-constructed item of property, plant or equipment, would form part of the cost of that asset. Subsequently these costs are expensed through the depreciation of that item of property, plant and equipment during its useful life. *[IAS 2.35]*.

Any write-downs or losses of inventory must be recognised as an expense when the write-down or loss occurs. Reversals of previous write-downs are recognised as a reduction in the inventory expense recognised in the period in which the reversal occurs. *[IAS 2.34]*.

6 DISCLOSURE REQUIREMENTS OF IAS 2

6.1 General requirements

The financial statements should disclose:

(a) the accounting policies adopted in measuring inventories, including the cost formula used;

(b) the total carrying amount of inventories and the carrying amount in classifications appropriate to the entity;

(c) the carrying amount of inventories carried at fair value less costs to sell;

(d) the amount of inventories recognised as an expense during the period;

(e) the amount of any write-down of inventories recognised as an expense in the period;

(f) the amount of any reversal of any write-down that is recognised as a reduction in the amount of inventories recognised as expense in the period;

(g) the circumstances or events that led to the reversal of a write-down of inventories; and

(h) the carrying amount of inventories pledged as security for liabilities. *[IAS 2.36]*.

IAS 2 does not specify the precise classifications that must be used to comply with (b) above. However it states that 'information about the carrying amounts held in different classifications of inventories and the extent of the changes in these assets is useful to financial statement users', and suggests suitable examples of common classifications such as merchandise, production supplies, materials, work-in-progress, and finished goods. *[IAS 2.37]*.

Extract 22.3 below shows how the Unilever Group disclosed the relevant information.

Extract 22.3: Unilever PLC and Unilever N.V. (2019)
Consolidated Financial Statements Unilever Group [extract]
Notes to the Consolidated Financial Statements Unilever Group [extract]
12.   Inventories [extract]

Inventories	€ million 2019	€ million 2018
Raw materials and consumables	1,399	1,454
Finished goods and goods for resale	3,053	3,052
Total inventories	4,452	4,506
Provision for inventories	(288)	(205)
	4,164	4,301

Provisions for inventories	€ million 2019	€ million 2018
1 January	205	194
Charge to income statement	153	92
Reduction/releases	(71)	(72)
Currency translations	–	(7)
Others[(a)]	1	(2)
31 December	288	205

(a) Others mainly include the amount towards the acquisition/ disposal of business and transfers.

Inventories with a value of €159 million (2018: €124 million) are carried at net realisable value, this being lower than cost. During 2019 a total expense of €363 million (2018: €227 million) was recognised in the income statement for inventory write downs and losses.

The amount of inventory recognised as an expense in the period is normally included in cost of sales; this category includes unallocated production overheads and abnormal costs as well as the costs of inventory that has been sold. The circumstances of the entity may warrant the inclusion of distribution or other costs in cost of sales. *[IAS 2.38]*. Hence when a company presents its profit or loss based upon this IAS 1 'function of expense' or 'cost of sales' method it will normally be disclosing costs that are greater than those that have previously been classified as inventory.

Extract 22.4 below shows how Stora Enso classified its inventories in its 2019 financial statements.

Extract 22.4: Stora Enso Oyj (2019)
Consolidated financial statements [extract]
Notes to the consolidated financial statements [extract]
Note 16   Inventories [extract]

EUR million	As at 31 December	
	2019	2018
Materials and supplies	372	438
Work in progress	84	98
Finished goods	672	752
Spare parts and consumables	317	298
Other inventories	17	17
Advance payments and cutting rights	53	83
Obsolescence allowance – spare parts and consumables	–101	–98
Obsolescence allowance – finished goods	–16	–15
Net realisable value allowance	–6	–5
Total	1 391	1 567

EUR 4 693 (EUR 4 872) million of inventories have been expensed during the year, which are included in the materials and supplies line and relate to materials. EUR 14 (EUR 16) million of inventory write-downs have been recognised as an expense. EUR 8 (EUR 3) million have been recognised as a reversal of previous write-downs.

Some entities adopt a format for profit or loss that results in amounts other than the cost of inventories being disclosed as an expense during the period. This will happen if an entity presents an analysis of expenses using a classification based on the nature of expenses. The entity then discloses the costs recognised as an expense for raw materials and consumables, labour costs and other costs together with the amount of the net change in inventories for the period. *[IAS 2.39]*.

Formats for the presentation of profit or loss are discussed in Chapter 3.

The requirement to disclose the amount of any write-down of inventories recognised as an expense in the period in (e) above only relates to write-downs of inventory held at the end of the reporting period. The notion of 'write-down' is used in the context of the lower of cost and net realisable value test. An entity only performs this test at a reporting date.

6.2 Additional disclosure requirements for crypto-assets

In June 2019, the IFRS Interpretations Committee noted the following disclosure requirements in the context of holdings of cryptocurrencies in addition to the disclosures required by IAS 2 for cryptocurrencies held for sale in the ordinary course of business (see 6 above):

- IAS 38 disclosures for holdings of cryptocurrencies to which it applies IAS 38 (see Chapter 17).
- IFRS 13 disclosures if an entity measures its holdings of cryptocurrencies at fair value less costs to sell (see Chapter 14).
- IAS 1 disclosures when an entity has made judgements regarding its accounting for holdings of cryptocurrencies, if they are part of the judgements that had the most significant effect on the amounts recognised in the financial statements.
- IAS 10 disclosures for any material non-adjusting events after the reporting period, including information about the nature of the event and an estimate of its financial effect (or a statement that such an estimate cannot be made). (See Chapter 38). For example, an entity holding cryptocurrencies would consider whether changes in the fair value of those holdings after the reporting period are of such significance that non-disclosure could influence the economic decisions that users of the financial statements make on the basis of the financial statements.[10]

References

1 *IFRIC Update*, March 2014.
2 *IFRIC Update*, November 2014.
3 *IFRIC Update*, June 2019.
4 *IFRIC Update*, June 2019.
5 *IFRIC Update*, July 2015.
6 *IFRIC Update*, March 2019.
7 Exposure Draft ED/2017/5 – *Accounting Policies and Accounting Estimates – Proposed amendments to IAS 8*, paragraph 32B.
8 *IFRIC Update*, June 2019.
9 *IFRIC Update*, June 2019.
10 *IFRIC Update*, June 2019.

Index of extracts from financial statements

3i Group plc 956
A.P. Møller – Mærsk A/S 1530, 3174
Accelerate Property Fund Ltd 1487
adidas AG 683
AEGON N.V. 4631
African Rainbow Minerals Limited 3149
AGF Mutual Funds 233
Airbus SE 2419
Akzo Nobel N.V. 1395, 1840, 1992
Alkane Resources Limited 3475
Allianz SE 3184, 4576, 4580, 4626
Allied Electronics Corporation 684
AMP Limited 4572, 4636, 4646
Angel Mining plc 3425
Anglo American Platinum Limited 3482
Anglo American plc 3459, 3465, 3484, 3485, 3522
AngloGold Ashanti Limited 1683, 1980, 3416, 3489, 3491
Anheuser-Busch InBev NV/SA 1314, 1841, 3150, 3217, 3257
ArcelorMittal 1413
Ardagh Group S.A. 3216
ARINSO International SA 383
ASML Holding N.V. 2421, 2426
ASOS Plc 1328
Assicurazioni Generali S.p.A. 4598
AstraZeneca PLC 3146, 4514
Aveng Limited 816
Aviva plc 986, 2849, 3681, 4624, 4638, 4642, 4656, 4665

Index of extracts from financial statements

AXA SA	4573, 4590
BAE Systems plc	3014, 3015
Barclays PLC	981
Barrick Gold Corporation	3456, 3554
Bayer Aktiengesellschaft	976, 1326, 3076
BBA Aviation plc	1241
Beazley plc	4646
Belarusian National Reinsurance Organisation	1276
Berendsen plc	4456
BHP Billiton plc	3477
BHP Group Plc	3366, 3389, 3430, 3515, 3560
BMW Group	3225
Bombardier Inc	344, 348, 364, 2393, 2429
BP p.l.c.	955, 977, 1154, 2619, 2620, 3120, 3127, 3208, 3359, 3370, 3438, 3478, 3488, 3493, 3647, 4470, 4508
Brit Limited	4653
British Airways Plc	1396
British Sky Broadcasting Group plc	3126
BT Group plc	2960, 2963
Canadian Imperial Bank of Commerce	362
Capita plc	2413, 2438
Capital & Counties Properties PLC	1506
Centrais Elétricas Brasileiras S.A. – Eletrobras	320
Centrica plc	1940, 4031
China Mobile Limited	3167
CNP Assurances	4629, 4640
Coca-Cola FEMSA S.A.B. de C.V.	305
Coca-Cola HBC AG	3260
Cranswick plc	3084
CRH plc	1693
Daimler AG	3001, 3006, 3215, 3222
Dairy Crest Group plc	2846
Deutsche Bank Aktiengesellschaft	962, 3212
Deutsche Lufthansa AG	3139, 3210
Deutsche Post AG	1777, 1816

Downer EDI Limited 3214
E.ON SE 1398
Enersource Corporation 300
ENGIE SA 428, 1883, 3487, 3555
Eni S.p.A. 1431
Equinor ASA 3004, 3013, 3209, 3390, 3452, 3463, 3468
Eskom Holdings SOC Ltd 1844
Fédération Internationale de Football Association 2398, 2416
Ferrovial, S.A. 2406
Forthnet S.A. 3210
Fortum Oyj 1989
Glencore plc 3369, 3413
Greencore Group plc 1840
Groupe Renault 3624
Harmony Gold Mining Company Limited 3400, 3481
Heineken N.V. 1389
Hochschild Mining PLC 2620
HOCHTIEF Aktiengesellschaft 2990, 3007
Hongkong Land Holdings Limited 3173
HSBC Holdings plc 964, 983, 1942, 3214, 3709, 4028
Hunting PLC 4436, 4468
Husky Energy Inc. 269
IAMGOLD Corporation 3490
Icade 1488
Infosys Technologies Limited 235
ING Groep N.V. 1082, 1137, 1196
Inspired Energy PLC 3172
InterContinental Hotels Group PLC 2944, 3145
International Consolidated Airlines Group, S.A. 1354, 3211, 3248
Intrepid Mines Limited 3398
ITV plc 1300
J Sainsbury plc 3126
KAZ Minerals PLC 1666, 1671
Kendrion N.V. 1401
Kinross Gold Corporation 3491

Klépierre	1484, 1485
Koninklijke Philips N.V.	2004, 2424
LafargeHolcim Ltd	3075
Land Securities Group PLC	1481, 1489, 1492
Legal & General Group plc	4649
Liverpool Victoria Friendly Society Limited	4546
Lloyds Banking Group plc	1208, 3144
Lonmin Plc	3516
Lucas Bols N.V.	1432
Manulife Financial Corporation	289
MERCK Kommanditgesellschaft auf Aktien	1310, 1325
MOL Hungarian Oil and Gas Plc.	1363
Mondi plc	3314
Mowi ASA	3320
MS Amlin plc	4650
Münchener Rückversicherungs – Gesellschaft Aktiengesellschaft	4628
Naspers Limited	3176
National Australia Bank Limited	3008
Nestlé S.A.	884, 1357, 1779, 3010, 3218, 3224, 4460
Netcare Limited	3186
Newcrest Mining Limited	3439
Nexen Inc.	293
Nine Entertainment Co. Holdings Limited	3219
Nokia Corporation	883
Norsk Hydro ASA	3557
Old Mutual plc	4589, 4594
Pearson plc	1228
PGS ASA	3085
Ping An Insurance	4634, 4666
Poste Italiane SpA	1812, 1817
Premier Oil plc	3364, 3389
Priorbank JSC	1282
ProSiebenSat.1 Media SE	2420
Proton Power Systems plc	3197
Prudential plc	4576, 4630, 4637, 4662

PSA Peugeot Citroën 1833
QBE Insurance Group 4651
Quilter plc 980
RAI – Radiotelevisione italiana SpA 1344
RELX PLC 1298
Repsol, S.A. 1364
Rio Tinto plc 1155, 3423, 3459, 3464, 3468, 3470, 3484, 3512, 3523
Robert Bosch Gesellschaft mit beschränkter Haftung 961
Roche Holding Ltd 2010, 2985, 3015, 3220
Rolls-Royce Holdings plc 3220, 3599
Royal Dutch Shell plc 2618, 3520
Royal Schiphol Group N.V. 3143
RSA Insurance Group plc 4586, 4631
RWE Aktiengesellschaft 883
Sanofi 1324
SAP SE 2430, 2434
Sappi Limited 3318
Sberbank of Russia 1211
Schroders plc 3125
Siemens Aktiengesellschaft 3003
Sirius Minerals Plc 3233
Skanska AB 1388, 1409
Slater and Gordon Limited 2405, 2436
Société nationale SNCF 2415
Spotify Technology S.A. 2423
Stagecoach Group plc 1845
Stora Enso Oyj 1699
Suncor Energy Inc 293
T&G Global Limited 3310
Telefónica, S.A. 1283
Telenor ASA 1901
The British Land Company PLC 1464, 1477
The Crown Estate 1479
The Go-Ahead Group plc 2984
The Rank Group Plc 678

Index of extracts from financial statements

The Royal Bank of Scotland Group plc 3129, 4461
The Toronto-Dominion Bank 270
The Village Building Co. Limited 2405
thyssenkrupp, AG 3218
TOTAL S.A. 975, 3380
Tullow Oil plc 3375, 3521
UBS Group AG 958, 985, 988, 1151, 1240, 2962, 3805, 4432
Unibail-Rodamco-Westfield SE 1470, 1499, 1507
Unilever PLC and Unilever N.V. 1698, 4459
Vivendi SE 1304, 1345
Vodafone Group Plc 1636, 3002, 3011, 4421
Volkswagen Aktiengesellschaft 4452, 4460
VTech Holdings Limited 3139
Woodside Petroleum Ltd 3424, 3560
Yorkshire Building Society 3211
Zargon Oil & Gas Ltd 299
Zurich Insurance Group, Zurich 4660

Index of standards

SP 1

SP 1.1 .... Ch.2, p.48
SP 1.2 .... Ch.2, p.48
SP 1.3 .... Ch.2, p.48
SP 1.4 .... Ch.2, p.48
SP 1.5 .... Ch.2, p.48

Conceptual Framework (2001)

CF(2001) 4.4 .... Ch.9, p.667

Conceptual Framework (2010)

CF(2010) 4.29 .... Ch.27, p.2018
CF(2010) 4.29 .... Ch.27, p.2027
CF(2010) 4.29 .... Ch.32, p.2406
CF(2010) 4.31 .... Ch.27, p.2018
CF(2010) 4.55(b) Ch.16, p.1260
CF(2010) 4.59(a) Ch.16, p.1251
CF(2010) BC3.28 .... Ch.26, p.1949
CF(2018) BC4.96 .... Ch.32, p.2406
CF(2010) QC12 .... Ch.26, p.1949
CF(2010) QC14 .... Ch.26, p.1949

Conceptual Framework

CF 1.1 .... Ch.2, p.49
CF 1.1-1.2 .... Ch.2, p.59
CF 1.2 .... Ch.2, p.49
CF 1.2 .... Ch.5, p.231
CF 1.3 .... Ch.2, p.50
CF 1.4 .... Ch.2, p.50
CF 1.5 .... Ch.2, p.49
CF 1.6 .... Ch.2, p.50
CF 1.7 .... Ch.2, p.50
CF 1.8 .... Ch.2, p.50
CF 1.9 .... Ch.2, p.50
CF 1.9 .... Ch.5, p.231
CF 1.10 .... Ch.2, p.49
CF 1.11 .... Ch.2, p.50
CF 1.12 .... Ch.2, p.50
CF 1.13 .... Ch.2, p.51
CF 1.14 .... Ch.2, p.51
CF 1.15 .... Ch.2, p.51
CF 1.16 .... Ch.2, p.51
CF 1.17 .... Ch.2, p.52
CF 1.17 .... Ch.3, p.156
CF 1.18 .... Ch.2, p.51
CF 1.19 .... Ch.2, p.52
CF 1.20 .... Ch.2, p.52
CF 1.20 .... Ch.40, p.3136
CF 1.21 .... Ch.2, p.51
CF 1.22 .... Ch.2, p.52
CF 1.23 .... Ch.2, p.52
CF 2.1 .... Ch.2, p.52
CF 2.2 .... Ch.2, p.53
CF 2.3 .... Ch.2, p.53
CF 2.4 .... Ch.2, p.53
CF 2.4 .... Ch.2, p.56
CF 2.4 .... Ch.2, p.92
CF 2.5 .... Ch.2, p.52
CF 2.6 .... Ch.2, p.54
CF 2.7 .... Ch.2, p.54
CF 2.8 .... Ch.2, p.54
CF 2.9 .... Ch.2, p.54
CF 2.10 .... Ch.2, p.54
CF 2.11 .... Ch.2, p.54
CF 2.12 .... Ch.2, p.54
CF 2.12 .... Ch.46, p.3654
CF 2.13 .... Ch.2, p.54
CF 2.13 .... Ch.26, p.1949
CF 2.14 .... Ch.2, p.55
CF 2.15 .... Ch.2, p.55
CF 2.15 .... Ch.3, p.165
CF 2.15 .... Ch.26, p.1949
CF 2.16 .... Ch.2, p.55
CF 2.16 .... Ch.3, p.165
CF 2.17 .... Ch.2, p.55
CF 2.18 .... Ch.2, p.55
CF 2.19 .... Ch.2, p.53
CF 2.20 .... Ch.2, p.56
CF 2.21 .... Ch.2, p.56
CF 2.22 .... Ch.2, p.56
CF 2.23 .... Ch.2, p.52
CF 2.23 .... Ch.2, p.56
CF 2.24 .... Ch.2, p.57
CF 2.25-2.27 .... Ch.2, p.57
CF 2.26-2.28 .... Ch.2, p.57
CF 2.29 .... Ch.2, p.57
CF 2.30 .... Ch.2, p.57
CF 2.31 .... Ch.2, p.57
CF 2.32 .... Ch.2, p.57
CF 2.33 .... Ch.2, p.57
CF 2.34 .... Ch.2, p.58

Index of standards

CF 2.35	Ch.2, p.58
CF 2.36	Ch.2, p.49
CF 2.36	Ch.2, p.58
CF 2.37	Ch.2, p.58
CF 2.38	Ch.2, p.58
CF 2.39	Ch.2, p.52
CF 2.39	Ch.2, p.58
CF 2.40	Ch.2, p.58
CF 2.41	Ch.2, p.58
CF 2.42	Ch.2, p.58
CF 2.42	Ch.2, p.59
CF 2.43	Ch.2, p.59
CF 3.1	Ch.2, p.59
CF 3.2	Ch.2, p.59
CF 3.3	Ch.2, p.59
CF 3.4	Ch.2, p.60
CF 3.5	Ch.2, p.60
CF 3.6	Ch.2, p.60
CF 3.7	Ch.2, p.60
CF 3.8	Ch.2, p.60
CF 3.9	Ch.2, p.60
CF 3.9	Ch.38, p.3083
CF 3.10	Ch.2, p.59
CF 3.10	Ch.2, p.60
CF 3.10	Ch.6, p.391
CF 3.10	Ch.6, p.402
CF 3.10	Ch.9, p.752
CF 3.10	Ch.10, p.774
CF 3.11	Ch.2, p.61
CF 3.12	Ch.2, p.61
CF 3.12	Ch.6, p.401
CF 3.13	Ch.2, p.61
CF 3.13-14	Ch.6, p.403
CF 3.14	Ch.2, p.61
CF 3.15	Ch.2, p.62
CF 3.16	Ch.2, p.62
CF 3.17	Ch.2, p.62
CF 3.18	Ch.2, p.62
CF 4.1-4.4	Ch.2, p.62
CF 4.2	Ch.2, p.70
CF 4.2	Ch.55, p.4569
CF 4.3	Ch.25, p.1862
CF 4.5	Ch.2, p.66
CF 4.6	Ch.2, p.66
CF 4.7	Ch.2, p.67
CF 4.8	Ch.2, p.67
CF 4.9	Ch.2, p.67
CF 4.10	Ch.2, p.67
CF 4.11	Ch.2, p.67
CF 4.12	Ch.2, p.67
CF 4.13	Ch.2, p.68
CF 4.14	Ch.2, p.68
CF 4.15	Ch.2, p.68
CF 4.16	Ch.2, p.68
CF 4.17	Ch.2, p.68
CF 4.18	Ch.2, p.68
CF 4.19	Ch.2, p.69
CF 4.20	Ch.2, p.69
CF 4.21	Ch.2, p.69
CF 4.22	Ch.2, p.69
CF 4.23	Ch.2, p.69
CF 4.24	Ch.2, p.69
CF 4.25	Ch.2, p.69
CF 4.26	Ch.2, p.62
CF 4.26	Ch.2, p.70
CF 4.26	Ch.26, p.1932
CF 4.26	Ch.55, p.4569
CF 4.27	Ch.2, p.70
CF 4.27	Ch.26, p.1932
CF 4.28	Ch.2, p.70
CF 4.28	Ch.55, p.4569
CF 4.29	Ch.2, p.70
CF 4.29	Ch.55, p.4569
CF 4.30	Ch.2, p.70
CF 4.31	Ch.2, p.70
CF 4.32	Ch.2, p.70
CF 4.33	Ch.2, p.70
CF 4.34	Ch.2, p.71
CF 4.35	Ch.2, p.71
CF 4.36	Ch.2, p.71
CF 4.37	Ch.2, p.71
CF 4.38	Ch.2, p.71
CF 4.39	Ch.2, p.71
CF 4.40	Ch.2, p.71
CF 4.41	Ch.2, p.71
CF 4.42	Ch.2, p.72
CF 4.43	Ch.2, p.72
CF 4.44	Ch.2, p.72
CF 4.45	Ch.2, p.72
CF 4.46	Ch.2, p.72
CF 4.46	Ch.43, p.3473
CF 4.47	Ch.2, p.72
CF 4.48	Ch.2, p.63
CF 4.49	Ch.2, p.63
CF 4.49	Ch.3, p.160
CF 4.50	Ch.2, p.63
CF 4.51	Ch.2, p.64
CF 4.52	Ch.2, p.64
CF 4.53	Ch.2, p.64
CF 4.54	Ch.2, p.64
CF 4.55	Ch.2, p.65
CF 4.56	Ch.2, p.65
CF 4.56	Ch.17, p.1302
CF 4.57	Ch.2, p.65
CF 4.57	Ch.17, p.1302
CF 4.58	Ch.2, p.65
CF 4.58	Ch.17, p.1302
CF 4.59	Ch.2, p.65
CF 4.60	Ch.2, p.66
CF 4.61	Ch.2, p.66
CF 4.62	Ch.2, p.66
CF 4.63	Ch.2, p.62
CF 4.63	Ch.2, p.72
CF 4.63-4.64	Ch.7, p.540
CF 4.64	Ch.2, p.72
CF 4.65	Ch.2, p.73

Index of standards 9

CF 4.66	Ch.2, p.73
CF 4.67	Ch.2, p.73
CF 4.68	Ch.2, p.62
CF 4.68	Ch.3, p.160
CF 4.68	Ch.27, p.2018
CF 4.68-70	Ch.2, p.73
CF 4.69	Ch.2, p.62
CF 4.71	Ch.2, p.73
CF 4.72	Ch.2, p.73
CF 5.1	Ch.2, p.74
CF 5.2	Ch.2, p.74
CF 5.2	Ch.2, p.101
CF 5.3	Ch.2, p.74
CF 5.3	Ch.2, p.103
CF 5.4	Ch.2, p.75
CF 5.5	Ch.2, p.75
CF 5.6	Ch.2, p.75
CF 5.7	Ch.2, p.75
CF 5.8	Ch.2, p.76
CF 5.9	Ch.2, p.76
CF 5.10	Ch.2, p.76
CF 5.11	Ch.2, p.76
CF 5.12	Ch.2, p.76
CF 5.13	Ch.2, p.76
CF 5.14	Ch.2, p.77
CF 5.15	Ch.2, p.77
CF 5.16	Ch.2, p.77
CF 5.17	Ch.2, p.77
CF 5.18	Ch.2, p.77
CF 5.19	Ch.2, p.77
CF 5.20	Ch.2, p.78
CF 5.21	Ch.2, p.78
CF 5.22	Ch.2, p.78
CF 5.23	Ch.2, p.78
CF 5.24	Ch.2, p.79
CF 5.25	Ch.2, p.79
CF 5.26	Ch.2, p.79
CF 5.27	Ch.2, p.79
CF 5.27	Ch.2, p.80
CF 5.28	Ch.2, p.80
CF 5.29	Ch.2, p.80
CF 5.30	Ch.2, p.80
CF 5.31	Ch.2, p.81
CF 5.32	Ch.2, p.81
CF 5.33	Ch.2, p.81
CF 6.1	Ch.2, p.81
CF 6.2	Ch.2, p.82
CF 6.3	Ch.2, p.82
CF 6.4	Ch.2, p.82
CF 6.5	Ch.2, p.82
CF 6.6	Ch.2, p.83
CF 6.7	Ch.2, p.83
CF 6.8	Ch.2, p.83
CF 6.9	Ch.2, p.83
CF 6.10	Ch.2, p.83
CF 6.11	Ch.2, p.83
CF 6.12	Ch.2, p.84
CF 6.13	Ch.2, p.84
CF 6.14	Ch.2, p.84
CF 6.15	Ch.2, p.84
CF 6.16	Ch.2, p.84
CF 6.17	Ch.2, p.85
CF 6.18	Ch.2, p.85
CF 6.19	Ch.2, p.85
CF 6.20	Ch.2, p.85
CF 6.21	Ch.2, p.85
CF 6.22	Ch.2, p.85
CF 6.23	Ch.2, p.86
CF 6.24	Ch.2, p.90
CF 6.25	Ch.2, p.90
CF 6.26	Ch.2, p.90
CF 6.27	Ch.2, p.90
CF 6.28	Ch.2, p.90
CF 6.29	Ch.2, p.90
CF 6.30	Ch.2, p.91
CF 6.31	Ch.2, p.91
CF 6.32	Ch.2, p.91
CF 6.33	Ch.2, p.91
CF 6.34	Ch.2, p.91
CF 6.35	Ch.2, p.91
CF 6.36	Ch.2, p.91
CF 6.37	Ch.2, p.91
CF 6.38	Ch.2, p.91
CF 6.39	Ch.2, p.92
CF 6.40	Ch.2, p.92
CF 6.41	Ch.2, p.92
CF 6.42	Ch.2, p.92
CF 6.43	Ch.2, p.92
CF 6.44	Ch.2, p.92
CF 6.45	Ch.2, p.92
CF 6.46	Ch.2, p.93
CF 6.47	Ch.2, p.92
CF 6.48	Ch.2, p.93
CF 6.49	Ch.2, p.93
CF 6.50	Ch.2, p.93
CF 6.51	Ch.2, p.93
CF 6.52	Ch.2, p.93
CF 6.53	Ch.2, p.94
CF 6.54	Ch.2, p.94
CF 6.55	Ch.2, p.94
CF 6.56	Ch.2, p.94
CF 6.57	Ch.2, p.94
CF 6.58	Ch.2, p.95
CF 6.59	Ch.2, p.95
CF 6.60	Ch.2, p.95
CF 6.61	Ch.2, p.95
CF 6.62	Ch.2, p.95
CF 6.63	Ch.2, p.95
CF 6.64	Ch.2, p.95
CF 6.65	Ch.2, p.95
CF 6.66	Ch.2, p.96
CF 6.67	Ch.2, p.96
CF 6.68	Ch.2, p.96
CF 6.69	Ch.2, p.96
CF 6.70	Ch.2, p.96
CF 6.71	Ch.2, p.96

CF 6.72	Ch.2, p.96	CF 8.7	Ch.2, p.106
CF 6.73	Ch.2, p.96	CF 8.8	Ch.2, p.106
CF 6.74	Ch.2, p.97	CF 8.9	Ch.2, p.105
CF 6.75	Ch.2, p.97	CF 8.10	Ch.2, p.105
CF 6.76	Ch.2, p.97	CF Appendix	Ch.6, p.391
CF 6.77	Ch.2, p.93	CF Appendix	Ch.6, p.400
CF 6.78	Ch.2, p.98	CF Appendix	Ch.6, p.402
CF 6.79	Ch.2, p.98	CF BC0.27	Ch.2, p.46
CF 6.80	Ch.2, p.98	CF BC0.28	Ch.2, p.47
CF 6.81	Ch.2, p.98	CF BC3.21	Ch.2, p.61
CF 6.82	Ch.2, p.98	CF BC3.21	Ch.6, p.401
CF 6.83	Ch.2, p.98	CF BC4.96	Ch.27, p.2018
CF 6.84	Ch.2, p.98	CF BC6.1	Ch.2, p.82
CF 6.85	Ch.2, p.99	CF BC6.10	Ch.2, p.82
CF 6.86	Ch.2, p.99	CF BC7.29	Ch.2, p.104
CF 6.87	Ch.2, p.99	CF BC7.24	Ch.2, p.103
CF 6.88	Ch.2, p.99		
CF 6.89	Ch.2, p.99		
CF 6.90	Ch.2, p.100	**IFRS 1**	
CF 6.91	Ch.2, p.100		
CF 6.92	Ch.2, p.100	IFRS 1.1	Ch.5, p.227
CF 6.93	Ch.2, p.100	IFRS 1.2-3	Ch.5, p.233
CF 6.94	Ch.2, p.100	IFRS 1.2(a)	Ch.5, p.232
CF 6.95	Ch.2, p.100	IFRS 1.2(b)	Ch.5, p.232
CF 7.1	Ch.2, p.101	IFRS 1.3	Ch.5, p.229
CF 7.2	Ch.2, p.101	IFRS 1.3(a)	Ch.5, p.229
CF 7.3	Ch.2, p.101	IFRS 1.3(b)	Ch.5, p.232
CF 7.4	Ch.2, p.101	IFRS 1.3(b)-(c)	Ch.5, p.231
CF 7.5	Ch.2, p.102	IFRS 1.3(d)	Ch.5, p.232
CF 7.6	Ch.2, p.102	IFRS 1.4	Ch.5, p.230
CF 7.7	Ch.2, p.102	IFRS 1.5	Ch.5, p.232
CF 7.8	Ch.2, p.102	IFRS 1.6	Ch.5, p.236
CF 7.9	Ch.2, p.102	IFRS 1.7	Ch.5, p.238
CF 7.10	Ch.2, p.102	IFRS 1.7	Ch.5, p.266
CF 7.10	Ch.43, p.3550	IFRS 1.7	Ch.5, p.268
CF 7.11	Ch.2, p.102	IFRS 1.7	Ch.5, p.291
CF 7.12	Ch.2, p.102	IFRS 1.7	Ch.5, p.302
CF 7.13	Ch.2, p.103	IFRS 1.7	Ch.5, p.364
CF 7.14	Ch.2, p.103	IFRS 1.7	Ch.33, p.2599
CF 7.15	Ch.2, p.103	IFRS 1.8	Ch.5, p.238
CF 7.16	Ch.2, p.103	IFRS 1.9	Ch.5, p.240
CF 7.17	Ch.2, p.103	IFRS 1.9	Ch.5, p.249
CF 7.18	Ch.2, p.104	IFRS 1.10	Ch.5, p.239
CF 7.19	Ch.2, p.104	IFRS 1.10	Ch.5, p.281
CF 7.20	Ch.2, p.104	IFRS 1.10	Ch.5, p.296
CF 7.21	Ch.2, p.104	IFRS 1.11	Ch.5, p.239
CF 7.22	Ch.2, p.101	IFRS 1.11	Ch.5, p.367
CF 7.22	Ch.2, p.104	IFRS 1.11	Ch.5, p.368
CF 8.1	Ch.2, p.105	IFRS 1.11	Ch.33, p.2572
CF 8.2	Ch.2, p.105	IFRS 1.12	Ch.5, p.241
CF 8.3(a)	Ch.2, p.105	IFRS 1.12(b)	Ch.5, p.266
CF 8.3(b)	Ch.2, p.106	IFRS 1.13	Ch.5, p.238
CF 8.4	Ch.2, p.104	IFRS 1.13	Ch.5, p.240
CF 8.5	Ch.2, p.105	IFRS 1.13-17	Ch.5, p.241
CF 8.5	Ch.2, p.106	IFRS 1.14	Ch.5, p.244
CF 8.6	Ch.2, p.104	IFRS 1.14	Ch.5, p.377
CF 8.6	Ch.2, p.105	IFRS 1.14	Ch.5, p.379
CF 8.7	Ch.2, p.105	IFRS 1.14-15	Ch.5, p.369

Index of standards

IFRS 1.14-17	Ch.5, p.365
IFRS 1.14-17	Ch.5, p.377
IFRS 1.4(a)	Ch.5, p.235
IFRS 1.4A	Ch.5, p.233
IFRS 1.4B	Ch.5, p.233
IFRS 1.15	Ch.5, p.244
IFRS 1.16	Ch.5, p.244
IFRS 1.17	Ch.5, p.245
IFRS 1.18	Ch.5, p.238
IFRS 1.18	Ch.5, p.240
IFRS 1.18	Ch.5, p.243
IFRS 1.20	Ch.5, p.342
IFRS 1.21	Ch.5, p.237
IFRS 1.21	Ch.5, p.342
IFRS 1.21-30	Ch.5, p.290
IFRS 1.22	Ch.5, p.343
IFRS 1.23	Ch.5, p.343
IFRS 1.23	Ch.5, p.347
IFRS 1.23	Ch.5, p.360
IFRS 1.23	Ch.5, p.365
IFRS 1.23-28	Ch.5, p.322
IFRS 1.23A	Ch.5, p.233
IFRS 1.23B	Ch.5, p.233
IFRS 1.24(a)	Ch.5, p.345
IFRS 1.24(a)	Ch.5, p.358
IFRS 1.24(a)-(b)	Ch.5, p.365
IFRS 1.24(b)	Ch.5, p.345
IFRS 1.24(b)	Ch.5, p.358
IFRS 1.24(c)	Ch.5, p.356
IFRS 1.24(c)	Ch.5, p.376
IFRS 1.25	Ch.5, p.345
IFRS 1.25	Ch.5, p.358
IFRS 1.25	Ch.5, p.364
IFRS 1.26	Ch.5, p.245
IFRS 1.26	Ch.5, p.345
IFRS 1.26	Ch.5, p.358
IFRS 1.26	Ch.5, p.365
IFRS 1.27	Ch.5, p.346
IFRS 1.27	Ch.5, p.365
IFRS 1.27A	Ch.5, p.347
IFRS 1.27A	Ch.5, p.365
IFRS 1.28	Ch.5, p.345
IFRS 1.29	Ch.5, p.314
IFRS 1.29-29A	Ch.5, p.356
IFRS 1.29A	Ch.5, p.315
IFRS 1.30	Ch.5, p.295
IFRS 1.30	Ch.5, p.296
IFRS 1.31	Ch.5, p.357
IFRS 1.32	Ch.5, p.360
IFRS 1.32	Ch.43, p.3550
IFRS 1.33	Ch.5, p.361
IFRS 1.30, D5	Ch.5, p.357
IFRS 1.31A	Ch.5, p.298
IFRS 1.31A	Ch.5, p.357
IFRS 1.31B	Ch.5, p.300
IFRS 1.31B	Ch.5, p.357
IFRS 1.31C	Ch.5, p.358
IFRS 1.32(a)	Ch.5, p.358
IFRS 1.32(b)	Ch.5, p.358
IFRS 1.32(c)	Ch.5, p.365
IFRS 1.32-33	Ch.5, p.356
IFRS 1 Appendix A	Ch.5, p.228
IFRS 1 Appendix A	Ch.5, p.229
IFRS 1 Appendix A	Ch.5, p.232
IFRS 1 Appendix A	Ch.5, p.234
IFRS 1 Appendix A	Ch.5, p.236
IFRS 1 Appendix A	Ch.5, p.240
IFRS 1 Appendix B	Ch.5, p.241
IFRS 1 Appendix C	Ch.5, p.242
IFRS 1 Appendix C	Ch.5, p.266
IFRS 1 Appendix C	Ch.5, p.267
IFRS 1 Appendix C	Ch.5, p.307
IFRS 1 Appendix D	Ch.5, p.242
IFRS 1.B2	Ch.5, p.247
IFRS 1.B2	Ch.5, p.271
IFRS 1.B3	Ch.5, p.247
IFRS 1.B4(a)	Ch.5, p.250
IFRS 1.B4(b)	Ch.5, p.250
IFRS 1.B5	Ch.5, p.248
IFRS 1.B5	Ch.5, p.252
IFRS 1.B6	Ch.5, p.248
IFRS 1.B6	Ch.5, p.252
IFRS 1.B6	Ch.5, p.253
IFRS 1.B6	Ch.5, p.256
IFRS 1.B7	Ch.5, p.262
IFRS 1.B7	Ch.5, p.268
IFRS 1.B8	Ch.5, p.262
IFRS 1.B8A	Ch.5, p.262
IFRS 1.B8A	Ch.5, p.356
IFRS 1.B8B	Ch.5, p.263
IFRS 1.B8B	Ch.5, p.357
IFRS 1.B8C	Ch.5, p.263
IFRS 1.B8D	Ch.5, p.264
IFRS 1.B8E	Ch.5, p.264
IFRS 1.B8F	Ch.5, p.264
IFRS 1.B8F(a)	Ch.5, p.264
IFRS 1.B8G	Ch.5, p.264
IFRS 1.B9	Ch.5, p.265
IFRS 1.B10	Ch.5, p.265
IFRS 1.B11	Ch.5, p.265
IFRS 1.B12	Ch.5, p.265
IFRS 1.B13	Ch.5, p.266
IFRS 1.C1	Ch.5, p.262
IFRS 1.C1	Ch.5, p.268
IFRS 1.C1	Ch.5, p.271
IFRS 1.C1	Ch.5, p.283
IFRS 1.C2	Ch.5, p.282
IFRS 1.C2	Ch.5, p.283
IFRS 1.C3	Ch.5, p.283
IFRS 1.C4(a)	Ch.5, p.271
IFRS 1.C4(a)	Ch.5, p.276
IFRS 1.C4(b)	Ch.5, p.271
IFRS 1.C4(b)	Ch.5, p.273
IFRS 1.C4(b)	Ch.5, p.277
IFRS 1.C4(b)	Ch.5, p.281
IFRS 1.C4(b)	Ch.5, p.286

IFRS 1.C4(b)(ii)	Ch.5, p.278
IFRS 1.C4(b)(ii)	Ch.5, p.280
IFRS 1.C4(b)(ii)	Ch.5, p.281
IFRS 1.C4(b)(ii)	Ch.5, p.378
IFRS 1.C4(c)	Ch.5, p.272
IFRS 1.C4(c)	Ch.5, p.281
IFRS 1.C4(c)(i)	Ch.5, p.277
IFRS 1.C4(c)(i)	Ch.5, p.278
IFRS 1.C4(c)(ii)	Ch.5, p.281
IFRS 1.C4(d)	Ch.5, p.276
IFRS 1.C4(d)	Ch.5, p.277
IFRS 1.C4(e)	Ch.5, p.263
IFRS 1.C4(e)	Ch.5, p.274
IFRS 1.C4(e)	Ch.5, p.277
IFRS 1.C4(f)	Ch.5, p.272
IFRS 1.C4(f)	Ch.5, p.273
IFRS 1.C4(f)	Ch.5, p.277
IFRS 1.C4(f)	Ch.5, p.278
IFRS 1.C4(f)	Ch.5, p.280
IFRS 1.C4(f)	Ch.5, p.281
IFRS 1.C4(f)	Ch.5, p.286
IFRS 1.C4(f)	Ch.5, p.378
IFRS 1.C4(g)	Ch.5, p.272
IFRS 1.C4(g)	Ch.5, p.276
IFRS 1.C4(g)	Ch.5, p.277
IFRS 1.C4(g)	Ch.5, p.279
IFRS 1.C4(g)(i)	Ch.5, p.273
IFRS 1.C4(g)(i)	Ch.5, p.278
IFRS 1.C4(g)(i)	Ch.5, p.281
IFRS 1.C4(g)(i)	Ch.5, p.286
IFRS 1.C4(g)(ii)	Ch.5, p.375
IFRS 1.C4(g)(ii)	Ch.5, p.376
IFRS 1.C4(h)	Ch.5, p.279
IFRS 1.C4(h)	Ch.5, p.280
IFRS 1.C4(h)	Ch.5, p.281
IFRS 1.C4(h)(i)	Ch.5, p.275
IFRS 1.C4(i)	Ch.5, p.281
IFRS 1.C4(i)(i)	Ch.5, p.281
IFRS 1.C4(i)(i)	Ch.5, p.282
IFRS 1.C4(i)(ii)	Ch.5, p.282
IFRS 1.C4(j)	Ch.5, p.283
IFRS 1.C4(j)	Ch.5, p.284
IFRS 1.C4(j)	Ch.5, p.306
IFRS 1.C4(k)	Ch.5, p.273
IFRS 1.C4(k)	Ch.5, p.277
IFRS 1.C4(k)	Ch.5, p.278
IFRS 1.C4(k)	Ch.5, p.281
IFRS 1.C4(k)	Ch.5, p.285
IFRS 1.C4(k)	Ch.5, p.286
IFRS 1.C5	Ch.5, p.271
IFRS 1.C5	Ch.5, p.279
IFRS 1.C5	Ch.5, p.285
IFRS 1.C5	Ch.5, p.375
IFRS 1.D2	Ch.5, p.287
IFRS 1.D2	Ch.5, p.289
IFRS 1.D2	Ch.34, p.2884
IFRS 1.D3	Ch.5, p.287
IFRS 1.D4	Ch.5, p.290
IFRS 1.D5	Ch.5, p.292
IFRS 1.D5	Ch.5, p.293
IFRS 1.D5	Ch.5, p.375
IFRS 1.D5-D7	Ch.5, p.295
IFRS 1.D5-D8	Ch.5, p.294
IFRS 1.D5-D8	Ch.5, p.296
IFRS 1.D6	Ch.5, p.292
IFRS 1.D6	Ch.5, p.293
IFRS 1.D7	Ch.5, p.292
IFRS 1.D7	Ch.5, p.294
IFRS 1.D7	Ch.5, p.296
IFRS 1.D7	Ch.5, p.357
IFRS 1.D7	Ch.5, p.375
IFRS 1.D8	Ch.5, p.295
IFRS 1.D8	Ch.5, p.296
IFRS 1.D8	Ch.5, p.297
IFRS 1.D9	Ch.5, p.273
IFRS 1.D9	Ch.5, p.302
IFRS 1.D12	Ch.5, p.304
IFRS 1.D12	Ch.5, p.305
IFRS 1.D12	Ch.5, p.310
IFRS 1.D13	Ch.5, p.304
IFRS 1.D13	Ch.5, p.305
IFRS 1.D13	Ch.5, p.310
IFRS 1.D13	Ch.5, p.311
IFRS 1.D13	Ch.5, p.312
IFRS 1.D13A	Ch.5, p.304
IFRS 1.D13A	Ch.5, p.310
IFRS 1.D13A	Ch.5, p.312
IFRS 1.D14	Ch.5, p.306
IFRS 1.D15	Ch.5, p.284
IFRS 1.D15	Ch.5, p.306
IFRS 1.D15	Ch.5, p.307
IFRS 1.D15	Ch.5, p.357
IFRS 1.D15	Ch.8, p.597
IFRS 1.D15A	Ch.5, p.307
IFRS 1.D15A	Ch.8, p.598
IFRS 1.D16	Ch.5, p.307
IFRS 1.D16	Ch.5, p.308
IFRS 1.D16-D17	Ch.5, p.307
IFRS 1.D16(a)	Ch.5, p.304
IFRS 1.D16(a)	Ch.5, p.313
IFRS 1.D17	Ch.5, p.277
IFRS 1.D17	Ch.5, p.283
IFRS 1.D17	Ch.5, p.306
IFRS 1.D17	Ch.5, p.307
IFRS 1.D17	Ch.5, p.311
IFRS 1.D17	Ch.5, p.313
IFRS 1.D17	Ch.5, p.314
IFRS 1.D18	Ch.5, p.314
IFRS 1.D19	Ch.5, p.315
IFRS 1.D19	Ch.5, p.356
IFRS 1.D19-D19C	Ch.5, p.265
IFRS 1.D19A	Ch.5, p.314
IFRS 1.D19A	Ch.5, p.356
IFRS 1.D19B	Ch.5, p.315
IFRS 1.D19C	Ch.5, p.315
IFRS 1.D20	Ch.5, p.316

IFRS 1.D21	Ch.5, p.316	IFRS 1.IG27(a)	Ch.5, p.306
IFRS 1.D21A	Ch.5, p.298	IFRS 1.IG27(b)	Ch.5, p.306
IFRS 1.D21A	Ch.5, p.319	IFRS 1.IG27(c)	Ch.5, p.284
IFRS 1.D22	Ch.5, p.319	IFRS 1.IG27(c)	Ch.5, p.306
IFRS 1.D23	Ch.5, p.320	IFRS 1.IG28	Ch.5, p.306
IFRS 1.D25	Ch.5, p.321	IFRS 1.IG30	Ch.5, p.312
IFRS 1.D26	Ch.5, p.321	IFRS 1.IG31	Ch.5, p.309
IFRS 1.D26-D30	Ch.5, p.358	IFRS 1.IG32	Ch.5, p.375
IFRS 1.D27	Ch.5, p.321	IFRS 1.IG33	Ch.5, p.375
IFRS 1.D27	Ch.16, p.1276	IFRS 1.IG34	Ch.5, p.375
IFRS 1.D28	Ch.5, p.321	IFRS 1.IG35	Ch.47, p.3699
IFRS 1.D29	Ch.5, p.321	IFRS 1.IG35-IG36	Ch.5, p.314
IFRS 1.D30	Ch.5, p.322	IFRS 1.IG36	Ch.47, p.3699
IFRS 1.D31	Ch.5, p.285	IFRS 1.IG37	Ch.5, p.358
IFRS 1.D31	Ch.5, p.322	IFRS 1.IG39	Ch.5, p.376
IFRS 1.D32	Ch.5, p.322	IFRS 1.IG40	Ch.5, p.376
IFRS 1.D33	Ch.5, p.342	IFRS 1.IG40	Ch.5, p.377
IFRS 1.D34	Ch.5, p.335	IFRS 1.IG41	Ch.5, p.376
IFRS 1.D34	Ch.5, p.336	IFRS 1.IG41	Ch.5, p.377
IFRS 1.D34	Ch.5, p.371	IFRS 1.IG43	Ch.5, p.376
IFRS 1.D35	Ch.5, p.335	IFRS 1.IG44	Ch.5, p.378
IFRS 1.D35	Ch.5, p.336	IFRS 1.IG46	Ch.5, p.378
IFRS 1.D35	Ch.5, p.337	IFRS 1.IG47	Ch.5, p.378
IFRS 1.D35	Ch.5, p.371	IFRS 1.IG48	Ch.5, p.378
IFRS 1.D36	Ch.5, p.342	IFRS 1.IG49	Ch.5, p.378
IFRS 1.D8(b)	Ch.5, p.297	IFRS 1.IG51	Ch.5, p.379
IFRS 1.D8A	Ch.5, p.298	IFRS 1.IG53	Ch.5, p.247
IFRS 1.D8A(b)	Ch.5, p.357	IFRS 1.IG53	Ch.5, p.248
IFRS 1.D8B	Ch.5, p.299	IFRS 1.IG54	Ch.5, p.247
IFRS 1.D8B	Ch.5, p.300	IFRS 1.IG55	Ch.5, p.264
IFRS 1.D8B	Ch.5, p.357	IFRS 1.IG56	Ch.5, p.262
IFRS 1.D9B	Ch.5, p.302	IFRS 1.IG57	Ch.5, p.263
IFRS 1.D9B	Ch.5, p.303	IFRS 1.IG58A	Ch.5, p.250
IFRS 1.D9B-D9E	Ch.5, p.273	IFRS 1.IG58A	Ch.5, p.263
IFRS 1.D9C	Ch.5, p.303	IFRS 1.IG58B	Ch.5, p.245
IFRS 1.D9D	Ch.5, p.303	IFRS 1.IG58B	Ch.5, p.250
IFRS 1.D9E	Ch.5, p.303	IFRS 1.IG59	Ch.5, p.263
IFRS 1.IG3	Ch.5, p.244	IFRS 1.IG60	Ch.5, p.248
IFRS 1.IG4	Ch.5, p.245	IFRS 1.IG60	Ch.5, p.256
IFRS 1.IG7	Ch.5, p.277	IFRS 1.IG60	Ch.5, p.257
IFRS 1.IG7	Ch.5, p.369	IFRS 1.IG60	Ch.5, p.258
IFRS 1.IG9	Ch.5, p.295	IFRS 1.IG60A	Ch.5, p.254
IFRS 1.IG10	Ch.5, p.370	IFRS 1.IG60B	Ch.5, p.253
IFRS 1.IG11	Ch.5, p.294	IFRS 1.IG60B	Ch.5, p.254
IFRS 1.IG11	Ch.5, p.296	IFRS 1.IG60B	Ch.5, p.255
IFRS 1.IG12	Ch.5, p.292	IFRS 1.IG60B	Ch.5, p.256
IFRS 1.IG12	Ch.5, p.371	IFRS 1.IG62	Ch.5, p.369
IFRS 1.IG13	Ch.5, p.316	IFRS 1.IG201	Ch.5, p.316
IFRS 1.IG14	Ch.5, p.371	IFRS 1.IG201-IG203	Ch.5, p.316
IFRS 1.IG17	Ch.5, p.372	IFRS 1.IG Example 1	Ch.5, p.246
IFRS 1.IG19	Ch.5, p.372	IFRS 1.IG Example 10	Ch.5, p.359
IFRS 1.IG20	Ch.5, p.373	IFRS 1.IG Example 11	Ch.5, p.345
IFRS 1.IG21	Ch.5, p.372	IFRS 1.IG Example 12	Ch.5, p.265
IFRS 1.IG21A	Ch.5, p.282	IFRS 1.IG Example 2	Ch.5, p.276
IFRS 1.IG23	Ch.5, p.320	IFRS 1.IG Example 3	Ch.5, p.272
IFRS 1.IG24	Ch.5, p.320	IFRS 1.IG Example 4	Ch.5, p.285
IFRS 1.IG26	Ch.5, p.305	IFRS 1.IG Example 4	Ch.5, p.286
IFRS 1.IG27(a)	Ch.5, p.283	IFRS 1.IG Example 5	Ch.5, p.281

IFRS 1.IG Example 6	Ch.5, p.284
IFRS 1.IG Example 7	Ch.5, p.273
IFRS 1.IG Example 8	Ch.5, p.308
IFRS 1.IG Example 9	Ch.5, p.277
IFRS 1.IG Example 9	Ch.5, p.311
IFRS 1.IG5-IG6	Ch.5, p.365
IFRS 1.BC3	Ch.5, p.227
IFRS 1.BC5	Ch.5, p.230
IFRS 1.BC6	Ch.5, p.230
IFRS 1.BC9	Ch.5, p.228
IFRS 1.BC10	Ch.5, p.228
IFRS 1.BC11	Ch.5, p.238
IFRS 1.BC14	Ch.5, p.240
IFRS 1.BC36	Ch.5, p.274
IFRS 1.BC39	Ch.5, p.279
IFRS 1.BC43	Ch.5, p.302
IFRS 1.BC45	Ch.5, p.292
IFRS 1.BC45	Ch.5, p.376
IFRS 1.BC47	Ch.5, p.294
IFRS 1.BC62	Ch.5, p.309
IFRS 1.BC63	Ch.5, p.311
IFRS 1.BC67	Ch.5, p.375
IFRS 1.BC75	Ch.5, p.252
IFRS 1.BC84	Ch.5, p.244
IFRS 1.BC91	Ch.5, p.343
IFRS 1.BC94	Ch.5, p.356
IFRS 1.BC97	Ch.5, p.347
IFRS 1.BC11A	Ch.5, p.238
IFRS 1.BC12(a)	Ch.5, p.242
IFRS 1.BC12(b)	Ch.5, p.241
IFRS 1.BC3B	Ch.5, p.228
IFRS 1.BC46B	Ch.5, p.297
IFRS 1.BC47A	Ch.5, p.298
IFRS 1.BC47B	Ch.5, p.298
IFRS 1.BC47D	Ch.5, p.298
IFRS 1.BC47F	Ch.5, p.299
IFRS 1.BC47G	Ch.5, p.300
IFRS 1.BC47H	Ch.5, p.300
IFRS 1.BC47I	Ch.5, p.299
IFRS 1.BC55C	Ch.5, p.310
IFRS 1.BC63CA	Ch.5, p.319
IFRS 1.BC63J	Ch.5, p.322
IFRS 1.BC6C	Ch.5, p.233
IFRS 1.BC83A	Ch.5, p.316
IFRS 1.BC89B	Ch.5, p.342

IFRS 2

IFRS 2.1	Ch.34, p.2642
IFRS 2.2	Ch.34, p.2643
IFRS 2.2	Ch.34, p.2651
IFRS 2.2	Ch.34, p.2662
IFRS 2.2	Ch.34, p.2855
IFRS 2.2(c)	Ch.34, p.2794
IFRS 2.3A	Ch.34, p.2644
IFRS 2.4	Ch.34, p.2654
IFRS 2.5	Ch.8, p.619

IFRS 2.5	Ch.34, p.2644
IFRS 2.5	Ch.34, p.2654
IFRS 2.5	Ch.34, p.2655
IFRS 2.6	Ch.34, p.2655
IFRS 2.6A	Ch.34, p.2674
IFRS 2.6A	Ch.34, p.2693
IFRS 2.6A	Ch.34, p.2740
IFRS 2.6A	Ch.34, p.2775
IFRS 2.7	Ch.34, p.2663
IFRS 2.7	Ch.34, p.2709
IFRS 2.8	Ch.34, p.2663
IFRS 2.9	Ch.34, p.2663
IFRS 2.10	Ch.8, p.615
IFRS 2.10	Ch.9, p.750
IFRS 2.10	Ch.34, p.2674
IFRS 2.11	Ch.34, p.2676
IFRS 2.11	Ch.34, p.2677
IFRS 2.12	Ch.34, p.2677
IFRS 2.13	Ch.9, p.750
IFRS 2.13	Ch.34, p.2691
IFRS 2.13A	Ch.9, p.750
IFRS 2.13A	Ch.34, p.2651
IFRS 2.13A	Ch.34, p.2662
IFRS 2.13A	Ch.34, p.2794
IFRS 2.14	Ch.34, p.2693
IFRS 2.15	Ch.34, p.2694
IFRS 2.15(b)	Ch.34, p.2699
IFRS 2.15(b)	Ch.34, p.2708
IFRS 2.16	Ch.34, p.2692
IFRS 2.17	Ch.34, p.2692
IFRS 2.18	Ch.34, p.2692
IFRS 2.19	Ch.34, p.2695
IFRS 2.19-20	Ch.34, p.2695
IFRS 2.19-21	Ch.34, p.2707
IFRS 2.19-21A	Ch.34, p.2693
IFRS 2.21	Ch.34, p.2704
IFRS 2.21A	Ch.34, p.2712
IFRS 2.22	Ch.34, p.2693
IFRS 2.23	Ch.34, p.2696
IFRS 2.24(a)	Ch.34, p.2766
IFRS 2.24(b)	Ch.34, p.2767
IFRS 2.25	Ch.34, p.2768
IFRS 2.25(a)	Ch.34, p.2768
IFRS 2.25(b)	Ch.34, p.2768
IFRS 2.26	Ch.34, p.2714
IFRS 2.26-28	Ch.34, p.2734
IFRS 2.26-29	Ch.5, p.287
IFRS 2.26-29	Ch.5, p.289
IFRS 2.27	Ch.34, p.2715
IFRS 2.27	Ch.34, p.2716
IFRS 2.27	Ch.34, p.2725
IFRS 2.28	Ch.34, p.2726
IFRS 2.28	Ch.34, p.2727
IFRS 2.28	Ch.34, p.2732
IFRS 2.28	Ch.34, p.2734
IFRS 2.28(a)	Ch.34, p.2729
IFRS 2.28(b)	Ch.47, p.3743
IFRS 2.28(c)	Ch.34, p.2731

IFRS 2.28A	Ch.34, p.2713	IFRS 2.63D	Ch.34, p.2638
IFRS 2.28A	Ch.34, p.2714	IFRS 2 Appendix A	Ch.34, p.2642
IFRS 2.29	Ch.34, p.2726	IFRS 2 Appendix A	Ch.34, p.2664
IFRS 2.30	Ch.34, p.2777	IFRS 2 Appendix A	Ch.34, p.2671
IFRS 2.30-33D	Ch.34, p.2775	IFRS 2 Appendix A	Ch.34, p.2674
IFRS 2.31	Ch.34, p.2770	IFRS 2 Appendix A	Ch.34, p.2676
IFRS 2.31	Ch.34, p.2775	IFRS 2 Appendix A	Ch.34, p.2677
IFRS 2.32	Ch.34, p.2777	IFRS 2 Appendix A	Ch.34, p.2678
IFRS 2.32-33	Ch.34, p.2777	IFRS 2 Appendix A	Ch.34, p.2692
IFRS 2.33	Ch.34, p.2775	IFRS 2 Appendix A	Ch.34, p.2693
IFRS 2.33A-33B	Ch.34, p.2777	IFRS 2 Appendix A	Ch.34, p.2704
IFRS 2.33C	Ch.34, p.2779	IFRS 2 Appendix A	Ch.34, p.2727
IFRS 2.33D	Ch.34, p.2777	IFRS 2 Appendix A	Ch.34, p.2771
IFRS 2.33D	Ch.34, p.2779	IFRS 2 Appendix A	Ch.34, p.2789
IFRS 2.33E	Ch.34, p.2860	IFRS 2.B1	Ch.34, p.2739
IFRS 2.33F	Ch.34, p.2860	IFRS 2.B2	Ch.34, p.2765
IFRS 2.33G	Ch.34, p.2860	IFRS 2.B3	Ch.34, p.2765
IFRS 2.33H(a)	Ch.34, p.2861	IFRS 2.B4-5	Ch.34, p.2744
IFRS 2.33H(b)	Ch.34, p.2860	IFRS 2.B5	Ch.34, p.2746
IFRS 2.34	Ch.34, p.2788	IFRS 2.B6	Ch.34, p.2754
IFRS 2.35	Ch.34, p.2788	IFRS 2.B7-9	Ch.34, p.2754
IFRS 2.35	Ch.34, p.2789	IFRS 2.B10	Ch.34, p.2754
IFRS 2.35	Ch.34, p.2794	IFRS 2.B11-12	Ch.34, p.2755
IFRS 2.36	Ch.34, p.2789	IFRS 2.B13-15	Ch.34, p.2755
IFRS 2.37	Ch.34, p.2790	IFRS 2.B16-17	Ch.34, p.2755
IFRS 2.38	Ch.34, p.2790	IFRS 2.B18	Ch.34, p.2757
IFRS 2.39-40	Ch.34, p.2792	IFRS 2.B19-21	Ch.34, p.2758
IFRS 2.40	Ch.34, p.2792	IFRS 2.B22-24	Ch.34, p.2759
IFRS 2.41	Ch.34, p.2795	IFRS 2.B25	Ch.34, p.2760
IFRS 2.41-42	Ch.34, p.2795	IFRS 2.B26	Ch.34, p.2761
IFRS 2.43	Ch.34, p.2796	IFRS 2.B27-29	Ch.34, p.2761
IFRS 2.43A	Ch.34, p.2644	IFRS 2.B30	Ch.34, p.2659
IFRS 2.43A	Ch.34, p.2815	IFRS 2.B30	Ch.34, p.2761
IFRS 2.43B	Ch.34, p.2647	IFRS 2.B31	Ch.34, p.2765
IFRS 2.43B	Ch.34, p.2648	IFRS 2.B31-32	Ch.34, p.2762
IFRS 2.43B	Ch.34, p.2811	IFRS 2.B33-34	Ch.34, p.2765
IFRS 2.43B	Ch.34, p.2815	IFRS 2.B34	Ch.34, p.2762
IFRS 2.43B-43C	Ch.34, p.2645	IFRS 2.B35	Ch.34, p.2762
IFRS 2.43B-43C	Ch.34, p.2648	IFRS 2.B36	Ch.34, p.2763
IFRS 2.43C	Ch.34, p.2649	IFRS 2.B37	Ch.34, p.2763
IFRS 2.43C	Ch.34, p.2816	IFRS 2.B38-39	Ch.34, p.2764
IFRS 2.43D	Ch.34, p.2815	IFRS 2.B40-41	Ch.34, p.2764
IFRS 2.44	Ch.5, p.287	IFRS 2.B42	Ch.34, p.2715
IFRS 2.44	Ch.34, p.2845	IFRS 2.B42	Ch.34, p.2716
IFRS 2.45	Ch.5, p.287	IFRS 2.B42	Ch.34, p.2725
IFRS 2.45	Ch.34, p.2845	IFRS 2.B42-43	Ch.34, p.2716
IFRS 2.46	Ch.34, p.2846	IFRS 2.B42-44	Ch.34, p.2716
IFRS 2.47	Ch.34, p.2847	IFRS 2.B43	Ch.34, p.2715
IFRS 2.48	Ch.34, p.2848	IFRS 2.B43(a)	Ch.34, p.2717
IFRS 2.49	Ch.34, p.2848	IFRS 2.B43(a)	Ch.34, p.2718
IFRS 2.50	Ch.34, p.2848	IFRS 2.B43(b)	Ch.34, p.2718
IFRS 2.51	Ch.34, p.2848	IFRS 2.B43(c)	Ch.34, p.2718
IFRS 2.52	Ch.34, p.2848	IFRS 2.B43-44	Ch.34, p.2725
IFRS 2.52	Ch.34, p.2861	IFRS 2.B44	Ch.34, p.2715
IFRS 2.62	Ch.34, p.2638	IFRS 2.B44	Ch.34, p.2725
IFRS 2.63	Ch.34, p.2638	IFRS 2.B44(a)	Ch.34, p.2720
IFRS 2.64	Ch.34, p.2638	IFRS 2.B44(b)	Ch.34, p.2721
IFRS 2.63A	Ch.34, p.2643	IFRS 2.B44(b)	Ch.34, p.2724

IFRS 2.B44(c)	Ch.34, p.2720	IFRS 2.IG Example 9	Ch.34, p.2792
IFRS 2.B44(c)	Ch.34, p.2721	IFRS 2.IG Example 9A	Ch.34, p.2713
IFRS 2.B44A	Ch.34, p.2786	IFRS 2.IG Example 10	Ch.34, p.2767
IFRS 2.B44B	Ch.34, p.2787	IFRS 2.IG Example 12	Ch.34, p.2775
IFRS 2.B44C	Ch.34, p.2787	IFRS 2.IG Example 12A	Ch.34, p.2775
IFRS 2.B45	Ch.34, p.2815	IFRS 2.IG Example 12A	Ch.34, p.2778
IFRS 2.B45	Ch.34, p.2816	IFRS 2.IG Example 12B	Ch.34, p.2860
IFRS 2.B45-46	Ch.34, p.2815	IFRS 2.IG Example 12C	Ch.34, p.2787
IFRS 2.B48-49	Ch.34, p.2772	IFRS 2.IG Example 13	Ch.34, p.2791
IFRS 2.B48(b)	Ch.34, p.2646	IFRS 2.BC8-17	Ch.34, p.2653
IFRS 2.B49	Ch.34, p.2648	IFRS 2.BC18C	Ch.34, p.2652
IFRS 2.B50	Ch.34, p.2648	IFRS 2.BC18D	Ch.34, p.2652
IFRS 2.B50	Ch.34, p.2817	IFRS 2.BC22E	Ch.34, p.2643
IFRS 2.B52	Ch.34, p.2817	IFRS 2.BC22G	Ch.34, p.2647
IFRS 2.B52(a)	Ch.34, p.2645	IFRS 2.BC24	Ch.34, p.2739
IFRS 2.B52(b)	Ch.34, p.2647	IFRS 2.BC54-BC57	Ch.37, p.3049
IFRS 2.B52(b)	Ch.34, p.2811	IFRS 2.BC70-74	Ch.34, p.2822
IFRS 2.B53	Ch.34, p.2817	IFRS 2.BC88-96	Ch.34, p.2675
IFRS 2.B53-B54	Ch.34, p.2645	IFRS 2.BC109	Ch.34, p.2641
IFRS 2.B54	Ch.34, p.2817	IFRS 2.BC109	Ch.47, p.3704
IFRS 2.B55	Ch.34, p.2647	IFRS 2.BC110	Ch.34, p.2641
IFRS 2.B55	Ch.34, p.2811	IFRS 2.BC110	Ch.47, p.3704
IFRS 2.B55	Ch.34, p.2817	IFRS 2.BC126	Ch.34, p.2675
IFRS 2.B56-B57	Ch.34, p.2818	IFRS 2.BC126-127	Ch.34, p.2676
IFRS 2.B56-B58	Ch.34, p.2649	IFRS 2.BC130	Ch.34, p.2740
IFRS 2.B58	Ch.34, p.2818	IFRS 2.BC131	Ch.34, p.2744
IFRS 2.B59	Ch.34, p.2840	IFRS 2.BC152	Ch.34, p.2744
IFRS 2.B60	Ch.34, p.2840	IFRS 2.BC153-169	Ch.34, p.2753
IFRS 2.B61	Ch.34, p.2841	IFRS 2.BC171A	Ch.34, p.2668
IFRS 2.IG1-3	Ch.34, p.2678	IFRS 2.BC171B	Ch.34, p.2669
IFRS 2.IG2	Ch.34, p.2678	IFRS 2.BC171B	Ch.34, p.2670
IFRS 2.IG4	Ch.34, p.2679	IFRS 2.BC183-184	Ch.34, p.2705
IFRS 2.IG5	Ch.34, p.2691	IFRS 2.BC188-192	Ch.34, p.2769
IFRS 2.IG5D	Ch.34, p.2651	IFRS 2.BC218-221	Ch.34, p.2696
IFRS 2.IG6-7	Ch.34, p.2691	IFRS 2.BC222-237	Ch.34, p.2715
IFRS 2.IG11	Ch.34, p.2696	IFRS 2.BC233	Ch.34, p.2732
IFRS 2.IG11	Ch.34, p.2698	IFRS 2.BC237A	Ch.34, p.2713
IFRS 2.IG12	Ch.34, p.2699	IFRS 2.BC237H	Ch.34, p.2787
IFRS 2.IG12	Ch.34, p.2702	IFRS 2.BC237K	Ch.34, p.2782
IFRS 2.IG13	Ch.34, p.2704	IFRS 2.BC246-251	Ch.34, p.2775
IFRS 2.IG13	Ch.34, p.2707	IFRS 2.BC255G	Ch.34, p.2858
IFRS 2.IG14	Ch.34, p.2708	IFRS 2.BC255G-I	Ch.34, p.2860
IFRS 2.IG15	Ch.34, p.2717	IFRS 2.BC255J	Ch.34, p.2861
IFRS 2.IG15	Ch.34, p.2721	IFRS 2.BC256	Ch.34, p.2803
IFRS 2.IG19	Ch.34, p.2775	IFRS 2.BC268H-268K	Ch.34, p.2818
IFRS 2.IG24	Ch.34, p.2669	IFRS 2.BC311-BC329	Ch.33, p.2589
IFRS 2.IG24	Ch.34, p.2713	IFRS 2.BC311-BC329	Ch.33, p.2593
IFRS 2.IG24	Ch.34, p.2714	IFRS 2.BC330-333	Ch.34, p.2673
IFRS 2.IG Example 1	Ch.34, p.2651	IFRS 2.BC341	Ch.34, p.2670
IFRS 2.IG Example 1	Ch.34, p.2652	IFRS 2.BC353-BC358	Ch.34, p.2669
IFRS 2.IG Example 2	Ch.34, p.2700	IFRS 2.BC364	Ch.34, p.2668
IFRS 2.IG Example 3	Ch.34, p.2701		
IFRS 2.IG Example 4	Ch.34, p.2700		
IFRS 2.IG Example 4	Ch.34, p.2702		
IFRS 2.IG Example 5	Ch.34, p.2707		
IFRS 2.IG Example 6	Ch.34, p.2708		
IFRS 2.IG Example 7	Ch.34, p.2717		
IFRS 2.IG Example 8	Ch.34, p.2721		

IFRS 3 (2000)

IFRS 3(2000).21B Ch.9, p.669

IFRS 3 (2007)

IFRS 3(2007).B8	Ch.8, p.595
IFRS 3(2007).B8	Ch.9, p.744
IFRS 3(2007).BC28	Ch.10, p.771

IFRS 3 (2022)

IFRS 3(2022).11	Ch.9, p.668
IFRS 3(2022).11	Ch.9, p.686
IFRS 3(2022).23A	Ch.9, p.686
IFRS 3(2022).BC114D	Ch.9, p.686

IFRS 3

IFRS 3.1	Ch.10, p.768
IFRS 3.2	Ch.9, p.647
IFRS 3.2	Ch.9, p.648
IFRS 3.2	Ch.10, p.766
IFRS 3.2	Ch.12, p.932
IFRS 3.2	Ch.46, p.3652
IFRS 3.2(a)	Ch.11, p.856
IFRS 3.2(a)	Ch.12, p.893
IFRS 3.2(b)	Ch.6, p.393
IFRS 3.2(b)	Ch.7, p.504
IFRS 3.2(b)	Ch.8, p.620
IFRS 3.2(b)	Ch.18, p.1397
IFRS 3.2(b)	Ch.19, p.1457
IFRS 3.2(b)	Ch.33, p.2516
IFRS 3.2(b)	Ch.33, p.2609
IFRS 3.2(b)	Ch.43, p.3418
IFRS 3.2(b)	Ch.49, p.3857
IFRS 3.2(b)	Ch.56, p.4864
IFRS 3.2(c)	Ch.6, p.393
IFRS 3.2(c)	Ch.10, p.768
IFRS 3.2(c)	Ch.56, p.4870
IFRS 3.2A	Ch.5, p.267
IFRS 3.2A	Ch.9, p.647
IFRS 3.3	Ch.5, p.267
IFRS 3.3	Ch.7, p.504
IFRS 3.3	Ch.7, p.514
IFRS 3.3	Ch.9, p.650
IFRS 3.3	Ch.10, p.768
IFRS 3.4	Ch.5, p.271
IFRS 3.4	Ch.9, p.659
IFRS 3.5	Ch.5, p.271
IFRS 3.5	Ch.9, p.659
IFRS 3.5	Ch.10, p.777
IFRS 3.6	Ch.9, p.659
IFRS 3.7	Ch.9, p.659
IFRS 3.7	Ch.9, p.752
IFRS 3.8	Ch.6, p.393
IFRS 3.8	Ch.7, p.503
IFRS 3.8	Ch.9, p.665
IFRS 3.9	Ch.9, p.665
IFRS 3.10	Ch.7, p.541
IFRS 3.10	Ch.9, p.666
IFRS 3.10	Ch.9, p.710
IFRS 3.10	Ch.33, p.2605
IFRS 3.11	Ch.2, p.47
IFRS 3.11	Ch.9, p.667
IFRS 3.11	Ch.43, p.3414
IFRS 3.12	Ch.9, p.667
IFRS 3.12	Ch.9, p.726
IFRS 3.13	Ch.9, p.667
IFRS 3.14	Ch.9, p.666
IFRS 3.15	Ch.9, p.670
IFRS 3.15	Ch.46, p.3652
IFRS 3.15	Ch.53, p.4277
IFRS 3.15	Ch.56, p.4863
IFRS 3.16	Ch.9, p.670
IFRS 3.16(b)	Ch.53, p.4277
IFRS 3.16(c)	Ch.46, p.3652
IFRS 3.17	Ch.9, p.670
IFRS 3.17(b)	Ch.55, p.4549
IFRS 3.18	Ch.9, p.666
IFRS 3.18	Ch.17, p.1365
IFRS 3.18	Ch.33, p.2605
IFRS 3.18	Ch.49, p.3857
IFRS 3.18	Ch.51, p.4016
IFRS 3.19	Ch.7, p.504
IFRS 3.19	Ch.7, p.541
IFRS 3.19	Ch.7, p.554
IFRS 3.19	Ch.9, p.666
IFRS 3.19	Ch.9, p.710
IFRS 3.19	Ch.9, p.714
IFRS 3.19	Ch.20, p.1602
IFRS 3.20	Ch.9, p.666
IFRS 3.20	Ch.9, p.669
IFRS 3.21	Ch.9, p.690
IFRS 3.22	Ch.9, p.690
IFRS 3.23	Ch.9, p.691
IFRS 3.23	Ch.26, p.1935
IFRS 3.23	Ch.26, p.1942
IFRS 3.23	Ch.26, p.1961
IFRS 3.24	Ch.9, p.692
IFRS 3.24	Ch.33, p.2562
IFRS 3.24	Ch.33, p.2605
IFRS 3.25	Ch.9, p.692
IFRS 3.25	Ch.33, p.2605
IFRS 3.26	Ch.9, p.692
IFRS 3.26	Ch.20, p.1584
IFRS 3.27	Ch.9, p.693
IFRS 3.27	Ch.45, p.3606
IFRS 3.27-28	Ch.9, p.693
IFRS 3.28	Ch.9, p.693
IFRS 3.29	Ch.9, p.695
IFRS 3.30	Ch.7, p.541
IFRS 3.30	Ch.9, p.695
IFRS 3.30	Ch.20, p.1584
IFRS 3.30	Ch.34, p.2804
IFRS 3.31	Ch.9, p.695
IFRS 3.31A	Ch.56, p.4863
IFRS 3.32	Ch.9, p.697

IFRS 3.32	Ch.9, p.708	IFRS 3.56	Ch.9, p.691
IFRS 3.32	Ch.10, p.777	IFRS 3.56	Ch.26, p.1942
IFRS 3.33	Ch.9, p.699	IFRS 3.56	Ch.26, p.1962
IFRS 3.33	Ch.9, p.709	IFRS 3.57	Ch.9, p.693
IFRS 3.33	Ch.9, p.741	IFRS 3.57	Ch.51, p.3959
IFRS 3.33	Ch.10, p.779	IFRS 3.58	Ch.5, p.287
IFRS 3.34	Ch.9, p.697	IFRS 3.58	Ch.7, p.539
IFRS 3.34	Ch.9, p.724	IFRS 3.58	Ch.9, p.707
IFRS 3.34	Ch.10, p.777	IFRS 3.58	Ch.40, p.3178
IFRS 3.35	Ch.9, p.724	IFRS 3.58	Ch.55, p.4542
IFRS 3.36	Ch.9, p.724	IFRS 3.58	Ch.56, p.4691
IFRS 3.36	Ch.51, p.4016	IFRS 3.58(b)(i)	Ch.45, p.3602
IFRS 3.37	Ch.8, p.584	IFRS 3.59	Ch.9, p.753
IFRS 3.37	Ch.9, p.698	IFRS 3.59(b)	Ch.41, p.3207
IFRS 3.37	Ch.10, p.779	IFRS 3.60	Ch.9, p.753
IFRS 3.37	Ch.11, p.828	IFRS 3.61	Ch.9, p.756
IFRS 3.38	Ch.9, p.698	IFRS 3.62	Ch.9, p.756
IFRS 3.39	Ch.7, p.539	IFRS 3.63	Ch.9, p.757
IFRS 3.39	Ch.9, p.700	IFRS 3.64	Ch.20, p.1602
IFRS 3.39	Ch.40, p.3178	IFRS 3.64N	Ch.56, p.4863
IFRS 3.39-40	Ch.9, p.703	IFRS 3.64N	Ch.56, p.4922
IFRS 3.40	Ch.5, p.287	IFRS 3.67	Ch.20, p.1597
IFRS 3.40	Ch.7, p.539	IFRS 3 Appendix A	Ch.5, p.267
IFRS 3.40	Ch.9, p.704	IFRS 3 Appendix A	Ch.6, p.393
IFRS 3.40	Ch.9, p.706	IFRS 3 Appendix A	Ch.7, p.503
IFRS 3.40	Ch.40, p.3178	IFRS 3 Appendix A	Ch.7, p.504
IFRS 3.41	Ch.9, p.717	IFRS 3 Appendix A	Ch.7, p.514
IFRS 3.41-42	Ch.11, p.836	IFRS 3 Appendix A	Ch.8, p.619
IFRS 3.41-42	Ch.11, p.870	IFRS 3 Appendix A	Ch.9, p.639
IFRS 3.42	Ch.9, p.717	IFRS 3 Appendix A	Ch.9, p.650
IFRS 3.42A	Ch.9, p.723	IFRS 3 Appendix A	Ch.9, p.665
IFRS 3.42A	Ch.12, p.937	IFRS 3 Appendix A	Ch.9, p.672
IFRS 3.43	Ch.9, p.708	IFRS 3 Appendix A	Ch.9, p.694
IFRS 3.44	Ch.9, p.709	IFRS 3 Appendix A	Ch.9, p.697
IFRS 3.45	Ch.9, p.736	IFRS 3 Appendix A	Ch.9, p.699
IFRS 3.45	Ch.9, p.737	IFRS 3 Appendix A	Ch.9, p.703
IFRS 3.45	Ch.20, p.1589	IFRS 3 Appendix A	Ch.9, p.709
IFRS 3.45	Ch.43, p.3562	IFRS 3 Appendix A	Ch.9, p.710
IFRS 3.46	Ch.9, p.736	IFRS 3 Appendix A	Ch.9, p.752
IFRS 3.46	Ch.20, p.1589	IFRS 3 Appendix A	Ch.10, p.768
IFRS 3.47	Ch.9, p.737	IFRS 3 Appendix A	Ch.10, p.789
IFRS 3.48	Ch.9, p.738	IFRS 3 Appendix A	Ch.17, p.1296
IFRS 3.49	Ch.9, p.737	IFRS 3 Appendix A	Ch.43, p.3412
IFRS 3.50	Ch.9, p.738	IFRS 3 Appendix A	Ch.55, p.4598
IFRS 3.51	Ch.9, p.726	IFRS 3 Appendix A	Ch.56, p.4870
IFRS 3.51-53	Ch.9, p.708	IFRS 3.B1	Ch.10, p.768
IFRS 3.52	Ch.9, p.727	IFRS 3.B1	Ch.20, p.1623
IFRS 3.52	Ch.9, p.731	IFRS 3.B1-B4	Ch.9, p.649
IFRS 3.52	Ch.34, p.2804	IFRS 3.B1-B4	Ch.10, p.768
IFRS 3.53	Ch.9, p.707	IFRS 3.B2	Ch.10, p.769
IFRS 3.53	Ch.14, p.1051	IFRS 3.B2	Ch.39, p.3114
IFRS 3.53	Ch.40, p.3148	IFRS 3.B3	Ch.10, p.769
IFRS 3.53	Ch.40, p.3177	IFRS 3.B4	Ch.10, p.769
IFRS 3.53	Ch.41, p.3238	IFRS 3.B4	Ch.10, p.787
IFRS 3.53	Ch.47, p.3739	IFRS 3.B5	Ch.9, p.650
IFRS 3.54	Ch.9, p.690	IFRS 3.B6	Ch.9, p.650
IFRS 3.54	Ch.9, p.739	IFRS 3.B7	Ch.9, p.651
IFRS 3.55	Ch.9, p.695	IFRS 3.B7	Ch.55, p.4598

IFRS 3.B7-B12D	Ch.7, p.514	IFRS 3.B37	Ch.9, p.685
IFRS 3.B7A	Ch.9, p.651	IFRS 3.B37	Ch.20, p.1584
IFRS 3.B7A	Ch.19, p.1454	IFRS 3.B38	Ch.9, p.686
IFRS 3.B7A	Ch.19, p.1456	IFRS 3.B38	Ch.20, p.1584
IFRS 3.B7B	Ch.9, p.652	IFRS 3.B39	Ch.9, p.739
IFRS 3.B7B	Ch.19, p.1455	IFRS 3.B40	Ch.9, p.686
IFRS 3.B7C	Ch.9, p.653	IFRS 3.B41	Ch.9, p.687
IFRS 3.B7-B8	Ch.56, p.4870	IFRS 3.B41	Ch.49, p.3857
IFRS 3.B7-B12D	Ch.7, p.504	IFRS 3.B41	Ch.51, p.4017
IFRS 3.B8	Ch.9, p.651	IFRS 3.B42	Ch.9, p.671
IFRS 3.B8	Ch.9, p.654	IFRS 3.B43	Ch.9, p.687
IFRS 3.B8	Ch.9, p.655	IFRS 3.B44	Ch.9, p.711
IFRS 3.B8A	Ch.9, p.654	IFRS 3.B45	Ch.9, p.711
IFRS 3.B9	Ch.9, p.651	IFRS 3.B46	Ch.9, p.709
IFRS 3.B11	Ch.9, p.655	IFRS 3.B47	Ch.9, p.709
IFRS 3.B11	Ch.19, p.1454	IFRS 3.B47	Ch.9, p.710
IFRS 3.B12B	Ch.9, p.654	IFRS 3.B48	Ch.9, p.710
IFRS 3.B12B	Ch.9, p.658	IFRS 3.B49	Ch.9, p.710
IFRS 3.B12C	Ch.9, p.655	IFRS 3.B50	Ch.9, p.727
IFRS 3.B12D(a)	Ch.9, p.654	IFRS 3.B50	Ch.34, p.2805
IFRS 3.B12D(b)	Ch.9, p.655	IFRS 3.B51	Ch.9, p.728
IFRS 3.B12D(c)	Ch.9, p.655	IFRS 3.B52	Ch.9, p.728
IFRS 3.B13	Ch.9, p.659	IFRS 3.B53	Ch.9, p.730
IFRS 3.B14	Ch.9, p.660	IFRS 3.B54	Ch.9, p.731
IFRS 3.B14	Ch.9, p.748	IFRS 3.B55	Ch.9, p.732
IFRS 3.B15	Ch.9, p.660	IFRS 3.B55(a)	Ch.9, p.732
IFRS 3.B16	Ch.9, p.660	IFRS 3.B55(a)	Ch.9, p.733
IFRS 3.B17	Ch.9, p.660	IFRS 3.B55(e)	Ch.9, p.733
IFRS 3.B18	Ch.9, p.661	IFRS 3.B56	Ch.9, p.707
IFRS 3.B18	Ch.10, p.789	IFRS 3.B56	Ch.34, p.2805
IFRS 3.B19	Ch.5, p.271	IFRS 3.B56	Ch.34, p.2808
IFRS 3.B19	Ch.9, p.740	IFRS 3.B56-B62	Ch.9, p.707
IFRS 3.B19	Ch.9, p.750	IFRS 3.B56-B62	Ch.9, p.734
IFRS 3.B19	Ch.9, p.752	IFRS 3.B56-B62	Ch.9, p.749
IFRS 3.B19	Ch.10, p.789	IFRS 3.B57-59	Ch.34, p.2805
IFRS 3.B20	Ch.9, p.740	IFRS 3.B59	Ch.34, p.2805
IFRS 3.B21	Ch.9, p.742	IFRS 3.B59	Ch.34, p.2809
IFRS 3.B22	Ch.9, p.743	IFRS 3.B60	Ch.34, p.2806
IFRS 3.B23	Ch.9, p.745	IFRS 3.B60	Ch.34, p.2809
IFRS 3.B24	Ch.9, p.745	IFRS 3.B61-62	Ch.34, p.2806
IFRS 3.B25	Ch.9, p.746	IFRS 3.B62A	Ch.7, p.541
IFRS 3.B25	Ch.37, p.3033	IFRS 3.B62A	Ch.9, p.707
IFRS 3.B26	Ch.9, p.747	IFRS 3.B62A	Ch.9, p.714
IFRS 3.B26	Ch.37, p.3033	IFRS 3.B62A-B62B	Ch.34, p.2811
IFRS 3.B27	Ch.9, p.747	IFRS 3.B62B	Ch.7, p.541
IFRS 3.B27	Ch.37, p.3033	IFRS 3.B62B	Ch.9, p.707
IFRS 3.B31	Ch.9, p.672	IFRS 3.B62B	Ch.9, p.714
IFRS 3.B31	Ch.9, p.673	IFRS 3.B63	Ch.9, p.698
IFRS 3.B32	Ch.9, p.673	IFRS 3.B63	Ch.9, p.739
IFRS 3.B32	Ch.17, p.1315	IFRS 3.B63(a)	Ch.7, p.498
IFRS 3.B32(b)	Ch.17, p.1299	IFRS 3.B63(a)	Ch.20, p.1582
IFRS 3.B33	Ch.9, p.672	IFRS 3.B63(d)	Ch.34, p.2809
IFRS 3.B33	Ch.17, p.1315	IFRS 3.B64	Ch.9, p.753
IFRS 3.B34	Ch.9, p.672	IFRS 3.B64(g)	Ch.54, p.4433
IFRS 3.B34	Ch.17, p.1315	IFRS 3.B64(h)	Ch.54, p.4433
IFRS 3.B35	Ch.9, p.684	IFRS 3.B64(o)(i)	Ch.9, p.753
IFRS 3.B36	Ch.9, p.685	IFRS 3.B65	Ch.9, p.755
IFRS 3.B36	Ch.9, p.695	IFRS 3.B65	Ch.41, p.3207

IFRS 3.B66	Ch.9, p.756	IFRS 3.BC149-BC156	Ch.9, p.679
IFRS 3.B66	Ch.41, p.3207	IFRS 3.BC178	Ch.9, p.685
IFRS 3.B67	Ch.9, p.756	IFRS 3.BC180	Ch.9, p.685
IFRS 3.B69(e)	Ch.5, p.281	IFRS 3.BC182-BC184	Ch.9, p.685
IFRS 3.IE1-IE5	Ch.9, p.740	IFRS 3.BC217	Ch.9, p.712
IFRS 3.IE9	Ch.9, p.747	IFRS 3.BC218	Ch.9, p.713
IFRS 3.10	Ch.9, p.747	IFRS 3.BC245	Ch.9, p.691
IFRS 3.IE11-IE15	Ch.9, p.745	IFRS 3.BC258	Ch.54, p.4432
IFRS 3.IE16	Ch.17, p.1315	IFRS 3.BC260	Ch.54, p.4433
IFRS 3.IE16-IE44	Ch.9, p.673	IFRS 3.BC275	Ch.9, p.691
IFRS 3.IE16-44	Ch.17, p.1315	IFRS 3.BC276	Ch.9, p.686
IFRS 3.IE23-31	Ch.17, p.1297	IFRS 3.BC276	Ch.20, p.1584
IFRS 3.IE28	Ch.9, p.676	IFRS 3.BC296-BC300	Ch.9, p.692
IFRS 3.IE30	Ch.9, p.675	IFRS 3.BC298	Ch.9, p.696
IFRS 3.IE30	Ch.17, p.1317	IFRS 3.BC302-BC303	Ch.9, p.693
IFRS 3.IE30(d)	Ch.55, p.4600	IFRS 3.BC 303	Ch.9, p.694
IFRS 3.IE30(d)	Ch.56, p.4871	IFRS 3.BC308	Ch.9, p.695
IFRS 3.IE34	Ch.9, p.675	IFRS 3.BC310	Ch.9, p.695
IFRS 3.IE45-IE49	Ch.9, p.725	IFRS 3.BC311	Ch.9, p.696
IFRS 3.IE50-IE53	Ch.9, p.737	IFRS 3.BC311B	Ch.34, p.2808
IFRS 3.IE54-IE57	Ch.9, p.729	IFRS 3.BC313	Ch.9, p.697
IFRS 3.IE57	Ch.9, p.729	IFRS 3.BC313	Ch.20, p.1584
IFRS 3.IE58-IE60	Ch.9, p.733	IFRS 3.BC316	Ch.9, p.697
IFRS 3.IE61-IE71	Ch.9, p.734	IFRS 3.BC317	Ch.20, p.1584
IFRS 3.IE61-71	Ch.34, p.2806	IFRS 3.BC323	Ch.20, p.1583
IFRS 3.IE72	Ch.9, p.758	IFRS 3.BC328	Ch.9, p.697
IFRS 3.IE73-123	Ch.9, p.653	IFRS 3.BC337-342	Ch.9, p.699
IFRS 3.IE74	Ch.19, p.1456	IFRS 3.BC338-BC342	Ch.9, p.699
IFRS 3.IE75-76	Ch.19, p.1456	IFRS 3.BC342	Ch.9, p.699
IFRS 3.IE77	Ch.19, p.1456	IFRS 3.BC347	Ch.9, p.701
IFRS 3.IE78	Ch.19, p.1457	IFRS 3.BC348	Ch.9, p.701
IFRS 3.BC21F	Ch.9, p.655	IFRS 3.BC349	Ch.9, p.701
IFRS 3.BC21G	Ch.19, p.1454	IFRS 3.BC357	Ch.9, p.706
IFRS 3.BC21H-21I	Ch.9, p.655	IFRS 3.BC360I	Ch.9, p.707
IFRS 3.BC21M	Ch.9, p.654	IFRS 3.BC370	Ch.9, p.708
IFRS 3.BC21Q	Ch.9, p.658	IFRS 3.BC370	Ch.9, p.734
IFRS 3.BC21V	Ch.19, p.1455	IFRS 3.BC371	Ch.9, p.724
IFRS 3.BC21W	Ch.19, p.1455	IFRS 3.BC372-BC375	Ch.9, p.724
IFRS 3.BC21Y	Ch.19, p.1456	IFRS 3.BC376-BC377	Ch.9, p.724
IFRS 3.BC23	Ch.10, p.773	IFRS 3.BC379	Ch.9, p.724
IFRS 3.BC58	Ch.9, p.647	IFRS 3.BC384	Ch.8, p.589
IFRS 3.BC60	Ch.9, p.647	IFRS 3.BC384	Ch.9, p.717
IFRS 3.BC61B-BC61D	Ch.9, p.647	IFRS 3.BC384	Ch.11, p.836
IFRS 3.BC71-BC72	Ch.9, p.647	IFRS 3.BC392	Ch.9, p.736
IFRS 3.BC79	Ch.9, p.647	IFRS 3.BC393	Ch.9, p.736
IFRS 3.BC110	Ch.9, p.665		
IFRS 3.BC112	Ch.9, p.667		
IFRS 3.BC120	Ch.9, p.734		
IFRS 3.BC122	Ch.9, p.728		
IFRS 3.BC125-BC130	Ch.9, p.667		
IFRS 3.BC132	Ch.9, p.667		
IFRS 3.BC132	Ch.9, p.734		
IFRS 3.BC137	Ch.9, p.667		
IFRS 3.BC137	Ch.9, p.734		
IFRS 3.BC146	Ch.9, p.671		
IFRS 3.BC148	Ch.9, p.671		
IFRS 3.BC148	Ch.19, p.1461		
IFRS 3.BC149-BC156	Ch.9, p.673		

IFRS 4

IFRS 4.1	Ch.55, p.4537
IFRS 4.1	Ch.55, p.4621
IFRS 4.2	Ch.55, p.4538
IFRS 4.2(b)	Ch.45, p.3594
IFRS 4.2(b)	Ch.55, p.4539
IFRS 4.2(b)	Ch.55, p.4574
IFRS 4.3	Ch.55, p.4540
IFRS 4.4(a)	Ch.55, p.4540
IFRS 4.4(b)	Ch.55, p.4541

IFRS 4.4(c)	Ch.55, p.4541	IFRS 4.20Q	Ch.11, p.861
IFRS 4.4(d)	Ch.45, p.3598	IFRS 4.20Q	Ch.55, p.4609
IFRS 4.4(d)	Ch.55, p.4541	IFRS 4.20R	Ch.55, p.4617
IFRS 4.4(e)	Ch.55, p.4542	IFRS 4.20S	Ch.55, p.4617
IFRS 4.4(f)	Ch.45, p.3599	IFRS 4.21	Ch.55, p.4587
IFRS 4.4(f)	Ch.51, p.3958	IFRS 4.22	Ch.55, p.4587
IFRS 4.4(f)	Ch.55, p.4542	IFRS 4.23	Ch.55, p.4588
IFRS 4.5	Ch.55, p.4538	IFRS 4.24	Ch.55, p.4590
IFRS 4.5	Ch.55, p.4600	IFRS 4.25	Ch.55, p.4588
IFRS 4.6	Ch.55, p.4539	IFRS 4.25(a)	Ch.55, p.4588
IFRS 4.7	Ch.55, p.4560	IFRS 4.25(b)	Ch.55, p.4589
IFRS 4.7	Ch.56, p.4713	IFRS 4.25(c)	Ch.7, p.503
IFRS 4.8	Ch.55, p.4561	IFRS 4.25(c)	Ch.55, p.4589
IFRS 4.8	Ch.55, p.4562	IFRS 4.26	Ch.55, p.4590
IFRS 4.8	Ch.56, p.4713	IFRS 4.27	Ch.55, p.4591
IFRS 4.9	Ch.55, p.4561	IFRS 4.28	Ch.55, p.4592
IFRS 4.10	Ch.55, p.4563	IFRS 4.29	Ch.55, p.4592
IFRS 4.10-12	Ch.56, p.4715	IFRS 4.30	Ch.55, p.4593
IFRS 4.10(a)	Ch.55, p.4564	IFRS 4.31	Ch.55, p.4596
IFRS 4.10(b)	Ch.55, p.4564	IFRS 4.31	Ch.56, p.4924
IFRS 4.10(c)	Ch.55, p.4564	IFRS 4.31(a)	Ch.55, p.4596
IFRS 4.11	Ch.55, p.4564	IFRS 4.31(b)	Ch.55, p.4596
IFRS 4.12	Ch.55, p.4564	IFRS 4.32	Ch.55, p.4597
IFRS 4.13	Ch.55, p.4576	IFRS 4.33	Ch.55, p.4597
IFRS 4.14	Ch.55, p.4577	IFRS 4.33	Ch.55, p.4599
IFRS 4.14(a)	Ch.55, p.4577	IFRS 4.34(a)-(b)	Ch.55, p.4571
IFRS 4.14(c)	Ch.55, p.4582	IFRS 4.34(b)	Ch.56, p.4839
IFRS 4.14(d)	Ch.55, p.4583	IFRS 4.34(c)	Ch.55, p.4571
IFRS 4.15	Ch.55, p.4578	IFRS 4.34(c)	Ch.55, p.4572
IFRS 4.16	Ch.55, p.4579	IFRS 4.34(d)-(e)	Ch.55, p.4572
IFRS 4.17	Ch.55, p.4580	IFRS 4.35(b)	Ch.55, p.4581
IFRS 4.18	Ch.55, p.4579	IFRS 4.35(d)	Ch.54, p.4411
IFRS 4.18	Ch.55, p.4580	IFRS 4.35(d)	Ch.55, p.4574
IFRS 4.19	Ch.55, p.4580	IFRS 4.35A	Ch.55, p.4600
IFRS 4.20	Ch.55, p.4584	IFRS 4.35B	Ch.55, p.4617
IFRS 4.20A	Ch.26, p.1935	IFRS 4.35B	Ch.55, p.4618
IFRS 4.20A	Ch.55, p.4601	IFRS 4.35C	Ch.55, p.4600
IFRS 4.20A	Ch.55, p.4616	IFRS 4.35C	Ch.55, p.4617
IFRS 4.20B	Ch.26, p.1935	IFRS 4.35C(b)	Ch.55, p.4601
IFRS 4.20B	Ch.55, p.4601	IFRS 4.35D	Ch.55, p.4618
IFRS 4.20B	Ch.55, p.4603	IFRS 4.35E	Ch.55, p.4619
IFRS 4.20C	Ch.55, p.4603	IFRS 4.35F	Ch.55, p.4619
IFRS 4.20D	Ch.55, p.4603	IFRS 4.35G	Ch.55, p.4619
IFRS 4.20E	Ch.55, p.4604	IFRS 4.35H	Ch.55, p.4619
IFRS 4.20F	Ch.55, p.4604	IFRS 4.35I	Ch.55, p.4620
IFRS 4.20G	Ch.55, p.4606	IFRS 4.35J	Ch.55, p.4620
IFRS 4.20H	Ch.55, p.4607	IFRS 4.35K	Ch.55, p.4620
IFRS 4.20I	Ch.55, p.4607	IFRS 4.35L	Ch.55, p.4618
IFRS 4.20J	Ch.55, p.4607	IFRS 4.35M	Ch.55, p.4619
IFRS 4.20K	Ch.55, p.4608	IFRS 4.35N	Ch.5, p.291
IFRS 4.20L	Ch.55, p.4608	IFRS 4.35N	Ch.55, p.4620
IFRS 4.20L-20N	Ch.5, p.291	IFRS 4.36	Ch.55, p.4623
IFRS 4.20M	Ch.55, p.4608	IFRS 4.37	Ch.55, p.4623
IFRS 4.20N	Ch.55, p.4608	IFRS 4.37(a)	Ch.55, p.4623
IFRS 4.20O	Ch.11, p.861	IFRS 4.37(b)	Ch.40, p.3185
IFRS 4.20O	Ch.55, p.4609	IFRS 4.37(b)	Ch.40, p.3186
IFRS 4.20P	Ch.11, p.861	IFRS 4.37(b)	Ch.55, p.4626
IFRS 4.20P	Ch.55, p.4609	IFRS 4.37(b)(i)-(ii)	Ch.55, p.4633

Index of standards

IFRS 4.37(c)	Ch.55, p.4633
IFRS 4.37(d)	Ch.55, p.4637
IFRS 4.37(e)	Ch.55, p.4639
IFRS 4.38	Ch.55, p.4643
IFRS 4.39	Ch.55, p.4643
IFRS 4.39(a)	Ch.55, p.4645
IFRS 4.39(c)	Ch.55, p.4648
IFRS 4.39(c)(i)	Ch.55, p.4650
IFRS 4.39(c)(ii)	Ch.55, p.4652
IFRS 4.39(c)(iii)	Ch.55, p.4654
IFRS 4.39(d)	Ch.55, p.4658
IFRS 4.39(d)(i)	Ch.55, p.4661
IFRS 4.39(d)(ii)	Ch.55, p.4663
IFRS 4.39(e)	Ch.55, p.4664
IFRS 4.39D	Ch.55, p.4612
IFRS 4.39A	Ch.55, p.4651
IFRS 4.39B	Ch.55, p.4609
IFRS 4.39C	Ch.55, p.4610
IFRS 4.39E	Ch.55, p.4613
IFRS 4.39F	Ch.55, p.4613
IFRS 4.39G	Ch.55, p.4613
IFRS 4.39H	Ch.55, p.4615
IFRS 4.39I	Ch.55, p.4615
IFRS 4.39J	Ch.55, p.4615
IFRS 4.39K	Ch.55, p.4620
IFRS 4.39L	Ch.55, p.4620
IFRS 4.39M	Ch.55, p.4621
IFRS 4.40-45	Ch.5, p.290
IFRS 4.41	Ch.55, p.4535
IFRS 4.42	Ch.40, p.3185
IFRS 4.42	Ch.40, p.3186
IFRS 4.44	Ch.5, p.290
IFRS 4.45	Ch.55, p.4595
IFRS 4.46	Ch.55, p.4600
IFRS 4.46-49	Ch.5, p.291
IFRS 4.47	Ch.55, p.4610
IFRS 4.48	Ch.55, p.4600
IFRS 4.49	Ch.55, p.4618
IFRS 4.50	Ch.55, p.4616
IFRS 4.50	Ch.55, p.4617
IFRS 4.51	Ch.55, p.4617
IFRS 4 Appendix A	Ch.45, p.3593
IFRS 4 Appendix A	Ch.45, p.3594
IFRS 4 Appendix A	Ch.45, p.3596
IFRS 4 Appendix A	Ch.55, p.4537
IFRS 4 Appendix A	Ch.55, p.4543
IFRS 4 Appendix A	Ch.55, p.4551
IFRS 4 Appendix A	Ch.55, p.4563
IFRS 4 Appendix A	Ch.55, p.4568
IFRS 4 Appendix B	Ch.45, p.3593
IFRS 4.B2	Ch.55, p.4550
IFRS 4.B3	Ch.55, p.4550
IFRS 4.B4	Ch.55, p.4550
IFRS 4.B5	Ch.55, p.4550
IFRS 4.B6	Ch.55, p.4550
IFRS 4.B7	Ch.55, p.4551
IFRS 4.B8	Ch.55, p.4551
IFRS 4.B9	Ch.55, p.4551
IFRS 4.B10	Ch.55, p.4552
IFRS 4.B11	Ch.55, p.4552
IFRS 4.B12	Ch.55, p.4548
IFRS 4.B13	Ch.55, p.4552
IFRS 4.B14	Ch.55, p.4553
IFRS 4.B15	Ch.55, p.4553
IFRS 4.B16	Ch.55, p.4553
IFRS 4.B17	Ch.55, p.4547
IFRS 4.B18	Ch.55, p.4555
IFRS 4.B18(l)	Ch.45, p.3594
IFRS 4.B19	Ch.55, p.4557
IFRS 4.B19(a)	Ch.45, p.3594
IFRS 4.B19(f)	Ch.45, p.3596
IFRS 4.B19(g)	Ch.45, p.3594
IFRS 4.B20	Ch.55, p.4554
IFRS 4.B21	Ch.55, p.4554
IFRS 4.B22	Ch.55, p.4544
IFRS 4.B23	Ch.55, p.4544
IFRS 4.B24	Ch.55, p.4548
IFRS 4.B25	Ch.55, p.4546
IFRS 4.B25 fn7	Ch.55, p.4547
IFRS 4.B26	Ch.55, p.4548
IFRS 4.B27	Ch.55, p.4549
IFRS 4.B28	Ch.55, p.4547
IFRS 4.B29	Ch.55, p.4549
IFRS 4.B30	Ch.55, p.4549
IFRS 4.IG2 E 1.3	Ch.55, p.4545
IFRS 4.IG2 E 1.3	Ch.56, p.4702
IFRS 4.IG2 E 1.6	Ch.55, p.4556
IFRS 4.IG2 E 1.7	Ch.55, p.4549
IFRS 4.IG2 E 1.10	Ch.55, p.4557
IFRS 4.IG2 E 1.11	Ch.45, p.3599
IFRS 4.IG2 E 1.12	Ch.55, p.4557
IFRS 4.IG2 E 1.13	Ch.55, p.4556
IFRS 4.IG2 E 1.14	Ch.55, p.4558
IFRS 4.IG2 E 1.15	Ch.55, p.4551
IFRS 4.IG2 E 1.18	Ch.55, p.4558
IFRS 4.IG2 E 1.19	Ch.55, p.4558
IFRS 4.IG2 E 1.20	Ch.55, p.4552
IFRS 4.IG2 E 1.21	Ch.35, p.2909
IFRS 4.IG2 E 1.21	Ch.55, p.4558
IFRS 4.IG2 E 1.22	Ch.55, p.4556
IFRS 4.IG2 E 1.23	Ch.55, p.4548
IFRS 4.IG2 E 1.25	Ch.55, p.4556
IFRS 4.IG2 E 1.26	Ch.55, p.4556
IFRS 4.IG2 E 1.29	Ch.55, p.4553
IFRS 4.IG2 E 1.27	Ch.55, p.4559
IFRS 4.IG4 E 2.1	Ch.55, p.4561
IFRS 4.IG4 E 2.3	Ch.55, p.4562
IFRS 4.IG4 E 2.12	Ch.55, p.4562
IFRS 4.IG4 E 2.14	Ch.55, p.4562
IFRS 4.IG4 E 2.17	Ch.55, p.4562
IFRS 4.IG4 E 2.18	Ch.55, p.4562
IFRS 4.IG5	Ch.55, p.4567
IFRS 4.IG5 E 3	Ch.55, p.4567
IFRS 4.IG8	Ch.55, p.4593
IFRS 4.IG9	Ch.55, p.4594
IFRS 4.IG10	Ch.55, p.4593

IFRS 4.IG10	Ch.55, p.4594	IFRS 4.IG65B	Ch.55, p.4661
IFRS 4.IG10 E 4	Ch.55, p.4594	IFRS 4.IG65C	Ch.55, p.4661
IFRS 4.IG12	Ch.55, p.4622	IFRS 4.IG65D	Ch.55, p.4663
IFRS 4.IG13	Ch.55, p.4622	IFRS 4.IG65E	Ch.55, p.4663
IFRS 4.IG15-16	Ch.55, p.4622	IFRS 4.IG65F	Ch.55, p.4664
IFRS 4.IG17	Ch.55, p.4624	IFRS 4.IG65G	Ch.55, p.4663
IFRS 4.IG18	Ch.55, p.4626	IFRS 4.IG65G	Ch.55, p.4664
IFRS 4.IG19	Ch.55, p.4633	IFRS 4.IG66	Ch.55, p.4664
IFRS 4.IG20	Ch.55, p.4627	IFRS 4.IG67	Ch.55, p.4664
IFRS 4.IG21	Ch.55, p.4627	IFRS 4.IG68	Ch.55, p.4664
IFRS 4.IG22	Ch.55, p.4627	IFRS 4.IG69	Ch.55, p.4665
IFRS 4.IG23	Ch.55, p.4627	IFRS 4.IG70	Ch.55, p.4665
IFRS 4.IG23A	Ch.55, p.4629	IFRS 4.IG71	Ch.55, p.4667
IFRS 4.IG24	Ch.55, p.4630	IFRS 4.BC2	Ch.55, p.4533
IFRS 4.IG25	Ch.55, p.4632	IFRS 4.BC3	Ch.55, p.4533
IFRS 4.IG26	Ch.55, p.4632	IFRS 4.BC3	Ch.55, p.4534
IFRS 4.IG27	Ch.55, p.4632	IFRS 4.BC10(c)	Ch.55, p.4540
IFRS 4.IG28	Ch.55, p.4632	IFRS 4.BC12	Ch.55, p.4544
IFRS 4.IG29	Ch.55, p.4633	IFRS 4.BC13	Ch.55, p.4544
IFRS 4.IG30	Ch.55, p.4628	IFRS 4.BC26-28	Ch.55, p.4552
IFRS 4.IG30	Ch.55, p.4632	IFRS 4.BC29	Ch.55, p.4552
IFRS 4.IG31	Ch.55, p.4633	IFRS 4.BC32	Ch.55, p.4545
IFRS 4.IG32	Ch.55, p.4634	IFRS 4.BC33	Ch.55, p.4545
IFRS 4.IG33	Ch.55, p.4633	IFRS 4.BC34	Ch.55, p.4545
IFRS 4.IG34	Ch.55, p.4637	IFRS 4.BC34	Ch.55, p.4546
IFRS 4.IG35	Ch.55, p.4637	IFRS 4.BC35	Ch.55, p.4545
IFRS 4.IG36	Ch.55, p.4638	IFRS 4.BC38	Ch.55, p.4549
IFRS 4.IG37	Ch.55, p.4639	IFRS 4.BC39	Ch.55, p.4549
IFRS 4.IG38	Ch.55, p.4639	IFRS 4.BC40	Ch.55, p.4563
IFRS 4.IG39	Ch.55, p.4642	IFRS 4.BC41	Ch.55, p.4564
IFRS 4.IG40	Ch.55, p.4643	IFRS 4.BC44-46	Ch.55, p.4564
IFRS 4.IG41	Ch.55, p.4644	IFRS 4.BC54	Ch.55, p.4567
IFRS 4.IG42	Ch.55, p.4644	IFRS 4.BC69	Ch.55, p.4541
IFRS 4.IG43	Ch.55, p.4644	IFRS 4.BC71	Ch.55, p.4541
IFRS 4.IG45	Ch.55, p.4644	IFRS 4.BC73	Ch.55, p.4542
IFRS 4.IG46	Ch.55, p.4644	IFRS 4.BC77	Ch.55, p.4575
IFRS 4.IG47	Ch.55, p.4645	IFRS 4.BC79	Ch.55, p.4577
IFRS 4.IG48	Ch.55, p.4645	IFRS 4.BC81	Ch.55, p.4575
IFRS 4.IG51	Ch.55, p.4648	IFRS 4.BC82	Ch.55, p.4575
IFRS 4.IG51A	Ch.55, p.4649	IFRS 4.BC83	Ch.55, p.4575
IFRS 4.IG52	Ch.55, p.4651	IFRS 4.BC87	Ch.55, p.4577
IFRS 4.IG52A	Ch.55, p.4651	IFRS 4.BC89(d)	Ch.55, p.4578
IFRS 4.IG53	Ch.55, p.4651	IFRS 4.BC90	Ch.55, p.4578
IFRS 4.IG53A	Ch.55, p.4651	IFRS 4.BC92(a)	Ch.55, p.4578
IFRS 4.IG54A	Ch.55, p.4651	IFRS 4.BC93	Ch.55, p.4578
IFRS 4.IG55	Ch.55, p.4652	IFRS 4.BC94	Ch.55, p.4578
IFRS 4.IG56	Ch.55, p.4653	IFRS 4.BC95	Ch.55, p.4580
IFRS 4.IG57	Ch.55, p.4653	IFRS 4.BC101	Ch.55, p.4579
IFRS 4.IG58	Ch.55, p.4666	IFRS 4.BC104	Ch.55, p.4580
IFRS 4.IG59	Ch.55, p.4654	IFRS 4.BC105	Ch.55, p.4582
IFRS 4.IG60	Ch.55, p.4654	IFRS 4.BC105	Ch.55, p.4584
IFRS 4.IG61	Ch.55, p.4654	IFRS 4.BC106	Ch.55, p.4583
IFRS 4.IG61 IE 5	Ch.55, p.4654	IFRS 4.BC107-108	Ch.55, p.4583
IFRS 4.IG62	Ch.55, p.4658	IFRS 4.BC110	Ch.55, p.4585
IFRS 4.IG64	Ch.55, p.4658	IFRS 4.BC111	Ch.55, p.4585
IFRS 4.IG64A	Ch.55, p.4658	IFRS 4.BC113	Ch.55, p.4585
IFRS 4.IG64B	Ch.55, p.4666	IFRS 4.BC116	Ch.55, p.4586
IFRS 4.IG65A	Ch.55, p.4667	IFRS 4.BC120	Ch.55, p.4586

IFRS 4.BC122	Ch.55, p.4586
IFRS 4.BC123	Ch.55, p.4587
IFRS 4.BC125	Ch.55, p.4587
IFRS 4.BC126	Ch.55, p.4588
IFRS 4.BC128	Ch.55, p.4588
IFRS 4.BC129	Ch.55, p.4589
IFRS 4.BC131	Ch.55, p.4589
IFRS 4.BC132	Ch.7, p.503
IFRS 4.BC132	Ch.55, p.4589
IFRS 4.BC133	Ch.55, p.4590
IFRS 4.BC138	Ch.55, p.4591
IFRS 4.BC140	Ch.55, p.4537
IFRS 4.BC141	Ch.55, p.4592
IFRS 4.BC142	Ch.55, p.4591
IFRS 4.BC144	Ch.55, p.4592
IFRS 4.BC145	Ch.55, p.4595
IFRS 4.BC147	Ch.55, p.4596
IFRS 4.BC148	Ch.55, p.4597
IFRS 4.BC149	Ch.55, p.4597
IFRS 4.BC153	Ch.55, p.4596
IFRS 4.BC154	Ch.55, p.4569
IFRS 4.BC155	Ch.55, p.4569
IFRS 4.BC157	Ch.55, p.4571
IFRS 4.BC158	Ch.55, p.4571
IFRS 4.BC160	Ch.55, p.4570
IFRS 4.BC161	Ch.55, p.4570
IFRS 4.BC162	Ch.55, p.4569
IFRS 4.BC163	Ch.55, p.4573
IFRS 4.BC164	Ch.55, p.4571
IFRS 4.BC183	Ch.55, p.4593
IFRS 4.BC190	Ch.55, p.4560
IFRS 4.BC193	Ch.55, p.4561
IFRS 4.BC212	Ch.55, p.4633
IFRS 4.BC217	Ch.55, p.4648
IFRS 4.BC220	Ch.55, p.4654
IFRS 4.BC222	Ch.55, p.4653
IFRS 4.BC229	Ch.55, p.4600
IFRS 4.BC240	Ch.55, p.4617
IFRS 4.BC240(b)(i)	Ch.55, p.4619
IFRS 4.BC240(b)(ii)	Ch.55, p.4619
IFRS 4.BC241	Ch.55, p.4617
IFRS 4.BC252	Ch.55, p.4602
IFRS 4.BC255(a)	Ch.55, p.4604
IFRS 4.BC255(b)	Ch.55, p.4604
IFRS 4.BC256	Ch.55, p.4605
IFRS 4.BC258	Ch.55, p.4603
IFRS 4.BC264	Ch.55, p.4606
IFRS 4.BC265	Ch.55, p.4606
IFRS 4.BC266	Ch.55, p.4607
IFRS 4.BC273	Ch.55, p.4601
IFRS 4.BC277D	Ch.55, p.4616
IFRS 4.BC277E-F	Ch.55, p.4616
IFRS 4.BC277F	Ch.55, p.4616
IFRS 4.BC279	Ch.55, p.4609
IFRS 4.BC282	Ch.55, p.4608

IFRS 5

IFRS 5.1	Ch.4, p.189
IFRS 5.2	Ch.4, p.189
IFRS 5.2	Ch.4, p.191
IFRS 5.2	Ch.4, p.198
IFRS 5.3	Ch.3, p.122
IFRS 5.3	Ch.4, p.205
IFRS 5.4	Ch.4, p.190
IFRS 5.4	Ch.4, p.198
IFRS 5.5	Ch.4, p.189
IFRS 5.5	Ch.4, p.198
IFRS 5.5	Ch.7, p.532
IFRS 5.5	Ch.8, p.602
IFRS 5.5A	Ch.4, p.189
IFRS 5.5A	Ch.4, p.191
IFRS 5.5A	Ch.4, p.193
IFRS 5.5A	Ch.7, p.532
IFRS 5.5A	Ch.7, p.533
IFRS 5.5A	Ch.8, p.602
IFRS 5.5B	Ch.4, p.214
IFRS 5.5B	Ch.33, p.2621
IFRS 5.5B	Ch.36, p.3010
IFRS 5.5B	Ch.45, p.3606
IFRS 5.6	Ch.4, p.190
IFRS 5.6	Ch.4, p.191
IFRS 5.6	Ch.18, p.1427
IFRS 5.7	Ch.4, p.191
IFRS 5.7	Ch.18, p.1427
IFRS 5.8	Ch.4, p.193
IFRS 5.8	Ch.18, p.1427
IFRS 5.8A	Ch.4, p.196
IFRS 5.8A	Ch.5, p.262
IFRS 5.9	Ch.4, p.194
IFRS 5.10	Ch.4, p.191
IFRS 5.11	Ch.4, p.191
IFRS 5.12	Ch.4, p.191
IFRS 5.12	Ch.4, p.213
IFRS 5.12	Ch.38, p.3080
IFRS 5.12A	Ch.4, p.193
IFRS 5.12A	Ch.7, p.532
IFRS 5.12A	Ch.8, p.602
IFRS 5.13	Ch.4, p.191
IFRS 5.13	Ch.4, p.196
IFRS 5.13	Ch.4, p.207
IFRS 5.14	Ch.4, p.196
IFRS 5.14	Ch.4, p.207
IFRS 5.15	Ch.4, p.198
IFRS 5.15	Ch.11, p.824
IFRS 5.15	Ch.19, p.1486
IFRS 5.15A	Ch.4, p.199
IFRS 5.15A	Ch.7, p.532
IFRS 5.15A	Ch.8, p.602
IFRS 5.16	Ch.4, p.199
IFRS 5.17	Ch.4, p.198
IFRS 5.18	Ch.4, p.198
IFRS 5.18	Ch.20, p.1545
IFRS 5.19	Ch.4, p.200

IFRS 5.20	Ch.4, p.200	IFRS 5.IG8	Ch.4, p.196
IFRS 5.21	Ch.4, p.200	IFRS 5.IG9	Ch.4, p.207
IFRS 5.22	Ch.4, p.200	IFRS 5.IG10	Ch.4, p.200
IFRS 5.23	Ch.4, p.200	IFRS 5.IG11	Ch.4, p.209
IFRS 5.24	Ch.4, p.202	IFRS 5.IG12	Ch.4, p.203
IFRS 5.25	Ch.4, p.199	IFRS 5.IG13	Ch.4, p.199
IFRS 5.25	Ch.19, p.1486	IFRS 5.BC24B-24C	Ch.4, p.197
IFRS 5.26	Ch.4, p.191	IFRS 5.BC58	Ch.4, p.203
IFRS 5.26	Ch.4, p.205		
IFRS 5.26A	Ch.4, p.206		
IFRS 5.27	Ch.4, p.205		
IFRS 5.28	Ch.4, p.206		
IFRS 5.28	Ch.4, p.212		
IFRS 5.28	Ch.12, p.938		

IFRS 6 (2010)

IFRS 6(2010).IN1 .... Ch.43, p.3338

IFRS 6

IFRS 5.29	Ch.4, p.205		
IFRS 5.30	Ch.3, p.123		
IFRS 5.30	Ch.4, p.202	IFRS 6.2(b)	Ch.20, p.1521
IFRS 5.31	Ch.4, p.207	IFRS 6.3	Ch.43, p.3401
IFRS 5.32	Ch.4, p.207	IFRS 6.4	Ch.43, p.3393
IFRS 5.33	Ch.5, p.327	IFRS 6.4	Ch.43, p.3397
IFRS 5.33	Ch.33, p.2611	IFRS 6.5	Ch.43, p.3360
IFRS 5.33	Ch.37, p.3062	IFRS 6.6	Ch.43, p.3361
IFRS 5.33(a)	Ch.4, p.208	IFRS 6.7	Ch.43, p.3361
IFRS 5.33(a)(ii)	Ch.3, p.136	IFRS 6.7	Ch.43, p.3401
IFRS 5.33(b)	Ch.4, p.208	IFRS 6.8	Ch.43, p.3367
IFRS 5.33(b)(ii)	Ch.33, p.2584	IFRS 6.8	Ch.43, p.3418
IFRS 5.33(c)	Ch.4, p.210	IFRS 6.9	Ch.43, p.3362
IFRS 5.33(c)	Ch.40, p.3185	IFRS 6.9	Ch.43, p.3368
IFRS 5.33(d)	Ch.4, p.208	IFRS 6.10	Ch.43, p.3362
IFRS 5.33A	Ch.4, p.208	IFRS 6.10	Ch.43, p.3368
IFRS 5.34	Ch.4, p.208	IFRS 6.11	Ch.43, p.3369
IFRS 5.34	Ch.4, p.211	IFRS 6.12	Ch.43, p.3367
IFRS 5.35	Ch.4, p.210	IFRS 6.13	Ch.43, p.3367
IFRS 5.36	Ch.4, p.213	IFRS 6.14	Ch.43, p.3367
IFRS 5.36A	Ch.4, p.196	IFRS 6.15	Ch.43, p.3365
IFRS 5.37	Ch.4, p.206	IFRS 6.15	Ch.43, p.3370
IFRS 5.37	Ch.4, p.208	IFRS 6.15	Ch.43, p.3373
IFRS 5.37	Ch.4, p.212	IFRS 6.16	Ch.43, p.3371
IFRS 5.38	Ch.4, p.203	IFRS 6.17	Ch.43, p.3363
IFRS 5.38-39	Ch.3, p.124	IFRS 6.17	Ch.43, p.3365
IFRS 5.39	Ch.4, p.203	IFRS 6.17	Ch.43, p.3371
IFRS 5.40	Ch.4, p.211	IFRS 6.17	Ch.43, p.3373
IFRS 5.41	Ch.4, p.213	IFRS 6.18	Ch.43, p.3372
IFRS 5.42	Ch.4, p.214	IFRS 6.18-20	Ch.43, p.3372
IFRS 5 Appendix A	Ch.4, p.190	IFRS 6.20	Ch.43, p.3372
IFRS 5 Appendix A	Ch.4, p.193	IFRS 6.20	Ch.43, p.3373
IFRS 5 Appendix A	Ch.4, p.195	IFRS 6.20	Ch.43, p.3563
IFRS 5 Appendix A	Ch.4, p.198	IFRS 6.21	Ch.43, p.3372
IFRS 5 Appendix A	Ch.4, p.205	IFRS 6.22	Ch.43, p.3372
IFRS 5 Appendix A	Ch.4, p.207	IFRS 6.23	Ch.43, p.3374
IFRS 5 Appendix A	Ch.17, p.1301	IFRS 6.24	Ch.43, p.3374
IFRS 5 Appendix A	Ch.26, p.1944	IFRS 6.24(b)	Ch.40, p.3187
IFRS 5 Appendix A	Ch.29, p.2180	IFRS 6.25	Ch.43, p.3376
IFRS 5 Appendix A	Ch.33, p.2491	IFRS 6 Appendix A	Ch.43, p.3338
IFRS 5 Appendix B	Ch.4, p.194	IFRS 6 Appendix A	Ch.43, p.3360
IFRS 5.IG1-3	Ch.4, p.192	IFRS 6.BC6	Ch.43, p.3361
IFRS 5.IG4	Ch.4, p.194	IFRS 6.BC17	Ch.43, p.3361
IFRS 5.IG5-7	Ch.4, p.195		

IFRS 6.BC17	Ch.43, p.3362	IFRS 7.11A	Ch.54, p.4426
IFRS 6.BC19	Ch.43, p.3361	IFRS 7.11A(d)	Ch.54, p.4486
IFRS 6.BC22	Ch.43, p.3362	IFRS 7.11B	Ch.54, p.4427
IFRS 6.BC23	Ch.43, p.3362	IFRS 7.12B	Ch.54, p.4427
IFRS 6.BC23B	Ch.43, p.3376	IFRS 7.12C	Ch.54, p.4427
IFRS 6.BC27	Ch.43, p.3368	IFRS 7.12D	Ch.54, p.4427
IFRS 6.BC28	Ch.43, p.3368	IFRS 7.13A	Ch.54, p.4500
IFRS 6.BC29-BC30	Ch.43, p.3368	IFRS 7.13B	Ch.54, p.4500
IFRS 6.BC33	Ch.43, p.3371	IFRS 7.13C	Ch.54, p.4501
IFRS 6.BC37	Ch.43, p.3371	IFRS 7.13D	Ch.54, p.4502
IFRS 6.BC40-BC47	Ch.43, p.3372	IFRS 7.13E	Ch.54, p.4503
IFRS 6.BC48	Ch.43, p.3374	IFRS 7.13F	Ch.54, p.4503
IFRS 6.BC49	Ch.43, p.3367	IFRS 7.14	Ch.54, p.4428
IFRS 6.BC53	Ch.43, p.3376	IFRS 7.14-15	Ch.55, p.4629
		IFRS 7.15	Ch.54, p.4428
		IFRS 7.16A	Ch.54, p.4424

IFRS 7 (2010)

IFRS 7(2010).IG3	Ch.54, p.4408

IFRS 7

IFRS 7.1	Ch.44, p.3577	IFRS 7.17	Ch.54, p.4428
IFRS 7.1	Ch.54, p.4406	IFRS 7.18	Ch.54, p.4428
IFRS 7.2	Ch.54, p.4406	IFRS 7.19	Ch.54, p.4429
IFRS 7.3	Ch.14, p.1010	IFRS 7.20	Ch.54, p.4410
IFRS 7.3	Ch.45, p.3591	IFRS 7.20(a)(i)	Ch.54, p.4489
IFRS 7.3	Ch.45, p.3594	IFRS 7.20(a)(vii)	Ch.54, p.4489
IFRS 7.3(a)	Ch.45, p.3592	IFRS 7.20(a)(viii)	Ch.54, p.4489
IFRS 7.3(a)	Ch.45, p.3593	IFRS 7.20(b)	Ch.54, p.4411
IFRS 7.3(a)	Ch.45, p.3602	IFRS 7.20(c)	Ch.54, p.4411
IFRS 7.3(b)	Ch.45, p.3605	IFRS 7.20A	Ch.54, p.4410
IFRS 7.3(d)	Ch.45, p.3593	IFRS 7.21	Ch.54, p.4409
IFRS 7.3(d)	Ch.45, p.3595	IFRS 7.21A	Ch.54, p.4412
IFRS 7.3(d)	Ch.45, p.3598	IFRS 7.21A(a)	Ch.53, p.4273
IFRS 7.3(d)	Ch.56, p.4918	IFRS 7.21B	Ch.54, p.4413
IFRS 7.3(e)	Ch.45, p.3605	IFRS 7.21C	Ch.54, p.4413
IFRS 7.4	Ch.45, p.3600	IFRS 7.21D	Ch.54, p.4412
IFRS 7.4	Ch.54, p.4406	IFRS 7.22A	Ch.54, p.4413
IFRS 7.5	Ch.45, p.3607	IFRS 7.22B	Ch.54, p.4413
IFRS 7.5	Ch.45, p.3608	IFRS 7.22C	Ch.54, p.4414
IFRS 7.5A	Ch.45, p.3607	IFRS 7.23A	Ch.54, p.4415
IFRS 7.6	Ch.54, p.4408	IFRS 7.23B	Ch.54, p.4415
IFRS 7.6	Ch.54, p.4409	IFRS 7.23C	Ch.53, p.4277
IFRS 7.7	Ch.54, p.4409	IFRS 7.23C	Ch.53, p.4278
IFRS 7.8	Ch.54, p.4424	IFRS 7.23C	Ch.54, p.4415
IFRS 7.9	Ch.54, p.4426	IFRS 7.23D	Ch.54, p.4416
IFRS 7.10(a)	Ch.54, p.4425	IFRS 7.23E	Ch.54, p.4416
IFRS 7.10(b)	Ch.54, p.4425	IFRS 7.23F	Ch.54, p.4416
IFRS 7.10(c)	Ch.54, p.4425	IFRS 7.24A	Ch.54, p.4416
IFRS 7.10(d)	Ch.54, p.4425	IFRS 7.24B	Ch.54, p.4417
IFRS 7.10A(a)	Ch.54, p.4425	IFRS 7.24C	Ch.54, p.4418
IFRS 7.10A(b)	Ch.54, p.4425	IFRS 7.24D	Ch.54, p.4415
IFRS 7.11	Ch.54, p.4426	IFRS 7.24E	Ch.54, p.4420
IFRS 7.11(a)	Ch.54, p.4425	IFRS 7.24F	Ch.54, p.4421
IFRS 7.11(b)	Ch.54, p.4425	IFRS 7.24G	Ch.53, p.4388
IFRS 7.11(c)	Ch.54, p.4425	IFRS 7.24G	Ch.54, p.4423
		IFRS 7.24H	Ch.54, p.4423
		IFRS 7.24I	Ch.54, p.4473
		IFRS 7.24J	Ch.54, p.4473
		IFRS 7.25	Ch.14, p.1009
		IFRS 7.25	Ch.14, p.1010
		IFRS 7.25	Ch.41, p.3223
		IFRS 7.25	Ch.54, p.4429

IFRS 7.26	Ch.41, p.3223	IFRS 7.35H(c)	Ch.51, p.3931
IFRS 7.26	Ch.54, p.4429	IFRS 7.35I	Ch.51, p.4074
IFRS 7.28	Ch.41, p.3223	IFRS 7.35I	Ch.54, p.4442
IFRS 7.28	Ch.54, p.4430	IFRS 7.35J	Ch.54, p.4442
IFRS 7.29	Ch.14, p.1009	IFRS 7.35K	Ch.51, p.4074
IFRS 7.29(a)	Ch.14, p.1010	IFRS 7.35K	Ch.54, p.4444
IFRS 7.29(a)	Ch.41, p.3223	IFRS 7.35K(a)	Ch.56, p.4917
IFRS 7.29(a)	Ch.54, p.4430	IFRS 7.35K(c)	Ch.51, p.3928
IFRS 7.29(c)	Ch.41, p.3223	IFRS 7.35L	Ch.51, p.4070
IFRS 7.29(c)	Ch.54, p.4430	IFRS 7.35L	Ch.51, p.4075
IFRS 7.29(c)	Ch.55, p.4574	IFRS 7.35L(c)	Ch.54, p.4446
IFRS 7.29(c)	Ch.55, p.4667	IFRS 7.35M	Ch.51, p.4075
IFRS 7.29(d)	Ch.14, p.1010	IFRS 7.35M	Ch.54, p.4446
IFRS 7.29(d)	Ch.54, p.4430	IFRS 7.35N	Ch.54, p.4446
IFRS 7.30	Ch.54, p.4430	IFRS 7.36	Ch.13, p.987
IFRS 7.30	Ch.55, p.4667	IFRS 7.36-38	Ch.55, p.4659
IFRS 7.31	Ch.54, p.4433	IFRS 7.36(a)	Ch.51, p.4050
IFRS 7.31-42	Ch.15, p.1244	IFRS 7.36(a)	Ch.54, p.4449
IFRS 7.32	Ch.54, p.4433	IFRS 7.36(b)	Ch.54, p.4449
IFRS 7.32A	Ch.54, p.4433	IFRS 7.38	Ch.54, p.4449
IFRS 7.33(a)	Ch.54, p.4435	IFRS 7.39	Ch.40, p.3152
IFRS 7.33(b)	Ch.54, p.4435	IFRS 7.39	Ch.40, p.3158
IFRS 7.33(c)	Ch.54, p.4436	IFRS 7.39	Ch.55, p.4661
IFRS 7.33-35	Ch.40, p.3158	IFRS 7.39(a)	Ch.54, p.4454
IFRS 7.34(a)	Ch.54, p.4438	IFRS 7.39(b)	Ch.54, p.4454
IFRS 7.34(b)	Ch.54, p.4438	IFRS 7.39(c)	Ch.54, p.4462
IFRS 7.34(c)	Ch.54, p.4471	IFRS 7.40	Ch.54, p.4463
IFRS 7.35	Ch.54, p.4438	IFRS 7.40	Ch.55, p.4663
IFRS 7.35A	Ch.54, p.4439	IFRS 7.41	Ch.54, p.4469
IFRS 7.35A(a)	Ch.32, p.2399	IFRS 7.41	Ch.55, p.4663
IFRS 7.35A(a)	Ch.54, p.4444	IFRS 7.42	Ch.54, p.4470
IFRS 7.35A(b)	Ch.54, p.4445	IFRS 7.42	Ch.55, p.4663
IFRS 7.35B	Ch.51, p.4074	IFRS 7.42A	Ch.54, p.4474
IFRS 7.35B	Ch.54, p.4439	IFRS 7.42B	Ch.54, p.4474
IFRS 7.35C	Ch.54, p.4439	IFRS 7.42C	Ch.54, p.4477
IFRS 7.35D	Ch.54, p.4439	IFRS 7.42D	Ch.54, p.4475
IFRS 7.35E	Ch.54, p.4439	IFRS 7.42E	Ch.54, p.4478
IFRS 7.35F	Ch.54, p.4440	IFRS 7.42F	Ch.54, p.4480
IFRS 7.35F(a)	Ch.51, p.3969	IFRS 7.42G	Ch.54, p.4480
IFRS 7.35F(a)	Ch.51, p.4074	IFRS 7.42G	Ch.54, p.4481
IFRS 7.35F(b)	Ch.51, p.4074	IFRS 7.42H	Ch.54, p.4474
IFRS 7.35F(c)	Ch.51, p.4074	IFRS 7.42R	Ch.5, p.262
IFRS 7.35F(d)	Ch.51, p.4074	IFRS 7.42R	Ch.5, p.356
IFRS 7.35F(e)	Ch.51, p.4070	IFRS 7.42S	Ch.5, p.263
IFRS 7.35F(e)	Ch.51, p.4075	IFRS 7.42S	Ch.5, p.357
IFRS 7.35F(f)	Ch.51, p.4034	IFRS 7.44DE	Ch.54, p.4520
IFRS 7.35F(f)	Ch.51, p.4075	IFRS 7.44DF	Ch.54, p.4520
IFRS 7.35G	Ch.51, p.4050	IFRS 7.44GG	Ch.54, p.4520
IFRS 7.35G	Ch.54, p.4440	IFRS 7.44HH	Ch.54, p.4520
IFRS 7.35G(a)(i)	Ch.51, p.4074	IFRS 7 Appendix A	Ch.50, p.3872
IFRS 7.35G(a)(ii)	Ch.51, p.3969	IFRS 7 Appendix A	Ch.53, p.4285
IFRS 7.35G(a)(ii)	Ch.51, p.4074	IFRS 7 Appendix A	Ch.54, p.4428
IFRS 7.35G(a)(iii)	Ch.51, p.4074	IFRS 7 Appendix A	Ch.54, p.4434
IFRS 7.35G(b)	Ch.51, p.4074	IFRS 7 Appendix A	Ch.54, p.4448
IFRS 7.35G(c)	Ch.51, p.3969	IFRS 7 Appendix A	Ch.56, p.4915
IFRS 7.35G(c)	Ch.51, p.4074	IFRS 7.B1	Ch.54, p.4408
IFRS 7.35H	Ch.51, p.4074	IFRS 7.B2	Ch.54, p.4409
IFRS 7.35H	Ch.54, p.4441	IFRS 7.B3	Ch.54, p.4408

IFRS 7.B5	Ch.54, p.4410	IFRS 7.B29	Ch.54, p.4478
IFRS 7.B5(a)	Ch.54, p.4409	IFRS 7.B30	Ch.54, p.4478
IFRS 7.B5(c)	Ch.54, p.4409	IFRS 7.B30A	Ch.54, p.4478
IFRS 7.B5(e)	Ch.54, p.4409	IFRS 7.B31	Ch.54, p.4478
IFRS 7.B5(f)	Ch.54, p.4409	IFRS 7.B32	Ch.54, p.4475
IFRS 7.B5(g)	Ch.54, p.4409	IFRS 7.B33	Ch.54, p.4480
IFRS 7.B5(aa)	Ch.54, p.4409	IFRS 7.B34	Ch.54, p.4479
IFRS 7.B6	Ch.54, p.4435	IFRS 7.B35	Ch.54, p.4479
IFRS 7.B6-B24	Ch.15, p.1244	IFRS 7.35J	Ch.51, p.4034
IFRS 7.B7	Ch.54, p.4438	IFRS 7.35J	Ch.51, p.4075
IFRS 7.B8	Ch.54, p.4472	IFRS 7.B36	Ch.54, p.4479
IFRS 7.B8A	Ch.51, p.4074	IFRS 7.B37	Ch.54, p.4479
IFRS 7.B8A	Ch.54, p.4440	IFRS 7.B38	Ch.54, p.4481
IFRS 7.B8B	Ch.51, p.4034	IFRS 7.B39	Ch.54, p.4474
IFRS 7.B8B	Ch.51, p.4075	IFRS 7.B40	Ch.54, p.4500
IFRS 7.B8B	Ch.54, p.4440	IFRS 7.B41	Ch.54, p.4501
IFRS 7.B8C	Ch.54, p.4441	IFRS 7.B42	Ch.54, p.4503
IFRS 7.B8D	Ch.54, p.4442	IFRS 7.B43	Ch.54, p.4501
IFRS 7.B8E	Ch.51, p.4073	IFRS 7.B44	Ch.54, p.4502
IFRS 7.B8E	Ch.54, p.4442	IFRS 7.B45	Ch.54, p.4502
IFRS 7.B8F	Ch.51, p.4074	IFRS 7.B46	Ch.54, p.4502
IFRS 7.B8F	Ch.54, p.4445	IFRS 7.B47	Ch.54, p.4502
IFRS 7.B8G	Ch.51, p.4074	IFRS 7.B48	Ch.54, p.4502
IFRS 7.B8G	Ch.54, p.4445	IFRS 7.B49	Ch.54, p.4503
IFRS 7.B8H	Ch.51, p.4075	IFRS 7.B50	Ch.54, p.4503
IFRS 7.B8H	Ch.54, p.4448	IFRS 7.B51	Ch.54, p.4503
IFRS 7.B8I	Ch.51, p.4075	IFRS 7.B52	Ch.54, p.4503
IFRS 7.B8I	Ch.54, p.4448	IFRS 7.B53	Ch.54, p.4500
IFRS 7.B8J	Ch.54, p.4448	IFRS 7.IG1	Ch.54, p.4407
IFRS 7.B9	Ch.54, p.4445	IFRS 7.IG2	Ch.54, p.4407
IFRS 7.B10	Ch.54, p.4445	IFRS 7.IG5	Ch.54, p.4408
IFRS 7.B10A	Ch.54, p.4454	IFRS 7.IG6	Ch.54, p.4408
IFRS 7.B11	Ch.54, p.4454	IFRS 7.IG12	Ch.54, p.4429
IFRS 7.B11A	Ch.54, p.4458	IFRS 7.IG13	Ch.54, p.4483
IFRS 7.B11B	Ch.54, p.4454	IFRS 7.IG13C	Ch.54, p.4416
IFRS 7.B11C(a)	Ch.54, p.4455	IFRS 7.IG13D	Ch.54, p.4417
IFRS 7.B11C(b)	Ch.54, p.4456	IFRS 7.IG13E	Ch.54, p.4418
IFRS 7.B11C(c)	Ch.54, p.4456	IFRS 7.IG14	Ch.54, p.4430
IFRS 7.B11C(c)	Ch.54, p.4458	IFRS 7.IG14	Ch.54, p.4431
IFRS 7.B11D	Ch.54, p.4456	IFRS 7.IG15	Ch.54, p.4436
IFRS 7.B11D	Ch.55, p.4661	IFRS 7.IG16	Ch.54, p.4436
IFRS 7.B11E	Ch.54, p.4462	IFRS 7.IG17	Ch.54, p.4436
IFRS 7.B11E	Ch.55, p.4661	IFRS 7.IG18	Ch.54, p.4472
IFRS 7.B11F	Ch.40, p.3158	IFRS 7.IG19	Ch.54, p.4471
IFRS 7.B11F	Ch.54, p.4462	IFRS 7.IG20	Ch.54, p.4438
IFRS 7.B17	Ch.54, p.4464	IFRS 7.IG20B	Ch.54, p.4443
IFRS 7.B18	Ch.54, p.4465	IFRS 7.IG20C	Ch.54, p.4446
IFRS 7.B19	Ch.54, p.4467	IFRS 7.IG20D	Ch.54, p.4446
IFRS 7.B20	Ch.54, p.4469	IFRS 7.IG21	Ch.54, p.4439
IFRS 7.B21	Ch.54, p.4463	IFRS 7.IG22	Ch.54, p.4449
IFRS 7.B22	Ch.54, p.4434	IFRS 7.IG31A	Ch.54, p.4455
IFRS 7.B23	Ch.54, p.4434	IFRS 7.IG32	Ch.54, p.4434
IFRS 7.B24	Ch.54, p.4464	IFRS 7.IG32	Ch.54, p.4464
IFRS 7.B25	Ch.54, p.4434	IFRS 7.IG33	Ch.54, p.4466
IFRS 7.B25	Ch.54, p.4467	IFRS 7.IG34	Ch.54, p.4466
IFRS 7.B26	Ch.54, p.4434	IFRS 7.IG35	Ch.54, p.4467
IFRS 7.B27	Ch.54, p.4464	IFRS 7.IG36	Ch.54, p.4467
IFRS 7.B28	Ch.54, p.4463	IFRS 7.IG37(a)	Ch.54, p.4470

IFRS 7.IG37(b)	Ch.54, p.4471	IFRS 8.2	Ch.36, p.2982
IFRS 7.IG37(c)	Ch.54, p.4471	IFRS 8.2(b)	Ch.36, p.2982
IFRS 7.IG38	Ch.54, p.4471	IFRS 8.3	Ch.36, p.2983
IFRS 7.IG39	Ch.54, p.4471	IFRS 8.4	Ch.36, p.2983
IFRS 7.IG40	Ch.54, p.4471	IFRS 8.5	Ch.20, p.1587
IFRS 7.IG40C	Ch.54, p.4476	IFRS 8.5	Ch.20, p.1588
IFRS 7.IG40C	Ch.54, p.4480	IFRS 8.5	Ch.36, p.2978
IFRS 7.IG40D	Ch.54, p.4503	IFRS 8.5	Ch.36, p.2980
IFRS 7.BC6	Ch.54, p.4406	IFRS 8.5	Ch.36, p.2984
IFRS 7.BC8	Ch.45, p.3602	IFRS 8.5	Ch.36, p.2996
IFRS 7.BC9	Ch.54, p.4406	IFRS 8.5(a)	Ch.36, p.2979
IFRS 7.BC10	Ch.54, p.4406	IFRS 8.5(b)	Ch.32, p.2411
IFRS 7.BC10	Ch.54, p.4408	IFRS 8.5(b)	Ch.36, p.2987
IFRS 7.BC11	Ch.54, p.4406	IFRS 8.5(b)	Ch.36, p.2989
IFRS 7.BC13	Ch.54, p.4409	IFRS 8.5(c)	Ch.36, p.2987
IFRS 7.BC14	Ch.54, p.4424	IFRS 8.6	Ch.36, p.2984
IFRS 7.BC15	Ch.54, p.4424	IFRS 8.7	Ch.36, p.2980
IFRS 7.BC22	Ch.54, p.4425	IFRS 8.7	Ch.36, p.2984
IFRS 7.BC25	Ch.54, p.4428	IFRS 8.7	Ch.36, p.2985
IFRS 7.BC31	Ch.54, p.4428	IFRS 8.8	Ch.36, p.2983
IFRS 7.BC32	Ch.54, p.4428	IFRS 8.8	Ch.36, p.2986
IFRS 7.BC33	Ch.54, p.4411	IFRS 8.8	Ch.36, p.2988
IFRS 7.BC34	Ch.54, p.4411	IFRS 8.9	Ch.36, p.2980
IFRS 7.BC35	Ch.54, p.4412	IFRS 8.9	Ch.36, p.2985
IFRS 7.BC35C	Ch.54, p.4412	IFRS 8.9	Ch.36, p.2988
IFRS 7.BC35O	Ch.54, p.4520	IFRS 8.10	Ch.20, p.1587
IFRS 7.BC35P	Ch.54, p.4412	IFRS 8.10	Ch.36, p.2979
IFRS 7.BC35U	Ch.54, p.4416	IFRS 8.10	Ch.36, p.2988
IFRS 7.BC35W	Ch.54, p.4416	IFRS 8.11	Ch.36, p.2981
IFRS 7.BC35X	Ch.54, p.4416	IFRS 8.11	Ch.36, p.3000
IFRS 7.BC36	Ch.54, p.4429	IFRS 8.11-12	Ch.20, p.1587
IFRS 7.BC40(b)	Ch.54, p.4435	IFRS 8.12	Ch.20, p.1588
IFRS 7.BC41	Ch.54, p.4435	IFRS 8.12	Ch.36, p.2981
IFRS 7.BC42	Ch.54, p.4435	IFRS 8.12	Ch.36, p.2986
IFRS 7.BC43	Ch.54, p.4435	IFRS 8.12	Ch.36, p.2992
IFRS 7.BC44	Ch.54, p.4435	IFRS 8.12	Ch.36, p.2995
IFRS 7.BC45	Ch.54, p.4435	IFRS 8.13	Ch.36, p.2981
IFRS 7.BC46	Ch.54, p.4435	IFRS 8.13	Ch.36, p.2996
IFRS 7.BC47	Ch.54, p.4438	IFRS 8.13	Ch.36, p.2997
IFRS 7.BC47A	Ch.54, p.4408	IFRS 8.14	Ch.36, p.2997
IFRS 7.BC48	Ch.54, p.4438	IFRS 8.15	Ch.36, p.2998
IFRS 7.BC56	Ch.54, p.4449	IFRS 8.16	Ch.36, p.2997
IFRS 7.BC57	Ch.54, p.4455	IFRS 8.16	Ch.36, p.2998
IFRS 7.BC58A(a)	Ch.54, p.4457	IFRS 8.16	Ch.36, p.3001
IFRS 7.BC58A(b)	Ch.54, p.4454	IFRS 8.16	Ch.36, p.3007
IFRS 7.BC58D	Ch.54, p.4462	IFRS 8.17	Ch.36, p.2990
IFRS 7.BC59	Ch.54, p.4463	IFRS 8.18	Ch.36, p.2998
IFRS 7.BC61	Ch.54, p.4469	IFRS 8.19	Ch.36, p.2998
IFRS 7.BC65	Ch.54, p.4472	IFRS 8.20	Ch.32, p.2411
IFRS 7.BC72B	Ch.54, p.4407	IFRS 8.20	Ch.36, p.3000
IFRS 7.BC72C	Ch.54, p.4407	IFRS 8.21	Ch.36, p.3000
		IFRS 8.22	Ch.36, p.2979

IFRS 8

		IFRS 8.22	Ch.36, p.3001
		IFRS 8.22(aa)	Ch.36, p.3001
IFRS 8.1	Ch.36, p.2981	IFRS 8.23	Ch.36, p.2979
IFRS 8.1	Ch.36, p.2989	IFRS 8.23	Ch.36, p.2997
IFRS 8.1	Ch.36, p.3012	IFRS 8.23	Ch.36, p.3002

IFRS 8.23	Ch.36, p.3003	IFRS 9.2.1	Ch.45, p.3591
IFRS 8.23-24	Ch.36, p.3004	IFRS 9.2.1	Ch.51, p.4046
IFRS 8.23(g)	Ch.36, p.2989	IFRS 9.2.1(a)	Ch.7, p.499
IFRS 8.24	Ch.36, p.3005	IFRS 9.2.1(a)	Ch.7, p.550
IFRS 8.24(a)	Ch.36, p.2989	IFRS 9.2.1(a)	Ch.11, p.876
IFRS 8.25	Ch.36, p.2999	IFRS 9.2.1(a)	Ch.11, p.877
IFRS 8.25	Ch.36, p.3010	IFRS 9.2.1(a)	Ch.45, p.3592
IFRS 8.26	Ch.36, p.2999	IFRS 9.2.1(a)	Ch.45, p.3593
IFRS 8.27	Ch.36, p.3005	IFRS 9.2.1(b)	Ch.45, p.3593
IFRS 8.27	Ch.36, p.3006	IFRS 9.2.1(b)	Ch.51, p.4046
IFRS 8.27-28	Ch.36, p.3000	IFRS 9.2.1(b)(i)	Ch.52, p.4088
IFRS 8.27(f)	Ch.36, p.2999	IFRS 9.2.1(b)(ii)	Ch.52, p.4088
IFRS 8.28	Ch.36, p.3007	IFRS 9.2.1(c)	Ch.45, p.3605
IFRS 8.29	Ch.36, p.3009	IFRS 9.2.1(d)	Ch.45, p.3602
IFRS 8.30	Ch.36, p.3009	IFRS 9.2.1(e)	Ch.26, p.1935
IFRS 8.31	Ch.36, p.2979	IFRS 9.2.1(e)	Ch.45, p.3593
IFRS 8.31	Ch.36, p.3012	IFRS 9.2.1(e)	Ch.45, p.3594
IFRS 8.32	Ch.36, p.3013	IFRS 9.2.1(e)	Ch.45, p.3595
IFRS 8.32-34	Ch.36, p.2979	IFRS 9.2.1(e)(iv)	Ch.45, p.3595
IFRS 8.32-33	Ch.36, p.3012	IFRS 9.2.1(e)	Ch.45, p.3598
IFRS 8.33	Ch.36, p.3013	IFRS 9.2.1(e)	Ch.45, p.3599
IFRS 8.33	Ch.36, p.3014	IFRS 9.2.1(e)(iv)	Ch.48, p.3837
IFRS 8.34	Ch.36, p.3014	IFRS 9.2.1(e)	Ch.51, p.3958
IFRS 8.34	Ch.36, p.3015	IFRS 9.2.1(e)	Ch.55, p.4539
IFRS 8.35	Ch.36, p.2977	IFRS 9.2.1(e)(iv)	Ch.56, p.4692
IFRS 8.36	Ch.36, p.2981	IFRS 9.2.1(f)	Ch.45, p.3603
IFRS 8 Appendix A	Ch.36, p.2980	IFRS 9.2.1(g)	Ch.45, p.3600
IFRS 8.D01-D04	Ch.36, p.2977	IFRS 9.2.1(g)	Ch.49, p.3861
IFRS 8.IG7	Ch.36, p.2991	IFRS 9.2.1(g)	Ch.50, p.3879
IFRS 8.BC22	Ch.36, p.2983	IFRS 9.2.1(g)	Ch.51, p.3924
IFRS 8.BC23	Ch.36, p.2982	IFRS 9.2.1(g)	Ch.51, p.4049
IFRS 8.BC27	Ch.36, p.2988	IFRS 9.2.1(g)	Ch.52, p.4088
IFRS 8.BC30	Ch.36, p.2992	IFRS 9.2.1(h)	Ch.45, p.3605
IFRS 8.BC32	Ch.36, p.2992	IFRS 9.2.1(i)	Ch.45, p.3606
IFRS 8.BC43-45	Ch.36, p.2979	IFRS 9.2.1(j)	Ch.45, p.3606
IFRS 8.BC43-45	Ch.36, p.2992	IFRS 9.2.1(j)	Ch.52, p.4089
IFRS 8.BC44	Ch.36, p.3012	IFRS 9.2.3	Ch.50, p.3879
IFRS 8.BC46-47	Ch.36, p.3012	IFRS 9.2.3	Ch.51, p.3924
IFRS 8.BC Appendix A 72	Ch.36, p.2979	IFRS 9.2.3	Ch.51, p.4049
IFRS 8.BC Appendix A 73	Ch.36, p.2992	IFRS 9.2.3(a)	Ch.45, p.3600
		IFRS 9.2.3(b)	Ch.45, p.3600
		IFRS 9.2.3(b)	Ch.45, p.3601

IFRS 9 (2012)

IFRS 9(2012).B5.4.12	Ch.14, p.1009

IFRS 9 (2022)

IFRS 9(2022).7.1.9	Ch.52, p.4158
IFRS 9(2022).7.2.35	Ch.52, p.4158
IFRS 9(2022).B3.3.6	Ch.52, p.4158
IFRS 9(2022).B3.3.6A	Ch.52, p.4161

IFRS 9

IFRS 9.1.1	Ch.44, p.3577

IFRS 9.2.3(c)	Ch.45, p.3600
IFRS 9.2.3(c)	Ch.50, p.3879
IFRS 9.2.3(c)	Ch.51, p.4049
IFRS 9.2.4	Ch.17, p.1366
IFRS 9.2.4	Ch.42, p.3297
IFRS 9.2.4	Ch.43, p.3456
IFRS 9.2.4	Ch.43, p.3473
IFRS 9.2.4	Ch.45, p.3607
IFRS 9.2.4	Ch.45, p.3608
IFRS 9.2.4	Ch.45, p.3609
IFRS 9.2.4	Ch.53, p.4388
IFRS 9.2.5	Ch.5, p.342
IFRS 9.2.5	Ch.43, p.3474
IFRS 9.2.5	Ch.45, p.3613
IFRS 9.2.5	Ch.53, p.4389
IFRS 9.2.6	Ch.43, p.3473

IFRS 9.2.6	Ch.43, p.3474
IFRS 9.2.6	Ch.45, p.3608
IFRS 9.2.6	Ch.45, p.3609
IFRS 9.2.6(b)	Ch.43, p.3457
IFRS 9.2.6(c)	Ch.43, p.3457
IFRS 9.2.7	Ch.43, p.3474
IFRS 9.2.7	Ch.45, p.3610
IFRS 9.3.1.1	Ch.15, p.1188
IFRS 9.3.1.1	Ch.48, p.3812
IFRS 9.3.1.1	Ch.49, p.3841
IFRS 9.3.1.1	Ch.49, p.3845
IFRS 9.3.1.1	Ch.50, p.3880
IFRS 9.3.1.2	Ch.50, p.3880
IFRS 9.3.2.1	Ch.53, p.4364
IFRS 9.3.2.2	Ch.52, p.4093
IFRS 9.3.2.2	Ch.52, p.4098
IFRS 9.3.2.2(b)	Ch.52, p.4105
IFRS 9.3.2.3	Ch.50, p.3880
IFRS 9.3.2.3	Ch.52, p.4099
IFRS 9.3.2.4	Ch.52, p.4103
IFRS 9.3.2.5	Ch.52, p.4108
IFRS 9.3.2.6	Ch.52, p.4114
IFRS 9.3.2.6(a)	Ch.52, p.4114
IFRS 9.3.2.6(b)	Ch.52, p.4114
IFRS 9.3.2.6(c)	Ch.52, p.4114
IFRS 9.3.2.6(c)	Ch.52, p.4119
IFRS 9.3.2.7	Ch.52, p.4114
IFRS 9.3.2.7	Ch.52, p.4115
IFRS 9.3.2.8	Ch.52, p.4114
IFRS 9.3.2.9	Ch.52, p.4119
IFRS 9.3.2.10	Ch.52, p.4132
IFRS 9.3.2.11	Ch.52, p.4129
IFRS 9.3.2.12	Ch.51, p.4015
IFRS 9.3.2.12	Ch.52, p.4129
IFRS 9.3.2.13	Ch.52, p.4130
IFRS 9.3.2.13	Ch.52, p.4140
IFRS 9.3.2.14	Ch.52, p.4131
IFRS 9.3.2.15	Ch.52, p.4134
IFRS 9.3.2.16	Ch.52, p.4138
IFRS 9.3.2.16(a)	Ch.52, p.4138
IFRS 9.3.2.16(b)-(c)	Ch.52, p.4139
IFRS 9.3.2.17	Ch.52, p.4139
IFRS 9.3.2.18	Ch.52, p.4139
IFRS 9.3.2.19	Ch.52, p.4139
IFRS 9.3.2.21	Ch.52, p.4140
IFRS 9.3.2.22	Ch.40, p.3155
IFRS 9.3.2.22	Ch.52, p.4151
IFRS 9.3.2.23	Ch.52, p.4152
IFRS 9.3.3.1	Ch.47, p.3671
IFRS 9.3.3.1	Ch.49, p.3847
IFRS 9.3.3.1	Ch.52, p.4099
IFRS 9.3.3.1	Ch.52, p.4154
IFRS 9.3.3.1	Ch.55, p.4582
IFRS 9.3.3.2	Ch.52, p.4099
IFRS 9.3.3.2	Ch.52, p.4157
IFRS 9.3.3.3	Ch.52, p.4166
IFRS 9.3.3.4	Ch.52, p.4166
IFRS 9.3.3.5	Ch.52, p.4171
IFRS 9.3.3.5	Ch.56, p.4695
IFRS 9.4.1.1	Ch.48, p.3771
IFRS 9.4.1.1	Ch.50, p.3869
IFRS 9.4.1.2	Ch.5, p.262
IFRS 9.4.1.2	Ch.48, p.3774
IFRS 9.4.1.2	Ch.48, p.3780
IFRS 9.4.1.2	Ch.51, p.3924
IFRS 9.4.1.2-2A	Ch.51, p.3974
IFRS 9.4.1.2(b)	Ch.50, p.3889
IFRS 9.4.1.2(b)	Ch.53, p.4289
IFRS 9.4.1.2A	Ch.5, p.262
IFRS 9.4.1.2A	Ch.5, p.263
IFRS 9.4.1.2A	Ch.33, p.2579
IFRS 9.4.1.2A	Ch.48, p.3774
IFRS 9.4.1.2A	Ch.48, p.3783
IFRS 9.4.1.2A	Ch.51, p.3924
IFRS 9.4.1.2A	Ch.51, p.4036
IFRS 9.4.1.2A	Ch.51, p.4074
IFRS 9.4.1.2A	Ch.53, p.4220
IFRS 9.4.1.2A(b)	Ch.53, p.4289
IFRS 9.4.1.3(a)	Ch.48, p.3791
IFRS 9.4.1.3(b)	Ch.48, p.3792
IFRS 9.4.1.4	Ch.43, p.3410
IFRS 9.4.1.4	Ch.48, p.3774
IFRS 9.4.1.4	Ch.53, p.4289
IFRS 9.4.1.5	Ch.5, p.314
IFRS 9.4.1.5	Ch.48, p.3774
IFRS 9.4.1.5	Ch.48, p.3826
IFRS 9.4.2.1	Ch.7, p.555
IFRS 9.4.2.1	Ch.48, p.3777
IFRS 9.4.2.1	Ch.50, p.3869
IFRS 9.4.2.1-2	Ch.7, p.539
IFRS 9.4.2.1(a)	Ch.51, p.3924
IFRS 9.4.2.1(a)	Ch.50, p.3879
IFRS 9.4.2.1(b)	Ch.50, p.3881
IFRS 9.4.2.1(c)	Ch.50, p.3879
IFRS 9.4.2.1(c)	Ch.51, p.4048
IFRS 9.4.2.1(c)-(d)	Ch.53, p.4388
IFRS 9.4.2.1(d)	Ch.51, p.3924
IFRS 9.4.2.1(d)	Ch.50, p.3879
IFRS 9.4.2.1(d)	Ch.51, p.4049
IFRS 9.4.2.1(d)	Ch.45, p.3600
IFRS 9.4.2.1(d)	Ch.51, p.4048
IFRS 9.4.2.1(d)	Ch.51, p.4050
IFRS 9.4.2.1(e)	Ch.7, p.539
IFRS 9.4.2.2	Ch.5, p.315
IFRS 9.4.2.2	Ch.7, p.555
IFRS 9.4.2.2	Ch.48, p.3776
IFRS 9.4.2.2(a)	Ch.48, p.3826
IFRS 9.4.2.2(b)	Ch.48, p.3784
IFRS 9.4.2.2(b)	Ch.48, p.3826
IFRS 9.4.2.2(b)	Ch.48, p.3828
IFRS 9.4.3.1	Ch.43, p.3475
IFRS 9.4.3.1	Ch.46, p.3629
IFRS 9.4.3.1	Ch.46, p.3630
IFRS 9.4.3.1	Ch.46, p.3653
IFRS 9.4.3.1	Ch.55, p.4559
IFRS 9.4.3.1	Ch.56, p.4713

IFRS 9.4.3.2	Ch.46, p.3629	IFRS 9.5.4.1	Ch.51, p.3927
IFRS 9.4.3.2	Ch.46, p.3631	IFRS 9.5.4.1(b)	Ch.51, p.4070
IFRS 9.4.3.2	Ch.46, p.3641	IFRS 9.5.4.2	Ch.51, p.3928
IFRS 9.4.3.2	Ch.48, p.3774	IFRS 9.5.4.3	Ch.50, p.3871
IFRS 9.4.3.3	Ch.5, p.264	IFRS 9.5.4.3	Ch.50, p.3894
IFRS 9.4.3.3	Ch.46, p.3629	IFRS 9.5.4.3	Ch.50, p.3897
IFRS 9.4.3.3	Ch.46, p.3630	IFRS 9.5.4.3	Ch.51, p.4034
IFRS 9.4.3.3	Ch.50, p.3889	IFRS 9.5.4.3	Ch.51, p.4035
IFRS 9.4.3.3	Ch.55, p.4560	IFRS 9.5.4.3	Ch.52, p.4100
IFRS 9.4.3.3	Ch.56, p.4712	IFRS 9.5.4.4	Ch.51, p.3928
IFRS 9.4.3.4	Ch.54, p.4488	IFRS 9.5.4.4	Ch.51, p.4036
IFRS 9.4.3.4	Ch.54, p.4509	IFRS 9.5.4.4	Ch.51, p.4068
IFRS 9.4.3.5	Ch.48, p.3776	IFRS 9.5.4.4	Ch.52, p.4103
IFRS 9.4.3.5	Ch.48, p.3826	IFRS 9.5.4.4	Ch.54, p.4440
IFRS 9.4.3.5	Ch.48, p.3829	IFRS 9.5.4.5	Ch.52, p.4101
IFRS 9.4.3.6	Ch.5, p.264	IFRS 9.5.4.5	Ch.52, p.4159
IFRS 9.4.3.6	Ch.46, p.3630	IFRS 9.5.4.5-7	Ch.53, p.4370
IFRS 9.4.3.7	Ch.46, p.3630	IFRS 9.5.4.7	Ch.50, p.3899
IFRS 9.4.4.1	Ch.48, p.3832	IFRS 9.5.4.7	Ch.52, p.4101
IFRS 9.4.4.1	Ch.55, p.4595	IFRS 9.5.4.7	Ch.52, p.4159
IFRS 9.5.1.1	Ch.7, p.509	IFRS 9.5.4.8(a)	Ch.50, p.3899
IFRS 9.5.1.1	Ch.8, p.627	IFRS 9.5.4.8	Ch.52, p.4102
IFRS 9.5.1.1	Ch.8, p.629	IFRS 9.5.4.8	Ch.52, p.4159
IFRS 9.5.1.1	Ch.14, p.1052	IFRS 9.5.4.8	Ch.53, p.4370
IFRS 9.5.1.1	Ch.24, p.1832	IFRS 9.5.4.9	Ch.52, p.4102
IFRS 9.5.1.1	Ch.25, p.1875	IFRS 9.5.4.9	Ch.52, p.4159
IFRS 9.5.1.1	Ch.25, p.1909	IFRS 9.5.4.9	Ch.52, p.4160
IFRS 9.5.1.1	Ch.25, p.1910	IFRS 9.5.5	Ch.51, p.4017
IFRS 9.5.1.1	Ch.25, p.1913	IFRS 9.5.5.1	Ch.33, p.2579
IFRS 9.5.1.1	Ch.26, p.2007	IFRS 9.5.5.1	Ch.51, p.3924
IFRS 9.5.1.1	Ch.32, p.2399	IFRS 9.5.5.2	Ch.33, p.2579
IFRS 9.5.1.1	Ch.49, p.3854	IFRS 9.5.5.2	Ch.50, p.3871
IFRS 9.5.1.1	Ch.49, p.3859	IFRS 9.5.5.2	Ch.51, p.4036
IFRS 9.5.1.1	Ch.51, p.4015	IFRS 9.5.5.2	Ch.51, p.4074
IFRS 9.5.1.1A	Ch.7, p.509	IFRS 9.5.5.3	Ch.33, p.2579
IFRS 9.5.1.1A	Ch.49, p.3855	IFRS 9.5.5.3	Ch.51, p.3925
IFRS 9.5.1.2	Ch.7, p.509	IFRS 9.5.5.3	Ch.51, p.3926
IFRS 9.5.1.2	Ch.49, p.3860	IFRS 9.5.5.3	Ch.51, p.3929
IFRS 9.5.1.3	Ch.7, p.509	IFRS 9.5.5.3	Ch.51, p.4015
IFRS 9.5.1.3	Ch.32, p.2399	IFRS 9.5.5.3	Ch.51, p.4017
IFRS 9.5.1.3	Ch.49, p.3854	IFRS 9.5.5.4	Ch.51, p.3926
IFRS 9.5.2.1	Ch.11, p.835	IFRS 9.5.5.5	Ch.33, p.2579
IFRS 9.5.2.1	Ch.50, p.3870	IFRS 9.5.5.5	Ch.51, p.3925
IFRS 9.5.2.1	Ch.50, p.3872	IFRS 9.5.5.5	Ch.51, p.3926
IFRS 9.5.2.1	Ch.50, p.3877	IFRS 9.5.5.5	Ch.51, p.3929
IFRS 9.5.2.1	Ch.51, p.4017	IFRS 9.5.5.5	Ch.51, p.4015
IFRS 9.5.2.2	Ch.50, p.3870	IFRS 9.5.5.5(a)	Ch.51, p.4017
IFRS 9.5.2.2	Ch.50, p.3871	IFRS 9.5.5.6	Ch.5, p.264
IFRS 9.5.2.2	Ch.51, p.4017	IFRS 9.5.5.6	Ch.51, p.4047
IFRS 9.5.2.3	Ch.50, p.3880	IFRS 9.5.5.7	Ch.51, p.3926
IFRS 9.5.3.1	Ch.50, p.3871	IFRS 9.5.5.8	Ch.51, p.3925
IFRS 9.5.3.1	Ch.50, p.3872	IFRS 9.5.5.8	Ch.51, p.4017
IFRS 9.5.3.2	Ch.50, p.3880	IFRS 9.5.5.8	Ch.51, p.4068
IFRS 9.5.4.1	Ch.5, p.338	IFRS 9.5.5.9	Ch.51, p.3944
IFRS 9.5.4.1	Ch.27, p.2039	IFRS 9.5.5.9	Ch.51, p.3970
IFRS 9.5.4.1	Ch.50, p.3871	IFRS 9.5.5.9	Ch.51, p.3972
IFRS 9.5.4.1	Ch.50, p.3882	IFRS 9.5.5.9	Ch.51, p.3973
IFRS 9.5.4.1	Ch.51, p.3916	IFRS 9.5.5.9	Ch.51, p.4047

IFRS 9.5.5.10	Ch.5, p.264	IFRS 9.5.7.5	Ch.11, p.835
IFRS 9.5.5.10	Ch.51, p.3990	IFRS 9.5.7.5	Ch.48, p.3775
IFRS 9.5.5.11	Ch.5, p.264	IFRS 9.5.7.5	Ch.48, p.3830
IFRS 9.5.5.11	Ch.51, p.3979	IFRS 9.5.7.5	Ch.50, p.3877
IFRS 9.5.5.11	Ch.51, p.3980	IFRS 9.5.7.5	Ch.50, p.3900
IFRS 9.5.5.11	Ch.51, p.3994	IFRS 9.5.7.6	Ch.5, p.338
IFRS 9.5.5.12	Ch.51, p.4034	IFRS 9.5.7.6	Ch.48, p.3831
IFRS 9.5.5.12	Ch.51, p.4036	IFRS 9.5.7.6	Ch.50, p.3877
IFRS 9.5.5.13	Ch.51, p.3929	IFRS 9.5.7.7	Ch.14, p.1076
IFRS 9.5.5.13	Ch.51, p.3930	IFRS 9.5.7.7	Ch.48, p.3776
IFRS 9.5.5.13	Ch.51, p.4015	IFRS 9.5.7.7	Ch.50, p.3872
IFRS 9.5.5.14	Ch.51, p.3930	IFRS 9.5.7.7-8	Ch.5, p.315
IFRS 9.5.5.15	Ch.51, p.3928	IFRS 9.5.7.8	Ch.48, p.3776
IFRS 9.5.5.15	Ch.51, p.3932	IFRS 9.5.7.8	Ch.50, p.3872
IFRS 9.5.5.15(a)	Ch.51, p.4043	IFRS 9.5.7.9	Ch.50, p.3872
IFRS 9.5.5.15(a)(i)	Ch.51, p.3928	IFRS 9.5.7.10	Ch.50, p.3871
IFRS 9.5.5.15(a)(i)	Ch.51, p.3932	IFRS 9.5.7.10	Ch.52, p.4129
IFRS 9.5.5.15(a)(ii)	Ch.51, p.3929	IFRS 9.5.7.11	Ch.50, p.3871
IFRS 9.5.5.15(b)	Ch.51, p.3929	IFRS 9.5.7.11	Ch.53, p.4388
IFRS 9.5.5.15(b)	Ch.51, p.4044	IFRS 9.5.7.11	Ch.54, p.4482
IFRS 9.5.5.16	Ch.51, p.3929	IFRS 9.6.1.1	Ch.53, p.4185
IFRS 9.5.5.17	Ch.51, p.3934	IFRS 9.6.1.1	Ch.53, p.4187
IFRS 9.5.5.17	Ch.51, p.3952	IFRS 9.6.1.1	Ch.53, p.4191
IFRS 9.5.5.17	Ch.51, p.4043	IFRS 9.6.1.1	Ch.53, p.4274
IFRS 9.5.5.17(a)	Ch.51, p.3947	IFRS 9.6.1.1	Ch.53, p.4280
IFRS 9.5.5.17(b)	Ch.51, p.3943	IFRS 9.6.1.1	Ch.53, p.4394
IFRS 9.5.5.17(c)	Ch.51, p.3962	IFRS 9.6.1.1	Ch.53, p.4395
IFRS 9.5.5.18	Ch.51, p.3947	IFRS 9.6.1.2	Ch.53, p.4188
IFRS 9.5.5.18	Ch.51, p.4036	IFRS 9.6.1.2	Ch.53, p.4275
IFRS 9.5.5.19	Ch.51, p.3944	IFRS 9.6.1.2	Ch.53, p.4289
IFRS 9.5.5.19	Ch.51, p.3946	IFRS 9.6.1.3	Ch.53, p.4186
IFRS 9.5.5.19	Ch.51, p.4047	IFRS 9.6.1.3	Ch.53, p.4382
IFRS 9.5.5.20	Ch.51, p.3945	IFRS 9.6.1.3	Ch.53, p.4385
IFRS 9.5.5.20	Ch.51, p.3946	IFRS 9.6.1.3	Ch.53, p.4386
IFRS 9.5.5.20	Ch.51, p.4047	IFRS 9.6.2.1	Ch.53, p.4234
IFRS 9.5.5.20	Ch.51, p.4051	IFRS 9.6.2.1	Ch.53, p.4238
IFRS 9.5.5.20	Ch.51, p.4054	IFRS 9.6.2.2	Ch.53, p.4234
IFRS 9.5.6.1	Ch.48, p.3835	IFRS 9.6.2.2	Ch.53, p.4240
IFRS 9.5.6.1	Ch.50, p.3878	IFRS 9.6.2.2	Ch.53, p.4241
IFRS 9.5.6.2	Ch.50, p.3879	IFRS 9.6.2.2	Ch.53, p.4396
IFRS 9.5.6.3	Ch.50, p.3879	IFRS 9.6.2.3	Ch.53, p.4234
IFRS 9.5.7.1	Ch.48, p.3775	IFRS 9.6.2.3	Ch.53, p.4248
IFRS 9.5.7.1	Ch.50, p.3872	IFRS 9.6.2.3	Ch.53, p.4249
IFRS 9.5.7.1(b)	Ch.48, p.3775	IFRS 9.6.2.4	Ch.53, p.4235
IFRS 9.5.7.1(d)	Ch.50, p.3871	IFRS 9.6.2.4	Ch.53, p.4243
IFRS 9.5.7.1A	Ch.5, p.338	IFRS 9.6.2.4	Ch.53, p.4247
IFRS 9.5.7.1A	Ch.27, p.2039	IFRS 9.6.2.4	Ch.53, p.4330
IFRS 9.5.7.1A	Ch.38, p.3081	IFRS 9.6.2.4(a)	Ch.53, p.4246
IFRS 9.5.7.1A	Ch.50, p.3877	IFRS 9.6.2.4(a)	Ch.53, p.4278
IFRS 9.5.7.2	Ch.50, p.3870	IFRS 9.6.2.4(a)	Ch.53, p.4330
IFRS 9.5.7.2	Ch.50, p.3871	IFRS 9.6.2.4(b)	Ch.53, p.4247
IFRS 9.5.7.3	Ch.50, p.3880	IFRS 9.6.2.4(c)	Ch.53, p.4243
IFRS 9.5.7.4	Ch.49, p.3848	IFRS 9.6.2.5	Ch.53, p.4234
IFRS 9.5.7.4	Ch.50, p.3880	IFRS 9.6.2.5	Ch.53, p.4242
IFRS 9.5.7.4	Ch.51, p.4016	IFRS 9.6.2.5	Ch.53, p.4306
IFRS 9.5.7.4	Ch.51, p.4047	IFRS 9.6.2.6	Ch.53, p.4235
IFRS 9.5.7.5	Ch.5, p.263	IFRS 9.6.3.1	Ch.53, p.4189
IFRS 9.5.7.5	Ch.5, p.315	IFRS 9.6.3.2	Ch.53, p.4189

IFRS 9.6.3.3	Ch.53, p.4189	IFRS 9.6.5.8	Ch.53, p.4221
IFRS 9.6.3.3	Ch.53, p.4216	IFRS 9.6.5.8	Ch.53, p.4290
IFRS 9.6.3.4	Ch.53, p.4189	IFRS 9.6.5.8	Ch.53, p.4344
IFRS 9.6.3.4	Ch.53, p.4224	IFRS 9.6.5.8	Ch.53, p.4345
IFRS 9.6.3.4	Ch.53, p.4226	IFRS 9.6.5.8	Ch.53, p.4380
IFRS 9.6.3.4	Ch.53, p.4233	IFRS 9.6.5.8(b)	Ch.53, p.4292
IFRS 9.6.3.5	Ch.53, p.4189	IFRS 9.6.5.8(b)	Ch.53, p.4355
IFRS 9.6.3.5	Ch.53, p.4248	IFRS 9.6.5.8(b)	Ch.53, p.4380
IFRS 9.6.3.5	Ch.53, p.4259	IFRS 9.6.5.9	Ch.53, p.4293
IFRS 9.6.3.6	Ch.53, p.4189	IFRS 9.6.5.10	Ch.5, p.258
IFRS 9.6.3.6	Ch.53, p.4259	IFRS 9.6.5.10	Ch.51, p.4019
IFRS 9.6.3.6	Ch.53, p.4260	IFRS 9.6.5.10	Ch.53, p.4292
IFRS 9.6.3.7	Ch.53, p.4190	IFRS 9.6.5.10	Ch.53, p.4355
IFRS 9.6.3.7(a)	Ch.53, p.4190	IFRS 9.6.5.11	Ch.53, p.4295
IFRS 9.6.3.7(c)	Ch.53, p.4201	IFRS 9.6.5.11	Ch.53, p.4344
IFRS 9.6.4.1	Ch.5, p.248	IFRS 9.6.5.11(a)	Ch.53, p.4232
IFRS 9.6.4.1	Ch.5, p.252	IFRS 9.6.5.11(a)	Ch.53, p.4288
IFRS 9.6.4.1	Ch.5, p.256	IFRS 9.6.5.11(a)	Ch.53, p.4352
IFRS 9.6.4.1	Ch.53, p.4271	IFRS 9.6.5.11(a)(ii)	Ch.53, p.4228
IFRS 9.6.4.1	Ch.53, p.4275	IFRS 9.6.5.11(a)(ii)	Ch.53, p.4329
IFRS 9.6.4.1(a)	Ch.5, p.248	IFRS 9.6.5.11(d)	Ch.53, p.4297
IFRS 9.6.4.1(a)	Ch.5, p.252	IFRS 9.6.5.11(d)	Ch.53, p.4379
IFRS 9.6.4.1(b)	Ch.5, p.248	IFRS 9.6.5.11(d)(i)	Ch.53, p.4298
IFRS 9.6.4.1(b)	Ch.5, p.252	IFRS 9.6.5.11(d)(i)	Ch.53, p.4343
IFRS 9.6.4.1(b)	Ch.53, p.4272	IFRS 9.6.5.11(d)(i)	Ch.53, p.4379
IFRS 9.6.4.1(b)	Ch.53, p.4275	IFRS 9.6.5.11(d)(ii)	Ch.53, p.4379
IFRS 9.6.4.1(b)	Ch.53, p.4306	IFRS 9.6.5.12	Ch.5, p.253
IFRS 9.6.4.1(b)	Ch.53, p.4308	IFRS 9.6.5.12	Ch.53, p.4298
IFRS 9.6.4.1(c)	Ch.5, p.248	IFRS 9.6.5.12	Ch.53, p.4355
IFRS 9.6.4.1(c)	Ch.5, p.252	IFRS 9.6.5.12(b)	Ch.5, p.253
IFRS 9.6.4.1(c)	Ch.53, p.4279	IFRS 9.6.5.13	Ch.5, p.255
IFRS 9.6.4.1(c)(ii)	Ch.53, p.4325	IFRS 9.6.5.13	Ch.53, p.4300
IFRS 9.6.4.1(c)(iii)	Ch.53, p.4288	IFRS 9.6.5.13	Ch.53, p.4301
IFRS 9.6.5.1	Ch.5, p.256	IFRS 9.6.5.13	Ch.53, p.4303
IFRS 9.6.5.1	Ch.53, p.4289	IFRS 9.6.5.13	Ch.53, p.4305
IFRS 9.6.5.2	Ch.53, p.4187	IFRS 9.6.5.14	Ch.53, p.4300
IFRS 9.6.5.2	Ch.53, p.4220	IFRS 9.6.5.14	Ch.53, p.4364
IFRS 9.6.5.2	Ch.53, p.4221	IFRS 9.6.5.15	Ch.5, p.259
IFRS 9.6.5.2	Ch.53, p.4222	IFRS 9.6.5.15	Ch.53, p.4246
IFRS 9.6.5.2	Ch.53, p.4262	IFRS 9.6.5.15	Ch.53, p.4330
IFRS 9.6.5.2(b)	Ch.53, p.4329	IFRS 9.6.5.15	Ch.53, p.4331
IFRS 9.6.5.2(c)	Ch.53, p.4307	IFRS 9.6.5.15	Ch.53, p.4332
IFRS 9.6.5.3	Ch.53, p.4220	IFRS 9.6.5.15	Ch.53, p.4338
IFRS 9.6.5.3	Ch.53, p.4221	IFRS 9.6.5.15(b)	Ch.53, p.4381
IFRS 9.6.5.3	Ch.53, p.4345	IFRS 9.6.5.15(c)	Ch.53, p.4333
IFRS 9.6.5.3	Ch.53, p.4396	IFRS 9.6.5.15(c)	Ch.53, p.4341
IFRS 9.6.5.5	Ch.53, p.4349	IFRS 9.6.5.15(c)	Ch.53, p.4342
IFRS 9.6.5.6	Ch.5, p.248	IFRS 9.6.5.15(c)	Ch.53, p.4382
IFRS 9.6.5.6-7	Ch.5, p.253	IFRS 9.6.5.16	Ch.5, p.259
IFRS 9.6.5.6-7	Ch.5, p.256	IFRS 9.6.5.16	Ch.53, p.4247
IFRS 9.6.5.6	Ch.53, p.4344	IFRS 9.6.5.16	Ch.53, p.4299
IFRS 9.6.5.6	Ch.53, p.4347	IFRS 9.6.5.16	Ch.53, p.4304
IFRS 9.6.5.6	Ch.53, p.4353	IFRS 9.6.5.16	Ch.53, p.4336
IFRS 9.6.5.6	Ch.53, p.4359	IFRS 9.6.5.16	Ch.53, p.4338
IFRS 9.6.5.6	Ch.53, p.4362	IFRS 9.6.5.16	Ch.53, p.4339
IFRS 9.6.5.7	Ch.5, p.248	IFRS 9.6.6.1	Ch.5, p.252
IFRS 9.6.5.8	Ch.5, p.258	IFRS 9.6.6.1	Ch.53, p.4211
IFRS 9.6.5.8	Ch.51, p.4019	IFRS 9.6.6.1(c)	Ch.53, p.4213

IFRS 9.6.6.1(c)(ii)	Ch.53, p.4215
IFRS 9.6.6.2	Ch.53, p.4211
IFRS 9.6.6.3	Ch.53, p.4212
IFRS 9.6.6.3(c)	Ch.53, p.4287
IFRS 9.6.6.4	Ch.53, p.4213
IFRS 9.6.6.4	Ch.53, p.4381
IFRS 9.6.6.4	Ch.54, p.4487
IFRS 9.6.6.5	Ch.53, p.4381
IFRS 9.6.6.6	Ch.53, p.4216
IFRS 9.6.7.1	Ch.53, p.4387
IFRS 9.6.7.2	Ch.53, p.4387
IFRS 9.6.7.3	Ch.53, p.4387
IFRS 9.6.7.4	Ch.53, p.4387
IFRS 9.6.8.1	Ch.53, p.4366
IFRS 9.6.8.4	Ch.53, p.4366
IFRS 9.6.8.5	Ch.53, p.4366
IFRS 9.6.8.6	Ch.53, p.4366
IFRS 9.6.8.7	Ch.53, p.4367
IFRS 9.6.8.8	Ch.53, p.4367
IFRS 9.6.8.9	Ch.53, p.4368
IFRS 9.6.8.10	Ch.53, p.4368
IFRS 9.6.8.11	Ch.53, p.4368
IFRS 9.6.8.12	Ch.53, p.4368
IFRS 9.6.8.13	Ch.53, p.4368
IFRS 9.6.9.1	Ch.53, p.4370
IFRS 9.6.9.2	Ch.53, p.4371
IFRS 9.6.9.3	Ch.53, p.4371
IFRS 9.6.9.3-4	Ch.53, p.4370
IFRS 9.6.9.5	Ch.53, p.4371
IFRS 9.6.9.6	Ch.53, p.4372
IFRS 9.6.9.7	Ch.53, p.4372
IFRS 9.6.9.8	Ch.53, p.4372
IFRS 9.6.9.9	Ch.53, p.4372
IFRS 9.6.9.10	Ch.53, p.4372
IFRS 9.6.9.11	Ch.53, p.4372
IFRS 9.6.9.12	Ch.53, p.4372
IFRS 9.7.1.8	Ch.53, p.4366
IFRS 9.7.1.9	Ch.52, p.4102
IFRS 9.7.1.9	Ch.52, p.4160
IFRS 9.7.1.9	Ch.53, p.4377
IFRS 9.7.2.1	Ch.53, p.4391
IFRS 9.7.2.1	Ch.56, p.4941
IFRS 9.7.2.2	Ch.53, p.4390
IFRS 9.7.2.2	Ch.53, p.4391
IFRS 9.7.2.14A	Ch.45, p.3613
IFRS 9.7.2.15	Ch.53, p.4390
IFRS 9.7.2.15	Ch.56, p.4941
IFRS 9.7.2.19(a)	Ch.5, p.264
IFRS 9.7.2.20	Ch.5, p.264
IFRS 9.7.2.21	Ch.5, p.249
IFRS 9.7.2.21	Ch.50, p.3880
IFRS 9.7.2.21	Ch.53, p.4186
IFRS 9.7.2.21	Ch.53, p.4386
IFRS 9.7.2.21	Ch.53, p.4389
IFRS 9.7.2.21-26	Ch.53, p.4390
IFRS 9.7.2.22	Ch.53, p.4390
IFRS 9.7.2.23	Ch.53, p.4391
IFRS 9.7.2.24	Ch.53, p.4391
IFRS 9.7.2.25	Ch.53, p.4391
IFRS 9.7.2.26(a)	Ch.53, p.4391
IFRS 9.7.2.26(b)	Ch.53, p.4392
IFRS 9.7.2.26(b)	Ch.53, p.4393
IFRS 9.7.2.26(d)	Ch.53, p.4367
IFRS 9.7.2.36	Ch.53, p.4377
IFRS 9.7.2.37(b)	Ch.53, p.4377
IFRS 9.7.2.37	Ch.53, p.4377
IFRS 9.7.2.39	Ch.56, p.4941
IFRS 9.7.2.40	Ch.56, p.4941
IFRS 9.7.2.43	Ch.52, p.4102
IFRS 9.7.2.43	Ch.52, p.4160
IFRS 9.7.2.46	Ch.52, p.4102
IFRS 9.7.2.46	Ch.52, p.4160
IFRS 9 Appendix A	Ch.5, p.338
IFRS 9 Appendix A	Ch.27, p.2039
IFRS 9 Appendix A	Ch.33, p.2579
IFRS 9 Appendix A	Ch.39, p.3122
IFRS 9 Appendix A	Ch.40, p.3142
IFRS 9 Appendix A	Ch.45, p.3596
IFRS 9 Appendix A	Ch.46, p.3620
IFRS 9 Appendix A	Ch.46, p.3624
IFRS 9 Appendix A	Ch.46, p.3628
IFRS 9 Appendix A	Ch.47, p.3667
IFRS 9 Appendix A	Ch.47, p.3740
IFRS 9 Appendix A	Ch.48, p.3776
IFRS 9 Appendix A	Ch.48, p.3777
IFRS 9 Appendix A	Ch.48, p.3835
IFRS 9 Appendix A	Ch.49, p.3845
IFRS 9 Appendix A	Ch.49, p.3860
IFRS 9 Appendix A	Ch.50, p.3878
IFRS 9 Appendix A	Ch.50, p.3881
IFRS 9 Appendix A	Ch.50, p.3882
IFRS 9 Appendix A	Ch.50, p.3883
IFRS 9 Appendix A	Ch.50, p.3887
IFRS 9 Appendix A	Ch.51, p.3916
IFRS 9 Appendix A	Ch.51, p.3924
IFRS 9 Appendix A	Ch.51, p.3925
IFRS 9 Appendix A	Ch.51, p.3926
IFRS 9 Appendix A	Ch.51, p.3927
IFRS 9 Appendix A	Ch.51, p.3930
IFRS 9 Appendix A	Ch.51, p.3934
IFRS 9 Appendix A	Ch.51, p.3935
IFRS 9 Appendix A	Ch.51, p.3936
IFRS 9 Appendix A	Ch.51, p.3937
IFRS 9 Appendix A	Ch.51, p.3944
IFRS 9 Appendix A	Ch.51, p.3947
IFRS 9 Appendix A	Ch.51, p.3956
IFRS 9 Appendix A	Ch.51, p.4034
IFRS 9 Appendix A	Ch.51, p.4035
IFRS 9 Appendix A	Ch.51, p.4036
IFRS 9 Appendix A	Ch.51, p.4045
IFRS 9 Appendix A	Ch.51, p.4067
IFRS 9 Appendix A	Ch.51, p.4068
IFRS 9 Appendix A	Ch.51, p.4070
IFRS 9 Appendix A	Ch.51, p.4073
IFRS 9 Appendix A	Ch.51, p.4074
IFRS 9 Appendix A	Ch.52, p.4088

IFRS 9 Appendix A	Ch.53, p.4285	IFRS 9.B3.2.13(c)	Ch.52, p.4144
IFRS 9 Appendix A	Ch.54, p.4515	IFRS 9.B3.2.13(d)	Ch.52, p.4145
IFRS 9 Appendix A	Ch.55, p.4559	IFRS 9.B3.2.13(e)	Ch.52, p.4147
IFRS 9 Appendix A	Ch.56, p.4690	IFRS 9.B3.2.13(a)	Ch.52, p.4150
IFRS 9 Appendix A	Ch.56, p.4713	IFRS 9.B3.2.14	Ch.49, p.3843
IFRS 9.B1	Ch.45, p.3587	IFRS 9.B3.2.14	Ch.52, p.4152
IFRS 9.B2	Ch.46, p.3628	IFRS 9.B3.2.15	Ch.48, p.3825
IFRS 9.B2.1	Ch.45, p.3594	IFRS 9.B3.2.15	Ch.49, p.3843
IFRS 9.B2.1	Ch.46, p.3622	IFRS 9.B3.2.16(r)	Ch.51, p.4068
IFRS 9.B2.3	Ch.45, p.3593	IFRS 9.B3.2.16(r)	Ch.52, p.4103
IFRS 9.B2.4	Ch.45, p.3594	IFRS 9.B3.2.16(h)-(i)	Ch.52, p.4116
IFRS 9.B2.5	Ch.45, p.3598	IFRS 9.B3.2.16(a)	Ch.52, p.4121
IFRS 9.B2.5(a)	Ch.45, p.3594	IFRS 9.B3.2.16(b)	Ch.52, p.4121
IFRS 9.B2.5(a)	Ch.45, p.3598	IFRS 9.B3.2.16(c)	Ch.52, p.4122
IFRS 9.B2.5(a)	Ch.49, p.3857	IFRS 9.B3.2.16(d)	Ch.52, p.4122
IFRS 9.B2.5(b)	Ch.45, p.3596	IFRS 9.B3.2.16(e)	Ch.52, p.4122
IFRS 9.B2.5(c)	Ch.45, p.3599	IFRS 9.B3.2.16(j)	Ch.52, p.4122
IFRS 9.B2.6	Ch.45, p.3599	IFRS 9.B3.2.16(k)	Ch.52, p.4122
IFRS 9.B2.6	Ch.55, p.4542	IFRS 9.B3.2.16(f)	Ch.52, p.4123
IFRS 9.B2.6	Ch.56, p.4690	IFRS 9.B3.2.16(g)	Ch.52, p.4123
IFRS 9.B3.1.1	Ch.49, p.3843	IFRS 9.B3.2.16(h)	Ch.52, p.4124
IFRS 9.B3.1.2(b)	Ch.15, p.1188	IFRS 9.B3.2.16(h)-(i)	Ch.52, p.4124
IFRS 9.B3.1.2(a)	Ch.49, p.3842	IFRS 9.B3.2.16(i)	Ch.52, p.4124
IFRS 9.B3.1.2(b)	Ch.49, p.3842	IFRS 9.B3.2.16(j)	Ch.52, p.4125
IFRS 9.B3.1.2(c)	Ch.49, p.3842	IFRS 9.B3.2.16(k)	Ch.52, p.4125
IFRS 9.B3.1.2(d)	Ch.49, p.3842	IFRS 9.B3.2.16(l)	Ch.52, p.4125
IFRS 9.B3.1.2(e)	Ch.49, p.3842	IFRS 9.B3.2.16(m)	Ch.52, p.4125
IFRS 9.B3.1.2(d)	Ch.52, p.4123	IFRS 9.B3.2.16(n)	Ch.52, p.4127
IFRS 9.B3.1.2(e)	Ch.53, p.4235	IFRS 9.B3.2.16(o)	Ch.52, p.4128
IFRS 9.B3.1.3	Ch.49, p.3845	IFRS 9.B3.2.16(p)	Ch.52, p.4128
IFRS 9.B3.1.3	Ch.50, p.3880	IFRS 9.B3.2.16(q)	Ch.52, p.4128
IFRS 9.B3.1.4	Ch.49, p.3845	IFRS 9.B3.2.16(g)	Ch.54, p.4477
IFRS 9.B3.1.5	Ch.49, p.3845	IFRS 9.B3.2.16(h)	Ch.54, p.4477
IFRS 9.B3.1.5	Ch.49, p.3848	IFRS 9.B3.2.17	Ch.52, p.4116
IFRS 9.B3.1.5	Ch.50, p.3880	IFRS 9.B3.2.17	Ch.52, p.4142
IFRS 9.B3.1.6	Ch.49, p.3845	IFRS 9.B3.2.17	Ch.52, p.4149
IFRS 9.B3.1.6	Ch.49, p.3848	IFRS 9.B3.3.1	Ch.52, p.4154
IFRS 9.B3.1.6	Ch.50, p.3880	IFRS 9.B3.3.1(b)	Ch.52, p.4154
IFRS 9.B3.2.1	Ch.52, p.4090	IFRS 9.B3.3.2	Ch.52, p.4154
IFRS 9.B3.2.1	Ch.52, p.4091	IFRS 9.B3.3.3	Ch.52, p.4156
IFRS 9.B3.2.2	Ch.52, p.4103	IFRS 9.B3.3.4	Ch.52, p.4154
IFRS 9.B3.2.3	Ch.52, p.4108	IFRS 9.B3.3.4	Ch.52, p.4155
IFRS 9.B3.2.4	Ch.52, p.4115	IFRS 9.B3.3.5	Ch.52, p.4156
IFRS 9.B3.2.4(c)	Ch.52, p.4123	IFRS 9.B3.3.6	Ch.50, p.3897
IFRS 9.B3.2.5	Ch.52, p.4115	IFRS 9.B3.3.6	Ch.52, p.4099
IFRS 9.B3.2.5(d)	Ch.52, p.4123	IFRS 9.B3.3.6	Ch.52, p.4157
IFRS 9.B3.2.6	Ch.52, p.4114	IFRS 9.B3.3.6	Ch.52, p.4162
IFRS 9.B3.2.6	Ch.52, p.4126	IFRS 9.B3.3.7	Ch.52, p.4167
IFRS 9.B3.2.6	Ch.52, p.4152	IFRS 9.B4.1.1	Ch.48, p.3779
IFRS 9.B3.2.7	Ch.52, p.4120	IFRS 9.B4.1.2	Ch.48, p.3779
IFRS 9.B3.2.8(a)	Ch.52, p.4120	IFRS 9.B4.1.2	Ch.48, p.3780
IFRS 9.B3.2.8(b)	Ch.52, p.4120	IFRS 9.B4.1.2A	Ch.48, p.3778
IFRS 9.B3.2.9	Ch.52, p.4120	IFRS 9.B4.1.2A	Ch.48, p.3779
IFRS 9.B3.2.10	Ch.52, p.4132	IFRS 9.B4.1.2B	Ch.48, p.3779
IFRS 9.B3.2.11	Ch.52, p.4131	IFRS 9.B4.1.2C	Ch.48, p.3780
IFRS 9.B3.2.12	Ch.52, p.4134	IFRS 9.B4.1.3	Ch.48, p.3781
IFRS 9.B3.2.13(a)	Ch.52, p.4141	IFRS 9.B4.1.3A	Ch.48, p.3781
IFRS 9.B3.2.13(b)	Ch.52, p.4142	IFRS 9.B4.1.3B	Ch.48, p.3781

IFRS 9.B4.1.3B	Ch.48, p.3782	IFRS 9.B4.1.18	Ch.48, p.3791
IFRS 9.B4.1.3B	Ch.48, p.3787	IFRS 9.B4.1.18	Ch.48, p.3797
IFRS 9.B4.1.4A	Ch.48, p.3784	IFRS 9.B4.1.18	Ch.48, p.3804
IFRS 9.B4.1.4B	Ch.48, p.3784	IFRS 9.B4.1.18	Ch.48, p.3808
IFRS 9.B4.1.4 Example 1	Ch.48, p.3786	IFRS 9.B4.1.18	Ch.48, p.3814
IFRS 9.B4.1.4 Example 2	Ch.48, p.3787	IFRS 9.B4.1.19	Ch.48, p.3794
IFRS 9.B4.1.4 Example 3	Ch.48, p.3787	IFRS 9.B4.1.20	Ch.48, p.3816
IFRS 9.B4.1.4 Example 4	Ch.48, p.3788	IFRS 9.B4.1.20	Ch.48, p.3817
IFRS 9.B4.1.4C Example 5	Ch.48, p.3788	IFRS 9.B4.1.20	Ch.48, p.3820
IFRS 9.B4.1.4C Example 6	Ch.48, p.3788	IFRS 9.B4.1.20-26	Ch.51, p.3974
IFRS 9.B4.1.4C Example 7	Ch.48, p.3789	IFRS 9.B4.1.21	Ch.48, p.3816
IFRS 9.B4.1.5	Ch.48, p.3785	IFRS 9.B4.1.21	Ch.48, p.3817
IFRS 9.B4.1.5	Ch.48, p.3790	IFRS 9.B4.1.21(b)	Ch.48, p.3820
IFRS 9.B4.1.6	Ch.48, p.3784	IFRS 9.B4.1.21(b)-(c)	Ch.48, p.3819
IFRS 9.B4.1.6	Ch.48, p.3785	IFRS 9.B4.1.22	Ch.48, p.3816
IFRS 9.B4.1.6	Ch.53, p.4219	IFRS 9.B4.1.22	Ch.48, p.3819
IFRS 9.B4.1.7A	Ch.25, p.1876	IFRS 9.B4.1.23-25	Ch.48, p.3816
IFRS 9.B4.1.7A	Ch.48, p.3791	IFRS 9.B4.1.25	Ch.48, p.3817
IFRS 9.B4.1.7A	Ch.48, p.3792	IFRS 9.B4.1.26	Ch.48, p.3817
IFRS 9.B4.1.7B	Ch.48, p.3791	IFRS 9.B4.1.26	Ch.48, p.3821
IFRS 9.B4.1.8	Ch.48, p.3809	IFRS 9.B4.1.27	Ch.48, p.3826
IFRS 9.B4.1.9	Ch.48, p.3809	IFRS 9.B4.1.28	Ch.48, p.3826
IFRS 9.B4.1.9	Ch.48, p.3811	IFRS 9.B4.1.29	Ch.48, p.3827
IFRS 9.B4.1.9A	Ch.48, p.3792	IFRS 9.B4.1.30	Ch.48, p.3827
IFRS 9.B4.1.9B	Ch.48, p.3799	IFRS 9.B4.1.31	Ch.48, p.3828
IFRS 9.B4.1.9B-9D	Ch.5, p.262	IFRS 9.B4.1.32	Ch.48, p.3828
IFRS 9.B4.1.9B-9D	Ch.5, p.356	IFRS 9.B4.1.33	Ch.48, p.3784
IFRS 9.B4.1.9C	Ch.48, p.3799	IFRS 9.B4.1.33	Ch.48, p.3828
IFRS 9.B4.1.9C	Ch.48, p.3801	IFRS 9.B4.1.34	Ch.48, p.3828
IFRS 9.B4.1.9D	Ch.48, p.3801	IFRS 9.B4.1.35	Ch.48, p.3826
IFRS 9.B4.1.9D	Ch.48, p.3802	IFRS 9.B4.1.35	Ch.48, p.3828
IFRS 9.B4.1.9E	Ch.48, p.3795	IFRS 9.B4.1.36	Ch.48, p.3784
IFRS 9.B4.1.9E	Ch.48, p.3802	IFRS 9.B4.1.36	Ch.48, p.3829
IFRS 9.B4.1.10	Ch.48, p.3803	IFRS 9.B4.3.1	Ch.47, p.3699
IFRS 9.B4.1.11	Ch.48, p.3803	IFRS 9.B4.3.2	Ch.46, p.3630
IFRS 9.B4.1.11(b)	Ch.48, p.3807	IFRS 9.B4.3.3	Ch.46, p.3649
IFRS 9.B4.1.12	Ch.5, p.263	IFRS 9.B4.3.3	Ch.46, p.3650
IFRS 9.B4.1.12	Ch.5, p.357	IFRS 9.B4.3.3	Ch.49, p.3860
IFRS 9.B4.1.12	Ch.48, p.3806	IFRS 9.B4.3.4	Ch.46, p.3651
IFRS 9.B4.1.12	Ch.50, p.3889	IFRS 9.B4.3.5(a)	Ch.46, p.3641
IFRS 9.B4.1.12(c)	Ch.48, p.3807	IFRS 9.B4.3.5(b)	Ch.46, p.3635
IFRS 9.B4.1.12A	Ch.48, p.3804	IFRS 9.B4.3.5(b)	Ch.46, p.3637
IFRS 9.B4.1.12A	Ch.48, p.3806	IFRS 9.B4.3.5(c)-(d)	Ch.46, p.3639
IFRS 9.B4.1.13 Instrument C	Ch.48, p.3794	IFRS 9.B4.3.5(c)-(d)	Ch.56, p.4714
IFRS 9.B4.1.13 Instrument D	Ch.48, p.3794	IFRS 9.B4.3.5(e)	Ch.46, p.3633
IFRS 9.B4.1.13 Instrument A	Ch.48, p.3796	IFRS 9.B4.3.5(e)	Ch.46, p.3637
IFRS 9.B4.1.13 Instrument B	Ch.48, p.3801	IFRS 9.B4.3.5(e)	Ch.47, p.3727
IFRS 9.B4.1.13 Instrument E	Ch.48, p.3811	IFRS 9.B4.3.5(e)	Ch.47, p.3734
IFRS 9.B4.1.13 Instrument A	Ch.48, p.3812	IFRS 9.B4.3.5(e)	Ch.55, p.4561
IFRS 9.B4.1.14	Ch.48, p.3808	IFRS 9.B4.3.5(e)(ii)	Ch.46, p.3636
IFRS 9.B4.1.14 Instrument F	Ch.48, p.3810	IFRS 9.B4.3.5(f)	Ch.46, p.3640
IFRS 9.B4.1.14 Instrument G	Ch.48, p.3810	IFRS 9.B4.3.5(f)	Ch.51, p.4022
IFRS 9.B4.1.14 Instrument H	Ch.48, p.3810	IFRS 9.B4.3.6	Ch.46, p.3641
IFRS 9.B4.1.15	Ch.48, p.3814	IFRS 9.B4.3.7	Ch.46, p.3641
IFRS 9.B4.1.16	Ch.48, p.3814	IFRS 9.B4.3.7	Ch.55, p.4563
IFRS 9.B4.1.17	Ch.48, p.3794	IFRS 9.B4.3.7	Ch.56, p.4715
IFRS 9.B4.1.17	Ch.48, p.3814	IFRS 9.B4.3.8	Ch.46, p.3630
IFRS 9.B4.1.18	Ch.25, p.1876	IFRS 9.B4.3.8(a)	Ch.46, p.3631

IFRS 9.B4.3.8(a)	Ch.46, p.3633	IFRS 9.B5.4.6	Ch.47, p.3724
IFRS 9.B4.3.8(b)	Ch.46, p.3637	IFRS 9.B5.4.6	Ch.50, p.3887
IFRS 9.B4.3.8(b)	Ch.46, p.3647	IFRS 9.B5.4.6	Ch.50, p.3894
IFRS 9.B4.3.8(c)	Ch.46, p.3631	IFRS 9.B5.4.6	Ch.51, p.3931
IFRS 9.B4.3.8(d)	Ch.43, p.3476	IFRS 9.B5.4.7	Ch.50, p.3882
IFRS 9.B4.3.8(d)	Ch.46, p.3642	IFRS 9.B5.4.7	Ch.51, p.3929
IFRS 9.B4.3.8(d)	Ch.46, p.3651	IFRS 9.B5.4.7	Ch.51, p.3930
IFRS 9.B4.3.8(e)	Ch.46, p.3637	IFRS 9.B5.4.8	Ch.47, p.3740
IFRS 9.B4.3.8(f)(i)	Ch.46, p.3648	IFRS 9.B5.4.8	Ch.49, p.3860
IFRS 9.B4.3.8(f)(ii)	Ch.46, p.3648	IFRS 9.B5.4.9	Ch.51, p.4036
IFRS 9.B4.3.8(f)(iii)	Ch.46, p.3648	IFRS 9.B5.4.9	Ch.51, p.4069
IFRS 9.B4.3.8(g)	Ch.46, p.3648	IFRS 9.B5.4.9	Ch.52, p.4103
IFRS 9.B4.3.8(g)	Ch.55, p.4563	IFRS 9.B5.5.1	Ch.51, p.3926
IFRS 9.B4.3.8(g)	Ch.56, p.4715	IFRS 9.B5.5.1-6	Ch.5, p.264
IFRS 9.B4.3.8(h)	Ch.46, p.3648	IFRS 9.B5.5.2	Ch.51, p.3979
IFRS 9.B4.3.8(h)	Ch.56, p.4712	IFRS 9.B5.5.4	Ch.51, p.4000
IFRS 9.B4.3.8(h)	Ch.56, p.4714	IFRS 9.B5.5.5	Ch.51, p.4002
IFRS 9.B4.3.9	Ch.48, p.3829	IFRS 9.B5.5.6	Ch.51, p.4002
IFRS 9.B4.3.10	Ch.48, p.3829	IFRS 9.B5.5.7	Ch.51, p.3969
IFRS 9.B4.3.11	Ch.5, p.265	IFRS 9.B5.5.8	Ch.51, p.3970
IFRS 9.B4.3.11	Ch.43, p.3477	IFRS 9.B5.5.8	Ch.51, p.4047
IFRS 9.B4.3.11	Ch.46, p.3630	IFRS 9.B5.5.9	Ch.51, p.3988
IFRS 9.B4.3.11	Ch.46, p.3652	IFRS 9.B5.5.10	Ch.51, p.3988
IFRS 9.B4.3.12	Ch.46, p.3652	IFRS 9.B5.5.11	Ch.51, p.3972
IFRS 9.B4.4.1	Ch.48, p.3832	IFRS 9.B5.5.11	Ch.51, p.3988
IFRS 9.B4.4.2	Ch.48, p.3835	IFRS 9.B5.5.12	Ch.51, p.3971
IFRS 9.B4.4.3	Ch.48, p.3833	IFRS 9.B5.5.12	Ch.51, p.3975
IFRS 9.B4.4.3(a)	Ch.48, p.3833	IFRS 9.B5.5.13	Ch.51, p.3995
IFRS 9.B5.1.1	Ch.8, p.627	IFRS 9.B5.5.14	Ch.51, p.3995
IFRS 9.B5.1.1	Ch.24, p.1832	IFRS 9.B5.5.15	Ch.51, p.3975
IFRS 9.B5.1.1	Ch.46, p.3638	IFRS 9.B5.5.16	Ch.51, p.3967
IFRS 9.B5.1.1	Ch.49, p.3854	IFRS 9.B5.5.16	Ch.51, p.3975
IFRS 9.B5.1.1	Ch.49, p.3855	IFRS 9.B5.5.17	Ch.51, p.3973
IFRS 9.B5.1.1	Ch.50, p.3883	IFRS 9.B5.5.17	Ch.51, p.3976
IFRS 9.B5.1.2	Ch.49, p.3856	IFRS 9.B5.5.17(f)	Ch.51, p.4067
IFRS 9.B5.1.2A	Ch.49, p.3854	IFRS 9.B5.5.17(g)	Ch.51, p.4067
IFRS 9.B5.1.2A	Ch.49, p.3855	IFRS 9.B5.5.17(i)	Ch.51, p.4067
IFRS 9.B5.1.2A(b)	Ch.5, p.316	IFRS 9.B5.5.17(j)	Ch.51, p.3973
IFRS 9.B5.2.1	Ch.50, p.3872	IFRS 9.B5.5.17(k)	Ch.51, p.3973
IFRS 9.B5.2.2	Ch.49, p.3859	IFRS 9.B5.5.17(l)	Ch.51, p.3973
IFRS 9.B5.2.2	Ch.49, p.3860	IFRS 9.B5.5.18	Ch.51, p.3975
IFRS 9.B5.2.2A	Ch.49, p.3855	IFRS 9.B5.5.19	Ch.51, p.3980
IFRS 9.B5.2.3	Ch.50, p.3877	IFRS 9.B5.5.19	Ch.51, p.4006
IFRS 9.B5.2.4	Ch.50, p.3878	IFRS 9.B5.5.20	Ch.51, p.3980
IFRS 9.B5.2.5	Ch.50, p.3878	IFRS 9.B5.5.21	Ch.51, p.3969
IFRS 9.B5.2.6	Ch.50, p.3878	IFRS 9.B5.5.21	Ch.51, p.3980
IFRS 9.B5.4.1	Ch.50, p.3882	IFRS 9.B5.5.22	Ch.51, p.3990
IFRS 9.B5.4.1-3	Ch.5, p.338	IFRS 9.B5.5.22-24	Ch.5, p.264
IFRS 9.B5.4.1-7	Ch.5, p.338	IFRS 9.B5.5.23	Ch.51, p.3990
IFRS 9.B5.4.1-7	Ch.27, p.2039	IFRS 9.B5.5.24	Ch.51, p.3990
IFRS 9.B5.4.2	Ch.50, p.3882	IFRS 9.B5.5.25	Ch.51, p.4033
IFRS 9.B5.4.3	Ch.50, p.3882	IFRS 9.B5.5.26	Ch.51, p.3930
IFRS 9.B5.4.4	Ch.50, p.3886	IFRS 9.B5.5.26	Ch.51, p.4033
IFRS 9.B5.4.4	Ch.50, p.3891	IFRS 9.B5.5.27	Ch.51, p.4034
IFRS 9.B5.4.4	Ch.51, p.4070	IFRS 9.B5.5.28	Ch.51, p.3935
IFRS 9.B5.4.5	Ch.50, p.3883	IFRS 9.B5.5.28	Ch.51, p.3952
IFRS 9.B5.4.5	Ch.50, p.3885	IFRS 9.B5.5.28	Ch.51, p.4047
IFRS 9.B5.4.6	Ch.43, p.3394	IFRS 9.B5.5.28	Ch.51, p.3947

IFRS 9.B5.5.29	Ch.32, p.2399	IFRS 9.B5.7.1	Ch.48, p.3830
IFRS 9.B5.5.29	Ch.51, p.3935	IFRS 9.B5.7.1	Ch.49, p.3859
IFRS 9.B5.5.30	Ch.51, p.3936	IFRS 9.B5.7.1	Ch.50, p.3877
IFRS 9.B5.5.30	Ch.51, p.4047	IFRS 9.B5.7.1A	Ch.50, p.3871
IFRS 9.B5.5.31	Ch.51, p.3936	IFRS 9.B5.7.2	Ch.50, p.3871
IFRS 9.B5.5.31	Ch.51, p.3944	IFRS 9.B5.7.2	Ch.50, p.3880
IFRS 9.B5.5.32	Ch.51, p.3936	IFRS 9.B5.7.2	Ch.50, p.3900
IFRS 9.B5.5.32	Ch.51, p.4047	IFRS 9.B5.7.2-2A	Ch.50, p.3900
IFRS 9.B5.5.32	Ch.51, p.4048	IFRS 9.B5.7.2A	Ch.50, p.3871
IFRS 9.B5.5.33	Ch.51, p.4019	IFRS 9.B5.7.2A	Ch.50, p.3900
IFRS 9.B5.5.34	Ch.51, p.4044	IFRS 9.B5.7.3	Ch.11, p.835
IFRS 9.B5.5.35	Ch.51, p.3932	IFRS 9.B5.7.3	Ch.15, p.1197
IFRS 9.B5.5.35	Ch.51, p.4043	IFRS 9.B5.7.3	Ch.15, p.1198
IFRS 9.B5.5.37	Ch.51, p.3935	IFRS 9.B5.7.3	Ch.16, p.1258
IFRS 9.B5.5.37	Ch.51, p.3938	IFRS 9.B5.7.3	Ch.50, p.3877
IFRS 9.B5.5.38	Ch.51, p.3945	IFRS 9.B5.7.3	Ch.50, p.3900
IFRS 9.B5.5.38	Ch.51, p.4047	IFRS 9.B5.7.5	Ch.50, p.3875
IFRS 9.B5.5.39	Ch.51, p.3945	IFRS 9.B5.7.6	Ch.50, p.3875
IFRS 9.B5.5.39	Ch.51, p.4047	IFRS 9.B5.7.7	Ch.50, p.3875
IFRS 9.B5.5.39	Ch.51, p.4051	IFRS 9.B5.7.8	Ch.50, p.3872
IFRS 9.B5.5.39	Ch.51, p.4052	IFRS 9.B5.7.8	Ch.50, p.3876
IFRS 9.B5.5.40	Ch.51, p.3945	IFRS 9.B5.7.9	Ch.50, p.3872
IFRS 9.B5.5.40	Ch.51, p.4047	IFRS 9.B5.7.10	Ch.48, p.3776
IFRS 9.B5.5.40	Ch.51, p.4055	IFRS 9.B5.7.10	Ch.50, p.3876
IFRS 9.B5.5.41	Ch.51, p.3947	IFRS 9.B5.7.11	Ch.50, p.3876
IFRS 9.B5.5.42	Ch.51, p.3947	IFRS 9.B5.7.12	Ch.50, p.3876
IFRS 9.B5.5.43	Ch.51, p.3936	IFRS 9.B5.7.13	Ch.50, p.3872
IFRS 9.B5.5.43	Ch.51, p.3935	IFRS 9.B5.7.14	Ch.50, p.3873
IFRS 9.B5.5.44	Ch.51, p.3952	IFRS 9.B5.7.15	Ch.50, p.3873
IFRS 9.B5.5.44	Ch.51, p.3953	IFRS 9.B5.7.16	Ch.50, p.3873
IFRS 9.B5.5.44	Ch.51, p.4047	IFRS 9.B5.7.16(b)	Ch.50, p.3875
IFRS 9.B5.5.44	Ch.51, p.4064	IFRS 9.B5.7.17	Ch.50, p.3873
IFRS 9.B5.5.45	Ch.51, p.3930	IFRS 9.B5.7.18	Ch.50, p.3873
IFRS 9.B5.5.45	Ch.51, p.3953	IFRS 9.B5.7.19	Ch.50, p.3875
IFRS 9.B5.5.46	Ch.51, p.3953	IFRS 9.B5.7.20	Ch.50, p.3875
IFRS 9.B5.5.46	Ch.51, p.4044	IFRS 9.B6.2.1	Ch.53, p.4238
IFRS 9.B5.5.47	Ch.48, p.3813	IFRS 9.B6.2.2	Ch.53, p.4242
IFRS 9.B5.5.47	Ch.51, p.3953	IFRS 9.B6.2.3	Ch.53, p.4241
IFRS 9.B5.5.47	Ch.51, p.4047	IFRS 9.B6.2.3	Ch.53, p.4303
IFRS 9.B5.5.47	Ch.51, p.4063	IFRS 9.B6.2.3	Ch.53, p.4306
IFRS 9.B5.5.48	Ch.51, p.3953	IFRS 9.B6.2.4	Ch.53, p.4235
IFRS 9.B5.5.48	Ch.51, p.4047	IFRS 9.B6.2.4	Ch.53, p.4236
IFRS 9.B5.5.49	Ch.51, p.3962	IFRS 9.B6.2.5	Ch.53, p.4241
IFRS 9.B5.5.49-54	Ch.51, p.3967	IFRS 9.B6.2.6	Ch.53, p.4243
IFRS 9.B5.5.50	Ch.51, p.3964	IFRS 9.B6.3.1	Ch.9, p.698
IFRS 9.B5.5.51	Ch.51, p.3962	IFRS 9.B6.3.1	Ch.53, p.4221
IFRS 9.B5.5.51	Ch.51, p.3963	IFRS 9.B6.3.1	Ch.53, p.4343
IFRS 9.B5.5.51	Ch.51, p.3967	IFRS 9.B6.3.2	Ch.53, p.4263
IFRS 9.B5.5.51	Ch.51, p.3944	IFRS 9.B6.3.2	Ch.53, p.4267
IFRS 9.B5.5.52	Ch.51, p.3964	IFRS 9.B6.3.3	Ch.53, p.4234
IFRS 9.B5.5.52	Ch.51, p.3965	IFRS 9.B6.3.4	Ch.53, p.4226
IFRS 9.B5.5.53	Ch.51, p.3965	IFRS 9.B6.3.4	Ch.53, p.4227
IFRS 9.B5.5.54	Ch.51, p.3964	IFRS 9.B6.3.5	Ch.53, p.4260
IFRS 9.B5.5.55	Ch.45, p.3599	IFRS 9.B6.3.6	Ch.53, p.4298
IFRS 9.B5.5.55	Ch.51, p.3955	IFRS 9.B6.3.7	Ch.53, p.4191
IFRS 9.B5.5.55	Ch.51, p.3973	IFRS 9.B6.3.7	Ch.53, p.4193
IFRS 9.B5.6.2	Ch.50, p.3879	IFRS 9.B6.3.7	Ch.53, p.4202
IFRS 9.B5.7.1	Ch.11, p.835	IFRS 9.B6.3.8	Ch.53, p.4190

IFRS 9.B6.3.8	Ch.53, p.4191
IFRS 9.B6.3.8	Ch.53, p.4197
IFRS 9.B6.3.8	Ch.53, p.4201
IFRS 9.B6.3.9	Ch.53, p.4191
IFRS 9.B6.3.9	Ch.53, p.4194
IFRS 9.B6.3.9	Ch.53, p.4197
IFRS 9.B6.3.9	Ch.53, p.4201
IFRS 9.B6.3.9	Ch.53, p.4373
IFRS 9.B6.3.10	Ch.53, p.4191
IFRS 9.B6.3.10	Ch.53, p.4192
IFRS 9.B6.3.10(b)	Ch.53, p.4195
IFRS 9.B6.3.10(c)	Ch.53, p.4196
IFRS 9.B6.3.10(c)(i)	Ch.53, p.4208
IFRS 9.B6.3.10(d)	Ch.53, p.4194
IFRS 9.B6.3.10(d)	Ch.53, p.4373
IFRS 9.B6.3.11	Ch.53, p.4191
IFRS 9.B6.3.11	Ch.53, p.4198
IFRS 9.B6.3.11	Ch.53, p.4290
IFRS 9.B6.3.11	Ch.53, p.4308
IFRS 9.B6.3.12	Ch.53, p.4246
IFRS 9.B6.3.12	Ch.53, p.4306
IFRS 9.B6.3.12	Ch.53, p.4327
IFRS 9.B6.3.12	Ch.53, p.4328
IFRS 9.B6.3.12	Ch.53, p.4329
IFRS 9.B6.3.13	Ch.53, p.4200
IFRS 9.B6.3.14	Ch.53, p.4200
IFRS 9.B6.3.15	Ch.53, p.4200
IFRS 9.B6.3.16	Ch.53, p.4201
IFRS 9.B6.3.17	Ch.53, p.4201
IFRS 9.B6.3.18	Ch.53, p.4202
IFRS 9.B6.3.18	Ch.53, p.4203
IFRS 9.B6.3.19	Ch.53, p.4202
IFRS 9.B6.3.20	Ch.53, p.4203
IFRS 9.B6.3.21	Ch.53, p.4206
IFRS 9.B6.3.21	Ch.53, p.4210
IFRS 9.B6.3.21-22	Ch.53, p.4206
IFRS 9.B6.3.23	Ch.53, p.4209
IFRS 9.B6.3.23	Ch.53, p.4210
IFRS 9.B6.3.24	Ch.53, p.4206
IFRS 9.B6.3.25	Ch.53, p.4207
IFRS 9.B6.4.1	Ch.53, p.4191
IFRS 9.B6.4.1	Ch.53, p.4198
IFRS 9.B6.4.1	Ch.53, p.4276
IFRS 9.B6.4.1	Ch.53, p.4280
IFRS 9.B6.4.1	Ch.53, p.4290
IFRS 9.B6.4.1	Ch.53, p.4307
IFRS 9.B6.4.1	Ch.53, p.4308
IFRS 9.B6.4.1	Ch.53, p.4325
IFRS 9.B6.4.2	Ch.53, p.4276
IFRS 9.B6.4.3	Ch.53, p.4362
IFRS 9.B6.4.4	Ch.53, p.4200
IFRS 9.B6.4.4	Ch.53, p.4281
IFRS 9.B6.4.5	Ch.53, p.4281
IFRS 9.B6.4.6	Ch.53, p.4281
IFRS 9.B6.4.6	Ch.53, p.4283
IFRS 9.B6.4.6	Ch.53, p.4344
IFRS 9.B6.4.7	Ch.53, p.4284
IFRS 9.B6.4.7	Ch.53, p.4286
IFRS 9.B6.4.8	Ch.53, p.4284
IFRS 9.B6.4.10	Ch.53, p.4288
IFRS 9.B6.4.11(a)	Ch.53, p.4288
IFRS 9.B6.4.11(a)	Ch.53, p.4296
IFRS 9.B6.4.11(b)	Ch.53, p.4289
IFRS 9.B6.4.12	Ch.53, p.4280
IFRS 9.B6.4.12	Ch.53, p.4283
IFRS 9.B6.4.12	Ch.53, p.4346
IFRS 9.B6.4.13	Ch.53, p.4280
IFRS 9.B6.4.14	Ch.53, p.4281
IFRS 9.B6.4.15	Ch.53, p.4277
IFRS 9.B6.4.15	Ch.53, p.4282
IFRS 9.B6.4.15	Ch.53, p.4310
IFRS 9.B6.4.16	Ch.53, p.4280
IFRS 9.B6.4.16	Ch.53, p.4282
IFRS 9.B6.4.17	Ch.53, p.4276
IFRS 9.B6.4.17	Ch.53, p.4280
IFRS 9.B6.4.18	Ch.53, p.4280
IFRS 9.B6.4.18	Ch.53, p.4282
IFRS 9.B6.4.18	Ch.53, p.4283
IFRS 9.B6.4.18	Ch.53, p.4344
IFRS 9.B6.4.19	Ch.53, p.4276
IFRS 9.B6.4.19	Ch.53, p.4280
IFRS 9.B6.5.1	Ch.53, p.4262
IFRS 9.B6.5.2	Ch.53, p.4218
IFRS 9.B6.5.2	Ch.53, p.4264
IFRS 9.B6.5.3	Ch.53, p.4263
IFRS 9.B6.5.3	Ch.53, p.4266
IFRS 9.B6.5.3	Ch.53, p.4343
IFRS 9.B6.5.4	Ch.53, p.4241
IFRS 9.B6.5.4	Ch.53, p.4309
IFRS 9.B6.5.4	Ch.53, p.4312
IFRS 9.B6.5.4	Ch.53, p.4329
IFRS 9.B6.5.5	Ch.53, p.4304
IFRS 9.B6.5.5	Ch.53, p.4305
IFRS 9.B6.5.5	Ch.53, p.4310
IFRS 9.B6.5.5	Ch.53, p.4312
IFRS 9.B6.5.5	Ch.53, p.4313
IFRS 9.B6.5.5	Ch.53, p.4325
IFRS 9.B6.5.5	Ch.53, p.4326
IFRS 9.B6.5.5	Ch.53, p.4328
IFRS 9.B6.5.5	Ch.53, p.4339
IFRS 9.B6.5.7	Ch.53, p.4347
IFRS 9.B6.5.7	Ch.53, p.4348
IFRS 9.B6.5.8	Ch.53, p.4350
IFRS 9.B6.5.9	Ch.53, p.4347
IFRS 9.B6.5.10	Ch.53, p.4347
IFRS 9.B6.5.11	Ch.53, p.4295
IFRS 9.B6.5.11	Ch.53, p.4350
IFRS 9.B6.5.12	Ch.53, p.4350
IFRS 9.B6.5.13	Ch.53, p.4349
IFRS 9.B6.5.14	Ch.53, p.4349
IFRS 9.B6.5.16	Ch.53, p.4350
IFRS 9.B6.5.16-20	Ch.53, p.4352
IFRS 9.B6.5.21	Ch.53, p.4353
IFRS 9.B6.5.24	Ch.53, p.4273
IFRS 9.B6.5.24	Ch.53, p.4356
IFRS 9.B6.5.24(a)	Ch.53, p.4357

IFRS 9.B6.5.26(a)	Ch.53, p.4393	IFRS 9.IE66-IE73 Example 11	Ch.51, p.4034
IFRS 9.B6.5.27(a)	Ch.53, p.4352	IFRS 9.IE74-IE77 Example 12	Ch.51, p.4043
IFRS 9.B6.5.24(b)	Ch.53, p.4277	IFRS 9.IE78-IE81 Example 13	Ch.33, p.2580
IFRS 9.B6.5.24(b)	Ch.53, p.4359	IFRS 9.IE78-IE81 Example 13	Ch.51, p.4036
IFRS 9.B6.5.28	Ch.53, p.4190	IFRS 9.IE82-IE102	Ch.51, p.4037
IFRS 9.B6.5.28	Ch.53, p.4209	IFRS 9.IE115-147	Ch.53, p.4225
IFRS 9.B6.5.28	Ch.53, p.4234	IFRS 9.IE116-127	Ch.53, p.4231
IFRS 9.B6.5.28	Ch.53, p.4276	IFRS 9.IE119(b)	Ch.53, p.4231
IFRS 9.B6.5.28	Ch.53, p.4310	IFRS 9.IE119(b)	Ch.53, p.4232
IFRS 9.B6.5.29	Ch.53, p.4331	IFRS 9.IE122	Ch.53, p.4232
IFRS 9.B6.5.29-39	Ch.5, p.259	IFRS 9.IE123	Ch.53, p.4232
IFRS 9.B6.5.29(b)	Ch.53, p.4303	IFRS 9.IE128-137	Ch.53, p.4227
IFRS 9.B6.5.29(b)	Ch.53, p.4338	IFRS 9.IE131(b)	Ch.53, p.4227
IFRS 9.B6.5.30	Ch.53, p.4331	IFRS 9.IE134	Ch.53, p.4229
IFRS 9.B6.5.31	Ch.53, p.4334	IFRS 9.IE134(a)	Ch.53, p.4228
IFRS 9.B6.5.32	Ch.53, p.4334	IFRS 9.IE138-147	Ch.53, p.4229
IFRS 9.B6.5.33	Ch.53, p.4334	IFRS 9.IE139(b)	Ch.53, p.4230
IFRS 9.B6.5.34-36	Ch.53, p.4336	IFRS 9.IE143	Ch.53, p.4230
IFRS 9.B6.5.37	Ch.53, p.4337	IFRS 9.IG A.1	Ch.45, p.3609
IFRS 9.B6.5.37	Ch.53, p.4338	IFRS 9.IG A.2	Ch.45, p.3611
IFRS 9.B6.5.37	Ch.53, p.4343	IFRS 9.IG B.3	Ch.46, p.3627
IFRS 9.B6.5.38	Ch.53, p.4343	IFRS 9.IG B.4	Ch.46, p.3625
IFRS 9.B6.6.1	Ch.53, p.4211	IFRS 9.IG B.5	Ch.46, p.3626
IFRS 9.B6.6.7	Ch.53, p.4213	IFRS 9.IG B.6	Ch.46, p.3628
IFRS 9.B6.6.7	Ch.53, p.4215	IFRS 9.IG B.6	Ch.53, p.4235
IFRS 9.B6.6.8	Ch.53, p.4215	IFRS 9.IG B.7	Ch.46, p.3627
IFRS 9.B6.6.12	Ch.53, p.4212	IFRS 9.IG B.8	Ch.46, p.3621
IFRS 9.B6.6.13	Ch.54, p.4487	IFRS 9.IG B.9	Ch.46, p.3625
IFRS 9.B6.6.13-15	Ch.53, p.4380	IFRS 9.IG B.9	Ch.46, p.3626
IFRS 9.B6.6.14	Ch.54, p.4487	IFRS 9.IG B.10	Ch.46, p.3626
IFRS 9.B6.6.15	Ch.53, p.4215	IFRS 9.IG B.11	Ch.48, p.3778
IFRS 9.B6.6.15	Ch.54, p.4487	IFRS 9.IG B.24	Ch.50, p.3889
IFRS 9.B6.6.16	Ch.53, p.4381	IFRS 9.IG B.25	Ch.50, p.3889
IFRS 9.B6.6.16	Ch.54, p.4487	IFRS 9.IG B.26	Ch.50, p.3884
IFRS 9.B7.2.2	Ch.5, p.264	IFRS 9.IG B.26	Ch.50, p.3888
IFRS 9.B7.2.2-3	Ch.5, p.264	IFRS 9.IG B.27	Ch.50, p.3884
IFRS 9.B7.2.3	Ch.5, p.264	IFRS 9.IG B.28	Ch.49, p.3846
IFRS 9.BA.1	Ch.46, p.3621	IFRS 9.IG B.29	Ch.49, p.3846
IFRS 9.BA.2	Ch.46, p.3627	IFRS 9.IG B.30	Ch.49, p.3846
IFRS 9.BA.3	Ch.46, p.3624	IFRS 9.IG B.31	Ch.49, p.3847
IFRS 9.BA.3	Ch.46, p.3625	IFRS 9.IG C.1	Ch.46, p.3649
IFRS 9.BA.4	Ch.46, p.3629	IFRS 9.IG C.2	Ch.46, p.3650
IFRS 9.BA.4	Ch.49, p.3860	IFRS 9.IG C.2	Ch.46, p.3651
IFRS 9.BA.5	Ch.46, p.3622	IFRS 9.IG C.4	Ch.46, p.3641
IFRS 9.BA.6	Ch.48, p.3778	IFRS 9.IG C.6	Ch.46, p.3653
IFRS 9.BA.7	Ch.48, p.3778	IFRS 9.IG C.6	Ch.46, p.3654
IFRS 9.BA.7(d)	Ch.48, p.3778	IFRS 9.IG C.7	Ch.46, p.3645
IFRS 9.BA.8	Ch.48, p.3778	IFRS 9.IG C.8	Ch.46, p.3645
IFRS 9.IE1-IE5	Ch.50, p.3874	IFRS 9.IG C.9	Ch.46, p.3643
IFRS 9.IE7-11 Example 1	Ch.51, p.3982	IFRS 9.IG C.10	Ch.46, p.3631
IFRS 9.IE12-17 Example 2	Ch.51, p.3982	IFRS 9.IG D.1.1	Ch.49, p.3844
IFRS 9.IE18-IE23 Example 3	Ch.51, p.3972	IFRS 9.IG D.2.1	Ch.49, p.3848
IFRS 9.IE24-IE28 Example 4	Ch.51, p.3992	IFRS 9.IG D.2.2	Ch.49, p.3848
IFRS 9.IE29-IE39 Example 5	Ch.51, p.4004	IFRS 9.IG D.2.2	Ch.50, p.3881
IFRS 9.IE40-IE42 Example 6	Ch.51, p.3998	IFRS 9.IG D.2.3	Ch.49, p.3853
IFRS 9.IE43-IE47 Example 7	Ch.51, p.3997	IFRS 9.IG E.1.1	Ch.49, p.3859
IFRS 9.IE53-IE57 Example 9	Ch.51, p.3942	IFRS 9.IG E.3.2	Ch.50, p.3900
IFRS 9.IE58-IE65 Example 10	Ch.51, p.4055	IFRS 9.IG E.3.3	Ch.50, p.3902

IFRS 9.IG E.3.4	Ch.50, p.3900
IFRS 9.IG G.2	Ch.40, p.3161
IFRS 9.IG G.2	Ch.54, p.4520
IFRS 9.BCZ2.2	Ch.45, p.3600
IFRS 9.BCZ2.2	Ch.45, p.3601
IFRS 9.BCZ2.2	Ch.51, p.4045
IFRS 9.BCZ2.2	Ch.51, p.4046
IFRS 9.BCZ2.3	Ch.45, p.3600
IFRS 9.BCZ2.3	Ch.49, p.3862
IFRS 9.BCZ2.6	Ch.45, p.3601
IFRS 9.BCZ2.7	Ch.45, p.3601
IFRS 9.BCZ2.12	Ch.45, p.3598
IFRS 9.BCZ2.14	Ch.45, p.3600
IFRS 9.BCZ2.18	Ch.43, p.3474
IFRS 9.BCZ2.18	Ch.45, p.3608
IFRS 9.BCZ2.18	Ch.45, p.3609
IFRS 9.BCZ2.18	Ch.45, p.3610
IFRS 9.BCZ2.24	Ch.45, p.3613
IFRS 9.BCZ2.39	Ch.45, p.3603
IFRS 9.BCZ2.40	Ch.45, p.3603
IFRS 9.BCZ2.41	Ch.45, p.3603
IFRS 9.BCZ2.42	Ch.11, p.827
IFRS 9.BCZ2.42	Ch.45, p.3604
IFRS 9.BCZ3.4-12	Ch.52, p.4138
IFRS 9.BC4.23	Ch.48, p.3790
IFRS 9.BC4.26	Ch.48, p.3817
IFRS 9.BC4.28	Ch.48, p.3818
IFRS 9.BC4.29	Ch.48, p.3818
IFRS 9.BC4.33	Ch.48, p.3818
IFRS 9.BC4.34	Ch.48, p.3818
IFRS 9.BC4.35(d)	Ch.48, p.3822
IFRS 9.BCZ4.61	Ch.48, p.3827
IFRS 9.BCZ4.66	Ch.48, p.3829
IFRS 9.BCZ4.68-70	Ch.48, p.3830
IFRS 9.BCZ4.70	Ch.48, p.3830
IFRS 9.BCZ4.74-76	Ch.48, p.3826
IFRS 9.BCZ4.92	Ch.46, p.3629
IFRS 9.BCZ4.92	Ch.46, p.3619
IFRS 9.BCZ4.94	Ch.46, p.3643
IFRS 9.BCZ4.97	Ch.46, p.3636
IFRS 9.BCZ4.99	Ch.46, p.3651
IFRS 9.BCZ4.100	Ch.46, p.3651
IFRS 9.BCZ4.100-101	Ch.46, p.3652
IFRS 9.BCZ4.105	Ch.46, p.3653
IFRS 9.BCZ4.106	Ch.46, p.3652
IFRS 9.BC4.117	Ch.48, p.3834
IFRS 9.BC4.150	Ch.48, p.3774
IFRS 9.BC4.150	Ch.50, p.3871
IFRS 9.BC4.158	Ch.48, p.3790
IFRS 9.BC4.171	Ch.48, p.3790
IFRS 9.BC4.172	Ch.48, p.3790
IFRS 9.BC4.178	Ch.48, p.3793
IFRS 9.BC4.180	Ch.48, p.3791
IFRS 9.BC4.180	Ch.48, p.3802
IFRS 9.BC4.182(a)	Ch.48, p.3791
IFRS 9.BC4.182(b)	Ch.48, p.3791
IFRS 9.BC4.182(b)	Ch.48, p.3792
IFRS 9.BC4.182(b)	Ch.48, p.3793
IFRS 9.BC4.193	Ch.48, p.3806
IFRS 9.BC4.194	Ch.48, p.3807
IFRS 9.BC4.206(a)	Ch.48, p.3821
IFRS 9.BC4.225	Ch.48, p.3805
IFRS 9.BC4.232	Ch.48, p.3805
IFRS 9.BC4.252	Ch.52, p.4163
IFRS 9.BC4.252-253	Ch.50, p.3894
IFRS 9.BC4.253	Ch.52, p.4163
IFRS 9.BC5.13	Ch.50, p.3878
IFRS 9.BC5.16	Ch.50, p.3878
IFRS 9.BC5.18	Ch.50, p.3878
IFRS 9.BC5.21	Ch.48, p.3830
IFRS 9.BC5.25(a)	Ch.48, p.3832
IFRS 9.BC5.25(c)	Ch.48, p.3831
IFRS 9.BC5.40	Ch.48, p.3776
IFRS 9.BC5.41	Ch.48, p.3776
IFRS 9.BCZ5.67	Ch.50, p.3881
IFRS 9.BC5.75	Ch.51, p.4070
IFRS 9.BC5.78	Ch.51, p.4071
IFRS 9.BC5.87	Ch.51, p.3912
IFRS 9.BC5.89	Ch.51, p.3912
IFRS 9.BC5.92	Ch.51, p.3912
IFRS 9.BC5.93	Ch.51, p.3913
IFRS 9.BC5.95	Ch.51, p.3913
IFRS 9.BC5.96	Ch.51, p.3913
IFRS 9.BC5.104	Ch.51, p.3929
IFRS 9.BC5.111	Ch.51, p.3913
IFRS 9.BC5.112	Ch.51, p.3913
IFRS 9.BC5.114	Ch.51, p.3915
IFRS 9.BC5.116	Ch.51, p.3915
IFRS 9.BC5.123	Ch.51, p.3976
IFRS 9.BC5.135	Ch.51, p.3937
IFRS 9.BC5.141	Ch.51, p.3926
IFRS 9.BC5.154	Ch.32, p.2398
IFRS 9.BC5.157	Ch.51, p.3970
IFRS 9.BC5.157	Ch.51, p.3975
IFRS 9.BC5.160	Ch.51, p.3971
IFRS 9.BC5.161	Ch.51, p.3971
IFRS 9.BC5.162	Ch.51, p.3971
IFRS 9.BC5.163	Ch.51, p.3971
IFRS 9.BC5.164	Ch.51, p.3971
IFRS 9.BC5.165	Ch.51, p.3971
IFRS 9.BC5.168	Ch.51, p.3997
IFRS 9.BC5.171	Ch.51, p.3987
IFRS 9.BC5.172	Ch.51, p.3987
IFRS 9.BC5.178	Ch.51, p.3995
IFRS 9.BC5.181	Ch.51, p.3989
IFRS 9.BC5.182	Ch.51, p.3989
IFRS 9.BC5.183	Ch.51, p.3989
IFRS 9.BC5.184	Ch.51, p.3989
IFRS 9.BC5.188	Ch.51, p.3990
IFRS 9.BC5.190	Ch.51, p.3980
IFRS 9.BC5.192	Ch.51, p.3980
IFRS 9.BC5.199	Ch.51, p.3937
IFRS 9.BC5.214	Ch.51, p.3930
IFRS 9.BC5.216	Ch.52, p.4099
IFRS 9.BC5.217	Ch.51, p.3930
IFRS 9.BC5.225	Ch.51, p.3929

IFRS 9.BC5.227	Ch.52, p.4099	IFRS 9.BC6.380	Ch.54, p.4490
IFRS 9.BC5.248	Ch.51, p.3935	IFRS 9.BC6.387	Ch.53, p.4329
IFRS 9.BC5.249	Ch.51, p.3935	IFRS 9.BC6.398	Ch.53, p.4335
IFRS 9.BC5.252	Ch.51, p.3935	IFRS 9.BC6.399	Ch.53, p.4333
IFRS 9.BC5.252	Ch.51, p.3938	IFRS 9.BC6.416	Ch.53, p.4337
IFRS 9.BC5.254-261	Ch.51, p.4053	IFRS 9.BC6.422	Ch.53, p.4336
IFRS 9.BC5.259	Ch.51, p.4054	IFRS 9.BC6.435	Ch.53, p.4211
IFRS 9.BC5.260	Ch.51, p.4064	IFRS 9.BC6.436	Ch.53, p.4211
IFRS 9.BC5.260	Ch.51, p.4061	IFRS 9.BC6.438	Ch.53, p.4212
IFRS 9.BC5.260	Ch.51, p.3944	IFRS 9.BC6.439	Ch.53, p.4212
IFRS 9.BC5.265	Ch.51, p.3938	IFRS 9.BC6.455	Ch.53, p.4213
IFRS 9.BC5.281	Ch.51, p.3964	IFRS 9.BC6.457	Ch.53, p.4380
IFRS 9.BC5.306	Ch.50, p.3898	IFRS 9.BC6.461	Ch.53, p.4380
IFRS 9.BC5.309	Ch.50, p.3899	IFRS 9.BC6.470	Ch.53, p.4387
IFRS 9.BC5.311	Ch.50, p.3899	IFRS 9.BC6.470	Ch.53, p.4192
IFRS 9.BC5.312	Ch.50, p.3899	IFRS 9.BC6.491	Ch.53, p.4387
IFRS 9.BC5.318	Ch.50, p.3899	IFRS 9.BC6.504	Ch.53, p.4387
IFRS 9.BC6.327	Ch.53, p.4354	IFRS 9.BC6.517	Ch.53, p.4192
IFRS 9.BC6.330	Ch.53, p.4354	IFRS 9.BC6.560	Ch.53, p.4367
IFRS 9.BC6.82	Ch.53, p.4187	IFRS 9.BC6.567	Ch.53, p.4367
IFRS 9.BC6.91-95	Ch.53, p.4385	IFRS 9.BC6.568	Ch.53, p.4367
IFRS 9.BC6.93-95	Ch.53, p.4394	IFRS 9.BC6.575	Ch.53, p.4367
IFRS 9.BC6.93-95	Ch.53, p.4187	IFRS 9.BC6.594	Ch.53, p.4368
IFRS 9.BC6.94-95	Ch.53, p.4265	IFRS 9.BC6.619	Ch.53, p.4375
IFRS 9.BC6.97	Ch.53, p.4394	IFRS 9.BC6.647	Ch.53, p.4374
IFRS 9.BC6.97-101	Ch.53, p.4274	IFRS 9.BC6.587-593	Ch.53, p.4368
IFRS 9.BC6.98	Ch.53, p.4275	IFRS 9.BC6.616-619	Ch.53, p.4371
IFRS 9.BC6.98	Ch.53, p.4381	IFRS 9.BC7.44-51	Ch.53, p.4393
IFRS 9.BC6.98	Ch.53, p.4394	IFRS 9.BC7.49	Ch.53, p.4393
IFRS 9.BC6.100(a)	Ch.53, p.4381	IFRS 9.BC7.49	Ch.53, p.4392
IFRS 9.BC6.100(a)	Ch.53, p.4275	IFRS 9.BC7.52	Ch.5, p.249
IFRS 9.BC6.100(b)	Ch.53, p.4394	IFRS 9.BC7.52	Ch.5, p.252
IFRS 9.BC6.100(b)	Ch.53, p.4275	IFRS 9.BC7.88	Ch.53, p.4377
IFRS 9.BC6.104	Ch.54, p.4412		
IFRS 9.BC6.104	Ch.53, p.4386		
IFRS 9.BC6.104	Ch.53, p.4390	**IFRS 10**	
IFRS 9.BC6.117-122	Ch.53, p.4238		
IFRS 9.BC6.142-150	Ch.53, p.4250	IFRS 10.1	Ch.6, p.394
IFRS 9.BC6.151	Ch.53, p.4236	IFRS 10.2	Ch.6, p.394
IFRS 9.BC6.153	Ch.53, p.4236	IFRS 10.2	Ch.27, p.2035
IFRS 9.BC6.167	Ch.53, p.4233	IFRS 10.3	Ch.6, p.394
IFRS 9.BC6.174	Ch.53, p.4193	IFRS 10.4	Ch.5, p.313
IFRS 9.BC6.331	Ch.53, p.4354	IFRS 10.4	Ch.6, p.394
IFRS 9.BC6.176	Ch.53, p.4198	IFRS 10.4	Ch.8, p.577
IFRS 9.BC6.176	Ch.53, p.4191	IFRS 10.4-4B	Ch.27, p.2035
IFRS 9.BC6.200	Ch.53, p.4361	IFRS 10.4(a)	Ch.6, p.395
IFRS 9.BC6.226-228	Ch.53, p.4206	IFRS 10.4(a)	Ch.8, p.577
IFRS 9.BC6.238	Ch.53, p.4281	IFRS 10.4A	Ch.6, p.398
IFRS 9.BC6.269	Ch.53, p.4282	IFRS 10.4B	Ch.6, p.399
IFRS 9.BC6.297	Ch.53, p.4330	IFRS 10.5	Ch.6, p.405
IFRS 9.BC6.301	Ch.53, p.4350	IFRS 10.6	Ch.6, p.405
IFRS 9.BC6.303	Ch.53, p.4347	IFRS 10.6	Ch.9, p.659
IFRS 9.BC6.310	Ch.53, p.4350	IFRS 10.7	Ch.6, p.405
IFRS 9.BC6.324	Ch.53, p.4354	IFRS 10.7	Ch.6, p.410
IFRS 9.BC6.332-337	Ch.52, p.4102	IFRS 10.7	Ch.6, p.436
IFRS 9.BC6.333	Ch.52, p.4167	IFRS 10.7	Ch.6, p.439
IFRS 9.BC6.335	Ch.52, p.4155	IFRS 10.7	Ch.6, p.445
IFRS 9.BC6.380	Ch.54, p.4421	IFRS 10.7	Ch.7, p.508

IFRS 10.8	Ch.6, p.406	IFRS 10.24	Ch.7, p.546
IFRS 10.8	Ch.6, p.410	IFRS 10.24	Ch.7, p.547
IFRS 10.8	Ch.6, p.467	IFRS 10.24	Ch.7, p.548
IFRS 10.8	Ch.7, p.508	IFRS 10.24	Ch.7, p.549
IFRS 10.8	Ch.52, p.4153	IFRS 10.25	Ch.6, p.405
IFRS 10.9	Ch.6, p.406	IFRS 10.25	Ch.6, p.488
IFRS 10.10	Ch.6, p.408	IFRS 10.25	Ch.7, p.509
IFRS 10.10	Ch.6, p.409	IFRS 10.25	Ch.7, p.514
IFRS 10.10	Ch.6, p.432	IFRS 10.25	Ch.7, p.518
IFRS 10.11	Ch.6, p.413	IFRS 10.25	Ch.7, p.519
IFRS 10.11	Ch.6, p.434	IFRS 10.25	Ch.7, p.520
IFRS 10.12	Ch.6, p.415	IFRS 10.25	Ch.7, p.565
IFRS 10.13	Ch.6, p.409	IFRS 10.25	Ch.11, p.857
IFRS 10.14	Ch.6, p.409	IFRS 10.25	Ch.12, p.933
IFRS 10.14	Ch.6, p.414	IFRS 10.26	Ch.7, p.509
IFRS 10.14	Ch.6, p.416	IFRS 10.26	Ch.7, p.514
IFRS 10.15	Ch.6, p.439	IFRS 10.26	Ch.7, p.518
IFRS 10.16	Ch.6, p.439	IFRS 10.26	Ch.7, p.519
IFRS 10.17	Ch.6, p.445	IFRS 10.26	Ch.7, p.520
IFRS 10.18	Ch.6, p.445	IFRS 10.26	Ch.7, p.524
IFRS 10.18	Ch.6, p.446	IFRS 10.26	Ch.7, p.525
IFRS 10.19	Ch.5, p.335	IFRS 10.26	Ch.7, p.526
IFRS 10.19	Ch.7, p.497	IFRS 10.26	Ch.7, p.527
IFRS 10.19	Ch.55, p.4589	IFRS 10.26	Ch.7, p.531
IFRS 10.20	Ch.6, p.399	IFRS 10.26	Ch.7, p.565
IFRS 10.20	Ch.6, p.405	IFRS 10.27	Ch.6, p.473
IFRS 10.20	Ch.7, p.497	IFRS 10.28	Ch.6, p.473
IFRS 10.20	Ch.7, p.503	IFRS 10.29	Ch.6, p.473
IFRS 10.20	Ch.8, p.578	IFRS 10.30	Ch.6, p.474
IFRS 10.20	Ch.27, p.2035	IFRS 10.30	Ch.6, p.488
IFRS 10.21	Ch.7, p.497	IFRS 10.31	Ch.5, p.313
IFRS 10.21	Ch.7, p.498	IFRS 10.31	Ch.6, p.485
IFRS 10.21	Ch.7, p.499	IFRS 10.31	Ch.8, p.583
IFRS 10.21	Ch.7, p.501	IFRS 10.31	Ch.45, p.3592
IFRS 10.21	Ch.7, p.502	IFRS 10.31-33	Ch.7, p.497
IFRS 10.21	Ch.7, p.503	IFRS 10.31-33	Ch.7, p.540
IFRS 10.21	Ch.7, p.523	IFRS 10.32	Ch.5, p.313
IFRS 10.21	Ch.7, p.547	IFRS 10.32	Ch.6, p.475
IFRS 10.21	Ch.7, p.549	IFRS 10.32	Ch.6, p.485
IFRS 10.21	Ch.7, p.550	IFRS 10.33	Ch.5, p.313
IFRS 10.22	Ch.7, p.498	IFRS 10.33	Ch.6, p.489
IFRS 10.22	Ch.7, p.545	IFRS 10 Appendix A	Ch.5, p.285
IFRS 10.22	Ch.11, p.840	IFRS 10 Appendix A	Ch.5, p.313
IFRS 10.22	Ch.11, p.867	IFRS 10 Appendix A	Ch.6, p.394
IFRS 10.23	Ch.5, p.262	IFRS 10 Appendix A	Ch.6, p.405
IFRS 10.23	Ch.7, p.498	IFRS 10 Appendix A	Ch.6, p.416
IFRS 10.23	Ch.7, p.533	IFRS 10 Appendix A	Ch.7, p.497
IFRS 10.23	Ch.7, p.538	IFRS 10 Appendix A	Ch.7, p.498
IFRS 10.23	Ch.8, p.623	IFRS 10 Appendix A	Ch.7, p.540
IFRS 10.23	Ch.10, p.788	IFRS 10 Appendix A	Ch.7, p.544
IFRS 10.23	Ch.11, p.868	IFRS 10 Appendix A	Ch.8, p.577
IFRS 10.23	Ch.20, p.1606	IFRS 10 Appendix A	Ch.12, p.898
IFRS 10.23	Ch.33, p.2600	IFRS 10 Appendix A	Ch.13, p.951
IFRS 10.23	Ch.47, p.3741	IFRS 10 Appendix A	Ch.13, p.959
IFRS 10.24	Ch.7, p.498	IFRS 10 Appendix A	Ch.27, p.2035
IFRS 10.24	Ch.7, p.499	IFRS 10 Appendix A	Ch.39, p.3102
IFRS 10.24	Ch.7, p.533	IFRS 10 Appendix A	Ch.39, p.3104
IFRS 10.24	Ch.7, p.538	IFRS 10 Appendix A	Ch.40, p.3174

IFRS 10.B1	Ch.6, p.457	IFRS 10.B35	Ch.6, p.421
IFRS 10.B2	Ch.6, p.406	IFRS 10.B36	Ch.6, p.421
IFRS 10.B2	Ch.6, p.410	IFRS 10.B37	Ch.6, p.421
IFRS 10.B2	Ch.6, p.436	IFRS 10.B38	Ch.6, p.421
IFRS 10.B3	Ch.6, p.406	IFRS 10.B39	Ch.6, p.433
IFRS 10.B3	Ch.12, p.897	IFRS 10.B40	Ch.6, p.433
IFRS 10.B4	Ch.6, p.406	IFRS 10.B41	Ch.6, p.423
IFRS 10.B5	Ch.6, p.407	IFRS 10.B42	Ch.6, p.423
IFRS 10.B6	Ch.6, p.406	IFRS 10.B42	Ch.6, p.429
IFRS 10.B6	Ch.6, p.408	IFRS 10.B43	Ch.6, p.424
IFRS 10.B6	Ch.6, p.409	IFRS 10.B43 Example 4	Ch.6, p.424
IFRS 10.B6	Ch.6, p.420	IFRS 10.B43 Example 5	Ch.6, p.433
IFRS 10.B7	Ch.6, p.408	IFRS 10.B44	Ch.6, p.424
IFRS 10.B8	Ch.6, p.408	IFRS 10.B44 Example 6	Ch.6, p.424
IFRS 10.B8	Ch.6, p.441	IFRS 10.B45	Ch.6, p.425
IFRS 10.B9	Ch.6, p.408	IFRS 10.B45 Example 7	Ch.6, p.425
IFRS 10.B10	Ch.6, p.409	IFRS 10.B45 Example 8	Ch.6, p.426
IFRS 10.B11-B12	Ch.6, p.409	IFRS 10.B46	Ch.6, p.423
IFRS 10.B13	Ch.6, p.409	IFRS 10.B47	Ch.6, p.428
IFRS 10.B13 Example 1	Ch.6, p.409	IFRS 10.B47	Ch.6, p.430
IFRS 10.B13 Example 1	Ch.12, p.898	IFRS 10.B48	Ch.6, p.428
IFRS 10.B13 Example 2	Ch.6, p.410	IFRS 10.B49	Ch.6, p.429
IFRS 10.B14	Ch.6, p.413	IFRS 10.B50	Ch.6, p.429
IFRS 10.B14	Ch.6, p.430	IFRS 10.B50 Example 9	Ch.6, p.431
IFRS 10.B15	Ch.6, p.414	IFRS 10.B50 Example 10	Ch.6, p.429
IFRS 10.B16	Ch.6, p.414	IFRS 10.B51	Ch.6, p.438
IFRS 10.B17	Ch.6, p.434	IFRS 10.B52	Ch.6, p.434
IFRS 10.B18	Ch.6, p.437	IFRS 10.B53	Ch.6, p.435
IFRS 10.B19	Ch.6, p.437	IFRS 10.B53 Example 11	Ch.6, p.436
IFRS 10.B19	Ch.6, p.440	IFRS 10.B53 Example 12	Ch.6, p.436
IFRS 10.B20	Ch.6, p.420	IFRS 10.B54	Ch.6, p.420
IFRS 10.B20	Ch.6, p.438	IFRS 10.B54	Ch.6, p.436
IFRS 10.B20	Ch.6, p.440	IFRS 10.B55	Ch.6, p.439
IFRS 10.B21	Ch.6, p.437	IFRS 10.B56	Ch.6, p.439
IFRS 10.B22	Ch.6, p.414	IFRS 10.B56	Ch.6, p.440
IFRS 10.B22	Ch.6, p.430	IFRS 10.B56	Ch.13, p.947
IFRS 10.B23	Ch.6, p.414	IFRS 10.B56	Ch.13, p.948
IFRS 10.B23	Ch.6, p.451	IFRS 10.B57	Ch.6, p.439
IFRS 10.B23(a)	Ch.6, p.431	IFRS 10.B57	Ch.6, p.444
IFRS 10.B23(a)(ii)	Ch.6, p.430	IFRS 10.B57(c)	Ch.6, p.444
IFRS 10.B23(a)(vi)	Ch.6, p.451	IFRS 10.B58	Ch.6, p.446
IFRS 10.B23(b)	Ch.6, p.450	IFRS 10.B58	Ch.6, p.447
IFRS 10.B24	Ch.6, p.415	IFRS 10.B59	Ch.6, p.447
IFRS 10.B24	Ch.6, p.430	IFRS 10.B59	Ch.6, p.454
IFRS 10.B24	Ch.6, p.432	IFRS 10.B60	Ch.6, p.447
IFRS 10.B24 Example 3-3D	Ch.6, p.415	IFRS 10.B60	Ch.6, p.457
IFRS 10.B25	Ch.6, p.416	IFRS 10.B61	Ch.6, p.447
IFRS 10.B26	Ch.6, p.416	IFRS 10.B62	Ch.6, p.448
IFRS 10.B26-27	Ch.12, p.898	IFRS 10.B63	Ch.6, p.448
IFRS 10.B27	Ch.6, p.416	IFRS 10.B64	Ch.6, p.449
IFRS 10.B28	Ch.6, p.416	IFRS 10.B64	Ch.6, p.451
IFRS 10.B29	Ch.6, p.417	IFRS 10.B65	Ch.6, p.450
IFRS 10.B30	Ch.6, p.418	IFRS 10.B66	Ch.6, p.449
IFRS 10.B31	Ch.6, p.418	IFRS 10.B67	Ch.6, p.450
IFRS 10.B32	Ch.6, p.418	IFRS 10.B68	Ch.6, p.452
IFRS 10.B33	Ch.6, p.418	IFRS 10.B69	Ch.6, p.453
IFRS 10.B34	Ch.6, p.420	IFRS 10.B70	Ch.6, p.453
IFRS 10.B34	Ch.6, p.421	IFRS 10.B71	Ch.6, p.454

IFRS 10.B72	Ch.6, p.455	IFRS 10.B85U	Ch.6, p.481
IFRS 10.B72 Example 13	Ch.6, p.449	IFRS 10.B85V	Ch.6, p.481
IFRS 10.B72 Example 13	Ch.6, p.453	IFRS 10.B85W	Ch.6, p.482
IFRS 10.B72 Example 13	Ch.6, p.457	IFRS 10.B86	Ch.7, p.498
IFRS 10.B72 Example 14	Ch.6, p.453	IFRS 10.B86	Ch.11, p.846
IFRS 10.B72 Example 14	Ch.6, p.457	IFRS 10.B86	Ch.11, p.847
IFRS 10.B72 Example 14-14A	Ch.6, p.449	IFRS 10.B86	Ch.40, p.3174
IFRS 10.B72 Example 14A	Ch.6, p.458	IFRS 10.B86	Ch.53, p.4248
IFRS 10.B72 Example 14B	Ch.6, p.458	IFRS 10.B86(c)	Ch.7, p.501
IFRS 10.B72 Example 14C	Ch.6, p.458	IFRS 10.B86(c)	Ch.7, p.502
IFRS 10.B72 Example 15	Ch.6, p.450	IFRS 10.B87	Ch.7, p.497
IFRS 10.B72 Example 15	Ch.6, p.453	IFRS 10.B87	Ch.7, p.503
IFRS 10.B72 Example 15	Ch.6, p.459	IFRS 10.B87	Ch.10, p.780
IFRS 10.B72 Example 16	Ch.6, p.460	IFRS 10.B88	Ch.7, p.497
IFRS 10.B72 Example 16	Ch.13, p.982	IFRS 10.B88	Ch.7, p.498
IFRS 10.B73	Ch.6, p.462	IFRS 10.B88	Ch.7, p.503
IFRS 10.B73	Ch.6, p.463	IFRS 10.B88	Ch.7, p.523
IFRS 10.B74	Ch.6, p.462	IFRS 10.B88	Ch.10, p.783
IFRS 10.B74	Ch.6, p.463	IFRS 10.B88	Ch.40, p.3174
IFRS 10.B75	Ch.6, p.462	IFRS 10.B89	Ch.7, p.499
IFRS 10.B75(f)	Ch.6, p.463	IFRS 10.B89	Ch.7, p.547
IFRS 10.B76	Ch.6, p.464	IFRS 10.B89	Ch.7, p.549
IFRS 10.B77	Ch.6, p.464	IFRS 10.B90	Ch.7, p.499
IFRS 10.B78	Ch.6, p.467	IFRS 10.B90	Ch.7, p.547
IFRS 10.B79	Ch.6, p.467	IFRS 10.B90	Ch.7, p.549
IFRS 10.B80	Ch.6, p.467	IFRS 10.B91	Ch.7, p.499
IFRS 10.B80	Ch.7, p.508	IFRS 10.B91	Ch.7, p.550
IFRS 10.B81	Ch.6, p.467	IFRS 10.B91	Ch.45, p.3592
IFRS 10.B82	Ch.6, p.467	IFRS 10.B92	Ch.7, p.502
IFRS 10.B82	Ch.6, p.471	IFRS 10.B93	Ch.7, p.503
IFRS 10.B83	Ch.6, p.467	IFRS 10.B94	Ch.5, p.262
IFRS 10.B84	Ch.6, p.467	IFRS 10.B94	Ch.7, p.498
IFRS 10.B85	Ch.6, p.468	IFRS 10.B94	Ch.7, p.499
IFRS 10.B85A	Ch.6, p.473	IFRS 10.B94	Ch.7, p.546
IFRS 10.B85A	Ch.6, p.485	IFRS 10.B94	Ch.7, p.547
IFRS 10.B85B	Ch.6, p.474	IFRS 10.B94	Ch.7, p.548
IFRS 10.B85C	Ch.6, p.475	IFRS 10.B94	Ch.7, p.549
IFRS 10.B85D	Ch.6, p.475	IFRS 10.B94	Ch.11, p.840
IFRS 10.B85E	Ch.6, p.475	IFRS 10.B94	Ch.11, p.867
IFRS 10.B85F	Ch.6, p.477	IFRS 10.B95	Ch.7, p.547
IFRS 10.B85G	Ch.6, p.477	IFRS 10.B96	Ch.5, p.262
IFRS 10.B85H	Ch.6, p.477	IFRS 10.B96	Ch.7, p.533
IFRS 10.B85H	Ch.6, p.485	IFRS 10.B96	Ch.7, p.538
IFRS 10.B85I	Ch.6, p.478	IFRS 10.B96	Ch.7, p.548
IFRS 10.B85J	Ch.6, p.479	IFRS 10.B96	Ch.10, p.788
IFRS 10.B85K	Ch.6, p.479	IFRS 10.B96	Ch.11, p.868
IFRS 10.B85L	Ch.6, p.479	IFRS 10.B96	Ch.33, p.2600
IFRS 10.B85L	Ch.12, p.892	IFRS 10.B97	Ch.7, p.524
IFRS 10.B85L	Ch.12, p.929	IFRS 10.B97	Ch.7, p.525
IFRS 10.B85L(b)	Ch.11, p.820	IFRS 10.B97	Ch.9, p.715
IFRS 10.B85M	Ch.6, p.479	IFRS 10.B97-B99	Ch.5, p.262
IFRS 10.B85N	Ch.6, p.473	IFRS 10.B98	Ch.7, p.509
IFRS 10.B85O	Ch.6, p.480	IFRS 10.B98	Ch.7, p.514
IFRS 10.B85P	Ch.6, p.480	IFRS 10.B98	Ch.7, p.518
IFRS 10.B85Q	Ch.6, p.480	IFRS 10.B98	Ch.7, p.565
IFRS 10.B85R	Ch.6, p.480	IFRS 10.B98(a)	Ch.7, p.527
IFRS 10.B85S	Ch.6, p.480	IFRS 10.B98(b)	Ch.7, p.531
IFRS 10.B85T	Ch.6, p.481	IFRS 10.B98(b)(i)	Ch.45, p.3605

IFRS 10.B98(d)	Ch.7, p.527	IFRS 10.BC240F	Ch.6, p.475
IFRS 10.B99	Ch.7, p.509	IFRS 10.BC240H	Ch.6, p.476
IFRS 10.B99	Ch.7, p.518	IFRS 10.BC242	Ch.6, p.478
IFRS 10.B99	Ch.7, p.526	IFRS 10.BC243	Ch.6, p.479
IFRS 10.B99	Ch.7, p.527	IFRS 10.BC248	Ch.6, p.477
IFRS 10.B99	Ch.7, p.565	IFRS 10.BC250	Ch.6, p.479
IFRS 10.B99A	Ch.7, p.514	IFRS 10.BC251	Ch.6, p.479
IFRS 10.B99A	Ch.7, p.519	IFRS 10.BC252	Ch.6, p.478
IFRS 10.B99A	Ch.7, p.520	IFRS 10.BC260	Ch.6, p.480
IFRS 10.B99A	Ch.7, p.565	IFRS 10.BC261	Ch.6, p.481
IFRS 10.B100	Ch.6, p.489	IFRS 10.BC263	Ch.6, p.481
IFRS 10.B101	Ch.6, p.488	IFRS 10.BC264	Ch.6, p.481
IFRS 10.C1A	Ch.6, p.393	IFRS 10.BC266	Ch.6, p.481
IFRS 10.C1B	Ch.6, p.393	IFRS 10.BC271	Ch.8, p.589
IFRS 10.C1B	Ch.6, p.472	IFRS 10.BC272	Ch.6, p.476
IFRS 10.C1C	Ch.7, p.514	IFRS 10.BC276-278	Ch.6, p.489
IFRS 10.C1C	Ch.7, p.565	IFRS 10.BC280	Ch.6, p.489
IFRS 10.C1D	Ch.6, p.393	IFRS 10.BC281	Ch.6, p.489
IFRS 10.C1D	Ch.6, p.397	IFRS 10.BC282	Ch.6, p.489
IFRS 10.C1D	Ch.6, p.473	IFRS 10.BC283	Ch.6, p.489
IFRS 10.IE1-IE6	Ch.6, p.483	IFRS 10.BC298-BC300	Ch.6, p.472
IFRS 10.IE7-IE8	Ch.6, p.483		
IFRS 10.IE12-IE15	Ch.6, p.485		

IFRS 11

IFRS 10.BCZ18	Ch.6, p.396		
IFRS 10.BCZ21	Ch.6, p.471	IFRS 11.1	Ch.12, p.892
IFRS 10.BC28A-B	Ch.6, p.397	IFRS 11.2	Ch.12, p.892
IFRS 10.BC28A-28B	Ch.8, p.578	IFRS 11.3	Ch.12, p.892
IFRS 10.BC28D	Ch.6, p.398	IFRS 11.4	Ch.12, p.891
IFRS 10.BC37-BC39	Ch.6, p.445	IFRS 11.4	Ch.43, p.3403
IFRS 10.BC63	Ch.6, p.456	IFRS 11.5	Ch.12, p.891
IFRS 10.BC66	Ch.6, p.442	IFRS 11.5	Ch.43, p.3543
IFRS 10.BC69	Ch.6, p.406	IFRS 11.5(a)	Ch.43, p.3404
IFRS 10.BC124	Ch.6, p.431	IFRS 11.6	Ch.12, p.891
IFRS 10.BC124	Ch.6, p.469	IFRS 11.6	Ch.12, p.904
IFRS 10.BC130	Ch.6, p.455	IFRS 11.7	Ch.12, p.895
IFRS 10.BC132	Ch.6, p.454	IFRS 11.7	Ch.43, p.3404
IFRS 10.BC152	Ch.6, p.468	IFRS 11.7	Ch.43, p.3543
IFRS 10.BCZ162-164	Ch.7, p.548	IFRS 11.8	Ch.12, p.898
IFRS 10.BCZ165	Ch.7, p.548	IFRS 11.8	Ch.43, p.3404
IFRS 10.BCZ168	Ch.40, p.3175	IFRS 11.9	Ch.12, p.901
IFRS 10.BCZ173	Ch.7, p.533	IFRS 11.10	Ch.12, p.897
IFRS 10.BCZ173	Ch.33, p.2600	IFRS 11.10	Ch.12, p.901
IFRS 10.BCZ175	Ch.7, p.500	IFRS 11.11	Ch.12, p.895
IFRS 10.BCZ180	Ch.7, p.509	IFRS 11.11	Ch.13, p.953
IFRS 10.BCZ182	Ch.7, p.512	IFRS 11.12	Ch.12, p.896
IFRS 10.BCZ185	Ch.7, p.524	IFRS 11.13	Ch.12, p.897
IFRS 10.BCZ186	Ch.7, p.525	IFRS 11.13	Ch.12, p.931
IFRS 10.BC190I	Ch.7, p.518	IFRS 11.14	Ch.12, p.904
IFRS 10.BC190I	Ch.7, p.565	IFRS 11.15	Ch.12, p.904
IFRS 10.BC190J	Ch.7, p.520	IFRS 11.16	Ch.12, p.904
IFRS 10.BC190L-190O	Ch.7, p.565	IFRS 11.17	Ch.12, p.906
IFRS 10.BC190M-190N	Ch.7, p.565	IFRS 11.18	Ch.12, p.894
IFRS 10.BC190N	Ch.18, p.1429	IFRS 11.19	Ch.12, p.931
IFRS 10.BC190O	Ch.7, p.514	IFRS 11.20	Ch.8, p.580
IFRS 10.BC190O	Ch.18, p.1429	IFRS 11.20	Ch.12, p.923
IFRS 10.BC239	Ch.6, p.475	IFRS 11.20	Ch.27, p.2037
IFRS 10.BC240B	Ch.6, p.476	IFRS 11.20	Ch.40, p.3180
IFRS 10.BC240E	Ch.6, p.475		

IFRS 11.20-23	Ch.5, p.375	IFRS 11.B15	Ch.12, p.906
IFRS 11.20-23	Ch.12, p.929	IFRS 11.B16	Ch.12, p.923
IFRS 11.21	Ch.12, p.923	IFRS 11.B17	Ch.12, p.923
IFRS 11.21	Ch.27, p.2037	IFRS 11.B18	Ch.12, p.923
IFRS 11.21	Ch.43, p.3450	IFRS 11.B19	Ch.12, p.906
IFRS 11.21A	Ch.12, p.936	IFRS 11.B20	Ch.12, p.906
IFRS 11.21A	Ch.40, p.3181	IFRS 11.B21	Ch.12, p.907
IFRS 11.22	Ch.7, p.523	IFRS 11.B22	Ch.12, p.908
IFRS 11.22	Ch.12, p.928	IFRS 11.B23	Ch.12, p.908
IFRS 11.23	Ch.8, p.580	IFRS 11.B24	Ch.12, p.907
IFRS 11.23	Ch.12, p.927	IFRS 11.B25	Ch.12, p.909
IFRS 11.23	Ch.18, p.1430	IFRS 11.B26	Ch.12, p.909
IFRS 11.23	Ch.43, p.3399	IFRS 11.B27	Ch.12, p.908
IFRS 11.23	Ch.43, p.3407	IFRS 11.B27	Ch.12, p.910
IFRS 11.23	Ch.43, p.3408	IFRS 11.B27	Ch.12, p.913
IFRS 11.24	Ch.12, p.929	IFRS 11.B28	Ch.12, p.910
IFRS 11.25	Ch.12, p.929	IFRS 11.B29	Ch.12, p.911
IFRS 11.25	Ch.43, p.3408	IFRS 11.B30	Ch.12, p.911
IFRS 11.26	Ch.8, p.580	IFRS 11.B31	Ch.12, p.911
IFRS 11.26(a)	Ch.12, p.929	IFRS 11.B31-B32	Ch.12, p.914
IFRS 11.26(b)	Ch.12, p.930	IFRS 11.B31-B32	Ch.12, p.916
IFRS 11.27(a)	Ch.12, p.929	IFRS 11.B32	Ch.12, p.912
IFRS 11.27(b)	Ch.12, p.930	IFRS 11.B32	Ch.12, p.916
IFRS 11 Appendix A	Ch.6, p.410	IFRS 11.B32-B33	Ch.12, p.914
IFRS 11 Appendix A	Ch.6, p.433	IFRS 11.B32 Example 5	Ch.12, p.911
IFRS 11 Appendix A	Ch.12, p.891	IFRS 11.B33A	Ch.12, p.936
IFRS 11 Appendix A	Ch.12, p.892	IFRS 11.B33B	Ch.12, p.936
IFRS 11 Appendix A	Ch.12, p.893	IFRS 11.B33C	Ch.12, p.936
IFRS 11 Appendix A	Ch.12, p.895	IFRS 11.B33CA	Ch.12, p.937
IFRS 11 Appendix A	Ch.12, p.906	IFRS 11.B33D	Ch.12, p.936
IFRS 11 Appendix A	Ch.13, p.951	IFRS 11.B34	Ch.7, p.523
IFRS 11 Appendix A	Ch.39, p.3102	IFRS 11.B34	Ch.12, p.928
IFRS 11 Appendix A	Ch.39, p.3105	IFRS 11.B34	Ch.18, p.1429
IFRS 11 Appendix A	Ch.43, p.3403	IFRS 11.B35	Ch.7, p.523
IFRS 11 Appendix A	Ch.43, p.3404	IFRS 11.B35	Ch.12, p.928
IFRS 11 Appendix A	Ch.43, p.3406	IFRS 11.B36	Ch.12, p.928
IFRS 11 Appendix C	Ch.5, p.322	IFRS 11.B37	Ch.12, p.928
IFRS 11.B2	Ch.10, p.769	IFRS 11.C14	Ch.12, p.897
IFRS 11.B2	Ch.12, p.893	IFRS 11.C14	Ch.12, p.929
IFRS 11.B2	Ch.43, p.3404	IFRS 11.C14	Ch.43, p.3408
IFRS 11.B3	Ch.12, p.893	IFRS 11.IE1	Ch.12, p.917
IFRS 11.B4	Ch.12, p.893	IFRS 11.IE2-IE52	Ch.12, p.917
IFRS 11.B5	Ch.12, p.897	IFRS 11 Examples 1-6	Ch.12, p.917
IFRS 11.B5	Ch.12, p.898	IFRS 11 Example 4	Ch.12, p.909
IFRS 11.B5	Ch.43, p.3404	IFRS 11 Example 5	Ch.12, p.916
IFRS 11.B6	Ch.12, p.901	IFRS 11.BC14	Ch.12, p.897
IFRS 11.B7	Ch.12, p.901	IFRS 11.BC15-18	Ch.12, p.892
IFRS 11.B8	Ch.12, p.902	IFRS 11.BC20	Ch.12, p.894
IFRS 11.B8 Example 1	Ch.12, p.902	IFRS 11.BC24	Ch.12, p.891
IFRS 11.B8 Example 2	Ch.12, p.902	IFRS 11.BC25	Ch.12, p.891
IFRS 11.B8 Example 3	Ch.12, p.902	IFRS 11.BC27	Ch.12, p.907
IFRS 11.B9	Ch.12, p.901	IFRS 11.BC28	Ch.12, p.891
IFRS 11.B9	Ch.43, p.3404	IFRS 11.BC29	Ch.12, p.906
IFRS 11.B10	Ch.12, p.896	IFRS 11.BC31	Ch.12, p.907
IFRS 11.B10	Ch.12, p.903	IFRS 11.BC32	Ch.12, p.907
IFRS 11.B11	Ch.12, p.897	IFRS 11.BC35	Ch.12, p.894
IFRS 11.B14	Ch.12, p.906	IFRS 11.BC36	Ch.12, p.894
IFRS 11.B14	Ch.12, p.914	IFRS 11.BC38	Ch.12, p.923

IFRS 11.BC43	Ch.12, p.908	IFRS 12.21	Ch.13, p.971
IFRS 11.BC43	Ch.12, p.915	IFRS 12.21A	Ch.13, p.971
IFRS 11.BC45A	Ch.43, p.3417	IFRS 12.22	Ch.13, p.971
IFRS 11.BC45E	Ch.12, p.936	IFRS 12.22	Ch.15, p.1244
IFRS 11.BC45F	Ch.12, p.936	IFRS 12.22(a)	Ch.40, p.3187
IFRS 11.BC45H	Ch.43, p.3417	IFRS 12.24	Ch.13, p.978
IFRS 11.BC45I	Ch.43, p.3417	IFRS 12.25	Ch.13, p.979
		IFRS 12.25A	Ch.13, p.978
		IFRS 12.26	Ch.13, p.979

IFRS 12

IFRS 12.1	Ch.13, p.945	IFRS 12.27	Ch.13, p.982
IFRS 12.2	Ch.13, p.945	IFRS 12.28	Ch.13, p.982
IFRS 12.3	Ch.13, p.946	IFRS 12.29	Ch.13, p.987
IFRS 12.4	Ch.13, p.951	IFRS 12.30	Ch.13, p.989
IFRS 12.5	Ch.13, p.946	IFRS 12.31	Ch.13, p.989
IFRS 12.5A	Ch.4, p.214	IFRS 12 Appendix A	Ch.6, p.407
IFRS 12.5A	Ch.13, p.950	IFRS 12 Appendix A	Ch.6, p.435
IFRS 12.6(a)	Ch.13, p.953	IFRS 12 Appendix A	Ch.13, p.983
IFRS 12.6(b)	Ch.8, p.604	IFRS 12 Appendix A	Ch.13, p.992
IFRS 12.6(b)	Ch.13, p.953	IFRS 12.B3	Ch.13, p.951
IFRS 12.6(c)	Ch.13, p.953	IFRS 12.B4	Ch.13, p.950
IFRS 12.6(d)	Ch.13, p.954	IFRS 12.B5	Ch.13, p.951
IFRS 12.7	Ch.12, p.896	IFRS 12.B6	Ch.13, p.951
IFRS 12.7	Ch.12, p.906	IFRS 12.B7	Ch.13, p.947
IFRS 12.7	Ch.13, p.954	IFRS 12.B8	Ch.13, p.947
IFRS 12.8	Ch.13, p.954	IFRS 12.B8	Ch.13, p.948
IFRS 12.9	Ch.13, p.954	IFRS 12.B9	Ch.6, p.442
IFRS 12.9A	Ch.6, p.473	IFRS 12.B9	Ch.13, p.948
IFRS 12.9A	Ch.13, p.956	IFRS 12.B10	Ch.5, p.333
IFRS 12.9B	Ch.13, p.968	IFRS 12.B10	Ch.13, p.959
IFRS 12.9(d)	Ch.11, p.816	IFRS 12.B10(b)	Ch.40, p.3187
IFRS 12.9(e)	Ch.11, p.816	IFRS 12.B11	Ch.13, p.959
IFRS 12.10	Ch.13, p.957	IFRS 12.B11	Ch.40, p.3187
IFRS 12.10	Ch.15, p.1244	IFRS 12.B12	Ch.13, p.972
IFRS 12.11	Ch.13, p.957	IFRS 12.B12(a)	Ch.40, p.3187
IFRS 12.12	Ch.5, p.333	IFRS 12.B12-13	Ch.5, p.333
IFRS 12.12	Ch.13, p.959	IFRS 12.B13	Ch.13, p.973
IFRS 12.12(e)	Ch.5, p.332	IFRS 12.B13(a)	Ch.40, p.3187
IFRS 12.13	Ch.13, p.962	IFRS 12.B14	Ch.13, p.973
IFRS 12.13	Ch.15, p.1244	IFRS 12.B15	Ch.13, p.974
IFRS 12.14	Ch.13, p.964	IFRS 12.B16	Ch.5, p.333
IFRS 12.15	Ch.13, p.965	IFRS 12.B16	Ch.13, p.976
IFRS 12.16	Ch.13, p.966	IFRS 12.B17	Ch.4, p.214
IFRS 12.17	Ch.13, p.966	IFRS 12.B17	Ch.13, p.950
IFRS 12.18	Ch.13, p.966	IFRS 12.B17	Ch.13, p.976
IFRS 12.19	Ch.5, p.333	IFRS 12.B18	Ch.13, p.977
IFRS 12.19	Ch.13, p.967	IFRS 12.B18	Ch.39, p.3122
IFRS 12.19A	Ch.13, p.968	IFRS 12.B19	Ch.13, p.977
IFRS 12.19B	Ch.13, p.968	IFRS 12.B19-20	Ch.39, p.3123
IFRS 12.19C	Ch.13, p.968	IFRS 12.B22	Ch.6, p.435
IFRS 12.19D	Ch.13, p.969	IFRS 12.B22	Ch.13, p.949
IFRS 12.19E	Ch.13, p.969	IFRS 12.B23	Ch.6, p.435
IFRS 12.19F	Ch.13, p.969	IFRS 12.B23	Ch.13, p.949
IFRS 12.19G	Ch.13, p.969	IFRS 12.B24	Ch.6, p.435
IFRS 12.20	Ch.13, p.970	IFRS 12.B24	Ch.13, p.950
IFRS 12.20	Ch.15, p.1244	IFRS 12.B25-26	Ch.13, p.990
IFRS 12.21	Ch.5, p.333	IFRS 12.BC16	Ch.13, p.956
		IFRS 12.BC19	Ch.13, p.956
		IFRS 12.BC27	Ch.13, p.959

IFRS 12.BC28	Ch.13, p.959
IFRS 12.BC29	Ch.13, p.959
IFRS 12.BC31	Ch.13, p.962
IFRS 12.BC32	Ch.13, p.962
IFRS 12.BC33	Ch.13, p.962
IFRS 12.BC34	Ch.13, p.963
IFRS 12.BC35	Ch.13, p.963
IFRS 12.BC38-39	Ch.13, p.967
IFRS 12.BC49	Ch.13, p.974
IFRS 12.BC50-51	Ch.13, p.974
IFRS 12.BC52	Ch.13, p.974
IFRS 12.BC52	Ch.39, p.3106
IFRS 12.BC60	Ch.13, p.974
IFRS 12.BC61C	Ch.13, p.969
IFRS 12.BC61I	Ch.13, p.968
IFRS 12.BC69	Ch.13, p.952
IFRS 12.BC72	Ch.13, p.979
IFRS 12.BC77	Ch.13, p.952
IFRS 12.BC82	Ch.13, p.949
IFRS 12.BC83	Ch.13, p.950
IFRS 12.BC83-85	Ch.13, p.950
IFRS 12.BC87	Ch.13, p.982
IFRS 12.BC90	Ch.13, p.983
IFRS 12.BC94	Ch.13, p.986
IFRS 12.BC96	Ch.13, p.979
IFRS 12.BC96	Ch.13, p.980
IFRS 12.BC97	Ch.13, p.987
IFRS 12.BC98-99	Ch.13, p.987
IFRS 12.BC100	Ch.13, p.987
IFRS 12.BC104	Ch.13, p.966
IFRS 12.BC105-106	Ch.13, p.965
IFRS 12.BC113-114	Ch.13, p.990

IFRS 13

IFRS 13.1	Ch.14, p.1003
IFRS 13.1	Ch.24, p.1838
IFRS 13.2	Ch.9, p.669
IFRS 13.2	Ch.9, p.682
IFRS 13.2	Ch.14, p.1006
IFRS 13.2	Ch.14, p.1007
IFRS 13.2	Ch.14, p.1017
IFRS 13.2	Ch.18, p.1419
IFRS 13.2	Ch.19, p.1469
IFRS 13.2	Ch.20, p.1546
IFRS 13.3	Ch.14, p.1007
IFRS 13.3	Ch.14, p.1045
IFRS 13.4	Ch.14, p.1008
IFRS 13.5	Ch.10, p.779
IFRS 13.5	Ch.14, p.1007
IFRS 13.5	Ch.24, p.1830
IFRS 13.6	Ch.9, p.695
IFRS 13.6	Ch.14, p.1007
IFRS 13.6	Ch.20, p.1546
IFRS 13.6(c)	Ch.19, p.1473
IFRS 13.6(c)	Ch.20, p.1581
IFRS 13.7	Ch.14, p.1008
IFRS 13.7(c)	Ch.20, p.1546
IFRS 13.8	Ch.14, p.1008
IFRS 13.9	Ch.4, p.198
IFRS 13.9	Ch.10, p.779
IFRS 13.9	Ch.14, p.1016
IFRS 13.9	Ch.19, p.1468
IFRS 13.9	Ch.24, p.1830
IFRS 13.9	Ch.42, p.3277
IFRS 13.9	Ch.52, p.4088
IFRS 13.11	Ch.14, p.1025
IFRS 13.11	Ch.14, p.1110
IFRS 13.11	Ch.20, p.1546
IFRS 13.11	Ch.42, p.3304
IFRS 13.12	Ch.14, p.1025
IFRS 13.13	Ch.14, p.1019
IFRS 13.14	Ch.14, p.1019
IFRS 13.15	Ch.14, p.1017
IFRS 13.15	Ch.14, p.1038
IFRS 13.16	Ch.14, p.1029
IFRS 13.16	Ch.14, p.1033
IFRS 13.17	Ch.14, p.1030
IFRS 13.17	Ch.42, p.3304
IFRS 13.18	Ch.14, p.1029
IFRS 13.18	Ch.42, p.3300
IFRS 13.18	Ch.42, p.3306
IFRS 13.19	Ch.14, p.1031
IFRS 13.20	Ch.14, p.1031
IFRS 13.20	Ch.14, p.1038
IFRS 13.21	Ch.14, p.1030
IFRS 13.22	Ch.14, p.1034
IFRS 13.22	Ch.14, p.1035
IFRS 13.22	Ch.19, p.1469
IFRS 13.23	Ch.14, p.1034
IFRS 13.23	Ch.42, p.3304
IFRS 13.24	Ch.14, p.1050
IFRS 13.25	Ch.14, p.1017
IFRS 13.25	Ch.14, p.1050
IFRS 13.25	Ch.19, p.1469
IFRS 13.25	Ch.19, p.1476
IFRS 13.25	Ch.42, p.3292
IFRS 13.25	Ch.42, p.3305
IFRS 13.26	Ch.14, p.1050
IFRS 13.27	Ch.14, p.1053
IFRS 13.27	Ch.18, p.1419
IFRS 13.27	Ch.19, p.1460
IFRS 13.27	Ch.20, p.1546
IFRS 13.27	Ch.42, p.3299
IFRS 13.27-28	Ch.19, p.1482
IFRS 13.28	Ch.14, p.1053
IFRS 13.28	Ch.18, p.1419
IFRS 13.28	Ch.42, p.3299
IFRS 13.29	Ch.14, p.1056
IFRS 13.29	Ch.14, p.1057
IFRS 13.29	Ch.18, p.1419
IFRS 13.29	Ch.19, p.1481
IFRS 13.29	Ch.20, p.1546
IFRS 13.29	Ch.42, p.3299
IFRS 13.30	Ch.14, p.1057

IFRS 13.31	Ch.42, p.3299
IFRS 13.31(a)-(b)	Ch.18, p.1420
IFRS 13.31(a)(i)	Ch.14, p.1059
IFRS 13.31(a)(ii)	Ch.14, p.1062
IFRS 13.31(a)(iii)	Ch.14, p.1060
IFRS 13.31(b)	Ch.14, p.1059
IFRS 13.32	Ch.14, p.1062
IFRS 13.32	Ch.42, p.3300
IFRS 13.34	Ch.9, p.699
IFRS 13.34	Ch.14, p.1064
IFRS 13.34(a)	Ch.9, p.700
IFRS 13.36	Ch.10, p.779
IFRS 13.36	Ch.14, p.1066
IFRS 13.37	Ch.9, p.701
IFRS 13.37	Ch.14, p.1066
IFRS 13.38	Ch.14, p.1066
IFRS 13.39	Ch.14, p.1067
IFRS 13.40	Ch.14, p.1066
IFRS 13.40	Ch.14, p.1069
IFRS 13.41	Ch.14, p.1070
IFRS 13.42	Ch.9, p.704
IFRS 13.42-44	Ch.14, p.1073
IFRS 13.44	Ch.14, p.1078
IFRS 13.45	Ch.14, p.1087
IFRS 13.46	Ch.14, p.1087
IFRS 13.47	Ch.7, p.552
IFRS 13.47	Ch.14, p.1088
IFRS 13.47	Ch.47, p.3712
IFRS 13.47	Ch.53, p.4222
IFRS 13.48	Ch.14, p.1085
IFRS 13.48	Ch.14, p.1088
IFRS 13.48	Ch.14, p.1092
IFRS 13.48	Ch.14, p.1094
IFRS 13.49	Ch.14, p.1089
IFRS 13.50	Ch.14, p.1090
IFRS 13.51	Ch.14, p.1090
IFRS 13.52	Ch.14, p.1089
IFRS 13.53	Ch.14, p.1096
IFRS 13.54	Ch.14, p.1091
IFRS 13.54	Ch.14, p.1095
IFRS 13.55	Ch.14, p.1095
IFRS 13.56	Ch.14, p.1096
IFRS 13.57	Ch.14, p.1096
IFRS 13.57-59	Ch.42, p.3305
IFRS 13.58	Ch.14, p.1096
IFRS 13.58	Ch.49, p.3854
IFRS 13.59	Ch.14, p.1096
IFRS 13.60	Ch.14, p.1097
IFRS 13.60	Ch.49, p.3854
IFRS 13.60	Ch.49, p.3855
IFRS 13.61	Ch.9, p.682
IFRS 13.61	Ch.14, p.1100
IFRS 13.61	Ch.18, p.1420
IFRS 13.61	Ch.20, p.1546
IFRS 13.62	Ch.9, p.681
IFRS 13.62	Ch.14, p.1100
IFRS 13.62	Ch.18, p.1420
IFRS 13.62	Ch.19, p.1471
IFRS 13.62	Ch.20, p.1546
IFRS 13.62	Ch.42, p.3305
IFRS 13.63	Ch.14, p.1101
IFRS 13.63	Ch.42, p.3305
IFRS 13.64	Ch.14, p.1105
IFRS 13.65	Ch.14, p.1105
IFRS 13.65	Ch.14, p.1106
IFRS 13.65	Ch.14, p.1114
IFRS 13.66	Ch.14, p.1106
IFRS 13.66	Ch.18, p.1421
IFRS 13.66	Ch.20, p.1547
IFRS 13.67	Ch.14, p.1109
IFRS 13.67	Ch.19, p.1472
IFRS 13.67	Ch.42, p.3300
IFRS 13.68	Ch.14, p.1109
IFRS 13.69	Ch.14, p.1109
IFRS 13.69	Ch.14, p.1111
IFRS 13.69	Ch.14, p.1112
IFRS 13.69	Ch.14, p.1113
IFRS 13.70	Ch.14, p.1114
IFRS 13.71	Ch.14, p.1114
IFRS 13.72	Ch.14, p.1117
IFRS 13.72	Ch.18, p.1421
IFRS 13.72	Ch.20, p.1547
IFRS 13.73	Ch.14, p.1119
IFRS 13.73	Ch.14, p.1120
IFRS 13.74	Ch.14, p.1100
IFRS 13.74	Ch.14, p.1118
IFRS 13.74	Ch.42, p.3305
IFRS 13.75	Ch.14, p.1119
IFRS 13.75	Ch.14, p.1121
IFRS 13.75	Ch.14, p.1126
IFRS 13.75	Ch.42, p.3307
IFRS 13.76	Ch.14, p.1125
IFRS 13.76	Ch.18, p.1421
IFRS 13.77	Ch.14, p.1125
IFRS 13.78	Ch.14, p.1126
IFRS 13.79	Ch.14, p.1125
IFRS 13.79(a)	Ch.14, p.1126
IFRS 13.79(b)	Ch.14, p.1127
IFRS 13.79(c)	Ch.14, p.1126
IFRS 13.80	Ch.14, p.1112
IFRS 13.80	Ch.14, p.1127
IFRS 13.81	Ch.14, p.1127
IFRS 13.82	Ch.14, p.1127
IFRS 13.83	Ch.14, p.1130
IFRS 13.84	Ch.14, p.1130
IFRS 13.86	Ch.14, p.1131
IFRS 13.87	Ch.14, p.1131
IFRS 13.87	Ch.14, p.1132
IFRS 13.87-89	Ch.20, p.1547
IFRS 13.88	Ch.14, p.1132
IFRS 13.89	Ch.14, p.1049
IFRS 13.89	Ch.14, p.1131
IFRS 13.89	Ch.14, p.1132
IFRS 13.89	Ch.20, p.1548
IFRS 13.91	Ch.9, p.669
IFRS 13.91	Ch.14, p.1134

IFRS 13.91	Ch.41, p.3223	IFRS 13 Appendix A	Ch.14, p.1043
IFRS 13.91	Ch.42, p.3292	IFRS 13 Appendix A	Ch.14, p.1050
IFRS 13.91(a)	Ch.9, p.753	IFRS 13 Appendix A	Ch.14, p.1053
IFRS 13.92	Ch.14, p.1134	IFRS 13 Appendix A	Ch.14, p.1115
IFRS 13.92	Ch.19, p.1505	IFRS 13 Appendix A	Ch.14, p.1118
IFRS 13.92	Ch.41, p.3224	IFRS 13 Appendix A	Ch.17, p.1293
IFRS 13.93	Ch.7, p.533	IFRS 13 Appendix A	Ch.17, p.1335
IFRS 13.93	Ch.14, p.1138	IFRS 13 Appendix A	Ch.18, p.1419
IFRS 13.93	Ch.14, p.1139	IFRS 13 Appendix A	Ch.19, p.1497
IFRS 13.93	Ch.14, p.1140	IFRS 13 Appendix A	Ch.20, p.1534
IFRS 13.93	Ch.14, p.1146	IFRS 13 Appendix A	Ch.20, p.1547
IFRS 13.93	Ch.18, p.1434	IFRS 13 Appendix A	Ch.24, p.1825
IFRS 13.93	Ch.18, p.1435	IFRS 13 Appendix A	Ch.42, p.3301
IFRS 13.93	Ch.41, p.3223	IFRS 13 Appendix A	Ch.42, p.3304
IFRS 13.93	Ch.42, p.3320	IFRS 13 Appendix A	Ch.52, p.4088
IFRS 13.93	Ch.55, p.4667	IFRS 13.B2	Ch.14, p.1017
IFRS 13.93(a)	Ch.14, p.1136	IFRS 13.B2	Ch.42, p.3298
IFRS 13.93(b)	Ch.19, p.1498	IFRS 13.B3	Ch.14, p.1061
IFRS 13.93(b)	Ch.38, p.3085	IFRS 13.B4(a)-(b)	Ch.14, p.1097
IFRS 13.93(c)	Ch.14, p.1122	IFRS 13.B4(c)	Ch.14, p.1096
IFRS 13.93(c)	Ch.14, p.1144	IFRS 13.B4(c)	Ch.14, p.1099
IFRS 13.93(c)	Ch.19, p.1498	IFRS 13.B4(d)	Ch.14, p.1097
IFRS 13.93(d)	Ch.14, p.1137	IFRS 13.B5	Ch.14, p.1106
IFRS 13.93(d)	Ch.14, p.1146	IFRS 13.B5	Ch.18, p.1420
IFRS 13.93(d)	Ch.19, p.1498	IFRS 13.B5	Ch.20, p.1547
IFRS 13.93(d)	Ch.38, p.3085	IFRS 13.B6	Ch.14, p.1106
IFRS 13.93(e)	Ch.19, p.1498	IFRS 13.B6	Ch.18, p.1420
IFRS 13.93(e)(iv)	Ch.14, p.1122	IFRS 13.B6	Ch.20, p.1547
IFRS 13.93(e)(iv)	Ch.14, p.1144	IFRS 13.B7	Ch.14, p.1106
IFRS 13.93(f)	Ch.19, p.1499	IFRS 13.B8	Ch.9, p.682
IFRS 13.93(g)	Ch.19, p.1499	IFRS 13.B8	Ch.14, p.1107
IFRS 13.93(g)	Ch.38, p.3086	IFRS 13.B8	Ch.18, p.1421
IFRS 13.93(h)	Ch.19, p.1499	IFRS 13.B8	Ch.20, p.1547
IFRS 13.93(i)	Ch.14, p.1056	IFRS 13.B9	Ch.9, p.682
IFRS 13.93(i)	Ch.14, p.1156	IFRS 13.B9	Ch.14, p.1107
IFRS 13.93(i)	Ch.19, p.1498	IFRS 13.B9	Ch.18, p.1421
IFRS 13.93(i)	Ch.38, p.3086	IFRS 13.B9	Ch.20, p.1547
IFRS 13.94	Ch.14, p.1135	IFRS 13.B10	Ch.14, p.1108
IFRS 13.94	Ch.19, p.1504	IFRS 13.B10	Ch.18, p.1421
IFRS 13.94	Ch.19, p.1505	IFRS 13.B10	Ch.20, p.1547
IFRS 13.94-96	Ch.41, p.3223	IFRS 13.B11	Ch.14, p.1108
IFRS 13.95	Ch.14, p.1122	IFRS 13.B11	Ch.18, p.1421
IFRS 13.95	Ch.14, p.1137	IFRS 13.B11	Ch.20, p.1547
IFRS 13.95	Ch.14, p.1144	IFRS 13.B12	Ch.14, p.1160
IFRS 13.96	Ch.14, p.1137	IFRS 13.B13	Ch.14, p.1161
IFRS 13.97	Ch.14, p.1156	IFRS 13.B13(c)	Ch.14, p.1162
IFRS 13.97	Ch.55, p.4667	IFRS 13.B14	Ch.14, p.1162
IFRS 13.98	Ch.14, p.1156	IFRS 13.B15	Ch.14, p.1162
IFRS 13.98	Ch.41, p.3223	IFRS 13.B16	Ch.9, p.703
IFRS 13.99	Ch.7, p.533	IFRS 13.B16	Ch.14, p.1115
IFRS 13.99	Ch.14, p.1135	IFRS 13.B16	Ch.14, p.1162
IFRS 13.99	Ch.38, p.3086	IFRS 13.B17	Ch.14, p.1163
IFRS 13.99	Ch.41, p.3224	IFRS 13.B18	Ch.14, p.1163
IFRS 13 Appendix A	Ch.5, p.292	IFRS 13.B19	Ch.14, p.1163
IFRS 13 Appendix A	Ch.14, p.1014	IFRS 13.B19	Ch.14, p.1164
IFRS 13 Appendix A	Ch.14, p.1030	IFRS 13.B20-21	Ch.14, p.1165
IFRS 13 Appendix A	Ch.14, p.1033	IFRS 13.B22	Ch.14, p.1164
IFRS 13 Appendix A	Ch.14, p.1034	IFRS 13.B23	Ch.14, p.1166

IFRS 13.B24	Ch.14, p.1166	IFRS 13.IE66	Ch.14, p.1153
IFRS 13.B25	Ch.14, p.1167	IFRS 13.BC6	Ch.14, p.1170
IFRS 13.B25-B29	Ch.14, p.1115	IFRS 13.BC8	Ch.14, p.1011
IFRS 13.B26	Ch.14, p.1167	IFRS 13.BC21	Ch.14, p.1010
IFRS 13.B27-B29	Ch.14, p.1168	IFRS 13.BC22	Ch.14, p.1010
IFRS 13.B30	Ch.14, p.1168	IFRS 13.BC24	Ch.19, p.1473
IFRS 13.B31	Ch.14, p.1070	IFRS 13.BC29	Ch.14, p.1016
IFRS 13.B32	Ch.14, p.1070	IFRS 13.BC31	Ch.14, p.1017
IFRS 13.B33	Ch.14, p.1070	IFRS 13.BC36	Ch.14, p.1016
IFRS 13.B34	Ch.14, p.1109	IFRS 13.BC39	Ch.14, p.1017
IFRS 13.B34	Ch.36, p.2983	IFRS 13.BC40	Ch.14, p.1017
IFRS 13.B35	Ch.14, p.1128	IFRS 13.BC46	Ch.14, p.1025
IFRS 13.B35(g)	Ch.19, p.1497	IFRS 13.BC52	Ch.14, p.1030
IFRS 13.B36	Ch.14, p.1132	IFRS 13.BC52	Ch.14, p.1033
IFRS 13.B37	Ch.14, p.1040	IFRS 13.BC55-BC59	Ch.14, p.1034
IFRS 13.B38	Ch.14, p.1046	IFRS 13.BC57	Ch.14, p.1035
IFRS 13.B39	Ch.14, p.1115	IFRS 13.BC63	Ch.14, p.1053
IFRS 13.B40	Ch.14, p.1045	IFRS 13.BC69	Ch.14, p.1055
IFRS 13.B40	Ch.14, p.1102	IFRS 13.BC81	Ch.14, p.1065
IFRS 13.B41	Ch.14, p.1017	IFRS 13.BC82	Ch.14, p.1065
IFRS 13.B42	Ch.14, p.1045	IFRS 13.BC88	Ch.14, p.1067
IFRS 13.B43	Ch.14, p.1039	IFRS 13.BC89	Ch.9, p.702
IFRS 13.B43	Ch.14, p.1043	IFRS 13.BC89	Ch.14, p.1067
IFRS 13.B43	Ch.14, p.1044	IFRS 13.BC91	Ch.14, p.1116
IFRS 13.B43	Ch.19, p.1472	IFRS 13.BC92	Ch.14, p.1075
IFRS 13.B43	Ch.20, p.1548	IFRS 13.BC93	Ch.14, p.1075
IFRS 13.B44	Ch.14, p.1043	IFRS 13.BC94	Ch.14, p.1075
IFRS 13.B44	Ch.14, p.1044	IFRS 13.BC95	Ch.14, p.1076
IFRS 13.B44	Ch.14, p.1046	IFRS 13.BC96-BC98	Ch.14, p.1076
IFRS 13.B44(c)	Ch.14, p.1044	IFRS 13.BC99	Ch.14, p.1028
IFRS 13.B45	Ch.14, p.1122	IFRS 13.BC99	Ch.14, p.1087
IFRS 13.B46	Ch.14, p.1116	IFRS 13.BC100	Ch.14, p.1028
IFRS 13.B47	Ch.14, p.1123	IFRS 13.BC100	Ch.14, p.1087
IFRS 13.C1	Ch.14, p.1003	IFRS 13.BCZ102-BCZ103	Ch.14, p.1088
IFRS 13.IE3-IE6	Ch.14, p.1036	IFRS 13.BC106	Ch.14, p.1063
IFRS 13.IE7-IE8	Ch.14, p.1056	IFRS 13.BC119A	Ch.14, p.1089
IFRS 13.IE7-IE8	Ch.18, p.1420	IFRS 13.BC119B	Ch.14, p.1089
IFRS 13.IE9	Ch.14, p.1057	IFRS 13.BC121	Ch.14, p.1090
IFRS 13.IE11-IE14	Ch.14, p.1103	IFRS 13.BC138	Ch.14, p.1097
IFRS 13.IE11-IE14	Ch.14, p.1108	IFRS 13.BC138	Ch.49, p.3854
IFRS 13.IE15-IE17	Ch.14, p.1102	IFRS 13.BC138A	Ch.14, p.1010
IFRS 13.IE19-IE20	Ch.14, p.1029	IFRS 13.BC138A	Ch.49, p.3854
IFRS 13.IE19.21-IE22	Ch.14, p.1033	IFRS 13.BC145	Ch.14, p.1105
IFRS 13.IE24-IE26	Ch.14, p.1098	IFRS 13.BC157	Ch.14, p.1113
IFRS 13.IE28-IE29	Ch.14, p.1026	IFRS 13.BC164	Ch.14, p.1114
IFRS 13.IE31	Ch.14, p.1073	IFRS 13.BC165	Ch.14, p.1099
IFRS 13.IE32	Ch.14, p.1074	IFRS 13.BC184	Ch.14, p.1133
IFRS 13.IE34	Ch.14, p.1074	IFRS 13.BC208	Ch.14, p.1170
IFRS 13.IE35-IE39	Ch.14, p.1070	IFRS 13.BC238(a)	Ch.14, p.1172
IFRS 13.IE40-IE42	Ch.14, p.1067	IFRS 13.BC238(b)	Ch.14, p.1172
IFRS 13.IE43-IE47	Ch.14, p.1068	IFRS 13.BC238(c)	Ch.14, p.1172
IFRS 13.IE49-IE58	Ch.14, p.1047		
IFRS 13.IE60	Ch.14, p.1142		
IFRS 13.IE61	Ch.14, p.1150		
IFRS 13.IE62	Ch.14, p.1151		
IFRS 13.IE63	Ch.14, p.1147		
IFRS 13.IE64(a)	Ch.14, p.1134		
IFRS 13.IE65	Ch.14, p.1152		

IFRS 14

IFRS 14.5	Ch.5, p.323
IFRS 14.5	Ch.26, p.1966
IFRS 14.6	Ch.5, p.323

IFRS 14.6	Ch.26, p.1966
IFRS 14.7	Ch.5, p.325
IFRS 14.8	Ch.5, p.323
IFRS 14.8	Ch.5, p.335
IFRS 14.9	Ch.5, p.324
IFRS 14.9	Ch.5, p.325
IFRS 14.9-10	Ch.5, p.324
IFRS 14.11	Ch.5, p.324
IFRS 14.11	Ch.5, p.326
IFRS 14.11	Ch.5, p.334
IFRS 14.12	Ch.5, p.334
IFRS 14.12-15	Ch.5, p.324
IFRS 14.13	Ch.2, p.47
IFRS 14.13	Ch.5, p.325
IFRS 14.13	Ch.5, p.326
IFRS 14.13	Ch.26, p.1966
IFRS 14.13-15	Ch.5, p.324
IFRS 14.14	Ch.5, p.325
IFRS 14.15	Ch.5, p.325
IFRS 14.16	Ch.5, p.333
IFRS 14.17	Ch.5, p.333
IFRS 14.18-19	Ch.5, p.324
IFRS 14.20	Ch.5, p.326
IFRS 14.20-24	Ch.5, p.328
IFRS 14.21	Ch.5, p.326
IFRS 14.22	Ch.5, p.326
IFRS 14.23	Ch.5, p.326
IFRS 14.24	Ch.5, p.326
IFRS 14.24	Ch.5, p.327
IFRS 14.24	Ch.5, p.331
IFRS 14.25	Ch.5, p.327
IFRS 14.26	Ch.5, p.327
IFRS 14.26	Ch.5, p.328
IFRS 14.27	Ch.5, p.331
IFRS 14.28	Ch.5, p.331
IFRS 14.29	Ch.5, p.331
IFRS 14.29(a)	Ch.5, p.332
IFRS 14.30	Ch.5, p.331
IFRS 14.31	Ch.5, p.332
IFRS 14.32	Ch.5, p.332
IFRS 14.33	Ch.5, p.327
IFRS 14.33	Ch.5, p.332
IFRS 14.34	Ch.5, p.332
IFRS 14.35	Ch.5, p.332
IFRS 14.35	Ch.5, p.333
IFRS 14.36	Ch.5, p.333
IFRS 14 Appendix A	Ch.5, p.299
IFRS 14 Appendix A	Ch.5, p.322
IFRS 14.B1	Ch.5, p.323
IFRS 14.B2	Ch.5, p.323
IFRS 14.B3	Ch.5, p.325
IFRS 14.B4	Ch.5, p.324
IFRS 14.B5	Ch.5, p.325
IFRS 14.B6	Ch.5, p.326
IFRS 14.B7-B28	Ch.5, p.333
IFRS 14.B8	Ch.5, p.333
IFRS 14.B9	Ch.5, p.334
IFRS 14.B10	Ch.5, p.334
IFRS 14.B11	Ch.5, p.326
IFRS 14.B12	Ch.5, p.327
IFRS 14.B12	Ch.5, p.331
IFRS 14.B14	Ch.5, p.327
IFRS 14.B15	Ch.5, p.334
IFRS 14.B15-B16	Ch.5, p.334
IFRS 14.B16	Ch.5, p.334
IFRS 14.B17-B18	Ch.5, p.334
IFRS 14.B19	Ch.5, p.334
IFRS 14.B20	Ch.5, p.327
IFRS 14.B21	Ch.5, p.327
IFRS 14.B22	Ch.5, p.327
IFRS 14.B23	Ch.5, p.335
IFRS 14.B24	Ch.5, p.335
IFRS 14.B25	Ch.5, p.332
IFRS 14.B26-B27	Ch.5, p.333
IFRS 14.B28	Ch.5, p.333
IFRS 14.C1	Ch.26, p.1966
IFRS 14.IE1	Ch.5, p.326
IFRS 14.IE1	Ch.5, p.328
IFRS 14.IE1	Ch.5, p.329
IFRS 14.IE1	Ch.5, p.333
IFRS 14.IE2	Ch.5, p.328
IFRS 14.BC10	Ch.2, p.47
IFRS 14.BC10	Ch.26, p.1966
IFRS 14.BC22	Ch.5, p.323
IFRS 14.BC23	Ch.5, p.323
IFRS 14.BC32	Ch.5, p.324
IFRS 14.BC33	Ch.5, p.325

IFRS 15 (2016)

IFRS 15(2016).IN5	Ch.27, p.2020

IFRS 15

IFRS 15.1	Ch.27, p.2021
IFRS 15.2	Ch.27, p.2021
IFRS 15.2	Ch.31, p.2345
IFRS 15.3	Ch.27, p.2022
IFRS 15.4	Ch.28, p.2068
IFRS 15.5	Ch.27, p.2024
IFRS 15.5(c)	Ch.27, p.2035
IFRS 15.5(d)	Ch.18, p.1406
IFRS 15.5(d)	Ch.43, p.3449
IFRS 15.5(d)	Ch.43, p.3450
IFRS 15.6	Ch.27, p.2028
IFRS 15.6	Ch.43, p.3450
IFRS 15.6	Ch.43, p.3453
IFRS 15.6	Ch.43, p.3460
IFRS 15.7	Ch.27, p.2029
IFRS 15.7	Ch.29, p.2249
IFRS 15.7	Ch.31, p.2327
IFRS 15.7	Ch.43, p.3457
IFRS 15.8	Ch.25, p.1896
IFRS 15.8	Ch.27, p.2026

IFRS 15.8	Ch.31, p.2358
IFRS 15.9	Ch.28, p.2053
IFRS 15.9	Ch.28, p.2054
IFRS 15.9(e)	Ch.28, p.2058
IFRS 15.10	Ch.25, p.1869
IFRS 15.10	Ch.25, p.1914
IFRS 15.10	Ch.28, p.2052
IFRS 15.10	Ch.28, p.2055
IFRS 15.11	Ch.28, p.2052
IFRS 15.11	Ch.28, p.2061
IFRS 15.12	Ch.28, p.2061
IFRS 15.13	Ch.28, p.2053
IFRS 15.14	Ch.28, p.2083
IFRS 15.15	Ch.28, p.2066
IFRS 15.15	Ch.28, p.2082
IFRS 15.16	Ch.28, p.2082
IFRS 15.18	Ch.28, p.2065
IFRS 15.18	Ch.28, p.2069
IFRS 15.18	Ch.28, p.2077
IFRS 15.18	Ch.29, p.2172
IFRS 15.19	Ch.28, p.2069
IFRS 15.20	Ch.28, p.2071
IFRS 15.20(a)	Ch.28, p.2072
IFRS 15.20(b)	Ch.28, p.2072
IFRS 15.20-21	Ch.5, p.335
IFRS 15.21	Ch.28, p.2073
IFRS 15.21(a)	Ch.29, p.2248
IFRS 15.22	Ch.25, p.1870
IFRS 15.22	Ch.25, p.1906
IFRS 15.22	Ch.28, p.2084
IFRS 15.22(b)	Ch.28, p.2109
IFRS 15.22(b)	Ch.28, p.2116
IFRS 15.23	Ch.28, p.2084
IFRS 15.23	Ch.28, p.2109
IFRS 15.23	Ch.28, p.2116
IFRS 15.24	Ch.28, p.2085
IFRS 15.24	Ch.28, p.2089
IFRS 15.25	Ch.28, p.2085
IFRS 15.25	Ch.28, p.2086
IFRS 15.25	Ch.28, p.2089
IFRS 15.26	Ch.25, p.1870
IFRS 15.26	Ch.25, p.1906
IFRS 15.26	Ch.28, p.2085
IFRS 15.26(e)	Ch.28, p.2087
IFRS 15.26(g)	Ch.28, p.2087
IFRS 15.27	Ch.25, p.1870
IFRS 15.27	Ch.25, p.1906
IFRS 15.28	Ch.28, p.2097
IFRS 15.29	Ch.28, p.2098
IFRS 15.29	Ch.28, p.2099
IFRS 15.29	Ch.28, p.2104
IFRS 15.29(a)	Ch.28, p.2100
IFRS 15.29(b)	Ch.28, p.2102
IFRS 15.29(c)	Ch.28, p.2102
IFRS 15.30	Ch.25, p.1870
IFRS 15.30	Ch.25, p.1906
IFRS 15.30	Ch.28, p.2095
IFRS 15.30	Ch.28, p.2120
IFRS 15.31	Ch.19, p.1492
IFRS 15.31	Ch.25, p.1908
IFRS 15.31	Ch.30, p.2257
IFRS 15.31	Ch.43, p.3450
IFRS 15.32	Ch.19, p.1492
IFRS 15.32	Ch.25, p.1908
IFRS 15.32	Ch.30, p.2258
IFRS 15.32	Ch.30, p.2259
IFRS 15.33	Ch.28, p.2125
IFRS 15.33	Ch.30, p.2257
IFRS 15.33	Ch.30, p.2258
IFRS 15.34	Ch.30, p.2298
IFRS 15.35	Ch.30, p.2259
IFRS 15.35(a)	Ch.25, p.1908
IFRS 15.35(a)	Ch.25, p.1916
IFRS 15.35(a)	Ch.28, p.2092
IFRS 15.35(b)	Ch.25, p.1908
IFRS 15.35(b)	Ch.25, p.1915
IFRS 15.35(c)	Ch.5, p.337
IFRS 15.35(c)	Ch.30, p.2264
IFRS 15.36	Ch.30, p.2264
IFRS 15.36	Ch.30, p.2266
IFRS 15.36	Ch.30, p.2276
IFRS 15.37	Ch.30, p.2267
IFRS 15.37	Ch.30, p.2276
IFRS 15.38	Ch.23, p.1802
IFRS 15.38	Ch.28, p.2126
IFRS 15.38	Ch.30, p.2291
IFRS 15.39	Ch.25, p.1898
IFRS 15.39	Ch.30, p.2278
IFRS 15.40	Ch.30, p.2278
IFRS 15.40	Ch.38, p.3088
IFRS 15.41	Ch.30, p.2279
IFRS 15.41	Ch.30, p.2280
IFRS 15.42	Ch.30, p.2278
IFRS 15.43	Ch.30, p.2278
IFRS 15.44	Ch.30, p.2279
IFRS 15.45	Ch.25, p.1908
IFRS 15.45	Ch.30, p.2279
IFRS 15.46	Ch.29, p.2164
IFRS 15.47	Ch.19, p.1493
IFRS 15.47	Ch.25, p.1871
IFRS 15.47	Ch.25, p.1907
IFRS 15.47	Ch.29, p.2164
IFRS 15.47	Ch.29, p.2166
IFRS 15.47	Ch.33, p.2459
IFRS 15.47	Ch.43, p.3458
IFRS 15.47	Ch.43, p.3558
IFRS 15.48	Ch.29, p.2164
IFRS 15.49	Ch.29, p.2164
IFRS 15.49	Ch.31, p.2384
IFRS 15.50	Ch.25, p.1871
IFRS 15.50	Ch.25, p.1907
IFRS 15.50	Ch.29, p.2175
IFRS 15.50-51	Ch.29, p.2167
IFRS 15.51	Ch.25, p.1871
IFRS 15.51	Ch.25, p.1907
IFRS 15.51	Ch.29, p.2167

IFRS 15.51	Ch.29, p.2172	IFRS 15.74	Ch.25, p.1908
IFRS 15.51	Ch.29, p.2174	IFRS 15.74	Ch.25, p.1915
IFRS 15.52	Ch.29, p.2167	IFRS 15.74	Ch.29, p.2222
IFRS 15.53	Ch.25, p.1871	IFRS 15.75	Ch.29, p.2222
IFRS 15.53	Ch.25, p.1907	IFRS 15.76	Ch.29, p.2222
IFRS 15.53	Ch.29, p.2176	IFRS 15.76	Ch.29, p.2235
IFRS 15.54	Ch.29, p.2176	IFRS 15.77	Ch.29, p.2222
IFRS 15.55	Ch.9, p.689	IFRS 15.77	Ch.29, p.2223
IFRS 15.55	Ch.26, p.2006	IFRS 15.77	Ch.29, p.2224
IFRS 15.55	Ch.29, p.2188	IFRS 15.77	Ch.29, p.2225
IFRS 15.56	Ch.25, p.1871	IFRS 15.78	Ch.29, p.2223
IFRS 15.56	Ch.25, p.1907	IFRS 15.78	Ch.29, p.2224
IFRS 15.56	Ch.29, p.2179	IFRS 15.78	Ch.29, p.2225
IFRS 15.57	Ch.29, p.2179	IFRS 15.78	Ch.29, p.2228
IFRS 15.58	Ch.29, p.2180	IFRS 15.79	Ch.25, p.1872
IFRS 15.59	Ch.29, p.2187	IFRS 15.79	Ch.25, p.1908
IFRS 15.60	Ch.29, p.2192	IFRS 15.79	Ch.25, p.1915
IFRS 15.60	Ch.51, p.3928	IFRS 15.79	Ch.29, p.2224
IFRS 15.60-65	Ch.40, p.3167	IFRS 15.79	Ch.29, p.2225
IFRS 15.61	Ch.29, p.2192	IFRS 15.79(c)	Ch.29, p.2226
IFRS 15.61(a)	Ch.29, p.2201	IFRS 15.80	Ch.29, p.2225
IFRS 15.62	Ch.25, p.1871	IFRS 15.80	Ch.29, p.2227
IFRS 15.62	Ch.25, p.1915	IFRS 15.81	Ch.29, p.2244
IFRS 15.62	Ch.29, p.2193	IFRS 15.82	Ch.29, p.2244
IFRS 15.62(a)	Ch.28, p.2154	IFRS 15.82(b)	Ch.29, p.2215
IFRS 15.62(c)	Ch.29, p.2201	IFRS 15.83	Ch.29, p.2244
IFRS 15.63	Ch.25, p.1909	IFRS 15.84	Ch.29, p.2237
IFRS 15.63	Ch.29, p.2193	IFRS 15.85	Ch.28, p.2153
IFRS 15.63	Ch.29, p.2202	IFRS 15.85	Ch.29, p.2237
IFRS 15.63	Ch.51, p.3928	IFRS 15.85	Ch.29, p.2238
IFRS 15.64	Ch.25, p.1872	IFRS 15.85	Ch.31, p.2347
IFRS 15.64	Ch.25, p.1876	IFRS 15.86	Ch.29, p.2237
IFRS 15.64	Ch.25, p.1907	IFRS 15.86	Ch.29, p.2246
IFRS 15.64	Ch.25, p.1909	IFRS 15.87	Ch.29, p.2222
IFRS 15.64	Ch.25, p.1911	IFRS 15.88	Ch.29, p.2223
IFRS 15.64	Ch.25, p.1913	IFRS 15.88-89	Ch.28, p.2079
IFRS 15.64	Ch.29, p.2193	IFRS 15.88-89	Ch.29, p.2247
IFRS 15.64	Ch.29, p.2196	IFRS 15.89	Ch.28, p.2152
IFRS 15.65	Ch.29, p.2205	IFRS 15.90	Ch.29, p.2248
IFRS 15.66	Ch.18, p.1402	IFRS 15.90(a)	Ch.29, p.2248
IFRS 15.66	Ch.25, p.1880	IFRS 15.90(b)	Ch.29, p.2249
IFRS 15.66	Ch.29, p.2206	IFRS 15.91	Ch.25, p.1896
IFRS 15.67	Ch.25, p.1880	IFRS 15.91-93	Ch.31, p.2359
IFRS 15.67	Ch.25, p.1915	IFRS 15.91-93	Ch.55, p.4586
IFRS 15.67	Ch.29, p.2206	IFRS 15.92	Ch.25, p.1896
IFRS 15.68	Ch.29, p.2207	IFRS 15.92	Ch.31, p.2359
IFRS 15.69	Ch.29, p.2207	IFRS 15.93	Ch.25, p.1896
IFRS 15.70	Ch.29, p.2210	IFRS 15.94	Ch.31, p.2363
IFRS 15.70	Ch.29, p.2214	IFRS 15.95	Ch.25, p.1897
IFRS 15.70	Ch.29, p.2215	IFRS 15.95	Ch.31, p.2365
IFRS 15.70-72	Ch.25, p.1864	IFRS 15.95	Ch.41, p.3243
IFRS 15.71	Ch.29, p.2210	IFRS 15.95-96	Ch.22, p.1687
IFRS 15.71	Ch.29, p.2214	IFRS 15.95-96	Ch.31, p.2365
IFRS 15.72	Ch.29, p.2211	IFRS 15.97	Ch.26, p.1974
IFRS 15.72	Ch.29, p.2212	IFRS 15.97	Ch.31, p.2367
IFRS 15.72	Ch.29, p.2215	IFRS 15.98	Ch.26, p.1974
IFRS 15.73	Ch.29, p.2222	IFRS 15.98	Ch.31, p.2368
IFRS 15.74	Ch.25, p.1872	IFRS 15.99	Ch.31, p.2375

IFRS 15.99	Ch.31, p.2376	IFRS 15.117	Ch.32, p.2417
IFRS 15.99	Ch.31, p.2380	IFRS 15.118	Ch.32, p.2417
IFRS 15.99	Ch.31, p.2384	IFRS 15.119	Ch.29, p.2168
IFRS 15.100	Ch.31, p.2376	IFRS 15.119-120	Ch.32, p.2422
IFRS 15.101	Ch.31, p.2384	IFRS 15.119(a)	Ch.30, p.2260
IFRS 15.101(a)	Ch.31, p.2384	IFRS 15.120	Ch.5, p.335
IFRS 15.102	Ch.31, p.2384	IFRS 15.120	Ch.32, p.2432
IFRS 15.102	Ch.31, p.2385	IFRS 15.121	Ch.32, p.2430
IFRS 15.103	Ch.31, p.2385	IFRS 15.121	Ch.32, p.2432
IFRS 15.104	Ch.31, p.2385	IFRS 15.122	Ch.32, p.2430
IFRS 15.105	Ch.9, p.689	IFRS 15.123	Ch.3, p.175
IFRS 15.105	Ch.32, p.2393	IFRS 15.123	Ch.29, p.2168
IFRS 15.105	Ch.32, p.2395	IFRS 15.123	Ch.32, p.2433
IFRS 15.105	Ch.52, p.4089	IFRS 15.123(a)	Ch.30, p.2260
IFRS 15.106	Ch.9, p.688	IFRS 15.124	Ch.30, p.2260
IFRS 15.106-107	Ch.32, p.2394	IFRS 15.124	Ch.32, p.2433
IFRS 15.107	Ch.9, p.689	IFRS 15.125	Ch.32, p.2433
IFRS 15.107	Ch.25, p.1876	IFRS 15.126	Ch.29, p.2168
IFRS 15.107	Ch.25, p.1883	IFRS 15.126	Ch.32, p.2435
IFRS 15.107	Ch.25, p.1910	IFRS 15.127-128	Ch.32, p.2437
IFRS 15.107	Ch.25, p.1912	IFRS 15.129	Ch.32, p.2439
IFRS 15.107	Ch.25, p.1913	IFRS 15 Appendix A	Ch.8, p.627
IFRS 15.107	Ch.25, p.1916	IFRS 15 Appendix A	Ch.9, p.689
IFRS 15.107	Ch.32, p.2395	IFRS 15 Appendix A	Ch.25, p.1869
IFRS 15.107	Ch.32, p.2398	IFRS 15 Appendix A	Ch.25, p.1905
IFRS 15.107	Ch.45, p.3607	IFRS 15 Appendix A	Ch.25, p.1906
IFRS 15.107	Ch.52, p.4089	IFRS 15 Appendix A	Ch.25, p.1914
IFRS 15.108	Ch.25, p.1875	IFRS 15 Appendix A	Ch.27, p.2018
IFRS 15.108	Ch.25, p.1876	IFRS 15 Appendix A	Ch.27, p.2023
IFRS 15.108	Ch.25, p.1877	IFRS 15 Appendix A	Ch.27, p.2027
IFRS 15.108	Ch.25, p.1885	IFRS 15 Appendix A	Ch.27, p.2033
IFRS 15.108	Ch.25, p.1909	IFRS 15 Appendix A	Ch.28, p.2057
IFRS 15.108	Ch.25, p.1910	IFRS 15 Appendix A	Ch.42, p.3315
IFRS 15.108	Ch.25, p.1911	IFRS 15 Appendix A	Ch.43, p.3452
IFRS 15.108	Ch.25, p.1912	IFRS 15 Appendix A	Ch.43, p.3467
IFRS 15.108	Ch.32, p.2395	IFRS 15 Appendix A	Ch.43, p.3469
IFRS 15.108	Ch.32, p.2399	IFRS 15 Appendix A	Ch.51, p.3924
IFRS 15.108	Ch.32, p.2404	IFRS 15 Appendix A	Ch.51, p.3928
IFRS 15.108	Ch.45, p.3606	IFRS 15.B3	Ch.30, p.2261
IFRS 15.108	Ch.49, p.3854	IFRS 15.B4	Ch.25, p.1908
IFRS 15.108	Ch.52, p.4089	IFRS 15.B4	Ch.30, p.2261
IFRS 15.109	Ch.32, p.2396	IFRS 15.B5	Ch.30, p.2263
IFRS 15.110	Ch.32, p.2408	IFRS 15.B6	Ch.30, p.2264
IFRS 15.111	Ch.32, p.2408	IFRS 15.B7	Ch.30, p.2264
IFRS 15.112	Ch.32, p.2408	IFRS 15.B7	Ch.30, p.2265
IFRS 15.112	Ch.32, p.2410	IFRS 15.B8	Ch.30, p.2265
IFRS 15.112	Ch.36, p.2980	IFRS 15.B9	Ch.30, p.2267
IFRS 15.113	Ch.32, p.2404	IFRS 15.B10	Ch.30, p.2268
IFRS 15.113	Ch.43, p.3458	IFRS 15.B11	Ch.30, p.2268
IFRS 15.113(a)	Ch.43, p.3450	IFRS 15.B12	Ch.30, p.2267
IFRS 15.113(b)	Ch.29, p.2206	IFRS 15.B12	Ch.30, p.2269
IFRS 15.113(b)	Ch.32, p.2399	IFRS 15.B13	Ch.30, p.2269
IFRS 15.113(b)	Ch.32, p.2400	IFRS 15.B14	Ch.30, p.2279
IFRS 15.114	Ch.32, p.2409	IFRS 15.B15	Ch.30, p.2279
IFRS 15.114	Ch.36, p.2980	IFRS 15.B16	Ch.30, p.2280
IFRS 15.115	Ch.32, p.2411	IFRS 15.B16	Ch.30, p.2281
IFRS 15.115	Ch.36, p.2980	IFRS 15.B17	Ch.30, p.2280
IFRS 15.116	Ch.32, p.2417	IFRS 15.B18	Ch.25, p.1908

IFRS 15.B18	Ch.25, p.1915
IFRS 15.B18	Ch.30, p.2280
IFRS 15.B19	Ch.25, p.1898
IFRS 15.B19	Ch.30, p.2283
IFRS 15.B19	Ch.30, p.2284
IFRS 15.B19(a)	Ch.30, p.2284
IFRS 15.B20	Ch.28, p.2154
IFRS 15.B20	Ch.29, p.2188
IFRS 15.B21	Ch.29, p.2188
IFRS 15.B21	Ch.29, p.2189
IFRS 15.B22	Ch.28, p.2154
IFRS 15.B22	Ch.29, p.2188
IFRS 15.B23	Ch.29, p.2189
IFRS 15.B24	Ch.29, p.2189
IFRS 15.B25	Ch.29, p.2189
IFRS 15.B25	Ch.32, p.2402
IFRS 15.B26	Ch.28, p.2154
IFRS 15.B26	Ch.29, p.2188
IFRS 15.B27	Ch.28, p.2154
IFRS 15.B27	Ch.29, p.2188
IFRS 15.B28	Ch.31, p.2350
IFRS 15.B28-B33	Ch.28, p.2096
IFRS 15.B29	Ch.31, p.2350
IFRS 15.B29	Ch.31, p.2353
IFRS 15.B30	Ch.25, p.1906
IFRS 15.B30	Ch.25, p.1914
IFRS 15.B30	Ch.26, p.1936
IFRS 15.B30	Ch.26, p.2003
IFRS 15.B30	Ch.31, p.2350
IFRS 15.B30	Ch.31, p.2354
IFRS 15.B31	Ch.31, p.2350
IFRS 15.B32	Ch.31, p.2353
IFRS 15.B32	Ch.31, p.2355
IFRS 15.B33	Ch.26, p.1936
IFRS 15.B33	Ch.31, p.2350
IFRS 15.B33	Ch.31, p.2351
IFRS 15.B34	Ch.28, p.2121
IFRS 15.B34	Ch.28, p.2123
IFRS 15.B34	Ch.28, p.2124
IFRS 15.B34A(a)	Ch.28, p.2123
IFRS 15.B34A(b)	Ch.28, p.2125
IFRS 15.B34A	Ch.28, p.2121
IFRS 15.B35	Ch.28, p.2121
IFRS 15.B35	Ch.28, p.2122
IFRS 15.B35A	Ch.28, p.2126
IFRS 15.B35B	Ch.28, p.2131
IFRS 15.B36	Ch.28, p.2121
IFRS 15.B36	Ch.28, p.2131
IFRS 15.B37	Ch.28, p.2129
IFRS 15.B37A	Ch.28, p.2129
IFRS 15.B38	Ch.28, p.2132
IFRS 15.B39	Ch.28, p.2140
IFRS 15.B39-B43	Ch.28, p.2096
IFRS 15.B40	Ch.28, p.2140
IFRS 15.B40	Ch.28, p.2148
IFRS 15.B40	Ch.28, p.2154
IFRS 15.B41	Ch.28, p.2141
IFRS 15.B41	Ch.28, p.2148
IFRS 15.B41	Ch.28, p.2150
IFRS 15.B42	Ch.29, p.2231
IFRS 15.B43	Ch.29, p.2231
IFRS 15.B43	Ch.29, p.2232
IFRS 15.B44-B47	Ch.28, p.2154
IFRS 15.B44-B47	Ch.43, p.3472
IFRS 15.B45	Ch.30, p.2309
IFRS 15.B46	Ch.28, p.2066
IFRS 15.B46	Ch.30, p.2309
IFRS 15.B46	Ch.30, p.2311
IFRS 15.B46	Ch.31, p.2348
IFRS 15.B48	Ch.29, p.2218
IFRS 15.B49	Ch.28, p.2089
IFRS 15.B49	Ch.29, p.2218
IFRS 15.B50	Ch.29, p.2218
IFRS 15.B51	Ch.29, p.2218
IFRS 15.B52	Ch.31, p.2320
IFRS 15.B53	Ch.31, p.2321
IFRS 15.B54	Ch.28, p.2096
IFRS 15.B54	Ch.31, p.2324
IFRS 15.B56	Ch.31, p.2320
IFRS 15.B58	Ch.31, p.2328
IFRS 15.B59	Ch.31, p.2328
IFRS 15.B59A	Ch.31, p.2329
IFRS 15.B60	Ch.31, p.2333
IFRS 15.B61	Ch.31, p.2333
IFRS 15.B61	Ch.31, p.2335
IFRS 15.B61	Ch.31, p.2336
IFRS 15.B62(a)	Ch.31, p.2324
IFRS 15.B62(b)	Ch.31, p.2326
IFRS 15.B63	Ch.31, p.2337
IFRS 15.B63	Ch.31, p.2348
IFRS 15.B63A	Ch.31, p.2338
IFRS 15.B63B	Ch.31, p.2340
IFRS 15.B64	Ch.30, p.2298
IFRS 15.B64	Ch.43, p.3466
IFRS 15.B65	Ch.30, p.2298
IFRS 15.B65	Ch.43, p.3466
IFRS 15.B66-B67	Ch.30, p.2299
IFRS 15.B68-B69	Ch.30, p.2300
IFRS 15.B70	Ch.30, p.2301
IFRS 15.B70	Ch.30, p.2302
IFRS 15.B70-B71	Ch.30, p.2301
IFRS 15.B72	Ch.30, p.2302
IFRS 15.B73	Ch.30, p.2302
IFRS 15.B74	Ch.30, p.2302
IFRS 15.B75	Ch.30, p.2301
IFRS 15.B76	Ch.30, p.2302
IFRS 15.B77	Ch.30, p.2304
IFRS 15.B77	Ch.30, p.2305
IFRS 15.B78	Ch.30, p.2304
IFRS 15.B79	Ch.30, p.2305
IFRS 15.B79-B82	Ch.43, p.3448
IFRS 15.B80	Ch.30, p.2305
IFRS 15.B81	Ch.30, p.2306
IFRS 15.B82	Ch.30, p.2306
IFRS 15.B82	Ch.43, p.3448
IFRS 15.B83	Ch.30, p.2295

IFRS 15.B84	Ch.30, p.2296	IFRS 15.IE238A-IE238G	Ch.28, p.2133
IFRS 15.B85	Ch.30, p.2296	IFRS 15.IE239-IE243	Ch.28, p.2134
IFRS 15.B86	Ch.30, p.2296	IFRS 15.IE244-IE248	Ch.28, p.2134
IFRS 15.B87	Ch.32, p.2410	IFRS 15.IE248A-IE248F	Ch.28, p.2135
IFRS 15.B87-B89	Ch.32, p.2410	IFRS 15.IE250-IE253	Ch.28, p.2141
IFRS 15.C1	Ch.27, p.2020	IFRS 15.IE257-IE266	Ch.28, p.2151
IFRS 15.C5	Ch.5, p.335	IFRS 15.IE267-IE270	Ch.30, p.2310
IFRS 15.C5(a)(ii)	Ch.5, p.339	IFRS 15.IE281	Ch.31, p.2322
IFRS 15.C5(a)(ii)	Ch.5, p.341	IFRS 15.IE281-IE284	Ch.31, p.2331
IFRS 15.C5(c)	Ch.5, p.336	IFRS 15.IE285-IE288	Ch.31, p.2322
IFRS 15.C6	Ch.5, p.336	IFRS 15.IE297-IE302	Ch.31, p.2334
IFRS 15.C10	Ch.27, p.2020	IFRS 15.IE303-IE306	Ch.31, p.2335
IFRS 15.IE3-IE6	Ch.28, p.2059	IFRS 15.IE307-IE308	Ch.31, p.2340
IFRS 15.IE7-IE9	Ch.29, p.2169	IFRS 15.IE309-IE313	Ch.31, p.2342
IFRS 15.IE14-IE17	Ch.28, p.2061	IFRS 15.IE315	Ch.30, p.2303
IFRS 15.IE17	Ch.28, p.2061	IFRS 15.IE315-IE318	Ch.30, p.2300
IFRS 15.IE19	Ch.28, p.2074	IFRS 15.IE319-IE321	Ch.30, p.2303
IFRS 15.IE19-IE21	Ch.28, p.2073	IFRS 15.IE323-IE327	Ch.30, p.2307
IFRS 15.IE22-IE24	Ch.28, p.2074	IFRS 15.BC32	Ch.28, p.2052
IFRS 15.IE33-IE36	Ch.28, p.2074	IFRS 15.BC32	Ch.28, p.2086
IFRS 15.IE37-IE41	Ch.28, p.2076	IFRS 15.BC33	Ch.28, p.2053
IFRS 15.IE42-IE43	Ch.28, p.2069	IFRS 15.BC34	Ch.28, p.2053
IFRS 15.IE45-IE48C	Ch.28, p.2116	IFRS 15.BC35	Ch.28, p.2055
IFRS 15.IE49-IE58	Ch.28, p.2117	IFRS 15.BC36	Ch.28, p.2056
IFRS 15.IE58A-IE58K	Ch.28, p.2118	IFRS 15.BC37	Ch.28, p.2056
IFRS 15.IE59-IE65A	Ch.28, p.2087	IFRS 15.BC40	Ch.28, p.2056
IFRS 15.IE67-IE68	Ch.28, p.2114	IFRS 15.BC43	Ch.28, p.2057
IFRS 15.IE67-IE68	Ch.30, p.2262	IFRS 15.BC45	Ch.28, p.2057
IFRS 15.IE69-IE72	Ch.30, p.2269	IFRS 15.BC46	Ch.28, p.2058
IFRS 15.IE73-IE76	Ch.30, p.2265	IFRS 15.BC46C	Ch.28, p.2058
IFRS 15.IE77-IE80	Ch.30, p.2270	IFRS 15.BC46E	Ch.28, p.2057
IFRS 15.IE81-IE90	Ch.30, p.2270	IFRS 15.BC46E	Ch.28, p.2058
IFRS 15.IE92-IE94	Ch.30, p.2286	IFRS 15.BC46H	Ch.28, p.2083
IFRS 15.IE95-IE100	Ch.30, p.2284	IFRS 15.BC46H	Ch.28, p.2084
IFRS 15.IE98	Ch.30, p.2286	IFRS 15.BC47	Ch.28, p.2083
IFRS 15.IE102-IE104	Ch.29, p.2173	IFRS 15.BC48	Ch.28, p.2066
IFRS 15.IE110-IE115	Ch.29, p.2190	IFRS 15.BC48	Ch.28, p.2083
IFRS 15.IE116-IE123	Ch.29, p.2182	IFRS 15.BC52-BC56	Ch.43, p.3450
IFRS 15.IE124-IE128	Ch.29, p.2167	IFRS 15.BC54	Ch.27, p.2028
IFRS 15.IE129-IE133	Ch.29, p.2184	IFRS 15.BC54	Ch.43, p.3453
IFRS 15.IE135-IE140	Ch.29, p.2197	IFRS 15.BC56	Ch.27, p.2028
IFRS 15.IE141-IE142	Ch.29, p.2198	IFRS 15.BC58	Ch.27, p.2026
IFRS 15.IE143-IE147	Ch.29, p.2199	IFRS 15.BC69	Ch.28, p.2068
IFRS 15.IE148-IE151	Ch.29, p.2199	IFRS 15.BC71	Ch.28, p.2067
IFRS 15.IE152-IE154	Ch.29, p.2200	IFRS 15.BC73	Ch.28, p.2068
IFRS 15.IE156-IE158	Ch.29, p.2207	IFRS 15.BC74	Ch.28, p.2067
IFRS 15.IE160-IE162	Ch.29, p.2216	IFRS 15.BC75	Ch.28, p.2067
IFRS 15.IE164-IE166	Ch.29, p.2227	IFRS 15.BC76	Ch.28, p.2070
IFRS 15.IE167-IE177	Ch.29, p.2244	IFRS 15.BC79	Ch.27, p.2024
IFRS 15.IE178-IE187	Ch.29, p.2242	IFRS 15.BC79	Ch.28, p.2071
IFRS 15.IE178-IE187	Ch.31, p.2340	IFRS 15.BC83	Ch.29, p.2248
IFRS 15.IE189-IE191	Ch.31, p.2362	IFRS 15.BC85	Ch.28, p.2084
IFRS 15.IE192-IE196	Ch.31, p.2368	IFRS 15.BC87	Ch.28, p.2086
IFRS 15.IE198-IE200	Ch.32, p.2396	IFRS 15.BC87	Ch.28, p.2088
IFRS 15.IE201-IE204	Ch.32, p.2397	IFRS 15.BC88	Ch.28, p.2086
IFRS 15.IE210-IE211	Ch.32, p.2412	IFRS 15.BC89	Ch.28, p.2086
IFRS 15.IE212-IE219	Ch.32, p.2430	IFRS 15.BC90	Ch.28, p.2090
IFRS 15.IE220-IE221	Ch.32, p.2432	IFRS 15.BC92	Ch.28, p.2087

IFRS 15.BC100	Ch.28, p.2097	IFRS 15.BC171	Ch.30, p.2286
IFRS 15.BC100	Ch.28, p.2104	IFRS 15.BC172	Ch.30, p.2284
IFRS 15.BC101	Ch.28, p.2097	IFRS 15.BC172	Ch.30, p.2285
IFRS 15.BC102	Ch.28, p.2096	IFRS 15.BC172	Ch.30, p.2286
IFRS 15.BC102	Ch.28, p.2099	IFRS 15.BC174	Ch.30, p.2284
IFRS 15.BC105	Ch.28, p.2104	IFRS 15.BC174	Ch.30, p.2285
IFRS 15.BC107	Ch.28, p.2101	IFRS 15.BC179	Ch.30, p.2279
IFRS 15.BC108	Ch.28, p.2101	IFRS 15.BC180	Ch.30, p.2279
IFRS 15.BC109	Ch.28, p.2102	IFRS 15.BC185	Ch.29, p.2164
IFRS 15.BC110	Ch.28, p.2102	IFRS 15.BC187	Ch.29, p.2164
IFRS 15.BC112	Ch.28, p.2103	IFRS 15.BC188D	Ch.28, p.2136
IFRS 15.BC113	Ch.28, p.2109	IFRS 15.BC188D	Ch.29, p.2166
IFRS 15.BC113	Ch.28, p.2112	IFRS 15.BC191	Ch.29, p.2167
IFRS 15.BC114	Ch.28, p.2109	IFRS 15.BC194	Ch.28, p.2059
IFRS 15.BC115	Ch.28, p.2111	IFRS 15.BC194	Ch.29, p.2170
IFRS 15.BC116	Ch.28, p.2112	IFRS 15.BC200	Ch.29, p.2176
IFRS 15.BC116D	Ch.28, p.2090	IFRS 15.BC200	Ch.29, p.2177
IFRS 15.BC116J	Ch.28, p.2099	IFRS 15.BC201	Ch.29, p.2177
IFRS 15.BC116J	Ch.28, p.2104	IFRS 15.BC202	Ch.29, p.2176
IFRS 15.BC116J-BC116L	Ch.28, p.2100	IFRS 15.BC203	Ch.29, p.2179
IFRS 15.BC116K	Ch.28, p.2099	IFRS 15.BC204	Ch.29, p.2179
IFRS 15.BC116K	Ch.28, p.2104	IFRS 15.BC211	Ch.29, p.2180
IFRS 15.BC116L	Ch.28, p.2099	IFRS 15.BC212	Ch.29, p.2180
IFRS 15.BC116N	Ch.28, p.2100	IFRS 15.BC215	Ch.29, p.2185
IFRS 15.BC116N	Ch.28, p.2104	IFRS 15.BC219	Ch.31, p.2337
IFRS 15.BC116U	Ch.28, p.2090	IFRS 15.BC228	Ch.29, p.2187
IFRS 15.BC118	Ch.30, p.2257	IFRS 15.BC228	Ch.29, p.2249
IFRS 15.BC120	Ch.30, p.2257	IFRS 15.BC229	Ch.29, p.2193
IFRS 15.BC121	Ch.30, p.2258	IFRS 15.BC230	Ch.29, p.2193
IFRS 15.BC125	Ch.30, p.2260	IFRS 15.BC232	Ch.29, p.2194
IFRS 15.BC126	Ch.30, p.2261	IFRS 15.BC233	Ch.29, p.2194
IFRS 15.BC127	Ch.30, p.2262	IFRS 15.BC233	Ch.29, p.2195
IFRS 15.BC129	Ch.30, p.2263	IFRS 15.BC234	Ch.29, p.2196
IFRS 15.BC130	Ch.30, p.2263	IFRS 15.BC235	Ch.29, p.2194
IFRS 15.BC135	Ch.30, p.2265	IFRS 15.BC236	Ch.29, p.2194
IFRS 15.BC136	Ch.30, p.2266	IFRS 15.BC238	Ch.29, p.2195
IFRS 15.BC137	Ch.30, p.2265	IFRS 15.BC239	Ch.29, p.2196
IFRS 15.BC138	Ch.30, p.2265	IFRS 15.BC244	Ch.29, p.2205
IFRS 15.BC138-BC139	Ch.27, p.2025	IFRS 15.BC247	Ch.29, p.2206
IFRS 15.BC139	Ch.30, p.2266	IFRS 15.BC252	Ch.29, p.2209
IFRS 15.BC141	Ch.30, p.2266	IFRS 15.BC254C	Ch.29, p.2208
IFRS 15.BC142	Ch.30, p.2267	IFRS 15.BC254E	Ch.29, p.2208
IFRS 15.BC142	Ch.30, p.2268	IFRS 15.BC254H	Ch.29, p.2209
IFRS 15.BC144	Ch.30, p.2268	IFRS 15.BC257	Ch.29, p.2213
IFRS 15.BC145	Ch.30, p.2269	IFRS 15.BC266	Ch.29, p.2222
IFRS 15.BC145	Ch.30, p.2273	IFRS 15.BC272	Ch.29, p.2226
IFRS 15.BC146	Ch.30, p.2273	IFRS 15.BC273	Ch.29, p.2226
IFRS 15.BC148	Ch.30, p.2293	IFRS 15.BC278	Ch.29, p.2237
IFRS 15.BC154	Ch.30, p.2293	IFRS 15.BC279-BC280	Ch.29, p.2243
IFRS 15.BC155	Ch.30, p.2292	IFRS 15.BC280	Ch.29, p.2237
IFRS 15.BC160	Ch.30, p.2280	IFRS 15.BC283	Ch.29, p.2244
IFRS 15.BC161	Ch.30, p.2278	IFRS 15.BC296	Ch.31, p.2356
IFRS 15.BC161	Ch.30, p.2288	IFRS 15.BC307	Ch.31, p.2365
IFRS 15.BC163	Ch.30, p.2281	IFRS 15.BC307	Ch.31, p.2367
IFRS 15.BC165	Ch.30, p.2280	IFRS 15.BC308	Ch.25, p.1897
IFRS 15.BC166	Ch.30, p.2281	IFRS 15.BC308	Ch.31, p.2367
IFRS 15.BC171	Ch.30, p.2284	IFRS 15.BC309	Ch.31, p.2377
IFRS 15.BC171	Ch.30, p.2285	IFRS 15.BC312	Ch.31, p.2370

IFRS 15.BC313	Ch.31, p.2371	IFRS 15.BC414P	Ch.31, p.2326
IFRS 15.BC315	Ch.31, p.2371	IFRS 15.BC414Q	Ch.31, p.2325
IFRS 15.BC317	Ch.32, p.2400	IFRS 15.BC414S	Ch.31, p.2336
IFRS 15.BC323	Ch.32, p.2396	IFRS 15.BC414T	Ch.31, p.2337
IFRS 15.BC323-BC324	Ch.32, p.2395	IFRS 15.BC414U	Ch.31, p.2337
IFRS 15.BC325	Ch.32, p.2395	IFRS 15.BC414X	Ch.31, p.2321
IFRS 15.BC327	Ch.32, p.2408	IFRS 15.BC414X	Ch.31, p.2331
IFRS 15.BC331	Ch.32, p.2408	IFRS 15.BC414Y	Ch.31, p.2332
IFRS 15.BC332	Ch.32, p.2404	IFRS 15.BC415	Ch.31, p.2338
IFRS 15.BC334	Ch.32, p.2404	IFRS 15.BC416	Ch.31, p.2338
IFRS 15.BC336	Ch.32, p.2410	IFRS 15.BC421	Ch.31, p.2343
IFRS 15.BC340	Ch.32, p.2411	IFRS 15.BC421E	Ch.31, p.2338
IFRS 15.BC340	Ch.36, p.2980	IFRS 15.BC421F	Ch.31, p.2343
IFRS 15.BC341	Ch.32, p.2417	IFRS 15.BC421G	Ch.31, p.2338
IFRS 15.BC346	Ch.32, p.2417	IFRS 15.BC421I	Ch.31, p.2337
IFRS 15.BC347	Ch.32, p.2418	IFRS 15.BC421I	Ch.31, p.2341
IFRS 15.BC348	Ch.32, p.2428	IFRS 15.BC421J	Ch.31, p.2340
IFRS 15.BC350	Ch.32, p.2428	IFRS 15.BC423	Ch.30, p.2299
IFRS 15.BC354	Ch.32, p.2421	IFRS 15.BC425	Ch.30, p.2300
IFRS 15.BC355	Ch.32, p.2433	IFRS 15.BC427	Ch.30, p.2299
IFRS 15.BC355	Ch.32, p.2435	IFRS 15.BC427	Ch.30, p.2303
IFRS 15.BC364	Ch.28, p.2154	IFRS 15.BC431	Ch.30, p.2304
IFRS 15.BC371	Ch.31, p.2353	IFRS 15.BC441	Ch.5, p.338
IFRS 15.BC376	Ch.31, p.2353	IFRS 15.BC445D	Ch.5, p.338
IFRS 15.BC376	Ch.31, p.2354		
IFRS 15.BC383-BC385	Ch.28, p.2132		
IFRS 15.BC385B	Ch.28, p.2123		
IFRS 15.BC385D	Ch.28, p.2121		

IFRS 16

IFRS 15.BC385E	Ch.28, p.2121
IFRS 15.BC385H	Ch.28, p.2129
IFRS 15.BC385O	Ch.28, p.2123
IFRS 15.BC385O	Ch.28, p.2127
IFRS 15.BC385Q	Ch.28, p.2123
IFRS 15.BC385R	Ch.28, p.2128
IFRS 15.BC385S	Ch.28, p.2125
IFRS 15.BC385U	Ch.28, p.2126
IFRS 15.BC385V	Ch.28, p.2127
IFRS 15.BC385Z	Ch.28, p.2136
IFRS 15.BC386	Ch.28, p.2140
IFRS 15.BC390	Ch.29, p.2231
IFRS 15.BC391	Ch.28, p.2064
IFRS 15.BC394	Ch.29, p.2231
IFRS 15.BC 394	Ch.29, p.2232
IFRS 15.BC395	Ch.29, p.2232
IFRS 15.BC398	Ch.30, p.2309
IFRS 15.BC400	Ch.30, p.2309
IFRS 15.BC405-BC406	Ch.31, p.2325
IFRS 15.BC407	Ch.31, p.2320
IFRS 15.BC407	Ch.31, p.2330
IFRS 15.BC412(b)	Ch.28, p.2094
IFRS 15.BC413	Ch.31, p.2329
IFRS 15.BC414	Ch.31, p.2333
IFRS 15.BC414	Ch.31, p.2336
IFRS 15.BC414I	Ch.31, p.2329
IFRS 15.BC414K	Ch.31, p.2330
IFRS 15.BC414N	Ch.31, p.2330
IFRS 15.BC414O	Ch.31, p.2325
IFRS 15.BC414P	Ch.31, p.2325

IFRS 16.1	Ch.23, p.1710
IFRS 16.2	Ch.23, p.1710
IFRS 16.2	Ch.43, p.3540
IFRS 16.3	Ch.17, p.1294
IFRS 16.3	Ch.23, p.1710
IFRS 16.3	Ch.43, p.3528
IFRS 16.3(a)	Ch.43, p.3336
IFRS 16.3(a)	Ch.43, p.3361
IFRS 16.3(b)	Ch.42, p.3280
IFRS 16.3(c)	Ch.25, p.1857
IFRS 16.4	Ch.23, p.1710
IFRS 16.5	Ch.23, p.1710
IFRS 16.6	Ch.5, p.303
IFRS 16.6	Ch.23, p.1752
IFRS 16.6	Ch.23, p.1753
IFRS 16.6	Ch.43, p.3547
IFRS 16.7	Ch.23, p.1752
IFRS 16.8	Ch.23, p.1752
IFRS 16.8	Ch.23, p.1753
IFRS 16.9	Ch.17, p.1373
IFRS 16.9	Ch.23, p.1713
IFRS 16.9	Ch.23, p.1714
IFRS 16.9	Ch.25, p.1857
IFRS 16.9	Ch.43, p.3539
IFRS 16.9	Ch.43, p.3553
IFRS 16.9-11	Ch.5, p.302
IFRS 16.10	Ch.23, p.1714
IFRS 16.11	Ch.5, p.302
IFRS 16.11	Ch.23, p.1728
IFRS 16.12	Ch.23, p.1728

IFRS 16.12	Ch.27, p.2030	IFRS 16.47	Ch.18, p.1388
IFRS 16.12	Ch.43, p.3531	IFRS 16.47	Ch.23, p.1774
IFRS 16.12	Ch.43, p.3554	IFRS 16.48	Ch.18, p.1388
IFRS 16.13	Ch.23, p.1731	IFRS 16.48	Ch.19, p.1445
IFRS 16.14	Ch.23, p.1731	IFRS 16.48	Ch.23, p.1774
IFRS 16.15	Ch.23, p.1730	IFRS 16.49	Ch.23, p.1774
IFRS 16.15-16	Ch.26, p.1977	IFRS 16.50	Ch.23, p.1775
IFRS 16.16	Ch.23, p.1729	IFRS 16.50	Ch.40, p.3168
IFRS 16.17	Ch.23, p.1734	IFRS 16.50	Ch.40, p.3169
IFRS 16.17	Ch.27, p.2030	IFRS 16.51	Ch.23, p.1776
IFRS 16.18	Ch.23, p.1736	IFRS 16.52	Ch.23, p.1776
IFRS 16.19	Ch.23, p.1736	IFRS 16.53	Ch.23, p.1776
IFRS 16.20	Ch.23, p.1741	IFRS 16.53(i)	Ch.23, p.1807
IFRS 16.21	Ch.23, p.1742	IFRS 16.53(g)	Ch.23, p.1778
IFRS 16.22	Ch.23, p.1751	IFRS 16.53(g)	Ch.40, p.3168
IFRS 16.22	Ch.45, p.3587	IFRS 16.54	Ch.23, p.1776
IFRS 16.23	Ch.23, p.1754	IFRS 16.55	Ch.23, p.1778
IFRS 16.24	Ch.19, p.1463	IFRS 16.55	Ch.38, p.3080
IFRS 16.24	Ch.23, p.1754	IFRS 16.56	Ch.19, p.1445
IFRS 16.24(b)	Ch.19, p.1462	IFRS 16.56	Ch.23, p.1778
IFRS 16.24(b)	Ch.23, p.1743	IFRS 16.57	Ch.23, p.1778
IFRS 16.24(d)	Ch.26, p.1986	IFRS 16.58	Ch.23, p.1778
IFRS 16.25	Ch.23, p.1754	IFRS 16.58	Ch.54, p.4455
IFRS 16.25	Ch.26, p.1986	IFRS 16.59	Ch.23, p.1779
IFRS 16.26	Ch.23, p.1749	IFRS 16.60	Ch.23, p.1751
IFRS 16.26	Ch.23, p.1754	IFRS 16.61	Ch.23, p.1781
IFRS 16.26	Ch.45, p.3587	IFRS 16.62	Ch.23, p.1781
IFRS 16.27	Ch.23, p.1755	IFRS 16.63	Ch.23, p.1782
IFRS 16.27(a)	Ch.19, p.1462	IFRS 16.64	Ch.23, p.1782
IFRS 16.27(a)	Ch.23, p.1743	IFRS 16.65	Ch.23, p.1782
IFRS 16.28	Ch.23, p.1744	IFRS 16.66	Ch.5, p.371
IFRS 16.29	Ch.23, p.1755	IFRS 16.66	Ch.23, p.1783
IFRS 16.29-35	Ch.18, p.1426	IFRS 16.67	Ch.23, p.1784
IFRS 16.30	Ch.23, p.1755	IFRS 16.67	Ch.23, p.1796
IFRS 16.31	Ch.23, p.1755	IFRS 16.67	Ch.25, p.1856
IFRS 16.31	Ch.26, p.2003	IFRS 16.67-97	Ch.42, p.3280
IFRS 16.32	Ch.23, p.1755	IFRS 16.68	Ch.23, p.1785
IFRS 16.33	Ch.20, p.1521	IFRS 16.68	Ch.23, p.1799
IFRS 16.33	Ch.23, p.1756	IFRS 16.69	Ch.23, p.1751
IFRS 16.33	Ch.23, p.1773	IFRS 16.69	Ch.23, p.1785
IFRS 16.34	Ch.19, p.1444	IFRS 16.70	Ch.23, p.1785
IFRS 16.34	Ch.23, p.1756	IFRS 16.70(a)	Ch.23, p.1743
IFRS 16.35	Ch.23, p.1756	IFRS 16.70(c)	Ch.23, p.1745
IFRS 16.36	Ch.23, p.1756	IFRS 16.71	Ch.23, p.1785
IFRS 16.37	Ch.23, p.1756	IFRS 16.72	Ch.23, p.1786
IFRS 16.38	Ch.23, p.1756	IFRS 16.73	Ch.23, p.1786
IFRS 16.38(b)	Ch.23, p.1746	IFRS 16.74	Ch.23, p.1786
IFRS 16.39	Ch.23, p.1748	IFRS 16.75	Ch.23, p.1787
IFRS 16.39	Ch.23, p.1758	IFRS 16.76	Ch.23, p.1787
IFRS 16.40	Ch.23, p.1758	IFRS 16.77	Ch.23, p.1787
IFRS 16.41	Ch.23, p.1758	IFRS 16.77	Ch.23, p.1789
IFRS 16.42	Ch.23, p.1758	IFRS 16.77	Ch.51, p.4045
IFRS 16.42(a)	Ch.23, p.1745	IFRS 16.78	Ch.23, p.1788
IFRS 16.42(b)	Ch.23, p.1744	IFRS 16.79	Ch.23, p.1793
IFRS 16.43	Ch.23, p.1758	IFRS 16.80	Ch.23, p.1793
IFRS 16.44	Ch.23, p.1759	IFRS 16.81	Ch.19, p.1462
IFRS 16.45	Ch.23, p.1760	IFRS 16.81	Ch.23, p.1791
IFRS 16.46	Ch.23, p.1760	IFRS 16.81-88	Ch.42, p.3280

IFRS 16.82	Ch.23, p.1791	IFRS 16.B7	Ch.23, p.1753
IFRS 16.83	Ch.19, p.1463	IFRS 16.B7	Ch.23, p.1799
IFRS 16.83	Ch.23, p.1791	IFRS 16.B8	Ch.23, p.1753
IFRS 16.84	Ch.23, p.1791	IFRS 16.B9	Ch.17, p.1373
IFRS 16.85	Ch.23, p.1791	IFRS 16.B9	Ch.23, p.1714
IFRS 16.86	Ch.23, p.1791	IFRS 16.B9	Ch.25, p.1857
IFRS 16.87	Ch.23, p.1793	IFRS 16.B10	Ch.23, p.1714
IFRS 16.88	Ch.23, p.1796	IFRS 16.B11	Ch.23, p.1714
IFRS 16.89	Ch.23, p.1797	IFRS 16.B12	Ch.23, p.1714
IFRS 16.90	Ch.23, p.1797	IFRS 16.B13	Ch.23, p.1716
IFRS 16.91	Ch.23, p.1797	IFRS 16.B14	Ch.23, p.1720
IFRS 16.92	Ch.23, p.1797	IFRS 16.B14	Ch.43, p.3531
IFRS 16.93	Ch.23, p.1797	IFRS 16.B14	Ch.43, p.3541
IFRS 16.94	Ch.23, p.1797	IFRS 16.B14(a)-(b)	Ch.43, p.3531
IFRS 16.95	Ch.23, p.1798	IFRS 16.B15	Ch.23, p.1720
IFRS 16.96	Ch.23, p.1798	IFRS 16.B16	Ch.23, p.1720
IFRS 16.97	Ch.23, p.1798	IFRS 16.B17	Ch.23, p.1720
IFRS 16.98	Ch.23, p.1801	IFRS 16.B18	Ch.23, p.1721
IFRS 16.99	Ch.23, p.1801	IFRS 16.B19	Ch.23, p.1721
IFRS 16.99	Ch.40, p.3170	IFRS 16.B19	Ch.43, p.3531
IFRS 16.100	Ch.23, p.1803	IFRS 16.B19	Ch.43, p.3541
IFRS 16.100	Ch.40, p.3170	IFRS 16.B20	Ch.23, p.1717
IFRS 16.101	Ch.23, p.1805	IFRS 16.B21	Ch.23, p.1722
IFRS 16.101	Ch.40, p.3170	IFRS 16.B22	Ch.23, p.1722
IFRS 16.102	Ch.23, p.1805	IFRS 16.B23	Ch.23, p.1722
IFRS 16.103	Ch.23, p.1807	IFRS 16.B24	Ch.23, p.1722
IFRS 16.103	Ch.40, p.3170	IFRS 16.B24	Ch.23, p.1724
IFRS 16 Appendix A	Ch.5, p.303	IFRS 16.B24	Ch.43, p.3545
IFRS 16 Appendix A	Ch.17, p.1373	IFRS 16.B25	Ch.23, p.1723
IFRS 16 Appendix A	Ch.19, p.1462	IFRS 16.B26	Ch.23, p.1723
IFRS 16 Appendix A	Ch.19, p.1463	IFRS 16.B27	Ch.23, p.1724
IFRS 16 Appendix A	Ch.23, p.1711	IFRS 16.B28	Ch.23, p.1725
IFRS 16 Appendix A	Ch.23, p.1713	IFRS 16.B29	Ch.23, p.1726
IFRS 16 Appendix A	Ch.23, p.1720	IFRS 16.B30	Ch.23, p.1726
IFRS 16 Appendix A	Ch.23, p.1735	IFRS 16.B31	Ch.23, p.1726
IFRS 16 Appendix A	Ch.23, p.1742	IFRS 16.B32	Ch.23, p.1728
IFRS 16 Appendix A	Ch.23, p.1743	IFRS 16.B32	Ch.27, p.2030
IFRS 16 Appendix A	Ch.23, p.1749	IFRS 16.B33	Ch.23, p.1728
IFRS 16 Appendix A	Ch.23, p.1750	IFRS 16.B33	Ch.23, p.1729
IFRS 16 Appendix A	Ch.23, p.1751	IFRS 16.B33	Ch.27, p.2030
IFRS 16 Appendix A	Ch.23, p.1752	IFRS 16.B34	Ch.23, p.1739
IFRS 16 Appendix A	Ch.23, p.1759	IFRS 16.B35	Ch.23, p.1739
IFRS 16 Appendix A	Ch.23, p.1780	IFRS 16.B36	Ch.23, p.1736
IFRS 16 Appendix A	Ch.23, p.1784	IFRS 16.B37	Ch.23, p.1736
IFRS 16 Appendix A	Ch.23, p.1792	IFRS 16.B37	Ch.23, p.1737
IFRS 16 Appendix A	Ch.23, p.1798	IFRS 16.B38	Ch.23, p.1737
IFRS 16 Appendix A	Ch.23, p.1806	IFRS 16.B39	Ch.23, p.1738
IFRS 16 Appendix A	Ch.40, p.3169	IFRS 16.B40	Ch.23, p.1738
IFRS 16 Appendix A	Ch.43, p.3530	IFRS 16.B41	Ch.23, p.1741
IFRS 16 Appendix A	Ch.43, p.3553	IFRS 16.B42	Ch.23, p.1743
IFRS 16.B1	Ch.23, p.1773	IFRS 16.B43	Ch.23, p.1735
IFRS 16.B1	Ch.23, p.1796	IFRS 16.B44	Ch.23, p.1735
IFRS 16.B2	Ch.23, p.1734	IFRS 16.B45	Ch.23, p.1735
IFRS 16.B3	Ch.23, p.1753	IFRS 16.B46	Ch.23, p.1735
IFRS 16.B3-B8	Ch.5, p.303	IFRS 16.B47	Ch.23, p.1736
IFRS 16.B4	Ch.23, p.1753	IFRS 16.B48	Ch.23, p.1779
IFRS 16.B5	Ch.23, p.1753	IFRS 16.B49	Ch.23, p.1780
IFRS 16.B6	Ch.23, p.1753	IFRS 16.B50	Ch.23, p.1780

IFRS 16.B51	Ch.23, p.1780	IFRS 16.BC182	Ch.19, p.1445
IFRS 16.B52	Ch.23, p.1807	IFRS 16.BC199	Ch.23, p.1773
IFRS 16.B53	Ch.23, p.1781	IFRS 16.BC222	Ch.23, p.1778
IFRS 16.B54	Ch.23, p.1783	IFRS 16.BC235	Ch.23, p.1800
IFRS 16.B55	Ch.23, p.1783	IFRS 16.BC236	Ch.23, p.1800
IFRS 16.B56	Ch.23, p.1729	IFRS 16.BC262	Ch.23, p.1802
IFRS 16.B56	Ch.23, p.1783	IFRS 16.BC266	Ch.40, p.3170
IFRS 16.B57	Ch.23, p.1729	IFRS 16.BC287	Ch.23, p.1811
IFRS 16.B57	Ch.23, p.1783	IFRS 16.BC298	Ch.23, p.1808
IFRS 16.B58	Ch.23, p.1799		
IFRS 16.C1	Ch.23, p.1808		
IFRS 16.C1	Ch.41, p.3240		

IFRS 17

IFRS 16.C2	Ch.23, p.1809	IFRS 17.IN4	Ch.56, p.4681
IFRS 16.C3	Ch.23, p.1809	IFRS 17.IN5	Ch.56, p.4681
IFRS 16.C4	Ch.23, p.1809	IFRS 17.IN7	Ch.56, p.4682
IFRS 16.C4	Ch.25, p.1857	IFRS 17.IN8	Ch.56, p.4682
IFRS 16.C5	Ch.23, p.1809	IFRS 17.1	Ch.56, p.4683
IFRS 16.C6	Ch.23, p.1809	IFRS 17.1	Ch.56, p.4898
IFRS 16.C7	Ch.23, p.1810	IFRS 17.2	Ch.56, p.4696
IFRS 16.C8	Ch.23, p.1810	IFRS 17.3	Ch.56, p.4686
IFRS 16.C9	Ch.23, p.1811	IFRS 17.3(c)	Ch.45, p.3594
IFRS 16.C10	Ch.23, p.1811	IFRS 17.3(c)	Ch.56, p.4855
IFRS 16.C11	Ch.23, p.1816	IFRS 17.4	Ch.56, p.4687
IFRS 16.C12	Ch.23, p.1819	IFRS 17.5	Ch.56, p.4687
IFRS 16.C13	Ch.23, p.1819	IFRS 17.7	Ch.56, p.4688
IFRS 16.C14	Ch.23, p.1818	IFRS 17.7(a)	Ch.56, p.4689
IFRS 16.C15	Ch.23, p.1818	IFRS 17.7(b)	Ch.56, p.4689
IFRS 16.C16	Ch.23, p.1818	IFRS 17.7(c)	Ch.56, p.4689
IFRS 16.C17	Ch.23, p.1818	IFRS 17.7(d)	Ch.56, p.4689
IFRS 16.C18	Ch.23, p.1818	IFRS 17.7(e)	Ch.26, p.1935
IFRS 16.C19	Ch.23, p.1819	IFRS 17.7(e)	Ch.45, p.3598
IFRS 16.C20	Ch.23, p.1819	IFRS 17.7(e)	Ch.56, p.4690
IFRS 16.IE4	Ch.23, p.1732	IFRS 17.7(f)	Ch.56, p.4691
IFRS 16.IE7	Ch.23, p.1760	IFRS 17.7(g)	Ch.45, p.3599
IFRS 16.IE8	Ch.23, p.1800	IFRS 17.7(g)	Ch.51, p.3958
IFRS 16.IE11	Ch.23, p.1807	IFRS 17.7(g)	Ch.56, p.4691
IFRS 16.BC58-BC66	Ch.42, p.3280	IFRS 17.7(h)	Ch.45, p.3595
IFRS 16.BC68(a)	Ch.43, p.3528	IFRS 17.7(h)	Ch.48, p.3837
IFRS 16.BC68(b)	Ch.42, p.3280	IFRS 17.7(h)	Ch.56, p.4692
IFRS 16.BC69	Ch.25, p.1857	IFRS 17.8	Ch.27, p.2025
IFRS 16.BC100	Ch.23, p.1753	IFRS 17.8	Ch.56, p.4693
IFRS 16.BC113	Ch.23, p.1720	IFRS 17.8A	Ch.45, p.3596
IFRS 16.BC113	Ch.43, p.3531	IFRS 17.8A	Ch.48, p.3835
IFRS 16.BC120	Ch.23, p.1723	IFRS 17.8A	Ch.56, p.4694
IFRS 16.BC121	Ch.23, p.1724	IFRS 17.9	Ch.56, p.4703
IFRS 16.BC126	Ch.43, p.3542	IFRS 17.9	Ch.56, p.4710
IFRS 16.BC130-BC132	Ch.23, p.1734	IFRS 17.9	Ch.56, p.4718
IFRS 16.BC135 (b)	Ch.23, p.1730	IFRS 17.10	Ch.56, p.4710
IFRS 16.BC139-BC140	Ch.40, p.3168	IFRS 17.11	Ch.56, p.4710
IFRS 16.BC165	Ch.23, p.1744	IFRS 17.11(a)	Ch.45, p.3595
IFRS 16.BC170	Ch.23, p.1745	IFRS 17.11(b)	Ch.45, p.3595
IFRS 16.BC173	Ch.23, p.1736	IFRS 17.11(b)	Ch.56, p.4716
IFRS 16.BC178	Ch.19, p.1444	IFRS 17.12	Ch.56, p.4710
IFRS 16.BC178	Ch.19, p.1467	IFRS 17.12	Ch.56, p.4720
IFRS 16.BC179	Ch.19, p.1471	IFRS 17.13	Ch.56, p.4703
IFRS 16.BC179(b)	Ch.19, p.1443	IFRS 17.13	Ch.56, p.4710
IFRS 16.BC180	Ch.19, p.1471	IFRS 17.14	Ch.56, p.4722
IFRS 16.BC181	Ch.19, p.1471		

IFRS 17.14	Ch.56, p.4723	IFRS 17.54	Ch.56, p.4809
IFRS 17.14	Ch.56, p.4872	IFRS 17.55	Ch.56, p.4812
IFRS 17.16	Ch.56, p.4722	IFRS 17.55(b)	Ch.56, p.4814
IFRS 17.17	Ch.56, p.4726	IFRS 17.56	Ch.56, p.4809
IFRS 17.18	Ch.56, p.4732	IFRS 17.57	Ch.56, p.4813
IFRS 17.18	Ch.56, p.4813	IFRS 17.58	Ch.56, p.4813
IFRS 17.19	Ch.56, p.4726	IFRS 17.59(a)	Ch.56, p.4809
IFRS 17.20	Ch.56, p.4727	IFRS 17.59(b)	Ch.56, p.4816
IFRS 17.20	Ch.56, p.4728	IFRS 17.61	Ch.56, p.4819
IFRS 17.21	Ch.56, p.4722	IFRS 17.62	Ch.56, p.4733
IFRS 17.21	Ch.56, p.4727	IFRS 17.62A	Ch.56, p.4734
IFRS 17.22	Ch.56, p.4728	IFRS 17.63	Ch.56, p.4822
IFRS 17.23	Ch.56, p.4725	IFRS 17.63	Ch.56, p.4828
IFRS 17.24	Ch.56, p.4723	IFRS 17.64	Ch.56, p.4828
IFRS 17.24	Ch.56, p.4725	IFRS 17.65	Ch.56, p.4823
IFRS 17.24	Ch.56, p.4730	IFRS 17.65A	Ch.56, p.4823
IFRS 17.25	Ch.56, p.4732	IFRS 17.66	Ch.56, p.4829
IFRS 17.26	Ch.56, p.4732	IFRS 17.66A	Ch.56, p.4824
IFRS 17.28	Ch.56, p.4732	IFRS 17.66B	Ch.56, p.4825
IFRS 17.28	Ch.56, p.4733	IFRS 17.66(bb)	Ch.56, p.4833
IFRS 17.28	Ch.56, p.4764	IFRS 17.67	Ch.56, p.4832
IFRS 17.28A	Ch.56, p.4735	IFRS 17.68	Ch.56, p.4819
IFRS 17.28A	Ch.56, p.4749	IFRS 17.69	Ch.56, p.4836
IFRS 17.28B	Ch.56, p.4735	IFRS 17.70	Ch.56, p.4837
IFRS 17.28C	Ch.56, p.4862	IFRS 17.70A	Ch.56, p.4837
IFRS 17.28D	Ch.56, p.4735	IFRS 17.71	Ch.56, p.4737
IFRS 17.28E-F	Ch.56, p.4801	IFRS 17.71	Ch.56, p.4856
IFRS 17.28F	Ch.56, p.4802	IFRS 17.72	Ch.56, p.4858
IFRS 17.29	Ch.56, p.4738	IFRS 17.72	Ch.56, p.4859
IFRS 17.30	Ch.15, p.1190	IFRS 17.73	Ch.56, p.4858
IFRS 17.30	Ch.56, p.4739	IFRS 17.74	Ch.56, p.4859
IFRS 17.31	Ch.56, p.4749	IFRS 17.75	Ch.56, p.4859
IFRS 17.31	Ch.56, p.4765	IFRS 17.76	Ch.56, p.4860
IFRS 17.32	Ch.56, p.4737	IFRS 17.77	Ch.56, p.4860
IFRS 17.32	Ch.56, p.4740	IFRS 17.77	Ch.56, p.4861
IFRS 17.33	Ch.56, p.4749	IFRS 17.78	Ch.56, p.4872
IFRS 17.33	Ch.56, p.4750	IFRS 17.79	Ch.56, p.4872
IFRS 17.34	Ch.56, p.4740	IFRS 17.80	Ch.56, p.4874
IFRS 17.35	Ch.56, p.4741	IFRS 17.81	Ch.56, p.4775
IFRS 17.36	Ch.56, p.4762	IFRS 17.81	Ch.56, p.4881
IFRS 17.37	Ch.56, p.4770	IFRS 17.82	Ch.56, p.4874
IFRS 17.38	Ch.56, p.4776	IFRS 17.83	Ch.56, p.4876
IFRS 17.39	Ch.56, p.4776	IFRS 17.84	Ch.56, p.4880
IFRS 17.40	Ch.56, p.4777	IFRS 17.85	Ch.56, p.4715
IFRS 17.41	Ch.56, p.4779	IFRS 17.85	Ch.56, p.4719
IFRS 17.42	Ch.56, p.4780	IFRS 17.85	Ch.56, p.4878
IFRS 17.43	Ch.56, p.4780	IFRS 17.86	Ch.56, p.4874
IFRS 17.44	Ch.56, p.4780	IFRS 17.86	Ch.56, p.4880
IFRS 17.45	Ch.56, p.4849	IFRS 17.86(c)	Ch.56, p.4874
IFRS 17.46	Ch.56, p.4784	IFRS 17.87	Ch.56, p.4881
IFRS 17.47	Ch.56, p.4794	IFRS 17.88	Ch.56, p.4883
IFRS 17.48	Ch.56, p.4794	IFRS 17.88	Ch.56, p.4886
IFRS 17.49	Ch.56, p.4794	IFRS 17.89	Ch.56, p.4892
IFRS 17.50	Ch.56, p.4794	IFRS 17.90	Ch.56, p.4886
IFRS 17.51	Ch.56, p.4795	IFRS 17.91	Ch.56, p.4862
IFRS 17.52	Ch.56, p.4795	IFRS 17.91(a)	Ch.56, p.4887
IFRS 17.53	Ch.56, p.4808	IFRS 17.91(b)	Ch.56, p.4895
IFRS 17.53	Ch.56, p.4812	IFRS 17.92	Ch.56, p.4882

IFRS 17.93	Ch.56, p.4898	IFRS 17 Appendix A	Ch.56, p.4735
IFRS 17.93	Ch.56, p.4900	IFRS 17 Appendix A	Ch.56, p.4758
IFRS 17.93	Ch.56, p.4912	IFRS 17 Appendix A	Ch.56, p.4778
IFRS 17.93(b)	Ch.56, p.4909	IFRS 17 Appendix A	Ch.56, p.4779
IFRS 17.94	Ch.56, p.4899	IFRS 17 Appendix A	Ch.56, p.4791
IFRS 17.95	Ch.56, p.4872	IFRS 17 Appendix A	Ch.56, p.4796
IFRS 17.95	Ch.56, p.4899	IFRS 17 Appendix A	Ch.56, p.4817
IFRS 17.96	Ch.56, p.4899	IFRS 17 Appendix A	Ch.56, p.4851
IFRS 17.97	Ch.56, p.4906	IFRS 17 Appendix A	Ch.56, p.4855
IFRS 17.98	Ch.56, p.4872	IFRS 17.B2	Ch.56, p.4697
IFRS 17.98	Ch.56, p.4900	IFRS 17.B2-B30	Ch.45, p.3593
IFRS 17.99	Ch.56, p.4900	IFRS 17.B3	Ch.56, p.4697
IFRS 17.99	Ch.56, p.4906	IFRS 17.B4	Ch.56, p.4697
IFRS 17.100	Ch.56, p.4900	IFRS 17.B5	Ch.56, p.4697
IFRS 17.100	Ch.56, p.4906	IFRS 17.B5	Ch.56, p.4797
IFRS 17.100	Ch.56, p.4915	IFRS 17.B5	Ch.56, p.4835
IFRS 17.101	Ch.56, p.4902	IFRS 17.B5	Ch.56, p.4868
IFRS 17.102	Ch.56, p.4900	IFRS 17.B6	Ch.56, p.4698
IFRS 17.103	Ch.56, p.4900	IFRS 17.B7	Ch.56, p.4698
IFRS 17.103	Ch.56, p.4907	IFRS 17.B8	Ch.56, p.4698
IFRS 17.104	Ch.56, p.4902	IFRS 17.B9	Ch.56, p.4698
IFRS 17.105	Ch.56, p.4904	IFRS 17.B10	Ch.56, p.4699
IFRS 17.105	Ch.56, p.4907	IFRS 17.B11	Ch.56, p.4699
IFRS 17.105A	Ch.56, p.4904	IFRS 17.B12	Ch.56, p.4699
IFRS 17.105B	Ch.56, p.4904	IFRS 17.B13	Ch.56, p.4700
IFRS 17.106	Ch.56, p.4904	IFRS 17.B14	Ch.56, p.4700
IFRS 17.107	Ch.56, p.4905	IFRS 17.B15	Ch.56, p.4700
IFRS 17.108	Ch.56, p.4905	IFRS 17.B16	Ch.56, p.4703
IFRS 17.109	Ch.56, p.4906	IFRS 17.B17	Ch.56, p.4701
IFRS 17.109A	Ch.56, p.4906	IFRS 17.B18	Ch.56, p.4701
IFRS 17.110	Ch.56, p.4907	IFRS 17.B19	Ch.56, p.4701
IFRS 17.111	Ch.56, p.4908	IFRS 17.B20	Ch.56, p.4701
IFRS 17.112	Ch.56, p.4908	IFRS 17.B21	Ch.56, p.4704
IFRS 17.113	Ch.56, p.4908	IFRS 17.B22	Ch.56, p.4703
IFRS 17.114	Ch.56, p.4908	IFRS 17.B23	Ch.56, p.4704
IFRS 17.115	Ch.56, p.4908	IFRS 17.B24	Ch.56, p.4706
IFRS 17.116	Ch.56, p.4909	IFRS 17.B25	Ch.56, p.4705
IFRS 17.117	Ch.56, p.4909	IFRS 17.B25	Ch.56, p.4857
IFRS 17.118	Ch.56, p.4909	IFRS 17.B26	Ch.56, p.4706
IFRS 17.119	Ch.56, p.4910	IFRS 17.B26(k)	Ch.45, p.3594
IFRS 17.120	Ch.56, p.4910	IFRS 17.B27	Ch.56, p.4708
IFRS 17.121	Ch.56, p.4912	IFRS 17.B27(a)	Ch.45, p.3594
IFRS 17.122	Ch.56, p.4912	IFRS 17.B27(c)	Ch.56, p.4703
IFRS 17.123	Ch.56, p.4912	IFRS 17.B27(f)	Ch.45, p.3596
IFRS 17.124	Ch.56, p.4912	IFRS 17.B27(g)	Ch.45, p.3594
IFRS 17.125	Ch.56, p.4912	IFRS 17.B28	Ch.56, p.4709
IFRS 17.126	Ch.56, p.4918	IFRS 17.B29	Ch.56, p.4709
IFRS 17.127	Ch.56, p.4913	IFRS 17.B30	Ch.45, p.3596
IFRS 17.128	Ch.56, p.4914	IFRS 17.B30	Ch.56, p.4709
IFRS 17.129	Ch.56, p.4915	IFRS 17.B31	Ch.56, p.4717
IFRS 17.130	Ch.56, p.4915	IFRS 17.B32	Ch.56, p.4717
IFRS 17.131	Ch.56, p.4917	IFRS 17.B33	Ch.56, p.4721
IFRS 17.132	Ch.56, p.4917	IFRS 17.B34	Ch.56, p.4721
IFRS 17 Appendix A	Ch.45, p.3593	IFRS 17.B35	Ch.56, p.4721
IFRS 17 Appendix A	Ch.56, p.4684	IFRS 17.B35A	Ch.56, p.4736
IFRS 17 Appendix A	Ch.56, p.4695	IFRS 17.B35A	Ch.56, p.4749
IFRS 17 Appendix A	Ch.56, p.4698	IFRS 17.B35B	Ch.56, p.4749
IFRS 17 Appendix A	Ch.56, p.4715	IFRS 17.B35C	Ch.56, p.4737

IFRS 17.B35D	Ch.56, p.4802	IFRS 17.B91	Ch.56, p.4772
IFRS 17.B37	Ch.56, p.4750	IFRS 17.B92	Ch.56, p.4773
IFRS 17.B38	Ch.56, p.4750	IFRS 17.B93	Ch.56, p.4864
IFRS 17.B39	Ch.56, p.4751	IFRS 17.B94	Ch.56, p.4865
IFRS 17.B40	Ch.56, p.4751	IFRS 17.B95	Ch.56, p.4865
IFRS 17.B41	Ch.56, p.4751	IFRS 17.B95A	Ch.56, p.4865
IFRS 17.B42	Ch.56, p.4752	IFRS 17.B95B	Ch.56, p.4865
IFRS 17.B43	Ch.56, p.4752	IFRS 17.B95C	Ch.56, p.4866
IFRS 17.B44	Ch.56, p.4752	IFRS 17.B95D	Ch.56, p.4866
IFRS 17.B45	Ch.56, p.4752	IFRS 17.B95E	Ch.56, p.4867
IFRS 17.B46	Ch.56, p.4752	IFRS 17.B95F	Ch.56, p.4867
IFRS 17.B47	Ch.56, p.4752	IFRS 17.B96	Ch.56, p.4720
IFRS 17.B48	Ch.56, p.4753	IFRS 17.B96	Ch.56, p.4781
IFRS 17.B49	Ch.56, p.4753	IFRS 17.B97	Ch.56, p.4783
IFRS 17.B50	Ch.56, p.4753	IFRS 17.B98	Ch.56, p.4784
IFRS 17.B51	Ch.56, p.4754	IFRS 17.B99	Ch.56, p.4785
IFRS 17.B52	Ch.56, p.4754	IFRS 17.B100	Ch.56, p.4785
IFRS 17.B53	Ch.56, p.4754	IFRS 17.B101	Ch.56, p.4844
IFRS 17.B54	Ch.56, p.4754	IFRS 17.B102	Ch.56, p.4844
IFRS 17.B55	Ch.56, p.4755	IFRS 17.B103	Ch.56, p.4846
IFRS 17.B56	Ch.56, p.4755	IFRS 17.B104	Ch.56, p.4843
IFRS 17.B57	Ch.56, p.4755	IFRS 17.B105	Ch.56, p.4844
IFRS 17.B58	Ch.56, p.4755	IFRS 17.B106	Ch.56, p.4844
IFRS 17.B59	Ch.56, p.4755	IFRS 17.B107	Ch.56, p.4845
IFRS 17.B60	Ch.56, p.4755	IFRS 17.B107(b)(i)	Ch.56, p.4842
IFRS 17.B61	Ch.56, p.4740	IFRS 17.B108	Ch.56, p.4846
IFRS 17.B62	Ch.56, p.4756	IFRS 17.B109	Ch.56, p.4837
IFRS 17.B63	Ch.56, p.4741	IFRS 17.B109	Ch.56, p.4839
IFRS 17.B64	Ch.56, p.4741	IFRS 17.B111	Ch.56, p.4849
IFRS 17.B65	Ch.56, p.4757	IFRS 17.B112	Ch.56, p.4849
IFRS 17.B65(c)	Ch.56, p.4804	IFRS 17.B113	Ch.56, p.4850
IFRS 17.B66	Ch.56, p.4762	IFRS 17.B113(a)	Ch.56, p.4849
IFRS 17.B66A	Ch.56, p.4776	IFRS 17.B114	Ch.56, p.4850
IFRS 17.B67	Ch.56, p.4840	IFRS 17.B115	Ch.56, p.4852
IFRS 17.B68	Ch.56, p.4840	IFRS 17.B116	Ch.56, p.4853
IFRS 17.B69	Ch.56, p.4841	IFRS 17.B117	Ch.56, p.4852
IFRS 17.B70	Ch.56, p.4841	IFRS 17.B117A	Ch.56, p.4853
IFRS 17.B71	Ch.56, p.4841	IFRS 17.B117A	Ch.56, p.4883
IFRS 17.B72-B73	Ch.56, p.4763	IFRS 17.B118	Ch.56, p.4853
IFRS 17.B73	Ch.56, p.4764	IFRS 17.B119	Ch.56, p.4785
IFRS 17.B74	Ch.56, p.4765	IFRS 17.B119A	Ch.56, p.4792
IFRS 17.B75	Ch.56, p.4765	IFRS 17.B119A	Ch.56, p.4851
IFRS 17.B76	Ch.56, p.4765	IFRS 17.B119B	Ch.56, p.4792
IFRS 17.B77	Ch.56, p.4766	IFRS 17.B119D	Ch.56, p.4825
IFRS 17.B78	Ch.56, p.4766	IFRS 17.B119E	Ch.56, p.4825
IFRS 17.B79	Ch.56, p.4766	IFRS 17.B119E	Ch.56, p.4835
IFRS 17.B80	Ch.56, p.4767	IFRS 17.B119F	Ch.56, p.4833
IFRS 17.B81	Ch.56, p.4767	IFRS 17.B120	Ch.56, p.4876
IFRS 17.B82	Ch.56, p.4768	IFRS 17.B121	Ch.56, p.4877
IFRS 17.B83	Ch.56, p.4768	IFRS 17.B123	Ch.56, p.4759
IFRS 17.B84	Ch.56, p.4768	IFRS 17.B123	Ch.56, p.4760
IFRS 17.B85	Ch.56, p.4769	IFRS 17.B123	Ch.56, p.4877
IFRS 17.B86	Ch.56, p.4770	IFRS 17.B123A	Ch.56, p.4878
IFRS 17.B87	Ch.56, p.4770	IFRS 17.B124	Ch.56, p.4878
IFRS 17.B87	Ch.56, p.4771	IFRS 17.B125	Ch.56, p.4759
IFRS 17.B88	Ch.56, p.4771	IFRS 17.B125	Ch.56, p.4878
IFRS 17.B89	Ch.56, p.4771	IFRS 17.B126	Ch.56, p.4815
IFRS 17.B90	Ch.56, p.4771	IFRS 17.B126	Ch.56, p.4880

IFRS 17.B127	Ch.56, p.4815	IFRS 17.C25	Ch.56, p.4924
IFRS 17.B127	Ch.56, p.4880	IFRS 17.C26	Ch.56, p.4924
IFRS 17.B128	Ch.56, p.4881	IFRS 17.C27	Ch.56, p.4924
IFRS 17.B129	Ch.56, p.4883	IFRS 17.C28	Ch.56, p.4921
IFRS 17.B130	Ch.56, p.4887	IFRS 17.C29	Ch.56, p.4938
IFRS 17.B131	Ch.56, p.4887	IFRS 17.C30	Ch.56, p.4939
IFRS 17.B132(a)	Ch.56, p.4888	IFRS 17.C31	Ch.56, p.4939
IFRS 17.B132(b)	Ch.56, p.4889	IFRS 17.C32	Ch.56, p.4939
IFRS 17.B132(c)	Ch.56, p.4889	IFRS 17.C33	Ch.56, p.4939
IFRS 17.B133	Ch.56, p.4892	IFRS 17.C34	Ch.56, p.4919
IFRS 17.B134	Ch.56, p.4893	IFRS 17.IE43-51	Ch.56, p.4718
IFRS 17.B135	Ch.56, p.4895	IFRS 17.IE51-55	Ch.56, p.4721
IFRS 17.B136	Ch.56, p.4895	IFRS 17.IE95(c)	Ch.56, p.4795
IFRS 17.B137	Ch.56, p.4896	IFRS 17.IE124-129	Ch.56, p.4823
IFRS 17.B137	Ch.56, p.4924	IFRS 17.IE130-138	Ch.56, p.4830
IFRS 17.C1	Ch.56, p.4919	IFRS 17.IE138A-138K	Ch.56, p.4826
IFRS 17.C2	Ch.56, p.4919	IFRS 17.IE138L-138M	Ch.56, p.4833
IFRS 17.C3	Ch.56, p.4919	IFRS 17.IE139-151	Ch.56, p.4866
IFRS 17.C3(a)	Ch.56, p.4921	IFRS 17.IE155-IE172	Ch.56, p.4889
IFRS 17.C3(b)	Ch.56, p.4922	IFRS 17.IE173-IE185	Ch.56, p.4893
IFRS 17.C4	Ch.56, p.4923	IFRS 17.IE186-IE191	Ch.56, p.4930
IFRS 17.C5	Ch.56, p.4919	IFRS 17.IE192-IE199	Ch.56, p.4932
IFRS 17.C5A	Ch.56, p.4919	IFRS 17.BC34	Ch.56, p.4719
IFRS 17.C5B	Ch.56, p.4920	IFRS 17.BC63	Ch.56, p.4687
IFRS 17.C6	Ch.56, p.4925	IFRS 17.BC64	Ch.56, p.4687
IFRS 17.C6(a)	Ch.56, p.4920	IFRS 17.BC65(a)	Ch.45, p.3594
IFRS 17.C7	Ch.56, p.4925	IFRS 17.BC65(c)	Ch.18, p.1408
IFRS 17.C8	Ch.56, p.4925	IFRS 17.BC66	Ch.45, p.3599
IFRS 17.C9	Ch.56, p.4927	IFRS 17.BC66	Ch.56, p.4691
IFRS 17.C9A	Ch.56, p.4927	IFRS 17.BC67	Ch.56, p.4696
IFRS 17.C10	Ch.56, p.4927	IFRS 17.BC69	Ch.56, p.4696
IFRS 17.C11	Ch.56, p.4927	IFRS 17.BC73	Ch.56, p.4699
IFRS 17.C12	Ch.56, p.4928	IFRS 17.BC74	Ch.56, p.4699
IFRS 17.C13	Ch.56, p.4928	IFRS 17.BC75	Ch.56, p.4699
IFRS 17.C14	Ch.56, p.4928	IFRS 17.BC77	Ch.56, p.4702
IFRS 17.C14A	Ch.56, p.4929	IFRS 17.BC78	Ch.56, p.4701
IFRS 17.C14B	Ch.56, p.4928	IFRS 17.BC79	Ch.56, p.4702
IFRS 17.C14C	Ch.56, p.4929	IFRS 17.BC79	Ch.56, p.4703
IFRS 17.C14D	Ch.56, p.4929	IFRS 17.BC80	Ch.56, p.4702
IFRS 17.C15	Ch.56, p.4929	IFRS 17.BC80	Ch.56, p.4705
IFRS 17.C16	Ch.56, p.4929	IFRS 17.BC80	Ch.56, p.4706
IFRS 17.C16A	Ch.56, p.4930	IFRS 17.BC81	Ch.56, p.4706
IFRS 17.C16B	Ch.56, p.4930	IFRS 17.BC83	Ch.56, p.4855
IFRS 17.C16C	Ch.56, p.4930	IFRS 17.BC87(d)	Ch.56, p.4690
IFRS 17.C17	Ch.56, p.4931	IFRS 17.BC89	Ch.56, p.4689
IFRS 17.C17A	Ch.56, p.4930	IFRS 17.BC90	Ch.56, p.4689
IFRS 17.C18	Ch.56, p.4933	IFRS 17.BC91	Ch.56, p.4690
IFRS 17.C19	Ch.56, p.4934	IFRS 17.BC93	Ch.56, p.4690
IFRS 17.C20	Ch.56, p.4935	IFRS 17.BC94	Ch.56, p.4691
IFRS 17.C20A	Ch.56, p.4936	IFRS 17.BC94B	Ch.45, p.3595
IFRS 17.C20B	Ch.56, p.4936	IFRS 17.BC94B	Ch.48, p.3836
IFRS 17.C21-C22	Ch.56, p.4936	IFRS 17.BC94B	Ch.56, p.4692
IFRS 17.C22A	Ch.56, p.4936	IFRS 17.BC94C	Ch.45, p.3595
IFRS 17.C23	Ch.56, p.4936	IFRS 17.BC94C	Ch.56, p.4692
IFRS 17.C23	Ch.56, p.4937	IFRS 17.BC94E	Ch.56, p.4694
IFRS 17.C24	Ch.56, p.4937	IFRS 17.BC94F	Ch.56, p.4694
IFRS 17.C24A	Ch.56, p.4937	IFRS 17.BC95	Ch.56, p.4693
IFRS 17.C24B	Ch.56, p.4937	IFRS 17.BC96-97	Ch.56, p.4693

IFRS 17.BC99	Ch.56, p.4710	IFRS 17.BC236B-C	Ch.56, p.4898
IFRS 17.BC104	Ch.56, p.4712	IFRS 17.BC240	Ch.56, p.4843
IFRS 17.BC105(a)	Ch.56, p.4713	IFRS 17.BC241	Ch.56, p.4843
IFRS 17.BC105(b)	Ch.56, p.4713	IFRS 17.BC244	Ch.56, p.4843
IFRS 17.BC108	Ch.45, p.3595	IFRS 17.BC245(a)	Ch.56, p.4845
IFRS 17.BC108	Ch.56, p.4716	IFRS 17.BC245(b)	Ch.56, p.4845
IFRS 17.BC108(b)	Ch.56, p.4719	IFRS 17.BC245(b)(ii)	Ch.56, p.4848
IFRS 17.BC109	Ch.56, p.4716	IFRS 17.BC248	Ch.56, p.4837
IFRS 17.BC111	Ch.56, p.4720	IFRS 17.BC256B	Ch.56, p.4853
IFRS 17.BC112	Ch.56, p.4720	IFRS 17.BC256C	Ch.56, p.4854
IFRS 17.BC113	Ch.56, p.4721	IFRS 17.BC256D-F	Ch.56, p.4854
IFRS 17.BC114	Ch.56, p.4717	IFRS 17.BC265	Ch.56, p.4804
IFRS 17.BC114	Ch.56, p.4721	IFRS 17.BC265fn27	Ch.56, p.4804
IFRS 17.BC114	Ch.56, p.4806	IFRS 17.BC269B	Ch.56, p.4805
IFRS 17.BC119	Ch.56, p.4725	IFRS 17.BC277	Ch.56, p.4739
IFRS 17.BC129	Ch.56, p.4726	IFRS 17.BC278	Ch.56, p.4739
IFRS 17.BC132	Ch.56, p.4727	IFRS 17.BC279	Ch.56, p.4786
IFRS 17.BC133	Ch.56, p.4728	IFRS 17.BC280	Ch.56, p.4786
IFRS 17.BC136	Ch.56, p.4728	IFRS 17.BC282	Ch.56, p.4786
IFRS 17.BC137	Ch.56, p.4728	IFRS 17.BC283	Ch.56, p.4787
IFRS 17.BC138	Ch.56, p.4728	IFRS 17.BC283B	Ch.56, p.4791
IFRS 17.BC138	Ch.56, p.4841	IFRS 17.BC283C	Ch.56, p.4792
IFRS 17.BC139	Ch.56, p.4725	IFRS 17.BC283D-E	Ch.56, p.4792
IFRS 17.BC139J	Ch.56, p.4730	IFRS 17.BC283I	Ch.56, p.4761
IFRS 17.BC139K	Ch.56, p.4730	IFRS 17.BC287	Ch.56, p.4795
IFRS 17.BC139L	Ch.56, p.4731	IFRS 17.BC298	Ch.56, p.4818
IFRS 17.BC139M	Ch.56, p.4731	IFRS 17.BC302	Ch.56, p.4818
IFRS 17.BC139N	Ch.56, p.4731	IFRS 17.BC304	Ch.56, p.4734
IFRS 17.BC139O	Ch.56, p.4731	IFRS 17.BC305(a)	Ch.56, p.4734
IFRS 17.BC139P	Ch.56, p.4731	IFRS 17.BC305(b)	Ch.56, p.4734
IFRS 17.BC139T	Ch.56, p.4729	IFRS 17.BC308	Ch.56, p.4828
IFRS 17.BC162	Ch.56, p.4742	IFRS 17.BC309	Ch.56, p.4832
IFRS 17.BC163	Ch.56, p.4742	IFRS 17.BC309E	Ch.56, p.4820
IFRS 17.BC164	Ch.56, p.4743	IFRS 17.BC309F	Ch.56, p.4820
IFRS 17.BC166	Ch.56, p.4756	IFRS 17.BC312	Ch.56, p.4823
IFRS 17.BC168	Ch.56, p.4756	IFRS 17.BC314	Ch.56, p.4829
IFRS 17.BC169	Ch.56, p.4756	IFRS 17.BC315	Ch.56, p.4830
IFRS 17.BC170	Ch.56, p.4841	IFRS 17.BC315C	Ch.56, p.4825
IFRS 17.BC170A	Ch.56, p.4762	IFRS 17.BC315E	Ch.56, p.4825
IFRS 17.BC172	Ch.56, p.4840	IFRS 17.BC315F	Ch.56, p.4826
IFRS 17.BC182(a)	Ch.56, p.4757	IFRS 17.BC315G	Ch.56, p.4826
IFRS 17.BC183	Ch.56, p.4759	IFRS 17.BC315H	Ch.56, p.4825
IFRS 17.BC184B	Ch.56, p.4736	IFRS 17.BC322	Ch.56, p.4860
IFRS 17.BC184C-D	Ch.56, p.4736	IFRS 17.BC327A	Ch.56, p.4870
IFRS 17.BC184E	Ch.56, p.4736	IFRS 17.BC327B-C	Ch.56, p.4864
IFRS 17.BC184F	Ch.56, p.4736	IFRS 17.BC327E	Ch.56, p.4869
IFRS 17.BC184H	Ch.56, p.4764	IFRS 17.BC327G	Ch.56, p.4869
IFRS 17.BC184J	Ch.56, p.4802	IFRS 17.BC327I	Ch.56, p.4868
IFRS 17.BC184K	Ch.56, p.4802	IFRS 17.BC330B	Ch.56, p.4874
IFRS 17.BC184N	Ch.56, p.4776	IFRS 17.BC330C	Ch.56, p.4873
IFRS 17.BC209	Ch.56, p.4770	IFRS 17.BC330D	Ch.56, p.4873
IFRS 17.BC213	Ch.56, p.4772	IFRS 17.BC342A	Ch.56, p.4882
IFRS 17.BC214	Ch.56, p.4772	IFRS 17.BC347	Ch.56, p.4898
IFRS 17.BC217	Ch.56, p.4773	IFRS 17.BC348	Ch.56, p.4899
IFRS 17.BC228	Ch.56, p.4764	IFRS 17.BC349	Ch.56, p.4899
IFRS 17.BC235	Ch.56, p.4783	IFRS 17.BC369-371	Ch.56, p.4918
IFRS 17.BC235fn	Ch.56, p.4783	IFRS 17.BC373	Ch.56, p.4920
IFRS 17.BC236	Ch.56, p.4896	IFRS 17.BC374	Ch.56, p.4923

IFRS 17.BC377	Ch.56, p.4920	IAS 1.7(i)-(j)	Ch.56, p.4874
IFRS 17.BC378	Ch.56, p.4920	IAS 1.8	Ch.3, p.133
IFRS 17.BC380A	Ch.56, p.4926	IAS 1.9	Ch.3, p.116
IFRS 17.BC380B	Ch.56, p.4926	IAS 1.10	Ch.3, p.134
IFRS 17.BC380C	Ch.56, p.4925	IAS 1.10	Ch.40, p.3138
IFRS 17.BC380C	Ch.56, p.4926	IAS 1.10(f)	Ch.41, p.3232
IFRS 17.BC380D	Ch.56, p.4925	IAS 1.10-10A	Ch.3, p.121
IFRS 17.BC382A	Ch.56, p.4927	IAS 1.10-11	Ch.3, p.116
IFRS 17.BC384A-B	Ch.56, p.4935	IAS 1.10-11	Ch.3, p.121
IFRS 17.BC390	Ch.56, p.4921	IAS 1.10A	Ch.3, p.134
IFRS 17.BC391	Ch.56, p.4927	IAS 1.10A	Ch.37, p.3061
IFRS 17.BC392	Ch.56, p.4927	IAS 1.10A	Ch.41, p.3228
IFRS 17.BC393C	Ch.56, p.4922	IAS 1.11	Ch.40, p.3135
IFRS 17.BC393D-E	Ch.56, p.4922	IAS 1.13	Ch.3, p.117
IFRS 17.BC398A-B	Ch.56, p.4941	IAS 1.14	Ch.3, p.117
IFRS 17.BC407	Ch.5, p.266	IAS 1.15	Ch.3, p.152
		IAS 1.15	Ch.45, p.3606
		IAS 1.15-35	Ch.41, p.3203

IAS 1 (2023)

IAS 1(2023).74	Ch.38, p.3086	IAS 1.16	Ch.1, p.22
IAS 1(2023).76	Ch.38, p.3086	IAS 1.16	Ch.3, p.120
IAS 1(2023).76A	Ch.15, p.1219	IAS 1.16	Ch.41, p.3224
IAS 1(2023).76A	Ch.54, p.4516	IAS 1.17	Ch.3, p.153
IAS 1(2023).76B	Ch.54, p.4516	IAS 1.17	Ch.36, p.3012
IAS 1(2023).136U	Ch.54, p.4520	IAS 1.17(c)	Ch.43, p.3357
IAS 1(2023).139U	Ch.3, p.126	IAS 1.18	Ch.3, p.153
		IAS 1.19	Ch.3, p.154
		IAS 1.19	Ch.36, p.3012

IAS 1

IAS 1.1	Ch.3, p.114	IAS 1.20-21	Ch.3, p.154
IAS 1.2	Ch.3, p.114	IAS 1.22	Ch.3, p.154
IAS 1.2	Ch.5, p.231	IAS 1.23	Ch.3, p.155
IAS 1.3	Ch.3, p.114	IAS 1.24	Ch.3, p.153
IAS 1.4	Ch.3, p.114	IAS 1.25	Ch.3, p.155
IAS 1.4	Ch.41, p.3203	IAS 1.25	Ch.38, p.3083
IAS 1.4	Ch.41, p.3226	IAS 1.25	Ch.41, p.3226
IAS 1.5	Ch.3, p.114	IAS 1.26	Ch.3, p.155
IAS 1.6	Ch.3, p.114	IAS 1.26	Ch.41, p.3226
IAS 1.7	Ch.3, p.114	IAS 1.27	Ch.3, p.156
IAS 1.7	Ch.3, p.115	IAS 1.28	Ch.3, p.156
IAS 1.7	Ch.3, p.117	IAS 1.29	Ch.3, p.157
IAS 1.7	Ch.3, p.119	IAS 1.29	Ch.33, p.2568
IAS 1.7	Ch.3, p.133	IAS 1.29	Ch.54, p.4511
IAS 1.7	Ch.3, p.134	IAS 1.30	Ch.3, p.157
IAS 1.7	Ch.3, p.140	IAS 1.30	Ch.3, p.158
IAS 1.7	Ch.3, p.144	IAS 1.30A	Ch.2, p.50
IAS 1.7	Ch.3, p.157	IAS 1.30A	Ch.3, p.157
IAS 1.7	Ch.3, p.158	IAS 1.30A	Ch.3, p.161
IAS 1.7	Ch.5, p.231	IAS 1.31	Ch.3, p.158
IAS 1.7	Ch.7, p.502	IAS 1.31	Ch.39, p.3115
IAS 1.7	Ch.8, p.600	IAS 1.32	Ch.3, p.159
IAS 1.7	Ch.16, p.1278	IAS 1.32	Ch.23, p.1800
IAS 1.7	Ch.36, p.3012	IAS 1.32	Ch.24, p.1841
IAS 1.7	Ch.39, p.3115	IAS 1.32	Ch.32, p.2406
IAS 1.7	Ch.41, p.3235	IAS 1.32	Ch.42, p.3315
IAS 1.7	Ch.41, p.3239	IAS 1.32	Ch.43, p.3409
		IAS 1.32	Ch.54, p.4487
		IAS 1.32	Ch.54, p.4491
		IAS 1.32-33	Ch.24, p.1841
		IAS 1.33	Ch.3, p.159

IAS 1.33	Ch.54, p.4487	IAS 1.54(ma)	Ch.56, p.4872
IAS 1.33	Ch.54, p.4508	IAS 1.54(n)	Ch.33, p.2568
IAS 1.34	Ch.3, p.159	IAS 1.54(n)	Ch.33, p.2611
IAS 1.34	Ch.27, p.2018	IAS 1.54(o)	Ch.33, p.2568
IAS 1.34	Ch.32, p.2406	IAS 1.54(o)	Ch.33, p.2611
IAS 1.34	Ch.42, p.3315	IAS 1.54(q)	Ch.54, p.4517
IAS 1.34	Ch.54, p.4487	IAS 1.54(r)	Ch.54, p.4517
IAS 1.34(a)	Ch.32, p.2406	IAS 1.55	Ch.3, p.128
IAS 1.35	Ch.3, p.159	IAS 1.55	Ch.17, p.1356
IAS 1.35	Ch.54, p.4487	IAS 1.55	Ch.40, p.3163
IAS 1.36	Ch.3, p.116	IAS 1.55	Ch.54, p.4508
IAS 1.36	Ch.5, p.237	IAS 1.55	Ch.54, p.4511
IAS 1.37	Ch.3, p.116	IAS 1.55	Ch.54, p.4517
IAS 1.37	Ch.5, p.238	IAS 1.55	Ch.56, p.4873
IAS 1.38	Ch.3, p.117	IAS 1.55A	Ch.3, p.130
IAS 1.38	Ch.3, p.118	IAS 1.55A	Ch.54, p.4509
IAS 1.38	Ch.5, p.237	IAS 1.56	Ch.3, p.124
IAS 1.38	Ch.5, p.343	IAS 1.56	Ch.3, p.125
IAS 1.38	Ch.39, p.3115	IAS 1.57	Ch.3, p.128
IAS 1.38	Ch.40, p.3145	IAS 1.57	Ch.3, p.129
IAS 1.38	Ch.41, p.3198	IAS 1.57	Ch.33, p.2568
IAS 1.38	Ch.41, p.3231	IAS 1.57	Ch.54, p.4508
IAS 1.38A	Ch.3, p.118	IAS 1.57	Ch.54, p.4511
IAS 1.38A	Ch.41, p.3198	IAS 1.57(a)	Ch.54, p.4508
IAS 1.38B	Ch.3, p.119	IAS 1.57(b)	Ch.54, p.4509
IAS 1.38C	Ch.3, p.118	IAS 1.58	Ch.3, p.128
IAS 1.38D	Ch.3, p.118	IAS 1.58	Ch.3, p.130
IAS 1.40A	Ch.3, p.118	IAS 1.58	Ch.54, p.4509
IAS 1.40A-40D	Ch.41, p.3198	IAS 1.58	Ch.54, p.4511
IAS 1.40C	Ch.3, p.118	IAS 1.59	Ch.3, p.128
IAS 1.41	Ch.3, p.119	IAS 1.59	Ch.54, p.4509
IAS 1.41	Ch.36, p.3010	IAS 1.60	Ch.3, p.122
IAS 1.41	Ch.41, p.3242	IAS 1.60	Ch.3, p.123
IAS 1.42	Ch.3, p.119	IAS 1.60	Ch.17, p.1356
IAS 1.43	Ch.3, p.119	IAS 1.60	Ch.55, p.4627
IAS 1.45	Ch.3, p.156	IAS 1.61	Ch.3, p.123
IAS 1.45	Ch.41, p.3242	IAS 1.62	Ch.3, p.122
IAS 1.46	Ch.3, p.156	IAS 1.63	Ch.3, p.123
IAS 1.48	Ch.3, p.121	IAS 1.64	Ch.3, p.123
IAS 1.49-50	Ch.3, p.120	IAS 1.65	Ch.3, p.123
IAS 1.51	Ch.3, p.120	IAS 1.66	Ch.3, p.122
IAS 1.52	Ch.3, p.120	IAS 1.66	Ch.3, p.124
IAS 1.53	Ch.3, p.120	IAS 1.66	Ch.42, p.3309
IAS 1.54	Ch.3, p.128	IAS 1.66	Ch.54, p.4515
IAS 1.54	Ch.3, p.129	IAS 1.67	Ch.3, p.122
IAS 1.54	Ch.7, p.546	IAS 1.67	Ch.17, p.1356
IAS 1.54	Ch.13, p.961	IAS 1.68	Ch.3, p.122
IAS 1.54	Ch.13, p.970	IAS 1.68	Ch.3, p.124
IAS 1.54	Ch.17, p.1356	IAS 1.68	Ch.22, p.1678
IAS 1.54	Ch.33, p.2568	IAS 1.69	Ch.3, p.122
IAS 1.54	Ch.41, p.3199	IAS 1.69	Ch.3, p.125
IAS 1.54	Ch.42, p.3308	IAS 1.69	Ch.32, p.2398
IAS 1.54	Ch.54, p.4508	IAS 1.69	Ch.54, p.4515
IAS 1.54	Ch.54, p.4511	IAS 1.69(d)	Ch.54, p.4516
IAS 1.54	Ch.55, p.4626	IAS 1.69(d)	Ch.54, p.4517
IAS 1.54-56	Ch.33, p.2609	IAS 1.70	Ch.3, p.122
IAS 1.54(da)	Ch.56, p.4872	IAS 1.70	Ch.3, p.125
IAS 1.54(e)	Ch.11, p.882	IAS 1.70	Ch.54, p.4511

IAS 1.71	Ch.3, p.125
IAS 1.72	Ch.3, p.126
IAS 1.73	Ch.3, p.126
IAS 1.73	Ch.54, p.4516
IAS 1.73	Ch.54, p.4517
IAS 1.74	Ch.3, p.126
IAS 1.74	Ch.38, p.3086
IAS 1.75	Ch.3, p.126
IAS 1.76	Ch.3, p.126
IAS 1.76	Ch.3, p.183
IAS 1.76	Ch.38, p.3079
IAS 1.76	Ch.38, p.3080
IAS 1.76	Ch.38, p.3086
IAS 1.77	Ch.3, p.130
IAS 1.77	Ch.39, p.3124
IAS 1.77	Ch.54, p.4509
IAS 1.77	Ch.54, p.4517
IAS 1.78	Ch.3, p.130
IAS 1.78(b)	Ch.54, p.4509
IAS 1.78(e)	Ch.54, p.4517
IAS 1.79	Ch.3, p.131
IAS 1.79(a)	Ch.54, p.4518
IAS 1.79(a)(vi)	Ch.47, p.3742
IAS 1.79(b)	Ch.54, p.4517
IAS 1.80	Ch.3, p.131
IAS 1.80	Ch.54, p.4518
IAS 1.80A	Ch.3, p.131
IAS 1.80A	Ch.54, p.4518
IAS 1.81A	Ch.3, p.136
IAS 1.81A	Ch.3, p.140
IAS 1.81B	Ch.3, p.136
IAS 1.81B	Ch.3, p.141
IAS 1.81B	Ch.7, p.546
IAS 1.81B	Ch.13, p.961
IAS 1.81B(a)	Ch.54, p.4485
IAS 1.81B(b)	Ch.54, p.4490
IAS 1.82	Ch.3, p.135
IAS 1.82	Ch.13, p.970
IAS 1.82	Ch.41, p.3199
IAS 1.82(a)	Ch.51, p.4034
IAS 1.82(a)	Ch.53, p.4379
IAS 1.82(a)	Ch.54, p.4482
IAS 1.82(a)(ii)	Ch.56, p.4874
IAS 1.82(aa)	Ch.54, p.4410
IAS 1.82(aa)	Ch.54, p.4482
IAS 1.82(ab)-(ac)	Ch.56, p.4874
IAS 1.82(b)	Ch.54, p.4483
IAS 1.82(ba)	Ch.51, p.4068
IAS 1.82(ba)	Ch.51, p.4069
IAS 1.82(ba)	Ch.54, p.4482
IAS 1.82(bb)-(bc)	Ch.56, p.4874
IAS 1.82(c)	Ch.11, p.883
IAS 1.82(ca)	Ch.54, p.4483
IAS 1.82(cb)	Ch.54, p.4483
IAS 1.82A	Ch.3, p.140
IAS 1.82A	Ch.11, p.884
IAS 1.82A	Ch.54, p.4489
IAS 1.85	Ch.20, p.1612
IAS 1.85	Ch.40, p.3163
IAS 1.85	Ch.42, p.3283
IAS 1.85	Ch.54, p.4485
IAS 1.85	Ch.56, p.4875
IAS 1.85-86	Ch.3, p.134
IAS 1.85A	Ch.3, p.135
IAS 1.85A	Ch.54, p.4485
IAS 1.85B	Ch.3, p.135
IAS 1.86	Ch.3, p.134
IAS 1.86	Ch.3, p.135
IAS 1.86	Ch.54, p.4481
IAS 1.86	Ch.54, p.4485
IAS 1.87	Ch.3, p.148
IAS 1.87	Ch.54, p.4486
IAS 1.88	Ch.3, p.133
IAS 1.88	Ch.3, p.160
IAS 1.88	Ch.35, p.2947
IAS 1.88	Ch.40, p.3150
IAS 1.89	Ch.3, p.160
IAS 1.90	Ch.3, p.145
IAS 1.90	Ch.33, p.2611
IAS 1.90	Ch.33, p.2613
IAS 1.91	Ch.3, p.140
IAS 1.91	Ch.3, p.145
IAS 1.91	Ch.33, p.2611
IAS 1.92-93	Ch.3, p.144
IAS 1.92	Ch.53, p.4295
IAS 1.92	Ch.53, p.4297
IAS 1.92	Ch.53, p.4379
IAS 1.94	Ch.3, p.141
IAS 1.94	Ch.3, p.144
IAS 1.95	Ch.3, p.144
IAS 1.96	Ch.3, p.145
IAS 1.96	Ch.54, p.4490
IAS 1.97	Ch.3, p.119
IAS 1.97	Ch.3, p.148
IAS 1.97	Ch.19, p.1509
IAS 1.97	Ch.21, p.1671
IAS 1.97	Ch.40, p.3163
IAS 1.97	Ch.54, p.4486
IAS 1.98	Ch.3, p.148
IAS 1.98	Ch.54, p.4486
IAS 1.99	Ch.3, p.137
IAS 1.99	Ch.42, p.3283
IAS 1.99-100	Ch.3, p.136
IAS 1.100	Ch.3, p.137
IAS 1.101	Ch.3, p.137
IAS 1.102	Ch.3, p.138
IAS 1.103	Ch.3, p.140
IAS 1.104	Ch.3, p.140
IAS 1.105	Ch.3, p.137
IAS 1.105	Ch.3, p.138
IAS 1.106	Ch.3, p.148
IAS 1.106	Ch.7, p.546
IAS 1.106	Ch.13, p.961
IAS 1.106	Ch.47, p.3741
IAS 1.106	Ch.54, p.4490
IAS 1.106(d)	Ch.13, p.967

IAS 1.106A	Ch.3, p.149	IAS 1.125-129	Ch.33, p.2473
IAS 1.106A	Ch.54, p.4490	IAS 1.125-129	Ch.33, p.2540
IAS 1.107	Ch.3, p.149	IAS 1.125-133	Ch.15, p.1244
IAS 1.107	Ch.54, p.4490	IAS 1.126	Ch.3, p.177
IAS 1.108	Ch.3, p.149	IAS 1.127	Ch.3, p.178
IAS 1.109	Ch.3, p.149	IAS 1.128	Ch.3, p.178
IAS 1.109	Ch.7, p.538	IAS 1.129	Ch.3, p.178
IAS 1.109	Ch.47, p.3741	IAS 1.130	Ch.3, p.178
IAS 1.110	Ch.3, p.149	IAS 1.131	Ch.3, p.179
IAS 1.111	Ch.3, p.121	IAS 1.132	Ch.3, p.178
IAS 1.112	Ch.3, p.151	IAS 1.133	Ch.3, p.178
IAS 1.112	Ch.40, p.3158	IAS 1.134	Ch.3, p.180
IAS 1.112	Ch.54, p.4513	IAS 1.135	Ch.3, p.180
IAS 1.113	Ch.3, p.151	IAS 1.135	Ch.55, p.4665
IAS 1.114	Ch.3, p.151	IAS 1.135	Ch.56, p.4918
IAS 1.116	Ch.3, p.151	IAS 1.136	Ch.3, p.180
IAS 1.117	Ch.3, p.174	IAS 1.136	Ch.55, p.4666
IAS 1.117	Ch.17, p.1361	IAS 1.136	Ch.56, p.4918
IAS 1.117	Ch.21, p.1671	IAS 1.136A	Ch.3, p.182
IAS 1.117	Ch.23, p.1780	IAS 1.136A	Ch.54, p.4463
IAS 1.117	Ch.32, p.2391	IAS 1.137	Ch.3, p.182
IAS 1.117	Ch.43, p.3511	IAS 1.137	Ch.38, p.3081
IAS 1.117	Ch.56, p.4910	IAS 1.137	Ch.39, p.3121
IAS 1.117-121	Ch.15, p.1244	IAS 1.138	Ch.3, p.183
IAS 1.117-124	Ch.42, p.3283	IAS 1.138(b)	Ch.13, p.957
IAS 1.118	Ch.3, p.163	IAS 1.138(c)	Ch.39, p.3113
IAS 1.118	Ch.3, p.174	IAS 1.IG3	Ch.3, p.131
IAS 1.119	Ch.3, p.174	IAS 1.IG6	Ch.33, p.2611
IAS 1.121	Ch.3, p.174	IAS 1.IG10-11	Ch.3, p.180
IAS 1.121	Ch.17, p.1361	IAS 1.IG Part I	Ch.3, p.131
IAS 1.122	Ch.3, p.175	IAS 1.IG Part I	Ch.3, p.138
IAS 1.122	Ch.13, p.956	IAS 1.IG Part I	Ch.3, p.141
IAS 1.122	Ch.15, p.1244	IAS 1.IG Part I	Ch.3, p.144
IAS 1.122	Ch.16, p.1267	IAS 1.IG Part I	Ch.3, p.146
IAS 1.122	Ch.19, p.1453	IAS 1.IG Part I	Ch.3, p.150
IAS 1.122	Ch.21, p.1672	IAS 1.BC13L	Ch.3, p.161
IAS 1.122	Ch.23, p.1781	IAS 1.BC13Q	Ch.3, p.157
IAS 1.122	Ch.26, p.1936	IAS 1.BC30F	Ch.3, p.161
IAS 1.122	Ch.33, p.2475	IAS 1.BC32C	Ch.3, p.118
IAS 1.122	Ch.35, p.2895	IAS 1.BC33	Ch.41, p.3232
IAS 1.122	Ch.40, p.3158	IAS 1.BC38G	Ch.3, p.130
IAS 1.122	Ch.43, p.3379	IAS 1.BC38I	Ch.54, p.4515
IAS 1.122	Ch.43, p.3438	IAS 1.BC38J	Ch.54, p.4515
IAS 1.122	Ch.43, p.3441	IAS 1.BC38L-P	Ch.3, p.125
IAS 1.122	Ch.54, p.4513	IAS 1.BC55	Ch.3, p.137
IAS 1.122	Ch.56, p.4909	IAS 1.BC56	Ch.3, p.137
IAS 1.122-133	Ch.32, p.2433	IAS 1.BC64	Ch.3, p.148
IAS 1.123	Ch.3, p.175	IAS 1.BC76D	Ch.3, p.151
IAS 1.124	Ch.3, p.175	IAS 1.BC84	Ch.3, p.179
IAS 1.125	Ch.3, p.177	IAS 1.BC86	Ch.3, p.180
IAS 1.125	Ch.23, p.1781	IAS 1.BC86	Ch.54, p.4472
IAS 1.125	Ch.26, p.2009	IAS 1.BC88	Ch.54, p.4473
IAS 1.125	Ch.33, p.2475	IAS 1.BC100B	Ch.3, p.182
IAS 1.125	Ch.42, p.3292	IAS 1.BC103	Ch.37, p.3039
IAS 1.125	Ch.43, p.3438		
IAS 1.125	Ch.43, p.3441		
IAS 1.125	Ch.43, p.3511		
IAS 1.125	Ch.45, p.3606		

IAS 2

IAS 2.1	Ch.22, p.1675
IAS 2.2	Ch.22, p.1676
IAS 2.3	Ch.17, p.1366
IAS 2.3	Ch.22, p.1676
IAS 2.3(a)	Ch.43, p.3336
IAS 2.3(a)	Ch.43, p.3361
IAS 2.3(a)	Ch.43, p.3451
IAS 2.3(a)	Ch.43, p.3480
IAS 2.3(a)	Ch.43, p.3487
IAS 2.3(b)	Ch.22, p.1688
IAS 2.3(b)	Ch.22, p.1694
IAS 2.3(b)	Ch.43, p.3480
IAS 2.3(b)	Ch.43, p.3487
IAS 2.4	Ch.22, p.1676
IAS 2.4	Ch.43, p.3336
IAS 2.4	Ch.43, p.3361
IAS 2.5	Ch.22, p.1676
IAS 2.6	Ch.17, p.1299
IAS 2.6	Ch.17, p.1366
IAS 2.6	Ch.22, p.1676
IAS 2.6	Ch.22, p.1678
IAS 2.6	Ch.22, p.1682
IAS 2.6	Ch.32, p.2407
IAS 2.7	Ch.22, p.1683
IAS 2.8	Ch.22, p.1677
IAS 2.8	Ch.43, p.3481
IAS 2.9	Ch.17, p.1344
IAS 2.9	Ch.22, p.1682
IAS 2.9	Ch.29, p.2215
IAS 2.9	Ch.43, p.3451
IAS 2.9	Ch.43, p.3488
IAS 2.10	Ch.22, p.1683
IAS 2.10	Ch.43, p.3428
IAS 2.11	Ch.22, p.1683
IAS 2.12	Ch.22, p.1684
IAS 2.12	Ch.22, p.1696
IAS 2.12	Ch.22, p.1697
IAS 2.12	Ch.26, p.1974
IAS 2.13	Ch.22, p.1684
IAS 2.13	Ch.41, p.3243
IAS 2.14	Ch.22, p.1685
IAS 2.14	Ch.22, p.1696
IAS 2.14	Ch.43, p.3483
IAS 2.15	Ch.22, p.1685
IAS 2.15	Ch.22, p.1686
IAS 2.16	Ch.22, p.1685
IAS 2.16	Ch.22, p.1694
IAS 2.16	Ch.43, p.3428
IAS 2.16(b)	Ch.22, p.1685
IAS 2.16(c)	Ch.22, p.1686
IAS 2.16(c)	Ch.26, p.1974
IAS 2.17	Ch.22, p.1686
IAS 2.18	Ch.22, p.1687
IAS 2.20	Ch.22, p.1676
IAS 2.21	Ch.22, p.1689
IAS 2.22	Ch.22, p.1689
IAS 2.23	Ch.22, p.1690
IAS 2.24	Ch.22, p.1690
IAS 2.25	Ch.22, p.1690
IAS 2.25	Ch.43, p.3486
IAS 2.26	Ch.22, p.1690
IAS 2.27	Ch.22, p.1691
IAS 2.28	Ch.22, p.1692
IAS 2.28	Ch.29, p.2215
IAS 2.29	Ch.22, p.1692
IAS 2.30	Ch.22, p.1692
IAS 2.30	Ch.43, p.3488
IAS 2.31	Ch.22, p.1692
IAS 2.32	Ch.22, p.1692
IAS 2.32	Ch.22, p.1693
IAS 2.33	Ch.22, p.1693
IAS 2.34	Ch.22, p.1697
IAS 2.34	Ch.43, p.3447
IAS 2.35	Ch.22, p.1697
IAS 2.36	Ch.22, p.1697
IAS 2.37	Ch.22, p.1698
IAS 2.37	Ch.43, p.3481
IAS 2.38	Ch.22, p.1685
IAS 2.38	Ch.22, p.1698
IAS 2.39	Ch.22, p.1699
IAS 2.BC9	Ch.22, p.1691

IAS 7

IAS 7 Objective	Ch.40, p.3137
IAS 7.1	Ch.40, p.3182
IAS 7.3	Ch.40, p.3138
IAS 7.4	Ch.40, p.3137
IAS 7.5	Ch.40, p.3138
IAS 7.6	Ch.16, p.1272
IAS 7.6	Ch.40, p.3137
IAS 7.6	Ch.40, p.3138
IAS 7.6	Ch.40, p.3141
IAS 7.6	Ch.40, p.3147
IAS 7.6	Ch.40, p.3151
IAS 7.6	Ch.40, p.3152
IAS 7.6-8	Ch.5, p.363
IAS 7.7	Ch.40, p.3138
IAS 7.7	Ch.40, p.3140
IAS 7.7	Ch.40, p.3141
IAS 7.8	Ch.5, p.363
IAS 7.8	Ch.40, p.3142
IAS 7.9	Ch.40, p.3138
IAS 7.10	Ch.16, p.1272
IAS 7.10	Ch.40, p.3135
IAS 7.10	Ch.40, p.3145
IAS 7.11	Ch.40, p.3145
IAS 7.11	Ch.40, p.3152
IAS 7.12	Ch.40, p.3146
IAS 7.13	Ch.40, p.3147
IAS 7.13	Ch.40, p.3154
IAS 7.14	Ch.18, p.1427
IAS 7.14	Ch.27, p.2041

IAS 7.14	Ch.40, p.3147	IAS 7.35	Ch.40, p.3154
IAS 7.14	Ch.40, p.3148	IAS 7.36	Ch.33, p.2612
IAS 7.14	Ch.40, p.3153	IAS 7.36	Ch.40, p.3154
IAS 7.14	Ch.40, p.3159	IAS 7.37	Ch.40, p.3180
IAS 7.14	Ch.40, p.3160	IAS 7.37	Ch.40, p.3181
IAS 7.14	Ch.40, p.3161	IAS 7.38	Ch.40, p.3180
IAS 7.14(a)	Ch.40, p.3155	IAS 7.39	Ch.40, p.3176
IAS 7.14(d)	Ch.40, p.3155	IAS 7.39-42	Ch.9, p.757
IAS 7.15	Ch.40, p.3148	IAS 7.40	Ch.40, p.3176
IAS 7.15	Ch.40, p.3184	IAS 7.40-40A	Ch.40, p.3181
IAS 7.16	Ch.40, p.3148	IAS 7.41	Ch.40, p.3176
IAS 7.16	Ch.40, p.3151	IAS 7.42	Ch.40, p.3176
IAS 7.16	Ch.40, p.3161	IAS 7.42A	Ch.40, p.3153
IAS 7.16	Ch.40, p.3168	IAS 7.42A	Ch.40, p.3175
IAS 7.16	Ch.40, p.3177	IAS 7.42A	Ch.40, p.3176
IAS 7.16	Ch.40, p.3178	IAS 7.42B	Ch.40, p.3175
IAS 7.16	Ch.40, p.3179	IAS 7.43	Ch.40, p.3157
IAS 7.16	Ch.40, p.3180	IAS 7.43	Ch.40, p.3166
IAS 7.16	Ch.43, p.3376	IAS 7.43	Ch.40, p.3178
IAS 7.16(b)	Ch.40, p.3159	IAS 7.43	Ch.54, p.4512
IAS 7.16(e)	Ch.40, p.3184	IAS 7.44	Ch.40, p.3167
IAS 7.16(f)	Ch.40, p.3184	IAS 7.44A	Ch.40, p.3171
IAS 7.17	Ch.40, p.3152	IAS 7.44A	Ch.54, p.4513
IAS 7.17	Ch.40, p.3160	IAS 7.44B	Ch.40, p.3171
IAS 7.17	Ch.40, p.3162	IAS 7.44C	Ch.40, p.3171
IAS 7.17	Ch.40, p.3179	IAS 7.44D	Ch.40, p.3171
IAS 7.17	Ch.40, p.3180	IAS 7.44E	Ch.40, p.3172
IAS 7.17(a)	Ch.40, p.3161	IAS 7.45	Ch.40, p.3139
IAS 7.17(c)	Ch.40, p.3155	IAS 7.45	Ch.40, p.3143
IAS 7.17(e)	Ch.40, p.3169	IAS 7.46	Ch.40, p.3139
IAS 7.18	Ch.40, p.3148	IAS 7.48	Ch.15, p.1244
IAS 7.18	Ch.40, p.3165	IAS 7.48	Ch.40, p.3143
IAS 7.19	Ch.40, p.3148	IAS 7.49	Ch.15, p.1244
IAS 7.19	Ch.40, p.3175	IAS 7.49	Ch.40, p.3143
IAS 7.19	Ch.40, p.3185	IAS 7.50	Ch.40, p.3173
IAS 7.20	Ch.40, p.3149	IAS 7.51	Ch.40, p.3173
IAS 7.20	Ch.40, p.3150	IAS 7.52	Ch.40, p.3173
IAS 7.20	Ch.40, p.3175	IAS 7 Appendix A part D	Ch.40, p.3174
IAS 7.21	Ch.40, p.3152	IAS 7.IE Example A	Ch.3, p.138
IAS 7.21	Ch.40, p.3153	IAS 7.BC3	Ch.40, p.3152
IAS 7.21	Ch.40, p.3164	IAS 7.BC5-7	Ch.40, p.3179
IAS 7.22	Ch.40, p.3164	IAS 7.BC7	Ch.40, p.3152
IAS 7.23	Ch.40, p.3164	IAS 7.BC9	Ch.40, p.3171
IAS 7.23A	Ch.40, p.3164	IAS 7.BC11	Ch.54, p.4510
IAS 7.23A(c)	Ch.40, p.3155		
IAS 7.24	Ch.40, p.3185		
IAS 7.25	Ch.40, p.3165		
IAS 7.26	Ch.40, p.3165		
IAS 7.27	Ch.40, p.3165		
IAS 7.28	Ch.40, p.3140		
IAS 7.28	Ch.40, p.3165		
IAS 7.31	Ch.40, p.3153		
IAS 7.32	Ch.40, p.3154		
IAS 7.33	Ch.40, p.3153		
IAS 7.33	Ch.40, p.3184		
IAS 7.34	Ch.40, p.3153		
IAS 7.34	Ch.40, p.3154		
IAS 7.35	Ch.33, p.2612		

IAS 8

IAS 8.1	Ch.3, p.115
IAS 8.2	Ch.3, p.115
IAS 8.3	Ch.3, p.114
IAS 8.4	Ch.3, p.115
IAS 8.5	Ch.3, p.114
IAS 8.5	Ch.3, p.157
IAS 8.5	Ch.3, p.163
IAS 8.5	Ch.3, p.166
IAS 8.5	Ch.3, p.168
IAS 8.5	Ch.3, p.169

IAS 8.5	Ch.3, p.171
IAS 8.5	Ch.3, p.172
IAS 8.5	Ch.5, p.244
IAS 8.5	Ch.5, p.365
IAS 8.5	Ch.5, p.368
IAS 8.5	Ch.30, p.2279
IAS 8.5	Ch.33, p.2473
IAS 8.5	Ch.33, p.2540
IAS 8.5	Ch.33, p.2573
IAS 8.5	Ch.43, p.3498
IAS 8.5	Ch.43, p.3518
IAS 8.5	Ch.43, p.3563
IAS 8.5	Ch.51, p.4020
IAS 8.5	Ch.56, p.4920
IAS 8.7	Ch.3, p.164
IAS 8.7	Ch.10, p.765
IAS 8.7	Ch.43, p.3344
IAS 8.8	Ch.3, p.153
IAS 8.8	Ch.3, p.164
IAS 8.8	Ch.5, p.239
IAS 8.8	Ch.14, p.1010
IAS 8.8	Ch.49, p.3854
IAS 8.9	Ch.3, p.114
IAS 8.10	Ch.3, p.164
IAS 8.10	Ch.5, p.324
IAS 8.10	Ch.5, p.325
IAS 8.10	Ch.8, p.586
IAS 8.10	Ch.17, p.1309
IAS 8.10	Ch.18, p.1403
IAS 8.10	Ch.19, p.1465
IAS 8.10	Ch.43, p.3344
IAS 8.10	Ch.43, p.3361
IAS 8.10	Ch.43, p.3421
IAS 8.10	Ch.53, p.4295
IAS 8.10	Ch.55, p.4587
IAS 8.10-11	Ch.51, p.3958
IAS 8.10-12	Ch.5, p.239
IAS 8.10-12	Ch.7, p.517
IAS 8.10-12	Ch.31, p.2383
IAS 8.11	Ch.3, p.165
IAS 8.11	Ch.5, p.324
IAS 8.11	Ch.17, p.1308
IAS 8.11	Ch.43, p.3344
IAS 8.11	Ch.43, p.3514
IAS 8.11-12	Ch.55, p.4587
IAS 8.11(a)	Ch.7, p.504
IAS 8.12	Ch.3, p.165
IAS 8.13	Ch.42, p.3283
IAS 8.12	Ch.5, p.324
IAS 8.12	Ch.5, p.325
IAS 8.12	Ch.43, p.3344
IAS 8.13	Ch.3, p.157
IAS 8.13	Ch.24, p.1831
IAS 8.14	Ch.3, p.166
IAS 8.14	Ch.22, p.1690
IAS 8.14-15	Ch.5, p.325
IAS 8.14(b)	Ch.41, p.3240
IAS 8.15	Ch.3, p.157
IAS 8.16	Ch.3, p.167
IAS 8.17	Ch.18, p.1425
IAS 8.17	Ch.41, p.3241
IAS 8.17-18	Ch.3, p.167
IAS 8.19	Ch.55, p.4588
IAS 8.19-20	Ch.3, p.166
IAS 8.21	Ch.3, p.167
IAS 8.22	Ch.3, p.166
IAS 8.23	Ch.3, p.166
IAS 8.23	Ch.3, p.172
IAS 8.23	Ch.33, p.2572
IAS 8.24	Ch.3, p.172
IAS 8.25	Ch.3, p.172
IAS 8.26	Ch.3, p.166
IAS 8.26	Ch.3, p.172
IAS 8.27	Ch.3, p.172
IAS 8.28	Ch.3, p.176
IAS 8.28	Ch.56, p.4923
IAS 8.29	Ch.3, p.176
IAS 8.29	Ch.40, p.3148
IAS 8.29	Ch.41, p.3242
IAS 8.30	Ch.3, p.177
IAS 8.30	Ch.38, p.3087
IAS 8.30	Ch.55, p.4601
IAS 8.31	Ch.3, p.177
IAS 8.32-33	Ch.3, p.167
IAS 8.32-38	Ch.43, p.3518
IAS 8.32-40	Ch.5, p.245
IAS 8.32-40	Ch.5, p.250
IAS 8.32(d)	Ch.18, p.1415
IAS 8.34	Ch.3, p.167
IAS 8.34	Ch.20, p.1588
IAS 8.34	Ch.30, p.2279
IAS 8.35	Ch.3, p.163
IAS 8.35	Ch.3, p.164
IAS 8.35	Ch.3, p.167
IAS 8.36	Ch.3, p.168
IAS 8.36	Ch.17, p.1347
IAS 8.36	Ch.17, p.1349
IAS 8.36	Ch.18, p.1415
IAS 8.36	Ch.26, p.1957
IAS 8.36	Ch.33, p.2476
IAS 8.36	Ch.33, p.2567
IAS 8.36-37	Ch.30, p.2279
IAS 8.36-38	Ch.3, p.168
IAS 8.38	Ch.3, p.163
IAS 8.38	Ch.17, p.1347
IAS 8.39	Ch.3, p.179
IAS 8.40	Ch.3, p.179
IAS 8.41	Ch.3, p.168
IAS 8.42	Ch.3, p.169
IAS 8.42	Ch.33, p.2476
IAS 8.43	Ch.3, p.170
IAS 8.43	Ch.3, p.173
IAS 8.44	Ch.3, p.173
IAS 8.45	Ch.3, p.173
IAS 8.46	Ch.3, p.169
IAS 8.47	Ch.3, p.174

IAS 8.48	Ch.3, p.164	IAS 10.17	Ch.38, p.3086
IAS 8.48	Ch.3, p.168	IAS 10.17	Ch.41, p.3219
IAS 8.49	Ch.3, p.179	IAS 10.18	Ch.38, p.3086
IAS 8.50	Ch.3, p.171	IAS 10.19	Ch.38, p.3082
IAS 8.51	Ch.3, p.171	IAS 10.20	Ch.38, p.3082
IAS 8.52	Ch.3, p.172	IAS 10.21	Ch.33, p.2474
IAS 8.53	Ch.3, p.171	IAS 10.21	Ch.33, p.2476
IAS 8.IG1	Ch.3, p.169	IAS 10.21	Ch.33, p.2542
IAS 8.IG3	Ch.3, p.172	IAS 10.21	Ch.38, p.3074
		IAS 10.21	Ch.38, p.3083
		IAS 10.21	Ch.39, p.3115

IAS 10

		IAS 10.22	Ch.38, p.3079
IAS 10.1	Ch.38, p.3074	IAS 10.22(e)	Ch.26, p.1968
IAS 10.2	Ch.38, p.3073	IAS 10.22(f)	Ch.38, p.3079
IAS 10.3	Ch.33, p.2473	IAS 10.22(h)	Ch.33, p.2474
IAS 10.3	Ch.33, p.2541	IAS 10.22(h)	Ch.33, p.2475
IAS 10.3	Ch.33, p.2567	IAS 10.22(h)	Ch.33, p.2541
IAS 10.3	Ch.38, p.3073	IAS 10.22(h)	Ch.38, p.3090
IAS 10.3	Ch.38, p.3074	IAS 10.22(h)	Ch.41, p.3252
IAS 10.3	Ch.43, p.3518	IAS 10.BC4	Ch.38, p.3081
IAS 10.3	Ch.43, p.3561		
IAS 10.3(a)	Ch.38, p.3073		

IAS 12 (2018)

IAS 10.3(a)	Ch.38, p.3078		
IAS 10.3(a)	Ch.43, p.3419	IAS 12(2018).52A	Ch.33, p.2577
IAS 10.3(b)	Ch.38, p.3074		
IAS 10.3(b)	Ch.38, p.3079		

IAS 12

IAS 10.4	Ch.38, p.3074		
IAS 10.5	Ch.38, p.3074	IAS 12 Objective	Ch.33, p.2455
IAS 10.5-6	Ch.38, p.3075	IAS 12 Objective	Ch.33, p.2456
IAS 10.6	Ch.38, p.3074	IAS 12.1-2	Ch.33, p.2458
IAS 10.7	Ch.38, p.3077	IAS 12.1-2	Ch.43, p.3557
IAS 10.8	Ch.38, p.3073	IAS 12.2	Ch.33, p.2457
IAS 10.8	Ch.38, p.3082	IAS 12.2	Ch.33, p.2461
IAS 10.9	Ch.26, p.1939	IAS 12.4	Ch.24, p.1828
IAS 10.9	Ch.26, p.1945	IAS 12.4	Ch.33, p.2458
IAS 10.9	Ch.38, p.3078	IAS 12.4	Ch.33, p.2462
IAS 10.9(b)(i)	Ch.38, p.3088	IAS 12.5	Ch.33, p.2457
IAS 10.9(b)(ii)	Ch.22, p.1692	IAS 12.5	Ch.33, p.2471
IAS 10.9(b)(ii)	Ch.38, p.3087	IAS 12.5	Ch.33, p.2478
IAS 10.9(e)	Ch.38, p.3089	IAS 12.5	Ch.33, p.2482
IAS 10.10	Ch.5, p.244	IAS 12.5	Ch.33, p.2494
IAS 10.10	Ch.38, p.3074	IAS 12.5	Ch.33, p.2519
IAS 10.10	Ch.38, p.3083	IAS 12.5	Ch.33, p.2522
IAS 10.11	Ch.38, p.3079	IAS 12.5	Ch.33, p.2523
IAS 10.11	Ch.38, p.3080	IAS 12.5	Ch.33, p.2568
IAS 10.11	Ch.38, p.3089	IAS 12.7	Ch.33, p.2479
IAS 10.11	Ch.51, p.3966	IAS 12.7	Ch.33, p.2530
IAS 10.12	Ch.33, p.2535	IAS 12.8	Ch.33, p.2480
IAS 10.12	Ch.38, p.3079	IAS 12.9	Ch.33, p.2481
IAS 10.13	Ch.8, p.599	IAS 12.10	Ch.33, p.2456
IAS 10.13	Ch.38, p.3081	IAS 12.10	Ch.33, p.2481
IAS 10.14	Ch.38, p.3074	IAS 12.10	Ch.33, p.2546
IAS 10.14	Ch.38, p.3082	IAS 12.11	Ch.33, p.2478
IAS 10.14	Ch.38, p.3083	IAS 12.11	Ch.33, p.2560
IAS 10.15	Ch.38, p.3082	IAS 12.12	Ch.33, p.2471
IAS 10.16(a)	Ch.38, p.3083	IAS 12.12	Ch.33, p.2569
IAS 10.16(b)	Ch.38, p.3083		

IAS 12.13	Ch.41, p.3255	IAS 12.29(b)	Ch.33, p.2604
IAS 12.13-14	Ch.33, p.2471	IAS 12.29A	Ch.33, p.2522
IAS 12.15	Ch.5, p.365	IAS 12.30	Ch.33, p.2520
IAS 12.15	Ch.33, p.2491	IAS 12.31	Ch.33, p.2518
IAS 12.15	Ch.33, p.2516	IAS 12.32A	Ch.9, p.692
IAS 12.15	Ch.33, p.2531	IAS 12.32A	Ch.33, p.2495
IAS 12.15(a)	Ch.5, p.277	IAS 12.33	Ch.33, p.2488
IAS 12.15(b)	Ch.33, p.2515	IAS 12.33	Ch.33, p.2498
IAS 12.15(b)	Ch.33, p.2516	IAS 12.34	Ch.33, p.2464
IAS 12.16	Ch.33, p.2453	IAS 12.34	Ch.33, p.2526
IAS 12.16	Ch.33, p.2456	IAS 12.35	Ch.33, p.2526
IAS 12.17-20	Ch.33, p.2482	IAS 12.35	Ch.33, p.2527
IAS 12.19	Ch.55, p.4599	IAS 12.36	Ch.33, p.2527
IAS 12.20	Ch.33, p.2516	IAS 12.37	Ch.33, p.2528
IAS 12.20	Ch.33, p.2517	IAS 12.38	Ch.33, p.2531
IAS 12.20	Ch.33, p.2522	IAS 12.39	Ch.33, p.2534
IAS 12.20	Ch.33, p.2528	IAS 12.39	Ch.33, p.2535
IAS 12.21	Ch.33, p.2495	IAS 12.39	Ch.33, p.2537
IAS 12.21A	Ch.33, p.2495	IAS 12.39	Ch.33, p.2601
IAS 12.21A	Ch.33, p.2499	IAS 12.39(b)	Ch.33, p.2536
IAS 12.21A	Ch.33, p.2503	IAS 12.40	Ch.33, p.2534
IAS 12.21B	Ch.33, p.2496	IAS 12.41	Ch.15, p.1242
IAS 12.22	Ch.33, p.2497	IAS 12.41	Ch.33, p.2572
IAS 12.22(a)	Ch.20, p.1593	IAS 12.41	Ch.43, p.3421
IAS 12.22(c)	Ch.33, p.2493	IAS 12.42	Ch.33, p.2534
IAS 12.22(c)	Ch.33, p.2499	IAS 12.43	Ch.33, p.2534
IAS 12.22(c)	Ch.33, p.2508	IAS 12.44	Ch.33, p.2535
IAS 12.22(c)	Ch.33, p.2609	IAS 12.45	Ch.33, p.2535
IAS 12.23	Ch.33, p.2515	IAS 12.46	Ch.33, p.2471
IAS 12.24	Ch.5, p.365	IAS 12.46	Ch.33, p.2473
IAS 12.24	Ch.33, p.2488	IAS 12.46	Ch.33, p.2475
IAS 12.24	Ch.33, p.2491	IAS 12.46	Ch.33, p.2561
IAS 12.24	Ch.33, p.2492	IAS 12.46	Ch.33, p.2564
IAS 12.24	Ch.33, p.2516	IAS 12.46	Ch.33, p.2569
IAS 12.24	Ch.33, p.2531	IAS 12.47	Ch.33, p.2475
IAS 12.24	Ch.41, p.3256	IAS 12.47	Ch.33, p.2539
IAS 12.24-31	Ch.5, p.367	IAS 12.47	Ch.33, p.2540
IAS 12.25	Ch.33, p.2456	IAS 12.47	Ch.33, p.2561
IAS 12.26	Ch.33, p.2482	IAS 12.47	Ch.33, p.2564
IAS 12.26(d)	Ch.33, p.2522	IAS 12.47	Ch.41, p.3253
IAS 12.27	Ch.33, p.2492	IAS 12.48	Ch.33, p.2471
IAS 12.27	Ch.33, p.2517	IAS 12.48	Ch.33, p.2539
IAS 12.27	Ch.33, p.2523	IAS 12.48	Ch.41, p.3251
IAS 12.27A	Ch.33, p.2518	IAS 12.49	Ch.33, p.2539
IAS 12.27A	Ch.33, p.2524	IAS 12.51	Ch.33, p.2542
IAS 12.28	Ch.33, p.2518	IAS 12.51A	Ch.33, p.2544
IAS 12.28	Ch.33, p.2525	IAS 12.51A	Ch.33, p.2551
IAS 12.28	Ch.33, p.2526	IAS 12.51B	Ch.33, p.2547
IAS 12.28	Ch.33, p.2528	IAS 12.51C	Ch.33, p.2549
IAS 12.29	Ch.33, p.2512	IAS 12.51C	Ch.33, p.2550
IAS 12.29	Ch.33, p.2518	IAS 12.51D	Ch.33, p.2550
IAS 12.29	Ch.33, p.2525	IAS 12.51E	Ch.33, p.2547
IAS 12.29	Ch.33, p.2604	IAS 12.51E	Ch.33, p.2550
IAS 12.29(a)(i)	Ch.33, p.2519	IAS 12.52A	Ch.33, p.2536
IAS 12.29(a)(i)	Ch.33, p.2523	IAS 12.52A	Ch.33, p.2554
IAS 12.29(a)(ii)	Ch.33, p.2519	IAS 12.53	Ch.33, p.2477
IAS 12.29(b)	Ch.33, p.2542	IAS 12.53	Ch.33, p.2556
IAS 12.29(b)	Ch.33, p.2543	IAS 12.54	Ch.33, p.2556

IAS 12.55	Ch.33, p.2556	IAS 12.80(d)	Ch.33, p.2541
IAS 12.56	Ch.33, p.2528	IAS 12.81	Ch.33, p.2613
IAS 12.57	Ch.33, p.2570	IAS 12.81(c)	Ch.33, p.2460
IAS 12.57A	Ch.33, p.2536	IAS 12.81(c)	Ch.33, p.2617
IAS 12.57A	Ch.33, p.2554	IAS 12.81(d)	Ch.33, p.2474
IAS 12.57A	Ch.33, p.2574	IAS 12.81(d)	Ch.33, p.2541
IAS 12.58	Ch.15, p.1242	IAS 12.81(e)	Ch.33, p.2620
IAS 12.58	Ch.33, p.2570	IAS 12.81(f)	Ch.33, p.2620
IAS 12.58	Ch.33, p.2573	IAS 12.81(g)	Ch.33, p.2619
IAS 12.58	Ch.33, p.2582	IAS 12.82	Ch.33, p.2616
IAS 12.58	Ch.33, p.2601	IAS 12.82A	Ch.33, p.2617
IAS 12.58(a)	Ch.33, p.2600	IAS 12.84	Ch.33, p.2614
IAS 12.58(a)	Ch.33, p.2601	IAS 12.85	Ch.33, p.2615
IAS 12.60	Ch.33, p.2570	IAS 12.86	Ch.33, p.2613
IAS 12.60	Ch.33, p.2573	IAS 12.87	Ch.33, p.2616
IAS 12.61A	Ch.5, p.365	IAS 12.87A	Ch.33, p.2617
IAS 12.61A	Ch.5, p.366	IAS 12.87A-87C	Ch.33, p.2617
IAS 12.61A	Ch.5, p.368	IAS 12.88	Ch.26, p.1935
IAS 12.61A	Ch.33, p.2528	IAS 12.88	Ch.33, p.2541
IAS 12.61A	Ch.33, p.2541	IAS 12.88	Ch.33, p.2614
IAS 12.61A	Ch.33, p.2570	IAS 12.88	Ch.33, p.2619
IAS 12.61A	Ch.33, p.2571	IAS 12.98I	Ch.33, p.2455
IAS 12.61A	Ch.33, p.2580	IAS 12.98I	Ch.33, p.2577
IAS 12.61A	Ch.33, p.2581	IAS 12.IE.A-C	Ch.33, p.2482
IAS 12.61A	Ch.33, p.2582	IAS 12.IE.A.18	Ch.16, p.1266
IAS 12.61A(b)	Ch.33, p.2601	IAS 12 IE Example 4	Ch.33, p.2515
IAS 12.62	Ch.33, p.2570	IAS 12 IE Example 6	Ch.33, p.2597
IAS 12.62A	Ch.33, p.2570	IAS 12 IE Example 7	Ch.33, p.2524
IAS 12.62A(a)	Ch.33, p.2573	IAS 12.BC1A	Ch.33, p.2520
IAS 12.63	Ch.33, p.2571	IAS 12.BC6	Ch.33, p.2545
IAS 12.64	Ch.33, p.2571	IAS 12.BC6	Ch.33, p.2547
IAS 12.65	Ch.33, p.2571	IAS 12.BC37	Ch.33, p.2520
IAS 12.65A	Ch.33, p.2574	IAS 12.BC38	Ch.33, p.2521
IAS 12.65A	Ch.33, p.2575	IAS 12.BC39	Ch.33, p.2521
IAS 12.65A	Ch.33, p.2576	IAS 12.BC40	Ch.33, p.2522
IAS 12.66	Ch.33, p.2604	IAS 12.BC42-44	Ch.33, p.2522
IAS 12.67	Ch.33, p.2607	IAS 12.BC47	Ch.33, p.2521
IAS 12.68	Ch.9, p.692	IAS 12.BC49	Ch.33, p.2523
IAS 12.68	Ch.20, p.1597	IAS 12.BC50	Ch.33, p.2523
IAS 12.68	Ch.33, p.2607	IAS 12.BC52	Ch.33, p.2521
IAS 12.68A	Ch.33, p.2587	IAS 12.BC53	Ch.33, p.2521
IAS 12.68A-68C	Ch.5, p.367	IAS 12.BC53	Ch.33, p.2523
IAS 12.68A-68C	Ch.33, p.2570	IAS 12.BC55	Ch.33, p.2521
IAS 12.68B	Ch.33, p.2587	IAS 12.BC55	Ch.33, p.2523
IAS 12.68C	Ch.5, p.367	IAS 12.BC56	Ch.33, p.2519
IAS 12.68C	Ch.33, p.2587	IAS 12.BC56	Ch.33, p.2523
IAS 12.68C	Ch.33, p.2589	IAS 12.BC57	Ch.33, p.2521
IAS 12.68C	Ch.33, p.2593	IAS 12.BC58	Ch.33, p.2523
IAS 12.71	Ch.33, p.2610	IAS 12.BC59	Ch.33, p.2524
IAS 12.72	Ch.33, p.2610	IAS 12.BC67	Ch.33, p.2577
IAS 12.73	Ch.33, p.2610	IAS 12.BC69	Ch.33, p.2578
IAS 12.74	Ch.33, p.2610	IAS 12.BC70	Ch.33, p.2577
IAS 12.75	Ch.33, p.2611		
IAS 12.76	Ch.33, p.2611		
IAS 12.77	Ch.33, p.2611		
IAS 12.78	Ch.33, p.2612		
IAS 12.79-80	Ch.33, p.2613		
IAS 12.79-80	Ch.33, p.2617		

IAS 16 (2022)

IAS 16(2022).17(e)	Ch.18, p.1405
IAS 16(2022).BC16F-G	Ch.43, p.3448

IAS 16(2022).BC16J Ch.43, p.3448

IAS 16

IAS 16.1	Ch.18, p.1385
IAS 16.2	Ch.43, p.3513
IAS 16.2-3	Ch.18, p.1386
IAS 16.3	Ch.18, p.1386
IAS 16.3	Ch.43, p.3513
IAS 16.3(b)	Ch.18, p.1393
IAS 16.3(c)	Ch.43, p.3361
IAS 16.3(d)	Ch.43, p.3336
IAS 16.3(d)	Ch.43, p.3361
IAS 16.3(d)	Ch.43, p.3502
IAS 16.5	Ch.18, p.1386
IAS 16.5	Ch.18, p.1418
IAS 16.6	Ch.8, p.585
IAS 16.6	Ch.18, p.1387
IAS 16.6	Ch.18, p.1393
IAS 16.6	Ch.18, p.1410
IAS 16.6	Ch.18, p.1419
IAS 16.6	Ch.32, p.2407
IAS 16.6	Ch.33, p.2545
IAS 16.6	Ch.43, p.3395
IAS 16.6	Ch.43, p.3418
IAS 16.7	Ch.18, p.1388
IAS 16.7	Ch.18, p.1428
IAS 16.8	Ch.18, p.1389
IAS 16.9	Ch.5, p.292
IAS 16.9	Ch.5, p.371
IAS 16.9	Ch.18, p.1389
IAS 16.9	Ch.18, p.1428
IAS 16.10	Ch.18, p.1394
IAS 16.11	Ch.18, p.1390
IAS 16.12	Ch.5, p.371
IAS 16.12	Ch.18, p.1395
IAS 16.12	Ch.43, p.3492
IAS 16.13	Ch.5, p.371
IAS 16.13	Ch.18, p.1395
IAS 16.13	Ch.43, p.3492
IAS 16.14	Ch.18, p.1396
IAS 16.14	Ch.18, p.1397
IAS 16.14	Ch.43, p.3492
IAS 16.15	Ch.18, p.1397
IAS 16.15	Ch.21, p.1647
IAS 16.15	Ch.43, p.3367
IAS 16.15	Ch.43, p.3395
IAS 16.15	Ch.43, p.3398
IAS 16.16	Ch.18, p.1397
IAS 16.16	Ch.18, p.1399
IAS 16.16	Ch.18, p.1405
IAS 16.16	Ch.18, p.1414
IAS 16.16	Ch.26, p.1941
IAS 16.16	Ch.26, p.1979
IAS 16.16(a)	Ch.26, p.2001
IAS 16.16(b)	Ch.18, p.1403
IAS 16.16(b)	Ch.19, p.1457
IAS 16.16(b)	Ch.21, p.1647
IAS 16.16(b)	Ch.42, p.3285
IAS 16.16(b)	Ch.43, p.3443
IAS 16.16(b)	Ch.43, p.3486
IAS 16.16(c)	Ch.5, p.316
IAS 16.16(c)	Ch.26, p.1947
IAS 16.16(c)	Ch.26, p.1985
IAS 16.16(c)	Ch.33, p.2509
IAS 16.16(c)	Ch.43, p.3428
IAS 16.17	Ch.18, p.1399
IAS 16.17	Ch.18, p.1404
IAS 16.17(e)	Ch.43, p.3444
IAS 16.18	Ch.18, p.1398
IAS 16.18	Ch.26, p.1947
IAS 16.18	Ch.26, p.1986
IAS 16.18	Ch.43, p.3428
IAS 16.19	Ch.18, p.1400
IAS 16.20	Ch.18, p.1400
IAS 16.20	Ch.18, p.1404
IAS 16.20	Ch.43, p.3444
IAS 16.20A	Ch.17, p.1308
IAS 16.20A	Ch.18, p.1404
IAS 16.21	Ch.18, p.1403
IAS 16.21	Ch.18, p.1404
IAS 16.21	Ch.19, p.1466
IAS 16.21	Ch.43, p.3444
IAS 16.21	Ch.43, p.3445
IAS 16.22	Ch.18, p.1399
IAS 16.22	Ch.18, p.1400
IAS 16.22	Ch.42, p.3286
IAS 16.22A	Ch.18, p.1393
IAS 16.22A	Ch.42, p.3284
IAS 16.22A	Ch.42, p.3286
IAS 16.23	Ch.16, p.1261
IAS 16.23	Ch.18, p.1401
IAS 16.24	Ch.8, p.613
IAS 16.24	Ch.8, p.616
IAS 16.24	Ch.18, p.1406
IAS 16.24	Ch.18, p.1408
IAS 16.24	Ch.43, p.3402
IAS 16.25	Ch.11, p.852
IAS 16.25	Ch.18, p.1407
IAS 16.26	Ch.8, p.613
IAS 16.26	Ch.8, p.615
IAS 16.26	Ch.18, p.1408
IAS 16.28	Ch.18, p.1408
IAS 16.29	Ch.18, p.1408
IAS 16.29	Ch.18, p.1417
IAS 16.29	Ch.18, p.1418
IAS 16.29	Ch.42, p.3284
IAS 16.29A-29B	Ch.18, p.1409
IAS 16.30	Ch.18, p.1408
IAS 16.30	Ch.19, p.1483
IAS 16.31	Ch.14, p.1136
IAS 16.31	Ch.18, p.1417
IAS 16.31	Ch.21, p.1647
IAS 16.34	Ch.14, p.1136
IAS 16.34	Ch.18, p.1418

Index of standards

IAS 16.35	Ch.18, p.1423
IAS 16.36	Ch.18, p.1418
IAS 16.37	Ch.18, p.1418
IAS 16.37	Ch.42, p.3310
IAS 16.38	Ch.18, p.1418
IAS 16.39	Ch.18, p.1422
IAS 16.39	Ch.18, p.1424
IAS 16.40	Ch.18, p.1422
IAS 16.41	Ch.18, p.1422
IAS 16.41	Ch.18, p.1426
IAS 16.41	Ch.27, p.2040
IAS 16.42	Ch.18, p.1423
IAS 16.43	Ch.5, p.371
IAS 16.43	Ch.18, p.1394
IAS 16.43	Ch.18, p.1409
IAS 16.43	Ch.26, p.1963
IAS 16.43	Ch.43, p.3514
IAS 16.44	Ch.17, p.1299
IAS 16.44	Ch.18, p.1394
IAS 16.44	Ch.18, p.1409
IAS 16.44	Ch.19, p.1485
IAS 16.44	Ch.26, p.1964
IAS 16.44	Ch.26, p.2003
IAS 16.45	Ch.18, p.1392
IAS 16.45	Ch.18, p.1410
IAS 16.45	Ch.43, p.3514
IAS 16.46	Ch.18, p.1410
IAS 16.47	Ch.18, p.1410
IAS 16.48	Ch.18, p.1410
IAS 16.49	Ch.18, p.1410
IAS 16.50	Ch.18, p.1411
IAS 16.51	Ch.5, p.369
IAS 16.51	Ch.5, p.370
IAS 16.51	Ch.18, p.1410
IAS 16.51	Ch.18, p.1411
IAS 16.51	Ch.19, p.1483
IAS 16.51	Ch.42, p.3284
IAS 16.52	Ch.18, p.1411
IAS 16.53	Ch.18, p.1411
IAS 16.53	Ch.42, p.3293
IAS 16.54	Ch.18, p.1411
IAS 16.55	Ch.18, p.1414
IAS 16.55	Ch.18, p.1415
IAS 16.56	Ch.18, p.1412
IAS 16.56	Ch.18, p.1414
IAS 16.56(c)	Ch.18, p.1414
IAS 16.57	Ch.18, p.1411
IAS 16.57	Ch.18, p.1412
IAS 16.57	Ch.18, p.1414
IAS 16.58	Ch.18, p.1413
IAS 16.59	Ch.18, p.1413
IAS 16.59	Ch.18, p.1414
IAS 16.60-62	Ch.18, p.1415
IAS 16.61	Ch.5, p.369
IAS 16.61	Ch.18, p.1414
IAS 16.61	Ch.18, p.1415
IAS 16.62	Ch.18, p.1416
IAS 16.62	Ch.41, p.3244
IAS 16.62A	Ch.18, p.1415
IAS 16.63	Ch.18, p.1417
IAS 16.63	Ch.42, p.3284
IAS 16.65	Ch.18, p.1417
IAS 16.65	Ch.18, p.1431
IAS 16.66	Ch.18, p.1417
IAS 16.66	Ch.18, p.1431
IAS 16.66(c)	Ch.55, p.4542
IAS 16.67	Ch.18, p.1426
IAS 16.67	Ch.18, p.1428
IAS 16.67	Ch.43, p.3395
IAS 16.67	Ch.43, p.3399
IAS 16.68	Ch.18, p.1406
IAS 16.68	Ch.18, p.1426
IAS 16.68	Ch.27, p.2018
IAS 16.68	Ch.27, p.2040
IAS 16.68	Ch.36, p.2999
IAS 16.68A	Ch.3, p.122
IAS 16.68A	Ch.18, p.1406
IAS 16.68A	Ch.18, p.1427
IAS 16.68A	Ch.19, p.1509
IAS 16.68A	Ch.22, p.1677
IAS 16.68A	Ch.22, p.1681
IAS 16.68A	Ch.27, p.2040
IAS 16.68A	Ch.27, p.2041
IAS 16.68A	Ch.40, p.3159
IAS 16.69	Ch.18, p.1426
IAS 16.69	Ch.27, p.2040
IAS 16.70	Ch.18, p.1394
IAS 16.70	Ch.18, p.1426
IAS 16.71	Ch.18, p.1426
IAS 16.71	Ch.25, p.1865
IAS 16.71	Ch.27, p.2040
IAS 16.71	Ch.43, p.3399
IAS 16.72	Ch.18, p.1427
IAS 16.72	Ch.25, p.1865
IAS 16.72	Ch.27, p.2040
IAS 16.72	Ch.43, p.3400
IAS 16.72	Ch.45, p.3605
IAS 16.73	Ch.41, p.3232
IAS 16.73	Ch.42, p.3310
IAS 16.73(a)	Ch.18, p.1431
IAS 16.73(b)	Ch.18, p.1431
IAS 16.73(c)	Ch.18, p.1432
IAS 16.73(d)	Ch.18, p.1432
IAS 16.73(d)	Ch.20, p.1612
IAS 16.73(e)	Ch.18, p.1432
IAS 16.73(e)	Ch.41, p.3205
IAS 16.73(e)(iv)	Ch.20, p.1612
IAS 16.74	Ch.18, p.1433
IAS 16.74(c)	Ch.38, p.3080
IAS 16.74(c)	Ch.39, p.3123
IAS 16.74A	Ch.18, p.1434
IAS 16.75	Ch.18, p.1431
IAS 16.75	Ch.18, p.1432
IAS 16.76	Ch.18, p.1434
IAS 16.77	Ch.18, p.1434
IAS 16.78	Ch.18, p.1436

Index of standards

IAS 16.79	Ch.18, p.1436
IAS 16.80D	Ch.18, p.1405
IAS 16.81N	Ch.18, p.1405
IAS 16.BC19	Ch.18, p.1406
IAS 16.BC21	Ch.17, p.1311
IAS 16.BC21	Ch.18, p.1407
IAS 16.BC22	Ch.11, p.852
IAS 16.BC23	Ch.18, p.1408
IAS 16.BC29	Ch.18, p.1410
IAS 16.BC35C	Ch.27, p.2041
IAS 16.BC67	Ch.42, p.3293
IAS 16.BC81	Ch.42, p.3285
IAS 16.BC82	Ch.42, p.3286
IAS 16.BC83	Ch.42, p.3277

IAS 17

IAS 17.4	Ch.51, p.4044

IAS 18

IAS 18.12	Ch.43, p.3449
IAS 18.16	Ch.5, p.341

IAS 19

IAS 19.1	Ch.35, p.2891
IAS 19.2	Ch.35, p.2892
IAS 19.3	Ch.35, p.2892
IAS 19.4	Ch.35, p.2892
IAS 19.5	Ch.35, p.2892
IAS 19.6	Ch.35, p.2892
IAS 19.7	Ch.35, p.2892
IAS 19.8	Ch.34, p.2855
IAS 19.8	Ch.35, p.2892
IAS 19.8	Ch.35, p.2894
IAS 19.8	Ch.35, p.2895
IAS 19.8	Ch.35, p.2898
IAS 19.8	Ch.35, p.2908
IAS 19.8	Ch.35, p.2909
IAS 19.8	Ch.35, p.2910
IAS 19.8	Ch.35, p.2912
IAS 19.8	Ch.35, p.2929
IAS 19.8	Ch.35, p.2930
IAS 19.8	Ch.35, p.2941
IAS 19.8	Ch.35, p.2942
IAS 19.8	Ch.35, p.2943
IAS 19.8	Ch.35, p.2945
IAS 19.8	Ch.35, p.2946
IAS 19.8	Ch.35, p.2947
IAS 19.8	Ch.35, p.2951
IAS 19.8	Ch.35, p.2953
IAS 19.9	Ch.35, p.2948
IAS 19.9(a)	Ch.34, p.2855
IAS 19.10	Ch.35, p.2948
IAS 19.11	Ch.35, p.2948
IAS 19.13	Ch.41, p.3248
IAS 19.13(b)	Ch.35, p.2949
IAS 19.14	Ch.35, p.2948
IAS 19.15	Ch.35, p.2948
IAS 19.16	Ch.35, p.2949
IAS 19.17	Ch.35, p.2949
IAS 19.18	Ch.35, p.2949
IAS 19.19	Ch.35, p.2949
IAS 19.19	Ch.41, p.3246
IAS 19.20	Ch.35, p.2950
IAS 19.21	Ch.34, p.2864
IAS 19.21	Ch.35, p.2950
IAS 19.22	Ch.35, p.2950
IAS 19.23	Ch.35, p.2950
IAS 19.24	Ch.35, p.2950
IAS 19.25	Ch.35, p.2967
IAS 19.26	Ch.35, p.2894
IAS 19.27	Ch.35, p.2894
IAS 19.28	Ch.35, p.2895
IAS 19.29	Ch.35, p.2894
IAS 19.29(b)	Ch.35, p.2902
IAS 19.30	Ch.35, p.2894
IAS 19.30	Ch.35, p.2895
IAS 19.30	Ch.35, p.2897
IAS 19.32	Ch.35, p.2898
IAS 19.33	Ch.35, p.2898
IAS 19.34	Ch.35, p.2899
IAS 19.35	Ch.35, p.2898
IAS 19.36	Ch.35, p.2898
IAS 19.36	Ch.35, p.2899
IAS 19.37	Ch.35, p.2899
IAS 19.37	Ch.35, p.2907
IAS 19.38	Ch.35, p.2898
IAS 19.39	Ch.35, p.2900
IAS 19.40	Ch.35, p.2900
IAS 19.41	Ch.35, p.2900
IAS 19.42	Ch.35, p.2901
IAS 19.43	Ch.35, p.2901
IAS 19.44	Ch.35, p.2901
IAS 19.44	Ch.35, p.2902
IAS 19.45	Ch.35, p.2902
IAS 19.46	Ch.35, p.2896
IAS 19.47	Ch.35, p.2896
IAS 19.48	Ch.35, p.2896
IAS 19.48	Ch.35, p.2897
IAS 19.49	Ch.35, p.2896
IAS 19.50	Ch.35, p.2906
IAS 19.51	Ch.35, p.2906
IAS 19.52	Ch.35, p.2906
IAS 19.53	Ch.35, p.2957
IAS 19.54	Ch.35, p.2957
IAS 19.55	Ch.35, p.2907
IAS 19.56	Ch.35, p.2895
IAS 19.56	Ch.35, p.2907
IAS 19.57	Ch.35, p.2908
IAS 19.58	Ch.35, p.2928
IAS 19.59	Ch.5, p.372

IAS 19.59	Ch.35, p.2908
IAS 19.59	Ch.35, p.2924
IAS 19.59	Ch.35, p.2928
IAS 19.60	Ch.35, p.2908
IAS 19.60	Ch.35, p.2928
IAS 19.61	Ch.35, p.2912
IAS 19.62	Ch.35, p.2912
IAS 19.63	Ch.35, p.2929
IAS 19.64	Ch.35, p.2930
IAS 19.65	Ch.35, p.2929
IAS 19.66	Ch.35, p.2917
IAS 19.67	Ch.35, p.2917
IAS 19.67	Ch.35, p.2941
IAS 19.68	Ch.35, p.2917
IAS 19.69	Ch.35, p.2924
IAS 19.70	Ch.35, p.2918
IAS 19.70	Ch.35, p.2919
IAS 19.71	Ch.35, p.2918
IAS 19.71-74	Ch.35, p.2920
IAS 19.72	Ch.35, p.2918
IAS 19.73	Ch.35, p.2919
IAS 19.74	Ch.35, p.2922
IAS 19.75	Ch.35, p.2928
IAS 19.75-77	Ch.35, p.2923
IAS 19.76	Ch.15, p.1201
IAS 19.76	Ch.35, p.2922
IAS 19.76(b)	Ch.35, p.2947
IAS 19.78	Ch.35, p.2923
IAS 19.79	Ch.35, p.2925
IAS 19.80	Ch.35, p.2923
IAS 19.80	Ch.35, p.2928
IAS 19.81	Ch.35, p.2923
IAS 19.82	Ch.35, p.2923
IAS 19.83	Ch.15, p.1201
IAS 19.83	Ch.26, p.1952
IAS 19.83	Ch.35, p.2925
IAS 19.83	Ch.35, p.2926
IAS 19.83	Ch.35, p.2927
IAS 19.84	Ch.26, p.1952
IAS 19.84	Ch.35, p.2924
IAS 19.85	Ch.35, p.2924
IAS 19.86	Ch.26, p.1953
IAS 19.86	Ch.35, p.2926
IAS 19.87	Ch.35, p.2913
IAS 19.87	Ch.35, p.2923
IAS 19.87-90	Ch.35, p.2912
IAS 19.88	Ch.35, p.2913
IAS 19.89	Ch.35, p.2913
IAS 19.91	Ch.35, p.2913
IAS 19.92	Ch.35, p.2913
IAS 19.93	Ch.35, p.2913
IAS 19.93	Ch.35, p.2914
IAS 19.94	Ch.35, p.2916
IAS 19.95	Ch.35, p.2913
IAS 19.96-97	Ch.35, p.2923
IAS 19.97	Ch.35, p.2923
IAS 19.98	Ch.35, p.2923
IAS 19.99	Ch.35, p.2941
IAS 19.100	Ch.35, p.2941
IAS 19.101	Ch.35, p.2941
IAS 19.101A	Ch.35, p.2941
IAS 19.102	Ch.35, p.2942
IAS 19.103	Ch.5, p.373
IAS 19.103	Ch.35, p.2942
IAS 19.104	Ch.35, p.2942
IAS 19.105	Ch.35, p.2942
IAS 19.106	Ch.35, p.2942
IAS 19.107	Ch.35, p.2942
IAS 19.108	Ch.35, p.2943
IAS 19.109	Ch.35, p.2941
IAS 19.110	Ch.35, p.2941
IAS 19.111	Ch.35, p.2924
IAS 19.111	Ch.35, p.2943
IAS 19.112	Ch.35, p.2943
IAS 19.113	Ch.35, p.2910
IAS 19.114	Ch.35, p.2909
IAS 19.115	Ch.35, p.2910
IAS 19.116-118	Ch.35, p.2910
IAS 19.119	Ch.35, p.2910
IAS 19.120	Ch.15, p.1200
IAS 19.120	Ch.35, p.2940
IAS 19.121	Ch.35, p.2940
IAS 19.122	Ch.7, p.526
IAS 19.122	Ch.35, p.2940
IAS 19.122A	Ch.35, p.2941
IAS 19.123	Ch.35, p.2945
IAS 19.123A	Ch.35, p.2945
IAS 19.124	Ch.35, p.2945
IAS 19.125	Ch.35, p.2945
IAS 19.126	Ch.35, p.2945
IAS 19.127	Ch.35, p.2946
IAS 19.127(b)	Ch.15, p.1200
IAS 19.128	Ch.35, p.2924
IAS 19.128	Ch.35, p.2946
IAS 19.129	Ch.35, p.2946
IAS 19.130	Ch.35, p.2946
IAS 19.130	Ch.35, p.2947
IAS 19.131	Ch.35, p.2940
IAS 19.132	Ch.35, p.2939
IAS 19.133	Ch.3, p.125
IAS 19.133	Ch.35, p.2939
IAS 19.134	Ch.35, p.2940
IAS 19.135	Ch.35, p.2957
IAS 19.136	Ch.35, p.2957
IAS 19.136	Ch.35, p.2965
IAS 19.137	Ch.35, p.2958
IAS 19.137	Ch.35, p.2966
IAS 19.138	Ch.35, p.2958
IAS 19.139	Ch.35, p.2958
IAS 19.140	Ch.35, p.2959
IAS 19.141	Ch.35, p.2959
IAS 19.142	Ch.35, p.2961
IAS 19.142	Ch.35, p.2966
IAS 19.143	Ch.35, p.2961
IAS 19.143	Ch.35, p.2967
IAS 19.143	Ch.47, p.3742

IAS 19.144	Ch.35, p.2962	IAS 20.6	Ch.24, p.1825
IAS 19.145	Ch.5, p.372	IAS 20.7	Ch.24, p.1830
IAS 19.145	Ch.35, p.2963	IAS 20.7	Ch.24, p.1843
IAS 19.146	Ch.35, p.2963	IAS 20.8	Ch.24, p.1830
IAS 19.147	Ch.35, p.2963	IAS 20.9	Ch.24, p.1824
IAS 19.148	Ch.35, p.2964	IAS 20.9	Ch.24, p.1830
IAS 19.149	Ch.35, p.2965	IAS 20.10	Ch.24, p.1831
IAS 19.150	Ch.35, p.2967	IAS 20.10A	Ch.5, p.265
IAS 19.151	Ch.35, p.2967	IAS 20.10A	Ch.24, p.1823
IAS 19.152	Ch.35, p.2967	IAS 20.10A	Ch.24, p.1827
IAS 19.153	Ch.35, p.2951	IAS 20.10A	Ch.24, p.1832
IAS 19.154	Ch.35, p.2951	IAS 20.10A	Ch.24, p.1833
IAS 19.154	Ch.35, p.2953	IAS 20.10A	Ch.24, p.1836
IAS 19.155-156	Ch.35, p.2951	IAS 20.10A	Ch.49, p.3855
IAS 19.157	Ch.35, p.2952	IAS 20.11	Ch.24, p.1830
IAS 19.158	Ch.35, p.2967	IAS 20.12	Ch.24, p.1824
IAS 19.159	Ch.35, p.2954	IAS 20.12	Ch.24, p.1832
IAS 19.160	Ch.35, p.2954	IAS 20.12	Ch.24, p.1834
IAS 19.161	Ch.35, p.2954	IAS 20.12	Ch.24, p.1836
IAS 19.162	Ch.35, p.2954	IAS 20.13	Ch.24, p.1834
IAS 19.163	Ch.35, p.2954	IAS 20.15	Ch.24, p.1834
IAS 19.164	Ch.35, p.2955	IAS 20.16	Ch.24, p.1834
IAS 19.165	Ch.35, p.2955	IAS 20.16	Ch.24, p.1835
IAS 19.165(b)	Ch.41, p.3207	IAS 20.16	Ch.24, p.1836
IAS 19.166	Ch.35, p.2955	IAS 20.17	Ch.24, p.1824
IAS 19.167	Ch.35, p.2955	IAS 20.17	Ch.24, p.1834
IAS 19.168	Ch.35, p.2955	IAS 20.17	Ch.24, p.1835
IAS 19.169	Ch.35, p.2956	IAS 20.18	Ch.24, p.1835
IAS 19.170	Ch.35, p.2956	IAS 20.19	Ch.24, p.1835
IAS 19.171	Ch.35, p.2967	IAS 20.19	Ch.24, p.1837
IAS 19.BC29	Ch.35, p.2895	IAS 20.20	Ch.24, p.1837
IAS 19.BC48-49	Ch.35, p.2901	IAS 20.20-22	Ch.24, p.1835
IAS 19.BC127	Ch.35, p.2947	IAS 20.23	Ch.17, p.1310
IAS 19.BC130	Ch.35, p.2928	IAS 20.23	Ch.17, p.1361
IAS 19.BC200	Ch.3, p.125	IAS 20.23	Ch.17, p.1367
IAS 19.BC200	Ch.35, p.2939	IAS 20.23	Ch.24, p.1825
IAS 19.BC207	Ch.35, p.2957	IAS 20.23	Ch.24, p.1830
IAS 19.BC209	Ch.35, p.2957	IAS 20.24	Ch.24, p.1840
IAS 19.BC253	Ch.35, p.2904	IAS 20.25	Ch.24, p.1840
		IAS 20.26	Ch.24, p.1840
		IAS 20.27	Ch.24, p.1840
		IAS 20.28	Ch.24, p.1842
IAS 20		IAS 20.28	Ch.40, p.3164
		IAS 20.29	Ch.17, p.1367
IAS 20.1	Ch.24, p.1826	IAS 20.29	Ch.24, p.1840
IAS 20.2	Ch.24, p.1827	IAS 20.30	Ch.24, p.1841
IAS 20.2	Ch.33, p.2462	IAS 20.31	Ch.24, p.1841
IAS 20.2(b)	Ch.24, p.1828	IAS 20.32	Ch.24, p.1838
IAS 20.2(d)	Ch.24, p.1823	IAS 20.33	Ch.24, p.1838
IAS 20.3	Ch.24, p.1823	IAS 20.34	Ch.24, p.1824
IAS 20.3	Ch.24, p.1825	IAS 20.34	Ch.24, p.1826
IAS 20.3	Ch.24, p.1826	IAS 20.34	Ch.24, p.1838
IAS 20.3	Ch.24, p.1830	IAS 20.35	Ch.24, p.1824
IAS 20.3	Ch.24, p.1831	IAS 20.35	Ch.24, p.1826
IAS 20.3	Ch.25, p.1854	IAS 20.35	Ch.24, p.1834
IAS 20.4	Ch.24, p.1824	IAS 20.35	Ch.24, p.1839
IAS 20.4	Ch.24, p.1826	IAS 20.36	Ch.24, p.1824
IAS 20.5	Ch.24, p.1824	IAS 20.36	Ch.24, p.1839
IAS 20.6	Ch.24, p.1823		

IAS 20.38	Ch.24, p.1826	IAS 21.22	Ch.15, p.1188
IAS 20.38	Ch.24, p.1839	IAS 21.22	Ch.15, p.1190
IAS 20.39	Ch.24, p.1843	IAS 21.23	Ch.5, p.333
IAS 20.39(b)	Ch.24, p.1834	IAS 21.23	Ch.5, p.373
IAS 20.39(b)	Ch.24, p.1839	IAS 21.23	Ch.15, p.1193
IAS 20.39(b)	Ch.24, p.1845	IAS 21.23	Ch.26, p.1959
IAS 20.41	Ch.24, p.1823	IAS 21.23	Ch.50, p.3899
IAS 20.41	Ch.24, p.1838	IAS 21.23	Ch.53, p.4325
IAS 20.43	Ch.24, p.1823	IAS 21.23(a)	Ch.53, p.4322
IAS 20.45	Ch.24, p.1830	IAS 21.24	Ch.15, p.1193
		IAS 21.25	Ch.15, p.1193
		IAS 21.25	Ch.20, p.1558

IAS 21

		IAS 21.26	Ch.15, p.1191
		IAS 21.26	Ch.15, p.1192
IAS 21.1	Ch.15, p.1180	IAS 21.27	Ch.15, p.1181
IAS 21.2	Ch.15, p.1180	IAS 21.28	Ch.15, p.1194
IAS 21.3	Ch.15, p.1180	IAS 21.28	Ch.26, p.1959
IAS 21.4	Ch.15, p.1181	IAS 21.29	Ch.15, p.1194
IAS 21.5	Ch.15, p.1181	IAS 21.30	Ch.15, p.1195
IAS 21.6	Ch.15, p.1181	IAS 21.30	Ch.15, p.1196
IAS 21.7	Ch.15, p.1181	IAS 21.31	Ch.15, p.1195
IAS 21.7	Ch.40, p.3165	IAS 21.32	Ch.5, p.304
IAS 21.8	Ch.15, p.1181	IAS 21.32	Ch.15, p.1194
IAS 21.8	Ch.15, p.1196	IAS 21.32	Ch.15, p.1217
IAS 21.8	Ch.15, p.1217	IAS 21.32	Ch.15, p.1219
IAS 21.8	Ch.16, p.1258	IAS 21.33	Ch.15, p.1219
IAS 21.8	Ch.26, p.1959	IAS 21.33	Ch.15, p.1220
IAS 21.8	Ch.53, p.4307	IAS 21.34	Ch.15, p.1204
IAS 21.8-14	Ch.5, p.373	IAS 21.35	Ch.15, p.1202
IAS 21.9	Ch.15, p.1182	IAS 21.36	Ch.15, p.1202
IAS 21.9	Ch.15, p.1183	IAS 21.36	Ch.43, p.3425
IAS 21.9	Ch.43, p.3422	IAS 21.37	Ch.15, p.1202
IAS 21.10	Ch.15, p.1183	IAS 21.38	Ch.7, p.500
IAS 21.10	Ch.43, p.3422	IAS 21.38	Ch.15, p.1204
IAS 21.11	Ch.5, p.373	IAS 21.38	Ch.16, p.1277
IAS 21.11	Ch.15, p.1183	IAS 21.39	Ch.5, p.304
IAS 21.11	Ch.43, p.3422	IAS 21.39	Ch.15, p.1205
IAS 21.12	Ch.15, p.1183	IAS 21.39	Ch.16, p.1264
IAS 21.12	Ch.43, p.3422	IAS 21.39	Ch.16, p.1278
IAS 21.13	Ch.15, p.1184	IAS 21.39(b)	Ch.15, p.1216
IAS 21.14	Ch.16, p.1254	IAS 21.39(b)	Ch.53, p.4261
IAS 21.14	Ch.16, p.1277	IAS 21.40	Ch.15, p.1206
IAS 21.15	Ch.15, p.1217	IAS 21.40	Ch.15, p.1212
IAS 21.15	Ch.53, p.4269	IAS 21.41	Ch.15, p.1206
IAS 21.15A	Ch.15, p.1220	IAS 21.41	Ch.15, p.1208
IAS 21.16	Ch.15, p.1196	IAS 21.41	Ch.15, p.1216
IAS 21.16	Ch.15, p.1197	IAS 21.41	Ch.16, p.1278
IAS 21.16	Ch.16, p.1258	IAS 21.41	Ch.16, p.1279
IAS 21.17	Ch.15, p.1182	IAS 21.42	Ch.15, p.1209
IAS 21.18	Ch.15, p.1182	IAS 21.42	Ch.16, p.1264
IAS 21.18	Ch.15, p.1204	IAS 21.42	Ch.16, p.1277
IAS 21.19	Ch.15, p.1182	IAS 21.42	Ch.16, p.1278
IAS 21.20	Ch.15, p.1187	IAS 21.42(b)	Ch.16, p.1280
IAS 21.21	Ch.5, p.333	IAS 21.42(b)	Ch.16, p.1281
IAS 21.21	Ch.5, p.373	IAS 21.43	Ch.15, p.1209
IAS 21.21	Ch.15, p.1188	IAS 21.43	Ch.15, p.1210
IAS 21.21	Ch.26, p.1959	IAS 21.43	Ch.16, p.1277
IAS 21.21	Ch.53, p.4261	IAS 21.43	Ch.16, p.1279

IAS 21.44	Ch.15, p.1204
IAS 21.44	Ch.53, p.4307
IAS 21.45	Ch.15, p.1216
IAS 21.45	Ch.15, p.1217
IAS 21.45	Ch.15, p.1223
IAS 21.46	Ch.7, p.503
IAS 21.46	Ch.15, p.1225
IAS 21.47	Ch.5, p.282
IAS 21.47	Ch.15, p.1226
IAS 21.48	Ch.5, p.304
IAS 21.48	Ch.11, p.873
IAS 21.48	Ch.15, p.1227
IAS 21.48	Ch.53, p.4364
IAS 21.48-48B	Ch.7, p.527
IAS 21.48A	Ch.11, p.871
IAS 21.48A	Ch.15, p.1229
IAS 21.48B	Ch.7, p.534
IAS 21.48B	Ch.15, p.1229
IAS 21.48C	Ch.7, p.534
IAS 21.48C	Ch.11, p.872
IAS 21.48C	Ch.15, p.1230
IAS 21.48C	Ch.15, p.1231
IAS 21.48D	Ch.15, p.1230
IAS 21.49	Ch.15, p.1228
IAS 21.49	Ch.15, p.1230
IAS 21.50	Ch.15, p.1242
IAS 21.51	Ch.15, p.1243
IAS 21.52	Ch.15, p.1242
IAS 21.52	Ch.15, p.1243
IAS 21.52	Ch.15, p.1244
IAS 21.52(a)	Ch.54, p.4486
IAS 21.53	Ch.15, p.1243
IAS 21.54	Ch.15, p.1243
IAS 21.55	Ch.15, p.1243
IAS 21.56	Ch.15, p.1243
IAS 21.57	Ch.15, p.1243
IAS 21.BC6	Ch.15, p.1183
IAS 21.BC17	Ch.15, p.1208
IAS 21.BC18	Ch.7, p.500
IAS 21.BC18	Ch.15, p.1209
IAS 21.BC18	Ch.15, p.1214
IAS 21.BC19	Ch.15, p.1209
IAS 21.BC20	Ch.15, p.1208
IAS 21.BC27	Ch.15, p.1225
IAS 21.BC30	Ch.15, p.1226
IAS 21.BC31	Ch.15, p.1226
IAS 21.BC32	Ch.15, p.1226
IAS 21.BC33-34	Ch.11, p.872
IAS 21.BC35	Ch.15, p.1230

IAS 23

IAS 23.1	Ch.21, p.1645
IAS 23.2	Ch.21, p.1646
IAS 23.3	Ch.21, p.1646
IAS 23.3	Ch.21, p.1663
IAS 23.4	Ch.21, p.1646
IAS 23.4	Ch.22, p.1686
IAS 23.4(a)	Ch.21, p.1647
IAS 23.4(b)	Ch.21, p.1646
IAS 23.4(b)	Ch.29, p.2204
IAS 23.5	Ch.21, p.1646
IAS 23.5	Ch.21, p.1649
IAS 23.5	Ch.43, p.3370
IAS 23.5-6	Ch.29, p.2204
IAS 23.6	Ch.15, p.1195
IAS 23.6	Ch.21, p.1649
IAS 23.6(e)	Ch.21, p.1650
IAS 23.6(e)	Ch.21, p.1657
IAS 23.7	Ch.21, p.1646
IAS 23.7	Ch.21, p.1648
IAS 23.7	Ch.22, p.1686
IAS 23.7	Ch.29, p.2204
IAS 23.7	Ch.29, p.2205
IAS 23.8	Ch.21, p.1645
IAS 23.8	Ch.21, p.1650
IAS 23.8	Ch.21, p.1651
IAS 23.8	Ch.22, p.1686
IAS 23.8	Ch.29, p.2204
IAS 23.8	Ch.43, p.3370
IAS 23.9	Ch.21, p.1650
IAS 23.9	Ch.21, p.1651
IAS 23.9	Ch.21, p.1663
IAS 23.9	Ch.21, p.1665
IAS 23.9	Ch.43, p.3370
IAS 23.10	Ch.21, p.1651
IAS 23.10	Ch.21, p.1661
IAS 23.11	Ch.21, p.1651
IAS 23.12	Ch.21, p.1651
IAS 23.12	Ch.41, p.3245
IAS 23.13	Ch.21, p.1651
IAS 23.14	Ch.21, p.1652
IAS 23.14	Ch.41, p.3245
IAS 23.15	Ch.21, p.1652
IAS 23.16	Ch.5, p.320
IAS 23.16	Ch.21, p.1669
IAS 23.17	Ch.21, p.1664
IAS 23.18	Ch.21, p.1652
IAS 23.18	Ch.21, p.1656
IAS 23.18	Ch.21, p.1665
IAS 23.19	Ch.21, p.1665
IAS 23.20	Ch.21, p.1668
IAS 23.21	Ch.21, p.1668
IAS 23.22	Ch.21, p.1669
IAS 23.23	Ch.21, p.1669
IAS 23.24	Ch.21, p.1669
IAS 23.25	Ch.21, p.1669
IAS 23.25	Ch.21, p.1670
IAS 23.26	Ch.5, p.320
IAS 23.26	Ch.21, p.1671
IAS 23.29	Ch.21, p.1645
IAS 23.BC2	Ch.21, p.1645
IAS 23.BC6	Ch.21, p.1646
IAS 23.BC6	Ch.21, p.1647
IAS 23.BC14B	Ch.21, p.1653

IAS 23.BC14C	Ch.21, p.1653	IAS 24.25	Ch.39, p.3127
IAS 23.BC14D	Ch.21, p.1653	IAS 24.26	Ch.39, p.3128
IAS 23.BC14E	Ch.21, p.1654	IAS 24.27	Ch.39, p.3129
IAS 23.BC21	Ch.21, p.1661	IAS 24.BC10	Ch.39, p.3117
IAS 23.BC22	Ch.11, p.828	IAS 24.BC16-17	Ch.39, p.3099
		IAS 24.BC19(a)	Ch.39, p.3107
		IAS 24.BC41	Ch.39, p.3111
		IAS 24.BC45	Ch.39, p.3129
		IAS 24.BC46	Ch.39, p.3129
		IAS 24.BC47-48	Ch.39, p.3129

IAS 24

IAS 24.1	Ch.39, p.3098
IAS 24.2	Ch.39, p.3098
IAS 24.3	Ch.39, p.3099
IAS 24.4	Ch.39, p.3099
IAS 24.5	Ch.39, p.3097
IAS 24.6-7	Ch.39, p.3097
IAS 24.8	Ch.39, p.3098
IAS 24.9	Ch.10, p.769
IAS 24.9	Ch.39, p.3099
IAS 24.9	Ch.39, p.3100
IAS 24.9	Ch.39, p.3103
IAS 24.9	Ch.39, p.3108
IAS 24.9	Ch.39, p.3110
IAS 24.9	Ch.39, p.3114
IAS 24.9	Ch.39, p.3116
IAS 24.9	Ch.39, p.3117
IAS 24.9(b)	Ch.39, p.3104
IAS 24.9(b)	Ch.39, p.3105
IAS 24.9(b)	Ch.39, p.3107
IAS 24.9(b)	Ch.39, p.3108
IAS 24.9(b)	Ch.39, p.3109
IAS 24.9(b)	Ch.39, p.3110
IAS 24.10	Ch.39, p.3100
IAS 24.11	Ch.39, p.3111
IAS 24.12	Ch.39, p.3102
IAS 24.12	Ch.39, p.3105
IAS 24.12	Ch.39, p.3107
IAS 24.13	Ch.39, p.3112
IAS 24.14	Ch.39, p.3112
IAS 24.15	Ch.39, p.3114
IAS 24.16	Ch.39, p.3113
IAS 24.17	Ch.39, p.3116
IAS 24.17A	Ch.39, p.3104
IAS 24.17A	Ch.39, p.3110
IAS 24.17A	Ch.39, p.3116
IAS 24.18	Ch.13, p.977
IAS 24.18	Ch.39, p.3120
IAS 24.18	Ch.39, p.3123
IAS 24.18	Ch.51, p.4050
IAS 24.18A	Ch.39, p.3104
IAS 24.18A	Ch.39, p.3127
IAS 24.18-19	Ch.13, p.977
IAS 24.19	Ch.39, p.3124
IAS 24.20	Ch.39, p.3124
IAS 24.21	Ch.39, p.3121
IAS 24.21	Ch.51, p.4050
IAS 24.22	Ch.39, p.3121
IAS 24.23	Ch.39, p.3124
IAS 24.24	Ch.39, p.3122

IAS 27

IAS 27.2	Ch.6, p.395
IAS 27.2	Ch.8, p.575
IAS 27.3	Ch.8, p.575
IAS 27.4	Ch.8, p.575
IAS 27.7	Ch.8, p.575
IAS 27.7	Ch.8, p.577
IAS 27.7	Ch.13, p.953
IAS 27.8	Ch.6, p.395
IAS 27.8	Ch.6, p.400
IAS 27.8	Ch.8, p.578
IAS 27.8A	Ch.6, p.487
IAS 27.8A	Ch.8, p.576
IAS 27.8A	Ch.8, p.578
IAS 27.10	Ch.8, p.583
IAS 27.10	Ch.11, p.813
IAS 27.10	Ch.11, p.881
IAS 27.10	Ch.12, p.930
IAS 27.10	Ch.20, p.1625
IAS 27.10	Ch.45, p.3592
IAS 27.10	Ch.53, p.4307
IAS 27.10(a)	Ch.20, p.1625
IAS 27.10(c)	Ch.33, p.2533
IAS 27.11	Ch.8, p.583
IAS 27.11	Ch.11, p.881
IAS 27.11	Ch.12, p.930
IAS 27.11	Ch.45, p.3592
IAS 27.11A	Ch.6, p.487
IAS 27.11A	Ch.8, p.578
IAS 27.11A	Ch.8, p.583
IAS 27.11B	Ch.8, p.584
IAS 27.11B(a)	Ch.6, p.489
IAS 27.11B(b)	Ch.6, p.488
IAS 27.12	Ch.8, p.584
IAS 27.12	Ch.8, p.599
IAS 27.12	Ch.11, p.882
IAS 27.12	Ch.33, p.2533
IAS 27.12	Ch.38, p.3082
IAS 27.13	Ch.8, p.591
IAS 27.13	Ch.8, p.594
IAS 27.13(b)	Ch.8, p.593
IAS 27.13(c)	Ch.8, p.592
IAS 27.14	Ch.8, p.591
IAS 27.15	Ch.8, p.604
IAS 27.16	Ch.8, p.604

IAS 27.16(a)	Ch.6, p.397	IAS 28.19	Ch.11, p.821
IAS 27.16A	Ch.8, p.578	IAS 28.19	Ch.45, p.3592
IAS 27.16A	Ch.8, p.605	IAS 28.20	Ch.4, p.197
IAS 27.17	Ch.8, p.581	IAS 28.20	Ch.11, p.824
IAS 27.17	Ch.8, p.582	IAS 28.20	Ch.11, p.870
IAS 27.17	Ch.8, p.605	IAS 28.20	Ch.12, p.892
IAS 27.17	Ch.8, p.606	IAS 28.20	Ch.12, p.935
IAS 27.BC10D	Ch.8, p.579	IAS 28.21	Ch.4, p.197
IAS 27.BC24(a)	Ch.8, p.592	IAS 28.21	Ch.4, p.212
IAS 27.BC24(b)	Ch.8, p.592	IAS 28.21	Ch.11, p.824
IAS 27.BC25	Ch.8, p.594	IAS 28.21	Ch.12, p.935
IAS 27.BC27	Ch.8, p.591	IAS 28.22	Ch.11, p.870
		IAS 28.22	Ch.11, p.871
		IAS 28.22	Ch.12, p.935

IAS 28

IAS 28.1	Ch.11, p.813	IAS 28.23	Ch.11, p.871
IAS 28.2	Ch.8, p.579	IAS 28.23	Ch.12, p.935
IAS 28.2	Ch.9, p.722	IAS 28.24	Ch.11, p.837
IAS 28.2	Ch.11, p.814	IAS 28.24	Ch.11, p.870
IAS 28.3	Ch.6, p.409	IAS 28.24	Ch.11, p.872
IAS 28.3	Ch.11, p.814	IAS 28.24	Ch.12, p.934
IAS 28.3	Ch.11, p.824	IAS 28.25	Ch.11, p.872
IAS 28.3	Ch.11, p.828	IAS 28.25	Ch.12, p.934
IAS 28.3	Ch.11, p.868	IAS 28.25	Ch.15, p.1231
IAS 28.3	Ch.11, p.874	IAS 28.26	Ch.10, p.797
IAS 28.3	Ch.13, p.952	IAS 28.26	Ch.11, p.827
IAS 28.3	Ch.34, p.2843	IAS 28.26	Ch.11, p.830
IAS 28.3	Ch.39, p.3102	IAS 28.26	Ch.11, p.846
IAS 28.3	Ch.39, p.3105	IAS 28.26	Ch.11, p.847
IAS 28.4	Ch.11, p.814	IAS 28.26	Ch.11, p.885
IAS 28.4	Ch.11, p.881	IAS 28.27	Ch.11, p.839
IAS 28.5	Ch.11, p.815	IAS 28.27	Ch.11, p.840
IAS 28.5	Ch.11, p.816	IAS 28.27	Ch.11, p.868
IAS 28.5	Ch.55, p.4604	IAS 28.28	Ch.7, p.514
IAS 28.6	Ch.11, p.815	IAS 28.28	Ch.7, p.515
IAS 28.7	Ch.11, p.817	IAS 28.28	Ch.11, p.841
IAS 28.8	Ch.11, p.817	IAS 28.28-31	Ch.7, p.515
IAS 28.9	Ch.11, p.815	IAS 28.29	Ch.7, p.515
IAS 28.10	Ch.11, p.825	IAS 28.29	Ch.11, p.843
IAS 28.10	Ch.11, p.828	IAS 28.29	Ch.11, p.846
IAS 28.10	Ch.11, p.863	IAS 28.30	Ch.7, p.514
IAS 28.10	Ch.11, p.865	IAS 28.30	Ch.11, p.851
IAS 28.10	Ch.11, p.884	IAS 28.30	Ch.11, p.854
IAS 28.11	Ch.11, p.826	IAS 28.31	Ch.11, p.851
IAS 28.12	Ch.11, p.838	IAS 28.31A	Ch.11, p.857
IAS 28.13	Ch.11, p.838	IAS 28.31B	Ch.11, p.858
IAS 28.14	Ch.11, p.838	IAS 28.32	Ch.10, p.798
IAS 28.14A	Ch.11, p.878	IAS 28.32	Ch.11, p.825
IAS 28.14A	Ch.45, p.3592	IAS 28.32	Ch.11, p.830
IAS 28.15	Ch.11, p.882	IAS 28.32	Ch.11, p.854
IAS 28.16	Ch.11, p.818	IAS 28.32	Ch.11, p.883
IAS 28.17	Ch.11, p.818	IAS 28.32	Ch.20, p.1629
IAS 28.17	Ch.11, p.819	IAS 28.33	Ch.11, p.859
IAS 28.18	Ch.8, p.577	IAS 28.34	Ch.11, p.860
IAS 28.18	Ch.11, p.819	IAS 28.35	Ch.11, p.860
IAS 28.18	Ch.11, p.821	IAS 28.35-36	Ch.5, p.335
IAS 28.18	Ch.45, p.3592	IAS 28.36	Ch.11, p.860
		IAS 28.36A	Ch.11, p.820
		IAS 28.36A	Ch.11, p.861

IAS 28.37	Ch.11, p.838
IAS 28.37	Ch.11, p.865
IAS 28.38	Ch.11, p.846
IAS 28.38	Ch.11, p.862
IAS 28.38	Ch.11, p.882
IAS 28.39	Ch.11, p.862
IAS 28.40	Ch.11, p.876
IAS 28.40	Ch.11, p.877
IAS 28.40	Ch.11, p.884
IAS 28.40-41A	Ch.20, p.1627
IAS 28.40-43	Ch.20, p.1629
IAS 28.41A	Ch.11, p.877
IAS 28.41A	Ch.20, p.1627
IAS 28.41A	Ch.20, p.1628
IAS 28.41B	Ch.11, p.877
IAS 28.41C	Ch.11, p.878
IAS 28.42	Ch.11, p.874
IAS 28.42	Ch.11, p.878
IAS 28.42	Ch.20, p.1521
IAS 28.42	Ch.20, p.1626
IAS 28.42	Ch.20, p.1629
IAS 28.43	Ch.11, p.877
IAS 28.43	Ch.20, p.1628
IAS 28.44	Ch.8, p.579
IAS 28.44	Ch.11, p.881
IAS 28.44	Ch.45, p.3592
IAS 28.45C	Ch.7, p.514
IAS 28.45C	Ch.7, p.565
IAS 28.45G	Ch.11, p.878
IAS 28.45G	Ch.45, p.3592
IAS 28.45I	Ch.45, p.3592
IAS 28.BC12	Ch.11, p.820
IAS 28.BC13	Ch.11, p.820
IAS 28.BC16	Ch.11, p.817
IAS 28.BCZ18	Ch.11, p.815
IAS 28.BCZ19	Ch.11, p.860
IAS 28.BC22	Ch.11, p.822
IAS 28.BC23-27	Ch.11, p.824
IAS 28.BC30	Ch.12, p.934
IAS 28.BC37J	Ch.7, p.514
IAS 28.BC37J	Ch.7, p.565
IAS 28.BCZ39-40	Ch.11, p.862

IAS 29

IAS 29.1	Ch.16, p.1254
IAS 29.2	Ch.16, p.1253
IAS 29.3	Ch.16, p.1255
IAS 29.4	Ch.16, p.1255
IAS 29.4	Ch.41, p.3258
IAS 29.7	Ch.16, p.1282
IAS 29.8	Ch.16, p.1274
IAS 29.8-9	Ch.16, p.1253
IAS 29.10	Ch.16, p.1254
IAS 29.10	Ch.16, p.1260
IAS 29.11	Ch.16, p.1253
IAS 29.12	Ch.16, p.1258
IAS 29.13	Ch.16, p.1259
IAS 29.14	Ch.16, p.1260
IAS 29.15	Ch.16, p.1260
IAS 29.15	Ch.16, p.1263
IAS 29.16	Ch.16, p.1261
IAS 29.17	Ch.16, p.1256
IAS 29.18	Ch.16, p.1260
IAS 29.19	Ch.16, p.1257
IAS 29.19	Ch.16, p.1261
IAS 29.19	Ch.16, p.1262
IAS 29.19	Ch.16, p.1263
IAS 29.20	Ch.16, p.1263
IAS 29.20	Ch.16, p.1264
IAS 29.21	Ch.16, p.1261
IAS 29.21	Ch.16, p.1262
IAS 29.21	Ch.21, p.1663
IAS 29.22	Ch.16, p.1261
IAS 29.24	Ch.16, p.1266
IAS 29.25	Ch.16, p.1266
IAS 29.25	Ch.16, p.1279
IAS 29.26	Ch.16, p.1268
IAS 29.26	Ch.16, p.1269
IAS 29.27	Ch.16, p.1270
IAS 29.28	Ch.16, p.1259
IAS 29.28	Ch.16, p.1269
IAS 29.28	Ch.16, p.1270
IAS 29.29	Ch.16, p.1260
IAS 29.30	Ch.16, p.1268
IAS 29.31	Ch.16, p.1270
IAS 29.32	Ch.16, p.1266
IAS 29.33	Ch.16, p.1272
IAS 29.34	Ch.16, p.1273
IAS 29.35	Ch.16, p.1264
IAS 29.36	Ch.16, p.1264
IAS 29.37	Ch.16, p.1256
IAS 29.38	Ch.16, p.1275
IAS 29.38	Ch.41, p.3259
IAS 29.39	Ch.16, p.1281

IAS 32

IAS 32.2	Ch.44, p.3577
IAS 32.2	Ch.47, p.3665
IAS 32.3	Ch.47, p.3665
IAS 32.4	Ch.45, p.3591
IAS 32.4(a)	Ch.45, p.3592
IAS 32.4(a)	Ch.45, p.3593
IAS 32.4(b)	Ch.45, p.3605
IAS 32.4(d)	Ch.45, p.3593
IAS 32.4(d)	Ch.45, p.3598
IAS 32.4(e)	Ch.45, p.3594
IAS 32.4(f)(i)	Ch.45, p.3605
IAS 32.4(f)(ii)	Ch.45, p.3605
IAS 32.8	Ch.43, p.3456
IAS 32.8	Ch.43, p.3473
IAS 32.8	Ch.45, p.3607
IAS 32.8	Ch.45, p.3608

IAS 32.9	Ch.43, p.3473
IAS 32.9	Ch.43, p.3474
IAS 32.9	Ch.45, p.3608
IAS 32.9	Ch.45, p.3609
IAS 32.9(b)	Ch.43, p.3457
IAS 32.9(c)	Ch.43, p.3457
IAS 32.10	Ch.45, p.3610
IAS 32.11	Ch.7, p.540
IAS 32.11	Ch.9, p.705
IAS 32.11	Ch.26, p.2007
IAS 32.11	Ch.37, p.3023
IAS 32.11	Ch.43, p.3400
IAS 32.11	Ch.43, p.3454
IAS 32.11	Ch.45, p.3585
IAS 32.11	Ch.47, p.3665
IAS 32.11	Ch.47, p.3666
IAS 32.11	Ch.47, p.3667
IAS 32.11	Ch.47, p.3709
IAS 32.11	Ch.51, p.4046
IAS 32.11	Ch.52, p.4087
IAS 32.11	Ch.52, p.4088
IAS 32.11	Ch.55, p.4569
IAS 32.11(b)(i)	Ch.47, p.3731
IAS 32.11(b)(i)	Ch.47, p.3733
IAS 32.11(b)(ii)	Ch.47, p.3705
IAS 32.13	Ch.45, p.3585
IAS 32.13	Ch.47, p.3667
IAS 32.14	Ch.45, p.3585
IAS 32.14	Ch.47, p.3667
IAS 32.15	Ch.5, p.314
IAS 32.15	Ch.47, p.3668
IAS 32.15	Ch.47, p.3731
IAS 32.16	Ch.47, p.3668
IAS 32.16	Ch.47, p.3669
IAS 32.16(a)	Ch.43, p.3454
IAS 32.16b(i)	Ch.47, p.3737
IAS 32.16b(ii)	Ch.47, p.3737
IAS 32.16A	Ch.7, p.546
IAS 32.16A	Ch.47, p.3687
IAS 32.16A-16B	Ch.34, p.2661
IAS 32.16A-16B	Ch.47, p.3686
IAS 32.16B	Ch.7, p.546
IAS 32.16B	Ch.47, p.3687
IAS 32.16C	Ch.7, p.546
IAS 32.16C	Ch.47, p.3688
IAS 32.16C-16D	Ch.47, p.3688
IAS 32.16D	Ch.7, p.546
IAS 32.16D	Ch.47, p.3688
IAS 32.16E	Ch.47, p.3693
IAS 32.16F(a)	Ch.47, p.3693
IAS 32.16F(b)	Ch.47, p.3693
IAS 32.17	Ch.47, p.3669
IAS 32.18	Ch.47, p.3670
IAS 32.18(a)	Ch.47, p.3679
IAS 32.18(b)	Ch.47, p.3686
IAS 32.19	Ch.47, p.3670
IAS 32.20	Ch.47, p.3672
IAS 32.20	Ch.47, p.3709
IAS 32.20(a)	Ch.24, p.1831
IAS 32.21	Ch.47, p.3678
IAS 32.21	Ch.47, p.3707
IAS 32.22	Ch.47, p.3677
IAS 32.22	Ch.47, p.3678
IAS 32.22	Ch.47, p.3703
IAS 32.22	Ch.47, p.3720
IAS 32.22A	Ch.47, p.3677
IAS 32.22A	Ch.47, p.3703
IAS 32.22A	Ch.47, p.3711
IAS 32.22A	Ch.47, p.3714
IAS 32.23	Ch.7, p.552
IAS 32.23	Ch.7, p.555
IAS 32.23	Ch.47, p.3678
IAS 32.23	Ch.47, p.3711
IAS 32.23	Ch.47, p.3712
IAS 32.24	Ch.47, p.3678
IAS 32.24	Ch.47, p.3707
IAS 32.25	Ch.17, p.1308
IAS 32.25	Ch.18, p.1403
IAS 32.25	Ch.43, p.3419
IAS 32.25	Ch.47, p.3673
IAS 32.26	Ch.47, p.3705
IAS 32.26	Ch.47, p.3710
IAS 32.27	Ch.47, p.3710
IAS 32.28	Ch.5, p.314
IAS 32.28	Ch.47, p.3715
IAS 32.28	Ch.47, p.3716
IAS 32.29	Ch.47, p.3715
IAS 32.29	Ch.47, p.3716
IAS 32.30	Ch.47, p.3719
IAS 32.31	Ch.47, p.3717
IAS 32.31	Ch.47, p.3726
IAS 32.31-32	Ch.47, p.3717
IAS 32.33	Ch.40, p.3160
IAS 32.33	Ch.47, p.3742
IAS 32.33	Ch.47, p.3743
IAS 32.33A	Ch.47, p.3744
IAS 32.34	Ch.47, p.3743
IAS 32.34	Ch.54, p.4491
IAS 32.34	Ch.54, p.4518
IAS 32.35	Ch.7, p.538
IAS 32.35	Ch.40, p.3161
IAS 32.35	Ch.47, p.3739
IAS 32.35A	Ch.47, p.3742
IAS 32.36	Ch.47, p.3664
IAS 32.36	Ch.47, p.3740
IAS 32.37	Ch.7, p.538
IAS 32.37	Ch.47, p.3740
IAS 32.38	Ch.47, p.3741
IAS 32.38	Ch.49, p.3859
IAS 32.39	Ch.54, p.4491
IAS 32.40	Ch.47, p.3740
IAS 32.40	Ch.54, p.4486
IAS 32.41	Ch.47, p.3740
IAS 32.41	Ch.54, p.4488
IAS 32.42	Ch.14, p.1090
IAS 32.42	Ch.26, p.1991

Index of standards

IAS 32.42	Ch.40, p.3143
IAS 32.42	Ch.43, p.3409
IAS 32.42	Ch.52, p.4151
IAS 32.42	Ch.54, p.4491
IAS 32.42	Ch.55, p.4583
IAS 32.43	Ch.54, p.4492
IAS 32.44	Ch.54, p.4492
IAS 32.45	Ch.54, p.4492
IAS 32.46	Ch.54, p.4492
IAS 32.47	Ch.54, p.4495
IAS 32.48	Ch.54, p.4495
IAS 32.48	Ch.54, p.4496
IAS 32.49(a)	Ch.54, p.4497
IAS 32.49(b)	Ch.54, p.4497
IAS 32.49(c)	Ch.54, p.4497
IAS 32.49(d)	Ch.54, p.4497
IAS 32.49(e)	Ch.54, p.4497
IAS 32.50	Ch.54, p.4495
IAS 32.96C	Ch.34, p.2661
IAS 32.AG3	Ch.45, p.3586
IAS 32.AG4	Ch.45, p.3586
IAS 32.AG5	Ch.45, p.3586
IAS 32.AG6	Ch.45, p.3586
IAS 32.AG6	Ch.47, p.3695
IAS 32.AG7	Ch.45, p.3585
IAS 32.AG8	Ch.45, p.3587
IAS 32.AG9	Ch.14, p.1010
IAS 32.AG9	Ch.45, p.3587
IAS 32.AG10	Ch.45, p.3587
IAS 32.AG11	Ch.45, p.3588
IAS 32.AG12	Ch.45, p.3585
IAS 32.AG12	Ch.45, p.3586
IAS 32.AG13	Ch.45, p.3589
IAS 32.AG13	Ch.45, p.3591
IAS 32.AG13	Ch.47, p.3677
IAS 32.AG13	Ch.47, p.3678
IAS 32.AG13	Ch.47, p.3703
IAS 32.AG14	Ch.47, p.3678
IAS 32.AG14B	Ch.47, p.3690
IAS 32.AG14C	Ch.47, p.3690
IAS 32.AG14D	Ch.47, p.3690
IAS 32.AG14E	Ch.47, p.3687
IAS 32.AG14F	Ch.47, p.3692
IAS 32.AG14G	Ch.47, p.3692
IAS 32.AG14H	Ch.47, p.3693
IAS 32.AG14I	Ch.47, p.3693
IAS 32.AG14J	Ch.47, p.3692
IAS 32.AG15	Ch.45, p.3589
IAS 32.AG16	Ch.45, p.3589
IAS 32.AG16	Ch.45, p.3590
IAS 32.AG17	Ch.45, p.3590
IAS 32.AG18	Ch.45, p.3590
IAS 32.AG19	Ch.45, p.3591
IAS 32.AG20	Ch.43, p.3473
IAS 32.AG20	Ch.45, p.3588
IAS 32.AG20	Ch.45, p.3607
IAS 32.AG20	Ch.51, p.4046
IAS 32.AG21	Ch.45, p.3589
IAS 32.AG22	Ch.45, p.3588
IAS 32.AG23	Ch.45, p.3589
IAS 32.AG25	Ch.47, p.3670
IAS 32.AG25	Ch.47, p.3678
IAS 32.AG25	Ch.47, p.3679
IAS 32.AG26	Ch.47, p.3680
IAS 32.AG27	Ch.47, p.3711
IAS 32.AG27	Ch.47, p.3714
IAS 32.AG27(a)	Ch.47, p.3703
IAS 32.AG27(a)-(b)	Ch.47, p.3711
IAS 32.AG27(b)	Ch.7, p.552
IAS 32.AG27(b)	Ch.47, p.3712
IAS 32.AG27(c)	Ch.47, p.3711
IAS 32.AG27(c)	Ch.47, p.3714
IAS 32.AG27(d)	Ch.47, p.3707
IAS 32.AG27(d)	Ch.47, p.3710
IAS 32.AG28	Ch.47, p.3674
IAS 32.AG29	Ch.7, p.546
IAS 32.AG29	Ch.7, p.555
IAS 32.AG29	Ch.47, p.3695
IAS 32.AG29A	Ch.7, p.546
IAS 32.AG29A	Ch.47, p.3689
IAS 32.AG30	Ch.47, p.3715
IAS 32.AG30	Ch.47, p.3716
IAS 32.AG31(b)	Ch.47, p.3717
IAS 32.AG32	Ch.47, p.3720
IAS 32.AG33	Ch.47, p.3722
IAS 32.AG34	Ch.47, p.3722
IAS 32.AG35	Ch.47, p.3725
IAS 32.AG36	Ch.47, p.3742
IAS 32.AG36	Ch.47, p.3743
IAS 32.AG37	Ch.47, p.3679
IAS 32.AG37	Ch.47, p.3715
IAS 32.AG37	Ch.47, p.3739
IAS 32.AG38A	Ch.54, p.4493
IAS 32.AG38B	Ch.54, p.4493
IAS 32.AG38C	Ch.54, p.4493
IAS 32.AG38D	Ch.54, p.4493
IAS 32.AG38E	Ch.54, p.4492
IAS 32.AG38F	Ch.54, p.4496
IAS 32.AG39	Ch.54, p.4497
IAS 32.IE2-6	Ch.47, p.3746
IAS 32.IE7-11	Ch.47, p.3748
IAS 32.IE12-16	Ch.47, p.3752
IAS 32.IE17-21	Ch.47, p.3754
IAS 32.IE22-26	Ch.47, p.3756
IAS 32.IE27-31	Ch.47, p.3758
IAS 32.IE31	Ch.47, p.3761
IAS 32.IE32	Ch.54, p.4488
IAS 32.IE32	Ch.54, p.4518
IAS 32.IE33	Ch.54, p.4489
IAS 32.IE33	Ch.54, p.4519
IAS 32.IE34-36	Ch.47, p.3717
IAS 32.IE37-38	Ch.47, p.3727
IAS 32.IE39-46	Ch.47, p.3722
IAS 32.IE47-50	Ch.47, p.3725
IAS 32.BC4I	Ch.47, p.3709
IAS 32.BC4K	Ch.47, p.3709

IAS 32.BC7-BC8 .... Ch.47, p.3686
IAS 32.BC9 .... Ch.47, p.3682
IAS 32.BC12 .... Ch.47, p.3711
IAS 32.BC17 .... Ch.47, p.3674
IAS 32.BC21(a) Ch.47, p.3701
IAS 32.BC67 .... Ch.47, p.3689
IAS 32.BC68 .... Ch.47, p.3689
IAS 32.BC77 .... Ch.54, p.4500
IAS 32.BC80 .... Ch.54, p.4493
IAS 32.BC83 .... Ch.54, p.4494
IAS 32.BC84 .... Ch.54, p.4494
IAS 32.BC94 .... Ch.54, p.4492
IAS 32.BC94-BC100 .... Ch.54, p.4496
IAS 32.BC101 .... Ch.54, p.4497
IAS 32.BC103 .... Ch.54, p.4499
IAS 32.BC105-BC111 .... Ch.54, p.4500

IAS 33

IAS 33.1 .... Ch.37, p.3022
IAS 33.2 .... Ch.37, p.3022
IAS 33.3 .... Ch.37, p.3022
IAS 33.4 .... Ch.37, p.3023
IAS 33.4A Ch.37, p.3061
IAS 33.5 .... Ch.37, p.3023
IAS 33.5 .... Ch.37, p.3040
IAS 33.5 .... Ch.37, p.3042
IAS 33.5 .... Ch.37, p.3048
IAS 33.5 .... Ch.37, p.3055
IAS 33.6 .... Ch.37, p.3023
IAS 33.7 .... Ch.37, p.3040
IAS 33.8 .... Ch.37, p.3021
IAS 33.8 .... Ch.37, p.3023
IAS 33.9 .... Ch.37, p.3023
IAS 33.10 .... Ch.37, p.3023
IAS 33.11 .... Ch.37, p.3022
IAS 33.12 .... Ch.37, p.3023
IAS 33.13 .... Ch.37, p.3023
IAS 33.14(a) Ch.37, p.3035
IAS 33.14(b) Ch.37, p.3035
IAS 33.15 .... Ch.37, p.3035
IAS 33.16 .... Ch.37, p.3035
IAS 33.17 .... Ch.37, p.3035
IAS 33.18 .... Ch.37, p.3035
IAS 33.19 .... Ch.37, p.3024
IAS 33.20 .... Ch.37, p.3026
IAS 33.21 .... Ch.37, p.3024
IAS 33.21 .... Ch.37, p.3025
IAS 33.21(f) Ch.37, p.3033
IAS 33.22 .... Ch.37, p.3033
IAS 33.23 .... Ch.37, p.3024
IAS 33.24 .... Ch.37, p.3024
IAS 33.24 .... Ch.37, p.3025
IAS 33.26 .... Ch.37, p.3027
IAS 33.26 .... Ch.37, p.3032
IAS 33.26 .... Ch.37, p.3062
IAS 33.26-27 .... Ch.37, p.3029

IAS 33.27 .... Ch.37, p.3027
IAS 33.28 .... Ch.37, p.3027
IAS 33.29 .... Ch.37, p.3029
IAS 33.29 .... Ch.37, p.3031
IAS 33.29 .... Ch.37, p.3062
IAS 33.30 .... Ch.37, p.3040
IAS 33.31 .... Ch.37, p.3040
IAS 33.32 .... Ch.37, p.3022
IAS 33.32 .... Ch.37, p.3040
IAS 33.33 .... Ch.37, p.3041
IAS 33.33 .... Ch.37, p.3048
IAS 33.34 .... Ch.37, p.3041
IAS 33.35 .... Ch.37, p.3041
IAS 33.36 .... Ch.37, p.3041
IAS 33.36 .... Ch.37, p.3051
IAS 33.37 .... Ch.37, p.3041
IAS 33.38 .... Ch.37, p.3032
IAS 33.38 .... Ch.37, p.3041
IAS 33.38 .... Ch.37, p.3051
IAS 33.39 .... Ch.37, p.3042
IAS 33.40 .... Ch.37, p.3059
IAS 33.42 .... Ch.37, p.3043
IAS 33.43 .... Ch.37, p.3042
IAS 33.44 .... Ch.37, p.3043
IAS 33.44 .... Ch.37, p.3048
IAS 33.45 .... Ch.37, p.3050
IAS 33.45-46 .... Ch.37, p.3050
IAS 33.46 .... Ch.37, p.3050
IAS 33.46 .... Ch.37, p.3051
IAS 33.47 .... Ch.37, p.3062
IAS 33.47A Ch.37, p.3021
IAS 33.47A Ch.37, p.3055
IAS 33.48 .... Ch.37, p.3025
IAS 33.48 .... Ch.37, p.3054
IAS 33.48 .... Ch.37, p.3055
IAS 33.49 .... Ch.37, p.3045
IAS 33.50 .... Ch.37, p.3046
IAS 33.51 .... Ch.37, p.3047
IAS 33.52 .... Ch.37, p.3055
IAS 33.52 .... Ch.37, p.3062
IAS 33.53 .... Ch.37, p.3056
IAS 33.54 .... Ch.37, p.3058
IAS 33.55 .... Ch.37, p.3056
IAS 33.56 .... Ch.37, p.3058
IAS 33.56 .... Ch.37, p.3059
IAS 33.57 .... Ch.37, p.3061
IAS 33.58 .... Ch.37, p.3042
IAS 33.59 .... Ch.37, p.3042
IAS 33.59-60 .... Ch.37, p.3048
IAS 33.60 .... Ch.37, p.3042
IAS 33.61 .... Ch.37, p.3042
IAS 33.62 .... Ch.37, p.3053
IAS 33.63 .... Ch.37, p.3051
IAS 33.64 .... Ch.37, p.3027
IAS 33.64 .... Ch.37, p.3033
IAS 33.64 .... Ch.37, p.3036
IAS 33.64 .... Ch.37, p.3062
IAS 33.65 .... Ch.37, p.3041

IAS 33.65	Ch.37, p.3062	IAS 34.1	Ch.41, p.3196
IAS 33.65	Ch.41, p.3265	IAS 34.1	Ch.41, p.3197
IAS 33.66	Ch.37, p.3023	IAS 34.2	Ch.41, p.3196
IAS 33.66	Ch.37, p.3036	IAS 34.2	Ch.41, p.3197
IAS 33.66	Ch.37, p.3061	IAS 34.3	Ch.41, p.3197
IAS 33.66	Ch.37, p.3062	IAS 34.4	Ch.41, p.3196
IAS 33.67	Ch.37, p.3062	IAS 34.4	Ch.41, p.3208
IAS 33.67A	Ch.3, p.141	IAS 34.4	Ch.41, p.3232
IAS 33.67A	Ch.37, p.3061	IAS 34.4	Ch.41, p.3267
IAS 33.68	Ch.37, p.3061	IAS 34.5	Ch.41, p.3198
IAS 33.68	Ch.37, p.3062	IAS 34.5(f)	Ch.41, p.3240
IAS 33.68A	Ch.37, p.3061	IAS 34.6	Ch.41, p.3199
IAS 33.69	Ch.37, p.3061	IAS 34.6	Ch.41, p.3204
IAS 33.70	Ch.37, p.3063	IAS 34.7	Ch.41, p.3198
IAS 33.71	Ch.37, p.3063	IAS 34.7	Ch.41, p.3199
IAS 33.72	Ch.37, p.3063	IAS 34.7	Ch.41, p.3237
IAS 33.73	Ch.37, p.3039	IAS 34.8	Ch.41, p.3199
IAS 33.73A	Ch.37, p.3039	IAS 34.8A	Ch.41, p.3199
IAS 33.A1	Ch.37, p.3023	IAS 34.8A	Ch.41, p.3228
IAS 33.A2	Ch.37, p.3029	IAS 34.9	Ch.41, p.3198
IAS 33.A2	Ch.37, p.3030	IAS 34.10	Ch.41, p.3199
IAS 33.A3	Ch.37, p.3043	IAS 34.10	Ch.41, p.3242
IAS 33.A4	Ch.37, p.3051	IAS 34.10	Ch.41, p.3267
IAS 33.A5	Ch.37, p.3051	IAS 34.11	Ch.41, p.3203
IAS 33.A6	Ch.37, p.3052	IAS 34.11A	Ch.41, p.3203
IAS 33.A7	Ch.37, p.3048	IAS 34.14	Ch.41, p.3203
IAS 33.A7	Ch.37, p.3052	IAS 34.15	Ch.32, p.2440
IAS 33.A8	Ch.37, p.3052	IAS 34.15	Ch.41, p.3199
IAS 33.A9	Ch.37, p.3048	IAS 34.15	Ch.41, p.3204
IAS 33.A9	Ch.37, p.3053	IAS 34.15	Ch.41, p.3205
IAS 33.A10	Ch.37, p.3052	IAS 34.15	Ch.41, p.3207
IAS 33.A11	Ch.37, p.3059	IAS 34.15	Ch.41, p.3231
IAS 33.A12	Ch.37, p.3060	IAS 34.15	Ch.41, p.3236
IAS 33.A13	Ch.37, p.3036	IAS 34.15	Ch.41, p.3267
IAS 33.A14	Ch.37, p.3037	IAS 34.15	Ch.54, p.4407
IAS 33.A14	Ch.37, p.3047	IAS 34.15-15A	Ch.5, p.361
IAS 33.A15	Ch.37, p.3024	IAS 34.15A	Ch.41, p.3204
IAS 33.A16	Ch.37, p.3053	IAS 34.15A	Ch.41, p.3231
IAS 33.IE1	Ch.37, p.3035	IAS 34.15A	Ch.41, p.3236
IAS 33.IE2	Ch.37, p.3024	IAS 34.15A	Ch.54, p.4407
IAS 33.IE2	Ch.37, p.3026	IAS 34.15B	Ch.32, p.2440
IAS 33.IE3	Ch.37, p.3028	IAS 34.15B	Ch.41, p.3204
IAS 33.IE4	Ch.37, p.3030	IAS 34.15B	Ch.41, p.3205
IAS 33.IE5	Ch.37, p.3050	IAS 34.15B	Ch.54, p.4407
IAS 33.IE5A	Ch.37, p.3055	IAS 34.15B(a)	Ch.41, p.3208
IAS 33.IE6	Ch.37, p.3046	IAS 34.15B(a)	Ch.41, p.3209
IAS 33.IE7	Ch.37, p.3057	IAS 34.15B(b)	Ch.41, p.3209
IAS 33.IE8	Ch.37, p.3046	IAS 34.15B(c)	Ch.41, p.3207
IAS 33.IE9	Ch.37, p.3043	IAS 34.15B(d)	Ch.41, p.3210
IAS 33.IE10	Ch.37, p.3060	IAS 34.15B(e)	Ch.41, p.3210
IAS 33.IE11	Ch.37, p.3037	IAS 34.15B(f)	Ch.41, p.3210
IAS 33.IE12	Ch.37, p.3064	IAS 34.15B(g)	Ch.41, p.3232
		IAS 34.15B(h)	Ch.41, p.3211
		IAS 34.15B(i)	Ch.41, p.3212
		IAS 34.15B(j)	Ch.41, p.3212
		IAS 34.15B(k)	Ch.41, p.3214
		IAS 34.15B(k)	Ch.41, p.3267
		IAS 34.15B(m)	Ch.41, p.3214

IAS 34

IAS 34 Objective	Ch.19, p.1495
IAS 34 Objective	Ch.41, p.3196

Index of standards

IAS 34.15B(m) Ch.41, p.3268
IAS 34.15C Ch.41, p.3204
IAS 34.15C Ch.41, p.3205
IAS 34.15C Ch.54, p.4407
IAS 34.16A Ch.41, p.3203
IAS 34.16A Ch.41, p.3204
IAS 34.16A Ch.41, p.3206
IAS 34.16A Ch.41, p.3207
IAS 34.16A Ch.41, p.3208
IAS 34.16A(a) Ch.41, p.3199
IAS 34.16A(a) Ch.41, p.3215
IAS 34.16A(a) Ch.41, p.3232
IAS 34.16A(a) Ch.41, p.3267
IAS 34.16A(b) Ch.41, p.3216
IAS 34.16A(b) Ch.41, p.3243
IAS 34.16A(c) Ch.41, p.3216
IAS 34.16A(d) Ch.41, p.3207
IAS 34.16A(d) Ch.41, p.3239
IAS 34.16A(d) Ch.41, p.3252
IAS 34.16A(d) Ch.41, p.3267
IAS 34.16A(e) Ch.41, p.3217
IAS 34.16A(f) Ch.41, p.3218
IAS 34.16A(g) Ch.41, p.3221
IAS 34.16A(g) Ch.41, p.3268
IAS 34.16A(g)(iv) Ch.41, p.3268
IAS 34.16A(g)(v) Ch.41, p.3267
IAS 34.16A(h) Ch.41, p.3218
IAS 34.16A(h) Ch.41, p.3252
IAS 34.16A(i) Ch.9, p.753
IAS 34.16A(i) Ch.13, p.946
IAS 34.16A(i) Ch.41, p.3207
IAS 34.16A(i) Ch.41, p.3219
IAS 34.16A(j) Ch.41, p.3223
IAS 34.16A(j) Ch.54, p.4407
IAS 34.16A(k) Ch.13, p.946
IAS 34.16A(l) Ch.32, p.2439
IAS 34.19 .... Ch.41, p.3224
IAS 34.20 .... Ch.41, p.3227
IAS 34.20 .... Ch.41, p.3232
IAS 34.20 .... Ch.41, p.3234
IAS 34.20 .... Ch.41, p.3266
IAS 34.20(b) Ch.41, p.3228
IAS 34.21 .... Ch.41, p.3228
IAS 34.21 .... Ch.41, p.3234
IAS 34.21C Ch.41, p.3243
IAS 34.22 .... Ch.41, p.3228
IAS 34.23 .... Ch.41, p.3207
IAS 34.23 .... Ch.41, p.3235
IAS 34.23 .... Ch.41, p.3236
IAS 34.24 .... Ch.41, p.3235
IAS 34.25 .... Ch.41, p.3199
IAS 34.25 .... Ch.41, p.3200
IAS 34.25 .... Ch.41, p.3204
IAS 34.25 .... Ch.41, p.3205
IAS 34.25 .... Ch.41, p.3207
IAS 34.25 .... Ch.41, p.3235
IAS 34.25 .... Ch.41, p.3236
IAS 34.26 .... Ch.41, p.3237
IAS 34.26 .... Ch.41, p.3239
IAS 34.26 .... Ch.41, p.3252
IAS 34.27 .... Ch.41, p.3237
IAS 34.28 .... Ch.41, p.3195
IAS 34.28 .... Ch.41, p.3237
IAS 34.28 .... Ch.41, p.3239
IAS 34.28 .... Ch.41, p.3242
IAS 34.28 .... Ch.41, p.3245
IAS 34.29 .... Ch.41, p.3237
IAS 34.29 .... Ch.41, p.3238
IAS 34.29 .... Ch.41, p.3243
IAS 34.29 .... Ch.41, p.3253
IAS 34.30(a) Ch.41, p.3238
IAS 34.30(b) Ch.41, p.3238
IAS 34.30(c) Ch.41, p.3238
IAS 34.30(c) Ch.41, p.3249
IAS 34.30(c) Ch.41, p.3252
IAS 34.31 .... Ch.41, p.3243
IAS 34.32 .... Ch.41, p.3238
IAS 34.32 .... Ch.41, p.3243
IAS 34.32 .... Ch.41, p.3259
IAS 34.33 .... Ch.41, p.3238
IAS 34.34-36 .... Ch.41, p.3239
IAS 34.36 .... Ch.41, p.3245
IAS 34.37 .... Ch.41, p.3242
IAS 34.38 .... Ch.41, p.3242
IAS 34.39 .... Ch.41, p.3243
IAS 34.39 .... Ch.41, p.3260
IAS 34.40 .... Ch.41, p.3243
IAS 34.41 .... Ch.41, p.3236
IAS 34.41 .... Ch.41, p.3265
IAS 34.42 .... Ch.41, p.3265
IAS 34.43 .... Ch.41, p.3239
IAS 34.43 .... Ch.41, p.3240
IAS 34.43(a) Ch.41, p.3242
IAS 34.44 .... Ch.41, p.3239
IAS 34.44 .... Ch.41, p.3240
IAS 34.45 .... Ch.41, p.3240
IAS 34.B1 .... Ch.41, p.3246
IAS 34.B2 .... Ch.41, p.3260
IAS 34.B3 .... Ch.41, p.3259
IAS 34.B4 .... Ch.41, p.3259
IAS 34.B5 .... Ch.41, p.3246
IAS 34.B6 .... Ch.41, p.3246
IAS 34.B7 .... Ch.41, p.3260
IAS 34.B8 .... Ch.41, p.3244
IAS 34.B9 .... Ch.41, p.3247
IAS 34.B10 .... Ch.41, p.3248
IAS 34.B11 .... Ch.41, p.3260
IAS 34.B12 .... Ch.41, p.3249
IAS 34.B13 .... Ch.41, p.3249
IAS 34.B13 .... Ch.41, p.3250
IAS 34.B13 .... Ch.41, p.3251
IAS 34.B13 .... Ch.41, p.3252
IAS 34.B13 .... Ch.41, p.3253
IAS 34.B14 .... Ch.41, p.3250
IAS 34.B14 .... Ch.41, p.3251
IAS 34.B15 .... Ch.41, p.3250

IAS 34.B16	Ch.41, p.3250	IAS 36.10-11	Ch.20, p.1610
IAS 34.B17	Ch.41, p.3254	IAS 36.11	Ch.20, p.1522
IAS 34.B18	Ch.41, p.3254	IAS 36.11	Ch.20, p.1610
IAS 34.B19	Ch.41, p.3257	IAS 36.12	Ch.20, p.1523
IAS 34.B20	Ch.41, p.3255	IAS 36.12-13	Ch.20, p.1522
IAS 34.B21	Ch.41, p.3254	IAS 36.12(f)	Ch.18, p.1415
IAS 34.B22	Ch.41, p.3254	IAS 36.12(h)	Ch.8, p.599
IAS 34.B23	Ch.41, p.3249	IAS 36.13	Ch.8, p.600
IAS 34.B24	Ch.41, p.3244	IAS 36.13	Ch.20, p.1518
IAS 34.B25	Ch.41, p.3248	IAS 36.13	Ch.20, p.1628
IAS 34.B26	Ch.41, p.3248	IAS 36.14	Ch.20, p.1523
IAS 34.B28	Ch.41, p.3249	IAS 36.15	Ch.20, p.1522
IAS 34.B29	Ch.41, p.3257	IAS 36.15	Ch.20, p.1523
IAS 34.B30	Ch.41, p.3257	IAS 36.16	Ch.20, p.1525
IAS 34.B31	Ch.41, p.3257	IAS 36.16	Ch.20, p.1565
IAS 34.B32	Ch.16, p.1273	IAS 36.17	Ch.20, p.1523
IAS 34.B32	Ch.41, p.3258	IAS 36.18	Ch.19, p.1486
IAS 34.B33	Ch.16, p.1273	IAS 36.18	Ch.20, p.1544
IAS 34.B33	Ch.41, p.3258	IAS 36.18	Ch.43, p.3434
IAS 34.B34	Ch.16, p.1274	IAS 36.19	Ch.20, p.1544
IAS 34.B34	Ch.41, p.3258	IAS 36.19	Ch.43, p.3434
IAS 34.B35	Ch.41, p.3244	IAS 36.20	Ch.20, p.1544
IAS 34.B36	Ch.41, p.3244	IAS 36.20	Ch.20, p.1548
IAS 34.B36	Ch.41, p.3245	IAS 36.21	Ch.20, p.1545
IAS 34.IE A	Ch.41, p.3228	IAS 36.22	Ch.17, p.1350
IAS 34.IE C7	Ch.19, p.1495	IAS 36.22	Ch.20, p.1544
		IAS 36.22	Ch.43, p.3434
		IAS 36.23	Ch.20, p.1544

IAS 36

		IAS 36.24	Ch.20, p.1610
		IAS 36.24	Ch.20, p.1611
IAS 36.2	Ch.20, p.1521	IAS 36.28	Ch.20, p.1546
IAS 36.3	Ch.20, p.1521	IAS 36.29	Ch.20, p.1546
IAS 36.4	Ch.20, p.1521	IAS 36.30	Ch.20, p.1551
IAS 36.4	Ch.20, p.1625	IAS 36.30	Ch.20, p.1552
IAS 36.6	Ch.14, p.1051	IAS 36.30	Ch.20, p.1563
IAS 36.6	Ch.20, p.1525	IAS 36.31	Ch.20, p.1544
IAS 36.6	Ch.20, p.1544	IAS 36.31	Ch.20, p.1551
IAS 36.6	Ch.43, p.3431	IAS 36.31	Ch.43, p.3434
IAS 36.6	Ch.43, p.3432	IAS 36.32	Ch.20, p.1551
IAS 36.6	Ch.43, p.3434	IAS 36.33	Ch.20, p.1552
IAS 36.6	Ch.43, p.3440	IAS 36.33	Ch.20, p.1557
IAS 36.8-9	Ch.8, p.599	IAS 36.33(a)	Ch.43, p.3436
IAS 36.8-9	Ch.20, p.1522	IAS 36.33(b)	Ch.43, p.3435
IAS 36.8-9	Ch.42, p.3284	IAS 36.34	Ch.20, p.1552
IAS 36.8-17	Ch.43, p.3373	IAS 36.35	Ch.20, p.1553
IAS 36.9	Ch.17, p.1339	IAS 36.35	Ch.43, p.3435
IAS 36.9	Ch.20, p.1522	IAS 36.36	Ch.20, p.1553
IAS 36.9	Ch.20, p.1591	IAS 36.37	Ch.20, p.1553
IAS 36.9	Ch.20, p.1610	IAS 36.38	Ch.20, p.1553
IAS 36.10	Ch.9, p.680	IAS 36.39	Ch.20, p.1553
IAS 36.10	Ch.17, p.1319	IAS 36.39(b)	Ch.20, p.1526
IAS 36.10	Ch.17, p.1339	IAS 36.39(b)	Ch.20, p.1558
IAS 36.10	Ch.17, p.1347	IAS 36.40	Ch.20, p.1553
IAS 36.10	Ch.17, p.1350	IAS 36.41	Ch.20, p.1554
IAS 36.10	Ch.20, p.1522	IAS 36.41	Ch.20, p.1559
IAS 36.10	Ch.20, p.1595	IAS 36.42	Ch.20, p.1554
IAS 36.10	Ch.20, p.1610	IAS 36.42	Ch.43, p.3439
IAS 36.10-11	Ch.20, p.1531	IAS 36.43	Ch.20, p.1553

IAS 36.44	Ch.20, p.1554	IAS 36.78	Ch.20, p.1561
IAS 36.44	Ch.20, p.1556	IAS 36.78	Ch.43, p.3435
IAS 36.44	Ch.20, p.1559	IAS 36.79	Ch.20, p.1536
IAS 36.44	Ch.43, p.3439	IAS 36.79	Ch.20, p.1540
IAS 36.45	Ch.20, p.1556	IAS 36.79	Ch.20, p.1554
IAS 36.46	Ch.20, p.1556	IAS 36.79	Ch.43, p.3435
IAS 36.47	Ch.20, p.1556	IAS 36.80	Ch.20, p.1582
IAS 36.48	Ch.20, p.1554	IAS 36.80	Ch.20, p.1585
IAS 36.49	Ch.20, p.1555	IAS 36.80	Ch.20, p.1587
IAS 36.50	Ch.20, p.1554	IAS 36.80	Ch.20, p.1621
IAS 36.50	Ch.20, p.1584	IAS 36.80(b)	Ch.20, p.1588
IAS 36.51	Ch.20, p.1554	IAS 36.80(b)	Ch.36, p.2983
IAS 36.51	Ch.20, p.1584	IAS 36.81	Ch.20, p.1582
IAS 36.52	Ch.20, p.1556	IAS 36.81	Ch.20, p.1587
IAS 36.53	Ch.20, p.1556	IAS 36.82	Ch.20, p.1583
IAS 36.53A	Ch.20, p.1581	IAS 36.83	Ch.20, p.1583
IAS 36.53A	Ch.20, p.1582	IAS 36.84	Ch.20, p.1589
IAS 36.54	Ch.20, p.1557	IAS 36.84	Ch.20, p.1590
IAS 36.54	Ch.26, p.1959	IAS 36.84	Ch.20, p.1591
IAS 36.54	Ch.43, p.3440	IAS 36.85	Ch.20, p.1589
IAS 36.55	Ch.20, p.1564	IAS 36.86	Ch.20, p.1598
IAS 36.55	Ch.20, p.1567	IAS 36.87	Ch.20, p.1588
IAS 36.55	Ch.20, p.1577	IAS 36.87	Ch.20, p.1599
IAS 36.55	Ch.20, p.1578	IAS 36.88	Ch.20, p.1613
IAS 36.55	Ch.43, p.3436	IAS 36.89	Ch.20, p.1610
IAS 36.56	Ch.20, p.1564	IAS 36.89	Ch.20, p.1611
IAS 36.56	Ch.20, p.1568	IAS 36.90	Ch.20, p.1590
IAS 36.59	Ch.20, p.1612	IAS 36.90	Ch.20, p.1591
IAS 36.60	Ch.20, p.1612	IAS 36.96	Ch.20, p.1591
IAS 36.60	Ch.42, p.3284	IAS 36.97-98	Ch.20, p.1592
IAS 36.61	Ch.18, p.1422	IAS 36.99	Ch.20, p.1592
IAS 36.62	Ch.20, p.1612	IAS 36.100	Ch.20, p.1542
IAS 36.63	Ch.20, p.1612	IAS 36.101	Ch.20, p.1542
IAS 36.64	Ch.20, p.1613	IAS 36.102	Ch.20, p.1542
IAS 36.66	Ch.20, p.1551	IAS 36.104	Ch.17, p.1350
IAS 36.66	Ch.43, p.3431	IAS 36.104	Ch.20, p.1531
IAS 36.67	Ch.20, p.1551	IAS 36.104	Ch.20, p.1604
IAS 36.68	Ch.20, p.1525	IAS 36.104	Ch.20, p.1613
IAS 36.68-69	Ch.20, p.1528	IAS 36.105	Ch.20, p.1545
IAS 36.69	Ch.20, p.1525	IAS 36.105	Ch.20, p.1613
IAS 36.70	Ch.20, p.1534	IAS 36.105	Ch.20, p.1614
IAS 36.70	Ch.20, p.1558	IAS 36.106	Ch.20, p.1614
IAS 36.70	Ch.20, p.1620	IAS 36.107	Ch.20, p.1615
IAS 36.70	Ch.43, p.3432	IAS 36.108	Ch.20, p.1614
IAS 36.71	Ch.20, p.1534	IAS 36.108	Ch.26, p.1976
IAS 36.72	Ch.20, p.1531	IAS 36.109-123	Ch.43, p.3374
IAS 36.73	Ch.20, p.1531	IAS 36.109-125	Ch.31, p.2385
IAS 36.74	Ch.43, p.3434	IAS 36.110	Ch.20, p.1616
IAS 36.74-79	Ch.5, p.334	IAS 36.111	Ch.20, p.1616
IAS 36.75	Ch.20, p.1535	IAS 36.112	Ch.20, p.1616
IAS 36.75	Ch.43, p.3434	IAS 36.113	Ch.20, p.1616
IAS 36.76	Ch.20, p.1535	IAS 36.114-116	Ch.20, p.1617
IAS 36.76	Ch.43, p.3435	IAS 36.117	Ch.18, p.1424
IAS 36.77	Ch.20, p.1535	IAS 36.117	Ch.20, p.1617
IAS 36.78	Ch.20, p.1536	IAS 36.118	Ch.20, p.1617
IAS 36.78	Ch.20, p.1537	IAS 36.119	Ch.5, p.376
IAS 36.78	Ch.20, p.1538	IAS 36.119	Ch.20, p.1618
IAS 36.78	Ch.20, p.1546	IAS 36.119	Ch.20, p.1619

IAS 36.120	Ch.20, p.1619
IAS 36.121	Ch.20, p.1618
IAS 36.121	Ch.20, p.1619
IAS 36.122	Ch.20, p.1618
IAS 36.123	Ch.20, p.1618
IAS 36.124	Ch.20, p.1593
IAS 36.124	Ch.20, p.1615
IAS 36.124	Ch.20, p.1629
IAS 36.124	Ch.41, p.3245
IAS 36.125	Ch.20, p.1593
IAS 36.125	Ch.20, p.1615
IAS 36.126	Ch.20, p.1630
IAS 36.127	Ch.20, p.1630
IAS 36.128	Ch.20, p.1630
IAS 36.129	Ch.20, p.1630
IAS 36.130	Ch.20, p.1631
IAS 36.131	Ch.20, p.1632
IAS 36.132	Ch.20, p.1632
IAS 36.133	Ch.20, p.1632
IAS 36.134	Ch.20, p.1634
IAS 36.134(d)(i)-(ii)	Ch.43, p.3437
IAS 36.134(d)(v)	Ch.20, p.1575
IAS 36.134(e)(i)-(ii)	Ch.43, p.3437
IAS 36.134(f)	Ch.20, p.1524
IAS 36.134(f)(ii)	Ch.20, p.1635
IAS 36.135	Ch.20, p.1634
IAS 36.135	Ch.20, p.1635
IAS 36.A2	Ch.20, p.1563
IAS 36.A4	Ch.20, p.1563
IAS 36.A6	Ch.20, p.1563
IAS 36.A7	Ch.20, p.1563
IAS 36.A10	Ch.20, p.1563
IAS 36.A10-13	Ch.20, p.1564
IAS 36.A15	Ch.20, p.1578
IAS 36.A16	Ch.20, p.1564
IAS 36.A17	Ch.20, p.1564
IAS 36.A17	Ch.20, p.1580
IAS 36.A18	Ch.20, p.1565
IAS 36.A19	Ch.20, p.1565
IAS 36.A19	Ch.20, p.1579
IAS 36.A20	Ch.20, p.1565
IAS 36.A21	Ch.20, p.1565
IAS 36.C1	Ch.20, p.1602
IAS 36.C2	Ch.20, p.1602
IAS 36.C3	Ch.20, p.1604
IAS 36.C4	Ch.20, p.1604
IAS 36.C6	Ch.20, p.1602
IAS 36.C7	Ch.20, p.1602
IAS 36.C8	Ch.20, p.1604
IAS 36.IE5-10	Ch.20, p.1535
IAS 36.IE62-68	Ch.20, p.1604
IAS 36.IE69-IE79	Ch.20, p.1543
IAS 36.IE Example 1C	Ch.43, p.3433
IAS 36.BCZ28-BCZ29	Ch.20, p.1550
IAS 36.BCZ49	Ch.20, p.1557
IAS 36.BCZ49	Ch.43, p.3440
IAS 36.BCZ81	Ch.20, p.1568
IAS 36.BCZ84	Ch.20, p.1569
IAS 36.BCZ85	Ch.20, p.1567
IAS 36.BCZ85	Ch.20, p.1569
IAS 36.BCZ85	Ch.20, p.1576
IAS 36.BCZ88	Ch.20, p.1568
IAS 36.BC139	Ch.20, p.1585
IAS 36.BC156	Ch.20, p.1598
IAS 36.BC162	Ch.20, p.1591
IAS 36.BC173	Ch.20, p.1591
IAS 36.BC177	Ch.20, p.1593

IAS 37 (2022)

IAS 37(2022).68A	Ch.31, p.2357

IAS 1

IAS 37 Objective	Ch.26, p.1932
IAS 37.1	Ch.26, p.1929
IAS 37.1	Ch.26, p.1932
IAS 37.2	Ch.26, p.1935
IAS 37.3	Ch.26, p.1932
IAS 37.3	Ch.26, p.1934
IAS 37.3	Ch.26, p.1945
IAS 37.3	Ch.39, p.3122
IAS 37.5	Ch.26, p.1934
IAS 37.5	Ch.26, p.2006
IAS 37.5	Ch.33, p.2561
IAS 37.5(c)	Ch.26, p.1934
IAS 37.5(c)	Ch.26, p.1975
IAS 37.5(g)	Ch.26, p.1936
IAS 37.5(g)	Ch.26, p.1977
IAS 37.7	Ch.26, p.1936
IAS 37.8	Ch.26, p.1946
IAS 37.9	Ch.26, p.1935
IAS 37.9	Ch.26, p.1967
IAS 37.9	Ch.26, p.2012
IAS 37.10	Ch.9, p.690
IAS 37.10	Ch.13, p.978
IAS 37.10	Ch.26, p.1931
IAS 37.10	Ch.26, p.1932
IAS 37.10	Ch.26, p.1936
IAS 37.10	Ch.26, p.1938
IAS 37.10	Ch.26, p.1939
IAS 37.10	Ch.26, p.1943
IAS 37.10	Ch.26, p.1944
IAS 37.10	Ch.26, p.1965
IAS 37.10	Ch.26, p.1966
IAS 37.10	Ch.26, p.1972
IAS 37.10	Ch.26, p.1974
IAS 37.10	Ch.26, p.1979
IAS 37.10	Ch.35, p.2912
IAS 37.10	Ch.43, p.3398
IAS 37.10	Ch.55, p.4569
IAS 37.11	Ch.26, p.1936
IAS 37.11(a)	Ch.54, p.4511
IAS 37.12	Ch.26, p.1937

IAS 37.13	Ch.26, p.1937
IAS 37.13	Ch.26, p.1943
IAS 37.14	Ch.17, p.1361
IAS 37.14	Ch.26, p.1937
IAS 37.14	Ch.26, p.1943
IAS 37.14	Ch.26, p.1992
IAS 37.14	Ch.26, p.2005
IAS 37.14	Ch.26, p.2006
IAS 37.14	Ch.55, p.4547
IAS 37.14	Ch.56, p.4703
IAS 37.15	Ch.24, p.1830
IAS 37.15	Ch.26, p.1938
IAS 37.15	Ch.26, p.2005
IAS 37.16	Ch.26, p.1938
IAS 37.16	Ch.26, p.1939
IAS 37.16	Ch.26, p.2005
IAS 37.16(a)	Ch.26, p.1943
IAS 37.16(b)	Ch.26, p.1943
IAS 37.17	Ch.26, p.1939
IAS 37.17	Ch.26, p.1963
IAS 37.17	Ch.26, p.2002
IAS 37.18	Ch.26, p.1939
IAS 37.18	Ch.26, p.1963
IAS 37.18	Ch.26, p.1964
IAS 37.18	Ch.26, p.2002
IAS 37.19	Ch.26, p.1940
IAS 37.19	Ch.26, p.1962
IAS 37.19	Ch.26, p.1963
IAS 37.19	Ch.26, p.1964
IAS 37.19	Ch.26, p.1966
IAS 37.19	Ch.26, p.1969
IAS 37.19	Ch.26, p.1975
IAS 37.19	Ch.26, p.2002
IAS 37.20	Ch.26, p.1941
IAS 37.21	Ch.26, p.1941
IAS 37.22	Ch.26, p.1941
IAS 37.22	Ch.26, p.1992
IAS 37.23	Ch.17, p.1301
IAS 37.23	Ch.26, p.1941
IAS 37.23	Ch.26, p.1943
IAS 37.23	Ch.26, p.1945
IAS 37.23	Ch.33, p.2491
IAS 37.24	Ch.26, p.1941
IAS 37.24	Ch.26, p.2004
IAS 37.25	Ch.26, p.1942
IAS 37.25	Ch.26, p.2005
IAS 37.25	Ch.43, p.3429
IAS 37.26	Ch.26, p.1942
IAS 37.26	Ch.26, p.1943
IAS 37.26	Ch.43, p.3429
IAS 37.27-28	Ch.26, p.1942
IAS 37.29	Ch.26, p.1960
IAS 37.30	Ch.26, p.1944
IAS 37.31	Ch.26, p.1942
IAS 37.32	Ch.26, p.1944
IAS 37.33	Ch.9, p.686
IAS 37.33	Ch.26, p.1944
IAS 37.33	Ch.55, p.4542
IAS 37.34	Ch.26, p.1942
IAS 37.34	Ch.26, p.1945
IAS 37.35	Ch.26, p.1945
IAS 37.35	Ch.33, p.2569
IAS 37.35	Ch.38, p.3079
IAS 37.35	Ch.38, p.3081
IAS 37.36	Ch.17, p.1361
IAS 37.36	Ch.26, p.1947
IAS 37.36	Ch.26, p.1952
IAS 37.36	Ch.26, p.1958
IAS 37.36	Ch.43, p.3451
IAS 37.36-37	Ch.26, p.1947
IAS 37.36-47	Ch.55, p.4580
IAS 37.37	Ch.17, p.1364
IAS 37.37	Ch.26, p.1947
IAS 37.37	Ch.43, p.3451
IAS 37.38	Ch.26, p.1948
IAS 37.39	Ch.26, p.1942
IAS 37.39	Ch.26, p.1948
IAS 37.39	Ch.26, p.2004
IAS 37.40	Ch.26, p.1942
IAS 37.40	Ch.26, p.1949
IAS 37.41	Ch.26, p.1947
IAS 37.42	Ch.26, p.1949
IAS 37.43	Ch.26, p.1949
IAS 37.43	Ch.26, p.1950
IAS 37.43	Ch.26, p.1951
IAS 37.44	Ch.26, p.1950
IAS 37.45	Ch.26, p.1950
IAS 37.46	Ch.26, p.1950
IAS 37.47	Ch.26, p.1950
IAS 37.47	Ch.26, p.1951
IAS 37.47	Ch.26, p.1952
IAS 37.47	Ch.26, p.1954
IAS 37.47	Ch.26, p.1957
IAS 37.48	Ch.26, p.1958
IAS 37.49	Ch.26, p.1959
IAS 37.50	Ch.26, p.1959
IAS 37.51	Ch.26, p.1972
IAS 37.51-52	Ch.26, p.1961
IAS 37.53	Ch.17, p.1363
IAS 37.53	Ch.26, p.1959
IAS 37.53	Ch.51, p.3958
IAS 37.53	Ch.51, p.3959
IAS 37.54	Ch.26, p.1959
IAS 37.55	Ch.26, p.1959
IAS 37.56	Ch.26, p.1960
IAS 37.56	Ch.55, p.4542
IAS 37.57	Ch.26, p.1960
IAS 37.58	Ch.26, p.1960
IAS 37.59	Ch.26, p.1955
IAS 37.59	Ch.26, p.1961
IAS 37.59	Ch.26, p.1981
IAS 37.60	Ch.26, p.1954
IAS 37.60	Ch.26, p.1956
IAS 37.60	Ch.26, p.1961
IAS 37.61	Ch.26, p.1961
IAS 37.61	Ch.26, p.2009

IAS 37.61-62	Ch.43, p.3534	IAS 37.IE Example 4	Ch.26, p.1938
IAS 37.62	Ch.26, p.1961	IAS 37.IE Example 4	Ch.26, p.2005
IAS 37.63	Ch.26, p.1962	IAS 37.IE Example 5A	Ch.26, p.1968
IAS 37.63	Ch.26, p.1966	IAS 37.IE Example 5B	Ch.26, p.1969
IAS 37.63	Ch.26, p.1970	IAS 37.IE Example 6	Ch.26, p.1940
IAS 37.63	Ch.26, p.1972	IAS 37.IE Example 7	Ch.26, p.1939
IAS 37.64	Ch.26, p.1962	IAS 37.IE Example 10	Ch.26, p.1944
IAS 37.65	Ch.26, p.1963	IAS 37.IE Example 11A	Ch.18, p.1396
IAS 37.66	Ch.26, p.1972	IAS 37.IE Example 11A	Ch.26, p.1963
IAS 37.66	Ch.31, p.2356	IAS 37.IE Example 11B	Ch.18, p.1396
IAS 37.67	Ch.26, p.1972	IAS 37.IE Example 11B	Ch.26, p.1940
IAS 37.67-68	Ch.31, p.2357	IAS 37.IE Example 11B	Ch.26, p.1963
IAS 37.68	Ch.26, p.1960	IAS 37.IE Example 11B	Ch.43, p.3492
IAS 37.68	Ch.26, p.1972	IAS 37.IE D Examples:	
IAS 37.68	Ch.26, p.1977	disclosures Example 3	Ch.26, p.2013
IAS 37.68A	Ch.26, p.1973	IAS 37.BC7	Ch.26, p.1973
IAS 37.69	Ch.26, p.1975		
IAS 37.69	Ch.31, p.2356		
IAS 37.70	Ch.26, p.1967	**IAS 38**	
IAS 37.71	Ch.26, p.1967		
IAS 37.71	Ch.41, p.3207	IAS 38.1	Ch.17, p.1294
IAS 37.72	Ch.26, p.1967	IAS 38.2	Ch.17, p.1294
IAS 37.72	Ch.26, p.1969	IAS 38.2	Ch.43, p.3513
IAS 37.73	Ch.26, p.1968	IAS 38.2(c)	Ch.43, p.3336
IAS 37.74	Ch.26, p.1968	IAS 38.2(c)-(d)	Ch.43, p.3361
IAS 37.75	Ch.26, p.1968	IAS 38.3	Ch.17, p.1292
IAS 37.76	Ch.26, p.1969	IAS 38.3	Ch.17, p.1294
IAS 37.77	Ch.26, p.1969	IAS 38.3	Ch.17, p.1295
IAS 37.78	Ch.26, p.1969	IAS 38.3	Ch.17, p.1299
IAS 37.79	Ch.26, p.1970	IAS 38.3(a)	Ch.22, p.1677
IAS 37.80	Ch.26, p.1970	IAS 38.3(a)	Ch.22, p.1680
IAS 37.80	Ch.26, p.1971	IAS 38.3(a)	Ch.32, p.2407
IAS 37.81	Ch.26, p.1964	IAS 38.3(e)	Ch.22, p.1680
IAS 37.81	Ch.26, p.1970	IAS 38.3(g)	Ch.56, p.4868
IAS 37.82	Ch.26, p.1972	IAS 38.3(i)	Ch.31, p.2383
IAS 37.83	Ch.26, p.1972	IAS 38.4	Ch.17, p.1298
IAS 37.84	Ch.26, p.2009	IAS 38.4	Ch.18, p.1391
IAS 37.84(e)	Ch.26, p.1957	IAS 38.5	Ch.17, p.1295
IAS 37.85	Ch.26, p.2009	IAS 38.5	Ch.17, p.1299
IAS 37.86	Ch.13, p.978	IAS 38.6	Ch.17, p.1294
IAS 37.86	Ch.26, p.2012	IAS 38.6	Ch.17, p.1299
IAS 37.86	Ch.43, p.3429	IAS 38.7	Ch.17, p.1295
IAS 37.87	Ch.26, p.2012	IAS 38.8	Ch.9, p.672
IAS 37.88	Ch.26, p.2012	IAS 38.8	Ch.9, p.681
IAS 37.89	Ch.26, p.2013	IAS 38.8	Ch.17, p.1292
IAS 37.90	Ch.26, p.2013	IAS 38.8	Ch.17, p.1293
IAS 37.91	Ch.26, p.2012	IAS 38.8	Ch.17, p.1295
IAS 37.91	Ch.26, p.2013	IAS 38.8	Ch.17, p.1298
IAS 37.92	Ch.26, p.2013	IAS 38.8	Ch.17, p.1305
IAS 37.94A	Ch.26, p.1973	IAS 38.8	Ch.17, p.1312
IAS 37.105	Ch.26, p.1973	IAS 38.8	Ch.17, p.1320
IAS 37 Appendix C	Ch.43, p.3492	IAS 38.8	Ch.17, p.1329
IAS 37.IE Example 1	Ch.26, p.2004	IAS 38.8	Ch.17, p.1338
IAS 37.IE Example 2A	Ch.26, p.1992	IAS 38.8	Ch.17, p.1341
IAS 37.IE Example 2B	Ch.26, p.1938	IAS 38.8	Ch.17, p.1347
IAS 37.IE Example 2B	Ch.26, p.1992	IAS 38.8	Ch.17, p.1350
IAS 37.IE Example 3	Ch.26, p.1946	IAS 38.8	Ch.17, p.1368
IAS 37.IE Example 3	Ch.26, p.1979	IAS 38.8	Ch.17, p.1369

IAS 38.8	Ch.17, p.1374	IAS 38.33	Ch.17, p.1313
IAS 38.8	Ch.33, p.2545	IAS 38.33-35	Ch.9, p.679
IAS 38.8	Ch.43, p.3395	IAS 38.34	Ch.9, p.673
IAS 38.8	Ch.43, p.3418	IAS 38.34	Ch.9, p.679
IAS 38.9	Ch.17, p.1295	IAS 38.34	Ch.17, p.1318
IAS 38.10	Ch.17, p.1295	IAS 38.35	Ch.17, p.1314
IAS 38.11	Ch.9, p.672	IAS 38.36	Ch.9, p.678
IAS 38.11	Ch.17, p.1296	IAS 38.36	Ch.17, p.1314
IAS 38.12	Ch.9, p.672	IAS 38.37	Ch.9, p.678
IAS 38.12	Ch.17, p.1293	IAS 38.37	Ch.17, p.1314
IAS 38.12	Ch.17, p.1296	IAS 38.42	Ch.9, p.680
IAS 38.12	Ch.17, p.1313	IAS 38.42	Ch.17, p.1319
IAS 38.12(b)	Ch.17, p.1299	IAS 38.43	Ch.9, p.680
IAS 38.12(b)	Ch.17, p.1368	IAS 38.43	Ch.17, p.1319
IAS 38.13	Ch.17, p.1293	IAS 38.44	Ch.17, p.1310
IAS 38.13	Ch.17, p.1296	IAS 38.45	Ch.17, p.1311
IAS 38.13	Ch.17, p.1297	IAS 38.45	Ch.25, p.1881
IAS 38.13	Ch.17, p.1299	IAS 38.45	Ch.43, p.3402
IAS 38.13	Ch.17, p.1352	IAS 38.46	Ch.17, p.1311
IAS 38.13	Ch.17, p.1368	IAS 38.46	Ch.17, p.1312
IAS 38.13	Ch.17, p.1374	IAS 38.47	Ch.17, p.1311
IAS 38.13-14	Ch.17, p.1296	IAS 38.48	Ch.17, p.1295
IAS 38.15	Ch.17, p.1297	IAS 38.48	Ch.17, p.1319
IAS 38.15	Ch.31, p.2367	IAS 38.49	Ch.17, p.1319
IAS 38.16	Ch.17, p.1296	IAS 38.50	Ch.17, p.1319
IAS 38.16	Ch.17, p.1297	IAS 38.51	Ch.17, p.1320
IAS 38.17	Ch.17, p.1298	IAS 38.52	Ch.17, p.1320
IAS 38.17	Ch.17, p.1368	IAS 38.52	Ch.17, p.1322
IAS 38.18	Ch.17, p.1297	IAS 38.53	Ch.17, p.1320
IAS 38.18	Ch.17, p.1301	IAS 38.53	Ch.17, p.1321
IAS 38.19	Ch.17, p.1301	IAS 38.53	Ch.17, p.1322
IAS 38.20	Ch.17, p.1305	IAS 38.54	Ch.9, p.679
IAS 38.20	Ch.17, p.1326	IAS 38.54	Ch.17, p.1320
IAS 38.20	Ch.17, p.1352	IAS 38.54-55	Ch.17, p.1321
IAS 38.20	Ch.17, p.1369	IAS 38.55	Ch.17, p.1322
IAS 38.21	Ch.5, p.281	IAS 38.56	Ch.17, p.1320
IAS 38.21	Ch.9, p.679	IAS 38.56	Ch.17, p.1369
IAS 38.21	Ch.17, p.1301	IAS 38.57	Ch.9, p.679
IAS 38.21	Ch.17, p.1313	IAS 38.57	Ch.17, p.1321
IAS 38.21	Ch.17, p.1376	IAS 38.57	Ch.17, p.1369
IAS 38.21	Ch.43, p.3395	IAS 38.57(d)	Ch.24, p.1832
IAS 38.21	Ch.43, p.3398	IAS 38.58	Ch.17, p.1321
IAS 38.22	Ch.17, p.1301	IAS 38.59	Ch.17, p.1320
IAS 38.23	Ch.17, p.1301	IAS 38.60	Ch.9, p.679
IAS 38.24	Ch.17, p.1304	IAS 38.60	Ch.17, p.1321
IAS 38.24	Ch.17, p.1329	IAS 38.61	Ch.17, p.1322
IAS 38.24	Ch.43, p.3367	IAS 38.62	Ch.17, p.1322
IAS 38.25	Ch.17, p.1305	IAS 38.63	Ch.17, p.1292
IAS 38.26	Ch.17, p.1305	IAS 38.63	Ch.17, p.1305
IAS 38.27	Ch.17, p.1306	IAS 38.63-64	Ch.17, p.1326
IAS 38.28	Ch.17, p.1306	IAS 38.64	Ch.17, p.1292
IAS 38.29-30	Ch.17, p.1307	IAS 38.65	Ch.17, p.1329
IAS 38.30	Ch.17, p.1306	IAS 38.66	Ch.17, p.1330
IAS 38.31	Ch.17, p.1307	IAS 38.67	Ch.17, p.1328
IAS 38.31	Ch.17, p.1324	IAS 38.67	Ch.17, p.1330
IAS 38.32	Ch.17, p.1306	IAS 38.67(a)	Ch.26, p.1974
IAS 38.32	Ch.25, p.1892	IAS 38.68	Ch.17, p.1301
IAS 38.33	Ch.9, p.681	IAS 38.68	Ch.17, p.1329

IAS 38.68	Ch.17, p.1330	IAS 38.98	Ch.17, p.1342
IAS 38.68-69	Ch.31, p.2367	IAS 38.98	Ch.25, p.1881
IAS 38.69	Ch.17, p.1330	IAS 38.98	Ch.41, p.3244
IAS 38.69	Ch.17, p.1332	IAS 38.98A	Ch.17, p.1345
IAS 38.69	Ch.25, p.1898	IAS 38.98A	Ch.17, p.1346
IAS 38.69A	Ch.17, p.1331	IAS 38.98A	Ch.25, p.1882
IAS 38.69A	Ch.17, p.1332	IAS 38.98B	Ch.17, p.1346
IAS 38.70	Ch.17, p.1331	IAS 38.98B	Ch.25, p.1883
IAS 38.71	Ch.5, p.378	IAS 38.98C	Ch.17, p.1346
IAS 38.71	Ch.17, p.1301	IAS 38.98C	Ch.25, p.1883
IAS 38.71	Ch.17, p.1329	IAS 38.99	Ch.17, p.1342
IAS 38.71	Ch.17, p.1334	IAS 38.100	Ch.17, p.1348
IAS 38.71	Ch.41, p.3238	IAS 38.101	Ch.17, p.1348
IAS 38.71	Ch.41, p.3244	IAS 38.102	Ch.17, p.1348
IAS 38.72	Ch.17, p.1333	IAS 38.103	Ch.17, p.1348
IAS 38.72	Ch.43, p.3368	IAS 38.104	Ch.5, p.379
IAS 38.73	Ch.17, p.1333	IAS 38.104	Ch.17, p.1347
IAS 38.73	Ch.17, p.1335	IAS 38.105	Ch.17, p.1347
IAS 38.74	Ch.17, p.1333	IAS 38.106	Ch.17, p.1347
IAS 38.75	Ch.17, p.1333	IAS 38.107	Ch.17, p.1349
IAS 38.75	Ch.17, p.1334	IAS 38.108	Ch.17, p.1349
IAS 38.75	Ch.17, p.1335	IAS 38.109	Ch.17, p.1349
IAS 38.75	Ch.43, p.3368	IAS 38.109	Ch.33, p.2549
IAS 38.76	Ch.17, p.1334	IAS 38.110	Ch.17, p.1349
IAS 38.77	Ch.17, p.1334	IAS 38.111	Ch.17, p.1350
IAS 38.78	Ch.17, p.1334	IAS 38.112	Ch.17, p.1350
IAS 38.78	Ch.17, p.1335	IAS 38.112	Ch.17, p.1365
IAS 38.79	Ch.17, p.1335	IAS 38.112	Ch.43, p.3395
IAS 38.80	Ch.17, p.1337	IAS 38.112	Ch.43, p.3399
IAS 38.81-82	Ch.17, p.1333	IAS 38.113	Ch.17, p.1351
IAS 38.81-82	Ch.17, p.1334	IAS 38.113	Ch.17, p.1357
IAS 38.82	Ch.17, p.1335	IAS 38.113	Ch.17, p.1365
IAS 38.83	Ch.17, p.1335	IAS 38.113	Ch.27, p.2040
IAS 38.84	Ch.17, p.1335	IAS 38.113	Ch.43, p.3399
IAS 38.85	Ch.17, p.1335	IAS 38.114	Ch.17, p.1350
IAS 38.86	Ch.17, p.1336	IAS 38.114	Ch.27, p.2040
IAS 38.87	Ch.17, p.1337	IAS 38.115	Ch.17, p.1352
IAS 38.87	Ch.27, p.2040	IAS 38.115A	Ch.17, p.1351
IAS 38.88	Ch.17, p.1338	IAS 38.116	Ch.17, p.1351
IAS 38.88	Ch.33, p.2548	IAS 38.116	Ch.27, p.2040
IAS 38.88	Ch.33, p.2549	IAS 38.116	Ch.43, p.3400
IAS 38.89	Ch.17, p.1338	IAS 38.116	Ch.45, p.3605
IAS 38.90	Ch.17, p.1339	IAS 38.117	Ch.17, p.1342
IAS 38.91	Ch.17, p.1338	IAS 38.118	Ch.17, p.1353
IAS 38.91	Ch.20, p.1610	IAS 38.118	Ch.41, p.3232
IAS 38.91	Ch.33, p.2548	IAS 38.118(d)	Ch.17, p.1357
IAS 38.92	Ch.17, p.1338	IAS 38.119	Ch.17, p.1333
IAS 38.92	Ch.17, p.1339	IAS 38.119	Ch.17, p.1353
IAS 38.93	Ch.17, p.1339	IAS 38.120	Ch.17, p.1355
IAS 38.94	Ch.17, p.1340	IAS 38.121	Ch.17, p.1355
IAS 38.94-95	Ch.17, p.1340	IAS 38.122	Ch.17, p.1356
IAS 38.96	Ch.17, p.1340	IAS 38.122(e)	Ch.38, p.3080
IAS 38.97	Ch.17, p.1341	IAS 38.122(e)	Ch.39, p.3123
IAS 38.97	Ch.17, p.1342	IAS 38.123	Ch.17, p.1356
IAS 38.97	Ch.17, p.1344	IAS 38.124	Ch.17, p.1357
IAS 38.97	Ch.25, p.1880	IAS 38.125	Ch.17, p.1358
IAS 38.97	Ch.25, p.1881	IAS 38.126-127	Ch.17, p.1358
IAS 38.97-98	Ch.17, p.1344	IAS 38.128	Ch.17, p.1356

IAS 38.BC5	Ch.17, p.1295	IAS 39.91(b)	Ch.53, p.4397
IAS 38.BC7	Ch.17, p.1295	IAS 39.91(c)	Ch.53, p.4397
IAS 38.BC8	Ch.17, p.1295	IAS 39.96	Ch.53, p.4397
IAS 38.BC10	Ch.17, p.1296	IAS 39.101(b)	Ch.53, p.4397
IAS 38.BC13	Ch.17, p.1296	IAS 39.101(d)	Ch.53, p.4397
IAS 38.BC19A	Ch.17, p.1313	IAS 39.102A-102N	Ch.53, p.4369
IAS 38.BC19B	Ch.17, p.1313	IAS 39.102B	Ch.55, p.4616
IAS 38.BCZ40	Ch.17, p.1302	IAS 39.102F	Ch.53, p.4369
IAS 38.BCZ41	Ch.17, p.1302	IAS 39.102G	Ch.53, p.4369
IAS 38.BC46B	Ch.17, p.1331	IAS 39.102H	Ch.53, p.4369
IAS 38.BC46D	Ch.17, p.1331	IAS 39.102M	Ch.53, p.4378
IAS 38.BC46E	Ch.17, p.1331	IAS 39.102P(d)	Ch.53, p.4378
IAS 38.BC46G	Ch.17, p.1332	IAS 39.102V	Ch.53, p.4378
IAS 38.BC59	Ch.17, p.1348	IAS 39.108G	Ch.53, p.4369
IAS 38.BC62	Ch.17, p.1338	IAS 39.AG4A	Ch.55, p.4542
IAS 38.BC72H-72I	Ch.17, p.1346	IAS 39.AG5	Ch.51, p.3930
IAS 38.BC74	Ch.33, p.2548	IAS 39.AG30(g)	Ch.55, p.4561
IAS 38.BC82	Ch.9, p.679	IAS 39.AG32	Ch.55, p.4563
IAS 38.BC82	Ch.17, p.1319	IAS 39.AG33(g)	Ch.55, p.4563
		IAS 39.AG87	Ch.55, p.4584
		IAS 39.AG88	Ch.55, p.4584

IAS 39 (2006)

IAS 39(2006).BC222(v)(ii)	Ch.49, p.3855	IAS 39.AG94	Ch.53, p.4236
		IAS 39.AG94	Ch.53, p.4396
		IAS 39.AG98	Ch.9, p.698
		IAS 39.AG99F	Ch.53, p.4395

IAS 39 (2010)

		IAS 39.AG99F(a)	Ch.53, p.4194
IAS 39(2010).AG70	Ch.14, p.1114	IAS 39.AG99F(a)	Ch.53, p.4378
		IAS 39.AG100	Ch.53, p.4395
		IAS 39.AG105(b)	Ch.53, p.4396
		IAS 39.AG107	Ch.53, p.4283
		IAS 39.AG110	Ch.53, p.4221

IAS 39 (2017)

IAS 39(2017).AG84	Ch.14, p.1012	IAS 39.AG114-132	Ch.53, p.4382
		IAS 39.IG B.9	Ch.46, p.3625
		IAS 39.IG E.4.4	Ch.51, p.4018
		IAS 39.IG F.1.2	Ch.53, p.4238

IAS 39

		IAS 39.IG F.1.3(b)	Ch.53, p.4236
IAS 39.2(e)	Ch.55, p.4539	IAS 39.IG F.1.4	Ch.53, p.4248
IAS 39.9	Ch.51, p.4045	IAS 39.IG F.1.4	Ch.53, p.4249
IAS 39.9	Ch.55, p.4559	IAS 39.IG F.1.5	Ch.53, p.4251
IAS 39.10	Ch.55, p.4559	IAS 39.IG F.1.6	Ch.53, p.4252
IAS 39.11	Ch.55, p.4560	IAS 39.IG F.1.7	Ch.53, p.4252
IAS 39.39	Ch.55, p.4582	IAS 39.IG F.1.9	Ch.53, p.4283
IAS 39.50	Ch.55, p.4595	IAS 39.IG F.1.13	Ch.53, p.4243
IAS 39.50A(c)	Ch.55, p.4595	IAS 39.IG F.1.14	Ch.53, p.4235
IAS 39.72	Ch.53, p.4396	IAS 39.IG F.2.1	Ch.53, p.4220
IAS 39.74	Ch.53, p.4397	IAS 39.IG F.2.2	Ch.53, p.4264
IAS 39.81A	Ch.53, p.4382	IAS 39.IG F.2.3	Ch.53, p.4223
IAS 39.82	Ch.53, p.4395	IAS 39.IG F.2.3	Ch.53, p.4382
IAS 39.83	Ch.53, p.4395	IAS 39.IG F.2.5	Ch.53, p.4265
IAS 39.84	Ch.53, p.4395	IAS 39.IG F.2.5	Ch.53, p.4266
IAS 39.86	Ch.53, p.4390	IAS 39.IG F.2.6	Ch.53, p.4274
IAS 39.86	Ch.53, p.4396	IAS 39.IG F.2.8	Ch.53, p.4221
IAS 39.88	Ch.53, p.4396	IAS 39.IG F.2.12	Ch.53, p.4218
IAS 39.88(a)	Ch.53, p.4395	IAS 39.IG F.2.14	Ch.53, p.4261
IAS 39.89	Ch.53, p.4397	IAS 39.IG F.2.15	Ch.53, p.4252
IAS 39.89A	Ch.53, p.4382	IAS 39.IG F.2.17	Ch.53, p.4197
		IAS 39.IG F.3.5	Ch.53, p.4262
		IAS 39.IG F.3.6	Ch.53, p.4263

IAS 39.IG F.3.6	Ch.53, p.4264	IAS 40.19A	Ch.19, p.1444
IAS 39.IG F.3.6	Ch.53, p.4292	IAS 40.19A	Ch.19, p.1451
IAS 39.IG F.3.7	Ch.52, p.4123	IAS 40.20	Ch.14, p.1052
IAS 39.IG F.3.7	Ch.53, p.4217	IAS 40.20	Ch.19, p.1457
IAS 39.IG F.3.10	Ch.53, p.4202	IAS 40.20	Ch.19, p.1460
IAS 39.IG F.3.10	Ch.53, p.4361	IAS 40.21	Ch.19, p.1457
IAS 39.IG F.3.11	Ch.53, p.4360	IAS 40.21	Ch.19, p.1476
IAS 39.IG F.5.2	Ch.53, p.4296	IAS 40.23(a)	Ch.19, p.1459
IAS 39.IG F.5.5	Ch.53, p.4319	IAS 40.23(b)	Ch.19, p.1459
IAS 39.IG F.5.6	Ch.53, p.4324	IAS 40.23(c)	Ch.19, p.1459
IAS 39.IG F.5.6	Ch.53, p.4336	IAS 40.24	Ch.19, p.1460
IAS 39.IG F.6.1-3	Ch.53, p.4382	IAS 40.27	Ch.43, p.3402
IAS 39.IG F.6.1-3	Ch.53, p.4385	IAS 40.27-29	Ch.19, p.1461
IAS 39.BC15	Ch.51, p.4045	IAS 40.29A	Ch.19, p.1461
IAS 39.BC220O-Q	Ch.53, p.4362	IAS 40.30	Ch.19, p.1467
IAS 39.BC220R	Ch.53, p.4362	IAS 40.31	Ch.19, p.1467
IAS 39.BC220S	Ch.53, p.4362	IAS 40.32	Ch.19, p.1467
IAS 39.BC222(d)	Ch.49, p.3860	IAS 40.32	Ch.19, p.1469
		IAS 40.32A	Ch.19, p.1467
		IAS 40.32A	Ch.55, p.4540
		IAS 40.32A	Ch.56, p.4695
		IAS 40.32B	Ch.19, p.1467

IAS 40

IAS 40.1	Ch.19, p.1441	IAS 40.32C	Ch.19, p.1468
IAS 40.2	Ch.19, p.1441	IAS 40.33	Ch.14, p.1020
IAS 40.4	Ch.19, p.1443	IAS 40.33	Ch.19, p.1468
IAS 40.4(a)	Ch.19, p.1451	IAS 40.33	Ch.19, p.1474
IAS 40.4(b)	Ch.43, p.3336	IAS 40.35	Ch.19, p.1468
IAS 40.4(b)	Ch.43, p.3361	IAS 40.40	Ch.19, p.1469
IAS 40.5	Ch.19, p.1442	IAS 40.40	Ch.38, p.3089
IAS 40.5	Ch.19, p.1468	IAS 40.40A	Ch.19, p.1444
IAS 40.5	Ch.22, p.1695	IAS 40.40A	Ch.19, p.1472
IAS 40.5	Ch.43, p.3418	IAS 40.41	Ch.19, p.1472
IAS 40.7	Ch.19, p.1443	IAS 40.48	Ch.19, p.1472
IAS 40.7	Ch.19, p.1445	IAS 40.50	Ch.19, p.1473
IAS 40.7	Ch.19, p.1446	IAS 40.50(a)	Ch.19, p.1450
IAS 40.8	Ch.19, p.1445	IAS 40.50(a)	Ch.19, p.1477
IAS 40.8	Ch.19, p.1446	IAS 40.50(b)	Ch.19, p.1450
IAS 40.9	Ch.19, p.1445	IAS 40.50(b)	Ch.19, p.1477
IAS 40.9	Ch.19, p.1446	IAS 40.50(c)	Ch.19, p.1477
IAS 40.10	Ch.19, p.1447	IAS 40.50(d)	Ch.19, p.1479
IAS 40.10	Ch.19, p.1448	IAS 40.52	Ch.19, p.1482
IAS 40.11	Ch.9, p.657	IAS 40.53	Ch.19, p.1473
IAS 40.11	Ch.19, p.1448	IAS 40.53	Ch.19, p.1474
IAS 40.11-14	Ch.9, p.641	IAS 40.53	Ch.19, p.1475
IAS 40.11-14	Ch.9, p.657	IAS 40.53A	Ch.19, p.1475
IAS 40.12-13	Ch.19, p.1449	IAS 40.53B	Ch.19, p.1475
IAS 40.13	Ch.19, p.1449	IAS 40.54	Ch.19, p.1475
IAS 40.14	Ch.19, p.1443	IAS 40.55	Ch.19, p.1474
IAS 40.14	Ch.19, p.1447	IAS 40.56	Ch.19, p.1444
IAS 40.14	Ch.19, p.1448	IAS 40.56	Ch.19, p.1483
IAS 40.14	Ch.19, p.1449	IAS 40.56	Ch.19, p.1486
IAS 40.14A	Ch.9, p.657	IAS 40.57	Ch.19, p.1488
IAS 40.14A	Ch.19, p.1453	IAS 40.57	Ch.19, p.1490
IAS 40.15	Ch.19, p.1446	IAS 40.57	Ch.42, p.3277
IAS 40.16	Ch.19, p.1451	IAS 40.57(d)	Ch.19, p.1490
IAS 40.17	Ch.19, p.1451	IAS 40.58	Ch.19, p.1490
IAS 40.18	Ch.19, p.1452	IAS 40.59	Ch.19, p.1461
IAS 40.19	Ch.19, p.1452	IAS 40.59	Ch.19, p.1490

IAS 40.60	Ch.19, p.1491	IAS 41.5A	Ch.18, p.1393
IAS 40.61	Ch.19, p.1491	IAS 41.5A	Ch.42, p.3276
IAS 40.62	Ch.19, p.1491	IAS 41.5B	Ch.18, p.1393
IAS 40.63	Ch.19, p.1491	IAS 41.5B	Ch.42, p.3276
IAS 40.64	Ch.19, p.1491	IAS 41.5C	Ch.18, p.1393
IAS 40.65	Ch.19, p.1492	IAS 41.5C	Ch.42, p.3275
IAS 40.66	Ch.19, p.1492	IAS 41.5C	Ch.42, p.3289
IAS 40.67	Ch.19, p.1492	IAS 41.6	Ch.42, p.3274
IAS 40.67	Ch.27, p.2040	IAS 41.7	Ch.42, p.3274
IAS 40.68	Ch.19, p.1494	IAS 41.7	Ch.42, p.3287
IAS 40.69	Ch.19, p.1493	IAS 41.8	Ch.42, p.3277
IAS 40.69	Ch.27, p.2040	IAS 41.10	Ch.42, p.3281
IAS 40.70	Ch.19, p.1493	IAS 41.10	Ch.42, p.3288
IAS 40.70	Ch.27, p.2040	IAS 41.11	Ch.42, p.3281
IAS 40.71	Ch.19, p.1493	IAS 41.12	Ch.19, p.1443
IAS 40.72	Ch.19, p.1495	IAS 41.12	Ch.42, p.3282
IAS 40.73	Ch.19, p.1495	IAS 41.13	Ch.42, p.3283
IAS 40.74	Ch.19, p.1496	IAS 41.13	Ch.42, p.3284
IAS 40.75	Ch.19, p.1497	IAS 41.15	Ch.42, p.3295
IAS 40.76	Ch.19, p.1505	IAS 41.16	Ch.42, p.3297
IAS 40.77	Ch.19, p.1506	IAS 41.22	Ch.42, p.3296
IAS 40.78	Ch.19, p.1508	IAS 41.22	Ch.42, p.3298
IAS 40.79	Ch.19, p.1509	IAS 41.24	Ch.42, p.3305
IAS 40.79(e)	Ch.14, p.1008	IAS 41.25	Ch.42, p.3300
IAS 40.79(e)	Ch.19, p.1467	IAS 41.25	Ch.42, p.3303
IAS 40.79(e)(iii)	Ch.14, p.1012	IAS 41.26	Ch.42, p.3289
IAS 40.BC19-20	Ch.19, p.1453	IAS 41.27	Ch.42, p.3290
IAS 40.BC25	Ch.19, p.1489	IAS 41.28	Ch.42, p.3290
IAS 40.BC26	Ch.19, p.1489	IAS 41.29	Ch.42, p.3290
IAS 40.BC27	Ch.19, p.1489	IAS 41.30	Ch.14, p.1012
IAS 40.BC28	Ch.19, p.1489	IAS 41.30	Ch.42, p.3282
		IAS 41.30	Ch.42, p.3290
		IAS 41.30	Ch.42, p.3291
		IAS 41.30	Ch.42, p.3292

IAS 41 (2008)

IAS 41(2008).21	Ch.42, p.3306

		IAS 41.31	Ch.42, p.3292
		IAS 41.32	Ch.42, p.3283
		IAS 41.33	Ch.42, p.3292

IAS 41

		IAS 41.34	Ch.24, p.1843
		IAS 41.34	Ch.42, p.3294
IAS 41 Objective	Ch.42, p.3273	IAS 41.35	Ch.24, p.1843
IAS 41.1	Ch.42, p.3277	IAS 41.35	Ch.42, p.3294
IAS 41.1	Ch.42, p.3281	IAS 41.36	Ch.24, p.1843
IAS 41.1(a)	Ch.24, p.1842	IAS 41.36	Ch.42, p.3294
IAS 41.2	Ch.19, p.1443	IAS 41.37-38	Ch.24, p.1842
IAS 41.2	Ch.42, p.3278	IAS 41.37-38	Ch.42, p.3293
IAS 41.2(b)	Ch.42, p.3279	IAS 41.38	Ch.24, p.1842
IAS 41.2(e)	Ch.42, p.3281	IAS 41.40	Ch.42, p.3313
IAS 41.3	Ch.42, p.3278	IAS 41.41	Ch.42, p.3315
IAS 41.3	Ch.42, p.3279	IAS 41.42	Ch.42, p.3315
IAS 41.4	Ch.42, p.3275	IAS 41.43	Ch.42, p.3316
IAS 41.5	Ch.24, p.1825	IAS 41.44	Ch.42, p.3316
IAS 41.5	Ch.24, p.1842	IAS 41.45	Ch.42, p.3316
IAS 41.5	Ch.42, p.3274	IAS 41.46	Ch.42, p.3289
IAS 41.5	Ch.42, p.3275	IAS 41.46	Ch.42, p.3316
IAS 41.5	Ch.42, p.3277	IAS 41.49	Ch.42, p.3316
IAS 41.5	Ch.42, p.3287	IAS 41.50	Ch.42, p.3316
IAS 41.5	Ch.42, p.3295	IAS 41.51	Ch.42, p.3317
		IAS 41.52	Ch.42, p.3317

IAS 41.53	Ch.42, p.3318
IAS 41.54	Ch.42, p.3322
IAS 41.55	Ch.42, p.3322
IAS 41.56	Ch.42, p.3323
IAS 41.57	Ch.42, p.3323
IAS 41.B8	Ch.42, p.3278
IAS 41.B8	Ch.42, p.3284
IAS 41.B22	Ch.42, p.3296
IAS 41.B33	Ch.42, p.3296
IAS 41.B35	Ch.42, p.3292
IAS 41.B36	Ch.42, p.3292
IAS 41.B37	Ch.42, p.3293
IAS 41.B41	Ch.42, p.3278
IAS 41.B42	Ch.42, p.3284
IAS 41.B43	Ch.42, p.3283
IAS 41.B45	Ch.42, p.3278
IAS 41.B50-B54	Ch.42, p.3297
IAS 41.B55-B57	Ch.42, p.3278
IAS 41.B58-B60	Ch.42, p.3278
IAS 41.B62	Ch.42, p.3282
IAS 41.B66	Ch.24, p.1827
IAS 41.B66	Ch.24, p.1843
IAS 41.B66	Ch.42, p.3294
IAS 41.B67	Ch.24, p.1827
IAS 41.B69	Ch.24, p.1830
IAS 41.B74-B77	Ch.42, p.3317
IAS 41.B78-B79	Ch.42, p.3313
IAS 41.B81	Ch.42, p.3296
IAS 41.B82(n)	Ch.42, p.3280
IAS 41.IE1	Ch.42, p.3308
IAS 41.IE1	Ch.42, p.3314
IAS 41.IE2	Ch.42, p.3317
IAS 41.BC3	Ch.42, p.3296
IAS 41.BC4A-D	Ch.42, p.3279
IAS 41.BC4B	Ch.42, p.3279
IAS 41.BC4C	Ch.42, p.3291
IAS 41.BC4D	Ch.42, p.3288

IFRIC 1

IFRIC 1.1	Ch.25, p.1900
IFRIC 1.1	Ch.26, p.1981
IFRIC 1.2	Ch.18, p.1406
IFRIC 1.2	Ch.26, p.1982
IFRIC 1.2	Ch.26, p.1985
IFRIC 1.3	Ch.18, p.1406
IFRIC 1.3	Ch.26, p.1982
IFRIC 1.4-6	Ch.41, p.3259
IFRIC 1.4-7	Ch.26, p.1982
IFRIC 1.5	Ch.25, p.1900
IFRIC 1.5	Ch.26, p.1957
IFRIC 1.5	Ch.26, p.1982
IFRIC 1.5	Ch.33, p.2509
IFRIC 1.5	Ch.43, p.3501
IFRIC 1.6	Ch.26, p.1983
IFRIC 1.6	Ch.26, p.1984
IFRIC 1.7	Ch.18, p.1414
IFRIC 1.7	Ch.26, p.1957
IFRIC 1.7	Ch.26, p.1982
IFRIC 1.8	Ch.25, p.1900
IFRIC 1.8	Ch.26, p.1954
IFRIC 1.8	Ch.26, p.1961
IFRIC 1.8	Ch.26, p.1982
IFRIC 1.IE1-4	Ch.26, p.1983
IFRIC 1.IE5	Ch.26, p.1957
IFRIC 1.IE5	Ch.26, p.1985
IFRIC 1.IE6-10	Ch.26, p.1984
IFRIC 1.IE7	Ch.26, p.1985
IFRIC 1.IE11-12	Ch.26, p.1984
IFRIC 1.BC23	Ch.26, p.1985
IFRIC 1.BC26	Ch.26, p.1954
IFRIC 1.BC26-27	Ch.26, p.1982

IFRIC 2

IFRIC 2.1-4	Ch.47, p.3693
IFRIC 2.5	Ch.47, p.3694
IFRIC 2.6	Ch.47, p.3694
IFRIC 2.6-8	Ch.47, p.3694
IFRIC 2.8	Ch.47, p.3694
IFRIC 2.9	Ch.47, p.3694
IFRIC 2.10	Ch.47, p.3694
IFRIC 2.11	Ch.47, p.3694
IFRIC 2.BC10	Ch.47, p.3734

IFRIC 5

IFRIC 5.1	Ch.26, p.1986
IFRIC 5.2	Ch.26, p.1987
IFRIC 5.3	Ch.26, p.1987
IFRIC 5.4	Ch.26, p.1987
IFRIC 5.5	Ch.26, p.1987
IFRIC 5.5	Ch.45, p.3606
IFRIC 5.6	Ch.26, p.1988
IFRIC 5.7	Ch.26, p.1988
IFRIC 5.7	Ch.26, p.1990
IFRIC 5.8	Ch.26, p.1988
IFRIC 5.9	Ch.26, p.1988
IFRIC 5.10	Ch.26, p.1990
IFRIC 5.11	Ch.26, p.1991
IFRIC 5.12	Ch.26, p.1991
IFRIC 5.13	Ch.26, p.1991
IFRIC 5.BC7	Ch.26, p.1990
IFRIC 5.BC8	Ch.26, p.1991
IFRIC 5.BC14	Ch.26, p.1988
IFRIC 5.BC19-20	Ch.26, p.1988
IFRIC 5.BC19-20	Ch.26, p.1989

IFRIC 6

IFRIC 6.3	Ch.26, p.1995
IFRIC 6.4	Ch.26, p.1995

IFRIC 6.5	Ch.26, p.1996
IFRIC 6.6	Ch.26, p.1995
IFRIC 6.7	Ch.26, p.1996
IFRIC 6.8	Ch.26, p.1995
IFRIC 6.9	Ch.26, p.1996
IFRIC 6.BC5	Ch.26, p.1996
IFRIC 6.BC6	Ch.26, p.1996
IFRIC 6.BC7	Ch.26, p.1996

IFRIC 7

IFRIC 7.3	Ch.16, p.1263
IFRIC 7.3	Ch.16, p.1274
IFRIC 7.3	Ch.41, p.3258
IFRIC 7.4	Ch.16, p.1265
IFRIC 7.5	Ch.16, p.1265
IFRIC 7.IE1-IE6	Ch.16, p.1265
IFRIC 7.BC21-BC22	Ch.16, p.1264

IFRIC 10

IFRIC 10.2	Ch.41, p.3245
IFRIC 10.8	Ch.41, p.3245
IFRIC 10.9	Ch.41, p.3246
IFRIC 10.BC9	Ch.41, p.3245

IFRIC 12

IFRIC 12 references	Ch.2, p.47
IFRIC 12.1	Ch.5, p.319
IFRIC 12.1	Ch.25, p.1854
IFRIC 12.1	Ch.25, p.1855
IFRIC 12.1	Ch.25, p.1862
IFRIC 12.2	Ch.5, p.319
IFRIC 12.2	Ch.25, p.1853
IFRIC 12.3	Ch.25, p.1853
IFRIC 12.3	Ch.25, p.1854
IFRIC 12.3	Ch.25, p.1892
IFRIC 12.4	Ch.25, p.1854
IFRIC 12.4	Ch.25, p.1858
IFRIC 12.5	Ch.25, p.1854
IFRIC 12.5	Ch.25, p.1857
IFRIC 12.5	Ch.25, p.1858
IFRIC 12.5	Ch.25, p.1869
IFRIC 12.5(b)	Ch.25, p.1859
IFRIC 12.6	Ch.25, p.1854
IFRIC 12.6	Ch.25, p.1861
IFRIC 12.7	Ch.25, p.1853
IFRIC 12.7	Ch.25, p.1854
IFRIC 12.7	Ch.25, p.1862
IFRIC 12.7	Ch.25, p.1864
IFRIC 12.8	Ch.25, p.1862
IFRIC 12.8	Ch.25, p.1865
IFRIC 12.9	Ch.25, p.1854
IFRIC 12.9	Ch.25, p.1858
IFRIC 12.10	Ch.25, p.1917
IFRIC 12.11	Ch.25, p.1853
IFRIC 12.11	Ch.25, p.1858
IFRIC 12.11	Ch.25, p.1867
IFRIC 12.11	Ch.25, p.1879
IFRIC 12.11	Ch.25, p.1890
IFRIC 12.12	Ch.25, p.1868
IFRIC 12.12	Ch.25, p.1884
IFRIC 12.13	Ch.25, p.1868
IFRIC 12.13	Ch.25, p.1869
IFRIC 12.13	Ch.25, p.1884
IFRIC 12.14	Ch.25, p.1853
IFRIC 12.14	Ch.25, p.1857
IFRIC 12.14	Ch.25, p.1867
IFRIC 12.14	Ch.25, p.1869
IFRIC 12.14	Ch.25, p.1875
IFRIC 12.14	Ch.25, p.1879
IFRIC 12.14	Ch.25, p.1890
IFRIC 12.14	Ch.25, p.1899
IFRIC 12.15	Ch.25, p.1853
IFRIC 12.15	Ch.25, p.1873
IFRIC 12.15	Ch.25, p.1879
IFRIC 12.16	Ch.25, p.1873
IFRIC 12.16	Ch.25, p.1875
IFRIC 12.16	Ch.45, p.3589
IFRIC 12.17	Ch.25, p.1873
IFRIC 12.17	Ch.25, p.1879
IFRIC 12.18	Ch.25, p.1873
IFRIC 12.18	Ch.25, p.1885
IFRIC 12.19	Ch.25, p.1853
IFRIC 12.19	Ch.25, p.1868
IFRIC 12.19	Ch.25, p.1873
IFRIC 12.19	Ch.25, p.1875
IFRIC 12.19	Ch.25, p.1879
IFRIC 12.19	Ch.25, p.1883
IFRIC 12.19	Ch.25, p.1899
IFRIC 12.19	Ch.25, p.1909
IFRIC 12.19	Ch.25, p.1910
IFRIC 12.19	Ch.25, p.1912
IFRIC 12.19	Ch.25, p.1916
IFRIC 12.20	Ch.25, p.1853
IFRIC 12.20	Ch.25, p.1869
IFRIC 12.20	Ch.25, p.1899
IFRIC 12.20	Ch.25, p.1901
IFRIC 12.21	Ch.25, p.1899
IFRIC 12.21	Ch.25, p.1901
IFRIC 12.21	Ch.25, p.1906
IFRIC 12.21	Ch.25, p.1914
IFRIC 12.22	Ch.25, p.1876
IFRIC 12.22	Ch.25, p.1879
IFRIC 12.22	Ch.25, p.1916
IFRIC 12.23	Ch.25, p.1916
IFRIC 12.24	Ch.25, p.1876
IFRIC 12.25	Ch.25, p.1876
IFRIC 12.26	Ch.25, p.1881
IFRIC 12.27	Ch.25, p.1904
IFRIC 12.29	Ch.5, p.319
IFRIC 12.30	Ch.5, p.319

IFRIC 12.AG2	Ch.25, p.1859	IFRIC 14.21	Ch.35, p.2934
IFRIC 12.AG3	Ch.25, p.1859	IFRIC 14.22	Ch.35, p.2934
IFRIC 12.AG5	Ch.25, p.1858	IFRIC 14.23	Ch.35, p.2936
IFRIC 12.AG6	Ch.25, p.1858	IFRIC 14.24	Ch.35, p.2937
IFRIC 12.AG6	Ch.25, p.1860	IFRIC 14.IE1-2	Ch.35, p.2937
IFRIC 12.AG7	Ch.25, p.1855	IFRIC 14.IE3-8	Ch.35, p.2937
IFRIC 12.AG7	Ch.25, p.1866	IFRIC 14.IE9-27	Ch.35, p.2934
IFRIC 12.AG8	Ch.25, p.1866	IFRIC 14.BC10	Ch.35, p.2932
IFRIC 12.IE15	Ch.25, p.1879	IFRIC 14.BC30	Ch.35, p.2933
IFRIC 12.IE15	Ch.25, p.1916		
IFRIC 12.IE19	Ch.25, p.1902		
IFRIC 12.IE20	Ch.25, p.1902		

IFRIC 16

IFRIC 12.BC7	Ch.2, p.47		
IFRIC 12.BC11-13	Ch.25, p.1852	IFRIC 16.1	Ch.53, p.4266
IFRIC 12.BC11-13	Ch.25, p.1854	IFRIC 16.2	Ch.53, p.4267
IFRIC 12.BC13	Ch.25, p.1855	IFRIC 16.2	Ch.53, p.4306
IFRIC 12.BC14	Ch.25, p.1858	IFRIC 16.3	Ch.53, p.4300
IFRIC 12.BC15	Ch.25, p.1858	IFRIC 16.4	Ch.53, p.4266
IFRIC 12.BC16	Ch.25, p.1865	IFRIC 16.7	Ch.53, p.4267
IFRIC 12.BC20	Ch.2, p.47	IFRIC 16.7	Ch.53, p.4306
IFRIC 12.BC21	Ch.25, p.1858	IFRIC 16.8	Ch.53, p.4267
IFRIC 12.BC22	Ch.25, p.1858	IFRIC 16.10	Ch.53, p.4267
IFRIC 12.BC31	Ch.25, p.1867	IFRIC 16.11	Ch.53, p.4268
IFRIC 12.BC31	Ch.25, p.1869	IFRIC 16.11	Ch.53, p.4269
IFRIC 12.BC32	Ch.25, p.1880	IFRIC 16.12	Ch.53, p.4267
IFRIC 12.BC35	Ch.25, p.1884	IFRIC 16.13	Ch.53, p.4269
IFRIC 12.BC44	Ch.25, p.1873	IFRIC 16.13	Ch.53, p.4270
IFRIC 12.BC52	Ch.25, p.1874	IFRIC 16.14	Ch.53, p.4270
IFRIC 12.BC53	Ch.25, p.1885	IFRIC 16.14	Ch.53, p.4302
IFRIC 12.BC65	Ch.25, p.1881	IFRIC 16.14	Ch.53, p.4303
IFRIC 12.BC66	Ch.25, p.1900	IFRIC 16.15	Ch.53, p.4301
IFRIC 12.BC68	Ch.25, p.1900	IFRIC 16.15	Ch.53, p.4302
		IFRIC 16.16	Ch.53, p.4364
		IFRIC 16.17	Ch.7, p.500

IFRIC 14

		IFRIC 16.17	Ch.7, p.501
IFRIC 14.1	Ch.35, p.2930	IFRIC 16.17	Ch.15, p.1214
IFRIC 14.1-3	Ch.35, p.2930	IFRIC 16.17	Ch.53, p.4364
IFRIC 14.2	Ch.35, p.2930	IFRIC 16.17	Ch.53, p.4365
IFRIC 14.3	Ch.35, p.2930	IFRIC 16.AG1-3	Ch.53, p.4268
IFRIC 14.5	Ch.35, p.2933	IFRIC 16.AG2	Ch.53, p.4268
IFRIC 14.6	Ch.35, p.2930	IFRIC 16.AG2	Ch.53, p.4303
IFRIC 14.7	Ch.35, p.2931	IFRIC 16.AG2	Ch.53, p.4304
IFRIC 14.8	Ch.35, p.2931	IFRIC 16.AG4	Ch.53, p.4268
IFRIC 14.9	Ch.35, p.2931	IFRIC 16.AG4	Ch.53, p.4301
IFRIC 14.10	Ch.35, p.2967	IFRIC 16.AG5	Ch.53, p.4301
IFRIC 14.11-12	Ch.35, p.2931	IFRIC 16.AG5	Ch.53, p.4302
IFRIC 14.11-12	Ch.35, p.2932	IFRIC 16.AG6	Ch.53, p.4269
IFRIC 14.13	Ch.35, p.2931	IFRIC 16.AG6	Ch.53, p.4271
IFRIC 14.14	Ch.35, p.2931	IFRIC 16.AG7	Ch.53, p.4301
IFRIC 14.14	Ch.35, p.2969	IFRIC 16.AG8	Ch.53, p.4365
IFRIC 14.15	Ch.35, p.2932	IFRIC 16.AG10	Ch.53, p.4269
IFRIC 14.16	Ch.35, p.2933	IFRIC 16.AG11	Ch.53, p.4270
IFRIC 14.17	Ch.35, p.2933	IFRIC 16.AG12	Ch.53, p.4270
IFRIC 14.18	Ch.35, p.2934	IFRIC 16.AG12	Ch.53, p.4302
IFRIC 14.19	Ch.35, p.2934	IFRIC 16.AG13	Ch.53, p.4270
IFRIC 14.20	Ch.35, p.2934	IFRIC 16.AG14	Ch.53, p.4269
IFRIC 14.21	Ch.35, p.2933	IFRIC 16.AG15	Ch.53, p.4270
		IFRIC 16.BC24A	Ch.53, p.4270

IFRIC 16.BC24B	Ch.53, p.4270	IFRIC 19.10	Ch.47, p.3739
IFRIC 16.BC36	Ch.7, p.501	IFRIC 19.11	Ch.47, p.3738
		IFRIC 19.13	Ch.5, p.321
		IFRIC 19.BC16	Ch.2, p.47
		IFRIC 19.BC22	Ch.47, p.3738
		IFRIC 19.BC33	Ch.5, p.321

IFRIC 17

IFRIC 17.3	Ch.7, p.531
IFRIC 17.3	Ch.8, p.601
IFRIC 17.4	Ch.7, p.531

IFRIC 20

IFRIC 20 references	Ch.2, p.47
IFRIC 20.1	Ch.5, p.322
IFRIC 20.2	Ch.43, p.3502
IFRIC 20.3	Ch.5, p.322
IFRIC 20.3	Ch.43, p.3502
IFRIC 20.5	Ch.5, p.322
IFRIC 20.8	Ch.43, p.3502
IFRIC 20.9	Ch.43, p.3504
IFRIC 20.10	Ch.43, p.3504
IFRIC 20.12	Ch.43, p.3505
IFRIC 20.13	Ch.43, p.3505
IFRIC 20.14	Ch.43, p.3511
IFRIC 20.15	Ch.43, p.3506
IFRIC 20.15	Ch.43, p.3511
IFRIC 20.16	Ch.43, p.3511
IFRIC 20 Appendix A	Ch.5, p.322
IFRIC 20.BC4	Ch.43, p.3502
IFRIC 20.BC8	Ch.43, p.3510
IFRIC 20.BC10	Ch.43, p.3504
IFRIC 20.BC12	Ch.43, p.3505
IFRIC 20.BC15	Ch.43, p.3505
IFRIC 20.BC17	Ch.43, p.3510

IFRIC 17.4	Ch.8, p.602
IFRIC 17.5	Ch.7, p.531
IFRIC 17.5	Ch.8, p.602
IFRIC 17.5	Ch.8, p.617
IFRIC 17.6	Ch.7, p.531
IFRIC 17.6	Ch.8, p.602
IFRIC 17.7	Ch.7, p.531
IFRIC 17.7	Ch.8, p.602
IFRIC 17.8	Ch.7, p.531
IFRIC 17.10	Ch.7, p.531
IFRIC 17.10	Ch.8, p.599
IFRIC 17.10	Ch.8, p.602
IFRIC 17.10	Ch.38, p.3081
IFRIC 17.11	Ch.7, p.532
IFRIC 17.11	Ch.8, p.602
IFRIC 17.12	Ch.7, p.532
IFRIC 17.12	Ch.8, p.602
IFRIC 17.13	Ch.7, p.532
IFRIC 17.13	Ch.8, p.602
IFRIC 17.14-15	Ch.7, p.532
IFRIC 17.14-15	Ch.8, p.603
IFRIC 17.16	Ch.7, p.533
IFRIC 17.16	Ch.8, p.603
IFRIC 17.17	Ch.7, p.533
IFRIC 17.17	Ch.8, p.604
IFRIC 17.17	Ch.38, p.3085
IFRIC 17.BC5	Ch.8, p.602
IFRIC 17.BC18-20	Ch.38, p.3081
IFRIC 17.BC22	Ch.45, p.3591
IFRIC 17.BC27	Ch.45, p.3591
IFRIC 17.BC55	Ch.7, p.532
IFRIC 17.BC56	Ch.7, p.532

IFRIC 21

IFRIC 21.2	Ch.26, p.1997
IFRIC 21.2	Ch.41, p.3261
IFRIC 21.3	Ch.26, p.1997
IFRIC 21.3	Ch.26, p.2000
IFRIC 21.4	Ch.26, p.1932
IFRIC 21.4	Ch.26, p.1997
IFRIC 21.4	Ch.26, p.1998
IFRIC 21.5	Ch.26, p.1997
IFRIC 21.5	Ch.26, p.2001
IFRIC 21.6	Ch.26, p.1997
IFRIC 21.6	Ch.41, p.3261
IFRIC 21.7	Ch.26, p.1997
IFRIC 21.8	Ch.26, p.1997
IFRIC 21.8	Ch.26, p.1998
IFRIC 21.8	Ch.41, p.3261
IFRIC 21.9	Ch.26, p.1998
IFRIC 21.9-10	Ch.41, p.3261
IFRIC 21.10	Ch.26, p.1998
IFRIC 21.11	Ch.26, p.1998
IFRIC 21.11	Ch.41, p.3261
IFRIC 21.12	Ch.26, p.1998
IFRIC 21.14	Ch.26, p.1998

IFRIC 19

IFRIC 19 references	Ch.2, p.47
IFRIC 19.1	Ch.47, p.3737
IFRIC 19.2	Ch.5, p.321
IFRIC 19.2	Ch.47, p.3737
IFRIC 19.3	Ch.5, p.321
IFRIC 19.3	Ch.47, p.3738
IFRIC 19.5-7	Ch.47, p.3738
IFRIC 19.7	Ch.47, p.3738
IFRIC 19.8	Ch.47, p.3738
IFRIC 19.9	Ch.47, p.3738

IFRIC 21.14	Ch.26, p.2000	IFRIC 23.A3	Ch.33, p.2567
IFRIC 21.14	Ch.26, p.2001	IFRIC 23.A4(a)	Ch.33, p.2567
IFRIC 21.31	Ch.41, p.3261	IFRIC 23.A4(b)	Ch.33, p.2567
IFRIC 21.A1	Ch.26, p.1997	IFRIC 23.A5	Ch.33, p.2567
IFRIC 21.IE1	Ch.26, p.1999	IFRIC 23.B1	Ch.33, p.2455
IFRIC 21.IE1 Example 2	Ch.26, p.1998	IFRIC 23.B1	Ch.33, p.2561
IFRIC 21.IE1 Example 2	Ch.41, p.3261	IFRIC 23.B2	Ch.33, p.2561
IFRIC 21.IE1 Example 3	Ch.26, p.2000	IFRIC 23.IE1	Ch.33, p.2565
IFRIC 21.IE1 Example 4	Ch.41, p.3262	IFRIC 23.IE2-6	Ch.33, p.2564
IFRIC 21.BC4	Ch.26, p.1997	IFRIC 23.IE7-10	Ch.33, p.2565
IFRIC 21.BC4	Ch.26, p.2001	IFRIC 23.BC4	Ch.33, p.2569
		IFRIC 23.BC6	Ch.33, p.2561
		IFRIC 23.BC8	Ch.33, p.2562
		IFRIC 23.BC9	Ch.33, p.2562

IFRIC 22

		IFRIC 23.BC11	Ch.33, p.2563
		IFRIC 23.BC13	Ch.33, p.2563
IFRIC 22 references	Ch.2, p.47	IFRIC 23.BC23	Ch.9, p.691
IFRIC 22.4	Ch.5, p.341	IFRIC 23.BC23	Ch.33, p.2562
IFRIC 22.4	Ch.15, p.1189	IFRIC 23.BC24	Ch.9, p.692
IFRIC 22.5	Ch.15, p.1189	IFRIC 23.BC24	Ch.33, p.2562
IFRIC 22.6	Ch.15, p.1190		
IFRIC 22.7	Ch.5, p.342		
IFRIC 22.8	Ch.15, p.1189		

SIC-7

IFRIC 22.8-9	Ch.5, p.342	SIC-7.3	Ch.15, p.1241
IFRIC 22.9	Ch.15, p.1189	SIC-7.4	Ch.15, p.1242
IFRIC 22.BC8	Ch.15, p.1190	SIC-7.5	Ch.15, p.1241
IFRIC 22.BC17	Ch.2, p.47	SIC-7.6	Ch.15, p.1242
IFRIC 22.BC17	Ch.15, p.1197	SIC-7.7	Ch.15, p.1242

IFRIC 23

SIC-10

IFRIC 23.3	Ch.33, p.2458	SIC-10.3	Ch.24, p.1827
IFRIC 23.3	Ch.33, p.2476		
IFRIC 23.3	Ch.33, p.2542		
IFRIC 23.3	Ch.33, p.2562		

SIC-25

IFRIC 23.4	Ch.26, p.1935	SIC-25.4	Ch.33, p.2475
IFRIC 23.4	Ch.33, p.2561	SIC-25.4	Ch.33, p.2599
IFRIC 23.4	Ch.33, p.2568		
IFRIC 23.5	Ch.33, p.2561		
IFRIC 23.6	Ch.33, p.2563		

SIC-29

IFRIC 23.8	Ch.33, p.2563		
IFRIC 23.9	Ch.33, p.2564	SIC-29.1	Ch.25, p.1855
IFRIC 23.10	Ch.33, p.2564	SIC-29.1	Ch.25, p.1856
IFRIC 23.10	Ch.33, p.2567	SIC-29.1	Ch.25, p.1917
IFRIC 23.11	Ch.33, p.2564	SIC-29.2	Ch.25, p.1917
IFRIC 23.12	Ch.33, p.2563	SIC-29.2(a)	Ch.25, p.1855
IFRIC 23.12	Ch.33, p.2566	SIC-29.3	Ch.25, p.1917
IFRIC 23.13	Ch.33, p.2477	SIC-29.4	Ch.25, p.1852
IFRIC 23.13	Ch.33, p.2566	SIC-29.5	Ch.25, p.1917
IFRIC 23.13	Ch.38, p.3090	SIC-29.6	Ch.25, p.1917
IFRIC 23.14	Ch.33, p.2477	SIC-29.6	Ch.25, p.1918
IFRIC 23.14	Ch.33, p.2566	SIC-29.6A	Ch.25, p.1918
IFRIC 23.14	Ch.33, p.2567	SIC-29.7	Ch.25, p.1918
IFRIC 23.14	Ch.38, p.3078		
IFRIC 23.14	Ch.38, p.3080		
IFRIC 23.14	Ch.38, p.3090		
IFRIC 23.A2	Ch.33, p.2566		
IFRIC 23.A2	Ch.38, p.3090		

SIC-32

SIC-32.1	Ch.17, p.1326
SIC-32.2	Ch.17, p.1327
SIC-32.3	Ch.17, p.1327
SIC-32.5-6	Ch.17, p.1327
SIC-32.7	Ch.17, p.1326
SIC-32.8	Ch.17, p.1327
SIC-32.9	Ch.17, p.1327
SIC-32.10	Ch.17, p.1328

Management Commentary

MC.12	Ch.2, p.107
MC.13	Ch.2, p.107
MC.24	Ch.2, p.107
MC Appendix	Ch.2, p.106
MC.IN2	Ch.2, p.106
MC.IN3	Ch.2, p.106
MC.IN4	Ch.2, p.106
MC.IN5	Ch.2, p.107

PS 2

PS 2.2	Ch.3, p.160
PS 2.5-7	Ch.3, p.161
PS 2.8-10	Ch.3, p.161
PS 2.11-12	Ch.3, p.161
PS 2.13-23	Ch.3, p.161
PS 2.24-26	Ch.3, p.161
PS 2.28	Ch.3, p.161
PS 2.29-32	Ch.3, p.162
PS 2.35-39	Ch.3, p.162
PS 2.40-55	Ch.3, p.162
PS 2.56-59	Ch.3, p.162
PS 2.60-65	Ch.3, p.162
PS 2.66-71	Ch.3, p.162
PS 2.72-80	Ch.3, p.163
PS 2.81-83	Ch.3, p.163
PS 2.84-88	Ch.3, p.163

Index

Note: This index uses chapter number followed by section number for locators. A section number includes all its sub-sections. For example the locator Ch. 37, 2.7 will include subsections 2.7.1 and 2.7.2 in chapter 37. The locator Ch. 21, 5.3.1 will include subsections and 5.3.1.B. Where a range is indicated, for example, Ch. 3, 2–3, this means the topic starts from the beginning of section 2 to the end of section 3.

Accounting estimates
   vs. accounting policies, Ch. 3, 4.2
   changes in, Ch. 3, 4.5
   disclosures of, Ch. 3, 5.2
Accounting policies, Ch. 3, 4. *See also* IAS 1; IAS 8
   vs. accounting estimates, Ch. 3, 4.2
   accrual basis of accounting, Ch. 3, 4.1.3
   aggregation, Ch. 3, 4.1.5.A
   application of, Ch. 3, 4.3
   changes in, Ch. 3, 4.4
   consistency, Ch. 3, 4.1.4; Ch. 7, 2.6
   correction of errors, Ch. 3, 4.6
   definition of, Ch. 3, 4.2
   disclosures relating to, Ch. 3, 5.1
      changes in accounting policies, Ch. 3, 5.1.2
      changes pursuant to the initial application of an IFRS, Ch. 3, 5.1.2.A
      judgements made in applying accounting policies, Ch. 3, 5.1.1.B
      new IFRS, future impact of, Ch. 3, 5.1.2.C
      summary of significant accounting policies, Ch. 3, 5.1.1.A
      voluntary changes in accounting policy, Ch. 3, 5.1.2.B
   fair presentation, Ch. 3, 4.1.1
   general principles, Ch. 3, 4.1
   going concern, Ch. 3, 4.1.2
   interim financial reports, Ch. 41, 8.1
      measurement on a year-to-date basis, Ch. 41, 8.1.1
      new accounting pronouncements and other changes in accounting policies, Ch. 41, 8.1.2
      voluntary changes in presentation, Ch. 41, 8.1.3
   materiality, Ch. 3, 4.1.5.A
   offset, Ch. 3, 4.1.5.B
   Practice Statement 2, Ch. 3, 4.1.7
   profit or loss for the period, Ch. 3, 4.1.6
   selection of, Ch. 3, 4.3
Accounting Standards Advisory Forum (ASAF), Ch. 1, 2.8
Accounting Standards Board (AcSB), Ch. 1, 4.3.2
Accounting Standards Board of Japan (ASBJ), Ch. 1, 4.4.2
Accounting Standards Codification (ASC). *See under* ASC
Accounting Standards for Business Enterprises (ASBE), Ch. 1, 4.4.1.A
Accrual basis of accounting, Ch. 3, 4.1.3

Accrued operating lease income, Ch. 19, 6.6
   rental income and lease incentives, Ch. 19, 6.6.1
Acquired receivables, Ch. 49, 3.3.4; Ch. 54, 4.6.1
Acquirer's obligation to transfer proceeds from realisation of acquired contingent asset, Ch. 9, 5.6.4.A
Acquisition method of accounting, Ch. 9, 4. *See also* Business combinations; IFRS 3
   acquisition date determination, Ch. 9, 4.2
   business combinations under common control, application to, Ch. 10, 3.1–3.2
   identifying the acquirer, Ch. 9, 4.1
   'reverse acquisitions', Ch. 9, 4.1
Acquisition of cash flows, insurance contracts, Ch. 56, 8.2.3.E
Acquisition of insurance contracts, Ch. 56, 13
Acquisition-related costs, Ch. 9, 7.3; Ch. 40, 6.3.1
Active market, Ch. 14, 3, 8.1.1, 17; Ch. 20, 3.3
Active market identifying CGUs, Ch. 20, 3.3
Actuarial assumptions, Ch. 35, 7.5
Actuarial gains and losses, Ch. 35, 7.5
Actuarial methodology, Ch. 35, 7.3
Adjusting events, Ch. 38, 2.1.2
   determining value in use, Ch. 20, 7
   treatment of, Ch. 38, 2.2
Advisory bodies, Ch. 1, 2.9
   Accounting Standards Advisory Forum (ASAF), Ch. 1, 2.8
   Advisory Council, IFRS, Ch. 1, 2.7
   Capital Markets Advisory Committee, Ch. 1, 2.9
   Consultative Group for Rate Regulation, Ch. 1, 2.9
   Emerging Economies Group, Ch. 1, 2.9
   Global Preparers Forum, Ch. 1, 2.9
   IFRS Taxonomy Consultative Group, Ch. 1, 2.9
   Islamic Finance Consultative Group, Ch. 1, 2.9
   Management Commentary Consultative Group, Ch. 1, 2.9
   SME Implementation Group, Ch. 1, 2.9
   Transition Resource Group for IFRS 17 Insurance Contracts, Ch. 1, 2.9
   World Standard-setters Conferences, Ch. 1, 2.9
Agenda consultation 2011, Ch. 10, 6.1
Agenda consultation 2015, Ch. 10, 6.1; Ch. 43, 1.3.6, 8.4.1
Aggregated exposures, hedge accounting, Ch. 53, 2.7
Aggregation criteria, operating segments, Ch. 36, 1.3, 3.2.1

Index

Agriculture, Ch. 42, 1–5. *See also* IAS 41
'All employee' share plans, Ch. 34, 2.2.2.D
All-in-one hedges, hedge accounting, Ch. 53, 5.2.1
Americas, IFRS adoption in, Ch. 1, 4.3
Amortisation of intangible assets, Ch. 17, 9
 assessing the useful life of an intangible asset as finite/indefinite, Ch. 17, 9.1
  factors affecting the useful life, Ch. 17, 9.1.1
  useful life of contractual/other legal rights, Ch. 17, 9.1.2
 impairment losses, Ch. 17, 9.4; Ch. 20, 11
 intangible assets with a finite useful life, Ch. 17, 9.2
  amortisation period and method, Ch. 17, 9.2.1
   amortisation of programme and other broadcast rights, Ch. 17, 9.2.1.B
   amortising customer relationships and similar intangible assets, Ch. 17, 9.2.1.A
  residual value, Ch. 17, 9.2.4
  revenue-based amortisation, Ch. 17, 9.2.2
  review of amortisation period and amortisation method, Ch. 17, 9.2.3
 intangible assets with an indefinite useful life, Ch. 17, 9.3; Ch. 20, 10
 retirements and disposals, Ch. 17, 9.5
  derecognition of parts of intangible assets, Ch. 17, 9.5.1
Amortised cost, Ch. 50, 3; Ch. 51, 14.1
 financial assets measured at, Ch. 50, 2.1; Ch. 51, 14.1
 financial liabilities measured at, Ch. 50, 2.2
 transfers of assets measured at, Ch. 52, 5.4.2
Area-of-interest method, E&E expenditure, Ch. 43, 3.2.5
ASC 310–*Receivables*, Ch. 27, 3.5.1.C
ASC 405–*Liabilities*, Ch. 27, 3.5.1.B
ASC 460–*Guarantees*, Ch. 27, 3.5.1.B
ASC 718–*Compensation Stock Compensation*, Ch. 34, 1.1
ASC 815–*Derivatives and Hedging*, Ch. 27, 3.5.1.B
ASC 860–*Transfers and Servicing*, Ch. 27, 3.5.1.B
ASC 924–*Entertainment–Casinos*, Ch. 27, 3.5.1.F
ASC 958–605–*Not-for-Profit Entities–Revenue Recognition*, Ch. 27, 3.5.1.E
Asia, IFRS adoption in, Ch. 1, 4.4
Asset swap accounts, Ch. 43, 6.3
Associates. *See also* Equity method/accounting, IAS 28; Investments in associates and joint ventures
 cash flows of, Ch. 40, 6.4
 definition, Ch. 11, 3
 disclosure, Ch. 13, 5
  nature, extent and financial effects of interests in associates, Ch. 13, 5.1
  risks associated with interests in associates, Ch. 13, 5.2
 dividends from, Ch. 8, 2.4.1
 equity accounted associate or joint venture that is not a business becomes a subsidiary in an acquisition in stages, Ch. 7, 3.1.2
 first-time adoption
  assets and liabilities of, Ch. 5, 5.9
  investments in, Ch. 5, 5.8
 investments in, Ch. 11, 5.3; Ch. 20, 12.4
 loss of control – interest retained in former subsidiary is an associate, Ch. 7, 3.3.2, 7.1; Ch. 11, 7.4.1
 separate financial statements and interests in, Ch. 8, 1.1.1
 share-based payments to employee of, Ch. 34, 12.9
 significant influence, Ch. 11, 4
  fund managers, Ch. 11, 4.6
  holdings of less than 20% of the voting power, Ch. 11, 4.3
  lack of, Ch. 11, 4.2
  potential voting rights, Ch. 11, 4.4
  severe long-term restrictions impairing ability to transfer funds to the investor, Ch. 11, 4.1
  voting rights held in a fiduciary capacity, Ch. 11, 4.5
Assurance-type warranty, Ch. 31, 3.3
Australia, IFRS adoption in, Ch. 1, 4.5
Australian Accounting Standards (AAS), Ch. 1, 4.5
'Back-to-back' forward contracts, Ch. 47, 11.1.3
Balance sheet. *See* Statement of financial position
Bank overdrafts, Ch. 40, 3.2.4
Barter transactions, Ch. 29, 2.6.2
Basel Committee on Banking Supervision, Ch. 1, 2.5
'Basic' sensitivity analysis, Ch. 54, 5.5.1
Bearer plants, Ch. 18, 3.1.7; Ch. 42, 2.3.3
 definition, Ch. 18, 2.2; Ch. 42, 2.2.1.A
 requirements for produce growing on, Ch. 42, 3.2.3
 in scope of IAS 16, Ch. 18, 2.1; Ch. 42, 3.2.3.A
Bid-ask spread, Ch. 14, 15.3.2
Binomial model, Ch. 34, 8.3.2
Biological assets, Ch. 42, 2.3.1. *See also* IAS 41–*Agriculture*
 definition of, Ch. 42, 2.2.1
 disclosure of groups of, Ch. 42, 5.1.3
 fair value measurement, Ch. 42, 4.5.2, 4.6.2.A
 leases of, Ch. 42, 2.3.5
 measurement, Ch. 42, 3.2.1
Black economic empowerment (BEE) and share-based payment, Ch. 34, 15.5
Black-Scholes-Merton formula, Ch. 34, 8.3.1
Block caving, depreciation, depletion and amortisation (mining), Ch. 43, 16.2
Bonds. *See* Convertible bonds
Borrowing costs, Ch. 21. *See also* Capitalisation of borrowing costs; IAS 23
 definition of, Ch. 21, 4
 eligible for capitalisation, Ch. 17, 6.3.2; Ch. 21, 5
  accrued costs and trade payables, Ch. 21, 5.3.3
  calculation of capitalisation rate, Ch. 21, 5.3.2
  directly attributable, Ch. 21, 5.1
  exchange differences as, Ch. 21, 5.4
  general borrowings, Ch. 21, 5.3
   completed qualifying assets, related to, Ch. 21, 5.3.1.A
   specific non-qualifying assets, related to, Ch. 21, 5.3.1.B
  group considerations, Ch. 21, 5.7
  hyperinflationary economies, Ch. 21, 5.6
  specific borrowings, Ch. 21, 5.2
 intangible assets, Ch. 17, 4.2
 interim reporting, Ch. 41, 9.1.4
 inventory, Ch. 22, 3.1.3C
 investment property, Ch. 19, 4.8
 on 'land expenditures', Ch. 21, 6.3.1
 other finance costs as, Ch. 21, 4.2, 5.5
 property, plant and equipment, Ch. 18, 4.1.2

Branches, foreign exchange, Ch. 15, 4.4
Brazil, IFRS adoption in, Ch. 1, 4.3.3
Broadcast rights, intangible assets amortisation of, Ch. 17, 9.2.1.B
Business Advisory Council (BAC), Ch. 1, 4.4.2
Business combination exemption (first-time adoption), Ch. 5, 5.2
  associates and joint arrangements, Ch. 5, 5.2, 5.2.2.A
  classification of business combinations, Ch. 5, 5.2.3
  currency adjustments to goodwill, Ch. 5, 5.2.6
  goodwill previously deducted from equity, Ch. 5, 5.2.5.C
  goodwill, restatement of, Ch. 5, 5.2.5
  measurement of deferred taxes and non-controlling interests, Ch. 5, 5.2.9
  option to restate business combinations retrospectively, Ch. 5, 5.2.2
  previously consolidated entities that are not subsidiaries, Ch. 5, 5.2.8
  previously unconsolidated subsidiaries, Ch. 5, 5.2.7
  recognition of assets and liabilities, Ch. 5, 5.2.4
  subsequent measurement under IFRSs not based on cost, Ch. 5, 5.2.4.E
Business combinations, Ch. 9, 1–16. *See also* Common control business combinations; IFRS 3; Income taxes
  achieved in stages (step acquisitions), Ch. 9, 9
  accounting for previously held interests in a joint operation, Ch. 9, 9.1
  achieved without the transfer of consideration, Ch. 9, 7.4
  acquired receivables, Ch. 54, 4.6
  acquirer and a vendor in, contracts between, Ch. 44, 3.7.2
  acquirer, identifying the, Ch. 9, 4.1
  acquirer, new entity formed to effect business combination, Ch. 9, 4.1.1
  acquirer that is not a legal entity, Ch. 9, 4.1
  acquisition method of accounting, Ch. 9, 4
    determining the acquisition date, Ch. 9, 4.2
    identifying the acquirer, Ch. 9, 4.1
  acquisition of intangible assets in, Ch. 17, 5
    customer relationship intangible assets, Ch. 17, 5.4
    in-process research and development, Ch. 17, 5.5
    intangible assets acquired, examples, Ch. 17, 5.2
    measuring the fair value of intangible assets, Ch. 17, 5.3
    recognition of intangible assets, Ch. 17, 5.1
  acquisition related costs, Ch. 9, 7.3
    presentation in statement of cash flows, Ch. 40. 6.3.1
  acquisitions of investment property in or a, Ch. 19, 3.3
  apparent immediate impairment of goodwill created by deferred tax, Ch. 33, 12.3
  assessing whether acquired process is substantive, Ch. 9, 3.2.4
    bargain purchase transactions, Ch. 9, 10
    recognising and measuring goodwill or a gain in, Ch. 9, 6
  'business' under IFRSs, definition of, Ch. 9, 3.2; Ch. 19, 3.3.1
    assessment whether acquired set of activities and assets constitutes a, Ch. 9, 3.2.2
    'capable of' from the viewpoint of a market participant, Ch. 9, 3.2.5
  common control, Ch. 10, 1–6; Ch. 56, 13.3
  concentration test, Ch. 9, 3.2.3
  consideration transferred, Ch. 9, 7
  contingent consideration, Ch. 9, 7.1
    cash flows, Ch. 40. 6.3.3
    and indemnification assets, Ch. 54, 4.6.2
    payable by an acquirer, Ch. 45, 3.7.1.A
    receivable by a vendor, Ch. 45, 3.7.1.B
  contingent liabilities recognised in a business combination, Ch. 9, 5.6.1
    changes in, Ch. 26, 4.10
  by contract alone, Ch. 9, 7.4.1
  contracts between acquirer and vendor, Ch. 45, 3.7.2
  customer relationship intangible assets acquired in, Ch. 17, 5.4
  deferred taxes, Ch. 33, 6.2.1.E, 6.2.2.E,
    arising on a business combination, Ch. 33, 12.1.2
      assets of the acquiree, Ch. 33, 12.1.2.B
      assets of the acquirer, Ch. 33, 12.1.2.A
  development stage entities, Ch. 9, 3.2.7
  disclosures, Ch. 9, 16
    combinations during current reporting period, Ch. 9, 16.1.1
    combinations effected after the end of reporting period, Ch. 9, 16.1.2
    financial effects of adjustments, Ch. 9, 16.2
    nature and financial effect, Ch. 9, 16.1
  exceptions to recognition and/or measurement principles, Ch. 9, 5.6
    assets held for sale, Ch. 9, 5.6.6
    contingent liabilities, Ch. 9, 5.6.1
    employee benefits, Ch. 9, 5.6.3
    income taxes, Ch. 9, 5.6.2
    indemnification assets, Ch. 9, 5.6.4
    insurance contracts within the scope of IFRS 17, Ch. 9, 5.6.9
    leases in which the acquiree is a lessee, Ch. 9, 5.6.8
    reacquired rights, Ch. 9, 5.6.5
    share-based payment transactions, Ch. 9, 5.6.7
  fair value of intangible assets acquired in, measuring, Ch. 17, 5.3
  goodwill, Ch. 9, 6
  identifying a, Ch. 9, 3.1
  identifying the acquirer, Ch. 9, 4.1
  in-process research and development (IPR&D) acquired in, Ch. 17, 5.5
  insurance contracts acquired in, Ch. 55, 9
  intangible assets acquired in, recognition of
    identifiability in relation to an intangible asset, Ch. 17, 5.1.3
      contractual-legal rights, Ch. 17, 5.1.3.A
      separability, Ch. 17, 5.1.3.B
    probable inflow of benefits, Ch. 17, 5.1.1
    reliability of measurement, Ch. 17, 5.1.2
  involving a Newco, Ch. 9, 4.1.1; Ch. 10, 4
  involving mutual entities, Ch. 9, 7.5
  leases, Ch. 23, 9
  loans and receivables acquired in, Ch. 49, 3.3.4
  measurement and recognition of deferred tax in, Ch. 33, 12.1
    deferred tax assets arising on a business combination, Ch. 33, 12.1.2
    deferred tax liabilities of acquired entity, Ch. 33, 12.1.3
    manner of recovery of assets and settlement of liabilities, determining, Ch. 33, 12.1.1
      changes in tax base consequent on the business combination, Ch. 33, 12.1.1.A

Business combinations—*contd*
   measurement period, Ch. 9, 12
   non-controlling interest as part of a business combination under common control, Ch. 10, 3.3.5
   non-controlling interests, measurement in, Ch. 7, 3.2, 3.1.1, 3.1.2, 5.2, 5.3
   pre-existing relationships, Ch. 9, 11.1
   process, Ch. 9, 3.2.1
   push down accounting, Ch. 9, 15
   recognition and measurement of assets acquired, liabilities assumed and non-controlling interests, Ch. 9, 5
      assembled workforce, Ch. 9, 5.5.4.A
      assets and liabilities related to contacts with customers, Ch. 9, 5.5.8
      assets with uncertain cash flows, Ch. 9, 5.5.5
      equity-accounted entities, investments in, Ch. 9, 5.5.7
      future contract renewals, Ch. 9, 5.5.4.B
      items not qualifying as assets, Ch. 9, 5.5.4.B
      liabilities assumed, Ch. 9, 5
      non-controlling interests, Ch. 9, 5.1, 7.2, 7.4.1
      reacquired rights, Ch. 9, 5.5.3
   replacement share-based payment awards in, Ch. 9, 7.2; Ch. 34, 11
   reverse acquisitions, Ch. 9, 14, 14.8, 14.9
   spin-off transaction, Ch. 9, 4.1.1
   stapling arrangements, Ch. 9, 4.1.2
   subsequent measurement and accounting, Ch. 9, 13
   tax deductions for acquisition costs, Ch. 33, 12.4
   tax deductions for replacement share-based payment awards in a business combination, Ch. 33, 12.2
   temporary differences arising from the acquisition of a group of assets that is not a business, Ch. 33, 12.5
Business combinations under common control' (BCUCC) research project
   accounting methods and disclosures, Ch. 10, 6.2
   background and scope, Ch. 10, 6.1
   next steps, Ch. 10, 6.3
'Business model' assessment, financial assets, Ch. 48, 5
   anticipated capital expenditure, Ch. 48, 5.6
   applying in practice, Ch. 48, 5.6
   credit-impaired financial assets in a hold to collect business model, Ch. 48, 5.6
   credit risk management activities, Ch. 48, 5.6
   hedging activities in a hold to collect business model, Ch. 48, 5.6
   hold to collect contractual cash flows, Ch. 48, 5.2
   hold to collect contractual cash flows and selling financial assets, Ch. 48, 5.3
   impact of sales on the assessment, Ch. 48, 5.2.1
   level at which the business model assessment should be applied, Ch. 48, 5.1
   liquidity portfolio for every day liquidity needs, Ch. 48, 5.6
   liquidity portfolio for stress case scenarios, Ch. 48, 5.6
   loans that are to be sub-participated, Ch. 48, 5.6
   opportunistic portfolio management, Ch. 48, 5.6
   other business models, Ch. 48, 5.4
   portfolio managed on a fair value basis, Ch. 48, 5.6
   replication portfolios, Ch. 48, 5.6
   sales to manage concentration risk, Ch. 48, 5.6
   securitisation, Ch. 48, 5.6
   splitting portfolios, Ch. 48, 5.6
   subsidiary that is held for sale, Ch. 48, 5.5
   transferred financial assets that are not derecognised, Ch. 48, 5.2.2
Buying reinsurance, gains/losses on, Ch. 55, 7.2.6.C
By-products, extractive industries, Ch. 43, 12.6, 14.2.1, 16.1.3.D
Call options, Ch. 7, 6.1, 6.3, 6.4, 6.5; Ch. 34, 8.2.1; Ch. 47, 11.2
   over non-controlling interests, Ch. 7, 6.1, 6.3, 6.4, 6.5; Ch. 9, 8.5
      call and put options entered into in relation to existing non-controlling interests, Ch. 7, 6.4
      call options only, Ch. 7, 6.1
      combination of call and put options, Ch. 7, 6.3
      separate financial statements, Ch. 7, 6.5
   purchased call option, Ch. 47, 11.2.1
   share-based payment, Ch. 34, 8.2.1
      intrinsic value and time value, Ch. 34, 8.2.2
   written call option, Ch. 47, 11.2.2
Canada, IFRS adoption in, Ch. 1, 4.3.2
Capital commitments, Ch. 41, 4.3.4
Capital, disclosures about, Ch. 3, 5.4; Ch. 54, 5.6.3
   general capital disclosures, Ch. 3, 5.4.1
   puttable financial instruments classified as equity, Ch. 3, 5.4.2
Capital Markets Advisory Committee, Ch. 1, 2.9
Capitalisation of borrowing costs, Ch. 21, 1–7. *See also* IAS 23
   cessation of capitalisation, Ch. 21, 6.3
      borrowing costs on 'land expenditures', Ch. 21, 6.3.1
   commencement, Ch. 21, 6.1
      expenditures on a qualifying asset, Ch. 21, 6.1.1
   disclosure requirements, Ch. 21, 7
   group considerations, Ch. 21, 5.7
      borrowings in one company and development in another, Ch. 21, 5.7.1
      qualifying assets held by joint arrangements, Ch. 21, 5.7.2
   in hyperinflationary economies, Ch. 21, 5.6
   interim financial reporting, Ch. 41, 9.1.4
   suspension of, Ch. 21, 6.2
      impairment considerations, Ch. 21, 6.2.1
Carried interests/party, extractive industries, Ch. 43, 6.1
   in E&E phase, Ch. 43, 6.1.2
   financing-type, Ch. 43, 6.1.3
   purchase/sale-type, Ch. 43, 6.1.4
Carve-out financial statements. *See* Combined financial statements
Cash and cash equivalents, Ch. 40, 3. *See also* IAS 7
   components of, Ch. 40, 3.2
      bank overdrafts, Ch. 40, 3.2.4
      client money, Ch. 40, 3.2.6
      cryptocurrencies, Ch. 40, 3.2.5
      demand deposits, Ch. 40, 3.2.1
      investments with maturities greater than three months, Ch. 40, 3.2.3
      money market funds (MMF), Ch. 40, 3.2.2
      short-term investments, Ch. 40, 3.2.1
   restrictions on the use of, Ch. 40, 3.4
   statement of financial position items, reconciliation with, Ch. 40, 3.3
Cash flow hedges, Ch. 53, 1.5, 5.2, 7.2; Ch. 54, 4.3.3
   acquisition or disposal of subsidiaries, Ch. 53, 7.2.4

acquisitions, Ch. 53, 7.2.4
all-in-one hedges, Ch. 53, 5.2.1
discontinuation, Ch. 53, 8.3
of firm commitments, Ch. 53, 5.2.2
of foreign currency monetary items, Ch. 53, 5.2.3
hypothetical derivatives, Ch. 53, 7.4.4
leased assets, CGU identification, Ch. 20, 3.2
measuring ineffectiveness, Ch. 53, 7.4.6
of a net position, Ch. 53, 2.5.3
presentation, Ch. 53, 10.1
reclassification of gains and losses, Ch. 53, 7.2.2

Cash-generating units (CGUs). *See also* Impairment of assets; Value in use (VIU)
active markets, identifying, Ch. 20, 3.2
carrying amount of, identifying, Ch. 20, 4
dividing the entity into, Ch. 20, 3
estimating the future pre-tax cash flows of, Ch. 20, 7.1
and goodwill impairment, Ch. 20, 8
impairment losses, Ch. 20, 11.2
leased assets and CGUs, Ch. 20, 3.2
reversal of impairments, Ch. 20, 11.4

Cash-settled share-based payment transaction, Ch. 34, 9; Ch. 36, 2.2.1. *See also* Equity-settled share-based payment transaction; IFRS 2; Share-based payment transactions
accounting treatment, Ch. 34, 9.3
application of the accounting treatment, Ch. 34, 9.3.2
market conditions and non-vesting conditions, Ch. 34, 9.3.2.D
modification, cancellation and settlement, Ch. 34, 9.3.2.E
non-market vesting conditions, Ch. 34, 9.3.2.C
periodic allocation of cost, Ch. 34, 9.3.2.B
vesting period determination, Ch. 34, 9.3.2.A
basic accounting treatment, Ch. 34, 9.3.1
modification to or from equity-settlement, Ch. 34, 9.4
cash-settled award modified to equity-settled award, Ch. 34, 9.4.2
equity-settled award modified to cash-settled award, Ch. 34, 9.4.1
scope of requirements, Ch. 34, 9.1
transactions with equity and cash alternatives, Ch. 34, 10.1, 10.2, 10.3
what constitutes a cash-settled award?, Ch. 34, 9.2
arrangements to sell employees' shares including 'broker settlement,' Ch. 34, 9.2.4
economic compulsion for cash settlement (including unlisted company schemes), Ch. 34, 10.2.1.A
formal and informal arrangements for the entity to purchase illiquid shares or otherwise settle in cash, Ch. 34, 9.2.1
market purchases of own equity following equity-settlement of award, Ch. 34, 9.2.3
market purchases of own equity to satisfy awards, Ch. 34, 9.2.2

Catastrophe provisions, Ch. 55, 7.2.1
CCIRS. *See* Cross-currency interest rate swaps (CCIRS)
CCP. *See* Central clearing party (CCP)
Cedant, Ch. 55, 2.2.1
Chief operating decision maker (CODM), Ch. 36, 1.3, 3.1
China Accounting Standards Committee (CASC), Ch. 1, 4.4.1.A

China, IFRS adoption in, Ch. 1, 4.4.1
Clawback conditions, share-based payment, Ch. 34, 3.1.1
Clean-up call options, Ch. 52, 4.2.7
Client money, Ch. 40, 3.2.6; Ch. 52, 3.7
'Closely related,' meaning of, Ch. 46, 5
Cloud computing, Ch. 17, 11.6
implementation costs, Ch. 17, 11.6.2
'software as a service' cloud computing arrangements, Ch. 17, 11.6.1
'Collar' put and call options, Ch. 52, 5.4.3.C
Collateral, Ch. 51, 5.8.1; Ch. 52, 5.5.2
Collectability, revenue IFRS 15, Ch. 28, 2.1.6
assessing for a portfolio of contracts, Ch. 28, 2.1.6.A
determining when to reassess, Ch. 28, 2.1.6.B
Combined financial statements, Ch. 6, 2.2.6
common control, Ch. 6, 2.2.6.A
preparation of, Ch. 6, 2.2.6.C
purpose and users, Ch. 6, 2.2.6.B
reporting entity in, Ch. 6, 1.1; Ch. 6, 2.2.6.B; Ch. 6, 2.2.6.C; Ch. 6, 2.2.6.E
'special- purpose' vs 'general- purpose', Ch. 6, 2.2.6.D
Comissão de Valores Mobiliários (CVM), Ch. 1, 2.3, 4.3.3
Commencement of lease, Ch. 23, 4.2
Committee for Mineral Reserves International Reporting Standards (CRIRSCO), Ch. 43, 1.3
International Reporting Template, Ch. 43, 2.3.1
reporting terminology, Ch. 43, 2.3.1.B
scope, Ch. 43, 2.3.1.A
Commodity-based contracts, extractive industries
allocate the transaction price, Ch. 43, 12.15.4
definition of commodity contract, Ch. 43, 12.6.1
fixed consideration, Ch. 43, 12.15.4.B
forward-selling to finance development, Ch. 43, 12.6
modifications to, Ch. 43, 12.10
multi-period, Ch. 43, 12.15
normal purchase and sales exemption, Ch. 43, 13.1
principal *vs.* agent considerations in, Ch. 43, 12.11
revenue recognition, Ch. 43, 12.15.5
take-or-pay contracts, Ch. 43, 12.16, 17.2
trading activities, Ch. 43, 12.7
Commodity broker-traders, Ch. 45, 4.2.2
Commodity, equity-linked interest and principal payments, Ch. 46, 5.1.7
Commodity price assumptions, Ch. 43, 11.4.3, 11.5.2
Common control business combinations, Ch. 10, 1–6
accounting for, Ch. 10, 3
application of the acquisition method under IFRS 3, Ch. 10, 3.2
application of the pooling of interests method, Ch. 10, 3.3
acquisition of non-controlling interest as part of a business combination under common control, Ch. 10, 3.3.5
carrying amounts of assets and liabilities, Ch. 10, 3.3.2
equity reserves and history of assets and liabilities carried over, Ch. 10, 3.3.4
general requirements, Ch. 10, 3.3.1
restatement of financial information for periods prior to the date of the combination, Ch. 10, 3.3.3

Common control business combinations—*contd*
  accounting for—*contd*
    pooling of interests method versus acquisition method, Ch. 10, 3.1
  accounting for transactions under common control (or ownership) involving a Newco, Ch. 10, 4
    inserting a new intermediate parent within an existing group, Ch. 10, 4.3
    setting up a new top holding company, Ch. 10, 4.2
      transactions effected through issuing equity interests, Ch. 10, 4.2.1
      transactions involving consideration other than equity interests, Ch. 10, 4.2.2
    transferring businesses outside an existing group using a Newco, Ch. 10, 4.4
  accounting for transfers of associates/joint ventures under common control, Ch. 10, 5
  future developments, Ch. 10, 6
    BCUCC research project
      accounting methods and disclosures, Ch. 10, 6.2
      background and scope, Ch. 10, 6.1
      next steps, Ch. 10, 6.3
  group reorganisations, Ch. 10, 1.2
  IFRS 3 scope exclusion, Ch. 10, 2
    common control by an individual/group of individuals, Ch. 10, 2.1.1
    transitory control, Ch. 10, 2.1.2
  scope of chapter, Ch. 10, 1.3

Common control/group transactions, individual financial statements, Ch. 8, 4. *See also* Group reorganisations
  application of the principles in practice, Ch. 8, 4.4
    acquiring and selling businesses–transfers between subsidiaries, Ch. 8, 4.4.2
      accounting for a business that has been acquired, Ch. 8, 4.4.2.B
      accounting for transactions if net assets are not a business, Ch. 8, 4.4.2.D
      purchase and sale of a business for cash/equity not representative of fair value of business, Ch. 8, 4.4.2.C
    financial instruments within the scope of IFRS 9 (or IAS 39), Ch. 8, 4.4.5
      financial guarantee contracts, parent guarantee issued on behalf of subsidiary, Ch. 8, 4.4.5.B
      interest-free or non-market interest rate loans, Ch. 8, 4.4.5.A
    incurring expenses and settling liabilities without recharges, Ch. 8, 4.4.4
    transactions involving non-monetary assets, Ch. 8, 4.4.1
      acquisition of assets for shares, Ch. 8, 4.4.1.C
      contribution and distribution of assets, Ch. 8, 4.4.1.D
      parent exchanges PP&E for a non-monetary asset of the subsidiary, Ch. 8, 4.4.1.B
      sale of PP&E from parent to subsidiary for an amount of cash not representative of fair value of asset, Ch. 8, 4.4.1.A
      transfers between subsidiaries, Ch. 8, 4.4.1.E
    transfers of businesses between parent and subsidiary, Ch. 8, 4.4.3
      distributions of businesses without consideration, Ch. 8, 4.4.3.A
      legal merger of parent and subsidiary, Ch. 8, 4.4.3.B
      subsidiary as a surviving entity, Ch. 8, 4.4.3.B
  cost of investments acquired in, Ch. 8, 2.1.1.B
  disclosures, Ch. 8, 4.5
  measurement, Ch. 8, 4.3
    fair value in intra-group transactions, Ch. 8, 4.3.1
  recognition, Ch. 8, 4.2

Comparative information, Ch. 3, 2.4; Ch. 4, 4; Ch. 5, 6.1
  interim financial statements, Ch. 41, 5.1
  treatment on cessation of classification as held for sale, Ch. 4, 4.2
  treatment on initial classification as held for sale statement of comprehensive income, Ch. 4, 4.1.1

Compensation, related-party disclosures, Ch. 39. 2.6.1

Compound financial instruments, Ch. 47, 6
  background, Ch. 47, 6.1
  common forms of convertible bonds, Ch. 47, 6.6
    bond convertible into fixed percentage of equity, Ch. 47, 6.6.6
    contingent convertible bond, Ch. 47, 6.6.2
    convertible bonds with down round or ratchet features, Ch. 47, 6.6.7
    convertibles with cash settlement at the option of the issuer, Ch. 47, 6.6.5
    foreign currency convertible bond, Ch. 47, 6.6.4
    functional currency bond convertible into a fixed number of shares, Ch. 47, 6.6.1
    mandatorily convertible bond, Ch. 47, 6.6.3
  components of a compound instrument, Ch. 47, 6.4
    compound instruments with embedded derivatives, Ch. 47, 6.4.2
      issuer call option-'closely related' embedded derivatives, Ch. 47, 6.4.2.A
    determining, Ch. 47, 6.4.1
  conversion at maturity, Ch. 47, 6.3.1
    before maturity, Ch. 47, 6.3.2
      accounting treatment, Ch. 47, 6.3.2.B
      embedded derivatives, Ch. 47, 6.3.2.C
      'fixed stated principal' of a bond, Ch. 47, 6.3.2.A
  deferred tax, initial recognition exception, Ch. 33, 7.2.8
  early redemption/repurchase, Ch. 47, 6.3.3
    through exercising an embedded call option, Ch. 47, 6.3.3.B
    through negotiation with bondholders, Ch. 47, 6.3.3.A
  modification, Ch. 47, 6.3.4
  with multiple embedded derivatives, statement of financial position, Ch. 54, 4.4.7
  'split accounting', Ch. 47, 6.2
    initial recognition of a compound instrument, Ch. 47, 6.2
      accounting for the equity component, Ch. 47, 6.2.1
      temporary differences arising from, Ch. 47, 6.2.2
  treatment by holder and issuer contrasted, Ch. 47, 6.1.1

Comprehensive income, Ch. 3, 3.2

Comprehensive income statement. *See* Statement of comprehensive income

Concentration test, Ch. 9, 3.2.3

Concentrations of risk, Ch. 54, 5.6.1; Ch. 55, 11.2.4

Conceptual Framework for Financial Reporting 2010, Ch. 2, 2

Conceptual framework, IASB's, Ch. 1, 2.5; Ch. 2, 1–12. *See also* General purpose financial reporting
  contents, Ch. 2, 3.1
  derecognition, Ch. 2, 8.3
  development, Ch. 2, 2
  discussion paper on, Ch. 2, 1
  effective date, Ch. 2, 2
  enhancing qualitative characteristics, Ch. 2, 5.2
    applying, Ch. 2, 5.2.5
    comparability, Ch. 2, 5.2.1
    timeliness, Ch. 2, 5.2.3
    understandability, Ch. 2, 5.2.4
    verifiability, Ch. 2, 5.2.2
  financial capital maintenance, Ch. 2.11.1
  financial statements, Ch. 2.6.1
    assets, Ch. 2.7.2
    consolidated and unconsolidated, Ch. 2.6.2.1
    elements, Ch. 2.7
    equity, Ch. 2.7.4
    executory contracts, Ch. 2.7.1.2
    going concern assumption, Ch. 2.6.1.4
    income and expenses, Ch. 2.7.5
    liabilities, Ch. 2.7.3
    objective and scope, Ch. 2.6.1.1
    perspective adopted in financial statements, Ch. 2.6.1.3
    reporting period and comparative information, Ch. 2.6.1.2
    substance of contractual rights and contractual obligations, Ch. 2.7.1.3
    unit of account, Ch. 2.7.1.1
  fundamental qualitative characteristics, Ch. 2, 5.1
    applying, Ch. 2, 5.1.3
    cost constraint, Ch. 2, 5.3
    faithful representation, Ch. 2, 5.1.2
    relevance (including materiality), Ch. 2, 5.1.1
  general purpose financial reporting, Ch. 2, 4
    economic resources, Ch. 2, 4.2.1
    limitations, Ch. 2, 4.1.2
    objective and usefulness, Ch. 2, 4.1.1
  management commentary, Ch. 2, 12
  measurement, Ch. 2, 9
    bases, Ch. 2, 9.1
    cash-flow-based measurement techniques, Ch. 2, 9.5
    equity, Ch. 2, 9.4
    factors to consider in selecting measurement bases, Ch. 2, 9.3
    information provided by different measurement bases, Ch. 2, 9.2
  physical capital maintenance, Ch. 2, 11.2
  political and economic environment influences, Ch. 2, 1.2
  presentation and disclosure, Ch. 2, 10
    aggregation, Ch. 2, 10.3
    classification, Ch. 2, 10.2
    objectives and principles, Ch. 2, 10.1
  purpose, Ch. 2, 3.2
  recognition criteria, Ch. 2, 8.2
    faithful representation, Ch. 2, 8.2.2
    relevance, Ch. 2, 8.2.1
  recognition process, Ch. 2, 8.1
  reporting entity, Ch. 2, 6.2
  scope, Ch. 2, 3
  standard settings, Ch. 2, 1.2
  status, Ch. 2, 3.2
  useful financial information, qualitative characteristics of, Ch. 2, 5

Concession agreements. *See* Service concession arrangements (SCA)
  mineral reserves and resources, Ch. 43, 2

Concessionary agreements (concessions), extractive industries, Ch. 43, 5.2

Condensed interim financial statements, Ch. 41, 3.2. *See also under* IAS 34
  disclosures in, Ch. 41, 4
    accounting policies and methods of computation, Ch. 41, 4.3.11
    amounts that are unusual because of their nature, size or incidence, Ch. 41, 4.3.13
    capital commitments, Ch. 41, 4.3.4
    changes in circumstances affecting fair values, Ch. 41, 4.3.6
    changes in composition of the entity, Ch. 41, 4.3.17
    compliance with IFRS, Ch. 41, 4.6
    contingent liabilities, Ch. 41, 4.3.10
    debt and equity securities, Ch. 41, 4.3.14
    default or breach of loan covenants not remedied before end of interim period, Ch. 41, 4.3.7
    dividends paid Ch. 41, 4.3.15
    events after the interim reporting date, Ch. 41, 4.3.16
    fair value disclosures, Ch. 41, 4.5
    fair value hierarchy levels, transfers between, Ch. 41, 4.3.9
    inventory write-down and reversals, Ch. 41, 4.3.1
    litigation settlements, Ch. 41, 4.3.5
    PP&E, acquisition and disposal of, Ch. 41, 4.3.3
    recognition and reversal of impairment losses, Ch. 41, 4.3.2
    related party transactions, Ch. 41, 4.3.8
    seasonality or cyclicality of operations, Ch. 41, 4.3.12
    segment information, Ch. 41, 4.4
    significant events and transactions, Ch. 41, 4.1
    transfers between different levels of fair value hierarchy, , Ch. 41, 4.3.9
  first-time presentation, Ch. 41, 11.1
  requirements for interim financial information, Ch. 41, 3.3

Consideration transferred, Ch. 9, 7. *See also* Contingent consideration
  acquisition-related costs, Ch. 9, 7.3

Consignment stock and sale and repurchase agreements, Ch. 22, 2.3.1F

Consistency in application of IFRS, Ch. 1, 5

Consistent accounting policies, Ch. 7, 2.6; Ch. 11, 7.8. *See also* Financial statements, presentation of; IAS 1

Consolidated financial statements, Ch. 6, 1–11; Ch. 8, 1.1. *See also* consolidation procedures, IFRS 10
  continuous assessment, Ch. 6, 9
  control, Ch. 6, 3
  control of specified assets, Ch. 6, 8
  employee benefit trusts, Ch. 6, 2.2.2; Ch. 34, 12.3, 12.4.1, 12.5.1
  entity no longer a parent at the end of reporting period, Ch. 6, 2.2.4
  exemption from preparing
    consent of non-controlling shareholders, Ch. 6, 2.2.1.A

Consolidated financial statements—*contd*
   exemption from preparing—*contd*
      not filing financial statements for listing securities, Ch. 6, 2.2.1.C
      parent's IFRS financial statements are publicly available, Ch. 6, 2.2.1.D
      securities not traded in a public market, Ch. 6, 2.2.1.B
   exposure to variable returns, Ch. 6, 5
   future developments, Ch. 6, 11
   investment entities, Ch. 6, 10
   power over an investee, Ch. 6, 4
   principal-agency situations, Ch. 6, 6
   related parties and *de facto* agents, Ch. 6, 7

Consolidated statement of cash flows, preparing, Ch. 40, 6.1

Consolidation procedures, Ch. 7. *See also* non-controlling interests
   basic principles, Ch. 7, 2.1
   changes in control, Ch. 7, 3
      accounting for a loss of control Ch. 7, 3.2
      deemed disposal, Ch. 7, 3.6
      demergers and distributions of non-cash assets to owners, Ch. 7, 3.7, Ch. 8, 2.4.2. *See also* IFRIC 17
      interest retained in the former subsidiary, Ch. 7, 3.3
         associate or joint venture, Ch. 7, 3.3.2, 7.1
         financial asset, Ch. 7, 3.3.1
         joint operation, Ch. 7, 3.3.3, 7.2
         Interpretations Committee and IASB discussions about the sale of a single asset entity containing real estate, Ch. 7.3.2.1
      loss of control in multiple arrangements, Ch. 7, 3.4
      other comprehensive income, Ch. 7, 3.5
   changes in ownership interest without a loss of control, Ch. 7, 4
      contingent consideration on purchase of a noncontrolling interest, Ch. 7, 4.5
      goodwill attributable to non-controlling interests, Ch. 7, 4.2; Ch. 20, 9
      non-cash acquisition of non-controlling interests, Ch. 7, 4.3
      reattribution of other comprehensive income, Ch. 7, 4.1
      transaction costs, Ch. 7, 4.4
   commencement and cessation of consolidation, Ch. 7, 3.1
      acquisition in stages: associate or joint venture that is not a business becomes a subsidiary, Ch. 7, 3.1.2
      acquisition of a subsidiary that is not a business, Ch. 7, 3.1.1
      demergers and distributions of non-cash assets to owners, Ch. 7, 3.7
         presentation and disclosure, Ch. 7, 3.7.3
         recognition and measurement in IFRIC 17, Ch. 7, 3.7.2
         scope of IFRIC 17, Ch. 7, 3.7.1
   consistent accounting policies, Ch. 7, 2.6
   consolidating foreign operations, Ch. 7, 2.3
   intragroup eliminations, Ch. 7, 2.4
   non-coterminous accounting periods, Ch. 7, 2.5
   proportion consolidated, Ch. 7, 2.2, 5.6

Constructive obligation, Ch. 26, 3.1
   employee benefits, Ch. 37, 7.1
   provisions, Ch. 26, 3.1

Consultative Group for Rate Regulation, Ch. 1, 2.9

Contingent assets, Ch. 26, 3.2.2
   definition, Ch. 26, 3.2.2
   disclosure of, Ch. 26, 7.3
   relating to business combinations, Ch. 9, 5.5.4.B

Contingent consideration, Ch. 7, 4.5; Ch. 9, 7.1
   cash flows in business combinations, Ch. 40, 6.3.3.A
      payable by an acquirer, Ch. 45, 3.7.1.A
      receivable by a vendor, Ch. 45, 3.7.1.B
   initial recognition and measurement, Ch. 9, 7.1.1
   intangible assets acquired for, Ch. 17, 4.5
   on loss of control of a subsidiary, Ch. 7.3.2
   obligation, classification, Ch. 9, 7.1.2
   on purchase of non-controlling interest, Ch. 7, 4.5
   subsequent measurement and accounting, Ch. 9, 7.1.3

Contingent convertible bond, Ch. 47, 6.6.2

Contingent costs, investment property, Ch. 19, 4.10

Contingent liabilities, Ch. 26, 3.2.1
   business combinations, Ch. 9, 5.6.1
   definition, Ch. 26, 3.2.1
   disclosure of, Ch. 26, 7.2
   joint ventures and associates, Ch. 13, 5.2.2

Contingent resources, extractive industries, Ch. 43, 2.2.1

Contingent settlement provisions, Ch. 47, 4.3
   contingencies that are 'not genuine,' Ch. 47, 4.3.1
   liabilities that arise only on a change of control, Ch. 47, 4.3.3
   liabilities that arise only on liquidation, Ch. 47, 4.3.2
   some typical contingent settlement provisions, Ch. 47, 4.3.4

Contingently issuable shares (EPS), Ch. 37, 6.4.6
   earnings-based contingencies, Ch. 37, 6.4.6.A
   share-price-based contingencies, Ch. 37, 6.4.6.B

Continuous assessment of control, Ch. 6, 9; Ch. 12, 8
   bankruptcy filings, Ch. 6, 9.2
   changes in market conditions, Ch. 6, 9.1
   control re-assessment, Ch. 6, 9.3
   joint arrangements, Ch. 12, 8
   troubled debt restructurings, Ch. 6, 9.2

Contract asset, Ch. 32, 2.1
   presentation requirements for, Ch. 32, 2.1

Contract costs, Ch. 31, 5
   amortisation of capitalised costs, Ch. 31, 5.3
      classification and presentation of capitalised contract costs and related amortisation, Ch. 31, 5.3.6
   costs to fulfil a contract, Ch. 31, 5.2
      assets recognised from, Ch. 32, 3.2.3
   costs to obtain a contract, Ch. 31, 5.1
   impairment of capitalised costs, Ch. 31, 5.4

Contract liability, Ch. 32, 2.1
   presentation requirements for, Ch. 32, 2.1

Contract modifications, Ch. 28, 2.4
   not a separate contract, Ch. 28, 2.4.2
   represents a separate contract, Ch. 28, 2.4.1

Contractual arrangement, business combinations, Ch. 6, 4.4
   additional rights from, Ch. 6, 4.3.6
   with other vote holders, Ch. 6, 4.3.5
   structured entities, Ch. 6, 4.4.1

Contractual cash flows, financial instruments IFRS 9, Ch. 48, 6
   auction rate securities, Ch. 48, 6.4.4.B

bonds with a capped or floored interest rate, Ch. 48, 6.3.3
contractual features that may affect the classification, Ch. 48, 6.4
    de minimis and non-genuine features, Ch. 48, 6.4.1
    features that change the timing or amount of contractual cash flows, Ch. 48, 6.4.4
        prepayment – assets originated at a premium or discount, Ch. 48, 6.4.4.B
        prepayment – negative compensation, Ch. 48, 6.4.4.A
    features that modify the consideration for the time value of money, Ch. 48, 6.4.2
    features that normally do not represent payment of principal and interest, Ch. 48, 6.4.5
    regulated interest rates, Ch. 48, 6.4.3
contractual features that normally pass the test, Ch. 48, 6.3
    bonds with a capped or floored interest rate, Ch. 48, 6.3.3
    conventional subordination features, Ch. 48, 6.3.1
    features which compensate the lender for changes in tax or other related costs, Ch. 48, 6.3.6
    full recourse loans secured by collateral, Ch. 48, 6.3.2
    lender has discretion to change the interest rate, Ch. 48, 6.3.4
    unleveraged inflation-linked bonds, Ch. 48, 6.3.5
contractually linked instruments, Ch. 48, 6.6
    assessing the characteristics of the underlying pool, Ch. 48, 6.6.1
    assessing the exposure to credit risk in the tranche held, Ch. 48, 6.6.2
    conventional subordination features, Ch. 48, 6.3.1
convertible debt, Ch. 48, 6.4.5
de minimis features, Ch. 48, 6.4.1.A
debt covenants, Ch. 48, 6.4.4.B
dual currency instruments, Ch. 48, 6.4.5
five-year constant maturity bond, Ch. 48, 6.4.2
fixed rate bond prepayable by the issuer at fair value, Ch. 48, 6.4.5
full recourse loans secured by collateral, Ch. 48, 6.3.2
interest rate period, Ch. 48, 6.4.2
inverse floater, Ch. 48, 6.4.5
investment in open-ended money market or debt funds, Ch. 48, 6.4.5
lender has discretion to change the interest rate, Ch. 48, 6.3.4
loan commitments, Ch. 48, 6.4.6
meaning of 'interest,' Ch. 48, 6.2
meaning of 'principal', Ch. 48, 6.1
modified time value of money component, Ch. 48, 6.4.2
multiple of a benchmark interest rate, Ch. 48, 6.4.5
non-genuine features, Ch. 48, 6.4.1.B
non-recourse assets, Ch. 48, 6.5
non-recourse loans, Ch. 48, 6.5
perpetual instruments with potentially deferrable coupons, Ch. 48, 6.4.5
prepayment, assets originated at a premium or discount, Ch. 48, 6.4.4.B
prepayment, negative compensation, Ch. 48, 6.4.4.A
prepayment options, Ch. 48, 6.4.4
regulated interest rates, Ch. 48, 6.4.3
unleveraged inflation-linked bonds, Ch. 48, 6.3.5
Contractual-legal criterion (intangible assets), Ch. 9, 5.5.2

Contractual service margin (CSM), insurance contracts, Ch. 56, 8.5
    measurement of, using the variable fee approach, Ch. 56, 11.2.2
    recognition of in profit or loss, Ch. 56, 11.2.4
    release of, Ch. 56, 10.4.1
    subsequent measurement, Ch. 56, 8.6.2
Contractually linked instruments, Ch. 48, 6.6
    assessing the characteristics of the underlying pool, Ch. 48, 6.6.1
    assessing the exposure to credit risk in the tranche held, Ch. 48, 6.6.2
Control, Ch. 6, 3; Ch. 12, 4, Ch 30
    assessing control, Ch. 6, 3.1
    changes in control (*see* Consolidation procedures)
    common control, Ch. 6, 2.2.6.A
    de facto control, Ch. 6, 4.3.3
    joint, Ch. 12, 4
    potential voting rights, Ch. 6, 4.3.4
    purpose and design of investee, Ch. 6, 3.2
    of specified assets, Ch. 6, 8
        of silo, evaluating, Ch. 6, 8.2
    transfer of, Ch 30
Controlling relationships, disclosure of, Ch. 39, 2.4
Convergence, IFRS/US GAAP, Ch. 1, 3.2
Convertible bonds, Ch. 47, 6.6
    bond convertible into fixed percentage of equity, Ch. 47, 6.6.6
    with cash settlement at the option of the issuer, Ch. 47, 6.6.5
    contingent convertible bond, Ch. 47, 6.6.2
    with down round or ratchet features, Ch. 47, 6.6.7
    foreign currency convertible bond, Ch. 47, 6.6.4
    functional currency bond convertible into a fixed number of shares, Ch. 47, 6.6.1
    issued to acquire goods/services, Ch. 34, 10.1.6
    mandatorily convertible bond, Ch. 47, 6.6.3
Convertible debt instruments, Ch. 46, 5.1.9
Convertible instruments (EPS), Ch. 37, 6.4.1
    convertible debt, Ch. 37, 6.4.1.A
    convertible preference shares, Ch. 37, 6.4.1.B
    participating equity instruments, Ch. 37, 6.4.1.C
Convertible loans, Ch. 54, 7.4.4.B
Core deposits, Ch. 43, 2.6.7
Core inventories, extractive industries, Ch. 43, 14.3
Corporate assets, Ch. 20, 4.2, Ch. 20, 3.1.1
    leased corporate assets, Ch. 20, 4.2.1
Cost approach, Ch. 18, 6.1.1.C
Cost of investment, Ch. 8, 2.1.1
    acquired for own shares or other equity instruments, Ch. 8, 2.1.1.A
    acquired in a common control transactions, Ch. 8, 2.1.1.B
    formation of a new parent, Ch. 8, 2.1.1.E–F
    reverse acquisitions in the separate financial statements, Ch. 8, 2.1.1.G
    subsidiary accounted for at cost: partial disposal, Ch. 8, 2.1.1.D
    subsidiary, associate or joint venture acquired in stages, Ch. 8, 2.1.1.C

Cost model
  investment property, Ch. 19, 7
    impairment, Ch. 19, 7.3
    incidence of use of the cost model, Ch. 19, 7.2
    initial recognition, Ch. 19, 7.1
      non-physical parts, identification of, Ch. 19, 7.1.2
      physical parts, identification of, Ch. 19, 7.1.1
  property, plant and equipment, Ch. 18, 5
    depreciable amount, Ch. 18, 5.2
    depreciation charge, Ch. 18, 5.3
    depreciation methods, Ch. 18, 5.6
    impairment, Ch. 18, 5.7
    land, Ch. 18, 5.4.2
    repairs and maintenance, Ch. 18, 5.4.1
    residual values, Ch. 18, 5.2
    significant parts of assets, Ch. 18, 5.1
    technological change, Ch. 18, 5.4.3
    useful lives, Ch. 18, 5.4
    when depreciation starts, Ch. 18, 5.5

Costs of hedging, accounting for, Ch. 53, 7.5
  foreign currency basis spreads in financial instruments, Ch. 53, 7.5.3
    measurement of the costs of hedging for, Ch. 53, 7.5.3.A
    transition, Ch. 53, 13.3.3
  forward element of forward contracts, Ch. 53, 7.5.2
    forward element in net investment hedge, Ch. 53, 7.5.2.A
    transition, Ch. 53, 13.3.2
  time value of options, Ch. 53, 7.5.1
    aligned time value, Ch. 53, 7.5.1.A
    transition, Ch. 53, 13.3.1

Council of European Securities Regulators (CESR), Ch. 1, 5
Credit break clauses, Ch. 53, 3.2.4
Credit card arrangements, Ch. 27, 3.5.1.C
  and similar arrangements which give rise to insurance risk, Ch. 45, 3.3.4
Credit card-holder rewards programmes, Ch. 27, 3.5.1.D
Credit enhancements, Ch. 51, 6.1.1; Ch. 52, 3.3.1
Credit guarantees, Ch. 52, 4.3
Credit-linked notes, Ch. 46, 5.1.8
Credit losses. *See* Expected credit losses (ECLs)
Credit risk, Ch. 54, 5.3
  changes in, calculating gain/loss attributable to, Ch. 51, 6.2.1
  counterparty
    fair value measurement, Ch. 14, 12.2.2
    valuation of derivative transactions, Ch. 14, 11.3.2
  disclosures, Ch. 55, 11.2.6.A
  exposure, Ch. 54, 5.3.4
  of financial instrument, Ch. 54, 5.3
  hedging, Ch. 53, 12.1
  illustrative disclosures, Ch. 54, 5.3.6
  impact on hedged item, Ch. 53, 6.4.2.A
  impact on hedging instrument, Ch. 53, 6.4.2.B, 7.4.9
  incorporation into valuation of derivative contracts, Ch. 14, 11.3.3
  management practices, Ch. 54, 5.3.2
  significant increases in, determining, Ch. 51, 6
    change in the risk of a default occurring, Ch. 51, 6.1
      contractually linked instruments (CLIs) and subordinated interests, Ch. 51, 6.1.2
    determining change in risk of a default under loss rate approach, Ch. 51, 6.1.3
    impact of collateral, credit enhancements and financial guarantee contracts, Ch. 51, 6.1.1
  collective assessment, Ch. 51, 6.5
    basis of aggregation for collective assessment, Ch. 51, 6.5.2
    example of collective assessment ('bottom up' and 'top down' approach), Ch. 51, 6.5.3
    example of individual assessment of changes in credit risk, Ch. 51, 6.5.1
  determining the credit risk at initial recognition of an identical group of financial assets, Ch. 51, 6.6
  factors/indicators of changes in credit risk, Ch. 51, 6.2
    concessions granted to a wide range of customers, Ch. 51, 6.2.3
    examples, Ch. 51, 6.2.1
    illustrative examples when assessing significant increases in credit risk, Ch. 51, 6.2.4
    past due status and more than 30 days past due presumption, Ch. 51, 6.2.2
    use of behavioural factors, Ch. 51, 6.2.5
  operational simplifications, Ch. 51, 6.4
    assessment at the counterparty level, Ch. 51, 6.4.4
    delinquency, Ch. 51, 6.4.2
    determining maximum initial credit risk for a portfolio, Ch. 51, 6.4.5
    low credit risk, Ch. 51, 6.4.1
    12-month risk as an approximation for change in lifetime risk, Ch. 51, 6.4.3
  revolving credit facilities, Ch. 51, 12
  in the tranche held, Ch. 48, 6.6.2

Cross-currency interest rate swaps (CCIRS), Ch. 53, 3.2.4.A, 7.3.3.B, 7.5.3
Crypto-assets
  additional disclosure requirements for, Ch. 22, 6.2
  cost model, Ch. 17, 11.5.2.A
  Cryptocurrencies as cash, Ch. 40, 3.2.5
  In scope of IAS 2, Ch. 22, 2.3.1.D
  recognition and initial measurement, Ch. 17, 11.5.1
  revaluation model, Ch. 17, 11.5.2.B
  standard setter activity, Ch. 17, 11.5.3
  subsequent measurement, Ch. 17, 11.5.2
Cryptocurrencies, Ch. 40, 3.2.5
CSM. *See* Contractual service margin
Cumulative preference shares, Ch. 11, 7.5.2
Cumulative translation differences, foreign operations, Ch. 5, 5.7
Current assets, Ch. 3, 3.1.3
Current liabilities, Ch. 3, 3.1.4
  Subsequent rectification of a covenant breach, Ch. 38, 2.3.2
Current service cost, employee benefits, Ch. 35, 5, 10.1
Current tax, Ch. 33, 5. *See also* IAS 12
  definition, Ch. 33, 3
Customer, Ch. 28, 3.6
  definition, Ch. 27, 3.3
Customer relationship intangible assets, Ch. 9, 5.5.2.B
Customer-supplier relationship, Ch. 6, 7.1
DAC. *See* Deferred acquisition costs

Date of transition to IFRSs, Ch. 5, 1.3
'Day 1' profits, Ch. 49, 3.3
De facto **agents**, Ch. 12, 4.2.5
De facto **control**, Ch. 6, 4.3.3
Death-in-service benefits, Ch. 35, 3.6
Death waivers, loans with, Ch. 45, 3.3.5
Debt, extinguishment of, Ch. 52, 6.1
   gains and losses on, Ch. 52, 6.3
Debt instruments, Ch. 45, 3.4.1.B; Ch. 48, 2.1
   convertible and exchangeable, Ch. 37, 6.4.1.A; Ch. 46, 5.1.9
   measured at fair value through other comprehensive income, Ch. 51, 9
   term extension and similar call, put and prepayment options in, Ch. 46, 5.1.4
Debt investments, foreign currency, Ch. 51, 9.2
Decommissioning, Ch. 26, 6.3; Ch. 43, 10
   accounting for changes in costs, Ch. 18, 4.3
   in extractive industries, Ch. 43, 10
      foreign exchange differences, treatment of, Ch. 43, 10.2
      indefinite life assets, Ch. 43, 10.3
      recognition and measurement issues, Ch. 43, 10.1
   provisions, Ch. 26, 6.3
Deductible temporary differences, Ch. 33, 6.2.2. *See also* Temporary differences, Deferred tax assets
   business combinations and consolidation, Ch. 33, 6.2.2.E
   definition, Ch. 33, 3
   foreign currency differences, Ch. 33, 6.2.2.F
   recognition, Ch. 33, 7.1.2
      initial recognition of goodwill, Ch. 33, 7.2.2.B
   restrictions on recognition, Ch. 33, 7.4
      and future and 'probable' taxable profit, Ch. 33, 7.4.3
      and unrealised losses, Ch. 33, 7.4.5
   revaluations, Ch. 33, 6.2.2.C
   tax re-basing, Ch. 33, 6.2.2.D
   transactions that affect, Ch. 33, 6.2.2.A
      profit/loss, Ch. 33, 6.2.2.A
      statement of financial position, Ch. 33, 6.2.2.B
Deemed cost on first-time adoption, Ch. 5, 5.5
   for assets used in operations subject to rate regulation, Ch. 5, 5.5.4
   disclosures regarding, Ch. 5, 6.5
   event-driven fair value measurement as, Ch. 5, 5.5.2
      exemption for event-driven revaluations after the date of transition, Ch. 5, 5.5.2.C
      'fresh start' accounting, Ch. 5, 5.5.2.B
      'push down' accounting, Ch. 5, 5.5.2.A
   fair value or revaluation as, Ch. 5, 5.5.1
      determining deemed cost, Ch. 5, 5.5.1.A
      before the date of transition to IFRSs, Ch. 5, 5.5.1.B
   for oil and gas assets, Ch. 5, 5.5.3
   of subsidiary, on transition to IFRS, Ch. 8, 2.1.2
   use of
      after severe hyperinflation, Ch. 5, 6.5.5
      for assets used in operations subject to rate regulation, Ch. 5, 6.5.4
      fair value as, Ch. 5, 6.5.1
      for investments in subsidiaries, joint ventures and associates, Ch. 5, 6.5.2
      for oil and gas assets, Ch. 5, 6.5.3

Deemed disposals, Ch. 7, 3.6; Ch. 11, 7.12.6
Default
   change in the risk of a default occurring, Ch. 51, 6.1
      contractually linked instruments (CLIs) and subordinated interests, Ch. 51, 6.1.2
      determining change in risk of a default under loss rate approach, Ch. 51, 6.1.3
      impact of collateral, credit enhancements and financial guarantee contracts, Ch. 51, 6.1.1
   definition of, Ch. 51, 5.1
   exposure at default, revolving facilities, Ch. 51, 12.3
   losses expected in the event of default, Ch. 51, 5.8
      cash flows from the sale of a defaulted loan, Ch. 51, 5.8.2
      credit enhancements: collateral and financial guarantees, Ch. 51, 5.8.1
      treatment of collection costs paid to an external debt collection agency, Ch. 51, 5.8.3
   probability of default (PD) and loss rate approaches, Ch. 51, 5.4
      loss rate approach, Ch. 51, 5.4.2
      probability of default approach, Ch. 51, 5.4.1
Deferred acquisition costs (DAC), Ch. 55, 9.1.1.B
Deferred tax, Ch. 33, 6–8. *See also* IAS 12; Income taxes; Tax bases; Temporary differences
   assets, Ch. 33, 6.1.1; Ch. 33, 7.1.2
   investment property held by a 'single asset' entity, Ch. 19, 6.10
   liabilities, Ch. 33, 6.1.2, 7.1.1
   measurement, Ch. 33, 8
      different tax rates applicable to retained and distributed profits, Ch. 33, 8.5
         effectively tax-free entities, Ch. 33, 8.5.1
         withholding tax/distribution tax?, Ch. 33, 8.5.2
      discounting, Ch. 33, 8.6
      expected manner of recovery of assets/settlement of liabilities, Ch. 33, 8.4
         assets and liabilities with more than one tax base, Ch. 33, 8.4.3
         carrying amount, Ch. 33, 8.4.2
         change in expected manner of recovery of an asset/settlement of a liability, Ch. 33, 8.4.11
         depreciable PP&E and intangible assets, Ch. 33, 8.4.5
         determining the expected manner of recovery of assets, Ch. 33, 8.4.4
         investment properties, Ch. 19, 6.10; Ch. 33, 8.4.7
         non-depreciable PP&E and intangible assets, Ch. 33, 8.4.6
         non-amortised or indefinite life intangible assets, Ch. 33, 8.4.6.B
         PP&E accounted for using the revaluation model, Ch. 33, 8.4.6.A
         other assets and liabilities, Ch. 33, 8.4.8
         'outside' temporary differences relating to subsidiaries, branches, associates and joint arrangements, Ch. 33, 8.4.9
         'single asset' entities, Ch. 19, 4.1.2, 6.10; Ch. 33, 8.4.10
         tax planning strategies, Ch. 33, 8.4.1
   legislation at the end of the reporting period, Ch. 33, 8.1

Deferred tax—*contd*
  measurement—*contd*
    'prior year adjustments' of previously presented tax balances and expense (income), Ch. 33, 8.3
    uncertain tax treatments, Ch. 33, 8.2, 9
    unrealised intragroup profits and losses in consolidated financial, Ch. 33, 8.7
      intragroup transfers of goodwill and intangible assets, Ch. 33, 8.7.1
        consolidated financial statements, Ch. 7, 2.4, Ch. 33, 8.7.1.C
        individual financial statements of buyer, Ch. 33, 8.7.1.A
        individual financial statements of seller, Ch. 33, 8.7.1.B
        when the tax base of goodwill is retained by the transferor entity, Ch. 33, 8.7.1.D
  recognition, Ch. 33, 7
    assets carried at fair value/revalued amount, Ch. 33, 7.3
    basic principles, Ch. 33, 7.1
      deductible temporary differences (deferred tax assets), Ch. 33, 7.1.2
      taxable temporary differences (deferred tax liabilities), Ch. 33, 7.1.1
    deferred taxable gains, Ch. 33, 7.7
    initial recognition exception, Ch. 33, 7.2
      acquisition of an investment in a subsidiary, associate, branch or joint arrangement, Ch. 33, 7.2.10
      acquisition of subsidiary that does not constitute a business, Ch. 33, 7.2.9
      changes to temporary differences after initial recognition, Ch. 33, 7.2.4
        change in carrying value due to revaluation, Ch. 33, 7.2.4.B
        change in tax base due to deductions in tax return, Ch. 33, 7.2.4.C
        depreciation, amortisation/impairment of initial carrying value, Ch. 33, 7.2.4.A
        temporary difference altered by legislative change, Ch. 33, 7.2.4.D
      initial recognition of compound financial instruments by the issuer, Ch. 33, 7.2.8
      initial recognition of goodwill, Ch. 33, 7.2.2
      initial recognition of other assets and liabilities, Ch. 33, 7.2.3
      intragroup transfers of assets with no change in tax base, Ch. 33, 7.2.5
      partially deductible and super-deductible assets, Ch. 33, 7.2.6
      tax losses, acquisition of, Ch. 33, 7.2.1
      transactions involving the initial recognition of an asset and liability, Ch. 33, 7.2.7
        decommissioning costs, Ch. 33, 7.2.7.A
        finance leases under IFRS 16 taxed as operating leases, Ch. 33, 7.2.7.B
    interpretation issues, Ch. 33, 7.1.3
      accounting profit, Ch. 33, 7.1.3.A
      taxable profit 'at the time of the transaction,' Ch. 33, 7.1.3.B
    'outside' temporary differences relating to subsidiaries, branches, associates and joint arrangements, Ch. 33, 7.5
      calculation of, Ch. 33, 7.5.1
        consolidated financial statements, Ch. 33, 7.5.1.A
        separate financial statements of investor, Ch. 33, 7.5.1.B
      deductible temporary differences, Ch. 33, 7.5.3
      foreseeable future – anticipated intragroup dividend, Ch. 33, 7.5.4
        consolidated financial statements of receiving entity, Ch. 33, 7.5.4.A
        separate financial statements of paying entity, Ch. 33, 7.5.4.B
      taxable temporary differences, Ch. 33, 7.5.2
      unpaid intragroup interest, royalties, management charges etc., Ch. 33, 7.5.5
    restrictions on recognition of deferred tax assets, Ch. 33, 7.4
      effect of disposals on recoverability of tax losses, Ch. 33, 7.4.8
        tax losses of retained entity recoverable against profits of subsidiary disposed of, Ch. 33, 7.4.8.B
        tax losses of subsidiary disposed of recoverable against profits of retained entity, Ch. 33, 7.4.8.C
        tax losses of subsidiary disposed of recoverable against profits of that subsidiary, Ch. 33, 7.4.8.A
      re-assessment of deferred tax assets, Ch. 33, 7.4.7
      restrictions imposed by relevant tax laws, Ch. 33, 7.4.1
      sources of 'probable' taxable profit, estimates of future taxable profits, Ch. 33, 7.4.3
        ignore origination of new future deductible temporary differences, Ch. 33, 7.4.3.A
        ignore reversal of existing deductible temporary differences, Ch. 33, 7.4.3.B
      sources of 'probable' taxable profit, taxable temporary differences, Ch. 33, 7.4.2
      tax planning opportunities, Ch. 33, 7.4.4
      unrealised losses on debt securities measured at fair value, Ch. 33, 7.4.5
      unused tax losses and unused tax credits, Ch. 33, 7.4.6
    'tax-transparent' ('flow-through') entities, Ch. 33, 7.6
  tax bases and temporary differences, Ch. 33, 6

Deferred tax assets, Ch. 33, 3, 7.4
Deferred tax liabilities, Ch. 33, 3
Defined benefit plans, Ch. 35, 5–11. *See also* IAS 19; IFRIC 14
  costs of administering, Ch. 35, 11
  vs. defined contribution plans, Ch. 35, 3.1
  disclosure requirements, Ch. 35, 15.2
    amounts in financial statements, Ch. 35, 15.2.2
    characteristics and risks associated with, Ch. 35, 15.2.1
    future cash flows, amount, timing and uncertainty of, Ch. 35, 15.2.3
    multi-employer plans, Ch. 35, 15.2.4
    in other IFRSs, Ch. 35, 15.2.6
    sharing risks between entities under common control, Ch. 35, 15.2.5
  and insured benefits, Ch. 35, 3.2
  and multi-employer plans, Ch. 35, 3.3
  net defined benefit liability (asset), presentation of, Ch. 35, 9

plan assets, Ch. 35, 6
  contributions to defined benefit funds, Ch. 35, 6.5
  definition of, Ch. 35, 6.1
  longevity swaps, Ch. 35, 6.6
  measurement of, Ch. 35, 6.2
  qualifying insurance policies, Ch. 35, 6.3
  reimbursement rights, Ch. 35, 6.4
plan liabilities, Ch. 35, 7
  actuarial assumptions, Ch. 35, 7.5
  actuarial methodology, Ch. 35, 7.3
  attributing benefit to years of service, Ch. 35, 7.4
  contributions by employees and third parties, Ch. 35, 7.2
  discount rate, Ch. 35, 7.6
  frequency of valuations, Ch. 35, 7.7
  legal and constructive obligations, Ch. 35, 7.1
refund from, Ch. 35, 16.2.1
sharing risks between entities under common control, Ch. 35, 3.3.2
treatment in profit/loss and other comprehensive income, Ch. 35, 10
  acquisition of a qualifying insurance policy, Ch. 35, 10.2.2
  net interest on the net defined benefit liability (asset), Ch. 35, 10.2
  past service cost, Ch. 35, 10.1.1
  remeasurements, Ch. 35, 10.3
  service cost, Ch. 35, 10.1
  settlements, Ch. 35, 10.2.3
treatment of the plan surplus/deficit in the statement of financial position, Ch. 35, 8
  assets restriction to their recoverable amounts, Ch. 35, 8.2
    economic benefits available as reduced future contributions when no minimum funding requirements for future service, Ch. 35, 8.2.2
    IFRIC 14 requirements concerning limit on defined benefit asset, Ch. 35, 8.2.1
    minimum funding requirements, IFRIC interpretation effect on economic benefit available as a reduction in future contributions, Ch. 35, 8.2.3
    when the requirement may give rise to a liability, Ch. 35, 8.2.4
    pension funding payments contingent on future events within the control of the entity, Ch. 35, 8.2.5
  net defined benefit liability (asset), Ch. 35, 8.1
Defined contribution plans, Ch. 35, 4
  accounting requirements, Ch. 35, 4.1
  vs. defined benefit plans, Ch. 35, 3.1
  disclosure requirements, Ch. 35, 15
  with vesting conditions, Ch. 35, 4.1.2
Delegated decision making, Ch. 12, 4.2.4
Delegated power, Ch. 6, 6.1
Demand deposits, Ch. 40, 3.2.1
Deposit components unbundling, Ch. 55, 5
  illustration, Ch. 55, 5.2
  practical difficulties, Ch. 55, 5.3
  requirements, Ch. 55, 5.1
Depreciation, depletion and amortisation (DD&A), extractive industries, Ch. 43, 16
  block caving, Ch. 43, 16.2
  determining when production phase commences, Ch. 43, 15.5.2

requirements under IAS 16 and IAS 38, Ch. 43, 16.1
  assets depreciated using the straight-line method, Ch. 43, 16.1.2
  assets depreciated using the units of production method, Ch. 43, 16.1.3
    joint and by-products, Ch. 43, 16.1.3.D
    reserves base, Ch. 43, 16.1.3.B
    unit of measure, Ch. 43, 16.1.3.C
    units of production formula, Ch. 43, 16.1.3.A
  mineral reserves, Ch. 43, 16.1.1
Depreciation, property, plant and equipment (PP&E), Ch. 18, 5
charge, Ch. 18, 5.3
depreciable amount and residual values, Ch. 18, 5.2
methods, Ch. 18, 5.6
  diminishing balance methods, Ch. 18, 5.6.1
  sum of the digits method, Ch. 18, 5.6.1
  unit-of-production method, Ch. 18, 5.6.2
and useful life of asset, Ch. 18, 5.4
Derecognition, financial instruments, Ch. 52, 1–8
  accounting treatment, Ch. 52, 5
    collateral, Ch. 52, 5.5.2
    offset, Ch. 52, 5.5.1
    reassessing derecognition, Ch. 52, 5.6
    reassessment of consolidation of subsidiaries and SPEs, Ch. 52, 5.6.1
    rights/obligations over transferred assets that continue to be recognised, Ch. 52, 5.5.3
    transfers that do not qualifying for derecognition, through retention of risks and rewards, Ch. 52, 5.2
    transfers that qualify for derecognition, Ch. 52, 5.1
      servicing assets and liabilities, Ch. 52, 5.1.2
      transferred asset part of larger asset, Ch. 52, 5.1.1
    transfers with continuing involvement, Ch. 52, 5.3
      associated liability, Ch. 52, 5.3.3
      continuing involvement in part only of a larger asset, Ch. 52, 5.3.5
      guarantees, Ch. 52, 5.3.1
      options, Ch. 52, 5.3.2
      subsequent measurement of assets and liabilities, Ch. 52, 5.3.4
    transfers with continuing involvement–accounting examples, Ch. 52, 5.4
      continuing involvement in part only of a financial asset, Ch. 52, 5.4.4
      transfers of assets measured at amortised cost, Ch. 52, 5.4.2
      transfers of assets measured at fair value, Ch. 52, 5.4.3
        'collar' put and call options, Ch. 52, 5.4.3.C
        transferor's call option, Ch. 52, 5.4.3.A
        transferee's put option, Ch. 52, 5.4.3.B
      transfers with guarantees, Ch. 52, 5.4.1
  CUSIP 'netting', Ch. 52, 7
  definitions, Ch. 52, 2.1
  development of IFRS, Ch. 52, 2
  financial assets, Ch. 52, 3
    background, Ch. 52, 3.1
    client money, Ch. 52, 3.7
    contractual rights to receive cash flows from the asset, expiration of, Ch. 52, 3.4

Derecognition, financial instruments—*contd*
  financial assets—*contd*
    contractual rights to receive cash flows from the asset, expiration of—*contd*
      asset restructuring in the context of Greek government debt, Ch. 52, 3.4.2
      IBOR reform, Ch. 52, 3.4.3
      novation of contracts to intermediary counterparties, Ch. 52, 3.4.4
      renegotiation of the terms of an asset, Ch. 52, 3.4.1
      write-offs, Ch. 52, 3.4.5
    retention of rights subject to obligation to pay over to others (pass-through arrangement), Ch. 52, 3.5.2
    transfers of, Ch. 52, 3.5.1
    decision tree, Ch. 52, 3.2
      importance of applying tests in sequence, Ch. 52, 3.2.1
    groups of financial assets, Ch. 52, 3.3.2
      IASB's view and the Interpretations Committee's tentative conclusions, Ch. 52, 3.3.2.A
      similar assets, Ch. 52, 3.3.2.B
    principles, parts of assets and groups of assets, Ch. 52, 3.3
      credit enhancement through, Ch. 52, 3.3.1
      transfer of asset (or part of asset) for only part of its life, Ch. 52, 3.3.3
    securitisations, Ch. 52, 3.6
      'empty' subsidiaries or SPEs, Ch. 52, 3.6.6
      insurance protection, Ch. 52, 3.6.3
      non-optional derivatives along with a group of financial assets transfers, Ch. 52, 3.6.5
      recourse to originator, Ch. 52, 3.6.1
      short-term loan facilities, Ch. 52, 3.6.2
      treatment of collection proceeds, Ch. 52, 3.6.4
    transfer/retention of substantially all the risks and rewards of ownership, Ch. 52, 3.8
      evaluating extent to which risks and rewards are transferred, Ch. 52, 3.8.4
      transferee's 'practical ability' to sell the asset, Ch. 52, 3.9.1
      transfers, cumulative basis, Ch. 52, 3.8.5
      transfers, resulting in neither transfer nor retention of substantially all risks and rewards, Ch. 52, 3.8.3
      transfers, resulting in retention of substantially all risks and rewards, Ch. 52, 3.8.2
      transfers, resulting in transfer of substantially all risks and rewards, Ch. 52, 3.8.1
  financial liabilities, Ch. 52, 6
    derivatives that can be financial assets or financial liabilities, Ch. 52, 6.4
    exchange or modification of debt by original lender, Ch. 52, 6.2
      costs and fees, Ch. 52, 6.2.5
      examples, Ch. 52, 6.2.4
      IBOR reform, Ch. 52, 6.2.2
      loan syndications, Ch. 52, 6.2.3
      modification gains and losses, Ch. 52, 6.2.6
      settlement of financial liability with issue of new equity instrument, Ch. 52, 6.2.8
      'substantially' different, Ch. 52, 6.2.1
      through intermediary, Ch. 52, 6.2.4
    extinguishment of debt
      in exchange for transfer of assets not meeting the derecognition criteria, Ch. 52, 6.1.4
      'in-substance defeasance' arrangements, Ch. 52, 6.1.3
      legal release by creditor, Ch. 52, 6.1.2
      what constitutes 'part' of a liability, Ch. 52, 6.1.1
    gains and losses on extinguishment of debt, Ch. 52, 6.3
    supply-chain finance, Ch. 52, 6.5
  future developments, Ch. 52, 8
  off-balance sheet finance, Ch. 52, 1.1
  practical application factoring of trade receivables, Ch. 52, 4.5
  repurchase agreements ('repos') and securities lending, Ch. 52, 4.1
    agreement to repurchase at fair value, Ch. 52, 4.1.5
    agreements to return the same asset, Ch. 52, 4.1.1
    agreements with right of substitution, Ch. 52, 4.1.3
    agreements with right to return the same or substantially the same asset, Ch. 52, 4.1.2
    net cash-settled forward repurchase, Ch. 52, 4.1.4
    right of first refusal to repurchase at fair value, Ch. 52, 4.1.6
    wash sale, Ch. 52, 4.1.7
  scope, Ch. 52, 2.2
  subordinated retained interests and credit guarantees, Ch. 52, 4.3
  transfers by way of swaps, Ch. 52, 4.4
    interest rate swaps, Ch. 52, 4.4.2
    total return swaps, Ch. 52, 4.4.1
  transfers subject to put and call options, Ch. 52, 4.2
    changes in probability of exercise of options after initial transfer of asset, Ch. 52, 4.2.9
    clean-up call options, Ch. 52, 4.2.7
    deeply in the money put and call options, Ch. 52, 4.2.1
    deeply out of the money put and call options, Ch. 52, 4.2.2
    net cash-settled options, Ch. 52, 4.2.5
    option to put or call at fair value, Ch. 52, 4.2.4
    options that are neither deeply out of the money nor deeply in the money, Ch. 52, 4.2.3
    removal of accounts provision, Ch. 52, 4.2.6
    same (or nearly the same) price put and call options, Ch. 52, 4.2.8

Derivative(s), Ch. 46, 1–3. *See also* Embedded derivatives
  call and put options over non-controlling interest. Ch. 7, 6. *See also* 'Non-controlling interest'
  changes in value in response to changes in underlying, Ch. 46, 2.1
    non-financial variables specific to one party to the contract, Ch. 46, 2.1.3
    notional amounts, Ch. 46, 2.1.1
    underlying variables, Ch. 46, 2.1.2
  common derivatives, Ch. 46, 3.1
  contracts, cash flows on, Ch. 40, 4.4.12
  defining characteristics, Ch. 46, 2
    changes in value in response to changes in underlying, Ch. 46, 2.1
    future settlement, Ch. 46, 2.3
    initial net investment, Ch. 46, 2.2
  discount rates for calculating fair value of, Ch. 53, 7.4.5
  in-substance derivatives, Ch. 46, 3.2
  linked and separate transactions, Ch. 46, 8
  regular way contracts, Ch. 46, 3.3

restructuring of, Ch. 53, 3.6.3
'synthetic' instruments, Ch. 46, 8
Derivative financial instruments, Ch. 45, 2.2.8; Ch. 53, 3.2
    basis swaps, Ch. 53, 3.2.5
    credit break clauses, Ch. 53, 3.2.4
        principal resetting cross currency swaps, Ch. 53, 3.2.4.A
    embedded derivatives, Ch. 53, 3.2.3
    net written options, Ch. 53, 3.2.2
    offsetting external derivatives, Ch. 53, 3.2.1
Designation at fair value through profit or loss, Ch. 48, 7
Dilapidation provision, Ch. 26, 6.9
Diluted EPS, Ch. 37, 6. *See also* Earnings per share (EPS); IAS 33
    calculation of, Ch. 37, 6.2; Ch. 37, 8
        diluted earnings, Ch. 37, 6.2.1
        diluted number of shares, Ch. 37, 6.2.2
    contingently issuable potential ordinary shares, Ch. 37, 6.4.8
    contingently issuable shares, Ch. 37, 6.4.6
        earnings-based contingencies, Ch. 37, 6.4.6.A
        not driven by earnings or share price, Ch. 37, 6.4.6.C
        share-price-based contingencies, Ch. 37, 6.4.6.B
    convertible instruments, Ch. 37, 6.4.1
        convertible debt, Ch. 37, 6.4.1.A
        convertible preference shares, Ch. 37, 6.4.1.B
        participating equity instruments, Ch. 37, 6.4.1.C
    dilutive instruments, types, Ch. 37, 6.4
    dilutive potential ordinary shares, Ch. 37, 6.3
        judged by effect on profits from continuing operations, Ch. 37, 6.3.1
        judged by the cumulative impact of potential shares, Ch. 37, 6.3.2
    need for, Ch. 37, 6.1
    options, warrants and their equivalents, Ch. 37, 6.4.2
        forward purchase agreements, Ch. 37, 6.4.2.C
        numerator, Ch. 37, 6.4.2.A
        options over convertible instruments, Ch. 37, 6.4.2.D
        settlement of option exercise price, Ch. 37, 6.4.2.E
        specified application of option proceeds, Ch. 37, 6.4.2.F
        written call options, Ch. 37, 6.4.2.B
        written put options, Ch. 37, 6.4.2.C
    partly paid shares, Ch. 37, 6.4.4
    potentially ordinary shares of investees, Ch. 37, 6.4.7
    presentation, restatement and disclosure, Ch. 37, 7
    purchased options and warrants, Ch. 37, 6.4.3
    share-based payments, Ch. 37, 6.4.5
Diminishing balance methods, depreciation, Ch. 18, 5.6.1
Direct method of consolidation, foreign operations, Ch. 7, 2.3; Ch. 15, 6.6.3
Directly attributable borrowing costs, Ch. 21, 5.1
'Directly attributable' costs, Ch. 18, 4.1.1
'Dirty' fair values, Ch. 53, 7.4.10
Disclosure(s). *See also* individual entries for standards
    in annual financial statements, Ch. 32, 3
    business combinations, Ch. 9, 16
    capital disclosures, Ch. 3, 5.4; Ch. 54, 5.6.3
    capitalisation of borrowing costs, Ch. 21, 7
    of changes in ownership interests in subsidiaries, Ch. 13, 4.5
    common control transactions, Ch. 8, 4.3.1
    in condensed interim financial statements, Ch. 41, 4
    earnings per share (EPS), Ch. 37, 7.3
    employee benefits, Ch. 35, 15
    first-time adoption, Ch. 5, 6
    financial instruments
        qualitative disclosures, Ch. 54, 5.1
        quantitative disclosures, Ch. 54, 5.2, 5.6
    foreign exchange, Ch. 15, 10
    government assistance, Ch. 24, 6
    government grants, Ch. 24, 6
    of IFRS information before adoption of IFRSs, Ch. 5, 6.7
    of IFRS information in financial statements, Ch. 5, 6.3.1
    impairment of fixed assets and goodwill, Ch. 20, 13.3
    income taxes, Ch. 33, 14
    insurance contracts, Ch. 55, 11; Ch. 56, 16
    intangible assets, Ch. 17, 11
        additional disclosures when the revaluation model is applied, Ch. 17, 10.4
        general disclosures, Ch. 17, 10.1
        profit/loss presentation, Ch. 17, 10.3
        of research and development expenditure, Ch. 17, 10.5
        statement of financial position presentation, Ch. 17, 10.2
    inventories, Ch. 22, 6
        additional disclosure requirements for crypto-assets, Ch. 22, 6.2
        general disclosure requirements, Ch. 22, 6.1
    investment property, Ch. 19, 12
    investments in associates and joint ventures, Ch. 11, 10; Ch. 13, 5
    joint arrangements, Ch. 13, 5
    leases (IFRS 16), Ch. 23, 10.6
    of mineral reserves and resources, Ch. 43, 2.4
    objective and general requirements, Ch. 32, 3.1
    offsetting, Ch. 2, 10.2.1.A; Ch. 54, 7.4.2.D
    property, plant and equipment (PP&E), Ch. 18, 8–8.3
    provisions, contingent liabilities and contingent assets, Ch. 26, 7
    related party disclosures, Ch. 39, 1–2
    relating to accounting policies, Ch. 3, 5
        changes in accounting estimates, Ch. 3, 5.2.2
        changes in accounting policies, Ch. 3, 5.1.2
        changes pursuant to the initial application of an IFRS, Ch. 3, 5.1.2.A
        estimation uncertainty, Ch. 3, 5.2.1
        judgements made in applying accounting policies, Ch. 3, 5.1.1.B
        new IFRS, future impact of, Ch. 3, 5.1.2.C
        prior period errors, Ch. 3, 5.3
        significant accounting policies, Ch. 3, 5.1.1.A
        voluntary changes in accounting policy, Ch. 3, 5.1.2.B
    reportable segments, Ch. 36, 5
    revenue and contract cost disclosure requirements, Ch. 32, 3.2
    separate financial statements, Ch. 8, 3
    service concession arrangements (SCA), Ch. 25, 7
    share-based payment, Ch. 34, 13
Disclosure of interests in other entities, Ch. 13, 1–6. *See also* IFRS 12; Interests in joint arrangements and associates
    definitions, Ch. 13, 2.2.1
        interaction of IFRS 12 and IFRS 5, Ch. 13, 2.2.1.C
        interests in other entities, Ch. 13, 2.2.1.A
        structured entities, Ch. 13, 2.2.1.B
    interests disclosed under IFRS 12, Ch. 13, 2.2.2
    interests not within the scope of IFRS 12, Ch. 13, 2.2.3

Disclosure of interests in other entities—*contd*
  joint arrangements and associates, Ch. 13, 5
    nature, extent and financial effects, Ch. 13, 5.1
    risks associated, Ch. 13, 5.2
      commitments relating to joint ventures, Ch. 13, 5.2.1
      contingent liabilities relating to joint ventures and associates, Ch. 13, 5.2.2
  objective, Ch. 13, 2.1
  scope, Ch. 13, 2.2
  significant judgements and assumptions, Ch. 13, 3
  subsidiaries, Ch. 13, 4
    changes in ownership interests in subsidiaries, Ch. 13, 4.5
    composition of the group, Ch. 13, 4.1
    consolidated structured entities, nature of risks, Ch. 13, 4.4
      current intentions to provide financial or other support, Ch. 13, 4.4.4
      financial or other support to with no contractual obligation, Ch. 13, 4.4.2
      terms of contractual arrangements, Ch. 13, 4.4.1
    nature and extent of significant restrictions, Ch. 13, 4.3
    non-controlling interests, Ch. 13, 4.2
  unconsolidated structured entities, Ch. 13, 6
    nature of interests, Ch. 13, 6.1
    nature of risks, Ch. 13, 6.2
      actual and intended financial and other support to structured entities, Ch. 13, 6.2.2
      disclosure of funding difficulties, Ch. 13, 6.3.6
      disclosure of liquidity arrangements, Ch. 13, 6.3.5
      disclosure of losses, Ch. 13, 6.3.2
      disclosure of ranking and amounts of potential losses, Ch. 13, 6.3.4
      disclosure of support, Ch. 13, 6.3.1
      disclosure of the forms of funding of an unconsolidated structured entity, Ch. 13, 6.3.7
      disclosure of types of income received, Ch. 13, 6.3.3
      maximum exposure to loss from those interests, Ch. 13, 6.2.1

Discontinued operation, Ch. 3, 3.2.5; Ch. 4, 3.2. *See also* IFRS 5
  cash flows of, Ch. 40, 8.1
  definition of, Ch. 4, 3.1
  presentation of, Ch. 4, 3.2
  property, plant and equipment, derecognition and disposal, Ch. 18, 7.1
  trading with continuing operations, Ch. 4, 3.3

Discount rate
  for calculating fair value of derivatives, Ch. 53, 7.4.5
  employee benefits, Ch. 35, 7.6
    high quality corporate bonds, Ch. 35, 7.6.1
    no deep market, Ch. 35, 7.6.2
  estimated cash flows to a present value (provisions), Ch. 26, 4.3
    adjusting for risk and using a government bond rate, Ch. 26, 4.3.2
    effect of changes in interest rates on the discount rate applied, Ch. 26, 4.3.6
    own credit risk is not taken into account, Ch. 26, 4.3.3
    pre-tax discount rate, Ch. 26, 4.3.4
    real *vs.* nominal rate, Ch. 26, 4.3.1
    unwinding of the discount, Ch. 26, 4.3.5
  impairment of fixed assets and goodwill, Ch. 20, 7.2
    approximations and short cuts, Ch. 20, 7.2.4
    discount rates other than WACC, Ch. 20, 7.2.9
    entity-specific WACCs and capital structure, Ch. 20, 7.2.8
    entity-specific WACCs and different project risks within the entity, Ch. 20, 7.2.7
    pre-tax discount rate, calculating, Ch. 20, 7.2.2
    pre-tax discount rates disclosing when using a post-tax methodology, Ch. 20, 7.2.5
    pre-tax rates determination taking account of tax losses, Ch. 20, 7.2.6
    VIU calculation using post-tax cash flows, Ch. 20, 7.2.3
    WACC, Ch. 20, 7.2.1
  insurance contracts, Ch. 56, 8.3
  leases, Ch. 23, 4.6
  significant financing components, Ch. 29, 2.5

Discretionary participation feature (DPF), Ch. 55, 2.2.1, 6
  definition, Ch. 55, 2.2.1
  in financial instruments, Ch. 55, 6.2
  guaranteed benefits, Ch. 55, 6
  in insurance contracts, Ch. 55, 6.1
  investment contracts with, Ch. 55, 2.2.2, 6.1, 6.2, 7.2.2.C
  practical issues, Ch. 55, 6.3
    contracts with switching features, Ch. 55, 6.3.2
    negative DPF, Ch. 55, 6.3.1

Discussion Paper (DP)–*Accounting for Dynamic Risk Management*, Ch. 53, 11.1
Discussion Paper (DP)–*Extractive Activities*, Ch. 43, 1.3
Discussion Paper (DP)–*Preliminary Views on Insurance Contracts*, Ch. 55, 1.1
Discussion Paper (DP)–*A Review of the Conceptual Framework for Financial Reporting*, Ch. 2, 1

Disposal groups held for sale/distribution, Ch. 3, 3.1.2; Ch. 4, 1–6. *See also* IFRS 5
  changes to a plan of sale/plan of distribution, Ch. 4, 2.2.5
  classification as held for sale/held for distribution to owners, Ch. 4, 2.1.2
    abandonment, Ch. 4, 2.1.2.C
    available for immediate sale, meaning of, Ch. 4, 2.1.2.A
    criteria met after the reporting period, Ch. 38, 2.1.3
    highly probable, meaning of, Ch. 4, 2.1.2.B
  comparative information, Ch. 4, 4
  concept of disposal group, Ch. 4, 2.1.1
  disclosure requirements, Ch. 4, 5
  discontinued operations, Ch. 4, 3
  future developments, Ch. 4, 6
  measurement, Ch. 4, 2.2
    impairments and reversals of impairment, Ch. 4, 2.2.3
    presentation in statement of financial position, Ch. 4, 2.2.4
  partial disposals of operations, Ch. 4, 2.1.3
    of an associate or joint venture, Ch. 4, 2.1.3.B
    loss of control of a subsidiary, Ch. 4, 2.1.3.A; Ch. 7, 3.2, 3.4, 3.5, 3.7

'Dividend blocker' clause, Ch. 47, 4.5.3.A
Dividend discount model (DDM), Ch. 20, 12.2, 12.4.2.A
'Dividend pusher' clause, Ch. 47, 4.5.3.B
Dividends, Ch. 8, 2.4; Ch. 11, 7.11.1
  declared after the reporting period, Ch. 38, 2.1.3.A

and other distributions, Ch. 8, 2.4
  distributions of noncash assets to owners (IFRIC 17), Ch. 7, 3.7; Ch. 8, 2.4.2
  dividend exceeding total comprehensive income, Ch. 8, 2.4.1
  resulting in carrying amount of an investment exceeding consolidated net assets, Ch. 8, 2.4.1.B
  returns of capital, Ch. 8, 2.4.1.C
  from subsidiaries, joint ventures or associates, Ch. 8, 2.4.1
  payable on shares classified as financial liabilities, Ch. 21, 5.5.4
Divisions, foreign exchange, Ch. 15, 4.4
Downstream activities, extractive industries, Ch. 43, 1.6
'Downstream' transactions elimination, equity accounted investments, Ch. 11, 7.6.1
Downward valuations of property, plant and equipment, reversals of, Ch. 18, 6.3
DP. See under Discussion Paper
DPF. *See* Discretionary participation feature (DPF)
Due Process Handbook, Ch. 1, 2.6
Dynamic hedging strategies, Ch. 53, 6.3.2
Earnings-based contingencies (EPS), Ch. 37, 6.4.6.A
Earnings per share (EPS), Ch. 37, 1–8. *See also* Diluted EPS; IAS 33
  basic EPS, Ch. 37, 3
    earnings, Ch. 37, 3.1
    number of shares, Ch. 37, 3.2
  definitions, Ch. 37, 1.1
  disclosure, Ch. 37, 7.3
  interim financial reporting, Ch. 41, 9.8
  numerator, matters affecting, Ch. 37, 5
    earnings, Ch. 37, 5.1
    other bases, Ch. 37, 5.5
    participating equity instruments, Ch. 37, 5.4
    preference dividends, Ch. 37, 5.2
    retrospective adjustments, Ch. 37, 5.3
    tax deductible dividends on, Ch. 37, 5.4.1
  outstanding ordinary shares, changes in, Ch. 37, 4
  presentation, Ch. 37, 7.1
  restatement, Ch. 37, 7.2
  reverse acquisitions, business combinations, Ch. 9, 14.5; Ch. 37, 4.6.2
EBTs. *See* Employee benefit trusts (EBTs)
Economic relationship, hedge accounting, Ch. 53, 6.4.1
EDs. *See* Exposure Drafts (EDs)
Effective interest method, Ch. 50, 3
Effective interest rate (EIR), Ch. 50, 3.1
Effective tax rate, Ch. 33, 14.2
  changes in during the year, Ch. 41, 9.5.2
Embedded derivatives, Ch. 46, 4–7; Ch. 55, 4
  cash flows, Ch. 54, 5.4.2.E
  characteristics, Ch. 55, 4
  in commodity arrangements, Ch. 43, 12.8
  compound financial instruments with multiple, Ch. 54, 4.4.7
  compound instruments with, Ch. 47, 6.4.2
  contracts for the sale of goods or services, Ch. 46, 5.2
    floors and caps, Ch. 46, 5.2.4
    foreign currency derivatives, Ch. 46, 5.2.1
    fund performance fees, Ch. 46, 5.2.5
    inflation-linked features, Ch. 46, 5.2.3
    inputs, ingredients, substitutes and other proxy pricing mechanisms, Ch. 46, 5.2.2
  decision tree, Ch. 55, 4
  derivative and, Ch. 46, 4
  exposures to market risk from, Ch. 55, 11.2.7
  extractive industries, Ch. 43, 13.2
  financial instrument hosts, Ch. 46, 5.1
    commodity-and equity-linked interest and principal payments, Ch. 46, 5.1.7
    convertible and exchangeable debt instruments, Ch. 46, 5.1.9
    credit-linked notes, Ch. 46, 5.1.8
    fallback provisions relating to interest rate benchmark reform, Ch. 46, 5.1.3
    foreign currency monetary items, Ch. 46, 5.1.1
    inflation-linked debt instruments, Ch. 46, 5.1.6
    interest rate floors and caps, Ch. 46, 5.1.5
    interest rate indices, Ch. 46, 5.1.2
    puttable instruments, Ch. 46, 5.1.10
    term extension and similar call, put and prepayment options in debt instruments, Ch. 46, 5.1.4
  foreign currency embedded derivatives, Ch. 43, 13.2.1
  gains and losses recognised in profit/loss, Ch. 54, 7.1.4
  gas markets, development of, Ch. 43, 13.2.4
  hedging instruments, Ch. 53, 3.2.3
  and host contracts, identifying the terms, Ch. 46, 6
    embedded non-option derivatives, Ch. 46, 6.1
    embedded option-based derivative, Ch. 46, 6.2
    multiple embedded derivatives, Ch. 46, 6.3
  initial measurement, Ch. 49, 3.5
  insurance contracts, Ch. 46, 5.4
  leases, Ch. 46, 5.3
    contingent rentals based on related sales, Ch. 46, 5.3.3
    contingent rentals based on variable interest rates, Ch. 46, 5.3.4
    foreign currency derivatives, Ch. 46, 5.3.1
    inflation-linked features, Ch. 46, 5.3.2
  long-term supply contracts, Ch. 43, 13.2.3
  provisionally priced contracts, Ch. 43, 13.2.2
  reassessment, Ch. 46, 7
    acquisition of contracts, Ch. 46, 7.1
    business combinations, Ch. 46, 7.2
    remeasurement issues arising from, Ch. 46, 7.3
  unit-linked features, Ch. 55, 4.1
Embedded leases, extractive industries, Ch. 43, 17.1
Embedded value (EV) of insurance contract, Ch. 55, 1.4.3
Emerging Economies Group, Ch. 1, 2.9
Emission rights, Ch. 9, 5.5.2.E; Ch. 17, 11.2
  acquired in a business combination, Ch. 9, 5.5.2.E; Ch. 17, 11.2.5
  amortisation, Ch. 17, 11.2.4
  by brokers and traders, accounting for, Ch. 17, 11.2.7
  impairment testing, Ch. 17, 11.2.4
  sale of, Ch. 17, 11.2.6
Emissions trading schemes, intangible assets, Ch. 17, 11.2
  accounting for emission rights by brokers and traders, Ch. 17, 11.2.7
  amortisation and impairment testing of emission rights, Ch. 17, 11.2.4

Emissions trading schemes, intangible assets—*contd*
    emission rights acquired in a business combination, Ch. 17, 11.2.5
    government grant approach, Ch. 17, 11.2.3
    green certificates compared to, Ch. 26, 6.6 IFRIC 3, Ch. 17, 11.2.1
    liabilities associated with, Ch. 26, 6.5
    net liability approaches, Ch. 17, 11.2.2
    sale of emission rights, Ch. 17, 11.2.6

Employee benefit(s), Ch. 35, 1–16. *See also* Defined benefit plans; Defined contribution plans; IAS 19; Long-term employee benefits, Multi-employer plans; Short-term employee benefits
    costs of administering, Ch. 35, 11
    death-in-service benefits, Ch. 35, 3.6
    defined benefit plans, Ch. 35, 5–11
    defined contribution plans, Ch. 35, 4
    disclosure requirements, Ch. 35, 15
        defined benefit plans, Ch. 35, 15.2
        defined contribution plans, Ch. 35, 15.1
        multi-employer plans, Ch. 35, 15.2.4
    future developments, Ch. 35, 16
    insured benefits, Ch. 35, 3.2
    interim financial reporting, Ch. 41, 9.3
        employer payroll taxes and insurance contributions, Ch. 41, 9.3.1
        pensions, Ch. 41, 9.3.3
        vacations, holidays and other short-term paid absences, Ch. 41, 9.3.4
        year-end bonuses, Ch. 41, 9.3.2
    long-term employee benefits, Ch. 35, 13
    multi-employer plans, Ch. 35, 3.3
    objective of IAS 19, Ch. 35, 2.1
    pensions, Ch. 35, 3
    plans that would be defined contribution plans, Ch. 35, 3.5
    post-employment benefits, Ch. 35, 3
    scope of IAS 19, Ch. 35, 2.2
    short-term employee benefits, Ch. 35, 12
    state plans, Ch. 35, 3.4
    termination benefits, Ch. 35, 14

Employee benefit plans, Ch. 6, 2.2.2; Ch. 13, 2.2.3.A

Employee benefit trusts (EBTs) and similar arrangements, Ch. 34, 12.3
    accounting for, Ch. 34, 12.3.2
    awards satisfied by shares purchased by, or issued to, an EBT, Ch. 34, 12.3.3
    background, Ch. 34, 12.3.1
    EBT as extension of parent, Ch. 34, 12.4.2.B, 12.5.2.B
    financial statements of the EBT, Ch. 34, 12.3.5
    financial statements of the parent, Ch. 34, 12.4.2, 12.5.2
    group share scheme illustrative examples
        equity-settled award satisfied by fresh issue of shares, Ch. 34, 12.5
        equity-settled award satisfied by market purchase of shares, Ch. 34, 12.4
    separate financial statements of sponsoring entity, Ch. 34, 12.3.4

Employee, definition, Ch. 34, 5.2.1

'Empty' subsidiaries, Ch. 52, 3.6.6

'End-user' contracts, Ch. 45, 4.2.4

Enhanced Disclosure Task Force (EDTF), Ch. 54, 9.2

Entity's functional currency determination, Ch. 15, 4
    branches and divisions, Ch. 15, 4.4
    documentation of judgements made, Ch. 15, 4.5
    intermediate holding companies/finance subsidiaries, Ch. 15, 4.2
    investment holding companies, Ch. 15, 4.3

EPS. *See* Earnings per share

Equalisation provisions, Ch. 55, 7.2.1

Equity instruments, Ch. 8, 2.1.1.A; Ch. 45, 2.2.7, 3.6
    classification, Ch. 48, 2.2
    contracts to issue equity instruments, Ch. 47, 4.4.2
    contracts settled by delivery of the entity's own equity instruments, Ch. 47, 5
        contracts accounted for as equity instruments, Ch. 47, 5.1
            comparison with IFRS 2–share-based payment, Ch. 47, 5.1.1
            contracts to acquire non-controlling interests, Ch. 47, 5.3.2
            contracts to purchase own equity during 'closed' or 'prohibited' periods, Ch. 47, 5.3.1
            exchange of fixed amounts of equity (equity for equity), Ch. 47, 5.1.4
            number of equity instruments issued adjusted for capital restructuring or other event, Ch. 47, 5.1.2
            stepped up exercise price, Ch. 47, 5.1.3
        contracts accounted for as financial assets/liabilities, Ch. 47, 5.2
            derivative financial instruments with settlement options, Ch. 47, 5.2.8
            fixed amount of cash denominated in a currency other than entity's functional currency, Ch. 47, 5.2.3
                rights issues with a price fixed in a currency other than entity's functional currency, Ch. 47, 5.2.3.A
            fixed amount of cash determined by reference to share price Ch. 47, 5.2.6
            fixed number of equity instruments for variable consideration, Ch. 47, 5.2.2
            fixed number of equity instruments with variable value, Ch. 47, 5.2.5
            instrument with equity settlement alternative of significantly higher value than cash settlement alternative, Ch. 47, 5.2.4
            net-settled contracts over own equity, Ch. 47, 5.2.7
            variable number of equity instruments, Ch. 47, 5.2.1
        gross-settled contracts for the sale or issue of the entity's own equity instruments, Ch. 47, 5.4
        liabilities arising from gross-settled contracts for the purchase of the entity's own equity instruments, Ch. 47, 5.3
            contracts to acquire non-controlling interests, Ch. 47, 5.3.2
            contracts to purchase own equity during 'closed' or 'prohibited' periods, Ch. 47, 5.3.1
    definition, Ch. 34, 2.2.1; Ch. 45, 2.1; Ch. 47, 3
    determining fair value of, Ch. 14, 11.2; Ch. 34, 5.5
    holder, Ch. 45, 3.6.2
    investments in, designated at fair value through OCI, Ch. 51, 9
    issued instruments, Ch. 45, 3.6.1; Ch. 47, 4.4.1

Equity method/accounting, Ch. 11, 7
  application of the equity method, Ch. 11, 7
    consistent accounting policies, Ch. 11, 7.8
    date of commencement of equity accounting, Ch. 11, 7.3
    discontinuing the use of the equity method, Ch. 11, 7.12
      deemed disposals, Ch. 11, 7.12.6
      investment in associate becomes a joint venture (or vice versa), Ch. 11, 7.12.4
      investment in associate/joint venture that is a business becoming a subsidiary, Ch. 11, 7.12.1
      investment in associate or joint venture that is not a business becoming a subsidiary, Ch. 11, 7.12.2
      partial disposals of interests in associate/joint venture, Ch. 11, 7.12.4
      retained investment in the former associate or joint venture is a financial asset, Ch. 11, 7.12.3
    distributions received in excess of the carrying amount, Ch. 11, 7.10
    equity accounting and consolidation, comparison between, Ch. 11, 7.2
    equity transactions in an associate's/joint venture's financial statements, Ch. 11, 7.11
      dividends/other forms of distributions, Ch. 11, 7.11.1
      effects of changes in parent/non-controlling interests in subsidiaries, Ch. 11, 7.11.4
      equity-settled share-based payment transactions, Ch. 11, 7.11.3
      issues of equity instruments, Ch. 11, 7.11, 7.11.2
    impairment losses, Ch. 11, 8
      general, Ch. 11, 8.1
      investment in the associate or joint venture, Ch. 11, 8.2
      other interests that are not part of the net investment in the associate or joint venture, Ch. 11, 8.3
    impairment of investments in subsidiaries, associates and joint ventures, Ch. 20, 12.4
      equity accounted investments and CGU's, Ch. 20, 12.4.5
      equity accounted investments and goodwill for impairment, Ch. 20, 12.4.6
      indicators of impairment, Ch. 20, 12.4.3, 12.4.4
    initial carrying amount of an associate/joint venture, Ch. 11, 7.4
      cost-based approach, Ch. 11, 7.4.2.A
      fair value (IFRS 3) approach, Ch. 11, 7.4.2.A
      following loss of control of an entity, Ch. 7, 3.3.2, 7.1, 3.2; Ch. 11, 7.4.1, 7.6.5
      piecemeal acquisition, Ch. 11, 7.4.2
        common control transactions involving sales of associates, Ch. 11, 7.4.2.D
        existing associate that becomes a joint venture, or vice versa, Ch. 11, 7.4.2.C
        financial instrument becoming an associate/joint venture, Ch. 11, 7.4.2.A
        step increase in an existing associate/joint venture without a change in status of the investee, Ch. 11, 7.4.2.B
    loss-making associates/joint ventures, Ch. 11, 7.9
    non-coterminous accounting periods, Ch. 11, 7.7
    overview, Ch. 11, 7.1
    share of the investee, Ch. 11, 7.5
      accounting for potential voting rights, Ch. 11, 7.5.1
      cumulative preference shares held by parties other than the investor, Ch. 11, 7.5.2
      several classes of equity, Ch. 11, 7.5.3
      where the investee is a group, Ch. 11, 7.5.5
      where the reporting entity is a group, Ch. 11, 7.5.4
    transactions between the reporting entity and its associates/joint ventures, Ch. 11, 7.6
      contributions of non-monetary assets to an associate/a joint venture, Ch. 11, 7.6.5
        commercial substance, Ch. 11, 7.6.5.A
        conflict between IAS 28 and IFRS 10, Ch. 11, 7.6.5.C
        practical application, Ch. 11, 7.6.5.B
      elimination of 'upstream' and 'downstream' transactions, Ch. 11, 7.6.1
      loans and borrowings between the reporting entity, Ch. 11, 7.6.3
      reciprocal interests, Ch. 11, 7.6.2
      statement of cash flows, Ch. 11, 7.6.4
  exemptions from applying the equity method, Ch. 11, 5.3
    investments held in associates/joint ventures held by venture capital organisations, Ch. 11, 5.3
      application of IFRS 9 (or IAS 39) to exempt, Ch. 11, 5.3.2
      entities with a mixture of activities, Ch. 11, 5.3.2.A
    investment entities exception, Ch. 11, 5.3.1
  former subsidiary that becomes an equity-accounted investee, Ch. 7, 3.3.2, 7.1
    application of partial gain recognition where the gain exceeds the carrying amount of the investment in the associate or joint venture accounted using the equity method, Ch. 7, 3.3.2.D
    conflict between IFRS 10 and IAS 28 (September 2014 amendments applied), Ch. 7, 3.3.2.B, 3.3.2.E, 7.1
    conflict between IFRS 10 and IAS 28 (September 2014 amendments not applied), Ch. 7, 3.3.2.A, 3.3.2.E
    determination of the fair value of the retained interest in a former subsidiary that is an associate or joint venture, Ch. 7, 3.3.2.F
    examples of accounting for sales or contributions to an existing associate, Ch. 7, 3.3.2.E
    presentation of comparative information for a former subsidiary that becomes an investee for using the equity method, Ch. 7, 3.3.2.G
    reclassification of items of other comprehensive income where the interest retained in the former subsidiary is an associate or joint venture accounted using the equity method, Ch. 7, 3.3.2.C
  parents exempt from preparing consolidated financial statements, Ch. 11, 5.1
  partial use of fair value measurement of associates, Ch. 11, 5.4
  subsidiaries meeting certain criteria, Ch. 11, 5.2
  transfers of associates/joint ventures between entities under common control, Ch. 10, 5

Equity-settled share-based payment transactions, Ch. 34, 2.2.1, 4–8. *See also* Cash-settled share-based payment transactions; IFRS 2; Share-based payment/transactions; Vesting, share-based payment
  accounting treatment, summary, Ch. 34, 4.1

Equity-settled share-based payment transactions—*contd*
  allocation of expense, Ch. 34, 6
    market conditions, Ch. 34, 6.3
    non-vesting conditions, Ch. 34, 6.4
    overview, Ch. 34, 6.1
      accounting after vesting, Ch. 34, 6.1.3
      continuous estimation process of IFRS 2, Ch. 34, 6.1.1
      vesting and forfeiture, Ch. 34, 6.1.2
    vesting conditions other than market conditions, Ch. 34, 6.2
      'graded' vesting, Ch. 34, 6.2.2
      service conditions, Ch. 34, 6.2.1
      variable exercise price, Ch. 34, 6.2.5
      variable number of equity instruments, Ch. 34, 6.2.4
      variable vesting periods, Ch. 34, 6.2.3
  award modified to, or from, cash-settled, Ch. 34, 9.4
  cancellation, replacement and settlement, Ch. 34, 7.4
    calculation of the expense on cancellation, Ch. 34, 7.4.3
    cancellation and forfeiture, distinction between, Ch. 34, 7.4.1
      surrender of award by employee, Ch. 34, 7.4.1.B
      termination of employment by entity, Ch. 34, 7.4.1.A
    cancellation and modification, distinction between, Ch. 34, 7.4.2
    replacement awards, Ch. 34, 7.4.4
      designation, Ch. 34, 7.4.4.A
      incremental fair value of, Ch. 34, 7.4.4.B
      replacement of vested awards, Ch. 34, 7.4.4.C
    valuation requirements when an award is cancelled or settled, Ch. 34, 7.2
  cost of awards, Ch. 34, 5
    determining the fair value of equity instruments, Ch. 34, 5.5, 8
      reload features, Ch. 34, 5.5.1, 8.9
    grant date, Ch. 34, 5.3
    overview, Ch. 34, 5.1
    transactions with employees, Ch. 34, 5.2
    transactions with non-employees, Ch. 34, 5.4
  credit entry, Ch. 34, 4.2
  entity's plans for future modification/replacement of award, Ch. 34, 7.6
  grant date, Ch. 34, 5.3
  market conditions, Ch. 34, 6.3
    accounting treatment summary, Ch. 34, 6.3.2
    awards with a condition linked to flotation price, Ch. 34, 6.3.8
    definition, Ch. 34, 6.3.1
    hybrid/interdependent market conditions and non-market vesting conditions, Ch. 34, 6.3.7
    independent market conditions and non-market vesting conditions, Ch. 34, 6.3.6
    market conditions and known vesting periods, Ch. 34, 6.3.3
    multiple outcomes depending on market conditions, Ch. 34, 6.3.5
    transactions with variable vesting periods due to market conditions, Ch. 34, 6.3.4
  market purchases of own equity, Ch. 34, 9.2.2, 9.2.3
  modification, Ch. 34, 7.3
    altering vesting period, Ch. 34, 7.3.3
    decreasing the value of an award, Ch. 34, 7.3.2
      additional/more onerous non-market vesting conditions, Ch. 34, 7.3.2.C
      decrease in fair value of equity instruments granted, Ch. 34, 7.3.2.A
      decrease in number of equity instruments granted, Ch. 34, 7.3.2.B
    from equity-settled to cash-settled, Ch. 34, 7.3.5
    increasing the value of an award, Ch. 34, 7.3.1
      increase in fair value of equity instruments granted, Ch. 34, 7.3.1.A
      increase in number of equity instruments granted, Ch. 34, 7.3.1.B
      removal/mitigation of non-market vesting conditions, Ch. 34, 7.3.1.C
    that reduces the number of equity instruments granted but maintains or increases the value of an award, Ch. 34, 7.3.4
    share splits and consolidations, Ch. 34, 7.8
    two awards running 'in parallel', Ch. 34, 7.7
    valuation requirements when an award is modified, Ch. 34, 7.2
  non-vesting conditions, Ch. 34, 6.4
    awards with no conditions other than non-vesting conditions, Ch. 34, 6.4.1
    awards with non-vesting conditions and variable vesting periods, Ch. 34, 6.4.2
    failure to meet non-vesting conditions, Ch. 34, 6.4.3
  reload features, Ch. 34, 5.5.1, 8.9
  termination of employment by entity, Ch. 34, 7.4.1.A
    replacement and *ex gratia* awards, Ch. 34, 7.5
  transactions with employees, Ch. 34, 5.2
    basis of measurement, Ch. 34, 5.2.2
    employee definition, Ch. 34, 5.2.1
  transactions with non-employees, Ch. 34, 5.4
    effect of change of status from employee to non-employee (or vice versa), Ch. 34, 5.4.1
  transactions with equity and cash alternatives, Ch. 34, 10.1, 10.2, 10.3
    awards requiring cash settlement in specific circumstances (awards with contingent cash settlement), Ch. 34, 10.3
      change in manner of settlement where award is contingent on future events outside the control of the entity and the counterparty, Ch. 34, 10.3.4
      cash settlement on a change of control, Ch. 34, 10.3.3
      IASB discussion, Ch. 34, 10.3.5
      treat as cash-settled if contingency is outside entity's control, Ch. 34, 10.3.1
      contingency outside entity's control and probable, Ch. 34, 10.3.2
    cash settlement alternative not based on share price/value, Ch. 34, 10.4
  transactions where the counterparty has choice of settlement, Ch. 34, 10.1
    accounting treatment, during vesting period, Ch. 34, 10.1.3.A
    accounting treatment, settlement, Ch. 34, 10.1.3. B
    'backstop' cash settlement rights, Ch. 34, 10.1.5
    cash-settlement alternative for employee introduced after grant date, Ch. 34, 10.1.4

convertible bonds issued to acquire goods/services, Ch. 34, 10.1.6
transactions in which the fair value is measured directly, Ch. 34, 10.1.1
transactions in which the fair value is measured indirectly, Ch. 34, 10.1.2
transactions where the entity has choice of settlement, Ch. 34, 10.2
  change in entity's settlement policy/intention leading to change in classification of award after grant date, Ch. 34, 10.2.3
  transactions treated as cash-settled, Ch. 34, 10.2.1
    economic compulsion for cash settlement, Ch. 34, 10.2.1.A
  transactions treated as equity-settled, Ch. 34, 10.2.2
valuation, Ch. 34, 8
  awards of equity instruments to a fixed monetary value, Ch. 34, 8.10
  awards other than options, Ch. 34, 8.7
    non-recourse loans, Ch. 34, 8.7.2
    performance rights, Ch. 34, 8.7.4
    share appreciation rights (SAR), Ch. 34, 8.7.3
    shares, Ch. 34, 8.7.1
  awards whose fair value cannot be measured reliably, Ch. 34, 8.8
    intrinsic value method, Ch. 34, 8.8.1
    modification, cancellation and settlement, Ch. 34, 8.8.2
  awards with reload features, Ch. 34, 8.9
  capital structure effects and dilution, Ch. 34, 8.6
  option-pricing model, selection of, Ch. 34, 8.3
    binomial model, Ch. 34, 8.3.2
    Black-Scholes-Merton formula, Ch. 34, 8.3.1
    Monte Carlo Simulation, Ch. 34, 8.3.3
  option-pricing model, selecting appropriate assumptions, Ch. 34, 8.5
    exercise and termination behaviour, Ch. 34, 8.5.2
    expected dividends, Ch. 34, 8.5.4
    expected term of the option, Ch. 34, 8.5.1
    expected volatility of share price, Ch. 34, 8.5.3
    risk-free interest rate, Ch. 34, 8.5.5
  option-pricing models, adapting for share-based payment, Ch. 34, 8.4
    non-transferability, Ch. 34, 8.4.1
    vesting and non-vesting conditions, treatment of, Ch. 34, 8.4.2
  options, Ch. 34, 8.2
    call options, overview, Ch. 34, 8.2.1
    call options, valuation, Ch. 34, 8.2.2
    factors specific to employee share options, Ch. 34, 8.2.3
vesting conditions other than market conditions, Ch. 34, 6.2
  'graded' vesting, Ch. 34, 6.2.2
  service conditions, Ch. 34, 6.2.1
  variable exercise price, Ch. 34, 6.2.5
  variable number of equity instruments, Ch. 34, 6.2.4
  variable vesting periods, Ch. 34, 6.2.3

Equity transactions
in an associate's/joint venture's financial statements, Ch. 11, 7.11
  dividends/other forms of distributions, Ch. 11, 7.11.1
  effects of changes in parent/non-controlling interests in subsidiaries, Ch. 11, 7.11.4
  equity-settled share-based payment transactions, Ch. 11, 7.11.3
  issues of equity instruments, Ch. 11, 7.11.2
tax effects of, Ch. 47, 8.2
transaction costs of, Ch. 47, 8.1

Errors, prior period
correction of, Ch. 3, 4.6
disclosure of, Ch. 3, 5.3
discovery of fraud after the reporting period, Ch. 38, 3.5
impracticability of restatement, Ch. 3, 4.7.2

Estimates. *See* Accounting Estimates

Estimation uncertainty, Ch. 3, 5.2
disclosures of, Ch. 3, 5.2
sources of, Ch. 3, 5.2.1

Euro, introduction of, Ch. 15, 8

European Commission, Ch. 1, 1, 2.2–2.3, 2.5, 4.2.1

European Embedded Values (EEV), Ch. 55, 1.4.3

European Financial Reporting Advisory Group (EFRAG), Ch. 1, 4.2.1

European Securities and Markets Authority (ESMA), Ch. 1, 5

European Union
adoption of IRFS in the EU, Ch. 1, 4.2.1
EU directive on WE&EE (IFRIC 6), Ch. 26, 6.7
EU 'top up' for financial conglomerates, Ch. 1, 4.2.1
introduction of the euro, Ch. 15, 8
tax implications of UK withdrawal from the (EU), Ch. 33, 5.1.4

Events after the reporting period, Ch. 38, 1–3. *See also* IAS 10
adjusting events, Ch. 38, 2.1.2
  treatment of, Ch. 38, 2.2
extractive industries, Ch. 43, 20
  business combinations-application of the acquisition method, Ch. 43, 20.2
  completion of E&E activity after, Ch. 43, 20.3
  reserves proven after the reporting period, Ch. 43, 20.1
impairment, Ch. 20, 7.1.9
non-adjusting events, Ch. 38, 2.1.3
  dividend declaration, Ch. 38, 2.1.3.A
  treatment of, Ch. 38, 2.3
practical issues, Ch. 38, 3
  changes to estimates of uncertain tax treatments, Ch. 38, 3.6
  discovery of fraud after the reporting period, Ch. 38, 3.5
  insolvency of a debtor and IFRS 9 expected credit losses, Ch. 38, 3.3
  percentage of completion estimates, Ch. 38, 3.2
  valuation of inventory, Ch. 38, 3.1
  valuation of investment property at fair value and tenant insolvency, Ch. 38, 3.4

Evidence of power over an investee, Ch. 6, 4.5

Ex gratia **share-based payment award**, Ch. 34, 7.5

Exchanges of assets, Ch. 17, 4.7; Ch. 18, 4.4
commercial substance, Ch. 17, 4.7.2; Ch. 18, 4.4.1
measurement of assets exchanged, Ch. 17, 4.7.1
reliably measurable, Ch. 18, 4.4.2

Executory contract, Ch. 26, 2.2.1.A

Existing rights, investee
    budget approval rights, Ch. 6, 4.2.2.C
    evaluation whether rights are protective, Ch. 6, 4.2.2
    evaluation whether rights are substantive, Ch. 6, 4.2.1
    franchises, Ch. 6, 4.2.2.B
    incentives to obtain power, Ch. 6, 4.2.3
    independent directors, Ch. 6, 4.2.2.D
    veto rights, Ch. 6, 4.2.2.A

Expected credit losses (ECLs), Ch. 51, 14. *See also* Credit risk
    approaches, Ch. 51, 3
        general approach, Ch. 51, 3.1
        purchased/originated credit-impaired financial assets, Ch. 51, 3.3
        simplified approach, Ch. 51, 3.2
    background and history of impairment project, Ch. 51, 1.1
    calculations, Ch. 51, 7
        Basel guidance on accounting for ECLs, Ch. 51, 7.1
        date of derecognition and date of initial recognition, Ch. 51, 7.3.1
        Global Public Policy Committee (GPPC) guidance, Ch. 51, 7.2
        interaction between expected credit losses calculations and fair value hedge accounting, Ch. 51, 7.5; Ch. 53, 6.4.2.B
        interaction between the initial measurement of debt instruments acquired in a business combination and the impairment model of IFRS 9, Ch. 51, 7.4
        measurement dates of ECLs, Ch. 51, 7.3
        trade date and settlement date accounting, Ch. 51, 7.3.2
    derecognition of contract assets, Ch. 32, 2.1.4
    disclosures, Ch. 51, 15
    financial assets measured at fair value through other comprehensive income, Ch. 51, 9; Ch. 53, 2.6.3
        accounting treatment for debt instruments measured at fair value through other comprehensive income, Ch. 51, 9.1
        interaction between foreign currency translation, fair value hedge accounting and impairment, Ch. 51, 9.2
    financial guarantee contracts, Ch. 51, 11
    Global Public Policy Committee guidance, Ch. 51, 7.2
    IFRS Transition Resource Group for Impairment of Financial Instruments (ITG) and IASB webcasts, Ch. 51, 1.5
    impairment of contract assets, Ch. 32, 2.1.3
    impairment requirements (IFRS 9), Ch. 51, 1.2
    initial measurement of receivables, Ch. 32, 2.1.5
    intercompany loans, Ch. 51, 13
    key changes from the IAS 39 requirements and the main implications of these changes, Ch. 51, 1.3
    key differences from the FASB's requirements, Ch. 51, 1.4
    loan commitments, Ch. 51, 11
    measurement, Ch. 51, 5
        definition of default, Ch. 51, 5.1
        expected life *vs.* contractual period, Ch. 51, 5.5
        lifetime expected credit losses, Ch. 51, 5.2
        losses expected in the event of default, Ch. 51, 5.8
            cash flows from the sale of a defaulted loan, Ch. 51, 5.8.2
            credit enhancements: collateral and financial guarantees, Ch. 51, 5.8.1
            treatment of collection costs paid to an external debt collection agency, Ch. 51 5.8.3
        12-month expected credit losses, Ch. 51, 5.3
        probability of default (PD) and loss rate approaches, Ch. 51, 5.4
            loss rate approach, Ch. 51, 5.4.2
            probability of default approach, Ch. 51, 5.4.1
        probability-weighted outcome, Ch. 51, 5.6
        reasonable and supportable information, Ch. 51, 5.9
            information about past events, current conditions and forecasts of future economic conditions, Ch. 51, 5.9.3
            sources of information, Ch. 51, 5.9.2
            undue cost/effort, Ch. 51, 5.9.1
        time value of money, Ch. 51, 12.4
    modified financial assets, accounting treatment, Ch. 51, 8
        if assets are derecognised, Ch. 51, 8.1
        if assets are not derecognised, Ch. 51, 8.2
    other guidance on ECLs, Ch. 51, 1.6
    presentation of ECLs in the statement of financial position, Ch. 51, 14
        accumulated impairment amount for debt instruments measured at fair value through other comprehensive income, Ch. 51, 14.3
        allowance for financial assets measured at amortised cost, contract assets and lease receivables, Ch. 51, 14.1
            presentation of the gross carrying amount and ECL allowance for credit-impaired assets, Ch. 51, 14.1.2
            write-off, Ch. 51, 14.1.1
        provisions for loan commitments and financial guarantee contracts, Ch. 51, 14.2
    revolving credit facilities, Ch. 51, 12
        determining a significant increase in credit risk, Ch. 51, 12.5
        exposure at default, Ch. 51, 12.3
        period over which to measure ECLs, Ch. 51, 12.2
        scope of the exception, Ch. 51, 12.1
        time value of money, Ch. 51, 12.4
    scope of IFRS 9 impairment requirements, Ch. 51, 2
    trade receivables, contract assets and lease receivables, Ch. 51, 10
        lease receivables, Ch. 51, 10.2
        trade receivables and contract assets, Ch. 51, 10.1

Expenses analysis, Ch. 3, 3.2.3
    by function, Ch. 3, 3.2.3.B,
    by nature, Ch. 3, 3.2.3.A

Exploration and evaluation (E&E) assets. *See also* IFRS 6 asset swaps, Ch. 43, 6.3.1
    carried interest in E&E phase, Ch. 43, 6.1.2
    exchanges of E&E assets for other types of assets, Ch. 43, 6.3.3
    farm-in arrangements, Ch. 43, 6.2
    impairment of, Ch. 43, 3.5
        additional considerations if E&E assets are impaired, Ch. 43, 3.5.5
        cash-generating units comprising successful and unsuccessful E&E projects, Ch. 43, 3.5.3
        impairment testing 'triggers,' Ch. 43, 3.5.1

income statement treatment of E&E write downs, Ch. 43, 3.5.6
order of impairment testing, Ch. 43, 3.5.4
reversal of impairment losses, Ch. 43, 3.5.7
specifying the level at which E&E assets are assessed for impairment, Ch. 43, 3.5.2
measurement of, Ch. 43, 3.3
capitalisation of borrowing costs in the E&E phase, Ch. 43, 3.3.2
types of expenditure in the E&E phase, Ch. 43, 3.3.1
reclassification of, Ch. 43, 3.4.1
recognition of, Ch. 43, 3.2
area-of-interest method, Ch. 43, 3.2.5
changes in accounting policies, Ch. 43, 3.2.6
developing an accounting policy under IFRS 6, Ch. 43, 3.2.1
full cost method, Ch. 43, 3.2.4
options for an exploration and evaluation policy, Ch. 43, 3.2.2
successful efforts method, Ch. 43, 3.2.3

Exposure Drafts (EDs)
ED 5–*Insurance Contracts*, Ch. 55, 1.2
ED/2009/2–*Income Tax*, Ch. 33, 1.3, 8.5.1
ED/2014/4 – *Measuring Quoted Investments in Subsidiaries, Joint Ventures and Associates at Fair Value (Proposed amendments to IFRS 10, IFRS 12, IAS 27, IAS 28 and IAS 36 and Illustrative Examples for IFRS 13)*, Ch. 7, 3.3.2.F; Ch. 14, 5.1.1
ED/2017/5 – *Accounting Policies and Accounting Estimates – Proposed amendments to IAS 8*, Ch. 3, 6.2.1; Ch. 22, 3.2.2
ED/2019/5 – *Deferred Tax related to Assets and Liabilities arising from a Single Transaction: Proposed amendments to IAS 12*, Ch. 33, 7.2.7
ED/2019/6 – *Disclosure of Accounting Policies, Proposed amendments to IAS 1 and IFRS Practice Statement 2*, Ch. 3, 6.2.2
ED/2019/7 – *General Presentation and Disclosure*, Ch. 3, 6.1.2

External hedging instruments, offsetting, Ch. 53, 3.2.1

Extractive industries, Ch. 43, 1–20. *See also* IFRS 6; Mineral reserves and resources; Reserves
acquisitions, Ch. 43, 8
accounting for land acquisitions, Ch. 43, 8.4.2
acquisition of an interest in a joint operation that is a business, Ch. 43, 8.3
asset acquisitions and conditional purchase consideration, Ch. 43, 8.4.1
business combinations, Ch. 43, 8.2
events after the reporting period, Ch. 43, 22.2
goodwill in business combinations, Ch. 43, 8.2.1
impairment of assets and goodwill recognised on acquisition, Ch. 43, 8.2.2
value beyond proven and probable reserves (VBPP), Ch. 43, 8.2.3
business combinations *vs.* asset acquisitions, Ch. 43, 8.1
definition of a business, Ch. 43, 8.1.2
differences between asset purchase transactions and, Ch. 43, 8.1.1
April 2010 discussion paper, extractive activities, Ch. 43, 1.3
asset measurement, Ch. 43, 1.3.3
asset recognition, Ch. 43, 1.3.2
disclosure, Ch. 43, 1.3.4
Extractive Activities project, status of, Ch. 43, 1.3.6
project status, Ch. 43, 1.3.6
publish what you pay proposals, Ch. 43, 1.3.5
reserves and resources, definitions of, Ch. 43, 1.3.1
decommissioning and restoration/rehabilitation, Ch. 43, 10
indefinite life assets, Ch. 43, 10.3
recognition and measurement issues, Ch. 43, 10.1
treatment of foreign exchange differences, Ch. 43, 10.2
definitions, Ch. 43, 1.1, 21
depreciation, depletion and amortisation (DD&A), Ch. 43, 16
block caving, Ch. 43, 16.2
determining when production phase commences, Ch. 43, 15.5.2
requirements under IAS 16 and IAS 38, Ch. 43, 16.1
assets depreciated using the straight-line method, Ch. 43, 16.1.2
assets depreciated using the units of production method, Ch. 43, 16.1.3
mineral reserves, Ch. 43, 16.1.1
events after the reporting period, Ch. 43, 22
business combinations-application of the acquisition method, Ch. 43, 22.2
completion of E&E activity after, Ch. 43, 22.3
reserves proven after the reporting period, Ch. 43, 22.1
financial instruments, Ch. 43, 13
embedded derivatives, Ch. 43, 13.2
development of gas markets, Ch. 43, 13.2.4
foreign currency embedded derivatives, Ch. 43, 13.2.1
long-term supply contracts, Ch. 43, 13.2.3
provisionally priced sales contracts, Ch. 43, 13.2.2
hedging sales of metal concentrate (mining), Ch. 43, 13.4
normal purchase and sales exemption, Ch. 43, 13.1
volume flexibility in supply contracts, Ch. 43, 13.3
functional currency, Ch. 43, 9
changes in, Ch. 43, 9.2
determining, Ch. 43, 9.1
guidance under national accounting standards, Ch. 43, 1.5
impact of IFRS 15, Ch. 43, 12
commodity-based contracts, modifications to, Ch. 43, 12.10
embedded derivatives in commodity arrangements, Ch. 43, 12.8
forward-selling contracts to finance development, Ch. 43, 12.6
gold bullion sales (mining only), Ch. 43, 12.13
inventory exchanges with the same counterparty, Ch. 43, 12.3
multi-period commodity-based sales contracts, Ch. 43, 12.15
overlift and underlift (oil and gas), Ch. 43, 12.4
principal *vs.* agent considerations in commodity-based contracts, Ch. 43, 12.11
production sharing contracts/arrangements (PSCs), Ch. 43, 12.5
repurchase agreements, Ch. 43, 12.14
royalty income, Ch. 43, 12.9
sale of product with delayed shipment, Ch. 43, 12.2
shipping, Ch. 43, 12.12
take-or-pay contracts, Ch. 43, 12.16
trading activities, Ch. 43, 12.7

24 Index

Extractive industries—*contd*
- impact of IFRS 16, Ch. 43, 17, 18
  - allocating contract consideration, Ch. 43, 17.6
  - definition of a lease, Ch. 43, 17.2
  - identifying and separating lease and non-lease components, Ch. 43, 17.
  - identifying lease payments included in the measurement of the lease liability, Ch. 43, 17.5
  - interaction of IFRS 16 and IFRS 11, Ch. 43, 18
  - interaction of leases with asset retirement obligations, Ch. 43, 17.7
  - joint arrangements, Ch. 43, 18
  - land easements or rights of way, Ch. 43, 17.1.2
  - scope and scope exclusions, Ch. 43, 17.1
  - substitution rights, Ch. 43, 17.3
  - subsurface rights, Ch. 43, 17.1.3
- impairment of assets, Ch. 43, 11
  - basis of recoverable amount – value-in-use (VIU) or fair value less costs of disposal (FVLCD), Ch. 43, 11.3
  - calculation of FVLCD, Ch. 43, 11.5
  - calculation of VIU, Ch. 43, 11.4
  - cash flows from mineral reserves and resources and the appropriate discount rate, Ch. 43, 11.4.2.A
  - commodity price assumptions, Ch. 43, 11.4.3, 11.5.2
  - foreign currency cash flows, Ch. 43, 11.4.5, 11.5.4
  - future capital expenditure, Ch. 43, 11.4.4, 11.5.3
  - identifying cash-generating units (CGUs), Ch. 43, 11.2
  - impairment indicators, Ch. 43, 11.1
  - low mine or field profitability near end of life, Ch. 43, 11.6
  - projections of cash flows, Ch. 43, 11.4.2, 11.5.1
- inventories, Ch. 43, 14
  - carried at fair value, Ch. 43, 14.4
  - core inventories, Ch. 43, 14.3
  - heap leaching (mining), Ch. 43, 14.6
  - recognition of work in progress, Ch. 43, 14.1
  - sale of by-products and joint products, Ch. 43, 14.2
    - by-products, Ch. 43, 14.2.1
    - joint products, Ch. 43, 14.2.2
  - stockpiles of low grade ore (mining), Ch. 43, 14.5
- investments in the extractive industries, Ch. 43, 7
  - joint arrangements, Ch. 43, 7.1
    - assessing joint control, Ch. 43, 7.1.1
    - determining whether a manager has control, Ch. 43, 7.1.2
    - managers of joint arrangements, Ch. 43, 7.1.4
    - non-operators, Ch. 43, 7.1.5
    - parties without joint control/control, Ch. 43, 7.1.3
  - undivided interests, Ch. 43, 7.2
- legal rights to explore for, develop and produce mineral properties, Ch. 43, 5
  - concessionary agreements (concessions), Ch. 43, 5.2
  - different types of royalty interests, Ch. 43, 5.7
    - net profits interests, Ch. 43, 5.7.4
    - overriding royalties, Ch. 43, 5.7.2
    - production payment royalties, Ch. 43, 5.7.3
    - revenue and royalties: gross or net?, Ch. 43, 5.7.5
    - working interest and basic royalties, Ch. 43, 5.7.1
  - evolving contractual arrangements, Ch. 43, 5.5
  - how a mineral lease works, Ch. 43, 5.1
  - joint operating agreements, Ch. 43, 5.6
  - pure-service contract, Ch. 43, 5.4
  - traditional production sharing contracts, Ch. 43, 5.3
- long-term contracts and leases, Ch. 43, 19
  - embedded leases, Ch. 43, 19.1
  - impact of IFRS 16, Ch. 43, 19.3
  - take-or-pay contracts, Ch. 43, 19.2
    - make-up product and undertake, Ch. 43, 19.2.1
- mineral reserves and resources, Ch. 43, 2
  - disclosure of mineral reserves and resources, Ch. 43, 2.4
    - mining sector, Ch. 43, 2.4.2
    - oil and gas sector, Ch. 43, 2.4.1
    - value of reserves, Ch. 43, 2.4.3
  - international harmonisation of reserve reporting, Ch. 43, 2.1
  - mining resource and reserve reporting, Ch. 43, 2.3
    - CIRSCO International reporting template, Ch. 43, 2.3.1
  - petroleum reserve estimation and reporting, Ch. 43, 2.2
    - basic principles and definitions, Ch. 43, 2.2.1
    - classification and categorisation guidelines, Ch. 43, 2.2.2
- property, plant and equipment, Ch. 43, 15
  - care and maintenance, Ch. 43, 15.3
  - major maintenance and turnarounds/renewals and reconditioning costs, Ch. 43, 15.1
  - redeterminations, Ch. 43, 15.4.2
    - as capital reimbursements, Ch. 43, 15.4.2.A
    - decommissioning provisions, Ch. 43, 15.4.2.C
    - 'make-up' oil, Ch. 43, 15.4.2.B
  - stripping costs in the production phase of a surface mine (mining), Ch. 43, 15.5
    - determining when production phase commences, Ch. 43, 15.5.2
    - disclosures, Ch. 43, 15.5.6
    - initial recognition, Ch. 43, 15.5.4
    - recognition criteria-stripping activity asset, Ch. 43, 15.5.3
    - scope of IFRIC 20, Ch. 43, 15.5.1
    - subsequent measurement, Ch. 43, 15.5.5
  - unitisations, Ch. 43, 15.4
  - well workovers and recompletions (oil and gas), Ch. 43, 15.2
- revenue recognition, Ch. 43, 12
  - forward-selling contracts to finance development, Ch. 43, 12.6
  - inventory exchanges with the same counterparty, Ch. 43, 12.3
  - overlift and underlift (oil and gas), Ch. 43, 12.4
    - accounting for imbalances in revenue under IFRS 15, Ch. 43, 12.4.1
    - consideration of cost of goods sold where revenue is recognised in accordance with IFRS 15, Ch. 43, 12.4.2
    - facility imbalances, Ch. 43, 12.4.3
  - revenue in the development phase, Ch. 43, 12.1
    - incidental revenue, Ch. 43, 12.1.1
    - integral to development, Ch. 43, 12.1.2
  - sale of product with delayed shipment, Ch. 43, 12.2
  - trading activities, Ch. 43, 12.7
- risk-sharing arrangements, Ch. 43, 6
  - asset swaps, Ch. 43, 6.3

E&E assets, Ch. 43, 6.3.1
  Exchanges of E&E assets for other types of assets, Ch. 43, 6.3.3
  PP&E, intangible assets and investment property, Ch. 43, 6.3.2
 carried interests, Ch. 43, 6.1
  arrangements in E&E phase, Ch. 43, 6.1.2
  financing-type carried interest arrangements in the development phase, Ch. 43, 6.1.3
  purchase/sale-type carried interest arrangements in the development phase, Ch. 43, 6.1.4
  types of carried interests, Ch. 43, 6.1.1
 farm-ins and farm-outs, Ch. 43, 6.2
  farm-in arrangements in E&E phase, Ch. 43, 6.2.1
  farm-in arrangements outside the E&E phase: accounting by the farmee, Ch. 43, 6.2.2
  farm-in arrangements outside the E&E phase: accounting by the farmor, Ch. 43, 6.2.3
 status of the statement of recommended practice, UK Oil Industry Accounting Committee, June 2001 (OIAC SORP), Ch. 43, 1.4
 taxation, Ch. 43, 21
  excise duties, production taxes and severance taxes, Ch. 43, 21.1
   petroleum revenue tax (or resource rent tax), Ch. 43, 21.1.2
   production-based taxation, Ch. 43, 21.1.1
  grossing up of notional quantities withheld, Ch. 43, 21.2
  tolling arrangements, Ch. 43, 20
 unit of account, Ch. 43, 4
 upstream versus downstream activities, Ch. 43, 1.6
Fair presentation, Ch. 3, 4.1.1
 and compliance with IFRS, Ch. 3, 4.1.1.A
 override, Ch. 3, 4.1.1.B
Fair value. *See also* Fair value hedges; Fair value hierarchy; Fair value less costs of disposal (FVLCD);
Fair value measurement *under* **IFRS 13**. *See also* Fair value measurement and IFRS 13 below
 'clean' *vs.* 'dirty' values, Ch. 53, 7.4.10
 definition, Ch. 14, 3
 derivatives, discount rates for calculating, Ch. 53, 7.4.5
 designation of own use contracts at fair value through profit or loss, Ch. 53, 12.2
 financial assets and financial liabilities at, Ch. 50, 2.4
 financial assets designated at fair value through profit/loss, Ch. 54, 4.4.3
 financial liabilities designated at fair value through profit/loss, Ch. 54, 4.4.2
 first-time adoption, Ch. 5, 3.3
 future investment management fees in, Ch. 55, 8.2.1.B
 hedged items held at fair value through profit/loss, Ch. 53, 2.6.2
 hedging using instruments with non-zero fair value, Ch. 53, 7.4.3
 on initial recognition of financial instrument, measurement of, Ch. 49, 3.3.2
 of insurer's liabilities, Ch. 55, 9.1.1.B
 of intangible assets, determining, Ch. 9, 5.5.2.F
 in intra-group transactions, Ch. 8, 4.3.1
 investment property, fair value model, Ch. 19, 6

deferred taxation for property held by a 'single asset' entity, Ch. 19, 6.10
  estimating fair value, Ch. 19, 6.1
   comparison with value in use, Ch. 19, 6.1.3
   'double counting,' Ch. 19, 6.1.4
   methods of estimation, Ch. 19, 6.1.1
   observable data, Ch. 19, 6.1.2
  fair value of investment property under construction, Ch. 19, 6.3
  fair value of properties held under a lease, valuation adjustments to the, Ch. 19, 6.7
  fixtures and fittings subsumed within fair value, Ch. 19, 6.5
  future capital expenditure and development value ('highest and best use'), Ch. 19, 6.8
  inability to determine fair value of completed investment property, Ch. 19, 6.2
  negative present value, Ch. 19, 6.9
  prepaid and accrued operating lease income, Ch. 19, 6.6
   accrued rental income and lease incentives, Ch. 19, 6.6.1
   prepaid rental income, Ch. 19, 6.6.2
  transaction costs incurred by the reporting entity on acquisition, Ch. 19, 6.4
 property, plant and equipment, revaluation model, Ch. 18, 6
  meaning of fair value, Ch. 18, 6.1
   cost approach, Ch. 18, 6.1.1.C
   highest and best use, Ch. 18, 6.1.1.A
   revaluing assets under IFRS 13, Ch. 18, 6.1.1
   valuation approaches, Ch. 18, 6.1.1.B
 and value in use (VIU), differences between, Ch. 20, 7.3
Fair value hedges, Ch. 53, 1.5, 5.1, 7.1; Ch. 54, 4.3.3
 adjustments to the hedged item, Ch. 53, 7.1.2
 discontinuing, Ch. 53, 8.3
 firm commitments, Ch. 53, 5.1.1
 foreign currency monetary items, Ch. 53, 5.1.2
 layer components for, Ch. 53, 2.3.2
 presentation, Ch. 53, 9.2
Fair value hierarchy, Ch. 14, 16
 categorisation within, Ch. 14, 16.2
  over-the-counter derivative instruments, Ch. 14, 16.2.4
  significance of inputs, assessing, Ch. 14, 16.2.1
  third-party pricing services/brokers, Ch. 14, 16.2.3
  transfers between levels within, Ch. 14, 16.2.2
Fair value less costs of disposal (FVLCD), Ch. 20, 6
 calculation of (extractive industries), Ch. 43, 11.5
 depreciated replacement cost/current replacement cost as, Ch. 20, 6.1.2
 estimating, Ch. 20, 6.1
 investments in subsidiaries, associates and joint ventures, Ch. 20, 12.4.1
 and unit of account, Ch. 20, 6.1.1
Fair value measurement, Ch. 14, 1–23. *See also* Fair value; Fair value hierarchy; IFRS 13; Offsetting positions; Valuation techniques
 agriculture, Ch. 42, 4
  establishing what to measure, Ch. 42, 4.2
  determining costs to sell, Ch. 42, 4.4
  disclosures, Ch. 42, 5.2
   additional disclosures if fair value cannot be measured reliably, Ch. 42, 5.3

Fair value measurement—*contd*
  agriculture—*contd*
    IAS 41-specific requirements, Ch. 42, 4.5
    interaction between IAS 41 and IFRS 13, Ch. 42, 4.1
    overview of IFRS 13 requirements, Ch. 42, 4.6
    problem of measuring fair value for part-grown or immature biological assets, Ch. 42, 4.7
    when to measure fair value, Ch. 42, 4.3
  asset/liability, Ch. 14, 5
    characteristics
      condition and location, Ch. 14, 5.2.1
      restrictions on assets/liabilities, Ch. 14, 5.2.2
    unit of account
      asset's (or liability's) components, Ch. 14, 5.1.4
      and portfolio exception, Ch. 14, 5.1.2
      and PxQ, Ch. 7, 3.3.2.F; Ch. 14, 5.1.1
      vs. valuation premise, Ch. 14, 5.1.3
  of associates, partial use of, Ch. 11, 5.4
  convergence with US GAAP, Ch. 14, 22
    disclosures, Ch. 14, 22.2.4
    fair value of liabilities with demand feature, Ch. 14, 22.2.2
    IFRS 13, development of, Ch. 14, 22.1
    practical expedient for alternative investments, Ch. 14, 22.2.1
    recognition of day-one gains and losses, Ch. 14, 22.2.3
  day 1 profits, financial instruments, Ch. 54, 4.5.2
  definitions, Ch. 14, 3
  disclosures, Ch. 14, 20
    accounting policy, Ch. 14, 20.2
    objectives
      format of, Ch. 14, 20.1.1
      level of disaggregation, Ch. 14, 20.1.2
      'recurring' *vs.* 'non-recurring', Ch. 14, 20.1.3
    for recognised fair value measurements, Ch. 14, 20.3
      fair value hierarchy categorisation, Ch. 14, 20.3.3
      highest and best use, Ch. 14, 20.3.9
      level 3 reconciliation, Ch. 14, 20.3.6
      non-recurring fair value measurements, Ch. 14, 20.3.2
      recurring fair value measurements, Ch. 14, 20.3.1
      sensitivity of level 3 measurements to changes in significant unobservable inputs, Ch. 14, 20.3.8
      transfers between hierarchy levels for recurring fair value measurements, Ch. 14, 20.3.4
      of valuation processes for level 3 measurements, Ch. 14, 20.3.7
      valuation techniques and inputs, Ch. 14, 20.3.5
    regarding liabilities issued with an inseparable third-party credit enhancement, Ch. 14, 20.5
    for unrecognised fair value measurements, Ch. 14, 20.4
  effective date and transition, Ch. 14, 22
  fair value framework, Ch. 14, 4
    definition, Ch. 14, 4.1
    measurement, Ch. 14, 4.2
  financial assets and liabilities with offsetting positions, Ch. 14, 12
    criteria for using the portfolio approach for offsetting positions, Ch. 14, 12.1
      accounting policy considerations, Ch. 14, 12.1.1
      level 1 instruments in, Ch. 14, 12.1.4
      minimum level of offset, to use portfolio approach, Ch. 14, 12.1.3
      presentation considerations, Ch. 14, 12.1.2
    measuring fair value for offsetting positions, Ch. 14, 12.2
      exposure to market risks, Ch. 14, 12.2.1
      exposure to the credit risk of a particular counterparty, Ch. 14, 12.2.2
  hierarchy, Ch. 14, 16
    categorisation within, Ch. 14, 16.2
      over-the-counter derivative instruments, Ch. 14, 16.2.4
      significance of inputs, assessing, Ch. 14, 16.2.1
      third-party pricing services/brokers, Ch. 14, 16.2.3
      transfers between levels within, Ch. 14, 16.2.2
  IFRS 13, objective of, Ch. 14, 1.3
  IFRS 13, overview, Ch. 14, 1.2
  at initial recognition, Ch. 14, 13
    day 1 gains and losses, Ch. 14, 13.2
    exit price *vs.* entry price, Ch. 14, 13.1
    related party transactions, Ch. 14, 13.3
  inputs to valuation techniques, Ch. 14, 15
    broker quotes and pricing services, Ch. 14, 15.5
    general principles, Ch. 14, 15.1
    premiums and discounts, Ch. 14, 15.2
      blockage factors (or block discounts), Ch. 14, 15.2.1
    pricing within the bid-ask spread, Ch. 14, 15.3
      bid-ask spread, Ch. 14, 15.3.2
      mid-market pricing, Ch. 14, 15.3.1
    risk premiums, Ch. 14, 15.4
  of intangible assets, determining, Ch. 9, 5.5.2.F
  level 1 inputs, Ch. 14, 17
    alternative pricing methods, Ch. 14, 17.2
    quoted prices in active markets Ch. 14, 17.3
    unit of account, Ch. 14, 17.4
    use of, Ch. 14, 17.1
  level 2 inputs, Ch. 14, 18
    examples of, Ch. 14, 18.2
    making adjustments to, Ch. 14, 18.4
    market corroborated inputs, Ch. 14, 18.3
    recently observed prices in an inactive market, Ch. 14, 18.5
  level 3 inputs, Ch. 14, 19
    examples of, Ch. 14, 19.2
    use of, Ch. 14, 19.1
  liabilities and an entity's own equity, application to, Ch. 14, 11
    financial liability with demand feature, Ch. 14, 11.5
    general principles
      fair value of an entity's own equity, Ch. 14, 11.1.2
      fair value of liability, Ch. 14, 11.1.1
      settlement value *vs.* transfer value, Ch. 14, 11.1.3
    non-performance risk, Ch. 14, 11.1
      counterparty credit risk and its own credit risk, Ch. 14, 11.3.2
      derivative liabilities, Ch. 14, 11.3.4
      entity incorporate credit risk into the valuation of its derivative contracts, Ch. 14, 11.3.3
      with third-party credit enhancements, Ch. 14, 11.3.1
    not held by other parties as assets, Ch. 14, 11.2.2
    restrictions preventing the transfer of, Ch. 14, 11.4
    that are held by other parties as assets, Ch. 14, 11.2.1
  market participants, Ch. 14, 7
    assumptions, Ch. 14, 7.2
    characteristics, Ch. 14, 7.1

non-financial assets, application to, Ch. 14, 10
   highest and best use, Ch. 14, 10.1
      vs. current use, Ch. 14, 10.1.2
      vs. intended use, Ch. 14, 10.1.3
      legally permissible, Ch. 14, 10.1.1
   valuation premise, Ch. 14, 10.2
      in combination with other assets and/or liabilities, Ch. 14, 10.2.2
      liabilities association, Ch. 14, 10.2.3
      stand-alone basis, Ch. 14, 10.2.1
      unit of account *vs.*, Ch. 14, 10.2.4
for part-grown or immature biological assets, Ch. 42, 4.7
present value techniques, Ch. 14, 21
   components of, Ch. 14, 21.2
      risk and uncertainty in, Ch. 14, 21.2.2
      time value of money, Ch. 14, 21.2.1
   discount rate adjustment technique, Ch. 14, 21.3
   expected present value technique, Ch. 14, 21.4
   general principles for use of, Ch. 14, 21.1
price, Ch. 14, 9
   transaction costs, Ch. 14, 9.1
   transportation costs, Ch. 14, 9.2
principal (or most advantageous) market, Ch. 14, 6
scope, Ch. 14, 2
   exclusions, Ch. 14, 2.2
      exemptions from the disclosure requirements of IFRS 13, Ch. 14, 2.2.4
      fair value, measurements similar to, Ch. 14, 2.2.3
      lease transactions, Ch. 14, 2.2.2
      share-based payments, Ch. 14, 2.2.1
   fair value measurement exceptions, Ch. 14, 2.4
   IFRS 13, items in scope of, Ch. 14, 2.1
      fair value disclosures, Ch. 14, 2.1.1
      fair value measurements, Ch. 14, 2.1.2
      short-term receivables and payables, Ch. 14, 2.1.3
   practical expedient for impaired financial assets carried at amortised cost, Ch. 14, 2.4.2
   present value techniques, Ch. 14, 2.3
transaction, Ch. 14, 8
   estimation, Ch. 14, 8.3
   identification, Ch. 14, 8.2
   volume and level of activity for an asset/liability, Ch. 14, 8.1
unit of account, Ch. 14, 5.1
   asset's (or liability's) components, Ch. 14, 5.1.4
   level 1 assets and liabilities, Ch. 14, 17.4
   and portfolio exception, Ch. 14, 5.1.2
   and PxQ, Ch. 7, 3.3.2.F; Ch. 14, 5.1.1
   vs. valuation premise, Ch. 14, 5.1.3
valuation techniques, Ch. 14, 14
   cost approach, Ch. 14, 14.3
   income approach, Ch. 14, 14.4
   market approach, Ch. 14, 14.2
   selecting appropriate, Ch. 14, 14.1
      making changes to valuation techniques, Ch. 14, 14.1.4
      single *vs.* multiple valuation techniques, Ch. 14, 14.1.1
      using multiple valuation techniques to measure fair value, Ch. 14, 14.1.2
      valuation adjustments, Ch. 14, 14.1.3

Fair value model, investment property, Ch. 19, 6. *See also* Fair value; Investment property
   completed investment property, inability to determine fair value, Ch. 19, 6.2
   deferred taxation for property held by a 'single asset' entity, Ch. 19, 6.10
   estimating fair value, Ch. 19, 6.1
   fixtures and fittings subsumed, Ch. 19, 6.5
   future capital expenditure and development value ('highest and best use'), Ch. 19, 6.8
   negative present value, Ch. 19, 6.9
   prepaid and accrued operating lease income, Ch. 19, 6.6
   properties held under a lease, valuation adjustment to the, Ch. 19, 6.7
   property under construction, Ch. 19, 6.3
   transaction costs incurred on acquisition, Ch. 19, 6.4
Fair value through other comprehensive income (FVTOCI), Ch. 48, 8; Ch. 54, 7.2
   debt instruments, subsequent measurement accumulated impairment amount for, Ch. 51, 14.3
   financial assets measured at, Ch. 51, 9
   hedges of exposures classified as, Ch. 53, 2.6.3
   non-derivative equity investments designation at, Ch. 48, 8
Faithful representation, Ch. 2, 5.1.2
Farm-ins and farm outs, extractive industries, Ch. 43, 6.2
   farm-in arrangements in the E&E phase, Ch. 43, 6.2.1
   farm-in arrangements outside the E&E phase: accounting by the farmee, Ch. 43, 6.2.2
      farming into an asset, Ch. 43, 6.2.2.A
      farming into a business which is a joint operation or results in the formation of a joint operation, Ch. 43, 6.2.2.B
   farm-in arrangements outside the E&E phase: accounting by the farmor, Ch. 43, 6.2.3
Finance costs as a borrowing cost, Ch. 21, 5.5
   derecognition of borrowings, gains and losses on, Ch. 21, 5.5.2
   derivative financial instruments, Ch. 21, 5.5.1
   derivative financial instruments, gains or losses on termination of, Ch. 21, 5.5.3
   dividends payable on shares classified as financial liabilities, Ch. 21, 5.5.4
   unwinding discounts, Ch. 21, 4.2
Finance leases, accounting for, Ch. 23, 6.2
   accounting by lessors, Ch. 23, 6.2–6.2.4
      initial measurement, Ch. 23, 6.2.1
      presentation in the statement of cash flows, Ch. 40, 5.5.5
      remeasurement, Ch. 23, 6.2.4
      subsequent measurement, Ch. 23, 6.2.3
         unguaranteed residual values, Ch. 23, 6.2.3.A
   manufacturer/dealer lessors, Ch. 23, 6.2.2
Financial Accounting Standards Board (FASB), Ch. 1, 2.9, 3.2; Ch. 14, 22.2
Financial assets
   accounting for loss of control, interest retained in the former subsidiary is a financial asset, Ch. 7, 3.3.1
   call options over non-controlling interest, Ch. 7, 6.1, 6.3, 6.4, 6.5

Financial assets—contd
  classification and measurement on first-time adoption, Ch. 5, 4.9
  classifying, Ch. 48, 2
    debt instruments, Ch. 48, 2.1
    equity instruments and derivatives, Ch. 48, 2.2
  contractual obligation to deliver, Ch. 47, 4.2
  definition, Ch. 45, 2.1; Ch. 47, 3; Ch. 52, 2.1
  derecognition, Ch. 52, 3
  designated as measured at fair value through profit/loss, Ch. 54, 4.4.3
  at fair value through profit/loss, Ch. 50, 2.4
  held for trading, Ch. 48, 4
  and liabilities with offsetting positions, Ch. 14, 12
    criteria for using the portfolio approach for offsetting positions, Ch. 14, 12.1
    measuring fair value for offsetting positions, Ch. 14, 12.2
  measured at amortised cost, Ch. 51, 14.1
  measured at fair value through other comprehensive income, Ch. 51, 14.3
  measured at fair value through profit/loss, Ch. 51, 9.1
  modified financial assets, Ch. 51, 8.2
  offsetting, Ch. 54, 7.4.1
    cash pooling arrangements, Ch. 54, 7.4.1.E
    disclosure, Ch. 54, 7.4.2
    enforceable legal right of set-off, Ch. 54, 7.4.1.A
    intention to settle net, Ch. 54, 7.4.1.C
    master netting agreements, Ch. 54, 7.4.1.B
    offsetting collateral amounts, Ch. 54, 7.4.1.F
    situations where offset is not normally appropriate, Ch. 54, 7.4.1.D
    unit of account, Ch. 54, 7.4.1.G
  reclassifications of, Ch. 48, 9; Ch. 50, 2.7
  redesignation of, Ch. 55, 8.4
  that are either past due or impaired, Ch. 54, 5.3.3
  transfers of, Ch. 54, 6
    assets that are derecognised in their entirety, Ch. 54, 6.3
      disclosure requirements, Ch. 54, 6.3.2
      meaning of continuing involvement, Ch. 54, 6.3.1
    assets that are not derecognised in their entirety, Ch. 54, 6.2
    meaning of 'transfer,' Ch. 54, 6.1
Financial capital maintenance (framework), Ch. 2, 11.1
Financial guarantee(s), Ch. 51, 5.8.1
  to provide a loan at a below-market interest rate, Ch. 50, 2.8
Financial guarantee contracts, Ch. 45, 3.4; Ch. 49, 3.3.3; Ch. 55, 2.2.3.D
  between entities under common control, Ch. 45, 3.4.4
  definition, Ch. 45, 3.4.1; Ch. 51, 11.1
    debt instrument, Ch. 45, 3.4.1.B
    form and existence of contract, Ch. 45, 3.4.1.C
    reimbursement for loss incurred, Ch. 45, 3.4.1.A
  holders of, Ch. 45, 3.4.3
  IFRS 9 impairment requirements, Ch. 51, 1.2
  issuers of, Ch. 45, 3.4.2
  maturity analysis, Ch. 54, 5.4.2.F
Financial instrument(s). *See also* IAS 32, IAS 39, IFRS 7; IFRS 9
  contracts to buy or sell commodities and other non-financial items, Ch. 45, 4
  contracts that may be settled net, Ch. 45, 4.1
  definitions, Ch. 45, 2.1
    applying, Ch. 45, 2.2
    contingent rights and obligations, Ch. 45, 2.2.3
    derivative financial instruments, Ch. 45, 2.2.8
    dividends payable, Ch. 45, 2.2.9
    equity instruments, Ch. 45, 2.1; Ch. 45, 2.2.7
    financial asset, Ch. 45, 2.1
    financial instrument, Ch. 45, 2.1
    financial liability, Ch. 45, 2.1
    leases, Ch. 45, 2.2.4
    need for a contract, Ch. 45, 2.2.1
    non-financial assets and liabilities and contracts thereon, Ch. 45, 2.2.5
    payments for goods and services, Ch. 45, 2.2.6
    simple financial instruments, Ch. 45, 2.2.2
  discretionary participation feature in, Ch. 55, 6.2
  normal sales and purchases (or own use contracts), Ch. 45, 4.2
    commodity broker-traders and similar entities, Ch. 45, 4.2.2
    contracts containing volume flexibility, Ch. 45, 4.2.5
    electricity and similar 'end-user' contracts, Ch. 45, 4.2.4
    fair value option in IFRS 9, Ch. 45, 4.2.6
    net settlement of similar contracts, Ch. 45, 4.2.1
    written options that can be settled net, Ch. 45, 4.2.3
  scope, Ch. 45, 3
    business combinations, Ch. 45, 3.7
    contingent pricing of property, plant and equipment and intangible assets, Ch. 45, 3.8
    disposal groups classified as held for sale and discontinued operations, Ch. 45, 3.11
    employee benefit plans and share-based payment, Ch. 45, 3.9
    equity instruments, Ch. 45, 3.6
    financial guarantee contracts, Ch. 45, 3.4
    indemnification assets, Ch. 45, 3.12
    insurance and similar contracts, Ch. 45, 3.3
      contracts with discretionary participation features, Ch. 45, 3.3.2
      separating financial instrument components including embedded derivatives from insurance contracts, Ch. 45, 3.3.3
      weather derivatives, Ch. 45, 3.3.1
    leases, Ch. 45, 3.2
    loan commitments, Ch. 45, 3.5
    reimbursement rights in respect of provisions, Ch. 45, 3.10
    rights and obligations within the scope of IFRS 15, Ch. 45, 3.13
    subsidiaries, associates, joint ventures and similar investments, Ch. 45, 3.1
Financial instrument hosts, Ch. 49, 3.5
Financial instruments, classification, Ch. 48, 1–9
  'business model' assessment, Ch. 48, 5
    applying in practice, Ch. 48, 5.6
    consolidated and subsidiary accounts, Ch. 48, 5.5
    hold to collect contractual cash flows, Ch. 48, 5.2
    hold to collect contractual cash flows and selling financial assets, Ch. 48, 5.3
    impact of sales on the assessment, Ch. 48, 5.2.1
    level at which the business model assessment is applied, Ch. 48, 5.1

transferred financial assets that are not derecognised, Ch. 48, 5.2.2
contractual cash flows, Ch. 48, 6
   auction rate securities, Ch. 48, 6.4.4
   bonds with a capped or floored interest rate, Ch. 48, 6.3.3
   contractual features that change the timing or amount, Ch. 48, 6.4.4
   contractually linked instruments, Ch. 48, 6.6
   conventional subordination features, Ch. 48, 6.3.1
   convertible debt, Ch. 48, 6.4.5
   de minimis features, Ch. 48, 6.4.1.A
   debt covenants, Ch. 48, 6.4.4
   dual currency instruments, Ch. 48, 6.4.5
   five-year constant maturity bond, Ch. 48, 6.4.2
   fixed rate bond prepayable by the issuer at fair value, Ch. 48, 6.4.5
   full recourse loans secured by collateral, Ch. 48, 6.3.2
   interest rate period, Ch. 48, 6.4.2
   inverse floater, Ch. 48, 6.4.5
   investment in open-ended money market or debt funds, Ch. 48, 6.4.5
   lender has discretion to change the interest rate, Ch. 48, 6.3.4
   meaning of 'interest', Ch. 48, 6.2
   meaning of 'principal,' Ch. 48, 6.1
   modified time value of money component, Ch. 48, 6.4.2
   multiple of a benchmark interest rate, Ch. 48, 6.4.5
   non-genuine features, Ch. 48, 6.4.1.B
   non-recourse loans, Ch. 48, 6.5
   perpetual instruments with potentially deferrable coupons, Ch. 48, 6.4.5
   prepayment, assets originated at a premium or discount, Ch. 48, 6.4.4.B
   prepayment options, Ch. 48, 6.4.4
   prepayment, negative compensation, Ch. 48, 6.4.4.A
   regulated interest rates, Ch. 48, 6.4.3
   term extension options, Ch. 48, 6.4.4
   unleveraged inflation-linked bonds, Ch. 48, 6.3.5
   variable interest rate, Ch. 48, 6.4.4
designation at fair value through profit or loss, Ch. 48, 7
financial assets and liabilities held for trading, Ch. 48, 4
financial assets classification, Ch. 48, 2
   debt instruments, Ch. 48, 2.1
   equity instruments and derivatives, Ch. 48, 2.2
financial liabilities classification, Ch. 48, 3
reclassification of financial assets, Ch. 48, 9

Financial instruments, derecognition, Ch. 52, 1–8. *See also* Derecognition

Financial instruments, derivatives and embedded derivatives, Ch. 46, 1–8
   call and put options over noncontrolling interests, Ch. 7, 6. *See also* Non-controlling interests
   changes in value in response to changes in underlying, Ch. 46, 2.1
      non-financial variables specific to one party to the contract, Ch. 46, 2.1.3
      notional amounts, Ch. 46, 2.1.1
      underlying variables, Ch. 46, 2.1.2
   common derivatives, Ch. 46, 3.1
   embedded derivatives, Ch. 46, 4
      contracts for the sale of goods or services, Ch. 46, 5.2
      floors and caps, Ch. 46, 5.2.4
      foreign currency derivatives, Ch. 46, 5.2.1
      fund performance fees, Ch. 46, 5.2.5
      inflation-linked features, Ch. 46, 5.2.3
      inputs, ingredients, substitutes and other proxy pricing mechanisms, Ch. 46, 5.2.2
   financial instrument hosts, Ch. 46, 5.1
      commodity-and equity-linked interest and principal payments, Ch. 46, 5.1.7
      convertible and exchangeable debt instruments, Ch. 46, 5.1.9
      credit-linked notes, Ch. 46, 5.1.8
      foreign currency monetary items, Ch. 46, 5.1.1
      inflation-linked debt instruments, Ch. 46, 5.1.6
      interest rate floors and caps, Ch. 46, 5.1.5
      interest rate indices, Ch. 46, 5.1.2
      puttable instruments, Ch. 46, 5.1.10
      term extension and similar call, put and prepayment options in debt instruments, Ch. 46, 5.1.14
   identifying the terms of embedded derivatives and host contracts, Ch. 46, 6
      embedded non-option derivatives, Ch. 46, 6.1
      embedded option-based derivative, Ch. 46, 6.2
      multiple embedded derivatives, Ch. 46, 6.3
   insurance contracts, Ch. 46, 5.4
   leases, Ch. 46, 5.3
   reassessment, Ch. 46, 7
      acquisition of contracts, Ch. 46, 7.1
      business combinations, Ch. 46, 7.2
      remeasurement issues arising from reassessment, Ch. 46, 7.3
   future settlement, Ch. 46, 2.3
   initial net investment, Ch. 46, 2.2
   in-substance derivatives, Ch. 46, 3.2
   linked and separate transactions and 'synthetic' instruments, Ch. 46, 8
   prepaid forward purchase of shares, Ch. 46, 2.2
   prepaid interest rate swap, Ch. 46, 2.2
   regular way contracts, Ch. 46, 3.3

Financial Instruments: disclosures (IFRS 7), Ch. 54, 1–9

Financial instruments, extractive industries, Ch. 43, 13
   embedded derivatives, Ch. 43, 13.2
      development of gas markets, Ch. 43, 13.2.4
      foreign currency embedded derivatives, Ch. 43, 13.2.1
      long-term supply contracts, Ch. 43, 13.2.3
      provisionally priced sales contracts, Ch. 43, 13.2.2
   hedging sales of metal concentrate (mining), Ch. 43, 13.4
   normal purchase and sales exemption, Ch. 43, 13.1
   volume flexibility in supply contracts, Ch. 43, 13.3

Financial instruments: financial liabilities and equity, Ch. 47, 1–12
   background, Ch. 47, 1.1
   classification of instruments, Ch. 47, 4
      consolidated financial statements, Ch. 47, 4.8.1
      contingent settlement provisions, Ch. 47, 4.3
      contractual obligation to deliver cash or other financial assets, Ch. 47, 4.2
      definition of equity instrument, Ch. 47, 4.1
      examples of equity instruments, Ch. 47, 4.4

Financial instruments: financial liabilities and equity—*contd*
  classification of instruments—*contd*
    examples of equity instruments—*contd*
      contracts to issue equity instruments, Ch. 47, 4.4.2
      issued instruments, Ch. 47, 4.4.1
      instruments redeemable
        with a 'dividend blocker,' Ch. 47, 4.5.3.A
        with a 'dividend pusher,' Ch. 47, 4.5.3.B
        mandatorily or at the holder's option, Ch. 47, 4.5.1
        only at the issuer's option or not redeemable, Ch. 47, 4.5.2
      perpetual debt, Ch. 47, 4.7
      preference shares and similar instruments, Ch. 47, 4.5
      puttable instruments and instruments repayable only on liquidation, Ch. 47, 4.6.5
      reclassification of instruments
        change of circumstances, Ch. 47, 4.9.2
        change of terms, Ch. 47, 4.9.1
      single entity financial statements, Ch. 47, 4.8.2
    compound financial instruments, Ch. 47, 6
      background, Ch. 47, 6.1
      common forms of convertible bonds, Ch. 47, 6.6
        bond convertible into fixed percentage of equity, Ch. 47, 6.6.6
        contingent convertible bond, Ch. 47, 6.6.2
        convertible bonds with down round or ratchet features, Ch. 47, 6.6.7
        convertibles with cash settlement at the option of the issuer, Ch. 47, 6.6.5
        foreign currency convertible bond, Ch. 47, 6.6.4
        functional currency bond convertible into a fixed number of shares, Ch. 47, 6.6.1
        mandatorily convertible bond, Ch. 47, 6.6.3
      components, Ch. 47, 6.4
        compound instruments with embedded derivatives, Ch. 47, 6.4.2
        determining the components of a compound instrument, Ch. 47, 6.4.1
      conversion
        at maturity, Ch. 47, 6.3.1
        before maturity, Ch. 47, 6.3.2
        early redemption/repurchase, Ch. 47, 6.3.3
          exercising an embedded call option, Ch. 47, 6.3.3.B
          through negotiation with bondholders, Ch. 47, 6.3.3.A
        initial recognition–'split accounting,' Ch. 47, 6.2
          accounting for the equity component, Ch. 47, 6.2.1
          temporary differences arising from split accounting, Ch. 47, 6.2.2
      modification, Ch. 47, 6.3.4
      treatment by holder and issuer contrasted, Ch. 47, 6.1.1
    contracts accounted for as equity instruments, Ch. 47, 5.1
    contracts accounted for as financial assets or financial liabilities, Ch. 47, 5.2
    definitions, Ch. 47, 3
    derivatives over own equity instruments, Ch. 47, 11
      call options, Ch. 47, 11.2
        purchased call option, Ch. 47, 11.2.1
        written call option, Ch. 47, 11.2.2
      forward contracts, Ch. 47, 11.1
        'back-to-back' forward contracts, Ch. 47, 11.1.3
        forward purchase, Ch. 47, 11.1.1
        forward sale, Ch. 47, 11.1.2
      put options
        purchased put option, Ch. 47, 11.3.1
        written put option, Ch. 47, 11.3.2
    future developments, Ch. 47, 12
  Financial Instruments with Characteristics of Equity Research Project (FICE), Ch. 7, 7.3, 7.4, 7.5; Ch. 47, 1, 4.6.6, 5.1.2, 5.3.2A, 6.6.3B, 12
  gross-settled contracts for the sale or issue of the entity's own equity instruments, Ch. 47, 5.4
  'hedging' of instruments classified as equity, Ch. 47, 10
  interest, dividends, gains and losses, Ch. 47, 8
    tax effects, Ch. 47, 8.2
    transaction costs, Ch. 47, 8.1
  liabilities arising from gross-settled contracts for the purchase of the entity's own equity instruments, Ch. 47, 5.3
    contracts to acquire non-controlling interests, Ch. 47, 5.3.2
    contracts to purchase own equity during 'closed' or 'prohibited' periods, Ch. 47, 5.3.1
  objective, Ch. 47, 2.1
  scope, Ch. 47, 2.2
  settlement of financial liability with equity instrument, Ch. 47, 7
    debt for equity swaps with shareholders, Ch. 47, 7.3
    requirements of IFRIC 19, Ch. 47, 7.2
    scope and effective date of IFRIC 19, Ch. 47, 7.1
  treasury shares, Ch. 47, 9
    IFRS 17 Treasury share election, Ch. 47, 9.2
    transactions in own shares not at fair value, Ch. 47, 9.1
Financial instruments: hedge accounting, Ch. 53, 1–14
  accounting for the costs of hedging, Ch. 53, 7.5
    foreign currency basis spreads in financial instruments, Ch. 53, 7.5.3
    forward element of forward contracts, Ch. 53, 7.5.2
    time value of options, Ch. 53, 7.5.1
  aggregated exposures, Ch. 53, 2.7
    accounting for, Ch. 53, 2.7.3
  alternatives to hedge accounting, Ch. 53, 12
    credit risk exposures, Ch. 53, 12.1
    own use contracts, Ch. 53, 12.2
  background, Ch. 53, 1.1
  development of, Ch. 53, 1.3
  discontinuation, Ch. 53, 8.3, 14.5
    of cash flow hedges, Ch. 53, 8.3.2
    of fair value hedges, Ch. 53, 8.3.1
    hedging counterparty within the same consolidated group, Ch. 53, 8.3.7
    hedged net investment, disposal of, Ch. 53, 8.3.8
    novation to central clearing parties, Ch. 53, 8.3.5
    settle to market derivatives, Ch. 53, 8.3.6
  economic relationship, Ch. 53, 6.4.1
  effective hedges, accounting for, Ch. 53, 7
    cash flow hedges, Ch. 53, 7.2
      acquisition or disposal of subsidiaries, Ch. 53, 7.2.4
      all-in-one hedges, Ch. 53, 5.2.1
      discontinuing, Ch. 53, 8.3.2
      firm commitments, hedges of, Ch. 53, 5.2.2
      foreign currency monetary items, Ch. 53, 5.2.3

hypothetical derivatives, Ch. 53, 7.4.4
measuring ineffectiveness of, Ch. 53, 7.4.6
of a net position, Ch. 53, 2.5.3
novation of, due to central clearing regulations, Ch. 53, 8.3.5
ongoing accounting, Ch. 53, 7.2.1
presentation, Ch. 53, 10.1
reclassification of gains and losses, Ch. 53, 7.2.2
documented rollover hedging strategy, Ch. 53, 7.7
equity instrument designated at fair value through OCI, Ch. 53, 7.8
fair value hedges, Ch. 53, 1.5, 5.1, 7.1
adjustments to the hedged item, Ch. 53,7.1.2
discontinuing, Ch. 53, 8.3.1
firm commitments, Ch. 53, 5.1.1
foreign currency monetary items, Ch. 53, 5.1.2
layer components for, Ch. 53, 2.3.2
ongoing accounting, Ch. 53, 7.1.1
presentation, Ch. 53, 10.2
hedges of a firm commitment to acquire a business, Ch. 53, 7.6
hedges of a net investment in a foreign operation, accounting for, Ch. 7, 2.3; Ch. 53, 1.5, 5.3, 7.3, 8.3.7
effective date and transition, Ch. 53, 13
limited retrospective application, Ch. 53, 13.3
prospective application in general, Ch. 53, 13.2
effectiveness assessment, Ch. 53, 8.1, 6.4
credit risk dominance, Ch. 53, 6.4.2
economic relationship, Ch. 53, 6.4.1
hedge ratio, Ch. 53, 6.4.3
effectiveness measurement, Ch. 53, 7.4
calculation of, Ch. 53, 7.4.6
'clean' vs. 'dirty' values, Ch. 53, 7.4.10
comparison of spot rate and forward rate methods, Ch. 53, 7.4.7
discount rates for calculating the change in value of the hedged item, Ch. 53, 7.4.5
effectiveness of options, Ch. 53, 7.4.11
foreign currency basis spreads, Ch. 53, 7.4.8
hedged items with embedded optionality, Ch. 53, 7.4.12
hedging instrument's impact on credit quality, Ch. 53, 7.4.9
hedging using instruments with a non-zero fair value, Ch. 53, 7.4.3
hypothetical derivatives, Ch. 53, 7.4.4
time value of money, Ch. 53, 7.4.2
hedged items, Ch. 53, 2
core deposits, Ch. 53, 2.6.7
held at fair value through profit or loss, Ch. 53, 2.6.2
held at fair value through OCI, Ch. 53, 2.6.3
firm commitment to acquire a business, Ch. 53, 7.6
forecast acquisition/issuance of foreign currency monetary items, Ch. 53, 2.6.5
general requirements, Ch. 53, 2.1
groups of items, Ch. 53, 2.5
cash flow hedge of a net position, Ch. 53, 2.5.3
general requirements, Ch. 53, 2.5.1
hedging a component of a group, Ch. 53, 2.5.2
nil net positions, Ch. 53, 2.5.4
highly probable, Ch. 53, 2.6.1
internal, Ch. 53, 4.3

nominal components. Ch. 53, 2.3
general requirement, Ch. 53, 2.3.1
layer component for fair value hedge, Ch. 53, 2.3.2
own equity instruments, Ch. 53, 2.6.6
risk components, Ch. 53, 2.2
contractually specified, Ch. 53, 2.2.2
foreign currency as, Ch. 53, 2.2.5
general requirements, Ch. 53, 2.2.1
inflation as, Ch. 53, 2.2.6
interest rate, Ch. 53, 2.2.7
non-contractually specified, Ch. 53, 2.2.3
partial term hedging, Ch. 53, 2.2.4
sub-LIBOR issue, Ch. 53, 2.4
negative interest rates, Ch. 53, 2.4.2
hedge ratio, Ch. 53, 6.4.3
hedging instruments, Ch. 53, 3
combinations of instruments, Ch. 53, 3.5
derivatives, Ch. 53, 3.2
basis swaps, Ch. 53, 3.2.5
credit break clauses, Ch. 53, 3.2.4
principal resetting cross currency swaps, Ch. 53, 3.2.4.A
embedded derivatives, Ch. 53, 3.2.3
net written options, Ch. 53, 3.2.2
offsetting external derivatives, Ch. 53, 3.2.1
embedded derivatives, Ch. 53, 3.2.3
general requirements, Ch. 53, 3.1
hedging different risks with one instrument, Ch. 53, 3.6.2
non-derivative financial instruments, Ch. 53, 3.3
of foreign currency risk, Ch. 53, 3.3.1
non-derivative liabilities, Ch. 53, 3.3
own equity instruments, Ch. 53, 3.4
portions and proportions of, Ch. 53, 3.6
different risks with one instrument, Ch. 53, 3.6.2
foreign currency basis spread, Ch. 53, 3.6.5
interest elements of forwards, Ch. 53, 3.6.5
portion of a time period, Ch. 53, 3.6.6
proportions of instruments, Ch. 53, 3.6.1
restructuring of derivatives, Ch. 53, 3.6.3
time value of options, Ch. 53, 3.6.4
hedging relationships, types of, Ch. 53, 5
cash flow hedges, Ch. 53, 5.2
all-in-one hedges, Ch. 53, 5.2.1
firm commitments hedges, Ch. 53, 5.2.2
foreign currency monetary items, Ch. 53, 5.2.3
fair value hedges, Ch. 53, 5.1
firm commitments, hedges of, Ch. 53, 5.1.1
foreign currency monetary items, hedges of, Ch. 53, 5.1.2
hedges of net investments in foreign operations, Ch. 53, 5.3
amount of the hedged item for which a hedging relationship may be designated, Ch. 53, 5.3.2
nature of the hedged risk, Ch. 53, 5.3.1
where the hedging instrument can be held, Ch. 53, 5.3.3
ineffectiveness, measuring, Ch. 53, 7.4
interbank Offered Rate Reform (IBOR), Ch. 53, 9
internal hedges and other group accounting issues, Ch. 53, 4
central clearing parties, Ch. 53, 4.1.1
external hedging instruments, offsetting, Ch. 53, 4.2

Financial instruments: hedge accounting—*contd*
  internal hedges and other group accounting issues—*contd*
    hedged item and hedging instrument held by different group entities, Ch. 53, 4.4
    internal hedged items, Ch. 53, 4.3
    internal hedging instruments, Ch. 53, 4.1
    offsetting internal hedges instruments, Ch. 53, 4.2
  macro hedging, Ch. 53, 11
    accounting for dynamic risk management, Ch. 53, 11.1
    macro hedging strategies under IFRS 9, Ch. 53, 11.2
  main differences between IFRS 9 and IAS 39 hedge accounting requirements, Ch. 53, 14
    discontinuation, Ch. 53, 14.5
    effectiveness criteria, Ch. 53, 14.4
    eligible hedged items, Ch. 53, 14.2
    eligible hedging instruments, Ch. 53, 14.3
    hedge accounting mechanisms, Ch. 53, 14.6
    objective of hedge accounting, Ch. 53, 14.1
  portfolio/macro hedging, Ch. 53, 11
  objective of, Ch. 53, 1.4
  overview, Ch. 53, 1.5
  own use contracts, Ch. 53, 12.2
  presentation, Ch. 53, 10
    cash flow hedges, Ch. 53, 10.1
    cost of hedging, Ch. 53, 10.4
    fair value hedges, Ch. 53, 10.2
    hedges of groups of items, Ch. 53, 10.3
  proxy hedges, Ch. 53, 6.2.1
  qualifying criteria, Ch. 53, 6
    credit risk dominance, Ch. 53, 6.4.2
      on the hedged item, Ch. 53, 6.4.2.B
      on the hedging instrument, Ch. 53, 6.4.2.A
    designating 'proxy hedges', Ch. 53, 6.2.1
    documentation and designation, Ch. 53, 6.3
      business combinations, Ch. 53, 6.3.1
      dynamic hedging strategies, Ch. 53, 6.3.2
      forecast transactions, Ch. 53, 6.3.3
    economic relationship, Ch. 53, 6.4.1
    general requirements, Ch. 53, 6.1
    hedge effectiveness requirements, Ch. 53, 6.4
      credit risk dominance, Ch. 53, 6.4.2
      economic relationship, Ch. 53, 6.4.1
      hedge ratio, Ch. 53, 6.4.3
    proxy hedging, Ch. 53, 6.2.1
    risk management strategy, Ch. 53, 6.2
    risk management objective, Ch. 53, 6.2
    setting the hedge ratio, Ch. 53, 6.4.3
  rebalancing, Ch. 53, 8.2
    definition, Ch. 53, 8.2.1
    mechanics of, Ch. 53, 8.2.3
    requirement to rebalance, Ch. 53, 8.2.2
  risk management, Ch. 53, 6.2, 6.3
    proxy hedges, Ch. 53, 6.2.1
    risk management objective, Ch. 53, 6.2
      change in, Ch. 53, 8.3
    risk management strategy, Ch. 53, 6.2
  standards, development of, Ch. 53, 1.3

Financial instruments: presentation and disclosure, Ch. 54, 1–9
  disclosures, structuring, Ch. 54, 3
    classes of financial instrument, Ch. 54, 3.3
    level of detail, Ch. 54, 3.1
    materiality, Ch. 54, 3.2
  effective date and transitional provisions, Ch. 54, 8
  future developments, Ch. 54, 9
  interim reports, Ch. 54, 2.3
  nature and extent of risks arising from financial instruments, Ch. 54, 5
    credit risk, Ch. 54, 5.3
      collateral and other credit enhancements obtained, Ch. 54, 5.3.5
      credit risk exposure, Ch. 54, 5.3.4
      credit risk management practices, Ch. 54, 5.3.2
      illustrative disclosures, Ch. 54, 5.3.6
      quantitative and qualitative information about amounts arising from expected credit losses, Ch. 54, 5.3.3
      scope and objectives, Ch. 54, 5.3.1
    liquidity risk, Ch. 54, 5.4
      information provided to key management, Ch. 54, 5.4.1
      management of associated liquidity risk, Ch. 54, 5.4.3
      maturity analyses, Ch. 54, 5.4.2
      puttable financial instruments classified as equity, Ch. 54, 5.4.4
    market risk, Ch. 54, 5.5
      'basic' sensitivity analysis, Ch. 54, 5.5.1
      other market risk disclosures, Ch. 54, 5.5.3
      value-at-risk and similar analyses, Ch. 54, 5.5.2
    qualitative disclosures, Ch. 54, 5.1
    quantitative disclosures, Ch. 54, 5.2, 5.6
      capital disclosures, Ch. 54, 5.6.3
      concentrations of risk, Ch. 54, 5.6.1
      operational risk, Ch. 54, 5.6.2
  presentation on the face of the financial statements and related disclosures, Ch. 54, 7
    gains and losses recognised in other comprehensive income, Ch. 54, 7.2
    gains and losses recognised in profit/loss, Ch. 54, 7.1
      embedded derivatives, Ch. 54, 7.1.4
      entities whose share capital is not equity, Ch. 54, 7.1.5
      further analysis of gains and losses recognised in profit/loss, Ch. 54, 7.1.2
      offsetting and hedges, Ch. 54, 7.1.3
      presentation on the face of the statement of comprehensive income (or income statement), Ch. 54, 7.1.1
  significance of financial instruments for an entity's financial position/performance, Ch. 54, 4
    accounting policies, Ch. 54, 4.1
    business combinations, Ch. 54, 4.6
      acquired receivables, Ch. 54, 4.6.1
      contingent consideration and indemnification assets, Ch. 54, 4.6.2
    day 1 profits, Ch. 54, 4.5.2
    fair values, Ch. 54, 4.5
    general disclosure requirements, Ch. 54, 4.5.1
    hedge accounting, Ch. 54, 4.3
      amount, timing and uncertainty of future cash flows, Ch. 54, 4.3.2
      effects of hedge accounting on financial position and performance, Ch. 54, 4.3.3

option to designate a credit exposure as measured at fair value through profit/loss, Ch. 54, 4.3.4
risk management strategy, Ch. 54, 4.3.1
uncertainty arising from interest rate benchmark (or IBOR) reform, Ch. 54, 4.3.5
income, expenses, gains and losses, Ch. 54, 4.2
fee income and expense, Ch. 54, 4.2.3
gains and losses by measurement category, Ch. 54, 4.2.1
interest income and expense, Ch. 54, 4.2.2
statement of cash flows, Ch. 54, 7.5
statement of changes in equity, Ch. 54, 7.3
statement of financial position, Ch. 54, 7.4, , Ch. 54, 4.4
assets and liabilities, Ch. 54, 7.4.3
categories of financial assets and financial liabilities, Ch. 54, 4.4.1
collateral, Ch. 54, 4.4.6
compound financial instruments with multiple embedded derivatives, Ch. 54, 4.4.7
current and non-current assets and liabilities, distinction between, Ch. 54, 7.4.4
convertible loans, Ch. 54, 7.4.4.B
debt with refinancing or roll over agreements, Ch. 54, 7.4.4.D
derivatives, Ch. 54, 7.4.4.A
A loan covenants, Ch. 54, 7.4.4.E
long-term loans with repayment on demand terms, Ch. 54, 7.4.4.C
defaults and breaches of loans payable, Ch. 54, 4.4.8
disclosure requirements, Ch. 54, 7.4.2.C
enforceable legal right of set-off, Ch. 54, 7.4.1.A
entities whose share capital is not equity, Ch. 54, 7.4.6
equity, Ch. 54, 7.4.5
financial assets designated as measured at fair value through profit/loss, Ch. 54, 4.4.3
financial liabilities designated at fair value through profit/loss, Ch. 54, 4.4.2
intention to settle net, Ch. 54, 7.4.1.C
interests in associates and joint ventures accounted for in accordance with IFRS 9, Ch. 54, 4.4.9
investments in equity instruments designated at fair value through other comprehensive income (IFRS 9), Ch. 54, 4.4.4
master netting agreements, Ch. 54, 7.4.1.B
objective, Ch. 54, 7.4.2.A
offsetting collateral amounts, Ch. 54, 7.4.1.F
offsetting financial assets and financial liabilities, Ch. 54, 7.4.1
offsetting financial assets and financial liabilities: disclosure, Ch. 54, 7.4.2
reclassification, Ch. 54, 4.4.5
scope, Ch. 54, 7.4.2.B
situations where offset is not normally appropriate, Ch. 54, 7.4.1.D
unit of account, Ch. 54, 7.4.1.G
transfers of financial assets, Ch. 54, 6
meaning of 'transfer,' Ch. 54, 6.1
transferred financial assets that are derecognised in their entirety, Ch. 54, 6.3
disclosure requirements, Ch. 54, 6.3.2
meaning of continuing involvement, Ch. 54, 6.3.1
transferred financial assets that are not derecognised in their entirety, Ch. 54, 6.2
transitional provisions, Ch. 54, 8

Financial instruments: recognition and initial measurement, Ch. 49, 1–3
initial measurement (IFRS 9), Ch. 49, 3
assets and liabilities arising from loan commitments, Ch. 49, 3.7
embedded derivatives and financial instrument hosts, Ch. 49, 3.5
general requirements, Ch. 49, 3.1
initial fair value and 'day 1' profits, Ch. 49, 3.3
financial guarantee contracts and off-market loan commitments, Ch. 49, 3.3.3
interest-free and low-interest long-term loans, Ch. 49, 3.3.1
loans and receivables acquired in a business combination, Ch. 49, 3.3.4
measurement of financial instruments following modification of contractual terms, Ch. 49, 3.3.2
regular way transactions, Ch. 49, 3.6
transaction costs, Ch. 49, 3.4
recognition (IFRS 9), Ch. 49, 2
general requirements, Ch. 49, 2.1
cash collateral, Ch. 49, 2.1.7
firm commitments to purchase/sell goods/services, Ch. 49, 2.1.2
forward contracts, Ch. 49, 2.1.3
option contracts, Ch. 49, 2.1.4
planned future/forecast transactions, Ch. 49, 2.1.5
principal versus agent, Ch. 49, 2.1.8
receivables and payables, Ch. 49, 2.1.1
transfers of financial assets not qualifying for derecognition by transferor, Ch. 49, 2.1.6
'regular way' transactions, Ch. 49, 2.2
exchanges of non-cash financial assets, Ch. 49, 2.2.5.A
financial liabilities, Ch. 49, 2.2.2
general requirements, Ch. 49, 2.2.1
settlement date accounting, Ch. 49, 2.2.4
trade date accounting, Ch. 49, 2.2.3

Financial instruments: subsequent measurement
amortised cost and the effective interest method, Ch. 50, 3
fixed interest rate instruments, Ch. 50, 3.2
floating rate instruments, Ch. 50, 3.3
inflation-linked debt, Ch. 50, 3.6
more complex financial liabilities, Ch. 50, 3.7
perpetual debt instruments, Ch. 50, 3.5
prepayment, call and similar options, Ch. 50, 3.4
revisions to estimated cash flows, Ch. 50, 3.4.1
foreign currencies, Ch. 50, 4
foreign entities, Ch. 50, 4.2
instruments, Ch. 50, 4.1
and recognition of gains and losses, Ch. 50, 2
financial assets and financial liabilities at fair value through profit/loss, Ch. 50, 2.4
financial guarantees and commitments to provide a loan at a below-market interest rate, Ch. 50, 2.8
reclassification of financial assets, Ch. 50, 2.7

Financial liabilities and equity, Ch. 47, 1–12. *See also* Equity instruments; Financial assets; IAS 32

Financial liabilities and equity—*contd*
  background, Ch. 47, 1.1
  classification, Ch. 48, 3
  classification of instruments
    consolidated financial statements, Ch. 47, 4.8.1
    contingent settlement provisions, Ch. 47, 4.3
      contingencies that are 'not genuine,' Ch. 47, 4.3.1
      liabilities that arise only on a change of control, Ch. 47, 4.3.3
      liabilities that arise only on liquidation, Ch. 47, 4.3.2
      some typical contingent settlement provisions, Ch. 47, 4.3.4
    contractual obligation to deliver cash or other financial assets, Ch. 47, 4.2
      implied contractual obligation to deliver cash or other financial assets, Ch. 47, 4.2.2
      relationship between an entity and its members, Ch. 47, 4.2.1
    definition of equity instrument, Ch. 47, 4.1
    examples of equity instruments
      contracts to issue equity instruments, Ch. 47, 4.4.2
      issued instruments, Ch. 47, 4.4.1
    IFRS development on, Ch. 47, 12
    instruments redeemable
      with a 'dividend blocker,' Ch. 47, 4.5.3.A
      with a 'dividend pusher,' Ch. 47, 4.5.3.B
      mandatorily or at the holder's option, Ch. 47, 4.5.1
      only at the issuer's option or not redeemable, Ch. 47, 4.5.2
    perpetual debt, Ch. 47, 4.7
    preference shares and similar instruments, Ch. 47, 4.5
      'change of control,' 'taxation change' and 'regulatory change' clauses, Ch. 47, 4.5.8
      economic compulsion, Ch. 47, 4.5.6
      instruments redeemable mandatorily or at the holder's option, Ch. 47, 4.5.1
      'linked' instruments, Ch. 47, 4.5.7
      perpetual instruments with a 'step-up' clause, Ch. 47, 4.5.4
      relative subordination, Ch. 47, 4.5.5
    puttable instruments and instruments repayable only on liquidation IFRIC 2, Ch. 47, 4.6.6
      instruments entitling the holder to a pro rata share of net assets only on liquidation, Ch. 47, 4.6.3
      instruments issued by a subsidiary, Ch. 47, 4.6.4.A
      instruments that substantially fix or restrict the residual return to the holder of an instrument, Ch. 47, 4.6.4.E
      issue, Ch. 47, 4.6.1
      meaning of 'identical features,' Ch. 47, 4.6.4.C
      no obligation to deliver cash or another financial asset, Ch. 47, 4.6.4.D
      puttable instruments, Ch. 47, 4.6.2
      reclassification, Ch. 47, 4.6.5
      relative subordination of the instrument, Ch. 47, 4.6.4.B
      transactions entered into by an instrument holder other than as owner of the entity, Ch. 47, 4.6.4.F
    reclassification of instruments
      change of circumstances, Ch. 47, 4.9.2
      change of terms, Ch. 47, 4.9.1
    single entity financial statements, Ch. 47, 4.8.2
  compound financial instruments, Ch. 47, 6
    background, Ch. 47, 6.1
    common forms of convertible bonds, Ch. 47, 6.6
      bond convertible into fixed percentage of equity, Ch. 47, 6.6.6
      contingent convertible bond, Ch. 47, 6.6.2
      convertible bonds with down round or ratchet features, Ch. 47, 6.6.7
      convertibles with cash settlement at the option of the issuer, Ch. 47, 6.6.5
      foreign currency convertible bond, Ch. 47, 6.6.4
      functional currency bond convertible into a fixed number of shares, Ch. 47, 6.6.1
      mandatorily convertible bond, Ch. 47, 6.6.3
    components, Ch. 47, 6.4
      compound instruments with embedded derivatives, Ch. 47, 6.4.2
      determining the components of a compound instrument, Ch. 47, 6.4.1
    conversion
      at maturity, Ch. 47, 6.3.1
      before maturity, Ch. 47, 6.3.2
      early redemption/repurchase, Ch. 47, 6.3.3
      exercising an embedded call option, Ch. 47, 6.3.3.B
      through negotiation with bondholders, Ch. 47, 6.3.3.A
    initial recognition–'split accounting,' Ch. 47, 6.2
      accounting for the equity component, Ch. 47, 6.2.1
      temporary differences arising from split accounting, Ch. 47, 6.2.2
    modification, Ch. 47, 6.3.4
    treatment by holder and issuer contrasted, Ch. 47, 6.1.1
  contracts accounted for as equity instruments, Ch. 47, 5.1
    comparison with IFRS 2–share-based payment, Ch. 47, 5.1.1
    exchange of fixed amounts of equity (equity for equity), Ch. 47, 5.1.4
    number of equity instruments issued adjusted for capital, Ch. 47, 5.1.2
    restructuring or other event, Ch. 47, 5.1.2
    stepped up exercise price, Ch. 47, 5.1.3
  contracts accounted for as financial assets or financial liabilities, Ch. 47, 5.2
    derivative financial instruments with settlement options, Ch. 47, 5.2.8
    fixed amount of cash (or other financial assets) denominated in a currency other than the entity's functional currency, Ch. 47, 5.2.3
    fixed amount of cash determined by reference to share price, Ch. 47, 5.2.6
    fixed number of equity instruments for variable consideration, Ch. 47, 5.2.2
    fixed number of equity instruments with variable value, Ch. 47, 5.2.5
    instrument with equity settlement alternative of significantly higher value than cash settlement alternative, Ch. 47, 5.2.4
    net-settled contracts over own equity, Ch. 47, 5.2.7
    variable number of equity instruments, Ch. 47, 5.2.1
  definitions, Ch. 45, 2.1; Ch. 47, 3; Ch. 52, 2.1

derecognition, Ch. 52, 6. *See also* Derecognition
    derivatives that can be financial assets or financial liabilities, Ch. 52, 6.4
    exchange or modification of debt by original lender, Ch. 52, 6.2
        costs and fees, Ch. 52, 6.2.5
        examples, Ch. 52, 6.2.7
        exchange of debt through an intermediary, Ch. 52, 6.2.4
        Interbank Offered Rate (IBOR) Reform, Ch. 52, 6.2.2
        loan syndications, Ch. 52, 6.2.3
        modification gains and losses, Ch. 52, 6.2.6
        settlement of financial liability with issue of new equity instrument, Ch. 52, 6.2.8
    extinguishment of debt, Ch. 52, 6.1
        extinguishment in exchange for transfer of assets not meeting the derecognition criteria, Ch. 52, 6.1.4
        'in-substance defeasance' arrangements, Ch. 52, 6.1.3
        legal release by creditor, Ch. 52, 6.1.2
        what constitutes 'part' of a liability?, Ch. 52, 6.1.1
    gains and losses on extinguishment of debt, Ch. 52, 6.3
    supply-chain finance, Ch. 52, 6.5
derivatives over own equity instruments, Ch. 47, 11
    call options, Ch. 47, 11.2
        call options over non-controlling interest, Ch. 7, 6.1, 6.3, 6.4, 6.5
        purchased call option, Ch. 47, 11.2.1
        written call option, Ch. 47, 11.2.2
    forward contracts, Ch. 47, 11.1
        'back-to-back' forward contracts, Ch. 47, 11.1.3
        forward purchase, Ch. 47, 11.1.1
        forward sale, Ch. 47, 11.2
    put options, Ch. 47, 11.3
        purchased put option, Ch. 47, 11.3.1
        put options over noncontrolling interest, Ch. 7, 6.2, 6.3, 6.4, 6.5
        written put option, Ch. 47, 11.3.2
designated at fair value through profit/loss, Ch. 54, 4.4.2; Ch. 50, 2.4
dividends payable on shares classified as, Ch. 21, 5.5.4
Financial Instruments with Characteristics of Equity Research Project (FICE), Ch. 7, 7.3, 7.4, 7.5; Ch. 47, 1, 4.6.6, 5.1.2, 5.3.2A, 6.6.3B, 12
future developments, Ch. 47, 12
gross-settled contracts for the sale or issue of the entity's own equity instruments, Ch. 47, 5.4
'hedging' of instruments classified as equity, Ch. 47, 10
held for trading, Ch. 48, 4
interest, dividends, gains and losses, Ch. 47, 8
    tax effects, Ch. 47, 8.2
    transaction costs, Ch. 47, 8.1
liabilities arising from gross-settled contracts for the purchase of the entity's own equity instruments, Ch. 47, 5.3
    contracts to acquire non-controlling interests, Ch. 47, 5.3.2
    contracts to purchase own equity during 'closed' or 'prohibited' periods, Ch. 47, 5.3.1
non-controlling interests classified as, Ch. 7, 5.5, 6.2, 6.3, 6.4
objective, Ch. 47, 2.1
offsetting, Ch. 54, 7.4.1
    cash pooling arrangements, Ch. 54, 7.4.1.E
    disclosure, Ch. 54, 7.4.2
    enforceable legal right of set-off, Ch. 54, 7.4.1.A
    intention to settle net, Ch. 54, 7.4.1.C
    master netting agreements, Ch. 54, 7.4.1.B
    offsetting collateral amounts, Ch. 54, 7.4.1.F
    situations where offset is not normally appropriate, Ch. 54, 7.4.1.D
    unit of account, Ch. 54, 7.4.1.G
recognition, Ch. 49, 2.2.2
scope, Ch. 47, 2.2
settlement of financial liability with equity instrument, Ch. 47, 7
    debt for equity swaps with shareholders, Ch. 47, 7.3
    requirements of IFRIC 19, Ch. 47, 7.2
    scope and effective date of IFRIC 19, Ch. 47, 7.1
    shares/warrants issued in connection with, Ch. 34, 2.2.4.I
treasury shares, Ch. 47, 9
    IFRS 17 Treasury share election, Ch. 47, 9.2
    transactions in own shares not at fair value, Ch. 47, 9.1

Financial reporting in hyperinflationary economies, Ch. 16, 1–12. *See also* Hyperinflation

Financial Service Agency, Japan, Ch. 1, 2.3

Financial Service Commission, Republic of Korea, Ch. 1, 2.3

Financial statements, Ch. 3, 2–3.4. *See also* IAS 1; IAS 8; IAS 10; Income statement; Statement of comprehensive income; Statement of financial position comparative information, Ch. 3, 2.4
components of, Ch. 3, 2.3
conceptual framework, IASB's, Ch. 2.6.1
    assets, Ch. 2.7.2
    consolidated and unconsolidated, Ch. 2.6.2.1
    elements, Ch. 2.7
    equity, Ch. 2.7.4
    executory contracts, Ch. 2.7.1.2
    going concern assumption, Ch. 2.6.1.4
    income and expenses, Ch. 2.7.5
    liabilities, Ch. 2.7.3
    objective and scope, Ch. 2.6.1.1
    perspective adopted in financial statements, Ch. 2.6.1.3
    reporting period and comparative information, Ch. 2.6.1.2
    substance of contractual rights and contractual obligations, Ch. 2.7.1.3
    unit of account, Ch. 2.7.1.1
date when financial statements are authorised for issue, Ch. 38, 2.1.1
events requiring adjustment to the amounts recognised/disclosures in, Ch. 38, 2.2.1
first IFRS financial statements in scope of IFRS 1, Ch. 5, 2.1
frequency of reporting and period covered, Ch. 3, 2.2
identification of, Ch. 3, 2.5.1
notes to, Ch. 3, 3.4
purpose of, Ch. 3, 2.1
re-issuing (dual dating), Ch. 38, 2.1.1.B
statement of changes in equity, Ch. 3, 3.3
statement of compliance with IFRS, Ch. 3, 2.5.2
statement of comprehensive income and income statement, Ch. 3, 3.2
statement of financial position, Ch. 3, 3.1
structure of, Ch. 3, 3

Financial statements, presentation of, Ch. 3, 2–3. *See also* IAS 1

Financial statements, presentation of—*contd*
   comparative information, Ch. 3, 2.4
   components of a complete set of financial statements, Ch. 3, 2.3
   frequency of reporting and period covered, Ch. 3, 2.2 IAS 1, Ch. 3, 1.1
   IAS 8, Ch. 3, 1.2
   identification of, Ch. 3, 2.5.1
   purpose of, Ch. 3, 2.1
   statement of compliance with IFRS, Ch. 3, 2.5.2
   structure of financial statements, Ch. 3, 3
      notes to the financial statements, Ch. 3, 3.4
      statement of changes in equity, Ch. 3, 3.3
      statement of comprehensive income and the statement of profit or loss, Ch. 3, 3.2
         classification of expenses recognised in profit or loss by nature or function, Ch. 3, 3.2.3
         discontinued operations, Ch. 3, 3.2.5
         information required on the face of the statement of profit or loss, Ch. 3, 3.2.2
         material and extraordinary items, Ch. 3, 3.2.6
         operating profit, Ch. 3, 3.2.2.A
         profit and loss and comprehensive income, Ch. 3, 3.2.1
         statement of comprehensive income, Ch. 3, 3.2.4
      statement of financial position, Ch. 3, 3.1
         current assets, Ch. 3, 3.1.3
         current liabilities, Ch. 3, 3.1.4
         current/non-current assets and liabilities, distinction between, Ch. 3, 3.1.1
         information required either on the face of the statement of financial position or in the notes, Ch. 3, 3.1.6
         information required on the face of statement of financial position, Ch. 3, 3.1.5
         non-current assets and disposal groups held for sale/distribution, Ch. 3, 3.1.2
Financing activities, cash flows from, Ch. 40, 4.3
Firm commitments
   to acquire a business, hedges of, Ch. 53, 7.6
   hedges of, Ch. 53, 5.1.1, 5.2.2
   to purchase or sell goods or services, Ch. 49, 2.1.2
First-time adoption, Ch. 5, 1–8. *See also* IFRS 1
   actuarial assumptions, Ch. 5, 7.7.3
   authoritative literature, Ch. 5, 1.2
   business combinations, Ch. 5, 5.2
   classification and measurement of financial instruments, Ch. 5, 4.9
   compound financial instruments, Ch. 5, 5.10
   consolidated financial statements, Ch. 5, 5.8.1
   cumulative translation differences, Ch. 5, 5.7
   date of transition to IFRSs, Ch. 5, 5.5.1.B
   deemed cost, Ch. 5, 5.5
   defined terms, Ch. 5, 1.3
   derecognition of financial assets and financial liabilities, Ch. 5, 4.3
   embedded derivatives, Ch. 5, 4.11
   employee benefits, Ch. 5, 7.7
   estimates, Ch. 5, 4.2
   fair value, Ch. 5, 3.3, 5.5.1
   first IFRS financial statements, Ch. 5, 2.1
   first IFRS reporting period, Ch. 5, 7.2.1
   first-time adopter, identifying, Ch. 5, 2
      application of IFRS 1, Ch. 5, 2.2
      dual reporting entity, Ch. 5, 2.3
      first IFRS financial statements in scope of IFRS 1, Ch. 5, 2.1
      previous GAAP, determining, Ch. 5, 2.3
   full actuarial valuations, Ch. 5, 7.7.2
   full retrospective application, Ch. 5, 3.5
   government loans, Ch. 5, 4.12
   hedge accounting, Ch. 5, 4.4, 4.5, 4.6, 4.7
   insurance contracts, Ch. 5, 4.13, 5.4
   interim financial reports, Ch. 5, 6.6
   leases, Ch. 5, 5.6
   line-by-line reconciliations, Ch. 5, 6.3.2
   mandatory exceptions, Ch. 5, 3.5, 4.1
   measurement, Ch. 5, 4.9
   non-controlling interests, Ch. 5, 4.8
   objectives of, Ch. 5, 1.1
   opening IFRS statement of financial position, Ch. 5, 3
      accounting policies, applying, Ch. 5, 3.2
      timeline, Ch. 5, 3.1
   optional exemptions, Ch. 5, 5
   regulatory issues
      foreign private issuers that are SEC registrants, Ch. 5, 8.1
      International Practices Task Force (IPTF) guidance, Ch. 5, 8.1.2
   related hedges, gains and losses arising on, Ch. 5, 5.7.1
   restatement of goodwill, Ch. 5, 5.2.5
   revenue from contracts with customers, Ch. 5, 5.21
   separate financial statements, Ch. 5, 5.8.2
   timeline, Ch. 5, 3.1
   unrecognised past service costs, Ch. 5, 7.7.4
First-time presentation of interim reports, Ch. 41, 11.1
Fixed fee service contracts, Ch. 55, 3.5.1
Fixed interest rate instruments, Ch. 50, 3.2
'Fixed stated principal' of a bond, Ch. 47, 6.3.2.A
Floating interest rate instruments, Ch. 50, 3.3
Foreign currency basis spreads, Ch. 53, 3.6.5, 7.4.8, 7.5.3
   retrospective application, Ch. 53, 13.3.3
Foreign currency cash flows
   impairment, Ch. 20, 7.1.5
   statement of cash flows, Ch. 40, 5.3
Foreign currency convertible bond, Ch. 47, 6.6.4
   instrument issued by foreign subsidiary convertible into equity of parent, Ch. 47, 6.6.4.A
Foreign currency derivatives, Ch. 46, 5.2.1
   commonly used currencies, Ch. 46, 5.2.1.C
   functional currency of counterparty, Ch. 46, 5.2.1.A
   oil contract, Ch. 46, 5.2.1.D
   routinely denominated in commercial transactions, Ch. 46, 5.2.1.B
Foreign currency instruments, Ch. 50, 4.1
   debt security measured at fair value through other comprehensive income, Ch. 51, 14.3
Foreign currency translation, interim financial reporting, Ch. 41, 9.6

Foreign entities, subsequent measurement of financial instruments, Ch. 50, 4
IFRS 9, Ch. 51, 1.2
Foreign exchange, Ch. 15, 1–11. *See also* IAS 21
background, Ch. 15, 1.1
change in functional currency, Ch. 15, 5.5
change of presentation currency, Ch. 15, 7
disclosure requirements, Ch. 15, 10
    convenience translations of financial statements/other financial information, Ch. 15, 10.3
    exchange differences, Ch. 15, 10.1
    judgements made in applying IAS 21 and related disclosures, Ch. 15, 10.4
    presentation and functional currency, Ch. 15, 10.2
entity's functional currency determination, Ch. 15, 4
    branches and divisions, Ch. 15, 4.4
    documentation of judgements made, Ch. 15, 4.5
    general, Ch. 15, 4.1
    intermediate holding companies/finance subsidiaries, Ch. 15, 4.2
    investment holding companies, Ch. 15, 4.3
future developments, Ch. 15, 11
introduction of euro, Ch. 15, 8
monetary/non-monetary determination, Ch. 15, 5.4
    deferred tax, Ch. 15, 5.4.5
    deposits and advance payments for actively traded commodities, Ch. 15, 5.4.2
    deposits/progress payments, Ch. 15, 5.4.1
    foreign currency share capital, Ch. 15, 5.4.4
    investments in preference shares, Ch. 15, 5.4.3
    post-employment benefit plans-foreign currency assets, Ch. 15, 5.4.6
    post-employment benefit plans-foreign currency plans, Ch. 15, 5.4.7
presentation currency other than the functional currency, Ch. 15, 6
    average rate calculation, Ch. 15, 6.1.4
    disposal of a foreign operation, Ch. 15, 6.6; Ch. 7, 2.3, 3.5
        partial disposal, Ch. 15, 6.6.2; Ch. 7, 2.3, 4.1
        step-by-step and direct methods of consolidation, Ch. 15, 6.6.3; Ch. 7, 2.3
    exchange differences on intragroup balances, Ch. 15, 6.3
        becoming part of the net investment in a foreign operation, Ch. 15, 6.3.1.F
        ceasing to be part of the net investment in a foreign operation, Ch. 15, 6.3.61.G
        currency of monetary item, Ch. 15, 6.3.1.C dividends, Ch. 15, 6.3.2
        monetary items included as part of the net investment in a foreign operation, Ch. 15, 6.3.1
        transacted by other members of the group, Ch. 15, 6.3.1.E
        treatment in individual financial statements, Ch. 15, 6.3.1.D
        unrealised profits on intragroup transactions, Ch. 15, 6.3.3
    foreign operations where sub-groups exist, accounting for, Ch. 15, 6.1.5
    goodwill and fair value adjustments, Ch. 15, 6.5
    non-coterminous period ends, Ch. 15, 6.4
    partial disposal of a foreign operation, Ch. 15, 6.6.2
    translation of equity items, Ch. 15, 6.2
        equity balances resulting from income and expenses being recognised in other comprehensive income, Ch. 15, 6.2.3
        equity balances resulting from transactions with equity holders, Ch. 15, 6.2.2
        share capital, Ch. 15, 6.2.1
    translation to the presentation currency, Ch. 15, 6.1
        accounting for foreign operations where sub-groups exist, Ch. 15, 6.1.5
        calculation of average rate, Ch. 15, 6.1.4
        dual rates, suspension of rates and lack of exchangeability, Ch. 15, 6.1.3
        functional currency is not that of a hyperinflationary economy, Ch. 15, 6.1.1
        functional currency is that of a hyperinflationary economy, Ch. 15, 6.1.2; Ch. 16. 11
reporting foreign currency transactions in the functional currency of an entity, Ch. 15, 5
    books and records not kept in functional currency, Ch. 15, 5.6
    change in functional currency, Ch. 15, 5.5
    at ends of subsequent reporting periods, Ch. 15, 5.2
    exchange differences, treatment of, Ch. 15, 5.3
        monetary items, Ch. 15, 5.3.1
        non-monetary items, Ch. 15, 5.3.2
    initial recognition, Ch. 15, 5.1
        deposits and other consideration received or paid in advance, Ch. 15, 5.1.2
        dual rates, Ch. 15, 5.1.4.A
        identifying the date of transaction, Ch. 15, 5.1.1
        suspension of rates: longer term lack of exchangeability, Ch. 15, 5.1.4.C
        practical difficulties in determining exchange rates, Ch. 15, 5.1.4
        suspension of rates: temporary lack of exchangeability, Ch. 15, 5.1.4.B
        using average rates, Ch. 15, 5.1.3
tax effects of all exchange differences, Ch. 15, 9
Forfeiture, share-based payments, Ch. 34, 6.1.2, 7.4.1
Forward contracts, Ch. 47, 11.1; Ch. 49, 2.1.3
'back-to-back' forward contracts, Ch. 47, 11.1.3
forward purchase, Ch. 47, 11.1.1
forward sale, Ch. 47, 11.1.2
Forward currency contracts, Ch. 53, 3.6.5, 7.3.3.A, 7.5.2, 13.3.2
Forward purchase agreements (EPS), Ch. 37, 6.4.2.C
Forward rate method, Ch. 53, 7.4.7
'Fresh start' accounting, Ch. 5, 5.5.2.B
Full cost method, extractive industries, Ch. 43, 3.2.4
Functional currency, Ch. 5, 7.8.1; Ch. 15, 3–6; Ch. 43, 9. *See also* Foreign exchange
books and records not kept in, Ch. 15, 5.6
change in, Ch. 15, 5.5; Ch. 43, 9.2
definition of, Ch. 15, 2.3
determining, Ch. 15, 4; Ch. 43, 9.1
at ends of subsequent reporting periods, Ch. 15, 5.2
exchange differences, treatment of, Ch. 15, 5.3
    monetary items, Ch. 15, 5.3.1
    non-monetary items, Ch. 15, 5.3.2
initial recognition, Ch. 15, 5.1

Functional currency—*contd*
  initial recognition—*contd*
    deposits and other consideration received or paid in advance, Ch. 15, 5.1.2
    dual rates, Ch. 15, 5.1.4.A
    identifying the date of transaction, Ch. 15, 5.1.1
    suspension of rates: longer term lack of exchangeability, Ch. 15, 5.1.4.C
    practical difficulties in determining exchange rates, Ch. 15, 5.1.4
    suspension of rates: temporary lack of exchangeability, Ch. 15, 5.1.4.B
    using average rates, Ch. 15, 5.1.3
  monetary/non-monetary determination, Ch. 15, 5.4
    deferred tax, Ch. 15, 5.4.4
    deposits/progress payments, Ch. 15, 5.4.1
    foreign currency share capital, Ch. 15, 5.4.3
    investments in preference shares, Ch. 15, 5.4.2
    post-employment benefit plans-foreign currency assets, Ch. 15, 5.4.5
    post-employment benefit plans-foreign currency plans, Ch. 15, 5.4.6

Fund performance fees, Ch. 46, 5.2.5
FVTOCI. *See* Fair value through other comprehensive income
General price index, Ch. 16, 3
  not available for all periods, Ch. 16, 3.2
  selection of, Ch. 16, 3.1
General purpose financial reporting, Ch. 2, 4
  changes in economic resources and claims, Ch. 2, 4.2.2
  economic resources and claims, Ch. 2, 4.2.1
  information about the use of economic resources (stewardship), Ch. 2, 4.2.3
  objective and usefulness, Ch. 2, 4.1.1
  limitations, Ch. 2, 4.1.2
Global Preparers Forum, Ch. 1, 2.9
Global Public Policy Committee (GPPC) guidance, Ch. 51, 7.2
Going concern, Ch. 2, 6.1.4; Ch. 3, 4.1.2; Ch. 38, 2.2.2
  disclosure in relation to the going concern assumption, Ch. 41, 4.7
Gold bullion sales (mining), Ch. 43, 12.13
'Good leaver' arrangements, share-based payments, Ch. 34, 5.3.9
Goodwill, Ch. 9, 6
  and allocation to cash-generating units (CGUs), Ch. 20, 8.1
  attributable to non-controlling interests, changes in ownership interest without loss of control, Ch. 7, 4.2; Ch. 20, 9
  in business combinations, Ch. 9, 6;
  and fair value adjustments, foreign operations, Ch. 15, 6.5
  impairment of goodwill, Ch. 20, 8
    acquisitions by subsidiaries and determining the level at which the group tests goodwill for impairment, Ch. 20, 12.2.3
    effect of IFRS 8 – Operating Segments – on impairment tests, Ch. 20, 8.1.4
    goodwill initially unallocated to CGUs, Ch. 20, 8.1.5
    identifying synergies and CGUs/CGU groups for allocating goodwill, Ch. 20, 8.1.2, 12.2
    measuring the goodwill allocated to CGUs/GCU groups, Ch. 20, 8.1.3
    disposal of operation within a CGU to which goodwill has been allocated, Ch. 20, 8.5
    changes in composition of CGUs, Ch. 20, 8.5.1
    effect of IFRS 8 (operating segments) when allocating goodwill to CGU's in individual financial statements, Ch. 20, 12.2.2
    goodwill synergies arising outside of the reporting entity/subgroup, Ch. 20, 12.2.1
  impairment of assets and goodwill recognised on acquisition, Ch. 20, 8.3
    deferred tax assets and losses of acquired businesses, Ch. 20, 8.3.2
    testing goodwill 'created' by deferred tax for impairment, Ch. 20, 8.3.1; Ch. 33, 12.3
  impairment testing when a CGU crosses more than one operating segment, Ch. 20, 8.4
  in individual (or subgroup) financial statements and the interaction with the group financial statements, Ch. 20, 12.2
  when to test CGUs with goodwill for impairment, Ch. 20, 8.2
  internally generated, Ch. 17, 6.2
  measuring, Ch. 9, 6
  non-controlling interests (NCIs)
    goodwill attributable to, Ch. 7, 4.2, 5.2.1
    impact of impairment testing on, Ch. 20, 9
  recognising and measuring, Ch. 9, 6
    subsequent accounting for goodwill, Ch. 9, 6.1
  restatement of goodwill on first-time adoption, Ch. 5, 5.2.5
    derecognition of negative goodwill, Ch. 5, 5.2.5.B
    goodwill previously deducted from equity, Ch. 5, 5.2.5.C
    prohibition of other adjustments of goodwill, Ch. 5, 5.2.5.A
  tax deductible, Ch. 33, 7.2.2.C
  tax on initial recognition of, Ch. 33, 7.2.2
Government grants, Ch. 24, 1–6. *See also* IAS 20
  acquisition of intangible assets by way of, Ch. 17, 4.6
  acquisition of property, plant and equipment by way of, Ch. 18, 4.6
  agriculture, Ch. 42, 3.3
  definition, Ch. 24, 1.2
  disclosures, Ch. 24, 6
  presentation of grants, Ch. 24, 4
    cash flows, Ch. 24, 4.1.1
    related to assets, Ch. 24, 4.1
    related to income, Ch. 24, 4.2
  recognition and measurement, Ch. 24, 3
    forgivable loans, Ch. 24, 3.3
    general requirements of IAS 20, Ch. 24, 3.1
    government assistance, Ch. 24, 3.8
    in the income statement, Ch. 24, 3.6
    loans at lower than market rates of interest, Ch. 24, 3.4
    non-monetary grants, Ch. 24, 3.2
    repayment of government grants, Ch. 24, 3.7
  related to biological assets, IAS 41, Ch. 24, 5, Ch. 42, 3.3
  scope of IAS 20, Ch. 24, 2
Government-related entities, Ch. 39, 2.2.10
'Graded' vesting, Ch. 34, 6.2.2. *See also* Share-based payment transactions
Grant date, share-based payment, Ch. 34, 5.3

award of equity instruments to a fixed monetary value, Ch. 34, 5.3.5
awards over a fixed pool of shares (including 'last man standing' arrangements), Ch. 34, 5.3.6
awards subject to modification by entity after original grant date, Ch. 34, 5.3.8
   discretion to make further awards, Ch. 34, 5.3.8.C
   interpretation of general terms, Ch. 34, 5.3.8.B
   significant equity restructuring or transactions, Ch. 34, 5.3.8.A
awards with multiple service and performance periods, Ch. 34, 5.3.7
awards vesting or exercisable on an exit event or change of control, Ch. 34, 15.4.1
communication of awards to employees and services in advance of, Ch. 34, 5.3.2
determination of, Ch. 34, 5.3.1
exercise price paid in shares (net settlement of award), Ch. 34, 5.3.4
exercise price/performance target dependent on a formula/future share price, Ch. 34, 5.3.3
'good leaver' arrangements, Ch. 34, 5.3.9
   automatic full/pro rata entitlement on leaving employment, Ch. 34, 5.3.9.C
   discretionary awards to, Ch. 34, 5.3.9.B
   provision for 'good leavers' made in original terms of award, Ch. 34, 5.3.9.A
special purpose acquisition companies ('SPACs'), Ch. 34, 5.3.10

Gross/net presentation of cash flows, Ch. 40, 5.2

Gross-settled contracts for entity's own equity instruments, Ch. 47, 5.4

Group reorganisations, Ch. 10, 1.2
and the carrying value of investments in subsidiaries, Ch. 20, 12.3

Group share schemes, Ch. 34, 12. *See also* Employee benefit trusts (EBTs) and similar arrangements; Share-based payment transactions
accounting treatment of group share schemes, summary, Ch. 34, 12.2
   awards settled in equity of the subsidiary, Ch. 34, 12.2.5.A
   awards settled in equity of the parent, Ch. 34, 12.2.5.B
   cash-settled transactions not settled by the entity receiving goods/services, Ch. 34, 12.2.6, 12.6
   entity receiving goods or services, Ch. 34, 12.2.3
   entity settling the transaction, Ch. 34, 12.2.4
   intragroup recharges and management charges, Ch. 34, 12.2.7
   scope of IFRS 2 for group share schemes, Ch. 34, 12.2.2
cash-settled transactions not settled by the entity receiving goods/services, illustrative example, Ch. 34, 12.6
consolidated financial statements, Ch. 34, 12.6.1
employee benefit trusts ('EBTs') and similar arrangements, Ch. 34, 12.3
employee transferring between group entities, Ch. 34, 12.7
equity-settled award satisfied by fresh issue of shares, illustrative example, Ch. 34, 12.5
equity-settled award satisfied by market purchase of shares, illustrative example, Ch. 34, 12.4
features of a group share scheme, Ch. 34, 12.1
group reorganisations, Ch. 34, 12.8
joint ventures or associates, share-based payments to employees of, Ch. 34, 12.9
scope of IFRS 2 for group share schemes, Ch. 34, 12.2.2
timing of recognition of intercompany recharges, Ch. 34, 12.2.7.A

Group transactions. *See* Common control/group transactions

Group treasury arrangements, Ch. 40, 6.5.2

Groups of items, hedge accounting, Ch. 53, 2.5
cash flow hedge of a net position, Ch. 53, 2.5.3
general requirements, Ch. 53, 2.5.1
hedging a component of a group, Ch. 53, 2.5.2
layer component designation, Ch. 53, 2.3.2
macro hedging, Ch. 53, 11
   accounting for dynamic risk management, Ch. 53, 11.1
   applying hedge accounting for macro hedging strategies under IFRS 9, Ch. 53, 11.2
nil net positions, Ch. 53, 2.5.4

Guarantees, transferred assets, Ch. 52, 5.3.1, 5.4.1
parent guarantees issued on behalf of subsidiary, Ch. 8, 4.4.5.B

Heap leaching, mining, Ch. 43, 14.6

Hedge accounting
accounting for the costs of hedging, Ch. 53, 7.5
   foreign currency basis spreads in financial instruments, Ch. 53, 7.5.3
   forward element of forward contracts, Ch. 53, 7.5.2
   time value of options, Ch. 53, 7.5.1
aggregated exposures, Ch. 53, 2.7
   accounting for, Ch. 53, 2.7.3
alternatives to hedge accounting, Ch. 53, 12
   credit risk exposures, Ch. 53, 12.1
   own use contracts, Ch. 53, 12.2
background, Ch. 53, 1.1
development of, Ch. 53, 1.3
discontinuation, Ch. 53, 8.3, 14.5
   of cash flow hedges, Ch. 53, 8.3.2
   Documented hedged item no longer exists, Ch. 53, 8.3.4
   of fair value hedges, Ch. 53, 8.3.1
   hedged net investment, disposal of, Ch. 53, 8.3.8
   hedging counterparty within the same consolidated group, Ch. 53, 8.3.7
   novation to central clearing parties, Ch. 53, 8.3.5
   risk management objective, change in, Ch. 53, 8.3.3
   settle to market derivatives, Ch. 53, 8.3.6
economic relationship, Ch. 53, 6.4.1
effective hedges, accounting for, Ch. 53, 7
   cash flow hedges, Ch. 53, 7.2
      acquisition or disposal of subsidiaries, Ch. 53, 7.2.4
      all-in-one hedges, Ch. 53, 5.2.1
      discontinuing, Ch. 53, 8.3
      documented rollover hedging strategy, Ch. 53, 7.7
      equity instrument designated at fair value through OCI, Ch. 53, 7.8
   fair value hedges, Ch. 53, 1.5, 5.1, 7.1
      adjustments to the hedged item, Ch. 53, 7.1.2
      discontinuing, Ch. 53, 8.3.1
      firm commitments, Ch. 53, 5.1.1
      foreign currency monetary items, Ch. 53, 5.1.2
      layer components with prepayment risk for, Ch. 53, 2.3.2

Hedge accounting—*contd*
   effective hedges, accounting for—*contd*
      cash flow hedges—*contd*
         fair value hedges—*contd*
            ongoing accounting, Ch. 53, 7.1.1
            presentation, Ch. 53, 10.2
         firm commitments, hedges of, Ch. 53, 5.2.2
         foreign currency monetary items, Ch. 53, 5.2.3
         hedges of a firm commitment to acquire a business, Ch. 53, 7.6
         hedges of a net investment in a foreign operation, accounting for, Ch. 7, 2.3; Ch. 53, 1.5, 5.3, 7.3, 8.3.7
         hypothetical derivatives, Ch. 53, 7.4.4
         measuring ineffectiveness of, Ch. 53, 7.4
         of a net position, Ch. 53, 2.5.3
         novation of, due to central clearing regulations, Ch. 53, 8.3.5
         ongoing accounting, Ch. 53, 7.2.1
         presentation, Ch. 53, 10.1
         reclassification of gains and losses, Ch. 53, 7.2.2
   effective date and transition, Ch. 53, 13
      limited retrospective application, Ch. 53, 13.3
      prospective application in general, Ch. 53, 13.2
   effectiveness assessment, Ch. 53, 8.1, 6.4
      credit risk dominance, Ch. 53, 6.4.2
      economic relationship, Ch. 53, 6.4.1
      hedge ratio, Ch. 53, 6.4.3
   effectiveness measurement, Ch. 53, 7.4
      calculation of, Ch. 53, 7.4.6
      'clean' *vs.* 'dirty' values, Ch. 53, 7.4.10
      comparison of spot rate and forward rate methods, Ch. 53, 7.4.7
      detailed example of calculation of ineffectiveness for a cash flow hedge, Ch. 53, 7.4.6
      discount rates for calculating fair value of hypothetical derivatives, Ch. 53, 7.4.5
      effectiveness of options, Ch. 53, 7.4.11
      foreign currency basis spreads, Ch. 53, 7.4.8
      hedged items with embedded optionality, Ch. 53, 7.4.12
      hedging instrument's impact on credit quality, Ch. 53, 7.4.9
      hedging using instruments with a non-zero fair value, Ch. 53, 7.4.3
      hypothetical derivative, Ch. 53, 7.4.4
      time value of money, Ch. 53, 7.4.2
   hedge ratio, Ch. 53, 6.4.3
   hedged items, Ch. 53, 2
      core deposits, Ch. 53, 2.6.7
      firm commitment to acquire a business, Ch. 53, 7.64
      forecast acquisition/issuance of foreign currency monetary items, Ch. 53, 2.6.5
      general requirements, Ch. 53, 2.1
      groups of items, Ch. 53, 2.5
         cash flow hedge of a net position, Ch. 53, 2.5.3
         general requirements, Ch. 53, 2.5.1
         hedging a component of a group, Ch. 53, 2.5.2
         nil net positions, Ch. 53, 2.5.4
      held at fair value through profit or loss, Ch. 53, 2.6.2
      held at fair value through OCI, Ch. 53, 2.6.3
      highly probable, Ch. 53, 2.6.1
      internal, Ch. 53, 4.3
      nominal components, Ch. 53, 2.3
         general requirement, Ch. 53, 2.3.1
         layer component for fair value hedge with prepayment risk, Ch. 53, 2.3.2
      own equity instruments, Ch. 53, 2.6.6
      risk components, Ch. 53, 2.2
         contractually specified, Ch. 53, 2.2.2
         foreign currency as, Ch. 53, 2.2.5
         general requirements, Ch. 53, 2.2.1
         inflation as, Ch. 53, 2.2.6
         non-contractually specified, Ch. 53, 2.2.3
         partial term hedging, Ch. 53, 2.2.4
      sub-LIBOR issue, Ch. 53, 2.4
         negative interest rates, Ch. 53, 2.4.2
   hedging instruments, Ch. 53, 3
      combinations of instruments, Ch. 53, 3.5
      derivatives, Ch. 53, 3.2
         basis swaps, Ch. 53, 3.2.5
         credit break clauses, Ch. 53, 3.2.4
         embedded derivatives, Ch. 53, 3.2.3
         net written options, Ch. 53, 3.2.2
         offsetting external derivatives, Ch. 53, 3.2.1
      embedded derivatives, Ch. 53, 3.2.3
      general requirements, Ch. 53, 3.1
      hedging different risks with one instrument, Ch. 53, 3.7
      non-derivative financial instruments, Ch. 53, 3.3
         of foreign currency risk, Ch. 53, 3.3.1
      non-derivative liabilities, Ch. 53, 3.3
      own equity instruments, Ch. 53, 3.4
      portions and proportions of, Ch. 53, 3.6
         foreign currency basis spread, Ch. 53, 3.6.5
         interest elements of forwards, Ch. 53, 3.6.5
         notional decomposition, Ch. 53, 3.6.2
         portion of a time period, Ch. 53, 3.6.6
         proportions of instruments, Ch. 53, 3.6.1
         restructuring of derivatives, Ch. 53, 3.6.3
         time value of options, Ch. 53, 3.6.4
   hedging relationships, types of, Ch. 53, 5
      cash flow hedges, Ch. 53, 5.2
         all-in-one hedges, Ch. 53, 5.2.1
         firm commitments hedges, Ch. 53, 5.2.2
         foreign currency monetary items, Ch. 53, 5.2.3
      fair value hedges, Ch. 53, 5.1
         firm commitments, hedges of, Ch. 53, 5.1.1
         foreign currency monetary items, hedges of, Ch. 53, 5.1.2
      hedges of net investments in foreign operations, Ch. 53, 5.3
         amount of the hedged item for which a hedging relationship may be designated, Ch. 53, 5.3.2
         nature of the hedged risk, Ch. 53, 5.3.1
         where the hedging instrument can be held, Ch. 53, 5.3.3
   ineffectiveness, measuring, Ch. 53, 7.4
   internal hedges and other group accounting issues, Ch. 53, 4
      central clearing parties, Ch. 53, 4.1.1
      external hedging instruments, offsetting, Ch. 53, 4.2
      hedged item and hedging instrument held by different group entities, Ch. 53, 4.4
      internal hedged items, Ch. 53, 4.3

internal hedging instruments, Ch. 53, 4.1
    offsetting internal hedges instruments, Ch. 53, 4.2
macro hedging, Ch. 53, 11
    accounting for dynamic risk management, Ch. 53, 11.1
    macro hedging strategies under IFRS 9, Ch. 53, 11.2
main differences between IFRS 9 and IAS 39 hedge accounting requirements, Ch. 53, 14
    discontinuation, Ch. 53, 14.5
    effectiveness criteria, Ch. 53, 14.4
    eligible hedged items, Ch. 53, 14.2
    eligible hedging instruments, Ch. 53, 14.3
    hedge accounting mechanisms, Ch. 53, 14.5
    objective of hedge accounting, Ch. 53, 14.1
negative interest rates, Ch. 53, 2.4.2
portfolio/macro hedging, Ch. 53, 11
presentation, Ch. 53, 10
    cash flow hedges, Ch. 53, 10.1
    cost of hedging, Ch. 53, 10.4
    fair value hedges, Ch. 53, 10.2
    hedges of groups of items, Ch. 53, 10.3
proxy hedges, Ch. 53, 6.2.1
objective of, Ch. 53, 1.4
overview, Ch. 53, 1.5
own use contracts, Ch. 53, 12.2
qualifying criteria, Ch. 53, 6
    credit risk dominance, Ch. 53, 6.4.2
        on the hedged item, Ch. 53, 6.4.2.B
        on the hedging instrument, Ch. 53, 6.4.2.A
    designating 'proxy hedges', Ch. 53, 6.2.1
    documentation and designation, Ch. 53, 6.3
        business combinations, Ch. 53, 6.3.1
        dynamic hedging strategies, Ch. 53, 6.3.2
        forecast transactions, Ch. 53, 6.3.3
    economic relationship, Ch. 53, 6.4.1
    general requirements, Ch. 53, 6.1
    hedge effectiveness requirements, Ch. 53, 6.4
        credit risk dominance, Ch. 53, 6.4.2
        economic relationship, Ch. 53, 6.4.1
        hedge ratio, Ch. 53, 6.4.3
    proxy hedging, Ch. 53, 6.2.1
    risk management strategy, Ch. 53, 6.2
    risk management objective, Ch. 53, 6.2
    setting the hedge ratio, Ch. 53, 6.4.3
rebalancing, Ch. 53, 8.2
    definition, Ch. 53, 8.2.1
    mechanics of, Ch. 53, 8.2.3
    requirement to rebalance, Ch. 53, 8.2.2
risk management, Ch. 53, 6.2, 6.3
    proxy hedges, Ch. 53, 6.2.1
    risk management objective, Ch. 53, 6.2
        change in, Ch. 53, 8.3
    risk management strategy, Ch. 53, 6.2
standards, development of, Ch. 53, 1.3

Hedge ratio, setting, Ch. 53, 6.4.3

'Hedging' of instruments classified as equity, Ch. 47, 10

Hedging sales of metal concentrate (mining sector), Ch. 43, 13.4

High-Level Expert Group (HLEG), Ch. 1, 4.2.1.B

Hong Kong Accounting Standards (HKAS), Ch. 1, 4.4.1.B

Hong Kong Financial Reporting Standards (HKFRS), Ch. 1, 4.4.1.B

Hong Kong, IFRS adoption in, Ch. 1, 4.4.1.B

Hong Kong Institute of Certified Public Accountants (HKICPA), Ch. 1, 4.4.1.B

Hybrid taxes, Ch. 33, 4.1.2, 4.5
    minimum based on a measure other than taxable profits, Ch. 33, 4.5.1
    tax based on revenues, unless a profit measure gives a lower result, Ch. 33, 4.5.3
    tax is the higher of measures based on taxable profits and revenues, Ch. 33. 4.5.2

Hyperinflation, Ch. 16, 1–12. *See also* IAS 29–*Financial Reporting in Hyperinflationary Economies*
    background, Ch. 16, 1.1
    capitalisation of borrowing costs, Ch. 21, 5.6
    definition of, Ch. 16, 2.3
    disclosures, Ch. 16, 12
    general price index, selection of, Ch. 16, 3.1
    hyperinflationary economies, Ch. 16, 1.2
        capitalisation of borrowing costs in, Ch. 16, 4.1.4; Ch. 21, 5.6
        interim financial reporting in, Ch. 16.9; Ch. 41, 9.6.2
    restatement approach, Ch. 16, 1.3
    restatement of comparative figures, Ch. 16, 8
    restatement of the statement of cash flows, Ch. 16, 7
    restatement of the statement of changes in equity, Ch. 16, 5
    restatement of the statement of profit and loss and other comprehensive income, Ch. 16, 6
    restatement of the statement of financial position, Ch. 16, 4
    transition, Ch. 16, 10
    translation to a different presentation currency, Ch. 16, 11
        comparative information, Ch. 16, 11.2

Hypothetical derivative, hedge accounting, Ch. 53, 7.4.4

IAS 1–*Presentation of Financial Statements*, Ch. 3. *See also* Financial Statements, presentation of
    accrual basis of accounting, Ch. 3, 4.1.3
    capital disclosures, Ch. 3, 5.4.1
    consistency, Ch. 3, 4.1.4
    current assets criteria, Ch. 3, 3.1.3
    current liabilities criteria, Ch. 3, 3.1.4
    current *versus* non-current classification, Ch. 3, 3.1.1
    disclosures, Ch. 3, 5.1, 5.5; Ch. 54, 5.2
        capital disclosures, Ch. 3, 5.4.1; Ch. 54, 5.6.3
        going concern basis, Ch. 3, 4.1.2
        sources of estimation uncertainty, Ch. 3, 5.2.1
    fair presentation and compliance with IFRS, Ch. 3, 4.1.1.A
    fair presentation override, Ch. 3, 4.1.1.B
    future developments, Ch. 3, 6
    general principles, Ch. 3, 4.1
    going concern basis, Ch. 3, 4.1.2
    materiality concept, Ch. 3, 4.1.5; Ch. 54, 3.2
    objective of, Ch. 3, 1.1 offset, Ch. 3, 4.1.5.B
    profit or loss for the period, Ch. 3, 4.1.6 purpose of, Ch. 3, 2, Ch. 3, 2.1
    scope of, Ch. 3, 1.1
    statement of comprehensive income, Ch. 3, 3.2

IAS 2–*Inventories*, Ch. 22, 1–6
    definitions, Ch. 22, 2.2
    disclosure requirements of IAS 2, Ch. 22, 6
        crypto-assets, Ch. 22, 6.2
    measurement, Ch. 22, 3

IAS 2–*Inventories*—*contd*
  measurement—*contd*
    cost criteria, Ch. 22, 3.1
      borrowing costs and purchases on deferred terms, Ch. 22, 3.1.3.C
      costs of purchase, Ch. 22, 3.1.1
      costs of conversion, Ch. 22, 3.1.2
      drug production costs within the pharmaceutical industry, Ch. 22, 3.1.3.F
      forward contracts to purchase inventory, Ch. 22, 3.1.3.E
      general and administrative overheads, Ch. 22, 3.1.3.B
      other cost, Ch. 22, 3.1.3
      service providers, Ch. 22, 3.1.3.D
      storage and distribution costs, Ch. 22, 3.1.3.A
    cost formulas, Ch. 22, 3.2.2
      first-in, first-out (FIFO), Ch. 22, 3.2.2.A
      last-in, first-out (LIFO), Ch. 22, 3.2.2.C
      weighted average cost, Ch. 22, 3.2.2.B
    crypto-assets, Ch. 22, 3.4
      cost or lower net realisable value, Ch. 22, 3.4.1
      fair value less costs to sell, Ch. 22, 3.4.2
    net realisable value, Ch. 22, 3.4.1
      sale after the reporting period, Ch. 38, 3.3
    transfers of rental assets to inventory, Ch. 22, 2.3.1.E
  objective of, Ch. 22, 2
  real estate inventory, Ch. 22, 4
    classification, Ch. 22, 4.1
    costs of, Ch. 22, 4.2
      allocation to individual units in multi-unit developments, Ch. 22, 4.2.1
      property demolition and operating lease, Ch. 22, 4.2.2
  recognition in profit/loss, Ch. 22, 5
  scope and recognition issues, IAS 2/another IFRS, Ch. 22, 2.3
    crypto-assets, Ch. 22, 2.3.1.D
    broadcast rights - IAS 2/IAS 38, Ch. 22, 2.3.1.B
    consignment stock and sale and repurchase agreements, Ch. 22, 2.3.1.F
    core inventories and spare parts, Ch. 22, 2.3.1.A
    emission rights, Ch. 22, 2.3.1.C
    sales with a right of return, Ch. 22, 2.3.1.G
    transfers of rental assets to inventory, Ch. 22, 2.3.1.E
  techniques for the measurement of cost, Ch. 22, 3.2.1
    retail method, Ch. 22, 3.2.1.B
    standard cost, Ch. 22, 3.2.1.A

IAS 7–*Statement of Cash Flows*, Ch. 40, 1–8. *See also* Statement of cash flows
  additional IAS 7 considerations for financial institutions, Ch. 40, 7
    operating cash flows, Ch. 40, 7.1
    reporting cash flows on a net basis, Ch. 40, 7.2
  additional IAS 7 considerations for groups, Ch. 40, 6
    acquisitions and disposals, Ch. 40, 6.3
      acquisition-related costs, Ch. 40, 6.3.1
      contingent consideration, Ch. 40, 6.3.3
      deferred and other non-cash consideration, Ch. 40, 6.3.2
      settlement of amounts owed by the acquired entity, Ch. 40, 6.3.4
      settlement of intra-group balances on a demerger, Ch. 40, 6.3.5
    cash flows in separate financial statements, Ch. 40, 6.5
      cash flows of subsidiaries, associates and joint ventures, Ch. 40, 6.5.1
      cash pooling, Ch. 40, 6.5.4
        and cash sharing arrangements, Ch. 40, 6.5.2
        notional cash pooling, Ch. 40, 6.5.4.A
        physical cash pooling, Ch. 40, 6.5.4.B
      group treasury arrangements, Ch. 40, 6.5.3
    cash flows of subsidiaries, associates and joint ventures, Ch. 40, 6.4
      cash flows in investment entities, Ch. 40, 6.4.3
      cash flows of joint operations, Ch. 40, 6.4.2
      investments in associates and joint ventures, Ch. 40, 6.4.1
    preparing a consolidated statement of cash flows, Ch. 40, 6.1
    transactions with non-controlling interests, Ch. 40, 6.2
  background, Ch. 40, 1.1
  cash and cash equivalents, Ch. 40, 3
    cash management policies, Ch. 40, 3.1
    components of cash and cash equivalents, Ch. 40, 3.2
      bank overdrafts, Ch. 40, 3.2.4
      client money, Ch. 40, 3.2.6
      cryptocurrencies, Ch. 40, 3.2.5
      demand deposits and short-term investments, Ch. 40, 3.2.1
      investments with maturities greater than three months, Ch. 40, 3.2.3
      money market funds, Ch. 40, 3.2.2
    reconciliation with items in the statement of financial position, Ch. 40, 3.3
    restrictions on the use of cash and cash equivalents, Ch. 40, 3.4
  cash flow presentation issues, Ch. 40, 5
    exceptional and other material cash flows, Ch. 40, 5.1
    disclosure of accounting policies, Ch. 40, 5.7
    foreign currency cash flows, Ch. 40, 5.3
      entities applying the direct method, Ch. 40, 5.3.1
      entities applying the indirect method, Ch. 40, 5.3.2
      indirect method and foreign subsidiaries, Ch. 40, 5.3.2.C
      treatment of non-operating cash flows, Ch. 40, 5.3.2.B
      treatment of operating cash flows, Ch. 40, 5.3.2.A
    gross/net presentation of cash flows, Ch. 40, 5.2
    non-cash transactions and transactions on deferred terms, Ch. 40, 5.4
      asset disposals on deferred terms, Ch. 40, 5.4.2
      asset purchased on deferred terms from the supplier, Ch. 40, 5.4.1
      revenue contracts with deferred payment terms, Ch. 40, 5.4.3
      sale and leaseback transactions, Ch. 40, 5.5.4
    voluntary disclosures, Ch. 40, 5.7
      cash flows to increase and maintain operating capacity, Ch. 40, 5.7.1
      segment cash flow disclosures, Ch. 40, 5.7.2
  future developments, Ch. 40, 1.3
  liabilities arising from financing activities, changes in, Ch. 40, 5.6
  objective, Ch. 40, 2.1
  primary financial statement, Ch. 40, 1.2
  requirements of other standards, Ch. 40, 8

cash flows arising from insurance contracts, Ch. 40, 8.2
cash flows arising from interests in subsidiaries, joint ventures and associates, Ch. 40, 8.4
cash flows arising from the exploration of mineral resources, Ch. 40, 8.3
cash flows of discontinued operations, Ch. 40, 8.1
scope, Ch. 40, 2.2
terms used in IAS 7, Ch. 40, 1.5
transparency and consistency of cash flow presentation, Ch. 40, 1.3

IAS 8–*Accounting Policies, Changes in Accounting Estimates and Errors*, Ch. 3, 4; Ch. 5, 7.2. *See also* Accounting policies; Financial Statements
accounting policies defined by, Ch. 3, 4.2
changes in accounting estimates, Ch. 3, 4.5, 5.2.2, 6.2.2.6..C
changes in accounting policies, Ch. 3, 4.4, 6.2.2.6..C
changes in estimates, Ch. 3, 5.2.2
consistency of accounting policies, Ch. 3, 4.1.4
correction of errors, Ch. 3, 4.6
disclosure of prior period errors, Ch. 3, 5.3
during the first IFRS reporting period, Ch. 5, 7.2.1
materiality defined by, Ch. 3, 4.1.5.A
objective of, Ch. 3, 1.2
scope of, Ch. 3, 1.2

IAS 10–*Events after the Reporting Period*, Ch. 38, 1–3. *See also* Events after the reporting period
adjusting events, Ch. 38, 2.1.2
treatment of, Ch. 38, 2.2
date when financial statements are authorised for issue, Ch. 38, 2.1.1
impact of preliminary reporting, Ch. 38, 2.1.1.A
re-issuing (dual dating) financial statements, Ch. 38, 2.1.1.B
definitions, Ch. 38, 2.1
non-adjusting events, Ch. 38, 2.1.3
dividend declaration, Ch. 38, 2.1.3.A
treatment of, Ch. 38, 2.3
objective, Ch. 38, 2.1
other disclosures, Ch. 38, 2.4
practical issues, Ch. 38, 3
changes to estimates of uncertain tax treatments, Ch. 38, 3.6
discovery of fraud after the reporting period, Ch. 38, 3.5
insolvency of a debtor and IFRS 9 expected credit losses, Ch. 38, 3.3
percentage of completion estimates, Ch. 38, 3.2
valuation of inventory, Ch. 38, 3.1
valuation of investment property at fair value and tenant insolvency, Ch. 38, 3.4
scope, Ch. 38, 2.1
treatment of adjusting events, Ch. 38, 2.2
events indicating that the going concern basis is not appropriate, Ch. 38, 2.2.2
events requiring adjustment to the amounts recognised, or disclosures, in the financial statements, Ch. 38, 2.2.1
treatment of non-adjusting events, Ch. 38, 2.3
breach of a long-term loan covenant and its subsequent rectification, Ch. 38, 2.3.2
declaration to distribute non-cash assets to owners, Ch. 38, 2.3.1

IAS 12–*Income Taxes*, Ch. 33, 1–14. *See also* Deferred tax; Income taxes
allocation of tax charge or credit, Ch. 33, 10
business combinations, Ch. 33, 12
current tax, Ch. 33, 5
deferred tax
measurement, Ch. 33, 8
discounting, Ch. 33, 8.6
expected manner of recovery, Ch. 33, 8.4
recognition, Ch. 33, 7
assets carried at fair value or revalued amount, Ch. 33, 7.3
basic principles, Ch. 33, 7.1
initial recognition exception, Ch. 33, 7.2
'outside' temporary differences, Ch. 33, 7.5
restriction on recognition of deferred tax assets, Ch. 33, 7.4
'tax transparent' entities, Ch. 33, 7.6
tax bases and temporary differences, Ch. 33, 6
definitions, Ch. 33, 3
development of IAS 12, Ch. 33, 1.3
disclosure, Ch. 33, 14
first-time adoption, Ch. 5, 7.3
objective, Ch. 33, 2.1
overview, Ch. 33, 2.2
presentation, Ch. 33, 13
scope, Ch. 33, 4
uncertain tax treatments, Ch. 33, 9

IAS 16–*Property, Plant and Equipment*, Ch. 18, 1–8. *See also* Property, plant and equipment (PP&E)
definitions used in IAS 16, Ch. 18, 2.2
depreciation, Ch. 18, 5
derecognition and disposal, Ch. 18, 7
partial disposals and undivided interests, Ch. 18, 7.3
joint control, Ch. 18, 7.3.1
subsidiary that is a single asset entity, Ch. 19, 6.10
vendor retains control, Ch. 18, 7.3.2
and replacement of insured assets, Ch. 18, 7.4
sale of assets held for rental, Ch. 18, 7.2
disclosure requirements, Ch. 18, 8–8.3
additional disclosures for revalued assets, Ch. 18, 8.2
first-time adopter, Ch. 5, 7.4
general disclosures, Ch. 18, 8.1
other disclosures, Ch. 18, 8.3
measurement after recognition, cost model, Ch. 18, 5
depreciable amount and residual values, Ch. 18, 5.2
depreciation charge, Ch. 18, 5.3
depreciation methods, Ch. 18, 5.6
diminishing balance methods, Ch. 18, 5.6.1
unit-of-production method, Ch. 18, 5.6.2
impairment, Ch. 18, 5.7
significant parts of assets, Ch. 18, 5.1
useful lives, Ch. 18, 5.4
land, Ch. 18, 5.4.2
repairs and maintenance, Ch. 18, 5.4.1
technological change, Ch. 18, 5.4.3
when depreciation starts, Ch. 18, 5.5
measurement after recognition, revaluation model, Ch. 18, 6–6.5
accounting for valuation surpluses and deficits, Ch. 18, 6.2
adopting a policy of revaluation, Ch. 18, 6.4
assets held under finance leases, Ch. 18, 6.5

IAS 16–*Property, Plant and Equipment*—*contd*
  measurement after recognition, cost model—*contd*
    when depreciation starts—*contd*
      measurement after recognition, revaluation model—*contd*
        meaning of fair value, Ch. 18, 6.1
        reversals of downward valuations, Ch. 18, 6.3
  measurement at recognition, Ch. 18, 4
    accounting for changes in decommissioning and restoration costs, Ch. 18, 4.3
    assets acquired with the assistance of government grants, Ch. 18, 4.6
    assets held under finance leases, Ch. 18, 4.5
    elements of cost and cost measurement, Ch. 18, 4.1
      administration and other general overheads, Ch. 18, 4.1.3
      borrowing costs, Ch. 18, 4.1.2
      cessation of capitalisation, Ch. 18, 4.1.4
      deferred payment, Ch. 18, 4.1.6
      'directly attributable' costs, Ch. 18, 4.1.1
      land and buildings to be redeveloped, Ch. 18, 4.1.7
      self-built assets, Ch. 18, 4.1.5
      transfers of assets from customers (IFRIC 18), Ch. 18, 4.1.8
      variable and contingent consideration, Ch. 18, 4.1.9
    exchanges of assets, Ch. 18, 4.4
      commercial substance, Ch. 18, 4.4.1
      reliably measurable, Ch. 18, 4.4.2
    incidental and non-incidental income, Ch. 18, 4.2
      income earned while bringing the asset to the intended location and condition, Ch. 18, 4.2.1
      income received during the construction of property, Ch. 18, 4.2.2
      liquidated damages during construction, Ch. 18, 4.2.3
  and presentation of right-of-use assets, Ch. 18, 2.3
  recognition, Ch. 18, 3
    accounting for parts ('components') of assets, Ch. 18, 3.2
    aspects of recognition, Ch. 18, 3.1
      bearer plants, Ch. 18, 3.1.7, Ch. 42, 3.2.3.A
      classification of items as inventory or PP&E when minimum levels are maintained, Ch. 18, 3.1.5
      classification as PP&E/intangible asset, Ch. 18, 3.1.4
      environmental and safety equipment, Ch. 18, 3.1.2
      production stripping costs of surface mines, Ch. 18, 3.1.6
      property economic benefits and property developments, Ch. 18, 3.1.3
      spare parts and minor items, Ch. 18, 3.1.1
    initial and subsequent expenditure, Ch. 18, 3.3
      major inspections, Ch. 18, 3.3.2
      types of parts, Ch. 18, 3.3.1
  requirements of IAS 16, Ch. 18, 2
  scope, Ch. 18, 2.1

IAS 19–*Employee Benefits*, Ch. 35, 1–16. *See also* Defined benefit plans; Defined contribution plans; Employee benefits; Long-term employee benefits; short-term employee benefits
  defined contribution plans, Ch. 35, 4
    general accounting requirements, Ch. 35, 4.1
    with minimum return guarantee, Ch. 35, 3.5
    with vesting conditions, Ch. 35, 4.2
  disclosure requirements, Ch. 35, 15

  defined benefit plans, Ch. 35, 15.2
    amount, timing and uncertainty of future cash flows, Ch. 35, 15.2.3
    characteristics and risks associated with, Ch. 35, 15.2.1
    defined benefit plans that share risks between entities under common control, Ch. 35, 15.2.5
    disclosure requirements in other IFRSs, Ch. 35, 15.2.6
    explanation of amounts in financial statements, Ch. 35, 15.2.2
    multi-employer plans, Ch. 35, 15.2.4
    plans accounted for as defined benefit plans, Ch. 35, 15.2.5.A
    plans accounted for as defined contribution plans, Ch. 35, 15.2.5.B
  defined contribution plans, Ch. 35, 15.1
  first-time adopter, Ch. 5, 7.7
  future developments, Ch. 35, 16
  interpretations committee activities, Ch. 35, 16.2
    availability of refund from defined benefit plan, Ch. 35, 16.2.2
  long-term employee benefits other than post-employment benefits, Ch. 35, 13
    meaning of other long-term employee benefits, Ch. 35, 13.1
    recognition and measurement, Ch. 35, 13.2
      attribution to years of service, Ch. 35, 13.2.1
      long-term disability benefit, Ch. 35, 13.2.2
      long-term benefits contingent on a future event, Ch. 35, 13.2.3
  objective, Ch. 35, 2.1
  pensions and other post-employment benefits, defined contribution and defined benefit plans, Ch. 35, 3
    death-in-service benefits, Ch. 35, 3.6
    distinction between, Ch. 35, 3.1
    insured benefits, Ch. 35, 3.2
    multi-employer plans, Ch. 35, 3.3
    plans that would be defined contribution plans but for existence of minimum return guarantee, Ch. 35, 3.5
    state plans, Ch. 35, 3.4
  scope, Ch. 35, 2.2
    employee benefits settled by a shareholder or another group entity, Ch. 36, 2.2.2
    scope requirements of IAS 19, Ch. 35, 2.2.1
  short-term employee benefits, Ch. 35, 12
    general recognition criteria for, Ch. 35, 12.1
    profit-sharing and bonus plans, Ch. 35, 12.3
    short-term paid absences, Ch. 35, 12.2
  termination benefits, Ch. 35, 14

IAS 20–*Accounting for Government Grants and Disclosure of Government Assistance*, Ch. 24, 1–6
  definitions, Ch. 24, 1.2
  disclosures, Ch. 24, 6
    government assistance, Ch. 24, 6.2
    government grants, Ch. 24, 6.1
  government grants related to biological assets in the scope of IAS 41, Ch. 24, 5, Ch. 42, 3.3
  overview of IAS 20, Ch. 24, 1.1
  presentation of grants, Ch. 24, 4
    related to assets, Ch. 24, 4.1
      cash flows, Ch. 24, 4.1.1

impairment testing of assets that qualified for government grants, Ch. 24, 4.1.2
related to income, Ch. 24, 4.2
recognition and measurement, Ch. 24, 3
  forgivable loans, Ch. 24, 3.3
  general requirements of IAS 20, Ch. 24, 3.1
  government assistance, Ch. 24, 3.7
  loans at lower than market rates of interest, Ch. 24, 3
  non-monetary grants, Ch. 24, 3.2
  recognition in the income statement, Ch. 24, 3.6
    achieving the most appropriate matching, Ch. 24, 3.6.1
    loans at lower than market rates of interest, Ch. 24, 3.6.2
    period to be benefited by the grant, Ch. 24, 3.6.3
    separating grants into elements, Ch. 24, 3.6.4
  repayment of government grants, Ch. 24, 3.7
scope, Ch. 24, 2
  government assistance, Ch. 24, 2.1
  government grants, Ch. 24, 2.2
    definition, Ch. 24, 2.2.1
  scope exclusion, Ch. 24, 2.3
    general considerations, Ch. 24, 2.3.1
    investment tax credits, Ch. 24, 2.3.2

IAS 21–*The Effects of Changes in Foreign Exchange Rates*, Ch. 15, 1–11. *See also* Foreign exchange, Functional currency
background, Ch. 15, 1.1
change in functional currency, Ch. 15, 5.5
change of presentation currency, Ch. 15, 7
definitions of terms, Ch. 15, 2.3
disclosure requirements, Ch. 15, 10
  entity's functional currency determination, Ch. 15, 4
    branches and divisions, Ch. 15, 4.4
    documentation of judgements made, Ch. 15, 4.5
    general, Ch. 15, 4.1
    intermediate holding companies/finance subsidiaries, Ch. 15, 4.2
    investment holding companies, Ch. 15, 4.3
first-time adopter, Ch. 5, 7.8
future developments, Ch. 15, 11
introduction of euro, Ch. 15, 8
objective of the standard, Ch. 15, 2.1
presentation currency use other than the functional currency, Ch. 15, 6
  disposal or partial disposal of a foreign operation, Ch. 7, 2.3, 3.5, 4.1; Ch. 15, 6.6
    step-by-step and direct methods of consolidation, Ch. 7, 2.3; Ch. 15, 6.6.3
  exchange differences on intragroup balances, Ch. 15, 6.3
    monetary items included as part of the net investment in a foreign operation, Ch. 15, 6.3.1
      becoming part of the net investment in a foreign operation, Ch. 15, 6.3.1.F
      ceasing to be part of the net investment in a foreign operation, Ch. 15, 6.3.1.G
      currency of monetary item, Ch. 15, 6.3.1.C
      dividends, Ch. 15, 6.3.2
      manner of settlement of monetary, Ch. 15, 6.3.1.B
      trade receivables or payables included as part of the net investment in a foreign operation, Ch. 15, 6.3.1.A
      transacted by other members of the group, Ch. 15, 6.3.1.E
      treatment in individual financial statements, Ch. 15, 6.3.1.D
    unrealised profits on intragroup transactions, Ch. 15, 6.3.3
  goodwill and fair value adjustments, Ch. 15, 6.5
  non-coterminous period ends, Ch. 15, 6.4
  translation of equity items, Ch. 15, 6.2
    equity balances from income and expenses in OCI, Ch. 15, 6.2.3
    equity balances from transactions with equity holders, Ch. 15, 6.2.2
    share capital, Ch. 15, 6.2.1
  translation to the presentation currency, Ch. 15, 6.1
    accounting for foreign operations where sub-groups exist, Ch. 7, 2.3; Ch. 15, 6.1.5
    calculation of average rate, Ch. 15, 6.1.4
    dual rates, suspension of rates and lack of exchangeability, Ch. 15, 6.1.3
    functional currency is not that of a hyperinflationary economy, Ch. 15, 6.1.1
    functional currency is that of a hyperinflationary economy, Ch. 15, 6.1.2
relevant pronouncements, Ch. 15, 1.2
reporting foreign currency transactions in the functional currency of an entity, Ch. 15, 5
  books and records not kept in functional currency, Ch. 15, 5.6
  change in functional currency, Ch. 15, 5.5
  at ends of subsequent reporting periods, Ch. 15, 5.2
  exchange differences, treatment of, Ch. 15, 5.3
    monetary items, Ch. 15, 5.3.1
    non-monetary items, Ch. 15, 5.3.2
  initial recognition, Ch. 15, 5.1
    deposits and other consideration received or paid in advance, Ch. 15, 5.1.2
    dual rates, Ch. 15, 5.1.4.A
    identifying the date of transaction, Ch. 15, 5.1.1
    practical difficulties in determining exchange rates, Ch. 15, 5.1.4
    suspension of rates: longer term lack of exchangeability, Ch. 15, 5.1.4.C
    suspension of rates: temporary lack of exchangeability, Ch. 15, 5.1.4.B
    using average rates, Ch. 15, 5.1.3
  monetary/non-monetary determination, Ch. 15, 5.4
    deferred tax, Ch. 15, 5.4.5
    deposits and advance payments for actively traded commodities, Ch. 15, 5.4.2
    deposits or progress payments, Ch. 15, 5.4.1
    foreign currency share-capital, Ch. 15, 5.4.4
    investments in preference shares, Ch. 15, 5.4.3
    post-employment benefit plans-foreign currency assets, Ch. 15, 5.4.5
    post-employment benefit plans-foreign currency plans, Ch. 15, 5.4.6
summary of approach required by IAS 21, Ch. 15, 3
scope of IAS 21, Ch. 15, 2.2
tax effects of all exchange differences, Ch. 15, 9

IAS 23–*Borrowing Costs*, Ch. 21, 1–7. *See also* Borrowing costs

IAS 23–*Borrowing Costs*—contd
  borrowing costs eligible for capitalisation, Ch. 21, 5
    capitalisation of borrowing costs in hyperinflationary economies, Ch. 21, 5.6
    derivative financial instruments, Ch. 21, 5.5.1
    directly attributable borrowing costs, Ch. 21, 5.1
    dividends payable on shares classified as financial liabilities, Ch. 21, 5.5.4
    exchange differences as a borrowing cost, Ch. 21, 5.4
    gains and losses on derecognition of borrowings, Ch. 21, 5.5.2
    gains/losses on termination of derivative financial instruments, Ch. 21, 5.5.3
    general borrowings, Ch. 21, 5.3
      accrued costs and trade payables, Ch. 21, 5.3.3
      assets carried below cost in the statement of financial position, Ch. 21, 5.3.4
      calculation of capitalisation rate, Ch. 21, 5.3.2
      completed qualifying assets, related to, Ch. 21, 5.3.1.A
      definition of general borrowings, Ch. 21, 5.3.1
      specific non-qualifying assets, related to, Ch. 21, 5.3.1.B
    group considerations, Ch. 21, 5.7
      borrowings in one company and development in another, Ch. 21, 5.7.1
      qualifying assets held by joint arrangements, Ch. 21, 5.7.2
    specific borrowings, Ch. 21, 5.2
  commencement, suspension and cessation of capitalisation, Ch. 21, 6
    cessation, Ch. 21, 6.3
      borrowing costs on 'land expenditures', Ch. 21, 6.3.1
    commencement, Ch. 21, 6.1
      expenditures on a qualifying asset, Ch. 21, 6.1.1
    suspension, Ch. 21, 6.2
      impairment considerations, Ch. 21, 6.2.1
  definition of borrowing costs, Ch. 21, 4
    in IAS 23, Ch. 21, 4.1
    other finance costs, Ch. 21, 4.2
  disclosure requirements, Ch. 21, 7
  qualifying assets, Ch. 21, 3
    assets measured at fair value, Ch. 21, 3.2
    constructed good, over time transfer of, Ch. 21, 3.1
    financial assets, Ch. 21, 3.3
    inventories, Ch. 21, 3.1
  requirements of, Ch. 21, 2
    core principle, Ch. 21, 2.1
    scope, Ch. 21, 2.2

IAS 24–*Related Party Disclosures*, Ch. 39, 1–2. *See also* Key management personnel; Related party
  disclosable transactions, Ch. 39, 2.5
    materiality, Ch. 39, 2.5.1
  disclosure of controlling relationships, Ch. 39, 2.4
  disclosure of expense incurred with management entity, Ch. 39, 2.8
  disclosure of key management personnel compensation, Ch. 39, 2.6
    compensation, Ch. 39, 2.6.1
    key management personnel compensated by other entities, Ch. 39, 2.6.8
    post-employment benefits, Ch. 39, 2.6.3
    reporting entity part of a group, Ch. 39, 2.6.7
    share-based payment transactions, Ch. 39, 2.6.6
    short-term employee benefits, Ch. 39, 2.6.2
    termination benefits, Ch. 39, 2.6.5
  disclosure of other related party transactions, including commitments, Ch. 39, 2.7
    disclosures required for related party transactions, including commitments, Ch. 39, 2.7.2
    related party transactions requiring disclosure, Ch. 39, 2.7.1
      aggregation of items of a similar nature, Ch. 39, 2.7.1.A
      commitments, Ch. 39, 2.7.1.B
  disclosures with government-related entities, Ch. 39, 2.9
  objective, Ch. 39, 2.1.1
  parties that are not related parties, Ch. 39, 2.3
  possible solutions, Ch. 39, 1.2
    remeasurement of related party transactions at fair values, Ch. 39, 1.2.1
  related party and related party transactions, identification of, Ch. 39, 2.2
    entities that are associates/joint ventures, Ch. 39, 2.2.3
      joint operations, Ch. 39, 2.2.3.A
    entities that are joint ventures and associates of the same third entity, Ch. 39, 2.2.5
    entities that are joint ventures of the same third party, Ch. 39, 2.2.5
    entities that are members of the same group, Ch. 39, 2.2.2
    entities under control or joint control of certain persons/close members of their family, Ch. 39, 2.2.7
    entities under significant influence of certain persons/close members of their family, Ch. 39, 2.2.8
    government-related entities, Ch. 39, 2.2.10
    key management personnel services provided by a management entity, Ch. 39, 2.2.9
    persons/close members of a person's family that are related parties, Ch. 39, 2.2.1
      control, Ch. 39, 2.2.1.A
      joint control, Ch. 39, 2.2.1.B
      key management personnel, Ch. 39, 2.2.1.D
      significant influence, Ch. 39, 2.2.1.C
    post-employment benefit plans, Ch. 39, 2.2.6
  related party issue, Ch. 39, 1.1
  scope, Ch. 39, 2.1.2

IAS 27–*Separate Financial Statements*, Ch. 8, 1–3. *See also* Separate financial statements
  definitions, Ch. 8, 1
  disclosure, Ch. 8, 3
  requirements of separate financial statements, Ch. 8, 2
  scope, Ch. 8, 1

IAS 28–*Investments in Associates and Joint Ventures*, Ch. 11, 1–11. *See also* Investments in associates and joint ventures
  application of the equity method, Ch. 11, 7
  definitions, Ch. 11, 3
  entities with no subsidiaries but exempt from applying IAS 28, Ch. 8, 3.3.1
  exemptions from applying the equity method, Ch. 11, 5
    investments held in associates/joint ventures held by venture capital organisations, Ch. 11, 5.3
      application of IFRS 9 (or IAS 39) to exempt, Ch. 11, 5.3.2

designation of investments as 'at fair value through
    profit or loss', Ch. 11, 5.3.2.B
  entities with a mixture of activities, Ch. 11,
    5.3.2.A
  investment entities exception, Ch. 11, 5.3.1
  parents exempt from preparing consolidated financial
    statements, Ch. 11, 5.1
  partial use of fair value measurement of associates, Ch. 11,
    5.4
  subsidiaries meeting certain criteria, Ch. 11, 5.2
first-time adoption, Ch. 5, 7.9
and IFRS 10, conflict between, Ch. 7, 3.3.2, 7.1; Ch. 11,
    7.6.5.C; Ch. 12, 8.2.3
impairment losses, Ch. 11, 8, 9.1, 10.1.2
objective, Ch. 11, 2.1
scope, Ch. 11, 2.2
significant influence, Ch. 11, 4
  fund managers, Ch. 11, 4.6
  holdings of less than 20% of the voting power, Ch. 11, 4.3
  lack of, Ch. 11, 4.2
  potential voting rights, Ch. 11, 4.4
  severe long-term restrictions impairing ability to transfer
    funds to the investor, Ch. 11, 4.1
  voting rights held in a fiduciary capacity, Ch. 11, 4.5
IAS 29–*Financial Reporting in Hyperinflationary Economies,*
    Ch. 16, 1–12. *See also* Hyperinflation
  context of, Ch. 16, 2.1
  definition of hyperinflation, Ch. 16, 2.3
  disclosures, Ch. 16, 12
  restatement of comparative figures, Ch. 16, 8
  restatement of the statement of cash flows, Ch. 16, 7
  restatement of the statement of changes in equity, Ch. 16, 5
  restatement of the statement of profit and loss and other
    comprehensive income, Ch. 16, 6
    calculation of gain or loss on net monetary position,
      Ch. 16, 6.2
    interest and exchange differences, Ch. 16, 6.1
    measurement of reclassification adjustments within equity,
      Ch. 16, 6.3
  restatement process, Ch. 16, 2.4
  scope, Ch. 16, 2.2
  selection of general price index, Ch. 16, 3.1
  statement of financial position, analysis and restatement of,
    Ch. 16, 4
    deferred taxation, calculation of, Ch. 16, 4.4
    inventories, Ch. 16, 4.2
    monetary and non-monetary items, Ch. 16, 4.1
      distinguishing between, Ch. 16, 4.1.1
      monetary items, Ch. 16, 4.1.2
      non-monetary items carried at current cost, Ch. 16,
        4.1.3
      non-monetary items carried at historic cost, Ch. 16,
        4.1.4
    restatement of associates, joint ventures and subsidiaries,
      Ch. 16, 4.3
  transition
    economies becoming hyperinflationary, Ch. 16, 10.1
    economies ceasing to be hyperinflationary, Ch. 16, 10.2
    economies exiting severe hyperinflation, Ch. 16, 10.3
  translation to a different presentation currency, Ch. 16, 11
    comparative information, Ch. 16, 11.2

initial application and ceasing application of IAS 29,
    Ch. 16, 11.1
IAS 32–*Financial Instruments: Presentation*, Ch. 44, 2; Ch. 54,
    See also Financial instruments, financial liabilities and equity;
    Presentation and disclosure, financial instruments
  definitions, Ch. 47, 3
  objective, Ch. 47, 2.1
  options over puttable instruments classified as equity, Ch. 34,
    2.2.4.J
  presentation
    compound financial instruments, Ch. 47, 6
    interest, dividends, losses and gains, Ch. 47, 8
    liabilities and equity
      contingent settlement provisions, Ch. 47, 4.3
      contracts to issue equity instruments, Ch. 47, 4.4.2
      contractual obligation to deliver cash or other financial
        assets, Ch. 47, 4.2
      implied contractual obligation to deliver cash or other
        financial assets, Ch. 47, 4.2.2
      perpetual debt, Ch. 47, 4.7
      preference shares, Ch. 47, 4.5
      puttable instruments, Ch. 47, 4.6
    offsetting a financial asset and a financial liability, Ch. 54,
      7.4.1
    treasury shares, Ch. 47, 9
  scope, Ch. 47, 2.2
  transactions in financial assets outside the scope of, Ch. 34,
    2.2.3.F
  transactions not in the scope of (compared with IFRS 2),
    Ch. 34, 2.2.3.E
IAS 33–*Earnings per Share*, Ch. 37, 1–8. *See also* Diluted EPS
  basic EPS, Ch. 37, 3
    earnings, Ch. 37, 3.1
    number of shares, Ch. 37, 3.2
  changes in outstanding ordinary shares, Ch. 37, 4
    adjustments to EPS in historical summaries, Ch. 37, 4.7
    changes in ordinary shares without corresponding changes
      in resources, Ch. 37, 4.3
      B share schemes, Ch. 37, 4.3.4
      capitalisation, bonus issues and share splits, Ch. 37,
        4.3.1.A
      put warrants priced above market value, Ch. 37, 4.3.5
      rights issue, Ch. 37, 4.3.3
      share consolidation with a special dividend, Ch. 37,
        4.3.2
      share consolidations, Ch. 37, 4.3.1.C
      stock dividends, Ch. 37, 4.3.1.B
    issue to acquire another business, Ch. 37, 4.6
      acquisitions, Ch. 37, 4.6.1
      establishment of a new parent undertaking, Ch. 37,
        4.6.3
      reverse acquisitions, Ch. 37, 4.6.2
    options exercised during the year, Ch. 37, 4.4
    post balance sheet changes in capital, Ch. 37, 4.5
    purchase and redemption of own shares, Ch. 37, 4.2
    weighted average number of shares, Ch. 37, 4.1
  contingently issuable potential ordinary shares, Ch. 37, 6.4.8
  contingently issuable shares, Ch. 37, 6.4.6
    earnings-based contingencies, Ch. 37, 6.4.6.A
    share-price-based contingencies, Ch. 37, 6.4.6.B

IAS 33–*Earnings per Share*—contd
- convertible instruments, Ch. 37, 6.4.1
  - convertible debt, Ch. 37, 6.4.1.A
  - convertible preference shares, Ch. 37, 6.4.1.B
  - participating equity instruments, Ch. 37, 6.4.1.C
- definitions, Ch. 37, 1.1
- disclosure, Ch. 37, 7.3
- matters affecting the numerator, Ch. 37, 5
  - earnings, Ch. 37, 5.1
  - participating equity instruments and two class shares, Ch. 37, 5.4
  - preference dividends, Ch. 37, 5.2
  - retrospective adjustments, Ch. 37, 5.3
- objective, Ch. 37, 2.1
- options, warrants and their equivalents, Ch. 37, 6.4.2
  - forward purchase agreements, Ch. 37, 6.4.2.C
  - numerator, Ch. 37, 6.4.2.A
  - options over convertible instruments, Ch. 37, 6.4.2.D
  - settlement of option exercise price, Ch. 37, 6.4.2.E
  - specified application of option proceeds, Ch. 37, 6.4.2.F
  - written call options, Ch. 37, 6.4.2.B
  - written put options, Ch. 37, 6.4.2.C
- ordinary shares of investees, Ch. 37, 6.4.7
- partly paid shares, Ch. 37, 6.4.4
- presentation, Ch. 37, 7.1
- purchased options and warrants, Ch. 37, 6.4.3
- restatement, Ch. 37, 7.2
- scope, Ch. 37, 2.2
- share based payments, Ch. 37, 6.4.5

IAS 34–*Interim Financial Reporting*, Ch. 41, 1–11; Ch. 54, 2.3
- components, form and content, Ch. 41, 3
  - complete set of interim financial statements, Ch. 41, 3.1
  - condensed interim financial statements, Ch. 41, 3.2
  - management commentary, Ch. 41, 3.4
  - requirements for both complete and condensed interim financial information, Ch. 41, 3.3
- definitions, Ch. 41, 1.1
- disclosure in annual financial statements, Ch. 41, 7
- disclosures in condensed financial statements, Ch. 41, 4
  - disclosure of compliance with IFRS, Ch. 41, 4.6
  - examples of disclosures, Ch. 41, 4.3
    - accounting policies and methods of computation, Ch. 41, 4.3.11
    - acquisition and disposal of property, plant and equipment, Ch. 41, 4.3.3
    - amounts that are unusual because of their nature, size or incidence, Ch. 41, 4.3.14
    - capital commitments, Ch. 41, 4.3.4
    - changes in circumstances affecting fair values, Ch. 41, 4.3.6
    - changes in the composition of the entity, Ch. 41, 4.3.17
    - contingent liabilities, Ch. 41, 4.3.10
    - default/breach of loan covenants not remedied before the end of interim period, Ch. 41, 4.3.7
    - dividends paid, Ch. 41, 4.3.15
    - events after the interim reporting date, Ch. 41, 4.3.16
    - inventory write-down and reversals, Ch. 41, 4.3.1
    - issues, repurchases and repayments of debt and equity securities, Ch. 41, 4.3.14
    - litigation settlements, Ch. 41, 4.3.5
    - recognition and reversal of impairment losses, Ch. 41, 4.3.3
    - related party transactions, Ch. 41, 4.3.8
    - seasonality/cyclicality of operations, Ch. 41, 4.3.12
    - transfers between different levels of fair value hierarchy, Ch. 41, 4.3.9
  - fair value disclosures for financial instruments, Ch. 41, 4.5
  - going concern assumption, disclosure in relation to, Ch. 41, 4.7
  - other disclosures required by IAS 34, Ch. 41, 4.2
  - segment information, Ch. 41, 4.4
  - significant events and transactions, Ch. 41, 4.1
  - specified disclosures, location of, Ch. 41, 4.2.1
- effective dates and transitional rules, Ch. 41, 11
  - first-time presentation of interim reports complying with IAS 34, Ch. 41, 11.1
- estimates, use of, Ch. 41, 10
- materiality, Ch. 41, 6
- objective, Ch. 41, 2.1
- periods for which interim financial statements are required to be presented, Ch. 41, 5
  - change in financial year-end, Ch. 41, 5.3
  - comparatives following a financial period longer than a year, Ch. 41, 5.4
  - length of interim reporting period, Ch. 41, 5.2
  - other comparative information, Ch. 41, 5.1
  - when the comparative period is shorter than the current period, Ch. 41, 5.5
- recognition and measurement, Ch. 41, 8
  - examples of, Ch. 41, 9
    - contingent lease payments, Ch. 41, 9.7.4
    - contractual/anticipated purchase price changes, Ch. 41, 9.4.2
    - cost of sales, Ch. 41, 9.4
    - earnings per share, Ch. 41, 9.8
    - employee benefits, Ch. 41, 9.3
    - foreign currency translation, Ch. 41, 9.6
    - interim period manufacturing cost variances, Ch. 41, 9.4.3
    - inventories, Ch. 41, 9.4.1
    - levies charged by public authorities, Ch. 41, 9.7.5
    - periodic maintenance/overhaul, Ch. 41, 9.7.3
    - property, plant and equipment and intangible assets, Ch. 41, 9.1
    - provisions, contingencies and accruals for other costs, Ch. 41, 9.7
    - reversal of impairment losses recognised in a previous interim period (IFRIC 10), Ch. 41, 9.2
    - taxation, Ch. 41, 9.5
  - same accounting policies as in annual financial statements, Ch. 41, 8.1
    - measurement on a year-to-date basis, Ch. 41, 8.1.1
    - new accounting pronouncements and other changes in accounting policies, Ch. 41, 8.1.2
    - voluntary changes in presentation, Ch. 41, 8.1.3
  - seasonal businesses, Ch. 41, 8.2
    - costs incurred unevenly during the year, Ch. 41, 8.2.2
    - revenues received seasonally, cyclically, or occasionally, Ch. 41, 8.2.1
- scope, Ch. 41, 2.2
- use of estimates, Ch. 41, 10

IAS 36–*Impairment of Assets*, Ch. 20, 1–14. *See also* Goodwill; Impairment of assets; Value in use (VIU)
   carrying amount of CGU assets, identifying, Ch. 20, 4
      consistency and the impairment test, Ch. 20, 4.1
      corporate assets, Ch. 20, 4.2
         leased corporate assets, Ch. 20, 4.2.1
   developments, Ch. 20, 14
   disclosures required by IAS 36, Ch. 20, 13.3
      annual impairment disclosures for goodwill and intangible assets with an indefinite useful life, Ch. 20, 13.3
      for impairment losses or reversals, Ch. 20, 13.2.1
      material impairments, Ch. 20, 13.2.2
   dividing the entity into cash-generating units (CGUs), Ch. 20, 3
      active markets and identifying CGUs, Ch. 20, 3.3
      CGUs and intangible assets, Ch. 20, 3.1
   fair value less costs of disposal, Ch. 20, 6
      estimating, Ch. 20, 6.1
         Depreciated replacement costs or current replacement cost as FVLCD, Ch. 20, 6.1.2
      FVLCD and the unit of account, Ch. 20, 6.1.1
   first-time adopters of IAS 36, Ch. 5, 7.12
   goodwill and its allocation to CGUs, Ch. 20, 8.1
      composition of goodwill, Ch. 20, 8.1.1
         effect of IFRS 8 on impairment tests, Ch. 20, 8.1.4
            aggregation of operating segments for disclosure purposes, Ch. 20, 8.1.4.B
            changes to operating segments, Ch. 20, 8.1.4.A
      goodwill initially unallocated to CGUs, Ch. 20, 8.1.5
      identifying synergies and identifying CGUs/CGU groups for allocating goodwill, Ch. 20, 8.1.2
      measuring the goodwill allocated to CGUs/CGU groups, Ch. 20, 8.1.3
   group and separate financial statement issues, Ch. 20, 12
      goodwill in individual (or subgroup) financial statements and the interaction with the group financial statements, Ch. 20, 12.2
      group reorganisations and the carrying value of investments in subsidiaries, Ch. 20, 12.3
      VIU: relevant cash flows and non-arm's length prices, Ch. 20, 12.1
   investments in subsidiaries, associates and joint ventures, Ch. 20, 12.4
   impairment of intangible assets with an indefinite useful life, Ch. 20, 10
   impairment losses, recognising and reversing, Ch. 20, 11
      impairment losses and CGUs, Ch. 20, 11.2
      on individual assets, Ch. 20, 11.1
      reversal of impairment losses recognised in a previous interim period, Ch. 41, 9.2
         relating to goodwill prohibited, Ch. 20, 11.3
         relating to assets other than goodwill, Ch. 20, 11.4
   impairment of goodwill, Ch. 20, 8
      disposal of operation within a CGU to which goodwill has been allocated, Ch. 20, 8.5
         changes in composition of CGUs, Ch. 20, 8.5.1
      impairment of assets and goodwill recognised on acquisition, Ch. 20, 8.3
         deferred tax assets and losses of acquired businesses, Ch. 20, 8.3.2
         testing goodwill 'created' by deferred tax for impairment, Ch. 20, 8.3.1
      impairment testing when a CGU crosses more than one operating segment, Ch. 20, 8.4
      when to test CGUs with goodwill for impairment, Ch. 20, 8.2
         carry forward of a previous impairment test calculation, Ch. 20, 8.2.3
         reversal of impairment loss for goodwill prohibited, Ch. 20, 8.2.4
         sequence of impairment tests for goodwill and other assets, Ch. 20, 8.2.2
         timing of impairment tests, Ch. 20, 8.2.1
   impairment review, features of, Ch. 20, 1.2
   impairment testing requirements, Ch. 20, 2
      indicators of impairment, Ch. 20, 2.1
         (future) performance, Ch. 20, 2.1.2
         individual assets/part of CGU?, Ch. 20, 2.1.3
         interest rates, Ch. 20, 2.1.4
         market capitalisation, Ch. 20, 2.1.1
   non-controlling interests, impact on goodwill impairment testing, Ch. 7, 4.2, Ch. 20, 9
   recoverable amount, Ch. 20, 5
      impairment of assets held for sale, Ch. 20, 5.1
   scope of IAS 36, Ch. 20, 1.3
   theory behind, Ch. 20, 1.1
   value in use (VIU), determining, Ch. 20, 7
      appropriate discount rate and discounting the future cash flows, Ch. 20, 7.2
         approximations and short cuts, Ch. 20, 7.2.4
         calculating VIU using post-tax cash flows, Ch. 20, 7.2.3
         determining pre-tax rates taking account of tax losses, Ch. 20, 7.2.6
         disclosing pre-tax discount rates when using a post-tax methodology, Ch. 20, 7.2.5
         discount rates and the weighted average cost of capital, Ch. 20, 7.2.1
         entity-specific WACCs and capital structure, Ch. 20, 7.2.8
         entity-specific WACCs and different project risks within the entity, Ch. 20, 7.2.7
         pre-tax discount rate, calculating, Ch. 20, 7.2.2
         use of discount rates other than the WACC, Ch. 20, 7.2.9
      fair value and value in use, differences between, Ch. 20, 7.3
      future pre-tax cash flows of the CGU under review, estimating, Ch. 20, 7.1
         budgets and cash flows, Ch. 20, 7.1.1
         cash inflows and outflows from improvements and enhancements, Ch. 20, 7.1.2
         events after the reporting period, Ch. 20, 7.1.9
         foreign currency cash flows, Ch. 20, 7.1.5
         internal transfer pricing, Ch. 20, 7.1.6
         lease payments, Ch. 20, 7.1.8
         overheads and share-based payments, Ch. 20, 7.1.7
         restructuring, Ch. 20, 7.1.3
         terminal values, Ch. 20, 7.1.4

IAS 37–*Provisions, Contingent Liabilities and Contingent Assets*, Ch. 26, 1–7. *See also* Provisions, contingent liabilities and contingent assets
   cases in which no provision should be recognised, Ch. 26, 5
      future operating losses, Ch. 26, 5.1
      rate-regulated activities, Ch. 26, 5.4
      repairs and maintenance of owned assets, Ch. 26, 5.2
      staff training costs, Ch. 26, 5.3
   definitions, Ch. 26, 1.3
   disclosure requirements, Ch. 26, 7
      contingent assets, Ch. 26, 7.3
      contingent liabilities, Ch. 26, 7.2
      provisions, Ch. 26, 7.1
      reduced disclosure when information is seriously prejudicial, Ch. 26, 7.4
   first-time adopters, Ch. 5, 7.13
   interpretations related to the application of IAS 37, Ch. 26, 1.2
   measurement, Ch. 26, 4
      anticipating future events that may affect the estimate of cash flows, Ch. 26, 4.4
      best estimate of provision, Ch. 26, 4.1
      changes and uses of provisions, Ch. 26, 4.9
         changes in contingent liabilities recognised in a business combination, Ch. 26, 4.10
      dealing with risk and uncertainty in measuring a provision, Ch. 26, 4.2
      discounting the estimated cash flows to a present value, Ch. 26, 4.3
         adjusting for risk and using a government bond rate, Ch. 26, 4.3.2
         effect of changes in interest rates on the discount rate applied, Ch. 26, 4.3.6
         own credit risk is not taken into account, Ch. 26, 4.3.3
         pre-tax discount rate, Ch. 26, 4.3.4
         real *vs.* nominal rate, Ch. 26, 4.3.1
         unwinding of the discount, Ch. 26, 4.3.5
      joint and several liability, Ch. 26, 4.7
      provisions are not reduced for gains on disposal of related assets, Ch. 26, 4.8
      provisions that will be settled in a currency other than the entity's functional currency, Ch. 26, 4.5
      reimbursements, insurance and other recoveries from third parties, Ch. 26, 4.6
   objective of IAS 37, Ch. 26, 2.1
   recognition, Ch. 26, 3
      contingencies, Ch. 26, 3.2
         contingent assets, Ch. 26, 3.2.2
            obligations contingent on the successful recovery of, Ch. 26, 3.2.2.A
         contingent liabilities, Ch. 26, 3.2.1
         how probability determines whether to recognise or disclose, Ch. 26, 3.2.3
      determining when a provision should be recognised, Ch. 26, 3.1
         an entity has a present obligation as a result of a past event, Ch. 26, 3.1.1
         it is probable that an outflow of resources embodying economic benefits will be required to settle the obligation, Ch. 26, 3.1.2
         a reliable estimate can be made of the amount of the obligation, Ch. 26, 3.1.3
      recognising an asset when recognising a provision, Ch. 26, 3.3
   scope of IAS 37, Ch. 26, 2.2
      distinction between provisions and contingent liabilities, Ch. 26, 2.2.3
      items outside the scope of IAS 37, Ch. 26, 2.2.1
         executory contracts, except where the contract is onerous, Ch. 26, 2.2.1.A
         items covered by another standard, Ch. 26, 2.2.1.B
      provisions compared to other liabilities, Ch. 26, 2.2.2
   specific examples of provisions and contingencies, Ch. 26, 6
      decommissioning provisions, Ch. 26, 6.3
         changes in estimated decommissioning costs (IFRIC 1), Ch. 26, 6.3.1
         changes in legislation after construction of the asset, Ch. 26, 6.3.2
         funds established to meet an obligation (IFRIC 5), Ch. 26, 6.3.3
         interaction of leases with asset retirement obligations, Ch. 26.6.3.4
      dilapidation and other provisions relating to leased assets, Ch. 26, 6.9
      environmental provisions, general guidance in IAS 37, Ch. 26, 6.4
      EU Directive on 'Waste Electrical and Electronic Equipment' (IFRIC 6), Ch. 26, 6.7
      green certificates compared to emissions trading schemes, Ch. 26, 6.6
      levies imposed by governments, Ch. 26, 6.8
         payments relating to taxes other than income tax, Ch. 26, 6.8.4
         recognition and measurement of levy liabilities, Ch. 26, 6.8.2
         recognition of an asset/expense when a levy is recorded, Ch. 26, 6.8.3
         scope of IFRIC 21, Ch. 26, 6.8.1
      liabilities associated with emissions trading schemes, Ch. 26, 6.5
      litigation and other legal claims, Ch. 26, 6.11
      obligations to make donations to non-profit organisations, Ch. 26, 6.14
      onerous contracts, Ch. 26, 6.2
         contracts with customers that are, or have become, onerous, Ch. 26, 6.2.2
         onerous leases, Ch. 26, 6.2.1
      refunds policy, Ch. 26, 6.12
      restructuring provisions, Ch. 26, 6.1
         costs that can (and cannot) be included in a restructuring provision, Ch. 26, 6.1.4
         definition, Ch. 26, 6.1.1
         recognition of a restructuring provision, Ch. 26, 6.1.2
         recognition of obligations arising from the sale of an operation, Ch. 26, 6.1.3
      self insurance, Ch. 26, 6.13
      settlement payments, Ch. 26, 6.15
      warranty provisions, Ch. 26, 6.10

IAS 38–*Intangible Assets*, Ch. 17, 1–11. *See also* Intangible assets
   acquisition as part of a business combination, Ch. 17, 5
      customer relationship intangible assets, Ch. 17, 5.4

in-process research and development, Ch. 17, 5.5
intangible assets acquired, Ch. 17, 5.2
measuring the fair value of intangible assets, Ch. 17, 5.3
recognition of intangible assets acquired in a business combination, Ch. 17, 5.1
agile software development, Ch. 17, 6.2.6
amortisation of intangible assets, Ch. 17, 9
    assessing the useful life of an intangible asset as finite/indefinite, Ch. 17, 9.1
        factors affecting the useful life, Ch. 17, 9.1.1
        useful life of contractual/other legal rights, Ch. 17, 9.1.2
    impairment losses, Ch. 17, 9.4
    intangible assets with a finite useful life, Ch. 17, 9.2
        amortisation period and method, Ch. 17, 9.2.1
            amortisation of programme and other broadcast rights, Ch. 17, 9.2.1.B
            amortising customer relationships and similar intangible assets, Ch. 17, 9.2.1.A
        residual value, Ch. 17, 9.2.4
        revenue-based amortisation, Ch. 17, 9.2.2
        review of amortisation period and amortisation method, Ch. 17, 9.2.3
    intangible assets with an indefinite useful life, Ch. 17, 9.3
    retirements and disposals, Ch. 17, 9.5
        derecognition of parts of intangible assets, Ch. 17, 9.5.1
background, Ch. 17, 1.1
cloud computing, Ch. 17, 11.6
    implementation costs, Ch. 17, 11.6.2
    'software as a service' cloud computing arrangements, Ch. 17, 11.6.1
development phase, Ch. 17, 6.2.2
disclosure, Ch. 17, 10
    additional disclosures when the revaluation model is applied, Ch. 17, 10.4
    general disclosures, Ch. 17, 10.1
    profit/loss presentation, Ch. 17, 10.3
    of research and development expenditure, Ch. 17, 10.5
    statement of financial position presentation, Ch. 17, 10.2
first-time adoption, Ch. 5, 7.14
identifiability, Ch. 17, 2.1.1
    in relation to asset acquired in a business combination, Ch. 17, 5.1.3
impairment losses, Ch. 17, 9.4
intangible asset, definition, Ch. 17, 2.1–2.1.3
    control, Ch. 17, 2.1.2
    future economic benefits, Ch. 17, 2.1.3
    identifiability, Ch. 17, 2.1.1
internally generated intangible assets, Ch. 17, 6
    cost of an internally generated intangible asset, Ch. 17, 6.3
        determining the costs eligible for capitalisation, Ch. 17, 6.3.2
        establishing the time from which costs can be capitalised, Ch. 17, 6.3.1
    development phase, Ch. 17, 6.2.2
    internally generated brands, mastheads, publishing titles and customer lists, Ch. 17, 6.2.4
    internally generated goodwill, Ch. 17, 6.1
    pharmaceutical industry, research and development in, Ch. 17, 6.2.3

    research phase, Ch. 17, 6.2.1
    website costs (SIC-32), Ch. 17, 6.2.5
measurement, Ch. 17, 3.2
    asset exchanges, Ch. 17, 4.7.1
    assets acquired for contingent consideration, Ch. 17, 4.5
measurement after initial recognition, Ch. 17, 8
    cost model for measurement of intangible assets, Ch. 17, 8.1
    revaluation model for measurement of intangible assets, Ch. 17, 8.2
        accounting for revaluations, Ch. 17, 8.2.3
        frequency of revaluations, Ch. 17, 8.2.2
        revaluation is only allowed if there is an active market, Ch. 17, 8.2.1
objective, Ch. 17, 2
recognition, Ch. 17, 3.1
    assets acquired in a business combination, Ch. 17, 5.1
    of expense, Ch. 17, 7
        catalogues and other advertising costs, Ch. 17, 7.1
        programme and other broadcast rights, Ch. 17, 3.1.1
        separately acquired intangible assets, Ch. 17, 4.1
research and development in pharmaceutical industry, Ch. 17, 6.2.3
retirements and disposals, Ch. 17, 9.5
scope of, Ch. 17, 2
separate acquisition, Ch. 17, 4
    by way of government grant, Ch. 17, 4.6
    components of cost, Ch. 17, 4.2
    costs to be expensed, Ch. 17, 4.3
    exchanges of assets
        commercial substance, Ch. 17, 4.7.2
        measurement of assets exchanged, Ch. 17, 4.7.1
    income from incidental operations, Ch. 17, 4.4
    measurement of intangible assets acquired for contingent consideration, Ch. 17, 4.5
    recognition, Ch. 17, 4.1
specific regulatory and environmental issues regarding intangible assets, Ch. 17, 11
    accounting for green certificates/renewable energy certificates, Ch. 17, 11.3
    accounting for REACH costs, Ch. 17, 11.4
    crypto-assets, Ch. 17, 11.5
    emissions trading schemes, Ch. 17, 11.2
    rate-regulated activities, Ch. 17, 11.1
subsequent expenditure, Ch. 17, 3.3
terms used in, Ch. 17, 1.2
IAS 39–*Financial Instruments: Recognition and Measurement*, Ch. 44, 3. *See also* Financial instruments, recognition and initial measurement
    hedge accounting, Ch. 53, 1.3, 14
    requirements in IAS 39, Ch. 53, 14
IAS 40–*Investment Property*, Ch. 13, 4.3; Ch. 19, 1–12. *See also* Investment property
    cost model, Ch. 19, 7
    definitions, Ch. 19, 2
    disclosure requirements of, Ch. 19, 12
        for cost model, Ch. 19, 12.3
        direct operating expenses, Ch. 19, 12.1.3
        for fair value model, Ch. 19, 12.2
        level of aggregation for IFRS 13 disclosures, Ch. 19, 12.1.2

IAS 40–*Investment Property*—*contd*
   disclosure requirements of—*contd*
      methods and assumptions in fair value estimates, Ch. 19, 12.1.1
      presentation of changes in fair value, Ch. 19, 12.2.1
      presentation of sales proceeds, Ch. 19, 12.4
      under both fair value and cost models, Ch. 19, 12.1
      where fair value cannot be determined reliably, Ch. 19, 12.2.2
   disposal of, Ch. 19, 10
   fair value model, Ch. 19, 6
   held for sale, Ch. 19, 8
   initial measurement, Ch. 19, 4
   interim reporting, Ch. 19, 11
   measurement after initial recognition, Ch. 19, 5
   recognition, Ch. 19, 3
      business combination, Ch. 19, 3.3
         definition of business, Ch. 19, 3.3.1
      cost recognition, Ch. 19, 3.2
         allocation into parts, Ch. 19, 3.2.2
         repairs and maintenance, Ch. 19, 3.2.1
      expenditure prior to planning permissions/zoning consents, Ch. 19, 3.1
   scope, Ch. 19, 2
      group of assets leased out under a single operating lease, Ch. 19, 2.10
      investment property under construction, Ch. 19, 2.5
      land, Ch. 19, 2.2
      property held for own use ('owner-occupied'), Ch. 19, 2.4
      property held/under construction for sale in the ordinary course of business, Ch. 19, 2.6
      property interests held under a lease, Ch. 19, 2.1
      property leased to others, Ch. 19, 2.3
      property where rentals are determined by reference to the operations in the property, Ch. 19, 2.9
      property with dual uses, Ch. 19, 2.7
      property with the provision of ancillary services, Ch. 19, 2.8
   transfer of assets to/from investment property, Ch. 19, 9

IAS 41–*Agriculture*, Ch. 42, 1–5
   control, Ch. 42, 3.1.1
   definitions, Ch. 42, 2.2
      agriculture-related definitions, Ch. 42, 2.2.1
         bearer plants, Ch. 42, 2.2.1.A
      general definitions, Ch. 42, 2.2.2
   disclosure, Ch. 42, 5
      additional disclosures if fair value cannot be measured reliably, Ch. 42, 5.3
      fair value measurement disclosures, Ch. 42, 5.2
      government grants, Ch. 42, 5.4
      groups of biological assets, Ch. 42, 5.1.3
      income statement, Ch. 42, 5.1.2
      statement of financial position, Ch. 42, 5.1.1
         current *vs.* non-current classification, Ch. 42, 5.1.1.A
   government grants, Ch. 42, 3.3
   measurement, Ch. 42, 3.2
      agricultural produce, Ch. 42, 3.2.2
      biological assets within the scope of IAS 41, Ch. 42, 3.2.1
         initial and subsequent measurement, Ch. 42, 3.2.1.A
         subsequent expenditure, Ch. 42, 3.2.1.B
      gains and losses, Ch. 42, 3.2.4
      inability to measure fair value reliably, Ch. 42, 3.2.5
         cost model, Ch. 42, 3.2.5.B
         rebutting the presumption, Ch. 42, 3.2.5.A
      requirements for produce growing on a bearer plant, Ch. 42, 3.2.3
         agricultural produce growing on bearer plants, Ch. 42, 3.2.3.B
         requirements for bearer plants in the scope of IAS 16, Ch. 42, 3.2.3.A
   measurement of change, Ch. 42, 2.2.1
   measuring fair value less costs to sell, Ch. 42, 4
      determining costs to sell, Ch. 42, 4.4
      establishing what to measure, Ch. 42, 4.2
         grouping of assets, Ch. 42, 4.2.2
         unit of account, Ch. 42, 4.2.1
      interaction between IAS 41 and IFRS 13, Ch. 42, 4.1
      measuring fair value: IAS 41-specific requirements, Ch. 42, 4.5
         financing cash flows and taxation, Ch. 42, 4.5.5
         forward sales contracts, Ch. 42, 4.5.3
         obligation to re-establish a biological asset after harvest, Ch. 42, 4.5.2
         onerous contracts, Ch. 42, 4.5.4
         use of external independent valuers, Ch. 42, 4.5.1
   measuring fair value: overview of IFRS 13's requirements, Ch. 42, 4.6
      fair value measurement framework, Ch. 42, 4.6.1
      highest and best use and valuation premise, Ch. 42, 4.6.2
         biological assets attached to land, Ch. 42, 4.6.2.A
      selecting appropriate assumptions, Ch. 42, 4.6.3
         condition and location, Ch. 42, 4.6.3.A
      valuation techniques in IFRS 13, Ch. 42, 4.6.4
         cost as an approximation of fair value, Ch. 42, 4.6.4.A
   problem of measuring fair value for part-grown or immature biological assets, Ch. 42, 4.7
   when to measure fair value, Ch. 42, 4.3
   objective, Ch. 42, 2.1
   recognition, Ch. 42, 3.1
   scope, Ch. 42, 2.3
      agricultural produce before and after harvest, Ch. 42, 2.3.2
      bearer plants and produce growing on a bearer plant, Ch. 42, 2.3.3
      biological assets outside the scope of IAS 41, Ch. 42, 2.3.1
      concessions, Ch. 42, 2.3.6
      leases of biological assets (excluding bearer plants), Ch. 42, 2.3.5
      products that are the result of processing after harvest, Ch. 42, 2.3.4

Identifiable assets acquired in a business combination, Ch. 9, 5.2
   acquisition-date fair values of, Ch. 9, 5.3
   classifying, Ch. 9, 5.4
   intangible assets, Ch. 9, 5.5.2
   operating leases, recognising and measuring, Ch. 9, 5.5
   recognising, Ch. 9, 5

IFRIC 1–*Changes in Existing Decommissioning, Restoration and Similar Liabilities*, Ch. 26, 1.2.1, 6.3
   changes in estimated decommissioning costs, Ch. 26, 6.3.1

IFRIC 12–*Service Concession Arrangements*, Ch. 25, 1–7. *See also* Service concession arrangements
  accounting by the concession operator, financial asset and intangible asset models, Ch. 25, 4
    accounting for contractual payments to be made by an operator to a grantor, Ch. 25, 4.7
      under the financial asset model, Ch. 25, 4.7.2
      under the intangible asset model, Ch. 25, 4.7.3
      variable payments in a service concession, Ch. 25, 4.7.1
    accounting for residual interests, Ch. 25, 4.6
    allocating the consideration, Ch. 25, 4.1.1
      allocating the transaction price to the performance obligations in the contract, Ch. 25, 4.1.1.D
      determining the transaction price under the contract, Ch. 25, 4.1.1.C
      identifying the contract(s) with a customer, Ch. 25, 4.1.1.A
      identifying the performance obligations in the contract, Ch. 25, 4.1.1.B
    'bifurcation,' single arrangements that contain both financial and intangible assets, Ch. 25, 4.5
    determining the accounting model after the construction phase, Ch. 25, 4.1.2
    financial asset model, Ch. 25, 4.2
    intangible asset model, Ch. 25, 4.3
      amortisation of the intangible asset, Ch. 25, 4.3.1
      impairment during the construction phase, Ch. 25, 4.3.2
    revenue recognition implications of the two models, Ch. 25, 4.4
  application of IFRIC 12 and interactions with IFRS 15 and IFRS 9, Ch. 26, 6
  control model, Ch. 25, 3
    assets within scope, Ch. 25, 3.3
    control of the residual interest, Ch. 25, 3.2
    partially regulated assets, Ch. 25, 3.4
    regulation of services, Ch. 25, 3.1
  definitions, Ch. 25, 1.2
  disclosure requirements, SIC-29, Ch. 25, 7
  revenue and expenditure during the operations phase, Ch. 25, 5
    accounting for the operations phase, Ch. 25, 5.2
    additional construction and upgrade services, Ch. 25, 5.1
      subsequent construction services that are part of the initial infrastructure asset, Ch. 25, 5.1.1
      subsequent construction services that comprise additions to the initial infrastructure, Ch. 25, 5.1.2
    items provided to the operator by the grantor, Ch. 25, 5.3
  scope of IFRIC 12, Ch. 25, 2
    accounting by grantors, Ch. 25, 2.5
    arrangements that are not in the scope of IFRIC 12, Ch. 25, 2.2
      outsourcing arrangements, Ch. 25, 2.2.1
    interaction of IFRS 16 and IFRIC 12, Ch. 25, 2.3
    private-to-private arrangements, Ch. 25, 2.4
    public service nature of the obligation, Ch. 25, 2.1
IFRIC 14–IAS 19–*The Limit on a Defined Benefit Asset Minimum Funding Requirements and their Interaction*, Ch. 35, 8.2

IFRIC 16–*Hedges of a Net Investment in a Foreign Operation*, Ch. 7, 2.3; Ch. 15, 6.1.5. *See also* Net investment hedges
IFRIC 17–*Distributions of Non-cash Assets to Owners*, Ch. 7, 3.7; Ch. 8, 2.4.2
  demerger and, Ch. 7, 3.7
  measurement in, Ch. 7, 3.7.2; Ch. 8, 2.4.2.B
  recognition in, Ch. 7, 3.7.2; Ch. 8, 2.4.2.B
  scope of, Ch. 7, 3.7.1; Ch. 8, 2.4.2.A
IFRIC 19–*Extinguishing Financial Liabilities with Equity Instruments*, Ch. 5, 5.16; Ch. 47, 7
  effective date, Ch. 47, 7.1
  requirements, Ch. 47, 7.2
  scope, Ch. 47, 7.1
IFRIC 20–*Stripping Costs in the Production Phase of a Surface Mine*, Ch. 5, 5.19; Ch. 18, 3.1.6; Ch. 43, 15.5
  determining when production phase commences, Ch. 43, 15.5.2
  disclosures, Ch. 43, 15.5.6
  initial recognition, Ch. 43, 15.5.4
    allocating costs between inventory and the stripping activity asset, Ch. 43, 15.5.4.A
    identifying the component of the ore body, Ch. 43, 15.5.4.B
  recognition criteria-stripping activity asset, Ch. 43, 15.5.3
  scope of IFRIC 20, Ch. 43, 15.5.1
  subsequent measurement, Ch. 43, 15.5.5
IFRIC 21–*Levies*, Ch. 26, 6.8
IFRIC 22–*Foreign Currency Transactions and Advance Consideration*, Ch. 5, 5.22
IFRIC 23–*Uncertainty over Income Tax Treatments*, Ch. 33, 9
  changes to estimates of uncertain tax treatments, Ch. 38, 3.6
  events after the reporting period
    adjusting events, Ch. 38, 2.1.2
    non-adjusting events, Ch. 38, 2.1.3
IFRS 1–*First-time Adoption of International Financial Reporting Standards*, Ch. 5, 1–8. *See also* First-time adoption accounting policies and practical application issues, Ch. 5, 7
  authoritative literature, Ch. 5, 1.2
  borrowing costs, Ch. 5, 5.15
  compound financial instruments, Ch. 5, 5.10
  cumulative translation differences, Ch. 5, 5.7
  decommissioning liabilities included in the cost of property, plant and equipment, Ch. 5, 5.13
  deemed cost, Ch. 5, 5.5
  designation of contracts to buy or sell a non-financial item, Ch. 5, 5.23
  designation of previously recognised financial instruments, Ch. 5, 5.11
  disclosures, Ch. 5, 5.20.6.B, 6
  embedded derivatives, Ch. 5, 4.11
  employee benefits, Ch. 5, 7.7
  exceptions to retrospective application of other IFRSs, Ch. 5, 4
  estimates, Ch. 5, 4.2
  extinguishing financial liabilities with equity instruments, Ch. 5, 5.16
  fair value measurement of financial assets and liabilities at initial recognition, Ch. 5, 5.12
  financial assets or intangible assets accounted for in accordance with IFRIC 12, Ch. 5, 5.14

IFRS 1–*First-time Adoption of International Financial Reporting Standards*—contd
 financial instruments under IFRS 9, classification and measurement of, Ch. 5, 4.9
 first-time adopter, Ch. 5, 2
 foreign currency transactions and advance consideration, Ch. 5, 5.22
 future developments, Ch. 5, 1.4
 government loans, Ch. 5, 4.12
 hedge accounting, Ch. 5, 4.4–4.7
  in opening IFRS statement of financial position, Ch. 5, 4.5
  subsequent treatment, Ch. 5, 4.6
 impairment of financial instruments, Ch. 5, 4.10
 insurance contracts, Ch. 5, 4.13, 5.4
 investment entities, Ch. 5, 5.9.5
 investments in subsidiaries, joint ventures and associates, Ch. 5, 6.5.2
 joint arrangements, Ch. 5, 5.18
 leases, Ch. 5, 5.6, 7.5
 non-controlling interests, Ch. 5, 4.8
 objectives of, Ch. 5, 1.1
 opening IFRS statement of financial position, Ch. 5, 3
  and accounting policies, Ch. 5, 3.2
  defined terms, Ch. 5, 1.3
  departures from full retrospective application, Ch. 5, 3.5
  fair value and deemed cost, Ch. 5, 3.3
  first-time adoption timeline, Ch. 5, 3.1
  hedge accounting in, Ch. 5, 4.5
  transitional provisions in other standards, Ch. 5, 3.4
 optional exemptions from the requirements of certain IFRSs, Ch. 5, 5
  business combinations and acquisitions of associates and joint arrangements, Ch. 5, 5.2
   associates and joint arrangements, Ch. 5, 5.2.2.A
  business combinations and acquisitions of associates and joint ventures asset acquisitions, Ch. 5, 5.2.1.A
   assets and liabilities excluded, Ch. 5, 5.2.4.B
   assets and liabilities to be recognised in the opening IFRS statement of financial position, Ch. 5, 5.2.4
   classification of business combinations, Ch. 5, 5.2.3
   currency adjustments to goodwill, Ch. 5, 5.2.6
   deferred taxes and non-controlling interests, measurement of, Ch. 5, 5.2.9
   definition of a 'business' under IFRS 3, Ch. 5, 5.2.1
   derecognition of negative goodwill, Ch. 5, 5.2.5.B
   goodwill previously deducted from equity, Ch. 5, 5.2.5.C
   in-process research and development, Ch. 5, 5.2.4.D
   option to restate business combinations retrospectively, Ch. 5, 5.2.2
   previous GAAP carrying amount as deemed cost, Ch. 5, 5.2.4.C
   previously consolidated entities that are not subsidiaries, Ch. 5, 5.2.8
   previously unconsolidated subsidiaries, Ch. 5, 5.2.7
   prohibition of other adjustments of goodwill, Ch. 5, 5.2.5.A
   recognition and measurement requirements, Ch. 5, 5.2.4.F
   recognition of assets and liabilities, Ch. 5, 5.2.4.B
   restatement of goodwill, Ch. 5, 5.2.5
  subsequent measurement under IFRSs not based on cost, Ch. 5, 5.2.4.E
  transition accounting for contingent consideration, Ch. 5, 5.2.10
 presentation and disclosure, Ch. 5, 6
  comparative information, Ch. 5, 6.1 designation of financial instruments, Ch. 5, 6.4
  disclosure of IFRS information before adoption of IFRSs, Ch. 5, 6.7
  disclosures regarding deemed cost use, Ch. 5, 6.5
   after severe hyperinflation, Ch. 5, 6.5.5
   for assets used in operations subject to rate regulation, Ch. 5, 6.5.4
   for investments in subsidiaries, joint ventures and associates, Ch. 5, 6.5.2
   for oil and gas assets, Ch. 5, 6.5.3
   use of fair value as deemed cost, Ch. 5, 6.5.1
  explanation of transition to IFRSs, Ch. 5, 6.3
   disclosure of reconciliations, Ch. 5, 6.3.1
   inclusion of IFRS 1 reconciliations by cross reference, Ch. 5, 6.3.4
   line-by-line reconciliations and detailed explanations, Ch. 5, 6.3.2
   recognition and reversal of impairments, Ch. 5, 6.3.3
   reconciliation by a first-time adopter that continues to publish previous GAAP financial statements, Ch. 5, 6.3.1.A
  interim financial reports, Ch. 5, 6.6
   disclosures in, Ch. 5, 6.6.2
   reconciliations in, Ch. 5, 6.6.1
 regulatory deferral accounts, Ch. 5, 5.20
 regulatory issues, Ch. 5, 8
 revenue from contracts with customers (IFRS 15), Ch. 5, 5.21; Ch. 5, 7.6
 severe hyperinflation, Ch. 5, 5.17
 share-based payment transactions, Ch. 5, 5.3
 stripping costs in the production phase of a surface mine, Ch. 5, 5.19
IFRS 2 – *Share-based payment*, Ch. 34, 1–16. *See also* Cash-settled share based payment transactions; Equity-settled share-based payment transactions; Share-based payment transactions; Vesting
 awards entitled to dividends during the vesting period, Ch. 34, 15.3
 awards vesting/exercisable on an exit event/change of control, Ch. 34, 15.4
  awards 'purchased for fair value', Ch. 34, 15.4.5
  awards requiring achievement of a minimum price on flotation/sale, Ch. 34, 15.4.4
  'drag along' and 'tag along' rights, Ch. 34, 15.4.6
  is flotation/sale a vesting condition or a non-vesting condition?, Ch. 34, 15.4.3
  grant date, Ch. 34, 15.4.1
  vesting period, Ch. 34, 15.4.2
 business combination, replacement share-based payment awards issued, Ch. 34, 11
  acquiree award not replaced by acquirer, Ch. 34, 11.3
  background, Ch. 34, 11.1
  financial statements of the acquired entity, Ch. 34, 11.4
  replacement award, Ch. 34, 11.2

accounting for changes in vesting assumptions after the acquisition date, Ch. 34, 11.2.3
acquiree awards that the acquirer is not 'obliged' to replace, Ch. 34, 11.2.2
awards that the acquirer is 'obliged' to replace, Ch. 34, 11.2.1
cash-settled transactions, Ch. 34, 9
cost of awards, equity-settled transactions, Ch. 34, 5
development of IFRS 2, Ch. 34, 1.2
definitions, Ch. 34, 2.2.1
disclosures, Ch. 34, 13
equity-settled transactions
    allocation of expense, Ch. 34, 6
    cost of awards, Ch. 34, 5
    modification, cancellation and settlement, Ch. 34, 7
    overview, Ch. 34, 4
    valuation, Ch. 34, 8
first-time adoption, Ch. 34, 16.1
general recognition principles, Ch. 34, 3
grant date, Ch. 34, 5.3. *See also* Grant date
group share schemes, Ch. 34, 12. *See also* Group share schemes
loans to employees to purchase shares, Ch. 34, 15.2
market conditions, Ch. 34, 6.3
matching share awards, Ch. 34, 15.1
modification, cancellation and settlement of equity-settled transactions, Ch. 34, 7
non-compete agreements, Ch. 34, 3.2.3
Non-controlling interests in share-based payment transactions, Ch. 7, 5.1, 5.2, 5.6
objective of IFRS 2, Ch. 34, 2.1
overall approach of IFRS 2, Ch. 34, 1.4
    classification differences between IFRS 2 and IAS 32/IFRS 9, Ch. 34, 1.4.1
research project, Ch. 34, 1.2.1
scope, Ch. 34, 2.2
    definitions, Ch. 34, 2.2.1
    practical applications of scope requirements, Ch. 34, 2.2.4
        awards for which the counterparty has paid 'fair value', Ch. 34, 2.2.4.D
        awards with a foreign currency strike price, Ch. 34, 2.2.4.G
        cash bonus dependent on share price performance, Ch. 34, 2.2.4.E
        cash-settled awards based on an entity's 'enterprise value' or other formula, Ch. 34, 2.2.4.F
        equity-settled award of subsidiary with put option against the parent, Ch. 34, 2.2.4.B
        holding own shares to satisfy or 'hedge' awards, Ch. 34, 2.2.4.H
        increase in ownership interest with no change in number of shares held, Ch. 34, 2.2.4.C
        options over puttable instruments classified as equity under specific exception in IAS 32, Ch. 34, 2.2.4.J
        remuneration in non-equity shares and arrangements with put rights over equity shares, Ch. 34, 2.2.4.A
        shares/warrants issued in connection with a financial liability, Ch. 34, 2.2.4.I
        special discounts to certain categories of investor on a share issue, Ch. 34, 2.2.4.K
    transactions not within the scope of IFRS 2, Ch. 34, 2.2.3
        business combinations, Ch. 34, 2.2.3.C
        common control transactions and formation of joint arrangements, Ch. 34, 2.2.3.D
        transactions in financial assets outside the scope of IAS 32 and IFRS 9, Ch. 34, 2.2.3.F
        transactions in the scope of IAS 32 and IFRS 9, Ch. 34, 2.2.3.E
        transactions with shareholders in their capacity as such, Ch. 34, 2.2.3.A
        transfer of assets in group restructuring arrangements, Ch. 34, 2.2.3.B
    transactions within the scope of IFRS 2, Ch. 34, 2.2.2
        'all employee' share plans, Ch. 34, 2.2.2.D
        group schemes and transactions with group shareholders, Ch. 34, 2.2.2.A
        transactions where the identifiable consideration received appears to be less than the consideration given, Ch. 34, 2.2.2.C
        transactions with employee benefit trusts and similar vehicles, Ch. 34, 2.2.2.B
        vested transactions, Ch. 34, 2.2.2.E
South African black economic empowerment ('BEE') and similar arrangements, Ch. 34, 15.5
taxes related to share-based payment transactions, Ch. 34, 14
transactions with equity and cash alternatives, Ch. 34, 10
    awards requiring cash settlement in specific circumstances (awards with contingent cash settlement), Ch. 34, 10.3
        accounting for change in manner of settlement where award is contingent on future events outside the control of the entity and the counterparty, Ch. 34, 10.3.4
        cash settlement on a change of control, Ch. 34, 10.3.3
        cash-settled if contingency is outside entity's control, Ch. 34, 10.3.1
        cash-settled if contingency is outside entity's control and probable, Ch. 34, 10.3.2
        manner of settlement contingent on future events, Ch. 34, 10.3.5
    cash settlement alternative not based on share price/value, Ch. 34, 10.4
    transactions where the counterparty has choice of settlement, Ch. 34, 10.1
        accounting treatment, Ch. 34, 10.1.3
        'backstop' cash settlement rights, Ch. 34, 10.1.5
        cash-settlement alternative for employee introduced after grant date, Ch. 34, 10.1.4
        convertible bonds issued to acquire goods/services, Ch. 34, 10.1.6
        transactions in which the fair value is measured directly, Ch. 34, 10.1.1
        transactions in which the fair value is measured indirectly, Ch. 34, 10.1.2
    transactions where the entity has choice of settlement, Ch. 34, 10.2
        change in entity's settlement policy/intention leading to change in classification of award after grant date, Ch. 34, 10.2.3
        transactions treated as cash-settled, Ch. 34, 10.2.1
        transactions treated as equity-settled, Ch. 34, 10.2.2
valuation of equity-settled transactions, Ch. 34, 8
vesting conditions, Ch. 34, 3.1

IFRS 2 – *Share-based payment*—contd
- vesting conditions other than market conditions, Ch. 34, 6.2
- vesting period, Ch. 34, 3.3

IFRS 3–*Business Combinations*, Ch. 9, 1–16. *See also* Business combinations
- acquisition method of accounting, Ch. 9, 4
  - acquisition date determination, Ch. 9, 4.2
  - identifying the acquirer, Ch. 9, 4.1
    - new entity formed to effect a business combination, Ch. 9, 4.1.1
    - stapling arrangements, Ch. 9, 4.1.2
  - assessing what is part of the exchange for the acquiree, Ch. 9, 11
    - effective settlement of pre-existing relationships, Ch. 9, 11.1
    - reimbursement for paying the acquirer's acquisition-related costs, Ch. 9, 11.3
    - remuneration for future services of employees or former owners of the acquire, Ch. 9, 11.2
    - restructuring plans, Ch. 9, 11.4
- bargain purchase transactions, Ch. 9, 10
- business combinations achieved in stages ('step acquisitions'), Ch. 9, 9
- consideration transferred, Ch. 9, 7
  - acquisition-related costs, Ch. 9, 7.3
  - business combinations achieved without the transfer of consideration, Ch. 9, 7.4
    - business combinations by contract alone, Ch. 9, 7.4.1
  - combinations involving mutual entities, Ch. 9, 7.5
  - contingent consideration, Ch. 9, 7.1
    - classification of a contingent consideration obligation, Ch. 9, 7.1.2
    - initial recognition and measurement, Ch. 9, 7.1.1
    - subsequent measurement and accounting, Ch. 9, 7.1.3
  - replacement share-based payment awards, Ch. 9, 7; Ch. 34, 11.2, 11.3
- disclosures, Ch. 9, 16
  - financial effects of adjustments recognised in the current reporting period, Ch. 9, 16.2
  - illustrative example, Ch. 9, 16.4
  - nature and financial effect of business combinations, Ch. 9, 16.1
    - business combinations during the current reporting period, Ch. 9, 16.1.1
    - business combinations effected after the end of the reporting period, Ch. 9, 16.1.2
- identifying a business combination, Ch. 9, 3.2.3
  - definition of a business, Ch. 9, 3.2; Ch. 19, 3.3.1
    - assessing whether an acquired process is substantive, Ch. 9, 3.2.4
    - assessment whether acquired set of activities and assets constitutes a business, Ch. 9, 3.2.2
    - 'capable of' from the viewpoint of a market participant, Ch. 9, 3.2.5
    - concentration test, Ch. 9, 3.2.3
    - development stage entities, Ch. 9, 3.2.7
    - identifying business combinations, Ch. 9, 3.2.6
    - inputs, processes and outputs, Ch. 9, 3.2.1
- IFRS 3 (as revised in 2008) and subsequent amendments, Ch. 9, 1.1
  - post-implementation review, Ch. 9, 1.1.1
- measurement period, Ch. 9, 12
  - adjustments made after end of measurement period, Ch. 9, 12.2
  - adjustments made during measurement period to provisional amounts, Ch. 9, 12.1
- push down accounting, Ch. 9, 15
- recognising and measuring goodwill or a gain in a bargain purchase, Ch. 9, 6
  - subsequent accounting for goodwill, Ch. 9, 6.1
- recognising and measuring non-controlling interests, Ch. 7, 3.1.1, 3.1.2, 5, 6; Ch. 9, 8
  - call and put options over non-controlling interests, Ch. 7, 6; Ch. 9, 8.5
  - implications of method chosen for measuring non-controlling interests, Ch. 9, 8.3
  - measuring qualifying non-controlling interests at acquisition-date fair value, Ch. 9, 8.1
  - measuring qualifying non-controlling interests at the proportionate share of the value of net identifiable assets acquired, Ch. 9, 8.2
  - measuring share-based payment and other components of non-controlling interests, Ch. 7, 5.1, 5.2, 5.6; Ch. 9, 8.4
- recognition and measurement of assets acquired, liabilities assumed and non-controlling interests, Ch. 9, 5, 5.5
  - acquisition-date fair values of identifiable assets acquired and liabilities assumed, Ch. 9, 5.3
  - classifying or designating identifiable assets acquired and liabilities assumed, Ch. 9, 5.4
  - exceptions to recognition and/or measurement principles, Ch. 9, 5.6
    - assets held for sale, Ch. 9, 5.6.6
    - contingent liabilities, Ch. 9, 5.6.1; 9, 5.6.1.B
    - employee benefits, Ch. 9, 5.6.3
    - income taxes, Ch. 9, 5.6.2
    - indemnification assets, Ch. 9, 5.6.4
    - initial recognition and measurement, Ch. 9, 5.6.1.A
    - insurance contracts within the scope of IFRS 17, Ch. 9, 5.6.9
    - leases in which the acquiree is the lessee, Ch. 9, 5.6.8
    - reacquired rights, Ch. 9, 5.6.5
    - share-based payment transactions, Ch. 9, 5.6.7
  - recognising and measuring particular assets acquired and liabilities assumed, Ch. 9, 5.5
    - assembled workforce and other items that are not identifiable, Ch. 9, 5.5.4
    - assets and liabilities related to contacts with customers, Ch. 9, 5.5.8
    - assets that the acquirer does not intend to use or intends to use in a way that is different from other market participants, Ch. 9, 5.5.6
    - assets with uncertain cash flows (valuation allowances), Ch. 9, 5.5.5
    - combining an intangible asset with a related contract, identifiable asset or liability, Ch. 9, 5.5.2.C
    - customer relationship intangible assets, Ch. 9, 5.5.2.B
    - determining the fair values of intangible assets, Ch. 9, 5.5.2.F
    - emission rights, Ch. 9, 5.5.2.E
    - in-process research or development project expenditure, Ch. 9, 5.5.2.D

intangible assets, Ch. 9, 5.5.2.
investments in equity-accounted entities, Ch. 9, 5.5.7
items not qualifying as assets, Ch. 9, 5.5.4.B
operating leases in which the acquiree is the lessor, Ch. 9, 5.5.1
reacquired rights, Ch. 9, 5.5.3
recognising identifiable assets acquired and liabilities assumed, Ch. 9, 5.2
replacement awards in business combinations, Ch. 34, 11; Ch. 7, 5.2
reverse acquisitions, Ch. 9, 14
cash consideration, Ch. 9, 14.6
earnings per share, Ch. 9, 14.5
measuring goodwill, Ch. 9, 14.2
measuring the consideration transferred, Ch. 9, 14.1
non-controlling interest, Ch. 9, 14.4
preparation and presentation of consolidated financial statements, Ch. 9, 14.3
reverse acquisitions and acquirers that are not legal entities, Ch. 9, 14.9
reverse acquisitions involving a non-trading shell company, Ch. 9, 14.8
share-based payments, Ch. 9, 14.7
scope of IFRS 3, Ch. 9, 2
acquisition by an investment entity, Ch. 9, 2.3
arrangements out of scope of IFRS 3, Ch. 9, 2.2
acquisition of an asset or a group of assets that does not constitute a business, Ch. 9, 2.2.2, Ch. 19, 4.1.1
arrangements under common control, Ch. 9, 2.2.3
formation of a joint arrangement, Ch. 9, 2.2.1
mutual entities, Ch. 9, 2.1
subsequent measurement and accounting, Ch. 9, 13

IFRS 4–*Insurance Contracts*, Ch. 55, 1–12. *See also* Insurance contracts, IFRS 17
development of, Ch. 55, 1.2
objectives of, Ch. 55, 2
scope of, Ch. 55, 2.2
definitions, Ch. 55, 2.2.1
product classification process, Ch. 55, 2.2.4
transactions not within the scope of IFRS 4, Ch. 55, 2.2.3
assets and liabilities arising from employment benefit plans, Ch. 55, 2.2.3.B
contingent consideration payable/receivable in a business combination, Ch. 55, 2.2.3.E
contingent rights and obligations related to non-financial items, Ch. 55, 2.2.3.C
direct insurance contracts in which the entity is the policyholder, Ch. 55, 2.2.3.F
financial guarantee contracts, Ch. 55, 2.2.3.D
product warranties, Ch. 55, 2.2.3.A
transactions within the scope of IFRS 4, Ch. 55, 2.2.2

IFRS 5–*Non-current Assets Held for Sale and Discontinued Operations*, Ch. 4, 1–6. *See also* Discontinued operation
comparative information, Ch. 4, 4
treatment on cessation of classification as held for sale, Ch. 4, 4.2
treatment on initial classification as held for sale
statement of comprehensive income, Ch. 4, 4.1.1
statement of financial position, Ch. 4, 4.1.2
disclosure requirements, Ch. 4, 5
discontinued operation, Ch. 4, 3.2
definition of, Ch. 4, 3.1
presentation of, Ch. 4, 3.2
trading with continuing operations, Ch. 4, 3.3
future developments, Ch. 4, 6
interaction with IFRS 9, Ch. 51, 7.4
interaction of IFRS 12 and, Ch. 13, 2.2.1.C
non-current assets (and disposal groups) held for sale/distribution, Ch. 4, 2
classification, Ch. 4, 2.1, 2.1.1–2.1.3B
abandonment, Ch. 4, 2.1.2.C
classification as held for sale or as held for distribution to owners, Ch. 4, 2.1.2–2.1.2.C
concept of a disposal group, Ch. 4, 2.1.1
loss of control of a subsidiary, Ch. 4, 2.1.3.A; Ch. 7, 3.2, 3.7
meaning of available for immediate sale, Ch. 4, 2.1.2.A
meaning of highly probable, Ch. 4, 2.1.2.B
partial disposal of an associate or joint venture, Ch. 4, 2.1.3.B
partial disposals of operations, Ch. 4, 2.1.3
measurement, Ch. 4, 2.2
changes to a plan of sale/distribution, Ch. 4, 2.2.5
impairments and reversals of impairment, Ch. 4, 2.2.3
on initial classification as held for sale, Ch. 4, 2.2.2.A
presentation in the statement of financial position of, Ch. 4, 2.2.4
scope of the measurement requirements, Ch. 4, 2.2.1
subsequent remeasurement, Ch. 4, 2.2.2.B
objective and scope, Ch. 4, 1

IFRS 6–*Exploration for and Evaluation of Mineral Resources*, Ch. 43, 3. *See also* Extractive industries
disclosure, Ch. 43, 3.6
impairment, Ch. 43, 3.5
additional considerations if E&E assets are impaired, Ch. 43, 3.5.5
cash-generating units comprising successful and unsuccessful E&E projects, Ch. 43, 3.5.3
impairment testing 'triggers,' Ch. 43, 3.5.1
income statement treatment of E&E, Ch. 43, 3.5.6
order of impairment testing, Ch. 43, 3.5.4
reversal of impairment losses, Ch. 43, 3.5.7
specifying the level at which E&E assets are assessed for impairment, Ch. 43, 3.5.2
measurement of exploration and evaluation assets, Ch. 43, 3.3
capitalisation of borrowing costs, Ch. 43, 3.3.2
types of expenditure in, Ch. 43, 3.3.1
objective, Ch. 43, 3.1
presentation and classification, Ch. 43, 3.4
reclassification of E&E assets, Ch. 43, 3.4.1
recognition of exploration and evaluation assets, Ch. 43, 3.2
area-of-interest method, Ch. 43, 3.2.5
changes in accounting policies, Ch. 43, 3.2.6
developing an accounting policy under IFRS 6, Ch. 43, 3.2.1
full cost method, Ch. 43, 3.2.4
options for an exploration and evaluation policy, Ch. 43, 3.2.2
successful efforts method, Ch. 43, 3.2.3
scope, Ch. 43, 3.1
scope exclusions in other standards relating to the extractive industries, Ch. 43, 3.1.1

IFRS 7–*Financial Instruments: Disclosures*, Ch. 44, 4, Ch. 54, 1–9
  disclosures, structuring, Ch. 54, 3
    classes of financial instrument, Ch. 54, 3.3
    level of detail, Ch. 54, 3.1
    materiality, Ch. 54, 3.2
  future developments, Ch. 54, 9
  interim reports, Ch. 54, 2.3
  nature and extent of risks arising from financial instruments, Ch. 54, 5
    credit risk, Ch. 54, 5.3
      collateral and other credit enhancements obtained, Ch. 54, 5.3.5
      credit risk exposure, Ch. 54, 5.3.4
      credit risk management practices, Ch. 54, 5.3.2
      illustrative disclosures, Ch. 54, 5.3.6
      quantitative and qualitative information about amounts arising from expected credit losses, Ch. 54, 5.3.3
      scope and objectives, Ch. 54, 5.3.1
    liquidity risk, Ch. 54, 5.4
      information provided to key management, Ch. 54, 5.4.1
      management of associated liquidity risk, Ch. 54, 5.4.3
      maturity analyses, Ch. 54, 5.4.2
      puttable financial instruments classified as equity, Ch. 54, 5.4.4
    market risk, Ch. 54, 5.5
      'basic' sensitivity analysis, Ch. 54, 5.5.1
      other market risk disclosures, Ch. 54, 5.5.3
      value-at-risk and similar analyses, Ch. 54, 5.5.2
    qualitative disclosures, Ch. 54, 5.1
    quantitative disclosures, Ch. 54, 5.2, 5.6
      capital disclosures, Ch. 54, 5.6.3
      concentrations of risk, Ch. 54, 5.6.1
      operational risk, Ch. 54, 5.6.2
  presentation on the face of the financial statements and related disclosures, Ch. 54, 7
    gains and losses recognised in other comprehensive income, Ch. 54, 7.2
    gains and losses recognised in profit/loss embedded derivatives, Ch. 54, 7.1.4
      entities whose share capital is not equity, Ch. 54, 7.1.5
      further analysis of gains and losses recognised in profit/loss, Ch. 54, 7.1.2
      offsetting and hedges, Ch. 54, 7.1.3
      presentation on the face of the statement of comprehensive income (or income statement), Ch. 54, 7
    statement of cash flows, Ch. 54, 7.5
    statement of changes in equity, Ch. 54, 7.3
    statement of financial position, Ch. 54, 7.4
      assets and liabilities, Ch. 54, 7.4.3
      convertible loans, Ch. 54, 7.4.4.B
      current and non-current assets and liabilities, distinction between, Ch. 54, 7.4.4
      debt with refinancing or roll over agreements, Ch. 54, 7.4.4.D
      derivatives, Ch. 54, 7.4.4.A
      disclosure requirements, Ch. 54, 7.4.2.C
      enforceable legal right of set-off, Ch. 54, 7.4.1.A
      entities whose share capital is not equity, Ch. 54, 7.4.6
      equity, Ch. 54, 7.4.5
      intention to settle net, Ch. 54, 7.4.1.C
      loan covenants, Ch. 54, 7.4.4.E
      long-term loans with repayment on demand terms, Ch. 54, 7.4.4.C
      master netting agreements, Ch. 54, 7.4.1.B
      objective, Ch. 54, 7.4.2.A
      offsetting collateral amounts, Ch. 54, 7.4.1.F
      offsetting financial assets and financial liabilities, Ch. 54, 7.4.1
      offsetting financial assets and financial liabilities: disclosure, Ch. 54, 7.4.2
      scope, Ch. 54, 7.4.2.B
      situations where offset is not normally appropriate, Ch. 54, 7.4.1.D
      unit of account, Ch. 54, 7.4.1.G
  significance of financial instruments for an entity's financial position/performance, Ch. 54, 4
    accounting policies, Ch. 54, 4.1
    business combinations, Ch. 54, 4.6
      acquired receivables, Ch. 54, 4.6.1
      contingent consideration and indemnification assets, Ch. 54, 4.6.2
    fair values, Ch. 54, 4.5
      day 1 profits, Ch. 54, 4.5.2
      general disclosure requirements, Ch. 54, 4.5.1
    hedge accounting, Ch. 54, 4.3
      amount, timing and uncertainty of future cash flows, Ch. 54, 4.3.2
      effects of hedge accounting on financial position and performance, Ch. 54, 4.3.3
      option to designate a credit exposure as measured at fair value through profit/loss, Ch. 54, 4.3.4
      risk management strategy, Ch. 54, 4.3.1
      uncertainty arising from interest rate benchmark (or IBOR) reform, Ch. 54, 4.3.5
    income, expenses, gains and losses, Ch. 54, 4.2
      fee income and expense, Ch. 54, 4.2.3
      gains and losses by measurement category, Ch. 54, 4.2.1
      interest income and expense, Ch. 54, 4.2.2
    statement of financial position, Ch. 54, 4.4
      categories of financial assets and financial liabilities, Ch. 54, 4.4.1
      collateral, Ch. 54, 4.4.6
      compound financial instruments with multiple embedded derivatives, Ch. 54, 4.4.7
      defaults and breaches of loans payable, Ch. 54, 4.4.8
      financial assets designated as measured at fair value through profit/loss, Ch. 54, 4.4.3
      financial liabilities designated at fair value through profit/loss, Ch. 54, 4.4.2
      interests in associates and joint ventures accounted for in accordance with IFRS 9, Ch. 54, 4.4.9
      investments in equity instruments designated at fair value through other comprehensive income (IFRS 9), Ch. 54, 4.4.4
      reclassification, Ch. 54, 4.4.5
  transfers of financial assets, Ch. 54, 6
    meaning of 'transfer,' Ch. 54, 6.1

transferred financial assets that are derecognised in their entirety, Ch. 54, 6.3
    disclosure requirements, Ch. 54, 6.3.2
    meaning of continuing involvement, Ch. 54, 6.3.1
transferred financial assets that are not derecognised in their entirety, Ch. 54, 6.2
transitional provisions, Ch. 54, 8

IFRS 8–*Operating Segments*, Ch. 36, 1–6. *See also* Operating segments; Reportable segments
  definition of an operating segment, Ch. 36, 3.1.3
    availability of discrete financial information, Ch. 36, 1.3
    'chief operating decision maker' and 'segment manager,' Ch. 36, 3.1.2
    equity accounted investment can be an operating segment, Ch. 36, 3.1.5
    revenue earning business activities, Ch. 36, 3.1.1
    when a single set of components is not immediately apparent, Ch. 36, 3.1.4
  entity-wide disclosures for all entities, Ch. 36, 6
    information about geographical areas, Ch. 36, 6.2
    information about major customers, Ch. 36, 6.3
      customers known to be under common control, Ch. 36, 6.3.1
    information about products and services, Ch. 36, 6.1
  externally reportable segments, identifying, Ch. 36, 3.2
    aggregation criteria, Ch. 36, 3.2.1
    'all other segments,' Ch. 36, 3.2.4
    combining small operating segments into a larger reportable segment, Ch. 36, 3.2.3
    'practical limit' for the number of reported operating segments, Ch. 36, 3.2.5
    restatement of segments reported in comparative periods, Ch. 36, 3.2.6
    quantitative thresholds, operating segments which are reportable because of their size, Ch. 36, 3.2.2
  features of IFRS 8, Ch. 36, 1.2
  measurement, Ch. 36, 4
  objective of IFRS 8, Ch. 36, 2.1
  reportable segments, information to be disclosed, Ch. 36, 5
    additional disclosures relating to segment assets, Ch. 36, 5.4
    disclosures required by IFRS 15, Ch. 36, 1.3
    disclosure of commercially sensitive information, Ch. 36, 5.8
    disclosure of other elements of revenue, income and expense, Ch. 36, 5.3
    explanation of the measurements used in segment reporting, Ch. 36, 5.5
    general information about reportable segments, Ch. 36, 5.1
      disclosure of how operating segments are aggregated, Ch. 36, 5.1.1
    measure of segment profit or loss, total assets and total liabilities, Ch. 36, 5.2
    reconciliations, Ch. 36, 5.6
    restatement of previously reported information, Ch. 36, 5.7
      changes in organisation structure, Ch. 36, 5.7.1
      changes in segment measures, Ch. 36, 5.7.2
  scope of IFRS 8, Ch. 36, 2.2

    consolidated financial statements presented with those of the parent, Ch. 36, 2.2.2
    entities providing segment information on a voluntary basis, Ch. 36, 2.2.3
    meaning of 'traded in a public market', Ch. 36, 2.2.1
  single set of operating segments, identifying, Ch. 36, 3
  terms used in IFRS 8, Ch. 36, 1.4
  transitional provisions, Ch. 36, 1.5

IFRS 9–*Financial Instruments*, Ch. 44, 5; Ch. 48, 1–9; Ch. 49, 1–3. *See also* Financial instruments, classification (IFRS 9); Financial instruments, hedge accounting (IFRS 9); Financial instruments, subsequent measurement (IFRS 9)
  amortised cost and the effective interest method, Ch. 50, 3
    fixed interest, fixed term instruments, Ch. 50, 3.2
    floating rate instruments, Ch. 50, 3.3
    inflation-linked debt, Ch. 50, 3.6
    modified financial assets and liabilities, Ch. 50, 3.8
    more complex financial liabilities, Ch. 50, 3.7
    perpetual debt instruments, Ch. 50, 3.5
    prepayment, call and similar options, Ch. 50, 3.4
      estimated cash flows, revisions to, Ch. 50, 3.4.1
  'business model' assessment, Ch. 48, 5
    applying in practice, Ch. 48, 5.6
    consolidated and subsidiary accounts, Ch. 48, 5.5
    hold to collect contractual cash flows, Ch. 48, 5.2
      impact of sales on the assessment, Ch. 48, 5.2.1
    hold to collect contractual cash flows and selling financial assets, Ch. 48, 5.3
    level at which the business model assessment is applied, Ch. 48, 5.1
    transferred financial assets that are not derecognised, Ch. 48, 5.2.2
  classification, Ch. 48, 2
  contractual cash flows, Ch. 48, 6
    auction rate securities, Ch. 48, 6.4.4
    bonds with a capped or floored interest rate, Ch. 48, 6.3.3
    contractual features that change the timing or amount, Ch. 48, 6.4.4
    contractually linked instruments, Ch. 48, 6.6
      assessing the characteristics of the underlying pool, Ch. 48, 6.6.1
      assessing the exposure to credit risk in the tranche held, Ch. 48, 6.6.2
      characteristics of underlying pool, assessing, Ch. 48, 6.6.1
      exposure to credit risk in the tranche held, assessing, Ch. 48, 6.6.2
    conventional subordination features, Ch. 48, 6.3.1
    convertible debt, Ch. 48, 6.4.5
    de minimis features, Ch. 48, 6.4.1.A
    debt covenants, Ch. 48, 6.4.4
    dual currency instruments, Ch. 48, 6.4.5
    five-year constant maturity bond, Ch. 48, 6.4.2
    fixed rate bond prepayable by the issuer at fair value, Ch. 48, 6.4.5
    full recourse loans secured by collateral, Ch. 48, 6.3.2
    interest rate period, Ch. 48, 6.4.2
    inverse floater, Ch. 48, 6.4.5
    investment in open-ended money market or debt funds, Ch. 48, 6.4.5

IFRS 9–*Financial Instruments*—*contd*
  contractual cash flows—*contd*
    lender has discretion to change the interest rate, Ch. 48, 6.3.4
    loan commitments, Ch. 48, 6.4.6
    meaning of 'interest,' Ch. 48, 6.2
    meaning of 'principal,' Ch. 48, 6.1
    modified time value of money component, Ch. 48, 6.4.2
    multiple of a benchmark interest rate, Ch. 48, 6.4.5
    non-genuine features, Ch. 48, 6.4.1.B
    non-recourse loans, Ch. 48, 6.5
    perpetual instruments with potentially deferrable coupons, Ch. 48, 6.4.5
    prepayment, asset originated at a premium of discount, Ch. 48, 6.4.4.B
    prepayment, negative compensation, Ch. 48, 6.4.4.A
    prepayment options, Ch. 48, 6.4.4
    regulated interest rates, Ch. 48, 6.4.3
    term extension options, Ch. 48, 6.4.4
    unleveraged inflation-linked bonds, Ch. 48, 6.3.5
    variable interest rate, Ch. 48, 6.4.4
  designation at fair value through profit or loss, Ch. 48, 7
  designation of contracts to buy or sell a non-financial item, Ch. 5, 5.23
  designation of non-derivative equity investments at fair value through other comprehensive income, Ch. 48, 8
  fair value option for own use contracts, Ch. 45, 4.2.6
  financial assets and liabilities held for trading, Ch. 48, 4
  financial assets classification, Ch. 48, 2
    debt instruments, Ch. 48, 2.1
    equity instruments and derivatives, Ch. 48, 2.2
  financial instruments within the scope of, Ch. 8, 4.4.5
  financial liabilities classification, Ch. 48, 3
  IFRS 4 applying IFRS 9 with, Ch. 55, 10
    interest rate benchmark reform Ch. 55, 10.1.6
    overlay approach, Ch. 55, 10.2
    temporary exemption from IFRS 9, Ch. 55, 10.1
  impairment
    approaches, Ch. 51, 3
      general approach, Ch. 51, 3.1
        purchased/originated credit-impaired financial assets, Ch. 51, 3.3
        simplified approach, Ch. 51, 3.2
      calculation of expected credit losses (ECLs), other matters, Ch. 51, 7
        Basel guidance on accounting for ECLs, Ch. 51, 7.1
        changes in ECL methodologies – errors, changes in estimates or changes in accounting policies, Ch. 51, 7.6
        Global Public Policy Committee (GPPC) guidance, Ch. 51, 7.2
        interaction between expected credit losses calculations and fair value hedge accounting, Ch. 51, 7.5
        interaction between the initial and subsequent measurement of debt instruments acquired in a business combination and the impairment model of IFRS 9, Ch. 51, 7.4
        measurement dates of ECLs, Ch. 51, 7.3
          date of derecognition and date of initial recognition, Ch. 51, 7.3.1
          trade date and settlement date accounting, Ch. 51, 7.3.2
      determining significant increases in credit risk, Ch. 51, 6
        change in the risk of a default occurring, Ch. 51, 6.1
        collective assessment, Ch. 51, 6.5
        definition of significant, Ch. 51, 6.3
        factors/indicators of changes in credit risk, Ch. 51, 6.2
        at initial recognition of an identical group of financial assets, Ch. 51, 6.6
        multiple scenarios for 'staging' assessment, Ch. 51, 6.7
        operational simplifications, Ch. 51, 6.4
      disclosures, Ch. 51, 15
      expected credit losses measurement
        credit enhancements: collateral and financial guarantees, Ch. 51, 5.8.1
        definition of default, Ch. 51, 5.1
        expected life *vs.* contractual period, Ch. 51, 5.5
        information about past events, current conditions and forecasts of future economic conditions, Ch. 51, 5.9.3
        lifetime expected credit losses, Ch. 51, 5.2
        12-month expected credit losses, Ch. 51, 6.4.3
        probability-weighted outcome, Ch. 51, 5.6
        reasonable and supportable information, Ch. 51, 5.9
        sources of information, Ch. 51, 5.9.2
        time value of money, Ch. 51, 5.7
        undue cost/effort, Ch. 51, 5.9.1
      financial assets measured at fair value through other comprehensive income, Ch. 51, 9
        debt instruments measured at fair value through other comprehensive income, Ch. 51, 9.1
      financial guarantee contracts, Ch. 51, 11
      Global Public Policy Committee guidance, Ch. 51, 7.2
      history and background, Ch. 51, 1.1
      IFRS Transition Resource Group for Impairment of Financial Instruments (ITG), Ch. 51, 1.5
      intercompany loans, Ch. 51, 13
        determining the ECLs, Ch. 51, 13.3
        repayable on demand, Ch. 51, 13.2
        scope, Ch. 51, 13.1
      key changes from the IAS 39 impairment requirements and the main implications of these changes, Ch. 51, 1.3
      key differences from the FASB's standard, Ch. 51, 1.4 lease receivables, Ch. 51, 10.2
      lease receivables, Ch. 51, 10.2
      loan commitments and financial guarantee contracts, Ch. 51, 11
      measurement dates of expected credit losses, Ch. 51, 7.3
        date of derecognition and date of initial recognition, Ch. 51, 7.3.1
        trade date and settlement date accounting, Ch. 51, 7.3.2
      modified financial assets, Ch. 51, 8
      other guidance on expected credit losses, Ch. 51, 1.6
      presentation of expected credit losses in the statement of financial position, Ch. 51, 14
        accumulated impairment amount for debt instruments measured at fair value through other comprehensive income, Ch. 51, 14.3

allowance for financial assets measured at amortised cost, contract assets and lease receivables, Ch. 51, 14.1
provisions for loan commitments and financial guarantee contracts, Ch. 51, 14.2
requirements, Ch. 51, 1.2
revolving credit facilities, Ch. 51, 12
scope, Ch. 51, 2
trade receivables, contract assets and lease receivables, Ch. 51, 10
    lease receivables, Ch. 51, 10.2
    trade receivables and contract assets, Ch. 51, 10.1
initial measurement, Ch. 49, 3
acquisition of a group of assets that does not constitute a business, Ch. 49, 3.3.5
assets and liabilities arising from loan commitments, Ch. 49, 3.7
    loan commitments outside the scope of IFRS 9, Ch. 49, 3.7.1
    loan commitments within the scope of IFRS 9, Ch. 49, 3.7.2
embedded derivatives and financial instrument hosts, Ch. 49, 3.5
general requirements, Ch. 49, 3.1
initial fair value and 'day 1' profits, Ch. 49, 3.3
    financial guarantee contracts and off-market loan commitments, Ch. 49, 3.3.3
    interest-free and low-interest long-term loans, Ch. 49, 3.3.1
    loans and receivables acquired in a business combination, Ch. 49, 3.3.4
    measurement of financial instruments following modification of contractual terms that leads to initial recognition of a new instrument, Ch. 49, 3.3.2
regular way transactions, Ch. 49, 3.6
trade receivables without a significant financing component, Ch. 49, 3.2
transaction costs, Ch. 49, 3.4
interests in associates and joint ventures accounted for in accordance with IFRS 9, Ch. 54, 4.4.9
reclassification of financial assets, Ch. 48, 9
recognition, Ch. 49, 2
general requirements, Ch. 49, 2.1
    cash collateral, Ch. 49, 2.1.7
    firm commitments to purchase/sell goods/services, Ch. 49, 2.1.2
    forward contracts, Ch. 49, 2.1.3
    option contracts, Ch. 49, 2.1.4
    planned future/forecast transactions, Ch. 49, 2.1.5
    principal *vs.* agent, Ch. 49, 2.1.8
    receivables and payables, Ch. 49, 2.1.1
    transfers of financial assets not qualifying for derecognition by transferor, Ch. 49, 2.1.6
'regular way' transactions, Ch. 49, 2.2
    financial assets: general requirements, Ch. 49, 2.2.1
        contracts not settled according to marketplace convention: derivatives, Ch. 49, 2.2.1.B
        exercise of a derivative, Ch. 49, 2.2.1.D
        multiple active markets: settlement provisions, Ch. 49, 2.2.1.C
        no established market, Ch. 49, 2.2.1.A
    financial liabilities, Ch. 49, 2.2.2
    illustrative examples, Ch. 49, 2.2.5
    settlement date accounting, Ch. 49, 2.2.4
    trade date accounting, Ch. 49, 2.2.3

IFRS 10–*Consolidated Financial Statements*, Ch. 6, 1–11. *See also* Consolidated financial statements, consolidation procedures
continuous assessment, Ch. 6, 9
control, Ch. 6, 3
control of specified assets, Ch. 6, 8
development of IFRS 10, Ch. 6, 1.2
disclosure requirements, Ch. 6, 1.4
exposure to variable returns, Ch. 6, 5
future developments, Ch. 6, 11
investment entities, Ch. 6, 10
    accounting by a parent of an investment entity, Ch. 6, 10.4
    accounting by an investment entity, Ch. 6, 10.3
    definition, Ch. 6, 10.1
    determining whether an entity is an investment entity, Ch. 6, 10.2
        earnings from investments, Ch. 6, 10.2.3
        exit strategies, Ch. 6, 10.2.2
        fair value measurement, Ch. 6, 10.2.4
        having more than one investor, Ch. 6, 10.2.6
        holding more than one investment, Ch. 6, 10.2.5
        intermediate holding companies established for tax optimisation purposes, Ch. 6, 10.2.1.B
        investment entity illustrative examples, Ch. 6, 10.2.9
        investment-related services, Ch. 6, 10.2.1.A
        multi-layered fund structures, Ch. 6, 10.2.10
        ownership interests, Ch. 6, 10.2.8
        unrelated investors, Ch. 6, 10.2.7
objective of, Ch. 6, 2.1
power and returns, principal-agency situations, Ch. 6, 6
    application examples, Ch. 6, 6.6–6.7
    delegated power: principals and agents, Ch. 6, 6.1
    exposure to variability of returns from other interests, Ch. 6, 6.5
    remuneration, Ch. 6, 6.4
    rights held by other parties, Ch. 6, 6.3
    scope of decision-making, Ch. 6, 6.2
power over an investee, Ch. 6, 4
    contractual arrangements, Ch. 6, 4.4
    determining whether sponsoring (designing) a structured entity gives power, Ch. 6, 4.6
    existing rights, Ch. 6, 4.2
    relevant activities, Ch. 6, 4.1
    voting rights, Ch. 6, 4.3
related parties and de facto agents, Ch. 6, 7
scope, Ch. 6, 2.2
    combined and carve-out financial statements, Ch. 6, 2.2.6
    employee benefit plans and employee share trusts, Ch. 6, 2.2.2
    entity no longer a parent at the end of the reporting period, Ch. 6, 2.2.4
    exemption from preparing consolidated financial statements by an intermediate parent, Ch. 6, 2.2.1
    interaction of IFRS 10 and EU law, Ch. 6, 2.2.5
    investment entity exception, Ch. 6, 2.2.3

IFRS 11–*Joint Arrangements*, Ch. 12, 1–10. *See also* Joint arrangements
- accounting for joint operations, Ch. 12, 6
  - accounting for rights and obligations, Ch. 12, 6.2
  - determining the relevant IFRS, Ch. 12, 6.3
  - interest in a joint operation without joint control, Ch. 12, 6.4
  - not structured through a separate vehicle, Ch. 12, 6.1
  - in separate financial statements, Ch. 12, 6.7
  - transactions between a joint operator and a joint operation, Ch. 12, 6.6
- accounting for joint ventures, Ch. 12, 7
  - contributions of non-monetary assets to a joint venture, Ch. 12, 7.2
  - interest in a joint venture without joint control, Ch. 12, 7.1
  - in separate financial statements, Ch. 12, 7.3
- classification of, Ch. 12, 5
  - accompanying IFRS 11, illustrative examples, Ch. 12, 5.5
  - contractual terms, Ch. 12, 5.3
  - facts and circumstances, Ch. 12, 5.4
  - legal form of the separate vehicle, Ch. 12, 5.2
  - separate vehicle or not, Ch. 12, 5.1
- continuous assessment, Ch. 12, 8
  - changes in ownership of a joint arrangement that does not constitute a business, Ch. 12, 8.4
  - changes in ownership of a joint operation, Ch. 12, 8.3
    - acquisition of an interest in a joint operation, Ch. 12, 8.3.1
    - disposal of interest in a joint operation, Ch. 12, 8.3.5
    - former subsidiary becomes a joint operation, Ch. 7, 3.3.3, 7.2; Ch. 12, 8.3.3
    - obtaining control or joint control over a joint operation that is a business, Ch. 12, 8.3.2
    - other changes in ownership of a joint operation, Ch. 12, 8.3.4
  - changes in ownership of a joint venture, Ch. 12, 8.2
    - acquisition of an interest, Ch. 12, 8.2.1
    - becomes a financial asset (or vice versa), Ch. 12, 8.2.5
    - becomes an associate (or vice versa), Ch. 12, 8.2.4
    - control over a joint venture, Ch. 12, 8.3.2
    - disposal of interest in, Ch. 12, 8.2.6
    - former subsidiary becomes a joint venture, Ch. 7, 3.3.2, 7.1; Ch. 12, 8.3.3
    - interest in a joint venture held for sale, Ch. 12, 8.2.7
  - when to reassess under IFRS 11, Ch. 12, 8.1
- disclosures, Ch. 12, 9
- future developments, Ch. 12, 10
- joint control, Ch. 12, 4
  - practical issues with assessing, Ch. 12, 4.4
    - evaluate multiple agreements together, Ch. 12, 4.4.2
    - lease/joint arrangement, Ch. 12, 4.4.1
  - relevant activities in sequential activities, Ch. 12, 4.1.1
  - rights to control collectively, Ch. 12, 4.2
    - delegated decision-making, Ch. 12, 4.2.4
    - evidence of, Ch. 12, 4.2.3
    - government, role of, Ch. 12, 4.2.6
    - potential voting rights and joint control, Ch. 12, 4.2.2
    - protective rights, including some veto rights, Ch. 12, 4.2.1
    - related parties and de facto agents, Ch. 12, 4.2.5
  - sequential activities in, Ch. 12, 4.1.1
  - unanimous consent, Ch. 12, 4.3
    - arbitration, Ch. 12, 4.3.3
    - arrangements involving passive investors, Ch. 12, 4.3.1
    - statutory mechanisms, Ch. 12, 4.3.4
    - ultimate voting authority, Ch. 12, 4.3.2
- nature of joint arrangements, Ch. 12, 1.1
- objective, Ch. 12, 2.1
- scope, Ch. 12, 2.2
  - accounting by a joint operation, Ch. 12, 2.2.3
  - application by venture capital organisations and similar entities, Ch. 12, 2.2.1
  - application to joint arrangements held for sale, Ch. 12, 2.2.2

IFRS 12–*Disclosure of Interests in Other Entities*, Ch. 13, 1–6. *See also* Disclosure of interests in other entities
- definitions, Ch. 13, 2.2.1
  - interaction of IFRS 12 and IFRS 5, Ch. 13, 2.2.1.C
  - interests in other entities, Ch. 13, 2.2.1.A
  - structured entities, Ch. 13, 2.2.1, 2.2.1.B
- interests disclosed under, Ch. 13, 2.2.2
- interests not within the scope of, Ch. 13, 2.2.3
- joint arrangements and associates, Ch. 13, 5
  - nature, extent and financial effects, Ch. 13, 5.1
  - risks associated with, Ch. 13, 5.2
    - commitments relating to joint ventures, Ch. 13, 5.2.1
    - contingent liabilities relating to joint ventures and associates, Ch. 13, 5.2.2
- significant judgements and assumptions, Ch. 13, 3
- objective, Ch. 13, 2.1
- scope, Ch. 13, 2.2
- subsidiaries, Ch. 13, 4
  - changes in ownership interests in subsidiaries, Ch. 13, 4.5
  - composition of the group, Ch. 13, 4.1
  - consolidated structured entities, nature of risks, Ch. 13, 4.4
    - current intentions to provide financial or other support, Ch. 13, 4.4.4
    - financial or other support to, with no contractual obligation, Ch. 13, 4.4.2
    - terms of contractual arrangements, Ch. 13, 4.4.1
  - nature and extent of significant restrictions, Ch. 13, 4.3
  - non-controlling interests, Ch. 13, 4.2
- unconsolidated structured entities, Ch. 13, 6
  - nature of interests, Ch. 13, 6.1
    - nature, purpose, size, activities and financing of structured entities, Ch. 13, 6.1.1
    - sponsored structured entities for which no interest is held at the reporting date, Ch. 13, 6.1.2
  - nature of risks, Ch. 13, 6.2–6.3
    - actual and intended financial and other support to structured entities, Ch. 13, 6.2.2
    - disclosure of funding difficulties, Ch. 13, 6.3.6
    - disclosure of liquidity arrangements, Ch. 13, 6.3.5
    - disclosure of losses, Ch. 13, 6.3.2
    - disclosure of ranking and amounts of potential losses, Ch. 13, 6.3.4
    - disclosure of support, Ch. 13, 6.3.1
    - disclosure of the forms of funding of an unconsolidated structured entity, Ch. 13, 6.3.7

disclosure of types of income received, Ch. 13, 6.3.3
maximum exposure to loss from those interests, Ch. 13, 6.2.1

IFRS 13–*Fair Value Measurement*, Ch. 14, 1–23. *See also* Fair value; Fair value measurement; Valuation techniques
asset/liability, Ch. 14, 5
  characteristics, Ch. 14, 5.2
    condition and location, Ch. 14, 5.2.1
    restrictions on assets or liabilities, Ch. 14, 5.2.2
  unit of account, Ch. 14, 5.1
    asset's (or liability's) components, Ch. 14, 5.1.4
    and portfolio exception, Ch. 14, 5.1.2
    and PxQ, Ch. 7, 3.3.2.F; Ch. 14, 5.1.1
    vs. valuation premise, Ch. 14, 5.1.3
convergence with US GAAP, Ch. 14, 22
  disclosures, Ch. 14, 22.2.4
  fair value of liabilities with demand feature, Ch. 14, 22.2.2
  practical expedient for alternative investments, Ch. 14, 22.2.1
  recognition of day-one gains and losses, Ch. 14, 22.2.3
definitions, Ch. 14, 3
development of, Ch. 14, 22.1
disclosures, Ch. 14, 20
  accounting policy, Ch. 14, 20.2
  objectives, Ch. 14, 20.1
    format of, Ch. 14, 20.1.1
    level of disaggregation, Ch. 14, 20.1.2
    'recurring' *vs.* 'non-recurring', Ch. 14, 20.1.3
  proposed amendments resulting from the Targeted Standards-level, Ch. 14, 20.6
  for recognised fair value measurements, Ch. 14, 20.3
    fair value hierarchy categorisation, Ch. 14, 20.3.3
    highest and best use, Ch. 14, 20.3.9
    level 3 reconciliation, Ch. 14, 20.3.6
    non-recurring fair value measurements, Ch. 14, 20.3.2
    recurring fair value measurements, Ch. 14, 20.3.1
    sensitivity of level 3 measurements to changes in significant unobservable inputs, Ch. 14, 20.3.8
    transfers between hierarchy levels for recurring fair value measurements, Ch. 14, 20.3.4
    of valuation processes for level 3 measurements, Ch. 14, 20.3.7
    valuation techniques and inputs, Ch. 14, 20.3.5
  regarding liabilities issued with an inseparable third-party credit enhancement, Ch. 14, 20.5
  for unrecognised fair value measurements, Ch. 14, 20.4
fair value framework, Ch. 14, 4
  definition, Ch. 14, 4.1
  measurement, Ch. 14, 4.2
financial assets and liabilities with offsetting positions, Ch. 14, 12
  criteria for using the portfolio approach for offsetting positions
    accounting policy considerations, Ch. 14, 12.1.1
    level 1 instruments in, Ch. 14, 12.1.4
    minimum level of offset, to use portfolio approach, Ch. 14, 12.1.3
    presentation considerations, Ch. 14, 12.1.2
  measuring fair value for offsetting positions
    exposure to market risks, Ch. 14, 12.2.1
    exposure to the credit risk of a particular counterparty, Ch. 14, 12.2.2
hierarchy, Ch. 14, 16
  categorisation within, Ch. 14, 16.2
    over-the-counter derivative instruments, Ch. 14, 16.2.4
    significance of inputs, assessing, Ch. 14, 16.2.1
    third-party pricing services/brokers, Ch. 14, 16.2.3
    transfers between levels within, Ch. 14, 16.2.2
IFRS 13, objective of, Ch. 14, 1.3
IFRS 13, overview, Ch. 14, 1.2
at initial recognition, Ch. 14, 13
  day one gains and losses, Ch. 14, 13.2
    losses for over-the-counter derivative transactions, Ch. 14, 13.2.1
    when entry and exit markets are the same, Ch. 14, 13.2.2
  exit price *vs.* entry price, Ch. 14, 13.1
  related party transactions, Ch. 14, 13.3
inputs to valuation techniques, Ch. 14, 15
  broker quotes and pricing services, Ch. 14, 15.5
  general principles, Ch. 14, 15.1
  premiums and discounts, Ch. 14, 15.2
    blockage factors (or block discounts), Ch. 14, 15.2.1
  pricing within the bid-ask spread bid-ask spread, Ch. 14, 15.3
    mid-market pricing, Ch. 14, 15.3.1
  risk premiums, Ch. 14, 15.4
level 1 inputs, Ch. 14, 17
  alternative pricing methods, Ch. 14, 17.2
  quoted prices in active markets that are not representative of, Ch. 14, 17.3
  unit of account, Ch. 14, 17.4
  use of, Ch. 14, 17.1
level 2 inputs, Ch. 14, 18
  examples of, Ch. 14, 18.2
  making adjustments to, Ch. 14, 18.4
  market corroborated inputs, Ch. 14, 18.3
  recently observed prices in an inactive market, Ch. 14, 18.5
level 3 inputs, Ch. 14, 19
  examples of, Ch. 14, 19.2
  use of, Ch. 14, 19.1
liabilities and an entity's own equity, application to, Ch. 14, 11
  financial liability with demand feature, Ch. 14, 11.5
  non-performance risk, Ch. 14, 11.3
    counterparty credit risk and its own credit risk, Ch. 14, 11.3.2
    derivative liabilities, Ch. 14, 11.3.4
    entity incorporate credit risk into the valuation of its derivative contracts, Ch. 14, 11.3.3
    with third-party credit enhancements, Ch. 14, 11.3.1
  not held by other parties as assets, Ch. 14, 11.2.2
  principles, Ch. 14, 11.1
    fair value of an entity's own equity, Ch. 14, 11.1.2
    fair value of a liability, Ch. 14, 11.1.1
    settlement value *vs.* transfer value, Ch. 14, 11.1.3
  restrictions preventing the transfer of, Ch. 14, 11.1
  that are held by other parties as assets, Ch. 14, 11.2.1
market participants, Ch. 14, 7

IFRS 13–*Fair Value Measurement*—*contd*
market participants—*contd*
assumptions, Ch. 14, 7.2
characteristics, Ch. 14, 7.1
measurement exception to the fair value principles for financial instruments, Ch. 14, 2.5.2
non-financial assets, application to, Ch. 14, 10
highest and best use, Ch. 14, 10.1
vs. current use, Ch. 14, 10.1.2
vs. intended use, Ch. 14, 10.1.3
legally permissible, Ch. 14, 10.1.1
valuation premise, Ch. 14, 10.2
in combination with other assets and/or liabilities, Ch. 14, 10.2.2
liabilities association, Ch. 14, 10.2.3
stand-alone basis, Ch. 14, 10.2.1 unit of account *vs.*, Ch. 14, 10.2.4
practical expedient in, Ch. 14, 2.5.1
present value technique, Ch. 14, 21
components of, Ch. 14, 21.2
risk and uncertainty in, Ch. 14, 21.2.2
time value of money, Ch. 14, 21.2.1
discount rate adjustment technique, Ch. 14, 21.3
expected present value technique, Ch. 14, 21.4
general principles for use of, Ch. 14, 21.1
price, Ch. 14, 9
transaction costs, Ch. 14, 9.1
transportation costs, Ch. 14, 9.2
principal (or most advantageous) market, Ch. 14, 6
scope, Ch. 14, 2
exclusions, Ch. 14, 2.2
disclosure requirements of IFRS 13, exemptions from, Ch. 14, 2.2.4
lease transactions, Ch. 14, 2.2.2
measurements similar to fair value, Ch. 14, 2.2.3
share-based payments, Ch. 14, 2.2.1
fair value measurement exceptions, Ch. 14, 2.4
IFRS 13, items in, Ch. 14, 2.1
fair value disclosures, Ch. 14, 2.1.1
fair value measurements, Ch. 14, 2.1.2
short-term receivables and payables, Ch. 14, 2.1.3
practical expedient for impaired financial assets carried at amortised cost, Ch. 14, 2.4.2
present value techniques, Ch. 14, 2.3
transaction, Ch. 14, 8
estimation, Ch. 14, 8.3
identification, Ch. 14, 8.2
volume and level of activity for an asset/liability, Ch. 14, 8.1
unit of account, Ch. 14, 5
asset's (or liability's) components, Ch. 14, 5.1.4
level 1 assets and liabilities, Ch. 14, 17.4
and portfolio exception, Ch. 14, 5.1.2
and PxQ, Ch. 7, 3.3.2.F; Ch. 14, 5.1.1
vs. valuation premise, Ch. 14, 5.1.3
valuation techniques, Ch. 14, 14
cost approach, Ch. 14, 14.3
income approach, Ch. 14, 14.4
market approach, Ch. 14, 14.2
selecting appropriate, Ch. 14, 14.1

making changes to valuation techniques, Ch. 14, 14.1.4
single *vs.* multiple valuation techniques, Ch. 14, 14.1.1
using multiple valuation techniques to measure fair value, Ch. 14, 14.1.2
valuation adjustments, Ch. 14, 14.1.3
IFRS 14–*Regulatory Deferral Accounts*, Ch. 5, 5.20; Ch. 26, 5.4
changes in accounting policies, Ch. 5, 5.20.5
continuation of previous GAAP accounting policies, Ch. 5, 5.20.3
defined terms, Ch. 5, 5.20.1
disclosures, Ch. 5, 5.20.7
interaction with other standards, Ch. 5, 5.20.8
presentation, Ch. 5, 5.20.6
recognition of regulatory deferral account balances, Ch. 5, 5.20.4
scope, Ch. 5, 5.20.2
IFRS 15–*Revenue recognition*, Ch. 27, 1–4; Ch. 28, 1–3; Ch. 29, 1–3; Ch. 30, 1–11; Ch. 31, 1–5; Ch. 32, 1–4. *See also* Revenue recognition
allocate the transaction price to the performance obligations, Ch. 29, 3
allocating a discount, Ch. 29, 3.4
allocating variable consideration, Ch. 29, 3.3
allocation of transaction price to components outside the scope of IFRS 15, Ch. 29, 3.6
applying the relative stand-alone selling price method, Ch. 29, 3.2
changes in transaction price after contract inception, Ch. 29, 3.5
determining stand-alone selling prices, Ch. 29, 3.1
additional considerations for determining, Ch. 29, 3.1.4
factors to consider when estimating, Ch. 29, 3.1.1
measurement of options that are separate performance obligations, Ch. 29, 3.1.5
possible estimation approaches, Ch. 29, 3.1.2
updating estimated, Ch. 29, 3.1.3
relative stand-alone selling price method, Ch. 29, 3.2
variable consideration allocation, Ch. 29, 3.3
definitions, Ch. 27, 2.2
determine the transaction price, Ch. 29, 2
changes in the transaction price, Ch. 29, 2.9
consideration paid/payable to a customer, Ch. 29, 2.7
classification of different types and measurement of, Ch. 29, 2.7.3
determining who is an entity's customer when applying the requirements for consideration payable to a customer, Ch. 29, 2.7.1
forms of, Ch. 29, 2.7.2
timing of recognition of, Ch. 29, 2.7.4
non-cash consideration, Ch. 29, 2.6
non-refundable upfront fees, Ch. 29, 2.8
refund liabilities, Ch. 29, 2.3
rights of return, Ch. 29, 2.4
significant financing component, Ch. 29, 2.5
application questions on identifying and accounting for, Ch. 29, 2.5.2
examples of, Ch. 29, 2.5.1

financial statement presentation of financing component, Ch. 29, 2.5.3
    implementation questions on identifying and accounting for, Ch. 29, 2.5.2
  variable consideration, Ch. 29, 2.2
    constraining estimates of, Ch. 29, 2.2.3
    estimating, Ch. 29, 2.2.2
    forms, Ch. 29, 2.2.1
    reassessment of, Ch. 29, 2.2.4
disposal of non-financial assets not in the ordinary course of business, Ch. 27, 4.3
  sale of assets held for rental, Ch. 27, 4.3.1
extractive industries, Ch. 43, 12
income and distributable profits, Ch. 27, 4.1
interest and dividends, Ch. 27, 4.2
identify the contract with the customer, Ch. 28, 2
  arrangements not meeting the definition of a contract under the standard, Ch. 28, 2.5
  attributes of a contract, Ch. 28, 2.1
    collectability, Ch. 28, 2.1.6
    commercial substance, Ch. 28, 2.1.5
    consideration of side agreements, Ch. 28, 2.1.1.C
    each party's rights regarding the goods/services to be transferred can be identified, Ch. 28, 2.1.3
    free trial period, Ch. 28, 2.1.1.B
    master supply arrangements (MSA), Ch. 28, 2.1.1.A
    parties have approved the contract and are committed to perform their respective obligations, Ch. 28, 2.1.2
    payment terms can be identified, Ch. 28, 2.1.4
  combining contracts, Ch. 28, 2.3
    portfolio approach practical expedient, Ch. 28, 2.3.1
  contract enforceability and termination clauses, Ch. 28, 2.2
    consideration that was received from a customer, but not recognised as revenue, when contract is cancelled, accounting for, Ch. 28, 2.2.1 E
    evaluating termination clauses, Ch. 28, 2.2.1.A
    evaluating the contract term when an entity has a past practice of not enforcing termination payments, Ch. 28, 2.2.1.C
    partial termination of a contract, accounting for, Ch. 28, 2.2.1.D
    termination payments in determining the contract term, Ch. 28, 2.2.1.A
  contract modifications, Ch. 28, 2.4
    blend-and-extend, accounting for, Ch. 28, 2.4.3.F
    decrease scope of the contract, Ch. 28, 2.4.3.E
    marketing offer, Ch. 28. 2.4.3. D
    not a separate contract, Ch. 28, 2.4.2
    reassessing criteria if contract modified, Ch. 28, 2.4.3.B
    represents a separate contract, Ch. 28, 2.4.1
identify the performance obligations in the contract, Ch. 28, 3
  consignment arrangements, Ch. 28, 3.5
  customer options for additional goods/services, Ch. 28, 3.6
    accounting for the exercise of a material right, Ch. 28, 3.6.1.J
    considering whether prospective volume discounts determined to be customer options are material rights, Ch. 28, 3.6.1.G
    customer option as a separate performance obligation when there are no contractual penalties, Ch. 28, 3.6.1.D
  customer options that provide a material right: evaluating whether there is a significant financing component, Ch. 28, 3.6.1.K
    customer options that provide a material right: recognising revenue when there is no expiration date, Ch. 28, 3.6.1.L
    Considering the class of customer when evaluating whether a customer option is a material right, Ch. 28, 3.6.1.F
    Considering whether a loyalty or reward programme is a material right, Ch. 28, 3.6.1 I
    Considering whether a renewal option is a material right, Ch. 28, 3.6.1.H
    distinguishing between a customer option and variable consideration, Ch. 28, 3.6.1.C
    nature of evaluation of customer options: quantitative *versus* qualitative, Ch. 28, 3.6.1.B
    prospective volume discounts determined to be customer options are material rights, Ch. 28, 3.6.1.F
    transactions to consider when assessing customer options for additional goods/services, Ch. 28, 3.6.1.A
    volume rebates and/or discounts on goods or services: customer options *versus* variable consideration, Ch. 28, 3.6.1.E
  determining when promises are performance obligations, Ch. 28, 3.2
    determination of 'distinct,' Ch. 28, 3.2.1
    examples, Ch. 28, 3.2.3
    series of distinct goods and services that are substantially the same and have the same pattern of transfer, Ch. 28, 3.2.2
  identifying the promised goods and services in the contract, Ch. 28, 3.1
  principal *versus* agent considerations, Ch. 28, 3.4
    control of the specified good/service, Ch. 28, 3.4.2
    examples, Ch. 28, 3.4.4
    identifying the specified good/service, Ch. 28, 3.4.1
    recognising revenue as principal/agent, Ch. 28, 3.4.3
  promised goods and services that are not distinct, Ch. 28, 3.3
  sale of products with a right of return, Ch. 28, 3.7
interaction with IFRIC 12, Ch. 25, 6
licences of intellectual property, Ch. 31, 2
  identifying performance obligations in a licensing arrangement, Ch. 31, 2.1
    application questions on, Ch. 31, 2.1.5
    contracts that grant both permission for past use of intellectual property and a licence to use the intellectual property in the future, Ch. 31, 2.1.5.B
    contractual restrictions, Ch. 31, 2.1.3
    guarantees to defend or maintain a patent, Ch. 31, 2.1.4

IFRS 15–*Revenue recognition*–*contd*
- licences of intellectual property–*contd*
  - identifying performance obligations in a licensing arrangement–*contd*
    - licences of intellectual property that are distinct, Ch. 31, 2.1.1
    - licences of intellectual property that are not distinct, Ch. 31, 2.1.2
  - licence renewals, Ch. 31, 2.4
  - nature of the entity's promise in granting a licence, determining, Ch. 31, 2.2
    - applying the licensing application guidance to a single (bundled) performance obligation that includes a licence of intellectual property, Ch. 31, 2.2.1
  - sales-based/usage-based royalties on, Ch. 31, 2.5
    - application questions on the sales-based or usage-based royalty recognition constraint, Ch. 31, 2.5.2
  - transfer of control of licensed intellectual property, Ch. 31, 2.3
    - recognition of royalties for a licence that provides a right to access intellectual property, Ch. 31, 2.5.1
    - right to access, Ch. 31, 2.3.1
    - right to use, Ch. 31, 2.3.2
    - use and benefit requirement, Ch. 31, 2.3.3
- objective, Ch. 27, 2
  - contract costs, Ch. 31, 5
    - amortisation of capitalised costs, Ch. 31, 5.3
  - costs to obtain a contract, Ch. 31, 5.1
  - costs to fulfil a contract, Ch. 31, 5.2
  - impairment of capitalised costs, Ch. 31, 5.4
  - onerous contracts, Ch. 31, 4
  - warranties, Ch. 31, 3
    - assurance-type warranty, Ch. 31, 3.3
    - contracts that contain both assurance and service-type warranties, Ch. 31, 3.4
    - service-type warranties, Ch. 31, 3.2
- overview, Ch. 27, 2.1
- presentation and disclosure
  - disclosure objective and general requirements, Ch. 32, 3.1
  - disclosures in interim financial statements, Ch. 32, 4
  - presentation requirements for, Ch. 32, 2.2
    - presentation of income outside the scope of IFRS 15, Ch. 32, 2.2.1
    - presentation requirements for contract assets and contract liabilities, Ch. 32, 2.1
    - application questions on presentation of contract assets and liabilities, Ch. 32, 2.1.6
  - specific disclosure requirements, Ch. 32, 3.2
    - assets recognised from the costs to obtain or fulfil a contract, Ch. 32, 3.2.3
    - contracts with customers, Ch. 32, 3.2.1
      - contract balances, Ch. 32, 3.2.1.B
      - disaggregation of revenue, Ch. 32, 3.2.1.A
      - performance obligations, Ch. 32, 3.2.1.C
      - use of 'backlog' practical expedient when criteria to use 'right to invoice' expedient are not met, Ch. 32, 3.2.1.D
    - practical expedients, Ch. 32, 3.2.4
    - significant judgements, Ch. 32, 3.2.2
      - timing of satisfaction of performance obligations, Ch. 32, 3.2.2.A
      - transaction price and the amounts allocated to performance obligations, Ch. 32, 3.2.2.B
- satisfaction of performance obligations, Ch. 30, 1-11
  - bill-and-hold arrangements, Ch. 30, 7
  - breakage and prepayments for future goods/services, Ch. 30, 11
  - consignment arrangements, Ch. 30, 6
  - control transferred at a point in time, Ch. 30, 4
    - customer acceptance, Ch. 30, 4.2
    - effect of shipping terms when an entity has transferred control of a good to a customer, Ch. 30, 4.1
  - over time, Ch. 30, 2
    - asset with no alternative use and right to payment, Ch. 30, 2.3
      - enforceable right to payment for performance completed to date, Ch. 30, 2.3.2
        - considerations when assessing the over-time criteria for the sale of a real estate unit, Ch. 30, 2.3.2.F
        - determining whether an entity has an enforceable right to payment, Ch. 30, 2.3.2.A
        - determining whether an entity has an enforceable right to payment for a contract priced at a loss, Ch. 30, 2.3.2.D
        - enforceable right to payment: contemplating consideration an entity might receive from the potential resale of the asset, Ch. 30, 2.3.2.G
        - enforceable right to payment determination when not entitled to a reasonable profit margin on standard inventory materials purchased, but not yet used, Ch. 30, 2.3.2.E
        - enforceable right to payment: does an entity need a present unconditional right to payment, Ch. 30, 2.3.2.B
        - enforceable right to payment: non-refundable upfront payments that represent the full transaction price, Ch. 30, 2.3.2.C
      - no alternative use, Ch. 30, 2.3.1
    - customer controls asset as it is created/enhanced, Ch. 30, 2.2
    - customer simultaneously receives and consumes benefits as the entity performs, Ch. 30, 2.1
    - measuring progress over time, Ch. 30, 3
      - application questions, Ch. 30, 3.4
      - examples, Ch. 30, 3.3
      - input methods, Ch. 30, 3.2
      - output methods, Ch. 30, 3.1
  - recognising revenue for customer options for additional goods and services, Ch. 30, 10
  - recognising revenue for licences of intellectual property, Ch. 30, 8
  - recognising revenue when a right of return exists, Ch. 30, 9
  - repurchase agreements, Ch. 30, 5
    - forward/call option held by the entity, Ch. 30, 5.1
    - put option held by the customer, Ch. 30, 5.2
    - sales with residual value guarantees, Ch. 30, 5.3
- regulatory assets and liabilities, Ch. 27, 4.4
- scope, Ch. 27, 3

collaborative arrangements, Ch. 27, 3.4
definition of customer, Ch. 27, 3.3
interaction with other standards, Ch. 27, 3.5
    certain fee-generating activities of financial institutions, Ch. 27, 3.5.1.B
    contributions, Ch. 27, 3.5.1.E
    credit card arrangements, Ch. 27, 3.5.1.C
    credit card-holder rewards programmes, Ch. 27, 3.5.1.D
    determining whether IFRS 10 or IFRS 15 applies to the sale of a corporate wrapper to a customer, Ch. 7, 3.2.1; Ch. 27, 3.5.1.J
    equity instruments issued by an entity to a customer in connection with a revenue arrangement, Ch. 27, 3.5.1.L
    fixed-odds wagering contracts, Ch. 27, 3.5.1.F
    Islamic financing transactions, Ch. 27, 3.5.1.A
    prepaid gift cards, Ch. 27, 3.5.1.I
    pre-production activities related to long-term supply arrangements, Ch. 27, 3.5.1.G
    revenue arising from an interest in a joint operation, Ch. 27, 3.5.1.K
    sales of by-products or scrap materials, Ch. 27, 3.5.1.H
rights and obligations within, Ch. 45, 3.13

IFRS 16–Leases, Ch. 23, 1–10. *See also* Leases (IFRS 16)
business combinations, Ch. 23, 9, 10.5.2
    acquiree in a business combination is a lessee, Ch. 23, 9.1
    acquiree in a business combination is a lessor, Ch. 23, 9.2
commencement date of the lease, Ch. 23, 4.2
definition, Ch. 23, 3
    contract combinations, Ch. 23, 3.3
    determining whether an arrangement contains a lease, Ch. 23, 3.1
    identifying and separating lease and non-lease components of a contract, Ch. 23, 3.2
discount rates, Ch. 23, 4.6
    determination of the incremental borrowing rate by a subsidiary with centralised treasury functions, Ch. 23, 4.6.1
economic life, Ch. 23, 4.8
effective date and transition, Ch. 23, 10
    amounts previously recognised in a business combination, Ch. 23, 10.5.2
    disclosure, Ch. 23, 10.6
    effective date, Ch. 23, 10.1; Ch. 54, 8.4
    lessee transition, Ch. 23, 10.3
        full retrospective approach, Ch. 23, 10.3.1
        modified retrospective approach, Ch. 23, 10.3.2
            leases previously classified as operating leases, Ch. 23, 10.3.2.A
            leases previously classified as finance leases, Ch. 23, 10.3.2.C
            separating and allocating lease and non-lease components of a contract upon transition, Ch. 23, 10.3.2.B
        lessor transition, Ch. 23, 10.4
            subleases, Ch. 23, 10.4.1
    references to IFRS 9, Ch. 23, 10.5.3
    sale and leaseback transactions, Ch. 23, 10.5.1
    transition, Ch. 23, 10.2
fair value, Ch. 23, 4.9
inception of the lease (inception date), Ch. 23, 4.1
initial direct costs, Ch. 23, 4.7; Ch. 19, 4.9.2
    directly attributable costs other than initial direct costs incurred by lessees, Ch. 23, 4.7.1
lease liabilities under IFRS 16, Ch. 20, 4.1.2
lease payments, Ch. 23, 4.5
    amounts expected to be payable under residual value guarantees– lessees only, Ch. 23, 4.5.6
    amounts payable under residual value guarantees–lessors only, Ch. 23, 4.5.7
    exercise price of a purchase option, Ch. 23, 4.5.4 in-substance fixed lease payments, Ch. 23, 4.5.1
    lease incentives, Ch. 23, 4.5.2; Ch. 19, 4.9.1
        presentation in the statement of cash flows, Ch. 40, 5.5.3
    payments for penalties for terminating a lease, Ch. 23, 4.5.5
    reassessment of the lease liability, Ch. 23, 4.5.9
    remeasurement by lessors, Ch. 23, 4.5.13
    security deposits, Ch. 23, 4.5.9
    value added tax and property taxes, Ch. 23, 4.5.10
    variable lease payments that depend on an index/rate, Ch. 23, 4.5.3
    variable lease payments which do not depend on an index or rate, Ch. 23, 4.5.8
lease term and purchase options, Ch. 23, 4.4
    cancellable leases, Ch. 23, 4.4.1
    reassessment of lease term and purchase options–lessees, Ch. 23, 4.4.2
    reassessment of lease term and purchase options–lessors, Ch. 23, 4.4.3
lessee accounting, Ch. 23, 5
    disclosure, Ch. 23, 5.8
        additional, Ch. 23, 5.8.3
        of assets, liabilities, expenses and cash flows, Ch. 23, 5.8.2
        objective, Ch. 23, 5.8.1
    initial measurement, Ch. 23, 5.2
        lease liabilities, Ch. 23, 5.2.2
        right-of-use assets, Ch. 23, 5.2.1
    initial recognition, Ch. 23, 5.1
        leases of low-value assets, Ch. 23, 5.1.2
        short-term leases, Ch. 23, 5.1.1
    lease modifications, Ch. 23, 5.5
        amendment to IFRS 16 for covid-19 related rent concessions, Ch. 23, 5.5.4
        application of lease modification guidance to rent concessions, Ch. 23, 5.5.3
        determining whether a lease modification results in a separate lease, Ch. 23, 5.5.1
        lessee accounting for a modification that does not result in a separate lease, Ch. 23, 5.5.2
    lessee matters, Ch. 23, 5.6
        impairment of right-of-use assets, Ch. 23, 5.6.1
        income tax accounting, Ch. 23, 5.6.4
        leases denominated in a foreign currency, Ch. 23, 5.6.2
        portfolio approach, Ch. 23, 5.6.3
    presentation, Ch. 23, 5.7
    remeasurement of lease liabilities and right-of-use assets, Ch. 23, 5.4

IFRS 16–*Leases—contd*
  lessee accounting—*contd*
    subsequent measurement, Ch. 23, 5.3
      expense recognition, Ch. 23, 5.3.3
      lease liabilities, Ch. 23, 5.3.2
      right-of-use assets, Ch. 23, 5.3.1
  lessee involvement with the underlying asset before the commencement date, Ch. 23, 4.3
  lessor accounting, Ch. 23, 6
    cash flows, Ch. 40, 5.5.5
    disclosure, Ch. 23, 6.7
      for all lessors, Ch. 23, 6.7.2
      for finance leases, Ch. 23, 6.7.3
      objective, Ch. 23, 6.7.1
      for operating leases, Ch. 23, 6.7.4
    finance leases, Ch. 23, 6.2
      initial measurement, Ch. 23, 6.2.1
      manufacturer/dealer lessors, Ch. 23, 6.2.2
      remeasurement of the net investment in the lease, Ch. 23, 6.2.4
      subsequent measurement, Ch. 23, 6.2.3
      unguaranteed residual values, Ch. 23, 6.2.3.A
  lease classification, Ch. 23, 6.1
    criteria, Ch. 23, 6.1.1
    reassessment of, Ch. 23, 6.1.4
    residual value guarantees included in the lease classification test, Ch. 23, 6.1.3
    test for land and buildings, Ch. 23, 6.1.2
  lease modifications, Ch. 23, 6.4
    determining whether a modification to a finance lease results in a separate lease, Ch. 23, 6.4.1
    lessor accounting for a modification to a finance lease that does not result in a separate lease, Ch. 23, 6.4.2
    modification to an operating lease, Ch. 23, 6.4.3
  lessor matters, Ch. 23, 6.5
    portfolio approach, Ch. 23, 6.5
  operating leases, Ch. 23, 6.3
    income, Ch. 23, 6.3.1
  presentation, Ch. 23, 6.6
  objective, Ch. 23, 2.1
  recognition exemptions, Ch. 23, 2.3
  sale and leaseback transactions, Ch. 23, 8
    determining whether the transfer of an asset is a sale, Ch. 23, 8.1
    disclosures, Ch. 23, 8.4
    transactions in which the transfer of an asset is a sale, Ch. 23, 8.2
      accounting for the leaseback, Ch. 23, 8.2.2
      accounting for the sale, Ch. 23, 8.2.1
      adjustment for off-market terms, Ch. 23, 8.2.3
    transactions in which the transfer of an asset is not a sale, Ch. 23, 8.3
  scope, Ch. 23, 2.2
  service concession arrangements, Ch. 25, 2.3
  subleases, Ch. 23, 7
    definition, Ch. 23, 7.1
    disclosure, Ch. 23, 7.5
    intermediate lessor accounting, Ch. 23, 7.2
    presentation, Ch. 23, 7.4
    sublessee accounting, Ch. 23, 7.3
IFRS 17-**Insurance contracts**, Ch. 56. *See also* Insurance contracts
  acquisitions of insurance contracts, Ch. 56, 13
    cash flows acquired in a business combination within the scope of IFRS 3, Ch. 56, 13.1
    common control business combinations, Ch. 56, 13.3
    practical issues, Ch. 56, 13.4
    subsequent treatment of contracts acquired in their settlement period, Ch. 56, 13.2
  definitions in IFRS 17, Ch. 56, 2.2
  derecognition, Ch. 56, 12.2
    accounting for, Ch. 56, 12.3
  disclosure, Ch. 56, 16
    accounting policies, Ch. 56, 16.4
    explanation of recognised amounts, Ch. 56, 16.1
    nature and extent of risks arising from contracts within the scope of IFRS 17, Ch. 56, 16.5
    significant judgements in applying IFRS 17, Ch. 56, 16.3
    transition amounts, Ch. 56, 16.2
  effective date and transition, Ch. 56, 17
    effective date, Ch. 56, 17.1
    entities that have not previously applied IFRS 9, Ch. 56, 17.7
    fair value approach, Ch. 56, 17.5
    modified retrospective approach, Ch. 56, 17.4
    redesignation of financial assets – IFRS 9 previously applied, Ch. 56, 17.6
    retrospective application of transition, Ch. 56, 17.3
    transition, Ch. 56, 17.2
      disclosures about the effect of, Ch. 56, 17.2.2
  impairment of insurance acquisition cash flows, Ch. 56, 8.10
  insurance contract definition, Ch. 56, 3
    changes in the level of insurance risk, Ch. 56, 3.6
    the definition, Ch. 56, 3.1
    insurance and non-insurance contracts, Ch. 56, 3.7
    insurance risk *vs.* financial risk, Ch. 56, 3.4
    payments in kind, Ch. 56, 3.3
    significant insurance risk, Ch. 56, 3.5
    uncertain future events, Ch. 56, 3.2
  initial recognition, Ch. 56, 6
    insurance acquisition cash flows as assets, Ch. 56, 6.3
    investment components, Ch. 56, 4.2
      definition, Ch. 56, 4.2.1
      separability of, Ch. 56, 4.2.2
      measurement, Ch. 56, 4.2.3
      investment-return service, Ch. 56, 8.7.2
  level of aggregation, Ch. 56, 5
    identifying groups according to expected profitability, Ch. 56, 5.2
    identifying groups for contracts applying the premium allocation approach, Ch. 56, 5.3
    identifying portfolios, Ch. 56, 5.1
  measurement
    contracts with participation features, Ch. 56, 11
      cash flows that affect or are affected by cash flows to policyholders of other contracts (mutualisation), Ch. 56, 11.1
      direct participation features, Ch. 56, 11.2
        allocation of the contractual service margin to profit or loss, Ch. 56, 11.2.4
        definition, Ch. 56, 11.2.1
        disaggregation of finance income or expense between profit or loss and other comprehensive income, Ch. 56, 11.2.6

measurement of CSM using variable fee approach, Ch. 56, 11.2.3
risk adjustment for non-financial risk using the variable fee approach, Ch. 56, 11.2.2
risk mitigation, Ch. 56, 11.2.5
general model, Ch. 56, 8
   allocation of the contractual service margin to profit or loss, Ch. 56, 8.7
   contract boundary, Ch. 56, 8.1
      acquisition cash flows paid on an initially written contract, Ch. 56, 8.1.4
      constraints or limitations relevant in assessing repricing, Ch. 56, 8.1.2
      contracts between an entity and customers of an association or bank, Ch. 56, 8.1.3
      issues related to reinsurance contracts held, Ch. 56, 8.1.5
      options to add insurance coverage, Ch. 56, 8.1.1
   contractual service margin (CSM), Ch. 56, 8.5
      allocation to profit or loss, Ch. 56, 8.7
      discount rates, Ch. 56, 8.3
   estimates of expected future cash flows, Ch. 56, 8.2
      contract boundary, Ch. 56, 8.2.4
      excluded from the contract boundary, Ch. 56, 8.2.4
      market and non-market variables, Ch. 56, 8.2.1
      using current estimates, Ch. 56, 8.2.2
      within the contract boundary, Ch. 56, 8.2.3
   impairment of assets recognised for insurance acquisition cash flows, Ch. 56, 8.10
   insurance contracts issued by mutual entities, Ch. 56, 8.11
   onerous contracts, Ch. 56, 8.8
   other matters, Ch. 56, 8.12
      impairment of insurance receivables, Ch. 56, 8.12.1
      policyholder loans, Ch. 56, 8.12.2
   reinsurance contracts issued, Ch. 56, 8.9
      accounting for ceding commissions and reinstatement premiums, Ch. 56, 8.9.3
      boundary of, Ch. 56, 8.9.1
      determining the quantity of benefits for identifying coverage units, Ch. 56, 8.9.4
      issued adverse loss development covers, Ch. 56, 8.9.2
   risk adjustment for non-financial risk, Ch. 56, 8.4
      consideration of reinsurance held, Ch. 56, 8.4.3
      level, Ch. 56, 8.4.2
      statement of comprehensive income, Ch. 56, 8.4.4
      techniques, Ch. 56, 8.4.1
   subsequent measurement, Ch. 56, 8.6
      of CSM (for contracts without direct participation features), Ch. 56, 8.6.3
      liability for incurred claims, Ch. 56, 8.6.2
      liability for remaining coverage, Ch. 56, 8.6.1
investment contracts with discretionary participation features, Ch. 56, 11.3
   contracts with switching features, Ch. 56, 11.3.1
overview of measurement, Ch. 56, 7

insurance contracts in a foreign currency, Ch. 56, 7.3
modifications to the general model, Ch. 56, 7.2
overview of general model, Ch. 56, 7.1
premium allocation approach, Ch. 56, 9
   criteria for use of, Ch. 56, 9.1
      applying materiality for the premium allocation approach eligibility assessment, Ch. 56, 9.1.1
      main sources of difference between the premium allocation approach and the general approach, Ch. 56, 9.1.2
   initial measurement, Ch. 56, 9.2
   subsequent measurement, liability for incurred claims, Ch. 56, 9.4
   remaining coverage, Ch. 56, 9.3
reinsurance contracts held, Ch. 56, 10
   aggregation level, Ch. 56, 10.1
   allocation of the CSM to profit or loss, Ch. 56, 10.5
   boundary of, Ch. 56, 10.2
   initial recognition, Ch. 56, 10.3
   premium allocation approach for, Ch. 56, 10.6
   subsequent measurement, Ch. 56, 10.4
   and the variable fee approach, Ch. 56, 10.7
modification and derecognition, Ch. 56, 12
   accounting for derecognition, Ch. 56, 12.3
   derecognition, Ch. 56, 12.2
   modification, Ch. 56, 12.1
mutual entities, Ch. 56, 3.2.2.B, 8.11
objective of IFRS 17, Ch. 56, 2.1
presentation in the statement of financial performance, Ch. 56, 15
   insurance finance income or expenses, Ch. 56, 15.3
   insurance revenue, Ch. 56, 15.1
      and expense from reinsurance contracts held, Ch. 56, 15.1.3
      related to the provision of services in a period, Ch. 56, 15.1.1
      under the premium allocation approach, Ch. 56, 15.1.2
   insurance service expenses, Ch. 56, 15.2
   reporting the CSM in interim financial statements, Ch. 56, 15.4
presentation in the statement of financial position, Ch. 56, 14
scope of IFRS 17, Ch. 56, 2
separating components from an insurance contract, Ch. 56, 4
   embedded derivatives from an insurance contract, Ch. 56, 4.1
   investment components from an insurance contract, Ch. 56, 4.2
      definition, Ch. 56, 4.2.1
      measurement of the non-distinct, Ch. 56, 4.2.3
      separable, Ch. 56, 4.2.2
   a promise to provide distinct goods and non-insurance services from insurance contracts, Ch. 56, 4.3

IFRS Taxonomy, Ch. 1, 2.6, 2.9

IFRS Taxonomy Consultative Group, Ch. 1, 2.9

IFRS Transition Resource Group for Impairment of Financial Instruments (ITG), Ch. 51, 1.5

Impairment of assets, Ch. 20. *See also* IAS 36; Impairment of goodwill; Value in use (VIU)

Impairment of assets—*contd*
  basis of recoverable amount–value-in-use (VIU) or fair value less costs of disposal (FVLCD), Ch. 43, 11.3
  calculation of FVLCD, Ch. 20, 6.1, Ch. 43, 11.5
  calculation of VIU, Ch. 20, 7, Ch. 43, 11.4
  held for sale, Ch. 20, 5.1
  identifying cash-generating units (CGUs), Ch. 20, 3, Ch. 43, 11.2
    external users of processing assets, Ch. 43, 11.2.2
    fields/mines operated on a portfolio basis, Ch. 43, 11.2.4
    markets for intermediate products, Ch. 43, 11.2.1
    shared infrastructure, Ch. 43, 11.2.3
  impairment indicators, Ch. 20, 2.1, Ch. 43, 11.1
  intangible assets with an indefinite useful life, Ch. 20, 10
  low mine/field profitability near end of life, Ch. 43, 11.6
Impairment of goodwill, Ch. 20, 8 created by deferred tax, Ch. 33, 12.3
  disposal of operation within a cash-generating unit (CGU) to which goodwill has been allocated, Ch. 20, 8.5
    changes in composition of cash-generating units CGUs, Ch. 20, 8.5.1
  goodwill and its allocation to cash-generating unites, Ch. 20, 8.1
  recognised on acquisition, Ch. 20, 8.3
    deferred tax assets and losses of acquired businesses, Ch. 20, 8.3.2
    testing goodwill 'created' by deferred tax for impairment, Ch. 20, 8.3.1
  impairment testing when a CGU crosses more than one operating segment, Ch. 20, 8.4
  when to test CGUs with goodwill for impairment, Ch. 20, 8.2
    carry forward of a previous impairment test calculation, Ch. 20, 8.2.3
    reversal of impairment loss, Ch. 20, 5, 8.2.4
    sequence of tests, Ch. 20, 8.2.2
    timing of tests, Ch. 20, 8.2.1
Impairments. *See also* IAS 36; Impairment of assets; Impairment of goodwill
  associates or joint ventures, Ch. 11, 8
    in separate financial statements, Ch. 11, 9.1
  cost model, Ch. 18, 5; Ch. 19, 7.3
  of fixed assets and goodwill, Ch. 20, 1–14
    intangible assets, Ch. 17, 9.4
  of insurance assets, hierarchy exemption, Ch. 55, 7.2.6.B
  of reinsurance assets, hierarchy exemption, Ch. 55, 7.2.5
  suspension of capitalisation of borrowing costs, Ch. 21, 6.2
Income approach (fair value), Ch. 14, 14.4
  property, plant and equipment, Ch. 18, 6.1.1.B
Income, definition of, Ch. 27, 4.1
Income statement (statement of profit or loss), Ch. 3, 3.2.1. *See also* Statement of comprehensive income
  classification of expenses recognised in profit/loss, Ch. 3, 3.2.3
    analysis of expenses by function, Ch. 3, 3.2.3.B
    analysis of expenses by nature, Ch. 3, 3.2.3.A
  face of, information required on, Ch. 3, 3.2.2
Income taxes, Ch. 33, 1–14. *See also* IAS 12
  allocation between periods, Ch. 33, 1.2
    no provision for deferred tax ('flow through'), Ch. 33, 1.2.1
    provision for deferred tax (the temporary difference approach), Ch. 33, 1.2.2
  allocation of tax charge/credit, Ch. 33, 10
    change in tax status of entity/shareholders, Ch. 33, 10.9
    defined benefit pension plans, Ch. 33, 10.7
      tax on refund of pension surplus, Ch. 33, 10.7.1
    discontinued operations, Ch. 33, 10.6
    disposal of an interest in a subsidiary that does not result in a loss of control, Ch. 33, 10.11
    dividends and transaction costs of equity instruments, Ch. 33, 10.3
      dividend subject to differential tax rate, Ch. 33, 10.3.1
      dividend subject to withholding tax, Ch. 33, 10.3.2
      incoming dividends, Ch. 33, 10.3.4
      intragroup dividend subject to withholding tax, Ch. 33, 10.3.3
      tax benefits of distributions and transaction costs of equity instruments, Ch. 33, 10.3.5
    gain/loss in profit/loss and loss/gain outside profit/loss offset for tax purposes, Ch. 33, 10.5
    gains and losses reclassified ('recycled') to profit/loss, Ch. 33, 10.4
      debt instrument measured at fair value through OCI under IFRS 9, Ch. 33, 10.4.1
      recognition of expected credit losses with no change in fair value, Ch. 33, 10.4.2
    previous revaluation of PP&E treated as deemed cost on transition to IFRS, Ch. 33, 10.10
    retrospective restatements/applications, Ch. 33, 10.2
    revalued and rebased assets, Ch. 33, 10.1
      non-monetary assets with a tax base determined in a foreign currency, Ch. 33, 10.1.1
    share-based payment transactions, Ch. 33, 10.8
      allocation of tax deduction between profit/loss and equity, Ch. 33, 10.8.1
      allocation when more than one award is outstanding, Ch. 33, 10.8.3
      replacement awards in a business combination, Ch. 33, 10.8.5
      share-based payment transactions subject to transitional provisions of IFRS 1 and IFRS 2, Ch. 33, 10.8.6
      staggered exercise of awards, Ch. 33, 10.8.4
      tax base, determining, Ch. 33, 10.8.2
  business combinations, Ch. 33, 12
    apparent immediate impairment of goodwill created by deferred tax, Ch. 33, 12.3
    measurement and recognition of deferred tax in, Ch. 33, 12.1
      deferred tax assets rising on a business combination, Ch. 33, 12.1.2
      deferred tax liabilities of acquired entity, Ch. 33, 12.1.3
      manner of recovery of assets and settlement of liabilities, determining, Ch. 33, 12.1.1
    tax deductions for acquisition costs, Ch. 33, 12.4
    tax deductions for replacement share-based payment awards in a business combination, Ch. 33, 12.2
    temporary differences arising from the acquisition of a group of assets that is not a business, Ch. 33, 12.5

consolidated tax returns and offset of taxable profits and losses within groups, Ch. 33, 11
    examples of accounting by entities in a tax-consolidated group, Ch. 33, 11.1
    payments for intragroup transfer of tax losses, Ch. 33, 11.2
    recognition of deferred tax assets where tax losses are transferred in a group, Ch. 33, 11.3
current tax, Ch. 33, 5
    discounting of current tax assets and liabilities, Ch. 33, 5.4
    enacted/substantively enacted tax legislation, Ch. 33, 5.1
        changes to tax rates and laws enacted after the reporting date, Ch. 33, 5.1.3
        changes to tax rates and laws enacted before the reporting date, Ch. 33, 5.1.2
        implications of the decision by the UK's to withdrawal from the EU, Ch. 33, 5.1.4
        substantive enactment meaning, Ch. 33, 5.1.1
    intra-period allocation, presentation and disclosure, Ch. 33, 5.5
    'prior year adjustments' of previously presented tax balances and expense, Ch. 33, 5.3
    uncertain tax treatments, Ch. 33, 5.2
deferred tax, measurement, Ch. 33, 8
    different tax rates applicable to retained and distributed profits, Ch. 33, 8.5
        effectively tax-free entities, Ch. 33, 8.5.1
        withholding tax/distribution tax, Ch. 33, 8.5.2
    discounting, Ch. 33, 8.6
    expected manner of recovery of assets/settlement of liabilities, Ch. 33, 8.4
        assets and liabilities with more than one tax base, Ch. 33, 8.4.3
        carrying amount, Ch. 33, 8.4.2
        change in expected manner of recovery of an asset/settlement of a liability, Ch. 33, 8.4.11
        depreciable PP&E and intangible assets, Ch. 33, 8.4.5
        determining the expected manner of recovery of assets, Ch. 33, 8.4.4
        investment properties, Ch. 33, 8.4.7
        non-depreciable PP&E and intangible assets, Ch. 33, 8.4.6
            non-amortised or indefinite life intangible assets, Ch. 33, 8.4.6.B
            PP&E accounted for using the revaluation model, Ch. 33, 8.4.6.A
        other assets and liabilities, Ch. 33, 8.4.8
        'outside' temporary differences relating to subsidiaries, branches, associates and joint arrangements, Ch. 33, 8.4.9
        'single asset' entities, Ch. 33, 8.4.10
        tax planning strategies to reduce liabilities are not anticipated, Ch. 33, 8.4.1
    legislation at the end of the reporting period, Ch. 33, 8.1
        changes to tax rates and laws enacted after the reporting date, Ch. 33, 8.1.2
        changes to tax rates and laws enacted before the reporting date, Ch. 33, 8.1.1
            backward tracing of changes in deferred taxation, Ch. 33, 8.1.1.B
            disclosures relating to changes, Ch. 33, 8.1.1.C
            managing uncertainty in determining the effect of new tax legislation, Ch. 33, 8.1.1.A
    'prior year adjustments' of previously presented tax balances and expense (income), Ch. 33, 8.3
    uncertain tax treatments, Ch. 33, 8.2, 9
    unrealised intragroup profits and losses in consolidated financial, Ch. 33, 8.7
        intragroup transfers of goodwill and intangible assets, Ch. 33, 8.7.1
            consolidated financial statements, Ch. 33, 8.7.1.C
            individual financial statements of buyer, Ch. 33, 8.7.1.A
            individual financial statements of seller, Ch. 33, 8.7.1.B
            when the tax base of goodwill is retained by the transferor entity, Ch. 33, 8.7.1.D
deferred tax, recognition, Ch. 33, 7
    assets carried at fair value/revalued amount, Ch. 33, 7.3
    basic principles, Ch. 33, 7.1
        deductible temporary differences (deferred tax assets), Ch. 33, 7.1.2
        interpretation issues, Ch. 33, 7.1.3
            accounting profit, Ch. 33, 7.1.3.A
            taxable profit 'at the time of the transaction,' Ch. 33, 7.1.3.B
        taxable temporary differences (deferred tax liabilities), Ch. 33, 7.1.1
    gains, Ch. 33, 7.7
    initial recognition exception, Ch. 33, 7.2
        acquisition of an investment in a subsidiary, associate, branch or joint arrangement, Ch. 33, 7.2.10
        acquisition of subsidiary that does not constitute a business, Ch. 33, 7.2.9
        acquisition of tax losses, Ch. 33, 7.2.1
        changes to temporary differences after initial recognition, Ch. 33, 7.2.4
            change in carrying value due to revaluation, Ch. 33, 7.2.4.B
            change in tax base due to deductions in tax return, Ch. 33, 7.2.4.C
            depreciation, amortisation/impairment of initial carrying value, Ch. 33, 7.2.4.A
            temporary difference altered by legislative change, Ch. 33, 7.2.4.D
        initial recognition of compound financial instruments by the issuer, Ch. 33, 7.2.8
        initial recognition of goodwill, Ch. 33, 7.2.2
            deductible temporary differences, Ch. 33, 7.2.2.B
            taxable temporary differences, Ch. 33, 7.2.2.A
            tax deductible goodwill, Ch. 33, 7.2.2.C
        initial recognition of other assets and liabilities, Ch. 33, 7.2.3
        intragroup transfers of assets with no change in tax base, Ch. 33, 7.2.5
        partially deductible and super-deductible assets, Ch. 33, 7.2.6
        transactions involving the initial recognition of an asset and liability, Ch. 33, 7.2.7
            decommissioning costs, Ch. 33, 7.2.7.A
            leases under IFRS 16 taxed as operating leases, Ch. 33, 7.2.7.B

Income taxes—*contd*
  deferred tax, recognition—*contd*
    'outside' temporary differences relating to subsidiaries, branches, associates and joint arrangements, Ch. 33, 7.5
      calculation of, Ch. 33, 7.5.1
        consolidated financial statements, Ch. 33, 7.5.1.A
        separate financial statements of the investor, Ch. 33, 7.5.1.B
      deductible temporary differences, Ch. 33, 7.5.3
      foreseeable future – anticipated intragroup dividend, Ch. 33, 7.5.4
        consolidated financial statements of receiving entity, Ch. 33, 7.5.4.A
        separate financial statements of paying entity, Ch. 33, 7.5.4.B
      taxable temporary differences, Ch. 33, 7.5.2
      unpaid intragroup interest, royalties, management charges etc., Ch. 33, 7.5.5
    restrictions on recognition of deferred tax assets, Ch. 33, 7.4
      effect of disposals on recoverability of tax losses, Ch. 33, 7.4.8
        tax losses of retained entity recoverable against profits of subsidiary disposed of, Ch. 33, 7.4.8.B
        tax losses of subsidiary disposed of recoverable against profits of retained entity, Ch. 33, 7.4.8.C
        tax losses of subsidiary disposed of recoverable against profits of that subsidiary, Ch. 33, 7.4.8.A
      re-assessment of deferred tax assets, Ch. 33, 7.4.7
      restrictions imposed by relevant tax laws, Ch. 33, 7.4.1
      sources of 'probable' taxable profit, estimates of future taxable profits, Ch. 33, 7.4.3
        ignore the origination of new future deductible temporary differences, Ch. 33, 7.4.3.B
        ignore the reversal of existing deductible temporary differences, Ch. 33, 7.4.3.A
      sources of 'probable' taxable profit, taxable temporary differences, Ch. 33, 7.4.2
      tax planning opportunities, Ch. 33, 7.4.4
      unrealised losses on debt securities measured at fair value, Ch. 33, 7.4.5
      unused tax losses and unused tax credits, Ch. 33, 7.4.6
    'tax-transparent' ('flow-through') entities, Ch. 33, 7.6
  deferred tax–tax bases and temporary differences, Ch. 33, 6
    tax base, Ch. 33, 6.1
      of assets, Ch. 33, 6.1.1
      assets and liabilities whose tax base is not immediately apparent, Ch. 33, 6.1.3
      disclaimed/with no economic value, Ch. 33, 6.1.7
      equity items with a tax base, Ch. 33, 6.1.5
      of items not recognised as assets/liabilities in financial statements, Ch. 33, 6.1.4
      items with more than one tax base, Ch. 33, 6.1.6
      of liabilities, Ch. 33, 6.1.2
    temporary differences, examples, Ch. 33, 6.2
      assets and liabilities with no temporary difference, Ch. 33, 6.2.3
      business combinations and consolidation, Ch. 33, 6.2.1.E, 6.2.2.E
      deductible, Ch. 33, 6.2.2
        business combinations and consolidation, Ch. 33, 6.2.2.E
        foreign currency differences, Ch. 33, 6.2.1.F, 6.2.2.F
        hyperinflation, Ch. 33, 6.2.1.G
        revaluations, Ch. 33, 6.2.1.C, 6.2.2.C
        tax re-basing, Ch. 33, 6.2.1.D, 6.2.2.D
        transactions that affect profit of loss, Ch. 33, 6.2.2.A
        transactions that affect statement of financial position, Ch. 33, 6.2.2.B
      taxable, Ch. 33, 6.2.1
        business combinations and consolidation, Ch. 33, 6.2.1.E
        foreign currency differences, Ch. 33, 6.2.1.F
        hyperinflation, Ch. 33, 6.2.1.G
        revaluations, Ch. 33, 6.2.1.C
        tax re-basing, Ch. 33, 6.2.1.D
        transactions that affect profit of loss, Ch. 33, 6.2.1.A, 6.2.2.A
        transactions that affect statement of financial position, Ch. 33, 6.2.1.B, 6.2.2.B
  definitions, Ch. 33, 3, 4.1
    effectively tax-free entities, Ch. 33, 4.56
    hybrid taxes (including minimum taxes), Ch. 33, 4.1.2, 4.5
      minimum based on a measure other than taxable profits, Ch. 33, 4.5.1
      tax based on revenues, unless a profit measure gives a lower result, Ch. 33, 4.5.3
      tax is the higher of measures based on taxable profits and revenues, Ch. 33. 4.5.2
    interest and penalties, Ch. 33, 4.4
    investment tax credits, Ch. 33, 4.3
    levies, Ch. 33, 4.1.1, Ch. 26, 6.8
    withholding and similar taxes, Ch. 33, 4.2
  development of IAS 12, Ch. 33, 1.3
  disclosure, Ch. 33, 14
    components of tax expense, Ch. 33, 14.1
    discontinued operations–interaction with IFRS 5, Ch. 33, 14.6
    dividends, Ch. 33, 14.4
    examples, Ch. 33, 14.5
    other disclosures, Ch. 33, 14.2
      tax (or tax rate) reconciliation, Ch. 33, 14.2.1
      temporary differences relating to subsidiaries, associates, branches and joint arrangements, Ch. 33, 14.2.2
    reason for recognition of certain tax assets, Ch. 33, 14.3
  nature of taxation, Ch. 33, 1.1
  presentation, Ch. 33, 13
    statement of cash flows, Ch. 33, 13.3
    statement of comprehensive income, Ch. 33, 13.2
    statement of financial position, Ch. 33, 13.1
      offset current tax, Ch. 33, 13.1.1.A
      offset deferred tax, Ch. 33, 13.1.1.B
      no offset of current and deferred tax, Ch. 33, 13.1.1.C
  uncertain tax treatments, Ch. 33, 9

assumptions about the examination of tax treatments ('detection risk'), Ch. 33, 9.3
consideration of changes in facts and circumstances, Ch. 33, 9.5
  the expiry of a taxation authority's right to examine or re-examine a tax treatment, Ch. 33, 9.5.1
considered separately (unit of account), Ch. 33, 9.2
determining effects of, Ch. 33, 9.4
disclosures relating to, Ch. 33, 9.6
IFRIC 23, scope and definitions used, Ch. 33, 9.1
presentation of liabilities or assets for uncertain tax treatments, Ch. 33, 9.7
recognition of an asset for payments on account, Ch. 33, 9.8
transition to IFRIC 23, Ch. 33, 9.9

Indemnification assets, Ch. 9, 5.6.4; Ch. 45, 3.12
India, IFRS adoption in, Ch. 1, 4.4.3
Indian Accounting Standards (Ind AS), Ch. 1, 4.4.3
Individual financial statements, Ch. 8, 1–4. *See also* Separate and individual financial statements; Separate financial statements
common control or group transactions in, Ch. 8, 4
  application of the principles in practice, Ch. 8, 4.4
    acquiring and selling businesses, transfers between subsidiaries, Ch. 8, 4.4.2
    acquisition and sale of assets for shares, Ch. 8, 4.4.1.C
    contribution and distribution of assets, Ch. 8, 4.4.1.D
    financial guarantee contracts, Ch. 8, 4.4.5.B
    financial instruments within the scope of IFRS 9, Ch. 8, 4.4.5
    incurring expenses and settling liabilities without recharges, Ch. 8, 4.4.4
    interest-free or non-market interest rate loans, Ch. 8, 4.4.5.A
    legal merger of parent and subsidiary, Ch. 8, 4.4.3.B
    parent exchanges PP&E for a non-monetary asset of the subsidiary, Ch. 8, 4.4.1.B
    sale of PP&E from the parent to the subsidiary for an amount of cash not representative of the fair value of the asset, Ch. 8, 4.4.1.A
    subsidiary transferring business to the parent, Ch. 8, 4.4.3.A
    transactions involving non-monetary assets, Ch. 8, 4.4.1
    transfers between subsidiaries, Ch. 8, 4.4.1.E
    transfers of businesses between parent and subsidiary, Ch. 8, 4.4.3
disclosures, Ch. 8, 4.5
fair value in intra-group transactions, Ch. 8, 4.3.1
measurement, Ch. 8, 4.3
put and call options in separate financial statements, Ch. 7, 6.5
recognition, Ch. 8, 4.2

Inflation-linked debt, Ch. 50, 3.6; Ch. 53, 2.2.6
Inflation risk, hedges of, Ch. 53, 2.2.6
Infrastructure assets. *See* Service concession arrangements (SCA)
Initial measurement of financial instruments, Ch. 49, 3
acquisition of a group of assets that does not constitute a business, Ch. 49, 3.3.5
business combination, loans and receivables acquired in, Ch. 49, 3.3.4
'day 1' profits, Ch. 49, 3.3
embedded derivatives, Ch. 49, 3.5
financial guarantee contracts, Ch. 49, 3.3.3
financial instrument hosts, Ch. 49, 3.5
general requirements, Ch. 49, 3.1
initial fair value, transaction price and 'day 1' profits, Ch. 49, 3.3
  interest-free and low-interest long-term loans, Ch. 49, 3.3.1
  measurement of financial instruments following modification of contractual terms that leads to initial recognition of a new instrument, Ch. 49, 3.3.2
loan commitments, assets and liabilities arising from, Ch. 49, 3.7
off-market loan commitments, Ch. 49, 3.3.3
regular way transactions, Ch. 49, 3.6
trade receivables without a significant financing component, Ch. 49, 3.2
transaction costs, Ch. 49, 3.4
transaction price, Ch. 49, 3.3

In-process research and development (IPR&D), Ch. 9, 5.5.2.D; Ch. 17, 5.5
Institute of Chartered Accountants of India (ICAI), Ch. 1, 4.4.3
In-substance defeasance arrangements, Ch. 52, 6.1.3
In-substance derivatives, Ch. 46, 3.2
Insurance acquisition cash flows, Ch. 56, 8.2.3.E
Insurance assets, Ch. 55, 2.2.2
derecognition of, Ch. 55, 7.2.6.A
impairment of, Ch. 55, 7.2.6.B
reconciliations of changes in, Ch. 55, 11.1.6
Insurance contracts, Ch. 45, 3.3; Ch. 55, 1–12; Ch. 56, 1–18. *See also* IFRS 4–*Insurance Contracts*; IFRS 17–*Insurance Contracts*
acquired in business combinations and portfolio transfers, Ch. 55, 9; Ch. 56, 13
  customer lists and relationships not connected to contractual insurance rights and obligations, Ch. 55, 9.2
  expanded presentation of insurance contracts, Ch. 55, 9.1
  practical issues, Ch. 55, 9.1.1; Ch. 56, 13.4
applying IFRS 9 with IFRS 4, Ch. 55, 1.3, 10
  overlay approach, Ch. 55, 10.2
    designation and de-designation of eligible financial assets, Ch. 55, 10.2.1
    disclosures required for entities using the overlay approach, Ch. 55, 10.2.3
    first-time adopters, Ch. 55, 10.2.2
  temporary exemption from IFRS 9, Ch. 55, 10.1
    activities that are predominantly connected with insurance, Ch. 55, 10.1.1
    disclosures required for entities using the temporary exemption, Ch. 55, 10.1.5
    first-time adopters, Ch. 55, 10.1.3
    initial assessment and reassessment of the temporary exemption, Ch. 55, 10.1.2
    interest rate benchmark reform, Ch. 55, 10.1.6
    relief from investors in associates and joint ventures, Ch. 55, 10.1.4
cash flows excluded from the contract boundary, Ch. 56, 8.2.4
cash flows within the contract boundary, Ch. 56, 8.2.3

Insurance contracts—*contd*
- changes in accounting policies, Ch. 55, 8
  - criteria for, Ch. 55, 8.1
  - practical issues, Ch. 55, 8.5
    - changes to local GAAP, Ch. 55, 8.5.1
  - redesignation of financial assets, Ch. 55, 8.4; Ch. 56, 17.6
  - shadow accounting, Ch. 55, 8.3
  - specific issues, Ch. 55, 8.2
    - continuation of existing practices, Ch. 55, 8.2.1
    - current market interest rates, Ch. 55, 8.2.2
    - future investment margins, Ch. 55, 8.2.4
    - prudence, Ch. 55, 8.2.3
- contract boundary, Ch. 56, 8.2.3
- contractual service margin (CSM), Ch. 56, 8.5
  - measurement of using the variable fee approach, Ch. 56, 11.2.2
  - recognition of in profit or loss, Ch. 56, 11.2.5
  - release of, Ch. 56, 10.4.1
  - subsequent measurement, Ch. 56, 8.6.2
- definition of, Ch. 55, 3; Ch. 56, 3
  - accounting differences between insurance and non insurance contracts, Ch. 55, 3.7
  - adverse effect on the policyholder, Ch. 55, 3.7
    - insurance of non-insurance risks, Ch. 55, 3.7.2; Ch. 56, 3.4.3
    - lapse, persistency and expense risk, Ch. 55, 3.7.1; Ch. 56, 3.4.2
  - changes in the level of insurance risk, Ch. 55, 3.3; Ch. 56, 3.6
  - examples of insurance and non-insurance contracts, Ch. 55, 3.9; Ch. 56, 3.7
  - insurable interest, Ch. 56, 3.4.1
  - insurance risk and financial risk, distinction between, Ch. 55, 3.6; Ch. 56, 3.4
  - payments in kind, Ch. 55, 3.5; Ch. 56, 3.3
  - service contracts, Ch. 55, 3.5.1
  - significant insurance risk, Ch. 55, 3.2; Ch. 56, 3.5
  - uncertain future events, Ch. 55, 3.4; Ch. 56, 3.2
- derecognition of, Ch. 56, 12
- with direct participating features, Ch. 56, 11.2
- direct participation features, Ch. 56, 11.2
  - coverage period for insurance contracts with, Ch. 56, 11.2
  - definition, Ch. 56, 11.2.1
  - disaggregation of finance income or expense between profit/loss and OCI, Ch. 56, 11.2.6
  - measurement of contractual service margin using variable fee approach, Ch. 56, 11.2.3
  - risk mitigation, Ch. 56, 11.2.5
- disclosure, Ch. 55, 11; Ch. 56, 16
  - nature and extent of risks arising from insurance contracts, Ch. 55, 11.2; Ch. 56, 16.5
    - credit risk, liquidity risk and market risk disclosures, Ch. 55, 11.2.6; Ch. 56, 16.5.2, 16.5.4-16.5.5
    - exposures to market risk from embedded derivatives, Ch. 55, 11.2.7
    - insurance risk
      - claims development information, Ch. 55, 11.2.5; Ch. 56, 16.5.3
      - concentrations of risk, Ch. 55, 11.2.4; Ch. 56, 16.5.1
      - insurance risk–general matters, Ch. 55, 11.2.2
    - sensitivity information, Ch. 55, 11.2.3; Ch. 56, 16.5.2
    - objectives, policies and processes for managing insurance contract risks, Ch. 55, 11.2.1
  - other disclosure matters, Ch. 55, 11.2.8
    - fair value disclosures, Ch. 55, 11.2.8.C
    - financial guarantee contracts, Ch. 55, 11.2.8.B
    - IAS 1 capital disclosures, Ch. 55, 11.2.8.A
    - key performance indicators, Ch. 55, 11.2.8.D
  - recognised amounts, explanation of, Ch. 55, 11.1; Ch. 56, 16.1
    - disclosure of accounting policies, Ch. 55, 11.1.1; Ch. 56, 16.4
    - effects of changes in assumptions, Ch. 55, 11.1.5
    - gains/losses on buying reinsurance, Ch. 55, 11.1.3
    - insurance finance income or expenses, Ch. 56, 16.1.3
    - premium allocation approach, accounting policies adopted for, Ch. 56, 16.1.2
    - process used to determine significant assumptions, Ch. 55, 11.1.4
    - recognised assets, liabilities, income and expense, Ch. 55, 11.1.2
    - reconciliations of changes in insurance assets and liabilities, Ch. 55, 11.1.6
    - reconciliations required for contracts applying the general model, Ch. 56, 16.1.1
    - reconciliations required for contracts applying the premium allocation approach, Ch. 56, 16.1.2
  - regulatory, Ch. 56, 16.5.6
  - significant judgements in applying IFRS 17, Ch. 56, 16.3
  - transition amounts, Ch. 56, 16.2
- discount rates, Ch. 56, 8.3
- discretionary participation feature, Ch. 55, 6; Ch. 56, 11.3
  - in financial instruments, Ch. 55, 6.2; Ch. 56, 11.2
  - in insurance contracts, Ch. 55, 6.1
  - investment contracts with, Ch. 56, 11.3
  - practical issues, Ch. 55, 6.3
    - contracts with switching features, Ch. 55, 6.3.2
    - negative DPF, Ch. 55, 6.3.1
- embedded derivatives, Ch. 55, 4
  - unit-linked features, Ch. 55, 4.1
- estimates of expected future cash flows, Ch. 56, 8.2
- existing accounting practices for, Ch. 55, 1.4
  - embedded value, Ch. 55, 1.4.3
  - life insurance, Ch. 55, 1.4.2
  - non-life insurance, Ch. 55, 1.4.1
- first-time adoption, Ch. 5, 5.4
- foreign currency, Ch. 56, 7.3
- history of the IASB's insurance project, Ch. 55, 1.1
- liability for incurred claims, Ch. 56, 8.6.2
- liability for remaining coverage, Ch. 56, 8.6.1
- modification of, Ch. 56, 12.1
- with participating features, Ch. 56, 11
- premium allocation approach, criteria and measurement, Ch. 56, 9
- risk adjustment for non-financial risk, Ch. 56, 8.4
- selection of accounting policies, Ch. 55, 7
  - hierarchy exemption, Ch. 55, 7.1
  - limits on the hierarchy exemption, Ch. 55, 7.2

accounting policy matters not addressed by IFRS 4, Ch. 55, 7.2.6
catastrophe and equalisation provisions, Ch. 55, 7.2.1
impairment of reinsurance assets, Ch. 55, 7.2.5
insurance liability derecognition, Ch. 55, 7.2.3
liability adequacy testing, Ch. 55, 7.2.2
offsetting of insurance and related reinsurance contracts, Ch. 55, 7.2.4
unbundling of deposit components, Ch. 55, 5
illustration, Ch. 55, 5.2
practical difficulties, Ch. 55, 5.3
requirements, Ch. 55, 5.1
without direct participating features, Ch. 56, 8.6.3, 17.4.2
Insurance finance income or expense, Ch. 56, 15.3, 16.1.3, 17.5.1
Insurance liability, Ch. 55, 2.2.1
derecognition, Ch. 55, 7.2.3
reconciliations of changes in, Ch. 55, 11.1.6
on undiscounted basis, measuring, Ch. 55, 8.2.1.A
Insurance mutuals, Ch. 55, 3.2.2.B; Ch. 56, 3.5.2.B
Insurance protection, Ch. 52, 3.6.3
Insurance revenue, Ch. 56, 15.1
Insurance risk
changes in the level of, Ch. 55, 3.3; Ch. 56, 3.6
claims development information, Ch. 55, 11.2.5; Ch. 56, 16.5.3
concentrations of risk, Ch. 55, 11.2.4; Ch. 56, 16.5.1
financial risk, distinction from, Ch. 55, 3.6; Ch. 56, 3.4
general matters, Ch. 55, 11.2.2
sensitivity information, Ch. 55, 11.2.3
significant insurance risk, Ch. 55, 3.2; Ch. 56, 3.5
level of assessment, Ch. 55, 3.2.2
insurance mutuals, Ch. 55, 3.2.2.B
intragroup insurance contracts, Ch. 55, 3.2.2.C
self insurance, Ch. 55, 3.2.2.A
meaning of 'significant,' Ch. 55, 3.2.1
quantity of insurance risk, Ch. 56, 3.5.1
significant additional benefits, Ch. 55, 3.2.3
Insurance service expenses, Ch. 56, 15.2
Insured benefits, employee benefits, Ch. 35, 3.2
Insured event, Ch. 55, 2.2.1
Insurer, Ch. 55, 2, 2.2.1; Ch. 56, 2
Insurer's liabilities, fair value of, Ch. 55, 9.1.1.B
Intangible asset model, service concession arrangements, Ch. 25, 4.3
Intangible assets, Ch. 9, 5.5.2; Ch. 17, 1–11. *See also* Amortisation of intangible assets; IAS 38; Internally generated intangible assets
acquisition by way of government grant, Ch. 17, 4.6
agile software development, Ch. 17, 6.2.6
as corporate assets, Ch. 20, 3.1.1
cloud computing, Ch. 17, 11.6
accounting, intangible asset, Ch. 17, 11.6.4; Ch. 17, 11.6.5
arrangement contains a lease, Ch. 17, 11.6.2
arrangement contains an intangible asset, , Ch. 17, 11.6.3
arrangements that contain an intangible asset, accounting for, Ch. 17,11.6.4

fees in the arrangement, Ch. 17, 11.6.4.A; Ch. 17, 11.6.4.B
implementation costs, Ch. 17, 11.6.4.B; Ch. 17, 11.6.5.B
types of cloud computing arrangements and determination of applicable IFRSs, Ch. 17, 11.6.1
definition, Ch. 17, 2.1
classification of programme and other broadcast rights as inventory/intangible assets, Ch. 17, 2.2.2
control, Ch. 17, 2.1.2
future economic benefits, Ch. 17, 2.1.3
identifiability, Ch. 17, 2.1.1
whether to record a tangible/intangible asset, Ch. 17, 2.2.1
disclosure, Ch. 17, 10
additional disclosures when the revaluation model is applied, Ch. 17, 10.4
general disclosures, Ch. 17, 10.1
profit/loss presentation, Ch. 17, 10.3
of research and development expenditure, Ch. 17, 10.5
statement of financial position presentation, Ch. 17, 10.2
exchanges of assets
commercial substance, Ch. 17, 4.7.2
measurement of assets exchanged, Ch. 17, 4.7.1
impairment losses, Ch. 17, 9.4
impairment of intangibles with an indefinite useful life, Ch. 20, 10
interim financial reporting, depreciation and amortisation, Ch. 41, 9.1
issues regarding, Ch. 17, 11
accounting for green certificates/renewable energy certificates, Ch. 17, 11.3
accounting for REACH costs, Ch. 17, 11.4
crypto-assets, Ch. 17, 11.5
emissions trading schemes, Ch. 17, 11.2
accounting for emission rights by brokers and traders, Ch. 17, 11.2.7
amortisation and impairment testing of emission rights, Ch. 17, 11.2.4
emission rights acquired in a business combination, Ch. 17, 11.2.5
government grant approach, Ch. 17, 11.2.3
IFRIC 3, Ch. 17, 11.2.1
net liability approaches, Ch. 17, 11.2.2
sale of emission rights, Ch. 17, 11.2.6
rate-regulated activities, Ch. 17, 11.1
measurement, Ch. 17, 3.2
acquired for contingent consideration, Ch. 17, 4.5
after initial recognition, Ch. 17, 8
cost model for measurement of intangible assets, Ch. 17, 8.1
revaluation model for measurement of intangible assets, Ch. 17, 8.2
accounting for revaluations, Ch. 17, 8.2.3
frequency of revaluations, Ch. 17, 8.2.2
revaluation is only allowed if there is an active market, Ch. 17, 8.2.1
recognising and measuring assets acquired and liabilities assumed in a business combination, Ch. 9, 5.5
combining an intangible asset with a related contract, Ch. 9, 5.5.2.C
contractual-legal, Ch. 9, 5.5.2

Intangible assets—*contd*
  recognising and measuring assets acquired and liabilities assumed in a business combination—*contd*
    customer relationship intangible assets, Ch. 9, 5.5.2.B
    emission rights, Ch. 9, 5.5.2.E
    fair values of intangible assets, determining, Ch. 9, 5.5.2.F
    in-process research or development project expenditure, Ch. 9, 5.5.2.D
    Multi Period Excess Earnings Method (MEEM), Ch. 9, 5.5.2.F
    Relief from Royalty method, Ch. 9, 5.5.2.F
    separability, Ch. 9, 5.5.2; Ch. 17, 5.1.3.B
  recognition, Ch. 17, 3.1
    PP&E components classified as, Ch. 18, 3.1.4
  separate acquisition, Ch. 17, 4
    acquisition by way of government grant, Ch. 17, 4.6
    components of cost, Ch. 17, 4.2
    costs to be expensed, Ch. 17, 4.3
    exchanges of assets, Ch. 17, 4.7
      commercial substance, Ch. 17, 4.7.2
      measurement of assets exchanged, Ch. 17, 4.7.1
    income from incidental operations, Ch. 17, 4.4
    measurement of intangible assets acquired for contingent consideration, Ch. 17, 4.5
    recognition, Ch. 17, 4.1
  subsequent expenditure, Ch. 17, 3.3
  useful life of, assessing, Ch. 17, 9.1
    with an indefinite useful life, Ch. 17, 9.3
    contractual/other legal rights, Ch. 17, 9.1.2
    factors affecting, Ch. 17, 9.1.1
    with a finite useful life, Ch. 17, 9.2

Intellectual property licences, Ch. 31, 2
  identifying performance obligations in a licensing arrangement, Ch. 31, 2.1
    application questions, Ch. 31, 2.1.5
    contracts that grant both permission for past use of intellectual property and a licence to use the intellectual property in the future, Ch. 31, 2.1.5.B
    contractual restrictions, Ch. 31, 2.1.3
    guarantees to defend or maintain a patent, Ch. 31, 2.1.4
    licences of intellectual property that are distinct, Ch. 31, 2.1.1
    licences of intellectual property that are not distinct, Ch. 31, 2.1.2
  licence renewals, Ch. 31, 2.4
  nature of the entity's promise in granting a licence, determining, Ch. 31, 2.2
    applying the licensing application guidance to a single (bundled) performance obligation that includes a licence of intellectual property, Ch. 31, 2.2.1
  recognising revenue for, Ch. 30, 8
  sales-based/usage-based royalties on, Ch. 31, 2.5
    application questions on the sales-based or usage-based royalty recognition constraint, Ch. 31, 2.5.2
    recognition of royalties for a licence that provides a right to access intellectual property, Ch. 31, 2.5.1
  transfer of control of licensed intellectual property, Ch. 31, 2.3
    right to access, Ch. 31, 2.3.1
    right to use, Ch. 31, 2.3.2
    use and benefit requirement, Ch. 31, 2.3.3

Interbank Offered Rate Reform (IBOR), Ch. 50, 3.8.3; Ch. 53,9; Ch. 54, 4.3.5, 5.7; Ch. 55, 10.1.6
Intercompany. *See* Intragroup
Interest-free long-term loans, Ch. 49, 3.3.1
Interest rate
  floors and caps, Ch. 46, 5.1.5
  indices, Ch. 46, 5.1.2
  negative, Ch. 53, 2.4.2
Interest rate risk, Ch. 54, 5
  contractually specified portions of, Ch. 53, 2.2.2
  offsetting internal hedging instruments, Ch. 53, 4.2
  sensitivity analysis, Ch. 54, 5.5.1
Interest rate swaps (IRS), Ch. 6, 5.3.1; Ch. 21, 5.5.1; Ch. 52, 4.4.2
  future settlement, Ch. 46, 2.3
  initial net investment, Ch. 46, 2.2
  at initial recognition, Ch. 14, 13.2.1
Interests in consolidated structured entities
  disclosure of risks associated with, Ch. 13, 4.4
Interests in joint arrangements and associates, disclosure of, Ch. 13, 5. *See also* IFRS 12
  extent, Ch. 13, 5.1
  financial effects, Ch. 13, 5.1
  individually immaterial joint ventures and associates, Ch. 13, 5.1.2
  joint ventures, Ch. 13, 5.2
  nature, Ch. 13, 5.1
  risks associated, Ch. 13, 5.2
  summarised financial information, Ch. 13, 5.1.1
Interests in other entities, Ch. 13, 2.2.1.A, 2.2.3.D
Interests in subsidiaries, disclosure of, Ch. 13, 4
  changes in ownership interests in subsidiaries, Ch. 13, 4.5
  composition of the group, Ch. 13, 4.1
  interests of non-controlling interests, Ch. 13, 4.2
  of nature and extent of significant restrictions, Ch. 13, 4.3
  required by investment entities, Ch. 13, 4.6
  risks associated with interests in consolidated structured entities, Ch. 13, 4.4
  terms of contractual arrangements, Ch. 13, 4.4.1
Interests in unconsolidated structured entities, disclosure of, Ch. 13, 6. *See also* IFRS 12
  nature of interests, Ch. 13, 6.1
    nature, purpose, size, activities and financing of structured entities, Ch. 13, 6.1.1
    sponsored structured entities for which no interest is held at the reporting date, Ch. 13, 6.1.2
  nature of risks, Ch. 13, 6.2–6.3
Interim financial reporting, Ch. 41, 1–11. *See also* IAS 34
Interim income tax expense, measuring, Ch. 41, 9.5.1
Internal hedges
  held by other group entities, Ch. 53, 4
  internal hedged items, Ch. 53, 4.3
    forecast intragroup transactions, Ch. 53, 4.3.2
    intragroup monetary items, Ch. 53, 4.3.1
  internal hedging instruments, Ch. 53, 4.1
    central clearing parties and ring fencing, Ch. 53, 4.1.1
  offsetting instruments, Ch. 53, 4.2
    foreign exchange risk, Ch. 53, 4.2.2
    interest rate risk, Ch. 53, 4.2.1

Internally generated intangible assets, Ch. 17, 6
  brands, Ch. 17, 6.2.4
  cost of
    eligible for capitalisation, Ch. 17, 6.3.2
    establishing the time from, Ch. 17, 6.3.1
  customer lists, Ch. 17, 6.2.4
  development phase, Ch. 17, 6.2.2
  goodwill, Ch. 17, 6.1
  mastheads, Ch. 17, 6.2.4
  pharmaceutical industry, research and development in, Ch. 17, 6.2.3
  publishing titles, Ch. 17, 6.2.4
  research phase, Ch. 17, 6.2.1
  website costs (SIC-32), Ch. 17, 6.2.5
    application and infrastructure, Ch. 17, 6.2.5
    content development, Ch. 17, 6.2.5
    graphical design development, Ch. 17, 6.2.5
    operating stage, Ch. 17, 6.2.5
    planning, Ch. 17, 6.2.5
International Accounting Standards (IAS), Ch. 1, 2.1. *See also individual* IAS *entries*
International Accounting Standards Board (IASB), Ch. 1, 2.4. *See also* Conceptual framework, IASB's
  agenda consultation, Ch. 1, 2.2, 2.4, 3.1,3.2
  annual improvements, Ch. 1, 2.5
  convergence, Ch. 1, 3.2
  current priorities, Ch. 1, 3.1
  Due Process Handbook, Ch. 1, 2.5, 2.6
  future agenda, Ch. 1, 3.1
  maintenance projects, Ch. 3, 6.2
  primary financial statements, Ch. 3, 6.1.2
  Monitoring Board, Ch. 1, 2.3
  standard-setting projects, Ch. 3, 6.1
  standard setting structure, Ch. 1, 2.1
    advisory bodies, Ch. 1, 2.9
    IFRS Advisory Council, Ch. 1, 2.7
    IFRS Foundation, Ch. 1, 2.2
    IFRS Interpretations Committee, Ch. 1, 2,1-2.2, 2.5–2.7
International Financial Reporting Standards (IFRS), Ch. 1, 2.1. *See also individual* IFRS *entries*
  adoption, worldwide, Ch. 1, 4.1
    Americas, Ch. 1, 4.3
    Asia, Ch. 1, 4.4
    Australia, Ch. 1, 4.5
    Europe, Ch. 1, 4.2
    South Africa, Ch. 1, 4.6
  consistency in application of, Ch. 1, 5
International Organisation of Securities Commissions (IOSCO), Ch. 1, 1, 2.3, 5
Interpretations Committee, Ch. 1, 2.5
  agenda decisions Ch. 1, 2.5.1
Intragroup (Intercompany)
  deferred tax on foreseeable future – anticipated intragroup dividend, Ch. 33, 7.5.4
  dividend subject to withholding tax, Ch. 33, 10.3.3
  eliminations, Ch. 7, 2.4
  insurance contracts, Ch. 56, 3.5.2.C
  transactions, Ch. 8, 4.3.1
  transfer of assets with no change in tax base, Ch. 33, 7.2.5
  transfer of tax losses, payments for, Ch. 33, 11.2
  unpaid interest, royalties, management charges etc., Ch. 33, 7.5.5
  unrealised profits and losses in consolidated financial statements, Ch. 33, 8.7
Intrinsic value method, share-based payments Ch. 34, 8.8.1
Inventories, Ch. 22, 1–6. *See also* IAS 2–*Inventories*
  disclosure requirements, Ch. 22, 6
  interim financial reporting, Ch. 41, 9.4
  measurement, Ch. 22, 3
  real estate inventory, Ch. 22, 4
  recognition in profit/loss, Ch. 22, 5
Inventories, extractive industries, Ch. 43, 14
  carried at fair value, Ch. 43, 14.4
  core inventories, Ch. 43, 14.3
  heap leaching (mining), Ch. 43, 14.6
  recognition of work in progress, Ch. 43, 14.1
  sale of by-products and joint products, Ch. 43, 14.2
    by-products, Ch. 43, 14.2.1
    joint products, Ch. 43, 14.2.2
  stockpiles of low grade ore (mining), Ch. 43, 14.5
Investing activities, cash flows, Ch. 40, 4.2
Investment contracts, Ch. 55, 2.2.2, 3.9.2
Investment contracts with discretionary participation features, Ch. 55, 6.1–6.2, 7.2.2.C; Ch. 56, 11.3
Investment entity, Ch. 6, 10
  accounting by a parent of an investment entity, Ch. 6, 10.4
  accounting by an investment entity, Ch. 6, 10.3
  cash flows in, Ch. 40, 6.4.3
  definition, Ch. 6, 10.1
  determining whether an entity is an investment entity, Ch. 6, 10.2
    earnings from investments, Ch. 6, 10.2.3
    exit strategies, Ch. 6, 10.2.2
    fair value measurement, Ch. 6, 10.2.4
    having more than one investor, Ch. 6, 10.2.6
    holding more than one investment, Ch. 6, 10.2.5
    intermediate holding companies established for tax optimization purposes, Ch. 6, 10.2.1.B
    investment entity illustrative examples, Ch. 6, 10.2.9
    investment-related services, Ch. 6, 10.2.1.A
    multi-layered fund structures, Ch. 6, 10.2.10
    ownership interests, Ch. 6, 10.2.8
    unrelated investors, Ch. 6, 10.2.7
  disclosures required by, Ch. 13, 4.6
Investment property, Ch. 19, 1–12. *See also* IAS 40
  cost model, Ch. 19, 7
    impairment, Ch. 19, 7.3
    incidence of use of the cost model, Ch. 19, 7.2
    initial recognition, Ch. 19, 7.1
      identification of non-physical parts, Ch. 19, 7.1.2
      identification of physical parts, Ch. 19, 7.1.1
  definitions, Ch. 19, 2
  disclosure requirements of IAS 40, Ch. 19, 12
    additional disclosures for the cost model, Ch. 19, 12.3
    additional disclosures for the fair value model, Ch. 19, 12.2
      extra disclosures where fair value cannot be determined reliably, Ch. 19, 12.2.2
      presentation of changes in fair value, Ch. 19, 12.2.1

Investment property—*contd*
  disclosure requirements of IAS 4—*contd*
    disclosures under both fair value and cost models, Ch. 19, 12.1
      disclosure of direct operating expenses, Ch. 19, 12.1.3
      level of aggregation for IFRS 13 disclosures, Ch. 19, 12.1.2
      methods and assumptions in fair value estimates, Ch. 19, 12.1.1
      presentation of sales proceeds, Ch. 19, 12.4
  disposal of investment property, Ch. 19, 10
    calculation of gain/loss on disposal, Ch. 19, 10.1
    compensation from third parties, Ch. 19, 10.4
    replacement of parts of investment property, Ch. 19, 10.3
    sale prior to completion of construction, Ch. 19, 10.2
  fair value model, Ch. 19, 6
    deferred taxation for property held by a 'single asset' entity, Ch. 19, 6.10
    estimating fair value, Ch. 19, 6.1
      comparison with value in use, Ch. 19, 6.1.3
      'double counting,' Ch. 19, 6.1.4
      methods of estimation, Ch. 19, 6.1.1
      observable data, Ch. 19, 6.1.2
    fair value of investment property under construction, Ch. 19, 6.3
    fixtures and fittings subsumed within fair value, Ch. 19, 6.5
    future capital expenditure and development value ('highest and best use'), Ch. 19, 6.8
    inability to determine fair value of completed investment property, Ch. 19, 6.2
    negative present value, Ch. 19, 6.9
    prepaid and accrued operating lease income, Ch. 19, 6.6
      accrued rental income and lease incentives, Ch. 19, 6.6.1
      prepaid rental income, Ch. 19, 6.6.2
    transaction costs incurred by the reporting entity on acquisition, Ch. 19, 6.4
    valuation adjustment to the fair value of properties held under a lease, Ch. 19, 6.7
  IFRS 5 and investment property, Ch. 19, 8
  initial measurement, Ch. 19, 4
    assets acquired in exchange transactions, Ch. 19, 4.6
    attributable costs, Ch. 19, 4.1
      acquisition of a group of assets that does not constitute a business, Ch. 19, 4.1.1
      deferred taxes when acquiring a 'single asset' entity that is not a business, Ch. 19, 4.1.2
    borrowing costs, Ch. 19, 4.8
    contingent costs, Ch. 19, 4.10
    deferred payments, Ch. 19, 4.3
    income from tenanted property during development, Ch. 19, 4.11
    initial recognition of tenanted investment property subsequently measured using the cost model, Ch. 19, 4.7
    lease incentives and initial costs of leasing a property, Ch. 19, 4.9
      initial direct costs of obtaining a lease, Ch. 19, 4.9.2
      lease incentives, Ch. 19, 4.9.1
    payments by the vendor to the purchaser, Ch. 19, 4.12
    property held under a lease, Ch. 19, 4.5
    reclassifications from property, plant and equipment ('PP&E'/from inventory, Ch. 19, 4.4
    start-up costs and self-built property, Ch. 19, 4.2
      cost of a building to be demolished in connection with the construction of a new building, Ch. 19, 4.2.1
  interim reporting and IAS 40, Ch. 19, 11
  measurement after initial recognition, Ch. 19, 5
    by insurers and similar entities, Ch. 19, 5.1
  recognition, Ch. 19, 3
  scope, Ch. 19, 2
  transfer of assets to/from investment property, Ch. 19, 9
    accounting treatment of transfers, Ch. 19, 9.2
    transfers from investment property to inventory, Ch. 19, 9.1

Investment tax credits, Ch. 24, 2.3.2; Ch. 33, 4.3

Investments in associates and joint ventures, Ch. 11, 1–11. *See also* Equity method/accounting; IAS 28; Reciprocal interests in equity accounted entities
  application of the equity method, Ch. 11, 7
    consistent accounting policies, Ch. 11, 7.8
    date of commencement of equity accounting, Ch. 11, 7.3
    discontinuing the use of the equity method, Ch. 11, 7.12
      deemed disposals, Ch. 11, 7.12.6
      investment in associate becomes a joint venture (or vice versa), Ch. 11, 7.12.4
      investment in associate/joint venture that is a business becoming a subsidiary, Ch. 11, 7.12.1
      partial disposals of interests in associate/joint venture, Ch. 11, 7.12.5
      retained investment in associate or joint venture that is not a business becoming a subsidiary, Ch. 11, 7.12.2
      retained investment in the former associate or joint venture is a financial asset, Ch. 11, 7.12.3
    distributions received in excess of the carrying amount, Ch. 11, 7.10
    equity accounting and consolidation, comparison between, Ch. 11, 7.2
    equity transactions in an associate's/joint venture's financial statements, Ch. 11, 7.11
      dividends/other forms of distributions, Ch. 11, 7.11.1
      effects of changes in parent/non-controlling interests in subsidiaries, Ch. 11, 7.11.4
      equity-settled share-based payment transactions, Ch. 11, 7.11.3
      issues of equity instruments, Ch. 11, 7.11.2
    initial carrying amount of an associate/joint venture, Ch. 11, 7.4
      applying a cost-based approach, Ch. 11, 7.4.2.A
      applying a fair value (IFRS 3) approach, Ch. 11, 7.4.2.A
      following loss of control of an entity, Ch. 7, 3.3.2, 7.1; Ch. 11, 7.4.1
      piecemeal acquisition, Ch. 11, 7.4.2
        common control transactions involving sales of associates, Ch. 11, 7.4.2.D
        existing associate that becomes a joint venture, or vice versa, Ch. 11, 7.4.2.C
        financial instrument becoming an associate/joint venture, Ch. 11, 7.4.2.A

step increase in an existing associate/joint venture without a change in status of the investee, Ch. 11, 7.4.2.B
loss-making associates/joint ventures, Ch. 11, 7.9
non-coterminous accounting periods, Ch. 11, 7.7
overview, Ch. 11, 7.1
share of the investee, Ch. 11, 7.5
    accounting for potential voting rights, Ch. 11, 7.5.1
    cumulative preference shares held by parties other than the investor, Ch. 11, 7.5.2
    several classes of equity, Ch. 11, 7.5.3
    where the investee is a group, Ch. 11, 7.5.5
    where the reporting entity is a group, Ch. 11, 7.5.4
transactions between the reporting entity and its associates/joint ventures, Ch. 11, 7.6
    contributions of non-monetary assets to an associate/joint venture, Ch. 11, 7.6.5
        commercial substance, Ch. 11, 7.6.5.A
        conflict between IAS 28 and IFRS 10, Ch. 7, 3.3.2, 7.1; Ch. 11, 7.6.5.C
        practical application, Ch. 11, 7.6.5.B
    elimination of 'upstream' and 'downstream' transactions, Ch. 11, 7.6.1
    loans and borrowings between the reporting entity, Ch. 11, 7.6.3
    reciprocal interests, Ch. 11, 7.6.2
    statement of cash flows, Ch. 11, 7.6.4
classification as held for sale (IFRS 5), Ch. 11, 6
definitions, Ch. 11, 3
disclosures, Ch. 11, 10.2
exemptions from applying the equity method, Ch. 11, 5.3
    investments held in associates/joint ventures held by venture capital organisations, Ch. 11, 5.3
        application of IFRS 9 to exempt, Ch. 11, 5.3.2
            entities with a mixture of activities, Ch. 11, 5.3.2.A
        application of IFRS 9 to exempt investments in associates or joint ventures, Ch. 11, 5.3.2
        investment entities exception, Ch. 11, 5.3.1
future developments, Ch. 11, 11
impairment losses, Ch. 11, 8
objective, Ch. 11, 2.1
parents exempt from preparing consolidated financial statements, Ch. 11, 5.1
partial use of fair value measurement of associates, Ch. 11, 5.4
presentation, Ch. 11, 10.1
    other items of comprehensive income, Ch. 11, 10.1.3
    profit/loss, Ch. 11, 10.1.2
    statement of cash flows, Ch. 11, 10.1.4
    statement of financial position, Ch. 11, 10.1.1
scope, Ch. 11, 2.2
separate financial statements, Ch. 11, 9
significant influence, Ch. 11, 4
    fund managers, Ch. 11, 4.6
    holdings of less than 20% of the voting power, Ch. 11, 4.3
    lack of, Ch. 11, 4.2
    potential voting rights, Ch. 11, 4.4
    severe long-term restrictions impairing ability to transfer funds to the investor, Ch. 11, 4.1
    voting rights held in a fiduciary capacity, Ch. 11, 4.5
subsidiaries meeting certain criteria, Ch. 11, 5.2

transfers of associates/joint ventures between entities under common control, Ch. 10, 5

Investments in subsidiaries, associates and joint ventures, Ch. 8.2.1, Ch. 20, 12.4
equity accounted investment and indicators of impairment, Ch. 20, 12.4.3
equity accounted investments and CGUs, Ch. 20, 12.4.5
equity accounted investments and long term loans, Ch. 20, 12.4.4
equity accounted investments and testing goodwill for impairment, Ch. 20,12.4.6
exemptions from applying the equity method, Ch. 11, 5
fair value less costs of disposal (FVLCD), Ch. 20, 12.4.1
value in use (VIU) for, Ch. 20, 12.4.2
Islamic Finance Consultative Group, Ch. 1, 2.9
Islamic financial institutions (IFIs), Ch. 27, 3.5.1.A
Japan, IFRS adoption in, Ch. 1, 4.4.2
Joint arrangements, Ch. 12, 1–910. *See also* IFRS 11; Joint control; Joint operations
accounting for joint operations, Ch. 12, 6
    accounting for rights and obligations, Ch. 12, 6.2
    determining the relevant IFRS, Ch. 12, 6.3
    interest in a joint operation without joint control, Ch. 12, 6.4
    not structured through a separate vehicle, Ch. 12, 6.1
    with a party that participates in a joint arrangement but does not have joint control, Ch. 12, 6.5
    in separate financial statements, Ch. 12, 6.7
    transactions between a joint operator and a joint operation, Ch. 12, 6.6
accounting for joint ventures, Ch. 12, 7
    contributions of non-monetary assets to a joint venture, Ch. 12, 7.2
    interest in a joint venture without joint control, Ch. 12, 7.1
    in separate financial statements, Ch. 12, 7.3
applications to joint arrangements held for sale, Ch. 12, 2.2.2
cash flows of, Ch. 40, 6.4.2
classification of, Ch. 12, 5
    contractual terms, Ch. 12, 5.3
    facts and circumstances, Ch. 12, 5.4
    illustrative examples, Ch. 12, 5.5
    legal form of the separate vehicle, Ch. 12, 5.2
    separate vehicle or not, Ch. 12, 5.1
continuous assessment, Ch. 12, 8
changes in ownership of a joint arrangement that is not a business, Ch. 12, 8.4
    joint operator obtains control, Ch. 7, 3.1.2; Ch. 12, 8.4.1
    parties that participate in a joint arrangement but do not have joint control obtain joint control, Ch. 12, 8.4.1
changes in ownership of a joint operation that is a business, Ch. 12, 8.3
    acquisition of an interest in, Ch. 12, 8.3.1
    disposal of interest in, Ch. 12, 8.3.5
    former subsidiary becomes, Ch. 7, 3.3.3, 7.2; Ch. 12, 8.3.3
    obtaining control or joint control over a joint operation that is a business, Ch. 12, 8.3.2
    other changes in ownership of, Ch. 12, 8.3.4

Joint arrangements—*contd*
  continuous assessment—*contd*
    changes in ownership of a joint venture that is a business, Ch. 12, 8.2
      acquisition of an interest, Ch. 12, 8.2.1
      becomes a financial asset (or vice versa), Ch. 12, 8.2.5
      becomes an associate (or vice versa), Ch. 12, 8.2.4
      control over a former joint venture, Ch. 12, 8.2.2
      disposal of interest in, Ch. 12, 8.2.6
      former subsidiary becomes a joint venture, Ch. 7, 3.3.2, 7.1; Ch. 12, 8.2.3
      interest in a joint venture held for sale, Ch. 12, 8.2.7
      when to reassess under IFRS 11, Ch. 12, 8.1
  definition of, Ch. 12, 3; Ch. 13, 2.2.2.B
  disclosures, Ch. 12, 9
  guarantees, Ch. 12, 5.3.1
  nature of, Ch. 12, 1.1
  objective, Ch. 12, 2.1
  scope, Ch. 12, 2.2
    accounting by a joint operation, Ch. 12, 2.2.3
    application by venture capital organisations and similar entities, Ch. 12, 2.2.1
    application to joint arrangements held for sale, Ch. 12, 2.2.2
  unit of account, Ch. 12, 3.1

Joint control, Ch. 12, 4
  assessing in extractive industries, Ch. 43, 7.1.1
    meaning of unanimous consent, Ch. 43, 7.1.1.B
    relevant activities, Ch. 43, 7.1.1.A
  practical issues with assessing, Ch. 12, 4.4
    evaluate multiple agreements together, Ch. 12, 4.4.2
    undivided share/lease/joint arrangement, Ch. 12, 4.4.1
  rights to control collectively, Ch. 12, 4.2
    de facto agents, Ch. 12, 4.2.5
    delegated decision-making, Ch. 12, 4.2.4
    evidence of, Ch. 12, 4.2.3
    government, role of, Ch. 12, 4.2.6
    potential voting rights and joint control, Ch. 12, 4.2.2
    protective rights, including some veto rights, Ch. 12, 4.2.1
  sequential activities in, Ch. 12, 4.1.1
  unanimous consent, Ch. 12, 4.3
    arbitration, Ch. 12, 4.3.3
    arrangements involving passive investors, Ch. 12, 4.3.1
    ultimate voting authority, Ch. 12, 4.3.2

Joint operating agreement (JOA), Ch. 43, 5.6, 17.3.3

Joint operations
  accounting for, Ch. 12, 6
    accounting for rights and obligations, Ch. 12, 6.2
    determining the relevant IFRS, Ch. 12, 6.3
    interest in a joint operation without joint control, Ch. 12, 6.4
    not structured through a separate vehicle, Ch. 12, 6.1
    with a party that participates in a joint arrangement but does not have joint control, Ch. 12, 6.5
    in separate financial statements, Ch. 12, 6.7
    transactions between a joint operator and a joint operation, Ch. 12, 6.6
  changes in ownership of, Ch. 12, 8.3 acquisition of an interest in, Ch. 12, 8.3.1
    disposal of interest in, Ch. 12, 8.3.5
    former subsidiary becomes, Ch. 7, 3.3.3, 7.2; Ch. 12, 8.3.3
    obtaining control or joint control over a joint operation that is a business, Ch. 12, 8.3.2
  implications of controlling, Ch. 43, 7.1.2.A
  in separate financial statements, Ch. 8, 1.1.2

Joint products, extractive industries, Ch. 43, 14.2, 16.1.3.D

Joint ventures. *See also* IAS 28–*Investments in associates and joint ventures*
  accounting for, Ch. 12, 7
    contributions of non-monetary assets to a joint venture, Ch. 12, 7.2
    interest in a joint venture without joint control, Ch. 12, 7.1
    in separate financial statements, Ch. 8, 1.1.1; Ch. 12, 7.3
  cash flows, Ch. 40, 6.4
    arising from interests in, Ch. 40, 8.4
    cash flows of joint operations, Ch. 40, 6.4.2
    investments in associates and joint ventures, Ch. 40, 6.4.1
  changes in ownership, Ch. 12, 8.2
  disclosure of commitments relating to, Ch. 13, 5.2.1
  disclosure of contingent liabilities relating to, Ch. 13, 5.2.2
  equity transactions in, Ch. 11, 7.11
  FVLCD for investments in, Ch. 20, 12.4.1
  implications of controlling, Ch. 43, 7.1.2.B
  initial carrying amount of an associate/joint venture, Ch. 11, 7.4
    following loss of control of an entity, Ch. 7, 3.3.2, 7.1; Ch. 11, 7.4.1
    piecemeal acquisition, Ch. 11, 7.4.2
      common control transactions involving sales of associates, Ch. 11, 7.4.2.D
      existing associate that becomes a joint venture, or vice versa, Ch. 11, 7.4.2.C
      financial instrument becoming an associate/joint venture, Ch. 11, 7.4.2.A
      step increase in an existing associate/joint venture without a change in status of the investee, Ch. 11, 7.4.2.B
  investments held in, Ch. 11, 5.3
  loans and borrowings between the reporting entity and, Ch. 11, 7.6.3
  risks associated with interests in, Ch. 13, 5.2
  separate financial statements and interests in, Ch. 8, 1.1.1
  share-based payments to employees of, Ch. 34, 12.9
  transactions between the reporting entity and, Ch. 11, 7.6
  VIU for investments in, calculating, Ch. 20, 12.4.2
    based on cash flows generated by underlying assets, Ch. 20, 12.4.2.B
    using dividend discount models, Ch. 20, 12.4.2.A

Key management personnel, related party, Ch. 39, 2.2.1.D

Leases (IFRS 16), Ch. 23, 1–10. *See also* IFRS 16
  acquiree in a business combination is a lessee, Ch. 23, 9.1
  acquiree in a business combination is a lessor, Ch. 23, 9.2
  business combinations, Ch. 23, 9–9.2
  commencement date of the lease, Ch. 23, 4.2
  contract combinations, Ch. 23, 3.3
  definition, Ch. 23, 3–3.3
    determining whether an arrangement contains a lease, Ch. 23, 3.1

Index   81

flowchart of the decision making process, Ch. 23, 3.1.6
identified asset, Ch. 23, 3.1.2
joint arrangements, Ch. 23, 3.1.1
reassessment of the contract, Ch. 23, 3.1.7
right to direct the use of the identified asset, Ch. 23, 3.1.5
    how and for what purpose the asset is used, Ch. 23, 3.1.5.A
    protective rights, Ch. 23, 3.1.5.D
    relevant decisions about how and for what purpose the asset is used are predetermined, Ch. 23, 3.1.5.B
    specifying the output of an asset before the period of use, Ch. 23, 3.1.5.C
right to obtain substantially all of the economic benefits from use of the identified asset, Ch. 23, 3.1.4
substantive substitution rights, Ch. 23, 3.1.3
identifying and separating lease and non-lease components of a contract, Ch. 23, 3.2
    determining and allocating the consideration in the contract– lessees, Ch. 23, 3.2.3
    determining and allocating the consideration in the contract– lessors, Ch. 23, 3.2.4
    identifying and separating lease components of a contract, Ch. 23, 3.2.1
    identifying and separating lease from non-lease components of a contract, Ch. 23, 3.2.2
        lessee reimbursements, Ch. 23, 3.2.2.A
        practical expedient–lessees, Ch. 23, 3.2.2.B
discount rates, Ch. 23, 4.6
    determination of the incremental borrowing rate by a subsidiary with centralised treasury functions, Ch. 23, 4.6.1
economic life, Ch. 23, 4.8
effective date and transition, Ch. 23, 10
    amounts previously recognised in a business combination, Ch. 23, 10.5.2
    disclosure, Ch. 23, 10.6
    effective date, Ch. 23, 10.1
    lessee transition, Ch. 23, 10.3
        full retrospective approach, Ch. 23, 10.3.1
        modified retrospective approach, Ch. 23, 10.3.2
    lessor transition, Ch. 23, 10.4
        subleases, Ch. 23, 10.4.1
    sale and leaseback transactions, Ch. 23, 10.5.1
    transition, Ch. 23, 10.2
extractive industries, impact of IFRS 16 on, Ch. 43, 17, 18
    allocating contract consideration, Ch. 43, 17.6
    definition of a lease, Ch. 43, 17.2
    identifying and separating lease and non-lease components, Ch. 43, 17.
    identifying lease payments included in the measurement of the lease liability, Ch. 43, 17.5
    interaction of IFRS 16 and IFRS 11, Ch. 43, 18
    interaction of leases with asset retirement obligations, Ch. 43, 17.7
    joint arrangements, Ch. 43, 18
    scope and scope exclusions, Ch. 43, 17.1
    substitution rights, Ch. 43, 17.3

fair value, Ch. 23, 4.9
inception of a contract, Ch. 23, 4.1
initial direct costs, Ch. 23, 4.7; Ch. 19, 4.9.2
lease liabilities under IFRS 16, Ch. 20, 4.1.2
lease payments, Ch. 23, 4.5
    amounts expected to be payable under residual value guarantees lessees only, Ch. 23, 4.5.6
    co-tenancy clauses, Ch. 23, 4.5.11
    exercise price of a purchase option, Ch. 23, 4.5.4
    in-substance fixed lease payments, Ch. 23, 4.5.1
    lease incentives, Ch. 23, 4.5.2; Ch. 19, 4.9.1
    lessors only, Ch. 23, 4.5.7
    payments for penalties for terminating a lease, Ch. 23, 4.5.5
    reassessment of the lease liability, Ch. 23, 4.5.12
    remeasurement by lessors, Ch. 23, 4.5.13
    security deposits, Ch. 23, 4.5.9
    value added tax and property taxes, Ch. 23, 4.5.10
    variable lease payments that depend on an index/rate, Ch. 23, 4.5.3
    variable lease payments which do not depend on an index or rate, Ch. 23, 4.5.8
lease term and purchase options, Ch. 23, 4.4 cancellable leases, Ch. 23, 4.4.1
    reassessment of lease term and purchase options, lessees, Ch. 23, 4.4.2
    lessors, Ch. 23, 4.4.3
lessee accounting, Ch. 23, 5
    disclosure, Ch. 23, 5.8
        additional, Ch. 23, 5.8.3
        of assets, liabilities, expenses and cash flows, Ch. 23, 5.8.2 objective, Ch. 23, 5.8.1
    initial measurement, Ch. 23, 5.2
        lease liabilities, Ch. 23, 5.2.2
        right-of-use assets, Ch. 23, 5.2.1
    initial recognition, Ch. 23, 5.1
        leases of low-value assets, Ch. 23, 5.1.2
        short-term leases, Ch. 23, 5.1.1
    lease modifications, Ch. 23, 5.5
        amendment to IFRS 16 for covid-19 related rent concessions, Ch. 23, 5.5.4
            accounting for a concession in the form of a deferral of lease payments as if the lease is unchanged (Approach 3), Ch. 23, 5.5.4.C
            accounting for a concession, in the form of forgiveness or deferral of lease payments, as a negative variable lease payment (Approach 1), Ch. 23, 5.5.4.A
            accounting for a concession in the form of forgiveness or deferral of lease payments as a resolution of a contingency that fixes previously variable lease payments (Approach 2), Ch. 23, 5.5..B
            disclosure, Ch. 23, 5.5.4.D
            transition and effective date, Ch. 23, 5.5.4.E
        application of lease modification guidance to rent concessions, Ch. 23, 5.5.3
            lessee accounting for rent concessions as lease modifications, Ch. 23, 5.5.3.B
            rent concessions that change the consideration in the contract, Ch. 23, 5.5.3.A

Leases (IFRS 16)—*contd*
   lessee accounting—*contd*
      lease modifications—*contd*
         lessee accounting for a modification that does not result in a separate lease, Ch. 23, 5.5.2
         resulting in a separate lease, Ch. 23, 5.5.1
      lessee matters, Ch. 23, 5.6
         impairment of right-of-use assets, Ch. 23, 5.6.1
         income tax accounting, Ch. 23, 5.6.4
         leases denominated in a foreign currency, Ch. 23, 5.6.2
         portfolio approach, Ch. 23, 5.6.3
      presentation, Ch. 23, 5.7
      presentation in the statement of cash flows, Ch. 40, 5.5.1
      remeasurement of lease liabilities and right-of-use assets, Ch. 23, 5.4
      subsequent measurement, Ch. 23, 5.3
         expense recognition, Ch. 23, 5.3.3
         lease liabilities, Ch. 23, 5.3.2
         right-of-use assets, Ch. 23, 5.3.1
   lessee involvement with the underlying asset before the commencement date, Ch. 23, 4.3
   lessor accounting, Ch. 23, 6
      disclosure, Ch. 23, 6.7
         for all lessors, Ch. 23, 6.7.2
         for finance leases, Ch. 23, 6.7.3
         objective, Ch. 23, 6.7.1
         for operating leases, Ch. 23, 6.7.4
      finance leases, Ch. 23, 6.2
         initial measurement, Ch. 23, 6.2.1
         manufacturer/dealer lessors, Ch. 23, 6.2.2
         remeasurement of the net investment in the lease, Ch. 23, 6.2.4
         subsequent measurement, Ch. 23, 6.2.3
      lease classification, Ch. 23, 6.1
         criteria, Ch. 23, 6.1.1
         reassessment of, Ch. 23, 6.1.4
         residual value guarantees included in the lease classification test, Ch. 23, 6.1.3
         test for land and buildings, Ch. 23, 6.1.2
      lease modifications, Ch. 23, 6.4
         determining whether a modification to a finance lease results in a separate lease, Ch. 23, 6.4.1
         lessor accounting for a modification to a finance lease that does not result in a separate lease, Ch. 23, 6.4.2
         modification to an operating lease, Ch. 23, 6.4.3
      lessor matters, Ch. 23, 6.5
         portfolio approach, Ch. 23, 6.5.1
      operating leases, Ch. 23, 6.3
         income, Ch. 23, 6.3.1
      presentation, Ch. 23, 6.6
      presentation in the statement of cash flows, Ch. 40, 5.5.5
   sale and leaseback transactions, Ch. 23, 8
      determining whether the transfer of an asset is a sale, Ch. 23, 8.1
      disclosures, Ch. 23, 8.4
      transactions in which the transfer of an asset is a sale, Ch. 23, 8.2
         accounting for the leaseback, Ch. 23, 8.2.2
         accounting for the sale, Ch. 23, 8.2.1
         adjustment for off-market terms, Ch. 23, 8.2.3
      transactions in which the transfer of an asset is not a sale, Ch. 23, 8.3
   subleases, Ch. 23, 7
      definition, Ch. 23, 7.1
      disclosure, Ch. 23, 7.5
      intermediate lessor accounting, Ch. 23, 7.2
      presentation, Ch. 23, 7.4
      sublessee accounting, Ch. 23, 7.3
Leases of land, Ch. 23, 3.2
   separating land and buildings, Ch. 23, 6.1.2
Legal obligation, Ch. 26, 1.3, 3.1.1; Ch. 35, 7.1, 12.3.1
Legal right of set-off, enforceable, Ch. 54, 7.4.1.A
Lessee accounting (IFRS 16), Ch. 23, 5
   disclosure, Ch. 23, 5.8
      additional, Ch. 23, 5.8.3
      of assets, liabilities, expenses and cash flows, Ch. 23, 5.8.2
      objective, Ch. 23, 5.8.1
   initial measurement, Ch. 23, 5.2
      lease liabilities, Ch. 23, 5.2.2
      right-of-use assets, Ch. 23, 5.2.1
   initial recognition, Ch. 23, 5.1
      leases of low-value assets, Ch. 23, 5.1.2
      short-term leases, Ch. 23, 5.1.1
   lease liabilities under IFRS 16, Ch. 20, 4.1.2
   lease modifications, Ch. 23, 5.5
      determining whether a lease modification results in a separate lease, Ch. 23, 5.5.1
      lessee accounting for a modification that does not result in a separate lease, Ch. 23, 5.5.2
   lessee matters, Ch. 23, 5.6
      impairment of right-of-use assets, Ch. 23, 5.6.1
      income tax accounting, Ch. 23, 5.6.4
      leases denominated in a foreign currency, Ch. 23, 5.6.2
      portfolio approach, Ch. 23, 5.6.3
   presentation, Ch. 23, 5.7
   remeasurement of lease liabilities and right-of-use assets, Ch. 23, 5.4
   subsequent measurement, Ch. 23, 5.3
      expense recognition, Ch. 23, 5.3.3
      lease liabilities, Ch. 23, 5.3.2
      right-of-use assets, Ch. 23, 5.3.1
Lessor accounting (IFRS 16), Ch. 23, 6
   disclosure, Ch. 23, 6.7
      for all lessors, Ch. 23, 6.7.2
      for finance leases, Ch. 23, 6.7.3
      objective, Ch. 23, 6.7.1
      for operating leases, Ch. 23, 6.4.3
   finance leases, Ch. 23, 6.2
      initial measurement, Ch. 23, 6.2.1
      manufacturer/dealer lessors, Ch. 23, 6.2.2
      remeasurement of the net investment in the lease, Ch. 23, 6.2.4
      subsequent measurement, Ch. 23, 6.2.3
   lease classification, Ch. 23, 6.1
      criteria, Ch. 23, 6.1.1
      reassessment of, Ch. 23, 6.1.4
      residual value guarantees included in the lease classification test, Ch. 23, 6.1.3
      test for land and buildings, Ch. 23, 6.1.2

lease modifications, Ch. 23, 6.4
  determining whether a modification to a finance lease results in a separate lease, Ch. 23, 6.4.1
  lessor accounting for a modification to a finance lease that does not result in a separate lease, Ch. 23, 6.4.2
  modification to an operating lease, Ch. 23, 6.4.3
  lessor matters, Ch. 23, 6.5
    portfolio approach, Ch. 23, 6.5.1
  operating leases, Ch. 23, 6.3
  presentation, Ch. 23, 6.6
Level 1, 2 and 3 inputs, fair value measurement, Ch. 14, 17, 18, 19; Ch. 19, 12.1.1
Levies, Ch. 33, 4.1.1, Ch. 26, 6.8
  charged by public authorities, interim reports, Ch. 41, 9.7.5
Liability adequacy testing, Ch. 55, 7.2.2
  investment contracts with a discretionary participation feature. Ch. 55, 7.2.2.C
  and shadow accounting, interaction between, Ch. 55, 7.2.2.D
  specified in IFRS Ch. 55, 7.2.2.B
  under existing accounting policies, Ch. 55, 7.2.2.A
LIBOR
  LIBOR replacement, Ch. 53, 8.3.5
  'sub-LIBOR issue', Ch. 53, 2.4
Life insurance, Ch. 55, 1.4.2
'Linked' instruments, Ch. 47, 4.5.7
Liquidity risk, Ch. 54, 5.4
  associated liquidity risk, management of, Ch. 54, 5.4.3
  information provided to key management, Ch. 54, 5.4.1
  maturity analyses, Ch. 54, 5.4.2
    cash flows: borrowings, Ch. 54, 5.4.2.C
    cash flows: derivatives, Ch. 54, 5.4.2.D
    cash flows: embedded derivatives, Ch. 54, 5.4.2.E
    cash flows: financial guarantee contracts and written options, Ch. 54, 5.4.2.F
    cash flows: general requirements, Ch. 54, 5.4.2.B
    examples of disclosures in practice, Ch. 54, 5.4.2.G
    time bands, Ch. 54, 5.4.2.A
  puttable financial instruments classified as equity, Ch. 54, 5.4.4
Litigation, provisions and contingencies, Ch. 26, 6.11
Loan commitments, Ch. 48, 6.4.6
  assets and liabilities from, Ch. 49, 3.7
  IFRS 9 impairment requirements, Ch. 51, 11
  off-market, Ch. 49, 3.3.3
  outside the scope of and IFRS 9, Ch. 49, 3.7.1
  within the scope of and IFRS 9, Ch. 49, 3.7.2
Loans
  acquired in business combination, Ch. 49, 3.3.4
  at a below-market interest rate, Ch. 50, 2.8
  commitment, Ch. 45, 3.5
  intercompany loans, Ch. 51, 13
  low-interest long-term, Ch. 49, 3.3.1
  payable, defaults and breaches of, Ch. 54, 4.4.8
Longevity swaps, Ch. 35, 6.6
Long-term contracts and leases, extractive industries Ch. 43, 19
  embedded leases, Ch. 43, 19.1
  impact of IFRS 16, Ch. 43, 19.3
  take-or-pay contracts, Ch. 43, 19.2
    make-up product and undertake, Ch. 43, 19.2.1

Long-term employee benefits, Ch. 35, 13
  meaning of, Ch. 35, 13.1
  other than post-employment benefits, Ch. 35, 13.1
  recognition and measurement, Ch. 35, 13.2
    attribution to years of service, Ch. 35, 13.2.1
    long-term disability benefit, Ch. 35, 13.2.2
    long-term benefits contingent on a future event, Ch. 35, 13.2.3
Long-term loans with repayment on demand terms, Ch. 54, 7.4.4.C
Loss-making associates/joint ventures, Ch. 11, 7.9
Loss-making subsidiaries, Ch. 7, 5.6.1
Low-interest long-term loans, Ch. 49, 3.3.1
Macro hedge accounting, Ch. 53, 11
'Make-up' oil, Ch. 43, 15.4.2.B
Make-up product and undertake, Ch. 43, 17.2.1
'Malus' clauses, share-based payments, Ch. 34, 3.1.1
Management commentary, Ch. 2, 12
Management Commentary Consultative Group, Ch. 1, 2.9
Mandatorily convertible bond, Ch. 47, 6.6.3
  convertible into a variable number of shares
    upon a contingent 'non-viability' event, Ch. 47, 6.6.3.B
    with option for issuer to settle early for a maximum number of shares, Ch. 47, 6.6.3.A
Mandatory tender offers, Ch. 7, 6.2.4, 7.4
Market and non-market variables, insurance contracts, Ch. 56, 8.2.1
Market approach, valuation technique, Ch. 14, 14.2
Market Consistent Embedded Value Principles (MCEV), Ch. 55, 1.4.3
Market participants, Ch. 14, 7
  assumptions, Ch. 14, 7.2
  characteristics, Ch. 14, 7.1
Market risk, Ch. 54, 5.5
  'basic' sensitivity analysis, Ch. 54, 5.5.1
  other market risk disclosures, Ch. 54, 5.5.3
  value-at-risk and similar analyses, Ch. 54, 5.5.2
Market vesting conditions, share-based payments, Ch. 34, 6.3.
  See also Cash-settled share-based payment transactions; Equity-settled share-based payment transactions; IFRS 2; Share-based payment transactions
Master netting agreements, Ch. 54, 7.4.1.B
  and non-performance risk, Ch. 14, 11.3.4
Material cash flows, Ch. 40, 5.1
Materiality, Ch. 3, 4.1.5.A; Ch. 54, 3.2
  interim financial reporting, Ch. 41, 6
Maturity analyses, liquidity risk, Ch. 54, 5.4.2
  cash flows
    borrowings, Ch. 54, 5.4.2.C
    derivatives, Ch. 54, 5.4.2.D
    embedded derivatives, Ch. 54, 5.4.2.E
    examples of disclosures in practice, Ch. 54, 5.4.2.G
    financial guarantee contracts and written options, Ch. 54, 5.4.2.F
    general requirements, Ch. 54, 5.4.2.B
    time bands, Ch. 54, 5.4.2.A
Measurement period, business combinations, Ch. 9, 12

Measurement period, business combinations—*contd*
    adjustments made during, Ch. 9, 12.1
        to provisional amounts, Ch. 9, 12.1
    after end of measurement period, Ch. 9, 12.2

Measurements based on fair value. *See* Fair value measurements

Measuring ECLs during the coronavirus (covid-19) pandemic, Ch. 51, 7.8
    calculation of ECLs, Ch. 51, 7.8.3
    determining whether there has been a significant increase in credit risk, Ch. 51, 7.8.4
    disclosures, Ch. 51, 7.8.5
    guidance, Ch. 51, 7.8.2
    introduction, Ch. 51, 7.8.1

Mineral reserves and resources, extractive industries
    disclosure of mineral reserves and resources, Ch. 43, 2.4
        associates, joint arrangements and other investments, Ch. 43, 2.4
        commodity price, Ch. 43, 2.4
        mining sector, Ch. 43, 2.4.2
        non-controlling interests, Ch. 43, 2.4
        oil and gas sector, Ch. 43, 2.4.1
        production sharing contracts and risk service contracts, Ch. 43, 2.4
        proven and probable reserves, Ch. 43, 2.4 royalties, Ch. 43, 2.4
        standardised measure of oil and gas, Ch. 43, 2.4.3.A
        value of reserves, Ch. 43, 2.4.3
    international harmonisation of reserve reporting, Ch. 43, 2.1
    legal rights to explore for, develop and produce mineral properties, Ch. 43, 5
        concessionary agreements (concessions), Ch. 43, 5.2
        different types of royalty interests, Ch. 43, 5.7
        evolving contractual arrangements, Ch. 43, 5.5
        joint operating agreements, Ch. 43, 5.6
    mineral lease agreements, Ch. 43, 5.1
    pure-service contract, Ch. 43, 5.4
        basic principles and definitions, Ch. 43, 2.2.1
        classification and categorisation guidelines, Ch. 43, 2.2.2
        mining resource and reserve reporting, Ch. 43, 2.3
        petroleum reserve estimation and reporting, Ch. 43, 2.2
        traditional production sharing contracts, Ch. 43, 5.3

Mining sector disclosures, Ch. 43, 2.4.2. *See also* Extractive industries

Ministry of Finance, People's Republic of China, Ch. 1, 2.3, 4.4.1.A

Modifications in share-based payment, Ch. 34, 7.3
    cash-settled modified to equity-settled, Ch. 34, 9.4.2
    decrease the value of an award, Ch. 34, 7.3.2
        additional/more onerous non-market vesting conditions, Ch. 34, 7.3.2.C
        decrease in fair value of equity instruments granted, Ch. 34, 7.3.2.A
        decrease in number of equity instruments granted, Ch. 34, 7.3.2.B
    distinction between cancellation and modification, Ch. 34, 7.4.2
    entity's plans for future, Ch. 34, 7.6
    equity-settled modified to cash-settled, Ch. 34, 7.3.5, 9.4.1
    'give and take', Ch. 34, 7.3.4
    increase the value of an award, Ch. 34, 7.3.1
        increase in fair value of equity instruments granted, Ch. 34, 7.3.1.A
        increase in number of equity instruments granted, Ch. 34, 7.3.1.B
        removal/mitigation of non-market vesting conditions, Ch. 34, 7.3.1.C
    reduce the number of equity instruments granted but maintain or increase the value of an award, Ch. 34, 7.3.4
    share splits and consolidations, Ch. 34, 7.8
    two awards running 'in parallel', Ch. 34, 7.7
    valuation requirements, Ch. 34, 7.2
    'value for value', Ch. 34, 7.3.4
    of vesting period, Ch. 34, 7.3.3

Modified International Standards (JMIS), Japan, Ch. 1, 4.4.2

Monetary/non-monetary determination, foreign exchange, Ch. 15, 5.4
    deferred tax, Ch. 15, 5.4.5
    deposits and advance payments for actively traded commodities, Ch. 15, 5.4.2
    deposits/progress payments, Ch. 15, 5.4.1
    foreign currency share capital, Ch. 15, 5.4.4
    insurance contracts, Ch. 56, 7.3
    investments in preference shares, Ch. 15, 5.4.3
    post-employment benefit plans-foreign currency assets, Ch. 15, 5.4.6
    post-employment benefit plans-foreign currency plans, Ch. 15, 5.4.7

Monetary/non-monetary distinction
    hyperinflationary economies, Ch. 16, 4.1.1

Money market funds (MMF), Ch. 40, 3.2.2

Monitoring Board, Ch. 1, 2.3

Monte Carlo Simulation, Ch. 34, 8.3.3

Most advantageous market, Ch. 14, 6.2

Multi-employer plans, employee benefits, Ch. 35, 3.3
    defined benefit plans sharing risks between entities under common control, Ch. 35, 3.3.2
    disclosure requirements
        other than plans sharing risks between entities under common control, Ch. 35, 3.3.1
        plans accounted for as defined benefit plans, Ch. 35, 15.2.4.A
        plans accounted for as defined contribution plans, Ch. 35, 15.2.4.B

Multi-layered fund structures, Ch. 6, 10.2.10

Multi Period Excess Earnings Method (MEEM), Ch. 9, 5.5.2.F

Multiple valuation techniques, fair value measurement, Ch. 14, 14.1.2
    vs. single valuation techniques, Ch. 14, 14.1.1

Mutual entities, Ch. 9, 2.1, 7.5

Negative compensation, Ch. 48, 6.4.4.A

Negative discretionary participation feature, Ch. 55, 6.3.1

Negative intangible assets, Ch. 55, 9.1.1.D

Net cash-settled forward repurchase, Ch. 52, 4.1.4

Net defined benefit liability (asset), employee benefits, Ch. 35, 8.1
    net interest on, Ch. 35, 10.3.2
    presentation of, Ch. 35, 9

Net finance costs, Ch. 54, 7.1.1

Net investment hedges
   combination of derivatives and non-derivatives, Ch. 53, 7.3.4
   in foreign operations, Ch. 53, 1.5, 5.3, 7.3; Ch. 54, 4.3.3
      amount of the hedged item for which a hedging relationship may be designated, Ch. 53, 5.3.2
      nature of the hedged risk, Ch. 53, 5.3.1
      where the hedging instrument can be held, Ch. 53, 5.3.3
   identifying the effective portion, Ch. 53, 7.3.1
      cross-currency interest rate swaps, Ch. 53, 7.3.3.B
      derivatives used as the hedging instrument, Ch. 53, 7.3.3
      forward currency contracts, Ch. 53, 7.3.3.A
   individual/separate financial statements, Ch. 53, 7.3.5
      non-derivative liabilities used as the hedging instrument, Ch. 53, 7.3.2
      purchased options, Ch. 53, 7.3.3.C

Net realisable value, inventories, Ch. 22, 3.3

Net-settled contracts over own equity, Ch. 47, 5.2.7

Nominal amount components, Ch. 53, 2.3
   general requirement, Ch. 53, 2.3.1
   layer components for fair value hedges with prepayment risk, Ch. 53, 2.3.2

Non-adjusting events, Ch. 38, 2.1.3, 2.3

Non-cash assets to owners, Ch. 7, 3.7; Ch. 8, 2.4.2
   declaration to distribute, Ch. 38, 2.3.1.A
   distributions of, Ch. 7, 3.7; Ch. 8, 2.4.2

Non-cash transactions and transactions on deferred terms, Ch. 40, 5.4

Non-contractually specified risk components, Ch. 53, 2.2.3

Non-controlling interests (NCI), Ch. 7, 2.1, 3.1.1, 3.1.2, 4, 5, 6; Ch. 43, 2.4
   acquisition of, as part of a business combination under common control, Ch. 10, 3.3.5
   associate holds an interest in a subsidiary, Ch. 7, 5.3
   business combinations, recognising and measuring NCIs, Ch. 7, 5.2.1; Ch. 9, 8
      call and put options over NCIs, Ch. 7, 6; Ch. 9, 8.5
      implications of method chosen for measuring NCIs, Ch. 9, 8.3
      measuring qualifying NCIs at acquisition-date fair value, Ch. 7, 5.2.1; Ch. 9, 8.1
      measuring qualifying NCIs at the proportionate share of the value of net identifiable assets acquired, Ch. 7, 5.2.1; Ch. 9, 8.2
      measuring share-based payment and other components of NCIs, Ch. 7, 5.2.1, 5.6; Ch. 9, 8.4
   call and put options over, Ch. 7, 6.5
      call and put options, combination, Ch. 7, 6.3
      call and put options entered into in relation to existing NCIs, Ch. 7, 6.4
      call options only, Ch. 7, 6.1
         options giving the acquirer present access to returns associated with that ownership interest, Ch. 7, 6.1.1
         options not giving the acquirer present access to returns associated with that ownership interest, Ch. 7, 6.1.2
      exercisable in cash or shares, Ch. 7, 6.2
      put options only, Ch. 7, 6.2
         assessing whether multiple transactions should be accounted for as a single arrangement, Ch. 7, 6.2.4
         financial liability for the NCI put, Ch. 7, 6.2.1
         full recognition of NCI, Ch. 7, 6.2.3.B
         mandatory tender offers, Ch. 7, 6.2.4
         NCI is subsequently derecognized, Ch. 7, 6.2.3.D
         NCI put does not provide a present ownership interest, Ch. 7, 6.2.3
         NCI put provides a present ownership interest, Ch. 7, 6.2.2, 6.2.3.A
         partial recognition of NCI, Ch. 7, 6.2.3.C
         separate financial statements, Ch. 7, 6.5
   changes in ownership interest without loss of control (*see* Consolidation procedures)
   classified as financial liabilities, Ch. 7, 5.5
   definition of NCI, Ch. 7, 5.1
   disclosure of interests held by, Ch. 13, 4.2
   exceptions to retrospective application of other IFRSs, Ch. 5, 4.8
   future developments, Ch. 7, 7
      financial instruments with characteristics of equity project, Ch. 7, 7.3
      mandatory purchase of NCIs, Ch. 7, 7.4
      Post-implementation Reviews of IFRS 10, IFRS 11 and IFRS 12, Ch. 7, 7.5
   goodwill impairment testing, Ch. 7, 4.2; Ch. 20, 9
      acquisitions of NCIs measured at the proportionate share of net identifiable assets, Ch. 20, 9.1.1
      testing for impairment in entities with NCIs, alternative allocation methodologies, Ch. 20, 9.3
      testing for impairment in entities with NCIs initially measured at fair value, Ch. 20, 9.2
      testing for impairment in entities with NCIs measured at the proportionate share of net identifiable assets, Ch. 20, 9.1
   initial measurement of NCIs in a business combination, Ch. 7, 5.2.1, 5.2.2
   initial measurement of NCIs in a subsidiary that is not a business combination, Ch. 7, 3.1.1, 5.2.2
   mandatory tender offers in a business combination, Ch. 7, 6.2.4
   measurement in, Ch. 7, 2.1, 2.2, 3.1.1, 3.1.2, 5
   measurement of NCI where an associate holds an interest in a subsidiary, Ch. 7, 5.3
   non-cash acquisition of, Ch. 7, 4
   not recognized, Ch. 7, 6.2.3.A
   presentation of NCIs, Ch. 7, 5.4
   reverse acquisitions, business combinations, Ch. 9, 14.4
   subsequent measurement of, Ch. 7, 5.6
      loss-making subsidiaries, Ch. 7, 5.6.1
   transactions with, IAS 7, Ch. 40, 6.2

Non-coterminous accounting periods, Ch. 7, 2.5; Ch. 11, 7.7; Ch. 15, 6.4

Non-current assets (and disposal groups) held for sale/distribution, Ch. 4, 2
   classification, Ch. 4, 2.1
      abandonment, Ch. 4, 2.1.2.C
      classification as held for sale or as held for distribution to owners, Ch. 4, 2.1.2
      concept of a disposal group, Ch. 4, 2.1.1
      loss of control of a subsidiary, Ch. 4, 2.1.3.A
      meaning of available for immediate sale, Ch. 4, 2.1.2.A

Non-current assets (and disposal groups) held for sale/distribution—*contd*
  classification—*contd*
    meaning of highly probable, Ch. 4, 2.1.2.B
    partial disposal of an associate or joint venture, Ch. 4, 2.1.3.B
    partial disposals of operations, Ch. 4, 2.1.3
  comparative information, Ch. 4, 4
  disclosure requirements, Ch. 4, 5
  discontinued operation, Ch. 4, 3.2
  future developments, Ch. 4, 6
  measurement, Ch. 4, 2.2
    changes to a plan of sale/distribution, Ch. 4, 2.2.5
    impairments and reversals of impairment, Ch. 4, 2.2.3
    on initial classification as held for sale, Ch. 4, 2.2.2.A
    presentation in the statement of financial position of, Ch. 4, 2.2.4
    scope of the measurement requirements, Ch. 4, 2.2.1
    subsequent remeasurement, Ch. 4, 2.2.2.B
  property, plant and equipment, Ch. 18, 7.1
  statement of financial position presentation, Ch. 4, 4.1.2

Non-employees, share-based payment transactions with, Ch. 34, 5.4.1

Non-financial assets
  financial instruments definition, Ch. 45, 2.2.5
  hedged item, Ch. 53, 2.2.3.A; Ch. 53, 2.2.1
  non-contractual risk components, Ch. 53, 2.2.3.A

Non-financial risk, risk adjustment for, Ch. 56, 8.4

Non insurance contracts, Ch. 55, 3.8; Ch. 56, 3.7.2

Non-life insurance, Ch. 55, 1.4.1

Non-market interest rate loans, Ch. 8, 4.4.5.A

Non-monetary assets
  to an associate/a joint venture, contributions of, Ch. 7, 3.3.2, 7.1; Ch. 11, 7.6.5.B
  transactions involving, Ch. 8, 4.4.1

Non-performance risk
  counterparty credit risk and its own credit risk, Ch. 14, 11.3.2
  derivative liabilities, Ch. 14, 11.3.4
  entity incorporate credit risk into the valuation of its derivative contracts, Ch. 14, 11.3.3
  with third-party credit enhancements, Ch. 14, 11.3.1

Non-recourse loans, Ch. 34, 8.7.2; Ch. 48, 6.5

Non-vesting conditions, share-based payment, Ch. 34, 3.2
  background, Ch. 34, 3.2.1
  cash-settled transactions, Ch. 34, 9.3.2.D
  defining non-vesting condition, Ch. 34, 3.2.2
  equity-settled transactions, Ch. 34, 6.4
  non-compete agreements, Ch. 34, 3.2.3
  option pricing models, treatment of non-vesting condition, Ch. 34, 8.4.2

Notional decomposition, hedging instruments, Ch. 53, 3.6.2

Novation of contracts to intermediary counterparties, Ch. 52, 3.4.4

Numerator (EPS), Ch. 37, 6.4.2.A

Obligating event, Ch. 26, 1.3, 3.1

Observable inputs, Ch. 14, 8.3.2

OCI. *See* Other Comprehensive Income (OCI)

Off-balance sheet finance, Ch. 52, 1.1

Off-market loan commitments, Ch. 49, 3.3.3

Offsetting and hedges, Ch. 54, 7.1.3
  external instruments, Ch. 53, 3.2.1
  internal hedging instruments, Ch. 53, 4.2
    foreign exchange risk, Ch. 53, 4.2.2
    interest rate risk, Ch. 53, 4.2.1

Offsetting financial assets and financial liabilities, Ch. 54, 7.4.1
  cash pooling arrangements, Ch. 54, 7.4.1.E
    presentation in the statement of cash flows, Ch. 40, 6.5
  collateral amounts, Ch. 54, 7.4.1.F
  disclosures, Ch. 54, 7.4.2
    examples, Ch. 54, 7.4.2.D
    objective, Ch. 54, 7.4.2.A
    requirements, Ch. 54, 7.4.2.C
    scope, Ch. 54, 7.4.2.B
  enforceable legal right of set-off criterion, Ch. 54, 7.4.1.A
  master netting agreements, Ch. 54, 7.4.1.B
  net settlement criterion, Ch. 54, 7.4.1.C
  situations where offset is not normally appropriate, Ch. 54, 7.4.1.D
  unit of account, Ch. 54, 7.4.1.G

Oil and gas sector. *See also* Extractive industries
  disclosures by, Ch. 43, 2.4.1
  IFRIC 1 exemption for oil and gas assets at deemed cost, Ch. 5, 5.13.2

Oil Industry Accounting Committee (OIAC), Statement of Recommended Practice (SORP), Ch. 43, 1.4

Onerous contracts, Ch. 26, 6.2
  onerous leases, Ch. 23, 10.3.2.A

Operating activities, cash flows from, Ch. 40, 4.1

Operating segments, Ch. 36, 1–7. *See also* IFRS 8; Reportable segments
  aggregation criteria, Ch. 36, 3.2.1
  'chief operating decision maker' and 'segment manager', Ch. 36, 3.1.2
  combining small operating segments into a larger reportable segment, Ch. 36, 3.2.3
  entity-wide disclosures for all entities, Ch. 36, 6
    information about geographical areas, Ch. 36, 6.2
    information about major customers, Ch. 36, 6.3
    information about products and services, Ch. 36, 6.1
  equity accounted investment can be an operating segment, Ch. 36, 3.1.5
  identifying externally reportable segments, Ch. 36, 3.2
  measurement, Ch. 36, 4
  operating segments which are reportable because of their size, Ch. 36, 3.2.2
    proposed amendments to IFRS 8 and IAS 34 (ED/2017/2), Ch. 36, 7.1
  reportable segments, information to be disclosed, Ch. 36, 5
    additional disclosures relating to segment assets, Ch. 36, 5.4
    disclosure of commercially sensitive information, Ch. 36, 5.8
    disclosure of other elements of revenue, income and expense, Ch. 36, 5.3
    explanation of the measurements used in segment reporting, Ch. 36, 5.5
    general information about reportable segments, Ch. 36, 5.1

disclosure of how operating segments are aggregated, Ch. 36, 5.1.1
measure of segment profit or loss, total assets and total liabilities, Ch. 36, 5.2
reconciliations, Ch. 36, 5.6
restatement of previously reported information, Ch. 36, 5.7
changes in organisation structure, Ch. 36, 5.7.1
changes in segment measures, Ch. 36, 5.7.2
restatement of segments reported in comparative periods, Ch. 36, 3.2.6
revenue earning business activities, Ch. 36, 3.1.1
scope, Ch. 36, 2.2
consolidated financial statements presented with those of the parent, Ch. 36, 2.2.2
entities providing segment information on a voluntary basis, Ch. 36, 2.2.3
meaning of 'traded in a public market,' Ch. 36, 2.2.1
single set of operating segments, identifying, Ch. 36, 3
definition of an operating segment, Ch. 36, 3.1
terms used in IFRS 8, Ch. 36, 1.3
transitional provisions, Ch. 36, 1.4

Operational risk, Ch. 54, 5.6.2

Option contracts, Ch. 49, 2.1.4

Option-pricing models. *See also* Share-based payment transactions
accounting for share-based payment, Ch. 34, 8.4
market-based performance measures and non-vesting conditions, Ch. 34, 8.4.2.A
non-market vesting conditions, Ch. 34, 8.4.2.B
non-transferability, Ch. 34, 8.4.1
vesting and non-vesting conditions, treatment of, Ch. 34, 8.4.2
selecting appropriate assumptions for, Ch. 34, 8.5
binomial model and other lattice models, Ch. 34, 8.5.4.B
Black-Scholes-Merton formula, Ch. 34, 8.5.4.A
exercise and termination behaviour, Ch. 34, 8.5.2
expected dividends, Ch. 34, 8.5.4
expected term of the option, Ch. 34, 8.5.1
expected volatility of share price, Ch. 34, 8.5.3
risk-free interest rate, Ch. 34, 8.5.5
selection of model, Ch. 34, 8.3
binomial model, Ch. 34, 8.3.2
Black-Scholes-Merton formula, Ch. 34, 8.3.1
lattice models-number of time steps, Ch. 34, 8.3.2.A
Monte Carlo Simulation, Ch. 34, 8.3.3

Orderly transaction, Ch. 14, 8.2.2

Other Comprehensive Income (OCI), Ch. 3, 3.2.1
accounting for loss of control, Ch. 7, 2.3, 3.5
cash flow hedge accounting, Ch. 53, 7.2, 7.3
debt instrument measured at fair value through OCI under IFRS 9, Ch. 33, 10.4.1
defined benefit plans, Ch. 33, 10.7; Ch. 35, 9
remeasurements, Ch. 35, 10.4
actuarial gains and losses, Ch. 35, 10.4.1
return on plan assets, excluding amounts included in net interest on the net defined benefit liability (asset), Ch. 35, 10.4.2
gains and losses recognised in, Ch. 54, 7.2
hedges of exposures affecting, Ch. 53, 2.6.3

insurance contracts, allocating finance income or expenses on, Ch. 56, 15.3
non-derivative equity investments designation at, Ch. 48, 8
reattribution of, changes in ownership interest without a loss of control, Ch. 7, 4.1
tax on items of, Ch. 3, 3.2.4.C

Outside temporary differences, deferred tax recognition, Ch. 33, 7.5
anticipated intragroup dividends in future foreseeable future, Ch. 33, 7.5.4
consolidated financial statements of receiving entity, Ch. 33, 7.5.4.A
separate financial statements of paying entity, Ch. 33, 7.5.4.B
calculation of, Ch. 33, 7.5.1
consolidated financial statements, Ch. 33, 7.5.1.A
separate financial statements, Ch. 33, 7.5.1.B
deductible temporary differences, Ch. 33, 7.5.3
other overseas income taxed only on remittance, Ch. 33, 7.5.6
taxable temporary differences, Ch. 33, 7.5.2
'tax transparent' entities, Ch. 33, 7.6
unpaid intragroup interest, royalties, management charges etc., Ch. 33, 7.5.5

Outstanding ordinary shares, changes in, Ch. 37, 4
adjustments to EPS in historical summaries, Ch. 37, 4.7
issue to acquire another business, Ch. 37, 4.6
acquisitions, Ch. 37, 4.6.1
establishment of a new parent undertaking, Ch. 37, 4.6.3
reverse acquisitions, Ch. 37, 4.6.2
new parent undertaking, establishment of, Ch. 37, 4.6.3
options exercised during the year, Ch. 37, 4.4
ordinary shares without corresponding changes in resources, changes in, Ch. 37, 4.3
B share schemes, Ch. 37, 4.3.4
bonus issue, Ch. 37, 4.3.1.A
capitalisation, Ch. 37, 4.3.1.A
put warrants priced above market value, Ch. 37, 4.3.5
rights issue, Ch. 37, 4.3.3
share consolidation, Ch. 37, 4.3.1.C
share consolidation with a special dividend, Ch. 37, 4.3.2
share consolidations, Ch. 37, 4.3.1.C
share split, Ch. 37, 4.3.1.A
stock dividends, Ch. 37, 4.3.1.B
post balance sheet changes in capital, Ch. 37, 4.5
purchase and redemption of own shares, Ch. 37, 4.2
weighted average number of shares, Ch. 37, 4.1

Overlift and underlift (oil and gas), Ch. 43, 12.4

Over-the-counter (OTC) derivatives
categorisation, Ch. 14, 16.2.4

Own equity instruments, Ch. 53, 3.4

Own use contracts, Ch. 53, 12.2

Owner-occupied property, Ch. 19, 2.4. *See also* IAS 16; Property, plant and equipment

Ownership changes in a joint venture, Ch. 12, 8.2
acquisition of an interest in a joint venture, Ch. 12, 8.2.1
control over a joint venture, Ch. 12, 8.3.2
demergers and distributions of non-cash assets to owners, Ch. 7, 3.7
disposal of interest in a joint venture, Ch. 12, 8.2.6

Ownership changes in a joint venture—*contd*
   former subsidiary becomes a joint venture, Ch. 7, 3.3.2, 7.1; Ch. 12, 8.3.3
   interest in a joint venture held for sale, Ch. 12, 8.2.7
   joint venture becomes a financial asset (or vice versa), Ch. 12, 8.2.5
   joint venture becomes an associate (or vice versa), Ch. 12, 8.2.4

Ownership interests, changes in, Ch. 7, 3, 4, 5.2, 6
   accounting for a loss of control, Ch. 7 3.2, 3.3, 3.4, 3.5, 3.6, 3.7, 7.1, 7.2
   acquisition of a subsidiary that is not a business, Ch. 7, 3.1.1, 3.1.2
   deemed disposal, Ch. 7, 3.6. *See also* IFRIC 17
   interest retained in the former subsidiary, Ch. 7, 3.3
      interest retained in the former subsidiary-associate or joint venture, Ch. 7, 3.3.2, 7.1
      interest retained in the former subsidiary–financial asset, Ch. 7, 3.3.1
      interest retained in the former subsidiary–joint operation, Ch. 7, 3.3.3, 7.2
   loss of control in multiple arrangements Ch. 7, 3.4
   mandatory tender offers in a business combination, Ch. 7, 6.2.4, 7.4
   multiple arrangements, loss of control in, Ch. 7, 3.4
   non-cash assets to owners, Ch. 7, 3.5
   other comprehensive income, Ch. 7, 2.3, 3.5, 4.1
   without a loss of control, Ch. 7, 4.1, 4.2, 4.3, 4.4, 4.5

Partial disposals. *See also* Ownership interests, changes in
   of an associate or joint venture, Ch. 4, 2.1.3.B; Ch. 11, 7.12.5
   of foreign operation, Ch. 15, 2.3, 4.1, 6.6.2.
   of interests in associate/joint venture, Ch. 11, 7.12.5
   of operations, Ch. 4, 2.1.3
   of property, plant and equipment, Ch. 18, 7.3

Partial term hedging, Ch. 53, 2.2.4
Parts (components) approach, assets, accounting for, Ch. 18, 3.2
Past service cost, employee benefits, Ch. 35, 10.2.1
Payables, Ch. 49, 2.1.1
Pension, Ch. 35, 3. *See also* Defined benefit plans; Defined contribution plans; IAS 19; IFRIC 14
   defined benefit plans, Ch. 35, 3.1, 5
      funding payments contingent on future events within the control of the entity, Ch. 35, 8.2.5
   insured benefits, Ch. 35, 3.2

Performance condition, share-based payment, Ch. 34, 3.1, 6.2, 6.3
Performance obligation, IFRS 15, Ch. 28, 3
Performance rating, share-based payment, Ch. 34, 3.1.2
Performance target, share-based payment, Ch. 34, 3.1, 5.3.3
Perpetual debt, Ch. 47, 4.7; Ch. 50, 3.5
Perpetual instruments with a 'step-up' clause, Ch. 47, 4.5.4
Persistency risk, insurance contracts, Ch. 55, 3.7.1
Petroleum reserve estimation and reporting, Ch. 43, 2.2
   basic principles and definitions, Ch. 43, 2.2.1
   classification and categorisation guidelines, Ch. 43, 2.2.2
Phantom options, share-based payment, Ch. 34, 9.1
Physical capital maintenance (framework), Ch. 2, 11.2
Piecemeal acquisition of an associate/joint venture, Ch. 11, 7.4.2

common control transactions involving sales of associates, Ch. 11, 7.4.2.D
cost-based approach, Ch. 11, 7.4.2.A
existing associate that becomes a joint venture, or vice versa, Ch. 11, 7.4.2.C
fair value (IFRS 3) approach, Ch. 11, 7.4.2.A
financial instrument becoming an associate/joint venture, Ch. 11, 7.4.2.A
step increase in an existing associate/joint venture without a change in status of the investee, Ch. 11, 7.4.2.B

Plan assets, employee benefits, Ch. 35, 6
   contributions to defined benefit funds, Ch. 35, 6.5
   definition of, Ch. 35, 6.1
   longevity swaps, Ch. 35, 6.6
   measurement of, Ch. 35, 6.2
   qualifying insurance policies, Ch. 35, 6.3
   reimbursement rights, Ch. 35, 6.4

Plan liabilities, employee benefits, Ch. 35, 7
   actuarial assumptions, Ch. 35, 7.5
   actuarial methodology, Ch. 35, 7.3
   attributing benefit to years of service, Ch. 35, 7.4
   contributions by employees and third parties, Ch. 35, 7.2
   discount rate, Ch. 35, 7.6
   frequency of valuations, Ch. 35, 7.7
   legal and constructive obligations, Ch. 35, 7.1

Policy administration and maintenance costs (insurance contracts), Ch. 56, 8.2.3.H
Policyholder, Ch. 55, 2.2.1
   adverse effect on, Ch. 55, 3.7
      insurance of non-insurance risks, Ch. 55, 3.7.2
      lapse, persistency and expense risk, Ch. 55, 3.7.1
   of direct insurance contracts, Ch. 55, 2.2.3.F

Policyholder loans, Ch. 55, 7.2.6.F; Ch. 56, 8.12.2
Pooling of interests method, Ch. 10, 3.1, 3.3
Post-employment benefits, Ch. 35, 3. *See also* Pension
   defined benefit plans, Ch. 35, 3.1
   defined contribution plans, Ch. 35, 3.1
   disclosure of key management personnel compensation, Ch. 39, 2.6.3
   insured benefits, Ch. 35, 3.2
   multi-employer plans, Ch. 35, 3.3
   related parties, Ch. 39, 2.2.6
   state plans, Ch. 35, 3.4

Post-tax cash flows, VIU calculation using, Ch. 20, 7.2.3
Power and returns, principal-agency situations, Ch. 6, 6
   application examples in IFRS 10, Ch. 6, 6.6–6.7
   available replacements, Ch. 6, 6.3.1.A
   decision-making, scope of, Ch. 6, 6.2
   delegated power: principals and agents, Ch. 6, 6.1
   exercise period, Ch. 6, 6.3.1.B
   exposure to variability of returns from other interests, Ch. 6, 6.5
   liquidation rights and redemption rights, Ch. 6, 6.3.2
   remuneration, Ch. 6, 6.4
   rights held by other parties, Ch. 6, 6.3

Power over an investee, Ch. 6, 4. *See also* Existing rights, investee; Voting rights, investee
   contractual arrangements, Ch. 6, 4.4
   determining whether sponsoring (designing) a structured entity gives power, Ch. 6, 4.6

existing rights, Ch. 6, 4.2
management of defaults on assets, Ch. 6, 4.1.4
more than one relevant activity, Ch. 6, 4.1.1
no relevant activities, Ch. 6, 4.1.2
relevant activities, Ch. 6, 4.1
single asset, single lessee vehicles, Ch. 6, 4.1.3
voting rights, Ch. 6, 4.3

PP&E. *See* Property, Plant and Equipment

Pre-existing relationships, business combination, Ch. 9, 11.1
assessing part of exchange for the acquiree, Ch. 9, 11
contingent payments, arrangements for, Ch. 9, 11.2.1
effective settlement of, Ch. 9, 11.1
reimbursement for paying acquirer's acquisition-related costs, Ch. 9, 11.3
remuneration for future services, Ch. 9, 11.2
restructuring plans, Ch. 9, 11.4
share-based payment awards, Ch. 9, 7.2

Preference dividends (EPS), Ch. 37, 5.2

Preference shares, Ch. 47, 4.5
'change of control,' 'taxation change' and 'regulatory change' clauses, Ch. 47, 4.5.8
economic compulsion, Ch. 47, 4.5.6
instruments redeemable
    with a 'dividend blocker,' Ch. 47, 4.5.3.A
    with a 'dividend pusher,' Ch. 47, 4.5.3.B
    mandatorily or at the holder's option, Ch. 47, 4.5.1
    only at the issuer's option or not redeemable, Ch. 47, 4.5.2
'linked' instruments, Ch. 47, 4.5.7
perpetual instruments with a 'step-up' clause, Ch. 47, 4.5.4
relative subordination, Ch. 47, 4.5.5

Premium allocation approach, insurance contracts, Ch. 56, 9
accounting policies adopted for contracts applying, Ch. 56, 16.1.2.A
aggregation for contracts applying, Ch. 56, 5.3
allocating insurance finance income/expenses for incurred claims when applying, Ch. 56, 15.3.2
criteria for use of, Ch. 56, 9.1
derecognition contracts, Ch. 56, 12.3.4
initial measurement, Ch. 56, 9.2
insurance revenue under, Ch. 56, 15.1.2
reconciliations required for contracts applying, Ch. 56, 16.1.1
for reinsurance contracts held, Ch. 56, 10.7
subsequent measurement
    liability for incurred claims, Ch. 56, 9.4
    liability for remaining coverage, Ch. 56, 9.3

Premium cash flows, Ch. 56, 8.2.3.A

Prepaid and accrued operating lease income, Ch. 19, 6.6

Prepayment, negative compensation, Ch. 48, 6.4.4.A

Present value of future profits (PVFP), Ch. 55, 9.1

Present value of in-force business (PVIF), Ch. 55, 9.1

Presentation and disclosure, financial instruments, Ch. 54, 1–9
disclosures, structuring, Ch. 54, 3
    classes of financial instrument, Ch. 54, 3.3
    level of detail, Ch. 54, 3.1
    materiality, Ch. 54, 3.2
effective date and transitional provisions, Ch. 54, 8
future developments, Ch. 54, 9
interim reports, Ch. 54, 2.3
nature and extent of risks arising from financial instruments, Ch. 54, 5
    qualitative disclosures, Ch. 54, 5.1
    quantitative disclosures, Ch. 54, 5.2
    'basic' sensitivity analysis, Ch. 54, 5.5.1
    capital disclosures, Ch. 54, 5.6.3
    cash flows, Ch. 54, 5.4.2
    concentrations of risk, Ch. 54, 5.6.1
    credit risk, Ch. 54, 5.3
    credit risk exposure, Ch. 54, 5.3.4
    credit risk management practices, Ch. 54, 5.3.2
    illustrative disclosures, Ch. 54, 5.3.6
    information provided to key management, Ch. 54, 5.4.1
    liquidity risk, Ch. 54, 5.4
    management of associated liquidity risk, Ch. 54, 5.4.3
    market risk, Ch. 54, 5.5
    maturity analyses, Ch. 54, 5.4.2
    operational risk, Ch. 54, 5.6.2
    puttable financial instruments classified as equity, Ch. 54, 5.4.4
    quantitative and qualitative information about amounts arising from expected credit losses, Ch. 54, 5.3.3
    scope and objectives, Ch. 54, 5.3.1
    time bands, Ch. 54, 5.4.2.A
    value-at-risk and similar analyses, Ch. 54, 5.5.2
presentation on the face of the financial statements and related disclosures, Ch. 54, 7
    gains and losses recognised in other comprehensive income, Ch. 54, 7.2
    gains and losses recognised in profit/loss embedded derivatives, Ch. 54, 7.1.4
    entities whose share capital is not equity, Ch. 54, 7.1.4
    further analysis of gains and losses recognised in profit/loss, Ch. 54, 7.1.2
    offsetting and hedges, Ch. 54, 7.1.3
    presentation on the face of the statement of comprehensive income (or income statement), Ch. 54, 7.1.1
statement of cash flows, Ch. 54, 7.5
statement of changes in equity, Ch. 54, 7.3
statement of financial position, Ch. 54, 7.4
    assets and liabilities, Ch. 54, 7.4.3
    convertible loans, Ch. 54, 7.4.4.B
    current and non-current assets and liabilities, distinction between, Ch. 54, 7.4.4
    debt with refinancing or roll over agreements, Ch. 54, 7.4.4.D
    derivatives, Ch. 54, 7.4.4.A
    disclosure requirements, Ch. 54, 7.4.2.C
    enforceable legal right of set-off, Ch. 54, 7.4.1.A
    entities whose share capital is not equity, Ch. 54, 7.4.6
    equity, Ch. 54, 7.4.5
    intention to settle net, Ch. 54, 7.4.1.C
    loan covenants, Ch. 54, 7.4.4.E
    long-term loans with repayment on demand terms, Ch. 54, 7.4.4.C
    master netting agreements, Ch. 54, 7.4.1.B
    objective, Ch. 54, 7.4.2.A
    offsetting collateral amounts, Ch. 54, 7.4.1.F

Presentation and disclosure, financial instruments—*contd*
  presentation on the face of the financial statements and related disclosures—*contd*
    statement of financial position—*contd*
      offsetting financial assets and financial liabilities, Ch. 54, 7.4.1
      offsetting financial assets and financial liabilities: disclosure, Ch. 54, 7.4.2
      scope, Ch. 54, 7.4.2.B
      situations where offset is not normally appropriate, Ch. 54, 7.4.1.D
      unit of account, Ch. 54, 7.4.1.G
  significance of financial instruments for an entity's financial position/performance, Ch. 54, 4
    accounting policies, Ch. 54, 4.1
    business combinations, Ch. 54, 4.6
      acquired receivables, Ch. 54, 4.6.1
      contingent consideration and indemnification assets, Ch. 54, 4.6.2
    fair values, Ch. 54, 4.5
      day 1 profits, Ch. 54, 4.5.2
      general disclosure requirements, Ch. 54, 4.5.1
    hedge accounting, Ch. 54, 4.3
      amount, timing and uncertainty of future cash flows, Ch. 54, 4.3.2
      effects of hedge accounting on financial position and performance, Ch. 54, 4.3.3
      option to designate a credit exposure as measured at fair value through profit/loss, Ch. 54, 4.3.4
      risk management strategy, Ch. 54, 4.3.1
      uncertainty arising from interest rate benchmark (or IBOR) reform, Ch. 54, 4.3.5
    income, expenses, gains and losses, Ch. 54, 4.2
      fee income and expense, Ch. 54, 4.2.3
      gains and losses by measurement category, Ch. 54, 4.2.1
      interest income and expense, Ch. 54, 4.2.2
    statement of financial position, Ch. 54, 4.4
      categories of financial assets and financial liabilities, Ch. 54, 4.4.1
      collateral, Ch. 54, 4.4.6
      compound financial instruments with multiple embedded derivatives, Ch. 54, 4.4.7
      defaults and breaches of loans payable, Ch. 54, 4.4.8
      financial assets designated as measured at fair value through profit/loss, Ch. 54, 4.4.3
      financial liabilities designated at fair value through profit/loss, Ch. 54, 4.4.2
      interests in associates and joint ventures accounted for in accordance with IFRS 9, Ch. 54, 4.4.9
      investments in equity instruments designated at fair value through other comprehensive income (IFRS 9), Ch. 54, 4.4.4
      reclassification, Ch. 54, 4.4.5
  transfers of financial assets, Ch. 54, 6
    meaning of 'transfer,' Ch. 54, 6.1
    transferred financial assets that are derecognised in their entirety, Ch. 54, 6.3
      disclosure requirements, Ch. 54, 6.3.2
      meaning of continuing involvement, Ch. 54, 6.3.1
    transferred financial assets that are not derecognised in their entirety, Ch. 54, 6.2
  transitional provisions, Ch. 54, 8

Presentation currency. *See also* IAS 21
  average rate calculation, Ch. 15, 6.1.4
  change of, Ch. 15, 7
  disposal of a foreign operation, Ch. 15, 6.6
    step-by-step and direct methods of consolidation, Ch. 7, 2.3; Ch. 15, 6.6.3
  exchange differences on intragroup balances, Ch. 15, 6.3
    becoming part of the net investment in a foreign operation, Ch. 15, 6.3.1.F
    ceasing to be part of the net investment in a foreign operation, Ch. 15, 6.3.1.G
    currency of monetary item, Ch. 15, 6.3.1.C
    dividends, Ch. 15, 6.3.2
    manner of settlement of monetary, Ch. 15, 6.3.1.B
    monetary items included as part of the net investment in a foreign operation, Ch. 15, 6.3.1
    net investment in a foreign operation, Ch. 15, 6.3.1.F
    transacted by other members of the group, Ch. 15, 6.3.1.E
    treatment in individual financial statements, Ch. 15, 6.3.1.D
    unrealised profits on intragroup transactions, Ch. 15, 6.3.3
  foreign operations where sub-groups exist, accounting for, Ch. 15, 6.1.5
  goodwill and fair value adjustments, Ch. 15, 6.5
  non-coterminous period ends, Ch. 15, 6.4
  partial disposal of foreign operation, Ch. 7, 4.1 Ch. 15, 6.6.2
  translation of equity items, Ch. 15, 6.2
    equity balances resulting from income and expenses being recognised in other comprehensive income, Ch. 15, 6.2.3
    equity balances resulting from transactions with equity holders, Ch. 15, 6.2.2
    share capital, Ch. 15, 6.2.1
  translation to, Ch. 15, 6.1
    accounting for foreign operations where sub-groups exist, Ch. 15, 6.1.5
    calculation of average rate, Ch. 15, 6.1.4
    dual rates, suspension of rates and lack of exchangeability, Ch. 15, 6.1.3
    where functional currency is not that of a hyperinflationary economy, Ch. 15, 6.1.1
    where functional currency is that of a hyperinflationary economy, Ch. 15, 6.1.2
  use other than the functional currency, Ch. 15, 6

Presentation of financial statements and accounting policies, Ch. 3, 1–6. *See also* IAS 1; IAS 8

Previous GAAP, Ch. 5, 2.3
  carrying amount as deemed cost, Ch. 5, 5.2.4.C
  definition of, Ch. 5, 1.3
  determining, Ch. 5, 2.3
    transition to IFRSs from a similar GAAP, Ch. 5, 2.3.1
  restatement of costs recognised under, Ch. 5, 5.3.2

Price, fair value measurement, Ch. 14, 9
  transaction costs, Ch. 14, 9.1
  transportation costs, Ch. 14, 9.2

Price risk, Ch. 54, 5

Principal-agency situations, IFRS 10, Ch. 6, 6, IFRS 15, Ch. 28, 3.4
    application examples in IFRS 10, Ch. 6, 6.6–6.7
    delegated power: principals and agents, Ch. 6, 6.1
    exposure to variability of returns from other interests, Ch. 6, 6.5
    liquidation rights, Ch. 6, 6.3.2
    redemption rights, Ch. 6, 6.3.2
    remuneration, Ch. 6, 6.4
    rights held by other parties, Ch. 6, 6.3.
    scope of decision-making, Ch. 6, 6.2
Principal market, Ch. 14, 6
    entity-specific volume, Ch. 14, 6.1.2
    market-based volume and activity, Ch. 14, 6.1.2
    most advantageous market, Ch. 14, 6.2
Prior period errors
    correction of, Ch. 3, 4.6
    disclosure of, Ch. 3, 5.3
Probability-weighted outcome, Ch. 51, 5.6
Production sharing contracts (PSCs), Ch. 43, 5.3; Ch. 43, 12.5
Property, plant and equipment (PP&E), Ch. 18, 1–8. *See also* IAS 16; Investment property
    administration and other general overheads, Ch. 18, 4.1.3
    borrowing costs, Ch. 18, 4.1.2
    decommissioning and restoration costs, Ch. 18, 4.3
    deferred payment, Ch. 18, 4.1.6
    definitions, Ch. 18, 2.2
    depreciation, cost model, Ch. 18, 5
        charge, Ch. 18, 5.3
        depreciable amount, Ch. 18, 5.2
        methods, Ch. 18, 5.6
        significant 'parts' of asset, Ch. 18, 5.1
        start and finish, Ch. 18, 5.5
        and useful life of asset, Ch. 18, 5.4
    derecognition and disposal, Ch. 18, 7
        held for sale and discontinued operations (IFRS 5), Ch. 18, 7.1
        partial disposals and undivided interests, Ch. 18, 7.3
        of parts ('components') of an asset, Ch. 18, 3.2
        sale of assets held for rental, Ch. 18, 7.2
    disclosure, Ch. 18, 8
    environmental and safety equipment, Ch. 18, 3.1.2
    exchanges of assets, Ch. 18, 4.4
    extractive industries, Ch. 43, 15
        care and maintenance, Ch. 43, 15.3
        major maintenance and turnarounds/renewals and reconditioning costs, Ch. 43, 15.1
        redeterminations, Ch. 43, 15.4.2
            as capital reimbursements, Ch. 43, 15.4.2.A
            decommissioning provisions, Ch. 43, 15.4.2.C
            'make-up' oil, Ch. 43, 15.4.2.B
        stripping costs in the production phase of a surface mine (mining), Ch. 43, 15.5
        determining when production phase commences, Ch. 43, 15.5.2
        disclosures, Ch. 43, 15.5.6
        initial recognition, Ch. 43, 15.5.4
        recognition criteria-stripping activity asset, Ch. 43, 15.5.3
        scope of IFRIC 20, Ch. 43, 15.5.1
        subsequent measurement, Ch. 43, 15.5.5
        unitisations, Ch. 43, 15.4
        well workovers and recompletions (oil and gas), Ch. 43, 15.2
    fair value, Ch. 18, 6.1
    finance leases, assets held under, Ch. 18, 6.5
    first-time adoption, Ch. 5, 7.4
        depreciation method and rate, Ch. 5, 7.4.1
        IFRIC 1 exemptions, Ch. 5, 5.13.1
        parts approach, Ch. 5, 7.4.4
        residual value and useful life estimation, Ch. 5, 7.4.2
        revaluation model, Ch. 5, 7.4.3
    government grants, assets acquired with, Ch. 18, 4.6
    impairment, Ch. 18, 5.7
    income, Ch. 18, 4
        earned while bringing the asset to the intended location and condition, Ch. 18, 4.2.1
        received during the construction of property, Ch. 18, 4.2.2
    interim financial reporting, Ch. 41, 9.1
    inventory, classification as, Ch. 18, 3.1.5
    land, Ch. 18, 5.4.2
    measurement after recognition
        cost model, Ch. 18, 5
        revaluation model, Ch. 18, 6
    residual values, Ch. 18, 5.2
    revaluation
        assets held under finance leases, Ch. 18, 4.5
        revaluation policy, adopting, Ch. 18, 6.4
        reversals of downward valuations, Ch. 18, 6.3
        valuation surpluses and deficits, accounting for, Ch. 18, 6.2
    sale of assets held for rental, Ch. 18, 7.2 scope, Ch. 18, 2.1
    significant parts of assets, Ch. 18, 5.1
    spare parts and minor items, Ch. 18, 3.1.1
    technological change, Ch. 18, 5.4.3
    unit of production method, Ch. 18, 5.6.2
    useful lives, Ch. 18, 5.4
Prospective resources, Ch. 43, 2.2.1
Provisions, Contingent Liabilities and Contingent Assets, Ch. 26, 1–7. *See also* IAS 37; Restructuring provisions
    cases in which no provision should be recognised, Ch. 26, 5
        future operating losses, Ch. 26, 5.1
        rate-regulated activities, Ch. 26, 5.4
        repairs and maintenance of owned assets, Ch. 26, 5.2
        staff training costs, Ch. 26, 5.3
    disclosure requirements, Ch. 26, 7
        contingent assets, Ch. 26, 7.3
        contingent liabilities, Ch. 26, 7.2
        provisions, Ch. 26, 7.1
        reduced disclosure when information is seriously prejudicial, Ch. 26, 7.4
    examples of provisions and contingencies, Ch. 26, 6
        decommissioning provisions, Ch. 26, 6.3
            changes in estimated decommissioning costs (IFRIC 1), Ch. 26, 6.3.1
            changes in legislation after construction of the asset, Ch. 26, 6.3.2
            funds established to meet an obligation (IFRIC 5), Ch. 26, 6.3.3
        dilapidation and other provisions relating to leased assets, Ch. 26, 6.9

Provisions, Contingent Liabilities and Contingent Assets—*contd*
  examples of provisions and contingencies—*contd*
    environmental provisions–general guidance in IAS 37, Ch. 26, 6.4
    EU Directive on 'Waste Electrical and Electronic Equipment' (IFRIC 6), Ch. 26, 6.7
    green certificates compared to emissions trading schemes, Ch. 26, 6.6
    levies imposed by governments, Ch. 26, 6.8
      payments relating to taxes other than income tax, Ch. 26.6.8.4
      recognition and measurement of levy liabilities, Ch. 26, 6.8.2
      recognition of an asset/expense when a levy is recorded, Ch. 26, 6.8.3
      scope of IFRIC 21, Ch. 26, 6.8.1
    liabilities associated with emissions trading schemes, Ch. 26, 6.5
    litigation and other legal claims, Ch. 26, 6.11
    obligations to make donations to non-profit organisations, Ch. 26, 6.14
    onerous contracts, Ch. 26, 6.2
    refunds policy, Ch. 26, 6.12
    restructuring provisions, Ch. 26, 6.1
    self insurance, Ch. 26, 6.13
    settlement payments, Ch. 26.6.15
    warranty provisions, Ch. 26, 6.10
  measurement, Ch. 26, 4
    anticipating future events that may affect the estimate of cash flows, Ch. 26, 4.4
    best estimate of provision, Ch. 26, 4.1
    changes and uses of provisions, Ch. 26, 4.9
    changes in contingent liabilities recognised in a business combination, Ch. 26, 4.10
    dealing with risk and uncertainty in measuring a provision, Ch. 26, 4.2
    discounting the estimated cash flows to a present value, Ch. 26, 4.3
      adjusting for risk and using a government bond rate, Ch. 26, 4.3.2
      effect of changes in interest rates on the discount rate applied, Ch. 26, 4.3.6
      own credit risk is not taken into account, Ch. 26, 4.3.3
      pre-tax discount rate, Ch. 26, 4.3.4
      real *vs.* nominal rate, Ch. 26, 4.3.1
      unwinding of the discount, Ch. 26, 4.3.5
    disposal of related assets, Ch. 26, 4.8
    joint and several liability, Ch. 26, 4.7
    provisions are not reduced for gains on disposal of related assets, Ch. 26, 4.8
    provisions that will be settled in a currency other than the entity's functional currency, Ch. 26, 4.5
    reimbursements, insurance and other recoveries from third parties, Ch. 26, 4.6
    settlement in a foreign currency, Ch. 26, 4.5
  recognition, Ch. 26, 3
    contingencies, Ch. 26, 3.2
      contingent assets, Ch. 26, 3.2.2
        obligations contingent on the successful recovery of, Ch. 26, 3.2.2.A
      contingent liabilities, Ch. 26, 3.2.1
      how probability determines whether to recognise or disclose, Ch. 26, 3.2.3
    determining when a provision should be recognised, Ch. 26, 3.1
      an entity has a present obligation as a result of a past event, Ch. 26, 3.1.1
      it is probable that an outflow of resources embodying economic benefits will be required to settle the obligation, Ch. 26, 3.1.2
      a reliable estimate can be made of the amount of the obligation, Ch. 26, 3.1.3
    recognising an asset when recognising a provision, Ch. 26, 3.3

'Proxy hedges,' designating, Ch. 53, 6.2.1
Prudence, Ch. 55, 8.2.3
Public Company Accounting Oversight Board, Ch. 2, 1.2
Publicly accountable enterprises, Ch. 1, 4.3.2
Purchased options
  call option (EPS), Ch. 37, 6.4.3
  hedge accounting, Ch. 53, 3.2.2, 7.3.3.C
  put option (EPS), Ch. 37, 6.4.3
  and warrants (EPS), Ch. 37, 6.4.3
Pure-service contract, Ch. 43, 5.4
Push down accounting, Ch. 5, 5.5.2.A; Ch. 9, 15
Put option(s)
  held by the customer, Ch. 30, 5.2
  over non-controlling interests, Ch. 7, 6.2, 6.3, 6.4, 6.5, 6.6, 7.3, 7.4, 7.5;; Ch. 9, 8.5 (*see also* Noncontrolling interests, call and put options over)
  purchased put option, Ch. 47, 11.3.1
  written put option, Ch. 47, 11.3.2
Puttable instruments, Ch. 47, 4.6.2
  classified as equity, Ch. 3, 5.4.2; Ch. 47, 4.6; Ch. 54, 5.4.4
  options over, IAS 32 specific exception, Ch. 34, 2.2.4.J
  definitions, Ch. 47, 3
  embedded derivatives, Ch. 46, 5.1.10
  entitling the holder to a pro rata share of net assets only on liquidation, Ch. 47, 4.6.3
  IFRIC 2, Ch. 47, 4.6.6
  issue, Ch. 47, 4.6.1
  issued by a subsidiary, Ch. 47, 4.6.4.A
  meaning of 'identical features,' Ch. 47, 4.6.4.C
  no obligation to deliver cash or another financial asset, Ch. 47, 4.6.4.D
  reclassification, Ch. 47, 4.6.5
  relative subordination of the instrument, Ch. 47, 4.6.4.B
  substantially fix or restrict the residual return to the holder of an instrument, Ch. 47, 4.6.4.E
  transactions entered into by an instrument holder other than as owner of the entity, Ch. 47, 4.6.4.F
Qualifying assets, Ch. 21, 3. *See also* IAS 23
  assets measured at fair value, Ch. 21, 3.2
  constructed good, over time transfer of, Ch. 21, 3.4
  financial assets, Ch. 21, 3.3
  inventories, Ch. 21, 3.1
Qualitative disclosures, financial instruments, Ch. 54, 5.1
Quantitative disclosures, financial instruments, Ch. 54, 5.2, 5.6
  capital disclosures, Ch. 54, 5.6.3
  concentrations of risk, Ch. 54, 5.6.1
  operational risk, Ch. 54, 5.6.2

Quantitative thresholds, operating segments, Ch. 36, 1.3, 3.2.2
Quoted prices in active markets, Ch. 14, 17.3
    consideration of an entry price in measuring a liability or entity's own equity not held as an asset, Ch. 14, 11.2.2.B
    fair value of a liability or an entity's own equity, measuring when quoted prices for the liability or equity instruments are not available, Ch. 14, 11.2
    liabilities or an entity's own equity not held by other parties as assets, Ch. 14, 11.2.2
    liabilities or an entity's own equity that are held by other parties as assets, Ch. 14, 11.2.1
    use of present value techniques to measure fair value for liabilities and an entity's own equity instruments not held by other parties as asset, Ch. 14, 11.2.2.A

Rate-regulated activities, intangible assets, Ch. 17, 11.1
Reacquired rights, Ch. 9, 5.5.3
Real estate inventory, Ch. 22, 4
    classification of, Ch. 22, 4.1
    costs of, Ch. 22, 4.2
        individual units in multi-unit developments, Ch. 22, 4.2.1
        property demolition and operating lease costs, Ch. 22, 4.2.2
Real Estate Investment Trusts (REITs), Ch. 55, 6
Rebalancing, hedge accounting, Ch. 53, 8.2
    definition, Ch. 53, 8.2.1
    mechanics of, Ch. 53, 8.2.3
    requirement to rebalance, Ch. 53, 8.2.2
Receivables
    acquired in business combination, Ch. 49, 3.3.4; Ch. 54, 4.6.1
    distinction between contract assets and, Ch. 32, 2.1.1
    initial measurement of, Ch. 32, 2.1.5
    lease receivables, measurement of expected credit losses, Ch. 51, 10.2
    recognition, Ch. 49, 2.1.1
    trade receivables, measurement of expected credit losses, Ch. 51, 10.1
    trade receivables with no significant financing component initial measurement, Ch. 49, 3.2
Reciprocal interests in equity accounted entities, Ch. 11, 7.6.2
    measurement of noncontrolling interests where an associate holds and interest in a subsidiary, Ch. 7, 5.3
    in reporting entity accounted for, Ch. 11, 7.6.2.A
    in reporting entity not accounted for, Ch. 11, 7.6.2.B
Reclassification adjustments, financial statements, Ch. 3, 3.2.4.B
Recognition of financial instruments, Ch. 49, 2
    general requirements, Ch. 49, 2.1
        cash collateral, Ch. 49, 2.1.7
        firm commitments to purchase/sell goods/services, Ch. 49, 2.1.2
        forward contracts, Ch. 49, 2.1.3
        option contracts, Ch. 49, 2.1.4
        planned future/forecast transactions, Ch. 49, 2.1.5
        principal *vs.* agent, Ch. 49, 2.1.8
        receivables and payables, Ch. 49, 2.1.1
        transfers of financial assets not qualifying for derecognition by transferor, Ch. 49, 2.1.6
    'regular way' transactions, Ch. 49, 2.2
        exchanges of non-cash financial assets, Ch. 49, 2.2.5.A
        financial assets: general requirements, Ch. 49, 2.2.1
        contracts not settled according to marketplace convention: derivatives, Ch. 49, 2.2.1.B
        exercise of a derivative, Ch. 49, 2.2.1.D
        multiple active markets: settlement provisions, Ch. 49, 2.2.1.C
        no established market, Ch. 49, 2.2.1.A
        financial liabilities, Ch. 49, 2.2.2
        illustrative examples, Ch. 49, 2.2.5
        settlement date accounting, Ch. 49, 2.2.4
        trade date accounting, Ch. 49, 2.2.3
Recompletions, oil and gas wells, Ch. 43, 15.2
Reconciliation on first-time adoption, Ch. 5, 6.3.1.A
    inclusion of IFRS 1 reconciliations by cross reference, Ch. 5, 6.3.4
    line-by-line reconciliations, Ch. 5, 6.3.2
Recoverable amount, Ch. 20, 5. *See also* IAS 36.
Redesignation of financial assets, Ch. 55, 8.4; Ch. 56, 17.6
Redeterminations, Ch. 43, 15.4.2
Reduced Disclosure Requirements (RDRs), Ch. 1, 4.5
Registration, Evaluation, Authorisation and Restriction of Chemicals (REACH), Ch. 17, 11.4
Regression analysis, Ch. 53, 6.4.1
Regular way contracts, derivatives, Ch. 46, 3.3
'Regular way' transactions, Ch. 49, 2.2
    financial assets: general requirements, Ch. 49, 2.2.1
        contracts not settled according to marketplace convention: derivatives, Ch. 49, 2.2.1.B
        exercise of a derivative, Ch. 49, 2.2.1.D
        multiple active markets: settlement provisions, Ch. 49, 2.2.1.C
        no established market, Ch. 49, 2.2.1.A
    financial liabilities, Ch. 49, 2.2.2
    illustrative examples, Ch. 49, 2.2.5
    initial measurement, Ch. 49, 3.6
    settlement date accounting, Ch. 49, 2.2.4
    subsequent measurement exceptions, Ch. 50, 2.9.2
    trade date accounting, Ch. 49, 2.2.3
Reimbursement rights, Ch. 45, 3.10
Reinsurance assets
    definition, Ch. 55, 2.2.1
    impairments of, Ch. 55, 7.2.5; Ch. 56, 10.3
Reinsurance contract, Ch. 55, 2.2.1, 2.2.2, 3.7.2, 7.2.4; Ch. 56, 2.2, 2.3, 8.9
Reinsurance contracts held, Ch. 56, 10
    aggregation level, Ch. 56, 10.1
    allocation of the CSM to profit or loss, Ch. 56, 10.5
    boundary of, Ch. 56, 10.2
    measurement - initial recognition, Ch. 56, 10.3, 10.4
    premium allocation approach for, Ch. 56, 10.6
    subsequent measurement, Ch. 56, 10.4
    and the variable fee approach, Ch. 56, 10.7
Reinsurance contracts issued, Ch. 56, 8.9
    accounting for ceding commissions and reinstatement premiums, Ch. 56, 8.9.3
    boundary of, Ch. 56, 8.9.1
    determining the quantity of benefits for identifying coverage units, Ch. 56, 8.9.4
    issued adverse loss development covers, Ch. 56, 8.9.2

Reinsurer, Ch. 55, 2.2.1
Reissuing (dual dating) financial statements, Ch. 38, 2.1.1.B
  Related party disclosures, Ch. 39. *See also* IAS 24
  compensation, defined, Ch. 39, 2.6.1
  disclosure
    of controlling relationships, Ch. 39, 2.4
    expense incurred with management entity, Ch. 39, 2.8
    with government-related entities, Ch. 39, 2.9
    key management personnel compensation, Ch. 39, 2.6
    other related party transactions, including commitments, Ch. 39, 2.7
    transactions, Ch. 39, 2.5
  identification of a related party and related party transactions, Ch. 39, 2.2
    entities that are associates/joint ventures, Ch. 39, 2.2.3
    entities that are joint ventures and associates of the same third entity, Ch. 39, 2.2.5
    entities that are joint ventures of the same third party, Ch. 39, 2.2.4
      joint operations (IFRS 11), Ch. 39, 2.2.3.A
    entities that are members of same group, Ch. 39, 2.2.2
    entities under control/joint control of certain persons/close members of their family, Ch. 39, 2.2.7
    entities under significant influence of certain persons/close members of their family, Ch. 39, 2.2.8
    government-related entities, Ch. 39, 2.2.10
    persons/close members of a person's family that are related parties, Ch. 39, 2.2.1
      control, Ch. 39, 2.2.1.A
      joint control, Ch. 39, 2.2.1.B
      key management personnel, Ch. 39, 2.2.1.D
      significant influence, Ch. 39, 2.2.1.C
    post-employment benefit plans, Ch. 39, 2.2.6
  parties that are not related parties, Ch. 39, 2.3
  post-employment benefits, Ch. 39, 2.6.3
  related party issue, Ch. 39, 1.1
  reporting entity part of a group, Ch. 39, 2.6.7
  share-based payment transactions, Ch. 39, 2.6.6
  short-term employee benefits, Ch. 39, 2.6.2
  termination benefits, Ch. 39, 2.6.5
  transactions requiring disclosure, Ch. 39, 2.7.1
Relative subordination, Ch. 47, 4.5.5, 4.6.4.B
  preference shares, Ch. 47, 4.5.5
  of puttable instrument, Ch. 47, 4.6.4.B
Relevant activities, investee
  management of defaults on assets, Ch. 6, 4.1.4
  more than one relevant activity, Ch. 6, 4.1.1
  no relevant activities, Ch. 6, 4.1.2
  single asset, single lessee vehicles, Ch. 6, 4.1.3
Renewable energy certificates (RECs), Ch. 17, 11.3
Rental assets transferred to inventory, Ch. 22, 2.3.1.E
Rental income, Ch. 19, 6.6.1. *See also* IFRS 16
Replacement share-based payment awards, Ch. 34, 7.4.4, 11.
  See also Equity-settled share-based payment transactions
  in a business combination, Ch. 7, 5.2.1; Ch. 9, 7.2; Ch. 34, 11
    accounted for under IFRS 3, Ch. 34, 11.2
      accounting for changes in vesting assumptions after the acquisition date, Ch. 34, 11.2.3
      acquiree awards the acquirer is not 'obliged' to replace, Ch. 34, 11.2.2
      awards that the acquirer is 'obliged' to replace, Ch. 34, 11.2.1
    acquiree award not replaced by acquirer, Ch. 34, 11.3
    background, Ch. 34, 11.1
    financial statements of the acquired entity, Ch. 34, 11.4
  designation of award as, Ch. 34, 7.4.4.A
  incremental fair value of, Ch. 34, 7.4.4.B
  replacement of vested awards, Ch. 34, 7.4.4.C
  tax deductions for, Ch. 33, 12.2
  on termination of employment, Ch. 34, 7.5
Reportable segments. *See also* IFRS 8; Operating segments
  externally reportable segments, identifying, Ch. 36, 3.2
    aggregation criteria, Ch. 36, 3.2.1
    'all other segments,' Ch. 36, 3.2.4
    combining small operating segments into a larger reportable segment, Ch. 36, 3.2.3
    'practical limit' for the number of reported operating segments, Ch. 36, 3.2.5
    restatement of segments reported in comparative periods, Ch. 36, 3.2.6
    quantitative thresholds, operating segments which are reportable because of their size, Ch. 36, 3.2.2
  information to be disclosed about, Ch. 36, 5
    commercially sensitive information, Ch. 36, 5.8
    explanation of measurements used in segment reporting, Ch. 36, 5.5
    general information, Ch. 36, 5.1
    other elements of revenue, income and expense, Ch. 36, 5.3
    reconciliations, Ch. 36, 5.6
    restatement of previously reported information, Ch. 36, 5.7
      organisation structure, changes in, Ch. 36, 5.7.1
      segment measures, changes in, Ch. 36, 5.7.2
    segment profit or loss, measure of, Ch. 36, 5.2
    total assets and total liabilities, measure of, Ch. 36, 5.2
Repurchase agreements ('repos')
  agreement to repurchase at fair value, Ch. 52, 4.1.5
  agreements to return the same asset, Ch. 52, 4.1.1
  agreements with right of substitution, Ch. 52, 4.1.3
  agreements with right to return the same or substantially the same asset, Ch. 52, 4.1.2
  derecognition criteria, securities lending, Ch. 52, 4.1
  inventory, Ch. 22, 2.3.1.F
  net cash-settled forward repurchase, Ch. 52, 4.1.4
  revenue from contracts with customers (IFRS 15)
    forward/call option held by the entity, Ch. 30, 5.1
    put option held by the customer, Ch. 30, 5.2
    sales with residual value guarantees, Ch. 30, 5.3
  right of first refusal to repurchase at fair value, Ch. 52, 4.1.6
  sale and leaseback transactions, Ch. 23, 7.3
  wash sale, Ch. 52, 4.1.7
Reserves and resources. *See also* Extractive industries
  definitions, Ch. 43, 1.3.1
  disclosure, Ch. 43, 2.4
    mining sector, Ch. 43, 2.4.2
    oil and gas sector, Ch. 43, 2.4.1
    standardised measure of oil and gas, Ch. 43, 2.4.3.A
    value of reserves, Ch. 43, 2.4.3
  reporting, Ch. 43, 2.1–2.3

Residual values
  definition, Ch. 23, 6.1.3
  finance lease accounting, Ch. 23, 6.2.3
  property, plant and equipment, Ch. 18, 5.2
Restatement
  hyperinflation, Ch. 16, 8
  of prior periods, impracticability of, Ch. 3, 4.7
    for change in accounting policy, Ch. 3, 4.7.1
    for a material error, Ch. 3, 4.7.2
Restatement of goodwill on first-time adoption, Ch. 5, 5.2.5
  derecognition of negative goodwill, Ch. 5, 5.2.5.B
  previously deducted from equity, Ch. 5, 5.2.5.C
  prohibition of other adjustments of goodwill, Ch. 5, 5.2.5.A
Restructuring of derivatives, hedging instruments, Ch. 53, 3.6.3
Restructuring provisions, Ch. 26, 6.1
  costs that can (and cannot) be included in, Ch. 26, 6.1.4
  definition, Ch. 26, 6.1.1
  recognition of, Ch. 26, 6.1.2
  recognition of obligations arising from the sale of an operation, Ch. 26, 6.1.3
Retrospective application, first-time adoption
  departures from, Ch. 5, 3.5
  estimates, Ch. 5, 4.2
  exceptions to, Ch. 5, 4
  financial assets and liabilities, derecognition of, Ch. 5, 4.3
Returns of capital, Ch. 8, 2.4.1.C
Revaluation model
  assets held under finance leases, Ch. 18, 6.5
  downward valuations, reversals of, Ch. 18, 6.3
  fair value before the adoption of IFRS 13, Ch. 18, 6.1.1.A
  first-time adopter, Ch. 5, 7.4.3
  for intangible assets measurement, Ch. 17, 8.2
    accounting for revaluations, Ch. 17, 8.2.3
    frequency of revaluations, Ch. 17, 8.2.2
    revaluation is only allowed if there is an active market, Ch. 17, 8.2.1
  meaning of fair value, Ch. 18, 6.1
  policy of revaluation, adopting, Ch. 18, 6.4
  revalued assets, disclosures for, Ch. 18, 8.2
  revaluing assets under IFRS 13, Ch. 18, 6.1.1
    cost approach, Ch. 18, 6.1.1.C
    highest and best use, Ch. 18, 6.1.1.A
    income approach, Ch. 18, 6.1.1.B
    market approach, Ch. 18, 6.1.1.B
    valuation approaches, Ch. 18, 6.1.1.B
  valuation surpluses and deficits, accounting for, Ch. 18, 6.2
Revenue from contracts with customers. *See* IFRS 15
Revenue recognition, Ch. 28, 1–3, Ch. 30, 1–11. *See also* IFRS 15; IFRS 17
  and agency relationships, Ch. 28, 3.4
  disclosure, Ch. 32
  extractive industries, Ch. 43, 12
    accounting for imbalances in revenue under IFRS 15, Ch. 43, 12.4.2
      consideration of cost of goods sold where revenue is recognised in accordance with IFRS 15, Ch. 43, 12.4.3
      facility imbalances, Ch. 43, 12.4.4
      future developments, Ch. 43, 12.1.2.A
      historical industry practice, Ch. 43, 12.4.1
      incidental revenue, Ch. 43, 12.1.1
      integral to development, Ch. 43, 12.1.2
      revenue in the development phase, Ch. 43, 12.1
    forward-selling contracts to finance development, Ch. 43, 12.6
      accounting by the investor, Ch. 43, 12.6.2
      accounting by the producer, Ch. 43, 12.6.1
    impact of IFRS 15, Ch. 43, 12
    inventory exchanges with the same counterparty, Ch. 43, 12.3
    overlift and underlift (oil and gas), Ch. 43, 12.4
    sale of product with delayed shipment, Ch. 43, 12.2
    trading activities, Ch. 43, 12.7
  insurance revenue, Ch. 56, 15.1
Reversal of impairment losses, Ch. 20, 11
Reverse acquisitions, Ch. 9, 14
  cash consideration, Ch. 9, 14.6
  earnings per share, Ch. 9, 14.5
  measuring goodwill, Ch. 9, 14.2
  measuring the consideration transferred, Ch. 9, 14.1
  non-controlling interest, Ch. 9, 14.4
  preparation and presentation of consolidated financial statements, Ch. 9, 14.3
  reverse acquisitions and acquirers that are not legal entities, Ch. 9, 14.9
  reverse acquisitions involving a non-trading shell company, Ch. 9, 14.8
  share-based payments, Ch. 9, 14.7
Reverse factoring, *See* Supply-chain finance
Reverse indemnification liabilities, Ch. 9, 5.6.4.A
Rights issue, Ch. 37, 4.3.3
Risk components, hedge accounting, Ch. 53, 2.2
Risk, concentrations of, Ch. 54, 5.6.1; Ch. 55, 11.2.4
Risk management objective, hedge accounting, Ch. 53, 6.2
Risk management strategy, hedge accounting, Ch. 53, 6.2; Ch. 54, 4.3.1
Risk service contracts, Ch. 43, 5.5.1
Risk-sharing arrangements, extractive industries, Ch. 43, 6
  asset swaps, Ch. 43, 6.3
  carried interests, Ch. 43, 6.1
  E&E assets, Ch. 43, 6.3.1
  exchanges of E&E assets for other types of assets, Ch. 43, 6.3.3
  farm-ins and farm-outs, Ch. 43, 6.2
  PP&E, intangible assets and investment property, Ch. 43, 6.3.2
Rollover hedging strategy, Ch. 53, 7.7
Royalties
  extractive industries, Ch. 43, 5.7, 12.9
Russia, IFRS adoption in, Ch. 1, 4.2.2
Russian Accounting Principles (RAP), Ch. 1, 4.2.2
Sale and leaseback transactions, Ch. 23, 7; Ch. 23, 8–8.4
  determining whether the transfer of an asset is a sale, Ch. 23, 8.1
  disclosures, Ch. 23, 8.4
  finance leaseback, Ch. 23, 7.2
  operating leaseback, Ch. 23, 7.2

Sale and leaseback transactions—*contd*
   presentation in the statement of cash flows, Ch. 40, 5.4.3
   repurchase agreements and options, Ch. 23, 8.1
   transactions in which the transfer of an asset is a sale, Ch. 23, 8.2
      accounting for the leaseback, Ch. 23, 8.2.2
      accounting for the sale, Ch. 23, 8.2.1
      adjustment for off-market terms, Ch. 23, 8.2.3
   transactions in which the transfer of an asset is not a sale, Ch. 23, 8.3

Sale of goods
   sale and repurchase agreements, Ch. 30, 5.3

Sale of a mineral interest and a contract to provide extraction services, Ch. 43, 12.1.2

SARs. *See* Share appreciation rights

Seasonal businesses, Ch. 41, 8.2
   costs incurred, Ch. 41, 8.2.2
   revenues received, Ch. 41, 8.2.1

Seasonality or cyclicality of operations, Ch. 41, 4.3.12

Securities and Exchange Board of India (SEBI), Ch. 1, 4.4.3

Securities and Exchange Commission (SEC), US, Ch. 1, 2.3, 3.2
   first-time adoption by foreign private issuers, Ch. 5, 8.1

Securities lending, Ch. 52, 4.1

Securitisations, Ch. 52, 3.6
   'business model' assessment, Ch. 48, 5.6
   'empty' subsidiaries or SPEs, Ch. 52, 3.6.6
   group of assets transfer, Ch. 52, 3.6.5
   insurance protection, Ch. 52, 3.6.3
   recourse to originator, Ch. 52, 3.6.1
   short-term loan facilities, Ch. 52, 3.6.2
   treatment of collection, Ch. 52, 3.6.4
   vehicles, Ch. 13, 2.2.1.B

Securitisations and special purpose entities (SPEs), Ch. 51, 7.7
   accounting for a financial liability issued, Ch. 51, 7.7.2
   ECL requirements for the SPE, Ch. 51, 7.7.1

Segment cash flow disclosures, Ch. 40, 5.6.2

Segment manager, Ch. 36, 3.1.2

Self-built assets, Ch. 18, 4.1.5

Self insurance, Ch. 26, 6.13; Ch. 55, 3.2.2.A; Ch. 56, 3.5.2.A

Separability criterion
   intangible assets, Ch. 9, 5.5.2; Ch. 17, 5.1.3.B

Separate and individual financial statements, Ch. 8, 1
   consolidated financial statements and, Ch. 8, 1.1
      associates and joint ventures, separate financial statements and interests in, Ch. 8, 1.1.1
      joint operation, separate financial statements and interests in, Ch. 8, 1.1.2
      publishing without consolidated financial statements or financial statements in which investments in associates or joint ventures are equity accounted, Ch. 8, 1.1.3
   disclosure, Ch. 8, 3
   entities incorporated in EU and consolidated and separate financial statements, Ch. 8, 1.2
   entities with no subsidiaries but exempt from applying IAS 28, Ch. 8, 3.3.1
   prepared by an entity other than a parent electing not to prepare consolidated financial statements, Ch. 8, 1.2
   prepared by parent electing not to prepare consolidated financial statements, Ch. 8, 3.1
   put and call options in separate financial statements, Ch. 7, 6.5

Separate financial statements, Ch. 8, 1–3; Ch. 13, 2.2.3.B. *See also* Separate and individual financial statements; Individual financial statements
   disclosure, Ch. 8, 3
   requirements of, Ch. 8, 2
      cost method, Ch. 8, 2.1
         cost of investment, Ch. 8, 2.1.1
         cost of investment in subsidiary, associate or joint venture acquired in stages, Ch. 8, 2.1.1.C
         deemed cost on transition to IFRS, Ch. 8, 2.1.2
         formation of a new parent, Ch. 8, 2.1.1.E formation of a new parent: calculating the cost and measuring equity, Ch. 8, 2.1.1.F
         investment in a subsidiary accounted for at cost: partial disposal, Ch. 8, 2.1.1.D
         investments acquired for own shares or other equity instruments, Ch. 8, 2.1.1.A
         investments acquired in common control transactions, Ch. 8, 2.1.1.B
         reverse acquisitions in the separate financial statements, Ch. 8, 2.1.1.G
      dividends and other distributions, Ch. 8, 2.4
         carrying amount of investment exceeds the consolidated net assets, Ch. 8, 2.4.1.B
         distributions of non-cash assets to owners (IFRIC 17), Ch. 8, 2.4.2
         recognition, measurement and presentation, Ch. 8, 2.4.2.B
         scope, Ch. 8, 2.4.2.A
         dividend exceeds the total comprehensive income, Ch. 8, 2.4.1.A
         dividends from subsidiaries, joint ventures or associates, Ch. 8, 2.4.1
         returns of capital, Ch. 8, 2.4.1.C
      equity method, Ch. 8, 2.3
      IFRS 9 method, Ch. 8, 2.2

Service concession arrangements (SCA), Ch. 25, 1–7. *See also* IFRIC 12
   accounting by grantors, Ch. 25, 2.5
   additional construction and upgrade services, Ch. 25, 5.1
      that comprise a new infrastructure asset, Ch. 25, 5.1.2
      that are part of the initial infrastructure asset, Ch. 25, 5.1.1
   bifurcation, Ch. 25, 4.5
   cash flows for, Ch. 40, 4.4.9
   consideration for services provided, Ch. 25, 4.1
      allocating, Ch. 25, 4.1.1
      determining accounting model, Ch. 25, 4.1.2
   construction phase, impairment during, Ch. 25, 4.3.2
   contract acquisition and mobilisation costs, Ch. 25, 4.8
   contractual payments made by an operator to a grantor, Ch. 25, 4.7
      under financial asset model, Ch. 25, 4.7.2
      under intangible asset model, Ch. 25, 4.7.3
      variable payments, Ch. 25, 4.7.1
   control model, Ch. 25, 3
      assets within scope, control model, Ch. 25, 3.3
      partially regulated assets, Ch. 25, 3.4
      residual interest, control of, Ch. 25, 3.2
      regulation of services, Ch. 25, 3.1
   disclosure requirements, Ch. 25, 7
   expenditure during operations phase, Ch. 25, 5

financial asset model, Ch. 25, 4.2
grantor, Ch. 25, 5.3
intangible asset model, Ch. 25, 4.3
    amortisation of, Ch. 25, 4.3.1
    impairment during construction phase, Ch. 25, 4.3.2
interaction of IFRS 16 and IFRIC 12, Ch. 25, 2.3
Interpretations Committee's approach to, Ch. 25, 1.1
operations phase, accounting for, Ch. 25, 5.2
operations services, Ch. 25, 4.1.1
outsourcing arrangements and, Ch. 25, 2.2.1
previously held assets, Ch. 25, 3.3.3
private-to-private arrangements, Ch. 25, 2.4
public service nature of the obligation, Ch. 25, 2.1
residual interests
    accounting for, Ch. 25, 4.6
    control of, Ch. 25, 3.2
revenue recognition, Ch. 25, 4.4
upgrade services, Ch. 25, 5.1

Service condition, share-based payment, Ch. 34, 3.1

Service cost, defined benefit pension plans, Ch. 35, 10.1
    current service cost, Ch. 35, 10.1
    past service cost, Ch. 35, 10.2.1
    settlements, Ch. 35, 10.2.3

Service-type warranties, Ch. 31, 3.2

Set-off, enforceable legal right of, financial assets and liabilities, Ch. 54, 7.4.1.A

Settlement date accounting, Ch. 49, 2.2.4; Ch. 51, 7.3.2
    exchange of non-cash financial assets, Ch. 49, 2.2.5.A

Shadow accounting, insurance contracts, Ch. 55, 7.2.2.D, 8.3

Share appreciation rights (SARs), Ch. 34, 8.7.3, 9.1

Share-based payment arrangement, Ch. 34, 2.2.1

Share-based payment transactions, Ch. 34, 2.2.1. *See also* Cash-settled share-based payment transactions; Equity-settled share-based payment transactions; IFRS 2; Vesting, share-based payment
    allocation of expense for equity-settled transactions, overview, Ch. 34, 6.1
    awards entitled to dividends or dividend equivalents during the vesting period, Ch. 34, 15.3
    awards exchanged for awards held by acquiree's employees, Ch. 9, 11.2.2
    awards vesting/exercisable on an exit event/change of control, Ch. 34, 15.4
    cash-settled transactions, Ch. 34, 9
        accounting, Ch. 34, 9.3
        modification of award from equity-settled to cash-settled (or vice versa), Ch. 34, 9.4
    cost of awards, equity-settled, Ch. 34, 5
        determining the fair value of equity instruments, Ch. 34, 5.5
        grant date, Ch. 34, 5.3
        transactions with employees, Ch. 34, 5.2
        transactions with non-employees, Ch. 34, 5.4
    disclosures, Ch. 34, 13
        impact of share-based payment transactions on financial statements, Ch. 34, 13.3
        of key management personnel compensation, Ch. 39, 2.6.6
        nature and extent of share-based payment arrangements, Ch. 34, 13.1
        valuation of share-based payment arrangements, Ch. 34, 13.2
    equity-settled transactions, allocation of expense, Ch. 34, 6
        cost of awards, Ch. 34, 5
        modification, cancellation and settlement, Ch. 34, 7
        overview, Ch. 34, 4
        valuation, Ch. 34, 8
    first-time adoption, Ch. 34, 16.1
    group share schemes, Ch. 34, 12
    loans to employees to purchase shares (limited recourse and full recourse loans), Ch. 34, 15.2
    matching share awards, Ch. 34, 15.1
        cancellation and settlement, Ch. 34, 7.4
        future modification or replacement of award, Ch. 34, 7.6
        modification, cancellation and settlement of equity-settled transactions, Ch. 34, 7
    modifications, Ch. 34, 7.3
        replacement and ex-gratia awards on termination of employment, Ch. 34, 7.5
        share splits and consolidations, Ch. 34, 7.8
        two awards running 'in parallel', Ch. 34, 7.7
        valuation requirements, Ch. 34, 7.2
    recognition, general principles of, Ch. 34, 3
        non-vesting conditions, Ch. 34, 3.2
        vesting conditions, Ch. 34, 3.1
            market conditions, Ch. 34, 6.3
            non-vesting conditions, Ch. 34, 6.4
        vesting conditions other than market conditions, Ch. 34, 6.2
        vesting period, Ch. 34, 3.3
    replacement awards in business combination, Ch. 34, 11; Ch. 7, 5.2.1; Ch. 9, 7.2
        accounted for under IFRS 3, Ch. 34, 11.2
        acquiree award not replaced by acquirer, Ch. 34, 11.3
        financial statements of the acquired entity, Ch. 34, 11.4
    South African black economic empowerment ('BEE') and similar arrangements, Ch. 34, 15.5
    tax base, determining, Ch. 33, 10.8.2
    taxes related to, Ch. 33, 10.8; Ch. 34, 14
        employment taxes of the employer, Ch. 34, 14.2
        income tax deductions for the entity, Ch. 34, 14.1
        sale or surrender of shares by employee to meet employee's tax liability ('sell to cover' and net settlement), Ch. 34, 14.3
    transactions with equity and cash alternatives, Ch. 34, 10
        awards requiring cash or equity settlement in specific circumstances (awards with contingent cash or contingent equity settlement), Ch. 34, 10.3
        cash settlement alternative not based on share price or value, Ch. 34, 10.4
        transactions where counterparty has choice of settlement, Ch. 34, 10.1
        transactions where entity has choice of settlement, Ch. 34, 10.2
    valuation of equity-settled transactions, Ch. 34, 8
        adapting option-pricing models, Ch. 34, 8.4
        appropriate assumptions for option-pricing models, Ch. 34, 8.5
        awards to a fixed monetary value, Ch. 34, 8.10
        awards whose fair value cannot be measured reliably, Ch. 34, 8.8

Share-based payment transactions—*contd*
    valuation of equity-settled transactions—*contd*
        awards with reload features, Ch. 34, 8.9
        option-pricing model selection, Ch. 34, 8.3
        other awards requiring the use of option valuation models, Ch. 34, 8.7

Share option, Ch. 34, 2.2

Share price-based contingencies, Ch. 37, 6.4.6.B

Share splits and consolidations, Ch. 37, 4.3.1

Shipping of commodities, Ch. 43, 12.12
    identification of performance obligations, Ch. 43, 12.12.1
    sale of product with delayed shipment, Ch. 43, 12.2
    satisfaction of performance obligations – control assessment, Ch. 43, 12.12.2

Short-term employee benefits, Ch. 35, 12
    disclosure of key management personnel compensation, Ch. 39, 2.6.2
    general recognition criteria for, Ch. 35, 12.1
    profit-sharing and bonus plans, Ch. 35, 12.3
        present legal or constructive obligation, Ch. 35, 12.3.1
        reliable estimate of provision, Ch. 35, 12.3.2
        statutory profit-sharing based on taxable profit, Ch. 35, 12.3.3
    short-term paid absences, Ch. 35, 12.2
        accumulating absences, Ch. 35, 12.2.1
        non-accumulating absences, Ch. 35, 12.2.2

Short-term loan facilities, Ch. 52, 3.6.2

Short-term receivables and payables, Ch. 14, 2.1.3

SIC-5–*Classification of Financial Instruments–Contingent Settlement Provisions*, Ch. 47, 4.3.1

SIC-7–*Introduction of the Euro*, Ch. 15, 1.2, 8

SIC-10–*Government Assistance-No Specific Relation to Operating Activities*, Ch. 24, 2.2.2

SIC-12–*Consolidation-Special Purpose Entities*, Ch. 6,

SIC-16–*Share Capital – Reacquired Own Equity Instruments (Treasury Shares)*, Ch. 47, 9.1

SIC-21–*Income Taxes–Recovery of Revalued Non-Depreciable Assets*, Ch. 33, 8.4.6

SIC-25–*Income Taxes– Changes in the Tax Status of an Entity or its Shareholders*, Ch. 33, 10.9

SIC-29–*Service Concession Arrangements: Disclosures*, Ch. 25.1–7

SIC-32–*Intangible Assets-Web Site Costs*, Ch. 17, 6.2.5

Significant estimates and judgements, disclosure of, Ch. 13, 3

Significant influence, Ch. 11, 4
    fund managers, Ch. 11, 4.6
    holdings of less than 20% of the voting power, Ch. 11, 4.3
    lack of, Ch. 11, 4.2
    potential voting rights, Ch. 11, 4.4
    severe long-term restrictions impairing ability to transfer funds to the investor, Ch. 11, 4.1
    voting rights held in a fiduciary capacity, Ch. 11, 4.5

Significant insurance risk, Ch. 55, 3.2; Ch. 56, 3.5
    changes in level of, Ch. 56, 3.6
    level of assessment, Ch. 55, 3.2.2; Ch. 56, 3.5.2
        insurance mutuals, Ch. 55, 3.2.2.B; Ch. 56, 3.5.2.B
        intragroup insurance contracts, Ch. 55, 3.2.2.C; Ch. 56, 3.5.2.C
        self insurance, Ch. 55, 3.2.2.A; Ch. 56, 3.5.2.A
    meaning of 'significant', Ch. 55, 3.5.1
    quantity of insurance risk, Ch. 56, 3.5.1
    significant additional amounts, Ch. 56, 3.5.3
    significant additional benefits, Ch. 55, 3.5.3

Silo, Ch. 6, 8
    consolidation of, Ch. 6, 8.3
    evaluating control of, Ch. 6, 8.2
    identifying, Ch. 6, 8.1
        in insurance industry, Ch. 6, 8.1.1
        in investment funds industry, Ch. 6, 8.1.2

Simplified Disclosure Standard (SDS), Ch. 1, 4.5

SME Implementation Group, Ch. 1, 2.9

South Africa, IFRS adoption in, Ch. 1, 4.6

SPACs. *See* Special purpose acquisition companies (SPACs)

Special purpose acquisition companies (SPACs), Ch. 34, 5.3.10

Special purpose entities (SPEs), Ch. 52, 3.6.6, 5.6.1

Split accounting, compound financial instruments, Ch. 47, 6.2
    accounting for the equity component, Ch. 47, 6.2.1
    temporary differences arising from split accounting, Ch. 47, 6.2.2

Standing Interpretations Committee (SIC), Ch. 1, 2.1

Start-up costs, investment properties, Ch. 19, 4.2
    intangible assets, Ch. 17, 7

Statement of cash flows, Ch. 40, 1–8. *See also* IAS 7
    acquisition-related costs, Ch. 40, 6.3.1
    acquisitions, Ch. 40, 6.3
    classification, Ch. 40, 4
        allocating items to operating, investing and financing activities, Ch. 40, 4.4
        cash flows for service concession arrangements, Ch. 40, 4.4.9
        cash flows from factoring of trade receivables, Ch. 40, 4.4.5
        cash flows from supply-chain financing (reverse factoring), Ch. 40, 4.4.6
        cash flows on derivative contracts, Ch. 40, 4.4.12
        cash flows related to the costs of a share issue, Ch. 40, 4.4.11
        classification of cash flows-future developments, Ch. 40, 4.4.11
        compensation for an insured loss, Ch. 40, 4.4.8
        contributions to a log-term employee benefit fund, Ch. 40, 4.4.4
        debt instrument issued at a discount or redeemed at a premium, Ch. 40, 4.4.13
        early settlement of a debt instrument, Ch. 40, 4.4.14
        interest and dividends, Ch. 40, 4.4.1
        property, plant and equipment held for rental, Ch. 40, 4.4.7
        sales taxes and other non-income tax cash flows, Ch. 40, 4.4.3
        taxes on income, Ch. 40, 4.4.2
        treasury shares, Ch. 40, 4.4.10
    cash flows from financing activities, Ch. 40, 4.3
    cash flows from investing activities, Ch. 40, 4.2
    cash flows from operating activities, Ch. 40, 4.1
        direct method, Ch. 40, 4.1.1
        indirect method, Ch. 40, 4.1.2
    consolidated statement of cash flows, preparing, Ch. 40, 6.1

contingent consideration, Ch. 40, 6.3.3
deferred and other non-cash consideration, Ch. 40, 6.3.2
disposals, Ch. 40, 6.3
first-time adopter, Ch. 5, 7.1
foreign currency cash flows, Ch. 40, 5.3
    entities applying the direct method, Ch. 40, 5.3.1
    entities applying the indirect method, Ch. 40, 5.3.2
gross/net presentation of cash flows, Ch. 40, 5.2
group treasury arrangements, Ch. 40, 6.5.2
non-cash transactions and transactions on deferred terms, Ch. 40, 5.4
    asset disposals on deferred terms, Ch. 40, 5,4,2
    asset purchased on deferred terms from the supplier, Ch. 40, 5.4.1
    revenue contracts with deferred payment terms, Ch. 40, 5.4.3
    sale and leaseback transactions, Ch. 40, 5.5.4
operating, investing and financing activities, allocating items to, Ch. 40, 4.4
    accounting as lessee, Ch. 40, 5.5.1
    accounting as lessor, Ch. 40, 5.5.5
    cash flows for service concession arrangements, Ch. 40, 4.4.9
    cash flows from factoring of trade receivables, Ch. 40, 4.4.5
    cash flows from leasing transactions, Ch. 40, 5.5
    cash flows from supply-chain financing (reverse factoring), Ch. 40, 4.4.6
    cash flows on derivative contracts, Ch. 40, 4.4.12
    cash flows related to the costs of a share issue, Ch. 40, 4.4.11
    contributions to a log-term employee benefit fund, Ch. 40, 4.4.4
    debt instrument issued at a discount or redeemed at a premium, Ch. 40, 4.4.13
    interest and dividends, Ch. 40, 4.4.1
    lease incentives, Ch. 40, 5.5.3
    payments made by the lessee before commencement date, Ch. 40, 5.5.2
    property, plant and equipment held for rental, Ch. 40, 4.4.7
    received as compensation for an insured loss, Ch. 40, 4.4.9
    sales taxes, Ch. 40, 4.4.3
    taxes on income, Ch. 40, 4.4.2
    treasury shares, Ch. 40, 4.4.10
settlement of amounts owed by the acquired entity, Ch. 40, 6.3.4
settlement of intra-group balances on a demerger, Ch. 40, 6.3.5
in subsidiaries, associates and joint ventures, Ch. 40, 6.5.1
transactions with non-controlling interests, Ch. 40, 6.2
voluntary disclosures, Ch. 40, 5.7
    cash flows to increase and maintain operating capacity, Ch. 40, 5.7.1
    segment cash flow disclosures, Ch. 40, 5.7.2

Statement of changes in equity, Ch. 3, 3.3

Statement of comprehensive income, Ch. 3, 3.2
    cash flow hedges, Ch. 54, 4.3.3
    comparative information, Ch. 4, 4
    for co-operative, Ch. 54, 7.1.5
    discontinued operations, Ch. 3, 3.2.5
    expenses analysis, Ch. 3, 3.2.3
        by function, Ch. 3, 3.2.3.B
        by nature, Ch. 3, 3.2.3.A
    extraordinary items, Ch. 3, 3.2.6.B
    face of, information required on, Ch. 3, 3.2.2
    fair value hedges, Ch. 54, 4.3.3
    material items, Ch. 3, 3.2.6.A
    for mutual fund, Ch. 54, 7.1.5
    operating profit, Ch. 3, 3.2.2.A
    ordinary activities, Ch. 3, 3.2.6.B
    presentation on face of, Ch. 54, 7
    reclassification adjustments, Ch. 3, 3.2.4.B
    tax on items of other comprehensive income, Ch. 3, 3.2.4.C

Statement of financial position, Ch. 3, 3.1. *See also* IAS 1
    comparative information, Ch. 3, 2.4; Ch. 4, 4.2
    current assets, Ch. 3, 3.1.3
    current liabilities, Ch. 3, 3.1.4
    current/non-current assets and liabilities, distinction between, Ch. 3, 3.1.1
    hyperinflation, Ch. 16, 4
    IFRS statement of financial position, opening, Ch. 5, 3
        and accounting policies, Ch. 5, 3.2
        assets and liabilities to be recognised in, Ch. 5, 5.2.4
        defined terms, Ch. 5, 1.3
        departures from full retrospective application, Ch. 5, 3.5
        fair value and deemed cost, Ch. 5, 3.3
        first-time adoption timeline, Ch. 5, 3.1
        hedge accounting in, Ch. 5, 4.5
        transitional provisions in other standards, Ch. 5, 3.4
    information required either on the face of the statement of financial position or in the notes, Ch. 3, 3.1.6
    information required on the face of statement of financial position, Ch. 3, 3.1.5
    non-current assets and disposal groups held for sale, Ch. 3, 3.1.2
    plan surplus or deficit in, treatment of, Ch. 35, 8
        assets restriction to their recoverable amounts, Ch. 35, 8.2
        net defined benefit liability (asset), Ch. 35, 8.1

Step acquisitions, Ch. 9, 9

Step-by-step method, Ch. 7, 2.3; Ch. 15, 6.6.3
    in consolidating foreign operations, Ch. 7, 2.3

Step-disposal of a subsidiary, Ch. 7, 3.4
    advance payment, Ch. 7, 3.4
    immediate disposal, Ch. 7, 3.4

'Step-up' clause, perpetual instruments, Ch. 47, 4.5.4

Stepped up exercise price, Ch. 47, 5.1.3

Stewardship, Ch. 2, 4.2.3

Straight-line method, assets depreciated using, Ch. 43, 16.1.2

Streaming arrangements, forward-selling contracts to finance development, Ch. 43, 12.6

Stripping costs in the production phase of a surface mine, Ch. 43, 15.5
    determining when production phase commences, Ch. 43, 15.5.2
    disclosures, Ch. 43, 15.5.6
    initial recognition, Ch. 43, 15.5.4
        allocating costs between inventory and the stripping activity asset, Ch. 43, 15.5.4.A
        identifying components of the ore body, Ch. 43, 15.5.4.B

Stripping costs in the production phase of a surface mine—*contd*
   recognition criteria-stripping activity asset, Ch. 43, 15.5.3
   scope of IFRIC 20, Ch. 43, 15.5.1
   subsequent measurement, Ch. 43, 15.5.5
Structured entities, Ch. 13, 2.2.1, 2.2.1.B
   disclosure of interests in unconsolidated, Ch. 13, 6
   disclosure of the nature of the risks associated with consolidated, Ch. 13, 4.4
   unconsolidated, Ch. 13, 2.2.2.D
Subleases, Ch. 23, 7
   definition, Ch. 23, 7.1
   disclosure, Ch. 23, 7.5
   intermediate lessor accounting, Ch. 23, 7.2
   presentation, Ch. 23, 7.4
   sublessee accounting, Ch. 23, 7.3
Sub-LIBOR issue, Ch. 53, 2.4
Subordinated financial support, Ch. 13, 2.2.1.B
Subordinated retained interests, Ch. 52, 4.3
Subrogation, Ch. 55, 7.2.6.E
Subsequent measurement, financial instruments, Ch. 50, 1–4.
   See also Impairments
   amortised cost and the effective interest method, Ch. 50, 3
     effective interest rate, Ch. 50, 3.1
     fixed interest rate instruments, Ch. 50, 3.2
     floating interest rate instruments, Ch. 50, 3.3
     inflation-linked debt instruments, Ch. 50, 3.6
     modified financial assets and liabilities, Ch. 50, 3.8
       accounting for modifications that do not result in derecognition, Ch. 50, 3.8.1, 5.1.1
       treatment of modification fees, Ch. 50, 3.8.2
     more complex financial liabilities, Ch. 50, 3.7
     perpetual debt instruments, Ch. 50, 3.5
     prepayment, call and similar options, Ch. 50, 3.4
       revisions to estimated cash flows, Ch. 50, 3.4.1
   estimated cash flows, revisions to, Ch. 50, 3.4.1
   exceptions to the general principles, Ch. 50, 2.9
     hedging relationships, Ch. 50, 2.9.1
     liabilities arising from 'failed derecognition' transactions, Ch. 50, 2.9.3
     regular way transactions, Ch. 50, 2.9.2
   financial assets and financial liabilities at fair value through profit/loss, Ch. 50, 2.4
   financial guarantees and commitments to provide a loan at a below-market interest rate, Ch. 50, 2.8
   floating interest rate instruments, Ch. 50, 3.3
   foreign currencies
     foreign entities, Ch. 50, 4.2
     instruments, Ch. 50, 4.1
   impairment, Ch. 51, 1–15
     approaches, Ch. 51, 3
     for corporates, Ch. 51, 4
     disclosures, Ch. 51, 15
     financial assets measured at fair value through other comprehensive income, Ch. 51, 9
     general approach, Ch. 51, 6
     intercompany loans, Ch. 51, 13
     introduction, Ch. 51, 1
     loan commitments and financial guarantee contracts, Ch. 51, 11
     measurement of ECL's, Ch. 51, 5
     modified financial assets, Ch. 51, 8
     presentation of credit losses, Ch. 51, 14
     revolving credit facilities, Ch. 51, 12
     scope, Ch. 51, 2
     trade receivables, contract assets and lease receivables, Ch. 51, 10
   reclassification of financial assets, Ch. 50, 2.7
   and recognition of gains and losses, Ch. 50, 2
     debt financial assets measured at amortised cost, Ch. 50, 2.1
     debt financial assets measured at fair value through other comprehensive income, Ch. 50, 2.3
     exceptions to the general principles, Ch. 50, 2.9
       hedging relationships, Ch. 50, 2.9.1
       liabilities arising from 'failed derecognition' transactions, Ch. 50, 2.9.3
       regular way transactions, Ch. 50, 2.9.2
     financial assets and financial liabilities at fair value through profit/loss, Ch. 50, 2.4
     financial guarantees and commitments to provide a loan at a below-market interest rate, Ch. 50, 2.8
     financial liabilities measured at amortised cost, Ch. 50, 2.2
     reclassification of financial assets, Ch. 50, 2.7
     unquoted equity instruments and related derivatives, Ch. 50, 2.6
   unquoted equity instruments and related derivatives, Ch. 50, 2.6
Subsidiaries, Ch. 7; Ch. 13, 2.2.2.A. *See also* Ownership interests, changes in
   acquired in stages, cost of, Ch. 7, 3.1.1, 3.1.2; Ch. 8, 2.1.1.C
   acquisition, Ch. 8, 4.4.2
     deferred tax exemption, Ch. 33, 7.2.9
   becoming a first-time adopter later than its parent, Ch. 5, 5.9.1
   dividends from, Ch. 8, 2.4.1
   former subsidiary
     comparative information for, Ch. 7, 3.3.2.G
     interest retained in, Ch. 7, 3.3.1
   investments in, Ch. 5, 5.8; Ch. 20, 12.4
   parent becoming a first-time adopter later than, Ch. 5, 5.9.2
Substantive rights, Ch. 6, 4.2.1
Substantively enacted tax legislation, Ch. 33, 5.1
Successful efforts method, E&E expenditure, Ch. 43, 3.2.3
Super-deductible assets (tax), Ch. 33, 7.2.6
Supply-chain finance, Ch. 52, 6.5; Ch. 40, 4.4.6
'Synthetic' instruments, Ch. 46, 8
Take-or-pay contracts, Ch. 43, 12.7.14, 17.2
Tax bases, Ch. 33, 6.1
   of assets, Ch. 33, 6.1.1
   assets and liabilities whose tax base is not immediately apparent, Ch. 33, 6.1.3
   disclaimed or with no economic value, Ch. 33, 6.1.7
   equity items with, Ch. 33, 6.1.5
   of items not recognised as assets/liabilities in financial statements, Ch. 33, 6.1.4
   items with more than one tax base, Ch. 33, 6.1.6
   of liabilities, Ch. 33, 6.1.2
Tax expense (tax income)
   definition, Ch. 33, 3
Tax planning opportunities, Ch. 33, 7.4.4, 8.4.1

Taxable profit (tax loss)
  definition, Ch. 33, 3
Taxable temporary differences
  definition, Ch. 33, 3
Taxation, Ch. 33. *See also* Deferred tax; IAS 12–*Income taxes*; Income taxes
  extractive industries, Ch. 43, 19
  interim financial reporting, Ch. 41, 9.5
    changes in the effective tax rate during the year, Ch. 41, 9.5.2
    difference in financial year and tax year, Ch. 41, 9.5.3
    measuring interim income tax expense, Ch. 41, 9.5.1
    tax credits, Ch. 41, 9.5.5
    tax loss and tax credit carrybacks and carryforwards, Ch. 41, 9.5.4
Taxes related to share-based payment transactions, Ch. 34, 14
  employment taxes of the employer, Ch. 34, 14.2
    applicable standards, Ch. 34, 14.2.1
      holding of own shares to 'hedge' employment tax liabilities, Ch. 34, 14.2.3
      recovery of employer's taxes from employees, Ch. 34, 14.2.2
  income tax deductions for the entity, Ch. 34, 14.1
  sale or surrender of shares by employee to meet employee's tax liability ('sell to cover' and net settlement), Ch. 34, 14.3
    net settlement feature for withholding tax obligations, Ch. 34, 14.3.1
Temporal method, Ch. 15, 1.1
Temporary differences, Ch. 33, 6, 6.2, 7. *See also* Deferred tax
  changes after initial recognition Ch. 33, 7.42.4
    altered by legislative change, Ch. 33, 7.2.4.D
    amortisation, Ch. 33, 7.2.4.A
    in carrying value due to revaluation, Ch. 33, 7.2.4.B
    depreciation, Ch. 33, 7.2.4.A
    in tax base due to deductions in tax return, Ch. 33, 7.2.4.C
  deductible, Ch. 33, 3, 6, 6.1, 6.2.2, 7.2.2.B, 7.5.3
    business combinations and consolidation, Ch. 33, 6.2.2.E
    foreign currency differences, Ch. 33, 6.2.2.F
    revaluations, Ch. 33, 6.2.2.C
    tax re-basing, Ch. 33, 6.2.2.D
    transactions that affect profit of loss, Ch. 33, 6.2.2.A
    transactions that affect statement of financial position, Ch. 33, 6.2.2.B
  definition, Ch. 33, 3
  taxable, Ch. 33, 6.2.1
    business combinations and consolidation, Ch. 33, 6.2.1.E
    foreign currency differences, Ch. 33, 6.2.1.F
    hyperinflation, Ch. 33, 6.2.1.G
    revaluations, Ch. 33, 6.2.1.C
    tax re-basing, Ch. 33, 6.2.1.D
    transactions that affect profit of loss, Ch. 33, 6.2.1.A
    transactions that affect statement of financial position, Ch. 33, 6.2.1.B
Termination benefits, employee benefits, Ch. 35, 14
  measurement, Ch. 35, 14.3
  recognition, Ch. 35, 14.2
  statutory termination indemnities, Ch. 35, 14.1
Third-party credit enhancement, liabilities issued with
  by the issuer, Ch. 14, 11.3.1
  by a third-party, Ch. 14, 11.3.1.A

Time-period related hedged item, Ch. 53, 7.5.1
Time value of money, Ch. 51, 5.7
  hedge effectiveness, measurement of, Ch. 53, 7.4.2
Time value of options, Ch. 53, 3.6.4, 7.5.1
  aligned time value, Ch. 53, 7.5.1.A
  and effectiveness of options, Ch. 53, 7.4.12
  hedged items with embedded optionality, Ch. 53, 3.6.4
  retrospective application, Ch. 53, 12.3.1
Tolling arrangements, mining sector, Ch. 43, 20
Total Distributable Income (TDI), Ch. 55, 6
Total return swaps, Ch. 52, 4.4.1
Trade date accounting, Ch. 49, 2.2.3; Ch. 51, 7.3.2
  exchange of non-cash financial assets, Ch. 49, 2.2.5.A
Trade receivables. *See* Receivables
'Traded in a public market,' meaning of, Ch. 6, 2.2.1.B; Ch. 36, 2.2.1
Transaction-based taxes, Ch. 56, 8.2.3.I
Transaction costs
  changes in ownership interest without loss of control, Ch. 7, 4.4
  equity instruments, tax benefits, Ch. 33, 10.3.5
  equity transactions, Ch. 47, 8.1
  fair value measurement, Ch. 14, 9.1
  financial instruments, Ch. 49, 3.4
    accounting treatment, Ch. 49, 3.4.1
    identifying, Ch. 49, 3.4.2
  incurred by the reporting entity on acquisition of investment property, Ch. 19, 6.4
Transaction price, IFRS 15
  allocation of, Ch. 29, 3
  determination of, Ch. 29, 2
  initial measurement, Ch. 49, 3.3
Transaction related hedged item, Ch. 53, 7.5.1
Transfer of control, Ch 30. 2-4
Transferee's put option, Ch. 52, 5.4.3.B
Transferor's call option, Ch. 52, 5.4.3.A
Transfers of financial assets, Ch. 54, 6
  disclosure requirements, Ch. 54, 6.3.2
  meaning of continuing involvement, Ch. 54, 6.3.1
  meaning of 'transfer,' Ch. 54, 6.1
  transferred financial assets
    that are derecognised in their entirety, Ch. 54, 6.3
    that are not derecognised in their entirety, Ch. 54, 6.2
Transition Resource Group for Impairment of Financial Instruments, IFRS, Ch. 1, 2.9
Transition Resource Group for Insurance Contracts, Ch. 1, 2.9
Transition Resource Group for Revenue Recognition, Ch. 1, 2.9, 27, 28, 29, 30, 31, 32
Transportation costs, Ch. 14, 9.2
Treasury shares, Ch. 47, 9
  cash flow statement, Ch. 40, 4.4.10
  IFRS 17 Treasury share election, Ch. 47, 9.2
  transactions in own shares not at fair value, Ch. 47, 9.1
Trustees, IFRS Foundation, Ch. 1, 2,2–2.8, 3.2, 5
Unanimous consent, joint control, Ch. 12,4.3; Ch. 43, 7.1.1.B
Unbundling of deposit components, Ch. 55, 5
  illustration, Ch. 55, 5.2

Unbundling of deposit components—*contd*
  practical difficulties, Ch. 55, 5.3
  requirements, Ch. 55, 5.1
Uncertain future events, insurance contracts, Ch. 55, 3.4; Ch. 56, 3.2
Uncertain tax treatments, Ch. 33, 5.2, 8.2, 9
  assumptions about the examination of tax treatments ('detection risk'), Ch. 33, 9.3
  consideration of changes in facts and circumstances, Ch. 33, 9.5
  considered separately (unit of account), Ch. 33, 9.2
  determining effects of, Ch. 33, 9.4
  disclosures relating to, Ch. 33, 9.6
  IFRIC 23
    changes in estimates, Ch. 38, 3.6
    scope and definitions used, Ch. 33, 9.1
  presentation of liabilities or assets for, Ch. 33, 9.7
  recognition of an asset for payments on account, Ch. 33, 9.8
Unconsolidated structured entities, Ch. 13, 2.2.2.D
  disclosure of interests, Ch. 13, 6
  financial or other support to, Ch. 13, 4.4.3
Undivided interests, Ch. 18, 7.3; Ch. 43, 7.2
Unit of account, Ch. 14, 5.1
  extractive industries, Ch. 43, 4
  fair value measurement
    asset's (or liability's) components, Ch. 14, 5.1.4
    and portfolio exception, Ch. 14, 5.1.2
    and PxQ, Ch. 7, 3.3.2.F; Ch. 14, 5.1.1
    vs. valuation premise, Ch. 14, 5.1.3
  and FVLCD estimation, Ch. 20, 6.1.1
Unit of production method, Ch. 18, 5.6.2
United Kingdom (UK) adopted- IAS, Ch. 1, 4,.2.3
United Kingdom (UK), IFRS adoption in, Ch. 1, 4.2.3
United States of America (US), IFRS adoption in, Ch. 1, 3.2, 4.3.1
Unitisations, mineral properties, Ch. 43, 15.4.1
Unit-linked features, Ch. 55, 4.1
Units of production method, assets depreciated using, Ch. 43, 16.1.3
  joint and by-products, Ch. 43, 16.1.3.D
  reserves base, Ch. 43, 16.1.3.B
  unit of measure, Ch. 43, 16.1.3.C
  units of production formula, Ch. 43, 16.1.3.A
Unquoted equity instruments
  and related derivatives, Ch. 50, 2.6
Upstream activity phases, extractive industries, Ch. 43, 1.6.1
  acquisition of mineral rights, Ch. 43, 1.6.1
  appraisal/evaluation, Ch. 41, 1.6.1
  closure and decommissioning, Ch. 43, 1.6.1
  construction, Ch. 43, 1.6.1
  development, Ch. 43, 1.6.1
  exploration, Ch. 43, 1.6.1
  production, Ch. 43, 1.6.1
  prospecting, Ch. 43, 1.6.1
'Upstream' transactions elimination, equity accounted entities, Ch. 11, 7.6.1
US GAAP, convergence with IFRS, Ch. 1, 3.2
US, IFRS adoption in, Ch. 1, 3.2
Useful life, intangible assets, Ch. 17, 9.1.1
  contractual/other legal rights, Ch. 17, 9.1.2
  with a finite useful life, Ch. 17, 9.2
  with an indefinite useful life, Ch. 17, 9.3
Valuation techniques, fair value measurement, Ch. 14, 14
  cost approach, Ch. 14, 14.3
    use of depreciated replacement cost to measure fair value, Ch. 14, 14.3.1
  disclosure of, Ch. 14, 20.3.5
  income approach, Ch. 14, 14.4
  inputs to, Ch. 14, 15
    broker quotes and pricing services, Ch. 14, 15.5
    central clearing organisations, values from, Ch. 14, 15.5.1
    general principles, Ch. 14, 15.1
    premiums and discounts, Ch. 14, 15.2
      blockage factors (or block discounts), Ch. 14, 15.2.1
    pricing within the bid-ask spread, Ch. 14, 15.3
      bid-ask spread, Ch. 14, 15.3.2
      mid-market pricing, Ch. 14, 15.3.1
    risk premiums, Ch. 14, 15.4
  market approach, Ch. 14, 14.2
  property, plant and equipment, Ch. 18, 6.1.1.B
  selecting appropriate, Ch. 14, 14.1
    making changes to valuation techniques, Ch. 14, 14.1.4
    single *vs.* multiple valuation techniques, Ch. 14, 14.1.1
    using multiple valuation techniques to measure fair value, Ch. 14, 14.1.2
    valuation adjustments, Ch. 14, 14.1.3
Value-at-risk and similar analyses, Ch. 54, 5.5.2
Value beyond proven and probable reserves (VBPP), Ch. 43, 8.2.3
Value in use (VIU). *See also* IAS 36
  calculation of (extractive industries), Ch. 43, 11.4
    commodity price assumptions, Ch. 43, 11.4.3
    consistency in cash flows and book values attributed to the CGU, Ch. 43, 11.4.1
      environmental provisions and similar provisions and liabilities, Ch. 43, 11.4.1.A
    foreign currency cash flows, Ch. 43, 11.4.5
    future capital expenditure, Ch. 43, 11.4.4
    projections of cash flows, Ch. 43, 11.4.2
      cash flows from mineral reserves and resources and the appropriate discount rate, Ch. 43, 11.4.2.A
  differences between fair value and VIU, Ch. 20, 7.3
  estimating the future pre-tax cash flows of the CGU under review, Ch. 20, 7.1
    budgets and cash flows, Ch. 20, 7.1.1
    cash inflows and outflows from improvements and enhancements, Ch. 20, 7.1.2
    events after the reporting period, Ch. 20, 7.1.9
    foreign currency cash flows, Ch. 20, 7.1.5
    internal transfer pricing, Ch. 20, 7.1.6
    lease payments, Ch. 20, 7.1.8
    overheads and share-based payments, Ch. 20, 7.1.7
    restructuring, Ch. 20, 7.1.3
    terminal values, Ch. 20, 7.1.4
  identifying appropriate discount rate and discounting future cash flows, Ch. 20, 7.2
    approximations and short cuts, Ch. 20, 7.2.4
    calculating VIU using post-tax cash flows, Ch. 20, 7.2.3
    determining pre-tax rates taking account of tax losses, Ch. 20, 7.2.6

disclosing pre-tax discount rates when using a post-tax methodology, Ch. 20, 7.2.5
discount rates and the weighted average cost of capital, Ch. 20, 7.2.1
entity-specific WACCs and capital structure, Ch. 20, 7.2.8
entity-specific WACCs and different project risks within the entity, Ch. 20, 7.2.7
pre-tax discount rate, calculating, Ch. 20, 7.2.2
use of discount rates other than the WACC, Ch. 20, 7.2.9
for investment in subsidiaries, associates and joint ventures, Ch. 20, 12.4.2
based on cash flows generated by underlying assets, Ch. 20, 12.4.2.B
using dividend discount models, Ch. 20, 12.4.2.A
relevant cash flows and non-arm's length prices (transfer pricing), Ch. 20, 12.1

Value of business acquired (VOBA), Ch. 55, 9.1
Variable interest entity (VIE), Ch. 13, 2.2.1.B
Variable returns, exposure to
evaluating derivatives, Ch. 6, 5.3
as indicator of power, Ch. 6, 5.1
interest rate swaps, Ch. 6, 5.3.1
plain vanilla foreign exchange swaps, Ch. 6, 5.3.1
returns, Ch. 6, 5.2
total return swaps, Ch. 6, 5.3.2

Vested transactions, share-based payment, Ch. 34, 2.2.2.E
Vesting, share-based payment, Ch. 34, 3.1, 6.1, 9.3.2. *See also* Cash-settled share-based payment transactions; Equity-settled share-based payment transactions
market conditions, Ch. 34, 6.3
non-vesting conditions, Ch. 34, 3.2, 3.4, 6.4
background, Ch. 34, 3.2.1
defining, Ch. 34, 3.2.2
non-compete agreements Ch. 34, 3.2.3
treatment of, option-pricing models, Ch. 34, 8.4.2
overview, Ch. 34, 6.1
accounting after vesting, Ch. 34, 6.1.3
continuous estimation process of IFRS 2, Ch. 34, 6.1.1
vesting and forfeiture, Ch. 34, 6.1.2
shares used as a currency of payment, Ch. 34, 15.6
awards assessed on the market value of a subsidiary or business unit and settled by reference to the fair value of shares in the parent entity, Ch. 34, 15.6.1
vesting conditions, Ch. 34, 3.1, 3.4
employee's performance rating, Ch. 34, 3.1.2
'malus' clauses and clawback conditions, Ch. 34, 3.1.1
other than market conditions, Ch. 34, 6.2
service condition, Ch. 34, 6.2.1
vesting period, Ch. 34, 3.3
awards entitled to dividends during, Ch. 34, 15.3
determining, Ch. 34, 9.3.2.A
market conditions and known vesting periods, Ch. 34, 6.3.3
modifications with altered vesting period, Ch. 34, 7.3.3
non-vesting conditions and, Ch. 34, 6.4.2
variable vesting periods due to market conditions, Ch. 34, 6.3.4
variable vesting periods due to non-market vesting conditions, Ch. 34, 6.2.3
vesting in instalments ('graded vesting'), Ch. 34, 6.2.2

Veto rights, Ch. 6, 4.2.2.A
Voluntary changes of accounting policy, Ch. 3, 4.4; Ch. 41, 8.1.2.B
disclosures relating to, Ch. 3, 5.1.2
Voting power, Ch. 11, 4.3
Voting rights
held in fiduciary capacity, Ch. 11, 4.5
significant influence, potential, Ch. 11, 4.4
Voting rights, investee
additional rights from other contractual arrangements, Ch. 6, 4.3.6
contractual arrangement with other vote holders, Ch. 6, 4.3.5
de facto control, Ch. 6, 4.3.3
majority without power, Ch. 6, 4.3.3
potential voting rights, Ch. 6, 4.3.4
power with a majority, Ch. 6, 4.3.1

Warranties, Ch. 31, 3
assurance-type warranties, Ch. 31, 3.3
contracts that contain both assurance and service-type warranties, Ch. 31, 3.4
determining whether warranty is an assurance-type or service-type warranty, Ch. 31, 3.1
customer's return of defective item in exchange for compensation: right of return *vs.* assurance type warranty, Ch. 31, 3.1.3
evaluating whether a product warranty is a service-type warranty (i.e. a performance obligation) when it is not separately priced, Ch. 31, 3.1.1
how would an entity account for repairs provided outside the warranty period?, Ch. 31, 3.1.2
service-type warranties, Ch. 31, 3.2
Warranty provisions (IAS 37), Ch. 26, 6.10
Waste electrical and electronic equipment (WE&EE), EU directive, Ch. 26, 6.7
Weather derivatives, Ch. 45, 3.3.1
Website costs, Ch. 17, 6.2.5
application and infrastructure, Ch. 17, 6.2.5
content development, Ch. 17, 6.2.5
graphical design development, Ch. 17, 6.2.5
operating stage, Ch. 17, 6.2.5
planning, Ch. 17, 6.2.5
Weighted average cost of capital (WACC), Ch. 20, 7.2
discount rates and, Ch. 20, 7.2.1
entity-specific WACCs
and capital structure, Ch. 20, 7.2.8
and different project risks, Ch. 20, 7.2.7
Weighted average number of shares, Ch. 37, 4.1
Work in progress, recognition of, Ch. 43, 14.1
Workovers, oil and gas wells, Ch. 43, 15.2
World Standard-setters Conferences, Ch. 1, 2.9
Worldwide adoption of IFRS, Ch. 1, 4.1
Written options
call option, Ch. 37, 6.4.2.B; Ch. 47, 11.2.2
maturity analysis, Ch. 54, 5.4.2.F
net settlement, Ch. 45, 4.2.3
net written options, Ch. 53, 3.2.2
put option, Ch. 7, 6.2, 6.3, 6.4, 6.5, 7.3, 7.4; Ch. 37, 6.4.2.C; Ch. 47, 11.3.2

Notes

Notes

Notes

Notes

International GAAP® 2021

Generally Accepted Accounting Practice
under International Financial Reporting Standards

Cullum Allen
Jeremy Barnes
Anne-Cathrine Bernhoft
Martin Beyersdorff
Mike Bonham
David Bradbery
Rob Carrington
Jessica Cayadi
Victor Chan
Wei Li Chan
Larissa Connor
Pieter Dekker
Tim Denton
Alicia Edelstein
Prahalad Halgeri
Andrea Holmes

Lennart Hoogerwaard
Jane Hurworth
Ted Jones
Heather de Jongh
Parbin Khatun
Maria Kingston
Bernd Kremp
Dean Lockhart
Sharon MacIntyre
Anna Malcolm
Amanda Marrion
Emily Moll
Richard Moore
Ayesha Moosa
Tom Mullins
Mqondisi Ndlovu

Tina Patel
Claire Patra
Michael Pratt
Matthew Richardson
Tim Rogerson
Vadim Shelaginov
Yuta Shimomura
Anna Sirocka
Kirsty Smith
Sharanya Sreedaran
David Stolker
Michael Varila
Aikaterini Vatzaki
Jane Watson

EY
Building a better working world

WILEY

This edition first published in 2021 by John Wiley & Sons Ltd.
Cover, cover design and content copyright © 2021 Ernst & Young LLP.
The United Kingdom firm of Ernst & Young LLP is a member of Ernst & Young Global Limited.
International GAAP® is a registered trademark of Ernst & Young LLP.

This publication contains copyright © material and trademarks of the IFRS Foundation®. All rights reserved. Reproduced by Ernst & Young LLP with the permission of the IFRS Foundation. Reproduction and use rights are strictly limited. For more information about the IFRS Foundation and rights to use its material please visit www.ifrs.org.
Disclaimer: To the extent permitted by applicable law the Board and the IFRS Foundation expressly disclaims all liability howsoever arising from this publication or any translation thereof whether in contract, tort or otherwise (including, but not limited to, liability for any negligent act or omission) to any person in respect of any claims or losses of any nature including direct, indirect, incidental or consequential loss, punitive damages, penalties or costs.

Registered office
John Wiley & Sons Ltd, The Atrium, Southern Gate, Chichester, West Sussex, PO19 8SQ, United Kingdom

For details of our global editorial offices, for customer services and for information about how to apply for permission to reuse the copyright material in this book please see our website at www.wiley.com

The right of the author to be identified as the author of this work has been asserted in accordance with the Copyright, Designs and Patents Act 1988.

All rights reserved. No part of this publication may be reproduced, stored in a retrieval system, or transmitted, in any form or by any means, electronic, mechanical, photocopying, recording or otherwise, except as permitted by the UK Copyright, Designs and Patents Act 1988, without the prior permission of the publisher.

Wiley publishes in a variety of print and electronic formats and by print-on-demand. Some material included with standard print versions of this book may not be included in e-books or in print-on-demand. If this book refers to media such as a CD or DVD that is not included in the version you purchased, you may download this material at http://booksupport.wiley.com. For more information about Wiley products, visit www.wiley.com.

Designations used by companies to distinguish their products are often claimed as trademarks. All brand names and product names used in this book are trade names, service marks, trademarks or registered trademarks of their respective owners. The publisher is not associated with any product or vendor mentioned in this book.

Limit of Liability/Disclaimer of Warranty: While the publisher and author have used their best efforts in preparing this book, they make no representations or warranties with respect to the accuracy or completeness of the contents of this book and specifically disclaim any implied warranties of merchantability or fitness for a particular purpose. It is sold on the understanding that the publisher is not engaged in rendering professional services and neither the publisher nor the author shall be liable for damages arising herefrom. If professional advice or other expert assistance is required, the services of a competent professional should be sought.

This publication has been carefully prepared, but it necessarily contains information in summary form and is therefore intended for general guidance only, and is not intended to be a substitute for detailed research or the exercise of professional judgement. The publishers, Ernst & Young LLP, Ernst & Young Global Limited or any of its Member Firms or partners or staff can accept no responsibility for loss occasioned to any person acting or refraining from action as a result of any material in this publication. On any specific matter, reference should be made to the appropriate adviser.

ISBN 978-1-119-77243-9 (paperback)
[EY personnel only ISBN 978-1-119-77244-6]
ISBN 978-1-119-77245-3 (ebk)
ISBN 978-1-119-77266-8 (ebk)

A catalogue record for this book is available from the British Library.

Printed and bound by CPI Group (UK) Ltd, Croydon, CR0 4YY.

This book is printed on acid-free paper, responsibly manufactured from well-managed FSC®-certified forests and other controlled sources.

About this book

The 2021 edition of International GAAP® has been fully revised and updated in order to:
- Provide expanded discussion and practical illustrations on the many implementation issues arising as entities continue to apply IFRS 16 – *Leases*, including those related to recent rent concessions and the associated narrow scope amendment issued by the International Accounting Standards Board (IASB).
- Include an updated chapter on the new insurance contracts standard IFRS 17 – *Insurance Contracts*, which reflects the IASB's recently issued *Amendments to IFRS 17*, resulting in a number of significant changes as well as many other editorial alterations. The chapter also discusses implementation issues and explores other matters arising as insurers prepare for the adoption of the standard.
- Continue to investigate the many application issues arising as entities apply IFRS 9 – *Financial Instruments* – and IFRS 15 – *Revenue from Contracts with Customers*.
- Discuss the IASB's amendments to IFRS 9 and related standards to address the effects of the Interbank Offered Rates (IBOR) reform on financial reporting.
- Illustrate the application of IFRS to the accounting for natural disasters highlighted by the accounting issues related to the recent coronavirus pandemic.
- Discuss the new agenda decisions issued by the IFRS Interpretations Committee since the preparation of the 2020 edition.
- Address the amendments to standards and the many other initiatives that are currently being discussed by the IASB and the potential consequential changes to accounting requirements.
- Provide further insight on the many issues relating to the practical application of IFRS, based on the extensive experience of the book's authors in dealing with current issues.

The book is published in three volumes. The 56 chapters – listed on pages xi to xiii – are split between the three volumes as follows:
- Volume 1 - Chapters 1 to 22,
- Volume 2 - Chapters 23 to 43,
- Volume 3 - Chapters 44 to 56.

Each chapter includes a detailed list of contents and list of illustrative examples.

Each of the three volumes contains the following indexes covering all three volumes:
- an index of extracts from financial statements,
- an index of references to standards and interpretations,
- a general index.

Preface

The IASB noted in its 2018 analysis of the use of IFRS around the world that, other than China, India, Japan and the United States, the vast majority of the 166 jurisdictions they have researched require the use of IFRS for all or most domestic publicly accountable entities (listed companies and financial institutions) in their capital markets. Maintaining the current international alignment of accounting standards requires an ongoing commitment on the part of all jurisdictions involved, but the benefits of IFRS are clear when looking at the way in which the IASB was able to consider the impact of the coronavirus pandemic on financial reporting.

The coronavirus outbreak was first reported near the end of 2019, with the virus subsequently spreading worldwide. On 11 March 2020, the World Health Organisation classified the outbreak as a pandemic. While the coronavirus outbreak is first and foremost a public health concern, it has significantly impacted the world economy and, indirectly, financial reporting and the work of the IASB itself.

In response to the development, the IASB issued Amendments to IFRS 16 – *Leases: Covid-19-Related Rent Concessions*, deferred the effective date of Amendments to IAS 1 – *Presentation of Financial Statements: Classification of Liabilities as Current or Non-current*, decided to extend the consultation period of several consultation documents by three months, and decided to monitor the situation with a view to making further changes to its timelines, if necessary. As a result, the next milestones of many of the IASB's projects have been pushed out to accommodate the exceptional circumstances.

The economic impacts of the coronavirus outbreak can also be seen in the financial reports of companies where it has affected the accounting for and disclosure of going concern issues, impairment testing, government grants, leases, onerous contracts, income taxes and fair value measurement. While the economic uncertainty increased the need for the careful exercise of judgement, IFRS has offered an accounting framework that provides the necessary guidance to deal even with these unusual circumstances.

New standards

IFRS 16 became effective in 2019 and its interactions with other standards has given rise to a number of challenging implementation questions that continue to be addressed. The Interpretations Committee has published agenda decisions on the treatment of subsurface rights, determining the incremental borrowing rate, the definition of a lease and the interaction between the lease term and useful life of leasehold improvements. The IASB continues to work on its project that deals with the application of IAS 12 – *Income Taxes* – to right-of-use assets and lease liabilities, while the Interpretations

Committee is currently considering the accounting for the sale and leaseback of an asset in a single-asset entity.

IFRS 17 – *Insurance Contracts* – was amended in June 2020 and has an effective date of 1 January 2023. The IASB amended IFRS 17 in response to matters of concern raised primarily in Europe regarding the concepts and practical implementation of the standard that were raised by stakeholders. IFRS 17, together with IFRS 9 – *Financial Instruments*, will result in profound changes to the accounting in IFRS financial statements for insurance companies. This will also have a significant impact on data, systems and processes used to produce information for financial reporting purposes. The new model is likely to have a significant impact on the profit and total equity of some insurance entities, but IFRS 17 has been welcomed by the user community as it is expected to improve comparability between insurers and increase the transparency around the drivers of performance and source of earnings.

Current work plan

The IASB has deferred its agenda consultation until 2021 and is currently still working on the projects in its work plan for the period from 2017 until 2021. The work plan can be divided into three elements: the standard-setting and maintenance projects, the research projects, and the Better Communication in Financial Reporting initiative.

The IASB's standard-setting and maintenance agenda focuses almost exclusively on narrow scope projects that address certain aspects of existing standards. The exposure draft on the rate-regulated activities project – a more comprehensive project but limited in impact as it is industry-specific – was delayed by almost a year and is now expected to be published in early 2021.

As part of its active research agenda, the IASB's core model for dynamic risk management and discussion paper on business combinations under common control are expected in late 2020, while the comment period on the discussion paper on goodwill and impairment was extended to December 2020. The IASB is currently considering the direction on the projects on financial instruments with characteristics of equity and extractive activities. Although these technically complex but important projects are taking longer than expected, we encourage the IASB to continue its work as they deal with issues that have been the source of many accounting questions.

The IASB expects to publish, in late 2020, its request for information on the Post-Implementation Review of IFRS 10 – *Consolidated Financial Statements*, IFRS 11 – *Joint Arrangements* – and IFRS 12 – *Disclosure of Interests in Other Entities*. The Interpretations Committee has often discussed requests regarding the interpretation of IFRS 11 and it seems likely that the Post-Implementation Review will similarly give rise to questions from constituents.

Better communication and sustainability reporting

The IASB continues to work on the various aspects of its Better Communication in Financial Reporting initiative, such as the primary financial statements, management commentary and the taxonomy. The project to update the Management Commentary Practice Statement, for which an exposure draft is expected early in 2021, is seen by the

IASB as the cornerstone of the notion of 'broader financial information'. That said, there is an ongoing debate as to how 'broad' annual reporting, and by extension the IASB's own remit, should be.

In November 2019, Hans Hoogervorst, the Chairman of the IASB, noted in a speech that 'The popularity of non-GAAP has risen sharply and there is growing interest in broader reporting, particularly in the area of sustainability. [...] In the light of these developments, the IASB constantly asks itself how it can strengthen the relevance of IFRS Standards in this changing world.'[1] Sue Lloyd, the Vice-Chair of the IASB, noted in December 2019 that '[...] the IASB exists to write Standards that result in investors getting the information they need to make their investment decisions. We know that in order to make informed investment decisions, investors need information that goes beyond the boundaries of that captured within the traditional financial statements. Investors need information about items that are not recognised and measured for accounting purposes, but that can affect the company's future cash flows and the value of its equity.'[2]

Many of the non-financial issues that interest investors can be characterised as externalities, which are commonly defined as consequences of an industrial or commercial activity that affect other parties without being reflected in market prices. Traditional financial reporting has focused on how companies are affected by externalities that are inflicted upon them (i.e. the investor perspective), but far less on how their actions affect others (i.e. the societal perspective). In addressing these considerations, the IASB faces the challenge that it does not have the breadth of expertise that would allow it to cover the entire field of non-financial reporting and that its resources are limited.

In September 2020, Erik Thedéen, the Chair of IOSCO's Task Force on Sustainable Finance, noted in a speech that IOSCO is engaging with two initiatives that 'are both very interesting and very promising'.[3] Firstly, an alliance of five framework- and standard-setting institutions of international significance – CDP, the Climate Disclosure Standards Board (CDSB), the Global Reporting Initiative (GRI), the International Integrated Reporting Council (IIRC) and the Sustainability Accounting Standards Board (SASB) – announced a commitment to working towards a comprehensive corporate reporting system. Secondly, a working group of IFRS trustees is considering what role the IFRS Foundation can play in setting standards for sustainability reporting. The Trustees of the IFRS Foundation published a consultation paper on sustainability reporting to assess if there is sufficient demand for global sustainability standards and, if so, whether the development of a sustainability standards board under the governance structure of the IFRS Foundation would be an appropriate approach to achieving further consistency and global comparability in sustainability reporting.

---

1 Speech by Hans Hoogervorst, 5 November 2019 (IASB Chair delivers keynote at Eumedion Annual Symposium, Netherlands). IFRS Foundation website: http://www.ifrs.org/news-and-events/2019/11/the-iasb-from-financial-to-integrated-standard-setter/
2 Speech by Sue Lloyd, 9 December 2019 (Enhancing relevance in 2020 and beyond). IFRS Foundation website: http://www.ifrs.org/news-and-events/2019/12/enhancing-relevance-in-2020-and-beyond/
3 Speech by Erik Thedéen, 1 October 2020 (speech at the conference Driving Global Standards on Sustainable Finance). Swedish Finansinspektionen website: https://www.fi.se/en/published/presentations/2020/erik-thedeens-speech-at-driving-global-standards-on-sustainable-finance/

We commend the initiative of the Trustees of the IFRS Foundation in taking an active role in the efforts to improve the broader financial report, as non-financial reporting provides important information that allows users to put the financial statements in context and helps them in assessing future risks and opportunities. In addition to IOSCO, the International Federation of Accountants (IFAC) has also expressed support for the creation of a new sustainability standards board that would exist alongside the IASB under the IFRS Foundation. However, as legislators in some jurisdictions have already taken steps to ensure a minimum level of communication about sustainability issues, we believe it is crucial in the interest of broad acceptance to build as broad a base of support as possible.

This edition of *International GAAP®* covers the many interpretations, practices and solutions that have now been developed based on our work with clients, and discussions with regulators, standard-setters and other professionals. In particular, the edition has been revised to consider the many financial reporting issues that have arisen in the context of the coronavirus pandemic. We believe that *International GAAP®*, now in its sixteenth edition, plays an important role in ensuring consistent application of IFRS and helping companies as they address emerging issues (e.g. interest rate benchmark reform, application of IFRS 16 and implementation of IFRS 17). These issues are complex and give rise to many practical questions about the recognition, measurement, presentation and disclosure requirements.

Our team of authors and reviewers hails from all parts of the world and includes not only our global technical experts but also senior client-facing professionals. This gives us an in-depth knowledge of practice in many different countries and industry sectors, enabling us to go beyond mere recitation of the requirements of standards to explaining their application in many varied situations.

We are deeply indebted to many of our colleagues within the global organisation of EY for their selfless assistance and support in the publication of this book. It has been a truly international effort, with valuable contributions from EY people around the globe.

Our thanks go particularly to those who reviewed and edited the drafts, most notably: Elisa Alfieri, Mark Barton, Christian Baur, Paul Beswick, Silke Blaschke, Linzi Carr, Patrick Cavanagh, Larissa Clark, Tony Clifford, Angela Covic, Josh Forgione, Peter Gittens, Archibald Groenewald, Paul Hebditch, Lara Iob, Guy Jones, Steinar Kvifte, Michiel van der Lof, James Luke, Kerri Madden, Mark Mahar, Fernando Marticorena, John Offenbacher, John O'Grady, Christiana Panayidou, Pierre Phan Van Phi, Christoph Piesbergen, George Prieksaitis, Takeshi Saida, Gerard van Santen, Nicola Sawaki, Rachel Simons, Alison Spivey, Leo van der Tas, Daniel Trotman, Hans van der Veen, Tracey Waring, Arne Weber, Clare Wong and Luci Wright.

Our thanks also go to everyone who directly or indirectly contributed to the book's creation, including the following members of EY's IFRS desks: Thato Lengana, Steve Mwereria, Teresia Ng'ang'a, Anna Pickup and Tanay Rai.

We also thank Jeremy Gugenheim for his assistance with the production technology throughout the period of writing.

London,

October 2020

Cullum Allen	Lennart Hoogerwaard	Tina Patel
Jeremy Barnes	Jane Hurworth	Claire Patra
Anne-Cathrine Bernhoft	Ted Jones	Michael Pratt
Martin Beyersdorff	Heather de Jongh	Matthew Richardson
Mike Bonham	Parbin Khatun	Tim Rogerson
David Bradbery	Maria Kingston	Vadim Shelaginov
Rob Carrington	Bernd Kremp	Yuta Shimomura
Jessica Cayadi	Dean Lockhart	Anna Sirocka
Victor Chan	Sharon MacIntyre	Kirsty Smith
Wei Li Chan	Anna Malcolm	Sharanya Sreedaran
Larissa Connor	Amanda Marrion	David Stolker
Pieter Dekker	Emily Moll	Michael Varila
Tim Denton	Richard Moore	Aikaterini Vatzaki
Alicia Edelstein	Ayesha Moosa	Jane Watson
Prahalad Halgeri	Tom Mullins	
Andrea Holmes	Mqondisi Ndlovu	

Volume 2

23	Leases	1701
24	Government grants	1821
25	Service concession arrangements	1847
26	Provisions, contingent liabilities and contingent assets	1923
27	Revenue: Introduction and scope	2015
28	Revenue: Identify the contract and performance obligations	2045
29	Revenue: Determine and allocate the transaction price	2157
30	Revenue: Recognition	2253
31	Revenue: Licences, warranties and contract costs	2313
32	Revenue: Presentation and disclosure	2387
33	Income taxes	2441
34	Share-based payment	2623
35	Employee benefits	2887
36	Operating segments	2973
37	Earnings per share	3017
38	Events after the reporting period	3071
39	Related party disclosures	3093
40	Statement of cash flows	3131
41	Interim financial reporting	3189
42	Agriculture	3269
43	Extractive industries	3325

Index of extracts from financial statements	*index* 1
Index of standards	*index* 7
Index	*index* 111

The list of chapters in volume 3 follows overleaf.

Lists of chapters

Volume 1

1 International GAAP 1
2 The IASB's Conceptual Framework 39
3 Presentation of financial statements and accounting policies 109
4 Non-current assets held for sale and discontinued operations 187
5 First-time adoption 217
6 Consolidated financial statements 385
7 Consolidation procedures and non-controlling interests 491
8 Separate and individual financial statements 571
9 Business combinations 633
10 Business combinations under common control 761
11 Investments in associates and joint ventures 807
12 Joint arrangements 887
13 Disclosure of interests in other entities 941
14 Fair value measurement 995
15 Foreign exchange 1175
16 Hyperinflation 1249
17 Intangible assets 1285
18 Property, plant and equipment 1381
19 Investment property 1437
20 Impairment of fixed assets and goodwill 1511
21 Capitalisation of borrowing costs 1643
22 Inventories 1673

Index of extracts from financial statements ....*index* 1
Index of standards .... *index* 7
Index ....*index* 111

The lists of chapters in volumes 2 and 3 follow overleaf.

Volume 3

44	Financial instruments: Introduction	3571
45	Financial instruments: Definitions and scope	3579
46	Financial instruments: Derivatives and embedded derivatives	3615
47	Financial instruments: Financial liabilities and equity	3657
48	Financial instruments: Classification	3767
49	Financial instruments: Recognition and initial measurement	3839
50	Financial instruments: Subsequent measurement	3865
51	Financial instruments: Impairment	3905
52	Financial instruments: Derecognition	4079
53	Financial instruments: Hedge accounting	4173
54	Financial instruments: Presentation and disclosure	4399
55	Insurance contracts (IFRS 4)	4525
56	Insurance contracts (IFRS 17)	4669

Index of extracts from financial statements	*index* 1
Index of standards	*index* 7
Index	*index* 111

Abbreviations

The following abbreviations are used in this book:

Professional and regulatory bodies:

AASB	Australian Accounting Standards Board
AcSB	Accounting Standards Board of Canada
AICPA	American Institute of Certified Public Accountants
AOSSG	Asian-Oceanian Standard-Setters Group
APB	Accounting Principles Board (of the AICPA, predecessor of the FASB)
ARC	Accounting Regulatory Committee of representatives of EU Member States
ASAF	Accounting Standards Advisory Forum
ASB	Accounting Standards Board in the UK
ASBJ	Accounting Standards Board of Japan
ASU	Accounting Standards Update
CASC	China Accounting Standards Committee
CESR	Committee of European Securities Regulators, an independent committee whose members comprised senior representatives from EU securities regulators (replaced by ESMA)
CICA	Canadian Institute of Chartered Accountants
EC	European Commission
ECB	European Central Bank
ECOFIN	The Economic and Financial Affairs Council
EDTF	Enhanced Disclosure Task Force of the (FSB)
EFRAG	European Financial Reporting Advisory Group
EITF	Emerging Issues Task Force in the US
EPRA	European Public Real Estate Association
ESMA	European Securities and Markets Authority (see CESR)
EU	European Union
FAF	Financial Accounting Foundation
FASB	Financial Accounting Standards Board in the US
FCAG	Financial Crisis Advisory Group
FEE	Federation of European Accountants

FSB	Financial Stability Board (successor to the FSF)
FSF	Financial Stability Forum
G4+1	The (now disbanded) group of four plus 1, actually with six members, that comprised an informal 'think tank' of staff from the standard setters from Australia, Canada, New Zealand, UK, and USA, plus the IASC
G7	The Group of Seven Finance Ministers (successor to G8)
G8	The Group of Eight Finance Ministers
G20	The Group of Twenty Finance Ministers and Central Bank Governors
GPPC	Global Public Policy Committee of the six largest accounting networks
HKICPA	Hong Kong Institute of Certified Public Accountants
IASB	International Accounting Standards Board, or the Board
IASC	International Accounting Standards Committee. The former Board of the IASC was the predecessor of the IASB
IASCF	International Accounting Standards Committee Foundation (predecessor of the IFRS Foundation)
ICAEW	Institute of Chartered Accountants in England and Wales
ICAI	Institute of Chartered Accountants of India
ICAS	Institute of Chartered Accountants of Scotland
IFAC	International Federation of Accountants
IFASS	International Forum of Accounting Standard Setters
IFRIC	The IFRS Interpretations Committee (formerly the International Financial Reporting Interpretations Committee) of the IASB
IGC	Implementation Guidance Committee on IAS 39 (now disbanded)
IOSCO	International Organisation of Securities Commissions
IPSASB	International Public Sector Accounting Standards Board
IPTF	International Practices Task Force (a task force of the SEC Regulations Committee)
ISDA	International Swaps and Derivatives Association
IVSC	International Valuation Standards Council
KASB	Korea Accounting Standards Board
RICS	Royal Institution of Chartered Surveyors
SAC	Standards Advisory Council, predecessor of the IFRS Advisory Council which provides advice to the IASB on a wide range of issues
SEC	Securities and Exchange Commission (the US securities regulator)
SIC	Standing Interpretations Committee of the IASC (replaced by IFRIC)
TEG	Technical Expert Group, an advisor to the European Commission
TRG	Joint Transition Resource Group for Revenue Recognition

Accounting related terms:

ADS	American Depositary Shares
AFS	Available-for-sale investment
ARB	Accounting Research Bulletins (issued by the AICPA)
ARS	Accounting Research Studies (issued by the APB)
ASC	Accounting Standards Codification®. The single source of authoritative US GAAP recognised by the FASB, to be applied to non-governmental entities for interim and accounting periods ending after 15 September 2009
ASU	Accounting Standards Update
BCUCC	Business Combinations Under Common Control
CCIRS	Cross Currency Interest Rate Swap
CDO	Collateralised Debt Obligation
CLO	Collateralized Loan Obligation
CF	Conceptual Framework
CGU	Cash-generating Unit
CU	Currency Unit
DD&A	Depreciation, Depletion and Amortisation
DPF	Discretionary Participation Feature
E&E	Exploration and Evaluation
EBIT	Earnings Before Interest and Taxes
EBITDA	Earnings Before Interest, Taxes, Depreciation and Amortisation
EIR	Effective Interest Rate
EPS	Earnings per Share
FAS	Financial Accounting Standards (issued by the FASB). Superseded by Accounting Standards Codification® (ASC)
FC	Foreign currency
FICE	Financial Instruments with the Characteristics of Equity
FIFO	First-In, First-Out basis of valuation
FRS	Financial Reporting Standard (issued by the ASB)
FTA	First-time Adoption
FVLCD	Fair value less costs of disposal
FVLCS	Fair value less costs to sell (following the issue of IFRS 13, generally replaced by FVLCD)
FVPL	Fair value through profit and loss
FVOCI	Fair value through other comprehensive income

GAAP		Generally accepted accounting practice (as it applies under IFRS), or generally accepted accounting principles (as it applies to the US)
HTM		Held-to-maturity investment
IAS		International Accounting Standard (issued by the former board of the IASC)
IBOR		Interbank Offered Rate
IBNR		Incurred but not reported claims
IFRS		International Financial Reporting Standard (issued by the IASB)
IFRS for SMEs		International Financial Reporting Standard for Small and Medium-sized Entities
IGC Q&A		Implementation guidance to the original version of IAS 39 (issued by the IGC)
IPO		Initial Public Offering
IPR&D		In-process Research and Development
IPSAS		International Public Sector Accounting Standard
IRR		Internal Rate of Return
IRS		Interest Rate Swap
JA		Joint Arrangement
JCA		Jointly Controlled Asset
JCE		Jointly Controlled Entity
JCO		Jointly Controlled Operation
JO		Joint Operation
JV		Joint Venture
LAT		Liability Adequacy Test
LC		Local Currency
LIBOR		London Inter Bank Offered Rate
LIFO		Last-In, First-Out basis of valuation
NBV		Net Book Value
NCI		Non-controlling Interest
NPV		Net Present Value
NRV		Net Realisable Value
OCI		Other Comprehensive Income
PP&E		Property, Plant and Equipment
R&D		Research and Development
SCA		Service Concession Arrangement
SE		Structured Entity
SFAC		Statement of Financial Accounting Concepts (issued by the FASB as part of its conceptual framework project)

SFAS	Statement of Financial Accounting Standards (issued by the FASB). Superseded by Accounting Standards Codification® (ASC)
SME	Small or medium-sized entity
SPE	Special Purpose Entity
SPE-PRMS	Society of Petroleum Engineers – Petroleum Resources Management System
SV	Separate Vehicle
TSR	Total Shareholder Return
VIU	Value In Use
WACC	Weighted Average Cost of Capital

References to IFRSs, IASs, Interpretations and supporting documentation:

AG	Application Guidance
AV	Alternative View
BCZ	Basis for Conclusions on IASs
BC	Basis for Conclusions on IFRSs and IASs
DI	Draft Interpretation
DO	Dissenting Opinion
DP	Discussion Paper
ED	Exposure Draft
IE	Illustrative Examples on IFRSs and IASs
IG	Implementation Guidance
IN	Introduction to IFRSs and IASs
PIR	Post-implementation Review

Authoritative literature

The content of this book takes into account all accounting standards and other relevant rules issued up to September 2020. Consequently, it covers the IASB's *Conceptual Framework for Financial Reporting* and authoritative literature listed below.

References in the main text of each chapter to the pronouncements below are generally to the versions of those pronouncements as approved and expected to be included in the Blue Book edition of the Bound Volume 2021 International Financial Reporting Standards – IFRS – Consolidated without early application – Official pronouncements applicable on 1 January 2021, to be published by the IASB.

References to those pronouncements below which have an effective date after 1 January 2021 (such as IFRS 17 – *Insurance contracts*) are to the versions of those pronouncements that are expected to be included in the Red Book edition of the Bound Volume 2021 International Financial Reporting Standards – IFRS – Official pronouncements issued at 1 January 2021, to be published by the IASB.

US GAAP accounting standards are organised within a comprehensive FASB Accounting Standards Codification©, which is now the single source of authoritative US GAAP recognised by the FASB to be applied to non-governmental entities and has been applied in this publication.

† The standards and interpretations marked with a dagger have been withdrawn or superseded.

		IASB Framework
		The Conceptual Framework for Financial Reporting
		International Financial Reporting Standards (2021 Bound Volume)
	IFRS 1	First-time Adoption of International Financial Reporting Standards
	IFRS 2	Share-based Payment
	IFRS 3	Business Combinations
†	IFRS 4	Insurance Contracts
	IFRS 5	Non-current Assets Held for Sale and Discontinued Operations
	IFRS 6	Exploration for and Evaluation of Mineral Resources
	IFRS 7	Financial Instruments: Disclosures
	IFRS 8	Operating Segments
	IFRS 9	Financial Instruments
	IFRS 10	Consolidated Financial Statements

IFRS 11	Joint Arrangements
IFRS 12	Disclosure of Interests in Other Entities
IFRS 13	Fair Value Measurement
IFRS 14	Regulatory Deferral Accounts
IFRS 15	Revenue from Contracts with Customers
IFRS 16	Leases

International Financial Reporting Standards (mandatory after 1 January 2023)

| IFRS 17 | Insurance Contracts |

International Accounting Standards (2021 Bound Volume)

IAS 1	Presentation of Financial Statements
IAS 2	Inventories
IAS 7	Statement of Cash Flows
IAS 8	Accounting Policies, Changes in Accounting Estimates and Errors
IAS 10	Events after the Reporting Period
IAS 12	Income Taxes
IAS 16	Property, Plant and Equipment
IAS 19	Employee Benefits
IAS 20	Accounting for Government Grants and Disclosure of Government Assistance
IAS 21	The Effects of Changes in Foreign Exchange Rates
IAS 23	Borrowing Costs
IAS 24	Related Party Disclosures
IAS 26	Accounting and Reporting by Retirement Benefit Plans
IAS 27	Separate Financial Statements
IAS 28	Investments in Associates and Joint Ventures
IAS 29	Financial Reporting in Hyperinflationary Economies
IAS 32	Financial Instruments: Presentation
IAS 33	Earnings per Share
IAS 34	Interim Financial Reporting
IAS 36	Impairment of Assets
IAS 37	Provisions, Contingent Liabilities and Contingent Assets
IAS 38	Intangible Assets
IAS 39	Financial Instruments: Recognition and Measurement
IAS 40	Investment Property
IAS 41	Agriculture

IFRS Interpretations Committee Interpretations

IFRIC 1	Changes in Existing Decommissioning, Restoration and Similar Liabilities
IFRIC 2	Members' Shares in Co-operative Entities and Similar Instruments
IFRIC 5	Rights to Interests arising from Decommissioning, Restoration and Environmental Rehabilitation Funds
IFRIC 6	Liabilities arising from Participating in a Specific Market – Waste Electrical and Electronic Equipment
IFRIC 7	Applying the Restatement Approach under IAS 29 Financial Reporting in Hyperinflationary Economies
IFRIC 10	Interim Financial Reporting and Impairment
IFRIC 12	Service Concession Arrangements
IFRIC 14	IAS 19 – The Limit on a Defined Benefit Asset, Minimum Funding Requirements and their Interaction
IFRIC 16	Hedges of a Net Investment in a Foreign Operation
IFRIC 17	Distributions of Non-cash Assets to Owners
IFRIC 19	Extinguishing Financial Liabilities with Equity Instruments
IFRIC 20	Stripping Costs in the Production Phase of a Surface Mine
IFRIC 21	Levies
IFRIC 22	Foreign Currency Transactions and Advance Consideration
IFRIC 23	Uncertainty over Income Tax Treatments

Standing Interpretations Committee Interpretations

SIC-7	Introduction of the Euro
SIC-10	Government Assistance – No Specific Relation to Operating Activities
SIC-25	Income Taxes – Changes in the Tax Status of an Entity or its Shareholders
SIC-29	Service Concession Arrangements: Disclosures
SIC-32	Intangible Assets – Web Site Costs

IASB Exposure Drafts

ED/2015/5	Remeasurement on a Plan Amendment, Curtailment or Settlement/Availability of a Refund from a Defined Benefit Plan (Proposed amendments to IAS 19 and IFRIC 14)
ED/2017/5	Accounting Policies and Accounting Estimates (Proposed amendments to IAS 8)
ED/2019/5	Deferred Tax related to Assets and Liabilities arising from a Single Transaction (Proposed amendments to IAS 12)
ED/2019/6	Disclosure of Accounting Policies (Proposed amendments to IAS 1 and IFRS Practice Statement 2)
ED/2019/7	General Presentation and Disclosure

IASB Discussion Papers

DP/2014/1	Accounting for Dynamic Risk Management: a Portfolio Revaluation Approach to Macro Hedging
DP/2014/2	Reporting the Financial Effects of Rate Regulation
DP/2017/1	Disclosure Initiative – Principles of Disclosure
DP/2018/1	Financial Instruments with Characteristics of Equity
DP/2020/1	Business Combinations – Disclosures, Goodwill and Impairment

Other IASB publications

IFRS for SMEs	International Financial Reporting Standard (IFRS) for Small and Medium-sized Entities (SMEs)
Practice Statement 1	Management Commentary
Practice Statement 2	Making Materiality Judgements

Chapter 23 — Leases

1 INTRODUCTION 1709
2 OBJECTIVE AND SCOPE OF IFRS 16 1710
   2.1 Objective of IFRS 16 1710
   2.2 Scope of IFRS 16 1710
   2.3 Recognition exemptions 1710
   2.4 Definitions 1711
3 WHAT IS A LEASE? 1713
   3.1 Determining whether an arrangement contains a lease 1713
       3.1.1 Joint arrangements 1714
       3.1.2 Identified asset 1716
       3.1.3 Substantive substitution rights 1720
       3.1.4 Right to obtain substantially all of the economic benefits from use of the identified asset 1721
       3.1.5 Right to direct the use of the identified asset 1722
           3.1.5.A How and for what purpose the asset is used 1723
           3.1.5.B Relevant decisions about how and for what purpose the asset is used are predetermined 1724
           3.1.5.C Specifying the output of an asset before the period of use 1725
           3.1.5.D Protective rights 1726
       3.1.6 Flowchart of the decision-making process 1726
       3.1.7 Reassessment of the contract 1728
   3.2 Identifying and separating lease and non-lease components of a contract 1728
       3.2.1 Identifying and separating lease components of a contract 1728
       3.2.2 Identifying and separating lease from non-lease components of a contract 1729
           3.2.2.A Lessee reimbursements 1729
           3.2.2.B Practical expedient – lessees 1730

		3.2.3	Determining and allocating the consideration in the contract – lessees 1731
			3.2.3.A Determining the consideration in the contract 1731
			3.2.3.B Allocating the consideration in the contract – lessees 1731
		3.2.4	Determining and allocating the consideration in the contract – lessors 1733
			3.2.4.A Determining the consideration in the contract 1733
			3.2.4.B Allocating the consideration in the contract – lessors 1734
	3.3	Contract combinations 1734
4	KEY CONCEPTS 1734
	4.1	Inception date of the lease (inception date) 1734
	4.2	Commencement date of the lease 1735
	4.3	Lessee involvement with the underlying asset before the commencement date 1735
	4.4	Lease term and purchase options 1736
		4.4.1	Cancellable leases 1738
		4.4.2	Reassessment of lease term and purchase options – lessees 1741
		4.4.3	Reassessment of lease term and purchase options – lessors 1742
	4.5	Lease payments 1742
		4.5.1	In-substance fixed lease payments 1743
		4.5.2	Lease incentives 1743
		4.5.3	Variable lease payments that depend on an index or rate 1744
		4.5.4	The exercise price of a purchase option 1745
		4.5.5	Payments for penalties for terminating a lease 1745
		4.5.6	Amounts expected to be payable under residual value guarantees – lessees only 1745
		4.5.7	Amounts payable under residual value guarantees – lessors only 1745
		4.5.8	Variable lease payments which do not depend on an index or rate 1746
		4.5.9	Security deposits 1746
		4.5.10	Value added tax and property taxes 1747
		4.5.11	Co-tenancy clauses 1748
		4.5.12	Reassessment of the lease liability 1748
		4.5.13	Remeasurement by lessors 1748
	4.6	Discount rates 1748
		4.6.1	Determination of the incremental borrowing rate by a subsidiary with centralised treasury functions 1750

4.7	Initial direct costs		1750
	4.7.1	Directly attributable costs other than initial direct costs incurred by lessees	1751
4.8	Economic life		1751
4.9	Fair value		1751

5 LESSEE ACCOUNTING ... 1751

5.1	Initial recognition			1751
	5.1.1	Short-term leases		1752
	5.1.2	Leases of low-value assets		1753
5.2	Initial measurement			1754
	5.2.1	Right-of-use assets		1754
	5.2.2	Lease liabilities		1754
5.3	Subsequent measurement			1755
	5.3.1	Right-of-use assets		1755
		5.3.1.A	Cost model	1755
		5.3.1.B	Other measurement models	1756
	5.3.2	Lease liabilities		1756
	5.3.3	Expense recognition		1756
5.4	Remeasurement of lease liabilities			1758
5.5	Lease modifications			1759
	5.5.1	Determining whether a lease modification results in a separate lease		1759
	5.5.2	Lessee accounting for a modification that does not result in a separate lease		1760
	5.5.3	Application of lease modification guidance to rent concessions		1763
		I	A change in the scope of a lease	1764
		II	A change in the consideration for a lease	1764
		III	A change that is, or is not, part of the original terms and conditions of the lease	1765
		5.5.3.A	Rent concessions that change the consideration in the contract	1766
		5.5.3.B	Lessee accounting for rent concessions as lease modifications	1766
	5.5.4	Amendment to IFRS 16 for covid-19 related rent concessions		1767
		5.5.4.A	Accounting for a concession, in the form of forgiveness or deferral of lease payments, as a negative variable lease payment (Approach 1)	1769

		5.5.4.B	Accounting for a concession in the form of forgiveness or deferral of lease payments as a resolution of a contingency that fixes previously variable lease payments (Approach 2) 1769
		5.5.4.C	Accounting for a concession in the form of a deferral of lease payments as if the lease is unchanged (Approach 3) 1769
		5.5.4.D	Disclosure 1772
		5.5.4.E	Transition and effective date 1772
	5.6	Other lessee matters 1773	
		5.6.1	Impairment of right-of-use assets 1773
		5.6.2	Leases denominated in a foreign currency 1773
		5.6.3	Portfolio approach 1773
		5.6.4	Income tax accounting 1774
	5.7	Presentation 1774	
	5.8	Disclosure 1776	
		5.8.1	Disclosure objective 1776
		5.8.2	Disclosures of assets, liabilities, expenses and cash flows 1776
		5.8.3	Additional disclosures 1778
		5.8.4	Disclosures required by IAS 1 1780
6	LESSOR ACCOUNTING 1781		
	6.1	Lease classification 1781	
		6.1.1	Criteria for lease classification 1781
		6.1.2	Lease classification test for land and buildings 1783
		6.1.3	Residual value guarantees included in the lease classification test 1783
		6.1.4	Reassessment of lease classification 1783
	6.2	Finance leases 1784	
		6.2.1	Initial measurement 1785
		6.2.2	Manufacturer or dealer lessors 1785
		6.2.3	Subsequent measurement 1787
		6.2.3.A	Unguaranteed residual values 1789
		6.2.4	Remeasurement of the net investment in the lease 1790
	6.3	Operating leases 1791	
		6.3.1	Operating lease income 1791
	6.4	Lease modifications 1792	
		6.4.1	Determining whether a modification to a finance lease results in a separate lease 1793
		6.4.2	Lessor accounting for a modification to a finance lease that does not result in a separate lease 1793

		6.4.3	Modification to an operating lease	1793
	6.5	Other lessor matters – portfolio approach		1796
	6.6	Presentation		1796
	6.7	Disclosure		1797
		6.7.1	Disclosure objective	1797
		6.7.2	Disclosures for all lessors	1797
		6.7.3	Disclosures for finance leases	1797
		6.7.4	Disclosures for operating leases	1798
7	SUBLEASES			1798
	7.1	Definition		1798
	7.2	Intermediate lessor accounting		1798
	7.3	Sublessee accounting		1800
	7.4	Presentation		1800
	7.5	Disclosure		1801
8	SALE AND LEASEBACK TRANSACTIONS			1801
	8.1	Determining whether the transfer of an asset is a sale		1801
	8.2	Transactions in which the transfer of an asset is a sale		1803
		8.2.1	Accounting for the sale	1803
		8.2.2	Accounting for the leaseback	1805
		8.2.3	Adjustment for off-market terms	1805
	8.3	Transactions in which the transfer of an asset is not a sale		1807
	8.4	Disclosures		1807
9	BUSINESS COMBINATIONS			1807
	9.1	Acquiree in a business combination is a lessee		1807
	9.2	Acquiree in a business combination is a lessor		1808
10	EFFECTIVE DATE AND TRANSITION			1808
	10.1	Effective date		1808
	10.2	Transition		1809
	10.3	Lessee transition		1809
		10.3.1	Full retrospective approach	1809
		10.3.2	Modified retrospective approach	1810
		10.3.2.A	Leases previously classified as operating leases	1810
		10.3.2.B	Separating and allocating lease and non-lease components of a contract upon transition – leases previously classified as operating leases	1815
		10.3.2.C	Leases previously classified as finance leases	1816
	10.4	Lessor transition		1818
		10.4.1	Subleases	1818

1706 Chapter 23

    10.5   Other considerations 1818
          10.5.1   Sale and leaseback transactions 1818
          10.5.2   Amounts previously recognised in a business combination 1819
          10.5.3   References to IFRS 9 1819
    10.6   Disclosure 1819

List of examples

Example 23.1:	Implicitly specified asset	1717
Example 23.2:	Identified asset – implicitly specified at the time the asset is made available for use by the customer	1717
Example 23.3:	Identified asset – physically distinct portion of a larger asset	1717
Example 23.4:	Identified asset – capacity portion of an asset	1718
Example 23.5:	Substitution rights	1721
Example 23.6:	Right to direct the use of an asset	1726
Example 23.7:	Identifying and separating lease components	1728
Example 23.8:	Activities that are not components of a lease contract	1730
Example 23.9:	Allocating contract consideration to lease and non-lease components – lessees	1732
Example 23.10:	Lessee allocation of consideration to lease and non-lease components of a contract (IFRS 16 Example 12)	1732
Example 23.11:	Determining the lease term	1738
Example 23.12:	Cancellable leases	1741
Example 23.13:	Variable lease payment that depends on an index or rate	1744
Example 23.14:	Property leases with market rent reviews	1744
Example 23.15:	Residual value guarantee included in lease payments	1745
Example 23.16:	Variable lease payments which do not depend on an index or rate	1746
Example 23.17:	Short-term lease	1752
Example 23.18:	Lessee accounting	1757
Example 23.19:	Lease modifications (IFRS 16 Illustrative Examples 15 to 19)	1760
Example 23.20:	Deferral of lease payments	1764
Example 23.21:	Change of lease payments from fixed to partially variable	1766
Example 23.22:	Lessee accounting for rent concessions that are a lease modification	1766
Example 23.23:	Lease accounting for covid-19 related rent concessions on a forgiveness of lease payments applying the amendment to IFRS 16	1770

Example 23.24:	Lease accounting for covid-19 related rent concessions on a deferral of lease payments applying the amendment to IFRS 16	1771
Example 23.25:	The lessor's gross and net investment in the lease	1784
Example 23.26:	Manufacturer or dealer lessors	1786
Example 23.27:	Lessor accounting for a finance lease	1788
Example 23.28:	Reduction in residual value	1790
Example 23.29:	Operating lease income not expected to be fully collectible	1792
Example 23.30:	Forgiveness of future lease payments of an operating lease	1794
Example 23.31:	Waiver of a lease receivable in an operating lease	1794
Example 23.32:	Classification of a sublease	1799
Example 23.33:	Subleases (IFRS 16 Illustrative Examples 20 and 21)	1800
Example 23.34:	Sale and leaseback with variable payments (IFRIC Agenda Decision)	1804
Example 23.35:	Sale and leaseback transaction (IFRS 16 Illustrative Example 24)	1806
Example 23.36:	Accounting for lease contracts at transition using the full retrospective and modified retrospective approaches	1813

Chapter 23 Leases

1 INTRODUCTION

IFRS 16 – *Leases* – requires lessees to recognise assets and liabilities for most leases. The IASB issued the standard after joint deliberations with the US FASB, which issued a similar standard, ASC 842 – *Leases*. However, there are significant differences between the IASB and FASB standards (e.g. lessees classify leases as finance or operating leases under the FASB standard). These differences will result in certain transactions being accounted for differently under IFRS and US GAAP.

IFRS 16 replaces IAS 17 – *Leases* – and requires lessees to recognise most leases on their statements of financial position and provides enhanced disclosure requirements. The IASB believes this will result in a more faithful representation of lessees' assets and liabilities and greater transparency about lessees' financial obligations and leasing activities. Under IFRS 16, leases are accounted for based on a 'right-of-use model'. The model reflects that, at the commencement date, a lessee has a financial obligation to make lease payments to the lessor for its right to use the underlying asset during the lease term. The lessor conveys that right to use the underlying asset at lease commencement, which is the time when it makes the underlying asset available for use by the lessee.

Entities will need to focus on whether an arrangement contains a lease or a service agreement because there are significant differences in the accounting. Although IFRS 16 changes how the definition of a lease is applied, we believe that the assessment of whether a contract contains a lease will be straightforward in most arrangements. However, judgement may be required in applying the definition of a lease to certain arrangements, particularly those that include significant services.

Lessor accounting under IFRS 16 is substantially unchanged from the accounting under IAS 17. Lessors continue to classify all leases as operating or finance leases.

IFRS 16 is effective for annual periods beginning on or after 1 January 2019. Early application is permitted, provided the new revenue standard, IFRS 15 – *Revenue from Contracts with Customers* – has been applied, or is applied at the same date as IFRS 16.

2 OBJECTIVE AND SCOPE OF IFRS 16

2.1 Objective of IFRS 16

IFRS 16 sets out the principles for the recognition, measurement, presentation and disclosure of leases. The objective is to ensure that lessees and lessors provide relevant information in a manner that faithfully represents those transactions. This information gives a basis for users of financial statements to assess the effect that leases have on the financial position, financial performance and cash flows of an entity. *[IFRS 16.1]*.

IFRS 16 requires an entity to consider the terms and conditions of contracts and all relevant facts and circumstances, and to apply the standard consistently to contracts with similar characteristics and in similar circumstances. *[IFRS 16.2]*.

2.2 Scope of IFRS 16

IFRS 16 applies to all leases, including leases of right-of-use assets in a sublease, except for:
(a) Leases to explore for or use minerals, oil, natural gas and similar non-regenerative resources (see Chapter 43);
(b) Leases of biological assets within the scope of IAS 41 – *Agriculture* – held by a lessee (see Chapter 42 at 2.3.5);
(c) Service concession arrangements within the scope of IFRIC 12 – *Service Concession Arrangements* (see Chapter 25);
(d) Licences of intellectual property granted by a lessor within the scope of IFRS 15 (see Chapter 31 at 2); and
(e) Rights held by a lessee under licensing agreements within the scope of IAS 38 – *Intangible Assets* – for such items as motion picture films, video recordings, plays, manuscripts, patents and copyrights (see Chapter 17). *[IFRS 16.3]*.

A lessee may, but is not required to, apply IFRS 16 to leases of intangible assets other than those described in (e) above. *[IFRS 16.4]*.

There are differing views about whether a licence of software is excluded from the scope of IFRS 16 based on interpretations of paragraph 3(e) of IFRS 16. If an entity determines a licence of software is not excluded from the scope of IFRS 16, paragraph 4 of IFRS 16 permits, but does not require, an entity to account for the licence of software as a lease.

If the cloud computing arrangement contains a lease of an asset other than a licence of software (or the entity has determined a licence of software is not excluded from the scope of IFRS 16 and has elected to account for leases of intangible assets under IFRS 16), an entity should apply the provisions of IFRS 16 to the cloud computing arrangement. This includes identifying and separating lease and non-lease components and allocating contract consideration, which is discussed at 3.2 below.

2.3 Recognition exemptions

A lessee can elect not to apply the recognition requirements to:
(a) Short term leases; and
(b) Leases for which the underlying asset is of low value. *[IFRS 16.5]*.

These recognition exemptions are discussed in further detail at 5.1.1 and 5.1.2 below.

2.4 Definitions

The following table summarises the terms that are defined in IFRS 16. *[IFRS 16 Appendix A]*.

Term	Definition
Commencement date of the lease (commencement date)	The date on which a lessor makes an underlying asset available for use by a lessee.
Economic life	Either the period over which an asset is expected to be economically usable by one or more users or the number of production or similar units expected to be obtained from an asset by one or more users.
Effective date of the modification	The date when both parties agree to a lease modification.
Fair value	For the purpose of applying the lessor accounting requirements in this Standard, the amount for which an asset could be exchanged, or a liability settled, between knowledgeable, willing parties in an arm's length transaction.
Finance lease	A lease that transfers substantially all the risks and rewards incidental to ownership of an underlying asset.
Fixed payments	Payments made by a lessee to a lessor for the right to use an underlying asset during the lease term, excluding variable lease payments.
Gross investment in the lease	The sum of: • the lease payments receivable by a lessor under a finance lease; and • any unguaranteed residual value accruing to the lessor.
Inception date of the lease (inception date)	The earlier of the date of a lease agreement and the date of commitment by the parties to the principal terms and conditions of the lease.
Initial direct costs	Incremental costs of obtaining a lease that would not have been incurred if the lease had not been obtained, except for such costs incurred by a manufacturer or dealer lessor in connection with a finance lease.
Interest rate implicit in the lease	The rate of interest that causes the present value of (a) the lease payments and (b) the unguaranteed residual value to equal the sum of (i) the fair value of the underlying asset and (ii) any initial direct costs of the lessor.
Lease	A contract, or part of a contract, that conveys the right to use an asset (the underlying asset) for a period of time in exchange for consideration.
Lease incentives	Payments made by a lessor to a lessee associated with a lease, or the reimbursement or assumption by a lessor of costs of a lessee.
Lease modification	A change in the scope of a lease, or the consideration for a lease, that was not part of the original terms and conditions of the lease (for example, adding or terminating the right to use one or more underlying assets, of extending or shortening the contractual lease term).

Term	Definition
Lease payments	Payments made by a lessee to a lessor relating to the right to use an underlying asset during the lease term, comprising the following: (a) Fixed payments (including in-substance fixed payments), less any lease incentives; (b) Variable lease payments that depend on an index or a rate; (c) The exercise price of a purchase option if the lessee is reasonably certain to exercise that option; and (d) Payments of penalties for terminating the lease, if the lease term reflects the lessee exercising an option to terminate the lease. For the lessee, lease payments also include amounts expected to be payable by the lessee under residual value guarantees. Lease payments do not include payments allocated to non-lease components of a contract, unless the lessee elects to combine non-lease components with a lease component and to account for them as a single lease component. For the lessor, lease payments also include any residual value guarantees provided to the lessor by the lessee, a party related to the lessee or a third party unrelated to the lessor that is financially capable of discharging the obligations under the guarantee. Lease payments do not include payments allocated to non-lease components.
Lease term	The non-cancellable period for which a lessee has the right to use an underlying asset, together with both: (a) periods covered by an option to extend the lease if the lessee is reasonably certain to exercise that option; and (b) periods covered by an option to terminate the lease if the lessee is reasonably certain not to exercise that option.
Lessee	An entity that obtains the right to use an underlying asset for a period of time in exchange for consideration.
Lessee's incremental borrowing rate	The rate of interest that a lessee would have to pay to borrow over a similar term, and with a similar security, the funds necessary to obtain an asset of a similar value to the right-of-use asset in a similar economic environment.
Lessor	An entity that provides the right to use an underlying asset for a period of time in exchange for consideration.
Net investment in the lease	The gross investment in the lease discounted at the interest rate implicit in the lease.
Operating lease	A lease that does not transfer substantially all the risks and rewards incidental to ownership of an underlying asset.
Optional lease payments	Payments to be made by a lessee to a lessor for the right to use an underlying asset during periods covered by an option to extend or terminate a lease that are not included in the lease term.
Period of use	The total period of time that an asset is used to fulfil a contract with a customer (including any non-consecutive periods of time).
Residual value guarantee	A guarantee made to a lessor by a party unrelated to the lessor that the value (or part of the value) of an underlying asset at the end of a lease will be at least a specified amount.

Right-of-use asset	An asset that represents a lessee's right to use an underlying asset for the lease term.
Short-term lease	A lease that, at the commencement date, has a lease term of 12 months or less. A lease that contains a purchase option is not a short-term lease.
Sublease	A transaction for which an underlying asset is re-leased by a lessee ('intermediate lessor') to a third party, and the lease ('head lease') between the head lessor and the lessee remains in effect.
Underlying asset	An asset that is the subject of a lease, for which the right to use that asset has been provided by a lessor to a lessee.
Unearned finance income	The difference between: (a) the gross investment in the lease; and (b) the net investment in the lease.
Unguaranteed residual value	That portion of the residual value of the underlying asset, the realisation of which by a lessor is not assured or is guaranteed solely by a party related to the lessor.
Variable lease payments	The portion of payments made by a lessee to a lessor for the right to use an underlying asset during the lease term that varies because of changes in facts or circumstances occurring after the commencement date, other than the passage of time.

The following terms are defined in other standards and are used in IFRS 16 with the same meaning.

Term	Definition
Contract	An agreement between two or more parties that creates enforceable rights and obligations.
Useful life	The period over which an asset is expected to be available for use by an entity; or the number of production or similar units expected to be obtained from an asset by an entity.

3 WHAT IS A LEASE?

IFRS 16 defines a lease as 'a contract, or part of a contract, that conveys the right to use an asset (the underlying asset) for a period of time in exchange for consideration'. *[IFRS 16 Appendix A]*. The determination of whether an arrangement contains a lease is performed at the inception of the contract. *[IFRS 16.9]*.

The assessment of whether a contract is or contains a lease will be straightforward in most arrangements. However, judgement may be required in applying the definition of a lease to certain arrangements. For example, in contracts that include significant services, we believe that determining whether the contract conveys the right to direct the use of an identified asset may be challenging. We discuss this further at 3.1 below.

3.1 Determining whether an arrangement contains a lease

At inception of a contract, an entity assesses whether the contract is, or contains, a lease. A contract is, or contains, a lease if the contract conveys the right to control the use of an identified asset for a period of time in exchange for consideration. *[IFRS 16.9]*. See 3.1.2 below for additional discussion on identified assets.

A period of time may be described in terms of the amount of use of an identified asset (for example, the number of production units that an item of equipment will be used to produce). *[IFRS 16.10]*.

To assess whether a contract conveys the right to control the use of an identified asset for a period of time, an entity assesses whether, throughout the period of use, the customer has both of the following:

(a) the right to obtain substantially all of the economic benefits from use of the identified asset (see 3.1.4 below); and

(b) the right to direct the use of the identified asset (see 3.1.5 below). *[IFRS 16.B9]*.

If the customer has the right to control the use of an identified asset for only a portion of the term of the contract, the contract contains a lease for that portion of the term. *[IFRS 16.B10]*.

An entity assesses whether a contract contains a lease for each potential separate lease component. *[IFRS 16.B12]*. See 3.2 below.

3.1.1 Joint arrangements

Entities often enter into joint arrangements (JOAs) with other entities for certain activities. For example, the exploration of oil and gas fields, or the development of pharmaceutical products.

A contract for the use of an asset by a joint arrangement might be entered into in a number of different ways, including:

- directly by the joint arrangement, if the joint arrangement has its own legal identity;
- by each of the parties to the joint arrangement (i.e. the lead operator and the other parties, commonly referred to as the non-operators) individually signing the same arrangement;
- by one or more of the parties to the joint arrangement on behalf of the joint arrangement. Generally, this would be evidenced in the contract and the parties to the joint arrangement would have similar rights and obligations as they would if they individually signed the arrangement. In these situations, the facts and circumstances, as well as the legal position of each entity, need to be evaluated carefully; and
- by the lead operator of the joint arrangement in its own name, i.e. as principal. This may occur when the lead operator leases equipment which it then uses in fulfilling its obligations as the lead operator of the joint arrangement and/or across a range of unrelated activities, including other joint arrangements with unrelated activities, such as with other joint operating parties.

A contract to receive goods or services may be entered into by a joint arrangement or on behalf of a joint arrangement, as defined by IFRS 11 – *Joint Arrangements*. In this case, the joint arrangement is considered to be the customer in the contract. *[IFRS 16.B11]*. Accordingly, in determining whether such a contract contains a lease, an assessment needs to be made as to which party (e.g. the joint arrangement or the lead operator) has the right to control the use of an identified asset throughout the period of use.

If the parties to the joint arrangement collectively have the right to control the use of an identified asset throughout the period of use as a result of their collective control of the operation, the joint arrangement is the customer to the contract that may contain a lease. It would be inappropriate to conclude that the contract does not contain a lease on the grounds that each of the parties to the joint arrangement either has rights to a non-physically distinct portion of an underlying asset and, therefore, does not have the right to substantially all of the economic benefits from the use of that underlying asset or does not unilaterally direct its use. Determining if the parties to the joint arrangement collectively have the right to control the use of an identified asset throughout the period of use would require a careful analysis of the rights and obligations of each party.

In the first three scenarios above, if it has been determined that a contract is, or contains, a lease, each of the parties to the joint arrangement (i.e. the joint operators comprising the lead operator and the non-operators) will account for their respective interests in the joint arrangement (including any leases) under paragraphs 20-23 of IFRS 11. Therefore, they will account for their individual share of any right-of-use assets and lease liabilities, and associated depreciation and interest.

In the fourth scenario (i.e. where the lead operator enters the arrangement in its own name), the lead operator will need to assess whether the arrangement is, or contains, a lease. If the lead operator controls the use of the identified asset, it would recognise the entire right-of-use asset and lease liability on its balance sheet. This would be the case even if it is entitled to bill the non-operator parties their proportionate share of the costs under the joint operating agreement.

If the lead operator determines it is the lessee, it would also evaluate whether it has entered into a sublease with the joint arrangement (as the customer to the sublease). For example, the lead operator may enter into a five-year equipment lease with a supplier, but may then enter into a two-year arrangement with one of its joint arrangements, thereby yielding control of the right to use the equipment to the joint arrangement during the two-year period. In many cases, the lead operator will not meet the requirements to recognise a sublease because the arrangement does not create legally enforceable rights and obligations that convey the right to control the use of the asset to the joint arrangement. However, the conclusion as to whether the joint arrangement is a customer, i.e. the lessee in a contract with a lead operator, by virtue of the joint operating agreement, would be impacted by the individual facts and circumstances.

If there is a sublease with the operator, IFRS 11 would require the non-operators to recognise their respective share of the joint arrangement's right-of-use asset and lease liability and the lead operator would have to account for its sublease to the joint arrangement separately. However, if no sublease existed, the non-operators would recognise joint interest payables when incurred for their share of the costs incurred by the operator in respect of the leased asset.

In limited cases, the lead operator and non-operators will enter into a contract directly with the supplier in which the lead operator and non-operators are proportionately liable for their share of the arrangement. In this case, the parties with interests in the joint operation would recognise their proportionate share of the leased asset, liability and lease expense in accordance with IFRS 11.

There has been considerable debate as to how the term 'on behalf of the joint arrangement' should be interpreted and applied in practice. The IFRS Interpretations Committee discussed a question (in September 2018) relating to lease arrangements in a joint operation (JO) under IFRS 16. The question asked was how a lead operator (the party responsible for undertaking the operations on behalf of the other joint operators) of a JO which is not structured through a separate vehicle, recognises a lease liability. The question specifically focused on situations where the lead operator, as the sole signatory, enters into a lease contract with a third-party supplier (lessor) for an item of property, plant and equipment that will be operated jointly as part of the JO's activities. The lead operator has the right to recover a share of the lease costs from the other joint operators in accordance with the contractual and other arrangements governing the JO.

The Committee concluded, in the agenda decision published in March 2019,[1] that in accordance with IFRS 11, a joint operator identifies and recognises both:

(a) liabilities it incurs in relation to its interest in the JO; and
(b) its share of any liabilities incurred jointly with other parties to the joint arrangement.

The Committee observed that identifying the liabilities that a joint operator incurs and those incurred jointly, requires an assessment of the terms and conditions in all contractual arrangements that relate to the JO, including consideration of the laws pertaining to those agreements. The Committee further observed, in accordance with IFRS 11, the liabilities a joint operator recognises include those for which it has primary responsibility. Therefore, as sole signatory and where a lead operator has primary responsibility for a lease, the lead operator recognises 100% of the lease liability.

The Committee also highlighted the importance of disclosing information about joint operations that is sufficient for a user of financial statements to understand the activities of the joint operation and a joint operator's interest in that operation. Therefore, the Committee concluded that the principles and requirements in IFRS standards provide an adequate basis for the lead operator to identify and recognise its liabilities in relation to its interest in a JO and, did not to add this matter to its standard-setting agenda.

Joint arrangements are particularly common in extractive industries and the implications of this agenda decision are discussed further in Chapter 43 at 18.

3.1.2 Identified asset

An arrangement only contains a lease if there is an identified asset.

An asset is typically identified by being explicitly specified in a contract. However, an asset can also be identified by being implicitly specified at the time that the asset is made available for use by the customer. *[IFRS 16.B13]*.

Example 23.1:   Implicitly specified asset

Customer X enters into a five-year contract with Supplier Y for the use of rolling stock specifically designed for Customer X. The rolling stock is designed to transport materials used in Customer X's production process and is not suitable for use by other customers. The rolling stock is not explicitly specified in the contract, but Supplier Y owns only one rolling stock that is suitable for Customer X's use. If the rolling stock does not operate properly, the contract requires Supplier Y to repair or replace the rolling stock. Assume that Supplier Y does not have a substantive substitution right (see 3.1.3 below).

Analysis: The rolling stock is an identified asset. While the rolling stock is not explicitly specified in the contract (e.g. by serial number), it is implicitly specified because Supplier Y must use it to fulfil the contract.

Example 23.2:   Identified asset – implicitly specified at the time the asset is made available for use by the customer

Customer X enters into a five-year contract with Supplier Y for the use of a car. The specification of the car is contained in the contract (brand, type, colour, options, etc.). At inception of the contract the car is not yet built.

Analysis: The car is an identified asset. Although the car cannot be identified at inception of the contract, it is apparent that it will be identifiable at commencement of the lease. The car is identified by being implicitly specified at the time it is made available for use by the customer (i.e. at the commencement date).

A capacity portion of an asset is an identified asset if it is physically distinct (for example, a floor of a building). A capacity or other portion of an asset that is not physically distinct (for example, a capacity portion of a fibre optic cable) is not an identified asset, unless it represents substantially all of the capacity of the asset and thereby provides the customer with the right to obtain substantially all of the economic benefits from use of the asset. *[IFRS 16.B20]*.

Some contracts involve a dedicated cable that is part of the larger network infrastructure (e.g. unbundled network element arrangements for the 'last mile' to a customer location, 'special access' arrangements for a dedicated connection between two locations). IFRS 16 does not specify or provide examples that clarify whether these arrangements are identified assets. However, the FASB's standard, ASC 842, includes an additional example that is similar to a dedicated cable (i.e. a segment of a pipeline that connects a single customer to a larger pipeline). That example clarifies that such segments of a larger pipeline are identified assets. As the IASB has stated that it and the FASB have reached the same conclusions on the definition of a lease, we believe that, under IFRS 16, the last mile of a network that connects a single customer to a larger network may be an identified asset. However, such arrangements may or may not meet the definition of a lease. Entities will need to be sensitive to this matter in both these and similar arrangements.

Example 23.3:   Identified asset – physically distinct portion of a larger asset

Customer X enters into a 12-year contract with Supplier Y for the right to use three fibres within a fibre optic cable between New York and London. The contract identifies three of the cable's 20 fibres for use by Customer X. The three fibres are dedicated solely to Customer X's data for the duration of the contract term. Assume that Supplier Y does not have a substantive substitution right (see 3.1.3 below).

Analysis: The three fibres are identified assets because they are physically distinct and explicitly specified in the contract.

Example 23.4:   Identified asset – capacity portion of an asset

Scenario A:

Customer X enters into a five-year contract with Supplier Y for the right to transport oil from Country A to Country B through Supplier Y's pipeline. The contract provides that Customer X will have the right to use 95% of the pipeline's capacity throughout the term of the arrangement.

Analysis: The capacity portion of the pipeline is an identified asset. While 95% of the pipeline's capacity is not physically distinct from the remaining capacity of the pipeline, it represents substantially all of the capacity of the entire pipeline and thereby provides Customer X with the right to obtain substantially all of the economic benefits from use of the pipeline.

Scenario B:

Assume the same facts as in Scenario A, except that Customer X has the right to use 60% of the pipeline's capacity throughout the term of the arrangement.

Analysis: The capacity portion of the pipeline is not an identified asset because 60% of the pipeline's capacity is less than substantially all of the capacity of the pipeline. Customer X does not have the right to obtain substantially all of the economic benefits from use of the pipeline.

Land easements or rights of way are rights to use, access or cross another entity's land for a specified purpose. For example, a land easement might be obtained for the right to construct and operate a pipeline or other assets (e.g. railway line, utility pipes or telecommunication lines) over, under or through an existing area of land or body of water while allowing the landowner continued use of the land for other purposes (e.g. farming), as long as the landowner does not interfere with the rights conveyed in the land easement. A land easement may be perpetual or for a specified term. It may provide for exclusive or non-exclusive use of the land and may be prepaid or paid over a defined term.

Perpetual easements are outside the scope of IFRS 16, as the definition of a lease requires the contract to be for a period of time. Therefore, entities must carefully evaluate easement contracts to determine whether the contract is perpetual or for a period of time. Examples of contracts that may appear perpetual but are term based include:

- very long-term contracts (e.g. the FASB indicated in the Basis for Conclusions to ASC 842 (BC113) that very long-term leases of land (e.g. 999 years) are in the scope of ASC 842);
- contracts with a stated, non-cancellable lease term that 'automatically renews' if the lessee pays a periodic renewal fee. This is an in-substance fixed term contract with optional renewal periods; and
- contracts that define the period of use as the period over which the assets are used (e.g. as long as natural gas flows through a gathering system) is a fixed term contract (i.e. terminated when production ceases) rather than a perpetual contract because the gas reserves will ultimately be depleted.

When determining whether a contract for a land easement or right of way is a lease, entities will need to assess whether there is an identified asset and whether the customer obtains substantially all of the economic benefits of the identified asset and has the right to direct the use of that asset throughout the period of use.

In June 2019, the IFRS Interpretations Committee discussed a contract for subsurface rights.[2] In the contract described, a pipeline operator obtains the right to place an oil pipeline in underground space for 20 years in exchange for consideration. The contract specifies the exact location and dimensions (path, width and depth) of the underground space within which the pipeline will be placed. The landowner retains the right to use the surface of the land above the pipeline, but it has no right to access or otherwise change the use of the specified underground space throughout the 20-year period of use. The customer has the right to perform inspection, repairs and maintenance work (including replacing damaged sections of the pipeline when necessary).

The Committee noted the following in the agenda decision:

- Paragraph 3 of IFRS 16 requires an entity to apply IFRS 16 to all leases, with limited exceptions. In the contract described in the request, none of the exceptions in paragraphs 3 and 4 of IFRS 16 apply. In particular, the Committee noted that the underground space is tangible. Accordingly, if the contract contains a lease, IFRS 16 applies to that lease. If the contract does not contain a lease, the entity would then consider which other IFRS standard applies.

- Applying paragraph B9 of IFRS 16, to meet the definition of a lease, the customer must have both:
  (a) the right to obtain substantially all the economic benefits from use of an identified asset throughout the period of use; and
  (b) the right to direct the use of the identified asset throughout the period of use.

- The specified underground space is physically distinct from the remainder of the land. The contract's specifications include the path, width and depth of the pipeline, thereby defining a physically distinct underground space. The space being underground does not in itself affect whether it is an identified asset – the specified underground space is physically distinct in the same way that a specified area of space on the land's surface would be physically distinct. As the landowner does not have the right to substitute the underground space throughout the period of use, the Committee concluded that the specified underground space is an identified asset as described in paragraphs B13–B20 of IFRS 16.

- The customer has the right to obtain substantially all the economic benefits from use of the specified underground space throughout the 20-year period of use. The customer has exclusive use of the specified underground space throughout that period of use.

- The customer has the right to direct the use of the specified underground space throughout the 20-year period of use because the customer has the right to operate the asset throughout the period of use without the supplier having the right to change those operating instructions. How and for what purpose the specified underground space will be used (i.e. to locate the pipeline with specified dimensions through which oil will be transported) is predetermined in the contract. The customer has the right to operate the specified underground space by having the right to perform inspection, repairs and maintenance work. The customer makes all the decisions about the use of the specified underground space that can be made during the 20-year period of use.

Consequently, the Committee concluded that the contract described in the request contains a lease as defined in IFRS 16. The customer would therefore apply IFRS 16 in accounting for that lease.

3.1.3 Substantive substitution rights

Even if an asset is specified, a customer does not have the right to use an identified asset if, at inception of the contract, a supplier has the substantive right to substitute the asset throughout the period of use (i.e. the total period of time that an asset is used to fulfil a contract with a customer, including the sum of any non-consecutive periods of time). *[IFRS 16 Appendix A]*. A supplier's right to substitute an asset is substantive when both of the following conditions are met:

- the supplier has the practical ability to substitute alternative assets throughout the period of use (e.g. the customer cannot prevent the supplier from substituting an asset and alternative assets are readily available to the supplier or could be sourced by the supplier within a reasonable period of time); and
- the supplier would benefit economically from the exercise of its right to substitute the asset (i.e. the economic benefits associated with substituting the asset are expected to exceed the costs associated with substituting the asset). *[IFRS 16.B14]*.

The IASB indicated in the Basis for Conclusions to IFRS 16 that the conditions above are intended to differentiate between substitution rights that result in a supplier controlling the use of an asset, rather than the customer, and rights that do not change the substance or character of the contract. *[IFRS 16.BC113]*.

If the supplier has a right or an obligation to substitute the asset only on or after either a particular date or the occurrence of a specified event, the supplier's substitution right is not substantive because the supplier does not have the practical ability to substitute alternative assets throughout the period of use. *[IFRS 16.B15]*.

An entity's evaluation of whether a supplier's substitution right is substantive is based on facts and circumstances at inception of the contract. At inception of the contract, an entity should not consider future events that are not likely to occur. IFRS 16 provides the following examples of circumstances that, at inception of the contract, are not likely to occur and, thus, are excluded from the evaluation of whether a supplier's substitution right is substantive throughout the period of use:

- an agreement by a future customer to pay an above market rate for use of the asset;
- the introduction of new technology that is not substantially developed at inception of the contract;
- a substantial difference between the customer's use of the asset, or the performance of the asset, and the use or performance considered likely at inception of the contract; and
- a substantial difference between the market price of the asset during the period of use, and the market price considered likely at inception of the contract. *[IFRS 16.B16]*.

The requirement that a substitution right must benefit the supplier economically in order to be substantive is a new concept. In many cases, it will be clear that the supplier will not benefit from the exercise of a substitution right because of the costs associated with substituting an asset. *[IFRS 16.BC113]*. If an asset is located at the customer's premises or elsewhere, the costs associated with substitution are generally higher than when located at the supplier's premises, and therefore, are more likely to exceed the benefits associated with substituting the asset. *[IFRS 16.B17]*. However, simply because a supplier concludes that the cost of substitution is not significant does not automatically mean that it would economically benefit from the right of substitution.

IFRS 16 further clarifies that a customer should presume that a supplier's substitution right is not substantive when the customer cannot readily determine whether the supplier has a substantive substitution right. *[IFRS 16.B19]*. This requirement is intended to clarify that a customer is not expected to exert undue effort to provide evidence that a substitution right is not substantive. We believe that the Board did not include a similar provision for suppliers, because they should have sufficient information to make a determination of whether a substitution right is substantive.

Contract terms that allow or require a supplier to substitute alternative assets only when the underlying asset is not operating properly (e.g. a normal warranty provision) or when a technical upgrade becomes available do not create a substantive substitution right. *[IFRS 16.B18]*.

Example 23.5: Substitution rights

Scenario A:

Assume that an electronic data storage provider (supplier) provides services, through a centralised data centre, that involve the use of a specified server (Server No. 9). The supplier maintains many identical servers in a single, accessible location and determines, at inception of the contract, that it is permitted to and can easily substitute another server without the customer's consent throughout the period of use. Further, the supplier would benefit economically from substituting an alternative asset, because doing this would allow the supplier to optimise the performance of its network at only a nominal cost. In addition, the supplier has made clear that it has negotiated this right of substitution as an important right in the arrangement, and the substitution right affected the pricing of the arrangement.

Analysis: The customer does not have the right to use an identified asset because, at the inception of the contract, the supplier has the practical ability to substitute the server and would benefit economically from such a substitution. However, if the customer could not readily determine whether the supplier had a substantive substitution right (e.g. there is insufficient transparency into the supplier's operations), the customer would presume the substitution right is not substantive and conclude that there is an identified asset.

Scenario B:

Assume the same facts as in Scenario A except that Server No. 9 is customised, and the supplier does not have the practical ability to substitute the customised asset throughout the period of use. Additionally, it is unclear whether the supplier would benefit economically from sourcing a similar alternative asset.

Analysis: Because the supplier does not have the practical ability to substitute the asset and there is no evidence of economic benefit to the supplier from substituting the asset, the substitution right is non-substantive, and Server No. 9 would be an identified asset. In this case, neither of the conditions of a substitution right is met. As a reminder, both conditions must be met for the supplier to have a substantive substitution right.

3.1.4 Right to obtain substantially all of the economic benefits from use of the identified asset

To control the use of an identified asset, a customer is required to have the right to obtain substantially all of the economic benefits from use of the asset throughout the period of use (for example, by having exclusive use of the asset throughout that period). A customer can obtain economic benefits from use of an asset directly or indirectly in many ways, such as by using, holding or sub-leasing the asset. The economic benefits from use of an asset include its primary output and by-products (including potential cash flows derived from these items), and other economic benefits from using the asset that could be realised from a commercial transaction with a third party. *[IFRS 16.B21]*.

Economic benefits arising from construction or ownership of the identified asset (e.g. tax benefits related to excess tax depreciation and investment tax credits as discussed in paragraph BC118 of the Basis of Conclusions to IFRS 16) are not considered economic benefits derived from the use of the asset. Therefore, they are not considered when assessing whether a customer has the right to obtain substantially all of the economic benefits.

When assessing the right to obtain substantially all of the economic benefits from use of an asset, an entity considers the economic benefits that result from use of the asset within the defined scope of a customer's right to use the asset. For example:

(a) if a contract limits the use of a motor vehicle to only one particular territory during the period of use, an entity considers only the economic benefits from use of the motor vehicle within that territory, and not beyond; or

(b) if a contract specifies that a customer can drive a motor vehicle only up to a particular number of miles during the period of use, an entity considers only the economic benefits from use of the motor vehicle for the permitted mileage, and not beyond. *[IFRS 16.B22]*.

If a contract requires a customer to pay the supplier or another party a portion of the cash flows derived from use of an asset as consideration, those cash flows paid as consideration are considered to be part of the economic benefits that the customer obtains from use of the asset. For example, if the customer is required to pay the supplier a percentage of sales from use of retail space as consideration for that use, that requirement does not prevent the customer from having the right to obtain substantially all of the economic benefits from use of the retail space. This is because the cash flows arising from those sales are considered to be economic benefits that the customer obtains from use of the retail space, a portion of which it then pays to the supplier as consideration for the right to use that space. *[IFRS 16.B23]*.

3.1.5 Right to direct the use of the identified asset

A customer has the right to direct the use of an identified asset throughout the period of use when either:

- the customer has the right to direct how and for what purpose the asset is used throughout the period of use; or
- the relevant decisions about how and for what purpose an asset is used are predetermined; and
    - the customer either has the right to operate the asset, or to direct others to operate the asset in a manner that it determines, throughout the period of use, without the supplier having the right to change those operating instructions; or
    - the customer designed the asset, or specific aspects of the asset, in a way that predetermines how and for what purpose the asset will be used throughout the period of use. *[IFRS 16.B24]*.

Requiring a customer to have the right to direct the use of an identified asset is a change from IFRIC 4 – *Determining whether an Arrangement Contains a Lease*. A contract may have met IFRIC 4's control criterion if, for example, the customer obtained substantially all of the output of an underlying asset and met certain price-per-unit-of-output criteria even though the customer did not have the right to direct the use of the identified asset as contemplated by IFRS 16. Under IFRS 16, such arrangements are no longer considered leases.

3.1.5.A How and for what purpose the asset is used

A customer has the right to direct how and for what purpose the asset is used if, within the scope of its right of use defined in the contract, it can change how and for what purpose the asset is used throughout the period of use. In making this assessment, an entity considers the decision-making rights that are most relevant to changing how and for what purpose the asset is used throughout the period of use. Decision-making rights are relevant when they affect the economic benefits to be derived from use. The decision-making rights that are most relevant are likely to be different for different contracts, depending on the nature of the asset and the terms and conditions of the contract. *[IFRS 16.B25]*.

How and for what purpose an asset is used is a single concept (i.e. 'how' an asset is used is not assessed separately from 'for what purpose' an asset is used). *[IFRS 16.BC120]*.

The IASB have indicated that decisions about how and for what purpose an asset is used can be viewed as similar to the decisions made by a board of directors. Decisions made by a board of directors about the operating and financing activities of an entity are generally the most relevant decisions rather than the actions of individuals implementing those decisions. *[IFRS 16.BC120]*.

Examples of decision-making rights that, depending on the circumstances, grant the right to change how and for what purpose the asset is used, within the defined scope of the customer's right of use, include:

(a) rights to change the type of output that is produced by the asset (for example, to decide whether to use a shipping container to transport goods or for storage, or to decide upon the mix of products sold from retail space);

(b) rights to change when the output is produced (for example, to decide when an item of machinery or a power plant will be used);

(c) rights to change where the output is produced (for example, to decide upon the destination of a truck or a ship, or to decide where an item of equipment is used); and

(d) rights to change whether the output is produced, and the quantity of that output (for example, to decide whether to produce energy from a power plant and how much energy to produce from that power plant). *[IFRS 16.B26]*.

Examples of decision-making rights that do not grant the right to change how and for what purpose the asset is used include rights that are limited to operating or maintaining the asset. Such rights can be held by the customer or the supplier. Although rights such as those to operate or maintain an asset are often essential to the efficient use of an asset, they are not rights to direct how and for what purpose the asset is used and are often dependent on the decisions about how and for what purpose the asset is used. However, rights to operate an asset may grant the customer the right to direct the use of the asset if the relevant decisions about how and for what purpose the asset is used are predetermined. *[IFRS 16.B27]*.

The customer does not need the right to operate the underlying asset to have the right to direct its use. That is, the customer may direct the use of an asset that is operated by the supplier's personnel. However, as discussed at 3.1.5.B below, the right to operate an asset will often provide the customer the right to direct the use of the asset if the relevant decisions about how and for what purpose the asset is used are predetermined.

3.1.5.B Relevant decisions about how and for what purpose the asset is used are predetermined

In some cases, it will not be clear whether the customer has the right to direct the use of the identified asset. This could be the case when the most relevant decisions about how and for what purpose an asset is used are predetermined by contractual restrictions on the use of the asset (e.g. the decisions about the use of the asset are agreed to by the design of the asset or by contractual restrictions on the use of the asset). This may occur when the customer and the supplier in negotiating the contract predetermined the most relevant decisions and those decisions cannot be changed. The IASB indicated that it would expect decisions about how and for what purpose an asset is used to be predetermined in few cases. *[IFRS 16.BC121]*. In such cases, a customer has the right to direct the use of an identified asset throughout the period of use when the customer either:

- has the right to operate the asset, or direct others to operate the asset in a manner that it determines, throughout the period of use without the supplier having the right to change those operating instructions; or
- designed the asset (or specific aspects of the asset) in a way that predetermines how and for what purpose the asset will be used throughout the period of use.

[IFRS 16.B24].

Significant judgement may be required to assess whether a customer designed the asset (or specific aspects of the asset) in a way that predetermines how and for what purpose the asset will be used throughout the period of use.

In January 2020, the IFRS Interpretations Committee issued an Agenda Decision (AD) about whether the customer has the right to direct the use of a ship throughout the five-year term of a contract. In the fact pattern described in the request:

(a) there is an identified asset (the ship) applying paragraphs B13–B20 of IFRS 16.

(b) the customer has the right to obtain substantially all the economic benefits from use of the ship throughout the five-year period of use applying paragraphs B21–B23 of IFRS 16.

(c) many, but not all, decisions about how and for what purpose the ship is used are predetermined in the contract. The customer has the right to make the remaining decisions about how and for what purpose the ship is used throughout the period of use. In the fact pattern described in the request, the customer has determined that this decision-making right is relevant because it affects the economic benefits to be derived from use of the ship.

(d) the supplier operates and maintains the ship throughout the period of use.

The Committee observed that, in the fact pattern described in the request, because not all relevant decisions about how and for what purpose the ship is used are predetermined, the customer considers paragraph B24(a) of IFRS 16 in assessing whether it has the right to direct the use of the ship.

Paragraph B24(a) specifies that a customer has the right to direct the use of an identified asset throughout the period of use if it has 'the right to direct how and for what purpose the asset is used throughout the period of use (as described in paragraphs B25–B30)'. To have the right to direct how and for what purpose the asset is used, within the scope of its right of use defined in the contract, the customer must be able to change how and for what purpose the asset is used throughout the period of use (paragraph B25). In assessing whether that is the case, an entity considers rights to make decisions during the period of use that are most relevant to changing how and for what purpose the asset is used throughout that period. Decision-making rights are relevant when they affect the economic benefits to be derived from use (paragraph B25). An entity does not consider decisions that are predetermined before the period of use unless the conditions in paragraph B24(b)(ii) exist (paragraph B29).

The Committee observed that, in the fact pattern described in the request, the customer has the right to direct how and for what purpose the ship is used throughout the period of use. The customer has the right to make decisions about the use of the ship during the period of use that affect the economic benefits to be derived from that use. Therefore, within the scope of its right of use defined in the contract, the customer can change how and for what purpose the ship is used. The predetermination in the contract of many decisions about how and for what purpose the ship is used defines the scope of the customer's right of use – within that scope, the customer has the right to make the decisions that are most relevant to changing how and for what purpose the ship is used.

The Committee also observed that, although the operation and maintenance of the ship are essential to its efficient use, the supplier's decisions in this regard do not give it the right to direct how and for what purpose the ship is used.

The Committee concluded that, in the fact pattern described in the request, the customer has the right to direct the use of the ship throughout the period of use. Consequently, the contract contains a lease. The Committee concluded that the principles and requirements in IFRS 16 provide an adequate basis for an entity to determine whether the contract described in the request contains a lease and therefore decided not to add the matter to its standard-setting agenda.

3.1.5.C   Specifying the output of an asset before the period of use

As noted above, the relevant decisions about how and for what purpose the asset is used can be predetermined in a number of ways. For example, the relevant decisions can be predetermined by the design of the asset or by contractual restrictions on the use of the asset. *[IFRS 16.B28]*.

In assessing whether a customer has the right to direct the use of an asset, an entity considers only rights to make decisions about the use of the asset during the period of use, unless how and for what purpose an asset is used is predetermined.

See 3.1.5.B above. Consequently, unless the customer designed the asset (or specific aspects of the asset) in a way that predetermines how and for what purposes the asset will be used throughout the period of use, an entity does not consider decisions that are predetermined before the period of use. For example, if a customer is able only to specify the output of an asset before the period of use, the customer does not have the right to direct the use of that asset throughout the period of use. The ability to specify the output in a contract before the period of use, without any other decision-making rights relating to the use of the asset, gives a customer the same rights as any customer that purchases goods or services. *[IFRS 16.B29]*.

3.1.5.D Protective rights

A contract may include terms and conditions designed to protect the supplier's interest in the asset or other assets, to protect its personnel, or to ensure the supplier's compliance with laws or regulations. These are examples of protective rights. For example, a contract may (i) specify the maximum amount of use of an asset or limit where or when the customer can use the asset, (ii) require a customer to follow particular operating practices, or (iii) require a customer to inform the supplier of changes in how an asset will be used. Protective rights typically define the scope of the customer's right of use but do not, in isolation, prevent the customer from having the right to direct the use of an asset. *[IFRS 16.B30]*.

Example 23.6: Right to direct the use of an asset

Customer X enters into a contract with Supplier Y to use a vehicle for a three-year period. The vehicle is identified in the contract. Supplier Y cannot substitute another vehicle unless the specified vehicle is not operational (e.g. it breaks down).

Under the contract:

- Customer X operates the vehicle (i.e. drives the vehicle) or directs others to operate the vehicle (e.g. hires a driver);
- Customer X decides how to use the vehicle (within contractual limitations, discussed below). For example, throughout the period of use, Customer X decides where the vehicle goes as well as when or whether it is used and what it is used for. Customer X can also change these decisions throughout the period of use; and
- Supplier Y prohibits certain uses of the vehicle (e.g. moving it overseas) and modifications to the vehicle to protect its interest in the asset.

Analysis: Customer X has the right to direct the use of the identified vehicle throughout the period of use. Customer X has the right to direct the use of the vehicle because it has the right to change how the vehicle is used, when or whether the vehicle is used, where the vehicle goes and what the vehicle is used for.

Supplier Y's limits on certain uses for the vehicle and modifications to it are considered protective rights that define the scope of Customer X's use of the asset but do not affect the assessment of whether Customer X directs the use of the asset.

3.1.6 Flowchart of the decision-making process

IFRS 16 contains a flowchart that depicts the decision-making process for determining whether an arrangement contains a lease *[IFRS 16.B31]* and provides a summary of the discussion at 3.1.2 to 3.1.5.D above. This has been reproduced below.

Figure 23.1 Determining whether an arrangement contains a lease

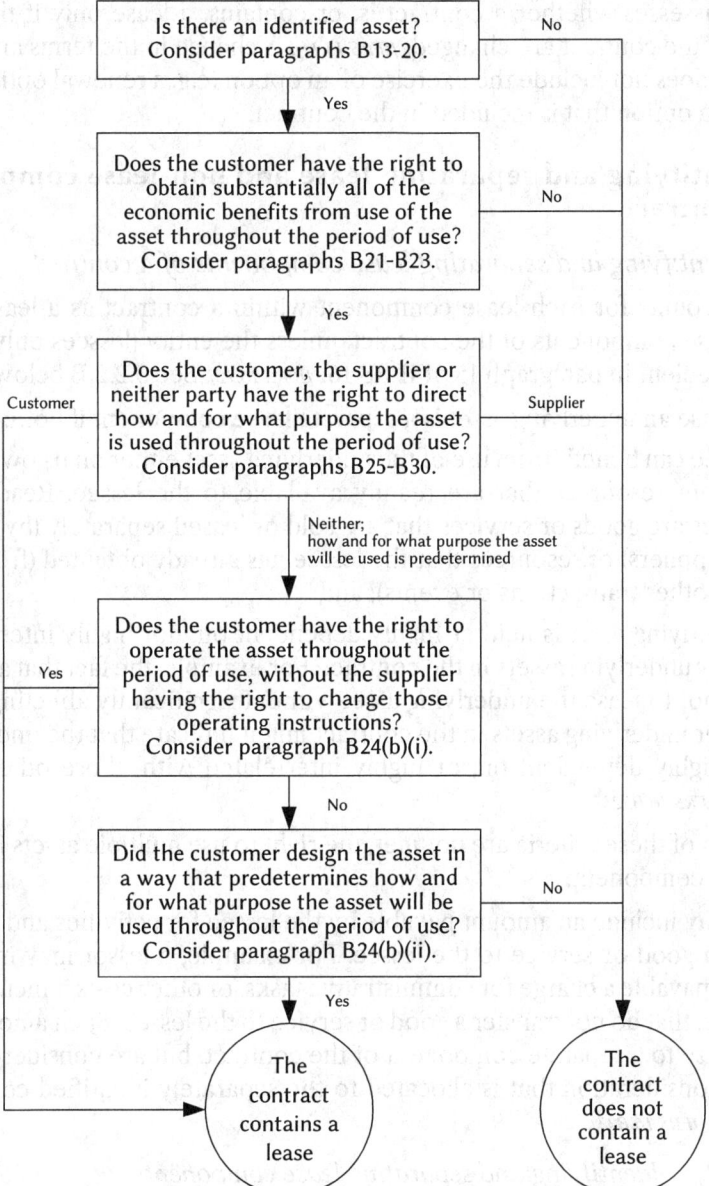

We believe that the assessment of whether a contract is or contains a lease will be straightforward in most arrangements. However, judgement may be required in applying the definition of a lease to certain arrangements.

3.1.7 Reassessment of the contract

An entity reassesses whether a contract is, or contains, a lease only if the terms and conditions of the contract are changed. *[IFRS 16.11]*. A change in the terms and conditions of a contract does not include the exercise of an option (e.g. a renewal option) or failure to exercise an option that is included in the contract.

3.2 Identifying and separating lease and non-lease components of a contract

3.2.1 Identifying and separating lease components of a contract

An entity accounts for each lease component within a contract as a lease separately from non-lease components of the contract, unless the entity (lessees only) applies the practical expedient in paragraph 15 of IFRS 16. *[IFRS 16.12]*. See 3.2.2.B below.

The right to use an underlying asset is a separate lease component if both:

(a) the lessee can benefit from use of the underlying asset either on its own or together with other resources that are readily available to the lessee. Readily available resources are goods or services that are sold or leased separately (by the lessor or other suppliers) or resources that the lessee has already obtained (from the lessor or from other transactions or events); and

(b) the underlying asset is neither highly dependent on, nor highly interrelated with, the other underlying assets in the contract. For example, the fact that a lessee could decide not to lease the underlying asset without significantly affecting its rights to use other underlying assets in the contract might indicate that the underlying asset is not highly dependent on, or highly interrelated with, those other underlying assets. *[IFRS 16.B32]*.

If one or both of these criteria are not met, the right to use multiple assets is considered a single lease component.

A contract may include an amount payable by the lessee for activities and costs that do not transfer a good or service to the lessee. For example, a lessor may include in the total amount payable a charge for administrative tasks, or other costs it incurs associated with the lease, that do not transfer a good or service to the lessee. Such amounts payable do not give rise to a separate component of the contract, but are considered to be part of the total consideration that is allocated to the separately identified components of the contract. *[IFRS 16.B33]*.

Example 23.7: Identifying and separating lease components

Scenario A

Assume that a lessee enters into a lease of an excavator and the related accessories (e.g. excavator attachments) that are used for mining purposes. The lessee is a local mining company that intends to use the excavator at a copper mine.

Analysis: From the perspective of the lessee, the contract contains one lease component. The lessee would be unable to benefit from the use of the excavator without also using the accessories. Therefore, the excavator is dependent upon the accessories.

Scenario B

Assume the same facts as in Scenario A, except that the contract also conveys the right to use an additional loading truck. This loading truck could be deployed by the lessee for other uses (e.g. to transport iron ores at another mine).

Analysis: From the perspective of the lessee, the contract contains two lease components: a lease of the excavator (together with the accessories) and a lease of the loading truck. Because the loading truck could be deployed for other uses independent of the excavator, the lessee can benefit from the loading truck on its own or together with other readily available resources. The lessee can also benefit from the use of the excavator on its own or together with other readily available resources.

For contracts that involve the right to use land and land improvements (e.g. buildings), IFRS 16 requires a lessor to classify (see 6.1 below) and account for the right to use land as a separate lease component, unless the accounting effect of doing so is immaterial to the lease. *[IFRS 16.B57]*. For example, separation of the land may not be necessary when the amount that would be recognised for the land lease component is immaterial to the lease. If the lease payments cannot be allocated reliably between the land and the buildings, the entire lease is classified as a finance lease, unless it is clear that both elements are operating leases (i.e. the entire lease is classified as an operating lease). *[IFRS 16.B56]*. An entity that leases an entire building (i.e. 100% of the building) is inherently leasing the land underneath the building and would potentially account for the land and building as separate lease components. However, this would not necessarily be the case when an entity only leases part of the building.

3.2.2 Identifying and separating lease from non-lease components of a contract

Many contracts contain a lease coupled with an agreement to purchase or sell other goods or services (non-lease components). The non-lease components are identified and accounted for separately from the lease component in accordance with other standards, unless the lessee applies the practical expedient as discussed at 3.2.2.B below. *[IFRS 16.16]*. For example, the non-lease components may be accounted for as executory arrangements by lessees (customers) or as contracts subject to IFRS 15 by lessors (suppliers).

Some contracts contain items that do not relate to the transfer of goods or services by the lessor to the lessee (e.g. fees or other administrative costs a lessor charges a lessee). These items are not considered separate lease or non-lease components, and lessees and lessors do not allocate consideration in the contract to these items. *[IFRS 16.B33]*. See 3.2.3.B below. However, if the lessor provides goods or services, such as maintenance, supply of utilities, including operating the underlying asset for the customer (e.g. vessel charter, aircraft wet lease), the contract would generally contain non-lease components.

3.2.2.A Lessee reimbursements

Under IFRS 16, payments for maintenance activities, including common area maintenance (e.g. cleaning the common areas of a building, removing snow from a car park for employees and customers) and other goods or services transferred to the tenant (e.g. providing utilities or rubbish removal) are considered non-lease components because they provide the lessee with a service.

In some leases, a lessee may also reimburse (or make certain payments on behalf of) the lessor that relate to the leased asset for activities and costs that do not transfer a good or service to the lessee (e.g. payments made for real estate taxes that would be owed by the lessor regardless of whether it leased the building and regardless of who the lessee is, payments made for insurance that protects the lessor's investment in the asset and the landlord will receive the proceeds from any claim). Under IFRS 16, such costs are not separate components of the contract because they do not represent payments for goods or services and are considered to be part of the total consideration that is allocated to the separately identified components of the contract (i.e. the lease and non-lease components). Entities also need to evaluate whether such payments are fixed (or in-substance fixed) lease payments or variable lease payments. See 4.5 below.

Example 23.8: Activities that are not components of a lease contract

Scenario A

A lessee enters into a three-year lease of equipment, with fixed annual payments of CU12,000. The contract itemises the fixed annual payments as follows: CU9,000 for rent, CU2,500 for maintenance and CU500 of administrative tasks.

Analysis: The contract contains two components – one lease component (lease of equipment) and a non-lease component (maintenance). The amount paid for administrative tasks does not transfer a good or service to the lessee. Therefore, the total consideration in the contract of CU36,000 will be allocated to the lease component (equipment) and the non-lease component (maintenance).

Scenario B

Assume the fact pattern as in scenario A except that, in addition, the contract requires the lessee to pay for the restoration of the equipment to its original condition.

Analysis: The contract still contains two components – one lease component (lease of equipment) and a non-lease component (maintenance). Similar to the amount paid for administrative tasks, the restoration does not transfer a good or service to the lessee as it is only performed at the end of the lease term. Therefore, the total consideration in the contract will be allocated to the lease component (equipment) and the non-lease component (maintenance). See 5.2.1 below for further discussion on the inclusion of restoration costs to the initial measurement of the right-of-use asset.

3.2.2.B Practical expedient – lessees

As a practical expedient, a lessee may elect, by class of underlying asset, not to separate non-lease components from lease components, and instead account for each lease component and any associated non-lease components as a single lease component. A lessee cannot apply this practical expedient to embedded derivatives that meet the criteria in paragraph 4.3.3 of IFRS 9 – *Financial Instruments*. [IFRS 16.15]. See Chapter 46 at 4.

IFRS 16 provides this expedient to alleviate concerns that the costs and administrative burden of allocating consideration to separate lease and non-lease components may not be justified by the benefit of more precisely reflecting the right-of-use asset and the lease liability. Furthermore, the IASB expects the practical expedient to most often be used when the non-lease components of a contract are not significant when compared with the lease components of a contract. [IFRS 16.BC135 (b)]. The practical expedient does not allow lessees to account for multiple lease components of a contract as a single lease component.

Although it is not explicitly stated, we believe that non-lease components relate to services contained within the lease contract. Paragraphs BC133 and BC135 of the Basis for Conclusions to IFRS 16 refer to non-lease components being service components. Therefore, when a lease includes a component related to the purchase of inventory or another asset such as property, plant and equipment or an intangible asset, we believe an entity should separate these asset components from other lease and non-lease components, even if it has elected to apply the practical expedient to the class of underlying asset to which the lease relates. For example, if a contract contains a lease as well as non-lease components related to a service and the purchase of sheet metal to be used in the construction of inventory, we believe the purchase of the sheet metal should be accounted for as a component of inventory rather than together with the lease component as the purchase of a physical good is not a 'non-lease component associated with that lease component'.

Lessees that make the policy election to account for each separate lease component of a contract and any associated non-lease components as a single lease component allocate all of the contract consideration to the lease component. Therefore, the initial and subsequent measurement of the lease liability and right-of-use asset is higher than if the policy election was not applied.

3.2.3 Determining and allocating the consideration in the contract – lessees

3.2.3.A Determining the consideration in the contract

IFRS 16 does not define 'consideration' in a contract, nor is 'consideration' defined in the IFRS Glossary. However, we believe that the consideration in a contract for a lessee would include all the lease payments described at 4.5 below, as well as certain other consideration in the contract regardless of whether it is labelled as lease payments or payments for non-lease components of a contract, including other fixed payments (e.g. monthly service charges) or in-substance fixed payments, variable payments that depend on an index or a rate, initially measured using the index or rate at the commencement date, less any incentives paid or payable to the lessee, other than those included in lease payments.

3.2.3.B Allocating the consideration in the contract – lessees

For a contract that contains a lease component and one or more additional lease or non-lease components, a lessee allocates the consideration in the contract to each lease component on the basis of the relative stand-alone price of the lease component and the aggregate stand-alone price of the non-lease components. *[IFRS 16.13]*.

The relative stand-alone price of lease and non-lease components is determined on the basis of the price the lessor, or a similar supplier, would charge an entity for that component, or a similar component, separately. If an observable stand-alone price is not readily available, the lessee estimates the stand-alone price, maximising the use of observable information. *[IFRS 16.14]*. A contractually stated price may be the stand-alone price for a good or service, but it is not presumed to be for accounting purposes.

Example 23.9: **Allocating contract consideration to lease and non-lease components – lessees**

A lessee enters into a lease of equipment. The contract stipulates the lessor will perform maintenance of the leased equipment and receive consideration for that maintenance service. The contract includes the following fixed prices for the lease and non-lease components:

Lease	CU80,000
Maintenance	CU10,000
Total	CU90,000

Assume the stand-alone prices cannot be readily observed, so the lessee makes estimates, maximising the use of observable information, of the lease and non-lease components, as follows:

Lease	CU85,000
Maintenance	CU15,000
Total	CU100,000

Analysis: The stand-alone price for the lease component represents 85% of total estimated stand-alone prices. The lessee allocates the consideration in the contract (CU90,000), as follows:

Lease	CU76,500	(1)
Maintenance	CU13,500	(2)
Total	CU90,000	

(1) 85% × CU90,000
(2) 15% × CU90,000

The following example from the IFRS 16 illustrative examples illustrates the allocation of consideration in a contract to lease and non-lease components by a lessee. *[IFRS 16.IE4]*.

Example 23.10: **Lessee allocation of consideration to lease and non-lease components of a contract (IFRS 16 Example 12)**

Lessor leases a bulldozer, a truck and a long-reach excavator to Lessee to be used in Lessee's mining operations for four years. Lessor also agrees to maintain each item of equipment throughout the lease term. The total consideration in the contract is CU600,000[a], payable in annual instalments of CU150,000, and a variable amount that depends on the hours of work performed in maintaining the long-reach excavator. The variable payment is capped at 2 per cent of the replacement cost of the long-reach excavator. The consideration includes the cost of maintenance services for each item of equipment.

[a] In these Illustrative Examples, currency amounts are denominated in 'currency units' (CU).

Lessee accounts for the non-lease components (maintenance services) separately from each lease of equipment applying paragraph 12 of IFRS 16. Lessee does not elect the practical expedient in paragraph 15 of IFRS 16. Lessee considers the requirements in paragraph B32 of IFRS 16 and concludes that the lease of the bulldozer, the lease of the truck and the lease of the long-reach excavator are each separate lease components. This is because:

(a) Lessee can benefit from use of each of the three items of equipment on its own or together with other readily available resources (for example, Lessee could readily lease or purchase an alternative truck or excavator to use in its operations); and

(b) Although Lessee is leasing all three items of equipment for one purpose (i.e. to engage in mining operations), the machines are neither highly dependent on, nor highly interrelated with, each other. Lessee's ability to derive benefit from the lease of each item of equipment is not significantly affected by its decision to lease, or not lease, the other equipment from Lessor.

Consequently, Lessee concludes that there are three lease components and three non-lease components (maintenance services) in the contract. Lessee applies the guidance in paragraphs 13–14 of IFRS 16 to allocate the consideration in the contract to the three lease components and the non-lease components.

Several suppliers provide maintenance services for a similar bulldozer and a similar truck. Accordingly, there are observable standalone prices for the maintenance services for those two items of leased equipment. Lessee is able to establish observable stand-alone prices for the maintenance of the bulldozer and the truck of CU32,000 and CU16,000, respectively, assuming similar payment terms to those in the contract with Lessor. The long-reach excavator is highly specialised and, accordingly, other suppliers do not lease or provide maintenance services for similar excavators. Nonetheless, Lessor provides four-year maintenance service contracts to customers that purchase similar long-reach excavators from Lessor. The observable consideration for those four-year maintenance service contracts is a fixed amount of CU56,000, payable over four years, and a variable amount that depends on the hours of work performed in maintaining the long-reach excavator.

That variable payment is capped at 2 per cent of the replacement cost of the long-reach excavator. Consequently, Lessee estimates the stand-alone price of the maintenance services for the long-reach excavator to be CU56,000 plus any variable amounts. Lessee is able to establish observable stand-alone prices for the leases of the bulldozer, the truck and the long-reach excavator of CU170,000, CU102,000 and CU224,000, respectively.

Lessee allocates the fixed consideration in the contract (CU600,000) to the lease and non-lease components as follows:

CU	Bulldozer	Truck	Long-reach excavator	Total
Lease	170,000	102,000	224,000	496,000
Non-lease				104,000
Total fixed consideration				600,000

Lessee allocates all of the variable consideration to the maintenance of the long-reach excavator, and, thus, to the non-lease components of the contract. Lessee then accounts for each lease component applying the guidance in IFRS 16, treating the allocated consideration as the lease payments for each lease component.

3.2.4 Determining and allocating the consideration in the contract – lessors

3.2.4.A Determining the consideration in the contract

As discussed at 3.2.3.A above, IFRS 16 does not define 'consideration' in a lease contract, nor is 'consideration' defined in the IFRS Glossary. However, we believe that the consideration in a lease contract for a lessor would include the following:

(a) lease payments as described at 4.5 below;

(b) the following other payments not labelled in the contract as lease payments:

   (i) any other fixed payments (e.g. monthly service charges, non-lease components such as maintenance) or in-substance fixed payments made during the lease term, less any incentives paid or payable to the lessee;

   (ii) any other variable payments that depend on an index or a rate made during the lease term and initially measured using the index or rate at the commencement date; and

   (iii) any other variable payment amounts that would be included in the transaction price in accordance with the requirements on variable consideration in IFRS 15 that specifically relate to either of the following:

   (A) the lessor's efforts to transfer one or more goods or services that are not leases; or

   (B) an outcome from transferring one or more goods or services that are not leases.

Variable consideration is described broadly in IFRS 15 and can take many forms. Consideration can vary because of discounts, rebates, refunds, credits, price concessions, incentives, performance bonuses, penalties or other similar items. It is important for lessors to appropriately identify the different types of variable consideration included in the contract because estimating variable consideration requires lessors to apply a constraint to each type of variable consideration. See Chapter 29 at 2.2 for further discussion on variable consideration under IFRS 15.

3.2.4.B   *Allocating the consideration in the contract – lessors*

For a contract that contains a lease component and one or more additional lease or non-lease components, a lessor allocates the consideration in the contract applying paragraphs 73 to 90 of IFRS 15. *[IFRS 16.17].*

Paragraphs 73 to 86 of IFRS 15 require the lessor to allocate the consideration in the contract between the lease and non-lease components on a relative stand-alone selling price basis. In addition, lessors are required to apply paragraphs 87-90 of IFRS 15 to allocate any subsequent changes in the consideration of the contract between the lease and non-lease components. The stand-alone selling price is the price at which an entity would sell a promised good or service separately to a customer. When stand-alone selling prices are not directly observable, the lessor must estimate the stand-alone selling price. Paragraph 79 of IFRS 15 provides suitable methods for estimating the stand-alone selling price. See Chapter 29 at 3.1 for further discussion on determining stand-alone selling prices under IFRS 15.

3.3   Contract combinations

An entity combines two or more contracts entered into at or near the same time with the same counterparty (or related parties of the counterparty), and accounts for the contracts as a single contract if one or more of the following criteria are met:

(a)   the contracts are negotiated as a package with an overall commercial objective that cannot be understood without considering the contracts together;

(b)   the amount of consideration to be paid in one contract depends on the price or performance of the other contract; or

(c)   the rights to use underlying assets conveyed in the contracts (or some rights to use underlying assets conveyed in each of the contracts) form a single lease component. *[IFRS 16.B2].*

The IASB developed these criteria to address concerns that separately accounting for multiple contracts may not result in a faithful representation of the combined transaction. *[IFRS 16.BC130-132].*

4   KEY CONCEPTS

4.1   Inception date of the lease (inception date)

IFRS 16 requires customers and suppliers to determine whether a contract is a lease at inception of the lease. The inception date is the earlier of the date of a lease agreement and the date of commitment by the parties to the principal terms and conditions of the lease. *[IFRS 16 Appendix A]*.

The underlying asset is the asset that is subject to a lease, for which the right to use that asset has been provided by a lessor to a lessee. *[IFRS 16 Appendix A]*.

4.2 Commencement date of the lease

The commencement date of the lease is the date on which the lessor makes an underlying asset available for use by a lessee. *[IFRS 16 Appendix A]*. In some cases, the commencement date of the lease may be before the date stipulated in the lease agreement (e.g. the date on which rent becomes due and payable). This often occurs when the leased space is modified by the lessee prior to commencing operations in the leased space (e.g. during the period a lessee uses the leased space to construct its own leasehold improvements). If a lessee takes possession of, or is given control over, the use of the underlying asset before it begins operations or making lease payments under the terms of the lease, the lease term has commenced even if the lessee is not required to pay rent or the lease arrangement states the lease commencement date is a later date. The timing of when lease payments begin under the contract does not affect the commencement date of the lease. For example, a lessee (except for a lessee applying the short-term lease or lease of low-value asset exemption discussed at 5.1.1 and 5.1.2 below) initially recognises a lease liability and related right-of-use asset on the commencement date and a lessor (for finance leases) initially recognises its net investment in the lease on the commencement date.

4.3 Lessee involvement with the underlying asset before the commencement date

An entity may negotiate a lease before the underlying asset is available for use by the lessee. For some leases, the underlying asset may need to be constructed or redesigned for use by the lessee. Depending on the terms and conditions of the contract, a lessee may be required to make payments relating to the construction or design of the asset. *[IFRS 16.B43]*.

If a lessee incurs costs relating to the construction or design of an underlying asset, the lessee accounts for those costs applying other IFRS, such as IAS 16 – *Property, Plant and Equipment*. Costs relating to the construction or design of an underlying asset do not include payments made by the lessee for the right to use the underlying asset. Payments for the right to use an underlying asset are payments for a lease, regardless of the timing of those payments. *[IFRS 16.B44]*.

A lessee may obtain legal title to an underlying asset before that legal title is transferred to the lessor and the asset is leased to the lessee. Obtaining legal title does not in itself determine how to account for the transaction. *[IFRS 16.B45]*.

If the lessee controls (or obtains control of) the underlying asset before that asset is transferred to the lessor, the transaction is a sale and leaseback transaction that is accounted for as described at 8 below. *[IFRS 16.B46]*.

However, if the lessee does not obtain control of the underlying asset before the asset is transferred to the lessor, the transaction is not a sale and leaseback transaction. For example, this may be the case if a manufacturer, a lessor and a lessee negotiate a transaction for the purchase of an asset from the manufacturer by the lessor, which is in turn leased to the lessee. The lessee may obtain legal title to the underlying asset before legal title transfers to the lessor. In this case, if the lessee obtains legal title to the underlying asset but does not obtain control of the asset before it is transferred to the lessor, the transaction is not accounted for as a sale and leaseback transaction, but as a lease. *[IFRS 16.B47]*.

4.4 Lease term and purchase options

An entity determines the lease term as the non-cancellable period of the lease, together with both:

- periods covered by an option to extend the lease if the lessee is reasonably certain to exercise that option; and
- periods covered by an option to terminate the lease if the lessee is reasonably certain not to exercise that option. *[IFRS 16.18]*.

The phrase 'reasonably certain' was also used in IAS 17 and is generally interpreted as a high threshold. Therefore, the IASB does not anticipate a change in practice.

Purchase options are assessed in the same way as options to extend or terminate the lease. The IASB indicated that an option to purchase an underlying asset is economically similar to an option to extend the lease term for the remaining economic life of the underlying asset. *[IFRS 16.BC173]*.

The lease term begins at the commencement date and includes any rent-free periods provided to the lessee by the lessor. *[IFRS 16.B36]*.

At the commencement date, an entity assesses whether the lessee is reasonably certain to exercise an option to extend the lease or to purchase the underlying asset, or not to exercise an option to terminate the lease. *[IFRS 16.19, IFRS 16.B37]*. The entity considers all relevant facts and circumstances that create an economic incentive for the lessee to exercise, or not to exercise, the option, including any expected changes in facts and circumstances from the commencement date until the exercise date of the option. Examples of factors to consider include, but are not limited to:

(a) contractual terms and conditions for the optional periods compared with market rates, such as:
  (i) the amount of payments for the lease in any optional period;
  (ii) the amount of any variable payments for the lease or other contingent payments, such as payments resulting from termination penalties and residual value guarantees; and
  (iii) the terms and conditions of any options that are exercisable after initial optional periods (for example, a purchase option that is exercisable at the end of an extension period at a rate that is currently below market rates).
(b) significant leasehold improvements undertaken (or expected to be undertaken) over the term of the contract that are expected to have significant economic benefit for the lessee when the option to extend or terminate the lease, or to purchase the underlying asset, becomes exercisable;
(c) costs relating to the termination of the lease, such as negotiation costs, relocation costs, costs of identifying another underlying asset suitable for the lessee's needs,

costs of integrating a new asset into the lessee's operations, or termination penalties and similar costs, including costs associated with returning the underlying asset in a contractually specified condition or to a contractually specified location;

(d) the importance of that underlying asset to the lessee's operations, considering, for example, whether the underlying asset is a specialised asset, the location of the underlying asset and the availability of suitable alternatives; and

(e) conditionality associated with exercising the option (i.e. when the option can be exercised only if one or more conditions are met), and the likelihood that those conditions will exist. *[IFRS 16.B37]*.

The longer the period from commencement of the lease to the exercise date of an option, the more difficult it will be, in certain cases, to determine whether the exercise of the option is reasonably certain. The difficulty arises from several factors. For example, a lessee's estimates of its future needs for the leased asset become less precise the further into the future the forecast goes. Also, the future fair value of certain assets such as those involving technology is more difficult to predict than the future fair value of a relatively stable asset, such as a fully leased commercial office building located in a prime area.

The further into the future that the option exercise date is, the lower the option price must be in relation to the estimated future fair value to conclude that the lessee is reasonably certain to exercise the option. For example, the difference between the option purchase price and the estimated future fair value of an asset that is subject to significant changes in value also should be greater than would be the case for an asset with a relatively stable value.

An artificially short lease term (e.g. a lease of a corporate headquarters, distribution facility, manufacturing plant or other key property with a four-year lease term), may effectively create a significant economic incentive for the lessee to exercise a purchase or renewal option. This may be evidenced by the significance of the underlying asset to the lessee's continuing operations and whether, absent the option, the lessee would have entered into such a lease.

Similarly, the significance of the underlying asset to the lessee's operations may affect a lessee's decisions about whether it is reasonably certain to exercise a purchase or renewal option. For example, a company that leases a specialised facility (e.g. manufacturing plant, distribution facility, corporate headquarters) and does not exercise a purchase or renewal option would face a significant economic penalty if an alternative facility is not readily available. This would potentially have an adverse effect on the company while it searched for a replacement asset.

An option to extend or terminate a lease may be combined with one or more other contractual features (for example, a residual value guarantee) such that the lessee guarantees the lessor a minimum or fixed cash return that is substantially the same regardless of whether the option is exercised. In such cases, and notwithstanding the guidance on in-substance fixed payments (see 4.5.1 below), an entity assumes that the lessee is reasonably certain to exercise the option to extend the lease, or not to exercise the option to terminate the lease. *[IFRS 16.B38]*.

The shorter the non-cancellable period of a lease, the more likely a lessee is to exercise an option to extend the lease or not to exercise an option to terminate the lease. This is because the costs associated with obtaining a replacement asset are likely to be proportionately higher the shorter the non-cancellable period. *[IFRS 16.B39]*.

A lessee's past practice regarding the period over which it has typically used particular types of assets (whether leased or owned), and its economic reasons for doing so, may provide information that is helpful in assessing whether the lessee is reasonably certain to exercise, or not to exercise, an option. For example, if a lessee has typically used particular types of assets for a particular period of time or if the lessee has a practice of frequently exercising options on leases of particular types of underlying assets, the lessee considers the economic reasons for that past practice in assessing whether it is reasonably certain to exercise an option on leases of those assets. *[IFRS 16.B40]*.

A lessee may enter into a lease contract for non-consecutive periods. This is seen in the retail industry when retailers enter into contracts with shopping centres to lease the same retail space for certain non-consecutive months of the year (e.g. during an annual holiday period). Similar arrangements also exist when sports teams lease a sports stadium for particular non-consecutive days of the year. These arrangements will usually meet the definition of a lease because during the agreed period of use, the customer controls the right to use the underlying asset. In these arrangements, the lease term is the aggregate of the non-consecutive periods, as shown in Example 23.11, Scenario C below.

Example 23.11:   Determining the lease term

Scenario A

Assume that Entity P enters into a lease for equipment that includes a non-cancellable term of four years and a two-year fixed-priced renewal option with future lease payments that are intended to approximate market rates at lease inception. There are no termination penalties or other factors indicating that Entity P is reasonably certain to exercise the renewal option.

Analysis: At the lease commencement date, the lease term is four years.

Scenario B

Assume that Entity Q enters into a lease for a building that includes a non-cancellable term of four years and a two-year, market-priced renewal option. Before it takes possession of the building, Entity Q pays for leasehold improvements. The leasehold improvements are expected to have significant value at the end of four years, and that value can only be realised through continued occupancy of the leased property.

Analysis: At lease commencement, Entity Q determines that it is reasonably certain to exercise the renewal option because it would suffer a significant economic penalty if it abandoned the leasehold improvements at the end of the initial non-cancellable period. At lease commencement, Entity Q concludes that the lease term is six years.

Scenario C

Assume that Entity R enters into a lease for an identified retail space in a shopping centre. The retail space will be available to Entity R for only the months of October, November and December during a non-cancellable term of five years. The lessor agrees to provide the same retail space for each of the five years.

Analysis: At the lease commencement date, the lease term is fifteen months (three months per year over the 5 annual periods specified in the contract).

4.4.1 Cancellable leases

In determining the lease term and assessing the length of the non-cancellable period of a lease, an entity applies the definition of a contract and determines the period for which the contract is enforceable. A lease is no longer enforceable when the lessee and the lessor each has the right to terminate the lease without permission from the other party with no more than an insignificant penalty. *[IFRS 16.B34]*.

Any non-cancellable periods (by the lessee and lessor) in contracts that meet the definition of a lease are considered part of the lease term. IFRS 16 further provides that, if only a lessee has the right to terminate a lease, that right is considered to be an option to terminate the lease available to the lessee that an entity considers when determining the lease term. If only a lessor has the right to terminate a lease, the non-cancellable period of the lease includes the period covered by the option to terminate the lease. *[IFRS 16.B35]*.

The question arises as to whether penalty should be interpreted to include only the contractual amount payable by one party to the other if the termination option is exercised (i.e. the narrow interpretation) or whether significant economic disincentives should also be considered a penalty (i.e. the wide interpretation). With respect to the determination of the lease term, IFRS 16 requires an entity to consider all relevant facts and circumstances that create an economic incentive for the lessee to exercise, or not to exercise, the option (see 4.4 above) and thus suggests that all aspects of termination penalties, whether contractual or financial in nature, should be considered. Although the guidance may not directly apply in this situation as the lessee is unable to exercise the option to renew the lease without the approval of the lessor, we believe, by analogy, it is appropriate to evaluate the existence of any significant economic disincentives taking into account all facts and circumstances.

The IFRS Interpretations Committee issued an Agenda Decision (AD) in November 2019 related to this issue. The Committee was asked how to determine the lease term of a cancellable lease or a renewable lease. Specifically, when applying paragraph B34 of IFRS 16 and assessing 'no more than an insignificant penalty' whether an entity considers the broader economics of the contract and not only contractual termination payments. Such considerations might include the cost of abandoning or dismantling leasehold improvements. Another example may be the importance of the asset to the lessee's operations.

To determine the lease term, an entity determines the non-cancellable period and the enforceable period. It then determines where the lease term falls, depending on the likelihood of exercising the options to extend or terminate using the reasonably certain threshold. The impact of extension options is shown in the diagram below, taken from the Committee's agenda paper.

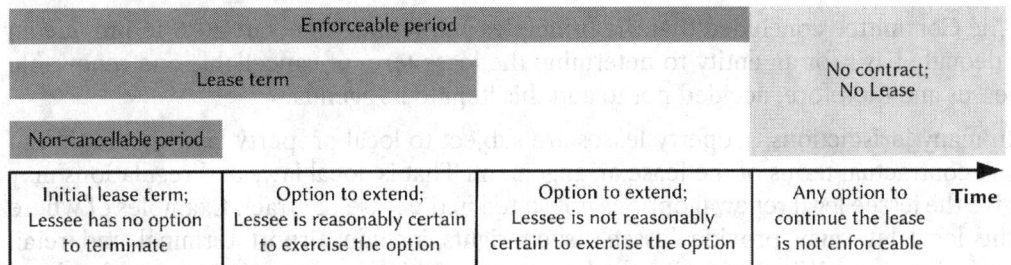

We believe the impact of termination options on the determination of the lease term would be similar. That is, the lease term includes the non-cancellable period, the periods covered by the options to extend if the lessee is reasonably certain to exercise that option and the periods covered by the option to terminate, if the lessee is reasonably certain not to exercise that option.

The Committee noted that in applying paragraph B34 and determining the enforceable period of the lease, an entity considers[3]:

- the broader economics of the contract and not only the contractual termination payments. For example, if either party has an economic incentive not to terminate the lease such that it would incur a penalty on termination that is more than insignificant, the contract is enforceable beyond the date on which the contract can be terminated; and
- whether each of the parties has the right to terminate the lease without permission from the other party with no more than an insignificant penalty. Applying paragraph B34, a lease is no longer enforceable only when both parties have such a right. Consequently, if only one party has the right to terminate the lease without permission from the other party with no more than an insignificant penalty, the contract is enforceable beyond the date on which the contract can be terminated by that party.

If an entity concludes that the contract is enforceable beyond the notice period of a cancellable lease, it then applies paragraphs 19 and B37-B40 of IFRS 16 to assess whether the lessee is reasonably certain not to exercise the option to terminate the lease.

The Committee noted that in assessing whether a lessee is reasonably certain to extend (or not to terminate) a lease, paragraph B37 of IFRS 16 requires an entity to consider all relevant facts and circumstances that create an economic incentive for the lessee. This includes significant leasehold improvements undertaken (or expected to be undertaken) over the term of the contract that are expected to have significant economic benefit for the lessee when an option to extend or terminate the lease becomes exercisable (paragraph B37(b) of IFRS 16). In addition, an entity considers the broader economics of the contract when determining the enforceable period of a lease. This includes, for example, the costs of abandoning or dismantling non-removable leasehold improvements. If an entity expects to use non-removable leasehold improvements beyond the date on which the contract can be terminated, the existence of those leasehold improvements indicates that the entity might incur a more than insignificant penalty if it terminates the lease. Consequently, applying paragraph B34 of IFRS 16, an entity considers whether the contract is enforceable for at least the period of expected utility of the leasehold improvements.

The Committee concluded that the principles and requirements in IFRS 16 provide an adequate basis for an entity to determine the lease term of cancellable and renewable leases and therefore, decided not to add this item to its agenda.

In many jurisdictions, property leases are subject to local property laws in addition to the contractual terms of the lease arrangement. That is, local laws and regulations may give the lessee legal renewal options not stated in the lease contract. Examples of where the local law may provide lessee's such rights include airport terminal and retail shopping space. When assessing the lease term, entities need to consider whether local laws and regulations create enforceable rights and obligations that need to be included in the evaluation of the lease term.

IFRS 16 also applies to contracts that are referred to as 'cancellable,' 'month-to-month,' 'at-will,' 'evergreen,' 'perpetual' or 'rolling' if they create enforceable rights and obligations. These types of leases generally allow for the contract to continue beyond a non-cancellable period until one party gives notice to terminate the contract (e.g. the contract will roll monthly until the lessee or the lessor elect to terminate the contract). If both the lessee and the lessor can terminate the contract without more than an insignificant penalty at any time at or after the end of the non-cancellable term, then there are no enforceable rights and obligations beyond the non-cancellable term (i.e. the lease term is limited to the non-cancellable term). However, if the lessee holds a renewal option, there may be other factors to consider in determining whether the lessee is reasonably certain to extend the lease, including economic disincentives discussed above.

Example 23.12: Cancellable leases

A lease contract has an initial non-cancellable period of one year and an extension for an additional year if both the lessee and the lessor agree. There is no penalty for either party if they do not agree to extend for the additional year. The initial one-year non-cancellable period meets the definition of a contract because it creates enforceable rights and obligations. However, the one-year extension period does not meet the definition of a contract because both the lessee and the lessor could unilaterally elect to not extend the arrangement without a more than insignificant penalty. That is, at lease commencement, neither party has enforceable rights and obligations beyond the initial non-cancellable period.

4.4.2   Reassessment of lease term and purchase options – lessees

After lease commencement, IFRS 16 requires lessees to monitor leases for significant changes that could trigger a change in the lease term. A lessee reassesses whether it is reasonably certain to exercise an extension option, or not to exercise a termination option, upon the occurrence of either a significant event or a significant change in circumstances that:

(a)   is within the control of the lessee; and

(b)   affects whether the lessee is reasonably certain to exercise an option not previously included in its determination of the lease term, or not to exercise an option previously included in its determination of the lease term. *[IFRS 16.20]*.

Examples of significant events or changes in circumstances that would trigger a reassessment include:

(a)   significant leasehold improvements not anticipated at the commencement date that are expected to have significant economic benefit for the lessee when the option to extend or terminate the lease, or to purchase the underlying asset, becomes exercisable;

(b)   a significant modification to, or customisation of, the underlying asset that was not anticipated at the commencement date;

(c)   the inception of a sublease of the underlying asset for a period beyond the end of the previously determined lease term; and

(d)   a business decision of the lessee that is directly relevant to exercising, or not exercising, an option (for example, a decision to extend the lease of a complementary asset, to dispose of an alternative asset or to dispose of a business unit within which the right-of-use asset is employed). *[IFRS 16.B41]*.

An entity revises the lease term if there is a change in the non-cancellable period of a lease. For example, the non-cancellable period of a lease will change if:

(a) the lessee exercises an option not previously included in the entity's determination of the lease term;

(b) the lessee does not exercise an option previously included in the entity's determination of the lease term;

(c) an event occurs that contractually obliges the lessee to exercise an option not previously included in the entity's determination of the lease term; or

(d) an event occurs that contractually prohibits the lessee from exercising an option previously included in the entity's determination of the lease term. *[IFRS 16.21].*

As a lessee is required to reassess the lease term upon the occurrence of either a significant event or a significant change in circumstances that is within the control of the lessee, the revision of the lease term often happens before the actual exercise of the option in these circumstances. Additionally, if the reassessment of lease term or the exercise of a purchase option results in a change, lessees would remeasure the lease liability, using revised inputs (e.g. discount rate) at the reassessment date, and would adjust the right-of-use asset. However, if the right-of-use asset is reduced to zero, a lessee would recognise any remaining amount in profit or loss. See 4.5.12 below.

4.4.3 Reassessment of lease term and purchase options – lessors

IFRS 16 requires a lessor to revise the lease term to account for a lessee's exercise of an option to extend or terminate the lease or purchase the underlying asset, when exercise of such options was not already included in the lease term.

4.5 Lease payments

Lease payments are payments made by a lessee to a lessor relating to the right to use an underlying asset during the lease term, comprising the following:

(a) fixed payments (including in-substance fixed payments), less any lease incentives;

(b) variable lease payments that depend on an index or a rate;

(c) the exercise price of a purchase option if the lessee is reasonably certain to exercise that option; and

(d) payments of penalties for terminating the lease, if the lease term reflects the lessee exercising an option to terminate the lease.

For the lessee, lease payments also include amounts expected to be payable by the lessee under residual value guarantees. Lease payments do not include payments allocated to non-lease components of a contract, unless the lessee elects to combine non-lease components with a lease component and to account for them as a single lease component.

For the lessor, lease payments also include any residual value guarantees provided to the lessor by the lessee, a party related to the lessee or a third party unrelated to the lessor that is financially capable of discharging the obligations under the guarantee. Lease payments do not include payments allocated to non-lease components. *[IFRS 16 Appendix A].*

4.5.1 In-substance fixed lease payments

Lease payments include any in-substance fixed lease payments. In-substance fixed lease payments are payments that may, in form, contain variability but that, in substance, are unavoidable. In-substance fixed lease payments exist, for example, if:

(a) payments are structured as variable lease payments, but there is no genuine variability in those payments. Those payments contain variable clauses that do not have real economic substance. Examples of those types of payments include:

   (i) payments that must be made only if an asset is proven to be capable of operating during the lease, or only if an event occurs that has no genuine possibility of not occurring; or

   (ii) payments that are initially structured as variable lease payments linked to the use of the underlying asset but for which the variability will be resolved at some point after the commencement date so that the payments become fixed for the remainder of the lease term. Those payments become in-substance fixed payments when the variability is resolved;

(b) there is more than one set of payments that a lessee could make, but only one of those sets of payments is realistic. In this case, an entity considers the realistic set of payments to be lease payments; or

(c) there is more than one realistic set of payments that a lessee could make, but it must make at least one of those sets of payments. In this case, an entity considers the set of payments that aggregates to the lowest amount (on a discounted basis) to be lease payments. *[IFRS 16.B42]*.

4.5.2 Lease incentives

Lease incentives are defined as 'payments made by a lessor to a lessee associated with a lease, or the reimbursement or assumption by a lessor of costs of a lessee'. *[IFRS 16 Appendix A]*.

A lease agreement with a lessor might include incentives for the lessee to sign the lease, such as an up-front cash payment to the lessee, payment of costs for the lessee (such as moving expenses) or the assumption by the lessor of the lessee's pre-existing lease with a third party.

For lessees, lease incentives that are received by the lessee at or before the lease commencement date reduce the initial measurement of a lessee's right-of-use asset. *[IFRS 16.24(b)]*. Lease incentives that are receivable by the lessee at lease commencement date, reduce a lessee's lease liability (and therefore the right-of-use asset as well). *[IFRS 16.27(a)]*.

For lessors, lease incentives that are paid or payable to the lessee are also deducted from lease payments and affect the lease classification test. For finance leases, lease incentives that are payable to the lessee reduce the expected lease receivables at the commencement date and thereby the initial measurement of the lessor's net investment in the lease. *[IFRS 16.70(a)]*. For operating leases, lessors should defer the cost of any lease incentives paid or payable to the lessee and recognise that cost as a reduction to lease income over the lease term.

In May 2020 the IASB issued *Annual Improvements to IFRS Standards 2018 – 2020*, which included an amendment to Illustrative Example 13 to remove the illustration of the reimbursement of leasehold improvements by the lessor. This was removed because of concerns that the example did not explain clearly enough the conclusion as to whether the reimbursement would meet the definition of a lease incentive in IFRS 16.

4.5.3 Variable lease payments that depend on an index or rate

Variable lease payments that depend on an index or a rate include, for example, payments linked to a consumer price index (CPI), payments linked to a benchmark interest rate (such as LIBOR) or payments that vary to reflect changes in market rental rates. *[IFRS 16.28]*. The payments are included in the lease payments and are measured using the prevailing index or rate at the measurement date (e.g. lease commencement date for initial measurement). The IASB indicated in the Basis for Conclusions that, despite the measurement uncertainty associated with changes to index- or rate-based payments, the payments meet the definition of an asset (lessor) and a liability (lessee) because they are unavoidable and do not depend on any future activity of the lessee. *[IFRS 16.BC165]*. Lessees subsequently remeasure the lease liability if there is a change in the cash flows (i.e. when the adjustment to the lease payments takes effect) for future payments resulting from a change in index or rate used to determine lease payments. *[IFRS 16.42(b)]*.

Example 23.13: Variable lease payment that depends on an index or rate

Entity A enters into a 10-year lease of property. The lease payment for the first year is CU1,000. The lease payments are linked to the consumer price index (CPI), i.e. not a floating interest rate. The CPI at the beginning of the first year is 100. Lease payments are updated at the end of every second year. At the end of year one, the CPI is 105. At the end of year two, the CPI is 108.

Analysis: At the lease commencement date, the lease payments are CU1,000 per year for 10 years. Entity A does not take into consideration the potential future changes in the index. At the end of year one the payments have not changed, so the liability is not updated. At the end of year two, when the lease payments change, Entity A updates the remaining eight lease payments to CU1,080 per year (CU1,000 ÷ 100 × 108) and does not change its discount rate to remeasure the lease liability (and right-of-use asset).

Lease contracts, particularly those relating to property, may include market rent reviews at future dates. The following example shows how these clauses may be treated.

Example 23.14: Property leases with market rent reviews

Entity A enters into a 5-year lease of property. The lease payment for the first year is CU1,000. In years 2 and 3, there is a fixed escalation of 4%. At the beginning of year 4 there is a market rent review that will determine the lease payment in years 4 and 5.

Analysis: The lease payments included in the lease liability and right-of-use asset at the lease commencement date are determined as follows:

Year 1 – CU1,000

Year 2 – CU1,000 + 4% fixed escalation = CU1,040

Year 3 – CU1,040 + 4% fixed escalation = CU1,082

The market rent review applicable to years 4 and 5 is a variable lease payment that depends on an index or a rate (as described in paragraph 28 of IFRS 16). Entity A assesses the market rent at commencement date for the lease of the property for a period of two years, which is the length of the remaining lease term. This is determined to be CU1,060 per annum for years 4 and 5.

4.5.4 The exercise price of a purchase option

If the lessee is reasonably certain to exercise a purchase option, the exercise price is included as a lease payment. That is, entities consider the exercise price of asset purchase options included in lease contracts consistently with the evaluation of lease renewal and termination options. See 4.4 above.

4.5.5 Payments for penalties for terminating a lease

If it is reasonably certain that the lessee will not terminate a lease, the lease term is determined assuming that the termination option would not be exercised, and any termination penalty is excluded from the lease payments. Otherwise, the lease termination penalty is included as a lease payment. The determination of whether to include lease termination penalties as lease payments is similar to the evaluation of lease renewal options.

4.5.6 Amounts expected to be payable under residual value guarantees – lessees only

IFRS 16 requires lessees to include amounts expected to be payable to the lessor under residual value guarantees as lease payments.

A lessee may provide a guarantee to the lessor that the value of the underlying asset it returns to the lessor at the end of the lease will be at least a specified amount. Such guarantees are unconditional obligations that the lessee has assumed by entering into the lease. Uncertainty related to a lessee's guarantee of a lessor's residual value affects the measurement of the obligation rather than the existence of an obligation. *[IFRS 16.BC170].*

A lessee is required to remeasure the lease liability if there is a change in the amounts expected to be payable under a residual value guarantee. *[IFRS 16.42(a)].*

Example 23.15: Residual value guarantee included in lease payments

Entity R (lessee) enters into a lease and guarantees that the lessor will realise CU15,000 from selling the asset to another party at the end of the lease. At lease commencement, based on Entity R's estimate of the residual value of the underlying asset, Entity R determines that it expects that it will owe CU6,000 at the end of the lease.

Analysis: Because it is expected that it will owe the lessor CU6,000 under the residual value guarantee, Entity R includes that amount as a lease payment.

IFRS 16 does not state how frequently reassessment should occur for expected changes under residual value guarantees. However, we would expect entities to apply judgement to determine the frequency of reassessment based on the relevant facts and circumstances.

4.5.7 Amounts payable under residual value guarantees – lessors only

IFRS 16 requires lessors to include in the lease payments, any residual value guarantees provided to the lessor by the lessee, a party related to the lessee, or a third party unrelated to the lessor that is financially capable of discharging the obligations under the guarantee. *[IFRS 16.70(c)].* This amount included in lease payments is different to that for a lessee which only includes the amount expected to be payable. See 4.5.6 above.

4.5.8 Variable lease payments which do not depend on an index or rate

Variable lease payments that do not depend on an index or rate and are not in-substance fixed (see 4.5.1 above), such as those based on performance (e.g. a percentage of sales) or usage of the underlying asset (e.g. the number of hours flown, the number of units produced), are not included as lease payments. Instead they are recognised in profit or loss (unless they are included in the carrying amount of another asset in accordance with other IFRS) in the period in which the event that triggers the payment occurs. [IFRS 16.38(b)].

In some cases, the variability may be resolved during the lease term, so that payments become fixed for the remainder of the lease term. The new fixed payments are then used to remeasure the lease liability (with an offset to the right-of-use asset). In some cases, the contract requires that when the contingency is resolved, the lessee is required to make an immediate catch up payment. The catch-up payment relates specifically to the lessee's prior use of the asset. In this case, we believe, when the contingency is resolved, the catch-up obligation is recognised as part of the lease liability and is expensed immediately (rather than adjusting the right-of-use asset).

Lease payments do not include payments allocated to the non-lease components of a contract. However, lease payments include amounts that would otherwise be allocable to the non-lease components of a contract when the lessee makes an accounting policy election to account for the lease and non-lease components as a single lease component. See 3.2.2.B above.

Example 23.16: Variable lease payments which do not depend on an index or rate

Entity A is a medical equipment manufacturer and a supplier of the related consumables. Customer B operates a medical centre. Under the agreement entered into by both parties, Entity A grants Customer B the right to use a medical laboratory machine at no cost and Customer B purchases consumables for use in the equipment from Entity A at CU100 each. The consumables can only be used for that equipment and Customer B cannot use other consumables as substitutes. There is no minimum purchase amount required in the contract.

Based on its historical experience, Customer B estimates that it is highly likely to purchase at least 8,000 units of consumables annually. Customer B has appropriately assessed that the arrangement contains a lease of medical equipment. There are no residual value guarantees or other forms of consideration included in the contract.

Analysis: There are two components in the arrangement, a lease of equipment and the purchase of consumables.

Even though Customer B may believe that it is highly unlikely to purchase fewer than 8,000 units of consumables every year, in this example, there are no lease payments for purposes of initial measurement (Entity A and Customer B) and lease classification (Entity A).

Entity A and Customer B would allocate the payments associated with the future payments to the lease and consumables component of the contract.

4.5.9 Security deposits

At the commencement of a lease, a lessee may be required to pay a security deposit to the lessor. As long as the deposit is a true deposit and not a prepaid lease payment, the deposit gives the lessee a right to receive the money back in cash from the lessor and is therefore a financial asset for the lessee and a financial liability for the lessor and is within the scope of IFRS 9. The deposit must initially be accounted for at fair value. The excess of the principal amount of the deposit over its fair value is a part of the lease payments within the scope of IFRS 16. It is therefore considered by the lessor in determining whether the lease is an operating or finance lease. The fair value of the deposit is determined based on the prevailing market rate of interest for a similar loan to the lessor, considering the lessor's credit-worthiness and, depending on facts and circumstances, any additional security available to the lessee.

When the deposit earns interest below the market rate, the excess of the principal amount of the deposit over its fair value is accounted for by both the lessee and lessor as a prepaid lease payment. The lessee includes this amount in the cost of its right-of-use asset at the lease commencement date. For the lessor, if the lease is classified as an operating lease, the prepaid lease payment is included in the total lease payments that are recognised as income on either a straight-line basis or another systematic basis if that basis is more representative of the pattern in which benefit from the use of the underlying asset is diminished. If the lease is classified as a finance lease, the lessor includes the prepaid lease payment in the consideration for the lease (i.e. lease payments) and, therefore, in the determination of the gain or loss on derecognition of the underlying asset, if any.

Interest on the deposit is accounted for using the effective interest method by both the lessee and the lessor.

4.5.10 Value added tax and property taxes

When a lessee enters into a lease contract the lessor may be required to charge the lessee VAT in accordance with the local tax regulations. In many jurisdictions, the lessor charges VAT on behalf of the tax authority and payment is remitted to the tax authority. In circumstances when the VAT is the obligation of the lessee (i.e. not the lessor's obligation) the VAT charged is not a lease payment from the perspective of the lessor. From a lessee's perspective, typically the lessee only incurs a liability for the VAT when the lessor invoices the lease payment. In some cases, VAT is not fully recoverable by the lessee, usually because either the activities of the lessee prohibit the recovery of VAT or recovery is prohibited due to the nature of the leased asset. Generally, we expect that lessees will not include VAT in lease payments in these situations. Non-recoverable VAT payments are in the scope of IFRIC 21 – *Levies*. See Chapter 26 at 6.8.

In some circumstances, a lessee may enter into a contract to lease property and the lessor is required to pay property taxes levied by a local government authority. The lease contract may specify that the lessee pays an additional amount to cover the lessors expected tax costs. Property tax that is reimbursable by the lessee to the lessor as the owner of the office building, according to the contract, does not transfer any goods or services to the lessee and as such it is not a separate component of the contract. Rather, it is part of the total consideration and should be allocated to the separately identified components of the contract. Unlike the non-recoverable VAT payments discussed above, the property tax reimbursable by the lessee to the lessor is not a collection of tax by the lessor on behalf of the tax authority. The obligation to pay the property tax rests with the lessor as the owner (regardless of whether the lessee ends up making any payments to the lessor). That is, the property tax is a cost of ownership and the lessee's payment to the lessor simply compensates the lessor for the use of the office building.

4.5.11 Co-tenancy clauses

A co-tenancy clause is a clause in a lease contract that could result in changes in a lessee's lease payments if certain events involving other tenants occur (e.g. if key tenants, or a certain number of tenants, leave a retail shopping centre). A co-tenancy clause, if triggered, may temporarily reduce a lessee's lease payments or contractually change the lease payments from fixed lease payments to variable lease payments (e.g. payments that were previously fixed are changed to a percentage of sales). Generally, when the co-tenancy clause is resolved (e.g. the anchor tenant is replaced or occupancy levels return to a stated percentage), the lease payments will revert back to the previous amounts.

If after lease commencement, a co-tenancy clause is triggered, we believe a lessee generally would not remeasure the lease payments. IFRS 16 requires a lessee to remeasure lease payments when a contingency, upon which some or all of the variable lease payments that will be paid over the remainder of the lease term are based, is resolved and those payments now meet the definition of lease payments. A co-tenancy clause would typically result in the inverse scenario because it would temporarily lower the lease payment or temporarily cause fixed payments to become variable. Therefore, we believe any temporary change in lease payments that results from a co-tenancy clause being triggered should be recognised in profit or loss similar to variable lease payments.

However, in certain circumstances, when it is likely the co-tenancy clause will not be resolved (e.g. the lease space is an aging shopping centre with a low likelihood of locating replacement tenants that comply with the clause), we believe a lessee may reasonably conclude it should remeasure the lease payments. In this example, the lease payments would be remeasured resulting in a reduction to the existing lease liability. The effect of a co-tenancy clause when reassessing lease payments will depend on facts and circumstances.

4.5.12 Reassessment of the lease liability

IFRS 16 contains specific requirements about how to remeasure the lease liability to reflect changes to the lease payments (see 5.4 below). A lessee recognises the amount of the remeasurement of the lease liability as an adjustment to the right-of-use asset. However, if the carrying amount of the right-of-use asset is reduced to zero and there is a further reduction in the measurement of the lease liability, a lessee recognises any remaining amount of the remeasurement in profit or loss. *[IFRS 16.39]*.

4.5.13 Remeasurement by lessors

Lessors remeasure the lease payments upon a modification (i.e. a change in the scope of a lease, or the consideration for a lease that was not part of its original terms and conditions) that is not accounted for as a separate contract. See 6.4 below.

4.6 Discount rates

Discount rates are used to determine the present value of the lease payments which are used to determine lease classification (see 6.1 below) and to measure a lessor's net investment in the lease and a lessee's lease liability.

The discount rate for lessors is the interest rate implicit in the lease, which is defined as the rate that causes the present value of (a) the lease payments and (b) the unguaranteed residual value to equal the sum of (i) the fair value of the underlying asset and (ii) any initial direct costs of the lessor. *[IFRS 16 Appendix A]*.

Initial direct costs, other than those incurred by manufacturer or dealer lessors, are included in the initial measurement of the net investment in the lease and reduce the amount of income recognised over the lease term.

For lessees, lease payments are discounted using the interest rate implicit in the lease if that rate can be readily determined. If that rate cannot be readily determined, the lessee uses the incremental borrowing rate. *[IFRS 16.26]*. The interest rate implicit in the lease is not necessarily the rate stated in the contract and reflects, among other things, the lessor's initial direct costs and estimates of residual value. Therefore, lessees may find it difficult to determine the interest rate implicit in the lease, in which case they will need to determine the incremental borrowing rate.

The term readily determinable is not equivalent to estimable. Therefore, when the interest rate implicit in the lease can only be determined by using estimates and/or assumptions, then the interest rate implicit in the lease is not readily determinable.

The lessee's incremental borrowing rate is the rate of interest that a lessee would have to pay to borrow over a similar term, and with a similar security, the funds necessary to obtain an asset of a similar value to the right-of-use asset in a similar economic environment. *[IFRS 16 Appendix A]*.

In determining the incremental borrowing rate, the lessee considers borrowings with a similar term and security to the right-of-use asset, not the underlying asset. For example, in the case of a five-year property lease, the lessee considers borrowings with a similar term to the five year right-of-use asset, not the property itself, which may have a significantly longer life. Observable rates, such as a property yield can be used as a starting point to determine the incremental borrowing rate, but adjustments need to be considered for an asset with a value similar to the right-of-use asset. Other potential sources of adjustment may include the credit profile of the lessee, the borrowing currency, or the length of the lease term. It is likely that in some cases significant judgement will be needed to determine the incremental borrowing rate.

Market interest rates, particularly risk-free rates, can be negative. IFRS 16 does not contain a floor of zero for the discount rate and therefore it is possible that a lessee's incremental borrowing rate could be below zero. However, as stated above, observable borrowings with negative nominal interest rates may be a starting point and entities will need to consider all potential sources of adjustment (e.g. its own credit rating, lease term, currency) to determine its own incremental borrowing rate.

The incremental borrowing rate is determined in accordance with the definition in IFRS 16 as described above. In certain cases, particularly for high value assets, the incremental borrowing rate may be lower than the lessee would expect the lessor's interest rate implicit in the lease to be, because the lessor is exposed to the residual value risk of the asset at the end of the lease term. This asset risk premium is not adjusted for as it does not meet the definition of the incremental borrowing rate in IFRS 16.

As explained above, the lessee's incremental borrowing rate reflects the rate of interest that a lessee would have to pay, among others, in a similar economic environment. This is generally a nominal discount rate. If the contract requires lease payments to be made in a currency other than the functional currency of the lessee, the incremental borrowing rate of the lessee should be determined based on a borrowing of a similar amount in that foreign currency. Leases denominated in a foreign currency are discussed further at 5.6.2 below.

In June and September 2019, the IFRS Interpretations Committee discussed whether a lessee's incremental borrowing rate is required to reflect the interest rate on a loan with both a similar maturity to the lease and a similar payment profile to the lease.[4] Specifically, whether an entity should use the interest rate for an amortising loan (whereby the principal and interest are paid down over time) or the interest rate for a bullet repayment loan (whereby the interest is paid over time with a single bullet payment of the principal at the end of the loan). Interest rates for bullet repayment loans are often higher than those for amortising loans.

The Committee noted that the lessee's incremental borrowing rate is a lease-specific rate that the Board defined 'to take into account the terms and conditions of the lease'.[5] The definition of a lessee's incremental borrowing rate in IFRS 16 does not explicitly require a lessee to determine its incremental borrowing rate to reflect the interest rate on a loan with a similar payment profile to the lease payments. Nonetheless, the Committee observed that it would be consistent with the Board's objective (when developing the definition of incremental borrowing rate) for a lessee to refer, as a starting point, to a readily observable rate for a loan with a similar payment profile to that of the lease.

The Committee concluded that the principles and requirements in IFRS 16 provide an adequate basis for a lessee to determine its incremental borrowing rate and decided not to add the matter to its standard setting agenda.

Given the lack of prescriptive guidance, we believe that the use of an amortising loan rate that has a similar payment profile to the lease is always acceptable. The use of other rates (e.g. bullet loan rates) may also be acceptable depending on the facts and circumstances (e.g. when the use of such rates aligns with the lessee's normal borrowing practices).

4.6.1 Determination of the incremental borrowing rate by a subsidiary with centralised treasury functions

Some groups maintain centralised treasury functions and all funding requirements for the group are managed by the parent entity. Under IFRS 16, subsidiaries participating in a centralised treasury function cannot default to their parent's incremental borrowing rate. Rather all facts and circumstances should be considered to determine the subsidiary/lessee's incremental borrowing rate. The existence of guarantees of the subsidiary's obligations may result in a rate that is similar to the parent's rate as if the parent had entered into the lease directly.

4.7 Initial direct costs

Initial direct costs are incremental costs of obtaining a lease that would not have been incurred if the lease had not been obtained, except for such costs incurred by a manufacturer or dealer lessor in connection with a finance lease. *[IFRS 16 Appendix A]*.

For lessors, initial direct costs, other than those incurred by manufacturer or dealer lessors, are included in the initial measurement of the net investment in the lease and reduce the amount of income recognised over the lease term. The interest rate implicit in the lease is defined in such a way that the initial direct costs are included automatically in the net investment in the lease and there is no need to add them separately. *[IFRS 16.69]*.

IFRS 16 requires lessees to include their initial direct costs in their initial measurement of the right-of-use asset. As noted above, initial direct costs are incremental costs that would not have been incurred if the lease had not been obtained (e.g. commissions, certain payments made to an existing lessee to incentivise that lessee to terminate its lease). Lessees and lessors apply the same definition of initial direct costs. The requirements under IFRS 16 for initial direct costs are consistent with the concept of incremental costs in IFRS 15. Under IAS 17, initial direct costs are incremental costs that are directly attributable to negotiating and arranging a lease, except for such costs incurred by manufacturer or dealer lessors. The revised definition under IFRS 16 could result in some changes in practice for lessors. Lessor's initial direct costs will now also exclude costs incurred regardless of whether the lease is obtained (e.g. certain legal advice).

4.7.1 Directly attributable costs other than initial direct costs incurred by lessees

Certain costs associated with acquiring an asset within the scope of IAS 16 are required to be capitalised upon initial recognition. See Chapter 18 at 4.1. However, IFRS 16 does not address the accounting for lessees' costs incurred directly attributable to bringing a right-of-use asset to the location and condition necessary for it to be capable of operating in the manner intended by management. To the extent that costs related to acquiring a right-of-use asset are not subject to capitalisation under other IFRS (e.g. IAS 16), it remains to be seen in practice whether they are charged to profit or loss when incurred or capitalised by analogy to IAS 16. For example, a lessee may incur costs when leasing an asset, by paying a third party to ship the asset, prepare the site and install the underlying asset. We believe lessees may analogise to IAS 16 to determine if such costs can be capitalised.

4.8 Economic life

The economic life is either the period over which an asset is expected to be economically usable by one or more users or the number of production or similar units expected to be obtained from an asset by one or more users. *[IFRS 16 Appendix A]*.

4.9 Fair value

The fair value for the purposes of applying the lessor accounting requirements in IFRS 16 is the amount for which an asset could be exchanged, or a liability settled, between knowledgeable, willing parties in an arm's length transaction. *[IFRS 16 Appendix A]*.

The fair value definition for lessors has been carried forward from IAS 17.

5 LESSEE ACCOUNTING

5.1 Initial recognition

At the commencement date, a lessee recognises a right-of-use asset and a lease liability. *[IFRS 16.22]*. This applies to all leases unless the lessee elects the short-term lease and/or lease of low-value asset recognition exemptions, discussed below. If an entity applies the exemptions it must disclose that fact. *[IFRS 16.60]*.

5.1.1 Short-term leases

A short-term lease is a lease that, at the commencement date, has a lease term of 12 months or less. A lease that contains a purchase option is not a short-term lease. *[IFRS 16 Appendix A]*.

The short-term lease exemption can be made by class of underlying asset to which the right of use relates. A class of underlying asset is a grouping of underlying assets of a similar nature and use in an entity's operations. *[IFRS 16.8]*.

A lessee that makes this accounting policy election does not recognise a lease liability or right-of-use asset on its balance sheet. Instead, the lessee recognises the lease payments associated with those leases as an expense on either a straight-line basis over the lease term or another systematic basis. The lessee applies another systematic basis if that basis is more representative of the pattern of the lessee's benefit. *[IFRS 16.6]*.

When determining whether a lease qualifies as a short-term lease, a lessee evaluates the lease term in the same manner as all other leases. That is, the lease term includes the non-cancellable term of the lease, periods covered by an option to extend the lease if the lessee is reasonably certain to exercise that option and periods covered by an option to terminate the lease if the lessee is reasonably certain not to exercise that option. As the determination is made at commencement date, a lease cannot be classified as short-term if the lease term is subsequently reduced to less than 12 months. In addition, to qualify as a short-term lease, the lease cannot include an option to purchase the underlying asset.

A lease that qualifies as a short-term lease at the commencement is a new lease if there is a lease modification or a change in a lessee's assessment of the lease term (e.g. the lessee exercises an option not previously included in the determination of the lease term). *[IFRS 16.7]*. The new lease is evaluated to determine whether it qualifies for the short-term exemption, similar to any other new lease.

The short-term lease accounting policy election is intended to reduce the cost and complexity of applying IFRS 16. However, a lessee that makes the election must make certain quantitative and qualitative disclosures about short-term leases (see 5.8.2 below).

Once a lessee establishes a policy for a class of underlying assets, all future short-term leases for that class are required to be accounted for in accordance with the lessee's policy. A lessee evaluates any potential change in its accounting policy in accordance with IAS 8 – *Accounting Policies, Changes in Accounting Estimates and Errors*.

Example 23.17: Short-term lease

Scenario A

A lessee enters into a lease with a nine-month non-cancellable term with an option to extend the lease for four months. The lease does not have a purchase option. At the lease commencement date, the lessee concludes that it is reasonably certain to exercise the extension option because the monthly lease payments during the extension period are significantly below market rates.

Analysis: The lease term is greater than 12 months i.e. 13 months. Therefore, the lessee may not account for the lease as a short-term lease.

Scenario B

Assume the same facts as Scenario A except, at the lease commencement date, the lessee concludes that it is not reasonably certain to exercise the extension option because the monthly lease payments during the optional extension period are at what the lessee expects to be market rates and there are no other factors that would make exercise of the renewal option reasonably certain.

Analysis: The lease term is 12 months or less, i.e. nine months. Therefore, the lessee may (subject to its accounting policy, by class of underlying asset) account for the lease under the short-term lease exemption, i.e. it recognises lease payments as an expense on either a straight-line basis over the lease term or another systematic basis and does not recognise a lease liability or right-of-use asset on its balance sheet, similar to an operating lease under IAS 17.

5.1.2 Leases of low-value assets

Lessees can also make an election for leases of low-value assets, which can be made on a lease-by-lease basis. *[IFRS 16.8]*. A lessee that makes this accounting policy election does not recognise a lease liability or right-of-use asset on its statement of financial position. Instead, the lessee recognises the lease payments associated with those leases as an expense on either a straight-line basis over the lease term or another systematic basis. The lessee applies another systematic basis if that basis is more representative of the pattern of the lessee's benefit. *[IFRS 16.6]*.

A lessee assesses the value of an underlying asset based on the value of the asset when it is new, regardless of the age of the asset being leased. *[IFRS 16.B3]*. The assessment of whether an underlying asset is of low value is performed on an absolute basis. Leases of low-value assets qualify for the exemption regardless of whether those leases are material to the lessee. The assessment is not affected by the size, nature or circumstances of the lessee. Accordingly, different lessees are expected to reach the same conclusion about whether a particular underlying asset is of low-value. *[IFRS 16.B4]*. At the time of reaching its decisions about the exemption, the IASB had in mind leases of underlying assets with a value, when new, of US$5,000 or less. *[IFRS 16.BC100]*. Examples of low-value assets include desktop and laptop computers, small items of office furniture, telephones and other low-value equipment *[IFRS 16.B8]* and excludes cars because a new car would typically not be of low value. *[IFRS 16.B6]*.

An underlying asset can only be of low-value if both:
- the lessee can benefit from use of the assets on their own, or together with, other resources that are readily available to the lessee; and
- the underlying asset is not dependent on, or highly interrelated with, other assets. *[IFRS 16.B5]*.

For example, an entity may lease a truck for use in its business and the lease includes the use of the tyres attached to the truck. To use the tyres for their intended purpose, they can only be used with the truck and therefore are dependent on, or highly interrelated with the truck. Therefore, the tyres would not qualify for the low-value asset exemption.

A lease of an underlying asset does not qualify as a lease of a low-value asset if the nature of the asset is such that, when new, the asset is typically not of low value. For example, leases of cars would not qualify as leases of low-value assets because a new car would typically not be of low value. *[IFRS 16.B6]*.

An intermediate lessor who subleases, or expects to sublease an asset, cannot account for the head lease as a lease of a low-value asset. *[IFRS 16.B7]*.

5.2 Initial measurement

5.2.1 Right-of-use assets

At commencement date, a lessee measures the right-of-use asset at cost. *[IFRS 16.23]*.

The cost of a right-of-use asset comprises:

- the amount of the initial measurement of the lease liability;
- any lease payments made at or before the commencement date, less any lease incentives received;
- any initial direct costs incurred by the lessee; and
- an estimate of costs to be incurred by the lessee in dismantling and removing the underlying asset, restoring the site on which it is located or restoring the underlying asset to the condition required by the terms and conditions of the lease, unless those costs are to produce inventories. The lessee incurs the obligation for those costs either at the commencement date or as a consequence of having used the underlying asset during a particular period. *[IFRS 16.24]*.

A lessee recognises dismantling, removal and restoration costs above as part of the cost of the right-of-use asset when it incurs an obligation for those costs. A lessee applies IAS 2 – *Inventories* – to costs that are incurred during a particular period as a consequence of having used the right-of-use asset to produce inventories during that period. The obligations for such costs are recognised and measured applying IAS 37 – *Provisions, Contingent Liabilities and Contingent Assets*. *[IFRS 16.25]*.

In certain retail property leases, a lessee may sign a lease contract with a lessor and also make a payment to the existing lessee in return for vacating the property. This is sometimes referred to as key money. The existing lessee is released from all obligations under the lease contract with the lessor (i.e. this is not a sublease arrangement). The new lessee also has the right to sell the lease contract to another party in exchange for payment, which would also release the new lessee from all obligations with the lessor. On initial recognition of the lease contract, the payment to the previous lessee is accounted for as an initial direct cost and is included in the measurement of the right-of-use asset. The payment is not in the scope of IAS 38. The new lessee applies the requirements described at 5.3.1 below to the subsequent measurement of the right-of-use asset.

5.2.2 Lease liabilities

At the commencement date, a lessee measures the lease liability at the present value of the lease payments that are not paid at that date. The lease payments are discounted using the interest rate implicit in the lease, if that rate can be readily determined. If that rate cannot be readily determined, the lessee uses the lessee's incremental borrowing rate. *[IFRS 16.26]*.

At the commencement date, the lease payments included in the measurement of the lease liability comprise the following payments for the right to use the underlying asset during the lease term that are not paid at the commencement date:

- fixed payments (including in-substance fixed payments), less any lease incentives receivable;

- variable lease payments that depend on an index or a rate, initially measured using the index or rate as at the commencement date;
- amounts expected to be payable by the lessee under residual value guarantees;
- the exercise price of a purchase option if the lessee is reasonably certain to exercise that option; and
- payments of penalties for terminating the lease, if the lease term reflects the lessee exercising an option to terminate the lease. *[IFRS 16.27]*.

5.3 Subsequent measurement

5.3.1 Right-of-use assets

After the commencement date, a lessee measures the right-of-use asset applying a cost model, unless it applies either of the measurement models described at 5.3.1.B below. *[IFRS 16.29]*.

5.3.1.A Cost model

To apply the cost model, the lessee measures the right-of-use asset at cost:
- less any accumulated depreciation and accumulated impairment losses; and
- adjusted for the remeasurement of the lease liability described at 5.4 below. *[IFRS 16.30]*.

A lessee applies the depreciation requirements in IAS 16 in depreciating the right-of-use asset, subject to the following requirements. *[IFRS 16.31]*.

If the lease transfers ownership of the underlying asset to the lessee by the end of the lease term or if the cost of the right-of-use asset reflects that the lessee will exercise a purchase option, the lessee depreciates the right-of-use asset from the commencement date to the end of the useful life of the underlying asset. Otherwise, the lessee depreciates the right-of-use asset from the commencement date to the earlier of the end of the useful life of the right-of-use asset or the end of the lease term. *[IFRS 16.32]*. The leased asset is depreciated from the commencement date of the lease even if the lessee chooses not to use the asset from the commencement date, for example, because leasehold improvements are being constructed.

Depreciation of the right-of-use asset is recognised in a manner consistent with existing standards for property, plant and equipment. IAS 16 is not prescriptive about the methods of depreciation, mentioning straight line, diminishing balance and units of production as possibilities. The overriding requirement of IAS 16 is that the depreciation charge reflects the pattern of consumption of the benefits the asset brings over its useful life and is applied consistently from period to period.

IAS 16 also requires that each part of an item of property, plant and equipment with a cost that is significant in relation to the total cost of the item be depreciated separately. An entity allocates the amount initially recognised with respect to an item of property, plant and equipment to its significant parts and depreciates separately each such part. For example, as noted in IAS 16, it may be appropriate to depreciate separately the airframe and engines of an aircraft. In many cases, the right-of-use asset will relate to one underlying asset or significant part and so a component approach may not be necessary.

However, entities will need to assess whether it should be applied for right-of-use assets that have significant parts with different useful economic lives.

A lessee applies IAS 36 – *Impairment of Assets* – to determine whether the right-of-use asset is impaired and to account for any impairment loss identified. *[IFRS 16.33]*.

5.3.1.B   Other measurement models

If a lessee applies the fair value model in IAS 40 – *Investment Property* – to its investment property, the lessee also applies that fair value model to right-of-use assets that meet the definition of investment property in IAS 40. *[IFRS 16.34]*.

If right-of-use assets relate to a class of property, plant and equipment to which the lessee applies the revaluation model in IAS 16, a lessee may elect to apply that revaluation model to all of the right-of-use assets that relate to that class of property, plant and equipment. *[IFRS 16.35]*.

5.3.2   Lease liabilities

After the commencement date, a lessee measures the lease liability by:

(a)   increasing the carrying amount to reflect interest on the lease liability;

(b)   reducing the carrying amount to reflect the lease payments made; and

(c)   remeasuring the carrying amount to reflect any reassessment or lease modifications specified, or to reflect revised in-substance fixed lease payments. *[IFRS 16.36]*.

Interest on the lease liability in each period during the lease term is the amount that produces a constant periodic rate of interest on the remaining balance of the lease liability. The periodic rate of interest is the discount rate described at commencement, unless a reassessment requiring a change in the discount rate has been triggered. *[IFRS 16.37]*.

5.3.3   Expense recognition

After the commencement date, the lessee recognises depreciation and impairment of the right-of-use asset in profit or loss, unless depreciation is permitted to be capitalised (e.g. to inventory) under other IFRS (or the lessee applies the fair value model described in at 5.3.1.B above).

A lessee also recognises in profit or loss, unless the costs are included in the carrying amount of another asset applying other IFRS, both:

(a)   interest on the lease liability; and

(b)   variable lease payments not included in the measurement of the lease liability in the period in which the event or condition that triggers those payments occurs.
[IFRS 16.38].

When a lessee depreciates the right-of-use asset on a straight-line basis, the total periodic expense (i.e. the sum of interest and depreciation expense) is generally higher in the early periods and lower in the later periods. Because a constant interest rate is applied to the lease liability, the interest expense decreases as cash payments are made during the lease term and the lease liability decreases. Therefore, more interest expense is incurred in the early periods and less in the later periods. This trend in the interest expense, combined with straight-line depreciation of the right-of-use asset, results in a front-loaded expense recognition pattern.

If a lessee determines that a right-of-use asset is impaired, it recognises an impairment loss and measures the right-of-use asset at its carrying amount immediately after the impairment. A lessee subsequently depreciates, generally on a straight-line basis, the right-of-use asset from the date of the impairment to the earlier of the end of the useful life of the right-of-use asset or the end of the lease term. However, the depreciation period is the remaining useful life of the underlying asset if the lessee is reasonably certain to exercise an option to purchase the underlying asset or if the lease transfers ownership of the underlying asset to the lessee by the end of the lease term. See 5.6.1 below for additional discussion of impairment of right-of-use assets.

Example 23.18: Lessee accounting

Entity H (lessee) enters into a three-year lease of equipment. Entity H agrees to make the following annual payments at the end of each year: CU10,000 in year one, CU12,000 in year two and CU14,000 in year three. For simplicity, there are no other elements to the lease payments (e.g. purchase options, lease incentives from the lessor, initial direct costs). The initial measurement of the right-of-use asset and lease liability is CU33,000 (present value of lease payments using a discount rate of approximately 4.235%). Entity H uses its incremental borrowing rate because the rate implicit in the lease cannot be readily determined. Entity H depreciates the right-of-use asset on a straight-line basis over the lease term.

Analysis: At lease commencement, Entity H would recognise the lease-related asset and liability:

Dr. Right-of-use asset	CU33,000	
Cr. Lease liability		CU33,000
To initially recognise the lease-related asset and liability		

The following journal entries would be recorded in the first year:

Dr. Interest expense	CU1,398	
Cr. Lease liability		CU1,398
To record interest expense and accrete the lease liability using the interest method (CU33,000 × 4.235%)		
Dr. Depreciation expense	CU11,000	
Cr. Right-of-use asset		CU11,000
To record depreciation expense on the right-of-use asset (CU33,000 ÷ 3 years)		
Dr. Lease liability	CU10,000	
Cr. Cash		CU10,000

A summary of the lease contract's accounting (assuming no changes due to reassessment) is as follows:

	Initial	Year 1	Year 2	Year 3
	CU	CU	CU	CU
Cash lease payments		10,000	12,000	14,000
Lease expense recognised				
Interest expense		1,398	1,033	569
Depreciation expense		11,000	11,000	11,000
Total periodic expense		12,398	12,033	11,569
Statement of financial position				
Right-of-use asset	33,000	22,000	11,000	–
Lease liability	(33,000)	(24,398)	(13,431)	–

5.4 Remeasurement of lease liabilities

After the commencement date, a lessee remeasures the lease liability to reflect changes to the lease payments. A lessee recognises the amount of the remeasurement of the lease liability as an adjustment to the right-of-use asset. However, if the carrying amount of the right-of-use asset is reduced to zero and there is a further reduction in the measurement of the lease liability, a lessee recognises any remaining amount of the remeasurement in profit or loss. *[IFRS 16.39]*.

A lessee remeasures the lease liability by discounting the revised lease payments using a revised discount rate, if:

(a) there is a change in the lease term. A lessee determines the revised lease payments on the basis of the revised lease term; or

(b) there is a change in the assessment of an option to purchase the underlying asset, assessed considering the events and circumstances in the context of a purchase option. A lessee determines the revised lease payments to reflect the change in amounts payable under the purchase option. *[IFRS 16.40]*.

The lessee determines the revised discount rate as the interest rate implicit in the lease for the remainder of the lease term, if that rate can be readily determined, or the lessee's incremental borrowing rate at the date of reassessment, if the interest rate implicit in the lease cannot be readily determined. *[IFRS 16.41]*.

A lessee remeasures the lease liability by discounting the revised lease payments, if either:

(a) there is a change in the amounts expected to be payable under a residual value guarantee. A lessee determines the revised lease payments to reflect the change in amounts expected to be payable under the residual value guarantee;

(b) there is a change in future lease payments resulting from a change in an index or a rate used to determine those payments, including for example a change to reflect changes in market rental rates following a market rent review. The lessee remeasures the lease liability to reflect those revised lease payments only when there is a change in the cash flows (i.e. when the adjustment to the lease payments takes effect). A lessee determines the revised lease payments for the remainder of the lease term based on the revised contractual payments. *[IFRS 16.42]*.

In applying the paragraph above, a lessee uses an unchanged discount rate, unless the change in lease payments results from a change in floating interest rates. In that case, the lessee uses a revised discount rate that reflects changes in the interest rate. *[IFRS 16.43]*.

When a lease includes a market rate adjustment (a market rent review), the negotiations between the lessee and the lessor may take some time to complete (the negotiation period). For example, consider a 10 year lease that has a market rate adjustment that applies from the end of year 5. The market rent review negotiations begin during year 5 but are not completed until later in year 6. During year 6, while the negotiation is ongoing, the lessee is required to pay the original contractual lease payments. At the conclusion of the negotiation period (i.e. upon a final determination of the lease payments for year 6 until year 10), the new lease payments apply retrospectively from the beginning of year 6.

In this example, the lessee does not adjust the lease payments at the beginning of year 6 for the expected increase in rent. Rather, any adjustment is recognised as an adjustment to lease payments when the market rent review is finalised and the change in contractual cash flows takes effect.

The accounting for changes in lease payments arising from rent concessions when the lessee applies *Covid-19-Related Rent Concessions – Amendment to IFRS 16* (the amendment), are discussed at 5.5.4 below.

5.5 Lease modifications

A lease modification is a change in the scope of a lease, or the consideration for a lease, that was not part of the original terms and conditions of the lease (for example, adding or terminating the right to use one or more underlying assets, or extending or shortening the contractual lease term). *[IFRS 16 Appendix A]*.

If a lease is modified, the modified contract is evaluated to determine whether it is or contains a lease (see 3.1 above). If a lease continues to exist, the lease modification can result in:

- a separate lease (see 5.5.1 below); or
- a change in the accounting for the existing lease (i.e. not a separate lease) (see 5.5.2 below).

The exercise of an existing purchase or renewal option or a change in the assessment of whether such options are reasonably certain to be exercised are not lease modifications but can result in the remeasurement of lease liabilities and right-of-use assets (see 5.4 above).

In April 2020, the IASB issued an educational document explaining how an entity evaluates whether a rent concession constitutes a lease modification. This is discussed further at 5.5.3 below. On 28 May 2020, the IASB issued *Covid-19-Related Rent Concessions – Amendment to IFRS 16* (the amendment). The Board amended the standard to provide a temporary optional relief to lessees from applying IFRS 16 guidance on lease modification accounting for rent concessions arising as a direct consequence of the coronavirus pandemic. See 5.5.4 below.

5.5.1 Determining whether a lease modification results in a separate lease

A lessee accounts for a lease modification as a separate lease when both of the following conditions are met:

- the modification increases the scope of the lease by adding the right to use one or more underlying assets; and
- the consideration for the lease increases by an amount commensurate with the stand-alone price for the increase in scope and any adjustments to that stand-alone price reflect the circumstances of the particular contract. *[IFRS 16.44]*.

If both of these conditions are met, the lease modification results in two separate leases, the unmodified original lease and a separate new lease. Lessees account for the separate contract that contains a lease in the same manner as other new leases. If either of the conditions are not met, the modified lease is not accounted for as a separate lease (see 5.5.2 below).

5.5.2 Lessee accounting for a modification that does not result in a separate lease

For a lease modification that is not accounted for as a separate lease, at the effective date of the lease modification the lessee:

(a) allocates the consideration in the modified contract;

(b) determines the lease term of the modified lease; and

(c) remeasures the lease liability by discounting the revised lease payments using a revised discount rate. The revised discount rate is determined as the interest rate implicit in the lease for the remainder of the lease term, if that rate can be readily determined, or the lessee's incremental borrowing rate at the effective date of the modification, if the interest rate implicit in the lease cannot be readily determined. *[IFRS 16.45]*.

For a lease modification that is not accounted for as a separate lease, the lessee accounts for the remeasurement of the lease liability by:

(a) decreasing the carrying amount of the right-of-use asset to reflect the partial or full termination of the lease for lease modifications that decrease the scope of the lease. The lessee recognises in profit or loss any gain or loss relating to the partial or full termination of the lease; or

(b) making a corresponding adjustment to the right-of-use asset for all other lease modifications. *[IFRS 16.46]*.

IFRS 16 contains a number of illustrative examples on modifications, which are reproduced below. *[IFRS 16.IE7]*.

Example 23.19: Lease modifications (IFRS 16 Illustrative Examples 15 to 19)

IFRS 16 Example 15 – Modification that is a separate lease

Lessee enters into a 10-year lease for 2,000 square metres of office space. At the beginning of Year 6, Lessee and Lessor agree to amend the original lease for the remaining five years to include an additional 3,000 square metres of office space in the same building. The additional space is made available for use by Lessee at the end of the second quarter of Year 6. The increase in total consideration for the lease is commensurate with the current market rate for the new 3,000 square metres of office space, adjusted for the discount that Lessee receives reflecting that Lessor does not incur costs that it would otherwise have incurred if leasing the same space to a new tenant (for example, marketing costs).

Lessee accounts for the modification as a separate lease, separate from the original 10-year lease. This is because the modification grants Lessee an additional right to use an underlying asset, and the increase in consideration for the lease is commensurate with the stand-alone price of the additional right-of-use adjusted to reflect the circumstances of the contract. In this example, the additional underlying asset is the new 3,000 square metres of office space. Accordingly, at the commencement date of the new lease (at the end of the second quarter of Year 6), Lessee recognises a right-of-use asset and a lease liability relating to the lease of the additional 3,000 square metres of office space. Lessee does not make any adjustments to the accounting for the original lease of 2,000 square metres of office space as a result of this modification.

IFRS 16 Example 16 – Modification that increases the scope of the lease by extending the contractual lease term

Lessee enters into a 10-year lease for 5,000 square metres of office space. The annual lease payments are CU100,000 payable at the end of each year. The interest rate implicit in the lease cannot be readily determined. Lessee's incremental borrowing rate at the commencement date is 6 per cent per annum. At the beginning of Year 7, Lessee and Lessor agree to amend the original lease by extending the contractual lease term by four years. The annual lease payments are unchanged (i.e. CU100,000 payable at the end of each year from Year 7 to Year 14). Lessee's incremental borrowing rate at the beginning of Year 7 is 7 per cent per annum.

At the effective date of the modification (at the beginning of Year 7), Lessee remeasures the lease liability based on: (a) an eight-year remaining lease term, (b) annual payments of CU100,000 and (c) Lessee's incremental borrowing rate of 7 per cent per annum. The modified lease liability equals CU597,130. The lease liability immediately before the modification (including the recognition of the interest expense until the end of Year 6) is CU346,511. Lessee recognises the difference between the carrying amount of the modified lease liability and the carrying amount of the lease liability immediately before the modification (CU250,619) as an adjustment to the right-of-use asset.

IFRS 16 Example 17 – Modification that decreases the scope of the lease

Lessee enters into a 10-year lease for 5,000 square metres of office space. The annual lease payments are CU50,000 payable at the end of each year. The interest rate implicit in the lease cannot be readily determined. Lessee's incremental borrowing rate at the commencement date is 6 per cent per annum. At the beginning of Year 6, Lessee and Lessor agree to amend the original lease to reduce the space to only 2,500 square metres of the original space starting from the end of the first quarter of Year 6. The annual fixed lease payments (from Year 6 to Year 10) are CU30,000. Lessee's incremental borrowing rate at the beginning of Year 6 is 5 per cent per annum.

At the effective date of the modification (at the beginning of Year 6), Lessee remeasures the lease liability based on: (a) a five-year remaining lease term, (b) annual payments of CU30,000 and (c) Lessee's incremental borrowing rate of 5 per cent per annum. This equals CU129,884.

Lessee determines the proportionate decrease in the carrying amount of the right-of-use asset on the basis of the remaining right-of-use asset (i.e. 2,500 square metres corresponding to 50 per cent of the original right-of-use asset).

50 per cent of the pre-modification right-of-use asset (CU184,002) is CU92,001. Fifty per cent of the pre-modification lease liability (CU210,618) is CU105,309. Consequently, Lessee reduces the carrying amount of the right-of-use asset by CU92,001 and the carrying amount of the lease liability by CU105,309. Lessee recognises the difference between the decrease in the lease liability and the decrease in the right-of-use asset (CU105,309 – CU92,001 = CU13,308) as a gain in profit or loss at the effective date of the modification (at the beginning of Year 6).

Lessee recognises the difference between the remaining lease liability of CU105,309 and the modified lease liability of CU129,884 (which equals CU24,575) as an adjustment to the right-of-use asset reflecting the change in the consideration paid for the lease and the revised discount rate.

IFRS 16 Example 18 – Modification that both increases and decreases the scope of the lease

Lessee enters into a 10-year lease for 2,000 square metres of office space. The annual lease payments are CU100,000 payable at the end of each year. The interest rate implicit in the lease cannot be readily determined. Lessee's incremental borrowing rate at the commencement date is 6 per cent per annum. At the beginning of Year 6, Lessee and Lessor agree to amend the original lease to (a) include an additional 1,500 square metres of space in the same building starting from the beginning of Year 6 and (b) reduce the lease term from 10 years to eight years. The annual fixed payment for the 3,500 square metres is CU150,000 payable at the end of each year (from Year 6 to Year 8). Lessee's incremental borrowing rate at the beginning of Year 6 is 7 per cent per annum.

The consideration for the increase in scope of 1,500 square metres of space is not commensurate with the stand-alone price for that increase adjusted to reflect the circumstances of the contract. Consequently, Lessee does not account for the increase in scope that adds the right to use an additional 1,500 square metres of space as a separate lease.

The pre-modification right-of-use asset and the pre-modification lease liability in relation to the lease are as follows.

	Lease liability				Right-of-use asset		
Year	Beginning balance CU	6% interest expense CU	Lease payment CU	Ending balance CU	Beginning balance CU	Depreciation charge CU	Ending balance CU
1	736,009	44,160	(100,000)	680,169	736,009	(73,601)	662,408
2	680,169	40,810	(100,000)	620,979	662,408	(73,601)	588,807
3	620,979	37,259	(100,000)	558,238	588,807	(73,601)	515,206
4	558,238	33,494	(100,000)	491,732	515,206	(73,601)	441,605
5	491,732	29,504	(100,000)	421,236	441,605	(73,601)	368,004
6	421,236				368,004		

At the effective date of the modification (at the beginning of Year 6), Lessee remeasures the lease liability on the basis of: (a) a three-year remaining lease term, (b) annual payments of CU150,000 and (c) Lessee's incremental borrowing rate of 7 per cent per annum. The modified liability equals CU393,647, of which (a) CU131,216 relates to the increase of CU50,000 in the annual lease payments from Year 6 to Year 8 and (b) CU262,431 relates to the remaining three annual lease payments of CU100,000 from Year 6 to Year 8.

Decrease in the lease term

At the effective date of the modification (at the beginning of Year 6), the pre-modification right-of-use asset is CU368,004. Lessee determines the proportionate decrease in the carrying amount of the right-of-use asset based on the remaining right-of-use asset balance for the original 2,000 square metres of office space (i.e. a remaining three-year lease term rather than the original five-year lease term). The remaining right-of-use asset for the original 2,000 square metres of office space is CU220,802 (i.e. CU368,004 ÷ 5 × 3 years).

At the effective date of the modification (at the beginning of Year 6), the pre-modification lease liability is CU421,236. The remaining lease liability for the original 2,000 square metres of office space is CU267,301 (i.e. present value of three annual lease payments of CU100,000, discounted at the original discount rate of 6 per cent per annum).

Consequently, Lessee reduces the carrying amount of the right-of-use asset by CU147,202 (CU368,004 – CU220,802), and the carrying amount of the lease liability by CU153,935 (CU421,236 – CU267,301). Lessee recognises the difference between the decrease in the lease liability and the decrease in the right-of-use asset (CU153,935 – CU147,202 = CU6,733) as a gain in profit or loss at the effective date of the modification (at the beginning of Year 6).

Dr. Lease liability	CU153,935	
Cr. Right-of-use asset		CU147,202
Cr. Gain		CU6,733

At the effective date of the modification (at the beginning of Year 6), Lessee recognises the effect of the remeasurement of the remaining lease liability reflecting the revised discount rate of 7 per cent per annum, which is CU4,870 (CU267,301 – CU262,431), as an adjustment to the right-of-use asset.

Dr. Lease liability	CU4,870	
Cr. Right-of-use asset		CU4,870

Increase in the leased space

At the commencement date of the lease for the additional 1,500 square metres of space (at the beginning of Year 6), Lessee recognises the increase in the lease liability related to the increase in scope of CU131,216 (i.e. present value of three annual lease payments of CU50,000, discounted at the revised interest rate of 7 per cent per annum) as an adjustment to the right-of-use asset.

Dr. Right-of-use asset	CU131,216	
Cr. Lease liability		CU131,216

The modified right-of-use asset and the modified lease liability in relation to the modified lease are as follows.

	Lease liability				Right-of-use asset		
Year	Beginning balance CU	7% interest expense CU	Lease payment CU	Ending balance CU	Beginning balance CU	Depreciation charge CU	Ending balance CU
6	393,647	27,556	(150,000)	271,203	347,148	(115,716)	231,432
7	271,203	18,984	(150,000)	140,187	231,432	(115,716)	115,716
8	140,187	9,813	(150,000)	–	115,716	(115,716)	–

IFRS 16 Example 19 – Modification that is a change in consideration only

Lessee enters into a 10-year lease for 5,000 square metres of office space. At the beginning of Year 6, Lessee and Lessor agree to amend the original lease for the remaining five years to reduce the lease payments from CU100,000 per year to CU95,000 per year. The interest rate implicit in the lease cannot be readily determined. Lessee's incremental borrowing rate at the commencement date is 6 per cent per annum. Lessee's incremental borrowing rate at the beginning of Year 6 is 7 per cent per annum. The annual lease payments are payable at the end of each year.

At the effective date of the modification (at the beginning of Year 6), Lessee remeasures the lease liability based on: (a) a five-year remaining lease term, (b) annual payments of CU95,000, and (c) Lessee's incremental borrowing rate of 7 per cent per annum. Lessee recognises the difference between the carrying amount of the modified liability (CU389,519) and the lease liability immediately before the modification (CU421,236) of CU31,717 as an adjustment to the right-of-use asset.

In some cases, the lessee and lessor may agree to a modification to the lease contract that starts at a later date (i.e. the terms of the modification take effect at a date later than the date when both parties agreed to the modification). For example, a lessee enters into a lease arrangement with a lessor to lease an asset for 10 years. At the beginning of year 8 the lessee and lessor agree to a modification to the contract that will take effect from the beginning of year 9.

- If the modification is an increase in the scope that does not result in a separate lease, the lessee will re-allocate the consideration in the modified contract to each existing lease component and non-lease component and remeasure the lease liability at the date both parties agreed to the modification (the beginning of year 8).
- If the modification results in a separate lease component, the lessee will allocate the consideration in the modified contract to each existing and new lease and non-lease component at the date both parties agreed to the modification (the beginning of year 8). The lessee will remeasure the lease liability for the existing lease components at that date as well. However, recognition of the lease liability and right-of-use asset for any new lease component occurs at the commencement date of the new lease component (the beginning of year 9).
- If the modification is a decrease in the scope, the lessee will re-allocate the consideration in the modified contract to each existing lease and non-lease component and remeasure the lease liability and right-of-use asset at the effective date of the modification (the beginning of year 8).

5.5.3 Application of lease modification guidance to rent concessions

As discussed above, a lease modification is defined in IFRS 16 as a change in the scope of a lease, or the consideration for a lease, that was not part of the original terms and conditions of the lease.

I A change in the scope of a lease

In assessing whether there has been a change in the scope of a lease, an entity considers whether there has been a change in the right of use conveyed to the lessee by the contract. A change in the scope of a lease includes adding or terminating the right to use one or more underlying assets or extending or shortening the contractual lease term. A lease payment deferral, lease payment holiday or lease payment reduction alone is a change in consideration for a lease and is not, in isolation, a change in the scope of a lease.

II A change in the consideration for a lease

In assessing whether there has been a change in the consideration for a lease, an entity considers the overall effect of any change in the lease payments. For example, a lessor-granted concession may allow a lessee not to make lease payments for a three-month period, but the lease payments for periods thereafter are increased proportionally in a way that means that the consideration for the lease is unchanged. Such a lease payment deferral, with no change in the total consideration for the lease, or the scope of the lease, would not be a lease modification. We believe that increases to subsequent lease payments to take account solely of the time value of money would not be a substantive change in the consideration for the lease. For example, if a lessor deferred a lease payment for June 2020 and required it to be paid in January 2021 plus an interest charge at a rate to reasonably compensate the lessor for the time value of money, that would not be a substantive change in the consideration for the lease. However, other changes in the consideration for a lease (e.g. a substantive forgiveness of rent payable/receivable) would be a change in the consideration for a lease.

Example 23.20: Deferral of lease payments

Restaurant A leases space in a shopping mall from Lessor B.

Under the terms of the lease, Restaurant A makes fixed lease payments of €100 to Lessor B at the beginning of each month. The non-cancellable lease term ends on 28 February 2022. The contract does not include any extension, termination or purchase options. For simplicity, the discount rate is assumed to be 0% at the commencement date and thus the lease liability at 30 June 2020 for the remaining 20 monthly lease payments is €2,000.

Assume that Restaurant A's right-of-use asset is not impaired before or during the periods described.

On 1 July 2020, Lessor B agrees to defer the three months of lease payments originally due in July, August and September 2020 to 1 January 2021. There are no non-lease components to the contract and there are no other changes to the terms and conditions of the lease.

Analysis: Under IFRS 16, a lease modification is defined as a change in the scope of a lease, or the consideration for a lease, that was not part of the original terms and conditions of the lease. Given that the only change is the timing of the cash outflows, there is no change in the scope of the lease. Restaurant A next considers whether there is a change in the consideration for the lease by reference to the overall effect of any change in the lease payments. In this fact pattern, Restaurant A does not make lease payments for a period of three months from July 2020 and will increase the lease payment due on 1 January 2021 by the same amount as the deferral. Therefore, the consideration for the lease remains substantively unchanged and the rent concession does not constitute a lease modification. The accounting consequences of this are considered at 5.5.4 below.

III   A change that is, or is not, part of the original terms and conditions of the lease

When evaluating if there has been a change in either the scope of, or the consideration for, the lease, an entity is required to consider the terms and conditions of contracts and all relevant facts and circumstances, including the applicable law governing such contracts. When a lessee and lessor agree to a change to a lease that is not contemplated by the original terms and conditions of the lease, the change is accounted for as a lease modification. In this case, lessees would follow paragraphs 44 to 46 of IFRS 16 (if the amendment discussed at 5.5.4 below is not applied) and lessors would consider the guidance in paragraphs 79 and 80 of IFRS 16 (for finance leases) or paragraph 87 of IFRS 16 (for operating leases).

However, if a change is limited solely to the changes contemplated in the existing terms and conditions of the lease, there is no lease modification for the purposes of IFRS 16.

Entities should carefully consider terms in their contracts as they may contain clauses (e.g. a force majeure clause) that result in changes to lease payments if particular events occur or circumstances arise. For example, a contract may include a clause providing the lessee with a right to reduced lease payments upon government action requiring the closure of retail stores for a period of time. Changes in lease payments that result from clauses in the original contract (or in applicable law) would not be lease modifications for the purposes of IFRS 16.

Existing contracts may not specifically contemplate particular circumstances (for example the effect of a global pandemic such as the coronavirus pandemic) and, as such, there could be legal ambiguities when evaluating lease contracts. Therefore, to determine the appropriate accounting for a lease concession, it is important to carefully identify and consider the rights and obligations of the lessee and lessor, taking into account the terms and conditions of the contract and the applicable legal framework.

Questions have been asked as to whether the lease concessions mandated by changes to applicable law constitute a lease modification. For example, when a government introduces new laws mandating certain rent concessions. Some stakeholders believe that, in these cases, there is a change in the consideration for the lease which was not part of the original terms and conditions of the lease and, thus, modification accounting is required. However, other stakeholders believe that when the lessee and lessor agree to a lease contract, subject to the law of a jurisdiction, the parties have also agreed to be bound by any future changes in the applicable law. Thus, any changes made to comply with a change in law are contemplated in the contract and should not be considered to constitute a lease modification. Given that IFRS 16 does not specifically address this circumstance, we believe there is likely to be diversity in practice and both approaches are acceptable. However, entities should consider the disclosure objectives in IFRS 16 and disclose their policies and the effect of such policies related to lease concessions.

Lessees generally account for rent concessions as a lease modification when the definition of a lease modification is met and the amendment to IFRS 16 is not applied (see 5.5.3.B below). However, in circumstances involving a voluntary forgiveness of a lease liability granted by the lessor without other changes to the lease, it might also be reasonable for the lessee to account for such rent concession as a (partial) derecognition of a lease liability applying paragraph 3.3.1 of IFRS 9 with a credit to profit or loss (i.e. rather than applying the IFRS 16 amendments or the IFRS 16 lease modification guidance). Therefore, diversity in practice may exist in this situation and it is important to consider the perspective of the local regulator. Lessees should apply their policy (i.e. to apply IFRS 16 or IFRS 9) consistently to contracts with similar characteristics and in similar circumstances.

5.5.3.A Rent concessions that change the consideration in the contract

Some forms of rent concessions may change the consideration of the lease beyond what was contemplated in the original terms and conditions of the lease and, thus, require lease modification accounting to be applied.

Example 23.21: Change of lease payments from fixed to partially variable

Restaurant A leases space in a shopping mall from Lessor B.

Under the terms of the lease, Restaurant A makes fixed lease payments of €100 to Lessor B at the beginning of each month. The non-cancellable lease term ends on 28 February 2022. The contract does not include any extension, termination or purchase options. For simplicity, the discount rate is assumed to be 0% at the commencement date and thus the lease liability at 30 June 2020 for the remaining 20 monthly lease payments is €2,000.

Assume that Restaurant A's right-of-use asset is not impaired before or during the periods described.

On 1 July 2020, Lessor B agrees to change the terms and conditions of the lease contract with Restaurant A, such that fixed lease payments are reduced to €25 per month, plus an additional variable lease payment based on 3% of the monthly turnover of Restaurant A at that shopping mall.

There are no other changes to the terms and conditions of the lease.

Analysis: In this fact pattern, the consideration for the lease has changed from solely fixed lease payments to a combination of fixed and variable lease payments, which were not part of the original terms and conditions of the contract. Therefore, the change constitutes a lease modification.

5.5.3.B Lessee accounting for rent concessions as lease modifications

As discussed at 5.5.2 above, for a lease modification that is not accounted for as a separate lease, a lessee applies modification accounting at the effective date of the lease modification. In such a case, a lessee allocates the consideration in the modified contract to the lease and non-lease components (where applicable), determines the lease term of the modified lease and remeasures the lease liability by discounting the revised lease payments using a revised discount rate determined on that date. The revised discount rate is the rate of interest implicit in the lease for the remainder of the lease term, or if that rate cannot be readily determined, the lessee's incremental borrowing rate.

If the modification decreases the scope of the lease (e.g. a change that reduces total leased space or shortens the lease term), the lessee remeasures the lease liability and reduces the right-of-use asset to reflect the partial or full termination of the lease (e.g. a 50% reduction in leased space would reduce the right-of-use asset by 50%). Any difference between those two adjustments is recognised in profit or loss at the effective date of the modification. For all other modifications, the lessee recognises the amount of the remeasurement of the lease liability as an adjustment to the right-of-use asset, without affecting profit or loss.

Example 23.22: Lessee accounting for rent concessions that are a lease modification

Scenario 1 – Forgiveness of lease payments and extension of the lease term

Restaurant A leases space in a shopping mall from Lessor B. Lessor B classifies the lease as an operating lease.

Under the terms of the lease, Restaurant A makes fixed lease payments of €100 to Lessor B at the beginning of each month. The non-cancellable lease term ends on 28 February 2022. The contract does not include any extension, termination or purchase options. For simplicity, the discount rate is assumed to be 0% at the commencement date and thus the lease liability at 30 June 2020 for the remaining 20 monthly lease payments is €2,000.

Assume that Restaurant A's right-of-use asset is not impaired before or during the periods described.

On 1 July 2020, Lessor B agrees to forgive the three months of lease payments originally due in July, August and September 2020. There are no non-lease components to the contract and there are no other changes to the terms and conditions of the lease.

Assume the parties agree to extend the lease term by three months at the same monthly lease payment of €100 per month. The lease term will now end on 31 May 2022.

Restaurant A does not apply the amendment to IFRS 16 not to assess whether a rent concession is a lease modification.

Analysis: There is no overall effect of any change in the lease payments in this scenario. Thus, there is no change in the consideration for the lease. However, the scope of the lease has changed as the lease term has been extended by three months, which was not part of the original terms and conditions of the lease. Therefore, the rent concession in this scenario constitutes a lease modification.

On the effective date of modification (i.e. 1 July 2020), Restaurant A applies lease modification accounting and remeasures the lease liability by discounting the revised lease payments using a revised discount rate, determined at the effective date of the modification. A corresponding adjustment is made to the right-of-use asset.

Depreciation of the right-of-use asset continues over the revised remaining lease term.

Scenario 2 – Forgiveness of lease payments

Assume the same fact pattern as above, except for the following:

On 1 July 2020, Lessor B agrees to waive the three months of lease payments originally due in July, August and September 2020. There are no other changes to the terms and conditions of the lease.

Restaurant A does not apply the amendment to IFRS 16 (see 5.5.4 below) not to assess whether a rent concession is a lease modification.

Analysis: In this fact pattern, there is a reduction in the consideration for the lease which was not part of the original terms and conditions of the lease. Therefore, there is a lease modification.

On the effective date of the modification (i.e. 1 July 2020), Restaurant A applies lease modification accounting and remeasures the lease liability by discounting the revised lease payments using a revised discount rate, determined at the effective date of the modification. Restaurant A accounts for the remeasurement of the lease liability by adjusting the carrying amount of the right-of-use asset, as follows (assuming the revised discount rate is 0%):

Dr Lease liability (100 × 3)	€300
Cr Right-of-use asset	€300

Depreciation of the revised right-of-use asset continues over the remaining lease term.

5.5.4 Amendment to IFRS 16 for covid-19 related rent concessions

On 28 May 2020, the IASB issued *Covid-19-Related Rent Concessions – Amendment to IFRS 16* (the amendment). The Board amended the standard to provide a temporary optional relief to lessees from applying IFRS 16 guidance on lease modification accounting for rent concessions arising as a direct consequence of the coronavirus pandemic. The amendments do not apply to lessors.

In providing the relief, the Board acknowledged, in the Basis for Conclusions paragraph BC205B that '... lessees could find it challenging to assess whether a potentially large volume of covid-19 related rent concessions are lease modifications and, for those that are, to apply the required accounting in IFRS 16, especially in the light of the many challenges lessees face during the pandemic.'

The objective of the amendment is to provide lessees that have been granted covid-19 related rent concessions with practical relief, while still providing useful information about leases to users of the financial statements.

As a practical expedient, a lessee may elect not to assess whether a covid-19 related rent concession from a lessor is a lease modification. A lessee that makes this election accounts for any qualifying change in lease payments resulting from the covid-19 related rent concession the same way it would account for the change under IFRS 16 if the change were not a lease modification. A lessee may elect to apply the practical expedient consistently to contracts with similar characteristics and in similar circumstances, as specified in paragraph 2 of IFRS 16.

The practical expedient applies only to rent concessions occurring as a direct consequence of the coronavirus pandemic and only if all of the following conditions described in IFRS 16 paragraph 46B are met:

- The change in lease payments results in revised consideration for the lease that is substantially the same as, or less than, the consideration for the lease immediately preceding the change.
- Any reduction in lease payments affects only payments originally due on or before 30 June 2021 (for example, a rent concession would meet this condition if it results in reduced lease payments before 30 June 2021 and increased lease payments that extend beyond 30 June 2021).
- There is no substantive change to other terms and conditions of the lease.

In the Basis for Conclusions to the amendment, paragraph BC205D(a) states that 'The Board was of the view that a rent concession that increases total payments for the lease should not be considered a direct consequence of the covid-19 pandemic, except to the extent the increase reflects only the time value of money.' Therefore, a rent concession that defers payments to a future date and increases those payments to reflect the time value of money would be in the scope of the practical relief, provided all the other conditions were met.

The IASB further explained, in the Basis for Conclusions, paragraph BC205D(c), that qualitative and quantitative factors are considered in assessing whether there are no substantive changes to other terms and conditions of the lease. Other substantive changes beyond providing a covid-19 related rent concession, such as introducing or withdrawing extension, termination or purchase options, would make the entire modification to the lease ineligible to qualify for the relief provided by the practical expedient. Conversely, under the amendment, a change in the lease term, such as a three-month rent holiday before 30 June 2021 followed by three additional months of substantially equivalent payments at the end of the lease, would not constitute a substantive change to other terms and conditions of the lease.

The amendment to IFRS 16 does not provide explicit guidance about how a lessee accounts for a rent concession when applying the practical expedient. It states that a lessee making the election accounts for any change in lease payments resulting from the covid-19 related rent concession the same way it would account for the change under IFRS 16, if the change were not a lease modification.

We believe there are several potential approaches for accounting for a rent concession which is not accounted for as a lease modification, including:

- Accounting for a concession in the form of forgiveness or deferral of lease payments, as a negative variable lease payment (Approach 1).
- Accounting for a concession in the form of forgiveness or deferral of lease payments, as a resolution of a contingency that fixes previously variable lease payments (Approach 2).
- Accounting for a concession in the form of a deferral of payments as if the lease is unchanged (Approach 3).

There are many different forms of rent concessions obtained by lessees. Therefore, lessees need to evaluate the details of the rent concession granted carefully to determine an appropriate accounting approach. It is possible for more than one approach to be acceptable.

5.5.4.A   Accounting for a concession, in the form of forgiveness or deferral of lease payments, as a negative variable lease payment (Approach 1)

When a lessor grants a concession that contractually releases a lessee from certain lease payments or defers lease payments, we believe a lessee may account for the concession as a negative variable lease payment. In this case, the lessee would remeasure the remaining consideration in the contract and, if the contract contains multiple lease and non-lease components, reallocate the consideration to the lease and non-lease components (using unchanged allocation percentages). The lessee would also not update the discount rate used to measure the lease liability. In this case, the lessee would recognise the allocated portion of the forgiven payments as a negative variable lease expense in the period when changes in facts and circumstances on which the variable lease payments are based occur. This approach is similar to that used by the lessor to recognise variable lease income.

5.5.4.B   Accounting for a concession in the form of forgiveness or deferral of lease payments as a resolution of a contingency that fixes previously variable lease payments (Approach 2)

We believe that a lessee may account for a rent concession in the same manner as it would account for a resolution of a contingency that fixes previously variable lease payments. In this case, the lessee would remeasure the remaining consideration in the contract and, if the contract contains multiple lease and non-lease components, reallocate the consideration to the lease and non-lease components (using unchanged allocation percentages). The lessee would also not update the discount rate used to measure the lease liability. Therefore, the lessee would remeasure its lease liability, using the remeasured consideration (e.g. reflecting the lease payment reduction or lease payment deferral provided by the lessor), with a corresponding adjustment to the right-of-use asset.

5.5.4.C   Accounting for a concession in the form of a deferral of lease payments as if the lease is unchanged (Approach 3)

When a lessor permits a lessee to defer a lease payment, we believe the lessee may account for the concession by continuing to account for the lease liability and right-of-use asset using the rights and obligations of the existing lease and recognising a separate lease payable (that generally does not accrue interest) in the period that the allocated lease cash payment is due. In this case, the lessee would reduce the lease payable when it makes the lease payment at the revised payment date.

This approach of recording a lease payable for the future payment would allow the lease liability to be accreted using the original incremental borrowing rate and would result in a lease liability balance of zero at the end of the lease term (i.e. the lessee would not need to revisit the accretion of its lease liability based on the revised timing of payments). In many cases, this will allow a lessee to use its existing systems to account for the lease liability using the existing payment schedule and discount rate.

Example 23.23 illustrates how a lessee may account for lease payment forgiveness following Approaches 1 and 2 described above.

Example 23.23: **Lease accounting for covid-19 related rent concessions on a forgiveness of lease payments applying the amendment to IFRS 16**

Restaurant A leases space in a shopping mall from Lessor B. Lessor B classifies the lease as an operating lease.

Under the terms of the lease, Restaurant A makes fixed lease payments of £100 to Lessor B at the beginning of each month. The non-cancellable lease term ends on 28 February 2022. The contract does not include any non-lease components, extension, termination or purchase options. For simplicity, the discount rate is assumed to be 0% at the commencement date and thus the lease liability at 30 June 2020 for the remaining 20 monthly lease payments is £2,000.

Assume that Restaurant A's right-of-use asset is not impaired before or during the periods described.

Due to reduced customer traffic arising from the coronavirus pandemic, on 1 July 2020, Lessor B agrees to waive the three months of lease payments originally due in July, August and September 2020. There are no other changes to the terms and conditions of the lease.

Analysis: Restaurant A first assesses whether the rent concession qualifies for the practical relief provided by IFRS 16. The change in lease payments, granted as a direct consequence of the coronavirus pandemic, results in revised consideration for the lease that is less than the consideration for the lease immediately preceding the change. The reduction in lease payments affects only payments originally due on or before 30 June 2021. As there are no other changes to the terms and conditions of the contract, Restaurant A concludes that the conditions of paragraph 46B are met.

Approach 1 – account for the forgiveness as a negative variable lease payment

On 1 July 2020, Restaurant A treats the concession as an event or condition which triggers a negative variable payment. Restaurant A accounts for the reduction in future lease payments by derecognising the part of the lease liability which has been forgiven and recognising the adjustment in profit or loss.

Dr Lease liability (100 × 3)	£300
Cr Profit or loss	£300

Depreciation of the right-of-use asset continues over the remaining lease term.

Approach 2 – account for the forgiveness as a resolution of a contingency that fixes previously variable lease payments

On 1 July 2020, Restaurant A treats the concession as an event or condition which resolves uncertainty or conditionality on the previous lease payments. Restaurant A accounts for the reduction in future lease payments by derecognising the part of the lease liability which has been forgiven and adjusting the right-of-use asset.

Dr Lease liability (100 × 3)	£300	
Cr Right-of-use asset		£300

To record the reduction in lease liability arising from the rent concession

Depreciation of the revised right-of-use asset continues over the remaining lease term.

Note that if the fact pattern were changed such that the lessee is entitled to a reduction in lease payments for August and September on a month-by-month basis (i.e. if conditions related to the coronavirus pandemic continue to be present the monthly lease liability is contractually forgiven), the reduction in the lease obligation would also be recognised monthly. The corresponding credit to profit and loss or the right-of-use asset would depend on whether Approach 1 or Approach 2 is taken.

Example 23.24 below illustrates how a lessee may account for a lease payment deferral following Approaches 1 to 3 described above.

Example 23.24: Lease accounting for covid-19 related rent concessions on a deferral of lease payments applying the amendment to IFRS 16

Restaurant Y leases space in a shopping mall from Lessor Z.

Under the terms of the lease, Restaurant Y makes fixed lease payments to Lessor Z of £600 semi-annually in arrears. The non-cancellable lease term starts on 1 January 2020 and ends on 30 June 2021. The contract does not include any non-lease components, extension, termination or purchase options. The discount rate is 5% at the commencement date.

As a direct consequence of the coronavirus pandemic, on 1 July 2020, Lessor Z agrees to defer the lease payment originally due on 31 December 2020 to 30 June 2021. There are no other changes to the terms and conditions of the lease.

Assume that Restaurant Y's right-of-use asset is not impaired before or during the periods described.

Analysis: Restaurant Y first assesses whether the rent concession qualifies for the practical relief provided by IFRS 16. The rent concession is granted as a direct consequence of the coronavirus pandemic and results in no substantive change in the lease payments for the lease. The reduction in lease payments affects only payments originally due on or before 30 June 2021. As there are no other changes to the terms and conditions of the contract, Restaurant Y concludes that the conditions of paragraph 46B are met.

Approach 1 – account for the deferral as a negative variable lease payment

On 1 July 2020, Restaurant Y treats the concession as an event or condition which triggers a negative variable payment. Restaurant Y derecognises the part of the lease liability which is the time value of money of the lease payment deferred using the unchanged discount rate with the adjustment in profit or loss.

Lease liability immediately before the rent concession:

Present value of lease payments discounted at 5% = £1,157 ($600 \div (1.05)^{1/2} + 600 \div 1.05$)

Lease liability immediately after the rent concession:

Present value of lease payments discounted at 5% = £1,143 ($1,200 \div 1.05$)

Dr Lease liability (1,157 – 1,143)	£14	
Cr Profit or loss		£14

To record the reduction in lease liability arising from the rent concession

Depreciation of the right-of-use asset continues over the remaining lease term.

Approach 2 – account for the deferral as a resolution of a contingency that fixes previously variable lease payments

The accounting under this approach would be the same as under Approach 1 above, except that the credit of £14 would be recognised as an adjustment to the right-of-use asset, rather than a credit to profit or loss.

Approach 3 – account for the deferral of lease payments as if the lease is unchanged

In this approach, Restaurant Y continues to account for the lease liability and right-of-use asset using the rights and obligations of the existing lease. The lease payment originally due on 31 December 2020 will remain on the balance sheet until it is settled on 30 June 2021, but the amount will not accrue interest during the deferral period. Hence, the interest expense for the six months up to 30 June 2021 will remain the same as in the original amortisation schedule.

Depreciation of the right-of-use asset continues over the remaining lease term.

5.5.4.D Disclosure

A lessee that applies the practical expedient discloses that it has applied the practical expedient to all rent concessions that meet the conditions for it or, if not applied to all such rent concessions, information about the nature of the contracts to which it has applied the practical expedient.

In addition, a lessee discloses the amount recognised in profit or loss to reflect changes in lease payments that arise from such rent concessions to which the lessee has applied the practical expedient. The Basis for Conclusions to the amendment also notes that disclosure of the cash flow effects of rent concessions would be relevant regardless of whether a lessee applies the practical expedient.

As well as providing the specific disclosures required in the amendment, entities should be mindful of the disclosure objectives of IFRS 16 which require lessees to provide adequate disclosure that gives a basis for financial statement users to assess the effect that leases have on the financial position, financial performance and cash flows of the lessee. In addition, lessees need to consider the presentation and disclosure requirements in other standards such as those in IAS 1 – *Presentation of Financial Statements* – when accounting for rent concessions.

5.5.4.E Transition and effective date

Lessees apply the practical expedient retrospectively, recognising the cumulative effect of initially applying the amendment as an adjustment to the opening balance of retained earnings (or other component of equity, as appropriate) at the beginning of the annual reporting period in which the lessee first applies the amendment. In the reporting period in which a lessee first applies the amendment, the lessee is not required to disclose the amount of the adjustment for each financial statement line affected and earnings per share required by paragraph 28(f) of IAS 8.

A lessee applies the amendment for annual reporting periods beginning on or after 1 June 2020. Earlier application is permitted, including in financial statements not yet authorised for issue at 28 May 2020.

5.6 Other lessee matters

5.6.1 Impairment of right-of-use assets

A lessee applies IAS 36 to determine whether the right-of-use asset is impaired and to account for any impairment loss identified. *[IFRS 16.33]*.

IAS 36 requires an impairment indicator analysis at each reporting period. If any indicators are present, the entity is required to estimate the recoverable amount of the asset (or the cash-generating unit of which the asset is a part – the CGU). The entity has to recognise an impairment loss if the recoverable amount of the CGU is less than the carrying amount of the CGU. After an impairment loss is recognised, the adjusted carrying amount of the right-of-use asset would be its new basis for depreciation.

Subsequent reversal of a previously recognised impairment loss needs to be assessed if there is any indication that an impairment loss recognised in prior periods may no longer exist or may have decreased. In recognising any reversal, the increased carrying amount of the asset must not exceed the carrying amount that would have been determined after depreciation, had there been no impairment.

Lessees currently apply the same impairment analysis to assets held under finance leases. This analysis would be new for leases currently accounted for as operating leases and could significantly affect the timing of expense recognition.

5.6.2 Leases denominated in a foreign currency

Lessees apply IAS 21 – *The Effects of Changes in Foreign Exchange Rates* – to leases denominated in a foreign currency. As they do for other monetary liabilities, lessees remeasure the foreign currency-denominated lease liability using the exchange rate at each reporting date. Any changes to the lease liability due to exchange rate changes are recognised in profit or loss. Because the right-of-use asset is a non-monetary asset measured at historical cost, it is not affected by changes in the exchange rate.

The IASB acknowledged in the Basis for Conclusions that this approach could result in volatility in profit or loss from the recognition of foreign currency exchange gains or losses, but it will be clear to users of financial statements that the gains or losses result solely from changes in exchange rates. *[IFRS 16.BC199]*.

5.6.3 Portfolio approach

IFRS 16 specifies the accounting for an individual lease. However, as a practical expedient, an entity may apply it to a portfolio of leases with similar characteristics if the entity reasonably expects that the effects on the financial statements of applying IFRS 16 to the portfolio would not differ materially from applying it to the individual leases within that portfolio. If accounting for a portfolio, an entity uses estimates and assumptions that reflect the size and composition of the portfolio. *[IFRS 16.B1]*.

A decision to use the portfolio approach would be similar to a decision some entities make today to expense, rather than capitalise, certain assets when the accounting difference is, and would continue to be, immaterial to the financial statements.

5.6.4 Income tax accounting

IFRS 16 could affect lessees' accounting for income taxes. For lessees, IFRS 16 requires recognition of lease-related assets and liabilities and could change the measurement of other lease-related assets and liabilities. These changes affect certain aspects of accounting for income taxes such as the following:

(a) recognition and measurement of deferred tax assets and liabilities; and

(b) assessment of the recoverability of deferred tax assets.

Deferred tax assets and liabilities are further discussed in Chapter 33 at 7 and 8.

5.7 Presentation

A lessee presents either in the statement of financial position, or discloses in the notes:

(a) right-of-use assets separately from other assets. If a lessee does not present right-of-use assets separately in the statement of financial position, the lessee:

  (i) includes right-of-use assets within the same line item as that within which the corresponding underlying assets would be presented if they were owned; and

  (ii) discloses which line items in the statement of financial position include those right-of-use assets;

(b) lease liabilities separately from other liabilities. If the lessee does not present lease liabilities separately in the statement of financial position, the lessee discloses which line items in the statement of financial position include those liabilities. *[IFRS 16.47]*.

The requirement above does not apply to right-of-use assets that meet the definition of investment property, which is presented in the statement of financial position as investment property. *[IFRS 16.48]*.

Right-of-use assets and lease liabilities are subject to the same considerations as other assets and liabilities in classifying them as current and non-current in the statement of financial position.

In the statement of profit or loss and other comprehensive income, a lessee presents interest expense on the lease liability separately from the depreciation charge for the right-of-use asset. Interest expense on the lease liability is a component of finance costs, which paragraph 82(b) of IAS 1 requires to be presented separately in the statement of profit or loss and other comprehensive income. *[IFRS 16.49]*.

In the statement of cash flows, a lessee classifies:
(a) cash payments for the principal portion of the lease liability within financing activities;
(b) cash payments for the interest portion of the lease liability applying the requirements in IAS 7 – *Statement of Cash Flows* – for interest paid; and
(c) short-term lease payments, payments for leases of low-value assets and variable lease payments not included in the measurement of the lease liability within operating activities. *[IFRS 16.50]*.

The following table summarises the presentation requirements for lessees.

Financial statement	Lessee presentation
Statement of financial position	Right-of-use assets presented either: • separately from other assets (e.g. owned assets); or • together with other assets as if they were owned, with disclosures of the balance sheet line items that include right-of-use assets and their amounts. Right-of-use assets that meet the definition of investment property are presented as investment property. Lease liabilities presented either: • separately from other liabilities; or • together with other liabilities with disclosure of the balance sheet line items that include lease liabilities and their amounts.
Statement of profit or loss	Lease-related depreciation and lease-related interest expense are presented separately (i.e. lease-related depreciation and lease-related interest expense cannot be combined). Interest expense on the lease liability is a component of finance costs.
Statement of cash flows	Cash payments for the principal portion of the lease liability are presented within financing activities. Cash payments for the interest portion of the lease liability are presented based on an accounting policy election in accordance with IAS 7. Lease payments for short-term leases and leases of low-value assets not recognised on the balance sheet and variable lease payments not included in the lease liability are presented within operating activities. Non-cash activity (e.g. the initial recognition of the lease at commencement) is disclosed as a supplemental non-cash item.

5.8 Disclosure

5.8.1 Disclosure objective

The objective of the disclosures is for lessees to disclose information in the notes that, together with the information provided in the statement of financial position, statement of profit or loss and statement of cash flows, gives a basis for users of financial statements to assess the effect that leases have on the financial position, financial performance and cash flows of the lessee. *[IFRS 16.51]*.

A lessee discloses information about its leases for which it is a lessee in a single note or separate section in its financial statements. However, a lessee need not duplicate information that is already presented elsewhere in the financial statements, provided that the information is incorporated by cross-reference in the single note or separate section about leases. *[IFRS 16.52]*.

5.8.2 Disclosures of assets, liabilities, expenses and cash flows

To meet the disclosure objective, IFRS 16 includes a number of required disclosures.

Paragraph 53 of IFRS 16 includes the following disclosure requirements for lessees, for the reporting period:

(a) depreciation charge for right-of-use assets by class of underlying asset;

(b) interest expense on lease liabilities;

(c) the expense relating to short-term leases. This expense need not include the expense relating to leases with a lease term of one month or less;

(d) the expense relating to leases of low-value assets. This expense does not include the expense relating to short-term leases of low-value assets included in paragraph (c) above;

(e) the expense relating to variable lease payments not included in the measurement of lease liabilities;

(f) income from subleasing right-of-use assets;

(g) total cash outflow for leases;

(h) additions to right-of-use assets;

(i) gains or losses arising from sale and leaseback transactions; and

(j) the carrying amount of right-of-use assets at the end of the reporting period by class of underlying asset. *[IFRS 16.53]*.

A lessee provides the disclosures specified in paragraph 53, as shown above, in a tabular format, unless another format is more appropriate. The amounts disclosed include costs that a lessee has included in the carrying amount of another asset during the reporting period. *[IFRS 16.54]*.

In Extract 23.1 below Deutsche Post presents disclosures of right-of-use assets in the notes to the accounts.

Extract 23.1: Deutsche Post AG (2019)
NOTES TO THE CONSOLIDATED FINANCIAL STATEMENTS OF DEUTSCHE POST AG [extract]
Lease disclosures
40 Lease disclosures

Currency translation gains on lease liabilities totalled €30 million (previous year: €27 million), whilst the related losses amounted to €32 million (previous year: €56 million. The right-of-use assets carried as non-current assets resulting from leases are presented separately in the following table:

Right-of-use assets
€m

	Land and buildings	Technical equipment and machinery	IT systems, operating and office equipment	Aircraft	Transport equipment	Advance payments and assets under development	Total
31 December 2018							
Accumulated cost	9,003	186	9	1,476	731	2	11,407
of which additions	1,801	52	1	341	201	1	2,397
Accumulated depreciation and impairment losses	1,311	54	7	334	198	0	1,904
Carrying amount	7,692	132	2	1,142	533	2	9,503
31 December 2019							
Accumulated cost	10,538	232	9	1,644	866	0	13,289
of which additions	2,125	74	1	292	233	2	2,727
Accumulated depreciation and impairment losses	2,543	88	7	601	343	0	3,582
Carrying amount	7,995	144	2	1,043	523	0	9,707

In the real estate area, the Group primarily leases warehouses, office buildings and mail and parcel centres. The leased aircraft are predominantly deployed in the air network of the Express segment. Leased transport equipment also includes the leased vehicle fleet. The real estate leases in particular are long-term leases. The Group had around 64 real estate leases with remaining lease terms of more than twenty years as at 31 December 2019 (previous year: 65 leases). Aircraft leases have remaining lease terms of up to eleven years. Leases may include extension and termination options, note 6. The leases are negotiated individually and include a wide range of different conditions. Lease liabilities are presented in the following table:
€m

	2018	2019
Non-current lease liabilities	7,756	8,145
Current lease liabilities	2,103	2,156
Total	**9,859**	**10,301**

Financial liabilities under leases of €1,894 million (previous year: €1,722 million) was repaid and interest on leases of €416 million (previous year: €376 million) was paid in financial year 2019. Future cash outflows amounted to €13 billion (previous year: €12 billion) as at the reporting date, note 42.

Possible future cash outflows amounting to €1.5 billion (previous year €1.3 billion) were not included in lease liabilities because it is not reasonably certain that the leases will be extended (or not terminated).

Leases that the Group has entered into as a lessee but that have not yet commenced result in possible future payment outflows totalling €0.2 billion (previous year: €0.4 billion).

A lessee discloses the amount of its lease commitments for short-term leases if the portfolio of short-term leases to which it is committed at the end of the reporting period is dissimilar to the portfolio of short-term leases to which the short-term lease expense disclosed applying paragraph 53(c) of IFRS 16 relates. *[IFRS 16.55]*.

If right-of-use assets meet the definition of investment property, a lessee applies the disclosure requirements in IAS 40. In that case, a lessee is not required to provide the disclosures in paragraph 53(a), (f), (h) or (j) of IFRS 16, for those right-of-use assets. *[IFRS 16.56]*.

If a lessee measures right-of-use assets at revalued amounts applying IAS 16, the lessee discloses the information required by paragraph 77 of IAS 16 for those right-of-use assets. *[IFRS 16.57]*. Those disclosures include the effective date of the revaluation, whether an independent valuer was involved, the carrying amount of the class of asset that would have been recognised under the cost model and the revaluation surplus. These disclosures are discussed further in Chapter 18 at 8.2.

A lessee also discloses a maturity analysis of lease liabilities applying paragraphs 39 and B11 of IFRS 7 – *Financial Instruments: Disclosures* – separately from the maturity analyses of other financial liabilities. *[IFRS 16.58]*. The IASB indicated in the Basis for Conclusions to IFRS 16 that because the lessee accounting model is based on the premise that a lease liability is a financial liability, it is appropriate for lessees to apply the same maturity analysis disclosure requirements to lease liabilities as to those applied to other financial liabilities. *[IFRS 16.BC222]*.

IFRS 16 requires disclosure of the total cash outflow for leases. *[IFRS 16.53(g)]*. It does not explicitly state that leases of low-value assets and short-term leases are excluded. Therefore, we believe the cash outflows related to those leases should be included in the disclosure.

5.8.3 Additional disclosures

In addition to the disclosures described above, a lessee may need to disclose additional qualitative and quantitative information about its leasing activities necessary to meet the disclosure objective discussed at 5.8.1 above. Specifically, additional information relating to variable lease payments, extension options or termination options and residual value guarantees that, depending on the circumstances, may be needed to satisfy the disclosure objective. The additional information may also include, but is not limited to, information that helps users of financial statements to assess:

(a) the nature of the lessee's leasing activities;

(b) future cash outflows to which the lessee is potentially exposed that are not reflected in the measurement of lease liabilities. This includes exposure arising from:
  (i) variable lease payments;
  (ii) extension options and termination options;
  (iii) residual value guarantees; and
  (iv) leases not yet commenced to which the lessee is committed;

(c) restrictions or covenants imposed by leases; and
(d) sale and leaseback transactions. *[IFRS 16.59]*.

In Extract 23.2 below Nestle describe the nature of its leasing activities.

> *Extract 23.2: Nestlé S.A. (2019)*
>
> Notes [extract]
> 8   Property, plant and equipment
> 8.2a Description of lease activities [extract]
>
> **Real estate leases**
> The Group leases land and buildings for its office and warehouse space and retail stores. Lease terms are negotiated on an individual basis and contain a wide range of different terms and conditions. Leases are typically made for a fixed period of 5-15 years and may include extension options which provide operational flexibility. If the Group exercised all extension options not currently included in the lease liability, the additional payments would amount to CHF 0.8 billion (undiscounted) at December 31, 2019.
>
> **Vehicle leases**
> The Group leases trucks for distribution in specific businesses and cars for management and sales functions. The average contract duration is 6 years for trucks and 3 years for cars.
>
> **Other leases**
> The Group also leases Machinery and equipment and Tools, furniture and other equipment that combined are insignificant to the total leased asset portfolio.

In determining whether additional information about leasing activities is necessary to meet the disclosure objective, a lessee is required to consider:

(a) whether that information is relevant to users of financial statements. A lessee provides additional information specified in paragraph 59 of IFRS 16 only if that information is expected to be relevant to users of financial statements. In this context, this is likely to be the case if it helps those users to understand:

  (i) the flexibility provided by leases. Leases may provide flexibility if, for example, a lessee can reduce its exposure by exercising termination options or renewing leases with favourable terms and conditions;

  (ii) restrictions imposed by leases. Leases may impose restrictions, for example, by requiring the lessee to maintain particular financial ratios;

  (iii) sensitivity of reported information to key variables. Reported information may be sensitive to, for example, future variable lease payments;

  (iv) exposure to other risks arising from leases; and

  (v) deviations from industry practice. Such deviations may include, for example, unusual or unique lease terms and conditions that affect a lessee's lease portfolio; and

(b) whether that information is apparent from information either presented in the primary financial statements or disclosed in the notes. A lessee need not duplicate information that is already presented elsewhere in the financial statements. *[IFRS 16.B48]*.

Additional information relating to variable lease payments that, depending on the circumstances, may be needed to satisfy the disclosure objective (see 5.8.1 above) could include information that helps users of financial statements to assess, for example:

(a) the lessee's reasons for using variable lease payments and the prevalence of those payments;
(b) the relative magnitude of variable lease payments to fixed payments;
(c) key variables upon which variable lease payments depend and how payments are expected to vary in response to changes in those key variables; and
(d) other operational and financial effects of variable lease payments. *[IFRS 16.B49]*.

Additional information relating to extension options or termination options that, depending on the circumstances, may be needed to satisfy the disclosure objective (see 5.8.1 above) could include information that helps users of financial statements to assess, for example:

(a) the lessee's reasons for using extension options or termination options and the prevalence of those options;
(b) the relative magnitude of optional lease payments to lease payments;
(c) the prevalence of the exercise of options that were not included in the measurement of lease liabilities; and
(d) other operational and financial effects of those options. *[IFRS 16.B50]*.

Optional lease payments are payments made by a lessee to a lessor for the right to use an underlying asset during periods covered by an option to extend or terminate a lease that are not included in the lease term. *[IFRS 16 Appendix A]*.

Additional information relating to residual value guarantees that, depending on the circumstances, may be needed to satisfy the disclosure objective (see 5.8.1 above) could include information that helps users of financial statements to assess, for example:

(a) the lessee's reasons for providing residual value guarantees and the prevalence of those guarantees;
(b) the magnitude of a lessee's exposure to residual value risk;
(c) the nature of underlying assets for which those guarantees are provided; and
(d) other operational and financial effects of those guarantees. *[IFRS 16.B51]*.

5.8.4 Disclosures required by IAS 1

In addition to the disclosure requirements under IFRS 16 described above, an entity is required to make disclosures in accordance with IAS 1. An entity is required to disclose its significant accounting policies comprising:

(a) the measurement basis (or bases) used in preparing the financial statements; and
(b) the other accounting policies used that are relevant to an understanding of the financial statements. *[IAS 1.117]*.

An entity discloses, along with its significant accounting policies or other notes, the judgements, apart from those involving estimations (see below), that management has made in the process of applying the entity's accounting policies and that have the most significant effect on the amounts recognised in the financial statements. *[IAS 1.122]*. An entity discloses information about the assumptions it makes about the future, and other major sources of estimation uncertainty at the end of the reporting period, that have a significant risk of resulting in a material adjustment to the carrying amounts of assets and liabilities within the next financial year. In respect of those assets and liabilities, the notes include details of:

(a)   their nature, and

(b)   their carrying amount as at the end of the reporting period. *[IAS 1.125]*.

There are a number of judgements and estimates that entities may make in applying IFRS 16, which may require disclosure in accordance with IAS 1. These include, but are not limited to, application of the definition of a lease, determination of the lease term and determination of the incremental borrowing rate.

6   LESSOR ACCOUNTING

IFRS 16 substantially carries forward the lessor accounting model in IAS 17. The significant differences between the lessor accounting requirements in IFRS 16 and those in IAS 17 are primarily a consequence of decisions reached about the lessee accounting model in IFRS 16. IFRS 16 does change certain aspects of the lessor accounting model, including changes to the accounting for subleases, initial direct costs and lessor disclosures.

6.1   Lease classification

At inception date of the lease, a lessor classifies each of its leases as either an operating lease or a finance lease. *[IFRS 16.61]*. The classification of leases under IFRS 16 is the same as under IAS 17. A lease is classified as a finance lease if it transfers substantially all the risks and rewards incidental to ownership of an underlying asset. A lease is classified as an operating lease if it does not transfer substantially all the risks and rewards of ownership of an underlying asset. *[IFRS 16.62]*.

6.1.1   Criteria for lease classification

The classification of leases is based on the extent to which the lease transfers the risks and rewards incidental to ownership of an underlying asset. Risks include the possibilities of losses from idle capacity or technological obsolescence and of variations in return because of changing economic conditions. Rewards may be represented by the expectation of profitable operation over the underlying asset's economic life and of gain from appreciation in value or realisation of a residual value. *[IFRS 16.B53]*.

Whether a lease is a finance lease or an operating lease depends on the substance of the transaction rather than the form of the contract. Examples of situations that individually or in combination would normally lead to a lease being classified as a finance lease are:

(a) the lease transfers ownership of the underlying asset to the lessee by the end of the lease term;

(b) the lessee has the option to purchase the underlying asset at a price that is expected to be sufficiently lower than the fair value at the date the option becomes exercisable for it to be reasonably certain, at the inception date, that the option will be exercised;

(c) the lease term is for the major part of the economic life of the underlying asset even if title is not transferred;

(d) at the inception date, the present value of the lease payments amounts to at least substantially all of the fair value of the underlying asset; and

(e) the underlying asset is of such a specialised nature that only the lessee can use it without major modifications. *[IFRS 16.63]*.

IFRS 16 does not provide quantitative indicators or thresholds for the assessment of the terms 'major part' and 'substantially all' to determine that a lease should be classified as a finance lease rather than as an operating lease. Under IFRS 16 entities apply qualitative, rather than quantitative assessments to determine whether the risks and rewards incident to ownership of a leased asset lie with the lessor or the lessee. Accordingly, assessing whether a lease term is for the major part of the economic life of an asset or whether the present value of the minimum lease payments amounts to at least substantially all of the fair value of a leased asset is a matter of judgement.

Indicators of situations that individually or in combination could also lead to a lease being classified as a finance lease are:

(a) if the lessee can cancel the lease, the lessor's losses associated with the cancellation are borne by the lessee;

(b) gains or losses from the fluctuation in the fair value of the residual accrue to the lessee (for example, in the form of a rent rebate equalling most of the sales proceeds at the end of the lease); and

(c) the lessee has the ability to continue the lease for a secondary period at a rent that is substantially lower than market rent. *[IFRS 16.64]*.

The examples and indicators above are not always conclusive. If it is clear from other features that the lease does not transfer substantially all the risks and rewards incidental to ownership of an underlying asset, the lease is classified as an operating lease. For example, this may be the case if ownership of the underlying asset transfers at the end of the lease for a variable payment equal to its then fair value, or if there are variable lease payments, as a result of which the lessor does not transfer substantially all such risks and rewards. *[IFRS 16.65]*.

In our view, other considerations that could be made in determining the economic substance of the lease arrangement include the following:

(a) Are the lease rentals based on a market rate for use of the asset (which would indicate an operating lease) or a financing rate for use of the funds, which would be indicative of a finance lease?

(b) Is the existence of put and call options a feature of the lease? If so, are they exercisable at a predetermined price or formula (indicating a finance lease) or are they exercisable at the market price at the time the option is exercised (indicating an operating lease)?

A lease contract may include terms and conditions to adjust the lease payments for particular changes that occur between the inception date and the commencement date (such as a change in the lessor's cost of the underlying asset or a change in the lessor's cost of financing the lease). In that case, for the purposes of classifying the lease, the effect of any such changes is deemed to have taken place at the inception date. [IFRS 16.B54].

6.1.2 Lease classification test for land and buildings

When a lease includes both land and buildings elements, a lessor assesses the classification of each element as a finance lease or an operating lease separately. In determining whether the land element is an operating lease or a finance lease, an important consideration is that land normally has an indefinite economic life. [IFRS 16.B55].

Whenever necessary in order to classify and account for a lease of land and buildings, a lessor allocates lease payments (including any lump-sum upfront payments) between the land and the buildings elements in proportion to the relative fair values of the leasehold interests in the land element and buildings element of the lease at the inception date. If the lease payments cannot be allocated reliably between these two elements, the entire lease is classified as a finance lease, unless it is clear that both elements are operating leases, in which case the entire lease is classified as an operating lease. [IFRS 16.B56].

For a lease of land and buildings in which the amount for the land element is immaterial to the lease, a lessor may treat the land and buildings as a single unit for the purpose of lease classification and classify it as a finance lease or an operating lease. In such a case, a lessor regards the economic life of the buildings as the economic life of the entire underlying asset. [IFRS 16.B57].

6.1.3 Residual value guarantees included in the lease classification test

In evaluating IFRS 16's lease classification criteria, lessors are required to include in the 'substantially all' test any (i.e. the maximum obligation) residual value guarantees provided by both lessees and any other third party unrelated to the lessor.

6.1.4 Reassessment of lease classification

Lease classification is made at the inception date and is reassessed only if there is a lease modification. Changes in estimates (for example, changes in estimates of the economic life or of the residual value of the underlying asset), or changes in circumstances (for example, default by the lessee), do not give rise to a new classification of a lease for accounting purposes. [IFRS 16.66].

Lessors reassess lease classification as at the effective date of the modification using the modified conditions at that date. Lease modifications are discussed at 6.4 below. If a lease modification results in a separate new lease, that new lease would be classified in the same manner as any new lease. See 6.1.1 above.

6.2 Finance leases

At commencement date, a lessor recognises assets held under a finance lease in its statement of financial position and presents them as a receivable at an amount equal to the net investment in the lease. *[IFRS 16.67]*.

The net investment in the lease is defined as 'the gross investment in the lease discounted at the interest rate implicit in the lease'. *[IFRS 16 Appendix A]*. The gross investment in the lease is 'the sum of (a) the lease payments receivable by a lessor under a finance lease and (b) any unguaranteed residual value accruing to the lessor.' *[IFRS 16 Appendix A]*.

Example 23.25: The lessor's gross and net investment in the lease

Details of a non-cancellable lease are as follows:

- The asset has a fair value of CU10,000
- The lessee is required to make five annual rentals payable in advance of CU2,100
- The unguaranteed estimated residual value at the end of five years is CU1,000.

The lessor's direct costs have been excluded for simplicity.

The interest rate implicit in the lease is that which gives a present value of CU10,000 for the five rentals plus the total estimated residual value at the end of year 5. This rate of 6.62% is calculated as follows:

Year	Receivable at start of period CU	Rental received CU	Finance income (6.62% per annum) CU	Gross investment at end of period CU	Gross earnings allocated to future periods CU	Receivable at end of period CU
1	10,000	2,100	523	9,400	977	8,423
2	8,423	2,100	419	7,300	558	6,742
3	6,742	2,100	307	5,200	251	4,949
4	4,949	2,100	189	3,100	62	3,038
5	3,038	2,100	62	1,000	–	1,000
		10,500	1,500			

The lessor's gross investment in the lease is the total rent receivable of CU10,500 and the unguaranteed residual value of CU1,000. The gross earnings are therefore CU1,500. The initial carrying value of the receivable is its fair value of CU10,000, which is also the present value of the gross investment discounted at the interest rate implicit in the lease of 6.62%.

The gross investment in the lease at any point in time comprises the aggregate of the rentals receivable in future periods and the unguaranteed residual value, e.g. at the end of year 2, the gross investment of CU7,300 is three years' rental of CU2,100 plus the unguaranteed residual of CU1,000. The net investment, which is the amount at which the debtor will be recorded in the statement of financial position, is CU7,300 less the earnings allocated to future periods of CU558 = CU6,742.

6.2.1 Initial measurement

At lease commencement, a lessor accounts for a finance lease, as follows:

(a) derecognises the carrying amount of the underlying asset;
(b) recognises the net investment in the lease; and
(c) recognises, in profit or loss, any selling profit or selling loss.

The lessor uses the interest rate implicit in the lease to measure the net investment in the lease. In the case of a sublease, if the interest rate implicit in the sublease cannot be readily determined, an intermediate lessor may use the discount rate used for the head lease (adjusted for any initial direct costs associated with the sublease) to measure the net investment in the sublease. *[IFRS 16.68]*.

Initial direct costs, other than those incurred by manufacturer or dealer lessors, are included in the initial measurement of the net investment in the lease and reduce the amount of income recognised over the lease term. The interest rate implicit in the lease is defined in such a way that the initial direct costs are included automatically in the net investment in the lease; there is no need to add them separately. *[IFRS 16.69]*.

At the commencement date, the lease payments included in the measurement of the net investment in the lease comprise the following payments for the right to use the underlying asset during the lease term that are not received at the commencement date:

(a) fixed payments (including in-substance fixed payments), less any lease incentives payable;
(b) variable lease payments that depend on an index or a rate, initially measured using the index or rate as at the commencement date;
(c) any residual value guarantees provided to the lessor by the lessee, a party related to the lessee or a third party unrelated to the lessor that is financially capable of discharging the obligations under the guarantee;
(d) the exercise price of a purchase option if the lessee is reasonably certain to exercise that option; and
(e) payments of penalties for terminating the lease, if the lease term reflects the lessee exercising an option to terminate the lease. *[IFRS 16.70]*.

6.2.2 Manufacturer or dealer lessors

At the commencement date, a manufacturer or dealer lessor recognises the following for each of its finance leases:

(a) revenue being the fair value of the underlying asset, or, if lower, the present value of the lease payments accruing to the lessor, discounted using a market rate of interest;
(b) the cost of sale being the cost, or carrying amount if different, of the underlying asset less the present value of the unguaranteed residual value; and
(c) selling profit or loss (being the difference between revenue and the cost of sale) in accordance with its policy for outright sales to which IFRS 15 applies. A manufacturer or dealer lessor recognises selling profit or loss on a finance lease at the commencement date, regardless of whether the lessor transfers the underlying asset as described in IFRS 15. *[IFRS 16.71]*.

Manufacturers or dealers often offer to customers the choice of either buying or leasing an asset. A finance lease of an asset by a manufacturer or dealer lessor gives rise to profit or loss equivalent to that resulting from an outright sale of the underlying asset, at normal selling prices, reflecting any applicable volume or trade discounts. *[IFRS 16.72].*

Manufacturer or dealer lessors sometimes quote artificially low rates of interest in order to attract customers. The use of such a rate would result in a lessor recognising an excessive portion of the total income from the transaction at the commencement date. If artificially low rates of interest are quoted, a manufacturer or dealer lessor restricts selling profit to that which would apply if a market rate of interest were charged. *[IFRS 16.73].*

A manufacturer or dealer lessor recognises as an expense costs incurred in connection with obtaining a finance lease at the commencement date because they are mainly related to earning the manufacturer or dealer's selling profit. Costs incurred by manufacturer or dealer lessors in connection with obtaining a finance lease are excluded from the definition of initial direct costs and, thus, are excluded from the net investment in the lease. *[IFRS 16.74].*

Example 23.26: Manufacturer or dealer lessors

A company manufactures specialised machinery. The company offers customers the choice of either buying or leasing the machinery. A customer chooses to lease the machinery. Details of the arrangement are as follows:

(i) The lease commences on 1 January 20X1 and lasts for three years.

(ii) The lessee is required to make three annual rentals payable in arrears of €57,500.

(iii) The leased machinery is returned to the lessor at the end of the lease.

(iv) The fair value of the machinery is CU150,000, which is equivalent to the selling price of the machinery.

(v) The machinery cost CU100,000 to manufacture. The lessor incurred costs of CU2,500 to negotiate and arrange the lease.

(vi) The expected useful life of the machinery is 3 years. The machinery has an expected residual value of CU10,000 at the end of year three. The estimated residual value does not change over the term of the lease.

(vii) The interest rate implicit in the lease is 10.19%.

The lessor classifies the lease as a finance lease.

The cost to the lessor of providing the machinery for lease consists of the book value of the machinery (CU100,000), plus the initial direct costs associated with entering into the lease (CU2,500), less the future income expected from disposing of the machinery at the end of the lease (the present value of the unguaranteed residual value of CU10,000, being CU7,475). This gives a cost of sale of CU95,025.

The lessor records the following entries at the commencement of the lease:

	Debit CU	Credit CU
Lease receivable	150,000	
Cost of sales	95,025	
Inventory		100,000
Revenue		142,525
Creditors / cash (initial direct costs)		2,500

The sales profit recognised by the lessor at the commencement of the lease is therefore CU47,500 (CU142,525 − CU95,025). This is equal to the fair value of the machinery of CU150,000, less the book value of the machinery (CU100,000) and the initial direct costs of entering into the lease (CU2,500). Revenue is equal to the lease receivable (CU150,000), less the present value of the unguaranteed residual value (CU7,475).

Lease payments received from the lessee will then be allocated over the lease term as follows:

Year	Lease receivable at the start of the year (CU)	Lease payments (CU)	Interest income (10.19% per annum) (CU)	Decrease in lease receivable (CU)	Lease receivable at the end of the year (CU)
	(a)	(b)	(c)	(d)=(b)–(c)	(e)=(a)–(d)
1	150,000	57,500	15,280	42,220	107,780
2	107,780	57,500	10,979	46,521	61,260
3	61,260	57,500	6,240	51,260	10,000

The lessor will record the following entries:

		Debit CU	Credit CU
Year 1	Cash	57,500	
	Lease receivable		42,220
	Interest income		15,280

		Debit CU	Credit CU
Year 2	Cash	57,500	
	Lease receivable		46,521
	Interest income		10,979
Year 3	Cash	57,500	
	Lease receivable		51,260
	Interest income		6,240

At the end of the three-year lease term, the leased machinery will be returned to the lessor, who will record the following entries:

Inventory	10,000	
Lease receivable		10,000

6.2.3 Subsequent measurement

After commencement a lessor recognises finance income over the lease term, based on a pattern reflecting a constant periodic rate of return on the lessor's net investment in the lease. *[IFRS 16.75]*. A lessor aims to allocate finance income over the lease term on a systematic and rational basis. A lessor applies the lease payments relating to the period against the gross investment in the lease to reduce both the principal and the unearned finance income. *[IFRS 16.76]*. Thus, the lessor reduces the net investment in the lease for lease payments received (net of interest income calculated above).

The lessor also recognises income from variable payments that are not included in the net investment in the lease (e.g. performance or usage based variable payments) separately in the period in which the income is earned.

A lessor applies the derecognition and impairment requirements in IFRS 9 to the net investment in the lease. The lessor reviews regularly estimated unguaranteed residual values used in computing the gross investment in the lease. If there has been a reduction in the estimated unguaranteed residual value, the lessor revises the income allocation over the lease term and recognise immediately any reduction in respect of amounts accrued. *[IFRS 16.77]*.

The question arises as to whether the finance income should be calculated based on the gross lease receivable or the net amount of the lease receivable less any expected credit loss? We believe the staging approach[6] in IFRS 9 (see Chapter 51 at 3.1) can be applied to determine how finance income recognised over the lease term is calculated:

- on a gross basis (excluding the effect of expected credit losses) for lease receivables in stages 1 or 2 of the expected credit loss model in IFRS 9), and
- on a net basis (based on the net investment in the lease less expected credit losses) for lease receivables in stage 3 of the expected credit loss model in IFRS 9).

The election (or non-election) of the simplified approach allowed by IFRS 9 does not affect this conclusion.

In the absence of prescriptive guidance in IFRS, entities may apply the above accounting as an accounting policy choice. Alternative approaches may also be acceptable.

Credit losses should be presented separately in the income statement in accordance with paragraph 82 of IAS 1.

The net investment in the lease should generally be presented net of the loss allowance. However, a separate presentation of the net investment in the lease, gross of the lease allowance and the loss allowance itself may be appropriate when the presentation is relevant to understanding the entity's financial position. For example, where the loss allowance has significantly reduced an otherwise material net investment in the lease.

A lessor that classifies an asset under a finance lease as held for sale (or includes it in a disposal group that is classified as held for sale) applies IFRS 5 – *Non-current Assets Held for Sale and Discontinued Operations*. [IFRS 16.78].

Example 23.27: Lessor accounting for a finance lease

Assume Lessor enters into a 10-year lease of equipment with Lessee. The equipment is not specialised in nature and is expected to have alternative use to Lessor at the end of the 10-year lease term. Under the lease:

- Lessor receives annual lease payments of CU15,000, payable at the end of the year.
- Lessor expects the residual value of the equipment to be CU50,000 at the end of the 10-year lease term.
- Lessee provides a residual value guarantee that protects Lessor from the first CU30,000 of loss for a sale at a price below the estimated residual value at the end of the lease term (i.e. CU50,000).
- The equipment has an estimated remaining economic life of 15 years, a carrying amount of CU100,000 and a fair value of CU111,000.
- The lease does not transfer ownership of the underlying asset to Lessee at the end of the lease term or contain an option to purchase the underlying asset.
- The interest rate implicit in the lease is 10.078%.

Lessor classifies the lease as a finance lease because the sum of the present value of lease payments amounts to substantially all of the fair value of the underlying asset.

At lease commencement, Lessor accounts for the finance lease, as follows:

To record the net investment in the finance lease and derecognise the underlying asset:

Dr. Net investment in the lease	CU111,000 (a)	
Dr. Cost of goods sold	CU92,344 (b)	
Cr. Revenue		CU103,344 (c)
Cr. Property held for lease		CU100,000 (d)

(a) The net investment in the lease consists of (1) the present value of the 10 annual payments of CU15,000 plus the guaranteed residual value of CU30,000, both discounted at the interest rate implicit in the lease, which equals CU103,344 (i.e. the lease payment) and (2) the present value of unguaranteed residual asset of CU20,000, which equals CU7,656. Note that the net investment in the lease is subject to the same considerations as other assets in classification as current or non-current assets in a classified balance sheet (see 6.6 below).

(b) Cost of goods sold is the carrying amount of the equipment of CU100,000 less the present value of the unguaranteed residual asset of CU7,656.

(c) Revenue equals the lease receivable.

(d) The carrying amount of the underlying asset.

At lease commencement, Lessor recognises selling profit of CU11,000 which is calculated as revenue (i.e. the lease payments of CU103,344) less the cost of goods sold which is the carrying amount of the asset (CU100,000), net of any unguaranteed residual asset (CU7,656), which equals CU92,344.

Year 1 journal entries for a finance lease:

Dr. Cash	CU15,000 (a)	
Cr. Net investment in the lease		CU3,813 (b)
Cr. Interest income		CU11,187 (c)

(a) Receipt of annual lease payments at the end of the year.

(b) Reduction of the net investment in the lease for lease payments received of (CU15,000), net of interest income of CU11,187.

(c) Interest income is the amount that produces a constant periodic discount rate on the remaining balance of the net investment in the lease. See computation below.

The following table summarises the interest income from this lease and the related amortisations of the net investment over the lease term:

Year	Annual rental payment	Annual interest income (a)	Net investment at end of year
Initial net investment	CU –	CU –	CU 111,000
1	15,000	11,187	107,187
2	15,000	10,803	102,990
3	15,000	10,380	98,370
4	15,000	9,914	93,284
5	15,000	9,401	87,685
6	15,000	8,837	81,522
7	15,000	8,216	74,738
8	15,000	7,532	67,270
9	15,000	6,780	59,050
10	15,000	5,950	(b) 50,000

(a) Interest income equals 10.078% of the net investment in the lease at the beginning of each year. For example, Year 1 annual interest income is calculated as (CU111,000 initial net investment × 10.078%).

(b) The estimated residual value of the equipment at the end of the lease term.

6.2.3.A Unguaranteed residual values

Income recognition by lessors can be extremely sensitive to the amount recognised as the asset's residual value. This is because the amount of the residual directly affects the computation of the amount of finance income earned over the lease term – this is illustrated in Example 23.28 below. The standard gives no guidance regarding the estimation of unguaranteed residual values, but it does require them to be reviewed regularly. If there has been a reduction in the estimated value, the income allocation over the lease term is revised and any reduction in respect of amounts accrued is recognised immediately. *[IFRS 16.77]*.

Example 23.28: Reduction in residual value

Details of a non-cancellable lease are as follows:
- The asset has a fair value of €10,000.
- The lessee is required to make five annual rentals payable in advance of €2,100.
- The unguaranteed estimated residual value at the end of five years is €1,000.

The lessor's direct costs have been excluded for simplicity.

Year	Receivable at start of period €	Rental received €	Finance income (6.62% per annum) €	Gross investment at end of period €	Gross earnings allocated to future periods €	Receivable at end of period €
1	10,000	2,100	523	9,400	977	8,423
2	8,423	2,100	419	7,300	558	6,742
3	6,742	2,100	307	5,200	251	4,949
4	4,949	2,100	189	3,100	62	3,038
5	3,038	2,100	62	1,000	–	1,000
		10,500	1,500			

The gross investment in the lease at any point in time comprises the aggregate of the rentals receivable in future periods and the unguaranteed residual value, e.g. at the end of year 2, the gross investment of €7,300 is three years' rental of €2,100 plus the unguaranteed residual of €1,000. The net investment, which is the amount that will be recorded in the statement of financial position, is €7,300 less the earnings allocated to future periods of €558 = €6,742. The gross earnings allocated to future periods is the total finance income of €1,500 less the finance income already recognised.

The lessor concludes at the end of year 2 that the residual value of the asset is only €500 and revises the income allocation over the lease term accordingly.

Year	Receivable at start of period €	Rental received €	Finance income (6.62% per annum) €	Gross investment at end of period* €	Gross earnings allocated to future periods €	Receivable at end of period €
2	8,423	2,100	419	6,800	471	6,329
3	6,329	2,100	280	4,700	191	4,509
4	4,509	2,100	160	2,600	31	2,569
5	2,569	2,100	31	500	–	500

* The gross investment in the lease now takes account of the revised unguaranteed residual of €500, rather than the original €1,000.

The lessor will have to write off €413, being the difference between the carrying amount of the receivable and the revised balance above (€6,742 – €6,329). This is the present value as at the end of year 2 of €500 and represents the part of the unguaranteed residual written off.

6.2.4 Remeasurement of the net investment in the lease

After lease commencement, the net investment in a lease is remeasured when:
- the lease is modified (i.e. a change in the scope of the lease, or the consideration for the lease, that was not part of the original terms and conditions of the lease) and the modified lease is not accounted for as a separate contract (see 6.4 below); or

- the lease term is revised when there is a change in the non-cancellable period of the lease (see 4.4 above); or
- there is a change in the estimated unguaranteed residual value (see 6.2.3.A above).

A lessor includes in its initial measurement of the net investment in the lease, variable lease payments that depend on an index or rate. IFRS 16 is silent on the accounting for any subsequent changes in future cash flows resulting from a change in an index or rate or variable lease payments becoming in-substance fixed. In the absence of further guidance, we believe lessors have an accounting policy choice regarding whether variable lease payments that do not depend on an index or rate are remeasured.

6.3 Operating leases

Under IFRS 16, lessors account for operating leases in a manner similar to the requirements under IAS 17. That is, they continue to recognise the underlying asset and do not recognise a net investment in the lease on the balance sheet or initial profit (if any) on the income statement. The underlying asset continues to be accounted for in accordance with applicable accounting standards (e.g. IAS 16).

Lessors recognise lease payments as income on either a straight-line basis or another systematic basis if that basis is more representative of the pattern in which benefit derived from the use of the underlying asset is diminished. *[IFRS 16.81]*. After lease commencement, lessors recognise variable lease payments that do not depend on an index or rate (e.g. performance- or usage-based payments) as they are earned. If the lessor pays the lessee an incentive to enter the lease, this is accounted for as described in 4.5.2 above.

A lessor recognises costs, including depreciation, incurred in earning the lease income as an expense. *[IFRS 16.82]*. A lessor adds initial direct costs incurred in obtaining an operating lease to the carrying amount of the underlying asset and recognises those costs as an expense over the lease term on the same basis as the lease income. *[IFRS 16.83]*.

The depreciation policy for depreciable underlying assets subject to operating leases must be consistent with the lessor's normal depreciation policy for similar assets. A lessor calculates depreciation in accordance with IAS 16 and IAS 38. *[IFRS 16.84]*. A lessor applies IAS 36 to determine whether an underlying asset subject to an operating lease is impaired and to account for any impairment loss identified. *[IFRS 16.85]*.

A manufacturer or dealer lessor does not recognise any selling profit on entering into an operating lease because it is not the equivalent of a sale. *[IFRS 16.86]*.

6.3.1 Operating lease income

Unlike other standards such as IFRS 15, IFRS 16 does not refer to collectability to determine whether (and when) lease income should be recognised. Therefore, we believe that a lessor may continue to recognise operating lease income even when collectability is not probable. However, other approaches may also be appropriate when there is significant doubt about collectability. Therefore, there could be diversity in practice, and it is important to consider the views of local regulators. Regardless of the approach followed, IFRS 9's guidance on credit losses continues to be applicable to recognised lease receivables (see Chapter 51 at 10.2).

Example 23.29: Operating lease income not expected to be fully collectible

Restaurant A leases space in a shopping mall from Lessor B. Lessor B classifies the lease as an operating lease.

Under the terms of the lease, Restaurant A makes fixed lease payments of $100 to Lessor B at the beginning of each month. The non-cancellable lease term ends on 28 February 2022. The contract does not include any non-lease components, extension, termination or purchase options. For simplicity, the discount rate is assumed to be 0% at the commencement date.

Due to significant financial difficulties, at the end of June, Restaurant A has indicated that it will only pay 25% of the lease receivable due for the month of July 2020. Up to 31 July 2020, $25 has been collected and Lessor B does not expect the remaining amount of $75 due in respect of July to be recovered considering Restaurant A's financial condition.

Analysis

Approach 1 – Recognising the full operating lease income

Lessor B recognises the full operating lease income on a straight-line basis of $100 per month in accordance with paragraph 81 of IFRS 16.

Lessor B recognises a lease receivable and an impairment loss of $75 reflecting the remote likelihood of collection in accordance with IFRS 9.

Under this approach, Lessor B records the following entries:

Dr Lease receivable	$100	
Cr Operating lease income		$100
To record the operating lease income and lease receivable for July 2020		
Dr Cash	$25	
Cr Lease receivable		$25
To record receipt of $25 from the lessee		
Dr Impairment loss on lease receivable	$75	
Cr Impairment allowance on lease receivable		$75
To record an impairment loss against the lease receivable		

Approach 2 – Recognition of operating lease income to the extent collectable

Under this approach, Lessor B accounts for the monthly lease income to the extent collectable. This approach reflects the high uncertainty related to the collectability of the full lease payments and Lessor B's concerns about the appropriateness of reporting income when the likelihood of collecting the full amount is considered to be remote.

Under this approach, Lessor B records the following entries:

Dr Lease receivable	$25	
Cr Operating lease income		$25
To record the operating lease income for July 2020		
Dr Cash	$25	
Cr Lease receivable		$25
To record receipt of $25 from the lessee		

6.4 Lease modifications

A lease modification is a change in the scope of a lease, or the consideration for a lease, that was not part of the original terms and conditions of the lease (for example, adding or terminating the right to use one or more underlying assets, or extending or shortening the contractual lease term). *[IFRS 16 Appendix A].*

If a lease is modified, the modified contract is evaluated to determine whether it is or contains a lease (see 3.1 above). If a lease continues to exist, the lease modification can result in:
- a separate lease (see 6.4.1 below); or
- a change in the accounting for the existing lease (i.e. not a separate lease) (see 6.4.2 and 6.4.3 below).

6.4.1 Determining whether a modification to a finance lease results in a separate lease

A lessor accounts for a modification to a finance lease as a separate lease if both:
(a) the modification increases the scope of the lease by adding the right to use one or more underlying assets; and
(b) the consideration for the lease increases by an amount commensurate with the stand-alone price for the increase in scope and any appropriate adjustments to that stand-alone price to reflect the circumstances of the particular contract. [IFRS 16.79].

If both of the conditions above are met, the lease modification results in two separate leases, the unmodified original finance lease and a separate lease. Lessors account for the separate lease in the same manner as other new leases. If either of the conditions is not met, the lease modification does not result in a separate lease.

6.4.2 Lessor accounting for a modification to a finance lease that does not result in a separate lease

For a modification to a finance lease that is not accounted for as a separate lease, a lessor accounts for the modification as follows:
(a) if the lease would have been classified as an operating lease had the modification been in effect at the inception date, the lessor:
    (i) accounts for the lease modification as a new lease from the effective date of the modification; and
    (ii) measures the carrying amount of the underlying asset as the net investment in the lease immediately before the effective date of the lease modification;
(b) otherwise, the lessor applies the requirements of IFRS 9. [IFRS 16.80].

6.4.3 Modification to an operating lease

A lessor accounts for a modification to an operating lease as a new lease from the effective date of the modification, considering any prepaid or accrued lease payments relating to the original lease as part of the lease payments for the new lease. [IFRS 16.87].

Accounting for the new lease includes identifying and separating the lease and non-lease components of the contract as discussed at 3.2 above.

Example 23.30 shows how the modification guidance is applied for a concession that involves the forgiveness of future lease payments.

Example 23.30: Forgiveness of future lease payments of an operating lease

Restaurant A leases space in a shopping mall from Lessor B. Lessor B classifies the lease as an operating lease.

Under the terms of the lease, Restaurant A makes fixed lease payments of €100 to Lessor B at the beginning of each month. The non-cancellable lease term ends on 28 February 2022. The contract does not include any non-lease components, extension, termination or purchase options. For simplicity, the discount rate is assumed to be 0% at the commencement date.

All lease payments due up to 30 June 2020 have been received in a timely manner. On 30 June 2020, in compensation for the closure of the shopping mall, Lessor B agrees to forgive Restaurant A's future lease payments for the months of July, August and September 2020.

Analysis: The rent concession results in a decrease in the total lease payments. Thus, there has been a change in the consideration for a lease that was not part of the original terms and conditions of the contract. Therefore, the rent concession constitutes a lease modification. The modification does not change the classification of the lease as an operating lease.

On the effective date of the modification (i.e. 30 June 2020), Lessor B accounts for the modification as a new lease, as follows:

- The remaining lease payments under the modified lease comprise €1,700 (lease payments of €100 per month from October 2020 to February 2022).
- The remaining lease term is 20 months.

The monthly operating lease income to be recognised over the remaining lease term is therefore €1,700 ÷ 20 months = €85.

In some cases, a lessor may forgive past lease payments that are recognised as a lease receivable in an operating lease. The rent concession results in a change in the consideration for the lease that was not part of the original terms of the lease and therefore may be viewed as a lease modification. An alternative view may be to consider that the forgiveness of the past lease payments is an extinguishment of the operating lease receivable and the derecognition requirements of IFRS 9 apply. Paragraph 2.1(b)(i) of IFRS 9 clarifies that operating lease receivables recognised by a lessor are subject to the derecognition and impairment requirements of IFRS 9. When IFRS 9 is applied in these situations, we believe the lessor has an accounting policy choice, to be applied consistently, to either include or exclude the expected forgiveness of lease payments in the ECL assessment of operating lease receivables (see Chapter 51 at 10.2 and 14.1.1). The approaches applying IFRS 9 and IFRS 16 are illustrated below.

Example 23.31: Waiver of a lease receivable in an operating lease

Restaurant A leases space in a shopping mall from Lessor B. Lessor B classifies the lease as an operating lease.

Under the terms of the lease, Restaurant A makes fixed lease payments of US$100 to Lessor B at the beginning of each month. The non-cancellable lease term ends on 28 February 2022. The contract does not include any non-lease components, extension, termination or purchase options. For simplicity, the discount rate is assumed to be 0% at the commencement date.

Due to financial difficulties, Restaurant A did not pay the lease payment for June 2020. Consequently, Lessor B recognised, in accordance with IFRS 9, an impairment loss of US$20 on 30 June 2020, which takes into consideration the collateral in the contract.

On 1 July 2020, Lessor B grants a rent concession that waives US$60 of the outstanding amount for June 2020. The remaining amount (US$40) is paid shortly after.

Analysis

Approach 1 – Lease modification under IFRS 16.

The rent concession results in a decrease in the total lease payments and, thus, there has been a change in the consideration for a lease that was not part of the original terms and conditions of the contract. Therefore, the rent concession constitutes a lease modification. Assume the modification does not change the classification of the lease as an operating lease.

Lessor B records the following entries for June 2020:

Dr Lease receivable	US$100	
Cr Operating lease income		US$100
To record the operating lease income and lease receivable for June 2020		
Dr Impairment loss on lease receivable	US$20	
Cr Impairment allowance on lease receivable		US$20
To record an impairment loss against the lease receivable		

Paragraph 87 of IFRS 16 requires that a lessor accounts for a modification to an operating lease as a new lease from the effective date of the modification, considering any prepaid or accrued lease payments relating to the original lease as part of the lease payments for the new lease.

Therefore, at the effective date of the modification (i.e. 1 July 2020), Lessor B accounts for the new lease with a lease term that ends in February 2022. The remaining lease payments after taking into account the partial forgiveness of the June lease payment amount to US$1,940 (US$2,000 – US$60).

Lessor B records the following entries for July 2020:

Dr Lease incentive	US$60	
Cr Lease receivable		US$60
Dr Impairment allowance on lease receivable	US$20	
Cr Profit/loss		US$20
To recognise the lease incentive (forgiveness of US$60) to enter into the modified lease and reverse the IFRS 9 allowance recognised in June 2020		
Dr Cash	US$40	
Cr Lease receivable		US$40
To record receipt of partial payment		
Dr Lease receivable	US$100	
Cr Operating lease income		US$100
Dr Operating lease income	US$3	
Cr Lease incentive		US$3
To recognise July 2020 lease income of US$100 (based on the monthly US$100 payments) less amortisation of the lease incentive of US$3 (US$60 divided by 20 months).		

Therefore, operating lease income of US$97 will be recognised each month for the remainder of the new lease term. The IFRS 9 impairment loss of US$20 is written back to profit or loss when the US$60 of the receivable is forgiven.

Under this approach, since the remaining US$40 recognised receivable of the pre-modified lease has already been recognised in income and will be received, it is not carried forward to the new lease.

Approach 2 – Derecognition of past lease receivable under IFRS 9

Lessor B records the following entries for June 2020:

Dr Lease receivable	US$100	
Cr Operating lease income		US$100
To record the operating lease income and lease receivable for June 2020		
Dr Impairment loss on lease receivable	US$20	
Cr Impairment allowance on lease receivable		US$20
To record an impairment loss against the lease receivable		

Lessor B records the following entries for July 2020:

Dr Impairment allowance on lease receivable	US$20	
Dr Derecognition loss on lease receivable	US$40	
Cr Lease receivable		US$60
To derecognise the past lease receivable that is forgiven		

Under this approach, the forgiveness of the lease receivables that were previously impaired under IFRS 9 do not impact the lease modification accounting. Therefore, the lessor in this illustration would continue to recognise US$100 of lease income over the new lease term (i.e. based on the regular payments of US$100 over the new lease term).

6.5 Other lessor matters – portfolio approach

IFRS 16 specifies the accounting for an individual lease. However, as a practical expedient, an entity may apply it to a portfolio of leases with similar characteristics if the entity reasonably expects that the effects on the financial statements of applying IFRS 16 to the portfolio would not differ materially from applying it to the individual leases within that portfolio. If accounting for a portfolio, an entity uses estimates and assumptions that reflect the size and composition of the portfolio. *[IFRS 16.B1]*.

A decision to use the portfolio approach would be similar to a decision some entities already make to expense, rather than capitalise, certain assets when the accounting difference is, and would continue to be, immaterial to the financial statements.

6.6 Presentation

IFRS 16 requires lessors to recognise assets held under a finance lease in the statements of financial position and present them as a receivable at an amount equal to the net investment in the lease. *[IFRS 16.67]*. In addition, lessors are required under IFRS 16 to present underlying assets subject to operating leases according to the nature of that asset in the statement of financial position. *[IFRS 16.88]*.

The net investment in the lease is subject to the same considerations as other assets in classification as current or non-current assets in the statement of financial position.

6.7 Disclosure

6.7.1 Disclosure objective

The objective of the disclosures for lessors is to disclose information in the notes that, together with the information provided in the statement of financial position, statement of profit or loss and statement of cash flows, gives a basis for users of financial statements to assess the effect that leases have on the financial position, financial performance and cash flows of the lessor. *[IFRS 16.89]*.

6.7.2 Disclosures for all lessors

A lessor discloses the following amounts for the reporting period:

(a) for finance leases:
 (i) selling profit or loss;
 (ii) finance income on the net investment in the lease; and
 (iii) income relating to variable lease payments not included in the measurement of the net investment in the lease;

(b) for operating leases, lease income, separately disclosing income relating to variable lease payments that do not depend on an index or a rate. *[IFRS 16.90]*.

The disclosures specified above are provided in a tabular format, unless another format is more appropriate. *[IFRS 16.91]*.

A lessor discloses additional qualitative and quantitative information about its leasing activities necessary to meet the disclosure objective discussed at 6.7.1 above. This additional information includes, but is not limited to, information that helps users of financial statements to assess:

(a) the nature of the lessor's leasing activities; and

(b) how the lessor manages the risk associated with any rights it retains in underlying assets. In particular, a lessor discloses its risk management strategy for the rights it retains in underlying assets, including any means by which the lessor reduces that risk. Such means may include, for example, buy-back agreements, residual value guarantees or variable lease payments for use in excess of specified limits. *[IFRS 16.92]*.

6.7.3 Disclosures for finance leases

A lessor provides a qualitative and quantitative explanation of the significant changes in the carrying amount of the net investment in finance leases. *[IFRS 16.93]*.

A lessor discloses a maturity analysis of the lease payments receivable, showing the undiscounted lease payments to be received on an annual basis for a minimum of each of the first five years and a total of the amounts for the remaining years. A lessor reconciles the undiscounted lease payments to the net investment in the lease. The reconciliation must identify the unearned finance income relating to the lease payments receivable and any discounted unguaranteed residual value. *[IFRS 16.94]*.

6.7.4 Disclosures for operating leases

For items of property, plant and equipment subject to an operating lease, a lessor applies the disclosure requirements of IAS 16. In doing so, the lessor disaggregates each class of property, plant and equipment into assets subject to operating leases and assets not subject to operating leases. Therefore, a lessor provides the disclosures required by IAS 16 for assets subject to an operating lease (by class of underlying asset) separately from owned assets held and used by the lessor. *[IFRS 16.95]*.

A lessor applies the disclosure requirements in IAS 36, IAS 38, IAS 40 and IAS 41 for assets subject to operating leases. *[IFRS 16.96]*.

A lessor discloses a maturity analysis of lease payments, showing the undiscounted lease payments to be received on an annual basis for a minimum of each of the first five years and a total of the amounts for the remaining years. *[IFRS 16.97]*.

7 SUBLEASES

7.1 Definition

A sublease is a transaction for which an underlying asset is re-leased by a lessee ('intermediate lessor') to a third party, and the lease ('head lease') between the head lessor and lessee remains in effect. *[IFRS 16 Appendix A]*.

Lessees often enter into arrangements to sublease a leased asset to a third party while the original lease contract is in effect. In these arrangements, one party acts as both the lessee and lessor of the same underlying asset. The original lease is often referred to as a head lease, the original lessee is often referred to as an intermediate lessor or sub-lessor and the ultimate lessee is often referred to as the sublessee.

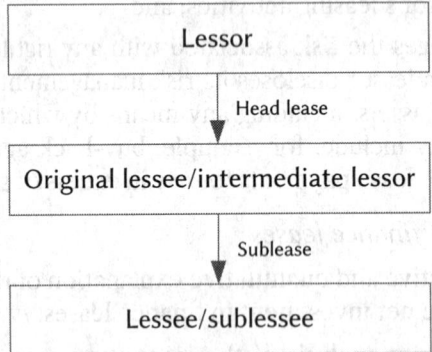

In some cases, the sublease is a separate lease agreement. In other cases, a third party assumes the original lease, but the original lessee remains the primary obligor under the original lease.

7.2 Intermediate lessor accounting

If an underlying asset is re-leased by a lessee to a third party and the original lessee retains the primary obligation under the original lease, the transaction is a sublease. That is, the original lessee generally continues to account for the original lease (the head lease) as a lessee and accounts for the sublease as the lessor (intermediate lessor).

The intermediate lessor classifies the sublease as a finance lease or an operating lease as follows:

(a) if the head lease is a short-term lease and the entity, as a lessee, has applied the short-term recognition exemption, the sublease is classified as an operating lease; or

(b) otherwise, the sublease is classified by reference to the right-of-use asset arising from the head lease, rather than by reference to the underlying asset (for example, the item of property, plant, or equipment that is the subject of the lease). *[IFRS 16.B58]*.

Example 23.32: Classification of a sublease

Entity F (original lessee/intermediate lessor) leases a building for five years. The building has an economic life of 30 years. Entity F subleases the building for four years. The sublease is classified with reference to the right-of-use asset in the head lease (and not the underlying building). For example, when assessing the useful life criterion, the sublease term of four years is compared with five year right-of-use asset in the head lease and not with 30-year economic life of the building, which may result in the sublease being classified as a finance lease.

The intermediate lessor accounts for the sublease as follows:

- if the sublease is classified as an operating lease, the original lessee continues to account for the lease liability and right-of-use asset on the head lease like any other lease. If the total remaining lease cost on the head lease exceeds the anticipated sublease income, this may indicate that the right-of-use asset associated with the head lease is impaired. A right-of-use asset is assessed for impairment under IAS 36; or

- if the sublease is classified as a finance lease, the original lessee derecognises the right-of-use asset on the head lease at the sublease commencement date and continues to account for the original lease liability in accordance with the lessee accounting model. The original lessee, as the sublessor, recognises a net investment in the sublease and evaluates it for impairment.

In a sublease, if the interest rate implicit in the sublease cannot be readily determined, an intermediate lessor may use the discount rate used for the head lease (adjusted for any initial direct costs associated with the sublease) to measure the net investment in the sublease. *[IFRS 16.68]*.

If a lessee subleases, or expects to sublease an asset, the head lease does not qualify as a lease of a low-value asset. *[IFRS 16.B7]*.

When contracts are entered into at or near the same time with the same counterparty (or related parties of the counterparties), an intermediate lessor is required to consider the criteria for combining contracts (e.g. when the contracts are negotiated with the same counterparty (or related parties of the counterparties) as a package with a single commercial objective, or when the consideration to be paid in one contract depends on the price or performance of the other contract). If the contracts are required to be combined, the intermediate lessor accounts for the head lease and sublease as a single combined transaction.

Example 23.33: Subleases (IFRS 16 Illustrative Examples 20 and 21)

IFRS 16 Example 20 – Sublease classified as a finance lease [IFRS 16.IE8]

Head lease – An intermediate lessor enters into a five-year lease for 5,000 square metres of office space (the head lease) with Entity A (the head lessor).

Sublease – At the beginning of Year 3, the intermediate lessor subleases the 5,000 square metres of office space for the remaining three years of the head lease to a sublessee.

The intermediate lessor classifies the sublease by reference to the right-of-use asset arising from the head lease. The intermediate lessor classifies the sublease as a finance lease, having considered the requirements in paragraphs 61-66 of IFRS 16.

When the intermediate lessor enters into the sublease, the intermediate lessor:

(a) derecognises the right-of-use asset relating to the head lease that it transfers to the sublessee and recognises the net investment in the sublease;

(b) recognises any difference between the right-of-use asset and the net investment in the sublease in profit or loss; and

(c) retains the lease liability relating to the head lease in its statement of financial position, which represents the lease payments owed to the head lessor.

During the term of the sublease, the intermediate lessor recognises both finance income on the sublease and interest expense on the head lease.

IFRS 16 Example 21 – Sublease classified as an operating lease [IFRS 16.IE8]

Head lease – An intermediate lessor enters into a five-year lease for 5,000 square metres of office space (the head lease) with Entity A (the head lessor).

Sublease – At commencement of the head lease, the intermediate lessor subleases the 5,000 square metres of office space for two years to a sublessee.

The intermediate lessor classifies the sublease by reference to the right-of-use asset arising from the head lease. The intermediate lessor classifies the sublease as an operating lease, having considered the requirements in paragraphs 61-66 of IFRS 16.

When the intermediate lessor enters into the sublease, the intermediate lessor retains the lease liability and the right-of-use asset relating to the head lease in its statement of financial position.

During the term of the sublease, the intermediate lessor:

(a) recognises a depreciation charge for the right-of-use asset and interest on the lease liability; and

(b) recognises lease income from the sublease.

7.3 Sublessee accounting

A sublessee accounts for its lease in the same manner as any other lease under IFRS 16. See 5 above.

7.4 Presentation

According to IAS 1, an entity cannot offset assets and liabilities or income and expenses, unless required or permitted by an IFRS. *[IAS 1.32]*. Therefore, intermediate lessors are not permitted to offset lease liabilities and lease assets that arise from a head lease and a sublease, respectively, unless those liabilities and assets meet the requirements in IAS 1 for offsetting. *[IFRS 16.BC235]*. Similarly, intermediate lessors are not permitted to offset depreciation and interest expenses and lease income relating to a head lease and a sublease of the same underlying asset, respectively, unless the requirements for offsetting in IAS 1 are met. *[IFRS 16.BC236]*. For example, intermediate lessors apply the principal-versus-agent application guidance in IFRS 15 to determine whether sublease revenue needs to be presented on a gross or net basis (i.e. reduced for head lease expenses). We believe that intermediate lessors generally will not meet the principal-versus-agent application guidance in IFRS 15 to present sublease income on a net basis and therefore will generally present sublease revenue on a gross basis. See Chapter 28 at 3.4.

7.5 Disclosure

Intermediate lessors, like all lessors, are required to disclose qualitative and quantitative information which gives a basis for users of financial statements to assess the effect that leases have on the financial position, financial performance and cash flows of the lessor.

8 SALE AND LEASEBACK TRANSACTIONS

A sale and leaseback transaction involves the transfer of an asset by an entity (the seller-lessee) to another entity (the buyer-lessor) and the leaseback of the same asset by the seller-lessee. Because IFRS 16 requires lessees to recognise most leases on the balance sheet (i.e. all leases except for leases of low-value assets and short-term leases depending on the lessee's accounting policy election), sale and leaseback transactions may no longer provide lessees with a source of off-balance sheet financing.

If an entity (the seller-lessee) transfers an asset to another entity (the buyer-lessor) and leases that asset back from the buyer-lessor, both the seller-lessee and the buyer-lessor assess whether the transfer of the asset is a sale and account for it as described below. *[IFRS 16.98].*

The presentation in the statement of cash flows of sale and leaseback transactions is discussed in Chapter 40 at 5.5.4.

8.1 Determining whether the transfer of an asset is a sale

An entity applies the requirements for determining when a performance obligation is satisfied in IFRS 15 to determine whether the transfer of an asset is accounted for as a sale of that asset. *[IFRS 16.99].* If control of an underlying asset passes to the buyer-lessor, the transaction is accounted for as a sale or purchase of the asset and a lease. If not, both the seller-lessee and the buyer-lessor account for the transaction as a financing transaction. See Chapter 30 for determining when a performance obligation is satisfied under requirements of IFRS 15.

Paragraph 38 of IFRS 15 includes the following indicators of the transfer of the control:

(a) the entity has a present right to payment for the asset – if a customer is presently obliged to pay for an asset, then that may indicate that the customer has obtained the ability to direct the use of, and obtain substantially all of the remaining benefits from, the asset in exchange;

(b) the customer has legal title to the asset – legal title may indicate which party to a contract has the ability to direct the use of, and obtain substantially all of the remaining benefits from, an asset or to restrict the access of other entities to those benefits. Therefore, the transfer of legal title of an asset may indicate that the customer has obtained control of the asset. If an entity retains legal title solely as a protection against the customer's failure to pay, those rights of the entity would not preclude the customer from obtaining control of an asset;

(c) the entity has transferred physical possession of the asset – the customer's physical possession of an asset may indicate that the customer has the ability to direct the use of, and obtain substantially all of the remaining benefits from, the asset or to restrict the access of other entities to those benefits. However, physical possession may not coincide with control of an asset. For example, in some repurchase agreements and in some consignment arrangements, a customer or consignee may have physical possession of an asset that the entity controls. Conversely, in some bill-and-hold arrangements, the entity may have physical possession of an asset that the customer controls;

(d) the customer has the significant risks and rewards of ownership of the asset – the transfer of the significant risks and rewards of ownership of an asset to the customer may indicate that the customer has obtained the ability to direct the use of, and obtain substantially all of the remaining benefits from, the asset. However, when evaluating the risks and rewards of ownership of a promised asset, an entity is required to exclude any risks that give rise to a separate performance obligation in addition to the performance obligation to transfer the asset. For example, an entity may have transferred control of an asset to a customer but not yet satisfied an additional performance obligation to provide maintenance services related to the transferred asset; and

(e) the customer has accepted the asset – the customer's acceptance of an asset may indicate that it has obtained the ability to direct the use of, and obtain substantially all of the remaining benefits from, the asset. *[IFRS 15.38]*.

None of these indicators individually determine whether the buyer-lessor has obtained control of the underlying asset. Both the seller-lessee and the buyer-lessor must consider all relevant facts and circumstances to determine whether control has transferred. Furthermore, not all of the indicators must be present to determine that the buyer-lessor has gained control. Rather, the indicators are factors that are often present when a customer has obtained control of an asset and the list is meant to help entities apply the principle of control. See Chapter 30.

The IASB noted that the existence of a leaseback, in isolation, does not preclude a sale. This is because a lease is different from the sale or purchase of an underlying asset, as a lease does not transfer control of the underlying asset. Instead, it transfers the right to control the use of the underlying asset for the period of the lease. However, if the seller-lessee has a substantive repurchase option for the underlying asset (i.e. a right to repurchase the asset), no sale has occurred because the buyer-lessor has not obtained control of the asset. *[IFRS 16.BC262]*.

These requirements are a significant change from current practice for seller-lessees as they must apply the requirements of IFRS 15 to determine whether a sale has occurred.

IFRS 16 does not address whether a lessee's renewal options (e.g. fixed price, fair value at the date of exercise) permitting the seller-lessee to extend the lease for substantially all of the remaining economic life of the underlying asset precludes sale accounting. We believe that a lessee that has an option to extend a lease for substantially all of the remaining economic life of the underlying asset is, economically, in a similar position to a lessee that has an option to purchase the underlying asset. Therefore, when the renewal price is not fair value – at the time the renewal option is exercised – the renewal option would prohibit sale accounting under IFRS 15 and IFRS 16.

8.2 Transactions in which the transfer of an asset is a sale

8.2.1 Accounting for the sale

If the transfer of an asset by the seller-lessee satisfies the requirements of IFRS 15 to be accounted for as a sale of the asset:

(a) the seller-lessee measures the right-of-use asset arising from the leaseback at the proportion of the previous carrying amount of the asset that relates to the right of use retained by the seller-lessee. Accordingly, the seller-lessee recognises only the amount of any gain or loss that relates to the rights transferred to the buyer-lessor; and

(b) the buyer-lessor accounts for the purchase of the asset applying applicable Standards, and for the lease applying the lessor accounting requirements in this Standard. *[IFRS 16.100]*.

Although not explicitly stated in IFRS 16, we believe that if the sale and leaseback transaction results in a loss to the seller-lessee, that loss will not be deferred. In addition, the seller-lessee may also need to consider whether a) the underlying asset may have been impaired prior to the sale and leaseback and the transaction would require the asset to have been classified as held-for-sale under IFRS 5 (see Chapter 4) and hence subject to potential impairment prior to the transaction.

The IFRS Interpretations Committee issued an agenda decision in June 2020 related to a sale and leaseback transaction with variable payments. In the transaction described in the request, an entity (seller-lessee) enters into a sale and leaseback transaction whereby it transfers an item of property to another entity (buyer-lessor) and leases the asset back for five years. The transfer of the property satisfies the requirements in IFRS 15 to be accounted for as a sale of the property. The amount paid by the buyer-lessor to the seller-lessee in exchange for the property equals the property's fair value at the date of the transaction. Payments for the lease (which are at market rates) include variable payments, calculated as a percentage of the seller-lessee's revenue generated using the property during the five-year lease term. The seller-lessee has determined that the variable payments are not in-substance fixed payments as described in IFRS 16. The request asked how, in the transaction described, the seller-lessee measures the right-of-use asset arising from the leaseback and determines the amount of any gain or loss recognised at the date of the transaction.

The Committee observed that the requirements applicable to the transaction described in the request are in paragraph 100 of IFRS 16. Paragraph 100 states that 'if the transfer of an asset by the seller-lessee satisfies the requirements of IFRS 15 to be accounted for as a sale of the asset: (a) the seller-lessee shall measure the right-of-use asset arising from the leaseback at the proportion of the previous carrying amount of the asset that relates to the right of use retained by the seller-lessee. Accordingly, the seller-lessee shall recognise only the amount of any gain or loss that relates to the rights transferred to the buyer-lessor. ...'.

Consequently, to measure the right-of-use asset arising from the leaseback, the seller-lessee determines the proportion of the property transferred to the buyer-lessor that relates to the right of use retained – it does so by comparing, at the date of the transaction, the right of use it retains via the leaseback to the rights comprising the entire property. IFRS 16 does not prescribe a method for determining that proportion. In the transaction described in the request, the seller-lessee could determine the proportion by comparing, for example, (a) the present value of expected payments for the lease (including those that are variable), with (b) the fair value of the property at the date of the transaction.

The gain or loss the seller-lessee recognises at the date of the transaction is a consequence of its measurement of the right-of-use asset arising from the leaseback. Because the right of use the seller-lessee retains is not remeasured as a result of the transaction (it is measured as a proportion of the property's previous carrying amount), the amount of the gain or loss recognised relates only to the rights transferred to the buyer-lessor. Applying paragraph 53(i) of IFRS 16, the seller-lessee discloses gains or losses arising from sale and leaseback transactions.

The seller-lessee also recognises a liability at the date of the transaction, even if all the payments for the lease are variable and do not depend on an index or rate. The initial measurement of the liability is a consequence of how the right-of-use asset is measured – and the gain or loss on the sale and leaseback transaction determined – applying paragraph 100(a) of IFRS 16. Example 23.34 is taken from the Committee's agenda decision in the June 2020 IFRIC Update.

Example 23.34:   Sale and leaseback with variable payments (IFRIC Agenda Decision)

Seller-lessee enters into a sale and leaseback transaction whereby it transfers an asset (PPE) to buyer-lessor, and leases that PPE back for five years. The transfer of the PPE satisfies the requirements in IFRS 15 to be accounted for as a sale of the PPE.

The carrying amount of the PPE in Seller-lessee's financial statements at the date of the transaction is CU1,000,000, and the amount paid by Buyer-lessor for the PPE is CU1,800,000 (the fair value of the PPE at that date). All the payments for the lease (which are at market rates) are variable, calculated as a percentage of Seller-lessee's revenue generated using the PPE during the five-year lease term. At the date of the transaction, the present value of the expected payments for the lease is CU450,000. There are no initial direct costs.

Seller-lessee determines that it is appropriate to calculate the proportion of the PPE that relates to the right of use retained using the present value of expected payments for the lease. On this basis, the proportion of the PPE that relates to the right of use retained is 25%, calculated as CU450,000 (present value of expected payments for the lease) ÷ CU1,800,000 (fair value of the PPE). Consequently, the proportion of the PPE that relates to the rights transferred to Buyer-lessor is 75%, calculated as (CU1,800,000 – CU450,000) ÷ CU1,800,000.

Applying paragraph 100(a), Seller-lessee:

a. measures the right-of-use asset at CU250,000, calculated as CU1,000,000 (previous carrying amount of the PPE) × 25% (proportion of the PPE that relates to the right of use it retains).

b. recognises a gain of CU600,000 at the date of the transaction, which is the gain that relates to the rights transferred to Buyer-lessor. This gain is calculated as CU800,000 (total gain on sale of the PPE (CU1,800,000 – CU1,000,000)) × 75% (proportion of the PPE that relates to rights transferred to Buyer-lessor).

Applying paragraph 100(a), the right-of-use asset would not be measured at zero at the date of the transaction because zero would not reflect the proportion of the previous carrying amount of the PPE (CU1,000,000) that relates to the right of use retained by Seller-lessee.

At the date of the transaction, Seller-lessee accounts for the transaction as follows:

Dr Cash	CU 1,800,000	
Dr Right-of-use asset	CU 250,000	
Cr PPE		CU 1,000,000
Cr Liability		CU 450,000
Cr Gain on rights transferred		CU 600,000

The Committee concluded that the principles and requirements in IFRS 16 provide an adequate basis for an entity to determine, at the date of the transaction, the accounting for the sale and leaseback transaction described in the request and decided not to add the matter to its standard-setting agenda.

The Committee's discussions above highlighted that IFRS 16 does not specify the measurement of the liability that arises in such a sale and leaseback transaction. Therefore, the Board decided to amend IFRS 16 to specify how a seller-lessee should apply the subsequent measurement requirements in IFRS 16 to the liability that arises in the sale and leaseback transaction. At the time of writing, an exposure draft of the amendment is expected in the third quarter of 2020.

At the time of writing, the Interpretations Committee expected to discuss, in September 2020, a question about the applicability of the sale and leaseback requirements in IFRS 16 to a transaction in which an entity sells its equity interest in a subsidiary that holds only a real estate asset and then leases that real estate asset back. Further guidance may be issued as a result of that discussion.

8.2.2 Accounting for the leaseback

When a sale occurs, both the seller-lessee and the buyer-lessor account for the leaseback in the same manner as any other lease, with adjustments for off-market terms. Specifically, a seller-lessee recognises a lease liability and right-of-use asset for the leaseback (subject to the optional exemptions for short-term leases and leases of low-value assets).

8.2.3 Adjustment for off-market terms

The sale transaction and the ensuing lease are generally interdependent and negotiated as a package. Consequently, some transactions could be structured with a negotiated sales price that is above or below the asset's fair value and with lease payments for the ensuing lease that are above or below the market rates. These off-market terms could distort the gain or loss on the sale and the recognition of lease expense and lease income for the lease. To ensure that the gain or loss on the sale and the lease-related assets and liabilities associated with such transactions are neither understated nor overstated, IFRS 16 requires adjustments for any off-market terms of sale and leaseback transactions, on the more readily determinable basis of the difference between the fair value of the consideration for the sale and the fair value of the asset and the difference between the present value of the contractual payments for the lease and the present value of payments for the lease at market rates. *[IFRS 16.102]*. An entity is required to account for any below-market and above-market terms as a prepayment of lease payments and additional financing provided by the buyer-lessor to the seller-lessee, respectively. *[IFRS 16.101]*.

IFRS 16 defines fair value solely for the purpose of applying lessor accounting requirements but not for the purpose of applying sale and leaseback accounting in the standard. *[IFRS 16 Appendix A]*. Since IFRS 16 does not address fair value outside of lessor accounting, we believe it is appropriate to look to IFRS 13 – *Fair Value Measurement*, for sale and leaseback accounting (i.e. for determining the fair value of the asset sold and determining the resulting gain or loss), given IFRS 13 is also applicable to the measurement of fair value under IFRS 15. The IASB also acknowledged this linkage between IFRS 13 and IFRS 15 in IFRS 16's Basis for Conclusion paragraph 266.

Example 23.35:   Sale and leaseback transaction (IFRS 16 Illustrative Example 24)

An entity (Seller-lessee) sells a building to another entity (Buyer-lessor) for cash of CU2,000,000. Immediately before the transaction, the building is carried at a cost of CU1,000,000. At the same time, Seller-lessee enters into a contract with Buyer-lessor for the right to use the building for 18 years, with annual payments of CU120,000 payable at the end of each year. The terms and conditions of the transaction are such that the transfer of the building by Seller-lessee satisfies the requirements for determining when a performance obligation is satisfied in IFRS 15.

Accordingly, Seller-lessee and Buyer-lessor account for the transaction as a sale and leaseback. This example ignores any initial direct costs.

The fair value of the building at the date of sale is CU1,800,000. Because the consideration for the sale of the building is not at fair value Seller-lessee and Buyer-lessor make adjustments to measure the sale proceeds at fair value. The amount of the excess sale price of CU200,000 (CU2,000,000 – CU1,800,000) is recognised as additional financing provided by Buyer-lessor to Seller-lessee.

The interest rate implicit in the lease is 4.5 per cent per annum, which is readily determinable by Seller-lessee. The present value of the annual payments (18 payments of CU120,000, discounted at 4.5 per cent per annum) amounts to CU1,459,200, of which CU200,000 relates to the additional financing and CU1,259,200 relates to the lease – corresponding to 18 annual payments of CU16,447 and CU103,553, respectively.

Buyer-lessor classifies the lease of the building as an operating lease.

Seller-lessee

At the commencement date, Seller-lessee measures the right-of-use asset arising from the leaseback of the building at the proportion of the previous carrying amount of the building that relates to the right-of-use retained by Seller-lessee, which is CU699,555. This is calculated as: CU1,000,000 (the carrying amount of the building) ÷ CU1,800,000 (the fair value of the building) × CU1,259,200 (the discounted lease payments for the 18-year right-of-use asset).

Seller-lessee recognises only the amount of the gain that relates to the rights transferred to Buyer-lessor of CU240,355 calculated as follows. The gain on sale of building amounts to CU800,000 (CU1,800,000 – CU1,000,000), of which:

(a) CU559,645 (CU800,000 ÷ CU1,800,000 × CU1,259,200) relates to the right to use the building retained by Seller-lessee; and

(b) CU240,355 (CU800,000 ÷ CU1,800,000 × (CU1,800,000 – CU1,259,200)) relates to the rights transferred to Buyer-lessor.

At the commencement date, Seller-lessee accounts for the transaction as follows.

Dr. Cash	CU2,000,000	
Dr. Right-of-use asset	CU699,555	
Cr. Building		CU1,000,000
Cr. Financial liability		CU1,459,200
Cr. Gain on rights transferred		CU240,355

Buyer-lessor

At the commencement date, Buyer-lessor accounts for the transaction as follows.

Dr. Building	CU1,800,000	
Dr. Financial asset	CU200,000*	
Cr. Cash		CU2,000,000

* 18 payments of CU16,447, discounted at 4.5 per cent per annum

After the commencement date, Buyer-lessor accounts for the lease by treating CU103,553 of the annual payments of CU120,000 as lease payments. The remaining CU16,447 of annual payments received from Seller-lessee are accounted for as (a) payments received to settle the financial asset of CU200,000 and (b) interest revenue. *[IFRS 16.IE11]*.

8.3 Transactions in which the transfer of an asset is not a sale

If the transfer of an asset by the seller-lessee does not satisfy the requirements of IFRS 15 to be accounted for as a sale of the asset:

(a) the seller-lessee continues to recognise the transferred asset and recognises a financial liability equal to the transfer proceeds. It accounts for the financial liability applying IFRS 9; and

(b) the buyer-lessor does not recognise the transferred asset and recognises a financial asset equal to the transfer proceeds. It accounts for the financial asset applying IFRS 9. *[IFRS 16.103]*.

8.4 Disclosures

A seller-lessee may need to provide additional information relating to sale and leaseback transactions to satisfy the disclosure objective. This could include information that helps users of financial statements to assess, for example:

(a) the lessee's reasons for sale and leaseback transactions and the prevalence of those transactions;

(b) key terms and conditions of individual sale and leaseback transactions;

(c) payments not included in the measurement of lease liabilities; and

(d) the cash flow effect of sale and leaseback transactions in the reporting period. *[IFRS 16.B52]*.

A seller-lessee is also required to disclose any gains and losses arising from sale and leaseback transactions separately from gains and losses on disposals of other assets. *[IFRS 16.53(i)]*.

9 BUSINESS COMBINATIONS

9.1 Acquiree in a business combination is a lessee

Consequential amendments to IFRS 3 – *Business Combinations* – specify the initial measurement requirements for leases that are acquired in a business combination.

Paragraph 28A has been added to IFRS 3 to clarify that the acquirer recognises right-of-use assets and lease liabilities for leases identified in accordance with IFRS 16 in which the acquiree is the lessee. The acquirer is not required to recognise right-of-use assets and lease liabilities for:

(a) leases for which the lease term ends within 12 months of the acquisition date; or

(b) leases for which the underlying asset is of low-value.

As part of the consequential amendments to other standards arising from IFRS 16, paragraph 28B has been added to IFRS 3 to clarify that the acquirer measures the lease liability at the present value of the remaining lease payments as if the acquired lease were a new lease at the acquisition date. The acquirer measures the right-of-use asset at the same amount as the lease liability, adjusted to reflect favourable or unfavourable terms of the lease when compared with market terms. Because the off-market nature of the lease is captured in the right-of-use asset, the acquirer does not separately recognise an intangible asset or liability for favourable or unfavourable lease terms relative to market. The discount rate is determined from the perspective of the acquiree, as the acquiree is the customer in lease contract. However, the determination of the lessee's incremental borrowing rate will take into account that the acquiree is now part of the new group. This is discussed further at 4.6.1 above. The acquirer is not required to recognise assets and liabilities relating to off-market terms for short-term leases and leases of low-value assets, as the IASB expect that the effect of off-market terms will rarely be material for these contracts. *[IFRS 16.BC298]*.

The subsequent measurement requirements for an acquired lease liability and right-of-use asset are the same as the requirements for any other existing lease arrangement.

9.2 Acquiree in a business combination is a lessor

Paragraph 17 of IFRS 3 has been amended to require an acquirer to classify acquired lessor leases as either finance or operating leases using the contractual terms and conditions at the inception of the lease, or, if the terms of the contract have been modified in a manner that would change its classification, at the date of that modification. Therefore, the classification is not changed as a result of a business combination unless a lease is modified.

10 EFFECTIVE DATE AND TRANSITION

10.1 Effective date

An entity applied IFRS 16 for annual periods beginning on or after 1 January 2019. Earlier application was permitted for entities that apply IFRS 15 at or before the date of initial application of IFRS 16. If an entity applied IFRS 16 earlier, it must disclose that fact. *[IFRS 16.C1]*.

The application date for IFRS 15 was for annual periods beginning on or after 1 January 2018.

10.2 Transition

The transition provisions of IFRS 16 are applied at the initial date of application. For this purpose, the date of initial application is the beginning of the annual reporting period in which an entity first applies IFRS 16. *[IFRS 16.C2]*.

As a practical expedient, an entity is not required to reassess whether a contract is, or contains a lease at the date of initial application. Instead, an entity is permitted:

(a) to apply IFRS 16 to contracts that were previously identified as leases applying IAS 17 and IFRIC 4; or

(b) not to apply IFRS 16 to contracts that were not previously identified as containing a lease applying IAS 17 and IFRIC 4. *[IFRS 16.C3]*.

If an entity chooses to apply the practical expedient, it discloses that fact and applies the practical expedient to all of its contracts. As a result, entities apply the requirements in paragraphs 9 to 11 of IFRS 16 (identifying a lease) only to contracts entered into after the date of initial application. *[IFRS 16.C4]*.

As the accounting for operating leases under IAS 17 was similar to the accounting for service contracts, entities may not always have focussed on determining whether an arrangement is a lease or a service contract. Some entities may need to revisit assessments made under IAS 17 and IFRIC 4 because, under IFRS 16, most leases are recognised on lessees' balance sheets and the effects of treating an arrangement as a service instead of a lease may be material. IFRS 16's practical expedient that allows an entity not to reassess whether a contract contains a lease, only applies to arrangements that were appropriately assessed under IAS 17 and IFRIC 4.

10.3 Lessee transition

A lessee applies IFRS 16 to its leases either:

(a) retrospectively to each prior reporting period presented applying IAS 8 (see 10.3.1 below); or

(b) retrospectively with the cumulative effect of initially applying IFRS 16 recognised at the date of initial application (see 10.3.2 below). *[IFRS 16.C5]*.

A lessee applies its elected transition approach consistently to all leases in which it is a lessee. *[IFRS 16.C6]*.

10.3.1 Full retrospective approach

Under the full retrospective approach, an entity applies IFRS 16 as if it had been applied since the inception of all lease contracts that are presented in the financial statements. If the standard was applied at 1 January 2019, this means that, in the 31 December 2019 financial statements, the comparative period to 31 December 2018 (assuming that this is the only comparative period presented) must have been restated. A restated opening balance sheet at 1 January 2018 would also need to have been disclosed as required by IAS 1.

10.3.2 Modified retrospective approach

When applying the modified retrospective approach, a lessee does not restate comparative figures. Instead, a lessee recognises the cumulative effect of initially applying IFRS 16 as an adjustment to the opening balance of retained earnings (or other component of equity, as appropriate) at the date of initial application. *[IFRS 16.C7]*.

10.3.2.A Leases previously classified as operating leases

For leases previously classified as operating leases by applying IAS 17, a lessee:

(a) recognises a lease liability at the date of initial application for leases previously classified as an operating lease applying IAS 17. The lessee measures that lease liability at the present value of the remaining lease payments, discounted using the lessee's incremental borrowing rate at the date of initial application;

(b) recognises a right-of-use asset at the date of initial application for leases previously classified as an operating lease applying IAS 17. The lessee chooses, on a lease-by-lease basis, to measure that right-of-use asset at either:

  (i) its carrying amount as if IFRS 16 had been applied since the commencement date, but discounted using the lessee's incremental borrowing rate at the date of initial application; or

  (ii) an amount equal to the lease liability, adjusted by the amount of any prepaid or accrued lease payments relating to that lease recognised in the statement of financial position immediately before the date of initial application; and

(c) applies IAS 36 to right-of-use assets at the date of initial application, unless the lessee applies the practical expedient below. *[IFRS 16.C8]*.

IFRS 16 does not specify whether the lessee's incremental borrowing rate at the date of initial application should be determined based on the original lease term or the remaining lease term. We believe that both approaches are acceptable and an entity has an accounting policy choice to use either the original lease term or the remaining lease term. The policy chosen should be disclosed in the financial statements and consistently applied.

Notwithstanding the requirement in paragraph C8 of IFRS 16, a lessee:

(a) is not required to make any adjustments on transition for leases for which the underlying asset is of low value. The lessee accounts for those leases applying IFRS 16 from the date of initial application;

(b) is not required to make any adjustments on transition for leases previously accounted for as investment property using the fair value model in IAS 40. The lessee accounts for those leases applying IAS 40 and IFRS 16 from the date of initial application; and

(c) measures the right-of-use asset at fair value at the date of initial application for leases previously accounted for as operating leases under IAS 17 and that will be accounted for as investment property using the fair value model in IAS 40 from the date of initial application. The lessee accounts for those leases applying IAS 40 and IFRS 16 from the date of initial application. *[IFRS 16.C9]*.

A lessee may use one or more of the following practical expedients when applying the modified retrospective approach to leases previously classified as operating leases applying IAS 17. A lessee is permitted to apply these practical expedients on a lease-by-lease basis:

(a) a lessee may apply a single discount rate to a portfolio of leases with reasonably similar characteristics (such as leases with a similar remaining lease term for a similar class of underlying asset in a similar economic environment);

(b) a lessee may rely on its assessment of whether leases are onerous applying IAS 37 immediately before the date of initial application as an alternative to performing an impairment review. If a lessee chooses this practical expedient, the lessee adjusts the right-of-use asset at the date of initial application by the amount of any provision for onerous leases recognised in the statement of financial position immediately before the date of initial application. In the Basis for Conclusions, the IASB explained that it could be costly for a lessee to perform an impairment review of each of its right-of-use assets on transition to IFRS 16. In addition, any onerous operating lease liability identified applying IAS 37 is likely to reflect impairment of the right-of-use asset. *[IFRS 16.BC287]*. Thus, even when the provision for an onerous lease, immediately before the date of initial application, is nil we believe a lessee is able to rely on this practical expedient and not perform impairment reviews on that date;

(c) a lessee may elect not to recognise a lease liability and a right-of-use asset for leases for which the lease term ends within 12 months of the date of initial application. In this case, a lessee:

    (i) accounts for those leases in the same way as short-term leases; and

    (ii) includes the cost associated with those leases within the disclosure of short-term lease expense in the annual reporting period that includes the date of initial application;

(d) a lessee may exclude initial direct costs from the measurement of the right-of-use asset at the date of initial application; and

(e) a lessee may use hindsight, such as in determining the lease term if the contract contains options to extend or terminate the lease. *[IFRS 16.C10]*. IFRS 16 does not provide detailed guidance on the use of hindsight. However, we believe, similarly to the requirements of IAS 8 (paragraph 53) that hindsight can only be applied to matters of judgement and estimates and therefore would not apply to matters of fact such as changes to an index or rate.

In Extract 23.3 below Poste Italiane describe the transition method and main assumptions used on transition.

Extract 23.3: Poste Italiane SpA (2018)

Poste Italiane Financial Statements for the year ended 31 December 2018 [extract]

2. Basis of preparation and significant accounting policies [extract]

2.7 New accounting standards and interpretations and those soon to be effective [extract]

New International Financial Reporting Standards: Transitional provisions and ESMA disclosures [extract]

Transition method and main assumptions [extract]

Of the methods allowed for the transition to IFRS 16, the Poste Italiane Group opted for the simplified retrospective approach that requires the recognition of:
- the financial liability of the lease starting from the date of initial application and taking into account future lease payments until contract expiration;
- the right of use at an amount equal to the financial liability of the lease as adjusted for any deferred income or accrued income related to the leases reported in the statement of financial position immediately preceding the date of initial application.

The approach does not require the restatement of comparative data and allows the use of practical expedients to calculate the financial liability and the right of use at the transition date. Specifically, the Group used such practical expedients for:
- identifying the contracts in scope (IFRS 16, para. C3);[52]
- setting the discount rate for minimum future payments (IFRS 16 para. C10, point a);[53]
- determining the lease term (IFRS 16 para. C10, point e.);
- not applying the standard to low value and short-term leases (IFRS 16 para. 5),[54] and those where the underlying asset is an intangible asset, other than copyrights and similar (IFRS 16 paragraphs 3 and 4).[55]

Regarding the identification of contracts in scope, the Group elected not to remeasure contracts outstanding at the date of transition that had (or had not been) classified previously as leases or as containing a lease component. As a result of this expedient, lease contracts or contracts containing a lease component, which had been accounted for in accordance with IAS 17, now fall within the scope of IFRS 16.

---

52. As a practical expedient, an entity is not required to reassess whether a contract is, or contains, a lease at the date of initial application. instead, the entity is permitted:
    a) to apply this standard to contracts that were previously identified as leases applying IAS 17 – *Leases* and IFRIC 4 – Determining Whether an Arrangement Contains a Lease.
    b) not to apply this standard to contracts that were not previously identified as containing a lease, applying IAS 17 and IFRIC 4.
53. A lessee may use one or more of the following practical expedients when applying this standard retrospectively in accordance with paragraph C5(b) to leases previously classified as operating leases applying IAS 17. A lessee is permitted to apply these practical expedients on a lease-by-lease basis:
    a) a lessee may apply a single discount rate to a portfolio of leases with reasonably similar characteristics (such as leases with a similar remaining lease term for a similar class of underlying asset in a similar economic environment;
    b) Omissis;
    c) Omissis;
    d) Omissis;
    e) a lessee may use hindsight, such as in determining the lease term if the contract contains options to extend or terminate the lease.
54. A lessee may elect not to apply the requirements of the standard to:
    a) short-term leases; and
    b) leases for which the underlying asset is of low value (omissis).
55. An entity shall apply this standard to all leases, including leases of right-of-use assets in a sublease, except for: omissis; e) rights held by a lessee under licensing agreements within the scope of IAS 38 – *Intangible Assets* for such items as motion picture films, video recordings, plays, manuscripts, patents and copyrights (para. 3). A lessee may, but is not require to, apply this standard to leases of intangible assets other than those describe in paragraph 3 e) (par. 4).

Leases

Example 23.36: *Accounting for lease contracts at transition using the full retrospective and modified retrospective approaches*

A retailer (lessee) entered into 3-year lease of retail space beginning at 1 January 2017 with three annual lease payments of CU1,000 due on 31 December 2017, 2018 and 2019, respectively. The lease is classified as an operating lease under IAS 17. The retailer initially applies IFRS 16 for the first time in the annual period beginning at 1 January 2019.

The incremental borrowing rate at the date of the initial application is 3% p.a. The incremental borrowing rate at the commencement of the lease was 6% p.a. The right-of-use asset is subject to straight-line depreciation over the lease term. The present values of the remaining lease payments as of 1 January 2017 at 6% p.a., 1 January 2018 at 3% p.a. and 1 January 2019 at 3% p.a. are CU2,673, CU2,829 and CU971, respectively. Assume no practical expedients are elected.

For simplicity, this example assumes the lessee did not incur initial direct costs, there were no lease incentives and there were no requirements for the lessee to dismantle and remove the underlying asset, restore the site on which it is located or restore the underlying asset to the condition under the terms and conditions of the lease.

The following example illustrates the lease liability, the right-of-use asset at the date of initial application and expenses applying both the full retrospective and the modified retrospective approaches:

Full retrospective approach

Analysis: Under the full retrospective approach, the lease liability and the right-of-use asset are measured on the commencement date using the incremental borrowing rate at that date. The lease liability is accounted for by the interest method subsequently and the right-of-use asset is subject to depreciation on the straight-line basis over the lease term of three years. The following table shows account balances under this method beginning at lease commencement:

	Right-of-use asset	Lease liability	Interest expense	Amortisation expense	Retained earnings
1 January 2017	2,673[1]	2,673[1]	–	–	–
31 December 2017	1,782[2]	1,833[3]	160[4]	891[5]	(51)
31 December 2018	891[6]	943[7]	110[8]	891	–
1 January 2019	891	943	–	–	–
31 December 2019	–	–	57[9]	891	–

1. Present value of three CU1,000 payments at 6%
2. CU2,673 – (CU2,673 / 3 years) = CU1,782
3. CU2,673 (prior period ending lease liability) – CU1,000 (cash payment) + CU160 (current period interest expense) = CU1,833
4. CU2,673 × 6% = 160
5. CU2,673 / 3 years = 891
6. CU1,782 – (CU2,673 / 3 years) = CU891
7. CU1,833 (prior period ending lease liability) – CU1,000 (cash payment) + CU110 (current period interest expense) = CU943
8. CU1,833 × 6% = CU110
9. CU943 × 6% = CU57

At adoption, lessee would record the right-of-use asset and lease liability at the 31 December 2017 values from the above table, with the difference between the right-of-use asset and lease liability going to retained earnings as of 1 January 2018 (assuming that only the 2018 financial information is included as comparatives).

Dr Right-of-use asset	CU1,782	
Dr Retained earnings	CU51	
Cr Lease liability		CU1,833

To initially recognise the lease-related asset and liability as of 1 January 2018

1814 Chapter 23

The following journal entries would be recorded during 2018:

Dr Interest expense	CU110	
Cr Lease liability		CU110

To record interest expense and accrete the lease liability using the interest method

Dr Depreciation expense	CU891	
Cr Right-of-use asset		CU891

To record depreciation expense on the right-of-use asset

Dr Lease liability	CU1,000	
Cr Cash		CU1,000

To record lease payment

The following journal entries would be recorded during 2019:

Dr Interest expense	CU57	
Cr Lease liability		CU57

To record interest expense and accrete the lease liability using the interest method

Dr Depreciation expense	CU891	
Cr Right-of-use asset		CU891

To record depreciation expense on the right-of-use asset

Dr Lease liability	CU1,000	
Cr Cash		CU1,000

To record lease payment

Modified retrospective approach (alternative 1)

Analysis. Under the modified retrospective approach (alternative 1), the lease liability is measured based on the remaining lease payments discounted using the incremental borrowing rate as of the date of initial application (i.e. 3% per p.a.). The right-of-use asset is at its carrying amount as if the standard had been applied since the commencement date. The right-of-use asset is subject to depreciation on the straight-line basis over the lease term of three years:

Dr Right-of-use asset	CU943[10]	
Dr Retained earnings	CU28[11]	
Cr Lease liability		CU971[12]

To initially recognise the lease-related asset and liability as of 1 January 2019

The following journal entries would be recorded during 2019:

Dr Interest expense	CU29[13]	
Cr Lease liability		CU29

To record interest expense and accrete the lease liability using the interest method

Dr Depreciation expense	CU943	
Cr Right-of-use asset		CU943

To record depreciation expense on the right-of-use asset

Dr Lease liability	CU1,000	
Cr Cash		CU1,000

To record lease payment

Modified retrospective approach (alternative 2)

Analysis. Under the modified retrospective approach (alternative 2), the lease liability is also measured based on the remaining lease payments discounted using the incremental borrowing rate as of the date of initial application. In this example, the carrying amount of the right-of-use asset is an amount equal to the carrying amount of the lease liability on the date of initial application as there are no prepayments or accrual items:

Dr Right-of-use asset   CU971[12]
   Cr Lease liability   CU971[12]
To initially recognise the lease-related asset and liability as of 1 January 2019

The following journal entries would be recorded during 2019:

Dr Interest expense   CU29[13]
   Cr Lease liability   CU29
To record interest expense and accrete the lease liability using the interest method
Dr Depreciation expense   CU971[12]
   Cr Right-of-use asset   CU971
To record depreciation expense on the right-of-use asset
Dr Lease liability   CU1,000
   Cr Cash   CU1,000
To record lease payment

10 CU2,829 (present value of three CU1,000 payments at 3%) – (CU2,829 / 3 years) × 2 = CU943
11 CU971 – CU943 = CU28
12 Present value of one CU1,000 payment at 3%
13 CU971 × 3% = CU29

A summary of the lease contract's accounting (assuming no changes due to reassessments) is, as follows:

	Full retrospective approach	Modified retrospective approach (alternative 1)	Modified retrospective approach (alternative 2)
Opening balance sheet impact as of 1 January 2019			
Right-of-use asset	CU891	CU943	CU971
Lease liability	CU943	CU971	CU971
Period ended 31 December 2019 activity			
Cash lease payments	CU1,000	CU1,000	CU1,000
Lease expense recognised			
Interest expense	CU57	CU29	CU29
Depreciation expense	CU891	CU943	CU971
Total periodic expense	CU948	CU972	CU1,000

Immaterial differences may rise in the computation of amounts in the example above due to rounding.

10.3.2.B   Separating and allocating lease and non-lease components of a contract upon transition – leases previously classified as operating leases

IFRS 16 does not specify how a lessee would separate and allocate lease and non-lease components of a contract upon transition when the modified retrospective approach is adopted. We believe lessees could apply IFRS 16.13-16 and allocate the consideration in the contract, determined at lease commencement, to each lease and non-lease component on the basis of the relative stand-alone price of the lease component on that same date unless the practical expedient to account for each lease component and any associated non-lease components as a single lease component is elected. See 3.2 above. Other approaches with similar results may also be acceptable.

10.3.2.C Leases previously classified as finance leases

For a lessee that applies the modified retrospective approach to leases that were classified as finance leases applying IAS 17, the carrying amount of the right-of-use asset and the lease liability at the date of initial application are the carrying amounts of the lease asset and lease liability immediately before that date measured applying IAS 17. For those leases, a lessee accounts for the right-of-use asset and the lease liability applying IFRS 16 from the date of initial application. *[IFRS 16.C11]*. However, the guidance will not be applicable beyond the date of initial application and thus a reassessment and remeasurement may be necessary soon after the date of initial application. See 5.4 and 5.5 above.

In Extract 23.4 below Deutsche Post disclose the adjustments made on application of IFRS 16.

Extract 23.4: Deutsche Post AG (2018)

NOTES TO THE CONSOLIDATED FINANCIAL STATEMENTS OF DEUTSCHE POST AG [extract]

4   Adjustment of opening balances [extract]

Effects of IFRS 16, Leases [extract]

In the context of the transition to IFRS 16, right-of-use assets of €9.1 billion and lease liabilities of €9.2 billion were recognised as at 1 January 2018. Of these lease liabilities, €1.6 billion was due within one year. The Group transitioned to IFRS 16 in accordance with the modified retrospective approach. The prior-year figures were not adjusted. As part of the initial application of IFRS 16, the Group chooses to apply the relief option, which allows it to adjust the right-of-use asset by the amount of any provision for onerous leases recognised in the balance sheet immediately before the date of initial application. In addition, the Group has decided not to apply the new guidance to leases whose term will end within twelve months of the date of initial application. In such cases, the leases are accounted for as short-term leases and the lease payments associated with them are recognised as an expense from short-term leases. The following reconciliation to the opening balance for the lease liabilities as at 1 January 2018 is based upon the operating lease obligations as at 31 December 2017:

Reconciliation

€m	1 Jan. 2018
Operating lease obligations at 31 December 2017	11,298
Minimum lease payments (notional amount) on finance lease liabilities at 31 December 2017	237
Relief option for short-term leases	–225
Relief option for low value asset leases	–27
Lease-type obligations (service components)	2
Other	50
Gross lease liabilities at 1 January 2018	**11,335**
Discounting	–1,919
Lease liabilities at 1 January 2018	**9,416**
Present value of finance lease liabilities at 31 December 2017	–181
Additional lease liabilities as a result of the initial application of IFRS 16 as at 1 January 2018	**9,235**

Poste Italiane disclose the quantitative impact of first-time adoption of IFRS 16.

> **Extract 23.5: Poste Italiane SpA (2018)**
>
> **Poste Italiane Financial Statements for the year ended 31 December 2018** [extract]
> **2.7 New accounting standards and interpretations and those soon to be effective** [extract]
> **New International Financial Reporting Standards: Transitional provisions and ESMA disclosures** [extract]
> **Quantitative impacts of first-time adoption of IFRS 16** [extract]
>
> At the date of transition, the types of contract falling within the scope of IFRS 16 regard:
> - Properties used in operations (approximately 10,600 contracts);
> - Corporate fleet rented for the delivery of postal products and vehicles for business and personal use given to employees (plus contracts for approximately 19,200 vehicles);
> - Properties used as accommodation for employees (approximately 250 contracts);
> - Aircraft used by the Group's airline (6 contracts);
> - Other types of asset (7 contracts)
>
> The tables below show the main preliminary effects on the financial position at 1 January 2019 resulting from the application of IFRS 16, for both the Group and the Parent Company, Poste Italiane SpA. However, the figures shown are still being reviewed.
>
> **EFFECTS OF FIRST-TIME ADOPTION OF IFRS 16**
>
> | (€m) Poste Italiane Group | Right of use | Financial liability |
> |---|---|---|
> | Properties used in operations | 1,235 | 1,234 |
> | Other assets | 139 | 139 |
> | **Total at 1 January 2019** | **1,374** | **1,373** |
>
> **EFFECTS OF FIRST-TIME ADOPTION OF IFRS 16**
>
> | (€m) Poste Italiane SpA | Right of use | Financial liability |
> |---|---|---|
> | Properties used in operations | 1,114 | 1,114 |
> | Other assets | 114 | 114 |
> | **Total at 1 January 2019** | **1,228** | **1,228** |
>
> Lastly, the tables below show the reconciliation between the lease commitments at 31 December 2018 (on the basis of IAS 17) and the amount of the lease liability recognised at 1 January 2019 (in accordance with IFRS 16).
>
> **POSTE ITALIANE GROUP**
>
> | (€m) | |
> |---|---|
> | Operating lease commitments at 31 December 2018 | 780 |
> | Short-term lease exemption 31 December 2018 | (5) |
> | Low value exemption at 31 December 2018 | (5) |
> | **Lease liabilities at 31 December 2018 within scope of IFRS 16** | **770** |
> | Adjustment following different treatment of extension and termination options | 760 |
> | **Undiscounted lease liabilities at 1 January 2019** | **1,530** |
> | Adjustment for discounted lease liabilities at 1 January 2019 | (157) |
> | **Lease liabilities resulting from application of IFRS 16 at 1 January 2019** | **1,373** |

10.4 Lessor transition

With the exception of subleases (see 10.4.1. below), a lessor is not required to make any adjustments on transition for leases in which it is a lessor and accounts for those leases applying IFRS 16 from the date of initial application. *[IFRS 16.C14]*.

10.4.1 Subleases

An intermediate lessor (an entity that is both a lessee and a lessor of the same underlying asset):

- reassesses subleases that were classified as operating leases applying IAS 17 and are ongoing at the date of initial application, to determine whether each sublease should be classified as an operating lease or a finance lease. The intermediate lessor performs this assessment at the date of initial application on the basis of the remaining contractual terms and conditions of the head lease and sublease at that date; and
- for subleases that were classified as operating leases applying IAS 17 but finance leases applying IFRS 16, account for the sublease as a new finance lease entered into at the date of initial application. *[IFRS 16.C15]*.

10.5 Other considerations

IFRS 16 provides specific guidance on transition for sale and leaseback transactions and amounts previously recognised in a business combination. Such specific guidance is applicable irrespective of the transition approach adopted (i.e. full retrospective and modified retrospective approaches). Thus, lessees are required to follow the specific guidance below even when adopting the full retrospective approach.

10.5.1 Sale and leaseback transactions

An entity does not reassess sale and leaseback transactions entered into before the date of initial application to determine whether the transfer of the underlying asset satisfies the requirements in IFRS 15 to be accounted for as a sale. *[IFRS 16.C16]*.

If a sale and leaseback transaction was accounted for as a sale and a finance lease applying IAS 17, the seller-lessee:

- accounts for the leaseback in the same way as it accounts for any other finance lease that exists at the date of initial application; and
- continues to amortise any gain on sale over the lease term. *[IFRS 16.C17]*.

If a sale and leaseback transaction was accounted for as a sale and operating lease applying IAS 17, the seller-lessee:

- accounts for the leaseback in the same way as it accounts for any other operating lease that exists at the date of initial application; and
- adjusts the leaseback right-of-use asset for any deferred gains or losses that relate to off-market terms recognised in the statement of financial position immediately before the date of initial application. *[IFRS 16.C18]*.

10.5.2 Amounts previously recognised in a business combination

If a lessee previously recognised an asset or liability applying IFRS 3 relating to favourable or unfavourable terms of an operating lease acquired as part of a business combination, the lessee derecognises that asset or liability and adjusts the carrying amount of the right-of-use asset by a corresponding amount at the date of initial application. [IFRS 16.C19]. As discussed at 10.5 above, this paragraph applies to all entities. Therefore, even when an entity applies the standard retrospectively (in accordance with IFRS 16.C5(a)), the acquirer does not reopen the purchase price allocation for a business combination, but rather goes back to the date of acquisition of the acquiree and determines the lease liability and right of use asset as if the lease were a new lease at that date.

10.5.3 References to IFRS 9

If an entity applies IFRS 16 but does not yet apply IFRS 9, any reference in IFRS 16 to IFRS 9 should be read as a reference to IAS 39 – *Financial Instruments: Recognition and Measurement*. [IFRS 16.C20].

10.6 Disclosure

If an entity applies IFRS 16 in full retrospectively, it is required to apply certain disclosures under IAS 8 regarding the effect of the initial application (see Chapter 3 at 4.4).

If an entity applies the modified retrospective approach above, the lessee discloses information about initial application required by paragraph 28 of IAS 8, except for the information specified in paragraph 28(f) of IAS 8, which relates to the amount of the adjustments. Instead of the information specified in paragraph 28(f) of IAS 8, the lessee discloses:

- the weighted average lessee's incremental borrowing rate applied to lease liabilities recognised in the statement of financial position at the date of initial application; and
- an explanation of any difference between:
  - operating lease commitments disclosed applying IAS 17 at the end of the annual reporting period immediately preceding the date of initial application, discounted using the incremental borrowing rate at the date of initial application; and
  - lease liabilities recognised in the statement of financial position at the date of initial application. [IFRS 16.C12].

If a lessee uses one or more of the specified practical expedients in paragraph C10 (see 10.3.2.A above), it discloses that fact. [IFRS 16.C13].

References

1 *IFRIC Update*, March 2019.
2 *IFRIC Update*, June 2019.
3 *IFRIC Update*, November 2019.
4 *IFRIC Update*, September 2019.
5 IFRS 16 Basis for Conclusions, para. BC162.
6 IFRS 9, para. 5.4.1.

Chapter 24   Government grants

1 INTRODUCTION 1823
    1.1   Overview of IAS 20 1823
    1.2   Terms used in this chapter 1825
2 SCOPE OF IAS 20 1826
    2.1   Government assistance 1826
    2.2   Government grants 1826
           2.2.1   Definitions 1826
           2.2.2   Grants with no specific relation to operating activities (SIC-10) 1827
    2.3   Scope exclusions 1827
           2.3.1   General considerations 1827
           2.3.2   Investment tax credits 1828
3 RECOGNITION AND MEASUREMENT 1830
    3.1   General requirements of IAS 20 1830
    3.2   Non-monetary grants 1830
    3.3   Forgivable loans 1831
    3.4   Loans at lower than market rates of interest 1832
    3.5   Government guarantees 1833
    3.6   Recognition in the income statement 1834
           3.6.1   Achieving the most appropriate matching 1835
           3.6.2   Loans at lower than market rates of interest 1836
           3.6.3   The period to be benefited by the grant 1837
           3.6.4   Separating grants into elements 1837
    3.7   Repayment of government grants 1838
    3.8   Government assistance 1838
    3.9   Impairment testing of assets that qualified for government grants 1839
4 PRESENTATION OF GRANTS 1840

	4.1 Presentation of grants related to assets in the statement of financial position	1840
	4.2 Presentation of grants related to income in the statement of profit or loss	1840
	4.3 Statement of cash flows	1842
5	GOVERNMENT GRANTS RELATED TO BIOLOGICAL ASSETS IN THE SCOPE OF IAS 41	1842
6	DISCLOSURES	1843

List of examples

Example 24.1:	Government grant by way of forgivable loan	1831
Example 24.2:	Interest-free loan from a government agency	1832
Example 24.3:	Entity allowed to retain amounts owed to government	1833
Example 24.4:	Grant associated with investment property	1836
Example 24.5:	Below-market interest rate loan from the government	1837
Example 24.6:	Government assistance	1839
Example 24.7:	Presentation of grants with different characteristics	1841
Example 24.8:	Grant relating to biological assets carried at fair value	1843

Chapter 24   Government grants

1   INTRODUCTION

IAS 20 – *Accounting for Government Grants and Disclosure of Government Assistance* – applied for the first time in 1984. *[IAS 20.41]*. The only substantive amendment since issue was in 2008, requiring entities to quantify the benefit of a government loan at a below-market rate of interest. *[IAS 20.10A, 43]*.

IAS 20 defines government grants in terms of transfers of resources to an entity in return for meeting certain conditions relating to the operating activities of the entity. *[IAS 20.3]*. SIC-10 – *Government Assistance – No Specific Relation to Operating Activities* – was issued in 1998 to clarify that IAS 20 applies even if the only condition is a requirement to operate in certain regions or industry sectors (see 2.2.2 below).

Government grants related to biological assets are excluded from the scope of IAS 20 and are dealt with in IAS 41 – *Agriculture*, which has different accounting requirements (see 5 below and Chapter 42 at 3.3). *[IAS 20.2(d)]*.

1.1   Overview of IAS 20

Government grants are transfers of resources to an entity in return for past or future compliance with certain conditions relating to the entity's operating activities. *[IAS 20.3]*.

Such assistance has been available to businesses for many years, although the exact nature of such support will vary from country to country and over time as governments and their priorities change.

For example, in 2020 governments all over the world introduced measures to provide financial assistance to businesses in an effort to mitigate the significant impact of the coronavirus pandemic on their economies. These measures included direct subsidies, tax exemptions, tax reductions and credits, extended expiry periods for utilising unused tax losses, reductions in public levies, rental reductions or deferrals, low-interest loans and legal protections from eviction or insolvency proceedings. Whilst not all these measures are accounted for as government grants, the pandemic has caused a significant increase in the prominence of government grants and other forms of government assistance.

IAS 20 states that the purpose of government grants, which may be called subsidies, subventions or premiums, *[IAS 20.6]*, and other forms of government assistance is often to encourage a private sector entity to take a course of action that it would not normally have taken if the assistance had not been provided. [IAS 20.4].

As the standard notes, the receipt of government assistance by an entity may be significant for the preparation of the financial statements for two reasons:

- if resources have been transferred, an appropriate method of accounting for the transfer must be found; and
- it is desirable to give an indication of the extent to which an entity has benefited from such assistance during the reporting period, because this facilitates comparison of its financial statements with those of prior periods and with those of other entities. [IAS 20.5].

The main accounting issue that arises from government grants is how to deal with the benefit that the grant represents. IAS 20 adopts an income approach, whereby grants are recognised in profit or loss in the same periods as the entity recognises as expenses the costs that the grants are intended to compensate. [IAS 20.12]. Accordingly, grants relating to specific expenses are recognised in profit or loss in the same periods as those expenses, and grants relating to depreciable assets are recognised in profit or loss in the same periods as the related depreciation expense. [IAS 20.17]. Government grants are accounted for similarly regardless of whether they are received in cash or as a reduction of a liability to the government. [IAS 20.9]. When a grant is received in the form of a transfer of a non-monetary asset, the standard allows an alternative accounting treatment, which is detailed in 3.2 below.

The standard pre-dates the IASB's *Conceptual Framework* and, as the IASB itself has noted, it is inconsistent with it,[1] resulting in the recognition in the statement of financial position of deferred credits that do not meet the *Framework's* definitions of liabilities and allowing alternatives to initial measurement at fair value that could result in an asset being understated by reference to the *Framework*. Now that IAS 11 – *Construction Contracts* – and IAS 18 – *Revenue* – have been replaced by IFRS 15 – *Revenue from Contracts with Customers*, IAS 20 is the only standard left that takes an income approach instead of the balance sheet approach for the recognition of assets and liabilities applied in the rest of the IFRS literature.

The standard recognises that an entity may receive other forms of government assistance which cannot reasonably have a value placed upon them. Rather than prescribe how these should be accounted for, it requires disclosure about such assistance. [IAS 20.34, 36]. However, since the issue of IFRS 13 – *Fair Value Measurement* – the challenge of placing a value on forms of assistance has reduced (see 3.8 below). For example, IAS 20 cites free technical or marketing advice and the provision of guarantees as examples of government assistance that cannot reasonably have a value placed on them and hence are excluded from the definition of grants. [IAS 20.35]. Nevertheless, where it can be demonstrated that a fair value can be determined for these items, then they should be accounted as a government grant (see 3.5 below for further discussion about guarantees).

1.2 Terms used in this chapter

The following terms are used in this chapter with the meanings specified:

Term	Definition
Government	Government, government agencies and similar bodies whether local, national or international. *[IAS 20.3]*.
Government assistance	Action by government designed to provide an economic benefit specific to an entity or a range of entities qualifying under certain criteria. Government assistance does not include benefits provided only indirectly through action affecting general trading conditions, such as the provision of infrastructure in development areas or the imposition of trading constraints on competitors. *[IAS 20.3]*.
Government grants	Assistance by government in the form of transfers of resources to an entity in return for past or future compliance with certain conditions relating to the operating activities of the entity. This excludes those forms of government assistance which cannot reasonably have a value placed upon them and transactions with government which cannot be distinguished from the normal trading transactions of the entity. *[IAS 20.3]*. Government grants are sometimes called by other names such as subsidies, subventions, or premiums. *[IAS 20.6]*.
Grants related to assets	Government grants whose primary condition is that an entity qualifying for them should purchase, construct or otherwise acquire long-term assets. Subsidiary conditions may also be attached restricting the type or location of the assets or the periods during which they are required to be acquired or held. *[IAS 20.3]*.
Grants related to income	Government grants other than those related to assets. *[IAS 20.3]*.
Forgivable loans	Loans which the lender undertakes to waive repayment under certain prescribed conditions. *[IAS 20.3]*.
Fair value	The price that would be received to sell an asset or paid to transfer a liability in an orderly transaction between market participants at the measurement date. *[IAS 20.3, IFRS 13 Appendix A]*.
Non-monetary government grant	A government grant that takes the form of a transfer of a non-monetary asset, such as land or other resources, for the use of the entity. *[IAS 20.23]*.
Biological asset	A living animal or plant. *[IAS 41.5]*.
Bearer plant	A bearer plant is a living plant that: *[IAS 41.5]* (a) is used in the production or supply of agricultural produce; (b) is expected to bear produce for more than one period; and (c) has a remote likelihood of being sold as agricultural produce, except for incidental scrap sales.
Costs to sell	The incremental costs directly attributable to the disposal of an asset, excluding finance costs and income taxes. *[IAS 41.5]*.

2 SCOPE OF IAS 20

IAS 20 applies in accounting for, and in the disclosure of, government grants and in the disclosure of other forms of government assistance. *[IAS 20.1]*. The distinction between government grants and other forms of government assistance is important because the standard's accounting requirements only apply to the former.

The standard regards the term 'government' to include government agencies and similar bodies whether local, national or international. *[IAS 20.3]*.

2.1 Government assistance

Government assistance is defined as action by government designed to provide an economic benefit to an entity or range of entities qualifying under certain criteria. *[IAS 20.3]*. Government assistance takes many forms 'varying both in the nature of the assistance given and in the conditions which are usually attached to it'. *[IAS 20.4]*.

However, such assistance does not include benefits provided indirectly through action affecting general trading conditions, such as the provision of infrastructure (e.g. transport, communications networks or utilities) in development areas or that are available for the benefit of an entire local community or the imposition of trading constraints on competitors (see 3.8 below). *[IAS 20.3, 38]*.

2.2 Government grants

2.2.1 Definitions

Government grants are a specific form of government assistance. Under IAS 20, government grants represent assistance by government in the form of transfers of resources to an entity in return for past or future compliance with certain conditions relating to the operating activities of the entity. *[IAS 20.3]*. The standard identifies the following types of government grants:

- grants related to assets are government grants whose primary condition is that an entity qualifying for them should purchase, construct or otherwise acquire long-term assets. Subsidiary conditions may also be attached restricting the type or location of the assets or the periods during which they are to be acquired or held; and

- grants related to income are government grants other than those related to assets. *[IAS 20.3]*.

Government grants exclude:

(a) assistance to which no value can reasonably be assigned; and

(b) transactions with government that cannot be distinguished from the normal trading transactions of the entity, e.g. where the entity is being favoured by a government's procurement policy. *[IAS 20.3, 34, 35]*.

Such excluded items are to be treated as falling only within the standard's disclosure requirements for government assistance (see 3.8 below).

Loans at below-market interest rates are also deemed to be a form of government grant and the standard requires entities to measure and record the benefit of the below-market rate of interest in accordance with IFRS 9 – *Financial Instruments*. *[IAS 20.10A]*. The accounting consequences are discussed at 3.4 below.

While grants of emission rights and renewable energy certificates typically meet the definition of government grants under IAS 20, the rights and certificates themselves are intangible assets. Accounting for emission rights and renewable energy certificates is discussed in Chapter 17 at 11.2 and 11.3.

2.2.2 Grants with no specific relation to operating activities (SIC-10)

SIC-10 addresses the situation in some countries where government assistance is provided to entities, but without there being any conditions specifically relating to their operating activities, other than to operate in certain regions or industry sectors. It determined that such forms of government assistance are to be treated as government grants. *[SIC-10.3]*. This ruling was made to avoid any suggestion that such forms of assistance were not governed by IAS 20 and could be credited directly to equity.

2.3 Scope exclusions

2.3.1 General considerations

IAS 20 does not deal with:

(a) accounting for government grants if the entity prepares financial information that reflect the effects of changing prices, whether as financial statements or in supplementary information of a similar nature;

(b) government assistance in the form of benefits that are available in determining taxable profit or loss or are determined or limited on the basis of income tax liability, e.g. income tax holidays, investment tax credits, accelerated depreciation allowances and reduced income tax rates;

(c) government participation in the ownership of the entity; and

(d) government grants covered by IAS 41. *[IAS 20.2]*.

The accounting treatment of government assistance either provided by way of a reduction in taxable profit or loss; or determined or limited according to an entity's income tax liability is discussed in the context of investment tax credits at 2.3.2 below and in Chapter 33 at 4.3.

In the case of exclusion (c) above, for an entity in which the government is a shareholder, it will be necessary to determine whether any assistance being provided to the entity is being given by the government acting in its capacity as a shareholder. If so, such assistance will not be within the scope of IAS 20 and will be accounted for in equity, in common with other shareholder transactions (see Chapter 3 at 3.3).

The reason for exclusion (d) above is that the presentation permitted by IAS 20 of deducting government grants from the carrying amount of the asset (see 4.1 below) was considered inconsistent with a fair value model, which must be used in the measurement of biological assets. *[IAS 41.B66]*. The IASB decided to deal with government grants related to agricultural activity in IAS 41 rather than initiate a wider review of IAS 20. *[IAS 41.B67]*. The requirements of IAS 41 in relation to government grants are set out at 5 below and in Chapter 42 at 3.3.

There are no similar exclusions for government grants in IAS 40 – *Investment Property* – which includes a similar fair value model (see Chapter 19), nor was IAS 20 revised to deal with the matter. This is probably because government grants in the investment property sector are relatively rare compared to the agricultural sector. However, governments do on occasion provide grants and subsidised loans to finance the acquisition of social housing that meets the definition of investment property. The discount on these subsidised loans is considered to be a government grant, as described at 3.4 below.

2.3.2 Investment tax credits

IAS 20 excludes from its scope government assistance either provided by way of a reduction in taxable profit or determined or limited according to an entity's income tax liability, citing income tax holidays, investment tax credits, accelerated depreciation allowances and reduced income tax rates as examples. *[IAS 20.2(b)]*. IAS 12 – *Income Taxes* – states that it does not deal with the methods of accounting for government grants or investment tax credits, although any temporary differences that arise from them are in the scope of the standard. *[IAS 12.4]*. Accordingly, if government assistance is described as an investment tax credit, but it is neither determined or limited by reference to the entity's income tax liability nor provided in the form of an income tax deduction, the requirements of IAS 20 apply.

This raises the question as to how an entity should account for those forms of government incentives for specific kinds of investment that are delivered through the tax system. Sometimes, a tax credit is given as a deduction from the entity's income tax liability, and sometimes as a deductible expense in computing the liability. Entitlement to assistance can be determined in a variety of ways. Some investment tax credits may relate to direct investment in property, plant and equipment. Other entities may receive investment tax credits relating to research and development activities. Some credits may be realisable only through a reduction in current or future income taxes payable, while others may be settled directly in cash if the entity does not have sufficient income taxes payable to offset the credit within a certain period. Access to the credit may be limited according to the total of all taxes paid (i.e. including taxes such as payroll and sales taxes remitted to government in addition to income taxes). There may be other conditions associated with receiving the investment tax credit, for example with respect to the conduct and continuing activities of the entity, and the credit may become repayable if ongoing conditions are not met.

The fact that both IAS 20 and IAS 12 use the term 'investment tax credits' to describe items excluded from their scope requires entities to carefully consider the nature of such incentives and the conditions attached to them to determine which standard the particular tax credit is excluded from and, therefore, whether they fall in the scope of IAS 20 or IAS 12.

In our view, the determination of which framework to apply to a particular investment tax credit is a matter of judgement and all facts and circumstances relating to the specific incentive need to be considered in assessing the substance of the arrangement. The following factors will often be relevant, but this list of factors should not be considered exhaustive, and entities may identify other factors which they consider to be more important than those listed below:

Feature of credit	Indicator of IAS 20 treatment	Indicator of IAS 12 treatment
Method of realisation	Directly settled in cash where there are insufficient taxable profits to allow credit to be fully recovered, or available for set off against non-income taxes, such as payroll taxes, sales taxes or other amounts owed to government.	Only available as a reduction in income taxes payable (i.e. benefit is forfeited if there are insufficient income taxes payable). However, a lengthy period allowed for carrying forward unused credits may make this indicator less relevant.
Number of conditions not related to tax position (e.g. minimum employment, ongoing use of purchased assets)	Many	None or few
Restrictions as to nature of expenditure required to receive the grant	Highly specific	Broad criteria encompassing many different types of qualifying expenditure
Tax status of grant income	Taxable	Not taxable

In group accounts, in which entities from several different jurisdictions may be consolidated, it may be desirable that all 'investment tax credits' should be consistently accounted for, either as an IAS 20 government grant or as an income tax under IAS 12. However, the judgment as to which standard applies is made by reference to the nature of each type of investment tax credit and the conditions attached to it. This may mean that the predominant practice in a particular jurisdiction for a specific type of investment tax credit has evolved differently from the consensus in another jurisdiction for what could appear to be a substantially similar credit. We believe that, in determining whether the arrangement is of a type that falls within the scope of IAS 20 or IAS 12, an entity should consider the following factors in the order listed below:

- if there is a predominant local treatment for a specific investment tax credit as to whether a specific credit in the relevant tax jurisdiction falls within the scope of IAS 20 or IAS 12, this should take precedence;
- if there is no predominant local treatment, the group-wide approach to determining the standard that applies to such a credit should be applied; and
- in the absence of a predominant local consensus or a group-wide approach to making the determination, the indicators listed in the table above should provide guidance.

This may mean that an entity operating in several territories adopts different accounting treatments for apparently similar arrangements in different countries, but it at least ensures a measure of comparability between different entities operating in the same tax jurisdiction.

The treatment of investment tax credits accounted under IAS 12 is discussed in Chapter 33 at 4.3.

3 RECOGNITION AND MEASUREMENT

3.1 General requirements of IAS 20

IAS 20 requires that government grants should be recognised only when there is reasonable assurance that:

(a) the entity will comply with the conditions attaching to them; and

(b) the grants will be received. *[IAS 20.7]*.

The standard does not define 'reasonable assurance', which raises the question of whether or not it means the same as 'probable' (or 'more likely than not' *[IAS 37.15]*). When developing IAS 41 the Board noted that 'it would inevitably be a subjective decision as to when there is reasonable assurance that the conditions are met and that this subjectivity could lead to inconsistent income recognition.' *[IAS 41.B69]*. The phrase 'reasonable assurance' is generally interpreted as being a high threshold which we would suggest implies a significantly higher probability than 'more likely than not'. Therefore, we would not expect an entity to recognise government grants before it was significantly more likely than probable that the entity would comply with the conditions attached to them and that the grants would be received. In assessing the likelihood of compliance with conditions attached to the grant it is acknowledged the conditions may relate to future performance and other future events. However, for a grant related to an asset, we would not expect a grant to be recognised before the asset is acquired, regardless of how likely the acquisition of the asset is. If the grant is also conditional on maintaining a number of jobs to operate the asset, the grant should be recognised as soon as the asset is acquired as long as there is reasonable assurance that the jobs will be maintained as required. The standard notes that receiving a grant does not of itself provide conclusive evidence that the conditions attaching to the grant have been or will be fulfilled. *[IAS 20.8]*.

After an entity has recognised a government grant, any related contingent liability or contingent asset should be accounted for under IAS 37 – *Provisions, Contingent Liabilities and Contingent Assets*. *[IAS 20.11]*.

Government grants are accounted for similarly regardless of whether they are received in cash or as a reduction of a liability to the government. *[IAS 20.9]*. When a grant is received in the form of a transfer of a non-monetary asset, the standard allows an alternative accounting treatment, which is detailed in 3.2 below.

3.2 Non-monetary grants

A government grant in the form of a transfer of a non-monetary asset, such as land or other resources, which is intended for use by the entity, is usually recognised at the fair value of that asset. *[IAS 20.23]*. Fair value is defined in IFRS 13 and applies when another IFRS requires or permits fair value measurement, including IAS 20. *[IFRS 13.5, IAS 20.45]*. Fair value is the price that would be received to sell an asset or paid to transfer a liability in an orderly transaction between market participants at the measurement date. *[IAS 20.3, IFRS 13.9]*. The requirements of IFRS 13 are discussed in Chapter 14.

An alternative of recognising such assets, and the related grant, at a nominal amount is permitted, effectively leading to no recognition and a pure disclosure approach. *[IAS 20.23]*.

This alternative is available even if the fair value of the asset differs materially from the nominal amount. Under IAS 8 – *Accounting Policies, Changes in Accounting Estimates and Errors* – an entity should select an accounting policy and apply it consistently to all non-monetary government grants. *[IAS 8.13].*

3.3 Forgivable loans

A forgivable loan from government, the repayment of which will be waived under certain prescribed conditions, *[IAS 20.3]*, is to be treated as a government grant when there is reasonable assurance that the entity will meet the terms for forgiveness of the loan. *[IAS 20.10].*

Example 24.1:   Government grant by way of forgivable loan

An entity participates in a government-sponsored research and development programme under which it is entitled to receive a government grant of up to 50% of the costs incurred for a particular project. The government grant is interest-bearing and fully repayable based on a percentage ('royalty') of the sales revenue of any products developed. Although the repayment period is not limited, no repayment is required if there are no sales of the products.

The entity should account for this type of government grant as follows:

- initially recognise the forgivable loan as a liability at nominal amount;
- apply the principles underlying the effective interest rate method in subsequent periods, which would involve estimating the amount and timing of future cash flows;
- review at each reporting date whether there is reasonable assurance that the entity will meet the terms for forgiveness of part or all of the loan based on expected future royalty repayments. If this is the case, then derecognise part or all of the liability initially recorded with a corresponding profit in the income statement; and
- if the entity subsequently revises its estimates of future sales upwards, it recognises a liability for any amounts previously included in profit and recognises a corresponding loss in the income statement.

However, an arrangement only meets the definition of a forgivable loan if its terms provide for circumstances where repayment would be waived (i.e. forgiven), without any other form of settlement. In Example 24.1 above, the entity either repays some or all of the loan if the project generates any sales or, if no sales are made, its liability is waived in full, with no further recourse to the government. In May 2016, the Interpretations Committee concluded on a request to clarify whether cash received to help an entity finance a research and development project would be treated as a forgivable loan in the following specific circumstances:[2]

- the loan was repayable only if the entity decided to exploit and commercialise the results of the research phase of the project;
- otherwise, the loan was not repayable in cash but instead the entity was required to transfer to the government the rights to the research.

The Interpretations Committee noted that, in this arrangement, the cash received did not meet the definition of a forgivable loan under IAS 20, because the government did not undertake to waive repayment of the loan but instead required settlement in cash or by the transfer of rights to the research. In other words, the entity could only avoid repayment by settling a non-financial obligation (to hand over the rights to the research). This requirement confirms the status of the cash receipt as a financial liability under IAS 32 – *Financial Instruments: Presentation*. *[IAS 32.20(a)].* The Committee also noted that the financial liability should be measured under IFRS 9. Any difference between the cash receipt and the fair value of the liability would need to be accounted for under IAS 20 as discussed at 3.4 below. The Interpretations Committee decided not to add this issue to its agenda on the basis that existing standards provide an adequate basis of accounting.[3]

Where an entity receives a loan to finance a research and development project and the loan will be forgiven if the project is not successful then the existence of the forgivable loan has no bearing on assessing the project for capitalisation under the criteria in IAS 38 – *Intangible Assets* (see Chapter 17 at 6.2). One of the criteria for capitalisation of development costs is that the entity must demonstrate that the intangible asset will generate probable economic benefits. *[IAS 38.57(d)]*. The existence of the forgivable loan does not mean that this requirement is always met. The criteria in IAS 38 should be assessed on their own merits.

3.4 Loans at lower than market rates of interest

IAS 20 requires government loans that have a below-market rate of interest to be recognised and measured in accordance with IFRS 9. *[IAS 20.10A, IFRS 9.5.1.1]*. The loans could be interest-free. The difference between the initial carrying value of the loan (its fair value) and the proceeds received is treated as a government grant. *[IAS 20.10A, IFRS 9.B5.1.1]*.

Example 24.2: Interest-free loan from a government agency

Company A secures an interest-free loan of €1,000 from a local government agency to ensure that the company invests in new equipment at its manufacturing facility. The loan is repayable at the end of five years and carries no interest. Company A can draw down the loan on demonstrating that it has incurred qualifying expenditure on property, plant and equipment.

On initial recognition, the market rate of interest for a similar five-year loan is 10% per year. The initial fair value of the loan is the present value of the future payment of €1,000, discounted using the market rate of interest for a similar loan of 10% for five years. This equates to €621.

The value of the government incentive to Company A to invest in its factory is €379, the difference between the total consideration received of €1,000 and the loan's initial fair value of €621. This difference is treated as a government grant.

Subsequently, interest will be imputed to the loan using the effective interest method, taking account of any transaction costs (see Chapter 49 at 3.3.1). IAS 20 requires that the grant is recognised in profit or loss on a systematic basis that matches it with the related costs it is intended to compensate. *[IAS 20.12]*. The standard stresses that the entity must consider the conditions and obligations that have been, or must be, met when 'identifying the costs for which the benefit of the loan is intended to compensate'. *[IAS 20.10A]*. In this example, the benefit of the loan is to help fund the purchase of new equipment. Therefore, it would be appropriate to recognise the grant as the new equipment is depreciated, rather than as the interest on the loan is recognised. Recognition in the income statement of the benefit of loans at below-market interest rates is discussed further at 3.6.2 below.

As well as routine subsidised lending to meet specific objectives, loans made as part of government rescue plans are generally within scope of IAS 20 if they are at a lower than market rate of interest. In 2009 PSA Peugeot Citroën received assistance from the European Investment Bank as described in Extract 24.1 below.

> Extract 24.1: PSA Peugeot Citroën (2009)
>
> Half-Year Financial Report 2009 [extract]
>
> 17.2. REFINANCING TRANSACTIONS [extract]
>
> – *EIB loan*
>
> In April 2009, Peugeot Citroën Automobiles S.A. obtained a €400 million 4-year bullet loan from the European Investment Bank (EIB). Interest on the loan is based on the 3-month Euribor plus 179 bps. At June 30, 2009 the government bonds (OATs) given by Peugeot S.A. as collateral for all EIB loans to Group companies had a market value of €160 million. In addition, 4,695,000 Faurecia shares held by Peugeot S.A. were pledged to the EIB as security for the loans. The interest rate risk on the new EIB loan has not been specifically hedged.
>
> This new loan is at a reduced rate of interest. The difference between the market rate of interest for an equivalent loan at the inception date and the rate granted by the EIB has been recognised as a government grant in accordance with IAS 20. The grant was originally valued at €38 million and was recorded as a deduction from the capitalized development costs financed by the loan. It is being amortised on a straight-line basis over the life of the underlying projects. The loan is measured at amortised cost, in the amount of €362 million at June 30, 2009. The effective interest rate is estimated at 5.90%.

Governments sometimes provide assistance in arrangements that are similar in substance to loans by allowing entities to retain sums that they collect on behalf of the government (e.g. value added taxes) until a future event, as in the following example:

Example 24.3:   Entity allowed to retain amounts owed to government

The local government of an underdeveloped region is trying to stimulate investment by allowing local companies to delay payment of the value added tax (VAT) on their sales. An entity participating in this scheme is entitled to retain an amount up to 40% of its investment in fixed assets. The retained VAT must be paid to the local government after 5 years and does not bear interest.

In this example, the fact that amounts retained by the entity are required to be repaid after 5 years makes this arrangement similar in nature to an interest-free loan. Accordingly, the entity would determine a value for the government assistance by comparing the amounts retained to the fair value of a 5-year loan at market rates of interest, as illustrated in Example 24.2 above. In determining an appropriate basis for recognising the benefit of the grant in profit or loss, the entity must consider the conditions and obligations that have been, or must be, met when 'identifying the costs for which the benefit of the loan is intended to compensate'. *[IAS 20.10A]*. In the example above, because the grant is intended to stimulate investment in fixed assets, it would be appropriate to recognise the grant in income in line with depreciation of the relevant assets. The judgement involved in matching the benefit to costs is discussed at 3.6 below.

3.5   Government guarantees

Governments sometimes provide support to an entity, indirectly, in the form of guarantees to lenders to the entity.

For example, a government may offer to guarantee loans taken out by entities that meet certain conditions. The government does not charge the lender a fee for this guarantee and consequently with the credit enhancement provided by the guarantee the lender is able to reduce the interest rate charged to the borrower.

IAS 20 cites guarantees as an example of government assistance that cannot reasonably have a value placed on them and hence are excluded from the definition of grants. *[IAS 20.35]*. Nevertheless, where it can be demonstrated that a fair value can be determined for the guarantee, and the guarantee is not integral to the loan then it could be accounted for separately as a government grant.

This determination will depend on the facts and circumstances of the guarantee. Assessing whether the guarantee is integral to the loan is a matter of judgement (see Chapter 51 at 5.8.1). This may include consideration as to whether the loan together with the guarantee is capable of being transferred.

If it is determined that grant accounting is appropriate, then the approach for below-market rate loans would apply (see 3.4 above and 3.6.2 below). In this case, the fair value of the loan reflects the present value of cash flows discounted using the market rate as if no guarantee were in place. The difference between the proceeds received and the fair value of the loan is accounted for as a government grant. If it is determined that the guarantee is government assistance, then the nature of that government assistance should be disclosed. *[IAS 20.39(b)]*.

3.6 Recognition in the income statement

Grants should be recognised in the income statement on a systematic basis that matches them with the related costs that they are intended to compensate. *[IAS 20.12]*. They should not be credited directly to equity. *[IAS 20.15]*. Income recognition on a receipts basis, which is not in accordance with the accruals accounting assumption, is only acceptable if there is no basis for allocating a grant to periods other than the one in which it is received. *[IAS 20.16]*.

IAS 20 rejects a 'capital approach', under which a grant is recognised outside profit or loss (typically credited directly to equity), *[IAS 20.13]*, in favour of the 'income approach', under which grants are taken to income over one or more periods, because:

(a) government grants are receipts from a source other than shareholders. As such, they should not be credited directly to equity but should be recognised in profit or loss in appropriate periods;

(b) government grants are rarely gratuitous. An entity earns them through compliance with their conditions and meeting the envisaged obligations. They should therefore be recognised in profit or loss over the periods in which the entity recognises the associated costs which the grant is intended to compensate; and

(c) as income and other taxes are expenses, it is logical to deal also with government grants, which are an extension of fiscal policies, in profit or loss. *[IAS 20.15]*.

IAS 20 envisages that in most cases, the periods over which an entity recognises the costs or expenses related to the government grant are readily ascertainable and thus grants in recognition of specific expenses are recognised as income in the same period as the relevant expense. *[IAS 20.17]*.

Grants related to depreciable assets are recognised as income over the periods, and in the proportions, in which depreciation on those assets is charged. *[IAS 20.17]*. Grants related to non-depreciable assets may also require the fulfilment of certain obligations, in which case they would be recognised as income over the periods in which the costs of meeting the obligations are incurred. For example, a grant of land may be conditional upon the erection of a building on the site and it may be appropriate to recognise it as income over the life of the building. *[IAS 20.18]*.

IAS 20 acknowledges that grants may be received as part of a package of financial or fiscal aids to which a number of conditions are attached. In such cases, the standard indicates that care is needed in identifying the conditions giving rise to the costs and expenses which determine the periods over which the grant will be recognised as income. It may also be appropriate to allocate part of the grant on one basis and part on another. *[IAS 20.19]*.

Where a grant relates to expenses or losses already incurred or becomes receivable for the purpose of giving immediate financial support to the entity with no future related costs, the grant should be recognised in income when it becomes receivable and the entity should disclose its effects to ensure that these are clearly understood. *[IAS 20.20-22]*.

Many of the problems in accounting for government grants relate to that of interpreting the requirement to match the grant with the related costs, particularly because of the international context in which IAS 20 is written. It does not address specific questions that relate to particular types of grant that are available in individual countries.

3.6.1 Achieving the most appropriate matching

The requirement to match the grant against the costs that it is intended to compensate can be difficult to apply in practice, because grants are sometimes given for a particular kind of expenditure that forms an element of a larger project. For example, in trying to determine an appropriate accounting policy for government assistance that is in the form of a grant against training costs incurred as part of a larger project, an entity might consider recognition in income in one of the following ways:

(a) matching against direct training costs; or

(b) matching rateably against total project costs.

Determining a reasonable approach is dependent on the specific facts and circumstances, including those relating to the context in which the grant was offered; the conditions attached to it; and the consequences of failing to meet those conditions.

Recognition of a grant in income when received in cash is unlikely to be an appropriate method, because it is not obviously linked to the recognition of the related expenditure and would be acceptable only if no basis existed for allocating a grant to periods other than the one in which it was received. *[IAS 20.16]*.

In some jurisdictions, grants are taxed as income on receipt; consequently, this is often the argument advanced for taking grants to income when received in cash. However, it is clear that the treatment of an item for tax purposes does not necessarily determine its treatment for accounting purposes, and immediate recognition in the income statement may result in an unacceptable departure from the principle that government grants should be matched with the costs that they are intended to compensate. *[IAS 20.16]*. The recognition of a grant in the income statement in a different period from that in which it is taxed, gives rise to a temporary difference that should be accounted for in accordance with IAS 12 (see Chapter 33). The example below illustrates that the determination of a systematic basis for recognition under the standard is not always straightforward.

Example 24.4: Grant associated with investment property

The government provides a grant to an entity that owns an investment property that is let for social housing. The grant is intended to compensate the entity for the lower rent it will receive when the property is let as social housing at below-market rates. That means that future rental income will be lower over the period of the lease which, at the same time, reduces the fair value of the investment property.

If the entity accounts for the investment property under the IAS 40 cost model, then it could be argued that the government grant should be recognised over the term of the lease to offset the lower rental income.

Alternatively, if the entity applied the IAS 40 fair value model then the cost being compensated is the reduction in fair value of the investment property. In that case it is more appropriate to recognise the benefit of the government grant immediately.

If, instead of a grant, the government subsidises a loan used by the entity to acquire the property, then the loan will be brought in at its fair value. The difference between the face value and fair value will be a government grant and the arguments at 3.6.2 below will apply to its treatment.

If the government imposes conditions, e.g. that the building must be used for social housing for ten years, this does not necessarily mean that the grant should be taken to income over that period. Rather, it should apply a process like that in Example 24.1 above. The entity assesses whether there is reasonable assurance that it will meet the terms of the grant and, to that extent, treat an appropriate amount as a grant as above. This should be reviewed at each reporting date and adjustments made if it appears that the conditions will not be met (see 3.7 below).

In the face of the problems described above of attributing a grant to related costs, it is difficult to offer definitive guidance; entities will have to make their own determination as to how the matching principle is to be applied in light of the specific facts and circumstances of the case. The only overriding considerations are that the method should be systematically and consistently applied, and that the policy adopted in respect of both capital and revenue grants, if material, should be adequately disclosed.

3.6.2 Loans at lower than market rates of interest

As discussed at 3.4 above, IAS 20 requires that the difference between the initial fair value of a government loan that has a below-market rate of interest and the proceeds received is treated as a government grant. *[IAS 20.10A]*.

The issue that then arises is how to recognise the grant in profit or loss. As noted at 3.6 above, IAS 20 requires that the grant is recognised in profit or loss on a systematic basis that matches it with the related costs it is intended to compensate, *[IAS 20.12]*, i.e. the emphasis in IAS 20 is on matching the benefit of a grant with the related costs as they are recognised in the income statement, rather than on the recognition of liquidity or cash flows.

The assessment of an appropriate method of allocation requires the entity to identify the costs intended to be compensated by the grant and is driven by a careful analysis of the facts and circumstances. The final determination as to which treatment is appropriate should reflect not only the terms of the arrangement but also other facts that might highlight the purpose of the loan, e.g.:

- Where it is determined that the grant is a grant related to an asset, as in Example 24.2 above, recognition as the asset is depreciated would be appropriate.
- Where the grant is a grant related to income and is intended to compensate for a specific expense, then recognition at the same time as that expense is recognised in profit or loss would be appropriate. This could include immediate recognition for expenses or losses that had already been incurred. *[IAS 20.20]*. Where the grant is intended to compensate for the cost of funding, then recognition on the same basis as the interest is charged (i.e. over the term of the loan) would be appropriate. This is illustrated in the following example.

Example 24.5: Below-market interest rate loan from the government

Company A secures a low interest loan of €1,000 from the government as part of its support measures for the coronavirus pandemic. The loan is repayable at the end of five years and carries an interest rate of 5%, demonstrably below the market rate. There are no conditions attached regarding the expenditure that the loan should be used for. Also, the grant benefit of the below-market rate loan cannot be attributed to any specific costs, past or future, neither based on the terms of the arrangement nor on other facts and circumstances, other than the cost of funding. The purpose of the grant is to provide the entity with immediate liquidity support by allowing it to borrow more money than it could have based on the market rate.

On initial recognition, the market rate of interest for a similar five-year loan is 10% per year. The initial fair value of the loan is the present value of the future payments for the loan, discounted using the market rate of interest for a similar loan of 10% for five years. This equates to €828.

The value of the government incentive to Company A is €172, being the difference between the total consideration received of €1,000 and the loan's initial fair value of €828. This difference is treated as a government grant.

In this example, the grant is compensating Company A for the higher market rate of interest that would otherwise have been charged as an expense on the loan. Company A recognises the grant benefit on the same basis as the interest is charged, over the term of the loan, thereby matching the benefit with the interest cost.

3.6.3 The period to be benefited by the grant

IAS 20 cautions that care is needed in identifying the conditions giving rise to the costs and expenses which determine the periods over which the grant will be earned. *[IAS 20.19]*. The qualifying conditions that must be satisfied are not necessarily conclusive evidence of the period to be benefited by the grant. For example, certain grants may become repayable if assets cease to be used for a qualifying purpose within a certain period; notwithstanding this condition, the grant may need to be recognised over the whole life of the asset, not over the qualifying period.

3.6.4 Separating grants into elements

The grant received may relate to a package of activities, the elements of which have different costs and conditions. In such cases, it is common that the elements for which the grant is given are not specifically identified or quantified. It might be appropriate to treat these different elements on different bases rather than accounting for the entire grant in one way, *[IAS 20.19]*, however, this will not always be practical. For example, a grant may be given on the basis that an entity makes approved capital expenditure in a particular area and employs a specified number of local people for an agreed period of time. In general, the most straightforward way of recognising such a grant is by linking it to long-term assets where this is a possible interpretation, particularly where the receipt of the grant depends on the cost of acquisition of long-term assets. However, this approach can only be taken if there is no clear indication to the contrary.

The assessment of an appropriate method of allocation requires the entity to identify the costs intended to be compensated by the grant and is driven by a careful analysis of the facts and circumstances. The final determination as to which treatment is appropriate should reflect not only the terms of the arrangement but also other facts that might highlight the purpose of the loan. Allocation of a grant between the elements will often involve judgement and entities may place more stress on some features than on others. In these cases, and where the effect is material, the financial statements should explicitly state what judgment has been made when applying the standard and disclose the corresponding financial effect.

3.7 Repayment of government grants

A government grant that becomes repayable after recognition should be accounted for as a revision of an accounting estimate. Repayment of a grant related to income should be charged first against the related unamortised deferred credit and any excess should be recognised as an expense immediately. *[IAS 20.32]*.

Repayment of a grant related to an asset should be recognised by increasing the carrying amount of the related asset or reducing the related unamortised deferred credit. The cumulative additional depreciation that would have been recognised to date as an expense in the absence of the grant should be charged immediately to profit or loss. *[IAS 20.32]*.

IAS 20 emphasises that the circumstances giving rise to the repayment of a grant related to an asset may require that consideration be given to the possible impairment of the asset. *[IAS 20.33]*.

3.8 Government assistance

IAS 20 excludes from the definition of government grants 'certain forms of government assistance which cannot reasonably have a value placed upon them and transactions with government which cannot be distinguished from the normal trading transactions of the entity'. *[IAS 20.34]*.

In the period since 1984, when IAS 20 first became effective, *[IAS 20.41]*, the use of fair values in financial reporting and the range of techniques used to determine reliable measures of fair value have increased. IFRS 13, issued in 2011, defines fair value, provides a principles-based framework for measuring fair value under IFRS and requires information about those fair value measurements to be disclosed. *[IFRS 13.1]*. IFRS 13 provides guidance for selecting appropriate valuation techniques and therefore one should now expect the occurrence of government assistance that cannot reasonably have a value placed on it to be a relatively rare occurrence (see Chapter 14).

IAS 20 cites a government procurement policy as an example of assistance that cannot be distinguished from the normal trading transactions of the entity. In this case, the 'existence of the benefit might be unquestioned but any attempt to segregate the trading activities from government assistance could well be arbitrary'. *[IAS 20.35]*. The standard therefore requires disclosure of significant government assistance. *[IAS 20.36, 39(b)]*.

The following example describes two different forms of government assistance:

Example 24.6:   Government assistance

(a)   Assistance in the form of priority bidding status

A government specifies that entities below a certain size are to be given priority in bidding for a particular type of government contract by mandating a minimum number of such entities to obtain bidding status. Although the entities will benefit from the quota, the value cannot be identified, and the effects of the assistance cannot be segregated from the trading activities of the qualifying entities.

(b)   Assistance in the form of credit facilities at market rates

Three governments that between themselves own just over 50% of the shares in an airline participate in granting it a revolving credit facility at a market rate of interest. This is not a government grant as it is on terms that a private market participant might have accepted but it is government assistance as the benefit cannot be distinguished from normal trading activities of the airline.

Under IAS 20, 'government assistance does not include the provision of infrastructure by improvement to the general transport and communication network and the supply of improved facilities such as irrigation or water reticulation that is available on an ongoing indeterminate basis for the benefit of an entire local community.' *[IAS 20.38]*.

3.9   Impairment testing of assets that qualified for government grants

When an asset is tested for impairment under IAS 36 – *Impairment of Assets* – the value of any government grants received in relation to those assets is taken into account regardless of whether the entity elected to deduct the grants in arriving at the carrying amount of the related assets or decided to set up the grant as deferred income.

Where grants had been deducted from the initial carrying amount of the related assets, no further adjustment is required before commencing the impairment test. However, when grants relating to assets are classified as deferred income, the unamortised balance carried in the statement of financial position should be deducted from the carrying amount of the assets or cash generating unit being tested.

If the impairment test requires the carrying value of the asset or related CGU to be reduced (because it exceeds the recoverable amount determined under IAS 36), the amount of the impairment is deducted from the carrying amount of the asset. However, no adjustment should be made to the balance presented as deferred income, which would continue to be recognised as income over the useful life of the asset. When the asset that is tested for impairment has been financed partly or fully by forgivable loans, the recognition of an impairment loss would generally be a trigger for the reassessment of whether there is reasonable assurance that the entity will meet the terms for forgiveness of part or all the related forgivable loan (see 3.3 above). The requirements of IAS 36 are discussed in Chapter 20.

4 PRESENTATION OF GRANTS

4.1 Presentation of grants related to assets in the statement of financial position

Grants that are related to assets (i.e. those whose primary condition is that an entity qualifying for them should purchase, construct or otherwise acquire long-term assets) should be presented in the statement of financial position either: *[IAS 20.24]*

(a) by setting up the grant as deferred income, which is recognised as income on a systematic basis over the useful life of the asset; *[IAS 20.26]* or

(b) by deducting the grant in arriving at the carrying amount of the asset, in which case the grant is recognised in profit or loss as a reduction of depreciation. *[IAS 20.27]*.

IAS 20 regards both these methods of presenting grants in financial statements as acceptable alternatives. *[IAS 20.25]*. The presentation approach should be applied consistently to all similar grants and appropriately disclosed.

Greencore Group plc adopted the former treatment, as shown below:

> **Extract 24.2: Greencore Group plc (2019)**
>
> Notes to the Group Financial Statements [extract]
>
> 1. Group Statement of Accounting Policies [extract]
>
> Government Grants
>
> Government grants for the acquisition of assets are recognised at their fair value when there is reasonable assurance that the grant will be received and any conditions attached to them have been fulfilled. The grant is held on the Statement of Financial Position as a deferred credit and released to the profit or loss over the periods necessary to match the related depreciation charges, or other expenses of the asset, as they are incurred.

An example of a company adopting a policy of deducting grants related to assets from the cost of the assets is shown below:

> **Extract 24.3: Akzo Nobel N.V. (2019)**
>
> NOTES TO THE CONSOLIDATED FINANCIAL STATEMENTS [extract]
>
> Note 1: Summary of significant accounting policies [extract]
>
> GOVERNMENT GRANTS
>
> Government grants related to costs are deducted from the relevant costs to be compensated in the same period. Government grants to compensate for the cost of an asset are deducted from the cost of the related asset. Emission rights granted by the government are recorded at cost. A provision is recorded if the actual emission is higher than the emission rights granted.

4.2 Presentation of grants related to income in the statement of profit or loss

Grants related to income should be presented either as:

(a) a credit in the income statement, either separately or under a general heading such as 'other income'; or

(b) a deduction in reporting the related expense. *[IAS 20.29]*.

The presentation approach should be applied consistently to all similar grants and appropriately disclosed. Grants that have the same characteristics should follow the same presentational approach on a consistent basis.

Example 24.7:   Presentation of grants with different characteristics

Company A has been receiving government grants to fund research activities for a number of years that it presents as 'other operating income'. In its current financial year, it has also received government support to compensate for the salaries of furloughed employees due to the coronavirus pandemic. Company A judges the R&D credits and the furlough grant to have different characteristics. It continues to present the grants to fund research activities separately in other operating income and recognises the furlough grant as a deduction from employment costs.

The standard points out that supporters of method (a) above consider it inappropriate to present income and expense items on a net basis and that 'separation of the grant from the expense facilitates comparison with other expenses not affected by a grant'. *[IAS 20.30]*. Furthermore, method (a) is consistent with the general prohibition of offsetting in IAS 1 – *Presentation of Financial Statements*. *[IAS 1.32-33]*. However, supporters of method (b) above would argue that 'the expenses might well not have been incurred by the entity if the grant had not been available and presentation of the expense without offsetting the grant may therefore be misleading'. *[IAS 20.30]*. The standard regards both methods as acceptable for the presentation of grants related to income. *[IAS 20.31]*. When offsetting is permitted by another standard, the general prohibition in IAS 1 does not apply. *[IAS 1.32]*. In any case, IAS 20 considers that disclosure of the grant is necessary when material for a proper understanding of the financial statements. Furthermore, disclosure of the effect of grants on any item of income or expense, which should be disclosed separately, is usually appropriate. *[IAS 20.31]*.

As illustrated below, Anheuser-Busch InBev has adopted a policy of presenting grants within other operating income, although not separately on the face of the income statement, rather than as a deduction from the related expense.

> Extract 24.4: Anheuser-Busch InBev NV/SA (2019)
>
> Notes to the consolidated financial statements [extract]
>
> 3. Summary of significant accounting policies [extract]
>
> (X) INCOME RECOGNITION [extract]
>
> Government grants
>
> A government grant is recognized in the balance sheet initially as deferred income when there is reasonable assurance that it will be received and that the company will comply with the conditions attached to it. Grants that compensate the company for expenses incurred are recognized as other operating income on a systematic basis in the same periods in which the expenses are incurred. Grants that compensate the company for the acquisition of an asset are presented by deducting them from the acquisition cost of the related asset.

Refer to Extract 24.3 above for an example of a company presenting the grant as a deduction from the related expense in the income statement.

4.3 Statement of cash flows

The receipt of grants can cause major movements in the cash flows of an entity.

However, neither IAS 20 nor IAS 7 – *Statement of Cash Flows* – provide guidance on where in the statement of cash flows to present the cash inflows from the receipt of government grants.

The Interpretations Committee discussed the presentation of cash flows for several fact patterns including government grants related to assets. in July 2012.[4] The issue was further discussed in March 2013. In the course of the discussions held, staff suggested that grants were providing a source of financing to the entity, and consequently cash received would be part of the entity's financing activities. Eventually, the Committee could not conclude on all fact patterns discussed and discontinued its work.[5]

Consequently, there is likely to be diversity in practice for the presentation of all grants in the statement of cash flows, whether related to assets or to income. Cash flows received from grants could be considered to be financing by nature. Alternatively, cash flows received from grants (or only those from grants related to income) could be presented as operating cash flows by default since they do not seem to meet the definition of financing activities. Another view would be to classify cash flows from grants in accordance with the nature of the activity to which they relate, following the definitions of operating, investing and financing activities in paragraph 6 of IAS 7.

Selecting the most appropriate presentation will be a matter of judgment. Once adopted, the presentation principles should be applied consistently and clear disclosure of the principles and the impact thereof on the cash flow statement should be provided in accordance with IAS 1.

IAS 20 does makes clear, however, that cash flows from government grants should be disclosed as separate items in the cash flow statement, even as regards grants related to assets when such grants are deducted from the related assets for the purpose of presentation in the statement of financial position. *[IAS 20.28]*.

Lastly, cash flows from refundable advances should be presented as financing cash flows, whereas their transformation into a grant, if and when the entity meets the conditions for forgiveness of the loan, is a non-cash transaction.

5 GOVERNMENT GRANTS RELATED TO BIOLOGICAL ASSETS IN THE SCOPE OF IAS 41

A different accounting treatment to that prescribed in IAS 20 is required if a government grant relates to a biological asset measured at its fair value less costs to sell, in accordance with IAS 41, or a government grant requires an entity not to engage in specified agricultural activity. *[IAS 41.38]*. In this context, the term 'biological asset' excludes bearer plants as defined in IAS 41 (see 1.2 above). *[IAS 41.1(a), 5]*. Government grants involving biological assets should only be accounted for under IAS 20 if the biological asset is 'measured at its cost less any accumulated depreciation and any accumulated impairment losses' (see Chapter 42 at 3.3). *[IAS 41.37-38]*. For government grants relating to biological assets measured at fair value less costs to sell, the requirements of IAS 41 apply as follows.

An unconditional government grant related to a biological asset measured at its fair value less costs to sell is recognised in profit or loss when, and only when, the grant becomes receivable. *[IAS 41.34]*. An entity is therefore not permitted under IAS 41 to deduct a government grant from the carrying amount of the related asset. The IASB determined that any adjustment to the carrying value of the asset would be inconsistent with a fair value model and would give rise to no difference in the treatment of unconditional and conditional government grants, with both effectively recognised in income immediately. *[IAS 41.B66]*.

A conditional government grant related to a biological asset measured at its fair value less costs to sell is recognised only when the conditions attaching to the grant are met. *[IAS 41.35]*. IAS 41 permits an entity to recognise a government grant as income only to the extent that it (i) has met the terms and conditions of the grant and (ii) has no obligation to return the grant. *[IAS 41.36]*. This would generally be later than the point of recognition in IAS 20, where reasonable assurance that these criteria will be met is sufficient. *[IAS 20.7]*. The following example, which is taken from IAS 41, illustrates how an entity should apply these requirements. *[IAS 41.36]*.

Example 24.8:   Grant relating to biological assets carried at fair value

Entity A receives a government grant under terms that require it to farm in a particular location for five years. The entire government grant must be returned if it farms for less than five years. In this case the government grant is not recognised as income until the five years have passed.

Entity B receives a government grant on a similar basis, except it allows part of the government grant to be retained based on the passage of time. Entity B recognises that part of the government grant as income as time passes.

6   DISCLOSURES

IAS 20 requires that entities should disclose the following information regarding government grants:

(a)   the accounting policy, including the methods of presentation adopted in the statement of financial position, the statement of profit or loss and the cash flows statement;

(b)   a description of the nature and extent of the grants recognised in the financial statements and an indication of other forms of government assistance from which the entity has directly benefited; and

(c)   unfulfilled conditions or other contingencies attaching to government assistance that has been recognised. *[IAS 20.39]*.

The extracts below illustrate how companies typically satisfy the disclosure requirements of IAS 20. It should be noted that disclosures concerning the nature and conditions of government grants are sometimes relatively minimal, possibly because the amounts involved are immaterial.

Extract 24.5: Eskom Holdings SOC Ltd (2019)

NOTES TO THE FINANCIAL STATEMENTS [extract]

2. Summary of significant accounting policies [extract]

2.16 Payments received in advance, contract liabilities and deferred income [extract]

Grants

Government grants for electrification are initially recognised in payments received in advance and allocated to deferred income when the related asset has been connected to the electricity network. The deferred income is recognised in profit or loss within depreciation and amortisation expense on a straight-line basis over the expected useful lives of the related assets.

27. Payments received in advance and contract liabilities and deferred income [extract]

		2019 Government grant Rm
27.2	Contract liabilities and deferred income [extract]	
	Group and company	
	Balance at beginning of the year	18 589
	Transfers from payments received in advance	2 790
	Income recognised	(1 209)
	Balance at end of the year	20 170
	Maturity analysis	20 170
	Non-current	18 878
	Current	1 292

		Group 2019 Rm	2018 Rm
38.	Depreciation and amortisation expense [extract]		
	Depreciation of property, plant and equipment	30 511	23 721
	Amortisation of intangible assets	454	461
	Contract liabilities and deferred income recognised (government grant)	(1 209)	(1 050)
		29 756	23 132

Eskom Holdings also provided information relating to the parent company and for other items of deferred income that, for brevity, is not reproduced above. Additional examples of accounting policies for government grants can be found in Extracts 24.2, 24.3 and 24.4 above.

In Extract 24.6 below, Stagecoach Group plc provides an indication of other forms of government assistance from which the entity has directly benefited, *[IAS 20.39(b)]*, in this case in the form of additional support from government bodies and local authorities to whom the Group provides concessionary travel and other tendered transport services.

> Extract 24.6: Stagecoach Group plc (2020)
>
> **Notes to the consolidated financial statements** [extract]
>
> **Note 3 Operating costs and other operating income** [extract]
>
> COVID-19 related grants receivable reflects the amounts receivable in respect of government grants provided to organisations in light of the ongoing COVID-19 situation. The amounts principally reflect grants receivable in respect of the year ended 2 May 2020 under the Coronavirus Job Retention Scheme ("CJRS") and under the COVID-19 Bus Services Support Grant ("CBSSG") scheme.
>
> [...]
>
> In addition to the COVID–19 related grants receivable shown above, some government bodies have agreed to continue certain levels of payments of concessionary revenue, tender revenue and Bus Service Operators Grant ("BSOG") to help support the continuing operation of bus services. The payment rates of these items during the period affected by COVID-19 are higher than they would ordinarily be for the relevant levels of patronage, mileage and fuel consumption. Consistent with previous years, all amounts of concessionary revenue and tender revenue are reported within revenue and an analysis of revenue for the year ended 2 May 2020 is provided in note 2(a) to these consolidated financial statements. Also consistent with previous years, all amounts of BSOG receivable, essentially rebates of fuel duty, are included net within materials and consumables costs shown above.
>
> Had the average rate of concessionary revenue per journey for the year ended 2 May 2020 as a whole been consistent with the rate for the period from 28 April 2019 to 29 February 2020, the concessionary revenue for the year would have been £234.3m, £22.3m lower than £256.6m reported in note 2(a). While not all concessionary revenue is ordinarily determined on a "per journey" basis, that illustrates the extent to which concessionary payments were maintained notwithstanding the COVID-19 related reductions in journey numbers.

References

1 IASB Completed projects, IASB archive site, Work plan for IFRSs, All projects since 2006 in alphabetical order, Government grants (Deferred), IASB website, http://archive.ifrs.org/Current-Projects/IASB-Projects/Government-Grants/Pages/Government-Grants.aspx (accessed on 16 September 2020).

2 *IFRIC Update*, May 2016.
3 *IFRIC Update*, May 2016.
4 *IFRIC Update*, July 2012.
5 *IFRIC Update*, March 2013.

Chapter 25   Service concession arrangements

1 INTRODUCTION 1851
   1.1   The Interpretations Committee's approach to accounting for service concessions 1852
   1.2   Terms used in this chapter 1853
2 SCOPE OF IFRIC 12 1854
   2.1   Public service nature of the obligation 1855
   2.2   Arrangements that are not in the scope of IFRIC 12 1855
         2.2.1   Outsourcing arrangements 1856
   2.3   Interaction of IFRS 16 and IFRIC 12 1857
   2.4   Private-to-private arrangements 1857
   2.5   Accounting by grantors 1858
3 THE CONTROL MODEL 1858
   3.1   Regulation of services 1858
   3.2   Control of the residual interest 1859
   3.3   Assets within scope 1862
         3.3.1   Accounting for service concession arrangements for which the infrastructure is leased from a party other than the grantor 1862
         3.3.2   Periodic payments to the grantor for the right to use assets 1864
         3.3.3   Previously held assets used for the concession 1865
   3.4   Partially regulated assets 1866
4 ACCOUNTING BY THE CONCESSION OPERATOR: THE FINANCIAL ASSET AND INTANGIBLE ASSET MODELS 1867
   4.1   Consideration for services provided and the determination of the appropriate model 1868

		4.1.1 Allocating the consideration..1869	
			4.1.1.A Identifying the contract(s) with a customer.............1869
			4.1.1.B Identifying the performance obligations in the contract...1870
			4.1.1.C Determining the transaction price under the contract...1871
			4.1.1.D Allocating the transaction price to the performance obligations in the contract...................1872
		4.1.2 Determining the accounting model after the construction phase..1873	
	4.2	The financial asset model...1875	
	4.3	The intangible asset model.. 1879	
		4.3.1 Amortisation of the intangible asset...1881	
		4.3.2 Impairment during the construction phase................................. 1883	
	4.4	Revenue recognition implications of the two models 1884	
	4.5	'Bifurcation' – single arrangements that contain both financial and intangible assets...1885	
	4.6	Accounting for residual interests..1889	
	4.7	Accounting for contractual payments to be made by an operator to a grantor..1891	
		4.7.1 Accounting for variable payments in a service concession........1892	
		4.7.2 Accounting for contractual payments under the financial asset model...1893	
		4.7.3 Accounting for contractual payments under the intangible asset model..1894	
	4.8	Contract acquisition and mobilisation costs...1896	
		4.8.1 Costs to obtain a contract..1896	
		4.8.2 Pre-contract costs 1897	
		4.8.3 Mobilisation costs 1897	
			4.8.3.A Mobilisation costs are excluded from input measures of contract progress 1898
5	REVENUE AND EXPENDITURE DURING THE OPERATIONS PHASE OF THE CONCESSION AGREEMENT 1898		
	5.1	Additional construction and upgrade services......................................1899	
		5.1.1 Subsequent construction or upgrade services that are part of the initial infrastructure asset..1900	
		5.1.2 Subsequent construction services that comprise additions to the initial infrastructure...1900	
	5.2	Accounting for the operations phase..1901	
	5.3	Items provided to the operator by the grantor 1904	

6 FURTHER EXAMPLES ILLUSTRATING THE APPLICATION OF
    IFRIC 12 AND INTERACTIONS WITH IFRS 15 AND IFRS 9 1905
7 DISCLOSURE REQUIREMENTS: SIC-29 1916

List of examples

Example 25.1:	Residual arrangements	1860
Example 25.2:	Payment mechanisms for service concessions	1868
Example 25.3:	The Financial Asset Model	1877
Example 25.4:	The Intangible Asset Model – recording the construction asset	1880
Example 25.5:	Output-based versus revenue-based amortisation when prices change	1882
Example 25.6:	Revenue under the financial asset and intangible models	1884
Example 25.7:	The bifurcated model	1885
Example 25.8:	Contractual rights to cash in termination arrangements	1890
Example 25.9:	Contractual payments made to a grantor under the financial asset model	1893
Example 25.10:	Contractual payments made to a grantor under the intangible asset model	1895
Example 25.11:	Executory and contractual obligations to maintain and restore the infrastructure	1902
Example 25.12:	The Intangible Asset Model – recording the operations phase	1902
Example 25.13:	Financial asset model – Receivable recognised once construction is complete and no change in discount rate on recognition of receivable	1905
Example 25.14:	Financial asset model – Receivable recognised once construction is complete and a change in discount rate on recognition of receivable	1910
Example 25.15:	Financial Asset Model – Contract asset relating to construction services unwinds to a receivable over the period in which the other performance obligations in the contract are satisfied	1912
Example 25.16:	Intangible asset model	1914

Chapter 25 Service concession arrangements

1 INTRODUCTION

Service concession arrangements (SCAs) have been developed as a mechanism for governments to procure public services using private capital and management expertise. The rights and obligations of the public sector body procuring the services and the private sector entity providing the services are set out in a contract, the terms of which can be complex depending upon the nature of the SCA. The most common forms of arrangement are as follows:

- 'Build-operate-transfer' SCA – where a private sector entity takes responsibility for building and operating infrastructure assets such as roads, bridges, railways, hospitals, prisons, power stations and schools, in consideration for a long-term contract from the public sector body giving the entity the right to charge for services to the public using that infrastructure;

- 'Rehabilitate-operate-transfer' SCA – where the private sector entity restores or improves an existing facility or public service up to an agreed standard and continues to maintain and operate the related infrastructure for a contracted period. This type of arrangement includes a range of projects from the refurbishment of social housing and street lighting to major civil engineering projects to restore a city's underground rail system; and

- 'Operate-only' SCA – where a private sector entity becomes responsible for the operational management and maintenance of an existing infrastructure asset that is used to provide services to the public. This last variant, together with the development of similar arrangements between private sector bodies, has at times obscured the boundary between service concessions and outsourcing arrangements (see 2.2.1 below).

The accounting challenge is to reflect the substance of these arrangements fairly in the financial statements of both of the contracting parties, because the various transactions between the parties to a SCA range across a number of accounting standards and interpretations, including:

- accounting for the rights of the parties over the infrastructure assets (IAS 16 – *Property, Plant and Equipment*, and IFRS 16 – *Leases*);
- construction or refurbishment of the infrastructure assets (IFRS 15 – *Revenue from Contracts with Customers*);
- accounting for the various performance obligations under the contract during the operations period of the concession (IFRS 15 and IAS 37 – *Provisions, Contingent Liabilities and Contingent Assets*); and
- recognition and measurement of the amounts payable or receivable under the arrangement (IAS 20 – *Accounting for Government Grants and Disclosure of Government Assistance*, IAS 23 – *Borrowing Costs*, IAS 32 – *Financial Instruments: Presentation*, IAS 37, IAS 38 – *Intangible Assets* – and IFRS 9 – *Financial Instruments*).

This makes it difficult to develop a coherent accounting model that deals with all the features of service concessions simultaneously, and from the position of both the private sector (i.e. the 'operator') and public sector (i.e. the 'grantor'). Moreover, prior to the issue of IFRIC 12 – *Service Concession Arrangements*, entrenched national positions had developed and differing accounting treatments had been widely adopted in various jurisdictions, with or without a basis in specific local accounting standards. Also, some jurisdictions accepted more than one accounting treatment for broadly similar arrangements, some of which are influenced by a taxation basis that has been agreed with the jurisdictional taxation authorities. All this resulted in considerable diversity in the accounting by IFRS reporters of seemingly similar arrangements.

In 2001, SIC-29 – *Service Concession Arrangements: Disclosures* – was issued. This did not attempt to address the accounting issues but considered the information that should be disclosed in the notes to the financial statements of an 'operator' and 'grantor' under a service concession arrangement. *[SIC-29.4]*. Its requirements are described further at 7 below.

IFRIC 12 addresses the accounting issues from the perspective of the operator and was approved by the IASB in November 2006. The fact that the Interpretation took more than three years to develop indicates the complexity of the issues and the difficulty that the Committee encountered in fitting a solution into the existing accounting framework.

1.1 The Interpretations Committee's approach to accounting for service concessions

The Interpretations Committee views the primary accounting determination for the operator as being whether control over the infrastructure assets rests with the operator or whether any new or existing assets under the concession arrangement are controlled by the grantor.

The Interpretations Committee suggests that arrangements where control does not rest with the grantor, and the asset is either derecognised by the grantor or is an asset constructed for the concession that the grantor never controls, can be dealt with adequately by other accounting standards or interpretations. *[IFRIC 12.BC11-BC13]*. The interrelationship with other accounting standards is discussed further at 2.2 below.

Infrastructure assets controlled by the grantor are the subject of IFRIC 12. This applies whether the assets are constructed or acquired by the operator for the concession, that become those of the grantor because it controls them, or existing assets that remain under the grantor's control and to which the operator is granted access. *[IFRIC 12.7]*.

'Control' is therefore a central concept in IFRIC 12. Control is not determined by attributing risks and benefits to identify the 'owner' of the infrastructure. Instead, IFRIC 12 regards control in terms of the operator's ability (or lack thereof) to decide how to use the asset during the concession term and how it will be deployed thereafter. Its definition and consequences are discussed further at 3 below.

Thus, any infrastructure that is under the control of the grantor will be accounted for using IFRIC 12. In doing so, the Interpretations Committee establishes the following principles for accounting by the operator of a concession falling within its scope:

- the infrastructure is not recognised as property, plant and equipment by the operator; *[IFRIC 12.11]*
- the operator recognises revenue from construction services when assets are built or upgraded during the concession term; *[IFRIC 12.14]*
- a financial asset or an intangible asset is recognised as consideration for these construction services, depending upon the way in which the operator is paid for services under the contract; *[IFRIC 12.15]*
- however, both types of consideration are classified as a contract asset during the construction or upgrade period in accordance with IFRS 15; *[IFRIC 12.19]* and
- revenues and costs for the provision of operating services are recognised over the term of the concession arrangement. *[IFRIC 12.20]*.

The requirement to recognise an asset as consideration for construction services gives rise to three service concession models – the 'financial asset' model, the 'intangible asset' model and a hybrid model. These are considered further at 4 below. However, under all models the operator is required to recognise a contract asset during the construction or upgrade period in accordance with IFRS 15. The recognition of revenue and costs in the operations phase is discussed at 5 below.

1.2 Terms used in this chapter

The following terms are used in this chapter with the meanings specified:

Term	Definition
Grantor	A public sector body (including a governmental body, or a private sector entity to which responsibility for a public service has been devolved) that grants the service arrangement. *[IFRIC 12.3]*.
Operator	A private sector entity that is contractually obliged to construct and/or upgrade, operate and maintain infrastructure used to provide services to the public on behalf of the public sector entity. The operator is responsible for at least some of the management of the infrastructure and related services and does not merely act as an agent on behalf of the grantor. *[IFRIC 12.2, 3]*.

Term	Definition
Service concession arrangement	A contract that obliges the operator to construct and/or upgrade, operate and maintain infrastructure used to provide the services to the public on behalf of the grantor. The contract sets the initial prices to be levied by the operator and regulates price revisions over the period of the service arrangement. *[IFRIC 12.3]*.
Infrastructure	Assets used in the provision of services to the public. Examples include roads, bridges, tunnels, prisons, hospitals, airports, water distribution facilities, energy supply and telecommunications networks. *[IFRIC 12.1]*. Infrastructure can be constructed or acquired by the operator for the purpose of the service arrangement; or can be existing assets to which the grantor gives the operator access for the purpose of the service arrangement. *[IFRIC 12.7]*.
Control criteria	(a) the grantor controls or regulates what services the operator must provide with the infrastructure, to whom it must provide them, and at what price; and (b) the grantor controls any significant residual interest in the infrastructure at the end of the term of the arrangement, through ownership, beneficial entitlement or otherwise. *[IFRIC 12.5]*.
Government	Refers to government, government agencies and similar bodies whether local, national or international. *[IAS 20.3]*.

2 SCOPE OF IFRIC 12

The scope of IFRIC 12 is specific and relatively narrow. The Interpretations Committee decided to address only public-to-private service concession arrangements in which:

(a) the grantor controls or regulates the services that the operator must provide using the infrastructure, to whom it must provide them, and at what price; and

(b) the grantor controls any significant residual interest in the property at the end of the concession term through ownership, beneficial entitlement or otherwise. (Infrastructure used in a service concession for its entire useful life is deemed to meet this second condition because there is no significant residual interest). *[IFRIC 12.5, 6]*.

The Committee also decided to restrict its guidance to the accounting by operators in public-to-private service concession arrangements. *[IFRIC 12.4]*. Accordingly, the Interpretation does not specify the accounting by grantors. *[IFRIC 12.9]*.

The Committee acknowledged that these restrictions would exclude many arrangements that are found in practice for private sector participation in the provision of public services. However, it concluded that the above conditions were likely to be met in most of the public-to-private service concession arrangements for which guidance had been sought and that other standards apply when these conditions are not a feature of the arrangement. *[IFRIC 12.BC11-13]*. The standards that might apply for arrangements outside the scope of IFRIC 12 are set out at 2.2 below.

2.1 Public service nature of the obligation

Initially, as described in the exposure draft D12, the interpretation was intended to apply only to arrangements that involved a 'public service obligation', i.e. a contractual obligation for the operator to 'keep available to the public the services related to the infrastructure'.

Having agreed that 'the concept of a public service obligation was not in itself robust enough to form the basis for the scope',[1] the IFRIC did not retain this condition. This is understandable, since different governments will have a range of political or ideological views of what activities should be provided by the state and the definition of a 'public service obligation' may vary across jurisdictions and, sometimes, over time within the same jurisdiction.

As a result, the reference to 'the public service nature of the obligation undertaken by the operator' now only appears as a common feature of a service concession in the background section of the interpretation, without defining what is meant by the term. Instead, the Committee refers to examples of service concession arrangements. IFRIC 12 identifies roads, bridges, tunnels, prisons, hospitals, airports, water distribution facilities, energy supply and telecommunications networks as examples of infrastructure used for public services. *[IFRIC 12.1]*. SIC-29 refers to water treatment and supply facilities, motorways, car parks, tunnels, bridges, airports and telecommunications networks. *[SIC-29.1]*. It also states that a service concession arrangement generally involves the grantor conveying to the concession operator the right to provide services that give the public access to major economic and social facilities for the period of the concession. *[SIC-29.2(a)]*.

It is at least clear that it is not necessary for the operator to have direct involvement with the public as evidenced by the example in the Application Guidance of the interpretation of a 'hospital [which] is used by the grantor to treat public patients'. *[IFRIC 12.AG7]*.

2.2 Arrangements that are not in the scope of IFRIC 12

The Committee acknowledged that in practice there are arrangements for private sector participation in the provision of public services that will not fall in the scope of IFRIC 12. However, it was satisfied that the Interpretation would apply to most of the public-to-private service concession arrangements for which guidance had been sought. Nevertheless, the Committee did consider a range of typical arrangements and decided that it could provide references to the standards that apply to those that fall outside the scope of IFRIC 12 without giving any guidance as to their application. *[IFRIC 12.BC13]*.

These references are presented in Information Note 2 to IFRIC 12 (on which the following table is based) and which shows a range of arrangements between the public and private sectors. The Interpretations Committee's view is that IFRIC 12 is interpreting IFRSs for the transactions in the middle of this range, where the application of standards was previously unclear. These are described in the table below as 'Rehabilitate-operate-transfer' and 'Build-operate-transfer' arrangements. The table also demonstrates how other standards, namely IFRS 16, IFRS 15 and IAS 16, apply to arrangements that do not contain the features of a public-to-private service concession as defined in the Interpretation.

Category	Lessee	Service Provider			Owner	
Typical arrangement types	Lease, e.g. Operator leases asset from grantor	Service and/or maintenance contract (specific tasks e.g. debt collection)	Rehabilitate-operate-transfer	Build-operate-transfer	Build-own-operate	100% Divestment Privatisation, Corporation
Asset Ownership	Grantor				Operator	
Capital Investment	Grantor		Operator			
Demand Risk	Shared	Grantor	Operator and/or Grantor		Operator	
Typical Duration	8-20 years	1-5 years	25-30 years		Indefinite (or may be limited by licence)	
Residual Interest	Grantor				Operator	
Relevant IFRSs	IFRS 16	IFRS 15	IFRIC 12		IAS 16	

2.2.1 Outsourcing arrangements

Service concessions are not the only contractual arrangements between public sector bodies and private sector providers of services. Public sector bodies lease buildings or other property, plant and equipment from private sector entities for their own use. The private sector entity might also be engaged to construct the buildings or other property before it is occupied by the public sector body. The public sector also engages independent subcontractors to perform procurement services or to outsource the operation of its internal activities and functions.

It is important to consider whether the infrastructure is being used by the operator to provide services for the benefit of the public (such as in the case of a water treatment facility, for example), rather than to the grantor for its own benefit.

SIC-29 identifies examples of activities that are not service concession arrangements, citing an entity outsourcing the operation of its internal services, such as employee cafeteria, building maintenance, and accounting or information technology functions. *[SIC-29.1].*

The Interpretations Committee noted in September 2005 that it would not expect an information technology outsourcing arrangement for a government department to be dealt with under IFRIC 12.[2]

The assessment of whether an arrangement is a service concession within scope of IFRIC 12 or an outsourcing arrangement could give rise to differences in accounting for the private sector entity. Treating an arrangement as an outsourcing arrangement could result in the private sector entity recognising PP&E in its financial statements in respect of the assets subject to the arrangement. This would be the case if the arrangement were accounted for as the provision of goods and services under IFRS 15. When the private sector entity is considered to be the lessor, given the length of typical service concession arrangements, it is likely that a finance lease receivable would be recognised under IFRS 16. *[IFRS 16.67].*

Although for an arrangement accounted for under IFRIC 12, the private sector entity (operator) would in this case normally recognise a financial asset, an important distinction is that in an IFRIC 12 service concession, the private sector entity would recognise revenue in the period during which any infrastructure asset was being constructed. *[IFRIC 12.14]*. A lessor would record an IAS 16 asset under construction and only recognise revenue if the terms of the lease required that asset to be derecognised.

2.3 Interaction of IFRS 16 and IFRIC 12

IFRS 16 was issued by the IASB in January 2016 and became effective for annual reporting periods beginning on or after 1 January 2019. Unlike IAS 17 – *Leases*, IFRS 16 clearly excludes from its scope service concession arrangements falling within scope of IFRIC 12. *[IFRS 16.3(c)]*.

IFRS 16 defines an arrangement as containing a lease if the contract conveys the right to control the use of an identified asset for a period of time in exchange for consideration. *[IFRS 16.9]*. A right to control the use of an identified asset is then described in terms of the right to direct the use of the asset. *[IFRS 16.B9]*. Since IFRS 16 now also clearly applies a control model, like IFRIC 12, any arrangement that meets the control criteria in paragraph 5 of IFRIC 12 cannot meet the definition of a lease in IFRS 16, *[IFRS 16.BC69]*, as a conclusion that the grantor controls or regulates what services the operator must provide with the infrastructure, to whom, and at what price, *[IFRIC 12.5]*, is not compatible with the assertion that the private sector entity has a leasehold interest in the same assets under IFRS 16. The control criteria in IFRIC 12 are discussed at 3 below.

In light of this, the IASB had considered whether it was necessary to explicitly exclude from the scope of IFRS 16 service concession arrangements within the scope of IFRIC 12. However, stakeholders informed the IASB that including a scope exclusion for service concession arrangements in IFRS 16 would provide clarity in this respect. *[IFRS 16.BC69]*.

We believe that there is no requirement for entities to reassess whether arrangements entered into before the date of initial application of IFRS 16 that were previously determined to be leases fall in scope of IFRIC 12 or IFRS 16. This is because the transitional provisions of IFRS 16 allow a practical expedient whereby entities are not required to reassess whether a contract is, or contains, a lease at the date of initial application of the standard if they had previously determined whether the contract contained a lease under IFRIC 4 – *Determining whether an Arrangement contains a Lease*. The transitional provisions of IFRS 16 are discussed in Chapter 23 at 10.

However, entities must assess contracts that may fall within scope of IFRIC 12 and are entered into after the date of initial application of IFRS 16 *[IFRS 16.C4]* to determine whether a past practice to treat such contracts as leases is still appropriate.

2.4 Private-to-private arrangements

While the Interpretations Committee expects IFRIC 12 to be applied primarily to public-to-private arrangements, its application to private-to-private arrangements is neither required nor prohibited. The Basis for Conclusions notes that application by analogy could be appropriate under the hierarchy in IAS 8 – *Accounting Policies, Changes in Accounting Estimates and Errors* – if the arrangement met the control criteria quoted at 2 above. *[IFRIC 12.BC14]*. Accordingly, the application of IFRIC 12 to other arrangements would be regarded as an accounting policy choice, rather than a treatment that could be determined on a case by case basis. However, this choice would not be possible if it was determined that the arrangement falls within the scope of other standards, such as IFRS 15 and IFRS 16.

2.5 Accounting by grantors

The Interpretation applies only to accounting by the operator, not the grantor. *[IFRIC 12.4, 9]*. Grantor accounting was determined not to be a priority for the Committee, who noted that grantors are government bodies that do not necessarily apply IFRS. *[IFRIC 12.BC15]*. In 2011, the International Public Sector Accounting Standards Board (IPSASB) approved a new standard, IPSAS 32 – *Service Concession Arrangements: Grantor* – that addresses the grantor's accounting in such arrangements. Its approach is consistent with that used for the operator's accounting in IFRIC 12, in that an infrastructure asset is recognised by the grantor, together with an obligation comprising either a financial liability to the operator or, where an unconditional to pay cash to the operator is not a feature of the arrangement, a deferred revenue balance.[3] This chapter does not address accounting by grantors.

3 THE CONTROL MODEL

A contractual arrangement that is within the scope of IFRIC 12 includes the following features, commonly referred to as the 'control criteria':

(a) the grantor controls or regulates the services that the operator must provide using the infrastructure, to whom it must provide them, and at what price; and

(b) the grantor controls any significant residual interest in the infrastructure at the end of the concession term through ownership, beneficial entitlement or otherwise. *[IFRIC 12.5]*.

The Interpretations Committee considers that, taken together, these conditions identify when the infrastructure is controlled by the grantor for the whole of its economic life, *[IFRIC 12.AG6]*, in which case an operator is only managing the infrastructure on the grantor's behalf. Crucially, it has concluded from this that an infrastructure asset controlled by the grantor cannot be the property, plant and equipment of the operator. *[IFRIC 12.11, BC21, BC22]*. Control should be distinguished from management. If the grantor retains both the degree of control described in (a) above and any significant residual interest in the infrastructure, the operator is only managing the infrastructure on the grantor's behalf – even though, in many cases, it may have wide managerial discretion. *[IFRIC 12.AG5]*.

3.1 Regulation of services

The control or regulation of services does not have to be governed by contract as it could include control via an industry regulator. Control also extends to circumstances in which the grantor buys all the output as well as those in which it is bought by other users.

The grantor and relevant related parties must be considered together. If the grantor is a public sector entity, the public sector as a whole, together with any independent regulators acting in the public interest, are to be regarded as related to the grantor. *[IFRIC 12.AG2]*. 'Price' can mean the amount at which the grantor buys the service or the amount that the operator charges members of the public or a combination of both.

This means that many regulated public utilities (water, sewage, electricity supply etc.) will fall within (a) at 3 above. Other arrangements that fall within (a) include public health facilities that are free to users and subsidised transport facilities (rail, some toll roads and bridges) that are partly paid by public sector grant and partly by passenger fares. Of course, all of these will only be within scope of IFRIC 12 if there is also a contract between grantor and operator for the arrangement and any significant residual interest is also 'controlled' by the grantor under (b) above.

The Interpretations Committee stresses that the grantor does not need to have complete control of the price. It is sufficient for the price to be regulated, which could be by way of a capping mechanism (regulated utilities are usually free to charge lower prices). Other 'caps' may not be so apparent. A contract may give the operator freedom to set its prices but any excess is clawed back by the grantor, e.g. through setting a maximum return on an agreed investment in the infrastructure. In such a case, the operator's return is capped and the price element of the control test is substantively met. *[IFRIC 12.AG3]*.

Care should be taken to look to the substance of the agreements, so a cap that only applies in remote circumstances will be ignored.

Some arrangements only allow the grantor to control prices for part of the life of the infrastructure. For example, an operator may construct clinical facilities that are used by a government health care provider (the grantor) for a five-year contract term. At the end of the term, the health care provider may extend the contract by renegotiation. If it does not do so, the operator can run the facilities for private health care. Although the prices are controlled for the first five years, this arrangement is unlikely to meet the control condition in (a) at 3 above.

Alternatively, the contract might allow regulation of the prices of some but not all the services provided with the infrastructure. Judgement is required in determining whether arrangements involving partially regulated assets fall within the scope of IFRIC 12 (see 3.4 below).

3.2 Control of the residual interest

In order for an arrangement to be within scope of IFRIC 12, the grantor must control not only the services provided with the infrastructure but also any significant residual interest in the property at the end of the concession term through ownership, beneficial entitlement or otherwise. *[IFRIC 12.5(b)]*. The grantor's control over any significant residual interest should restrict the operator's ability to sell or pledge the infrastructure. As discussed below, control over the residual interest does not require the infrastructure to be returned to the grantor. It is sufficient that the grantor controls how access to the infrastructure is awarded after the concession term.

The control approach requires consideration of the infrastructure as a whole (what the IFRIC refers to as a 'holistic' approach), thereby avoiding the piecemeal accounting for the different components of the infrastructure as required by IAS 16. If the operator has to replace part of an item of infrastructure during the life of the concession, e.g. the top layer of a road or the roof of a building, the item of infrastructure is to be considered as a whole, so that condition (b) will be met for the whole of the infrastructure, including the part that is replaced, if the grantor has the residual interest in the final replacement of that part. *[IFRIC 12.AG6]*.

The Interpretation does not expand on what is regarded as 'significant'. Some infrastructure assets such as toll roads and bridges generate cash flows directly and it may be possible to use estimated future cash flows to calculate the significance of the residual value, whether or not the grantor will charge tolls after reversion of the asset. It may not be possible to base the assessment of 'significance' on the cash flows received by the operator on handing back the asset to the grantor as these may be nominal amounts; indeed, the grantor may pay nothing. The remaining useful life of the asset when it reverts may give a good indication, e.g. if a hospital is handed back to the public sector with a remaining useful life of twenty years, this residual interest is likely to be significant.

There are a number of features that indicate whether the grantor controls the residual interest. There are usually several contractual alternatives: the operator is granted a second concession term, a new operator is allowed to acquire the assets or the grantor acquires the assets and brings the arrangement 'in house'. The grantor still controls the residual as it will determine which of these alternatives applies and the option exercise price (if it or a new operator acquires the infrastructure) is irrelevant.

In some arrangements the grantor only has an option to reacquire the asset at the end of the concession term. The operator cannot control the infrastructure until the grantor decides what to do with the option. An option at fair value at the date of exercise may by itself be enough to give the grantor control over the residual under IFRIC 12 if it is sufficient to restrict the operator's ability to sell or pledge the infrastructure. This is a clear difference between a 'risks and rewards' and a 'control' model as under the former, the operator would be seen as keeping the risks and rewards of ownership if another party had the right to acquire the asset at fair value.

Example 25.1: Residual arrangements

A gas transmission system is being operated under a concession arrangement with the State Gas Authority. At the end of the term, the grantor will either acquire the infrastructure assets at their net book value, determined on the basis of the contract, or it may decide to grant a new SCA on the basis of a competitive tender, which will exclude the current operator. If the grantor elects to do the latter, the operator will be entitled to the lower of the following two amounts:

(a) the net book value of the infrastructure, determined on the basis of the contract; and

(b) the proceeds of a new competitive bidding process to acquire a new contract.

Although the operator cannot enter the competitive tender, it also has the right to enter into a new concession term but, in order to do so, it must match the best tender offer made. It has to pay to the grantor the excess of the best offer (b) above the amount in (a); should the tender offer be lower than (a), it will receive an equivalent refund.

In this arrangement, the grantor will control the residual. It can choose to take over the activities of the concession itself or it can allow potential operators, including the incumbent, to bid for a second term. The price that might be received by the operator, or paid by the grantor, is not relevant.

What if the arrangement is for the whole life of the infrastructure? Assets in service concession arrangements may revert to the grantor at the end of the concession term but they may not have much, if any, remaining useful life. Many modern buildings, for example, only have a useful life of thirty years or so and this is a common concession term. Consequently, infrastructure used in a service concession arrangement for its entire useful life ('whole of life infrastructure') is included within the scope of IFRIC 12 if the grantor controls or regulates the services that the operator must provide using the infrastructure, to whom it must provide them, and at what price. *[IFRIC 12.6]*.

The Interpretations Committee noted that one reason for including the 'significant residual interest' requirement was to differentiate between privatised, but still regulated, industries and service concession arrangements, thereby seeming to confirm that it had not intended regulated industries to be in scope.[4] The Interpretations Committee considers that privatised regulated industries should generally be out of scope, because they are divestitures or privatisations where it is more appropriate to treat the infrastructure as the property, plant and equipment of the operator. This is indicated in the table included as Information Note 2 to IFRIC 12 (reproduced at 2.2 above). It is usually the case in a privatisation that the infrastructure only reverts to the grantor in the event of a major breach of the conditions of the regulatory framework as otherwise the right of the operator to provide the regulated services may roll over indefinitely into a new term. In other cases, it may require legislative change to bring the assets back into the control of the public sector. This means that the grantor does not control the residual interest in the property as required by IFRIC 12.

ENGIE discloses that some of its concessions are not considered to be within scope of IFRIC 12 as the grantor has no rights over the infrastructure at the end of the contract. These assets (for gas distribution) are likely to have an economic life significantly in excess of the contract term.

Extract 25.1: ENGIE SA (2019)

NOTES TO THE CONSOLIDATED FINANCIAL STATEMENTS [extract]

NOTE 14   INTANGIBLE ASSETS [extract]

Intangible rights arising on concession contracts [extract]

For a concession arrangement to fall within the scope of IFRIC 12, usage of the infrastructure must be controlled by the concession grantor. This requirement is satisfied when the following two conditions are met:

- the grantor controls or regulates what services the operator must provide with the infrastructure, to whom it must provide them, and at what price; and
- the grantor controls any residual interest in the infrastructure at the end of the term of the arrangement, for example retains the right to take back the infrastructure at the end of the concession.

[...]

Concession infrastructures that do not meet the requirements of IFRIC 12 are presented as property, plant and equipment. This is the case of gas distribution infrastructures in France. The related assets are recognized in accordance with IAS 16, given that GRDF operates its network under long-term concession arrangements, most of which are mandatorily renewed upon expiration pursuant to French law No. 46-628 of April 8, 1946.

3.3 Assets within scope

There are two groups of assets within scope of IFRIC 12:

(a) the infrastructure that the operator constructs or acquires from a third party for the purpose of the concession; and

(b) existing infrastructure to which the grantor gives the operator access for the purpose of the concession. *[IFRIC 12.7]*.

Generally, 'infrastructure' is interpreted broadly and it is accepted that 'the infrastructure' used to provide services can include moveable assets. Although IFRIC 12 uses the word 'infrastructure' and includes examples traditionally regarded as such, including roads, bridges, hospitals and airports, *[IFRIC 12.1]*, the Interpretation is based on the definition of an asset under IFRS. An asset is 'a present economic resource controlled by the entity as a result of past events', *[CF 4.3]*, and is therefore considered to apply to all assets, including items such as buses or railway rolling stock that are made available by the grantor to the operator of the public service.

It is usually relatively straightforward to apply (a) above to infrastructure that the operator constructs or acquires from a third party for the purpose of the concession. The accounting for service concession arrangements in which infrastructure is leased from a party other than the grantor is discussed at 3.3.1 below.

However, there are some issues of interpretation relating to infrastructure to which the grantor has given access to the operator for the purpose of the SCA. Infrastructure under (b) above could include other arrangements in the form of leases from the grantor over assets. As part of a SCA, in addition to receiving payments for the construction and/or operation of the infrastructure, an operator may make payments to a grantor, e.g. in respect of the land on which a facility is to be built. These issues are discussed at 3.3.2 below.

A third group of assets comprises property, plant and equipment previously held by the operator and then used in connection with the provision of services under the SCA. The Interpretations Committee's view is that accounting for these types of assets is already covered by existing accounting standards, principally IAS 16, and therefore it does not specify how the operator should account for its previously existing assets that now form part of the infrastructure. *[IFRIC 12.8]*. The treatment of existing assets is discussed further at 3.3.3 below.

3.3.1 Accounting for service concession arrangements for which the infrastructure is leased from a party other than the grantor

As noted at 3.3 above, assets within the scope of IFRIC 12 include infrastructure that the operator constructs or acquires from a third party for the purpose of the service arrangement and existing infrastructure to which the grantor gives the operator access for the purpose of the service arrangement. *[IFRIC 12.7]*. In some cases, an operator may enter into an arrangement with the grantor to provide a public service using infrastructure that is leased. For example, an operator may lease trains in order to provide rail transportation services to the public. The accounting for arrangements in which infrastructure is leased from the grantor are addressed at 3.3.2 below. Where the lessor and grantor are controlled by the same governmental body and are related parties, lease payments made by the operator to the lessor are, in substance, payments made to a grantor in a service concession arrangement[5] which are covered at 3.3.2 below. For arrangements in which infrastructure is leased from a third party, the first question that arises is whether such arrangements are in scope of IFRIC 12. If so, how should the operator account for any assets and liabilities arising from the arrangement with the lessor?

The Interpretations Committee has discussed these questions in respect of an arrangement where infrastructure is leased from a third party lessor, unrelated to the grantor, and the operator is not required to provide any construction or upgrade services with respect to the infrastructure. In the fact pattern discussed, the operator is contractually required to pay the lessor for the lease of the infrastructure, and has an unconditional contractual right to receive cash from the grantor to reimburse those payments. In September 2016, the Interpretations Committee observed that:

(a) Assessing whether an arrangement is in scope of IFRIC 12 requires consideration of all facts and circumstances, in particular whether the control conditions in paragraph 5 of IFRIC 12 are met (see 3 above), and whether the infrastructure falls within one of the groups of assets set out in paragraph 7 of IFRIC 12 as in scope of IFRIC 12 (see 3.3 above). However, an operator is not required to provide construction or upgrade services with respect to the infrastructure for the arrangement to be in scope of IFRIC 12.

(b) If the arrangement is in scope of IFRIC 12, then it is the grantor, not the operator, that controls the right to use the infrastructure. Accordingly, the operator should assess whether it has the obligation to make payments to the lessor for the lease, or whether the grantor has this obligation.

   (i) If the grantor has the obligation to make payments to the lessor, the operator is collecting cash from the grantor that it remits to the lessor on behalf of the grantor.

   (ii) If the operator has the obligation to make payments to the lessor as part of the service concession arrangement, the operator should recognise a liability for this obligation when it is committed to the service concession arrangement and the infrastructure is made available by the lessor. At the time the operator recognises the liability, it should also recognise a financial asset because the operator has a contractual right to receive cash from the grantor to reimburse those payments. The operator should offset the liability to make payments to the lessor against the corresponding receivable from the grantor only when the criteria for offsetting a financial asset and financial liability in IAS 32 are met.[6] The offsetting criteria in IAS 32 are discussed in Chapter 54 at 7.4.1.

In contrast to the fact pattern discussed by the Committee, if the operator is contractually required to pay the lessor for the lease of the infrastructure, but does not have an unconditional contractual right to receive cash from the grantor to reimburse those payments, then in effect it is paying the lease payments on behalf of the grantor. Therefore, the operator should recognise a liability for this obligation and treat this obligation either as an additional cost of the concession right asset under the intangible asset model or as a reduction to the overall consideration the financial asset model applies (see section 3.3.2 below).

3.3.2 Periodic payments to the grantor for the right to use assets

Assets within the scope of IFRIC 12 include infrastructure that the operator constructs or acquires from a third party for the purpose of the service arrangement and existing infrastructure to which the grantor gives the operator access for the purpose of the service arrangement. *[IFRIC 12.7]*. IFRIC 12 contains no explicit guidance regarding periodic payments made to the grantor in connection with the right to use assets. The issue is whether these costs should be treated as lease costs in accordance with IFRS 16, treated as executory in nature with costs expensed as incurred or otherwise recognised as a liability. If they are considered to be within scope of IFRIC 12, what are the accounting consequences? Are they part of the overall consideration paid by the grantor or recognised as an asset and, if an asset, did they form part of the 'concession asset' at the start of the concession, with an obligation to make the related payments?

This has been discussed by the Interpretations Committee. The Committee decided in March 2016 that the treatment of variable payments for asset purchases, including payments that vary in relation to future activity by the purchaser, was too broad an issue for it to address, and consequently decided not to add the issue to its agenda.[7]

For fixed payments made by the operator to the grantor, the Committee observed in July 2016 that IFRIC 12 would apply, unless:

(a) they are payments for the right to a good or service that is separate from the service concession arrangement, which should be accounted for under other applicable IFRSs; or

(b) they are payments for the right to use an asset that is separate from the infrastructure within the scope of IFRIC 12, in which case the operator should assess whether the arrangement contains a lease. If the arrangement contains a lease, the operator should account for those payments by applying IFRS 16.[8]

This approach is consistent with the requirements in IFRS 15 to determine whether consideration payable to a customer gives rise to goods or services distinct from the customer contract (see Chapter 29 at 2.7). *[IFRS 15.70-72]*. Payments that are part of the overall concession agreement but do not fall within these two exceptions will be accounted for as part of the SCA. In this case the accounting treatment will depend on whether the SCA falls within the financial asset model, the intangible asset model or is a hybrid. If the financial asset model applies, payments to the grantor would be treated as reductions to the overall consideration received and therefore be offset against the financial asset receivable under the SCA. In contrast, under the intangible asset model the payments to the grantor should be recognised as a liability that increases the cost of the concession right asset. This is discussed further at 4.7 below.

3.3.3 Previously held assets used for the concession

IFRIC 12 does not apply to infrastructure held and recognised as property, plant and equipment by the operator before entering into the SCA. If such assets of the operator become part of the infrastructure in the SCA, the operator must apply the derecognition requirements of IAS 16 to determine whether it should derecognise those previously held assets. *[IFRIC 12.8]*. The Interpretations Committee's view is that accounting for assets is already covered by existing accounting standards, principally IAS 16, and therefore it is not necessary to specify how the operator should account for its previously existing assets that now form part of the infrastructure. *[IFRIC 12.BC16]*.

The implication is that losing control of a previously held asset by contractually giving control of its use to the grantor may be a disposal of the asset under IAS 16. The existing asset would be derecognised and any consideration on the disposal established in accordance with the requirements for determining the transaction price in IFRS 15. *[IAS 16.72]*. This means that the total consideration received under the contract would be allocated between an amount receivable for construction and upgrade services and an amount to reflect the transfer of the asset to the control of the grantor. What was previously recorded by the operator as property, plant and equipment would be replaced by an element of either an intangible asset or a financial asset, depending on the accounting model determined to be appropriate to the particular SCA (see 4.1.2 below). Gains and losses must be calculated as the difference between any net disposal proceeds and the carrying value of the item of property, plant and equipment, *[IAS 16.71]*, and recognised in profit or loss. Derecognition of assets within scope of IAS 16 in general is discussed in Chapter 18 at 7.

The operator may use some of its existing assets for the purpose of the concession without transferring control to the grantor. Unless the contract transfers the residual interest in these pre-existing assets to the grantor (and thereby both of the control criteria laid out at 3 above are met), these assets are out of scope of IFRIC 12. If an infrastructure asset is itself out of scope, the SCA might include, for example, extensions to that asset, upgrades to it and a contractual period of using the infrastructure asset to provide services. In this case, the total consideration payable under the concession will be allocated between the extension, upgrade and operating services within scope of IFRIC 12. Accordingly, construction revenue would be recognised at the time of the extension or upgrade work, with an additional financial asset or intangible asset recognised as appropriate.

3.4 Partially regulated assets

IFRIC 12 notes that it is not uncommon for the use of infrastructure to be partly regulated and partly unregulated and gives examples while noting that these activities take a variety of forms:

'(a) any infrastructure that is physically separable and capable of being operated independently and meets the definition of a cash generating unit as defined in IAS 36 – *Impairment of Assets* – shall be analysed separately if it is used wholly for unregulated purposes. For example, this might apply to a private wing of a hospital, where the remainder of the hospital is used by the grantor to treat public patients.

(b) where purely ancillary activities (such as a hospital shop) are unregulated, the control tests shall be applied as if those services did not exist, because in cases in which the grantor controls the services described in paragraph 5, the existence of ancillary activities does not detract from the grantor's control of the relevant infrastructure.' *[IFRIC 12.AG7]*.

In both cases, the grantor may have given to the operator a right to use the unregulated asset in question. This right may be in substance a lease from the grantor to the operator; if so, this is to be accounted for in accordance with IFRS 16. *[IFRIC 12.AG8]*. Determining whether the right is, in substance, a lease would involve using the principles in IFRS 16 (see Chapter 23 at 3.1). The interaction of IFRIC 12 and IFRS 16 is discussed at 2.3 above.

The Interpretation gives no further guidance on how an entity might interpret the term 'purely ancillary' in evaluating whether an unregulated activity is ignored for the purposes of determining if the control criteria are met or considered to detract from the grantor's control of the asset. The hospital shop is clearly insignificant by virtue of its size relative to the whole hospital, the proportion of cash flows attributable to it and the fact that the existence of a shop has no direct impact on the function of the infrastructure in the provision of regulated services. However, it is not clear at what point a secondary activity would become or cease to be 'purely ancillary'. This will be a matter of judgement.

In addition, there are many concession agreements that include unregulated services that are neither purely ancillary nor delivered by using a physically separable portion of the total infrastructure, a situation not addressed by AG 7. For example, a grantor may control prices charged to children, pensioners and the unemployed who use a sports facility but the amounts charged to other adults are not controlled. The same facility is being used by all, regardless of the amount that they pay. Alternatively, price regulation could apply only to services provided at certain times of the day rather than to different classes of user. In such cases it will be a matter of judgement whether enough of the service is unregulated in order to demonstrate that the grantor is not considered to control the asset, which would lead to the arrangement as a whole falling out of the scope of IFRIC 12. This assessment will be made at the beginning of the contract and will not be revisited unless errors were made in the original assessment. In practice, partial price regulation is often a reason for an arrangement to fall outside the scope of IFRIC 12.

However, if it transpires that there are significantly fewer unregulated users than anticipated then it is likely that the contract will be renegotiated. This is because of the public service obligation, which means that the grantor will want the service to continue to be provided to the public albeit under new terms. The new contract may be within scope of IFRIC 12. If a toll bridge has had fewer users than anticipated, the grantor might subsidise the tolls under a new arrangement.

4 ACCOUNTING BY THE CONCESSION OPERATOR: THE FINANCIAL ASSET AND INTANGIBLE ASSET MODELS

The Interpretations Committee's accounting framework for public-to-private arrangements is summarised in the following diagram from Information Note 1 in IFRIC 12. The diagram starts with the presumption that the arrangement has already been determined to be a service concession (see 2 above):

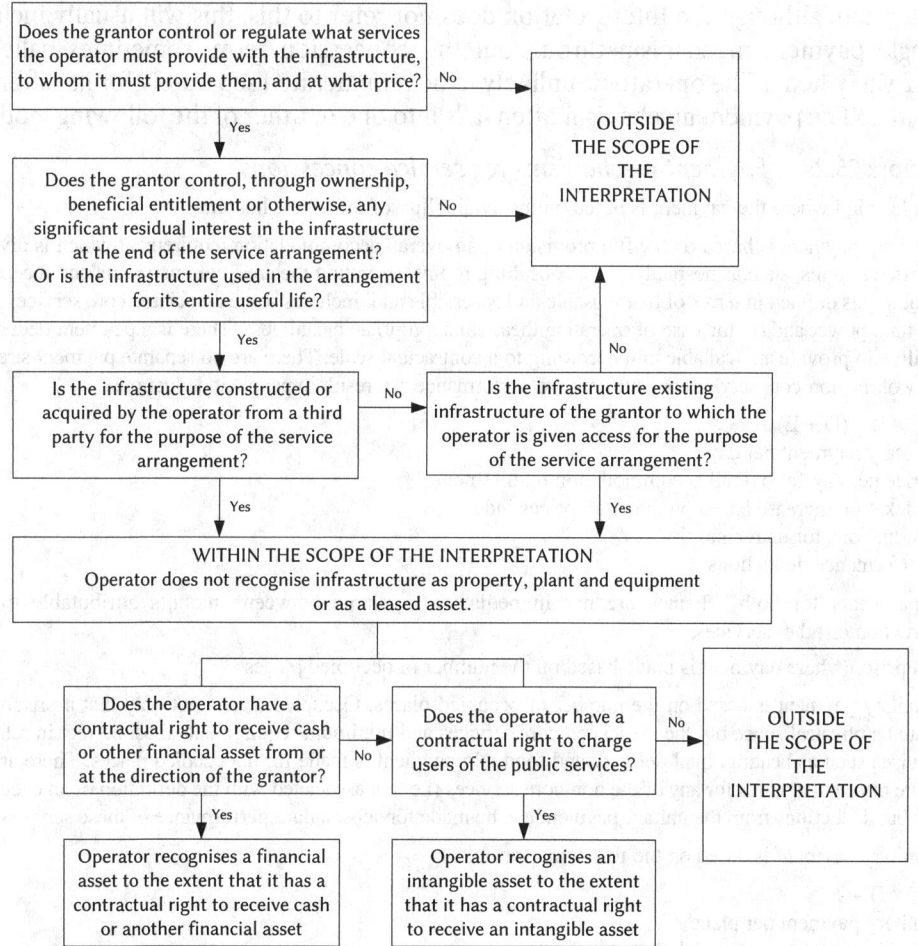

The two accounting models in IFRIC 12 apply several decisions of principle:

- the control model applies as described at 3 above, which means that the operator will not recognise infrastructure assets as its property, plant and equipment; *[IFRIC 12.11]* and

- the operator is providing 'construction services' and not, for example, constructing an item of property, plant and equipment for sale. Construction services are to be accounted for separately from 'operation services' in the operations phase of the contract. *[IFRIC 12.14, BC31]*.

There is a third important point of principle: although the nature of the consideration determines the subsequent accounting (as discussed at 4.1.2 below), both types of consideration give rise to a contract asset during the construction or upgrade period. *[IFRIC 12.19]*. The point at which the consideration is subsequently classified as a receivable or intangible asset is discussed at 4.2 and 4.3 below, respectively.

4.1 Consideration for services provided and the determination of the appropriate model

Most service concession agreements are for both construction (or upgrade) services and operations services. Operators almost always negotiate a single contract with the grantor and, although the Interpretation does not refer to this, this will usually include a single payment mechanism throughout the concession term, sometimes called a 'unitary payment'. The operator is unlikely to be remunerated separately for its different activities. The payment mechanism often falls into one or other of the following models:

Example 25.2:   Payment mechanisms for service concessions

(a)   a hospital where the payment is based on the availability of the whole hospital

The unitary payment is based on the full provision of an overall accommodation requirement which is divided into different units, such as hospital wards, consulting rooms, operating theatres, common parts and reception. Availability is defined in terms of being usable and accessible and, includes some associated core services such as heating, power and (in the case of operating theatres) appropriate cleanliness. There is a payment deduction for failure to provide an available unit according to a contractual scale. There are no separate payment streams for any of the non-core services but substandard performance can result in payment deductions.

$P = (F \times I) - (D + E)$
P = unitary payment per day
F = price per day for overall accommodation requirement
I = Indexation increase based on the retail prices index
D = deductions for unavailability
E = performance deductions

The payments for both schemes are not immediately separable between amounts attributable to the construction or other services.

b)   a prison where payment is made based on the number of occupied places

The unitary payment is based on the number of occupied places. Occupied means not only that a prisoner is allocated a physical space but the associated core services and minimum requirements must be met in relation to services such as heating, mail delivery and food. No payment is made for unoccupied places. There are no separate payment streams for any of the non-core services (i.e. not associated with the definition of an occupied place) but deductions from the unitary payment can be made for substandard performance of these services.

The unitary payment is based on the following formula:

$P = (F \times I) - Z$
P = unitary payment per place
F = Fixed amount per occupied place per day
I = Indexation increase based on the retail prices index
Z = Performance deductions

The operator acts as a service provider. It constructs or upgrades infrastructure used to provide a public service and operates and maintains that infrastructure for a specified period of time. *[IFRIC 12.12]*. IFRIC 12 clarifies that the operator should recognise and measure revenue in accordance with IFRS 15 for the services it performs. *[IFRIC 12.13]*. This requires the operator to allocate the consideration receivable to each performance obligation in proportion to their relative stand-alone selling prices. The exercise to separate the consideration receivable for the distinct services (i.e. construction, upgrade or operating services) provided by the operator is expanded at 4.1.1 below. The nature of the consideration determines the accounting model, *[IFRIC 12.13]*, as described at 4.1.2 below.

Payments often start only when the infrastructure asset has been completed and accepted as suitable for purpose by the grantor. Operators usually seek payment during the construction phase but whether or not they receive any is inevitably a result of negotiation between the parties. Payments that are received are normally for services provided and not directly to meet construction costs; any amounts received will be allocated to the relevant service activity as described below.

4.1.1 Allocating the consideration

The Interpretation argues that the separate services within a service concession arrangement, i.e. 'construction services', 'upgrade services' or 'operations services', should be disaggregated 'because each separate phase or element has its own distinct skills, requirements and risks'. *[IFRIC 12.BC31]*.

The allocation of revenue for the provision of these separate services is determined in accordance with IFRS 15. *[IFRIC 12.14, 20]*. This involves identifying who is the customer(s) of the service concession arrangement (see 4.1.1.A below), identifying the performance obligations under the contract with the customer (see 4.1.1.B below), determining the transaction price under the contract(s) (see 4.1.1.C below), and allocating that transaction price to the performance obligations in the contract (see 4.1.1.D below).

4.1.1.A Identifying the contract(s) with a customer

The first step in allocating consideration in accordance with IFRS 15 is to identify the contract with the customer. Under IFRS 15, a contract is defined as an agreement between two parties that creates enforceable rights and obligations. *[IFRS 15 Appendix A]*. Whether the customer in a service concession arrangement is the grantor and/or the user of the infrastructure will depend on the terms and conditions of the service concession arrangement. Because the grantor of the concession retains control over the infrastructure asset, *[IFRIC 12.5]*, it is likely that the grantor will be identified as the customer for any construction or upgrade services.

Because of the public service nature of the obligation undertaken by the operator, the operating services are provided to the public. This suggests that the public may be the customer for the operating services. A customer is defined in IFRS 15 as a party that has contracted with an entity to obtain goods or services that are an output of an entity's ordinary activities in exchange for consideration. *[IFRS 15 Appendix A]*. IFRS 15 does not require the existence of a written contract; a contract may be oral or implied, although it must be legally enforceable. *[IFRS 15.10]*. Therefore, where a written or implied contract exist between the operator and users of the infrastructure, the operator receives consideration from those users of the infrastructure, and is collecting that consideration as principal (rather than as agent for the grantor), we believe that the users of the infrastructure may be identified as the customers for the operation services.

Identification of the contract with the customer under IFRS 15 is discussed in Chapter 28.

4.1.1.B Identifying the performance obligations in the contract

Most service concession agreements are for both construction (or upgrade) services and operations services. Many service concessions also require the operator to perform some level of maintenance of the infrastructure asset over the term of the service concession arrangement. IFRS 15 provides guidance on the types of items that may be goods or services promised in the contract. Examples given by the standard include performing a contractually agreed-upon task (or tasks) for a customer, and providing a service of standing ready to provide goods or services. *[IFRS 15.26]*.

A promised good or service is a performance obligation if it is either:

(a) a good or service that is distinct; or

(b) a series of distinct goods or services that are substantially the same and have the same pattern of transfer to the customer. *[IFRS 15.22]*.

In order to be distinct, a promised good or service must be:

(a) capable of being distinct – i.e. provide a benefit to the customer either on its own or together with other resources that are readily available to the customer; and

(b) distinct within the context of the contract – i.e. the entity's promise to transfer the good or service to the customer is separately identifiable from other promises in the contract. *[IFRS 15.27]*.

If a promised good or service is not distinct, IFRS 15 requires that the entity should combine those goods or services with other promised goods or services until it identifies a bundle of goods or services that is distinct. *[IFRS 15.30]*.

Where an operator has identified only one contract with the grantor, the operator would typically identify, at least, construction services, upgrade services and operation services as separate performance obligations. Whether the operator has identified a contract with the users of the infrastructure as the customer for the operating services will impact the identification of performance obligations within the contract(s) with customers.

It could be argued that because major maintenance enhances an asset that the grantor owns, then it is providing a benefit to the grantor. In addition, contractual terms often require an operator to repay an element advanced by the grantor for maintenance services if the operator does not incur contracted levels of maintenance spend. This may also support the argument that maintenance is a separate performance obligation. In practice, there is likely to be some judgement involved in determining whether maintenance is a separate performance obligation, based on how it is defined in the contractual arrangement. To the extent that the contract requires the operator to provide major maintenance, similar in nature to an upgrade, that enhances the infrastructure asset, maintenance could be a separate performance obligation. However, minor maintenance necessary to preserve the infrastructure in a condition required for the operator to operate the infrastructure safely and to return it to the grantor in a certain condition at the end of the arrangement could be argued as not transferring a distinct good or service to the grantor. In other cases, it may be less clear whether a contractual obligation represents a performance obligation under IFRS 15 or an obligation that should be accounted for under IAS 37. For example, a water supply operator may be contractually required to replace all lead pipes for environmental and health reasons; similarly, a gas supply operator may be required to replace all cast-iron pipes for safety reasons. If an entity exercises significant judgement in determining whether major maintenance is a separate performance obligation, consideration should be given to the disclosure requirements in paragraph 122 of IAS 1 – *Presentation of Financial Statements*. See Chapter 3 at 5.1.1.B.

In practice, operators may often sub-contract some or all the construction activities under a service concession arrangement. In such cases, the operator should apply the guidance in IFRS 15 to determine whether it is acting as principal or agent for the provision of construction services. This determination will impact whether the operator's performance obligation under the contract is to provide construction services, or to arrange for another party to provide construction services. Principal versus agent considerations under IFRS 15 are discussed in Chapter 28 at 3.4.

4.1.1.C   Determining the transaction price under the contract

Transaction price is defined in IFRS 15 as the amount of consideration to which an entity expects to be entitled in exchange for transferring promised goods or services to a customer, excluding amounts collected on behalf of third parties. *[IFRS 15.47]*.

The determination of transaction price must take into account any elements of variable consideration. It is often the case within service concession arrangements that the operator will be required to pay penalties if their performance under the contract does not meet specified standards. The element of revenue that is subject to such penalties would be considered a form of variable consideration under IFRS 15. *[IFRS 15.51]*. IFRS 15 requires that, if the consideration promised in a contract includes a variable amount, an entity should estimate the amount of consideration to which they will be entitled. *[IFRS 15.50]*. IFRS 15 requires that variable consideration should be estimated using either an expected value or most likely amount basis, depending on which method the entity expects to better predict the amount of consideration to which it will be entitled. *[IFRS 15.53]*. The assessment of which approach is most appropriate will depend upon the facts and circumstances of the service concession arrangement and the penalty regime. In practice, it may be that the expected value approach better predicts the amount of consideration to which the operator expects to be entitled in many service concession arrangements. Estimates of variable consideration are then included in the transaction price only to the extent that it is highly probable that a significant reversal of revenue will not occur when the uncertainty associated with the variable consideration is subsequently resolved. *[IFRS 15.56]*.

Payments often start under a service concession arrangement only when the infrastructure asset has been completed and accepted as suitable for purpose by the grantor. In these cases, the delay between the timing of payments from the grantor compared to the provision of construction services by the operator, may require a significant financing component to be taken into account in determining the transaction price. However, where the reason for the difference between the cash selling price of the construction services and the promised consideration arises for reasons other than the provision of finance, and the difference between those amounts is proportional to the reason given for the difference, the contract does not contain a significant financing component. *[IFRS 15.62]*. This may be the case where the form of the consideration for the construction services necessitates a delay between the provision of the services and the receipt of the consideration, such as where the operator receives an intangible asset in return for construction services.

When it is determined that the contract contains a significant financing component, the amount of promised consideration should be discounted at a rate that the operator would use if it were to enter into a separate financing transaction with the grantor at contract inception. The discount rate should reflect the credit characteristics of the grantor, as well as any collateral or security provided, including assets transferred in the contract, [IFRS 15.64], i.e. the discount rate is a rate specific to the contract. IFRS 15 also notes that the discount rate could be derived by discounting the contractual cash flows to a cash selling price for the promised good or service. [IFRS 15.64]. In Illustrative Example 1 to IFRIC 12, the implied interest rate in the contract is assumed to be the rate that would be reflected in a financing transaction between the operator and the grantor, although this may not always be the case in a service concession arrangement. Some may argue that the rate implicit in the contract more appropriately reflects the economic substance. However, in our view, primacy should be given to the rate that the operator would use if it were to enter into a separate financing transaction with the grantor at contract inception. Whilst the rate implicit in the contract may be used in determining that rate, we believe that that the use of the rate implicit in the contract may not always be consistent with the objective of paragraph 64 of IFRS 15, being to use a discount rate that would be reflected in a separate financing transaction between the entity and the customer. When determining the discount rate to use, the factors that the operator might take into account include:

- the expected duration and repayment pattern of the service payments, noting that SCA payments may extend significantly longer than the duration of government bonds;
- the credit profile of the government entity;
- borrowing rates that may be offered by the central treasury function of the government;
- credit risks specific to the terms of the SCA, including security or guarantees provided by the government, whether express or implied by statute or legislation, and to the extent it impacts the rate that would be negotiated between the parties; and
- any administration costs and profit margin related to financing.

The effect of financing is excluded from the transaction price prior to the allocation of the transaction price to the performance obligations in the contract.

Determination of the transaction price under IFRS 15 is discussed in Chapter 29.

An operator may also be contractually required to make payments to the grantor. These may take the form of payments for the right of access to infrastructure or other assets, for the construction of assets or additional fees for the right to operate the concession. If the SCA falls within the financial asset model, the payments made may reduce the consideration received from the grantor. This is considered further at 4.7 below.

4.1.1.D   Allocating the transaction price to the performance obligations in the contract

IFRS 15 generally requires the transaction price to be allocated to each performance obligation in proportion to their relative stand-alone selling prices. [IFRS 15.74].

If stand-alone selling prices are not readily observable, they must be estimated, considering all information that is reasonably available to the entity. The operator may choose to estimate stand-alone selling prices using an expected cost-plus margin approach, [IFRS 15.79], although other approaches are permitted.

Although most service concessions apply a single payment mechanism, it is often straightforward in practice to identify the underlying cash flows that relate to different activities within the arrangement. This may be based on the original contract negotiations or because the contract contains terms allowing for subsequent price adjustments by 'market testing' or benchmarking. However, the cash flows may not reflect the stand-alone prices of the underlying services so care will have to be taken. There may be practical problems when it comes to apportioning the total contract consideration between the elements of the contract and the allocation will be a matter of judgement.

Allocation of the transaction price to performance obligations under IFRS 15 is discussed in Chapter 29.

4.1.2 Determining the accounting model after the construction phase

IFRIC 12 states that the operator may receive a financial asset or an intangible asset as consideration for its construction services and the asset that it receives determines the subsequent treatment. *[IFRIC 12.15, 19]*. The nature of the consideration given by the grantor to the operator shall be determined by reference to the contract terms and, when it exists, relevant contract law. However, the Interpretation is clear that both types of consideration give rise to a contract asset during the construction or upgrade period. *[IFRIC 12.19]*.

The Interpretations Committee decided that the boundary between the financial and the intangible asset models should be based on the operator's unconditional contractual right to receive cash from, or at the direction of, the grantor. *[IFRIC 12.16]*. The grantor does not need to pay the cash to the operator directly. Fees or tolls received from users are viewed as essentially no more than collections on behalf of the grantor if they are part of an overall arrangement under which the grantor bears ultimate responsibility. If the grantor pays but the amounts are wholly based on usage of the infrastructure and there is no minimum guaranteed payment, the entity has no unconditional contractual right to receive cash, as the amounts receivable are contingent on the extent to which the public uses the service. In this case the intangible asset model will apply.

The operator will recognise a financial asset to the extent that it has a contractual right to receive cash or other financial assets from the grantor for the construction services, where the grantor has little, if any, discretion to avoid payment. This is usually because the agreement is legally enforceable. *[IFRIC 12.16]*. The recognition of a financial asset is not affected by the fact that the operator's contractual right to receive cash may be contingent on performance standards, as in the example of a unitary charge for a hospital in Example 25.2 above. The Interpretations Committee points out that this is no different from other circumstances and other financial assets where the payment for goods and services depends on the subsequent performance of the asset. *[IFRIC 12.BC44]*.

The operator will recognise an intangible asset to the extent that it receives a licence to charge users of the public service. *[IFRIC 12.17]*.

Sometimes it is necessary to 'bifurcate' the operator's right to cash flows for construction services into a financial asset and an intangible asset and account separately for each component of the operator's consideration. This, the Interpretations Committee argues, is because the operator is paid for its services partly by a financial asset and partly by an intangible asset. *[IFRIC 12.18]*.

The analysis between the different models can be seen in the following table:

	Arrangement	Applicable model
1	Grantor pays – fixed payments	Financial asset
2	Grantor pays – payments vary with demand	Intangible asset
3	Grantor retains demand risk – users pay but grantor guarantees amounts	Financial asset or bifurcated (part financial, part intangible)
4	Grantor retains demand risk – operator collects revenues from users until it achieves specified return	Intangible asset
5	Users pay – no grantor guarantees	Intangible asset

Of the two arrangements in Example 25.2 above, the hospital is an example of (1) above: the payments are contractually fixed if all obligations and services are provided. The prison, as described in Example 25.2 above, would fall within (2) and be accounted for as an intangible asset. However, the prison operator might be paid on a different basis, e.g. it might be paid for 1,000 'available places' and receive this as long as heating and food were capable of being provided. In this case it would be no different to the hospital and be a financial asset. There are, of course, many potential variations and a combination of fixed and variable demand could lead to bifurcation.

Common examples of arrangements that fall within (3) above are transport concessions where the operator collects revenue from users but is entitled to an agreed return on capital invested in the infrastructure. The fees or tolls up to this amount are considered to be collections on behalf of the grantor. There will be a financial asset to the extent of the guaranteed return. There may be an intangible asset as well if the value of the financial asset is less than the fair value of the construction services.

However, arrangements of the type in (4) above remain to be treated as intangible assets even if the overall risk to the operator of not obtaining a specified result is very low. An arrangement that effectively caps revenue collected from users once an agreed level of return is reached, it is argued, is not a contractual right to cash but a right to collect revenues from users and it is not relevant that the risk is low or that the operator will, in effect, get a fixed return. [IFRIC 12.BC52].

The following are examples of arrangements that will be accounted for using the intangible asset model:

(a) A municipality grants the operator a contract to treat all its waste collections for which it will be paid per unit processed. The arrangement does not provide for any guaranteed volume of waste to be treated by the operator (so it does not contain a take-or-pay arrangement) or any form of guarantee by the grantor. Historically, however, the annual volume of waste has never been less than 40,000 tons and the average annual volume over the last 20 years has been 75,000 tons.

(b) An operator enters into a toll bridge concession. The operator is permitted to collect revenues from users or the grantor until it achieves a 6% return on its agreed infrastructure spend, at which point the arrangement comes to an end.

In commercial terms, the toll bridge concession may be virtually identical to a transaction that falls within (3) above, e.g. where the users pay tolls but the grantor guarantees a minimum 6% return. The crucial difference is the grantor's guarantee. The arrangement with the guarantee, which will contain a financial asset, is likely to leave more of the rewards of ownership with the operator than the intangible arrangement in (b) as the operator will be entitled to benefits in excess of the 6% return. This demonstrates that the distinction between the financial asset and intangible asset models is linked less to the transfer of commercial risk, but more by the existence (or not) of an unconditional contractual right to cash flows.

There are jurisdictions where public-to-private contract laws or the concession arrangements themselves allow an operator to ask the grantor for a revision of the tariffs for the public service when the operator's actual return is below initial expectations. Although this feature in the concession arrangement is included to reduce the operator's risk, it only gives the operator a right to re-negotiate and the outcome of that is not certain. As a result, the operator does not have an unconditional right to receive cash and, therefore, the existence of these features would not allow the operator to apply the financial asset model.

Many payment mechanisms include deductions for substandard performance of services. These do not affect the analysis of the contract as a financial asset or intangible asset and are discussed further below.

4.2 The financial asset model

Under the financial asset model, which applies if the entity has an unconditional contractual right to receive cash or another financial asset, *[IFRIC 12.16]*, the service element that relates to the construction of the infrastructure asset ('construction services') is accounted for in accordance with IFRS 15. *[IFRIC 12.14]*. For the avoidance of doubt, an asset is not recognised for the discounted present value of all amounts payable by the grantor under the service concession arrangement. The entity recognises an asset for construction services performed up to the reporting date; subsequently it may recognise an asset on the same basis for upgrade services; the carrying value of the asset does not include future services yet to be performed or maintenance services that are accounted for as expenses. The consideration received by the operator for other services is addressed at 5 below.

IFRIC 12 requires the consideration due to the operator to be classified as a contract asset rather than a receivable during the construction activity. *[IFRIC 12.19]*. IFRS 15 requires that a receivable is recognised only when the operator has an unconditional right to receive consideration. This is the case only if nothing other than the passage of time is required before payment of the consideration is due. *[IFRS 15.108]*. The right to consideration would not be unconditional if the operator must first satisfy another performance obligation in the contract before it is entitled to payment from the customer. Therefore, we believe that the operator should recognise a receivable in scope of IFRS 9 only when, and to the extent that, payment is not conditional on future delivery of operation services. Due to the nature of contractual penalties imposed in service concession arrangements, we believe that, in practice, the amount due to the operator in exchange for construction services will often unwind from a contract asset to a receivable over the period in which the other performance obligations in the contract are satisfied by the operator, rather than at the point when construction activity is completed.

On initial recognition, IFRS 9 requires a financial asset to be measured at its fair value (plus or minus transaction costs). *[IFRS 9.5.1.1]*. As a result, the receivable is initially recognised at fair value. In our view, the discount rate used to determine the initial measurement of the receivable under IFRS 9 should be determined considering the passage of time before payment is due and counterparty credit risk. The discount rate should not be risk adjusted to reflect the risk that payments to be received over the operating period may be subject to penalties. This is consistent with the requirement in IFRS 15 that a receivable is recognised only when there is an unconditional right to consideration, i.e. when only the passage of time is required before payment is due. *[IFRS 15.108]*. To the extent that the right to payment does depend upon the operator's future performance, the operator does not have an unconditional right to consideration and therefore should continue to recognise a contract asset, rather than a receivable. The fair value of the financial asset is impacted by changes in market interest rates. Where construction or upgrade activity takes a significant time (as is common in many infrastructure projects), it is possible that market interest rates will have moved between the date of commencement of construction services and the point at which the receivable is initially recognised, such that there is a difference between the initial measurement of the receivable in accordance with IFRS 9 and the amount of construction revenue and accrued interest recognised as a contract asset in accordance with IFRS 15 up to that point. In addition, whilst fair value under IFRS 9 is based on market interest rates, accrued interest recognised as part of the contract asset under IFRS 15 is determined using the rate 'that would be reflected in a separate financing transaction between the entity and its customer at contract inception', *[IFRS 15.64]*, i.e. a rate specific to the contract. This may also lead to differences between the amount recognised as a contract asset under IFRS 15 and the initial measurement of the receivable under IFRS 9. IFRS 15 requires any difference between the initial measurement of the financial asset in accordance with IFRS 9 and the corresponding amount of revenue recognised under IFRS 15 to be presented as an expense. *[IFRS 15.108]*.

As required by IFRS 9, the receivable would subsequently be recognised at amortised cost, at fair value through other comprehensive income, or at fair value through profit or loss, depending upon how it is classified under IFRS 9. *[IFRIC 12.24]*. Measurement at amortised cost requires the receivable to be held in a business model whose objective is to hold financial assets in order to collect contractual cash flows, and requires that those contractual cash flows represent solely payments of principal and interest. Any features that introduce more than *de minimis* exposure to risks or volatility in the contractual cash flows that are inconsistent with a basic lending arrangement would mean that the receivable would not be measured at amortised cost. *[IFRS 9.B4.1.7A, B4.1.18]*. If the amount due from the grantor is measured at amortised cost or fair value through other comprehensive income, interest income will be recognised, calculated using the effective interest method. *[IFRIC 12.25]*. Classification of financial assets under IFRS 9 is discussed in Chapter 48 at 2.

The financial asset recognised by the operator will be subject to the impairment requirements of IFRS 9. IFRS 15 also requires that contract assets are assessed for impairment in accordance with IFRS 9. *[IFRS 15.107]*. The impairment requirements of IFRS 9 are discussed in Chapter 51.

Borrowing costs incurred by the operator during the construction phase cannot be capitalised under the financial asset model. *[IFRIC 12.22]*.

Example 25.3 below is based on Illustrative Example 1 in IFRIC 12 and illustrates how the financial asset model may be applied. It should, however, be noted that this example deals with only one of many possible types of arrangements seen in practice and is based on an uncomplicated fact pattern. It is important that entities understand and assess all the facts and circumstances of their own service concession arrangements in order to determine the appropriate accounting.

In the example below, the operator recognises a receivable once construction services are complete. As discussed above, IFRS 15 requires that a receivable is recognised only when the operator has an unconditional right to receive consideration, which will be the case only when nothing other than the passage of time is required before payment of the consideration is due. *[IFRS 15.108]*. The example below contains an unstated assumption that this is the case at completion of construction services. However, this may not always be the case in practice.

Example 25.3:   The Financial Asset Model

Table 1 Concession terms

The terms of the arrangement require an operator to construct a road – completing construction within two years – and maintain and operate the road to a specified standard for eight years (i.e. years 3-10). The terms of the concession also require the operator to resurface the road at the end of year 8. At the end of year 10, the arrangement will end. Assume that the operator identified three performance obligations for construction services, operation services and road resurfacing. The operator estimates that the costs it will incur to fulfil its obligations will be:

	Year	€
Construction services (per year)	1-2	500
Operation services (per year)	3-10	10
Road resurfacing	8	100

The terms of the concession require the grantor to pay the operator €200 per year in years 3-10 for making the road available to the public.

For the purpose of this illustration, it is assumed that all cash flows take place at the end of the year.

Table 2 Contract revenue

The operator recognises contract revenue in accordance with IFRS 15. Revenue – the amount of consideration to which the operator expects to be entitled from the grantor for the services provided – is recognised when (or as) the performance obligations are satisfied.

The total consideration (€200 in each of years 3-8) is allocated to the performance obligations based on the relative stand-alone selling prices of the construction services, operating services and road resurfacing, taking into the significant financing component, as follows:

	Transaction price allocation (including effect of the significant financing component)
	€
Construction services (a)	1,050
Operation services (b)	96
Road resurfacing services (c)	110
Total	1,256
Implied interest rate (d)	6.18% per year

(a) The operator estimates the relative stand-alone selling price by reference to the forecast cost plus 5 per cent.
(b) The operator estimates the relative stand-alone selling price by reference to the forecast cost plus 20 per cent.
(c) The operator estimates the relative stand-alone selling price by reference to the forecast cost plus 10 per cent.
(d) The implied interest rate is assumed to be the rate that would be reflected in a financing transaction between the operator and the grantor.

Financial asset

During the first two years, the entity recognises a contract asset and accounts for the significant financing component in the arrangement in accordance with IFRS 15. Once the construction is complete, the amounts due from the grantor are accounted for in accordance with IFRS 9 as receivables.

Table 3 Measurement of contract asset / receivable

	€
Amount due for construction in year 1	525
Contract asset at end of year 1*	525
Effective interest in year 2 on contract asset at the end of year 1 (6.18% × €525)	32
Amount due for construction in year 2	525
Receivable at end of year 2	1,082
Effective interest in year 3 on receivable at the end of year 2 (6.18% × €1,082)	67
Amount due for operation in year 3 (€10 × (1 + 20%))	12
Cash receipts in year 3	(200)
Receivable at end of year 3	961

* No effective interest arises in year 1 because the cash flows are assumed to take place at the end of the year.

Overview of cash flows, statement of comprehensive income and statement of financial position

For the purposes of this example, it is assumed that the operator finances the arrangement wholly with debt and retained profits. It pays interest at 6.7 per cent per year on outstanding debt. If the cash flows and fair values remain the same as those forecast, the operator's cash flows, statement of comprehensive income and statement of financial position over the duration of the arrangement will be as follows.

Table 4 Cash flows (€)

Year	1	2	3	4	5	6	7	8	9	10	Total
Receipts	–	–	200	200	200	200	200	200	200	200	1,600
Contract costs (a)	(500)	(500)	(10)	(10)	(10)	(10)	(10)	(110)	(10)	(10)	(1,180)
Borrowing costs (b)	–	(34)	(69)	(61)	(53)	(43)	(33)	(23)	(19)	(7)	(342)
Net inflow / (outflow)	(500)	(534)	121	129	137	147	157	67	171	183	78

(a) Table 1
(b) Debt at start of year (table 6) × 6.7%

Table 5 Statement of comprehensive income (€)

Year	1	2	3	4	5	6	7	8	9	10	Total
Revenue	525	525	12	12	12	12	12	122	12	12	1,256
Contract costs	(500)	(500)	(10)	(10)	(10)	(10)	(10)	(110)	(10)	(10)	(1,180)
Finance income (a)	–	32	67	59	51	43	34	25	22	11	344
Borrowing costs (b)	–	(34)	(69)	(61)	(53)	(43)	(33)	(23)	(19)	(7)	(342)
Net profit	25	23	–	–	–	2	3	14	5	6	78

(a) Amount due from grantor at start of year (table 6) × 6.18%
(b) Cash / (debt) (table 6) × 6.7%

Table 6 Statement of financial position (€)

End of year	1	2	3	4	5	6	7	8	9	10
Amount due from grantor (a)	525	1,082	961	832	695	550	396	343	177	–
Cash / (debt) (b)	(500)	(1,034)	(913)	(784)	(647)	(500)	(343)	(276)	(105)	78
Net assets	25	48	48	48	48	50	53	67	72	78

(a) Amount due from grantor at start of year, plus revenue and finance income earned in year (table 5), less receipts in year (table 4).

(b) Debt at start of year plus net cash flow in year (table 4).

4.3 The intangible asset model

If the financial asset model does not apply (i.e. there is no unconditional contractual right to cash or other financial assets), the operator's consideration for its construction services will be an intangible asset. *[IFRIC 12.15]*. As with the financial asset model, the operator cannot have an item of property, plant and equipment because the physical infrastructure is controlled by the grantor (see 3 above). *[IFRIC 12.11]*. Therefore, the Interpretations Committee has concluded that the right of an operator to charge users of the public service, for example the right to collect tolls from a road or a bridge, meets the definition of an intangible asset, that should be accounted for in accordance with IAS 38. It is, in effect, a licence 'bought' in exchange for construction services. *[IFRIC 12.17]*.

Consideration is classified as a contract asset during the construction or upgrade period. *[IFRIC 12.19]*. and revenue for construction or upgrade services will be recorded in accordance with IFRS 15. *[IFRIC 12.14]*.

Under the intangible assets model, borrowing costs must be capitalised during the period of construction. *[IFRIC 12.22]*. However, as noted above, IFRIC 12 requires consideration to be classified as a contract asset, rather than an intangible asset, during the construction period. *[IFRIC 12.19]*. In March 2019, the Interpretations Committee issued an agenda decision relating to the capitalisation of borrowing costs on a constructed good for which revenue was recognised over time. In that agenda decision, the Interpretations Committee noted that, in the particular fact pattern considered, a contract asset is not a qualifying asset as the intended use of the contract asset is not a use for which it necessarily takes a substantial period of time to get ready. IAS 23 requires capitalisation of borrowing costs that are directly attributable to the acquisition, construction or production of an asset that necessarily takes a substantial period of time to get ready for is intended use or sale. Some may argue that there is a tension between the requirement in IFRIC 12 to capitalise interest during the construction phase under the intangible asset model and this agenda decision. However, we believe that the agenda decision does not override the requirements of IFRIC 12 paragraph 22.

Whilst IFRIC 12 requires consideration to be classified as a contract asset during the construction or upgrade period, Illustrative Example 2 to IFRIC 12 shows that the contract asset is presented as an intangible asset during the construction phase. *[IFRIC 12.IE15]*.

It is argued that an inevitable consequence of applying the intangible asset model is that there must be an exchange transaction in which the operator receives the intangible right in exchange for its construction services. As this is an exchange of dissimilar assets, revenue must be recognised in accordance with IFRS 15, which requires the recognition of revenue based on the fair value of the assets received, unless the fair value of the assets received cannot be reasonably estimated. *[IFRIC 12.BC32, IFRS 15.66, 67]*. This means that the operator must establish the fair value of either the intangible asset it receives or the stand-alone selling price of the construction services. *[IFRS 15.67]*.

Under IAS 38, amortisation of an intangible asset should begin when the asset is available for use, i.e. when it is in the location and condition necessary for it to be capable of operating in the manner intended by management. *[IAS 38.97]*. We believe that this would likely be the case once construction is complete and the operator can begin using the license received in exchange for construction services in order to generate revenues.

In the following example, based on Illustrative Example 2 in IFRIC 12, the operator determines the fair value of the intangible asset indirectly by reference to the stand-alone selling price of the construction services delivered. As with Example 25.3 above, it should be noted that this relatively simple example deals with only one of many possible types of arrangements seen in practice and it is important that entities understand and assess the facts and circumstances of their own service concession arrangements in order to determine the appropriate accounting.

Example 25.4:   The Intangible Asset Model – recording the construction asset

Arrangement terms

The terms of a service arrangement require an operator to construct a road – completing construction within two years – and maintain and operate the road to a specified standard for eight years (i.e. years 3-10). The terms of the arrangement also require the operator to resurface the road when the original surface has deteriorated below a specified condition. The operator estimates that it will have to undertake the resurfacing at the end of the year 8. At the end of year 10, the service arrangement will end. The operator estimates that the costs it will incur to fulfil its obligations will be:

Table 1 Contract costs

	Year	€
Construction services (per year)	1-2	500
Operation services (per year)	3-10	10
Road resurfacing	8	100

The terms of the arrangement allow the operator to collect tolls from drivers using the road. The operator forecasts that vehicle numbers will remain constant over the duration of the contract and that it will receive tolls of €200 in each of years 3-10.

For the purpose of this illustration, it is assumed that all cash flows take place at the end of the year.

Intangible asset

The operator provides construction services to the grantor in exchange for an intangible asset, i.e. a right to collect tolls from road users in years 3-10. In accordance with IFRS 15, the operator measures this non-cash consideration at fair value. In this case the operator determines the fair value indirectly by reference to the stand-alone selling price of the construction services delivered.

During the construction phase of the arrangement the operator's contract asset (representing its accumulating right to be paid for providing construction services) is presented as an intangible asset (licence to charge users of the infrastructure). The operator estimates the stand-alone selling price of the construction services to be equal to the forecast construction costs plus 5 per cent margin, which the operator concludes is consistent with the rate a market participant would require as compensation for providing the construction services and for assuming the risk associated with the construction costs. The operator also capitalises borrowing costs during the construction phase as required by IAS 23, at an estimated rate of 6.7 per cent:

Table 2 Initial measurement of intangible asset

	€
Construction services in year 1 (€500 × (1 + 5%))	525
Capitalisation of borrowing costs	34
Construction services in year 2 (€500 × (1 + 5%))	525
Intangible asset at end of year 2	1,084

The intangible asset is amortised over the period in which it is expected to be available for use by the operator, i.e. years 3-10. In this case, the directors determine that it is appropriate to amortise using a straight-line method. The annual amortisation charge is therefore €1,084 divided by 8 years, i.e. €135 per year.

Construction costs and revenue

The operator accounts for the construction services in accordance with IFRS 15. It measures revenue at the fair value of the non-cash consideration received or receivable. Thus in each of years 1 and 2 it recognises in its income statement construction costs of €500, construction revenue of €525 (cost plus 5 per cent) and, hence, construction profit of €25.

Toll revenue

The road users pay for the public services at the same time as they receive them, i.e. when they use the road. The operator therefore recognises toll revenue when it collects the tolls.

The accounting for the operations phase of this example service concession arrangement is discussed in Example 25.12 at 5.2 below.

4.3.1 Amortisation of the intangible asset

The intangible asset will subsequently be accounted for in accordance with IAS 38, *[IFRIC 12.26]*, and the amount at which it is measured initially, i.e. after the exchange transaction, is its cost. *[IAS 38.45]*. It will be amortised on a systematic basis over its useful life, using a method that reflects 'the pattern in which the asset's future economic benefits are expected to be consumed by the entity'. *[IAS 38.97]*. This means that the methods permitted by IAS 38 are available (straight line, diminishing balance or unit-of-production). *[IAS 38.98]*. The requirements of IAS 38 are discussed in detail in Chapter 17. Interest methods of amortisation are forbidden. *[IFRIC 12.BC65]*.

The Interpretations Committee expressly considered unit-of-production methods to be appropriate in some circumstances; in March 2006, it was noted in the *IFRIC Update* that the Basis of Conclusions had been redrafted to avoid the impression that these methods were not allowed.[9] There were still concerns that a unit-of-production method could result in lower amortisation in the early years of the asset's operation so IAS 38 itself was amended to remove a statement discouraging methods that might have such a result.[10] This clarifies that there is no prohibition when the method is the most appropriate, whatever the resulting profile of amortisation.

Unit-of-production methods are typically considered in the context of toll roads and bridges. Obviously, the method might apply if there is a right to charge a specified number of users. It might also be used using the estimated number of users, e.g. the number of vehicles that might use a particular road during the concession term, as a basis.

The remaining issue regarding amortisation methods has been whether they could be based on revenue generated by the asset; this depends on the meaning of 'consumption of economic benefits' in the context of intangible assets with finite lives. In May 2014, the IASB issued amendments to IAS 38 to introduce a rebuttable presumption that a method of amortisation based on the revenue expected to be generated from an activity that includes the use of an intangible asset is not appropriate. This is because this method typically reflects factors that are not directly linked to the consumption of the economic benefits embodied in the asset. [IAS 38.98A]. See Chapter 17 at 9.2.2. The amendment became effective in 2016.

Example 25.5 below demonstrates the potentially distorting effects for a SCA of basing amortisation on revenue.

However, the Board did acknowledge certain 'limited circumstances' that would give rise to an exception to this presumption. Revenue generated can be used to amortise an intangible asset when: [IAS 38.98A]

- the rights embodied in that intangible asset are expressed as a measure of revenue; or
- when it can be demonstrated that revenue and the consumption of economic benefits are 'highly correlated'.

The Board did not define what is meant by 'highly correlated', but it describes situations where the asset is 'expressed as a measure of revenue'. A 'highly correlated' outcome would only be achieved where a revenue-based method of amortisation is expected to give the same answer as one of the other methods permitted by IAS 38. For example, if revenue is earned evenly over the expected life of the asset, the pattern of amortisation would be similar to a straight-line basis. In situations where unit prices are fixed and all production is sold, the pattern of amortisation would replicate the use of the units-of-production method. However, when unit prices are not fixed, revenue would not provide the same answer and its use would therefore be inappropriate. The following example illustrates how a revenue-based method of amortisation diverges from the units-of-production method when the price per unit is not fixed.

Example 25.5: Output-based versus revenue-based amortisation when prices change

Entity Z enters into a twenty-five year SCA over a toll bridge. It recognises an intangible asset of £20 million and expects the bridge to be used at its full capacity of 500,000 vehicles per year. Tolls will commence at £10 per vehicle and, under the terms of the SCA, it is allowed to raise prices by 10% every five years. On this basis, the profile of amortisation on a units-of-production method (UoP) and on a revenue-based method would be as follows:

	Units	Charge UoP basis £	Revenue £	Charge Revenue basis £
Years 1-5	500,000	4,000,000	5,000,000	3,276,000
Years 6-10	500,000	4,000,000	5,500,000	3,604,000
Years 11-15	500,000	4,000,000	6,050,000	3,964,000
Years 16-20	500,000	4,000,000	6,655,000	4,360,000
Years 21-25	500,000	4,000,000	7,320,500	4,796,000
Total	2,500,000	20,000,000	30,525,500	20,000,000

Despite an expected constant level of consumption of the asset in the example above, the revenue-based method results in amortisation being delayed until the later periods of the asset's use. This distortion is caused by the increase in price rather than any factor related to the use of the intangible asset.

The Board permits revenue-based amortisation to be used when revenue is 'the predominant limiting factor that is inherent in the intangible asset'. *[IAS 38.98B]*. In other words, revenue determines the useful life of the asset, rather than, for example, a number of years or the number of units produced.

The IASB provided two examples of this circumstance in which revenue earned can be regarded as a measure of consumption of an intangible asset: *[IAS 38.98C]*

(a) a contract may allow the extraction of gold from a mine until total cumulative revenue from the sale of gold reaches $2 billion; or

(b) the right to operate a toll road could be based on a fixed total amount of revenue generated, based on cumulative tolls that have been charged.

An example of (b) is a SCA, described at 4.1.2 above, in which an operator enters into a toll bridge concession under which it is permitted to collect revenues from users or the grantor until it achieves a 6% return on its agreed infrastructure spend, at which point the arrangement comes to an end. As explained at 4.1.2, this will be accounted for as an intangible asset because the operator bears demand risk and may never achieve the revenue target. In this case the operator could calculate amortisation based on cumulative revenue as a percentage of total revenue.

The choice of amortisation method is a matter of judgement. In the following extract from its accounting policies, ENGIE indicates that it amortises its intangible assets mainly on a straight-line basis.

Extract 25.2: ENGIE SA (2019)

NOTES TO THE CONSOLIDATED FINANCIAL STATEMENTS [extract]

NOTE 14 INTANGIBLE ASSETS [extract]

Accounting standards [extract]

Amortization

Intangible assets are amortized on the basis of the expected pattern of consumption of the estimated future economic benefits embodied in the asset. Amortization is calculated mainly on a straight-line basis over the following useful lives:

Main depreciation periods (years)	Useful life	
	Minimum	Maximum
Concession rights	10	30
Customer portfolio	10	40
Other intangible assets	1	50

Intangible assets with an indefinite useful life are not amortized but are tested for impairment annually.

4.3.2 Impairment during the construction phase

As noted at 4.3 above IFRS 15 requires the operator to classify the consideration given by the grantor as a contract asset during the construction phase. *[IFRIC 12.19]*. Contract assets are subject to the impairment requirements of IFRS 9. *[IFRS 15.107]*.

Operators may need to apply judgement in determining how to test the contract asset for impairment, given that the contract asset is expected to be realised in the form of an intangible asset, rather than as a receivable or cash. Operators may need to consider whether and how they can use the value of the underlying asset to which they are entitled as a proxy for cash flows in order to determine expected credit losses on the contract asset. The impairment requirements of IFRS 9 are discussed in Chapter 51, and impairment of non-cash consideration contract assets is discussed in Chapter 32 at 2.1.3.

4.4 Revenue recognition implications of the two models

Under the terms of arrangements within the scope of IFRIC 12, the operator provides services to construct or upgrade infrastructure (construction or upgrade services) used to provide the service, and operates and maintains that infrastructure for a specified period of time (operating services). *[IFRIC 12.12]*. The operator recognises and measures revenue in accordance with IFRS 15 for the services it performs.

While the nature of the consideration (i.e. a financial asset, an intangible asset or a mixture of the two) determines how revenue is recognised during the operating phase, *[IFRIC 12.13]*, under both models, the revenue that is recognised by the operator for the construction or upgrade services is the same and equals the fair value of these construction services.

There is nonetheless a major difference in the way in which revenue is measured under the two models during the operating phase of the arrangement. Under the financial asset model, total revenue over the concession term will be the same as the total cash inflows under the contract. By contrast, the fair value of the intangible asset is recognised as revenue under the intangible asset model, so total revenue measured using this model will be higher by this amount. The consequences of the two models can be demonstrated by the following simple example:

Example 25.6:   Revenue under the financial asset and intangible models

An operator builds a road at a cost of 100. The construction profit is 10 and total cash inflows over the life of the concession are 200. Assume that there is no significant financing component in the arrangement.

Under the financial asset model, the operator will recognise construction revenue of 110 and a receivable of 110. Of the future cash inflows of 200, 110 will be treated as repaying the receivable, with the remaining 90 being recognised as revenue over the life of the concession. Total revenue will be 200.

Under the intangible asset model, the operator will recognise construction revenue of 110, an intangible of 110, and a construction profit of 10. Over the life of the concession, the intangible asset of 110 would be amortised against revenues (which in this case would be from users) of 200. The net position is the same as in the financial asset case, but total revenues will be 310 rather than 200.

It is fair to say that this proved highly controversial. In fact, the September 2004 *IFRIC Update* stated that 'the majority of the Interpretations Committee strongly disliked this outcome'.[11] However, the Interpretations Committee maintained that this is the appropriate application of accounting standards to the arrangements and is consistent with the treatment generally accorded to barter transactions, *[IFRIC 12.BC35]*, although, of course, there are no other sectors where barter transactions are fundamental to the arrangement.

4.5 'Bifurcation' – single arrangements that contain both financial and intangible assets

The Interpretations Committee concluded that it may be necessary in certain circumstances to divide the operator's right to cash flows into a financial asset and an intangible asset. *[IFRIC 12.18]*. The *IFRIC Update* (March 2006) reported that 'With this change, the proposed amendment would better reflect the economic reality of concession arrangements: to the extent that the operator is remunerated for its construction services by obtaining a contractual right to receive cash from, or at the direction of, the grantor, the operator would recognise a financial asset and, to the extent that the operator receives only a licence to charge users, it would recognise an intangible asset.'

The Basis for Conclusions to IFRIC 12 explains more of the reasoning and potential impact. In some arrangements both parties to the contract share the risk (demand risk) that the cash flows generated by the project will not be sufficient to recover the operator's capital investment. A common mechanism for achieving this is where the grantor pays partly by a financial asset (i.e. the grantor will pay cash for the services provided) but gives the operator the right to charge for services (i.e. the operator has an intangible asset). The operator's infrastructure asset is to be split into a financial asset component for any guaranteed amount of cash and an intangible asset for the remainder. *[IFRIC 12.18, BC53]*.

This is common in transport concessions, e.g. a rail system paid for partly by grantor subsidy and partly by the payment of fares. This gives rise to difficult matters of judgement. It may not be clear how much of the arrangement is a financial asset and, therefore, where to draw the boundary between the two assets.

The following example, based on Illustrative Example 3 in IFRIC 12, illustrates how an entity may account for a service concession arrangement under the bifurcated model. As with Examples 25.3 and 25.4 above, it should be noted that this example deals with only one of many possible types of arrangements seen in practice and it is important that entities understand and assess the facts and circumstances of their own service concession arrangements in order to determine the appropriate accounting. In the example below, the operator recognises a receivable and an intangible asset once construction services are complete. As discussed at 4.2 above, IFRS 15 requires that a receivable is recognised only when the operator has an unconditional right to receive consideration, which will be the case only when nothing other than the passage of time is required before payment of the consideration is due. *[IFRS 15.108]*. We therefore assume that the example below contains an unstated assumption that this is the case at completion of construction services. However, this may not always be the situation in practice.

Example 25.7: The bifurcated model

Arrangement terms

The terms of a service arrangement require an operator to construct a road – completing construction within two years – and maintain and operate the road to a specified standard for eight years (i.e. years 3-10). The terms of the arrangement also require the operator to resurface the road when the original surface has deteriorated below a specified condition. The operator estimates that it will have to undertake the resurfacing at the end of the year 8. At the end of year 10, the service arrangement will end. The operator estimates that the costs it will incur to fulfil its obligations will be:

Table 1 Contract costs

	Year	€
Construction services (per year)	1-2	500
Operation services (per year)	3-10	10
Road resurfacing	8	100

The operator estimates the consideration in respect of construction services to be €1,050 by reference to the stand-alone selling price of those services, which it estimates at forecast cost plus 5 per cent. The terms of the arrangement allow the operator to collect tolls from drivers using the road. In addition, the grantor guarantees the operator a minimum amount of €700 and interest at a specified rate of 6.18 per cent to reflect the timing of cash receipts. The operator forecasts that vehicle numbers will remain constant over the duration of the contract and that it will receive tolls of €200 in each of years 3 to 10.

Dividing the arrangement

The contractual right to receive cash from the grantor for the services and the right to charge users for the public services should be regarded as two separate assets under IFRSs. Therefore, in this arrangement it is necessary to divide the operator's contract asset during the construction phase into two components – a financial asset component based on the guaranteed amount and an intangible asset for the remainder. When the construction services are complete, the two components of the contract asset would be classified and measured as a financial asset and an intangible asset accordingly.

Table 2 Dividing the operator's consideration

Year	Total	Financial asset		Intangible asset
Construction services in year 1	525	350		175
Construction services in year 2	525	350		175
Total construction services	1,050	700		350
	100%	67%	(a)	33%
Finance income, at specified rate of 6.18% (see table 3)	22	22		–
Borrowing costs capitalised (interest paid in years 1 and 2 × 33) (see table 7)	11	–		11
Total fair value of the operator's consideration	1,083	722		361

(a) Amount guaranteed by the grantor as a proportion of the construction services.

Financial asset

During the first two years, the entity recognises a contract asset and accounts for the significant financing component in the arrangement in accordance with IFRS 15. Once the construction is complete, the amount due from, or at the direction of, the grantor in exchange for the construction services is accounted for in accordance with IFRS 9 as a receivable. The example assumes that there has been no change in market interest rates during the construction phase of the arrangement.

Table 3 Measurement of the contract asset / receivable

	€
Construction services in year 1 allocated to the contract asset	350
Contract asset at end of year 1	350
Construction services in year 2 allocated to the contract asset	350
Interest in year 2 on contract asset at end of year 1 (6.18% × €350)	22

	€
Receivable at end of year 2	722
Interest in year 3 on receivable at end of year 2 (6.18% × €722)	45
Cash receipts in year 3 (see table 5)	(117)
Receivable at end of year 3	650

Intangible asset

In accordance with IAS 38, the operator recognises the intangible asset at cost, i.e. the fair value of the consideration received or receivable. During the construction phase of the arrangement, the portion of the operator's contract asset that represents its accumulating right to be paid amounts in excess of the guaranteed amount for providing construction services is presented as a right to receive a license to charge users of the infrastructure. The operator estimates the stand-alone selling price of the construction services as equal to the forecast construction costs plus 5 per cent, which the operator concludes is consistent with the rate that a market participant would require as compensation for providing the construction services and for assuming the risk associated with the construction costs. It is also assumed that, in accordance with IAS 23, the operator capitalises the borrowing costs, estimated at 6.7 per cent, during the construction phase.

Table 4 Initial measurement of the intangible asset

	€
Construction services in year 1	175
Borrowing costs (interest paid in years 1 and 2 × 33%) (see table 7)	11
Construction services in year 2	175
Intangible asset at the end of year 2	361

In accordance with IAS 38, the intangible asset is amortised over the period in which it is expected to be available for use by the operator, i.e. years 3-10. The depreciable amount of the intangible asset (€361 including borrowing costs) is allocated using a straight-line method. The annual amortisation charge is therefore €361 divided by 8 years, i.e. €45 per year.

Revenue and costs

The operator provides construction services to the grantor in exchange for a financial asset and an intangible asset. Under both the financial asset model and intangible asset model, the operator accounts for the construction services in accordance with IFRS 15. Thus in each of years 1 and 2 it recognises in profit or loss construction costs of €500 and construction revenue of €525.

Toll revenue

The road users pay for the public services at the same time as they receive them, i.e. when they use the road. Under the terms of this arrangement the cash flows are allocated to the financial asset and intangible asset in proportion, so the operator allocates the receipts from tolls between repayment of the financial asset and revenue earned from the intangible asset.

Table 5 Allocation of toll receipts

Year	€
Guaranteed receipt from grantor	700
Finance income (see table 8)	237
Total	937
Cash allocated to realisation of the financial asset per year (€937 / 8 years)	117
Receipts attributable to intangible asset (€200 × 8 years – €937)	663
Annual receipt from intangible asset (€663 / 8 years)	83

Resurfacing obligations

The operator's resurfacing obligation arises as a consequence of use of the road during the operation phase. It is recognised and measured in accordance with IAS 37, i.e. at the best estimate of the expenditure required to settle the present obligation at the end of the reporting period. It is assumed that the terms of the operator's contractual obligation are such that the best estimate of the expenditure required to settle the obligation at any date is proportionate to the number of vehicles that have used the road by that date and increased by €17 each year. The operator discounts the provision to its present value in accordance with IAS 37. The charge recognised each period in profit or loss is:

Table 6 Resurfacing obligation (€)

Year	3	4	5	6	7	8	Total
Obligation arising in year (€17 discounted at 6%)	12	13	14	15	16	17	87
Increase in earlier years' provision arising from passage of time	0	1	1	2	4	5	13
Total expense recognised in profit or loss	12	14	15	17	20	22	100

Overview of cash flows, statement of comprehensive income and statement of financial position

For the purposes of this example, it is assumed that the operator finances the arrangement wholly with debt and retained profits. It pays interest at 6.7 per cent per year on outstanding debt. If the cash flows are fair values remain the same as those forecast, the operator's cash flows, statement of comprehensive income and statement of financial position over the duration of the arrangement will be as follows.

Table 7 Cash flows (€)

Year	1	2	3	4	5	6	7	8	9	10	Total
Receipts	–	–	200	200	200	200	200	200	200	200	1,600
Contract costs (a)	(500)	(500)	(10)	(10)	(10)	(10)	(10)	(110)	(10)	(10)	(1,180)
Borrowing costs (b)	–	(34)	(69)	(61)	(53)	(43)	(33)	(23)	(19)	(7)	(342)
Net inflow / (outflow)	(500)	(534)	121	129	137	147	157	67	171	183	78

(a) Table 1
(b) Debt at start of year (table 9) × 6.7%

Table 8 Statement of comprehensive income (€)

Year	1	2	3	4	5	6	7	8	9	10	Total
Revenue on construction	525	525	–	–	–	–	–	–	–	–	1,050
Revenue allocated to operation services	–	–	83	83	83	83	83	83	83	83	663
Finance income (a)	–	22	45	40	35	30	25	19	13	7	237
Amortisation	–	–	(45)	(45)	(45)	(45)	(45)	(45)	(45)	(46)	(361)
Resurfacing expense	–	–	(12)	(14)	(15)	(17)	(20)	(22)	–	–	(100)
Construction costs	(500)	(500)	–	–	–	–	–	–	–	–	(1,000)
Other contract costs (b)	–	–	(10)	(10)	(10)	(10)	(10)	(10)	(10)	(10)	(80)
Borrowing costs (c) (table 7)	–	(23)	(69)	(61)	(53)	(43)	(33)	(23)	(19)	(7)	(331)
Net profit	25	24	(8)	(7)	(5)	(2)	–	2	22	27	78

(a) Interest on receivable
(b) Table 1
(c) In year 2, borrowing costs are stated net of amount capitalised in the intangible (see table 4).

Table 9 Statement of financial position (€)

End of year	1	2	3	4	5	6	7	8	9	10
Receivable	350	722	650	573	491	404	312	214	110	–
Intangible asset	175	361	316	271	226	181	136	91	46	–
Cash / (debt) (a)	(500)	(1,034)	(913)	(784)	(647)	(500)	(343)	(276)	(105)	78
Resurfacing obligation	–	–	(12)	(26)	(41)	(58)	(78)	–	–	–
Net assets	25	49	41	34	29	27	27	29	51	78

(a) Debt at start of year plus net cash flow in year (table 7)

The example above shows the operator's contractual obligation to resurface the road being recognised and measured in accordance with IAS 37. The accounting for maintenance costs during the operations phase is discussed at 5.2 below.

4.6 Accounting for residual interests

Unless the infrastructure in a service concession arrangement is used for the whole of its useful life (within scope of IFRIC 12 – see 3.2 above), there will be a residual interest at the end of the contract that will be controlled by the grantor. The way in which the grantor controls the residual interest will affect the way in which the operator accounts for it. If the operator has an unconditional contractual right to cash (or another financial asset) for the residual interest in the infrastructure, this right will be a financial asset. This is unaffected by the basis on which the consideration is calculated.

There are many different arrangements over residual interests in the infrastructure at the end of the concession term but broadly they depend on whether the grantor has a right or an option to acquire the residual interest and on the rights or options of the operator:

(a) The grantor may control the residual via an obligation to purchase the infrastructure from the operator but this could be at fair value, net book value, a notional amount or zero.

(b) It may only have an option to acquire the assets, on similar bases to (a), but it also has a right to put in place other arrangements, e.g. granting the operator a new term or selecting a new party to take on the assets. Payment might be made by the grantor or by the new operator but always at the direction of the grantor.

(c) The grantor has an option to acquire the assets but if this is not exercised then the operator may retain them.

The implications of grantor options and control of the residual interest have been discussed at 3.2 above.

If the terminal arrangements fall within (a) above the operator will have an unconditional contractual right to cash. It will recognise a financial asset, initially at fair value, which will then be accounted for according to the relevant classification under IFRS 9 (see 4.2 above). If the financial asset measured at amortised cost or fair value through other comprehensive income under IFRS 9, then interest will be calculated using the effective interest method. At the end of the contract the financial asset in respect of the residual interest will be stated at the operator's best estimate of the amount receivable.

Where the grantor has a right to put in place other arrangements, as in (b) above, the operator would only have an unconditional right to cash (i.e. a financial asset) after the grantor terminates the operator's involvement in the concession (by letting the contract lapse or by selecting a new party to take on the assets) if such termination will result in a payment to the operator. To the extent that the grantor can avoid any obligation to pay cash by allowing the concession term to continue, the operator has an intangible asset. The existence of such extension rights would have to be considered when determining the term of the concession arrangement.

If the arrangement is of the type described in (c), then the operator's residual interest is not a financial asset. Nor does it have a residual interest in the underlying property, plant and equipment because this is an arrangement within scope of IFRIC 12 and the entity cannot recognise the underlying assets, in whole or in part. *[IFRIC 12.11]*. The only option is to recognise an intangible right to receive cash or the residual interest in the assets. By contrast to the residual financial asset, it is most unlikely that the operator would be able to restate the value of this right over the term to its best estimate of the amount receivable at the end of the contract. IAS 38 only allows intangible assets to be revalued in very restricted circumstances; see Chapter 17 at 8.2.

The operator will have to account for its residual interests as described above based on the contractual rights, whatever model is being applied to its construction services. This is similar to the explicit requirements for upgrade services described at 5.1 below: IFRIC 12 recognises that upgrade services should be recognised as revenue on the basis of their individual contract terms regardless of the model applied. *[IFRIC 12.14]*. The result is that an entity that has recognised an intangible asset for the major part of its construction services might have to recognise a financial asset for the residual interests – or *vice versa* if its construction services have been accounted for as a financial asset. This treatment is a variation of the bifurcation described at 4.5 above except that the financial asset relates only to the residual interest in the infrastructure rather than to a portion of the consideration receivable for the infrastructure as a whole. The residual rights will be taken into account in calculating the revenue receivable under the contract, which are described at 4.2 and 4.3 above.

As the termination arrangements can be complex, care will have to be taken to ensure that the effects are fully analysed.

Example 25.8: Contractual rights to cash in termination arrangements

The facts of the SCA are as in Example 25.1 above. At the end of the term, the grantor will either pay for the infrastructure assets at their net book value, determined on the basis of the contract, or it may decide to grant a new SCA on the basis of a competitive tender, which will exclude the current operator. If the grantor elects to do the latter, the operator will be entitled to the lower of the following two amounts:

(a) the net book value of the infrastructure, determined on the basis of the contract; and

(b) the proceeds of a new competitive bidding process to acquire a new contract.

Although the operator cannot enter the competitive tender, it also has the right to enter into a new concession term but in order to do so, it must match the best tender offer made. It has to pay to the grantor the excess of the best offer (b) above the amount in (a); should the tender offer be lower than (a), it will receive an equivalent refund.

In this arrangement, the operator has a contractual right to cash that should be recognised as a financial asset. It has a right to receive the lower of (a) and (b). It may choose to use its right to cash to settle part or all of the price of a new concession agreement but this does not affect the fact that it has a right to cash. This example also illustrates that calculating the fair value of the contractual right to cash may be complex as it must take account of a number of different estimates, including the net book value of the infrastructure at the end of the contract, as well as the options available to the parties to the contract.

4.7 Accounting for contractual payments to be made by an operator to a grantor

Many arrangements require an entity to make payments to the grantor during the course of the SCA. These payments take two main forms:

(a) payments related to the use of tangible assets, including:

  (i) payments to the grantor or third parties for making assets available (such as trains and buses) in order to provide the services required by the concession contract;

  (ii) payments to a third party for the construction and making available of assets (such as rolling stock) that pass to the grantor at the end of the concession term; and

  (iii) payments to the grantor for making available land on which the infrastructure assets are constructed or situated; or

(b) fees payable to the grantor for the right to operate the concession, which can be described as concession fees, development fees or access charges.

It is possible that some of these payments could be for the right to use assets controlled by the operator itself or the concession payment could relate to a distinct good or service that is separate from the concession arrangement. In July 2016, the Interpretations Committee observed:

(a) if payments made by an operator to a grantor are for a right to a good or service that is separate from the service concession arrangement, the operator should account for those payments by applying the applicable IFRS Standards; and

(b) if payments are for the right to use an asset that is separate from the infrastructure within the scope of IFRIC 12, the operator should assess whether the arrangement contains a lease. If the arrangement contains a lease, the operator should account for those payments by applying IFRS 16.[12]

The application guidance in AG7 and AG8 of IFRIC 12 may be relevant to an operator in assessing whether an asset is separate from the infrastructure within scope of IFRIC 12. This application guidance is considered at 3.4 above, in the context of partially regulated assets.

The Interpretations Committee observed that if payments made by an operator to a grantor are not for the right to a separate good or service or a right to use an asset that is a lease, the accounting for those payments should depend on whether the SCA falls within the financial asset model, the intangible asset model or is a hybrid. This means that the payments will be reflected in the carrying value of the appropriate concession asset:

- if the SCA is accounted for under the financial asset model, then the concession payment is an adjustment to the transaction price, applying the requirements in paragraphs 70-72 of IFRS 15, illustrated at 4.7.2 below;
- if the intangible asset model applies, then the concession payment is part of the cost of acquiring the intangible asset recognised for the right to charge users of the service, illustrated at 4.7.3 below; and
- if the operator has both a right to charge users of the public service and a contractual right to receive cash from the grantor, then the entity should assess the extent to which the concession payment represents an adjustment to the overall consideration receivable or whether it is consideration for the intangible asset element.[13] This is determined by comparing the amount of the contractual right to receive cash from the grantor with the fair value of the operator's services.

The recommended treatment under the financial asset model is predicated on the fact that the operator has a contractual right to receive cash from the grantor and that payments between the parties are all part of this single relationship, however described. In this regard, payments to the grantor will include amounts paid to a related private sector entity to which responsibility for the service has been devolved. *[IFRIC 12.3]*.

Under the Interpretations Committee's approach for the intangible asset model, payments to the grantor that are not for a right to a good or service that is separate from the SCA, and are not an embedded lease, represent consideration for the concession, i.e. part of the cost of the intangible asset recognised. It is clearly a requirement of IAS 38 that an intangible asset be recognised when it meets the definition and other recognition criteria (see Chapter 17 at 2 and 3) and it must be recognised at its present value if payment is deferred. *[IAS 38.32]*.

Therefore, fixed fees payable over the life of a concession generate an intangible asset and give rise to a financial liability on inception, as the fixed fee will only be avoided by the operator if it withdraws from the concession, which in most circumstances is contractually and economically unfeasible.

4.7.1 Accounting for variable payments in a service concession

Some contracted payments, particularly concession fees, vary with a measure of usage of the concession asset or with another feature of the arrangement. Whilst the Interpretations Committee was able to reach a consensus on the treatment of concession fees that do not depend on future activity, as noted at 4.7 above, it has found the issue of variable payments more challenging.

In July 2013, the Committee tentatively agreed that, in cases where the variable payments do not depend on the purchaser's future activity, the fair value of those variable payments should be recognised as a liability and included as appropriate in the measurement of the related asset. The Committee was unable to reach a consensus on the treatment of payments that vary in relation to future activity and on the question of whether subsequent changes to the estimate of contingent consideration should be capitalised or expensed.[14] In March 2016, the Committee determined that the issue of variable payments for asset purchases is too broad for it to address within the confines of existing IFRS standards, and consequently decided not to add the issue to its agenda.[15] The Committee's deliberations on the treatment of variable payments for the separate acquisition of PP&E and intangible assets are also discussed in Chapter 17 at 4.5 and Chapter 18 at 4.1.9. At present, the usual treatment for an operator in a service concession is to treat contingent payments that vary in relation to future activity as executory and expense them as incurred.

4.7.2 Accounting for contractual payments under the financial asset model

If the financial asset model applies then the Interpretations Committee agreed that unless the contractual payments relate to the right to use assets controlled by the operator itself or relate to a distinct good or service that is distinct from the service concession arrangement, the contractual payment is accounted for as a reduction in the overall consideration received, i.e. it is an adjustment to the fair value of the consideration given by the grantor[16] (see 4.7 above). Another way of expressing this is that payments from the grantor reduce the financial asset while payments to the grantor increase that asset; both will also affect the amount of interest accrued on the outstanding balance. This applies whether the payment is for the right of access to an asset or described as a concession fee.

Example 25.9: Contractual payments made to a grantor under the financial asset model

Entity A enters into a 10 year concession agreement requiring it to construct a school and be responsible for operations services (including maintenance, utilities, cleaning and catering). After a 2 year construction period, the entity will receive €300 per year during years 3-10, to operate the asset, after which the concession will cease. The entity must pay €30 per year for the use of the land on which the school is built. Entity A concludes that the land use charge does not relate to a distinct good or service that is distinct from the service concession itself and does not give the entity a right to use an asset that is separate from the infrastructure.

The entity's estimated contract costs and contractual payments are as follows:

	Year	Annual charge €	Total €
Construction services	1-2	500	1,000
Operation services	3-10	100	800
Land use charge	1-10	30	300
Total cash paid	1-10		2,100

The operating cash flows under the contract are as follows:

Year	1 €	2 €	3 €	4 €	5 €	6 €	7 €	8 €	9 €	10 €
Concession consideration	–	–	300	300	300	300	300	300	300	300
Construction and operation costs	(500)	(500)	(100)	(100)	(100)	(100)	(100)	(100)	(100)	(100)
Land use charge	(30)	(30)	(30)	(30)	(30)	(30)	(30)	(30)	(30)	(30)
Net cash flow	(530)	(530)	170	170	170	170	170	170	170	170

The entity recognises revenue in accordance with IFRS 15 and estimates that the stand-alone selling price of its services and total revenue from those services is as follows:

	Estimated stand-alone selling price	Total
		€
Construction	Forecast cost + 5%	1,050
Operation and maintenance	" " + 15%	920
Total revenue		1,970
Lending rate to grantor	2.25% per year	

Under the financial asset model, the land use charge is treated as an adjustment to the transaction price and is not treated as an expense. Accordingly, the gross concession profit is calculated as follows:

Year	1	2	3	4	5	6	7	8	9	10	Total
	€	€	€	€	€	€	€	€	€	€	€
Concession revenue*	525	525	115	115	115	115	115	115	115	115	1,970
Construction costs	(500)	(500)	(100)	(100)	(100)	(100)	(100)	(100)	(100)	(100)	(1,800)
Finance income	6	19	24	21	18	15	12	8	5	3	130
Concession profit**	31	44	39	36	33	30	27	23	20	18	300

* Concession revenue comprises revenue from construction and operation and maintenance services, less the land use charge.

** Concession profit totals €300, which represents the total consideration received for services (€2,400), less the land use charge of €300, and construction costs of €1,800. In the income statement this is analysed as:

	€
Concession revenue	1,970
Construction costs	(1,800)
Finance income	130
Total	300

The contract asset / financial asset is computed as follows, applying an effective interest rate of 2.25%.

Year	1	2	3	4	5	6	7	8	9	10
	€	€	€	€	€	€	€	€	€	€
Opening balance	0	561	1,135	1,004	870	733	592	449	302	152
Additions	525	525	115	115	115	115	115	115	115	115
Net cash	30	30	(270)	(270)	(270)	(270)	(270)	(270)	(270)	(270)
Finance income*	6	19	24	21	18	15	12	8	5	3
Closing balance	561	1,135	1,004	870	733	592	449	302	152	–

* Finance income is calculated on the average debtor balance outstanding and assumes that the same interest rate is applied to both the contract asset and receivable.

4.7.3 Accounting for contractual payments under the intangible asset model

Under the intangible asset model, concession payments would be treated in accordance with IAS 38 as part of the consideration for the intangible asset.

While lease-type costs and land use charges can be part of any concession arrangement, concession fees (however called) are much more commonly a feature of arrangements which follow the intangible asset model. This is unsurprising as they are in substance payments made by the operator for the right to charge users of the concession infrastructure.

The Interpretations Committee have noted that unless the contractual payments relate to the right to use assets controlled by the operator itself or relate to a distinct good or service that is distinct from the service concession arrangement, the concession payment represents consideration for the concession right (i.e. part of the cost of the intangible asset recognised)[17] (see 4.7 above). However, the effects on reported revenues were not addressed directly. In the following illustration, the concession fee is regarded as a distinct cost in addition to the fair value of the construction services. Alternatively, the concession fee could be regarded as a cost of the construction services, for example if the concession payments were for access to the land on which the infrastructure was to be constructed or for an asset used in the delivery of the construction services. In that case, the estimate of the stand-alone selling price of the construction services would include an appropriate margin on top of the concession fee (see 4.3 above).

Example 25.10: Contractual payments made to a grantor under the intangible asset model

Entity B enters into a 10 year concession agreement to construct a toll road and be responsible for operations services. After a 2 year construction period, the entity expects to receive tolls of €300 per year, which it expects to remain at the same level for the duration of the concession. The entity must pay a concession fee of €50 per year in years 5-10.

The entity concludes that the obligation for the concession fee is incurred in year 1 and estimates that its present value is €209, using a discount rate of 5%. The contract costs and contractual payments are as follows:

	Year	Annual charge €	Total €
Construction services	1-2	500	1,000
Operation services	3-10	100	800
Concession fee	5-10	50	300
Total cash paid	1-10		2,100

The entity assesses the fair value of its intangible asset to be the stand-alone selling price of the construction services, which it determines as the cost of construction services plus a margin of 5%. To this it adds an amount to reflect the present value of the obligation to pay the concession fee. This means that it will record construction revenue and additions to its intangible asset in years 1 and 2 as follows.

Year	1 €	2 €
Construction services	500	500
Revenue (uplift costs by 5%)	525	525
Concession fee (present value of obligation)	209	–
Intangible asset additions	734	525

This means that the entity recognises concession revenue for construction services totalling €1,050 (525+525) and an intangible asset of €1,259 (734+525). It concludes that, as usage is expected to be the same throughout the term, the intangible asset should be amortised in equal annual instalments commencing in year 3. The concession gross profit (revenue – contract costs – unwinding discount on the concession fee – amortisation of the intangible asset) is calculated as follows:

Year	1 €	2 €	3 €	4 €	5 €	6 €	7 €	8 €	9 €	10 €
Concession revenue	525	525	300	300	300	300	300	300	300	300
Contract costs	(500)	(500)	(100)	(100)	(100)	(100)	(100)	(100)	(100)	(100)
Unwinding discount	(10)	(11)	(12)	(12)	(12)	(11)	(9)	(7)	(5)	(2)
Amortisation*	–	–	(157)	(157)	(158)	(158)	(158)	(157)	(157)	(157)
Concession profit**	15	14	31	31	30	31	33	36	38	41

* The amortisation is adjusted for rounding

** Concession profit totals €300, which represents the total consideration received from users for services (€2,400) less the total costs including the concession fee of €2,100. In the income statement this is analysed as:

	€
Concession revenue (525+525+2,400)	3,450
Contract costs	(1,800)
Unwinding discount	(91)
Amortisation	(1,259)
Total	300

4.8 Contract acquisition and mobilisation costs

Given the scale of many service concession arrangements, operators often incur significant bid costs, pre-contract costs and mobilisation costs.

IFRS 15 specifies the accounting treatment for costs that an entity incurs to obtain and fulfil a contract to provide goods or services to customers, if those costs are not within the scope of another standard. *[IFRS 15.8]*.

4.8.1 Costs to obtain a contract

IFRS 15 requires that incremental costs of obtaining a contract with a customer are recognised as an asset if the entity expects to recover them, either directly (i.e. reimbursement under the contract), or indirectly (i.e. through the margin inherent under the contract). *[IFRS 15.91, 93]*. Incremental costs of obtaining a contract are those that the entity would not have incurred if the contract had not been obtained, such as sales commission. *[IFRS 15.92]*. Costs incurred to obtain a contract that are not incremental costs must be expensed as incurred, unless they are explicitly chargeable to the customer regardless of whether the contract is obtained. *[IFRS 15.93]*. Many of the costs that an operator incurs in bidding for a service concession contract, such as the fixed salaries of employees involved in drafting the tender document, and legal due diligence fees, may not meet the definition of incremental costs under IFRS 15 and therefore must be expensed as incurred, even if the operator expects to be successful in bidding for the service concession and expects to be able to indirectly recover those costs through the margin in the service concession contract over the term of the arrangement.

In determining the appropriate accounting treatment for costs to obtain a service concession that are not explicitly chargeable regardless of obtaining the contract, the key judgements are made in the following order:
- Are the costs within the scope of another standard? If so, apply that standard.
- Are the costs incremental (i.e. would not have occurred if the contract had not been obtained)? Costs that are not incremental should be expensed.
- Are the incremental costs expected to be recovered? To the extent that incremental costs are not expected to be recoverable, they are expensed as incurred.

Costs to obtain a contract with a customer are discussed in Chapter 31 at 5.1.

4.8.2 Pre-contract costs

Pre-contract costs incurred by the operator of a service concession may include costs incurred in designing financial models and planning infrastructure improvements for tender purposes, costs incurred in undertaking site surveys, and similar expenses. Such costs will often result in no future economic benefit for the operator unless the contract is obtained. As discussed in Chapter 31 at 5.2.4, pre-contract costs that are incurred in anticipation of a specific contract should first be evaluated for capitalisation under other standards (e.g. IAS 2 – *Inventories*, IAS 16, or IAS 38). Costs not addressed under other standards should be capitalised under IFRS 15 only if they meet the criteria of a cost incurred to fulfil a contract, that is:

(a) the costs relate directly to a contract or to an anticipated contract that the entity can specifically identify (e.g. costs relating to services to be provided under renewal of an existing contract or costs of designing an asset to be transferred under a specific contract that has not yet been approved);

(b) the costs generate or enhance resources of the entity that will be used in satisfying performance obligations in the future; and

(c) the costs are expected to be recovered. *[IFRS 15.95]*.

The need to consider first the requirement of other relevant standards is significant, for example where another standard requires costs of a similar nature to be expensed. As noted at 4.8.3 below, these requirements are not overridden on the basis that the costs were incurred in the context of a service concession arrangement.

Criterion (b) above is to ensure that only those costs that meet the definition of an asset are recognised as such. *[IFRS 15.BC308]*. In the context of service concessions, costs for pre-designing a bespoke piece of equipment or infrastructure for the concession (e.g. a tramway or a depot for electrical buses) are an example of such costs.

4.8.3 Mobilisation costs

An operator may also incur significant mobilisation costs in moving personnel, equipment and supplies as it takes on the service concession. These costs are incurred to ensure that the entity is able to fulfil its promise to the customer in a contract, rather than transferring a good or service to the customer. That is, they do not represent a promised good or service in its own right. The assessment of whether mobilisation costs can be capitalised will depend on the specific facts and circumstances and may require significant judgement. Entities need to ensure that the costs are within the scope of IFRS 15; and meet all of the criteria of a cost incurred to fulfil a contract set out at 4.8.2 above.

Particular care must be taken where costs of a similar nature to those being considered in the service concession arrangement fall under the scope of another standard. For example, IAS 38 cites training costs, expenditure on advertising and promotional activities, and expenditure on start-up activities as examples of expenditure that should be recognised as an expense when it is incurred. *[IAS 38.69]*. In March 2020, the Interpretations Committee considered a question about the interaction of the above requirements in relation to staff training to deliver outsourced services for a customer. The Committee concluded that, in the fact pattern described in the request, the entity recognises the training costs to fulfil the contract with the customer as an expense when incurred. The Committee noted that the entity's ability to charge to the customer the costs of training does not affect that conclusion.[18]

Mobilisation costs are discussed in Chapter 31 at 5.2.5.

4.8.3.A Mobilisation costs are excluded from input measures of contract progress

Where an operator determines that a performance obligation is satisfied over time, IFRS 15 requires selection of a revenue recognition method to measure progress. *[IFRS 15.39]*. If the operator selects a method based on costs incurred, they must exclude from their measure of progress those costs that do not depict the entity's performance in transferring a good or service to the customer. *[IFRS 15.B19]*. An example may be costs incurred in mobilisation activities that do not transfer a good or service to the grantor and from which the grantor receives little or no benefit. Measurement of revenue recognised over time is discussed in Chapter 30 at 3.

5 REVENUE AND EXPENDITURE DURING THE OPERATIONS PHASE OF THE CONCESSION AGREEMENT

So far, we have described the recognition and measurement of the infrastructure asset in the accounts of the operator under the two models. A significant issue in practice is that service concession arrangements are composite transactions. They usually have a long duration (twenty-five to thirty years is not uncommon) during which time the operator has a variety of obligations. These may be in connection with the infrastructure asset itself and include:

- enhancement of the infrastructure or construction of new infrastructure;
- infrastructure components that must be replaced in their entirety;
- infrastructure subject to major cyclical repairs; and
- regular repairs and maintenance.

In addition, many service concession arrangements involve the provision of services. In the case of a hospital, for example, this could include utilities (such as water and electricity) and a wide range of 'soft' services such as cleaning, laundry, meals, portering, security and grounds maintenance, amongst others. All of these might be paid for as a single unitary charge that would probably be adjusted according to performance as in

Example 25.2 above. The accounting models for service concessions must be able to deal with all of these issues.

IFRIC 12 identifies two principle revenue-generating activities in a service concession arrangement, construction or upgrade services and operation services, requiring that both are accounted for in accordance with IFRS 15. *[IFRIC 12.14, 20].* The Interpretation also states that, during the construction phase, both accounting models (intangible asset and financial asset) give rise to a contract asset in accordance with IFRS 15. *[IFRIC 12.19].* The point at which the consideration is subsequently classified as a receivable, or an intangible asset, is discussed at 4.2 and 4.3 above, respectively. Whilst the Interpretation includes examples to illustrate how these requirements might be applied to a relatively simple set of facts and circumstances, it does set out any special treatments in relation to how IFRS 15 is applied for an SCA. Any questions about how IFRS 15 should be applied in accounting for revenue from construction, upgrade or operation services or for the contract assets and liabilities arising during the construction phase of an SCA will be answered by reference to that Standard (see Chapters 27 to 32), rather than to IFRIC 12.

5.1 Additional construction and upgrade services

The concession may include obligations to construct new infrastructure (construction services) or to enhance either new or existing infrastructure to a condition better than at the start of the concession (upgrade services). IFRIC 12 does not deal in detail with the treatment to be adopted other than to say that revenue and costs relating to construction or upgrade services are recognised in accordance with IFRS 15. *[IFRIC 12.14].* This means that all construction or upgrade services are accounted for in accordance with the appropriate model, regardless of when they take place. Contractual obligations to maintain or restore infrastructure may also include an upgrade element. *[IFRIC 12.21].*

Upgrade or construction services are separate performance obligations. This means that the contract has to require the particular service to be carried out at a specified time. This is not the same as a general requirement to maintain the asset in a specified condition.

It would be unusual for a toll road concession, for example, to require resurfacing to take place according to a predetermined schedule as road surfaces degrade with usage (based on both the number of vehicles and weight per axle) as well as weather conditions. However, the contract might require a new bridge or access road after a specified period of time and either of these would be separate upgrade services.

Upgrade services must be recognised in accordance with IFRS 15. *[IFRIC 12.14].* IFRS 15 is discussed in Chapters 27 to 32.

The entity must determine the consideration receivable for the upgrade services. This may be part of the allocation at inception of the contract, as shown in Example 25.3 above where part of the contract revenue is attributed to road resurfacing, or the contract may specify a separate payment when the upgrade is performed. In either case, the entity would allocate the transaction price for the arrangement as a whole to each of the performance obligations in proportion to their stand-alone selling prices in accordance with IFRS 15. *[IFRIC 12.14].* The entity would recognise revenue for the upgrade service only as the obligation to provide those services is fulfilled.

5.1.1 Subsequent construction or upgrade services that are part of the initial infrastructure asset

In some circumstances, the 'enhancement' spend is a component of the original intangible asset and should be recognised as part of the exchange transaction to secure the right to charge users described at 4.3 above. An example of this is the construction of an additional water treatment facility for an existing water distribution network to which the operator is given immediate access to charges users for water supply.

Assuming that the intangible asset model is the relevant one, the intangible asset received in exchange for such construction or upgrade services should be recognised in accordance with the general principles applicable to contracts for the exchange of goods or services. Therefore, service concession contracts should not be recognised to the extent that they remain executory, which is generally the case when they are signed. *[IFRIC 12.BC66, BC68]*. The contract is no longer executory if:

- the operator has started to fulfil its contractual obligations by constructing the infrastructure concerned or enhancing an existing infrastructure before being entitled to derive benefits from its right to charge for the public service; or
- the operator starts deriving benefits from its right to charge for the public service before fulfilling its obligations (e.g. when the contract provides for a new item to be constructed some time ahead in the concession period).

Therefore, if the operator starts charging users before the upgrade services are performed, the present value of these expenditures should be included in the measure of the consideration given for the intangible asset and therefore recognised as part of its carrying value on initial recognition. This would require the recognition of a liability for the present value of the best estimate of the amount required to construct the additional water treatment facility for the existing water distribution network.

The Interpretations Committee did not address the accounting treatment of subsequent variations in the amount of the liability for the operator's unfulfilled obligations that is recognised as part of the cost of the intangible asset (the licence) e.g. when the estimated amount of the expenditures to be incurred is revised. The situation may be regarded as analogous to the situation addressed by IFRIC Interpretation 1 – *Changes in Existing Decommissioning, Restoration and Similar Liabilities* – where the obligation is recognised as a liability in accordance with IAS 37 and as part of the cost of an asset. *[IFRIC 1.1]*. Therefore, the principles set out in IFRIC 1 – *Changes in Existing Decommissioning, Restoration and Similar Liabilities* – should be applied, i.e. a change in the measurement of the liability should be added to, or deducted from the cost of the intangible asset, subject to impairment testing and to the extent that the amount deducted from the cost of the asset does not exceed the carrying amount of the intangible asset. *[IFRIC 1.5]*. The periodic unwinding of the discount must be recognised in profit or loss. *[IFRIC 1.8]*. IFRIC 1 is discussed in Chapter 26 at 6.3.1.

5.1.2 Subsequent construction services that comprise additions to the initial infrastructure

An operator may be contractually required to add to the infrastructure and from this generate additional revenues. For example, it is common in developing countries that the operator of a water distribution network incurs an obligation to extend the distribution network. The operator will obtain revenues from newly connected users under its right to charge for the services. There is an example of such a right in Extract 25.3 below, in which Telenor ASA disclosed in its 2017 financial statements that it had a right 'to arrange, expand, operate and provide the cellular telephone services in various areas in Thailand'.

> Extract 25.3: Telenor ASA (2017)
> Notes to the Financial Statements / Telenor Group [extract]
> NOTE 17 Intangible assets [extract]
> dtac operates under a concession right to operate and deliver mobile services in Thailand granted by CAT Telecom Public Company Limited (CAT). CAT allows dtac to arrange, expand, operate and provide the cellular telephone services in various areas in Thailand. The concession originally covered a 15-year period but the agreement was amended on 23 July 1993 and 22 November 1996 with the concession period being extended to 22 and 27 years, respectively. Accordingly, the concession period under the amended agreement expires in September 2018.

Revenues generated by the new infrastructure will be determined under the terms of the original licence granted to the operator. In this case, the extension work will add to the initial infrastructure asset, meaning that it will only be recognised when the expenditure is made. Accordingly, that new cost is not an additional component of the cost of the original intangible asset but will be a new intangible asset in its own right, giving rise to new construction revenues and recognised using the same principles as the original as described at 4.3 above.

5.2 Accounting for the operations phase

Both the financial and intangible asset models apply the same accounting in the operations phase of the SCA. According to the September 2006 *IFRIC Update*, 'the nature of the asset recognised by the operator as consideration for providing construction services (a financial asset or an intangible asset) does not determine the accounting for the operation phase of the arrangement'.[19]

Revenue and costs for the operation services will be recognised in accordance with IFRS 15. *[IFRIC 12.20]*. This means that most operating costs are likely to be executory and will be accounted for as incurred. Contractual obligations, including obligations to maintain, replace or restore infrastructure to a specified level of serviceability during its operation or to a specified condition at the end of the concession, are to be recognised and measured in accordance with IAS 37, *[IFRIC 12.21]*, as shown in Example 25.11 below, when such obligations do not include any upgrade element (which is treated as an additional construction service, see 5.1 above).

Distinguishing between executory maintenance expenditure and contractual obligations is not always straightforward. A concession arrangement may provide for a specified total amount of expenditure to be incurred by the operator throughout the contract. Sometimes, the contract provides for mechanisms whereby at the end of the contract, any shortfall in the agreed amount is paid in cash to the grantor by the operator. Particularly in the case of older contracts, it is common for the maintenance and repair obligation to be expressed in very general terms such as keeping the infrastructure in 'good working condition' or 'state of the art' working condition.

The obligation may include the requirement that the asset be handed over with a certain number of years' useful life remaining.

Local regulations or laws also change over time. Some operators are obliged to report annually to the grantor on the level of maintenance and renewal expenditure incurred during the year and on a cumulative basis from inception of the contract. Sometimes, the operator must report on expected expenditures over some future period of time (e.g. over the next 12 months or two years) as well. In these situations, more often than not the grantor compares the cumulative expenditure at any point in time with either the operator's prior estimates of expenditures or with the level of expenditure that had been anticipated at the outset of the arrangement and was factored into the level of usage charges. In such circumstances, judgement is required in deciding whether expenditure on renewals is an obligation requiring recognition or an executory contract.

Example 25.11: Executory and contractual obligations to maintain and restore the infrastructure

The operator under a water supply service concession is required as part of the overall contractual arrangement to replace four water pumps as soon as their performance drops below certain quality levels. The operator expects this to be the case after 15 years of service. The expected cost of replacing the pumps is $1,000. The operator's best estimate is that the service potential of the pumps is consumed evenly over time and provision for the costs is made on this basis from inception of the service concession arrangement until the date of expected replacement. The provision is measured at the net present value of the amounts expected to be paid, using the operator's discount rate of 5%. The amount provided in the first year can be calculated as $33.67. Assuming no changes to estimates, in 15 years $1,000 would have been provided and would be utilised in replacing the pumps. The provision would be adjusted on a cumulative basis to take account of changes in estimates to the cost of replacement pumps, the manner in which they are wearing out or changes to the operator's discount rate.

The Interpretations Committee has also provided an example in Illustrative Example 2, the intangible asset model, of how operational expenditure might be accounted for in accordance with IAS 37. Although this illustration is in the context of an intangible asset, IAS 37 can apply to maintenance and other obligations whichever model applies. Major maintenance, in this case the requirement to resurface the road, will be recognised as the best estimate of the expenditure required to settle the present obligation at the reporting date and it is suggested that this might 'arise as a consequence of use of the road', therefore increasing in measurable annual increments. *[IFRIC 12.IE19, IE20]*. The basis for accounting for such obligations is discussed further in Chapter 26.

Example 25.12: The Intangible Asset Model – recording the operations phase

The terms of the arrangement are the same as in Example 25.4 above. The contract costs and initial measurement of the intangible asset are set out in Table 1 and Table 2 in that example.

Resurfacing obligations

The operator's resurfacing obligation arises as a consequence of use of the road during the operating phase. It is recognised and measured in accordance with IAS 37, i.e. at the best estimate of the expenditure required to settle the present obligation at the reporting date.

For the purpose of this illustration, it is assumed that the terms of the operator's contractual obligation are such that the best estimate of the expenditure required to settle the obligation at any date is proportional to the number of vehicles that have used the road by that date and increases by €17 (discounted to a current value) each year. The operator discounts the provision to its present value in accordance with IAS 37. The income statement charge each period is:

Table 3 Resurfacing obligation

Year	3 €	4 €	5 €	6 €	7 €	8 €	Total €
Obligation arising in year (€17 discounted at 6%)	12	13	14	15	16	17	87
Increase in earlier years' provision arising from passage of time	–	1	1	2	4	5	13
Total expense recognised in income statement	12	14	15	17	20	22	100

Overview of cash flows, income statement and statement of financial position

For the purpose of this illustration, it is assumed that the operator finances the arrangement wholly with debt and retained profits. It pays interest at 6.7% a year on outstanding debt. If the cash flows and fair values remain the same as those forecast, the operator's cash flows, income statement and statement of financial position over the duration of the arrangement will be:

Table 4 Cash flows

Year	1 €	2 €	3 €	4 €	5 €	6 €	7 €	8 €	9 €	10 €	Total €
Receipts	–	–	200	200	200	200	200	200	200	200	1,600
Contract costs	(500)	(500)	(10)	(10)	(10)	(10)	(10)	(110)	(10)	(10)	(1,180)
Borrowing costs†	–	(34)	(69)	(61)	(53)	(43)	(33)	(23)	(19)	(7)	(342)
Net inflow/(outflow)	(500)	(534)	121	129	137	147	157	67	171	183	78

† Debt at start of year (table 6) × 6.7%

Table 5 Income statement

Year	1 €	2 €	3 €	4 €	5 €	6 €	7 €	8 €	9 €	10 €	Total €
Revenue	525	525	200	200	200	200	200	200	200	200	2,650
Amortisation	–	–	(135)	(135)	(136)	(136)	(136)	(136)	(135)	(135)	(1,084)
Resurfacing expense	–	–	(12)	(14)	(15)	(17)	(20)	(22)	–	–	(100)
Other operating costs†	(500)	(500)	(10)	(10)	(10)	(10)	(10)	(10)	(10)	(10)	(1,080)
Borrowing costs* (table 4)	–	–	(69)	(61)	(53)	(43)	(33)	(23)	(19)	(7)	(308)
Net profits	25	25	(26)	(20)	(14)	(6)	1	9	36	48	78

* Borrowing costs are capitalised during the construction phase

† Table 1

Table 6 Statement of financial position

End of Year	1 €	2 €	3 €	4 €	5 €	6 €	7 €	8 €	9 €	10 €
Intangible asset	525	1,084	949	814	678	542	406	270	135	–
Cash/(debt)*	(500)	(1,034)	(913)	(784)	(647)	(500)	(343)	(276)	(105)	78
Resurfacing obligation	–	–	(12)	(26)	(41)	(58)	(78)	–	–	–
Net assets	25	50	24	4	(10)	(16)	(15)	(6)	30	78

* Debt at start of year plus net cash flow in year (table 4)

To make this illustration as clear as possible, it has been assumed that the arrangement period is only ten years and that the operator's annual receipts are constant over the period. In practice, arrangement periods may be much longer and annual revenue may increase with time. In such circumstances, the changes in net profit from year to year could be greater.

In the following extract, Vinci explains how provisions are recognised for contractual obligations to maintain the condition of concession assets.

> *Extract 25.4: VINCI SA (2019)*
>
> Notes to the consolidated financial statements at 31 December 2019 [extract]
> H.   Other balance sheet items and business-related commitments [extract]
> 19.   Working capital requirements and current provisions [extract]
> 19.3   Breakdown of current provisions [extract]
>
> Provisions are taken for contractual obligations to maintain the condition of concession assets. They concern the motorway concession operating companies and cover the expense of major road repairs (surface courses, restructuring of slow lanes, etc.), bridges, tunnels and hydraulic infrastructure. They also include expenses to be incurred by airport concession companies (repairs to runways, traffic lanes and other paved surfaces) and are calculated on the basis of maintenance expense plans spanning several years, which are updated annually. These expenses are reassessed on the basis of appropriate indexes (mainly the TP01, TP02 and TP09 indexes in France). Provisions are also taken whenever signs of defects are encountered on certain infrastructure.
>
> [...]
>
> At 31 December 2019, contractual obligations to maintain the condition of concession assets mainly comprised €453 million for the ASF group (€418 million at 31 December 2018), €269 million for Cofiroute (€258 million at 31 December 2018), and €194 million for VINCI Airports (€189 million at 31 December 2018) including €85 million for the ANA group (€74 million at 31 December 2018).

5.3 Items provided to the operator by the grantor

Following the basic principles underlying the accounting treatment under both models, infrastructure items to which the operator is given access by the grantor for the purpose of the service concession are not recognised as its property, plant and equipment. *[IFRIC 12.27]*. This is because they remain under the control of the grantor.

There is a different treatment for assets that are given to the operator as part of the consideration for the concession that can be kept or dealt with as the operator wishes. These assets are not to be treated as government grants as defined in IAS 20. Instead, an operator should account for these assets as part of the transaction price and in accordance with IFRS 15. *[IFRIC 12.27]*. (See Chapter 29 at 2.)

What this means is that an operator that has been given a licence or similar arrangement over a piece of land on which a hospital is to be built does not recognise the land as an asset.

If, on the other hand, the operator has been given a piece of surplus land on which it can build private housing for sale, it will recognise an asset. The consideration, which is the fair value of that land, will be aggregated with the remainder of the consideration for the transaction and accounted for according to the model being used.

6 FURTHER EXAMPLES ILLUSTRATING THE APPLICATION OF IFRIC 12 AND INTERACTIONS WITH IFRS 15 AND IFRS 9

IFRIC 12 was not significantly amended upon issue of IFRS 15 and IFRS 9 and the illustrative examples to IFRIC 12 were largely unchanged. However, it should be noted that the illustrative examples in IFRIC 12 are intended simply to demonstrate the principal features of the financial asset and intangible asset models. In doing so, they reflect some aspects of service concession arrangements that are commonly seen in practice, but the examples are not intended to be exhaustive. It is important that entities understand and assess the facts and circumstances of their own arrangements in order to determine whether their existing service concession accounting is supported under the 5-step model within IFRS 15 and the requirements of IFRS 9 as appropriate.

In the examples below, we have considered the fact patterns set out in Illustrative Examples 1 and 2 from IFRIC 12 (which are reproduced in Examples 25.3 at 4.2 above, 25.4 at 4.3 above and 25.12 at 5.2 above), in the context of the 5-step model in IFRS 15, and suggested how the accounting for the same basic fact pattern may be impacted by certain changes to the terms within the concession arrangement, the operator's assessment of those terms, and the introduction of other facts and circumstances.

Example 25.13: Financial asset model – Receivable recognised once construction is complete and no change in discount rate on recognition of receivable

Arrangement terms

The terms of the arrangement are the same as in Example 25.3 at 4.2 above.

The operator's annual receipts do not vary over the concession period, cash flows and fair values remain the same as forecast, no contract modifications occur over the concession period, and there is no change to the timing of delivery from that anticipated at contract inception. In addition, for the purposes of this example, we assume that the operator may be subject to penalties for substandard performance, with any penalties being deducted from the €200 per annum to which the operator is entitled in years 3 to 10 of the arrangement. However, in this case the operator has not deducted any potential penalties when determining the transaction price under the contract on the basis that it is highly probable that significant penalties will not be incurred (see Step 3 below – Determining the transaction price). In addition, we assume that there is no difference between the discount rate used by the operator in determining the transaction price in accordance with IFRS 15 and the discount rate used to determine the fair value of the receivable on initial recognition in accordance with IFRS 9 (see Step 5 below – Recognise revenue when (or as) the entity satisfies a performance obligation).

Any changes in these assumptions or facts and circumstances would need to be assessed by reference to the requirements of IFRIC 12 and IFRS 15 and could result in a change to the accounting discussed below.

Step 1 – Identify the contract with the customer

Under IFRS 15, a contract is defined as an agreement between two parties that creates enforceable rights and obligations. *[IFRS 15 Appendix A].*

Because the public-sector grantor of the concession retains control over the infrastructure asset, construction and upgrade (resurfacing) services are provided to the grantor. The grantor pays cash consideration to the operator in exchange for those services. The grantor is the only party with which the operator has a contract.

Because of the public service nature of the obligation undertaken by the operator, the operating services (operation of the road) are provided to the public. However, a customer is defined in IFRS 15 as a party that has contracted with an entity to obtain goods or services that are an output of an entity's ordinary activities in exchange for consideration. *[IFRS 15 Appendix A]*. Under the terms of the arrangement, the operator does not collect any tolls so the end user of the road is not passing consideration to the operator and therefore is not considered a customer. The grantor is therefore considered to be the only customer of the operator in this arrangement.

Identification of the contract(s) with the customer under IFRS 15 is discussed in Chapter 28.

Step 2 – Identify the performance obligations in the contract

Example 25.3 at 4.2 above identifies construction services, operation services and road resurfacing as performance obligations within the contract with the grantor.

IFRS 15 provides guidance on the types of items that may be goods or services promised in the contract. Examples given by the standard include performing a contractually agreed-upon task (or tasks) for a customer, and providing a service of standing ready to provide goods or services. *[IFRS 15.26]*. This introduces the possibility that maintenance may also be a performance obligation within the contract with the grantor.

A promised good or service is a performance obligation if it is either:

(a) a good or service that is distinct; or

(b) a series of distinct goods or services that are substantially the same and have the same pattern of transfer to the customer. *[IFRS 15.22]*.

In order to be distinct, a promised good or service must be:

(a) capable of being distinct – i.e. provide a benefit to the customer either on its own or together with other resources that are readily available to the customer; and

(b) distinct within the context of the contract – i.e. the entity's promise to transfer the good or service to the customer is separately identifiable from other promises in the contract. *[IFRS 15.27]*.

If a promised good or service is not distinct, IFRS 15 requires that the entity should combine those goods or services with other promised goods or services until it identifies a bundle of goods or services that is distinct. *[IFRS 15.30]*.

It could be argued that because major maintenance enhances an asset that the grantor owns, then it is providing a benefit to the grantor. In addition, contractual terms often require an operator to repay an element advanced by the grantor for maintenance services if the operator does not incur contracted levels of maintenance spend. This may also support the argument that maintenance is a separate performance obligation. In practice, there is likely to be some judgement involved in determining whether maintenance is a separate performance obligation, based on how it is defined in the contractual arrangement. To the extent that the contract requires the operator to provide major maintenance, similar in nature to an upgrade, that enhances the infrastructure asset, maintenance could be a separate performance obligation. However, minor maintenance necessary to preserve the road in a condition required for the operator to operate the road safely and to return the road to the grantor in a certain condition at the end of the arrangement could be argued as not transferring a distinct good or service to the grantor.

Maintenance has not been identified as a separate performance obligation in Example 25.3 at 4.2 above. This may be on the basis that the operator is required to return the road to the grantor in a specified condition at the end of the concession arrangement. IFRIC 12 requires contractual obligations to maintain infrastructure to a specified level of serviceability or to return infrastructure to the grantor in a specified condition at the end of the service concession arrangement to be recognised and measured in accordance with IAS 37. *[IFRIC 12.21]*. This treatment is akin to that required for assurance-type warranties under IFRS 15. An assurance-type warranty provides the customer with assurance that the product complies with agreed-upon specifications and is not a separate performance obligation. *[IFRS 15.B30]*. IFRS 15 requires the estimated cost of satisfying assurance warranty obligations to be accrued in accordance with the requirements in IAS 37. *[IFRS 15.B30]*. In many arrangements other than service concessions, the 8 year term of the maintenance promise would likely indicate that treatment as an assurance-type warranty may not be appropriate. However, common warranty practices within the industry and the entity's business practices relating to warranties should be considered when identifying assurance-type warranties under IFRS 15. The accounting for warranties under IFRS 15 is discussed in Chapter 31 at 3.

Alternatively, it may be, that in Example 25.3 at 4.2 above, maintenance is considered to be a promised service that is not distinct in the context of the contract, as the operator would not be able to fulfil its promise to operate the road without maintaining the road in a safe condition. As such, maintenance may have been bundled with operation services into a single performance obligation.

Identification of performance obligations in a contract under IFRS 15 is discussed in Chapter 28.

Step 3 – Determine the transaction price

Transaction price is defined in IFRS 15 as the amount of consideration to which an entity expects to be entitled in exchange for transferring promised goods or services to a customer, excluding amounts collected on behalf of third parties. *[IFRS 15.47]*.

The determination of transaction price must also take into account any elements of variable consideration. The element of revenue that is subject to penalties would be considered a form of variable consideration under IFRS 15. *[IFRS 15.51]*. IFRS 15 requires that, if the consideration promised in a contract includes a variable amount, an entity should estimate the amount of consideration to which they will be entitled. *[IFRS 15.50]*. Estimates of variable consideration are then included in the transaction price only to the extent that it is highly probable that a significant reversal of revenue will not occur when the uncertainty associated with the variable consideration is subsequently resolved. *[IFRS 15.56]*. As noted in the arrangement terms section above, for the purposes of this example we assume that the operator is subject to penalties for substandard performance, with any penalties being deducted from the €200 per annum to which the operator is entitled in years 3 to 10 of the service concession arrangement. IFRS 15 requires that variable consideration should be estimated using either an expected value or most likely amount basis, depending on which method the entity expects to better predict the amount of consideration to which it will be entitled. *[IFRS 15.53]*. The assessment of which approach is most appropriate will depend upon the facts and circumstances of the service concession arrangement and the penalty regime. In practice, it may be that the expected value approach better predicts the amount of consideration to which the operator expects to be entitled in many service concession arrangements. In this example, the operator concludes that the most-likely amount is the most appropriate approach due to the nature of the penalties. Based on their previous experience in the sector, the operator concludes that they are most likely to receive the full amount of €200 per annum (i.e. €1600 in total, and not incur any penalties) and that it is highly probable that they will not incur significant penalties. The operator concludes that if they include the full €200 per annum in the transaction price for the contract, it is highly probable that a significant revenue reversal will not occur when the uncertainty is resolved. The operator therefore does not deduct any potential penalties when determining the transaction price under the contract. The assessment of the impact of penalties on the IFRS 15 transaction price will depend on facts and circumstances. Whilst an experienced concession operator may be able to meet the requirements for not constraining revenue in some concessions, this will not hold true in all cases, for example if they were to enter into a concession involving an infrastructure asset with which they had little experience.

The difference between the timing of payments from the grantor compared to the provision of construction services by the operator is likely to require a significant financing component to be taken into account in determining the transaction price. The gross amount of consideration should be discounted at a rate that the operator would use if it were to enter into a separate financing transaction with the grantor at contract inception. The discount rate should reflect the credit characteristics of the grantor, as well as any collateral or security provided, including assets transferred in the contract, *[IFRS 15.64]*, i.e. the discount rate is a rate specific to the contract. IFRS 15 also notes that an entity may be able to determine that rate by identifying the rate that discounts the nominal amount of the promised consideration to the price that the customer would pay in cash for the goods or services when (or as) they transfer to the customer. *[IFRS 15.64]*. In Example 25.3 at 4.2 above, the implied interest rate in the contract is assumed to be the rate that would be reflected in a financing transaction between the operator and the grantor, although this may not always be the case in a service concession arrangement. Some may argue that the rate implicit in the contract more appropriately reflects the economic substance. However, in our view, primacy should generally be given to the rate that the operator would use if it were to enter into a separate financing transaction with the grantor at contract inception. Whilst the rate implicit in the contract may be used in determining that rate, we believe that that the use of the rate implicit in the contract may not always be consistent with the objective of paragraph 64 of IFRS 15, being to use a discount rate that would be reflected in a separate financing transaction.

The effect of financing is excluded from the transaction price prior to the allocation of transaction price to performance obligations.

Based on the arrangement terms in this example, the total amount of consideration to which the operator expects to be entitled in exchange for transferring promised construction, operating, maintenance and upgrade services to the grantor is €200 per year for 8 years, i.e. €1600. The financing component is €344, based on a rate of 6.18% per year. This gives a net transaction price of €1256 (being €1600 – €344). This is consistent with the transaction price in Example 25.3 at 4.2 above.

Step 4 – Allocate the transaction price to the performance obligations in the contract

IFRS 15 generally requires the transaction price to be allocated to each performance obligation in proportion to their relative stand-alone selling prices. *[IFRS 15.74].*

If stand-alone selling prices are not readily observable, they must be estimated, considering all information that is reasonably available to the entity. The operator may choose to estimate stand-alone selling prices using an expected cost plus margin approach, *[IFRS 15.79],* although other approaches are permitted. Example 25.3 at 4.2 above shows the operator estimating stand-alone selling prices for each performance obligation using an expected cost plus margin approach.

In Example 25.3 at 4.2 above, the transaction price allocated to each performance obligation is equal to the estimated stand-alone selling price for each distinct service (i.e. construction, operations, upgrade), and as such, there is no discount in the contract to allocate between the performance obligations.

Allocation of the transaction price to performance obligations under IFRS 15 is discussed in Chapter 29.

Step 5 – Recognise revenue when (or as) the entity satisfies a performance obligation

IFRS 15 requires that revenue is recognised when an identified performance obligation is satisfied, by transferring a promised good or service to a customer, i.e. when the customer obtains control. *[IFRS 15.31].* Performance obligations will be satisfied either over time or at a point in time. *[IFRS 15.32].*

In Example 25.3 at 4.2 above, revenue is recognised over time for construction, resurfacing and operating services. As discussed at Step 2 above, maintenance is assumed not to be a separate performance obligation within this example and therefore no revenue is recognised in respect of maintenance.

One of the criteria in IFRS 15 for recognising revenue over time is that an entity's performance creates or enhances an asset that the customer controls. *[IFRS 15.35(b)].* In order to be in scope of IFRIC 12, the grantor to a service concession arrangement must control the infrastructure asset, including any significant residual interest. It therefore appears reasonable to conclude that this criteria for recognising revenue over time is met for construction and resurfacing services because they create and then enhance the grantor's asset.

In some circumstances, an entity may be unable to reasonably measure the outcome of the construction performance obligation. They may be able to determine that a loss will not be incurred, but may not be able to reasonably estimate the amount of profit. Until the entity can reasonably measure the outcome, IFRS 15 requires the entity to recognise revenue, but only up to the amount of costs incurred. *[IFRS 15.45].* This could result in an operator recognising no margin on construction services until they are able to reasonably estimate the amount of profit.

An alternative criterion in IFRS 15 for recognising revenue over time is that the customer simultaneously receives and consumes the benefit as the entity performs. *[IFRS 15.35(a)].* i.e. a performance obligation is satisfied over time if an entity determines that another entity would not need to substantially re-perform the work that the entity has completed to date if that other entity were to fulfil the remaining performance obligation to the customer. *[IFRS 15.B4].* It would seem reasonable to conclude that this criterion is met for operating services in Illustrative Example 25.3 at 4.2 above.

Progress over time may be measured using an input method to recognise revenue on the basis of the operator's inputs to the satisfaction of the performance obligation (e.g. costs incurred or time elapsed) relative to the total expected efforts to the satisfaction of that performance obligation. *[IFRS 15.B18].* Other methods are also permitted, although the entity should determine the best method that faithfully depicts the entity's performance.

In Example 25.3 at 4.2 above, construction revenue appears to be recognised over time by reference to costs incurred relative to total expected costs required to satisfy the construction services performance obligation. Revenue from operation services is also recognised using an input method. In Example 25.3 above, operating costs are incurred evenly over the operating phase of the service concession arrangement and so the recognition pattern shown in the example may have been derived using either a time elapsed input method or by reference to costs incurred relative to total expected costs required to satisfy the performance obligation. Entities do not have a free choice in determining how to measure progress over time. IFRS 15 requires that, in measuring progress over time, an entity should select a revenue recognition method that faithfully depicts its performance in satisfying the performance obligation. Although upgrade revenue appears to meet the criteria to be recognised over time as it enhances an asset owned and controlled by the grantor, all upgrade services occur in year 8 and hence the revenue allocated to this performance obligation is all recognised in year 8.

With regards the recognition of finance income, IFRIC 12 requires consideration given by the grantor to be classified as a contract asset during the construction activity. *[IFRIC 12.19]*. The operator would recognise a receivable, rather than a contract asset, only once the operator has an unconditional right to receive consideration from the customer. The operator's right to consideration is unconditional only if nothing other than the passage of time is required before payment of that consideration is due. *[IFRS 15.108]*. The right to consideration would not be unconditional if the operator must first satisfy another performance obligation in the contract before it is entitled to payment from the customer.

In this example, the operator receives payment of €200 per annum in years 3 to 10 of the service concession arrangement, i.e. once construction is complete and the operator starts providing operating services. As noted in the arrangement terms section above, for the purposes of this example we assume that the operator is subject to penalties for substandard performance, with any penalties being deducted from the €200 per annum to which the operator is entitled in years 3 to 10 of the service concession arrangement. Although the amounts the operator will receive may be reduced by penalties in the event of substandard performance, or failure to meet specified quality or efficiency requirements, for the purposes of this example, we assume that the operator determines that even in the event that the maximum penalties possible under the contract were incurred, the total consideration to which they would be entitled in years 3 to 10 would exceed the amount recognised as revenue for satisfying the construction performance obligation. Because the operator will receive payment for their construction services regardless of whether they deliver the other performance obligations within the contract, the operator therefore concludes that they have an unconditional right to consideration from the grantor for construction services as soon as construction activity is complete. The operator therefore recognises a receivable in respect of the construction performance obligation once construction is complete. This is consistent with the treatment in Example 25.3 at 4.2 above.

Until a receivable is recognised, the operator accounts for the significant financing component in the arrangement in accordance with IFRS 15. Under IFRS 15 a significant financing component would be recorded if the consideration was paid more than a year after construction is complete, which is the case in Example 25.3 above, and this example, as noted at step 3 above. Example 25.3 does not identify any significant financing component in respect of upgrade services delivered in year 8. Based on the entity's chosen approach to allocating the consideration receivable under the arrangement to the various performance obligations, at contract inception, the entity may expect the period between delivery of the upgrade services and the date on which payment will be received to be one year or less. *[IFRS 15.63]*.

Once a receivable is recognised, the amounts due from the grantor are accounted for in accordance with IFRS 9. On initial recognition, IFRS 9 requires a financial asset to be measured at its fair value (plus or minus transaction costs). *[IFRS 9.5.1.1]*. As a result, the financial asset will initially be recognised at fair value, in this example, once construction is complete. The fair value of the financial asset is impacted by changes in market interest rates. Where construction or upgrade activity takes a significant time (as is common in many infrastructure projects), it is possible that market interest rates will have moved over the construction phase of the arrangement, such that there is a difference between the initial measurement of the financial asset in accordance with IFRS 9 and the amount of construction revenue and accrued interest recognised as a contract asset in accordance with IFRS 15. In addition, whilst fair value under IFRS 9 is based on market interest rates, accrued interest recognised as part of the contract asset under IFRS 15 is determined using the rate 'that would be reflected in a separate financing transaction between the entity and its customer at contract inception', *[IFRS 15.64]*, i.e. a rate specific to the contract. This may also lead to differences between the amount recognised as a contract asset under IFRS 15 and the initial measurement of the financial asset under IFRS 9. IFRS 15 requires any difference between the initial measurement of the financial asset in accordance with IFRS 9 and the corresponding amount of revenue recognised under IFRS 15 to be presented as an expense. *[IFRS 15.108]*. For the purposes of this example, we assume no difference between these two amounts. Therefore, the fair value of the receivable at initial recognition is equal to the carrying value of the contract asset at completion of construction, and interest is recognised on the financial asset at 6.18%. This is consistent with Example 25.3 at 4.2 above.

In our view, the interest rate used to determine the initial measurement of the receivable under IFRS 9 should be determined considering the passage of time before payment is due and counterparty credit risk. The discount rate should not be risk adjusted to reflect the risk that payments to be received over the operating period may be subject to penalties. This is consistent with the requirement in IFRS 15 that a receivable is recognised only when there is an unconditional right to consideration, i.e. when only the passage of time is required before payment is due. *[IFRS 15.108]*. As noted above, based on the arrangement terms set out above, the operator has determined that even if the maximum penalties possible under the contract were incurred, the total consideration to which they would be entitled in years 3 to 10 of the arrangement would exceed the amount recognised as revenue for satisfying the construction performance obligation. To the extent that the right to payment does depend upon the operator's future performance, the operator does not have an unconditional right to consideration and therefore should continue to recognise a contract asset, rather than a receivable.

IFRS 9 requires the receivable to be subsequently measured at amortised cost, fair value through other comprehensive income or fair value through profit or loss, depending on the operator's business model for managing the receivable, and the contractual cash flow characteristics of the receivable. We assume for the purpose of this example that the operator has a business model whose objective is to collect the contractual cash flows of the receivable. As noted above, the operator has determined that recoverability of the receivable recognised for construction services is not dependent upon their future performance of the service concession arrangement. The operator has not identified any other features that would cause the receivable to fail the SPPI test (that confirms that the cash flows are 'solely payments of principal and interest on the principal amount outstanding'). Therefore, the receivable is subsequently measured at amortised cost. This is consistent with Example 25.3 at 4.2 above. Subsequent measurement of financial assets under IFRS 9 is discussed in Chapter 50.

Under the arrangement terms in this Example, as set out above, the overview of the operator's Statement of cash flows, statement of comprehensive income and statement of financial position will be consistent with those in Illustrative Example 1 to IFRIC 12, which are shown in Example 25.3 at 4.2 above. Although the operator in this arrangement may be subject to penalties for substandard performance, the contractual terms of the penalties do not impact the accounting in the operator's primary statements, for reasons explained above.

Both the contract asset recognised during the construction phase, and the receivable recognised once construction is complete will be subject to the impairment requirements of IFRS 9. *[IFRS 15.107]*. Impairment of financial assets under IFRS 9 is discussed in Chapter 51.

Example 25.14: Financial asset model – Receivable recognised once construction is complete and a change in discount rate on recognition of receivable

Arrangement terms

The terms of the arrangement are the same as in Example 25.13 above. However, in this example we assume that there is a change in discount rates between the inception of the service concession contract and the point at which the operator recognises a receivable. This will result in changes to the income statement and statement of financial position of the operator compared to the results shown in Example 25.3 at 4.2 above.

Any changes in these assumptions or facts and circumstances would need to be assessed by reference to the requirements of IFRIC 12 and IFRS 15 and could result in a change to the accounting discussed below.

Initial recognition of the receivable

IFRIC 12 requires consideration due from the grantor to be classified as a contract asset during the construction activity. *[IFRIC 12.19]*. The operator should recognise a receivable, rather than a contract asset, only once the operator has an unconditional right to receive consideration from the customer. The operator's right to consideration is unconditional only if nothing other than the passage of time is required before payment of that consideration is due. *[IFRS 15.108]*. Consistent with Examples 25.3 and 25.13 above, under the arrangement terms in this example, the operator recognises a receivable in respect of the construction performance obligation once construction is complete.

Once a receivable is recognised, the amounts due from the grantor are accounted for in accordance with IFRS 9. On initial recognition, IFRS 9 requires a financial asset to be measured at its fair value (plus or minus transaction costs). *[IFRS 9.5.1.1]*. As a result, the financial asset will initially be recognised at fair value. The fair value of the financial asset is impacted by changes in market interest rates. Where construction or upgrade activity takes a significant time (as is common in many infrastructure projects), it is possible that market interest rates will have moved over the construction phase of the arrangement, such that there is a difference between the initial measurement of the financial asset in accordance with IFRS 9 and the amount of construction revenue and accrued interest recognised as a contract asset in accordance with IFRS 15. In addition, whilst fair value under

IFRS 9 is based on market interest rates, accrued interest recognised as part of the contract asset under IFRS 15 is determined using the rate 'that would be reflected in a separate financing transaction between the entity and its customer at contract inception', *[IFRS 15.64]*, i.e. a rate specific to the contract. This may also lead to differences between the amount recognised as a contract asset under IFRS 15 and the initial measurement of the financial asset under IFRS 9. IFRS 15 requires any difference between the initial measurement of the financial asset in accordance with IFRS 9 and the corresponding amount of revenue recognised under IFRS 15 to be presented as an expense. *[IFRS 15.108]*. Examples 25.3 and 25.13 above assume no difference between these two amounts. In this example, we assume that the interest rate applied in the initial recognition of the receivable on completion of construction (being 6.73%), differs from the rate that was applied under IFRS 15 (being 6.18%), resulting in the recognition of a receivable at a lower value than the IFRS 15 contact asset.

In our view, the interest rate used to determine the initial measurement of the receivable under IFRS 9 should be determined considering the passage of time before payment is due and counterparty credit risk. The discount rate should not be risk adjusted to reflect the risk that payments to be received over the operating period may be subject to penalties. This is consistent with the requirement in IFRS 15 that a receivable is recognised only when there is an unconditional right to consideration, i.e. when only the passage of time is required before payment is due. *[IFRS 15.108]*. In this example, the operator has determined that even if the maximum penalties possible under the contract were incurred, the total consideration to which they would be entitled in years 3 to 10 of the arrangement would exceed the amount recognised as revenue for satisfying the construction performance obligation. To the extent that the right to payment does depend upon the operator's future performance, the operator does not have an unconditional right to consideration and therefore should continue to recognise a contract asset, rather than a receivable.

The operator's statement of comprehensive income and statement of financial position will be as follows. The operator's statement of cash flows will be the same as that shown in Example 25.3 at 4.2 above.

Statement of comprehensive income (€)

Year	1	2	3	4	5	6	7	8	9	10	Total
Revenue (a)	525	525	12	12	12	12	12	122	12	12	1,256
Contract costs (a)	(500)	(500)	(10)	(10)	(10)	(10)	(10)	(110)	(10)	(10)	(1,180)
Finance income (b)	–	32	71	64	55	46	37	26	23	12	366
Expense on initial recognition of receivable (c)	–	(22)	–	–	–	–	–	–	–	–	(22)
Borrowing costs (a)	–	(34)	(69)	(61)	(53)	(43)	(33)	(23)	(19)	(7)	(342)
Net profit	25	2	4	4	5	5	5	15	6	7	78

(a) Revenue, contract costs and borrowing costs are the same as in Example 25.3 at 4.2 above.
(b) Finance income on the contract asset in year 2 is recognised at a rate of 6.18%, determined in accordance with IFRS 15. Finance income on the receivable in years 3 to 10 is based on the effective interest rate of 6.73%, determined in accordance with IFRS 9.
(c) Being the difference between the fair value of the receivable on initial recognition (€1,060), and the corresponding amount of revenue and finance income recognised under IFRS 15 (€1,082).

Statement of financial position (€)

End of year	1	2	3	4	5	6	7	8	9	10
Amount due from grantor (a)	–	1,060	943	818	686	544	393	341	176	–
Contract asset	525	–	–	–	–	–	–	–	–	–
Cash / (debt) (b)	(500)	(1,034)	(913)	(784)	(647)	(500)	(343)	(276)	(105)	78
Net assets	25	26	30	34	39	44	50	65	71	78

(a) Amount due from grantor at start of year, plus revenue and finance income earned in year (statement of comprehensive income), less receipts of €200 in years 3-10.
(b) Cash / debt and Statement of cash flows are the same as in Example 25.3 at 4.2 above.

Prior to derecognition at completion of construction, the contract asset was carried at €1,082, being the contract asset of €525 at the end of year 1, plus revenue of €525 in year 2 and interest accrued at a rate of 6.18% in year 2 of €32. The operator determined that the fair value of the receivable at initial recognition was €1,060, based on a discount rate of 6.73%. The operator recognises a charge to the income statement of €22 (being €1,082 – €1,060) at the end of year 2 on initial recognition of the receivable. IFRS 15 requires any difference between the initial measurement of the financial asset in accordance with IFRS 9 and the corresponding amount of revenue recognised under IFRS 15 to be presented as an expense (for example, as an impairment loss). *[IFRS 15.108]*.

IFRS 9 requires the receivable to be subsequently measured at amortised cost, fair value through other comprehensive income or fair value through profit or loss, depending on the operator's business model for managing the receivable, and the contractual cash flow characteristics of the receivable. In this example, the operator has a business model whose objective is to collect the contractual cash flows of the receivable and has not identified any features that would cause the receivable to fail the SPPI test. Therefore, the receivable is subsequently measured at amortised cost and interest on the receivable is recognised at the effective interest rate of 6.73%. This results in the operator recognising a higher finance income over the operating period than if the interest rate had not changed. In this example, this offsets the impairment on initial recognition of the financial asset over the remaining term of the service concession, so that overall net profit from the concession is €78, consistent with Example 25.13 above. Subsequent measurement of financial assets under IFRS 9 is discussed in Chapter 50.

Both the contract asset recognised during the construction phase, and the receivable recognised once construction is complete will be subject to the impairment requirements of IFRS 9. *[IFRS 15.107]*. Impairment of financial assets under IFRS 9 is discussed in Chapter 51.

Example 25.15: Financial Asset Model – Contract asset relating to construction services unwinds to a receivable over the period in which the other performance obligations in the contract are satisfied

Arrangement terms

The terms of the arrangement are the same as in Example 25.13 above, except that in this example we assume that in the event of total non-performance by the operator of operating, maintenance and upgrade services, the penalties incurred in years 3 to 10 of the arrangement could be up to €200 per annum. Therefore, if the operator were to incur maximum penalties, the total amount the operator would receive in years 3 to 10 would be nil. This will result in changes to the income statement and statement of financial position of the operator compared to those shown in the previous examples.

Any changes in these assumptions or facts and circumstances would need to be assessed by reference to the requirements of IFRIC 12 and IFRS 15 and could result in a change to the accounting discussed below.

Initial recognition of the receivable

IFRIC 12 requires consideration due from the grantor to be classified as a contract asset during the construction activity. *[IFRIC 12.19]*. The operator would recognise a receivable, rather than a contract asset, only once the operator has an unconditional right to receive consideration from the customer. The operator's right to consideration is unconditional only if nothing other than the passage of time is required before payment of that consideration is due. *[IFRS 15.108]*. The right to consideration would not be unconditional if the operator must first satisfy another performance obligation in the contract before it is entitled to payment from the customer.

In this example, the operator is entitled to payment of €200 per annum in each of years 3 to 10, i.e. once construction is complete and the operator starts providing operating services. However, this amount may be reduced by penalties in the event of substandard performance by the operator, or failure to meet specified quality or efficiency requirements. In the event of total non-performance by the operator of operating, maintenance and upgrade services, the penalties would be €200 per annum, such that the total amount the operator would receive in years 3-10 would be nil. Although the operator does not expect to incur a significant amount of penalties, the operator does not have an unconditional right to consideration once construction is complete because it is not only the passage of time that is required before payment of consideration for construction services is due. Instead, the operator must provide other services, and to a satisfactory standard, in order to receive payment for the construction services. Because the operator must first satisfy another performance obligation in the contract before it is entitled to receive consideration for the construction services, the operator continues to recognise a contract asset even after construction is complete. Each year, as the operator satisfies the operations and maintenance performance obligation, €200 of the operator's right to consideration becomes unconditional (i.e. nothing other than the passage of time is required before payment of the €200 becomes due). The amount due for construction services therefore unwinds from a contract asset to a receivable over the period in which the other performance obligations in the contact are satisfied by the operator. Due to the nature of contractual penalties imposed in service concession arrangements, we believe that, in practice, the amount due to the operator in exchange for construction services will often unwind from a contract asset to a receivable over the period in which the other performance obligations in the contract are satisfied by the operator.

IFRS 9 requires the receivable to be initially recognised at fair value. *[IFRS 9.5.1.1].* However, because the consideration due to the operator does not qualify for recognition as a receivable until the point at which the annual instalment is payable by the grantor, there is considered to be no material difference between the fair value of each instalment and its face value, i.e. €200. Therefore, no interest income is recognised in respect of the receivable balance.

The operator continues to accrue interest on the remaining portion of the contract asset in accordance with IFRS 15 at the original interest rate of 6.18%. Whilst it is possible that market interest rates may have moved since construction services were provided by the operator, IFRS 15 requires that an entity should not update the discount rate (used to discount promised consideration) for changes in circumstances or interest rates after contract inception. *[IFRS 15.64].*

Both the contract asset and the receivable will be subject to the impairment requirements of IFRS 9. *[IFRS 15.107].*

The operator's statement of comprehensive income and statement of financial position will be as follows. The operator's statement of cash flows will be the same as that shown in Example 25.3 at 4.2 above.

Statement of comprehensive income (€)

Year	1	2	3	4	5	6	7	8	9	10	Total
Revenue (a)	525	525	12	12	12	12	12	122	12	12	1,256
Contract costs (a)	(500)	(500)	(10)	(10)	(10)	(10)	(10)	(110)	(10)	(10)	(1,180)
Finance income (b)	–	32	67	59	51	43	34	25	21	11	344
Borrowing costs (a)	–	(34)	(69)	(61)	(53)	(43)	(33)	(23)	(19)	(7)	(342)
Net profit	25	24	–	–	1	2	3	14	5	8	78

(a) Revenue, contract costs and borrowing costs are the same as in Illustrative Example 1 to IFRIC 12, as shown in Example 25.3 at 4.2 above.

(b) Finance income on the contract asset continued to be recognised at a rate of 6.18%, determined in accordance with IFRS 15 at inception of the contract.

Statement of financial position (€)

End of year	1	2	3	4	5	6	7	8	9	10
Amount due from grantor (a)	–	–	–	–	–	–	–	–	–	–
Contract asset	525	1,082	961	832	695	550	396	343	177	–
Cash / (debt) (b)	(500)	(1,034)	(913)	(784)	(647)	(500)	(343)	(276)	(105)	78
Net assets	25	48	48	48	48	50	53	67	72	78

(a) Contract asset at the start of year, plus revenue and finance income earned in year (statement of comprehensive income), less receipts of €200 in years 3-10.

(b) Cash / debt and Statement of cash flows are the same as in Illustrative Example 1 to IFRIC 12, as shown in Example 25.3 at 4.2 above.

Example 25.16: Intangible asset model

Arrangement terms

The terms of the arrangement are the same as in Example 25.4 at 4.3 above and Example 25.12 at 5.2 above. Examples 25.4 and 25.12 are based on Illustrative Example 2 in IFRIC 12 and assume that that the operator's annual receipts are constant over the concession period, that cash flows and fair values remain the same as forecast, that no contract modifications occur over the concession period, and that there is no change to the timing of delivery from that anticipated at contract inception. Any changes in these assumptions or facts and circumstances would need to be assessed by reference to the requirements of IFRIC 12 and IFRS 15 and could result in a change to the accounting illustrated in Examples 25.4 and 25.12 above.

Step 1 – Identify the contract(s) with a customer

Under IFRS 15, a contract is defined as an agreement between two parties that creates enforceable rights and obligations. *[IFRS 15 Appendix A]*. A customer is defined in IFRS 15 as a party that has contracted with an entity to obtain goods or services that are an output of an entity's ordinary activities in exchange for consideration. *[IFRS 15 Appendix A]*.

Because the public sector grantor of the concession retains control over the infrastructure asset, construction and upgrade (resurfacing) services are provided to the grantor. The grantor pays consideration, in the form of an intangible asset, to the operator in exchange for those services.

Because of the public service nature of the obligation undertaken by the operator, the operating services are provided to the public users the road. There could be a written contract between the operator and each road user, if, for example, the road user takes a ticket from the toll booth on entering the road. Even in the absence of a written contract, the public users of the road transfer consideration to the operator in exchange for using the road, and therefore could be considered to have an implied contract with the operator. IFRS 15 does not require the existence of a written contract; a contract may be oral or implied, although it must be legally enforceable. *[IFRS 15.10]*. The specified good or service in the contract between the operator and the road user is the provision of access to the toll road. Access is physically controlled by the operator through the operating services that they provide.

Examples 25.4 and 25.12 above reflect two contractual customer relationships within the arrangement, being (1) a contract with the grantor for the provision of construction services to build toll road; and (2) many contracts with individual public road users to provide access to the toll road by way of a service fulfilled by the operator, and reflect the operator acting as principal in both contractual customer relationships.

Identification of the contract(s) with the customer under IFRS 15 is discussed in Chapter 28.

Step 2 – Identify the performance obligations in the contract

In Examples 25.4 and 25.12 above, the operator recognises revenue in respect of the following performance obligations:

- contract with the grantor – a distinct performance obligation, being construction services; and
- many contracts with road users – a distinct performance obligation for operation services.

The contract with the grantor requires the operator to resurface the road when the original surface has deteriorated below a specified condition. Resurfacing is not identified as a separate performance obligation. Because the resurfacing is required when the original surface has deteriorated below a specific condition, rather than being required at a specified point in time, the operator treats this as a contractual obligation to maintain or restore the infrastructure, with the contractual obligation to restore the road recognised and measured in accordance with IAS 37. *[IFRIC 12.21]*. This is similar to the treatment required for assurance-type warranties under IFRS 15. An assurance-type warranty is a warranty that provides the customer (the public users of the road in this example) with assurance that the product complies with agreed-upon specifications and is not a separate performance obligation. *[IFRS 15.B30]*.

Identification of performance obligations in a contract under IFRS 15 is discussed in Chapter 28.

Step 3 – Determine the transaction price

The consideration in the contract with the grantor is the amount that the operator expects to be entitled to in exchange for construction services. The consideration is a right to charge toll road users, i.e. non-cash consideration which would be measured at fair value, unless the entity cannot reasonably estimate the fair value of the non-cash consideration, in which case it should be measured indirectly by reference to the stand-alone selling price of the promised goods or services. *[IFRS 15.67]*. In Examples 25.4 and 25.12 above, the fair value of the intangible asset has been measured indirectly by reference to the stand-alone selling price of the promised construction services.

Examples 25.4 and 25.12 above do not identify a significant financing component related to the provision of construction services by the operator, despite the timing difference between the operator providing construction services in years 1 and 2, and delivery of the intangible asset once construction is complete at the end of year 2. This may be because the operator has concluded that the reason for the difference between the cash selling price of the construction services and the promised consideration arises for reasons other than the provision of finance, and the difference between those amounts is proportional to the reason for the difference. *[IFRS 15.62]*. The operator may have reached this conclusion because the promised consideration in this example is an intangible asset, representing a right to charge users of the toll road, and that right cannot be exercised until the toll road is constructed. Therefore, in this example, the nature of the consideration necessitates a delay between provision of the construction services by the operator, and receipt of the promised consideration, being the intangible asset.

The operator will receive cash consideration from each toll road user in exchange for operating services. The total amount of consideration for operating services will vary depending upon how many vehicles use the toll road. However, as each contract is with a separate road user (customer), it would seem appropriate to consider each contract in isolation. The transaction price for each contract is the cash toll paid by each road user.

Determination of the transaction price under IFRS 15 is discussed in Chapter 29.

Step 4 – Allocate the transaction price to the performance obligations in the contract

IFRS 15 requires the transaction price to be allocated to each performance obligation in proportion to their relative stand-alone selling prices. *[IFRS 15.74]*. If stand-alone selling prices are not readily observable, they must be estimated, considering all information that is reasonably available to the entity. The operator may choose to estimate stand-alone selling prices using an expected cost-plus margin approach, *[IFRS 15.79]*, although other approaches are permitted.

As discussed at Step 2 above, there is only one distinct performance obligation in the contract with the grantor, being construction services. The transaction price is therefore allocated to construction services. Similarly, each contract with individual road users has one distinct performance obligation, being the provision of operating services.

Allocation of the transaction price to performance obligations under IFRS 15 is discussed in Chapter 29.

Step 5 – Recognise revenue when (or as) the entity satisfied a performance obligation

Examples 25.4 and 25.12 above show revenue being recognised over time for construction and operating services.

One criterion within IFRS 15 for recognising revenue over time is that an entity's performance creates or enhances an asset that the customer controls. *[IFRS 15.35(b)]*. To be in scope of IFRIC 12, the grantor to a service concession arrangement must control the infrastructure asset, including any significant residual interest. It therefore appears reasonable to conclude that this criteria for recognising revenue over time is met for construction services. Progress over time may be measured using an input method to recognise revenue based on the operator's inputs to the satisfaction of the performance obligation (e.g. costs incurred or time elapsed) relative to the total expected efforts to the satisfaction of that performance obligation. *[IFRS 15.B18]*. Other methods are also permitted, although the entity should determine the best method that faithfully depicts the entity's performance. In Examples 25.4 and 25.12 above, construction revenue appears to be recognised over time by reference to costs incurred relative to total expected costs required to satisfy the construction services performance obligation.

An alternative criterion in IFRS 15 for recognising revenue over time is that the customer simultaneously receives and consumes the benefit as the entity performs. *[IFRS 15.35(a)]*. Each road-user simultaneously receives and consumes the benefits provided by the operator as the operator provides the road operating services and therefore the operator recognises revenue over time. However, given the short time period over which the operator provides road operating services to each road user in this fact pattern (i.e. the duration of the time it takes the road user to travel the length of the toll road), the operator recognises toll revenue when it collects the tolls.

Under the arrangement terms in this Example, as set out above, the overview of the operator's Statement of cash flows, statement of comprehensive income and statement of financial position will be consistent with those in Illustrative Example 2 to IFRIC 12, which are shown in Example 25.4 at 4.3 above and Example 25.12 at 5.2 above.

Satisfaction of performance obligations under IFRS 15 is discussed in Chapter 30.

Classification as contract asset or intangible asset, and impairment testing

IFRIC 12 requires that, during the construction or upgrade period, consideration is classified as a contract asset by the operator. *[IFRIC 12.19]*.

Whilst IFRIC 12 requires consideration to be classified as a contract asset during the construction or upgrade period, Illustrative Example 2 to IFRIC 12 shows that the contract asset may still be presented as an intangible asset during the construction phase. *[IFRIC 12.IE15]*.

Under IAS 38, amortisation of an intangible asset should begin when the asset is available for use, i.e. when it is in the location and condition necessary for it to be capable of operating in the manner intended by management. This would likely be the case once construction of the road is complete and the operator can begin using their right to operate the road to generate revenue.

As noted above, IFRIC 12 requires that during the construction or upgrade period, consideration is classified as a contract asset by the operator. Contract assets are subject to the impairment requirements of IFRS 9. *[IFRS 15.107]*. Operators may need to apply judgement in determining how to test the contract asset for impairment, given that the contract asset is expected to be realised in the form of an intangible asset, rather than as a receivable or cash. Operators may consider whether and how they can use the value of the underlying intangible asset to which they are entitled as a proxy for cash flows in order to determine expected credit losses on the contract asset.

Capitalisation of borrowing costs

Under the intangible assets model, borrowing costs must be capitalised during the period of construction. *[IFRIC 12.22]*. However, as noted above IFRIC 12 requires consideration to be classified as a contract asset, rather than an intangible asset, during the construction period. *[IFRIC 12.19]*. In March 2019, the Interpretations Committee issued an agenda decision relating to the capitalisation of borrowing costs on a constructed good for which revenue was recognised over time. In that agenda decision, the Interpretations Committee noted that, in the particular fact pattern considered, a contract asset is not a qualifying asset as the intended use of the contract asset is not a use for which it necessarily takes a substantial period of time to get ready. IAS 23 requires capitalisation of borrowing costs that are directly attributable to the acquisition, construction or production of an asset that necessarily takes a substantial period of time to get ready for its intended use or sale. Some may argue that there is a tension between the requirement in IFRIC 12 to capitalise interest during the construction phase under the intangible asset model and this agenda decision. However, we believe that the agenda decision does not override the requirements of IFRIC 12 paragraph 22.

7 DISCLOSURE REQUIREMENTS: SIC-29

IFRIC 12 has no specific disclosure requirements, although the disclosure requirements of the various applicable standards (such as IFRS 9, IFRS 7 – *Financial Instruments: Disclosures*, *[IFRIC 12.23]*, and IAS 38) will have to be applied as appropriate. SIC-29, which pre-dates IFRIC 12 by several years, includes additional disclosure requirements. *[IFRIC 12.10]*. It is important to note that the scope of SIC-29 is not defined in terms of IFRIC 12 and is potentially broader in scope than IFRIC 12. It applies to a type of transaction that is described although not really defined and which does not depend on the control criteria described at 3 above. It also applies to both sides of the transaction, whereas IFRIC 12 applies only to the operator under the concession agreement.

SIC-29 describes service concessions as arrangements in which an entity (the operator) provides services on behalf of another entity (the grantor, which may be a public or private sector entity, including a governmental body) that give the public access to major economic and social facilities. The examples of service concession arrangements given by SIC-29 include water treatment and supply facilities, motorways, car parks, tunnels, bridges, airports and telecommunication networks. *[SIC-29.1]*.

SIC-29 states that the common characteristic of all service concession arrangements is that the operator both receives a right and incurs an obligation to provide public services. *[SIC-29.3]*. It excludes from its scope an entity outsourcing the operation of its internal services (e.g. employee cafeteria, building maintenance, and accounting or information technology functions). *[SIC-29.1]*. This means that some of the arrangements that do not include the construction of a major capital asset, as discussed above, may not be caught by the requirements of the SIC, although there is no hard-and-fast dividing line between service concessions and outsourcing arrangements. For example, a contract between a government department and an operator to maintain the existing computer system, including replacement of hardware and software as appropriate, may be outside the scope of SIC-29.

SIC-29 summarises the rights and obligations as follows:

For the period of the concession, the operator has received from the grantor:

(a) the right to provide services that give the public access to major economic and social facilities; and

(b) in some cases, the right to use specified tangible assets, intangible assets, and/or financial assets;

in exchange for the operator:

(a) committing to provide the services according to certain terms and conditions during the concession period; and

(b) when applicable, committing to return at the end of the concession period the rights received at the beginning of the concession period and/or acquired during the concession period. *[SIC-29.2]*.

The disclosure requirements in respect of such projects are set out below:

SIC-29 requires disclosure in addition to that required by other standards that may cover part of the transaction, such as IAS 16 (see Chapter 18), IFRS 16 (see Chapter 23) and IAS 38 (see Chapter 17). *[SIC-29.5]*. All aspects of a service concession arrangement should be considered in determining the appropriate disclosures in the notes to the financial statements. *[SIC-29.6]*.

An operator and a grantor should disclose the following in each period:
(a) a description of the arrangement;
(b) significant terms of the arrangement that may affect the amount, timing and certainty of future cash flows (e.g. the period of the concession, re-pricing dates and the basis upon which re-pricing or re-negotiation is determined);
(c) the nature and extent (e.g. quantity, time period or amount as appropriate) of:
    (i) rights to use specified assets;
    (ii) obligations to provide or rights to expect provision of services;
    (iii) obligations to acquire or build items of property, plant and equipment;
    (iv) obligations to deliver or rights to receive specified assets at the end of the concession period;
    (v) renewal and termination options; and
    (vi) other rights and obligations (e.g. major overhauls);
(d) changes in the arrangement occurring during the period; and
(e) how the service arrangement has been classified. [SIC-29.6].

These disclosures should be provided individually for each service concession arrangement or in aggregate for each class of service concession arrangements. A class is a grouping of service concession arrangements involving services of a similar nature (e.g. toll collections, telecommunications and water treatment services). [SIC-29.7].

IFRIC 12 added a requirement to disclose 'the amount of revenue and profits or losses recognised in the period on exchanging construction services for a financial asset and an intangible asset'. [SIC-29.6A].

Vinci has made aggregate disclosures for the principal terms of its arrangements. The following extract is part only of the disclosures that address concession arrangements.

Extract 25.5: VINCI SA (2019)

Notes to the consolidated financial statements at 31 December 2019 [extract]
F. Concession business: PPP contracts, concession contracts and other infrastructure [extract]
12 Features of the main contracts in the Concessions business [extract]

	Country	Concession end date	Model	Consolidation method
VINCI Autoroutes[*] **[extract]**				
ASF group				
ASF	France	2036	Intangible asset	FC
2,730 km of toll motorways				
Escota	France	2032	Intangible asset	FC
471 km of toll motorways [...]				

VINCI Airports[**] [extract]				
[...]				
ANA Group 10 airports [...]	Portugal	2063	Intangible asset	FC
Liberia International Airport Daniel Oduber Quiros International Airport	Costa Rica	2030	Bifurcated model: intangible asset and financial asset	EM

FC Full consolidation; EM Equity method
[*] *Remuneration is based on the pricing law as defined in the concession contract, and price increases must be validated by the grantor.*
[**] *Remuneration comes from both users and from airlines. Air tariffs are generally regulated.*

[...]

When the contracts end, the concession infrastructure is generally returned to the grantor for no consideration. In the event that the contract is terminated or the concession asset is bought out early by the grantor, compensation is generally payable to the concession holders. Its amount is determined in accordance with contractual or statutory provisions.

[...]

15. Off-balance sheet commitments made under concession and PPP contracts

15.1 Commitments made in respect of companies controlled by the Group

Contractual investment and renewal or financing obligations

(in € millions)	31/12/2019	31/12/2018
ASF group	1,024	1,245
Cofiroute	762	869
Belgrade airport (Serbia)	441	460
ANA group (Portugal)	220	79
Arcos	143	403
Cambodia Airports	132	32
Lamsac (Peru)	127	154
London Gatwick Airport (United Kingdom)	96	3,220[*]
ADL – Aéroports de Lyon (France)	36	1
Société Concessionaire Aéroport du Grand Ouest (Scago)	35	35
Salvador airport (Brazil)	2	116
Other	43	35
Total	**3,060**	**6,648**

[*] *Commitment to purchase a 50.01% stake in London Gatwick Airport*

Contractual investment obligations of motorway concession companies consist mainly of undertakings made under concession contracts, multi-year master contracts as part of the 2015 motorway stimulus plan and the motorway investment plan approved in 2018. In 2019, progress with works by VINCI Autoroutes companies led to a €587 million reduction in their commitments to €1,930 million at 31 December 2019.

The above amounts do not include obligations relating to maintenance expenditure on infrastructure under concession, in respect of which specific provisions based on maintenance plans are set aside (see Note H.19.3, "Breakdown of current provisions").

Where the financial asset or bifurcated model applies, subsidiaries receive a guarantee of payment from the concession grantor in return for their investment commitment.

Collateral security connected with financing

Collateral security (in the form of pledges of shares) is generally granted to secure financing arranged with subsidiaries, and breaks down as follows:

(in € millions)	Start date	End date	Amount at 31/12/2019
London Gatwick Airport	2011	2049	2,744
Arcour	2008	2047	646
Lamsac	2016	2037	364
Aerodom	2017	2029	358
ADL – Aéroports de Lyon	2016	2032	225
Gefyra	1997	2029	188
Belgrade airport	2018	2035	183
Caraibus	2015	2035	66
Arcos	2018	2045	61
Belfast airport (United Kingdom)	2016	2023	36
Park Azur	2008	2036	35
Le Mans Stadium	2008	2043	31
Other concession operating companies			18

In addition to the disclosures required by SIC-29, the disclosure requirements of IFRS 15 will need to be considered. See Chapter 32. Vinci also disclosed the revenue and profit earned from its concession arrangements. The following extract discloses revenue from concessions as a component of revenue by business line. The extract is not intended to illustrate the disclosures requirements of IFRS 15.

Extract 25.6: VINCI SA (2019)

Notes to the consolidated financial statements at 31 December 2019 [extract]
C. Financial indicators by business line and geographical area [extract]
1. Information by operating segment [extract]
1.2 Information relating to the Concessions business [extract]

2019

(in € millions)	VINCI Autoroutes	VINCI Airports	VINCI Highways and other concessions	Total
Income statement				
Revenue (*)	5,593	2,631	319	8,544
Concession subsidiaries' works revenue	834	198	6	1,038
Total revenue	6,427	2,829	325	9,581
Operating income from ordinary activities	2,967	1,016	6	3,989
% of revenue (*)	53.0%	38.6%	2.0%	46.7%
Recurring operating income	2,948	1,187	11	4,146
Operating income	2,948	1,179	41	4,167

(*) Excluding concession subsidiaries' revenue derived from works carried out by non-Group companies.

References

1 *IFRIC Update*, September 2005.
2 *IFRIC Update*, September 2005.
3 IPSAS 32, *Service Concession Arrangements: Grantor*, International Public Sector Accounting Standards Board, October 2011.
4 *IFRIC Update*, September 2005.
5 *IFRIC Staff paper*, March 2016, IFRIC 12 – *Service Concession Arrangements* – Service concession arrangements with leased infrastructure, p.11.
6 *IFRIC Update*, September 2016, Interpretations Committee's agenda decision.
7 *IFRIC Update*, March 2016.
8 *IFRIC Update*, July 2016.
9 *IFRIC Update*, March 2006.
10 IAS 38 (2007), *Intangible Assets*, IASB, 2007 Bound Volume, para. 98 stated that 'there is rarely, if ever, persuasive evidence to support an amortisation method for intangible assets with finite useful lives that results in a lower amount of accumulated amortisation than under the straight-line method.' This was removed by *Improvements to IFRSs*, May 2008.
11 *IFRIC Update*, September 2004.
12 *IFRIC Update*, July 2016.
13 *IFRIC Update*, July 2016.
14 *IASB Update*, July 2013.
15 *IFRIC Update*, March 2016.
16 *IFRIC Update*, July 2016.
17 *IFRIC Update*, July 2016.
18 *IFRIC Update*, March 2020.
19 *IFRIC Update*, September 2006.

Chapter 26
Provisions, contingent liabilities and contingent assets

1 INTRODUCTION 1929
   1.1 Background 1929
   1.2 Interpretations related to the application of IAS 37 1930
      1.2.1 IFRIC 1 1930
      1.2.2 IFRIC 3 1930
      1.2.3 IFRIC 5 1930
      1.2.4 IFRIC 6 1930
      1.2.5 IFRIC 21 1931
   1.3 Terms used in this chapter 1931
2 OBJECTIVE AND SCOPE OF IAS 37 1932
   2.1 Objective 1932
   2.2 Scope of IAS 37 1932
      2.2.1 Items outside the scope of IAS 37 1934
           2.2.1.A Executory contracts, except where the contract is onerous 1934
           2.2.1.B Items covered by another standard 1934
      2.2.2 Provisions compared to other liabilities 1936
      2.2.3 Distinction between provisions and contingent liabilities 1937
3 RECOGNITION 1937
   3.1 Determining when a provision should be recognised 1937
      3.1.1 'An entity has a present obligation (legal or constructive) as a result of a past event' 1938
      3.1.2 'It is probable that an outflow of resources embodying economic benefits will be required to settle the obligation' 1941

		3.1.3	'A reliable estimate can be made of the amount of the obligation'	1942

- 3.2 Contingencies 1942
  - 3.2.1 Contingent liabilities 1943
  - 3.2.2 Contingent assets 1944
    - 3.2.2.A Obligations contingent on the successful recovery of a contingent asset 1945
  - 3.2.3 How probability determines whether to recognise or disclose 1946
- 3.3 Recognising an asset when recognising a provision 1946

4 MEASUREMENT 1947

- 4.1 Best estimate of provision 1947
- 4.2 Dealing with risk and uncertainty in measuring a provision 1949
- 4.3 Discounting the estimated cash flows to a present value 1950
  - 4.3.1 Real versus nominal rate 1950
  - 4.3.2 Adjusting for risk and using a government bond rate 1951
  - 4.3.3 Own credit risk 1953
  - 4.3.4 Pre-tax discount rate 1954
  - 4.3.5 Unwinding of the discount 1954
  - 4.3.6 The effect of changes in interest rates on the discount rate applied 1957
- 4.4 Anticipating future events that may affect the estimate of cash flows 1958
- 4.5 Provisions that will be settled in a currency other than the entity's functional currency 1959
- 4.6 Reimbursements, insurance and other recoveries from third parties 1959
- 4.7 Joint and several liability 1960
- 4.8 Provisions are not reduced for gains on disposal of related assets 1961
- 4.9 Changes and uses of provisions 1961
- 4.10 Changes in contingent liabilities recognised in a business combination 1961

5 CASES IN WHICH NO PROVISION SHOULD BE RECOGNISED 1962

- 5.1 Future operating losses 1962
- 5.2 Repairs and maintenance of owned assets 1963
- 5.3 Staff training costs 1964
- 5.4 Rate-regulated activities 1965

6 SPECIFIC EXAMPLES OF PROVISIONS AND CONTINGENCIES 1966

- 6.1 Restructuring provisions 1966
  - 6.1.1 Definition 1966

	6.1.2	Recognition of a restructuring provision........................... 1967		
	6.1.3	Recognition of obligations arising from the sale of an operation 1969		
	6.1.4	Costs that can (and cannot) be included in a restructuring provision 1970		
6.2	Onerous contracts 1972			
	6.2.1	Onerous leases 1975		
	6.2.2	Contracts with customers that are, or have become, onerous 1977		
6.3	Decommissioning provisions 1979			
	6.3.1	Changes in estimated decommissioning costs (IFRIC 1) 1981		
	6.3.2	Changes in legislation after construction of the asset 1985		
	6.3.3	Funds established to meet an obligation (IFRIC 5) 1986		
		6.3.3.A	Accounting for an interest in a fund 1988	
		6.3.3.B	Accounting for obligations to make additional contributions 1990	
		6.3.3.C	Gross presentation of interest in the fund and the decommissioning liability 1990	
		6.3.3.D	Disclosure of interests arising from decommissioning, restoration and environmental rehabilitation funds 1991	
	6.3.4	Interaction of leases with asset retirement obligations 1991		
6.4	Environmental provisions – general guidance in IAS 37 1991			
6.5	Liabilities associated with emissions trading schemes 1992			
6.6	Green certificates compared to emissions trading schemes 1994			
6.7	EU Directive on 'Waste Electrical and Electronic Equipment' (IFRIC 6) 1995			
6.8	Levies imposed by governments 1997			
	6.8.1	Scope of IFRIC 21 1997		
	6.8.2	Recognition and measurement of levy liabilities 1998		
	6.8.3	Recognition of an asset or expense when a levy is recorded 2000		
	6.8.4	Payments relating to taxes other than income tax 2001		
6.9	Dilapidation and other provisions relating to leased assets 2002			
6.10	Warranty provisions 2003			
6.11	Litigation and other legal claims 2004			
6.12	Refunds policy 2005			
6.13	Self insurance 2006			
6.14	Obligations to make donations to non-profit organisations 2006			
6.15	Settlement payments 2008			

7	Disclosure requirements	2008
7.1	Provisions	2009
7.2	Contingent liabilities	2012
7.3	Contingent assets	2013
7.4	Reduced disclosure when information is seriously prejudicial	2013

List of examples

Example 26.1:	Recognising a provision because of a constructive obligation	1938
Example 26.2:	No provision without a past obligating event	1939
Example 26.3:	Obligations must exist independently of an entity's future actions	1940
Example 26.4:	When the likelihood of an outflow of benefits becomes probable	1944
Example 26.5:	When the recognition of a provision gives rise to an asset	1946
Example 26.6:	Calculation of expected value	1948
Example 26.7:	Calculation of a risk-adjusted rate	1951
Example 26.8:	Use of discounting and tax effect	1954
Example 26.9:	Effect on future profits of choosing a real or nominal discount rate	1954
Example 26.10:	Effect on future profits of choosing a risk-free or risk-adjusted rate	1956
Example 26.11:	Accounting for the effect of changes in the discount rate	1958
Example 26.12:	Prohibition on maintenance provisions relating to owned assets	1963
Example 26.13:	The effect of timing of the creation of a constructive obligation on the recognition of a restructuring provision	1968
Example 26.14:	Distinguishing restructuring costs from ongoing expenses	1970
Example 26.15:	Onerous supply contract	1975
Example 26.16:	Onerous contract with several 'over time' performance obligations that are satisfied consecutively	1977
Example 26.17:	Changes in decommissioning costs – related asset measured at cost	1982
Example 26.18:	Changes in decommissioning costs – related asset carried at revaluation amount	1983
Example 26.19:	Illustration of IFRIC 6 requirements	1996
Example 26.20:	A levy is triggered in full as soon as the entity generates revenues	1998

Example 26.21:	Recognising a liability for levies that are triggered progressively	2000
Example 26.22:	Recognition of a provision for warranty costs	2004
Example 26.23:	Accounting for donations to non-profit organisations	2006
Example 26.24:	Reduced disclosure when information is seriously prejudicial	2013

Chapter 26

Provisions, contingent liabilities and contingent assets

1 INTRODUCTION

1.1 Background

IAS 37 – *Provisions, Contingent Liabilities and Contingent Assets* – applies to all provisions, contingent liabilities and contingent assets, except those relating to executory contracts that are not onerous and those provisions covered by another Standard. *[IAS 37.1]*.

For some time the IASB has considered amending IAS 37 and an exposure draft was issued in June 2005. Subsequent deliberation, including round-table meetings held with constituents to discuss their views, resulted in the Board revising its proposals and issuing a second exposure draft in January 2010. However, IAS 37 was not revised. Instead, in 2010, the Board suspended the project to allow it to focus on higher priority projects, and pending completion of its project to revise the Conceptual Framework. The IASB again began discussions on a Provisions, Contingent Liabilities and Contingent Assets research project in 2015. Whilst stakeholders have told the Board that IAS 37 generally works well in practice, problems have been identified with some aspects of the Standard. It is often difficult to determine whether an entity has a liability if an entity has an obligation that has arisen from its past actions but is also dependent on a future action of the entity. Some stakeholders have argued that the principles underlying IFRIC 21 – *Levies*, an interpretation of IAS 37, are inconsistent with other requirements in IAS 37, and have argued that IFRIC 21 results in information that is not useful to investors. In addition, the measurement requirements in IAS 37 for provisions are not clear on which costs should be included as part of 'the expenditure required to settle' an obligation, and do not specify whether the rate used to discount provisions should reflect the risk that the entity may fail to fulfil its liability (i.e. the entity's own credit risk). This leads to diversity in practice in the measurement of provisions. At the time of writing, the Board is developing proposals for three targeted improvements to IAS 37. These would involve aligning the definition of a liability and requirements for identifying liabilities with the Conceptual Framework for Financial Reporting, clarifying which costs to include in the measurement of a provision, and specifying whether the rate at which an entity discounts a provision should reflect the entity's own credit risk.[1]

1.2 Interpretations related to the application of IAS 37

The Interpretations Committee has issued a number of pronouncements relating to the application of IAS 37 (although one of them was subsequently withdrawn).

1.2.1 IFRIC 1

IFRIC 1 – *Changes in Existing Decommissioning, Restoration and Similar Liabilities* – provides guidance on how to account for the effect of changes in the measurement of existing provisions for obligations to dismantle, remove or restore items of property, plant and equipment. This is discussed at 6.3 below.

1.2.2 IFRIC 3

Another issue considered by the Interpretations Committee was how to account for a 'cap and trade' emission rights scheme. In December 2004, the Interpretations Committee issued IFRIC 3 – *Emission Rights* – but this was later withdrawn in June 2005. This interpretation, *inter alia*, required that as emissions are made, a liability was to be recognised for the obligation to deliver allowances equal to the emissions that had been made by the entity. Such a liability was a provision within the scope of IAS 37, and was to be measured at the present market value of the number of allowances required to cover emissions made up to the end of the reporting period. Accounting for liabilities associated with emissions trading schemes is discussed at 6.5 below.

1.2.3 IFRIC 5

IFRIC 5 – *Rights to Interests arising from Decommissioning, Restoration and Environmental Rehabilitation Funds* – deals with the accounting by an entity when it participates in a 'decommissioning fund', the purpose of which is to segregate assets to fund some or all of the costs of its decommissioning or environmental liabilities for which it has to make a provision under IAS 37. This is discussed at 6.3.3 below.

1.2.4 IFRIC 6

IFRIC 6 – *Liabilities arising from Participating in a Specific Market – Waste Electrical and Electronic Equipment* – provides guidance on the accounting for liabilities for waste management costs. This clarifies when certain producers of electrical goods will need to recognise a liability for the cost of waste management relating to the decommissioning of waste electrical and electronic equipment (historical waste) supplied to private households. This is discussed at 6.7 below.

1.2.5 IFRIC 21

IFRIC 21 addresses the recognition of a liability to pay a levy imposed by government if that liability is within the scope of IAS 37. It also addresses the accounting for a liability to pay a levy whose timing and amount is certain (see 6.8 below).

Although they are not interpretations of the standard as such, the IAS 37 guidance on non-financial liabilities is also referred to in IFRIC 12 – *Service Concession Arrangements* (see Chapter 25); and IFRIC 14 – *IAS 19 – The Limit on a Defined Benefit Asset, Minimum Funding Requirements and their Interaction* (see Chapter 35).

1.3 Terms used in this chapter

The following terms are used in this chapter with the meanings specified:

Term	Definition
Provision	A liability of uncertain timing or amount. *[IAS 37.10]*.
Liability	A present obligation of the entity arising from past events, the settlement of which is expected to result in an outflow from the entity of resources embodying economic benefits. *[IAS 37.10]*.
Obligating event	An event that creates a legal or constructive obligation that results in an entity having no realistic alternative to settling that obligation. *[IAS 37.10]*.
Legal obligation	An obligation that derives from a contract (through its explicit or implicit terms); legislation; or other operation of law. *[IAS 37.10]*.
Constructive obligation	An obligation that derives from an entity's actions where: (a) by an established pattern of past practice, published policies or a sufficiently specific current statement, the entity has indicated to other parties that it will accept certain responsibilities; and (b) as a result, the entity has created a valid expectation on the part of those other parties that it will discharge those responsibilities. *[IAS 37.10]*.

Contingent liability	(a) a possible obligation that arises from past events and whose existence will be confirmed only by the occurrence or non-occurrence of one or more uncertain future events not wholly within the control of the entity; or
	(b) a present obligation that arises from past events but is not recognised because:
	  (i) it is not probable that an outflow of resources embodying economic benefits will be required to settle the obligation; or
	  (ii) the amount of the obligation cannot be measured with sufficient reliability. *[IAS 37.10]*.

Contingent asset	A possible asset that arises from past events and whose existence will be confirmed only by the occurrence or non-occurrence of one or more uncertain future events not wholly within the control of the entity. *[IAS 37.10]*.

Term	Definition
Onerous contract	A contract in which the unavoidable costs of meeting the obligations under the contract exceed the economic benefits expected to be received under it. *[IAS 37.10]*.
Restructuring	A programme that is planned and controlled by management, and materially changes either: (a) the scope of a business undertaken by an entity; or (b) the manner in which that business is conducted. *[IAS 37.10]*.
Executory contract	A contract under which neither party has performed any of its obligations or both parties have partially performed their obligations to an equal extent. *[IAS 37.3]*.
Levy	An outflow of resources embodying economic benefits that is imposed by governments on entities in accordance with legislation (i.e. laws and or regulations), other than: (a) those outflows of resources that are within the scope of other Standards (such as income taxes that are within the scope of IAS 12); and (b) fines or other penalties that are imposed for breaches of the legislation. *[IFRIC 21.4]*.
Government	Refers to government, government agencies and similar bodies whether local, national or international. *[IFRIC 21.4]*.

As noted at 1.1 above, the IASB is developing proposals for three targeted improvements to IAS 37. One of the proposed improvements would involve aligning the definition of a liability in IAS 37 and the requirements for identifying liabilities with the Conceptual Framework. The Conceptual Framework defines a liability as a present obligation of the entity to transfer an economic resource as a result of past events, *[CF 4.26]*, and requires that for a liability to exist, three criteria must be satisfied:

(a) the entity has an obligation;

(b) the obligation is to transfer an economic resource; and

(c) the obligation is a present obligation that exists as a result of past events. *[CF 4.27]*.

2 OBJECTIVE AND SCOPE OF IAS 37

2.1 Objective

The objective of IAS 37 'is to ensure that appropriate recognition criteria and measurement bases are applied to provisions, contingent liabilities and contingent assets and that sufficient information is disclosed in the notes to enable users to understand their nature, timing and amount'. *[IAS 37 Objective]*.

2.2 Scope of IAS 37

The standard is required to be applied by all entities in accounting for provisions, contingent liabilities and contingent assets, except those arising from executory contracts (unless the contract is onerous) and those covered by another standard. *[IAS 37.1]*.

Provisions, contingent liabilities and contingent assets

The following table lists the specific types of transaction or circumstances referred to in the standard that might give rise to a provision, contingent liability or contingent asset. In some cases, the transaction is identified in IAS 37 only to prohibit recognition of any liability, such as for future operating losses and repairs and maintenance of owned assets (see 5 below). This chapter does not address those items identified below as falling outside the scope of the standard.

Types of transaction or circumstances referred to	In scope	Out of scope	Another standard
Restructuring costs	•		
Environmental penalties or clean-up costs	•		
Decommissioning costs	•		
Product warranties / refunds	•		
Legal claims	•		
Reimbursement rights	•		
Future operating costs (training, relocation, etc.)	•		
Future operating losses	•		
Onerous contracts (including onerous contracts under IFRS 15)	•		
Repairs and maintenance costs	•		
Provisions for depreciation, impairment or doubtful debts		•	IAS 16 / IAS 38 / IAS 36 / IFRS 9
Executory contracts (unless onerous)		•	
Income taxes		•	IAS 12
Leases (unless onerous)		•	IFRS 16
Employee benefits		•	IAS 19
Insurance contracts issued by insurers to policyholders		•	IFRS 4 / IFRS 17
Contingent liabilities acquired in a business combination		•	IFRS 3
Contingent consideration of an acquirer in a business combination		•	IFRS 3
Financial instruments and financial guarantees within the scope of IFRS 9		•	IFRS 9
Trade payables		•	IFRS 9
Accruals		•	

2.2.1 Items outside the scope of IAS 37

2.2.1.A Executory contracts, except where the contract is onerous

The standard uses the term executory contracts to mean 'contracts under which neither party has performed any of its obligations, or both parties have partially performed their obligations to an equal extent'. *[IAS 37.3]*. This means that contracts such as supplier purchase contracts and capital commitments, which would otherwise fall within the scope of the standard, are exempt.

This exemption prevents the statement of financial position from being grossed up for all manner of commitments that an entity has entered into, and in respect of which it is debatable whether (or at what point) such contracts give rise to items that meet the definition of a liability or an asset. In particular, the need for this exemption arises because the liability framework on which this standard is based includes the concept of a constructive obligation (see 3.1.1 below) which, when applied to executory contracts would otherwise give rise to an inordinate number of contingent promises requiring recognition or disclosure.

An executory contract will still require recognition as a provision if the contract becomes onerous. *[IAS 37.3]*. Onerous contracts are dealt with at 6.2 below.

2.2.1.B Items covered by another standard

Where another standard deals with a specific type of provision, contingent liability or contingent asset, it should be applied instead of IAS 37. Examples given in the standard are:

- income taxes (dealt with in IAS 12 – *Income Taxes* – see Chapter 33);
- leases (dealt with in IFRS 16 – *Leases* – see Chapter 23). However, IAS 37 applies to any lease that becomes onerous before the commencement date of the lease, as defined in IFRS 16. IAS 37 also applies to onerous short-term leases and onerous leases of low value assets that are accounted for under paragraph 6 of IFRS 16; *[IAS 37.5(c)]*
- employee benefits (dealt with in IAS 19 – *Employee Benefits* – see Chapter 35);
- insurance contracts dealt with in IFRS 4 – *Insurance Contracts* – see Chapter 55, or insurance and other contracts in scope of IFRS 17 – *Insurance Contracts* – if that standard has been adopted (see Chapter 56). However, IAS 37 requires an insurer to apply the standard to provisions, contingent liabilities and contingent assets, other than those arising from its contractual obligations and rights under insurance contracts within the scope of IFRS 4, or IFRS 17 if that Standard has been adopted;
- contingent consideration of an acquirer in a business combination (dealt with in IFRS 3 – *Business Combinations* – see Chapter 9); and
- revenue from contracts with customers (dealt with in IFRS 15 – *Revenue from Contracts with Customers* – see Chapters 27-32). However, as IFRS 15 contains no specific requirements to address contracts with customers that are, or have become, onerous, IAS 37 applies to such cases. *[IAS 37.5]*.

Contingent consideration of an acquirer in a business combination is excluded from the scope of IAS 37. See Chapter 9 at 7.1.

As noted above, the scope of IAS 37 excludes income taxes that fall in the scope of IAS 12. The Interpretations Committee confirmed in July 2014 that the recognition of tax-related contingent liabilities and contingent assets should also be assessed using the guidance in IAS 12 rather than IAS 37.[2] In addition, IFRIC 23 – *Uncertainty over Income Tax Treatments* – was issued in June 2017 and clarifies how to apply the recognition and measurement requirements in IAS 12 when there is uncertainty over tax treatments. *[IFRIC 23.4]*. IAS 37 remains relevant to the disclosure of tax-related contingent liabilities and contingent assets. *[IAS 12.88]*. However, as discussed at 6.8 below, IAS 37 in general and IFRIC 21 in particular, applies to taxes or levies outside the scope of IAS 12. As regards interest and penalties imposed by taxation authorities the position is unclear. Neither IAS 12 nor IFRIC 23 contain a specific reference to interest and penalties, and, in September 2017, the Interpretations Committee decided not to add a project on interest and penalties to its agenda.[3] However, notwithstanding their decision to exclude interest and penalties from the scope of IFRIC 23 and their decision not to add a project on interest and penalties to its agenda, the Interpretations Committee observed that if an entity determines that amounts payable or receivable for interest and penalties are income taxes, then the entity applies IAS 12 to those amounts. If an entity does not apply IAS 12 to interest and penalties, then it applies IAS 37 to those amounts. Uncertain tax treatments are discussed further in Chapter 33 at 9. The circumstances in which interest and penalties might fall within the scope of IAS 12 are considered in Chapter 33 at 4.4. Levies imposed by governments are examined at 6.8 below.

Whilst IAS 37 contains no reference to it, IFRS 3 states that the requirements in IAS 37 do not apply in determining which contingent liabilities to recognise as of the acquisition date (see 4.10 below and Chapter 9 at 5.6.1). *[IFRS 3.23]*.

In addition, the standard does not apply to financial instruments (including guarantees) that are within the scope of IFRS 9 – *Financial Instruments*. *[IAS 37.2]*. This means that guarantees of third party borrowings (including those of subsidiaries, associates and joint arrangements) are not covered by IAS 37. However, the guarantee contract may meet the definition of an insurance contract in IFRS 4 and the issuer may have previously asserted that it regards such contracts as insurance contracts. In such cases, the issuer may elect to apply either IFRS 9 (or, for annual reporting periods beginning before 1 January 2021, IAS 39 – *Financial Instruments: Recognition and Measurement*, for those entities whose predominant activity is issuing contracts in scope of IFRS 4 and who previously have not applied any version of IFRS 9 *[IFRS 4.20A, 20B]*) or IFRS 4 *[IFRS 9.2.1(e)]* and the accounting policy applied by the issuer may result in the issuer providing for probable payments under the guarantee. A similar accounting policy choice exists for entities that apply IFRS 17, *[IFRS 17.7(e)]*, although entities applying IFRS 17 do not have the option to apply IAS 39 rather than IFRS 9. (See Chapter 55 for IFRS 4 and Chapter 56 for IFRS 17).

The standard applies to provisions for restructurings, including discontinued operations. However, it emphasises that when a restructuring meets the definition of a discontinued operation under IFRS 5 – *Non-current Assets Held for Sale and Discontinued Operations*, additional disclosures may be required under that standard (see Chapter 4 at 3). *[IAS 37.9]*.

As noted above, IAS 37 applies to contracts in scope of IFRS 15 that are, or have become, onerous. *[IAS 37.5(g)]*. IFRS 15 adds that IAS 37 applies to other obligations under a contract with a customer that do not give rise to a performance obligation. For example, a law that requires an entity to pay compensation if its products cause harm or damage does not give rise to a performance obligation and IAS 37 would apply. Similarly, an entity would account for customer indemnities arising from claims of patent, copyright, trademark or other infringement in relation to its products in accordance with IAS 37. *[IFRS 15.B33]*. Furthermore, whilst an entity would apply IFRS 15 to separately purchased warranties, if a customer does not have the option to purchase a warranty separately, an entity would consider IAS 37 (see 6.10 below), unless the promised warranty, or a part of the promised warranty, provides the customer with a service in addition to the assurance that the product complies with agreed-upon specifications. *[IFRS 15.B30]*.

The standard defines a provision as 'a liability of uncertain timing or amount'. *[IAS 37.10]*. Thus it only deals with provisions that are shown as liabilities in a statement of financial position. The term 'provision' is also used widely in the context of items such as depreciation, impairment of assets and doubtful debts. Such 'provisions' are not addressed in IAS 37, since these are adjustments to the carrying amounts of assets. *[IAS 37.7]*.

2.2.2 Provisions compared to other liabilities

IAS 37 states that the feature distinguishing provisions from other liabilities, such as trade payables and accruals, is the existence of 'uncertainty about the timing or amount of the future expenditure required in settlement'. *[IAS 37.11]*. The standard compares provisions to:

(a) trade payables – liabilities to pay for goods or services that have been received or supplied and have been invoiced or formally agreed with the supplier; and

(b) accruals – liabilities to pay for goods or services that have been received or supplied but have not been paid, invoiced or formally agreed with the supplier, including amounts due to employees (for example, amounts relating to accrued vacation pay). Although it is sometimes necessary to estimate the amount or timing of accruals, the uncertainty is generally much less than for provisions.

IAS 37 also notes that accruals are often reported as part of trade and other payables whereas provisions are reported separately. *[IAS 37.11]*.

For trade payables and their associated accruals, there is little uncertainty regarding either the amount of the obligation (which would be determined by the contracted price for the goods and services being provided) or of the timing of settlement (which would normally occur within an agreed period following transfer of the goods and services in question and the issue of an invoice). In practice, however, contracts can be more complex and give rise to a wide range of possible outcomes in terms of the amount or timing of payment. In these circumstances, the difference between provisions and other liabilities is less obvious and judgement may be required to determine where the requirement to make an estimate of an obligation indicates a level of uncertainty about timing or amount that is more indicative of a provision. Such judgements, if significant to the amounts recognised in the financial statements, would merit disclosure (see Chapter 3 at 5.1.1.B). *[IAS 1.122]*.

One reason why this distinction matters is that provisions are subject to narrative disclosure requirements regarding the nature of the obligation and the uncertainties over timing and amount; and to quantitative disclosures of movements arising from their use, remeasurement or release that do not apply to other payables (see 7.1 below). In fact, although questions of recognition and measurement are important, transparency of disclosure is also a very significant matter in relation to accounting for provisions and ensuring that their effect is properly understood by users of the financial statements.

2.2.3 Distinction between provisions and contingent liabilities

There is an area of overlap between provisions and contingent liabilities. Although contingent liabilities are clearly not as likely to give rise to outflows, similar judgements are made in assessing the nature of the uncertainties, the need for disclosures and ultimately the recognition of a liability in the financial statements. The standard notes that in a general sense, all provisions are contingent because they are uncertain in timing or amount. However, in IAS 37 the term 'contingent' is used for liabilities and assets that are not recognised because their existence will be confirmed only by the occurrence of one or more uncertain future events not wholly within the entity's control. In addition, the term 'contingent liability' is used for liabilities that do not meet the recognition criteria for provisions. [IAS 37.12].

Accordingly, the standard distinguishes between:

(a) provisions – which are recognised as liabilities (assuming that a reliable estimate can be made) because they are present obligations and it is probable that an outflow of resources embodying economic benefits will be required to settle the obligations; and

(b) contingent liabilities – which are not recognised as liabilities because they are either:
   (i) possible obligations, as it has yet to be confirmed whether the entity has a present obligation that could lead to an outflow of resources embodying economic benefits; or
   (ii) present obligations that do not meet the recognition criteria in the standard because either it is not probable that an outflow of resources embodying economic benefits will be required to settle the obligation, or a sufficiently reliable estimate of the amount of the obligation cannot be made. [IAS 37.13].

3 RECOGNITION

3.1 Determining when a provision should be recognised

IAS 37 requires that a provision should be recognised when:

(a) an entity has a present obligation (legal or constructive) as a result of a past event;

(b) it is probable that an outflow of resources embodying economic benefits will be required to settle the obligation; and

(c) a reliable estimate can be made of the amount of the obligation.

No provision should be recognised unless all of these conditions are met. [IAS 37.14].

Each of these three conditions is discussed separately below.

3.1.1 'An entity has a present obligation (legal or constructive) as a result of a past event'

The standard defines both legal and constructive obligations. The definition of a legal obligation is fairly straightforward and uncontroversial; it refers to an obligation that derives from a contract (through its explicit or implicit terms), legislation or other operation of law. *[IAS 37.10]*.

The definition of a constructive obligation, on the other hand, may give rise to more problems of interpretation. A constructive obligation is defined as an obligation that derives from an entity's actions where:

(a) by an established pattern of past practice, published policies or a sufficiently specific current statement, the entity has indicated to other parties that it will accept certain responsibilities; and

(b) as a result, the entity has created a valid expectation on the part of those other parties that it will discharge those responsibilities. *[IAS 37.10]*.

The following examples in IAS 37 illustrate how a constructive obligation is created.

Example 26.1: Recognising a provision because of a constructive obligation

Scenario 1: Environmental policy – contaminated land

An entity in the oil industry operates in a country with no environmental legislation. However, it has a widely published environmental policy in which it undertakes to clean up all contamination that it causes and it has a record of honouring this published policy. During the period the entity causes contamination to some land in this country.

In these circumstances, the contamination of the land gives rise to a constructive obligation because the entity (through its published policy and record of honouring it) has created a valid expectation on the part of those affected by it that the entity will clean up the site. *[IAS 37 IE Example 2B]*.

Scenario 2: Refunds policy – product returns

A retail store has a generally known policy of refunding purchases by dissatisfied customers, even though it is under no legal obligation to do so.

In these circumstances, the sale of its products gives rise to a constructive obligation because the entity (through its reputation for providing refunds) has created a valid expectation on the part of customers that a refund will be given if they are dissatisfied with their purchase. *[IAS 37 IE Example 4]*.

These examples demonstrate that the essence of a constructive obligation is the creation of a valid expectation that the entity is irrevocably committed to accepting and discharging its responsibilities.

The standard states that in almost all cases it will be clear whether a past event has given rise to a present obligation. However, it acknowledges that there will be some rare cases, such as a lawsuit against an entity, where this will not be so because the occurrence of certain events or the consequences of those events are disputed. *[IAS 37.16]*. When it is not clear whether there is a present obligation, a 'more likely than not' evaluation (taking into account all available evidence) is deemed to be sufficient to require recognition of a provision at the end of the reporting period. *[IAS 37.15]*.

The evidence to be considered includes, for example, the opinion of experts together with any additional evidence provided by events after the reporting period. If on the basis of such evidence it is concluded that a present obligation is more likely than not to exist at the end of the reporting period, a provision will be required (assuming that the other recognition criteria are met). *[IAS 37.16]*. This is an apparent relaxation of the standard's first criterion for the recognition of a provision as set out at 3.1 above, which requires there to be a definite obligation, not just a probable one. It also confuses slightly the question of the existence of an obligation with the probability criterion, which strictly speaking relates to whether it is more likely than not that there will be an outflow of resources (see 3.1.2 below). However, this interpretation is confirmed in IAS 10 – *Events after the Reporting Period*, which includes 'the settlement after the reporting period of a court case that confirms that the entity had a present obligation at the end of the reporting period' as an example of an adjusting event. *[IAS 10.9]*.

The second half of this condition uses the phrase 'as a result of a past event'. This is based on the concept of an obligating event, which the standard defines as 'an event that creates a legal or constructive obligation and that results in an entity having no realistic alternative to settling that obligation'. *[IAS 37.10]*. The standard says that this will be the case only:

(a) where the settlement of the obligation can be enforced by law; or

(b) in the case of a constructive obligation, where the event (which may be an action of the entity) creates valid expectations in other parties that the entity will discharge the obligation. *[IAS 37.17]*.

This concept of obligating event is used in the standard when discussing specific examples of recognition, which we consider further at 6 below. However, it is worth mentioning here that this concept, like that of a constructive obligation, is open to interpretation and requires the exercise of judgement, as the obligating event is not always easy to identify.

The standard emphasises that the financial statements deal with the financial position of an entity at the end of its reporting period, not its possible position in the future. Accordingly, no provision should be recognised for costs that need to be incurred to operate in the future. The only liabilities to be recognised are those that exist at the end of the reporting period. *[IAS 37.18]*. It is not always easy to distinguish between the current state at the reporting date and the entity's future possible position, especially where IAS 37 requires an assessment to be made based on the probability of obligations and expectations as to their outcome. However, when considering these questions it is important to ensure that provisions are not recognised for liabilities that arise from events after the reporting period (see Chapter 38 at 2).

Example 26.2: No provision without a past obligating event

The government introduces a number of changes to the income tax system. As a result of these changes, an entity in the financial services sector will need to retrain a large proportion of its administrative and sales staff in order to ensure continued compliance with financial services regulation. At the end of the reporting period, no training has taken place.

In these circumstances, no event has taken place at the reporting date to create an obligation. Only once the training has taken place will there be a present obligation as a result of a past event. *[IAS 37 IE Example 7]*.

IAS 37 prohibits certain provisions that might otherwise qualify to be recognised by stating that it 'is only those obligations arising from past events existing independently of an entity's future actions (i.e. the future conduct of its business) that are recognised as provisions'. In contrast to situations where the entity's past conduct has created an obligation to incur expenditure (such as to rectify environmental damage already caused), a commercial or legal requirement to incur expenditure in order to operate in a particular way in the future, will not of itself justify the recognition of a provision. It argues that because the entity can avoid the expenditure by its future actions, for example by changing its method of operation, there is no present obligation for the future expenditure. *[IAS 37.19]*.

Example 26.3:   Obligations must exist independently of an entity's future actions

Under legislation passed in 2020, an entity is required to fix smoke filters in its factories by 30 June 2022. The entity has not fitted the smoke filters.

At 31 December 2021, the end of the reporting period, no event has taken place to create an obligation. Only once the smoke filters are fitted or the legislation takes effect, will there be a present obligation as a result of a past event, either for the cost of fitting smoke filters or for fines under the legislation.

At 31 December 2022, there is still no obligating event to justify provision for the cost of fitting the smoke filters required under the legislation because the filters have not been fitted. However, an obligation may exist as at the reporting date to pay fines or penalties under the legislation because the entity is operating its factory in a non-compliant way. However, a provision would only be recognised for the best estimate of any fines and penalties if, as at 31 December 2022, it is determined to be more likely than not that such fines and penalties will be imposed. *[IAS 37 IE Example 6]*.

The standard expects strict application of the requirement that, to qualify for recognition, an obligation must exist independently of an entity's future actions. Even if a failure to incur certain costs would result in a legal requirement to discontinue an entity's operations, no provision can be recognised. As discussed at 5.2 below, IAS 37 considers the example of an airline required by law to overhaul its aircraft once every three years. It concludes that no provision is recognised because the entity can avoid the requirement to perform the overhaul, for example by replacing the aircraft before the three year period has expired. *[IAS 37 IE Example 11B]*.

Centrica plc describes its interpretation of the group's obligations under UK legislation to install energy efficiency improvement measures in domestic households in a manner consistent with Example 26.3 above.

> *Extract 26.1: Centrica plc (2018)*
>
> **Notes to the Financial Statements** [extract]
>
> **3.   Critical accounting judgements and key sources of estimation uncertainty** [extract]
>
> **(a)   Critical judgements in applying the Group's accounting policies** [extract]
>
> **Energy Company Obligation**
>
> The Energy Company Obligation (ECO) order requires UK-licensed energy suppliers to improve the energy efficiency of domestic households. Targets are set in proportion to the size of historic customer bases. ECO phase 1 and ECO phase 2 had delivery dates of 31 March 2015 and 30 September 2018 (extended from 31 March 2017), respectively. ECO phase 3 is currently effective with a delivery date of 31 March 2022. Although this phase includes certain sub-obligations, there are no interim targets and, consistent with previous years, the Group continues to judge that it is not legally obligated by the order until delivery date. Accordingly, the costs of delivery are recognised as incurred, when cash has been spent or unilateral commitments made, resulting in obligations that could not be avoided.

Significantly, however, such considerations do not apply in the case of obligations to dismantle or remove an asset at the end of its useful life, where an obligation is recognised despite the entity's ability to dispose of the asset before its useful life has expired. Such costs are required to be included by IAS 16 – *Property, Plant and Equipment* – as part of the measure of an asset's initial cost. *[IAS 16.16]*. Decommissioning provisions are discussed at 6.3 below. Accordingly, the determination of whether an obligation exists independently of an entity's future actions can be a matter of judgement that depends on the particular facts and circumstances of the case.

There is no requirement for an entity to know to whom an obligation is owed. The obligation may be to the public at large. It follows that the obligation could be to one party, but the amount ultimately payable will be to another party. For example, in the case of a constructive obligation for an environmental clean-up, the obligation is to the public, but the liability will be settled by making payment to the contractors engaged to carry out the clean-up. However, the principle is that there must be another party for the obligation to exist. It follows from this that a management or board decision will not give rise to a constructive obligation unless it is communicated in sufficient detail to those affected by it before the end of the reporting period. *[IAS 37.20]*. The most significant application of this requirement relates to restructuring provisions, which is discussed further at 6.1 below.

The standard discusses the possibility that an event that does not give rise to an obligation immediately may do so at a later date, because of changes in the law or an act by the entity (such as a sufficiently specific public statement) which gives rise to a constructive obligation. *[IAS 37.21]*. Changes in the law will be relatively straightforward to identify. The only issue that arises will be to determine exactly when that change in the law should be recognised. IAS 37 states that an obligation arises only when the legislation is virtually certain to be enacted as drafted and suggests that in many cases, this will not be until it is enacted. *[IAS 37.22]*.

The more subjective area is the possibility that an act by the entity will give rise to a constructive obligation. The example given is of an entity publicly accepting responsibility for rectification of previous environmental damage in a way that creates a constructive obligation. *[IAS 37.21]*. This seems to introduce a certain amount of flexibility to management when reporting results. By bringing forward or delaying a public announcement of a commitment that management had always intended to honour, it can affect the reporting period in which a provision is recognised. Nevertheless, the existence of a public announcement provides a more transparent basis for recognising a provision than, for example, a decision made behind the closed doors of a boardroom.

3.1.2 'It is probable that an outflow of resources embodying economic benefits will be required to settle the obligation'

This requirement has been included as a result of the standard's attempt to incorporate contingent liabilities within the definition of provisions. This is discussed at 3.2 below.

The meaning of probable in these circumstances is that the outflow of resources is more likely than not to occur; that is, it has a probability of occurring that is greater than 50%. *[IAS 37.23]*. The standard also makes it clear that where there are a number of similar obligations, the probability that an outflow will occur is based on the class of obligations as a whole. This is because in the case of certain obligations such as warranties, the possibility of an outflow for an individual item may be small (likely to be much less than 50%) whereas the possibility of at least some outflow of resources for the population as a whole will be much greater (almost certainly greater than 50%). *[IAS 37.24]*. With regard to the measurement of a provision arising from a number of similar obligations, the standard refers to the calculation of an 'expected value', whereby the obligation is estimated by weighting all the possible outcomes by their associated probabilities. *[IAS 37.39]*. Where the obligation being measured relates to a single item, the standard suggests that the best estimate of the liability may be the individual most likely outcome. *[IAS 37.40]*. For the purposes of recognition, a determination that it is more likely than not that *any* outflow of resources will be required is sufficient. The measurement of provisions is discussed at 4 below.

3.1.3 'A reliable estimate can be made of the amount of the obligation'

The standard takes the view that a sufficiently reliable estimate can almost always be made for a provision where an entity can determine a range of possible outcomes. Hence, the standard contends that it will only be in extremely rare cases that a range of possible outcomes cannot be determined and therefore no sufficiently reliable estimate of the obligation can be made. *[IAS 37.25]*. In these extremely rare circumstances, no liability is recognised. Instead, the liability should be disclosed as a contingent liability (see disclosure requirements at 7.2 below). *[IAS 37.26]*. Whether such a situation is as rare as the standard asserts is open to question, especially for entities trying to determine estimates relating to potential obligations that arise from litigation and other legal claims (see 6.11 below).

In the extract below, HSBC explains that it cannot reliably estimate the amount it may be liable to pay under the UK's Financial Services Compensation Scheme.

> **Extract 26.2: HSBC Holdings plc (2019)**
> **Notes on the Financial Statements** [extract]
> 32.   **Contingent liabilities, contractual commitments and guarantees** [extract]
> **Financial Services Compensation Scheme**
> The Financial Services Compensation Scheme ('FSCS') has provided compensation to customers of financial services firms that have failed. Following the financial crisis, the compensation paid out to customers was initially funded through loans from HM Treasury, which were fully repaid in 2018 by the FSCS. The Group could be liable to pay a proportion of any future amounts that the FSCS borrows from HM Treasury to the extent the industry levies imposed to date are not sufficient to cover the compensation due to customers in any future possible collapse. The ultimate FSCS levy to the industry as a result of a collapse cannot currently be estimated reliably. It is dependent on various uncertain factors including the potential recoveries of assets by the FSCS, changes in the level of protected products (including deposits and investments) and the population of FSCS members at the time.

3.2 Contingencies

IAS 37 says that contingent liabilities and contingent assets should not be recognised, but only disclosed. *[IAS 37.27-28, 31, 34]*.

Contingent liabilities that are recognised separately as part of allocating the cost of a business combination are covered by the requirements of IFRS 3. *[IFRS 3.23]*. Such liabilities continue to be measured after the business combination at the higher of:

(a)   the amount that would be recognised in accordance with IAS 37, and

(b)   the amount initially recognised less, if appropriate, the cumulative amount of income recognised in accordance with the principles of IFRS 15. *[IFRS 3.56]*.

The requirements in respect of contingent liabilities identified in a business combination are discussed in Chapter 9 at 5.6.1.

3.2.1 Contingent liabilities

A contingent liability is defined in the standard as:

(a) a possible obligation that arises from past events and whose existence will be confirmed only by the occurrence or non-occurrence of one or more uncertain future events not wholly within the control of the entity; or

(b) a present obligation that arises from past events but is not recognised because:

   (i) it is not probable that an outflow of resources embodying economic benefits will be required to settle the obligation; or

   (ii) the amount of the obligation cannot be measured with sufficient reliability. [IAS 37.10].

At first glance, this definition is not easy to understand because a natural meaning of 'contingent' would include any event whose outcome depends on future circumstances. The meaning is perhaps clearer when considering the definition of a liability and the criteria for recognising a provision in the standard. A possible obligation whose existence is yet to be confirmed does not meet the definition of a liability; and a present obligation in respect of which an outflow of resources is not probable, or which cannot be measured reliably does not qualify for recognition. [IAS 37.14]. On that basis a contingent liability under IAS 37 means one of the following:

(a) an obligation that is estimated to be less than 50+% likely to exist (i.e. it does not meet the definition of a liability). Where it is more likely than not that a present obligation exists at the end of the reporting period, a provision is recognised. [IAS 37.16(a)]. Where it is more likely than not that no present obligation exists, a contingent liability is disclosed (unless the possibility is remote); [IAS 37.16(b)]

(b) a present obligation that has a less than 50+% chance of requiring an outflow of economic benefits (i.e. it meets the definition of a liability but does not meet the recognition criteria). Where it is not probable that there will be an outflow of resources, an entity discloses a contingent liability (unless the possibility is remote); [IAS 37.23] or

(c) a present obligation for which a sufficiently reliable estimate cannot be made (i.e. it meets the definition of a liability but does not meet the recognition criteria). In these rare circumstances, a liability cannot be recognised and it is disclosed as a contingent liability. [IAS 37.26].

The term 'possible' is not defined, but literally it could mean any probability greater than 0% and less than 100%. However, the standard effectively divides this range into four components, namely 'remote', 'possible but not probable', 'probable' and 'virtually certain'. The standard requires a provision to be recognised if 'it is more likely than not that a present obligation exists at the end of the reporting period'. [IAS 37.16(a)]. Therefore, IAS 37 distinguishes between a 'probable' obligation (which is more likely than not to exist and, therefore requires recognition as a provision) and a 'possible' obligation (for which either the existence of a present obligation is yet to be confirmed or where the probability of an outflow of resources is 50% or less). [IAS 37.13]. Appendix A to IAS 37, in summarising the main requirements of the standard, uses the phrase 'a possible obligation ... that may, but probably will not, require an outflow of resources'. Accordingly, the definition restricts contingent liabilities to those where either the existence of the liability or the transfer of economic benefits arising is less than 50+% probable (or where the obligation cannot be measured at all, but as noted at 3.1.3 above, this would be relatively rare).

The standard requires that contingent liabilities are assessed continually to determine whether circumstances have changed, in particular whether an outflow of resources embodying economic benefits has become probable. Where this becomes the case, then provision should be made in the period in which the change in probability occurs (except in the rare circumstances where no reliable estimate can be made). *[IAS 37.30]*. Other changes in circumstances might require disclosure of a previously remote obligation on the grounds that an outflow of resources has become possible (but not probable).

Example 26.4:   When the likelihood of an outflow of benefits becomes probable

After a wedding in 2021, ten people died, possibly as a result of food poisoning from products sold by the entity. Legal proceedings are started seeking damages from the entity. The entity disputes any liability and, up to the date on which its financial statements for the year ended 31 December 2021 are authorised for issue, its lawyers have advised that is probable that the entity will not be found liable. However, when the entity prepares its financial statements for the year ended 31 December 2022, its lawyers advise that, owing to developments in the case, it is probable that the entity will be found liable.

At 31 December 2021, no provision is recognised and the matter is disclosed as a contingent liability unless the probability of any outflow is regarded as remote. On the basis of the evidence available when the financial statements were approved, there is no obligation as a result of a past event.

At 31 December 2022, a provision is recognised for the best estimate of the amount required to settle the obligation. The fact that an outflow of economic benefits is now believed to be probable means that there is a present obligation. *[IAS 37 IE Example 10]*.

3.2.2   Contingent assets

A contingent asset is defined in a more intuitive way. It is 'a possible asset that arises from past events and whose existence will be confirmed only by the occurrence or non-occurrence of one or more uncertain future events not wholly within the control of the entity'. *[IAS 37.10]*. In this case, the word 'possible' is not confined to a level of probability of 50% or less, which may further increase the confusion over the different meaning of the term in the definition of contingent liabilities.

Contingent assets usually arise from unplanned or other unexpected events that give rise to the possibility of an inflow of economic benefits to the entity. An example is a claim that an entity is pursuing through legal process, where the outcome is uncertain. *[IAS 37.32]*.

The standard states that a contingent asset should not be recognised, as this could give rise to recognition of income that may never be realised. However, when the realisation of income is virtually certain, then the related asset is no longer regarded as contingent and recognition is appropriate. *[IAS 37.33]*.

Virtual certainty is not defined in the standard, but it is certainly a much higher hurdle than 'probable' and indeed more challenging than the term 'highly probable', defined in IFRS 5 as 'significantly more likely than probable'. *[IFRS 5 Appendix A]*. We think it reasonable that virtual certainty is interpreted as being as close to 100% as to make any remaining uncertainty insignificant. What this means in practice requires each case to be decided on its merits and any judgement should be made in the knowledge that, in any event, it is rarely possible to accurately assess the probability of the outcome of a particular event.

The standard requires disclosure of the contingent asset when the inflow of economic benefits is probable. *[IAS 37.34]*. For the purposes of the standard 'probable' means that the event is more likely than not to occur; that is, it has a probability greater than 50%. *[IAS 37.23]*. The disclosure requirements are detailed at 7.3 below.

As with contingent liabilities, any contingent assets should be assessed continually to ensure that developments are appropriately reflected in the financial statements. If it has become virtually certain that an inflow of economic benefits will arise, the asset and the related income should be recognised in the period in which the change occurs. If a previously unlikely inflow becomes probable, then the contingent asset should be disclosed. *[IAS 37.35]*.

The requirement to recognise the effect of changing circumstances in the period in which the change occurs extends to the analysis of information available after the end of the reporting period and before the date of approval of the financial statements. In our view, such information would not give rise to an adjusting event after the reporting period. In contrast to contingent liabilities (in respect of which IAS 10 includes as a specific example of an adjusting event 'the settlement after the reporting period of a court case that confirms that the entity had a present obligation at the end of the reporting period' *[IAS 10.9]*), no adjustment should be made to reflect the subsequent settlement of a legal claim in favour of the entity. In this instance, the period in which the change occurs is subsequent to the reporting period. There is also no suggestion that the example in IAS 10 is referring to anything but liabilities. An asset could only be recognised if, at the end of the reporting period, the entity could show that it was virtually certain that its claim would succeed.

3.2.2.A   Obligations contingent on the successful recovery of a contingent asset

Entities may sometimes be required to pay contingent fees to a third party dependent upon the successful recovery of a contingent asset. For example, the payment of fees to a legal advisor in a contract agreed on a 'no win, no fee' basis will depend upon the successful outcome of a legal claim. In such cases, we believe that the obligation for the success fee arises from an executory contract that should be evaluated separately from the legal claim. The liability for the success fee would therefore only be recognised by the entity upon winning the claim.

IAS 37 uses the term executory contracts to mean 'contracts under which neither party has performed any of its obligations, or both parties have partially performed their obligations to an equal extent'. *[IAS 37.3]*. When a contract for services is wholly contingent on recovering a contingent asset, no service requiring payment is deemed to be provided until or unless the matter is resolved successfully. Unless the contract also required payment to be made in the event of failure, the amount of work put in by the lawyer to prepare a case and argue for recovery of the contingent asset is irrelevant to the existence of a liability to pay fees.

If the entity has deemed it appropriate to recognise an asset in respect of the claim, it would be appropriate to take account of any such fees in the measurement of that asset (in determining the net amount recoverable); but no accrual should be made for the legal fees themselves unless a successful outcome is confirmed.

This analysis is specific to a no win-no fee arrangement related to a contingent asset and may not be appropriate in other circumstances.

3.2.3 How probability determines whether to recognise or disclose

The following matrix summarises the treatment of contingencies under IAS 37:

Likelihood of outcome	Accounting treatment: contingent liability	Accounting treatment: contingent asset
Virtually certain	Recognise	Recognise
Probable	Recognise	Disclose
Possible but not probable	Disclose	No disclosure permitted
Remote	No disclosure required	No disclosure permitted

The standard does not put a numerical measure of probability on either 'virtually certain' or 'remote'. In our view, the use of such measures would downgrade a process requiring the exercise of judgement into a mechanical exercise. It is difficult to imagine circumstances when an entity could reliably determine an obligation to be, for example, 92%, 95% or 99% likely, let alone be able to compare those probabilities objectively. Accordingly, we think it reasonable to regard 'virtually certain' as describing a likelihood that is as close to 100% as to make any remaining uncertainty insignificant; to see 'remote' as meaning a likelihood of an outflow of resources that is not significant; and for significance to be a matter for judgement and determined according to the merits of each case.

3.3 Recognising an asset when recognising a provision

In most cases, the recognition of a provision results in an immediate expense in profit or loss. Nevertheless, in some cases it may be appropriate to recognise an asset. These issues are not discussed in IAS 37, which neither prohibits nor requires capitalisation of the costs recognised when a provision is made. It states that other standards specify whether expenditures are treated as assets or expenses. *[IAS 37.8]*.

Whilst the main body of IAS 37 is silent on the matter, the standard contains the following example which concludes that an asset should be recognised when a decommissioning provision is established.

Example 26.5: When the recognition of a provision gives rise to an asset

An entity operates an offshore oilfield where its licensing agreement requires it to remove the oil rig at the end of production and restore the seabed. 90% of the eventual costs relate to the removal of the oil rig and restoration of damage caused by building it, with 10% expected to arise through the extraction of oil. At the end of the reporting period, the rig has been constructed but no oil has been extracted.

A provision is recognised in respect of the probable costs relating to the removal of the rig and restoring damage caused by building it. This is because the construction of the rig, combined with the requirement under the licence to remove the rig and restore the seabed, creates an obligating event as at the end of the reporting period. These costs are included as part of the cost of the oil rig.

However, there is no obligation to rectify any damage that will be caused by the future extraction of oil. *[IAS 37 IE Example 3]*.

This conclusion is supported by IAS 16, which requires the cost of an item of property, plant and equipment to include the initial estimate of the costs of dismantling and removing an asset and restoring the site on which it is located, the obligation for which an entity incurs either when the item is acquired or as a consequence of having used the item during a particular period for purposes other than to produce inventories during that period. *[IAS 16.16(c), 18]*. The treatment of decommissioning costs is discussed further at 6.3 below.

4 MEASUREMENT

4.1 Best estimate of provision

IAS 37 requires the amount to be recognised as a provision to be the best estimate of the expenditure required to settle the present obligation at the end of the reporting period. *[IAS 37.36]*. This measure is determined before tax, as the tax consequences of the provision, and changes to it, are dealt with under IAS 12. *[IAS 37.41]*.

The standard equates this 'best estimate' with 'the amount that an entity would rationally pay to settle the obligation at the end of the reporting period or to transfer it to a third party at that time'. *[IAS 37.37]*. It is interesting that a hypothetical transaction of this kind should be proposed as the conceptual basis of the measurement required, rather than putting the main emphasis upon the actual expenditure that is expected to be incurred in the future.

The standard does acknowledge that it would often be impossible or prohibitively expensive to settle or transfer the obligation at the end of the reporting period. However, it goes on to state that 'the estimate of the amount that an entity would rationally pay to settle or transfer the obligation gives the best estimate of the expenditure required to settle the present obligation at the end of the reporting period'. *[IAS 37.37]*.

During the Provisions research project, stakeholders have noted that the measurement objective in IAS 37 is not precise and, in practice, is interpreted in different ways.[4] Paragraph 36 of IAS 37 requires an entity to measure a provision at the best estimate of the expenditure required to settle the obligation, implying a 'fulfilment value' measurement basis. However, paragraph 37 of the standard states that the best estimate may be the amount that the entity would rationally pay to transfer the obligation to a third party at the reporting date, suggesting a 'transfer value' measurement basis. *[IAS 37.36-37]*. The assumptions that an entity makes regarding derecognition of the liability may influence how the entity determines the best estimate of the expenditure required to settle the obligation. In practice, there are several ways in which an IAS 37 obligation may be derecognised. For example:

(a) The obligation is settled by the entity performing the obligation itself (for example, the entity uses its own personnel to clean up a site to satisfy an environmental clean-up obligation);

(b) The entity employs a third party to perform the work required to settle the obligation (for example, the entity hires a third party company to clean up the site);

(c) The entity transfers the obligation to a third party (for example, another entity takes on the obligation to clean up the site, the entity pays the transferee, and is relieved of the obligation); or

(d) The obligation is cash settled by negotiation with the party to whom the obligation is owed (for example, the entity negotiates a cash settlement with the local municipality in order to be relieved of the obligation).

In January 2020, the IASB decided that clarification of the measurement objective of IAS 37 would not be included in the scope of the current project to amend aspects of IAS 37.[5] In our view, any of the assumptions above are acceptable bases for measurement provided that they appropriately reflect the facts and circumstances of the situation. If an entity exercises significant judgement in determining the most appropriate approach, consideration should be given to the disclosure requirements in paragraph 122 of IAS 1 – *Presentation of Financial Statements*. See Chapter 3 at 5.1.1.B.

The estimates of outcome and financial effect are determined by the judgement of the entity's management, supplemented by experience of similar transactions and, in some cases, reports from independent experts. The evidence considered will include any additional evidence provided by events after the reporting period. *[IAS 37.38]*. The standard suggests that there are various ways of dealing with the uncertainties surrounding the amount to be recognised as a provision. It mentions three, an expected value (or probability-weighted) method; the mid-point of the range of possible outcomes; and an estimate of the individual most likely outcome. An expected value approach would be appropriate when a large population of items is being measured, such as warranty costs. This is a statistical computation which weights the cost of all the various possible outcomes according to their probabilities, as illustrated in the following example taken from IAS 37. *[IAS 37.39]*.

Example 26.6: Calculation of expected value

An entity sells goods with a warranty under which customers are covered for the cost of repairs of any manufacturing defects that become apparent within the first six months after purchase. If minor defects were detected in all products sold, repair costs of £1 million would result. If major defects were detected in all products sold, repair costs of £4 million would result. The entity's past experience and future expectations indicate that, for the coming year, 75 per cent of the goods sold will have no defects, 20 per cent of the goods sold will have minor defects and 5 per cent of the goods sold will have major defects. In accordance with paragraph 24 of IAS 37 (see 3.1.2 above) an entity assesses the probability of a transfer for the warranty obligations as a whole.

The expected value of the cost of repairs is:

(75% of nil) + (20% of £1m) + (5% of £4m) = £400,000.

In a situation where there is a continuous range of possible outcomes and each point in that range is as likely as any other, IAS 37 requires that the mid-point of the range is used. *[IAS 37.39]*. This is not a particularly helpful way of setting out the requirement, as it does not make it clear what the principle is meant to be. The mid-point in this case represents the median as well as the expected value. The latter may have been what was intended, but the median could be equally well justified on the basis that it is 50% probable that at least this amount will be payable, while anything in excess of that constitutes a possible but not a probable liability, that should be disclosed rather than accrued. Interestingly, US GAAP has a different approach to this issue in relation to contingencies. FASB ASC Topic 450 – *Contingencies* – states that where a contingent loss could fall within a range of amounts then, if there is a best estimate within the range, it should be accrued, with the remainder noted as a contingent liability. However, if there is no best estimate then the lowest figure within the range should be accrued, with the remainder up to the maximum potential loss noted as a contingent liability.[6]

Where the obligation being measured relates to a single item, the standard suggests that the best estimate of the liability may be the individual most likely outcome. However, even in such a case, it notes that consideration should be given to other possible outcomes and where these are predominantly higher or mainly lower than the most likely outcome, the resultant 'best estimate' will be a higher or lower amount than the individual most likely outcome. To illustrate this, the standard gives an example of an entity that has to rectify a fault in a major plant that it has constructed for a customer. The most likely outcome is that the repair will succeed at the first attempt. However, a provision should be made for a larger amount if there is a significant chance that further attempts will be necessary. *[IAS 37.40]*.

As noted at 1.1 above, in January 2020, the IASB decided to add to its work plan a project to amend aspects of IAS 37. The scope of this project includes three targeted improvements to the Standard, one of which is to clarify which costs are included in the measurement of a provision.[7]

4.2 Dealing with risk and uncertainty in measuring a provision

It is clear from the definition of a provision as a liability of uncertain timing or amount that entities will have to deal with risk and uncertainty in estimating an appropriate measure of the obligation at the end of the reporting period. It is therefore interesting to consider how the measurement rules detailed in IAS 37 help entities achieve a faithful representation of the obligation in these circumstances. A faithful representation requires estimates that are neutral, that is, without bias. *[CF(2010) QC12, QC14]*. The *Conceptual Framework (2010)* warns against the use of conservatism or prudence in estimates because this is 'likely to lead to a bias'. It adds that the exercise of prudence can be counterproductive, in that the overstatement of liabilities in one period frequently leads to overstated financial performance in later periods, 'a result that cannot be described as prudent or neutral'. *[CF(2010) BC3.28]*. In March 2018, the IASB issued a revised *Conceptual Framework for Financial Reporting*. The revised framework became effective immediately for the IASB and IFRS Interpretations Committee and became effective from 1 January 2020 for entities that use the Conceptual Framework to develop accounting policies when no IFRS standard applies to a particular transaction. The revised Conceptual Framework also notes that a faithful representation requires estimates that are neutral, i.e. without bias. *[CF 2.13, 2.15]*.

The standard does not refer to neutrality as such; however, it does discuss the concept of risk and the need for exercising caution and care in making judgements under conditions of uncertainty. It states that 'the risks and uncertainties that inevitably surround many events and circumstances shall be taken into account in reaching the best estimate of a provision'. *[IAS 37.42]*. It refers to risk as being variability of outcome and suggests that a risk adjustment may increase the amount at which a liability is measured. *[IAS 37.43]*. Whilst the standard provides an example of a case in which the best estimate of an obligation might have to be larger than the individual most likely outcome, *[IAS 37.40]*, it gives no indication of how this increment should be determined. It warns that caution is needed in making judgements under conditions of uncertainty, so that expenses or liabilities are not understated. However, it says that uncertainty does not justify the creation of excessive provisions or a deliberate overstatement of liabilities. Accordingly, care is needed to avoid duplicating adjustments for risk and uncertainty, for example by estimating the costs of a particularly adverse outcome and then overestimating its probability. *[IAS 37.43]*. Any uncertainties surrounding the amount of the expenditure are to be disclosed (see 7.1 below). *[IAS 37.44]*.

The overall result of all this is somewhat confusing. Whilst a best estimate based solely on the expected value approach or the mid-point of a range addresses the uncertainties relating to there being a variety of possible outcomes, it does not fully reflect risk, because the actual outcome could still be higher or lower than the estimate. Therefore, the discussion on risk suggests that an additional adjustment should be made. However, apart from indicating that the result may be to increase the recognised liability and pointing out the need to avoid duplicating the effect of risk in estimates of cash flows and probability, *[IAS 37.43]*, it is not clear quite how this might be achieved. This leaves a certain amount of scope for variation in the estimation of provisions and is further complicated when the concept of risk is combined with considerations relating to the time value of money (see 4.3.2 below).

4.3 Discounting the estimated cash flows to a present value

The standard requires that where the effect of the time value of money is material, the amount of a provision should be the present value of the expenditures expected to be required to settle the obligation. *[IAS 37.45]*. The discount rate (or rates) to be used in arriving at the present value should be 'a pre-tax rate (or rates) that reflect(s) current market assessments of the time value of money and the risks specific to the liability. The discount rate(s) shall not reflect risks for which the future cash flow estimates have been adjusted.' *[IAS 37.47]*. However, it is worth noting that no discounting is required for provisions where the cash flows will not be sufficiently far into the future for discounting to have a material impact. *[IAS 37.46]*.

The main types of provision where the impact of discounting will be significant are those relating to decommissioning and other environmental restoration liabilities. IFRIC 1 addresses some of the issues relating to the use of discounting (in the context of provisions for obligations to dismantle, remove or restore items of property, plant and equipment, referred to as 'decommissioning, restoration and similar liabilities') which are discussed at 6.3.1 below.

4.3.1 Real versus nominal rate

IAS 37 does not indicate whether the discount rate should be a real discount rate or a nominal discount rate (although a real discount rate is referred to in Example 2 in Appendix D which illustrates the narrative disclosure for decommissioning costs). The discount rate to be used depends on whether:

(a) the future cash flows are expressed in current prices, in which case a real discount rate (which excludes the effects of general inflation) should be used; or

(b) the future cash flows are expressed in expected future prices, in which case a nominal discount rate (which includes a return to cover expected inflation) should be used.

Either alternative is acceptable, and these methods may produce the same figure for the initial present value of the provision. However, the effect of the unwinding of the discount may be different in each case (see 4.3.5 below).

4.3.2 Adjusting for risk and using a government bond rate

IAS 37 also requires that risk is taken into account in the calculation of a provision, but gives little guidance as to how this should be done. Where discounting is concerned, it merely says that the discount rate should not reflect risks for which the future cash flow estimates have been adjusted. *[IAS 37.47]*. One may use a discount rate that reflects the risk associated with the liability (a risk-adjusted rate). The following example, taken from the UK Accounting Standards Board's (ASB) Working Paper – *Discounting in Financial Reporting*,[8] shows how an entity might calculate such a risk adjusted rate.

Example 26.7: Calculation of a risk-adjusted rate[9]

A company has a provision for which the expected value of the cash outflow in three years' time is £150, and the risk-free rate (i.e. the nominal rate unadjusted for risk) is 5%. However, the possible outcomes from which the expected value has been determined lie within a range between £100 and £200. The company is risk averse and would settle instead for a certain payment of, say, £160 in three years' time rather than be exposed to the risk of the actual outcome being as high as £200. The effect of risk in calculating the present value can be expressed as either:

(a) discounting the risk-adjusted cash flow of £160 at the risk-free (unadjusted) rate of 5%, giving a present value of £138; or

(b) discounting the expected cash flow (which is unadjusted for risk) of £150 at a risk-adjusted rate that will give the present value of £138, i.e. a rate of 2.8%.

As can be seen from this example, the risk-adjusted discount rate is a lower rate than the unadjusted (risk-free) discount rate. This may seem counter-intuitive initially, because the experience of most borrowers is that banks and other lenders will charge a higher rate of interest on loans that are assessed to be higher risk to the lender. However, in the case of a provision a risk premium is being suffered to eliminate the possibility of the actual cost being higher (thereby capping a liability), whereas in the case of a loan receivable a premium is required to compensate the lender for taking on the risk of not recovering its full value (setting a floor for the value of the lender's financial asset). In both cases the actual cash flows incurred by the paying entity are higher to reflect a premium for risk. In other words, the discount rate for an asset is increased to reflect the risk of recovering less and the discount rate for a liability is reduced to reflect the risk of paying more.

A problem with changing the discount rate to account for risk is that this adjusted rate is a theoretical rate, as it is unlikely that there would be a market assessment of the risks specific to the liability alone. *[IAS 37.47]*. However the lower discount rate in the above example is consistent with the premise that a risk-adjusted liability should be higher than a liability without accounting for the risk that the actual settlement amount is different to the estimate. *[IAS 37.43]*. It is also difficult to see how a risk-adjusted rate could be obtained in practice. In the above example, it was obtained only by reverse-engineering; it was already known that the net present value of a risk-adjusted liability was £138, so the risk-adjusted rate was just the discount rate applied to unadjusted cash flow of £150 to give that result.

IAS 37 offers an alternative approach – instead of using a risk-adjusted discount rate, the estimated future cash flows themselves can be adjusted for risk. *[IAS 37.47]*. This does of course present the problem of how to adjust the cash flows for risk (see 4.2 above). However, this may be easier than attempting to risk-adjust the discount rate.

For the purposes of discounting post-employment benefit obligations, IAS 19 requires the discount rate to be determined by reference to market yields at the end of the reporting period on high quality corporate bonds (although in countries where there is no deep market in such bonds, the market yields on government bonds should be used). [IAS 19.83]. Although IAS 19 indicates that this discount rate reflects the time value of money (but not the actuarial or investment risk), [IAS 19.84], we do not believe it is appropriate to use the yield on a high quality corporate bond for determining a risk-free rate to be used in discounting provisions under IAS 37. Accordingly, in our view, where an entity is using a risk-free discount rate for the purposes of calculating a provision under IAS 37, that rate should be based on a government bond rate with a similar currency and remaining term as the provision. It follows that because a risk-adjusted rate is always lower than the risk-free rate, an entity cannot justify the discounting of a provision at a rate that is higher than a government bond rate with a similar currency and term to the provision.

Whichever method of reflecting risk is adopted, IAS 37 emphasises that care must be taken that the effect of risk is not double-counted by inclusion in both the cash flows and the discount rate. [IAS 37.47].

In recent years, government bond rates have been more volatile as markets have changed rates to reflect (among other factors) heightened perceptions of sovereign debt risk. In some cases, government bond yields may be negative. The question has therefore arisen whether government bond rates, at least in certain jurisdictions, should continue to be regarded as the default measure of a risk-free discount rate. Whilst the current volatility in rates has highlighted the fact that no debt (even government debt) is totally risk free, the challenge is to find a more reliable measure as an alternative. Any adjustment to the government bond rate to 'remove' the estimate of sovereign debt risk is conceptually flawed, as it not possible to isolate one component of risk from all the other variables that influence the setting of an interest rate. Another approach might be to apply some form of average bond rate over a period of 3, 6 or 12 months to mitigate the volatility inherent in applying the spot rate at the period end. However, this is clearly inappropriate given the requirements in IAS 37 to determine the best estimate of an obligation by reference to the expenditure required to settle it 'at the end of the reporting period', [IAS 37.36], and to determine the discount rate on the basis of 'current market assessments' of the time value of money. [IAS 37.47].

With 'risk' being a measure of potential variability in returns, it remains the case that in most countries a government bond will be subject to the lowest level of variability in that jurisdiction. As such, in most countries it remains the most suitable of all the observable measures of the time value of money in a particular country. Where government bond rates are negative or, more likely, result in a negative discount rate once adjusted for risk, we believe that it is not appropriate to apply a floor of zero to the discount rate as this would result in an understatement of the liability. As discussed above, and at 4.3.1 above, IAS 37 offers various approaches to determining an appropriate discount rate. It may sometimes be the case that one or more of the allowed approaches result in a negative discount rate whereas the application of an alternative permitted approach would not. In order to avoid some of the presentational difficulties associated with a negative discount rate, entities faced with a negative real discount rate before risk adjustment may wish to consider the alternative approach of discounting expected future cash flows expressed in future prices, at a nominal discount rate (see 4.3.1 above), if the nominal rate is not negative. Similarly, entities that are faced with a negative risk-adjusted discount rate only because of risk adjustment (i.e. where risk free rates themselves are not negative) may wish to adopt the alternative approach of adjusting the estimated future cash flows to reflect the risks associated with the liability, rather than risk-adjusting the discount rate.

A difficulty that can arise in certain countries is finding a government bond with a similar term to the provision, for example when measuring a decommissioning provision expected to be settled in 30 years in a country where there are no government bonds with a term exceeding 10 years. In such cases, the government bond rate might be adjusted and the techniques adopted by actuaries for measuring retirement obligations with long maturities, that involve extrapolating current market rates along a yield curve, *[IAS 19.86]*, might be considered. The difficulties of finding an appropriate discount rate in the context of retirement benefit obligations are discussed in Chapter 35 at 7.6.

4.3.3 Own credit risk

IAS 37 does not address whether an entity's own credit risk should be considered a risk specific to a liability when determining a risk-adjusted discount rate. In March 2011, the Interpretations Committee decided not to take to its agenda a request for interpretation of the phrase 'the risks specific to the liability' and whether this means that an entity's own credit risk should be excluded from any adjustments made to the discount rate used to measure liabilities. In doing so, the Interpretations Committee acknowledged that IAS 37 is not explicit on the question of own credit risk; but understood that the predominant practice was to exclude it for the reason that credit risk is generally viewed as a risk of the entity rather than a risk specific to the liability.[10]

Whether own credit risk is considered a risk specific to a liability may depend, at least in part, on the way in which an entity measures a provision (i.e. how an entity determines the best estimate of the expenditure required to settle the obligation). As discussed at 4.1 above, the measurement objective in IAS 37 is not precise, and the term 'best estimate' may be interpreted in different ways. For example, an entity may determine the best estimate by assuming that the obligation will be cash settled by negotiation with the party to whom the obligation is owed. In this case, own credit risk might be considered relevant if the party to whom the obligation is owed would be willing to negotiate a lower settlement amount if the entity risks defaulting in the future. If an entity has exercised significant judgement in determining the best estimate of the expenditure required to settle an obligation, and whether own credit risk is taken into account, consideration should be given to the disclosure requirements in paragraph 122 of IAS 1. See Chapter 3 at 5.1.1.B.

As noted at 1.1 above, in January 2020, the IASB decided to add to its work plan a project to amend aspects of IAS 37. The scope of this project includes three targeted improvements to the Standard, one of which is to specify whether the rate at which an entity discounts a provision should reflect the entity's own credit risk.[11]

4.3.4 Pre-tax discount rate

Since IAS 37 requires provisions to be measured before tax, it follows that cash flows should be discounted at a pre-tax discount rate. *[IAS 37.47]*. No further explanation of this is given in the standard.

This is probably because, in reality, the use of a pre-tax discount rate will be most common. Supposing, for example, that the risk-free rate of return is being used, then the discount rate used will be a government bond rate. This rate will be obtained gross. Thus, the idea of trying to determine a pre-tax rate (for example by obtaining a required post-tax rate of return and adjusting it for the tax consequences of different cash flows) will seldom be relevant.

The calculation is illustrated in the following example.

Example 26.8: Use of discounting and tax effect

It is estimated that the settlement of an environmental provision will give rise to a gross cash outflow of £500,000 in three years' time. The gross interest rate on a government bond maturing in three years' time is 6%. The tax rate is 30%.

The net present value of the provision is £419,810 (£500,000 × 1 ÷ $(1.06)^3$). Hence, a provision of £419,810 should be booked in the statement of financial position. A corresponding deferred tax asset of £125,943 (30% of £419,810) would be set up if it met the criteria for recognition in IAS 12 (see Chapter 33 at 7.4).

4.3.5 Unwinding of the discount

IAS 37 indicates that where discounting is used, the carrying amount of a provision increases in each period to reflect the passage of time, and that this increase is recognised as a borrowing cost. *[IAS 37.60]*. This is the only guidance that the standard gives on the unwinding of the discount. IFRIC 1 in relation to provisions for decommissioning, restoration and similar liabilities requires that the periodic unwinding of the discount is recognised in profit or loss as a finance cost as it occurs. The Interpretations Committee concluded that the unwinding of the discount is not a borrowing cost for the purposes of IAS 23 – *Borrowing Costs* – and thus cannot be capitalised under that standard. *[IFRIC 1.8]*. It noted that IAS 23 addresses funds borrowed specifically for the purpose of obtaining a particular asset and agreed that a decommissioning liability does not fall within this description since it does not reflect funds borrowed. Accordingly, the Interpretations Committee concluded that the unwinding of the discount is not a borrowing cost as defined in IAS 23. *[IFRIC 1.BC26]*.

However, there is no discussion of the impact that the original selection of discount rate can have on its unwinding, that is, the selection of real versus nominal rates, and risk-free versus risk-adjusted rates and the fact that these different discount rates will unwind differently. This is best illustrated by way of an example.

Example 26.9: Effect on future profits of choosing a real or nominal discount rate

A provision is required to be set up for an expected cash outflow of €100,000 (estimated at current prices), payable in three years' time. The appropriate nominal discount rate is 7.5%, and inflation is estimated at 5%. If the provision is discounted using the nominal rate, the expected cash outflow has to reflect future prices. Accordingly, if prices increase at the rate of inflation, the cash outflow will be €115,762 (€100,000 × 1.05^3). The net present value of €115,762, discounted at 7.5%, is €93,184 (€115,762 × 1 ÷ $(1.075)^3$). If all assumptions remain valid throughout the three-year period, the movement in the provision would be as follows:

	Undiscounted cash flows	Provision
	€	€
Year 0	115,762	93,184
Unwinding of discount (€93,184 × 0.075)		6,989
Revision to estimate		–
Year 1	115,762	100,173
Unwinding of discount (€100,173 × 0.075)		7,513
Revision to estimate		–
Year 2	115,762	107,686
Unwinding of discount (€107,686 × 0.075)		8,076
Revision to estimate		–
Year 3	115,762	115,762

If the provision is calculated based on the expected cash outflow of €100,000 (estimated at current prices), then it needs to be discounted using a real discount rate. This may be thought to be 2.5%, being the difference between the nominal rate of 7.5% and the inflation rate of 5%. However, it is more accurately calculated as 2.381%, being (1.075 ÷ 1.05) – 1. Accordingly, the net present value of €100,000, discounted at 2.381%, is €93,184 (€100,000 × 1 ÷ (1.02381)^3), the same as the calculation using future prices discounted at the nominal rate.

If all assumptions remain valid throughout the three-year period, the movement in the provision comprises both the unwinding of the discount and the increase in the level of current prices used to determine the estimate of cost, as follows:

	Undiscounted cash flows	Provision
	€	€
Year 0	100,000	93,184
Unwinding of discount (€93,184 × 0.02381)		2,219
Revision to estimate (€100,000 × 0.05)	5,000	4,770
Year 1	105,000	100,173
Unwinding of discount (€100,173 × 0.02381)		2,385
Revision to estimate (€105,000 × 0.05)	5,250	5,128
Year 2	110,250	107,686
Unwinding of discount (€107,686 × 0.02381)		2,564
Revision to estimate (€110,250 × 0.05)	5,512	5,512
Year 3	115,762	115,762

Although the total expense in each year is the same under either method, what will be different is the allocation of the change in provision between operating costs (assuming the original provision was treated as an operating expense) and finance charges. It can be seen from the second table in the above example that using the real discount rate will give rise to a much lower finance charge each year. However, this does not lead to a lower provision in the statement of financial position at the end of each year. Provisions have to be revised annually to reflect the current best estimate of the obligation. *[IAS 37.59]*. Thus, the provision in the above example at the end of each year needs to be adjusted to reflect current prices at that time (and any other adjustments that arise from changes in the estimate of the provision), as well as being adjusted for the unwinding of the discount. For example, the revised provision at the end of Year 1 is €100,173, being €105,000 discounted for two years at 2.381%. After allowing for the unwinding of the discount, this required an additional provision of €4,770. Alternatively, entities may take the view that the amount included as a borrowing cost should be based on the nominal discount rate. The basis for this argument is that IAS 37 requires the increase in a provision due to the passage of time to be recognised as a borrowing cost [IAS 37.60] and inflation, which is reflected in the nominal rate but not the real rate, is part of the time value of money.

A more significant difference will arise where the recognition of the original provision is included as part of the cost of property, plant or equipment, rather than as an expense, such as when a decommissioning provision is recognised. In that case, using a real discount rate will result initially in a lower charge to the income statement, since under IFRIC 1 any revision to the estimate of the provision is not taken to the income statement but is treated as an adjustment to the carrying value of the related asset, which is then depreciated prospectively over the remaining life of the asset (see 6.3.1 below).

A similar issue arises with the option of using the risk-free or the risk-adjusted discount rate. However, this is a more complex problem, because it is not clear what to do with the risk-adjustment built into the provision. This is illustrated in the following example.

Example 26.10: Effect on future profits of choosing a risk-free or risk-adjusted rate

A company is required to make a provision for which the estimated value of the cash outflow in three years' time is £150, when the risk-free rate (i.e. the rate unadjusted for risk) is 5%. However, the possible outcomes from which the expected value has been determined lie within a range between £100 and £200. The reporting entity is risk averse and would settle instead for a certain payment of, say, £160 in three years' time rather than be exposed to the risk of the actual outcome being as high as £200. The measurement options to account for risk can be expressed as either:

(a) discounting the risk-adjusted cash flow of £160 at the risk-free (unadjusted) rate of 5%, giving a present value of £138; or

(b) discounting the expected cash flow (which is unadjusted for risk) of £150 at a risk-adjusted rate that will give the present value of £138, i.e. a rate of 2.8%.

If no changes in estimate were made to the provision during the three-year period, alternative (a) will unwind to give an overall finance charge of £22 and a final provision of £160. Alternative (b) will unwind to give an overall finance charge of £12 and a final provision of £150.

In this example, the unwinding of different discount rates gives rise to different provisions. The difference of £10 (£22 – £12) relates to the risk adjustment that has been made to the provision. However, as the actual date of settlement comes closer, the estimates of the range of possible outcomes (and accordingly the expected value of the outflow) and the premium the entity would accept for certainty would need to be re-estimated. As such, the effect of any initial difference related to the decision to apply a risk-free or risk-adjusted rate will be lost in the other estimation adjustments that would be made over time.

In circumstances where a provision has been discounted using a negative discount rate (see 4.3.2 above), entities will need to give some consideration to how the unwinding of the discount should be presented in the statement of comprehensive income. The presentation of income and expense resulting from negative interest has been discussed by the Interpretations Committee in the context of financial instruments. Whilst that topic was not taken on to the Interpretations Committee's agenda, the Committee noted in their agenda decision that the expense arising on a financial asset because of a negative interest rate should not be presented as interest revenue, but in an appropriate expense classification.[12] Whilst negative interest rates on financial liabilities were not explicitly addressed in the agenda decision, the Interpretations Committee noted during discussions that an inflow of economic benefits arising from a liability cannot be characterised as revenue.[13] In our view, similar considerations are appropriate to the presentation of the unwinding of the discount on a provision that has been discounted using a negative nominal discount rate.

4.3.6 The effect of changes in interest rates on the discount rate applied

The standard requires the discount rate to reflect current market assessments of the time value of money. *[IAS 37.47]*. This means that where interest rates change, the provision should be recalculated on the basis of revised interest rates (see Example 26.11 below).

Any revision in the interest rate will give rise to an adjustment to the carrying value of the provision in addition to the unwinding of the previously estimated discount. The standard requires these movements to be disclosed in the notes to the financial statements (see 7.1 below). *[IAS 37.84(e)]*. However, the standard does not explicitly say how the effect of changes in interest rates should be classified in the income statement. We believe that this element should be treated separately from the effect of the passage of time, with only the charge for unwinding of the discount being classified as a finance cost. Any adjustment to the provision as a result of revising the discount rate is a change in accounting estimate, as defined in IAS 8 – *Accounting Policies, Changes in Accounting Estimates and Errors* (see Chapter 3 at 4.5). Accordingly, it should be reflected in the line item of the income statement to which the expense establishing the provision was originally taken and not as a component of the finance cost. Indeed, this is the approach required by IFRIC 1 in relation to provisions for decommissioning, restoration and similar liabilities in relation to assets measured using the cost model (see 6.3.1 below). However, in that case the original provision gives rise to an asset rather than an expense, so any subsequent adjustment is not included in profit or loss, *[IAS 8.36]*, but added to or deducted from the cost of the asset to which it relates. *[IFRIC 1.5]*. The adjusted depreciable amount of the asset is then depreciated prospectively over its remaining useful life. *[IFRIC 1.7]*. Nevertheless, the effect is distinguished from the unwinding of the discount.

In addition, the standard gives no specific guidance on how or when this adjustment should be made. For example, it is unclear whether the new discount rate should be applied during the year or just at the year-end, and whether the rate should be applied to the new estimate of the provision or the old estimate. IFRIC 1 implies that the finance cost is adjusted prospectively from the date on which the liability is remeasured. Example 1 to IFRIC 1 states that if the change in the liability had resulted from a change in discount rate, instead of a change in the estimated cash flows, the change would still have been reflected in the carrying value of the related asset, but next year's finance cost would have reflected the new discount rate. *[IFRIC 1.IE5]*. This conclusion is consistent with the requirement in IAS 37 for the value of a provision to reflect the best estimate of the expenditure required to settle the obligation as at the end of the reporting period, *[IAS 37.36]*, as illustrated in the following example.

Example 26.11: Accounting for the effect of changes in the discount rate

A provision is required to be set up for an expected cash outflow of €100,000 (estimated at current prices), payable in three years' time. The appropriate nominal discount rate is 7.5%, and inflation is estimated at 5%. At future prices the cash outflow will be €115,762 (€100,000 × 1.05³). The net present value of €115,762, discounted at 7.5%, is €93,184 (€115,762 × 1 ÷ 1.075³).

At the end of Year 2, all assumptions remain valid, except it is determined that a current market assessment of the time value of money and the risks specific to the liability would require a decrease in the discount rate to 6.5%. Accordingly, at the end of Year 2, the revised net present value of €115,762, discounted at 6.5%, is €108,697 (€115,762 ÷ 1.065).

The movement in the provision would be reflected as follows:

	Undiscounted cash flows	Provision
	€	€
Year 0	115,762	93,184
Unwinding of discount (€93,184 × 0.075)		6,989
Revision to estimate		–
Year 1	115,762	100,173
Unwinding of discount (€100,173 × 0.075)		7,513
	115,762	107,686
Revision to estimate (€108,697 – €107,686)		1,011
Year 2	115,762	108,697
Unwinding of discount (€108,697 × 0.065)		7,065
Revision to estimate		–
Year 3	115,762	115,762

In Year 2, the finance charge is based on the previous estimate of the discount rate and the revision to the estimate of the provision would be charged to the same line item in the income statement that was used to establish the provision of €93,184 at the start of Year 1.

Where market rates of interest are more volatile, entities may decide to reassess the applicable discount rate for a provision during an annual reporting period. Equally, it would be appropriate to revise this assessment as at the end of any interim reporting period during the financial year to the extent that the impact is material.

4.4 Anticipating future events that may affect the estimate of cash flows

The standard states that 'future events that may affect the amount required to settle an obligation shall be reflected in the amount of a provision where there is sufficient objective evidence that they will occur'. *[IAS 37.48]*. The types of future events that the standard has in mind are advances in technology and changes in legislation.

The requirement for objective evidence means that it is not appropriate to reduce the best estimate of future cash flows simply by assuming that a completely new technology will be developed before the liability is required to be settled. There will need to be sufficient objective evidence that such future developments are likely. For example, an entity may believe that the cost of cleaning up a site at the end of its life will be reduced by future changes in technology. The amount recognised has to reflect a reasonable expectation of technically qualified, objective observers, taking account of all available evidence as to the technology that will be available at the time of the clean-up. Thus it is appropriate to include, for example, expected cost reductions associated with increased experience in applying existing technology or the expected cost of applying existing technology to a larger or more complex clean-up operation than has previously been carried out. [IAS 37.49].

Similarly, if new legislation is to be anticipated, there will need to be evidence both of what the legislation will demand and whether it is virtually certain to be enacted and implemented. In many cases sufficient objective evidence will not exist until the new legislation is enacted. [IAS 37.50].

These requirements are most likely to impact provisions for liabilities that will be settled some distance in the future, such as decommissioning costs (see 6.3 below).

4.5 Provisions that will be settled in a currency other than the entity's functional currency

Entities may sometimes expect to settle an obligation in a currency other than their functional currency. In such cases, the provision would be measured in the currency in which settlement is expected and then discounted using a discount rate appropriate for that currency. This approach is consistent with that required by IAS 36 – *Impairment of Assets* – for foreign currency cash flows in value in use calculations. [IAS 36.54]. The present value would be translated into functional currency at the spot exchange rate at the date at which the provision is recognised. [IAS 21.21]. If the provision is considered to be a monetary liability, i.e. it is expected to be paid in a fixed or determinable number of units of currency, [IAS 21.8], it would thereafter be retranslated at the spot exchange rate at each reporting date. [IAS 21.23]. In most cases, exchange differences arising on provisions will be taken to profit or loss in the period in which they arise, in accordance with the general rule for monetary items in IAS 21 – *The Effects of Changes in Foreign Exchange Rates*. [IAS 21.28].

Exchange differences arising on decommissioning provisions recognised under IAS 37 and capitalised as part of the cost of an asset under IAS 16 are considered in Chapter 43 at 10.2.

4.6 Reimbursements, insurance and other recoveries from third parties

In some circumstances an entity is able to look to a third party to reimburse part of the costs required to settle a provision or to pay the amounts directly to a third party. Examples are insurance contracts, indemnity clauses and suppliers' warranties. [IAS 37.55]. A reimbursement asset is recognised only when it is virtually certain to be received if the entity settles the obligation. The asset cannot be greater than the amount of the provision. No 'netting off' is allowed in the statement of financial position, with any asset classified separately from any provision. [IAS 37.53]. However, the expense relating to a provision can be shown in the income statement net of reimbursement. [IAS 37.54]. This means that if an entity has insurance cover in relation to a specific potential obligation, this is treated as a reimbursement right under IAS 37. It is not appropriate to record no provision (where the recognition criteria in the standard are met) on the basis that the entity's net exposure is expected to be zero.

The main area of concern with these requirements is whether the 'virtually certain' criterion that needs to be applied to the corresponding asset might mean that some reimbursements will not be capable of recognition at all. For items such as insurance contracts, this may not be an issue, as entities will probably be able to confirm the existence of cover for the obligation in question and accordingly be able to demonstrate that a recovery on an insurance contract is virtually certain if the entity is required to settle the obligation. Of course, it may be more difficult in complex situations for an entity to confirm it has cover against any loss. For other types of reimbursement, it may be more difficult to establish that recovery is virtually certain.

Except when an obligation is determined to be joint and several (see 4.7 below), any form of net presentation in the statement of financial position is prohibited. This is because the entity would remain liable for the whole cost if the third party failed to pay for any reason, for example as a result of the third party's insolvency. In such situations, the provision should be made gross and any reimbursement should be treated as a separate asset (but only when it is virtually certain that the reimbursement will be received if the entity settles the obligation). *[IAS 37.56]*.

If the entity has no liability in the event that the third party cannot pay, then these costs are excluded from the estimate of the provision altogether because, by its very nature, there is no liability. *[IAS 37.57]*.

In contrast, where an entity is assessing an onerous contract, it is common for entities to apply what looks like a net approach. However, because an onerous contract provision relates to the excess of the unavoidable costs over the expected economic benefits, *[IAS 37.68]*, there is no corresponding asset to be recognised. This is discussed further at 6.2 below.

4.7 Joint and several liability

It is interesting to contrast the approach of IAS 37 to reimbursements with the case where an entity is jointly and severally liable for an obligation. Joint and several liability arises when a number of entities are liable for a single obligation (for example, to damages), both individually and collectively. The holder of the obligation in these circumstances can collect the entire amount from any single member of the group or from any and all of the members in various amounts until the liability is settled in full. Even when the members have an agreement between themselves as to how the total obligation should be divided, each member remains liable to make good any deficiency on the part of the others. This situation is different from proportionate liability, where individual members of a group might be required to bear a percentage of the total liability, but without any obligation to make good any shortfall by another member. Joint and several liability can be established in a contract, by a court judgement or under legislation.

An entity that is jointly and severally liable recognises only its own share of the obligation, based on the amount it is probable that the entity will pay. The remainder that is expected to be met by other parties is treated only as a contingent liability. *[IAS 37.29, 58]*.

The fact that the other third parties in this situation have a direct (albeit shared) obligation for the past event itself, rather than only a contractual relationship with the entity, is enough of a difference in circumstances to allow a form of net determination of the amount to recognise. Arguably, the economic position is no different, because the entity is exposed to further loss in the event that the third parties are unable or unwilling to pay. However, IAS 37 does not treat joint and several liability in the same way as reimbursement, which would have required a liability to be set up for the whole amount with a corresponding asset recognised for the amount expected to be met by other parties.

4.8 Provisions are not reduced for gains on disposal of related assets

IAS 37 states that gains from the expected disposal of assets should not be taken into account in measuring a provision, even if the expected disposal is closely linked to the event giving rise to the provision. Such gains should be recognised at the time specified by the Standard dealing with the assets concerned. *[IAS 37.51-52]*. This is likely to be of particular relevance in relation to restructuring provisions (see 6.1.4 below). However, it may also apply in other situations. Extract 26.3 at 6.3 below illustrates an example of a company excluding gains from the expected disposal of assets in determining its provision for decommissioning costs.

4.9 Changes and uses of provisions

After recognition, a provision will be re-estimated, used and released over the period up to the eventual determination of a settlement amount for the obligation. IAS 37 requires that provisions should be reviewed at the end of each reporting period and adjusted to reflect the current best estimate. If it is no longer probable that an outflow of resources embodying economic benefits will be required to settle the obligation, the provision should be reversed. *[IAS 37.59]*. Where discounting is applied, the carrying amount of a provision increases in each period to reflect the passage of time. This increase is recognised as a borrowing cost. *[IAS 37.60]*. As discussed at 4.3.5 above, the periodic unwinding of the discount is recognised as a finance cost in the income statement, and it is not a borrowing cost capable of being capitalised under IAS 23. *[IFRIC 1.8]*.

The standard does not allow provisions to be redesignated or otherwise used for expenditures for which the provision was not originally recognised. *[IAS 37.61]*. In such circumstances, a new provision is created and the amount no longer needed is reversed, as to do otherwise would conceal the impact of two different events. *[IAS 37.62]*. This means that the questionable practice of charging costs against a provision that was set up for a different purpose is specifically prohibited.

4.10 Changes in contingent liabilities recognised in a business combination

In a business combination, the usual requirements of IAS 37 do not apply and the acquirer recognises a liability at the acquisition date for those contingent liabilities of the acquiree that represent a present obligation arising as a result of a past event and in respect of which the fair value can be measured reliably. *[IFRS 3.23]*. After initial recognition, and until the liability is settled, cancelled or expires, the acquirer measures the contingent liability recognised in a business combination at the higher of:

(a) the amount that would be recognised in accordance with IAS 37; and

(b) the amount initially recognised less, if appropriate, the cumulative amount of income recognised in accordance with the principles of IFRS 15. *[IFRS 3.56]*.

This requirement does not apply to contracts accounted for in accordance with IFRS 9. See Chapter 9 at 5.6.1.B.

This requirement prevents the immediate release to post acquisition profit of any contingency recognised in a business combination.

5 CASES IN WHICH NO PROVISION SHOULD BE RECOGNISED

IAS 37 sets out three particular cases in which the recognition of a provision is prohibited. They are: future operating losses, repairs and maintenance of owned assets and staff training costs. The Interpretations Committee has also considered repeated requests relating to obligations arising on entities operating in a rate-regulated environment. The Interpretations Committee concluded that there is no justification for the recognition of a special regulatory liability, although IFRS 14 – *Regulatory Deferral Accounts* – provides some relief for first-time adopters of IFRS who have recognised regulatory deferral account balances under their previous GAAP (see 5.4 below). The common theme in these cases is that the potential obligation does not exist independently of an entity's future actions. In other words, the entity is able to change the future conduct of its business in a way that avoids the future expenditure. Only those obligations that exist independently of an entity's future actions are recognised as provisions. *[IAS 37.19]*. This principle is also relevant to determining the timing of recognition of a provision, whereby no liability is recognised until the obligation cannot otherwise be avoided by the entity. Examples include those arising from participation in a particular market under IFRIC 6 (see 6.7 below) and an obligation for levies imposed by government under IFRIC 21 (see 6.8 below).

5.1 Future operating losses

IAS 37 explicitly states that 'provisions shall not be recognised for future operating losses'. *[IAS 37.63]*. This is because such losses do not meet the definition of a liability and the general recognition criteria of the standard. *[IAS 37.64]*. In particular there is no present obligation as a result of a past event. Such costs should be left to be recognised as they occur in the future in the same way as future profits.

However, it would be wrong to assume that this requirement has effectively prevented the effect of future operating losses from being anticipated, because they are sometimes recognised as a result of requirements in another standard, either in the measurement of an asset of the entity or to prevent inappropriate recognition of revenue. For example:

- under IAS 2 – *Inventories* – inventories are written down to the extent that they will not be recovered from future revenues, rather than leaving the non-recovery to show up as future operating losses (see Chapter 22 at 3.3); and

- under IAS 36 impairment is assessed on the basis of the present value of future operating cash flows, meaning that the effect of not only future operating losses but also sub-standard operating profits will be recognised (see Chapter 20). IAS 37 specifically makes reference to the fact that an expectation of future operating losses may be an indication that certain assets are impaired. *[IAS 37.65]*.

This is therefore a rather more complex issue than IAS 37 acknowledges. Indeed, IAS 37 itself has to navigate closely the dividing line between the general prohibition of the recognition of future losses and the recognition of contractual or constructive obligations that are expected to give rise to losses in future periods.

5.2 Repairs and maintenance of owned assets

Repairs and maintenance provisions in respect of owned assets are generally prohibited under IAS 37. Under the standard, the following principles apply:

(a) provisions are recognised only for obligations existing independently of the entity's future actions (i.e. the future conduct of its business) and in cases where an entity can avoid future expenditure by its future actions, for example by changing its method of operation, it has no present obligation; *[IAS 37.19]*

(b) financial statements deal with an entity's position at the end of the reporting period and not its possible position in the future. Therefore, no provision is recognised for costs that need to be incurred to operate in the future; *[IAS 37.18]* and

(c) for an event to be an obligating event, the entity can have no realistic alternative to settling the obligation created by the event. *[IAS 37.17]*.

These principles are applied strictly in the case of an obligation to incur repairs and maintenance costs in the future, even when this expenditure is substantial, distinct from what may be regarded as routine maintenance and essential to the continuing operations of the entity, such as a major refit or refurbishment of the asset. This is illustrated by two examples in an appendix to the standard.

Example 26.12: Prohibition on maintenance provisions relating to owned assets

Scenario 1: Re-lining costs of a furnace

An entity operates a furnace, the lining of which needs to be replaced every five years for technical reasons. At the end of the reporting period, the lining has been in use for three years. In these circumstances, a provision for the cost of replacing the lining is not recognised because, at the end of the reporting period, no obligation to replace the lining exists independently of the entity's future actions. Even the intention to incur the expenditure depends upon the entity deciding to continue operating the furnace or to replace the lining. Instead of a provision being recognised, the initial cost of the lining is treated as a significant part of the furnace asset and depreciated over a period of five years. *[IAS 16.43]*. The re-lining costs are then capitalised when incurred and depreciated over the next five years. *[IAS 37 IE Example 11A]*.

Scenario 2: Overhaul costs of an aircraft

An airline is required by law to overhaul its aircraft once every three years. Even with the legal requirement to perform the overhaul, there is no obligating event until the three year period has elapsed. As with Scenario 1, no obligation exists independently of the entity's future actions. The entity could avoid the cost of the overhaul by selling the aircraft before the three year period has elapsed. Instead of a provision being recognised, the overhaul cost is identified as a separate part of the aircraft asset under IAS 16 and is depreciated over three years. *[IAS 37 IE Example 11B]*.

Entities might try to argue that a repairs and maintenance provision should be recognised on the basis that there is a clear intention to incur the expenditure at the appointed time and that this means it is more likely than not, as at the end of the reporting period, that an outflow of resources will occur. However, the application of the three principles noted above, particularly that an entity should not provide for future operating costs, make an entity's intentions irrelevant. In the example above, recognition was not allowed because the entity could do all manner of things to avoid the obligation, including selling the asset, however unlikely that might be in the context of the entity's business or in terms of the relative cost of replacement as compared to repair. The existence of a legal requirement, probably resulting in the aircraft being grounded, was still not enough. This detachment from intention or even commercial reality, regarded by some as extreme, is also exhibited in the Interpretations Committee's approach to the recognition of levies imposed by government under IFRIC 21 (see 6.8 below).

The effect of the prohibition on setting up provisions for repairs obviously has an impact on presentation in the statement of financial position. It may not always, however, have as much impact on the statement of comprehensive income. This is because it is stated in the examples that depreciation would be adjusted to take account of the repairs. For example, in the case of the furnace lining, the lining should be depreciated over five years in advance of its expected repair. Similarly, in the case of the aircraft overhaul, the example in the standard states that an amount equivalent to the expected maintenance costs is depreciated over three years. The result of this is that the depreciation charge recognised in profit or loss over the life of the component of the asset requiring regular repair may be equivalent to that which would previously have arisen from the combination of depreciation and a provision for repair. This is the way IAS 16 requires entities to account for significant parts of an item of property, plant and equipment which have different useful lives (see Chapter 18 at 5.1). *[IAS 16.44]*.

5.3 Staff training costs

In the normal course of business it is unlikely that provisions for staff training costs would be permissible, because it would normally contravene the general prohibition in the standard on the recognition of provisions for future operating costs. *[IAS 37.18]*. In the context of a restructuring, IAS 37 identifies staff retraining as an ineligible cost because it relates to the future conduct of the business. *[IAS 37.81]*. Example 26.2 at 3.1.1 above reproduces an example in the standard where the government introduces changes to the income tax system, such that an entity in the financial services sector needs to retrain a large proportion of its administrative and sales workforce in order to ensure continued compliance with financial services regulation. The standard argues that there is no present obligation until the actual training has taken place and so no provision should be recognised. We also note that in many cases the need to incur training costs is not only future operating expenditure but also fails the 'existing independently of an entity's future actions' criterion, *[IAS 37.19]*, in that the cost could be avoided by the entity, for example, if it withdrew from that market or hired new staff who were already appropriately qualified.

This example again illustrates how important it is to properly understand the nature of any potential 'constructive obligation' or 'obligating event' and to determine separately its financial effect in relation to past transactions and events on the one hand and in relation to the future operation of the business on the other. Otherwise, it can be easy to mistakenly argue that a provision is required, such as for training costs to ensure that staff comply with new legal requirements, on the basis that the entity has a constructive obligation to ensure staff are appropriately skilled to adequately meet the needs of its customers. However, the obligation, constructive or not, declared or not, relates to the entity's future conduct, is a future cost of operation and is therefore ineligible for recognition under the standard until the training takes place.

5.4 Rate-regulated activities

In many countries, the provision of utilities (e.g. water, natural gas or electricity) to consumers is regulated by the national government. Regulations differ between countries but often regulators operate a cost-plus system under which a utility provider is allowed to make a fixed return on investment. Under certain national GAAPs, an entity may account for the effects of regulation by recognising a 'regulatory asset' that reflects the increase in future prices approved by the regulator or a 'regulatory liability' that reflects a requirement from the regulator to reduce tariffs or improve services so as to return the benefit of earlier excess profits to customers. This issue has for a long time been a matter of significant interest as entities in those countries adopt IFRS, because the recognition of these regulatory assets and liabilities is prohibited under IFRS. Just as the ability to charge higher prices for goods services to be rendered in the future does not meet the definition of an intangible asset in IAS 38 – *Intangible Assets* (see Chapter 17 at 11.1), the requirement to charge a lower price for the delivery of goods and services in the future does not meet the definition of a past obligating event, or a liability, in IAS 37.

A liability is defined in IAS 37 as 'a present obligation of the entity arising from past events, the settlement of which is expected to result in an outflow from the entity of resources embodying economic benefits'. *[IAS 37.10]*. The return to customers of amounts mandated by a regulator depends on future events including:

- future rendering of services;
- future volumes of output (generally consisting of utilities such as water or electricity) consumed by users; and
- the continuation of regulation.

Similar considerations apply to actions that a regulator may require entities to complete in the future, such as an obligation to invest in equipment to improve efficiency. Other than decommissioning obligations (see 6.3 below), such items do not meet the definition of a liability because there needs to be a present obligation at the end of the reporting period before a liability can be recognised. Such a regulatory obligation that fails to qualify for recognition under IAS 37 is illustrated in Extract 26.1 at 3.1.1 above.

Whilst the requirements of IAS 37 and the *Conceptual Framework* issued in 2010 are clear in this respect, their perceived inflexibility in this regard has been identified as a significant barrier that prevents the entities affected by it from adopting IFRS as a whole.[14] In 2012, the IASB decided on a two-tier approach to address this.[15] As a result, in January 2014, the IASB issued IFRS 14, an interim Standard on the accounting for regulatory deferral accounts that would apply for first-time adopters of IFRS until the completion of a more comprehensive project. *[IFRS 14.BC10]*. IFRS 14 became effective for annual periods beginning on or after 1 January 2016, with early application permitted. *[IFRS 14.C1]*.

The Standard can be applied in only very limited circumstances. A first-time adopter is permitted (but not required) to apply IFRS 14 in its first IFRS financial statements if, and only if, it conducts rate-regulated activities (as defined in the Standard) and recognised amounts that qualify as regulatory deferral account balances in its financial statements prepared under its previous GAAP. *[IFRS 14.5]*. An entity shall not change its accounting policies in order to start to recognise regulatory deferral account balances. *[IFRS 14.13]*.

Entities can apply IFRS 14 after first-time adoption if, and only if, they had elected to apply the Standard in their first IFRS financial statements and had recognised regulatory deferral account balances in those financial statements. *[IFRS 14.6]*. Therefore, the scope for applying this standard does not extend to existing IFRS reporters; nor to first-time adopters whose previous GAAP did not allow for the recognition of regulatory assets and liabilities; nor even to first-time adopters whose previous GAAP allowed such recognition but the entity chose not to do so.

The requirements of first-time adoption of IFRS are discussed further in Chapter 5.

As regards its comprehensive standard-setting project, the Board aims to publish an exposure draft in the fourth quarter of 2020.[16]

6 SPECIFIC EXAMPLES OF PROVISIONS AND CONTINGENCIES

IAS 37 expands on its general recognition and measurement requirements by including more specific requirements for particular situations, i.e. future restructuring costs and onerous contracts. This section discusses those situations, looks at other examples, including those addressed in an appendix to the Standard and other areas where the Interpretations Committee has considered how the principles of IAS 37 should be applied.

6.1 Restructuring provisions

IAS 37 allows entities to recognise restructuring provisions, but it has specific rules on the nature of obligations and the types of cost that are eligible for inclusion in such provisions, as discussed below. These rules ensure that entities recognise only obligations that exist independently of their future actions, *[IAS 37.19]*, and that provisions are not made for future operating costs and losses. *[IAS 37.63]*.

6.1.1 Definition

IAS 37 defines a restructuring as 'a programme that is planned and controlled by management, and materially changes either:

(a) the scope of a business undertaken by an entity; or

(b) the manner in which that business is conducted'. *[IAS 37.10]*.

This is said to include:
(a) the sale or termination of a line of business;
(b) the closure of business locations in a country or region or the relocation of business activities from one country or region to another;
(c) changes in management structure, for example, eliminating a layer of management; and
(d) fundamental reorganisations that have a material effect on the nature and focus of the entity's operations. *[IAS 37.70]*.

This definition is very wide and whilst it may be relatively straightforward to establish whether an operation has been sold, closed or relocated, the determination of whether an organisational change is fundamental, material or just part of a process of continuous improvement is a subjective judgement. Whilst organisational change is a perennial feature in most business sectors, entities could be tempted to classify all kinds of operating costs as restructuring costs and thereby invite the user of the financial statements to perceive them in a different light from the 'normal' costs of operating in a dynamic business environment. Even though the requirements in IAS 37 prevent such costs being recognised too early, the standard still leaves the question of classification open to judgement. As such there can be a tension between the permitted recognition of expected restructuring costs, subject to meeting the criteria set out at 6.1.2 below, and the general prohibition in IAS 37 against provision for future operating losses, which is discussed at 5.1 above.

IAS 37 emphasises that when a restructuring meets the definition of a discontinued operation under IFRS 5, additional disclosures may be required under that standard (see Chapter 4 at 3). *[IAS 37.9]*.

6.1.2 Recognition of a restructuring provision

IAS 37 requires that restructuring costs are recognised only when the general recognition criteria in the standard are met, i.e. there is a present obligation (legal or constructive) as a result of a past event, in respect of which a reliable estimate can be made of the probable cost. *[IAS 37.71]*. The standard's specific requirements for the recognition of a provision for restructuring costs seek to define the circumstances that give rise to a constructive obligation and thereby restrict the recognition of a provision to cases when an entity:

(a) has a detailed formal plan for the restructuring identifying at least:
  (i) the business or part of a business concerned;
  (ii) the principal locations affected;
  (iii) the location, function, and approximate number of employees who will be compensated for terminating their services;
  (iv) the expenditures that will be undertaken; and
  (v) when the plan will be implemented; and
(b) has raised a valid expectation in those affected that it will carry out the restructuring by starting to implement that plan or announcing its main features to those affected by it. *[IAS 37.72]*.

The standard gives examples of the entity's actions that may provide evidence that the entity has started to implement a plan, quoting the dismantling of plant or selling of assets, or the public announcement of the main features of the plan. However, it also emphasises that the public announcement of a detailed plan to restructure will not automatically create an obligation; the important principle is that the announcement is made in such a way and in sufficient detail to give rise to valid expectations in other parties such as customers, suppliers and employees that the restructuring will be carried out. *[IAS 37.73]*.

The standard also suggests that for an announced plan to give rise to a constructive obligation, its implementation needs to be planned to begin as soon as possible and to be completed in a timeframe that makes significant changes to the plan unlikely. Any extended period before commencement of implementation, or if the restructuring will take an unreasonably long time, will mean that recognition of a provision is premature, because the entity is still likely to have a chance of changing the plan. *[IAS 37.74]*.

In summary, these conditions require the plan to be detailed and specific, to have gone beyond the directors' powers of recall and to be put into operation without delay or significant alteration.

The criteria set out above for the recognition of provisions mean that a board decision, if it is the only relevant event arising before the end of the reporting period, is not sufficient. This message is reinforced specifically in the standard, the argument being made that a constructive obligation is not created by a management decision. There will only be a constructive obligation where the entity has, before the end of the reporting period:

(a) started to implement the restructuring plan; or

(b) announced the main features of the restructuring plan to those affected by it in a sufficiently specific manner to raise a valid expectation in them that the entity will carry out the restructuring. *[IAS 37.75]*.

If the restructuring is not started or announced in detail until after the end of the reporting period, no provision is recognised. Instead, the entity discloses a non-adjusting event after the reporting period. *[IAS 37.75, IAS 10.22(e)]*.

The following examples in IAS 37 illustrate how a constructive obligation for a restructuring may or may not be created.

Example 26.13: The effect of timing of the creation of a constructive obligation on the recognition of a restructuring provision

Scenario 1: Closure of a division – no implementation before end of the reporting period

On 12 December 2021, the board of Entity A decided to close down a division. No announcement was made before the end of the reporting period (31 December 2021) and no other steps were taken to implement the decision before that date.

In these circumstances, no provision is recognised because management's actions are insufficient to create a constructive obligation before the end of the reporting period. *[IAS 37 IE Example 5A]*.

Scenario 2: Closure of a division – communication/implementation before end of the reporting period

In another case, the board of Entity B decides on 12 December 2021 to close down one of its manufacturing divisions. On 20 December 2021 a detailed plan for closure was agreed by the board; letters were sent to customers warning them to seek an alternative source of supply and redundancy notices were sent to the staff of the division.

The communication of management's decision to customers and employees on 20 December 2021 creates a valid expectation that the division will be closed, thereby giving rise to a constructive obligation from that date. Accordingly, a provision is recognised at 31 December 2021 for the best estimate of the costs of closing the division. *[IAS 37 IE Example 5B]*.

The standard acknowledges that there will be circumstances where a board decision could trigger recognition, but not on its own. Only if earlier events, such as negotiations with employee representatives for termination payments or with purchasers for the sale of an operation, have been concluded subject only to board approval would the decision of the board create an obligation. In such circumstances, it is reasoned that when board approval has been obtained and communicated to the other parties, the entity is committed to restructure, assuming all other conditions are met. *[IAS 37.76]*.

There is also discussion in the standard of the situation that may arise in some countries where, for example, employee representatives may sit on the board, so that a board decision effectively communicates the decision to them, which may result in a constructive obligation to restructure. *[IAS 37.77]*.

In practice it can be very difficult to determine whether it is appropriate to recognise a provision for the future costs of a restructuring programme. The determination of whether an organisational change is fundamental, material or just part of a process of continuous improvement is a subjective judgement. Once it has been established that the activities in question constitute a restructuring rather than an ongoing operating cost, it can be difficult to determine whether management's actions before the reporting date have been sufficient to have 'raised a valid expectation in those affected'. *[IAS 37.72]*. Even if a trigger point is easily identifiable, such as the date of an appropriately detailed public announcement, it might not necessarily commit management to the whole restructuring, but only to specific items of expenditure such as redundancy costs. When the announcement is less clear, referring for example to consultations, negotiations or voluntary arrangements, particularly with employees, judgement is required. Furthermore, taken on its own, the 'valid expectation' test is at least as open to manipulation as one based on the timing of a board decision. Entities anxious to accelerate or postpone recognition of a liability could do so by advancing or deferring an event that signals such a commitment, such as a public announcement, without any change to the substance of their position.

In these situations it is important to consider all the related facts and circumstances and not to 'home in' on a single recognition criterion. The objective of the analysis is to determine whether there is a past obligating event at the reporting date. The guidance in the standard about restructuring, referring as it does to constructive obligations and valid expectations is ultimately aimed at properly applying the principle in IAS 37 that only those obligations arising from past events and existing independently of an entity's future actions are recognised as provisions. *[IAS 37.19]*. In essence, a restructuring provision qualifies for recognition if, as at the reporting date, it relates to a detailed plan of action from which management cannot realistically withdraw.

6.1.3 Recognition of obligations arising from the sale of an operation

IAS 37 has some further specific rules governing when to recognise an obligation arising on the sale of an operation, stating that no obligation arises for the sale of an operation until the entity is committed to the sale, i.e. there is a binding sale agreement. *[IAS 37.78]*.

Thus a provision cannot be made for a loss on sale unless there is a binding sale agreement by the end of the reporting period. The standard says that this applies even when an entity has taken a decision to sell an operation and announced that decision publicly, it cannot be committed to the sale until a purchaser has been identified and there is a binding sale agreement. Until there is such an agreement, the entity will be able to change its mind and indeed will have to take another course of action if a purchaser cannot be found on acceptable terms. [IAS 37.79].

Even in cases where it is part of a larger restructuring that qualifies for recognition under IAS 37, an obligation arising from the sale is not recognised until there is a binding sale agreement. Instead, the assets of the operation must be reviewed for impairment under IAS 36. This may therefore mean that an expense is recorded in the income statement; it is just that the expense gives rise to a reduction of the carrying amount of assets rather than the recognition of a liability. The standard also recognises that where a sale is only part of a restructuring, the entity could be committed to the other parts of restructuring before a binding sale agreement is in place. [IAS 37.79]. Hence, the costs of the restructuring will be recognised over different reporting periods.

6.1.4 Costs that can (and cannot) be included in a restructuring provision

Having met the specific tests in the standard for the recognition of a restructuring provision at the end of the reporting period, IAS 37 imposes further criteria to restrict the types of cost that can be provided for. Presumably these additional restrictions are intended to ensure that the entity does not contravene the general prohibition in IAS 37 against provision for future operating losses. [IAS 37.63].

A restructuring provision should include only the direct expenditures arising from the restructuring, which are those that are both:

(a) necessarily entailed by the restructuring; and
(b) not associated with the ongoing activities of the entity. [IAS 37.80].

The standard gives specific examples of costs that may not be included within the provision, because they relate to the future conduct of the business. Such costs include:

(a) retraining or relocating continuing staff;
(b) marketing; or
(c) investment in new systems and distribution networks. [IAS 37.81].

Because these costs relate to the future conduct of the business, they are recognised on the same basis as if they arose independently of a restructuring. [IAS 37.81]. In most cases, this means that the costs are recognised as the related services are provided.

Example 26.14: Distinguishing restructuring costs from ongoing expenses

On 15 November 2021, management announced its intention to close down its operation in the North of the country and relocate to a new site in the South, primarily to be closer to its key customers. Before the end of the reporting period (31 December 2021), the principal elements of the plan were agreed with employee representatives, a lease signed for a building at the new location, and a decision was made to market the existing facility for sale; all on the basis that production would start at the new location on 31 March 2022 and the existing site would be vacated on 30 April 2022. Production would cease at the existing site on 28 February 2022 to allow plant and equipment to be relocated. Inventory levels would be increased up to that date so that customers could be supplied with goods sent from the Northern facility until 31 March.

Whilst the majority of the 600 existing staff was expected to take redundancy on 28 February 2022, 50 had agreed to accept the entity's offer of relocation, including an incentive of €3,000 each towards relocation costs. Of those employees taking redundancy, 20 had agreed to continue to work for the entity until 30 June 2022, to dismantle plant and equipment at the Northern site; install it at the new facility in the South; and train new staff on its operation. A bonus of €4,500 per employee would be payable if they remained until 30 June. A further 60 had agreed to stay with the entity until 31 March 2022, to ensure that inventory was sent out to customers before the new site was operational, of which 10 would remain until 30 April 2022 to complete the decommissioning of the Northern facility. These employees would also receive a bonus for staying until the promised date.

The announcement of management's decision on 15 November 2021 and the fact that the key elements of the plan were understood by employees and customers of the Northern site before the end of the reporting period give rise to a constructive obligation that requires a provision to be recognised at 31 December 2021 for the best estimate of the costs of the reorganisation.

However, only those direct costs of the restructuring not associated with ongoing activities can be included in the provision. For example, as follows:

Type of expense	Direct cost of restructuring	Associated with ongoing activities
Redundancy payments to 550 staff	•	
Payroll costs to 28 February 2022 (all 600 staff)		•
Relocation incentive of €3,000 per employee (50 staff)		•
Payroll costs – to 31 March 2022 (60 staff dispatching goods)		•
Payroll costs – March to June 2022 (20 staff relocating plant) Note 1	•	
Payroll costs – April 2022 (10 staff decommissioning site)	•	
Costs of dismantling plant and equipment Note 1	•	•
Cost of transporting PP&E and inventory to the new site		•
Costs of recruiting and training staff for the Southern site		•
Rent of new site to 31 March 2022 (pre-production)		•
Cost of invoices, forms and stationery showing new address		•

Note 1: Costs relating to dismantling plant and equipment that is no longer intended for use in the business could be regarded as a direct cost of restructuring. However, costs relating to the dismantling and installation of equipment at the new site and training staff to operate it are costs associated with ongoing operations and, therefore, ineligible for inclusion in the restructuring provision.

The entity will need to consider whether the existing facility should be classified as a non-current asset held for sale. On the basis that management had decided to market the facility for sale, but had not yet actively begun to do so, it is unlikely that the criteria in IFRS 5 would be met as at 31 December 2021. Classification of non-current assets held for sale is discussed in Chapter 4 at 2.

This example shows that individual classes of expenditure should be disaggregated into components that distinguish those elements associated with ongoing activities. Even if expenditure would not have been incurred without the restructuring activity, its association with ongoing activities means that it is ineligible for inclusion in a provision. IAS 37 requires the cost to be both necessarily entailed by the restructuring and not associated with the ongoing activities of the entity. [IAS 37.80].

For that reason, whilst the cost of making employees redundant is an eligible restructuring cost, any incremental amounts paid to retain staff to ensure a smooth transition of operations from one location to another are not eligible because they are incurred to facilitate ongoing activities. IAS 19 requires these to be treated as short-term employee benefits to the extent that they are expected to be settled within 12 months after the end of the reporting period.[17] Similarly, whilst the costs of dismantling plant and equipment intended to be scrapped is an eligible restructuring cost, the costs of dismantling plant and equipment intended to be relocated and installed at the new site is ineligible, because it is associated with ongoing activities.

A further rule in IAS 37 is that the provision should not include identifiable future operating losses up to the date of the restructuring, unless they relate to an onerous contract. *[IAS 37.82]*. This means that even if the operation being reorganised is loss-making, its ongoing costs are not provided for. This is consistent with the general prohibition against the recognition of provisions for future operating losses. *[IAS 37.63]*.

The general requirement in the standard that gains from the expected disposal of assets cannot be taken into account in the measurement of provisions, *[IAS 37.51]*, is also relevant to the measurement of restructuring provisions, even if the sale of the asset is envisaged as part of the restructuring. *[IAS 37.83]*. Whilst the expected disposal proceeds from asset sales might have been a significant element of the economic case for a restructuring, the income from disposal is not anticipated just because it is part of a restructuring plan.

6.2 Onerous contracts

Although future operating losses in general cannot be provided for, IAS 37 requires that 'if an entity has a contract that is onerous, the present obligation under the contract shall be recognised and measured as a provision'. *[IAS 37.66]*.

The standard notes that many contracts (for example, some routine purchase orders) can be cancelled without paying compensation to the other party, and therefore there is no obligation. However, other contracts establish both rights and obligations for each of the contracting parties. Where events make such a contract onerous, the contract falls within the scope of the standard and a liability exists which is recognised. Executory contracts that are not onerous fall outside the scope of the standard. *[IAS 37.67]*.

IAS 37 defines an onerous contract as 'a contract in which the unavoidable costs of meeting the obligations under the contract exceed the economic benefits expected to be received under it'. *[IAS 37.10]*. This requires that the contract is onerous to the point of being directly loss-making, not simply uneconomic by reference to current prices.

IAS 37 considers that 'the unavoidable costs under a contract reflect the least net cost of exiting from the contract, which is the lower of the cost of fulfilling it and any compensation or penalties arising from failure to fulfil it'. *[IAS 37.68]*. This evaluation does not require an intention by the entity to fulfil or to exit the contract. It does not even require there to be specific terms in the contract that apply in the event of its termination or breach. Its purpose is to recognise only the unavoidable costs to the entity, which in the absence of specific clauses in the contract relating to termination or breach could include an estimation of the cost of ceasing to honour the contract and having the other party go to court for compensation for the resultant breach.

There is some diversity in practice in how entities determine the unavoidable costs of fulfilling their obligations under a contract. In May 2020, the IASB issued *Onerous Contracts – Cost of Fulfilling a Contract (Amendments to IAS 37)* that clarifies that the costs of fulfilling a contract comprise the costs that relate directly to the contract. Costs that relate directly to a contract consist of both:

(a) the incremental costs of fulfilling that contract – for example, direct labour and materials; and

(b) an allocation of other costs that relate directly to fulfilling contracts – for example, an allocation of the depreciation charge for an item of property, plant and equipment used in fulfilling that contract among others. *[IAS 37.68A]*.

The amendment is effective for annual reporting periods beginning on or after 1 January 2022. Earlier application is permitted. If an entity applies the amendments for an earlier period, it should disclose that fact. *[IAS 37.105]*. The amendments apply to contracts for which an entity has not yet fulfilled all its obligations at the beginning of the annual reporting period in which it first applies the amendments. Comparative information should not be restated. Instead, the entity should recognise the cumulative effect of initially applying the amendments as an adjustment to the opening balance of retained earnings or other component of equity, as appropriate, at the date of initial application. *[IAS 37.94A]*.

Entities that previously applied the incremental costs approach to determining the unavoidable costs of fulfilling obligations under a contract (i.e. considering only the costs that the entity would avoid if it did not have the contract) may be required to recognise additional provisions as a result of the requirement to also include costs directly related to contract activities when determining whether an onerous contract provision should be recognised. Entities that previously recognised contract loss provisions using a 'full-costs' approach, based on the guidance in the former standard IAS 11 – *Construction Contracts* – will be required to exclude the allocation of indirect overheads when determining whether to recognise an onerous contract provision. General overhead or administrative costs typically would not relate directly to fulfilling contracts.

Whilst the amendment to IAS 37 is intended to clarify how to determine the unavoidable costs of fulfilling obligations under a contract, judgement will be required in determining which costs are directly related to contract activities. The Board noted in the Basis for Conclusions to the amendment that several IFRS Standards, such as IAS 2, specify the costs to include in measuring a non-monetary asset. Although the detailed requirements differ, they all require an entity to include both the incremental costs of purchasing or constructing the asset, and an allocation of other directly related or directly attributable costs, such as production overheads. The Board concluded that, in assessing whether a contract to deliver goods is onerous, the way in which an entity determines the cost of fulfilling the contract should be broadly consistent with the way it measures the costs of the goods when it holds them. *[IAS 37.BC7]*. Therefore, entities may look to other standards, such as IAS 2 (see Chapter 22 at 3.1), IAS 16 (see Chapter 18 at 4.1), and IAS 38 (see Chapter 17 at 3.2) when considering which costs should be included or excluded when assessing whether an onerous contract provision should be recognised. In addition, we believe that the guidance in IFRS 15 on costs to fulfil a contract will be relevant (see Chapter 31 at 5.2). All of these Standards specify that entities exclude 'general overhead' or 'administrative' costs when measuring the cost of an asset, although with some exceptions:

(a) Under IFRS 15, general and administrative costs that are explicitly chargeable to customers may be costs to fulfil a contract that the entity recognises as an asset, subject to meeting certain criteria [IFRS 15.98] (see Chapter 31 at 5.2);

(b) Under IAS 2, administrative overheads that contribute to bringing inventories to their present condition and location are included in the cost of inventories [IAS 2.16(c)] (see Chapter 22 at 3.1.3.B); and

(c) Under IAS 38, selling, administrative and other general overheads expenditure that can be directly attributed to preparing an internally generated intangible asset for use are included in the cost of the intangible asset [IAS 38.67(a)] (see Chapter 17 at 6.3.2).

Therefore, whilst we believe that general overhead or administrative costs typically would not relate directly to fulfilling contracts, judgement may sometimes be required in making this assessment. In addition, whilst IAS 2 refers to indirect costs of production being included in the cost of inventories, the examples the Standard gives of such costs include depreciation and maintenance of factory buildings, and the cost of factory management and administration. [IAS 2.12]. These are similar to the depreciation and contract management and supervision costs that IFRS 15 gives as examples of costs that relate directly to a contract. [IFRS 15.97]. Therefore, an entity may determine that such costs do relate directly to fulfilling contracts for the sale of inventory when assessing whether an onerous contract provision should be recognised.

Whilst the clarification regarding costs to fulfil a contract is part of IAS 37's recognition requirements for onerous contracts, rather than its measurement requirements, entities may reasonably decide that the same costs should also be used to measure any onerous contract provision recognised.[18] As noted at 1.1 above, in January 2020, the IASB decided to add to its work plan a project to amend aspects of IAS 37. The scope of this project includes three targeted improvements to the Standard, one of which is to clarify which costs are included in the measurement of a provision.[19]

As noted above, IAS 37 defines an onerous contract as 'a contract in which the unavoidable costs of meeting the obligations under the contract exceed the economic benefits expected to be received under it'. [IAS 37.10]. There is also some diversity in practice in how entities determine the economic benefits expected to be received under a contract. However, in January 2020, the Board decided not to address this matter as part the planned targeted improvements to IAS 37.[20]

There is a subtle yet important distinction between making a provision in respect of the unavoidable costs under a contract (reflecting the least net cost of what the entity has to do) compared to making an estimate of the cost of what the entity intends to do. The first is an obligation, which merits the recognition as a provision, whereas the second is a choice of the entity, which fails the recognition criteria because it does not exist independently of the entity's future actions, *[IAS 37.19]*, and is therefore akin to a future operating loss.

Example 26.15: Onerous supply contract

Entity P negotiated a contract in 2018 for the supply of components when availability in the market was scarce. It agreed to purchase 100,000 units per annum for 5 years commencing 1 January 2019 at a price of $20 per unit. Since then, new suppliers have entered the market and the typical price of a component is now $5 per unit. Whilst its activities are still profitable (Entity P makes a margin of $6 per unit of finished product sold) changes to the entity's own business means that it will not use all of the components it is contracted to purchase. As at 31 December 2021, Entity P expects to use 150,000 units in future and has 55,000 units in inventory. The contract requires 200,000 units to be purchased before the agreement expires in 2023. If the entity terminates the contract before 2023, compensation of $1 million per year is payable to the supplier. Each finished product contains one unit of the component.

Therefore, the entity expects to achieve a margin of $900,000 (150,000 × $6) on the units it will produce and sell; but will make a loss of $15 ($20 – $5) per unit on each of the 105,000 components (55,000 + 200,000 – 150,000) it is left with at the end of 2022 and now expects to sell in the components market.

In considering the extent to which the contract is onerous, Entity P in the example above should not concentrate solely on the net cost of the excess units of $1,575,000 (105,000 × $15) that it is contracted to purchase but which are expected to be left unsold. Instead, the entity should consider all of the related benefits of the contract, which includes the profits earned as a result of having a secure source of supply of components. Therefore the supply contract is onerous (directly loss making) only to the extent of the costs not covered by related revenues, justifying a provision of $675,000 ($1,575,000 – $900,000).

IAS 37 requires that any impairment loss that has occurred on assets dedicated to an onerous contact is recognised before establishing a provision for the onerous contract. *[IAS 37.69]*. Once the amendment to IAS 37 in respect of onerous contracts becomes effective, paragraph 69 will instead require that an impairment loss that has occurred on assets used in fulfilling the contract be recognised before establishing a provision for the onerous contract.

6.2.1 Onerous leases

As discussed at 2.2.1.B above, IAS 37 specifically applies to leases only in limited circumstances. IAS 37 specifically applies only to:

- leases that become onerous before the commencement date of the lease; and
- short-term leases (as defined in IFRS 16) and leases for which the underlying asset is of low value that are accounted for in accordance with paragraph 6 of IFRS 16 and that have become onerous. *[IAS 37.5(c)]*.

The IASB noted in paragraph BC 72 of IFRS 16 that it '...decided not to specify any particular requirements in IFRS 16 for onerous contracts. The IASB made this decision because ...(a) for leases that have already commenced, no requirements are necessary. After the commencement date, an entity will appropriately reflect an onerous lease contract by applying the requirements of IFRS 16. For example, a lessee will determine and recognise any impairment of right-of-use assets applying IAS 36 *Impairment of Assets*.' However, this raises the question how an entity should account for onerous variable lease payments that are not included in the measurement of right-of-use assets or lease liabilities under IFRS 16 (including variable payments related to non-lease components that have not been separated from the lease components, in accordance with paragraph 15 of IFRS 16). It is not immediately obvious whether such onerous variable lease payments fall within the scope of IFRS 16 (and IAS 36), or IAS 37.

As discussed in Chapter 20, at 7.1.8.A, we believe that contractual variable lease payments that are not included in the lease liability (such as those that are not based on an index or rate, and are not in substance fixed) should be reflected in cash flow forecasts used for value-in-use calculations for impairment testing purposes. In many cases, leased assets will be tested for impairment at a cash-generating-unit (CGU) level rather than at an individual asset level, as many leased assets are used as an input to the operating activities of an entity rather than generating largely independent cash flows. IAS 36 sets out requirements for the allocation of an impairment loss to assets within a CGU, and requires that the allocation of the impairment loss does not reduce the carrying amount of an individual asset within the CGU below the highest of its fair value less costs of disposal, or value-in-use (if these can be established), or zero (see Chapter 20 at 11.2). It is therefore logically possible, after all assets and goodwill are either written off or down to their fair value less costs of disposal or value-in-use, for the carrying amount of a CGU to be higher than the computed recoverable amount. IAS 36 requires that a liability should be recognised for any remaining amount of an impairment loss for a CGU only if that is required by another IFRS. *[IAS 36.108]*.

A question therefore arises as to whether, in such situations, an onerous lease provision should be recognised under the requirements of IAS 37, for any variable lease payments not included in the measurement of any right-of-use assets that are part of the CGU. A similar question arises for a right-of-use asset tested for impairment at the asset level rather than as part of a CGU. The answers will depend upon the interpretation of the scope exemption in paragraph 5 of IAS 37.

One view is that paragraph 5 of IAS 37 does not explicitly state that provisions for onerous leases are outside the scope of IAS 37, it merely provides examples of cases where other Standards address provisions, including IFRS 16. The general requirements of IFRS 16 are applied to the extent that there is a right-of-use asset and liability recognised and measured in accordance with the requirements of that standard. Any other lease payments not included in the measurement of the lease liability or right-of-use asset, such as variable lease payments that do not depend on an index or rate and are not in substance fixed, are in scope of the requirements of IAS 37 on onerous contracts. An onerous lease provision would be recognised for onerous variable lease payments that are not included in the measurement of right-of-use assets or lease liabilities under IFRS 16.

An alternative view is that the scope exemption in paragraph 5 of IAS 37 applies to all leases and lease payments other than the specific exceptions set out in paragraph 5(c) of IAS 37. An onerous lease provision would not be recognised for onerous variable lease payments not included in the measurement of right-of-use assets or lease liabilities under IFRS 16.

In any case, where a lease contract contains non-lease components that have been accounted for separately from the lease components in accordance with paragraph 12 of IFRS 16, these non-lease components are in scope of IAS 37. This is because IFRS 16 specifies that once lease and non-lease components are elected not to be combined, a lessee accounts for non-lease components applying other applicable standards. [IFRS 16.15-16].

6.2.2 Contracts with customers that are, or have become, onerous

As IFRS 15 contains no specific requirements to address contracts with customers that are, or have become, onerous, IAS 37 applies to such contracts. [IAS 37.5(g)]. In assessing whether a contract is onerous, an entity should compare the unavoidable costs of meeting the obligations under the contract to the economic benefits expected to be received under it. The unavoidable costs under the contract are the lower of the cost of fulfilling the contract and any compensation or penalties arising from failure to fulfil the contract. [IAS 37.68]. As discussed at 6.2 above, in May 2020, the IASB issued an amendment to IAS 37 that clarifies that the costs of fulfilling a contract comprise the costs that relate directly to the contract, rather than only the incremental costs of the contract.[21]

One question that may arise, is how an entity should account for an onerous contract with a customer when the contract includes several 'over time' performance obligations that are satisfied consecutively. Since the requirements for onerous contracts are outside the scope of IFRS 15, an entity's accounting for onerous contracts does not affect the accounting for its revenue from contracts with customers in accordance with IFRS 15. Therefore, an entity must use an 'overlay' approach, which consists of two steps:

(a) apply the requirements of IFRS 15 to measure progress in satisfying each performance obligation, and account for the related costs when incurred in accordance with the applicable standards; and

(b) at the end of each reporting period, apply IAS 37 to determine if the remaining contract as a whole is onerous. If the entity concludes that the remaining contract as a whole is onerous, it recognises a provision only to the extent that the amount of the remaining unavoidable costs under the contract exceed the remaining economic benefits to be received under it.

This approach is illustrated below.

Example 26.16: Onerous contract with several 'over time' performance obligations that are satisfied consecutively

Entity A enters into a contract that consists of two distinct performance obligations, which are satisfied consecutively. Revenue is recognised over time for both performance obligations. Entity A expects to satisfy the first performance obligation (PO1) during Years 1-4 and the second performance obligation (PO2) in Years 5-6. Entity A measures progress towards the satisfaction of both performance obligations based on costs incurred compared to the total expected costs (i.e. it applies an input method under IFRS 15).

If Entity A terminates the contract, a penalty of €100,000 is payable.

The expected revenues and costs at the inception of the contract and the updated expectations at the beginning of Year 2 are as follows:

	At contract inception		Update in Year 2		
PO1	Expected costs	Expected revenue	Expected costs	Expected revenue	Expected progress
Year 1	24,000	30,000	24,000	30,000	25%
Year 2	24,000	30,000	24,000	30,000	25%
Year 3	24,000	30,000	24,000	30,000	25%
Year 4	24,000	30,000	24,000	30,000	25%
Total PO1	96,000	120,000	96,000	120,000	
PO2					
Year 5	10,000	15,000	32,000	15,000	50%
Year 6	10,000	15,000	32,000	15,000	50%
Total PO2	20,000	30,000	64,000	30,000	
Total contract	116,000	150,000	160,000	150,000	
Gross profit (loss)		34,000		(10,000)	

At contract inception, Entity A expects a positive margin for both performance obligations. At the beginning of Year 2, its estimates of the cost to fulfil the second performance obligation are increased by €44,000. Therefore, Entity A now expects to incur a loss of €34,000 for the second performance obligation, resulting in a negative margin for the entire contract of €10,000.

The contract as a whole is only onerous to the extent that the remaining costs to be incurred exceed the remaining benefits to be recognised. This is not the €34,000 loss relating to the second performance obligation, because at the beginning of Year 2, Entity A has yet to recognise profits of €18,000 for the completion of the first performance obligation. As a result, the net cost of fulfilling the contract at Year 2 is €16,000. This cost is less than the termination penalty of €100,000 and therefore, applying the 'overlay' approach explained above, Entity A recognises a provision under IAS 37 of €16,000 in Year 2.

In Years 2 to 4, as the first performance obligation is being completed, the provision increases to reflect the higher net cost of satisfying the remaining performance obligations in the contract. As at the end of Year 4, only the revenues and costs relating to the second performance obligation remain, such that the provision now stands at €34,000 and is utilised in Years 5 and 6 as the related losses are incurred.

The table below illustrates the effect of this accounting treatment (assuming that the actual outcome of the contract is the same as the updated estimates). This example ignores the time value of money for simplicity reasons.

	Costs	Revenue	Provision Additions/ Utilisations	Balance	Profit or loss for the period
Year 1	24,000	30,000	–	–	6,000
Year 2 (change in estimated total costs)	–	–	16,000	16,000	(16,000)
Year 2	24,000	30,000	6,000	22,000	–
Year 3	24,000	30,000	6,000	28,000	–
Year 4	24,000	30,000	6,000	34,000	–
Year 5	32,000	15,000	(17,000)	17,000	–
Year 6	32,000	15,000	(17,000)	–	–
Total	160,000	150,000	–	–	(10,000)

The effect of an onerous contract provision, or a change in the provision, is recognised as an expense in profit or loss and not as an adjustment to revenue.

As provisions for onerous contracts with customers are in the scope of IAS 37, they should be classified as provisions in the balance sheet and disclosed in accordance with IAS 37 (see 7.1 below). Onerous contract provisions are outside the scope of IFRS 15 and should not be included within contract liabilities.

Since the definition of an onerous contract in IAS 37 refers only to a contract, the unit of account to determine whether an onerous contract exists is the contract itself, rather than the performance obligations identified in accordance with IFRS 15. *[IAS 37.10]*. As a result, the entity must consider the entire remaining contract, including remaining revenue to be recognised for unsatisfied, or partially unsatisfied, performance obligations and the remaining costs to fulfil those performance obligations.

As discussed at 6.2 above, there is diversity in practice in how entities determine the economic benefits expected to be received under a contract for the purposes of assessing whether a contract is onerous. Where a contract with a customer contains an element of variable consideration, it is likely that judgement will be required in assessing the economic benefits expected to be received under a contract. This may particularly be the case where an entity is required to constrain the estimate of variable consideration to be included in the transaction price for revenue recognition purposes under IFRS 15. Variable consideration under IFRS 15 is discussed further in Chapter 29 at 2.2.

6.3 Decommissioning provisions

Decommissioning costs arise when an entity is required to dismantle or remove an asset at the end of its useful life and to restore the site on which it has been located, for example, when an oil rig or nuclear power station reaches the end of its economic life.

Rather than allowing an entity to build up a provision for the required costs over the life of the facility, IAS 37 requires that the liability is recognised as soon as the obligation arises. This is because the construction of the asset (and the environmental damage caused by it) creates the past obligating event requiring restoration in the future. *[IAS 37 IE Example 3]*.

The accounting for decommissioning costs is dealt with in IAS 37 by way of an example relating to an oil rig in an offshore oilfield (see Example 26.5 at 3.3 above). A provision is recognised at the time of constructing the oil rig in relation to the eventual costs that relate to its removal and the restoration of damage caused by building it. Additional provisions are recognised over the life of the oil field to reflect the need to reverse damage caused during the extraction of oil. *[IAS 37 IE Example 3]*. The total decommissioning cost is estimated, discounted to its present value and it is this amount which forms the initial provision. This 'initial estimate of the costs of dismantling and removing the item and restoring the site' is added to the corresponding asset's cost. *[IAS 16.16]*. Thereafter, the asset is depreciated over its useful life, while the discounted provision is progressively unwound, with the unwinding charge shown as a finance cost, as discussed at 4.3.5 above.

The effect of discounting on the statement of comprehensive income is to split the cost of the eventual decommissioning into two components: an expense based on the present value of the expected future cash outflows; and a finance element representing the unwinding of the discount. The overall effect is to produce a rising pattern of cost over the life of the facility, often with much of the total cost of the decommissioning classified as a finance cost.

AngloGold Ashanti's accounting policies and provisions note in respect of decommissioning obligations and restoration obligations are shown in the following extract.

Extract 26.3: AngloGold Ashanti Limited (2019)
ANNEXURE A [extract]
SUMMARY OF SIGNIFICANT ACCOUNTING POLICIES [extract]

ENVIRONMENTAL EXPENDITURE

The group has long-term remediation obligations comprising decommissioning and restoration liabilities relating to its past operations which are based on the group's environmental management plans, in compliance with current environmental and regulatory requirements. Provisions for non-recurring remediation costs are made when there is a present obligation, it is probable that expenditure on remediation work will be required and the cost can be estimated within a reasonable range of possible outcomes. The costs are based on currently available facts, technology expected to be available at the time of the clean-up, laws and regulations presently or virtually certain to be enacted and prior experience in remediation of contaminated sites.

Decommissioning costs

The provision for decommissioning represents the cost that will arise from rectifying damage caused before production commences. Accordingly, a provision and a decommissioning asset is recognised and included within mine infrastructure.

Decommissioning costs are provided at the present value of the expenditures expected to settle the obligation, using estimated cash flows based on current prices. The unwinding of the decommissioning obligation is included in the income statement. Estimated future costs of decommissioning obligations are reviewed regularly and adjusted as appropriate for new circumstances or changes in law or technology. Changes in estimates are capitalised or reversed against the relevant asset. Estimates are discounted at a pre-tax rate that reflects current market assessments of the time value of money.

Gains or losses from the expected disposal of assets are not taken into account when determining the provision.

Restoration costs

The provision for restoration represents the cost of restoring site damage after the start of production. Changes in the provision are recorded in the income statement as a cost of production.

Restoration costs are estimated at the present value of the expenditures expected to settle the obligation, using estimated cash flows based on current prices and adjusted for risks specific to the liability. The estimates are discounted at a pre-tax rate that reflects current market assessments of the time value of money.

GROUP – NOTES TO THE FINANCIAL STATEMENTS [extract]		
US dollar millions	2019	2018
27 ENVIRONMENTAL REHABILITATION AND OTHER PROVISIONS [extract]		
Environmental rehabilitation obligations [extract]		
Provision for decommissioning		
Balance at beginning of year	237	286
Charge to income statement	–	1
Change in estimates[1]	29	(47)
Unwinding of decommissioning obligation	10	12
Transfer to assets and liabilities held for sale	(81)	–
Utilised during the year	(1)	(1)
Translation	2	(14)
Balance at end of year	**196**	**237**
Provision for restoration		
Balance at beginning of year	385	409
Charge to income statement	(1)	2
Change in estimates[1]	50	(28)
Unwinding of restoration obligation	9	12
Transfer to assets and liabilities held for sale	(15)	–
Transfer to current portion	–	–
Utilised during the year	(5)	(3)
Translation	–	(7)
Balance at end of year	**423**	**385**

[1] *The change in estimates is attributable to changes in discount rates due to changes in global economic assumptions and changes in mine plans resulting in a change in cash flows and changes in design of tailings storage facilities and in methodology following requests from the environmental regulatory authorities. These provisions are expected to unwind beyond the end of the life of mine.*

6.3.1 Changes in estimated decommissioning costs (IFRIC 1)

IAS 37 requires provisions to be revised annually to reflect the current best estimate of the provision. *[IAS 37.59]*. However, the standard gives no guidance on accounting for changes in the decommissioning provision. Similarly, IAS 16 is unclear about the extent to which an item's carrying amount should be affected by changes in the estimated amount of dismantling and site restoration costs that occur after the estimate made upon initial measurement. This was addressed by the IASB with the publication of IFRIC 1 in May 2004. *[IFRIC 1.1]*.

IFRIC 1 applies to any decommissioning, restoration or similar liability that has been both included as part of the cost of an asset measured in accordance with IAS 16 or as part of the cost of a right-of-use asset in accordance with IFRS 16 and recognised as a liability in accordance with IAS 37. *[IFRIC 1.2]*. It addresses how the effect of the following events that change the measurement of an existing decommissioning, restoration or similar liability should be accounted for:

(a) a change in the estimated outflow of resources embodying economic benefits (e.g. cash flows) required to settle the obligation;

(b) a change in the current market-based discount rate (this includes changes in the time value of money and the risks specific to the liability); and

(c) an increase that reflects the passage of time (also referred to as the unwinding of the discount). *[IFRIC 1.3]*.

IFRIC 1 requires that (c) above, the periodic unwinding of the discount, is recognised in profit or loss as a finance cost as it occurs. *[IFRIC 1.8]*. The Interpretations Committee concluded that the unwinding of the discount is not a borrowing cost as defined in IAS 23, and thus cannot be capitalised under that standard. *[IFRIC 1.BC26-27]*.

For a change caused by (a) or (b) above, however, the adjustment is taken to the income statement only in specific circumstances. Any revision to the provision (other than to reflect the passage of time) is first recognised in the carrying value of the related asset or in other comprehensive income, depending on whether the asset is measured at cost or using the revaluation model. *[IFRIC 1.4-7]*.

If the related asset is measured using the cost model, the change in the liability should be added to or deducted from the cost of the asset to which it relates. Where the change gives rise to an addition to cost, the entity should consider the need to test the new carrying value for impairment. This is particularly relevant for assets approaching the end of their useful life, as their remaining economic benefits are often small compared to the potential changes in the related decommissioning liability. Reductions over and above the remaining carrying value of the asset are recognised immediately in profit or loss. *[IFRIC 1.5]*. The adjusted depreciable amount of the asset is then depreciated prospectively over its remaining useful life. *[IFRIC 1.7]*. IFRIC 1 includes the following illustrative example.

Example 26.17: Changes in decommissioning costs – related asset measured at cost

An entity has a nuclear power plant and a related decommissioning liability. The nuclear power plant started operating on 1 January 2012. The plant has a useful life of 40 years. Its initial cost was $120,000,000; this included an amount for decommissioning costs of $10,000,000, which represented $70,400,000 in estimated cash flows payable in 40 years discounted at a risk-adjusted rate of 5%. The entity's financial year ends on 31 December.

On 31 December 2021, the plant is 10 years old. Accumulated depreciation is $30,000,000. Because of the unwinding of discount over the 10 years, the decommissioning liability has grown from $10,000,000 to $16,300,000.

On 31 December 2021, the discount rate has not changed. However, the entity estimates that, as a result of technological advances, the net present value of the expected cash flows has decreased by $8,000,000. Accordingly, the entity reduces the decommissioning liability from $16,300,000 to $8,300,000 and reduces the carrying amount of the asset by the same amount.

Following this adjustment, the carrying amount of the asset is $82,000,000 ($120,000,000 − $8,000,000 − $30,000,000), which will be depreciated over the remaining 30 years of the asset's life to give a depreciation expense for 2021 of $2,733,333 ($82,000,000 ÷ 30). The next year's finance cost for the unwinding of the discount will be $415,000 ($8,300,000 × 5%). *[IFRIC 1.IE1-4]*.

In illustrating the requirements of the Interpretation, the example in IFRIC 1 reduces the carrying value of the whole asset (comprising its construction cost and decommissioning cost) by the reduction in the present value of the decommissioning provision. The solution set out in the example does not treat the decommissioning element as a separate component of the asset. Had this been the case, the component would have had accumulated depreciation as at 31 December 2021 of $2,500,000 ($10,000,000 × 10/40), giving a carrying amount of $7,500,000 at that date and a gain of $500,000 when reduced by the decrease in the provision of $8,000,000. Accordingly, we believe that the example in IFRIC 1 indicates that it would not be appropriate to recognise any gain until the carrying value of the whole asset is extinguished.

If the related asset is measured using the revaluation model, changes in the liability alter the revaluation surplus or deficit previously recognised for that asset. Decreases in the provision are recognised in other comprehensive income and increase the value of the revaluation surplus in respect of the asset, except that:

(a) a decrease in the provision should be recognised in profit or loss to the extent that it reverses a previous revaluation deficit on that asset that was recognised in profit or loss; and

(b) if a decrease in the provision exceeds the carrying amount of the asset that would have been recognised under the cost model, the excess should be recognised in profit or loss. *[IFRIC 1.6]*.

Increases in the provision are recognised in profit or loss, except that they should be recognised in other comprehensive income, and reduce the revaluation surplus, to the extent of any credit balance existing in the revaluation surplus in respect of that asset. Changes in the provision might also indicate the need for the asset (and therefore all assets in the same class) to be revalued. *[IFRIC 1.6]*.

The illustrative examples in IFRIC 1 address this alternative.

Example 26.18: Changes in decommissioning costs – related asset carried at revaluation amount

Assume that the entity in Example 26.17 above instead adopts the revaluation model in IAS 16, and its policy is to eliminate accumulated depreciation at the revaluation date against the gross carrying amount of the asset.

The entity first revalues the asset as at 31 December 2014 when the nuclear power plant is 3 years old. The valuation of $115,000,000 comprises a gross valuation of $126,600,000 and an allowance of $11,600,000 for decommissioning costs, which represents no change to the original estimate, after the unwinding of three years' discount. The amounts included in the statement of financial position at 31 December 2014 and the related revaluation reserve movements are therefore:

	Net book value	Valuation	Revaluation reserve
	$'000	$'000	$'000
Cost or valuation	120,000	126,600	6,600
Accumulated depreciation (3/40)	(9,000)	–	9,000
Carrying amount of asset	111,000	126,600	15,600
Original provision	10,000		
Unwinding of discount (3 years @ 5%)	1,600		
	11,600	11,600	
Carrying amount less provision	99,400	115,000	15,600

The depreciation expense for 2015 is therefore $3,420,000 ($126,600,000 ÷ 37) and the discount expense for 2014 is $580,000 (5% of $11,600,000). On 31 December 2015, the decommissioning liability (before any adjustment) is $12,180,000 and the discount rate has not changed. However, on that date, the entity estimates that, as a result of technological advances, the present value of the decommissioning liability has decreased by $5,000,000. Accordingly, the entity adjusts the decommissioning liability to $7,180,000. To determine the extent to which any of the change to the provision is recognised in profit or loss, the entity has to keep a record of revaluations previously recognised in profit or loss; the carrying amount of the asset that would have been recognised under the cost model; and the previous revaluation surplus relating to that asset. *[IFRIC 1.6]*. In this example, the whole of the adjustment is taken to revaluation surplus, because it does not exceed the carrying amount that would have been recognised for the asset under the cost model of $103,000 (see below). *[IFRIC 1.IE6-10]*.

In addition, the entity decides that a full valuation of the asset is needed at 31 December 2015, in order to ensure that the carrying amount does not differ materially from fair value. Suppose that the asset is now valued at $107,000,000, which is net of an allowance of $7,180,000 for the reduced decommissioning obligation. The valuation of the asset for financial reporting purposes, before deducting this allowance, is therefore $114,180,000. The effect on the revaluation reserve of the revision to the estimate of the decommissioning provision and the new valuation can be illustrated in the table below. *[IFRIC 1.IE11-12]*.

	Cost model	Revaluation	Revaluation reserve
	$'000	$'000	$'000
Carrying amount as at 31 December 2014	111,000	126,600	15,600
Depreciation charge for 2015	(3,000)	(3,420)	
Carrying amount as at 31 December 2015	108,000	123,180	
Revision to estimate of provision	(5,000)		
Revaluation adjustment in 2015		(9,000)	(9,000)
	103,000	114,180	
Provision as at 31 December 2014	11,600	11,600	
Unwinding of discount @ 5%	580	580	
Revision to estimate	(5,000)	(5,000)	5,000
Provision as at 31 December 2015	7,180	7,180	
Carrying amount less provision	95,820	107,000	11,600

As indicated at 4.3.6 above, IAS 37 is unclear whether a new discount rate should be applied during the year or just at the year-end, and whether the rate should be applied to the new estimate of the provision or the old estimate. Although IFRIC 1 requires that changes in the provision resulting from a change in the discount rate is added to, or deducted from, the cost of the related asset in the current period, it does not deal specifically with these points. However, Example 1 in the illustrative examples to IFRIC 1 indicates that a change in discount rate would be accounted for in the same way as other changes affecting the estimate of a provision for decommissioning, restoration and similar liabilities. That is, it is reflected as a change in the liability at the time the revised estimate is made and the new estimate is discounted at the revised discount rate from that point on. *[IFRIC 1.IE5]*.

When accounting for revalued assets to which decommissioning liabilities attach, the illustrative example in IFRIC 1 states that it is important to understand the basis of the valuation obtained. For example:

(a) if an asset is valued on a discounted cash flow basis, some valuers may value the asset without deducting any allowance for decommissioning costs (a 'gross' valuation), whereas others may value the asset after deducting an allowance for decommissioning costs (a 'net' valuation), because an entity acquiring the asset will generally also assume the decommissioning obligation. For financial reporting purposes, the decommissioning obligation is recognised as a separate liability, and is not deducted from the asset. Accordingly, if the asset is valued on a net basis, it is necessary to adjust the valuation obtained by adding back the allowance for the liability, so that the liability is not counted twice. This is the case in Example 26.18 above;

(b) if an asset is valued on a depreciated replacement cost basis, the valuation obtained may not include an amount for the decommissioning component of the asset. If it does not, an appropriate amount will need to be added to the valuation to reflect the depreciated replacement cost of that component. *[IFRIC 1.IE7]*.

6.3.2 Changes in legislation after construction of the asset

The scope of IFRIC 1 is set out in terms of any existing decommissioning, restoration or similar liability that is both recognised as part of the cost of the asset under IAS 16 or as part of the cost of a right-of-use asset in accordance with IFRS 16; and recognised as a liability in accordance with IAS 37. *[IFRIC 1.2]*. The Interpretation does not address the treatment of obligations arising after the asset has been constructed, for example as a result of changes in legislation. *[IFRIC 1.BC23]*. Nevertheless, in our opinion the cost of the related asset should be measured in accordance with the principles set out in IFRIC 1 regardless of whether the obligation exists at the time of constructing the asset or arises later in its life.

As discussed at 3.3 in Chapter 18, IAS 16 makes no distinction in principle between the initial costs of acquiring an asset and any subsequent expenditure upon it. In both cases any and all expenditure has to meet the recognition rules, and be expensed in profit or loss if it does not. IAS 16 states that the cost of an item of property, plant and equipment includes 'the initial estimate of the costs of dismantling and removing the item and restoring the site on which it is located, the obligation for which an entity incurs either when the item is acquired or as a consequence of having used the item during a particular period for purposes other than to produce inventories during that period.' *[IAS 16.16(c)]*. For example, the introduction of new legislation to require the clean-up of sites that cease to be used as gasoline filling stations would give rise to the recognition of a decommissioning provision and, to the extent that the clean-up obligation arose as a result of the construction of the filling stations, an increase in the carrying value of the properties. Similarly, IFRS 16 states that the cost of a right-of-use asset includes 'an estimate of costs to be incurred by the lessee in dismantling and removing the underlying asset, restoring the site on which it is located or restoring the underlying asset to the condition required by the terms and conditions of the lease, unless those costs are incurred to produce inventories. The lessee incurs the obligation for those costs either at the commencement date or as a consequence of having used the underlying asset during a particular period.' *[IFRS 16.24(d)].*

Both IAS 16 and IFRS 16 require an entity to apply IAS 2 to the costs of obligations for dismantling, removing and restoring the site on which an item is located that are incurred during a particular period as a consequence of having used the item to produce inventories during that period. *[IAS 16.18, IFRS 16.25].* For example, the cost of restoring the site of a quarry would be reflected as part of the cost of the aggregate extracted from it, and not added to the carrying value of the site. Accordingly, if an entity previously had no obligation to restore the site and new legislation was introduced after 25% of the site had been excavated and 80% of that output had been sold, then 80% of the new estimate of the restoration cost would be expensed; 20% added to the cost of inventory; and none added to the carrying value of the site.

When changes in legislation give rise to a new decommissioning, restoration or similar liability that is added to the carrying amount of the related asset, it would be appropriate to perform an impairment review in accordance with IAS 36 (see Chapter 20).

6.3.3 Funds established to meet an obligation (IFRIC 5)

Some entities may participate in a decommissioning, restoration or environmental rehabilitation fund, the purpose of which is to segregate assets to fund some or all of the costs of decommissioning for which the entity has to make a provision under IAS 37. IFRIC 5 was issued in December 2004 to address this issue, referring to decommissioning to mean not only the dismantling of plant and equipment but also the costs of undertaking environmental rehabilitation, such as rectifying pollution of water or restoring mined land. *[IFRIC 5.1].*

Contributions to these funds may be voluntary or required by regulation or law, and the funds may have one of the following common structures:

- funds that are established by a single contributor to fund its own decommissioning obligations, whether for a particular site, or for a number of geographically dispersed sites;

- funds that are established with multiple contributors to fund their individual or joint decommissioning obligations, where contributors are entitled to reimbursement for decommissioning expenses to the extent of their fund contributions plus any actual earnings on those contributions less their share of the costs of administering the fund. Contributors may have an obligation to make potential additional contributions, for example, in the event of the bankruptcy of another contributor;
- funds that are established with multiple contributors to fund their individual or joint decommissioning obligations when the required level of contributions is based on the current activity of a contributor, but the benefit obtained by that contributor is based on its past activity. In such cases there is a potential mismatch in the amount of contributions made by a contributor (based on current activity) and the value realisable from the fund (based on past activity). *[IFRIC 5.2]*.

Such funds generally have the following features:
- the fund is separately administered by independent trustees;
- entities (contributors) make contributions to the fund, which are invested in a range of assets that may include both debt and equity investments, and are available to help pay the contributors' decommissioning costs. The trustees determine how contributions are invested, within the constraints set by the fund's governing documents and any applicable legislation or other regulations;
- the contributors retain the obligation to pay decommissioning costs. However, contributors are able to obtain reimbursement of decommissioning costs from the fund up to the lower of the decommissioning costs incurred and the entity's share of assets of the fund; and
- the contributors may have restricted or no access to any surplus of assets of the fund over those used to meet eligible decommissioning costs. *[IFRIC 5.3]*.

IFRIC 5 applies to accounting in the financial statements of a contributor for interests arising from decommissioning funds that have both the following features:
- the assets are administered separately (either by being held in a separate legal entity or as segregated assets within another entity); and
- a contributor's right to access the assets is restricted. *[IFRIC 5.4]*.

A residual interest in a fund that extends beyond a right to reimbursement, such as a contractual right to distributions once all the decommissioning has been completed or on winding up the fund, may be an equity instrument within the scope of IFRS 9, and is not within the scope of IFRIC 5. *[IFRIC 5.5]*.

The issues addressed by IFRIC 5 are:

(a) How should a contributor account for its interest in a fund?

(b) When a contributor has an obligation to make additional contributions, for example, in the event of the bankruptcy of another contributor, how should that obligation be accounted for? *[IFRIC 5.6]*

6.3.3.A   Accounting for an interest in a fund

IFRIC 5 requires the contributor to recognise its obligations to pay decommissioning costs as a liability and recognise its interest in the fund separately, unless the contributor is not liable to pay decommissioning costs even if the fund fails to pay. *[IFRIC 5.7]*.

The contributor determines whether it has control, joint control or significant influence over the fund by reference to IFRS 10 – *Consolidated Financial Statements*, IFRS 11 – *Joint Arrangements* – and IAS 28 – *Investments in Associates and Joint Ventures*. If the contributor determines that it has such control, joint control or significant influence, it should account for its interest in the fund in accordance with those standards (see Chapters 6, 12 and 11 respectively). *[IFRIC 5.8]*.

Otherwise, the contributor should recognise the right to receive reimbursement from the fund as a reimbursement in accordance with IAS 37 (see 4.6 above). This reimbursement should be measured at the lower of:

- the amount of the decommissioning obligation recognised; and
- the contributor's share of the fair value of the net assets of the fund attributable to contributors. *[IFRIC 5.9]*.

This 'asset cap' means that the asset recognised in respect of the reimbursement rights can never exceed the recognised liability. Accordingly, rights to receive reimbursement to meet decommissioning liabilities that have yet to be recognised as a provision are not recognised. *[IFRIC 5.BC14]*. Although many respondents expressed concern about this asset cap and argued that rights to benefit in excess of this amount give rise to an additional asset, separate from the reimbursement asset, the Interpretations Committee, despite having sympathy with the concerns, concluded that to recognise such an asset would be inconsistent with the requirement in IAS 37 that 'the amount recognised for the reimbursement should not exceed the amount of the provision'. *[IFRIC 5.BC19-20]*.

Changes in the carrying value of the right to receive reimbursement other than contributions to and payments from the fund should be recognised in profit or loss in the period in which these changes occur. *[IFRIC 5.9]*.

The effect of this requirement is that the amount recognised in the statement of comprehensive income relating to the reimbursement bears no relation to the expense recognised in respect of the provision, particularly for decommissioning liabilities where most changes in the measurement of the provision are not taken to the profit or loss immediately, but are recognised prospectively over the remaining useful life of the related asset (see 6.3.1 above).

One company that has been affected by the 'asset cap' is Fortum as shown below. In this extract, the company observes that because IFRS does not allow the asset to exceed the amount of the provision, *[IFRIC 5.BC19-20]*, it recognises a reimbursement asset in its statement of financial position that is lower than its actual share of the fund.

Extract 26.4: Fortum Oyj (2019)

Notes [extract]
Balance sheet [extract]
29 Nuclear related assets and liabilities [extract]
ACCOUNTING POLICIES [extract]

Fortum owns Loviisa nuclear power plant in Finland. In Fortum's consolidated balance sheet, Share in the State Nuclear Waste Management Fund and the Nuclear provisions relate to Loviisa nuclear power plant. Fortum's nuclear related provisions and the related part of the State Nuclear Waste Management Fund are both presented separately on the balance sheet. Fortum's share in the State Nuclear Waste Management Fund is accounted for according to IFRIC 5, Rights to interests arising from decommissioning, restoration and environmental rehabilitation funds which states that the fund assets are measured at the lower of fair value or the value of the related liabilities since Fortum does not have control or joint control over the State Nuclear Waste Management Fund. The Nuclear Waste Management Fund is managed by governmental authorities. The related provisions are the provision for decommissioning and the provision for disposal of spent fuel.

[...]

Fortum's actual share of the State Nuclear Waste Management Fund, related to Loviisa nuclear power plant, is higher than the carrying value of the Fund on the balance sheet. The legal nuclear liability should, according to the Finnish Nuclear Energy Act, be fully covered by payments and guarantees to the State Nuclear Waste Management Fund. The legal liability is not discounted while the provisions are, and since the future cash flow is spread over a very long time horison, the difference between the legal liability and the provisions are material.

29.1 Nuclear related assets and liabilities for 100% owned nuclear power plant, Loviisa [extract]

EUR million	2019	2018
Carrying values on the balance sheet		
BS Nuclear provisions	813	899
BS Share in State Nuclear Waste Management Fund	813	899
Short term receivable from the State Nuclear Waste Management Fund	51	-
Legal liability and actual share of the State Nuclear Waste Management Fund		
Liability for nuclear waste management according to the Nuclear Energy Act	1,214	1,180
Funding obligation target	1,135	1,180
Fortum's share in the State Nuclear Waste Management Fund	1,180	1,153
Share of the fund not recognised on the balance sheet	316	254

Legal liability for Loviisa nuclear power plant

Finnish nuclear operators have submitted updated technical plan and cost estimates to the Ministry of Economic Affairs and Employment in June 2019. The legal liability on 31 December 2019, decided by the Ministry of Economic Affairs and Employment in November 2019, was EUR 1,214 million.

The legal liability is based on a cost estimate, which is done every year, and a technical plan, which is made every third year. The cost estimate and technical plan was updated in 2019. The legal liability is determined by assuming that the decommissioning would start at the beginning of the year following the assessment year. The provisions are based on the same cash flows for future costs as the legal liability, but the legal liability is not discounted to net present value.

Fortum's share in the State Nuclear Waste Management Fund

According to Nuclear Energy Act, Fortum is obligated to contribute funds in full to the State Nuclear Waste Management Fund to cover the legal liability. Fortum contributes funds to the Finnish State Nuclear Waste Management Fund based on the yearly funding obligation target decided by the governmental authorities in connection with the decision of size of the legal liability. Based on the law, Fortum applied for a periodisation of the fund target, due to a change in the legal liability. The application was approved by the Ministry of Economic Affairs and Employment in November 2019 confirming the fund target at EUR 1,135 million.

Nuclear provisions EUR million	2019	2018
BS 1 January	899	858
Additional provisions	10	29
Provision used	−29	−26
Provision reversed	−100	–
Unwinding of discount	32	38
BS 31 December	813	899
Fortum's share in the State Nuclear Waste Management Fund	813	899

Nuclear provision and fund accounted according to IFRS

Nuclear provisions include the provision for decommissioning and the provision for disposal of spent fuel. The carrying value of the nuclear provisions, calculated according to IAS 37, decreased by EUR 86 million compared to 31 December 2018, totalling EUR 813 million on 31 December 2019. The decrease in provision during 2019 was arising from the updated cost estimate. The decrease was EUR 100 million, of which the part relating to spent fuel was recognised immediately to the income statement and the part relating to decommissioning was capitalised as property, plant and equipment. The reduced provision led to negative nuclear fund adjustment of EUR 54 million and positive effect to other financial expenses – net of EUR 40 million. The periodisation of the fund target led to a positive fund adjustment of EUR 51 million, but did not have any impact on the provision. The increase of provision in 2018 is mainly arising from changes in assumptions used for the provision.

The carrying value of the Fund on the balance sheet cannot exceed the carrying value of the nuclear provisions according to IFRIC 5. The Fund is from an IFRS perspective overfunded with EUR 316 million, since Fortum's share of the Fund on 31 December 2019 was EUR 1,180 million, while the carrying value of the fund on the balance sheet was EUR 813 million and the short-term receivable from the fund EUR 51 million, see Note 23 Trade and other receivables.

Fortum's share of the Finnish Nuclear Waste Management Fund in Fortum's balance sheet can in maximum be equal to the amount of the provisions according to IFRS. As long as the Fund is overfunded from an IFRS perspective, the effects to operating profit from this adjustment will be positive if the provisions increase more than the Fund and negative if actual value of the fund increases more than the provisions. This accounting effect is not included in Comparable operating profit in Fortum's financial reporting. For more information see Note 7 Items affecting comparability.

6.3.3.B   Accounting for obligations to make additional contributions

IFRIC 5 requires that when a contributor has an obligation to make potential additional contributions, for example, in the event of the bankruptcy of another contributor or if the value of the investments held by the fund decreases to an extent that they are insufficient to fulfil the fund's reimbursement obligations, this obligation is a contingent liability that is within the scope of IAS 37. The contributor shall recognise a liability only if it is probable that additional contributions will be made. *[IFRIC 5.10]*.

6.3.3.C   Gross presentation of interest in the fund and the decommissioning liability

IFRIC 5 requires the contributor to a fund to recognise its obligations to pay decommissioning costs as a liability and recognise its interest in the fund separately, unless the contributor is not liable to pay decommissioning costs even if the fund fails to pay. *[IFRIC 5.7]*. Accordingly, in most cases it would not be appropriate to offset the decommissioning liability and the interest in the fund.

The Interpretations Committee reached this conclusion because IAS 37 requires an entity that remains liable for expenditure to recognise a provision even where reimbursement is available and to recognise a separate reimbursement asset only when the entity is virtually certain that it will be received when the obligation is settled. *[IFRIC 5.BC7]*.

The Interpretations Committee also noted that the conditions in IAS 32 – *Financial Instruments: Presentation* – for offsetting a financial asset and a financial liability would rarely be met because of the absence of a legal right of set off and the likelihood that settlement will not be net or simultaneous. *[IAS 32.42]*. Arguments that the existence of a fund allows derecognition of the liability by analogy to IAS 39;[22] or a net presentation similar to a pension fund, were also rejected. *[IFRIC 5.BC8]*.

6.3.3.D Disclosure of interests arising from decommissioning, restoration and environmental rehabilitation funds

IFRIC 5 requires the following disclosures:

- a contributor should disclose the nature of its interest in a fund and any restrictions on access to the assets in the fund; *[IFRIC 5.11]*
- when a contributor has an obligation to make potential additional contributions that is not recognised as a liability (see 6.3.3.B above), it should provide the contingent liability disclosures required by IAS 37 (see 7.2 below); *[IFRIC 5.12]* and
- when a contributor accounts for its right to receive reimbursement from the fund as a reimbursement right under IAS 37 in accordance with paragraph 9 of IFRIC 5 (see 6.3.3.A above), it should disclose the amount of the expected reimbursement and the amount of any asset that has been recognised for that expected reimbursement. *[IFRIC 5.13]*.

6.3.4 Interaction of leases with asset retirement obligations

An entity may sometimes (expect to) use a leased asset to carry out decommissioning or remediation work for which it has recognised a decommissioning, remediation or asset retirement provision. For example, at the end of life of an oil field, an entity may use a leased ship or rig to undertake the plugging and abandonment of oil wells. The entity may have included the estimated cost of plugging and abandonment of the wells in the decommissioning provision set up at the commencement of oil production. If an entity uses leased assets to carry out decommissioning or remediation work for which it recognised a decommissioning, remediation, or asset retirement provision, the question arises as to whether, at lease commencement, the entity's recognition of a lease liability for the leased assets in accordance with IFRS 16 results in derecognition of the asset retirement obligation recognised in the balance sheet. Given that, prior to the commencement of any asset retirement obligation related activities, the entity still has an obligation to rehabilitate under IAS 37, it cannot derecognise the asset retirement obligation. Instead, it now has a separate lease liability for the financing of the lease of the asset. Accordingly, acquiring the right-of-use asset does not result in the derecognition of the asset retirement obligation liability, rather it would be the activity undertaken or output of the asset which would ultimately settle the asset retirement obligation. This is discussed further in Chapter 43 at 17.7.

6.4 Environmental provisions – general guidance in IAS 37

The standard illustrates its recognition requirements in two examples relating to environmental provisions. The first deals with the situation where it is virtually certain that legislation will be enacted which will require the clean-up of land already contaminated. In these circumstances, the virtual certainty of new legislation being enacted means that the entity has a present legal obligation as a result of the past event (contamination of the land), requiring a provision to be recognised. *[IAS 37 IE Example 2A]*. However, in its discussion about what constitutes an obligating event, the standard notes that 'differences in circumstances surrounding enactment make it impossible to specify a single event that would make the enactment of a law virtually certain. In many cases, it will be impossible to be virtually certain of the enactment of a law until it is enacted.' *[IAS 37.22]*. The second example deals with a similar situation, except that the entity is not expected to be legally required to clean it up. Nevertheless, the entity has a widely publicised environmental policy undertaking to clean up all contamination that it causes, and has a record of honouring this policy. In these circumstances a provision is still required because the entity has created a valid expectation that it will clean up the land, meaning that the entity has a present constructive obligation as a result of past contamination. *[IAS 37 IE Example 2B]*. It is therefore clear that where an entity causes environmental damage and has a present legal or constructive obligation to make it good; it is probable that an outflow of resources will be required to settle the obligation; and a reliable estimate can be made of the amount, a provision will be required. *[IAS 37.14]*.

One company making provision for environmental costs is AkzoNobel, which describes some of the uncertainties relating to its measurement in the extract below.

> *Extract 26.5: Akzo Nobel N.V. (2019)*
>
> NOTES TO THE CONSOLIDATED FINANCIAL STATEMENTS [extract]
>
> 19   Other provisions and contingent liabilities [extract]
>
> **Environmental liabilities**
>
> We are confronted with costs arising out of environmental laws and regulations, which include obligations to eliminate or limit the effects on the environment of the disposal or release of certain wastes or substances at various sites. Proceedings involving environmental matters, such as the alleged discharge of chemicals or waste materials into the air, water, or soil, are pending against us in various countries. In some cases, this concerns sites divested in prior years or derelict sites belonging to companies acquired in the past.
>
> Environmental liabilities can change substantially due to the emergence of additional information on the nature or extent of the contamination, the geological circumstances, the necessity of employing particular methods of remediation, actions by governmental agencies or private parties, or other factors.
>
> The provisions for environmental costs amounted to €75 million at year-end 2019 (2018: €91 million). The provision has been discounted using an average pre-tax discount rate of 1.4% (2018: 1.9%). While it is not feasible to predict the outcome of all pending environmental exposures, it is reasonably possible that there will be a need for future provisions for environmental costs which, in management's opinion, based on information currently available, would not have a material effect on the company's financial position but could be material to the company's results of operations in any one accounting period.

If the expenditure relating to an environmental obligation is not expected to be incurred for some time, a significant effect of the standard is its requirement that provisions should be discounted, which can have a material impact.

6.5   Liabilities associated with emissions trading schemes

A number of countries around the world either have, or are developing, schemes to encourage reduced emissions of pollutants, in particular of greenhouse gases. These schemes comprise tradable emissions allowances or permits, an example of which is a 'cap and trade' model whereby participants are allocated emission rights or allowances equal to a cap (i.e. a maximum level of allowable emissions) and are permitted to trade those allowances. A cap and trade emission rights scheme typically has the following features:[23]

- an entity participating in the scheme (participant) is set a target to reduce its emissions to a specified level (the cap). The participant is issued allowances equal in number to its cap by a government or government agency. Allowances may be issued free of charge, or participants may pay the government for them;
- the scheme operates for defined compliance periods;
- participants are free to buy and sell allowances;
- if at the end of the compliance period a participant's actual emissions exceeded its emission rights, the participant will incur a penalty;
- in some schemes emission rights may be carried forward to future periods; and
- the scheme may provide for brokers – who are not themselves participants – to buy and sell emission rights.

In response to diversity in the accounting for cap and trade emission rights schemes, the Interpretations Committee added this matter to its agenda. Accordingly, in December 2004 the IASB issued IFRIC 3 to address the accounting for emission allowances that arise from cap and trade emission rights schemes.

IFRIC 3 took the view that a cap and trade scheme did not give rise to a net asset or liability, but that it gave rise to various items that were to be accounted for separately:[24]

(a) *an asset for allowances held* – Allowances, whether allocated by government or purchased, were to be regarded as intangible assets and accounted for under IAS 38. Allowances issued for less than fair value were to be measured initially at their fair value;[25]

(b) *a government grant* – When allowances are issued for less than fair value, the difference between the amount paid and fair value was a government grant that should be accounted for under IAS 20 – *Accounting for Government Grants and Disclosure of Government Assistance*. Initially the grant was to be recognised as deferred income in the statement of financial position and subsequently recognised as income on a systematic basis over the compliance period for which the allowances were issued, regardless of whether the allowances were held or sold;[26]

(c) *a liability for the obligation to deliver allowances equal to emissions that have been made* – As emissions are made, a liability was to be recognised as a provision that falls within the scope of IAS 37. The liability was to be measured at the best estimate of the expenditure required to settle the present obligation at the end of the reporting period. This would usually be the present market price of the number of allowances required to cover emissions made up to the end of the reporting period.[27]

However, the interpretation met with significant resistance because application of IFRIC 3 would result in a number of accounting mismatches:[28]

- a measurement mismatch between the assets and liabilities recognised in accordance with IFRIC 3;
- a mismatch in the location in which the gains and losses on those assets are reported; and
- a possible timing mismatch because allowances would be recognised when they are obtained – typically at the start of the year – whereas the emission liability would be recognised during the year as it is incurred.

Consequently, the IASB decided in June 2005 to withdraw IFRIC 3 despite the fact that it considered it to be 'an appropriate interpretation of existing IFRSs'.[29] The IASB activated its project on emission trading schemes in December 2007 but work was suspended in November 2010. In May 2012, IASB members gave their unanimous support to giving priority to restarting research on emission trading schemes.[30] In February 2015, the project was renamed from 'Emission trading schemes' to 'Pollutant pricing mechanisms'. This change was to reflect a decision by the Board in January 2015 to broaden the scope of the project to consider a variety of schemes that use emission allowances and other financial tools to manage the emission of pollutants. The Board also decided in January 2015 that they would take a 'fresh start' approach to the project rather than starting from the tentative decisions made in the previous project.[31] The project is currently included in the Board's research pipeline but is not yet on the active work plan.[32]

In the meantime, entities can either:

(a) apply IFRIC 3, which despite having been withdrawn, is considered to be an appropriate interpretation of existing IFRS; or

(b) develop its own accounting policy for cap and trade schemes based on the hierarchy of authoritative guidance in IAS 8.

A more detailed discussion of the issues and methods applied in practice is covered in Chapter 17 at 11.2.

6.6 Green certificates compared to emissions trading schemes

Some countries have launched schemes to promote the production of power from renewable sources based on green certificates – also known as renewable energy certificates (RECs), green tags, or tradable renewable certificates.

In a green certificates system, a producer of electricity from renewable sources is granted certificates by the government based on the power output (kWh) of green electricity produced. These certificates may be used in the current and future compliance periods as defined by the particular scheme. The certificates can be sold separately. Generally the cost to produce green electricity is higher than the cost of producing an equivalent amount of electricity generated from non-renewable sources, although this is not always the case. Distributors of electricity sell green electricity at the same price as other electricity.

In a typical green certificates scheme, distributors of electricity to consumers (businesses, households etc.) are required to remit a number of green certificates based on the kWh of electricity sold on an annual basis. Distributors must therefore purchase green certificates in the market (such certificates having been sold by producers). If a distribution company does not have the number of required certificates, it is required to pay a penalty to the environmental agency. Once the penalty is paid, the entity is discharged of its obligations to remit certificates.

It is this requirement to remit certificates that creates a market in and gives value to green certificates (the value depends on many variables but primarily on the required number of certificates that have to be delivered relative to the amount of power that is produced from renewable sources, and the level of penalty payable if the required number of certificates are not remitted).

There are similarities between green certificates and emission rights. However, green certificates are granted to generators of cleaner energy as an incentive for 'good' production achieved, irrespective of whether or not there is a subsequent sale of that cleaner energy to an end consumer. For a distributor of energy, a green certificate gives a similar 'right to pollute' as an emission right except that a distributor of energy under a green certificate regime must acquire the certificates from the market (i.e. they are not granted to the distributor by the government). As with emission rights, the topic of green certificates cuts across a number of different areas of accounting, not just provisions. A more detailed discussion of the issues and methods applied in practice is covered in Chapter 17 at 11.3.

6.7 EU Directive on 'Waste Electrical and Electronic Equipment' (IFRIC 6)

This Directive regulates the collection, treatment, recovery and environmentally sound disposal of waste electrical or electronic equipment (WE&EE).[33] It applies to entities involved in the manufacture and resale of electrical or electronic equipment, including entities (both European and Non-European) that import such equipment into the EU. As member states in the EU began to implement this directive into their national laws, it gave rise to questions about when the liability for the decommissioning of WE&EE should be recognised. The Directive distinguishes between 'new' and 'historical' waste and between waste from private households and waste from sources other than private households. New waste relates to products sold after 13 August 2005. All household equipment sold before that date is deemed to give rise to historical waste for the purposes of the Directive. *[IFRIC 6.3]*.

The Directive states that the cost of waste management for historical household equipment should be borne by producers of that type of equipment that are in the market during a period to be specified in the applicable legislation of each Member State (the measurement period). The Directive states that each Member State shall establish a mechanism to have producers contribute to costs proportionately 'e.g. in proportion to their respective share of the market by type of equipment.' *[IFRIC 6.4]*.

The Interpretations Committee was asked to determine in the context of the decommissioning of WE&EE what constitutes the obligating event in accordance with paragraph 14(a) of IAS 37 (discussed at 3.1.1 above) for the recognition of a provision for waste management costs:

- the manufacture or sale of the historical household equipment?
- participation in the market during the measurement period?
- the incurrence of costs in the performance of waste management activities?
[IFRIC 6.8]

IFRIC 6 was issued in September 2005 and provides guidance on the recognition, in the financial statements of producers, of liabilities for waste management under the EU Directive on WE&EE in respect of sales of historical household equipment. *[IFRIC 6.6]*. The interpretation addresses neither new waste nor historical waste from sources other than private households. The Interpretations Committee considers that the liability for such waste management is adequately covered in IAS 37. However, if, in national legislation, new waste from private households is treated in a similar manner to historical waste from private households, the principles of IFRIC 6 are to apply by reference to the hierarchy set out in IAS 8 (see Chapter 3 at 4.3). The IAS 8 hierarchy is also stated to be relevant for other regulations that impose obligations in a way that is similar to the cost attribution model specified in the EU Directive. *[IFRIC 6.7]*.

IFRIC 6 regards participation in the market during the measurement period as the obligating event in accordance with paragraph 14(a) of IAS 37. Consequently, a liability for waste management costs for historical household equipment does not arise as the products are manufactured or sold. Because the obligation for historical household equipment is linked to participation in the market during the measurement period, rather than to production or sale of the items to be disposed of, there is no obligation unless and until a market share exists during the measurement period. It is also noted that the timing of the obligating event may also be independent of the particular period in which the activities to perform the waste management are undertaken and the related costs incurred. *[IFRIC 6.9]*.

The following example, which is based on one within the accompanying Basis for Conclusions on IFRIC 6, illustrates its requirements.

Example 26.19: Illustration of IFRIC 6 requirements

An entity selling electrical equipment in 2019 has a market share of 4 per cent for that calendar year. It subsequently discontinues operations and is thus no longer in the market when the waste management costs for its products are allocated to those entities with market share in 2021. With a market share of 0 per cent in 2021, the entity's obligation is zero. However, if another entity enters the market for electronic products in 2021 and achieves a market share of 3 per cent in that period, then that entity's obligation for the costs of waste management from earlier periods will be 3 per cent of the total costs of waste management allocated to 2021, even though the entity was not in the market in those earlier periods and has not produced any of the products for which waste management costs are allocated to 2021. *[IFRIC 6.BC5]*.

The Interpretations Committee concluded that the effect of the cost attribution model specified in the Directive is that the making of sales during the measurement period is the 'past event' that requires recognition of a provision under IAS 37 over the measurement period. Aggregate sales for the period determine the entity's obligation for a proportion of the costs of waste management allocated to that period. The measurement period is independent of the period when the cost allocation is notified to market participants. *[IFRIC 6.BC6]*.

Some constituents asked the Interpretations Committee to consider the effect of the following possible national legislation: the waste management costs for which a producer is responsible because of its participation in the market during a specified period (for example 2021) are not based on the market share of the producer during that period but on the producer's participation in the market during a previous period (for example 2020). The Interpretations Committee noted that this affects only the measurement of the liability and that the obligating event is still participation in the market during 2020. *[IFRIC 6.BC7]*.

IFRIC 6 notes that terms used in the interpretation such as 'market share' and 'measurement period' may be defined very differently in the applicable legislation of individual Member States. For example, the length of the measurement period might be a year or only one month. Similarly, the measurement of market share and the formulae for computing the obligation may differ in the various national legislations. However, all of these examples affect only the measurement of the liability, which is not within the scope of the interpretation. *[IFRIC 6.5]*.

6.8 Levies imposed by governments

When governments or other public authorities impose levies on entities in relation to their activities, as opposed to income taxes and fines or other penalties, it is not always clear when the liability to pay a levy arises and a provision should be recognised. In May 2013, the Interpretations Committee issued IFRIC 21 to address this question. *[IFRIC 21.2, 7].* The Interpretation does not address the accounting for the costs arising out of an obligation to pay a levy, for example to determine whether an asset or expense should be recorded. Other standards should be applied in this regard. *[IFRIC 21.3].*

The Interpretation became mandatory for accounting periods beginning on or after 1 January 2014, although it permitted earlier application. *[IFRIC 21.A1].* It requires that, for levies within its scope, an entity should recognise a liability only when the activity that triggers payment, as identified by the relevant legislation, occurs. *[IFRIC 21.8].*

6.8.1 Scope of IFRIC 21

A levy is defined as an outflow of resources embodying economic benefits that is imposed by governments on entities in accordance with legislation, other than:

(a) those outflows of resources that are within the scope of other Standards (such as income taxes that are within the scope of IAS 12); and

(b) fines or other penalties that are imposed for breaches of the legislation. *[IFRIC 21.4].*

In addition to income taxes (see Chapter 33) and fines, the Interpretation does not apply to contractual arrangements with government in which the entity acquires an asset (see Chapters 17 and 18) or receives services; and it is not required to be applied to liabilities that arise from emission trading schemes (see 6.5 above). *[IFRIC 21.5, 6].* Although IFRIC 21 does not apply to income taxes in scope of IAS 12, the Interpretations Committee concluded in 2006 that any taxes not within the scope of other standards (such as IAS 12) are within the scope of IAS 37. Therefore such taxes may be within the scope of IFRIC 21. *[IFRIC 21.BC4].*

IFRIC 21 was developed to address concerns over the timing of recognition for government-imposed levies in which the obligation to pay depended upon participation in a particular market on a specified date. However, the definition of levy in IFRIC 21 has resulted in the scope of the interpretation being broader than entities might have expected. The term 'levy' may not be widely used across jurisdictions, and may be referred to as a charge, duty or a tax, for example. However, it is not the terminology, but the nature of the payment, that should be considered when determining if it is in the scope of IFRIC 21.

Entities should consider all payments imposed by governments pursuant to legislation to determine whether they are in scope of IFRIC 21. The interpretation provides a broad definition of government, including municipal, provincial, state, federal or international governments or government agencies or organisations controlled or administered by government. *[IFRIC 21.4].*

IFRIC 21 clarifies that both levies that give rise to a liability under IAS 37, and levies whose timing or amounts are certain are within scope of the interpretation. *[IFRIC 21.2].* Therefore, the scope of IFRIC 21 is broader than IAS 37. For example, a non-refundable fixed fee imposed by government payable at a specific date may be a levy within the scope of IFRIC 21.

In some cases, payments may pass through one or more non-governmental bodies or entities before being received by the government. In our view, IFRIC 21 does not distinguish between recipients of the payment; the key factor is whether the payment is required by law. Therefore, as long as the payments are required by law, they are generally considered to be imposed by the government. *[IFRIC 21.4]*.

Some of the legislation relating to payments imposed by governments can be complex, so entities should carefully analyse the facts and circumstances to determine whether a payment falls within the scope of IFRIC 21. However, where entities are making payments for any of the following items, it may be necessary to assess for any potential IFRIC 21 impacts:

- taxes other than income taxes, e.g. property tax, land tax and capital-based tax;
- certain fees, concessions, contributions or royalty fees imposed on industries which are regulated by government, e.g. telecommunications, mining, airline, banking, insurance, dairy produce and energy and natural resources; and
- transaction taxes based on activity in a specified market, e.g. banking and insurance.

6.8.2 Recognition and measurement of levy liabilities

For levies within the scope of the Interpretation, the activity that creates the obligation under the relevant legislation to pay the levy is the obligating event for recognition purposes. *[IFRIC 21.8]*. In many cases this activity is related to the entity's participation in a relevant market at a specific date or dates. The Interpretation states that neither a constructive nor a present obligation arises as a result of being economically compelled to continue operating; or from any implication of continuing operations in the future arising from the use of the going concern assumption in the preparation of financial statements. *[IFRIC 21.9, 10]*.

When a levy is payable progressively, for example as the entity generates revenues, the entity recognises a liability over a period of time on that basis. This is because the obligating event is the activity that generates revenues. *[IFRIC 21.11]*. If an obligation to pay a levy is triggered in full as soon as a minimum threshold is reached, such as when the entity commences generating sales or achieves a certain level of revenue, the liability is recognised in full on the first day that the entity reaches that threshold. *[IFRIC 21.12]*. If an entity pays over amounts to government before it is determined that an obligation to pay that levy exists, it recognises an asset. *[IFRIC 21.14]*.

Example 26.20: A levy is triggered in full as soon as the entity generates revenues

An entity with a calendar year end generates revenues in a specific market in 2021. The amount of the levy is determined by reference to revenues generated by the entity in the market in 2020 although the levy is only payable when revenues are generated in 2021. The entity generated revenues in the market in 2020 and starts to generate revenues in the market in 2021 on 3 January 2021.

In this example, the liability is recognised in full on 3 January 2021 because the obligating event, as identified by the legislation, is the first generation of revenues in 2021. The generation of revenues in 2020 is necessary, but not sufficient, to create a present obligation to pay a levy. Before 3 January 2021, the entity has no obligation. In other words, the activity that triggers the payment of the levy as identified by the legislation is the first generation of revenues at a point in time in 2020. The generation of revenues in 2020 is not the activity that triggers the payment of the levy. The amount of revenues generated in 2020 only affects the measurement of the liability. *[IFRIC 21.IE1 Example 2]*.

The table below summarises the illustrative examples that accompany IFRIC 21, which provide guidelines on how to account for the timing of the recognition for the various types of levies: *[IFRIC 21.IE1]*

Illustrative examples	Obligating event	Recognition of liability
Levy triggered progressively as revenue is generated in a specified period.	Generation of revenue in the specified period.	Recognise progressively. A liability must be recognised progressively because, at any point in time during the specified period, the entity has a present obligation to pay a levy on revenues generated to date.
Levy triggered in full as soon as revenue is generated in one period, based on revenues from a previous period.	First generation of revenue in subsequent period.	Full recognition at that point in time. Where an entity generates revenue in one period, which serves as the basis for measuring the amount of the levy, the entity does not become liable for the levy, and therefore cannot recognise a liability, until it first starts generating revenue in the subsequent period.
Levy triggered in full if the entity operates as a bank at the end of the annual reporting period.	Operating as a bank at the end of the reporting period.	Full recognition at the end of the annual reporting period. Before the end of the annual reporting period, the entity has no present obligation to pay a levy, even if it is economically compelled to continue operating as a bank in the future. The liability is recognised only at the end of the annual reporting period.
Levy triggered if revenues are above a minimum specified threshold (e.g. when a certain level of revenue has been achieved)	Reaching the specified minimum threshold.	Recognise an amount consistent with the obligation at that point of time. A liability is recognised only at the point that the specified minimum threshold is reached. For example, a levy is triggered when an entity generates revenues above specified thresholds: 0% for the first $50 million and 2% above $50 million. In this example, no liability is accrued until the entity's revenues reach the revenue threshold of $50 million.

As set out in the table above, when a levy is triggered progressively, for example, as the entity generates revenues, the entity recognises a liability over the period of time on that basis. Some examples of progressive-type levies are set out below.

Example 26.21: **Recognising a liability for levies that are triggered progressively**

Scenario 1: Minimums

The legislation prescribes that no levy is triggered until revenues reach a certain threshold. There is a 0% tax rate on revenues until they reach $50 million, with a payment of 2% of revenues in excess of that amount.

For an entity that earns $49 million as at 30 June 2021, $51 million as at 31 July 2021 and $100 million as at 31 December 2021, the following liabilities should be recognised:

30 June 2021 – No provision is recognised;

31 July 2021 – $20,000 provision is recognised (2% × $1 million); and

31 December 2021 – $1 million provision is recognised (2% × $50 million).

Scenario 2: Progressive tax rates

The legislation prescribes that the tax rate is escalating. There is a 2% tax rate on the first $50 million in revenues and 3% for revenues in excess of $50 million.

For an entity that earns $49 million as at 30 June 2021, $51 million as at 31 July 2021 and $100 million as at 31 December 2021, the following liabilities should be recognised:

30 June 2021 – $980,000 provision is recognised (2% × $49 million);

31 July 2021 – $1,030,000 provision is recognised ((2% × $50 million) + (3% × $1 million)); and

31 December 2021 – $2.5 million provision is recognised ((2% × $50 million) + (3% × $50 million)).

Scenario 3: Specified formula

The legislation prescribes that the levy is calculated based on a specified formula that does not match the actual activity for the period. A calendar year-end entity has to pay a monthly levy based on 0.1% of a 12-month rolling average of gross profit.

Under the legislation, the 12-month period which the rolling average of the gross profit would be based on relates to the preceding 12 months, for example:

Date	Preceding 12 months	12 month rolling average ($)	Liability to be recognised ($)
30 June 2021	1 July 2020 – 30 June 2021	50 million	50,000
31 July 2021	1 August 2020 – 31 July 2021	60 million	60,000
31 December 2021	1 January 2021 – 31 December 2021	40 million	40,000

When the legislation provides that a levy is triggered by an entity operating in a market only at the end of its annual reporting period, no liability is recognised until the last day of the annual reporting period. No amount is recognised before that date in anticipation of the entity still operating in the market. Accordingly, a provision would not be permitted to be recognised in interim financial statements if the obligating event occurs only at the end of the annual reporting period. *[IFRIC 21.IE1 Example 3].* The accounting treatment in interim reports is discussed in Chapter 41 at 9.7.5.

6.8.3 Recognition of an asset or expense when a levy is recorded

IFRIC 21 only provides guidance on when to recognise a liability, which is the credit side of the journal entry. The interpretation specifically states that it does not address whether the debit side of the journal entry is an asset or an expense, *[IFRIC 21.3],* except in the case of prepaid levies. *[IFRIC 21.14].*

Prepayments may be fairly common in arrangements in which the legislation requires entities to pay levies in advance and where the obligating events for these levies are progressive. For example, property taxes that are paid in advance at a specified date (e.g. 1 January) for an obligating event that relates to future periods (e.g. 1 January to 31 December). In such instances, the entity would recognise the prepaid levy as an asset. *[IFRIC 21.14]*. In this scenario, the prepaid levy would then be amortised over the period.

Aside from prepaid levies, there are also instances when the assessment of expensing the liability or recognising a corresponding asset requires the application of other standards, such as IAS 2, IAS 16 or IAS 38. Given that levies are imposed by government and arise from non-exchange transactions, there would not typically be a clear linkage to future economic benefits. Consequentially, if the incurrence of the liability does not give rise to an identifiable future economic benefit to the entity, the recognition of an asset would be inappropriate as the definition of an asset would not be met. In such cases, the debit side would therefore be to an expense account.

In the case where asset recognition is appropriate under other IFRS standards, levies are generally not expected to give rise to a stand-alone asset in its own right, given that payments for the acquisition of goods or services are scoped out of IFRIC 21. *[IFRIC 21.5]*. However, a levy may form part of the acquisition costs of some other asset, provided it meets the asset recognition criteria in other IFRS standards. For example, an entity may be required to pay an import duty to the government under legislation for any large cargo trucks purchased from overseas. The entity uses the large cargo trucks as part of their operations to transport their goods to customers locally and therefore capitalises the trucks as part of property, plant and equipment under IAS 16. The import duty that is payable under the legislation may give rise to an IFRIC 21 levy, which would also be capitalised as part of the cost of the asset. *[IAS 16.16(a)]*.

6.8.4 Payments relating to taxes other than income tax

As discussed at 6.8.1 above, IFRIC 21 does not apply to income taxes in scope of IAS 12. However, the Interpretations Committee concluded in 2006 that any taxes not within the scope of other standards (such as IAS 12) are within the scope of IAS 37. Therefore such taxes may be within the scope of IFRIC 21. *[IFRIC 21.BC4]*.

In 2018, the Interpretations Committee began discussing a fact pattern where an entity is in dispute with a tax authority in respect of a tax other than income tax. The entity determines that it is probable that it does not have an obligation for the disputed amount and consequently, it does not recognise a liability applying IAS 37. The entity nonetheless pays the disputed amount to the tax authority, either voluntarily or because it is required to do so. The entity has no right to a refund of the amount before resolution of the dispute. Upon resolution, either the tax authority returns the payment to the entity (if the outcome of the dispute is favourable to the entity) or the payment is used to settle the tax liability (if the outcome of the dispute is unfavourable to the entity).

In January 2019, the Interpretations Committee observed that the payment made by the entity gives rise to an asset as defined in both the *Conceptual Framework for Financial Reporting* issued in March 2018, and the definition in the previous Conceptual Framework that was in place when many existing IFRS Standards were developed.

The tax deposit gives the entity a right to receive future economic benefits, either in the form of a cash refund or by using the payment to settle the tax liability. The nature of the tax deposit, either voluntary or required, does not affect the conclusion that there is an asset. The right is not a contingent asset as defined in IAS 37 because it is an asset, and not a possible asset, of the entity. The entity therefore recognises an asset when it makes the payment to the tax authority.[34]

6.9 Dilapidation and other provisions relating to leased assets

As discussed at 5.2 above, it is not appropriate to recognise provisions that relate to repairs and maintenance of owned assets. However, the position can be different in the case of obligations relating to assets held under leases. Nevertheless, the same principles under IAS 37 apply:

(a) provisions are recognised only for obligations existing independently of the entity's future actions (i.e. the future conduct of its business) and in cases where an entity can avoid future expenditure by its future actions, for example by changing its method of operation, it has no present obligation; *[IAS 37.19]*

(b) financial statements deal with an entity's position at the end of the reporting period and not its possible position in the future. Therefore, no provision is recognised for costs that need to be incurred to operate in the future; *[IAS 37.18]* and

(c) for an event to be an obligating event, the entity must have no realistic alternative to settling the obligation created by the event. *[IAS 37.17]*.

Leases often contain clauses which specify that the lessee should incur periodic charges for maintenance, make good dilapidations or other damage occurring during the rental period or return the asset to the configuration that existed as at inception of the lease. These contractual provisions may restrict the entity's ability to change its future conduct to avoid the expenditure. For example, the entity might not be able to transfer the asset in its existing condition. Alternatively, the entity could return the asset to avoid the risk of incurring costs relating to any future damage, but would have to make a payment in relation of dilapidations incurred to date. Therefore the contractual obligations in a lease could create an environment in which a present obligation could exist as at the reporting date from which the entity cannot realistically withdraw.

Under principle (b) above, any provision should reflect only the conditions as at the reporting date. This means that a provision for specific damage done to the leased asset would merit recognition, as the event giving rise to the obligation under the lease has certainly occurred. For example, if an entity has erected partitioning or internal walls in a leasehold property and under the lease these must be removed at the end of the term, then provision should be made for this cost (on a discounted basis, if material) at the time of putting up the partitioning or the walls. In this case, an equivalent asset would be recognised and depreciated over the term of the lease. This is similar to a decommissioning provision discussed at 6.3 above. Another example would be where an airline company leases aircraft, and upon delivery of the aircraft has made changes to the interior fittings and layout, but under the leasing arrangements must return the asset to the configuration that existed as at inception of the lease.

What is less clear is whether a more general provision can be built up over time for maintenance charges and dilapidation costs in relation to a leased asset. It might be argued that in this case, the event giving rise to the obligation under the lease is simply the passage of time, and so a provision can be built up over time. However, in our view the phrase 'the event giving rise to the obligation under the lease' indicates that a more specific event must occur; there has to be specific evidence of dilapidation etc. before any provision can be made. That is, it cannot be assumed that the condition of a leased asset has deteriorated simply because time has passed. However, in practice, it will often be the case that dilapidations do occur over time, in which case a dilapidations provision should be recognised as those dilapidations occur over the lease term. Example 26.12 at 5.2 above dealt with an owned aircraft that by law needs overhauling every three years, but no provision could be recognised for such costs. Instead, IAS 37 suggests that an amount equivalent to the expected maintenance costs is treated as a separate part of the asset and depreciated over three years. Airworthiness requirements for the airline industry are the same irrespective of whether the aircraft is owned or leased. So, if an airline company leases the aircraft, should a provision be made for the overhaul costs? The answer will depend on the terms of the lease.

For a lessee, the accounting for contractual overhaul obligations will require careful consideration. IFRS 16 requires the depreciation requirements of IAS 16 to be applied in the subsequent measurement of a right-of-use asset. *[IFRS 16.31]*. Under the depreciation requirements of IAS 16, each part of an asset with a cost that is significant in relation to the total cost of the item must be depreciated separately. *[IAS 16.44]*. The application of this 'component approach' to the right-of-use asset could imply an approach similar to that suggested in Example 26.12 at 5.2 above for owned assets. An entity should apply judgement in determining an appropriate accounting policy for how the application of component accounting for the right-of-use asset would interact with the recognition of provisions for regulatory overhauls under IAS 37.

The fact that a provision for repairs can be made at all for leased assets might appear inconsistent with the case where the asset is owned by the entity. In that case, as discussed at 5.2 above, no provision for repairs could be made. There is, however, a difference between the two situations. Where the entity owns the asset, it has the choice of selling it rather than repairing it, and so the obligation is not independent of the entity's future actions. However, in the case of an entity leasing the asset, it can have a contractual obligation to repair any damage from which it cannot walk away.

6.10 Warranty provisions

Warranty provisions are specifically addressed in one of the examples appended to IAS 37. However, as noted at 2.2.1.B above, an entity would apply IFRS 15 to separately purchased warranties and to those warranties determined to provide the customer with a service in addition to the assurance that the product complies with agreed-upon specifications. Only if a customer does not have the option to purchase a warranty separately and the warranty is determined only to provide assurance that the product complies with agreed-upon specifications would an entity consider IAS 37. *[IFRS 15.B30]*. The requirements for warranties falling within the scope of IFRS 15 are considered further in Chapter 31.

The following example illustrates how warranty costs are addressed if IAS 37 applies.

Example 26.22:   Recognition of a provision for warranty costs

A manufacturer gives warranties at the time of sale to purchasers of its product. Under the terms of the contract for sale, the manufacturer undertakes to make good, by repair or replacement, manufacturing defects that become apparent within three years from the date of sale. On past experience, it is probable (i.e. more likely than not) that there will be some claims under the warranties.

In these circumstances the obligating event is the sale of the product with a warranty, which gives rise to a legal obligation. Because it is more likely than not that there will be an outflow of resources for some claims under the warranties as a whole, a provision is recognised for the best estimate of the costs of making good under the warranty for those products sold before the end of the reporting period. *[IAS 37 IE Example 1].*

The assessment of the probability of an outflow of resources is made across the population as a whole, and not using each potential claim as the unit of account. *[IAS 37.24].* On past experience, it is probable that there will be some claims under the warranties, so a provision is recognised.

The assessment over the class of obligations as a whole makes it more likely that a provision will be recognised, because the probability criterion is considered in terms of whether at least one item in the population will give rise to a payment. Recognition then becomes a matter of reliable measurement and entities calculate an expected value of the estimated warranty costs. IAS 37 discusses this method of 'expected value' and illustrates how it is calculated in an example of a warranty provision. *[IAS 37.39].* See Example 26.6 at 4.1 above.

An example of a company that makes a warranty provision is Philips Group as shown below:

Extract 26.6: Koninklijke Philips N.V. (2019)

10.9   Notes [extract]

1   **Significant accounting policies** [extract]

Provisions [extract]

Product warranty – A provision for assurance-type product warranty is recognized when the underlying products or services are sold. The provision is based on historical warranty data and a weighing of possible outcomes against their associated probabilities.

19   **Provisions** [extract]

Assurance-type product warranty [extract]

The provisions for assurance-type product warranty reflect the estimated costs of replacement and free-of-charge services that will be incurred by the company with respect to products sold.

The Company expects the provisions to be utilized mainly within the next year.

6.11   Litigation and other legal claims

IAS 37 includes an example of a court case in its appendix to illustrate how its principles distinguish between a contingent liability and a provision in such situations. See Example 26.4 at 3.2.1 above. However, the assessment of the particular case in the example is clear-cut. In most situations, assessing the need to provide for legal claims is one of the most difficult tasks in the field of provisioning. This is due mainly to the inherent uncertainty in the judicial process itself, which may be very long and drawn out. Furthermore, this is an area where either provision or disclosure might risk prejudicing the outcome of the case, because they give an insight into the entity's own view on the strength of its defence that can assist the claimant.

In principle, whether a provision should be made will depend on whether the three conditions for recognising a provision are met, i.e.

(a) there is a present obligation as a result of a past event;

(b) it is probable that an outflow of resources embodying economic benefits will be required to settle the obligation; and

(c) a reliable estimate can be made of the amount of the obligation. *[IAS 37.14]*.

In situations such as these, a past event is deemed to give rise to a present obligation if, taking account of all available evidence (including, for example, the opinion of experts), it is more likely than not that a present obligation exists at the end of the reporting period. *[IAS 37.15]*. The evidence to be considered includes any additional evidence occurring after the end of the reporting period. Accordingly, if on the basis of the evidence it is concluded that a present obligation is more likely than not to exist, a provision will be required, assuming the other conditions are met. *[IAS 37.16]*.

Condition (b) will be met if the transfer of economic benefits is more likely than not to occur, that is, it has a probability greater than 50%. In making this assessment, it is likely that account should be taken of any expert advice.

As far as condition (c) is concerned, the standard takes the view that a reasonable estimate can generally be made and it is only in extremely rare cases that this will not be the case. *[IAS 37.25]*.

Clearly, whether an entity should make provision for the costs of settling a case or to meet any award given by a court will depend on a reasoned assessment of the particular circumstances, based on appropriate legal advice.

6.12 Refunds policy

Example 26.1 at 3.1.1 above reflects an example given in the appendix of IAS 37 of a retail store that has a policy of refunding goods returned by dissatisfied customers. There is no legal obligation to do so, but the company's policy of making refunds is generally known. The example argues that the conduct of the store has created a valid expectation on the part of its customers that it will refund purchases. The obligating event is the original sale of the item, and the probability of some economic outflow is greater than 50%, as there will nearly always be some customers demanding refunds. Hence, a provision should be made, *[IAS 37 IE Example 4]*, presumably calculated on the 'expected value' basis.

This example is straightforward when the store has a very specific and highly publicised policy on refunds. However, some stores' policies on refunds might not be so clear cut. A store may offer refunds under certain conditions, but not widely publicise its policy. In these circumstances, there might be doubt as to whether the store has created a valid expectation on the part of its customers that it will honour all requests for a refund.

As with warranty costs (discussed at 6.10 above), the accounting treatment of refunds impinges into the area of revenue recognition. Under IFRS 15, an entity recognises the amount of expected returns as a refund liability, representing its obligation to return the customer's consideration. *[IFRS 15.55]*. As noted at 2.2.1.B above, other than contracts with customers that are, or have become onerous, contracts in scope of IFRS 15 are outside the scope of IAS 37. *[IAS 37.5]*.

6.13 Self insurance

Another situation where entities sometimes make provisions is self insurance which arises when an entity decides not to take out external insurance in respect of a certain category of risk because it would be uneconomic to do so. The same position may arise when a group insures its risks with a captive insurance subsidiary, the effects of which have to be eliminated on consolidation. In fact, the term 'self insurance' is potentially misleading, since it really means that the entity is not insured at all and will settle claims from third parties from its own resources in the event that it is found to be liable. Accordingly, the recognition criteria in IAS 37 should be applied, with a provision being justified only if there is a present obligation as a result of a past event; if it is probable that an outflow of resources will occur; and a reliable estimate can be determined. *[IAS 37.14]*.

Therefore, losses are recognised based on their actual incidence and any provisions that appear in the statement of financial position should reflect only the amounts expected to be paid in respect of those incidents that have occurred by the end of the reporting period.

In certain circumstances, a provision will often be needed not simply for known incidents, but also for those which insurance companies call IBNR – Incurred But Not Reported – representing an estimate of claims that have occurred at the end of the reporting period but which have not yet been notified to the reporting entity. We believe that it is appropriate that provision for such expected claims is made to the extent that such items can be measured reliably.

6.14 Obligations to make donations to non-profit organisations

When an entity promises to make donations to a non-profit organisation it can be difficult to determine whether a past obligating event exists that requires a provision to be recognised or whether it is appropriate instead to account for the gift as payments are made.

Example 26.23: Accounting for donations to non-profit organisations

An entity decides to enter into an arrangement to 'donate' €1m in cash to a university. A number of different options are available for the arrangement and the entity's management want to determine whether the terms of these options make any difference to the timing, measurement or presentation of the €1m expenditure, as follows:

Option 1:
The entity enters into an unenforceable contract to contribute €1m for general purposes. The benefits to the entity are deemed only to relate to its reputation as a 'good corporate citizen'; the entity does not receive any consideration or significant benefit from the university in return for the donation.

Option 2:
As per Option 1 except the entity publishes a press release in relation to the donation and announcing that payment is to be made in equal instalments of €200,000 over 5 years.

Option 3:
As per Option 2, except that the contract is legally enforceable in the event that the entity does not pay all the instalments under the contract.

Option 4:
As per Option 2, except that the entity is only required to make the donation if the university raises €4m from other sources.

Option 5:
As per Option 2, except that the contract is legally enforceable and the funds will be used for research and development activities specified by the entity. The entity will retain proprietary rights over the results of the research.

The following principles are relevant in determining when a promise to make a donation should be recognised as an obligation:

- to the extent that there is an enforceable contract, the donor should recognise an expense and a liability upon entry into that contract;
- where the agreement is not enforceable, the donor recognises an expense and a liability when a constructive obligation arises. The timing of recognition depends on whether the donation is conditional, whether it is probable that those conditions are substantially met and whether a past event has occurred; and
- if the donor expects to receive benefits commensurate with the value of the donation, the arrangement should be treated as an exchange transaction. Such transactions are in some cases executory contracts and may also give rise to the recognition of an asset rather than an expense.

In cases where the 'donation' is made under an enforceable contract, a present obligation is created when the entity enters into that contract. When payment is required in cash, the signing of an enforceable contract gives rise to a financial liability, *[IAS 32.11]*, which is measured initially at fair value. *[IFRS 9.5.1.1]*.

Where there is no legal obligation to make the payments, a liability is recognised when a constructive obligation arises. It is a matter of judgement whether and when a constructive obligation exists. In many unenforceable contracts, a signed contract would not, in itself, be sufficient to create a constructive obligation. Hence, in the absence of other facts and circumstances that would create a constructive obligation, the donor would recognise the expenditure when the cash or other assets are transferred.

By contrast, an exchange transaction is a reciprocal transfer in which each party receives and sacrifices approximately equal value. Assets and liabilities are not recognised until each party performs their obligations under the arrangement.

Applying these principles to the options listed in Example 26.23 above:

- In Option 1, the contract is unenforceable, there is no announcement or conditions preceding payment and there is no exchange of benefits. Accordingly, an expense would be recognised only when the entity transfers cash to the university.
- For Option 2, it may be appropriate for the entity to conclude that the entity's announcement of the donation to be paid by instalments indicates that there is a constructive obligation because the entity has a created a valid expectation that it will make all of the payments promised. Alternatively, it could determine that once the first instalment is paid, the entity has created a valid expectation that it will make the remaining payments. This is a matter of judgement. In this case the entity

- would recognise an expense and a liability, measured at the net present value of the 5 instalments of €200,000, at the point when it is determined that a constructive obligation exists.
- Option 3 involves an enforceable contract with no exchange of benefits. Therefore a liability and an expense is recognised on signing the enforceable contract, measured at the fair value of the 5 instalments of €200,000.
- Under Option 4, the contract is unenforceable and the donation is subject to a condition. In these circumstances, whether there is a constructive obligation to make the donation is a matter of judgement. Management might conclude that no constructive obligation exists until it is probable that the condition is met (which might not be until the additional funds have been collected). Only then would a liability and expense be recognised, measured at the net present value of the €1m promised.
- Option 5 involves an enforceable contract which may give rise to a liability when the contract is signed. However, there is an exchange of benefits relating to the research and development activities performed on behalf of the entity. Whether these benefits have a value of at least the present value of the 5 instalments of €200,000 is a matter of judgement. If it is determined that this is an exchange transaction that is not onerous, the entity could regard the signing of the contract as executory and could apply the criteria in IAS 38 to determine whether an asset or expense would be recognised for the related research and development costs as incurred (see Chapter 17 at 6.2).

Where the arrangement gives rise to an exchange transaction rather than a donation, the expenditure incurred by the donor is recorded in accordance with the relevant IFRS.

6.15 Settlement payments

A similar issue to that discussed at 6.14 above arises when an entity promises to make a settlement payment in cases where an entity believes that there is no present legal obligation. For example, an entity dismisses an employee for behaving in a manner which breaches their employment contract. The entity determines that it has no present legal obligation under the terms of the employment contract or employment law, but promises to make a settlement payment to the former employee in order to avoid future possible lawsuits and unfavourable publicity. It can be difficult to determine whether a past obligating event exists that requires a provision to be recognised before payment to the employee is made.

Where there is no legal obligation to make the payments, a liability is recognised when a constructive obligation arises. It is a matter of judgement whether and when a constructive obligation exists. A binding agreement to make a payment to the former employee could give rise to a legal obligation. In the absence of facts and circumstances that would create a constructive or legal obligation prior to settlement, the entity would recognise the settlement as an expense when the cash is transferred.

7 DISCLOSURE REQUIREMENTS

A significant distinction between the accounting treatment of provisions and other liabilities, such as trade payables and accruals, is the level of disclosure required.

7.1 Provisions

For each class of provision an entity should provide a reconciliation of the carrying amount of the provision at the beginning and end of the period showing:

(a) additional provisions made in the period, including increases to existing provisions;
(b) amounts used, i.e. incurred and charged against the provision, during the period;
(c) unused amounts reversed during the period; and
(d) the increase during the period in the discounted amount arising from the passage of time and the effect of any change in the discount rate.

Comparative information is not required. *[IAS 37.84].*

It is not clear whether disclosure (d) allows a single amount to be provided for the sum of the unwinding of the discount and any change in the provision resulting from a reassessment of the discount rate to be used or it requires these amounts to be given separately. However, given our view (discussed at 4.3.6 above) that only the charge for unwinding of the discount should be classified as a finance cost, with any further charge or credit that arises if discount rates have changed being recorded in the same line item that was used to establish the provision, it would make sense to disclose these items separately. It is also interesting that there is no specific requirement in the standard to disclose the discount rate used, especially where the effect of using a different discount rate could be material, such as in the measurement of a decommissioning provision. However, entities should remember that IAS 1 requires disclosure of information about major sources of estimation uncertainty that have a significant risk of resulting in a material adjustment to the carrying amounts of assets and liabilities within the next financial year. *[IAS 1.125].*

One of the important disclosures which is reinforced here is the requirement to disclose the release of provisions found to be unnecessary. This disclosure, along with the requirement in the standard that provisions should be used only for the purpose for which the provision was originally recognised, *[IAS 37.61]*, is designed to prevent entities from concealing expenditure by charging it against a provision that was set up for another purpose.

In addition, for each class of provision an entity should disclose the following:

(a) a brief description of the nature of the obligation and the expected timing of any resulting outflows of economic benefits;
(b) an indication of the uncertainties about the amount or timing of those outflows. Where necessary to provide adequate information, an entity should disclose the major assumptions made concerning future events, as addressed in paragraph 48 of the standard (discussed at 4.4 above). This refers to future developments in technology and legislation and is of particular relevance to environmental liabilities; and
(c) the amount of any expected reimbursement, stating the amount of any asset that has been recognised for that expected reimbursement. *[IAS 37.85].*

Section D of the implementation guidance to the standard provides examples of suitable disclosures in relation to warranties and decommissioning costs.

Most of the above disclosures are illustrated in the extract below, which includes the disclosure of provisions determined in accordance with IAS 37, contingent consideration provisions which would be determined in accordance with IFRS 3, and employee provisions (included within Other provisions) which would be determined in accordance with IAS 19.

Extract 26.7: Roche Holding Ltd (2019)

Notes to the Roche Group Consolidated Financial Statements [extract]

20. Provisions and contingent liabilities [extracts]

Provisions: movements in recognised liabilities in millions of CHF

	Legal provisions	Environ- mental provisions	Restruct- uring provisions	Contingent consideration provisions	Other provisions	Total
Year ended 31 December 2018						
At 1 January 2018	485	523	822	591	1,169	3,590
Additional provisions created	133	33	624	51	866	1,707
Unused amounts reversed	(15)	(3)	(111)	(130)	(336)	(595)
Utilised	(24)	(61)	(451)	(14)	(351)	(901)
Discount unwind[4]	0	9	0	15	2	26
Business combinations						
– Acquired companies	0	0	0	0	2	2
– Deferred consideration	–	–	–	–	0	0
– Contingent consideration	–	–	–	0	–	0
Asset acquisitions	1	0	0	0	0	1
Divestment of subsidiaries	(1)	0	0	0	(10)	(11)
Currency translation effects	(1)	(10)	(16)	(2)	(9)	(38)
At 31 December 2018	578	491	868	511	1,333	3,781
Current	570	83	535	180	961	2,329
Non-current	8	408	333	331	372	1,452
At 31 December 2018	578	491	868	511	1,333	3,781
Year ended 31 December 2019						
At 1 January 2019	578	491	868	511	1,333	3,781
Reclassification to lease liabilities on implementation of IFRS 16 'Leases'[28]	–	–	(22)	–	–	(22)
At 1 January 2019 (revised)	578	491	846	511	1,333	3,759
Additional provisions created	402	65	812	6	801	2,086
Unused amounts reversed	(33)	(5)	(91)	(152)	(111)	(392)
Utilised	(48)	(50)	(350)	(172)	(383)	(1,003)
Discount unwind[4]	0	17	0	14	0	31
Business combinations						
– Acquired companies	0	0	0	0	0	0
– Deferred consideration	–	–	–	–	0	0
– Contingent consideration	–	–	–	0	–	0
Asset acquisitions	–	–	–	–	–	–
Divestment of subsidiaries	0	0	0	0	0	0
Currency translation effects	(17)	(15)	(23)	(2)	(24)	(81)
At 31 December 2019	882	503	1,194	205	1,616	4,400

Current	858	99	668	18	1,242	2,885
Non-current	24	404	526	187	374	1,515
At 31 December 2019	882	503	1,194	205	1,616	4,400
Expected outflow of resources						
Within one year	858	99	668	18	1,242	2,885
Between one and two years	4	157	228	28	45	462
Between two and three years	1	104	199	37	75	416
More than three years	19	143	99	122	254	637
At 31 December 2019	882	503	1,194	205	1,616	4,400

[...]

Legal provisions

Legal provisions consist of a number of separate legal matters, including claims arising from trade, in various Group companies. By their nature the amounts and timings of any outflows are difficult to predict.

As part of the regular review of litigation matters, management has reassessed the provisions recorded for certain litigation matters. Based on the development of the various litigations, notably the Avastin/Lucentis investigations and the Meso case, there was a net increase in provisions of CHF 369 million. This was a major element of the 2019 expenses for legal cases of CHF 422 million (2018: net expense of CHF 128 million). Details of the major legal cases outstanding are disclosed below.

Environmental provisions [extract]

Provisions for environmental matters include various separate environmental issues in a number of countries. By their nature the amounts and timings of any outflows are difficult to predict. Significant provisions are discounted by between 1% and 3% where the time value of money is material. The significant provisions relate to the US site in Nutley, New Jersey, which was divested in September 2016, the estimated remediation costs for a landfill site near Grenzach, Germany, that was used by manufacturing operations that were closed some years ago and the estimated remediation costs for the manufacturing site at Clarecastle, Ireland. In 2019 the expected costs of environmental remediation at the Clarecastle site and other matters were reassessed. Accordingly, in 2019 environmental provisions increased by CHF 60 million, net. The net environmental expenses were CHF 59 million (2018: net expense of CHF 31 million).

Restructuring provisions

These arise from planned programmes that materially change the scope of business undertaken by the Group or the manner in which business is conducted. Such provisions include only the costs necessarily entailed by the restructuring which are not associated with the recurring activities of the Group. The timings of these cash outflows are reasonably certain. These provisions are not discounted as the time value of money is not material in these matters.

In the Pharmaceuticals Division the significant provisions relate to the strategic realignment of its manufacturing network and the resourcing flexibility plans. In the Diagnostics Division the significant provisions are associated with programmes to address long-term strategy, while in Corporate they relate to plans for outsourcing of IT and other functions to shared service centres and external providers. Further details are given in Note 7.

Other provisions

Other provisions relate to the items shown in the table below. With the exception of employee provisions, the timing of cash outflows is by its nature uncertain.

Other provisions in millions of CHF

	2019	2018	2017
Sales returns	616	497	366
Employee provisions	389	398	362
Other items	611	438	441
Total other provisions	**1,616**	**1,333**	**1,169**

The standard states that in determining which provisions may be aggregated to form a class, it is necessary to consider whether the nature of the items is sufficiently similar for a single statement about them to fulfil the requirements of (a) and (b) above. An example is given of warranties: it is suggested that, while it may be appropriate to treat warranties of different products as a single class of provision, it would not be appropriate to aggregate normal warranties with amounts that are subject to legal proceedings. [IAS 37.87]. For entities disclosing restructuring costs, this requirement could result in material components of the costs being disclosed separately. However, materiality will be an important consideration in judging how much analysis is required.

As indicated at 6.1.1 above, IAS 37 emphasises that when a restructuring meets the definition of a discontinued operation under IFRS 5, additional disclosures may be required under that standard (see Chapter 4 at 3). [IAS 37.9].

7.2 Contingent liabilities

Unless the possibility of any outflow in settlement is remote, IAS 37 requires the disclosure for each class of contingent liability at the end of the reporting period to include a brief description of the nature of the contingent liability, and where practicable:

(a) an estimate of its financial effect, measured in accordance with paragraphs 36-52 of IAS 37 (discussed at 4 above);

(b) an indication of the uncertainties relating to the amount or timing of any outflow; and

(c) the possibility of any reimbursement. [IAS 37.86].

Where any of the information above is not disclosed because it is not practicable to do so, that fact should be stated. [IAS 37.91].

The guidance given in the standard on determining which provisions may be aggregated to form a class referred to at 7.1 above also applies to contingent liabilities.

A further point noted in the standard is that where a provision and a contingent liability arise from the same circumstances, an entity should ensure that the link between the provision and the contingent liability is clear. [IAS 37.88]. This situation may occur, for instance, when an entity stratifies a population of known and potential claimants between different classes of obligation, and accounts for each class separately. For example, an entity's actions may have resulted in environmental damage. The entity identifies the geographical area over which that damage is likely to have occurred and recognises a provision based on its 'best estimate' of value of claims it expects to be submitted from residents in that geographical area. In addition, there is a chance (albeit possible rather than probable) that the pollution is found to have had an effect beyond the geographical area established by the entity. As noted at 3.2.1 above, the latter, 'possible but not probable' obligation meets the definition of a contingent liability for which disclosure is required.

Another example of when a provision and a contingent liability may arise from the same circumstance would be where an entity is jointly and severally liable for an obligation. As noted at 4.7 above, in these circumstances the part of the obligation that is expected to be met by other parties is treated as a contingent liability.

It is not absolutely clear what is meant by 'financial effect' in (a) above. Is it the potential amount of the loss or is it the *expected* amount of the loss? The cross-reference to the measurement principles in paragraphs 36-52 might imply the latter, but in any event, disclosure of the potential amount is likely to be relevant in explaining the uncertainties in (b) above.

7.3 Contingent assets

IAS 37 requires disclosure of contingent assets where an inflow of economic benefits is probable. The disclosures required are:

(a) a brief description of the nature of the contingent assets at the end of the reporting period; and

(b) where practicable, an estimate of their financial effect, measured using the principles set out for provisions in paragraphs 36-52 of IAS 37. *[IAS 37.89]*.

Where any of the information above is not disclosed because it is not practicable to do so, that fact should be stated. *[IAS 37.91]*. The standard goes on to emphasise that the disclosure must avoid giving misleading indications of the likelihood of income arising. *[IAS 37.90]*.

One problem that arises with IAS 37 is that it requires the disclosure of an estimate of the potential financial effect for contingent assets to be measured in accordance with the measurement principles in the standard. Unfortunately, the measurement principles in the standard are all set out in terms of the settlement of obligations, and these principles cannot readily be applied to the measurement of contingent assets. Hence, judgement will have to be used as to how rigorously these principles should be applied.

7.4 Reduced disclosure when information is seriously prejudicial

IAS 37 contains an exemption from disclosure of information in the following circumstances. It says that, 'in extremely rare cases, disclosure of some or all of the information required by [the disclosure requirements at 7.1 to 7.3 above] can be expected to prejudice seriously the position of the entity in a dispute with other parties on the subject matter of the provision, contingent liability or contingent asset'. *[IAS 37.92]*.

In such circumstances, the information need not be disclosed. However, disclosure will still need to be made of the general nature of the dispute, together with the fact that, and the reason why, the required information has not been disclosed. *[IAS 37.92]*.

The following example, from the implementation guidance to the Standard, provides an example of the disclosures required where some of the information required by the standard is not given because it is expected to prejudice seriously the position of the entity.

Example 26.24: Reduced disclosure when information is seriously prejudicial

An entity is involved in a dispute with a competitor, who is alleging that the entity has infringed patents and is seeking damages of $100 million. The entity recognises a provision for its best estimate of the obligation, but discloses none of the information required by paragraphs 84 and 85 of IAS 37. The following information is disclosed:

Litigation is in process against the company relating to a dispute with a competitor who alleges that the company has infringed patents and is seeking damages of $100 million. The information usually required by IAS 37 is not disclosed on the grounds that it can be expected to prejudice seriously the outcome of the litigation. The directors are of the opinion that the claim can be successfully resisted by the company.

[IAS 37 IE D Examples: disclosures Example 3].

As it can be seen in the above example, an entity applying the 'seriously prejudicial' exemption is still required to describe the general nature of the dispute, resulting in a level of disclosure that many entities might find uncomfortable in the circumstances.

References

1 *IASB Work Plan*, July 2020.
2 *IFRIC Update*, July 2014, p.7.
3 *IFRIC Update*, September 2017.
4 *IASB Agenda Paper 22 Provisions – Education Session – Scope of possible project to amend IAS 37*, May 2019.
5 *IASB Update*, January 2020.
6 FASB ASC Topic 450, Contingencies, para. 450-20-30-1.
7 *IASB Update*, January 2020.
8 *Discounting in Financial Reporting*, ASB, April 1997.
9 *Discounting in Financial Reporting*, ASB, April 1997, para. 2.10.
10 *IFRIC Update*, March 2011, p.4.
11 *IASB Update*, January 2020.
12 *IFRIC Update*, January 2015.
13 *IFRIC Staff Paper – Negative interest rates: implication for presentation in the statement of comprehensive income*, January 2015, p.6.
14 Exposure Draft ED/2013/5: *Regulatory Deferral Accounts*, IASB, April 2013, para. BC15.
15 *IASB Update*, September 2012, December 2012.
16 *IASB work plan*, July 2020.
17 IAS 19, *Employee Benefits*, Example illustrating paras. 159-170.
18 *IASB Staff Paper – Provisions – Research summary*, January 2020, para. 3.20.
19 *IASB Update*, January 2020.
20 *IASB Update*, January 2020, *IASB Staff paper – Provisions – Project proposal*, January 2020, para. 12.
21 *Onerous Contracts – Cost of Fulfilling a Contract (Amendments to IAS 37)*.
22 IFRS 9 replaced IAS 39, effective for annual periods beginning on or after 1 January 2018. IFRS 9 applies to items that were previously within the scope of IAS 39.
23 IFRIC 3, *Emission Rights*, IASB, December 2004, para. 6.
24 IFRIC 3.5.
25 IFRIC 3.6.
26 IFRIC 3.7.
27 IFRIC 3.8.
28 *IASB Update*, June 2005, p.1.
29 *IASB Update*, June 2005, p.1.
30 *IASB Update*, May 2012, p.8.
31 *IASB Update*, January 2015, p.10.
32 *IASB Work Plan*, July 2020.
33 Directive 2002/96/EC of the European Parliament and of the Council of 27 January 2003 on waste electrical and electronic equipment and Directive 2003/108/EC of the European Parliament and of the Council of 8 December 2003 amending Directive 2002/96/EC on waste electrical and electronic equipment.
34 *IFRIC Update*, January 2019.

Chapter 27   Revenue: introduction and scope

1 INTRODUCTION 2017
  1.1 The distinction between income, revenue and gains 2018
2 IFRS 15 – OBJECTIVE AND OVERVIEW.. 2018
  2.1 Overview of the standard 2020
    2.1.1 Core principle of the standard 2021
    2.1.2 Changes to the standard since issuance 2022
  2.2 Definitions... 2023
3 IFRS 15 – SCOPE 2024
  3.1 Scope of IFRS 15 2024
    3.1.1 Non-monetary exchanges 2025
  3.2 Other scope considerations.. 2026
  3.3 Definition of a customer 2027
  3.4 Collaborative arrangements 2028
  3.5 Interaction with other standards 2029
    3.5.1 Application questions on scope 2030
      3.5.1.A Islamic financing transactions 2030
      3.5.1.B Certain fee-generating activities of financial institutions.. 2031
      3.5.1.C Credit card arrangements 2032
      3.5.1.D Credit card-holder rewards programmes 2032
      3.5.1.E Contributions... 2032
      3.5.1.F Fixed-odds wagering contracts 2033
      3.5.1.G Pre-production activities related to long-term supply arrangements..2033
      3.5.1.H Sales of by-products or scrap materials 2033
      3.5.1.I Prepaid gift cards 2034

		3.5.1.J	Determining whether IFRS 10 or IFRS 15 applies to the sale of a corporate wrapper to a customer	2035
		3.5.1.K	Revenue arising from an interest in a joint operation	2037
		3.5.1.L	Are equity instruments issued by an entity to a customer in connection with a revenue arrangement within the scope of the revenue standard?	2038

4 OTHER INCOME AND OTHER REVENUE 2039
   4.1 Income and distributable profits 2039
   4.2 Interest and dividends 2039
   4.3 Disposal of non-financial assets not in the ordinary course of business 2039
      4.3.1 Sale of assets held for rental 2041
   4.4 Regulatory assets and liabilities 2041

List of examples

Example 27.1: Non-monetary exchange outside the scope of IFRS 15 2026
Example 27.2: Non-monetary exchange in the scope of IFRS 15 2026
Example 27.3: Identification of a customer 2027
Example 27.4: Interaction between IFRS 11 and IFRS 15 in recognising revenue relating to an interest in a joint operation 2037

Chapter 27   Revenue: introduction and scope

1   INTRODUCTION

Revenue is, arguably, one of most important indicators of an entity's performance. It may be perceived as an indicator of the desirability of an entity's products and services, and the growth or decline over time of a business. However, revenue does not represent all income for an entity. As discussed at 1.1 below, revenue is a subset of income, it is derived from the ordinary activities of an entity and may be referred to by a variety of different names, including sales, fees, interest, dividends, royalties and rent.

Identifying what is revenue and specifying how and when to measure and report it is critical to any accounting framework. Within IFRS, several standards deal with the recognition of revenue, for example IFRS 16 – *Leases* – covers lease revenue and IFRS 9 – *Financial Instruments* – covers dividends and interest, which would represent revenue if part of an entity's ordinary activities.

This chapter and Chapters 28-32 primarily cover IFRS 15 – *Revenue from Contracts with Customers*. As discussed further at 1.1 below, IFRS 15 only covers a subset of revenue – specifically, revenue that arises from a contract when the counterparty to that contract is a customer (as defined, see 3.3 below) and the contract is not specifically excluded from the standard (e.g. lease contracts within the scope of IFRS 16 or financial instruments within the scope of IFRS 9, see 3.1 below for a complete list of scope exclusions).

This chapter deals with the core principle in IFRS 15, its definitions and scope. Refer to the following chapters for requirements of IFRS 15 that are not covered in this chapter:

- Chapter 28 – Identifying the contract and identifying performance obligations.
- Chapter 29 – Determining the transaction price and allocating the transaction price.
- Chapter 30 – Recognising revenue.
- Chapter 31 – Licences, warranties and contract costs.
- Chapter 32 – Presentation and disclosure requirements.

Other revenue items that are not within the scope of IFRS 15, but arise in the course of the ordinary activities of an entity, as well as the disposal of non-financial assets that are not part of the ordinary activities of the entity, for which IFRS 15's requirements are relevant, are addressed at 4 below.

1.1 The distinction between income, revenue and gains

Income is defined in IFRS 15 as 'increases in economic benefits during the accounting period in the form of inflows or enhancements of assets or decreases of liabilities that result in increases in equity, other than those relating to contributions from equity participants'. *[IFRS 15 Appendix A]*. The *Conceptual Framework for Financial Reporting* similarly defines income. *[CF 4.68]*.

This definition encompasses both, 'revenue' and 'gains'. IFRS 15 defines revenue as income that arises in the course of the ordinary activities of an entity. *[IFRS 15 Appendix A]*. As discussed at 1 above, according to the International Accounting Standards Board's (IASB or the Board) 2010 *Conceptual Framework for Financial Reporting* (which applied when IFRS 15 was issued), it can include sales, fees, interest, dividends, royalties and rent. *[CF(2010) 4.29]*. Gains represent other items that meet the definition of income and may, or may not, arise in the course of the ordinary activities of an entity. Gains include, for example, those arising on the disposal of non-current assets. The definition of income also includes unrealised gains; for example, those arising on the revaluation of marketable securities and those resulting from increases in the carrying amount of long-term assets. *[CF(2010) 4.31]*. The 2018 *Conceptual Framework for Financial Reporting* no longer contains a discussion about revenue and gains and losses. However, the definition of revenue in IFRS 15 remains unchanged. The Board does not expect the removal of that discussion to cause any changes in practice. *[CF BC4.96]*.

The rules on offset in IAS 1 – *Presentation of Financial Statements* – distinguish between revenue and gains. That standard states that an entity undertakes, in the course of its ordinary activities, other transactions that do not generate revenue but are incidental to the main revenue-generating activities. When this presentation reflects the substance of the transaction or other event, the results of such transactions are presented by netting any income with related expenses arising on the same transaction. For example, gains and losses on the disposal of non-current assets, including investments and operating assets, are reported by deducting from the proceeds on disposal the carrying amount of the asset and related selling expenses. *[IAS 1.34]*. IAS 16 – *Property, Plant and Equipment* – has a general rule that 'gains shall not be classified as revenue'. *[IAS 16.68]*. The only exception to this rule is where an entity routinely sells property, plant and equipment (PP&E) that it has held for rental to others, which is discussed further at 4.3.1 below.

2 IFRS 15 – OBJECTIVE AND OVERVIEW

IFRS 15 provides accounting requirements for all revenue arising from contracts with customers. It affects all entities that enter into contracts to provide goods or services to their customers, unless the contracts are in the scope of other IFRSs, such as the leasing standard. The standard, which is largely converged with the revenue guidance in US GAAP, also specifies the accounting for costs an entity incurs to obtain and fulfil a contract to provide goods or services to customers (see Chapter 31 at 5) and provides a model for the measurement and recognition of gains and losses on the sale of certain non-financial assets, such as property, plant or equipment (see 4.3 below).

As a result, entities that adopted the standard often found implementation to be a significant undertaking. This is because the standard requires entities to make more judgements and estimates and affects entities' financial statements, business processes and internal controls over financial reporting.

While entities are now more familiar with its requirements, application of IFRS 15 continues to be challenging for them when business practices evolve and operating environments change, raising new implementation questions. For example, during and because of the coronavirus pandemic, areas that may be affected for revenue contracts include, but are not limited to, variable consideration, contract modifications and terminations, collectability and any extended payment terms, customer incentives and changes to selling prices, onerous contracts and capitalised contract costs.

Following the issuance of their revenue standards, the IASB and the US Financial Accounting Standards Board (FASB) (collectively, the Boards) created the Joint Transition Resource Group for Revenue Recognition (TRG) to help them determine whether more application guidance was needed. TRG members included financial statement preparers, auditors and other users from a variety of industries and countries, as well as public and private entities. Members of the joint TRG met six times in 2014 and 2015, and members of the FASB TRG met twice in 2016. TRG members' views are non-authoritative, but entities should consider them as they implement the standards. In its July 2016 public statement, the European Securities and Markets Authority (ESMA) encouraged issuers to consider the TRG discussions when implementing IFRS 15. Furthermore, the former Chief Accountant of the US Securities and Exchange Commission (SEC) encouraged SEC registrants, including foreign private issuers (that may report under IFRS), to consult with his office if they are considering applying the standard in a manner that differs from the discussions in which TRG members reached general agreement.[1]

We have incorporated our summaries of topics on which TRG members generally agreed throughout this chapter. Unless otherwise specified, these summaries represent the discussions of the joint TRG. Where possible, we indicate if members of the IASB or its staff commented on the FASB TRG discussions.

This chapter discusses the IASB's standard (including all amendments) and highlights significant differences from the FASB's standard, Accounting Standards Codification (ASC) 606 – *Revenue from Contracts with Customers*. Throughout this chapter and Chapters 28-32, when we refer to the FASB's standard, we mean ASC 606 (including any amendments), unless otherwise noted. It also addresses topics on which the members of the TRG reached general agreement and our views on certain topics.

The views we express in this chapter may evolve as application issues are identified and discussed among stakeholders. The conclusions we describe in our illustrations are also subject to change as views evolve. Conclusions in seemingly similar situations may differ from those reached in the illustrations due to differences in the underlying facts and circumstances.

2.1 Overview of the standard

The revenue standards that the Boards issued in May 2014 were largely converged and superseded virtually all legacy revenue recognition requirements in IFRS and US GAAP, respectively. The Boards' goal in the joint deliberations was to develop new revenue standards that:

- remove inconsistencies and weaknesses in the legacy revenue recognition literature;
- provide a more robust framework for addressing revenue recognition issues;
- improve comparability of revenue recognition practices across industries, entities within those industries, jurisdictions and capital markets;
- reduce the complexity of applying revenue recognition requirements by reducing the volume of the relevant standards and interpretations; and
- provide more useful information to users through expanded disclosure requirements. [IFRS 15(2016).IN5].[2]

The standards provide accounting requirements for all revenue arising from contracts with customers. They affect all entities that enter into contracts to provide goods or services to their customers, unless the contracts are in the scope of other IFRSs or US GAAP requirements, such as those for leasing. The standards also specify the accounting for costs an entity incurs to obtain and fulfil a contract to provide goods or services to customers (see Chapter 31 at 5) and provide a model for the measurement and recognition of gains and losses on the sale of certain non-financial assets, such as property, plant or equipment (see 4.3 below). IFRS 15 replaced all of the legacy revenue standards and interpretations in IFRS, including IAS 11 – *Construction Contracts*, IAS 18 – *Revenue*, IFRIC 13 – *Customer Loyalty Programmes*, IFRIC 15 – *Agreements for the Construction of Real Estate*, IFRIC 18 – *Transfers of Assets from Customers* – and SIC-31 – *Revenue – Barter Transactions Involving Advertising Services* (legacy revenue requirements or legacy IFRS). [IFRS 15.C10].

IFRS 15 became effective for annual reporting periods beginning on or after 1 January 2018. Early adoption was permitted, provided that fact was disclosed. [IFRS 15.C1].

IFRS 15 required retrospective application. However, it allowed either a 'full retrospective' adoption (in which the standard was applied retrospectively to all of the periods presented in accordance with IAS 8 – *Accounting Policies, Changes in Accounting Estimates and Errors*) or a 'modified retrospective' adoption (in which the standard was applied retrospectively to only the most current period presented in the financial statements). Under both transition methods, the IASB granted transition practical expedients to provide relief.

Depending on the manner in which an entity elected to transition to IFRS 15, it may not have needed to apply the standard to contracts if they had completed performance before the date of initial application or the beginning of the earliest period presented (depending on the practical expedient and the transition method), even if they had not yet received the consideration and that consideration was still subject to variability. Applying a completed contract practical expedient might also have affected an entity's revenue recognition in subsequent reporting periods. That is, if an entity applied a practical expedient for completed contracts, it continued to apply its legacy revenue policy to its completed contracts, instead of IFRS 15. In some cases, even though an entity will have fully transferred its identified goods or services, there may still be revenue to recognise in accordance with its legacy revenue policy in reporting periods after adoption of IFRS 15.

The FASB's standard became effective for public entities, as defined,[3] for annual reporting periods beginning after 15 December 2017 and interim periods therein. Non-public entities (i.e. an entity that does not meet the definition of a public entity in the FASB's standard) were required to adopt the standard for annual reporting periods beginning after 15 December 2018 and for interim periods within annual reporting periods beginning after 15 December 2019. That is, non-public entities were not required to apply the standard in interim periods in the year of adoption.

However, in June 2020, the FASB deferred by one year the effective date for entities that had not yet issued financial statements or made financial statements available for issuance that reflected the standard as of 3 June 2020 (i.e. certain non-public and not-for-profit entities). These entities are now required to adopt the standard for annual reporting periods beginning after 15 December 2019, and interim periods within annual reporting periods beginning after 15 December 2020. Early adoption is permitted.

After issuing the standards, the Boards issued converged amendments on certain topics (e.g. principal versus agent considerations) and different amendments on other topics (e.g. licences of intellectual property). The FASB also issued several amendments that the IASB has not issued (e.g. non-cash consideration). See 2.1.2 below for a discussion of the changes to the standards since issuance. While we address the significant differences between the IASB's final standard and the FASB's final standard throughout this chapter and in Chapters 28-32, the primary purpose of this chapter, and Chapters 28-32, is to describe the IASB's standard, including all amendments to date, and focus on the effects for IFRS preparers. As such, we generally refer to the 'standard' in the singular in this chapter and in Chapters 28-32.

2.1.1 Core principle of the standard

The standard describes the principles an entity must apply to measure and recognise revenue and the related cash flows. *[IFRS 15.1]*. The core principle is that an entity recognises revenue at an amount that reflects the consideration to which the entity expects to be entitled in exchange for transferring goods or services to a customer. *[IFRS 15.2]*.

The principles in IFRS 15 are applied using the following five steps:
1. Identify the contract(s) with a customer.
2. Identify the performance obligations in the contract.
3. Determine the transaction price.
4. Allocate the transaction price to the performance obligations in the contract.
5. Recognise revenue when (or as) the entity satisfies a performance obligation.

Entities need to exercise judgement when considering the terms of the contract(s) and all of the facts and circumstances, including implied contract terms. Entities also have to apply the requirements of the standard consistently to contracts with similar characteristics and in similar circumstances. *[IFRS 15.3]*. To assist entities, IFRS 15 includes detailed application guidance. The IASB also published more than 60 illustrative examples that accompany IFRS 15.

2.1.2 Changes to the standard since issuance

Since the issuance of the standards, the Boards have issued various amendments to their respective standards, as summarised below. The Boards did not agree on the nature and breadth of all of the changes to their respective revenue standards. However, the Boards have said they expect the amendments to result in similar outcomes in many circumstances. No further changes to the standard are currently expected.

In September 2015, the IASB deferred the effective date of IFRS 15 by one year to give entities more time to implement it.[4] In addition, in April 2016, the IASB issued *Clarifications to IFRS 15 – Revenue from Contracts with Customers* (the IASB's amendments) that addressed several implementation issues (many of which were discussed by the TRG) on key aspects of the standard.

The IASB's amendments:

- clarified when a promised good or service is separately identifiable from other promises in a contract (i.e. distinct within the context of the contract), which is part of an entity's assessment of whether a promised good or service is a performance obligation (see Chapter 28 at 3.2);
- clarified how to apply the principal versus agent application guidance to determine whether the nature of an entity's promise is to provide a promised good or service itself (i.e. the entity is a principal) or to arrange for goods or services to be provided by another party (i.e. the entity is an agent) (see Chapter 28 at 3.4);
- clarified for a licence of intellectual property when an entity's activities significantly affect the intellectual property to which the customer has rights, which is a factor in determining whether the entity recognises revenue over time or at a point in time (see Chapter 31 at 2);
- clarified the scope of the exception for sales-based and usage-based royalties related to licences of intellectual property (the royalty recognition constraint) when there are other promised goods or services in the contract (see Chapter 31 at 2.5); and
- added two practical expedients to the transition requirements of IFRS 15 for: (a) completed contracts under the full retrospective transition method; and (b) contract modifications at transition.

The FASB also deferred the effective date of its standard by one year for US GAAP public and non-public entities, as defined, which kept the standards' effective dates converged under IFRS and US GAAP. However, as discussed at 2.1 above, in June 2020, the FASB deferred by one year the effective date for entities that had not yet issued financial statements or made financial statements available for issuance that reflected the standard as of 3 June 2020 (i.e. certain non-public and not-for-profit entities).

Like the IASB, the FASB also amended its revenue standard to address principal versus agent considerations, identifying performance obligations, licences of intellectual property and certain practical expedients on transition.[5] The FASB's amendments for principal versus agent considerations and clarifying when a promised good or service is separately identifiable when identifying performance obligations were converged with those of the IASB discussed above. However, the FASB's other amendments were not the same as those of the IASB. The FASB also issued amendments, which the IASB did not, relating to immaterial goods or services in a contract, accounting for shipping and handling, collectability, non-cash consideration, consideration payable to a customer, the presentation of sales and other similar taxes, the measurement and recognition of gains and losses on the sale of non-financial assets (e.g. PP&E) and other technical corrections. We describe the significant differences between the IASB's final standard and the FASB's final standard throughout this chapter and in Chapters 28-32.

2.2 Definitions

The following table summarises the terms that are defined in IFRS 15. *[IFRS 15 Appendix A].*

Figure 27.1:   IFRS 15 Definitions

Term	Definition
Contract	An agreement between two or more parties that creates enforceable rights and obligations.
Contract asset	An entity's right to consideration in exchange for goods or services that the entity has transferred to a customer when that right is conditioned on something other than the passage of time (for example, the entity's future performance).
Contract liability	An entity's obligation to transfer goods or services to a customer for which the entity has received consideration (or the amount is due) from the customer.
Customer	A party that has contracted with an entity to obtain goods or services that are an output of the entity's ordinary activities in exchange for consideration.
Income	Increases in economic benefits during the accounting period in the form of inflows or enhancements of assets or decreases of liabilities that result in an increase in equity, other than those relating to contributions from equity participants.
Performance obligation	A promise in a contract with a customer to transfer to the customer either: (a) a good or service (or a bundle of goods or services) that is distinct; or (b) a series of distinct goods or services that are substantially the same and that have the same pattern of transfer to the customer.
Revenue	Income arising in the course of an entity's ordinary activities.
Stand-alone selling price (of a good or service)	The price at which an entity would sell a promised good or service separately to a customer.
Transaction price (for a contract with a customer)	The amount of consideration to which an entity expects to be entitled in exchange for transferring promised goods or services to a customer, excluding amounts collected on behalf of third parties.

3 IFRS 15 – SCOPE

3.1 Scope of IFRS 15

IFRS 15 applies to all entities and all contracts with customers to provide goods or services in the ordinary course of business, except for the following contracts, which are specifically excluded: *[IFRS 15.5]*

- lease contracts within the scope of IFRS 16;
- insurance contracts within the scope of IFRS 4 – *Insurance Contracts* (or, when effective, contracts within the scope of IFRS 17 – *Insurance Contracts* – except when an entity elects to apply IFRS 15 to certain service contracts in accordance with paragraph 8 of IFRS 17);
- financial instruments and other contractual rights or obligations within the scope of IFRS 9, IFRS 10 – *Consolidated Financial Statements*, IFRS 11 – *Joint Arrangements*, IAS 27 – *Separate Financial Statements* – and IAS 28 – *Investments in Associates and Joint Ventures*; and
- non-monetary exchanges between entities in the same line of business to facilitate sales to customers or potential customers.

Arrangements must meet the criteria set out in paragraph 9 of IFRS 15, which are discussed in Chapter 28 at 2.1, to be accounted for as a revenue contract under the standard.

For certain arrangements, entities have to evaluate their relationship with the counterparty to the contract in order to determine whether a vendor-customer relationship exists. Some collaboration arrangements, for example, are more akin to a partnership, while others have a vendor-customer relationship. Only transactions that are determined to be with a customer are within the scope of IFRS 15. The definition of a customer is discussed at 3.3 below. See 3.4 below for a discussion on collaborative arrangements.

The interaction between IFRS 15 and other standards can be challenging and may require significant judgement. Such interactions with IFRS 15 include when:

- an entity needs to apply other standards' requirements to assets and liabilities arising from a revenue contract (e.g. applying certain requirements in IFRS 9 to contract assets, determining an entity's right to consideration becomes unconditional (i.e. a receivable) such that IFRS 9 applies to that asset instead of IFRS 15, discussed in Chapter 32 at 2.1);
- other standards refer to guidance in IFRS 15 (e.g. the accounting for disposals of certain non-financial assets (as discussed at 4.3 below), applying requirements in IFRS 15 to service concession arrangements that are within the scope of IFRIC 12 – *Service Concession Arrangements* – See Chapter 25);
- two or more contracts need to be assessed together to determine the appropriate standard(s) to apply (e.g. sales with repurchase agreements (discussed in Chapter 30 at 5), sale and leaseback arrangements within the scope of IFRS 16) or the legal form of the arrangement is not consistent with the substance. When developing IFRS 16, the IASB noted that constituents had questions about how to distinguish between a lease and a sale or purchase when legal title to the underlying asset is not transferred. *[IFRS 15.BC79]*. If an arrangement does not meet the definition of a lease because the

'lessor' has a substantive right to substitute the underlying asset throughout the period of use and hence is out of scope of IFRS 16 (see Chapter 23 at 2.2), that entity may be providing a service within the scope of IFRS 15. The IASB decided not to provide requirements in this area and noted that the accounting for such leases would be similar to the sale or purchase of the respective asset and that the accounting also depends on the substance of the transaction and not its legal form. [IFRS 15.BC138-BC139]. Refer to Chapter 23, for more information on IFRS 16; and

- a contract falls within the scope of more than one standard (e.g. lease with a non-lease revenue component, a contract that includes the issuance of a financial instrument and a revenue component within the scope of IFRS 15). When entities enter into transactions that are partially within the scope of IFRS 15 and partially within the scope of other standards, the standard requires an entity to apply any separation and/or measurement requirements in the other standard first, before applying the requirements in IFRS 15. See 3.5 below for further discussion.

As noted above, when effective, IFRS 17 could change the applicable standard for certain service contracts, specifically fixed-fee service contracts, which are contracts in which the level of service depends on an uncertain event. Examples include roadside assistance programmes and maintenance contracts in which the service provider agrees to repair specified equipment after a malfunction for a fixed fee. IFRS 17 indicates that these are insurance contracts and, therefore, when it is effective, that standard would apply. However, if their primary purpose is the provision of services for a fixed fee, IFRS 17 permits entities the choice of applying IFRS 15 instead of IFRS 17 to such contracts if, and only if, all of the following conditions are met: [IFRS 17.8]

- the entity does not reflect an assessment of the risk associated with an individual customer in setting the price of the contract with that customer;
- the contract compensates the customer by providing services, rather than by making cash payments to the customer; and
- the insurance risk transferred by the contract arises primarily from the customer's use of services rather than from uncertainty over the cost of those services.

The entity may make that choice on a contract by contract basis, but the choice for each contract is irrevocable. IFRS 17 is effective for annual periods beginning on or after 1 January 2023. See Chapter 56 at 2.3.2 for further discussion.

IFRS 9 became effective for annual periods beginning on or after 1 January 2018, superseding IAS 39 – *Financial Instruments: Recognition and Measurement*. However, entities that are applying IFRS 4, have an optional temporary exemption that permits an insurance company whose activities are predominantly connected with insurance to defer adoption of IFRS 9. If an entity uses this optional exemption, it continues to apply IAS 39 until it first applies IFRS 17. References to IFRS 9 in this chapter, and Chapters 28-32, are generally also relevant for IAS 39.

3.1.1 Non-monetary exchanges

IFRS 15 does not apply to non-monetary exchanges between entities in the same line of business to facilitate sales to (potential) customers. For example, the standard does not apply to a contract between two oil companies that swap oil to fulfil demand from their respective customers in different locations on a timely basis and to reduce transportation costs. This scope exclusion applies even though the party exchanging goods or services with the entity might meet the definition of a customer on the basis that it has contracted with the entity to obtain an output of the entity's ordinary activities. As discussed in the Basis for Conclusions, this type of scenario may be common in industries with homogeneous products. [IFRS 15.BC58]. Not all non-monetary exchanges between entities are outside the scope of IFRS 15 and the standard does provide requirements for contracts involving non-cash consideration in exchange for goods or services (see Chapter 29 at 2.6 on non-cash consideration and at 2.6.2 on barter transactions). Therefore, determining whether an exchange is to facilitate a sale to a customer may require judgement. Judgement may also be needed to determine whether entities are in the same line of business.

The following examples illustrate some of these considerations:

Example 27.1:   Non-monetary exchange outside the scope of IFRS 15

An automobile dealer exchanges new model automobiles with another dealer to obtain the colour ordered by a customer. This non-monetary exchange is intended to facilitate a sale to a customer who is not a party to the exchange. In addition, it involves the exchange of inventory that both dealers hold for sale in the same line of business. Accordingly, this transaction is outside the scope of IFRS 15.

Example 27.2:   Non-monetary exchange in the scope of IFRS 15

An office supply retailer provides office equipment and supplies to an automobile dealer in exchange for an automobile. The automobile dealer will use the office equipment and supplies in its financing department. The new equipment is an upgrade from the automobile dealer's old equipment and will allow the automobile dealer to reduce administrative expenses. The office supply retailer will use the car received in its repair department, allowing the department to reduce response times and meet service level commitments. Although the exchange involves inventory held for sale by each entity, the transaction is not an exchange of a product held for sale in the ordinary course of business for a product to be sold in the same line of business to facilitate sales to customers. Accordingly, this transaction is within the scope of IFRS 15 for each entity.

3.2   Other scope considerations

Certain arrangements executed by entities include repurchase provisions, either as a component of a sales contract or as a separate contract that relates to the same or similar goods in the original agreement. The form of the repurchase agreement and whether the customer obtains control of the asset will determine whether the agreement is within the scope of the standard. See Chapter 30 at 5 for a discussion on repurchase agreements.

IFRS 15 also specifies the accounting for certain costs, such as the incremental costs of obtaining a contract and the costs of fulfilling a contract. However, the standard is clear that these requirements only apply if there are no other applicable requirements in IFRS for those costs. [IFRS 15.8]. See Chapter 31 at 5 for further discussion on the requirements relating to contract costs in the standard.

Certain requirements in IFRS 15 are also relevant for the recognition and measurement of a gain or loss on the disposal of a non-financial asset not in the ordinary course of business. See 4.3 below for further discussion.

3.3 Definition of a customer

The standard defines a customer as 'a party that has contracted with an entity to obtain goods or services that are an output of the entity's ordinary activities in exchange for consideration'. *[IFRS 15 Appendix A]*. IFRS 15 does not define the term 'ordinary activities' because it was derived from the definitions of revenue in the respective conceptual frameworks of the IASB and the FASB in effect when the standards were developed. In particular, the description of revenue in the IASB's *Conceptual Framework for Financial Reporting* at that time referred specifically to the 'ordinary activities' of an entity – *[CF(2010) 4.29, IFRS 15 Appendix A]* – and the definition of revenue in the FASB's Statement of Financial Accounting Concepts No. 6 refers to the notion of an entity's 'ongoing major or central operations'.[6] In many transactions, a customer is easily identifiable. However, in transactions involving multiple parties, it may be less clear which counterparties are customers of the entity. For some arrangements, multiple parties could all be considered customers of the entity. However, for other arrangements, only some of the parties involved are considered customers.

During the coronavirus pandemic, governments often granted additional and wide-ranging assistance, particularly during periods involving restrictions on business activities. Any entity will need to evaluate whether there is a vendor-customer relationship even when the counterparty is a government or similar body. To determine the appropriate standard to apply, an entity needs to consider all relevant facts and circumstances to understand whether there is an exchange transaction arising from a vendor-customer relationship (to which IFRS 15 applies) or if, for example, the entity is receiving government assistance or a grant (as defined in IAS 20 – *Accounting for Government Grants and Disclosure of Government Assistance* – see Chapter 24). Factors to consider would include, but not be limited to, whether the government (or similar body) is providing assistance to the entity or to its customer (e.g. by paying the entity on a customer's behalf), and whether the government (or similar body) is providing assistance in their capacity as the government (or similar body) or as the entity's customer. An entity with an existing vendor-customer relationship with a government or similar body also needs to evaluate whether any additional assistance is a modification of a customer contract under IFRS 15. See Chapter 28 at 2.4 for contract modifications.

Example 27.3 below shows how the party considered to be the customer may differ, depending on the specific facts and circumstances.

Example 27.3: Identification of a customer

An entity provides internet-based advertising services to companies. As part of those services, the entity purchases banner-space on various websites from a selection of publishers. For certain contracts, the entity provides a sophisticated service of matching the ad placement with the pre-identified criteria of the advertising party (i.e. the customer). In addition, the entity pre-purchases the banner-space from the publishers before it finds advertisers for that space. Assume that the entity appropriately concludes it is acting as the principal in these contracts (see Chapter 28 at 3.4 for further discussion on principal versus agent considerations). Accordingly, the entity identifies that its customer is the advertiser to whom it is providing services.

In other contracts, the entity simply matches advertisers with the publishers in its portfolio, but the entity does not provide any sophisticated ad-targeting services or purchase the advertising space from the publishers before it finds advertisers for that space. Assume that the entity appropriately concludes it is acting as the agent in these contracts. Accordingly, the entity identifies that its customer is the publisher to whom it is providing services.

In addition, the identification of the performance obligations in a contract (discussed further in Chapter 28 at 3) can have a significant effect on the determination of which party is the entity's customer. Also see the discussion of the identification of an entity's customer when applying the application guidance on consideration paid or payable to a customer in Chapter 29 at 2.7.

3.4 Collaborative arrangements

Entities often enter into collaborative arrangements to, for example, jointly develop and commercialise intellectual property (such as a drug candidate in the life sciences industry or a motion picture in the entertainment industry). In such arrangements, a counterparty may not always be a 'customer' of the entity. Instead, the counterparty may be a collaborator or partner that shares in the risks and benefits of developing a product to be marketed. *[IFRS 15.6]*. This is common in the pharmaceutical, bio-technology, oil and gas, and health care industries. However, depending on the facts and circumstances, these arrangements may also contain a vendor-customer relationship component. Such contracts could still be within the scope of IFRS 15, at least partially, if the collaborator or partner meets the definition of a customer for some, or all, aspects of the arrangement. If the collaborator or partner is not a customer, the transaction is not within the scope of IFRS 15. An example of transactions between collaborators or partners not being within the scope of IFRS 15 was discussed by the IFRS Interpretations Committee in March 2019; it related to the output to which an entity is entitled from a joint operation, but which the entity has not yet received and sold to its customers (see 3.5.1.K below).

The IASB decided not to provide additional application guidance for determining whether certain revenue-generating collaborative arrangements are within the scope of IFRS 15. In the Basis for Conclusions, the IASB explained that it would not be possible to provide application guidance that applies to all collaborative arrangements. *[IFRS 15.BC54]*. Therefore, the parties to such arrangements need to consider all facts and circumstances to determine whether a vendor-customer relationship exists that is subject to the standard.

However, the IASB did determine that, in some circumstances, it may be appropriate for an entity to apply the principles in IFRS 15 to collaborations or partnerships (e.g. when there are no applicable or more relevant requirements that could be applied). *[IFRS 15.BC56]*.

Identifying the customer can be difficult, especially when multiple parties are involved in a transaction. This evaluation may require significant judgement and IFRS 15 does not provide many factors to consider.

Furthermore, transactions among partners in collaboration arrangements are not within the scope of IFRS 15. Therefore, entities need to use judgement to determine whether transactions are between partners acting in their capacity as collaborators or reflect a vendor-customer relationship.

3.5 Interaction with other standards

The standard provides requirements for arrangements partially within the scope of IFRS 15 and partially within the scope of other standards. IFRS 15 states that if the other standards specify how to separate and/or initially measure one or more parts of the contract, then an entity shall first apply the separation and/or measurement requirements in those standards. An entity shall exclude from the transaction price (as discussed in Chapter 29 at 2) the amount of the part (or parts) of the contract that are initially measured in accordance with other standards and shall apply the allocation requirements in IFRS 15 (as discussed in Chapter 29 at 3) to allocate the amount of the transaction price that remains (if any) to each performance obligation within the scope of IFRS 15. If the other standards do not specify how to separate and/or initially measure one or more parts of the contract, then the entity shall apply IFRS 15 to separate and/or initially measure the part (or parts) of the contract. *[IFRS 15.7]*. Figure 27.2 illustrates these requirements.

Figure 27.2: Interactions with other standards

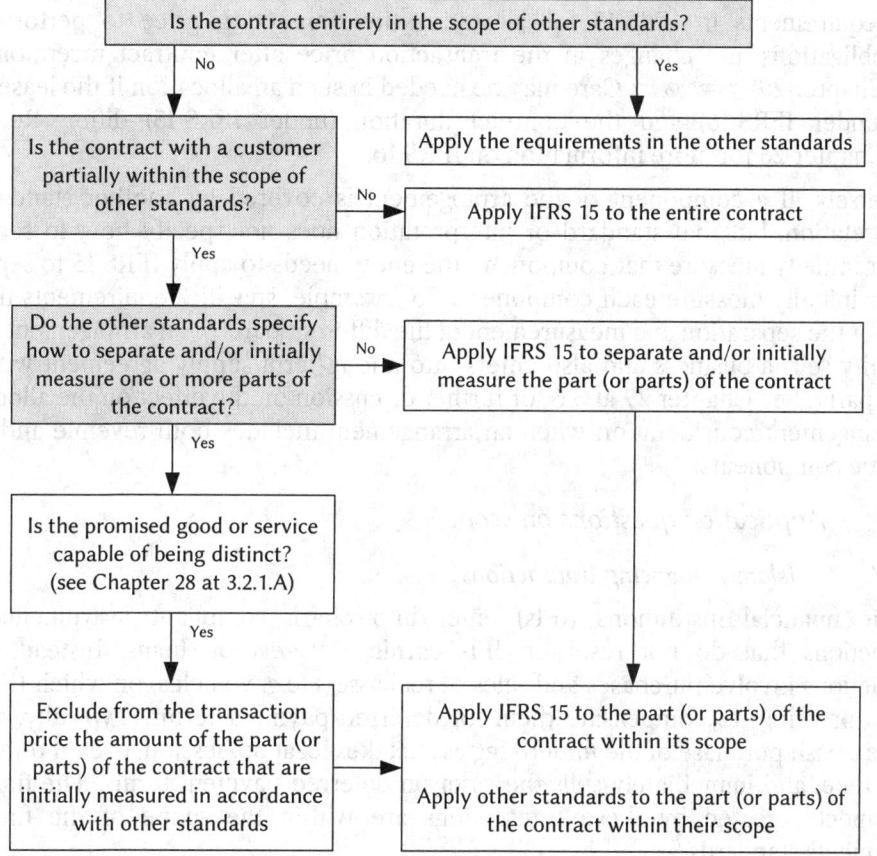

If a component of the arrangement is covered by another standard or interpretation that specifies how to separate and/or initially measure that component, the entity needs to apply IFRS 15 to the remaining components of the arrangement.

Some examples of where separation and/or initial measurement are addressed in other IFRS include the following:

- IFRS 9 generally requires that a financial instrument be recognised at fair value at initial recognition. For contracts that include the issuance of a financial instrument and revenue components within the scope of IFRS 15 and the financial instrument is required to be initially recognised at fair value, the fair value of the financial instrument is first measured and the remainder of the estimated contract consideration is allocated among the other components in the contract in accordance with IFRS 15.

- A contract may contain a lease coupled with an agreement to sell other goods or services (e.g. subject to IFRS 15). IFRS 16 requires that a lessor accounts separately for the lease component (in accordance with IFRS 16) and any non-lease components (in accordance with other standards) and provides application guidance on separating the components of such a contract. *[IFRS 16.12, B32, B33]*. A lessor allocates the consideration in a contract that contains a lease component and one or more additional lease or non-lease components by applying the requirements in IFRS 15 for allocating the transaction price to performance obligations and changes in the transaction price after contract inception (see Chapter 29). *[IFRS 16.17]*. Care may be needed in such an allocation if the lease term (under IFRS 16) and the contract duration (under IFRS 15) differ. Refer to Chapter 23 for more information on IFRS 16.

Conversely, if a component of the arrangement is covered by another standard or interpretation, but that standard or interpretation does not specify how to separate and/or initially measure that component, the entity needs to apply IFRS 15 to separate and/or initially measure each component. For example, specific requirements do not exist for the separation and measurement of the different parts of an arrangement when an entity sells a business and also enters into a long-term supply agreement with the other party. See Chapter 29 at 3.6 for further discussion on the effect on the allocation of arrangement consideration when an arrangement includes both revenue and non-revenue components.

3.5.1 Application questions on scope

3.5.1.A Islamic financing transactions

Islamic financial institutions (IFIs) enter into Sharia-compliant instruments and transactions that do not result in IFIs earning interest on loans. Instead, these transactions involve purchases and sales of real assets (e.g. vehicles) on which IFIs can earn a premium to compensate them for deferred payment terms. Typically, an IFI makes a cash purchase of the underlying asset, takes legal possession, even if only for a short time, and immediately sells the asset on deferred payment terms. The financial instruments created by these transactions are within the scope of the financial instruments standards.[7]

At the January 2015 TRG meeting, the IASB TRG members discussed whether (before applying the financial instruments standards) deferred-payment transactions that are part of Sharia-compliant instruments and transactions are within the scope of IFRS 15.

The IASB TRG members generally agreed that Sharia-compliant instruments and transactions may be outside the scope of the standard. However, the analysis depends on the specific facts and circumstances. This may require significant judgement as contracts often differ within and between jurisdictions. The FASB TRG members did not discuss this issue.[8]

3.5.1.B Certain fee-generating activities of financial institutions

The TRG considered an issue raised by US GAAP stakeholders whether certain fee-generating activities of financial institutions are in the scope of the revenue standard (i.e. servicing and sub-servicing financial assets, providing financial guarantees and providing deposit-related services).[9]

The FASB TRG members generally agreed that the standard provides a framework for determining whether certain contracts are in the scope of the FASB's standard, ASC 606, or other standards. As discussed above, the standard's scope includes all contracts with customers to provide goods or services in the ordinary course of business, except for contracts with customers that are within the scope of certain other ASC topics that are listed as scope exclusions. If another standard specifies the accounting for the consideration (e.g. a fee) received in the arrangement, the consideration is outside the scope of ASC 606. If other standards do not specify the accounting for the consideration and there is a separate good or service provided, the consideration is in (or at least partially in) the scope of ASC 606. The FASB staff applied this framework in the TRG agenda paper to arrangements to service financial assets, provide financial guarantees and provide deposit-related services.

The FASB TRG members generally agreed that income from servicing financial assets (e.g. loans) is not within the scope of ASC 606. An asset servicer performs various services, such as communication with the borrower and payment collection, in exchange for a fee. The FASB TRG members generally agreed that an entity should look to ASC 860 – *Transfers and Servicing* – to determine the appropriate accounting for these fees. This is because ASC 606 contains a scope exception for contracts that fall under ASC 860, which provides requirements on the recognition of the fees (despite not providing explicit requirements on revenue accounting).

The FASB TRG members generally agreed that fees from providing financial guarantees are not within the scope of ASC 606. A financial institution may receive a fee for providing a guarantee of a loan. These types of financial guarantees are generally within the scope of ASC 460 – *Guarantees* – or ASC 815 – *Derivatives and Hedging*. The FASB TRG members generally agreed that an entity should look to ASC 460 or ASC 815 to determine the appropriate accounting for these fees. This is because ASC 606 contains a scope exception for contracts that fall within those topics, which provide principles an entity can follow to determine the appropriate accounting to reflect the financial guarantor's release from risk (and credit to earnings).

The FASB TRG members also generally agreed that fees from deposit-related services are within the scope of ASC 606. In contrast to the decisions for servicing income and financial guarantees, the guidance in ASC 405 – *Liabilities* – that financial institutions apply to determine the appropriate liability accounting for customer deposits, does not provide a model for recognising fees related to customer deposits (e.g. ATM fees, account maintenance or dormancy fees). Accordingly, the FASB TRG members generally agreed that deposit fees and charges are within the scope of ASC 606, even though ASC 405 is listed as a scope exception in ASC 606, because of the lack of guidance on the accounting for these fees in ASC 405.

It should be noted that, while this was not specifically discussed by the IASB TRG, IFRS preparers may find the FASB TRG's discussions helpful in assessing whether certain contracts are within the scope of IFRS 15 or other standards.

3.5.1.C   Credit card arrangements

A bank that issues credit cards can have various income streams (e.g. annual fees) from a cardholder under various credit card arrangements. Some of these fees may entitle cardholders to ancillary services (e.g. concierge services, airport lounge access). The card issuer may also provide rewards to cardholders based on their purchases. At the July 2015 TRG meeting, the TRG members discussed a question raised by US GAAP stakeholders regarding whether such fees and programmes are within the scope of the revenue standard, particularly when a good or service is provided to a cardholder.[10]

While this question was only raised by US GAAP stakeholders, IASB TRG members generally agreed that an IFRS preparer first needs to determine whether the credit card fees are within the scope of IFRS 9. IFRS 9 requires that any fees that are an integral part of the effective interest rate for a financial instrument be treated as an adjustment to the effective interest rate. Conversely, any fees that are not an integral part of the effective interest rate of the financial instrument are generally accounted for under IFRS 15.

The FASB TRG members generally agreed that credit card fees that are accounted for under ASC 310 – *Receivables* – are not in the scope of ASC 606. This includes annual fees that may entitle cardholders to ancillary services. The FASB TRG members noted that this conclusion is consistent with legacy US GAAP requirements for credit card fees. However, the observer from the US SEC noted that the nature of the arrangement must truly be that of a credit card lending arrangement in order to be in the scope of ASC 310. As such, entities need to continue evaluating their arrangements as new programmes develop. Credit card fees could, therefore, be treated differently under IFRS and US GAAP.

3.5.1.D   Credit card-holder rewards programmes

The FASB TRG members also discussed whether cardholder rewards programmes are within the scope of ASC 606. The FASB TRG members generally agreed that if all consideration (i.e. credit card fees discussed at 3.5.1.C above) related to the rewards programme is determined to be within the scope of ASC 310, the rewards programme is not in the scope of ASC 606. However, this determination has to be made based on the facts and circumstances due to the wide variety of credit card reward programmes offered. The IASB TRG members did not discuss this issue because the question was only raised in relation to US GAAP.[11]

3.5.1.E   Contributions

The FASB amended ASC 606 to clarify that an entity needs to consider the requirements in ASC 958-605 – *Not-for-Profit Entities – Revenue Recognition* – when determining whether a transaction is a contribution (as defined in the ASC Master Glossary) within the scope of ASC 958-605 or a transaction within the scope of ASC 606.[12] The requirements for contributions received in ASC 958-605 generally apply to all entities that receive contributions (i.e. not just not-for-profit entities), unless otherwise indicated.

Before the amendment, FASB TRG members discussed this issue in March 2015 and generally agreed that contributions are not within the scope of ASC 606 because they are non-reciprocal transfers. That is, contributions generally do not represent consideration given in exchange for goods or services that are an output of the entity's ordinary activities. The IASB TRG members did not discuss this issue because the question was only raised in the context of US GAAP.[13]

3.5.1.F   Fixed-odds wagering contracts

In fixed-odds wagering contracts, the payout for wagers placed on gambling activities (e.g. table games, slot machines, sports betting) is known at the time the wager is placed.

Under IFRS, consistent with a July 2007 IFRS Interpretations Committee agenda decision, wagers that meet the definition of a derivative are within the scope of IFRS 9. Those that do not meet the definition of a derivative are within the scope of IFRS 15.

Under US GAAP, the FASB added scope exceptions in ASC 815 and ASC 924 – *Entertainment – Casinos* – in December 2016 to clarify that fixed-odds wagering arrangements are within the scope of ASC 606.

3.5.1.G   Pre-production activities related to long-term supply arrangements

In some long-term supply arrangements, entities perform upfront engineering and design activities to create new technology or adapt existing technology according to the needs of the customer. These pre-production activities are often a prerequisite to delivering any units under a production contract.

Entities need to evaluate whether the pre-production activities are promises in a contract with a customer (and potentially performance obligations) under IFRS 15. When making this evaluation, entities need to determine whether the activities transfer a good or service to a customer. Refer to Chapter 28 at 3.1.1.A for further discussion on determining whether pre-production activities are promised goods or services under IFRS 15. If an entity determines that these activities are promised goods or services, it will apply the requirements in IFRS 15 to those goods or services.

3.5.1.H   Sales of by-products or scrap materials

Consider an example in which a consumer products entity sells by-products or accumulated scrap materials that are produced as a result of its manufacturing process. In determining whether the sale of by-products or scrap materials to third parties is in the scope of IFRS 15, an entity first determines whether the sale of such items is an output of the entity's ordinary activities. This is because IFRS 15 defines revenue as 'income arising in the course of an entity's ordinary activities'. *[IFRS 15 Appendix A]*. If an entity determines the sale of such items represents revenue from a contract with a customer, it would generally recognise the sale under IFRS 15.

If an entity determines that such sales are not in the course of its ordinary activities, the entity would recognise those sales separately from revenue from contracts with customers because they represent sales to non-customers.

We do not believe that it would be appropriate for an entity to recognise the sale of by-products or scrap materials as a reduction of cost of goods sold. This is because recognising the sale of by-products or scrap materials as a reduction of cost of goods sold may inappropriately reflect the cost of raw materials used in manufacturing the main product. However, this interpretation would not apply if other accounting standards allow for recognition as a reduction of costs.

IAS 2 – *Inventories* – requires that the costs of conversion of the main product and the by-product be allocated between the products on a rational and consistent basis. However, IAS 2 mentions that most by-products, by their nature, are immaterial. When this is the case, they are often measured at net realisable value and this value is deducted from the cost of the main product. As a result, the carrying amount of the main product is not materially different from its cost. We believe that the language in IAS 2 only relates to the allocation of the costs of conversion between the main product and by-product and does not allow the proceeds from the sale of by-products to be presented as a reduction of cost of goods sold.

3.5.1.1 Prepaid gift cards

Entities may sell prepaid gift cards in their normal course of business in exchange for cash. The prepaid gift cards typically provide the customer with the right to redeem those cards in the future for goods or services of the entity and/or third parties. For any unused balance of the prepaid gift cards, entities need to recognise a liability that will be released upon redemption of that unused balance. However, the features of each prepaid gift card may vary and the nature of the liability depends on the assessment of these features. Entities may need to use judgement in order to determine whether the prepaid gift card is within the scope of IFRS 15 or another standard.

Prepaid gift cards that give rise to financial liabilities are within the scope of IFRS 9. If a prepaid gift card does not give rise to a financial liability it is likely to be within the scope of IFRS 15. For further information on applying IFRS 15 to prepaid gift cards within its scope refer to Chapter 30 at 11.

An example of a prepaid gift card that is within the scope of IFRS 9 was discussed by the IFRS Interpretations Committee at its March 2016 meeting. The issue related to the accounting treatment of any unused balance on a prepaid card issued by an entity in exchange for cash as well as the classification of the relevant liability that arises. The discussion was limited to prepaid cards that have the specific features described in the request to the IFRS Interpretations Committee.[14] In particular, the prepaid card:

(a) has no expiry date and no back-end fees. That is, any unspent balance does not reduce unless it is spent by the cardholder;

(b) is non-refundable, non-redeemable and non-exchangeable for cash;

(c) can be redeemed only for goods or services to a specified monetary amount; and

(d) can be redeemed only at specified third-party merchants (the range of merchants accepting the specific card could vary depending on the card programme) and, upon redemption, the entity delivers cash to the merchant(s).

The IFRS Interpretations Committee observed that when an entity issues a prepaid card with the above features, it is contractually obliged to deliver cash to the merchants on behalf of the cardholder. Although this obligation is conditional upon the cardholder redeeming the card by purchasing goods or services, the entity's right to avoid delivering cash to settle this contractual obligation is not unconditional. On this basis, the IFRS Interpretations Committee concluded that the entity's liability for such a prepaid card meets the definition of a financial liability and would fall within the scope of IFRS 9 and IAS 32 – *Financial Instruments: Presentation*. Entities need to apply judgement to determine which standard applies depending upon the specific facts and circumstances for scenarios other than the one discussed by the IFRS Interpretations Committee in its March 2016 meeting. The IFRS Interpretations Committee also noted in its agenda decision that its discussion on this issue did not include customer loyalty programmes.[15]

3.5.1.J   Determining whether IFRS 10 or IFRS 15 applies to the sale of a corporate wrapper to a customer

As part of their ordinary activities, entities may enter into contracts with customers to sell an asset by selling their equity interest in a separate entity (commonly referred to as a 'corporate wrapper' or 'single-asset entity') holding that asset (e.g. real estate), rather than by selling the asset itself. Entities may sell assets via a sale of equity interest in a corporate wrapper for tax or legal reasons or because of local regulation or business practice. Facts and circumstances may differ, for example, in relation to:

- when the corporate wrapper is created and the asset transferred into it;
- when the entity enters into a contract with a customer;
- if the asset is constructed by the entity, when construction starts; and
- when the equity interest in the corporate wrapper is legally transferred to the customer.

In addition, a corporate wrapper could include only one asset (plus a related deferred tax asset or liability) or one or more other assets or liabilities, such as a financing liability.

Whether an entity needs to apply IFRS 10 or IFRS 15 to the sale of a corporate wrapper to a customer depends on facts and circumstances and may require significant judgement, including consideration of the following:

- IFRS 10 requires an entity that controls one or more entities (i.e. the parent) to present consolidated financial statements, with some limited exceptions, and sets out the requirements to determine whether, as an investor, it controls (and, therefore, must consolidate) an investee. A parent consolidates an entity that it controls (i.e. the subsidiary) from the date on which it first obtains control. It ceases consolidating that subsidiary on the date on which it loses control. *[IFRS 10.2, 4-4B, 20, Appendix A]*. IFRS 10 also specifies how a parent accounts for the full or partial sale of a subsidiary. See Chapters 6 and 7 for further discussion.
- IFRS 15 excludes from its scope '... financial instruments and other contractual rights or obligations within the scope of ... IFRS 10' (see 3.1 above). *[IFRS 15.5(c)]*.

In practice, some entities apply IFRS 15 to all such contracts with customers because the transactions are part of the entity's ordinary activities and they believe doing so would better reflect the 'substance' of each transaction (e.g. the entity is 'in substance' selling the asset and not the equity interest; the structure is for legal, tax or risk reasons and they believe it should not affect the recognition of revenue).[16]

Judgement may also be needed in determining whether an investor controls the corporate wrapper. For example, the (selling) entity may act as an agent (in accordance with IFRS 10) in relation to the corporate wrapper based on the terms and conditions in the customer contract. IFRS 10 would not apply to the sale, if the entity does not control the corporate wrapper prior to sale.

In June 2019, the IFRS Interpretations Committee discussed a request about the accounting for a transaction in which an entity, as part of its ordinary activities, enters into a contract with a customer to sell real estate by selling its equity interest in a subsidiary. The entity established the subsidiary some time before it enters into the contract with the customer; the subsidiary has one asset (real estate inventory) and a related tax asset or liability. The entity has applied IFRS 10 in consolidating the subsidiary before it loses control of the subsidiary as a result of the transaction with the customer. The IFRS Interpretations Committee discussed this issue, but did not reach any decisions, at its June 2019 meeting.[17] At the time of writing, the IFRS Committee had not issued an agenda decision on this matter. Instead, the issue was referred to the IASB.

In October 2019, the IASB directed its staff to research the feasibility of narrow-scope standard setting. In June 2020, the IASB discussed a possible narrow-scope amendment that would have required an entity to apply IFRS 15, instead of IFRS 10, to sales of subsidiaries where all of the following apply:

- the entity contracts with a customer for goods or services that are the output of its ordinary activities in exchange for consideration;
- the subsidiary contains only inventory and any related income tax asset or liability; and
- the entity retains no interest in the inventory transferred to the customer.

the Board decided against proposing this amendment.[18]

During the discussions held by both the IFRS Interpretations Committee and the IASB, a number of members of the Committee and the Board considered that, absent an amendment, IFRS 10 (rather than IFRS 15) would apply to the transaction considered. During the June 2020 discussion, some Board members thought there was merit in a narrow-scope amendment. However, concerns were raised about potential unintended consequences of proposing a narrow-scope amendment without a more comprehensive discussion. Any narrow-scope amendment would affect the scope of both IFRS 10 and IFRS 15 and, as such, Board members wanted to learn more from stakeholders about the need for, and the consequences of, such a project.[19] However, these considerations were not noted in the relevant *IFRIC Update* and *IASB Update* that were issued as summaries of the meetings. At the time of writing, this matter was expected to be considered as part of phase 2 of the post-implementation review (PIR) of IFRS 10, which was scheduled to commence in Q4 of 2020.[20]

Until the deliberation process on this question is completed, there may continue to be some diversity in practice. However, in the meantime, entities may need to consider the discussions on this matter as they determine the appropriate standard to apply to transactions with customers involving the loss of control of a single asset entity.

It should be noted that the applicable standard (i.e. IFRS 10 or IFRS 15) is not just a matter of presentation. That is, it may also affect, for example, the timing of recognition (i.e. point in time versus over time and, if point in time, the specific point in time) and the measurement of consideration (e.g. IFRS 10 does not constrain variable consideration). Furthermore, IFRS 10 provides specific requirements for the derecognition of all assets and liabilities of the former subsidiary on loss of control, which would not apply if the contract with the customer is within the scope of IFRS 15.

Under US GAAP, the sale of a corporate wrapper to a customer generally will be in the scope of ASC 606. ASC 810 – *Consolidation* – indicates that its deconsolidation and derecognition guidance does not apply to a loss of control of a subsidiary that is a business if that transaction is within the scope of ASC 606. Loss of control of a subsidiary that is not a business is equally excluded from the scope of ASC 810 if the substance of the transaction is within the scope of another standard (e.g. ASC 606, ASC 610-20 – *Other Income – Gains and Losses from Derecognition of Nonfinancial Assets*). Therefore, the sale of a corporate wrapper to a counterparty that is not a customer may be in the scope of ASC 610-20, which applies to the recognition of gains or losses on transfers of non-financial assets and in-substance non-financial assets, including transfers of these assets when included in a consolidated subsidiary, that are not businesses to counterparties that are not customers.

3.5.1.K Revenue arising from an interest in a joint operation

Revenue recognised in accordance with IFRS 15 must reflect an entity's performance in transferring a good or service to a customer.

Under IFRS 11, a joint operator is required to account for revenue relating to its interest in the joint operation (as defined in IFRS 11; see Chapter 12) by applying the standards that are applicable to the particular revenue. *[IFRS 11.21]*. Therefore, while contracts with joint operators are excluded from the scope of IFRS 15, if revenue relating to an interest in a joint operation under IFRS 11 arises from a contract with a customer, it is recognised in accordance with IFRS 15.

As discussed at 3.1 above, IFRS 15 applies only to contracts with customers. In addition, IFRS 11 requires a joint operator to recognise 'its revenue from the sale of its share of the output arising from the joint operation'. *[IFRS 11.20]*. Therefore, revenue recognised by a joint operator must depict the output it has received from the joint operation and sold to customers, rather than the production of output or entitlement to output, as shown in Example 27.4 below.

This is consistent with the conclusion reached by the IFRS Interpretations Committee in March 2019. The IFRS Interpretations Committee discussed this issue using the following example:[21]

Example 27.4: Interaction between IFRS 11 and IFRS 15 in recognising revenue relating to an interest in a joint operation

Operators A and B establish an unincorporated joint operation (JO) that they expect will produce output over a 2-year period. According to the joint operating agreement, each operator is entitled to receive 50% of the output arising from the JO's activities and obliged to pay for 50% of the production costs incurred. For operational reasons, the output received by each joint operator and transferred to its customers in any one reporting period is different from the output to which it is entitled. Any difference between the operators' entitlement and the output received will be settled through future deliveries of output arising from the JO, not in cash.

Output from the JO's activities was £100,000 in year 1 and £150,000 in year 2. In Years 1 and 2, both operators paid for 50% of the production costs incurred.

(in £000s)	Operator A	Operator B
Year 1		
Entitlement to output	50	50
Output received and transferred to customers	48	52
Asset / (liability)	2	(2)
Year 2		
Entitlement to output	75	75
Output received and transferred to customers	77	73
	–	–

Operators A and B consider whether to recognise as revenue in each period: the entitlement to the output produced from the joint operation's activities; or the output that was received and transferred to its customers.

In this fact pattern, the IFRS Interpretations Committee concluded that, in accordance with IFRS 15, each joint operator recognises revenue to depict only the transfer of output to its customers in each reporting period. As such, if Operators A and B are entitled to output, but that output has not been received and sold to customers, they do not recognise revenue.

Therefore, Operator A recognises revenue from contracts with customers of £48,000 in Year 1 and £77,000 in Year 2. Similarly, Operator B recognises revenue from contracts with customers of £52,000 in Year 1 and £73,000 in Year 2.

3.5.1.L Are equity instruments issued by an entity to a customer in connection with a revenue arrangement within the scope of the revenue standard?

Whether or not an entity needs to apply IFRS 15 to a transaction in which equity instruments (e.g. shares) are issued to a customer in connection with a revenue arrangement depends on the substance and purpose of the transaction.

Many entities make payments to their customers. In some cases, the consideration paid or payable represents purchases by the entity of goods or services offered by the customer that satisfy a business need of the entity. In other cases, the consideration paid or payable represents incentives given by the entity to entice the customer to purchase, or continue purchasing, its goods or services.

According to paragraph 7 of IFRS 15, a contract with a customer may be partially within the scope of IFRS 15 and partially within the scope of other standards. IFRS 15 does not specify whether equity instruments issued by an entity to a customer are a type of consideration paid or payable to customer. Nor does IFRS 2 – *Share-based Payment* – specifically address such transactions. Depending on the facts and circumstances, several standards (or a combination of standards) may be applicable (e.g. IFRS 2, IFRS 15, IAS 32). To determine the substance of the transaction and which standard(s) apply, entities will need to consider all relevant facts and circumstances, including the purpose of the transaction. Such determinations may require significant judgement.

In 2018, the FASB amended ASC 606 to clarify that equity instruments granted to customers in conjunction with the sale of goods or services (e.g. shares, options) are within the scope of the requirements for consideration payable to customers.[22] The IASB has not proposed any similar amendments to IFRS 15. Therefore, entities applying IFRS could reach a different accounting conclusion from those applying US GAAP.

4 OTHER INCOME AND OTHER REVENUE

As income and revenue are defined broadly, not all income-generating transactions are in the scope of IFRS 15. As discussed at 3.1 above, an entity applies IFRS 15 only to a contract in which the counterparty to the contract meets the definition of a customer (unless the contract is specifically excluded from the scope of IFRS 15 (see 3.1 above for a list of scope exclusions)).

Below, we highlight some other items of income that are not within the scope of IFRS 15 and note whether they are covered by another standard. Some of these items of income may represent other revenue (i.e. non-IFRS 15 revenue) if part of the entity's ordinary activities.

4.1 Income and distributable profits

In general, IFRS does not address the issue of the distribution of profit. Whether or not revenue and gains recognised in accordance with IFRS are distributable to shareholders of an entity will depend entirely on the national laws and regulations with which the entity needs to comply. Thus, income reported in accordance with IFRS does not necessarily imply that such income would either be realised or distributable under a reporting entity's applicable national legislation.

4.2 Interest and dividends

Entities (e.g. financial institutions) may earn interest or dividends in the course of their ordinary activities and, therefore, present these transactions as revenue. The relevant recognition and measurement requirements are included in IFRS 9. These transactions are recognised as follows:

- *Interest:* calculated by using the effective interest method *[IFRS 9 Appendix A, IFRS 9.5.4.1, B5.4.1-B5.4.7]* as discussed in Chapter 50 at 3;
- *Dividends:* when the shareholder's right to receive payment is established, it is probable that the economic benefits associated with the dividend will flow to the entity and the amount of the dividend can be measured reliably. *[IFRS 9.5.7.1A].* See Chapter 50 at 2.

4.3 Disposal of non-financial assets not in the ordinary course of business

When an entity disposes of an asset that is within the scope of IAS 16, IAS 38 – *Intangible Assets* – and IAS 40 – *Investment Property* – and that disposal is not part of the entity's ordinary activities, the transaction is within the scope of those standards, not IFRS 15. However, IAS 16, IAS 38 and IAS 40 require entities to use certain of the requirements of IFRS 15 when recognising and measuring gains or losses arising from the sale or disposal of non-financial assets.

IAS 16, IAS 38 and IAS 40 require that the gain or loss arising from the disposal of a non-financial asset be included in profit or loss when the item is derecognised, unless IFRS 16 requires otherwise on a sale and leaseback. IAS 16 and IAS 38 specifically prohibit classification of any such gain as revenue. *[IAS 16.68, IAS 38.113, IAS 40.69]*. This was reiterated by the IFRS Interpretations Committee in June 2020 in relation to the presentation of player transfer payments resulting from the sale of an intangible asset within the scope of IAS 38.[23] However, IAS 16 mentions an exception in the case of entities that are in the business of renting and subsequently selling the same assets (discussed at 4.3.1 below). *[IAS 16.68A]*. IFRS 16 applies to disposal via a sale and leaseback. *[IAS 16.69, IAS 38.113, IAS 40.67]*.

The gain or loss on disposal of a non-financial asset is the difference between the net disposal proceeds, if any, and the carrying amount of the item. *[IAS 16.71, IAS 38.113, IAS 40.69]*. Under IAS 16 or IAS 38, if an entity applies the revaluation model for measurement after initial recognition, any revaluation surplus relating to the asset disposed of is transferred within equity to retained earnings when the asset is derecognised and not reflected in profit or loss. *[IAS 16.41, IAS 38.87]*.

As noted above, IAS 16, IAS 38 and IAS 40 provide a consistent model for the measurement and recognition of gains or losses on the sale or disposal of non-financial assets to non-customers (i.e. not in the ordinary course of business) by referring to the requirements in IFRS 15. For sales of non-financial assets to non-customers, IAS 16, IAS 38 and IAS 40 require entities to:

- determine the date of disposal (and, therefore, derecognition of the asset) using the requirements in IFRS 15 for determining when a performance obligation is satisfied (i.e. Step 5 requirements, see Chapter 30); *[IAS 16.69, IAS 38.114, IAS 40.67]* and
- measure the consideration that is included in the calculation of the gain or loss on disposal in accordance with the requirements for determining the transaction price (i.e. Step 3 requirements, see Chapter 29 at 2). Any subsequent changes to the estimate of the consideration (e.g. updates of variable consideration estimates, including reassessment of the constraint) are recognised in accordance with the requirements for changes in the transaction price. *[IAS 16.72, IAS 38.116, IAS 40.70]*. For example, if variable consideration is constrained at the time of disposal, it would not be recognised in profit or loss until it is no longer constrained, which could be in a subsequent period.

IFRS 5 – *Non-current Assets Held for Sale and Discontinued Operations* – provides additional requirements for assets that meet that standard's criteria to be classified as held for sale. These requirements include measurement provisions, which may affect the measurement of the amount of the subsequent gain or loss on disposal. These are discussed in Chapter 4 at 2.2.

IFRS 10 specifies how a parent accounts for the full or partial disposal of a subsidiary (see Chapter 7 for further discussion).[24] The accounting treatment may, therefore, differ depending on whether a non-financial asset is sold on its own (in which case, IAS 16, IAS 38 or IAS 40 would apply) or included within a full or partial disposal of a subsidiary (in which case IFRS 10 would apply). Where there is a retained interest in a former subsidiary, other IFRSs (such as IAS 28, IFRS 11 or IFRS 9) may also apply in accounting for the transaction.

Similar considerations may apply to disposals of non-financial assets held in a corporate wrapper that are in the ordinary course of business, since IFRS 15 excludes transactions within the scope of IFRS 10. See 3.5.1.J above for further discussion.

The FASB's ASC 610-20 provides guidance on how to account for any gain or loss resulting from the sale of non-financial assets or in-substance non-financial assets that are not an output of an entity's ordinary activities and are not a business. This includes the sale of intangible assets and PP&E, including real estate, as well as materials and supplies. ASC 610-20 requires entities to apply certain recognition and measurement principles of ASC 606. Thus, under US GAAP, the accounting for a contract that includes the sale of a non-financial asset to a non-customer will generally be consistent with a contract to sell a non-financial asset to a customer, except for financial statement presentation and disclosure. Sales or transfers of businesses or subsidiaries that do not contain solely non-financial assets and in-substance non-financial assets to non-customers are accounted for using the deconsolidation guidance in ASC 810.

As discussed above, IAS 16, IAS 38 and IAS 40 require entities to use certain of the requirements of IFRS 15 when recognising and measuring gains or losses arising from the sale or disposal of non-financial assets when it is not in the ordinary course of business. Changes in a parent's ownership interest in a subsidiary (including loss of control through sale or disposal) are generally accounted for under IFRS 10 (see 3.5.1.J above). Unlike US GAAP, IFRS does not contain specific requirements regarding the sale of in-substance non-financial assets.

4.3.1 Sale of assets held for rental

In general, IAS 16 prohibits the classification of gains arising from the derecognition of PP&E as revenue. *[IAS 16.68A]*. However, for entities that are in the business of renting and subsequently selling the same asset, the IASB has agreed that the presentation of revenue, rather than a net gain or loss on the sale of the assets, would better reflect the ordinary activities of such entities. *[IAS 16.BC35C]*. See Chapter 18 at 7.2 for further discussion.

Therefore, where an entity, in the course of its ordinary activities, routinely sells items of PP&E that it has held for rental to others, it is required to transfer the assets to inventories at their carrying amount when they cease to be rented and become held for sale. The proceeds from the sale of such assets are recognised as revenue in accordance with IFRS 15 on a gross basis. IFRS 5 does not apply when assets that are held for sale in the ordinary course of business are transferred to inventories. *[IAS 16.68A]*.

IAS 7 – *Statement of Cash Flows* – requires presentation within operating activities of cash payments to manufacture or acquire such assets and cash receipts from rents and sales of such assets. *[IAS 7.14]*. The requirements of IAS 7 are discussed further in Chapter 40.

4.4 Regulatory assets and liabilities

In many countries, the provision of utilities (e.g. water, natural gas or electricity) to consumers is regulated by a government agency (regulators). The objective of this rate regulation is to ensure 'quality, quantity and availability of supply', as well as 'stability, predictability and affordability of pricing' for 'goods or services that governments consider essential for a reasonable quality of life for their citizens and for which there are significant barriers to effective competition for supply'. Regulations differ between countries, but regulators may operate a cost-plus system under which a utility is allowed to make a fixed return on investment. Consequently, there is rate-adjustment mechanism to adjust the future price that a utility is allowed to charge its customers for variances between estimated and actual inputs to the rate calculation. Hence, this adjustment creates timing differences as the future price may be influenced by past cost levels and investment levels.

Under some national GAAPs (including US GAAP) accounting practices have been developed that allow an entity to account for the effects of regulation by recognising a 'regulatory liability' or 'regulatory asset' that reflects the decrease in future prices required by the regulator to compensate for an excessive return on investment, and *vice versa* where an increase would be permitted.

In September 2012, the Board decided to restart its rate-regulated activities project and issued a discussion paper in September 2014 aiming to develop an accounting model so that investors can compare the effects of rate regulation on the financial position, performance and cash flows of any entity with significant rate-regulated revenue.[25] As an interim measure, the IASB issued IFRS 14 – *Regulatory Deferral Accounts* – to help entities who currently recognise rate-regulated assets and liabilities under their national GAAP adopt IFRS. That standard permits a first-time adopter of IFRS to continue to use its previous accounting policies for rate-regulated assets and liabilities, with specific disclosure requirements (see Chapter 5 for discussion on first-time adoption).

The Board is currently undertaking a standard-setting project to develop a new accounting model to provide users of financial statements with useful information about an entity's rights and obligations arising from a defined rate regulation that are not captured by existing IFRS requirements.

The possible accounting model being discussed by the IASB provides explanations for the term 'defined rate regulation' and proposes a 'supplementary approach'. Under this approach, an entity would continue to apply existing IFRS standards, including IFRS 15, without modification (i.e. customer contracts perspective). The model would then be applied to provide information about the effects of the timing differences between when a transaction or event takes place and when some of the effects of that transaction or event are reflected in the rate (i.e. regulatory agreement perspective). The rights and obligations reflecting these timing differences that are incremental to those reported using existing IFRS standards (e.g. IFRS 15) would then be recognised in the statement of financial position as an asset or liability.[26]

At its July 2019 meeting, the Board decided to publish its proposal for a new accounting model as an exposure draft of a new standard that would replace IFRS 14.[27] In its September 2019 meeting, the Board discussed application guidance to include in the exposure draft to assist entities when determining the boundary of a regulatory agreement. It also discussed transition considerations.[28] In March 2020, the Board discussed its planned proposals for the elements of 'target profit' (i.e. the profit an entity is entitled to include in the regulated rate) and the composition of the total allowed compensation for the goods or services supplied.[29] At the time of writing, the Board was expected to issue the exposure draft in Q4 of 2020.[30] Until any new standard is issued and becomes effective, regulatory assets and liabilities are not eligible for recognition under IFRS, unless the entity is a first-time adopter that can apply IFRS 14. For further details see Chapter 17 at 11.1.

References

1. Speech by Wesley R. Bricker, 5 May 2016. Refer to SEC website at https://www.sec.gov/news/speech/speech-bricker-05-05-16.html (accessed 10 September 2018).
2. Paragraph IN5 was part of the Introduction that accompanied IFRS 15 when the standard was issued in May 2014. This Introduction was last included in the 2016 edition of the IFRS Red Book, which contained all IFRSs issued (but not necessarily effective) at 1 January 2016.
3. The FASB's standard defines a public entity as one of the following: A public business entity (as defined); A not-for-profit entity that has issued, or is a conduit bond obligor for, securities that are traded, listed or quoted on an exchange or an over-the-counter market; An employee benefit plan that files or furnishes financial statements with the US SEC. An entity may meet the definition of a public business entity solely because its financial statements or financial information is included in another entity's filing with the SEC. The SEC staff said it would not object if these entities adopt the new revenue standard using the effective date for non-public entities rather than the effective date for public entities.
4. *Effective Date of IFRS 15*, September 2015.
5. The FASB's amendments to its standard were effected through the following: ASU 2015-14, *Revenue from Contracts with Customers (Topic 606): Deferral of the Effective Date*; ASU 2016-08, *Revenue from Contracts with Customers (Topic 606): Principal versus Agent Considerations (Reporting Revenue Gross versus Net)*; ASU 2016-10, *Revenue from Contracts with Customers (Topic 606): Identifying Performance Obligations and Licensing* (April 2016); ASU 2016-12, *Revenue from Contracts with Customer (Topic 606): Narrow-Scope Improvements and Practical Expedients* (May 2016); and ASU 2016-20, *Technical Corrections and Improvements to Topic 606, Revenue From Contracts With Customers* (December 2016).
6. US GAAP, *Statement of Financial Accounting Concepts No. 6*, para. 78.
7. TRG Agenda paper 17, *Application of IFRS 15 to permitted Islamic Finance Transactions*, dated 26 January 2015.
8. TRG Agenda paper 25, *January 2015 Meeting – Summary of Issues Discussed and Next Steps*, dated 30 March 2015.
9. FASB TRG Agenda paper 52, *Scoping Considerations for Financial Institutions*, dated 18 April 2016.
10. TRG Agenda paper 36, *Scope: Credit Cards*, dated 13 July 2015.
11. TRG Agenda paper 36, *Scope: Credit Cards*, dated 13 July 2015.
12. ASU 2018-08, *Accounting Standards Update 2018-08 – Not-For-Profit Entities (Topic 958): Clarifying The Scope And Accounting Guidance For Contributions Received And Contributions Made*.
13. TRG Agenda paper 26, *Whether Contributions are Included or Excluded from the Scope*, dated 30 March 2015 and TRG Agenda paper 34, *March 2015 Meeting – Summary of Issues Discussed and Next Steps*, dated 13 July 2015.
14. *IFRIC Update*, March 2016.
15. *IFRIC Update*, March 2016.
16. Agenda paper 6, *Sale of a single asset entity containing real estate (IFRS 10)*, paras 15-16, dated June 2019.
17. *IFRIC Update*, June 2019.
18. *IASB Update*, June 2020 and IASB *agenda paper 12A, Maintenance and Consistent Application: Sale of a Subsidiary to a Customer*, dated June 2020.
19. Project summary: *Sales of Subsidiary to a customer*, website of the IFRS Foundation and IASB, https://www.ifrs.org/projects/2020/sale-of-a-single-asset-entity-containing-real-estate-ifrs-10/ (accessed 17 August 2020).
20. IASB work plan, website of the IFRS Foundation and IASB, https://www.ifrs.org/projects/2020/sale-of-a-single-asset-entity-containing-real-estate-ifrs-10/ (accessed 17 August 2020).
21. *IFRIC Update*, March 2019 and Agenda Paper 2, *Output received by a joint operator (IFRS 11)*, dated November 2018.
22. ASU 2018-07 *Compensation – Stock Compensation (718): Improvements to Nonemployee Share-Based Payment accounting*.
23. *IFRIC Update*, June 2020.
24. Para. 25 of IFRS 10 applies if a parent loses control of a subsidiary. Para. 23 of IFRS 10 applies if a parent's ownership interest in a subsidiary changes without the parent losing control of that subsidiary.

25 Discussion Paper DP/2014/2, *Reporting the Financial Effects of Rate Regulation*.
26 IASB Agenda paper 9A *Rate-regulated Activities*, July 2018.
27 *IASB Update*, July 2019.
28 *IASB Update*, September 2019.
29 *IASB Update*, March 2020.
30 Website of the IFRS Foundation and IASB, https://www.ifrs.org/projects/work-plan/ (accessed 20 August 2020).

Chapter 28 Revenue: identify the contract and performance obligations

1	INTRODUCTION			2051
2	IDENTIFY THE CONTRACT WITH THE CUSTOMER			2052
	2.1	Attributes of a contract		2053
		2.1.1	Application questions on attributes of a contract	2053
			2.1.1.A Master supply arrangements (MSA)	2053
			2.1.1.B Free trial period	2054
			2.1.1.C Consideration of side agreements	2055
		2.1.2	Parties have approved the contract and are committed to perform their respective obligations	2055
		2.1.3	Each party's rights regarding the goods or services to be transferred can be identified	2056
		2.1.4	Payment terms can be identified	2056
		2.1.5	Commercial substance	2056
		2.1.6	Collectability	2057
			2.1.6.A Assessing collectability for a portfolio of contracts	2060
			2.1.6.B Determining when to reassess collectability	2060
	2.2	Contract enforceability and termination clauses		2061
		2.2.1	Application questions on contract enforceability and termination clauses	2062
			2.2.1.A Evaluating termination clauses and termination payments in determining the contract duration	2062
			2.2.1.B Evaluating the contract term when only the customer has the right to cancel the contract without cause	2063

		2.2.1.C	Evaluating the contract term when an entity has a past practice of not enforcing termination payments	2064
		2.2.1.D	Accounting for a partial termination of a contract	2065
		2.2.1.E	Accounting for consideration that was received from a customer, but not recognised as revenue, when the contract is cancelled	2065
		2.2.1.F	Services provided during a period after contract expiration	2066
	2.3	Combining contracts		2067
		2.3.1	Portfolio approach practical expedient	2068
	2.4	Contract modifications		2068
		2.4.1	Contract modification represents a separate contract	2071
		2.4.2	Contract modification is not a separate contract	2073
		2.4.3	Application questions on contract modifications	2077
		2.4.3.A	When to evaluate the contract under the contract modification requirements	2077
		2.4.3.B	Reassessing the contract criteria if a contract is modified	2078
		2.4.3.C	Distinguishing between a contract modification and a change in the estimated transaction price due to variable consideration after contract inception	2078
		2.4.3.D	Distinguishing between a contract modification and a marketing offer	2079
		2.4.3.E	Contract modification that decreases the scope of the contract	2079
		2.4.3.F	Accounting for a 'blend-and-extend' contract modification	2080
	2.5	Arrangements that do not meet the definition of a contract under the standard		2081
		2.5.1	Application questions on arrangements that do not meet the definition of a contract under the standard	2083
		2.5.1.A	Determining when a contract is terminated for the purpose of applying paragraph 15(b) of IFRS 15	2083
3	IDENTIFY THE PERFORMANCE OBLIGATIONS IN THE CONTRACT			2084
	3.1	Identifying the promised goods or services in the contract		2084
		3.1.1	Application questions on identifying promised goods or services	2091
		3.1.1.A	Assessing whether pre-production activities are a promised good or service	2091

		3.1.1.B	The nature of the promise in a typical stand-ready obligation 2092
		3.1.1.C	Considering whether contracts with a stand-ready element include a single performance obligation that is satisfied over time 2093
		3.1.1.D	Evaluating whether an exclusivity provision in a contract with customer represents a promised good or service 2094
3.2	Determining when promises are performance obligations 2095
	3.2.1	Determination of 'distinct' 2096
		3.2.1.A	Capable of being distinct 2096
		3.2.1.B	Distinct within the context of the contract 2097
		3.2.1.C	How should an entity determine whether 'connected' hardware sold with cloud services represent one or more performance obligations? 2106
		3.2.1.D	How would entities determine whether implementation services are distinct? 2107
	3.2.2	Series of distinct goods or services that are substantially the same and have the same pattern of transfer 2109
		3.2.2.A	The series requirement: Consecutive transfer of goods or services 2112
		3.2.2.B	The series requirement versus treating the distinct goods or services as separate performance obligations 2112
		3.2.2.C	Assessing whether a performance obligation consists of distinct goods or services that are 'substantially the same' 2113
		3.2.2.D	When to apply the series requirement 2116
		3.2.2.E	Do all stand-ready obligations meet the criteria to be accounted for as a series? 2116
	3.2.3	Examples of identifying performance obligations 2116
3.3	Promised goods or services that are not distinct 2120
3.4	Principal versus agent considerations 2121
	3.4.1	Identifying the specified good or service 2123
	3.4.2	Control of the specified good or service 2125
		3.4.2.A	Principal indicators 2128
	3.4.3	Recognising revenue as principal or agent 2131
	3.4.4	Examples of principal versus agent considerations 2132
	3.4.5	Application questions on principal versus agent considerations 2137
		3.4.5.A	Considerations when there is only momentary transfer of legal title and absence of physical possession 2137

		3.4.5.B	Presentation of amounts billed to customers (e.g. shipping and handling, expenses or cost reimbursements and taxes or other assessments) 2138
3.5	Consignment arrangements.. 2140
3.6	Customer options for additional goods or services.................................... 2140
	3.6.1	Application questions on customer options for additional goods or services 2142
		3.6.1.A	Which transactions to consider when assessing customer options for additional goods or services 2142
		3.6.1.B	Nature of evaluation of customer options: quantitative versus qualitative 2142
		3.6.1.C	Distinguishing between a customer option and variable consideration.. 2142
		3.6.1.D	When, if ever, to consider the goods or services underlying a customer option as a separate performance obligation when there are no contractual penalties 2146
		3.6.1.E	Volume rebates and/or discounts on goods or services: customer options versus variable consideration 2147
		3.6.1.F	Considering the class of customer when evaluating whether a customer option is a material right.. 2148
		3.6.1.G	Considering whether prospective volume discounts determined to be customer options are material rights 2149
		3.6.1.H	Considering whether a renewal option is a material right.. 2150
		3.6.1.I	Considering whether a loyalty or reward programme is a material right 2152
		3.6.1.J	Accounting for the exercise of a material right........ 2152
		3.6.1.K	Customer options that provide a material right: Evaluating whether there is a significant financing component... 2153
		3.6.1.L	Customer options that provide a material right: recognising revenue when there is no expiration date... 2154
3.7	Sale of products with a right of return... 2154

List of examples

Example 28.1:	Oral contract	2052
Example 28.2:	Collectability of the consideration	2059
Example 28.3:	Assessing collectability for a portfolio of contracts	2060
Example 28.4:	Duration of a contract with a termination penalty	2063
Example 28.5:	Duration of a contract without a termination penalty	2063
Example 28.6:	Partial termination of a contract	2065
Example 28.7:	Services provided during a period after contract expiration	2066
Example 28.8:	Unapproved change in scope and price	2069
Example 28.9:	Determining whether the amount of consideration reflects the stand-alone selling price of additional goods or services	2072
Example 28.10:	Modification of a contract for goods	2073
Example 28.11:	Modification of a services contract	2074
Example 28.12:	Modification of a contract for goods	2074
Example 28.13:	Modification resulting in a cumulative catch-up adjustment to revenue	2076
Example 28.14:	Contract modification that decreases the scope of the promised goods or services in a contract	2080
Example 28.15:	Blend-and-extend contract modification	2081
Example 28.16:	Explicit and implicit promises in a contract	2087
Example 28.17:	Identification of promised good or service in a contract by a stock exchange that provides listing service to a customer	2089
Example 28.18:	Determining the nature of the promise in a contract with a stand-ready element	2094
Example 28.19:	Significant integration service	2101
Example 28.20:	Significant customisation service	2102
Example 28.21:	Highly interdependent and highly interrelated	2103
Example 28.22:	Identification of performance obligations in a contract for the sale of a real estate unit that includes the transfer of land	2105
Example 28.23:	Hardware sold with cloud services	2106
Example 28.24:	Implementation services are distinct	2108
Example 28.25:	Implementation services are not distinct	2108
Example 28.26:	Allocation of variable consideration for a series versus a single performance obligation comprising non-distinct goods and/or services	2111
Example 28.27:	A series in which the goods or services need not be consecutively transferred	2112
Example 28.28:	A series for which the accounting result would be different if not treated as a series	2113

Example 28.29:	IT outsourcing	2114
Example 28.30:	Transaction processing	2114
Example 28.31:	Hotel management	2115
Example 28.32:	Determining whether promised goods and services represent a series	2115
Example 28.33:	Goods and services are not distinct	2116
Example 28.34:	Determining whether goods or services are distinct (Case A and Case B)	2117
Example 28.35:	Determining whether goods or services are distinct (Case C – Case E)	2119
Example 28.36:	Entity is both a principal and an agent	2124
Example 28.37:	Entity is an agent	2130
Example 28.38:	Entity is a principal	2131
Example 28.39:	Promise to provide goods or services (entity is a principal) (office maintenance service)	2133
Example 28.40:	Promise to provide goods or services (entity is a principal) (airline tickets)	2134
Example 28.41:	Arranging for the provision of goods or services (entity is an agent)	2134
Example 28.42:	Entity is a principal and an agent in the same contract	2135
Example 28.43:	Option that provides the customer with a material right (discount voucher)	2141
Example 28.44:	Evaluating a customer option when the stand-alone selling price is highly variable	2141
Example 28.45:	Variable consideration (IT outsourcing arrangement)	2144
Example 28.46:	Customer option that is not a material right	2145
Example 28.47:	Customer option that is a material right	2145
Example 28.48:	Customer option	2145
Example 28.49:	Variable consideration (variable quantities of goods or services)	2146
Example 28.50:	Customer option with no contractual penalties	2146
Example 28.51:	Customer option with contractual penalties	2147
Example 28.52:	Class of customer evaluation	2148
Example 28.53:	Volume discounts	2149
Example 28.54:	Evaluating a customer option with volume discounts	2149
Example 28.55:	Option that provides the customer with a material right (renewal option)	2151
Example 28.56:	Exercise of a material right under the requirements for changes in the transaction price	2153

Chapter 28 Revenue: identify the contract and performance obligations

1 INTRODUCTION

Revenue is a broad concept that is dealt with in several standards. This chapter and Chapters 27-32 primarily cover the requirements for revenue arising from contracts with customers that are within the scope of IFRS 15 – *Revenue from Contracts with Customers*. This chapter deals with identifying the contract and identifying performance obligations. Refer to the following chapters for other requirements of IFRS 15:

- Chapter 27 – Core principle, definitions and scope.
- Chapter 29 – Determining the transaction price and allocating the transaction price.
- Chapter 30 – Recognising revenue.
- Chapter 31 – Licences, warranties and contract costs.
- Chapter 32 – Presentation and disclosure requirements.

Other revenue items that are not within the scope of IFRS 15, but arise in the course of the ordinary activities of an entity, as well as the disposal of non-financial assets that are not part of the ordinary activities of the entity, for which IFRS 15's requirements are relevant, are addressed in Chapter 27.

In addition, this chapter:

- Highlights significant differences from the equivalent US GAAP standard, Accounting Standards Codification (ASC) 606 – *Revenue from Contracts with Customers* (together with IFRS 15, the standards) issued by the US Financial Accounting Standards Board (FASB) (together with the International Accounting Standards Board (IASB), the Boards).
- Addresses topics on which the members of the Joint Transition Resource Group for Revenue Recognition (TRG) reached general agreement and our views on certain topics. TRG members' views are non-authoritative, but entities should consider them as they apply the standards. Unless otherwise specified, these summaries represent the discussions of the joint TRG.

The views we express in this chapter may evolve as application issues are identified and discussed among stakeholders. The conclusions we describe in our illustrations are also subject to change as views evolve. Conclusions in seemingly similar situations may differ from those reached in the illustrations due to differences in the underlying facts and circumstances.

2 IDENTIFY THE CONTRACT WITH THE CUSTOMER

To apply the five-step model in IFRS 15, an entity must first identify the contract, or contracts, to provide goods or services to customers. A contract must create enforceable rights and obligations to fall within the scope of the model in the standard. Such contracts may be written, oral or implied by an entity's customary business practices. For example, if an entity has an established practice of starting performance based on oral agreements with its customers, it may determine that such oral agreements meet the definition of a contract. *[IFRS 15.10]*.

As a result, an entity may need to account for a contract as soon as performance begins, rather than delay revenue recognition until the arrangement is documented in a signed contract. Certain arrangements may require a written contract to comply with laws or regulations in a particular jurisdiction. These requirements must be considered when determining whether a contract exists.

In the Basis for Conclusions, the Board acknowledged that entities need to look at the relevant legal framework to determine whether the contract is enforceable because factors that determine enforceability may differ among jurisdictions. *[IFRS 15.BC32]*. The Board also clarified that, while the contract must be legally enforceable to be within the scope of the model in the standard, all of the promises do not have to be enforceable to be considered performance obligations (see 3.1 below). That is, a performance obligation can be based on the customer's valid expectations (e.g. due to the entity's business practice of providing an additional good or service that is not specified in the contract). In addition, the standard clarifies that some contracts may have no fixed duration and can be terminated or modified by either party at any time. Other contracts may automatically renew on a specified periodic basis. Entities are required to apply IFRS 15 to the contractual period in which the parties have present enforceable rights and obligations. *[IFRS 15.11]*. Contract enforceability and termination clauses are discussed at 2.2 below.

Example 28.1: Oral contract

IT Support Co. provides online technology support for customers remotely via the internet. For a fixed fee, IT Support Co. will scan a customer's personal computer (PC) for viruses, optimise the PC's performance and solve any connectivity problems. When a customer calls to obtain the scan services, IT Support Co. describes the services it can provide and states the price for those services. When the customer agrees to the terms stated by the representative, payment is made over the telephone. IT Support Co. then gives the customer the information it needs to obtain the scan services (e.g. an access code for the website). It provides the services when the customer connects to the internet and logs onto the entity's website (which may be that day or a future date).

In this example, IT Support Co. and its customer are entering into an oral agreement, which is legally enforceable in this jurisdiction, for IT Support Co. to repair the customer's PC and for the customer to provide consideration by transmitting a valid credit card number and authorisation over the telephone. The required criteria for a contract with a customer (discussed further at 2.1 below) are all met. As such, this agreement is within the scope of the model in the standard at the time of the telephone conversation, even if the entity has not yet performed the scanning services.

2.1 Attributes of a contract

To help entities determine whether (and when) their arrangements with customers are contracts within the scope of the model in the standard, the Board identified certain attributes that must be present. The Board noted in the Basis for Conclusions that the criteria are similar to those in previous revenue recognition requirements and in other existing standards and are important in an entity's assessment of whether the arrangement contains enforceable rights and obligations. *[IFRS 15.BC33]*.

IFRS 15 requires an entity to account for a contract with a customer that is within the scope of the model in the standard only when all of the following criteria are met: *[IFRS 15.9]*

(a) the parties to the contract have approved the contract (in writing, orally or in accordance with other customary business practices) and are committed to perform their respective obligations;

(b) the entity can identify each party's rights regarding the goods or services to be transferred;

(c) the entity can identify the payment terms for the goods or services to be transferred;

(d) the contract has commercial substance (i.e. the risk, timing or amount of the entity's future cash flows is expected to change as a result of the contract); and

(e) it is probable that the entity will collect the consideration to which it will be entitled in exchange for the goods or services that will be transferred to the customer. In evaluating whether collectability of an amount of consideration is probable, an entity shall consider only the customer's ability and intention to pay that amount of consideration when it is due. The amount of consideration to which the entity will be entitled may be less than the price stated in the contract if the consideration is variable because the entity may offer the customer a price concession.

These criteria are assessed at the inception of the arrangement. If the criteria are met at that time, an entity does not reassess these criteria unless there is an indication of a significant change in facts and circumstances. *[IFRS 15.13]*. For example, as noted in paragraph 13 of IFRS 15, if the customer's ability to pay significantly deteriorates, an entity would have to reassess whether it is probable that the entity will collect the consideration to which it is entitled in exchange for transferring the remaining goods or services under the contract. The updated assessment is prospective in nature and would not change the conclusions associated with goods or services already transferred. That is, an entity would not reverse any receivables, revenue or contract assets already recognised under the contract. *[IFRS 15.BC34]*.

If the criteria are not met (and until the criteria are met), the arrangement is not considered a revenue contract under the standard and the requirements discussed at 2.5 below must be applied.

2.1.1 Application questions on attributes of a contract

2.1.1.A Master supply arrangements (MSA)

An entity may use an MSA to govern the overall terms and conditions of a business arrangement between itself and a customer (e.g. scope of services, pricing, payment terms, warranties and other rights and obligations). Typically, when an entity and a customer enter into an MSA, purchases are subsequently made by the customer by issuing a non-cancellable purchase order or an approved online authorisation that explicitly references the MSA and specifies the products, services and quantities to be delivered.

In such cases, the MSA is unlikely to create enforceable rights and obligations, which are needed to be considered a contract within the scope of the model in IFRS 15. This is because, while the MSA may specify the pricing or payment terms, it usually does not specify the specific goods or services, or quantities thereof, to be transferred. Therefore, each party's rights and obligations regarding the goods or services to be transferred are not identifiable. It is likely that the MSA and the customer order, taken together, would constitute a contract under IFRS 15. As such, entities need to evaluate both the MSA and the subsequent customer order(s) together to determine whether and when the criteria in paragraph 9 of IFRS 15 are met. *[IFRS 15.9]*.

If an MSA includes an enforceable clause requiring the customer to purchase a minimum quantity of goods or services, the MSA alone may constitute a contract under the standard because enforceable rights and obligations exist for this minimum amount of goods or services.

2.1.1.B   Free trial period

Free trial periods are common in certain subscription arrangements (e.g. magazines, streaming services). A customer may receive a number of 'free' months of goods or services at the inception of an arrangement; before the paid subscription begins; or as a bonus period at the beginning or end of a paid subscription period.

Under IFRS 15, revenue is not recognised until an entity determines that a contract within the scope of the model exists. Once an entity determines that an IFRS 15 contract exists, it is required to identify the promises in the contract. Therefore, if the entity has transferred goods or services prior to the existence of an IFRS 15 contract, we believe that the free goods or services provided during the trial period would generally be accounted for as marketing incentives.

Consider an example in which an entity has a marketing programme to provide a three-month free trial period of its services to prospective customers. The entity's customers are not required to pay for the services provided during the free trial period and the entity is under no obligation to provide the services under the marketing programme. If a customer enters into a contract with the entity at the end of the free trial period that obliges the entity to provide services in the future (e.g. signing up for a subsequent 12-month period) and obliges the customer to pay for the services, the services provided as part of the marketing programme may not be promises that are part of an enforceable contract with the customer.

However, if an entity, as part of a negotiation with a prospective customer, agrees to provide three free months of services if the customer agrees to pay for 12 months of services (effectively providing the customer a discount on 15 months), the entity would identify the free months as promises in the contract because the contract requires it to provide them.

The above interpretation applies if the customer is not required to pay any consideration for the additional goods or services during the trial period (i.e. they are free). If the customer is required to pay consideration in exchange for the goods or services received during the trial period (even if it is only a nominal amount), a different accounting conclusion could be reached. Entities need to apply judgement to evaluate whether a contract exists that falls within the scope of the standard.

2.1.1.C Consideration of side agreements

All terms and conditions that create or negate enforceable rights and obligations must be considered when determining whether a contract exists under the standard. Understanding the entire contract, including any side agreements or other amendments, is critical to this determination.

Side agreements are amendments to a contract that can be either undocumented or documented separately from the main contract. The potential for side agreements is greater for complex or material transactions or when complex arrangements or relationships exist between an entity and its customers. Side agreements may be communicated in many forms (e.g. oral agreements, email, letters or contract amendments) and may be entered into for a variety of reasons.

Side agreements may provide an incentive for a customer to enter into a contract near the end of a financial reporting period or to enter into a contract that it would not enter into in the normal course of business. Side agreements may entice a customer to accept delivery of goods or services earlier than required or may provide the customer with rights in excess of those customarily provided by the entity. For example, a side agreement may extend contractual payment terms; expand contractually stated rights; provide a right of return; or commit the entity to provide future products or functionality not contained in the contract or to assist resellers in selling a product. Therefore, if the provisions in a side agreement differ from those in the main contract, an entity should assess whether the side agreement creates new rights and obligations or changes existing rights and obligations. See 2.3 and 2.4 below, respectively, for further discussion of the standard's requirements on combining contracts and contract modifications.

2.1.2 Parties have approved the contract and are committed to perform their respective obligations

Before applying the model in IFRS 15, the parties must have approved the contract. As indicated in the Basis for Conclusions, the Board included this criterion because a contract might not be legally enforceable without the approval of both parties. *[IFRS 15.BC35]*. Furthermore, the Board decided that the form of the contract (i.e. oral, written or implied) is not determinative, in assessing whether the parties have approved the contract. Instead, an entity must consider all relevant facts and circumstances when assessing whether the parties intend to be bound by the terms and conditions of the contract. In some cases, the parties to an oral or implied contract may have the intent to fulfil their respective obligations. However, in other cases, a written contract may be required before an entity can conclude that the parties have approved the arrangement. *[IFRS 15.10]*.

In addition to approving the contract, the entity must be able to conclude that both parties are committed to perform their respective obligations. That is, the entity must be committed to providing the promised goods or services. In addition, the customer must be committed to purchasing those promised goods or services. In the Basis for Conclusions, the Board clarified that an entity and a customer do not always have to be committed to fulfilling all of their respective rights and obligations for a contract to meet this requirement. *[IFRS 15.BC36]*. The Board cited, as an example, a supply agreement between two parties that includes stated minimums. The customer does not always buy the required minimum quantity and the entity does not always enforce its right to require the customer to purchase the minimum quantity. In this situation, the Board stated that it may still be possible for the entity to determine that there is sufficient evidence to demonstrate that the parties are substantially committed to the contract. This criterion does not address a customer's intent and ability to pay the consideration (i.e. collectability). Collectability is a separate criterion and is discussed at 2.1.6 below.

Termination clauses are also an important consideration when determining whether both parties are committed to perform under a contract and, consequently, whether a contract exists. See 2.2 below for further discussion of termination clauses and how they affect contract duration.

2.1.3 Each party's rights regarding the goods or services to be transferred can be identified

This criterion is relatively straightforward. If the goods or services to be provided in the arrangement cannot be identified, it is not possible to conclude that an entity has a contract within the scope of the model in IFRS 15. The Board indicated that if the promised goods or services cannot be identified, the entity cannot assess whether those goods or services have been transferred because the entity would be unable to assess each party's rights with respect to those goods or services. *[IFRS 15.BC37]*.

2.1.4 Payment terms can be identified

Identifying the payment terms does not require that the transaction price be fixed or stated in the contract with the customer. As long as there is an enforceable right to payment (i.e. enforceability as a matter of law) and the contract contains sufficient information to enable the entity to estimate the transaction price (see further discussion in Chapter 29 at 2), the contract would qualify for accounting under the standard (assuming the remaining criteria set out in paragraph 9 of IFRS 15 have been met – see 2.1 above).

2.1.5 Commercial substance

The Board included a criterion that requires arrangements to have commercial substance (i.e. the risk, timing or amount of the entity's future cash flows is expected to change as a result of the contract) to prevent entities from artificially inflating revenue. *[IFRS 15.BC40]*. The model in IFRS 15 does not apply if an arrangement does not have commercial substance. Historically, some entities in high-growth industries allegedly engaged in transactions in which goods or services were transferred back and forth between the same entities in an attempt to show higher transaction volume and gross revenue (sometimes known as 'round-tripping'). This is also a risk in arrangements that involve non-cash consideration.

Determining whether a contract has commercial substance for the purposes of IFRS 15 may require significant judgement. In all situations, the entity must be able to demonstrate a substantive business purpose exists, considering the nature and structure of its transactions.

IFRS 15 does not contain requirements specific to advertising barter transactions. Entities need to carefully consider the commercial substance criterion when evaluating these types of transactions (see Chapter 29 at 2.6.2 for further discussion on barter transactions).

2.1.6 Collectability

Under IFRS 15, collectability refers to the customer's ability and intent to pay the amount of consideration to which the entity will be entitled in exchange for the goods or services that will be transferred to the customer. An entity needs to assess a customer's ability to pay based on the customer's financial capacity and its intention to pay considering all relevant facts and circumstances, including past experiences with that customer or customer class. *[IFRS 15.BC45]*.

In the Basis for Conclusions, the Board noted that the purpose of the criteria in paragraph 9 of IFRS 15 is to require an entity to assess whether a contract is valid and represents a genuine transaction. The collectability criterion (i.e. determining whether the customer has the ability and the intention to pay the promised consideration) is a key part of that assessment. In addition, the Board noted that, in general, entities only enter into contracts in which it is probable that the entity will collect the amount to which it will be entitled. *[IFRS 15.BC43]*. That is, in most instances, an entity would not enter into a contract with a customer if there was significant credit risk associated with that customer without also having adequate economic protection to ensure that it would collect the consideration. The IASB expects that only a small number of arrangements may fail to meet the collectability criterion. *[IFRS 15.BC46E]*.

Paragraph 9(e) of IFRS 15 requires an entity to evaluate at contract inception whether it is *probable* that it will collect the *consideration to which it will be entitled in exchange for the goods or services that will be transferred to a customer*. An entity is also required to reassess collectability after contract inception, when significant facts and circumstances change (see 2.1.6.A below for further discussion). We discuss each of the italicised concepts below.

Probable – For purposes of this analysis, the meaning of the term 'probable' is consistent with the existing definition in IFRS, i.e. 'more likely than not'. *[IFRS 15 Appendix A]*. If it is not probable that the entity will collect amounts to which it is entitled, the model in IFRS 15 is not applied to the contract until the concerns about collectability have been resolved. However, other requirements in IFRS 15 apply to such arrangements (see 2.5 below for further discussion). ASC 606 also uses the term 'probable' for the collectability assessment. However, 'probable' under US GAAP is a higher threshold than under IFRS.[1]

Consideration to which it will be entitled in exchange for the goods or services that will be transferred to a customer – The amount of consideration that is assessed for collectability is the amount to which the entity will be entitled for the goods or services that will be transferred to the customer. That is, the amount of consideration assessed for collectability is often the transaction price, but it may be a lesser amount in certain circumstances, as discussed further below.

It is important to note that the transaction price might be less than the stated contract price for the goods or services in the contract. Entities need to determine the transaction price in Step 3 of the model (as discussed in Chapter 29 at 2) before assessing the collectability of that amount. The contract price and transaction price most often will differ because of variable consideration (e.g. rebates, discounts or explicit or implicit price concessions) that reduces the amount of consideration stated in the contract. For example, the transaction price for the items expected to be transferred may be less than the stated contract price for those items if an entity concludes that it has offered, or is willing to accept, a price concession on products sold to a customer. See Chapter 29 at 2.2.1.A for further discussion on price concessions.

An entity deducts from the contract price any variable consideration that would reduce the amount of consideration to which it expects to be entitled (e.g. an estimated price concession) at contract inception in order to derive the transaction price for those items. The collectability assessment is then performed on the determined transaction price.

Paragraph 9(e) of IFRS 15 specifies that an entity should assess only the consideration to which it will be entitled in exchange for the goods or services that will be transferred to the customer (rather than the total amount promised for all goods or services in the contract). *[IFRS 15.9(e)]*. In the Basis for Conclusions, the Board noted that, if the customer were to fail to perform as promised and the entity were able to stop transferring additional goods or services to the customer in response, the entity would not consider the likelihood of payment for those goods or services that would not be transferred in its assessment of collectability. *[IFRS 15.BC46]*.

In the Basis for Conclusions, the Board also noted that the assessment of collectability criteria requires an entity to consider how the entity's contractual rights to the consideration relate to its performance obligations. That assessment considers the business practices available to the entity to manage its exposure to credit risk throughout the contract (e.g. through advance payments or the right to stop transferring additional goods or services). *[IFRS 15.BC46C]*. The FASB's standard includes additional guidance to clarify the intention of the collectability assessment. However, the IASB stated in the Basis for Conclusions on IFRS 15 that it does not expect differences in outcomes under IFRS and US GAAP in relation to the evaluation of the collectability criterion. *[IFRS 15.BC46E]*.

In addition to the IFRS 15 collectability assessment, an entity has to assess any contract assets or trade receivables arising from an IFRS 15 contract under the expected credit loss model in IFRS 9 – *Financial Instruments* (for further discussion see Chapter 32 at 2.1.3 and Chapter 51).

At contract inception, significant judgement is required to determine when an expected partial payment indicates that: (1) there is an implied price concession in the contract that affects the determination of the transaction price and the amount assessed for collectability under IFRS 15; (2) there is an expected credit loss (accounted for as an impairment loss under IFRS 9); or (3) the arrangement lacks sufficient substance to be considered a contract under the standard. See Chapter 29 at 2.2.1.A for further discussion on implicit price concessions.

(i) *Variable consideration versus credit risk*

In the Basis for Conclusions on IFRS 15, the IASB acknowledged that in some cases, it may be difficult to determine whether the entity has implicitly offered a price concession (i.e. variable consideration) or whether the entity has chosen to accept the risk of default by the customer of the contractually agreed-upon consideration (i.e. impairment losses under IFRS 9, see Chapter 51). *[IFRS 15.BC194]*. The Board did not develop detailed guidance for distinguishing between price concessions (recognised as variable consideration through revenue) and an expected credit loss to be accounted for as an impairment loss under IFRS 9 (i.e. outside of revenue). Therefore, entities need to consider all relevant facts and circumstances when analysing situations in which, at contract inception, an entity is willing to accept a lower price than the amount stated in the contract. In Chapter 29 at 2.2.1.A, we discuss certain factors that may suggest the entity has implicitly offered a price concession to the customer.

After the entity has determined the amount to assess for collectability under paragraph 9(e) of IFRS 15, it also has to apply the requirements in IFRS 9 to account for any expected credit loss for the receivable (or contract asset) that is recorded (i.e. after consideration of any variable consideration, such as an implicit price concession). Also, it should present any resulting impairment loss as an expense under IFRS 9 (i.e. not as a reduction of the transaction price).

Examples 2 (included as Example 29.2 in Chapter 29 at 2.2.1.A), 3 and 23 (included as Example 29.7 in Chapter 29 at 2.2.3) from the standard illustrate situations where the transaction price that is evaluated for collectability is not the amount stated in the contract. In contrast, the TRG discussed an example (included at 2.1.6.A below) in which an entity, at contract inception, believes it is probable that its customers will pay amounts owed and the transaction price (i.e. revenue recorded) equals the contract price, even though, on a portfolio basis, 2% is not expected to be collected.

(ii) *Example of assessing the collectability criterion*

The standard provides the following example of how an entity would assess the collectability criterion. *[IFRS 15.IE3-IE6]*.

Example 28.2: Collectability of the consideration

An entity, a real estate developer, enters into a contract with a customer for the sale of a building for €1 million. The customer intends to open a restaurant in the building. The building is located in an area where new restaurants face high levels of competition and the customer has little experience in the restaurant industry.

The customer pays a non-refundable deposit of €50,000 at inception of the contract and enters into a long-term financing agreement with the entity for the remaining 95 per cent of the promised consideration. The financing arrangement is provided on a non-recourse basis, which means that if the customer defaults, the entity can repossess the building, but cannot seek further compensation from the customer, even if the collateral does not cover the full value of the amount owed. The entity's cost of the building is €600,000. The customer obtains control of the building at contract inception.

In assessing whether the contract meets the criteria in paragraph 9 of IFRS 15, the entity concludes that the criterion in paragraph 9(e) of IFRS 15 is not met because it is not probable that the entity will collect the consideration to which it is entitled in exchange for the transfer of the building. In reaching this conclusion, the entity observes that the customer's ability and intention to pay may be in doubt because of the following factors:

- the customer intends to repay the loan (which has a significant balance) primarily from income derived from its restaurant business (which is a business facing significant risks because of high competition in the industry and the customer's limited experience);
- the customer lacks other income or assets that could be used to repay the loan; and
- the customer's liability under the loan is limited because the loan is non-recourse.

Because the criteria in paragraph 9 of IFRS 15 are not met, the entity applies paragraphs 15-16 of IFRS 15 to determine the accounting for the non-refundable deposit of €50,000. The entity observes that none of the events described in paragraph 15 have occurred – that is, the entity has not received substantially all of the consideration and it has not terminated the contract. Consequently, in accordance with paragraph 16, the entity accounts for the non-refundable €50,000 payment as a deposit liability. The entity continues to account for the initial deposit, as well as any future payments of principal and interest, as a deposit liability, until such time that the entity concludes that the criteria in paragraph 9 are met (i.e. the entity is able to conclude that it is probable that the entity will collect the consideration) or one of the events in paragraph 15 has occurred. The entity continues to assess the contract in accordance with paragraph 14 to determine whether the criteria in paragraph 9 are subsequently met or whether the events in paragraph 15 of IFRS 15 have occurred.

2.1.6.A   Assessing collectability for a portfolio of contracts

At the January 2015 TRG meeting, the TRG members considered how an entity would assess collectability if it has a portfolio of contracts. The TRG members generally agreed that if an entity has determined it is probable that a customer will pay amounts owed under a contract, but the entity has historical experience that it will not collect consideration from some of the customers within a portfolio of contracts (see 2.3.1 below), it would be appropriate for the entity to record revenue for the contract in full and separately evaluate the corresponding contract asset or receivable for impairment.[2] That is, the entity would not conclude the arrangement contains an implicit price concession and would not reduce revenue for the uncollectable amounts. See Chapter 29 at 2.2.1.A for a discussion of evaluating whether an entity has offered an implicit price concession.

Consider the following example included in the TRG agenda paper:

Example 28.3:   Assessing collectability for a portfolio of contracts

An entity has a large volume of similar customer contracts for which it invoices its customers in arrears, on a monthly basis. Before accepting a customer, the entity performs procedures designed to determine if it is probable that the customer will pay the amounts owed. It does not accept customers if it is not probable that the customer will pay the amounts owed. Because these procedures are only designed to determine whether collection is probable (and, thus, not a certainty), the entity anticipates that it will have some customers that will not pay all of the amounts owed. While the entity collects the entire amount due from the vast majority of its customers, on average, the entity's historical evidence (which is representative of its expectations for the future) indicates that the entity will only collect 98% of the amounts invoiced. In this case, the entity would recognise revenue for the full amount due. That is, when the entity satisfies the performance obligations in the contracts, it would recognise revenue of 100% of the amount due and a corresponding receivable for the same amount representing its unconditional right to the full consideration. It would then recognise an impairment loss in accordance with IFRS 9 for 2% of the amount due (i.e. the amount the entity does not expect to collect).[3]

In this example, the entity concludes that collectability is probable for each customer based on procedures it performed prior to accepting each customer and on its historical experience with this customer class, while also accepting that there is some credit risk inherent with this customer class. Furthermore, the entity concludes that any amounts not collected do not represent implied price concessions. Instead, they are due to credit risk that is present in a limited number of customer contracts.

Some TRG members cautioned that the analysis to determine whether to recognise an impairment loss for a contract in the same period in which revenue is recognised (instead of reducing revenue for an anticipated price concession) will require judgement.

2.1.6.B   Determining when to reassess collectability

As discussed at 2.1 above, paragraph 13 of IFRS 15 requires an entity to reassess whether it is probable that it will collect the consideration to which it will be entitled when significant facts and circumstances change. Example 4 in IFRS 15 illustrates a situation in which a customer's financial condition declines and its current access to credit and available cash on hand is limited. In this case, the entity does not reassess the collectability criterion. However, in a subsequent year, the customer's financial condition further declines after losing access to credit and its major customers. Example 4 in IFRS 15 illustrates that this subsequent change in the customer's financial condition is so significant that a reassessment of the criteria for identifying a contract is required, resulting in the collectability criterion not being met. *[IFRS 15.IE14-IE17]*. As noted in the TRG agenda paper, this example illustrates that it was not the Board's intent to require an entity to reassess collectability when changes occur that are relatively minor in nature (i.e. those that do not call into question the validity of the contract). The TRG members generally agreed that entities need to exercise judgement to determine whether changes in the facts and circumstances are significant enough to indicate that a contract no longer exists under the standard.[4]

Example 4 in the standard also notes that the entity accounts for any impairment of the existing receivable in accordance with IFRS 9 (see Chapter 51). *[IFRS 15.IE17]*.

2.2 Contract enforceability and termination clauses

An entity has to determine the duration of the contract (i.e. the stated contractual term or a shorter period) before applying certain aspects of the revenue model (e.g. identifying performance obligations, determining the transaction price). The contract duration under IFRS 15 is the period in which parties to the contract have present enforceable rights and obligations. An entity cannot assume that there are present enforceable rights and obligations for the entire term stated in the contract and it is likely that an entity will have to consider enforceable rights and obligations in individual contracts, as described in the standard.

The standard states that entities are required to apply IFRS 15 to the contractual period in which the parties have present enforceable rights and obligations. *[IFRS 15.11]*. For the purpose of applying IFRS 15, a contract does not exist if each party has the unilateral enforceable right to terminate a wholly unperformed contract without compensating each other or other parties. The standard defines a wholly unperformed contract as one for which 'both of the following criteria are met: (a) the entity has not yet transferred any promised goods or services to the customer; and (b) the entity has not yet received, and is not yet entitled to receive, any consideration in exchange for promised goods or services.' *[IFRS 15.12]*.

The period in which enforceable rights and obligations exist may be affected by termination provisions in the contract. Significant judgement is required to determine the effect of termination provisions on the contract duration. Entities need to review the overall contractual arrangements, including any master service arrangements, wind-down provisions and business practices to identify terms or conditions that might affect the enforceable rights and obligations in their contracts.

Under the standard, this determination is critical because the contract duration to which the standard is applied may affect the number of performance obligations identified and the determination of the transaction price. It may also affect the amounts disclosed in some of the required disclosures. See 2.2.1.A below for further discussion on how termination provisions may affect the contract duration.

If each party has the unilateral right to terminate a 'wholly unperformed' contract (as defined in paragraph 12 of IFRS 15) without compensating the counterparty,

IFRS 15 states that, for purposes of the standard, a contract does not exist and its accounting and disclosure requirements would not apply. This is because the contracts would not affect an entity's financial position or performance until either party performs. Any arrangement in which the entity has not provided any of the contracted goods or services and has not received or is not entitled to receive any of the contracted consideration is considered to be a 'wholly unperformed' contract.

The requirements for 'wholly unperformed' contracts do not apply if the parties to the contract have to compensate the other party if they exercise their right to terminate the contract and that termination payment is considered substantive.

Under IFRS 15, entities are required to account for contracts with longer stated terms as month-to-month (or possibly a shorter duration) contracts if the parties can terminate the contract without penalty.

Entities need to consider all facts and circumstances to determine the contract duration. For example, entities may need to use significant judgement to determine whether a termination payment is substantive and the effect of a termination provision on contract duration.

2.2.1 Application questions on contract enforceability and termination clauses

2.2.1.A Evaluating termination clauses and termination payments in determining the contract duration

Entities need to carefully evaluate termination clauses and any related termination payments to determine how they affect contract duration (i.e. the period in which there are enforceable rights and obligations). TRG members generally agreed that enforceable rights and obligations exist throughout the term in which each party has the unilateral enforceable right to terminate the contract by compensating the other party. For example, if a contract includes a substantive termination payment, the duration of the contract would equal the period through which a termination penalty would be due. This could be the stated contractual term or a shorter duration if the termination penalty does not extend to the end of the contract. However, the TRG members observed that the determination of whether a termination penalty is substantive, and what constitutes enforceable rights and obligations under a contract, requires judgement and consideration of the facts and circumstances. The TRG agenda paper also noted that, if an entity concludes that the duration of the contract is less than the stated term because of a termination clause, any termination penalty needs to be included in the transaction price. If the termination penalty is variable, the requirements for variable consideration, including the constraint (see Chapter 29 at 2.2.3), apply.

The TRG members also agreed that if a contract with a stated contractual term can be terminated by either party at any time for no consideration, the contract duration ends when control of the goods or services that have already been provided transfers to the customer (e.g. a month-to-month service contract), regardless of the contract's stated contractual term. In this case, entities also need to consider whether a contract includes a notification or cancellation period (e.g. the contract can be terminated with 90 days' notice) that would cause the contract duration to extend beyond the date when control of the goods or services that have already been provided were transferred to the customer. If such a period exists, the contract duration would be shorter than the stated contractual term, but would extend beyond the date when control of the goods or services that have already been provided were transferred to the customer.[5] Consider the following examples that illustrate how termination provisions affect the duration of a contract.

Example 28.4: Duration of a contract with a termination penalty

Entity A enters into a four-year service contract with a customer. The customer is required to pay a non-refundable annual fee of $100,000, which is the stand-alone selling price for each year of service.

To determine the duration of the contract in each of the scenarios below, the entity considers these facts and whether the contract provides cancellation rights and termination penalties.

Scenario A: Assume no cancellation rights are provided to either party. In this case, the enforceable rights and obligations exist for the entire stated contractual term and the contract duration is four years.

Scenario B: Assume the contract provides the customer with a right to cancel the contract at the end of each year without cause, but with a termination penalty. The penalty decreases annually throughout the contract term at the end of each year. The following illustrates the payments under the contract:

	Year 1	Year 2	Year 3	Year 4
Annual fee	$100,000	$100,000	$100,000	$100,000
Termination penalty	$225,000	$150,000	$75,000	$–

If Entity A determines that the penalty is substantive in each period, enforceable rights and obligations exist for the stated contractual term of four years.

Scenario C: Assume the contract provides the customer with a right to cancel at the end of each year, with no termination penalty.

In this case, Entity A determines that the contract duration is one year, with options to renew for each of the following three years because the customer can choose whether to receive the service during those years. That is, Entity A determines that enforceable rights and obligations do not exist throughout the entire stated contractual term because there is no substantive termination penalty. The options to renew are not material rights because they are offered at the stand-alone selling price of $100,000.

Example 28.5: Duration of a contract without a termination penalty

Entity A enters into a three-year contract with a customer to provide maintenance services. Entity A begins providing the services immediately. Consideration is payable in equal monthly instalments and each party has the unilateral right to terminate the contract without compensating the other party if it provides 30 days' notice.

While the stated contractual term is three years, Entity A's rights and obligations are enforceable only for 30 days. Therefore, under IFRS 15, the contract is accounted for as a one-month contract with a renewal option for additional months of maintenance services. This is because the customer or Entity A could cancel the agreement with 30 days' notice without paying a substantive termination payment.

Entity A also needs to evaluate the accounting for the renewal option(s) to determine whether it is a material right (see 3.6 below).

2.2.1.B Evaluating the contract term when only the customer has the right to cancel the contract without cause

Enforceable rights and obligations exist throughout the term in which each party has the unilateral enforceable right to terminate the contract by compensating the other party. The TRG members did not view a customer-only right to terminate sufficient to warrant a different conclusion than one in which both parties have the right to terminate, as discussed in 2.2.1.A above.

The TRG members generally agreed that a substantive termination penalty payable by a customer to the entity is evidence of enforceable rights and obligations of both parties throughout the period covered by the termination penalty. For example, consider a four-year service contract in which the customer has the right to cancel without cause at the end of each year, but for which the customer would incur a termination penalty that decreases each year and is determined to be substantive. The TRG members generally agreed that the arrangement would be treated as a four-year contract (see Example 28.4, Scenario B at 2.2.1.A above).

The TRG members also discussed situations in which a contractual penalty would result in including optional goods or services in the accounting for the original contract (see 3.6.1.D below).

The TRG members observed that the determination of whether a termination penalty is substantive, and what constitutes enforceable rights and obligations under a contract, requires judgement and consideration of the facts and circumstances. In addition, it is possible that payments that effectively act as a termination penalty and create or negate enforceable rights and obligations may not be labelled as such in a contract. The TRG agenda paper included an illustration in which an entity sells equipment and consumables. The equipment is sold at a discount, but the customer is required to repay some or all of the discount if it does not purchase a minimum number of consumables. The TRG paper concludes that the penalty (i.e. forfeiting the upfront discount) is substantive and is evidence of enforceable rights and obligations up to the minimum quantity. This example is discussed further at 3.6.1.D below. See 2.2.1.D below for another example.

If enforceable rights and obligations do not exist throughout the entire term stated in the contract the TRG members generally agreed that customer cancellation rights would be treated as customer options. Examples include, when there are no (or non-substantive) contractual penalties that compensate the entity upon cancellation and when the customer has the unilateral right to terminate the contract for reasons other than cause or contingent events outside the customer's control. In the Basis for Conclusions, the Board noted that a cancellation option or termination right can be similar to a renewal option. *[IFRS 15.BC391]*. An entity would need to determine whether a cancellation option indicates that the customer has a material right that would need to be accounted for as a performance obligation (e.g. there is a discount for goods or services provided during the cancellable period that provides the customer with a material right) (see 3.6 below).[6]

2.2.1.C Evaluating the contract term when an entity has a past practice of not enforcing termination payments

A TRG agenda paper for the October 2014 TRG meeting noted that the evaluation of the termination payment in determining the duration of a contract depends on whether the law (which may vary by jurisdiction) considers past practice as limiting the parties' enforceable rights and obligations. An entity's past practice of allowing customers to terminate the contract early without enforcing collection of the termination payment only affects the contract duration in cases in which the parties' legally enforceable rights and obligations are limited because of the lack of enforcement by the entity. If that past practice does not change the parties' legally enforceable rights and obligations, the contract duration equals the period throughout which a substantive termination penalty would be due (which could be the stated contractual term or a shorter duration if the termination penalty did not extend to the end of the contract).[7]

2.2.1.D   Accounting for a partial termination of a contract

We believe an entity should account for the partial termination of a contract (e.g. a change in the contract term from three years to two years prior to the beginning of year two) as a contract modification (see 2.4 below) because it results in a change in the scope of the contract. IFRS 15 states that 'a contract modification exists when the parties to a contract approve a modification that either creates new or changes existing enforceable rights and obligations of the parties to the contract'. *[IFRS 15.18]*. A partial termination of a contract results in a change to the enforceable rights and obligations in the existing contract (see also further below 2.4.3.E for a contract modification that decreases the scope of a contract). This conclusion is consistent with TRG agenda paper no. 48, which states, 'a substantive termination penalty is evidence of enforceable rights and obligations throughout the contract term. The termination penalty is ignored until the contract is terminated at which point it is accounted for as a modification'.[8]

Consider the following example:

Example 28.6:   Partial termination of a contract

An entity enters into a contract with a customer to provide monthly maintenance services for three years at a fixed price of £500 per month (i.e. total consideration of £18,000). The contract includes a termination clause that allows the customer to cancel the third year of the contract by paying a termination penalty of £1,000 (which is considered substantive for the purpose of this example). The penalty would effectively result in an adjusted price per month for two years of £542 (i.e. total consideration of £13,000). At the end of the first year, the customer decides to cancel the third year of the contract and pays the £1,000 termination penalty specified in the contract.

In this example, the modification is not accounted for as a separate contract because it does not result in the addition of distinct goods or services (see 2.4.2 below). Since the remaining services are distinct, the entity applies the requirements in paragraph 21(a) of IFRS 15 and accounts for the modification prospectively. The remaining consideration of £7,000 (£6,000 per year under the original contract for the second year, plus the £1,000 payment upon modification) is recognised over the remaining revised contract period of one year. That is, the entity recognises the £1,000 termination penalty over the remaining performance period.

2.2.1.E   Accounting for consideration that was received from a customer, but not recognised as revenue, when the contract is cancelled

When a contract is cancelled (by either the customer or the entity) it is a contract modification that reduces the scope of the contract. As discussed at 2.2.1.D above and 2.4.3.E below such a modification would not be accounted for as a separate contract because it does not result in the addition of distinct goods or services. Rather, the accounting will depend on whether there are any remaining goods and services to be provided after the cancellation and, if so, whether they are distinct from the goods and services already provided.

If there are no remaining goods and services to be provided after the cancellation, the accounting depends on whether the consideration is refundable or non-refundable. To determine whether consideration is refundable or non-refundable, entities may need to consider termination penalties, legal requirements for refund, customary business practices of providing refunds or statements made to customers that create a constructive or legal obligation to provide a refund.

If the consideration received from the customer is refundable and there are no remaining goods and services to be provided after the cancellation, the entity has a refund liability. This might require the entity to reclassify any existing contract liability to refund liability.

In some cases, the entity might ask the customer to waive their right to a refund of the consideration in exchange for vouchers, for example, and/or discounts on future goods or services. The accounting for such offers (including the accounting for the liability) depends on the specific facts and circumstances and may require judgement.

If the consideration received from the customer is non-refundable and there are no remaining goods and services to be provided after the cancellation, we believe that the entity can recognise revenue for the consideration received when the contract is cancelled, and the related contract liability would also be derecognised. This accounting treatment is similar to the application guidance for breakage (e.g. for gift cards, see Chapter 30 at 11 and the recognition of revenue for arrangements that fail the IFRS 15 contract criteria in accordance with paragraph 15 of IFRS 15 (see 2.5 below). In both of those situations, IFRS 15 provides guidance that permits an entity to derecognise a liability and recognise revenue, provided the relevant criteria are met, when: the entity expects the customer will not exercise its contractual rights (for breakage); *[IFRS 15.B46]* or the contract is effectively completed or cancelled (for contracts that do not meet the contract criteria in paragraph 9 of IFRS 15). *[IFRS 15.15, BC48]*.

In some cases, an entity may be entitled to termination fees in the event of cancellation. The accounting for termination fees is discussed at 2.2.1.D above.

2.2.1.F   Services provided during a period after contract expiration

If an entity continues to provide services to a customer during a period when a contract does not exist because a previous contract has expired and the contract has not yet been renewed, we believe that the entity would need to recognise revenue for providing those services on a cumulative catch-up basis at the time the contract is renewed (i.e. when enforceable rights and obligations exist between the entity and its customer). As discussed at 2 above, determining whether an enforceable contract exists under the model may require judgement and an evaluation of the relevant legal framework.

This approach to record revenue on a cumulative catch-up basis reflects the performance obligations that are partially satisfied at the time enforceable rights and obligations exist and is consistent with the overall principle of the standard that requires revenue to be recognised when (or as) an entity transfers control of goods or services to a customer under an enforceable contract. This conclusion is also consistent with the discussion in Chapter 30 at 3.4.6 on the accounting for goods or services provided to a customer before the contract establishment date.

Consider the following example:

Example 28.7:   Services provided during a period after contract expiration

Entity A enters into a non-cancellable one-year contract with a customer on 1 January 20X1 to provide web-hosting services that are transferred to the customer over time. The total consideration of £1,200 is payable upfront and is non-refundable. After the expiration of the contract, at its discretion, Entity A continues to provide web-hosting services to the customer for a limited time to allow the customer to contemplate renewing the contract. If the customer renews the contract, the pricing would include the web-hosting services provided during the period between the original contract expiration and the contract renewal.

The customer agrees to renew the contract on 1 February 20X2. Entity A agrees to provide web-hosting services from 1 January 20X2 to 31 December 20X2 for total consideration of £1,200, which is payable on the renewal date. Entity A determines that enforceable rights and obligations exist on 1 February 20X2 and a contract modification, an entity shall continue to apply this Standard to the existing contract until the contract modification is approved.' *[IFRS 15.18]*.

The standard goes on to state 'a contract modification may exist even though the parties to the contract have a dispute about the scope or price (or both) of the modification or the parties have approved a change in the scope of the contract but have not yet determined the corresponding change in price. In determining whether the rights and obligations that are created or changed by a modification are enforceable, an entity shall consider all relevant facts and circumstances including the terms of the contract and other evidence.' *[IFRS 15.19]*. If the parties to a contract have approved a change in the scope of the contract but have not yet determined the corresponding change in price, an entity shall estimate the change to the transaction price arising from the modification in accordance with the requirements for estimating and constraining estimates of variable consideration. *[IFRS 15.19]*.

These requirements illustrate that the Board intended these requirements to apply more broadly than only to finalised modifications. That is, IFRS 15 indicates that an entity may have to account for a contract modification prior to the parties reaching final agreement on changes in scope or pricing (or both). Instead of focusing on the finalisation of a modification, IFRS 15 focuses on the enforceability of the changes to the rights and obligations in the contract. Once an entity determines the revised rights and obligations are enforceable, it accounts for the contract modification. Contract terminations (either partial or full) are also considered a form of contract modification under IFRS 15.

The standard provides the following example to illustrate the accounting for an unapproved modification. *[IFRS 15.IE42-IE43]*.

Example 28.8: Unapproved change in scope and price

An entity enters into a contract with a customer to construct a building on customer-owned land. The contract states that the customer will provide the entity with access to the land within 30 days of contract inception. However, the entity was not provided access until 120 days after contract inception because of storm damage to the site that occurred after contract inception. The contract specifically identifies any delay (including *force majeure*) in the entity's access to customer-owned land as an event that entitles the entity to compensation that is equal to actual costs incurred as a direct result of the delay. The entity is able to demonstrate that the specific direct costs were incurred as a result of the delay in accordance with the terms of the contract and prepares a claim. The customer initially disagreed with the entity's claim.

The entity assesses the legal basis of the claim and determines, on the basis of the underlying contractual terms, that it has enforceable rights. Consequently, it accounts for the claim as a contract modification in accordance with paragraphs 18-21 of IFRS 15. The modification does not result in any additional goods and services being provided to the customer. In addition, all of the remaining goods and services after the modification are not distinct and form part of a single performance obligation. Consequently, the entity accounts for the modification in accordance with paragraph 21(b) of IFRS 15 by updating the transaction price and the measure of progress towards complete satisfaction of the performance obligation. The entity considers the constraint on estimates of variable consideration in paragraphs 56-58 of IFRS 15 when estimating the transaction price.

Once an entity has determined that a contract has been modified, the entity determines the appropriate accounting treatment for the modification. Certain modifications are treated as separate stand-alone contracts (discussed at 2.4.1 below), while others are combined with the original contract (discussed at 2.4.2 below) and accounted for in that manner. In addition, an entity accounts for some modifications on a prospective basis and others on a cumulative catch-up basis. The Board developed different approaches to account for different types of modifications with an overall objective of faithfully depicting an entity's rights and obligations in each modified contract. [IFRS 15.BC76].

The following figure illustrates these requirements.

Figure 28.1: Contract modifications

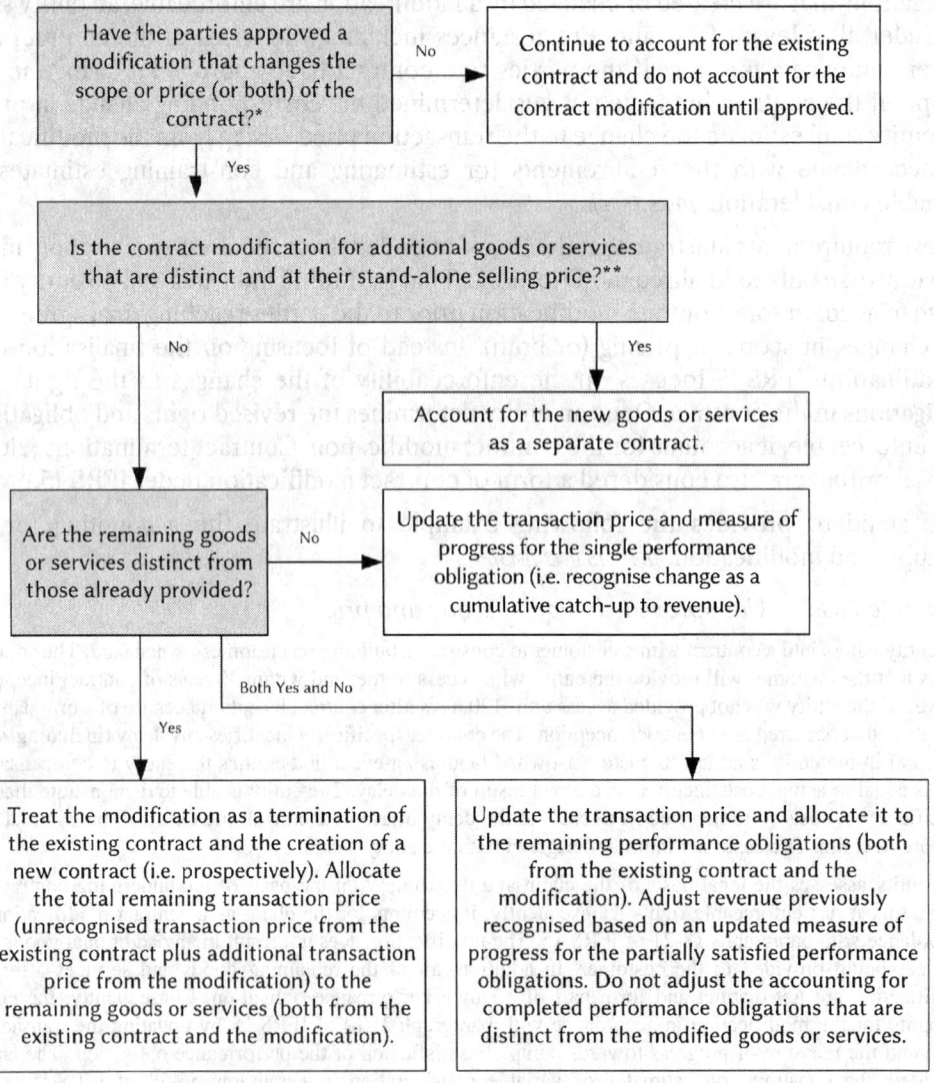

*   Under IFRS 15, a contract modification can be approved in writing, by oral agreement or implied by customary business practices. Paragraph 19 of IFRS 15 states that an entity may have to account for a contract modification prior to the parties reaching final agreement on changes in scope or pricing (or both), provided the rights and obligations that are created or changed by a modification are enforceable.

** In accordance with paragraph 20 of IFRS 15, an entity may make appropriate adjustments to the stand-alone selling price to reflect the circumstances of the contract and still meet the criteria to account for the modification as a separate contract.

When determining how to account for a contract modification, an entity must consider whether any additional goods or services are distinct, often giving careful consideration to whether those goods or services are distinct within the context of the modified contract (see 3.2.1 below for further discussion on evaluating whether goods or services are distinct). That is, although a contract modification may add a new good or service that would be distinct in a stand-alone transaction, that new good or service may not be distinct when considered in the context of the contract, as modified. For example, in a building renovation project, a customer may request a contract modification to add a new room. The construction firm may commonly sell the construction of an added room on a stand-alone basis, which would indicate that the service is capable of being distinct. However, when that service is added to an existing contract and the entity has already determined that the entire project is a single performance obligation, the added goods or services would normally be combined with the existing bundle of goods or services.

In contrast to the construction example (for which the addition of otherwise distinct goods or services are combined with the existing single performance obligation and accounted for in that manner), a contract modification that adds distinct goods or services to a single performance obligation that comprise a series of distinct goods or services (see 3.2.2 below) is accounted for either as a separate contract or as the termination of the old contract and the creation of a new contract (i.e. prospectively). In the Basis for Conclusions, the Board explained that it clarified the accounting for modifications that affect a single performance obligation that is made up of a series of distinct goods or services (e.g. repetitive service contracts) to address some stakeholders' concerns that an entity otherwise would have been required to account for these modifications on a cumulative catch-up basis. *[IFRS 15.BC79]*.

As illustrated in Example 28.12 at 2.4.2 below, a contract modification may include compensation to a customer for performance issues (e.g. poor service by the entity, defects present in transferred goods). An entity may need to account for the compensation to the customer as a change in the transaction price (see Chapter 29 at 3.5) separate from other modifications to the contract.

2.4.1 Contract modification represents a separate contract

Certain contract modifications are treated as separate, new contracts. *[IFRS 15.20]*. For these modifications, the accounting for the original contract is not affected by the modification and the revenue recognised to date on the original contract is not adjusted. Furthermore, any performance obligations remaining under the original contract continue to be accounted for under the original contract. The accounting for this type of modification reflects the fact that there is no economic difference between a separate contract for additional goods or services and a modified contract for those same items, provided the two criteria required for this type of modification are met.

The first criterion that must be met for a modification to be treated as a separate contract is that the additional promised goods or services in the modification must be distinct from the promised goods or services in the original contract. This assessment is done in accordance with IFRS 15's general requirements for determining whether promised goods or services are distinct (see 3.2.1 below). Only modifications that add distinct goods or services to the arrangement can be treated as separate contracts.

Arrangements that reduce the amount of promised goods or services or change the scope of the original promised goods or services cannot, by their very nature, be considered separate contracts. Instead, they are modifications of the original contract (see 2.4.2 below). *[IFRS 15.20(a)]*.

The second criterion is that the amount of consideration expected for the added promised goods or services must reflect the stand-alone selling prices of those promised goods or services at the contract modification date. However, when determining the stand-alone selling price entities have some flexibility to adjust the stand-alone selling price, depending on the facts and circumstances. For example, a vendor may give an existing customer a discount on additional goods because the vendor would not incur selling-related costs that it would typically incur for new customers. In this example, the entity (vendor) may determine that the additional transaction consideration meets the criterion, even though the discounted price is less than the stand-alone selling price of that good or service for a new customer. In another example, an entity may conclude that, with the additional purchases, the customer qualifies for a volume-based discount (see 3.6.1.E and 3.6.1.G below on volume discounts). *[IFRS 15.20(b)]*.

The following example illustrates considerations for determining whether the amount of consideration expected for the additional goods and services reflects the stand-alone selling price:

Example 28.9: Determining whether the amount of consideration reflects the stand-alone selling price of additional goods or services

Entity E agrees to construct a manufacturing facility on a customer's land for €10 million. During construction, the customer determines that a separate storage facility is needed at the location. The parties agree to modify the contract to include the construction of the storage facility, which is to be completed within three months of completing the manufacturing facility, for a total price of €11 million (i.e. when the contract is modified, an additional €1 million is added to the consideration Entity E will receive). Assume that Entity E determines that the construction of the separate storage facility is distinct (i.e. a performance obligation) and that it transfers control of each facility over time. Entity E must determine whether the €1 million represents the stand-alone selling price of the separate storage facility.

Scenario A – Contract modification is accounted for as a separate contract

Entity E determines that €1.1 million is the stand-alone selling price at the contract modification date for the construction of a similar facility. However, much of the equipment and labour force necessary to complete construction of the storage facility is already onsite and available for use by Entity E. Thus, Entity E concludes that the additional €1 million reflects the stand-alone selling price at contract modification, adjusted for the circumstances of the contract.

Scenario B – Contract modification is not accounted for as a separate contract

Entity E determines that €1.5 million is the stand-alone selling price at the contract modification date for the construction of a similar facility. While Entity E can attribute some of the discount to its ability to use equipment and labour that are already onsite, the price reduction was primarily driven by other factors (e.g. a desire to maintain the customer relationship). Therefore, the additional €1 million does not reflect the stand-alone selling price at contract modification.

In situations with highly variable pricing, determining whether the additional consideration in a modified contract reflects the stand-alone selling price for the additional goods or services may not be straightforward. Entities need to apply judgement when making this assessment. Evaluating whether the price in the modified contract is within a range of prices for which the goods or services are typically sold to similar customers may be an acceptable approach.

The following example illustrates a contract modification that represents a separate contract. *[IFRS 15.IE19-IE21].*

Example 28.10: Modification of a contract for goods

An entity promises to sell 120 products to a customer for $12,000 ($100 per product). The products are transferred to the customer over a six-month period. The entity transfers control of each product at a point in time. After the entity has transferred control of 60 products to the customer, the contract is modified to require the delivery of an additional 30 products (a total of 150 identical products) to the customer. The additional 30 products were not included in the initial contract.

Case A – Additional products for a price that reflects the stand-alone selling price

When the contract is modified, the price of the contract modification for the additional 30 products is an additional $2,850 or $95 per product. The pricing for the additional products reflects the stand-alone selling price of the products at the time of the contract modification and the additional products are distinct (in accordance with paragraph 27 of IFRS 15) from the original products.

In accordance with paragraph 20 of IFRS 15, the contract modification for the additional 30 products is, in effect, a new and separate contract for future products that does not affect the accounting for the existing contract. The entity recognises revenue of $100 per product for the 120 products in the original contract and $95 per product for the 30 products in the new contract.

2.4.2 Contract modification is not a separate contract

If the criteria discussed at 2.4.1 above are not met (i.e. distinct goods or services are not added or the distinct goods or services are not priced at their stand-alone selling price), the contract modifications are accounted for as changes to the original contract and not as separate contracts. This includes contract modifications that modify or remove previously agreed-upon goods or services or reduce the price of the contract. An entity accounts for the effects of these modifications differently, depending on which of the following three scenarios ((A)-(C) below) described in paragraph 21 of IFRS 15 most closely aligns with the facts and circumstances of the modification. *[IFRS 15.21].*

(A) *If the remaining goods or services after the contract modification are distinct from the goods or services transferred on, or before, the contract modification, the entity accounts for the modification as if it were a termination of the old contract and the creation of a new contract.*

The amount of consideration to be allocated to the remaining performance obligations (or to the remaining distinct goods or services in a single performance obligation identified in accordance with paragraph 22(b) of IFRS 15, see 3.2.2 below) is the sum of:

(i) the consideration promised by the customer (including amounts already received from the customer) that was included in the estimate of the transaction price and that had not been recognised as revenue; and

(ii) the consideration promised as part of the contract modification.

For these modifications, the revenue recognised to date on the original contract (i.e. the amount associated with the completed performance obligations) is not adjusted. Instead, the remaining portion of the original contract and the modification are accounted for, together, on a prospective basis by allocating the remaining consideration (i.e. the unrecognised transaction price from the existing contract plus the additional transaction price from the modification) to the remaining performance obligations, including those added in the modification.

Example 28.11 from the standard illustrates the accounting for a contract modification of a services contract that is determined to be a series of distinct goods or services (see 3.2.2 below) and meets the criteria in paragraph 21(a) of IFRS 15 to be accounted for as a termination of the existing contract and the creation of a new contract. As the performance obligation is a series, the services provided after the contract modification are distinct from those provided before the contract modification. *[IFRS 15.IE33-IE36]*.

Example 28.11: Modification of a services contract

An entity enters into a three-year contract to clean a customer's offices on a weekly basis. The customer promises to pay £100,000 per year. The stand-alone selling price of the services at contract inception is £100,000 per year. The entity recognises revenue of £100,000 per year during the first two years of providing services. At the end of the second year, the contract is modified and the fee for the third year is reduced to £80,000. In addition, the customer agrees to extend the contract for three additional years for consideration of £200,000 payable in three equal annual instalments of £66,667 at the beginning of years 4, 5 and 6. After the modification, the contract has four years remaining in exchange for total consideration of £280,000. The stand-alone selling price of the services at the beginning of the third year is £80,000 per year. The entity's stand-alone selling price at the beginning of the third year, multiplied by the remaining number of years to provide services, is deemed to be an appropriate estimate of the stand-alone selling price of the multi-year contract (i.e. the stand-alone selling price is 4 years × £80,000 per year = £320,000).

At contract inception, the entity assesses that each week of cleaning service is distinct in accordance with paragraph 27 of IFRS 15. Notwithstanding that each week of cleaning service is distinct, the entity accounts for the cleaning contract as a single performance obligation in accordance with paragraph 22(b) of IFRS 15. This is because the weekly cleaning services are a series of distinct services that are substantially the same and have the same pattern of transfer to the customer (the services transfer to the customer over time and use the same method to measure progress – that is, a time-based measure of progress).

At the date of the modification, the entity assesses the remaining services to be provided and concludes that they are distinct. However, the amount of remaining consideration to be paid (£280,000) does not reflect the stand-alone selling price of the services to be provided (£320,000).

Consequently, the entity accounts for the modification in accordance with paragraph 21(a) of IFRS 15 as a termination of the original contract and the creation of a new contract with consideration of £280,000 for four years of cleaning service. The entity recognises revenue of £70,000 per year (£280,000 ÷ 4 years) as the services are provided over the remaining four years.

The following example from the standard also illustrates a modification that is treated as a termination of an existing contract and the creation of a new contract. *[IFRS 15.IE19, IE22-IE24]*.

Example 28.12: Modification of a contract for goods

An entity promises to sell 120 products to a customer for $12,000 ($100 per product). The products are transferred to the customer over a six-month period. The entity transfers control of each product at a point in time. After the entity has transferred control of 60 products to the customer, the contract is modified to require the delivery of an additional 30 products (a total of 150 identical products) to the customer. The additional 30 products were not included in the initial contract.

Case B – Additional products for a price that does not reflect the stand-alone selling price

During the process of negotiating the purchase of an additional 30 products, the parties initially agree on a price of $80 per product. However, the customer discovers that the initial 60 products transferred to the customer contained minor defects that were unique to those delivered products. The entity promises a partial credit of $15 per product to compensate the customer for the poor quality of those products. The entity and the customer agree to incorporate the credit of $900 ($15 credit × 60 products) into the price that the entity charges for the additional 30 products. Consequently, the contract modification specifies that the price of the additional 30 products is $1,500 or $50 per product. That price comprises the agreed-upon price for the additional 30 products of $2,400, or $80 per product, less the credit of $900.

At the time of modification, the entity recognises the $900 as a reduction of the transaction price and, therefore, as a reduction of revenue for the initial 60 products transferred. In accounting for the sale of the additional 30 products, the entity determines that the negotiated price of $80 per product does not reflect the stand-alone selling price of the additional products. Consequently, the contract modification does not meet the conditions in paragraph 20 of IFRS 15 to be accounted for as a separate contract. Because the remaining products to be delivered are distinct from those already transferred, the entity applies the requirements in paragraph 21(a) of IFRS 15 and accounts for the modification as a termination of the original contract and the creation of a new contract.

Consequently, the amount recognised as revenue for each of the remaining products is a blended price of $93.33 {[($100 × 60 products not yet transferred under the original contract) + ($80 × 30 products to be transferred under the contract modification)] ÷ 90 remaining products}.

In Example 28.12 above, the entity attributed a portion of the discount provided on the additional products to the previously delivered products because they contained defects. This is because the compensation provided to the customer for the previously delivered products is a discount on those products, which results in variable consideration (i.e. a price concession) for them. The new discount on the previously delivered products was recognised as a reduction of the transaction price (and, therefore, revenue) on the date of the modification. Changes in the transaction price after contract inception are accounted for in accordance with paragraphs 88-90 of IFRS 15 (see Chapter 29 at 3.5).

In similar situations, it may not be clear from the change in the contract terms whether an entity has offered a price concession on previously transferred goods or services to compensate the customer for performance issues related to those items (that would be accounted for as a reduction of the transaction price) or has offered a discount on future goods or services (that would be included in the accounting for the contract modification). An entity needs to apply judgement when performance issues exist for previously transferred goods or services to determine whether to account for any compensation to the customer as a change in the transaction price for those previously transferred goods or services.

(B) *The remaining goods or services to be provided after the contract modification may not be distinct from those goods or services already provided and, therefore, form part of a single performance obligation that is partially satisfied at the date of modification.*

If this is the case, the entity accounts for the contract modification as if it were part of the original contract. The entity adjusts revenue previously recognised (either up or down) to reflect the effect that the contract modification has on the transaction price and updates the measure of progress (i.e. the revenue adjustment is made on a cumulative catch-up basis). This scenario is illustrated, as follows. *[IFRS 15.IE37-IE41].*

Example 28.13: Modification resulting in a cumulative catch-up adjustment to revenue

An entity, a construction company, enters into a contract to construct a commercial building for a customer on customer-owned land for promised consideration of £1 million and a bonus of £200,000 if the building is completed within 24 months. The entity accounts for the promised bundle of goods and services as a single performance obligation satisfied over time in accordance with paragraph 35(b) of IFRS 15 (discussed in Chapter 30 at 2.2) because the customer controls the building during construction. At the inception of the contract, the entity expects the following:

	£
Transaction price	1,000,000
Expected costs	700,000
Expected profit (30%)	300,000

At contract inception, the entity excludes the £200,000 bonus from the transaction price because it cannot conclude that it is highly probable that a significant reversal in the amount of cumulative revenue recognised will not occur. Completion of the building is highly susceptible to factors outside the entity's influence, including weather and regulatory approvals. In addition, the entity has limited experience with similar types of contracts.

The entity determines that the input measure, on the basis of costs incurred, provides an appropriate measure of progress towards complete satisfaction of the performance obligation. By the end of the first year, the entity has satisfied 60 per cent of its performance obligation on the basis of costs incurred to date (£420,000) relative to total expected costs (£700,000). The entity reassesses the variable consideration and concludes that the amount is still constrained in accordance with paragraphs 56-58 of IFRS 15. Consequently, the cumulative revenue and costs recognised for the first year are as follows:

	£
Revenue	600,000
Costs	420,000
Gross profit	180,000

In the first quarter of the second year, the parties to the contract agree to modify the contract by changing the floor plan of the building. As a result, the fixed consideration and expected costs increase by £150,000 and £120,000, respectively. Total potential consideration after the modification is £1,350,000 (£1,150,000 fixed consideration + £200,000 completion bonus). In addition, the allowable time for achieving the £200,000 bonus is extended by 6 months to 30 months from the original contract inception date. At the date of the modification, on the basis of its experience and the remaining work to be performed, which is primarily inside the building and not subject to weather conditions, the entity concludes that it is highly probable that including the bonus in the transaction price will not result in a significant reversal in the amount of cumulative revenue recognised in accordance with paragraph 56 of IFRS 15 and includes the £200,000 in the transaction price.

In assessing the contract modification, the entity evaluates paragraph 27(b) of IFRS 15 and concludes (on the basis of the factors in paragraph 29 of IFRS 15) that the remaining goods and services to be provided using the modified contract are not distinct from the goods and services transferred on or before the date of contract modification; that is, the contract remains a single performance obligation.

Consequently, the entity accounts for the contract modification as if it were part of the original contract (in accordance with paragraph 21(b) of IFRS 15). The entity updates its measure of progress and estimates that it has satisfied 51.2 per cent of its performance obligation (£420,000 actual costs incurred ÷ £820,000 total expected costs). The entity recognises additional revenue of £91,200 [(51.2 per cent complete × £1,350,000 modified transaction price) – £600,000 revenue recognised to date] at the date of the modification as a cumulative catch-up adjustment.

(C) Finally, a change in a contract may also be treated as a combination of the two: a modification of the existing contract and the creation of a new contract.

In this case, an entity would not adjust the accounting treatment for completed performance obligations that are distinct from the modified goods or services. However, the entity would adjust revenue previously recognised (either up or down) to reflect the effect of the contract modification on the estimated transaction price allocated to performance obligations that are not distinct from the modified portion of the contract and would update the measure of progress.

2.4.3 Application questions on contract modifications

See 2.2.1.D above for a discussion on how an entity would account for a partial termination of a contract (e.g. a change in the contract term from three years to two years prior to the beginning of year two). See Chapter 32 at 2.1.6.E for a discussion on how an entity would account for a contract asset that exists when a contract is modified if the modification is treated as the termination of an existing contract and the creation of a new contract.

2.4.3.A When to evaluate the contract under the contract modification requirements

An entity typically enters into a separate contract with a customer to provide additional goods or services. Stakeholders had questioned whether a new contract with an existing customer needs to be evaluated under the contract modification requirements.

A new contract with an existing customer needs to be evaluated under the contract modification requirements if the new contract results in a change in the scope or price of the original contract. Paragraph 18 of IFRS 15 states that 'a contract modification exists when the parties to a contract approve a modification that either creates new or changes existing enforceable rights and obligations of the parties to the contract'. *[IFRS 15.18]*. Therefore, an entity needs to evaluate whether a new contract with an existing customer represents a legally enforceable change in scope or price to an existing contract. A legally enforceable change in scope or price to an existing contract could also be accomplished by terminating the existing contract and entering into a new contract with the same customer. In those situations, entities also need to consider the contract modification requirements in IFRS 15.

In some cases, the determination of whether a new contract with an existing customer creates new or changes existing enforceable rights and obligations is straightforward because the new contract does not contemplate goods or services in the existing contract, including the pricing of those goods or services. Purchases of additional goods or services under a separate contract that do not modify the scope or price of an existing contract do not need to be evaluated under the contract modification requirements. Rather, they are accounted for as new (separate) contract.

In other cases, the determination of whether a new contract is a modification of an existing contract requires judgement. In such circumstances, we believe an entity should consider the specific facts and circumstances surrounding the new contract in order to determine whether it represents a contract modification. This could include considering factors such as those included in the contract combination requirements (see 2.3 above):

- whether the contracts were negotiated as a package with a single commercial objective (this might be the case in situations where the existing contract contemplates future modifications);
- whether the amount of consideration to be paid in one contract depends on the price or performance of the other contract; or
- whether the goods or services promised in the contracts (or some goods or services promised in each of the contracts) are a single performance obligation.

If the pricing in the new contract is dependent on the original contract, or if the terms of the new contract are in some other way negotiated based on the original contract, it is likely that the new contract needs to be evaluated under the contract modification requirements.

2.4.3.B Reassessing the contract criteria if a contract is modified

When an arrangement that has already been determined to meet the standard's contract criteria is modified, would an entity need to reassess whether that arrangement still meets the criteria to be considered a contract within the scope of the five-step model in the standard? There is no specific requirement in the standard to reconsider whether a contract meets the definition of a contract when it is modified. However, if a contract is modified, we believe that may indicate that 'a significant change in facts and circumstances' has occurred (see 2.1 above) and that the entity should reassess the criteria in paragraph 9 of IFRS 15 for the modified contract. Any reassessment is prospective in nature and would not change the conclusions associated with goods or services already transferred. That is, an entity would not reverse any receivables, revenue or contract assets already recognised under the contract because of the reassessment of the contract criteria in paragraph 9 of IFRS 15. However, due to the contract modification accounting (see 2.4.2 above), the entity may need to adjust contract assets or cumulative revenue recognised in the period of the contract modification.

See 3.6.1.J below for a discussion on how an entity would account for the exercise of a material right. See Chapter 31 at 2.1.5.A for a discussion on how entities would account for modifications to licences of intellectual property.

2.4.3.C Distinguishing between a contract modification and a change in the estimated transaction price due to variable consideration after contract inception

An entity may need to apply judgement to determine whether a change in the transaction price is the result of a contract modification (due to a change in the parties' enforceable rights and obligations after contract inception) or the result of new information obtained about variable consideration that existed (and was estimated) at contract inception. While a contract modification may result in a change in the transaction price, not all changes in the transaction price are due to contract modifications.

When a contract with a customer includes variable consideration (see Chapter 29 at 2.2), the entity is generally required to estimate, at contract inception and throughout the contract term, the amount of consideration to which it will be entitled in exchange for transferring promised goods or services. Changes to the transaction price that are related to a change in estimates of variable consideration (because they result in the resolution of variability that existed at contract inception), are allocated to the performance obligations in the contract on the same basis as at contract inception (see Chapter 29 at 3.5). *[IFRS 15.88-89]*. In contrast, changes in the transaction price that are related to a contract modification are accounted for in accordance with the contract modification requirements (as described above, in paragraphs 18-21 of IFRS 15).

2.4.3.D   Distinguishing between a contract modification and a marketing offer

An entity may provide incentives to customers to encourage demand. Customer incentives may include, free goods or services, options for additional goods and services at a discount (e.g. additional loyalty points, prospective coupons or discounts) or cash payments to customers. The accounting for these incentives will depend on the facts and circumstances of the offer. An offer to a current customer that creates new enforceable rights and obligations or changes the enforceable rights and obligations of the parties to an existing contract is accounted for as a contract modification. In some cases, an offer may not result in a contract modification and would be accounted for as a marketing offer (i.e. expense).

An offer that is the result of negotiations with a specific customer or group of customers may indicate the addition of new enforceable rights and obligations to an existing contract or changes to existing ones. However, the following circumstances may indicate that the entity has made a marketing offer:

- the same offer is available to both existing customers and counterparties that do not meet the definition of a customer;
- the offer is available to a broad group of (or all) current customers and is not the result of negotiations with individual customers; or
- the entity has the right to rescind the offer.

Entities need to carefully consider the terms and conditions of any customer incentive to determine whether the offer needs to be accounted for as a contract modification or a marketing offer.

In addition, as discussed at 2.4.3.A above we believe that the accounting principles for determining when contracts have to be combined under paragraph 17 of IFRS 15 be helpful when determining whether an offer of free goods or services to an existing customer is a contract modification.

For any payments to customers, entities will need to consider the requirements for consideration paid or payable to a customer (see Chapter 29 at 2.7). Such payments would be accounted for as a reduction of the transaction price (and, therefore, revenue) unless the payment to the customer is in exchange for a distinct good or service that the customer transfers to the entity.

2.4.3.E   Contract modification that decreases the scope of the contract

A modification that decreases the scope of a contract is not accounted for as a separate contract because it does not result in the addition of distinct goods or services (see 2.4.2 above). The accounting will depend on whether the remaining goods and services to be provided after the contract modification are distinct from the goods and services already provided. If the remaining goods and services are distinct, the contract modification is accounted for as a termination of the old contract and the creation of a new contract (i.e. prospectively). If the remaining goods and services are not distinct, the contract modification is accounted for as if it were part of the original contract (i.e. cumulative catch-up). See above 2.2.1.D regarding a partial termination of a contract.

Furthermore, to modify a contract, a customer may agree to pay a fee. We believe that such a fee is additional consideration that needs to be included in the modified transaction price and allocated to the remaining goods and services to be provided to the customer.

Consider the following example:

Example 28.14: Contract modification that decreases the scope of the promised goods or services in a contract

Entity X enters into a non-cancellable contract with a customer to provide information technology (IT) outsourcing services continuously for a three-year period. Entity X determines that the arrangement contains a single performance obligation comprising a series of distinct services that is transferred to the customer over time. Entity X bills the customer a fixed price of $500 per month (i.e. the total consideration is $18,000).

At the end of the second year, Entity X and the customer modify the contract to remove certain discrete services from the overall outsourcing service. As part of the modification, the customer agrees to pay a contract modification fee of $500 and reduce the monthly payments to $400 per month.

The services provided after the contract modification are distinct from those provided before the contract modification. This is because the performance obligation is a series of distinct services. Accordingly, Entity X applies the requirements in paragraph 21(a) of IFRS 15 and accounts for the modification prospectively. The remaining consideration of $5,300 ($4,800 for the services to be provided in the third year, plus the $500 payment upon modification) is recognised over the remaining contract period of one year. That is, Entity X recognises the $500 contract modification fee over the remaining performance period.

2.4.3.F   Accounting for a 'blend-and-extend' contract modification

A 'blend-and-extend' contract modification typically is one in which an entity, in exchange for a customer extending the term of the contract (and, therefore, purchasing additional units of a good or service), agrees to decrease the price per unit for all units to be provided (i.e. the new units, as well as the remaining units on the existing contract), resulting in a new blended price per unit. These types of contracts often occur in the power and utilities industry when market prices for the good or service decline after contract inception.

These arrangements are subject to the contract modification requirements in IFRS 15. Since these arrangements typically include the addition of distinct goods or services, the next step is for entities to evaluate whether the additional distinct goods or services are added at their stand-alone selling price in order to determine the accounting for the contract modification (i.e. as a separate contract or as a termination of the existing contract and the creation of a new contract).

When making this evaluation, stakeholders have questioned whether an entity should compare the blended contractual cash selling price or the overall contract price increase to the stand-alone selling price of the additional promised goods or services. We believe that entities should establish an approach based on the facts and circumstances of their modifications and apply that approach consistently to similar fact patterns.

Consider the following example:

Example 28.15: Blend-and-extend contract modification

Entity N enters into a four-year non-cancellable contract with Customer A to provide 100,000 widgets per year at a fixed price of ¥100 per widget. Each widget is a distinct good transferred at a point in time.

At the end of the second year, Entity N and Customer A modify the contract to extend the term of the contract by another two years (i.e. Entity N will continue to provide 100,00 widgets in years 5 and 6). The stand-alone selling price of the widget has declined and is now ¥80 per widget. As part of the modification, Entity N agrees to reduce the price to a blended rate of ¥90 per widget (¥100 in years 3 and 4 and ¥80 in years 5 and 6) in exchange for Customer A extending the contract term.

Entity N determines that each widget provided after the modification date is distinct from the widgets provided before the modification date.

Approach A – Compare the overall contract price increase to the stand-alone selling price of the additional promised goods or services

Since the price of the contract increases by an amount of consideration that reflects the stand-alone selling prices of the additional widgets (i.e. ¥80 per widget in years 5 and 6), Entity N determines that the contract modification is accounted for as a separate contract in accordance with paragraph 20 of IFRS 15. Entity N will continue to recognise revenue of ¥100 per widget for the remaining period in the initial contract (i.e. years 3 and 4) and recognise revenue of ¥80 per widget in years 5 and 6.

Approach B – Compare the blended contractual cash selling price to the stand-alone selling price of the additional promised goods or services

Since the blended price of ¥90 per widget does not reflect the stand-alone selling price of widgets at the modification date (i.e. ¥80 per widget), Entity N applies the requirements in paragraph 21(a) of IFRS 15 and accounts for the modification as if it were a termination of the original contract and the creation of a new contract. Total consideration of ¥36,000,000 (¥20,000,000 for the widgets to be provided the years 3 and 4, plus ¥16,000,000 for the widgets to be provided in years 5 and 6) is allocated to each of the remaining widgets to be provided (400,000 widgets). Entity N will recognise revenue for each widget at a blended rate of ¥90 per widget (¥36,000,000 ÷ 400,000 widgets).

The accounting will be different in contract modifications where an entity determines that the remaining goods or services to be provided after the modification date are not distinct from those goods or services provided before the modification date.

There is no presumption that such contract modifications contain a financing component that would be required to be accounted for separately. That is, the mere act of blending the rate in connection with a contract extension in which the customer pays more cash consideration for the same amount of goods or services at the beginning of the contract than the end of the contract does not automatically create a financing. However, each contract's facts and circumstances would need to be evaluated to determine whether a significant financing component exists (see Chapter 29 at 2.5 for further discussion on significant financing components).

2.5 Arrangements that do not meet the definition of a contract under the standard

If an arrangement does not meet the criteria to be considered a contract under the standard, the standard specifies how to account for it. The standard states that when a contract with a customer does not meet the criteria in paragraph 9 of IFRS 15 (i.e. the criteria discussed at 2.1 above) and an entity receives consideration from the customer, the entity shall recognise the consideration received as revenue only when either of the following events has occurred:

(a) the entity has no remaining obligations to transfer goods or services to the customer and all, or substantially all, of the consideration promised by the customer has been received by the entity and is non-refundable; or

(b) the contract has been terminated and the consideration received from the customer is non-refundable. *[IFRS 15.15]*.

The standard goes on to specify that an entity shall recognise the consideration received from a customer as a liability until one of the events described above occurs or until the contract meets the criteria to be accounted for within the revenue model. *[IFRS 15.16]*. Figure 28.2 illustrates this requirement:

Figure 28.2: Arrangements that do not meet the definition of a contract under the standard

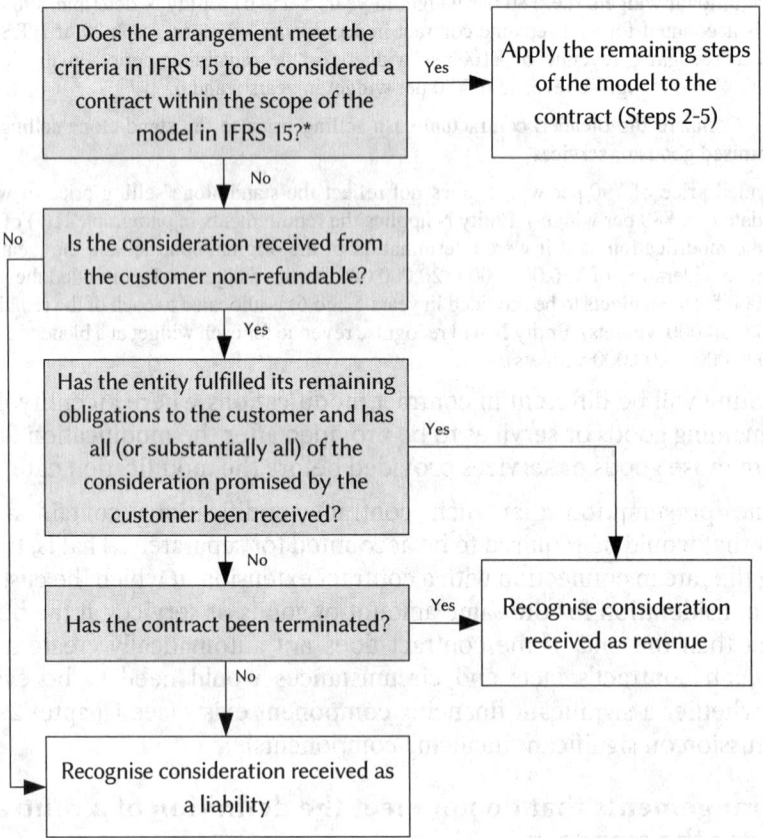

* Entities need to continue to assess the criteria throughout the term of the arrangement to determine whether they are subsequently met.

Entities are required to continue to assess the criteria in paragraph 9 of IFRS 15 throughout the term of the arrangement to determine whether they are subsequently met. Once the criteria are met, the model in the standard applies, rather than the requirements discussed below. *[IFRS 15.14]*. If an entity determines that the criteria in paragraph 9 of IFRS 15 are subsequently met, revenue is recognised on a cumulative catch-up basis as at the date when a contract exists within the scope of the model (i.e. at the 'contract establishment date', reflecting the performance obligations that are partially, or fully, satisfied at that date. This accounting is consistent with the discussion in TRG agenda paper no. 33, which states that the cumulative catch-up method 'best satisfies the core principle' in paragraph 2 of IFRS 15.[9] See Chapter 30 at 3.4.6 for further discussion.

If an arrangement does not meet the criteria in paragraph 9 of IFRS 15 (and until the criteria are met), an entity only recognises non-refundable consideration received as revenue when one of the events outlined above has occurred (i.e. full performance and all (or substantially all) consideration received or the contract has been terminated) or the arrangement subsequently meets the criteria in paragraph 9 of IFRS 15.

Until one of these events happens, any consideration received from the customer is initially accounted for as a liability (not revenue) and the liability is measured at the amount of consideration received from the customer.

In the Basis for Conclusions, the Board indicated that it intended this accounting to be 'similar to the "deposit method" that was previously included in US GAAP and applied when there was no consummation of a sale.' *[IFRS 15.BC48]*.

As noted in the Basis for Conclusions, the Board decided to include the requirements in paragraphs 14-16 of IFRS 15 (discussed above) to prevent entities from seeking alternative guidance or improperly analogising to the five-step revenue recognition model in IFRS 15 in circumstances in which an executed contract does not meet the criteria in paragraph 9 of IFRS 15. *[IFRS 15.BC47]*.

Under the FASB's standard, when the arrangement does not meet the criteria to be accounted for as a revenue contract under the standard, an entity can also recognise revenue (at the amount of the non-refundable consideration received) when the entity has transferred control of the goods or services and has stopped transferring (and has no obligation to transfer) additional goods or services.

IFRS 15 does not include a similar requirement. However, the IASB states in the Basis for Conclusions on IFRS 15 that contracts often specify that an entity has a right to terminate the contract in the event of non-payment. Furthermore, such clauses would not generally affect the entity's legal rights to recover any amounts due. Therefore, the IASB concluded that the requirements in IFRS 15 would allow an entity to conclude that a contract is terminated when it stops providing goods or services to the customer. *[IFRS 15.BC46H]*.

2.5.1 Application questions on arrangements that do not meet the definition of a contract under the standard

2.5.1.A Determining when a contract is terminated for the purpose of applying paragraph 15(b) of IFRS 15

Determining whether a contract is terminated may require significant judgement. In the Basis for Conclusions on IFRS 15, 'the IASB noted that contracts often specify that an entity has the right to terminate the contract in the event of non-payment by the customer and that this would not generally affect the entity's rights to recover any amounts owed by the customer. The IASB also noted that an entity's decision to stop pursuing collection would not typically affect the entity's rights and the customer's obligations under the contract with respect to the consideration owed by the customer. On this basis, ... the existing requirements in IFRS 15 are sufficient for an entity to conclude ... that a contract is terminated when it stops providing goods or services to the customer.' *[IFRS 15.BC46H].*

3 IDENTIFY THE PERFORMANCE OBLIGATIONS IN THE CONTRACT

To apply the standard, an entity must identify the promised goods or services within the contract and determine which of those goods or services are separate performance obligations. As noted in the Basis for Conclusions, the Board developed the notion of a 'performance obligation' to assist entities with appropriately identifying the unit of account for the purposes of applying the standard. *[IFRS 15.BC85].* Because the standard requires entities to allocate the transaction price to performance obligations, identifying the correct unit of account is fundamental to recognising revenue on a basis that faithfully depicts the entity's performance in transferring the promised goods or services to the customer.

With respect to identifying the performance obligations in a contract, the standard states that, at contract inception, an entity is required to assess the goods or services promised in a contract to identify performance obligations. A performance obligation is either: *[IFRS 15.22]*

(a) a good or service (or a bundle of goods or services) that is distinct; or

(b) a series of distinct goods or services that are substantially the same and that have the same pattern of transfer to the customer.

The standard goes on to clarify that a series of distinct goods or services has the same pattern of transfer to the customer if both of the following criteria are met: *[IFRS 15.23]*

- each distinct good or service in the series that the entity promises to transfer to the customer would meet the criteria to be a performance obligation satisfied over time (see Chapter 30 at 2); and
- the same method would be used to measure the entity's progress towards complete satisfaction of the performance obligation to transfer each distinct good or service in the series to the customer.

3.1 Identifying the promised goods or services in the contract

As a first step in identifying the performance obligation(s) in the contract, the standard requires an entity to identify, at contract inception, the promised goods or services in the contract. The standard provides guidance on the types of items that may be goods or services promised in the contract.

'A contract with a customer generally explicitly states the goods or services that an entity promises to transfer to a customer. However, the performance obligations identified in a contract with a customer may not be limited to the goods or services that are explicitly stated in that contract. This is because a contract with a customer may also include promises that are implied by an entity's customary business practices, published policies or specific statements if, at the time of entering into the contract, those promises create a valid expectation of the customer that the entity will transfer a good or service to the customer.' *[IFRS 15.24]*.

'Performance obligations do not include activities that an entity must undertake to fulfil a contract unless those activities transfer a good or service to a customer. For example, a services provider may need to perform various administrative tasks to set up a contract. The performance of those tasks does not transfer a service to the customer as the tasks are performed. Therefore, those setup activities are not a performance obligation.' *[IFRS 15.25]*.

Identifying which promised goods or services are distinct is very important. The standard includes the following examples of promised goods or services: *[IFRS 15.26]*

- sale of goods produced by an entity (e.g. inventory of a manufacturer);
- resale of goods purchased by an entity (e.g. merchandise of a retailer);
- resale of rights to goods or services purchased by an entity (e.g. a ticket resold by an entity acting as a principal – see 3.4 below);
- performing a contractually agreed-upon task (or tasks) for a customer;
- providing a service of standing ready to provide goods or services (e.g. unspecified updates to software that are provided on a when-and-if-available basis – see 3.1.1.B below) or of making goods or services available for a customer to use as and when the customer decides;
- providing a service of arranging for another party to transfer goods or services to a customer (e.g. acting as an agent of another party – see 3.4 below);
- granting rights to goods or services to be provided in the future that a customer can resell or provide to its customer (e.g. an entity selling a product to a retailer promises to transfer an additional good or service to an individual who purchases the product from the retailer);
- constructing, manufacturing or developing an asset on behalf of a customer;
- granting licences (see Chapter 31 at 2); and
- granting options to purchase additional goods or services when those options provide a customer with a material right (see 3.6 below).

In order for an entity to identify the promised goods or services in a contract, paragraph 24 of IFRS 15 indicates that an entity considers whether there is a valid expectation on the part of the customer that the entity will provide a good or service. *[IFRS 15.24]*. If the customer has a valid expectation that it will receive certain goods or services, it is likely that the customer would view those promises as part of the negotiated exchange. This expectation is most commonly created from an entity's explicit promises in a contract to transfer a good(s) or service(s) to the customer.

However, in other cases, promises to provide goods or services might be implied by the entity's customary business practices or standard industry norms (i.e. outside of the written contract). As discussed at 2 above, the Board clarified that, while the contract must be legally enforceable to be within the scope of the revenue model, not all of the promises (explicit or implicit) have to be legally enforceable to be considered when determining the entity's performance obligations. *[IFRS 15.BC32, BC87]*. That is, a performance obligation can be based on a customer's valid expectations (e.g. due to the entity's business practice of providing an additional good or service that is not specified in the contract).

In addition, some items commonly considered to be marketing incentives have to be evaluated under IFRS 15 to determine whether they represent promised goods or services in the contract. Such items may include 'free' handsets provided by telecommunication entities, 'free' maintenance provided by automotive manufacturers and customer loyalty points awarded by supermarkets, airlines, and hotels. *[IFRS 15.BC88]*. Although an entity may not consider those goods or services to be the 'main' items that the customer contracts to receive, the Board concluded that they are goods or services for which the customer pays and to which the entity would allocate consideration for the purpose of recognising revenue. *[IFRS 15.BC89]*.

Paragraph 25 of IFRS 15 states that promised goods or services do *not* include activities that an entity must undertake to fulfil a contract unless those activities transfer control of a good or service to a customer. *[IFRS 15.25]*. For example, internal administrative activities that an entity must perform to satisfy its obligation to deliver the promised goods or services, but do not transfer control of a good or service to a customer, would not be promised goods or services. The IFRS Interpretations Committee reiterated this point during its January 2019 meeting (see below for further discussion).

An entity may have to apply judgement when determining whether an activity it will perform is a promised good or service that will be transferred to a customer. The following questions may be relevant for an entity to consider when making this judgement:

- Is the activity identified as a good or service to be provided in the contractual arrangement with the customer? Activities that are not specifically identified could relate to an internal process of the entity, but they could also relate to implicit promises to the customer.
- Does the activity relate to the entity establishing processes and procedures or training its employees, so that it can render the contracted goods or services to the customer (e.g. set-up activities)?
- Is the activity administrative in nature (e.g. tasks performed to determine whether to accept or reject a customer, establishing the customer's account, invoicing the customer)?
- Is the customer aware of when the activity will be performed?

Paragraph 26 of IFRS 15 provides examples of promised goods or services that may be included in a contract with a customer. Several of them were considered deliverables under legacy IFRS, including a good produced by an entity or a contractually agreed-upon task (or service) performed for a customer. However, the IASB also included other examples that may not have been considered deliverables in the past. For example, paragraph 26(e) of IFRS 15 describes a stand-ready obligation as a promised service that consists of standing ready to provide goods or services or making goods or services available for a customer to use as and when it decides to use it. *[IFRS 15.26(e)]*. That is, a stand-ready obligation is the promise that the customer has access to a good or service, rather than a promise to transfer the underlying good or service itself. Stand-ready obligations are common in the software industry (e.g. unspecified updates to software on a when-and-if-available basis) and may be present in other industries. See 3.1.1.B and 3.1.1.C below for further discussion on stand-ready obligations.

Paragraph 26(g) of IFRS 15 notes that a promise to a customer may include granting rights to goods or services to be provided in the future that the customer can resell or provide to its own customers. *[IFRS 15.26(g)]*. Such a right may represent promises to the customer if it existed at the time that the parties agreed to the contract. As noted in the Basis for Conclusions, the Board thought it was important to clarify that a performance obligation may exist for a promise to provide a good or service in the future (e.g. when an entity makes a promise to provide goods or services to its customer's customer). *[IFRS 15.BC92]*. These types of promises exist in distribution networks in various industries and are common in the automotive industry.

After identifying the promised goods or services in the contract, an entity then determines which of these promised goods or services (or bundle of goods or services) represent separate performance obligations. The standard includes the following example to illustrate how an entity would identify the promised goods or services in a contract (including both explicit and implicit promises). *[IFRS 15.IE59-IE65A]*. The example also evaluates whether the identified promises are performance obligations, which we discuss at 3.2 below.

Example 28.16: Explicit and implicit promises in a contract

An entity, a manufacturer, sells a product to a distributor (i.e. its customer) who will then resell it to an end customer.

Case A – Explicit promise of service

In the contract with the distributor, the entity promises to provide maintenance services for no additional consideration (i.e. 'free') to any party (i.e. the end customer) that purchases the product from the distributor. The entity outsources the performance of the maintenance services to the distributor and pays the distributor an agreed-upon amount for providing those services on the entity's behalf. If the end customer does not use the maintenance services, the entity is not obliged to pay the distributor.

The contract with the customer includes two promised goods or services – (a) the product and (b) the maintenance services. The promise of maintenance services is a promise to transfer goods or services in the future and is part of the negotiated exchange between the entity and the distributor. The entity assesses whether each good or service is distinct in accordance with paragraph 27 of IFRS 15. The entity determines that both the product and the maintenance services meet the criterion in paragraph 27(a) of IFRS 15. The entity regularly sells the product on a stand-alone basis, which indicates that the customer can benefit from the product on its own. The customer can benefit from the maintenance services together with a resource the customer already has obtained from the entity (i.e. the product).

The entity further determines that its promises to transfer the product and to provide the maintenance services are separately identifiable (in accordance with paragraph 27(b) of IFRS 15) on the basis of the principle and the factors in paragraph 29 of IFRS 15. The product and the maintenance services are not inputs to a combined item in the contract. The entity is not providing a significant integration service because the presence of the product and the services together in this contract do not result in any additional or combined functionality. In addition, neither the product nor the services modify or customise the other. Lastly, the product and the maintenance services are not highly interdependent or highly interrelated because the entity would be able to fulfil each of the promises in the contract independently of its efforts to fulfil the other (i.e. the entity would be able to transfer the product even if the customer declined maintenance services and would be able to provide maintenance services in relation to products sold previously through other distributors). The entity also observes, in applying the principle in paragraph 29 of IFRS 15, that the entity's promise to provide maintenance is not necessary for the product to continue to provide significant benefit to the customer. Consequently, the entity allocates a portion of the transaction price to each of the two performance obligations (i.e. the product and the maintenance services) in the contract.

Case B – Implicit promise of service

The entity has historically provided maintenance services for no additional consideration (i.e. 'free') to end customers that purchase the entity's product from the distributor. The entity does not explicitly promise maintenance services during negotiations with the distributor and the final contract between the entity and the distributor does not specify terms or conditions for those services.

However, on the basis of its customary business practice, the entity determines at contract inception that it has made an implicit promise to provide maintenance services as part of the negotiated exchange with the distributor. That is, the entity's past practices of providing these services create valid expectations of the entity's customers (i.e. the distributor and end customers) in accordance with paragraph 24 of IFRS 15. Consequently, the entity assesses whether the promise of maintenance services is a performance obligation. For the same reasons as in Case A, the entity determines that the product and maintenance services are separate performance obligations.

Case C – Services are not a promised service

In the contract with the distributor, the entity does not promise to provide any maintenance services. In addition, the entity typically does not provide maintenance services and, therefore, the entity's customary business practices, published policies and specific statements at the time of entering into the contract have not created an implicit promise to provide goods or services to its customers. The entity transfers control of the product to the distributor and, therefore, the contract is completed. However, before the sale to the end customer, the entity makes an offer to provide maintenance services to any party that purchases the product from the distributor for no additional promised consideration.

The promise of maintenance is not included in the contract between the entity and the distributor at contract inception. That is, in accordance with paragraph 24 of IFRS 15, the entity does not explicitly or implicitly promise to provide maintenance services to the distributor or the end customers. Consequently, the entity does not identify the promise to provide maintenance services as a performance obligation. Instead, the obligation to provide maintenance services is accounted for in accordance with IAS 37 – *Provisions, Contingent Liabilities and Contingent Assets*.

Although the maintenance services are not a promised service in the current contract, in future contracts with customers the entity would assess whether it has created a business practice resulting in an implied promise to provide maintenance services.

In 2018, the IFRS Interpretations Committee received a request regarding the recognition of revenue by a stock exchange that provides listing services to customers. The request asked whether the stock exchange is providing an admission service that is distinct from an ongoing listing service. At its January 2019 meeting, the IFRS Interpretations Committee concluded that the principles and requirements in IFRS 15 provide sufficient guidance for an entity to assess the promised goods and services in a contract with a customer. Consequently, the IFRS Interpretations Committee decided not to add this matter to its agenda. *[IFRS 15.BC87]*.[10]

In considering this request, the IFRS Interpretations Committee noted that the main question relates to the assessment of the promised goods or services in the contract, rather than the assessment of whether the admission and the listing service are 'distinct' based on paragraphs 27-30 of IFRS 15. In their agenda decision, the IFRS Interpretations Committee highlighted that:

- before identifying its performance obligations, an entity needs to identify the goods and services promised in the contract; *[IFRS 15.24]*
- performing various tasks (e.g. set-up activities) that do not transfer a good or service to a customer is not a performance obligation – a performance obligation does not include activities that an entity must undertake to fulfil a contract, unless those activities transfer a good or service to a customer; *[IFRS 15.25]* and
- if a non-refundable upfront fee relates to an activity that is undertaken at or near contract inception to fulfil the contract, but does not result in transfer of a promised good or service to a customer (i.e. the activities only represent tasks to set up a contract), the fee is an advance payment for future goods or services. *[IFRS 15.B49]*.[11]

The IFRS Interpretations Committee discussed what the promised goods and services are in the contract using the following example.[12]

Example 28.17: **Identification of promised good or service in a contract by a stock exchange that provides listing service to a customer**

A stock exchange entity provides its customers with access to the capital markets by admitting them for listing in the stock exchange. The entity charges its customers a non-refundable upfront admission fee and an ongoing listing fee. The non-refundable upfront fee relates to various activities that are undertaken by the entity at or near contract inception to enable admission to the exchange, including:

- Performing due diligence for new applications.
- Reviewing the customer's listing application forms, including determining whether the application should be accepted.
- Issuing tickers and reference numbers for the new security.
- Processing of the listing on, and admission to, the exchange.
- Publishing the security on the order book.
- Issuing the dealing notice on the applicable admission date.

Once the customer has been admitted, the entity provides ongoing market access and maintains the listing. The listing service transferred to the customer is the same on initial listing and on all subsequent days for which the customer remains listed.

As part of identifying the goods and services promised to the customer in the contract, the stock exchange considers whether the above activities undertaken at or near contract inception transfer a service to the customer as the activities are performed. This assessment depends on the facts and circumstances of the contract.

In this fact pattern, the IFRS Interpretations Committee concluded that, while the activities undertaken at or near contract inception are required to fulfil the contract with the customer (which promises to provide the customer with the service of being listed on the exchange), it is likely that the stock exchange would conclude that the activities do not transfer separate services to the customer as they are performed. Accordingly, they are not promised goods or services to be identified under Step 2 of the model.

Entities may need to use judgement to identify promised goods or services in a contract. For example, some 'free' goods or services that may seem like marketing incentives have to be evaluated under the standard to determine whether they represent promised goods or services in a contract. In addition, the standard makes it clear that certain activities are not promised goods or services, such as activities that an entity must perform to satisfy its obligation to deliver the promised goods or services (e.g. internal administrative activities).

The Board noted in the Basis for Conclusions that it intentionally 'decided not to exempt an entity from accounting for performance obligations that the entity might regard as being perfunctory or inconsequential. Instead, an entity should assess whether those performance obligations are immaterial to its financial statements'. [IFRS 15.BC90].

In January 2015, the TRG members noted that entities may not disregard items that they deem to be perfunctory or inconsequential and need to consider whether 'free' goods or services represent promises to a customer. For example, telecommunications entities may have to allocate consideration to the 'free' handsets that they provide. Likewise, automobile manufacturers may have to allocate consideration to 'free' maintenance that may have been considered a marketing incentive in the past. However, entities would consider materiality in determining whether items are promised goods or services.[13]

The FASB's standard allows entities to disregard promises that are deemed to be immaterial in the context of a contract. That is, ASC 606 permits entities to disregard items that are immaterial at the contract level and does not require that the items be aggregated and assessed for materiality at the entity level. However, ASC 606 also emphasises that entities still need to evaluate whether customer options for additional goods or services are material rights to be accounted for in accordance with the related requirements (see 3.6 below).

IFRS 15 does not include explicit language to indicate an entity can disregard promised goods or services that are immaterial in the context of the contract. However, in the Basis for Conclusions, the IASB noted that it did not intend for entities to identify every possible promised good or services in a contract and that entities should consider materiality and the overall objective of IFRS 15 when assessing promised goods or services and identifying performance obligations. [IFRS 15.BC116D].

The FASB's standard also allows entities to elect to account for shipping and handling activities performed after the control of a good has been transferred to the customer as a fulfilment cost (i.e. an expense). Without such an accounting policy choice, a US GAAP entity that has shipping arrangements after the customer has obtained control may determine that the act of shipping is a performance obligation under the standard. If that were the case, the entity would be required to allocate a portion of the transaction price to the shipping service and recognise it when (or as) the shipping occurs.

The IASB has not permitted a similar policy choice in IFRS 15. In the Basis for Conclusions, the IASB noted that paragraph 22 of IFRS 15 requires an entity to assess the goods or services promised in a contract with a customer in order to identify performance obligations. Such a policy choice would override that requirement. Furthermore, a policy choice is applicable to all entities and it is possible that entities with significant shipping operations may make different policy choices. Therefore, it could also reduce comparability between entities, including those within the same industry. [IFRS 15.BC116U]. Since the FASB's standard includes a policy choice that IFRS 15 does not, it is possible that diversity between IFRS and US GAAP entities may arise in practice.

Another difference is that FASB uses different language in relation to implied contractual terms and whether those implied terms represent a promised good or service to a customer. IFRS 15 states that promised goods or services are not limited to explicit promises in a contract, but could be created by a 'valid expectation of the customer'.

ASC 606 refers to a 'reasonable expectation of the customer'. The FASB used this language in order to avoid confusion with the term 'valid expectation' because ASC 606 states that promises to provide goods or services do not need to be legally enforceable (although the overall arrangement needs to be enforceable). The use of the term 'valid' in IFRS 15 is consistent with the requirements for constructive obligations in IAS 37. While the terms used in IFRS 15 and ASC 606 are different, we do not expect this to result in a difference in practice.

3.1.1 Application questions on identifying promised goods or services

3.1.1.A Assessing whether pre-production activities are a promised good or service

Manufacturing and production entities in various industries had asked the TRG how they should account for activities and costs incurred prior to the production of goods under a long-term supply arrangement when they adopt IFRS 15. The questions arose because some long-term supply arrangements require an entity to incur upfront engineering and design costs to create new technology or adapt existing technology to the needs of the customer.

These pre-production activities are often a prerequisite to delivering any units under a production contract. For example, a manufacturer may incur costs to perform certain services related to the design and development of products it will sell under long-term supply arrangements. It may also incur costs to design and develop moulds, dies and other tools that will be used to produce those products. A contract may require the customer to reimburse the manufacturer for these costs. Alternatively, reimbursement may be implicitly guaranteed as part of the price of the product or by other means.

At the meeting in November 2015, the TRG members generally agreed that the determination of whether pre-production activities are a promised good or service or fulfilment activities requires judgement and consideration of the facts and circumstances. When making this evaluation, entities need to determine whether the activity transfers a good or service to a customer. If an entity determines that these activities are promised goods or services, it applies the requirements in IFRS 15 to those goods or services.

The TRG members generally agreed that if an entity is having difficulty determining whether a pre-production activity is a promised good or service in a contract, the entity needs to consider whether control of that good or service transfers to the customer. For example, if an entity is performing engineering and development services as part of developing a new product for a customer and the customer will own the resulting intellectual property (e.g. patents), it is likely that the entity would conclude that it is transferring control of the intellectual property and that the engineering and development activities are a promised good or service in the contract.

The TRG members noted that assessing whether control transfers in such arrangements may be challenging. In some arrangements, legal title of the good or service created from the pre-production activity is transferred to the customer. However, the TRG members generally agreed that an entity has to consider all indicators of control transfer under IFRS 15 and that the transfer of legal title is not a presumptive indicator.

The IASB staff noted in the TRG agenda paper that, when an entity is determining whether control transfers to a customer in such arrangements, one of the three over-time revenue recognition criteria may be applicable to pre-production activities. That criterion is whether the customer simultaneously receives and consumes the benefits provided by the entity's performance as the entity performs. *[IFRS 15.35(a)]*. As further discussed in Chapter 30 at 2.1, paragraph B3 of IFRS 15 notes that if an entity cannot readily identify whether this criterion is met, it should consider whether another entity would need to re-perform the work the entity had completed to date if that other entity were required to fulfil the remaining performance obligation.

For example, assume an entity is performing engineering and development as part of developing a new product for a customer. If the entity provided the customer with periodic progress reports in a level of detail that would not require the customer to contract with another entity to re-perform the work, or if the entity were required to provide the customer with the design information completed to date in the case of a termination, it is likely that the entity would conclude that control of that service transfers to the customer as the entity performs.

If a pre-production activity is determined to be a promised good or service, an entity allocates a portion of the transaction price to that good or service (as a single performance obligation or as part of a combined performance obligation that includes the pre-production activities along with other goods or services). If the pre-production activities are included in a performance obligation satisfied over time, they are considered when measuring progress toward satisfaction of that performance obligation (see Chapter 30 at 3).[14]

If a pre-production activity does not result in the transfer of control of a good or service to a customer, an entity should consider other requirements that may be applicable (e.g. IAS 16 – *Property, Plant and Equipment*, IAS 38 – *Intangible Assets*, paragraphs 95-98 of IFRS 15 on costs to fulfil a contract with a customer).

3.1.1.B   The nature of the promise in a typical stand-ready obligation

Stakeholders raised questions about the nature of the promise in a 'typical' stand-ready obligation.

At the January 2015 TRG meeting, the TRG members discussed numerous examples of stand-ready obligations and generally agreed that the nature of the promise in a stand-ready obligation is the promise that the customer will have access to a good or service, not the delivery of the underlying good or service.[15] The standard describes a stand-ready obligation as a promised service that consists of standing ready to provide goods or services or making goods or services available for a customer to use as and when it decides to do so. Stand-ready obligations are common in the software industry (e.g. unspecified updates to software on a when-and-if-available basis) and may be present in other industries.

The TRG agenda paper included the following types of promises to a customer that could be considered stand-ready obligations, depending on the facts and circumstances:[16]

- obligations for which the delivery of the good, service or intellectual property is within the control of the entity, but is still being developed (e.g. a software entity's promise to transfer unspecified software upgrades at its discretion);
- obligations for which the delivery of the underlying good or service is outside the control of the entity and the customer (e.g. an entity's promise to remove snow from an airport runway in exchange for a fixed fee for the year);
- obligations for which the delivery of the underlying good or service is within the control of the customer (e.g. an entity's promise to provide periodic maintenance on a when-and-if needed basis on a customer's equipment after a pre-established amount of usage by the customer); and
- obligations to make a good or service available to a customer continuously (e.g. a gym membership that provides unlimited access to a customer for a specified period of time).

An entity needs to carefully evaluate the facts and circumstances of its contracts to appropriately identify whether the nature of a promise to a customer is the delivery of the underlying good(s) or service(s) or the service of standing ready to provide goods or services. Entities also have to consider other promises in a contract that includes a stand-ready obligation to appropriately identify the performance obligations in the contract. The TRG members generally agreed that all contracts with a stand-ready element do not necessarily include a single performance obligation (see 3.1.1.C below).[17]

See 3.2.2.E below for a discussion on whether stand-ready obligations are generally considered to be a series of distinct goods or services.

At the TRG meeting, a FASB staff member also indicated that the staff does not believe that the FASB intended to change previous practice under US GAAP for determining when software or technology transactions include specified upgrade rights (i.e. a separate performance obligation) or unspecified upgrade rights (i.e. a stand-ready obligation).[18] For details of TRG members' discussion on measuring progress toward satisfaction for a stand-ready obligation that is satisfied over time see Chapter 30 at 3.4.1.

3.1.1.C   Considering whether contracts with a stand-ready element include a single performance obligation that is satisfied over time

At the November 2015 TRG meeting, the TRG members considered whether all contracts with a stand-ready element include a single performance obligation that is satisfied over time.

The TRG members generally agreed that the stand-ready element in a contract does not always represent a single performance obligation satisfied over time. This conclusion is consistent with the discussion in 3.1.1.B above that, when identifying the nature of a promise to a customer, an entity may determine that a stand-ready element exists, but it is not the promised good or service for revenue recognition purposes. Instead, the underlying goods or services are the goods or services promised to the customer and accounted for by the entity.

Consider the following example in the TRG agenda paper:[19]

Example 28.18:   *Determining the nature of the promise in a contract with a stand-ready element*

An entity is required to stand ready to produce a part for a customer under an MSA. The customer is not obligated to purchase any parts (i.e. there is no minimum guaranteed volume). However, it is highly likely the customer will purchase parts because the part is required to manufacture the customer's product and it is not practical for the customer to buy parts from multiple suppliers. The TRG members generally agreed that the nature of the promise in this example is the delivery of the parts, rather than a service of standing ready. When the customer submits a purchase order under the master supply arrangement, it is contracting for a specific number of distinct goods and the purchase order creates new performance obligations for the entity. However, if the entity determined that the nature of the promise is a service of standing ready, the contract would be accounted for as a single performance obligation satisfied over time. In that situation, the entity may be required to estimate the number of purchases to be made throughout the contract term (i.e. make an estimate of variable consideration and apply the constraint on variable consideration) and continually update the transaction price and its allocation among the transferred goods or services.

The TRG agenda paper also noted that, in this example, the entity is not obligated to transfer any parts until the customer submits a purchase order (i.e. the customer makes a separate purchasing decision). This contrasts with a stand-ready obligation, which requires the entity to make a promised service available to the customer and does not require the customer to make any additional purchasing decisions.

See 3.6.1.C below for further discussion on determining whether a contract involving variable quantities of goods or services should be accounted for as variable consideration (i.e. if the nature of the promise is to transfer one overall service to the customer, such as a stand-ready obligation) or a contract containing customer options (i.e. if the nature of the promise is to transfer the underlying distinct goods or services).

3.1.1.D   Evaluating whether an exclusivity provision in a contract with customer represents a promised good or service

We generally believe that an exclusivity provision does not represent a promised good or service. Contracts with customers involving the sale of products or services may contain exclusivity clauses whereby the entity agrees that it will not provide the products or services to others or will do so only on a limited basis. Such provisions may restrict the distribution of the products or services in certain geographical areas and/or prohibit the sale of the products or services to a customer's competitors. For example, an entity that provides advertising on its website may agree to run a banner advertisement for one customer for a specified period of time and exclude advertisements for similar products or services from the advertiser's competitors.

In the Basis for Conclusions on IFRS 15, the IASB discussed exclusivity in relation to licences of intellectual property and concluded that exclusivity is a restriction that represents an attribute of a licence, rather than the nature of the underlying intellectual property or the entity's promise in granting the licence. That is, exclusivity provisions define the scope of the customer's rights to intellectual property and would not be accounted for separately (see Chapter 31 at 2.1.3 for further discussion). *[IFRS 15.BC412(b)].*

We believe that the same principles would apply when evaluating exclusivity provisions in contracts that do not contain a licence of intellectual property. That is, exclusivity is an attribute of the promise to the customer, rather than a separate promised good or service. This is because exclusivity does not change the nature of the entity's performance to provide the underlying goods or services to the customer.

Any upfront payment received from a customer related to an exclusivity provision would need to be evaluated to determine whether it represents a material right (see further discussion in Chapter 29 at 2.8). Conversely, any payment made by the entity to the customer would need to be evaluated in accordance with the requirements for consideration paid or payable to a customer (see further discussion in Chapter 29 at 2.7).

3.2 Determining when promises are performance obligations

After identifying the promised goods or services within a contract, an entity determines which of those goods or services will be treated as separate performance obligations. That is, the entity identifies the individual units of account. Promised goods or services represent separate performance obligations if the goods or services are distinct (by themselves, or as part of a bundle of goods or services) (see 3.2.1 below) or if the goods or services are part of a series of distinct goods or services that are substantially the same and have the same pattern of transfer to the customer (see 3.2.2 below).

If a promised good or service is not distinct, an entity is required to combine that good or service with other promised goods or services until it identifies a bundle of goods or services that, together, is distinct. *[IFRS 15.30]*.

An entity is required to account for all the goods or services promised in a contract as a single performance obligation if the entire bundle of promised goods or services is the only performance obligation identified. See 3.3 below for further discussion. Figure 28.3 illustrates these requirements:

Figure 28.3: Determining when promises are performance obligations

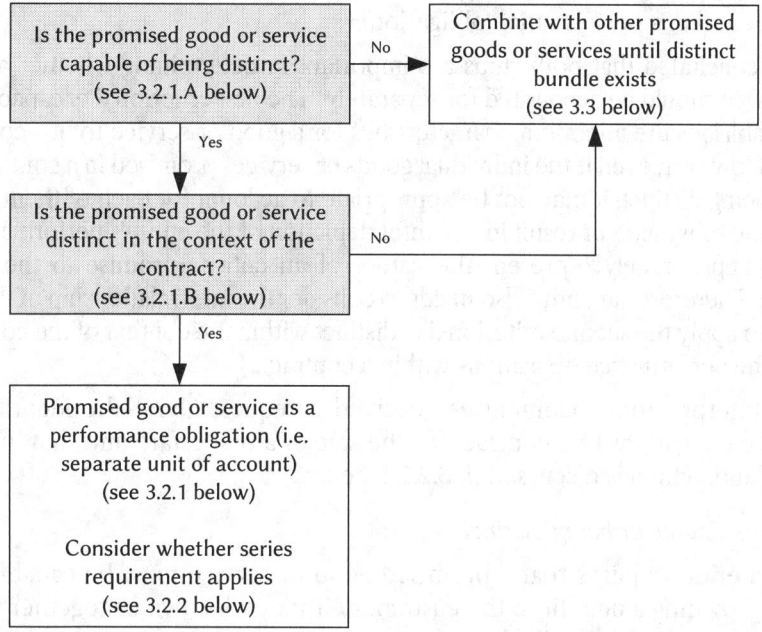

A single performance obligation may include a licence of intellectual property and other promised goods or services. IFRS 15 identifies two examples of licences of intellectual property that are not distinct from other promised goods or services in a contract: (1) a licence that is a component of a tangible good and that is integral to the functionality of the tangible good; and (2) a licence that the customer can benefit from only in conjunction with a related service (e.g. an online hosting service that enables a customer to access the content provided by the licence of intellectual property). *[IFRS 15.B54]*. See Chapter 31 at 2.1.2 for further discussion on these two examples.

The standard also specifies that the following items are performance obligations:

- Customer options for additional goods or services that provide material rights to customers (see 3.6 below). *[IFRS 15.B39-B43]*.
- Service-type warranties (see Chapter 31 at 3.2). *[IFRS 15.B28-B33]*.

Entities do not apply the general model to determine whether these goods or services are performance obligations because the Board deemed them to be performance obligations if they are identified as promises in a contract.

3.2.1 Determination of 'distinct'

IFRS 15 outlines a two-step process for determining whether a promised good or service (or a bundle of goods or services) is distinct:

- Consideration at the level of the individual good or service (i.e. the good or service is capable of being distinct).
- Consideration of whether the good or service is separable from other promises in the contract (i.e. the good or service is distinct within the context of the contract).

Both of these criteria must be met to conclude that the good or service is distinct. If these criteria are met, the individual good or service must be accounted for as a separate unit of account (i.e. a performance obligation).

The Board concluded that both steps are important in determining whether a promised good or service should be accounted for separately. The first criterion (i.e. capable of being distinct) establishes the minimum characteristics for a good or service to be accounted for separately. However, even if the individual goods or services promised in a contract may be capable of being distinct, it may not be appropriate to account for each of them separately because doing so would not result in a faithful depiction of the entity's performance in that contract or appropriately represent the nature of an entity's promise to the customer. *[IFRS 15.BC102]*. Therefore, an entity also needs to consider the interrelationship of those goods or services to apply the second criterion (i.e. distinct within the context of the contract) and determine the performance obligations within a contract.

The IFRS Interpretations Committee received a request about the identification of performance obligations in a contract for the sale of a real estate unit that includes the transfer of land, which is discussed in 3.2.1.B below.

3.2.1.A Capable of being distinct

The first criterion requires that a promised good or service must be capable of being distinct by providing a benefit to the customer either on its own or together with other resources that are readily available to the customer.

The standard states that a customer can benefit from a good or service if the good or service could be used, consumed, sold for an amount greater than scrap value or otherwise held in a way that generates economic benefits. A customer may be able to benefit from some goods or services on their own or in conjunction with other readily available resources. A readily available resource is a good or service that is sold separately (by the entity or another entity) or a resource that the customer has already obtained from the entity (including goods or services that the entity will have already transferred to the customer under the contract) or from other transactions or events. The fact that an entity regularly sells a good or service separately indicates that a customer can benefit from that good or service on its own or with readily available resources. *[IFRS 15.28]*.

Determining whether a good or service is capable of being distinct is straightforward in many situations. For example, if an entity regularly sells a good or service separately, this fact would demonstrate that the good or service provides benefit to a customer on its own or with other readily available resources.

The evaluation may require more judgement in other situations, particularly when the good or service can only provide benefit to the customer with readily available resources provided by other entities. These are resources that meet either of the following conditions:

- they are sold separately by the entity (or another entity); or
- the customer has already obtained them from the entity (including goods or services that the entity has already transferred to the customer under the contract) or from other transactions or events.

As noted in the Basis for Conclusions, the assessment of whether the customer can benefit from the goods or services (either on its own or with other readily available resources) is based on the characteristics of the goods or services themselves instead of how the customer might use the goods or services. *[IFRS 15.BC100]*. Consistent with this notion, an entity disregards any contractual limitations that may prevent the customer from obtaining those readily available resources from a party other than the entity when making this assessment (as illustrated below in Example 28.35 at 3.2.3 below). The IFRS Interpretations Committee also reiterated this point during its March 2018 meeting (see 3.2.1.B below for further discussion).

In the Basis for Conclusions, the Board explained that 'the attributes of being distinct are comparable to the previous revenue recognition requirements for identifying separate deliverables in a multiple-element arrangement, which specified that a delivered item must have "value to the customer on a stand-alone basis" for an entity to account for that item separately.' However, the Board did not use similar terminology in IFRS 15 so as to avoid implying that an entity must assess a customer's intended use for a promised good or service when it is identifying performance obligations. It observed that it would be difficult, if not impossible, for an entity to know a customer's intent. *[IFRS 15.BC101]*.

3.2.1.B   Distinct within the context of the contract

Once an entity has determined whether a promised good or service is capable of being distinct based on the individual characteristics of the promise, the entity considers the second criterion of whether the good or service is separately identifiable from other promises in the contract (i.e. whether the promise to transfer the good or service is distinct within the context of the contract). The standard states that, when assessing whether an entity's promises to transfer goods or services to the customer are separately identifiable from other promises in the contract, the objective is 'to determine whether the nature of the promise, within the context of the contract, is to transfer each of those goods or services individually or, instead, to transfer a combined item or items to which the promised goods or services are inputs. Factors that indicate that two or more promises to transfer goods or services to a customer are not separately identifiable include, but are not limited to, the following:

(a) The entity provides a significant service of integrating the goods or services with other goods or services promised in the contract into a bundle of goods or services that represent the combined output or outputs for which the customer has contracted. In other words, the entity is using the goods or services as inputs to produce or deliver the combined output or outputs specified by the customer. A combined output or outputs might include more than one phase, element or unit.

(b) One or more of the goods or services significantly modifies or customises, or are significantly modified or customised by, one or more of the other goods or services promised in the contract.

(c) The goods or services are highly interdependent or highly interrelated. In other words, each of the goods or services is significantly affected by one or more of the other goods or services in the contract. For example, in some cases, two or more goods or services are significantly affected by each other because the entity would not be able to fulfil its promise by transferring each of the goods or services independently.' *[IFRS 15.29]*.

Figure 28.4 depicts the above requirements:

Figure 28.4: Distinct in the context of the contract

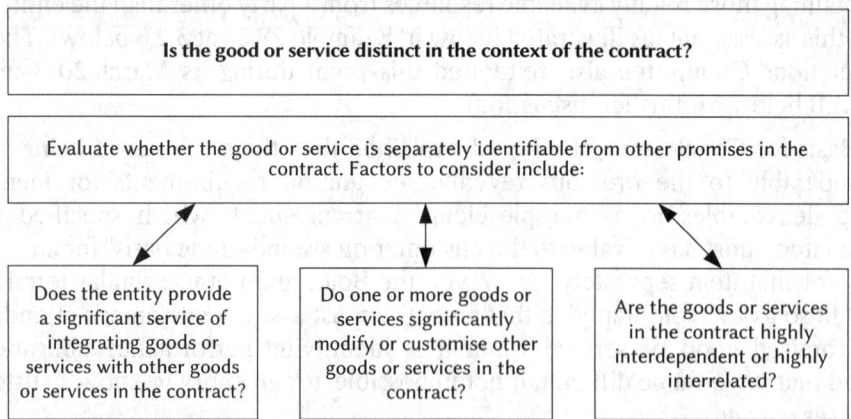

(a) *Separately identifiable principle*

To determine whether promised goods or services are separately identifiable (i.e. whether a promise to transfer a good or service is distinct within the context of the contract), an entity needs to evaluate whether its promise is to transfer each good or service individually or a combined item (or items) that comprises the individual goods or services promised in the contract. Therefore, an entity would evaluate whether the promised goods or services in the contract are outputs or they are inputs to a combined item (or items). In the Basis for Conclusions, the Board noted that, in many cases, a combined item (or items) is more than (or substantially different from) the sum of the underlying promised goods or services. *[IFRS 15.BC116J]*.

The evaluation of whether an entity's promise is separately identifiable considers the relationship between the various goods or services in the context of the process to fulfil the contract. Therefore, an entity considers the level of integration, interrelation or interdependence among the promises to transfer goods or services. In the Basis for Conclusions, the Board observed that, rather than considering whether one item, by its nature, depends on the other (i.e. whether two items have a functional relationship), an entity evaluates whether there is a transformative relationship between the two or more items in the process of fulfilling the contract. *[IFRS 15.BC116K]*. The point was also reiterated by the IFRS Interpretations Committee during its March 2018 meeting (see the discussion below).

The Board also emphasised that the separately identifiable principle is applied within the context of the bundle of promised goods or services in the contract. It is not within the context of each individual promised good or service. That is, the separately identifiable principle is intended to identify when an entity's performance in transferring a bundle of goods or services in a contract is fulfilling a single promise to a customer. Therefore, to apply the 'separately identifiable' principle, an entity evaluates whether two or more promised goods or services significantly affect each other in the contract (and are, therefore, highly interdependent or highly interrelated). *[IFRS 15.BC116L]*.

As an example of this evaluation, the IASB discussed in the Basis for Conclusions a typical construction contract that involves transferring to the customer many goods or services that are capable of being distinct (e.g. various building materials, labour, project management services). In this example, the IASB concluded that identifying all of the individual goods or services as separate performance obligations would be impractical and would not faithfully represent the nature of the entity's promise to the customer. That is, the entity would recognise revenue when the materials and other inputs to the construction process are provided rather than when it performs (and uses those inputs) in the construction of the item the customer has contracted to receive (e.g. a building, a house). As such, when determining whether a promised good or service is distinct, an entity not only determines whether the good or service is capable of being distinct but also whether the promise to transfer the good or service is distinct within the context of the contract. *[IFRS 15.BC102]*.

Paragraph 29 of IFRS 15 includes three factors (discussed individually below) that are intended to help entities identify when the promises in a bundle of promised goods or services are not separately identifiable and, therefore, need to be combined into a single performance obligation. *[IFRS 15.29]*. In the Basis for Conclusions, the IASB noted that these three factors are not an exhaustive list and that not all of the factors need to exist in order to conclude that the entity's promises to transfer goods or services are not separately identifiable. As emphasised by the IFRS Interpretations Committee during its March 2018 meeting (see the discussion below), the three factors also are not intended to be criteria that are evaluated independently of the separately identifiable principle.

Given the wide variety of arrangements that are within the scope of IFRS 15, the Board expects that there are some instances in which the factors are less relevant to the evaluation of the separately identifiable principle. *[IFRS 15.BC116N]*. Entities may need to apply significant judgement to evaluate whether a promised good or service is separately identifiable. The evaluation requires a thorough understanding of the facts and circumstances present in each contract. An entity should consider the following questions, which summarise what is discussed in the Basis for Conclusions: *[IFRS 15.BC116J-BC116L]*

- Is the combined item greater than, or substantively different from, the sum of the promised goods or services?
- Is an entity, in substance, fulfilling a single promise to the customer?
- Is the risk an entity assumes to fulfil its obligation to transfer a promised good or service inseparable from the risk relating to the transfer of the other promised goods or services in the bundle?
- Do two or more promised goods or services each significantly affect the other?
- Does each promised good or service significantly affect the other promised good or service's utility to the customer?

In a speech, a member of the staff from the US Securities and Exchange Commission (SEC) focused on considerations for determining whether a promise to transfer a good or service to a customer is separately identifiable from other promises in the contract, which could require significant judgement, as noted above. The SEC staff member emphasised the importance of supporting a registrant's conclusions by providing a well-reasoned analysis of the guidance in the revenue standard, rather than just referring to the manner in which the goods and services are sold to customers. The SEC staff member stated that the SEC staff are not persuaded that promises should be combined into a single performance obligation simply because they are provided as part of a 'solution'. Instead, they expect registrants to provide a robust assessment of the requirements in the revenue standard to support an assertion that the promises to transfer goods are not separately identifiable.

To illustrate this, the SEC staff member described a consultation with the Office of the Chief Accountant (OCA) in which the staff did not object to a registrant's conclusion that software and software updates represent a combined performance obligation. The registrant was able to demonstrate that the software updates were integral to maintaining the utility of the software. That is, without the software updates, the customer's ability to benefit from the software would be significantly limited over the contract term. Based on this point and other facts and circumstances, the registrant was able to demonstrate that the combined output was greater than, or substantively different from, the individual promises of the software and software updates.[20]

(i) Significant integration service

The first factor (included in paragraph 29(a) of IFRS 15) is the presence of a significant integration service. *[IFRS 15.29(a)]*. The IASB determined that, when an entity provides a significant service of integrating a good or service with other goods or services in a contract, the bundle of integrated goods or services represents a combined output or outputs. In other words, when an entity provides a significant integration service, the risk of transferring individual goods or services is inseparable from the bundle of integrated goods or services because a substantial part of an entity's promise to the customer is to make sure the individual goods or services are incorporated into the combined output or outputs. *[IFRS 15.BC107].* When evaluating this factor, entities need to consider whether they are providing a significant integration service that effectively transforms the individual promised goods or services (the inputs) into a combined output(s), as discussed in Example 28.35, Case E (included in 3.2.3 below). This is consistent with the notion discussed above that a combined item (or items) would be greater than (or substantially different from) the sum of the underlying promised goods or services.

This factor applies even if there is more than one output. Furthermore, as described in the standard, a combined output or outputs may include more than one phase, element or unit.

In the Basis for Conclusions, the IASB noted that this factor may be relevant in many construction contracts in which a contractor provides an integration (or contract management) service to manage and coordinate the various construction tasks and to assume the risks associated with the integration of those tasks. An integration service provided by the contractor often includes coordinating the activities performed by any subcontractors and making sure the quality of the work performed is in compliance with contract specifications and that the individual goods or services are appropriately integrated into the combined item that the customer has contracted to receive. *[IFRS 15.BC107].* This type of construction contract and the analysis of whether it contains a significant integration service is illustrated in Example 28.33, Case A (see 3.2.3 below) and in the example below.

Example 28.19: Significant integration service

Contractor Q, a construction firm, enters into a contract with a customer to design and construct a concert hall. The project has two phases, design and construction and the contract provides separate compensation for each phase.

For purposes of this example, assume that the individual goods and services provided in each phase are capable of being distinct. Contractor Q must then determine whether each of the individual goods and services in each phase are distinct in the context of the contract. Contractor Q provides a significant service of: (1) integrating the various design services to produce project plans in the design phase; and (2) integrating the various materials and construction services to build the concert hall in the construction phase. Contractor Q then evaluates whether the aggregated goods and services in the design phase (i.e. project plans) and aggregated goods and services in the construction phase (i.e. concert hall) are distinct in the context of the contract and, therefore, are two performance obligations or whether together they represent a single performance obligation.

In this illustration, the design and construction of a concert hall is necessary to satisfy Contractor Q's contract with the customer. Given the complex nature of the project, assume Contractor Q will be required to frequently alter the design of the concert hall during construction and to continually assess the propriety of the materials to be used. These changes may cause Contractor Q to rework the construction of the concert hall. Contractor Q determines it is providing a significant service of integrating goods and services into the combined output for which the customer has contracted (i.e. a completed concert hall). Contractor Q concludes that the design services and construction services are not distinct in the context of the contract and instead should be combined and accounted for as one performance obligation.

The Board observed that this factor could apply to other industries as well. *[IFRS 15.BC108].* In a speech, a member of the SEC staff described a consultation with the OCA in which an entity concluded that it was providing a significant integration service that transformed equipment (e.g. cameras, sensors) and monitoring services into a combined output (i.e. a 'smart' security solution) that provided its customers with an overall service offering that was greater than the customer could receive from each individual promise. In this consultation, OCA did not object to the entity's conclusion that its promises comprised a single performance obligation.[21]

(ii) Significant modification or customisation

The second factor in paragraph 29(b) of IFRS 15 is the presence of significant modification or customisation. *[IFRS 15.29(b)]*. In the Basis for Conclusions, the IASB explained that in some industries, the notion of inseparable risks is more clearly illustrated by assessing whether one good or service significantly modifies or customises another. This is because if a good or service modifies or customises another good or service in a contract, each good or service is being assembled together (as an input) to produce a combined output. *[IFRS 15.BC109]*.

In the Basis for Conclusions on IFRS 15, the Board provided the following example. *[IFRS 15.BC110]*.

Example 28.20: Significant customisation service

Assume that an entity promises to provide a customer with software that it will significantly customise to make the software function with the customer's existing infrastructure. Based on its facts and circumstances, the entity determines that it is providing the customer with a fully integrated system and that the customisation service requires it to significantly modify the software in such a way that the risks of providing it and the customisation service are inseparable (i.e. the software and customisation service are not separately identifiable).

The significance of modification or customisation services can affect an entity's conclusion about the number of identified performance obligations for similar fact patterns. Consider Example 28.34, Case A and Case B (included in 3.2.3 below). In Case A, each of the promised goods or services are determined to be distinct because the installation services being provided to the customer do not significantly modify the software. In Case B, two of the promised goods or services are combined into one performance obligation because one promise (the installation) significantly customises another promise (the software).

(iii) Highly interdependent or highly interrelated

The third factor in paragraph 29(c) of IFRS 15 is whether the promised goods or services are highly interdependent or highly interrelated. *[IFRS 15.29(c)]*. This is often the most difficult distinct factor for entities to assess and it is expected to be an area of focus for entities and their stakeholders. Promised goods or services are highly interdependent or highly interrelated if each of the promised goods or services is significantly affected by one or more of the other goods or services in the contract. As discussed above, the Board clarified that an entity would evaluate how two or more promised goods or services affect each other and not just evaluate whether one item, by its nature, depends on the other. That is, an entity needs to evaluate whether there is a significant two-way dependency or transformative relationship between the promised goods or services to determine whether the promises are highly interdependent or highly interrelated. Determining whether a two-way dependency is significant such that the promises are highly interdependent or highly interrelated with each other is a judgement that requires careful consideration.

In the Basis for Conclusions on IFRS 15, the Board provided the following example. [IFRS 15.BC112].

Example 28.21: Highly interdependent and highly interrelated

An entity promises to design an experimental new product for a customer and to manufacture ten prototype units of that product. Because the product and manufacturing process is unproven, the entity is required to continue to revise the design of the product during the construction and test of the prototypes and make any necessary modifications to in-progress or completed prototypes. The entity expects that most, or all, of the units to be produced will require some rework because of design changes made during the production process. That is, the customer is not likely to be able to choose whether to purchase only the design service or the manufacturing service without one significantly affecting the other. The entity determines that the design and manufacturing promises are highly interdependent on, and highly interrelated with, the other promises in the contract. Consequently, although each promise may provide a benefit on its own, the promises are not separately identifiable within the context of the contract.

Conversely, if the design was similar to that of a previous product and/or the entity did not expect to have to rework the prototypes due to design changes, the entity might determine that the two promises are not highly interdependent or highly interrelated and might conclude the contract contains multiple performance obligations.

Goods or services may not be separately identifiable if they are so highly interdependent, on or highly interrelated with, other goods or services under the contract. This may occur when the customer's decision not to purchase one promised good or service would significantly affect the other promised goods or services. In other words, the promised goods or services are so highly interrelated or highly interdependent with each other that the entity could not fulfil an individual promise independently from the other promises in the contract.

One aspect on which this evaluation should focus is the specific utility that can only be delivered through the combination of the goods or services. That is, it is important to establish that the utility each good or service can provide on its own is significantly less than the utility of the combined goods or services. Often, gaining sufficient understanding of the specific utility of the individual goods or services, as well as the combined offering, may involve discussion with employees from various departments (e.g. engineering, sales), in addition to those in the accounting and finance departments. An entity also needs to consider how its products and services are described in publicly available information (e.g. the entity's website, investor relations reports, financial statement filings). Those descriptions may indicate which functionalities are critical to the overall offering and influence customer expectations and whether those functionalities significantly affect the utility of other goods or services in the contract. Overall, the specific facts and circumstances of each offering and contract have to be carefully considered.

The concept regarding an entity's ability to separately fulfil a promise to a customer is highlighted in Example 28.35, Case E (see 3.2.3 below). Example 28.35, Case E, includes a contract for the sale of equipment and specialised consumables to be used with the equipment. In this example, the entity determines that the equipment and consumables are not highly interdependent or highly interrelated because the two promises do not significantly affect each other. As part of its analysis, the entity concludes that it would be able to fulfil each of its promises in the contract independently of the other promises.

(b) March 2018 IFRS Interpretations Committee discussion

In 2017, the IFRS Interpretations Committee received a request regarding the identification of performance obligations in a contract for the sale of a real estate unit that includes the transfer of land. The request also asked about the timing of revenue recognition for each performance obligation (either over-time or at a point in time), which is discussed in Chapter 30 at 2.3.2.D. At its March 2018 meeting, the IFRS Interpretations Committee concluded that the principles and requirements in IFRS 15 provide sufficient guidance for an entity to recognise revenue in a contract for the sale of a real estate unit that includes the transfer of land. Consequently, the IFRS Interpretations Committee decided not to add this matter to its agenda.[22]

In considering this request, the IFRS Interpretations Committee noted that the assessment of the distinct criteria requires judgement. Furthermore:

- The assessment of the first criterion is 'based on the characteristics of the goods or services themselves. Accordingly, an entity disregards any contractual limitations that might preclude the customer from obtaining readily available resources from a source other than the entity' (see 3.2.1.A above). *[IFRS 15.BC100].*

- The objective underlying the second criterion is to determine the nature of the promise within the context of the contract. That is, whether the entity has promised to transfer either the promised goods or services individually or a combined item to which those goods or services are inputs. IFRS 15 also includes some factors that indicate that two or more promises to transfer goods or services are not separately identifiable. *[IFRS 15.29].* However, these factors are not intended to be criteria that an entity evaluates independently of the 'separately identifiable' principle because, in some instances, one or more of the factors may be less relevant to the evaluation of that principle (see the discussion above). *[IFRS 15.BC116N].*

In the Basis for Conclusion, the Board indicated that the separately identifiable concept is influenced by the idea of separable risks. That is, whether the risk assumed to fulfil the obligation to transfer one of the promised goods or services to the customer is separable from the risk relating to the transfer of the other promised goods or services. Evaluating whether an entity's promise is separately identifiable considers the interrelationship between the goods or services within the contract in the context of the process to fulfil the contract. Accordingly, an entity considers the level of integration, interrelation or interdependence among the promises in the contract to transfer goods or services. An entity evaluates whether, in the process of fulfilling the contract, there is a transformative relationship between the promises, rather than considering whether one item, by its nature, depends upon another (i.e. whether the promises have a functional relationship). *[IFRS 15.BC105, 116J, 116K].* That is, the conclusion about whether the promised goods or services are separately identifiable hinges on whether there is a significant two-way dependency between the items. Determining whether a two-way dependency is significant such that the promises are separately identifiable is a judgement that requires careful consideration.

The IFRS Interpretations Committee discussed the identification of performance obligations in its March 2018 meeting using the following example from the IFRS Interpretations Committee agenda paper:[23]

Example 28.22: *Identification of performance obligations in a contract for the sale of a real estate unit that includes the transfer of land*

Entity A enters into a non-cancellable contract with a customer for the sale of a real estate unit that involves the transfer of a plot of land and a building that Entity A constructs on that land. The land represents all of the area on which the building will be constructed and the contract is for the entire building.

At contract inception, Entity A transfers the legal title of the land and the customer pays the price specified in the contract for it. The transfer of legal title to the customer cannot be revoked, regardless of what happens during the construction of the building. Throughout the construction period, the customer makes milestone payments that do not necessarily correspond to the amount of work completed to date.

The design and specification of the building were agreed between the counterparties before the contract was signed. However, during the construction of the building, the customer can request changes to the design and specification that are priced by Entity A based on a methodology specified in the contract. If the customer decides to proceed with the proposed changes, Entity A can reject them only for a limited number of reasons (e.g. when the change would breach planning permission). Entity A can only request changes if not doing so would lead to an unreasonable increase in costs or delay construction. However, the customer must approve those changes.

Entity A first assesses whether the land and the building are each capable of being distinct in accordance with paragraph 27(a) of IFRS 15. Entity A determines that the customer could benefit from the land on its own or together with other resources readily available to it (e.g. by hiring another developer to construct a building on the land). Also, Entity A determines that the customer could benefit from the construction of the building on its own or together with other resources readily available to it (e.g. by obtaining the construction services from Entity A or another developer without transferring the land). Therefore, Entity A concludes that the land and the building are each capable of being distinct.

The criterion in paragraph 27(b) of IFRS 15 is then assessed by Entity A in order to determine whether the land and the building are distinct in the context of the contract. In making this assessment, Entity A considers the factors in paragraph 29 of IFRS 15, including the following:

a. Whether it provides a significant service of integrating the land and the building into a combined output. Entity A analyses the transformative relationship between the transfer of the land and the construction of the building in the process of fulfilling the contract. As part of this analysis, it considers whether its performance in constructing the building would be different if it did not also transfer the land and *vice versa*. Despite the functional relationship between the land and the building (because the building cannot exist without the land on which its foundations will be built), the risks assumed by Entity A in transferring the land may, or may not, be separable from those assumed in constructing the building.

b. Whether the land and the building are highly interdependent or highly interrelated. Entity A determines whether its promise to transfer the land could be fulfilled if it did not also construct the building and *vice versa*.

The IFRS Interpretations Committee concluded that the two promises would be separately identifiable if Entity A concluded that '(a) its performance in constructing the building would be the same regardless of whether it also transferred the land; and (b) it would be able to fulfil its promise to construct the building even if it did not also transfer the land, and would be able to fulfil its promise to transfer the land even if it did not also construct the building.'[24]

The assessment of whether a good or service is distinct must consider the specific contract with a customer. That is, an entity cannot assume that a particular good or service is distinct (or not distinct) in all instances. The manner in which promised goods or services are bundled within a contract can affect the conclusion of whether a good or service is distinct. As a result, entities may account the same goods or services differently, depending on how those goods or services are bundled within a contract.

(c) Examples

The IASB included a number of examples in the standard that illustrate the application of the requirements for identifying performance obligations. The examples include analysis of how an entity may determine whether the promises to transfer goods or services are distinct within the context of the contract. See 3.2.3 below for full extracts of several of these examples.

3.2.1.C   *How should an entity determine whether 'connected' hardware sold with cloud services represent one or more performance obligations?*

To identify performance obligations in contracts containing connected hardware and cloud services, entities must determine whether the hardware and cloud services are each capable of being distinct and whether they are distinct within the context of the contract (as discussed at 3.2.1 above). An increasing number of connected hardware devices are now available (e.g. security cameras, home equipment). In contracts where a customer purchases hardware, the hardware may require the installation of an app or the purchase of a cloud service subscription in order to be used. Alternatively, the hardware may provide additional functionalities when paired with the cloud service.

In evaluating the distinct criteria, entities need to consider: whether the hardware can be used without the cloud service; how the hardware and cloud service affect each other (e.g. whether the cloud service enables the hardware to 'learn' or perform its intended function better over time); whether there are additional functionalities that result from using the hardware with the cloud service; and other details of how the hardware and cloud services function and are sold.

Consider the following example where an entity concludes that the connected hardware and cloud services are separately identifiable:

Example 28.23:   Hardware sold with cloud services

Entity L enters into a contract with a customer to provide a smart home security camera bundled with cloud services, which enable the customer to view live images from the camera in an app on internet-connected devices (e.g. tablets, phones). Entity L also provides the cloud services to customers who purchase the camera through secondary markets.

Entity L concludes that the customer can benefit from each of the goods and services either on its own or together with other goods or services that are readily available. That is, each good or service is capable of being distinct under paragraph 27(a) of IFRS 15.

The camera is capable of being distinct because the customer can benefit from it together with the cloud services, which are a readily available resource since they can be obtained separately. Furthermore, the customer can benefit from the camera because it can be resold through secondary markets for more than scrap value.

The cloud services are capable of being distinct because the customer can benefit from them together with the camera transferred at the outset of the contract or the customer can purchase the camera separately through the secondary markets and obtain the cloud services from the entity.

Entity L then considers the factors in paragraph 29 of IFRS 15 and determines that the promise to transfer each good and service is distinct within the context of the contract. In reaching this conclusion, the entity notes that it does not provide a significant service of integrating the cloud services with the camera into a combined output, and the cloud services and the camera do not significantly modify or customise one another.

Entity L also determines that the camera and the cloud services are not highly interdependent or highly interrelated because it can fulfil its promise to transfer the cloud services independently from its promise to provide the camera (i.e. since customers can purchase the camera in secondary markets). The cloud services provide only the basic functionality of connecting the camera to a personal device using Wi-Fi (instead of a traditional electrical cable). Therefore, the utility the customer can derive from the camera and the cloud services (when transferred together) is not greater than, or substantially different from, the utility the customer would receive if the camera and cloud services had been transferred separately.

As a result, Entity L identifies two performance obligations: the camera and the cloud services.

Entities will need to evaluate the specific features and functionality of the cloud services in arrangements that include connected hardware devices. Evaluating whether hardware and cloud services are separate performance obligations in arrangements for connected devices may be complex and require significant judgement when the cloud service has sophisticated features or functionality that the device cannot do independently. In these cases, there may be a high degree of interdependency between the hardware and the cloud service or a significant integration service may be present.

To conclude that hardware and a cloud service are a single performance obligation, entities will need to demonstrate that the functionality of both the hardware and the service is significantly elevated when they are used together. Many technology entities have concluded that they have separate performance obligations because the hardware and the cloud service do not significantly affect each other and because the hardware can be sold separately from the cloud service.

3.2.1.D   How would entities determine whether implementation services are distinct?

Entities will need to assess their implementation services and consider all relevant facts and circumstances to determine whether they are separate performance obligations (i.e. they are capable of being distinct and are distinct within the context of a contract, as discussed at 3.2.1 above). Entities may include promises to provide implementation services to customers as part of their product or service contracts (i.e. the implementation activities have been determined to transfer a service to the customer, as discussed at 3.1 above). For example, these services may include training of customer personnel and data conversion.

When assessing whether implementation services are capable of being distinct, an entity first considers whether the customer can benefit from those services on their own. There is strong evidence to suggest that implementation services are capable of being distinct if third party vendors offer (or are capable of offering) implementation services for the entity's products or services, or if the customer could perform these services on its own. This evidence would demonstrate that the implementation services provide benefit to the customer on their own (i.e. apart from the other promised products or services purchased from the entity).

If an entity concludes that the customer is not able to benefit from the implementation services on their own, the entity considers whether the customer can benefit from the services together with other readily available resources. Readily available resources include the other promised products or services from the contract if they are sold separately by the entity or if they are transferred to the customer before the implementation services. An entity disregards any contractual limitations that prevent the customer from obtaining readily available resources from a party other than the entity when making this assessment. That is, contractually restricting a customer from using another vendor to perform the installation services would not preclude an entity from determining that the implementation services are capable of being distinct.

In assessing whether the implementation services are distinct within the context of the contract, an entity needs to consider whether: the implementation services modify or customise the other promised products or services; the entity is providing a significant service of integrating the promised products or services with the implementation services into one combined output; or the entity would be able to fulfil its promise to transfer the other promised products or services in the contract independently from its promise to provide the implementation services (i.e. whether the implementation services are highly interdependent or interrelated with the other products or services). This evaluation may require judgement and is based on the facts and circumstances of the entity's contracts.

The following example depict implementation services that are distinct and are not distinct, respectively:

Example 28.24: Implementation services are distinct

Technology entity P enters into an arrangement with a customer to perform implementation services and to provide software as a service (SaaS) for a three-year period. The entity sells the SaaS and implementation services separately. The implementation services include changing the layout of the main dashboard for each type of user (e.g. marketing, finance) and do not alter the source code of the underlying software or add any new functionality. The implementation service is routinely performed by third parties and does not significantly modify or customise the SaaS.

Technology entity P evaluates the promised goods and services to determine which promises would be accounted for as separate performance obligations.

Technology entity P concludes that the implementation services are capable of being distinct because they can be used with the SaaS, a readily available resource, and because they can be purchased from third parties. Furthermore, the implementation services are distinct within the context of the contract for the following reasons: they are routine; they do not significantly modify or customise the SaaS; they are not integrated with the SaaS into a combined output; and they are not highly interdependent or interrelated with the SaaS since the entity can fulfil its promise to transfer the SaaS independently from its promise to provide the implementation services.

Based on this assessment, Technology entity P identifies two performance obligations: the SaaS and the implementation services.

Example 28.25: Implementation services are not distinct

Consider the same promised goods or services as in Example 28.24 above, except that the nature of the implementation services is to set up data feeds and interfaces with third-party applications and to connect the customer's SaaS account to Technology entity P's infrastructure.

Technology entity P does not sell the SaaS without the implementation services, and the customer cannot use the SaaS until the implementation services are complete, which may be up to nine months after entering into a contract. The implementation services cannot be provided by other entities because they require access to Technology entity P's systems.

Technology entity P evaluates the promised goods and services to determine which promises would be accounted for as separate performance obligations. The SaaS is capable of being distinct because it can be used together with the implementation services that are provided at the outset of the contract. However, the implementation services are not capable of being distinct because they are not sold separately by the Technology entity P; they cannot be provided by a third party; and they do not provide benefit to the customer without SaaS (which is not a readily available resource).

Based on this assessment, Technology entity P identifies one performance obligation: the implemented SaaS (comprised of the SaaS and implementation services).

3.2.2 Series of distinct goods or services that are substantially the same and have the same pattern of transfer

As discussed above, paragraph 22(b) of IFRS 15 defines, as a second type of performance obligation, a promise to transfer to the customer a series of distinct goods or services that are substantially the same and that have the same pattern of transfer, if both of the following criteria from paragraph 23 of IFRS 15 are met: *[IFRS 15.22(b), 23]*

- each distinct good or service in the series that the entity promises to transfer represents a performance obligation that would be satisfied over time in accordance with paragraph 35 of IFRS 15 (see 3.2.2.A below and Chapter 30 at 2), if it were accounted for separately; and
- the entity would measure its progress toward satisfaction of the performance obligation using the same measure of progress for each distinct good or service in the series (see Chapter 30 at 3).

Figure 28.5: The series requirement criteria

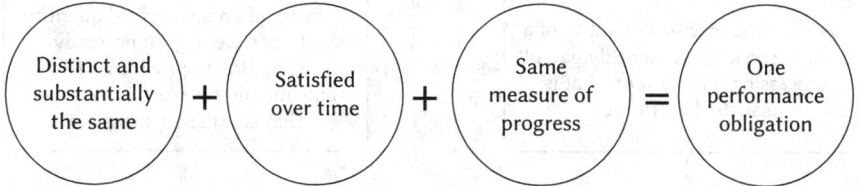

If a series of distinct goods or services meets the criteria in paragraph 22(b) of IFRS 15 and paragraph 23 of IFRS 15 (i.e. the series requirement), an entity is required to treat that series as a single performance obligation (i.e. it is not optional). The Board incorporated this requirement to simplify the model and promote consistent identification of performance obligations in cases when an entity provides the same good or service over a period of time. *[IFRS 15.BC113]*. Without the series requirement, the Board noted that applying the revenue model might present operational challenges because an entity would have to identify multiple distinct goods or services, allocate the transaction price to each distinct good or service on a stand-alone selling price basis and then recognise revenue when those performance obligations are satisfied. The IASB determined that this would not be cost effective. Instead, an entity identifies a single performance obligation and allocates the transaction price to that performance obligation. It will then recognise revenue by applying a single measure of progress to that performance obligation. *[IFRS 15.BC114]*.

For distinct goods or services to be accounted for as a series, one of the criteria is that they must be substantially the same. This is often the most difficult criterion for entities to assess. In the Basis for Conclusions, the Board provided three examples of repetitive services (i.e. cleaning, transaction processing and delivering electricity) that meet the series requirement. *[IFRS 15.BC114]*. In addition, the TRG members generally agreed that when determining whether distinct goods or services are substantially the same, entities need to first determine the nature of their promise. This is because a series could consist of either specified quantities of the underlying good or service delivered (e.g. each unit of a good) or distinct time increments (e.g. an hourly service), depending on the nature of the promise. That is, if the nature of the promise is to deliver a specified quantity of service (e.g. monthly payroll services over a defined contract period), the evaluation considers whether each service is distinct and substantially the same. In contrast, if the nature of the entity's promise is to stand ready or provide a single service for a period of time (i.e. because there is an unspecified quantity to be delivered), the evaluation considers whether each time increment (e.g. hour, day), rather than the underlying activities, is distinct and substantially the same.[25]

Figure 28.6 illustrates how the determination of the nature of the promise might affect whether the series requirement applies:

Figure 28.6:   The series requirement: determining the nature of the promise

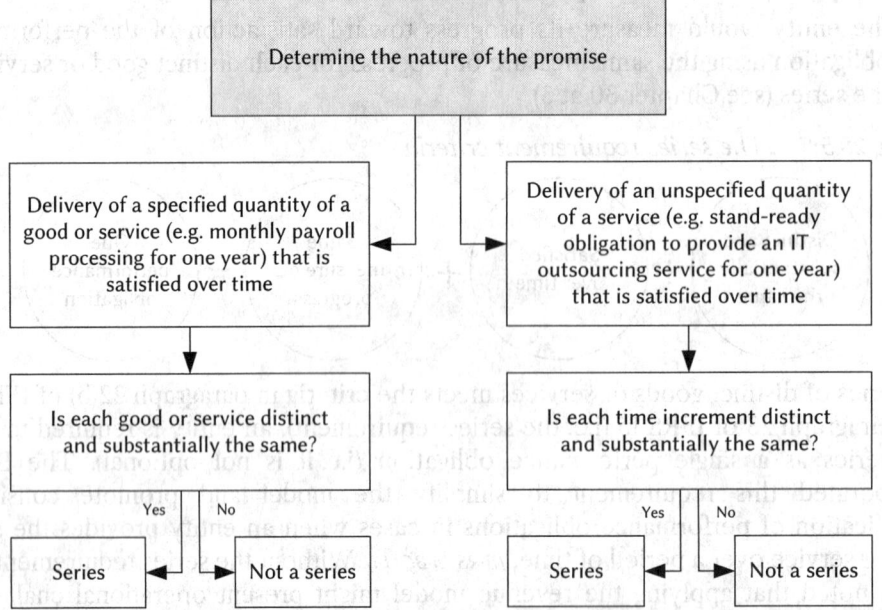

It is important to highlight that even if the underlying activities an entity performs to satisfy a promise vary significantly throughout the day and from day to day, that fact, by itself, does not mean the distinct goods or services are not substantially the same. Consider an example where the nature of the promise is to provide a daily hotel management service. The service is comprised of activities that may vary each day (e.g. cleaning services, reservation services or property maintenance). However, the entity determines that the daily hotel management services are substantially the same because the nature of the entity's promise is the same each day and the entity is providing the same overall management service each day. See 3.2.2.C below for further discussion on determining the nature of an entity's promise and evaluating the 'substantially the same' criterion.

A July 2015 TRG agenda paper explained that, when considering the nature of the entity's promise and the applicability of the series requirement (including whether a good or service is distinct), it may be helpful to consider which over-time criterion in paragraph 35 of IFRS 15 was met (i.e. why the entity concluded that the performance obligation is satisfied over time).[26] As discussed further in Chapter 30 at 2, a performance obligation is satisfied over time if one of three criteria are met. For example, if a performance obligation is satisfied over time because the customer simultaneously receives and consumes the benefits provided as the entity performs (i.e. the first over-time criterion in paragraph 35(a) of IFRS 15), that may indicate that each increment of service is capable of being distinct. If that is the case, the entity would need to evaluate whether each increment of service is separately identifiable (and substantially the same). If a performance obligation is satisfied over time based on the other two criteria in paragraph 35 of IFRS 15 (i.e. (1) the entity's performance creates or enhances an asset that the customer controls as the asset is created or enhanced; or (2) the entity's performance does not create an asset with an alternative use to the entity and the entity has an enforceable right to payment for performance completed to date), the nature of that promise might be to deliver a single specified good or service (e.g. a contract to construct a single piece of equipment), which would not be considered a series because the individual goods or services within that performance obligation are not distinct.

An entity's determination of whether a performance obligation is a single performance obligation comprising a series of distinct goods or services or a single performance obligation comprising goods or services that are not distinct from one another affects the accounting in the following areas: (1) allocation of variable consideration (see Chapter 29 at 3); (2) contract modifications (see 2.4 above); and (3) changes in transaction price (see Chapter 29 at 3.5). As the IASB discussed in the Basis for Conclusions an entity considers the underlying distinct goods or services in the contract, rather than the single performance obligation identified under the series requirement, when applying the requirements for these three areas of the model. *[IFRS 15.BC115].*

The following example, included in a March 2015 TRG agenda paper, illustrates how the allocation of variable consideration may differ for a single performance obligation identified under the series requirement and a single performance obligation comprising non-distinct goods and/or services.[27]

Example 28.26: Allocation of variable consideration for a series versus a single performance obligation comprising non-distinct goods and/or services

Consider a five-year service contract that includes payment terms of a fixed annual fee plus a performance bonus upon completion of a milestone at the end of year two. If the entire service period is determined to be a single performance obligation comprising a series of distinct services, the entity may be able to conclude that the variable consideration (i.e. the bonus amount) should be allocated directly to its efforts to perform the distinct services up to the date that the milestone is achieved (e.g. the underlying distinct services in years one and two). This could result in the entity recognising the entire bonus amount at the end of year two (when it is highly probable that a significant revenue reversal will not occur). See 3.2.2.C below for several examples of services for which it would be reasonable to conclude that they meet the series requirement.

In contrast, if the entity determines that the entire service period is a single performance obligation that is comprised of non-distinct services, the bonus would be included in the transaction price (subject to the constraint on variable consideration – see Chapter 29 at 2.2.3) and recognised based on the measure of progress determined for the entire service period. For example, assume the bonus becomes part of the transaction price at the end of year two (when it is highly probable that a significant revenue reversal will not occur). In that case, a portion of the bonus would be recognised at that the end of year two based on performance completed to date and a portion would be recognised as the remainder of the performance obligation is satisfied. As a result, the bonus amount would be recognised as revenue through to the end of the five-year service period.

We believe that entities may need to apply significant judgement when determining whether a promised good or service in a contract with a customer meets the criteria to be accounted for as a series of distinct goods or services. As illustrated in 3.2.2.C below, promised goods or services that meet the series criteria are not limited to a particular industry and can encompass a wide array of promised goods or services.

3.2.2.A The series requirement: Consecutive transfer of goods or services

In March 2015, the TRG members discussed whether the goods or services must be consecutively transferred to be considered under the series requirement. The TRG members generally agreed that a series of distinct goods or services need not be consecutively transferred. That is, the series requirement must be applied even when there is a gap or an overlap in an entity's transfer of goods or services, provided that the other criteria are met.[28] The IASB TRG members also noted that entities may need to carefully consider whether the series requirement applies, depending on the length of the gap between an entity's transfer of goods or services.

Stakeholders had asked this question because the Basis for Conclusions uses the term 'consecutively' when it discusses the series requirement. *[IFRS 15.BC113, BC116]*. However, the TRG agenda paper concluded that the Board's discussion was not meant to imply that the series requirement only applies to circumstances in which the entity provides the same good or service consecutively over a period of time.

Consider the following example from the TRG agenda paper:[29]

Example 28.27: A series in which the goods or services need not be consecutively transferred

An entity has a contract with a customer to provide a manufacturing service producing 24,000 units of a product over a two-year period. The units produced under the service arrangement are distinct, substantially the same and are manufactured to meet the customer's specifications. The entity determines that the service is satisfied over time (see Chapter 30 at 2) because its performance does not create an asset with alternative use to the entity (i.e. the units are manufactured to specific to the customer). Furthermore, if the contract were to be cancelled, the entity would have an enforceable right to payment (cost plus a reasonable profit margin). Therefore, the criteria for the series requirement in paragraph 23 of IFRS 15 have both been met.

The conclusion in the TRG agenda paper was not influenced by whether the entity would perform the service evenly over the two-year period (e.g. produce 1,000 units per month). That is, the entity could produce 2,000 units in some months and none in others, but this would not be a determining factor in concluding whether the contract met the criteria to be accounted for as a series.

3.2.2.B The series requirement versus treating the distinct goods or services as separate performance obligations

At the March 2015 TRG meeting, the TRG members were asked whether, in order to apply the series requirement, the accounting result needs to be the same as if the underlying distinct goods or services were accounted for as separate performance obligations.

The TRG members generally agreed that the accounting result does not need to be the same. Furthermore, an entity is not required to prove that the result would be the same as if the goods or services were accounted for as separate performance obligations.[30]

Consider the following example from the TRG agenda paper to illustrate this point:[31]

Example 28.28: A series for which the accounting result would be different if not treated as a series

An entity contracts with a customer to perform a manufacturing service that results in the production of 10 widgets. The manufacturing service will be performed over a three-year period. The contract price is $100 million, and the stand-alone selling price for each widget is $10 million.

Total expected costs are $80 million. The service the entity will provide to the customer in producing each widget is substantially the same. However, the design is new, so the entity expects a decline in production costs over time. Production of the first five units is expected to cost £9 million per widget. The costs to produce the other five widgets are expected to be £7 million per widget.

For purposes of this example, the entity determines that each service that it will provide to produce one of the 10 widgets is distinct and meets the criteria to be satisfied over time and that the same cost-based measure of progress would be used (i.e. the series requirement criteria in paragraph 23 of IFRS 15 are met). The following table demonstrates the difference in accounting between concluding that the series requirement applies and concluding that the contract is for 10 separate performance obligations:

(in $ millions)	Total contract	Series requirement (one performance obligation)		10 separate performance obligations	
		Units 1-5	Units 6-10	Units 1-5	Units 6-10
Revenue	100	56	44	50	50
Cost	80	45	35	45	35
Margin	20	11	9	5	15

Although $20 million in margin is recognised for the contract under both scenarios, there is a difference in the timing of revenue recognition (and margin) because more revenue is recognised in relation to the service to produce the first five widgets (and less in relation to its service to produce the final five widgets) when the series is accounted for as a single performance obligation using a single measure of progress towards complete satisfaction.

Also see Chapter 31 at 5.2.3 on how the effect of learning curve costs are addressed in IFRS 15.

3.2.2.C Assessing whether a performance obligation consists of distinct goods or services that are 'substantially the same'

At the July 2015 TRG meeting, the TRG members were asked to consider how an entity would assess whether a performance obligation consists of distinct goods or services that are 'substantially the same' in order to apply the series requirement.[32]

As discussed above, the TRG members generally agreed that the TRG paper, which primarily focused on the application of the series requirement to service contracts, will help entities understand how to determine whether a performance obligation consists of distinct goods or services that are 'substantially the same' under IFRS 15.

The TRG agenda paper noted that, when making the evaluation of whether goods or services are distinct and substantially the same, an entity first needs to determine the nature of the entity's promise in providing services to the customer. That is, if the nature of the promise is to deliver a specified quantity of service (e.g. monthly payroll services over a defined contract period), the evaluation should consider whether each service is distinct and substantially the same. In contrast, if the nature of the entity's promise is to stand ready or provide a single service for a period of time (i.e. because there is an unspecified quantity to be delivered), the evaluation would consider whether each time increment (e.g. hour, day), rather than the underlying activities, is distinct and substantially the same. The TRG agenda paper noted that the Board intended that a series could consist of either specified quantities of the underlying good or service delivered (e.g. each unit of a good) or distinct time increments (e.g. an hourly service), depending on the nature of the promise.

As discussed at 3.2.2 above, it is important to highlight that the underlying activities an entity performs to satisfy a performance obligation could vary significantly throughout a day and from day to day. However, the TRG agenda paper noted that this is not determinative in the assessment of whether a performance obligation consists of goods or services that are distinct and substantially the same. Consider an example where the nature of the promise is to provide a daily hotel management service. The hotel management service comprises various activities that may vary each day (e.g. cleaning services, reservation services, property maintenance). However, the entity determines that the daily hotel management services are substantially the same because the nature of the entity's promise is the same each day and the entity is providing the same overall management service each day.

The TRG agenda paper included several examples of promised goods or services that may meet the series requirement and the analysis that supports that conclusion. The evaluation of the nature of the promise for each example is consistent with Example 13 of IFRS 15, [IFRS 15.IE67-IE68], on monthly payroll processing. Below we have summarised some of the examples and analysis in the TRG agenda paper.

Example 28.29: IT outsourcing[33]

A vendor and customer execute a 10-year IT outsourcing arrangement in which the vendor continuously delivers the outsourced activities over the contract term (e.g. it provides server capacity, manages the customer's software portfolio, runs an IT help desk). The total monthly invoice is calculated based on different units consumed for the respective activities. The vendor concludes that the customer simultaneously receives and consumes the benefits provided by its services as it performs (meeting the over-time criterion in paragraph 35(a) of IFRS 15).

The vendor first considers the nature of its promise to the customer. Because the vendor has promised to provide an unspecified quantity of activities, rather than a defined number of services, the TRG agenda paper noted that the vendor could reasonably conclude that the nature of the promise is an obligation to stand ready to provide the integrated outsourcing service each day. If the nature of the promise is the overall IT outsourcing service, each day of service could be considered distinct because the customer can benefit from each day of service on its own and each day is separately identifiable. The TRG agenda paper also noted that the vendor could reasonably conclude that each day of service is substantially the same. That is, even if the individual activities that comprise the performance obligation vary from day to day, the nature of the overall promise is the same from day to day. Accordingly, it would be reasonable for an entity to conclude that this contract meets the series requirement.

Example 28.30: Transaction processing[34]

A vendor enters into a 10-year contract with a customer to provide continuous access to its system and to process all transactions on behalf of the customer. The customer is obliged to use the vendor's system, but the ultimate quantity of transactions is unknown. The vendor concludes that the customer simultaneously receives and consumes the benefits as it performs.

If the vendor concludes that the nature of its promise is to provide continuous access to its system, rather than process a particular quantity of transactions, it might conclude that there is a single performance obligation to stand ready to process as many transactions as the customer requires. If that is the case, the TRG agenda paper noted that it would be reasonable to conclude that there are multiple distinct time increments of the service. Each day of access to the service provided to the customer could be considered substantially the same since the customer is deriving a consistent benefit from the access each day, even if a different number of transactions are processed each day.

If the vendor concludes that the nature of the promise is the processing of each transaction, the TRG agenda paper noted that each transaction processed could be considered substantially the same even if there are multiple types of transactions that generate different payments. Furthermore, the TRG agenda paper noted that each transaction processed could be a distinct service because the customer could benefit from each transaction on its own and each transaction could be separately identifiable. Accordingly, it would be reasonable for an entity to conclude that this contract meets the series requirement.

Example 28.31: Hotel management[35]

A hotel manager (HM) enters into a 20-year contract to manage properties on behalf of a customer. HM receives monthly consideration of 1% of the monthly rental revenue, as well as reimbursement of labour costs incurred to perform the service and an annual incentive payment. HM concludes that the customer simultaneously receives and consumes the benefits of its services as it performs.

HM considers the nature of its promise to the customer. If the nature of its promise is the overall management service (because the underlying activities are not distinct from each other), the TRG agenda paper noted that each day of service could be considered distinct because the customer can benefit from each day of service on its own and each day of service is separately identifiable.

Assuming the nature of the promise is the overall management service, the TRG agenda paper noted that the service performed each day could be considered distinct and substantially the same. This is because, even if the individual activities that comprise the performance obligation vary significantly throughout the day and from day to day, the nature of the overall promise to provide the management service is the same from day to day. Accordingly, it would be reasonable for an entity to conclude that this contract meets the series requirement.

The following is another example of promised goods and services that may meet the series requirement and the analysis that supports that conclusion:

Example 28.32: Determining whether promised goods and services represent a series

A SaaS provider enters into a three-year contract with Customer X to provide access to its SaaS basic customer relationship management (CRM) application for £300,000. The contract also includes professional services that will personalise the user's interface based on the user's role. These services are sold separately from the CRM application and can be provided by third party vendors. The customer can benefit from the CRM application without the professional services, which do not significantly customise or modify the CRM application.

The SaaS provider determines that the CRM application and professional services are distinct (i.e. the CRM application and the professional services should not be combined into a single performance obligation). The two services are each capable of being distinct because Customer X can benefit from them on their own. The services are distinct within the context of the contract because they are not highly interdependent or interrelated and each service does not significantly modify or customise the other.

The SaaS provider first determines that the nature of the CRM application promise is to provide continuous access to its CRM application for the three-year period. Although the activities that Customer X may be able to perform via the CRM application may vary from day to day, the overall promise is to provide continuous access to the CRM application to Customer X for a period of three years.

The SaaS provider determines that access to the CRM application represents a series of distinct services that are substantially the same and have the same pattern of transfer to Customer X. Each day of service is capable of being distinct because Customer X benefits each day from access to the CRM application. Each day is distinct within the context of the contract because there are no significant integration services, each day does not modify or customise another day and each day is not highly interdependent or interrelated. Each day of service is substantially the same because Customer X derives a consistent benefit from the access to the CRM application and has the same pattern of transfer over the term of the contract. Each distinct service represents a performance obligation that is satisfied over time and has the same measure of progress (e.g. time-elapsed). Therefore, the criteria to account for access to the CRM application as a series of distinct services (i.e. a single performance obligation) are met.

The SaaS provider also considers whether the professional services meet the criteria to be accounted for as a series. As part of this assessment, the entity considers whether each day of the professional services is distinct from the other days or whether the nature of the promise for the professional services is for a combined output from all of the days. The entity also considers the complexity of the professional services and whether the activity of each day builds on one another or if each day is substantially the same. This analysis requires judgement and is based on the facts and circumstances of the professional services performed.

3.2.2.D When to apply the series requirement

As discussed above, if a series of distinct goods or services meets the criteria in paragraphs 22(b) and 23 of IFRS 15, an entity is required to treat that series as a single performance obligation (i.e. it is not an optional requirement). *[IFRS 15.22(b), 23].*

3.2.2.E Do all stand-ready obligations meet the criteria to be accounted for as a series?

We generally believe that stand-ready obligations will meet the criteria and, therefore, need to be accounted for as a series of distinct goods or services. As discussed at 3.1.1.B and 3.1.1.C above, entities may need to apply judgement to determine whether the nature of a promise to a customer is the service of standing ready to provide goods or services (i.e. a stand-ready obligation) or the delivery of the underlying goods or services (i.e. not a stand-ready obligation).

3.2.3 Examples of identifying performance obligations

The standard includes several examples that illustrate the application of the requirements for identifying performance obligations. The examples explain the judgements made to determine whether the promises to transfer goods or services are capable of being distinct and distinct within the context of the contract. We have extracted these examples below.

The following example illustrates contracts with promised goods or services that, while capable of being distinct, are not distinct within the context of the contract because of a significant integration service that combines the inputs (the underlying goods or services) into a combined output. *[IFRS 15.IE45-IE48C].*

Example 28.33: Goods and services are not distinct

Case A – Significant integration service

An entity, a contractor, enters into a contract to build a hospital for a customer. The entity is responsible for the overall management of the project and identifies various promised goods and services, including engineering, site clearance, foundation, procurement, construction of the structure, piping and wiring, installation of equipment and finishing.

The promised goods and services are capable of being distinct in accordance with paragraph 27(a) of IFRS 15. That is, the customer can benefit from the goods and services either on their own or together with other readily available resources. This is evidenced by the fact that the entity, or competitors of the entity, regularly sells many of these goods and services separately to other customers. In addition, the customer could generate economic benefit from the individual goods and services by using, consuming, selling or holding those goods or services.

However, the promises to transfer the goods and services are not separately identifiable in accordance with paragraph 27(b) of IFRS 15 (on the basis of the factors in paragraph 29 of IFRS 15). This is evidenced by the fact that the entity provides a significant service of integrating the goods and services (the inputs) into the hospital (the combined output) for which the customer has contracted.

Because both criteria in paragraph 27 of IFRS 15 are not met, the goods and services are not distinct. The entity accounts for all of the goods and services in the contract as a single performance obligation.

Case B – Significant integration service

An entity enters into a contract with a customer that will result in the delivery of multiple units of a highly complex, specialised device. The terms of the contract require the entity to establish a manufacturing process in order to produce the contracted units. The specifications are unique to the customer, based on a custom design that is owned by the customer and that were developed under the terms of a separate contract that is not part of the current negotiated exchange. The entity is responsible for the overall management of the contract, which requires the performance and integration of various activities including procurement of materials, identifying and managing subcontractors, and performing manufacturing, assembly and testing.

The entity assesses the promises in the contract and determines that each of the promised devices is capable of being distinct in accordance with paragraph 27(a) of IFRS 15 because the customer can benefit from each device on its own. This is because each unit can function independently of the other units.

The entity observes that the nature of its promise is to establish and provide a service of producing the full complement of devices for which the customer has contracted in accordance with the customer's specifications. The entity considers that it is responsible for overall management of the contract and for providing a significant service of integrating various goods and services (the inputs) into its overall service and the resulting devices (the combined output) and, therefore, the devices and the various promised goods and services inherent in producing those devices are not separately identifiable in accordance with paragraph 27(b) and paragraph 29 of IFRS 15. In this case, the manufacturing process provided by the entity is specific to its contract with the customer. In addition, the nature of the entity's performance and, in particular, the significant integration service of the various activities means that a change in one of the entity's activities to produce the devices has a significant effect on the other activities required to produce the highly complex, specialised devices such that the entity's activities are highly interdependent and highly interrelated. Because the criterion in paragraph 27(b) of IFRS 15 is not met, the goods and services that will be provided by the entity are not separately identifiable and, therefore, are not distinct. The entity accounts for all of the goods and services promised in the contract as a single performance obligation.

The determination of whether a 'significant integration service' exists within a contract, as illustrated in Case A and Case B above, requires significant judgement and is heavily dependent on the unique facts and circumstances for each individual contract with a customer.

The following example illustrates how the significance of installation services can affect an entity's conclusion about the number of identified performance obligations for similar fact patterns. *[IFRS 15.IE49-IE58]*. In Case A, each of the promised goods and services are determined to be distinct. In Case B, two of the promised goods or services are combined into a single performance obligation because one promise (the installation) significantly customises another promise (the software).

Example 28.34:   Determining whether goods or services are distinct (Case A and Case B)

Case A – Distinct goods or services

An entity, a software developer, enters into a contract with a customer to transfer a software licence, perform an installation service and provide unspecified software updates and technical support (online and telephone) for a two-year period. The entity sells the licence, installation service and technical support separately. The installation service includes changing the web screen for each type of user (for example, marketing, inventory management and information technology). The installation service is routinely performed by other entities and does not significantly modify the software. The software remains functional without the updates and the technical support.

The entity assesses the goods and services promised to the customer to determine which goods and services are distinct in accordance with paragraph 27 of IFRS 15. The entity observes that the software is delivered before the other goods and services and remains functional without the updates and the technical support. The customer can benefit from the updates together with the software licence transferred at the start of the contract. Thus, the entity concludes that the customer can benefit from each of the goods and services either on their own or together with the other goods and services that are readily available and the criterion in paragraph 27(a) of IFRS 15 is met.

The entity also considers the principle and the factors in paragraph 29 of IFRS 15 and determines that the promise to transfer each good and service to the customer is separately identifiable from each of the other promises (thus the criterion in paragraph 27(b) of IFRS 15 is met). In reaching this determination, the entity considers that, although it integrates the software into the customer's system, the installation services do not significantly affect the customer's ability to use and benefit from the software licence because the installation services are routine and can be obtained from alternative providers. The software updates do not significantly affect the customer's ability to use and benefit from the software licence during the licence period. The entity further observes that none of the promised goods or services significantly modify or customise one another, nor is the entity providing a significant service of integrating the software and the services into a combined output. Lastly, the entity concludes that the software and the services do not significantly affect each other and, therefore, are not highly interdependent or highly interrelated, because the entity would be able to fulfil its promise to transfer the initial software licence independently from its promise to subsequently provide the installation service, software updates or technical support.

On the basis of this assessment, the entity identifies four performance obligations in the contract for the following goods or services:

(a) the software licence;
(b) an installation service;
(c) software updates; and
(d) technical support.

The entity applies paragraphs 31-38 of IFRS 15 to determine whether each of the performance obligations for the installation service, software updates and technical support are satisfied at a point in time or over time. The entity also assesses the nature of the entity's promise to transfer the software licence in accordance with paragraph B58 of IFRS 15 (see Example 54 in paragraphs IE276-IE277).

Case B – Significant customisation

The promised goods and services are the same as in Case A, except that the contract specifies that, as part of the installation service, the software is to be substantially customised to add significant new functionality to enable the software to interface with other customised software applications used by the customer. The customised installation service can be provided by other entities.

The entity assesses the goods and services promised to the customer to determine which goods and services are distinct in accordance with paragraph 27 of IFRS 15. The entity first assesses whether the criterion in paragraph 27(a) has been met. For the same reasons as in Case A, the entity determines that the software licence, installation, software updates and technical support each meet that criterion. The entity next assesses whether the criterion in paragraph 27(b) has been met by evaluating the principle and the factors in paragraph 29 of IFRS 15. The entity observes that the terms of the contract result in a promise to provide a significant service of integrating the licensed software into the existing software system by performing a customised installation service as specified in the contract. In other words, the entity is using the licence and the customised installation service as inputs to produce the combined output (i.e. a functional and integrated software system) specified in the contract (see paragraph 29(a) of IFRS 15). The software is significantly modified and customised by the service (see paragraph 29(b) of IFRS 15). Consequently, the entity determines that the promise to transfer the licence is not separately identifiable from the customised installation service and, therefore, the criterion in paragraph 27(b) of IFRS 15 is not met. Thus, the software licence and the customised installation service are not distinct.

On the basis of the same analysis as in Case A, the entity concludes that the software updates and technical support are distinct from the other promises in the contract.

On the basis of this assessment, the entity identifies three performance obligations in the contract for the following goods or services:

(a) software customisation (which comprises the licence for the software and the customised installation service;
(b) software updates; and
(c) technical support.

The entity applies paragraphs 31-38 of IFRS 15 to determine whether each performance obligation is satisfied at a point in time or over time.

The following examples illustrate contracts that include multiple promised goods or services, all of which are determined to be distinct. The examples highlight the importance of considering both the separately identifiable principle and the underlying factors in paragraph 29 of IFRS 15. *[IFRS 15.IE58A-IE58K].*

Case C illustrates a contract that includes the sale of equipment and installation services. The equipment can be operated without any customisation or modification. The installation is not complex and can be performed by other entities. The entity determines that the two promises in the contract are distinct.

Case D illustrates that certain types of contractual restrictions, including those that require a customer to only use the entity's services, should not affect the evaluation of whether a promised good or service is distinct.

Case E illustrates a contract that includes the sale of equipment and specialised consumables to be used with the equipment. Even though the consumables can only be produced by the entity, they are sold separately. The entity determines that the two promises in the contract are distinct and the example walks through the analysis for determining whether the promises are capable of being distinct and distinct in the context of the contract. As part of this analysis, the entity concludes that the equipment and consumables are not highly interrelated nor highly interdependent because the two promises do not significantly affect each other. That is, the entity would be able to fulfil each of its promises in the contract independently of the other promises.

Example 28.35: Determining whether goods or services are distinct (Case C – Case E)

Case C – Promises are separately identifiable (installation)

An entity contracts with a customer to sell a piece of equipment and installation services. The equipment is operational without any customisation or modification. The installation required is not complex and is capable of being performed by several alternative service providers.

The entity identifies two promised goods and services in the contract: (a) equipment and (b) installation. The entity assesses the criteria in paragraph 27 of IFRS 15 to determine whether each promised good or service is distinct. The entity determines that the equipment and the installation each meet the criterion in paragraph 27(a) of IFRS 15. The customer can benefit from the equipment on its own, by using it or reselling it for an amount greater than scrap value, or together with other readily available resources (for example, installation services available from alternative providers). The customer also can benefit from the installation services together with other resources that the customer will already have obtained from the entity (i.e. the equipment).

The entity further determines that its promises to transfer the equipment and to provide the installation services are each separately identifiable (in accordance with paragraph 27(b) of IFRS 15). The entity considers the principle and the factors in paragraph 29 of IFRS 15 in determining that the equipment and the installation services are not inputs to a combined item in this contract. In this case, each of the factors in paragraph 29 of IFRS 15 contributes to, but is not individually determinative of, the conclusion that the equipment and the installation services are separately identifiable as follows:

(a) The entity is not providing a significant integration service. That is, the entity has promised to deliver the equipment and then install it; the entity would be able to fulfil its promise to transfer the equipment separately from its promise to subsequently install it. The entity has not promised to combine the equipment and the installation services in a way that would transform them into a combined output.

(b) The entity's installation services will not significantly customise or significantly modify the equipment.

(c) Although the customer can benefit from the installation services only after it has obtained control of the equipment, the installation services do not significantly affect the equipment because the entity would be able to fulfil its promise to transfer the equipment independently of its promise to provide the installation services. Because the equipment and the installation services do not each significantly affect the other, they are not highly interdependent or highly interrelated.

On the basis of this assessment, the entity identifies two performance obligations in the contract for the following goods or services:

(i) the equipment; and

(ii) installation services.

The entity applies paragraphs 31–38 of IFRS 15 to determine whether each performance obligation is satisfied at a point in time or over time.

Case D – Promises are separately identifiable (contractual restrictions)

Assume the same facts as in Case C, except that the customer is contractually required to use the entity's installation services.

The contractual requirement to use the entity's installation services does not change the evaluation of whether the promised goods and services are distinct in this case. This is because the contractual requirement to use the entity's installation services does not change the characteristics of the goods or services themselves, nor does it change the entity's promises to the customer. Although the customer is required to use the entity's installation services, the equipment and the installation services are capable of being distinct (i.e. they each meet the criterion in paragraph 27(a) of IFRS 15) and the entity's promises to provide the equipment and to provide the installation services are each separately identifiable, i.e. they each meet the criterion in paragraph 27(b) of IFRS 15. The entity's analysis in this regard is consistent with that in Case C.

Case E – Promises are separately identifiable (consumables)

An entity enters into a contract with a customer to provide a piece of off-the-shelf equipment (i.e. the equipment is operational without any significant customisation or modification) and to provide specialised consumables for use in the equipment at predetermined intervals over the next three years. The consumables are produced only by the entity, but are sold separately by the entity.

The entity determines that the customer can benefit from the equipment together with the readily available consumables. The consumables are readily available in accordance with paragraph 28 of IFRS 15, because they are regularly sold separately by the entity (i.e. through refill orders to customers that previously purchased the equipment). The customer can benefit from the consumables that will be delivered under the contract together with the delivered equipment that is transferred to the customer initially under the contract. Therefore, the equipment and the consumables are each capable of being distinct in accordance with paragraph 27(a) of IFRS 15.

The entity determines that its promises to transfer the equipment and to provide consumables over a three-year period are each separately identifiable in accordance with paragraph 27(b) of IFRS 15. In determining that the equipment and the consumables are not inputs to a combined item in this contract, the entity considers that it is not providing a significant integration service that transforms the equipment and consumables into a combined output. In addition, neither the equipment nor the consumables are significantly customised or modified by the other. Lastly, the entity concludes that the equipment and the consumables are not highly interdependent or highly interrelated because they do not significantly affect each other. Although the customer can benefit from the consumables in this contract only after it has obtained control of the equipment (i.e. the consumables would have no use without the equipment) and the consumables are required for the equipment to function, the equipment and the consumables do not each significantly affect the other. This is because the entity would be able to fulfil each of its promises in the contract independently of the other. That is, the entity would be able to fulfil its promise to transfer the equipment even if the customer did not purchase any consumables and would be able to fulfil its promise to provide the consumables, even if the customer acquired the equipment separately.

On the basis of this assessment, the entity identifies two performance obligations in the contract for the following goods or services:

(a) the equipment; and
(b) the consumables.

The entity applies paragraphs 31–38 of IFRS 15 to determine whether each performance obligation is satisfied at a point in time or over time.

3.3 Promised goods or services that are not distinct

If a promised good or service does not meet the criteria to be considered distinct, an entity is required to combine that good or service with other promised goods or services until the entity identifies a bundle of goods or services that, together, is distinct. This could result in an entity combining a good or service that is not considered distinct with another good or service that, on its own, would meet the criteria to be considered distinct (see 3.2.1 above). *[IFRS 15.30]*.

The standard provides two examples of contracts with promised goods or services that, while capable of being distinct, are not distinct in the context of the contract because of a significant integration service that combines the inputs (the underlying goods or services) into a combined output – see Example 28.33 at 3.2.3 above.

3.4 Principal versus agent considerations

When more than one party is involved in providing goods or services to a customer, the standard requires an entity to determine whether it is a principal or an agent in these transactions by evaluating the nature of its promise to the customer. An entity is a principal (and, therefore, records revenue on a gross basis) if it controls a promised good or service before transferring that good or service to the customer. *[IFRS 15.B35]*. An entity is an agent (and, therefore, records as revenue the net amount that it retains for its agency services) if its role is to arrange for another entity to provide the goods or services. *[IFRS 15.B36]*.

In the Basis for Conclusions, the Board explained that in order for an entity to conclude that it is providing the good or service to the customer, it must first control that good or service. That is, the entity cannot provide the good or service to a customer if the entity does not first control it. If an entity controls the good or service, the entity is a principal in the transaction. If an entity does not control the good or service before it is transferred to the customer, the entity is an agent in the transaction. *[IFRS 15.B36, BC385D]*.

In the Basis for Conclusions, the Board noted that an entity that itself manufactures a good or performs a service is always a principal if it transfers control of that good or service to another party. There is no need for such an entity to evaluate the principal versus agent application guidance because it transfers control of or provides its own good or service directly to its customer without the involvement of another party. For example, if an entity transfers control of a good to an intermediary that is a principal in providing that good to an end-customer, the entity records revenue as a principal in the sale of the good to its customer (the intermediary). *[IFRS 15.BC385E]*.

Entities need to carefully evaluate whether they are acting as principal or as an agent. The application guidance in IFRS 15 focuses on control of the specified goods or services as the overarching principle for entities to consider in determining whether they are acting as a principal or an agent. That is, an entity first evaluates whether it controls the specified good or service before reviewing the standard's principal indicators.

The standard states that when other parties are involved in providing the specified goods or services to an entity's customer, the entity must determine whether its performance obligation is to provide the specified good or service itself (i.e. the entity is a principal) or to arrange for another party to provide the specified good or service (i.e. the entity is an agent). An entity makes this determination for each specified good or service promised to the customer. The standard also notes that, if a contract includes more than one specified good or service, an entity could be a principal for some and an agent for others. *[IFRS 15.B34]*.

In order to determine the nature of its promise (as a principal or an agent), the entity must (a) identify the specified goods or services to be provided to the customer; and (b) assess whether it controls each specified good or service before that good or service is transferred to the customer. *[IFRS 15.B34A]*. As noted above, an entity is a principal if it controls a promised good or service before transferring that good or service to the customer. However, an entity may not necessarily control a specified good if it only momentarily obtains legal title to that good before legal title is transferred to a customer. Furthermore, the standard notes that a principal may satisfy its performance obligation to provide the specified good or service itself or it may engage another party to satisfy some, or all, of the performance obligation on its behalf. *[IFRS 15.B35]*.

Figure 28.7 illustrates the process for performing a principal versus agent evaluation.

Figure 28.7: *Principal versus agent evaluation*

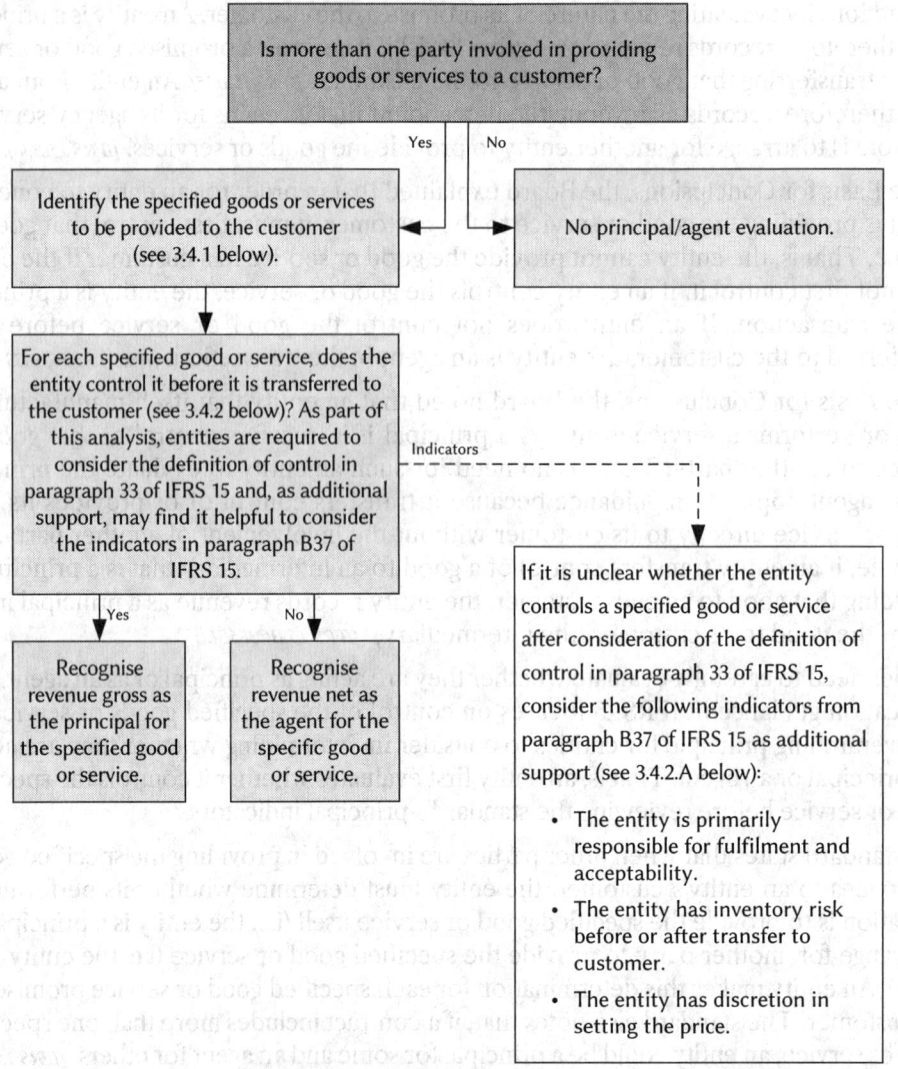

The principal versus agent application guidance applies regardless of the type of transaction under evaluation or the industry in which the entity operates. Entities that: (a) do not stock inventory and may employ independent warehouses or fulfilment houses to drop-ship merchandise to customers on their behalf; or (b) offer services to be provided by an independent service provider (e.g. travel agents, magazine subscription brokers and retailers that sell goods through catalogues or that

3.4.1 Identifying the specified good or service

In accordance with paragraph B34A of IFRS 15, an entity must first identify the specified good or service (or unit of account for the principal versus agent evaluation) to be provided to the customer in the contract in order to determine the nature of its promise (i.e. whether it is to provide the specified goods or services or to arrange for those goods or services to be provided by another party). A specified good or service is defined as 'a distinct good or service (or a distinct bundle of goods or services) to be provided to the customer'. *[IFRS 15.B34]*. While this definition is similar to that of a performance obligation (see 3.2 above), the IASB noted in the Basis for Conclusions that it created this new term because using 'performance obligation' would have been confusing in agency relationships. *[IFRS 15.BC385B]*. That is, because an agent's performance obligation is to arrange for goods or services to be provided by another party, providing the specified goods or services to the end-customer is not the agent's performance obligation.

A specified good or service may be a distinct good or service or a distinct bundle of goods or services. In the Basis for Conclusions, the Board noted that if individual goods or services are not distinct from one another, they may be inputs to a combined item and each good or service may represent only a part of a single promise to the customer. For example, in a contract in which goods or services provided by another party are inputs to a combined item (or items), the entity would assess whether it controls the combined item (or items) before that item (or items) is transferred to the customer. *[IFRS 15.BC385Q]*. That is, in determining whether it is a principal or an agent, an entity should evaluate that single promise to the customer, rather than the individual inputs that make up that promise.

Appropriately identifying the good or service to be provided is a critical step in determining whether an entity is a principal or an agent in a transaction. In many situations, especially those involving tangible goods, identifying the specified good or service is relatively straightforward. For example, if an entity is reselling laptop computers, the specified good that is transferred to the customer is a laptop computer.

However, the assessment may require significant judgement in other situations, such as those involving intangible goods or services. In accordance with paragraph B34A(a) of IFRS 15, the specified good or service may be the underlying good or service a customer ultimately wants to obtain (e.g. a flight, a meal) or a right to obtain that good or service (e.g. in the form of a ticket or voucher). *[IFRS 15.B34A(a)]*. In the Basis for Conclusions, the Board noted that when the specified good or service is a right to a good or service that will be provided by another party, the entity would determine whether its performance obligation is a promise to provide that right (and it is, therefore, a principal) or whether it is arranging for the other party to provide that right (and it is, therefore, an agent). The fact that the entity does not provide the underlying goods or services itself is not determinative. *[IFRS 15.BC385O]*.

The Board acknowledged that it may be difficult in some cases to determine whether the specified good or service is the underlying good or service, or a right to obtain that good or service. Therefore, it provided examples in the standard. Example 28.40 at 3.4.4 below involves an airline ticket reseller. In this example, the entity pre-purchases airline tickets that it will later sell to customers. While the customer ultimately wants airline travel, the conclusion in Example 28.40 is that the specified good or service is the right to fly on a specified flight (in the form of a ticket) and not the underlying flight itself. The entity itself does not fly the plane and it cannot change the service (e.g. change the flight time or destination). However, the entity obtained the ticket prior to identifying a specific customer to purchase the ticket. As a result, the entity holds an asset (in the form of a ticket) that represents a right to fly. The entity could, therefore, transfer that right to a customer (as depicted in the example) or decide to use the right itself.

Example 28.39 at 3.4.4 below involves an office maintenance service provider. In this example, the entity concludes that the specified good or service is the underlying office maintenance service (rather than a right to that service). While the entity obtained the contract with the customer prior to engaging a third party to perform the requested services, the right to the subcontractor's services never transfers to the customer. Instead, the entity retains the right to direct the service provider. That is, the entity can direct the right to use the subcontractor's services as it chooses (e.g. to fulfil the customer contract, to fulfil another customer contract, to service its own facilities). Furthermore, the customer in Example 28.39 is indifferent as to who carries out the office maintenance services. This is not the case in Example 28.40, in which the customer wants the ticket reseller to sell one of its tickets on a specific flight.

If a contract with a customer includes more than one specified good or service, IFRS 15 clarifies that an entity may be a principal for some specified goods or services and an agent for others. *[IFRS 15.B34]*. Example 28.42 at 3.4.4 below provides an illustration of this. Also consider the following example:

Example 28.36: Entity is both a principal and an agent

A software reseller sells software licences bundled with post-contract support (PCS) and other IT solutions to end-users. The reseller has entered into contracts with several software manufacturers that provide the reseller with the right to sell licences to the software with PCS to end-users during non-cancellable periods of time in exchange for fixed fees per licence sold. The reseller can set the prices it charges end-users, but is contractually required to pay the software manufacturer the fixed fee, regardless of the price paid by end-users. The software reseller does not have a commitment to make a minimum number of purchases from the software manufacturer and does not make purchases in advance.

The software reseller is responsible for identifying which software will address the customer's needs (including the feasibility of integrating it with the customer's existing technology environment), ordering the software from the manufacturer, assisting customers if they encounter issues downloading the software (all software is provided electronically) and with other basic technical support. The software manufacturer provides higher levels of technical support and provides PCS directly to the customer.

As part of its principal-versus-agent evaluation for these contracts, the software reseller determines that the software licence and PCS are separate specified goods or services.

When assessing control for the software licence, the reseller concludes that it controls the software licence before the licence is provided to the end-user. This is because the reseller has the right to direct the software manufacturer to provide the software to the end-user on the reseller's behalf. As part of this assessment, the software reseller also considers the three indicators of control in the standard and makes the following determinations that support its overall control evaluation:

- the software reseller is responsible for fulfilling the promise to the customer and the entity takes responsibility for much of the purchasing process, as described above;
- there is no inventory risk associated with the software provided electronically; and
- the software reseller has discretion to establish prices.

Conversely, the reseller concludes that it does not control the PCS before it is provided to the end-user because the software manufacturer creates the updates that it delivers electronically to end-users of the software directly through the internet and all but the most basic level of technical support will be provided by the software manufacturer. As part of this assessment, the software reseller also considers the three indicators of control in the standard and makes the following determinations that support its overall control evaluation:

- the software manufacturer is responsible for fulfilling the promise to the customer because it provides the updates directly to the end-users;
- there is no inventory risk associated with the PCS provided electronically; and
- the software reseller has discretion to establish prices.

The software reseller believes that the first of the indicators is the most relevant to consider in this assessment and that it supports its overall control assessment. Therefore, the software reseller concludes that it is the principal for the software licence, but is an agent for the PCS, because it does not control the PCS before it is transferred to the end-user.

As discussed above, appropriately identifying the specified good or service to be provided to the customer is a critical step in identifying whether the nature of an entity's promise is to act as a principal or an agent. Entities need to carefully examine their contract terms and may need to apply significant judgement to determine whether the specified good or service is the underlying good or service or a right to obtain that good or service.

3.4.2 Control of the specified good or service

In accordance with paragraph B34A of IFRS 15, the second step in determining the nature of the entity's promise (i.e. whether it is to provide the specified goods or services or to arrange for those goods or services to be provided by another party) is for the entity to determine whether the entity controls the specified good or service before it is transferred to the customer. An entity cannot provide the specified good or service to a customer (and, therefore, be a principal) unless it controls that good or service prior to its transfer. That is, as the Board noted in the Basis for Conclusions, control is the determining factor when assessing whether an entity is a principal or an agent. *[IFRS 15.BC385S]*.

In assessing whether an entity controls the specified good or service prior to transfer to the customer, paragraph B34A(b) of IFRS 15 requires the entity to consider the definition of control that is included in Step 5 of the model, in accordance with paragraph 33 of IFRS 15 (discussed further in Chapter 30). *[IFRS 15.B34A(b)]*. 'Control of an asset refers to the ability to direct the use of, and obtain substantially all of the remaining benefits from, the asset. Control includes the ability to prevent other entities from directing the use of, and obtaining the benefits from, an asset. The benefits of an asset are the potential cash flows (inflows or savings in outflows) that can be obtained directly or indirectly in many ways, such as by:

(a) using the asset to produce goods or provide services (including public services);

(b) using the asset to enhance the value of other assets;

(c) using the asset to settle liabilities or reduce expenses;

(d) selling or exchanging the asset;

(e) pledging the asset to secure a loan; and

(f) holding the asset.' *[IFRS 15.33]*.

When evaluating the definition of control in paragraph 33 of IFRS 15, we believe it could be helpful for entities to consider the indicators in paragraph 38 of IFRS 15 (discussed further in Chapter 30 at 4) that the IASB included to help determine the point in time when a customer obtains control of a particular good or service (e.g. legal title, physical possession, risks and rewards of ownership). *[IFRS 15.38]*.

If, after evaluating the requirement in paragraph 33 of IFRS 15, an entity concludes that it controls the specified good or service before it is transferred to the customer, the entity is a principal in the transaction. If the entity does not control that good or service before transfer to the customer, it is an agent.

Stakeholder feedback indicated that the control principle was easier to apply to tangible goods than to intangible goods or services because intangible goods or services generally exist only at the moment they are delivered. To address this concern, the standard includes application guidance on how the control principle applies to certain types of arrangements (including service transactions) by explaining what a principal controls before the specified good or service is transferred to the customer. Specifically, the standard states that '[w]hen another party is involved in providing goods or services to a customer, an entity that is a principal obtains control of any one of the following:

(a) a good or another asset from the other party that it then transfers to the customer.

(b) a right to a service to be performed by the other party, which gives the entity the ability to direct that party to provide the service to the customer on the entity's behalf.

(c) a good or service from the other party that it then combines with other goods or services in providing the specified good or service to the customer. For example, if an entity provides a significant service of integrating goods or services (see paragraph 29(a)) provided by another party into the specified good or service for which the customer has contracted, the entity controls the specified good or service before that good or service is transferred to the customer. This is because the entity first obtains control of the inputs to the specified good or service (which includes goods or services from other parties) and directs their use to create the combined output that is the specified good or service.' *[IFRS 15.B35A]*.

In the Basis for Conclusions, the Board observed that an entity can control a service to be provided by another party when it controls the right to the specified service that will be provided to the customer. *[IFRS 15.BC385U]*. Generally, the entity then either transfers the right (in the form of an asset, such as a ticket) to its customer, in accordance with paragraph B35A(a) of IFRS 15 (as in Example 28.40 at 3.4.4 below involving the airline ticket reseller that is discussed at 3.4.1 above), or uses its right to direct the other party to provide the specified service to the customer on the entity's behalf, in accordance with paragraph B35A(b) of IFRS 15 (as in Example 28.39 at 3.4.4 below involving the office maintenance services that is discussed at 3.4.1 above).

The condition described in paragraph B35A(a) of IFRS 15 includes contracts in which an entity transfers to the customer a right to a future service to be provided by another party. If the specified good or service is a right to a good or service to be provided by another party, the entity evaluates whether it controls the right to the goods or services before that right is transferred to the customer (rather than whether it controls the underlying goods or services). In the Basis for Conclusions, the Board noted that, in assessing such rights, it is often relevant to assess whether the right is created only when it is obtained by the customer or whether the right exists before the customer obtains it. If the right does not exist before the customer obtains it, an entity would not be able to control right before it is transferred to the customer. [IFRS 15.BC385O].

The standard includes two examples to illustrate this point. In Example 28.40 (discussed at 3.4.1 above and included at 3.4.4 below), which involves an airline ticket reseller, the specified good or service is determined to be the right to fly on a specified flight (in the form of a ticket). One of the determining factors for the principal-agent evaluation in this example is that the entity pre-purchases the airline tickets before a specific customer is identified. Accordingly, the right existed prior to a customer obtaining it. The example concludes that the entity controls the right before it is transferred to the customer (and is, therefore, a principal).

In Example 28.41 (included at 3.4.4 below), an entity sells vouchers that entitle customers to future meals at specified restaurants selected by the customer. The specified good or service is determined to be the right to a meal (in the form of a voucher). One of the determining factors for the principal-agent evaluation is that the entity does not control the voucher (the right to a meal) at any time. It does not pre-purchase or commit itself to purchase the vouchers from the restaurants before they are sold to a customer. Instead, the entity waits to purchase the voucher until a customer requests a voucher for a particular restaurant. In addition, vouchers are created only at the time that they are transferred to a customer and do not exist before that transfer. Accordingly, the right does not exist before the customer obtains it. Therefore, the entity does not at any time have the ability to direct the use of the vouchers or obtain substantially all of the remaining benefits from the vouchers before they are transferred to customers. The example concludes that the entity does not control the right before it is transferred to the customer (and is, therefore, an agent).

In the Basis for Conclusions, the IASB acknowledged that determining whether an entity is a principal or an agent may be more difficult when evaluating whether a contract falls under paragraph B35A(b) of IFRS 15. That is, it may be difficult to determine whether an entity has the ability to direct another party to provide the service on its behalf (and is, therefore, a principal) or is only arranging for the other party to provide the service (and is, therefore, an agent). As depicted in Example 28.39 (as discussed at 3.4.1 above and included at 3.4.4 below), an entity could control the right to the specified service and be a principal by entering into a contract with the subcontractor in which the entity defines the scope of service to be performed by the subcontractor on its behalf. This situation is equivalent to the entity fulfilling the contract using its own resources. Furthermore, the entity remains responsible for the satisfactory provision of the specified service in accordance with the contract with the customer. In contrast, when the specified service is provided by another party and the entity does not have the ability to direct those services, the entity typically is an agent because the entity is facilitating, rather than controlling the rights to, the service. [IFRS 15.BC385V].

In a speech, a member of the SEC staff described a consultation with OCA regarding a registrant that had performed some of the specified services for its customer, but had fully relied on another service provider for others, due to certain regulatory restrictions. The SEC staff member noted that it was critical to evaluate whether the entity could control the specified services before transferring them to the customer. In this case, the registrant was able to demonstrate that it had the contractual ability to control the other service provider by determining when the service provider delivered the services because the service provider could not contractually deny services to the customer, even though the service provider had discretion in how it fulfilled its obligations. The registrant concluded, and the SEC staff did not object, that the registrant was the principal in the arrangement, based on this analysis and an analysis of the other relevant indicators of control (e.g. the registrant was responsible for handling most customer concerns that arose from the services provided by the other service provider).[36]

In accordance with paragraph B35A(c) of IFRS 15, if an entity provides a significant service of integrating two or more goods or services into a combined item that is the specified good or service the customer contracted to receive, the entity controls that specified good or service before it is transferred to the customer. This is because the entity first obtains control of the inputs to the specified good or service (which can include goods or services from other parties) and directs their use to create the combined item that is the specified good or service. The inputs would be a fulfilment cost to the entity. However, as noted by the Board in the Basis for Conclusions, if a third party provides the significant integration service, the entity's customer for its good or services (which would be inputs to the specified good or service) is likely to be the third party. *[IFRS 15.BC385R]*.

3.4.2.A   Principal indicators

After considering the application guidance discussed above, it still may not be clear whether an entity controls the specified good or service. Therefore, the standard provides three indicators of when an entity controls the specified good or service (and is, therefore, a principal):

'Indicators that an entity controls the specified good or service before it is transferred to the customer (and is therefore a principal (see paragraph B35)) include, but are not limited to, the following:

(a)   the entity is primarily responsible for fulfilling the promise to provide the specified good or service. This typically includes responsibility for the acceptability of the specified good or service (for example, primary responsibility for the good or service meeting customer specifications). If the entity is primarily responsible for fulfilling the promise to provide the specified good or service, this may indicate that the other party involved in providing the specified good or service is acting on the entity's behalf.

(b)   the entity has inventory risk before the specified good or service has been transferred to a customer or after transfer of control to the customer (for example, if the customer has a right of return). For example, if the entity obtains, or commits itself to obtain, the specified good or service before obtaining a contract with a customer, that may indicate that the entity has the ability to direct the use of, and obtain substantially all of the remaining benefits from, the good or service before it is transferred to the customer.

(c)   the entity has discretion in establishing the price for the specified good or service. Establishing the price that the customer pays for the specified good or service may indicate that the entity has the ability to direct the use of that good or service and obtain substantially all of the remaining benefits. However, an agent can have discretion in establishing prices in some cases. For example, an agent may have some flexibility in setting prices in order to generate additional revenue from its service of arranging for goods or services to be provided by other parties to customers.' *[IFRS 15.B37]*.

The principal indicators above are meant to support an entity's assessment of control, not to replace it. Each indicator explains how it supports the assessment of control. As emphasised in the Basis for Conclusions, the indicators do not override the assessment of control, should not be viewed in isolation and do not constitute a separate or additional evaluation. Furthermore, they should not be considered a checklist of criteria to be met or factors to be considered in all scenarios. Paragraph B37A of IFRS 15 notes that considering one or more of the indicators will often be helpful and, depending on the facts and circumstances, individual indicators will be more or less relevant or persuasive to the assessment of control. *[IFRS 15.B37A, BC385H]*. If an entity reaches different conclusions about whether it controls the specified good or service by applying the standard's definition of control versus the principal indicators, the entity should re-evaluate its assessment, considering the facts and circumstances of its contract. This is because an entity's conclusions about control and the principal indicators should align.

The first indicator that an entity is a principal, in paragraph B37(a) of IFRS 15, is that the entity is primarily responsible for fulfilling the promise to provide the specified good or service to the customer, which typically includes responsibility for the acceptability of the specified good or service. We believe that one of the reasons that this indicator supports the assessment of control of the specified good or service is because an entity generally controls a specified good or service that it is responsible for transferring control to a customer.

The terms of the contract and representations (written or otherwise) made by an entity during marketing generally provide evidence of which party is responsible for fulfilling the promise to provide the specified good or service and for the acceptability of that good or service.

It is possible that one entity may not be solely responsible for both providing the specified good or service and for the acceptability of that same good or service. For example, a reseller may sell goods or services that are provided to the customer by a supplier. However, if the customer is dissatisfied with the goods or services it receives, the reseller may be solely responsible for providing a remedy to the customer. The reseller may promote such a role during the marketing process or may agree to such a role as claims arise in order to maintain its relationship with its customer. In this situation, both the reseller and the supplier possess characteristics of this indicator. Therefore, it is likely that other indicators will need to be considered to determine which entity is the principal. However, if the reseller is responsible for providing a remedy to a dissatisfied customer, but can then pursue a claim against the supplier to recoup any remedies it provides, that may indicate that the reseller is not ultimately responsible for the acceptability of the specified good or service.

The second indicator that an entity is a principal, in paragraph B37(b) of IFRS 15, is that the entity has inventory risk (before the specified good or service is transferred to the customer or upon customer return). Inventory risk is the risk normally taken by an entity that acquires inventory in the hope of reselling it at a profit. Inventory risk exists if a reseller obtains (or commits to obtain) the specified good or service before it is ordered by a customer. Inventory risk also exists if a customer has a right of return and the reseller will take back the specified good or service if the customer exercises that right.

This indicator supports the assessment of control of the specified good or service because when an entity obtains (or commits to obtain) the specified good or service before it has contracted with a customer, it is likely that the entity has the ability to direct the use of and obtain substantially all of the remaining benefits from the good or service. For example, inventory risk can exist in a customer arrangement involving the provision of services if an entity is obliged to compensate the individual service provider(s) for work performed, regardless of whether the customer accepts that work. However, this indicator often does not apply to intangible goods or services.

Factors may exist that mitigate a reseller's inventory risk. For example, a reseller's inventory risk may be significantly reduced or eliminated if it has the right to return to the supplier goods it cannot sell or goods that are returned by customers. Another example is if a reseller receives inventory price protection from the supplier. In these cases, the inventory risk indicator may be less relevant or persuasive to the assessment of control.

The third principal indicator, in paragraph B37(c) of IFRS 15, is that the entity has discretion in establishing the price of the specified good or service. Reasonable latitude, within economic constraints, to establish the price with a customer for the product or service may indicate that the entity has the ability to direct the use of that good or service and obtain substantially all of the remaining benefits (i.e. the entity controls the specified good or service). However, because an agent may also have discretion in establishing the price of the specified good or service, the facts and circumstances of the transaction need to be carefully evaluated.

The example below, which is similar to Example 45 in the standard, shows how an entity might conclude that it is an agent:

Example 28.37: Entity is an agent

An entity operates a website that provides a marketplace for customers to purchase goods from a variety of suppliers who deliver the goods directly to the customers. The entity's website facilitates customer payments to suppliers at prices that are set by the suppliers. The entity requires payment from customers before orders are processed, and all orders are non-refundable. The entity has no further obligations to the customers after arranging for the products to be provided to them; the entity is not responsible for the acceptability of goods provided to customers.

First, the entity evaluates the specified goods and concludes that there are no other goods or services provided to the customer except for those provided directly by the suppliers. Next, the entity considers whether it controls the specified goods before they are transferred to the customers. Since the entity does not at any time have the ability to direct the use of the goods transferred to the customers, the entity concludes that it does not control the specified goods before they are transferred. As part of this assessment, the entity considers the three indicators of control in the standard and makes the following determinations that support its overall control evaluation:

- The suppliers are responsible for fulfilling the promise to the customer, and the entity does not take responsibility for the acceptability of the goods.
- The entity does not have inventory risk because it does not obtain the goods at any time.
- The entity does not have discretion to establish prices because they are set by the suppliers.

The entity concludes that it is an agent for the goods sold through its website because the nature of its performance obligation is to arrange for goods to be provided to the customers.

Revenue: identify the contract and performance obligations

In contrast, consider the following example of an entity that concludes it is acting as a principal:

Example 28.38:   Entity is a principal

An entity operates a website that provides a marketplace for customers to purchase digital content. The entity has entered into contracts with suppliers that provide it with the right to sell the digital content during a non-cancellable period of time in exchange for a fixed fee per unit of content. The entity can set the price for the content to be sold to customers on its website. The entity is contractually required to pay the supplier a fixed price or rate for any digital content it sells to its customers and that price or rate is unaffected by the price paid by the end-customers. The entity is responsible for assisting customers if they encounter issues downloading the content or with the user experience, and customers do not interact with the suppliers.

The entity first evaluates the specified goods and concludes that the digital content is the only specified good or service. Next, the entity considers whether it controls the digital content before it is transferred to the customer. The entity concludes that it controls the specified goods before they are transferred because it has entered into a non-cancellable distribution agreement that permits the entity to sell the digital content to its customers. This conclusion differs from the entity's conclusion in Example 28.37 above because that entity provided a platform to connect suppliers to customers and did not have the ability to sell the suppliers' goods. As part of this assessment, the entity also considers the three indicators of control in the standard and makes the following determinations that support its overall control evaluation:

- The entity is responsible for fulfilling the promise to the customer and the entity takes responsibility for the acceptability of the digital content.
- There is no inventory risk associated with digital content.
- The entity has discretion to establish prices.

The entity concludes that it is a principal for the digital content sold through its website because it controls the content before it is transferred to the customer.

3.4.3   Recognising revenue as principal or agent

The determination of whether the entity is acting as a principal or an agent affects the amount of revenue the entity recognises. When the entity is the principal in the arrangement, the revenue recognised is the gross amount to which the entity expects to be entitled. *[IFRS 15.B35B]*. When the entity is the agent, the revenue recognised is the net amount that the entity is entitled to retain in return for its services as the agent. The entity's fee or commission may be the net amount of consideration that the entity retains after paying the other party the consideration received in exchange for the goods or services to be provided by that party. *[IFRS 15.B36]*.

After an entity determines whether it is the principal or the agent and the amount of gross or net revenue that would be recognised, the entity recognises revenue when or as it satisfies its performance obligation. An entity satisfies its performance obligation by transferring control of the specified good or service underlying the performance obligation, either at a point in time or over time (as discussed in Chapter 30). That is, a principal would recognise revenue when (or as) it transfers the specified good or service to the customer. An agent would recognise revenue when its performance obligation to arrange for the specified good or service is complete.

In the Basis for Conclusions, the Board noted that, in some contracts in which the entity is the agent, control of specified goods or services promised by the agent may transfer before the customer receives related goods or services from the principal. For example, an entity might satisfy its promise to provide customers with loyalty points when those points are transferred to the customer if:

- the entity's promise is to provide loyalty points to customers when the customer purchases goods or services from the entity;
- the points entitle the customers to future discounted purchases with another party (i.e. the points represent a material right to a future discount); or
- the entity determines that it is an agent (i.e. its promise is to arrange for the customers to be provided with points) and the entity does not control those points (i.e. the specified good or service) before they are transferred to the customer.

In contrast, if the points entitle the customers to future goods or services to be provided by the entity, the entity may conclude it is not an agent. This is because the entity's promise is to provide those future goods or services and, therefore, the entity controls both the points and the future goods or services before they are transferred to the customer. In these cases, the entity's performance obligation may only be satisfied when the future goods or services are provided.

In other cases, the points may entitle customers to choose between future goods or services provided by either the entity or another party. For example, many airlines allow loyalty programme members to redeem loyalty points for goods or services provided by a partner (e.g. travel on another airline, hotel accommodation). In this situation, the nature of the entity's performance obligation may not be known until the customer makes its choice. That is, until the customer has chosen the goods or services to be provided (and, therefore, whether the entity or the third party will provide those goods or services), the entity is obliged to stand ready to deliver goods or services. Therefore, the entity may not satisfy its performance obligation until it either delivers the goods or services or is no longer obliged to stand ready. If the customer subsequently chooses to receive the goods or services from another party, the entity would need to consider whether it was acting as an agent and would, therefore, only recognise revenue for a fee or commission that it received for arranging the ultimate transaction between the customer and the third party. *[IFRS 15.BC383-BC385]*.

The above discussion illustrates that control of specified goods or services promised by an agent may transfer before the customer receives related goods or services from the principal. An entity needs to assess each loyalty programme in accordance with the principles of the principal versus agent application guidance to determine if revenue would be reported on a gross or net basis.

Although an entity may be able to transfer its obligation to provide its customer specified goods or services, the standard says that such a transfer may not always satisfy the performance obligation. Specifically, it states that '[i]f another entity assumes the entity's performance obligations and contractual rights in the contract so that the entity is no longer obliged to satisfy the performance obligation to transfer the specified good or service to the customer (i.e. the entity is no longer acting as the principal), the entity shall not recognise revenue for that performance obligation. Instead, the entity shall evaluate whether to recognise revenue for satisfying a performance obligation to obtain a contract for the other party (i.e. whether the entity is acting as an agent).' *[IFRS 15.B38]*.

3.4.4 Examples of principal versus agent considerations

The standard includes six examples to illustrate the principal versus agent application guidance discussed above. We have extracted four of them below.

The standard includes the following example of when the specified good or service (see 3.4.1 above) is the underlying service, rather than the right to obtain that service. The entity in this example is determined to be a principal. [IFRS 15.IE238A-IE238G].

Example 28.39: **Promise to provide goods or services (entity is a principal) (office maintenance service)**

An entity enters into a contract with a customer to provide office maintenance services. The entity and the customer define and agree on the scope of the services and negotiate the price. The entity is responsible for ensuring that the services are performed in accordance with the terms and conditions in the contract. The entity invoices the customer for the agreed-upon price on a monthly basis with 10-day payment terms.

The entity regularly engages third-party service providers to provide office maintenance services to its customers. When the entity obtains a contract from a customer, the entity enters into a contract with one of those service providers, directing the service provider to perform office maintenance services for the customer. The payment terms in the contracts with the service providers are generally aligned with the payment terms in the entity's contracts with customers. However, the entity is obliged to pay the service provider even if the customer fails to pay.

To determine whether the entity is a principal or an agent, the entity identifies the specified good or service to be provided to the customer and assesses whether it controls that good or service before the good or service is transferred to the customer.

The entity observes that the specified services to be provided to the customer are the office maintenance services for which the customer contracted, and that no other goods or services are promised to the customer. While the entity obtains a right to office maintenance services from the service provider after entering into the contract with the customer, that right is not transferred to the customer. That is, the entity retains the ability to direct the use of, and obtain substantially all the remaining benefits from, that right. For example, the entity can decide whether to direct the service provider to provide the office maintenance services for that customer, or for another customer, or at its own facilities. The customer does not have a right to direct the service provider to perform services that the entity has not agreed to provide. Therefore, the right to office maintenance services obtained by the entity from the service provider is not the specified good or service in its contract with the customer.

The entity concludes that it controls the specified services before they are provided to the customer. The entity obtains control of a right to office maintenance services after entering into the contract with the customer but before those services are provided to the customer. The terms of the entity's contract with the service provider give the entity the ability to direct the service provider to provide the specified services on the entity's behalf (see paragraph B35A(b)). In addition, the entity concludes that the following indicators in paragraph B37 of IFRS 15 provide further evidence that the entity controls the office maintenance services before they are provided to the customer:

(a) the entity is primarily responsible for fulfilling the promise to provide office maintenance services. Although the entity has hired a service provider to perform the services promised to the customer, it is the entity itself that is responsible for ensuring that the services are performed and are acceptable to the customer (i.e. the entity is responsible for fulfilment of the promise in the contract, regardless of whether the entity performs the services itself or engages a third-party service provider to perform the services).

(b) the entity has discretion in setting the price for the services to the customer.

The entity observes that it does not commit itself to obtain the services from the service provider before obtaining the contract with the customer. Thus, the entity has mitigated inventory risk with respect to the office maintenance services. Nonetheless, the entity concludes that it controls the office maintenance services before they are provided to the customer on the basis of the evidence in paragraph IE238E.

Thus, the entity is a principal in the transaction and recognises revenue in the amount of consideration to which it is entitled from the customer in exchange for the office maintenance services.

The standard also includes the following example of when the specified good or service is the right to obtain a service and not the underlying service itself. The entity in this example is determined to be a principal. *[IFRS 15.IE239-IE243]*.

Example 28.40: Promise to provide goods or services (entity is a principal) (airline tickets)

An entity negotiates with major airlines to purchase tickets at reduced rates compared with the price of tickets sold directly by the airlines to the public. The entity agrees to buy a specific number of tickets and must pay for those tickets regardless of whether it is able to resell them. The reduced rate paid by the entity for each ticket purchased is negotiated and agreed in advance.

The entity determines the prices at which the airline tickets will be sold to its customers. The entity sells the tickets and collects the consideration from customers when the tickets are purchased.

The entity also assists the customers in resolving complaints with the service provided by the airlines. However, each airline is responsible for fulfilling obligations associated with the ticket, including remedies to a customer for dissatisfaction with the service.

To determine whether the entity's performance obligation is to provide the specified goods or services itself (i.e. the entity is a principal) or to arrange for those goods or services to be provided by another party (i.e. the entity is an agent), the entity identifies the specified good or service to be provided to the customer and assesses whether it controls that good or service before the good or service is transferred to the customer.

The entity concludes that, with each ticket that it commits itself to purchase from the airline, it obtains control of a right to fly on a specified flight (in the form of a ticket) that the entity then transfers to one of its customers (see paragraph B35A(a)). Consequently, the entity determines that the specified good or service to be provided to its customer is that right (to a seat on a specific flight) that the entity controls. The entity observes that no other goods or services are promised to the customer.

The entity controls the right to each flight before it transfers that specified right to one of its customers because the entity has the ability to direct the use of that right by deciding whether to use the ticket to fulfil a contract with a customer and, if so, which contract it will fulfil. The entity also has the ability to obtain the remaining benefits from that right by either reselling the ticket and obtaining all of the proceeds from the sale or, alternatively, using the ticket itself.

The indicators in paragraphs B37(b)–(c) of IFRS 15 also provide relevant evidence that the entity controls each specified right (ticket) before it is transferred to the customer. The entity has inventory risk with respect to the ticket because the entity committed itself to obtain the ticket from the airline before obtaining a contract with a customer to purchase the ticket. This is because the entity is obliged to pay the airline for that right regardless of whether it is able to obtain a customer to resell the ticket to or whether it can obtain a favourable price for the ticket. The entity also establishes the price that the customer will pay for the specified ticket.

Thus, the entity concludes that it is a principal in the transactions with customers. The entity recognises revenue in the gross amount of consideration to which it is entitled in exchange for the tickets transferred to the customers.

In the following example, the entity also determines that the specified good or service is the right to obtain a service and not the underlying service itself. However, the entity in this example is determined to be an agent. *[IFRS 15.IE244-IE248]*.

Example 28.41: Arranging for the provision of goods or services (entity is an agent)

An entity sells vouchers that entitle customers to future meals at specified restaurants. The sales price of the voucher provides the customer with a significant discount when compared with the normal selling prices of the meals (for example, a customer pays CU100 for a voucher that entitles the customer to a meal at a restaurant that would otherwise cost CU200). The entity does not purchase or commit itself to purchase vouchers in advance of the sale of a voucher to a customer; instead, it purchases vouchers only as they are requested by the customers. The entity sells the vouchers through its website and the vouchers are non-refundable.

The entity and the restaurants jointly determine the prices at which the vouchers will be sold to customers. Under the terms of its contracts with the restaurants, the entity is entitled to 30 per cent of the voucher price when it sells the voucher.

The entity also assists the customers in resolving complaints about the meals and has a buyer satisfaction programme. However, the restaurant is responsible for fulfilling obligations associated with the voucher, including remedies to a customer for dissatisfaction with the service.

To determine whether the entity is a principal or an agent, the entity identifies the specified good or service to be provided to the customer and assess whether it controls the specified good or service before that good or service is transferred to the customer.

A customer obtains a voucher for the restaurant that it selects. The entity does not engage the restaurants to provide meals to customers on the entity's behalf as described in the indicator in paragraph B37(a) of IFRS 15. Therefore, the entity observes that the specified good or service to be provided to the customer is the right to a meal (in the form of a voucher) at a specified restaurant or restaurants, which the customer purchases and then can use itself or transfer to another person. The entity also observes that no other goods or services (other than the vouchers) are promised to the customers.

The entity concludes that it does not control the voucher (right to a meal) at any time. In reaching this conclusion, the entity principally considers the following:

(a) the vouchers are created only at the time that they are transferred to the customers and, thus, do not exist before that transfer. Therefore, the entity does not at any time have the ability to direct the use of the vouchers, or obtain substantially all of the remaining benefits from the vouchers, before they are transferred to customers.

(b) the entity neither purchases, nor commits itself to purchase, vouchers before they are sold to customers. The entity also has no responsibility to accept any returned vouchers. Therefore, the entity does not have inventory risk with respect to the vouchers as described in the indicator in paragraph B37(b) of IFRS 15.

Thus, the entity concludes that it is an agent with respect to the vouchers. The entity recognises revenue in the net amount of consideration to which the entity will be entitled in exchange for arranging for the restaurants to provide vouchers to customers for the restaurants' meals, which is the 30 per cent commission it is entitled to upon the sale of each voucher.

Paragraph B34 of IFRS 15 clarifies that an entity may be a principal for some specified goods or services in a contract and an agent for others. The standard includes the following example of a contract in which an entity is both a principal and an agent. [IFRS 15.IE248A-IE248F].

Example 28.42: Entity is a principal and an agent in the same contract

An entity sells services to assist its customers in more effectively targeting potential recruits for open job positions. The entity performs several services itself, such as interviewing candidates and performing background checks. As part of the contract with a customer, the customer agrees to obtain a licence to access a third party's database of information on potential recruits. The entity arranges for this licence with the third party, but the customer contracts directly with the database provider for the licence. The entity collects payment on behalf of the third-party database provider as part of the entity's overall invoicing to the customer. The database provider sets the price charged to the customer for the licence, and is responsible for providing technical support and credits to which the customer may be entitled for service down time or other technical issues.

To determine whether the entity is a principal or an agent, the entity identifies the specified goods or services to be provided to the customer, and assesses whether it controls those goods or services before they are transferred to the customer.

For the purpose of this example, it is assumed that the entity concludes that its recruitment services and the database access licence are each distinct on the basis of its assessment of the requirements in paragraphs 27-30 of IFRS 15. Accordingly, there are two specified goods or services to be provided to the customer – access to the third party's database and recruitment services.

The entity concludes that it does not control the access to the database before it is provided to the customer. The entity does not at any time have the ability to direct the use of the licence because the customer contracts for the licence directly with the database provider. The entity does not control access to the provider's database – it cannot, for example, grant access to the database to a party other than the customer, or prevent the database provider from providing access to the customer.

As part of reaching that conclusion, the entity also considers the indicators in paragraph B37 of IFRS 15. The entity concludes that these indicators provide further evidence that it does not control access to the database before that access is provided to the customer:

(a) the entity is not responsible for fulfilling the promise to provide the database access service. The customer contracts for the licence directly with the third-party database provider and the database provider is responsible for the acceptability of the database access (for example, by providing technical support or service credits).

(b) the entity does not have inventory risk because it does not purchase, or commit itself to purchase, the database access before the customer contracts for database access directly with the database provider.

(c) the entity does not have discretion in setting the price for the database access with the customer because the database provider sets that price.

Thus, the entity concludes that it is an agent in relation to the third party's database service. In contrast, the entity concludes that it is the principal in relation to the recruitment services because the entity performs those services itself and no other party is involved in providing those services to the customer.

The FASB's standard allows an entity to make an accounting policy choice to present revenue net of certain types of taxes collected from a customer (including sales, use, value-added and some excise taxes). The FASB included this policy choice to address a concern expressed by stakeholders in the US as to the operability of the requirements under US GAAP. IFRS 15 does not provide a similar accounting policy choice for the following reasons: it would reduce comparability; the requirements in IFRS 15 are consistent with those in legacy IFRS; and it would create an exception to the five-step model. *[IFRS 15.BC188D]*. Since entities do not have a similar accounting policy choice under IFRS, differences could arise between IFRS and US GAAP.

Another difference relates to determining the transaction price when an entity is the principal, but is unable to determine the ultimate price charged to the customer. In the Basis for Conclusions on its May 2016 amendments, the FASB stated that, if uncertainty related to the transaction price is not ultimately expected to be resolved, it would not meet the definition of variable consideration and, therefore, should not be included in the transaction price.[37] Stakeholders had raised a question about how an entity that is a principal would estimate the amount of revenue to recognise if it were not aware of the amounts being charged to end-customers by an intermediary that is an agent. The IASB did not specifically consider how the transaction price requirements would be applied in these situations (i.e. when an entity that is a principal does not know and expects not to know the price charged to its customer by an agent), but concluded in the Basis for Conclusions that an entity that is a principal would generally be able to apply judgement and determine the consideration to which it is entitled using all information available to it. *[IFRS 15.BC385Z]*. Accordingly, we believe that it is possible that IFRS and US GAAP entities will reach different conclusions on estimating the gross transaction price in these situations.

3.4.5 Application questions on principal versus agent considerations

3.4.5.A Considerations when there is only momentary transfer of legal title and absence of physical possession

An entity's determination of whether it is a principal or an agent in a transaction for a specified good for which it only takes title momentarily or never has physical possession requires significant judgement and careful consideration of the facts and circumstances.

Entities may enter into contracts with third-party vendors (the vendors) to provide goods or services to be sold through their sales channels to their customers. In these arrangements, the entity may take legal title to the good only momentarily before the good is transferred to the customer, such as in scan-based trading or 'flash title' contracts (e.g. vendor is responsible for stocking, rotating and otherwise managing the product until the final point of sale). Alternatively, the entity may never take physical possession or legal title to the good (e.g. 'drop shipment arrangements' when goods are shipped directly from a vendor to the customer). In these situations, the entity needs to carefully evaluate whether it obtains control of the specified good and, therefore, is the principal in the transaction with the end-consumer. When evaluating the control principle and the principal indicators provided in the standard, we believe some questions an entity may consider when making this judgement could include:

- Does the entity take title to the goods at any point in the order-to-delivery process? If not, why?
- Is the vendor the party that the customer will hold responsible for the acceptability of the product (e.g. handling of complaints and returns)? If so, why?
- Does the entity have a return-to-vendor agreement with the vendor or have a history of returning goods to the vendor after a customer returns the good(s)? If so, why?
- Does the vendor have discretion in establishing the price for the goods (e.g. setting the floor or ceiling)? If so, why?
- Is the vendor responsible for the risk of loss or damage (e.g. shrinkage) while the goods are in the entity's store? If so, why?
- Does the vendor have the contractual right to take back the goods delivered to the entity and, if so, has the vendor exercised that right in situations other than when the goods were at the end of their useful lives?
- Can the entity move goods between their stores or relocate goods within their stores without first obtaining permission from the vendor? If not, why?
- Does the entity have any further obligation to the customer after remitting the customer's order to the vendor? If not, why?
- Once a customer order is placed, can the entity direct the product to another entity or prevent the product from being transferred to the customer? If not, why?

An SEC staff member said in a speech that the application of the principal-versus-agent application guidance can be especially challenging when an entity never obtains physical possession of a good. While noting that the staff has seen these types of fact patterns with conclusions of both principal and agent, the staff member further discussed certain facts and circumstances of a registrant consultation with OCA in which the SEC staff did not object to a principal determination in a transaction in which certain specialised goods were shipped directly to the end-customer by the vendor (not the registrant). In reaching this conclusion, the SEC staff member reiterated that the determination requires consideration of the definition of control in the standard, which often includes consideration of the indicators in paragraph B37 of IFRS 15. However, inventory risk is only one of those indicators and it is possible that physical possession will not coincide with control of a specified good.[38]

Understanding the business purpose and rationale for the contractual terms between the vendor and the entity may help the entity assess whether it controls the specified goods prior to the transfer to the end-consumer and is, therefore, the principal in the sale to the end-consumer.

3.4.5.B   Presentation of amounts billed to customers (e.g. shipping and handling, expenses or cost reimbursements and taxes or other assessments)

In July 2014, the TRG members were asked to consider how an entity would determine the presentation of amounts billed to customers (e.g. shipping and handling, reimbursement of out-of-pocket expenses and taxes) under the standard (i.e. as revenue or as a reduction of costs).[39]

The TRG members generally agreed that the standard is clear that any amounts not collected on behalf of third parties would be included in the transaction price (i.e. revenue). As discussed in Chapter 29 at 2, paragraph 47 of IFRS 15 says that 'the transaction price is the amount of consideration to which an entity expects to be entitled in exchange for transferring promised goods or services to a customer, excluding amounts collected on behalf of third parties (for example, some sales taxes)'. Therefore, if the amounts were earned by the entity in fulfilling its performance obligations, the amounts are included in the transaction price and recorded as revenue.

Shipping and handling

The appropriate presentation of amounts billed to customers for shipping and handling activities would depend on whether they entity is a principal or an agent in the shipping arrangement (see Chapter 32 at 2.3.1 for further discussion on presentation of shipping and handling costs incurred by the entity).

Expense or cost reimbursements

Many service providers routinely incur incidental expenses, commonly referred to as 'out-of-pocket' expenses, in the course of conducting their normal operations. Those expenses often include, but are not limited to, airfare, other travel-related costs (such as car rentals and hotel accommodation) and telecommunications charges. The entity (i.e. the service provider) and the customer may agree that the customer will reimburse the entity for the actual amount of such expenses incurred. Alternatively, the parties may negotiate a single fixed fee that is intended to compensate the service provider for both professional services rendered and out-of-pocket expenses incurred.

Out-of-pocket expenses are often costs incurred by an entity in fulfilling its performance obligation(s) (i.e. the out-of-pocket expenses are fulfilment costs) and do not transfer a good or service to the customer. In these situations, reimbursement for such costs generally should be included in the entity's estimate of the transaction price and recognised as revenue when (or as) the performance obligation(s) is (are) satisfied, even if the entity is reimbursed at 'cost' (i.e. at zero margin. Alternatively, if an entity concludes that the costs do transfer a good or service to the customer, it should consider the principal-versus-agent application guidance when determining whether reimbursement amounts received from its customer need to be recorded on a gross or net basis.

In some cases, it may be appropriate to include the reimbursement in the transaction price and recognise that amount as revenue when the applicable expense is incurred. That is, an entity may not have to estimate out-of-pocket expenses in its determination of the transaction price at contract inception. This was discussed in a US Private Company Council meeting under US GAAP. The FASB staff observed in the related staff paper the following situations in which this would be the case:[40]

- The entity is an agent as it relates to the specified good or service identified (see 3.4 above). That is, in cases in which the entity is an agent and the reimbursement is equal to the cost, the net effect on revenue would be zero and, therefore, no estimation would be required.

- The variable consideration is constrained (see Chapter 29 at 2.2.3). That is, if a portion of the transaction price related to reimbursements of out-of-pocket expenses is constrained, an entity would not include an estimate in the transaction price for that amount until it becomes highly probable that a significant revenue reversal will not occur, which may be when the underlying out-of-pocket expenses are incurred in some cases. For example, an entity may not be able to make reliable estimates of expenses and the related reimbursements that will not be subject to a significant revenue reversal due to a lack of historical evidence.

- The variable consideration relates specifically to a performance obligation or a distinct good or service in a series and the entity meets the variable consideration exception (see Chapter 29 at 3.3).

- The entity qualifies to apply the 'right to invoice' practical expedient (see Chapter 30 at 3.1.1).

- The entity applies a 'costs incurred' measure of progress when recognising revenue for over-time performance obligations (see Chapter 30 at 3). That is, if an entity selects a 'costs incurred' method, the timing of the costs being incurred and the revenue recognition associated with those costs would align.

Taxes or other assessments

Several TRG members noted that this would require entities to evaluate taxes collected in all jurisdictions in which they operate to determine whether a tax is levied on the entity or the customer. TRG members generally agreed that an entity would apply the principal versus agent application guidance when it is not clear whether the amounts are collected on behalf of third parties. This could result in amounts billed to a customer being recorded as an offset to costs incurred (i.e. on a net basis).

The issue of how an entity allocates the transaction price in a contract with multiple performance obligations in which the entity acts as both a principal and an agent is discussed in Chapter 29 at 3.2.1.

3.5 Consignment arrangements

The standard provides specific application guidance for a promise to deliver goods on a consignment basis to other parties. See Chapter 30 at 6.

3.6 Customer options for additional goods or services

Many sales contracts give customers the option to acquire additional goods or services. These additional goods or services may be priced at a discount or may even be free of charge. Options to acquire additional goods or services at a discount can come in many forms, including sales incentives, volume-tiered pricing structures, customer award credits (e.g. frequent flyer points) or contract renewal options (e.g. waiver of certain fees, reduced future rates). *[IFRS 15.B39].* See the application questions at 3.6.1, which discuss many of these different types of customer options.

When an entity grants a customer the option to acquire additional goods or services, that option is only a separate performance obligation if it provides a material right to the customer that the customer would not receive without entering into the contract (e.g. a discount that exceeds the range of discounts typically given for those goods or services to that class of customer in that geographical area or market). Refer to 3.6.1.F below for further discussion on the evaluation of class of customer. If the option provides a material right to the customer, the customer has, in effect, paid in advance for future goods or services. As such, the entity recognises revenue when those future goods or services are transferred or when the option expires. *[IFRS 15.B40].* In the Basis for Conclusions, the IASB indicated that the purpose of this requirement is to identify and account for options that customers are paying for (often implicitly) as part of the current transaction. *[IFRS 15.BC386].*

The Board did not provide any bright lines as to what constitutes a 'material' right. However, the standard requires that an option to purchase additional goods or services at their stand-alone selling prices does not provide a material right and, instead, is a marketing offer. This is the case even if the customer has obtained the option only as a result of entering into a previous contract. However, an option to purchase additional goods or services in the future at the current stand-alone selling price could be a material right if prices are highly likely to significantly increase. This could also be the case if a renewal option at the current stand-alone selling price is offered for an extended period of time and the stand-alone selling price for the product is highly likely to significantly increase, depending on the facts and circumstances of the contract. This is because the customer is being offered a discount on future goods or services compared to what others will have to pay in the future as a result of entering into the previous contract. The standard states that this is the case even if the option can only be exercised because the customer entered into the earlier transaction. An entity that has made a marketing offer accounts for it in accordance with IFRS 15 only when the customer exercises the option to purchase the additional goods or services. *[IFRS 15.B41]*.

Significant judgement may be required to determine whether a customer option represents a material right. This determination is important because it affects the accounting and disclosures for the contract at inception and throughout the life of the contract.

The standard includes the following example to illustrate the determination of whether an option represents a material right (see Chapter 29 at 3.1.5 for a discussion of the measurement of options that are separate performance obligations). *[IFRS 15.IE250-IE253]*.

Example 28.43: Option that provides the customer with a material right (discount voucher)

An entity enters into a contract for the sale of Product A for £100. As part of the contract, the entity gives the customer a 40 per cent discount voucher for any future purchases up to £100 in the next 30 days. The entity intends to offer a 10 per cent discount on all sales during the next 30 days as part of a seasonal promotion. The 10 per cent discount cannot be used in addition to the 40 per cent discount voucher.

Because all customers will receive a 10 per cent discount on purchases during the next 30 days, the only discount that provides the customer with a material right is the discount that is incremental to that 10 per cent (i.e. the additional 30 per cent discount). The entity accounts for the promise to provide the incremental discount as a performance obligation in the contract for the sale of Product A.

To estimate the stand-alone selling price of the discount voucher in accordance with paragraph B42 of IFRS 15, the entity estimates an 80 per cent likelihood that a customer will redeem the voucher and that a customer will, on average, purchase £50 of additional products. Consequently, the entity's estimated stand-alone selling price of the discount voucher is £12 (£50 average purchase price of additional products × 30 per cent incremental discount × 80 per cent likelihood of exercising the option). The stand-alone selling prices of Product A and the discount voucher and the resulting allocation of the £100 transaction price are as follows:

Performance obligations	Stand-alone selling price
	£
Product A	100
Discount voucher	12
Total	112

	Allocated transaction price	
Product A	89	(£100 ÷ £112 × £100)
Discount voucher	11	(£12 ÷ £112 × £100)
Total	100	

The entity allocates £89 to Product A and recognises revenue for Product A when control transfers. The entity allocates £11 to the discount voucher and recognises revenue for the voucher when the customer redeems it for goods or services or when it expires.

Evaluating whether an option provides a material right may be more complex when the stand-alone selling price of the good or service is highly variable, as illustrated below.

Example 28.44: Evaluating a customer option when the stand-alone selling price is highly variable

Technology entity Y enters into a contract with Customer Z for a perpetual licence of software A, with one year of PCS. The contract also includes an option to purchase additional licences of software A at 40% off the list price.

The entity does not sell software A separately, but it sells PCS separately in the form of renewals that are consistently priced at 20% of the net licence fee. Assume that Technology entity Y uses the residual method to estimate the stand-alone selling price of the perpetual licence for software A (see Chapter 29 at 3.1.2). Also assume that the price Technology entity Y charges for the bundle of the perpetual licence and PCS is highly variable. That is because the price Technology entity Y charges to customers in the same class and same market as Customer Z who have not made prior purchases ranges from the list price to a discounted price of up to 70% off the list price for the bundle. Assume that the entity has appropriately stratified its contracts/customers to evaluate the range of discounts and has a sufficient amount of transactions to support that this is the range of discounts it offers.

Since the 40% discount Technology entity Y offered to Customer Z is within the range of discounts it typically offers to customers in the same class as Customer Z, Technology entity Y concludes that this option does not represent a material right.

While the customer option is determined not to be a material right in this example, that might not always be the case. An entity would need to evaluate all customer options, even those for which the price of the good or service that is subject to the option is highly variable and for which the residual approach was used.

3.6.1 Application questions on customer options for additional goods or services

3.6.1.A Which transactions to consider when assessing customer options for additional goods or services

At their October 2014 meeting, the TRG members discussed whether entities should consider only the current transaction or also past and future transactions with the same customer when determining whether an option for additional goods or services provides the customer with a material right.

The TRG members generally agreed that entities should consider all relevant transactions with a customer (i.e. current, past and future transactions), including those that provide accumulating incentives, such as loyalty programmes, when determining whether an option represents a material right. That is, the evaluation is not solely performed in relation to the current transaction.[41]

3.6.1.B Nature of evaluation of customer options: quantitative versus qualitative

In October 2014, the TRG members considered whether the material right evaluation is solely a quantitative evaluation or whether it should also consider qualitative factors.

The TRG members generally agreed that the evaluation should consider both quantitative and qualitative factors that would be known to the entity (e.g. what a new customer would pay for the same service, the availability and pricing of competitors' service alternatives, whether the average customer life indicates that the fee provides an incentive for customers to remain beyond the stated contract term, whether the right accumulates). This is because a customer's perspective on what constitutes a 'material right' may consider qualitative factors. This is consistent with the notion that when identifying promised goods or services in Step 2, an entity considers reasonable expectations of the customer that the entity will transfer a good or service to it.[42]

3.6.1.C Distinguishing between a customer option and variable consideration

In November 2015, the TRG members were asked to consider how an entity would distinguish between a contract that contains an option to purchase additional goods or services and a contract that includes variable consideration (see Chapter 29 at 2.2) based on a variable quantity (e.g. a usage-based fee).[43]

Entities have found it challenging to distinguish between a contract that includes customer options to purchase additional goods or services and one that includes variable consideration based on a variable quantity (e.g. a usage-based fee). This is because, under both types of contracts, the ultimate quantity of goods or services to be transferred to the customer is often unknown at contact inception. The TRG members generally agreed that this determination requires judgement and consideration of the facts and circumstances. They also generally agreed that the TRG agenda paper on this question provides a framework that helps entities to make this determination.

This determination is important because it affects the accounting for the contract at inception and throughout the life of the contract, as well as disclosures. If an entity concludes that a customer option for additional goods or services provides a material right, the option itself is deemed to be a performance obligation in the contract, but the underlying goods or services are not accounted for until the option is exercised (as discussed at 3.6.1.D below). As a result, the entity is required to allocate a portion of the transaction price to the material right at contract inception and to recognise that revenue when or as the option is exercised or the option expires. If an entity, instead, concludes that an option for additional goods or services is not a material right, there is no accounting for the option and no accounting for the underlying optional goods or services until those subsequent purchases occur.

However, if the contract includes variable consideration (rather than a customer option), an entity has to estimate at contract inception the variable consideration expected over the life of the contract and update that estimate each reporting period (subject to the constraint on variable consideration) (see Chapter 29 at 2.2). There are also more disclosures required for variable consideration (e.g. the requirement to disclose the remaining transaction price for unsatisfied performance obligations) (see Chapter 32 at 3.2.1.C) than for options that are not determined to be material rights.

The TRG agenda paper explained that the first step (in determining whether a contract involving variable quantities of goods or services should be accounted for as a contract containing customer options or variable consideration) is for the entity to determine the nature of its promise in providing goods or services to the customer and the rights and obligations of each party.

In a contract in which the variable quantity of goods or services results in variable consideration, the nature of the entity's promise is to transfer to the customer an overall service. In providing this overall service, an entity may perform individual tasks or activities. At contract inception, the entity is presently obliged by the terms and conditions of the contract to transfer all promised goods or services provided under the contract and the customer is obliged to pay for those promised goods or services. This is because the customer entered into a contract that obliges the entity to transfer those goods or services. The customer's subsequent actions to utilise the service affect the measurement of revenue (in the form of variable consideration), but do not oblige the entity to provide additional distinct goods or services beyond those promised in the contract.

For example, consider a contract between a transaction processor and a customer in which the processor will process all of the customer's transactions in exchange for a fee paid for each transaction processed. The ultimate quantity of transactions that will be processed is not known. The nature of the entity's promise is to provide the customer with continuous access to the processing platform so that submitted transactions are processed. By entering into the contract, the customer has made a purchasing decision that obliges the entity to provide continuous access to the transaction processing platform. The consideration paid by the customer results from events (i.e. additional transactions being submitted for processing to the processor) that occur after (or as) the entity transfers the payment processing service. The customer's actions do not oblige the processor to provide additional distinct goods or services because the processor is already obliged (starting at contract inception) to process all transactions submitted to it.

Another example described in the TRG agenda paper of contracts that may include variable consideration was related to certain IT outsourcing contracts. Under this type of contract (similar to the transaction processing contract, discussed above), the entity provides continuous delivery of a service over the contract term and the amount of service provided is variable.

Example 28.45: Variable consideration (IT outsourcing arrangement)

An entity enters into a 10-year IT outsourcing arrangement with a customer in which it provides continuous delivery of outsourced activities over the contract term. The entity provides server capacity, manages the customer's software portfolio and runs an IT help desk. The total monthly invoice is calculated based on the units consumed for each activity. For example, the billings might be based on millions of instructions per second of computing power, the number of software applications used or the number of employees supported. The price per unit differs for each type of activity.

At contract inception, it is unknown how many outsourced activities the entity will perform for the customer throughout the life of the contract. The question that arises is whether the customer makes optional purchases when it sends activities to the entity to be performed or whether its use of the service affects the measurement of revenue (in the form of variable consideration).

The conclusion in the TRG agenda paper was that it is likely that this contract contains variable consideration because of the nature of the entity's promise. The customer is paying for the entity to stand ready to perform in an outsourcing capacity on any given day. The customer does not make a separate purchasing decision each time it sends a unit for processing. Instead, the customer made its purchasing decision when it entered into the outsourcing contract with the entity. Therefore, the customer's actions to use the service also do not oblige the entity to provide any additional distinct goods or services.

In contrast, when an entity provides a customer option, the nature of its promise is to provide the quantity of goods or services specified in the contract, if any, and a right for the customer to choose the amount of additional distinct goods or services the customer will purchase. That is, the entity is not obliged to provide any additional distinct goods or services until the customer exercises the option. The customer has a contractual right that allows it to choose the amount of additional distinct goods or services to purchase, but the customer has to make a separate purchasing decision to obtain those additional distinct goods or services. Prior to the customer's exercise of that right, the entity is not obliged to provide (nor does it have a right to consideration for transferring) those goods or services.

Since an option that is a marketing offer is considered a new contract if it is exercised, the IASB staff noted in the TRG agenda paper that an analogy to the contract modification requirements in paragraphs 20-21 of IFRS 15 (see 2.4 above) could be

Revenue: identify the contract and performance obligations 2145

helpful when an entity is distinguishing between optional purchases and variable consideration. For a modification to be considered a separate contract, one of the criteria is that the modification results in the addition of promised goods or services that are distinct. Similarly, the IASB staff noted that the exercise of a customer option would typically result in the addition of promised goods or services that are distinct.

The TRG agenda paper included the following example of a contract that includes a customer option (rather than variable consideration).

Example 28.46:   Customer option that is not a material right

Entity B enters into a contract to provide 100 widgets to Customer Y in return for consideration of $10 per widget. Each widget is a distinct good transferred at a point in time. The contract also gives Customer Y the right to purchase additional widgets at the stand-alone selling price of $10 per widget. Therefore, the quantity that may be purchased by Customer Y is variable.

The conclusion in the TRG agenda paper was that, while the quantity of widgets that may be purchased is variable, the transaction price for the existing contract is fixed at $1,000 [100 widgets × $10 per widget]. That is, the transaction price only includes the consideration for the 100 widgets specified in the contract and the customer's decision to purchase additional widgets is an option. While Entity B may be required to deliver additional widgets in the future, Entity B is not legally obligated to provide the additional widgets until Customer Y exercises the option. In this example, the option is accounted for as a separate contract because there is no material right, since the pricing of the option is at the stand-alone selling price of the widgets.

Contrast the above example with another contract that includes a customer option that is determined to be a material right:

Example 28.47:   Customer option that is a material right

Entity B enters into a contract to provide 100 widgets to Customer Y at $10 per widget (which is the widget's stand-alone selling price at contract inception). Each widget is a distinct good transferred at a point in time. The contract also gives Customer Y the right to purchase additional widgets at $9 per widget. Therefore, the quantity that may be purchased by Customer Y is variable.

While the quantity of widgets that may be purchased is variable, the transaction price for the existing contract is fixed at $1,000 [100 widgets x $10 per widget]. That is, the transaction price only includes the consideration for the 100 widgets specified in the contract, and the customer's decision to purchase additional widgets is an option. While Entity B may be required to deliver additional widgets in the future, Entity B is not legally obligated to provide the additional widgets until Customer Y exercises the option.

Entity B determines that Customer Y obtained a discount on future widgets because $9 per widget is lower than the stand-alone selling price of each widget at contract inception (i.e. $10 per widget), as well as being lower than the expected stand-alone selling price at renewal. In this example, the option is accounted for as a material right.

The TRG agenda paper also included the following example of a contract in which the variable quantity of goods or services includes a customer option.

Example 28.48:   Customer option[44]

A supplier enters into a five-year master supply arrangement in which the supplier is obliged to produce and sell parts to a customer at the customer's request. That is, the supplier is not obliged to transfer any parts until the customer submits a purchase order. In addition, the customer is not obliged to purchase any parts; however, it is highly likely it will do so because the part is required to manufacture the customer's product and it is not practical to obtain parts from multiple suppliers. Each part is determined to be a distinct good that transfers to the customer at a point in time.

The conclusion in the TRG agenda paper was that the nature of the promise in this example is the delivery of parts (and not a service of standing ready to produce and sell parts). That is, the contract provides the customer with a right to choose the quantity of additional distinct goods (i.e. it provides a customer option), rather than a right to use the services for which control to the customer has (or is currently being) transferred (such as in the transaction processor example above). Similarly, the supplier is not obliged to transfer any parts until the customer submits the purchase order (another important factor in distinguishing a customer option from variable consideration). In contrast, in certain other fact patterns the supplier is obliged to make the promised services available to the customer without any additional decisions made by the customer.

The TRG agenda paper contrasted this example with other contracts that may include a stand-ready obligation (e.g. a customer's use of a health club). When the customer submits a purchase order under the master supply arrangement, it is contracting for a specific number of distinct goods, which creates new performance obligations for the supplier. In contrast, a customer using services in a health club is using services that the health club is already obliged to provide under the present contract. That is, there are no new obligations arising from the customer's usage.

The TRG agenda paper also included the following example of a contract in which the variable quantity of goods or services results in variable consideration.

Example 28.49: Variable consideration (variable quantities of goods or services)[45]

Entity A enters into a contract to provide equipment to Customer X. The equipment is a single performance obligation transferred at a point in time. Entity A charges Customer X based on its usage of the equipment at a fixed rate per unit of consumption. The contract has no minimum payment guarantees. Customer X is not contractually obliged to use the equipment. However, Entity A is contractually obliged to transfer the equipment to Customer X.

The conclusion in the TRG agenda paper was that the usage of the equipment by Customer X is a variable quantity that affects the amount of consideration owed to Entity A. It does not affect Entity A's performance obligation, which is to transfer the piece of equipment. That is, Entity A has performed by transferring the distinct good. Customer X's actions, which result in payment to Entity A, occur after the equipment has been transferred and do not require Entity A to provide additional goods or services.

3.6.1.D When, if ever, to consider the goods or services underlying a customer option as a separate performance obligation when there are no contractual penalties

At their November 2015 meeting, TRG members generally agreed that an entity does not need to identify the additional goods or services underlying the option as promised goods or services (or performance obligations) if there are no contractual penalties (e.g. termination fees, monetary penalties for not meeting contractual minimums), even if it believes that it is virtually certain that a customer will exercise its option for additional goods or services. Only the option is assessed to determine whether it represents a material right (and accounted for as a performance obligation). As a result, any consideration that would be received in return for optional goods or services is not included in the transaction price at contract inception.[46]

The TRG agenda paper included the following example of a contract in which it is virtually certain that a customer will exercise its option for additional goods or services:

Example 28.50: Customer option with no contractual penalties[47]

An entity sells equipment and consumables, both of which are determined to be distinct goods that are recognised at a point in time. The stand-alone selling price of the equipment and each consumable is €10,000 and €100, respectively. The equipment costs €8,000 and each consumable costs €60. The entity sells the equipment for €6,000 (i.e. at a 40% discount on its stand-alone selling price) with a customer option to purchase each consumable for €100 (i.e. equal to its stand-alone selling price). There are no contractual minimums, but the entity estimates the customer will purchase 200 parts over the next two years. This is an exclusive contract in which the customer cannot purchase the consumables from any other vendors during the contract term.

TRG members generally agreed that the consumables underlying each option would not be considered part of the contract. Furthermore, the option does not represent a material right because it is priced at the stand-alone selling price for the consumable. This is the case even though the customer is compelled to exercise its option for the consumables because the equipment cannot function without the consumables and the contract includes an exclusivity clause that requires the customer to acquire the consumables only from the entity. Accordingly, the transaction price is €6,000 and it is entirely attributable to the equipment. This would result in a loss for the entity of €2,000 when it transfers control of the equipment to the customer.

However, contractual minimums may represent fixed consideration in a contract, even if the contract also contains optional purchases. For example, an MSA may set minimum purchase quantities that the entity is obliged to provide, but any quantities above the minimum may require the customer to make a separate purchasing decision (i.e. exercise a customer option). If contractual penalties exist (e.g. termination fees, monetary penalties assessed for not meeting contractual minimums), it may be appropriate to include some or all of the goods or services underlying customer options as part of the contract at inception. This is because the penalty effectively creates a minimum purchase obligation for the goods or services that would be purchased if the penalty were enforced.

Example 28.51: Customer option with contractual penalties[48]

Consider the same facts as in Example 28.50 above, except that the customer will incur a penalty if it does not purchase at least 200 consumables. That is, the customer will be required to repay some or all of the £4,000 discount provided on the equipment. Per the contract terms, the penalty decreases as each consumable is purchased at a rate of £20 per consumable.

The conclusion in the TRG agenda paper was that the penalty is substantive and it effectively creates a minimum purchase obligation. As a result, the entity concludes that the minimum number of consumables required to avoid the penalty would be evidence of enforceable rights and obligations. The entity would then calculate the transaction price as £26,000 [(200 consumables × £100/consumable) + £6,000 (the selling price of the equipment)]. Furthermore, the conclusion in the TRG agenda paper was that, if the customer failed to purchase 200 consumables, the entity accounts for the resulting penalty as a contract modification.

3.6.1.E Volume rebates and/or discounts on goods or services: customer options versus variable consideration

Should volume rebates and/or discounts on goods or services be accounted for as variable consideration or as customer options to acquire additional goods or services at a discount? It depends on whether rebate or discount programme is applied retrospectively or prospectively.

Generally, if a volume rebate or discount is applied prospectively, we believe the rebate or discount would be accounted for as a customer option (not variable consideration). This is because the consideration for the goods or services in the present contract is not contingent upon or affected by any future purchases. Rather, the discounts available from the rebate programme affect the price of future purchases. Entities need to evaluate whether the volume rebate or discount provides the customer with an option to purchase goods or services in the future at a discount that represents a material right (and is, therefore, accounted for as a performance obligation) (see 3.6.1.F below).

However, we believe a volume rebate or discount that is applied retrospectively is accounted for as variable consideration (see Chapter 29 at 2.2). This is because the final price of each good or service sold depends upon the customer's total purchases that are subject to the rebate programme. That is, the consideration is contingent upon the occurrence or non-occurrence of future events. This view is consistent with Example 24 in the standard (which is included as Example 29.1 in Chapter 29 at 2.2.1).

Entities should keep in mind that they need to evaluate whether contract terms, other than those specific to the rebate or discount programme, create variable consideration that needs to be separately evaluated (e.g. if the goods subject to the rebate programme are also sold with a right of return).

3.6.1.F Considering the class of customer when evaluating whether a customer option is a material right

At its meeting in April 2016, the FASB TRG discussed the issue how an entity should consider the class of customer when evaluating whether a customer option is a material right. FASB TRG members generally agreed that an entity should consider 'class of customer' when determining whether a customer option to acquire additional goods or services represents a material right. In addition, in making this evaluation, they agreed that an entity first determines whether the customer option exists independently of the existing contract. That is, would the entity offer the same pricing to a similar customer independent of a prior contract with the entity? If the pricing is independent, the option is considered a marketing offer and there is no material right. FASB TRG members also generally agreed that it is likely that the determination will require an entity to exercise significant judgement and consider all facts and circumstances.

As discussed above, paragraph B40 of IFRS 15 states that when an entity grants a customer the option to acquire additional goods or services, that option is a separate performance obligation if it provides a material right that the customer would not receive without entering into the contract (e.g. a discount that exceeds the range of discounts typically given for those goods or services to that class of customer in that region or market). *[IFRS 15.B40]*. Furthermore, paragraph B41 of IFRS 15 states that an option to purchase additional goods or services at their stand-alone selling prices does not provide a material right and instead is a marketing offer. *[IFRS 15.B41]*. The FASB staff noted in the TRG agenda paper that these requirements are intended to make clear that a customer option to acquire additional goods or services would not give rise to a material right if a customer could execute a separate contract to obtain the goods or services at the same price. That is, customer options that would exist independently of an existing contract with a customer do not constitute performance obligations in that existing contract.

The TRG agenda paper provided several examples of the FASB staff's views on this topic, including the following:

Example 28.52: Class of customer evaluation

Retailer owns and operates several electronic stores and currently provides customers who purchase a 50-inch television with a coupon for 50% off the purchase of a stereo system. The coupon must be redeemed at one of Retailer's stores and is valid for one year. Retailer has never offered a discount of this magnitude to a customer that does not purchase a television (or another item of similar value).

Customer A purchases a 50-inch television from Retailer. At the time of purchase, Customer A receives a coupon for 50% off a stereo system. In evaluating whether the 50% discount provided to Customer A exists independently of its existing contract to purchase a television, Retailer needs to compare the discount offered to Customer A (50%) with the discount typically offered to other customers independent of a prior contract (purchase) with Retailer. For customers that do not purchase a 50-inch television, the only promotion Retailer is running on the stereo system is offering a 5% off coupon to all customers walking into the store. It would not be appropriate for Retailer to compare the discount offered to Customer A with a discount offered to another customer that also purchased a 50-inch television. This is because the objective of the requirements in paragraphs B40-B41 of IFRS 15 is to determine whether a customer option exists independently of an existing contract with a customer.

Retailer determines that the discount offered to Customer A is not comparable to the discount typically offered to customers without a prior contract (purchase). Rather, Customer A is receiving an incremental discount that it would not have received had it not entered into a contract to purchase a 50-inch television. The incremental discount provided to Customer A represents a material right.

3.6.1.G   Considering whether prospective volume discounts determined to be customer options are material rights

At the April 2016 FASB TRG meeting, the FASB TRG members were asked to consider how an entity should consider whether prospective volume discounts determined to be customer options are material rights.[49]

The FASB TRG members generally agreed that in making this evaluation, similar to the discussion in 3.6.1.F above, an entity would first evaluate whether the option exists independently of the existing contract. That is, would the entity offer the same pricing to a similar high-volume customer independent of a prior contract with the entity? If yes, it indicates that the volume discount is not a material right, as it is not incremental to the discount typically offered to a similar high-volume customer. If the entity typically charges a higher price to a similar customer, it may indicate that the volume discount is a material right as the discount is incremental.

The TRG agenda paper included the following example:

Example 28.53:   Volume discounts

Entity enters into a long-term master supply arrangement with Customer A to provide an unspecified volume of non-customised parts. The price of the parts in subsequent years is dependent upon Customer A's purchases in the current year. That is, Entity charges Customer A $1.00 per part in year one and if Customer A purchases more than 100,000 parts, the year two price will be $0.90 per part.

When determining whether the contract between Entity and Customer A includes a material right, Entity first evaluates whether the option provided to Customer A exists independently of the existing contract. To do this, Entity compares the discount offered to Customer A with the discount typically offered to a similar high-volume customer that receives a discount independent of a prior contract with Entity. Such a similar customer could be Customer B who places a single order with Entity for 105,000 parts. Comparing the price offered to Customer A in year two with offers to other customers that also receive pricing that is contingent on prior purchases would not help Entity determine whether Customer A would have been offered the year two price had it not entered into the original contract.

Volume discounts or tiered pricing can make an entity's assessment of whether a customer option to purchase additional goods or services is a material right more complex. It is likely that this assessment will require significant judgement, as illustrated below:

Example 28.54:   Evaluating a customer option with volume discounts

Semi-conductor Entity S sells microchips for use in cell phones. The entity executes a contract with a customer to sell one million units of microchip M for €0.50 each (or €500,000). The contract provides the right for the customer to purchase an additional 200,000 microchips for €0.40 each.

The entity concludes that it has provided the customer with an option to purchase the additional microchips since the entity is not obligated to provide the additional goods until the customer makes a purchasing decision. Furthermore, the volume discount is applied prospectively and does not affect the transaction price in the original contract.

Scenario A

For microchip M, Semi-conductor Entity S provides volume discounts as part of its standard pricing practices and typically prices the first one million microchips at €0.50 each, the second million at €0.40 each and any additional amounts at €0.35 each.

Semi-conductor Entity S considers whether the option provides the customer with a material right. To make this evaluation, the entity compares the discount offered in this option with the discount it typically offers to a similar high-volume customer that receives a discount without having had a prior contract. In other words, the entity compares the pricing in this contract to the pricing it typically offers to customers that purchase between one million and two million units of microchip M without having made any prior purchases.

The entity has sold, and continues to sell, the same volume of microchip M at the same price to other customers in the same class of customer who have not made prior purchases (i.e. similar customers pay €0.50 each for the first one million microchips and €0.40 each for the second million). That is, the price offered to the customer in the option exists independently of the existing contract. Therefore, Semi-conductor Entity S concludes that it has not provided the customer with a material right.

Scenario B

For microchip M, Semi-conductor Entity S provides volume discounts as part of its standard pricing practices and typically prices the first three million microchips at €0.50 each and any additional amounts at €0.30 each.

Semi-conductor Entity S considers whether the option provides the customer with a material right. To make this evaluation, the entity compares the discount offered in this option with the discount it typically offers to a similar high-volume customer that receives a discount without having had a prior contract.

For similar high-volume customers of the same customer class who have not made prior purchases, the entity typically does not provide this pricing (e.g. similar customers would pay €0.50 per microchip for all 1.2 million microchips). Therefore, the entity concludes that it has provided the customer with a material right.

3.6.1.H   Considering whether a renewal option is a material right

An entity assesses whether a renewal option represents a material right in the same manner as other customer options discussed above. That is, an entity would determine whether the customer renewal option would be offered at the same price to a similar class of customer, independent of a prior contract with the entity. Customer renewal options may be explicitly included in the original contract or, as discussed in Chapter 29 at 2.8, the existence of a non-refundable upfront fee may indicate that the contract includes a renewal option for future goods or services (e.g. if the customer renews the contract without the payment of an additional upfront fee).

As discussed above at 3.6, paragraph B41 of IFRS 15 specifies that if a customer has the option to purchase additional goods or services (e.g. by exercising a renewal option) at a price that would reflect the stand-alone selling prices of those goods or services, the renewal option would not provide a material right and, instead, is a marketing offer. *[IFRS 15.B41]*. Determining the stand-alone selling price of a renewal option may require significant judgement. For example, a renewal option offered at the current stand-alone selling price may or may not be determined to be a material right. That is, if the pricing for the goods and service are expected to remain stable, it would be appropriate for a renewal option offered at a current stand-alone selling price to be considered a marketing offer. In contrast, a renewal option at the current stand-alone selling price could be a material right if, for example, prices are highly likely to significantly increase or the renewal option is offered for an extended period of time.

The following example from the standard describes the accounting for a renewal option that is a material right. This example also includes guidance on how to allocate a portion of the transaction price to the material right, which is further discussed in Chapter 29 at 3.1.5. *[IFRS 15.IE257-IE266]*.

Example 28.55:   Option that provides the customer with a material right (renewal option)

An entity enters into 100 separate contracts with customers to provide one year of maintenance services for €1,000 per contract. The terms of the contracts specify that at the end of the year, each customer has the option to renew the maintenance contract for a second year by paying an additional €1,000. Customers who renew for a second year are also granted the option to renew for a third year for €1,000. The entity charges significantly higher prices for maintenance services to customers that do not sign up for the maintenance services initially (i.e. when the products are new). That is, the entity charges €3,000 in Year 2 and €5,000 in Year 3 for annual maintenance services if a customer does not initially purchase the service or allows the service to lapse.

The entity concludes that the renewal option provides a material right to the customer that it would not receive without entering into the contract, because the price for maintenance services are significantly higher if the customer elects to purchase the services only in Year 2 or 3. Part of each customer's payment of €1,000 in the first year is, in effect, a non-refundable prepayment of the services to be provided in a subsequent year. Consequently, the entity concludes that the promise to provide the option is a performance obligation.

The renewal option is for a continuation of maintenance services and those services are provided in accordance with the terms of the existing contract. Instead of determining the stand-alone selling prices for the renewal options directly, the entity allocates the transaction price by determining the consideration that it expects to receive in exchange for all the services that it expects to provide, in accordance with paragraph B43 of IFRS 15.

The entity expects 90 customers to renew at the end of Year 1 (90 per cent of contracts sold) and 81 customers to renew at the end of Year 2 (90 per cent of the 90 customers that renewed at the end of Year 1 will also renew at the end of Year 2, that is 81 per cent of contracts sold).

At contract inception, the entity determines the expected consideration for each contract is €2,710 [€1,000 + (90 per cent × €1,000) + (81 per cent × €1,000)]. The entity also determines that recognising revenue on the basis of costs incurred relative to the total expected costs depicts the transfer of services to the customer. Estimated costs for a three-year contract are as follows:

	€
Year 1	600
Year 2	750
Year 3	1,000

Accordingly, the pattern of revenue recognition expected at contract inception for each contract is as follows:

	Expected costs adjusted for likelihood of contract renewal		Allocation of consideration expected	
	€		€	
Year 1	600	(€600 × 100%)	780	[(€600 ÷ €2,085) × €2,710]
Year 2	675	(€750 × 90%)	877	[(€675 ÷ €2,085) × €2,710]
Year 3	810	(€1,000 × 81%)	1,053	[(€810 ÷ €2,085) × €2,710]
Total	2,085		2,710	

Consequently, at contract inception, the entity allocates to the option to renew at the end of Year 1 €22,000 of the consideration received to date [cash of €100,000 – revenue to be recognised in Year 1 of €78,000 (€780 × 100)].

Assuming there is no change in the entity's expectations and the 90 customers renew as expected, at the end of the first year, the entity has collected cash of €190,000 [(100 × €1,000) + (90 × €1,000)], has recognised revenue of €78,000 (€780 × 100) and has recognised a contract liability of €112,000.

Consequently, upon renewal at the end of the first year, the entity allocates €24,300 to the option to renew at the end of Year 2 [cumulative cash of €190,000 less cumulative revenue recognised in Year 1 and to be recognised in Year 2 of €165,700 (€78,000 + €877 × 100)].

If the actual number of contract renewals was different than what the entity expected, the entity would update the transaction price and the revenue recognised accordingly.

3.6.1.I   Considering whether a loyalty or reward programme is a material right

Entities frequently offer loyalty or reward programmes under which customers accumulate points that they can redeem for 'free' or discounted products or services. Under paragraph B40 of IFRS 15, an entity typically concludes that such a loyalty or reward programme provides a material right to customers that they would not receive without entering into a contract. This is because the customer effectively pays in advance for the right to obtain a future good or service (e.g. travel, upgrades, products) or a discount on that good or service.

This is also consistent with the discussion of the TRG members, as noted at 3.6.1.A and 3.6.1.B above, that entities should consider all relevant transactions with a customer (i.e. current, past and future transactions) and both quantitative and qualitative factors, including those that provide accumulating incentives, when determining whether an option represents a material right. Example 52 in the standard (included as Example 30.17 in Chapter 30 at 11) illustrates the accounting for a loyalty programme.

3.6.1.J   Accounting for the exercise of a material right

At the March 2015 TRG meeting, the TRG members were asked to consider how an entity would account for the exercise of an option for additional goods or services that provides the customer with a material right (a material right).[50]

The TRG members generally agreed that it is reasonable for an entity to account for the exercise of a material right as either a contract modification or as a continuation of the existing contract (i.e. a change in the transaction price). TRG members also generally agreed that it is not appropriate to account for the exercise of a material right as variable consideration.

Under the approach that treats the exercise of a material right as a continuation of the existing contract (i.e. because the customer decided to purchase additional goods or services contemplated in the original contract), an entity would update the transaction price of the contract to include any consideration to which the entity expects to be entitled as a result of the exercise, in accordance with the requirements for changes in the transaction price included in paragraphs 87-90 of IFRS 15 (see Chapter 29 at 3.5).

Under these requirements, changes in the total transaction price are generally allocated to the separate performance obligations on the same basis as the initial allocation. However, paragraph 89 of IFRS 15 requires an entity to allocate a change in the transaction price entirely to one or more, but not all, performance obligations if the criteria in paragraph 85 of IFRS 15 are met. *[IFRS 15.89]*. These criteria (discussed further in Chapter 29 at 3.3) are that the additional consideration specifically relates to the entity's efforts to satisfy the performance obligation(s) and that allocating the additional consideration entirely to one or more, but not all, performance obligation(s) is consistent with the standard's allocation objective (see Chapter 29 at 3). The additional consideration received for the exercise of the option is likely to meet the criteria to be allocated directly to the performance obligation(s) underlying the material right. Revenue would be recognised when (or as) the performance obligation(s) is (are) satisfied. *[IFRS 15.85]*.

The TRG agenda paper included the following example.

Example 28.56: Exercise of a material right under the requirements for changes in the transaction price[51]

Entity enters into a contract with Customer to provide two years of Service A for $100 and includes an option for Customer to purchase two years of Service B for $300. The stand-alone selling prices of Services A and B are $100 and $400, respectively. Entity concludes that the option represents a material right and its estimate of the stand-alone selling price of the option is $33. Entity allocates the $100 transaction price to each performance obligation as follows:

	Transaction price	Stand-alone selling price	%	Allocation
Service A		$100	75%	$75
Option		$33	25%	$25
Total	$100	$133	100%	$100

Upon executing the contract, Customer pays $100 and Entity begins transferring Service A to Customer. The consideration of $75 that is allocated to Service A is recognised over the two-year service period. The consideration of $25 that is allocated to the option is deferred until Service B is transferred to the customer or the option expires.

Six months after executing the contract, Customer exercises the option to purchase two years of Service B for $300. Following the requirements for changes in the transaction price, the consideration of $300 related to Service B is added to the amount previously allocated to the option to purchase Service B (i.e. $300 + 25 = $325). This is recognised as revenue over the two-year period in which Service B is transferred. Entity is able to allocate the additional consideration received for the exercise of the option to Service B because it specifically relates to Entity's efforts to satisfy the performance obligation and the allocation in this manner is consistent with the standard's allocation objective.

Under the second approach, which treats the exercise of a material right as a contract modification (i.e. because there a change in the scope and/or price of a contract), an entity follows the contract modification requirements in paragraphs 18-21 of IFRS 15 (see 2.4 above).

Since more than one approach would be acceptable, the TRG members generally agreed that an entity needs to consider which approach is most appropriate, based on the facts and circumstances, and consistently apply that approach to similar contracts.[52]

3.6.1.K   Customer options that provide a material right: Evaluating whether there is a significant financing component

At their March 2015 TRG meeting, the TRG members discussed whether an entity is required to evaluate a customer option that provides a material right to determine if it includes a significant financing component and, if so, how entities would perform this evaluation.

The TRG members generally agreed that an entity has to evaluate whether a material right includes a significant financing component (see Chapter 29 at 2.5) in the same way that it evaluates any other performance obligation. This evaluation requires judgement and consideration of the facts and circumstances.[53]

On this question, the TRG agenda paper discussed a factor that may be determinative in this evaluation. Paragraph 62(a) of IFRS 15 indicates that if a customer provides advance payment for a good or service, but the customer can choose when the good or service is transferred, no significant financing component exists. *[IFRS 15.62(a)]*. As a result, if the customer can choose when to exercise the option, it is unlikely that there will be a significant financing component.[54]

3.6.1.L Customer options that provide a material right: recognising revenue when there is no expiration date

Stakeholders have asked this question because paragraph B40 of IFRS 15 states that an entity should recognise revenue allocated to options that are material rights when the future goods or services resulting from the option are transferred or when the option expires. *[IFRS 15.B40]*. However, in some cases, options may be perpetual and not have an expiration date. For example, loyalty points likely provide a material right to a customer and, sometimes, these points do not expire. We believe an entity may apply the requirements in IFRS 15 on customers' unexercised rights (or breakage) discussed in Chapter 30 at 11 (i.e. paragraphs B44-B47 of IFRS 15). *[IFRS 15.B44-B47]*. That is, we believe it is appropriate for revenue allocated to a customer option that does not expire to be recognised at the earlier of when the future goods or services, resulting from the option, are transferred or, if the goods or services are not transferred, when the likelihood of the customer exercising the option becomes remote.

3.7 Sale of products with a right of return

An entity may provide its customers with a right to return a transferred product. A right of return may be contractual, an implicit right that exists due to the entity's customary business practice or a combination of both (e.g. an entity has a stated return period, but generally accepts returns over a longer period). A customer exercising its right to return a product may receive a full or partial refund, a credit that can be applied to amounts owed, a different product in exchange or any combination of these items. *[IFRS 15.B20]*.

Offering a right of return in a sales agreement obliges the selling entity to stand ready to accept any returned product. Paragraph B22 of IFRS 15 states that such an obligation does not represent a performance obligation. *[IFRS 15.B22]*. Instead, an entity makes an uncertain number of sales when it provides goods with a return right. That is, until the right of return expires, the entity is not certain how many sales will fail. Therefore, the Board concluded that an entity does not recognise revenue for sales that are expected to fail as a result of the customer exercising its right to return the goods. *[IFRS 15.BC364]*. Instead, the potential for customer returns needs to be considered when an entity estimates the transaction price because potential returns are a component of variable consideration. This concept is discussed further in Chapter 29 at 2.4.

Paragraph B26 of IFRS 15 clarifies that exchanges by customers of one product for another of the same type, quality, condition and price (e.g. one colour or size for another) are not considered returns for the purposes of applying the standard. *[IFRS 15.B26]*. Furthermore, contracts in which a customer may return a defective product in exchange for a functioning product need to be evaluated in accordance with the requirements on warranties included in IFRS 15. *[IFRS 15.B27]*. See further discussion on warranties in Chapter 31 at 3.

References

1. For US GAAP, the term "probable" is defined in the master glossary of the US Accounting Standards Codification as 'the future event or events are likely to occur'.
2. TRG Agenda paper 25, *January 2015 Meeting – Summary of Issues Discussed and Next Steps,* dated 30 March 2015.
3. TRG Agenda paper 13, *Collectibility,* dated 26 January 2015.
4. TRG Agenda paper 13, *Collectibility,* dated 26 January 2015 and TRG Agenda paper 25, *January 2015 Meeting – Summary of Issues Discussed and Next Steps,* dated 30 March 2015.
5. TRG Agenda paper 10, *Contract enforceability and termination clauses,* dated 31 October 2014 and TRG Agenda paper 11, *October 2014 Meeting – Summary of Issues Discussed and Next Steps,* dated 26 January 2015.
6. TRG Agenda paper 48, *Customer options for additional goods and services,* dated 9 November 2015.
7. TRG Agenda paper 10, *Contract enforceability and termination clauses,* dated 31 October 2014.
8. Paragraph 47a of TRG Agenda paper 48, *Customer options for additional goods and services,* dated 9 November 2015.
9. TRG Agenda paper 33, *Partial Satisfaction of Performance Obligations Prior to Identifying the Contract,* dated 30 March 2015.
10. *IFRIC Update,* January 2019.
11. *IFRIC Update,* January 2019.
12. IFRIC Agenda paper 3, January 2019 and IFRIC Agenda paper 2, *Assessment of promised goods or services (IFRS 15),* dated September 2018.
13. TRG Agenda paper 25, *January 2015 Meeting – Summary of Issues Discussed and Next Steps,* dated 30 March 2015.
14. TRG Agenda paper 46, *Pre-Production Activities,* dated 9 November 2015.
15. TRG Agenda paper 16, *Stand-Ready Performance Obligations,* dated 26 January 2015.
16. TRG Agenda paper 16, *Stand-Ready Performance Obligations,* dated 26 January 2015.
17. TRG Agenda paper 48, *Customer options for additional goods and services,* dated 9 November 2015.
18. TRG Agenda paper 25, *January 2015 Meeting – Summary of Issues Discussed and Next Steps,* dated 30 March 2015.
19. TRG Agenda paper 48, *Customer options for additional goods and services,* dated 9 November 2015.
20. Remarks by Susan M. Mercier, Professional Accounting Fellow, SEC Office of the Chief Accountant, 9 December 2019, at the 2019 AICPA Conference.
21. Remarks by Sheri L. York, Professional Accounting Fellow, SEC Office of the Chief Accountant, 10 December 2018, at the 2018 AICPA conference.
22. *IFRIC Update,* March 2018.
23. IFRIC Agenda paper 2D, March 2018.
24. *IFRIC Update,* March 2018.
25. TRG Agenda paper 39, *Application of the Series Provision and Allocation of Variable Consideration,* dated 13 July 2015.
26. TRG Agenda paper 39, *Application of the Series Provision and Allocation of Variable Consideration,* dated 13 July 2015.
27. TRG Agenda paper 27, *Series of Distinct Goods or Services,* dated 30 March 2015.
28. TRG Agenda paper 34, *March 2015 Meeting – Summary of Issues Discussed and Next Steps,* dated 13 July 2015.
29. TRG Agenda paper 27, *Series of Distinct Goods or Services,* dated 30 March 2015.
30. TRG Agenda paper 27, *Series of Distinct Goods or Services,* dated 30 March 2015 and TRG Agenda paper 34, *March 2015 Meeting – Summary of Issues Discussed and Next Steps,* dated 13 July 2015.
31. TRG Agenda paper 27, *Series of Distinct Goods or Services,* dated 30 March 2015.
32. TRG Agenda paper 39, *Application of the Series Provision and Allocation of Variable Consideration,* dated 13 July 2015.
33. TRG Agenda paper 39, *Application of the Series Provision and Allocation of Variable Consideration,* dated 13 July 2015.
34. TRG Agenda paper 39, *Application of the Series Provision and Allocation of Variable Consideration,* dated 13 July 2015.
35. TRG Agenda paper 39, *Application of the Series Provision and Allocation of Variable Consideration,* dated 13 July 2015.
36. Remarks by Lauren K. Alexander, Professional Accounting Fellow, SEC Office of the Chief Accountant, 9 December 2019, at the 2019 AICPA Conference.

37 FASB ASU 2016-08, *Revenue from Contracts with Customers (Topic 606): Principal versus Agent Considerations* (March 2016), para. BC38.
38 Remarks by Sheri L. York, Professional Accounting Fellow, SEC Office of the Chief Accountant, 10 December 2018 at the 2018 AICPA conference.
39 TRG Agenda paper 2, *Gross versus Net Revenue: Amounts Billed to Customers,* dated 18 July 2014.
40 FASB staff Private Company Council Memo, *Reimbursement of Out-of-Pocket Expenses,* dated 26 June 2018.
41 TRG Agenda paper 6, *Customer options for additional goods and services and nonrefundable upfront fees,* dated 31 October 2014 and TRG Agenda paper 11, *October 2014 Meeting – Summary of Issues Discussed and Next Steps,* dated 26 January 2015.
42 TRG Agenda paper 6, *Customer options for additional goods and services and nonrefundable upfront fees,* dated 31 October 2014 and TRG Agenda paper 11, *October 2014 Meeting – Summary of Issues Discussed and Next Steps,* dated 26 January 2015.
43 TRG Agenda paper 48, *Customer options for additional goods and services,* dated 9 November 2015.
44 TRG Agenda paper 48, *Customer options for additional goods and services,* dated 9 November 2015.
45 TRG Agenda paper 48, *Customer options for additional goods and services,* dated 9 November 2015.
46 TRG Agenda paper 48, *Customer options for additional goods and services,* dated 9 November 2015.
47 TRG Agenda paper 48, *Customer options for additional goods and services,* dated 9 November 2015.
48 TRG Agenda paper 48, *Customer options for additional goods and services,* dated 9 November 2015.
49 FASB TRG Agenda paper 54, *Considering Class of Customer When Evaluating Whether a Customer Option Gives Rise to a Material Right,* dated 18 April 2016.
50 TRG Agenda paper 32, *Accounting for a Customer's Exercise of a Material Right,* dated 30 March 2015.
51 TRG Agenda paper 32, *Accounting for a Customer's Exercise of a Material Right,* dated 30 March 2015.
52 TRG Agenda paper 34, *March 2015 Meeting – Summary of Issues Discussed and Next Steps,* dated 13 July 2015.
53 TRG Agenda paper 34, *March 2015 Meeting – Summary of Issues Discussed and Next Steps,* dated 13 July 2015.
54 TRG Agenda paper 32, *Accounting for a Customer's Exercise of a Material Right,* dated 30 March 2015.

Chapter 29

Revenue: determine and allocate the transaction price

1	INTRODUCTION			2163
2	DETERMINE THE TRANSACTION PRICE			2164
	2.1	Presentation of sales (and other similar) taxes		2165
	2.2	Variable consideration		2166
		2.2.1	Forms of variable consideration	2167
			2.2.1.A Implicit price concessions	2168
			2.2.1.B Liquidated damages, penalties or compensation from other similar clauses: variable consideration versus warranty provisions	2172
			2.2.1.C Identifying variable consideration: undefined quantities with fixed per unit contractual prices	2173
			2.2.1.D If a contract is denominated in a currency other than that of the entity's functional currency, should changes in the contract price due to exchange rate fluctuations be accounted for as variable consideration?	2174
			2.2.1.E Price protection or price matching clauses	2174
			2.2.1.F Early payment (or prompt payment) discounts	2175
		2.2.2	Estimating variable consideration	2175
			2.2.2.A Situations in which an entity would not have to estimate variable consideration at contract inception under IFRS 15	2178
		2.2.3	Constraining estimates of variable consideration	2179

		2.2.3.A	Applying the constraint on variable consideration: contract level versus performance obligation level	2185
		2.2.3.B	Would an entity be required to follow a two-step approach to estimate variable consideration?	2185
		2.2.3.C	Applying the constraint on variable consideration to milestone payments	2185
	2.2.4		Reassessment of variable consideration	2187
2.3	Refund liabilities			2187
2.4	Rights of return			2188
	2.4.1		Is an entity applying the portfolio approach practical expedient when accounting for rights of return?	2191
	2.4.2		Accounting for restocking fees for goods that are expected to be returned	2191
	2.4.3		Accounting for restocking costs for goods that are expected to be returned	2192
2.5	Significant financing component			2192
	2.5.1		Examples of significant financing components	2197
	2.5.2		Application questions on identifying and accounting for significant financing components	2200
		2.5.2.A	Payment terms reflect reasons other than the provision of finance	2201
		2.5.2.B	Existence of a financing component when the promised consideration is equal to the cash selling price	2201
		2.5.2.C	Accounting for financing components that are not significant	2202
		2.5.2.D	Determining whether the significant financing component practical expedient applies to contracts with a single payment stream for multiple performance obligations	2202
		2.5.2.E	Calculating the adjustment to revenue for significant financing components	2203
		2.5.2.F	Allocating a significant financing component when there are multiple performance obligations in a contract	2203
		2.5.2.G	Significant financing components: considering whether interest expense can be borrowing costs eligible for capitalisation	2204
	2.5.3		Financial statement presentation of financing component	2205
2.6	Non-cash consideration			2206
	2.6.1		Non-cash consideration application considerations	2207
	2.6.2		Barter transactions	2209

	2.7	Consideration paid or payable to a customer		2210
		2.7.1	Determining who is an entity's customer when applying the requirements for consideration payable to a customer	2212
		2.7.2	Forms of consideration paid or payable to a customer	2212
			2.7.2.A Payments to a customer that are within the scope of the requirements for consideration payable to a customer	2213
		2.7.3	Classification and measurement of consideration paid or payable to a customer	2214
		2.7.4	Timing of recognition of consideration paid or payable to a customer	2215
			2.7.4.A Accounting for upfront payments to a customer	2217
			2.7.4.B Accounting for negative revenue resulting from consideration paid or payable to a customer	2217
	2.8	Non-refundable upfront fees		2218
		2.8.1	Application questions on non-refundable upfront fees	2219
			2.8.1.A Recognition period for a non-refundable upfront fee that does not relate to the transfer of a good or service	2219
			2.8.1.B Determining whether a contract that includes a non-refundable upfront fee for establishing a connection to a network is within the scope of IFRS 15	2220
			2.8.1.C Factors to consider when non-refundable upfront fees received for establishing a connection to a network are within the scope of IFRS 15	2220
	2.9	Changes in the transaction price		2222
3	ALLOCATE THE TRANSACTION PRICE TO THE PERFORMANCE OBLIGATIONS			2222
	3.1	Determining stand-alone selling prices		2222
		3.1.1	Factors to consider when estimating the stand-alone selling price	2224
		3.1.2	Possible estimation approaches	2224
		3.1.3	Updating estimated stand-alone selling prices	2228
		3.1.4	Additional considerations for determining the stand-alone selling price	2228
			3.1.4.A When estimating the stand-alone selling price, does an entity have to consider its historical pricing for the sale of the good or service involved?	2228

		3.1.4.B	When using an expected cost plus margin approach to estimate a stand-alone selling price, how would an entity determine an appropriate margin?..................................2229
		3.1.4.C	Estimating the stand-alone selling price of a good or service: estimating a range of prices versus identifying a point estimate..........................2229
		3.1.4.D	Evaluating a contract where the total transaction price exceeds the sum of the stand-alone selling prices 2230
	3.1.5	\multicolumn{2}{l	}{Measurement of options that are separate performance obligations .... 2231}
		3.1.5.A	Could the form of an option (e.g. a gift card versus a coupon) affect how an option's stand-alone selling price is estimated?................................2234
		3.1.5.B	Use of the practical alternative when not all of the goods or services in the original contract are subject to a renewal option 2234
3.2	\multicolumn{3}{l	}{Applying the relative stand-alone selling price method..........................2235}
	3.2.1	\multicolumn{2}{l	}{Allocating the transaction price in a contract with multiple performance obligations in which the entity acts as both a principal and an agent .... 2235}
3.3	\multicolumn{3}{l	}{Allocating variable consideration.. 2237}
	3.3.1	\multicolumn{2}{l	}{Application questions on the variable consideration allocation exception ....2243}
		3.3.1.A	In order to meet the criteria to allocate variable consideration entirely to a specific part of a contract, must the allocation be made on a relative stand-alone selling price basis?...........2243
3.4	\multicolumn{3}{l	}{Allocating a discount ....2244}
	3.4.1	\multicolumn{2}{l	}{Application questions on the discount allocation exception...2246}
		3.4.1.A	Interaction between the two allocation exceptions: variable discounts..................................2246
3.5	\multicolumn{3}{l	}{Changes in transaction price after contract inception................................. 2247}
3.6	\multicolumn{3}{l	}{Allocation of transaction price to components outside the scope of IFRS 15 ....2249}

List of examples

Example 29.1:	Volume discount incentive	2168
Example 29.2:	Consideration is not the stated price – implicit price concession	2169
Example 29.3:	Penalty gives rise to variable consideration	2173
Example 29.4:	Estimating the transaction price using the expected value method	2177
Example 29.5:	Estimating the transaction price using the most likely amount method	2177
Example 29.6:	Evaluating the factors that could increase the likelihood or magnitude of a significant revenue reversal	2181
Example 29.7:	Price concessions	2182
Example 29.8:	Estimating variable consideration using the expected value method	2183
Example 29.9:	Management fees subject to the constraint	2184
Example 29.10:	Milestone payments	2186
Example 29.11:	Right of return	2190
Example 29.12:	Restocking fees	2192
Example 29.13:	Significant financing component and right of return	2197
Example 29.14:	Withheld payments on a long-term contract	2198
Example 29.15:	Determining the discount rate	2199
Example 29.16:	Advance payment and assessment of discount rate	2199
Example 29.17:	Advance payment	2200
Example 29.18:	Entitlement to non-cash consideration	2207
Example 29.19:	Consideration paid to a customer in exchange for a distinct good or service	2214
Example 29.20:	Consideration payable to a customer	2216
Example 29.21:	Non-refundable upfront fees	2219
Example 29.22:	Allocation methodology	2227
Example 29.23:	Estimating the stand-alone selling price of options that are separate performance obligations	2231
Example 29.24:	Measuring an option	2233
Example 29.25:	Relative stand-alone selling price allocation	2235
Example 29.26:	Allocation when an entity is both a principal and an agent in a contract	2236
Example 29.27:	Variable fee service arrangement based on usage	2240
Example 29.28:	Fixed-fee service arrangement with overages	2241
Example 29.29:	Allocation of variable consideration	2242
Example 29.30:	Allocating a discount	2245
Example 29.31:	Change in transaction price after contract inception	2247
Example 29.32:	Arrangements with components outside the scope of the standard	2249

Chapter 29

Revenue: determine and allocate the transaction price

1 INTRODUCTION

Revenue is a broad concept that is dealt with in several standards. This chapter and Chapters 27-28 and 30-32, primarily cover the requirements for revenue arising from contracts with customers that are within the scope of IFRS 15 – *Revenue from Contracts with Customers*. This chapter deals with determining the transaction price and allocating the transaction price. Refer to the following chapters for other requirements of IFRS 15:

- Chapter 27 – Core principle, definitions and scope.
- Chapter 28 – Identifying the contract and identifying performance obligations.
- Chapter 30 – Recognising revenue.
- Chapter 31 – Licences, warranties and contract costs.
- Chapter 32 – Presentation and disclosure requirements.

Other revenue items that are not within the scope of IFRS 15, but arise in the course of the ordinary activities of an entity, as well as the disposal of non-financial assets that are not part of the ordinary activities of the entity, for which IFRS 15's requirements are relevant, are addressed in Chapter 27.

In addition, this chapter:

- Highlights significant differences from the equivalent US GAAP standard, Accounting Standards Codification (ASC) 606 – *Revenue from Contracts with Customers* (together with IFRS 15, the standards) issued by the US Financial Accounting Standards Board (FASB) (together with the International Accounting Standards Board (IASB), the Boards).
- Addresses topics on which the members of the Joint Transition Resource Group for Revenue Recognition (TRG) reached general agreement and our views on certain topics. TRG members' views are non-authoritative, but entities should consider them as they apply the standards. Unless otherwise specified, these summaries represent the discussions of the joint TRG.

The views we express in this chapter may evolve as application issues are identified and discussed among stakeholders. The conclusions we describe in our illustrations are also subject to change as views evolve. Conclusions in seemingly similar situations may differ from those reached in the illustrations due to differences in the underlying facts and circumstances.

2 DETERMINE THE TRANSACTION PRICE

When (or as) an entity satisfies a performance obligation, an entity recognises revenue at the amount of the transaction price (which excludes constrained estimates of variable consideration – see 2.2.3 below) that is allocated to that performance obligation. *[IFRS 15.46]*. The standard states that 'an entity shall consider the terms of the contract and its customary business practices to determine the transaction price. The transaction price is the amount of consideration to which an entity expects to be entitled in exchange for transferring promised goods or services to a customer, excluding amounts collected on behalf of third parties (for example, some sales taxes). The consideration promised in a contract with a customer may include fixed amounts, variable amounts, or both.' *[IFRS 15.47]*.

The nature, timing and amount of consideration promised by a customer affect the estimate of the transaction price. When determining the transaction price, an entity shall consider the effects of all of the following: *[IFRS 15.48]*

(a) variable consideration;

(b) constraining estimates of variable consideration;

(c) the existence of a significant financing component in the contract;

(d) non-cash consideration; and

(e) consideration payable to a customer.

For the purpose of determining the transaction price, an entity shall assume that the goods or services will be transferred to the customer as promised in accordance with the existing contract and that the contract will not be cancelled, renewed or modified. *[IFRS 15.49]*.

The transaction price is based on the amount to which the entity expects to be 'entitled'. This is meant to reflect the amount to which the entity has rights under the present contract (see Chapter 28 at 2.2 on contract enforceability and termination clauses). That is, the transaction price does not include estimates of consideration resulting from future change orders for additional goods or services. The amount to which the entity expects to be entitled also excludes amounts collected on behalf of another party, such as sales taxes. As noted in the Basis for Conclusions, the Board decided that the transaction price would not include the effects of the customer's credit risk, unless the contract includes a significant financing component (see 2.5 below). *[IFRS 15.BC185]*.

The IASB also clarified in the Basis for Conclusions that entities may have rights under the present contract to amounts that are to be paid by parties other than the customer and, if so, these amounts would be included in the transaction price. For example, in the healthcare industry, an entity may be entitled under the present contract to payments from the patient, insurance companies and/or government organisations. If that is the case, the total amount to which the entity expects to be entitled needs to be included in the transaction price, regardless of the source. *[IFRS 15.BC187]*.

Determining the transaction price is an important step in applying IFRS 15 because this amount is allocated to the identified performance obligations and is recognised as revenue when (or as) those performance obligations are satisfied. In many cases, the transaction price is readily determinable because the entity receives payment when it transfers promised goods or services and the price is fixed (e.g. a restaurant's sale of food with a no refund policy). Determining the transaction price is more challenging when it is variable, when payment is received at a time that differs from when the entity provides the promised goods or services or when payment is in a form other than cash. Consideration paid or payable by the entity to the customer may also affect the determination of the transaction price.

Figure 29.1 illustrates how an entity would determine the transaction price if the consideration to be received is fixed or variable:

Figure 29.1: Fixed versus variable consideration

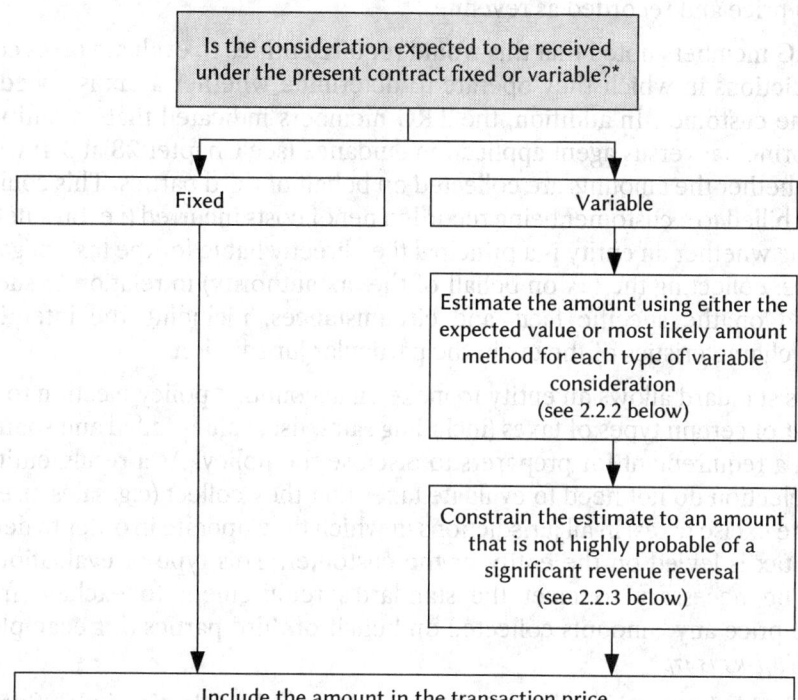

* Consideration expected to be received under the contract can be variable even when the stated price in the contract is fixed. This is because the entity may be entitled to consideration only upon the occurrence or non-occurrence of a future event (see 2.2.1 below).

See Chapter 28 at 3.4.5.B for a discussion on the presentation of amounts billed to customers (e.g. shipping and handling, expenses or cost reimbursements and taxes).

2.1 Presentation of sales (and other similar) taxes

Sales and excise taxes are those levied by taxing authorities on the sales of goods or services. Although various names are used for these taxes, sales taxes generally refer to taxes levied on the purchasers of the goods or services, and excise taxes refer to those levied on the sellers of goods or services.

The standard includes a general principle that an entity determines the transaction price exclusive of amounts collected on behalf of third parties (e.g. some sales taxes). Following the issuance of the standard, some stakeholders informed the Board's staff that there could be multiple interpretations regarding whether certain items that are billed to customers need to be presented as revenue or as a reduction of costs. Examples of such amounts include shipping and handling fees, reimbursements of out-of-pocket expenses and taxes or other assessments collected and remitted to government authorities.

At the July 2014 TRG meeting, the TRG members generally agreed that the standard is clear that any amounts that are not collected on behalf of third parties would be included in the transaction price (i.e. revenue). That is, if the amounts were earned by the entity in fulfilling its performance obligations, the amounts are included in the transaction price and recorded as revenue.

Several TRG members noted that this would require entities to evaluate taxes collected in all jurisdictions in which they operate to determine whether a tax is levied on the entity or the customer. In addition, the TRG members indicated that an entity would apply the principal versus agent application guidance (see Chapter 28 at 3.4) when it is not clear whether the amounts are collected on behalf of third parties. This could result in amounts billed to a customer being recorded net of costs incurred (i.e. on a net basis).[1] Determining whether an entity is a principal (i.e. directly liable for the tax obligation) or an agent (i.e. collecting the tax on behalf of the tax authority) in relation to such taxes will depend on the specific facts and circumstances, including the intention and underlying characteristics of the tax in the particular jurisdiction.

The FASB's standard allows an entity to make an accounting policy election to present revenue net of certain types of taxes (including sales, use, value-added and some excise taxes) with a requirement for preparers to disclose the policy. As a result, entities that make this election do not need to evaluate taxes that they collect (e.g. sales, use, value-added, some excise taxes) in all jurisdictions in which they operate in order to determine whether a tax is levied on the entity or the customer. This type of evaluation would otherwise be necessary to meet the standard's requirement to exclude from the transaction price any 'amounts collected on behalf of third parties (for example, some sales taxes)'. *[IFRS 15.47]*.

The IASB decided not to include a similar accounting policy election in IFRS 15, noting that the requirements of IFRS 15 are consistent with legacy IFRS requirements. *[IFRS 15.BC188D]*. As a result, differences may arise between entities applying IFRS 15 and those applying ASC 606.

2.2 Variable consideration

The transaction price reflects an entity's expectations about the consideration to which it will be entitled to receive from the customer. 'If the consideration promised in a contract includes a variable amount, an entity shall estimate the amount of consideration to which the entity will be entitled in exchange for transferring the promised goods or services to a customer.'

'An amount of consideration can vary because of discounts, rebates, refunds, credits, price concessions, incentives, performance bonuses, penalties or other similar items. The promised consideration can also vary if an entity's entitlement to the consideration is contingent on the occurrence or non-occurrence of a future event. For example, an amount of consideration would be variable if either a product was sold with a right of return or a fixed amount is promised as a performance bonus on achievement of a specified milestone.' *[IFRS 15.50-51].*

In some cases, the variability relating to the promised consideration may be explicitly stated in the contract. In addition to the terms of the contract, the standard states that the promised consideration is variable if either of the following circumstances exists:

- the customer has 'a valid expectation arising from an entity's customary business practices, published policies or specific statements that the entity will accept an amount of consideration that is less than the price stated in the contract. That is, it is expected that the entity will offer a price concession. Depending on the jurisdiction, industry or customer this offer may be referred to as a discount, rebate, refund or credit.'
- other facts and circumstances that indicate 'the entity's intention, when entering into the contract with the customer, is to offer a price concession to the customer.' *[IFRS 15.52].*

These concepts are discussed in more detail below.

2.2.1 Forms of variable consideration

Paragraph 51 of IFRS 15 describes 'variable consideration' broadly to include discounts, rebates, refunds, credits, price concessions, incentives, performance bonuses (e.g. meeting specified performance conditions where there is uncertainty about the outcome) and penalties. *[IFRS 15.51].* Variable consideration can result from explicit terms in a contract to which the parties to the contract agreed or can be implied by an entity's past business practices or intentions under the contract. It is important for entities to appropriately identify the different instances of variable consideration included in a contract because the second step of estimating variable consideration requires entities to apply a constraint (as discussed further at 2.2.3 below) to all variable consideration.

The Board noted in the Basis for Conclusions that consideration can be variable even when the stated price in the contract is fixed. This is because the entity may be entitled to consideration only upon the occurrence or non-occurrence of a future event. *[IFRS 15.BC191].* For example, IFRS 15's description of variable consideration includes amounts resulting from variability due to customer refunds or returns. As a result, a contract to provide a customer with 100 widgets at a fixed price per widget would be considered to include a variable component if the customer has the right to return the widgets (see 2.4 below).

In many transactions, entities have variable consideration as a result of rebates and/or discounts on the price of products or services they provide to customers once the customers meet specific volume thresholds. The standard contains the following example relating to volume discounts. *[IFRS 15.IE124-IE128].*

Example 29.1: Volume discount incentive

An entity enters into a contract with a customer on 1 January 20X8 to sell Product A for €100 per unit. If the customer purchases more than 1,000 units of Product A in a calendar year, the contract specifies that the price per unit is retrospectively reduced to €90 per unit. Consequently, the consideration in the contract is variable.

For the first quarter ended 31 March 20X8, the entity sells 75 units of Product A to the customer. The entity estimates that the customer's purchases will not exceed the 1,000-unit threshold required for the volume discount in the calendar year.

The entity considers the requirements in paragraphs 56–58 of IFRS 15 on constraining estimates of variable consideration, including the factors in paragraph 57 of IFRS 15. The entity determines that it has significant experience with this product and with the purchasing pattern of the entity. Thus, the entity concludes that it is highly probable that a significant reversal in the cumulative amount of revenue recognised (i.e. €100 per unit) will not occur when the uncertainty is resolved (i.e. when the total amount of purchases is known). Consequently, the entity recognises revenue of €7,500 (75 units × €100 per unit) for the quarter ended 31 March 20X8.

In May 20X8, the entity's customer acquires another company and in the second quarter ended 30 June 20X8 the entity sells an additional 500 units of Product A to the customer. In the light of the new fact, the entity estimates that the customer's purchases will exceed the 1,000-unit threshold for the calendar year and therefore it will be required to retrospectively reduce the price per unit to €90.

Consequently, the entity recognises revenue of €44,250 for the quarter ended 30 June 20X8. That amount is calculated from €45,000 for the sale of 500 units (500 units × €90 per unit) less the change in transaction price of €750 (75 units × €10 price reduction) for the reduction of revenue relating to units sold for the quarter ended 31 March 20X8 (see paragraphs 87 and 88 of IFRS 15).

IFRS 15 requires entities to disclose how they estimate variable consideration when determining the transaction price in contracts with customers, including the following:

- significant payment terms (including whether the consideration is variable and whether the estimate is typically constrained, rights of return, etc.); and
- significant judgements used in determining the transaction price, including information about methods, inputs and assumptions used to estimate variable consideration and assess whether the estimate is constrained.

As a result, entities may need to explain the different forms of variable consideration included in their contracts with customers. Entities, therefore, need to carefully consider and identify all forms of variable consideration when they determine the transaction price for their customer contracts and review their disclosures to verify that they meet the disclosure requirements in paragraphs 119, 123 and 126 of IFRS 15 (see Chapter 32 for further discussion of disclosure requirements). *[IFRS 15.119, 123, 126].*

See Chapter 28 at 3.6.1.E for discussion on whether volume rebates and/or discounts on goods or services should be accounted for as variable consideration or as customer options to acquire additional goods or services at a discount. See Chapter 28 at 3.6.1.C for a discussion on distinguishing between a contract that contains an option to purchase additional goods or services and a contract that includes variable consideration based on a variable quantity (e.g. a usage-based fee).

2.2.1.A Implicit price concessions

For some contracts, the stated price has easily identifiable variable components. However, for other contracts, the consideration may be variable because the facts and circumstances indicate that the entity may accept a lower price than the amount stated in the contract (i.e. it expects to provide an implicit price concession). This could be a result of the customer having a valid expectation that the entity will reduce its price based on the entity's customary business practices, published policies or statements made by the entity.

An implicit price concession could also result from other facts and circumstances indicating that the entity intended to offer a price concession to the customer when it entered into the contract. For example, an entity may accept a lower price than the amount stated in the contract to develop or enhance a customer relationship or because the incremental cost of providing the service to the customer is not significant and the consideration it expects to collect provides a sufficient margin.

An entity deducts from its contract price any estimated price concessions to derive the transaction price at contract inception (i.e. the amount the entity expects to be entitled in exchange for the goods or services that will be transferred to the customer). The IFRS 15 collectability assessment is then performed on the transaction price (see Chapter 28 at 2.1.6). An entity also has to assess any contract assets or trade receivables arising from an IFRS 15 contract under the expected credit loss model in IFRS 9 – *Financial Instruments* (see Chapter 51).

The standard provides the following example of when an implicit price concession exists and, as a result, the transaction price is not the amount stated in the contract. *[IFRS 15.IE7-IE9].*

Example 29.2: Consideration is not the stated price – implicit price concession

An entity sells 1,000 units of a prescription drug to a customer for promised consideration of €1 million. This is the entity's first sale to a customer in a new region, which is experiencing significant economic difficulty. Thus, the entity expects that it will not be able to collect from the customer the full amount of the promised consideration. Despite the possibility of not collecting the full amount, the entity expects the region's economy to recover over the next two to three years and determines that a relationship with the customer could help it to forge relationships with other potential customers in the region.

When assessing whether the criterion in paragraph 9(e) of IFRS 15 is met, the entity also considers paragraphs 47 and 52(b) of IFRS 15. Based on the assessment of the facts and circumstances, the entity determines that it expects to provide a price concession and accept a lower amount of consideration from the customer. Accordingly, the entity concludes that the transaction price is not €1 million and, therefore, the promised consideration is variable. The entity estimates the variable consideration and determines that it expects to be entitled to €400,000.

The entity considers the customer's ability and intention to pay the consideration and concludes that even though the region is experiencing economic difficulty, it is probable that it will collect €400,000 from the customer. Consequently, the entity concludes that the criterion in paragraph 9(e) of IFRS 15 is met based on an estimate of variable consideration of €400,000. In addition, on the basis of an evaluation of the contract terms and other facts and circumstances, the entity concludes that the other criteria in paragraph 9 of IFRS 15 are also met. Consequently, the entity accounts for the contract with the customer in accordance with the requirements in IFRS 15.

Example 3 and Example 23 from the standard (included as Example 29.7 at 2.2.3 below) also illustrate situations where an implicit price concession exists at contract inception and, therefore, the transaction price evaluated for collectability is not the amount stated in the contract due to implicit price concessions that exist at contract inception.

Variable consideration may also result from extended payment terms in a contract and any resulting uncertainty about whether the entity will be willing to accept a lower payment amount in the future. That is, an entity has to evaluate whether the extended payment terms represent an implied price concession because the entity does not intend to collect all amounts due in future periods. Offering extended payment terms may also indicate that the contract includes a significant financing component (see 2.5 below).

- *Variable consideration versus credit risk*

As discussed in Chapter 28 at 2.1.6, entities need to determine at contract inception whether they expect to collect a lower amount of consideration than the amount stated in the contract. In the Basis for Conclusions, the IASB acknowledged that in some cases, it may be difficult to determine whether the entity has implicitly offered a price concession (i.e. variable consideration) or whether the entity has chosen to accept the risk of the customer defaulting on the contractually agreed consideration (i.e. impairment losses under IFRS 9, see Chapter 51). *[IFRS 15.BC194]*. The Board did not develop detailed application guidance to assist in distinguishing between price concessions (recognised as variable consideration, within revenue) and an expected credit loss to be accounted for as an impairment loss under IFRS 9 (i.e. outside of revenue). Therefore, entities need to consider all relevant facts and circumstances when analysing situations in which an entity is willing to accept a lower price than the amount stated in the contract.

We believe the following factors may suggest that the entity has implicitly offered a price concession to the customer:

- The entity has an established business practice that indicates it is willing to accept consideration less than contractually stated prices. For example, an entity routinely accepts reduced payments on services for which it earns high margins, indicating that it is willing to accept an amount of consideration that is less than the contract price.
- The entity has a history of not enforcing its contractual rights to promised consideration in similar contracts under similar circumstances such that customers expect the entity to offer price concessions. For example, the customer has a valid expectation that the entity is willing to accept a lower amount of consideration than the contractually stated price based on its past experience with the entity.
- The entity is willing to enter into a contract with a customer even though facts and circumstances indicate that the customer intends to pay an amount of consideration that is less than the contractually stated price. For example, the entity willingly enters into a contract expecting that it will receive less than the stated contract price, implicitly reducing the transaction price to the expected lesser consideration.

Appropriately distinguishing between price concessions (i.e. reductions of revenue) and customer credit risk (i.e. impairment loss) for collectability concerns, that were known at contract inception, is also important because it affects whether a valid contract exists (see Chapter 28 at 2.1.6). If an entity determines at contract inception that a contract includes a price concession (i.e. variable consideration), the estimated amount of the concession is reflected in the transaction price (i.e. as a reduction to the stated contract price). As illustrated in Example 29.2 above (and also in Example 3 and Example 23 from the standard (included as Example 29.7 at 2.2.3 below), entities may estimate a transaction price that is significantly lower than the stated invoice or contractual amount, but still consider the difference between those amounts to be variable consideration (e.g. a price concession), rather than a collectability issue that would result in expected credit losses.

After the entity has determined the amount to assess for collectability under paragraph 9(e) of IFRS 15, it also has to apply the requirements in IFRS 9 to account for any expected credit losses for the receivable (or contract asset) that is recorded (i.e. after consideration of any variable consideration, such as an implicit price concession). Also, it should present any resulting impairment loss as an expense under IFRS 9 (i.e. not as a reduction of the transaction price). This is illustrated in an example from a January 2015 TRG agenda paper included as Example 28.3 in Chapter 28 at 2.1.6.A.[2]

After contract inception, entities need to update both their estimate of variable consideration under IFRS 15 (see 2.2.4 below) and their assessment of expected credit losses under IFRS 9, respectively, at the end of each reporting period. When the amount an entity expects to collect changes after contract inception, the entity may need to exercise significant judgement to determine whether that change is due to: (1) a change in estimate of the variable consideration identified at contract inception (and, therefore, would be accounted for as a change in the transaction price, as discussed at 3.5 below); or (2) an identifiable credit event (e.g. a known or expected decline in a customer's operations, a known or expected bankruptcy filing or other financial reorganisation, or the request for a concession on payment terms due to economic reasons) that would trigger a credit loss to be accounted for as an impairment loss under IFRS 9 (i.e. outside revenue). It is likely that this determination will require entities to establish policies to differentiate between price concessions and customer credit events, both at contract inception and as facts and circumstances change over the life of the contract. Such assessments may have been needed during the coronavirus pandemic because customers' ability and intent to pay were affected and/or entities were more willing to accept partial payment or extended payment terms. Importantly, if the parties need to change the terms of contracts with existing customers as a result, entities need to determine whether there is a contract modification (see Chapter 28 at 2.4).

When making this evaluation, the entity needs to consider the facts and circumstances that led to its change in expectation about the amount it expects to collect. For example, if an entity that had contemplated an implicit price concession at contract inception decides to increase the amount of the concession it is willing to provide to further enhance the relationship with its customer, it may conclude that this is variable consideration. Therefore, it would be a reduction of the transaction price, i.e. revenue. In contrast, if the entity determines it will collect less consideration than it originally estimated due to its customer filing for bankruptcy, it is likely the entity would conclude that this is an impairment loss to be accounted for outside of IFRS 15 (i.e. there would be no adjustment to revenue).

An entity may need to make the following assessments when evaluating changes in expectations about the amount it expects to collect after contract inception:

- reassess collectability of the remaining contract consideration if the entity concludes that the change in expectation is due to a significant change in facts and circumstances (see Chapter 28 at 2.1.6.B);
- consider whether the change in expectation is due to a contract modification. A contract modification is defined in IFRS 15 as 'a change in scope or price (or both) of a contract that is approved by the parties to a contract'. *[IFRS 15.18]*. See Chapter 28 at 2.4 for further discussion on contract modifications; and
- consider whether the change in expectation indicates that the entity needs to assess related capitalised costs to obtain or fulfil a contract for impairment (see Chapter 31 at 5).

2.2.1.B Liquidated damages, penalties or compensation from other similar clauses: variable consideration versus warranty provisions

Should liquidated damages, penalties or compensation from other similar clauses be accounted for as variable consideration or warranty provisions under the standard? Most liquidated damages, penalties and similar payments are accounted for as variable consideration. However, in limited situations, we believe that amounts that are based on the actual performance of a delivered good or service may be considered similar to warranty payments (e.g. in situations in which an entity pays the customer's direct costs to remedy a defect).

Some contracts provide for liquidated damages, penalties or other damages if an entity fails to deliver future goods or services or if the goods or services fail to meet certain specifications. Paragraph 51 of IFRS 15 includes 'penalties' as an example of variable consideration and describes how promised consideration in a contract can be variable if the right to receive the consideration is contingent on the occurrence or non-occurrence of a future event (e.g. the contract specifies that an entity pays a penalty if it fails to perform according to the agreed upon terms). *[IFRS 15.51]*.

Penalties and other clauses that are considered similar to warranty provisions would be accounted for as:

(a) consideration paid or payable to a customer (which may be variable consideration, see 2.7 below); or

(b) an assurance-type or service-type warranty (see Chapter 31 at 3 on warranties).

Cash fines or penalties paid to a customer would generally be accounted for under the requirements on consideration payable to a customer. However, we believe there may be situations in which it is appropriate to account for cash payments as an assurance-type warranty (e.g. an entity's direct reimbursement to the customer for costs paid by the customer to a third party for the repair of a product).

The following example (Example 20 from the standard) illustrates a performance penalty that is a form of variable consideration. *[IFRS 15.IE102-IE104].*

Example 29.3: Penalty gives rise to variable consideration

An entity enters into a contract with a customer to build an asset for £1 million. In addition, the terms of the contract include a penalty of £100,000 if the construction is not completed within three months of a date specified in the contract.

The entity concludes that the consideration promised in the contract includes a fixed amount of £900,000 and a variable amount of £100,000 (arising from the penalty).

The entity estimates the variable consideration in accordance with paragraphs 50–54 of IFRS 15 and considers the requirements in paragraphs 56–58 of IFRS 15 on constraining estimates of variable consideration.

In 2019, the IFRS Interpretations Committee received a request asking whether an airline accounts for its obligation to compensate customers for delayed or cancelled flights as variable consideration or, separate from the contract, by applying IAS 37 – *Provisions, Contingent Liabilities and Contingent Assets.*

When the issue was discussed at the September 2019 meeting, the Committee observed that the compensation for delays or cancellations gives rise to variable consideration because it:

- relates directly to the entity's fulfilment of its performance obligation (i.e. failure to perform as promised triggers the compensation payment); and
- does not represent compensation for harm or damage caused by the entity's products (and, therefore, paragraph B33 of IFRS 15 does not apply).

The Committee also observed that the compensation payment was similar to penalties for delayed transfer of an asset, which also gives rise to variable consideration, as is illustrated in Example 20 of the standard.[3]

2.2.1.C Identifying variable consideration: undefined quantities with fixed per unit contractual prices

At the July 2015 TRG meeting, the TRG members were asked whether the consideration is variable in a contract that includes a promise to provide an undefined quantity of outputs or to perform an undefined quantity of tasks, but has a contractual rate per unit that is fixed. The TRG members generally agreed that if a contract includes an unknown quantity of tasks throughout the contract period, for which the entity has enforceable rights and obligations (i.e. the unknown quantity of tasks is not an option to purchase additional goods or services, as described in Chapter 28 at 3.6.1.C) and the consideration received is contingent upon the quantity completed, the total transaction price would be variable. This is because the contract has a range of possible transaction prices and the ultimate consideration depends on the occurrence or non-occurrence of a future event (e.g. customer usage), even though the rate per unit is fixed.

The TRG agenda paper on this topic noted that an entity would need to consider contractual minimums (or other clauses) that would make some or all of the consideration fixed.[4]

2.2.1.D   If a contract is denominated in a currency other than that of the entity's functional currency, should changes in the contract price due to exchange rate fluctuations be accounted for as variable consideration?

We believe that changes to the contract price due to exchange rate fluctuations do not result in variable consideration. These price fluctuations are a consequence of entering into a contract that is denominated in a foreign currency, rather than a result of a contract term like a discount or rebate or one that depends on the occurrence or non-occurrence of a future event, as described in paragraph 51 of IFRS 15. *[IFRS 15.51]*.

The variability resulting from changes in foreign exchange rates relates to the form of the consideration (i.e. it is in a currency other than the entity's functional currency). As such, we believe that it would not be considered variable consideration when determining the transaction price. This variability may, instead, need to be accounted for in accordance with IFRS 9 if it is a separable embedded derivative. Otherwise, an entity would account for this variability in accordance with IAS 21 – *The Effects of Changes in Foreign Exchange Rates*.

IFRIC 22 – *Foreign Currency Transactions and Advance Consideration* – specifies that when consideration denominated in a foreign currency is recognised in advance of the associated revenue, the appropriate application of IAS 21 is to measure the revenue using the exchange rate at the date the advanced receipt is recognised, normally the payment date (see Chapter 15 at 5.1.2).

2.2.1.E   Price protection or price matching clauses

Consideration subject to price protection or price matching clauses that require an entity to refund a portion of the consideration to the customer in certain situations must be accounted for as variable consideration under IFRS 15. That is, we believe that, if an entity is required to retrospectively apply lower prices to previous purchases made by a customer (or has a past business practice of doing so, even if the contractual terms would only require prospective application), the consideration would be accounted for as variable consideration.

Examples include contracts between an entity and a customer that provide, either as a matter of formal agreement or due to an entity's business practices, that the entity will refund or provide a credit equal to a portion of the original purchase price towards future purchases if the entity subsequently reduces its price for a previously delivered product and the customer still has inventory of that product on hand. An entity may also offer to match a competitor's price and provide a refund of the difference if the customer finds the same product offered by one of the entity's competitors for a lower price during a specified period of time following the sale.

Contracts with customers also may contain 'most favoured nation' or 'most favoured customer' clauses under which the entity guarantees that the price of any products sold to the customer after contract inception will be the lowest price the entity offers to any other customer. How consideration from such contracts would be accounted for under IFRS 15 depends on the terms of the clause (i.e. whether the price protection is offered prospectively or retrospectively).

We believe that clauses that require an entity to prospectively provide a customer with its best prices on any purchases of products after the execution of a contract have no effect on the revenue recognised for goods or services already transferred to the customer (i.e. the consideration would not be accounted for as variable consideration).

However, if an entity is required to retrospectively apply lower prices to previous purchases made by a customer (or has a past business practice of doing so even if the written contractual terms would only require prospective application), we believe the contract includes a form of price protection and the consideration subject to this provision would be accounted for as variable consideration, as discussed above. We note that these clauses may be present in arrangements with governmental agencies. For example, an entity may be required to monitor discounts given to comparable customers during the contract period and to refund the difference between what was paid by the government and the price granted to comparable commercial customers.

2.2.1.F   Early payment (or prompt payment) discounts

Contracts with customers may include a discount for early payment (or 'prompt payment' discount) under which the customer can pay less than an invoice's stated amount if the payment is made within a certain period of time. For example, a customer might receive a 2% discount if the payment is made within 15 days of receipt (if payment is otherwise due within 45 days of receipt). Because the amount of consideration to be received by the entity would vary depending on whether the customer takes advantage of the discount, the transaction price is variable.

2.2.2   Estimating variable consideration

If a contract with a customer includes variable consideration, paragraph 50 of IFRS 15 (see 2.2 above) states that 'an entity shall estimate the amount of consideration to which the entity will be entitled in exchange for transferring the promised goods or services to a customer'. *[IFRS 15.50]*. Entities are generally required to estimate variable consideration at contract inception and at the end of each reporting period (see 2.2.4 below for reassessment requirements). At 2.2.2.A below, we discuss limited situations in which the estimation of variable consideration may not be required.

Variable consideration generally needs to be estimated, instead of waiting for the variable consideration to be received or known with a high degree of certainty (e.g. upon receipt of a report from a customer detailing the amount of revenue due to the entity). For example, it would not be acceptable for entities that sell their products through distributors or resellers to wait until the end-sale has occurred if the only uncertainty is the variability in the pricing. This is because IFRS 15 requires an entity to estimate the variable consideration (the end-sales price in our example) based on the information available, taking into consideration the effect of the constraint on variable consideration (see at 2.2.3 below), unless one of the limited situations discussed at 2.2.2.A below occurs.

An entity is required to estimate an amount of variable consideration by using either of the following methods, depending on which method the entity expects to better predict the amount of consideration to which it will be entitled:

- *The expected value* – 'the expected value is the sum of probability-weighted amounts in a range of possible consideration amounts. An expected value may be an appropriate estimate of the amount of variable consideration if an entity has a large number of contracts with similar characteristics.'
- *The most likely amount* – 'the most likely amount is the single most likely amount in a range of possible consideration amounts (i.e. the single most likely outcome of the contract). The most likely amount may be an appropriate estimate of the amount of variable consideration if the contract has only two possible outcomes' (e.g. an entity either achieves a performance bonus or does not). [IFRS 15.53].

An entity applies one method consistently throughout the contract when estimating the effect of an uncertainty on an amount of variable consideration to which the entity will be entitled. In addition, an entity is required to consider all the information (historical, current and forecast) that is reasonably available to the entity and identify a reasonable number of possible consideration amounts. The standard states that the information an entity uses to estimate the amount of variable consideration would typically be similar to the information that the entity's management uses during the bid-and-proposal process and in establishing prices for promised goods or services. [IFRS 15.54].

An entity is required to choose between the expected value method and the most likely amount method based on which method better predicts the amount of consideration to which it will be entitled. That is, the method selected is not meant to be a 'free choice'. Rather, an entity must select the method that is best suited, based on the specific facts and circumstances of the contract. [IFRS 15.53].

An entity applies the selected method consistently to each type of variable consideration throughout the contract term and updates the estimated variable consideration at the end of each reporting period. Once it selects a method, an entity is required to apply that method consistently for similar types of variable consideration in similar types of contracts. In the Basis for Conclusions, the Board noted that a contract may contain different types of variable consideration. [IFRS 15.BC202]. As such, it may be appropriate for an entity to use different methods (i.e. expected value or most likely amount) for estimating different types of variable consideration within a single contract.

Entities determine the expected value of variable consideration using the sum of probability-weighted amounts in a range of possible amounts under the contract. To do this, an entity identifies the possible outcomes of a contract and the probabilities of those outcomes. The Board indicated in the Basis for Conclusions that the expected value method may better predict expected consideration when an entity has a large number of contracts with similar characteristics. [IFRS 15.BC200]. This method may also better predict consideration when an entity has a single contract with a large number of possible outcomes. The IASB clarified that an entity preparing an expected value calculation is not required to consider all possible outcomes, even if the entity has extensive data and can identify many possible outcomes. Instead, the IASB noted in the

Basis for Conclusions that, in many cases, a limited number of discrete outcomes and probabilities can provide a reasonable estimate of the expected value. *[IFRS 15.BC201]*.

Example 29.4: Estimating the transaction price using the expected value method

Entity A enters into contracts with customers to construct commercial buildings. The contracts include similar terms and conditions and contain a fixed fee plus variable consideration for a performance bonus related to the timing of Entity A's completion of the construction. Based on Entity A's historical experience, the expected bonus amounts and associated probabilities for achieving each bonus are, as follows:

Bonus amount	Probability of outcome
$0	25%
$100,000	50%
$150,000	25%

Entity A determines that using the expected value method would better predict the amount of consideration to which it will be entitled because it has a large number of contracts that have characteristics that are similar to the new contract. Under the expected value method, Entity A estimates variable consideration of $87,500, as follows:

Bonus amount (a)	Probability of outcome (b)	Expected value amount (a × b)
$0	25%	$0
$100,000	50%	$50,000
$150,000	25%	$37,500
	Total	$87,500

Entity A needs to consider the effect of applying the constraint on variable consideration (see 2.2.3 below).

Entities determine the most likely amount of variable consideration using the single most likely amount in a range of possible consideration amounts. The Board indicated in the Basis for Conclusions that the most likely amount method may be the better predictor when the entity expects to be entitled to one of two possible amounts. *[IFRS 15.BC200]*. For example, a contract in which an entity is entitled to receive all or none of a specified performance bonus, but not a portion of that bonus.

Example 29.5: Estimating the transaction price using the most likely amount method

Entity A enters into a six-month advertising campaign agreement (€500,000 fixed fee) that also includes a potential €100,000 performance bonus linked to certain goals. Entity A estimates that it is 90% likely to receive the entire performance bonus and 10% likely to receive none of the bonus.

Because of the binary nature of the outcome (i.e. the entity will either receive the performance bonus or not receive it), Entity A determines that the most likely amount method is the better predictor of the amount to which it expects to be entitled. Because it is 90% probable that Entity A will receive the €100,000 performance bonus, Entity A estimates the most likely amount it will receive is €600,000 (i.e. €500,000 fixed fee plus the entire €100,000 bonus).

However, Entity A also needs to consider the effect of applying the constraint on variable consideration (see 2.2.3 below) and determine whether it is highly probable that a significant reversal will not occur if it includes the entire €100,000 performance bonus in the transaction price.

The standard requires that when applying either of these methods, an entity considers all information (historical, current and forecast) that is reasonably available to the entity. Some stakeholders questioned whether an entity would be applying the portfolio approach practical expedient in paragraph 4 of IFRS 15 (see Chapter 28 at 2.3.1) when considering evidence from other, similar contracts to develop an estimate of variable consideration using an expected value method. The TRG members discussed this question and generally agreed that an entity would not be applying the portfolio approach practical expedient if it used a portfolio of data from its historical experience with similar customers and/or contracts. The TRG members noted that an entity could choose to apply the portfolio approach practical expedient, but would not be required to do so.[5] Use of this practical expedient requires an entity to assert that it does not expect the use of the expedient to differ materially from applying the standard to an individual contract. The TRG agenda paper noted that using a portfolio of data is not equivalent to using the portfolio approach practical expedient, so entities that use the expected value method to estimate variable consideration would not be required to assert that the outcome from the portfolio is not expected to materially differ from an assessment of individual contracts.

2.2.2.A   Situations in which an entity would not have to estimate variable consideration at contract inception under IFRS 15

An entity may not have to estimate variable consideration at the inception of a contract in the following situations:

- *Allocation of variable consideration exception* – When the terms of a variable payment relate to an entity's efforts to satisfy a specific part of a contract (i.e. one or more, but not all, performance obligations or distinct goods or services promised in a series) and allocating the consideration to this specific part is consistent with the overall allocation objectives of the standard, IFRS 15 requires variable consideration to be allocated entirely to that specific part of a contract. As a result, variable consideration would not be estimated for the purpose of recognising revenue. For example, an entity that provides a series of distinct hotel management services and receives a variable fee based on a fixed percentage of rental revenue would need to allocate the percentage of monthly rental revenue entirely to the period in which the consideration is earned if the criteria to use this allocation exception are met. See 3.3 below for further discussion of the variable consideration allocation exception.

- *The 'right to invoice' practical expedient* – When an entity recognises revenue over time, the right to invoice practical expedient allows it to recognise revenue as invoiced if the entity's right to payment is for an amount that corresponds directly with the value to the customer of the entity's performance to date. For example, an entity may not be required to estimate the variable consideration for a three-year service contract under which it has a right to invoice the customer a fixed amount for each hour of service rendered, provided that fixed amount reflects the value to the customer. See Chapter 30 at 3.1.1 for further discussion of the right to invoice practical expedient.

- *Sales-based and usage-based royalties on licences of intellectual property recognition constraint* – The standard provides explicit application guidance for recognising consideration from sales-based and usage-based royalties provided in exchange for licences of intellectual property. The standard states that an entity recognises sales-based and usage-based royalties as revenue at the later of when: (1) the subsequent sales or usage occurs; or (2) the performance obligation to which some, or all, of the sales-based or usage-based royalty has been allocated has been satisfied (or partially satisfied). In many cases, using this application guidance results in the same pattern of revenue recognition as fully constraining the estimate of variable consideration associated with the future royalty stream. However, in cases where an entity is required to allocate sales-based or usage-based royalties to separate performance obligations in a contract, it may need to include expected royalties in its estimate of the stand-alone selling price of one or more of the performance obligations. See Chapter 31 at 2.5 for further discussion about sales-based and usage-based royalties related to licences of intellectual property.

2.2.3 Constraining estimates of variable consideration

Before an entity can include any amount of variable consideration in the transaction price, it must consider whether the amount of variable consideration is required to be constrained. Applying the constraint is an integral part of the evaluation of the variable consideration and it applies to all types of variable consideration that must be estimated in all transactions. The Board explained in the Basis for Conclusions that it created this constraint on variable consideration to address concerns raised by many constituents that the standard could otherwise require recognition of revenue before there was sufficient certainty that the amounts recognised would faithfully depict the consideration to which an entity expects to be entitled in exchange for the goods or services transferred to a customer. *[IFRS 15.BC203].*

The IASB explained in the Basis for Conclusions that it did not intend to eliminate the use of estimates from the revenue recognition standard. Instead, it wanted to make sure the estimates are robust and result in useful information. *[IFRS 15.BC204].* Following this objective, the Board concluded that it was appropriate to include estimates of variable consideration in revenue only when an entity has a 'high degree of confidence' that revenue will not be reversed in a subsequent reporting period. Therefore, the constraint is aimed at preventing the over-recognition of revenue (i.e. the standard focuses on potential significant reversals of revenue). The standard requires an entity to include in the transaction price some or all of an amount of variable consideration estimated only to the extent that it is highly probable that a significant reversal in the amount of cumulative revenue recognised will not occur when the uncertainty associated with the variable consideration is subsequently resolved. *[IFRS 15.56].*

In making this assessment, an entity is required to consider both the likelihood and the magnitude of the revenue reversal. The standard includes factors that could increase the likelihood or the magnitude of a revenue reversal. These include, but are not limited to, any of the following: *[IFRS 15.57]*

'(a) the amount of consideration is highly susceptible to factors outside the entity's influence. Those factors may include volatility in a market, the judgement or actions of third parties, weather conditions and a high risk of obsolescence of the promised good or service.

(b) the uncertainty about the amount of consideration is not expected to be resolved for a long period of time.

(c) the entity's experience (or other evidence) with similar types of contracts is limited, or that experience (or other evidence) has limited predictive value.

(d) the entity has a practice of either offering a broad range of price concessions or changing the payment terms and conditions of similar contracts in similar circumstances.

(e) the contract has a large number and broad range of possible consideration amounts.'

The standard does have an exception 'for consideration in the form of a sales or usage-based royalty that is promised in exchange for a licence of intellectual property.' *[IFRS 15.58]*.

To include variable consideration in the estimated transaction price, the entity has to conclude that it is 'highly probable' that a significant revenue reversal will not occur in future periods once the uncertainty related to the variable consideration is resolved. For the purpose of this analysis, the meaning of the term 'highly probable' is consistent with the existing definition in IFRS 5 – *Non-current Assets Held for Sale and Discontinued Operations*, i.e. 'significantly more likely than probable'. *[IFRS 5 Appendix A]*. For US GAAP preparers, ASC 606 uses the term 'probable' as the confidence threshold for applying the constraint, rather than 'highly probable', which is defined as 'the future event or events are likely to occur'.[6] However, the meaning of 'probable' under US GAAP is intended to be the same as 'highly probable' under IFRS. *[IFRS 15.BC211]*.

Furthermore, the IASB noted that an entity's analysis to determine whether its estimate of variable consideration should be constrained is largely qualitative. *[IFRS 15.BC212]*. That is, an entity needs to use judgement to evaluate whether it has met the objective of the constraint (i.e. it is highly probable that a significant revenue reversal will not occur in future periods) considering the factors provided in the standard that increase the probability of a significant revenue reversal (discussed further below). In addition, conclusions about amounts that may result in a significant revenue reversal may change as an entity satisfies a performance obligation.

An entity needs to consider both the likelihood and magnitude of a revenue reversal to apply the constraint.

- *Likelihood* – assessing the likelihood of a future reversal of revenue requires significant judgement. Entities want to ensure they adequately document the basis for their conclusions. The presence of any one of the indicators cited above does not necessarily mean that a reversal will occur if the variable consideration is included in the transaction price. The standard includes 'factors', rather than 'criteria', to signal that the list of items to consider is not a checklist for which all items need to be met. In addition, the factors provided are not meant to be an all-inclusive list and entities may consider additional factors that are relevant to their facts and circumstances.

- *Magnitude* – when assessing the probability of a significant revenue reversal, an entity is also required to assess the magnitude of that reversal. The constraint is based on the probability of a reversal of an amount that is 'significant' relative to the cumulative revenue recognised for the contract. When assessing the significance of the potential revenue reversal, the cumulative revenue recognised at the date of the potential reversal includes both fixed and variable consideration and includes revenue recognised from the entire contract, not just the transaction price allocated to a single performance obligation.

An entity must carefully evaluate the factors that could increase the likelihood or the magnitude of a revenue reversal, including those listed in paragraph 57 of IFRS 15:

- the amount of consideration is highly susceptible to factors outside the entity's influence (e.g. volatility in a market, judgement or actions of third parties, weather conditions, high risk of obsolescence of the promised good or service);
- the uncertainty about the amount of consideration is not expected to be resolved for a long period of time;
- the entity's experience (or other evidence) of similar types of contracts is limited, or that experience (or other evidence) has limited predictive value;
- the entity has a practice of either offering a broad range of price concessions or changing the payment terms and conditions of similar contracts in similar circumstances; or
- the contract has a large number and broad range of possible consideration amounts.

Example 29.6:   *Evaluating the factors that could increase the likelihood or magnitude of a significant revenue reversal*

Assume that an insurance broker receives 'trailing commissions' of £100 every time a consumer signs up for a new insurance policy and £50 whenever one of those consumers renews a policy.

In this fact pattern, the broker has a large pool of historical data about customer renewal patterns, given its significant experience with similar contracts. The broker considers the above factors and notes that the amount of consideration is highly susceptible to factors outside its influence and the uncertainty could remain over several years. However, it also has significant experience with similar types of contracts and its experience has predictive value.

As a result, even though the amount of consideration the entity will be entitled to is uncertain and depends on the actions of third parties (i.e. customer renewals), it is likely that the entity can estimate a minimum amount of variable consideration for which it is highly probable that a significant reversal of cumulative revenue will not occur. Assuming the broker's performance is complete upon initial signing of a contract, the broker would recognise the initial £100 fee plus the minimum amount related to future renewals that is not constrained.

There are some types of variable consideration that are frequently included in contracts that have significant uncertainties. It is likely to be more difficult for an entity to assert it is highly probable that these types of estimated amounts will not be subsequently reversed. Examples of the types of variable consideration include the following:

- payments contingent on regulatory approval (e.g. regulatory approval of a new drug);
- long-term commodity supply arrangements that are settled based on market prices at the future delivery date; or
- contingency fees based on litigation or regulatory outcomes (e.g. fees based on the positive outcome of litigation or the settlement of claims with government agencies).

When an entity determines that it cannot meet the highly probable threshold if it includes all of the variable consideration in the transaction price, the amount of variable consideration that must be included in the transaction price is limited to the amount that would not result in a significant revenue reversal. That is, the estimate of variable consideration is reduced until it reaches an amount that can be included in the transaction price that, if subsequently reversed when the uncertainty associated with the variable consideration is resolved, would not result in a significant reversal of cumulative revenue recognised. When there is significant uncertainty about the ultimate pricing of a contract, entities should not default to constraining the estimate of variable consideration to zero.

The standard includes an example in which the application of the constraint limits the amount of variable consideration included in the transaction price and one in which it does not. *[IFRS 15.IE116-IE123]*.

Example 29.7: Price concessions

An entity enters into a contract with a customer, a distributor, on 1 December 20X7. The entity transfers 1,000 products at contract inception for a price stated in the contract of CU100 per product (total consideration is CU100,000). Payment from the customer is due when the customer sells the products to the end customers. The entity's customer generally sells the products within 90 days of obtaining them. Control of the products transfers to the customer on 1 December 20X7.

On the basis of its past practices and to maintain its relationship with the customer, the entity anticipates granting a price concession to its customer because this will enable the customer to discount the product and thereby move the product through the distribution chain. Consequently, the consideration in the contract is variable.

Case A – Estimate of variable consideration is not constrained

The entity has significant experience selling this and similar products. The observable data indicate that historically the entity grants a price concession of approximately 20 per cent of the sales price for these products. Current market information suggests that a 20 per cent reduction in price will be sufficient to move the products through the distribution chain. The entity has not granted a price concession significantly greater than 20 per cent in many years.

To estimate the variable consideration to which the entity will be entitled, the entity decides to use the expected value method (see paragraph 53(a) of IFRS 15) because it is the method that the entity expects to better predict the amount of consideration to which it will be entitled. Using the expected value method, the entity estimates the transaction price to be CU80,000 (CU80 × 1,000 products).

The entity also considers the requirements in paragraphs 56–58 of IFRS 15 on constraining estimates of variable consideration to determine whether the estimated amount of variable consideration of CU80,000 can be included in the transaction price. The entity considers the factors in paragraph 57 of IFRS 15 and determines that it has significant previous experience with this product and current market information that supports its estimate. In addition, despite some uncertainty resulting from factors outside its influence, based on its current market estimates, the entity expects the price to be resolved within a short time frame. Thus, the entity concludes that it is highly probable that a significant reversal in the cumulative amount of revenue recognised (i.e. CU80,000) will not occur when the uncertainty is resolved (i.e. when the total amount of price concessions is determined). Consequently, the entity recognises CU80,000 as revenue when the products are transferred on 1 December 20X7.

Case B – Estimate of variable consideration is constrained

The entity has experience selling similar products. However, the entity's products have a high risk of obsolescence and the entity is experiencing high volatility in the pricing of its products. The observable data indicate that historically the entity grants a broad range of price concessions ranging from 20–60 per cent of the sales price for similar products. Current market information also suggests that a 15–50 per cent reduction in price may be necessary to move the products through the distribution chain.

To estimate the variable consideration to which the entity will be entitled, the entity decides to use the expected value method (see paragraph 53(a) of IFRS 15) because it is the method that the entity expects to better predict the amount of consideration to which it will be entitled. Using the expected value method, the entity estimates that a discount of 40 per cent will be provided and, therefore, the estimate of the variable consideration is CU60,000 (CU60 × 1,000 products).

The entity also considers the requirements in paragraphs 56–58 of IFRS 15 on constraining estimates of variable consideration to determine whether some or all of the estimated amount of variable consideration of CU60,000 can be included in the transaction price. The entity considers the factors in paragraph 57 of IFRS 15 and observes that the amount of consideration is highly susceptible to factors outside the entity's influence (i.e. risk of obsolescence) and it is likely that the entity may be required to provide a broad range of price concessions to move the products through the distribution chain. Consequently, the entity cannot include its estimate of CU60,000 (i.e. a discount of 40 per cent) in the transaction price because it cannot conclude that it is highly probable that a significant reversal in the amount of cumulative revenue recognised will not occur. Although the entity's historical price concessions have ranged from 20–60 per cent, market information currently suggests that a price concession of 15–50 per cent will be necessary. The entity's actual results have been consistent with then-current market information in previous, similar transactions. Consequently, the entity concludes that it is highly probable that a significant reversal in the cumulative amount of revenue recognised will not occur if the entity includes CU50,000 in the transaction price (CU100 sales price and a 50 per cent price concession) and therefore, recognises revenue at that amount. Therefore, the entity recognises revenue of CU50,000 when the products are transferred and reassesses the estimates of the transaction price at each reporting date until the uncertainty is resolved in accordance with paragraph 59 of IFRS 15.

In some situations, it is appropriate for an entity to include in the transaction price an estimate of variable consideration that is not a possible outcome of an individual contract. The TRG discussed this topic using the following example from the TRG agenda paper.[7]

Example 29.8:   Estimating variable consideration using the expected value method

Entity A develops websites for customers. The contracts include similar terms and conditions and contain a fixed fee, plus variable consideration for a performance bonus related to the timing of Entity A completing the website. Based on Entity A's historical experience, the bonus amounts and associated probabilities for achieving each bonus are as follows:

Bonus amount	Probability of outcome
–	15%
$50	40%
$100	45%

Entity A determines that using the expected value method would better predict the amount of consideration to which it will be entitled than using the most likely amount method because it has a large number of contracts that have characteristics that are similar to the new contract.

Under the expected value method, Entity A estimates variable consideration of $65,000 [(0 × 15%) + (50,000 × 40%) + (100,000 × 45%)]. Entity A must then consider the effect of applying the constraint on variable consideration. To do this, Entity A considers the factors that could increase the likelihood of a revenue reversal in paragraph 57 of IFRS 15 and concludes that it has relevant historical experience with similar types of contracts and that the amount of consideration is not highly susceptible to factors outside of its influence.

In determining whether the entity would include $50,000 or $65,000 in the transaction price, TRG members generally agreed that when an entity has concluded that the expected value approach is the appropriate method to estimate variable consideration, the constraint is also applied based on the expected value method. That is, the entity is not required to switch from an expected value method to a most likely amount for purposes of applying the constraint. As a result, if an entity applies the expected value method for a particular contract, the estimated transaction price may not be a possible outcome in an individual contract. Therefore, the entity could conclude that, in this example, $65,000 is the appropriate estimate of variable consideration to include in the transaction price. It is important to note that in this example, the entity had concluded that none of the factors in paragraph 57 of IFRS 15 or any other factors indicate a likelihood of a significant revenue reversal.

When an entity uses the expected value method and determines that the estimated amount of variable consideration is not a possible outcome in the individual contract, the entity must still consider the constraint on variable consideration. Depending on the facts and circumstances of each contract, an entity may need to constrain its estimate of variable consideration, even though it has used an expected value method, if the factors in paragraph 57 of IFRS 15 indicate a likelihood of a significant revenue reversal. However, using the expected value method and considering probability-weighted amounts sometimes achieves the objective of the constraint on variable consideration.

When an entity estimates the transaction price using the expected value method, the entity reduces the probability of a revenue reversal because the estimate does not include all of the potential consideration due to the probability weighting of the outcomes. In some cases, the entity may not need to constrain the estimate of variable consideration if the factors in paragraph 57 of IFRS 15 do not indicate a likelihood of a significant revenue reversal.

The standard provides the following example of a situation in which a qualitative analysis of the factors in paragraph 57 of IFRS 15 indicates that it is not highly probable that a significant reversal would not occur if an entity includes a performance-based incentive fee in the transaction price of an investment management contract. [IFRS 15.IE129-IE133].

Example 29.9:   Management fees subject to the constraint

On 1 January 20X8, an entity enters into a contract with a client to provide asset management services for five years. The entity receives a two per cent quarterly management fee based on the client's assets under management at the end of each quarter. In addition, the entity receives a performance-based incentive fee of 20 per cent of the fund's return in excess of the return of an observable market index over the five-year period. Consequently, both the management fee and the performance fee in the contract are variable consideration.

The entity accounts for the services as a single performance obligation in accordance with paragraph 22(b) of IFRS 15, because it is providing a series of distinct services that are substantially the same and have the same pattern of transfer (the services transfer to the customer over time and use the same method to measure progress – that is, a time-based measure of progress).

At contract inception, the entity considers the requirements in paragraphs 50–54 of IFRS 15 on estimating variable consideration and the requirements in paragraphs 56–58 of IFRS 15 on constraining estimates of variable consideration, including the factors in paragraph 57 of IFRS 15. The entity observes that the promised consideration is dependent on the market and thus is highly susceptible to factors outside the entity's influence. In addition, the incentive fee has a large number and a broad range of possible consideration amounts. The entity also observes that although it has experience with similar contracts, that experience is of little predictive value in determining the future performance of the market. Therefore, at contract inception, the entity cannot conclude that it is highly probable that a significant reversal in the cumulative amount of revenue recognised would not occur if the entity included its estimate of the management fee or the incentive fee in the transaction price.

At each reporting date, the entity updates its estimate of the transaction price. Consequently, at the end of each quarter, the entity concludes that it can include in the transaction price the actual amount of the quarterly management fee because the uncertainty is resolved. However, the entity concludes that it cannot include its estimate of the incentive fee in the transaction price at those dates. This is because there has not been a change in its assessment from contract inception – the variability of the fee based on the market index indicates that the entity cannot conclude that it is highly probable that a significant reversal in the cumulative amount of revenue recognised would not occur if the entity included its estimate of the incentive fee in the transaction price. At 31 March 20X8, the client's assets under management are ¥100 million. Therefore, the resulting quarterly management fee and the transaction price is ¥2 million.

At the end of each quarter, the entity allocates the quarterly management fee to the distinct services provided during the quarter in accordance with paragraphs 84(b) and 85 of IFRS 15. This is because the fee relates specifically to the entity's efforts to transfer the services for that quarter, which are distinct from the services provided in other quarters, and the resulting allocation will be consistent with the allocation objective in paragraph 73 of IFRS 15. Consequently, the entity recognises ¥2 million as revenue for the quarter ended 31 March 20X8.

See 3 below for a discussion of allocating the transaction price.

2.2.3.A Applying the constraint on variable consideration: contract level versus performance obligation level

At the January 2015 TRG meeting, the TRG members were asked whether an entity was required to apply the constraint on variable consideration at the contract level or at the performance obligation level.

The TRG members generally agreed that the constraint would be applied at the contract level and not at the performance obligation level. That is, the significance assessment of the potential revenue reversal would consider the total transaction price of the contract (and not the portion of transaction price allocated to a performance obligation).[8]

2.2.3.B Would an entity be required to follow a two-step approach to estimate variable consideration?

The Board noted in the Basis for Conclusions that an entity is not required to strictly follow a two-step process (i.e. first estimate the variable consideration and then apply the constraint to that estimate) if its internal processes incorporate the principles of both steps in a single step. *[IFRS 15.BC215].* For example, if an entity already has a single process to estimate expected returns when calculating revenue from the sale of goods in a manner consistent with the objectives of applying the constraint, the entity would not need to estimate the transaction price and then separately apply the constraint.

A TRG agenda paper also noted that applying the expected value method, which requires an entity to consider probability-weighted amounts, may sometimes achieve the objective of the constraint on variable consideration.[9] That is, in developing its estimate of the transaction price in accordance with the expected value method, an entity reduces the probability of a revenue reversal and may not need to further constrain its estimate of variable consideration. However, to meet the objective of the constraint, the entity's estimated transaction price would need to incorporate its expectations of the possible consideration amounts (e.g. products not expected to be returned) at a level at which it is highly probable that including the estimate of variable consideration in the transaction price would not result in a significant revenue reversal (e.g. such that it is highly probable that additional returns above the estimated amount would not result in a significant reversal).

2.2.3.C Applying the constraint on variable consideration to milestone payments

An entity may need to apply significant judgement to determine whether and, if so, how much of a milestone payment is constrained. Assuming the payment is not subject to the sales-based or usage-based royalty recognition constraint (see Chapter 31 at 2.5), a milestone payment is a form of variable consideration that needs to be estimated and included in the transaction price subject to the variable consideration constraint.

Milestone payments are often binary (i.e. the entity will either achieve the target or desired outcome and become entitled to the milestone payment or not). In these situations, entities generally conclude that the most likely amount method is the better predictor of the amount to which it expects to be entitled. The entity will then consider the constraint on variable consideration to determine whether it is highly probable that a significant reversal in the amount of cumulative revenue recognised will not occur when the uncertainties related to the milestone payments have been resolved. When assessing the significance of the potential revenue reversal of a future milestone payment, the cumulative revenue recognised at the date of the potential reversal would include any fixed consideration in addition to the variable consideration for the entire contract.

Applying the constraint to milestone payments often requires significant judgement, especially when uncertainty exists about the underlying activities necessary to meet the target or desired outcome that entitle the entity to the milestone payment. Entities need to analyse the facts and circumstances of each milestone payment and consider all information (historical, current and forecast) that is reasonably available to them to assess whether the revenue needs to be constrained. In addition, there could be external factors that affect an entity's assessment of the contract and the probability of entitlement to milestone payments. For example, we expect entities to conclude in many instances that milestone payments contingent on regulatory approval (e.g. regulatory approval of a new drug) are constrained, preventing them from recognising these payments until the uncertainty associated with the payments is resolved.

Consider the following example:

Example 29.10: Milestone payments

Biotech enters into an arrangement with Pharma under which Biotech provides a licence to a product candidate that is starting phase II clinical studies and performs research and development services for a specified period of time. Assume that these two promises are determined to be distinct. Biotech receives an upfront payment upon execution of the arrangement and may receive milestone payments upon: (1) enrolment of a specified number of patients in a phase II clinical study; (2) completion of phase III clinical studies; (3) regulatory approval in the US; and (4) regulatory approval in the European Union.

Under the standard, Biotech includes in the transaction price the upfront payment and its estimate of the milestone payments it expects to receive. The amount of consideration that Biotech can include in the transaction price is limited to amounts for which it is highly probable that a significant reversal of cumulative revenues recognised under the contract will not occur in future periods.

The milestone for patient enrolment only has two possible outcomes (e.g. Biotech enrols or does not enrol the specified number of patients). Therefore, Biotech determines that the most likely amount method is the better predictor of the milestone payment. It then determines that it can include the amount associated with the enrolment milestone in the transaction price because it is highly probable that doing so will not result in a significant revenue reversal, based on: its prior experience with enrolling participants in similar studies; clinical trial results on the product candidate to date; and the significance of the milestone payment compared to the cumulative revenues expected to be recognised under the contract at the time of the enrolment milestone.

Due to the significant uncertainty associated with the other future events that would result in milestone payments, however, Biotech initially determines that it cannot include these amounts in the transaction price (i.e. the other milestone payments are fully constrained at contract inception). At the end of each reporting period, Biotech updates its assessment of whether the milestone payments are constrained by considering both the likelihood and magnitude of a potential revenue reversal.

The evaluation of the constraint considers the probability of reversal (i.e. not achieving the target or desired outcome) and whether any such reversal would be significant in relation to cumulative revenue recognised to date on the total contract. There are many variables that need to be factored into this assessment. Thus, entities should carefully evaluate each milestone to determine when it is appropriate to include the milestone in the transaction price.

For example, an entity may consider the variable consideration constraint and conclude that the milestone payment is not constrained at contract inception because including the milestone payment in the transaction price would not result in a significant reversal of cumulative revenue in the event that the milestone requirements are not achieved (i.e. the entity is not entitled to the consideration). This may be the case when an entity expects to recognise a significant amount of the contract revenue early in the life of the contract and the milestone payment amount is not significant in relation to the cumulative revenue that will be recognised by the time the uncertainties related to the milestone have been resolved.

As discussed in 2.2.4 below, an entity is required to update its estimate of variable consideration (including any amounts that are constrained) at the end of each reporting period to reflect its revised expectations of the amount of consideration to which it expects to be entitled. For example, an entity may initially conclude that a milestone payment is constrained and, therefore, exclude it from the transaction price. However, in a later reporting period, when reassessing the amount of variable consideration that should be included in the transaction price, the entity may conclude a milestone payment is no longer constrained even though the target or desired outcome has not been achieved. That is, based on new information, an entity may conclude that it expects to achieve the target or desired outcome and, therefore, concludes that it is now highly probable that a significant revenue reversal will not occur.

2.2.4 Reassessment of variable consideration

The standard specifies that at the end of each reporting period, an entity must 'update the estimated transaction price (including updating its assessment of whether an estimate of variable consideration is constrained) to represent faithfully the circumstances present at the end of the reporting period and the changes in circumstances during the reporting period.' The entity accounts for changes in the transaction price in accordance with paragraphs 87–90 of IFRS 15. *[IFRS 15.59]*.

When a contract includes variable consideration, an entity needs to update its estimate of the transaction price throughout the term of the contract to depict conditions that exist at the end of each reporting period. This involves updating the estimate of the variable consideration (including any amounts that are constrained) to reflect an entity's revised expectations about the amount of consideration to which it expects to be entitled, considering uncertainties that are resolved or new information that is gained about remaining uncertainties. As discussed at 2.2.3 above, conclusions about amounts that may result in a significant revenue reversal may change as an entity satisfies a performance obligation. See 3.5 below for a discussion of allocating changes in the transaction price after contract inception.

The IASB noted in the Basis for Conclusions that, in some cases, an estimate of variable consideration made at the end of an accounting period could be affected by information that arises after the end of the reporting period, but before the release of the financial statements. The Board decided not to include guidance in IFRS 15 on accounting in these situations, because it noted that the accounting for subsequent events is already addressed in IAS 10 – *Events after the Reporting Period* (see Chapter 38). *[IFRS 15.BC228]*.

2.3 Refund liabilities

An entity may receive consideration that it will need to refund to the customer in the future because the consideration is not an amount to which the entity ultimately will be entitled under the contract. If an entity expects to refund some or all of that consideration, the amounts received (or receivable) need to be recorded as refund liabilities.

A refund liability is measured 'at the amount of consideration received (or receivable) for which the entity does not expect to be entitled (i.e. amounts not included in the transaction price).' An entity is required to update its estimates of refund liabilities (and the corresponding change in the transaction price) at the end of each reporting period. The standard also notes that, if a refund liability relates to a sale with a right of return, an entity applies the specific application guidance for sales with a right of return. [IFRS 15.55].

While the most common form of refund liabilities may be related to sales with a right of return, the refund liability requirements also apply when an entity expects that it will need to refund consideration received due to poor customer satisfaction with a service provided (i.e. there was no good delivered or returned) and/or if an entity expects to have to provide retrospective price reductions to a customer (e.g. if a customer reaches a certain threshold of purchases, the unit price is retrospectively adjusted). For a discussion of the accounting for sales with a right of return, see 2.4 below. We address the question of whether a refund liability is a contract liability (and, therefore, subject to the presentation and disclosure requirements of a contract liability) in Chapter 32 at 2.1.6.D.

2.4 Rights of return

The standard notes that, in some contracts, an entity may transfer control of a product to a customer, but grant the customer a right of return. In return, the customer may receive a full or partial refund of any consideration paid; a credit that can be applied against amounts owed, or that will be owed, to the entity; another product in exchange; or any combination thereof. [IFRS 15.B20]. As discussed in Chapter 28 at 3.7, the standard states that a right of return does not represent a separate performance obligation. [IFRS 15.B22]. Instead, a right of return affects the transaction price and the amount of revenue an entity can recognise for satisfied performance obligations. In other words, rights of return create variability in the transaction price.

Under IFRS 15, rights of return do not include exchanges by customers of one product for another of the same type, quality, condition and price (e.g. one colour or size for another). [IFRS 15.B26]. Nor do rights of return include situations where a customer may return a defective product in exchange for a functioning product; these are, instead, evaluated in accordance with the application guidance on warranties (see Chapter 31 at 3). [IFRS 15.B27].

'To account for the transfer of products with a right of return (and for some services that are provided subject to a refund), an entity shall recognise all of the following:

(a) revenue for the transferred products in the amount of consideration to which the entity expects to be entitled (therefore, revenue would not be recognised for the products expected to be returned);

(b) a refund liability; and

(c) an asset (and corresponding adjustment to cost of sales) for its right to recover products from customers on settling the refund liability.' [IFRS 15.B21].

Under the standard, an entity estimates the transaction price and applies the constraint to the estimated transaction price to determine the amount of consideration to which the entity expects to be entitled. In doing so, it considers the products expected to be returned in order to determine the amount to which the entity expects to be entitled (excluding consideration for the products expected to be returned). The entity recognises revenue based on the amount to which it expects to be entitled through to the end of the return period (considering expected product returns). An entity does not recognise the portion of the revenue subject to the constraint until the amount is no longer constrained, which could be at the end of the return period. The entity recognises the amount received or receivable that is expected to be returned as a refund liability, representing its obligation to return the customer's consideration (see 2.3 above). Subsequently, at the end of each reporting period, the entity updates its assessment of amounts for which it expects to be entitled and makes a corresponding change to the transaction price (and, therefore, to the amount of revenue recognised). [IFRS 15.B23].

As part of updating its estimate, an entity must update its assessment of expected returns and the related refund liabilities. [IFRS 15.B24]. This remeasurement is performed at the end of each reporting period and reflects any changes in assumptions about expected returns. Any adjustments made to the estimate result in a corresponding adjustment to amounts recognised as revenue for the satisfied performance obligations (e.g. if the entity expects the number of returns to be lower than originally estimated, it would have to increase the amount of revenue recognised and decrease the refund liability). [IFRS 15.B23, B24].

Finally, when customers exercise their rights of return, the entity may receive the returned product in a saleable or repairable condition. Under the standard, at the time of the initial sale (i.e. when recognition of revenue is deferred due to the anticipated return), the entity recognises a return asset (and adjusts the cost of goods sold) for its right to recover the goods returned by the customer. [IFRS 15.B21]. The entity initially measures this asset at the former carrying amount of the inventory, less any expected costs to recover the goods, including any potential decreases in the value of the returned goods. The consideration of potential decreases in value of the returned products is important because the returned products may not be in the same condition they were in when they were sold (e.g. due to damage or use) and this helps to ensure that the value of the return asset is not impaired.

Along with remeasuring the refund liability at the end of each reporting period (as discussed above), the entity updates the measurement of the asset recorded for any revisions to its expected level of returns, as well as any additional potential decreases in the value of the returned products. [IFRS 15.B25].

Because the standard includes specific remeasurement requirements for the return asset, an entity applies those requirements, rather than other impairment models (e.g. inventory). The standard also requires the refund liability to be presented separately from the corresponding asset (i.e. on a gross basis, rather than a net basis). [IFRS 15.B25]. While the standard does not explicitly state this, we believe that the return asset would generally be presented separately from inventory.

The standard provides the following example of rights of return. [IFRS 15.IE110-IE115].

Example 29.11: Right of return

An entity enters into 100 contracts with customers. Each contract includes the sale of one product for CU100 (100 total products × CU100 = CU10,000 total consideration). Cash is received when control of a product transfers. The entity's customary business practice is to allow a customer to return any unused product within 30 days and receive a full refund. The entity's cost of each product is CU60.

The entity applies the requirements in IFRS 15 to the portfolio of 100 contracts because it reasonably expects that, in accordance with paragraph 4, the effects on the financial statements from applying these requirements to the portfolio would not differ materially from applying the requirements to the individual contracts within the portfolio.

Because the contract allows a customer to return the products, the consideration received from the customer is variable. To estimate the variable consideration to which the entity will be entitled, the entity decides to use the expected value method (see paragraph 53(a) of IFRS 15) because it is the method that the entity expects to better predict the amount of consideration to which it will be entitled. Using the expected value method, the entity estimates that 97 products will not be returned.

The entity also considers the requirements in paragraphs 56-58 of IFRS 15 on constraining estimates of variable consideration to determine whether the estimated amount of variable consideration of CU9,700 (CU100 × 97 products not expected to be returned) can be included in the transaction price. The entity considers the factors in paragraph 57 of IFRS 15 and determines that although the returns are outside the entity's influence, it has significant experience in estimating returns for this product and customer class. In addition, the uncertainty will be resolved within a short time frame (i.e. the 30-day return period). Thus, the entity concludes that it is highly probable that a significant reversal in the cumulative amount of revenue recognised (i.e. CU9,700) will not occur as the uncertainty is resolved (i.e. over the return period).

The entity estimates that the costs of recovering the products will be immaterial and expects that the returned products can be resold at a profit.

Upon transfer of control of the 100 products, the entity does not recognise revenue for the three products that it expects to be returned. Consequently, in accordance with paragraphs 55 and B21 of IFRS 15, the entity recognises the following:

- revenue of CU9,700 (CU100 × 97 products not expected to be returned);
- a refund liability of CU300 (CU100 refund × 3 products expected to be returned); and
- an asset of CU180 (CU60 × 3 products for its right to recover products from customers on settling the refund liability).

In ASC 606, the same example includes the following journal entries to illustrate how the entity accounts for the contract in this example in accordance with the US GAAP equivalent of paragraphs 55 and B21 of IFRS 15 when the product is transferred to the customer:[10]

Dr. Cash	$10,000(a)	
Cr. Revenue		$9,700(b)
Cr. Refund liability		$300(c)
Dr. Cost of sales	$5,820(d)	
Dr. Asset	$180(e)	
Cr. Inventory		$6,000(f)

(a) $100 × 100 products transferred.
(b) $100 × 97 products not expected to be returned.
(c) $100 refund × 3 products expected to be returned.
(d) $60 × 97 products not expected to be returned.
(e) $60 × 3 products for its right to recover products from customers on settling the refund liability.
(f) $60 × 100 products.

See Chapter 30 at 5.1.1 for a discussion on evaluating a conditional call option to repurchase an asset.

2.4.1 Is an entity applying the portfolio approach practical expedient when accounting for rights of return?

An entity can, but would not be required to, apply the portfolio approach practical expedient to estimate variable consideration for expected returns using the expected value method. Similar to the discussion at 2.2.2 above on estimating variable consideration, the July 2015 TRG agenda paper noted that an entity can consider evidence from other, similar contracts to develop an estimate of variable consideration using the expected value method without applying the portfolio approach practical expedient. In order to estimate variable consideration in a contract, an entity frequently makes judgements considering its historical experience with other, similar contracts. Considering historical experience does not necessarily mean the entity is applying the portfolio approach practical expedient.[11]

This question arises, in part, because Example 22 in IFRS 15 (see Example 29.11 at 2.4 above) states that the entity is using the portfolio approach practical expedient in paragraph 4 of IFRS 15 to calculate its estimate of returns. Use of this practical expedient requires an entity to assert that it does not expect the use of the expedient to differ materially from applying the standard to an individual contract.

We expect that entities often use the expected value method to estimate variable consideration related to returns because doing so would likely better predict the amount of consideration to which the entities will be entitled. This is despite the fact that there are two potential outcomes for each contract from the variability of product returns: the product either will be returned or will not be returned. That is, the revenue for each contract ultimately either will be 100% or will be 0% of the total contract value (assuming returns create the only variability in the contract). However, entities may conclude that the expected value is the appropriate method for estimating variable consideration because they have a large number of contracts with similar characteristics. The TRG agenda paper noted that using a portfolio of data is not equivalent to using the portfolio approach practical expedient, so entities that use the expected value method to estimate variable consideration for returns would not be required to assert that the outcome from the portfolio is not expected to materially differ from an assessment of individual contracts.

2.4.2 Accounting for restocking fees for goods that are expected to be returned

Entities sometimes charge customers a 'restocking fee' when a product is returned. This fee may be levied by entities to compensate them for the costs of repackaging, shipping and/or reselling the item at a lower price to another customer. Stakeholders had raised questions about how to account for restocking fees and related costs.[12]

At the July 2015 TRG meeting, the TRG members generally agreed that restocking fees for goods that are expected to be returned would be included in the estimate of the transaction price at contract inception and recorded as revenue when (or as) control of the good transfers. That is, selling a product subject to a restocking fee if it is returned is not different from providing a partial return right and should be accounted for similarly.

Example 29.12: Restocking fees

Entity A enters into a contract with a customer to sell 10 widgets for £100 each. The customer has the right to return the widgets, but if it does so, it will be charged a 10% restocking fee (or £10 per returned widget). The entity estimates that 10% of all widgets that are sold will be returned. Upon transfer of control of the 10 widgets, the entity will recognise revenue of £910 [(9 widgets not expected to be returned × £100 selling price) + (1 widget expected to be returned × £10 restocking fee)]. A refund liability of £90 will also be recorded [1 widget expected to be returned × (£100 selling price – £10 restocking fee)].

2.4.3 Accounting for restocking costs for goods that are expected to be returned

At the July 2015 TRG meeting, the TRG members generally agreed that restocking costs (e.g. shipping and repackaging costs) would be recorded as a reduction of the amount of the return asset when (or as) control of the good is transferred to the customer. This accounting treatment is consistent with the requirement in paragraph B25 of IFRS 15 that the return asset be initially measured at the former carrying amount of the inventory, less any expected costs to recover the goods (e.g. restocking costs).[13]

2.5 Significant financing component

For some transactions, the receipt of the consideration does not match the timing of the transfer of goods or services to the customer (e.g. the consideration is prepaid or is paid after the services are provided). When the customer pays in arrears, the entity is effectively providing financing to the customer. Conversely, when the customer pays in advance, the entity has effectively received financing from the customer.

IFRS 15 states that 'in determining the transaction price, an entity shall adjust the promised amount of consideration for the effects of the time value of money if the timing of payments agreed to by the parties to the contract (either explicitly or implicitly) provides the customer or the entity with a significant benefit of financing the transfer of goods or services to the customer. In those circumstances, the contract contains a significant financing component. A significant financing component may exist regardless of whether the promise of financing is explicitly stated in the contract or implied by the payment terms agreed to by the parties to the contract.' *[IFRS 15.60]*.

The standard goes on to clarify that 'the objective when adjusting the promised amount of consideration for a significant financing component is for an entity to recognise revenue at an amount that reflects the price that a customer would have paid for the promised goods or services if the customer had paid cash for those goods or services when (or as) they transfer to the customer (i.e. the cash selling price). An entity shall consider all relevant facts and circumstances in assessing whether a contract contains a financing component and whether that financing component is significant to the contract, including both of the following:

(a) the difference, if any, between the amount of promised consideration and the cash selling price of the promised goods or services; and

(b) the combined effect of both of the following:

   (i) the expected length of time between when the entity transfers the promised goods or services to the customer and when the customer pays for those goods or services; and

   (ii) the prevailing interest rates in the relevant market.' *[IFRS 15.61]*

Notwithstanding this assessment, a contract with a customer would not have a significant financing component if any of the following factors exist: [IFRS 15.62]
- the customer paid for the goods or services in advance and the timing of the transfer of those goods or services is at the discretion of the customer;
- a substantial amount of the consideration promised by the customer is variable and the amount or timing of that consideration varies on the basis of the occurrence or non-occurrence of a future event that is not substantially within the control of the customer or the entity (e.g. if the consideration is a sales-based royalty); or
- the difference between the promised consideration and the cash selling price of the good or service (as described in (a) above) arises for reasons other than the provision of finance to either the customer or the entity, and the difference between those amounts is proportional to the reason for the difference. For example, the payment terms might provide the entity or the customer with protection from the other party failing to adequately complete some or all of its obligations under the contract.

This assessment may be difficult in some circumstances, so the Board provided a practical expedient. An entity 'need not adjust the promised amount of consideration for the effects of a significant financing component if the entity expects, at contract inception, that the period between when the entity transfers a promised good or service to a customer and when the customer pays for that good or service will be one year or less.' [IFRS 15.63].

When an entity concludes that a financing component is significant to a contract, it determines the transaction price by discounting the amount of promised consideration. The entity uses the same discount rate that it would use if it were to enter into a separate financing transaction with the customer at contract inception. The discount rate has to reflect the credit characteristics of the borrower in the contract, as well as any collateral or security provided by the customer or the entity, including assets transferred in the contract. The standard notes that an entity 'may be able to determine that rate by identifying the rate that discounts the nominal amount of the promised consideration to the price that the customer would pay in cash for the goods or services when (or as) they transfer to the customer.' The entity does not update the discount rate for changes in circumstances or interest rates after contract inception. [IFRS 15.64].

The Board explained in the Basis for Conclusions that, conceptually, a contract that includes a financing component is comprised of two transactions – one for the sale of goods and/or services and one for the financing. [IFRS 15.BC229]. Accordingly, the Board decided to require entities to adjust the amount of promised consideration for the effects of financing only if the timing of payments specified in the contract provides the customer or the entity with a significant benefit of financing. The IASB's objective in requiring entities to adjust the promised amount of consideration for the effects of a significant financing component is for entities to recognise as revenue the cash selling price of the underlying goods or services at the time of transfer. [IFRS 15.BC230].

(a) Practical expedient

As a practical expedient, an entity is not required to adjust the promised amount of consideration for the effects of a significant financing component if the entity expects, at contract inception, that the period between when the entity transfers a promised good or service to a customer and when the customer pays for that good or service will be one year or less. The Board added this practical expedient to the standard because it simplifies the application of this aspect of IFRS 15 and because the effect of accounting for a significant financing component (or of not doing so) should be limited in financing arrangements with a duration of less than 12 months. *[IFRS 15.BC236]*. If an entity uses this practical expedient, it would apply the expedient consistently to similar contracts in similar circumstances. *[IFRS 15.BC235]*.

It is important to note that if the period between when the entity transfers a promised good or service to a customer and the customer pays for that good or service is more than one year and the financing component is deemed to be significant, the entity must account for the entire financing component. That is, an entity cannot exclude the first 12 months of the period between when the entity transfers a promised good or service to a customer and when the customer pays for that good or service from the calculation of the potential adjustment to the transaction price. An entity also cannot exclude the first 12 months in its determination of whether the financing component of a contract is significant.

Entities may need to apply judgement to determine whether the practical expedient applies to some contracts. For example, the standard does not specify whether entities should assess the period between payment and performance at the contract level or at the performance obligation level. In addition, the TRG discussed how an entity should consider whether the practical expedient applies to contracts with a single payment stream for multiple performance obligations. See 2.5.2.D below.

(b) *Existence of a significant financing component*

Absent the use of the practical expedient, to determine whether a significant financing component exists, an entity needs to consider all relevant facts and circumstances, including:

(1) the difference between the cash selling price and the amount of promised consideration for the promised goods or services; and

(2) the combined effect of the expected length of time between the transfer of the goods or services and the receipt of consideration and the prevailing market interest rates. The Board acknowledged that a difference in the timing between the transfer of and payment for goods or services is not determinative, but the combined effect of timing and the prevailing interest rates may provide a strong indication that an entity is providing or receiving a significant benefit of financing. *[IFRS 15.BC232]*.

Even if conditions in a contract would otherwise indicate that a significant financing component exists, the standard includes several situations that the Board has determined do not provide the customer or the entity with a significant benefit of financing. These situations, as described in paragraph 62 of IFRS 15, include the following:

- The customer has paid for the goods or services in advance and the timing of the transfer of those goods or services is at the discretion of the customer. In these situations (e.g. prepaid phone cards, customer loyalty programmes), the Board noted in the Basis for Conclusions that the payment terms are not related to a financing arrangement between the parties and the costs of requiring an entity to account for a significant financing component would outweigh the benefits because an entity would need to continually estimate when the goods or services will transfer to the customer. *[IFRS 15.BC233]*.

- A substantial amount of the consideration promised by the customer is variable and is based on factors outside the control of the customer or entity. In these situations, the Board noted in the Basis for Conclusions that the primary purpose of the timing or terms of payment may be to allow for the resolution of uncertainties that relate to the consideration, rather than to provide the customer or the entity with the significant benefit of financing. In addition, the terms or timing of payment in these situations may be to provide the parties with assurance of the value of the goods or services (e.g. an arrangement for which consideration is in the form of a sales-based royalty). *[IFRS 15.BC233]*.

- The difference between the promised consideration and the cash selling price of the good or service arises for reasons other than the provision of financing to either the customer or the entity (e.g. a payment is made in advance or in arrears in accordance with the typical payment terms of the industry or jurisdiction) and the difference between those amounts is proportional to the reason for the difference. In certain situations, the Board determined the purpose of the payment terms may be to provide the customer with assurance that the entity will complete its obligations under the contract, rather than to provide financing to the customer or the entity. Examples include a customer withholding a portion of the consideration until the contract is complete (illustrated in Example 29.14 at 2.5.1 below) or a milestone is reached, or an entity requiring a customer to pay a portion of the consideration upfront in order to secure a future supply of goods or services. See 2.5.2.A below for further discussion.

(c) *Advance payments*

As explained in the Basis for Conclusions, the Board decided not to provide an overall exemption from accounting for the effects of a significant financing component arising from advance payments. This is because ignoring the effects of advance payments may skew the amount and timing of revenue recognised if the advance payment is significant and the purpose of the payment is to provide the entity with financing. *[IFRS 15.BC238]*. For example, an entity may require a customer to make advance payments to avoid obtaining the financing from a third party. If the entity obtained third-party financing, it would likely charge the customer additional amounts to cover the finance costs incurred. The Board decided that an entity's revenue should be consistent regardless of whether it receives the significant financing benefit from a customer or from a third party because, in either scenario, the entity's performance is the same.

In order to conclude that an advance payment does not represent a significant financing component, we believe that an entity needs to support why the advance payment does not provide a significant financing benefit and describe its substantive business purpose.[14] As a result, it is important that entities analyse all of the relevant facts and circumstances. Example 29.16 at 2.5.1 below illustrates an entity's determination that a customer's advance payment represents a significant financing component. In a 2018 speech, a member of the SEC staff discussed a consultation with the Office of the Chief Accountant (OCA) in which a registrant concluded that a contract with a large upfront payment did not have a significant financing component because: (1) the upfront payment was made for reasons other than to provide a significant financing benefit; and (2) the difference between the upfront payment and what the customer would have paid, had the payments been made over the term of the arrangement, was proportional to the reason identified for the difference. The SEC staff member noted, like other consultations that OCA has evaluated in relation to the revenue standard, the evaluation was based on the facts and circumstances. In this fact pattern, the staff did not object to the registrant's conclusion that the contract did not have a significant financing component based on the nature of the transaction and the purpose of the upfront payment.[15]

Example 29.17 at 2.5.1 below illustrates an entity's determination that a customer's advance payment does not represent a significant financing component.

(d) Assessment of significance

The assessment of significance is made at the individual contract level. As noted in the Basis for Conclusions, the Board decided that it would be an undue burden to require an entity to account for a financing component if the effects of the financing component are not significant to the individual contract, but the combined effects of the financing components for a portfolio of similar contracts would be material to the entity as a whole. *[IFRS 15.BC234].*

(e) Determination of the discount rate

When an entity concludes that a financing component is significant to a contract, in accordance with paragraph 64 of IFRS 15, it determines the transaction price by applying a discount rate to the amount of promised consideration. *[IFRS 15.64].* As stated above, the objective of requiring entities to adjust the promised consideration for the effects of a significant financing component is for the revenue recognised to approximate an amount that reflects the cash selling price that a customer would have paid for the promised goods or services. However, to achieve this objective, the entity does not need to estimate that cash selling price. Rather, the entity determines an interest rate and applies it to the amount of the promised consideration.

The entity uses the same interest rate that it would use if it were to enter into a separate financing transaction with the customer at contract inception. The interest rate needs to reflect the credit characteristics of the borrower in the contract, which could be either the entity or the customer (depending on who receives the financing). Using the risk-free rate or a rate explicitly stated in the contract that does not correspond with a separate financing rate would not be acceptable. *[IFRS 15.BC239].* Example 29.15 Case B at 2.5.1 below illustrates a contractual discount rate that does not reflect the rate in a separate financing transaction. Furthermore, using a contract's implicit interest rate (i.e. the interest rate that would make alternative payment options economically equivalent) would also not be acceptable if that rate does not reflect the rate in a separate financing transaction (as illustrated in Example 29.16 at 2.5.1 below).

While not explicitly stated in the standard, we believe an entity would consider the expected term of the financing when determining the interest rate in light of current market conditions at contract inception. In addition, paragraph 64 of IFRS 15 is clear that an entity does not update the interest rate for changes in circumstances or market interest rates after contract inception.

The standard requires that the interest rate be a rate similar to one that the entity would have used in a separate financing transaction with the customer. Because most entities are not in the business of entering into free-standing financing arrangements with their customers, they may find it difficult to identify an appropriate rate. However, most entities perform some level of credit analysis before financing purchases for a customer, so they likely have some information about the customer's credit risk. For entities that have different pricing for products depending on the time of payment (e.g. cash discounts), the standard indicates that the appropriate interest rate, in some cases, could be determined by identifying the rate that discounts the nominal amount of the promised consideration to the cash sales price of the good or service.

Entities likely have to exercise significant judgement to determine whether a significant financing component exists when there is more than one year between the transfer of goods or services and the receipt of contract consideration. Entities should consider sufficiently documenting their analyses to support their conclusions.

2.5.1 Examples of significant financing components

The standard includes several examples to illustrate these concepts. Example 29.13 illustrates a contract that contains a significant financing component because the cash selling price at contract inception differs from the promised amount of consideration payable after delivery and there are no other factors present that would indicate that this difference arises for reasons other than financing. In this example, the implicit interest rate in the contract is determined to be commensurate with the rate that would be reflected in a separate financing transaction between the entity and its customer at contract inception. *[IFRS 15.IE135-IE140].*

Example 29.13: Significant financing component and right of return

An entity sells a product to a customer for CU121 that is payable 24 months after delivery. The customer obtains control of the product at contract inception. The contract permits the customer to return the product within 90 days. The product is new and the entity has no relevant historical evidence of product returns or other available market evidence.

The cash selling price of the product is CU100, which represents the amount that the customer would pay upon delivery for the same product sold under otherwise identical terms and conditions as at contract inception. The entity's cost of the product is CU80.

The entity does not recognise revenue when control of the product transfers to the customer. This is because the existence of the right of return and the lack of relevant historical evidence means that the entity cannot conclude that it is highly probable that a significant reversal in the amount of cumulative revenue recognised will not occur in accordance with paragraphs 56-58 of IFRS 15. Consequently, revenue is recognised after three months when the right of return lapses.

The contract includes a significant financing component, in accordance with paragraphs 60-62 of IFRS 15. This is evident from the difference between the amount of promised consideration of CU121 and the cash selling price of CU100 at the date that the goods are transferred to the customer.

The contract includes an implicit interest rate of 10 per cent (i.e. the interest rate that over 24 months discounts the promised consideration of CU121 to the cash selling price of CU100). The entity evaluates the rate and concludes that it is commensurate with the rate that would be reflected in a separate financing transaction between the entity and its customer at contract inception. The following journal entries illustrate how the entity accounts for this contract in accordance with paragraphs B20-B27 of IFRS 15.

- When the product is transferred to the customer, in accordance with paragraph B21 of IFRS 15:

Asset for right to recover product to be returned	CU80[(a)]	
Inventory		CU80

    (a) This example does not consider expected costs to recover the asset.

- During the three-month right of return period, no interest is recognised in accordance with paragraph 65 of IFRS 15 because no contract asset or receivable has been recognised.

- When the right of return lapses (the product is not returned):

Receivable	CU100[(a)]	
Revenue		CU100
Cost of sales	CU80	
Asset for product to be returned		CU80

    (a) The receivable recognised would be measured in accordance with IFRS 9. This example assumes there is no material difference between the fair value of the receivable at contract inception and the fair value of the receivable when it is recognised at the time the right of return lapses. In addition, this example does not consider the impairment accounting for the receivable.

Until the entity receives the cash payment from the customer, interest revenue would be recognised in accordance with IFRS 9. In determining the effective interest rate in accordance with IFRS 9, the entity would consider the remaining contractual term.

Example 29.13 also illustrates the requirement in paragraph 65 of IFRS 15, which provides that interest income or interest expense is recognised only to the extent that a contract asset (or receivable) or a contract liability is recognised in accounting for a contract with a customer. See further discussion in 2.5.3 below.

In Example 29.14, the difference between the promised consideration and the cash selling price of the good or service arises for reasons other than the provision of financing. In this example, the customer withholds a portion of each payment until the contract is complete in order to protect itself from the entity failing to complete its obligations under the contract, as follows. *[IFRS 15.IE141-IE142].*

Example 29.14: Withheld payments on a long-term contract

An entity enters into a contract for the construction of a building that includes scheduled milestone payments for the performance by the entity throughout the contract term of three years. The performance obligation will be satisfied over time and the milestone payments are scheduled to coincide with the entity's expected performance. The contract provides that a specified percentage of each milestone payment is to be withheld (i.e. retained) by the customer throughout the arrangement and paid to the entity only when the building is complete.

The entity concludes that the contract does not include a significant financing component. The milestone payments coincide with the entity's performance and the contract requires amounts to be retained for reasons other than the provision of finance in accordance with paragraph 62(c) of IFRS 15. The withholding of a specified percentage of each milestone payment is intended to protect the customer from the contractor failing to adequately complete its obligations under the contract.

Example 29.15 illustrates two situations. *[IFRS 15.IE143-IE147].* In Case A, a contractual discount rate reflects the rate in a separate financing transaction. In Case B, it does not.

Example 29.15: Determining the discount rate

An entity enters into a contract with a customer to sell equipment. Control of the equipment transfers to the customer when the contract is signed. The price stated in the contract is CU1 million plus a five per cent contractual rate of interest, payable in 60 monthly instalments of CU18,871.

Case A – Contractual discount rate reflects the rate in a separate financing transaction

In evaluating the discount rate in the contract that contains a significant financing component, the entity observes that the five per cent contractual rate of interest reflects the rate that would be used in a separate financing transaction between the entity and its customer at contract inception (i.e. the contractual rate of interest of five per cent reflects the credit characteristics of the customer).

The market terms of the financing mean that the cash selling price of the equipment is CU1 million. This amount is recognised as revenue and as a loan receivable when control of the equipment transfers to the customer. The entity accounts for the receivable in accordance with IFRS 9.

Case B – Contractual discount rate does not reflect the rate in a separate financing transaction

In evaluating the discount rate in the contract that contains a significant financing component, the entity observes that the five per cent contractual rate of interest is significantly lower than the 12 per cent interest rate that would be used in a separate financing transaction between the entity and its customer at contract inception (i.e. the contractual rate of interest of five per cent does not reflect the credit characteristics of the customer). This suggests that the cash selling price is less than CU1 million.

In accordance with paragraph 64 of IFRS 15, the entity determines the transaction price by adjusting the promised amount of consideration to reflect the contractual payments using the 12 per cent interest rate that reflects the credit characteristics of the customer. Consequently, the entity determines that the transaction price is CU848,357 (60 monthly payments of CU18,871 discounted at 12 per cent). The entity recognises revenue and a loan receivable for that amount. The entity accounts for the loan receivable in accordance with IFRS 9.

Example 29.16 illustrates a contract with an advance payment from the customer that the entity concludes represents a significant benefit of financing. It also illustrates a situation in which the implicit interest rate does not reflect the interest rate that would be used in a separate financing transaction between the entity and its customer at contract inception, as follows. *[IFRS 15.IE148-IE151].*

Example 29.16: Advance payment and assessment of discount rate

An entity enters into a contract with a customer to sell an asset. Control of the asset will transfer to the customer in two years (i.e. the performance obligation will be satisfied at a point in time). The contract includes two alternative payment options: payment of CU5,000 in two years when the customer obtains control of the asset or payment of CU4,000 when the contract is signed. The customer elects to pay CU4,000 when the contract is signed.

The entity concludes that the contract contains a significant financing component because of the length of time between when the customer pays for the asset and when the entity transfers the asset to the customer, as well as the prevailing interest rates in the market.

The interest rate implicit in the transaction is 11.8 per cent, which is the interest rate necessary to make the two alternative payment options economically equivalent. However, the entity determines that, in accordance with paragraph 64 of IFRS 15, the rate to be used in adjusting the promised consideration is six per cent, which is the entity's incremental borrowing rate.

The following journal entries illustrate how the entity would account for the significant financing component:
- recognise a contract liability for the CU4,000 payment received at contract inception:

    Cash   CU4,000
        Contract liability   CU4,000

- during the two years from contract inception until the transfer of the asset, the entity adjusts the promised amount of consideration (in accordance with paragraph 65 of IFRS 15) and accretes the contract liability by recognising interest on CU4,000 at six per cent for two years:

    Interest expense   CU494[a]
        Contract liability   CU494

    (a) CU494 = CU4,000 contract liability × (6 per cent interest per year for two years).

- recognise revenue for the transfer of the asset:

    Contract liability   CU4,494
        Revenue   CU4,494

In Example 29.17, involving a contract with an advance payment from the customer, the entity determines that a significant financing component does not exist because the difference between the amount of promised consideration and the cash selling price of the good or service arises for reasons other than the provision of financing, as follows. [IFRS 15.IE152-IE154].

Example 29.17: Advance payment

An entity, a technology product manufacturer, enters into a contract with a customer to provide global telephone technology support and repair coverage for three years along with its technology product. The customer purchases this support service at the time of buying the product. Consideration for the service is an additional CU300. Customers electing to buy this service must pay for it upfront (i.e. a monthly payment option is not available).

To determine whether there is a significant financing component in the contract, the entity considers the nature of the service being offered and the purpose of the payment terms. The entity charges a single upfront amount, not with the primary purpose of obtaining financing from the customer but, instead, to maximise profitability, taking into consideration the risks associated with providing the service. Specifically, if customers could pay monthly, they would be less likely to renew and the population of customers that continue to use the support service in the later years may become smaller and less diverse over time (i.e. customers that choose to renew historically are those that make greater use of the service, thereby increasing the entity's costs). In addition, customers tend to use services more if they pay monthly rather than making an upfront payment. Finally, the entity would incur higher administration costs such as the costs related to administering renewals and collection of monthly payments.

In assessing the requirements in paragraph 62(c) of IFRS 15, the entity determines that the payment terms were structured primarily for reasons other than the provision of finance to the entity. The entity charges a single upfront amount for the services because other payment terms (such as a monthly payment plan) would affect the nature of the risks assumed by the entity to provide the service and may make it uneconomical to provide the service. As a result of its analysis, the entity concludes that there is not a significant financing component.

2.5.2 Application questions on identifying and accounting for significant financing components

See Chapter 28 at 3.6.1.K for discussion on whether an entity is required to evaluate if a customer option that provides a material right includes a significant financing component.

2.5.2.A Payment terms reflect reasons other than the provision of finance

According to IFRS 15, a significant financing component does not exist if the difference between the promised consideration and the cash selling price of the good or service arises for reasons other than the provision of finance. *[IFRS 15.62(c)]*. At the March 2015 TRG meeting, the TRG members discussed whether this factor should be broadly or narrowly applied.

The TRG members generally agreed that there is likely significant judgement involved in determining whether either party is providing financing or the payment terms are for another reason. The TRG members also generally agreed that the Board did not seem to intend to create a presumption that a significant financing component exists if the cash selling price differs from the promised consideration (or there is a long period of time between transfer of the goods and payment).

The TRG agenda paper noted that, although paragraph 61 of IFRS 15 states that the measurement objective for a significant financing component is to recognise revenue for the goods or services at an amount that reflects the cash selling price, this measurement objective is only followed when an entity has already determined that a significant financing component exists. The fact that there is a difference in the promised consideration and the cash selling price is not a principle for determining whether a significant financing component actually exists. It is only one factor to consider.[16]

Many of the TRG members noted that it requires significant judgement in some circumstances to determine whether a transaction includes a significant financing component.[17] The TRG members also acknowledged that when entities consider whether the difference between the promised consideration and cash selling price is for a reason other than financing, they must consider whether the difference between those amounts is proportional to the reason for the difference as contemplated in paragraph 62(c) of IFRS 15.

2.5.2.B Existence of a financing component when the promised consideration is equal to the cash selling price

Under IFRS 15, an entity must consider the difference, if any, between the amount of promised consideration and the cash selling price of a promised good or service when determining whether a significant financing component exists in a contract. *[IFRS 15.61(a)]*. At the March 2015 TRG meeting, the TRG members were asked to consider whether a financing component exists if the promised consideration is equal to the cash selling price.

The TRG members generally agreed that even if the list price, cash selling price and promised consideration of a good or service are all equal, an entity should not automatically assume that a significant financing component does not exist. This would be a factor to consider, but it would not be determinative.[18]

As discussed at 2.5.2.A above, while paragraph 61 of IFRS 15 states that the measurement objective for a significant financing component is to recognise revenue for the goods or services at an amount that reflects the cash selling price, this measurement objective is only followed when an entity has already determined that a significant financing component exists. The fact that there is no difference between the promised consideration and the cash selling price is not determinative in the evaluation of whether a significant financing component actually exists. It is a factor to consider, but it is not the only factor and is not determinative. As discussed above, an entity needs to consider all facts and circumstances in this evaluation.

The TRG agenda paper noted that the list price may not always equal the cash selling price (i.e. the price that a customer would have paid for the promised goods or services if the customer had paid cash for those goods or services when (or as) they transfer to the customer, as defined in paragraph 61 of IFRS 15). For example, if a customer offers to pay cash upfront when the entity is offering 'free' financing to customers, the customer that offers the upfront payment may be able to pay less than the list price. Determining a cash selling price may require judgement and the fact that an entity provides 'interest-free financing' does not necessarily mean that the cash selling price is the same as the price another customer would pay over time. Entities would have to consider the cash selling price in comparison to the promised consideration in making the evaluation based on the overall facts and circumstances of the arrangement.

This notion is consistent with paragraph 77 of IFRS 15 on allocating the transaction price to performance obligations based on stand-alone selling prices (see 3.1 below), which indicates that a contractually stated price or a list price for a good or service may be (but is not presumed to be) the stand-alone selling price of that good or service. The TRG agenda paper noted that it may be possible for a financing component to exist, but that it may not be significant. As discussed at 2.5 above, entities need to apply judgement in determining whether the financing component is significant.[19]

2.5.2.C Accounting for financing components that are not significant

At the March 2015 TRG meeting, the TRG members generally agreed that the standard does not preclude an entity from deciding to account for a financing component that is not significant. For example, an entity may have a portfolio of contracts in which there is a mix of significant and insignificant financing components. An entity could choose to account for all of the financing components as if they were significant in order to avoid having to apply different accounting methods to each.

An entity electing to apply the requirements for significant financing components to an insignificant financing component would need to be consistent in its application to all similar contracts with similar circumstances.[20]

2.5.2.D Determining whether the significant financing component practical expedient applies to contracts with a single payment stream for multiple performance obligations

The standard includes a practical expedient that allows an entity not to assess a contract for a significant financing component if the period between the customer's payment and the entity's transfer of the goods or services is one year or less. *[IFRS 15.63]*. The TRG members were asked, at the March 2015 TRG meeting, how entities should consider whether the practical expedient applies to contracts with a single payment stream for multiple performance obligations.

The TRG members generally agreed that entities either apply an approach of allocating any consideration received:

(1) to the earliest good or service delivered; or

(2) proportionately between the goods or services depending on the facts and circumstances.

The TRG agenda paper on this topic provided an example of a telecommunications entity that enters into a two-year contract to provide a device at contract inception and related data services over 24 months in exchange for 24 equal monthly instalments.[21] Under approach (1) above, an entity would be allowed to apply the practical expedient because the period between transfer of the good or service and customer payment would be less than one year for both the device and the related services. This is because, in the example provided, the device would be 'paid off' after five months. Under approach (2) above, an entity would not be able to apply the practical expedient because the device would be deemed to be paid off over the full 24 months (i.e. greater than one year).

Approach (2) above may be appropriate in circumstances similar to the example in the TRG agenda paper, when the cash payment is not directly tied to the earliest good or service in a contract. Approach (1) may be appropriate when the cash payment is directly tied to the earliest good or service delivered in a contract. However, the TRG members noted it may be difficult to tie a cash payment directly to a good or service because cash is fungible. Accordingly, judgement is required based on the facts and circumstances.[22]

2.5.2.E Calculating the adjustment to revenue for significant financing components

At the March 2015 TRG meeting, the TRG members discussed how an entity would calculate the adjustment to revenue for contracts that include a significant financing component.

The TRG members generally agreed that the standard does not contain requirements for how to calculate the adjustment to the transaction price due to a significant financing component. A financing component is recognised as interest expense (when the customer pays in advance) or interest income (when the customer pays in arrears). Entities need to consider requirements outside IFRS 15 to determine the appropriate accounting treatment (i.e. IFRS 9).[23]

2.5.2.F Allocating a significant financing component when there are multiple performance obligations in a contract

At the March 2015 TRG meeting, the TRG members discussed how an entity would allocate a significant financing component when there are multiple performance obligations in a contract.

The standard is clear that, when determining the transaction price in Step 3 of the model, the effect of financing is excluded from the transaction price prior to the allocation of the transaction price to performance obligations (which occurs in Step 4). However, stakeholders had questioned whether an adjustment for a significant financing component could ever be attributed to only one or some of the performance obligations in the contract, rather than to all of the performance obligations in the contract. This is because the standard only includes examples in which there is a single performance obligation.

The TRG members generally agreed that it may be reasonable for an entity to attribute a significant financing component to one or more, but not all, of the performance obligations in the contract. In doing so, the entity may analogise to the exceptions for allocating variable consideration and/or discounts to one or more (but not all) performance obligations, if specified criteria are met (see 3.3 and 3.4 below, respectively).[24] However, attribution of a financing component to one (or some) of the performance obligations requires the use of judgement, especially because cash is fungible.

2.5.2.G Significant financing components: considering whether interest expense can be borrowing costs eligible for capitalisation

IAS 23 – *Borrowing Costs* – requires borrowing costs to be capitalised if they are directly attributable to the acquisition, construction or production of a qualifying asset (whether or not the funds have been borrowed specifically for that purpose, see Chapter 21 for further discussion on IAS 23). *[IAS 23.8]*. IAS 23 and IFRS 15 do not specifically address whether interest expense arising from a customer contract with a significant financing component can be considered as borrowing costs eligible for capitalisation.

According to IAS 23, borrowing costs are 'interest and other costs that an entity incurs in connection with the borrowing of funds.' *[IAS 23.5 – IAS 23.6]*. Interest expense arising from customer contracts with a significant financing component might qualify as borrowing costs eligible for capitalisation if they are directly attributable to the acquisition, construction or production of a qualifying asset.

For most revenue transactions, it is likely that entities would be considering inventory when determining whether there is a qualifying asset. According to IAS 23, inventory can be a qualifying asset, but '... inventories that are manufactured, or otherwise produced, over a short period of time, are not qualifying assets. Assets that are ready for their intended use or sale when acquired are also not qualifying assets.' *[IAS 23.7]*. Significant judgement may be needed to determine whether inventories take a substantial period of time to manufacture or produce before being ready for their intended use or sale. However, it may be helpful for an entity to consider how it satisfies its performance obligations as part of this determination. In particular, entities should note that, if a performance obligation is satisfied over time, by definition, the customer obtains control of the good or service (and the entity derecognises any related inventory) as the entity performs. As discussed in Chapter 30 at 3.4.4, its performance should not result in the creation of a material asset in the entity's accounts (e.g. work in progress).

It is also important to note that capitalisation of borrowing costs is not required by IAS 23 for inventories that are manufactured, or otherwise produced, in large quantities on a repetitive basis even if they meet the definition of a qualifying asset. *[IAS 23.4(b)]*.

In late 2018 the IFRS Interpretations Committee received a request about the capitalisation of borrowing costs in relation to assets being developed for sale for which revenue is recognised over time as control transfers to the customer as the asset is constructed.

At its March 2019 meeting, the Committee noted that, when applying IAS 23 an entity assesses whether there is a qualifying asset (i.e. an asset that necessarily takes a substantial period of time to get ready for its intended use or sale). The request referred to real estate units, which may take a substantial period of time to construct. However, the Committee concluded that:

- *For any sold units* – there is no qualifying asset. When any of the criteria in paragraph 35 of IFRS 15 are met (and revenue is recognised over time), control transfers to the customer as the entity performs. Therefore, the entity holds no inventory. Instead, it recognises a receivable or contract asset for its right to receive consideration in exchange for its performance to date. IAS 23 explicitly states that receivables are not a qualifying asset. *[IAS 23.7]*. Like receivables, the intended use of a contract assets is to collect cash (or another asset), which is not a use for which it necessarily takes a substantial period of time to get ready. Therefore, the Committee observed that contract assets are also not qualifying assets.
- *For any unsold units* – any inventory (work-in-progress) for unsold units under construction is not a qualifying asset if: (i) the entity intends to sell the part-completed units as soon as it finds suitable customers – this is because the units are already ready for sale in their part-completed state; and (ii) control of the part-completed units transfers to the customer on signing the contract (which is the case if revenue is recognised over time).[25]

2.5.3 Financial statement presentation of financing component

As discussed at 2.5 above, when a significant financing component exists in a contract, the transaction price is adjusted so that the amount recognised as revenue is the 'cash selling price' of the underlying goods or services at the time of transfer. Essentially, a contract with a customer that has a significant financing component would be separated into a revenue component (for the notional cash sales price) and a loan component (for the effect of the deferred or advance payment terms). *[IFRS 15.BC244]*. Consequently, the accounting for accounts receivable arising from a contract that has a significant financing component should be comparable to the accounting for a loan with the same features. *[IFRS 15.BC244]*.

The amount allocated to the significant financing component would have to be presented separately from revenue recognised from contracts with customers. The financing component is recognised as interest expense (when the customer pays in advance) or interest income (when the customer pays in arrears). The interest income or expense is recognised over the financing period using the effective interest method described in IFRS 9. The standard notes that interest is only recognised to the extent that a contract asset, contract liability or receivable is recognised in accordance with IFRS 15. *[IFRS 15.65]*.

As discussed in Chapter 32 at 2.1, a contract asset (or receivable) or contract liability is generated (and presented on the balance sheet) when either party to a contract performs, depending on the relationship between the entity's performance and the customer's payment. Example 29.13 (see 2.5.1 above) illustrates a situation in which an entity transfers control of a good to a customer, but the customer is not required to pay for the good until two years after delivery. The contract includes a significant financing component.

Furthermore, the customer has the right to return the good for 90 days. The product is new and the entity does not have historical evidence of returns activity. Therefore, the entity is not able to recognise revenue (or a contract asset or receivable) upon delivery because it cannot assert that it is highly probable that a significant revenue reversal will not occur (i.e. it cannot assert that it is highly probable that the product will not be returned). Accordingly, during the 90-day return period, the entity also cannot record interest income. However, as depicted in the example, once the return period lapses, the entity can record revenue and a receivable, as well as begin to recognise interest income.

The IASB noted in the Basis for Conclusions that an entity may present interest income as revenue only when interest income represents income from an entity's ordinary activities. *[IFRS 15.BC247]*.

Although there are two components within the transaction price when there is a significant financing component (i.e. the revenue component and the significant financing component), it is only in the case of deferred payment terms that there are two cash flow components. In that case, the revenue component cash flows should be classified as cash flows from operating activities, and the cash flows related to the significant financing component should be classified consistent with the entity's choice to present cash flows from interests received/paid in accordance with paragraph 33 of IAS 7 – *Statement of Cash Flows* – (i.e. as cash flows from operating or investing/financing activities). If the customer pays in advance, the sum of the cash amount and the accrued interest represent revenue, and thus there is only one cash flow component. Accordingly, the cash received should be classified as cash flows from operating activities.

Impairment losses on receivables, with or without a significant financing component, are presented in line with the requirements of IAS 1 – *Presentation of Financial Statements* – and disclosed in accordance with IFRS 7 – *Financial Instruments: Disclosures*. However, IFRS 15 makes it clear that such amounts are 'disclosed separately from impairment losses from other contracts.' *[IFRS 15.113(b)]*.

We believe entities may need to expend additional effort to track impairment losses on assets arising from contracts that are within the scope of IFRS 15 separately from impairment losses on assets arising from other contracts. Entities need to ensure that they have the appropriate systems, internal controls, policies and procedures in place to collect and separately present this information.

2.6 Non-cash consideration

Customer consideration may be in the form of goods, services or other non-cash consideration (e.g. property, plant and equipment, a financial instrument). When an entity (i.e. the seller or vendor) receives, or expects to receive, non-cash consideration, the fair value of the non-cash consideration is included in the transaction price. *[IFRS 15.66]*.

An entity likely applies the requirements of IFRS 13 – *Fair Value Measurement* – or IFRS 2 – *Share-based Payment* – when measuring the fair value of any non-cash consideration. If an entity cannot reasonably estimate the fair value of non-cash consideration, it measures the non-cash consideration indirectly by reference to the stand-alone selling price of the promised goods or services. *[IFRS 15.67]*. Significant judgement and consideration of specific facts and circumstances may be required in such situations (e.g. advertising barter transactions – see 2.6.2 below for further discussion on barter transactions).

For contracts with both non-cash consideration and cash consideration, an entity needs to measure the fair value of the non-cash consideration and it looks to other requirements within IFRS 15 to account for the cash consideration. For example, for a contract in which an entity receives non-cash consideration and a sales-based royalty, the entity would measure the fair value of the non-cash consideration and refer to the requirements within the standard for the sales-based royalties.

The fair value of non-cash consideration may change both because of the form of consideration (e.g. a change in the price of a share an entity is entitled to receive from a customer) and for reasons other than the form of consideration (e.g. a change in the exercise price of a share option because of the entity's performance). Under IFRS 15, if an entity's entitlement to non-cash consideration promised by a customer is variable for reasons other than the form of consideration (i.e. there is uncertainty as to whether the entity receives the non-cash consideration if a future event occurs or does not occur), the entity considers the constraint on variable consideration. *[IFRS 15.68]*.

In some transactions, a customer contributes goods or services, such as equipment or labour, to facilitate the fulfilment of the contract. If the entity obtains control of the contributed goods or services, it would consider them non-cash consideration and account for that consideration as described above. *[IFRS 15.69]*. Assessing whether the entity obtains control of the contributed goods or services by the customer may require judgement.

The Board also noted that any assets recognised as a result of non-cash consideration are accounted for in accordance with other relevant standards (e.g. IAS 16 – *Property, Plant and Equipment*).

The standard provides the following example of a transaction for which non-cash consideration is received in exchange for services provided. *[IFRS 15.IE156-IE158]*.

Example 29.18: Entitlement to non-cash consideration

An entity enters into a contract with a customer to provide a weekly service for one year. The contract is signed on 1 January 20X1 and work begins immediately. The entity concludes that the service is a single performance obligation in accordance with paragraph 22(b) of IFRS 15. This is because the entity is providing a series of distinct services that are substantially the same and have the same pattern of transfer (the services transfer to the customer over time and use the same method to measure progress – that is, a time-based measure of progress).

In exchange for the service, the customer promises 100 shares of its common stock per week of service (a total of 5,200 shares for the contract). The terms in the contract require that the shares must be paid upon the successful completion of each week of service.

The entity measures its progress towards complete satisfaction of the performance obligation as each week of service is complete. To determine the transaction price (and the amount of revenue to be recognised), the entity measures the fair value of 100 shares that are received upon completion of each weekly service. The entity does not reflect any subsequent changes in the fair value of the shares received (or receivable) in revenue.

2.6.1 Non-cash consideration application considerations

Stakeholders raised questions about the date that should be used when measuring the fair value of non-cash consideration for inclusion within the transaction price. In addition, constituents noted that the variability of non-cash consideration could arise both from its form (e.g. shares) and for other reasons (e.g. performance factors that affect the amount of consideration to which the entity will be entitled). Consequently, they questioned how the constraint on variable consideration would be applied in such circumstances.

At the January 2015 TRG meeting, the TRG members discussed these questions and agreed that, while the standard requires non-cash consideration (e.g. shares, advertising provided as consideration from a customer) to be measured at fair value, it is unclear when that fair value must be measured (i.e. the measurement date). The TRG members discussed three measurement date options: contract inception; when it is received; or when the related performance obligation is satisfied. Each view received support from some TRG members. Since IFRS 15 does not specify the measurement date, an entity needs to use its judgement to determine the most appropriate measurement date when measuring the fair value of non-cash consideration. However, in accordance with paragraph 126 of IFRS 15, information about the methods, inputs and assumptions used to measure non-cash consideration needs to be disclosed. [IFRS 15.BC254E].

IFRS 15 requires that the constraint on variable consideration be applied to non-cash consideration only if the variability is due to factors other than the form of consideration (i.e. variability arising for reasons other than changes in the price of the non-cash consideration). The constraint does not apply if the non-cash consideration varies because of its form (e.g. listed shares for which the share price changes). However, the standard does not address how the constraint would be applied when the non-cash consideration is variable due to both its form and other reasons. While some of the TRG members said the standard could be interpreted to require an entity to split the consideration based on the source of the variability, other TRG members highlighted that this approach would be overly complex and would not provide useful information.

The FASB's standard specifies that the fair value of non-cash consideration needs to be measured at contract inception when determining the transaction price. Any subsequent changes in the fair value of the non-cash consideration due to its form (e.g. changes in share price) are not included in the transaction price and would be recognised, if required, as a gain or loss in accordance with other accounting standards, but would not be recognised as revenue from contracts with customers. However, in the Basis for Conclusions, the IASB observed that this issue has important interactions with other standards (including IFRS 2 and IAS 21) and there was a concern about the risk of unintended consequences. Therefore, the Board decided that, if needed, these issues would be considered more comprehensively in a separate project. [IFRS 15.BC254C]. The IASB acknowledged in the Basis for Conclusions, that the use of a measurement date other than contract inception would not be precluded under IFRS. Consequently, it is possible that diversity between IFRS and US GAAP entities may arise in practice. Unlike US GAAP, legacy IFRS did not contain specific requirements regarding the measurement date for non-cash consideration related to revenue transactions. As such, the IASB does not expect IFRS 15 to create more diversity than previously existed in relation to this issue. [IFRS 15.BC254E].

The FASB's standard also specifies that when the variability of non-cash consideration is due to both the form of the consideration and for other reasons, the constraint on variable consideration would apply only to the variability for reasons other than its form. While IFRS 15 does not have a similar requirement, the Board noted in the Basis for Conclusions that it decided to constrain variability in the estimate of the fair value of the non-cash consideration if that variability relates to changes in the fair value for reasons other than the form of the consideration. It also noted the view of some TRG members that, in practice, it might be difficult to distinguish between variability in the fair value due to the form of the consideration and other reasons, in which case applying the variable consideration constraint to the whole estimate of the non-cash consideration might be more practical. *[IFRS 15.BC252]*. However, for reasons similar to those on the measurement date for non-cash consideration, the IASB decided not to have a similar requirement to that of the FASB's standard. Consequently, the IASB acknowledged that differences may arise between an entity reporting under IFRS and an entity reporting under US GAAP. *[IFRS 15.BC254H]*.

2.6.2 Barter transactions

An entity may enter into barter transactions to provide goods or services in exchange for receiving similar or dissimilar goods or services from its customers. In some cases, barter transactions may include cash consideration in addition to the non-cash consideration. Therefore, significant judgement and consideration of the specific facts and circumstances will be needed when accounting for such transactions.

Aspects of the standard that will be particularly important to consider include, but are not limited to:

- *Understanding whether the transaction is within the scope of the standard* – barter transactions involve non-monetary exchanges. Therefore, an entity first needs to determine whether the barter transaction involves a non-monetary exchange between entities in the same line of business to facilitate sales to (potential) customers. If it does, it is excluded from the scope of IFRS 15 (see Chapter 27 at 3.1.1). For barter transactions not subject to this scope exclusion (i.e. they are within the scope of IFRS 15), an entity needs to understand whether there is vendor-customer relationship with the counterparty and whether the transaction is in the ordinary course of its business. This is because IFRS 15 only applies to contracts that provide goods or services to customers in the ordinary course of business (see Chapter 27 at 3.1 and 3.3).

- *Determining whether the transaction has commercial substance (such that the contract meets the criteria to be considered a contract under the five-step model in IFRS 15)* – exchanging goods or services in a barter transaction may lack commercial substance. An entity needs to determine whether the risk, timing or amount of an entity's future cash flows change as a result of the barter transaction (see Chapter 28 at 2.1.5).

- *Identifying the promised goods or services to be transferred to the customer* – barter transactions may involve the exchange of a good or service, but not necessarily the transfer of its control. An entity needs to understand whether the customer will obtain control of a good or service (see Chapter 30). That is, whether there is a promised good or service in the contract (see Chapter 28 at 3.1).

- *Determining whether the entity will obtain control of any non-cash consideration* – barter transactions involve the exchange of non-cash items. Only non-cash items of which the entity obtains control from the customer would be non-cash consideration for purposes of applying the standard (as noted above).

- *Determining the fair value of any non-cash consideration received from the customer* (see 2.6 above) – in order to recognise revenue in the barter transaction, the non-cash consideration obtained from a customer needs to be measured either: (a) directly, at its fair value if it can be reasonably estimated; or (b) indirectly, by reference to the stand-alone selling price of the promised good or service transferred to the customer if the fair value of the non-cash consideration cannot be reasonably estimated. IFRS 15 does not permit an entity to avoid recognising revenue if the fair value cannot be estimated reliably. Therefore, if the transaction is within the scope of IFRS 15, revenue must be recognised.

2.7 Consideration paid or payable to a customer

Many entities make payments to their customers. In some cases, the consideration paid or payable represents purchases by the entity of goods or services offered by the customer that satisfy a business need of the entity. In other cases, the consideration paid or payable represents incentives given by the entity to entice the customer to purchase, or continue purchasing, its goods or services.

The standard states that consideration payable to a customer includes 'cash amounts that an entity pays, or expects to pay, to the customer (or to other parties that purchase the entity's goods or services from the customer). Consideration payable to a customer also includes credit or other items (e.g. a coupon or voucher) that can be applied against amounts owed to the entity (or to other parties that purchase the entity's goods or services from the customer).' *[IFRS 15.70].*

To determine the appropriate accounting treatment, an entity must first determine whether the consideration paid or payable to a customer is: a payment for a distinct good or service; a reduction of the transaction price; or a combination of both. For a payment by the entity to a customer to be treated as something other than a reduction of the transaction price, the good or service provided by the customer must be distinct (as discussed in Chapter 28 at 3.2.1). The standard also states that, if the consideration payable to a customer includes a variable amount, an entity must estimate the transaction price in accordance with the requirements for estimating (and constraining) variable consideration (see 2.2 above). *[IFRS 15.70].*

If consideration payable to a customer is a payment for a distinct good or service from the customer, an entity is required to account for the purchase of the good or service in the same way that it accounts for other purchases from suppliers. If the amount of consideration payable to the customer exceeds the fair value of the distinct good or service that the entity receives from the customer, the entity is required to account for the excess as a reduction of the transaction price. If the entity cannot reasonably estimate the fair value of the good or service received from the customer, it is required to account for all of the consideration payable to the customer as a reduction of the transaction price. *[IFRS 15.71].*

If consideration payable to a customer is accounted for as a reduction of the transaction price, it is recognised as a reduction of revenue when (or as) the later of when:

(a) the entity recognises revenue for the transfer of the related goods or services to the customer; and

(b) the entity pays or promises to pay the consideration (even if the payment is conditional on a future event), which might be implied by the entity's customary business practices. [IFRS 15.72].

Figure 29.2 illustrates these requirements:

Figure 29.2: Consideration payable to a customer

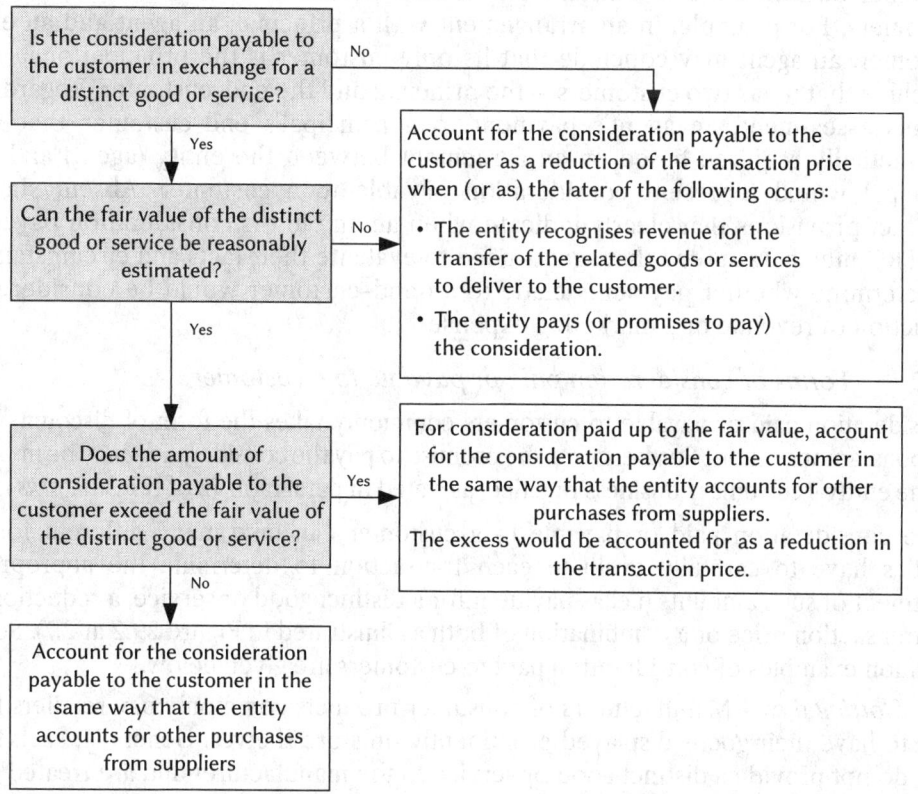

The standard indicates that an entity accounts for the consideration payable to a customer, regardless of whether the purchaser receiving the consideration is a direct or indirect customer of the entity. This includes consideration to any purchasers of the entity's products at any point along the distribution chain. This would include entities that make payments to the customers of resellers or distributors that purchase directly from the entity (e.g. manufacturers of breakfast cereals may offer coupons to end-consumers, even though their direct customers are the grocery stores that sell to end-consumers). The requirements in IFRS 15 apply to entities that derive revenue from sales of services, as well as entities that derive revenue from sales of goods.

2.7.1 Determining who is an entity's customer when applying the requirements for consideration payable to a customer

When applying the requirements for consideration payable to a customer, it is important to determine who is an entity's customer. This was considered by the TRG members at both the March 2015 and July 2015 TRG meetings.

The TRG members generally agreed that the requirements for consideration payable to a customer apply to all payments made to entities/customers in the distribution chain for that contract. However, they agreed that there could also be situations in which the requirements would apply to payments made to any customer of an entity's customer outside the distribution chain if both parties are considered the entity's customers. For example, in an arrangement with a principal, an agent and an end-customer, an agent may conclude that its only customer is the principal or it may conclude that it has two customers – the principal and the end-customer. Regardless of this assessment, an agent's payment to a principal's end-customer that was contractually required based on an agreement between the entity (agent) and the principal would represent consideration payable to a customer. Absent similar contract provisions that clearly indicate when an amount is consideration payable, the TRG members agreed that agents need to evaluate their facts and circumstances to determine whether payments made to an end-customer would be considered a reduction of revenue or a marketing expense.[26]

2.7.2 Forms of consideration paid or payable to a customer

Consideration paid or payable to customers commonly takes the form of discounts and coupons, among others. Furthermore, the promise to pay the consideration may be implied by the entity's customary business practice, as stated in paragraph 72 of IFRS 15. *[IFRS 15.72].*

Since consideration paid or payable to a customer can take many different forms, entities have to carefully evaluate each transaction to determine the appropriate treatment of such amounts (i.e. as payment for a distinct good or service, a reduction of the transaction price or a combination of both as illustrated in Figure 29.2 at 2.7). Some common examples of consideration paid to customers are given below.

- *Slotting fees* – Manufacturers of consumer products commonly pay retailers fees to have their goods displayed prominently on store shelves. Generally, such fees do not provide a distinct good or service to the manufacturer and are treated as a reduction of the transaction price.

- *Co-operative advertising arrangements* – In some arrangements, an entity agrees to reimburse a reseller for a portion of costs incurred by the reseller to advertise the entity's products. The determination of whether the payment from the vendor is in exchange for a distinct good or service at fair value depends on a careful analysis of the facts and circumstances of the contract.

- *Price protection* – An entity may agree to reimburse a retailer up to a specified amount for shortfalls in the sales price received by the retailer for the entity's products over a specified period of time. Normally such fees do not provide a distinct good or service to the manufacturer and are treated as a reduction of the transaction price (see 2.2.1.E above).

- *Coupons and rebates* – An indirect customer of an entity may receive a refund of a portion of the purchase price of the product or service acquired by returning a form to the retailer or the entity. Generally, such fees do not provide a distinct good or service to the manufacturer and are treated as a reduction of the transaction price.
- *'Pay-to-play' arrangements* – In some arrangements, an entity pays an upfront fee to the customer prior to, or in conjunction with, entering into a contract. In most cases, these payments are not associated with any distinct good or service to be received from the customer and are treated as a reduction of the transaction price.
- *Purchase of goods or services* – Entities often enter into supplier-vendor arrangements with their customers in which the customers provide them with a distinct good or service. For example, a software entity may buy its office supplies from one of its software customers. In such situations, the entity has to carefully determine whether the payment made to the customer is solely for the goods or services received, or whether part of the payment is actually a reduction of the transaction price for the goods or services the entity is transferring to the customer.

In 2018, the FASB issued an amendment to simplify the accounting for share-based payment awards to non-employees, including an amendment to ASC 606 to clarify that equity instruments granted to customers in conjunction with selling goods or services (e.g. shares, options) are within the scope of the requirements for consideration payable to customers.[27] The IASB has not proposed any similar amendments to IFRS 15. Therefore, entities applying IFRS could reach different accounting conclusions from those applying US GAAP. For further discussion, see Chapter 27 at 3.5.1.L.

In 2019, the FASB issued another amendment that requires entities to measure and classify share-based payment awards (both equity-classified and liability-classified) granted to a customer in a revenue arrangement and are not in exchange for a distinct good or service in accordance with ASC 718 – *Compensation – Stock Compensation*.[28] The IASB has not proposed any similar amendments to IFRS 15.

2.7.2.A Payments to a customer that are within the scope of the requirements for consideration payable to a customer

At both the March 2015 and July 2015 TRG meetings, the TRG members discussed which payments made to a customer would be within the scope of the requirements for consideration payable to a customer.

The TRG members generally agreed that an entity may not need to separately analyse each payment to a customer if it is apparent that the payment is for a distinct good or service acquired in the normal course of business at a market price. However, if the business purpose of a payment to a customer is unclear or the goods or services are acquired in a manner that is inconsistent with market terms that other entities would receive when purchasing the customer's good or services, the payment needs to be evaluated under these requirements.[29] In the Basis for Conclusions, the IASB noted that the amount of consideration received from a customer for goods or services and the amount of any consideration paid to that customer for goods or services may be linked even if they are separate events. *[IFRS 15.BC257]*.

2.7.3 Classification and measurement of consideration paid or payable to a customer

To determine the appropriate accounting treatment (and as illustrated in Figure 29.2 at 2.7 above), an entity must first determine whether the consideration paid or payable to a customer is a payment for a distinct good or service. If it is not in exchange for a distinct good or service, an entity accounts for consideration payable to a customer as a reduction in the transaction price. This is because paragraph 70 of IFRS 15 states that 'an entity shall account for consideration payable to a customer as a reduction of the transaction price and, therefore, of revenue unless the payment is for a distinct good or service' (see 2.7 above). *[IFRS 15.70]*. That is, for a payment by the entity to a customer to be treated as something other than a reduction of the transaction price, the good or service provided by the customer must be distinct (as discussed in Chapter 28 at 3.2.1).

If it is in exchange for a distinct good or service at fair value, an entity accounts for consideration payable to a customer in the same way it accounts for other purchases from suppliers. However, as noted in paragraph 71 of IFRS 15, if the payment to the customer is in excess of the fair value of the distinct good or service received, the entity must account for such excess as a reduction of the transaction price. In the event that the entity cannot reasonably estimate the fair value of the good or service received from the customer, it will need to account for all of the consideration payable to the customer as a reduction in the transaction price. *[IFRS 15.71]*.

Example 29.19: Consideration paid to a customer in exchange for a distinct good or service

Entity A enters into a contract to sell goods to Customer B in the ordinary course of business in exchange for cash consideration. Separately, Entity A enters into an agreement to purchase market research from Customer B related to the launch of a new product in exchange for cash consideration. The two contracts were not negotiated in contemplation of one another.

Entity A elects to purchase the market research, rather than internally developing such knowledge because of Customer's B expertise in this area. Entity A could purchase similar services from a non-customer.

Based on an evaluation of the circumstances, the cash consideration paid to the customer is in return for Customer B providing distinct services to Entity A. To reach this conclusion, Entity A considers the requirements in paragraphs 27-30 of IFRS 15 and concludes that the market research services are capable of being distinct, as well as separately identifiable (or distinct within the context of the contract), from Entity A's sale of its goods to Customer B.

Entity A determines that market research is capable of being distinct from the sale of its goods to Customer B because the market research could be purchased from a non-customer. Therefore, Entity A is able to demonstrate that the market research can provide benefits on its own or with other readily available resources.

Entity A determines that the market research is distinct within the context of the contract because of the following:

- Customer B is not providing a significant service of integrating the market research with the purchases of Entity A's goods because the promises to Entity A are not a combined output of integrated goods or services.
- The market research provided by Customer B does not modify or customise the purchases of Entity A's goods. The market research and the purchases of goods are not being assembled together to produce a combined output.
- The market research is not highly interrelated or interdependent with the sale of Entity A's goods because the market research is not needed for Customer B to purchase the goods. That is, there is no significant two-way dependency between the promises.

Entity A accounts for the cash consideration paid to Customer B in the same way that it accounts for other purchases from suppliers, provided that the cash consideration paid does not exceed the fair value of the distinct services received from Customer B. If the amount of cash consideration paid by Entity A exceeds the fair value of the distinct services, that excess amount would be characterised as a reduction of the transaction price of the goods sold to Customer B in Entity A's income statement.

In many cases, determining the amount of consideration payable to a customer (e.g. cash amounts an entity pays to a customer) will be straightforward. However, if the consideration paid or payable to a customer includes a variable amount, paragraph 70 of IFRS 15 notes that an entity would estimate the amount using the variable consideration requirements in paragraphs 50-58 of IFRS 15 (see 2.2 above). *[IFRS 15.70].*

2.7.4   Timing of recognition of consideration paid or payable to a customer

If the consideration paid or payable to a customer accounted for as a reduction of the transaction price, paragraph 72 of IFRS 15 states that this reduction of the transaction price (and, ultimately, revenue) is recognised at the later of when: (1) the entity recognises revenue for the transfer of the related promised goods or services to the customer; or (2) the entity pays or promises to pay the consideration (even if the payment is conditional on a future event) (see 2.7 above). *[IFRS 15.72].* For example, if goods subject to a discount through a coupon are already delivered to the retailers, the discount would be recognised when the coupons are issued. However, if a coupon is issued that can be used on a new line of products that have not yet been sold to retailers, the discount would be recognised upon sale of the products to a retailer. Paragraph 82(b) of IFRS 15 also notes that the promise to pay the consideration might be implied by an entity's customary business practices. *[IFRS 15.82(b)].*

Certain sales incentives, such as mail-in rebates and manufacturer coupons, entitle a customer to receive a reduction in the price of goods or services by submitting a form or claim for a refund of a specified amount of the price charged to the customer at the point of sale. An entity must recognise a liability for those sales incentives at the later of: (a) when it recognises revenue on the goods or services; or (b) the date at which the sales incentive was offered. The amount of liability will be based on the estimated amount of discounts or refunds that will be claimed by customers, similar to how the entity would estimate variable consideration (see 2.2.2 above).

Even if the sales incentives would result in a loss on the sale of the product or service, an entity would also recognise a liability for those sales incentives at the later of: (a) when it recognises revenue on the goods or services; or (b) the date at which the sales incentive was offered. That is, an entity would not recognise the loss before either date. However, an entity would need to consider whether the offer indicates that the net realisable value of inventories are lower than costs which will require write-down of inventories to net realisable value. *[IAS 2.9, IAS 2.28].*

To determine the appropriate timing of recognition of consideration payable to a customer, entities also need to consider the requirements for variable consideration. That is, the standard's description of variable consideration is broad and includes amounts such as coupons or other forms of credits that can be applied to the amounts owed to an entity by the customer (see 2.2.1 above). IFRS 15 requires that all potential variable consideration be considered and reflected in the transaction price at contract inception and reassessed as the entity performs. In other words, if an entity has a history of providing this type of consideration to its customers, the requirements on estimating variable consideration would require that such amounts be considered at contract inception, even if the entity has not yet provided or explicitly promised this consideration to the customer.

The TRG discussed the potential inconsistency that arises between the requirements on consideration payable to a customer and variable consideration, as the requirements specific to consideration payable to a customer indicate that such amounts are not recognised as a reduction of revenue until the later of when:

- the related sales are recognised, or
- the entity promises to provide such consideration.[30]

A literal read of these requirements seems to suggest that an entity need not anticipate offering these types of programmes, even if it has a history of doing so, and would only recognise the effect of these programmes at the later of when the entity transfers the promised goods or services or makes a promise to pay the customer. The TRG members generally agreed that if an entity has historically provided or intends to provide this type of consideration to customers, the requirements on estimating variable consideration (i.e. paragraphs 50-52 of IFRS 15) would require the entity to consider such amounts at contract inception when the transaction price is estimated, even if the entity has not yet provided or promised to provide this consideration to the customer.[31] If the consideration paid or payable to a customer includes variable consideration (e.g. in the form of a discount or refund for goods or services provided), an entity would use either the expected value method or most likely amount method to estimate the amount to which the entity expects to be entitled and apply the constraint to the estimate (see 2.2.3 above for further discussion) to determine the effect of the variable consideration payable to the customer.

There was general agreement by TRG members that entities need to consider the requirements for variable consideration to determine the appropriate timing of recognition of consideration payable to a customer. Therefore, significant judgement may be needed to determine the appropriate timing of recognition.

The standard includes the following example of consideration paid to a customer. [IFRS 15.IE160-IE162].

Example 29.20: Consideration payable to a customer

An entity that manufactures consumer goods enters into a one-year contract to sell goods to a customer that is a large global chain of retail stores. The customer commits to buy at least €15 million of products during the year. The contract also requires the entity to make a non-refundable payment of €1.5 million to the customer at the inception of the contract. The €1.5 million payment will compensate the customer for the changes it needs to make to its shelving to accommodate the entity's products.

The entity considers the requirements in paragraphs 70–72 of IFRS 15 and concludes that the payment to the customer is not in exchange for a distinct good or service that transfers to the entity. This is because the entity does not obtain control of any rights to the customer's shelves. Consequently, the entity determines that, in accordance with paragraph 70 of IFRS 15, the €1.5 million payment is a reduction of the transaction price.

The entity applies the requirements in paragraph 72 of IFRS 15 and concludes that the consideration payable is accounted for as a reduction in the transaction price when the entity recognises revenue for the transfer of the goods. Consequently, as the entity transfers goods to the customer, the entity reduces the transaction price for each good by 10 per cent (€1.5 million ÷ €15 million). Therefore, in the first month in which the entity transfers goods to the customer, the entity recognises revenue of €1.8 million (€2.0 million invoiced amount less €0.2 million of consideration payable to the customer).

2.7.4.A   Accounting for upfront payments to a customer

At the November 2016 FASB TRG meetings, the TRG members discussed how an entity should account for upfront payments to a customer. While the requirements for consideration payable to a customer clearly apply to payments to customers under current contracts, stakeholders have raised questions about how to account for upfront payments to potential customers and payments that relate to both current and anticipated contracts.

The FASB TRG members discussed two views. Under View A, an entity would recognise an asset for the upfront payment and reduce revenue as the related goods or services (or as the expected related goods or services) are transferred to the customer. As a result, the payment may be recognised in profit or loss over a period that is longer than the contract term. Entities would determine the amortisation period based on facts and circumstances and would assess the asset for recoverability using the principles in asset impairment models in other standards. Under View B, entities would reduce revenue in the current contract by the amount of the payment. If there is no current contract, entities would immediately recognise the payment in profit or loss.[32]

The FASB TRG members generally agreed that an entity needs to apply the view that best reflects the substance and economics of the payment to the customer; it would not be an accounting policy choice. Entities would evaluate the nature of the payment, the rights and obligations under the contract and whether the payment meets the definition of an asset. Some FASB TRG members noted that this evaluation was consistent with legacy US GAAP requirements for payments to customers and, therefore, similar conclusions may be reached under the revenue standard. The FASB TRG members also noted that an entity's decision on which view is appropriate may be a significant judgement in the determination of the transaction price that would require disclosure under the revenue standard.[33]

We believe an entity has to carefully evaluate all facts and circumstances of payments made to customers to determine the appropriate accounting treatment. However, if an entity expects to generate future revenue associated with the payment, we believe an entity generally applies View A (assuming any asset recorded is recoverable). If no revenue is expected as a result of the payment, View B may be appropriate.

2.7.4.B   Accounting for negative revenue resulting from consideration paid or payable to a customer

In certain arrangements, consideration paid or payable to a customer could exceed the consideration to which the entity expects to be entitled in exchange for transferring promised goods or services in a contract with a customer. In these situations, recognition of payments to the customer as a reduction of revenue could result in 'negative revenue'. IFRS 15 does not specifically address how entities should present negative revenue.

Stakeholders had asked the TRG whether an entity should reclassify negative revenue resulting from consideration paid or payable to a customer to expense and, if so, in what circumstances. The TRG did not discuss this question in detail and no additional application guidance was provided.

As discussed at 2.7 above, paragraph 70 of IFRS 15 states that an entity shall account for consideration payable to a customer as a reduction of the transaction price (and, therefore, of revenue), unless the payment to the customer is in exchange for a distinct good or service that the customer transfers to the entity. Therefore, we believe it is appropriate for an entity to present payments to a customer in excess of the transaction price that are not in exchange for a distinct good or service within revenue. The question of whether negative revenue can be reclassified to expense in the income statement was raised in comment letters to the IFRS Interpretations Committee in September 2019. However, the Committee did not consider this question.[34]

2.8 Non-refundable upfront fees

In certain circumstances, entities may receive payments from customers before they provide the contracted service or deliver a good. Upfront fees generally relate to the initiation, activation or set-up of a good to be used or a service to be provided in the future. Upfront fees may also be paid to grant access to or to provide a right to use a facility, product or service. In many cases, the upfront amounts paid by the customer are non-refundable. Examples include fees paid for membership to a health club or buying club and activation fees for phone, cable or internet services. *[IFRS 15.B48]*.

Entities must evaluate whether a non-refundable upfront fee relates to the transfer of a promised good or service. If it does, the entity is required to determine whether to account for the promised good or service as a separate performance obligation (see Chapter 28 at 3). *[IFRS 15.B49, B50]*.

The standard notes that, even though a non-refundable upfront fee relates to an activity that the entity is required to undertake at or near contract inception in order to fulfil the contract, in many cases that activity does not result in the transfer of a promised good or service to the customer. Instead, in many situations, an upfront fee represents an advance payment for future goods or services.

The existence of a non-refundable upfront fee may indicate that the contract includes a renewal option for future goods or services at a reduced price (if the customer renews the agreement without the payment of an additional upfront fee). In such circumstances, an entity would need to assess whether the option is a material right (i.e. another performance obligation in the contract) (see Chapter 28 at 3.6). *[IFRS 15.B49]*. If the entity concludes that the non-refundable upfront fee does not provide a material right, the fee would be part of the consideration allocable to the goods or services in the contract and would be recognised when (or as) the good or service to which the consideration was allocated is transferred to the customer. If an entity concludes that the non-refundable upfront fee provides a material right, the amount of the fee allocated to the material right would be recognised over the period of benefit of the fee, which may be the estimated customer life.

In some cases, an entity may charge a non-refundable fee in part as compensation for costs incurred in setting up a contract (or other administrative tasks). If those set-up activities do not satisfy a performance obligation, the entity is required to disregard those activities (and related costs) when measuring progress (see Chapter 30 at 3). This is because the costs of set-up activities do not depict the transfer of services to the customer. In addition, the entity is required to assess whether costs incurred in setting up a contract are costs incurred to fulfil a contract that meet the requirements for capitalisation in IFRS 15 (see Chapter 31 at 5.2). *[IFRS 15.B51]*.

The following illustration depicts the allocation of a non-refundable upfront fee determined to be a material right.

Example 29.21: Non-refundable upfront fees

A customer signs a one-year contract with a health club and is required to pay both a non-refundable initiation fee of $150 and an annual membership fee in monthly instalments of $40. At the end of each year, the customer can renew the contract for an additional year without paying an additional initiation fee. The customer is then required to pay an annual membership fee in monthly instalments of $40 for each renewal period. The club's activity of registering the customer does not transfer any service to the customer and, therefore, is not a performance obligation. By not requiring the customer to pay the upfront membership fee again upon renewal, the club is effectively providing a discounted renewal rate to the customer.

The club determines that the renewal option is a material right because it provides a renewal option at a lower price than the range of prices typically charged for new customers. Therefore, it is a separate performance obligation. Based on its experience, the club determines that its customers, on average, renew their annual memberships twice before terminating their relationship with the club. As a result, the club determines that the option provides the customer with the right to two annual renewals at a discounted price. In this scenario, the club would allocate the total transaction consideration of $630 ($150 upfront membership fee + $480 ($40 × 12 months)) to the identified performance obligations (monthly services for the one-year contract and renewal option) based on the relative stand-alone selling price method. In accordance with paragraph B40 of IFRS 15, the amount allocated to the renewal option would be recognised when, or as, the future goods or services are transferred (e.g. years two and three of the services if the renewal option is fully exercised) or when the renewal option expires.

Alternatively, the club could value the option by 'looking through' to the optional goods or services using the practical alternative provided in paragraph B42 of IFRS 15 (see 3.1.5 below). In that case, the club would determine that the total hypothetical transaction price (for purposes of allocating the transaction price to the option) is the sum of the upfront fee plus three years of service fees (i.e. $150 + $1,440) and would allocate that amount to all of the services expected to be delivered or 36 months of membership (or $44.17 per month). Therefore, the total consideration in the contract of $630 would be allocated to the 12 months of service ($530 ($44.17 × 12 months)) with the remaining amount being allocated to the renewal option ($100 ($630 – 530)). Assuming the renewal option is exercised for year 2 and year 3, the amount allocated to the renewal option ($100) would be recognised as revenue over each renewal period. One acceptable approach would be to reduce the initial $100 deferred revenue balance for the material right by $4.17 each month ($100/24 months remaining), assuming that the estimated renewal period of two years remains unchanged.

See Chapter 28 at 3.6 and 3.1.5 below for a more detailed discussion of the treatment of options (including the practical alternative allowed under paragraph B42 of IFRS 15) and 3.1 and 3.2 below for a discussion of estimating stand-alone selling prices and allocating consideration using the relative stand-alone selling price method.

2.8.1 Application questions on non-refundable upfront fees

See Chapter 28 at 2.2.1.E for a discussion on how consideration received from a customer, but not yet recognised as revenue, is accounted for when the contract is cancelled.

2.8.1.A Recognition period for a non-refundable upfront fee that does not relate to the transfer of a good or service

At the March 2015 TRG meeting, the TRG members were asked over what period an entity should recognise a non-refundable upfront fee (e.g. fees paid for membership to a club, activation fees for phone, cable or internet services) that does not relate to the transfer of a good or service.

The TRG members generally agreed that the period over which a non-refundable upfront fee is recognised depends on whether the fee provides the customer with a material right with respect to future contract renewals (see Chapter 28 at 3.6).[35] For example, assume that an entity charges a one-time activation fee of £50 to provide £100 of services to a customer on a month-to-month basis. If the entity concludes that the activation fee provides a material right, the fee would be recognised over the service period during which the customer is expected to benefit from not having to pay an activation fee upon renewal of the service. That period may be the estimated customer life in some situations. If the entity concludes that the activation fee does not provide a material right, the fee would be recognised over the contract duration (i.e. one month).

2.8.1.B Determining whether a contract that includes a non-refundable upfront fee for establishing a connection to a network is within the scope of IFRS 15

Utility entities are often responsible for constructing infrastructure (e.g. a pipe) that will physically connect a building to its network (i.e. connection) and for providing ongoing services (e.g. delivery of electricity, gas, water). In exchange, a utility entity generally charges the customer a non-refundable upfront connection fee and a separate fee for the ongoing services. Furthermore, the connection fee and/or the fee for ongoing services are often subject to rate regulation established through a formal regulatory framework that affects the rates that a utility entity is allowed to charge to its customers.

Utility entities first need to assess whether some or all of the contract is within the scope of another standard (e.g. IFRS 16 – *Leases*, IAS 16). If the contract is partially within the scope of IFRS 15, the entity would need to separate the non-revenue components, in accordance with paragraph 7 of IFRS 15, and account for the remainder within the scope of IFRS 15 (see Chapter 27 at 3.5 for further discussion).

To be within the scope of IFRS 15, a vendor-customer relationship needs to exist. Provided such goods or services are an output of the ordinary activities of the entity, we believe a vendor-customer relationship would exist (and the contract would be wholly, or partially, within the scope of the standard) if:

- the ongoing service is part of the contract or part of an associated contract for ongoing services that is combined with the contract to establish the connection if the combined contract criteria in paragraph 17 of IFRS 15 are met. In a rate-regulated environment, the contract to transfer ongoing services to a customer (e.g. delivery of energy) may be implied as the customer has no alternative other than purchasing the good or service from the entity that is responsible for creating the connection; or
- the customer obtains control of the infrastructure asset (e.g. a pipe) or the connection.

2.8.1.C Factors to consider when non-refundable upfront fees received for establishing a connection to a network are within the scope of IFRS 15

As discussed in 2.8.1.B above, utility entities are often responsible for constructing infrastructure (e.g. a pipe) that will physically connect a building to its network (i.e. connection) and may receive a non-refundable upfront connection fee in exchange. Applying the non-refundable upfront fee application guidance in such contracts often requires significant judgement and depends on the facts and circumstances. For example, if more than one party is involved, the utility entity may need to consider the principal versus agent application guidance (see Chapter 28 at 3.4) in addition to the non-refundable upfront fee application guidance.

The non-refundable upfront fee application guidance requires an entity to determine if the upfront fee is related to a distinct good or service. As part of this assessment:

- a utility entity needs to determine whether the connection is a promised good or service in the contract. It considers explicit promises in the contract and implied promises that create a valid expectation of the customer that it will transfer control of the connection to the customer. This is likely to require significant judgement if the infrastructure asset remains an asset of the utility entity; and
- if the connection is a promised good or service, a utility entity needs to determine whether the promise is distinct. In particular, the assessment of whether the connection is distinct in the context of the contract is highly judgemental and must consider the specific contract with the customer, including all relevant facts and circumstances. Entities should not assume that a particular type of good or service is distinct (or not distinct) in all instances. The manner in which the promised goods or services have been bundled within a contract, if any, will affect the entity's assessment.

As part of assessing whether the promise is distinct within the context of the contract, a utility entity considers the three factors described in paragraph 29 of IFRS 15, as follows:

- *Factor (a):* the utility entity needs to understand the promise(s) it has made to its customers and whether it integrates them to satisfy its promise(s). For example, if it promised its customer the ongoing supply of services, it might also bear the risk for distribution of these services (including ensuring continued connection). Therefore, it may be providing a significant service of integrating promised goods or services to provide a combined output;
- *Factor (b):* this factor is unlikely to be relevant in the assessment of whether connection is distinct within the context of the contract because the ongoing service and the connection are unlikely to modify or customise each other; and
- *Factor (c):* the utility entity has to determine whether the connection is highly interdependent and highly interrelated with the ongoing service (e.g. supply of electricity). For example, whether there is more than just a functional relationship (i.e. one item, by its nature, depends on the other) because the utility entity cannot provide ongoing services (its main output, e.g. electricity, gas, water) without the connection and the customer cannot benefit from the connection without the ongoing services (i.e. is there two-way dependency?).

If the utility entity concludes that connection is not a distinct good or service, the non-refundable upfront fee is advanced payment for future goods or services and is recognised as revenue when (or as) the future goods or services are provided. As discussed above, in such situations, an entity must determine whether the non-refundable upfront fee represents an option to renew the contract at a lower price and must assesses whether the option to renew represents a material right.

Significant judgement may be needed to determine whether the customer has a material right. However, the fact that the customer remains connected to the network and does not to pay the connection fee again while in the same property, for example, might indicate that a material right exists.

If the renewal option represents a material right, the period over which the upfront fee is recognised is longer than the initial contract duration. It is likely that significant judgement will be needed to determine the appropriate period over which to recognise the upfront fee in such circumstances (see 2.8.1.A above).

2.9 Changes in the transaction price

Changes in the transaction price can occur for various reasons, including 'the resolution of uncertain events or other changes in circumstances that change the amount of consideration to which an entity expects to be entitled in exchange for the promised goods or services'. *[IFRS 15.87]*. See 3.5 below for additional requirements on accounting for a change in transaction price.

3 ALLOCATE THE TRANSACTION PRICE TO THE PERFORMANCE OBLIGATIONS

The standard's allocation objective is to allocate the transaction price to each performance obligation (or distinct good or service) in an amount that depicts the amount of consideration to which the entity expects to be entitled in exchange for transferring the promised goods or services to the customer. *[IFRS 15.73]*. As noted above, the allocation is generally done in proportion to the stand-alone selling prices (i.e. on a relative stand-alone selling price basis). *[IFRS 15.74]*.

Once the separate performance obligations are identified and the transaction price has been determined, the standard generally requires an entity to allocate the transaction price to the performance obligations in proportion to their stand-alone selling prices (i.e. on a relative stand-alone selling price basis). The Board noted in the Basis for Conclusions that, in most cases, an allocation based on stand-alone selling prices will faithfully depict the different margins that may apply to promised goods or services. *[IFRS 15.BC266]*.

When allocating on a relative stand-alone selling price basis, any discount within the contract is generally allocated proportionately to all of the performance obligations in the contract. However, as discussed further below, there are some exceptions. For example, an entity could allocate variable consideration to a single performance obligation in some situations. IFRS 15 also contemplates the allocation of any discount in a contract only to certain performance obligations, if specified criteria are met. *[IFRS 15.74]*. An entity would not apply the allocation requirements if the contract has only one performance obligation (except for a single performance obligation that is made up of a series of distinct goods or services and includes variable consideration). *[IFRS 15.75]*.

3.1 Determining stand-alone selling prices

To allocate the transaction price on a relative stand-alone selling price basis, an entity must first determine the stand-alone selling price of the distinct good or service underlying each performance obligation. *[IFRS 15.76]*. Under the standard, this is the price at which an entity would sell a good or service on a stand-alone (or separate) basis at contract inception. *[IFRS 15.77]*.

IFRS 15 indicates the observable price of a good or service sold separately provides the best evidence of stand-alone selling price. *[IFRS 15.77]*. However, in many situations, stand-alone selling prices are not readily observable. In those cases, the entity must estimate the stand-alone selling price. *[IFRS 15.78]*.

When estimating a stand-alone selling price, an entity is required to consider all information (including market conditions, entity-specific factors and information about the customer or class of customer) that is reasonably available to the entity. In doing so, an entity maximises the use of observable inputs and applies estimation methods consistently in similar circumstances. *[IFRS 15.78]*.

Figure 29.3 illustrates how an entity might determine the stand-alone selling price of a good or service, which may include estimation:

Figure 29.3: Determining the stand-alone selling price of a good or service

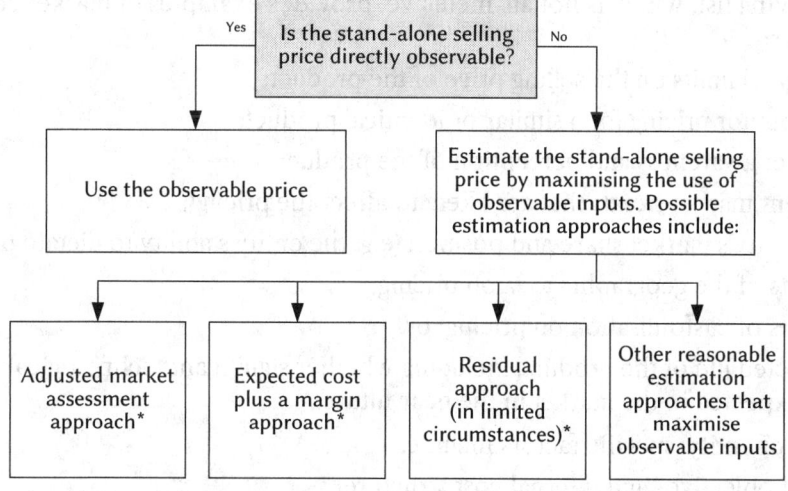

* See 3.1.2 below for further discussion of these estimation approaches, including when it might be appropriate to use a combination of approaches.

Stand-alone selling prices are determined at contract inception and are not updated to reflect changes between contract inception and when performance is complete. *[IFRS 15.88]*. For example, assume an entity determines the stand-alone selling price for a promised good using the expected cost plus a margin approach and, before it can finish manufacturing and deliver that good, the underlying cost of the materials doubles. In such a situation, the entity would not revise its stand-alone selling price used for this contract. However, for future contracts involving the same good, the entity would need to determine whether the change in circumstances (i.e. the significant increase in the cost to produce the good) warrants a revision of the stand-alone selling price. If so, the entity would use that revised price for allocations in future contracts (see 3.1.3 below).

Furthermore, if the contract is modified and that modification is treated as a termination of the existing contract and the creation of a new contract (see Chapter 28 at 2.4.2), the entity would update its estimate of the stand-alone selling price at the time of the modification. If the contract is modified and the modification is treated as a separate contract (see Chapter 28 at 2.4.1), the accounting for the original contact would not be affected (and the stand-alone selling prices of the underlying goods or services would not be updated), but the stand-alone selling prices of the distinct goods or services of the new, separate contract would have to be determined at the time of the modification.

3.1.1 Factors to consider when estimating the stand-alone selling price

To estimate the stand-alone selling price (if not readily observable), an entity may consider the stated prices in the contract. However, the standard says an entity cannot presume that a contractually stated price, or a list price, for a good or service is the stand-alone selling price. *[IFRS 15.77]*. In estimating a stand-alone selling price, an 'entity shall consider all information (including market conditions, entity-specific factors and information about the customer or class of customer) that is reasonably available to the entity'. *[IFRS 15.78]*. An entity also needs to maximise the use of observable inputs in its estimate. This is a very broad requirement for which an entity needs to consider a variety of data sources.

The following list, which is not all-inclusive, provides examples of market conditions to consider:

- potential limits on the selling price of the product;
- competitor pricing for a similar or identical product;
- market awareness and perception of the product;
- current market trends that are likely to affect the pricing;
- the entity's market share and position (e.g. the entity's ability to dictate pricing);
- effects of the geographic area on pricing;
- effects of customisation on pricing; or
- expected life of the product, including whether significant technological advances are expected in the market in the near future.

Examples of entity-specific factors include:

- profit objectives and internal cost structure;
- pricing practices and pricing objectives (including desired gross profit margin);
- effects of customisation on pricing;
- pricing practices used to establish pricing of bundled products;
- effects of a proposed transaction on pricing (e.g. the size of the deal, the characteristics of the targeted customer); or
- expected life of the product, including whether significant entity-specific technological advances are expected in the near future.

To document its estimated stand-alone selling price, an entity should consider describing the information that it has considered (e.g. the factors listed above), especially if there is limited observable data or none at all.

3.1.2 Possible estimation approaches

Paragraph 79 of IFRS 15 discusses three estimation approaches: (1) the adjusted market assessment approach; (2) the expected cost plus a margin approach; and (3) a residual approach. *[IFRS 15.79]*. All of these are discussed further below. When applying IFRS 15, an entity may need to use a different estimation approach for each of the distinct goods or services underlying the performance obligations in a contract. In addition, an entity may need to use a combination of approaches to estimate the stand-alone selling prices of goods or services promised in a contract if two or more of those goods or services have highly variable or uncertain stand-alone selling prices.

Furthermore, these are not the only estimation approaches permitted. IFRS 15 allows any reasonable estimation approach: as long as it is consistent with the notion of a stand-alone selling price; maximises the use of observable inputs and is applied on a consistent basis for similar goods or services and customers. *[IFRS 15.80]*.

In some cases, an entity may have sufficient observable data to determine the stand-alone selling price. For example, an entity may have sufficient stand-alone sales of a particular good or service that provide persuasive evidence of the stand-alone selling price of that particular good or service. In such situations, no estimation would be necessary. *[IFRS 15.77]*.

In many instances, an entity may not have sufficient stand-alone sales data to determine the stand-alone selling price based solely on those sales. In those instances, it must maximise the use of whatever observable inputs it has available in order to make its estimate. That is, an entity would not disregard any observable inputs when estimating the stand-alone selling price of a good or service. *[IFRS 15.78]*. An entity should consider all factors contemplated in negotiating the contract with the customer and the entity's normal pricing practices factoring in the most objective and reliable information that is available. While some entities may have robust practices in place regarding the pricing of goods or services, some may need to improve their processes to develop estimates of stand-alone selling prices.

The standard includes the following estimation approaches. *[IFRS 15.79]*.

- *Adjusted market assessment approach* – this approach focuses on the amount that the entity believes the market in which it sells goods or services is willing to pay for a good or service. For example, an entity might refer to competitors' prices for similar goods or services and adjust those prices, as necessary, to reflect the entity's costs and margins. When using the adjusted market assessment approach, an entity considers market conditions, such as those listed at 3.1.1 above. Applying this approach is likely to be easiest when an entity has sold the good or service for a period of time (such that it has data about customer demand), or a competitor offers similar goods or services that the entity can use as a basis for its analysis. Applying this approach may be difficult when an entity is selling an entirely new good or service because it may be difficult to anticipate market demand. In these situations, entities may want to use the market assessment approach, with adjustments as necessary, to reflect the entity's costs and margins, in combination with other approaches to maximise the use of observable inputs (e.g. using competitors' pricing, adjusted based on the market assessment approach in combination with an entity's planned internal pricing strategies if the performance obligation has never been sold separately).
- *Expected cost plus margin approach* – this approach focuses more on internal factors (e.g. the entity's cost basis), but has an external component as well. That is, the margin included in this approach must reflect the margin the market would be willing to pay, not just the entity's desired margin. The margin may have to be adjusted for differences in products, geographies, customers and other factors. The expected cost plus margin approach may be useful in many situations, especially

when the performance obligation has a determinable direct fulfilment cost (e.g. a tangible product or an hourly service). However, this approach may be less helpful when there are no clearly identifiable direct fulfilment costs or the amount of those costs is unknown (e.g. a new software licence or specified upgrade rights).

- *Residual approach* – this approach allows an entity to estimate the stand-alone selling price of a promised good or service as the difference between the total transaction price and the observable (i.e. not estimated) stand-alone selling prices of other promised goods or services in the contract, provided one of two criteria in paragraph 79(c) of IFRS 15 are met. *[IFRS 15.79(c)]*. The standard indicates that this approach can only be used for contracts with multiple promised goods or services when the selling price of one or more of the promised goods or services is unknown (either because the historical selling price is highly variable or because the goods or services have not yet been sold). As a result, we expect that the use of this approach is likely to be limited. However, allowing entities to use a residual technique provides relief to entities that rarely, or never, sell goods or services on a stand-alone basis, such as entities that sell intellectual property only with physical goods or services.

  The Board noted in the Basis for Conclusions that the use of the residual approach cannot result in a stand-alone selling price of zero if the good or service is distinct. *[IFRS 15.BC273]*. This is because a good or service must have value on a stand-alone basis to be distinct. The Board also stated that, if use of the residual approach results in very little, or no, consideration being allocated to a good or service or a bundle of goods or services, an entity should re-evaluate whether the use of the residual approach is appropriate.

  An example of an appropriate use of the residual approach would be an entity that frequently sells software, professional services and maintenance, bundled together, at prices that vary widely. However, the entity also sells the professional services and maintenance individually at relatively stable prices. The Board indicated that it may be appropriate to estimate the stand-alone selling price for the software as the difference between the total transaction price and the observable selling prices of the professional services and maintenance. See Cases B and C in Example 29.30, at 3.4 below, for examples of when the residual approach may or may not be appropriate.

  The Board clarified in the Basis for Conclusions that an entity could also use the residual approach if there are two or more goods or services in the contract with highly variable or uncertain stand-alone selling prices, provided that at least one of the other promised goods or services in the contract has an observable stand-alone selling price. The Board observed that, in such an instance, an entity may need to use a combination of techniques to estimate the stand-alone selling prices. *[IFRS 15.BC272]*. For example, an entity may apply the residual approach to estimate the aggregate of the stand-alone selling prices for all of the promised goods or services with highly variable or uncertain stand-alone selling prices, but then use another approach (e.g. adjusted market assessment, expected cost plus margin) to estimate the stand-alone selling prices of each of those promised goods or services with highly variable or uncertain stand-alone selling prices.

The standard includes the following example in which two estimation approaches are used to estimate stand-alone selling prices of two different goods in a contract. *[IFRS 15.IE164-IE166].*

Example 29.22: Allocation methodology

An entity enters into a contract with a customer to sell Products A, B and C in exchange for CU100. The entity will satisfy the performance obligations for each of the products at different points in time. The entity regularly sells Product A separately and therefore the stand-alone selling price is directly observable. The stand-alone selling prices of Products B and C are not directly observable.

Because the stand-alone selling prices for Products B and C are not directly observable, the entity must estimate them. To estimate the stand-alone selling prices, the entity uses the adjusted market assessment approach for Product B and the expected cost plus a margin approach for Product C. In making those estimates, the entity maximises the use of observable inputs (in accordance with paragraph 78 of IFRS 15). The entity estimates the stand-alone selling prices as follows:

Product	Stand-alone selling price	Method
	CU	
Product A	50	Directly observable (see paragraph 77 of IFRS 15)
Product B	25	Adjusted market assessment approach (see paragraph 79(a) of IFRS 15)
Product C	75	Expected cost plus a margin approach (see paragraph 79(b) of IFRS 15)
Total	150	

The customer receives a discount for purchasing the bundle of goods because the sum of the stand-alone selling prices (CU150) exceeds the promised consideration (CU100). The entity considers whether it has observable evidence about the performance obligation to which the entire discount belongs (in accordance with paragraph 82 of IFRS 15) and concludes that it does not. Consequently, in accordance with paragraphs 76 and 81 of IFRS 15, the discount is allocated proportionately across Products A, B and C. The discount, and therefore the transaction price, is allocated as follows:

Product	Allocated transaction price	
	CU	
Product A	33	(CU50 ÷ CU150 × CU100)
Product B	17	(CU25 ÷ CU150 × CU100)
Product C	50	(CU75 ÷ CU150 × CU100)
Total	100	

Given the flexibility provided by the standard to estimate stand-alone selling prices, it is both appropriate and necessary for entities to tailor the approach(es) used to their specific facts and circumstances. However, regardless of whether the entity uses a single approach or a combination of approaches, it must evaluate whether the resulting allocation of the transaction price is consistent with the overall allocation objective in paragraph 73 of IFRS 15 and the requirements for estimating stand-alone selling prices. *[IFRS 15.80].*

In accordance with IFRS 15, an entity must make a reasonable estimate of the stand-alone selling price for the distinct good or service underlying each performance obligation if an observable selling price is not readily available. We believe entities should have sufficient information to develop a reasonable estimate, even in instances in which limited information is available.

Entities need robust processes to estimate stand-alone selling prices. If those estimates have limited underlying observable data, it is important for entities to be able to demonstrate the reasonableness of the calculations they make in estimating stand-alone selling prices.

3.1.3 Updating estimated stand-alone selling prices

As discussed at 3.1 above, stand-alone selling prices are determined at contract inception and are not updated to reflect changes between contract inception and when performance is complete. However, an entity needs to update its estimates of stand-alone selling prices for future transactions to reflect changes in circumstances.

IFRS 15 does not specifically address how frequently estimated stand-alone selling prices must be updated. Instead, it indicates that an entity must make this estimate for each distinct good or service underlying each performance obligation in each contract with a customer, which suggests that an entity needs to constantly update its estimates.

In practice, we expect that entities will be able to consider their own facts and circumstances in order to determine how frequently they will need to update their estimates. If, for example, the information used to estimate the stand-alone selling price for similar transactions has not changed, an entity may determine that it is reasonable to use the previously determined stand-alone selling price.

However, in order for the changes in circumstances to be reflected in the estimate in a timely manner, we expect that an entity would formally update the estimate on a regular basis (e.g. monthly, quarterly, semi-annually). The frequency of updates should be based on the facts and circumstances of the distinct good or service underlying each performance obligation for which the estimate is made. An entity uses current information each time it develops or updates its estimate. While the estimates may be updated, the approach used to estimate a stand-alone selling price does not change (i.e. an entity must use a consistent approach), unless facts and circumstances change. [IFRS 15.78].

3.1.4 Additional considerations for determining the stand-alone selling price

While not explicitly stated in IFRS 15, we expect that a single good or service could have more than one stand-alone selling price. That is, the entity may be willing to sell goods or services at different prices to different customers. Furthermore, an entity may use different prices in different geographies or in markets where it uses different methods to distribute its products (e.g. it may use a distributor or reseller, rather than selling directly to the end-customer) or for other reasons (e.g. different cost structures or strategies in different markets). Accordingly, an entity may need to stratify its analysis to determine its stand-alone selling price for each class of customer, geography and/or market, as applicable.

3.1.4.A When estimating the stand-alone selling price, does an entity have to consider its historical pricing for the sale of the good or service involved?

We believe that an entity should consider its historical pricing in all circumstances, but it may not be determinative. Historical pricing is likely to be an important input as it may reflect both market conditions and entity-specific factors and can provide supporting evidence about the reasonableness of management's estimate. For example, if management determines, based on its pricing policies and competition in the market, that the stand-alone selling price of its good or service is X, historical transactions within a reasonable range of X would provide supporting evidence for management's estimate. However, if historical pricing was only 50% of X, this may indicate that historical pricing is no longer relevant due to changes in the market, for example, or that management's estimate is flawed.

Depending on the facts and circumstances, an entity may conclude that other factors such as internal pricing policies are more relevant to its determination of a stand-alone selling price. When historical pricing has been established using the entity's normal pricing policies and procedures, it is more likely that this information will be relevant in the estimation.

If the entity has sold the product separately or has information on competitors' pricing for a similar product, it is likely that the entity would find historical data relevant to its estimate of stand-alone selling prices, among other factors. In addition, we believe it may be appropriate for entities to stratify stand-alone selling prices based on: the type or size of customer; the amount of product or services purchased; the distribution channel; the geographic location; or other factors.

3.1.4.B   When using an expected cost plus margin approach to estimate a stand-alone selling price, how would an entity determine an appropriate margin?

When an entity elects to use the expected cost plus margin approach, it is important for the entity to use an appropriate margin. Determining an appropriate margin may require the use of significant judgement and involve the consideration of many market conditions and entity-specific factors, discussed at 3.1.1 above. For example, it would not be appropriate to determine that the entity's estimate of stand-alone selling price is equivalent to cost plus a 30% margin if a review of market conditions demonstrates that customers are only willing to pay the equivalent of cost plus a 12% margin for a comparable product. Similarly, it would be inappropriate to determine that cost plus a specified margin represents the stand-alone selling price if competitors are selling a comparable product at twice the determined estimate. Furthermore, the determined margin may have to be adjusted for differences in products, geographic locations, customers and other factors.

3.1.4.C   Estimating the stand-alone selling price of a good or service: estimating a range of prices versus identifying a point estimate

Entities might use a range of prices to help estimate the stand-alone selling price of a good or service. We believe it is reasonable for an entity to use such a range for the purpose of assessing whether a stand-alone selling price (i.e. a single price) that the entity intends to use is reasonably within that range. That is, we do not believe that an entity is required to determine a point estimate for each estimated stand-alone selling price if a range is a more practical means of estimating the stand-alone selling price for a good or service.

The objective of the standard is to allocate the transaction price to each performance obligation in 'an amount that depicts the amount of consideration for which the entity expects to be entitled in exchange for transferring the promised good or service to the customer'. While the standard does not address ranges of estimates, using a range of prices would not be inconsistent with the objective of the standard. The only requirements in the standard are that an entity maximise its use of observable inputs and apply the estimation approaches consistently. Therefore, the use of a range would also be consistent with these principles.

Practices we have observed include an entity establishing that a large portion of the stand-alone selling prices falls within a narrow range (e.g. by reference to historical pricing). We believe the use of a narrow range is acceptable for determining estimates of stand-alone selling prices under the standard because it is consistent with the standard's principle that an entity must maximise its use of observable inputs.

While the use of a range may be appropriate for estimating the stand-alone selling price, we believe that some approaches to identifying this range do not meet the requirements of IFRS 15. For example, it would not be appropriate for an entity to determine a range by estimating a single price point for the stand-alone selling price and then adding an arbitrary range on either side of that point estimate, nor would it be appropriate to take the historical prices and expand the range around the midpoint until a significant portion of the historical transactions fall within that band. The wider the range necessary to capture a high proportion of historical transactions, the less relevant it is in terms of providing a useful data point for estimating stand-alone selling prices.

Management's analysis of market conditions and entity-specific factors could support it in determining the best estimate of the stand-alone selling price. The historical pricing data from transactions, while not necessarily determinative, could be used as supporting evidence for management's conclusion. This is because it is consistent with the standard's principle that an entity must maximise its use of observable inputs. However, management would need to analyse the transactions that fall outside the range to determine whether they have similar characteristics and, therefore, need to be evaluated as a separate class of transactions with a different estimated selling price.

If the entity has established a reasonable range for the estimated stand-alone selling prices and the stated contractual price falls within that range, it may be appropriate to use the stated contractual price as the stand-alone selling price in the allocation calculation. However, if the stated contractual price for the good or service falls outside of the range, the stand-alone selling price needs to be adjusted to a point within the established range in order to allocate the transaction price on a relative stand-alone selling price basis. In these situations, the entity would need to determine which point in the range is most appropriate to use (e.g. the midpoint of the range or the outer limit nearest to the stated contractual price) when performing the allocation calculation.

3.1.4.D Evaluating a contract where the total transaction price exceeds the sum of the stand-alone selling prices

If the total transaction price exceeds the sum of the stand-alone selling prices it may indicate that the customer is paying a premium for bundling the goods or services in the contract. This situation is likely to be rare because most customers expect to receive a discount for purchasing a bundle of goods or services. If a premium exists after determining the stand-alone selling prices of each good or service, the entity needs to evaluate whether it properly identified both the estimated stand-alone selling prices (i.e. are they too low?) and the number of performance obligations in the contract. However, if the entity determines that a premium does exist after this evaluation, we believe the entity would need to allocate the premium in a manner consistent with the standard's allocation objective, which would typically be on a relative stand-alone selling price basis.

3.1.5 Measurement of options that are separate performance obligations

An entity that determines that a customer option for additional goods or services is a separate performance obligation (because the option provides the customer with a material right, as discussed at Chapter 28 at 3.6) needs to determine the stand-alone selling price of the option. *[IFRS 15.B42]*.

If the option's stand-alone selling price is not directly observable, the entity needs to estimate it. In doing so, paragraph B42 of IFRS 15 requires an entity to take into consideration any discount the customer would receive in a stand-alone transaction and the likelihood that the customer would exercise the option. *[IFRS 15.B42]*. Generally, option pricing models consider both the intrinsic value of the option (i.e. the value of the option if it were exercised today) and its time value (e.g. the option may be more or less valuable based on the amount of time until its expiration date and/or the volatility of the price of the underlying good or service). However, an entity is only required to measure the intrinsic value of the option when estimating the stand-alone selling price of the option. In the Basis for Conclusions, the Board noted that the benefits of valuing the time value component of an option would not justify the cost of doing so. *[IFRS 15.BC390]*. Example 28.43 in Chapter 28 at 3.6 illustrates the measurement of an option determined to be a material right under paragraph B42 of IFRS 15. The following example also illustrates this concept:

Example 29.23: Estimating the stand-alone selling price of options that are separate performance obligations

Publisher A sells a physical textbook for $10 and offers the customer an option to purchase the digital version of the publication at 50% off the retail price of $8. The typical discount for digital versions is 15%. Therefore, Publisher A concludes that this discount exceeds the typical discount offered to customers and that it provides the customer with a material right.

To estimate the stand-alone selling price of the option, Publisher A estimates there is a 50% likelihood that a customer will redeem the discount option. Therefore, Publisher A's estimated stand-alone selling price of the discount option is $1.40 ($8 digital price × 35% incremental discount × 50% likelihood of exercising the option).

Publisher A allocates $1.23 ($10 × [$1.40 / ($1.40 + $10)]) of the transaction price to the discount option and recognises revenue for the option when the customer exercises its right for the digital version or when the option expires. Publisher A allocates $8.77 ($10 – $1.23) to the physical book and recognises revenue for the physical book when it transfers control of the book to the customer.

Paragraph B43 of IFRS 15 provides an alternative to estimating the stand-alone selling price of an option. This practical alternative applies when the additional goods or services are both: (1) similar to the original goods or services in the contract (i.e. the entity continues to provide what it was already providing); *[IFRS 15.BC394]* and (2) provided in accordance with the terms of the original contract. The standard indicates that this practical alternative generally applies to options for contract renewals (i.e. the renewal option approach). *[IFRS 15.B43]*.

The Basis for Conclusions states that customer loyalty points and discount vouchers typically do not meet the criteria for use of this practical alternative. This is because customer loyalty points and discount vouchers are redeemable for goods or services that may differ in nature from those offered in the original contract and the terms of the original contract do not restrict the pricing of the additional goods or services. For example, if an airline offers flights to customers in exchange for points from its frequent flyer programme, the airline is not restricted because it can subsequently determine the number of points that are required to be redeemed for any particular flight. [IFRS 15.BC 394, BC395].

Under the practical alternative, a portion of the transaction price is allocated to the option (i.e. the material right that is a performance obligation) by reference to the total goods or services expected to be provided to the customer (including expected renewals) and the corresponding expected consideration. That is, the total amount of consideration expected to be received from the customer (including consideration from expected renewals) is allocated to the total goods or services expected to be provided to the customer, including those from the expected contract renewals. The amount allocated to the goods or services that the entity is required to transfer to the customer under the contract (i.e. excluding the optional goods or services that will be transferred if the customer exercises the renewal option(s)) is then subtracted from the total amount of consideration received (or that will be received) for transferring those goods or services. The difference is the amount that is allocated to the option at contract inception. An entity using this alternative needs to apply the constraint on variable consideration (as discussed at 2.2.3 above) to the estimated consideration for the optional goods or services prior to performing the allocation (see Example 29.24, Scenario B, below). [IFRS 15.B43].

It is important to note that the calculation of total expected consideration (i.e. the hypothetical transaction price), including consideration related to expected renewals, is only performed for the purpose of allocating a portion of the hypothetical transaction price to the option at contract inception. It does not change the enforceable rights or obligations in the contract, nor does it affect the actual transaction price for the goods or services that the entity is presently obliged to transfer to the customer (which would not include expected renewals). Accordingly, the entity would not include any remaining hypothetical transaction price in its disclosure of remaining performance obligations (see Chapter 32 at 3.2.1.C). In this respect, the practical alternative is consistent with the conclusion in Chapter 28 at 3.6.1.D. That is, even if an entity may think that it is almost certain that a customer will exercise an option to buy additional goods or services, an entity does not include the additional goods or services underlying the option as promised goods or services (or performance obligations), unless there are substantive contractual penalties.

Subsequent to contract inception, if the actual number of contract renewals is different from an entity's initial expectations, the entity updates the hypothetical transaction price and allocation. However, as discussed at 3.1 above, the estimate of the stand-alone selling price at contract inception is not updated. See Example 29.24, Scenario B below for an example of how an entity could update its practical alternative calculation based on a change in expectations.

The following example illustrates the two possible approaches for measuring options included in a contract.

Example 29.24: Measuring an option

A machinery maintenance contract provider offers a promotion to new customers who pay full price for the first year of maintenance coverage that grants them an option to renew the services for up to two years at a discount. The entity regularly sells maintenance coverage for $750 per year. With the promotion, the customer may renew the one-year maintenance at the end of each year for $600. The entity concludes that the ability to renew is a material right because the customer would receive a discount that exceeds any discount available to other customers. The entity also determines that no directly observable stand-alone selling price exists for the option to renew at a discount.

Scenario A – Estimate the stand-alone selling price of the option directly (paragraph B42 of IFRS 15)

Since the entity has no directly observable evidence of the stand-alone selling price for the renewal option, it estimates the stand-alone selling price of an option for a $150 discount on the renewal of service in years two and three. When developing its estimate, the entity considers factors such as the likelihood that the option will be exercised and the price of comparable discounted offers. For example, the entity may consider the selling price of an offer for a discounted price of similar services found on a 'deal of the day' website.

The option will then be included in the relative stand-alone selling price allocation. In this example, there are two performance obligations: one-year of maintenance services; and an option for discounted renewals. The consideration of $750 is allocated between these two performance obligations based on their relative stand-alone selling prices.

Example 28.43 in Chapter 28 at 3.6 illustrates the estimation of the stand-alone selling price of an option determined to be a material right under paragraph B42 of IFRS 15.

Scenario B – Practical alternative to estimating the stand-alone selling price of the option using the renewal option approach (paragraph B43 of IFRS 15)

If the entity chooses to use the renewal option approach, it allocates the transaction price to the option for maintenance services by reference to the maintenance services expected to be provided (including expected renewals) and the corresponding expected consideration. Since there is a discount offered on renewal of the maintenance service, this calculation will result in less revenue being allocated to the first year of the maintenance service when compared to the amount of consideration received for the first year of service (i.e. an amount less than $750). The difference between the consideration received (or that will be received) for the first year of maintenance service and the revenue allocated to the first year of maintenance service (i.e. $750) will represent the amount allocated to the option using the renewal option approach.

Assume the entity obtained 100 new customers under the promotion. Based on its experience, the entity anticipates approximately 50% attrition annually, after giving consideration to the anticipated effect that the $150 discount will have on attrition. The entity considers the constraint on variable consideration and concludes that it is not highly probable that a significant revenue reversal will not occur. Therefore, the entity concludes that, for this portfolio of contracts, it will ultimately sell 175 contracts, each contract providing one-year of maintenance services (i.e. 100 customers in the first year, 50 customers in the second year and 25 customers in the third year).

Therefore, the total consideration the entity expects to receive is $120,000 [(100 × $750) + (50 × $600) + (25 × $600)] (i.e. the hypothetical transaction price). Assuming the stand-alone selling price for each maintenance contract period is the same, the entity allocates $685.71 ($120,000/175) to each maintenance contract sold.

During the first year, the entity will recognise revenue of $68,571 (100 one-year maintenance service contracts sold × the allocated price of $685.71 per maintenance service contract). Consequently, at contract inception, the entity would allocate $6,429 to the option to renew ($75,000 cash received – $68,571 revenue to be recognised in the first year).

If the actual renewals in years two and three differ from expectations, the entity would have to update the hypothetical transaction price and allocation accordingly. However, beyond stating, as discussed at 3.1 above, that the estimate of the stand-alone selling prices at contract inception would not be updated, the standard is not explicit about how the entity would update the hypothetical transaction price and allocation. Below is an illustration of how an entity could update its practical alternative calculation based on a change in expectations.

For example, assume that the entity experiences less attrition than expected (e.g. 40% attrition annually, instead of 50%). Therefore, the entity's revised estimate is that it will ultimately sell 196 one-year maintenance services (100 + 60 renewals after year one + 36 renewals after year two). Accordingly, the total consideration that the entity expects to receive is $132,600 [(100 × $750) + (60 × $600) + (36 × $600)] (i.e. the updated hypothetical transaction price). The entity would not update its estimates of the stand-alone selling prices (which were assumed to be the same for each maintenance period). As such, the entity allocates $676.53 ($132,600/196) to each maintenance period. The entity would reduce the amount of revenue it recognises in year one by $918 ($68,571 − (100 × $676.53)) because the amount allocated to the option would have been higher at contract inception.

See Example 29.21 at 2.8 above for another example of applying the practical alternative when the contract includes a non-refundable upfront fee that is deemed to be a material right.

3.1.5.A Could the form of an option (e.g. a gift card versus a coupon) affect how an option's stand-alone selling price is estimated?

We believe that the form of an option should not affect how the stand-alone selling price is estimated. Consider, for example, a retailer that gives customers who spend more than €100 during a specified period a €15 discount on a future purchase in the form of a coupon or a gift card that expires two weeks from the sale date. If the retailer determines that this type of offer represents a material right (see Chapter 28 at 3.6), it will need to allocate a portion of the transaction price to the option on a relative stand-alone selling price basis.

As discussed at 3.1 above, the standard requires that an entity first look to any directly observable stand-alone selling price. This requires the retailer to consider the nature of the underlying transaction. In this example, while a customer can purchase a €15 gift card for its face value, that transaction is not the same in substance as a transaction in which the customer is given a €15 gift card or coupon in connection with purchasing another good or service. As such, the retailer could conclude that there is no directly observable stand-alone selling price for a 'free' gift card or coupon obtained in connection with the purchase of another good or service. It would then need to estimate the stand-alone selling price in accordance with paragraph B42 of IFRS 15.

The estimated stand-alone selling price of an option given in the form of a gift card or a coupon would be the same because both estimates would reflect the likelihood that the option will be exercised (i.e. breakage, as discussed in Chapter 30 at 11).

3.1.5.B Use of the practical alternative when not all of the goods or services in the original contract are subject to a renewal option

In certain instances, it might be appropriate to apply the practical alternative even if not all of the goods or services in the original contract are subject to renewal, provided that the renewal is of a good or service that is similar to that included in the original contract and follows the renewal terms included in the original contract. Consider a contract to sell hardware and a service-type warranty where the customer has the option to renew the warranty only. Furthermore, assume that the renewal option is determined to be a material right. If the terms of any future warranty renewals are consistent with the terms provided in the original contract, we believe it is reasonable to use the practical alternative when allocating the transaction price of the contract.

3.2 Applying the relative stand-alone selling price method

Once an entity has determined the stand-alone selling price for the separate goods or services in a contract, the entity allocates the transaction price to those performance obligations. *[IFRS 15.76]*. The standard requires an entity to use the relative stand-alone selling price method to allocate the transaction price, except in the two specific circumstances (variable consideration and discounts), which are described at 3.3 and 3.4 below.

Under the relative stand-alone selling price method, the transaction price is allocated to each performance obligation based on the proportion of the stand-alone selling price of each performance obligation to the sum of the stand-alone selling prices of all of the performance obligations in the contract, as described in Example 29.25 below. *[IFRS 15.76]*.

Example 29.25: Relative stand-alone selling price allocation

Manufacturing Co. entered into a contract with a customer to sell a machine for £100,000. The total contract price included installation of the machine and a two-year extended warranty. Assume that Manufacturing Co. determined there were three performance obligations and the stand-alone selling prices of those performance obligations were as follows: machine – £75,000, installation services – £14,000 and extended warranty – £20,000.

The aggregate of the stand-alone selling prices (£109,000) exceeds the total transaction price of £100,000, indicating there is a discount inherent in the contract. That discount must be allocated to each of the individual performance obligations based on the relative stand-alone selling price of each performance obligation. Therefore, the amount of the £100,000 transaction price is allocated to each performance obligation as follows:

Machine – £68,807 (£100,000 × (£75,000 / £109,000))

Installation – £12,844 (£100,000 × (£14,000 / £109,000))

Warranty – £18,349 (£100,000 × (£20,000 / £109,000))

The entity would recognise as revenue the amount allocated to each performance obligation when (or as) each performance obligation is satisfied.

3.2.1 Allocating the transaction price in a contract with multiple performance obligations in which the entity acts as both a principal and an agent

As discussed in the June 2014 TRG meeting, the standard does not illustrate the allocation of the transaction price for a contract with multiple performance obligations in which the entity acts as both a principal and an agent (see Chapter 28 at 3.4 for a discussion of principal versus agent considerations).[36] Example 29.26 below illustrates two acceptable ways to perform the allocation for this type of contract that are consistent with the standard's objective for allocating the transaction price. Entities need to evaluate the facts and circumstances of their contracts to make sure that the allocation involving multiple performance obligations in which an entity acts as both a principal and an agent meets the allocation objectives in IFRS 15.

Example 29.26: *Allocation when an entity is both a principal and an agent in a contract*

Entity X sells two distinct products (i.e. Product A and Product B) to Customer Y, along with a distinct service for an aggregate contract price of $800. Entity X is the principal for the sale of Product A and Product B, but is an agent for the sale of the service.

The stand-alone selling price of each good and service in the contract is, as follows:

Contract	Stand-alone selling price
	$
Product A	500
Product B	300
Service	200
Total	1,000

Entity X earns a 20% commission from the third-party service provider based on the stand-alone selling price of the service. That is, Entity X earns $40 of commission (i.e. $200 × 20%) and remits the remaining $160 to the third-party service provider.

Method A – Entity X determines that it has provided a single discount of $200 (i.e. sum of stand-alone selling prices of $1,000 less the contract price of $800) on the bundle of goods and services sold to Customer Y in the contract (i.e. Products A and B and the service provided by the third-party). Assume that the criteria for allocating the discount to one or more, but not all, performance obligations in accordance with paragraph 82 of IFRS 15 are not met – see 3.4 above.

In order to allocate the discount to all of the goods and services in the contract, Entity X considers the performance obligation for the agency service as part of the contract with Customer Y for purposes of allocating the transaction price. Entity X determines the stand-alone selling prices of Products A and B and the agency service and allocates the transaction price of $640 (i.e. $800 contract price less $160 to be remitted to the third-party service provider) for Products A and B and the service on a relative stand-alone selling price basis. This method is illustrated, as follows:

Contract	Stand-alone selling price		Allocated transaction price
	$		$
Product A	500	(500 ÷ 840 × 640)	381
Product B	300	(300 ÷ 840 × 640)	229
Service	40	(40 ÷ 840 × 640)	30
Total	840		640

Method B – Entity X determines that it has provided a discount of $200 on Products A and B since it is the principal for the transfer of those goods to Customer Y. Entity X believes the third-party service provider is a separate customer for its agency services and the commission Entity X expects to be entitled to receive for the agency service is not part of the transaction price in the contract with Customer Y. Entity X allocates a transaction price of $600 (i.e. $800 contract price less $200 stand-alone selling price of service) to Product A and B on a relative stand-alone selling price basis. This method is illustrated, as follows:

Contract	Stand-alone selling price		Allocated transaction price
	$		$
Product A	500	(500 ÷ 800 × 600)	375
Product B	300	(300 ÷ 800 × 600)	225
Total	800		600

The entity would recognise $40 separately for its earned commission on the service contract when the performance obligation for the agency service has been satisfied.

In either method, the same amount of revenue is ultimately recognised (i.e. $640). However, the timing of revenue recognition would be different if the products and agency service are transferred to the customer at different times.

3.3 Allocating variable consideration

The relative stand-alone selling price method is the default method for allocating the transaction price. However, the Board noted in the Basis for Conclusions on IFRS 15 that this method may not always result in a faithful depiction of the amount of consideration to which an entity expects to be entitled from the customer. *[IFRS 15.BC280]*. Therefore, the standard provides two exceptions to the relative selling price method of allocating the transaction price.

The first relates to the allocation of variable consideration (see 3.4 below for the second exception on the allocation of a discount). This exception requires variable consideration to be allocated entirely to a specific part of a contract such as one or more (but not all) performance obligations in the contract (e.g. a bonus may be contingent on an entity transferring a promised good or service within a specified period of time) or one or more (but not all) distinct goods or services promised in a series of distinct goods or services that form part of a single performance obligation (see Chapter 28 at 3.2.2). For example, the consideration promised for the second year of a two-year cleaning contract will increase on the basis of movements in a specified index. This exception will be applied to a single performance obligation, a combination of performance obligations or distinct goods or services that make up part of a performance obligation depending on the facts and circumstances of each contract. *[IFRS 15.84]*.

Two criteria must be met to apply this exception, as follows:

(a) the terms of a variable payment relate specifically to the entity's efforts to satisfy the performance obligation or transfer the distinct good or service (or to a specific outcome from satisfying the performance obligation or transferring the distinct good or service); and

(b) allocating the variable amount of consideration entirely to the performance obligation or the distinct good or service is consistent with the allocation objective (see 3 above) when considering all of the performance obligations and payment terms in the contract. *[IFRS 15.85]*.

The general allocation requirements (see 3.1 above) must then be applied to allocate the remaining amount of the transaction price that does not meet the above criteria. *[IFRS 15.86]*.

While the language in above criteria (from paragraph 85 of IFRS 15) implies that this exception is limited to allocating variable consideration to a single performance obligation or a single distinct good or service within a series, paragraph 84 of IFRS 15 indicates that the variable consideration can be allocated to 'one or more, but not all' performance obligations or distinct goods or services within a series. We understand it was not the Board's intent to limit this exception to a single performance obligation or a single distinct good or service within a series, even though the standard uses a singular construction for the remainder of the discussion and does not repeat 'one or more, but not all'.

The Board noted in the Basis for Conclusions that this exception is necessary because allocating contingent amounts to all performance obligations in a contract may not reflect the economics of a transaction in all cases. *[IFRS 15.BC278]*. Allocating variable consideration entirely to a distinct good or service may be appropriate when the result is that the amount allocated to that particular good or service is reasonable relative to all other performance obligations and payment terms in the contract. Subsequent changes in variable consideration must be allocated in a consistent manner.

It is important to note that allocating variable consideration to one or more, but not all, performance obligations or distinct goods or services in a series is a requirement, not a policy choice. If the above criteria are met, the entity must allocate the variable consideration to the related performance obligation(s) or distinct goods or services in a series. *[IFRS 15.85]*.

Entities may need to exercise significant judgement to determine whether they meet the requirements to allocate variable consideration to specific performance obligations or distinct goods or services within a series. Firstly, entities need to determine whether they meet the first criterion in paragraph 85 of IFRS 15, which requires that the terms of a variable payment relate specifically to either an entity's efforts to satisfy a performance obligation (or to transfer a distinct good or service that is part of a series) or a specific outcome from satisfying the performance obligation (or transferring the distinct good or service).

In performing this assessment, an entity needs to consider the nature of its promise and how the performance obligation has been defined. In addition, the entity needs to clearly understand the variable payment terms and how they align with the entity's promise. This includes evaluating any clawbacks or other potential adjustments to the variable payment. For example, an entity may conclude that the nature of its promise in a contract is to provide hotel management services (including management of the hotel employees, accounting services, training and procurement, etc.) that comprise a series of distinct services (i.e. daily hotel management). For providing this service, the entity receives a variable fee (based on a percentage of occupancy rates). It is likely that the entity would determine that it meets the first criterion to allocate the daily variable fee to the distinct service performed that day because the uncertainty related to the consideration is resolved on a daily basis as the entity satisfies its obligation to perform daily hotel management services. This is because the variable payments specifically relate to transferring the distinct service that is part of a series of distinct goods or services (i.e. the daily management service). The fact that the payments do not directly correlate with each of the underlying activities performed each day does not affect this assessment. See Chapter 28 at 3 for further discussion on identifying the nature of the goods or services promised in a contract, including whether they meet the series requirement.

In contrast, consider an entity that has a contract to sell equipment and maintenance services for that equipment. The maintenance services have been determined to be a series of distinct services because the customer benefits from the entity standing ready to perform in case the equipment breaks down. The consideration for the maintenance services is based on usage of the equipment and is, therefore, variable. In this example, the payment terms do not align with the nature of the entity's promise. This is because the payment terms are usage-based, but the nature of the entity's promise is to stand ready each day to perform any maintenance that may be needed, regardless of how much the customer uses the equipment. Since the entity does not meet the criteria to apply the allocation exception, it must estimate the variable consideration over the life of the contract, including consideration of the constraint. The entity would then recognise revenue based on its selected measure of progress (see Chapter 30 at 3).

After assessment of the first criterion, entities need to determine whether they meet the second criterion in paragraph 85 of IFRS 15; to confirm that allocating the consideration in this manner is consistent with the overall allocation objective of the standard in paragraph 73 of IFRS 15. That is, an entity should allocate to each performance obligation (or distinct good or service in a series) the portion of the transaction price that reflects the amount of consideration the entity expects to be entitled in exchange for transferring those goods or services to the customer.

The TRG discussed four types of contracts with different variable payment terms that may be accounted for as a series of distinct goods or services (see Chapter 28 at 3.2.2) and for which an entity may reasonably conclude that the allocation objective has been met (and the variable consideration could be allocated to each distinct period of service, such as day, month or year), which are detailed below:[37]

- *Declining prices* – The TRG agenda paper included an IT outsourcing contract in which the events that trigger the variable consideration are the same throughout the contract, but the per unit price declines over the life of the contract. The allocation objective could be met if the pricing is based on market terms (e.g. if the contract contains a benchmarking clause) or the changes in price are substantive and linked to changes in an entity's cost to fulfil the obligation or value provided to the customer;

- *Consistent fixed prices* – The TRG agenda paper included a transaction processing contract with an unknown quantity of transactions, but a fixed contractual rate per transaction. The allocation objective could be met if the fees are priced consistently throughout the contract and the rates charged are consistent with the entity's standard pricing practices with similar customers;

- *Consistent variable fees, cost reimbursements and incentive fees* – The TRG agenda paper included a hotel management contract in which monthly consideration is based on a percentage of monthly rental revenue, reimbursement of labour costs and an annual incentive payment. The allocation objective could be met for each payment stream as follows. The base monthly fees could meet the allocation objective if the consistent measure throughout the contract period (e.g. 1% of monthly rental revenue) reflects the value to the customer. The cost reimbursements could meet the allocation objective if they are commensurate with an entity's efforts to fulfil the promise each day. The annual incentive fee could also meet the allocation objective if it reflects the value delivered to the customer for the annual period and is reasonable compared with incentive fees that could be earned in other periods; and

- *Sales-based and usage-based royalty for licences of intellectual property* – The TRG agenda paper included a franchise agreement in which franchisor will receive a sales-based royalty of 5% in addition to a fixed fee. The allocation objective could be met if the consistent formula throughout the licence period reasonably reflects the value to the customer of its access to the franchisor's intellectual property (e.g. reflected by the sales that have been generated by the customer).

Beyond these four types of contracts discussed by the TRG, entities may also need to use judgement to determine whether contracts with usage-based variable consideration provisions meet the variable consideration allocation exception criteria, as follows:

(a) Variable fee arrangements based on usage

Consideration for some service contracts is based entirely on customer usage, and an entity has a stand-ready obligation to perform, regardless of how often the customer uses the service. Therefore, the usage-based fees are variable consideration.

It is important to note that, while these usage-based transactions may be economically similar to licensing arrangements that include sales-based or usage-based royalties, the accounting may be different. As described in Chapter 31 at 2.5, sales-based and usage-based royalties on licences of intellectual property are subject to the royalty recognition constraint and that requirement must be applied to the overall royalty stream when the sole or predominant item to which the royalty relates is a licence of intellectual property. Entities cannot analogise to the royalty recognition constraint for other situations.

If the usage-based fees relate specifically to the entity's effort to satisfy the performance obligation to provide services (or to a specific outcome from satisfying the performance obligation) and allocating the variable consideration to each distinct day is consistent with the allocation objective, the variable consideration allocation exception is met and the consideration is allocated to the period in which the usage occurred.

If the usage-based fees do not relate to an entity's effort to satisfy the performance obligation (or to a specific outcome from satisfying the performance obligation) or if the allocation of the usage-based fees is not consistent with the allocation exception, the allocation exception is not met. For example, the allocation exception would not be met if the fees decline over the contract term as an incentive for the customer to achieve certain volume thresholds, if, as discussed above, such pricing is not based on market terms or not linked to changes in the entity's cost to fulfil the obligation or value provided to the customer. In this situation, the variable consideration is estimated at contract inception and it is to be recognised over the contract duration. These estimates of variable consideration must be updated at the end of each reporting period and are subject to the constraint on variable consideration. See 2.2.2 above for further discussion on estimating variable consideration.

Consider the following example of a contract with variable usage-based fees calculated daily that is likely to meet the variable consideration allocation exception:

Example 29.27: Variable fee service arrangement based on usage

Provider C enters into a contract for cloud storage in which a customer agrees to pay daily fees based on the amount of storage space it uses (i.e. a fixed daily rate of $0.025 per gigabyte of storage is multiplied by the number of gigabytes used). Provider C invoices the customer at the end of each month. Assume that the entity has appropriately concluded that the nature of the entity's performance obligation is to stand ready to provide any amount of storage space the customer needs at any time during the contract term and the consideration in the contract is variable based on the number of gigabytes of storage used (and, therefore, each gigabyte used is not an optional purchase – refer to Chapter 28 at 3.6.1.C).

Provider C determines that the service provided to the customer in this contract meets the criteria to be accounted for as a series of distinct goods or services (see Chapter 28 at 3.2.2). This is because the performance obligation to stand ready to provide any amount of storage space represents a series of distinct services that are substantially the same and have the same pattern of transfer to the customer.

Provider C then considers whether the variable consideration allocation exception would apply to the daily usage-based fees. Provider C determines that it meets the first criterion to allocate the daily variable fee to the distinct service performed that day because the uncertainty related to the consideration is resolved on a daily basis as the entity satisfies its obligation to provide cloud storage. This is because the variable payments specifically relate to transferring the distinct service: access to any amount of cloud storage that the customer chooses to use each day.

Provider C concludes that allocating the variable payments to each day is consistent with the allocation objective because the fixed-rate-per-gigabyte fees reflect the value to the customer based on the amount of storage the customer uses each day. Further, the rates charged are consistent with Provider C's standard pricing practices.

Therefore, Provider C determines that it needs to apply the variable consideration allocation exception and recognises each day's fee for the day in which it occurs. That is, if the customer uses 250 gigabytes of storage the first day and 300 gigabytes the second, Provider C will recognise $6.25 and $7.50 of revenue for the respective days.

(b) Fixed-fee arrangements with overages

Some service contracts may have fixed fees (including any minimum amounts guaranteed) but also require customers to pay overage fees when they exceed certain thresholds based on usage. When an entity's performance obligation is to stand ready to perform, regardless of customer usage, the overage fee is considered variable consideration that the entity needs to estimate at contract inception, unless the variable consideration allocation exception is met.

Consider the following example of a contract with fixed fees and annual overages:

Example 29.28: Fixed-fee service arrangement with overages

Entity X enters into a three-year contract with a customer to provide access to its software as a service (SaaS) application, which allows the customer to process transactions, among other functions. The customer agrees to pay an annual fee of $100,000, plus overage fees at a rate of $0.10 per transaction for transactions processed through the application during the year that exceed one million (i.e. overage fees are only paid if the customer processes more than one million transactions during the year).

Assume that Entity X has determined that the nature of its performance obligation is to provide continuous access to the SaaS application, regardless of the number of transactions processed. Entity X determines that the $100,000 annual fee is fixed consideration and all additional consideration received as overage fees is variable consideration.

Also assume that Entity X has determined that the fixed component of the consideration should be recognised rateably over the contract term because the service is provided to the customer on a consistent basis (i.e. the performance obligation is satisfied evenly over the period). Entity X will then need to determine whether the variable consideration allocation exception applies to the overage fees, which are calculated based on annual usage.

Evaluating the allocation exception for distinct daily periods

We believe that, for the entity to apply the variable consideration allocation exception by allocating overage fees to a particular day, the entity would have to conclude that the overage fees relate to its performance on that particular day. Therefore, Entity X may conclude that it cannot apply the variable consideration allocation exception to the daily reporting periods for the overage fees because those payments do not relate to its efforts to satisfy the performance obligation to provide continuous access to the platform. That is, the nature of the performance obligation is a series of daily stand-ready obligations that are satisfied evenly over time, and the overage fees are additional consideration for satisfying that performance obligation over the course of each year.

Since the overage fees are only incurred after the annual minimum is reached, recognising revenue when the fees are incurred would result in more revenue recognised for the periods after the minimum is reached (i.e. backloading the revenue recognition), which is inconsistent with the allocation objective in paragraph 73 of IFRS 15. Therefore, the criteria for using the variable consideration allocation exception would not be met for each day of service, and Entity X would not recognise revenue for the overages on the days when the fees are incurred. However, we believe that if the overages in this example were calculated based on a short period of usage (e.g. daily or monthly (instead of annually)), Entity X may be able to demonstrate that it meets the criteria to apply the variable consideration allocation exception. This is because of the relatively short period of time between Entity X's performance and when it is entitled to the variable consideration such that Entity X could reasonably conclude that the allocation objective in paragraph 73 of IFRS 15 has been met.

Evaluating the allocation exception for annual periods

Since Entity X earns overage fees over a period of time that is less than the contract term (i.e. a three-year contract where overage fees are accrued and reset on an annual basis), Entity X would evaluate whether the overages need to be allocated to the period in which the overage fees are earned (e.g. to the annual period in which overages accrue).

To do so, Entity X evaluates whether it meets the criteria to apply the variable consideration allocation exception to the overage fees earned in each annual period in the three-year contract. Entity X may conclude that it needs to apply the variable consideration allocation exception to the overage fees earned in annual periods, which would require the entity to allocate the annual overage fees to each respective year (since the overages can be attributed to a single year). Therefore, Entity X will need to estimate overage fees only for each annual period (also considering the variable consideration constraint, as discussed at 2.2 above), rather than for the full three-year period at contract inception (which would be required if the variable consideration allocation exception was not met for any period). This would result in recognition of revenue from the overage fees only in the annual period to which the overages relate and not over the entire contract term.

For example, if the entity estimated that the overage fees for the first year would be $20,000, it would recognise this amount rateably over the year (i.e. $5,000 in each quarter), in addition to the fixed consideration that is also recognised rateably. The estimates of variable consideration must be updated at the end of each reporting period, as discussed at 2.2.4 above.

(c) *Illustrative example*

The standard provides the following example to illustrate when an entity may or may not be able to allocate variable consideration to a specific part of a contract. Note that the example focuses on licences of intellectual property, which are discussed at Chapter 31 at 2. *[IFRS 15.IE178-IE187]*.

Example 29.29: Allocation of variable consideration

An entity enters into a contract with a customer for two intellectual property licences (Licences X and Y), which the entity determines to represent two performance obligations each satisfied at a point in time. The stand-alone selling prices of Licences X and Y are €800 and €1,000, respectively.

Case A – Variable consideration allocated entirely to one performance obligation

The price stated in the contract for Licence X is a fixed amount of €800 and for Licence Y the consideration is three per cent of the customer's future sales of products that use Licence Y. For purposes of allocation, the entity estimates its sales-based royalties (i.e. the variable consideration) to be €1,000, in accordance with paragraph 53 of IFRS 15.

To allocate the transaction price, the entity considers the criteria in paragraph 85 of IFRS 15 and concludes that the variable consideration (i.e. the sales-based royalties) should be allocated entirely to Licence Y. The entity concludes that the criteria in paragraph 85 of IFRS 15 are met for the following reasons:

(a) the variable payment relates specifically to an outcome from the performance obligation to transfer Licence Y (i.e. the customer's subsequent sales of products that use Licence Y); and

(b) allocating the expected royalty amounts of €1,000 entirely to Licence Y is consistent with the allocation objective in paragraph 73 of IFRS 15. This is because the entity's estimate of the amount of sales-based royalties (€1,000) approximates the stand-alone selling price of Licence Y and the fixed amount of €800 approximates the stand-alone selling price of Licence X. The entity allocates €800 to Licence X in accordance with paragraph 86 of IFRS 15. This is because, based on an assessment of the facts and circumstances relating to both licences, allocating to Licence Y some of the fixed consideration in addition to all of the variable consideration would not meet the allocation objective in paragraph 73 of IFRS 15.

The entity transfers Licence Y at inception of the contract and transfers Licence X one month later. Upon the transfer of Licence Y, the entity does not recognise revenue because the consideration allocated to Licence Y is in the form of a sales-based royalty. Therefore, in accordance with paragraph B63 of IFRS 15, the entity recognises revenue for the sales-based royalty when those subsequent sales occur.

When Licence X is transferred, the entity recognises as revenue the €800 allocated to Licence X.

Case B – Variable consideration allocated on the basis of stand-alone selling prices

The price stated in the contract for Licence X is a fixed amount of €300 and for Licence Y the consideration is five per cent of the customer's future sales of products that use Licence Y. The entity's estimate of the sales-based royalties (i.e. the variable consideration) is €1,500 in accordance with paragraph 53 of IFRS 15.

To allocate the transaction price, the entity applies the criteria in paragraph 85 of IFRS 15 to determine whether to allocate the variable consideration (i.e. the sales-based royalties) entirely to Licence Y. In applying the criteria, the entity concludes that even though the variable payments relate specifically to an outcome from the performance obligation to transfer Licence Y (i.e. the customer's subsequent sales of products that use Licence Y), allocating the variable consideration entirely to Licence Y would be inconsistent with the principle for allocating the transaction price. Allocating €300 to Licence X and €1,500 to Licence Y does not reflect a reasonable allocation of the transaction price on the basis of the stand-alone selling prices of Licences X and Y of €800 and €1,000, respectively. Consequently, the entity applies the general allocation requirements in paragraphs 76-80 of IFRS 15.

The entity allocates the transaction price of €300 to Licences X and Y on the basis of relative stand-alone selling prices of €800 and €1,000, respectively. The entity also allocates the consideration related to the sales-based royalty on a relative stand-alone selling price basis. However, in accordance with paragraph B63 of IFRS 15, when an entity licenses intellectual property in which the consideration is in the form of a sales-based royalty, the entity cannot recognise revenue until the later of the following events: the subsequent sales occur; or the performance obligation is satisfied (or partially satisfied).

Licence Y is transferred to the customer at the inception of the contract and Licence X is transferred three months later. When Licence Y is transferred, the entity recognises as revenue the €167 (€1,000 ÷ €1,800 × €300) allocated to Licence Y. When Licence X is transferred, the entity recognises as revenue the €133 (€800 ÷ €1,800 × €300) allocated to Licence X.

In the first month, the royalty due from the customer's first month of sales is €200. Consequently, in accordance with paragraph B63 of IFRS 15, the entity recognises as revenue the €111 (€1,000 ÷ €1,800 × €200) allocated to Licence Y (which has been transferred to the customer and is therefore a satisfied performance obligation). The entity recognises a contract liability for the €89 (€800 ÷ €1,800 × €200) allocated to Licence X. This is because although the subsequent sale by the entity's customer has occurred, the performance obligation to which the royalty has been allocated has not been satisfied.

3.3.1 Application questions on the variable consideration allocation exception

3.3.1.A *In order to meet the criteria to allocate variable consideration entirely to a specific part of a contract, must the allocation be made on a relative stand-alone selling price basis?*

The TRG members generally agreed that a relative stand-alone selling price allocation is not required to meet the allocation objective when it relates to the allocation of variable consideration to a specific part of a contract (e.g. a distinct good or service in a series). The Basis for Conclusions notes that stand-alone selling price is the default method for meeting the allocation objective, but other methods could be used in certain instances (e.g. in allocating variable consideration). *[IFRS 15.BC279-BC280].*

Stakeholders had questioned whether the variable consideration exception would have limited application to a series of distinct goods or services (see Chapter 28 at 3.2.2). That is, they wanted to know whether the standard would require that each distinct service that is substantially the same be allocated the same amount (absolute value) of variable consideration.[38] While the standard does not state what other allocation methods could be used beyond the relative stand-alone selling price basis, the TRG members generally agreed that an entity would apply reasonable judgement to determine whether the allocation results in a reasonable outcome (and, therefore, meets the allocation objective in the standard), as discussed at 3.3 above.

3.4 Allocating a discount

The second exception to the relative stand-alone selling price allocation (see 3.3 above for the first exception) relates to discounts inherent in contracts. When an entity sells a bundle of goods or services, the selling price of the bundle is often less than the sum of the stand-alone selling prices of the individual elements. Under the relative stand-alone selling price allocation method, this discount would be allocated proportionately to all performance obligations. *[IFRS 15.81]*. However, if an entity determines that a discount is not related to all of the promised goods or services in the contract, the entity must allocate the contract's entire discount only to the goods or services to which it relates.

An entity makes this determination when the price of certain goods or services is largely independent of other goods or services in the contract. In these situations, an entity is able to effectively 'carve out' an individual performance obligation, or some of the performance obligations in the contract, and allocate the contract's entire discount to one or more, but not all, performance obligations, provided the criteria below are met. However, an entity cannot use this exception to allocate only a portion of the discount to one or more, but not all, performance obligations in the contract.

The standard requires an entity to allocate a discount entirely to one or more, but not all, performance obligations in the contract if all of the following criteria are met: *[IFRS 15.82]*

(a) the entity regularly sells each distinct good or service (or each bundle of distinct goods or services) on a stand-alone basis;

(b) the entity also regularly sells on a stand-alone basis a bundle (or bundles) of some of those distinct goods or services at a discount to the stand-alone selling prices of the goods or services in each bundle; and

(c) the discount attributable to each bundle of goods or services described in (b) is substantially the same as the discount in the contract and an analysis of the goods or services in each bundle provides observable evidence of the performance obligation (or performance obligations) to which the entire discount in the contract belongs.

The Board noted in the Basis for Conclusions that the requirements in paragraph 82 of IFRS 15 generally apply to contracts that include at least three performance obligations. While the standard contemplates that an entity may allocate the entire discount to as few as one performance obligation, the Board noted that such situations are expected to be rare. *[IFRS 15.BC283]*. Instead, the Board believes it is more likely that an entity will be able to demonstrate that a discount relates to two or more performance obligations. This is because an entity is likely to have observable information that the stand-alone selling price of a group of promised goods or services is lower than the price of those items when sold separately. It may be more difficult for an entity to have sufficient evidence to demonstrate that a discount is associated with a single performance obligation. When an entity applies a discount to one or more performance obligations in accordance with the above criteria, the standard states that the discount is allocated first before using the residual approach to estimate the stand-alone selling price of a good or service (see 3.1.2 above). *[IFRS 15.83]*.

The standard includes the following example to illustrate this exception and when the use of the residual approach for estimating stand-alone selling prices may or may not be appropriate. *[IFRS 15.IE167-IE177]*.

Example 29.30: Allocating a discount

An entity regularly sells Products A, B and C individually, thereby establishing the following stand-alone selling prices:

Product	Stand-alone selling price
	£
Product A	40
Product B	55
Product C	45
Total	140

In addition, the entity regularly sells Products B and C together for £60.

Case A – Allocating a discount to one or more performance obligations

The entity enters into a contract with a customer to sell Products A, B and C in exchange for £100. The entity will satisfy the performance obligations for each of the products at different points in time.

The contract includes a discount of £40 on the overall transaction, which would be allocated proportionately to all three performance obligations when allocating the transaction price using the relative stand-alone selling price method (in accordance with paragraph 81 of IFRS 15). However, because the entity regularly sells Products B and C together for £60 and Product A for £40, it has evidence that the entire discount should be allocated to the promises to transfer Products B and C in accordance with paragraph 82 of IFRS 15.

If the entity transfers control of Products B and C at the same point in time, then the entity could, as a practical matter, account for the transfer of those products as a single performance obligation. That is, the entity could allocate CU60 of the transaction price to the single performance obligation and recognise revenue of £60 when Products B and C simultaneously transfer to the customer.

If the contract requires the entity to transfer control of Products B and C at different points in time, then the allocated amount of £60 is individually allocated to the promises to transfer Product B (stand-alone selling price of £55) and Product C (stand-alone selling price of £45) as follows:

Product	Allocated transaction price	
	£	
Product B	33	(£55 ÷ £100 total stand-alone selling price × £60)
Product C	27	(£45 ÷ £100 total stand-alone selling price × £60)
Total	60	

Case B – Residual approach is appropriate

The entity enters into a contract with a customer to sell Products A, B and C as described in Case A. The contract also includes a promise to transfer Product D. Total consideration in the contract is £130. The stand-alone selling price for Product D is highly variable (see paragraph 79(c) of IFRS 15) because the entity sells Product D to different customers for a broad range of amounts (£15-£45). Consequently, the entity decides to estimate the stand-alone selling price of Product D using the residual approach.

Before estimating the stand-alone selling price of Product D using the residual approach, the entity determines whether any discount should be allocated to the other performance obligations in the contract in accordance with paragraphs 82 and 83 of IFRS 15.

As in Case A, because the entity regularly sells Products B and C together for £60 and Product A for £40, it has observable evidence that £100 should be allocated to those three products and a £40 discount should be allocated to the promises to transfer Products B and C in accordance with paragraph 82 of IFRS 15. Using the residual approach, the entity estimates the stand-alone selling price of Product D to be £30 as follows:

Product	Stand-alone selling price	Method
	£	
Product A	40	Directly observable (see paragraph 77 of IFRS 15)
Products B and C	60	Directly observable with discount (see Paragraph 82 of IFRS 15)
Product D	30	Residual approach (see paragraph 79(c) of IFRS 15)
Total	130	

The entity observes that the resulting £30 allocated to Product D is within the range of its observable selling prices (£15-£45). Therefore, the resulting allocation (see above table) is consistent with the allocation objective in paragraph 73 of IFRS 15 and the requirements in paragraph 78 of IFRS 15.

Case C – Residual approach is inappropriate

The same facts as in Case B apply to Case C except the transaction price is £105 instead of £130. Consequently, the application of the residual approach would result in a stand-alone selling price of £5 for Product D (£105 transaction price less £100 allocated to Products A, B and C). The entity concludes that £5 would not faithfully depict the amount of consideration to which the entity expects to be entitled in exchange for satisfying its performance obligation to transfer Product D, because £5 does not approximate the stand-alone selling price of Product D, which ranges from £15-£45. Consequently, the entity reviews its observable data, including sales and margin reports, to estimate the stand-alone selling price of Product D using another suitable method. The entity allocates the transaction price of £105 to Products A, B, C and D using the relative stand-alone selling prices of those products in accordance with paragraphs 73-80 of IFRS 15.

The exception allowing allocation of a discount to some, but not all, performance obligations within a contract gives entities the ability to better reflect the economics of the transaction in certain circumstances. However, the criteria that must be met to demonstrate that a discount is associated with only some of the performance obligations in the contract is likely to limit the number of transactions that are eligible for this exception.

3.4.1 Application questions on the discount allocation exception

3.4.1.A Interaction between the two allocation exceptions: variable discounts

A discount that is variable in amount and/or contingent on the occurrence or non-occurrence of future events will also meet the definition of variable consideration (see 2.2 above). As a result, some stakeholders had questioned which exception would apply – allocating a discount or allocating variable consideration.

At the March 2015 TRG meeting, the TRG members generally agreed that an entity will first determine whether a variable discount meets the variable consideration exception (see 3.3 above). *[IFRS 15.86]*. If it does not, the entity then considers whether it meets the discount exception (see 3.4 above).

In reaching that conclusion, the TRG agenda paper noted that paragraph 86 of IFRS 15 establishes a hierarchy for allocating variable consideration that requires an entity to identify variable consideration and then determine whether it should allocate variable consideration to one or some, but not all, performance obligations (or distinct goods or services that comprise a single performance obligation) based on the exception for allocating variable consideration. The entity would consider the requirements for allocating a discount only if the discount is not variable consideration (i.e. the amount of the discount is fixed and not contingent on future events) or the entity does not meet the criteria to allocate variable consideration to a specific part of the contract.[39]

3.5 Changes in transaction price after contract inception

The standard requires entities to determine the transaction price at contract inception. However, there could be changes to the transaction price after contract inception. For example, as discussed in 2.2.4 above, when a contract includes variable consideration, entities need to update their estimate of the transaction price at the end of each reporting period to reflect any changes in circumstances. Changes in the transaction price can also occur due to contract modifications (see Chapter 28 at 2.4).

As stated in paragraphs 88-89 in IFRS 15, changes in the total transaction price are generally allocated to the performance obligations on the same basis as the initial allocation, whether they are allocated based on the relative stand-alone selling price (i.e. using the same proportionate share of the total) or to individual performance obligations under the variable consideration exception discussed at 3.3 above. Amounts allocated to a satisfied performance obligation should be recognised as revenue, or a reduction in revenue, in the period that the transaction price changes.

As discussed at 3.1 above, stand-alone selling prices are not updated after contract inception, unless the contract has been modified. Furthermore, any amounts allocated to satisfied (or partially satisfied) performance obligations should be recognised in revenue in the period in which the transaction price changes (i.e. on a cumulative catch-up basis). This could result in either an increase or decrease to revenue in relation to a satisfied performance obligation or to cumulative revenue recognised for a partially satisfied over time performance obligation (see Chapter 30 at 2). *[IFRS 15.88-89]*.

The following example illustrates this concept for a partially satisfied over-time performance obligation:

Example 29.31: Change in transaction price after contract inception

Entity A, a construction company, enters into a contract with a customer on 1 January 20X1 to build three specific amenities at a community centre, a swimming pool, playground and a parking lot, for £3,000,000. Entity A will earn a bonus of £250,000 if it completes the swimming pool by 1 May 20X1.

At contract inception, Entity A concludes that the swimming pool, playground and parking lot are each distinct and, therefore, represent separate performance obligations. Entity A also concludes that the £250,000 bonus needs to be allocated entirely to the swimming pool because the criteria in paragraph 85 of IFRS 15 for the variable consideration allocation are met. However, Entity A does not expect it will be entitled to the £250,000 bonus related to the completion of the swimming pool by 1 May 20X1 due to factors outside of Entity A's control, including inclement winter weather and the swimming pool supplier's backlog. Therefore, Entity A uses the most likely amount method to estimate variable consideration and does not include the bonus in the transaction price.

As at 1 January 20X1, Entity A allocates the transaction price to the performance obligations on a relative stand-alone selling price basis as follows:

Performance obligations	Allocation of the transaction price
	£
Swimming pool	2,000,000
Playground	750,000
Parking lot	250,000
Total	3,000,000

Entity A concludes that each of the performance obligations are satisfied over time because they meet the criteria in paragraph 35 of IFRS 15 (see Chapter 30 at 2 for further discussion on evaluating whether performance obligations are satisfied over time). Due to the nature of Entity A's business, it determines that an input method based on costs incurred is an appropriate measure of progress over time.

As at 31 March 20X1, Entity A determines that it has incurred 60% of the total expected costs to complete each of its performance obligations. Therefore, Entity A recognises £1,800,000 (£3,000,000 × 60%) as revenue.

In addition, as at 31 March 20X1, Entity A reassesses its estimate of variable consideration in the contract (including the constraint) and believes it will be able to complete the swimming pool by 1 May 20X1 because the significant uncertainties related to the weather and the supplier have been resolved. Entity A updates its transaction price to include the £250,000 bonus related to the swimming pool in accordance with paragraph 59 of IFRS 15. Therefore, Entity A updates the transaction price as at 31 March 20X1 as follows:

Performance obligations	Allocation of the transaction price
	£
Swimming pool	2,250,000
Playground	750,000
Parking lot	250,000
Total	3,250,000

Due to the change in the transaction price related to the swimming pool performance obligation, Entity A recognises £150,000 (£250,000 × 60%) as revenue on a cumulative catch-up basis as at 31 March 20X1.

If the change in the transaction price is due to a contract modification, the contract modification requirements in paragraphs 18-21 of IFRS 15 must be followed (see Chapter 28 at 2.4 for a discussion on contract modifications). *[IFRS 15.90]*.

However, when contracts include variable consideration, it is possible that changes in the transaction price that arise after a modification may (or may not) be related to performance obligations that existed before the modification. For changes in the transaction price arising after a contract modification that is not treated as a separate contract, an entity must apply one of the two approaches: *[IFRS 15.90]*

- if the change in transaction price is attributable to an amount of variable consideration promised before the modification and the modification was considered a termination of the existing contract and the creation of a new contract, the entity allocates the change in transaction price to the performance obligations that existed before the modification; or
- in all other cases, the change in the transaction price is allocated to the performance obligations in the modified contract (i.e. the performance obligations that were unsatisfied and partially unsatisfied immediately after the modification).

The first approach is applicable to a change in transaction price that occurs after a contract modification that is accounted for in accordance with paragraph 21(a) of IFRS 15 (i.e. as a termination of the existing contract and the creation of a new contract) and the change in the transaction price is attributable to variable consideration promised before the modification. For example, an estimate of variable consideration in the initial contract may have changed or may no longer be constrained. *[IFRS 15.21(a), 90(a)]*. In this scenario, the Board decided that an entity should allocate the corresponding change in the transaction price to the performance obligations identified in the contract before the modification (e.g. the original contract), including performance obligations that were satisfied prior to the modification. *[IFRS 15.BC83]*. That is, it would not be appropriate for an entity to allocate the corresponding change in the transaction price to the performance obligations that are in the modified contract if the promised variable consideration (and the resolution of the associated uncertainty) were not affected by the contract modification.

The second approach is applicable in all other cases when a modification is not treated as a separate contract (e.g. when the change in the transaction price is not attributable to variable consideration promised before the modification). *[IFRS 15.90(b)].*

The IASB noted in the Basis for Conclusions on IFRS 15 that in some cases, an estimate of variable consideration made at the end of a reporting period could be affected by information that arises after the end of the reporting period, but before the release of the financial statements. The Board decided not to include guidance in IFRS 15 to address this circumstance because an entity would follow the accounting requirements for subsequent events in IAS 10 (see Chapter 38). *[IFRS 15.BC228].*

3.6 Allocation of transaction price to components outside the scope of IFRS 15

Revenue arrangements may include components that are not within the scope of IFRS 15. As discussed in Chapter 27 at 3.5, the standard indicates that in such situations, an entity must first apply the other standards if those standards address separation and/or measurement. *[IFRS 15.7].*

For example, some standards require certain components, such as financial liabilities, to be accounted for at fair value. As a result, when a revenue contract includes that type of component, the fair value of that component must be separated from the total transaction price. The remaining transaction price is then allocated to the remaining performance obligations. The following example illustrates this concept.

Example 29.32: Arrangements with components outside the scope of the standard

Retailer sells products to customers and often bundles them with prepaid gift cards when the customer buys multiple units of its products. The prepaid gift cards are non-refundable, non-redeemable and non-exchangeable for cash and do not have an expiry date or back-end fees. That is, any remaining balance on the prepaid gift cards does not reduce, unless it is spent by the customer. Customers can redeem prepaid gift cards only at third-party merchants specified by Retailer (i.e. the prepaid gift card cannot be redeemed at the Retailer) in exchange for goods or services up to a specified monetary amount. When a customer uses the prepaid gift cards at a merchant(s) to purchase goods or services, Retailer delivers cash to the merchant(s).

Customer X enters into a contract to purchase 100 units of a product and a prepaid gift card for total consideration of €1,000. Because it bought 100 units, Retailer gives Customer X a discount on the bundle. The stand-alone selling price of the product and the fair value of the prepaid gift card are €950 and €200, respectively.

Retailer determines that it has a contractual obligation to deliver cash to specified merchants on behalf of the prepaid gift card owner (Customer X) and that this obligation is conditional upon Customer X using the prepaid gift card to purchase goods or services. Also, Retailer does not have an unconditional right to avoid delivering cash to settle this contractual obligation. Therefore, Retailer concludes that the liability for the prepaid gift card meets the definition of a financial liability and applies the requirements in IFRS 9 to account for it. In accordance with paragraph 7 of IFRS 15, because IFRS 9 provides measurement requirements for initial recognition (i.e. requires that financial liabilities within its scope be initially recognised at fair value), Entity A excludes from the IFRS 15 transaction price the fair value of the prepaid gift card. Entity A allocates the remaining transaction price to the products purchased. The allocation of the total transaction price is, as follows:

	Stand-alone selling price and fair value	% Allocated discount	Allocated discount	Arrangement consideration allocation
Products (100 units)	€950	100%	€150	€800
Prepaid gift card	€200	0%	–	€200
	€1,150		€150	€1,000

For components that must be recognised at fair value at inception, any subsequent remeasurement would be pursuant to other IFRSs (e.g. IFRS 9). That is, subsequent adjustments to the fair value of those components have no effect on the amount of the transaction price previously allocated to any performance obligations included within the contract or on revenue recognised.

References

1 TRG Agenda paper 5, *July 2014 Meeting – Summary of Issues Discussed and Next Steps*, originally dated 31 October 2014, reissued 18 March 2015.
2 TRG Agenda paper 13, *Collectibility*, dated 26 January 2015.
3 *IFRIC Update*, September 2019.
4 TRG Agenda paper 39, *Application of the Series Provision and Allocation of Variable Consideration*, dated 13 July 2015.
5 TRG Agenda paper 38, *Portfolio Practical Expedient and Application of Variable Consideration Constraint*, dated 13 July 2015.
6 As defined in US GAAP in the master glossary of the Accounting Standards Codification.
7 TRG Agenda paper 38, *Portfolio Practical Expedient and Application of Variable Consideration Constraint*, dated 13 July 2015.
8 TRG Agenda paper 14, *Variable Consideration*, dated 26 January 2015 and TRG Agenda paper 25, *January 2015 Meeting – Summary of Issues Discussed and Next Steps*, dated 30 March 2015.
9 TRG Agenda paper 38, *Portfolio Practical Expedient and Application of Variable Consideration Constraint*, dated 13 July 2015.
10 ASC 606-10-55-207.
11 TRG Agenda paper 38, *Portfolio Practical Expedient and Application of Variable Consideration Constraint*, dated 13 July 2015.
12 TRG Agenda paper 35, *Accounting for Restocking Fees and Related Costs*, dated 13 July 2015.
13 TRG Agenda paper 35, *Accounting for Restocking Fees and Related Costs*, dated 13 July 2015.
14 Consistent with the discussions within TRG Agenda paper 30, *Significant Financing Components*, dated 30 March 2015.
15 Speech by Sarah N. Esquivel, Associate Chief Accountant, SEC Office of the Chief Accountant, 10 December 2018.
16 TRG Agenda paper 30, *Significant Financing Components*, dated 30 March 2015.
17 TRG Agenda paper 34, *March 2015 Meeting – Summary of Issues Discussed and Next Steps*, dated 13 July 2015.
18 TRG Agenda paper 34, *March 2015 Meeting – Summary of Issues Discussed and Next Steps*, dated 13 July 2015.
19 TRG Agenda paper 30, *Significant Financing Components*, dated 30 March 2015.
20 TRG Agenda paper 30, *Significant Financing Components*, dated 30 March 2015 and TRG Agenda paper 34, *March 2015 Meeting – Summary of Issues Discussed and Next Steps*, dated 13 July 2015.
21 TRG Agenda paper 30, *Significant Financing Components*, dated 30 March 2015.

22 TRG Agenda paper 34, *March 2015 Meeting – Summary of Issues Discussed and Next Steps,* dated 13 July 2015.
23 TRG Agenda paper 30, *Significant Financing Components,* dated 30 March 2015 and TRG Agenda paper 34, *March 2015 Meeting – Summary of Issues Discussed and Next Steps,* dated 13 July 2015.
24 TRG Agenda paper 30, *Significant Financing Components,* dated 30 March 2015 and TRG Agenda paper 34, *March 2015 Meeting – Summary of Issues Discussed and Next Steps,* dated 13 July 2015.
25 *IFRIC Update,* March 2019.
26 TRG Agenda paper 28, *Consideration Payable to a Customer,* dated 30 March 2015, TRG Agenda paper 34, *March 2015 Meeting – Summary of Issues Discussed and Next Steps,* dated 13 July 2015 and TRG Agenda paper 37, *Consideration Payable to a Customer,* dated 13 July 2015.
27 FASB ASU 2018-07 – *Compensation – Stock Compensation (718): Improvements to Nonemployee Share-Based Payment accounting.*
28 FASB ASU *2019-08 – Compensation – Stock Compensation (Topic 718) and Revenue from Contracts with Customers (Topic 606): Codification Improvements – Share-Based Consideration Payable to a Customer.*
29 TRG Agenda paper 28, *Consideration Payable to a Customer,* dated 30 March 2015, TRG Agenda paper 34, *March 2015 Meeting – Summary of Issues Discussed and Next Steps,* dated 13 July 2015 and TRG Agenda paper 37, *Consideration Payable to a Customer,* dated 13 July 2015.
30 TRG Agenda paper 37, *Consideration Payable to a Customer,* dated 13 July 2015.
31 TRG Agenda paper 44, *July 2015 Meeting – Summary of Issues Discussed and Next Steps,* dated 9 November 2015.
32 FASB TRG Agenda paper 59, *Payments to Customers,* dated 7 November 2016.
33 FASB TRG Agenda paper 60, *November 2016 Meeting – Summary of Issues Discussed and Next Steps,* dated 31 January 2017.
34 *IFRIC Update,* September 2019.
35 TRG Agenda paper 32, *Accounting for a Customer's Exercise of a Material Right,* dated 30 March 2015 and TRG Agenda paper 34, *March 2015 Meeting – Summary of Issues Discussed and Next Steps,* dated 13 July 2015.
36 TRG Agenda paper 1, *Gross versus Net Revenue,* dated 18 July 2014.
37 TRG Agenda paper 39, *Application of the Series Provision and Allocation of Variable Consideration,* dated 13 July 2015.
38 TRG Agenda paper 39, *Application of the Series Provision and Allocation of Variable Consideration,* dated 13 July 2015.
39 TRG Agenda paper 31, *Allocation of the Transaction Price for Discounts and Variable Consideration,* dated 30 March 2015 and TRG Agenda paper 34, *March 2015 Meeting – Summary of Issues Discussed and Next Steps,* dated 13 July 2015.

Chapter 30   Revenue: recognition

1 INTRODUCTION 2257
2 PERFORMANCE OBLIGATIONS SATISFIED OVER TIME 2259
    2.1 Customer simultaneously receives and consumes benefits as the entity performs 2260
        2.1.1 Evaluating whether a customer simultaneously receives and consumes the benefits of a commodity as the entity performs 2262
    2.2 Customer controls the asset as it is created or enhanced 2263
        2.2.1 Evaluating a customer's right to sell (or pledge) a right to obtain an asset when determining whether the customer controls the asset as it is created or enhanced 2263
    2.3 Asset with no alternative use and right to payment 2264
        2.3.1 No alternative use 2264
            2.3.1.A What to consider when assessing whether performance creates an asset with no alternative use 2266
        2.3.2 Enforceable right to payment for performance completed to date 2267
            2.3.2.A Determining whether an entity has an enforceable right to payment 2272
            2.3.2.B Enforceable right to payment: does an entity need a present unconditional right to payment? 2272
            2.3.2.C Enforceable right to payment: non-refundable upfront payments that represent the full transaction price 2273
            2.3.2.D Determining whether an entity has an enforceable right to payment for a contract priced at a loss 2273

		2.3.2.E	Enforceable right to payment determination when not entitled to a reasonable profit margin on standard inventory materials purchased, but not yet used 2274

		2.3.2.F	Considerations when assessing the over-time criteria for the sale of a real estate unit 2275
		2.3.2.G	Enforceable right to payment: contemplating consideration an entity might receive from the potential resale of the asset 2277
3	MEASURING PROGRESS OVER TIME 2278
	3.1	Output methods 2280
		3.1.1	Practical expedient for measuring progress towards satisfaction of a performance obligation 2281
	3.2	Input methods 2282
		3.2.1	Adjustments to the measure of progress based on an input method 2283
	3.3	Examples of measures of progress 2286
	3.4	Application questions on measuring progress over time 2287
		3.4.1	Measuring progress toward satisfaction of a stand-ready obligation that is satisfied over time 2287
		3.4.2	Selecting a measure of progress when there is more than one promised good or service within a performance obligation 2287
		3.4.3	Determining the appropriate single measure of progress for a combined performance obligation that is satisfied over time 2288
		3.4.4	Can control of a good or service underlying a performance obligation satisfied over time be transferred at discrete points in time? 2289
		3.4.5	Use of the 'right to invoice' practical expedient for a contract that includes rates that change over the contractual term 2289
		3.4.6	Recognising revenue when fulfilment costs are incurred prior to the contract establishment date for a specifically anticipated contract 2290
4	CONTROL TRANSFERRED AT A POINT IN TIME 2291
	4.1	Effect of shipping terms when an entity has transferred control of a good to a customer 2294
	4.2	Customer acceptance 2295
5	REPURCHASE AGREEMENTS 2298
	5.1	Forward or call option held by the entity 2299
		5.1.1	Conditional call options to repurchase an asset 2300

	5.2	Put option held by the customer	2301
	5.3	Sales with residual value guarantees	2303
6	CONSIGNMENT ARRANGEMENTS		2304
7	BILL-AND-HOLD ARRANGEMENTS		2305
8	RECOGNISING REVENUE FOR LICENCES OF INTELLECTUAL PROPERTY		2307
9	RECOGNISING REVENUE WHEN A RIGHT OF RETURN EXISTS		2308
10	RECOGNISING REVENUE FOR CUSTOMER OPTIONS FOR ADDITIONAL GOODS OR SERVICES		2308
11	BREAKAGE AND PREPAYMENTS FOR FUTURE GOODS OR SERVICES		2309
	11.1	Are customers' unexercised rights (i.e. breakage) a form of variable consideration?	2311

List of examples

Example 30.1:	Customer simultaneously receives and consumes the benefits	2262
Example 30.2:	Asset has no alternative use to the entity	2265
Example 30.3:	No alternative use	2267
Example 30.4:	Assessing alternative use and right to payment	2269
Example 30.5:	Enforceable right to payment for performance completed to date	2270
Example 30.6:	Assessing whether a performance obligation is satisfied at a point in time or over time	2271
Example 30.7:	Determination of enforceable right to payment for a contract priced at a loss	2274
Example 30.8:	Determining whether an enforceable right to payment exists when cancellation by a customer obliges an entity to resell the asset	2277
Example 30.9:	Uninstalled materials	2284
Example 30.10:	Choosing the measure of progress	2286
Example 30.11:	Measuring progress when making goods or services available	2287
Example 30.12:	Combined licence and installation service performance obligation	2289
Example 30.13:	Applying the indicators of the transfer of control to a performance obligation satisfied at a point in time	2294
Example 30.14:	Repurchase agreements (call option)	2300
Example 30.15:	Repurchase agreements (put option)	2303

Example 30.16:	Bill-and-hold arrangement	2307
Example 30.17:	Accounting for the sale of a gift card	2310
Example 30.18:	Customer loyalty programme	2310

Chapter 30   Revenue: recognition

1   INTRODUCTION

This chapter and Chapters 27-29 and 31-32, primarily cover the requirements for revenue arising from contracts with customers that are within the scope of IFRS 15 – *Revenue from Contracts with Customers*. This chapter deals with recognising revenue under IFRS 15.

Under IFRS 15, an entity only recognises revenue when it satisfies an identified performance obligation by transferring a promised good or service to a customer. A good or service is considered to be transferred when the customer obtains control. *[IFRS 15.31].*

IFRS 15 states that 'control of an asset refers to the ability to direct the use of and obtain substantially all of the remaining benefits from the asset'. Control also means the ability to prevent others from directing the use of, and receiving the benefit from, a good or service. *[IFRS 15.33].* The International Accounting Standards Board (IASB or Board) noted that both goods and services are assets that a customer acquires (even if many services are not recognised as an asset because those services are simultaneously received and consumed by the customer). *[IFRS 15.BC118].* The IASB explained the key terms in the definition of control in the Basis for Conclusions, which are, as follows: *[IFRS 15.BC120].*

- *Ability* – a customer must have the present right to direct the use of, and obtain substantially all of the remaining benefits from, an asset for an entity to recognise revenue. For example, in a contract that requires a manufacturer to produce an asset for a customer, it might be clear that the customer will ultimately have the right to direct the use of, and obtain substantially all of the remaining benefits from, the asset. However, the entity should not recognise revenue until the customer has actually obtained that right (which, depending on the contract, may occur during production or afterwards).

- *Direct the use of* – a customer's ability to direct the use of an asset refers to the customer's right to deploy or to allow another entity to deploy that asset in its activities or to restrict another entity from deploying that asset.

- *Obtain the benefits from* – the customer must have the ability to obtain substantially all of the remaining benefits from an asset for the customer to obtain control of it. Conceptually, the benefits from a good or service are potential cash flows (either an increase in cash inflows or a decrease in cash outflows). A customer can obtain the benefits directly or indirectly in many ways, such as: using the asset to produce goods or services (including public services); using the asset to enhance the value of other assets; using the asset to settle a liability or reduce an expense; selling or exchanging the asset; pledging the asset to secure a loan; or holding the asset. *[IFRS 15.33]*.

Under IFRS 15, the transfer of control to the customer represents the transfer of the rights with regard to the good or service. The customer's ability to receive the benefit from the good or service is represented by its right to substantially all of the cash inflows, or the reduction of the cash outflows, generated by the goods or services. *[IFRS 15.33]*. Upon transfer of control, the customer has sole possession of the right to use the good or service for the remainder of its economic life or to consume the good or service in its own operations.

The IASB explained in the Basis for Conclusions that control should be assessed primarily from the customer's perspective. While a seller often surrenders control at the same time the customer obtains control, the Board required the assessment of control to be from the customer's perspective to minimise the risk of an entity recognising revenue from activities that do not coincide with the transfer of goods or services to the customer. *[IFRS 15.BC121]*.

The standard indicates that an entity must determine, at contract inception, whether it will transfer control of a promised good or service over time. If an entity does not satisfy a performance obligation over time, the performance obligation is satisfied at a point in time. *[IFRS 15.32]*. These concepts are explored further at 2 and 4 below.

Refer to the following chapters for requirements of IFRS 15 that are not covered in this chapter:

- Chapter 27 – Core principle, definitions and scope.
- Chapter 28 – Identifying the contract and identifying performance obligations.
- Chapter 29 – Determining the transaction price and allocating the transaction price.
- Chapter 31 – Licences, warranties and contract costs.
- Chapter 32 – Presentation and disclosure requirements.

Other revenue items that are not within the scope of IFRS 15, but arise in the course of the ordinary activities of an entity, as well as the disposal of non-financial assets that are not part of the ordinary activities of the entity, for which IFRS 15's requirements are relevant, are addressed in Chapter 27.

This chapter:

- Highlights significant differences from the equivalent US GAAP standard, Accounting Standards Codification (ASC) 606 – *Revenue from Contracts with Customers* (together with IFRS 15, the standards) issued by the US Financial Accounting Standards Board (FASB) (together with the IASB, the Boards).
- Addresses topics on which the members of the Joint Transition Resource Group for Revenue Recognition (TRG) reached general agreement and our views on certain topics. TRG members' views are non-authoritative, but entities should consider them as they implement the standards. Unless otherwise specified, these summaries represent the discussions of the joint TRG.

The views we express in this chapter may evolve as application issues are identified and discussed among stakeholders. The conclusions we describe in our illustrations are also subject to change as views evolve. Conclusions in seemingly similar situations may differ from those reached in the illustrations due to differences in the underlying facts and circumstances.

2 PERFORMANCE OBLIGATIONS SATISFIED OVER TIME

Frequently, entities transfer the promised goods or services to the customer over time. While the determination of whether goods or services are transferred over time is straightforward in some contracts (e.g. many service contracts), it is more difficult in other contracts.

To help entities determine whether control transfers over time (rather than at a point in time), the standard states that an entity transfers control of a good or service over time (and, therefore, satisfies a performance obligation and recognises revenue over time) if one of the following criteria is met: *[IFRS 15.35]*

(a) the customer simultaneously receives and consumes the benefits provided by the entity's performance as the entity performs (see 2.1 below);

(b) the entity's performance creates or enhances an asset (e.g. work in progress) that the customer controls as the asset is created or enhanced (see 2.2 below); or

(c) the entity's performance does not create an asset with an alternative use to the entity and the entity has an enforceable right to payment for performance completed to date (see 2.3 below).

Examples of each of the criteria above are included below. If an entity is unable to demonstrate that control transfers over time, the presumption is that control transfers at a point in time (see 4 below). *[IFRS 15.32]*.

Figure 30.1 below illustrates how to evaluate whether control transfers over time:

Figure 30.1:   Evaluating whether control transfers over time

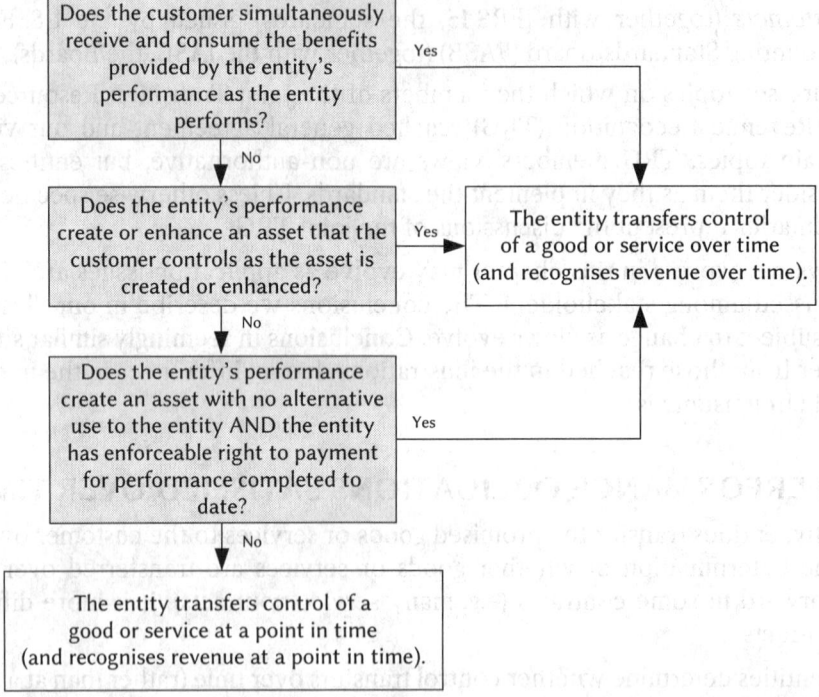

Determining when performance obligations are satisfied requires judgement. Paragraph 119(a) of IFRS 15 requires an entity to disclose when it typically satisfies its performance obligations (e.g. upon shipment, as services are delivered). See Chapter 32 at 3.2.1.C for more information. Paragraph 123(a) of IFRS 15 requires entities to disclose significant judgements made in determining the timing of satisfaction of performance obligations and paragraph 124 of IFRS 15 requires entities to disclose the method used to recognise revenue (e.g. a description of the input or output method used and how that method is applied) and why the method selected provides a faithful depiction of the transfer of goods or services. See Chapter 32 at 3.2.2.A for more information on these disclosure requirements. Entities should review their disclosures to verify that they not only meet the specific requirements of paragraphs 119(a), 123(a) and 124 of IFRS 15, but they also meet the overall disclosure objective in paragraph 110 of IFRS 15. *[IFRS 15.119(a), 123(a), 124]*.

2.1   Customer simultaneously receives and consumes benefits as the entity performs

As the Board explained in the Basis for Conclusions, in many service contracts the entity's performance creates an asset, momentarily, because that asset is simultaneously received and consumed by the customer. In these cases, the customer obtains control of the entity's output as the entity performs. Therefore, the performance obligation is satisfied over time. *[IFRS 15.BC125]*. While this criterion most often applies to service contracts, the TRG discussed instances in which commodity contracts (e.g. electricity, natural gas, heating oil) could be recognised over time. These situations could arise if the facts and circumstances of the contract indicate that the customer will simultaneously receive and consume the benefits (e.g. a continuous supply contract to meet immediate demands).[1] See 2.1.1 below for further information.

There may be contracts in which it is unclear whether the customer simultaneously receives and consumes the benefit of the entity's performance over time. IFRS 15 states that, for some types of performance obligations, the assessment of whether a customer receives the benefits of an entity's performance as the entity performs and simultaneously consumes those benefits as they are received will be straightforward. Examples given by the standard include routine or recurring services (e.g. a cleaning service) in which the receipt and simultaneous consumption by the customer of the benefits of the entity's performance can be readily identified. *[IFRS 15.B3]*.

For other types of performance obligations, an entity may not be able to readily identify whether a customer simultaneously receives and consumes the benefits from the entity's performance as the entity performs. In those circumstances, IFRS 15 states that 'a performance obligation is satisfied over time if an entity determines that another entity would not need to substantially re-perform the work that the entity has completed to date if that other entity were to fulfil the remaining performance obligation to the customer'. *[IFRS 15.B4]*.

In determining whether another entity would not need to substantially re-perform the work the entity has completed to date, the standard requires an entity to make both of the following assumptions: *[IFRS 15.B4]*

- disregard potential contractual restrictions or practical limitations that otherwise would prevent the entity from transferring the remaining performance obligation to another entity; and
- presume that another entity fulfilling the remainder of the performance obligation would not have the benefit of any asset that is presently controlled by the entity (and that would remain controlled by the entity if the performance obligation were to transfer to another entity).

The IASB added this application guidance because the notion of 'benefit' can be subjective. As discussed in the Basis for Conclusions, the Board provided an example of a freight logistics contract. Assume that the entity has agreed to transport goods from Vancouver to New York City. Some stakeholders had suggested that the customer receives no benefit from the entity's performance until the goods are delivered to, in this case, New York City. However, the Board said that the customer benefits as the entity performs. This is because, if the goods were only delivered part of the way (e.g. to Chicago), another entity would not need to substantially re-perform the entity's performance to date. The Board observed that in these cases, the assessment of whether another entity would need to substantially re-perform the entity's performance to date is an objective way to assess whether the customer receives benefit from the entity's performance as it occurs. *[IFRS 15.BC126]*.

In assessing whether a customer simultaneously receives and consumes the benefits provided by an entity's performance, all relevant facts and circumstances need to be considered. This includes considering the inherent characteristics of the good or service, the contract terms and information about how the good or service is transferred or delivered. However, as noted in paragraph B4(a) of IFRS 15 (the first bullet above), an entity disregards any contractual or practical restrictions when it assesses this criterion. In the Basis for Conclusions, the IASB explained that the assessment of whether control of the goods or services has transferred to the customer is performed by making a hypothetical assessment of what another entity would need to do if it were to take over the remaining performance. Therefore, actual practical or contractual restrictions would have no bearing on the assessment of whether the entity had already transferred control of the goods or services provided to date. *[IFRS 15.BC127]*.

The standard provides the following example that illustrates a customer simultaneously receiving and consuming the benefits as the entity performs in relation to a series of distinct payroll processing services. *[IFRS 15.IE67-IE68]*.

Example 30.1: Customer simultaneously receives and consumes the benefits

An entity enters into a contract to provide monthly payroll processing services to a customer for one year.

The promised payroll processing services are accounted for as a single performance obligation in accordance with paragraph 22(b) of IFRS 15. The performance obligation is satisfied over time in accordance with paragraph 35(a) of IFRS 15 because the customer simultaneously receives and consumes the benefits of the entity's performance in processing each payroll transaction as and when each transaction is processed. The fact that another entity would not need to re-perform payroll processing services for the service that the entity has provided to date also demonstrates that the customer simultaneously receives and consumes the benefits of the entity's performance as the entity performs. (The entity disregards any practical limitations on transferring the remaining performance obligation, including setup activities that would need to be undertaken by another entity.) The entity recognises revenue over time by measuring its progress towards complete satisfaction of that performance obligation in accordance with paragraphs 39-45 and B14-B19 of IFRS 15.

The IASB clarified, in the Basis for Conclusions, that an entity does not evaluate this criterion (to determine whether a performance obligation is satisfied over time) if the entity's performance creates an asset that the customer does not consume immediately as the asset is received. The IFRS Interpretations Committee reiterated this point at its meeting in March 2018, in relation to a contract for the sale of a real estate unit (see 2.3.2.F below for further discussion).[2] Instead, an entity assesses that performance obligation using the criteria discussed at 2.2 and 2.3 below.

For some service contracts, the entity's performance will not satisfy its obligation over time because the customer does not consume the benefit of the entity's performance until the entity's performance is complete. The standard provides an example (Example 14 of IFRS 15, included as Example 30.4 at 2.3.2 below) of an entity providing consulting services that will take the form of a professional opinion upon the completion of the services. In this situation, an entity cannot conclude that the services are transferred over time based on this criterion. Instead, the entity must consider the remaining two criteria in paragraph 35 of IFRS 15 (see 2.2 and 2.3, and Example 30.4 below).

2.1.1 Evaluating whether a customer simultaneously receives and consumes the benefits of a commodity as the entity performs

In July 2015, the TRG members discussed the factors that an entity should consider when evaluating whether a customer simultaneously receives and consumes the benefits of a commodity (e.g. electricity, natural gas, heating oil) as the entity performs.[3]

The TRG members generally agreed that an entity would consider all known facts and circumstances when evaluating whether a customer simultaneously receives and consumes the benefits of a commodity. These may include the inherent characteristics of the commodity (e.g. whether the commodity can be stored), contract terms (e.g. a continuous supply contract to meet immediate demands) and information about infrastructure or other delivery mechanisms.

As such, revenue related to the sale of a commodity may or may not be recognised over time, depending on whether the facts and circumstances of the contract indicate that the customer simultaneously receives and consumes the benefits. This evaluation may require the use of significant judgement.

Whether a commodity meets this criterion and is transferred over time is important in determining whether the sale of a commodity meets the criteria to apply the series requirement (see Chapter 28 at 3.2.2). This, in turn, affects how an entity allocates variable consideration and apply the requirements for contract modifications and changes in the transaction price.

2.2 Customer controls the asset as it is created or enhanced

The second criterion to determine whether control of a good or service is transferred over time requires entities to evaluate whether the customer controls the asset as it is being created or enhanced. An entity applies the requirements for control in paragraphs 31-34 and 38 of IFRS 15. *[IFRS 15.B5]*.

For the purpose of this determination, the definition of 'control' is the same as previously discussed (i.e. the ability to direct the use of and obtain substantially all of the remaining benefits from the asset). The IASB explained in the Basis for Conclusions that this criterion addresses situations in which the customer clearly controls any work in progress arising from the entity's performance. *[IFRS 15.BC129]*. The Board provided an example in which the entity has entered into a construction contract to build on the customer's land, stating that any work in progress arising from the entity's performance is generally controlled by the customer. *[IFRS 15.BC129]*. The IFRS Interpretations Committee also reiterated the overall intent of the criterion and referred to this example from the Basis for Conclusions during its March 2018 meeting (see 2.3.2.F below).[4] In addition, some construction contracts may also contain clauses indicating that the customer owns any work in progress as the contracted item is being built. Furthermore, the asset being created or enhanced can be either tangible or intangible. *[IFRS 15.B5]*.

The Board observed in the Basis for Conclusions that the second over-time criterion (related to the customer's control of the asset as it is being created or enhanced) is consistent with the notion that, in effect, the entity has agreed to sell its rights to the asset (i.e. work in progress) as the entity performs (i.e. a continuous sale). *[IFRS 15.BC130]*.

2.2.1 Evaluating a customer's right to sell (or pledge) a right to obtain an asset when determining whether the customer controls the asset as it is created or enhanced

We believe that an entity needs to assess control of the asset that the entity's performance creates or enhances, rather than any contractual rights to obtain the completed asset in the future. For example, and as discussed by the IFRS Interpretations Committee (see 2.3.2.F below), in a contract for the sale of real estate that the entity constructs, the asset created is the real estate itself and not the customer's right to obtain the completed real estate in the future. That is, an entity would evaluate whether the customer controls the partially constructed real estate as it is being constructed to determine whether the criterion in paragraph 35(b) of IFRS 15 is met. The customer's right to sell (or pledge) a right to obtain a completed asset in the future is not evidence that the customer controls the asset itself as it is being created or enhanced.[5]

2.3 Asset with no alternative use and right to payment

In some cases, it may be unclear whether the asset that an entity creates or enhances is controlled by the customer when considering the first two criteria (discussed at 2.1 and 2.2 above) for evaluating whether control transfers over time. Therefore, the Board added a third criterion, which requires revenue to be recognised over time if both of the following two requirements are met: *[IFRS 15.35(c)]*

- the entity's performance does not create an asset with alternative use to the entity (see 2.3.1 below); and
- the entity has an enforceable right to payment for performance completed to date (see 2.3.2 below).

2.3.1 No alternative use

The IASB explained in the Basis for Conclusions that it had developed the notion of 'alternative use' to prevent over time revenue recognition when the entity's performance does not transfer control of the goods or services to the customer over time. When the entity's performance creates an asset with an alternative use to the entity (e.g. standard inventory items), the entity can readily direct the asset to another customer. In those cases, the entity (not the customer) controls the asset as it is created because the customer does not have the ability to direct the use of the asset or restrict the entity from directing that asset to another customer. The standard states that an asset created by an entity's performance 'does not have an alternative use to an entity if the entity is either restricted contractually from readily directing the asset for another use during the creation or enhancement of that asset or limited practically from readily directing the asset in its completed state for another use'. The assessment of whether an asset has an alternative use to the entity is made at contract inception. *[IFRS 15.36]*.

In assessing whether an asset has an alternative use, an entity is required to consider the effects of contractual restrictions and practical limitations on its ability to readily direct that asset for another use (e.g. selling it to a different customer). The standard clarifies that the possibility of the contract with the customer being terminated is not a relevant consideration in this assessment. *[IFRS 15.B6]*.

In making the assessment of whether a good or service has an alternative use, an entity must consider any substantive contractual restrictions. A contractual restriction is substantive if a customer could enforce its rights to the promised asset if the entity sought to direct the asset for another use. *[IFRS 15.B7]*. Contractual restrictions that are not substantive, such as protective rights for the customer, are not considered. The Board explained in the Basis for Conclusions that a protective right typically gives an entity the practical ability to physically substitute or redirect the asset without the customer's knowledge or objection to the change. For example, a contract may specify that an entity cannot transfer a good to another customer because the customer has legal title to the good.

Such a contractual term would not be substantive if the entity could physically substitute that good for another and could redirect the original good to another customer for little cost. In that case, the contractual restriction would merely be a protective right and would not indicate that control of the asset has transferred to the customer. *[IFRS 15.BC138]*. As an example, the standard notes that contractual restrictions are not substantive if an asset is largely interchangeable with other assets that the entity could transfer to another customer without breaching the contract and without incurring significant costs that otherwise would not have been incurred in relation to that contract. *[IFRS 15.B7]*.

An entity also needs to consider any practical limitations on directing the asset for another use. A significant economic loss could arise because the entity either would incur significant costs to rework the asset or would only be able to sell the asset at a significant loss. For example, an entity may be practically limited from redirecting assets that either have design specifications that are unique to a customer or are located in remote areas. *[IFRS 15.B8]*. In making this determination, the Board clarified that an entity considers the characteristics of the asset that ultimately will be transferred to the customer and assesses whether the asset in its completed state could be redirected without a significant cost of rework. The Board provided an example of manufacturing contracts in which the basic design of the asset is the same across all contracts, but substantial customisation is made to the asset. As a result, redirecting the finished asset would require significant rework and the asset would not have an alternative use because the entity would incur significant economic losses to direct the asset for another use. *[IFRS 15.BC138]*.

Considering the level of customisation of an asset may help entities assess whether an asset has an alternative use. The IASB noted in the Basis for Conclusions that, when an entity is creating an asset that is highly customised for a particular customer, it is less likely that the entity could use that asset for any other purpose. *[IFRS 15.BC135]*. That is, it is likely that the entity would need to incur significant rework costs to redirect the asset to another customer or sell the asset at a significantly reduced price. As a result, the asset would not have an alternative use to the entity and the customer could be regarded as receiving the benefit of the entity's performance as the entity performs (i.e. having control of the asset), provided that the entity also has an enforceable right to payment (discussed at 2.3.2 below). However, the Board clarified that the level of customisation is a factor to consider, but it should not be a determinative factor. For example, in some real estate contracts, the asset may be standardised (i.e. not highly customised), but it still may not have an alternative use to the entity because of substantive contractual restrictions that preclude the entity from readily directing the asset to another customer. *[IFRS 15.BC137]*.

The standard provides the following example to illustrate an evaluation of practical limitations on directing an asset for another use. *[IFRS 15.IE73-IE76]*.

Example 30.2: Asset has no alternative use to the entity

An entity enters into a contract with a customer, a government agency, to build a specialised satellite. The entity builds satellites for various customers, such as governments and commercial entities. The design and construction of each satellite differ substantially, on the basis of each customer's needs and the type of technology that is incorporated into the satellite.

At contract inception, the entity assesses whether its performance obligation to build the satellite is a performance obligation satisfied over time in accordance with paragraph 35 of IFRS 15.

As part of that assessment, the entity considers whether the satellite in its completed state will have an alternative use to the entity. Although the contract does not preclude the entity from directing the completed satellite to another customer, the entity would incur significant costs to rework the design and function of the satellite to direct that asset to another customer. Consequently, the asset has no alternative use to the entity (see paragraphs 35(c), 36 and B6–B8 of IFRS 15) because the customer-specific design of the satellite limits the entity's practical ability to readily direct the satellite to another customer.

For the entity's performance obligation to be satisfied over time when building the satellite, paragraph 35(c) of IFRS 15 also requires the entity to have an enforceable right to payment for performance completed to date. This condition is not illustrated in this example.

Requiring an entity to assess contractual restrictions when evaluating this criterion may seem to contradict the requirements in paragraph B4 of IFRS 15 to ignore contractual and practical restrictions when evaluating whether another entity would need to substantially reperform the work the entity has completed to date (see 2.1 above). The Board explained that this difference is appropriate because each criterion provides a different method for assessing when control transfers and the criteria were designed to apply to different situations. *[IFRS 15.BC139]*.

After contract inception, an entity does not update its assessment of whether an asset has an alternative use for any subsequent changes in facts and circumstances, unless the parties approve a contract modification that substantively changes the performance obligation. *[IFRS 15.36]*. The IASB also decided that an entity's lack of an alternative use for an asset does not, by itself, mean that the customer effectively controls the asset. The entity would also need to determine that it has an enforceable right to payment for performance to date, as discussed at 2.3.2 below. *[IFRS 15.BC141]*.

2.3.1.A What to consider when assessing whether performance creates an asset with no alternative use

In November 2016, members of the FASB TRG were asked to consider whether an entity should consider the completed asset or the work in progress when assessing whether its performance creates an asset with no alternative use under paragraph 35(c) of IFRS 15.[6] The FASB TRG members generally agreed that when an entity evaluates whether its performance creates an asset with no alternative use, it should consider whether it could sell the completed asset to another customer without incurring a significant economic loss (i.e. whether it could sell the raw materials or work in process to another customer is not relevant). This conclusion is supported by the Board's comment in the Basis for Conclusions 'that an entity should consider the characteristics of the asset that will ultimately be transferred to the customer'. *[IFRS 15.BC136]*.

However, as discussed at 2.3.1. above and in accordance with paragraph 36 of IFRS 15, if the entity is contractually restricted or has a practical limitation on its ability to direct the asset for another use, the asset would not have an alternative use, regardless of the characteristics of the completed asset. A contractual restriction is substantive if a customer could enforce its rights to the promised asset if the entity sought to direct the asset for another use. A practical limitation exists if an entity would incur a significant economic loss to direct the asset for another use.[7]

The FASB TRG agenda paper included the following example:

Example 30.3: No alternative use

An entity enters into a contract with a customer to build customised equipment. The customisation of the equipment occurs when the manufacturing process is approximately 75% complete. That is, for approximately the first 75% of the manufacturing process, the in-process asset could be redirected to fulfil another customer's equipment order (assuming no contractual restrictions). However, the equipment cannot be sold in its completed state to another customer without incurring a significant economic loss. The design specifications of the equipment are unique to the customer and the entity would only be able to sell the completed equipment at a significant economic loss.

The entity would evaluate, at contract inception, whether there is any contractual restriction or practical limitation on its ability to readily direct the asset (in its completed state) for another use. Because the entity cannot sell the completed equipment to another customer without incurring a significant economic loss, the entity has a practical limitation on its ability to direct the equipment in its completed state and, therefore, the asset does not have an alternative use. However, before concluding that revenue should be recognised over time, an entity must evaluate whether it has an enforceable right to payment.

2.3.2 Enforceable right to payment for performance completed to date

To evaluate whether it has an enforceable right to payment for performance completed to date, the entity is required to consider the terms of the contract and any laws or regulations that relate to it. *[IFRS 15.37, B12]*. The standard states that the right to payment for performance completed to date need not be for a fixed amount. However, at any time during the contract term, an entity must be entitled to an amount that at least compensates the entity for performance completed to date (as defined in paragraph B9 of IFRS 15), even if the contract is terminated by the customer (or another party) for reasons other than the entity's failure to perform as promised. *[IFRS 15.37, B9]*. The IASB concluded that a customer's obligation to pay for the entity's performance is an indicator that the customer has obtained benefit from the entity's performance. *[IFRS 15.BC142]*.

The standard clarifies that an amount that would compensate an entity for performance completed to date would be an amount that approximates the selling price of the goods or services transferred to date (e.g. recovery of the costs incurred by an entity in satisfying the performance obligation plus a reasonable profit margin), rather than compensation for only the entity's potential loss of profit if the contract were to be terminated. *[IFRS 15.B9]*.

Compensation for a reasonable profit margin need not equal the profit margin expected if the contract was fulfilled as promised, but the standard states that an entity should be entitled to compensation for either of the following amounts: *[IFRS 15.B9]*

- a proportion of the expected profit margin in the contract that reasonably reflects the extent of the entity's performance under the contract before termination by the customer (or another party); or
- a reasonable return on the entity's cost of capital for similar contracts (or the entity's typical operating margin for similar contracts) if the contract-specific margin is higher than the return the entity usually generates from similar contracts.

An entity's right to payment for performance completed to date need not be a present unconditional right to payment. In many cases, an entity will have an unconditional right to payment only at an agreed-upon milestone or upon complete satisfaction of the performance obligation. Therefore, when assessing whether it has a right to payment for performance completed to date, an entity is required to consider whether it would have an enforceable right to demand or retain payment for performance completed to date if the contract were to be terminated before completion (for reasons other than the entity's failure to perform as promised). [IFRS 15.B10].

In some contracts, a customer may have a right to terminate the contract only at specified times during the life of the contract or the customer might not have any right to terminate the contract. The standard states that, if a customer acts to terminate a contract without having the right to terminate the contract at that time (including when a customer fails to perform its obligations as promised), the contract (or other laws) might entitle the entity to continue to transfer the promised goods or services in the contract to the customer and require the customer to pay the promised consideration. In those circumstances, an entity has a right to payment for performance completed to date because the entity has a right to continue to perform its obligations in accordance with the contract and to require the customer to perform its obligations (which include paying the promised consideration). [IFRS 15.B11].

The IASB described in the Basis for Conclusions how the factors of 'no alternative use' and the 'right to payment' relate to the assessment of control. Since an entity is constructing an asset with no alternative use to the entity, the entity is effectively creating an asset at the direction of the customer. That asset would have little or no value to the entity if the customer were to terminate the contract. As a result, the entity will seek economic protection from the risk of customer termination by requiring the customer to pay for the entity's performance to date in the event of customer termination. The customer's obligation to pay for the entity's performance to date (or, the inability to avoid paying for that performance) suggests that the customer has obtained the benefits from the entity's performance. [IFRS 15.BC142].

The enforceable right to payment criterion has two components that an entity must assess:

- the amount that the customer would be required to pay; and
- what it means to have the enforceable right to payment.

The Board provided additional application guidance on how to evaluate each of these components.

Firstly, the Board explained in the Basis for Conclusions that the focus of the analysis should be on the amount to which the entity would be entitled upon termination. [IFRS 15.BC144]. This amount is not the amount the entity would settle for in a negotiation and it does not need to reflect the full contract margin that the entity would earn if the contract were completed. The Board clarified in paragraph B9 of IFRS 15 that a 'reasonable profit margin' would either be a proportion of the entity's expected profit margin that reasonably reflects the entity's performance to date or a reasonable return on the entity's cost of capital. In addition, in paragraph B13 of IFRS 15, the standard clarifies that including a payment schedule in a contract does not, in and of itself, indicate that the entity has the right to payment for performance completed to date. This is because, in some cases, the contract may specify that the consideration received from the customer is refundable for reasons other than the entity failing to perform as promised in the contract. The entity must examine information that may contradict the payment schedule and may represent the entity's actual right to payment for performance completed to date. As highlighted in Example 30.5 below, payments from a customer must approximate the selling price of the goods or services transferred to date to be considered a right to payment for performance to date. A fixed payment schedule may not meet this requirement. *[IFRS 15.B13]*.

Secondly, the IASB added application guidance to help an entity assess the existence and enforceability of a right to payment. In making this assessment, entities need to consider any laws, legislation or legal precedent that could supplement or override the contractual terms. More specifically, IFRS 15 states that the assessment includes consideration of:

'(a) legislation, administrative practice or legal precedent confers upon the entity a right to payment for performance to date even though that right is not specified in the contract with the customer;

(b) relevant legal precedent indicates that similar rights to payment for performance completed to date in similar contracts have no binding legal effect; or

(c) an entity's customary business practices of choosing not to enforce a right to payment has resulted in the right being rendered unenforceable in that legal environment. However, notwithstanding that an entity may choose to waive its right to payment in similar contracts, an entity would continue to have a right to payment to date if, in the contract with the customer, its right to payment for performance to date remains enforceable.' *[IFRS 15.B12]*.

Furthermore, the standard indicates that an entity may have an enforceable right to payment even when the customer terminates the contract without having the right to terminate. This would be the case if the contract (or other law) entitles the entity to continue to transfer the goods or services promised in the contract and require the customer to pay the consideration promised for those goods or services (often referred to as 'specific performance'). *[IFRS 15.BC145]*. The standard also states that even when an entity chooses to waive its right to payment in other similar contracts, an entity would continue to have a right to payment for the contract if, in the contract, its right to payment for performance to date remains enforceable.

The standard provides the following example to illustrate the concepts described at 2.3 above. It depicts an entity providing consulting services that will take the form of a professional opinion upon the completion of the services. In this example, the entity's performance obligation meets the no alternative use and right to payment criterion in paragraph 35(c) of IFRS 15, as follows. *[IFRS 15.IE69-IE72]*.

Example 30.4: Assessing alternative use and right to payment

An entity enters into a contract with a customer to provide a consulting service that results in the entity providing a professional opinion to the customer. The professional opinion relates to facts and circumstances that are specific to the customer. If the customer were to terminate the consulting contract for reasons other than the entity's failure to perform as promised, the contract requires the customer to compensate the entity for its costs incurred plus a 15 per cent margin. The 15 per cent margin approximates the profit margin that the entity earns from similar contracts.

The entity considers the criterion in paragraph 35(a) of IFRS 15 and the requirements in paragraphs B3 and B4 of IFRS 15 to determine whether the customer simultaneously receives and consumes the benefits of the entity's performance. If the entity were to be unable to satisfy its obligation and the customer hired another consulting firm to provide the opinion, the other consulting firm would need to substantially re-perform the work that the entity had completed to date, because the other consulting firm would not have the benefit of any work in progress performed by the entity. The nature of the professional opinion is such that the customer will receive the benefits of the entity's performance only when the customer receives the professional opinion. Consequently, the entity concludes that the criterion in paragraph 35(a) of IFRS 15 is not met.

However, the entity's performance obligation meets the criterion in paragraph 35(c) of IFRS 15 and is a performance obligation satisfied over time because of both of the following factors:

(a) in accordance with paragraphs 36 and B6-B8 of IFRS 15, the development of the professional opinion does not create an asset with alternative use to the entity because the professional opinion relates to facts and circumstances that are specific to the customer. Therefore, there is a practical limitation on the entity's ability to readily direct the asset to another customer.

(b) in accordance with paragraphs 37 and B9-B13 of IFRS 15, the entity has an enforceable right to payment for its performance completed to date for its costs plus a reasonable margin, which approximates the profit margin in other contracts.

Consequently, the entity recognises revenue over time by measuring the progress towards complete satisfaction of the performance obligation in accordance with paragraphs 39-45 and B14-B19 of IFRS 15.

Example 30.5 below illustrates a contract in which the fixed payment schedule is not expected to correspond, at all times throughout the contract, to the amount that would be necessary to compensate the entity for performance completed to date. Accordingly, the entity concludes that it does not have an enforceable right to payment for performance completed to date as follows. *[IFRS 15.IE77-IE80].*

Example 30.5: Enforceable right to payment for performance completed to date

An entity enters into a contract with a customer to build an item of equipment. The payment schedule in the contract specifies that the customer must make an advance payment at contract inception of 10 per cent of the contract price, regular payments throughout the construction period (amounting to 50 per cent of the contract price) and a final payment of 40 per cent of the contract price after construction is completed and the equipment has passed the prescribed performance tests. The payments are non-refundable unless the entity fails to perform as promised. If the customer terminates the contract, the entity is entitled only to retain any progress payments received from the customer. The entity has no further rights to compensation from the customer.

At contract inception, the entity assesses whether its performance obligation to build the equipment is a performance obligation satisfied over time in accordance with paragraph 35 of IFRS 15.

As part of that assessment, the entity considers whether it has an enforceable right to payment for performance completed to date in accordance with paragraphs 35(c), 37 and B9–B13 of IFRS 15 if the customer were to terminate the contract for reasons other than the entity's failure to perform as promised. Even though the payments made by the customer are non-refundable, the cumulative amount of those payments is not expected, at all times throughout the contract, to at least correspond to the amount that would be necessary to compensate the entity for performance completed to date. This is because at various times during construction the cumulative amount of consideration paid by the customer might be less than the selling price of the partially completed item of equipment at that time. Consequently, the entity does not have a right to payment for performance completed to date.

Because the entity does not have a right to payment for performance completed to date, the entity's performance obligation is not satisfied over time in accordance with paragraph 35(c) of IFRS 15. Accordingly, the entity does not need to assess whether the equipment would have an alternative use to the entity. The entity also concludes that it does not meet the criteria in paragraph 35(a) or (b) of IFRS 15 and thus, the entity accounts for the construction of the equipment as a performance obligation satisfied at a point in time in accordance with paragraph 38 of IFRS 15.

Example 30.6 below contrasts similar situations and illustrates when revenue would be recognised over time (see 2 above) versus at a point in time (see 4 below). Specifically, this example illustrates the evaluation of the 'no alternative use' and 'right to payment for performance to date' concepts, as follows. *[IFRS 15.IE81-IE90].*

Example 30.6: Assessing whether a performance obligation is satisfied at a point in time or over time

An entity is developing a multi-unit residential complex. A customer enters into a binding sales contract with the entity for a specified unit that is under construction. Each unit has a similar floor plan and is of a similar size, but other attributes of the units are different (for example, the location of the unit within the complex).

Case A – Entity does not have an enforceable right to payment for performance completed to date

The customer pays a deposit upon entering into the contract and the deposit is refundable only if the entity fails to complete construction of the unit in accordance with the contract. The remainder of the contract price is payable on completion of the contract when the customer obtains physical possession of the unit. If the customer defaults on the contract before completion of the unit, the entity only has the right to retain the deposit.

At contract inception, the entity applies paragraph 35(c) of IFRS 15 to determine whether its promise to construct and transfer the unit to the customer is a performance obligation satisfied over time. The entity determines that it does not have an enforceable right to payment for performance completed to date because, until construction of the unit is complete, the entity only has a right to the deposit paid by the customer. Because the entity does not have a right to payment for work completed to date, the entity's performance obligation is not a performance obligation satisfied over time in accordance with paragraph 35(c) of IFRS 15. Instead, the entity accounts for the sale of the unit as a performance obligation satisfied at a point in time in accordance with paragraph 38 of IFRS 15.

Case B – Entity has an enforceable right to payment for performance completed to date

The customer pays a non-refundable deposit upon entering into the contract and will make progress payments during construction of the unit. The contract has substantive terms that preclude the entity from being able to direct the unit to another customer. In addition, the customer does not have the right to terminate the contract unless the entity fails to perform as promised. If the customer defaults on its obligations by failing to make the promised progress payments as and when they are due, the entity would have a right to all of the consideration promised in the contract if it completes the construction of the unit. The courts have previously upheld similar rights that entitle developers to require the customer to perform, subject to the entity meeting its obligations under the contract.

At contract inception, the entity applies paragraph 35(c) of IFRS 15 to determine whether its promise to construct and transfer the unit to the customer is a performance obligation satisfied over time. The entity determines that the asset (unit) created by the entity's performance does not have an alternative use to the entity because the contract precludes the entity from transferring the specified unit to another customer. The entity does not consider the possibility of a contract termination in assessing whether the entity is able to direct the asset to another customer.

The entity also has a right to payment for performance completed to date in accordance with paragraphs 37 and B9-B13 of IFRS 15. This is because if the customer were to default on its obligations, the entity would have an enforceable right to all of the consideration promised under the contract if it continues to perform as promised.

Therefore, the terms of the contract and the practices in the legal jurisdiction indicate that there is a right to payment for performance completed to date. Consequently, the criteria in paragraph 35(c) of IFRS 15 are met and the entity has a performance obligation that it satisfies over time. To recognise revenue for that performance obligation satisfied over time, the entity measures its progress towards complete satisfaction of its performance obligation in accordance with paragraphs 39-45 and B14-B19 of IFRS 15.

In the construction of a multi-unit residential complex, the entity may have many contracts with individual customers for the construction of individual units within the complex. The entity would account for each contract separately. However, depending on the nature of the construction, the entity's performance in undertaking the initial construction works (i.e. the foundation and the basic structure), as well as the construction of common areas, may need to be reflected when measuring its progress towards complete satisfaction of its performance obligations in each contract.

Case C – Entity has an enforceable right to payment for performance completed to date

The same facts as in Case B apply to Case C, except that in the event of a default by the customer, either the entity can require the customer to perform as required under the contract or the entity can cancel the contract in exchange for the asset under construction and an entitlement to a penalty of a proportion of the contract price.

Notwithstanding that the entity could cancel the contract (in which case the customer's obligation to the entity would be limited to transferring control of the partially completed asset to the entity and paying the penalty prescribed), the entity has a right to payment for performance completed to date because the entity could also choose to enforce its rights to full payment under the contract. The fact that the entity may choose to cancel the contract in the event the customer defaults on its obligations would not affect that assessment (see paragraph B11 of IFRS 15), provided that the entity's rights to require the customer to continue to perform as required under the contract (i.e. pay the promised consideration) are enforceable.

2.3.2.A Determining whether an entity has an enforceable right to payment

In November 2016, members of the FASB TRG were asked to consider how an entity should determine whether it has an enforceable right to payment.[8] The FASB TRG members generally agreed that entities need to evaluate the contractual provisions to determine whether the right to payment compensates the entity for performance completed to date. For example, a contract may not explicitly provide an entity with an enforceable right to payment for anything other than finished goods. However, if the termination provisions in the contract allow for a notice period (e.g. 60 days) that would provide sufficient time for an entity to move all work in progress to the finished goods stage, it is likely that an entity would conclude that the contract provides for an enforceable right to payment for performance completed to date. In addition, an entity should consider any legislation or legal precedent that could supplement or override any contractual terms.

The FASB TRG also discussed the linkage amongst right to payment, measure of progress and the timing of the customisation of a good. For example, the FASB TRG noted an entity may not always have an enforceable right to payment at contract inception, such as when an entity is producing standard goods (i.e. inventory) that may be customised for a customer towards the end of the production process. The FASB TRG members generally agreed that an entity would need to consider whether it has an enforceable right to payment related to its performance completed to date. If the entity's performance obligation is to customise its standard goods for a customer, FASB TRG members generally agreed that an entity would evaluate whether it has an enforceable right to payment at the point that the entity begins to satisfy the performance obligation to customise the goods for the customer. That is, because the right to payment is for performance completed to date, an entity's performance should coincide with how it defines the nature of its performance obligation and its measure of progress toward satisfaction of that performance obligation.[9]

2.3.2.B Enforceable right to payment: does an entity need a present unconditional right to payment?

In order to have an enforceable right to payment for performance completed to date, does an entity need to have a present unconditional right to payment? In the Basis for Conclusions, the IASB clarified that the contractual payment terms in a contract may not always align with an entity's enforceable rights to payment for performance completed to date. As a result, an entity does not need to have a present unconditional right to payment. Instead, it must have an enforceable right to demand and/or retain payment for performance completed to date upon customer termination without cause. To illustrate this point, the Board included an example of a consulting contract that requires an entity to provide a report at the end of the project. In return, the entity earns a fixed amount, which is due and payable to the entity when it delivers the report. Assume that the entity is performing under the contract and that the contract (or the law) requires the customer to compensate the entity for its performance completed to date. In that situation, the entity would have an enforceable right to payment for performance completed to date, even though an unconditional right to the fixed amount only exists at the time the report is provided to the customer. This is because the entity has a right to demand and retain payment for performance completed to date. [IFRS 15.BC145].

2.3.2.C Enforceable right to payment: non-refundable upfront payments that represent the full transaction price

If the entity receives a non-refundable upfront payment that represents the full transaction price, an entity has a right to payment for performance completed to date. The Board explained in the Basis for Conclusions that such a payment would represent an entity's right to payment for performance completed to date provided that the entity's right to retain and not refund the payment is enforceable upon termination by the customer. This is because a full upfront payment would at least compensate an entity for the work completed to date throughout the contract. [IFRS 15.BC146]. If the non-refundable upfront payment does not represent the full transaction price, an entity will have to apply judgement to determine whether the upfront payment provides the entity with a right to payment for performance completed to date in the event of a contract termination.

2.3.2.D Determining whether an entity has an enforceable right to payment for a contract priced at a loss

An entity may have an enforceable right to payment for performance completed to date even though the contract is priced at a loss. However, the specific facts and circumstances of the contract must be considered. As discussed above, the standard states that, if a contract is terminated for reasons other than the entity's failure to perform as promised, the entity must be entitled to an amount that at least compensates it for its performance to date. Furthermore, paragraph B9 of IFRS 15 states that 'an amount that would compensate an entity for performance completed to date would be an amount that approximates the selling price of the goods or services transferred to date (for example, recovery of the costs incurred by an entity in satisfying the performance obligation plus a reasonable profit margin).' Accordingly, stakeholders had asked whether an entity could have an enforceable right to payment for performance completed to date if the contract was priced at a loss.

We believe that the example in paragraph B9 of IFRS 15 of cost recovery plus a reasonable profit margin does not preclude an entity from having an enforceable right to payment even if the contract is priced at a loss. Rather, we believe an entity should evaluate whether it has an enforceable right to receive an amount that approximates the selling price of the goods or services for performance completed to date in the event the customer terminates the contract.

Consider the following example from the American Institute of Certified Public Accountants (AICPA) Audit and Accounting Guide on revenue recognition.[10]

Example 30.7:   Determination of enforceable right to payment for a contract priced at a loss

Customer X requests bids for the design of a highly customised system. The customer expects to award subsequent contracts for systems over the next 10 years to the entity that wins the design contract. Contractor A is aware of the competition and knows that in order to win the design contract it must bid the contract at a loss. That is, Contractor A is willing to bid the design contract at a loss due to the significant value in future expected orders.

Contractor A wins the contract with a value of €100 and estimated costs to complete of €130. Contractor A has determined that the contract contains a single performance obligation and that its performance does not create an asset with an alternative use. The contract is non-cancellable, however, the contract terms stipulate that if the customer terminates the contract, Contractor A would be entitled to payment for work completed to date. The payment amount would be equal to a proportional amount of the price of the contract based upon the performance of work done to date. For example, if at the termination date Contractor A was 50% complete (i.e. incurred €65 of costs), it would be entitled to a €50 payment from Customer X (i.e. 50% of €100 contract value).

In this example, we believe Contractor A has an enforceable right to payment for performance completed to date. This is in accordance with paragraph 35(c) of IFRS 15 because Contractor A is entitled to an amount that approximates the selling price of the good or service for performance completed to date in the event the customer terminates the contract.

See Chapter 31 at 4 regarding accounting for anticipated losses on contracts.

2.3.2.E   Enforceable right to payment determination when not entitled to a reasonable profit margin on standard inventory materials purchased, but not yet used

An entity may have an enforceable right to payment for performance completed to date even if it is not entitled to a reasonable profit margin on standard inventory materials that were purchased but not yet used in completing the performance obligation. Consider an example in which an entity agrees to construct a specialised asset for a customer that has no alternative use to the entity. The construction of this asset requires the use of standard inventory materials that could be used interchangeably on other projects of the entity until they are integrated into the production of the customer's asset. The contract with the customer entitles the entity to reimbursement of costs incurred plus a reasonable profit margin if the contract is terminated. However, the contract specifically excludes reimbursement of standard inventory purchases before they are integrated into the customer's asset. As previously discussed, the standard states that, at any time during the contract, an entity must be entitled to an amount that compensates the entity for performance completed to date (as defined in paragraph B9 of IFRS 15) if the contract is terminated for reasons other than the entity's failure to perform. However, in this example, the standard inventory materials have not yet been used in fulfilling the performance obligation, so the entity does not need to have an enforceable right to payment in relation to these materials. The entity could also repurpose the materials for use in other contracts with customers.

The entity will still need to evaluate whether it has an enforceable right to payment for performance completed to date once the standard inventory materials are used in fulfilling the performance obligation.

2.3.2.F   Considerations when assessing the over-time criteria for the sale of a real estate unit

The IFRS Interpretations Committee received three requests regarding the assessment of the over-time criteria in relation to contracts for the sale of a real estate unit. At its March 2018 meeting, the IFRS Interpretations Committee concluded that the principles and requirements in IFRS 15 provide an adequate basis for an entity to determine whether to recognise revenue over time, or at a point in time, including whether it has an enforceable right to payment for performance completed to date for a contract for the sale of a real estate unit. Consequently, the IFRS Interpretations Committee decided not to add these matters to its agenda.

After considering these requests, the IFRS Interpretations Committee decided that the agenda decisions should discuss the requirements of IFRS 15, as well as how the requirements apply to the fact patterns within the requests. The agenda decisions included the following reminders:

- an entity accounts for contracts within the scope of IFRS 15 only when all the criteria in paragraph 9 of IFRS 15 are met (which includes the collectability criterion);
- before considering the over-time criteria, an entity is required to apply paragraphs 22-30 of IFRS 15 to identify whether each promise to transfer a good or service to the customer is a performance obligation (see Chapter 28 at 3.2 for further discussion); and
- an entity assesses the over-time criteria in paragraph 35 of IFRS 15 at contract inception. Paragraph 35 of IFRS 15 specifies that an entity transfers control of a good or service over time and, therefore, satisfies a performance obligation and recognises revenue over time, if any of the three criteria is met. If an entity does not satisfy a performance obligation over time, it satisfies the performance obligation at a point in time.

The agenda decisions also noted the following in relation to the over-time criteria.[11]

Criterion (a)

According to paragraph 35(a) of IFRS 15, an entity recognises revenue over time if the customer simultaneously receives and consumes the benefits provided by the entity's performance as the entity performs. This criterion is not applicable in a contract for the sale of a real estate unit that the entity constructs because the real estate unit created by the entity's performance is not consumed immediately.

Criterion (b)

Paragraph 35(b) of IFRS 15 specifies that an entity recognises revenue over time if the customer controls the asset that an entity's performance creates or enhances as the asset is created or enhanced. Control refers to the ability to direct the use of, and obtain substantially all of the remaining benefits from, the asset. The Board included this criterion to 'address situations in which an entity's performance creates or enhances an asset that a customer clearly controls as the asset is created or enhanced'. Therefore, all relevant facts and circumstances need to be considered by an entity when assessing whether there is evidence that the customer clearly controls the asset that is being created or enhanced (e.g. the part-constructed real estate unit) as it is created or enhanced. None of the facts and circumstances is determinative.

The IFRS Interpretations Committee observed that 'in a contract for the sale of real estate that the entity constructs, the asset created is the real estate itself. It is not, for example, the right to obtain the real estate in the future. The right to sell or pledge a right to obtain real estate in the future is not evidence of control of the real estate itself'. That is, it is important to apply the requirements for control to the asset that the entity's performance creates or enhances (see 2.2.1 above).

Criterion (c)

The Board developed this third criterion because, in some cases, it may not be clear whether the asset that is created or enhanced is controlled by the customer. Paragraph 35(c) of IFRS 15 requires an entity to determine whether: (a) the asset created by an entity's performance does not have an alternative use to the entity; and (b) the entity has an enforceable right to payment for performance completed to date. However, the underlying objective of this criterion is still to determine whether the entity is transferring control of goods or services to the customer as it is creating the asset for that customer. The agenda decisions reiterate that:

- the asset being created does not have an alternative use to the entity if the entity is restricted contractually from readily directing the asset for another use during the asset's creation or if it is limited practically from readily directing the asset in the completed state for another use; *[IFRS 15.36]* and
- the entity has an enforceable right to payment if it is entitled to an amount that at least compensates it for performance completed to date were the contract to be terminated by the customer for reasons other than the entity's failure to perform as promised. *[IFRS 15.37]*. The entity must be entitled to this amount at all times throughout the duration of the contract and this amount should at least approximate the selling price of the goods or services transferred to date. That is, it is not meant to refer to compensation for only the entity's potential loss of profit were the contract to be terminated. The IFRS Interpretations Committee observed that 'it is the payment the entity is entitled to receive under the contract with the customer relating to performance under that contract that is relevant in determining whether the entity has an enforceable right to payment for performance completed to date'. As discussed at 2.3.2.G below, the IFRS Interpretations Committee also observed that an entity does not consider consideration it might receive upon resale of the asset if the original customer were to terminate the contract.

In determining whether it has an enforceable right to payment, an entity considers the contractual terms as well as any legislation or legal precedent that could supplement or override those contractual terms. While an entity does not need to undertake an exhaustive search for evidence, it is not appropriate for an entity to ignore evidence of relevant legal precedent that is available to it or to anticipate evidence that may become available in the future. The IFRS Interpretations Committee also observed that 'the assessment ... is focused on the existence of the right and its enforceability. The likelihood that the entity would exercise the right is not relevant to this assessment. Similarly, if a customer has the right to terminate the contract, the likelihood that the customer would terminate the contract is not relevant to this assessment'.

2.3.2.G Enforceable right to payment: contemplating consideration an entity might receive from the potential resale of the asset

We believe that only the payment the entity is entitled to receive relating to performance under the current customer contract is relevant in determining whether the entity has an enforceable right to payment for performance completed to date. For example, and as discussed by the IFRS Interpretations Committee (see 2.3.2.F above), an entity would not look to potential consideration it might receive upon resale of the asset if the original customer were to terminate the contract. This is because the resale of an asset typically represents a separate contract with a different customer and, therefore, is not relevant to determining the existence and enforceability of a right to payment with the existing customer.

Consider the following example discussed by the IFRS Interpretations Committee.[12]

Example 30.8:   Determining whether an enforceable right to payment exists when cancellation by a customer obliges an entity to resell the asset

Entity X, a construction company, enters into a contract with a customer to sell a real estate unit in a residential multi-unit complex before the entity constructs the unit. The entity determines that it has a single performance obligation to construct and deliver the real estate unit. The customer pays 10% of the purchase price at contract inception and the remainder after construction is complete. The entity retains legal title to the real estate unit (and any land attributed to it) until the customer has paid the purchase price after construction is complete.

Under the contract, the customer has the right to cancel the contract at any time before construction is complete. However, if it does, the entity is legally required to make reasonable efforts to resell the real estate unit to a third party. If the entity finds a new buyer, a new contract is executed and the original contract is not novated to the third party. If the resale price in the contract with the third party is less than the original purchase price (plus selling costs), the customer is legally obliged to pay the difference to the entity.

The entity concludes that the over-time criteria in paragraph 35(a) and (b) of IFRS 15 are not met. In considering the over-time criterion in paragraph 35(c) of IFRS 15, the entity determines that its performance does not create an asset with an alternative use to the entity. It, therefore, considers whether it has an enforceable right to payment.

The IFRS Interpretations Committee observed that, when determining whether an entity has an enforceable right to payment, an entity considers the payment to which it is entitled under the existing contract with the customer, which relates to its performance under that contract. It does not consider the consideration it would receive from a third party in a potential resale contract. Such consideration relates to that resale contract and is not payment for performance under the existing contract with the customer.

Since Entity X cannot consider the resale contract, the only future payment to which it has rights under the existing contract with the customer is for the difference between the resale price of the unit, if any, and its original purchase price (plus selling costs). That payment, together with the deposit received, does not (at all times throughout the duration of the contract) entitle the entity to an amount that at least approximates the selling price of the part-constructed real estate unit (i.e. it does not compensate for performance completed to date). Therefore, Entity X does not have an enforceable right to payment for performance completed to date. The IFRS Interpretations Committee concluded that none of the over-time criteria are met and the entity would recognise revenue at a point in time in accordance with paragraph 38 of IFRS 15.

3 MEASURING PROGRESS OVER TIME

When an entity has determined that a performance obligation is satisfied over time, the standard requires the entity to select a single revenue recognition method for the relevant performance obligation. The objective is to faithfully depict an entity's performance in transferring control of goods or services promised to a customer (i.e. the satisfaction of an entity's performance obligation). *[IFRS 15.39]*.

The standard requires the entity to select a single revenue recognition method to measure progress. The selected method must be applied consistently to similar performance obligations and in similar circumstances. At the end of each reporting period, an entity remeasures its progress towards complete satisfaction of a performance obligation satisfied over time. *[IFRS 15.40]*. Regardless of which method an entity selects, it excludes from its measure of progress any goods or services for which control has not transferred. *[IFRS 15.42]*.

As circumstances change over time, an entity updates its measure of progress to reflect any changes in the outcome of the performance obligation. Such changes to an entity's measure of progress are accounted for as a change in accounting estimate in accordance with IAS 8 – *Accounting Policies, Changes in Accounting Estimates and Errors*. *[IFRS 15.43]*.

While the standard (i.e. paragraph 40 of IFRS 15) requires an entity to remeasure its progress towards satisfaction of an over-time performance obligation at the end of each reporting period related to the measure of progress selected, it does not permit a change in method. A performance obligation is accounted for using the method the entity selects (i.e. either the specific input or output method it has chosen) from inception until the performance obligation has been fully satisfied. It would not be appropriate for an entity to start recognising revenue based on an input measure and later switch to an output measure (or to switch from one input method to a different input method). Furthermore, the standard requires that the selected method be applied to similar contracts in similar circumstances. It also requires that a single method of measuring progress be used for each performance obligation. *[IFRS 15.40]*. The Board noted that applying more than one method to measure performance would effectively override the guidance on identifying performance obligations. *[IFRS 15.BC161]*.

When measuring progress of an over-time performance obligation, paragraph 42 of IFRS 15 requires an entity to exclude any goods or services for which the entity does not transfer control to a customer. Conversely, an entity must include in the measure of progress any goods or services for which the entity does transfer control to a customer when satisfying that performance obligation. *[IFRS 15.42]*.

Paragraph 43 of IFRS 15 notes that changes in circumstances over time may require an entity to update its measure of progress to reflect any changes in the outcome of the performance obligation. *[IFRS 15.43]*. For example, an entity may determine that total expected costs are greater than its original expectation. If the entity was using an input method based on costs incurred, it would need to update its measure-of-progress calculation with this new information.

Changes to an entity's measure of progress are accounted for in accordance with the requirements in IAS 8 for changes in accounting estimates. IAS 8 requires a change in accounting estimate to be accounted for prospectively, i.e. by adjusting the carrying amount of an asset, liability or item of equity in the statement of financial position; and recognising the change by including it 'in profit or loss in: (1) the period of the change, if the change affects that period only; or (2) the period of the change and future periods, if the change affects both'. *[IAS 8.5, 36-37]*. IAS 8 is clear that a change in accounting estimate, by its nature, does not relate to prior periods and is not the correction of an error. *[IAS 8.34]*. The disclosure requirements in IAS 8 related to changes in accounting estimates are also applicable (see Chapter 3 at 4.5 and 5.2.2).

If an entity does not have a reasonable basis to measure its progress, revenue cannot be recognised until progress can be reasonably measured in accordance with paragraph 44 of IFRS 15. *[IFRS 15.44]*. However, if an entity can determine that a loss will not be incurred, the standard (i.e. paragraph 45 of IFRS 15) requires the entity to recognise revenue up to the amount of the costs incurred. *[IFRS 15.45]*. The IASB explained that an entity would need to stop using this method once it is able to reasonably measure its progress towards satisfaction of the performance obligation. *[IFRS 15.BC180]*. A cumulative catch-up adjustment would be recognised in the period in which the entity is able to reasonably measure its progress.

Finally, stakeholders had asked whether an entity's inability to measure progress would mean that costs incurred would also be deferred. The Board clarified that costs cannot be deferred in these situations, unless they meet the criteria for capitalisation under paragraph 95 of IFRS 15 (see Chapter 31 at 5.2). *[IFRS 15.BC179]*.

The standard provides two methods for recognising revenue on contracts involving the transfer of goods or services over time: input methods and output methods. *[IFRS 15.41, B14]*. The standard contains the following application guidance on these methods.

- *Output methods*

    Output methods recognise revenue on the basis of direct measurements of the value to the customer of the goods or services transferred to date relative to the remaining goods or services promised under the contract. Output methods include methods such as surveys of performance completed to date, appraisals of results achieved, milestones reached, time elapsed and units produced or units delivered. *[IFRS 15.B15]*.

    When an entity evaluates whether to apply an output method to measure its progress, the standard requires that an entity consider whether the output selected would faithfully depict the entity's performance towards complete satisfaction of the performance obligation. This would not be the case if the output selected would fail to measure some of the goods or services for which control has transferred to the customer. For example, output methods based on units produced or units delivered would not faithfully depict an entity's performance in satisfying a performance obligation if, at the end of the reporting period, the entity's performance has produced work in progress or finished goods controlled by the customer that are not included in the measurement of the output. *[IFRS 15.B15]*.

    As a practical expedient, if an entity has a right to consideration from a customer in an amount that corresponds directly with the value to the customer of the entity's performance completed to date (e.g. a service contract in which an entity bills a fixed amount for each hour of service provided), the entity may recognise revenue in the amount to which the entity has a right to invoice ('right to invoice' practical expedient, see 3.4.5 below and Chapter 32 at 3.2.1.D for further discussion). *[IFRS 15.B16]*.

The disadvantages of output methods are that the outputs used to measure progress may not be directly observable and the information required to apply them may not be available to an entity without undue cost. Therefore, an input method may be necessary. *[IFRS 15.B17]*.

- *Input methods*

    Input methods recognise revenue on the basis of the entity's efforts or inputs to the satisfaction of a performance obligation (e.g. resources consumed, labour hours expended, costs incurred, time elapsed or machine hours used) relative to the total expected inputs to the satisfaction of that performance obligation. If the entity's efforts or inputs are expended evenly throughout the performance period, it may be appropriate for the entity to recognise revenue on a straight-line basis. *[IFRS 15.B18]*.

In determining the best method for measuring progress that faithfully depicts an entity's performance, an entity needs to consider both the nature of the promised goods or services and the nature of the entity's performance. *[IFRS 15.41]*. In other words, an entity's selection of a method to measure its performance needs to be consistent with the nature of its promise to the customer and what the entity has agreed to transfer to the customer. To illustrate this concept, the Basis for Conclusions cites, as an example, a contract for health club services. *[IFRS 15.BC160]*. Regardless of when, or how frequently, the customer uses the health club, the entity's obligation to stand ready for the contractual period does not change. Furthermore, the customer is required to pay the fee regardless of whether the customer uses the health club. As a result, the entity would need to select a measure of progress based on its service of standing ready to make the health club available. Example 30.11 at 3.3 below illustrates how a health club might select this measure of progress.

3.1 Output methods

While there is no preferable measure of progress, the IASB stated in the Basis for Conclusions that, conceptually, an output measure is the most faithful depiction of an entity's performance. This is because it directly measures the value of the goods or services transferred to the customer. *[IFRS 15.BC160]*. However, the Board discussed two output methods that may not be appropriate in many instances if the entity's performance obligation is satisfied over time: units of delivery and units of production. *[IFRS 15.BC165]*.

Units-of-delivery or units-of-production methods may not result in the best depiction of an entity's performance over time if there is material work in progress at the end of the reporting period. In these cases, the IASB observed that using a units-of-delivery or units-of-production method would distort the entity's performance because it would not recognise revenue for the customer-controlled assets that are created before delivery or before construction is complete. This is because, when an entity determines control transfers to the customer over time, it has concluded that the customer controls any resulting asset as it is created. Therefore, the entity must recognise revenue related to those goods or services for which control has transferred. The IASB also stated, in the Basis for Conclusions, that a units-of-delivery or units-of-production method may not be appropriate if the contract provides both design and production services because each item produced 'may not transfer an equal amount of value to the customer'. *[IFRS 15.BC166]*. That is, it is likely that the items produced earlier have a higher value than those that are produced later.

It is important to note that 'value to the customer' in paragraph B15 of IFRS 15 refers to an objective method of measuring the entity's performance in the contract. This is not intended to be assessed by reference to the market prices, stand-alone selling prices or the value a customer perceives to be embodied in the goods or services. *[IFRS 15.BC163]*. The TRG agenda paper noted that this concept of value is different from the concept of value an entity uses to determine whether it can use the 'right to invoice' practical expedient, as discussed below. When an entity determines whether items individually transfer an equal amount of value to the customer (i.e. when applying paragraph B15 of IFRS 15), the evaluation related to how much, or what proportion, of the goods or services (i.e. quantities) have been delivered (but not the price). For example, for the purpose of applying paragraph B15 of IFRS 15, an entity might consider the amount of goods or services transferred to date in proportion to the total expected goods or services to be transferred when measuring progress. However, if this measure of progress results in material work in progress at the end of the reporting period, it would not be appropriate, as discussed above.[13] See the discussion at 3.1.1 below regarding the evaluation of 'value to the customer' in the context of evaluating the 'right to invoice' practical expedient in paragraph B16 of IFRS 15.

3.1.1 Practical expedient for measuring progress towards satisfaction of a performance obligation

The Board provided a practical expedient in paragraph B16 of IFRS 15 for an entity that is using an output method to measure progress towards completion of a performance obligation that is satisfied over time. The practical expedient only applies if an entity can demonstrate that the invoiced amount corresponds directly with the value to the customer of the entity's performance completed to date. *[IFRS 15.B16]*. In that situation, the practical expedient allows an entity to recognise revenue in the amount for which it has the right to invoice (i.e. the 'right to invoice' practical expedient). An entity may be able to use this practical expedient for a service contract in which an entity bills a fixed amount for each hour of service provided.

A TRG agenda paper noted that paragraph B16 of IFRS 15 is intended as an expedient to some aspects of Step 3, Step 4 and Step 5 in the standard. Because this practical expedient allows an entity to recognise revenue on the basis of invoicing, revenue is recognised by multiplying the price (assigned to the goods or services delivered) by the measure of progress (i.e. the quantities or units transferred). Therefore, an entity effectively bypasses the steps in the model for determining the transaction price, allocating that transaction price to the performance obligations and determining when to recognise revenue. However, it does not permit an entity to bypass the requirements for identifying the performance obligations in the contract and evaluating whether the performance obligation is satisfied over time, which is a requirement to use this expedient.[14]

To apply the practical expedient, an entity must also be able to assert that the right to consideration from a customer corresponds directly with the value to the customer of the entity's performance to date. When determining whether the amount that has been invoiced to the customer corresponds directly with the value to the customer of an entity's performance completed to date, the entity could evaluate the amount that has been invoiced in comparison to market prices, stand-alone selling prices or another reasonable measure of value to the customer. See 3.4.5 below for the TRG discussion on evaluating value to the customer in contracts with changing rates.

Furthermore, the TRG members also noted in their discussion of the TRG agenda paper that an entity would have to evaluate all significant upfront payments or retrospective adjustments (e.g. accumulating rebates) in order to determine whether the amount the entity has a right to invoice for each good or service corresponds directly to the value to the customer of the entity's performance completed to date. That is, if an upfront payment or retrospective adjustment significantly shifts payment for value to the customer to the front or back-end of a contract, it may be difficult for an entity to conclude that the amount invoiced corresponds directly with the value provided to the customer for goods or services.[15]

The TRG agenda paper also stated that the presence of an agreed-upon customer payment schedule does not mean that the amount an entity has the right to invoice corresponds directly with the value to the customer of the entity's performance completed to date. In addition, the TRG agenda paper stated that the existence of specified contract minimums (or volume discounts) would not always preclude the application of the practical expedient, provided that these clauses are deemed non-substantive (e.g. the entity expects to receive amounts in excess of the specified minimums).[16]

3.2 Input methods

Input methods recognise revenue based on an entity's efforts or inputs towards satisfying a performance obligation relative to the total expected efforts or inputs to satisfy the performance obligation. Examples of input methods mentioned in the standard include costs incurred, time elapsed, resources consumed or labour hours expended. An entity is required to select a single measure of progress for each performance obligation that depicts the entity's performance in transferring control of the goods or services promised to a customer. If an entity's efforts or inputs are used evenly throughout the entity's performance period, a time-based measure that results in a straight-line recognition of revenue may be appropriate. However, there may be a disconnect between an entity's inputs (e.g. cost of non-distinct goods included in a single performance obligation satisfied over time) and the depiction of an entity's performance to date. The standard includes specific application guidance on adjustments to the measure of progress that may be necessary in those situations. See 3.2.1 below for additional discussion.

Regardless of which method an entity selects, it excludes from its measure of progress any goods or services for which control has not transferred to the customer. Likewise, if an entity uses an input method based on costs incurred, it excludes from its measure of progress those costs that do not reflect its performance in transferring a good or service to the customer (e.g. borrowing costs incurred, which it incurs to fund its activities, rather than to fulfil a performance obligation).

3.2.1 Adjustments to the measure of progress based on an input method

If an entity applies an input method that uses costs incurred to measure its progress towards completion (e.g. cost to cost), the cost incurred may not always be proportionate to the entity's progress in satisfying the performance obligation. To address this shortcoming of input methods, the standard notes that a shortcoming of input methods is that there may not be a direct relationship between an entity's inputs and the transfer of control of goods or services to a customer. Therefore, an entity is required to exclude the effects of any inputs that do not depict the entity's performance (in transferring control of goods or services to the customer) from an input method. For instance, when using a cost-based input method, the standard suggests an adjustment to the measure of progress may be required in the following circumstances: *[IFRS 15.B19]*

(a) When a cost incurred does not contribute to an entity's progress in satisfying the performance obligation.

As an example, the standard states that an entity would not recognise revenue on the basis of costs incurred that are attributable to significant inefficiencies in the entity's performance that were not reflected in the price of the contract (e.g. the costs of unexpected amounts of wasted materials, labour or other resources that were incurred to satisfy the performance obligation).

(b) When a cost incurred is not proportionate to the entity's progress in satisfying the performance obligation.

In those circumstances, the standard states that the best depiction of the entity's performance may be to adjust the input method to recognise revenue only to the extent of that cost incurred. For example, a faithful depiction of an entity's performance might be to recognise revenue at an amount equal to the cost of a good used to satisfy a performance obligation if the entity expects at contract inception that all of the following conditions would be met:

(i) the good is not distinct;

(ii) the customer is expected to obtain control of the good significantly before receiving services related to the good;

(iii) the cost of the transferred good is significant relative to the total expected costs to completely satisfy the performance obligation; and

(iv) the entity procures the good from a third party and is not significantly involved in designing and manufacturing the good (but the entity is acting as a principal, see Chapter 28 at 3.4).

In a combined performance obligation comprised of non-distinct goods or services, the customer may obtain control of some of the goods before the entity provides the services related to those goods. This could be the case when goods are delivered to a customer site, but the entity has not yet integrated the goods into the overall project (e.g. the materials are 'uninstalled'). The Board concluded that, if an entity were using a percentage-of-completion method based on costs incurred to measure its progress (i.e. cost-to-cost), the measure of progress may be inappropriately affected by the delivery of these goods and that a pure application of such a measure of progress would result in overstated revenue. *[IFRS 15.BC171]*.

Paragraph B19 of IFRS 15 indicates that, in such circumstances, (e.g. when control of the individual goods has transferred to the customer, but the integration service has not yet occurred), the best depiction of the entity's performance may be to recognise revenue at an amount equal to the cost of the goods used to satisfy the performance obligation (i.e. a zero margin). This is because the costs incurred are not proportionate to an entity's progress in satisfying the performance obligation. It is also important to note that determining when control of the individual goods (that are part of a performance obligation) have transferred to the customer requires judgement. *[IFRS 15.B19]*.

The Board noted that the adjustment to the cost-to-cost measure of progress for uninstalled materials is generally intended to apply to a subset of construction-type goods that have a significant cost relative to the contract and for which the entity is effectively providing a simple procurement service to the customer. *[IFRS 15.BC172]*. By applying the adjustment to recognise revenue at an amount equal to the cost of uninstalled materials, an entity is recognising a margin similar to the one the entity would have recognised if the customer had supplied the materials. The IASB clarified that the outcome of recognising no margin for uninstalled materials is necessary to adjust the cost-to-cost calculation to faithfully depict an entity's performance. *[IFRS 15.BC174]*.

In addition, situations may arise in which not all of the costs incurred contribute to the entity's progress in completing the performance obligation. Paragraph B19(a) of IFRS 15 requires that, under an input method, an entity exclude these types of costs (e.g. costs related to significant inefficiencies, wasted materials, required rework) from the measure of progress, unless such costs were reflected in the price of the contract. *[IFRS 15.B19(a)]*.

The standard includes the following example, illustrating how uninstalled materials are considered in measuring progress towards complete satisfaction of a performance obligation. *[IFRS 15.IE95-IE100]*.

Example 30.9: Uninstalled materials

In November 20X1, an entity contracts with a customer to refurbish a 3-storey building and install new elevators for total consideration of $5 million. The promised refurbishment service, including the installation of elevators, is a single performance obligation satisfied over time. Total expected costs are $4 million, including $1.5 million for the elevators. The entity determines that it acts as a principal in accordance with paragraphs B34-B38 of IFRS 15, because it obtains control of the elevators before they are transferred to the customer.

A summary of the transaction price and expected costs is as follows:

	$
Transaction price	5,000,000
Expected costs	
Elevators	1,500,000
Other costs	2,500,000
Total expected costs	4,000,000

The entity uses an input method based on costs incurred to measure its progress towards complete satisfaction of the performance obligation. The entity assesses whether the costs incurred to procure the elevators are proportionate to the entity's progress in satisfying the performance obligation, in accordance with paragraph B19 of IFRS 15. The customer obtains control of the elevators when they are delivered to the site in December 20X1, although the elevators will not be installed until June 20X2. The costs to procure the elevators ($1.5 million) are significant relative to the total expected costs to completely satisfy the performance obligation ($4 million). The entity is not involved in designing or manufacturing the elevators.

The entity concludes that including the costs to procure the elevators in the measure of progress would overstate the extent of the entity's performance. Consequently, in accordance with paragraph B19 of IFRS 15, the entity adjusts its measure of progress to exclude the costs to procure the elevators from the measure of costs incurred and from the transaction price. The entity recognises revenue for the transfer of the elevators in an amount equal to the costs to procure the elevators (i.e. at a zero margin).

As at 31 December 20X1 the entity observes that:

(a) other costs incurred (excluding elevators) are $500,000; and

(b) performance is 20 per cent complete (i.e. $500,000 ÷ $2,500,000).

Consequently, at 31 December 20X1, the entity recognises the following:

	$	
Revenue	2,200,000	(a)
Cost of goods sold	2,000,000	(b)
Profit	200,000	

(a) Revenue recognised is calculated as (20 per cent × $3,500,000) + $1,500,000. ($3,500,000 is $5,000,000 transaction price − $1,500,000 costs of elevators).

(b) Cost of goods sold is $500,000 of costs incurred + $1,500,000 costs of elevators.

When costs for uninstalled materials are excluded from the measure of progress and those materials are subsequently installed, an entity will need to apply significant judgement, based on its assessment of which treatment best depicts its performance in the contract, to determine whether the costs should be: (a) included in the measure of progress upon installation; or (b) excluded from the measure of progress for the duration of the contract.

- *Approach (a) – once the materials have been installed, the costs for those materials are included in the measure of progress*

    Paragraph B19(b) of IFRS 15 can be read to apply only while materials are uninstalled. Once installed, it no longer applies to the materials and the entity reverts to the general requirements for measuring progress over time. The Basis for Conclusions indicates that recognising the profit margin for the performance obligation as a whole before the goods are installed could result in overstated revenue, and that paragraph B19(b) of IFRS 15 applies to uninstalled materials and that it is only those materials that are *not yet installed* that attract a zero margin. [IFRS 15.BC171, BC172, BC174]. Furthermore, Example 19 of IFRS 15 (included as Example 30.9 above) illustrates the accounting for materials before they are installed (at the point in time that control of those materials has passed to the customer) and not after being installed.

    When the profit margin applicable to the procured item(s) differs significantly from the profit margin attributable to other goods and services to be provided in accordance with the contract, the application of the profit margin for the performance obligation as a whole may overstate the amount of revenue and profit that is attributed to the procured item(s). Entities will need to consider whether the outcome of applying this approach is consistent with the underlying principle in paragraph 39 of IFRS 15, that the amount of revenue recognised depict its performance, as it satisfies its performance obligation.

If this approach is used, an entity needs to ensure it does not use a profit margin that differs from the profit margin for the performance obligation as a whole. That is, it should not attribute different profit margins to each component within a single performance obligation. This would effectively treat each component as a separate performance obligation when they are not distinct (and, therefore, inappropriately bypass the requirements for identifying performance obligations). *[IFRS 15.BC171]*.

- *Approach (b) - the costs for uninstalled materials are excluded from the measure of progress for the duration of the contract*

    Paragraph B19(b) of IFRS 15 does not distinguish goods that have been installed from those that have not yet been installed and the adjustments to the measure of progress in Example 19 of IFRS 15 (included as Example 30.9 above) can be read to apply for the duration of the contract. *[IFRS 15.IE98]*. As discussed above, paragraph B19(b) of IFRS 15 is generally intended to apply to a subset of construction-type goods that have a significant cost relative to the contract and for which the entity is effectively providing a simple procurement service to the customer or if the customer had supplied the materials themselves. *[IFRS 15.BC172]*.

    Approach (b) shifts the margin from uninstalled materials to the other components within the single performance obligation, which is recognised as the related costs are incurred (and included in the measure of progress). Entities may need to consider whether this reflects their performance if they typically charge a margin for procurement of similar materials.

3.3 Examples of measures of progress

The following example illustrates some possible considerations when determining an appropriate measure of progress.

Example 30.10: Choosing the measure of progress

A ship-building entity enters into a contract to build 15 vessels for a customer over a three-year period. The contract includes both design and production services. The entity has not built a vessel of this type in the past. In addition, the entity expects that the first vessels may take longer to produce than the last vessels because, as the entity gains experience building the vessels, it expects to be able to construct the vessels more efficiently.

Assume that the entity has determined that the design and production services represent a single performance obligation. In this situation, it is likely that the entity would not choose a 'units-of-delivery' method as a measure of progress because that method would not accurately capture the level of performance. That is, such a method would not reflect the entity's efforts during the design phase of the contract because no revenue would be recognised until a vessel was shipped. In such situations, an entity would likely determine that an input method is more appropriate, such as a percentage-of-completion method based on costs incurred.

The standard also includes the following example on selecting an appropriate measure of progress towards satisfaction of a performance obligation. *[IFRS 15.IE92-IE94]*.

Example 30.11: Measuring progress when making goods or services available

An entity, an owner and manager of health clubs, enters into a contract with a customer for one year of access to any of its health clubs. The customer has unlimited use of the health clubs and promises to pay £100 per month.

The entity determines that its promise to the customer is to provide a service of making the health clubs available for the customer to use as and when the customer wishes. This is because the extent to which the customer uses the health clubs does not affect the amount of the remaining goods and services to which the customer is entitled. The entity concludes that the customer simultaneously receives and consumes the benefits of the entity's performance as it performs by making the health clubs available. Consequently, the entity's performance obligation is satisfied over time in accordance with paragraph 35(a) of IFRS 15.

The entity also determines that the customer benefits from the entity's service of making the health clubs available evenly throughout the year. (That is, the customer benefits from having the health clubs available, regardless of whether the customer uses it or not.) Consequently, the entity concludes that the best measure of progress towards complete satisfaction of the performance obligation over time is a time-based measure and it recognises revenue on a straight-line basis throughout the year at CU100 per month.

3.4 Application questions on measuring progress over time

3.4.1 Measuring progress toward satisfaction of a stand-ready obligation that is satisfied over time

At the January 2015 TRG meeting, the TRG members discussed questions raised regarding how an entity would measure progress for a stand-ready obligation that is a performance obligation satisfied over time.

The TRG members generally agreed that an entity should not default to a straight-line revenue attribution model. However, they also generally agreed that if an entity expects the customer to receive and consume the benefits of its promise throughout the contract period, a time-based measure of progress (e.g. straight-line) would be appropriate. The TRG agenda paper noted that this is generally the case for unspecified upgrade rights, help-desk support contracts and cable or satellite television contracts. In contrast, the TRG members generally agreed that rateable recognition may not be appropriate if the benefits are not spread evenly over the contract period (e.g. an annual snow removal contract that provides most benefits in winter).[17]

See Chapter 28 at 3.1.1.C for a discussion on whether contracts with a stand-ready element include a single performance obligation that is satisfied over time.

As discussed in Chapter 28 at 3.2.2.E, we generally believe that a stand-ready obligation that is satisfied over time will meet the criteria to be accounted for as a series of distinct goods and services. Similar to the discussion above, while it is not appropriate to default to a straight-line revenue attribution model for a series, straight-line revenue recognition may be reasonable in many cases. Management should select the measure of progress that faithfully depicts the entity's performance in transferring the goods or services promised in a series.

3.4.2 Selecting a measure of progress when there is more than one promised good or service within a performance obligation

In July 2015, the TRG members were asked to consider whether an entity can use more than one measure of progress in order to depict an entity's performance in transferring a performance obligation comprised of two or more goods and/or services that is satisfied over time. Note that, under Step 2 of the new model, a single performance obligation may contain multiple non-distinct goods or services and/or distinct goods or services that were required to be combined with non-distinct goods or services in order to identify a distinct bundle. This bundled performance obligation is referred to as a 'combined performance obligation' for the purpose of this discussion.

The TRG members agreed that when an entity has determined that a combined performance obligation is satisfied over time, the entity has to select a single measure of progress that faithfully depicts the entity's performance in transferring the goods or services. For example, using different measures of progress for different non-distinct goods or services in the combined performance obligation would be inappropriate because doing so ignores the unit of account that has been identified under the standard (i.e. the single combined performance obligation). Furthermore, it would also be inappropriate because the entity would recognise revenue in a way that overrides the separation and allocation requirements in the standard. *[IFRS 15.BC161].*

The TRG agenda paper noted that a single method of measuring progress should not be broadly interpreted to mean an entity may apply multiple measures of progress as long as all measures used are either output or input measures.[18]

3.4.3 Determining the appropriate single measure of progress for a combined performance obligation that is satisfied over time

At the July 2015 TRG meeting, the TRG members discussed how an entity would determine the appropriate single measure of progress for a combined performance obligation that is satisfied over time.

The TRG members acknowledged that it may be difficult to appropriately determine a single measure of progress when the entity transfers goods or services that make up the combined performance obligation over different points of time and/or the entity would otherwise use a different measure of progress (e.g. a time-based method versus a labour-based input method) if each promise was a separate performance obligation. Such a determination requires significant judgement, but the TRG members generally agreed that the measure of progress selected is not meant to be a 'free choice'. Entities need to consider the nature of the overall promise for the combined performance obligation in determining the measure of progress to use. For example, entities should not default to a 'final deliverable' methodology such that all revenue would be recognised over the performance period of the last promised good or service. Rather, an entity is required to select the single measure of progress that most faithfully depicts the entity's performance in satisfying its combined performance obligation.[19]

Some of the TRG members observed that an entity would need to consider the reasons why goods or services were bundled into a combined performance obligation in order to determine the appropriate pattern of revenue recognition. For example, if a good or service was combined with other goods or services because it was not capable of being distinct, that may indicate that it does not provide value or use to the customer on its own. As such, the entity would not contemplate the transfer of that good or service when determining the pattern of revenue recognition for the combined performance obligation.

The TRG members also generally agreed that, if an appropriately selected single measure of progress does not faithfully depict the economics of the arrangement, the entity should challenge whether the performance obligation was correctly combined (i.e. there may be more than one performance obligation).

Consider the following example included in the TRG paper:[20]

Example 30.12: Combined licence and installation service performance obligation

An entity promises to provide a software licence and installation services that will substantially customise the software to add significant new functionality that enables the software to interface with other customised applications used by the customer.

The entity concludes that the software and services are not separately identifiable from the customised installation service, and the criterion in paragraph 27(b) of IFRS 15 is not met (see Chapter 28 at 3.2.1). Therefore, the software licence and installation service are combined into a single performance obligation and the entity concludes that the combined performance obligation is satisfied over time. If the licence was distinct, it would be considered a right-to-use licence and revenue would be recognised at a point in time.

The entity further determines that the nature of its overall promise is to develop the customised software over time. Accordingly, the entity determines that it should use a measure of progress that depicts the performance of completing the customised software solution. Therefore, all of the revenue for this contract would be recognised over the period that the customisation services are performed.

3.4.4 Can control of a good or service underlying a performance obligation satisfied over time be transferred at discrete points in time?

The FASB TRG members generally agreed that, if a performance obligation meets the criteria for revenue to be recognised over time (rather than at a point in time), control of the underlying good or service is not transferred at discrete points in time. Because control transfers as an entity performs, an entity's performance (as reflected using an appropriate measure of progress) should not result in the creation of a material asset in the entity's accounts (e.g. work in progress).

Stakeholders had queried whether control of a good or service underlying a performance obligation that is satisfied over time can be transferred at discrete points in time because the standard highlights several output methods, including 'milestones reached', as potentially acceptable methods for measuring progress towards satisfaction of an over-time performance obligation. The FASB TRG members generally agreed that an entity could use an output method only if that measure of progress correlates to the entity's performance to date.[21]

At the May 2016 IASB meeting, the IASB staff indicated support for the conclusions reached in the TRG agenda paper on this issue, noting that it provides some clarity about when to use milestones reached as a measure of progress. Furthermore, the members of the IASB who observed the FASB TRG meeting indicated that the FASB TRG discussion on the topic was helpful.

3.4.5 Use of the 'right to invoice' practical expedient for a contract that includes rates that change over the contractual term

At the July 2015 TRG meeting, the TRG members were asked to consider whether the 'right to invoice' practical expedient could apply to a contract that includes rates that change over the contractual term.

The TRG members generally agreed that determining whether an entity can apply the 'right to invoice' practical expedient requires judgement. They also generally agreed that it is possible for entities to meet the requirements for the practical expedient in contracts with changing rates, provided that the changes in rates correspond directly to changes in value to the customer. That is, a contract does not need to have a fixed price per unit for the duration of a contract in order to qualify for the practical expedient. Examples of contracts that might qualify include an IT outsourcing arrangement with rates that decrease over the contract term as the level of effort to the customer decreases or a multi-year electricity contract that contemplates the forward market price of electricity. However, the SEC staff observer also noted that entities need to have strong evidence that variable prices reflect the value to the customer in order to recognise variable amounts of revenue for similar goods or services.[22]

See Chapter 32 at 3.2.1.D for a discussion on whether an entity can still use the practical expedient (under which an entity can decide not to disclose the amount of transaction price allocated to remaining performance obligation) if it determines that it has not met the criteria to use the 'right to invoice' practical expedient (e.g. because there is a substantive contractual minimum payment or a volume discount).

3.4.6 Recognising revenue when fulfilment costs are incurred prior to the contract establishment date for a specifically anticipated contract

An entity cannot begin to recognise revenue on a contract until it meets all five criteria to be considered a contract under IFRS 15 (as discussed in Chapter 28 at 2.1), regardless of whether it has received any consideration or has begun performing under the terms of the arrangement.

At the March 2015 TRG meeting, the TRG members were asked to consider how an entity would recognise revenue at the date a contract exists if an entity begins activities on a specifically anticipated contract either:

- before it agrees to the contract with the customer; or
- before the arrangement meets the criteria to be considered a contract under the standard.[23]

The TRG members generally agreed that if the goods or services that ultimately will be transferred meet the criteria to be recognised over time, revenue would be recognised on a cumulative catch-up basis at the 'contract establishment date', reflecting the performance obligation(s) that are partially or fully satisfied at that time. The TRG agenda paper noted that the cumulative catch-up method is considered to be consistent with the overall principle of the standard that revenue is recognised when (or as) an entity transfers control of goods or services to a customer.[24]

When recording revenue on a cumulative catch-up basis in these circumstances, an entity needs to consider the requirements in Step 5 of the model to determine the goods or services that the customer controls. This determines what portion of costs incurred before the contract establishment date would be included in any measure of progress used to calculate the cumulative catch-up adjustment. If, for example, costs incurred prior to the contract establishment date relate to uninstalled materials or any goods or services that the customer does not control, the inclusion of those costs in determining how much revenue to recognise might not be appropriate (see 3.2.1 above for further discussion on uninstalled materials).

See Chapter 31 at 5.2.2 for the TRG members' discussion regarding contract fulfilment costs incurred prior to the contract establishment date.

4 CONTROL TRANSFERRED AT A POINT IN TIME

For performance obligations in which control is not transferred over time, control is transferred as at a point in time. *[IFRS 15.38]*. In many situations, the determination of when that point in time occurs is relatively straightforward. However, in other circumstances, this determination is more complex.

To help entities determine the point in time when a customer obtains control of a particular good or service, the standard requires an entity to consider the general requirements for control in paragraphs 31-34 of IFRS 15 (see 1 above). In addition, an entity is required to consider indicators of the transfer of control, which include, but are not limited to, the following: *[IFRS 15.38]*.

(a) *The entity has a present right to payment for the asset* – if a customer is presently obliged to pay for an asset, then that may indicate that the customer has obtained the ability to direct the use of, and obtain substantially all of the remaining benefits from, the asset in exchange.

(b) *The customer has legal title to the asset* – legal title may indicate which party to a contract has the ability to direct the use of, and obtain substantially all of the remaining benefits from, an asset or to restrict the access of other entities to those benefits. Therefore, the transfer of legal title of an asset may indicate that the customer has obtained control of the asset. If an entity retains legal title solely as protection against the customer's failure to pay, those rights of the entity would not preclude the customer from obtaining control of an asset.

(c) *The entity has transferred physical possession of the asset* – the customer's physical possession of an asset may indicate that the customer has the ability to direct the use of, and obtain substantially all of the remaining benefits from, the asset or to restrict the access of other entities to those benefits. However, physical possession may not coincide with control of an asset. For example, in some repurchase agreements (see 5 below) and in some consignment arrangements, a customer or consignee may have physical possession of an asset that the entity controls (see 6 below and Chapter 28 at 3.5). Conversely, in some bill-and-hold arrangements (see 7 below), the entity may have physical possession of an asset that the customer controls.

(d) *The customer has the significant risks and rewards of ownership of the asset* – the transfer of the significant risks and rewards of ownership of an asset to the customer may indicate that the customer has obtained the ability to direct the use of, and obtain substantially all of the remaining benefits from, the asset. However, when evaluating the risks and rewards of ownership of a promised asset, an entity is required to exclude any risks that give rise to a separate performance obligation in addition to the performance obligation to transfer the asset. For example, an entity may have transferred control of an asset to a customer but not yet satisfied an additional performance obligation to provide maintenance services related to the transferred asset.

(e) *The customer has accepted the asset* – the customer's acceptance of an asset may indicate that it has obtained the ability to direct the use of, and obtain substantially all of the remaining benefits from, the asset (see 4.2 below).

None of the indicators above are meant to individually determine whether the customer has gained control of the good or service. For example, while shipping terms may provide information about when legal title to a good transfers to the customer, they are not determinative when evaluating the point in time at which the customer obtains control of the promised asset. See 4.1 below for further discussion on shipping terms. An entity must consider all relevant facts and circumstances to determine whether control has transferred. The IASB also made it clear that the indicators are not meant to be a checklist. Furthermore, not all of them must be present for an entity to determine that the customer has gained control. Rather, the indicators are factors that are often present when a customer has obtained control of an asset and the list is meant to help entities apply the principle of control. *[IFRS 15.BC155]*.

Paragraph 38 of IFRS 15 also states that indicators of control transfer are not limited to those listed above. For example, channel stuffing is a practice that entities sometimes use to increase sales by inducing distributors or resellers to buy substantially more goods than can be promptly resold. To induce the distributors to make such purchases, an entity may offer deep discounts that it would have to evaluate as variable consideration in estimating the transaction price (see Chapter 29 at 2.2). Channel stuffing also may be accompanied by side agreements with the distributors that provide a right of return for unsold goods that is in excess of the normal sales return privileges offered by the entity. Significant increases in, or excess levels of, inventory in a distribution channel due to channel stuffing may affect or preclude the ability to conclude that control of such goods has transferred. Entities need to carefully consider the expanded rights of returns offered to customers in connection with channel stuffing in order to determine whether they prevent the entity from recognising revenue at the time of the sales transaction.

If an entity uses channel stuffing practices, it should consider whether disclosure in its financial statements is required when it expects these practices to materially affect future operating results. For example, if an entity sold excess levels into a certain distribution channel at, or near, the end of a reporting period, it is likely that those sales volumes would not be sustainable in future periods. That is, sales into that channel may, in fact, slow down in future periods as the excess inventory takes longer to entirely sell through the channel. In such a case, the entity should consider whether disclosure of the effect of the channel stuffing practice on its current and future earnings is required, if material.

In determining when control transfers, it is important that the entity consider the good or service it is transferring, not the right to obtain that good or service in the future. In its March 2018 meeting, the IFRS Interpretations Committee noted that the right to sell (or pledge) a right to obtain an asset (e.g. real estate) in the future is not evidence of control of the asset itself (see 2.2.1 above and 2.3.2.F above for further discussion).[25]

We discuss the indicators in paragraph 38 of IFRS 15 that an entity considers when determining when it transfers control of the promised good or service to the customer in more detail below.

- *Present right to payment for the asset*

    As noted in the Basis for Conclusions, the IASB considered, but rejected specifying a right to payment as an overarching criterion for determining when revenue would be recognised. Therefore, while the date at which the entity has a right to payment for the asset may be an indicator of the date the customer obtained control of the asset, it does not always indicate that the customer has obtained control of the asset. *[IFRS 15.BC148]*. For example, in some contracts, a customer is required to make a non-refundable upfront payment, but receives no goods or services in return at that time.

- *Legal title and physical possession*

    The term 'title' is often associated with a legal definition denoting the ownership of an asset or legally recognised rights that preclude others' claim to the asset. Accordingly, the transfer of title often indicates that control of an asset has been transferred. Determination of which party has title to an asset does not always depend on which party has physical possession of the asset, but without contractual terms to the contrary, title generally passes to the customer at the time of the physical transfer. For example, in a retail store transaction, there is often no clear documentation of the transfer of title. However, it is generally understood that the title to a product is transferred at the time it is purchased by the customer.

    While the retail store transaction is relatively straightforward, determining when title has transferred may be more complicated in other arrangements. Transactions that involve the shipment of products may have varying shipping terms and may involve third-party shipping agents. In such cases, a clear understanding of the seller's practices and the contractual terms is required in order to make an assessment of when title transfers. As indicated in paragraph 38(b) of IFRS 15, legal title and/or physical possession may be an indicator of which party to a contract has the ability to direct the use of, and obtain substantially all of the remaining benefits from, an asset or to restrict the access of other entities to those benefits. See 4.1 below for further discussion on how shipping terms affect when an entity has transferred control of a good to a customer.

- *Risks and rewards of ownership*

    Although the Board included the risks and rewards of ownership as one factor to consider when evaluating whether control of an asset has transferred, it emphasised, in the Basis for Conclusions, that this factor does not change the principle of determining the transfer of goods or services on the basis of control. *[IFRS 15.BC154]*. The concept of the risks and rewards of ownership is based on how the seller and the customer share both the potential gain (the reward) and the potential loss (risk) associated with owning an asset. Rewards of ownership include the following:

    - rights to all appreciation in value of the asset;
    - unrestricted usage of the asset;
    - ability to modify the asset;
    - ability to transfer or sell the asset; and
    - ability to grant a security interest in the asset.

Conversely, the risks of ownership include the following:
- absorbing all of the declines in market value;
- incurring losses due to theft or damage of the asset; and
- incurring losses due to changes in the business environment (e.g. obsolescence, excess inventory, effect of retail pricing environment).

However, as noted in paragraph 38(d) of IFRS 15, an entity does not consider risks that give rise to a separate performance obligation when evaluating whether the entity has the risks of ownership of an asset. For example, an entity does not consider warranty services that represent a separate performance obligation when evaluating whether it retains the risks of ownership of the asset sold to the customer.

- *Customer acceptance*

See the discussion of this indicator in 4.2 below.

The following example illustrates application of the indicators of the transfer of control in paragraph 38 of IFRS 15 to a performance obligation that is satisfied at a point in time:

Example 30.13: Applying the indicators of the transfer of control to a performance obligation satisfied at a point in time

BCB Liquors (BCB) uses a distribution network to sell its product to end-consumers. Upon receipt of the product, a distributor receives legal title to the goods and is required to pay BCB for the product. In this example, BCB has determined its relationship with the distributor is not a consignment agreement (see 6 below). Rather, the distributor is BCB's customer.

BCB determines that its performance obligation for the sale of product to the distributor is satisfied at a point in time. BCB considers the indicators of the transfer of control and concludes that control transfers to the distributor when the product is delivered to the distributor. At this point in time, BCB has a present right to payment and the distributor has legal title and physical possession of the product, as well as the risks and rewards of ownership. BCB concludes customer acceptance is a formality as BCB can objectively determine that the goods meet the agreed-upon specifications before shipment to the distributor.

Alternatively, if BCB sold the product to the distributor on consignment or determined that the end-consumer was its customer, the distributor was not obligated to pay for the product until it was sold to the end-consumer and BCB had the ability to require the return of any unsold product or the distributor had an unlimited amount of time to return any unsold products, then BCB may have concluded that control of the product would not transfer until it is sold to the end-consumer. Therefore, BCB would not recognise revenue until the product was sold to the end-consumer.

4.1 Effect of shipping terms when an entity has transferred control of a good to a customer

Under the standard, an entity recognises revenue only when it satisfies an identified performance obligation by transferring a promised good or service to a customer. While shipping terms may provide information about when legal title to a good transfers to the customer, they are not determinative when evaluating the point in time at which the customer obtains control of the promised asset. Entities must consider all relevant facts and circumstances to determine whether control has transferred.

For example, when the shipping terms are free on board (FOB), entities need to carefully consider whether the customer or the entity has the ability to control the goods during the shipment period. Furthermore, if the entity has the legal or constructive obligation to replace goods that are lost or damaged in transit, it needs to evaluate whether that obligation influences the customer's ability to direct the use, and obtain substantially all of the remaining benefits from the goods. A selling entity's historical practices also need to be considered when evaluating whether control of a good has transferred to a customer because the entity's practices may override the contractual terms of the arrangement.

Contractually specified shipping terms may vary depending on factors such as the mode of transport (e.g. by sea, inland waterway, road, air) and whether the goods are shipped locally or internationally. A selling entity may utilise International Commerce Terms (Incoterms®) to clarify when delivery occurs. Incoterms® are a series of pre-defined commercial terms published by the International Chamber of Commerce (ICC) relating to international commercial law. For example, 'EXW' or 'Ex Works' in Incoterms® 2010 means that the selling entity 'delivers' when it places the goods at the disposal of the customer, either at the seller's premises or at another named location (e.g. a factory, warehouse). The selling entity is not required to load the goods on any collecting vehicle, nor does it need to clear the goods for export (if applicable, see further discussion on Ex Works at 7 below). The Incoterm FOB means 'the seller delivers the goods on board the vessel nominated by the buyer at the named port of shipment or procures the goods already so delivered. The risk of loss of or damage to the goods passes when the goods are on board the vessel, and the buyer bears all costs from that moment onwards'.[26]

4.2 Customer acceptance

When determining whether the customer has obtained control of the goods or services, an entity must consider any customer acceptance clauses that require the customer to approve the goods or services before it is obliged to pay for them. If a customer does not accept the goods or services, the entity may not be entitled to consideration, may be required to take remedial action or may be required to take back the delivered good.

The standard states that a customer's acceptance of an asset may indicate that the customer has obtained control of the asset. Customer acceptance clauses allow a customer to cancel a contract or require an entity to take remedial action if a good or service does not meet agreed-upon specifications. As such, an entity needs to consider such clauses when evaluating when a customer obtains control of a good or service. [IFRS 15.B83].

If an entity can objectively determine that control of a good or service has been transferred to the customer in accordance with the agreed-upon specifications in the contract, then customer acceptance is a formality that would not affect the entity's determination of when the customer has obtained control of the good or service. The standard gives the example of a clause that is based on meeting specified size and weight characteristics. In that situation, an entity would be able to determine whether those criteria have been met before receiving confirmation of the customer's acceptance. The entity's experience with contracts for similar goods or services may provide evidence that a good or service provided to the customer is in accordance with the agreed-upon specifications in the contract. If revenue is recognised before customer acceptance, the entity still needs to consider whether there are any remaining performance obligations (e.g. installation of equipment) and evaluate whether to account for them separately. *[IFRS 15.B84].*

Conversely, if an entity cannot objectively determine that the good or service provided to the customer is in accordance with the agreed-upon specifications in the contract, it would not be able to conclude that the customer has obtained control until the entity receives the customer's acceptance. In that circumstance, the entity cannot determine that the customer has the ability to direct the use of, and obtain substantially all of the remaining benefits from, the good or service. *[IFRS 15.B85].*

If an entity delivers products to a customer for trial or evaluation purposes and the customer is not committed to pay any consideration until the trial period lapses, the standard clarifies that control of the product is not transferred to the customer until either the customer accepts the product or the trial period lapses. *[IFRS 15.B86].*

Some acceptance provisions may be straightforward, giving a customer the ability to accept or reject the transferred products based on objective criteria specified in the contract (e.g. the goods function at a specified speed). Other acceptance clauses may be subjective or may appear in parts of the contract that do not typically address acceptance matters, such as warranty provisions or indemnification clauses. Professional judgement may be required to determine the effect on revenue recognition of the latter types of acceptance clauses.

Acceptance criteria that an entity cannot objectively evaluate against the agreed-upon specifications in the contract preclude an entity from concluding that a customer has obtained control of a good or service until formal customer sign-off is obtained or the acceptance provisions lapse. However, the entity would consider its experience with other contracts for similar goods or services because that experience may provide evidence about whether the entity is able to objectively determine that a good or service provided to the customer is in accordance with the agreed-upon specifications in the contract. We believe one or more of the following would represent circumstances in which the entity may not be able to objectively evaluate the acceptance criteria.

- The acceptance provisions are unusual or 'non-standard'. Indicators of 'non-standard' acceptance terms are:
  - the duration of the acceptance period is longer than in contracts for similar goods or services;
  - the majority of the entity's contracts lack similar acceptance terms; and
  - the contract contains explicit customer-specified requirements that must be met prior to acceptance.
- The contract contains a requirement for explicit notification of acceptance (not just deemed acceptance). Explicit notification requirements may indicate that the criteria with which the customer is assessing compliance are not objective. In addition, such explicit notification clauses may limit the time period within which the customer can reject transferred products and may require the customer to provide, in writing, the reasons for the rejection of the products by the end of a specified period. When such clauses exist, acceptance can be deemed to have

occurred at the end of the specified time period if notification of rejection has not been received from the customer, as long as the customer has not indicated it will reject the products.

In determining whether compliance with the criteria for acceptance can be objectively assessed (and acceptance is only a formality), the following should be considered:

- whether the acceptance terms are standard in arrangements entered into by the entity; and
- whether the acceptance is based on the transferred product performing to standard, published, specifications and whether the entity can demonstrate that it has an established history of objectively determining that the product functions in accordance with those specifications.

As discussed above, customer acceptance should not be deemed a formality if the acceptance terms are unusual or non-standard. If a contract contains acceptance provisions that are based on customer-specified criteria, it may be difficult for the entity to objectively assess compliance with the criteria and the entity may not be able to recognise revenue prior to obtaining evidence of customer acceptance. However, determining that the acceptance criteria have been met (and, therefore, acceptance is merely a formality) may be appropriate if the entity can demonstrate that its product meets all of the customer's acceptance specifications by replicating, before shipment, those conditions under which the customer intends to use the product.

If it is reasonable to expect that the product's performance (once it has been installed and is operating at the customer's facility) will be different from the performance when it was tested prior to shipment, this acceptance provision will not have been met. The entity, therefore, would not be able to conclude that the customer has obtained control until customer acceptance occurs. Factors indicating that specifications cannot be tested effectively prior to shipment include:

- the customer has unique equipment, software or environmental conditions that can reasonably be expected to make performance in that customer's environment different from testing performed by the entity. If the contract includes customer acceptance criteria or specifications that cannot be effectively tested before delivery or installation at the customer's site, revenue recognition would be deferred until it can be demonstrated that the criteria are met;
- the products that are transferred are highly complex; and
- the entity has a limited history of testing products prior to control transferring to the customer or a limited history of having customers accept products that it has previously tested.

Determining when a customer obtains control of an asset in a contract with customer-specified acceptance criteria requires the use of professional judgement and depends on the weight of the evidence in the particular circumstances. The conclusion could change based on an analysis of an individual factor, such as the complexity of the equipment, the nature of the interface with the customer's environment, the extent of the entity's experience with this type of transaction or a particular clause in the agreement. An entity may need to discuss the situation with knowledgeable project managers or engineers in making such an assessment.

In addition, each contract containing customer-specified acceptance criteria may require a separate compliance assessment of whether the acceptance provisions have been met prior to confirmation of the customer's acceptance. That is, since different customers may specify different acceptance criteria, an entity may not be able to make one compliance assessment that applies to all contracts because of the variations in contractual terms and customer environments.

Even if a contract includes a standard acceptance clause, if the clause relates to a new product or one that has only been sold on a limited basis previously, an entity may be required to initially defer revenue recognition for the product until it establishes a history of successfully obtaining acceptance.

Paragraph B86 of IFRS 15 states that, if an entity delivers products to a customer for trial or evaluation purposes and the customer is not committed to pay any consideration until the trial period lapses, control of the product is not transferred to the customer until either the customer accepts the product or the trial period lapses. See further discussion of 'free' trial periods in Chapter 28 at 2.1.1.B, including when such arrangements may meet the criteria to be considered a contract within the scope of the model in IFRS 15.

5 REPURCHASE AGREEMENTS

Some agreements include repurchase provisions, either as part of a sales contract or as a separate contract that relates to the goods in the original agreement or similar goods. These provisions affect how an entity applies the requirements on control to affected transactions. That is, when evaluating whether a customer obtains control of an asset, an entity shall consider any agreement to repurchase the asset. *[IFRS 15.34]*.

The standard clarifies the types of arrangements that qualify as repurchase agreements. It defines a repurchase agreement as 'a contract in which an entity sells an asset and also promises or has the option (either in the same contract or in another contract) to repurchase the asset. The repurchased asset may be the asset that was originally sold to the customer, an asset that is substantially the same as that asset, or another asset of which the asset that was originally sold is a component'. *[IFRS 15.B64]*.

The standard states that repurchase agreements generally come in three forms: *[IFRS 15.B65]*

- an entity's obligation to repurchase the asset (a forward);
- an entity's right to repurchase the asset (a call option); and
- an entity's obligation to repurchase the asset at the customer's request (a put option).

In order for an obligation or right to purchase an asset to be accounted for as a repurchase agreement under IFRS 15, it needs to exist at contract inception, either as a part of the same contract or in another contract. The IASB clarified that an entity's subsequent decision to repurchase an asset (after transferring control of that asset to a customer) without reference to any pre-existing contractual right, would not be accounted for as a repurchase agreement under the standard. That is, the customer is not obliged to resell that good to the entity as a result of the initial contract. Therefore, any subsequent decision to repurchase the asset does not affect the customer's ability to control the asset upon initial transfer. However, in cases in which an entity decides to repurchase a good after transferring control of the good to a customer, the Board observed that the entity should carefully consider whether the customer obtained control in the initial transaction. Furthermore, it may need to consider the application guidance on principal versus agent considerations (see Chapter 28 at 3.4). *[IFRS 15.BC423]*.

5.1 Forward or call option held by the entity

When an entity has the obligation or right to repurchase an asset (i.e. a forward or a call option), the standard indicates that the customer has not obtained control of the asset. That is, the customer is limited in its ability to direct the use of, and obtain substantially all of the remaining benefits from, the asset even though the customer may have physical possession of the asset.

Consequently, the standard requires that an entity account for a transaction including a forward or a call option based on the relationship between the repurchase price and the original selling price. The standard indicates that if the entity has the right or obligation to repurchase the asset at a price less than the original sales price (taking into consideration the effects of the time value of money), the entity would account for the transaction as a lease in accordance with IFRS 16 – *Leases*, unless the contract is part of a sale and leaseback transaction. If the entity has the right or obligation to repurchase the asset at a price equal to or greater than the original sales price (considering the effects of the time value of money) or if the contract is part of a sale and leaseback transaction, the entity would account for the contract as a financing arrangement in accordance with paragraph B68 of IFRS 15. *[IFRS 15.B66-B67]*.

The following figure depicts this application guidance for transactions that are not sale and leaseback transaction.

Figure 30.2:   Forward or call options

Repurchase price	<	Original selling price	=	Lease
Repurchase price	≥	Original selling price	=	Financing

Under the standard, a transaction in which a seller has an option to repurchase the product is treated as a lease or a financing arrangement (i.e. not a sale). This is because the customer does not have control of the product and is constrained in its ability to direct the use of and obtain substantially all of the remaining benefits from the good. The Board noted in the Basis for Conclusions that entities would not need to consider the likelihood that a call option will be exercised in determining the accounting for the repurchase provision. However, the Board also stated that non-substantive call options are ignored and would not affect when a customer obtains control of an asset. *[IFRS 15.BC427]*. See also 5.1.1 below for how an entity might consider conditional call options and an example of a conditional call option that may qualify to be treated as a sale.

In the Basis for Conclusions, the Board also observed that 'theoretically, a customer is not constrained in its ability to direct the use of and obtain substantially all of the benefits from, the asset if an entity agrees to repurchase, at the prevailing market price, an asset from the customer that is substantially the same and is readily available in the marketplace.' *[IFRS 15.BC425]*. That is, in such a situation, a customer could sell the original asset (thereby exhibiting control over it) and then re-obtain a similar asset in the market place prior to the asset being repurchased by the entity.

If a transaction is considered a financing arrangement under the IFRS 15, in accordance with paragraph B68 of IFRS 15, the selling entity continues to recognise the asset. In addition, it records a financial liability for the consideration received from the customer. The difference between the consideration received from the customer and the consideration subsequently paid to the customer (upon repurchasing the asset) represents the interest and holding costs (as applicable) that are recognised over the term of the financing arrangement. If the option lapses unexercised, the entity derecognises the liability and recognises revenue at that time. *[IFRS 15.B68-B69]*.

Also note that paragraph B66(a) of IFRS 15 specifies that, if the contract is part of a sale and leaseback transaction, the entity continues to recognise the asset. Furthermore, the entity recognises a financial liability for any consideration received from the customer to which IFRS 9 – *Financial Instruments* – would apply.

Entities may find the requirements challenging to apply in practice as the standard treats all forwards and call options the same way and does not consider the likelihood that they will be exercised. In addition, since the standard provides lease requirements, it is important for entities to understand the interaction between the lease and revenue standards.

The standard provides the following example of a call option. *[IFRS 15.IE315-IE318]*.

Example 30.14: Repurchase agreements (call option)

An entity enters into a contract with a customer for the sale of a tangible asset on 1 January 20X7 for $1 million.

Case A – Call option: financing

The contract includes a call option that gives the entity the right to repurchase the asset for $1.1 million on or before 31 December 20X7.

Control of the asset does not transfer to the customer on 1 January 20X7 because the entity has a right to repurchase the asset and therefore the customer is limited in its ability to direct the use of, and obtain substantially all of the remaining benefits from, the asset. Consequently, in accordance with paragraph B66(b) of IFRS 15, the entity accounts for the transaction as a financing arrangement, because the exercise price is more than the original selling price. In accordance with paragraph B68 of IFRS 15, the entity does not derecognise the asset and instead recognises the cash received as a financial liability. The entity also recognises interest expense for the difference between the exercise price ($1.1 million) and the cash received ($1 million), which increases the liability.

On 31 December 20X7, the option lapses unexercised; therefore, the entity derecognises the liability and recognises revenue of $1.1 million.

5.1.1 Conditional call options to repurchase an asset

The standard does not specifically address conditional call options. We believe that if the entity controls the outcome of the condition that causes the call option to become active, then the presence of the call option indicates that control has not transferred because the customer is limited in its ability to direct the use of and obtain substantially all of the remaining benefits from the asset. That is, the entity would be required to treat the contract as a lease or a financing arrangement as required by paragraph B66 of IFRS 15.

We also believe that if the entity does not control the condition that causes the call option to become active, then it would be acceptable for the entity to apply judgement to determine whether the call option limits the customer's ability to direct the use of, and obtain substantially all of the remaining benefits from, the asset. For example, if neither the entity nor the customer controls the outcome of the contingency, the entity could evaluate the nature of the contingency, together with the likelihood of the contingency becoming active, to determine whether it limits the customer's ability to obtain control of the asset.

Furthermore, we believe that if the customer controls the outcome of the contingency, then the conditional call option may not prevent the customer from obtaining control of the asset if the customer can direct the use of, and obtain substantially all the remaining benefits from, the asset. The application guidance in paragraphs B70-B76 of IFRS 15 may be helpful for an entity to consider when determining whether the customer obtains control of the asset when it controls the outcome of the contingency.

In the case of perishable products, we believe that an entity's conditional right to remove and replace expired goods does not necessarily constrain the customer's ability to direct the use of and obtain substantially all of the remaining benefits from the products. That is, the entity is not able to remove and replace the products until they expire. Furthermore, the customer has control of the products over their entire useful life. Consequently, it may be reasonable for an entity to conclude that control of the initial product does transfer to the customer in this situation and that an entity could consider this right to be a form of a right of return (see Chapter 29 at 2.4).

5.2 Put option held by the customer

IFRS 15 indicates that if the customer has the ability to require an entity to repurchase an asset (i.e. a put option) at a price lower than its original selling price, the entity considers, at contract inception, whether the customer has a significant economic incentive to exercise that right. *[IFRS 15.B70]*. That is, this determination influences whether the customer truly has control over the asset received.

The determination of whether an entity has a significant economic incentive to exercise its right determines whether the arrangement is treated as a lease or a sale with the right of return (discussed in Chapter 29 at 2.4). An entity must consider all relevant facts and circumstances to determine whether a customer has a significant economic incentive to exercise its right, including the relationship between the repurchase price to the expected market value (taking into consideration the effects of the time value of money) of the asset at the date of repurchase and the amount of time until the right expires. The standard notes that if the repurchase price is expected to significantly exceed the market value of the asset the customer may have a significant economic incentive to exercise the put option. *[IFRS 15.B70-B71, B75]*.

- If a customer has a significant economic incentive to exercise its right, the customer is expected to ultimately return the asset. The entity accounts for the agreement as a lease because the customer is effectively paying the entity for the right to use the asset for a period of time. *[IFRS 15.B70]*. However, one exception to this would be if the contract is part of a sale and leaseback, in which case the contract would be accounted for as a financing arrangement (financing arrangements are discussed at 5.1 above). *[IFRS 15.B73]*. If the contract is part of a sale and leaseback transaction, the entity continues to recognise the asset. Furthermore, the entity recognises a financial liability for any consideration received from the customer to which IFRS 9 would apply.
- If a customer does not have a significant economic incentive to exercise its right, the entity accounts for the agreement in a manner similar to a sale of a product with a right of return. *[IFRS 15.B72]*.

The repurchase price of an asset that is equal to or greater than the original selling price, but less than or equal to the expected market value of the asset, must also be accounted for as a sale of a product with a right of return, if the customer does not have a significant economic incentive to exercise its right. *[IFRS 15.B74]*. See Chapter 29 at 2.4 for a discussion on sales with a right of return.

If the customer has the ability to require an entity to repurchase the asset at a price equal to, or more than, the original selling price and the repurchase price is more than the expected market value of the asset, the contract is in effect a financing arrangement.

If the option lapses unexercised, an entity derecognises the liability and recognises revenue. *[IFRS 15.B76]*.

The following figure depicts this application guidance.

Figure 30.3: Put options held by the customer

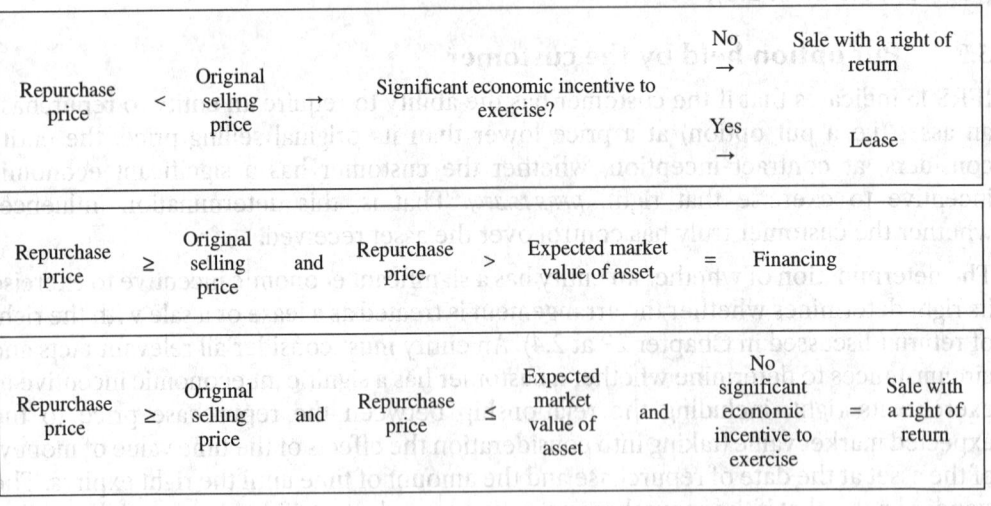

IFRS 15 does not provide any guidance on determining whether 'a significant economic incentive' exists and judgement may be required to make this determination.

The standard provides the following example of a put option. *[IFRS 15.IE315, IE319-IE321].*

Example 30.15: Repurchase agreements (put option)

An entity enters into a contract with a customer for the sale of a tangible asset on 1 January 20X7 for £1 million.

Case B – Put option: lease

Instead of having a call option, the contract includes a put option that obliges the entity to repurchase the asset at the customer's request for £900,000 on or before 31 December 20X7. The market value is expected to be £750,000 on 31 December 20X7.

At the inception of the contract, the entity assesses whether the customer has a significant economic incentive to exercise the put option, to determine the accounting for the transfer of the asset (see paragraphs B70-B76 of IFRS 15). The entity concludes that the customer has a significant economic incentive to exercise the put option because the repurchase price significantly exceeds the expected market value of the asset at the date of repurchase. The entity determines there are no other relevant factors to consider when assessing whether the customer has a significant economic incentive to exercise the put option. Consequently, the entity concludes that control of the asset does not transfer to the customer, because the customer is limited in its ability to direct the use of, and obtain substantially all of the remaining benefits from, the asset.

In accordance with paragraphs B70-B71 of IFRS 15, the entity accounts for the transaction as a lease in accordance with IFRS 16.

5.3 Sales with residual value guarantees

An entity that sells equipment may use a sales incentive programme under which it guarantees that the customer will receive a minimum resale amount when it disposes of the equipment (i.e. a residual value guarantee). If the customer holds a put option and has a significant economic incentive to exercise, the customer is effectively restricted in its ability to consume, modify or sell the asset. In contrast, when the entity guarantees that the customer will receive a minimum amount of sales proceeds, the customer is not constrained in its ability to direct the use of, and obtain substantially all of the benefits from, the asset. Accordingly, the Board decided that it was not necessary to expand the application guidance on repurchase agreements to consider guaranteed amounts of resale. *[IFRS 15.BC427].*

Therefore, it is important for an entity to review all its contracts and make sure that the residual value guarantee is not accomplished through a repurchase provision, such as a put within the contract (e.g. the customer has the right to require the entity to repurchase equipment two years after the date of purchase at 85% of the original purchase price). If a put option is present, the entity would have to use the application guidance in the standard discussed in 5.2 above to determine whether the existence of the put option precludes the customer from obtaining control of the acquired item. In such circumstances, the entity would determine whether the customer has a significant economic incentive to exercise the put. If the entity concludes that there is no significant economic incentive, the transaction would be accounted for as a sale with a right of return. Alternatively, if the entity concludes there is a significant economic incentive for the customer to exercise its right, the transaction would be accounted for as a lease.

However, assume the transaction includes a residual value guarantee in which no put option is present. If the entity guarantees that it will compensate the customer (or 'make whole') on a qualifying future sale if the customer receives less than 85% of the initial sale price, the application guidance on repurchase agreements in IFRS 15 would not apply. That is because the entity is not repurchasing the asset.

In such situations, judgement is needed to determine the appropriate accounting treatment, which will depend on the specific facts and circumstances. In some cases, an entity may need to consider the requirements of other IFRSs to appropriately account for the residual value guarantee. In other situations, IFRS 15 may apply to the entire transaction. If IFRS 15 applies, an entity would need to assess whether the guarantee affects control of the asset transferring, which will depend on the promise to the customer. In some cases, it may not affect the transfer of control. In the Basis for Conclusions, the Board noted that 'when the entity guarantees that the customer will receive a minimum amount of sales proceeds, the customer is not constrained in its ability to direct the use of, and obtain substantially all of the benefits from, the asset.' *[IFRS 15.BC431]*. However, while a residual value guarantee may not affect the transfer of control, an entity would need to consider whether it affects the transaction price (see Chapter 29 at 2). While the economics of a repurchase agreement and a residual value guarantee may be similar, the accounting could be quite different.

6 CONSIGNMENT ARRANGEMENTS

Entities frequently deliver inventory on a consignment basis to other parties (e.g. distributor, dealer). A consignment sale is one in which physical delivery of a product to a counterparty has occurred, but the counterparty is not required to pay until the product is either resold to an end customer or used by the counterparty. Under such arrangements, the seller (or consignor) retains the legal title to the merchandise and the counterparty (or consignee) acts as a selling agent. The consignee earns a commission on the products that have been sold and periodically remits the cash from those sales, net of the commission it has earned, to the consignor. In addition, consigned products that are not sold or used generally can be returned to the consignor. By shipping on a consignment basis, consignors are able to better market products by moving them closer to the end-customer. However, they do so without selling the goods to the intermediary (consignee). *[IFRS 15.B77]*.

The Board included indicators that an arrangement is a consignment arrangement include, but are not limited to, the following: *[IFRS 15.B78]*

'(a) the product is controlled by the entity until a specified event occurs, such as the sale of the product to a customer of the dealer or until a specified period expires;

(b) the entity is able to require the return of the product or transfer the product to a third party (such as another dealer); and

(c) the dealer does not have an unconditional obligation to pay for the product (although it might be required to pay a deposit).'

Entities entering into a consignment arrangement need to determine the nature of the performance obligation (i.e. whether the obligation is to transfer the product to the consignee or to transfer the product to the end-customer). This determination would be based on whether control of the product passes to the consignee. Typically, a consignor does not relinquish control of the consigned product until the product is sold to the end-customer or, in some cases, when a specified period expires. Consignees commonly do not have any obligation to pay for the product, other than to pay the consignor the agreed-upon portion of the sale price once the consignee sells the product to a third party. As a result, for consignment arrangements, revenue generally would not be recognised when the products are delivered to the consignee because control has not transferred (i.e. the performance obligation to deliver goods to the end-customer has not yet been satisfied). *[IFRS 15.B77].*

While some transactions are clearly identified as consignment arrangements, there are other, less transparent transactions, in which the seller has retained control of the goods, despite no longer having physical possession. Such arrangements may include the shipment of products to distributors that are not required (either explicitly or implicitly), or do not have the wherewithal, to pay for the product until it is sold to the end-customer. Judgement is necessary in assessing whether the substance of a transaction is a consignment arrangement. The identification of such arrangements often requires a careful analysis of the facts and circumstances of the transaction, as well as an understanding of the rights and obligations of the parties and the seller's customary business practices in such arrangements. While not required by IFRS 15 or IAS 2 – *Inventories*, we would encourage entities to separately disclose the amount of their consigned inventory, if material.

7   BILL-AND-HOLD ARRANGEMENTS

In some sales transactions, the selling entity fulfils its obligations and bills the customer for the work performed, but does not ship the goods until a later date. These transactions, often called bill-and-hold transactions, are usually designed this way at the request of the purchaser for a number of reasons, including a lack of storage capacity or its inability to use the goods until a later date. Whereas in a consignment sale (discussed in 6 above), physical delivery has occurred, but control of the goods has not transferred to the customer, the opposite may be true in a bill-and-hold transaction. For example, a customer may request an entity to enter into such a contract because of the customer's lack of available space for the product or because of delays in the customer's production schedules. *[IFRS 15.B79].*

An entity determines when it has satisfied its performance obligation to transfer a product by evaluating when a customer obtains control of that product. For some contracts, control transfers either when the product is delivered to the customer's site or when the product is shipped, depending on the terms of the contract (including delivery and shipping terms). However, for some contracts, a customer may obtain control of a product even though that product remains in an entity's physical possession. In that case, the customer has the ability to direct the use of, and obtain substantially all of the remaining benefits from, the product even though it has decided not to exercise its right to take physical possession of that product. Consequently, the entity does not control the product. Instead, the entity provides custodial services to the customer over the customer's asset. *[IFRS 15.B80].*

In addition to applying the general requirements for assessing whether control has transferred, for a customer to have obtained control of a product in a bill-and-hold arrangement, all of the following criteria must be met: *[IFRS 15.B81]*

(a) the reason for the bill-and-hold arrangement must be substantive (e.g. the customer has requested the arrangement);

(b) the product must be identified separately as belonging to the customer;

(c) the product currently must be ready for physical transfer to the customer; and

(d) the entity cannot have the ability to use the product or to direct it to another customer.

If an entity recognises revenue for the sale of a product on a bill-and-hold basis, the standard requires that it consider whether it has remaining performance obligations (e.g. for custodial services) to which it is required to allocate a portion of the transaction price. *[IFRS 15.B82]*.

When evaluating whether revenue recognition is appropriate for a bill-and-hold transaction, an entity must evaluate the application guidance in both paragraphs 38 of IFRS 15 (to determine whether control has been transferred to the customer – see 4 above) and B81 of IFRS 15 (to determine whether all four bill-and-hold criteria are met). That is, in addition to paragraph 38 of IFRS 15, the criteria that must be met for bill-and-hold transaction are:

- *the reason for the bill-and-hold arrangement must be substantive (e.g. the customer has requested the arrangement)*. A bill-and-hold transaction initiated by the selling entity typically indicates that a bill-and-hold arrangement is not substantive. We would generally expect the customer to request such an arrangement and the selling entity would need to evaluate the reasons for the request to determine whether the customer has a substantive business purpose. Judgement is required when assessing this criterion. For example, a customer with an established buying history that places an order in excess of its normal volume and requests that the entity retains the product needs to be evaluated carefully because the request may not appear to have a substantive business purpose;

- *the product must be identified separately as belonging to the customer*. Even if the entity's inventory is homogenous, the customer's product must be segregated from the entity's ongoing fulfilment operations;

- *the product currently must be ready for physical transfer to the customer*. In any revenue transaction recognised at a point in time, revenue is recognised when an entity has satisfied its performance obligation to transfer control of the product to the customer. If an entity has remaining costs or effort to develop, manufacture or refine the product, the entity may not have satisfied its performance obligation. This criterion does not include the actual costs to deliver a product, which would be normal and customary in most revenue transactions, or if the entity identifies a separate performance obligation for custodial services, as discussed below; and

- *the entity cannot have the ability to use the product or to direct it to another customer*. If the entity has the ability to freely substitute goods to fill other orders, control of the goods has not passed to the buyer. That is, the entity has retained the right to use the customer's product in a manner that best suits the entity.

If an entity concludes that it can recognise revenue for a bill-and-hold transaction, paragraph B82 of IFRS 15 states that the entity needs to further consider whether it is also providing custodial services for the customer that would be identified as a separate performance obligation in the contract.

As discussed in 4.1 above, certain entities may use Ex Works from Incoterms® 2010 in contracts with customers. Under an Ex Works arrangement, the entity's responsibility is to make ordered goods available to the customer at the entity's premises or another named location. The customer is responsible for arranging, and paying for, shipment of the goods to the desired location and bears all of the risks related to them once they are made available.

We believe that all Ex Works arrangements need to be evaluated using the bill-and-hold criteria discussed above to determine whether revenue recognition is appropriate prior to shipment.

The standard provides the following example to illustrate the application guidance on bill-and-hold arrangements. *[IFRS 15.IE323-IE327]*.

Example 30.16: Bill-and-hold arrangement

An entity enters into a contract with a customer on 1 January 20X8 for the sale of a machine and spare parts. The manufacturing lead time for the machine and spare parts is two years.

Upon completion of manufacturing, the entity demonstrates that the machine and spare parts meet the agreed-upon specifications in the contract. The promises to transfer the machine and spare parts are distinct and result in two performance obligations that each will be satisfied at a point in time. On 31 December 20X9, the customer pays for the machine and spare parts, but only takes physical possession of the machine. Although the customer inspects and accepts the spare parts, the customer requests that the spare parts be stored at the entity's warehouse because of its close proximity to the customer's factory. The customer has legal title to the spare parts and the parts can be identified as belonging to the customer. Furthermore, the entity stores the spare parts in a separate section of its warehouse and the parts are ready for immediate shipment at the customer's request. The entity expects to hold the spare parts for two to four years and the entity does not have the ability to use the spare parts or direct them to another customer.

The entity identifies the promise to provide custodial services as a performance obligation because it is a service provided to the customer and it is distinct from the machine and spare parts. Consequently, the entity accounts for three performance obligations in the contract (the promises to provide the machine, the spare parts and the custodial services). The transaction price is allocated to the three performance obligations and revenue is recognised when (or as) control transfers to the customer.

Control of the machine transfers to the customer on 31 December 20X9 when the customer takes physical possession. The entity assesses the indicators in paragraph 38 of IFRS 15 to determine the point in time at which control of the spare parts transfers to the customer, noting that the entity has received payment, the customer has legal title to the spare parts and the customer has inspected and accepted the spare parts. In addition, the entity concludes that all of the criteria in paragraph B81 of IFRS 15 are met, which is necessary for the entity to recognise revenue in a bill-and-hold arrangement. The entity recognises revenue for the spare parts on 31 December 20X9 when control transfers to the customer.

The performance obligation to provide custodial services is satisfied over time as the services are provided. The entity considers whether the payment terms include a significant financing component in accordance with paragraphs 60-65 of IFRS 15.

8 RECOGNISING REVENUE FOR LICENCES OF INTELLECTUAL PROPERTY

IFRS 15 provides application guidance for recognising of revenue from licences of intellectual property that differs in some respects from the general requirements for other promised goods or services. We discuss licensing in detail in Chapter 31 at 2.

9 RECOGNISING REVENUE WHEN A RIGHT OF RETURN EXISTS

As discussed in Chapter 28 at 3.7, a right of return does not represent a separate performance obligation. Instead, the existence of a right of return affects the transaction price and the entity must determine whether the customer will return the transferred product.

Under IFRS 15, as discussed in Chapter 29 at 2, an entity estimates the transaction price and applies the constraint to the estimated transaction price. In doing so, it considers the products expected to be returned in order to determine the amount to which the entity expects to be entitled (excluding consideration for the products expected to be returned). The entity recognises revenue based on the amounts to which the entity expects to be entitled through to the end of the return period (considering expected product returns). An entity does not recognise the portion of the revenue that is subject to the constraint until the amount is no longer constrained, which could be at the end of the return period or earlier if the entity's expectations about the products expected to be returned change prior to the end of the return period. The entity recognises the amount received or receivable that is expected to be returned as a refund liability, representing its obligation to return the customer's consideration. An entity also updates its estimates at the end of each reporting period. See Chapter 28 at 3.7 and Chapter 29 at 2.4 for further discussion on this topic.

10 RECOGNISING REVENUE FOR CUSTOMER OPTIONS FOR ADDITIONAL GOODS OR SERVICES

As discussed in Chapter 28 at 3.6, when an entity grants a customer the option to acquire additional goods or services, that option is a separate performance obligation if it provides a material right to the customer that the customer would not receive without entering into the contract (e.g. a discount that exceeds the range of discounts typically given for those goods or services to that class of customer in that geographical area or market). If the option provides a material right to the customer, the customer has, in effect, paid the entity in advance for future goods or services. IFRS 15 requires the entity to allocate a portion of the transaction price to the material right at contract inception (see Chapter 29 at 3.1.5). The revenue allocated to the material right is recognised when (or as) the option is exercised (and the underlying future goods or services are transferred) or when the option expires.

In contrast, if a customer option is not deemed to be a material right and is instead a marketing offer, the entity does not account for the option and waits to account for the underlying goods or services until those subsequent purchases occur.

See Chapter 28 at 3.6.1.J for discussion on how an entity would account for the exercise of a material right.

11 BREAKAGE AND PREPAYMENTS FOR FUTURE GOODS OR SERVICES

In certain industries, an entity collects non-refundable payments from its customers for goods or services that the customer has a right to receive in the future. However, a customer may ultimately leave that right unexercised (often referred to as 'breakage'). *[IFRS 15.B45]*. Retailers, for example, frequently sell gift cards that may not be partially redeemed or completely redeemed and airlines sometimes sell non-refundable tickets to passengers who allow the tickets to expire unused.

Under paragraph B44 of IFRS 15, when an entity receives consideration that is attributable to a customer's unexercised rights, the entity recognises a contract liability equal to the full amount prepaid by the customer for the performance obligation to transfer, or to stand ready to transfer, goods or services in the future. As discussed further below, an entity derecognises that contract liability (and recognises revenue) when it transfers those goods or services and, therefore, satisfies its performance obligation. The Board noted that this application guidance requires the same pattern of revenue recognition as the requirements for customer options (see Chapter 29 at 3.1.5). *[IFRS 15.BC398]*.

However, since entities may not be required by customers to fully satisfy their performance obligations, paragraph B46 of IFRS 15 requires that when an entity expects to be entitled to a breakage amount, the expected breakage would be recognised as revenue in proportion to the pattern of rights exercised by the customer. If an entity does not expect to be entitled to a breakage amount, it would not recognise any breakage amounts as revenue until the likelihood of the customer exercising its right becomes remote. *[IFRS 15.B46, BC398]*.

When estimating any breakage amount, an entity has to consider the constraint on variable consideration, as discussed in Chapter 29 at 2.2.3. *[IFRS 15.B46]*. That is, if it is highly probable that a significant revenue reversal would occur for any estimated breakage amounts, an entity would not recognise those amounts until the breakage amounts are no longer constrained.

Entities cannot recognise estimated breakage as revenue immediately upon receipt of prepayment from the customer. The Board noted that it rejected such an approach because the entity has not performed under the contract. That is, recognising revenue would not be a faithful depiction of the entity's performance and would understate its obligation to stand ready to provide future goods or services. *[IFRS 15.BC400]*. This would be the case even if an entity has historical evidence to support the view that no further performance will be required for some portion of the customer contract(s).

Furthermore, in accordance with paragraph B47 of IFRS 15, regardless of whether an entity can demonstrate the ability to reliably estimate breakage, entities would not estimate or recognise any amounts attributable to a customer's unexercised rights in income (e.g. an unused gift card balance) if the amounts are required to be remitted to another party (e.g. the government). Such an amount is recognised as a liability.

Consider the following example to illustrate how an entity would apply the above application guidance to the sale of a gift card that is within the scope of IFRS 15 (see Chapter 27 at 3.5.1.I for further discussion):

Example 30.17: Accounting for the sale of a gift card

Entity A sells a €500 non-refundable gift card that can be redeemed at any of its retail locations. Any unused balance is not subject to laws that require from the entity to remit the payment to another party. When the gift card is sold, Entity A recognises a contract liability of €500 (i.e. the full amount that was prepaid by the customer). No breakage is recognised as revenue upon sale of the gift card.

Scenario A – Entity expects to be entitled to a breakage amount

Based on historical redemption rates, Entity A expects 90% of the gift card (or €450) to be redeemed. That is, Entity A expects breakage of 10% (or €50). Upon its first use, the customer redeems €225 of the gift card. That is, 50% of the expected redemption has occurred (i.e. €225 redemption / €450 total expected redemption). Upon this redemption, Entity A recognises revenue and reduces the contract liability by €250. This is equal to €225 for the transfer of goods or services purchased by the customer, as well as breakage of €25 (50% redemption × €50 breakage estimate) that is recognised in proportion to the exercise of the customer's rights. Similar accounting would occur for future redemptions.

Scenario B – Entity does not expect to be entitled to a breakage amount

Based on historical redemption experiences that customers fully redeem similar gift cards (or possibly the lack of historical experience due to a new gift card programme that means Entity A is unable to estimate the redemption rates), Entity A does not expect to be entitled to a breakage amount. Upon its first use of the gift card, the customer redeems €225. Entity A recognises revenue and reduces the contract liability by the same amount as the redemption (or €225). That is, no additional amounts are recognised for breakage. Similar accounting would occur for future redemptions.

If no further redemptions occur, Entity A recognises the remaining gift card balance (or €275) as revenue (and reduces the contract liability by the same amount) when the likelihood of the customer exercising its remaining rights becomes remote.

As discussed above, the application guidance on breakage requires that an entity recognise a liability for the full amount of the prepayment. It would then recognise breakage on that liability proportionate to the pattern of rights exercised by the customer. If the prepayment element (e.g. the sale of a gift card, loyalty points) is part of a multiple-element arrangement, an entity needs to allocate the transaction price between the identified performance obligations. As a result, the deferred revenue associated with this element would be less than the 'prepaid' amount received for the unsatisfied performance obligations.

The following example depicts the sale of goods with loyalty points. In this example, the amount allocated to the points (i.e. the 'prepaid' element) is less than the stand-alone selling price of those points because of the allocation of the transaction price among the two performance obligations. *[IFRS 15.IE267-IE270]*.

Example 30.18: Customer loyalty programme

An entity has a customer loyalty programme that rewards a customer with one customer loyalty point for every £10 of purchases. Each point is redeemable for a £1 discount on any future purchases of the entity's products. During a reporting period, customers purchase products for £100,000 and earn 10,000 points that are redeemable for future purchases. The consideration is fixed and the stand-alone selling price of the purchased products is £100,000. The entity expects 9,500 points to be redeemed. The entity estimates a stand-alone selling price of £0.95 per point (totalling £9,500) on the basis of the likelihood of redemption in accordance with paragraph B42 of IFRS 15.

The points provide a material right to customers that they would not receive without entering into a contract. Consequently, the entity concludes that the promise to provide points to the customer is a performance obligation. The entity allocates the transaction price (£100,000) to the product and the points on a relative stand-alone selling price basis as follows:

	£	
Product	91,324	[£100,000 × (£100,000 stand-alone selling price ÷ £109,500)]
Points	8,676	[£100,000 × (£9,500 stand-alone selling price ÷ £109,500)]

At the end of the first reporting period, 4,500 points have been redeemed and the entity continues to expect 9,500 points to be redeemed in total. The entity recognises revenue for the loyalty points of £4,110 [(4,500 points ÷ 9,500 points) × £8,676] and recognises a contract liability of £4,566 (£8,676 – £4,110) for the unredeemed points at the end of the first reporting period.

At the end of the second reporting period, 8,500 points have been redeemed cumulatively. The entity updates its estimate of the points that will be redeemed and now expects that 9,700 points will be redeemed. The entity recognises revenue for the loyalty points of £3,493 {[(8,500 total points redeemed ÷ 9,700 total points expected to be redeemed) × £8,676 initial allocation] – £4,110 recognised in the first reporting period}. The contract liability balance is £1,073 (£8,676 initial allocation – £7,603 of cumulative revenue recognised).

As depicted in Example 30.18 above (i.e. paragraphs IE269-IE270 of IFRS 15), entities need to routinely refine and evaluate estimates of breakage.

Refer to Chapter 28 at 3.6.1.L for a discussion on recognising revenue for customer options for additional goods or services that represent a material right, but do not have an expiration date (i.e. whether an entity can recognise breakage for these options).

11.1 Are customers' unexercised rights (i.e. breakage) a form of variable consideration?

Although the breakage application guidance in paragraph B46 of IFRS 15 specifically refers to the constraint on variable consideration, we do not believe breakage is a form of variable consideration (see Chapter 29 at 2.2). This is because it does not affect the transaction price. Breakage is a recognition concept (Step 5) that could affect the timing of revenue recognition. It is not a measurement concept (Step 3). For example, the transaction price for a sale of a £20 gift card is fixed at £20 regardless of the expected breakage amount. The expected breakage, however, could affect the timing of revenue recognition because an entity is required under paragraph B46 of IFRS 15 to 'recognise the expected breakage amount as revenue in proportion to the pattern of rights exercised by the customer' if it expects to be entitled to a breakage amount. *[IFRS 15.B46]*.

References

1 TRG Agenda paper 43, *Determining When Control of a Commodity Transfers*, dated 13 July 2015.
2 *IFRIC Update*, March 2018.
3 TRG Agenda paper 43, *Determining When Control of a Commodity Transfers*, dated 13 July 2015.
4 *IFRIC Update*, March 2018.
5 *IFRIC Update*, March 2018.
6 FASB TRG Agenda paper 56, *Over Time Revenue Recognition*, dated 7 November 2016.
7 FASB TRG Agenda paper 60, *November 2016 Meeting – Summary of Issues Discussed and Next Steps*, dated 31 January 2017.
8 FASB TRG Agenda paper 56, *Over Time Revenue Recognition*, dated 7 November 2016.

9 FASB TRG Agenda paper 60, *November 2016 Meeting – Summary of Issues Discussed and Next Steps*, dated 31 January 2017.
10 AICPA Audit and Accounting Guide, *Revenue Recognition*, Chapter 3, *Aerospace and Defense Entities*, paras. 3.5.18-3.5.23.
11 *IFRIC Update*, March 2018.
12 *IFRIC Update*, March 2018.
13 TRG Agenda paper 40, *Practical Expedient for Measuring Progress toward Complete Satisfaction of a Performance Obligation*, dated 13 July 2015.
14 TRG Agenda paper 40, *Practical Expedient for Measuring Progress toward Complete Satisfaction of a Performance Obligation*, dated 13 July 2015.
15 TRG Agenda paper 40, *Practical Expedient for Measuring Progress toward Complete Satisfaction of a Performance Obligation*, dated 13 July 2015.
16 TRG Agenda paper 44, *July 2015 Meeting – Summary of Issues Discussed and Next Steps*, dated 9 November 2015.
17 TRG Agenda paper 16, *Stand-Ready Performance Obligations*, dated 26 January 2015 and TRG Agenda paper 25, *January 2015 Meeting – Summary of Issues Discussed and Next Steps*, dated 30 March 2015.
18 TRG Agenda paper 41, *Measuring progress when multiple goods or services are included in a single performance obligation*, dated 13 July 2015.
19 TRG Agenda paper 41, *Measuring progress when multiple goods or services are included in a single performance obligation*, dated 13 July 2015.
20 TRG Agenda paper 41, *Measuring progress when multiple goods or services are included in a single performance obligation*, dated 13 July 2015.
21 FASB TRG Agenda paper 53, *Evaluating How Control Transfers Over Time*, dated 18 April 2016.
22 TRG Agenda paper 40, *Practical Expedient for Measuring Progress toward Complete Satisfaction of a Performance Obligation*, dated 13 July 2015.
23 TRG Agenda paper 33, *Partial Satisfaction of Performance Obligations Prior to Identifying the Contract*, dated 30 March 2015.
24 TRG Agenda paper 34, *March 2015 Meeting – Summary of Issues Discussed and Next Steps*, dated 13 July 2015.
25 *IFRIC Update*, March 2018.
26 ICC website https://iccwbo.org/resources-for-business/incoterms-rules/incoterms-rules-2010/ (accessed 10 September 2019).

Chapter 31

Revenue: licences, warranties and contract costs

1 INTRODUCTION 2319
2 LICENCES OF INTELLECTUAL PROPERTY 2320
    2.1 Identifying performance obligations in a licensing arrangement 2321
        2.1.1 Licences of intellectual property that are distinct 2321
        2.1.2 Licences of intellectual property that are not distinct 2324
        2.1.3 Contractual restrictions 2324
        2.1.4 Guarantees to defend or maintain a patent 2326
        2.1.5 Application questions on identifying performance obligations in a licensing arrangement 2327
            2.1.5.A Accounting for modifications to licences of intellectual property 2327
            2.1.5.B Contracts that grant both permission for past use of intellectual property and a licence to use the intellectual property in the future 2327
    2.2 Determining the nature of the entity's promise in granting a licence 2328
        2.2.1 Applying the licensing application guidance to a single (bundled) performance obligation that includes a licence of intellectual property 2330
    2.3 Transfer of control of licensed intellectual property 2332
        2.3.1 Right to access 2333
            2.3.1.A Is a licence that provides a right to access intellectual property a series of distinct goods or services that would be accounted for as a single performance obligation? 2334
        2.3.2 Right to use 2335
        2.3.3 Use and benefit requirement 2336

2.4	Licence renewals		2336
2.5	Sales-based or usage-based royalties on licences of intellectual property		2337
	2.5.1	Recognition of royalties for a licence that provides a right to access intellectual property	2341
	2.5.2	Application questions on the sales-based or usage-based royalty recognition constraint	2343
		2.5.2.A Can the recognition constraint for sales-based or usage-based royalties be applied to royalties that are paid in consideration for sales of intellectual property (rather than just licences of intellectual property)?	2343
		2.5.2.B If a contract for a licence of intellectual property includes payments with fixed amounts (e.g. milestone payments) that are determined by reference to sales-based or usage-based thresholds, would the royalty recognition constraint need to be applied?	2343
		2.5.2.C If a contract for a licence of intellectual property includes a milestone payment based on the first commercial sale, should the royalty recognition constraint be applied?	2344
		2.5.2.D Can an entity recognise revenue for sales-based or usage-based royalties for licences of intellectual property on a lag if actual sales or usage data is not available at the end of a reporting period?	2344
		2.5.2.E Recognition of royalties with minimum guarantees promised in exchange for a licence of intellectual property that is satisfied at a point in time	2345
		2.5.2.F Recognition of royalties with minimum guarantees promised in exchange for a licence of intellectual property that is satisfied over time	2345
		2.5.2.G Application of the royalty recognition constraint for sales-based or usage-based royalties when an entity does not own the intellectual property or control the intellectual property as a principal in the arrangement	2348
		2.5.2.H Can entities recognise sales-based or usage-based royalties before the sale or usage of the intellectual property occurs if they have historical information that is highly predictive of future royalty amounts?	2349

| | | 2.5.2.I | Should an entity apply the royalty recognition constraint when the royalty is calculated on a financial metric that is not solely based on sales or usage?...2349 |

3 WARRANTIES..2349

   3.1 Determining whether a warranty is an assurance-type or service-type warranty...2350

      3.1.1 Evaluating whether a product warranty is a service-type warranty (i.e. a performance obligation) when it is not separately priced 2352

      3.1.2 How would an entity account for repairs provided outside the warranty period?...2352

      3.1.3 Customer's return of a defective item in exchange for compensation: right of return versus assurance-type warranty...2353

   3.2 Service-type warranties..2353

   3.3 Assurance-type warranties...2354

   3.4 Contracts that contain both assurance and service-type warranties 2355

4 ONEROUS CONTRACTS 2356

   4.1 Accounting for an onerous revenue contract when the contract includes more than one performance obligation that is satisfied over time consecutively 2358

5 CONTRACT COSTS 2358

   5.1 Costs to obtain a contract...2359

      5.1.1 Does the timing of commission payments affect whether they are incremental costs?..2363

      5.1.2 Commission payments subject to a threshold..........................2364

      5.1.3 Would an entity capitalise commissions paid on contract modifications?...2364

      5.1.4 Would fringe benefits on commission payments be included in the capitalised amounts?.......................................2364

      5.1.5 Must an entity apply the practical expedient to expense contract acquisition costs to all of its qualifying contracts across the entity or can it apply the practical expedient to individual contracts?...2365

      5.1.6 How would an entity account for capitalised commissions upon a modification of the contract that is treated as the termination of an existing contract and the creation of a new contract?..2365

   5.2 Costs to fulfil a contract..2365

      5.2.1 Can an entity defer costs of a transferred good or service that would otherwise generate an upfront loss because variable consideration is fully or partially constrained? 2369

	5.2.2	Accounting for fulfilment costs incurred prior to the contract establishment date that are outside the scope of another standard 2370
	5.2.3	Learning curve costs 2370
	5.2.4	Accounting for pre-contract or setup costs 2371
	5.2.5	Capitalisation of mobilisation costs as costs to fulfil a contract with a customer under IFRS 15 2372
	5.2.6	Accounting for loss leader contracts 2373
	5.2.7	Costs associated with installation or implementation activities 2373
5.3	Amortisation of capitalised contract costs 2375	
	5.3.1	Determining whether a commission on a renewal contract is commensurate with the commission on the initial contract 2377
	5.3.2	Determining the amortisation period of an asset recognised for the incremental costs of obtaining a contract with a customer 2378
	5.3.3	Can an entity attribute the capitalised contract costs to the individual performance obligations in the contract to determine the appropriate amortisation period? 2380
	5.3.4	Over what period would an entity amortise a sales commission (that is only paid once a threshold is met) that is determined to be an incremental cost to obtain a contract? 2381
	5.3.5	Determining when to begin to amortise an asset recognised for the incremental cost of obtaining a renewal contract 2382
	5.3.6	Classification and presentation of capitalised contract costs and related amortisation in the statement of financial position and statement of profit and loss and other comprehensive income 2383
5.4	Impairment of capitalised contract costs 2384	

List of examples

Example 31.1:	Identifying a distinct licence (licence is distinct) 2323
Example 31.2:	Identifying a distinct licence (licence is not distinct) 2331
Example 31.3:	Access to intellectual property 2334
Example 31.4:	Right to use intellectual property 2335
Example 31.5:	Sales-based royalty for a licence of intellectual property 2340
Example 31.6:	Licensing contract with a declining royalty rate 2341
Example 31.7:	Access to intellectual property 2342

Revenue: licences, warranties and contract costs 2317

Example 31.8:	Application of the royalty recognition constraint to a milestone payment	2343
Example 31.9:	Application of the royalty recognition constraint to a milestone payment based on the first commercial sale	2344
Example 31.10:	Accounting for a licence of intellectual property that is satisfied over time in exchange for a minimum guarantee and sales-based royalty	2346
Example 31.11:	Application of the royalty recognition constraint as an agent	2348
Example 31.12:	Consideration of service-type warranty factors	2352
Example 31.13:	Service-type and assurance-type warranties	2355
Example 31.14:	Service-type and assurance-type warranty costs	2356
Example 31.15:	Fixed employee salaries	2360
Example 31.16:	Commissions paid to different levels of employees	2360
Example 31.17:	Commissions paid to a pool of funds	2361
Example 31.18:	Incremental and non-incremental costs for same contract	2362
Example 31.19:	Incremental costs of obtaining a contract	2362
Example 31.20:	Timing of commission payments	2363
Example 31.21:	Commission payments subject to a threshold	2364
Example 31.22:	Cost to fulfil a contract related to past performance	2368
Example 31.23:	Costs that give rise to an asset	2369
Example 31.24:	Implementation services are not capitalised costs to fulfil a contract	2374
Example 31.25:	Implementation services are capitalised costs to fulfil a contract	2374
Example 31.26:	Amortisation period	2376
Example 31.27:	Methods for amortising capitalised contract costs	2380
Example 31.28:	Allocation of capitalised contract costs	2381
Example 31.29:	Amortisation of capitalised commission payments subject to a threshold	2382
Example 31.30:	Amortisation of a capitalised contract costs	2382

Chapter 31

Revenue: licences, warranties and contract costs

1 INTRODUCTION

Revenue is a broad concept that is dealt with in several standards. This chapter and Chapters 27-30 and 32 primarily cover the requirements for revenue arising from contracts with customers that are within the scope of IFRS 15 – *Revenue from Contracts with Customers*. This chapter deals with licences, warranties and contract costs. Refer to the following chapters for other requirements of IFRS 15:

- Chapter 27 – Core principle, definitions and scope.
- Chapter 28 – Identifying the contract and identifying performance obligations.
- Chapter 29 – Determining the transaction price and allocating the transaction price.
- Chapter 30 – Recognising revenue.
- Chapter 32 – Presentation and disclosure requirements.

Other revenue items that are not within the scope of IFRS 15, but arise in the course of the ordinary activities of an entity, as well as the disposal of non-financial assets that are not part of the ordinary activities of the entity, for which IFRS 15's requirements are relevant, are addressed in Chapter 27.

In addition, this chapter:

- highlights significant differences from the equivalent US GAAP standard, Accounting Standards Codification (ASC) 606 – *Revenue from Contracts with Customers* (together with IFRS 15, the standards) issued by the US Financial Accounting Standards Board (FASB) (together with the International Accounting Standards Board (IASB), the Boards).
- addresses topics on which the members of the Joint Transition Resource Group for Revenue Recognition (TRG) reached general agreement and our views on certain topics. TRG members' views are non-authoritative, but entities should consider them as they apply the standards. Unless otherwise specified, these summaries represent the discussions of the joint TRG.

The views we express in this chapter may evolve as application issues are identified and discussed among stakeholders. The conclusions we describe in our illustrations are also subject to change as views evolve. Conclusions in seemingly similar situations may differ from those reached in the illustrations due to differences in the underlying facts and circumstances.

2 LICENCES OF INTELLECTUAL PROPERTY

IFRS 15 provides application guidance for recognising revenue from licences of intellectual property that differs in some respects from the requirements for other promised goods or services.

Given that licences include a wide array of features and economic characteristics, the Board decided that an entity needs to evaluate the nature of its promise to grant a licence of intellectual property in order to determine whether the promise is satisfied (and revenue is recognised) over time or at a point in time. A licence provides either: *[IFRS 15.B56]*

- a right to access the entity's intellectual property throughout the licence period, which results in revenue that is recognised over time; or
- a right to use the entity's intellectual property as it exists at the point in time in which the licence is granted, which results in revenue that is recognised at a point in time.

The standard states that licences of intellectual property establish a customer's rights to the intellectual property of an entity and may include licences for any of the following: software and technology, media and entertainment (e.g. motion pictures and music), franchises, patents, trademarks and copyrights. *[IFRS 15.B52]*.

The application guidance provided on licences of intellectual property is only applicable to licences that are distinct. When the licence is the only promised item (either explicitly or implicitly) in the contract, the application guidance is clearly applicable to that licence. The assessment as to whether the contract includes a distinct licence of intellectual property may be straightforward for many contracts. However, if there are multiple promises in a contract, entities may have to more carefully evaluate the nature of the rights conveyed.

Licences of intellectual property are frequently included in multiple-element arrangements with promises for additional goods or services that may be explicit or implicit. In these situations, an entity first applies the requirements of Step 2 of the model to determine whether the licence of intellectual property is distinct, as discussed at 2.1 below and in Chapter 28 at 3.

For most licences that are not distinct, an entity would follow the general requirements in Step 5 of the model to account for the recognition of revenue for the performance obligation that includes the licence (i.e. the requirements in paragraphs 31-36 of IFRS 15 to determine whether the performance obligation transfers over time or at a point in time, as discussed in Chapter 30 at 2 and 4). Furthermore, the IASB noted in the Basis for Conclusions that there may be some situations in which, even though the licence is not distinct from the good or service transferred with the licence, the licence is the primary or dominant component (i.e. the predominant item) of the combined performance obligation. *[IFRS 15.BC407]*. In such situations, the IASB indicated that the application guidance for licences still applies. The Board provided no application guidance or bright lines for determining when a licence is the primary or dominant component. However, the IASB referred to an example in the Basis for Conclusions to illustrate this concept further. *[IFRS 15.BC414X]*. See 2.2.1 below for further discussion. The determination of whether a licence is the predominant component may be obvious in some cases, but not in others. Therefore, entities may need to exercise significant judgement and consider both qualitative and quantitative factors.

2.1 Identifying performance obligations in a licensing arrangement

Contracts for licences of intellectual property frequently include explicit or implicit promises for additional goods or services (e.g. equipment, when-and-if available upgrades, maintenance and installation). Consistent with Step 2 of the general model (see Chapter 28 at 3), entities need to apply the requirements on identifying performance obligations in paragraphs 22-30 of IFRS 15, when a contract with a customer includes a licence of intellectual property and other promised goods or services, in order to appropriately determine whether the licence of intellectual property and the other promises are distinct (i.e. are separate performance obligations).

In respect of identifying performance obligations in a licensing arrangement, the standard states that '[i]n addition to a promise to grant a licence to a customer, an entity may also promise to transfer other goods or services to the customer. Those promises may be explicitly stated in the contract or implied by an entity's customary business practices, published policies or specific statements (see paragraph 24). As with other types of contracts, when a contract with a customer includes a promise to grant a licence in addition to other promised goods or services, an entity applies paragraphs 22–30 to identify each of the performance obligations in the contract.' *[IFRS 15.B53]*.

As discussed in Chapter 28 at 3.2, the standard outlines a two-step process for determining whether a promised good or service (including a licence of intellectual property) is distinct and, therefore, is a performance obligation as follows:

(1) consideration of the individual good or service (i.e. whether the good or service is capable of being distinct); and

(2) consideration of whether the good or service is separately identifiable from other promises in the contract (i.e. whether the promise to transfer the good or service is distinct in the context of the contract).

To conclude that a good or service is distinct, an entity needs to determine that the good or service is both capable of being distinct and distinct in the context of the contract. These requirements need to be applied to determine whether a promise to grant a licence of intellectual property is distinct from other promised goods or services in the contract. Therefore, entities are required to assess whether the customer can benefit from a licence of intellectual property on its own or together with readily available resources (i.e. whether it is capable of being distinct) and whether the entity's promise to transfer a licence of intellectual property is separately identifiable from other promises in the contract (i.e. whether it is distinct in the context of the contract). The assessment of whether a licence of intellectual property is distinct needs to be based on the facts and circumstances of each contract.

2.1.1 Licences of intellectual property that are distinct

Licences are frequently capable of being distinct (i.e. the first criteria of a distinct good or service) as a customer can often obtain at least some benefit from the licence of intellectual property on its own or with other readily available resources. Consider Example 28.34, Case A, in Chapter 28 at 3.2.3, which includes a contract for a software licence that is transferred along with installation services, technical support and unspecified software updates. The installation service is routinely performed by other entities and does not significantly modify the software. The software licence is delivered before the other goods or services and remains functional without the updates and technical support. The entity concludes that the customer can benefit from each of the goods or services either on their own or together with other goods or services that are readily available. That is, each good or service, including the software licence, is capable of being distinct under paragraph 27 of IFRS 15.

If an entity determines that a licence of intellectual property and other promised goods or services are capable of being distinct, the second step in the evaluation is to determine whether they are distinct in the context of the contract. As part of this evaluation, an entity considers the indicators for whether the goods or services are not separately identifiable, including whether:

(1) the entity provides a significant service of integrating the licence and other goods or services into a combined output or outputs;

(2) the licence and other goods or services significantly modify or customise each other; or

(3) the licence and other goods or services are highly interdependent or highly interrelated, such that the entity would not be able to fulfil its promise to transfer the licence independently of fulfilling its promise to transfer the other goods or services to the customer.

Continuing with Example 28.34, Case A, in Chapter 28 at 3.2.3, which is discussed above, the entity considers the separately identifiable principle and factors in paragraph 29 of IFRS 15 and determines that the promise to transfer each good and service, including the software licence, is separately identifiable. In reaching this determination, the entity considers that the installation services are routine and can be obtained from other providers. In addition, the entity considers that, although it integrates the software into the customer's system, the software updates do not significantly affect the customer's ability to use and benefit from the software licence during the licence period. Therefore, neither the installation services nor the software updates significantly affect the customer's ability to use and benefit from the software licence. The entity further observes that none of the promised goods or services significantly modify or customise one another and the entity is not providing a significant service of integrating the software and services into one combined output. Lastly, the software and the services are not deemed to be highly interdependent or highly interrelated because the entity would be able to fulfil its promise to transfer the initial software licence independent from its promise to subsequently provide the installation service, software updates and the technical support.

The following example from the standard also illustrates a contract for which a licence of intellectual property is determined to be distinct from other promised goods or services. *[IFRS 15.IE281, IE285-IE288].*

Example 31.1:   Identifying a distinct licence (licence is distinct)

An entity, a pharmaceutical company, licenses to a customer its patent rights to an approved drug compound for 10 years and also promises to manufacture the drug for the customer. The drug is a mature product; therefore the entity will not undertake any activities to support the drug, which is consistent with its customary business practices.

Case B – Licence is distinct

In this case, the manufacturing process used to produce the drug is not unique or specialised and several other entities can also manufacture the drug for the customer.

The entity assesses the goods and services promised to the customer to determine which goods and services are distinct, and it concludes that the criteria in paragraph 27 of IFRS 15 are met for each of the licence and the manufacturing service. The entity concludes that the criterion in paragraph 27(a) of IFRS 15 is met because the customer can benefit from the licence together with readily available resources other than the entity's manufacturing service (because there are other entities that can provide the manufacturing service), and can benefit from the manufacturing service together with the licence transferred to the customer at the start of the contract.

The entity also concludes that its promises to grant the licence and to provide the manufacturing service are separately identifiable (i.e. the criterion in paragraph 27(b) of IFRS 15 is met). The entity concludes that the licence and the manufacturing service are not inputs to a combined item in this contract on the basis of the principle and the factors in paragraph 29 of IFRS 15. In reaching this conclusion, the entity considers that the customer could separately purchase the licence without significantly affecting its ability to benefit from the licence. Neither the licence, nor the manufacturing service, is significantly modified or customised by the other and the entity is not providing a significant service of integrating those items into a combined output. The entity further considers that the licence and the manufacturing service are not highly interdependent or highly interrelated because the entity would be able to fulfil its promise to transfer the licence independently of fulfilling its promise to subsequently manufacture the drug for the customer. Similarly, the entity would be able to manufacture the drug for the customer even if the customer had previously obtained the licence and initially utilised a different manufacturer. Thus, although the manufacturing service necessarily depends on the licence in this contract (i.e. the entity would not provide the manufacturing service without the customer having obtained the licence), the licence and the manufacturing service do not significantly affect each other. Consequently, the entity concludes that its promises to grant the licence and to provide the manufacturing service are distinct and that there are two performance obligations:

(a)   licence of patent rights; and

(b)   manufacturing service.

The entity assesses, in accordance with paragraph B58 of IFRS 15, the nature of the entity's promise to grant the licence. The drug is a mature product (i.e. it has been approved, is currently being manufactured and has been sold commercially for the last several years). For these types of mature products, the entity's customary business practices are not to undertake any activities to support the drug. The drug compound has significant stand-alone functionality (i.e. its ability to produce a drug that treats a disease or condition). Consequently, the customer obtains a substantial portion of the benefits of the drug compound from that functionality, rather than from the entity's ongoing activities. The entity concludes that the criteria in paragraph B58 of IFRS 15 are not met because the contract does not require, and the customer does not reasonably expect, the entity to undertake activities that significantly affect the intellectual property to which the customer has rights. In its assessment of the criteria in paragraph B58 of IFRS 15, the entity does not take into consideration the separate performance obligation of promising to provide a manufacturing service. Consequently, the nature of the entity's promise in transferring the licence is to provide a right to use the entity's intellectual property in the form and the functionality with which it exists at the point in time that it is granted to the customer. Consequently, the entity accounts for the licence as a performance obligation satisfied at a point in time.

The entity applies paragraphs 31-38 of IFRS 15 to determine whether the manufacturing service is a performance obligation satisfied at a point in time or over time.

2.1.2 Licences of intellectual property that are not distinct

The licences of intellectual property included in the examples above were determined to be distinct, as they met the two criteria of paragraph 27 of IFRS 15. In other situations, a licence of intellectual property may not be distinct from other promised goods or services in a contract, either because it is not capable of being distinct and/or it is not separately identifiable.

Paragraph B54 of IFRS 15 requires that a licence that is not distinct from other promised goods or services in a contract be combined into a single performance obligation. It also identifies two examples of licences of intellectual property that are not distinct from other goods or services, as follows: [IFRS 15.B54]

'(a) a licence that forms a component of a tangible good and that is integral to the functionality of the good; and

(b) a licence that the customer can benefit from only in conjunction with a related service (such as an online service provided by the entity that enables, by granting a licence, the customer to access content).'

In both examples, a customer only benefits from the combined output of the licence of intellectual property and the related good or service. Therefore, the licence is not distinct and would be combined with those other promised goods or services in the contract.

The standard includes other examples of licences of intellectual property that are not distinct, which are combined with other promised goods or services because the customer can only benefit from the licence in conjunction with a related service (as described in paragraph B54(b) of IFRS 15). For example, Example 55 in IFRS 15 and Example 56, Case A, in IFRS 15 (included as Example 31.2 at 2.2.1 below) illustrate contracts that include licences of intellectual property that are not distinct from other goods or services promised to the customer.

When an entity is required to bundle a licence of intellectual property with other promised goods or services in a contract, it often needs to consider the licensing application guidance to help determine the nature of its promise to the customer when the licence is the predominant item in the combined performance obligation. See 2.2.1 below for further discussion on applying the licensing application guidance to such performance obligations.

2.1.3 Contractual restrictions

Some licences contain substantive contractual restrictions on how the customer may employ a licence. Paragraph B62(a) of IFRS 15 explicitly states an entity must disregard restrictions of time, geography or use when determining whether the promise to transfer a licence is satisfied over time or at a point in time; such restrictions define the attributes of the promised licence, rather than define whether the entity satisfies its performance obligation at a point in time or over time. [IFRS 15.B62(a)].

While stakeholders acknowledged that paragraph B62 of IFRS 15 is clear that restrictions of time, geographical region or use do not affect the licensor's determination about whether the promise to transfer a licence is satisfied over time or at a point in time, some stakeholders thought that the standard was unclear about whether particular types of contractual restrictions would affect the identification of the promised goods or services in the contract. For example, an arrangement might grant a customer a licence to a well-known television programme or movie for a period of time (e.g. three years), but the customer might be restricted in how often it can show that licensed content to only once per year during each of those three years. In this instance, stakeholders thought that it may be unclear whether contractual restrictions affect the entity's identification of its promises in the contract (i.e. do the airing restrictions affect whether the entity has granted one licence or three licences?). [IFRS 15.BC414O].

In considering this issue further, the IASB explained that contracts that include a promise to grant a licence to a customer require an assessment of the promises in the contract using the criteria for identifying performance obligations, as is the case with other contracts. [IFRS 15.BC405-BC406]. This assessment is done before applying the criteria to determine the nature of an entity's promise in granting a licence. [IFRS 15.BC414P].

In the Basis for Conclusions, the IASB further explained that they considered Example 59 in IFRS 15 (see Example 31.4 at 2.3.2 below) in the context of this issue. The entity concludes that its only performance obligation is to grant the customer a right to use the music recording. When, where and how the right can be used is defined by the attributes of time (i.e. two years), geographical scope (i.e. Country A) and permitted use (i.e. in commercials). If, instead, the entity had granted the customer rights to use the recording for two different time periods in two geographical locations, for example, years X1-X3 in Country A and years X2-X4 in Country B, the entity would need to use the criteria for identifying performance obligations in paragraphs 27-30 of IFRS 15 to determine whether the contract included one licence that covers both countries or separate licences for each country. [IFRS 15.BC414Q].

Consequently, the entity considers all of the contractual terms to determine whether the promised rights result in the transfer to the customer of one or more licences. In making this determination, judgement is needed to distinguish between contractual provisions that create promises to transfer rights to use the entity's intellectual property from contractual provisions that establish when, where and how those rights may be used. Therefore, in the Board's view, the clarifications made to the requirements on identifying performance obligations in paragraphs 22-30 of IFRS 15 provide sufficient guidance to entities. [IFRS 15.BC414P].

We believe a critical part of the evaluation of contractual restrictions is whether the lifting of a restriction at a future date requires an entity to grant additional rights to the customer at that future date in order to fulfil its promises under the contract. The presence of a requirement to grant additional rights to the customer indicates that there may be multiple performance obligations that need to be accounted for under Step 2 of the model.

Entities may need to use significant judgement to distinguish between a single promised licence with multiple attributes and a licence that contains multiple promises to the customer that may be separate performance obligations.

ASC 606 requires that entities distinguish between contractual provisions that define the attributes of a single promised licence (e.g. restrictions of time, geography or use) and contractual provisions that require them to transfer additional goods or services to customers (e.g. additional rights to use or access intellectual property).

Contractual provisions that are attributes of a promised licence define the scope of a customer's rights to intellectual property and do not affect whether a performance obligation is satisfied at a point in time or over time. Nor do they affect the number of performance obligations in the contract.

The IASB decided not to clarify the requirements for identifying performance obligations in a contract containing one or more licences since it had clarified the general requirements for identifying performance obligations. *[IFRS 15.BC414P].*

As a result, ASC 606 includes guidance on contractual restrictions that differs from the requirements in IFRS 15. However, the IASB noted in the Basis for Conclusions that, consistent with the ASC 606, an entity needs to apply the requirements in Step 2 of the general model on identifying performance obligations when distinguishing between contractual provisions that create promises to transfer additional rights from those that are merely attributes of a licence that establish when, where and how the right may be used. *[IFRS 15.BC414P].* Under both IFRS 15 and ASC 606, an entity may need to apply significant judgement to distinguish between a single promised licence with multiple attributes and a licence that contains multiple promises to the customer that may be separate performance obligations.

2.1.4 Guarantees to defend or maintain a patent

IFRS 15 states that a guarantee provided by an entity that it has a valid patent to intellectual property and that it will defend or maintain a patent does not represent a performance obligation in a licensing contract. This is because 'the act of defending a patent protects the value of the entity's intellectual property assets and provides assurance to the customer that the licence transferred meets the specifications of the licence promised in the contract'. Furthermore, this type of guarantee does not affect the licensor's determination as to whether the licence provides a right to access intellectual property (satisfied over time) or a right to use intellectual property (satisfied at a point in time). *[IFRS 15.B62(b)].*

It is not unusual for intellectual property arrangements to include a clause that requires a licensor to defend and maintain related patents. While patent defence and maintenance is a continuing obligation, it is an obligation to ensure the licensee can continue to use the intellectual property as intended, and, as discussed above, is not a promised good or service under IFRS 15 that should be evaluated under Step 2. However, if there are questions regarding the validity of a patent at the time a licence arrangement is entered into, licensors need to consider whether that component of the arrangement meets the attributes to be considered a contract within the scope of the model (see Chapter 28 at 2.1).

Furthermore, as discussed above, because such a provision is to ensure that the licensee can continue to use the intellectual property as intended, it is similar to an assurance-type warranty discussed at 3 below (i.e. a warranty that promises the customer that the delivered product is as specified in the contract). Assurance-type warranties are not within the scope of IFRS 15 and, as stated in paragraph B30 of IFRS 15, would be accounted for in accordance with the requirements for product warranties in IAS 37 – *Provisions, Contingent Liabilities and Contingent Assets.*

2.1.5 Application questions on identifying performance obligations in a licensing arrangement

2.1.5.A Accounting for modifications to licences of intellectual property

A licence provides a customer with a right to use or a right to access the intellectual property of an entity. The terms of each licence of intellectual property are defined by the contract, which establishes the customer's rights (e.g. period of time, area of use). We believe that when a contract that only includes a licence of intellectual property is modified, the additional and/or modified licence of intellectual property is distinct from the original licence because the new and/or modified rights will always differ from those conveyed by the original licence.

The standard contains requirements on accounting for contract modification (see Chapter 28 at 2.4) and requires that a modification in which the additional promised goods or services are distinct be accounted for on a prospective basis, as follows:

- the modification is accounted for as a separate contract if the additional consideration from the modification reflects the new licence's stand-alone selling price in accordance with paragraph 20(b) of IFRS 15; or
- if the additional consideration does not reflect the stand-alone selling price of the new licence, the modification is accounted for in accordance with paragraph 21(a) of IFRS 15.

For a modification accounted for as a termination of the original contract and creation of a new contract in accordance with paragraph 21(a) of IFRS 15, any revenue recognised to date under the original contract is not adjusted. At the date of the modification, the remaining unrecognised transaction price from the original contract (if any) and the additional transaction price from the new contract are allocated to the remaining performance obligation(s) in the new contract. Any revenue allocated to a performance obligation created at the modification date for the renewal or extension of a licence would be recognised when (or as) that performance obligation is satisfied, which may not be until the beginning of the renewal or extension period (see 2.4 below).

2.1.5.B Contracts that grant both permission for past use of intellectual property and a licence to use the intellectual property in the future

An entity may enter into a contract with a customer that grants the right to use an IP and the customer also agrees to pay consideration for past use of that intellectual property. Such an agreement may be partially a settlement for the use of the intellectual property in the past without the entity's permission.

In such circumstances, it may require judgement to determine what aspects of the contract are within the scope of IFRS 15.

If the contract is partially within the scope of IFRS 15, an entity may need to use judgement when applying the requirements in paragraph 7 of IFRS 15 (see Chapter 27 at 3.5) to separate the consideration between the revenue in exchange for the licence, any amount received for the past use and any other components. *[IFRS 15.7]*.

2.2 Determining the nature of the entity's promise in granting a licence

Entities need to evaluate the nature of a promise to grant a licence of intellectual property in order to determine whether the promise is satisfied (and revenue is recognised) over time or at a point in time. In order to help entities in determining whether a licence provides a customer with a right to access or a right to use the intellectual property (which is important when determining the period of performance and, therefore, the timing of revenue recognition – see 2.3 below), the Board provided application guidance that clarifies that an entity's promise is to provide a right to access the entity's intellectual property if all of the following criteria are met: *[IFRS 15.B58]*

(a) the contract requires, or the customer reasonably expects, that the entity will undertake activities that significantly affect the intellectual property to which the customer has rights;

(b) the rights granted by the licence directly expose the customer to any positive or negative effects of the entity's activities identified in (a); and

(c) those activities do not result in the transfer of a good or a service to the customer as those activities occur.

The standard lists an entity's customary business practices, published policies or specific statements as factors that may indicate that a customer could reasonably expect that an entity will undertake activities that significantly affect the intellectual property. Although not determinative, the existence of a shared economic interest (that is related to the intellectual property to which the customer has rights) between the entity and the customer (e.g. a sales-based royalty) may also provide such an indication. *[IFRS 15.B59]*.

In providing this application guidance, the Board decided to focus on the characteristics of a licence that provides a right to access the entity's intellectual property. If the licensed intellectual property does not have those characteristics, it provides a right to use the entity's intellectual property, by default. This analysis is focused on situations in which the underlying intellectual property is subject to change over the licence period.

The key determinants of whether the nature of an entity's promise is a right to access the entity's intellectual property are whether: (1) the entity is required to undertake activities that affect the licensed intellectual property (or the customer has a reasonable expectation that the entity will do so); and (2) the customer is exposed to positive or negative effects resulting from those changes.

It is important to note that when an entity is making this assessment, it excludes the effect of any other performance obligations in the contract. For example, if an entity enters into a contract to license software and provide access to any future upgrades to that software during the licence period, the entity first determines whether the licence and the promise to provide future updates are separate performance obligations. If they are separate, when the entity considers whether it has a contractual (explicit or implicit) obligation to undertake activities to change the software during the licence period, it excludes any changes and activities associated with the performance obligation to provide future upgrades.

While the activities considered in this assessment do not include those that are a performance obligation, these activities can be part of an entity's ongoing ordinary activities and customary business practices (i.e. they do not have to be activities the entity is undertaking specifically as a result of the contract with the customer). In addition, the IASB noted, in the Basis for Conclusions, that the existence of a shared economic interest between the parties (e.g. sales-based or usage-based royalties) may be an indicator that the customer has a reasonable expectation that the entity will undertake such activities. *[IFRS 15.BC413]*.

After an entity has identified the activities for this assessment, it must determine if those activities significantly affect the intellectual property to which the customer has rights. The standard clarifies that such activities significantly affect the intellectual property if they: *[IFRS 15.B59A]*

- significantly change the form (e.g. design or content) or functionality (e.g. the ability to perform a function or task) of the intellectual property; or
- affect the ability of the customer to obtain benefit from the intellectual property (e.g. the benefit from a brand is often derived from, or dependent upon, the entity's ongoing activities that support or maintain the value of the intellectual property).

If the intellectual property has significant stand-alone functionality, the standard clarifies that the customer derives a substantial portion of the benefit of that intellectual property from that functionality. As such, 'the ability of the customer to obtain benefit from that intellectual property would not be significantly affected by the entity's activities unless those activities significantly change its form or functionality.' Therefore, if the intellectual property has significant stand-alone functionality, revenue is recognised at a point in time. Examples of types of intellectual property that may have significant stand-alone functionality that are mentioned in the standard include software, biological compounds or drug formulas, and completed media content. *[IFRS 15.B59A]*.

The IASB has not defined the term 'significant stand-alone functionality', but has made clarifications to the examples in the standard to illustrate when the intellectual property to which the customer has rights may have significant stand-alone functionality. In some cases, it will be clear when intellectual property has significant stand-alone functionality. If there is no significant stand-alone functionality, the benefit to the customer might be substantially derived from the value of the intellectual property and the entity's activities to support or maintain that value. The IASB noted, however, that an entity may need to apply judgement to determine whether the intellectual property to which the customer has rights has significant stand-alone functionality. *[IFRS 15.BC414I]*.

It is important for entities that provide licences of intellectual property to their customers to appropriately identify the performance obligations as part of Step 2 of the model because those conclusions may directly affect their evaluation of whether the entity's activities significantly change the form or functionality of the intellectual property or affect the ability of the customer to obtain benefit from the intellectual property.

Unlike IFRS 15, the FASB's standard requires entities to classify intellectual property in one of two categories to determine the nature of the entity's promise in granting a licence as detailed below:

- *Functional:* This intellectual property has significant stand-alone functionality (e.g. many types of software, completed media content such as films, television shows and music). Revenue for these licences is recognised at the point in time when the intellectual property is made available for the customer's use and benefit if the functionality is not expected to change substantively as a result of the licensor's ongoing activities that do not transfer another good or service to the customer. If the functionality of the intellectual property is expected to substantively change because of the activities of the licensor that do not transfer promised goods or services and the customer is contractually or practically required to use the latest version of the intellectual property, revenue for the licence is recognised over time. The FASB noted in its Basis for Conclusions on ASU 2016-10 that it expects entities to meet the criteria to recognise licences of functional intellectual property over time infrequently, if at all.

- *Symbolic:* This intellectual property does not have significant stand-alone functionality (e.g. brands, team and trade names, character images). The utility of symbolic intellectual property is derived from the licensor's ongoing or past activities (e.g. activities that support the value of character images licensed from an animated film). Revenue from these licences is recognised over time as the performance obligation is satisfied (e.g. over the licence period).

The IASB and FASB agreed that their approaches will generally result in consistent answers, but the Boards acknowledged that different outcomes may arise due to the different approaches when entities license brand names that no longer have any related ongoing activities (e.g. the licence to the brand name of a defunct sports team, such as the Brooklyn Dodgers). Under the FASB's approach, a licence of a brand name would be classified as symbolic intellectual property and revenue would be recognised over time, regardless of whether there are any related ongoing activities. Under the IASB's approach, revenue is recognised at a point in time if there are no ongoing activities that significantly affect the intellectual property. *[IFRS 15.BC414K, BC414N].*

2.2.1 Applying the licensing application guidance to a single (bundled) performance obligation that includes a licence of intellectual property

IFRS 15 does not explicitly state that an entity needs to consider the nature of its promise in granting a licence when applying the general revenue recognition model to performance obligations that are comprised of both a licence (that is not distinct) and other goods or services. However, the Board clarified in the Basis for Conclusions that to the extent that an entity is required to combine a licence with other promised goods or services in a single performance obligation and the licence is the primary or dominant component (i.e. the predominant item) of that performance obligation, the entity needs to consider the licensing application guidance to help determine the nature of its promise to the customer. *[IFRS 15.BC407].*

If the licence is a predominant item of a single performance obligation, entities need to consider the licensing application guidance when:

- determining whether the performance obligation is satisfied over time or at a point in time; and
- selecting an appropriate method for measuring progress of that performance obligation if it is satisfied over time.

Considering the nature of an entity's promise in granting a licence that is part of a single combined performance obligation is not a separate step or evaluation in the revenue model. Rather, it is part of the overall requirements in Step 5 of the model to determine whether that single performance obligation is satisfied over time or at a point in time and the appropriate measure of progress toward the satisfaction, if it is satisfied over time.

The Board did not provide application guidance or bright lines for determining when a licence is the primary or dominant (i.e. the predominant) component. However, the IASB explained in the Basis for Conclusions that, in some instances, not considering the nature of the entity's promise in granting a licence that is combined with other promised goods or services in a single performance obligation would result in accounting that does not best reflect the entity's performance. For example, consider a situation where an entity grants a 10-year licence that is not distinct from a one-year service arrangement. The IASB noted that a distinct licence that provides access to an entity's intellectual property over a 10-year period could not be considered completely satisfied before the end of the access period. The IASB observed in that example that it is, therefore, inappropriate to conclude that a single performance obligation that includes that licence is satisfied over the one-year period of the service arrangement. *[IFRS 15.BC414X].*

The standard includes examples that illustrate how an entity applies the licensing application guidance to help determine the nature of a performance obligation that includes a licence of intellectual property and other promised goods or services.

In Example 31.2 below an entity licences the patent rights for an approved drug compound to its customer and also promises to manufacture the drug for the customer. The entity considers that no other entity can perform the manufacturing service because of the highly specialised nature of the manufacturing process. Therefore, the licence cannot be purchased separately from the manufacturing service and the customer cannot benefit from the licence on its own or with other readily available resources (i.e. the licence and the manufacturing service are not capable of being distinct). Accordingly, the entity's promises to grant the licence and to manufacture the drug are accounted for as a single performance obligation, as follows. *[IFRS 15.IE281-IE284].*

Example 31.2: Identifying a distinct licence (licence is not distinct)

An entity, a pharmaceutical company, licenses to a customer its patent rights to an approved drug compound for 10 years and also promises to manufacture the drug for the customer. The drug is a mature product; therefore the entity will not undertake any activities to support the drug, which is consistent with its customary business practices.

Case A – Licence is not distinct

In this case, no other entity can manufacture this drug because of the highly specialised nature of the manufacturing process. As a result, the licence cannot be purchased separately from the manufacturing services.

The entity assesses the goods and services promised to the customer to determine which goods and services are distinct in accordance with paragraph 27 of IFRS 15. The entity determines that the customer cannot benefit from the licence without the manufacturing service; therefore, the criterion in paragraph 27(a) of

IFRS 15 is not met. Consequently, the licence and the manufacturing service are not distinct and the entity accounts for the licence and the manufacturing service as a single performance obligation.

The entity applies paragraphs 31–38 of IFRS 15 to determine whether the performance obligation (i.e. the bundle of the licence and the manufacturing services) is a performance obligation satisfied at a point in time or over time.

Example 31.2 above illustrates the importance of applying the licensing application guidance when determining the nature of an entity's promise in granting a licence that is combined into a single performance obligation with other promised goods or services. This is because the conclusion of whether a non-distinct licence provides the customer with a right to use intellectual property or a right to access intellectual property may have a significant effect on the timing of revenue recognition for the single combined performance obligation. In Example 31.2, the entity needs to determine the nature of its promise in granting the licence within the single performance obligation (comprising the licence and the manufacturing service) to appropriately apply the general principle of recognising revenue when (or as) it satisfies its performance obligation to the customer. If the licence in this example provided a right to use the entity's intellectual property that on its own would be recognised at the point in time in which control of the licence is transferred to the customer, it is likely that the combined performance obligation would only be fully satisfied when the manufacturing service is complete. In contrast, if the licence provided a right to access the entity's intellectual property, the combined performance obligation would not be fully satisfied until the end of the 10-year licence period, which could extend the period of revenue recognition beyond the date when the manufacturing service is complete.

ASC 606 explicitly states that an entity considers the nature of its promise in granting a licence when applying the general revenue recognition model to a single performance obligation that includes a licence and other goods or services (i.e. when applying the general requirements, consistent with those in paragraphs 31-45 of IFRS 15, to assess whether the performance obligations are satisfied at a point in time or over time). Consequently, when the licence is not the predominant item in a single performance obligation, this may result in a US GAAP preparer considering the nature of its promise in granting a licence in a greater number of circumstances than an IFRS preparer. [IFRS 15.BC414Y]. The determination of whether a licence is the predominant component may be obvious in some cases, but not in others. Therefore, entities may need to exercise significant judgement and consider both qualitative and quantitative factors.

2.3 Transfer of control of licensed intellectual property

When determining whether a licence of intellectual property transfers to a customer (and revenue is recognised) over time or at a point in time, the standard states that an entity provides a customer with either:

- a right to access the entity's intellectual property throughout the licence period for which revenue is recognised over the licence period; or
- a right to use the entity's intellectual property as it exists at the point in time the licence is granted, for which revenue is recognised at the point in time, the customer can first use and benefit from the licensed intellectual property.

On the timing of revenue recognition for right-to-access and right-to-use licences, the standard states that, if the criteria in paragraph B58 of IFRS 15 are met, 'an entity shall account for the promise to grant a licence as a performance obligation satisfied over time because the customer will simultaneously receive and consume the benefit from the entity's performance of providing access to its intellectual property as the performance occurs (see paragraph 35(a)). An entity shall apply paragraphs 39–45 to select an appropriate method to measure its progress towards complete satisfaction of that performance obligation to provide access.' *[IFRS 15.B60]*.

If, instead, the criteria in paragraph B58 of IFRS 15 are not met, the standard explains that 'the nature of an entity's promise is to provide a right to use the entity's intellectual property as that intellectual property exists (in terms of form and functionality) at the point in time at which the licence is granted to the customer.' As a result, the customer will be able to direct the use of, and obtain substantially all of the remaining benefits from, the licence at the point in time at which the licence transfers. Therefore, an entity is required to account for the promise to provide a right to use the entity's intellectual property as a performance obligation satisfied at a point in time. *[IFRS 15.B61]*.

An entity applies paragraph 38 of IFRS 15 to determine the point in time at which the licence transfers to the customer. However, 'revenue cannot be recognised for a licence that provides a right to use the entity's intellectual property before the beginning of the period during which the customer is able to use and benefit from the licence. For example, if a software licence period begins before an entity provides (or otherwise makes available) to the customer a code that enables the customer to immediately use the software, the entity would not recognise revenue before that code has been provided (or otherwise made available).' *[IFRS 15.B61]*.

2.3.1 Right to access

The Board concluded that a licence that provides an entity with the right to access intellectual property is satisfied over time 'because the customer simultaneously receives and consumes the benefit from the entity's performance as the performance occurs', including the related activities undertaken by entity. *[IFRS 15.B60, BC414]*. This conclusion is based on the determination that when a licence is subject to change (and the customer is exposed to the positive or negative effects of that change), the customer is not able to fully gain control over the licence of intellectual property at any given point in time, but rather gains control over the licence period. Entities need to apply the general Step 5 requirements in paragraphs 39-45 of IFRS 15 to determine the appropriate method to measure progress (see Chapter 30 at 3), in addition to paragraph B61 of IFRS 15 (i.e. the use and benefit requirement, discussed at 2.3.3 below). In performing this analysis, an entity should not default to a straight-line revenue attribution model. However, the customer may often receive and consume the benefits of a right-to-access licence evenly over the contract period and, therefore, a time-based measure of progress that results in a straight-line recognition of revenue would be appropriate.

The standard includes the following example of a right-to-access licence. [IFRS 15.IE297-IE302].

Example 31.3: Access to intellectual property

An entity, a creator of comic strips, licenses the use of the images and names of its comic strip characters in three of its comic strips to a customer for a four-year term. There are main characters involved in each of the comic strips. However, newly created characters appear regularly and the images of the characters evolve over time. The customer, an operator of cruise ships, can use the entity's characters in various ways, such as in shows or parades, within reasonable guidelines. The contract requires the customer to use the latest images of the characters.

In exchange for granting the licence, the entity receives a fixed payment of $1 million in each year of the four-year term.

In accordance with paragraph 27 of IFRS 15, the entity assesses the goods and services promised to the customer to determine which goods and services are distinct. The entity concludes that it has no other performance obligations other than the promise to grant a licence. That is, the additional activities associated with the licence do not directly transfer a good or service to the customer because they are part of the entity's promise to grant a licence.

The entity assesses the nature of the entity's promise to transfer the licence in accordance with paragraph B58 of IFRS 15. In assessing the criteria the entity considers the following:

(a) the customer reasonably expects (arising from the entity's customary business practices) that the entity will undertake activities that will significantly affect the intellectual property to which the customer has rights (i.e. the characters). This is because the entity's activities (i.e. development of the characters) change the form of the intellectual property to which the customer has rights. In addition, the ability of the customer to obtain benefit from the intellectual property to which the customer has rights is substantially derived from, or dependent upon, the entity's ongoing activities (i.e. the publishing of the comic strip);

(b) the rights granted by the licence directly expose the customer to any positive or negative effects of the entity's activities because the contract requires the customer to use the latest characters; and

(c) even though the customer may benefit from those activities through the rights granted by the licence, they do not transfer a good or service to the customer as those activities occur.

Consequently, the entity concludes that the criteria in paragraph B58 of IFRS 15 are met and that the nature of the entity's promise to transfer the licence is to provide the customer with access to the entity's intellectual property as it exists throughout the licence period. Consequently, the entity accounts for the promised licence as a performance obligation satisfied over time (i.e. the criterion in paragraph 35(a) of IFRS 15 is met).

The entity applies paragraphs 39-45 of IFRS 15 to identify the method that best depicts its performance in the licence. Because the contract provides the customer with unlimited use of the licensed characters for a fixed term, the entity determines that a time-based method would be the most appropriate measure of progress towards complete satisfaction of the performance obligation.

2.3.1.A   Is a licence that provides a right to access intellectual property a series of distinct goods or services that would be accounted for as a single performance obligation?

Step 2 of the model requires an entity to identify the performance obligations in a contract. This includes determining whether multiple distinct goods or services would be accounted for as a single performance obligation under the series requirement (see Chapter 28 at 3.2.2). It is likely that many licences that provide a right to access intellectual property may be a series of distinct goods or services that are substantially the same and have the same pattern of transfer to the customer (e.g. a series of distinct periods of access to intellectual property, such as monthly access or quarterly access).

A TRG agenda paper included an example of a licence that provides a right to access intellectual property that is accounted for as a series of distinct goods or services.[1] In the example, a franchisor grants a licence of intellectual property to a franchisee allowing the franchisee to use its trade name and sell its product for a period of 10 years. As discussed in Chapter 28 at 3.2.2.C, if the nature of an entity's promise is to provide a single service for a period of time, the evaluation of whether goods or services are distinct and substantially the same considers whether each time increment of access to the intellectual property (e.g. hour, day) is distinct and substantially the same. In this example, the nature of the franchisor's promise is to provide a right to access the intellectual property throughout the licence period. Each time increment is distinct because the customer benefits from the right to access each day on its own (i.e. each time increment is capable of being distinct). In addition, each day is separately identifiable (i.e. each time increment is distinct in the context of the contract) because: there is no integration service provided between the days of access provided; no day modifies or customises another; and the days of access are not highly interdependent or highly interrelated. In addition, each distinct daily service is substantially the same because the customer receives access to the intellectual property each day.

If a licence meets the criteria to be accounted for as a series of distinct goods or services, an entity needs to consider whether any variable consideration in the contract (e.g. royalties, milestone payments) should be allocated to the distinct periods of access, if certain allocation criteria are met. See Chapter 29 at 3.3 for a discussion of the variable consideration allocation exception and 2.5 below for a discussion of the accounting for sales-based or usage-based royalties.

2.3.2 Right to use

In contrast, when the licence represents a right to use the intellectual property as it exists at a specific point in time, the customer gains control over that intellectual property at the beginning of the period for which it has the right to use the intellectual property. *[IFRS 15.B61].* This timing may differ from when the licence was granted. For example, an entity may provide a customer with the right to use intellectual property, but indicate that right to use does not start until 30 days after the agreement is finalised. For the purpose of determining when control transfers for the right-to-use licence, the Board was clear that the assessment is from the customer's perspective (i.e. when the customer can use the licensed intellectual property), rather than the entity's perspective (i.e. when the entity transfers the licence). Entities need to apply the general Step 5 requirements in paragraph 38 of IFRS 15 to determine the point in time that control of the licence transfers to the customer (see Chapter 30 at 4) in addition to paragraph B61 of IFRS 15 (i.e. the use and benefit requirement, discussed at 2.3.3 below).

The standard includes the following example of a right-to-use licence. *[IFRS 15.IE303-IE306].*

Example 31.4: Right to use intellectual property

An entity, a music record label, licenses to a customer a 1975 recording of a classical symphony by a noted orchestra. The customer, a consumer products company, has the right to use the recorded symphony in all commercials, including television, radio and online advertisements for two years in Country A. In exchange for providing the licence, the entity receives fixed consideration of €10,000 per month. The contract does not include any other goods or services to be provided by the entity. The contract is non-cancellable.

The entity assesses the goods and services promised to the customer to determine which goods and services are distinct in accordance with paragraph 27 of IFRS 15. The entity concludes that its only performance obligation is to grant the licence. The entity determines that the term of the licence (two years), its geographical scope (the customer's right to use the recording only in Country A), and the defined permitted use for the recording (in commercials) are all attributes of the promised licence in the contract.

In accordance with paragraph B58 of IFRS 15, the entity assesses the nature of the entity's promise to grant the licence. The entity does not have any contractual or implied obligations to change the licensed recording. The licensed recording has significant stand-alone functionality (i.e. the ability to be played) and, therefore, the ability of the customer to obtain the benefits of the recording is not substantially derived from the entity's ongoing activities. The entity therefore determines that the contract does not require, and the customer does not reasonably expect, the entity to undertake activities that significantly affect the licensed recording (i.e. the criterion in paragraph B58(a) is not met). Consequently, the entity concludes that the nature of its promise in transferring the licence is to provide the customer with a right to use the entity's intellectual property as it exists at the point in time that it is granted. Therefore, the promise to grant the licence is a performance obligation satisfied at a point in time. The entity recognises all of the revenue at the point in time when the customer can direct the use of, and obtain substantially all of the remaining benefits from, the licensed intellectual property.

Because of the length of time between the entity's performance (at the beginning of the period) and the customer's monthly payments over two years (which are non-cancellable), the entity considers the requirements in paragraphs 60-65 of IFRS 15 to determine whether a significant financing component exists.

2.3.3 Use and benefit requirement

IFRS 15 states that revenue from a right-to-use licence cannot be recognised before the beginning of the period during which 'the customer is able to use and benefit from the licence'. *[IFRS 15.B61]*. The IASB explained in the Basis for Conclusions that if the customer cannot use and benefit from the licensed intellectual property then, by definition, it does not control the licence. *[IFRS 15.BC414]*. See 2.4 below for discussion on licence renewals.

Consider an example where an entity provides a customer with a right to use its software, but the customer requires a code before the software will function, which the entity will not provide until 30 days after the agreement is finalised. In this example, it is likely that the entity would conclude that control of the licence does not transfer until 30 days after the agreement is finalised because that is when the customer has the right to use and can benefit from the software.

2.4 Licence renewals

As discussed at 2.3.3 above, IFRS 15 states that revenue cannot be recognised for a licence that provides a right to use the entity's intellectual property before the beginning of the period during which the customer is able to use and benefit from the licence. *[IFRS 15.B61]*. Some stakeholders questioned whether paragraph B61 of IFRS 15 applies to the renewal of an existing licence or whether the entity could recognise revenue for the renewal when the parties agree to the renewal. Therefore, the TRG discussed the application of paragraph B61 of IFRS 15 within the context of renewals or extensions of existing licences. *[IFRS 15.BC414S]*. The discussion at the TRG indicated that this is an area in which judgement is needed and, therefore, this topic was further discussed by the IASB.[2]

The IASB decided that a clarification about the application of the contract modification requirements specifically for renewals of licensing arrangements was not necessary. The Board noted that, although some diversity may arise, IFRS 15 provides an extensive framework for applying judgement (see 2.1.5.A above for further discussion on modifications of licences).

Therefore, when an entity and a customer enter into a contract to renew (or extend the period of) an existing licence, the entity needs to evaluate whether the renewal or extension should be treated as a new licence or as a modification of the existing contract.

A modification would be accounted for in accordance with the contract modifications requirements in paragraphs 18-21 of IFRS 15 (see Chapter 28 at 2.4). *[IFRS 15.BC414T]*.

Under ASC 606, revenue related to the renewal of a licence of intellectual property may not be recognised earlier than the beginning of the renewal period. This is the case even if the entity provides a copy of the intellectual property in advance or the customer has a copy of the intellectual property from another transaction. The FASB also provided an additional example to illustrate this point.

IFRS 15 does not include similar requirements. Therefore, the IASB noted in the Basis for Conclusions that entities that report under IFRS might recognise revenue for contract renewals or extensions earlier than those that report under US GAAP. *[IFRS 15.BC414U]*.

In May 2019, the FASB added a project to the agenda of the Emerging Issues Task Force (EITF) on contract modifications of licences of intellectual property. The EITF's ongoing discussions are focused on two issues related to contract modifications for licences of intellectual property: (1) accounting for modifications that extend a licence term, but are not solely a renewal of the terms and conditions of the original licence; and (2) accounting for the revocation of a licence, including the conversion of a term software licence to a software as a service (SaaS) arrangement.

2.5 Sales-based or usage-based royalties on licences of intellectual property

The standard provides application guidance on the recognition of revenue for sales-based or usage-based royalties on licences of intellectual property, which differs from the requirements that apply to other revenue from licences. IFRS 15 requires that sales-based or usage-based royalties received in exchange for licences of intellectual property are recognised at the later of when: *[IFRS 15.B63]*

(1) the subsequent sale or usage occurs; and
(2) the performance obligation to which some or all of the sales-based or usage-based royalty has been allocated is satisfied (or partially satisfied).

That is, an entity recognises the royalties as revenue for such arrangements when (or as) the customer's subsequent sales or usage occurs, unless that pattern of recognition accelerates revenue recognition ahead of the entity's satisfaction of the performance obligation to which the royalty solely or partially relates, based on an appropriate measure of progress (see Chapter 30 at 3). *[IFRS 15.BC421]*.

The Board explained in the Basis for Conclusions that for a licence of intellectual property for which the consideration is based on the *customer's* subsequent sales or usage, an entity does not recognise any revenue for the variable amounts until the uncertainty is resolved (i.e. when a customer's subsequent sales or usage occurs). *[IFRS 15.BC219]*.

The IASB also explained in the Basis for Conclusions that the application guidance in paragraphs B63-B63B of IFRS 15 addresses the recognition of sales-based or usage-based royalties received in exchange for a licence of intellectual property, rather than when such amounts are included in the transaction price of the contract. *[IFRS 15.BC421]*. As a result, this exception is a recognition constraint and the constraint on variable consideration (see Chapter 29 at 2.2.3) does not apply.

While the variable consideration constraint does not apply, the other requirements for variable consideration still apply (see Chapter 29 at 2.2.2). However, as mentioned in Chapter 29 at 2.2.2.A, this may be one of the situations where an entity may not need to estimate variable consideration at contract inception. This is because, in many cases, using this application guidance will result in the same pattern of revenue recognition as fully constraining the estimate of variable consideration associated with the future royalty stream (also see 2.5.1 below for more information about recognition of royalties for a licence that provides a right to access the entity's intellectual property). However, in cases where an entity is required to allocate sales-based or usage-based royalties to separate performance obligations in a contract, it may need to include expected royalties in its estimate of the stand-alone selling price of one or more of the performance obligations.

The Board explained that it added the royalty recognition constraint because both users and preparers of financial statements indicated that it would not be useful for entities to recognise a minimum amount of revenue for sales-based or usage-based royalties received in exchange for licences of intellectual property (following the requirements in the general model on estimating the transaction price). This is because that approach would inevitably require the entity to report significant adjustments to the amount of revenue recognised throughout the life of the contract as a result of changes in circumstances that are not related to the entity's performance. The Board observed that this would not result in relevant information, especially for contracts in which the sales-based or usage-based royalties are paid over a long period of time. *[IFRS 15.BC415]*.

In some contracts, a sales-based or usage-based royalty may be related to both a licence of intellectual property and another good or service that may, or may not, be distinct. Paragraph B63A of IFRS 15 requires that the royalty recognition constraint be applied to the overall royalty stream when the sole or predominant item to which the royalty relates is a licence of intellectual property (including when no single licence of intellectual property is the predominant item to which the royalty relates, but the royalty predominantly relates to two or more licences of intellectual property in the contract). *[IFRS 15.B63A, BC421G]*. That is, this application guidance is applicable to all licences of intellectual property, regardless of whether they have been determined to be distinct. The standard does not provide a bright line for determining the 'predominant' item in a contract that includes a licence of intellectual property. The Board acknowledged in the Basis for Conclusions that significant judgement may be required to determine when a licence is the predominant item to which a royalty relates. However, the judgement for determining whether a licence is the predominant item is likely to be less than the judgement needed to apply the general requirements for variable consideration to such contracts. *[IFRS 15.BC421E]*.

It is important to note that the application guidance in paragraphs B63-B63B of IFRS 15 applies only to licences of intellectual property for which some or all of the consideration is in the form of a sales-based or usage-based royalty. The Board said in the Basis for Conclusions that the royalty recognition constraint was structured to apply only to a particular type of transaction (i.e. a licence of intellectual property). Therefore, other transactions that may be economically similar would be accounted for differently. *[IFRS 15.BC416]*. That is, entities cannot analogise to the royalty recognition constraint for other types of transactions. For example, it cannot be applied if consideration in a contract is in the form of a sales-based or usage-based royalty, but there is either: (a) no licence of intellectual property; or (b) the licence of intellectual property to which the sales-based or usage-based royalty relates is not the predominant item in the contract (e.g. the sale of a tangible good that includes a significant amount of intellectual property). When the royalty recognition constraint cannot be applied an entity follows the requirements in the general model on estimating variable consideration and applying the constraint on variable consideration (see Chapter 29 at 2.2). In some cases, it may not be obvious as to whether the arrangement is an in-substance sale of intellectual property (i.e. a promise that is in the form of a licence, but, in substance, has the characteristics of a sale) or a licence of intellectual property. In such instances, entities would have to exercise judgement to determine whether the control over the underlying intellectual property has been transferred from the entity to the customer and therefore, has been sold.

The following figure illustrates an entity's evaluation when determining whether the royalty recognition constraint should be applied to a royalty stream:

Figure 31.1: Determining whether the royalty recognition constraint applies to a royalty stream

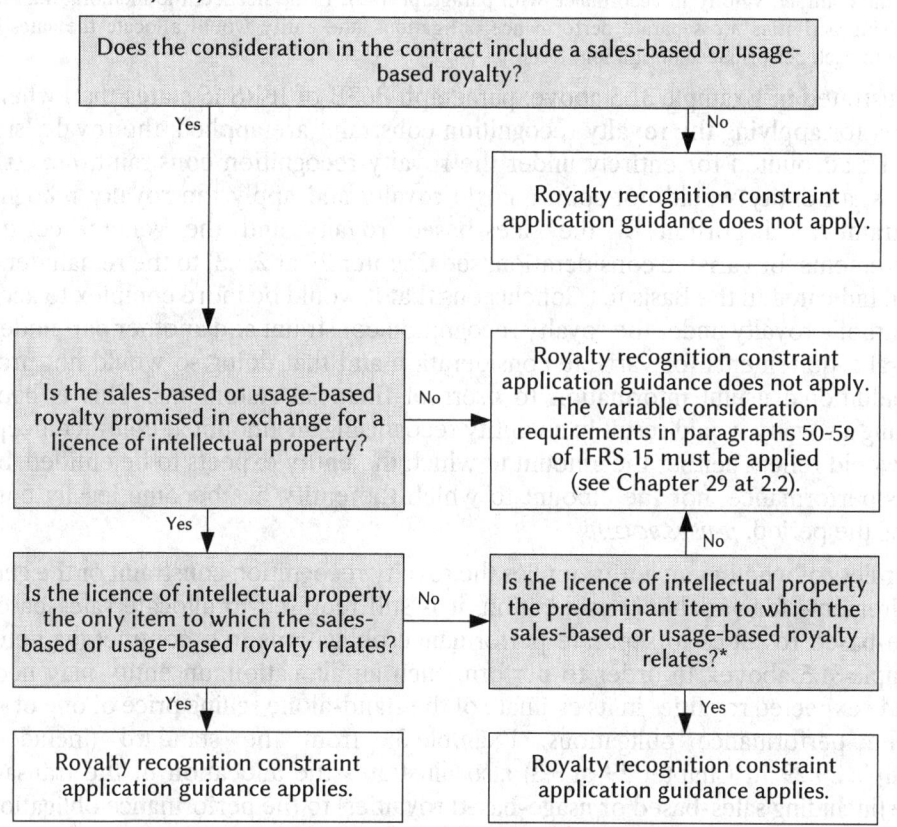

* This includes situations in which no single licence is the predominant item to which the sales-based or usage-based royalty relates, but the sales-based or usage-based royalty predominantly relates to two or more licences in the contract.

The standard provides the following example of a contract that includes two performance obligations, including a licence that provides a right to use the entity's intellectual property and consideration in the form of sales-based royalties. In the example, the licence is determined to be the predominant item to which the royalty relates. *[IFRS 15.IE307-IE308]*.

Example 31.5: Sales-based royalty for a licence of intellectual property

An entity, a movie distribution company, licenses Movie XYZ to a customer. The customer, an operator of cinemas, has the right to show the movie in its cinemas for six weeks. Additionally, the entity has agreed to: (a) provide memorabilia from the filming to the customer for display at the customer's cinemas before the beginning of the six-week screening period; and (b) sponsor radio advertisements for Movie XYZ on popular radio stations in the customer's geographical area throughout the six-week screening period. In exchange for providing the licence and the additional promotional goods and services, the entity will receive a portion of the operator's ticket sales for Movie XYZ (i.e. variable consideration in the form of a sales-based royalty).

The entity concludes that the licence to show Movie XYZ is the predominant item to which the sales-based royalty relates because the entity has a reasonable expectation that the customer would ascribe significantly more value to the licence than to the related promotional goods or services. The entity recognises revenue from the sales-based royalty, the only consideration to which the entity is entitled under the contract, wholly in accordance with paragraph B63. If the licence, the memorabilia and the advertising activities are separate performance obligations, the entity would allocate the sales-based royalty to each performance obligation.

As illustrated in Example 31.5 above, paragraph B63B of IFRS 15 states that, when the criteria for applying the royalty recognition constraint are applied, the royalty stream must be accounted for entirely under the royalty recognition constraint. *[IFRS 15.B63B]*. That is, an entity would not split a single royalty and apply the royalty recognition constraint to a portion of the sales-based royalty and the general constraint requirements for variable consideration (see Chapter 29 at 2.2.3) to the remainder. The Board indicated in the Basis for Conclusions that it would be more complex to account for part of a royalty under the royalty recognition constraint and another part under the general requirements for variable consideration and that doing so would not provide any additional useful information to users of financial statements. This is because splitting a royalty would result in an entity recognising an amount at contract inception that would reflect neither the amount to which the entity expects to be entitled, based on its performance, nor the amount to which the entity has become legally entitled during the period. *[IFRS 15.BC421J]*.

Regardless of whether an entity applies the royalty recognition constraint or the general requirements for variable consideration, it is still required to allocate sales-based or usage-based royalties to separate performance obligations in a contract (as noted in Example 31.5 above). In order to perform such an allocation, an entity may need to include expected royalties in its estimate of the stand-alone selling price of one or more of the performance obligations. Example 35 from the standard (included as Example 29.29 in Chapter 29 at 3.3) also illustrates the allocation of the transaction price (including sales-based or usage-based royalties) to the performance obligations in the contract. *[IFRS 15.IE178-IE187]*.

2.5.1 Recognition of royalties for a licence that provides a right to access intellectual property

The IASB explained in the Basis for Conclusions that the royalty recognition constraint is intended to align the recognition of sales or usage-based royalties with the standard's key principle that revenue should be recognised when (or as) an entity satisfies a performance obligation. As discussed above, IFRS 15 requires that royalties received in exchange for licences of intellectual property are recognised at the later of when: (1) the subsequent sales or usage occurs; and (2) the performance obligation to which the sales-based or usage-based royalties relates has been satisfied (or partially satisfied). That is, an entity recognises the royalties as revenue when (or as) the customer's subsequent sales or usage occurs, unless that pattern of recognition accelerates revenue recognition ahead of the entity's satisfaction of the performance obligation to which the royalty solely or partially relates, based on an appropriate measure of progress (see Chapter 30 at 3). *[IFRS 15.BC421I]*.

Consider the following example, which was provided by the FASB, that illustrates when revenue recognition may be inappropriately accelerated ahead of an entity's performance, if revenue was recognised under paragraph B63(a) of IFRS 15 for a right-to-access licence.

Example 31.6:   Licensing contract with a declining royalty rate[3]

A contract provides a customer with the right to access an entity's intellectual property and the entity receives royalties of 8% on total sales up to £1 million, 4% on the next £3 million in sales and 2% on all sales above £4 million. The declining royalty rate does not reflect changing value to the customer.

In this example, the FASB noted that recognising royalties as they are due (i.e. according to the contractual formula) would not be aligned with the principle of recognising revenue only when (or as) an entity satisfies a performance obligation because the right to access the intellectual property is provided evenly over the licence term while the declining royalty rate does not reflect the value to the customer. However, the FASB stated that the existence of a declining royalty rate in a contract does not always mean that recognising revenue for sales-based or usage-based royalties as the customer's underlying sales or usage occur is inappropriate. In fact, it would be appropriate if the declining royalty rate reflects the changing value to the customer.

The above example notwithstanding, for many contracts with licences that provide a right to access an entity's intellectual property, applying the royalty recognition constraint results in an entity recognising revenue from sales-based or usage-based royalties when (or as) the customer's underlying sales or usage occurs in accordance with paragraph B63(a) of IFRS 15. An output-based measure of progress that is the same as, or similar to, the application of the practical expedient in paragraph B16 of IFRS 15 (i.e. when the right to consideration corresponds directly with the value to the customer of the entity's performance to date) is appropriate because the entity's right to consideration (i.e. the sales-based or usage-based royalties earned) often corresponds directly with the value to the customer of the entity's performance completed to date. The practical expedient in paragraph B16 of IFRS 15 is discussed further in Chapter 30 at 3.1.1.

In addition, an output-based measure could also be appropriate for a licence that provides a right to access intellectual property in which the consideration is in the form of a fixed fee and royalties. The following example from the standard illustrates this. *[IFRS 15.IE309-IE313].*

Example 31.7: Access to intellectual property

An entity, a well-known sports team, licenses the use of its name and logo to a customer. The customer, an apparel designer, has the right to use the sports team's name and logo on items including t-shirts, caps, mugs and towels for one year. In exchange for providing the licence, the entity will receive fixed consideration of $2 million and a royalty of five per cent of the sales price of any items using the team name or logo. The customer expects that the entity will continue to play games and provide a competitive team.

The entity assesses the goods and services promised to the customer to determine which goods and services are distinct in accordance with paragraph 27 of IFRS 15. The entity concludes that its only performance obligation is to transfer the licence. The additional activities associated with the licence (i.e. continuing to play games and provide a competitive team) do not directly transfer a good or service to the customer because they are part of the entity's promise to grant the licence.

The entity assesses the nature of the entity's promise to transfer the licence in accordance with paragraph B58 of IFRS 15. In assessing the criteria the entity considers the following:

(a) the entity concludes that the customer would reasonably expect that the entity will undertake activities that will significantly affect the intellectual property (i.e. the team name and logo) to which the customer has rights. This is on the basis of the entity's customary business practice to undertake activities that support and maintain the value of the name and logo such as continuing to play and providing a competitive team. The entity determines that the ability of the customer to obtain benefit from the name and logo is substantially derived from, or dependent upon, the expected activities of the entity. In addition, the entity observes that because some of its consideration is dependent on the success of the customer (through the sales-based royalty), the entity has a shared economic interest with the customer, which indicates that the customer will expect the entity to undertake those activities to maximise earnings;

(b) the entity observes that the rights granted by the licence (i.e. the use of the team's name and logo) directly expose the customer to any positive or negative effects of the entity's activities; and

(c) the entity also observes that even though the customer may benefit from the activities through the rights granted by the licence, they do not transfer a good or service to the customer as those activities occur.

The entity concludes that the criteria in paragraph B58 of IFRS 15 are met and the nature of the entity's promise to grant the licence is to provide the customer with access to the entity's intellectual property as it exists throughout the licence period. Consequently, the entity accounts for the promised licence as a performance obligation satisfied over time (i.e. the criterion in paragraph 35(a) of IFRS 15 is met).

The entity then applies paragraphs 39–45 of IFRS 15 to determine a measure of progress that will depict the entity's performance. For the consideration that is in the form of a sales-based royalty, paragraph B63 of IFRS 15 applies because the sales-based royalty relates solely to the licence, which is the only performance obligation in the contract. The entity concludes that recognition of the $2 million fixed consideration as revenue rateably over time plus recognition of the royalty as revenue as and when the customer's sales of items using the team name or logo occur reasonably depicts the entity's progress towards complete satisfaction of the licence performance obligation.

In Example 31.7 above, the fixed consideration of $2 million is an explicit term in the contract with the customer. In some contracts, fixed consideration may be implied, such as when a guaranteed minimum amount of royalties is part of the transaction price.

In addition, as discussed in 2.3.1.A above, many licences that provide a right to access intellectual property may constitute a series of distinct goods or services that are substantially the same and have the same pattern of transfer to the customer (e.g. a series of distinct periods of access to intellectual property, such as monthly access or quarterly access). In cases where the criteria for a performance obligation to be accounted for as a series of distinct goods or services have been met, an entity needs to consider whether any variable consideration in the contract (e.g. sales-based or usage-based royalties) should be allocated directly to the distinct periods of access, if the criteria for certain allocation exceptions are met. The allocation of sales-based or usage-based royalties in this manner generally results in the recognition of royalties as revenue when (or as) the customer's underlying sales or usage occurs.

An entity may need to apply significant judgement to determine the appropriate pattern of revenue recognition for royalties received on a licence that provides a right to access intellectual property.

2.5.2 Application questions on the sales-based or usage-based royalty recognition constraint

2.5.2.A Can the recognition constraint for sales-based or usage-based royalties be applied to royalties that are paid in consideration for sales of intellectual property (rather than just licences of intellectual property)?

As noted in the Basis for Conclusions, the Board discussed but decided not to expand the scope of the royalty recognition constraint to include sales of intellectual property. The Board also stated that the royalty recognition constraint is intended to apply only to limited circumstances (i.e. those circumstances involving licences of intellectual property) and, therefore, entities cannot apply it by analogy to other types of transactions. [IFRS 15.BC421, BC421F].

2.5.2.B If a contract for a licence of intellectual property includes payments with fixed amounts (e.g. milestone payments) that are determined by reference to sales-based or usage-based thresholds, would the royalty recognition constraint need to be applied?

We generally believe the royalty recognition constraint would apply to fixed amounts of variable consideration (i.e. fixed amounts of consideration that are contingent on the occurrence of a future event), such as milestone payments, provided the amounts are determined by reference to sales-based or usage-based thresholds. This is the case even if those payments are not referred to as 'royalties' under the terms of the contract. However, entities need to apply judgement and carefully evaluate the facts and circumstances of their contracts for licences of intellectual property to determine whether these types of payments should be accounted for using the royalty recognition constraint.

Consider the following example.

Example 31.8: Application of the royalty recognition constraint to a milestone payment

An entity enters into a contract to grant a customer a right to use the entity's intellectual property. The contract contains payment terms that include a ¥100 million milestone payment that is payable to the entity once the customer has achieved sales of ¥1 billion associated with the licence.

The entity determines that the milestone payment is based on the customer's subsequent sales and represents variable consideration because it is contingent on the customer's sales reaching ¥1 billion. The entity accounts for the ¥100 million milestone payment in accordance with the royalty recognition constraint and only recognises revenue for the milestone payment once the customer's sales reach ¥1 billion.

2.5.2.C   If a contract for a licence of intellectual property includes a milestone payment based on the first commercial sale, should the royalty recognition constraint be applied?

We generally believe it would be acceptable for an entity to apply the royalty recognition constraint to a milestone payment that is contingent on the customer's first commercial sale of a product using the entity's intellectual property. This is because the milestone payment is linked to a sales-based or usage-based threshold (i.e. the milestone payment is based on the customer's sales).

Consider the following example.

Example 31.9:   Application of the royalty recognition constraint to a milestone payment based on the first commercial sale

An entity enters into a contract to grant a customer a right to use the entity's intellectual property. The contract contains payment terms that include a €10 million milestone payment that is payable to the entity upon the customer's first commercial sale of a product that uses the entity's intellectual property.

The entity determines that the milestone payment is based on the customer's subsequent sales and represents variable consideration because it is contingent on the customer's first commercial sale. It accounts for the €10 million milestone payment in accordance with the royalty recognition constraint and only recognises revenue for the milestone payment upon the customer's first commercial sale.

In contrast, if a milestone payment is contingent on metrics that are not determined by reference to sales-based or usage-based thresholds and that are substantive (e.g. regulatory approval), the royalty recognition constraint must not be applied because it is not linked to a sales-based or usage-based threshold (i.e. the milestone payment is not based on the customer's sales). Rather, the general variable consideration requirements need to be applied.

As discussed in Chapter 29 at 2.2.3.C, we expect entities to conclude, in many instances, that milestone payments contingent on regulatory approval (e.g. regulatory approval of a new drug) are constrained, preventing them from recognising these payments until the uncertainty associated with the payments is resolved.

2.5.2.D   Can an entity recognise revenue for sales-based or usage-based royalties for licences of intellectual property on a lag if actual sales or usage data is not available at the end of a reporting period?

The standard requires that sales-based or usage-based royalties promised in exchange for licences of intellectual property be recognised as revenue at the later of when: (1) the subsequent sales or usage occurs; and (2) the performance obligation to which the sales-based or usage-based royalties relates has been satisfied (or partially satisfied). Therefore, after the conditions in the royalty recognition constraint application guidance have been met (i.e. the underlying sales or usage has occurred and the performance obligation to which the royalties relate has been satisfied, or partially satisfied), we believe that licensors without actual sales or usage data from the licensee need to make an estimate of royalties earned in the current reporting period.

2.5.2.E   Recognition of royalties with minimum guarantees promised in exchange for a licence of intellectual property that is satisfied at a point in time

In November 2016, FASB TRG members were asked to consider how a minimum guarantee affects the recognition of sales-based or usage-based royalties promised in exchange for a licence of intellectual property that is satisfied at a point in time.[4] The FASB TRG members generally agreed that a minimum guaranteed amount of sales based or usage-based royalties promised in exchange for a licence of intellectual property that is satisfied at a point in time (IFRS: right-to-use licence; US GAAP: licence of functional intellectual property) would need to be recognised as revenue at the point in time that the entity transfers control of the licence to the customer (see 2.3.2 above). Any royalties above the fixed minimum would be recognised in accordance with the royalty recognition constraint (i.e. at the later of when the sale or usage occurs or when the entity satisfies the performance obligation to which some or all of the royalty has been allocated).[5]

2.5.2.F   Recognition of royalties with minimum guarantees promised in exchange for a licence of intellectual property that is satisfied over time

In November 2016, FASB TRG members were asked to consider how a minimum guarantee affects the recognition of sales-based or usage-based royalties promised in exchange for a licence of intellectual property that is satisfied over time.[6] The FASB TRG members generally agreed that various recognition approaches could be acceptable for minimum guarantees promised in exchange for licences of intellectual property that are satisfied over time (IFRS: right-to-access licences; US GAAP: licences of symbolic intellectual property, see 2.3.1 above). This is because, as the FASB staff noted in the TRG agenda paper, this question is asking what is an appropriate measure of progress for such contracts and the standard permits reasonable judgement when selecting a measure of progress. Because the standard does not prescribe a single approach that must be applied in all circumstances in which a sales-based or usage-based royalty is promised in exchange for a licence of intellectual property and the contract includes a minimum guaranteed amount, an entity should consider the nature of its arrangements and make sure that the measure of progress it selects does not override the core principle of the standard that 'an entity shall recognise revenue to depict the transfer of promised goods or services to customers in an amount that reflects the consideration to which the entity expects to be entitled in exchange for those goods or services'. *[IFRS 15.2]*. An entity would need to disclose the accounting policy it selects because it is likely that this would affect the timing of revenue recognised.

The agenda paper describes two approaches. Under one approach, an entity would estimate the total consideration (i.e. the fixed minimum and the variable consideration from future royalties) and apply an appropriate measure of progress to recognise revenue as the entity satisfies the performance obligation, subject to the royalty recognition constraint. Alternatively, under the other approach, an entity could apply a measure of progress to the fixed consideration and begin recognising the variable component after exceeding the fixed amount on a cumulative basis.

The first approach can be applied in two different ways, as follows:

- *View A*: If an entity expects royalties to exceed the minimum guarantee, the entity may determine that an output-based measure is an appropriate measure of progress and apply the right-to-invoice practical expedient (i.e. paragraph B16 of IFRS 15, see Chapter 30 at 3.1.1) because the royalties due for each period correlate directly with the value to the customer of the entity's performance each period. As a result of applying the practical expedient for recognising revenue, the entity would not need to estimate the expected royalties beyond determining whether it expects, at contract inception, that the royalties will exceed the minimum guarantee. However, the entity would be required to update that assessment at the end of each reporting period. It is important to note that this view is likely to be appropriate if the entity expects cumulative royalties to exceed the minimum guarantee.
- *View B*: An entity estimates the transaction price for the performance obligation (including both fixed and variable consideration) and recognises revenue using an appropriate measure of progress, subject to the royalty recognition constraint. If an entity does not expect cumulative royalties to exceed the minimum guarantee, the measure of progress is applied to the minimum guarantee since the transaction price will at least equal the fixed amount.

The second approach can be summarised, as follows:

- *View C*: An entity recognises the minimum guarantee (i.e. the fixed consideration) using an appropriate measure of progress and recognises royalties only when cumulative royalties exceed the minimum guarantee.

The FASB staff noted in the TRG agenda paper that, in order for an entity to apply View C, the over-time licence would have to be considered a series of distinct goods or services (i.e. a series of distinct time periods) and the variable consideration (i.e. the royalties in excess of the minimum guarantee) would have to be allocated to the distinct time periods to which they relate.

To illustrate the application of these views, the following example has been adapted from one included in the FASB TRG agenda paper.

Example 31.10:   Accounting for a licence of intellectual property that is satisfied over time in exchange for a minimum guarantee and sales-based royalty

An entity enters into a five-year arrangement to licence a trademark. The trademark is determined to be a licence of intellectual property that is satisfied over time (IFRS: right-to-access licence; US GAAP: licence of symbolic intellectual property). The licence requires the customer to pay a sales-based royalty of 5% of its gross sales associated with the trademark. However, the contract includes a guarantee that the entity will receive a minimum of £5 million for the entire five-year period.

The customer's actual gross sales associated with the trademark and the related royalties each year are, as follows (this information is not known at the beginning of the contract):

Year 1 – £15 million (royalties equal £750,000)

Year 2 – £30 million (royalties equal £1.5 million)

Year 3 – £40 million (royalties equal £2 million)

Year 4 – £20 million (royalties equal £1 million)

Year 5 – £60 million (royalties equal £3 million)

Total royalties equal £8.25 million.

View A: The entity expects total royalties to exceed the minimum guarantee. The entity determines that an output-based measure is an appropriate measure of progress and applies the right-to-invoice practical expedient because the royalties due for each period correlate directly with the value to the customer of the entity's performance for each period. The entity recognises revenue from the sales-based royalty when the customer's subsequent sales occur.

(in £000s)	Year 1	Year 2	Year 3	Year 4	Year 5
Royalties received	750	1,500	2,000	1,000	3,000
Annual revenue	750	1,500	2,000	1,000	3,000
Cumulative revenue	750	2,250	4,250	5,250	8,250

View B: The entity estimates the transaction price (including fixed and variable consideration) for the contract. The entity determines that time elapsed is an appropriate measure of progress and recognises revenue rateably over the five-year term of the contract, subject to the royalty recognition constraint (i.e. cumulative revenue recognised cannot exceed the cumulative royalties received once the minimum guarantee has been met).

(in £000s)	Year 1	Year 2	Year 3	Year 4	Year 5
Royalties received	750	1,500	2,000	1,000	3,000
Royalties (cumulative)	750	2,250	4,250	5,250	8,250
Fixed + Variable (rateable)[a]	1,650	1,650	1,650	1,650	1,650
Annual revenue	1,650	1,650	1,650	300	3,000
Cumulative revenue	1,650	3,300	4,950	[b]5,250	8,250

(a) Assuming the entity's estimated transaction price (including both fixed and variable consideration) is £8.25 million, the annual revenue that could be recognised is £1.65 million (£8.25 million divided by five years, being contract term).

(b) In Year 4, the cumulative revenue using a time-elapsed measure of progress of £6.6 million (£4.95 million plus £1.65 million) exceeds the cumulative royalties received (£5.25 million). As such, the total cumulative revenue recognised through to the end of Year 4 is constrained to the total cumulative royalties received of £5.25 million.

View C: The entity recognises the minimum guarantee (i.e. the fixed consideration) using an appropriate measure of progress and recognises royalties only when cumulative royalties exceed the minimum guarantee. The entity determines that time elapsed is an appropriate measure of progress.

The entity applies the royalty recognition constraint to the sales-based royalties that are in excess of the minimum guarantee (i.e. recognise the royalties as revenue when the minimum guarantee is exceeded on a cumulative basis). The variable consideration (royalties in excess of the minimum guarantee) is allocated to the distinct periods using the variable consideration allocation exception (see Chapter 29 at 3.3). *[IFRS 15.85]*. As previously discussed, the FASB staff noted in the TRG agenda paper that, in order for an entity to apply View C, the over-time licence would have to be considered a series of distinct goods or services (i.e. a series of distinct time periods) and the variable consideration (i.e. the royalties that are in excess of the minimum guarantee) would have to be allocated to the distinct time periods to which they relate.

(in £000s)	Year 1	Year 2	Year 3	Year 4	Year 5
Royalties received	750	1,500	2,000	1,000	3,000
Royalties (cumulative)	750	2,250	4,250	5,250	8,250
Fixed (rateable)[a]	1,000	1,000	1,000	1,000	1,000
Annual revenue	1,000	1,000	1,000	[b]1,250	[c]4,000
Cumulative revenue	1,000	2,000	3,000	4,250	8,250

(a) Because the minimum guarantee is £5 million over the contract term, the annual revenue (excluding royalties that are in excess of the minimum guarantee) is £1 million (£5 million divided by five years, being the contract term).

(b) In Year 4, the cumulative royalties received (£5.25 million) exceed the total minimum guarantee (£5 million) by £250,000. As such, the annual revenue recognised in Year 4 is £1.25 million (£1 million annual revenue plus £250,000 of royalties in excess of the minimum guarantee).

(c) In Year 5, the annual revenue recognised (£4 million) is calculated as the £1 million annual revenue plus the royalties for that year (£3 million) since the royalties exceeded the minimum guarantee in Year 4.

The FASB staff noted in the TRG agenda paper that other measures of progress, in addition to those set out above, could be acceptable because the standard permits entities to use judgement in selecting an appropriate measure of progress and that judgement is not limited to the views in the TRG agenda paper. However, the staff emphasised that it would not be acceptable for entities to apply any measure of progress in any circumstance. For example, the FASB staff noted it would not be acceptable to apply multiple measures of progress to a single performance obligation, such as one measure for fixed consideration and a different one for variable consideration. The staff also thought it would not be appropriate for an entity to apply the breakage model in paragraph B46 of IFRS 15 (see Chapter 30 at 11) because it is likely that a customer would not have an unexercised right in a licence arrangement if the entity is providing the customer with access to its intellectual property over the entire term of the arrangement. *[IFRS 15.B46]*. Another approach that would not be appropriate, according to the FASB staff, is one that ignores the royalties recognition constraint application guidance in paragraph B63 of IFRS 15, which requires revenue to be recognised at the later of when: (1) the subsequent sale or usage occurs; or (2) the performance obligation to which some or all of the sales-based or usage-based royalty has been allocated is satisfied (in whole or in part) (discussed at 2.5 above). *[IFRS 15.B63]*.

2.5.2.G   Application of the royalty recognition constraint for sales-based or usage-based royalties when an entity does not own the intellectual property or control the intellectual property as a principal in the arrangement

We generally believe entities can apply the royalty recognition constraint if their revenue is based on a sales-based or usage-based royalty from a licence of intellectual property, but they do not own or control the intellectual property as a principal in the arrangement.

Consider the following example:

Example 31.11:   Application of the royalty recognition constraint as an agent

University U has intellectual property for its logo. Company Z, acting as an agent for University U, identifies an apparel company looking to license University U's logo to put it on merchandise. University U is paid a royalty based on sales and usage of its intellectual property (the logo) by the licensee (the apparel company). Company Z receives a portion of the royalty earned by University U. Company Z does not control the intellectual property at any point during the arrangement and its ability to receive consideration from University U depends on the licensing of University U's intellectual property. We believe that application of the royalty recognition constraint may be appropriate in this example because the royalties earned by University U and, in effect, the amount Company Z expects to be entitled to receive, are directly tied to the usage of the intellectual property.

It is important to note that this view applies only to licences of intellectual property for which some or all of the consideration received by both the licensor and the agent is in the form of a sales-based or usage-based royalty. Entities cannot analogise to this view for other situations. Entities should disclose their use of the royalty recognition constraint because it is likely to affect the amount and timing of revenue recognised.

2.5.2.H   Can entities recognise sales-based or usage-based royalties before the sale or usage of the intellectual property occurs if they have historical information that is highly predictive of future royalty amounts?

Entities cannot recognise sales-based or usage-based royalties before the sale or usage of the intellectual property occurs even if they have historical information that is highly predictive of future royalty amounts. In accordance with paragraphs B63-B63B of IFRS 15, revenue from a sales-based or usage-based royalty promised in exchange for a licence of intellectual property is recognised at the later of when: (1) the subsequent sale or usage occurs; or (2) the performance obligation to which some or all of the sales-based or usage-based royalty has been allocated has been satisfied (in whole or in part). Revenue recognition cannot be accelerated even if an entity has historical information that is highly predictive of future royalty amounts. That is, the use of the royalty recognition constraint is not optional.

2.5.2.I   Should an entity apply the royalty recognition constraint when the royalty is calculated on a financial metric that is not solely based on sales or usage?

In certain circumstances, we believe the royalty recognition constraint can be applied when the royalty is calculated on a financial metric that is not solely based on sales or usage. For example, a licensor may be entitled to a fee based on a fixed percentage of gross profit generated by the licensee for the entire term of the contract. We believe that a metric such as gross profit, (commonly defined as sales less cost of goods sold) is largely attributable to sales. Therefore, if the royalty is calculated using gross profit, the royalty recognition constraint may be applied.

Judgement will be required to determine whether the royalty recognition constraint can be applied if the royalty is based on a different financial metric that is not solely based on sales or usage.

3 WARRANTIES

Warranties are commonly included in arrangements to sell goods or services. They may be explicitly included in the contractual arrangement with a customer or may be required by law or regulation. In addition, an entity may have established an implicit policy of providing warranty services to maintain a desired level of satisfaction among its customers. Whether explicit or implicit, warranty obligations extend an entity's obligations beyond the transfer of control of the good or service to the customer, requiring it to stand ready to perform under the warranty over the life of the warranty obligation.

The price of a warranty may be included in the overall purchase price or listed separately as an optional product. While the standard notes that the nature of a warranty can vary significantly across industries and contracts, it identifies two types of warranties: *[IFRS 15.B28]*

- warranties that promise the customer that the delivered product is as specified in the contract (called 'assurance-type warranties'); and
- warranties that provide a service to the customer in addition to assurance that the delivered product is as specified in the contract (called 'service-type warranties').

3.1 Determining whether a warranty is an assurance-type or service-type warranty

If the customer has the option to purchase the warranty separately or if the warranty provides a service to the customer, beyond fixing defects that existed at the time of sale paragraph B29 of IFRS 15 states that the entity is providing a service-type warranty. *[IFRS 15.B29]*. Otherwise, it is an assurance-type warranty, which provides the customer with assurance that the product complies with agreed-upon specifications. *[IFRS 15.B30]*. In some cases, it may be difficult to determine whether a warranty provides a customer with a service in addition to the assurance that the delivered product is as specified in the contract. In assessing whether a warranty provides a customer with a service (in addition to the assurance that the product complies with agreed-upon specifications), an entity is required to consider factors such as: *[IFRS 15.B31]*

- whether the warranty is required by law – if the entity is required by law to provide a warranty, the existence of that law indicates that the promised warranty is not a performance obligation because such requirements typically exist to protect customers from the risk of purchasing defective products;
- the length of the warranty coverage period – the longer the coverage period, the more likely it is that the promised warranty is a performance obligation because it is more likely to provide a service in addition to the assurance that the product complies with agreed-upon specifications; and
- the nature of the tasks that the entity promises to perform – if it is necessary for an entity to perform specified tasks to provide the assurance that a product complies with agreed-upon specifications (e.g. a return shipping service for a defective product), then those tasks likely do not give rise to a performance obligation.

The standard specifies that the following do not give rise to performance obligations:

- 'a law that requires an entity to pay compensation if its products cause harm or damage' – the standard gives the example of a manufacturer that sells products in a jurisdiction that, by law, holds the manufacturer liable for any damages arising if a consumer has used a product for its intended purpose; and
- 'an entity's promise to indemnify a customer for liabilities and damages arising from claims of patent, copyright, trademark or other infringement by the entity's products'. *[IFRS 15.B33]*.

The following figure illustrates these requirements:

Figure 31.2: Determining whether a warranty is an assurance-type or service-type warranty

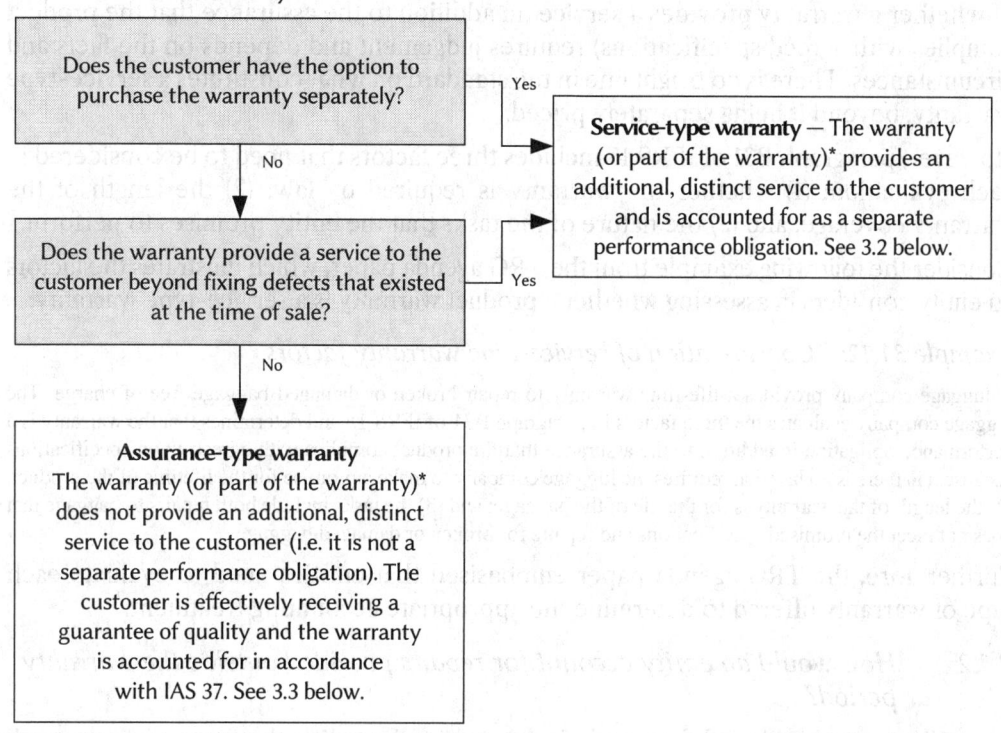

* Some contracts may include both as assurance-type warranty and a service-type warranty. See 3.4 below for further discussion

Entities may need to exercise significant judgement when determining whether a warranty is an assurance-type or service-type warranty. An entity's evaluation may be affected by several factors including common warranty practices within its industry and the entity's business practices related to warranties. For example, consider an automotive manufacturer that provides a five-year warranty on a luxury vehicle and a three-year warranty on a standard vehicle. The manufacturer may conclude that the longer warranty period is not an additional service because it believes the materials used to construct the luxury vehicle are of a higher quality and that latent defects would take longer to appear. In contrast, the manufacturer may also consider the length of the warranty period and the nature of the services provided under the warranty and conclude that the five-year warranty period, or some portion of it, is an additional service that needs to be accounted for as a service-type warranty. The standard excludes assurance-type warranties, which are accounted for in accordance with IAS 37. [IFRS 15.B33].

See Chapter 29 at 2.2.1.B for a discussion on whether liquidated damages, penalties or compensation from other similar clauses should be accounted for as variable consideration or warranty provisions under the standard.

3.1.1 Evaluating whether a product warranty is a service-type warranty (i.e. a performance obligation) when it is not separately priced

At the March 2015 TRG meeting, the TRG members generally agreed that the evaluation of whether a warranty provides a service (in addition to the assurance that the product complies with agreed specifications) requires judgement and depends on the facts and circumstances. There is no bright line in the standard on what constitutes a service-type warranty, beyond it being separately priced.

However, paragraph B31 of IFRS 15 includes three factors that need to be considered in each evaluation: (1) whether the warranty is required by law; (2) the length of the warranty coverage; and (3) the nature of the tasks that the entity promises to perform.

Consider the following example from the TRG agenda paper, which illustrates the factors an entity considers in assessing whether a product warranty is a service-type warranty:

Example 31.12: Consideration of service-type warranty factors

A luggage company provides a life-time warranty to repair broken or damaged baggage free of charge. The luggage company evaluates the three factors in paragraph B31 of IFRS 15 and determines that the warranty is a performance obligation in addition to the assurance that the product complies with agreed-upon specifications because: (1) there is no law that requires the luggage company to make a promise for the lifetime of the product; (2) the length of the warranty is for the life of the baggage; and (3) the tasks include both repairs to baggage that does not meet the promised specifications and repairs for broken or damaged baggage.

Furthermore, the TRG agenda paper emphasised that entities need to evaluate each type of warranty offered to determine the appropriate accounting treatment.[7]

3.1.2 How would an entity account for repairs provided outside the warranty period?

An entity must consider all facts and circumstances, including the factors in paragraph B31 of IFRS 15 (e.g. the nature of the services provided, the length of the implied warranty period) to determine whether repairs provided outside the warranty period need to be accounted for as an assurance-type or service-type warranty. Sometimes, entities provide these services as part of their customary business practices, in addition to providing assurance-type warranties for specified periods of time. For example, an equipment manufacturer may give its customers a standard product warranty that provides assurance that the product complies with agreed-upon specifications for one year from the date of purchase. However, the entity may also provide an implied warranty by frequently repairing products for free after the one-year standard warranty period has ended. See Chapter 28 at 3.1 for a discussion of implied promises in a contract with a customer.

If the entity determines that the repairs made during the implied warranty period generally involve defects that existed when the product was sold and the repairs occur shortly after the assurance warranty period, the entity may conclude that the repairs are covered by an assurance-type warranty. That is, the term of the assurance-type warranty may be longer than that stated in the contract. However, all facts need to be considered to reach a conclusion.

If the entity determines that the repairs provided outside the warranty period are covered by a service-type warranty (because the entity is providing a service to the customer beyond fixing defects that existed at the time of sale), it also needs to consider whether the term of the service-type warranty is longer than that stated in the contract.

3.1.3 Customer's return of a defective item in exchange for compensation: right of return versus assurance-type warranty

Should an entity account for a customer's return of a defective item in exchange for compensation (i.e. not for a replacement item) as a right of return or an assurance-type warranty? We believe that an entity should account for the right to return a defective item in return for cash (instead of a replacement item) under the right of return application guidance in paragraphs B20-B27 of IFRS 15, rather than as an assurance-type warranty. The Basis for Conclusions states that '... the boards decided that an entity should recognise an assurance-type warranty as a separate liability to replace or repair a defective product'. *[IFRS 15.BC376]*. This description of an assurance-type warranty does not include defective products that are returned for a refund. It only contemplates defective products that are replaced or repaired. See Chapter 29 at 2.4 for a discussion of rights of return.

However, there may be limited circumstances in which the cash paid to a customer for a defective item would need to be accounted for in accordance with the warranty application guidance, instead of as a right of return. For example, an entity may pay cash to a customer as reimbursement for third-party costs incurred to repair a defective item. In this case, the cash payment to the customer was incurred to fulfil the entity's warranty obligation. This assessment requires judgement and depend on the facts and circumstances.

3.2 Service-type warranties

The Board determined that a service-type warranty represents a distinct service and is a separate performance obligation. *[IFRS 15.BC371]*. Therefore, using the relative stand-alone selling price of the warranty, an entity allocates a portion of the transaction price to the service-type warranty (see Chapter 29 at 3). The entity then recognises the allocated revenue over the period in which the service-type warranty service is provided. *[IFRS 15.B29, B32]*. This is because it is likely that the customer receives and consumes the benefits of the warranty as the entity performs (i.e. it is likely that the warranty performance obligation is satisfied over time in accordance with paragraph 35(a) of IFRS 15, see Chapter 30 at 2.1).

Judgement may be required to determine the appropriate pattern of revenue recognition associated with service-type warranties. For example, an entity may determine that it provides the warranty service continuously over the warranty period (i.e. the performance obligation is an obligation to 'stand ready to perform' during the stated warranty period). An entity that makes this determination is likely to recognise revenue rateably over the warranty period. An entity may also conclude that a different pattern of recognition is appropriate based on data it has collected about when it provides such services. For example, an entity may recognise little or no revenue in the first year of a three-year service-type warranty if its historical data indicates that it only provides warranty services in the second and third years of the warranty period.

The American Institute of Certified Public Accountants (AICPA) Audit and Accounting Guide, *Revenue Recognition*, provides non-authoritative guidance on how to determine the appropriate pattern of recognition for service-type warranties. The guidance says that, if an entity determines that it is standing ready to provide protection against damage, loss or malfunction of a product caused by various risks for the specified coverage period (i.e. provides assurance of use for the covered product for the coverage period that would include some level of involvement with the repair or replacement), it recognises revenue over the coverage period.

If an entity determines that it has promised to repair, arrange to repair or replace the product, it recognises revenue over the period in which it is expected to repair or replace the product. The period could extend beyond the coverage period if services to repair or replace the product are expected to be provided after the coverage period ends.

For example, a claim may be filed at the end of a one-year period, but it is fulfilled after the coverage period ends. While the activities in both instances may be similar, the nature of the promise to the customer determines the period of recognition.[8] Considerations for determining the appropriate pattern of revenue recognition are described in Chapter 30 at 3, including those for stand-ready obligations. If payment for the service-type warranty is received upfront, an entity should also evaluate whether a significant financing component exists (see Chapter 29 at 2.5).

In some instances, entities that sell service-type warranties will buy insurance to protect themselves against the potential costs of performing under such warranties. Although the anticipated insurance proceeds might offset any costs that the entity might incur, immediate revenue recognition for the price of the service-type warranty is not appropriate. The entity has not been relieved of its obligation to perform under the terms of the warranty contract and, therefore, a liability still exists. Accordingly, the warranty obligation and any proceeds related to the insurance coverage need to be accounted for separately (unless the insurer has legally assumed the warranty obligation and the customer has acknowledged that fact).

As discussed in Chapter 29 at 3.1, stand-alone selling prices are determined at contract inception and are not updated to reflect changes between contract inception and when performance is complete. Accordingly, an entity would not change the amount of transaction price it originally allocated to the service-type warranty at contract inception. This would be the case, even if, for example, an entity may discover two months after a product is shipped that the cost of a part acquired from a third-party manufacturer has tripled and that, as a result, it will cost the entity significantly more to replace that part if a warranty claim is made. However, for future contracts involving the same warranty, the entity would need to determine whether to revise the stand-alone selling price because of the increase in the costs to satisfy the warranty and, if so, use that revised price for future allocations (see Chapter 29 at 3.1.3).

3.3 Assurance-type warranties

The Board concluded that assurance-type warranties do not provide an additional good or service to the customer (i.e. they are not separate performance obligations). By providing this type of warranty, the selling entity has effectively provided a guarantee of quality. In accordance with paragraph B30 of IFRS 15, these types of warranties are accounted for as warranty obligations and the estimated cost of satisfying them is accrued in accordance with the requirements in IAS 37. *[IFRS 15.B30, BC376]*. Once recorded, the warranty liability is assessed on an ongoing basis in accordance with IAS 37.

An entity might recognise revenue for sales of goods or services including assurance-type warranties when control of the goods or services is transferred to the customer, assuming that the arrangement meets the criteria to be considered a contract under IFRS 15 (see Chapter 28 at 2.1) and the entity's costs of honouring its warranty obligations are reasonably estimable.

Assurance-type warranties are accounted for outside of the scope of IFRS 15. Therefore, if an entity elects to use a costs incurred measure of progress for over time revenue recognition of the related good or service, the costs of satisfying an assurance-type warranty are excluded (i.e. excluded from both the numerator and the denominator in the measure of progress calculation. See Chapter 30 at 3 for further discussion on measuring progress over time).

3.4 Contracts that contain both assurance and service-type warranties

Some contracts may include both an assurance-type warranty and a service-type warranty. However, if an entity provides both an assurance-type and service-type warranty within a contract and the entity cannot reasonably account for them separately, the warranties are accounted for as a single performance obligation (i.e. revenue would be allocated to the combined warranty and recognised over the period the warranty services are provided). *[IFRS 15.B32]*.

When an assurance-type warranty and a service-type warranty are both present in a contract with a customer, an entity is required to accrue for the expected costs associated with the assurance-type warranty and defer the revenue for the service-type warranty, as illustrated in Example 31.13.

Example 31.13: Service-type and assurance-type warranties

An entity manufactures and sells computers that include an assurance-type warranty for the first 90 days. The entity offers an optional 'extended coverage' plan under which it will repair or replace any defective part for three years from the expiration of the assurance-type warranty. Since the optional 'extended coverage' plan is sold separately, the entity determines that the three years of extended coverage represent a separate performance obligation (i.e. a service-type warranty).

The total transaction price for the sale of a computer and the extended warranty is $3,600. The entity determines that the stand-alone selling prices of the computer and the extended warranty are $3,200 and $400, respectively. The inventory value of the computer is $1,440. Furthermore, the entity estimates that, based on its experience, it will incur $200 in costs to repair defects that arise within the 90-day coverage period for the assurance-type warranty. As a result, the entity will record the following entries:

Dr. Cash/Trade receivables	$3,600	
Dr. Warranty expense	$200	
Cr. Accrued warranty costs (assurance-type warranty)		$200
Cr. Contract liability (service-type warranty)		$400
Cr. Revenue		$3,200

To record revenue and contract liabilities related to warranties.

Dr. Cost of goods sold	$1,440	
Cr. Inventory		$1,440

To derecognise inventory and recognise cost of goods sold.

The entity derecognises the accrued warranty liability associated with the assurance-type warranty as actual warranty costs are incurred during the first 90 days after the customer receives the computer. The entity recognises the contract liability associated with the service-type warranty as revenue during the contract warranty period and recognises the costs associated with providing the service-type warranty as they are incurred. The entity would need to be able to determine whether the repair costs incurred are applied against the warranty reserve it had already established for claims that occur during the first 90 days or recognised as an expense as incurred.

Accounting for both assurance-type warranties and service-type warranties in the same transaction may be complex. Entities may need to develop processes to match individual warranty claims with the specific warranty plans so that claims can be analysed for the appropriate accounting treatment. This individual assessment of warranty claims is necessary because the assurance-type warranty costs will have been accrued previously, while the service-type warranty costs are expenses that need to be recognised in the period in which they are incurred, as illustrated in Example 31.14.

Example 31.14: Service-type and assurance-type warranty costs

Assume the same facts as in Example 31.13, but assume the entity has sold 500 computers during the year. In January of the following year, $10,000 of warranty claims are submitted by customers. The entity analyses each claim and identifies the specific computer sale to which the claims relate. The entity needs to do this in order to determine eligibility under the warranty plans and the appropriate accounting treatment.

The entity determines that a portion of the claims, costing $2,500 for repair and replacement parts, are covered by the assurance-type warranty plan. As shown above in Example 31.13, the expected cost of each assurance-type warranty was accrued at the time of the sale. The entity records the following entry to derecognise a portion of the warranty liability:

Dr. Accrued warranty costs (assurance-type warranty)	$2,500	
Cr. Cash		$2,500

To derecognise the assurance-type warranty liability as the costs are incurred.

The entity also determines that a portion of the claims, costing $7,000 for repair and replacement parts, are eligible under the 'extended coverage' plan (i.e. the service-type warranty). The entity records the following entry to recognise the costs associated with the service-type warranty:

Dr. Warranty expense	$7,000	
Cr. Cash		$7,000

To record the costs of the service-type warranty as the costs are incurred.

The entity also determines that $500 of the claims are not eligible under either warranty plan. This is because the claims relate to incidents that occurred after the 90-day coverage period for the assurance-type warranty and the customers in those transactions did not purchase the extended warranty coverage. The entity rejects these customer claims.

4 ONEROUS CONTRACTS

Entities are required to use the existing requirements in IAS 37 to identify and measure onerous revenue contracts. *[IFRS 15.BC296]*.

IAS 37 requires that, if an entity has a contract that is onerous, the present obligation under the contract must be recognised and measured as a provision. However, before a separate provision for an onerous contract is established, an entity recognises any impairment loss that has occurred on assets dedicated to that contract in accordance with IAS 36 – *Impairment of Assets*. *[IAS 37.66, 69]*.

IAS 37 clarifies that many contracts (e.g. some routine purchase orders) can be cancelled without paying compensation to the other party, and therefore there is no obligation. Other contracts establish both rights and obligations for each of the contracting parties. Where events make such a contract onerous, the contract falls within the scope of IAS 37 and a liability exists which is recognised. In addition, executory contracts that are not onerous fall outside its scope. IAS 37 goes on to define an onerous contract as 'a contract in which the unavoidable costs of meeting the obligations under the contract exceed the economic benefits expected to be received under it. The unavoidable costs under a contract reflect the least net cost of exiting from the contract, which is the lower of the cost of fulfilling it and any compensation or penalties arising from failure to fulfil it'. *[IAS 37.67-68]*. See Chapter 26 for further discussion.

In May 2020, the IASB issued amendments to IAS 37 clarifying that, when assessing whether a contract is onerous, 'the cost of fulfilling a contract comprises the costs that relate directly to the contract' and consist of both 'the incremental costs of fulfilling that contract' and 'an allocation of other costs that relate directly to fulfilling contract'. The amendments are effective for periods beginning on or after 1 January 2022. Earlier application is permitted. *[IAS 37(2022).68A]*. See Chapter 26 at 6.2.2 for further discussion. One significant impact of the coronavirus pandemic is the disruption to the global supply chain. For example, assume a manufacturing entity has contracts to sell goods at a fixed price and, because of the shutdown of its manufacturing facilities, as required by the local government, it cannot deliver the goods itself without procuring them from a third party at a significantly higher cost. If the entity determines the contract is onerous under IAS 37, the provision for the onerous contract will reflect the lower of the penalty for terminating the contract or the present value of the net cost of fulfilling the contract (i.e. the excess of the cost to procure the goods over the consideration to be received). Contracts need to be reviewed to determine whether there are any special terms that may relieve an entity of its obligations (e.g. force majeure). Contracts that can be cancelled without paying compensation to the other party do not become onerous as there is no obligation.

Under US GAAP, while requirements exist for some industries or for certain types of transactions, there is no general authoritative standard for when to recognise losses on onerous contracts and, if a loss is to be recognised, how to measure the loss. Accordingly, there is diversity in practice when such contracts are not within the scope of specific authoritative literature. The FASB retained existing requirements for situations in which an entity is expected to incur a loss on a contract (with certain consequential amendments to reflect the terminology of, and cross-references to, ASC 606, where appropriate).

In addition, the FASB clarified that the assessment is performed at the contract level, but that an entity can perform it at the performance obligation level as an accounting policy election. As the FASB's requirements on onerous contracts are not the same as those in IAS 37, the accounting treatment in this area is not converged.

4.1 Accounting for an onerous revenue contract when the contract includes more than one performance obligation that is satisfied over time consecutively

Since the requirements for onerous contracts are outside the scope of IFRS 15, an entity's accounting for onerous contracts does not affect the accounting for its revenue from contracts with customers in accordance with IFRS 15.

Therefore, we believe that entities must use an 'overlay' approach, which consists of two steps:

1. apply the requirements of IFRS 15 to measure progress in satisfying each performance obligation over time and account for the related costs when incurred in accordance with the applicable standards; and
2. at the end of each reporting period, apply IAS 37 to determine if the remaining contract as a whole is onerous (i.e. considering whether the revenue still to be recognised is less than the costs yet to be incurred). If an entity concludes that the remaining contract is onerous, it recognises a provision to the extent that the amount of the unavoidable costs under the contract exceed the economic benefits to be received under it.

The effect of the provision is recognised as an expense, not as an adjustment to revenue. A change in the provision is recognised in profit or loss in accordance with paragraph 59 of IAS 37.

Since the definition of an onerous contract in paragraph 10 of IAS 37 refers to a contract, the unit of account in determining whether an onerous contract exists is the contract itself, rather than the performance obligations identified in accordance with IFRS 15. As a result, the entity must consider the entire remaining contract, including remaining revenue to be recognised for unsatisfied, or partially unsatisfied, performance obligations and the remaining costs to fulfil those performance obligations.

5 CONTRACT COSTS

IFRS 15 specifies the accounting treatment for costs an entity incurs to obtain and fulfil a contract to provide goods or services to customers. An entity only applies those requirements to costs incurred that relate to a contract with a customer that is within the scope of IFRS 15 (see Chapter 27 at 3). *[IFRS 15.8]*.

When an entity recognises capitalised contract costs under IFRS 15, any such assets must be presented separately from contract assets and contract liabilities (see Chapter 32 at 2.1) in the statement of financial position or disclosed separately in the notes to the financial statements (assuming they are material). Furthermore, entities must consider the requirements in IAS 1 – *Presentation of Financial Statements* – on classification of current assets when determining whether their contract cost assets are presented as current or non-current. See Chapter 32 at 2.1.2 for a discussion on classification as current or non-current.

5.1 Costs to obtain a contract

Before applying the cost requirements in IFRS 15, entities need to consider the scoping provisions of the standard. Specifically, an entity needs to first consider whether the requirements on consideration payable to a customer under IFRS 15 apply to the costs (see Chapter 29 at 2.7 for a discussion on accounting for consideration paid or payable to a customer).

For costs that are within the scope of the cost requirements in IFRS 15, the standard requires that incremental costs of obtaining a contract with a customer are recognised as an asset if the entity expects to recover them. *[IFRS 15.91-93]*. An entity can expect to recover contract acquisition costs through direct recovery (i.e. reimbursement under the contract) or indirect recovery (i.e. through the margin inherent in the contract). Incremental costs are those that an entity would not have incurred if the contract had not been obtained. *[IFRS 15.92]*.

Costs incurred to obtain a contract that are not incremental costs must be expensed as incurred, unless they are explicitly chargeable to the customer (regardless of whether the contract is obtained).

The following figure illustrates the requirements in IFRS 15:

Figure 31.3:   Costs to obtain a contract

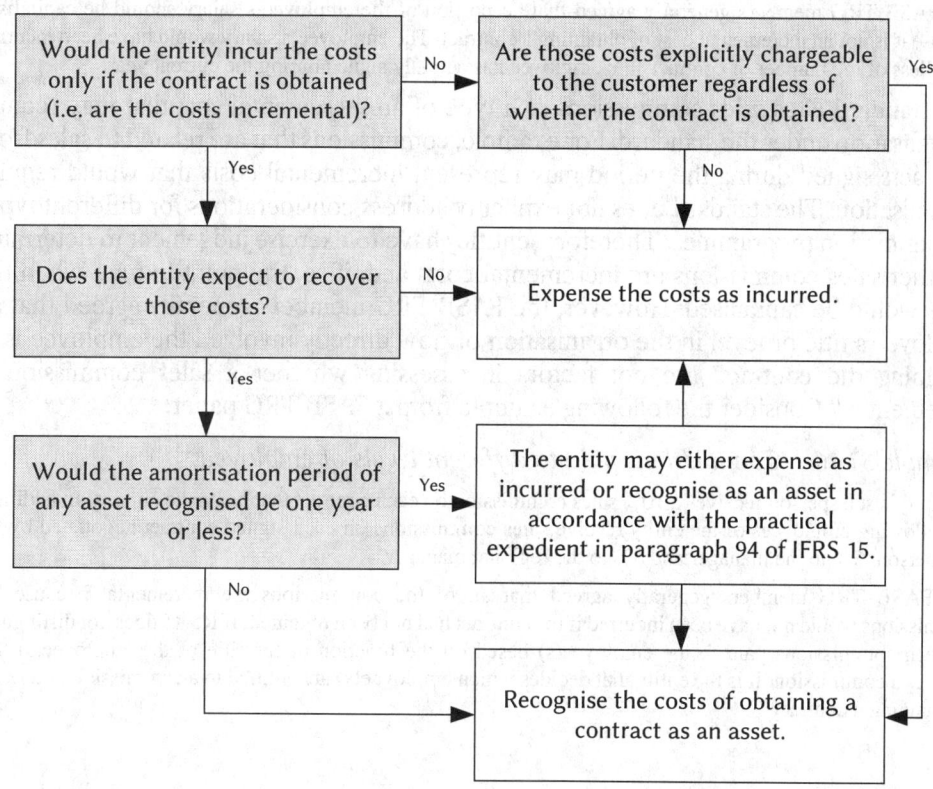

In a FASB TRG agenda paper, the FASB staff suggested that, to determine whether a cost is incremental, an entity should consider whether it would incur the cost if the customer (or the entity) decides, just as the parties are about to sign the contract, that it will not enter into the contract. If the costs would have been incurred even if the contract is not executed, the costs are not incremental to obtaining that contract. The FASB staff also noted that the objective of this requirement is not to allocate costs that are associated in some manner with an entity's marketing and sales activity, but only to identify those costs that an entity would not have incurred if the contract had not been obtained. For example, salaries and benefits of sales employees that are incurred regardless of whether a contract is obtained are not incremental costs.[9]

Consider the following example from the FASB TRG agenda paper:

Example 31.15: Fixed employee salaries[10]

An entity pays an employee an annual salary of £100,000. The employee's salary is based on the number of contracts he or she signed for the prior year, as well as the number of contracts the employee is expected to sign for the current year. The employee's current year salary will not change if the number of contracts the employee actually signs differs from the projected number. However, any difference would affect the employee's salary in the following year.

The FASB TRG members generally agreed that no portion of the employee's salary should be capitalised because it is not an incremental cost of obtaining a contract. The employee's salary would have been incurred regardless of the number of contracts the employee has actually signed during the current year.

The standard cites sales commissions as a type of an incremental cost that may require capitalisation under the standard. For example, commissions that are related to sales from contracts signed during the period may represent incremental costs that would require capitalisation. The standard does not explicitly address considerations for different types of commission programmes. Therefore, entities have to exercise judgement to determine whether sales commissions are incremental costs and, if so, the point in time when the costs would be capitalised. However, the FASB TRG members generally agreed that an employee's title or level in the organisation or how directly involved the employee is in obtaining the contract, are not factors in assessing whether a sales commission is incremental.[11] Consider the following example from a FASB TRG paper:

Example 31.16: Commissions paid to different levels of employees[12]

An entity's salesperson receives a 10% sales commission on each contract that he or she obtains. In addition, the following employees of the entity receive sales commissions on each signed contract negotiated by the salesperson: 5% to the manager and 3% to the regional manager.

The FASB TRG members generally agreed that all of the commissions are incremental because the commissions would not have been incurred if the contract had not been obtained. IFRS 15 does not distinguish between commissions paid to the employee(s) based on the function or the title of the employee(s) that receives a commission. It is the entity that decides which employee(s) are entitled to a commission as a result of obtaining a contract.

We believe that commissions that are paid to a third party in relation to sales from contracts that were signed during the period may also represent incremental costs that would require capitalisation. That is, commissions paid to third parties should be evaluated in the same manner as commissions paid to employees in order to determine whether they are required to be capitalised.

See 5.1.1 and 5.1.2 below for additional examples on how to apply the incremental cost requirements. In addition, entities need to carefully evaluate all compensation plans, not just sales commission plans, to determine whether any plans contain incremental costs that need to be capitalised. For example, payments under a compensation 'bonus' plan may be solely tied to contracts that are obtained. Such costs would be capitalised if they are incremental costs of obtaining a contract, irrespective of the title of the plan.

Example 31.17: Commissions paid to a pool of funds

Assume that an entity has a compensation plan for support personnel in its sales department. As a group, the employees are entitled to a pool of funds calculated based on 2% of all new contracts signed during the monthly period. Once the amount of the pool is known, the amount paid to each individual employee is determined based on each employee's rating.

While the amount paid to each employee is discretionary (based on each employee's rating), the total amount of the pool is considered an incremental cost to obtain a contract because the entity owes that amount to the employees (as a group) simply because a contract was signed.

The TRG members discussed the underlying principle for capitalising costs under the standard and generally agreed that entities first need to refer to the applicable liability standard (e.g. IAS 37, IFRS 9 – *Financial Instruments*) to determine when they are required to accrue for certain costs. Entities then use the requirements in IFRS 15 to determine whether the related costs need to be capitalised. The TRG members acknowledged that certain aspects of the cost requirements require entities to apply significant judgement in analysing the facts and circumstances and determining the appropriate accounting treatment.[13]

In addition, the IASB staff observed in a TRG agenda paper that incremental costs of obtaining a contract are not limited to initial incremental costs. Commissions recognised subsequent to contract inception (e.g. commissions paid on modifications, commissions subject to contingent events or clawback) because they did not meet the recognition criteria for liabilities at contract inception would still be considered for capitalisation as costs to obtain the contract when the liability is recognised. This would include costs related to contract renewals because, as mentioned in the TRG agenda paper, a renewal is a contract and there is nothing in the requirements for costs to obtain a contract that suggests a different treatment for contracts that are renewals of existing contracts. That is, the only difference between the two costs would be the timing of recognition based on when a liability has been incurred.[14] See 5.1.3 below for additional discussion of capitalising commissions paid on contract modifications.

Unlike many commissions, some incentive payments, such as bonuses and other compensation that are based on quantitative or qualitative metrics that are not related to contracts obtained (e.g. profitability, earnings per share (EPS), performance evaluations) are unlikely to meet the criteria for capitalisation because they are not incremental to obtaining a contract. However, a legal contingency cost may be an incremental cost of obtaining a contract, for example, when a lawyer is entitled to be paid only upon the successful completion of a negotiation. Determining which costs must be capitalised under the standard may require judgement and it is possible that some contract acquisition costs are determined to be incremental and others are not. Consider the following example from a FASB TRG agenda paper:

Example 31.18: Incremental and non-incremental costs for same contract[15]

An entity pays a 5% sales commission to its employees when they obtain contracts with customers. An employee begins negotiating a contract with a prospective customer and the entity incurs £5,000 in legal and travel costs in the process of trying to obtain the contract. The customer ultimately enters into a £500,000 contract and, as a result, the employee receives a sales commission of £25,000.

The FASB TRG members generally agreed that the entity should only capitalise the commission paid to the employee of £25,000. This cost is the only one that is incremental to obtaining the contract. While the entity incurs other costs that are necessary to facilitate a sale (e.g. legal, travel), those costs would have been incurred even if the contract had not been obtained.

The standard provides the following example regarding incremental costs of obtaining a contract. *[IFRS 15.IE189-IE191].*

Example 31.19: Incremental costs of obtaining a contract

An entity, a provider of consulting services, wins a competitive bid to provide consulting services to a new customer. The entity incurred the following costs to obtain the contract:

	€
External legal fees for due diligence	15,000
Travel costs to deliver proposal	25,000
Commissions to sales employees	10,000
Total costs incurred	50,000

In accordance with paragraph 91 of IFRS 15, the entity recognises an asset for the €10,000 incremental costs of obtaining the contract arising from the commissions to sales employees because the entity expects to recover those costs through future fees for the consulting services. The entity also pays discretionary annual bonuses to sales supervisors based on annual sales targets, overall profitability of the entity and individual performance evaluations. In accordance with paragraph 91 of IFRS 15, the entity does not recognise an asset for the bonuses paid to sales supervisors because the bonuses are not incremental to obtaining a contract. The amounts are discretionary and are based on other factors, including the profitability of the entity and the individuals' performance. The bonuses are not directly attributable to identifiable contracts.

The entity observes that the external legal fees and travel costs would have been incurred regardless of whether the contract was obtained. Therefore, in accordance with paragraph 93 of IFRS 15, those costs are recognised as expenses when incurred, unless they are within the scope of another Standard, in which case, the relevant provisions of that Standard apply.

As a practical expedient, the standard permits an entity to immediately expense contract acquisition costs when the asset that would have resulted from capitalising such costs would have been amortised within one year or less. *[IFRS 15.94]*. It is important to note that the amortisation period for incremental costs may not always be the initial contract term. See 5.3 below for discussion of the amortisation of capitalised contract costs.

5.1.1 Does the timing of commission payments affect whether they are incremental costs?

At their November 2016 meeting, FASB TRG members generally agreed that the timing of commission payments does not affect whether the costs would have been incurred if the contract had not been obtained. However, there could be additional factors or contingencies that would need to be considered in different commission plans that could affect the determination of whether all (or a portion) of a cost is incremental.[16] Consider the following example from a FASB TRG agenda paper:

Example 31.20: Timing of commission payments[17]

An entity pays an employee a 4% sales commission on a £50,000 signed contract with a customer. For cash flow management purposes, the entity pays the employee half of the commission (i.e. 2% of the total contract value) upon completion of the sale and the remainder in six months' time. The employee is entitled to receive the unpaid commission even if he or she is no longer employed by the entity when payment is due.

The FASB TRG members generally agreed that the entity would capitalise the entire commission in this example (the timing of which would coincide with the recognition of the related liability). That is, the entity would not just capitalise the portion it paid immediately and expense the rest.

In this fact pattern, only the passage of time is required for the entity to pay the second half of the commission. For example, in some commission plans, the employee will only be entitled to the second half of the commission payment if the employee is still employed by the entity when the commission is due. For such plans, an entity needs to carefully evaluate whether the requirement to remain employed in order to receive the commission (i.e. the service vesting condition) is substantive. We believe that the second half of the commission payment would not be incremental if the service condition is substantive because other conditions are necessary, beyond simply obtaining the contract, for the entity to incur the cost.

If the entity's payment of a commission is only 'contingent' on a customer paying the amount due in the obtained contract, we do not believe this would influence the determination of whether the commission is an incremental cost, provided the contract meets the Step 1 criteria to be accounted for as a contract under the five-step model. However, if there is an extended payment term (i.e. there is a significant amount of time between contract signing and the date in which the contract consideration is due), the entity should consider whether there is a service condition or other contingency, as discussed above.

5.1.2 Commission payments subject to a threshold

In November 2016, the FASB TRG members were asked to consider if commission payments subject to a threshold could be considered incremental costs. FASB TRG members generally agreed that basing a commission on a pool of contracts, rather than paying a set percentage for each contract, would not affect the determination of whether the commissions would have been incurred if the entity did not obtain the contracts with those customers.[18] Consider the following example from a FASB TRG agenda paper:

Example 31.21: Commission payments subject to a threshold[19]

An entity has a commission programme that increases the amount of commission a salesperson receives based on how many contracts the salesperson has obtained during an annual period, as follows:

0-9 contracts	0% commission
10-19 contracts	2% of value of contracts 1-19
20+ contracts	5% of value of contracts 1-20+

The FASB TRG members generally agreed that these costs are incremental costs of obtaining a contract with a customer. Therefore, the costs should be capitalised when the entity incurs a liability to pay these commissions. The costs are incremental because the entity will pay the commission under the programme terms as a result of entering into the contracts. See 5.3.4 below for discussion about the period over which an entity would amortise a sales commission that is subject to a threshold and is considered an incremental cost of obtaining a contract.

5.1.3 Would an entity capitalise commissions paid on contract modifications?

An entity would capitalise commissions paid on contract modifications if they are incremental (i.e. they would not have been incurred if there had not been a modification) and recoverable. Contract modifications are accounted for in one of three ways: (1) as a separate contract; (2) as a termination of the existing contract and the creation of a new contract; or (3) as part of the existing contract (see Chapter 28 at 2.4 for further requirements on contract modifications). In all three cases, commissions paid on contract modifications are incremental costs of obtaining a contract and should be capitalised if they are recoverable. In the first two cases, a new contract is created, so the costs of obtaining that contract would be incremental. A January 2015 TRG agenda paper noted that commissions paid on the modification of a contract that is accounted for as part of the existing contract are incremental costs even though they are not initial incremental costs.[20]

5.1.4 Would fringe benefits on commission payments be included in the capitalised amounts?

Fringe benefits should be capitalised as part of the incremental cost of obtaining a contract if the additional costs are based on the amount of commissions paid and the commissions qualify as costs to obtain a contract. However, if the costs of fringe benefits would have been incurred regardless of whether the contract had been obtained (e.g. health insurance premiums), the fringe benefits should not be capitalised. That is, an entity cannot allocate fringe benefits to the commission and, therefore, capitalise a portion of the costs of benefits it would provide regardless of whether the commission was paid.[21]

5.1.5 Must an entity apply the practical expedient to expense contract acquisition costs to all of its qualifying contracts across the entity or can it apply the practical expedient to individual contracts?

We believe the practical expedient to expense contract acquisition costs (that would, otherwise, be amortised over a period of one year or less) must be applied consistently to contracts with similar characteristics and in similar circumstances.

5.1.6 How would an entity account for capitalised commissions upon a modification of the contract that is treated as the termination of an existing contract and the creation of a new contract?

We believe an asset recognised for incremental costs to obtain a contract that exists when the related contract is modified should be carried forward into the new contract, if the modification is treated as the termination of an existing contract and the creation of a new contract and the goods or services to which the original contract cost asset relates are part of the new contract. This is because the contract cost asset relates to goods or services that have not yet been transferred and the accounting for the modification is prospective. This conclusion is similar to the one reached by the FASB TRG members in relation to the accounting for contract assets upon a contract modification, as discussed in Chapter 32 at 2.1.6.E.

The contract cost asset that remains on the entity's statement of financial position at the date of modification would continue to be evaluated for impairment in accordance with IFRS 15 (see 5.4 below). In addition, an entity should determine an appropriate amortisation period for the contract cost asset (see 5.3 below).

5.2 Costs to fulfil a contract

The standard divides contract fulfilment costs into two categories: (1) costs that give rise to an asset; and (2) costs that are expensed as incurred. When determining the appropriate accounting treatment for such costs, IFRS 15 makes it clear that any other applicable standards (e.g. IAS 2 – *Inventories*, IAS 16 – *Property, Plant and Equipment* – and IAS 38 – *Intangible Assets*) are considered first. That is, if costs incurred in fulfilling a contract are within the scope of another standard, an entity accounts for those costs in accordance with those other standards. [IFRS 15.95-96]. If those other standards preclude capitalisation of a particular cost, then an asset cannot be recognised under IFRS 15. [IFRS 15.BC307].

If the costs incurred to fulfil a contract are not within the scope of another standard, an entity capitalises such costs only if they meet all of the following criteria: [IFRS 15.95]

(a) the costs relate directly to a contract or to an anticipated contract that the entity can specifically identify (e.g. costs relating to services to be provided under renewal of an existing contract or costs of designing an asset to be transferred under a specific contract that has not yet been approved);

(b) the costs generate or enhance resources of the entity that will be used in satisfying (or in continuing to satisfy) performance obligations in the future; and

(c) the costs are expected to be recovered.

If all of the criteria are met, an entity is required to capitalise the costs.

The following figure illustrates these requirements:

Figure 31.4: Costs to fulfil a contract

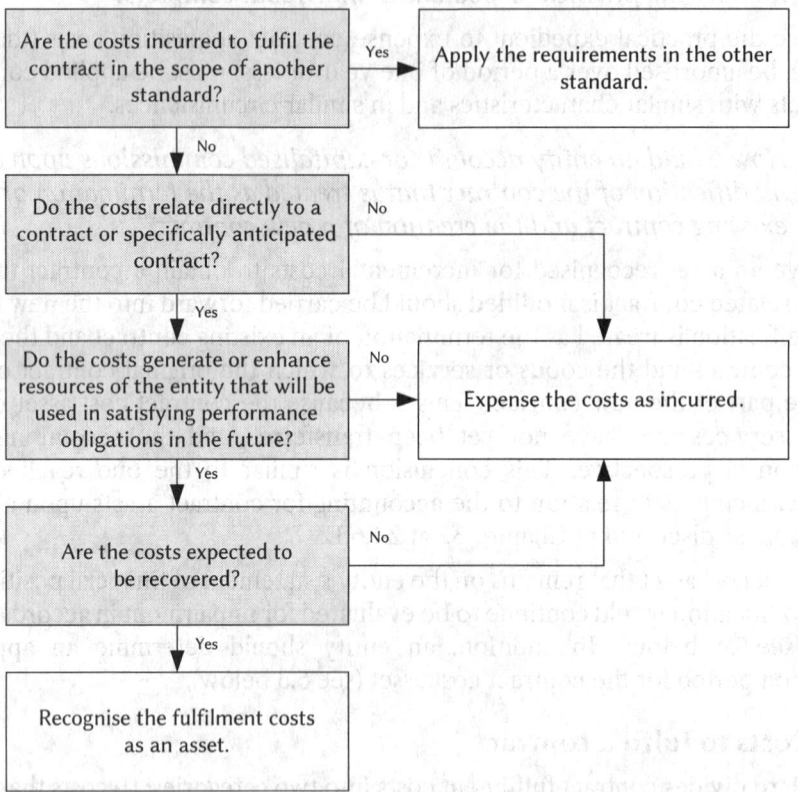

Standards that may be applicable to costs to fulfil a contract with a customer include, but are not limited to, the following:

- inventory costs within the scope of IAS 2;
- costs related to the acquisition of an intangible asset within the scope of IAS 38;
- costs attributable to the acquisition or construction of property, plant and equipment within the scope of IAS 16 or an investment property within the scope of IAS 40 – *Investment Property*; or
- costs related to biological assets or agricultural produce within the scope of IAS 41 – *Agriculture* – or bearer plants within the scope of IAS 16.

Example 31.23 below illustrates some costs that are accounted for under other standards.

The IFRS Interpretations Committee received a request about the recognition of training costs incurred to fulfil a contract with a customer in relation to an entity that supplies outsourced services and incurs costs to train its employees so that they understand the customer's equipment and processes. In March 2020, the Committee concluded that, before assessing the criteria in paragraph 95 of IFRS 15, an entity first considers whether the training costs incurred to fulfil the contract are within the scope of another IFRS standard. In relation to the request, since IAS 38 explicitly includes expenditure on training within its scope, the entity would apply the IAS 38 requirements and not IFRS 15. IAS 38 requires an entity to expense training costs as incurred and states that 'an entity usually has insufficient control over the expected future economic benefits arising from a team of skilled staff and from training for these items to meet the definition of an intangible asset'. *[IAS 38.15, 68-69]*. The Committee noted that the Basis for Conclusions on IFRS 15 states that 'if the other Standards preclude the recognition of any asset arising from a particular cost, an asset cannot then be recognised under IFRS 15'. *[IFRS 15.BC307]*. Therefore, since IAS 38 requires those costs to be expensed as incurred, they cannot be capitalised under IFRS 15. The Committee concluded that IFRS 15 and IAS 38 provide an adequate basis for an entity to determine its accounting for training costs incurred to fulfil a contract with a customer and decided not to add the matter to its agenda.[22]

When determining whether costs meet the criteria for capitalisation in IFRS 15, an entity must consider its specific facts and circumstances.

With regard to the first criterion, IFRS 15 states that costs can be capitalised even if the contract with the customer is not yet finalised. However, rather than allowing costs to be related to any potential future contract, the standard requires that the costs relate directly to a specifically anticipated contract.

The standard provides examples of costs that may meet the first criterion for capitalisation (i.e. costs that relate directly to the contract or a specifically anticipated contract) as follows: *[IFRS 15.97]*

(a) direct labour (e.g. salaries and wages of employees who provide the promised services directly to the customer);

(b) direct materials (e.g. supplies used in providing the promised services to a customer);

(c) allocations of costs that relate directly to the contract or to contract activities (e.g. costs of contract management and supervision, insurance and depreciation of tools, equipment and right-of-use assets used in fulfilling the contract);

(d) costs that are explicitly chargeable to the customer under the contract; and

(e) other costs that are incurred only because an entity entered into the contract (e.g. payments to subcontractors).

Significant judgement may be required to determine whether costs meet the second criterion for capitalisation (i.e. the costs generate or enhance resources of the entity that will be used in satisfying performance obligations in the future). In the Basis for Conclusions, the IASB explained that the standard only results in the capitalisation of costs that meet the definition of an asset and precludes an entity from deferring costs merely to normalise profit margins throughout a contract (by allocating revenue and costs evenly over the contract term). *[IFRS 15.BC308]*.

For costs to meet the third criterion (i.e. the 'expected to be recovered' criterion), they need to be either explicitly reimbursable under the contract, or reflected through the pricing on the contract and recoverable through margin. Determining whether the costs are expected to be recovered may be challenging and require significant judgement if some, or all, of the transaction price is contingent (e.g. success-based fees).

If the criteria are not met, the costs incurred in fulfilling a contract do not give rise to an asset and must be expensed as incurred. The standard provides some common examples of costs that must be expensed as incurred, as follows: [IFRS 15.98]

(a) general and administrative costs (unless those costs are explicitly chargeable to the customer under the contract, in which case an entity shall evaluate those costs in accordance with the above criteria for capitalising costs to fulfil a contract);

(b) costs of wasted materials, labour or other resources to fulfil the contract that were not reflected in the price of the contract;

(c) costs that relate to satisfied (or partially satisfied) performance obligations (i.e. costs that relate to past performance); and

(d) costs for which an entity cannot distinguish whether the costs relate to unsatisfied performance obligations or to satisfied (or partially satisfied) performance obligations.

Paragraph 98(c) of IFRS 15 specifies that, if a performance obligation (or a portion of a performance obligation that is satisfied over time) has been satisfied, fulfilment costs related to that performance obligation (or portion thereof) can no longer be capitalised. This is true even if the associated revenue has not yet been recognised (e.g. the contract consideration is variable and has been fully or partially constrained). Once an entity has begun satisfying a performance obligation that is satisfied over time, it only capitalises fulfilment costs that relate to future performance. Accordingly, it may be challenging for an entity to capitalise costs that are related to a performance obligation that an entity has already started to satisfy. Similarly, paragraph 98(d) of IFRS 15 specifies that, if an entity is unable to determine whether certain costs relate to past or future performance and the costs are not eligible for capitalisation under other IFRSs, the costs are expensed as incurred.

The IFRS Interpretations Committee received a request about the recognition of costs incurred to fulfil a contract in relation to a performance obligation that is satisfied over time. In June 2019, the Committee concluded that IFRS 15 provides an adequate basis for an entity to determine how to recognise the costs in the fact pattern provided and decided not to add the matter to its agenda.[23]

The IFRS Interpretations Committee discussed this issue using the following example.[24]

Example 31.22: Cost to fulfil a contract related to past performance

An entity enters into a contract with a customer to construct a building. It identifies a single performance obligation, being the promise to transfer the building to the customer, which it expects will take three years to complete. The entity satisfies this performance obligation (and recognises revenue) over time in accordance with paragraph 35(c) of IFRS 15 because its performance does not create an asset with alternative use and it has an enforceable right to payment (see Chapter 30 at 2.3).

At the end of the reporting period, the entity has begun constructing the building and has incurred costs related to laying the foundation of the building.

The IFRS Interpretations Committee noted that the foundation costs relate to construction work done on the partly-constructed building, which has been transferred to the customer. Therefore, the costs relate to the entity's past performance in partially satisfying its performance obligation and in accordance with paragraph 98(c) of IFRS 15, should be expensed as incurred. That is, the costs do not meet the criteria to be recognised as an asset under paragraph 95 of IFRS 15.

The standard provides the following example that illustrates costs that are capitalised under other IFRSs, costs that meet the capitalisation criteria and costs that do not. [IFRS 15.IE192-IE196].

Example 31.23: Costs that give rise to an asset

An entity enters into a service contract to manage a customer's information technology data centre for five years. The contract is renewable for subsequent one-year periods. The average customer term is seven years. The entity pays an employee a $10,000 sales commission upon the customer signing the contract. Before providing the services, the entity designs and builds a technology platform for the entity's internal use that interfaces with the customer's systems. That platform is not transferred to the customer, but will be used to deliver services to the customer.

Incremental costs of obtaining a contract

In accordance with paragraph 91 of IFRS 15, the entity recognises an asset for the $10,000 incremental costs of obtaining the contract for the sales commission because the entity expects to recover those costs through future fees for the services to be provided. The entity amortises the asset over seven years in accordance with paragraph 99 of IFRS 15, because the asset relates to the services transferred to the customer during the contract term of five years and the entity anticipates that the contract will be renewed for two subsequent one-year periods.

Costs to fulfil a contract

The initial costs incurred to set up the technology platform are as follows:

	$
Design services	40,000
Hardware	120,000
Software	90,000
Migration and testing of data centre	100,000
Total costs	350,000

The initial setup costs relate primarily to activities to fulfil the contract but do not transfer goods or services to the customer. The entity accounts for the initial setup costs as follows:

(a) hardware costs – accounted for in accordance with IAS 16;

(b) software costs – accounted for in accordance with IAS 38; and

(c) costs of the design, migration and testing of the data centre – assessed in accordance with paragraph 95 of IFRS 15 to determine whether an asset can be recognised for the costs to fulfil the contract. Any resulting asset would be amortised on a systematic basis over the seven-year period (i.e. the five-year contract term and two anticipated one-year renewal periods) that the entity expects to provide services related to the data centre.

In addition to the initial costs to set up the technology platform, the entity also assigns two employees who are primarily responsible for providing the service to the customer. Although the costs for these two employees are incurred as part of providing the service to the customer, the entity concludes that the costs do not generate or enhance resources of the entity (see paragraph 95(b) of IFRS 15). Therefore, the costs do not meet the criteria in paragraph 95 of IFRS 15 and cannot be recognised as an asset using IFRS 15. In accordance with paragraph 98, the entity recognises the payroll expense for these two employees when incurred.

5.2.1 Can an entity defer costs of a transferred good or service that would otherwise generate an upfront loss because variable consideration is fully or partially constrained?

An entity should not defer the costs of a transferred good or service when the application of the constraint on variable consideration results in an upfront loss, even if the entity ultimately expects to recognise a profit on that good or service, unless other specific requirements allow or require a deferral of those costs. The criteria in IFRS 15 must be met to capitalise costs to fulfil a contract, including the criterion that the costs must generate or enhance resources of the entity that will be used in satisfying performance obligations in the future. An entity recognises such costs when control of a good or service transfers to the customer. As such, the cost of those sales would not generate or enhance resources of the entity used to satisfy future performance obligations.

Consider the following example: An entity sells goods with a cost of £500,000 for consideration of £600,000. The goods have a high risk of obsolescence, which may require the entity to provide price concessions in the future, resulting in variable consideration (see Chapter 29 at 2.2.1.A). The entity constrains the transaction price and concludes that it is highly probable that £470,000 will not result in a significant revenue reversal, even though the entity reasonably expects the contract to ultimately be profitable. When control transfers, the entity recognises revenue of £470,000 and costs of £500,000. It would not capitalise the loss of £30,000 because the loss does not generate or enhance resources of the entity that will be used in satisfying performance obligations in the future.

5.2.2 Accounting for fulfilment costs incurred prior to the contract establishment date that are outside the scope of another standard

Entities sometimes begin activities on a specifically anticipated contract before the contract establishment date (e.g. before agreeing to the contract with the customer, before the contract satisfies the criteria to be accounted for under IFRS 15) that are not within the scope of another standard (e.g. IAS 2).

At the March 2015 TRG meeting, the TRG members generally agreed that costs in respect of pre-contract establishment date activities that relate to a good or service that will transfer to the customer at or after the contract establishment date may be capitalised as costs to fulfil a specifically anticipated contract. However, the TRG members noted that such costs would still need to meet the criteria in paragraph 95 of IFRS 15 to be capitalised (e.g. they are expected to be recovered under the anticipated contract). Certain costs, such as general and administrative costs that are not explicitly chargeable to the customer under the contract, would not satisfy these criteria and would need to be expensed as incurred.

Subsequent to capitalisation, costs that relate to goods or services that are transferred to the customer at the contract establishment date would be expensed immediately. Any remaining capitalised contract costs would be amortised over the period that the related goods or services are transferred to the customer.[25]

For requirements on recognising revenue for a performance obligation satisfied over time when activities are completed before the contract establishment date, see Chapter 30 at 3.4.6.

5.2.3 Learning curve costs

As discussed in the Basis for Conclusions on IFRS 15, 'a "learning curve" is the effect of efficiencies realised over time when an entity's costs of performing a task (or producing a unit) decline in relation to how many times the entity performs that task (or produces that unit)'. *[IFRS 15.BC312]*. Learning curve costs usually consist of materials, labour, overhead, rework or other costs that must be incurred to complete the contract (but do not include research and development costs). These types of efficiencies generally can be predicted at inception of an arrangement and are often considered in the pricing of a contract between an entity and a customer.

The IASB noted that in situations where learning curve costs are incurred in relation to a contract with a customer accounted for as a single performance obligation that is satisfied over time to deliver a specified number of units, IFRS 15 requires an entity to select a method of progress that depicts the transfer over time of the good or service to the customer (see Chapter 30 at 3). *[IFRS 15.BC313]*. The IASB further noted that an entity would probably select a method (such as a costs incurred measure of progress) for these types of contracts, which would result in the entity recognising more revenue and expense at the beginning of the contract relative to the end. The IASB clarified that this would be appropriate as an entity would charge a higher price to a customer only purchasing one unit (rather than multiple units) in order to recover its learning curve costs.

Conversely, when learning curve costs are incurred for a performance obligation satisfied at a point in time (rather than over time), an entity needs to assess whether those costs are within the scope of another standard. The IASB noted that in situations in which an entity incurs cost to fulfil a contract without also satisfying a performance obligation over time, the entity is probably creating an asset that is within the scope of another standard (e.g. IAS 2). *[IFRS 15.BC315]*. For example, if within the scope of IAS 2, the costs of producing the components would accumulate as inventory in accordance with the requirements in IAS 2. The entity would then recognise revenue when control of the inventory transfers to the customer. In that situation, no learning curve costs would be capitalised under IFRS 15 as the costs would be in the scope of another standard.

If the learning curve costs are not within the scope of another standard, we believe they generally will not be eligible for capitalisation under IFRS 15 (e.g. because the costs relate to past (and not future) performance).

5.2.4 Accounting for pre-contract or setup costs

Pre-contract costs are often incurred in anticipation of a contract and will result in no future benefit unless the contract is obtained. Examples include: (1) engineering, design or other activities performed on the basis of commitments, or other indications of interest, by a customer; (2) costs for production equipment and materials relating to specifically anticipated contracts (e.g. costs for the purchase of production equipment, materials or supplies); and (3) costs incurred to acquire or produce goods in excess of contractual requirements in anticipation of subsequent orders for the same item.

Pre-contract costs that are incurred in anticipation of a specific contract should first be evaluated for capitalisation under other standards (e.g. IAS 2, IAS 16, IAS 38). For example, pre-contract costs incurred to acquire or produce goods in excess of contractual requirements for an existing contract in anticipation of subsequent orders for the same item would likely be evaluated under IAS 2. Some other examples include costs incurred to move newly acquired equipment to its intended location, which could be required to be capitalised under IAS 16 (see 5.2.5 below), and employee training costs that are expensed in accordance with IAS 38.[26]

Pre-contract costs incurred in anticipation of a specific contract that are not addressed under other standards are capitalised under IFRS 15 only if they meet all of the criteria of a cost incurred to fulfil a contract. Pre-contract costs that do not meet the criteria under IFRS 15 are expensed as incurred.

5.2.5 Capitalisation of mobilisation costs as costs to fulfil a contract with a customer under IFRS 15

Entities incur mobilisation costs when moving personnel, equipment and supplies to a project site either before, at or after inception of a contract with a customer. They are incurred in order to ensure that the entity is in a position to fulfil its promise(s) in a contract (or specifically anticipated contract) with a customer, rather than transferring a good or service to a customer (i.e. they are not a promised good or service).

The assessment of whether mobilisation costs can be capitalised depends on the specific facts and circumstances and may require significant judgement. Entities need to ensure that the costs are: (1) within the scope of IFRS 15; and (2) meet all of the criteria in paragraph 95 of IFRS 15 to be capitalised.

Are the costs within the scope of IFRS 15?

If the asset being moved (e.g. equipment in the scope of IAS 16, inventory in the scope of IAS 2) is in the scope of another standard, an entity should determine whether the mobilisation costs are specifically addressed by the other standard. If so, the cost is outside the scope of IFRS 15.

If the mobilisation costs are not specifically addressed in another standard, or it is not clear whether these are within the scope of another standard, an entity further analyses whether the mobilisation costs are:

- specific to the asset being moved or applicable to more than one customer under unrelated contracts; in the latter case it is likely that they would not be within the scope of IFRS 15. For example, moving an asset between different premises of the entity to better utilise the asset in preparation for future contracts with many customers; or
- specific to the contract with the customer, in which case, it would be within the scope of IFRS 15. For example, moving an asset to a remote location at the customer's request, which does not provide a benefit to the entity beyond ensuring it is in a position to fulfil its obligation(s) to the customer under the contract.

Do the costs meet the criteria in paragraph 95 of IFRS 15 to be capitalised?

As discussed above, IFRS 15 includes three criteria that must be met for costs to fulfil a contract within its scope can be capitalised:

(a) Entities may need to use judgement to determine if costs relate directly to a contract (or a specifically anticipated contract) as required in paragraph 95(a) of IFRS 15. Indicators that a cost, by function rather than by nature, may be directly related include, but are not limited to, the following:
- the costs are explicitly or implicitly chargeable to the customer under the contract;
- the costs are incurred only because the entity entered into the contract;
- the contract explicitly or implicitly refers to mobilisation activities (e.g. that the entity must move equipment to a specific location); or
- the location in which the entity must perform is explicitly or implicitly specified in the contract and the mobilisation costs are incurred in order for the entity to fulfil its promise(s) to the customer.

(b) Significant judgement may also be required to determine whether costs generate or enhance resources of the entity that will be used in satisfying performance obligations in the future as required by paragraph 95(b) of IFRS 15. This determination would include (but not be limited to) considering whether:
- the costs are incurred in order for the entity to be able to fulfil the contract; and
- location is implicitly or explicitly an attribute of the contract.

If a performance obligation (or a portion of a performance obligation that is satisfied over time) has been satisfied, fulfilment costs related to that performance obligation (or portion thereof) can no longer be capitalised (see 5.2 above for further discussion).

(c) For costs to meet the 'expected to be recovered' criterion as required by paragraph 95(c) of IFRS 15, they need to be either explicitly reimbursable under the contract or reflected through the pricing on the contract and recoverable through margin.

5.2.6 Accounting for loss leader contracts

Certain contracts may be executed as part of a loss leader strategy in which a good is sold at a loss with an expectation that future sales contracts will result in higher sales and/or profits. In determining whether these anticipated contracts should be part of the accounting for the existing loss leader contract, entities need to refer to the definition of a contract in IFRS 15, which is based on enforceable rights and obligations in the existing contract (see Chapter 28 at 2.1). While it may be probable that the customer will enter into a future contract or the customer may even be economically compelled, or compelled by regulation to do so, it would not be appropriate to account for an anticipated contract when there is an absence of enforceable rights and obligations.

In addition, if the fulfilment costs incurred during satisfying the initial contract are within the scope of other accounting standards (e.g. IAS 2), the entity must account for those costs under that relevant standard. Even if the costs are not within the scope of another standard, the costs would relate to a satisfied or partially satisfied performance obligation (i.e. the original contract priced at a loss) and, therefore, must be expensed as incurred. IFRS 15 does not permit an entity to defer fulfilment costs or losses incurred based on the expectation of profits in a future contract.

5.2.7 Costs associated with installation or implementation activities

Entities that provide installation or implementation services to customers incur costs to fulfil the services. To determine the appropriate accounting for these costs, entities first need to determine whether the costs are within the scope of another IFRS (e.g. IAS 16, IAS 38).

If they are not within the scope of another IFRS, entities need to determine whether the installation or implementation service is a separate performance obligation that is satisfied over time (see Chapter 28). If it is a performance obligation, then entities generally expense the costs associated with it as incurred because, as discussed at 5.2 above, it may be challenging to conclude that the costs only relate to the entity's satisfaction of performance obligations in the future, which is required for capitalisation by paragraph 95(b) of IFRS 15.

If the installation or implementation service is not a separate performance obligation, an entity needs to evaluate whether it is required to capitalise the costs to fulfil the contract under the IFRS 15 requirements mentioned above. That is, costs incurred to fulfil a contract are required to be capitalised only if they meet all of the criteria for capitalisation in paragraph 95 of IFRS 15.

The illustrations below contrast an example of implementation services that are determined to be a separate performance obligation (and, therefore, are not capitalised as costs to fulfil a contract) with an example of implementation services that meet the criteria for capitalisation as costs to fulfil a contract under IFRS 15.

Example 31.24: Implementation services are not capitalised costs to fulfil a contract

Technology entity M enters into a three-year SaaS contract with a customer for $4,000,000 for a subscription to an inventory management application beginning 1 June 20X1. The contract includes implementation services that will be performed at the beginning of the contract, starting on 1 June 20X1. The implementation services include data migration, creation of objects for the customer's products that will be inventoried, and customisation of the application's layout with the customer's logo and colour scheme. Several third-party service providers also sell implementation services for Technology entity M's application. Assume that the implementation services do not represent a significant integration service (i.e. the implementation services do not significantly modify or customise the SaaS) and the SaaS is fully functional without the implementation service. Under the contract, the customer receives access to the fully functional SaaS on 1 June 20X1.

Technology entity M determines that the costs incurred related to the implementation services are not within the scope of another IFRS (e.g. property, plant and equipment, intangibles).

Technology entity M then considers the implementation services and SaaS and determines that they are separate performance obligations that will be satisfied over time. This is because the implementation services and SaaS can be purchased separately. Technology entity M determines that it is able to fulfil its promise to transfer the SaaS separately from the implementation services, indicating that the two are not highly interdependent or interrelated. Therefore, Technology entity M determines that the costs incurred related to implementation services do not meet the criteria for capitalisation because they do not relate to the entity's satisfaction of performance obligations in the future (i.e. the costs are incurred as the performance obligation for implementation services is satisfied).

Example 31.25: Implementation services are capitalised costs to fulfil a contract

Technology entity N enters into a contract with a customer for $2,000,000 for a one-year SaaS subscription to an enterprise software application beginning when the customer obtains access to the SaaS. The contract includes implementation services that will be performed at the beginning of the contract, starting on 1 January 20X1. The implementation services, which will take approximately two months to complete, must be performed in order for the customer to access the SaaS because the services involve the creation of customer-specific interfaces. Technology entity N does not sell the SaaS without these implementation services, and no other vendors are able to perform the implementation services because they require the creation of code that will reside on Technology entity N's servers.

Technology entity N determines that the costs incurred related to the implementation services are not within the scope of another IFRS (e.g. IAS 16, IAS 38).

Technology entity N then determines that the implementation services are not capable of being distinct. This is because they cannot be purchased separately or provided by a third party and because the services do not provide benefit on their own or with other readily available resources (since the SaaS has not yet been provided and also cannot be sold separately). Therefore, the implementation services and SaaS subscription are a combined performance obligation.

Technology entity N also concludes that the combined performance obligation meets the requirements for recognition over time. It determines that revenue will be recognised over the contract term, beginning when the customer obtains access to the SaaS.

Therefore, Technology entity N considers whether the costs incurred related to the implementation services that will be provided at the outset of the contract (i.e. before the customer obtains access to the SaaS) meet the criteria to be capitalised as a cost to fulfil the contract, as follows:

- the costs relate specifically to the SaaS contract with this customer;
- the costs generate a resource (the interfaces) that will be used to provide the SaaS, the future performance obligation, to the customer; and
- the costs are expected to be recovered based on the margin included in the contract.

As such, Technology entity N determines that the costs should be capitalised as a cost to fulfil as the implementation services are performed. The costs will then be amortised over the estimated period of benefit beginning when the customer gains access to the SaaS.

5.3 Amortisation of capitalised contract costs

Any capitalised contract costs are amortised, with the expense recognised on a systematic basis that is consistent with the entity's transfer of the related goods or services to the customer. *[IFRS 15.99]*.

Paragraph 99 of IFRS 15 states that capitalised contract costs are amortised on a systematic basis that is consistent with the transfer to the customer of the goods or services to which the asset relates. When the timing of revenue recognition (e.g. at a point in time, over time) aligns with the transfer of the goods or services to the customer, the amortisation of the capitalised contract costs in a reporting period will correspond with the revenue recognition in that reporting period. However, the timing of revenue recognition may not always align with the transfer of the goods and services to the customer (e.g. when variable consideration is constrained at the time the related performance obligation is satisfied). When this occurs, the amortisation of the capitalised contract costs will not correspond with the revenue recognition in a reporting period.

For example, consider an entity that enters into a contract with a customer with two performance obligations: (a) a right-to-use licence; and (b) a related service for three years. Further assume that payment from the customer is based on the customer's usage of the intellectual property (i.e. a usage-based royalty). Revenue in respect of the licence of intellectual property would be recognised at a point in time (see 2.3.2 above) and revenue in respect of the related service would be recognised over time. The transaction price allocated to the performance obligation for the licence of intellectual property cannot be recognised at the point in time when control of the licence transfers to the customer due to the royalty recognition constraint (see 2.5 above). Accordingly, any capitalised contract costs that relate to the licence need to be fully amortised upon the transfer of control of that licence (i.e. at a point in time), regardless of when the related revenue will be recognised. Any capitalised contract costs that relate to the services need to be amortised over the period of time consistent with the transfer of control of the service. It is important to note that capitalised contract costs may relate to multiple goods or services (e.g. design costs to manufacture multiple distinct goods when design services are not a separate performance obligation) in a single contract. In such instances, the amortisation period could be the entire contract term. See 5.3.3 below for a discussion on how an entity might determine the appropriate amortisation period when capitalised contract costs relate to multiple performance obligations. The amortisation period could also extend beyond a single contract if the capitalised contract costs relate to goods or services being transferred under multiple contracts or to a specifically anticipated contract (e.g. certain contract renewals). *[IFRS 15.99]*. In these situations, the capitalised contract costs would be amortised over a period that is consistent with the transfer to the customer of the goods or services to which the asset relates. This can also be thought of as the expected period of benefit of the asset capitalised. The expected period of benefit may be the expected customer relationship period, but that is not always the case. To determine the appropriate amortisation period, an entity needs to evaluate the type of capitalised contract costs, what the costs relate to and other facts and circumstances of the specific arrangement. Furthermore, before including estimated renewals in the period of benefit, an entity needs to evaluate its history with renewals to conclude that such an estimate is supportable.

The following figure lists some factors that should be considered in the evaluation of the period of benefit:

Figure 31.5:   Evaluation of the period of benefit

Nature of entity's services
- Product/service offerings and differences in the related customer lives
- Variations in contract terms and product sales structure

Customer life
- Historical customer turnover
- Length of contract and renewal patterns
- Other factors that may affect customers' lives in the future

Product and competitive environment
- Historical product turnover
- Products/services roadmap and other future changes to products/service offerings
- Competitive landscape

Period of benefit
Assess the customer life, product and competitive environment data points to select a period of benefit for each customer and/or product category evaluated

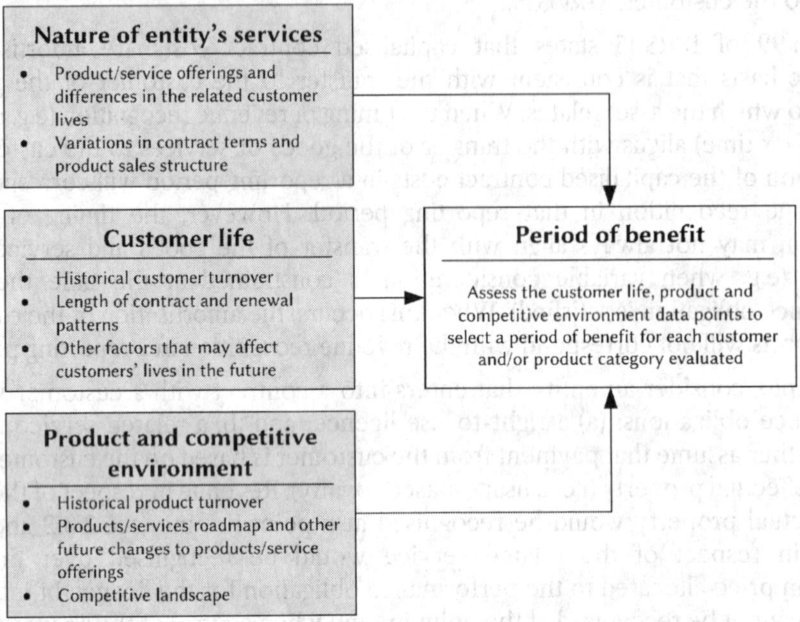

An entity updates the amortisation period when there is a significant change in the expected timing of transfer to the customer of the goods or services to which the asset relates (and accounts for such a change as a change in accounting estimate in accordance with IAS 8 – *Accounting Policies, Changes in Accounting Estimates and Errors*), *[IFRS 15.100]*, as illustrated in the following example:

Example 31.26:   Amortisation period

Entity A enters into a three-year contract with a new customer for transaction processing services. To fulfil the contract, Entity A incurred set-up costs of $60,000, which it capitalised in accordance with paragraphs 95-98 of IFRS 15 and will amortise over the term of the contract.

At the beginning of the third year, the customer renews the contract for an additional two years. Entity A will benefit from the initial set-up costs during the additional two-year period. Therefore, it changes the remaining amortisation period from one year to three years and adjusts the amortisation expense in the period of the change and future periods in accordance with the requirements in IAS 8 for changes in accounting estimates. The disclosure requirements of IAS 8 related to changes in accounting estimates are also applicable.

However, under IFRS 15, if Entity A had been in the position to anticipate the contract renewal at contract inception, Entity A would have amortised the set-up costs over the anticipated term of the contract including the expected renewal (i.e. five years).

Determining the amortisation period for incremental costs of obtaining a contract with a customer can be complicated, especially when contract renewals are expected and the commission rates are not constant throughout the entire life of the contract.

When evaluating whether the amortisation period for a sales commission extends beyond the original contract period, an entity would also evaluate whether an additional commission is paid for subsequent renewals. If so, it evaluates whether the renewal commission is considered 'commensurate' with the original commission. See 5.3.1 below for further discussion on whether a commission is commensurate. In the Basis for Conclusions, the IASB explained that amortising the asset over a longer period than the initial contract would not be appropriate if an entity pays a commission on a contract renewal that is commensurate with the commission paid on the initial contract. In that case, the costs of obtaining the initial contract do not relate to the subsequent contract. [IFRS 15.BC309]. An entity would also need to evaluate the appropriate amortisation period for any renewal commissions that are required to be capitalised under IFRS 15 in a similar manner. See 5.3.1 and 5.3.2 below for the FASB TRG's discussion of how an entity should determine the amortisation period of an asset recognised for the incremental costs of obtaining a contract with a customer.

Under IFRS 15, entities are required to evaluate whether the period of benefit is longer than the term of the initial contract. As discussed above, it is likely that an entity would be required to amortise the capitalised sales commission cost over a period longer than the initial contract if a renewal commission is not paid or a renewal commission is paid that is not commensurate with the original commission.

In determining the appropriate amortisation period or the period of benefit for capitalised contract costs, an entity considers its facts and circumstances and may use judgement similar to that used when estimating the amortisation period for intangible assets (e.g. a customer relationship intangible acquired in a business combination). This could include considering factors such as customer retention and how quickly the entity's products and services change.

It is important for entities to document the judgements they make when determining the appropriate amortisation period and disclose the same in their financial statements. IFRS 15 disclosure requirements (see Chapter 32 at 3.2.3) include judgements made in determining the amounts of costs that are capitalised, the amortisation method chosen and other quantitative disclosures.

5.3.1 Determining whether a commission on a renewal contract is commensurate with the commission on the initial contract

At their November 2016 meeting, FASB TRG members generally agreed that the commissions would have to be reasonably proportional to the contract values (e.g. 5% of both the initial and renewal contract values) to be considered commensurate. The FASB TRG members also generally agreed that it would not be reasonable for an entity to use a 'level of effort' analysis to determine whether a commission is commensurate. For example, a 6% commission on an initial contract and a 2% commission on a renewal would not be commensurate even if the declining commission rate corresponds to the level of effort required to obtain the contracts.[27]

As discussed at 5.3 above, if the renewal commission is considered to be commensurate with the commission on the initial contract, it would not be appropriate to amortise any asset for the initial commission over a longer period than the initial contract. In contrast, it is likely that it would be appropriate to amortise the asset over a longer period than the initial contract if the commissions are not considered to be commensurate (such as in the example above). See 5.3.2 below for discussion of how an entity determines this longer amortisation period.

Although the TRG did not discuss this, entities would also need to evaluate whether any expected subsequent renewal commissions are commensurate with prior renewal commissions to determine the appropriate amortisation period for any renewal commissions that are required to be capitalised under IFRS 15. Continuing the above example, assume the original three-year contract (for which a 6% commission is paid) and each subsequent renewal contract (for which a 2% renewal commission is paid) is for a one-year term. If the entity expects to renew the contract in years two through four and continue to pay a constant 2% commission upon each renewal, each renewal commission would be considered commensurate. As a result, it is likely that the appropriate amortisation period for each renewal required to be capitalised would be one year. See 5.3.5 below for discussion of when an entity would begin to amortise an asset recognised for the incremental cost of obtaining a renewal contract.

5.3.2 Determining the amortisation period of an asset recognised for the incremental costs of obtaining a contract with a customer

The FASB TRG members generally agreed that when an entity determines an amortisation period that is consistent with the transfer to the customer of the goods or services to which the asset relates, it must determine whether the capitalised contract costs relate only to goods or services that will be transferred under the initial contract, or whether the costs also relate to goods or services that will be transferred under a specifically anticipated contract. For example, if an entity only pays a commission based on the initial contract and does not expect the customer to renew the contract (e.g. based on its past experience or other relevant information), amortising the asset over the initial term would be appropriate.

However, if the entity's past experience indicates that the customer is likely to renew the contract, the amortisation period would be longer than the initial term if the renewal commission is not 'commensurate' with the initial commission. See 5.3.1 above for a discussion of commensurate.

The FASB TRG members generally agreed that an entity needs to evaluate its facts and circumstances to determine an appropriate amortisation period if it determines that the period should extend beyond the initial contract term, because the commission on the renewal contract is not commensurate with the commission on the initial contract. An entity might reasonably conclude that its average customer life is the best estimate of the amortisation period that is consistent with the transfer of the goods or services to which the asset relates (e.g. if the good or service does not change over time, such as a health club membership). However, FASB TRG members generally agreed that this approach is not required and that entities should not use this as a default. The FASB TRG members noted that entities would use judgement that is similar to judgement used when estimating the amortisation period for intangible assets (e.g. a customer relationship intangible acquired in a business combination) and could consider factors such as customer loyalty and how quickly their products and services change.[28]

Consider a technology entity that capitalises a commission earned on the sale of software, which the entity estimates it will maintain and support for only the next five years, and the estimated customer life is seven years. In evaluating the period of benefit, the entity may reasonably conclude the capitalised commission should be amortised over the five-year life of the software to which the commission relates.

However, in a TRG agenda paper the staff discussed two acceptable methods for amortising capitalised contract costs that relate to both the original contract and the renewals in cases in which the renewal commission is not commensurate with the initial commission:[29]

- The initial capitalised amount is amortised over the period of benefit that includes expected renewals, while amounts capitalised that relate to renewals are amortised over the renewal period.
- The portion of the initial capitalised amount that is commensurate is amortised over the original contract term and the additional amount that is not commensurate is amortised over the period of benefit that includes expected renewals. Capitalised amounts that relate to renewals are amortised over the renewal period.

Both methods are acceptable because they each meet the objective of amortising the costs on a systematic basis that is consistent with the transfer to the customer of the goods or services to which the asset relates. However, an entity needs to select one method and apply it consistently in similar circumstances. Other amortisation methods may also be acceptable if they are consistent with the pattern of transfer to the customer of the goods or services to which the asset relates.

The following example illustrates the two methods described in the TRG agenda paper:

Example 31.27: Methods for amortising capitalised contract costs

An entity has a commission plan that pays a 6% commission to a sales representative each time that a sales representative obtains a new contract with a customer and a 2% commission each time that customer renews. Based on the entity's assessment of the requirements in IFRS 15 for contract costs, it has concluded that the commissions earned as part of this commission plan are incremental costs to obtain a contract that are required to be capitalised. Furthermore, the entity has determined that the 2% commission paid for renewals is not commensurate with the 6% commission paid for initial contracts and, therefore, the period of benefit for capitalised commissions extends beyond the initial contract term.

The entity performs an assessment of average customer life, technology turnover and competitive factors and concludes that the period of benefit for capitalised commissions is five years.

The entity executes a three-year service contract with a customer for $600,000 and pays a 6% commission to the sales representative. At the end of the three-year term, the customer renews the contract for two more years for $400,000 and the entity pays a 2% commission to the sales representative.

The following are two acceptable methods for amortising the capitalised contract costs related to the $36,000 commission paid on the initial contract and the $8,000 commission paid on the renewal:

Method 1

The $36,000 commission related to the initial contract that was capitalised is amortised over the five-year period of benefit. When the contract is renewed, the $8,000 commission related to the renewal that was capitalised is amortised over the two-year renewal period. The commission would be amortised, as follows:

$	Year 1	Year 2	Year 3	Year 4	Year 5
Initial commission	7,200	7,200	7,200	7,200	7,200
Renewal commission	–	–	–	4,000	4,000
Total amortisation expense	7,200	7,200	7,200	11,200	11,200

Method 2

The $36,000 commission related to the initial contract that was capitalised is separated into two components: $12,000 that is commensurate with the commission paid on renewal (i.e. the amount of commission that the $600,000 initial contract earns at the commensurate rate of 2%) and $24,000 that is not commensurate. The entity amortises the $12,000 component over the three-year initial contract term and the $24,000 component over the five-year period of benefit. When the contract is renewed, the $8,000 commission related to the renewal that was capitalised is amortised over the two-year renewal period. The commission would be amortised, as follows:

$	Year 1	Year 2	Year 3	Year 4	Year 5
Initial commission (not commensurate)	4,800	4,800	4,800	4,800	4,800
Initial commission (commensurate)	4,000	4,000	4,000	–	–
Renewal commission	–	–	–	4,000	4,000
Total amortisation expense	8,800	8,800	8,800	8,800	8,800

5.3.3 Can an entity attribute the capitalised contract costs to the individual performance obligations in the contract to determine the appropriate amortisation period?

We believe an entity can attribute the capitalised contract costs to individual performance obligations in the contract to determine the appropriate amortisation period, but it is not required to do so. Paragraph 99 of IFRS 15 states that the asset recognised is amortised on a systematic basis 'that is consistent with the transfer to the customer of the goods or services to which the asset relates'. *[IFRS 15.99]*. A January 2015 TRG agenda paper noted that an entity may meet this objective by allocating the capitalised contract costs to performance obligations on a relative basis (i.e. in proportion to the transaction price allocated to each performance obligation) to determine the period of amortisation.[30]

Example 31.28: Allocation of capitalised contract costs

A technology entity executes a contract for $600,000 for a perpetual software licence and one year of post-contract support (PCS). Based on the stand-alone selling prices, the entity allocates $500,000 (83%) of the total transaction price to the licence and $100,000 (17%) to the PCS. The entity pays a 4% commission to the sales representative and has determined that the commission is required to be capitalised under IFRS 15 because it is an incremental cost of obtaining the contract. The entity concludes that the $24,000 sales commission needs to be allocated between the licence and the PCS and amortised over the expected period of benefit associated with each of those performance obligations. The entity allocates $20,000 (83%) to the licence and $4,000 (17%) to the PCS, consistent with the relative value of the performance obligations to the transaction price.

Other methods for allocating capitalised contract costs may be appropriate. For example, we believe an entity may also meet the objective by allocating specific capitalised contract costs to individual performance obligations when the costs relate specifically to certain goods or services.

An entity needs to have objective evidence to support a conclusion that a specified amount of the costs relates to a specific performance obligation and consistently apply any methods used for allocating capitalised contract costs to performance obligations.

In addition, as discussed at 5.3.2 above, an entity that attributes capitalised contract costs to individual performance obligations needs to consider whether the amortisation period for some or all of the performance obligations should extend beyond the original contract (see 5.3 above).

The TRG agenda paper also discussed another potentially acceptable amortisation pattern for capitalised contract costs. This pattern relates to multiple performance obligations that are satisfied over different periods that would not require allocation of the asset to individual performance obligations in the contract. That is, an entity may amortise a single capitalised contract cost using one measure of performance taking into consideration all of the performance obligations in the contract. The TRG paper noted that an entity that uses this method needs to select a measure that best reflects the 'use' of the asset as the goods and services are transferred to the customer. That is, the pattern of amortisation must meet the objective of paragraph 99 of IFRS 15 so that it is consistent with the transfer to the customer of the goods or services to which the asset relates.

5.3.4   Over what period would an entity amortise a sales commission (that is only paid once a threshold is met) that is determined to be an incremental cost to obtain a contract?

A January 2015 TRG agenda paper indicated that two of the alternatives discussed might meet the objective of amortising the costs on a systematic basis that is consistent with the transfer to the customer of the goods or services to which the asset relates. However, either alternative must be applied consistently to similar circumstances. In one alternative, an entity allocated the capitalised costs to all of the contracts that cumulatively resulted in the threshold being met and amortised the costs over the expected customer relationship period of each of those contracts. In the other alternative, an entity allocated the capitalised costs to the contract that resulted in the threshold being met and amortised the costs over the expected customer relationship period of that contract. The TRG agenda paper noted that the second alternative may result in a counterintuitive answer if the commission paid upon obtaining the contract that resulted in the threshold being met was large in relation to the transaction price for only that contract. While the first alternative may be easier to apply and result in a more intuitive answer than the second alternative in some situations, the TRG agenda paper noted that either approach is acceptable. The TRG agenda paper did not contemplate all possible alternatives. Consider the following example in the TRG agenda paper:[31]

Example 31.29: Amortisation of capitalised commission payments subject to a threshold

An entity has a commission programme that increases the amount of commission a salesperson receives based on how many contracts the salesperson has obtained during an annual period. In this example, the first commission is paid when the first contract is signed. Subsequently, once a cumulative threshold number of contracts is reached, a commission is paid on that threshold contract as a fixed escalating amount, taking into account any commission already paid, as follows:

1 contract £3,000 commission

10 contracts £5,000 cumulative commission (including £3,000 already paid)

15 contracts £10,000 cumulative commission (including £5,000 already paid)

Assume 11 new contracts are signed by a specific employee in that period.

As discussed in 5.1.2 above, FASB TRG members generally agreed that commission payments subject to a threshold are incremental costs of obtaining a contract with a customer and, therefore, the costs should be capitalised when the entity incurs a liability to pay these commissions.

In one acceptable alternative, an entity estimates the total amount of commission that is expected to be paid for the period and capitalises an equal amount as each contract is signed. In this example, because the entity estimates that the employee will sign 11 new contracts during the period, it expects the total amount of commission to be paid will be £5,000. The entity would capitalise £455 when each contract is signed (i.e. £5,000 cumulative commission divided by the 11 contracts). The capitalised amount would be amortised over the expected customer relationship period of each of those contracts. That is, the £455 capitalised for the first contract would be amortised over the expected customer relationship period of the first contract and the £455 capitalised for the second contract would be amortised over the expected customer relationship period of the second contract.

In the other acceptable alternative, an entity capitalises £3,000 in commission costs upon signing the first contract. This amount would be amortised over the expected customer relationship period of that contract (i.e. the first contract). The entity would not capitalise any additional costs upon signing the second contract through to the ninth contract because the next commission 'tier' has not been met. Once the tenth contract is signed, the entity capitalises an additional £2,000 in commission costs. This amount would be amortised over the expected customer relationship period for that contract (i.e. the tenth contract).

5.3.5 Determining when to begin to amortise an asset recognised for the incremental cost of obtaining a renewal contract

As discussed in 5.3.1 above, assets recognised for commensurate renewal commissions paid are amortised over the term of the contract renewal, with the expense recognised as the entity transfers the related goods or services to the customer.

We believe that the amortisation of the renewal commission should not begin earlier than the beginning of the renewal period. Consider the following illustration:

Example 31.30: Amortisation of a capitalised contract costs

On 1 January 2018, an entity enters into a three-year service contract with a customer that ends on 31 December 2020. Upon the customer signing the contract, the entity pays a sales employee a €50,000 sales commission for obtaining the contract. On 30 September 2020, the entity negotiates a three-year renewal term that will begin on 1 January 2021 and pays the sales employee a renewal commission that is commensurate with the initial sales commission paid. Since the entity does not begin to transfer services under the contract renewal until 1 January 2021, the entity would not begin amortising the asset related to the renewal commission until 1 January 2021.

5.3.6 Classification and presentation of capitalised contract costs and related amortisation in the statement of financial position and statement of profit and loss and other comprehensive income

As discussed at 5.1–5.3 above, IFRS 15 requires incremental costs of obtaining a contract and certain costs to fulfil a contract to be recognised as an asset and that asset to be amortised on a systematic basis. Paragraph 128 of IFRS 15 requires separate disclosure of closing balances and the amount of amortisation and impairment losses recognised during the period (see Chapter 32 at 3.2.3). However, the standard is silent on the classification of that asset and the related amortisation.

Under legacy IFRS, IAS 2 included the notion of work in progress (or 'inventory') of a service provider. However, this was consequentially removed from IAS 2 and replaced with the relevant requirements in IFRS 15. Furthermore, while these capitalised contract cost assets are intangible, in nature, IAS 38 specifically excludes from its scope intangible assets arising from contracts with customers that are recognised in accordance with IFRS 15. *[IAS 38.3(i)]*. In the absence of a standard that specifically deals with classification and presentation of contract costs, management would need to apply the requirements in IAS 8 to select an appropriate accounting policy. *[IAS 8.10-12]*.

In developing such an accounting policy, we believe that costs to obtain a contract and costs to fulfil a contract need to be considered separately for the purpose of classification and presentation in the financial statements.

- Considering the nature of *costs to obtain a contract* and the lack of guidance in IFRS, we believe that an entity may choose to classify and present these costs as either:
  - a separate class of asset (similar in nature to work in progress, or 'inventory') in the statement of financial position and its amortisation within cost of goods sold, changes in contract costs or similar; or
  - a separate class of intangible assets in the statement of financial position and its amortisation in the same line item as amortisation of intangible assets within the scope of IAS 38.

  In all cases, an entity needs to consider the aggregation requirements of IAS 1 when determining whether the separate classes of assets may be presented together with other assets.

  In addition, the entity needs to consider the requirements in IAS 7 – *Statement of Cash Flows*, in particular paragraph 16(a) of IAS 7, when determining the classification of cash flows arising from costs to obtain a contract (i.e. either as cash flow from operating activities or investing activities).

- In contrast, the nature of costs to fulfil a contract is such that they directly impact the entity's performance under the contract. Therefore, costs to fulfil a contract should be classified and presented as a separate class of asset in the statement of financial position and its amortisation within cost of goods sold, changes in contract costs or similar.

We do not believe it would be appropriate to analogise to the requirements for intangible assets in IAS 38. Instead, such costs are consistent in nature to costs incurred in the process of production, as is contemplated in IAS 2. That is, in nature, they are consistent with work in progress, or 'inventory', of a service provider. Therefore, whether costs to fulfil a contract meet the criteria for capitalisation in paragraph 95 of IFRS 15 or are expensed as incurred, we believe that classification and presentation of such costs in the statement of profit and loss and other comprehensive income, and the classification and presentation of related cash flows in the statement of cash flows needs to be consistent.

Capitalised contract costs are subject to impairment assessments (see 5.4 below). Impairment losses are recognised in profit or loss, but the standard is silent on where to classify and present such amounts within the primary financial statements. We believe it would be appropriate for the classification and presentation of any impairment losses to be consistent with the classification and presentation of the amortisation expense.

5.4 Impairment of capitalised contract costs

Capitalised contract costs must be tested for impairment. This is because the costs that give rise to an asset must be recoverable throughout the contract period (or period of benefit, if longer), to meet the criteria for capitalisation.

An impairment exists if the carrying amount of the asset exceeds the amount of consideration the entity expects to receive in exchange for providing the associated goods or services, less the remaining costs that relate directly to providing those goods or services. Impairment losses are recognised in profit or loss. *[IFRS 15.101]*. Refer to 5.3.6 above for further discussion on classifying and presenting impairment losses within profit or loss.

In July 2014, the TRG members generally agreed that an impairment test of capitalised contract costs should include future cash flows associated with contract renewal or extension periods, if the period of benefit of the costs under assessment is expected to extend beyond the present contract.[32] In other words, an entity should consider the total period over which it expects to receive economic benefits relating to the asset, for the purpose of both determining the amortisation period and estimating cash flows to be used in the impairment test. The question was raised because of an inconsistency within IFRS 15. IFRS 15 indicates that costs capitalised under the standard could relate to goods or services to be transferred under 'a specific anticipated contract' (e.g. goods or services to be provided under contract renewals and/or extensions). *[IFRS 15.99]*. The standard also indicates that an impairment loss would be recognised when the carrying amount of the asset exceeds the remaining amount of consideration expected to be received (determined by using principles in IFRS 15 for determining the transaction price, see Chapter 29 at 2). *[IFRS 15.101(a), 102]*. However, the requirements for measuring the transaction price in IFRS 15 indicate that an entity does not anticipate that the contract will be 'cancelled, renewed or modified' when determining the transaction price. *[IFRS 15.49]*.

In some instances, excluding renewals or extensions would trigger an immediate impairment of a contract asset because the consideration an entity expects to receive would not include anticipated cash flows from contract extensions or renewal periods. However, the entity would have capitalised contract costs on the basis that they would be recovered over the contract extension or renewal periods. When an entity determines the amount it expects to receive (see Chapter 29 at 2), the requirements for constraining estimates of variable consideration are not considered. That is, if an entity were required to reduce the estimated transaction price because of the constraint on variable consideration, it would use the unconstrained transaction price for the impairment test. *[IFRS 15.102]*. While unconstrained, this amount must be reduced to reflect the customer's credit risk before it is used in the impairment test.

IFRS 15 does not explicitly state how often an entity needs to assess its capitalised contract costs for impairment. We believe an entity needs to assess whether there is any indication that its capitalised contract costs may be impaired at the end of each reporting period. This is consistent with the requirement in paragraph 9 of IAS 36 to assess whether there are indicators that assets within the scope of that standard are impaired. For example, during 2020, the coronavirus pandemic may have affected customers' ability and intent to pay, and/or entities may be more willing to accept partial payment or extend payment terms. Such collectability concerns may indicate that entities need to assess related capitalised costs to obtain or fulfil a contract for impairment.

However, before recognising an impairment loss on capitalised contract costs incurred to obtain or fulfil a contract, entities need to consider impairment losses recognised in accordance with other standards (e.g. IAS 36). After applying the impairment test to the capitalised contract costs, an entity includes the resulting carrying amounts in the carrying amount of a cash-generating unit for purposes of applying the requirements in IAS 36. *[IFRS 15.103]*.

Under IFRS, IAS 36 permits the reversal of some or all of previous impairment losses on assets (other than goodwill) or cash-generating units if the estimates used to determine the assets' recoverable amount have changed. *[IAS 36.109-125]*. Consistent with IAS 36, IFRS 15 permits reversal of impairment losses when impairment conditions no longer exist or have improved. However, the increased carrying amount of the asset must not exceed the amount that would have been determined (net of amortisation) if no impairment loss had been recognised previously. *[IFRS 15.104]*.

Under US GAAP, the reversal of previous impairment losses is prohibited.

References

1 TRG Agenda paper 39, *Application of the Series Provision and Allocation of Variable Consideration*, dated 13 July 2015

2 TRG Agenda paper 45, *Licences – Specific Application Issues About Restrictions and Renewals*, dated 9 November 2015.

3 FASB ASU 2016-10, *Revenue from Contracts with Customers (Topic 606): Identifying Performance Obligations and Licensing*, April 2016, para. BC71.
4 FASB TRG Agenda paper 58, *Sales-Based or Usage-Based Royalty with Minimum Guarantee*, dated 7 November 2016.
5 FASB TRG Agenda paper 60, *November 2016 Meeting – Summary of Issues Discussed and Next Steps*, dated 31 January 2017.
6 FASB TRG Agenda paper 58, *Sales-Based or Usage-Based Royalty with Minimum Guarantee*, dated 7 November 2016.
7 TRG Agenda paper 29, *Warranties*, dated 30 March 2015 and TRG Agenda paper 34, *March 2015 Meeting – Summary of Issues Discussed and Next Steps*, dated 13 July 2015.
8 AICPA guide, *Revenue Recognition*, Chapter 1, *General Accounting Considerations*, paras. 1.63-1.75.
9 FASB TRG Agenda paper 57, *Capitalization and Amortization of Incremental Costs of Obtaining a Contract*, dated 7 November 2016.
10 FASB TRG Agenda paper 57, *Capitalization and Amortization of Incremental Costs of Obtaining a Contract*, dated 7 November 2016.
11 FASB TRG Agenda paper 60, *November 2016 Meeting – Summary of Issues Discussed and Next Steps*, dated 31 January 2017.
12 FASB TRG Agenda paper 57, *Capitalization and Amortization of Incremental Costs of Obtaining a Contract*, dated 7 November 2016.
13 TRG Agenda paper 23, *Incremental costs of obtaining a contract*, dated 26 January 2015.
14 TRG Agenda paper 23, *Incremental costs of obtaining a contract*, dated 26 January 2015.
15 FASB TRG Agenda paper 57, *Capitalization and Amortization of Incremental Costs of Obtaining a Contract*, dated 7 November 2016.
16 FASB TRG Agenda paper 60, *November 2016 Meeting – Summary of Issues Discussed and Next Steps*, dated 31 January 2017.
17 FASB TRG Agenda paper 57, *Capitalization and Amortization of Incremental Costs of Obtaining a Contract*, dated 7 November 2016.
18 FASB TRG Agenda paper 60, *November 2016 Meeting – Summary of Issues Discussed and Next Steps*, dated 31 January 2017.
19 FASB TRG Agenda paper 57, *Capitalization and Amortization of Incremental Costs of Obtaining a Contract*, dated 7 November 2016.
20 TRG Agenda paper 23, *Incremental costs of obtaining a contract*, dated 26 January 2015.
21 TRG Agenda paper 23, *Incremental costs of obtaining a contract*, dated 26 January 2015.
22 IFRS Interpretations Committee Agenda paper 2, *Training Costs to Fulfil a Contract (IFRS 15)*, dated 17 September 2019 and *IFRIC Update*, March 2020.
23 *IFRIC Update*, June 2019.
24 IFRS Interpretations Committee Agenda paper 2, *Costs to Fulfil a Contract (IFRS 15)*, dated March 2019 and *IFRIC Update*, June 2019.
25 TRG Agenda paper 33, *Partial Satisfaction of Performance Obligations Prior to Identifying the Contract*, dated 30 March 2015 and TRG Agenda paper 34, *March 2015 Meeting – Summary of Issues Discussed and Next Steps*, dated 13 July 2015.
26 IFRS Interpretations Committee Agenda paper 2, *Training Costs to Fulfil a Contract (IFRS 15)*, dated 17 September 2019 and *IFRIC Update*, March 2020.
27 FASB TRG Agenda paper 60, *November 2016 Meeting – Summary of Issues Discussed and Next Steps*, dated 31 January 2017 and FASB TRG Agenda paper 57, *Capitalization and Amortization of Incremental Costs of Obtaining a Contract*, dated 7 November 2016.
28 FASB TRG Agenda paper 60, *November 2016 Meeting – Summary of Issues Discussed and Next Steps*, dated 31 January 2017 and FASB TRG Agenda paper 57, *Capitalization and Amortization of Incremental Costs of Obtaining a Contract*, dated 7 November 2016.
29 TRG Agenda paper 23, *Incremental costs of obtaining a contract*, dated 26 January 2015.
30 TRG Agenda paper 23, *Incremental costs of obtaining a contract*, dated 26 January 2015.
31 TRG Agenda paper 23, *Incremental costs of obtaining a contract*, dated 26 January 2015.
32 TRG Agenda paper 4, *Impairment testing of capitalised contract costs*, dated 18 July 2014.

Chapter 32 Revenue: presentation and disclosure

1	INTRODUCTION		2391
2	PRESENTATION		2393
	2.1	Presentation requirements for contract assets and contract liabilities	2393
		2.1.1 Distinction between contract assets and receivables	2395
		2.1.2 Current versus non-current	2397
		2.1.3 Impairment of contract assets	2398
		2.1.4 Derecognition of contract assets	2399
		2.1.5 Initial measurement of receivables	2399
		2.1.6 Application questions on presentation of contract assets and liabilities	2400
		2.1.6.A Determining the presentation of contract assets and liabilities for contracts that contain multiple performance obligations	2400
		2.1.6.B Determining the presentation of two or more contracts that are required to be combined under the standards	2401
		2.1.6.C Offsetting contract assets and liabilities against other statement of financial position items (e.g. accounts receivable)	2401
		2.1.6.D Is a refund liability a contract liability (and, thus, subject to the presentation and disclosure requirements of a contract liability)?	2402
		2.1.6.E Accounting for a contract asset that exists when a contract is modified if the modification is treated as the termination of an existing contract and the creation of a new contract	2402

2388 *Chapter 32*

		2.1.6.F	Determining when an entity has an unconditional right to payment if it has not transferred a good or service	2404
	2.2	Presentation requirements for revenue from contracts with customers		2404
		2.2.1	Presentation of income outside the scope of IFRS 15	2406
	2.3	Other presentation considerations		2407
		2.3.1	Classifying shipping and handling costs in the income statement	2407
3	DISCLOSURES IN ANNUAL FINANCIAL STATEMENTS			2408
	3.1	Disclosure objective and general requirements		2408
	3.2	Specific disclosure requirements		2409
		3.2.1	Contracts with customers	2409
			3.2.1.A Disaggregation of revenue	2409
			3.2.1.B Contract balances	2416
			3.2.1.C Performance obligations	2421
			3.2.1.D Use of the 'backlog' practical expedient when the criteria to use the 'right to invoice' practical expedient are not met	2432
		3.2.2	Significant judgements	2433
			3.2.2.A Determining the timing of satisfaction of performance obligations	2433
			3.2.2.B Determining the transaction price and the amounts allocated to performance obligations	2435
		3.2.3	Assets recognised from the costs to obtain or fulfil a contract	2437
		3.2.4	Practical expedients	2439
4	DISCLOSURES IN INTERIM FINANCIAL STATEMENTS			2439

List of examples

Example 32.1:	Contract liability and receivable	2396
Example 32.2:	Contract asset recognised for the entity's performance	2397
Example 32.3:	Unbilled receivable	2397
Example 32.4:	Presentation of contract assets and liabilities	2400
Example 32.5:	Accounting for an existing contract asset when the contract is modified	2403
Example 32.6:	Disaggregation of revenue – quantitative disclosure	2412
Example 32.7:	Contract asset and liability disclosures	2418
Example 32.8:	Disclosure of the transaction price allocated to the remaining performance obligations	2431
Example 32.9:	Disclosure of the transaction price allocated to the remaining performance obligations – qualitative disclosure	2432

Chapter 32   Revenue: presentation and disclosure

1 INTRODUCTION

This chapter and Chapters 27-31 primarily cover the requirements for revenue arising from contracts with customers that are within the scope of IFRS 15 – *Revenue from Contracts with Customers*. This chapter deals with presentation and disclosure requirements.

IFRS 15 provides explicit presentation and disclosure requirements, which are more detailed than under legacy IFRS and increase the volume of required disclosures that entities have to include in their interim and annual financial statements.

While not part of the requirements in IFRS 15, entities also need to provide accounting policy disclosures. *[IAS 1.117]*. (See Chapter 3 for further discussion on the requirements of IAS 1 – *Presentation of Financial Statements*). Given the complexity of the requirements in IFRS 15, the policies that apply to revenues and costs within the scope of the standard may require entities to provide tailored and detailed disclosures.

Refer to the following chapters for requirements of IFRS 15 that are not covered in this chapter:

- Chapter 27 – Core principle, definitions and scope.
- Chapter 28 – Identifying the contract and identifying performance obligations.
- Chapter 29 – Determining the transaction price and allocating the transaction price.
- Chapter 30 – Recognising revenue.
- Chapter 31 – Licences, warranties and contract costs.

Other revenue items that are not within the scope of IFRS 15, but arise in the course of the ordinary activities of an entity, as well as the disposal of non-financial assets that are not part of the ordinary activities of the entity, for which IFRS 15's requirements are relevant, are addressed in Chapter 27.

As discussed more fully below, IFRS 15 requires extensive and detailed disclosures in entities' financial statements, particularly annual financial statements.

Entities may have to expend considerable effort when preparing the required disclosures for their interim and annual financial statements. For example, some entities operating in multiple segments with many different product lines may find it challenging to gather the data needed to provide the disclosures. Therefore, it is important for entities to have the appropriate systems, internal controls, policies and procedures in place to collect and disclose the required information.

This chapter:
- Highlights significant differences from the equivalent US GAAP standard, Accounting Standards Codification (ASC) 606 – *Revenue from Contracts with Customers* (together with IFRS 15, the standards) issued by the US Financial Accounting Standards Board (FASB) (together with the International Accounting Standards Board (IASB), the Boards).
- Addresses topics on which the members of the Joint Transition Resource Group for Revenue Recognition (TRG) reached general agreement and our views on certain topics. TRG members' views are non-authoritative, but entities should consider them as they apply the standards. Unless otherwise specified, these summaries represent the discussions of the joint TRG.

For US GAAP preparers, the FASB's standard provides requirements on presentation and disclosure that apply to both public and non-public entities and provide some relief on disclosure requirements for non-public entities. The FASB's standard defines a public entity as one of the following:

- a public business entity, as defined;
- a not-for-profit entity that has issued, or is a conduit bond obligor for, securities that are traded, listed or quoted on an exchange or an over-the-counter market; or
- an employee benefit plan that files or furnishes financial statements with the SEC.

An entity that does not meet any of the criteria above is considered a non-public entity for purposes of the FASB's standard.

IFRS 15 does not differentiate between public and non-public entities. Therefore, an entity that applies IFRS 15 must apply all of its requirements.

The extracts in this chapter illustrate possible formats entities might use to disclose information required by IFRS 15, using real-life examples from entities that have adopted the standard.

The views we express in this chapter may evolve as application issues are identified and discussed among stakeholders. The conclusions we describe in our illustrations are also subject to change as views evolve. Conclusions in seemingly similar situations may differ from those reached in the illustrations due to differences in the underlying facts and circumstances.

2 PRESENTATION

2.1 Presentation requirements for contract assets and contract liabilities

The revenue model is based on the notion that a contract asset or contract liability is generated when either party to a contract performs, depending on the relationship between the entity's performance and the customer's payment. The standard requires that an entity present these contract assets or contract liabilities in the statement of financial position. [IFRS 15.105]. In the following extract, Bombardier Inc. presents these amounts separately using the terminology from the standard.

Extract 32.1: Bombardier Inc. (2019)
CONSOLIDATED FINANCIAL STATEMENTS [extract]
For fiscal years 2019 and 2018
CONSOLIDATED STATEMENTS OF FINANCIAL POSITION [extract]
As at
(in millions of U.S. dollars)

	Notes	December 31 2019 [1]	December 31 2018	January 1 2018
Assets [extract]				
Cash and cash equivalents	15	$ 2,578	$ 3,187	$ 2,988
Trade and other receivables	16	1,844	1,575	1,174
Contract assets	17	2,485	2,617	2,460
Inventories	18	4,599	4,402	3,429
Other financial assets	20	195	210	415
Other assets	21	473	357	427
Assets held for sale	30	1,309	–	4,150
Current assets		13,483	12,348	15,043
Liabilities [extract]				
Trade and other payables	26	$ 4,682	$ 4,634	$ 3,964
Provisions	27	1,060	1,390	1,630
Contract liabilities	17	5,739	4,262	3,820
Other financial liabilities	27	518	607	342
Other liabilities	28	1,548	1,499	1,723
Liabilities directly associated with assets held for sale	30	1,768	–	2,686
Current liabilities		15,315	12,392	14,165

(1) Refer to Note 3 – Changes in accounting policies for the impact of the adoption of IFRS 16, *Leases*.

The following figure illustrates how an entity determines whether to recognise a receivable, a contract asset or a contract liability on the balance sheet:

Figure 32.1:   Recognition of a receivable, a contract asset or a contract liability

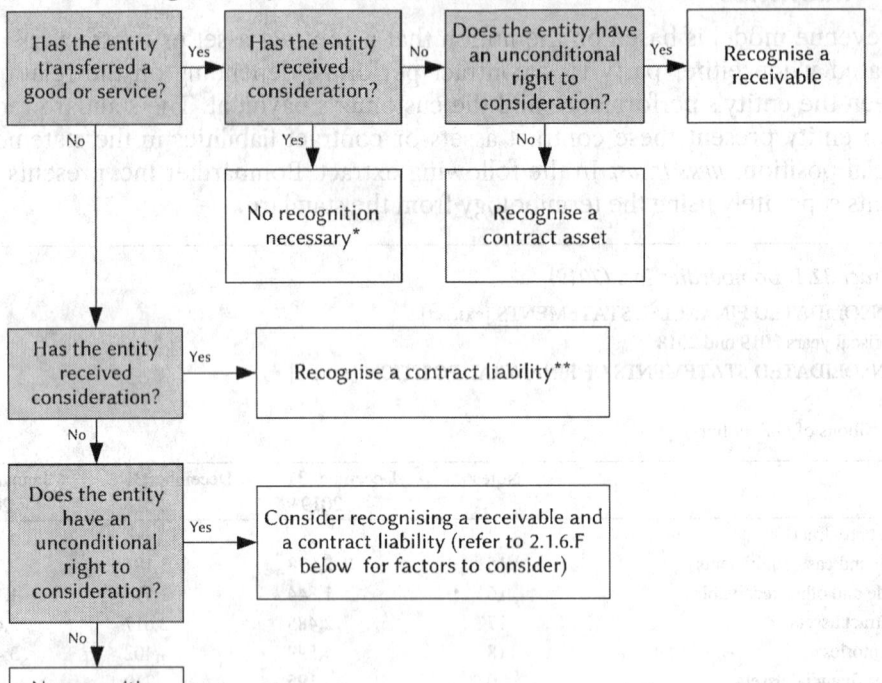

*   This assumes the consideration received is equal to the amount to which the entity is entitled for the good or service already transferred. If the consideration received is less than this amount, an entity may need to recognise a contract asset or a receivable for the difference. If the consideration received is more than this amount, an entity may need to recognise a contract liability or a refund liability.

** If the customer can cancel the contract and receive a refund of the advance payment, an entity would consider recognising a refund liability (separate from contract liabilities – see 2.1.6.D below).

When an entity satisfies a performance obligation by transferring a promised good or service, the entity has earned a right to consideration from the customer and, therefore, has a contract asset. When the customer performs first, for example, by prepaying its promised consideration, the entity has a contract liability. [IFRS 15.106-107].

An entity could also have recognised other assets related to contracts with a customer (e.g. the incremental costs of obtaining the contract and other costs incurred that meet the criteria for capitalisation). The standard requires that any such assets be presented separately from contract assets and contract liabilities in the statement of financial position or disclosed separately in the notes to the financial statements (assuming that they are material). These amounts are also assessed for impairment separately (see Chapter 31 at 5.4).

2.1.1 Distinction between contract assets and receivables

Contract assets may represent conditional or unconditional rights to consideration. The right is conditional, for example, when an entity must first satisfy another performance obligation in the contract before it is entitled to payment from the customer. If an entity has an unconditional right to receive consideration from the customer, the contract asset is accounted for as a receivable and presented separately from other contract assets. *[IFRS 15.105, BC323-BC324]*. A right is unconditional if nothing other than the passage of time is required before payment of that consideration is due. *[IFRS 15.108]*.

In the Basis for Conclusions on IFRS 15, the Board explains that in many cases an unconditional right to consideration (i.e. a receivable) arises when an entity satisfies a performance obligation, which could be before it invoices the customer (e.g. an unbilled receivable) if only the passage of time is required before payment of that consideration is due. It is also possible for an entity to have an unconditional right to consideration before it satisfies a performance obligation. *[IFRS 15.107, BC325]*.

In some industries, it is common for an entity to invoice its customers in advance of performance (and satisfaction of the performance obligation). For example, an entity that enters into a non-cancellable contract requiring payment a month before the entity provides the goods or services would recognise a receivable and a contract liability on the date the entity has an unconditional right to the consideration (see 2.1.6.F below for factors to consider when assessing whether an entity's right to consideration is considered unconditional). In this situation, revenue is not recognised until goods or services are transferred to the customer.

In December 2015, the IASB discussed application of IFRS 15 to contracts in which the entity has transferred control of a good to the customer at a point in time, but the consideration to which the entity is entitled is contingent upon a market price (e.g. a commodity price), which will be determined at a future date. The example assumed that there was no separable embedded derivative (i.e. the entire contract was within the scope of IFRS 15). In discussing this issue, the Board clarified the nature of conditions that might prevent recognition of a receivable. Specifically, the Board agreed that the variability arising solely from changes in the market price would not be a condition that prevents an entity to recognise a receivable. That is, since the entity has performed, '...nothing else (i.e. no future event) needs to happen before payment of the consideration is due. The existence of a price in the future requires no event to occur and depends solely on the passage of time. Changes in the price of Commodity do not affect the entity's right to consideration, even though the amount that the entity receives is known only on the payment date. In other words, there is no uncertainty with regards to the entity's entitlement to the consideration. The entity's right to consideration is therefore unconditional as understood by IFRS 15...'. Therefore, when the entity performs by transferring control of the good to the customer, it recognises a receivable in accordance with IFRS 9 – *Financial Instruments* (and is no longer subject to the requirements in IFRS 15 for the variable consideration constraint).[1]

In the Basis for Conclusions, the Board noted that making the distinction between a contract asset and a receivable is important because doing so provides users of financial statements with relevant information about the risks associated with the entity's rights in a contract. Although both are subject to credit risk, a contract asset is also subject to other risks (e.g. performance risk). [IFRS 15.BC323].

Under the standard, entities are not required to use the terms 'contract asset' or 'contract liability', but must disclose sufficient information so that users of the financial statements can clearly distinguish between unconditional rights to consideration (receivables) and conditional rights to receive consideration (contract assets). [IFRS 15.109].

The standard provides the following example of presentation of contract balances. [IFRS 15.IE198-IE200].

Example 32.1: Contract liability and receivable

Case A – Cancellable contract

On 1 January 20X1, an entity enters into a cancellable contract to transfer a product to a customer on 31 March 20X1. The contract requires the customer to pay consideration of £1,000 in advance on 31 January 20X1. The customer pays the consideration on 1 March 20X1. The entity transfers the product on 31 March 20X1. The following journal entries illustrate how the entity accounts for the contract:

- The entity receives cash of £1,000 on 1 March 20X1 (cash is received in advance of performance):

Cash	£1,000	
Contract liability		£1,000

- The entity satisfies the performance obligation on 31 March 20X1:

Contract liability	£1,000	
Revenue		£1,000

Case B – Non-cancellable contract

The same facts as in Case A apply to Case B except that the contract is non-cancellable. The following journal entries illustrate how the entity accounts for the contract:

- The amount of consideration is due on 31 January 20X1 (which is when the entity recognises a receivable because it has an unconditional right to consideration):

Receivable	£1,000	
Contract liability		£1,000

- The entity receives the cash on 1 March 20X1:

Cash	£1,000	
Receivable		£1,000

- The entity satisfies the performance obligation on 31 March 20X1:

Contract liability	£1,000	
Revenue		£1,000

If the entity issued the invoice before 31 January 20X1 (the due date of the consideration), the entity would not present the receivable and the contract liability on a gross basis in the statement of financial position because the entity does not yet have a right to consideration that is unconditional.

The standard includes another example of presentation of contract balances that illustrates when an entity has satisfied a performance obligation, but does not have an unconditional right to payment and, therefore, recognises a contract asset. *[IFRS 15.IE201-IE204].*

Example 32.2: Contract asset recognised for the entity's performance

On 1 January 20X1, an entity enters into a contract to transfer Products A and B to a customer in exchange for $1,000. The contract requires Product A to be delivered first and states that payment for the delivery of Product A is conditional on the delivery of Product B. In other words, the consideration of $1,000 is due only after the entity has transferred both Products A and B to the customer. Consequently, the entity does not have a right to consideration that is unconditional (a receivable) until both Products A and B are transferred to the customer:

The entity identifies the promises to transfer Products A and B as performance obligations and allocates $400 to the performance obligation to transfer Product A and $600 to the performance obligation to transfer Product B on the basis of their relative stand-alone selling prices. The entity recognises revenue for each respective performance obligation when control of the product transfers to the customer.

The entity satisfies the performance obligation to transfer Product A:

Contract asset	$400	
Revenue		$400

The entity satisfies the performance obligation to transfer Product B and to recognise the unconditional right to consideration:

Receivable	$1,000	
Contract asset		$400
Revenue		$600

Also consider the following example, which illustrates an unbilled receivable (rather than a contract asset):

Example 32.3: Unbilled receivable

On 14 September 20X1, Entity L enters into a contract to sell 100 widgets to Customer F at €10 per widget. All of the widgets are delivered to Customer F on 29 September 20X1. Entity L invoices Customer F on 12 October 20X1.

Entity L determines that revenue is recognised when control of the widgets transfers to Customer F on 29 September 20X1. Entity L records a corresponding receivable because only the passage of time is required before payment of that consideration is due. That is, Entity L has an unconditional right to consideration as at 29 September 20X1, even though Entity L has not yet issued an invoice. That is, even though the amount is 'unbilled', it is still considered a receivable, rather than a contract asset.

2.1.2 Current versus non-current

Unless an entity presents its statement of financial position on a liquidity basis, it needs to present contract assets or contract liabilities as current or non-current in the statement of financial position. Since IFRS 15 does not address this classification, entities need to consider the requirements in IAS 1.

The distinction between current and non-current items depends on the length of the entity's operating cycle. IAS 1 states that the operating cycle of an entity is the time between the acquisition of assets for processing and their realisation in cash or cash equivalents. However, when the entity's normal operating cycle is not clearly identifiable, it is assumed to be 12 months. IAS 1 does not provide guidance on how to determine whether an entity's operating cycle is 'clearly identifiable'. For some entities, the time involved in producing goods or providing services may vary significantly between contracts with one customer to another. In such cases, it may be difficult to determine what the normal operating cycle is. Therefore, entities need to consider all facts and circumstances and use judgement to determine whether it is appropriate to consider that the operating cycle is clearly identifiable, or whether to use the twelve-month default. This assessment is also relevant for other assets and liabilities arising from contracts with customers within the scope of IFRS 15 (e.g. capitalised contract costs to obtain and fulfil a contract).

Consequently, an entity assesses, based on the contract terms, facts and circumstances whether a contract asset or contract liability is classified as current or non-current. It considers:

- for a contract asset: when payment is due (e.g. based on payment schedule agreed with client); and
- for a contract liability: the timing of satisfaction of the performance obligation as a factor when applying the requirements of IAS 1. *[IAS 1.69].*

This assessment might lead to a separation of the contract asset or contract liability into a current and a non-current portion.

In Extract 32.2, Fédération Internationale de Football Association (FIFA) splits contract liabilities between current and non-current in its balance sheet and uses the terms from the standard.

Extract 32.2: Fédération Internationale de Football Association (2018)
CONSOLIDATED FINANCIAL STATEMENTS [extract]
CONSOLIDATED BALANCE SHEET [extract]

in TUSD	Note	31 Dec 2018	31 Dec 2017
Liabilities and reserves			
Payables	22	116,745	130,081
Derivative financial liabilities	28	6,220	12,681
Contract liabilities	24	258,048	2,392,143
Accrued expenses	23	785,767	520,333
Current liabilities		**1,166,780**	**3,055,238**
Contract liabilities	24	80,165	89,309
Accrued expenses	23	102,221	70,638
Post-employment benefit obligation	29	78,996	74,333
Derivative financial liabilities	28	386	322
Provisions	25	215,392	197,000
Non-current liabilities		**477,160**	**431,602**
Total liabilities		**1,643,940**	**3,486,840**

2.1.3 Impairment of contract assets

After initial recognition, contract assets, like receivables, are subject to impairment assessments in accordance with IFRS 9 (the impairment requirements are discussed in Chapter 51). *[IFRS 15.107].* The Basis for Conclusions on IFRS 9 clarifies that contract assets are in scope of IFRS 9 impairment because the IASB considered 'the exposure to credit risk on contract assets is similar to that of trade receivables'. *[IFRS 9.BC5.154].*

The expected credit loss model in IFRS 9 focuses on the difference between the contractual cash flows and expected cash flows. *[IFRS 9.B5.5.29]*. However, the right to receive non-cash consideration does not give rise to cash inflows. As such, judgement may be needed when the consideration to which the entity is entitled is non-cash. Since the entity does not yet hold the non-cash consideration, the impairment requirements in IAS 36 – *Impairment of Assets*, for example, do not directly apply.

When applying the impairment requirements of IFRS 9 to the contract asset, an entity considers the likelihood of not receiving the non-cash consideration (i.e. non-performance risk). However, this would not consider any potential impairment in the underlying asset to which the entity is entitled. As such, an entity may need to consider the value of the underlying non-cash consideration to which it is entitled to use as a proxy for the cash inflows when applying the impairment requirements of IFRS 9.

As discussed in Chapter 29 at 2.5.3, impairment losses on receivables are presented in line with the requirements of IAS 1 and the disclosure requirements in IFRS 7 – *Financial Instruments: Disclosures* – apply. *[IFRS 7.35A(a)]*. In addition, as discussed at 2.2 below, IFRS 15 requires that such amounts are disclosed separately from impairment losses from other contracts. *[IFRS 15.113(b)]*. These requirements also apply to impairment losses on contract assets.

2.1.4 Derecognition of contract assets

Contract assets will generally be derecognised when an entity's right to consideration becomes unconditional, and it is able to recognise a receivable in accordance with IFRS 9. IFRS 15 does not provide any additional requirements on derecognising contract assets and only the impairment requirements in IFRS 9 apply to contract assets. In theory, entities could also apply the derecognition requirements in IFRS 9 by analogy to contract assets. However, in practice, we believe that it is very unlikely that many contract assets would meet the requirements for derecognition in IFRS 9, particularly if they are still conditional on the entity's future performance.

2.1.5 Initial measurement of receivables

IFRS 9 includes different initial measurement requirements for receivables arising from IFRS 15 contracts depending on whether there is a significant financing component.

- If there is a significant financing component, the receivable is initially measured at fair value. *[IFRS 9.5.1.1]*.
- If there is no significant financing component (or the entity has used the practical expedient in paragraph 63 of IFRS 15), the receivable is initially recognised at the transaction price, measured in accordance with IFRS 15. *[IFRS 9.5.1.3]*.

If upon initial measurement there is a difference between the measurement of the receivable under IFRS 9 and the corresponding amount of revenue, that difference is presented immediately in profit or loss (e.g. as an impairment loss). *[IFRS 15.108]*.

If the initial measurement of a receivable is at fair value, there may be a number of reasons why differences from the IFRS 15 transaction price may arise (e.g. changes in the fair value of non-cash consideration not yet received). This is the case when the difference is attributable to customer credit risk, rather than an implied price concession. Implied price concessions are deducted from the contract price to derive the transaction price, which is the amount recognised as revenue. Distinguishing between implied price concessions and expense due to customer credit risk requires judgement (see Chapter 29 at 2.2.1.A). Impairment losses resulting from contracts with customers are presented separately from other impairment losses (see 2.1.3 above). *[IFRS 15.113(b)]*.

2.1.6 Application questions on presentation of contract assets and liabilities

2.1.6.A Determining the presentation of contract assets and liabilities for contracts that contain multiple performance obligations

At the October 2014 TRG meeting, the TRG members were asked how an entity would determine the presentation of contract assets and liabilities for contracts that contain multiple performance obligations. The TRG members generally agreed that contract assets and liabilities would be determined at the contract level and not at the performance obligation level. That is, an entity does not separately recognise an asset or liability for each performance obligation within a contract, but aggregates them into a single contract asset or liability.[2]

This question arose in part because, under the standard, the amount and timing of revenue recognition is determined based on progress toward complete satisfaction of each performance obligation. Therefore, some constituents questioned whether an entity could have a contract asset and a contract liability for a single contract. An example is when the entity has satisfied (or partially satisfied) one performance obligation in a contract for which consideration is not yet due, but has received a prepayment for another unsatisfied performance obligation in the contract. The TRG members generally agreed that the discussion in the Basis for Conclusions was clear that contract asset or contract liability positions are determined for each contract on a net basis. This is because the rights and obligations in a contract with a customer are interdependent – the right to receive consideration from a customer depends on the entity's performance and, similarly, the entity performs only as long as the customer continues to pay. The Board decided that those interdependencies are best reflected by accounting and presenting contract assets or liabilities on a net basis. *[IFRS 15.BC317]*.

Consider the following example.

Example 32.4: Presentation of contract assets and liabilities

Entity A has a contract with Customer B to transfer a licence on 1 January 20X0 for the right to use Entity A's intellectual property in exchange for a ¥200 million milestone payment that is contingent upon Customer B achieving a specific outcome. The contract also includes a one-year service to be provided by Entity A for fixed consideration of ¥100 million that is paid upfront by Customer B at contract inception. Assume Entity A concludes there are two performance obligations: one for the right to use licence of intellectual property that will be satisfied when the licence is delivered and one for the service that will be recognised over time using a time-elapsed measure of progress. On 1 January 20X0, the licence is delivered and the service commences.

Entity A determines that the milestone payment is variable consideration. Because of the binary nature of the outcome (i.e. the entity will either receive the milestone payment or not), Entity A determines that the most likely amount method (see Chapter 29 at 2.2.2) is the better predictor of the amount to which it expects to be entitled. Entity A believes it is 90% probable that it will receive the ¥200 million milestone payment. Therefore, using the most likely amount method, Entity A estimates that it will receive the full ¥200 million. Entity A then allocates the total transaction price of ¥300 million (variable consideration of ¥200 million plus the fixed consideration of ¥100 million) to the licence and the service based on their relative stand-alone selling prices (assume this arrangement does not meet the variable consideration allocation exception). Further assume that ¥200 million is allocated to the licence and ¥100 million is allocated to the service, i.e. the components were priced at their stand-alone selling price.

On 1 January 20X0, when Entity A satisfies the performance obligation related to the licence, it recognises revenue and a contract asset of ¥200 million. A contract asset is recorded (rather than a receivable) because Entity A's right to the consideration is contingent upon something other than the passage of time (i.e. Customer B achieving a specific outcome). The performance obligation associated with the service results in the recognition of a contract liability of ¥100 million as at 1 January 20X0 because Entity A paid upfront for the service.

On 31 March 20X0, related to the contract with Customer B, Entity A has a contract asset of ¥200 million (because the condition to receive consideration for the licence still has not been met) and a contract liability of ¥75 million (because ¥25 million of revenue has been recognised for one quarter of service). For presentation purposes at 31 March 20X0, Entity A nets the contract asset of ¥200 million and the contract liability of ¥75 million, and presents a net contract asset of ¥125 million.

After determining the net contract asset or contract liability position for a contract, entities consider the requirements in IAS 1 on classification as current or non-current in the statement of financial position, unless an entity presents its statement of financial position on a liquidity basis (see 2.1 above).

2.1.6.B Determining the presentation of two or more contracts that are required to be combined under the standards

At the October 2014 TRG meeting, the TRG members considered how an entity would determine the presentation of two or more contracts that are required to be combined under the standard. The TRG members generally agreed that the contract asset or liability would be combined (i.e. presented net) for different contracts with the same customer (or a related party of the customer) if an entity is otherwise required to combine those contracts under the standard (see Chapter 28 at 2.3 for discussion of the criteria for combining contracts).[3] When two or more contracts are required to be combined under the standard, the rights and obligations in the individual contracts are interdependent. Therefore, as discussed at 2.1.6.A above, this interdependency is best reflected by combining the individual contracts as if they were a single contract. However, the TRG members acknowledged that this analysis may be operationally difficult for some entities because their systems may capture data at the performance obligation level in order to comply with the recognition and measurement aspects of the standard.

2.1.6.C Offsetting contract assets and liabilities against other statement of financial position items (e.g. accounts receivable)

At the October 2014 TRG meeting, the TRG members considered when an entity would offset contract assets and liabilities against other statement of financial position items (e.g. accounts receivable). The TRG members generally agreed that, because the standard does not provide requirements for offsetting, entities need to apply the requirements of other standards to determine whether offsetting is appropriate (e.g. IAS 1, IAS 32 – *Financial Instruments: Presentation*).[4] For example, if an entity has recorded a contract asset (or a receivable) and a contract liability (or refund liability) from separate contracts with the same customer (that are not required to be combined under the standard), the entity needs to look to requirements outside IFRS 15 to determine whether offsetting is appropriate.

2.1.6.D Is a refund liability a contract liability (and, thus, subject to the presentation and disclosure requirements of a contract liability)?

An entity needs to determine whether a refund liability is characterised as a contract liability based on the specific facts and circumstances of the arrangement. We believe that a refund liability typically does not meet the definition of a contract liability. When an entity concludes that a refund liability is not a contract liability, it presents the refund liability separately from any contract liability (or asset) and the refund liability is not subject to the disclosure requirements in paragraphs 116-118 of IFRS 15 discussed at 3.2.1 below.

When a customer pays consideration (or consideration is unconditionally due) and the entity has an obligation to transfer goods or services to the customer, the entity recognises a contract liability. When the entity expects to refund some or all of the consideration received (or receivable) from the customer, it recognises a refund liability. A refund liability generally does not represent an obligation to transfer goods or services in the future. Similar to receivables (which are considered a subset of contract assets), refund liabilities could be considered a subset of contract liabilities. We believe refund liabilities are also similar to receivables in that they are extracted from the net contract position and presented separately (if material). This conclusion is consistent with the standard's specific requirement to present the corresponding asset for expected returns separately. *[IFRS 15.B25]*.

If an entity concludes, based on its specific facts and circumstances, that a refund liability represents an obligation to transfer goods or services in the future, the refund liability is a contract liability subject to the disclosure requirements in paragraphs 116-118 of IFRS 15. In addition, in that situation, the entity presents a single net contract liability or asset (i.e. including the refund liability) determined at the contract level, as discussed at 2.1.6.A above.

2.1.6.E Accounting for a contract asset that exists when a contract is modified if the modification is treated as the termination of an existing contract and the creation of a new contract

The FASB TRG members generally agreed that a contract asset that exists when a contract is modified would be carried forward into the new contract if the modification is treated as the termination of an existing contract and the creation of a new contract.

Some stakeholders questioned the appropriate accounting for contract assets when this type of modification occurs because the termination of the old contract could indicate that any remaining balances associated with the old contract must be written off.

FASB TRG members generally agreed that it is appropriate to carry forward the related contract asset in such modifications because the asset relates to a right to consideration for goods or services that have already been transferred and are distinct from those to be transferred in the future. As such, the revenue recognised to date is not reversed and the contract asset continues to be realised as amounts become due from the customer and are presented as a receivable. The contract asset that remains on the entity's statement of financial position at the date of modification continues to be subject to evaluation for impairment.[5]

Consider the following example included in the TRG agenda paper.

Example 32.5:   Accounting for an existing contract asset when the contract is modified

Vendor A enters into a contract to provide a good and one year of service. The transaction price is £4,200. The good and service are separate performance obligations, and the service is considered a series of distinct goods or services (see Chapter 28 at 3.2.2). The stand-alone selling price for the good is £3,000 and the stand-alone selling price for the services is £100 per month (£1,200 for one year). Therefore, Vendor A allocates £3,000 to the good and £1,200 to the services. Customer B will pay 12 equal instalments of £350. Vendor A will invoice Customer B at the end of each month.

At the beginning of the first month, the good is transferred to Customer B and the revenue allocated to that performance obligation (£3,000) is recognised. Vendor A also recognises a contract asset for £3,000 because payment of that £3,000 is conditional upon Vendor A's performance of future services.

At the end of the first month, Vendor A recognises revenue of £100 for progress toward complete satisfaction of the performance obligation related to the services (assuming the entity is using a time-based measure of progress). Vendor A also recognises accounts receivable of £350 because that amount is not conditional. The contract asset, which had a balance of £3,000 at the beginning of the month, would have a balance of £2,750 at the end of the first month.

Vendor A continues to make similar entries for the first nine months of the contract. After nine months, £3,900 of revenue has been recognised for the contract (£900 of revenue for the services and £3,000 for the good). Vendor A has a receivable for £350 (assuming Customer B already paid the first eight instalments). In addition, Vendor A has a contract asset for £750 (£3,000 – (9 × (£350 – £100))).

At the end of nine months, the contract is modified to include one additional year of service. The fee for the last three months of the initial one-year contract is unchanged, but the agreed fee for the additional one year of services is £50 per month, which is significantly below the stand-alone selling price of the services.

In addition, because the remaining services are a series of distinct services, Vendor A determines that the remaining services are distinct from the goods or services transferred prior to the modification. Therefore, the modification would be accounted for under paragraph 21(a) of IFRS 15 (i.e. as a termination of the existing contract and the creation of a new contract, as discussed in Chapter 28 at 2.4).

At the modification date, Vendor A retains the existing contract asset of £750 that relates to revenue previously recognised, but which has not been paid by the customer (and is not presented as a receivable). Vendor A also determines the total consideration to be allocated to the remaining performance obligations. The consideration promised by Customer B that was included in the transaction price, but not yet recognised as revenue under the original contract, is £300 (equal to £4,200 transaction price – £3,900 already recognised as revenue). The additional consideration promised as part of the contract modification is £600 (equal to 12 additional months × £50 per month). Therefore, the total amount of consideration allocated to the remaining distinct services is £900 (£300 + £600). Vendor A would allocate the £900 to the remaining performance obligations and recognise revenue over the remaining modified contract duration. Subsequent to the contract modification, the contract asset would be evaluated and accounted for in the same manner as any other contract asset.

While the FASB TRG members did not discuss this point, we believe a similar conclusion would be appropriate when accounting for an asset created under IFRS 15, such as capitalised commissions which exists immediately before a contract modification, that is treated as if it were a termination of the existing contract and creation of a new contract. See Chapter 31 at 5.1.6 for further discussion.

2.1.6.F Determining when an entity has an unconditional right to payment if it has not transferred a good or service

The standard states in paragraph 108 of IFRS 15 that a receivable is an entity's right to consideration that is unconditional. In general, we believe it may be difficult to assert that the entity has an unconditional right to payment when it has not transferred a good or service. *[IFRS 15.108]*. However, an entity may enter into non-cancellable contracts that provide unconditional rights to payment from the customer for services that the entity has not yet completed providing or services it will provide in the near future (e.g. amounts invoiced in advance related to a service or maintenance arrangement). When determining whether it is acceptable (or required) to recognise accounts receivable and a corresponding contract liability, the contractual terms and specific facts and circumstances supporting the existence of an unconditional right to payment should be evaluated. Factors to consider include:

- Does the entity have a contractual (or legal) right to invoice and receive payment from the customer for services being provided currently (and not yet completed) or being provided in the near future (e.g. amounts invoiced in advance related to a service or maintenance arrangement)?
- Is the advance invoice consistent with the entity's normal invoicing terms?
- Will the entity commence performance within a relatively short time frame of the invoice date?
- Is there more than one year between the advance invoice and performance?

2.2 Presentation requirements for revenue from contracts with customers

The Board decided to require entities to separately present or disclose the amount of revenue related to contracts with customers, as follows: *[IFRS 15.113, BC332]*

- Paragraph 113(a) of IFRS 15 requires an entity to disclose (or present in the statement of comprehensive income) the amount of revenue recognised from contracts with customers under IFRS 15 separately from other sources of revenue. For example, a large equipment manufacturer that both sells and leases its equipment should present (or disclose) amounts from these transactions separately.
- Paragraph 113(b) of IFRS 15 also requires an entity to disclose impairment losses from contracts with customers separately from other impairment losses if they are not presented in the statement of comprehensive income separately. As noted in the Basis for Conclusions, the Board felt that separately disclosing the impairment losses on contracts with customers provides the most relevant information to users of financial statements. *[IFRS 15.BC334]*.

In the following extract, Slater and Gordon Limited presents revenue from contracts with customers that are within the scope of IFRS 15, separately from other income, on the face of its consolidated statement of comprehensive income in its 2018 annual financial statements.

Extract 32.3: Slater and Gordon Limited (2018)

Financial Statements [extract]

Consolidated Statement of Profit or Loss and Other Comprehensive Income [extract]

For the Year Ended 30 June 2018

	Note	2018 $'000	Restated 2017 $'000
Revenue			
Fee revenue		162,166	194,024
Net movement in work in progress		(2,916)	(12,551)
Revenue from contracts with customers	3.1	159,250	181,473
Other income		1,026	1,541
Total revenue and other income		160,276	183,014

In the following extract, The Village Building Co. Limited presents a combined revenue number on the face of the statement of profit or loss which includes revenue recognised from contracts with customers in accordance with IFRS 15 and other revenue (e.g. rental income, dividends) in the same line item. It then presents customer contract revenues separately from other sources of revenue, in note 2.

Extract 32.4: The Village Building Co. Limited (2019)

CONSOLIDATED INCOME STATEMENT FOR THE YEAR ENDED 30 JUNE 2019 [extract]

	Note	2019 $'000	2018 $'000
Revenue	2	92,047	140,531
Cost of sales	3	(58,065)	(103,563)
Gross profit		33,982	36,968

NOTES TO THE CONSOLIDATED FINANCIAL STATEMENTS 30 JUNE 2019 [extract]

NOTE 2. REVENUE [extract]

	2019 $'000	2018 $'000
CUSTOMER CONTRACT REVENUES		
Land, house & land and units	83,859	133,216
Trading income – retail sales (Big Banana)	6,626	6,104
OTHER REVENUE		
Dividends	55	28
Unrealised gain on investments	138	27
Rental income	175	167
Other revenue	1,194	989
Total Revenue	92,047	140,531

Ferrovial, S.A. has applied a different approach by disclosing the amounts relating to contracts with customers in a narrative within the notes.

Extract 32.5: Ferrovial, S.A. (2019)

CONSOLIDATED FINANCIAL STATEMENTS 2019 [extract]

F. Notes to the consolidated annual accounts for 2019 [extract]

SECTION 2: PROFIT/(LOSS) FOR THE YEAR [extract]

NOTES ON PROFIT/(LOSS) FOR CONTINUING OPERATIONS [extract]

2.1. OPERATING INCOME [extract]

The detail of the Group's operating income at 31 December 2019 is as follows:

(Millions of euros)	2019	2018
Revenue	6,054	5,737
Other operating income	2	2
TOTAL OPERATING INCOME	6,056	5,738

The Group's revenue at 31 December 2019 relating to contracts with customers amounted to EUR 5,846 million (see Note 4.4).

Unless required, or permitted, by another standard, IAS 1 does not permit offsetting of income and expenses within profit or loss or the statement of comprehensive income. *[IAS 1.32]*.

After applying the requirements for determining the transaction price in IFRS 15, revenue recognised by an entity may include offsets, for example, for any trade discounts given and volume rebates paid by the entity to its customers. Similarly, in the ordinary course of business, an entity may undertake other transactions that do not generate revenue, but are incidental to the main revenue-generating activities. When this presentation reflects the substance of the transaction or other event, IAS 1 permits an entity to present 'the results of such transactions ... by netting any income with related expenses arising on the same transaction'. *[IAS 1.34]*. An example given in IAS 1 is the presentation of gains and losses on the disposal of non-current assets by deducting from the amount of consideration on disposal the carrying amount of the asset and related selling expenses. *[IAS 1.34(a)]*.

2.2.1 Presentation of income outside the scope of IFRS 15

Entities need to consider the definition of revenue. IFRS 15 defines revenue as 'Income arising in the course of an entity's ordinary activities', but the standard excludes some revenue contracts from its scope (e.g. leases). According to the *2010 Conceptual Framework for Financial Reporting* (which applied when IFRS 15 was issued), 'revenue arises in the course of the ordinary activities of an entity and is referred to by a variety of different names including sales, fees, interest, dividends, royalties and rent'. *[CF(2010) 4.29]*. The 2018 *Conceptual Framework for Financial Reporting* (which is effective for annual periods beginning on or after 1 January 2020) no longer contains a discussion about revenue and gains and losses. However, the definition of revenue in IFRS 15 will remain unchanged. The Board does not expect the removal of that discussion to cause any changes in practice. *[CF(2018) BC4.96]*.

While 'ordinary activities' is not defined, if the transaction involves the sale of an asset, the nature of the asset and the purpose for which it was held by the entity may be informative. For example, inventory accounted for under IAS 2 – *Inventories* – is, by definition, held for use in production or sale in the ordinary course of business. *[IAS 2.6]*. Therefore, the sale of that inventory is typically part of an entity's ordinary activities. Conversely, property, plant and equipment accounted for under IAS 16 – *Property, Plant and Equipment* – is, by definition, held for use by the entity for more than one period. *[IAS 16.6]*. Likewise, IAS 38 – *Intangible Assets* – excludes from its scope intangible assets held for sale in the ordinary course of business. *[IAS 38.3(a)]*. Therefore, their disposal is not typically part of an entity's ordinary activities and the difference between the net disposal proceeds and the carrying amount of the asset is not recognised as revenue under IFRS 15, but as a gain or loss on disposal. This was reiterated by the IFRS Interpretations Committee in June 2020, as is discussed in Chapter 27 at 4.3.[6]

If an entity receives consideration in the course of its ordinary activities that is outside the scope of IFRS 15, it may present that income as revenue in the income statement. However, this income will need to be presented either separately from revenue from contracts with customers on the income statement or separately disclosed within the notes. This is because, as mentioned at 2.2 above, entities are required to present in the statement of comprehensive income, or disclose within the notes, the amount of revenue recognised from contracts with customers separately from other sources of revenue.

IFRS 15 does not explicitly require an entity to use the term 'revenue from contracts with customers'. Therefore, entities might use a different terminology in their financial statements to describe revenue arising from transactions that are within the scope of IFRS 15. However, entities should ensure the terms used are not misleading and allow users to distinguish revenue from contracts with customers from other sources of revenue.

2.3 Other presentation considerations

The standard also includes presentation requirements for products expected to be returned and for those that contain a significant financing component. See Chapter 29 at 2.4 and 2.5.3 for presentation considerations related to rights of return and significant financing components, respectively. Also see Chapter 31 at 5.3.6 for classification and presentation considerations related to capitalised contract costs to obtain and fulfil a contract.

2.3.1 Classifying shipping and handling costs in the income statement

Under IFRS 15, an entity needs to determine whether shipping and handling is a separate promised service to the customer or if they are activities to fulfil the promise to transfer the good (see Chapter 28 at 3.1). Shipping and handling activities that are performed before the customer obtains control of the related good will be activities to fulfil its promise to transfer control of the good. If shipping and handling activities are performed after a customer obtains control of the related good, shipping and handling is a promised service to the customer and an entity needs to determine whether it acts as a principal or an agent in providing those services.

If an entity determines that the shipping and handling activities are related to a promised good or service to the customer (either the promise to transfer control of the good or the promise to provide shipping and handling services) and the entity is the principal (rather than the agent), we believe the related costs should be classified as cost of sales because the costs would be incurred to fulfil a revenue obligation. However, if the entity determines that shipping and handling is a separate promised service to the customer and it is acting as an agent in providing those services, the related revenue to be recognised for shipping and handling services would be net of the related costs.

We believe entities need to apply judgement to determine how to classify shipping and handling costs when it is not related to a promised good or service to the customer. This is because IFRS does not specifically address how entities should classify these costs. While not a requirement of IFRS 15, we would encourage entities to disclose the amount of these costs and the line item or items on the income statement that include them, if they are significant.

See Chapter 31 at 5.3.6 for a discussion on classification and presentation of capitalised contract costs and related amortisation in the statement of financial position and income statement, respectively.

3 DISCLOSURES IN ANNUAL FINANCIAL STATEMENTS

3.1 Disclosure objective and general requirements

In response to criticism that the legacy revenue recognition disclosures are inadequate, the Board sought to create a comprehensive and coherent set of disclosures. As a result, IFRS 15 described the overall objective of the disclosures, consistent with other recent standards, as detailed below.

The objective is for an entity to 'disclose sufficient information to enable users of financial statements to understand the nature, amount, timing and uncertainty of revenue and cash flows arising from contracts with customers'. To achieve that objective, an entity is required to disclose qualitative and quantitative information about all of the following: *[IFRS 15.110]*

(a) its contracts with customers (discussed further at 3.2.1 below);
(b) the significant judgements, and changes in the judgements, made in applying the standard to those contracts (discussed further at 3.2.2 below); and
(c) any assets recognised from the costs to obtain or fulfil a contract with a customer (discussed further at 3.2.3 below).

The standard requires that an entity consider the level of detail necessary to satisfy the disclosure objective and how much emphasis to place on each of the various requirements. The level of aggregation or disaggregation of disclosures requires judgement. Entities are required to ensure that useful information is not obscured (by either the inclusion of a large amount of insignificant detail or the aggregation of items that have substantially different characteristics). *[IFRS 15.111]*.

An entity does not need to disclose information in accordance with IFRS 15 if it discloses that information in accordance with another standard. *[IFRS 15.112]*.

As explained in the Basis for Conclusions, many preparers raised concerns that they would need to provide voluminous disclosures at a cost that may outweigh any potential benefits. *[IFRS 15.BC327, BC331]*. As summarised above, the Board clarified the disclosure objective and indicated that the disclosures described in the standard are not meant to be a checklist of minimum requirements. That is, entities do not need to include disclosures that are not relevant or are not material to them. In addition, the Board decided to require qualitative disclosures instead of tabular reconciliations for certain disclosures.

Entities should review their disclosures in each reporting period to determine whether they have met the standard's disclosure objective to enable users to understand the nature, amount, timing and uncertainty of revenue and cash flows arising from contracts with customers. For example, some entities may make large payments to customers that do not represent payment for a distinct good or service and therefore reduce the transaction price and affect the amount and timing of revenue recognised. Although there are no specific requirements in the standard to disclose balances related to consideration paid or payable to a customer, an entity may need to disclose qualitative and/or quantitative information about those arrangements to meet the objective of the disclosure requirements in the standard if the amounts are material.

The disclosures are required for (and as at) each annual period for which a statement of comprehensive income and a statement of financial position are presented.

Certain interim revenue disclosures are also required for entities preparing interim financial statements. When it issued IFRS 15, the IASB amended IAS 34 – *Interim Financial Reporting* – to require disclosure of disaggregated revenue information. However, none of the other annual disclosures are required for interim financial statements (see Chapter 41 for further discussion on interim financial reporting).

3.2 Specific disclosure requirements

3.2.1 Contracts with customers

The majority of the standard's disclosures relate to an entity's contracts with customers. These disclosures include disaggregation of revenue, information about contract asset and liability balances and information about an entity's performance obligations.

3.2.1.A Disaggregation of revenue

Entities are required to disclose disaggregated revenue information to illustrate how the nature, amount, timing and uncertainty about revenue and cash flows are affected by economic factors. *[IFRS 15.114].* This is the only revenue disclosure requirement that is required in both an entity's interim and annual financial statements.

As noted above, an entity is required to separately disclose any impairment losses recognised in accordance with IFRS 9 on receivables or contract assets arising from contracts with customers. However, IFRS 15 does not require entities to further disaggregate such losses for uncollectible amounts.

While the standard does not specify precisely how revenue should be disaggregated, the application guidance suggests categories for entities to consider. The application guidance indicates that the most appropriate categories for a particular entity depend on its facts and circumstances, but an entity needs to consider how it disaggregates revenue in other communications (e.g. press releases, information regularly reviewed by the chief operating decision maker) when determining which categories are most relevant and useful. These categories could include, but are not limited to: *[IFRS 15.B87-B89]*

- type of good or service (e.g. major product lines);
- geographical region (e.g. country or region);
- market or type of customer (e.g. government and non-government customers);
- type of contract (e.g. fixed-price and time-and-materials contracts);
- contract duration (e.g. short-term and long-term contracts);
- timing of transfer of goods or services (e.g. revenue from goods or services transferred to customers at a point in time and revenue from goods or services transferred over time); and
- sales channels (e.g. goods sold directly to consumers and goods sold through intermediaries).

As noted in the Basis for Conclusions, the Board decided not to prescribe a specific characteristic of revenue as the basis for disaggregation because it intended for entities to make this determination based on entity-specific and/or industry-specific factors that are the most meaningful for their businesses. The Board acknowledged that an entity may need to use more than one type of category to disaggregate its revenue. *[IFRS 15.B87, BC336]*.

We believe that, when determining categories for disaggregation of revenue, entities need to analyse specific risk factors for each of their revenue streams to determine the appropriate level of revenue disaggregation that will be beneficial to users of the financial statements. If certain risk factors could lead to changes in the nature, amount, timing and uncertainty of revenue recognition and cash flows, those factors will need to be considered as part of the evaluation. Different risk factors for revenue streams may indicate when disaggregation is required.

Paragraph 112 of IFRS 15 clarifies that an entity does not have to duplicate disclosures required by another standard. *[IFRS 15.112]*. For example, an entity that provides disaggregated revenue disclosures as part of its segment disclosures, in accordance with IFRS 8 – *Operating Segments*, does not need to separately provide disaggregated revenue disclosures if the segment-related disclosures are sufficient to illustrate how the nature, amount, timing and uncertainty about revenue and cash flows from contracts with customers are affected by economic factors and are presented on a basis consistent with IFRS.

However, segment disclosures may not be sufficiently disaggregated to achieve the disclosure objectives of IFRS 15. The IASB noted in the Basis for Conclusions that segment disclosures on revenue may not always provide users of financial statements with enough information to help them understand the composition of revenue recognised in the period. *[IFRS 15.BC340]*. If an entity applies IFRS 8, it is required under paragraph 115 of IFRS 15 to explain the relationship between the disaggregated revenue information and revenue information that is disclosed for each reportable segment. *[IFRS 15.115]*. Users of the financial statements believe this information is critical to their ability to understand not only the composition of revenue, but also how revenue relates to other information provided in the segment disclosures. Entities can provide this information in a tabular or a narrative form.

Regulators may review publicly provided information (e.g. investor presentations, press releases) in order to evaluate whether entities have met the objectives of this disclosure requirement. In accordance with paragraph B88 of IFRS 15, an entity needs to consider how information about its revenue has been presented for other purposes, including information disclosed outside the financial statements, information regularly reviewed by the chief operating decision maker (e.g. chief executive officer or chief operating officer) and other similar information used by the entity or users of the financial statements to evaluate the entity's financial performance or to make resource allocation decisions.

It is important to note that IFRS 15 and IFRS 8 have different objectives. The objective of the segment reporting requirements in IFRS 8 is to enable users of the financial statements to 'evaluate the nature and financial effects of the business activities in which an entity engages and the economic environment in which it operates'. *[IFRS 8.20]*. These disclosure requirements are largely based on how the chief operating decision maker allocates resources to the operating segments of the entity and assesses their performance. *[IFRS 8.5(b)]*. They also permit aggregation in certain situations. In contrast, IFRS 15 disclosure requirements focus on how the revenues and cash flows from contracts with customers are affected by economic factors and do not have similar aggregation criteria. As noted above, if an entity concludes that it is necessary to provide disaggregated revenue disclosures along with the segment disclosures required under IFRS 8, it is required under IFRS 15 to explain the relationship between the disclosures.

The Board provided an example of the disclosures for disaggregation of revenue, as follows. *[IFRS 15.IE210-IE211].*

Example 32.6: Disaggregation of revenue – quantitative disclosure

An entity reports the following segments: consumer products, transportation and energy, in accordance with IFRS 8. When the entity prepares its investor presentations, it disaggregates revenue into primary geographical markets, major product lines and timing of revenue recognition (i.e. goods transferred at a point in time or services transferred over time).

The entity determines that the categories used in the investor presentations can be used to meet the objective of the disaggregation disclosure requirement in paragraph 114 of IFRS 15, which is to disaggregate revenue from contracts with customers into categories that depict how the nature, amount, timing and uncertainty of revenue and cash flows are affected by economic factors. The following table illustrates the disaggregation disclosure by primary geographical market, major product line and timing of revenue recognition, including a reconciliation of how the disaggregated revenue ties in with the consumer products, transportation and energy segments, in accordance with paragraph 115 of IFRS 15.

Segments	Consumer products £	Transport £	Energy £	Total £
Primary geographical markets				
North America	990	2,250	5,250	8,490
Europe	300	750	1,000	2,050
Asia	700	260	–	960
	1,990	3,260	6,250	11,500
Major goods/service lines				
Office Supplies	600	–	–	600
Appliances	990	–	–	990
Clothing	400	–	–	400
Motorcycles	–	500	–	500
Automobiles	–	2,760	–	2,760
Solar Panels	–	–	1,000	1,000
Power Plant	–	–	5,250	5,250
	1,990	3,260	6,250	11,500
Timing of revenue recognition				
Goods transferred at a point in time	1,990	3,260	1,000	6,250
Services transferred over time	–	–	5,250	5,250
	1,990	3,260	6,250	11,500

Since entities are encouraged to tailor their disclosure of disaggregated revenue, they are unlikely to follow a single approach.

Consistent with the approach illustrated in Example 32.6 above, some entities provide disaggregated revenue information within their segment reporting disclosure. As shown in Extract 32.6 below, Capita plc discloses both revenue by major product line and segment revenue by contract type and geographical location in its segment note (Note 2.2.1). In the summary of significant accounting policies (Note 2), it specifically states that this approach is consistent with the objective of the IFRS 15 disclosure requirement and explains differences in the terminology used in previous financial statements.

Entities that are required to apply IFRS 8 might already provide adequate information that allows users to understand the composition of revenue. However, this information might be based on non-GAAP information (i.e. the revenue that is reported to the chief operating decision maker may be calculated on a basis that is not in accordance with IFRS 15). In such a situation, an entity may need to disclose additional information to meet the objective in paragraph 114 of IFRS 15.

Note that for brevity not all the segmental columns given in Capita plc's financial statements have been reproduced in Extract 32.6 below.

> Extract 32.6: Capita plc (2019)
>
> Financial statements [extract]
>
> Notes to the consolidated financial statements [extract]
>
> Section 2: Results for the year [extract]
>
> 2.2 Revenue including segmental revenue [extracts]
>
> Contract types [extract]
>
> The Group disaggregates revenue from contracts with customers by contract type, as management believe this best depicts how the nature, amount, timing and uncertainty of the Group's revenue and cash flows are affected by economic factors. Categories are: 'long-term contractual – greater than two years'; and 'short-term contractual – less than two years' and 'transactional'. Years based from service commencement date.
>
> 2.2.1 Segmental revenue [extract]
>
> The Group's operations are managed separately according to the nature of the services provided, with each segment representing a strategic business division offering a different package of client outcomes across the markets the Group serves. A description of the service provision for each segment can be found in the strategic report on pages 20-31.
>
> The tables below present revenue for the Group's business segments for the years 2019 and 2018. As discussed in the strategic report on pages 9-11, a new Consulting division was created in 2019. For segmental reporting, Consulting is aggregated within the 'Group trading and central services' segment. The division was formed following the transfer of businesses from the Software segment and the recruitment of additional resources. During 2019, there were transfers of businesses between the Specialist Services and Technology Solutions segments. Comparative information has been restated accordingly.
>
> Adjusted revenue, excluding results from businesses exited in both years (adjusting items), was £3,647.4m (2018: £3,814.7m), an organic decline of 4.4% (2018: 6.7%).

Year ended 31 December 2019	Notes	Software £m	People Solutions £m	Customer Management £m	Government Services £m	Group trading and central services £m	Total adjusted £m	Adjusting items £m	Total reported £m
Continuing operations									
Long-term contractual		331.8	313.3	552.6	673.7	14.7	2,615.4	23.5	2,638.9
Short-term contractual		37.9	34.8	248.1	14.6	2.4	563.2	0.4	563.6
Transactional (point in time)		5.7	152.4	1.7	89.6	0.3	468.8	7.3	476.1
Total segment revenue		375.4	500.5	802.4	777.9	17.4	3,647.4	31.2	3,678.6
Trading revenue		434.7	700.5	919.0	802.7	65.6	4,382.4	–	4,382.4
Inter-segment revenue		(59.3)	(200.0)	(116.6)	(24.8)	(48.2)	(735.0)	–	(735.0)
Total adjusted segment revenue		375.4	500.5	802.4	777.9	17.4	3,647.4	–	3,647.4
Business exits – trading	2.8	–	5.5	–	–	–	–	31.2	31.2
Total segment revenue		375.4	506.0	802.4	777.9	17.4	–	–	3,678.6

Geographical location

The table below presents revenue by geographical location.

	2019			2018		
	United Kingdom £m	Other £m	Total £m	United Kingdom £m	Other £m	Total £m
Revenue	3,358.4	320.2	3,678.6	3,609.7	308.7	3,918.4

In Extract 32.7 below, Société nationale SNCF discloses disaggregated revenue by main types of services provided, by type of customer, and by timing of transfer of services in the revenue note (Note 3.2) of its 2019 annual financial statements. The disaggregated revenue table below includes a column for Société nationale SNCF reportable segments and the amount of total revenue reconciles with the total revenue disclosed in the segment note. This is important because it helps users to understand the relationship between the disclosure of disaggregated revenue in the revenue note and the revenue information that is disclosed for each reportable segment in the segment note.

Extract 32.7: Société nationale SNCF (2019)
ANNUAL CONSOLIDATED FINANCIAL STATEMENTS [extract]
NOTES TO THE CONSOLIDATED FINANCIAL STATEMENTS [extract]
3. GROSS PROFIT [extract]
3.2 REVENUE [extract]

SNCF Group generates revenue from services provided at a given time or continuously over a certain period to public or private individuals under the following main service lines:

In € millions	31/12/2019	31/12/2018	Change	Segments
Revenue generated by passenger transport within Voyages activities	7,144	6,866	278	Voyages SNCF
Revenue generated from freight transport activities	7,043	6,832	212	SNCF Logistics
Other related transport activities	2,615	2,739	–124	Voyages SNCF, SNCF Logistics
Compensation collected from the Transport Organising Authorities in connection with regulated activities	13,914	12,927	987	SNCF Transilien & TER, Keolis, Intercités
Rail network management fees	2,205	2,096	110	SNCF Réseau
Revenue generated from station management	286	250	36	SNCF Gares & Connexions
Real estate leasing revenue (excluding rental payments generated by stations)	126	173	–47	SNCF Logistics, Voyages SNCF, Corporate
Transport equipment leasing revenue	352	312	39	SNCF Logistics, SNCF Transilien & TER, Keolis
Upkeep and maintenance services	254	194	60	All segments
Other revenue	1,182	923	259	All segments
Revenue by main service line	**35,120**	**33,311**	**1,809**	
Public sector customers (government authorities)	16,216	15,370	846	
Private individuals	7,440	6,901	539	
Private sector companies	11,464	11,041	424	
Revenue by customer type	**35,120**	**33, 311**	**1,809**	
Immediate or one-day transfer	10,116	9,968	148	
Point-in-time transfer over a period of less than one year (logistics, freight transport and compensation from OA)	24,391	22,745	1,647	
Over-time transfer over a period of more than one year (real estate activities, certain station management activities, etc.).	613	599	14	
Revenue by recognition rate	**35,120**	**33, 311**	**1,809**	

In Extract 32.8, Fédération Internationale de Football Association (FIFA) splits its disclosure of disaggregated revenue between the primary financial statements and the notes. In the statement of comprehensive income, FIFA presents revenue on a disaggregated basis, by the type of service. In the notes, FIFA further disaggregates each type of revenue into different categories, depending on the nature of the revenue. For example, in Note 1, FIFA disaggregates 'Revenue from television broadcasting rights' by geographical region, while presenting 'Revenue from marketing rights' by type of customer. Since FIFA does not need to comply with IFRS 8, it provides all disaggregation disclosures in accordance with paragraph 114 of IFRS 15 and the requirements in paragraph 115 of IFRS 15 do not apply.

Extract 32.8: Fédération Internationale de Football Association (2018)
CONSOLIDATED FINANCIAL STATEMENTS [extract]
CONSOLIDATED STATEMENT OF COMPREHENSIVE INCOME [extract]

in TUSD	Note	2018	2017
REVENUE			
Revenue from television broadcasting rights	1	2,543,968	228,645
Revenue from marketing rights	2	1,143,312	245,277
Revenue from licensing rights	3	184,573	160,211
Revenue from hospitality/accommodation rights and ticket sales	4	689,143	22,368
Other revenue	5	79,958	77,701
Total revenue		4,640,954	734,202

Notes to the consolidated statement of comprehensive income [extract]
1 REVENUE FROM TELEVISION BROADCASTING RIGHTS [extract]

in TUSD	2018	2017
Europe	897,748	6,395
Asia and North Africa	787,566	71,652
South and Central America	314,513	50,499
North America and the Caribbean	362,937	58,377
Rest of the world	85,075	13,863
Total revenue from television broadcasting rights by region	2,447,839	200,786
Other broadcasting revenue	92,352	13,799
Other FIFA event revenue	3,777	14,060
Total revenue from television broadcasting rights	2,543,968	228,645

2 REVENUE FROM MARKETING RIGHTS [extract]

in TUSD	2018	2017
FIFA Partners	695,054	185,411
FIFA World Cup Sponsors	301,620	41,030
FIFA Regional Supporters	143,488	7,382
FIFA National Supporters	3,150	11,454
Total revenue from marketing rights	1,143,312	245,277

3.2.1.B   Contract balances

The Board noted in the Basis for Conclusions that users of the financial statements need to understand the relationship between the revenue recognised and changes in the

overall balances of an entity's total contract assets and liabilities during a particular reporting period. *[IFRS 15.BC341]*. As a result, an entity is required to disclose: *[IFRS 15.116]*
- the opening and closing balances of receivables, contract assets and contract liabilities from contracts with customers, if not otherwise separately presented or disclosed;
- revenue recognised in the reporting period that was included in the contract liability balance at the beginning of the period; and
- revenue recognised in the reporting period from performance obligations satisfied (or partially satisfied) in previous periods (e.g. changes in transaction price).

In addition, an entity is required to explain how the timing of satisfaction of its performance obligations (see (a)(i) below at 3.2.1.C) relates to the typical timing of payment (see (a)(ii) below at 3.2.1.C) and the effect that those factors have on the contract asset and the contract liability balances. This explanation may use qualitative information. *[IFRS 15.117]*.

An entity is also required to provide an explanation of the significant changes in the contract asset and the contract liability balances during the reporting period. This explanation is required to include both qualitative and quantitative information. The standard identifies the following examples of changes in the entity's balances of contract assets and contract liabilities: *[IFRS 15.118]*
- changes due to business combinations;
- cumulative catch-up adjustments to revenue that affect the corresponding contract asset or contract liability, including adjustments arising from a change in the measure of progress, a change in an estimate of the transaction price (including any changes in the assessment of whether an estimate of variable consideration is constrained) or a contract modification;
- impairment of a contract asset;
- a change in the time frame for a right to consideration to become unconditional (i.e. for a contract asset to be reclassified to a receivable); and
- a change in the time frame for a performance obligation to be satisfied (i.e. for the recognition of revenue arising from a contract liability).

Entities are permitted to disclose information about contract balances, and changes therein, as they deem to be most appropriate, which would include a combination of tabular and narrative information. The IASB explained in the Basis for Conclusions that these disclosures are intended to provide financial statement users with information they requested on when contract assets are typically transferred to accounts receivable or collected as cash and when contract liabilities are recognised as revenue. *[IFRS 15.BC346]*.

In addition to the disclosures on contract balances and changes, the standard requires entities to disclose the amount of revenue recognised in the period that relates to amounts allocated to performance obligations that were satisfied (or partially satisfied) in previous periods (e.g. due to a change in transaction price or in estimates related to the constraint on revenue recognised). This disclosure requirement applies to sales-based and usage-based royalties received from a customer in exchange for a licence of intellectual property that are recognised as revenue in a reporting period, but relate to performance obligations satisfied (or partially satisfied) in previous periods (e.g. sales-based royalties recognised in the current period that are related to a right-to-use licence previously transferred to a customer). As noted in the Basis for Conclusions, the Board noted that this information is not required elsewhere in the financial statements and provides relevant information about the timing of revenue recognised that was not a result of performance in the current period. *[IFRS 15.BC347].*

The example below is an example of how an entity may fulfil these requirements.

Example 32.7: *Contract asset and liability disclosures*

Company A discloses receivables from contracts with customers separately in the statement of financial position. To comply with the other disclosure requirements for contract assets and liabilities, Company A includes the following information in the notes to the financial statements:

	20X1 $	20X0 $	20X9 $
Contract asset	1,500	2,250	1,800
Contract liability	(200)	(850)	(500)

	20X1 $	20X0 $	20X9 $
Revenue recognised in the period from:			
Amounts included in contract liability at the beginning of the period	650	200	100
Performance obligations satisfied in previous periods	200	125	200

We receive payments from customers based on a billing schedule, as established in our contracts. Contract asset relates to our conditional right to consideration for our completed performance under the contract. Accounts receivable are recognised when the right to consideration becomes unconditional. Contract liability relates to payments received in advance of performance under the contract. Contract liabilities are recognised as revenue as (or when) we perform under the contract. In addition, contract asset decreased in 20X1 due to a contract asset impairment of $400 relating to the early cancellation of a contract with a customer.

Paragraph 116(a) of IFRS 15 requires entities to separately disclose contract balances from contracts with customers. Therefore, it is necessary for entities that have material receivables from non-IFRS 15 contracts to separate these balances for disclosure purposes. For example, an entity may have accounts receivable relating to leasing contracts that would need to be disclosed separately from accounts receivable related to contracts with customers. Entities need to make sure they have appropriate systems, policies and procedures and internal controls in place to collect and disclose the required information.

Before providing its disclosure of significant changes in contract balances, Airbus SE provides the accounting policies for its contract balances in Extract 32.9 below. It then provides in a table the significant changes in the contract asset and the contract liability balances during the reporting period. The opening and closing balances are included in the primary financial statements.

> Extract 32.9: Airbus SE (2019)
>
> Notes to the IFRS Consolidated Financial Statements [extract]
>
> 2.5 Operational Assets and Liabilities [extract]
>
> 22. Contract Assets and Contract Liabilities, Trade Receivables and Trade Liabilities [extract]
>
> *Contract assets* represent the Company's right to consideration in exchange for goods or services that the Company has transferred to a customer when that right is conditioned by something other than the passage of time (*e.g.* revenue recognised from the application of the PoC method before the Company has a right to invoice).
>
> *Contract liabilities* represent the Company's obligation to transfer goods or services to a customer for which the Company has received consideration, or for which an amount of consideration is due from the customer (*e.g.* advance payments received).
>
> *Net contract assets and contract liabilities* are determined for each contract separately. For serial contracts, contract liabilities are presented in current contract liabilities, if revenues are expected within the next twelve months or material expenses for the manufacturing process have already occurred. For long-term production contracts (*e.g.* governmental contracts such as A400M, Tiger, NH90), contract liabilities are classified as current when the relating inventories or receivables are expected to be recognised within the normal operating cycle of the long-term contract.
>
> *Trade receivables* arise when the Company provides goods or services directly to a customer with no intention of trading the receivable. Trade receivables include claims arising from revenue recognition that are not yet settled by the debtor. Trade receivables are initially recognised at their transaction prices and are subsequently measured at amortised cost less any allowances for impairment. Gains and losses are recognised in the Consolidated Income Statement when the receivables are derecognised, impaired or amortised.
>
> *Impairment and allowances of trade receivables and contract assets* are measured at an amount equal to the life-time expected loss as described in "– Note 37: Information about Financial Instruments".
>
> Contract Assets, Contract Liabilities and Trade Receivables [extract]
>
> Significant changes in contract assets and contract liabilities during the period are as follows:
>
> | (in € million) | 2019 | |
> |---|---|---|
> | | Contract assets | Contract liabilities |
> | Revenue recognised that was included in the contract liability balance at 1 January | – | (37,303) |
> | Increases due to cash received, excluding amounts recognised as revenue | – | 38,312 |
> | Transfers from contract assets recognised at 1 January | (3,436) | – |
> | Increase as a result of changes in the measure of progress | 3,941 | – |
>
> As of 31 December 2019, trade receivables amounting to €203 million (2018: €583 million) will mature after more than one year.

ProSiebenSat.1 Media SE explains, in Extract 32.10 below, the nature of its contract assets and contract liabilities. In Note 5, it discloses the opening and closing balances of contract assets and contract liabilities in a table. Below the table, it explains significant changes in the contract asset and contract liability balances during the reporting period using a narrative format. In the same note, ProSiebenSat.1 Media SE discloses revenue recognised that was included in the contract liability balance at the beginning of the period.

Extract 32.10: ProSiebenSat.1 Media SE (2019)

CONSOLIDATED FINANCIAL STATEMENT [extract]

NOTES [extract]

NOTES TO THE INCOME STATEMENT [extract]

6 / Revenues [extract]

CONTRACT ASSETS AND LIABILITIES in EUR m

	12/31/2019	12/31/2018
Contract Assets	30	28
Contract Liabilities[1]	123	89

[1] Due to a necessary reclassification from contract liabilities, the previous year's figure was reduced by EUR 100 million. Of this amount, EUR 67 million were classified as obligations from event vouchers (see note 30 "Other liabilities"). The remaining EUR 33 million relate to accrued expenses for subsequent invoices.

Contract assets primarily relate to the Group's claims for consideration resulting from commissioned productions that have been completed but are yet to be invoiced as of the reporting date. These contract assets will be reclassified as trade receivables upon invoicing. In addition, contract assets also include services from multi-component transactions in the online dating services business that have already been provided but cannot yet be invoiced.

In financial year 2019, as in the previous year, changes in contract assets resulting from business combinations were immaterial. Expected losses to be recognized on contract assets were immaterial as well.

Contract liabilities primarily relate to advance payments received in connection with commissioned productions and the sale of program rights as well as to deferred income from online dating services and from media services not yet rendered.

In financial year 2019, contract liabilities increased by EUR 2 million as a result of business combinations (previous year: EUR 18 million). No effects resulted from deconsolidations in the financial year 2019 (previous year: EUR 9 million). Of the contract liabilities existing as of January 1, 2019, EUR 89 million were recognized as revenues in the 2019 financial year (previous year: EUR 90 million).

In financial year 2019, no material revenues were generated from performance obligations satisfied (or partially satisfied) in prior periods.

As permitted under IFRS 15, no disclosures are made for the remaining performance obligations at December 31, 2019 that have an original expected duration of one year or less. Performance obligations with an original expected duration of more than one year only exist to an insignificant extent as of December 31, 2019.

In connection with the "sale of goods" business model, inventories are recognized in the amount of EUR 48 million (previous year: EUR 42 million). Write-downs on inventories in the amount of EUR 4 million were recognized in financial year 2019 (previous year: EUR 2 million).

As shown in Extract 32.11 below, ASML Holding N.V. included a roll-forward of contract assets and contract liabilities to disclose significant changes in the balances during the reporting period. Although such a roll-forward is not required under IFRS 15, it may be an effective way to provide the disclosures required by paragraph 118 of IFRS 15. The requirement of the standard to disclose the 'revenue recognised in the reporting period that was included in the contract liability balance at the beginning of the period' was incorporated in the roll-forward. In addition, ASML Holding N.V. also provided a narrative explanation of the significant changes in the net contract balances during the reporting period.

> **Extract 32.11: ASML Holding N.V. (2019)**
> Consolidated financial statements [extract]
> Notes to the Consolidated Financial Statements [extract]
> 2. Revenue from contracts with customers [extract]
> Contract assets and liabilities
>
> The contract assets primarily relate to our rights to a consideration for goods or services delivered but not invoiced at the reporting date. The contract assets are transferred to the receivables when the receivables become unconditional. The contract liabilities primarily relate to remaining performance obligations for which consideration has been received such as down payments received for systems to be delivered, as well as deferred revenue from system shipments, based on the allocation of the consideration to the related performance obligations in the contract. This deferred revenue mainly consists of extended and enhanced warranties, installation and free goods or services provided as part of a volume purchase agreement.
>
> The majority of our customer contracts contain both asset and liability positions. At the end of each reporting period, these positions are netted on a contract basis and presented as either an asset or a liability in the Consolidated Balance Sheets. Consequently, a contract balance can change between periods from a net contract asset balance to a net contract liability balance in the balance sheet.
>
> Significant changes in the contract assets and the contract liabilities balances during the periods are as follows.
>
> | Year ended December 31 (in millions) | 2018 € Contract Assets | 2018 € Contract Liabilities | 2019 € Contract Assets | 2019 € Contract Liabilities |
> |---|---|---|---|---|
> | Balance at beginning of the year | 270.4 | 2,152.0 | 95.9 | 2,953.2 |
> | Transferred to receivables from contract assets from the beginning of the period | (456.2) | – | (167.4) | – |
> | Revenues recognized during the year, to be invoiced | 192.3 | – | 68.7 | – |
> | Revenue recognition that was included in the contract liability balance at the beginning of the period | – | (1,306.3) | – | (1,528.4) |
> | Changes as a result of cumulative catch-up adjustments arising from changes in estimates | – | (64.4) | – | (133.4) |
> | Remaining performance obligations for which considerations have been received | – | 2,082.5 | – | 2,760.8 |
> | Transfer between contract assets and liabilities | 89.4 | 89.4 | 233.8 | 233.8 |
> | Total | 95.9 | 2,953.2 | 231.0 | 4,286.0 |
>
> The increase in the net contract liability to €4,055.0 million as of December 31, 2019 compared to €2,857.3 million as of December 31, 2018 was mainly caused by an increase in contract liabilities related to the recognition of down payments related to unconditional receivables as well as regular down payments for systems to be shipped in 2020 or later. The cumulative catch-up adjustments recognized as revenues in 2019 mainly relate to changed estimates impacting discounts and credits related to system volumes as part of a volume purchase agreement that ended in 2019.

3.2.1.C Performance obligations

To help users of financial statements analyse the nature, amount, timing and uncertainty about revenue and cash flows arising from contracts with customers, the Board decided to require disclosures about an entity's performance obligations. As noted in the Basis for Conclusions, legacy IFRS required entities to disclose their accounting policies for recognising revenue, but users of financial statements had commented that many entities provided a 'boilerplate' description that did not explain how the policy related to the contracts they entered into with customers. *[IFRS 15.BC354]*. To address this criticism,

IFRS 15 requires an entity to provide more descriptive information about its performance obligations.

An entity is also required to disclose information about remaining performance obligations and the amount of the transaction price allocated to such obligations, including an explanation of when it expects to recognise the amount(s) in its financial statements.

Both quantitative and qualitative information are required, as follows: *[IFRS 15.119-120]*

(a) Information about its performance obligations, including a description of all of the following:
  (i) when the entity typically satisfies its performance obligations (e.g. upon shipment, upon delivery, as services are rendered or upon completion of service), including when performance obligations are satisfied in a bill-and-hold arrangement;
  (ii) the significant payment terms (e.g. when payment is typically due, whether the contract has a significant financing component, whether the consideration amount is variable and whether the estimate of variable consideration is typically constrained);
  (iii) the nature of the goods or services that the entity has promised to transfer, highlighting any performance obligations to arrange for another party to transfer goods or services (i.e. if the entity is acting as an agent);
  (iv) obligations for returns, refunds and other similar obligations; and
  (v) types of warranties and related obligations.

(b) For remaining performance obligations:
  (i) the aggregate amount of the transaction price allocated to the performance obligations that are unsatisfied (or partially unsatisfied) as at the end of the reporting period; and
  (ii) an explanation of when the entity expects to recognise as revenue the amount disclosed in accordance with (b)(i) above. An entity discloses this in either of the following ways:
    • on a quantitative basis using the time bands that would be most appropriate for the duration of the remaining performance obligations; or
    • by using qualitative information.

In Extract 32.12 below, Spotify Technology S.A. highlighted in its revenue note that the disclosures of its performance obligations are included in its significant accounting policy disclosures. In its summary of significant accounting policies, Spotify Technology S.A. discloses information about its performance obligations for subscription and advertising services. It describes when it typically satisfies its performance obligations and the significant payment terms.

Extract 32.12: Spotify Technology S.A. (2019)

Notes to the 2019 consolidated financial statements [extract]

4. Revenue recognition [extract]

Revenue from contracts with customers [extract]

(ii) Performance obligations

The Group discloses its policies for how it identifies, satisfies, and recognizes its performance obligations associated with its contracts with customers in Note 2.

2. Summary of significant accounting policies [extract]

(d) Revenue recognition

Premium revenue

The Group generates subscription revenue from the sale of the Premium Service in which customers can listen on-demand and offline. Premium Services are sold directly to end users and through partners who are generally telecommunications companies that bundle the subscription with their own services or collect payment for the stand-alone subscriptions from their end customers. The Group satisfies its performance obligation, and revenue from these services is recognized, on a straight-line basis over the subscription period. Typically, Premium Services are paid for monthly in advance.

Premium partner subscription revenue is based on a per-subscriber rate in a negotiated partner agreement. Under these arrangements, a premium partner may bundle the Premium Service with its existing product offerings or offer the Premium Service as an add-on. Payment is remitted to the Group through the premium partner. The Group assesses the facts and circumstances, including whether the partner is acting as a principal or agent, of all partner revenue arrangements and then recognizes revenues either gross or net. Premium partner services, whether recognized gross or net, have one material performance obligation, that being the delivery of the Premium Service.

Additionally, the Group bundles the Premium Service with third-party services and products. In bundle arrangements where the Group has multiple performance obligations, the transaction price is allocated to each performance obligation based on the relative stand-alone selling price. The Group generally determines stand-alone selling prices based on the prices charged to customers. For each performance obligation within the bundle, revenue is recognized either on a straight-line basis over the subscription period or at a point in time when control of the service or product is transferred to the customer.

Ad-Supported revenue

The Group's advertising revenue is primarily generated through display, audio, and video advertising delivered through advertising impressions and podcast downloads. The Group enters into arrangements with advertising agencies that purchase advertising on its platform on behalf of the agencies' clients. These advertising arrangements are typically sold on a cost-per-thousand basis and are evidenced by an Insertion Order ("IO") that specifies the terms of the arrangement such as the type of ad product, pricing, insertion dates, and number of impressions in a stated period. Revenue is recognized over time based on the number of impressions delivered. The Group also may offer cash rebates to advertising agencies based on the volume of advertising inventory purchased. These rebates are estimated based on expected performance and historical data and result in a reduction of revenue recognized.

Additionally, the Group generates Ad-Supported revenue through arrangements with certain advertising exchange platforms to distribute advertising inventory for purchase on a cost-per-thousand basis through their automated exchange. Revenue is recognized over time when impressions are delivered on the platform.

As part of its disclosure of information about its performance obligations, as presented in Extract 32.13 below, Koninklijke Philips N.V. provides information about the nature of its goods and services (e.g. consumer type-products, brand and technology licences), the timing of satisfaction of their performance obligations and the significant payment terms. It also provides information about the existence of sales returns and assurance-type warranties.

> *Extract 32.13: Koninklijke Philips N.V. (2019)*
>
> **10 Group financial statements**
>
> **10.9 Notes** [extract]
>
> **Notes to the Consolidated financial statements of Philips Group** [extract]
>
> **1. Significant accounting policies** [extract]
>
> **Policies that are more critical in nature** [extract]
>
> **Revenue recognition**
>
> Revenue from the sale of goods in the normal course of business is recognized at a point in time when the performance obligation is satisfied and it is based on the amount of the transaction price that is allocated to the performance obligation. The transaction price is the amount of the consideration to which the company expects to be entitled in exchange for transferring the promised goods to the customer. The consideration expected by the company may include fixed and/or variable amounts which can be impacted by sales returns, trade discounts and volume rebates. The company adjusts the consideration for the time value of money for the contracts where no explicit interest rate is mentioned if the period between the transfer of the promised goods or services to the customer and payment by the customer exceeds six months. Revenue for the sale of goods is recognized when control of the asset is transferred to the buyer and only when it is highly probable that a significant reversal of revenue will not occur when uncertainties related to a variable consideration are resolved.
>
> Transfer of control varies depending on the individual terms of the contract of sale. For consumer-type products in the segment Personal Health businesses, control is transferred when the product is shipped and delivered to the customer and title and risk have passed to the customer (depending on the delivery conditions) and acceptance of the product has been obtained. Examples of delivery conditions are 'Free on Board point of delivery' and 'Costs, Insurance Paid point of delivery', where the point of delivery may be the shipping warehouse or any other point of destination as agreed in the contract with the customer and where control is transferred to the customer.
>
> Revenues from transactions relating to distinct goods or services are accounted for separately based on their relative stand-alone selling prices. The stand-alone selling price is defined as the price that would be charged for the goods or service in a separate transaction under similar conditions to similar customers, which within the company is mainly the Country Target Price (CTP). The transaction price determined (taking into account variable considerations) is allocated to performance obligations based on relative stand-alone selling prices. These transactions mainly occur in the segments Diagnosis & Treatment businesses and Connected Care businesses and include arrangements that require subsequent installation and training activities in order to make distinct goods operable for the customer. As such, the related installation and training activities are part of equipment sales rather than separate performance obligations. Revenue is recognized when the performance obligation is satisfied, i.e. when the installation has been completed and the equipment is ready to be used by the customer in the way contractually agreed.

Revenues are recorded net of sales taxes. A variable consideration is recognized to the extent that it is highly probable that a significant reversal in the amount of cumulative revenue recognized will not occur when the uncertainty associated with the variable consideration is subsequently resolved. Such assessment is performed on each reporting date to check whether it is constrained. For products for which a right of return exists during a defined period, revenue recognition is determined based on the historical pattern of actual returns, or in cases where such information is not available revenue recognition is postponed until the return period has lapsed. Return policies are typically based on customary return arrangements in local markets.

A provision is recognized for assurance-type product warranty at the time of revenue recognition and reflects the estimated costs of replacement and free-of-charge services that will be incurred by the company with respect to the products sold. For certain products, the customer has the option to purchase the warranty separately, which is considered a separate performance obligation on top of the assurance-type product warranty. For such warranties which provide distinct service, revenue recognition occurs on a straight-line basis over the extended warranty contract period.

In the case of loss under a sales agreement, the loss is recognized immediately.

Expenses incurred for shipping and handling of internal movements of goods are recorded as cost of sales. Shipping and handling related to sales to third parties are recorded as selling expenses. When shipping and handling are part of a project and billed to the customer, then the related expenses are recorded as cost of sales. Shipping and handling billed to customers are distinct and separate performance obligations and recognized as revenues. Expenses incurred for sales commissions that are considered incremental to the contracts are recognized immediately in the Consolidated statements of income as selling expenses as a practical expedient under IFRS 15 Revenue from Contracts with Customers.

Revenue from services is recognized over a period of time as the company transfers control of the services to the customer which is demonstrated by the customer simultaneously receiving and consuming the benefits provided by the company. The amount of revenues is measured by reference to the progress made towards complete satisfaction of the performance obligation, which in general is evenly over time. Service revenue related to repair and maintenance activities for goods sold is recognized ratably over the service period or as services are rendered.

Royalty income from brand license arrangements is recognized based on a right to access the license, which in practice means over the contract period based on a fixed amount or reliable estimate of sales made by a licensee.

Royalty income from intellectual property rights such as technology licenses or patents is recognized based on a right to use the license, which in practice means at a point in time based on the contractual terms and substance of the relevant agreement with a licensee. However, revenue related to intellectual property contracts with variable consideration where a constraint in the estimation is identified, is recognized over the contract period and is based on actual or reliably estimated sales made by a licensee.

The company receives payments from customers based on a billing schedule or credit period, as established in our contracts. Credit periods are determined based on standard terms, which vary according to local market conditions. Amounts posted in deferred revenue for which the goods or services have not yet been transferred to the customer and amounts that have either been received or are due, are presented as Contract liabilities in the Consolidated balance sheets.

In its 2019 annual financial statements, ASML Holding N.V. provides a table that includes information about its performance obligations as shown in Extract 32.14 below. The first column details the various performance obligations. The second column provides information about the nature and satisfaction of these performance obligations and details of payment terms.

Extract 32.14: ASML Holding N.V. (2019)
Consolidated financial statements [extract]
Notes to the Consolidated Financial Statements [extract]
2. Revenue from contracts with customers [extract]

Accounting Policy – Revenue from contracts with customers [extract]

Goods or services	Nature, timing of satisfying the performance obligations, and significant payment terms
New systems (established technologies)	New systems sales include i-line, KrF, ArF, ArFi and EUV related systems, along with the related factory options ordered with the base system, as well as metrology and inspection systems. Prior to shipment, the majority of our systems undergo a Factory Acceptance Test (FAT) in our cleanroom facilities, effectively replicating the operating conditions that will be present on the customer's site, in order to verify whether the system meets its standard specifications and any additional technical and performance criteria agreed with the customer. A system is shipped only after all contractual specifications are met or discrepancies from agreed upon specifications are waived and customer sign-off is received for delivery. Each system's performance is re-tested through a Site Acceptance Test (SAT) after installation at the customer site. We have never failed to successfully complete installation of a system at a customer's premises; therefore, acceptance at FAT is considered to be proven for established technologies with a history of successful customer acceptances at SAT (equal or better than FAT).
	Transfer of control of a system undergoing FAT, and recognition of revenue related to this system, will occur upon delivery of the system, depending on the Incoterms.
	Transfer of control of a system not undergoing a FAT, and recognition of revenue related to this system, will occur upon customer acceptance of the system at SAT.
Used systems	We have no repurchase commitments in our general sales terms and conditions, however from time to time we repurchase systems that we have manufactured and sold and, following refurbishment, will resell to other customers. This repurchase decision is mainly driven by market demand expressed by other customers and less frequently by explicit or implicit contractual arrangements relating to the initial sale. We consider reasonable offers from any vendor, including customers, to repurchase used systems that we can refurbish, resell, and install as part of our normal business operations.
	Transfer of control of the sale of the repurchased and refurbished systems, and related revenue recognition, will occur either upon delivery of the system to the carrier or upon arrival of the system to the customer's loading dock, depending on the Incoterms and if a FAT was performed prior to shipment. If no FAT was performed, then transfer of control will be upon customer acceptance at SAT. If a FAT was performed, then transfer of control will be upon customer acceptance at FAT, refer to "New systems (established technologies)".

Field upgrades and options (system enhancements)	Field upgrades and options mainly relate to goods and services that are delivered for systems already installed in the customer factories. Certain upgrades require significant installation efforts, enhancing an asset the customer controls, therefore resulting in transfer of control over the period of installation, measured using the cost incurred method which is estimated using labor hours, as this best depicts the satisfaction of our obligation in transferring control. The options and other upgrades that do not require significant installation effort transfer control upon delivery, depending on the Incoterms.
	As long as we are not able to make a reliable estimate of the total efforts needed to complete the upgrade, we only recognize revenue to cover costs incurred. Margin will be realized at the earlier of us being able to make a reliable estimate or completion of the upgrade.
New product introduction	New product introductions are typically newly developed options to be used within our systems. Transfer of control and revenue recognition for new product introductions occurs upon customer acceptance (generally at SAT). Once there is an established history of successful installation and customer acceptance, revenue will be recognized consistent with other systems and goods after transfer of control.
Installation	Installation is provided within the selling price of a system. Installation is considered to be distinct as it does not significantly modify the system being purchased and the customer or a third party could be capable of performing the installation themselves if desired. Transfer of control takes place over the period of installation from delivery through SAT, measured on a straight-line basis, as our performance is satisfied evenly over this period of time.
	As long as we are not able to make a reliable estimate of the total efforts needed to complete the installation, we only recognize revenue to cover costs incurred. Margin will be realized at the earlier of us being able to make a reliable estimate or installation completion.
Warranties	We provide standard warranty coverage on our systems for 12 months and on certain optic parts for 60 months, providing labor and non-consumable parts necessary to repair our systems during these warranty periods. These standard warranties cannot be purchased and do not provide a service in addition to the general assurance the system will perform as promised. As a result, no revenue is allocated to these standard warranties.
	Both the extended and enhanced (optic) warranties on our systems are accounted for as a separate performance obligation, with transfer of control taking place over the warranty period, measured on a straight-line basis, as this is a stand-ready obligation.
Time-based licenses and related service	Time-based licenses relate to software licenses and the related service which are sold for a period of time. The licenses and the related service are not considered to be individually distinct and the transfer of control takes place over the license term, measured on a straight-line basis, as our performance is satisfied evenly over this period of time. Payments are made in instalments throughout the license term.
Application projects	Application projects are node transition and consulting projects which at times may be provided as free service within a volume purchase agreement. Measuring satisfaction of this performance obligation is performed through an input method based on the labor hours expended relative to the estimated total labor hours as this best depicts the transfer of control of these kind of services.
	As long as we are not able to make a reliable estimate of the total efforts needed to complete these kind of projects, we only recognize revenue to cover costs incurred. Margin will be realized at the earlier of us being able to make a reliable estimate or project completion.

Service contracts	Service contracts are entered into with our customers to support our systems used in their ongoing operations during the systems lifecycle, typically in the form of full-service agreements, limited manpower agreements, other labor agreements, parts availability or parts usage agreements. These services are typically for a specified period of time. Control transfers over this period of time, measured on a straight-line basis, as these are stand-ready obligations, with an exception for the labor hour pool service contracts for which we recognize revenue in line with invoicing, using the practical expedient in IFRS 15.B16. Invoicing is typically performed monthly or quarterly throughout the service period, typically payable within 15-45 days.
Billable parts and labor	Billable labor represents maintenance services to our systems installed in the customer's factories while in operation, through purchase orders from our customer. Control over these services is transferred to the customer upon receipt of customer sign-off. Billable parts represent spare parts including optical components relating to our systems installed in the customer's factories while in operation, through purchase orders from our customer. Billable parts can be: • Sold as direct spare parts, for which control transfers upon the relevant Incoterms; or • Sold as part of maintenance services, for which control transfers upon receipt of customer sign-off.
Field projects (relocations)	Field projects represent mainly relocation services. Measuring satisfaction of this performance obligation is performed through an input method based on the labor hours expended relative to the estimated total labor hours as this best depicts the transfer of control of our service.
OnPulse Maintenance	OnPulse maintenance services are provided over a specified period of time on our light source systems. Payment is determined by the amount of pulses counted from each light source system, which is variable. Invoicing is monthly based on the pulses counted. Revenue is recognized in line with invoicing using the practical expedient in IFRS 15.B16.

During the development of the standard, many users of financial statements commented that information about the amount and timing of revenue that an entity expects to recognise from its existing contracts would be useful in their analyses of revenue, especially for long-term contracts with significant unrecognised revenue. *[IFRS 15.BC348]*. In addition, the Board observed that a number of entities often voluntarily disclose such 'backlog' information. However, this information is typically presented outside the financial statements and may not be comparable across entities because there is no common definition of backlog. As summarised in the Basis for Conclusions, the Board's intention in including the disclosure requirements in paragraph 120 of IFRS 15 is to provide users of an entity's financial statements with additional information about the following: *[IFRS 15.BC350]*

- the amount and expected timing of revenue to be recognised from the remaining performance obligations in existing contracts;
- trends relating to the amount and expected timing of revenue to be recognised from the remaining performance obligations in existing contracts;
- risks associated with expected future revenue (e.g. some observe that revenue is more uncertain if an entity does not expect to satisfy a performance obligation until a much later date); and
- the effect of changes in judgements or circumstances on an entity's revenue.

This disclosure can be provided on either a quantitative basis (e.g. amounts to be recognised in given time bands, such as between one and two years and between two and three years) or by disclosing a mix of quantitative and qualitative information. In addition, this disclosure would only include amounts related to performance obligations in the current contract. For example, expected contract renewals that have not been executed and do not represent material rights are not performance obligations in the current contract. As such, an entity does not disclose amounts related to such renewals. However, if an entity concludes that expected contract renewals represents a material right to acquire goods or services in the future (and, therefore, was a separate performance obligation – see Chapter 28 at 3.6), the entity includes in its disclosure the consideration attributable to the material right for the options that have not yet been exercised (i.e. the unsatisfied performance obligation(s)).

The disclosure of the transaction price allocated to the remaining performance obligations does not include consideration that has been excluded from the transaction price. However, the standard requires entities to disclose qualitatively whether any consideration is not included in the transaction price and, therefore, is not included in the disclosure of the remaining performance obligations (e.g. variable consideration amounts that are constrained and, therefore, excluded from the transaction price).

Bombardier Inc. uses time bands to disclose information about remaining performance obligations. In Extract 32.15, it also explicitly discloses that constrained variable consideration is excluded from the amounts disclosed. This is a helpful reminder for users of financial statements and it indicates amounts recognised in future periods may be higher than those included in the table.

Extract 32.15: Bombardier Inc. (2019)

CONSOLIDATED FINANCIAL STATEMENTS [extract]

For fiscal years 2019 and 2018

NOTES TO THE CONSOLIDATED FINANCIAL STATEMENTS [extract]

19. BACKLOG

The following table presents the aggregate amount of the revenues expected to be realized in the future from partially or fully unsatisfied performance obligations as we perform under contracts at delivery or recognized over time. The amounts disclosed below represent the value of firm orders only. Such orders may be subject to future modifications that might impact the amount and/or timing of revenue recognition. The amounts disclosed below do not include constrained variable consideration, unexercised options or letters of intent.

Revenues expected to be recognized in:

(In billions of $)	December 31, 2019	December 31, 2018
Less than 24 months	$28.2	$26.8
Thereafter	23.9	26.3
Total	$52.1	$53.1

In contrast to the previous extract, SAP SE uses a non-tabular approach when disclosing information about remaining performance obligations. Extract 32.16 below illustrates this. SAP SE provides information about its remaining performance obligations to provide 'software support or cloud subscriptions and support'.

Extract 32.16: SAP SE (2019)

CONSOLIDATED FINANCIAL STATEMENTS IFRS [extract]

Notes [extract]

Section A – Customers [extract]

(A.1) Revenue [extract]

Remaining Performance Obligations

Amounts of a customer contract's transaction price that are allocated to the remaining performance obligations represent contracted revenue that has not yet been recognized. They include amounts recognized as contract liabilities and amounts that are contracted but not yet due.

The transaction price allocated to performance obligations that are unsatisfied or partially unsatisfied as at December 31, 2019, is €35.5 billion (December 31, 2018: €31.3 billion). This amount mostly comprises obligations to provide software support or cloud subscriptions services, as the respective contracts typically have durations of one or multiple years.

The majority of this amount is expected to be recognized as revenue over the next 12 months following the respective balance sheet date. This estimate is based on our best judgment, as it needs to consider estimates of possible future contract modifications. The amount of transaction price allocated to the remaining performance obligations, and changes in this amount over time, are impacted by, among others:

- Currency fluctuations
- The contract period of our cloud and software support contracts remaining at the balance sheet date and thus by the timing of contract renewals

---

The Board also provided a practical expedient under which an entity need not disclose the amount of the remaining performance obligations for contracts with an original expected duration of less than one year or those that meet the requirements of the right to invoice practical expedient in paragraph B16 IFRS 15 (see paragraph 121 of IFRS 15). As explained in Chapter 30 at 3.1.1, the right to invoice practical expedient permits an entity that is recognising revenue over time to recognise revenue as invoiced if the entity's right to payment is an amount that corresponds directly with the value to the customer of the entity's performance to date. *[IFRS 15.121]*. For example, an entity is not required to make the disclosure for a three-year service contract under which it has a right to invoice the customer a fixed amount for each hour of service provided. If an entity uses this disclosure practical expedient, it is required to qualitatively disclose that fact. *[IFRS 15.122]*.

Entities need to make sure they have appropriate systems, policies and procedures and internal controls in place to collect and disclose the required information.

ASC 606 contains optional exemptions that are consistent with the optional practical expedients included in paragraph 121 of IFRS 15. However, ASC 606 includes additional optional exemptions (that IFRS 15 does not) to allow entities not to make quantitative disclosures about remaining performance obligations in certain cases and require entities that use any of the new or existing optional exemptions (previously referred to as practical expedients) to expand their qualitative disclosures.

The standard provides the following examples of the required disclosures on remaining performance obligations. *[IFRS 15.IE212-IE219]*.

Example 32.8: Disclosure of the transaction price allocated to the remaining performance obligations

On 30 June 20X1, an entity enters into three contracts (Contracts A, B and C) with separate customers to provide services. Each contract has a two-year non-cancellable term. The entity considers the requirements in paragraphs 120-122 of IFRS 15 in determining the information in each contract to be included in the disclosure of the transaction price allocated to the remaining performance obligations at 31 December 20X1.

Contract A

Cleaning services are to be provided over the next two years typically at least once per month. For services provided, the customer pays an hourly rate of £25.

Because the entity bills a fixed amount for each hour of service provided, the entity has a right to invoice the customer in the amount that corresponds directly with the value of the entity's performance completed to date in accordance with paragraph B16 of IFRS 15. Consequently, no disclosure is necessary if the entity elects to apply the practical expedient in paragraph 121(b) of IFRS 15.

Contract B

Cleaning services and lawn maintenance services are to be provided as and when needed with a maximum of four visits per month over the next two years. The customer pays a fixed price of £400 per month for both services. The entity measures its progress towards complete satisfaction of the performance obligation using a time-based measure.

The entity discloses the amount of the transaction price that has not yet been recognised as revenue in a table with quantitative time bands that illustrates when the entity expects to recognise the amount as revenue. The information for Contract B included in the overall disclosure is as follows:

	20X2	20X3	Total
	£	£	£
Revenue expected to be recognised on this contract as at 31 December 20X1	4,800[a]	2,400[b]	7,200

(a) £4,800 = £400 × 12 months.
(b) £2,400 = £400 × 6 months.

Contract C

Cleaning services are to be provided as and when needed over the next two years. The customer pays fixed consideration of £100 per month plus a one-time variable consideration payment ranging from £0-£1,000 corresponding to a one-time regulatory review and certification of the customer's facility (i.e. a performance bonus). The entity estimates that it will be entitled to £750 of the variable consideration. On the basis of the entity's assessment of the factors in paragraph 57 of IFRS 15, the entity includes its estimate of £750 of variable consideration in the transaction price because it is highly probable that a significant reversal in the amount of cumulative revenue recognised will not occur. The entity measures its progress towards complete satisfaction of the performance obligation using a time-based measure.

The entity discloses the amount of the transaction price that has not yet been recognised as revenue in a table with quantitative time bands that illustrates when the entity expects to recognise the amount as revenue. The entity also includes a qualitative discussion about any significant variable consideration that is not included in the disclosure. The information for Contract C included in the overall disclosure is as follows:

	20X2	20X3	Total
	£	£	£
Revenue expected to be recognised on this contract as at 31 December 20X1	1,575[a]	788[b]	2,363

(a) Transaction price = £3,150 (£100 × 24 months + £750 variable consideration) recognised evenly over 24 months at £1,575 per year.
(b) £1,575 ÷ 2 = £788 (i.e. for 6 months of the year).

In addition, in accordance with paragraph 122 of IFRS 15, the entity discloses qualitatively that part of the performance bonus has been excluded from the disclosure because it was not included in the transaction price. That part of the performance bonus was excluded from the transaction price in accordance with the requirements for constraining estimates of variable consideration.

The standard also provides an example of how an entity could make the disclosure required by paragraph 120(b) of IFRS 15 using qualitative information (instead of quantitatively, using time bands) as follows. *[IFRS 15.IE220-IE221].*

Example 32.9: Disclosure of the transaction price allocated to the remaining performance obligations – qualitative disclosure

On 1 January 20X2, an entity enters into a contract with a customer to construct a commercial building for fixed consideration of €10 million. The construction of the building is a single performance obligation that the entity satisfies over time. As at 31 December 20X2, the entity has recognised €3.2 million of revenue. The entity estimates that construction will be completed in 20X3, but it is possible that the project will be completed in the first half of 20X4.

At 31 December 20X2, the entity discloses the amount of the transaction price that has not yet been recognised as revenue in its disclosure of the transaction price allocated to the remaining performance obligations. The entity also discloses an explanation of when the entity expects to recognise that amount as revenue. The explanation can be disclosed either on a quantitative basis using time bands that are most appropriate for the duration of the remaining performance obligation or by providing a qualitative explanation. Because the entity is uncertain about the timing of revenue recognition, the entity discloses this information qualitatively as follows:

> 'As at 31 December 20X2, the aggregate amount of the transaction price allocated to the remaining performance obligation is €6.8 million and the entity will recognise this revenue as the building is completed, which is expected to occur over the next 12-18 months.'

3.2.1.D Use of the 'backlog' practical expedient when the criteria to use the 'right to invoice' practical expedient are not met

At its July 2015 meeting, the TRG considered whether an entity can still use the disclosure practical expedient (regarding the amount of the transaction price allocated to remaining performance obligations) if it does not meet the criteria to use the 'right to invoice' practical expedient.

The TRG members generally agreed that the standard is clear that an entity can only use the practical expedient to avoid disclosing the amount of the transaction price allocated to remaining performance obligations for contracts: (a) with an original expected duration of less than one year; or (b) that qualify for the 'right to invoice' practical expedient. *[IFRS 15.121].* If a contract does not meet either of these criteria, an entity must disclose the information about remaining performance obligations that is required by Paragraph 120 of IFRS 15. *[IFRS 15.120].* However, under these requirements, an entity is able to qualitatively describe any consideration that is not included in the transaction price (e.g. any estimated amount of variable consideration that is constrained).

Stakeholders had questioned whether an entity can still use this disclosure practical expedient if it determines that it has not met the criteria to use the right to invoice practical expedient (e.g. because there is a substantive contractual minimum payment or a volume discount).[7]

3.2.2 Significant judgements

The standard specifically requires disclosure of significant accounting estimates and judgements (and changes in those judgements) made in determining the transaction price, allocating the transaction price to performance obligations and determining when performance obligations are satisfied. *[IFRS 15.123]*.

IFRS has general requirements requiring disclosures about significant accounting estimates and judgements made by an entity. Because of the importance placed on revenue by users of financial statements, as noted in the Basis for Conclusions on IFRS 15, the Board decided to require specific disclosures about the estimates used and the judgements made in determining the amount and timing of revenue recognition. *[IFRS 15.BC355]*. These requirements exceed those in the general requirements for significant judgements and accounting estimates required by IAS 1 and discussed in more detail below. *[IAS 1.122-133]*.

3.2.2.A Determining the timing of satisfaction of performance obligations

IFRS 15 requires entities to provide disclosures about the significant judgements made in determining the timing of satisfaction of performance obligations. The disclosure requirements for performance obligations that are satisfied over time differ from those satisfied at a point in time, but the objective is similar – to disclose the judgements made in determining the timing of revenue recognition. Entities must disclose: *[IFRS 15.124]*

- the methods used to recognise revenue (e.g. a description of the output methods or input methods used and how those methods are applied); and
- an explanation of why the methods used provide a faithful depiction of the transfer of goods or services.

For performance obligations that are satisfied at a point in time, entities must disclose the significant judgements made in evaluating the point in time when the customer obtains control of the goods or services. *[IFRS 15.125]*.

When an entity has determined that a performance obligation is satisfied over time, IFRS 15 requires the entity to select a single revenue recognition method for each performance obligation that best depicts the entity's performance in transferring the goods or services. Entities must disclose the method used to recognise revenue.

For example, assume an entity enters into a contract to refurbish a multi-level building for a customer and the work is expected to take two years. The entity concludes that the promised refurbishment service is a single performance obligation satisfied over time and it decides to measure progress using a percentage of completion method, based on the costs incurred. The entity discloses the method used, how it has been applied to the contract and why the method selected provides a faithful depiction of the transfer of goods or services.

When an entity has determined that a performance obligation is satisfied at a point in time, the standard requires the entity to disclose the significant judgements made in evaluating when the customer obtains control of the promised goods or services. For example, an entity needs to consider the indicators of the transfer of control listed in paragraph 38 of IFRS 15 to determine when control transfers and disclose the significant judgements made in reaching that conclusion.

In Extract 32.14 at 3.2.1.C above, ASML Holding N.V. describes the methods used to recognise its revenue over time and explains the relationship between the methods and the different types of services it provides. Koninklijke Philips N.V. recognises revenue at a point in time in relation its consumer type-products sales. Extract 32.13 at 3.2.1.C above provides a description of when control transfers to the customer for these sales.

In Extract 32.17 below, SAP SE provides disclosure of the significant judgement involved in determining the satisfaction of its performance obligations. It explains how it determines whether its software offerings provide customers with a right to use or a right to access its intellectual property. It also describes the judgement involved in identifying the appropriate method to measure the progress of its performance obligations satisfied overtime.

Extract 32.17: SAP SE (2019)

CONSOLIDATED FINANCIAL STATEMENTS IFRS [extract]

Notes [extract]

Section A – Customers [extract]

(A.1) Revenue [extract]

Accounting for Revenue from Contracts with Customers [extract]

Recognition of Revenue

Cloud revenue is recognized over time as the services are performed. Where our performance obligation is the grant of a right to continuously access and use a cloud offering for a certain term, revenue is recognized based on time elapsed and thus ratably over this term.

Software revenue is recognized at a point in time or over time depending on whether we deliver standard software, customer-specific software, or software subscription contracts that combine the delivery of software and the obligation to deliver, in the future, unspecified software products:

- Licenses for our standard on-premise software products are typically delivered by providing the customer with access to download the software. The license period starts when such access is granted. We recognize revenue for these on-premise licenses at the point in time when the customer has access to and thus control over the software. In judging whether our on-premise software offerings grant customers a right to use, rather than a right to access, our intellectual property, we have considered the usefulness of our software without subsequent updates to it.
- Typically, our customer-specific on-premise software development agreements:
    - Are for software developed for specific needs of individual customers and therefore it does not have any alternative use for us
    - Provide us with an enforceable right to payment for performance completed to date

  For such development agreements, we recognize revenue over time as the software development progresses. Judgment is required in identifying an appropriate method to measure the progress toward complete satisfaction of such performance obligations. We typically measure progress of our development agreements based on the direct costs incurred to date in developing the software as a percentage of the total reasonably estimated direct costs to fully complete the development work (percentage-of-completion method). This method of measuring progress faithfully depicts the transfer of the development services to the customer, as substantially all of these costs are cost of the staff or third parties performing the development work. In estimating the total cost to fully complete the development work, we consider our history with similar projects.
- For agreements that combine the delivery of software and the obligation to deliver, in the future, unspecific software products, we recognize revenue at a point in time for licenses that are made immediately accessible to the customer. We recognize revenue ratably over the term of the software subscription contract for the unspecified software products, as our performance obligation is to stand ready to deliver such products on a when-and-if-available basis.

Software support revenue is typically recognized based on time elapsed and thus ratably over the term of the support arrangement. Under our standardized support services, our performance obligation is to stand ready to provide technical product support and unspecified updates, upgrades, and enhancements on a when-and-if-available basis. Our customers simultaneously receive and consume the benefits of these support services as we perform.

Service revenue is typically recognized over time. Where we stand ready to provide the service (such as access to learning content), we recognize revenue based on time elapsed and thus ratably over the service period. Consumption-based services (such as separately identifiable consulting services and premium support services, messaging services, and classroom training services) are recognized over time as the services are utilized, typically following the percentage-of-completion method or ratably. When using the percentage-of-completion method, we typically measure the progress toward complete satisfaction of the performance obligation in the same way and with the same reasoning and judgment as we do for customer-specific on-premise software development agreements. We apply judgment in determining whether a service qualifies as a stand-ready service or as a consumption-based service.

Revenue for combined performance obligations is recognized over the longest period of all promises in the combined performance obligation.

Judgment is also required to determine whether revenue is to be recognized at a point in time or over time. For performance obligations satisfied over time, we need to measure progress using the method that best reflects SAP's performance. When using cost incurred as a measure of progress for recognizing revenue over time, we apply judgment in estimating the total cost to satisfy the performance obligation.

All of the judgments and estimates mentioned above can significantly impact the timing and amount of revenue to be recognized.

3.2.2.B Determining the transaction price and the amounts allocated to performance obligations

Entities often exercise significant judgement when estimating the transaction prices of their contracts, especially when those estimates involve variable consideration.

Furthermore, significant judgement may be required when allocating the transaction price, including estimating stand-alone selling prices; for example, it is likely that entities will need to exercise judgement when determining whether a customer option gives rise to a material right (see Chapter 28 at 3.6) and in estimating the stand-alone selling price for those material rights.

Given the importance placed on revenue by financial statement users, the standard requires entities to disclose qualitative information about the methods, inputs and assumptions used in their annual financial statements for all of the following:
[IFRS 15.126, BC355]

- determining the transaction price – includes, but is not limited to, estimating variable consideration, adjusting the consideration for the effects of the time value of money and measuring non-cash consideration;
- assessing whether an estimate of variable consideration is constrained;
- allocating the transaction price – includes estimating stand-alone selling prices of promised goods or services and allocating discounts and variable consideration to a specific part of the contract (if applicable); and
- measuring obligations for returns, refunds and other similar obligations.

Entities with diverse contracts need to ensure they have the processes and procedures in place to capture all of the different methods, inputs and assumptions used in determining the transaction price and allocating it to performance obligations.

In Extract 32.13 at 3.2.1.C above, Koninklijke Philips N.V. explains the need to estimate variable consideration in relation to returns.

Since fee arrangements often include contingencies (e.g. No Win-No Fee arrangements), Slater and Gordon Limited estimated variable consideration when determining the transaction price as presented in Extract 32.18. Therefore, it discloses information about the method (i.e. most likely amount approach), inputs and assumptions (i.e. management's assessment and the probability of success of each case). Furthermore, Slater and Gordon Limited discloses information about the assessment of whether a significant financing component exists. The entity concludes that contracts generally comprise only one performance obligation. As such, Slater and Gordon Limited does not disclose information about the allocation of the transaction price.

> **Extract 32.18: Slater and Gordon Limited (2018)**
> **Financial Statements** [extract]
> **Notes to the Financial Statements**[extract]
> For the Year Ended 30 June 2018
> **Note 3: Financial Performance** [extract]
> **3.1 Revenue from Contracts with Customers** [extract]
> **3.1.1 Accounting Policies** [extract]
>
> **Provision of Legal Services – Litigation and Emerging Services**
>
> The Group also earns revenue from provision of general legal services, incorporating project litigation. Revenue for general legal services is recognised over time in the accounting period when services are rendered.
>
> Fee arrangements from general legal services include fixed fee arrangements, unconditional fee for service arrangements ("time and materials"), and variable or contingent fee arrangements (including No Win – No Fee arrangements for services including project litigation, and some consumer and commercial litigation).
>
> For fixed fee arrangements, revenue is recognised based on the stage of completion with reference to the actual services provided as a proportion of the total services expected to be provided under the contract. The stage of completion is tracked on a contract by contract basis using a milestone based approach, which was explained above.
>
> In fee for service contracts, revenue is recognised up to the amount of fees that the Group is entitled to invoice for services performed to date based on contracted rates.
>
> The Group estimates fees for variable or conditional service fee arrangements using a most likely amount approach on a contract by contract basis. Management makes a detailed assessment of the amount of revenue expected to be received and the probability of success of each case. Variable consideration is included in revenue only to the extent that it is highly probable that the amount will not be subject to significant reversal when the uncertainty is resolved (generally when a matter is concluded).

> Certain project litigation matters are undertaken on a partially funded basis. The Group has arrangements with third party funders to provide a portion of the fees receivable on a matter over time as services are performed. In such arrangements, the funded portion of fees is billed regularly over time and is not contingent on the successful outcome of the litigation. The remaining portion of fees is variable consideration which is conditional on the successful resolution of the litigation. The variable consideration is included in revenue as services are performed only to the extent that it is highly probable that the amount will not be subject to significant reversal when the uncertainty is resolved.
>
> As in the case of personal injury claims, estimates of revenues, costs or extent of progress toward completion are revised if circumstances change. Any resulting increases or decreases in estimated revenues or costs are reflected in profit or loss in the period in which the circumstances that give rise to the revision become known by management.
>
> The Group has determined that no significant financing component exists in respect of the general law services revenue streams. This has been determined on fee for service and fixed fee arrangements as the period between when the entity transfers a promised good or service to a customer and when the customer pays for that good or service will be one year or less. For No Win – No Fee arrangements this has been determined because a significant amount of the consideration promised by the customer is variable subject to the occurrence or non-occurrence of a future event that is not substantially within the control of the customer or the Group.
>
> A receivable in relation to these services is recognised when a bill has been invoiced, as this is the point in time that the consideration is unconditional because only the passage of time is required before the payment is due.

3.2.3 Assets recognised from the costs to obtain or fulfil a contract

As discussed in Chapter 31 at 5, the standard specifies the accounting for costs an entity incurs to obtain and fulfil a contract to provide goods or services to customers. IFRS 15 requires entities to disclose information about the assets recognised to help users understand the types of costs recognised as assets and how those assets are subsequently amortised or impaired. These disclosure requirements are: *[IFRS 15.127-128]*

- A description of:
  (a) the judgements made in determining the amount of the costs incurred to obtain or fulfil a contract with a customer; and
  (b) the method it uses to determine the amortisation for each reporting period;
- the closing balances of assets recognised from the costs incurred to obtain or fulfil a contract with a customer, by main category of asset (for example, costs to obtain contracts with customers, pre-contract costs and setup costs); and
- the amount of amortisation and any impairment losses recognised in the reporting period.

Entities are required to disclose the judgements made in determining the amount of costs that were incurred to obtain or fulfil contracts with customers that meet the criteria for capitalisation, as well as the method the entity uses to amortise the assets recognised. For example, for costs to obtain a contract, an entity that capitalises commission costs upon the signing of each contract needs to describe the judgements used to determine the commission costs that qualified as costs incurred to obtain a contract with a customer, as well as the determination of the amortisation period. See the discussion in Chapter 31 at 5.3.6 on the classification and presentation requirements for contract cost assets and the related amortisation and impairment.

In Extract 32.19, Capita plc discloses its accounting policy on assets recognised from costs to fulfil and costs to obtain a contract in Note 3 on 'Operating assets and liabilities' in its 2019 annual financial statements. This is followed by a description of how it determines the amortisation period and assesses the assets for impairment. In the same Note, Capita plc provides quantitative disclosures of 'contract fulfilment assets', separately disclosing the closing balance, the amount that was utilised (i.e. amortisation expense) and the amount of impairment losses for each reporting period.

Extract 32.19: Capita plc (2019)

FINANCIAL STATEMENTS [extract]
Notes to the consolidated financial statements [extract]
Section 3: Operating assets and liabilities [extract]
3.1 Working Capital [extract]
3.1.3 Contract fulfilment assets [extract]

Accounting policies

The Group regularly incurs costs to deliver its outsourcing services in a more efficient way (often referred to as 'transformation' costs). These costs may include process mapping and design, system development, project management, hardware (generally in scope of the Group's accounting policy for property, plant and equipment), software licence costs (generally in scope of the Group's accounting policy for intangible assets), recruitment costs and training.

Contract fulfilment costs are divided into: (i) costs that give rise to an asset; and (ii) costs that are expensed as incurred.

When determining the appropriate accounting treatment for such costs, the Group firstly considers any other applicable standards. If those other standards preclude capitalisation of a particular cost, then an asset is not recognised under IFRS 15.

If other standards are not applicable to contract fulfilment costs, the Group applies the following criteria which, if met, result in capitalisation: (i) the costs directly relate to a contract or to a specifically identifiable anticipated contract; (ii) the costs generate or enhance resources of the entity that will be used in satisfying (or in continuing to satisfy) performance obligations in the future; and (iii) the costs are expected to be recovered.

The Group has determined that, where the relevant specific criteria are met, the costs for (i) process mapping and design; (ii) system development; and (iii) project management are likely to qualify to be capitalised as contract fulfilment assets.

The incremental costs of obtaining a contract with a customer are recognised as a contract fulfilment asset if the Group expects to recover them. The Group incurs costs such as bid costs, legal fees to draft a contract and sales commissions when it enters into a new contract.

The Group has determined that the following costs may be capitalised as contract fulfilment assets: (i) legal fees to draft a contract (once the Group has been selected as a preferred supplier for a bid); and (ii) sales commissions that are directly related to winning a specific contract.

Costs incurred prior to selection as preferred supplier are not capitalised but are expensed as incurred.

Utilisation: The utilisation charge is included within cost of sales. The Group utilises contract fulfilment assets over the expected contract period using a systematic basis that mirrors the pattern in which the Group transfers control of the service to the customer. Judgement is applied to determine this period.

Derecognition: A contract fulfilment asset is derecognised either when it is disposed of or when no further economic benefits are expected to flow from its use or disposal.

Impairment: At each reporting date, the Group determines whether or not the contract fulfilment assets are impaired by comparing the carrying amount of the asset to the remaining amount of consideration that the Group expects to receive less the costs that relate to providing services under the relevant contract. In determining the estimated amount of consideration, the Group uses the same principles as it does to determine the contract transaction price, except that any constraints used to reduce the transaction price will be removed for the impairment test.

Significant accounting judgements, estimates and assumptions

Judgement is applied by the Group when determining what costs qualify to be capitalised in particular when considering whether these costs are incremental and when considering if costs generate or enhance resources to be used to satisfy future performance obligations and whether costs are expected to be recoverable. For example, the Group considers which type of sales commissions are incremental to the cost of obtaining specific contracts and the point in time when the costs will be capitalised. See note 2.1 for further information.

Movements in non-current contract fulfilment assets were as follows¹:

	2019 £m	2018 £m
At 1 January	264.2	252.5
Additions	114.3	113.8
Prior year reclassification from current contract fulfilment assets	–	25.4
Impairment	(9.6)	(22.2)
Derecognition	(2.0)	(17.4)
Utilised during the year	(90.7)	(87.9)
Exchange movement	(0.4)	–
At 31 December	275.8	264.2

1. Refer to note 3.1.1 for current contract fulfilment assets.

Impairment: In 2019, the Group recognised an impairment of £9.6m (2018: £22.2m) within adjusted cost of sales, of which, £2.2m (2018: 22.2 relates to contract fulfilment assets added during the year.

Derecognition: In 2019, £2.0m (2018: £17.4m) was derecognised in relation to in year business exits. In the prior year, derecognition related to the Prudential and Marsh contracts which were terminated during 2018 and the Group had no further use for the assets.

3.2.4 Practical expedients

The standard allows entities to use several practical expedients. Paragraph 129 of IFRS 15 requires entities to disclose their use of two practical expedients: (a) the practical expedient in paragraph 63 of IFRS 15 associated with the determination of whether a significant financing component exists (see Chapter 29 at 2.5); and (b) the expedient in paragraph 94 of IFRS 15 for recognising an immediate expense for certain incremental costs of obtaining a contract with a customer (see Chapter 31 at 5.1). *[IFRS 15.129].*

In addition, entities are required to disclose the use of the disclosure practical expedient in paragraph 121 of IFRS 15 (which permits an entity not to disclose information about remaining performance obligations if one of the conditions in the paragraph are met, see 3.2.1.C above). IFRS 15 provides other practical expedients. Entities need to carefully consider the disclosure requirements of any other practical expedients it uses.

In Extract 32.10 at 3.2.1.B above, ProSiebenSat.1 Media SE discloses that it elected to use the practical expedient in paragraph 121(a) of IFRS 15 in relation to the remaining performance obligation disclosure requirement. Koninklijke Philips N.V. discloses its application of paragraph 94 of IFRS 15 relating to incremental costs of obtaining a contract in Extract 32.13 at 3.2.1.C above. In Extract 32.14 at 3.2.1.C above, ASML Holding N.V. discloses that it uses the 'right to invoice' practical expedient in paragraph B16 of IFRS 15 for its performance obligations relating to 'Service contracts' and 'OnPulse maintenance'.

4 DISCLOSURES IN INTERIM FINANCIAL STATEMENTS

IAS 34 requires disclosure of disaggregated revenue information, consistent with the requirement included in IFRS 15 for annual financial statements. *[IAS 34.16A(l)].* See 3.2.1.A above for further discussion on this disclosure requirement.

Although none of the other annual IFRS 15 disclosure requirements apply to condensed interim financial statements, entities need to comply with the general requirements in IAS 34. For example, an entity is required to include sufficient information to explain events and transactions that are significant to an understanding of the changes in the entity's financial position and performance since the end of the last annual reporting period. *[IAS 34.15]*. Information disclosed in relation to those events and transactions must update the relevant information presented in the most recent annual financial report. IAS 34 includes a non-exhaustive list of events and transactions for which disclosure would be required if they are significant, and which includes recognition of impairment losses on assets arising from contracts with customers, or reversals of such impairment losses. *[IAS 34.15B]*.

The required interim disclosures differ under IFRS and US GAAP. While the IASB requires only disaggregated revenue information to be disclosed for interim financial statements, the FASB requires the quantitative disclosures about revenue required for annual financial statements to also be disclosed in interim financial statements.

References

1 IASB meeting, December 2015, Agenda paper no. 7H, *Constraining estimates of variable consideration when the consideration varies based on a future market price*, and IASB Update, dated December 2015.
2 TRG Agenda paper 7, *Presentation of a contract as a contract asset or a contract liability*, dated 31 October 2014 and TRG Agenda paper 11, *October 2014 Meeting – Summary of Issues Discussed and Next Steps*, dated 26 January 2015.
3 TRG Agenda paper 7, *Presentation of a contract as a contract asset or a contract liability*, dated 31 October 2014 and TRG Agenda paper 11, *October 2014 Meeting – Summary of Issues Discussed and Next Steps*, dated 26 January 2015.
4 TRG Agenda paper 7, *Presentation of a contract as a contract asset or a contract liability*, dated 31 October 2014 and TRG Agenda paper 11, *October 2014 Meeting – Summary of Issues Discussed and Next Steps*, dated 26 January 2015.
5 FASB TRG Agenda paper 51, *Contract Asset Treatment in Contract Modifications*, dated 18 April 2016.
6 *IFRIC Update*, June 2020.
7 TRG Agenda paper 40, *Practical Expedient for Measuring Progress toward Complete Satisfaction of a Performance Obligation*, dated 13 July 2015.

Chapter 33 — Income taxes

1 INTRODUCTION 2451
   1.1   The nature of taxation 2451
   1.2   Allocation between periods 2451
        1.2.1   No provision for deferred tax ('flow through') 2452
        1.2.2   Provision for deferred tax (the temporary difference approach) 2453
   1.3   The development of IAS 12 2454
        1.3.1   References to taxes in standards other than IAS 12 2455
2 OBJECTIVE AND SCOPE OF IAS 12 2455
   2.1   Objective 2455
   2.2   Overview 2457
3 DEFINITIONS...2457
4 SCOPE 2458
   4.1   What is an 'income tax'? 2459
        4.1.1   Levies 2460
        4.1.2   Hybrid taxes (including minimum taxes) 2461
   4.2   Withholding and similar taxes 2461
   4.3   Investment tax credits 2462
   4.4   Interest and penalties 2464
   4.5   Hybrid taxes (including minimum taxes) 2467
        4.5.1   Hybrid taxes – minimum based on a measure other than taxable profits 2467
        4.5.2   Tax is the higher of measures based on taxable profits and revenues 2469
        4.5.3   Tax is based on revenues, unless a profit measure gives a lower result 2470
   4.6   Effectively tax-free entities 2471

Chapter 33

- 5 CURRENT TAX 2471
  - 5.1 Enacted or substantively enacted tax legislation 2471
    - 5.1.1 Meaning of substantive enactment in various jurisdictions 2472
    - 5.1.2 Changes to tax rates and laws enacted before the reporting date 2473
    - 5.1.3 Changes to tax rates and laws enacted after the reporting date 2474
    - 5.1.4 Implications of the UK's withdrawal from the EU 2474
  - 5.2 Uncertain tax treatments 2476
  - 5.3 'Prior year adjustments' of previously presented tax balances and expense (income) 2476
  - 5.4 Discounting of current tax assets and liabilities 2477
  - 5.5 Intra-period allocation, presentation and disclosure 2477
- 6 DEFERRED TAX – TAX BASES AND TEMPORARY DIFFERENCES 2477
  - 6.1 Tax base 2479
    - 6.1.1 Tax base of assets 2479
    - 6.1.2 Tax base of liabilities 2480
    - 6.1.3 Assets and liabilities whose tax base is not immediately apparent 2480
    - 6.1.4 Tax base of items not recognised as assets or liabilities in financial statements 2481
    - 6.1.5 Equity items with a tax base 2482
    - 6.1.6 Items with more than one tax base 2482
    - 6.1.7 Tax bases disclaimed or with no economic value 2482
  - 6.2 Examples of temporary differences 2482
    - 6.2.1 Taxable temporary differences 2483
      - 6.2.1.A Transactions that affect profit or loss 2483
      - 6.2.1.B Transactions that affect the statement of financial position 2484
      - 6.2.1.C Revaluations 2485
      - 6.2.1.D Tax re-basing 2485
      - 6.2.1.E Business combinations and consolidation 2486
      - 6.2.1.F Foreign currency differences 2486
      - 6.2.1.G Hyperinflation 2487
    - 6.2.2 Deductible temporary differences 2487
      - 6.2.2.A Transactions that affect profit of loss 2487
      - 6.2.2.B Transactions that affect the statement of financial position 2488
      - 6.2.2.C Revaluations 2489
      - 6.2.2.D Tax re-basing 2489
      - 6.2.2.E Business combinations and consolidation 2489

		6.2.2.F	Foreign currency differences	2489

- 6.2.3 Assets and liabilities with no temporary difference (because tax base equals carrying amount) 2490

7 DEFERRED TAX – RECOGNITION 2491

- 7.1 The basic principles 2491
  - 7.1.1 Taxable temporary differences (deferred tax liabilities) 2491
  - 7.1.2 Deductible temporary differences (deferred tax assets) 2491
  - 7.1.3 Interpretation issues 2492
    - 7.1.3.A Accounting profit 2492
    - 7.1.3.B Taxable profit 'at the time of the transaction' 2492
- 7.2 The initial recognition exception 2492
  - 7.2.1 Acquisition of tax losses 2494
  - 7.2.2 Initial recognition of goodwill 2494
    - 7.2.2.A Taxable temporary differences 2494
    - 7.2.2.B Deductible temporary differences 2495
    - 7.2.2.C Tax deductible goodwill 2496
  - 7.2.3 Initial recognition of other assets or liabilities 2496
  - 7.2.4 Changes to temporary differences after initial recognition 2498
    - 7.2.4.A Depreciation, amortisation or impairment of initial carrying value 2499
    - 7.2.4.B Change in carrying value due to revaluation 2499
    - 7.2.4.C Change in tax base due to deductions in tax return 2501
    - 7.2.4.D Temporary difference altered by legislative change 2502
  - 7.2.5 Intragroup transfers of assets with no change in tax base 2503
  - 7.2.6 Partially deductible and super-deductible assets 2504
  - 7.2.7 Transactions involving the initial recognition of an asset and liability 2507
    - 7.2.7.A Decommissioning costs 2509
    - 7.2.7.B Leases under IFRS 16 taxed as operating leases 2512
  - 7.2.8 Initial recognition of compound financial instruments by the issuer 2514
  - 7.2.9 Acquisition of subsidiary that does not constitute a business 2515
  - 7.2.10 Acquisition of an investment in a subsidiary, associate, branch or joint arrangement 2516
- 7.3 Assets carried at fair value or revalued amount 2516
- 7.4 Restrictions on recognition of deferred tax assets 2517
  - 7.4.1 Restrictions imposed by relevant tax laws 2517

7.4.2		Sources of 'probable' taxable profit – taxable temporary differences	2518
7.4.3		Sources of 'probable' taxable profit – estimates of future taxable profits	2518
	7.4.3.A	Ignore the origination of new future deductible temporary differences	2519
	7.4.3.B	Ignore the reversal of existing deductible temporary differences	2519
7.4.4		Tax planning opportunities and the recognition of deferred tax assets	2519
7.4.5		Unrealised losses on debt securities measured at fair value	2520
	7.4.5.A	The existence of a deductible temporary difference	2521
	7.4.5.B	Recovering an asset for more than its carrying amount	2522
	7.4.5.C	Excluding the reversal of existing deductible temporary differences	2523
	7.4.5.D	The basis for assessing the recoverability of deductible temporary differences	2523
7.4.6		Unused tax losses and unused tax credits	2526
	7.4.6.A	Where taxable temporary differences were recognised outside profit or loss	2527
7.4.7		Re-assessment of deferred tax assets	2528
	7.4.7.A	Previously recognised assets	2528
	7.4.7.B	Previously unrecognised assets	2528
7.4.8		Effect of disposals on recoverability of tax losses	2528
	7.4.8.A	Tax losses of subsidiary disposed of recoverable against profits of that subsidiary	2529
	7.4.8.B	Tax losses of retained entity recoverable against profits of subsidiary disposed of	2529
	7.4.8.C	Tax losses of subsidiary disposed of recoverable against profits of retained entity	2530
7.5		'Outside' temporary differences relating to subsidiaries, branches, associates and joint arrangements	2530
	7.5.1	Calculation of 'outside' temporary differences	2531
		7.5.1.A Consolidated financial statements	2533
		7.5.1.B Separate financial statements of investor	2533
	7.5.2	Taxable temporary differences	2534
	7.5.3	Deductible temporary differences	2535
	7.5.4	Foreseeable future – anticipated intragroup dividends	2535
		7.5.4.A Consolidated financial statements of receiving entity	2535
		7.5.4.B Separate financial statements of paying entity	2536

		7.5.5	Unpaid intragroup interest, royalties, management charges etc. 2536

- 7.6 'Tax-transparent' ('flow-through') entities 2537
- 7.7 Deferred taxable gains 2539

8 DEFERRED TAX – MEASUREMENT 2539

- 8.1 Legislation at the end of the reporting period 2539
  - 8.1.1 Changes to tax rates and laws enacted before the reporting date 2540
    - 8.1.1.A Managing uncertainty in determining the effect of new tax legislation 2540
    - 8.1.1.B Backward tracing of changes in deferred taxation 2541
    - 8.1.1.C Disclosures relating to changes in enacted tax rates and laws 2541
  - 8.1.2 Changes to tax rates and laws enacted after the reporting date 2541
- 8.2 Uncertain tax treatments 2542
- 8.3 'Prior year adjustments' of previously presented tax balances and expense (income) 2542
- 8.4 Expected manner of recovery of assets or settlement of liabilities 2542
  - 8.4.1 Tax planning strategies to reduce liabilities are not anticipated 2542
  - 8.4.2 Carrying amount 2543
  - 8.4.3 Assets and liabilities with more than one tax base 2544
  - 8.4.4 Determining the expected manner of recovery of assets 2544
  - 8.4.5 Depreciable PP&E and intangible assets 2545
  - 8.4.6 Non-depreciable PP&E and intangible assets 2547
    - 8.4.6.A PP&E accounted for using the revaluation model 2547
    - 8.4.6.B Non-amortised or indefinite-life intangible assets 2548
  - 8.4.7 Investment properties 2549
  - 8.4.8 Other assets and liabilities 2550
  - 8.4.9 'Outside' temporary differences relating to subsidiaries, branches, associates and joint arrangements 2551
  - 8.4.10 'Single asset' entities 2553
  - 8.4.11 Change in expected manner of recovery of an asset or settlement of a liability 2554
- 8.5 Different tax rates applicable to retained and distributed profits 2554
  - 8.5.1 Effectively tax-free entities 2555
  - 8.5.2 Withholding tax or distribution tax? 2556

8.6	Discounting		2556
8.7	Unrealised intragroup profits and losses in consolidated financial statements		2556
	8.7.1	Intragroup transfers of goodwill and intangible assets	2558
		8.7.1.A Individual financial statements of buyer	2558
		8.7.1.B Individual financial statements of seller	2558
		8.7.1.C Consolidated financial statements	2558
		8.7.1.D When the tax base of goodwill is retained by the transferor entity	2559

9 UNCERTAIN TAX TREATMENTS 2560

9.1	Scope of IFRIC 23 and definitions used		2561
	9.1.1	Business combinations	2562
9.2	Whether to consider uncertain tax treatments separately (unit of account)		2563
9.3	Assumptions about the examination of tax treatments ('detection risk')		2563
9.4	Determining the effect of an uncertain tax treatment or group of tax treatments		2564
9.5	Consideration of changes in facts and circumstances		2566
	9.5.1	The expiry of a taxation authority's right to examine or re-examine a tax treatment	2567
9.6	Disclosures relating to uncertain tax treatments		2567
9.7	Presentation of liabilities or assets for uncertain tax treatments		2568
9.8	Recognition of an asset for payments on account		2569

10 ALLOCATION OF TAX CHARGE OR CREDIT 2570

10.1	Revalued and rebased assets		2571
	10.1.1	Non-monetary assets or liabilities with a tax base determined in a different currency	2572
10.2	Retrospective restatements or applications		2572
10.3	Dividends and transaction costs of equity instruments		2574
	10.3.1	Dividend subject to differential tax rate	2574
	10.3.2	Dividend subject to withholding tax	2574
	10.3.3	Intragroup dividend subject to withholding tax	2575
	10.3.4	Incoming dividends	2575
	10.3.5	Tax benefits of distributions and transaction costs of equity instruments	2576
		10.3.5.A Tax benefits of transaction costs of equity instruments	2577
10.4	Gains and losses reclassified ('recycled') to profit or loss		2578

		10.4.1	Debt instrument measured at fair value through OCI under IFRS 9 2579
		10.4.2	Recognition of expected credit losses with no change in fair value 2581
	10.5	\multicolumn{2}{l	}{Gain/loss in profit or loss and loss/gain outside profit or loss offset for tax purposes .... 2582}
	10.6	\multicolumn{2}{l	}{Discontinued operations .... 2584}
	10.7	\multicolumn{2}{l	}{Defined benefit pension plans .... 2585}
		10.7.1	Tax on refund of pension surplus 2587
	10.8	\multicolumn{2}{l	}{Share-based payment transactions .... 2587}
		10.8.1	Allocation of tax deduction between profit or loss and equity 2587
		10.8.2	Determining the tax base 2590
		10.8.3	Allocation when more than one award is outstanding 2593
		10.8.4	Staggered exercise of awards 2594
		10.8.5	Replacement awards in a business combination 2597
		10.8.6	Share-based payment transactions subject to transitional provisions of IFRS 1 and IFRS 2 2598
	10.9	\multicolumn{2}{l	}{Change in tax status of entity or shareholders .... 2599}
	10.10	\multicolumn{2}{l	}{Previous revaluation of PP&E treated as deemed cost on transition to IFRS .... 2599}
	10.11	\multicolumn{2}{l	}{Disposal of an interest in a subsidiary that does not result in a loss of control .... 2600}
11	\multicolumn{3}{l	}{CONSOLIDATED TAX RETURNS AND OFFSET OF TAXABLE PROFITS AND LOSSES WITHIN GROUPS .... 2601}
	11.1	\multicolumn{2}{l	}{Examples of accounting by entities in a tax-consolidated group .... 2602}
	11.2	\multicolumn{2}{l	}{Payments for intragroup transfer of tax losses .... 2603}
	11.3	\multicolumn{2}{l	}{Recognition of deferred tax assets where tax losses are transferred in a group .... 2604}
12	\multicolumn{3}{l	}{BUSINESS COMBINATIONS .... 2604}
	12.1	\multicolumn{2}{l	}{Measurement and recognition of deferred tax in a business combination .... 2605}
		12.1.1	Determining the manner of recovery of assets and settlement of liabilities 2605
			12.1.1.A Changes in tax base consequent on the business combination 2606
		12.1.2	Deferred tax assets arising on a business combination 2607
			12.1.2.A Assets of the acquirer 2607
			12.1.2.B Assets of the acquiree 2607
		12.1.3	Deferred tax liabilities of acquired entity 2607

12.2		Tax deductions for replacement share-based payment awards in a business combination	2608
12.3		Apparent immediate impairment of goodwill created by deferred tax	2608
12.4		Tax deductions for acquisition costs	2608
12.5		Temporary differences arising from the acquisition of a group of assets that is not a business	2609

13 PRESENTATION 2609

13.1	Statement of financial position			2609
	13.1.1	Offset		2610
		13.1.1.A	Current tax	2610
		13.1.1.B	Deferred tax	2610
		13.1.1.C	No offset of current and deferred tax	2611
13.2	Statement of comprehensive income			2611
13.3	Statement of cash flows			2612

14 DISCLOSURE 2612

14.1	Components of tax expense		2612
14.2	Other disclosures		2613
	14.2.1	Tax (or tax rate) reconciliation	2614
	14.2.2	Temporary differences relating to subsidiaries, associates, branches and joint arrangements	2616
14.3	Reason for recognition of particular tax assets		2616
14.4	Dividends		2617
14.5	Examples of disclosures		2617
14.6	Discontinued operations – interaction with IFRS 5		2621

List of examples

Example 33.1:	PP&E attracting tax deductions in advance of accounting depreciation	2452
Example 33.2:	Minimum tax based on a specified amount – minimum treated as a levy	2468
Example 33.3:	Tax is the higher of measures based on taxable profits or revenues	2469
Example 33.4:	Tax based on revenues, unless a profit measure gives a lower result	2470
Example 33.5:	Rationale for initial recognition exception	2493
Example 33.6:	Deferred tax asset on initial recognition of goodwill	2495

Example 33.7:	Non-deductible PP&E	2497
Example 33.8:	Inception of loan with tax-deductible issue costs	2497
Example 33.9:	Inception of loan with non-deductible issue costs	2497
Example 33.10:	Purchase of PP&E subject to tax-free government grant	2498
Example 33.11:	Impairment of non-deductible goodwill	2499
Example 33.12:	Depreciation of non-deductible PP&E	2499
Example 33.13:	Amortisation of non-deductible loan issue costs	2499
Example 33.14:	Revaluation of non-deductible and non-depreciable asset	2500
Example 33.15:	Revaluation of non-deductible and depreciable asset	2500
Example 33.16:	Tax deduction for land	2501
Example 33.17:	Tax-deductible goodwill	2501
Example 33.18:	Asset non-deductible at date of acquisition later becomes deductible	2502
Example 33.19:	Partially deductible asset	2504
Example 33.20:	Super-deductible asset	2506
Example 33.21:	Asset and liability giving rise to equal temporary differences on initial recognition	2509
Example 33.22:	Compound financial instrument	2515
Example 33.23:	Acquired subsidiary accounted for as asset purchase	2516
Example 33.24:	Deductible temporary difference when the asset is valued below cost	2522
Example 33.25:	Debt instruments measured at fair value	2524
Example 33.26:	Temporary differences associated with subsidiaries, branches, associates and joint arrangements	2532
Example 33.27:	Tax-transparent entity (consolidated)	2537
Example 33.28:	Tax-transparent entity (equity-accounted)	2538
Example 33.29:	Measurement of deferred tax based on carrying amount of asset	2543
Example 33.30:	Calculation of deferred tax depending on method of realisation of asset	2544
Example 33.31:	Dual-based asset	2545
Example 33.32:	Convertible bond deductible if settled	2550
Example 33.33:	Deferred tax related to an investment in a subsidiary	2552
Example 33.34:	Different tax rates applicable to retained and distributed profits	2554
Example 33.35:	Elimination of intragroup profit (1)	2557
Example 33.36:	Elimination of intragroup profit (2)	2557
Example 33.37:	Intragroup transfer of goodwill	2558
Example 33.38:	Intragroup transfer of goodwill when tax base is retained by transferor	2559
Example 33.39:	Multiple treatments, expected value method	2565

Example 33.40:	Treatment relates to deferred tax asset, most likely amount is applied	2565
Example 33.41:	Remeasurement of deferred tax liability recognised as the result of retrospective application	2573
Example 33.42:	Tax deductible distribution on equity instrument	2576
Example 33.43:	Tax on reclassified ('recycled') items	2578
Example 33.44:	Debt instrument measured at fair value through other comprehensive income	2580
Example 33.45:	Debt instrument measured at fair value through other comprehensive income – tax effect	2581
Example 33.46:	Tax effect of expected credit losses with no change in fair value	2582
Example 33.47:	Loss in other comprehensive income and gain in profit or loss offset for tax purposes	2583
Example 33.48:	Recognition of deferred tax asset in profit or loss on the basis of tax liability accounted for outside profit or loss	2583
Example 33.49:	Profit in continuing operations and loss in discontinued operations offset for tax purposes	2584
Example 33.50:	Taxable profit on disposal of discontinued operation reduced by previously unrecognised tax losses	2584
Example 33.51:	Taxable profit on disposal of discontinued operation reduced by previously recognised tax losses	2585
Example 33.52:	Tax deductions for defined benefit pension plans	2585
Example 33.53:	Tax deductions for share-based payment transactions – allocation to profit or loss and equity	2588
Example 33.54:	Tax deductions for share-based payment transactions – 'multi-element' awards	2590
Example 33.55:	Tax deductions for share-based payment transactions – more than one award	2593
Example 33.56:	Tax deductions for share-based payment transactions – staggered exercise of award	2594
Example 33.57:	Deferred tax on replacement share-based awards in a business combination	2597
Example 33.58:	Tax effect of a disposal of an interest in a subsidiary that does not result in a loss of control	2600
Example 33.59:	Apparent 'day one' impairment arising from recognition of deferred tax in a business combination	2608
Example 33.60:	Alternative presentations of tax reconciliation	2615

Chapter 33   Income taxes

1 INTRODUCTION

1.1 The nature of taxation

Taxation has certain characteristics which set it apart from other business expenses and which might justify a different treatment, in particular:

- tax payments are not typically made in exchange for goods or services specific to the business (as opposed to access to generally available national infrastructure assets and services); and
- the business has no say in whether or not the payments are to be made.

1.2 Allocation between periods

The most significant accounting question which arises in relation to taxation is how to allocate tax expense between accounting periods. The recognition of transactions in the financial statements in a particular period is governed by the application of IFRS. However, the timing of the recognition of transactions for the purposes of measuring the taxable profit is governed by the application of tax law, which sometimes prescribes a treatment different from that used in the financial statements. The generally accepted view is that it is necessary for the financial statements to seek some reconciliation between these different treatments.

Accordingly, IFRS requires an entity to recognise, at each reporting date, the tax consequences expected to arise in future periods in respect of the recovery of its assets and settlement of its liabilities recognised at that date. Broadly speaking, those tax consequences that are legal assets or liabilities at the reporting date are referred to as current tax. The other consequences, which are expected to become, or (more strictly) form part of, legal assets or liabilities in a future period, are referred to as deferred tax.

This is illustrated by Example 33.1, which considers the treatment of tax deductions received against the cost of property, plant and equipment (PP&E), and the further discussion at 1.2.1 and 1.2.2 below.

Example 33.1: PP&E attracting tax deductions in advance of accounting depreciation

An item of equipment is purchased on 1 January 2021 for €50,000 and is estimated to have a useful life of five years, at the end of which it will be scrapped. There is no change to the estimated residual amount of zero over the life of the equipment. The depreciation charge will therefore be €10,000 per year for five years.

The entity is tax-resident in a jurisdiction where the corporate tax rate is 30%. No tax deductions are given for depreciation charged in the financial statements. Instead, the cost may be deducted from taxes payable in the year that the asset is purchased. The entity's profit before tax, including the depreciation charge, for each of the five years ended 31 December 2021 to 31 December 2025 is €100,000. All components of pre-tax profit, other than the accounting depreciation, are taxable or tax-deductible.

The entity's tax computations for each year would show the following (all figures in €s)[1]:

	2021	2022	2023	2024	2025
Accounting profit	100,000	100,000	100,000	100,000	100,000
Accounting depreciation	10,000	10,000	10,000	10,000	10,000
Tax depreciation	(50,000)	–	–	–	–
Taxable profit	60,000	110,000	110,000	110,000	110,000
Tax payable @ 30%	18,000	33,000	33,000	33,000	33,000

1.2.1 No provision for deferred tax ('flow through')

If the entity in Example 33.1 above were to account only for the tax legally due in respect of each year ('current tax'), it would report the amounts in the table below in profit or loss. Accounting for current tax only is generally known as the 'flow through' method.

€s	2021	2022	2023	2024	2025	Total
Profit before tax	100,000	100,000	100,000	100,000	100,000	500,000
Current tax	18,000	33,000	33,000	33,000	33,000	150,000
Profit after tax	82,000	67,000	67,000	67,000	67,000	350,000
Effective tax rate (%)	18	33	33	33	33	30

The 'effective tax rate' in the last row of the table above is the ratio, expressed as a percentage, of the profit before tax to the charge for tax in the financial statements, and is regarded as a key performance indicator by many preparers and users of financial statements. As can be seen from the table above, over the full five-year life of the asset, the entity pays tax at the statutory rate of 30% on its total profits of €500,000, but with considerable variation in the effective rate in individual accounting periods.

The generally held view is that simply to account for the tax legally payable as above is distortive, and that the tax should therefore be allocated between periods. Under IAS 12 – *Income Taxes* – this allocation is achieved by means of deferred taxation (see 1.2.2 below).

However, the flow-through method attracts the support of a number of commentators. They argue that the tax authorities impose a single annual tax assessment on the entity based on its profits as determined for tax purposes, not on accounting profits. That assessment is the entity's only liability to tax for that period, and any tax to be assessed in future years is not a present obligation and therefore not a liability as defined in the

IASB's *Conceptual Framework for Financial Reporting*. Supporters of flow-through acknowledge the distortive effect of transactions such as that in Example 33.1 above, but argue that this is better remedied by disclosure than by creating what they see as an 'imaginary' liability for deferred tax.

1.2.2 Provision for deferred tax (the temporary difference approach)

The approach currently required by IAS 12 is known as the temporary difference approach, which focuses on the difference between the carrying amount of an asset or liability in the financial statements and the amount attributed to it for tax purposes, known as its 'tax base'.

In Example 33.1 above, the carrying value of the PP&E in the financial statements at the end of each reporting period is:

€s	2021	2022	2023	2024	2025
PP&E	40,000	30,000	20,000	10,000	–

If the tax authority were to prepare financial statements based on tax law rather than IFRS, it would record PP&E of nil at the end of each period, since the full cost of €50,000 was written off in 2021 for tax purposes. There is therefore a difference, at the end of 2021, of €40,000 between the carrying amount of €40,000 of the asset in the financial statements and its tax base of nil. This difference is referred to as a 'temporary' difference because, by the end of 2025, the carrying value of the PP&E in the financial statements and its tax base are both nil, so that there is no longer a difference between them.

As discussed in more detail later in this Chapter, IAS 12 requires an entity to recognise a liability for deferred tax on the temporary difference arising on the asset (at 30%), as follows.

€s	2021	2022	2023	2024	2025
Net book value	40,000	30,000	20,000	10,000	–
Tax base	–	–	–	–	–
Temporary difference	40,000	30,000	20,000	10,000	–
Deferred tax	12,000	9,000	6,000	3,000	–
Movement in deferred tax in period	12,000	(3,000)	(3,000)	(3,000)	(3,000)

IAS 12 argues that, taking the position as at 31 December 2021 as an example, the carrying amount of the PP&E of €40,000 implicitly assumes that the asset will ultimately be recovered or realised by a cash inflow of at least €40,000. Any tax that will be paid on that inflow represents a present liability. In this case, the entity pays tax at 30% and will be unable to make any deduction in respect of the asset for tax purposes in a future period. It will therefore pay tax of €12,000 (30% of [€40,000 – nil]) as the asset is realised. This tax is as much a liability as the PP&E is an asset, since it would be internally inconsistent for the financial statements simultaneously to represent that the asset will be recovered at €40,000 while ignoring the tax consequences of doing so. *[IAS 12.16]*.

The deferred tax liability is recognised in the statement of financial position and any movement in the deferred tax liability during the period is recognised as deferred tax income or expense in profit or loss, with the following impact:

€s	2021	2022	2023	2024	2025	Total
Profit before tax	100,000	100,000	100,000	100,000	100,000	500,000
Current tax	18,000	33,000	33,000	33,000	33,000	150,000
Deferred tax	12,000	(3,000)	(3,000)	(3,000)	(3,000)	–
Total tax	30,000	30,000	30,000	30,000	30,000	150,000
Profit after tax	70,000	70,000	70,000	70,000	70,000	350,000
Effective tax rate (%)	30	30	30	30	30	30

It can be seen that the effect of accounting for deferred tax is to present an effective tax rate of 30% in profit or loss for each period. As will become apparent later in the Chapter, there is some tension in practice between the stated objective of IAS 12 (to recognise the appropriate amount of tax assets and liabilities in the statement of financial position) and what many users and preparers see as the real objective of IAS 12 (to match the tax effects of a transaction with the recognition of its pre-tax effects in the statement of comprehensive income or equity).

This tension arises in part because earlier methods of accounting for income tax, which explicitly focused on tax income and expense ('income statement approaches') rather than tax assets and liabilities ('balance sheet approaches'), remain part of the professional 'DNA' of many preparers and users. Moreover, as will be seen later in the Chapter, several aspects of IAS 12 are difficult to reconcile to the purported balance sheet approach of the standard, because, in reality, they are relics of the now superseded income statement approaches.

1.3 The development of IAS 12

The current version of IAS 12 was published in October 1996 and has been amended by a number of subsequent pronouncements. IAS 12 is based on the same principles as the US GAAP guidance (FASB ASC Topic 740 – *Income Taxes*). However, there are important differences of methodology between the two standards which can lead to significant differences between the amounts recorded under IAS 12 and US GAAP. Some of the main differences between the standards are noted at relevant points in the discussion below.

In July 2000, the SIC issued an interpretation of IAS 12, SIC-25 – *Income Taxes – Changes in the Tax Status of an Entity or its Shareholders* (see 10.9 below).[2]

In March 2009 the IASB issued an exposure draft (ED/2009/2 – *Income Tax*) of a standard to replace IAS 12. This was poorly received by commentators and there is no prospect of a new standard in this form being issued in the foreseeable future. Nevertheless, the IASB continues to consider possible limited changes to IAS 12 with the aim of improving it or clarifying its existing provisions.

In December 2010, the IASB issued an amendment to IAS 12 – *Deferred Tax: Recovery of Underlying Assets*. The amendment addressed the measurement of deferred tax associated with non-depreciable revalued property, plant and equipment and investment properties accounted for at fair value (see 8.4.6 and 8.4.7 below). *Recognition of Deferred Tax Assets for Unrealised Losses (Amendments to IAS 12)* – was issued in January 2016 in relation to the recognition of deferred tax assets for unrealised losses, for example on debt securities measured at fair value and related clarifications to the guidance on determining future taxable profits. It has been applied since annual periods beginning on or after 1 January 2017 (see 7.4.5 below).

In June 2017 the Interpretations Committee issued IFRIC 23 – *Uncertainty over Income Tax Treatments,* on the recognition and measurement of uncertain tax treatments. Annual Improvements to IFRS Standards 2015–2017 Cycle, issued in December 2017, clarifies that the income tax consequences of distributions relating to equity instruments should always be allocated to profit or loss, other comprehensive income or equity according to where the entity originally recognised the past transactions or events that generated distributable profits, and not only in situations where differential tax rates apply to distributed or undistributed earnings. This will require adjustment by those entities that previously allocated the related income tax to equity on the basis that it was linked more directly to the distribution to owners. Both changes became mandatory for annual periods beginning on or after 1 January 2019. *[IFRIC 23.B1, IAS 12.98I].* The treatment of uncertain tax positions is discussed at 9 below, with the allocation of tax on equity distributions set out at 10.3.5 below.

1.3.1 References to taxes in standards other than IAS 12

There are numerous references in other standards and interpretations to taxes, the more significant of which are noted later in this Chapter. The requirements of IFRS for accounting for income taxes in interim financial statements are discussed in Chapter 41 at 9.5. Other standards and interpretations also refer to taxes that are not necessarily income taxes within the scope of IAS 12. In some cases, such taxes are clearly outside the scope of IAS 12, such as sales taxes, payroll taxes and other taxes related to specific items of expenditure. These taxes often fall within the scope of IAS 37 – *Provisions, Contingent Liabilities and Contingent Assets* – and, in particular, IFRIC 21 – *Levies,* or by reference to the accounting standard most closely related to the item subject to such a non-income tax (such as IAS 19 – *Employee Benefits,* in the case of payroll taxes). In other cases, judgement is required to determine whether such taxes fall in the scope of IAS 12, as discussed at 4 below.

2 OBJECTIVE AND SCOPE OF IAS 12

2.1 Objective

The stated objective of IAS 12 is 'to prescribe the accounting treatment for income taxes. The principal issue in accounting for income taxes is how to account for the current and future tax consequences of:

(a) the future recovery (settlement) of the carrying amount of assets (liabilities) that are recognised in an entity's statement of financial position; and

(b) transactions and other events of the current period that are recognised in an entity's financial statements.' *[IAS 12 Objective].*

IAS 12 asserts that it is inherent in the recognition of an asset or liability that the reporting entity expects to recover or settle the carrying amount of that asset or liability. The Standard requires an entity to consider whether it is probable that recovery or settlement of that carrying amount will make future tax payments larger (or smaller) than they would be if such recovery or settlement had no tax consequences. *[IAS 12 Objective]*. If it is probable that such a larger or smaller tax payment will arise, IAS 12 requires an entity, with certain limited exceptions, to recognise a deferred tax liability or deferred tax asset. *[IAS 12.10, 16, 25]*. This is often referred to as the 'temporary difference approach' and is discussed further at 3 to 9 and 11 below.

IAS 12 also requires an entity to account for the tax consequences of transactions and other events in a manner consistent with the accounting treatment of the transactions and other events themselves. *[IAS 12 Objective]*. In other words:

- tax effects of transactions and other events recognised in profit or loss are also recognised in profit or loss;
- tax effects of transactions and other events recognised in other comprehensive income are also recognised in other comprehensive income;
- tax effects of transactions and other events recognised directly in equity are also recognised directly in equity; and
- deferred tax assets and liabilities recognised in a business combination affect:
  - the amount of goodwill arising in that business combination; or
  - the amount of the bargain purchase gain recognised.

This is discussed in more detail at 10 and 12 below.

The standard also deals with:

- the recognition of deferred tax assets arising for unused tax losses or unused tax credits (see 7.4.6 below);
- the presentation of income taxes in financial statements (see 13 below); and
- the disclosure of information relating to income taxes (see 14 below).

IAS 12 requires an entity to account for the tax consequences of recovering assets or settling liabilities at their carrying amount in the statement of financial position, not for the total tax expected to be paid (which will reflect the amount at which the asset or liability is actually settled, not its carrying amount at the reporting date).

IAS 12 may require an entity to recognise tax even on an accounting transaction that is not itself directly taxable, where the transaction gives rise to an asset (or liability) whose recovery (or settlement) will have tax consequences. For example, an entity might revalue a property. If (as is the case in many tax jurisdictions) no tax is payable on the revaluation, one might conclude that it has no tax effect. However, this is not the correct analysis under IAS 12, which focuses not on whether the revaluation itself is directly taxed, but rather on whether the profits out of which the increased carrying value of the property will be recovered will be subsequently taxed. This is discussed further at 8.4 below.

2.2 Overview

The overall requirements of IAS 12 can be summarised as follows:

- determine whether a tax is an 'income tax' (see 4 below);
- recognise income tax due or receivable in respect of the current and prior periods (current tax), measured using enacted or substantively enacted legislation (see 5 below), and having regard to any uncertain tax treatments (see 9 below);
- determine whether there are temporary differences between the carrying amount of assets and liabilities and their tax bases (see 6 below), having regard to the expected manner of recovery of assets or settlement of liabilities (see 8 below);
- determine whether there are unused tax losses or investment tax credits;
- determine whether IAS 12 prohibits or restricts recognition of deferred tax on any temporary differences or unused tax losses or investment tax credits (see 7 below);
- recognise deferred tax on all temporary differences, unused tax losses or investment tax credits not subject to such a prohibition or restriction (see 7 below), measured using enacted or substantively enacted legislation (see 8 below), and having regard to:
    - the expected manner of recovery of assets and settlement of liabilities (see 8 below); and
    - any uncertain tax treatments (see 9 below);
- allocate any income tax charge or credit for the period to profit or loss, other comprehensive income and equity (see 10 below);
- present income tax in the financial statements as required by IAS 12 (see 13 below); and
- make the disclosures required by IAS 12 (see 14 below).

3 DEFINITIONS

IAS 12 uses the following terms with the meanings specified below. *[IAS 12.2, 5]*.

Income taxes include all domestic and foreign taxes which are based on taxable profits. Income taxes also include taxes, such as withholding taxes, which are payable by a subsidiary, associate or joint arrangement on distributions to the reporting entity.

Accounting profit is profit or loss for a period before deducting tax expense.

Taxable profit (tax loss) is the profit (loss) for a period, determined in accordance with the rules established by the taxation authorities, upon which income taxes are payable (recoverable).

Tax expense (tax income) is the aggregate amount included in the determination of profit or loss for the period in respect of current tax and deferred tax.

Current tax is the amount of income taxes payable (recoverable) in respect of the taxable profit (tax loss) for a period.

Deferred tax liabilities are the amounts of income taxes payable in future periods in respect of *taxable temporary differences* (see below).

Deferred tax assets are the amounts of income taxes recoverable in future periods in respect of *deductible temporary differences* (see below), together with the carryforward of unused tax losses and unused tax credits.

Temporary differences are differences between the carrying amount of an asset or liability in the statement of financial position and its *tax base*. Temporary differences may be either:

- *taxable temporary differences*, which are temporary differences that will result in taxable amounts in determining taxable profit (tax loss) of future periods when the carrying amount of the asset or liability is recovered or settled; or
- *deductible temporary differences,* which are temporary differences that will result in amounts that are deductible in determining taxable profit (tax loss) of future periods when the carrying amount of the asset or liability is recovered or settled.

The *tax base* of an asset or liability is the amount attributed to that asset or liability for tax purposes.

IFRIC 23 uses the following terms in addition to those defined in IAS 12: *[IFRIC 23.3]*

Tax treatments refers to the treatments used or planned to be used by the entity in its income tax filings.

Taxation authority is the body or bodies that decide whether tax treatments are acceptable under the law. This might include a court.

Uncertain tax treatment is a tax treatment over which there is uncertainty concerning its acceptance under the law by the relevant taxation authority. For example, an entity's decision not to submit any tax filing in a particular tax jurisdiction or not to include specific income in taxable profit would be an uncertain tax treatment, if its acceptability is unclear under tax law.

4   SCOPE

IAS 12 should be applied in accounting for income taxes, defined as including:

- all domestic and foreign taxes which are based on taxable profits; and
- taxes, such as withholding taxes, which are payable by a subsidiary, associate or joint arrangement on distributions to the reporting entity. *[IAS 12.1-2]*.

IAS 12 does not apply to accounting for government grants, which fall within the scope of IAS 20 – *Accounting for Government Grants and Disclosure of Government Assistance*, or investment tax credits. However, it does deal with the accounting for any temporary differences that may arise from grants or investment tax credits. *[IAS 12.4]*.

A tax classified as an income tax is accounted for under IAS 12. Taxes other than income taxes are accounted for under IAS 37 and, in particular, IFRIC 21 or by reference to the accounting standard most closely related to the item subject to such a non-income tax (such as IAS 19, in the case of payroll taxes). The classification of a tax as an income tax affects its accounting treatment in several key respects:

- *Deferred tax*

    IAS 12 requires an entity to account for deferred tax in respect of income taxes. IAS 37 has no equivalent requirement for other taxes, recognising only legal or constructive obligations.

- *Recognition and measurement*

    IAS 12 requires tax to be recognised and measured according to a relatively tightly-defined accounting model. IAS 37 requires a provision to be recognised only where it is more likely than not that an outflow of resources will occur as a result of a past obligating event and measured at the best estimate of the amount expected to be paid. In the case of uncertain tax treatments (discussed at 9 below) an approach distinct from that in IAS 37 is required when IFRIC 23 is applied.

- *Presentation*

    IAS 1 – *Presentation of Financial Statements* – requires income tax assets, liabilities, income and expense to be presented in separate headings in profit or loss and the statement of financial position. There is no requirement for separate presentation of other taxes, but neither can they be included within the captions for 'income taxes'.

- *Disclosure*

    IAS 12 requires disclosures for income taxes significantly more detailed than those required by IAS 37 for other taxes.

4.1 What is an 'income tax'?

This is not as clear as might be expected, since the definition is circular. Income tax is defined as a tax based on 'taxable profits', which are in turn defined as profits 'upon which income taxes are payable' (see 3 above).

It seems clear that those taxes that take as their starting profit the reported net profit or loss are income taxes. However, several jurisdictions raise 'taxes' on sub-components of net profit. These include:

- sales taxes;
- goods and services taxes;
- value added taxes;
- levies on the sale or extraction of minerals and other natural resources;
- taxes on certain goods as they reach a given state of production or are moved from one location to another; or
- taxes on gross production margins.

Taxes that are simply collected by the entity from one third party (generally a customer or employee) on behalf of another third party (generally local or national government) are generally not regarded as 'income taxes' for the purposes of IAS 12. This view is supported by the requirement of IFRS 15 – *Revenue from Contracts with Customers* – that amounts which are collected from customers by the entity on behalf of third parties (for example, some sales taxes) do not form part of the entity's revenue, *[IFRS 15.47]*, (and, by implication, are not an expense of the entity either).

In cases where such taxes are a liability of the entity, they may often have some characteristics both of production or sales taxes (in that they are payable at a particular stage in the production or extraction process and may well be allowed as an expense in arriving at the tax on net profits) and of income taxes (in that they may be determined after deduction of certain allowable expenditure). This makes the classification of such taxes (as income taxes or not) difficult.

In March 2006 the Interpretations Committee considered whether to give guidance on which taxes are within the scope of IAS 12. The Committee noted that the definition of 'income tax' in IAS 12 (i.e. taxes that are based on taxable profit) implies that:

- not all taxes are within the scope of IAS 12; but
- because taxable profit is not the same as accounting profit, taxes do not need to be based on a figure that is exactly accounting profit to be within the scope of IAS 12.

The latter point is also implied by the requirement in IAS 12 to disclose an explanation of the relationship between tax expense and accounting profit – see 14.2 below. *[IAS 12.81(c)]*. The Interpretations Committee further noted that the term 'taxable profit' implies a notion of a net rather than gross amount, and that any taxes that are not in the scope of IAS 12 are in the scope of IAS 37 (see Chapter 26).

The Interpretations Committee drew attention to the variety of taxes that exist across the world and the need for judgement in determining whether some taxes are income taxes. The Committee therefore believed that guidance beyond the observations noted above could not be developed in a reasonable period of time and decided not to take a project on this issue onto its agenda.[3] This decision was confirmed in May 2009, when the Committee concluded that taxes based on tonnage transported or tonnage capacity or on notional income derived from tonnage capacity, being based on a gross amount, are not based on 'taxable profit' and, consequently, would not be considered income taxes in accordance with IAS 12.[4]

The Interpretations Committee's deliberations reinforce the difficulty of formulating a single view as to the treatment of taxes. The appropriate treatment will need to be addressed on a case-by-case basis depending on the particular terms of the tax concerned and the entity's own circumstances.

Where a tax is levied on multiple components of net income, it is more likely that the tax should be viewed as substantially a tax on income and therefore subject to IAS 12.

Even where such taxes are not income taxes, if they are deductible against current or future income taxes, they may nevertheless give rise to tax assets which do fall within the scope of IAS 12.

4.1.1 Levies

Several governments have introduced levies on certain types of entity, particularly those in the financial services sector. In many cases the levies are expressed as a percentage of a measure of revenue or net assets, or some component(s) of revenue or net assets, at a particular date. Such levies are not income taxes and should be accounted for in accordance with IAS 37 and IFRIC 21 (see Chapter 26 at 6.8).

4.1.2 Hybrid taxes (including minimum taxes)

Some jurisdictions impose income taxes which are charged as a percentage of taxable profits in the normal way, but are subject to a requirement that a minimum amount of tax must be paid. This minimum may be an absolute amount or a proportion of one or more components of the statement of financial position – for example, total equity as reported in the financial statements, or total share capital and additional paid-in capital (share premium). Another form of arrangement is where the amount of tax payable is the higher of one measure (based on profits) and another (for example based on: revenues; net assets; on total debt and equity).

Such 'hybrid taxes' raise the issue of how they should be accounted for; in particular whether they fall in the scope of IAS 12 or another standard. This issue is discussed at 4.5 below.

4.2 Withholding and similar taxes

As noted at 4.1 above, IAS 12 also includes in its scope those taxes, such as withholding taxes, which are payable by a subsidiary, associate or joint arrangement on distributions to the reporting entity. *[IAS 12.2]*. This gives rise to further questions of interpretation.

The most basic issue is what is meant by a 'withholding tax'. This is discussed at 10.3.2 and 10.3.4 below.

A second issue is whether the scope of IAS 12 covers only taxes on distributions from a subsidiary, associate or joint arrangement, or whether it extends to tax on distributions from other entities in which the reporting entity has an investment. Such an investment is typically accounted for at fair value under IFRS 9 – *Financial Instruments*.

The rationale for the treatment as income taxes of taxes payable by a subsidiary, associate or joint arrangement on distributions to the investor is discussed further at 7.5 below. Essentially, however, the reason for considering withholding taxes within the scope of income tax accounting derives from the accounting treatment of the investments themselves. The accounting treatment for such investments – whether by full consolidation or the equity method – results in the investor recognising profit that may be taxed twice: once as it is earned by the investee entity concerned, and again as that entity distributes the profit as dividend to the investor. IAS 12 ensures that the financial statements reflect both tax consequences.

Some argue that this indicates a general principle that an entity should account for all the tax consequences of realising the income of an investee as that income is recognised. On this analysis withholding taxes suffered on any investment income should be treated as income taxes. Others argue that the reference in IAS 12 to distributions from 'a subsidiary, associate or joint arrangement' should be read restrictively, and that no wider general principle is implied. In addition, because the amount of the tax relates to a single component of the investor entity's income, it can be argued that (without the specific reference to a 'withholding tax') such amounts are not within the scope of IAS 12 because they are not 'based on taxable profits', *[IAS 12.2]*, (see 4.1 above).

We believe that judgement is required to decide whether a tax deducted from investment income at the source of the income is a withholding tax in the scope of IAS 12. As well as the considerations noted above, the decision requires consideration of all the relevant facts and circumstances of the jurisdiction that levies the tax, especially the national tax legislation and the design of the investor entity. If it is determined that the tax withheld from investment income is a tax within the scope of IAS 12, any non-refundable portion of such withholding taxes is recognised as a tax expense in the statement of comprehensive income. In addition, the entity should apply all the provisions of IAS 12 for current and deferred taxes, including recognition, measurement, presentation and disclosure. An entity that determines that a withholding tax is in the scope of IAS 12 presents its related income as an amount gross of withholding taxes in the statement of comprehensive income.

Accordingly, an entity may determine that it should treat as income taxes the withholding taxes that could potentially be suffered on distributions from all investments, not just subsidiaries, associates and joint arrangements. Whether or not any tax liability is recognised will depend on an analysis of the facts and circumstances in each case, in particular whether the investment concerned is expected to be recovered through receipt of dividend income or through sale (see 8.4 below).

4.3 Investment tax credits

Investment tax credits are not defined in IAS 12, but for the purposes of the following discussion they are taken to comprise government assistance and incentives for specific kinds of business activity and investment delivered through the tax system. Investment tax credits can take different forms and be subject to different conditions. Sometimes a tax credit is given as a deductible expense in computing the entity's tax liability, and sometimes as a deduction from the entity's tax liability, rather than as a deductible expense. In some cases, the value of the credit is chargeable to income taxes and in others it is not.

Entitlement to receive investment tax credits can be determined in a variety of ways. Some investment tax credits may relate to direct investment in property, plant and equipment. Other entities may receive investment tax credits relating to research and development or other specific activities. Some credits may be realisable only through a reduction in current or future income taxes payable, while others may be settled directly in cash if the entity does not have sufficient income taxes payable to offset the credit within a certain period. Access to the credit may be limited according to total taxes paid (i.e. including taxes such as payroll and sales taxes remitted to government in addition to income taxes). There may be other conditions associated with receiving the investment tax credit, for example with respect to the conduct and continuing activities of the entity, and the credit may become repayable if ongoing conditions are not met.

As noted at 4 above, IAS 12 states that it does not deal with the methods of accounting for government grants or investment tax credits although any temporary differences that arise from them are in the scope of the Standard. *[IAS 12.4]*. At the same time, government assistance that is either provided in the form of benefits that are available in determining taxable profit or tax loss, or determined or limited according to an entity's income tax liability, is excluded from the scope of IAS 20. That Standard lists income tax holidays, investment tax credits, accelerated depreciation allowances and reduced income tax rates as examples of such benefits. *[IAS 20.2]*. Accordingly, if government assistance is described as an investment tax credit, but it is neither determined nor limited by reference to an entity's liability to income taxes, it falls within the scope of IAS 20 and should therefore be accounted for as a government grant (see Chapter 24 at 2.3.2).

The fact that both IAS 20 and IAS 12 use the term 'investment tax credits' to describe items excluded from their scope requires entities to carefully consider the nature of such incentives and the conditions attached to them to determine which standard the particular tax credit is excluded from and, therefore, whether they fall in the scope of IAS 12 or IAS 20.

In our view, the determination of which framework to apply to a particular investment tax credit is a matter of judgement and all facts and circumstances relating to the specific incentive need to be considered in assessing the substance of the arrangement. The following factors will often be relevant, but this list of factors should not be considered exhaustive, and entities may identify other factors which they consider to be more important than those listed below:

Feature of credit	Indicator of IAS 12 treatment	Indicator of IAS 20 treatment
Method of realisation	Only available as a reduction in income taxes payable (i.e. benefit is forfeit if there are insufficient income taxes payable). However, a lengthy period allowed for carrying forward unused credits may make this indicator less relevant.	Directly settled in cash where there are insufficient taxable profits to allow credit to be fully recovered, or available for set off against non-income taxes, such as payroll taxes, sales taxes or other amounts owed to government.
Number of non-tax conditions attached to the initial receipt of grant (e.g. minimum employment, ongoing use of purchased assets)	None or few	Many
Restrictions as to nature of expenditure required to receive the grant	Broad criteria encompassing many different types of qualifying expenditure	Highly specific
Tax treatment of grant income	Not taxable	Taxable

In group accounts, in which entities from several different jurisdictions may be consolidated, it may be desirable that all 'investment tax credits' should be consistently accounted for, either as an IAS 12 income tax or as a government grant under IAS 20. However, the judgment as to which standard applies is made by reference to the nature of each type of investment tax credit and the conditions attached to it. This may mean that the predominant practice in a particular jurisdiction for a specific type of investment tax credit has evolved differently from consensus in another jurisdiction for what could appear to be a substantially similar credit. We believe that, in determining whether the arrangement is of a type that falls within the scope of IAS 12 or IAS 20, an entity should consider the following factors in the order listed below:

- if there is a predominant local treatment for a specific investment tax credit as to whether a specific credit in the relevant tax jurisdiction falls within the scope of IAS 12 or IAS 20, this should take precedence;
- if there is no predominant local treatment, the group-wide approach to determining the standard that applies to such a credit should be applied; and
- in the absence of a predominant local treatment or a group-wide approach to making the determination, the indicators listed in the table above should provide guidance.

This may mean that an entity operating in several territories adopts different accounting treatments for apparently similar arrangements in different countries, but it at least ensures a measure of comparability between different entities operating in the same tax jurisdiction. Similar considerations apply in determining the meaning of 'substantively enacted' legislation in different jurisdictions (see 5.1 below).

Where a tax credit is determined to be in the nature of an income tax, the incentive should be recognised as an asset and a reduction in current income tax (to the extent of the incentive that has already been used) as soon as there is reasonable assurance that the entity will comply with the conditions of the tax credit and the tax credit becomes allowable against the income tax base of the current or preceding year.

A deferred tax asset will be recognised for any unused tax credits (up to the amount of incentive that has already been made available) to the extent that there is reasonable assurance that the entity will comply with the conditions of the tax credit and it is probable that future taxable profit will be available against which the unused tax losses and unused tax credits can be utilised. *[IAS 12.34]*. For incentives related to the initial recognition of assets (i.e. not relating to items expensed for accounting purposes), it would also be acceptable, as an alternative to immediate recognition in profit or loss, to treat the tax credit as an adjustment to the tax base of the asset. If this alternative approach is taken, the initial recognition exception would apply to prohibit recognition of the excess of the tax base over the accounting carrying value. The subsequent accounting would then be similar to the accounting followed for a super-deductible asset. The treatment of super-deductible assets is discussed further at 7.2.6 below.

Even if investment tax credits are recorded which will be realised in future periods, the related deferred tax asset should not be discounted.

4.4 Interest and penalties

Many tax regimes require interest and/or penalties to be paid on late payments of tax. This raises the question of whether or not such penalties fall within the scope of IAS 12. The answer can have consequences not only for the presentation of interest and penalties in the income statement; but also for the timing of recognition and on the measurement of amounts recognised. If such penalties and interest fall within the scope of IAS 12, they are presented as part of tax expense and measured in accordance with the requirements of that Standard. Where uncertainty exists as to whether interest and penalties will be applied by the tax authorities, IFRIC 23 on uncertain tax treatments would be relevant in determining how much should be recognised and when (see 9.1 below). If interest and penalties do not fall within the scope of IAS 12, they should be included in profit before tax, with recognition and measurement determined in accordance with another accounting standard, most likely to be IAS 37.

Some argue that penalties and interest have the characteristics of an income tax – they are paid to the tax authorities under specific tax legislation that has already been deemed to give rise to an IAS 12 income tax and therefore should be treated consistently. Others contend that penalties and interest are distinct from the main income tax liability, are not 'based on taxable profits' as required in paragraph 5 of the Standard and should not therefore form part of tax expense. Those who hold this view would point out, for example, that under IFRS the unwinding of the discount on discounted items is generally accounted for separately from the discounted expense.

The Interpretations Committee considered this issue most recently in 2017, as a result of comments received from respondents regarding the scope of what is now IFRIC 23. Notwithstanding their decision to exclude a specific reference to interest and penalties in IFRIC 23 and their decision in September 2017 not to add a project on interest and penalties to its agenda, the Committee observed that:[5]

(a) the determination of whether IAS 12 or IAS 37 should be applied is not an accounting policy choice. Instead, if an entity determines that a particular amount payable or receivable for interest and penalties is an income tax, then the entity applies IAS 12 to that amount. If an entity does not apply IAS 12 to interest and penalties, then it applies IAS 37 to those amounts;

(b) paragraph 79 of IAS 12 requires an entity to disclose the major components of tax expense (income); for each class of provision, and paragraphs 84 and 85 of IAS 37 require a reconciliation of the carrying amount at the beginning and end of the reporting period as well as various other pieces of information. Accordingly, regardless of whether an entity applies IAS 12 or IAS 37 when accounting for interest and penalties related to income taxes, the entity would disclose information about those interest and penalties if it is material; and

(c) paragraph 122 of IAS 1 requires disclosure of the judgements that management has made in the process of applying the entity's accounting policies and that have the most significant effect on the amounts recognised in the financial statements.

The Committee also observed that it had previously published agenda decisions discussing the scope of IAS 12 in March 2006 and May 2009 (as noted at 4.1 above).

The Interpretations Committee did not give any specific guidance as to how one might decide whether interest and penalties should be regarded as an IAS 12 income tax.

In our view, the judgement of whether IAS 12 or IAS 37 applies should be determined on a country-by-country and a tax-by-tax basis. The agenda decision is clear that this is not an accounting policy choice whereby an entity has 'free rein' to arbitrarily choose that one standard should be applied for all interest and penalties on taxes in all jurisdictions.

Instead, an entity should make a determination of the nature of the particular interest and penalties in question based on its understanding of the operation of the specific tax law and the way in which the charge or credit is calculated.

The following factors are relevant in determining whether an item is in scope of IAS 12, although we believe that no particular order should be applied and that no single factor is conclusive:

- whether there is a predominant local consensus in evidence or specific guidance issued locally by regulators as to the nature of interest and penalties applied to a specific tax in the relevant tax jurisdiction, leading to a predominant practice of accounting for these as income tax or not as income tax. Where a treatment may not otherwise be clear, entities often refer to local practice in determining whether a tax is an income tax; whether legislation has been substantively enacted; and in the treatment of investment tax credits. Determining whether interest and penalties are part of income tax requires careful consideration of the local legislation and hence entities would usually defer to local consensus where it exists. Since the judgement depends on the circumstances of the particular tax laws in a particular country, it should be accepted that an international group could encounter different conclusions in relation to interest and penalties arising in different jurisdictions. In particular, we would normally not expect a conclusion based on local consensus to be reversed in a subsequent consolidation by an overseas parent;
- whether the amounts are clearly identifiable as 'interest' or as 'penalty' making it more appropriate to not account for these as income tax. Does the tax legislation have specific rules and requirements that allow an entity to identify the amounts that are to be regarded as 'interest' and as 'penalties'? That is, if an entity pays a single lump sum to settle existing tax positions, it would only identify interest and penalty components to the extent that communications from the tax authorities and/or tax legislation allow the entity to identify such components. An entity would not bifurcate such a single payment to identify notional interest and penalty amounts as this would be too judgemental, but rather account for the whole as an income tax;
- the degree to which the entity believes it is certain that interest and penalties will be applied. A certain payment of interest for example would indicate it being a financing expense rather than an income tax. In some cases, an entity might decide to wait until a tax enquiry is concluded before settling an expected obligation. In others, the entity could be confident of recovering an overpayment of tax, with interest added to the expected refund. In these circumstances, it could be argued that interest and penalties result from an entity's conscious decision not to pay earlier the taxes due or to secure the later receipt of interest. Hence, those interest and penalties might be regarded as not directly related to taxable income, but rather the result of the entity's financing decisions;
- whether the amount is based on net taxable profit, indicating it is an income tax. As noted at 4.1 above, IAS 12 only applies to income taxes, which are based on 'taxable profits'. However, in many jurisdictions income tax legislation contains elements that, when looked at in isolation, are not strictly based on a notion of taxable profits. Examples include tax exempt amounts, deductibility caps and super-deductions for certain eligible expenditure. As a practical matter it is normally not considered helpful or necessary to account for such elements as a

separate unit of account, unless not doing so would significantly misrepresent the underlying substance of the arrangements; and

- whether the interest rate applied by the tax authorities reflects current market assessments of the time value of money, indicating it being a financing expense rather than income tax. If the applied rate clearly reflects the time value of money, it should be treated as interest. If the rate is largely punitive, the interest should be considered together with penalties. However, it would not be sensible to attempt to identify a notional time value component as this would be too judgemental.

Where the amounts involved are material, it will be appropriate for the entity to consider whether the judgements made and the amounts involved should be disclosed in accordance with the requirements of paragraph 122 of IAS 1.

4.5 Hybrid taxes (including minimum taxes)

The term 'hybrid taxes' is applied to arrangements in which:

(a) an entity's liability to tax is assessed on both a measure of its taxable profits and a non-profit measure; and

(b) the amount of tax to be paid in any period depends on the interaction between those two measures.

Examples of non-profit measures would include amounts based on particular types of revenue; on components of the statement of financial position, such as total equity, net assets or net debt; or to a non-financial measure such as physical output. Tax authorities might require entities to use the alternative measures to determine a minimum amount of tax to be paid in any period. Hybrid taxes do not include arrangements where an entity can elect to operate within one of a number of alternative tax regimes, for example to choose to be assessed on the basis of its taxable profits, or to have its profits exempt from tax and instead be assessed according to a non-profit measure such as revenues, net assets or physical output. In this case there is no interaction between taxable profits and the non-profit measure in determining the actual tax to be paid in a given period.

Such 'hybrid taxes' (where the tax to be paid depends on the interaction of a profit and a non-profit measure) raise the issue of how they should be accounted for. Does IAS 12 apply simply because one of the measures referred to in the tax legislation is based on taxable profits, or should a determination be made based on an assessment of which measure is most likely to influence the actual amount of tax to be incurred by the entity? Alternatively, should the tax charge be bifurcated between the component based on profits and the component based on another measure, with the former accounted as an income tax and the other as a levy under IAS 37 and IFRIC 21? This section considers some of the different arrangements seen in practice.

4.5.1 Hybrid taxes – minimum based on a measure other than taxable profits

In the case of a minimum tax, the authorities impose income taxes which are charged as a percentage of taxable profits in the normal way, but subject to a requirement that a minimum amount of tax must be paid. This minimum may be an absolute amount.

One approach would be to account for the fixed minimum element as a non-income tax under IAS 37 and IFRIC 21, with any excess above the fixed minimum element treated as an income tax under IAS 12.

An alternative approach would be to consider the overall substance of the tax. If it is apparent that the overall intention of the legislation is to charge taxes based on net profit, but subject to a floor, the tax should be accounted for as an income tax in its entirety, even if the floor would not be an income tax if considered in isolation.

This second approach appears to have some advantages over the first. A determination that the tax, in its entirety, is either in scope of IAS 12 or not is consistent with the Interpretation Committee's agenda decision in relation to interest and penalties (see 4.4 above). Having established the overall intention of the legislation, a consistent basis can be applied from period to period, for example to the identification of a tax rate for measuring deferred tax (should the entity have determined that IAS 12 should apply).

Under the first approach, an entity might have to account for current and deferred tax in periods where net profit results in a higher liability than the non-profit measure and apply a different basis when taxable profits give an assessment lower than the non-profit measure. Another practical disadvantage is that the effective rate of the element accounted for as income tax is unpredictable, as it will depend on the level of profit in future periods relative to the established minimum level of tax, as illustrated in the following example.

Example 33.2: Minimum tax based on a specified amount – minimum treated as a levy

Entity A is required to pay tax at 30% on its taxable profit, but subject to a minimum tax of €90,000 per year. No income tax relief is available for the minimum tax. If its taxable profits were less than or equal to €300,000, it would pay the minimum tax of €90,000. If taxable profits were €1 million, it would pay total tax of €300,000 (€1,000,000 at 30%). If the entity's taxable profits were €2,000,000 it would pay tax of €600,000 (€2,000,000 at 30%). Entity A applies the first approach above, treating the minimum amount as a levy under IAS 37 and IFRIC 21 and accounting for any excess as an income tax under IAS 12. On this basis, the effective rate of tax, for the purpose of measuring any deferred tax balances, would be derived as follows in each scenario:

	€	€	€
Total tax charge			
Taxable profit before minimum tax	300,000	1,000,000	2,000,000
Total tax (@ 30% or €90,000)	90,000	300,000	600,000
Minimum tax	90,000	90,000	90,000
Income tax (remainder)	–	210,000	510,000
Effective income tax rate			
Taxable profit before minimum tax	300,000	1,000,000	2,000,000
Minimum tax	90,000	90,000	90,000
Profit before income tax (A)	210,000	910,000	1,910,000
Income tax (B)	–	210,000	510,000
Profit after tax	210,000	700,000	1,400,000
Effective income tax rate (B/A)	n/a	23.1%	26.7%

In the circumstances illustrated above, in order to calculate deferred income taxes for the purposes of IAS 12, any future income tax rate would be subject to constant re-estimation, even if the 'headline' enacted rate had not changed.

In our view, either of these two approaches can be adopted so long as it is applied consistently.

4.5.2 Tax is the higher of measures based on taxable profits and revenues

Another form of hybrid tax is where the amount of tax payable is the higher of one measure (based on profits) and another (for example based on: revenues; net assets; or total debt and equity).

In these circumstances, treating the tax on an 'all-or-nothing' basis, e.g. wholly as a non-income tax could be problematic, especially in situations where the basis giving rise to the amount of total tax payable changes from period to period.

In these circumstances we believe that an entity could determine that the tax is primarily a non-income tax, with amounts in excess of that basis accounted under IAS 12; or that the tax is primarily an IAS 12 income tax, with any excess accounted as a non-income tax under IAS 37 and IFRIC 21. These two approaches are illustrated in Example 33.3 below.

Example 33.3: Tax is the higher of measures based on taxable profits or revenues

Entity B is required to pay tax at the higher of 40% on its taxable profit or 2% of its reported revenue. Income tax relief is not available for the revenue tax. The entity must therefore determine how much tax would be paid on each basis and incur the higher amount. The effective rate of income tax, for the purpose of measuring any deferred tax balances, would be derived as follows in the various scenarios below:

	€	€	€	€
Total tax charge				
Revenue (A)	20,000,000	20,000,000	20,000,000	20,000,000
Profit before tax (B)	500,000	900,000	1,200,000	2,400,000
Charge based on revenue (A @ 2%)	400,000	400,000	400,000	400,000
Charge based on profit (B @ 40%)	200,000	360,000	480,000	960,000
Tax charge under legislation	400,000	400,000	480,000	960,000
Approach 1 – Excess is IAS 12 tax				
Profit before revenue tax	500,000	900,000	1,200,000	2,400,000
Revenue tax	400,000	400,000	400,000	400,000
Profit before income tax (C)	100,000	500,000	800,000	2,000,000
Income tax (D)	–	–	80,000	560,000
Profit after tax	100,000	500,000	720,000	1,440,000
Effective income tax rate (D/C)	0%	0%	10%	28%
Approach 2 – Excess is revenue tax				
Profit before revenue tax	500,000	900,000	1,200,000	2,400,000
Revenue tax	200,000	40,000	–	–
Profit before income tax (E)	300,000	860,000	1,200,000	2,400,000
Income tax (F)	200,000	360,000	480,000	960,000
Profit after tax	100,000	500,000	720,000	1,040,000
Effective income tax rate (F/E)	66.7%	41.8%	40%	40%

In the example above, when the excess is accounted as an IAS 12 income tax, the effective income tax rate varies, requiring the entity to reassess its estimate for measuring deferred taxes in the future even when the enacted rate of income tax is unchanged. When the excess is treated as a revenue tax, the effective rate of income tax is equal to the enacted rate of income tax (40%), adjusted to reflect the disallowable revenue tax charge (effectively a permanent difference).

In our view, either of these approaches can be adopted so long as it is applied consistently.

4.5.3 Tax is based on revenues, unless a profit measure gives a lower result

As businesses have increasingly operated across international boundaries, national governments have sought to evolve their tax systems to ensure that the profit of a multinational group is taxed in the countries in which it creates value. The need for this development has become more urgent with the advent of the digital revolution, whereby companies can earn profits in a particular country without having any physical presence there.

As a result, governments are introducing taxes based primarily on measures of revenue earned in their jurisdiction by these entities. However, at the same time, governments do not wish to discourage local investment and innovation by businesses operating internationally or in the digital space, so they introduce reliefs and incentives. For example, the tax might be levied only on revenues above a certain threshold, or an entity might be permitted to elect to be taxed on its profits from that activity if it has a presence in the jurisdiction and it can show that a measure based on profits would give rise to a lower liability.

This is illustrated in the following example.

Example 33.4: Tax based on revenues, unless a profit measure gives a lower result

A government introduces a tax on the revenues of certain digital businesses (DST). A charge of 2% is levied on the digital revenues earned from customers in that country above an annual threshold. Where the local revenues received in connection with digital services activities exceed the annual threshold, the entity must submit DST returns to the local tax authority and will have to pay DST. No tax is payable for revenues up to the annual threshold.

Because the entities subject to this tax often have little or no physical presence in the country in question, DST normally applies at the rate of 2% on local digital services revenues above the annual threshold. However, an entity can elect to calculate its tax liability using an alternative basis. The alternative basis gives rise to a lower DST liability for entities making a loss or operating at a low margin on their local digital services activity.

This election is voluntary, applies for one year, and entities must make or renew the election at the time they submit their tax return for the period they wish to calculate their DST liability using the alternative method. Under the alternative basis, the DST is calculated by reference to the operating margin of the local digital services activity at a rate of 80% of that margin. In cases where the local digital services activity is loss making and the alternative basis is being applied, no DST needs to be paid on revenues attributable to that activity, but at the same time no relief is given in respect of those losses. That is, the DST is set at zero for the current period, but no losses are carried forward or back into other accounting periods.

How should entities account for this tax?

In these circumstances we believe that this type of arrangement should be treated wholly as a non-income tax outside the scope of IAS 12. In our view, it would not be appropriate to account for the tax as a non-income tax in those years when tax is paid on digital services revenues, and as an IAS 12 income tax when election is taken to apply the alternative basis, using a measure of profit. It would also be inappropriate to try to bifurcate the tax between a component based on revenue and a component based on the alternative profit measure regardless of whether the election is taken. Such bifurcation is only effective where the tax liability is the higher of one measure or another, as discussed at 4.5.2 above.

The nature of the arrangement in the example, in both design and operation, is a revenue-based tax that would fall outside the scope of IAS 12. The tax is designed to achieve a higher level of tax for entities that do not have a physical presence in the country in which revenues are generated; and in most cases it is this basis that will determine the amount of tax payable. The election to apply the alternative basis represents a relief for those particular entities with a low operating margin in the local jurisdiction (for example because they have a physical presence, employ staff or have other activities that would attract a liability to local taxes). In the example above, only if the entity's operating margin were below 2.5% (2% ÷ 0.8) would the alternative basis give rise to a lower charge than the levy on revenue.

4.6 Effectively tax-free entities

In several jurisdictions, certain classes of entity are exempt from income tax, and accordingly are not within the scope of IAS 12.

However, a more common, and more complex, situation is that tax legislation has the effect that certain classes of entities, whilst not formally designated as 'tax-free' in law, are nevertheless exempt from tax provided that they meet certain conditions that, in practice, they are almost certain to meet. A common example is that, in many jurisdictions, investment vehicles pay no tax, provided that they distribute all, or a minimum percentage, of their earnings to investors.

Accounting for the tax affairs of such entities raises a number of challenges, as discussed further at 8.5.1 below.

5 CURRENT TAX

Current tax is the amount of income taxes payable (recoverable) in respect of the taxable profit (tax loss) for a period. *[IAS 12.5]*.

Current tax for current and prior periods should, to the extent unpaid, be recognised as a liability. If the amount already paid in respect of current and prior periods exceeds the amount due for those periods, the excess should be recognised as an asset. *[IAS 12.12]*.

The benefit relating to a tax loss that can be carried back to recover current tax of a previous period should be recognised as an asset. When a tax loss is used to recover current tax of a previous period, an entity recognises the benefit as an asset in the period in which the tax loss occurs because it is probable that the benefit will flow to the entity and the benefit can be reliably measured. *[IAS 12.13-14]*.

Current tax should be measured at the amount expected to be paid to or recovered from the tax authorities by reference to tax rates and laws that have been enacted or substantively enacted by the end of the reporting period. *[IAS 12.46]*.

5.1 Enacted or substantively enacted tax legislation

IAS 12 requires current tax to be measured using tax rates or laws enacted 'or substantively enacted' at the end of the reporting period. *[IAS 12.46]*. The standard comments that, in some jurisdictions, announcements of tax rates (and tax laws) by the government have the substantive effect of actual enactment, which may follow the announcement by a period of several months. In these circumstances, tax assets and liabilities are measured using the announced tax rate (and tax laws). *[IAS 12.48]*.

IAS 12 gives no guidance as to how this requirement is to be interpreted in different jurisdictions. In most jurisdictions, however, a consensus has emerged as to the meaning of 'substantive enactment' for that jurisdiction (see 5.1.1 below). Nevertheless, apparently similar legislative processes in different jurisdictions may give rise to different treatments under IAS 12. For example, in most jurisdictions, tax legislation requires the formal approval of the head of state in order to become law. However, in some jurisdictions the head of state has real executive power (and could potentially not approve the legislation), whereas in others the head of state has a more ceremonial role (and cannot practically fail to approve the legislation).

The general principle tends to be that in those jurisdictions where the head of state has executive power, legislation is not substantively enacted until actually approved by the head of state. Where, however, the head of state's powers are more ceremonial, substantive enactment is generally regarded as occurring at the stage of the legislative process where no further amendment is possible.

5.1.1 Meaning of substantive enactment in various jurisdictions

The following table summarises the meaning of 'substantive enactment' in various jurisdictions as generally understood in those jurisdictions.[6]

Country	Point of substantive enactment
United Kingdom	A Finance Bill has been passed by the House of Commons and is awaiting only passage through the House of Lords and Royal Assent. Alternatively, a resolution having statutory effect has been passed under the Provisional Collection of Taxes Act 1968.
Canada	If there is a majority government, substantive enactment generally occurs with respect to proposed amendments to the Federal Income Tax Act when detailed draft legislation has been tabled for first reading in Parliament. If there is a minority government, proposed amendments to the Federal Income Tax Act would not normally be considered to be substantively enacted until the proposals have passed the third reading in the House of Commons.
Australia	The Bill has passed through both Houses of Parliament (but before Royal Assent).
France	Signature of the legislation by the executive.
Germany	The Bundestag and Bundesrat pass the legislation.
Japan	The Diet passes the legislation.
United States	The legislation is signed by the President or there is a successful override vote by both houses of Congress.
South Africa	Changes in tax rates not inextricably linked to other changes in tax law are substantively enacted when announced in the Minister of Finance's Budget statement. Other changes in tax rates and tax laws are substantively enacted when approved by Parliament and signed by the President.

5.1.2 Changes to tax rates and laws enacted before the reporting date

Current tax should be measured at the amount expected to be paid to or recovered from the tax authorities by reference to tax rates and laws that have been enacted, or substantively enacted, by the end of the reporting period. *[IAS 12.46]*. Accordingly, the effects of changes in tax rates and laws on current tax balances are required to be recognised in the period in which the legislation is substantively enacted. There is no relief from this requirement under IAS 12, even in circumstances when complex legislation is substantively enacted shortly before the end of an annual or interim reporting period. In cases where the effective date of any rate changes is not the first day of the entity's annual reporting period, current tax would be calculated by applying a blended rate to the taxable profits for the year.

Where complex legislation is enacted shortly before the end of the period, entities might encounter two distinct sources of uncertainty:

- uncertainty about the requirements of the law, which may give rise to uncertain tax treatments as defined by IFRIC 23 and discussed at 5.2 and 9 below; and
- uncertainties arising from incomplete information because entities may not have all the data required to process the effects of the changes in tax laws.

It is not necessary for entities to have a complete understanding of every aspect of the new tax law to arrive at reasonable estimates, and provided that entities make every effort to obtain and take into account all the information they could reasonably be expected to obtain up to the date when the financial statements for the period are authorised for issue, subsequent changes to those estimates would not be regarded as a prior period error under IAS 8 – *Accounting Policies, Changes in Accounting Estimates and Errors*. *[IAS 8.5]*. We expect that only in rare circumstances would it not be possible to determine a reasonable estimate. However, these uncertainties may require additional disclosure in the financial statements. IAS 1 requires entities to disclose information about major sources of estimation uncertainty at the end of the reporting period that have a significant risk of resulting in a material adjustment to the carrying amounts of assets and liabilities within the next financial year (see Chapter 3 at 5.2.1). *[IAS 1.125-129]*.

Whilst the effect of changes in tax laws enacted after the end of the reporting period are not taken into account (see 5.1.3 below), information and events that occur between the end of the reporting period and the date when the financial statements are authorised for issue are adjusting events after the reporting period if they provide evidence of conditions that existed as at the reporting date. *[IAS 10.3]*. Updated tax calculations, collection of additional data, clarifications issued by the tax authorities and gaining more experience with the tax legislation before the authorisation of the financial statements should be treated as adjusting events if they pertain to the position at the balance sheet date. Events that are indicative of conditions that arose after the reporting period should be treated as non-adjusting events. Judgement needs to be applied in determining whether technical corrections and regulatory guidance issued after year-end are to be considered adjusting events.

Where the effect of changes in the applicable tax rates compared to the previous accounting period are material, an explanation of those effects is required to be provided in the notes to the financial statements (see 14.1 below). *[IAS 12.81(d)]*.

5.1.3 Changes to tax rates and laws enacted after the reporting date

The requirement for substantive enactment by the end of the reporting period is quite clear in the literature. IAS 10 – *Events after the Reporting Period* – identifies the enactment or announcement of a change in tax rates and laws after the end of the reporting period as an example of a non-adjusting event. *[IAS 10.22(h)]*. For example, an entity with a reporting period ending on 31 December issuing its financial statements on 20 April the following year would measure its tax assets and liabilities by reference to tax rates and laws enacted or substantively enacted as at 31 December even if these had changed significantly before 20 April and even if those changes had retrospective effect. However, in these circumstances the entity would have to disclose the nature of those changes and provide an estimate of the financial effect of those changes if the impact is expected to be significant (see 14.2 below). *[IAS 10.21]*.

5.1.4 Implications of the UK's withdrawal from the EU

On 31 January 2020, the United Kingdom left the European Union (EU) and the Withdrawal Agreement concluded with the EU then came into force. That agreement established a transition period ending on 31 December 2020, during which the laws and regulations of the EU continue to apply in the UK. After that date, the UK will no longer be a part of the EU Single Market or the EU Customs Union and will acquire 'third country' status, the terms of which will be defined in a new arrangement. At the time of writing, this new arrangement has yet to be determined and there are no indications that the transition period will be extended.

Tax legislation in EU member states and other countries contains tax exemptions and tax reliefs (e.g. withholding tax and merger relief) that depend on whether or not one or more of the entities involved are EU domiciled. Once the transition period ends, these exemptions and reliefs may no longer apply to transactions between UK entities and entities in those EU member states and other countries. In those cases, additional tax liabilities may crystallise. For example, from 1 January 2021, some EU member states may start to deduct tax from dividends paid by EU subsidiaries to UK parent companies or from interest and royalty payments made into the UK, both of which used to be exempt. At the time of writing, it is still uncertain whether any of these exemptions and reliefs will continue to apply to the UK when the transition period ends. Unless new arrangements are agreed before the end of the transition period, entities would have to refer to the terms of any double taxation agreement between the relevant jurisdictions to determine what enacted legislation is in place.

Accordingly, the withdrawal process raises uncertainty about how the existing tax legislation in the UK and in other countries will apply after the end of the transition period. It has also raised uncertainty about the future tax status of entities, which may lead to changes in the accounting treatment.

Given the uncertainties on the outcome of negotiations for a new arrangement between the UK and the EU, we believe it is appropriate for entities to continue to apply their current accounting policies, until the position becomes clearer. However, these uncertainties will require additional disclosure in the financial statements of entities reporting in the period leading up to the end of the transition period, to reflect any progress between the parties in defining the terms of the new arrangement between the UK and the EU. IAS 1 requires entities to disclose the significant accounting policies used in preparing the financial statements, including the judgements that management has made in applying those accounting policies that have the most significant effect on the amounts recognised in the financial statements. [IAS 1.122]. IAS 1 also requires entities to disclose information about the assumptions they make about the future, and other major sources of estimation uncertainty at the end of the reporting period, that have a significant risk of resulting in a material adjustment to the carrying amounts of assets and liabilities within the next financial year. [IAS 1.125]. Therefore, entities will need to carefully consider the assumptions and estimates made about the future impact of tax positions and consider whether additional disclosure is needed of the uncertainties arising from UK withdrawal from the EU. An example would be the nature and extent of tax exposures should the status of the entity change.

At the same time, however, the recognition and measurement of current and deferred tax under IAS 12 is governed according to tax rates and laws that are (substantively) enacted as at the end of the reporting period (see 5.1.2 above and 8.1.1 below). [IAS 12.46, 47]. Unless there are earlier changes in enacted tax legislation, the effect of the change in status of the UK, from a member state to a third country, would be recognised in profit or loss for the period, unless those consequences relate to transactions and events that result, in the same or a different period, in a direct credit or charge to the recognised amount of equity or in amounts recognised in other comprehensive income (see 10.9 below). [SIC-25.4]. Therefore, an entity would account for the effects of the UK's change in status in its financial statements for the first period that ends on or after the end of the transition period.

As the negotiations establishing the arrangements that will apply after the transition period reach a conclusion, the uncertainties about tax legislation and the application of IAS 12 will be resolved as each jurisdiction confirms the appropriate tax treatment. Therefore, entities will need to consider the current position at each reporting date and may have to revise the accounting treatment and disclosures that have previously been applied. To the extent that, after the end of the transition period, uncertainties remain as to the effect of (substantively) enacted tax laws and regulations, this would include a requirement to make estimates of the expected outcomes and to measure related tax assets and liabilities in accordance with the requirements of IFRIC 23 (see 9 below). In summary, in our view:

- the effect of existing tax laws applying to entities in a different way as a result of the transition period ending is a change in tax status under SIC-25 and recognised in the financial reporting period in which the transition period ends; and
- the effect of any new legislation introduced as a consequence of the UK's withdrawal from the EU is recognised in the financial reporting period when it is (substantively) enacted, in the usual way (see 5.1.2 above).

Enactment of legislation after the end of the reporting period but before the date of approval of the financial statements is an example of a non-adjusting event, [IAS 10.22(h)], requiring entities to disclose the nature of any changes and provide an estimate of their financial effect if the impact is expected to be significant (see 5.1.3 above and 8.1.2 below). *[IAS 10.21]*.

5.2 Uncertain tax treatments

In recording the 'amount expected to be paid or recovered' as required by IAS 12, the entity will need to have regard to any uncertain tax treatments. 'Uncertain tax treatment' is defined as a tax treatment over which there is uncertainty concerning its acceptance under the law by the relevant taxation authority. For example, an entity's decision not to submit any tax filing in a particular tax jurisdiction or not to include specific income in taxable profit would be an uncertain tax treatment, if its acceptability is unclear under tax law. *[IFRIC 23.3]*. Entities might also have to address uncertainty in applying new tax legislation, especially when it is enacted shortly before the end of the reporting period, as discussed at 5.1.1 above.

Accounting for uncertain tax treatments is a particularly challenging aspect of accounting for tax. The requirements of IFRIC 23, which was issued in June 2017 and is mandatory for annual periods beginning on or after 1 January 2019, are discussed at 9 below.

5.3 'Prior year adjustments' of previously presented tax balances and expense (income)

The determination of the tax liability for all but the most straightforward entities is a complex process. It may be several years after the end of a reporting period before the tax liability for that period is finally agreed with the tax authorities and settled. Therefore, the tax liability initially recorded at the end of the reporting period to which it relates is no more than a best estimate at that time, which will usually require revision in subsequent periods until the liability is finally settled.

Tax practitioners often refer to such revisions as 'prior year adjustments' and regard them as part of the overall tax charge or credit for the current reporting period whatever their nature. However, for financial reporting purposes, the normal provisions of IAS 8 (see Chapter 3) apply to tax balances and the related expense (income). Therefore, the nature of any revision to a previously stated tax balance should be considered to determine whether the revision represents:

- a correction of a material prior period error (in which case it should be accounted for retrospectively, with a restatement of comparative amounts and, where applicable, the opening balance of assets, liabilities and equity at the start of the earliest period presented); *[IAS 8.42]* or

- a refinement in the current period of an estimate made in a previous period (in which case it should be accounted for in the current period). *[IAS 8.36]*.

In some cases the distinction is clear. If, for example, the entity used an incorrect substantively enacted tax rate (see 5.1 above) to calculate the liability in a previous period, the correction of that rate would – subject to materiality – be a prior year adjustment. A more difficult area is the treatment of accounting changes to reflect the resolution of uncertain tax treatments (see 5.2 above). These have in practice almost always been treated as measurement adjustments in the current period. However, a view could be taken that the eventual denial, or acceptance, by the tax authorities of a position taken by the taxpayer indicates that one or other party (or both) were previously misinterpreting the tax law. As with other aspects of accounting for uncertain tax treatments, this is an area where judgement may be required. IFRIC 23 suggests that entities would reassess judgements and estimates in response to a change in facts and circumstances, and that the financial effect would be recognised as a change in estimate under IAS 8, i.e. in the period of change (see 9.5 below). *[IFRIC 23.13, 14].*

5.4 Discounting of current tax assets and liabilities

In some jurisdictions, entities are permitted to settle current tax liabilities on deferred terms. Similarly, refunds of current tax might be receivable more than 12 months after the reporting date. IAS 12 specifically prohibits discounting of deferred tax assets and liabilities. *[IAS 12.53].* However, the Standard is silent on the discounting of current tax assets and liabilities. In June 2004, the Interpretations Committee decided not to add this issue to its agenda, but expressed a general view that current taxes payable should be discounted when the effects are material. However, the Committee also noted a potential conflict with the requirements of IAS 20, which at the time was intended to be withdrawn.[7] This has led to diversity in practice and it remains that entities are permitted, but not required, to discount current tax assets and liabilities. Accordingly, entities need to make an accounting policy choice and apply it consistently to all current taxes in all jurisdictions.

5.5 Intra-period allocation, presentation and disclosure

The allocation of current tax income and expense to components of total comprehensive income and equity is discussed at 10 below. The presentation and disclosure of current tax income expense and assets and liabilities are discussed at 13 and 14 below.

6 DEFERRED TAX – TAX BASES AND TEMPORARY DIFFERENCES

All deferred tax liabilities and many deferred tax assets represent the tax effects of temporary differences. Therefore, the first step in measuring deferred tax is to identify all temporary differences. The discussion below addresses only whether a temporary difference exists. It does not necessarily follow that deferred tax is recognised in respect of that difference, since there are a number of situations, discussed at 7 below, in which IAS 12 prohibits the recognition of deferred tax on a temporary difference.

Temporary differences are differences between the carrying amount of an asset or liability in the statement of financial position and its *tax base*. Temporary differences may be either:

- *taxable temporary differences*, which result in taxable amounts in determining taxable profit (tax loss) of future periods when the carrying amount of the asset or liability is recovered or settled; or
- *deductible temporary differences,* which result in amounts that are deductible in determining taxable profit (tax loss) of future periods when the carrying amount of the asset or liability is recovered or settled.

The *tax base* of an asset or liability is 'the amount attributed to that asset or liability for tax purposes'. *[IAS 12.5]*.

In consolidated financial statements, temporary differences are determined by comparing the carrying amounts of an asset or liability in the consolidated financial statements with the appropriate tax base. The appropriate tax base is determined:

- in those jurisdictions in which a consolidated tax return is filed, by reference to that return; and
- in other jurisdictions, by reference to the tax returns of each entity in the group. *[IAS 12.11]*.

As the definition of tax base is the one on which all the others relating to deferred tax ultimately depend, understanding it is key to a proper interpretation of IAS 12. A more detailed discussion follows at 6.1 and 6.2 below. However, the overall effect of IAS 12 can be summarised as follows:

A *taxable* temporary difference will arise when:

- *The carrying amount of an asset is higher than its tax base*

    For example, an item of PP&E is recorded in the financial statements at €8,000, but has a tax base of only €7,000. In future periods, tax will be paid on €1,000 more profit than will be recognised in the financial statements (since €1,000 of the remaining accounting depreciation is not tax-deductible).

- *The carrying amount of a liability is lower than its tax base*

    For example, a loan payable of €100,000 is recorded in the financial statements at €99,000, net of issue costs of €1,000 which have already been allowed for tax purposes (so that the loan is regarded as having a tax base of €100,000 – see 6.2.1.B below). In future periods, tax will be paid on €1,000 more profit than is recognised in the financial statements (since the €1,000 issue costs will be charged to the income statement but not be eligible for further tax deductions).

Conversely, a *deductible* temporary difference will arise when:

- *The carrying amount of an asset is lower than its tax base*

    For example, an item of PP&E is recorded in the financial statements at €7,000, but has a tax base of €8,000. In future periods, tax will be paid on €1,000 less profit than is recognised in the financial statements (since tax deductions will be claimed in respect of €1,000 more depreciation than is charged to the income statement in those future periods).

- *The carrying amount of a liability is higher than its tax base*

    For example, the financial statements record a liability for unfunded pension costs of €2 million. A tax deduction is available only as cash is paid to settle the liability (so that the liability is regarded as having a tax base of nil – see 6.2.2.A below). In future periods, tax will be paid on €2 million less profit than is recognised in the financial statements (since tax deductions will be claimed in respect of €2 million more expense than is charged to the income statement in those future periods).

This may be summarised in the following table.

Asset/liability	Carrying amount higher or lower than tax base?	Nature of temporary difference	Resulting deferred tax (if recognised)
Asset	Higher	Taxable	Liability
Asset	Lower	Deductible	Asset
Liability	Higher	Deductible	Asset
Liability	Lower	Taxable	Liability

6.1 Tax base

6.1.1 Tax base of assets

The tax base of an asset is the amount that will be deductible for tax purposes against any taxable economic benefits that will flow to an entity when it recovers the carrying amount of the asset. If those economic benefits will not be taxable, the tax base of the asset is equal to its carrying amount. *[IAS 12.7]*.

In some cases the 'tax base' of an asset is relatively obvious. In the case of a tax-deductible item of PP&E, it is the tax-deductible amount of the asset at acquisition less tax depreciation already claimed (see Example 33.1 at 1.2 above). Other items, however, require more careful analysis.

For example, an entity may have accrued interest receivable of €1,000 that will be taxed only on receipt. When the asset is recovered, all the cash received is subject to tax. In other words, the amount deductible for tax on recovery of the asset, and therefore its tax base, is nil. Another way of arriving at the same conclusion might be to consider the amount at which the tax authority would recognise the receivable in notional financial statements for the entity prepared under tax law. At the end of the reporting period the receivable would not be recognised in such notional financial statements, since the interest has not yet been recognised for tax purposes.

Conversely, an entity may have a receivable of €1,000 the recovery of which is not taxable. In this case, the tax base is €1,000 on the rule above that, where realisation of an asset will not be taxable, the tax base of the asset is equal to its carrying amount. This applies irrespective of whether the asset concerned arises from:

- a transaction already recognised in total comprehensive income and already subject to tax on initial recognition (e.g. in most jurisdictions, a sale);
- a transaction already recognised in total comprehensive income and exempt from tax (e.g. tax-free dividend income); or
- a transaction not affecting total comprehensive income at all (e.g. the principal of a loan receivable). *[IAS 12.7]*.

The effect of deeming the tax base of the €1,000 receivable to be equal to its carrying amount will be that the temporary difference associated with it is nil, and that no deferred tax is recognised in respect of it. This is appropriate given that, in the first case, the debtor represents a sale that has already been taxed and, in the second and third cases, the debtors represent items that are outside the scope of tax.

6.1.2 Tax base of liabilities

The tax base of a liability is its carrying amount, less any amount that will be deductible for tax purposes in respect of that liability in future periods. In the case of revenue which is received in advance, the tax base of the resulting liability is its carrying amount, less any amount of the revenue that will not be taxable in future periods. *[IAS 12.8]*.

As in the case of assets, the tax base of some items is relatively obvious. For example, an entity may have recognised a provision for environmental damage of CHF5 million, which will be deductible for tax purposes only on payment. The liability has a tax base of nil. Its carrying amount is CHF5 million, which is also the amount that will be deductible for tax purposes on settlement in future periods. The difference between these two (equal) amounts – the tax base – is nil. Another way of arriving at the same conclusion might be to consider the amount at which the tax authority would recognise the liability in notional financial statements for the entity prepared under tax law. At the end of the reporting period the liability would not be recognised in such notional financial statements, since the expense has not yet been recognised for tax purposes.

Likewise, if the entity records revenue of £1,000 received in advance that was taxed on receipt, its tax base is nil. Under the definition above, the carrying amount is £1,000, none of which is taxable in future periods. The tax base is the difference between the £1,000 carrying amount and the amount not taxed in future periods (£1,000) – i.e. nil.

Again, if we were to consider a notional statement of financial position of the entity drawn up by the tax authorities under tax law, this liability would not be included, since the relevant amount would, in the notional tax financial statements, have already been taken to income.

An entity may have a liability of (say) €1,000 that will attract no tax deduction when it is settled. In this case, the tax base is €1,000 (on the analogy with the rule in 6.1.1 above that where, realisation of an asset will not be taxable, the tax base of the asset is equal to its carrying amount). This applies irrespective of whether the liability concerned arises from:

- a transaction already recognised in total comprehensive income and already subject to a tax deduction on initial recognition (e.g. in most jurisdictions, the cost of goods sold or accrued expenses);
- a transaction already recognised in total comprehensive income and outside the scope of tax (e.g. non tax-deductible fines and penalties); or
- a transaction not affecting total comprehensive income at all (e.g. the principal of a loan payable). *[IAS 12.8]*.

This is appropriate given that, in the first case, the liability represents a cost that has already been deducted for tax purposes and, in the second and third cases, the liabilities represent items that are outside the scope of tax.

6.1.3 Assets and liabilities whose tax base is not immediately apparent

IAS 12 indicates that where the tax base of an asset or liability is not immediately apparent, it is helpful to consider the fundamental principle on which the standard is based: an entity should, with certain limited exceptions, recognise a deferred tax liability (asset) wherever recovery or settlement of the carrying amount of an asset or liability would make future tax payments larger (smaller) than they would be if such recovery or settlement were to have no tax consequences. *[IAS 12.10]*. In other words: provide for the tax that would be payable or receivable if the assets and liabilities in the statement of financial position were to be recovered or settled at book value.

The implication of this is that in the basic 'equation' of IAS 12, i.e.

carrying amount – tax base = temporary difference,

the true unknown is not in fact the temporary difference (as implied by the definitions of tax base and temporary difference) but the tax base (as implied by paragraph 10).

It will be apparent from the more detailed discussion at 6.2 below that this clarification is particularly relevant to determining the tax bases of certain financial liabilities, which often do not fit the general 'formula' of carrying amount less amount deductible on settlement.

6.1.4 Tax base of items not recognised as assets or liabilities in financial statements

Certain items are not recognised as assets or liabilities in financial statements, but may nevertheless have a tax base. Examples may include:

- research costs (which are required to be expensed immediately by IAS 38 – *Intangible Assets* – see Chapter 17);
- the cost of equity-settled share-based payment transactions (which under IFRS 2 – *Share-based Payment* – give rise to an increase in equity and not a liability – see Chapter 34); and
- goodwill deducted from equity under previous IFRS or national GAAP.

Where such items are tax-deductible, their tax base is the difference between their carrying amount (i.e. nil) and the amount deductible in future periods. *[IAS 12.9]*. This may seem somewhat contrary to the definition of tax base, in which it is inherent that, in order for an item to have a tax base, that item must be an asset or liability, whereas none of the items above was ever recognised as an asset.[8] The implicit argument is that all these items were initially (and very briefly) recognised as assets before being immediately written off in full.

Local tax legislation sometimes gives rise to liabilities that have a tax base but no carrying amount. For example, a subsidiary of the reporting entity may receive a tax deduction for a provision that has been recognised in the individual financial statements of that subsidiary prepared under local accounting principles. For the purposes of the entity's consolidated financial statements, however, the provision does not satisfy the recognition requirements of IAS 37. In such situations we consider it appropriate to regard the tax deduction received as giving rise to a deferred tax liability in the consolidated financial statements (by virtue of there being a provision with a tax base but no carrying amount) in addition to the current tax income recorded for the subsidiary.

Similar situations may arise where local tax legislation permits deductions for certain expenditure determined according to tax legislation without reference to any financial statements. Again, in those cases where an equivalent amount of expenditure is likely to be recognised in the financial statements at a later date, we would regard it as appropriate to regard the tax deduction received as giving rise to a deferred tax liability in the consolidated financial statements.

6.1.5 Equity items with a tax base

The definition of 'tax base' refers to the tax base of an 'asset or liability'. This begs the question of whether IAS 12 regards equity items as having a tax base and therefore whether deferred tax can be recognised in respect of equity instruments (since deferred tax is the tax relating to temporary differences which, by definition, can only arise on items with a tax base – see above).

In February 2003 the Interpretations Committee considered this issue. It drew attention to the IASB's proposal at that time to amend the definition of 'tax base' so as to refer not only to assets and liabilities but also equity instruments as supporting the view that deferred tax should be recognised where appropriate on equity instruments. This was effectively the approach proposed in the exposure draft ED/2009/2 (see 1.3 above).[9]

An alternative analysis might be that equity items do not have a tax base, but that any tax effects of them are to be treated as items that are not recognised as assets or liabilities but nevertheless have a tax base (see 6.1.4 above).

Given the lack of explicit guidance in the current version of IAS 12 either analysis may be acceptable, provided that it is applied consistently. This is reflected in a number of the examples in the remainder of this Chapter.

6.1.6 Items with more than one tax base

Some assets and liabilities have more than one tax base, depending on the manner in which they are realised or settled. These are discussed further at 8.4 below.

6.1.7 Tax bases disclaimed or with no economic value

In some situations an entity may choose not to claim an available deduction for an item as part of an overall tax planning strategy. In other cases, a deduction available as a matter of tax law may have no real economic effect – for example because the deduction will increase a pool of brought forward tax losses which the entity does not expect to recover in the foreseeable future.

In our view, the fact that the entity chooses not to take advantage of a potential tax deduction, or that such a deduction would have no real economic effect in the foreseeable future, does not mean that the asset to which the deduction relates has no tax base. While such considerations will be relevant to determining whether a deductible temporary difference gives rise to a recoverable deferred tax asset (see 7.4 below), the tax base of an asset is determined by reference to the amount attributed to the item by tax law. *[IAS 12.5]*.

6.2 Examples of temporary differences

The following are examples of taxable temporary differences, deductible temporary differences and items where the tax base and carrying value are the same so that there is no temporary difference. They are mostly based on those given in IAS 12, *[IAS 12.17-20, 26, IE.A-C]*, but include several others that are encountered in practice. It will be seen that a number of categories of assets and liabilities may give rise to either taxable or deductible temporary differences.

A temporary difference will not always result in a deferred tax asset or liability being recorded under IAS 12, since the difference may be subject to other provisions of the standard restricting the recognition of deferred tax assets and liabilities, which are discussed at 7 below. Moreover, even where deferred tax is recognised, it does not necessarily create tax income or expense, but may instead give rise to additional goodwill or bargain purchase gain in a business combination, or to a movement in equity.

6.2.1 Taxable temporary differences

6.2.1.A Transactions that affect profit or loss

- *Interest received in arrears*

    An entity with a financial year ending on 31 December 2021 holds a medium-term cash deposit on which interest of €10,000 is received annually on 31 March. The interest is taxed in the year of receipt. At 31 December 2021, the entity recognises a receivable of €7,000 in respect of interest accrued but not yet received. The receivable has a tax base of nil, since its recovery has tax consequences and no tax deductions are available in respect of it. The temporary difference associated with the receivable is €7,000 (€7,000 carrying amount less nil tax base).

- *Sale of goods taxed on a cash basis*

    An entity has recorded revenue from the sale of goods of €40,000, together with a cost of the goods sold of €35,000, since the goods have been delivered. However, the transaction is taxed in the following financial year when the cash from the sale is collected.

    The entity will have recognised a receivable of €40,000 for the sale. The receivable has a tax base of nil, since its recovery has tax consequences and no tax deductions are available in respect of it. The temporary difference associated with the receivable is €40,000 (€40,000 carrying amount less nil tax base).

    There is also a deductible temporary difference of €35,000 associated with the (now derecognised) inventory, which has a carrying amount of zero but a tax base of €35,000 (since it will attract a tax deduction of €35,000 when the sale is taxed) – see 6.2.2.A below.

- *Depreciation of an asset accelerated for tax purposes*

    An entity has an item of PP&E whose cost is fully tax deductible, but with deductions being given over a period shorter than the period over which the asset is being depreciated under IAS 16 – *Property, Plant and Equipment*. At the reporting date, the asset has been depreciated to £500,000 for financial reporting purposes but to £300,000 for tax purposes.

    Recovery of the PP&E has tax consequences since, although there is no deduction for accounting depreciation in the tax return, the PP&E is recovered through future taxable profits. There is a taxable temporary difference of £200,000 between the carrying value of the asset (£500,000) and its tax base (£300,000).

- *Capitalised development costs already deducted for tax*

    An entity incurred development costs of $1 million during the year ended 31 December 2021. The costs were fully deductible for tax purposes in the tax return for that period, but were recognised as an intangible asset under IAS 38 in the financial statements. The amount carried forward at 31 December 2021 is $800,000.

Recovery of the intangible asset through use has tax consequences since, although there is no deduction for accounting amortisation in the tax return, the asset is recovered through future profits which will be taxed. There is a taxable temporary difference of $800,000 between the carrying value of the asset ($800,000) and its tax base (nil). Although the expenditure to create the asset is tax-deductible in the current period, its tax base is the amount deductible in future periods, which is nil, since all deductions were made in the tax return for 2021.

A similar analysis would apply to prepaid expenses that have already been deducted on a cash basis in determining the taxable profit of the current or previous periods.

6.2.1.B Transactions that affect the statement of financial position

- *Non-deductible and partially deductible assets*

    An entity acquires a building for €1 million. Any accounting depreciation of the building is not deductible for tax purposes, and no deduction will be available for tax purposes when the asset is sold or scrapped.

    Recovery of the building, whether in use or on sale, nevertheless has tax consequences since the building is recovered through future taxable profits of €1 million. There is a taxable temporary difference of €1 million between the carrying value of the asset (€1 million) and its tax base of zero.

    A similar analysis applies to an asset which, when acquired, is deductible for tax purposes, but for an amount lower than its cost. The difference between the cost and the amount deductible for tax purposes is a taxable temporary difference.

- *Deductible loan transaction costs*

    A borrowing entity records a loan at £9.5 million, being the proceeds received of £10 million (which equal the amount due at maturity), less transaction costs of £500,000, which are deducted for tax purposes in the period when the loan was first recognised. For loans carried at amortised cost, IFRS 9 requires the costs, together with interest and similar payments, to be accrued over the period to maturity using the effective interest method.

    Inception of the loan gives rise to a taxable temporary difference of £500,000, being the difference between the carrying amount of the loan (£9.5 million) and its tax base (£10 million). This tax base does not conform to the general definition of the tax base of a liability – i.e. the carrying amount, less any amount that will be deductible for tax purposes in respect of that liability in future periods (see 6.1.2 above).

    The easiest way to derive the correct tax base is to construct a notional statement of financial position prepared by the tax authorities according to tax law. This would show a liability for the full £10 million (since the amortisation of the issue costs that has yet to occur in the financial statements has already occurred in the notional tax authority financial statements). This indicates that the tax base of the loan is £10 million.

    A far simpler analysis for the purposes of IAS 12 might have been that the £9.5 million carrying amount comprises a loan of £10 million (with a tax base of £10 million, giving rise to temporary difference of zero) offset by prepaid transaction costs of £500,000 (with a tax base of zero, giving rise to a taxable temporary difference of £500,000). However, this is inconsistent with the analysis in IFRS 9 that the issue costs are an integral part of the carrying value of the loan.

The consequence of recognising a deferred tax liability in this case is that the tax deduction for the transaction costs is recognised in profit or loss, not on inception of the loan, but as the costs are recognised through the effective interest method in future periods.

- *Non-deductible loan transaction costs*

    As in the immediately preceding example, a borrowing entity records a loan at £9.5 million, being the proceeds received of £10 million (which equal the amount due at maturity), less transaction costs of £500,000. In this case, however, the transaction costs are not deductible in determining the taxable profit of future, current or prior periods. For loans carried at amortised cost, IFRS 9 requires the costs to be accrued over the period to maturity using the effective interest method.

    Just as in the preceding example (and perhaps rather counter-intuitively, given that the costs are non-deductible) inception of the loan gives rise to a taxable temporary difference of £500,000, being the difference between the carrying amount of the loan (£9.5 million) and its tax base (£10 million). This is because a notional statement of financial position prepared by the tax authorities according to tax law would show a liability for the full £10 million, since the transaction costs would never have been recorded (as they never occurred for tax purposes).

- *Liability component of compound financial instrument*

    An entity issues a convertible bond for €5 million which, in accordance with the requirements of IAS 32 – *Financial Instruments: Presentation*, is analysed as comprising a liability component of €4.6 million and a residual equity component of €400,000. If the entity were to settle the liability for €4.6 million it would be liable to tax on €400,000 (€5 million less €4.6 million). Therefore, the tax base of the liability is €5 million and there is a taxable temporary difference of €400,000 between this and the carrying amount of the liability component. This is discussed further at 7.2.8 below.

6.2.1.C   Revaluations

- *Financial assets and property carried at valuation*

    An entity holds investments, accounted for at fair value through profit or loss, with a carrying amount of CHF2 million and an original cost (and tax base) of CHF1.3 million. There is a taxable temporary difference of CHF700,000 associated with the investments, being the amount on which the entity would pay tax if the investments were realised at their carrying value.

    A similar analysis would apply to investment property or PP&E carried at a value that exceeds cost, where no equivalent adjustment is made for tax purposes.

6.2.1.D   Tax re-basing

- *Withdrawal of tax depreciation for classes of PP&E*

    An entity holds buildings with a carrying amount of £15 million and a tax base of £12 million, giving rise to a taxable temporary difference of £3 million. As part of a general fiscal reform package introduced by the government, future tax deductions for the buildings (their tax base) are reduced to £1 million. This increases the taxable temporary difference by £11 million to £14 million.

6.2.1.E Business combinations and consolidation

- *Fair value adjustments*

  Where the carrying amount of an asset is increased to fair value in a business combination, but no equivalent adjustment is made for tax purposes, a taxable temporary difference arises just as on the revaluation of an asset (see 6.2.1.C above).

- *Non-deductible or partially-deductible goodwill*

  Where goodwill is not deductible, or only partially deductible, in determining taxable profit there will be a taxable temporary difference between the carrying amount of the goodwill and its tax base, similar to that arising on a non-deductible or partially-deductible asset (see 6.2.1.B above).

- *Intragroup transactions*

  Although intragroup transactions are eliminated in consolidated financial statements, they may give rise to temporary differences. An entity in a group (A) might sell inventory with a cost and tax base of £1,000 to another group entity (B) for £900, which becomes the cost and tax base to B. If the carrying value in the consolidated financial statements remains £1,000 (i.e. the inventory is not actually impaired, notwithstanding the intragroup sale at a loss), a new taxable temporary difference of £100 emerges in the consolidated financial statements between the carrying value of £1,000 and the new tax base of £900.

- *Undistributed earnings of group investments*

  A parent entity P holds an investment in subsidiary S. Retained earnings of $1 million relating to S are included in the consolidated financial statements of P. S must pay a non-refundable withholding tax on any distribution of earnings to P. There is therefore a taxable temporary difference in the consolidated financial statements of $1 million associated with the net assets representing the retained earnings, since their recovery (in the form of distribution to the parent) has tax consequences, with no offsetting tax deductions.

  Similar temporary differences may arise on the retained earnings of branches, associates and joint arrangements.

6.2.1.F Foreign currency differences

- *Translation of foreign subsidiary to presentation currency*

  A UK entity acquires the equity of a French entity, which therefore becomes its subsidiary, for €10 million. For UK tax purposes, the tax base of the investment is £8 million (the spot-rate equivalent of €10 million at the date of acquisition). The presentation currency of the UK entity's consolidated financial statements is sterling.

  Between the date of acquisition and the first reporting date, the French entity makes no gains or losses, such that its net assets and goodwill as included in the consolidated financial statements, expressed in euros, remain €10 million. However, the exchange rate has moved, so that the sterling equivalent of

€10 million at the reporting date, included in the consolidated statement of financial position, is £9 million.

This gives rise to a £1 million taxable temporary difference between the £9 million carrying value of the investment and its £8 million tax base.

- *Functional currency different from currency used to compute tax*

    On 1 January 2021 an entity which, under IAS 21 – *The Effects of Changes in Foreign Exchange Rates*, has determined its functional currency as US dollars (see Chapter 15), purchases plant for $1 million, which will be depreciated to its estimated residual value of zero over 10 years. The entity is taxed in the local currency LC, and is entitled to receive tax deductions for the depreciation charged in the financial statements. The exchange rate is $1=LC2 at 1 January 2021 (so that the cost of the asset for local tax purposes is LC2 million). The exchange rate at 31 December 2021 is $1=LC2.5.

    At 31 December 2021 there is a taxable temporary difference of $180,000, being the difference between the net book value of the plant of $900,000 (cost $1,000,000 less depreciation $100,000) and its tax base of $720,000 (cost LC2,000,000 less depreciation LC200,000 = LC1,800,000 translated at year end rate of $1=LC2.5).

6.2.1.G   Hyperinflation

A taxable temporary difference (similar to those in 6.2.1.F above) arises when non-monetary assets are restated in terms of the measuring unit current at the end of the reporting period under IAS 29 – *Financial Reporting in Hyperinflationary Economies* – but no equivalent adjustment is made for tax purposes.

6.2.2   Deductible temporary differences

6.2.2.A   Transactions that affect profit of loss

- *Expenses deductible for tax on cash basis*

    An entity records a liability of €1 million for retirement benefit costs which are tax deductible only when paid. The tax base of the liability is zero, being its carrying amount (€1 million) less the amount deductible for tax purposes when the liability is settled (also €1 million). There is therefore a deductible temporary difference of €1 million (€1 million carrying amount less zero tax base) associated with the liability.

- *Depreciation of an asset delayed for tax purposes*

    An entity has an item of PP&E that originally cost £1 million. The cost is fully tax deductible, with deductions being given over a period longer than the period over which the asset is being depreciated under IAS 16. At the reporting date, the asset has been depreciated to £300,000 for financial reporting purposes but to only £500,000 for tax purposes.

    Recovery of the PP&E has tax consequences since, although there is no deduction for accounting depreciation in the tax return, the PP&E is recovered through future taxable profits of £300,000. There is a deductible temporary difference of £200,000 between the carrying value of the asset (£300,000) and its tax base (£500,000).

- *Sale of goods taxed on a cash basis*

  An entity has recorded revenue from the sale of goods of €40,000, together with a cost of the goods sold of €35,000, since the goods have been delivered. However, the transaction is taxed in the following financial year when the cash from the sale is collected.

  There is a deductible temporary difference of €35,000 associated with the (now derecognised) inventory, which has a carrying amount of zero but a tax base of €35,000 (since it will attract a tax deduction of €35,000 when the sale is taxed).

  There is also a taxable temporary difference of €40,000 associated with the receivable (see 6.2.1.A above).

- *Write-down of asset not deductible for tax purposes until realised*

  An entity purchases inventory for $1,000, which is also its tax base. The inventory is later written down to a net realisable value of $800. However, no loss is recognised for tax purposes until the inventory is sold. There is a deductible temporary difference of $200 between the $800 carrying amount of the inventory and its $1,000 tax base.

- *Deferred income taxed on receipt*

  In the year ended 31 December 2021, an entity received €2 million, being 5 years' rent of an investment property received in advance. In the statement of financial position as at 31 December, €1,800,000 is carried forward as deferred income. However, the whole €2 million is taxed in the tax return for the period.

  There is a deductible temporary difference of €1,800,000 associated with the deferred income, being its carrying amount (€1,800,000), less its tax base of zero, computed as the carrying amount (€1,800,000) less the amount not taxable in future periods (also €1,800,000 since the income has already been taxed).

- *Deferred non-taxable income*

  An entity receives a non-taxable government grant of £1 million, of which £700,000 is carried forward in the statement of financial position as at the period end.

  There is a deductible temporary difference of £700,000 associated with the deferred income, being its carrying amount (£700,000), less its tax base of zero, computed as the carrying amount (£700,000) less the amount of income not taxable in future periods (also £700,000 since the income is tax free). In this case, while there is a deductible temporary difference, no deferred tax asset would be recognised, as discussed in Example 33.10 at 7.2.3. *[IAS 12.24, 33]*.

6.2.2.B   Transactions that affect the statement of financial position

- *Asset deductible for more than cost*

  An entity invests NOK10 million in PP&E for which tax deductions of NOK13 million may be claimed. There is a deductible temporary difference of NOK3 million between the NOK10 million carrying value of the PP&E and its tax base of NOK13 million.

6.2.2.C Revaluations

- *Financial assets and property carried at valuation*

    An entity holds investments, accounted for at fair value through profit or loss, with a carrying amount of CHF2 million and an original cost (and tax base) of CHF2.5 million. There is a deductible temporary difference of CHF500,000 associated with the investments, being the amount for which the entity would receive a tax deduction if the investments were realised at their carrying value.

    A similar analysis would apply to investment property or PP&E carried at a value below cost, where no equivalent adjustment is made for tax purposes.

6.2.2.D Tax re-basing

- *Indexation of assets for tax purposes*

    An entity acquires land for $5 million, which is also its tax base at the date of purchase. A year later, as part of a general fiscal reform package introduced by the government, future tax deductions for the land (its tax base) are increased to $6 million. This creates a deductible temporary difference of $1 million in respect of the land.

6.2.2.E Business combinations and consolidation

- *Fair value adjustments*

    Where a liability is recognised at fair value in a business combination, but the liability is deductible for tax purposes only on settlement, a deductible temporary difference arises similar to that arising on the initial recognition of a liability for an expense deductible for tax on a cash basis (see 6.2.2.A above).

- *Intragroup transactions*

    Although intragroup transactions are eliminated in consolidated financial statements, they may give rise to deductible temporary differences. An entity in a group (A) might sell inventory with a cost and tax base of £1,000 to another group entity (B) for £1,200, which becomes the cost and tax base to B. Since the carrying value in the consolidated financial statements remains £1,000, a new deductible temporary difference of £200 emerges in the consolidated financial statements between the carrying value of £1,000 and the new tax base of £1,200.

6.2.2.F Foreign currency differences

- *Translation of foreign subsidiary to presentation currency*

    A UK entity acquires the equity of a French entity, which therefore becomes its subsidiary, for €10 million. For UK tax purposes, the tax base of the investment is £8 million (the spot-rate equivalent of €10 million at the date of acquisition). The presentation currency of the UK entity's consolidated financial statements is sterling.

Between the date of acquisition and the first reporting date, the French entity makes no gains or losses, such that its net assets and goodwill as included in the consolidated financial statements, expressed in euros, remain €10 million. However, the exchange rate has moved, so that the sterling equivalent of €10 million at the reporting date, included in the consolidated statement of financial position, is £7 million.

This gives rise to a £1 million deductible temporary difference between the £7 million carrying value of the investment and its £8 million tax base.

- *Functional currency different from currency used to compute tax*

    On 1 January 2021 an entity which, under IAS 21 has determined its functional currency as US dollars (see Chapter 15), purchases plant for $1 million, which will be depreciated to its estimated residual value of zero over 10 years. The entity is taxed in the local currency LC, and is entitled to receive tax deductions for the depreciation charged in the financial statements. The exchange rate is $1=LC2 at 1 January 2021 (so that the cost of the asset for local tax purposes is LC2 million). The exchange rate at 31 December 2021 is $1=LC1.8.

    At 31 December 2021 there is a deductible temporary difference of $100,000, being the difference between the net book value of the plant of $900,000 (cost $1,000,000 less depreciation $100,000) and its tax base of $1,000,000 (cost LC2,000,000 less depreciation LC200,000 = LC1,800,000 translated at year end rate of $1=LC1.8).

6.2.3 Assets and liabilities with no temporary difference (because tax base equals carrying amount)

- *Liability for expense already deducted for tax*

    An entity accrues £200,000 for electricity costs in the year ended 31 March 2021. The expense is deductible for tax in that period. The temporary difference associated with the liability is zero. This is calculated as the carrying amount of £200,000 less the tax base of £200,000, being the carrying amount (£200,000) less amount deductible for tax in future periods (zero).

- *Liability for expense never deductible for tax*

    An entity accrues €400,000 for a fine for environmental pollution, which is not deductible for tax. The temporary difference associated with the liability is zero. This is calculated as the carrying amount of €400,000 less the tax base of €400,000, being the carrying amount (€400,000) less amount deductible for tax in future periods (zero).

- *Loan repayable at carrying amount*

    An entity borrows $2 million. This is the carrying amount of the loan on initial recognition, which is the same as the amount repayable on final maturity of the loan. The temporary difference associated with the liability is zero. This is calculated as the carrying amount of $2 million less the tax base of $2 million, being the carrying amount ($2 million) less amount deductible for tax in future periods (zero).

- *Receivable for non-taxable income*

    In its separate financial statements, an entity records a receivable for a £1 million dividend due from a subsidiary accounted for at cost. The dividend is not taxable. Accordingly, it gives rise to a temporary difference of zero, since the tax base of any asset, the recovery of the carrying amount of which is not taxable, is taken to be the same as its carrying amount.

7 DEFERRED TAX – RECOGNITION

7.1 The basic principles

7.1.1 Taxable temporary differences (deferred tax liabilities)

IAS 12 requires a deferred tax liability to be recognised in respect of all taxable temporary differences except those arising from:
- the initial recognition of goodwill; or
- the initial recognition of an asset or liability in a transaction that:
    - is not a business combination; and
    - at the time of the transaction, affects neither accounting profit nor taxable profit (tax loss).

These exceptions to the recognition principles do not apply to taxable temporary differences associated with investments in subsidiaries, branches and associates, and interests in joint arrangements, which are subject to further detailed provisions of IAS 12 (see 7.5 below). *[IAS 12.15]*.

Examples of taxable temporary differences are given in 6.2.1 above.

7.1.2 Deductible temporary differences (deferred tax assets)

IAS 12 requires a deferred tax asset to be recognised in respect of all deductible temporary differences to the extent that it is probable that taxable profit will be available against which the deductible temporary difference will be utilised except those arising from the initial recognition of an asset or liability in a transaction that:
- is not a business combination; and
- at the time of the transaction, affects neither accounting profit nor taxable profit (tax loss). *[IAS 12.24]*.

IAS 12 does not define 'probable' in this context. However, it is generally understood that, for example in IFRS 5 – *Non-current Assets Held for Sale and Discontinued Operations* – and IAS 37, it should be taken to mean 'more likely than not'. *[IFRS 5 Appendix A, IAS 37.23]*. The exposure draft ED/2009/2 (see 1.3 above) effectively clarified that this is the intended meaning.[10]

These exceptions to the recognition principles do not apply to deductible temporary differences associated with investments in subsidiaries, branches and associates, and interests in joint arrangements, which are subject to further detailed provisions of IAS 12 (see 7.5 below).

As noted above, IAS 12 restricts the recognition of deferred tax assets to the extent that it is probable that taxable profit will be available against which the underlying deductible temporary differences can be utilised. *[IAS 12.24, 27]*. This restriction is discussed at 7.4 below.

Examples of deductible temporary differences are given at 6.2.2 above.

7.1.3 Interpretation issues

7.1.3.A Accounting profit

The provisions of IAS 12 summarised above refer to a transaction that affects 'accounting profit'. In this context 'accounting profit' means any item recognised in total comprehensive income, whether recognised in profit or loss or in other comprehensive income.

7.1.3.B Taxable profit 'at the time of the transaction'

The provisions of IAS 12 summarised above also refer to a transaction which affects taxable profit 'at the time of the transaction'. Strictly speaking, no transaction affects taxable profit 'at the time of the transaction', since the taxable profit is affected only when the relevant item is included (some time later) in the tax return for the period. It is clear, however, that the intended meaning is that the transaction that gives rise to the initial recognition of the relevant asset or liability affects the current tax liability for the accounting period in which the initial recognition occurs.

Suppose that, in the year ended 31 December 2020, an entity received €2 million, being 5 years' prepaid rent of an investment property. In the statement of financial position as at 31 December, €1,800,000 is carried forward as deferred income. The whole €2 million is taxed on receipt and will therefore be included in the tax return for the period, which is not filed until 2021.

It could be argued that, in a literal legal sense, the transaction 'affects taxable profit' only in 2021. For the purposes of IAS 12, however, the transaction is regarded as affecting taxable profit during 2020 (since it affects the current tax for that period). This gives rise to the recognition, subject to the restrictions discussed at 7.4 below, of a deferred tax asset based on a deductible temporary difference of €1,800,000 (see 6.2.2.A above).

7.2 The initial recognition exception

The exceptions (summarised at 7.1 above) from recognising the deferred tax effects of certain temporary differences arising on the initial recognition of some assets and liabilities are generally referred to as the 'initial recognition exception' or 'initial recognition exemption', sometimes abbreviated to 'IRE'. 'Exception' is the more accurate description, since a reporting entity is required to apply it, rather than having the option to do so implicit in the term 'exemption'.

The initial recognition exception has its origins in the now superseded 'income statement' approaches to accounting for deferred tax. Under these approaches, deferred tax was not recognised on so-called 'permanent differences' – items of income or expense that appeared in either the financial statements or the tax return, but not in both. The majority of transactions to which the initial recognition exception applies would have been regarded as permanent differences under income statement approaches of accounting for deferred tax. For entities applying the temporary difference approach of IAS 12, the IRE avoids the need for entities to recognise an initial deferred tax liability or asset and adjust the carrying amount of the asset or liability by the same amount. The Standard argues that such adjustments would make the financial statements less transparent. Therefore, IAS 12 does not allow an entity to recognise the resulting deferred tax liability or asset, either on initial recognition or subsequently. *[IAS 12.22(c)]*. It would also be inappropriate to recognise any adjustment as a gain or loss in profit or loss, given that the transaction itself has no effect on profit or loss.

The purpose of the initial recognition exception is most easily understood by considering the accounting consequences that would follow if it did not exist, as illustrated in Example 33.5 below.

Example 33.5: Rationale for initial recognition exception

An entity acquires an asset for €1,000 which it intends to use for five years and then scrap (i.e. the residual value is nil). The tax rate is 40%. Depreciation of the asset is not deductible for tax purposes. On disposal, any capital gain would not be taxable and any capital loss would not be deductible.

Although the asset is non-deductible, its recovery has tax consequences, since it will be recovered out of taxable income of €1,000 on which tax of €400 will be paid. The tax base of the asset is therefore zero, and a temporary difference of €1,000 arises on initial recognition of the asset.

Absent the initial recognition exception, the entity would recognise a deferred tax liability of €400 on initial recognition of the asset, being the taxable temporary difference of €1,000 multiplied by the tax rate of 40%. A debit entry would then be required to balance the credit for the liability.

One possibility might be to recognise tax expense of €400 in the statement of total comprehensive income. This would be meaningless, since the entity has clearly not suffered a loss simply by purchasing a non-deductible asset in an arm's length transaction for a price that (economically) must reflect the asset's non-deductibility.

A second possibility would be to gross up the asset by €400 to €1,400. However, IAS 12 states that to make such adjustments to the carrying value of the asset would make the financial statements 'less transparent'. *[IAS 12.22(c)]*.

A third possibility (broadly the guidance provided under US GAAP) would be to gross up the asset to the amount that would rationally have been paid for it, had it been fully tax-deductible, and recognise a corresponding amount of deferred tax. As the asset is non-deductible, the €1,000 cost must theoretically represent the anticipated minimum *post*-tax return from the asset. In order to achieve a post-tax return of €1,000, an entity paying tax at 40% needs to earn pre-tax profits of €1,667 (€1,000 ÷ [1 − 0.4]). Therefore, the cost of an equivalent fully-deductible asset would, all else being equal, be €1,667. On this analysis, the entity would gross up the asset to €1,667 and recognise deferred tax of €667 (€1,667 @ 40%).

The fourth possibility, which is what is actually required by IAS 12, is not to provide for deferred tax at all, where to do so would lead to one of the three outcomes above. However, in cases where provision for the deferred tax on a temporary difference arising on initial recognition of an asset or liability would not lead to one of the outcomes above, the initial recognition exception does not apply. This is the case in a business combination or a transaction affecting taxable profit or accounting profit (or both).

- *Business combination*

    In a business combination, the corresponding accounting entry for a deferred tax asset or liability forms part of the goodwill arising or the bargain purchase gain recognised. No deferred tax income or expense is recorded.

- *Transaction affecting taxable profit or accounting profit*

    In a transaction affecting taxable profit or accounting profit (or both), the corresponding accounting entry for a deferred tax asset or liability is recorded as deferred tax income or expense.

    This ensures that the entity recognises all future tax consequences of recovering the assets, or settling the liabilities, recognised in the transaction. The effect of this on the statement of total comprehensive income is broadly to recognise the tax effects of the various components of income and expenditure in the same period(s) in which those items are recognised for financial reporting purposes (as illustrated at 1.2.2 above).

In short, the initial recognition exception may simply be seen as the least bad of the four theoretically possible options for dealing with 'day one' temporary differences.

7.2.1 Acquisition of tax losses

The initial recognition exception applies only to deferred tax relating to temporary differences. It does not apply to tax assets, such as purchased tax losses, that do not arise from deductible temporary differences. The definition of 'deferred tax assets' (see 3 above) explicitly distinguishes between deductible temporary differences and unused losses and tax credits. *[IAS 12.5]*. There is therefore no restriction on the recognition of acquired tax losses other than the general criteria of IAS 12 for recognition of tax assets (see 7.4 below).

Under the general principles of IAS 12, acquired tax losses are initially recognised at the amount paid, subsequently re-assessed for recoverability (see 7.4.6 below) and re-measured accordingly (see 8 below). Changes in the recognised amount of acquired tax losses are generally recognised in profit or loss, on the basis that, as acquired losses, they do not relate to any pre-tax transaction previously accounted for by the entity (see 10 below). However, in some limited circumstances, changes to tax losses acquired as part of a business combination are required to be treated as an adjustment to goodwill (see 12.1.2 below).

7.2.2 Initial recognition of goodwill

7.2.2.A Taxable temporary differences

In many jurisdictions, goodwill is not tax-deductible either as it is impaired or on ultimate disposal, such that it gives rise to a temporary difference equal to its carrying amount (representing its carrying amount less its tax base of zero).

It may well be that the shares in the acquired entity have a tax base equal to their cost so that, economically, an amount equal to the goodwill is deductible on disposal of those shares. However, accounting for the tax effects of the shares in an acquired subsidiary (or other significant group investment) is subject to separate provisions of IAS 12, which are discussed at 7.5 below.

The initial recognition exception for taxable temporary differences on goodwill prevents the grossing-up of goodwill that would otherwise occur. Goodwill is a function of all the net assets of the acquired business, including deferred tax. If deferred tax is provided for on goodwill, the goodwill itself is increased, which means that the deferred tax on the goodwill is increased further, which means that the goodwill increases again, and so on. Equilibrium is reached when the amount of goodwill originally recorded is grossed up by the fraction $1/(1 - t)$, where t is the entity's tax rate, expressed as a decimal fraction. For example, an entity that pays tax at 30% and recognises CU1,400 of goodwill before recognising deferred tax would (absent the initial recognition exception) increase the goodwill to CU2,000 and recognise a deferred tax liability of CU600 (which is 30% of the restated goodwill of CU2,000).

IAS 12 takes the view that this would not be appropriate, since goodwill is intended to be a residual arising after fair values have been determined for the assets and liabilities acquired in a business combination, and recognition of deferred tax liability would increase that goodwill. *[IAS 12.21]*. Subsequent reductions in a deferred tax liability that is unrecognised because it arises from the initial recognition of goodwill are also regarded as arising from the initial recognition of goodwill and are therefore not recognised. *[IAS 12.21A]*. This is illustrated in Example 33.11 at 7.2.4.A below.

7.2.2.B   Deductible temporary differences

Where the carrying amount of goodwill arising in a business combination is less than its tax base, a deductible temporary difference arises. In this case, IAS 12 requires a deferred tax asset to be recognised as part of the accounting for a business combination, to the extent that it is probable that taxable profit will be available against which the temporary difference could be utilised. *[IAS 12.32A]*. This contrasts with the prohibition against recognising a deferred tax liability on any taxable temporary difference on initial recognition of goodwill (see 7.2.2.A above). A more general discussion of the criteria in IAS 12 for assessing the recoverability of deferred tax assets may be found at 7.4 below.

IAS 12 gives no guidance on the method to be used in calculating the resulting deferred tax asset, which is not entirely straightforward, as illustrated by the following example.

Example 33.6:   Deferred tax asset on initial recognition of goodwill

An entity that pays tax at 40% recognises, in the initial accounting for a business combination, goodwill of €1,000 before recognising any related deferred tax asset. Tax deductions of €1,250 are given for the goodwill over a 5-year period.

One approach would be to adopt an iterative method similar to that described at 7.2.2.A above, whereby recognition of a deferred tax asset on goodwill leads to a reduction of the goodwill, which in turn will lead to a further increase in the deferred tax asset, and so on. Equilibrium is reached when the goodwill is adjusted to an amount equal to $(g - bt) / (1 - t)$, where:

- g is the amount of goodwill originally recorded (before recognising a deferred tax asset);
- b is the tax base of the goodwill; and
- t is the tax rate, expressed as a decimal fraction.

Under this method, the entity would record goodwill of €833 (being [€1,000 − 0.4 × €1,250] ÷ 0.6) and a deferred tax asset of €167. This represents a deductible temporary difference of €417 (comprising the tax base of €1,250 less the adjusted carrying amount of €833), multiplied by the tax rate of 40%. On any subsequent impairment or disposal of the goodwill, the entity would report an effective tax rate of 40% (the statutory rate), comprised of pre-tax expense of €833 and tax income of €333 (the real tax deduction of €500 (€1,250 @ 40%), less the write-off of the deferred tax asset of €167).

An alternative approach might be to record a deferred tax asset based on the carrying amount of goodwill before calculating the deferred tax asset, and adjust the goodwill only once, rather than undertaking the iterative reduction in the goodwill described in the previous paragraph. In the example above this would lead to the entity recording a deferred tax asset of €100 (representing 40% of the deductible temporary difference of €250 between the tax base of the goodwill of €1,250 and its original carrying amount of €1,000) and goodwill of €900. On any subsequent impairment or disposal of the goodwill the entity would report an effective tax rate of 44% (higher than the statutory rate), comprised of pre-tax expense of €900 and tax income of €400 (the real tax deduction of €500 (€1,250 @ 40%), less the write-off of the deferred tax asset of €100).

7.2.2.C Tax deductible goodwill

Where goodwill is tax-deductible, new temporary differences will arise after its initial recognition as a result of the interaction between tax deductions claimed and impairments (if any) of the goodwill in the financial statements. These temporary differences do not relate to the initial recognition of goodwill, and therefore deferred tax should be recognised on them, as illustrated by Example 33.17 at 7.2.4.C below. *[IAS 12.21B].*

7.2.3 Initial recognition of other assets or liabilities

Where a temporary difference arises on initial recognition of an asset or liability, its treatment depends on the circumstances which give rise to the recognition of the asset or liability.

If the temporary difference arises as the result of a business combination, deferred tax is recognised on the temporary difference with a corresponding adjustment to goodwill or any bargain purchase gain.

If the temporary difference arises in a transaction that gives rise to an accounting or taxable profit or loss, deferred tax is recognised on the temporary difference, giving rise to deferred tax expense or deferred tax income.

If the temporary difference arises in any other circumstances (i.e. neither in a business combination nor in a transaction that gives rise to an accounting or taxable profit or loss) no deferred tax is recognised. *[IAS 12.22]*.

The application of the initial recognition exception to assets and liabilities is illustrated in Examples 33.7 to 33.10 below.

Example 33.7:   Non-deductible PP&E

An entity acquires a building for €1 million. Any accounting depreciation of the building is not deductible for tax purposes, and no deduction will be available for tax purposes when the asset is sold or demolished.

Recovery of the building, whether in use or on sale, has tax consequences since the building is recovered through future taxable profits. There is a taxable temporary difference of €1 million between the €1 million carrying value of the asset and its tax base of zero.

Under the initial recognition exception, no deferred tax liability is provided for. The non-deductibility of the asset is reflected in an effective tax rate higher than the statutory rate (assuming that all other components of pre-tax profit are taxed at the statutory rate) as the asset is depreciated in future periods.

If the asset had been acquired as part of a business combination, the initial recognition exception would not have applied. Deferred tax of would have been provided for, with a corresponding increase in goodwill. As the asset is depreciated, the reduction in the deferred tax liability is released to deferred tax in the income statement, as illustrated in Example 33.1 above. This results in an effective tax rate equal to the statutory rate (assuming that all other components of pre-tax profit are taxed at the statutory rate).

Example 33.8:   Inception of loan with tax-deductible issue costs

A borrowing entity records a loan at £9.5 million, being the proceeds received of £10 million (which equal the amount due at maturity), less transaction costs of £500,000, which are deducted for tax purposes in the period when the loan is first recognised. For financial reporting purposes, under IFRS 9 the costs, together with interest and similar payments, are accrued over the period to maturity using the effective interest method.

Inception of the loan gives rise to a taxable temporary difference of £500,000, being the difference between the carrying amount of the loan (£9.5 million) and its tax base (£10 million). This analysis is explained in more detail at 6.2.1.B above.

Initial recognition of the transaction costs gives rise to no accounting loss (because they are included in the carrying amount of the loan). However, there is a tax loss (since the costs are included in the tax return for the period of inception). Accordingly, the initial recognition exception does not apply, and a deferred tax liability is recognised on the taxable temporary difference of £500,000.

Example 33.9:   Inception of loan with non-deductible issue costs

A borrowing entity records a loan at £9.5 million, being the proceeds received of £10 million (which equal the amount due at maturity), less transaction costs of £500,000, which are not deductible for tax purposes either in the period when the loan is first recognised or subsequently. For financial reporting purposes, under IFRS 9 the costs, together with interest and similar payments, are accrued over the period to maturity using the effective interest method.

Inception of the loan gives rise to a taxable temporary difference of £500,000, being the difference between the carrying amount of the loan (£9.5 million) and its tax base (£10 million). This analysis is explained in more detail at 6.2.1.B above.

Initial recognition of the transaction costs gives rise to no accounting loss (because they are included in the carrying amount of the loan) or tax loss (because in this case there is no deduction for the issue costs). Accordingly, the initial recognition exception applies and no deferred tax liability is recognised.

If the same loan (including the unamortised transaction costs) had been recognised as part of a larger business combination, the initial recognition exception would not have applied. Deferred tax would have been recognised on the taxable temporary difference of £500,000, with a corresponding increase in goodwill (or decrease in any bargain purchase gain).

Example 33.10: Purchase of PP&E subject to tax-free government grant

An entity acquires an item of PP&E for €1 million subject to a tax-free government grant of €350,000. The asset is also fully-tax deductible (at €1 million). IAS 20 permits the grant to be accounted for either as deferred income or by deduction from the cost of the asset. Whichever treatment is followed, a deductible temporary difference arises:

- If the grant is accounted for as deferred income, there is a deductible temporary difference between the liability of €350,000 and its tax base of nil (carrying amount €350,000 less amount not taxed in future periods, also €350,000).
- If the grant is accounted for as a reduction in the cost of the PP&E, there is a deductible temporary difference between the carrying amount of the PP&E (€650,000) and its tax base (€1 million).

IAS 12 emphasises that the initial recognition exception applies, and no deferred tax asset should be recognised. *[IAS 12.33]*.

7.2.4 Changes to temporary differences after initial recognition

The initial recognition exception applies only to temporary differences arising on initial recognition of an asset or liability. It does not apply to new temporary differences that arise on the same asset or liability after initial recognition. When the exception has been applied to the temporary difference arising on initial recognition of an asset or liability, and there is a different temporary difference associated with that asset or liability at a subsequent date, it is necessary to analyse the temporary difference at that date between:

- any amount relating to the original temporary difference (on which no deferred tax is recognised); and
- the remainder, which has implicitly arisen after initial recognition of the asset or liability (on which deferred tax is recognised).

IAS 12 does not set out comprehensive guidance to be followed in making this analysis, but it does give a number of examples, from which the following general principles may be inferred:

- the new temporary difference is treated as part of the temporary difference arising on initial recognition to the extent that any change from the original temporary difference is due to:
  - the write-down (through depreciation, amortisation or impairment) of the original carrying amount of an asset with no corresponding change in the tax base (see 7.2.4.A below); or
  - the increase in the original carrying amount of a liability arising from the amortisation of any discount recognised at the time of initial recognition of that liability, with no corresponding change in the tax base (see 7.2.4.A below);
- the new temporary difference is regarded as arising after initial recognition to the extent that any change from the original temporary difference is due to:
  - a change in the carrying value of the asset or liability, other than for the reasons set out above (see 7.2.4.B below); or
  - a change in the tax base due to items being recorded on the tax return (see 7.2.4.C below); and
- where the change in the temporary difference results from a change in the tax base due to legislative change, IAS 12 provides no specific guidance, and more than one treatment may be possible (see 7.2.4.D below).

7.2.4.A Depreciation, amortisation or impairment of initial carrying value

The following are examples of transactions where the initial temporary difference changes as the result of the amortisation of the original carrying amount, so that the adjusted temporary difference is regarded as part of the temporary difference arising on initial recognition, rather than a new difference.

Example 33.11: Impairment of non-deductible goodwill

Goodwill of £10 million (not tax-deductible) arose on a business combination in 2008. In accordance with IAS 12 no deferred tax liability was recognised on the taxable temporary difference of £10 million that arose on initial recognition of the goodwill. During the year ended 31 December 2021, following an impairment test, the carrying amount of the goodwill is reduced to £6 million.

No deferred tax is recognised on the new temporary difference of £6 million, because it has the effect of decreasing the value of the previously unrecognised deferred tax liability relating to the initial recognition of the goodwill. *[IAS 12.21A]*.

Example 33.12: Depreciation of non-deductible PP&E

During the year ended 31 March 2021 an entity acquires an item of PP&E for €1 million which it intends to use for 20 years, with no anticipated residual value. No tax deductions are available for the asset. In accordance with IAS 12 no deferred tax liability was recognised on the taxable temporary difference of €1 million that arises on initial recognition of the PP&E.

The entity's accounting policy is to charge a full year's depreciation in the year of purchase, so that the carrying amount of the asset at 31 March 2021 is €950,000. No deferred tax is recognised on the reduction to the temporary difference of €50,000, because IAS 12 prohibits the recognition of subsequent changes in the unrecognised deferred tax liability that arose on the initial recognition of the PP&E as the asset is depreciated. *[IAS 12.22(c)]*.

Example 33.13: Amortisation of non-deductible loan issue costs

A borrowing entity records a loan at £9.5 million, being the proceeds received of £10 million (which equal the amount due at maturity), less transaction costs of £500,000, which are not deductible for tax purposes either in the period when the loan is first recognised or subsequently. For financial reporting purposes, under IFRS 9 the costs, together with interest and similar payments, are accrued over the period to maturity using the effective interest method.

Inception of the loan gives rise to a taxable temporary difference of £500,000, being the difference between the carrying amount of the loan (£9.5 million) and its tax base (£10 million). This analysis is explained in more detail at 6.2.1.B above.

In accordance with IAS 12, no deferred tax liability was recognised on the taxable temporary difference of £10 million that arose on initial recognition of the loan.

One year later, the carrying amount of the loan is £9.7 million, comprising the proceeds received of £10 million (which equal the amount due at maturity), less unamortised transaction costs of £300,000. This gives rise to a current temporary difference of £300,000. No deferred tax is recognised on the current temporary difference, because it is part of the temporary difference arising on the initial recognition of the loan.

7.2.4.B Change in carrying value due to revaluation

As illustrated in Example 33.7 at 7.2.3 above, a temporary difference arises when a non tax-deductible asset is acquired. Where the asset is acquired separately (i.e. not as part of a larger business combination) in circumstances giving rise to neither an accounting nor a taxable profit or loss, no deferred tax liability is recognised for that temporary difference.

If such an asset is subsequently revalued, however, deferred tax is recognised on the new temporary difference arising as a result of the revaluation, since this does not arise on initial recognition of the asset, as illustrated in Examples 33.14 and 33.15.

Example 33.14: Revaluation of non-deductible and non-depreciable asset

On 1 January 2021 an entity paying tax at 30% acquires a non tax-deductible office building for €1,000,000 in circumstances in which IAS 12 prohibits recognition of the deferred tax liability associated with the temporary difference of €1,000,000.

Application of IAS 16 results in no depreciation being charged on the building.

On 1 January 2021 the entity revalues the building to €1,200,000. The temporary difference associated with the building is now €1,200,000, only €1,000,000 of which arose on initial recognition. Accordingly, the entity recognises a deferred tax liability based on the remaining temporary difference of €200,000 giving deferred tax expense at 30% of €60,000. This tax expense would be recognised in other comprehensive income (see 10 below).

Example 33.15: Revaluation of non-deductible and depreciable asset

On 1 January 2020 an entity paying tax at 30% acquires a non tax-deductible office building for €100,000 in circumstances in which IAS 12 prohibits recognition of the deferred tax liability associated with the temporary difference of €100,000. The building is depreciated over 10 years at €10,000 per year to a residual value of zero. The entity's financial year ends on 31 December.

At 1 January 2021, the carrying amount of the building is €90,000, and it is revalued upwards by €45,000 to its current market value of €135,000. As there is no change to the estimated residual value of zero, or to the life of the building, this will be depreciated over the next 9 years at €15,000 per year.

Following the revaluation, the temporary difference associated with the building is €135,000. Of this amount, only €90,000 arose on initial recognition, since €10,000 of the original temporary difference of €100,000 arising on initial recognition of the asset has been eliminated through depreciation of the asset (see 7.2.4.A above). The carrying amount (which equals the temporary difference, since the tax base is zero) and depreciation during the year ended 31 December 2021 and thereafter may then be analysed as follows.

Year	Carrying amount a	Tax base b	Gross temporary difference c (=a-b)	Unrecognised temporary difference[1] d	Recognised temporary difference e (=c-d)	Deferred tax liability e @ 30%
0	100,000	–	100,000	100,000	–	–
1	90,000	–	90,000	90,000	–	–
Reval	135,000	–	135,000	90,000	45,000	13,500
2	120,000	–	120,000	80,000	40,000	12,000
3	105,000	–	105,000	70,000	35,000	10,500
4	90,000	–	90,000	60,000	30,000	9,000
5	75,000	–	75,000	50,000	25,000	7,500
6	60,000	–	60,000	40,000	20,000	6,000
7	45,000	–	45,000	30,000	15,000	4,500
8	30,000	–	30,000	20,000	10,000	3,000
9	15,000	–	15,000	10,000	5,000	1,500
10	–	–	–	–	–	–

1   The depreciation is allocated *pro rata* to the cost element and revalued element of the total carrying amount.

On 1 January 2022 the entity recognises a deferred tax liability based on the temporary difference of €45,000 arising on the revaluation (i.e. after initial recognition) giving a deferred tax expense of €13,500 (€45,000 @ 30%), recognised in other comprehensive income (see 10 below). This has the result that the effective tax rate shown in the financial statements for the revaluation is 30% (€45,000 gain with deferred tax expense of €13,500).

As can be seen from the table above, as at 31 December 2022 (year 2), €40,000 of the total temporary difference arose after initial recognition. The entity therefore provides for deferred tax of €12,000 (€40,000 @ 30%), and a deferred tax credit of €1,500 (the reduction in the liability from €13,500 to €12,000) is recognised in profit or loss.

The deferred tax credit can be explained as the tax effect at 30% of the additional €5,000 depreciation relating to the revalued element of the building (see table above).

7.2.4.C   Change in tax base due to deductions in tax return

The following are examples of transactions where a new temporary difference emerges after initial recognition as the result of claiming tax deductions.

Example 33.16:   Tax deduction for land

An entity that pays tax at 35% acquires land with a fair value of €5 million. Tax deductions of €100,000 per year may be claimed for the land for the next 30 years (i.e. the tax base of the land is €3 million). In accordance with IAS 12, no deferred tax liability is recognised on the taxable temporary difference of €2 million that arises on initial recognition of the land.

In the period in which the land is acquired, the entity claims the first €100,000 annual tax deduction, and the original cost of the land is not depreciated or impaired. The taxable temporary difference at the end of the period is therefore €2.1 million (cost €5.0 million less tax base €2.9 million). Of this, €2 million arose on initial recognition and no deferred tax is recognised on this. However, the remaining €100,000 of the gross temporary difference arose after initial recognition. Accordingly the entity recognises a deferred tax liability of €35,000 (€100,000 @ 35%).

In subsequent years, the deferred tax liability is increased for the new temporary differences arising as a result of changes to the tax base as a result of claiming tax deductions, as illustrated in the following table:

Year	Carrying amount a	Tax base b	Gross temporary difference c (=a-b)	Unrecognised temporary difference d	Recognised temporary difference e (=c-d)	Deferred tax liability e @ 35%
0	5,000,000	3,000,000	2,000,000	2,000,000	–	–
1	5,000,000	2,900,000	2,100,000	2,000,000	100,000	35,000
2	5,000,000	2,800,000	2,200,000	2,000,000	200,000	70,000
3	5,000,000	2,700,000	2,300,000	2,000,000	300,000	105,000
4	5,000,000	2,600,000	2,400,000	2,000,000	400,000	140,000
5	5,000,000	2,500,000	2,500,000	2,000,000	500,000	175,000

The analysis if the land had later been impaired would be rather more complicated. The general issue of the treatment of assets that are tax-deductible, but for less than their cost, is discussed at 7.2.6 below.

Example 33.17:   Tax-deductible goodwill

On 1 January 2021 an entity with a tax rate of 35% acquires goodwill in a business combination with a cost of €1 million, which is deductible for tax purposes at a rate of 20% per year, starting in the year of acquisition.

During 2021 the entity claims the full 20% tax deduction and writes off €120,000 of the goodwill as the result of an impairment test. Thus, at the end of 2021 the goodwill has a carrying amount of €880,000 and a tax base of €800,000. This gives rise to a taxable temporary difference of €80,000 that does not relate to the initial recognition of goodwill, and accordingly the entity recognises a deferred tax liability at 35% of €28,000.

If, during 2021, there had been no impairment of the goodwill, but the full tax deduction had nevertheless been claimed, at the end of the year the entity would have had goodwill with a carrying amount of €1 million and a tax base of €800,000. This would have given rise to a taxable temporary difference of €200,000 that does not relate to the initial recognition of goodwill, and accordingly the entity would have recognised a deferred tax liability at 35% of €70,000.

7.2.4.D Temporary difference altered by legislative change

Any change to the basis on which an item is treated for tax purposes alters the tax base of the item concerned. For example, if the government decides that an item of PP&E that was previously tax-deductible is no longer eligible for tax deductions, the tax base of the PP&E is reduced to zero. Under IAS 12, any change in tax base normally results in an immediate adjustment of any associated deferred tax asset or liability, and the recognition of a corresponding amount of deferred tax income or expense.

However, where such an adjustment to the tax base occurs in respect of an asset or liability for which no deferred tax has previously been recognised because of the initial recognition exception, the treatment required by IAS 12 is not entirely clear. The issue is illustrated by Example 33.18 below.

Example 33.18: **Asset non-deductible at date of acquisition later becomes deductible**

At the beginning of the year ended 31 March 2021, an entity acquired an item of PP&E for €1 million which it intends to use for 20 years, with no anticipated residual value. No tax deductions were available for the asset. In accordance with IAS 12 no deferred tax liability was recognised on the taxable temporary difference of €1 million that arose on initial recognition of the PP&E. Then standard rate of income tax is 20%.

During the year ended 31 March 2022, the government announces that it will allow the cost of such assets to be deducted in arriving at taxable profit. The deductions will be allowed in equal annual instalments over a 10-year period. As at 31 March 2022, the carrying amount of the asset and its tax base are both €900,000. The carrying amount is the original cost of €1 million less two years' depreciation at €50,000 per year. The tax base is the original cost of €1 million less one year's tax deduction at €100,000 per year.

Prima facie, therefore, there is now no temporary difference associated with the asset, because its carrying amount and tax base are equal. However, the treatment illustrated in Examples 33.16 and 33.17 above would lead to the conclusion that this net temporary difference of nil should be analysed into:

- an original taxable temporary difference of €900,000 arising on initial recognition of the asset (being the €1 million difference arising on initial recognition less the €100,000 depreciation charged); and
- a new deductible temporary difference of €900,000 arising after initial recognition (representing the fact that, since initial recognition, the government increased the tax base by €1 million which has been reduced to €900,000 by the €100,000 tax deduction claimed in the current period).

This approach would indicate that no deferred tax liability should be recognised on the original taxable temporary difference (since this arose on initial recognition), but a deferred tax asset should be recognised on the new deductible temporary difference of €900,000 identified above, subject to confirming that there are sufficient future taxable profits available against which those deductions are expected to be utilised. The effect is illustrated as follows:

End of Year	Carrying amount a	Tax base b	Net temporary difference c (=a-b)	Unrecognised temporary difference d	Recognised temporary difference e (=c-d)	Deferred tax liability/(asset) e @ 20%
Acquisition	1,000,000	–	1,000,000	1,000,000	–	–
2021	950,000	–	950,000	950,000	–	–
2022	900,000	900,000	–	900,000	(900,000)	(180,000)
2023	850,000	800,000	50,000	850,000	(800,000)	(160,000)
2024	800,000	700,000	100,000	800,000	(700,000)	(140,000)
2025	750,000	600,000	150,000	750,000	(600,000)	(120,000)

An alternative approach would be that there is now no temporary difference as the granting of the tax base by the government simply eliminates a previously unrecognised assessable temporary difference, arguing:

- the change in tax law does not give rise to a 'new' temporary difference as would be the case for a revaluation of the asset (which is accompanied by the recognition of a gain in the financial statements) or a claim for tax deductions (which attracts a reduction to the tax charge for the period). Instead, the effect of the change in legislation is to reduce the original taxable temporary difference that arose on initial recognition of the asset. Such a reduction in the original temporary difference would not be recognised under IAS 12; *[IAS 12.21A]* and
- to account for only the deferred tax asset is effectively recognising a gain on the elimination of an income tax liability that was never previously recognised.

As far as the income tax charge or credit in profit or loss is concerned, the difference between the two approaches is one of timing. Where the overall temporary difference of zero is 'bifurcated' into an amount arising on initial recognition and an amount arising later, the change in legislation reduces income tax expense and the effective tax rate in the year of change. In the case where the net temporary difference of zero is considered as a whole, the reduction in income tax expense and the effective tax rate is recognised prospectively over the remaining life of the asset as those tax deductions are realised.

In our view, in the absence of specific guidance in the standard, either approach is acceptable, provided that it is applied consistently.

7.2.5 Intragroup transfers of assets with no change in tax base

In many tax jurisdictions the tax deductions for an asset are generally related to the cost of that asset to the legal entity that owns it. However, in some jurisdictions, where an asset is transferred between members of the same group within that jurisdiction, the tax base remains unchanged, irrespective of the consideration paid.

Therefore, where the consideration paid for an asset in such a case differs from its tax base, a temporary difference arises in the acquiring entity's separate financial statements on transfer of the asset. The initial recognition exception applies to any such temporary difference. A further complication can arise when the acquiring entity acquires an asset that is deductible for tax purposes, but for an amount different from its cost. The treatment of such assets in the context of the initial recognition exception is discussed more generally at 7.2.6 below.

In the consolidated financial statements of any parent of the buying entity, however, there is no change to the amount of deferred tax recognised provided that the tax rate of the buying and selling entity is the same. Where the tax rate differs, the deferred tax will be remeasured using the buying entity's tax rate.

Where an asset is transferred between group entities and the tax base of the asset changes as a result of the transaction, there will be deferred tax income or expense in the consolidated financial statements. This is discussed further at 8.7 below.

7.2.6 Partially deductible and super-deductible assets

In many tax jurisdictions the tax deductions for an asset are generally based on the cost of that asset to the legal entity that owns it. However, in some jurisdictions, certain categories of asset are deductible for tax but for an amount either less than the cost of the asset ('partially deductible') or more than the cost of the asset ('super-deductible').

IAS 12 provides no specific guidance on the treatment of partially deductible and super-deductible assets acquired in a transaction to which the initial recognition exception applies. The issues raised by such assets are illustrated in Examples 33.19 and 33.20 below.

Example 33.19: Partially deductible asset

An entity acquires an asset with a cost of €100,000 and a tax base of €60,000 in a transaction where IAS 12 prohibits recognition of deferred tax on the taxable temporary difference of €40,000 arising on initial recognition of the asset. The asset is depreciated to a residual value of zero over 10 years and qualifies for tax deductions of 20% per year over 5 years. The temporary differences associated with the asset over its life will therefore be as follows.

Year	Carrying amount €	Tax base €	Temporary difference €
0	100,000	60,000	40,000
1	90,000	48,000	42,000
2	80,000	36,000	44,000
3	70,000	24,000	46,000
4	60,000	12,000	48,000
5	50,000	–	50,000
6	40,000	–	40,000
7	30,000	–	30,000
8	20,000	–	20,000
9	10,000	–	10,000
10	–	–	–

These differences are clearly a function both of:

- the €40,000 temporary difference arising on initial recognition relating to the non-deductible element of the asset; and
- the emergence of temporary differences arising from the claiming of tax deductions for the €60,000 deductible element in advance of its depreciation.

Whilst IAS 12 does not explicitly mandate the treatment to be followed here, the general requirement to distinguish between these elements of the gross temporary difference (see 7.2.4 above) suggests the following approach.

On initial recognition, the entity should pro-rate the total carrying amount of the asset into a 60% deductible element and a 40% non-deductible element. The taxable temporary difference on the non-deductible element is not recognised (under the initial recognition exception). The 60% deductible element has a tax base equal to its carrying amount, such that there is no temporary difference for the deductible element on initial recognition. In subsequent periods, the entity would provide for deferred tax only on the temporary difference that subsequently emerges between the 60% deductible element and its tax base. On this basis, the temporary differences would be calculated as follows:

Year	Carrying amount a	40% non-deductible element b (40% of a)	60% deductible element c (60% of a)	Tax base d	Temporary difference c – d
0	100,000	40,000	60,000	60,000	–
1	90,000	36,000	54,000	48,000	6,000
2	80,000	32,000	48,000	36,000	12,000
3	70,000	28,000	42,000	24,000	18,000
4	60,000	24,000	36,000	12,000	24,000
5	50,000	20,000	30,000	–	30,000
6	40,000	16,000	24,000	–	24,000
7	30,000	12,000	18,000	–	18,000
8	20,000	8,000	12,000	–	12,000
9	10,000	4,000	6,000	–	6,000
10	–	–	–	–	–

Assuming that the entity pays tax at 30%, the amounts recorded for this transaction during year 1 (assuming that there are sufficient other taxable profits to absorb the tax loss created) would be as follows:

	€
Depreciation of asset	(10,000)
Current tax income[1]	3,600
Deferred tax charge[2]	(1,800)
Net tax credit	1,800
Post tax depreciation	(8,200)

[1] €100,000 [cost of asset] × 60% [deductible element] × 20% [tax depreciation rate] × 30% [tax rate]
[2] €6,000 [temporary difference] × 30% [tax rate] – brought forward balance [nil]

If this calculation is repeated for all 10 years, the following would be reported in the financial statements.

Year	Depreciation a	Current tax credit b	Deferred tax (charge)/ credit c	Total tax credit d (=b+c)	Effective tax rate e (=d/a)
1	(10,000)	3,600	(1,800)	1,800	18%
2	(10,000)	3,600	(1,800)	1,800	18%
3	(10,000)	3,600	(1,800)	1,800	18%
4	(10,000)	3,600	(1,800)	1,800	18%
5	(10,000)	3,600	(1,800)	1,800	18%
6	(10,000)	–	1,800	1,800	18%
7	(10,000)	–	1,800	1,800	18%
8	(10,000)	–	1,800	1,800	18%
9	(10,000)	–	1,800	1,800	18%
10	(10,000)	–	1,800	1,800	18%

This methodology has the result that the effective tax rate in each period corresponds to the effective tax rate for the transaction as a whole – i.e. cost of €100,000 attracting total tax deductions of €18,000 (€60,000 at 30%), an overall rate of 18%.

However, this approach cannot be said to be required by IAS 12 and other methodologies could well be appropriate, provided that they are applied consistently in similar circumstances.

Example 33.20: Super-deductible asset

The converse situation to that in Example 33.19 exists in some jurisdictions which seek to encourage certain types of investment by giving tax allowances for an amount in excess of the expenditure actually incurred. Suppose that an entity invests $1,000,000 in PP&E with a tax base of $1,200,000 in circumstances where IAS 12 prohibits recognition of deferred tax on the deductible temporary difference of $200,000 arising on initial recognition of the asset. The asset is depreciated to a residual value of zero over 10 years and qualifies for five annual tax deductions of 20% of its deemed tax cost of $1,200,000.

The approach adopted in Example 33.19 considered the deductible and non-deductible elements separately and recognised deferred tax on the temporary difference between the deductible element and its tax base. If a similar approach is applied, on initial recognition the entity would split the carrying amount of the asset into a 'cost' element and a 'super deduction' element, and recognise deferred tax on only the temporary difference between the 'cost' element and its tax base. Based on the fact pattern above the temporary differences associated with the 'super-deductible' asset would arise as follows.

Year	Book value a	Tax base b	'Super deduction' element c (=2/12 of b)	Cost element d (=10/12 of b)	Temporary difference a – d
0	1,000,000	1,200,000	200,000	1,000,000	–
1	900,000	960,000	160,000	800,000	100,000
2	800,000	720,000	120,000	600,000	200,000
3	700,000	480,000	80,000	400,000	300,000
4	600,000	240,000	40,000	200,000	400,000
5	500,000	–	–	–	500,000
6	400,000	–	–	–	400,000
7	300,000	–	–	–	300,000
8	200,000	–	–	–	200,000
9	100,000	–	–	–	100,000
10	–	–	–	–	–

Assuming that the entity pays tax at 30%, the amounts recognised for this transaction during year 1 (assuming that there are sufficient other taxable profits to absorb the tax loss created) are as follows:

	$
Depreciation of asset	(100,000)
Current tax income[1]	72,000
Deferred tax charge[2]	(30,000)
Net tax credit	42,000
Profit after tax	(58,000)

[1] $1,200,000 [deemed tax cost of asset] × 20% [tax depreciation rate] × 30% [tax rate]
[2] $100,000 [temporary difference] × 30% [tax rate] – brought forward balance [nil]

If this calculation is repeated for all 10 years, the following would be recognised in the financial statements.

Year	Depreciation a	Current tax credit b	Deferred tax (charge)/ credit c	Total tax credit d (=b+c)	Effective tax rate e (=d/a)
1	(100,000)	72,000	(30,000)	42,000	42%
2	(100,000)	72,000	(30,000)	42,000	42%
3	(100,000)	72,000	(30,000)	42,000	42%
4	(100,000)	72,000	(30,000)	42,000	42%
5	(100,000)	72,000	(30,000)	42,000	42%
6	(100,000)	–	30,000	30,000	30%
7	(100,000)	–	30,000	30,000	30%
8	(100,000)	–	30,000	30,000	30%
9	(100,000)	–	30,000	30,000	30%
10	(100,000)	–	30,000	30,000	30%

This accounting results in an effective 42% tax rate for this transaction being reported in years 1 to 5, and a rate of 30% in years 6 to 10, in contrast to the true effective rate of 36% for the transaction as a whole – i.e. cost of $1,000,000 attracting total tax deductions of $360,000 ($1,200,000 at 30%). This is because, whilst in the case of a partially deductible asset as in Example 33.19 above there is an accounting mechanism (i.e. depreciation) for allocating the non-deductible cost on a straight-line basis, in the case of a super-deductible asset there is no ready mechanism for spreading the additional $60,000 tax deductions on a straight-line basis.

In specific cases, the additional tax deductions might have sufficient characteristics of a government grant (e.g. if it were subject to conditions more onerous that those normally associated with tax deductions in the jurisdiction concerned) to allow application of the principles of IAS 20 which results in the allocation of the additional tax deductions over the life of the asset (see 4.4 above). However, such circumstances are rare.

Again, as in Example 33.19 above, no single approach can be said to be required by IAS 12 and other methodologies could well be appropriate, provided that they are applied consistently in similar circumstances.

7.2.7 Transactions involving the initial recognition of an asset and liability

As noted at 7.2 above, the initial recognition exception is essentially a pragmatic remedy to avoid accounting problems that would arise without it, particularly in transactions where one asset is exchanged for another (such as the acquisition of PP&E for cash).

However, experience has shown that the exception creates new difficulties of its own. In particular, it does not deal adequately with transactions involving the initial recognition of an equal and opposite asset and liability which subsequently unwind on different bases. Examples of such transactions include:

- recording a liability for decommissioning costs, for which the corresponding debit entry is an increase in PP&E (see 7.2.7.A below); and
- the commencement of a lease by a lessee, which involves the recording of an asset and a corresponding liability (see 7.2.7.B below).

In these circumstances there are three alternative approaches seen in practice:

(i) apply the initial recognition exception. Recognise nothing in respect of temporary differences arising at the time the asset and liability are first recognised. No deferred tax arises for any changes in those initial temporary differences;

(ii) recognise deferred tax on initial recognition – consider the asset and the liability separately. The entity recognises a deferred tax liability for any taxable temporary differences related to the asset component and a deferred tax asset for any deductible temporary differences related to the liability component. On initial recognition, the taxable temporary difference and the deductible temporary differences are equal and offset to zero. Deferred tax is recognised on subsequent changes to the taxable and deductible temporary differences; or

(iii) recognise deferred tax on initial recognition – consider the asset and the liability as in-substance linked to each other. Consider any temporary differences on a net basis and recognise deferred tax on that net amount. In this approach, the non-deductible asset and the tax-deductible liability are regarded as being economically the same as a tax-deductible asset that is acquired on deferred terms (where the repayment of the loan does not normally give rise to tax). On this basis, the net carrying value of the asset and liability is zero on initial recognition, as is the tax base. There is therefore no temporary difference and the initial recognition exception does not apply. Deferred tax is recognised on subsequent temporary differences that arise when the net asset or liability changes from zero.

These three approaches are illustrated in Example 33.21 below.

As can be seen below, applying the initial recognition exception results in significant fluctuations in effective tax rates reported in the periods over which the related asset is depreciated and the finance cost on the liability is recognised. In addition, it fails to reflect the economic reality that all expenditure is ultimately expected to be eligible for tax deductions at the standard tax rate. Indeed, it could be argued that the result of applying the initial recognition exception in these circumstances makes the financial statements less transparent, contrary to the stated reason in IAS 12 for requiring the exception to be applied. *[IAS 12.22(c)]*.

It has been argued that the Initial Recognition Exception (IRE) does not apply as paragraphs 15 and 24 of IAS 12 refer to the recognition of 'an asset or liability', but do not explicitly consider the simultaneous recognition of 'an asset and a liability'. Arguably a more informative result is achieved when the initial recognition exception is disregarded, as in the second and third approaches set out above. Both of these approaches eliminate the volatility in the reported effective tax rate, as demonstrated by Approach 2 and Approach 3 in Example 33.21 below. All three approaches give a result that is consistent with the implied intention of the initial recognition exception (that the reporting entity should provide for deferred tax on initial recognition unless to do so would create an immediate net tax expense or credit in the statement of comprehensive income).

As noted at 7.2.7.B below, in June 2018 the Interpretations Committee acknowledged the three approaches currently applied in the circumstances noted above and decided to recommend that the Board should develop a narrow-scope amendment to IAS 12.[11] In July 2019, the Board issued its Exposure Draft, ED/2019/5 – *Deferred Tax related to Assets and Liabilities arising from a Single Transaction: Proposed amendments to IAS 12*. The proposed amendments would require an entity to recognise deferred tax on initial recognition of particular transactions to the extent that the transaction gives rise to equal amounts of deferred tax assets and liabilities. The proposed amendments would apply to particular transactions for which an entity recognises both an asset and a liability, such as leases and decommissioning obligations.[12] The comment period for the Exposure Draft ended in November 2019. The Board discussed feedback on the Exposure Draft in April 2020. It made no decisions and will consider the project's direction at a future meeting.[13] As at the time of writing, these deliberations are expected to take place before the end of 2020.[14]

Notwithstanding that this recommendation could result in an approach that is similar to the second treatment above being required, we believe that any of the approaches described above continue to be acceptable until such an amendment is issued by the Board in its final form.

7.2.7.A Decommissioning costs

When an entity recognises a liability for decommissioning costs and the related asset is measured using the cost model, it adds to the carrying amount of the related item of PP&E an amount equal to the liability recognised. *[IAS 16.16(c), IFRIC 1.5]*. In many jurisdictions, no tax deduction is given in respect of this decommissioning component of the carrying value of the PP&E asset. However, payments made for decommissioning expenses are deductible for tax purposes. The effects of applying the three approaches in this situation are illustrated in Example 33.21 below.

Example 33.21: Asset and liability giving rise to equal temporary differences on initial recognition

On 1 January 2021 an entity paying tax at 40% recognises a provision for the clean-up costs of a mine that will require expenditure of €10 million at the end of 2025. A tax deduction for the expenditure will be given when it is incurred (i.e. as a reduction in the current tax liability for 2025).

In accordance with IAS 37, this provision is discounted (at a rate of 6%) to €7.5m, giving rise to the following accounting entry (see Chapter 26 at 6.3):

	€m	€m
PP&E	7.5	
Provision for clean-up costs		7.5

Under local tax legislation, no deductions are available for depreciation of the decommissioning component of the PP&E asset. However, payments made for decommissioning expenses are deductible for tax and capable of being carried forward or carried back against taxable profits.

On initial recognition, the tax base of the decommissioning component added to the carrying value of PP&E is nil, since no deductions are available and the €7.5 million carrying value of the asset is recovered through future taxable profits. The tax base of the provision is also nil (carrying amount of €7.5 million, less the amount deductible in future periods, also €7.5 million). Although deductions of €10 million are expected to be received in 2025 when the decommissioning costs are incurred, the tax base is determined by reference to the consequences of the liability being settled at its carrying amount of €7.5 million, which would result in a tax deduction of only €7.5 million.

There is therefore a taxable temporary difference of €7.5 million associated with the decommissioning component of the PP&E asset and a deductible temporary difference of the same amount associated with the provision.

Over the next five years, an expense of €10 million (equivalent to the ultimate cash spend) will be recognised in profit or loss, comprising depreciation of the €7.5 million decommissioning component of PP&E and accretion of €2.5 million finance costs on the provision. Given that this €10 million is fully tax-deductible, the entity expects to be entitled to a €4 million reduction in its current tax liability when the obligation for decommissioning costs is settled.

Approach 1: Apply the initial recognition exception

The initial recognition exception in IAS 12 would prohibit recognition of deferred tax on both the taxable temporary difference related to the decommissioning component of the asset and the deductible temporary difference on the decommissioning liability. Under the general approach of IAS 12 summarised at 7.2.4 above, the depreciation of the decommissioning component of PP&E is regarded as reducing the temporary difference that arose on initial recognition of the asset, and therefore gives rise to no tax effect. However, the accretion of €2.5 million finance costs on the provision gives rise to an additional deductible temporary difference arising after initial recognition of the liability, requiring recognition of a deferred tax asset (assuming that the general recognition criteria for assets are met – see 7.4 below). This gives rise to the following overall accounting entries for the year ended 31 December 2021.

	€m	€m
2021		
Depreciation (€7.5m ÷ 5)	1.50	
PP&E – decommissioning asset		1.50
Finance cost (€7.5m × 6%)	0.45	
Provision for clean-up costs		0.45
Deferred tax (statement of financial position)	0.18	
Deferred tax (profit or loss) (40% × €0.45m)		0.18

If equivalent entries are made for the following periods, the following amounts will be included in subsequent income statements (all figures in € millions):

	2021	2022	2023	2024	2025	Total
Depreciation	1.50	1.50	1.50	1.50	1.50	7.50
Finance costs	0.45	0.47	0.50	0.53	0.55	2.50
Cost before tax	1.95	1.97	2.00	2.03	2.05	10.00
Current tax (income)					(4.00)	(4.00)
Deferred tax (income)/charge[1]	(0.18)	(0.19)	(0.20)	(0.21)	0.78	–
Cost after tax	1.77	1.78	1.80	1.82	(1.17)	6.00
Effective tax rate	9.2%	9.6%	10.0%	10.3%	(157.1)%	40.0%

[1] In years 2021-2024 40% × finance cost for period. In 2025, reversal of cumulative deferred tax asset recognised in previous periods.

Approach 2: Recognise deferred tax on initial recognition – consider asset and liability separately

Under this approach, the entity would, on initial recognition of the provision and the addition to PP&E, establish a deferred tax asset of €3 million in respect of the provision (€7.5m @ 40%) and an equal liability in respect of the decommissioning component of PP&E. This would result in the following amounts being included in subsequent income statements (all figures in € millions):

	2021	2022	2023	2024	2025	Total
Depreciation	1.50	1.50	1.50	1.50	1.50	7.50
Finance costs	0.45	0.47	0.50	0.53	0.55	2.50
Cost before tax	1.95	1.97	2.00	2.03	2.05	10.00
Current tax (income)					(4.00)	(4.00)
Deferred tax (income)/charge[1]	(0.78)	(0.79)	(0.80)	(0.81)	3.18	–
Cost after tax	1.17	1.18	1.20	1.22	1.23	6.00
Effective tax rate	40.0%	40.0%	40.0%	40.0%	40.0%	40.0%

[1] In 2021, the sum of the reduction in deferred tax liability in respect of the decommissioning component of PP&E €0.6m (€1.5m @ 40%) and increase in deferred tax asset in respect of provision €0.18m (€0.45m @ 40%) – similarly for 2022-2024. The charge in 2025 represents the release of the remaining net deferred tax asset (equal to cumulative income statement credits in 2021-2024).

In the Statement of Financial Position, the related assets and liabilities would be recognised as follows:

	2021	2022	2023	2024	2025
PP&E – decommissioning asset	6.00	4.50	3.00	1.50	–
Decommissioning liability	(7.95)	(8.42)	(8.92)	(9.45)	–
Net decommissioning liability	(1.95)	(3.92)	(5.92)	(7.95)	–
Deferred tax asset	3.18	3.37	3.57	3.78	–
Deferred tax liability	(2.40)	(1.80)	(1.20)	(0.60)	–
Current tax recoverable					4.00

Approach 3: Recognise deferred tax – consider asset and liability as linked

Under this approach, the entity regards the decommissioning asset and liability as a single item. On this basis, the net asset or liability is compared to its tax base and deferred tax is recognised accordingly. On initial recognition of the provision and the addition to PP&E on 1 January 2021, the net carrying amount is zero so there is no temporary difference to recognise.

This would result in the following amounts being included in subsequent income statements (all figures in € millions):

	2021	2022	2023	2024	2025	Total
Depreciation	1.50	1.50	1.50	1.50	1.50	7.50
Finance costs	0.45	0.47	0.50	0.53	0.55	2.50
Cost before tax	1.95	1.97	2.00	2.03	2.05	10.00
Current tax (income)					(4.00)	(4.00)
Deferred tax (income)/charge[1]	(0.78)	(0.79)	(0.80)	(0.81)	3.18	–
Cost after tax	1.17	1.18	1.20	1.22	1.23	6.00
Effective tax rate	40.0%	40.0%	40.0%	40.0%	40.0%	40.0%

[1] In 2021, the net decommissioning liability increases from nil to €1.95m, resulting in a deferred tax asset €0.78m (€1.95m @ 40%) – similarly for 2022-2024. The charge in 2025 represents the release of the remaining net deferred tax asset (equal to cumulative income statement credits in 2021-2024).

If the deferred tax asset and deferred tax liability are capable of being offset in the statement of financial position (see 13.1.1 below), it would appear that Approach 2 and Approach 3 yield the same result. However, where Approach 2 is applied, the taxable temporary difference relating to the asset and the deductible temporary difference relating to the decommissioning liability are considered separately. Accordingly, a deferred tax asset will only be capable of recognition if it can be shown that there are probable taxable profits in future periods against which the entity can benefit from the tax deductions arising when the decommissioning obligation is settled. *[IAS 12.29]*. This might not be the case, for example where the liability is settled after the entity's revenue-generating activities have ceased and where tax losses incurred at this time are not permitted to be carried back to earlier periods.

7.2.7.B   Leases under IFRS 16 taxed as operating leases

In a number of jurisdictions, tax deductions are given for leases on the basis of lease payments made (i.e. regardless of whether a right-of-use asset is recognised under relevant accounting requirements). The total cost for both accounting and tax purposes is the same over the period of the lease, but in those cases where a right-of-use asset is recognised for accounting purposes, the cost recognised in the income statement comprises depreciation of the asset together with finance costs on the lease liability, rather than the lease payments made (on which tax relief is often given). Application of the initial recognition exception separately to the recognition of the right-of-use asset and the lease liability would lead to a result similar to that set out in the illustration of Approach 1 in Example 33.21 above, where the entity recognises neither a deferred tax asset for the deductible temporary difference on the lease liability nor the corresponding deferred tax liability for the taxable temporary difference on the right-of-use asset. However, the accretion of interest on the lease liability does create a deductible temporary difference, creating variability in the effective tax rate in the income statement.

As noted at 7.2.7 above, an alternative would be to disregard the initial recognition exception and consider the asset and liability recognised at the inception of a lease as a single transaction that gives rise to both a taxable temporary difference (on the asset) and a deductible temporary difference (on the liability). Under the second approach noted above, the amounts of the temporary differences are often equal and opposite. However, those temporary differences will only give rise to a net deferred tax position of zero if the entity is able to justify recognition of a separate deferred tax asset for the deductible temporary difference and the criteria for offset in the standard are met (see 13.1.1 below). Under the third approach noted above, the recording of a non-deductible right-of-use asset and a tax-deductible lease liability is regarded as being economically the same as the acquisition of a tax-deductible asset that is financed by a loan. Using this approach, the net temporary difference at initial recognition is zero. In both of these alternative approaches, the fact that the right-of-use asset is amortised at a different rate to the underlying lease liability does not result in any variation in the effective tax rate in the income statement (as illustrated in Approach 2 and Approach 3 in Example 33.21 above).

The Interpretations Committee considered this issue on two occasions in 2005 in relation to arrangements accounted as finance leases under IAS 17 – *Leases*.

IFRIC Update for April 2005 supported Approach 1:

'The [Interpretations Committee] noted that initial recognition exemption applies to each separate recognised element in the [statement of financial position], and no deferred tax asset or liability should be recognised on the temporary difference existing on the initial recognition of assets and liabilities arising from finance leases or subsequently.'[15]

However, only two months later in June 2005, the Committee added:

'The [Interpretations Committee] considered the treatment of deferred tax relating to assets and liabilities arising from finance leases.

While noting that there is diversity in practice in applying the requirements of IAS 12 to assets and liabilities arising from finance leases, the [Interpretations Committee] agreed not to develop any guidance because the issue falls directly within the scope of the Board's short-term convergence project on income taxes with the FASB.'[16]

At that meeting, the Committee had acknowledged that other approaches were applied in practice. However, it chose not to discuss the merits or problems relating to those approaches, because at that time the IASB had a project to replace IAS 12. This project resulted in the issue of the exposure draft (ED/2009/2 – *Income Tax*) noted at 1.1 above and was eventually abandoned.

As noted at 7.2.7 above, in July 2019 the Board issued its Exposure Draft, ED/2019/5 – *Deferred Tax related to Assets and Liabilities arising from a Single Transaction: Proposed amendments to IAS 12*. The proposed amendments would require an entity to recognise deferred tax on initial recognition of particular transactions to the extent that the transaction gives rise to equal amounts of deferred tax assets and liabilities. The proposed amendments would apply to particular transactions for which an entity recognises both an asset and a liability, such as leases and decommissioning obligations.[17]

Comparing the proposals in the Exposure Draft to the three approaches discussed at 7.2.7 above:

- The proposed amendment to IAS 12 would narrow the scope of the recognition exemption so that it would not apply to a transaction that gives rise to both an asset and a liability on initial recognition.[18]

- Entities would be required to recognise deferred tax assets and liabilities for temporary differences arising from the initial recognition of a lease and subsequently. An entity would typically offset these deferred tax assets and liabilities in the statement of financial position (applying paragraphs 74 to 75 of IAS 12).[19]

- At first glance, the proposals do not address the third approach noted above. However, in its Basis for Conclusions, the Exposure Draft states that the determination of whether tax deductions relate to the lease asset or lease liability is a judgment to be made by the entity, having considered the applicable tax law.[20] This would allow the entity to determine that, notwithstanding the fact that tax relief is given as lease payments are made, those tax deductions are attributable to the right-of-use asset (and interest expense), because the deductions relate to the expenses arising from the lease (that is, depreciation and interest expense).[21] In these circumstances there would be no temporary differences at initial recognition, because the tax bases of the right-of-use asset and lease liability equal their carrying amounts, reflecting that the entity will receive tax deductions equal to the carrying amount of the right-of-use asset and receive no tax deductions in respect of the lease liability. Accordingly, in cases where the tax legislation allows an interpretation that the benefit of deductions for lease payments are attributable to the right-of-use asset, the entity recognises no deferred tax on initial recognition, but does so if and when temporary differences arise after initial recognition.[22] While the argument presented for this treatment is not the same, the accounting outcome is the same as in Approach 3 above.

Therefore, under the amendments proposed in the Exposure Draft, on initial recognition of a right-of-use asset and lease liability, temporary differences would either:

(a) not arise, because the tax deductions are determined by the entity to relate to the right-of-use asset; or

(b) be equal and offsetting (that is, the resulting taxable and deductible temporary differences would be of the same amount), because the tax deductions are determined by the entity to relate to the lease liability.[23]

The comment period for the Exposure Draft ended in November 2019. The Board discussed feedback from respondents in April 2020. It made no decisions and will consider the project's direction at a future meeting.[24] As at the time of writing, these deliberations are expected to take place before the end of 2020.[25]

The review of feedback from the 68 respondents to the Exposure Draft identified concerns about particular aspects of the proposals relating to:

(i) the proposal to limit the recognition of deferred tax liabilities to the amount of the related deferred tax asset recognised;

(ii) the interaction of the proposed amendments with the requirement to reassess unrecognised deferred tax assets;

(iii) the proposed amendments' scope;

(iv) the attribution of tax deductions; and

(v) the requirements for advance lease payments and initial direct costs.[26]

Notwithstanding that the Exposure Draft could result in a treatment similar to that described as Approach 2 in Example 33.21 above being required, we believe that any of the existing approaches described at 7.2.7.A above continue to be acceptable until such an amendment is issued by the Board in its final form.

7.2.8 Initial recognition of compound financial instruments by the issuer

IAS 32 requires 'compound' financial instruments (those with both a liability feature and an equity feature, such as convertible bonds) to be accounted for by the issuer using so-called split accounting. This is discussed in more detail in Chapter 47 at 6, but in essence an entity is required to split the proceeds of issue of such an instrument (say €1 million) into a liability component, measured at its fair value based on real market rates for non-convertible debt rather than the nominal rate on the bond (say €750,000), with the balance being treated as an equity component (in this case €250,000).

Over the life of the instrument, the €750,000 carrying value of the liability element will be accreted back up to €1,000,000 (or such lower or higher sum as might be potentially repayable), so that the cumulative income statement interest charge will comprise:

(a) any actual cash interest payments made (which are tax-deductible in most jurisdictions); and

(b) the €250,000 accretion of the liability from €750,000 to €1,000,000 (which is not tax-deductible in most jurisdictions).

Where such an instrument is issued, IAS 12 requires the treatment in Example 33.22 to be adopted. [IAS 12 IE Example 4].

Example 33.22: Compound financial instrument

An entity issues a zero-coupon convertible loan of €1,000,000 on 1 January 2021 repayable at par on 1 January 2024. In accordance with IAS 32, the entity classifies the instrument's liability component as a liability and the equity component as equity. The entity assigns an initial carrying amount of €750,000 to the liability component of the convertible loan and €250,000 to the equity component. Subsequently, the entity recognises the imputed discount of €250,000 as interest expense at the effective annual rate of 10% on the carrying amount of the liability component at the beginning of the year. The tax authorities do not allow the entity to claim any deduction for the imputed discount on the liability component of the convertible loan. The tax rate is 40%.

Temporary differences arise on the liability element as follows (all figures in € thousands).

	1.1.21	31.12.21	31.12.22	31.12.23
Carrying value of liability component[1]	750	825	908	1,000
Tax base	1,000	1,000	1,000	1,000
Taxable temporary difference	250	175	92	–
Deferred tax liability @ 40%	100	70	37	–

1 Balance carried forward at end of previous period plus 10% accretion of notional interest less repayments.

The deferred tax arising at 1 January 2021 is deducted from equity. Subsequent reductions in the deferred tax balance are recognised in the income statement, resulting in an effective tax rate of 40%. For example, in 2021, the entity will accrete notional interest of €75,000 (closing loan liability €825,000 less opening balance €750,000) with deferred tax income of €30,000 (closing deferred tax liability €70,000 less opening liability €100,000).

This treatment causes some confusion in practice because it appears to contravene the prohibition on recognition of deferred tax on temporary differences arising on the initial recognition of assets and liabilities (other than in a business combination) that do not give rise to accounting or taxable profit or loss. [IAS 12.15(b)]. IAS 12 states that this temporary difference does not arise on initial recognition of a liability but as a result of the initial recognition of the equity component as a result of the requirement in IAS 32 to separate the instrument between its equity and liability components. [IAS 12.23].

7.2.9 Acquisition of subsidiary that does not constitute a business

Occasionally, an entity may acquire a subsidiary which is accounted for as the acquisition of an asset rather than as a business combination. This will most often be the case where the subsidiary concerned is a 'single asset entity' holding a single item of property, plant and equipment which is not considered to constitute a business.

Where an asset is acquired in such circumstances, the initial recognition exception applies, as illustrated by the following example.

Example 33.23: Acquired subsidiary accounted for as asset purchase

An entity (P) acquires all the shares of a subsidiary (S), whose only asset is an investment property, for $9 million. The transaction is accounted for as the acquisition of a property rather than as a business combination. The tax base of the property is $4.5 million and its carrying value (fair value) in the financial statements of S (under IFRS) is $12 million. The taxable temporary difference of $7.5 million in the financial records of S arose after the initial recognition by S of the property, and accordingly a deferred tax liability of $3 million has been recognised by S at its tax rate of 40%.

The question then arises as to whether any deferred tax should be recognised for the property in the financial statements of P.

Having determined that the acquisition does not constitute a business combination, the purchase price of $9 million is allocated to the assets acquired and liabilities assumed. *[IFRS 3.2(b)]*. The initial recognition exception applies to the difference between the cost of the property in the financial statements of P of $9 million and its tax base of $4.5 million, in exactly the same way as if the property had been legally acquired as a separate asset rather than through acquisition of the shares of S. *[IAS 12.15(b)]*. Therefore, no deferred tax is recognised by P in respect of the property at the time of its acquisition. At this point, P has an unrecognised taxable temporary difference of $4.5 million ($9 million less $4.5 million).

If P applies the fair value model in IAS 40 – *Investment Property*, the investment property is subsequently remeasured at its fair value of $12 million. This creates a new temporary difference in P of $3 million ($12 million less $9 million), in respect of which a taxable temporary difference of $1.2 million is recognised in profit and loss ($3 million @ 40%).

This conclusion was confirmed by the Interpretations Committee in March 2017. The Committee considered an example similar to Example 33.23 above and where the fair value of the property had been higher than the transaction price for the shares in S because of the associated deferred tax liability. Even in those circumstances, the Committee concluded that in a transaction that does not meet the definition of a business combination:[27]

(a) the entire purchase price is allocated to the investment property; *[IFRS 3.2(b)]* and

(b) no deferred tax liability is recognised by virtue of the initial recognition exception. *[IAS 12.15(b)]*.

7.2.10 Acquisition of an investment in a subsidiary, associate, branch or joint arrangement

The initial recognition exception does not apply to temporary differences associated with investments in subsidiaries, branches and associates, and interests in joint arrangements, which are subject to further detailed provisions of IAS 12 (see 7.5 below). *[IAS 12.15, 24]*.

7.3 Assets carried at fair value or revalued amount

IAS 12 notes that certain IFRSs permit or require assets to be carried at fair value or to be revalued. These include: *[IAS 12.20]*

- IAS 16 – *Property, Plant and Equipment;*
- IAS 38 – *Intangible Assets;*
- IAS 40 – *Investment Property;*
- IFRS 9 – *Financial Instruments;* and
- IFRS 16 – *Leases.*

In most jurisdictions, the revaluation or restatement of an asset does not affect taxable profit in the period of the revaluation or restatement. Nevertheless, the future recovery of the carrying amount will result in a taxable flow of economic benefits to the entity and the amount that will be deductible for tax purposes (i.e. the original tax base) will differ from the amount of those economic benefits.

The difference between the carrying amount of a revalued asset and its tax base is a temporary difference and gives rise to a deferred tax liability or asset. IAS 12 clarifies that this is the case even if:

- the entity does not intend to dispose of the asset. In such cases, the revalued carrying amount of the asset will be recovered through use and this will generate taxable income which exceeds the depreciation that will be allowable for tax purposes in future periods; or
- tax on capital gains is deferred if the proceeds of the disposal of the asset are invested in similar assets. In such cases, the tax will ultimately become payable on sale or use of the similar assets. *[IAS 12.20].* A discussion of the accounting for deferred taxable gains can be found at 7.7 below.

In some jurisdictions, the revaluation or other restatement of an asset to fair value affects taxable profit (tax loss) for the current period. In such cases, the tax base of the asset may be raised by an amount equivalent to the revaluation gain, so that no temporary difference arises.

7.4 Restrictions on recognition of deferred tax assets

There is an essential difference between deferred tax liabilities and deferred tax assets. An entity's deferred tax liabilities will crystallise if the entity recovers its existing net assets at their carrying amount. However, in order to realise its net deferred tax assets in full, an entity must earn profits in excess of those represented by the carrying amount of its net assets in order to generate sufficient taxable profits against which the deductions represented by deferred tax assets can be offset. Accordingly, IAS 12 restricts the recognition of deferred tax assets to the extent that it is probable that taxable profit will be available against which the underlying deductible temporary differences can be utilised. *[IAS 12.27].*

7.4.1 Restrictions imposed by relevant tax laws

When an entity assesses whether a deductible temporary difference is capable of being utilised, it must consider whether tax law restricts the sources of taxable profits against which deductions for this type of temporary difference are permitted. If tax law imposes no such restrictions, an entity can assess a deductible temporary difference in combination with all its other deductible temporary differences. However, if tax law restricts the utilisation of losses to deduction against a specific type of income, the recovery of a deductible temporary difference is assessed in combination only with other deductible temporary differences of the appropriate type. *[IAS 12.27A]*.

7.4.2 Sources of 'probable' taxable profit – taxable temporary differences

Before considering forecasts of future taxable profits, an entity should look to the deferred tax liabilities it has already recognised at the reporting date as a source of probable taxable profits that would allow any deductible temporary differences to be utilised. IAS 12 states that it is 'probable' that there will be sufficient taxable profit if a deductible temporary difference can be offset against a taxable temporary difference (deferred tax liability) relating to the same tax authority and the same taxable entity which will reverse in the same period as the asset, or in a period into which a loss arising from the asset may be carried back or forward. In such circumstances, a deferred tax asset is recognised. *[IAS 12.28]*.

There is no need at this stage to estimate the future taxable profits of the entity. If there are sufficient taxable temporary differences to justify the recognition of a deferred tax asset for deductible temporary differences, then the asset is recognised. The only condition to apply, as noted at 7.4.1 above, is that any deferred tax liability used as the basis for recognising a deferred tax asset represents a future tax liability against which the deductible temporary difference can actually be offset under the relevant tax law. *[IAS 12.27A]*. For example, in a tax jurisdiction where revenue and capital items are treated separately for tax purposes, a deferred tax asset representing a capital loss cannot be recognised by reference to a deferred tax liability relating to tax allowances received on PP&E in advance of the related depreciation expense.

7.4.3 Sources of 'probable' taxable profit – estimates of future taxable profits

Estimates of future taxable profits are only required to justify the recoverability of those deductible temporary differences in excess of the amounts already 'matched' against deferred tax liabilities recognised at the reporting date in the manner described at 7.4.2 above. Where there are insufficient taxable temporary differences relating to the same tax authority to offset deductible temporary differences, a deferred tax asset should be recognised to the extent that:

- it is probable that in future periods there will be sufficient taxable profits:
    - relating to the same tax authority;
    - relating to the same taxable entity; and
    - arising in the same period as the reversal of the deductible temporary difference or in a period into which a loss arising from the deferred tax asset may be carried back or forward; or
- tax planning opportunities are available that will create taxable profit in appropriate periods – see 7.4.4 below. *[IAS 12.29]*.

Where an entity has a history of recent losses it should also consider the guidance in IAS 12 for recognition of such losses (see 7.4.6 below). *[IAS 12.31]*.

7.4.3.A Ignore the origination of new future deductible temporary differences

In assessing the availability of future taxable profits, an entity must ignore taxable amounts arising from deductible temporary differences expected to originate in future periods. This is because those new deductible differences will themselves require future taxable profit in order to be utilised. *[IAS 12.29(a)(ii)]*.

For example, suppose that in 2021 an entity charges £100 to profit or loss for which a tax deduction is not available until 2022, when the amount is settled. However, in 2022 a further £100 is expected to be charged to profit or loss, for which a deduction will be available in 2023, and so on for the foreseeable future. This will have the effect that, in 2021, the entity will pay tax on the £100 for which no deduction is made on the 2021 tax return. In the tax return for 2022, there will be a deduction for that £100, but this will be offset by the add-back in the same tax return for the equivalent £100 charged for accounting purposes in 2022. If this cycle of '£100 deduction less £100 add-back' is expected to be perpetuated in each tax return for the foreseeable future, there is never any real recovery of the tax paid on the £100 in 2021 and, in the absence of any other taxable profits, no deferred tax asset would be recognised.

7.4.3.B Ignore the reversal of existing deductible temporary differences

In 2016, the IASB added text to the standard to clarify that the estimate of probable future taxable profit should exclude the tax deductions resulting from the reversal of the deductible temporary differences that are themselves being assessed for recognition as an asset. *[IAS 12.29(a)(i)]*. This amendment was made following the IASB's deliberations on the recognition of deferred tax assets for unrealised losses, as discussed at 7.4.5 below. The effect of the amendment is to clarify that the measure of taxable profit used for assessing the utilisation of deductible temporary differences is different from the taxable profit on which income taxes are payable. *[IAS 12.BC56]*.

The former is calculated before any allowances or deductions arising from the reversal of deductible temporary differences. The latter is the amount determined after the application of all applicable tax laws that gives rise to an entity's liability to pay income tax. *[IAS 12.5]*.

7.4.4 Tax planning opportunities and the recognition of deferred tax assets

'Tax planning opportunities' are actions that the entity would take in order to create or increase taxable income in a particular period before the expiry of a tax loss or tax credit carryforward. IAS 12 notes that, in some jurisdictions, taxable profit may be created or increased by:

- electing to have interest income taxed on either a received or receivable basis;
- deferring the claim for certain deductions from taxable profit;
- selling, and perhaps leasing back, assets that have appreciated but for which the tax base has not been adjusted to reflect such appreciation; and
- selling an asset that generates non-taxable income (such as, in some jurisdictions, a government bond) in order to purchase another investment that generates taxable income.

Where tax planning opportunities advance taxable profit from a later period to an earlier period, the utilisation of a tax loss or tax credit carryforward still depends on the existence of future taxable profit from sources other than future originating temporary differences. *[IAS 12.30]*.

The requirement to have regard to future tax planning opportunities applies only to the measurement of deferred tax assets. It does not apply to the measurement of deferred tax liabilities. Thus, for example, it would not be open to an entity subject to tax at 30% to argue that it should provide for deferred tax liabilities at some lower rate on the grounds that it intends to invest in assets attracting investment tax credits that will allow it to pay tax at that lower rate (see 8.4.1 below).

IAS 12 describes tax planning opportunities as actions that the entity 'would' take – not those it 'could' take. In other words, they are restricted to future courses of action that the entity would actually undertake to realise such a deferred tax asset, and do not include actions that are theoretically possible but practically implausible, such as the sale of an asset essential to the ongoing operations of the entity. Only if such actions are both capable of being taken and are intended to be taken by the entity can it be said that the resulting tax planning would give rise to a 'probable' future taxable profit.

Implementation of a tax planning opportunity may well entail significant direct costs or the loss of other tax benefits or both. Accordingly, any deferred tax asset recognised on the basis of a tax planning opportunity must be reduced by any cost of implementing that opportunity (measured, where applicable, on an after-tax basis).

Moreover, IAS 12 regards tax planning opportunities as a component of future net taxable profits. Thus, where a tax planning opportunity exists, but the entity is expected to remain loss-making (such that the opportunity effectively will simply reduce future tax losses), we believe that such an opportunity does not generally form the basis for recognising a deferred tax asset, except to the extent that it will create *net* future taxable profits (see also 7.4.6 below).

7.4.5 Unrealised losses on debt securities measured at fair value

In January 2016, the IASB issued *Recognition of Deferred Tax Assets for Unrealised Losses (Amendments to IAS 12)*. These amendments concluded deliberations started by the Interpretations Committee in May 2010 on the recognition of deferred tax assets for unrealised losses, for example on debt instruments measured at fair value. *[IAS 12.BC1A]*.

The Committee had been asked to provide guidance on how an entity determines whether to recognise a deferred tax asset under IAS 12 in the following circumstances: *[IAS 12.BC37]*

(a) the entity has a debt instrument measured at fair value under IAS 39 – *Financial Instruments: Recognition and Measurement* – and changes in market interest rates result in a decrease in the fair value of the debt instrument below its cost;

(b) it is probable that the issuer of the debt instrument will make all the contractual payments;

(c) the tax base of the debt instrument is its cost;

(d) tax law does not allow a loss to be deducted on a debt instrument until the loss is realised for tax purposes;

(e) the entity has the ability and intention to hold the debt instrument until the unrealised loss reverses (which may be at its maturity);

(f) tax law distinguishes between capital gains and losses and ordinary income tax losses. While capital losses can only be offset against capital gains, ordinary losses can be offset against both capital gains and ordinary income; and

(g) the entity has insufficient taxable temporary differences and no other probable taxable profits against which the entity can utilise those deductible temporary differences.

The Interpretations Committee had identified diversity in practice because of uncertainty about the application of some of the principles in IAS 12, in particular in relation to the following:

(a) The existence of a deductible temporary difference, when there are no tax consequences to the recovery of the principal on maturity; the holder of the debt instrument expects to hold it to maturity; and it is probable that the issuer will pay all the contractual cash flows. *[IAS 12.BC38, BC39]*.

(b) Whether it is appropriate for an entity to determine deductible temporary differences and taxable temporary differences on the basis of the asset's carrying amount when at the same time it assumes that the asset is recovered for more than its carrying amount for the purposes of estimating probable future taxable profit against which deductible temporary differences are assessed for utilisation. This question is relevant when taxable profit from other sources is insufficient for the utilisation of the deductible temporary differences arising when the asset is measured at fair value. *[IAS 12.BC38, BC47]*.

(c) Whether the estimate of probable future taxable profit should include or exclude the effects of reversing the deductible temporary differences that are being assessed for recognition as an asset. *[IAS 12.BC38, BC55]*.

(d) The basis for assessing the recoverability of deductible temporary differences, i.e. for each deductible temporary difference separately, or in combination with other deductible temporary differences. This question is relevant, for example, when tax law distinguishes capital gains and losses from other taxable gains and losses and capital losses can only be offset against capital gains. *[IAS 12.BC38, BC57]*.

Whilst the amendments to IAS 12 were framed around the above example of a fixed-rate debt instrument measured at fair value, the Board noted that the principle on which the amendments are based is not limited to any specific type or class of assets. *[IAS 12.BC52]*. However, as noted at 7.4.5.B below, the IASB acknowledged the concerns raised by respondents that the amendments could be applied too broadly and highlighted the need for particular caution where assets are measured at fair value. In response to that concern, the Board noted that entities will need to have sufficient evidence on which to base their estimate of probable future taxable profit, including when that estimate involves the recovery of an asset for more than its carrying amount. *[IAS 12.BC53]*.

7.4.5.A The existence of a deductible temporary difference

Because, in the case of many debt instruments, the collection of the principal on maturity does not give rise to any liability for tax, some believed that the collection of the principal is a non-taxable event. Consequently, proponents of this view argued that a deductible temporary difference cannot exist when an entity asserts that the contractual payments will be received, because any difference between the debt instrument's carrying amount and its higher tax base results from a loss that the entity expects never to realise for tax purposes. *[IAS 12.BC40].*

The IASB rejected this argument. IAS 12 already states that a deductible temporary difference arises if the tax base of an asset exceeds its carrying amount. *[IAS 12.20, 26(d)].* The calculation of a temporary difference is based on the premise that the carrying amount of the asset will be recovered. *[IAS 12.5].* The calculation of the temporary difference is not affected by possible future changes in the carrying amount of the asset. The Board considered that the economic benefit embodied in the related deferred tax asset results from the ability of the holder of the debt instrument to achieve future taxable gains in the amount of the deductible temporary difference without paying tax on those gains. This is the case where a previous impairment reverses, such that the entity recovers the original principal on the debt instrument. *[IAS 12.BC42-44].* Accordingly, the amendments add an example after paragraph 26 of IAS 12 to illustrate how a deductible temporary difference exists under paragraph 26(d).

Example 33.24: Deductible temporary difference when the asset is valued below cost

At the beginning of Year 1, Entity A purchases for $1,000 a debt instrument with a nominal value of $1,000 payable at the end of Year 5 and with an interest rate of 2% payable at the end of each year. The effective interest rate is determined to be 2% and the debt instrument is measured at fair value.

At the end of year 2, market interest rates have increased to 5%, causing the fair value of the debt instrument to decrease to $918. It is probable that Entity A will collect all the contractual cash flows if it continues to hold the debt instrument.

Any gains or losses on the debt instrument are taxable or deductible only when realised. Gains or losses arising on the sale or maturity of the instrument are calculated for tax purposes as the difference between the amount collected and the original cost of the debt instrument. Accordingly, the tax base of the debt instrument is its original cost.

The Example concludes that the difference between the carrying amount of the debt instrument of $918 and its tax base of $1,000 gives rise to a deductible temporary difference of $82 at the end of Year 2, *[IAS 12.20, 26(d)],* irrespective of whether Entity A expects to recover the carrying amount of the debt instrument by sale or by use, i.e. by holding it and collecting contractual cash flows, or a combination of both. Whether the asset is realised on sale or on maturity (i.e. through use), Entity A will obtain a tax deduction equivalent to the tax base of $1,000 in determining any resultant taxable profit.

7.4.5.B Recovering an asset for more than its carrying amount

The Board concluded that the estimate of probable future taxable profit may include the recovery of some of an entity's assets for more than their carrying amount, but only if there is sufficient evidence that it is probable that the entity will achieve this. In the case of a fixed-rate debt instrument measured at fair value, recovery for more than the carrying amount is probable if the entity expects to collect the contractual cash flows. *[IAS 12.29A].*

The determination of temporary differences and the estimation of probable future taxable profit are two separate steps, and the IASB concluded that the carrying amount of an asset is relevant only to determining the temporary differences. *[IAS 12.BC49]*. Indeed, the Board identified scenarios where an inappropriate outcome can arise if the possibility of realising a profit in excess of the carrying amount were limited. For example, a profitable manufacturing company relies on a business model that involves the sale of inventories and the recovery of property, plant and equipment for amounts exceeding their cost. Therefore, where such assets are recorded using the cost model, it would be inconsistent to assume that the entity will only recover these assets for their carrying amount. *[IAS 12.BC50]*. Nevertheless, in response to concerns raised by respondents that the amendment could be applied inappropriately, the Board acknowledged the need for caution where assets are measured at fair value. The risk of arbitrary estimates of future taxable profit is reduced where entities rely on evidence, such as the existence of contractual cash flows and an expectation of their recovery. *[IAS 12.BC53]*. For example, it would not be appropriate to assume recovery greater than an asset's carrying amount at fair value on the basis of an arbitrary assertion that fair value will inevitably recover in line with a longer-term improvement in the related market for the asset in question.

7.4.5.C   Excluding the reversal of existing deductible temporary differences

During its deliberations, the Interpretations Committee observed uncertainty about how entities should calculate the measure of taxable profit that is used for assessing the amounts available for the future utilisation of deductible temporary differences. In particular, there seemed to be diversity of opinion relating to whether entities should include or exclude deductions that will arise when those deductible temporary differences reverse. *[IAS 12.BC55]*. As discussed above at 7.4.3.B, the IASB concluded that the estimate of future taxable profit used to assess whether deductions can be utilised is not the same as 'taxable profit' (which is the amount determined after the application of all applicable tax laws that gives rise to an entity's liability to pay income tax). *[IAS 12.5]*.

Therefore, entities should exclude the effect of deductions arising from the reversal of the deductible temporary differences being assessed for recoverability, or they would be counted twice. *[IAS 12.29(a)(i), BC56]*.

7.4.5.D   The basis for assessing the recoverability of deductible temporary differences

As noted at 7.4 above, IAS 12 restricts the recognition of deferred tax assets to the extent that it is probable that taxable profit will be available against which the underlying deductible temporary differences can be utilised. *[IAS 12.27]*.

The Board noted that this is a matter for tax law; that IAS 12 defines taxable profit by reference to the application of the rules determined by tax authorities; and that no deferred tax is recognised if the reversal of the temporary difference will not lead to tax deductions. *[IAS 12.BC58]*. Therefore, the assessment of whether a deductible temporary difference can be utilised considers on a combined basis all deductible temporary differences relating to the same taxation authority and same taxable entity that are treated in a similar way under tax law. However, if tax law offsets specific types of losses against particular categories of income (for example when tax law allows capital losses to be deducted only against capital gains) such temporary differences are segregated according to their treatment under the relevant tax law. *[IAS 12.BC59]*.

IAS 12 was amended to clarify that entities making the assessment of the availability of taxable profits against which a deductible temporary difference can be utilised should do so in combination with all other deductible temporary differences, unless tax law restricts the sources of taxable profits against which that deductible temporary difference can be utilised. Where restrictions exist, the assessment is made together only with deductible temporary differences recoverable from the same sources. *[IAS 12.27A]*.

The amendments to IAS 12 add an example to illustrate how these requirements are applied to debt instruments measured at fair value, on which Example 33.25 below is based. *[IAS 12 Example 7]*.

Example 33.25: Debt instruments measured at fair value

At 31 December 2021 an entity holds a portfolio of three debt instruments, which are measured at fair value through other comprehensive income:

Debt instrument (All amounts in €)	Cost	Fair value	Contractual interest rate
Debt instrument A	2,000,000	1,942,857	2.00%
Debt instrument B	750,000	778,571	9.00%
Debt instrument C	2,000,000	1,961,905	3.00%

All the debt instruments were acquired for their nominal value. All three debt instruments mature on 31 December 2022, on which date repayment of the nominal value is due. Interest is paid at the end of each year. When the instruments were acquired, the contractually fixed interest rates were equal to the relevant market rates. However, at 31 December 2021 the market interest rate is 5%, resulting in the fair value of instruments A and C to be below their cost and the fair value of instrument B to be above its cost. It is probable that the entity would receive all the contractual cash flows if it continues to hold the debt instruments.

The entity expects to hold instruments A and B to maturity, collecting the cash flows as they fall due, and to sell instrument C in early 2022 for its fair value of €1,961,905.

The tax base of the debt instruments is cost, which is deductible either on maturity when the principal is paid or against any sale proceeds when the instruments are sold. Tax law specifies that gains (losses) on the debt instruments are taxable (deductible) only when realised. Tax law distinguishes ordinary gains and losses from capital gains and losses. Ordinary losses can be offset against both ordinary gains and capital gains. Capital losses can only be offset against capital gains. Capital losses can be carried forward for 5 years and ordinary losses can be carried forward for 20 years.

Ordinary gains are taxed at 30 per cent and capital gains are taxed at 10 per cent.

Tax law classifies interest income from the debt instruments as 'ordinary' and gains and losses arising on the sale of the debt instruments as 'capital'. Losses that arise if the issuer of the debt instrument fails to pay the principal on maturity are classified as ordinary by tax law.

In addition to the above, there are other taxable temporary differences of €50,000 and deductible temporary differences of €430,000 which are expected to reverse in ordinary taxable profit in 2022.

In summary, the following temporary differences are identified at 31 December 2021:

Temporary differences (All amounts in €)	Carrying amount	Tax base	Taxable temporary differences	Deductible temporary differences
Debt instrument A	1,942,857	2,000,000		57,143
Debt instrument B	778,571	750,000	28,571	
Debt instrument C	1,961,905	2,000,000		38,095
Other sources (not specified)			50,000	430,000
Total temporary differences			78,571	525.238
Expected to reverse in ordinary gains or losses			78,571	487,143
Expected to reverse as capital losses				38,095

The entity expects to report an ordinary tax loss of €200,000 for the year ending 31 December 2022. The deductible temporary difference on instrument C is classified as a capital loss because it is expected to be realised by sale. There are no other capital gains against which the entity could utilise capital losses in the current or future periods. What is the entity's deferred tax asset or liability as at 31 December 2021?

The entity assesses the availability of probable future taxable profits in two steps:

- Step 1: Determine the availability of taxable temporary differences at the reporting date. *[IAS 12.28]*.
- Step 2: Determine the availability of probable future taxable profits. *[IAS 12.29]*.

Step 1: Determine the availability of taxable temporary differences at the reporting date

All of the taxable temporary differences are expected to reverse in ordinary gains or losses and should therefore be compared to the deductible temporary differences of €487,143 that are capable of being utilised against ordinary gains. Accordingly, a deferred tax asset of €78,571 is justified at this stage, with €408,572 (487,143 – 78,571) of deductible temporary differences remaining to be utilised against ordinary gains or losses.

Step 2: Determine the availability of probable future taxable profits

The fact pattern states that the entity expects to report an ordinary tax loss of €200,000 for 2022. As noted at 7.4.5.C above, this figure is the amount determined after the application of all applicable tax laws that gives rise to an entity's liability to pay income tax. In order to calculate the available profits against which the deductible temporary differences can be utilised, the effect of deductions arising from the reversal of the deductible temporary differences must be excluded. The gives a probable future taxable profit of €208,572, as follows:

Excluding the reversal of existing temporary differences	Amount €
Expected tax loss reported for 2022	(200,000)
Reversal of taxable temporary differences (ordinary gains and losses)	(78,571)
Reversal of deductible temporary differences (ordinary gains and losses)	487,143
Probable taxable profit for 2022 excluding the effect of reversals	208,572

Accordingly, the entity recognises a deferred tax asset in respect of deductible temporary differences of €287,143, comprising €78,571 justified by reference to taxable temporary differences existing at the reporting date and €208,572 expected to be utilised against probable taxable profits in 2022. All of these deductible temporary differences are expected to reverse in ordinary gains or losses, for which the applicable tax rate is 30%.

Therefore, at 31 December 2021, the entity reports a deferred tax liability of €23,571, a deferred tax asset of €86,143 and unrecognised deductible temporary differences of €238,095, as follows:

Temporary differences (All amounts in €)	Amount	Tax rate	Deferred tax liability	Deferred tax asset
Taxable temporary differences	78,571	30%	23,571	
Total deductible temporary differences	525.238			
Less: eligible for recognition	(287,143)	30%		86,143
Unrecognised	238,095			

The unrecognised deductible temporary differences comprise €38,095 expected to reverse in capital gains and losses and €200,000 (487,143 – 287,143) expected to reverse in ordinary gains and losses.

7.4.6 Unused tax losses and unused tax credits

A deferred tax asset should be recognised for the carryforward of unused tax losses and unused tax credits to the extent that it is probable that future taxable profit will be available against which the unused tax losses and unused tax credits can be utilised. *[IAS 12.34]*.

The criteria for recognition are essentially the same as those for deductible temporary differences, as set out in 7.4.1 to 7.4.4 above, in particular that it is 'probable' that there will be sufficient taxable profit against which a deductible temporary difference can be utilised when there are sufficient taxable temporary differences relating to the same taxation authority and the same taxable entity which are expected to reverse in the same period as the asset, or in a period into which a loss arising from the asset may be carried back or forward. *[IAS 12.28]*.

However, IAS 12 emphasises that the existence of unused tax losses is strong evidence that taxable profits (other than those represented by deferred tax liabilities) may not be available. Therefore, an entity with a history of recent losses recognises a deferred tax asset arising from unused tax losses or tax credits only to the extent that: *[IAS 12.35]*

- it has sufficient taxable temporary differences; or
- there is other convincing evidence that sufficient taxable profit will be available against which the unused tax losses or unused tax credits can be utilised by the entity.

In May 2014, the Interpretations Committee confirmed that the consideration of available reversing taxable temporary differences is made independently of the assessment of an entity's expectations of future tax losses. Accordingly, a deferred tax asset is recognised for the carryforward of unused tax losses to the extent of the existing taxable temporary differences, of an appropriate type, that reverse in an appropriate period. The reversal of those taxable temporary differences enables the utilisation of the unused tax losses and justifies the recognition of deferred tax assets.[28]

In addition to the question noted above, the Interpretations Committee was asked to clarify how the guidance in IAS 12 is applied when tax laws limit the extent to which tax losses brought forward can be recovered against future taxable profits. In the tax systems considered for this issue, the amount of tax losses brought forward that can be recovered in each tax year is limited to a specified percentage of the taxable profits of that year.

In these circumstances, the Committee noted that the amount of deferred tax assets recognised from unused tax losses as a result of suitable existing taxable temporary differences should be restricted as specified by the tax law. This is because when the suitable taxable temporary differences reverse, the amount of tax losses that can be utilised by that reversal is reduced as specified by the tax law. Also, the Committee noted that in this case future tax losses are not considered.[29]

Consequently, the availability of future taxable profits is only required to be considered if the unused tax losses exceed the amount of suitable existing taxable temporary differences (after taking into account any restrictions). The Interpretations Committee also confirmed in May 2014 that an additional deferred tax asset is recognised only to the extent that the following requirements are met:[30] *[IAS 12.36]*

- whether the entity has sufficient taxable temporary differences relating to the same taxation authority and the same taxable entity, which will result in taxable amounts against which the unused tax losses or unused tax credits can be utilised before they expire;
- whether the entity will have taxable profits before the unused tax losses or unused tax credits expire;
- whether the unused tax losses result from identifiable causes which are unlikely to recur; and
- whether tax planning opportunities (see 7.4.4 above) are available to the entity that will create taxable profit in the period in which the unused tax losses or unused tax credits can be utilised.

To the extent that it is not probable that taxable profit will be available against which the unused tax losses or unused tax credits can be utilised, a deferred tax asset is not recognised. *[IAS 12.36]*. Additional disclosures are required when an entity recognises a deferred tax asset on the assumption that there will be future taxable profits available in excess of the amount of existing taxable temporary differences, and the entity has suffered a loss in either the current or preceding period in the tax jurisdiction to which the deferred tax asset relates (see 14.3 below). *[IAS 12.35]*.

Some have suggested that the IASB should set time limits on the foresight period used. We consider that such generalised guidance would be inappropriate, particularly in the context of an international standard, which must address the great variety of tax systems that exist worldwide, and which impose a wide range of restrictions on the carryforward of tax losses or tax credits. In any event, it may well be the case that a deferred tax asset recoverable in twenty years from profits from a currently existing long-term supply contract with a creditworthy customer may be more robust than one recoverable in one year from expected future trading by a start-up company.

7.4.6.A Where taxable temporary differences were recognised outside profit or loss

As noted above, where an entity has a history of recent losses, or even where it expects to continue to incur trading losses in the future, it still recognises a deferred tax asset for the carryforward of unused tax losses or tax credits to the extent that it has sufficient taxable temporary differences against which those tax losses and tax credits can be utilised. *[IAS 12.35]*. This will be the case for taxable temporary differences that relate to the same taxation authority and the same taxable entity, and which are expected to reverse in the same period as the asset, or in a period into which a loss arising from the asset may be carried back or forward. *[IAS 12.28]*.

It is irrelevant whether the taxable temporary differences were recognised in profit or loss, other comprehensive income or directly in equity, provided that offset is not restricted under local tax law. For example, a taxable temporary difference arises when assets are carried at fair value. *[IAS 12.20]*. For debt instruments classified as fair value through other comprehensive income and for property, plant and equipment the related taxable temporary difference is recognised in other comprehensive income together with the revaluation gain or loss. Deferred tax is also recorded outside profit and loss when the initial carrying value of a compound financial instrument is split between its liability and equity components, and a related taxable temporary difference is recognised in equity (see 7.2.8 above).

If local tax laws do not restrict the tax losses and tax credits to be utilised against the reversal of those taxable temporary differences, then a deferred tax asset is recognised. The deferred tax asset is recognised through profit or loss, except in those circumstances where the losses are related to transactions that were originally recognised outside profit or loss. *[IAS 12.61A]*. Example 33.47 at 10.5 below illustrates the recognition of a deferred tax asset in profit or loss on the basis of a deferred tax liability accounted for outside profit or loss.

7.4.7 Re-assessment of deferred tax assets

An entity must review its deferred tax assets, both recognised and unrecognised, at each reporting date.

7.4.7.A Previously recognised assets

An entity should reduce the carrying amount of a deferred tax asset to the extent that it is no longer probable that sufficient taxable profit will be available to enable the asset to be recovered. Any such reduction should be reversed if it subsequently becomes probable that sufficient taxable profit will be available. *[IAS 12.56]*.

7.4.7.B Previously unrecognised assets

An entity recognises a previously unrecognised deferred tax asset to the extent that it has become probable that sufficient taxable profit will be available to enable the asset to be recovered. For example, an improvement in trading conditions may make it more probable that the entity will be able to generate sufficient taxable profit in the future for the deferred tax asset to meet the recognition criteria. Special considerations apply when an entity re-appraises deferred tax assets of an acquired business at the date of the business combination or subsequently (see 12.1.2 below). *[IAS 12.37]*.

7.4.8 Effect of disposals on recoverability of tax losses

In consolidated financial statements, the disposal of a subsidiary may lead to the derecognition of a deferred tax asset in respect of tax losses because either:

- the entity disposed of had incurred those tax losses itself; or
- the entity disposed of was the source of probable future taxable profits against which the tax losses of another member of the group could be offset, allowing the group to recognise a deferred tax asset.

It is clear that, once the disposal has been completed, those tax losses will no longer appear in the disposing entity's statement of financial position. What is less clear is whether those tax losses should be derecognised before the disposal itself is accounted for – and if so, when. IAS 12 does not give any explicit guidance on this point, beyond the general requirement to recognise tax losses only to the extent that their recoverability is probable (see 7.4 above).

In our view, three broad circumstances need to be considered:
- the entity has recognised a deferred tax asset in respect of tax losses of the subsidiary to be disposed of, the recoverability of which is dependent on future profits of that subsidiary (see 7.4.8.A below);
- the entity has recognised a deferred tax asset in respect of tax losses of a subsidiary that is to remain in the group, the recoverability of which is dependent on future profits of the subsidiary to be disposed of (see 7.4.8.B below); and
- the entity has recognised a deferred tax asset in respect of tax losses of the subsidiary to be disposed of, the recoverability of which is dependent on future profits of one or more entities that are to remain in the group (see 7.4.8.C below).

7.4.8.A Tax losses of subsidiary disposed of recoverable against profits of that subsidiary

In this situation, we consider that the deferred tax asset for the losses should remain recognised until the point of disposal, provided that the expected proceeds of the disposal are expected at least to be equal to the total consolidated net assets of the entity to be disposed of, including the deferred tax asset. Whilst the group will no longer recover the tax losses through a reduction in its future tax liabilities, it will effectively recover their value through the disposal. Moreover, it would be expected that the disposal price would reflect the availability of usable tax losses in the disposed of entity, albeit that any price paid would reflect the fair value of such tax losses, rather than the undiscounted value required to be recorded by IAS 12 (see 8.6 below).

7.4.8.B Tax losses of retained entity recoverable against profits of subsidiary disposed of

In this case, we believe that IAS 12 requires the deferred tax asset to be derecognised once the disposal of the profitable subsidiary is probable (effectively meaning that the recoverability of losses by the retained entity is no longer probable). This derecognition threshold may be reached before the subsidiary to be disposed of is classified as held for sale under IFRS 5 (see Chapter 4). This is because the threshold for derecognising the deferred tax asset under IAS 12 (i.e. that the sale of the subsidiary is probable) is lower than the threshold for accounting for the net assets of the subsidiary under IFRS 5 (i.e. that the subsidiary is ready for sale, and the sale is highly probable).

7.4.8.C Tax losses of subsidiary disposed of recoverable against profits of retained entity

In this situation, we believe that more than one analysis is possible. One view would be that – as in 7.4.8.A above – a deferred tax asset for the losses should remain recognised until the point of disposal, provided that the expected proceeds of the disposal are at least equal to the total consolidated net assets of the entity to be disposed of, including the deferred tax asset. Another view would be that the asset should be derecognised. In contrast to the situation in 7.4.8.A above, it is not the case that the losses are of any benefit to the acquiring entity (since they are recognised by virtue of the expected profits of other entities in the group which are not being sold. Rather, as in 7.4.8.B above, the likely separation of the subsidiary from the profits available in one or more retained entities means that the utilisation of those losses by the retained subsidiary is no longer probable. A third view would be that it is necessary to determine whether or not the losses would be of value to the acquirer. If so, they should continue to be recognised to the extent that they are being recovered by the disposing entity through the sales proceeds (as in 7.4.8.A above). If not, they should be derecognised on the grounds that they will not be recovered either through a reduction in future taxable profits of the disposing entity, or through sale (as in 7.4.8.B above).

7.5 'Outside' temporary differences relating to subsidiaries, branches, associates and joint arrangements

Investments in subsidiaries, branches and associates or interests in joint arrangements can give rise to two types of temporary difference:

- Differences between the tax base of the investment or interest and its carrying amount. 'Tax base' refers to the amount that will be deductible for tax purposes against any taxable benefits arising when the carrying value of the asset is recovered. *[IAS 12.7]*. The tax base will be determined by the rules set in the relevant tax jurisdiction. It may be the original cost of the equity held in that investment or interest or its current fair value or even an historic amount excluding unremitted earnings. That will be determined by the local tax laws. 'Carrying amount' in this context means:

    - in separate financial statements, the carrying amount of the relevant investment or interest, and

    - in financial statements other than separate financial statements, the carrying amount of the net assets (including goodwill) relating to the relevant investment or interest, whether accounted for by consolidation or equity accounting.

These differences are generally referred to in practice as 'outside' temporary differences, and normally arise in the tax jurisdiction of the entity that holds the equity in the investment or interest. Accordingly, in general they directly affect the taxable profit of the investor entity.

- In financial statements other than separate financial statements, differences between the tax bases of the individual assets and liabilities of the investment or interest and the carrying amounts of those assets and liabilities (as included in those financial statements through consolidation or equity accounting).

  These differences are generally referred to in practice as 'inside' temporary differences. They normally arise in the tax jurisdiction of the investment or interest and affect the taxable profit of the investee entity.

This section is concerned with 'outside' temporary differences, the most common source of which is the undistributed profits of the investee entities, where distribution to the investor would trigger a tax liability. 'Outside' temporary differences may also arise from a change in the carrying value of an investment due to exchange movements, provisions, or revaluations; or from a change in the tax base of the investee in the jurisdiction of the investor.

The reversal of most 'inside' temporary differences is essentially inevitable as assets are recovered or liabilities settled at their carrying amount in the normal course of business. However, an entity may be able to postpone the reversal of some or all of its 'outside' differences more or less permanently. For example, if a distribution of the retained profits of a subsidiary would be subject to withholding tax, the parent may effectively be able to avoid such a tax by making the subsidiary reinvest all its profits into the business. IAS 12 recognises this essential difference in the nature of 'outside' and 'inside' temporary differences by setting different criteria for the recognition of 'outside' temporary differences.

As noted at 7.2.10 above, the initial recognition exception does not apply to temporary differences associated with investments in subsidiaries, branches and associates, and interests in joint arrangements. *[IAS 12.15, 24]*. The provisions of IAS 12 applicable to these temporary differences are set out at 7.5.2 and 7.5.3 below.

7.5.1 Calculation of 'outside' temporary differences

As noted above, 'outside' temporary differences arise in both consolidated and separate financial statements and may well be different, due to the different bases used to account for subsidiaries, branches and associates or interests in joint arrangements in consolidated and separate financial statements. *[IAS 12.38]*. This is illustrated by Example 33.26 below.

Example 33.26: Temporary differences associated with subsidiaries, branches, associates and joint arrangements

On 1 January 2021 entity H acquired 100% of the shares of entity S, whose functional currency is different from that of H, for €600m. The tax rate in H's tax jurisdiction is 30% and the tax rate in S's tax jurisdiction is 40%.

The fair value of the identifiable assets and liabilities (excluding deferred tax assets and liabilities) of S acquired by H is set out in the following table, together with their tax base in S's tax jurisdiction and the resulting temporary differences (all figures in € millions).

	Fair value	Tax base	(Taxable)/ Deductible temporary difference
PP&E	270	155	(115)
Accounts receivable	210	210	–
Inventory	174	124	(50)
Retirement benefit obligations	(30)	–	30
Accounts payable	(120)	(120)	–
Fair value of net assets acquired excluding deferred tax	504	369	(135)
Deferred tax (135 @ 40%)	(54)		
Fair value of identifiable assets acquired and liabilities assumed	450		
Goodwill (balancing figure)	150		
Carrying amount	600		

No deferred tax is recognised on the goodwill, in accordance with the requirements of IAS 12 as discussed at 7.2.2.A above.

At the date of combination, the tax base, in H's tax jurisdiction, of H's investment in S is €600 million. Therefore, in H's jurisdiction, no temporary difference is associated with the investment, either in the consolidated financial statements of H (where the investment is represented by net assets and goodwill of €600 million), or in its separate financial statements, if prepared (where the investment is shown as an investment at cost of €600 million).

During 2021:

- S makes a profit after tax, as reported in H's consolidated financial statements, of €150 million, of which €80 million is paid as a dividend (after deduction of withholding tax) before 31 December 2021, leaving a net retained profit of €70 million.

- In accordance with IAS 21, H's consolidated financial statements record a loss of €15 million on retranslation to the closing exchange rate of S's opening net assets and profit for the period.

- In accordance with IAS 36 – *Impairment of Assets*, H's consolidated financial statements record an impairment loss of €10 million in respect of goodwill.

Thus, in H's consolidated financial statements the carrying value of its investment in S is €645 million, comprising:

	€m
Carrying amount at 1.1.2021	600
Retained profit	70
Exchange loss	(15)
Impairment of goodwill	(10)
Carrying amount at 31.12.2021	645

7.5.1.A   Consolidated financial statements

Assuming that the tax base in H's jurisdiction remains €600 million, there is a taxable temporary difference of €45 million (carrying amount €645m less tax base €600m) associated with S in H's consolidated financial statements. Whether or not any deferred tax is required to be provided for on this difference is determined in accordance with the principles discussed at 7.5.2 below. Any tax provided for would be allocated to profit or loss, other comprehensive income or equity in accordance with the general provisions of IAS 12 (see 10 below). In this case, the foreign exchange loss, as a presentational rather than a functional exchange difference, would be recognised in other comprehensive income (see Chapter 15 at 6.1), as would any associated tax effect. The other items, and their associated effects, would be recognised in profit or loss.

Irrespective of whether provision is made for deferred tax, H would be required to make disclosures in respect of this difference (see 14.2.2 below).

7.5.1.B   Separate financial statements of investor

The amount of any temporary difference in H's separate financial statements would depend on the accounting policy adopted in those statements. IAS 27 – *Separate Financial Statements* – allows entities the choice of accounting for investments in group companies at either cost (less impairment), using the equity method or at fair value – see Chapter 8 at 2. Suppose that, notwithstanding the impairment of goodwill required to be recognised in the consolidated financial statements, the investment in S taken as a whole is not impaired, and indeed its fair value at 31 December 2021 is €660 million.

If, in its separate financial statements, H accounts for its investment at cost of €600 million, there would be no temporary difference associated with S in H's separate financial statements, since the carrying amount and tax base of S would both be €600 million.

If, however, in its separate financial statements, H accounts for its investment at its fair value of €660 million, there would be a taxable temporary difference of €60 million (carrying amount €660m less tax base €600m) associated with S in H's separate financial statements. Whether or not any deferred tax is required to be provided for on this difference is determined in accordance with the principles discussed at 7.5.2 and at 7.5.3 below. Any tax provided for would be allocated to profit or loss, other comprehensive income or equity in accordance with the general provisions of IAS 12 (see 10 below). Irrespective of whether provision is made for deferred tax, H would be required to make disclosures in respect of this difference (see 14.2.2 below).

IAS 27 also allows entities to use the equity method as described in IAS 28 – *Investments in Associates and Joint Ventures* – to account for investments in subsidiaries, joint ventures and associates in their separate financial statements. *[IAS 27.10(c)]*. Where the equity method is used, dividends from those investments are to be recognised as a reduction from the carrying value of the investment. *[IAS 27.12]*.

The same principles apply as those discussed above. Any difference between the carrying value of the entity's interest in its subsidiaries, joint ventures and associates, in this case determined using the equity method, and the tax base in the investor's jurisdiction gives rise to a temporary difference. Whether or not any deferred tax is required to be recognised on this difference is determined in accordance with the principles discussed at 7.5.2 below. Any tax provided for would be allocated to profit or loss, other comprehensive income or equity in accordance with the general provisions of IAS 12 (see 10 below).

7.5.2 Taxable temporary differences

IAS 12 requires a deferred tax liability to be recognised for all taxable temporary differences associated with investments in subsidiaries, branches and associates or interests in joint arrangements, unless:

(a) the parent, investor, joint venturer or joint operator is able to control the timing of the reversal of the temporary difference; and

(b) it is probable that the temporary difference will not reverse in the foreseeable future. *[IAS 12.39]*.

IAS 12 does not currently define the meaning of 'probable' in this context. However, we consider that, as in other IFRSs, it should be taken to mean 'more likely than not' (see 7.1.2 above). IAS 12 also does not elaborate on the meaning of 'foreseeable'. In our view, the period used will be a matter of judgement in individual circumstances and not limited by the setting of any arbitrary period.

What this means in practice is best illustrated by reference to its application to the retained earnings of subsidiaries, branches and joint arrangements on the one hand, and those of associates on the other.

In the case of a subsidiary or a branch, the parent is able to control when and whether the retained earnings are distributed. Therefore, no provision need be made for the tax consequences of distribution of profits that the parent has determined will not be distributed in the foreseeable future. *[IAS 12.40]*. In the case of a joint arrangement, provided that the joint venturer or joint operator can control the distribution policy, for example because any decision requires the consent of all or a group of the parties, similar considerations apply. *[IAS 12.43]*.

In the case of an associate, however, the investor cannot usually control the distribution policy. Therefore, provision should be made for the tax consequences of the distribution of the retained earnings of an associate, except to the extent that there is a shareholders' agreement that those earnings will not be distributed. *[IAS 12.42]*.

Some might consider this a counter-intuitive result. In reality, it is extremely unusual for any entity (other than one set up for a specific project) to pursue a policy of full distribution. To the extent that it occurs at all, it is much more likely in a wholly-owned subsidiary than in an associate; and yet IAS 12 seems to treat full distribution by associates as the norm and that by subsidiaries as the exception. Moreover, it seems to ignore the fact that equity accounting was developed as a regulatory response to the perceived ability of investors in associates to exert some degree of control over the amount and timing of dividends from them. However, the 'default' position in IAS 12 is that a deferred tax liability is recognised for *all* taxable temporary differences associated with investments in subsidiaries, branches and associates and interests in joint arrangements, with the exception applying only if the entity *both* controls the timing of reversal *and* it is probable that there will be no such reversal in the foreseeable future. *[IAS 12.39]*.

In some jurisdictions, some or all of the temporary differences associated with such investments in subsidiaries, branches and associates or interests in joint arrangements are taxed on disposal of that investment or interest. Clearly, where the entity is contemplating such a disposal, it would no longer be able to assert that it is probable that the relevant temporary difference will not reverse in the foreseeable future.

The measurement of any deferred tax liability recognised is discussed at 8.4.9 below.

7.5.3 Deductible temporary differences

IAS 12 requires a deferred tax asset to be recognised for all deductible temporary differences associated with investments in subsidiaries, branches and associates or interests in joint arrangements, only to the extent that it is probable that:

(a) the temporary difference will reverse in the foreseeable future; and

(b) taxable profit will be available against which the temporary difference can be utilised. *[IAS 12.44]*.

IAS 12 does not define the meaning of 'probable' in this context. However, we consider that, as in other IFRS, it should be taken to mean 'more likely than not' (see 7.1.2 above).

The guidance discussed at 7.4 above is used to determine whether or not a deferred tax asset can be recognised for such deductible temporary differences. *[IAS 12.45]*.

Any analysis of whether a deductible temporary difference gives rise to an asset must presumably make the same distinction between controlled and non-controlled entities as is required when assessing whether a taxable temporary difference gives rise to a liability (see 7.5.2 above). This may mean, in practical terms, that it is never possible to recognise a deferred tax asset in respect of a non-controlled investment (such as an associate), unless either the investee entity is committed to a course of action that would realise the asset or, where the asset can be realised by disposal, that it is probable that the reporting entity will undertake such a disposal.

The measurement of any deferred tax asset recognised is discussed at 8.4.9 below.

7.5.4 Foreseeable future – anticipated intragroup dividends

Under IAS 10, a dividend may be recognised as a liability of the paying entity and revenue of the receiving entity only if it has been declared by the paying entity before the end of the reporting period. *[IAS 10.12]*. This raises the question of when a reporting entity should account for the tax consequences of a dividend expected to be paid by a subsidiary or other investee out of its retained profits as at the reporting date.

7.5.4.A Consolidated financial statements of receiving entity

IAS 12 requires an investor to make provision for the taxes payable on the retained profits of its subsidiaries, branches, associates, and interests in joint arrangements as at each reporting date based on the best evidence available to it at the reporting date, subject only to the exception discussed at 7.5.2 above. *[IAS 12.39]*. For example, if in preparing its financial statements for 31 December 2021, an entity believes that, in order to meet the dividend expectations of its shareholders in 2022 and 2023, it will have to cause the retained earnings of certain overseas subsidiaries (as included in the group accounts at 31 December 2021) to be distributed, the group should provide for any tax consequences of such distributions in its consolidated financial statements for the period ended 31 December 2021. In these circumstances, the entity would be unable to assert that it is probable that the temporary difference associated with the retained earnings of these subsidiaries will not reverse in the foreseeable future. [IAS 12.39(b)]. Similarly, if the ability of the entity to settle financial liabilities as at the reporting date depends on the future receipt of dividends from other entities in the group, it should recognise the tax consequences of making those distributions in its consolidated financial statements for the current period.

It is not relevant that such dividends have not yet been recognised in the separate financial statements of the relevant members of the group. Indeed, such intragroup dividends will never be recognised in the group financial statements, as they will be eliminated on consolidation. IAS 12 requires recognition of the tax consequences of temporary differences as at the end of the reporting period, in this case the taxes ultimately payable on recovering the net assets of the group as at 31 December 2021. However, for this reason it would not be appropriate to recognise any liability for the tax anticipated to be paid out of an intragroup dividend in a future period that is likely to be covered by profits generated in future periods, since such profits do not form part of the carrying amount of the net assets of the group as at 31 December 2021.

This requirement was confirmed by the Interpretations Committee in June 2020, when it considered a question about how an entity, in its consolidated financial statements, accounts for deferred tax related to its investment in a subsidiary.[31] See 8.4.9 below.

7.5.4.B Separate financial statements of paying entity

Irrespective of whether a provision is made in the consolidated financial statements for the tax effects of an expected future intragroup dividend of the retained earnings of a subsidiary, the paying subsidiary would not recognise a liability for the tax effects of any distribution in its individual or separate financial statements until the liability to pay the dividend was recognised in those individual or separate financial statements. IAS 12 requires current and deferred taxes to be measured using the rate applicable to undistributed profits until a liability to pay a dividend is recognised, as discussed at 8.5 below. [IAS 12.52A, 57A].

7.5.5 Unpaid intragroup interest, royalties, management charges etc.

It is common for groups of companies to access the earnings of subsidiaries not only through distribution by way of dividend, but also by levying charges on subsidiaries such as interest, royalties or general management charges for central corporate services. In practice, such charges are often not settled but left outstanding on the intercompany account between the subsidiary and the parent. In some jurisdictions such income is taxed only on receipt.

This has led some to argue that, where settlement of such balances is within the control of the reporting entity, and it can be demonstrated that there is no foreseeable intention or need to settle outstanding amounts, such balances are economically equivalent to unremitted earnings, so that there is no need to provide for the tax consequences of settlement.

In February 2003 the Interpretations Committee considered the issue and indicated that it believes that the exemption from provision for deferred taxes on 'outside' temporary differences arising from subsidiaries, branches, associates and interests in joint arrangements is intended to address the temporary differences arising from the undistributed earnings of such entities. The exception does not apply to the 'inside' temporary differences that exist between the carrying amount and the tax base of individual assets and liabilities within the subsidiary, branch, associate or interest in a joint arrangement. Accordingly, the Interpretations Committee concluded that a deferred tax liability should be provided for the tax consequences of settling unpaid intragroup charges.[32]

7.6 'Tax-transparent' ('flow-through') entities

In many tax jurisdictions certain entities are not taxed in their own right. Instead the income of such entities is taxed in the hands of their owners as if it were income of the owners. An example might be a partnership which does not itself pay tax, but whose partners each pay tax on their share of the partnership's profits. Such entities are sometimes referred to as 'tax-transparent' or 'flow-through' entities.

The tax status of such an entity is of no particular relevance to the accounting treatment, in the investor's financial statements, of the current tax on the income of the entity. An investor in such an entity will determine whether the entity is a subsidiary, associate, joint arrangement, branch or a financial asset investment and account for it accordingly. The investor then accounts for its own current tax payable as it arises under the relevant tax legislation.

The investor will also determine whether the basis on which the investment has been accounted for (e.g. through consolidation or equity accounting) has led to the recognition of assets or liabilities which give rise to temporary differences and recognise deferred tax on these in the normal way.

Finally, the investor will also determine whether there are 'outside' temporary differences associated with the investment as a whole and account for these as above. However, in situations where the income from the investment is, under tax law, automatically regarded as income of the investor (for example, regardless of whether such income is distributed or not), there would be no 'outside' temporary differences associated with undistributed profits. As such, the criteria in paragraph 39 of IAS 12 that allow non-recognition of certain taxable temporary differences would not apply (see 7.5.2 above). *[IAS 12.39]*.

Examples 33.27 and 33.28 illustrate the accounting treatment for, respectively, a consolidated and an equity-accounted tax-transparent entity.

Example 33.27: Tax-transparent entity (consolidated)

An entity (A) acquires 60% of a tax-transparent partnership (P) for $100 million in a transaction accounted for as a business combination. The aggregate fair value of the identifiable net assets of the partnership is $80 million and their tax base is $60m. A is directly liable to tax at 25% on 60% of the taxable profits of the partnership, in computing which it is entitled to offset 60% of the tax base of the assets. A elects to measure the non-controlling interest at its proportionate share of the net assets of the partnership.

The accounting entry to record the business combination is:

	$m	$m
Net assets	80	
Goodwill (balancing figure)	55	
Consideration paid		100
Deferred tax*		3
Non-controlling interest†		32

* In recovering the carrying value of the net assets ($80m), A will pay tax on 60% of $20m ($80m – $60m) = $12m at 25% = $3m.
† 40% of $80m.

By contrast, if the partnership were a tax-paying entity, the accounting entry would be:

	$m	$m
Net assets	80	
Goodwill (balancing figure)	55	
Consideration paid		100
Deferred tax*		5
Non-controlling interest†		30

* In recovering the carrying value of the net assets ($80m), P will pay tax on $20m ($80m – $60m) at 25% = $5m.
† 40% of $75m (net assets excluding deferred tax $80m less deferred tax (as above) $5m).

Example 33.28: Tax-transparent entity (equity-accounted)

The facts are the same as in Example 33.27 above, except that, due to an agreement between A and the other partners, P is a jointly-controlled entity, rather than a subsidiary, of A, which accounts for P using the equity method. In this case it is less clear how to account for the deferred tax liability, which, it must be remembered, is not a liability of P, but of A and therefore does not form part of the net assets and goodwill underlying A's investment in P.

One analysis might be that the deferred tax relates to a temporary difference arising on the initial recognition of the investment in P in a transaction that gives rise to no accounting or taxable profit, and therefore is not recognised under the initial recognition exception (see 7.2.3 above). On this view, the initial accounting entry is simply:

	$m	$m
Investment in P	100	
Consideration		100

Another analysis might be that the true cost of the investment in P comprises both the consideration paid to the vendor and the assumption by A of the deferred tax liability associated with its share of the underlying assets (other than goodwill) of the investment. On this view the initial accounting entry is:

	$m	$m
Investment in P	103	
Deferred tax (see Example 33.27 above)		3
Consideration		100

This second method has the merit that it results in the same implied underlying goodwill as arises on full consolidation in Example 33.27 above: $103m – $48m [60% of $80m] = $55m. However, it does raise the issue of an apparent 'day one' impairment, as discussed in more detail at 12.3 below.

In our view, either analysis is acceptable so long as it is applied consistently.

Any income tax relating to a tax-transparent entity accounted for using equity accounting forms part of the investor's tax charge. It is therefore included in the income tax line in profit or loss and not shown as part of the investor's share of the results of the tax-transparent entity.

7.7 Deferred taxable gains

Some tax regimes mitigate the tax impact of significant asset disposals by allowing some or all of the tax liability on such transactions to be deferred, usually subject to conditions, such as a requirement to reinvest the proceeds from the sale of the asset disposed of in a similar 'replacement' asset. The postponement of tax payments achieved in this way may either be for a fixed period (e.g. the liability must be paid in any event no later than ten years after the original disposal) or for an indefinite period (e.g. the liability crystallises when, and only when, the 'replacement' asset is subsequently disposed of).

As noted at 7.3 above, IAS 12 makes it clear that the ability to postpone payment of the tax liability arising on disposal of an asset – even for a considerable period – does not extinguish the liability. In many cases, the effect of such deferral provisions in tax legislation is to reduce the tax base of the 'replacement' asset. This will increase any taxable temporary difference, or reduce any deductible temporary difference, associated with the asset.

8 DEFERRED TAX – MEASUREMENT

8.1 Legislation at the end of the reporting period

Deferred tax should be measured by reference to the tax rates and laws, as enacted or substantively enacted by the end of the reporting period, that are expected to apply in the periods in which the assets and liabilities to which the deferred tax relates are realised or settled. *[IAS 12.47]*.

When different tax rates apply to different levels of taxable income, deferred tax assets and liabilities are measured using the average rates that are expected to apply to the taxable profit (tax loss) of the periods in which the temporary differences are expected to reverse. *[IAS 12.49]*.

IAS 12 comments that, in some jurisdictions, announcements of tax rates (and tax laws) by the government have the substantive effect of actual enactment, which may follow the announcement by a period of several months. In these circumstances, tax assets and liabilities are measured using the announced tax rate (and tax laws). *[IAS 12.48]*.

IAS 12 gives no guidance as to how this requirement is to be interpreted in different jurisdictions. In most jurisdictions, however, a consensus has emerged as to the meaning of 'substantive enactment' for that jurisdiction. Nevertheless, in practice apparently similar legislative processes in different jurisdictions may give rise to different treatments under IAS 12. For example, in most jurisdictions, tax legislation requires the formal approval of the head of state in order to become law. However, in some jurisdictions the head of state has real executive power (and could potentially not approve the legislation), whereas in others the head of state has a more ceremonial role (and cannot practically fail to approve the legislation).

The general principle tends to be that, in those jurisdictions where the head of state has executive power, legislation is not substantively enacted until actually approved by the head of state. Where, however, the head of state's powers are more ceremonial, substantive enactment is generally regarded as occurring at the stage of the legislative process where no further amendment is possible.

Some examples of the interpretation of 'substantive enactment' in particular jurisdictions are given at 5.1.1 above.

8.1.1 Changes to tax rates and laws enacted before the reporting date

Deferred tax should be measured by reference to the tax rates and laws, as enacted or substantively enacted by the end of the reporting period. *[IAS 12.47]*. This requirement for substantive enactment is clear. Changes that have not been enacted by the end of the reporting period are ignored, but changes that are enacted before the reporting date must be applied, even in circumstances when complex legislation is substantively enacted shortly before the end of an annual or interim reporting period.

In cases where the effective date of any enacted changes is after the end of the reporting period, deferred tax should still be calculated by applying the new rates and laws to the deductible and taxable temporary differences that are expected to reverse in those later periods. *[IAS 12.47]*. When the effective date of any rate changes is not the first day of the entity's annual reporting period, deferred tax would be calculated by applying a blended rate to the taxable profits for each year.

In implementing any amendment to enacted tax rates and laws there will be matters to consider that are specific to the actual changes being made to the tax legislation. However, the following principles from IAS 12 and other standards are relevant in all cases where new tax legislation has been enacted before the end of the reporting period.

8.1.1.A Managing uncertainty in determining the effect of new tax legislation

Where complex legislation is enacted, especially if enactment is shortly before the end of the reporting period, entities might encounter two distinct sources of uncertainty:

- uncertainty about the requirements of the new law, which may give rise to uncertain tax treatments as defined by IFRIC 23 and discussed at 8.2 and 9 below;
- incomplete information because entities may not have all the data required to process the effects of the changes in tax laws.

It is not necessary for entities to have a complete understanding of every aspect of the new tax law to arrive at reasonable estimates, and provided that entities make every effort to obtain and take into account all the information they could reasonably be expected to obtain up to the date when the financial statements for the period are authorised for issue, subsequent changes to those estimates would not be regarded as a prior period error under IAS 8. *[IAS 8.5]*. Only in rare circumstances would it not be possible to determine a reasonable estimate. However, these uncertainties may require additional disclosure in the financial statements. IAS 1 requires entities to disclose information about major sources of estimation uncertainty at the end of the reporting period that have a significant risk of resulting in a material adjustment to the carrying amounts of assets and liabilities within the next financial year (see Chapter 3 at 5.2.1). *[IAS 1.125-129]*.

Whilst the effect of changes in tax laws enacted after the end of the reporting period are not taken into account (see 8.1.2 below), information and events that occur between the end of the reporting period and the date when the financial statements are authorised for issue are adjusting events after the reporting period if they provide evidence of conditions that existed as at the reporting date. *[IAS 10.3]*. Updated tax calculations, collection of additional data, clarifications issued by the tax authorities and gaining more experience with the previously enacted tax legislation before the authorisation of the financial statements should be treated as adjusting events if they pertain to the position at the balance sheet date. Events that are indicative of conditions that arose after the reporting period should be treated as non-adjusting events. Judgement needs to be applied in determining whether technical corrections and regulatory guidance issued after year-end are to be considered adjusting events.

Where the effect of changes in the applicable tax rates compared to the previous accounting period are material, an explanation of those effects is required to be provided in the notes to the financial statements (see 14.1 below). *[IAS 12.81(d)]*.

8.1.1.B   Backward tracing of changes in deferred taxation

IAS 12 requires tax relating to items not accounted for in profit or loss, whether in the same period or a different period, to be recognised:

(a)   in other comprehensive income, if it relates to an item accounted for in other comprehensive income; or

(b)   directly in equity, if it relates to an item accounted for directly in equity. *[IAS 12.61A]*.

If current and deferred taxes change as a result of new tax legislation, IAS 12 requires the impact to be attributed to the items in profit or loss, other comprehensive income and equity that gave rise to the tax in the first place. The requirement to have regard to the previous history of a transaction in accounting for its tax effects is commonly referred to as 'backward tracing' and is discussed at 10 below. The backward tracing requirements also apply to any subsequent changes in accounting estimates.

8.1.1.C   Disclosures relating to changes in enacted tax rates and laws

In addition to the disclosures noted at 8.1.1.A above concerning major sources of estimation uncertainty at the end of the reporting period, the following disclosures are required by IAS 12 (see 14 below):

- the amount of deferred tax expense (or income) relating to changes in tax rates or the imposition of new taxes; *[IAS 12.80(d)]*
- an explanation of changes in the applicable tax rate(s) compared to the previous accounting period; *[IAS 12.81(d)]* and
- information about tax-related contingent liabilities and contingent assets in accordance with the requirements of IAS 37 (see 9.6 below and Chapter 26 at 7). *[IAS 12.88]*.

8.1.2   Changes to tax rates and laws enacted after the reporting date

The requirement for substantive enactment as at the end of the reporting period is clear. IAS 10 identifies the enactment or announcement of a change in tax rates and laws after the end of the reporting period as an example of a non-adjusting event. *[IAS 10.22(h)]*. For example, an entity with a reporting period ending on 31 December issuing its financial statements on 20 April the following year would measure its tax assets and liabilities by reference to tax rates and laws enacted or substantively enacted as at 31 December even if these had changed significantly before 20 April and even if those changes have retrospective effect. However, in these circumstances the entity would have to disclose the nature of those changes and provide an estimate of the financial effect of those changes if the impact is expected to be significant (see 14.2 below). *[IAS 10.21]*.

8.2 Uncertain tax treatments

'Uncertain tax treatment' is defined as a tax treatment over which there is uncertainty concerning its acceptance under the law by the relevant taxation authority. For example, an entity's decision not to submit any tax filing in a particular tax jurisdiction or not to include specific income in taxable profit would be an uncertain tax treatment, if its acceptability is unclear under tax law. *[IFRIC 23.3]*.

Accounting for uncertain tax treatments is a particularly challenging aspect of accounting for tax. The requirements of IFRIC 23, which was issued in June 2017, are mandatory for annual reporting periods beginning on or after 1 January 2019 and are discussed at 9 below.

8.3 'Prior year adjustments' of previously presented tax balances and expense (income)

This is discussed in the context of current tax at 5.3 above. The comments there apply equally to adjustments to deferred tax balances and expense (income). Accordingly, for accounting purposes, the normal provisions of IAS 8 apply, which require an entity to determine whether the revision represents a correction of a material prior period error or a refinement in the current period of an earlier estimate.

8.4 Expected manner of recovery of assets or settlement of liabilities

Deferred tax should be measured by reference to the tax consequences that would follow from the manner in which the entity expects, at the end of the reporting period, to recover or settle the carrying amount of the asset or liability to which it relates. *[IAS 12.51]*.

8.4.1 Tax planning strategies to reduce liabilities are not anticipated

As discussed at 7.4.4 above, IAS 12 allows tax planning strategies to be taken into account in determining whether a deductible temporary difference as at the reporting date can be recognised as a deferred tax asset, provided that the entity will create taxable profit in appropriate periods. *[IAS 12.29(b)]*. This raises the question of the extent to which tax planning strategies may be taken into account more generally in applying IAS 12.

For example, some jurisdictions may offer incentives in the form of a significantly reduced tax rate for entities that undertake particular activities, or invest in particular plant, property and equipment, or create a certain level of employment.

Some have argued that, where an entity has the ability and intention to undertake transactions in the future that will lead to its being taxed at a lower rate, it may take this into account in measuring deferred tax liabilities relating to temporary differences that exist at the reporting date and will reverse in future periods when the lower rate is expected to apply.

We believe that this is not appropriate. IAS 12 only allows entities to consider tax planning opportunities available to the entity that will create taxable profits in appropriate periods for the purpose of determining whether deferred tax assets qualify for recognition. *[IAS 12.29(b)]*. However, entities are not permitted to take into account future tax planning opportunities in relation to the measurement of deferred tax liabilities as at the reporting date, nor are entities allowed to anticipate future tax deductions that are expected to become available. Such opportunities do not impact on the measurement of deferred tax until the entity has undertaken them, or is at least irrevocably committed to doing so.

8.4.2   Carrying amount

IAS 12 requires an entity to account for the tax consequences of recovering an asset or settling a liability at its carrying amount, and not, for example, the tax that might arise on a disposal at the current estimated fair value of the asset. This is illustrated by the example below.

Example 33.29:   Measurement of deferred tax based on carrying amount of asset

During 2013 an entity, which has an accounting date of 31 December and pays tax at 40%, purchased a business and assigned €3 million of the purchase consideration to goodwill. The goodwill originally had a tax base of €3 million, deductible only on disposal of the goodwill. Thus there was no temporary difference on initial recognition of the goodwill (and, even if there had been, no deferred tax would have been recognised under the initial recognition exception – see 7.2.2 above). During 2014 the entity disposed of another business giving rise to a taxable gain of €500,000. The tax law of the relevant jurisdiction allowed the gain to be deferred by deducting it from the tax base of the goodwill, which therefore became €2.5 million.

Since IFRS prohibits the amortisation of goodwill, but instead requires it to be measured at cost less impairment, in our view IAS 12 effectively requires any deferred tax to be measured at the amount that would arise if the goodwill were sold at its carrying amount. At the end of 2014, the goodwill was still carried at €3 million. The decrease in the tax base during the period through deferral of the taxable gain gave rise to a taxable temporary difference of €500,000 (€3 million carrying amount less €2.5 million tax base), which, since it arose after the initial recognition of the goodwill (see 7.2.4 above), gave rise to the recognition of a deferred tax liability of €200,000 (€500,000 @ 40%).

During 2015, the acquired business suffered a severe downturn in trading, such that the goodwill of €3 million was written off in its entirety. This gave rise to a deductible temporary difference of €2.5 million (carrying amount of zero less €2.5 million tax base). The deferred tax liability of €200,000 recognised at the end of 2014 was released. However, no deferred tax asset was recognised since it did not meet the criteria in IAS 12 for recognition of deferred tax assets, since there was no expectation of suitable taxable profits sufficient to enable recovery of the asset (see 7.4 above).

During 2021, a new trading opportunity arises in the acquired business, with the result that, at the end of 2021, the value of the goodwill of that business is once more €3 million. However, in accordance with IAS 36, which prohibits the reinstatement of previously impaired goodwill (see Chapter 20 at 8.2.4), no accounting adjustment is made to the carrying value of goodwill.

If the goodwill were disposed of for its current fair value of €3 million, tax of €200,000 would arise. However, the entity recognises no deferred tax liability at the end of 2021, since IAS 12 requires the entity to recognise the tax (if any) that would arise on disposal of the goodwill for its carrying amount of zero. If the asset were sold for zero, a tax loss of €2.5 million would arise but, in accordance with the general provisions of IAS 12 discussed at 7.4 above, a deferred tax asset could be recognised in respect of this deductible temporary difference only if there were an expectation of suitable taxable profits sufficient to enable that tax loss to be utilised.

This may mean that any deferred tax asset or liability recognised under IAS 12 will reflect the expected manner of recovery or settlement, but not the expected amount of recovery or settlement, where this differs from the current carrying amount.

8.4.3 Assets and liabilities with more than one tax base

IAS 12 notes that, in some jurisdictions, the manner in which an entity recovers (settles) the carrying amount of an asset (liability) may affect either or both of:

(a) the tax rate applicable when the entity recovers (settles) the carrying amount of the asset (or liability); and

(b) the tax base of the asset (or liability).

In such cases, an entity should measure deferred tax assets and liabilities using the tax rate and the tax base that are consistent with the expected manner of recovery or settlement. *[IAS 12.51A]*. Assets which are treated differently for tax purposes depending on whether their value is recovered through use or sale are commonly referred to as 'dual-based assets'. The basic requirements of IAS 12 for dual-based assets can be illustrated with an example.

Example 33.30: Calculation of deferred tax depending on method of realisation of asset

A building, which is fully tax-deductible, originally cost €1 million. At the end of the reporting period it is carried at €1,750,000, but tax allowances of €400,000 have been claimed in respect of it. If the building were sold the tax base of the building would be €1.5 million due to inflation-linked increases in its tax base.

Any gain on sale (calculated as sale proceeds less tax base of €1.5 million) would be taxed at 40%. If the asset is consumed in the business, its depreciation will be charged to profits that are taxed at 30%.

If the intention is to retain the asset in the business, its carrying amount will be recovered out of future income of €1.75 million, on which tax of €345,000 will be paid, calculated as:

	€000
Gross income (carrying amount of asset)	1,750
Future tax allowances for asset (£1m less €400,000 claimed to date)	(600)
	1,150
Tax at 30%	345

If, however, the intention is to sell the asset without further use, the required deferred tax liability is only €100,000 calculated as:

	€000
Sales proceeds (carrying amount of asset)	1,750
Tax base	(1,500)
	250
Tax at 40%	100

8.4.4 Determining the expected manner of recovery of assets

Example 33.30 above, like the various similar examples in IAS 12, assumes that an asset will either be used in the business or sold. In practice, however, many assets are acquired, used for part of their life and then sold before the end of that period. This is particularly the case with long-lived assets such as property. We set out below the approach which we believe should be adopted in assessing the manner of recovery of:

- depreciable PP&E, investment properties and intangible assets (see 8.4.5 below);
- non-depreciable PP&E, investment properties and intangible assets (see 8.4.6 and 8.4.7 below); and
- other assets and liabilities (see 8.4.8 below).

8.4.5 Depreciable PP&E and intangible assets

Depreciable PP&E and investment properties are accounted for in accordance with IAS 16. Amortisable intangibles are accounted for in accordance with IAS 38. IAS 16 and IAS 38, which are discussed in detail in Chapters 17 and 18, require the carrying amount of a depreciable asset to be separated into a 'residual value' and a 'depreciable amount'.

'Residual value' is defined as:

> '... the estimated amount that an entity would currently obtain from disposal of the asset, after deducting the estimated costs of disposal, if the asset were already of the age and condition expected at the end of its useful life'

and 'depreciable amount' as:

> '... the cost of an asset, or other amount substituted for cost, less its residual value'. *[IAS 16.6, IAS 38.8]*.

It is inherent in the definitions of 'residual value' and 'depreciable amount' that, in determining residual value, an entity is effectively asserting that it expects to recover the depreciable amount of an asset through use and its residual value through sale. If the entity does not expect to sell an asset, but to use and scrap it, then the residual value (i.e. the amount that would be obtained from sale) must be nil.

Accordingly, we believe that, in determining the expected manner of recovery of a depreciable asset for the purposes of IAS 12, an entity should assume that, in the case of an asset accounted for under IAS 16 or IAS 38, it will recover the residual value of the asset through sale and the depreciable amount through use. This view is reinforced by the Basis for Conclusions on IAS 12 which notes that 'recognition of depreciation implies that the carrying amount of a depreciable asset is expected to be recovered through use to the extent of its depreciable amount, and through sale at its residual value'. *[IAS 12.BC6]*.

Such an analysis is also consistent with the requirement of IAS 8 to account for similar transactions consistently (see Chapter 3 at 4.1.4). This suggests that consistent assumptions should be used in determining both the residual value of an asset for the purposes of IAS 16 and IAS 38 and the expected manner of its recovery for the purposes of IAS 12.

The effect of this treatment is illustrated as follows.

Example 33.31: Dual-based asset

As part of a business combination an entity purchases an opencast mine to which there is assigned a fair value of €10 million. The tax system of the jurisdiction where the mine is located provides that, if the site is sold (with or without the minerals *in situ*), €9 million will be allowed as a deduction in calculating the taxable profit on sale. The profit on sale of the land is taxed as a capital item. If the mine is exploited through excavation and sale of the minerals, no tax deduction is available.

The entity intends fully to exploit the mine and then to sell the site for retail development. Given the costs that any developer will need to incur in preparing the excavated site for development, the ultimate sales proceeds are expected to be €6 million. Thus, for the purposes of IAS 16, the quarry is treated as having a depreciable amount of €4 million and a residual value of €6 million.

On the analysis above, there is a taxable temporary difference of €4 million associated with the depreciable amount of the asset (carrying amount of €4 million less tax base in use of nil), and a deductible temporary difference of €3 million associated with the residual value (carrying amount of €6 million less tax base on disposal of €9 million).

The entity will therefore provide for a deferred tax liability on the taxable temporary difference. The extent to which a deferred tax asset is recognised in respect of the deductible temporary difference will depend on whether it is probable that taxable profits will be available against which that deductible temporary difference can be utilised (see 7.4 above). In some tax regimes, capital profits and losses are treated more or less separately from revenue profits and losses to a greater or lesser degree, so that it may be difficult to recognise such an asset due to a lack of suitable taxable profits.

This has not been the only interpretation of IAS 12 adopted in practice and there has been diversity as a result. However, in response to a request for guidance on this matter, the Interpretations Committee issued an agenda decision in April 2020 that supports the above analysis.[33]

The Committee was asked to consider an example in which an entity acquires an intangible asset with a finite useful life (a licence) as part of a business combination. The entity intends to recover the carrying amount of the licence through use, and the expected residual value of the licence at expiry is nil. Under the applicable tax law, two tax regimes are prescribed: an income tax regime and a capital gains tax regime. Any tax arising under each regime is not permitted to be offset in determining taxable profit. Tax paid under both regimes meets the definition of income taxes in IAS 12. Recovering the licence's carrying amount has both of the following tax consequences:

- under the income tax regime – the entity pays income tax on the economic benefits it receives from recovering the licence's carrying amount through use, but receives no tax deductions in respect of amortisation of the licence (taxable economic benefits from use); and

- under the capital gains tax regime – the entity receives a tax deduction when the licence expires that is equal to its initial carrying value (capital gain deduction).

In reaching its conclusion, the Committee cited the fundamental principle on which IAS 12 is based, that 'an entity shall, with certain limited exceptions, recognise a deferred tax liability (asset) whenever recovery or settlement of the carrying amount of an asset or liability would make future tax payments larger (smaller) than they would be if such recovery or settlement were to have no tax consequences'. *[IAS 12.10]*. The Committee determined that the entity should separately identify the temporary differences in a manner that reflects the distinct tax consequences under the two tax regimes of recovering the asset's carrying amount, by comparing:

(a) the portion of the asset's carrying amount that will be recovered under one tax regime; to

(b) the tax deductions the entity will receive under that same tax regime (which are reflected in the asset's tax base).

In the fact pattern described in the request, the Committee concluded that the entity identifies both:

(a) a taxable temporary difference under the income tax regime, reflecting the fact that it will receive no tax deductions as it recovers the asset through use; and

(b) a deductible temporary difference under the capital gains tax regime, representing the deduction received upon expiry of the licence.

The entity should then apply the requirements in IAS 12 considering the applicable tax law in recognising and measuring deferred tax for the identified temporary differences.

On this basis, the Committee concluded that the principles and requirements in IAS 12 provide an adequate basis for an entity to recognise and measure deferred tax in the fact pattern described in the request and consequently decided not to add the matter to its standard-setting agenda.[34]

8.4.6 Non-depreciable PP&E and intangible assets

During 2009 and 2010 the IASB received representations from various entities and bodies that it was often difficult and subjective to determine the manner of recovery of certain categories of asset for the purposes of IAS 12. This was particularly the case for investment properties accounted for at fair value under IAS 40 which are often traded opportunistically, without a specific business plan, but yield rental income until disposed of. In many jurisdictions rental income is taxed at the standard rate, while gains on asset sales are tax-free or taxed at a significantly lower rate. The principal difficulty was that the then extant guidance (SIC-21 – *Income Taxes – Recovery of Revalued Non-Depreciable Assets*) effectively required entities to determine what the residual amount of the asset would be if it were depreciated under IAS 16 rather than accounted for at fair value,[35] which many regarded as resulting in nonsensical tax effect accounting.

To deal with these concerns, in December 2010 the IASB amended IAS 12 so as to give more specific guidance on determining the expected manner of recovery for non-depreciable assets measured using the revaluation model in IAS 16 (see 8.4.6.A below) and for investment properties measured using the fair value model in IAS 40 (see 8.4.7 below). As noted at 8.4.6.B below, an indefinite-life intangible asset (that is not amortised because its useful economic life cannot be reliably determined) is not the same as a non-depreciable asset to which this amendment would apply.

8.4.6.A PP&E accounted for using the revaluation model

IAS 16 allows property, plant and equipment (PP&E) to be accounted for using a revaluation model under which PP&E is regularly revalued to fair value (see Chapter 18 at 6). IAS 12 clarifies that where a non-depreciable asset is revalued, any deferred tax on the revaluation should be calculated by reference to the tax consequences that would arise if the asset were sold at book value irrespective of the basis on which the carrying amount of the asset is measured. *[IAS 12.51B]*. The rationale for this treatment is that, in accounting terms, the asset is never recovered through use, as it is not depreciable. *[IAS 12.BC6]*.

IAS 12 clarifies that these requirements are subject to the general restrictions on the recognition of deferred tax assets (see 7.4 above). *[IAS 12.51E]*.

An issue not explicitly addressed in IAS 12 is whether the term 'non-depreciable' asset refers to an asset that is not currently being depreciated or to one that does not have a limited useful life. This is explored further in the discussion of non-amortised intangible assets immediately below.

8.4.6.B Non-amortised or indefinite-life intangible assets

Under IAS 38 an intangible asset with an indefinite life is not subject to amortisation.

The analysis at 8.4.5 and 8.4.6.A above would appear to lead to the conclusion that, where an intangible asset is not amortised, any deferred tax related to that asset should be measured on an 'on sale' basis. IAS 12 requires tax to be provided for based on the manner in which the entity expects to recover the 'carrying amount' of its assets. In this case it could be argued that if the asset is not amortised under IAS 38, the financial statements are asserting that the carrying amount is not recovered through use.

However, an alternative analysis would be that the fact that an intangible asset is not being amortised does not necessarily indicate that the expected manner of recovery is by sale or through use. The determination of an indefinite life under IAS 38 means that there is no foreseeable limit to the period over which the asset is expected to generate net cash inflows for the entity. *[IAS 38.88]*. This could still indicate an expectation of recovery through use.

This question was considered by the Interpretations Committee, which issued an agenda decision in November 2016, as follows:[36]

- the requirements in paragraph 51B of IAS 12 do not apply to indefinite-life intangible assets. An indefinite-life intangible asset is not a non-depreciable asset as envisaged by paragraph 51B of IAS 12. This is because a non-depreciable asset has an unlimited (or infinite) life. IAS 38 is clear that the term 'indefinite' does not mean 'infinite'; *[IAS 38.91]*

- the reason for not amortising an indefinite-life intangible asset is not because there is no consumption of the future economic benefits embodied in the asset. When the IASB amended IAS 38 in 2004, it observed that an indefinite-life intangible asset is not amortised because there is no foreseeable limit on the period during which the entity expects to consume the future economic benefits embodied in the asset and, hence, amortisation over an arbitrarily determined maximum period would not be representationally faithful; *[IAS 38.BC74]*

- the fact that an entity does not amortise an indefinite-life intangible asset does not necessarily mean that its carrying amount will be recovered only through sale and not through use. An entity recovers the carrying amount of an asset in the form of economic benefits that flow to the entity in future periods, which could be through use or sale of the asset; and

- accordingly, an entity should determine its expected manner of recovery of the carrying value of the indefinite-life intangible asset in accordance with the principle and requirements in paragraphs 51 and 51A of IAS 12 (as discussed at 8.4.3 above) and reflect the tax consequences that follow from that expected manner of recovery.

Whilst the agenda decision requires entities to review cases where they have previously applied paragraph 51B to indefinite-life intangible assets, it does not imply a presumption that the carrying amount of an indefinite-life intangible asset is always recovered through use (or for that matter through sale). The agenda decision emphasises that entities should apply the principle and requirements in paragraphs 51 and 51A that the tax consequences follow the expected manner of recovery of the asset. As noted above, this is a judgement made by reference to the entity's specific circumstances including its business model. Therefore, it remains possible that an entity could determine recovery through sale by applying the requirements of paragraphs 51 and 51A of IAS 12. However, such a conclusion would require an entity to be able to demonstrate that the facts and circumstances, including the entity's business model, support a realistic expectation that the specific intangible asset would be disposed of before any material recovery of its carrying amount had occurred through use.

It is possible that an entity applies the principle and requirements in paragraphs 51 and 51A and determines that, in its opinion, a portion of the indefinite-life intangible asset is expected to be recovered through use and another component is expected to be recovered through sale. In this case, the entity should challenge its original conclusion that the asset has an indefinite-life, in particular, that 'there is no foreseeable limit to the period over which the asset is expected to generate net cash inflows for the entity'. *[IAS 38.88]*.

Another question that often arises in the context of expected manner of recovery of an indefinite-life intangible asset is whether an entity should have a formal plan to sell the asset in order to determine an expected recovery through sale. Unlike other Standards (such as IFRS 5), IAS 12 does not require there to be a formal plan to sell the asset. Accordingly, judgement is required in deciding whether recovery is through sale if there are no immediate plans to sell the asset.

An impairment of an indefinite-life intangible asset or non-depreciable asset previously determined to be recovered through sale does not automatically change the expected manner of recovery of the asset. The recoverable amount under IAS 36 is defined as the higher of an asset's or cash-generating unit's fair value less costs to sell and its value in use regardless of the intent of management, whereas the expected manner of recovery will take management intent into account. Accordingly, an impairment charge can arise simply because of a change in the entity's estimate of the asset's recoverable amount. If an indefinite-life intangible asset is impaired, it is appropriate to challenge the validity of the entity's original determination that the asset life was indefinite. If it is determined that the asset is now depreciable, there is a change in the expected manner of recovery of at least the depreciable portion of the asset under paragraph 51 of IAS 12. When an entity starts to amortise the indefinite-life intangible asset, the asset ceases to be an indefinite life intangible asset, and the change is accounted as a change in estimate under IAS 8. *[IAS 38.109]*.

8.4.7 Investment properties

IAS 40 allows investment properties to be accounted for at fair value (see Chapter 19 at 6). IAS 12 requires any deferred tax asset or liability associated with such a property to be measured using a rebuttable presumption that the carrying amount of the investment property will be recovered through sale. *[IAS 12.51C]*. The same rebuttable presumption is used when measuring any deferred tax asset or liability associated with an investment property acquired in a business combination if the entity intends to adopt the fair value model in accounting for the property subsequently. *[IAS 12.51D]*.

The presumption is rebutted if the investment property is depreciable and the entity's business model is to consume substantially all the economic benefits embodied in the investment property over time, rather than through sale. The Interpretations Committee has clarified that the presumption can be rebutted in other circumstances, provided that sufficient evidence is available to support that rebuttal. However, the Committee neither gave any indication of, nor placed any restriction on, what those other circumstances might be.[37] If the presumption is rebutted, the entity applies the normal requirements of IAS 12 for determining the manner of recovery of assets (see 8.4.1 to 8.4.5 above). *[IAS 12.51C]*.

IAS 12 clarifies that these requirements are subject to the general restrictions on the recognition of deferred tax assets (see 7.4 above). *[IAS 12.51E]*.

8.4.8 Other assets and liabilities

In a number of areas of accounting IFRS effectively requires a transaction to be accounted for in accordance with an assumption as to the ultimate settlement of that transaction that may not reflect the entity's expectation of the actual outcome.

For example, if the entity enters into a share-based payment transaction with an employee that gives the employee the right to require settlement in either shares or cash, IFRS 2 requires the transaction to be accounted for on the assumption that it will be settled in cash, however unlikely this may be. IAS 19 may assert that an entity has a surplus on a defined benefit pension scheme on an accounting basis, when in reality it has a deficit on a funding basis. Similarly, if an entity issues a convertible bond that can also be settled in cash at the holder's option, IAS 32 requires the bond to be accounted for on the assumption that it will be repaid, however probable it is that the holders will actually elect for conversion. It may well be that such transactions have different tax consequences depending on the expected manner of settlement, as illustrated in Example 33.32 below.

Example 33.32: Convertible bond deductible if settled

An entity issues a convertible bond for €1 million. After three years, the holders can elect to receive €1.2 million or 100,000 shares of the entity. If the bond were settled in cash, the entity would receive a tax deduction for the €200,000 difference between its original issue proceeds and the amount payable on redemption. If the bond is converted, no tax deduction is available.

Under IAS 32, the bond would be accreted from €1 million to €1.2 million over the three year issue period. The tax base remains at €1 million throughout, so that a deductible temporary difference of €200,000 emerges over the issue period. It is assumed that the deferred tax asset relating to this difference would meet the recognition criteria in IAS 12 (see 7.4 above).

For various reasons, it is extremely unlikely that the bond will be redeemed in cash.

Example 33.32 raises the issue of whether any deferred tax asset should be recognised in respect of the €200,000 temporary difference.

One view would be that no deferred tax asset should be recognised on the basis that there is no real expectation that the transaction will be settled in cash, thus allowing the entity to claim a tax deduction. The contrary view would be that the underlying

Income taxes 2551

rationale of IAS 12 is that, in order for the financial statements to be internally consistent, the tax effects of recognised assets and liabilities must also be recognised (see 2.1 above). Accordingly, a deferred tax asset should be recognised.

8.4.9 'Outside' temporary differences relating to subsidiaries, branches, associates and joint arrangements

In this section, an 'outside' temporary difference means a difference between the tax base in the jurisdiction of the investor of an investment in a subsidiary, associate or branch or an interest in a joint arrangement and carrying amount of that investment or interest (or the net assets and goodwill relating to it) included in the financial statements. Such differences, and the special recognition criteria applied to them by IAS 12, are discussed in more detail at 7.5 above.

Where deferred tax is required to be recognised on such a temporary difference (see 7.5.2 to 7.5.4 above), the question arises as to how it should be measured. Broadly speaking, investors can realise an investment in one of two ways – either indirectly (by remittance of retained earnings or capital) or directly (through sale of the investment to a third party or by receiving residual assets upon liquidation of the associate). In many jurisdictions, the two means of realisation have very different tax consequences.

Having determined that a temporary difference should be recognised, the entity should apply the general rule (discussed in more detail above) that, where there is more than one method of recovering an investment, the entity should measure any associated deferred tax asset or liability by reference to the tax consequences associated with the expected manner of recovery of the investment. *[IAS 12.51A]*. In other words, to the extent that the investment is expected to be realised through sale, the deferred tax is measured according to the tax rules applicable on sale, but to the extent that the temporary difference is expected to reverse through a distribution of earnings or capital, the deferred tax is measured according to the tax rules applicable on distribution. In its decision in March 2015 not to take a question on this matter to its agenda, the Interpretations Committee confirmed this view. Accordingly, if one part of the temporary difference is expected to be received as dividends, and another part is expected to be recovered upon sale or liquidation (for example, an investor has a plan to sell the investment later and expects to receive dividends until the sale of the investment), different tax rates would be applied to the parts of the temporary difference in order to be consistent with the expected manner of recovery.[38]

Where the expected manner of recovery is through distribution, IAS 12 requires this to be reflected in the measurement of any related deferred tax assets and liabilities. *[IAS 12.51A]*. This includes proper consideration of the requirements of the standard where the rate at which tax is paid depends on whether profits are distributed or retained (see 8.5 below). This was confirmed in June 2020, when the Interpretations Committee considered a case where an entity and its subsidiary operate in a jurisdiction where profits are taxable only when distributed (i.e. the income tax rate applicable to undistributed profits is nil). The fact pattern considered is set out in Example 33.33 below.[39]

Example 33.33: Deferred tax related to an investment in a subsidiary

Entity A has determined that the undistributed profits of its subsidiary give rise to a taxable temporary difference associated with the entity's investment in the subsidiary and that it cannot rely on the recognition exemption in paragraph 39 of IAS 12 because it expects the subsidiary to distribute its profits (which are available for distribution) in the foreseeable future.

Both Entity A and its subsidiary operate in a jurisdiction in which:

(a) profits are taxable only when distributed, i.e. the income tax rate applicable to undistributed profits is nil (undistributed tax rate); and

(b) a 20% tax rate applies to profit distributions (distributed tax rate). However, profit distributions made by the entity are not taxable to the extent that the subsidiary has already been taxed on that profit, i.e. profit distributions are taxed only once.

The Committee was asked whether Entity A recognises a deferred tax liability for the taxable temporary difference associated with its investment in the subsidiary.

The Committee concluded that, in the fact pattern described, Entity A should recognise the deferred tax liability related to its investment in the subsidiary and measure it using the distributed tax rate of 20%. In making this determination, the Committee observed that:

- there is a taxable temporary difference associated with the entity's investment in the subsidiary. The entity has also determined that the recognition exception in paragraph 39 of IAS 12 does not apply because it is probable that the temporary difference will reverse in the foreseeable future when the subsidiary distributes its undistributed profits;
- paragraph 51 of IAS 12 requires an entity to reflect, in the measurement of deferred tax assets and deferred tax liabilities, 'the tax consequences that would follow from the manner in which the entity expects, at the end of the reporting period, to recover or settle the carrying amount of its assets and liabilities';
- the entity expects to recover the carrying amount of its investment in the subsidiary through distributions of profits by the subsidiary, which would be taxed at the distributed tax rate; and
- it is not appropriate to use the undistributed rate in paragraph 57A of IAS 12 to measure the deferred tax liability, because that paragraph applies only in the context of dividends payable by the reporting entity. Further, paragraph 52A of IAS 12 does not apply to the measurement of a current or deferred tax asset or liability that itself reflects the tax consequences of a distribution of profits.

The Committee concluded that the principles and requirements in IAS 12 provide an adequate basis for an entity to account for deferred tax in the fact pattern described in the request and consequently decided not to add the matter to its standard-setting agenda.[40]

In other cases, there may be tax consequences for more than one entity in the group when a distribution is made. For example, the paying company may suffer a withholding tax on the dividend paid and the receiving company may suffer income tax on the dividend received. In such cases, provision should be made for the cumulative effect of all tax consequences. As discussed further at 10.3.3 below, a withholding tax on an intragroup dividend is not accounted for in the consolidated financial statements as a withholding tax (i.e. within equity), but as a tax expense in profit or loss, since the group is not making a distribution but transferring assets from a group entity to a parent of that entity.

8.4.10 'Single asset' entities

In many jurisdictions it is common for certain assets (particularly properties) to be bought and sold by transferring ownership of a separate legal entity formed to hold the asset (a 'single asset' entity) rather than the asset itself.

A 'single asset' entity may be formed for a number of reasons. For example, the insertion of a 'single asset' entity between the 'real' owner and the property may limit the 'real' owner's liability for obligations arising from ownership of the property. It may also provide shelter from tax liabilities arising on disposal of the property since, in many jurisdictions, the sale of shares is taxed at a lower rate than the sale of property.

This raises the question whether, in determining the expected manner of recovery of an asset for the purposes of IAS 12, an entity may have regard to the fact that an asset held by a 'single asset' entity can be disposed of by selling the shares of the entity rather than the asset itself.

The Interpretations Committee has discussed this matter on a number of occasions since September 2011. In May 2012, the Committee noted the following significant diversity in practice:[41]

- some preparers recognise deferred tax on both the asset within, and the shares of, the 'single asset' entity;
- some preparers recognise tax on the shares only; and
- some preparers provide deferred tax on the difference between the asset within the entity and the tax base of its shares, using the tax rate applicable to a disposal of the shares.

The Interpretations Committee noted that IAS 12 requires the parent to recognise deferred tax on both the asset within, and the shares of, the 'single asset' entity, if tax law considers the asset and the shares as two separate assets and if no specific exemptions in IAS 12 apply. At that time, the Committee asked its staff to undertake more research with the possible outcome of an amendment to IAS 12 addressing this specific type of transaction. Such an amendment would, in the Committee's view, be beyond the scope of the Annual Improvements project.[42]

Following further deliberations, the Interpretations Committee decided in July 2014 not to take the issue onto its agenda but instead to recommend to the IASB that it should analyse and assess the concerns raised about the current requirements in IAS 12 in its research project on Income Taxes. In issuing its agenda decision, the Committee noted that:[43]

a) paragraph 11 of IAS 12 requires the entity to determine temporary differences in the consolidated financial statements by comparing the carrying amounts of assets and liabilities in the consolidated financial statements with the appropriate tax base. In the case of an asset or a liability of a subsidiary that files separate tax returns, this is the amount that will be taxable or deductible on the recovery (settlement) of the asset (liability) in the tax returns of the subsidiary; and

b) the requirement in paragraph 11 of IAS 12 is complemented by the requirement in paragraph 38 of IAS 12 to determine the temporary difference related to the shares held by the parent in the subsidiary by comparing the parent's share of the net assets of the subsidiary in the consolidated financial statements, including the carrying amount of goodwill, with the tax base of the shares for purposes of the parent's tax returns.

The Interpretations Committee also noted that these paragraphs require a parent to recognise both the deferred tax related to the asset inside and the deferred tax related to the shares, if:[44]

a) tax law attributes separate tax bases to the asset inside and to the shares;
b) in the case of deferred tax assets, the related deductible temporary differences can be utilised as specified in paragraphs 24 to 31 of IAS 12; and
c) no specific exceptions in IAS 12 apply.

Accordingly, in determining the expected manner of recovery of an asset for the purposes of IAS 12, the entity should have regard to both the asset itself and the shares (subject to the exemption relating to investments in subsidiaries in paragraph 39 of the Standard (see 7.5.2 above)).

8.4.11 Change in expected manner of recovery of an asset or settlement of a liability

A change in the expected manner of recovery of an asset or settlement of a liability should be dealt with as an item of deferred tax income or expense for the period in which the change of expectation occurs, and recognised in profit or loss or in other comprehensive income or movements in equity for that period as appropriate (see 10 below).

This may have the effect, in certain situations, that some tax consequences of a disposal transaction are recognised before the transaction itself. For example, an entity might own an item of PP&E which has previously been held for use but which the entity now expects to sell. In our view, any deferred tax relating to that item of PP&E should be measured on a 'sale' rather than a 'use' basis from that point, even though the disposal itself, and any related current tax, will not be accounted for until the disposal occurs. As noted at 7.4.8 above, which discusses the effect of disposals on the recoverability of tax losses, the change in measurement will be required even if the asset does not yet meet the criteria for being classified as held for sale in IFRS 5 (see Chapter 4 at 2.1.2). This is because those criteria set a higher hurdle for reclassification ('highly probable') than the requirement in IAS 12 to use the entity's expected manner of recovery of an asset.

8.5 Different tax rates applicable to retained and distributed profits

In some jurisdictions, the rate at which tax is paid depends on whether profits are distributed or retained. In other jurisdictions, distribution may lead to an additional liability to tax, or a refund of tax already paid. IAS 12 requires current and deferred taxes to be measured using the rate applicable to undistributed profits. *[IAS 12.52A]*. Only when an entity recognises a liability to pay a dividend should the tax consequences of that dividend also be recognised, as illustrated in Example 33.34 below. *[IAS 12.57A]*.

Example 33.34: Different tax rates applicable to retained and distributed profits

An entity operates in a jurisdiction where income taxes are payable at a higher rate on undistributed profits (50%) with an amount being refundable when profits are distributed. The tax rate on distributed profits is 35%. At the end of the reporting period, 31 December 2021, the entity does not recognise a liability for dividends proposed or declared after the end of the reporting period. As a result, no dividends are recognised in the year 2021. Taxable income for 2021 is €100,000. Net taxable temporary differences have increased during the year ended 31 December 2021 by €40,000.

The entity recognises a current tax liability and a current income tax expense of €50,000 (€100,000 taxable profit @ 50%). No asset is recognised for the amount potentially recoverable as a result of future dividends. The entity also recognises a deferred tax liability and deferred tax expense of €20,000 (€40,000 @ 50%) representing the income taxes that the entity will pay when it recovers or settles the carrying amounts of its assets and liabilities based on the tax rate applicable to undistributed profits.

Subsequently, on 15 March 2022 the entity declares, and recognises as a liability, dividends of €10,000 from previous operating profits. At that point, the entity recognises the recovery of income taxes of €1,500 (€10,000 @ [50% – 35%]), representing the refund of tax due in respect of the dividends recognised as a liability, as a current tax asset and as a reduction of current income tax expense for the year ended 31 December 2022.

As discussed at 10.3.5 below, the tax benefit of €1,500 in the example above will be recognised in profit or loss.

8.5.1 Effectively tax-free entities

In a number of jurisdictions certain types of entity, such as investment vehicles, are generally exempt from corporate income tax provided that they fulfil certain criteria, which generally include a requirement to distribute all, or a minimum percentage, of their annual income as a dividend to investors. This raises the question of how such entities should measure income taxes.

One view would be that, under the basic principle set out above, such an entity has a liability to tax at the undistributed rate until the dividend for a year becomes a liability. The liability for a dividend for an accounting period usually arises after the end of that period (as in Example 33.34 above). Under this analysis, therefore, such an entity would be required, at each period end, to record a liability for current tax at the standard corporate rate. That liability would be released in full when the dividend is recognised as a liability in the following period. This would mean that, on an ongoing basis, the income statement would show a current tax charge or credit comprising:

- a charge for a full liability for the current period; and
- a credit for the reversal of the corresponding liability for the prior period.

In addition, deferred tax would be recognised at the standard tax rate on all temporary differences.

A second view would be that the provisions of IAS 12 regarding different tax rates for distributed and undistributed tax rates are intended to apply where the only significant factor determining the differential tax rate is the retention or distribution of profit. By contrast, the tax status of an investment fund often depends on many more factors than whether or not profits are distributed, including restrictions on its activities and the nature of its investments. On this view, the analysis would be that such an entity can choose to operate within one of two tax regimes (a 'full tax' regime or a 'no tax' regime), rather than that it operates in a single tax regime with a dual tax rate depending on whether profits are retained or distributed. In these circumstances, it would be appropriate to infer a tax-free status for the entity until such time as it was evident that it no longer meets the conditions for retaining that status.

The IASB previously appeared to regard IAS 12 as favouring the first analysis, while accepting that the resulting accounting treatment – a cycle of raising full tax provisions and then reversing them – does not reflect economic reality. Accordingly, the exposure draft ED/2009/2 proposed that the measurement of tax assets and liabilities should include the effect of expected future distributions, based on the entity's past practices and expectations of future distributions.[45] Following the withdrawal of the exposure draft, the IASB intends to consider this issue further. However, no formal decision has been taken, nor proposals issued for comment.

8.5.2 Withholding tax or distribution tax?

In practice, it is sometimes difficult to determine whether a particular transaction should be accounted for under the provisions of IAS 12 relating to different tax rates for distributed and undistributed profits, or in accordance with the provisions of the standard relating to withholding taxes.

The classification can significantly affect tax expense, because IAS 12 requires a withholding tax to be accounted for as a deduction from equity, whereas a higher tax rate for distributed profits is usually accounted for as a charge to profit or loss.

This issue is discussed further at 10.3 below.

8.6 Discounting

IAS 12 prohibits discounting of deferred tax, on the basis that:

- it would be unreasonable to require discounting, given that it requires scheduling of the reversal of temporary differences, which can be impracticable or at least highly complex; and
- it would be inappropriate to permit discounting because of the lack of comparability between financial statements in which discounting was adopted and those in which it was not. *[IAS 12.53, 54]*.

Moreover, IAS 12 notes that when deferred tax is recognised in relation to an item that is itself discounted (such as a liability for post-employment benefits or a lease liability), the deferred tax, being based on the carrying amount of that item, is also effectively discounted. *[IAS 12.55]*.

8.7 Unrealised intragroup profits and losses in consolidated financial statements

As noted at 6.2.1 and 6.2.2 above, an unrealised intragroup profit or loss eliminated on consolidation will give rise to a temporary difference where the profit or loss arises on a transaction that alters the tax base of the item(s) subject to the transaction. Such an alteration in the tax base creates a temporary difference because there is no corresponding change in the carrying amount of the assets or liabilities in the consolidated financial statements, due to the intragroup eliminations.

IAS 12 does not specifically address the measurement of such items. However, IAS 12 generally requires an entity, in measuring deferred tax, to have regard to the expected manner of recovery or settlement of the tax. It would be consistent with this requirement to measure deferred tax on temporary differences arising from intragroup transfers at the tax rates and laws applicable to the 'transferee' company rather than those applicable to the 'transferor' company, since the 'transferee' company will be taxed when the asset or liability subject to the transfer is realised or sold.

There are some jurisdictions where the tax history of an asset or liability subject to an intragroup transfer remains with the 'transferor' company. In such cases, the general principles of IAS 12 should be used to determine whether any deferred tax should be measured at the tax rate of the 'transferor' or the 'transferee' company in the consolidated financial statements.

The effect of the treatment required by IAS 12 is that tax income or expense may be recognised on transactions eliminated on consolidation, as illustrated by Examples 33.35 and 33.36.

Example 33.35: Elimination of intragroup profit (1)

H, an entity taxed at 30%, has a subsidiary S, which is taxed at 34%. On 15 December 2021 S sells inventory with a cost of €100,000 to H for €120,000, giving rise to a taxable profit of €20,000 and current tax at 34% of €6,800. In the consolidated financial statements of H group for the year ended 31 December 2021, the profit made by S on the sale to H would be eliminated. However, whilst the carrying value of the inventory in the consolidated balance sheet is unchanged at €100,000, its tax base in H is now €120,000.

Under IAS 12, a deferred tax asset would be recognised in the consolidated financial statements on the unrealised profit of €20,000, based on H's 30% tax rate, i.e. €6,000. The additional €800 tax actually paid by S would be recognised in profit or loss for the period ended 31 December 2021, the accounting entry being:

	DR €	CR €
Current tax (profit or loss)	6,800	
Current tax (statement of financial position)		6,800
Deferred tax (statement of financial position)	6,000	
Deferred tax (profit or loss)		6,000

The net €800 tax charge to profit or loss (current tax charge €6,800 less deferred tax credit €6,000) reflects the fact that, by transferring the inventory from one tax jurisdiction to another with a lower tax rate, the group has effectively denied itself a tax deduction of €800 (i.e. €20,000 at the tax rate differential of 4%) for the inventory that would have been available had the inventory been sold by S, rather than H, to the ultimate third party customer.

Example 33.36: Elimination of intragroup profit (2)

H, an entity taxed at 34%, has a subsidiary S, which is taxed at 30%. On 15 December 2021 S sells inventory with a cost of €100,000 to H for €120,000, giving rise to a taxable profit of €20,000 and current tax at 30% of €6,000. In the consolidated financial statements of H group for the year ended 31 December 2021, the profit made by S on the sale to H would be eliminated. However, whilst the carrying value of the inventory in the consolidated balance sheet is unchanged at €100,000, its tax base in H is now €120,000.

In this case, the consolidated financial statements would record current tax paid by S of €6,000 and a deferred tax asset measured at H's effective tax rate of 34% of €6,800, giving rise to the following entry:

	DR €	CR €
Current tax (profit or loss)	6,000	
Current tax (statement of financial position)		6,000
Deferred tax (statement of financial position)	6,800	
Deferred tax (profit or loss)		6,800

In this case there is a net €800 tax credit to profit or loss (current tax charge €6,000 less deferred tax credit €6,800). This reflects the fact that, by transferring the inventory from one tax jurisdiction to another with a higher tax rate, the group has put itself in the position of being able to claim a tax deduction for the inventory of €800 (i.e. €20,000 at the tax rate differential of 4%) in excess of that which would have been available had the inventory been sold by S, rather than H, to the ultimate third party customer.

8.7.1 Intragroup transfers of goodwill and intangible assets

It is common in some jurisdictions to sell goodwill and intangible assets from one entity in a group to another in the same group, very often in order either to increase tax deductions on an already recognised asset or to obtain deductions for a previously unrecognised asset. This raises the issue of how the tax effects of such transactions should be accounted for in the financial statements both of the individual entities concerned and in the consolidated financial statements, as illustrated by Example 33.37 below.

Example 33.37: Intragroup transfer of goodwill

A parent company P has two subsidiaries – A, which was acquired some years ago and B, which was acquired during the period ended 31 December 2020 at a cost of €10 million. For the purposes of this discussion, it is assumed that B had negligible identifiable assets and liabilities. Accordingly, P recorded goodwill of €10 million in its consolidated financial statements.

During 2021, B sells its business to A for its then current fair value of €12.5 million. As the goodwill inherent in B's business was internally generated, it was not recognised in the financial statements of B. Hence, the entire consideration of €12.5 million represents a profit to B, which is subject to current tax at 20% (i.e. €2.5 million). However, as a result of this transaction, A will be entitled to claim tax deductions (again at 20%) for its newly-acquired goodwill of €12.5 million. The deductions will be received in ten equal annual instalments from 2021 to 2029. For the purposes of this discussion, it is assumed that A will have sufficient suitable taxable profits to be able to recover these deductions in full.

8.7.1.A Individual financial statements of buyer

The buyer (A) accounts for the acquisition of B's business. As the business still has negligible identifiable assets and liabilities, this gives rise to goodwill of €12.5 million within A's own financial statements. A has acquired an asset for €12.5 million with a tax base of the same amount. There is therefore no temporary difference (and thus no deferred tax) to be accounted for in the financial statements of A.

8.7.1.B Individual financial statements of seller

As described above, the individual financial statements of the seller (B) reflect a profit of €12.5 million and current tax of €2.5 million.

8.7.1.C Consolidated financial statements

In the consolidated financial statements of P, the sale of the business from B to A will be eliminated on consolidation. However, the €2.5 million current tax suffered by B will be reflected in the consolidated financial statements, since this is a transaction with a third party (the tax authority), not an intragroup transaction. The question is what, if any, deferred tax arises as the result of this transaction.

One analysis would be that the tax base of consolidated goodwill has effectively been increased from nil to €12.5 million. Compared to its carrying amount of €10 million, this creates a deductible temporary difference of €2.5 million on which a deferred tax asset at 20% (€500,000) may be recognised. It could also be argued that there is an analogy here with the general treatment of deferred tax on intragroup profits and losses eliminated on consolidation (see Examples 33.35 and 33.36 above).

Under this analysis, the consolidated income statement would show a net tax charge of €2.0 million (€2.5 million current tax expense arising in B, less €0.5 million deferred tax income arising on consolidation). However, this is arguably inconsistent with the fact that the entity is not in an overall tax-paying position (since it has incurred a current tax loss of €2.5 million, but expects to receive tax deductions of the same amount over the next ten years). Clearly, there is an economic loss since the entity has effectively made an interest free loan equal to the current tax paid to the tax authority, but this is not relevant, since tax is not measured on a discounted basis under IAS 12 (see 8.6 above).

An alternative analysis might therefore be to argue that the goodwill reflected in the consolidated statement of financial position still has no tax base. Rather, the tax base attaches to the goodwill recognised in the separate financial statements of A, which is eliminated on consolidation, and therefore has no carrying amount in the consolidated financial statements. Thus, applying the general principle illustrated in Examples 33.35 and 33.36 above, there is a deductible temporary difference of €12.5 million, being the difference between the carrying value of the goodwill (zero in the consolidated statement of financial position) and its tax base (€12.5 million). Alternatively, as noted at 6.1.4 above, certain items may have a tax base, but no carrying amount, and thus give rise to deferred tax.

This analysis would allow recognition of a deferred tax asset of €2.5 million on a temporary difference of €12.5 million, subject to the recognition criteria for deferred tax assets. This would result in a net tax charge of nil (€2.5 million current tax expense arising in B less €2.5 million deferred tax income arising on consolidation).

In our view, there are arguments for either analysis and entities need to take a view on their accounting policy for such transactions and apply it consistently.

8.7.1.D When the tax base of goodwill is retained by the transferor entity

In May 2014, the Interpretations Committee considered another example involving the internal reorganisation of a previously acquired business, as set out in Example 33.38 below.[46]

Example 33.38: Intragroup transfer of goodwill when tax base is retained by transferor

A parent company, H, recognised goodwill that had resulted from the acquisition of a group of assets (Business C) that meets the definition of a business in IFRS 3 – *Business Combinations*. Entity H subsequently recorded a deferred tax liability relating to goodwill deducted for tax purposes. Against this background, Entity H effects an internal reorganisation in which:

- Entity H set up a new wholly-owned subsidiary (Subsidiary A);
- Entity H transfers Business C, including the related (accounting) goodwill to Subsidiary A; and
- for tax purposes, however, the (tax) goodwill is retained by Entity H and not transferred to Subsidiary A.

How should Entity H calculate deferred tax following this internal reorganisation transaction in its consolidated financial statements in accordance with IAS 12?

The Interpretations Committee noted that when entities in the same consolidated group file separate tax returns, separate temporary differences will arise in those entities. Consequently, when an entity prepares its consolidated financial statements, deferred tax balances would be determined separately for those temporary differences, using the applicable tax rates for each entity's tax jurisdiction. *[IAS 12.11]*. The Interpretations Committee also noted that when calculating the deferred tax amount for the consolidated financial statements:

(a) the amount used as the carrying amount by the 'receiving' entity (in this case, Subsidiary A that receives the (accounting) goodwill) for an asset or a liability is the amount recognised in the consolidated financial statements; and

(b) the assessment of whether an asset or a liability is being recognised for the first time for the purpose of applying the initial recognition exception (see 7.2 above) is made from the perspective of the consolidated financial statements.

The Interpretations Committee noted that transferring the goodwill to Subsidiary A would not meet the initial recognition exception in the consolidated financial statements. Consequently, deferred tax would be recognised in the consolidated financial statements for any temporary differences arising in each separate entity by using the applicable tax rates for each entity's tax jurisdiction (subject to meeting the recoverability criteria for recognising deferred tax assets described at 7.4 above).

To the extent that there is a temporary difference between the carrying amount of the investment in Subsidiary A and the tax base of the investment (a so-called 'outside basis difference') in the consolidated financial statements, deferred tax for such a temporary difference would also be recognised subject to the limitations and exceptions discussed at 7.5.2 and 7.5.3 above.

The Interpretations Committee also noted that transferring assets between the entities in the consolidated group would affect the consolidated financial statements in terms of recognition, measurement and presentation of deferred tax, if the transfer affects the tax base of assets or liabilities, or the tax rate applicable to the recovery or settlement of those assets or liabilities. Such a transfer could also affect:

(a) the recoverability of any related deductible temporary differences and thereby affect the recognition of deferred tax assets; and

(b) the extent to which deferred tax assets and liabilities of different entities in the group are offset in the consolidated financial statements.

9 UNCERTAIN TAX TREATMENTS

The terms 'uncertain tax treatment' or 'uncertain tax position' refer to an item, the tax treatment of which is either unclear or is a matter of unresolved dispute between the reporting entity and the relevant tax authority. Uncertain tax treatments generally occur where there is an uncertainty as to the meaning of the law, or to the applicability of the law to a particular transaction, or both. For example, the tax legislation may allow the deduction of research and development expenditure, but there may be disagreement as to whether a specific item of expenditure falls within the definition of eligible research and development costs in the legislation. In some cases, it may not be clear how tax law applies to a particular transaction, if at all. In other situations, a tax return might have been submitted to the tax authorities, who are yet to opine on the treatment of certain transactions, or may even have indicated that they disagree with the entity's interpretation of tax law.

Estimating the outcome of an uncertain tax treatment is often one of the most complex and subjective areas in accounting for tax. However, IAS 12 does not specifically address the measurement of uncertain tax treatments, which are therefore implicitly subject to the general requirement of the standard to measure current tax and deferred tax at the amount expected to be paid or recovered, *[IAS 12.46, 47]*, (see 5 above).

Uncertain liabilities are generally accounted for under IAS 37 and historically entities have been drawn to this standard for guidance. However, IAS 37 does not apply to income taxes (see Chapter 26 at 2.2.1.B). *[IAS 37.5]*. In 2014, the Interpretations Committee was asked to consider the interaction between IAS 12 and IAS 37 in the situation where entities are required to make advance payments on account to the tax authorities before an uncertain tax treatment is resolved (see 9.7 below). The Committee concluded that IAS 12, not IAS 37, provides the relevant guidance on the recognition of current tax, in particular that probability of recovery (rather than virtual certainty) was the threshold for recognition of an asset for the advance payment.[47] It then embarked on a project to give guidance on the recognition and measurement of income tax assets and liabilities in circumstances where there is uncertainty, in particular in relation to how probability and detection risk should be reflected.[48]

In June 2017, the Committee issued IFRIC 23. The Interpretation is mandatory for annual reporting periods beginning on or after 1 January 2019. *[IFRIC 23.B1]*. On initial application, entities can either apply the Interpretation with full retrospective effect, in accordance with IAS 8, provided that this is possible without the use of hindsight, or by an adjustment to the opening balance of equity at the beginning of the first annual reporting period of application and without restating comparative information (see 9.8 below). *[IFRIC 23.B2]*.

9.1 Scope of IFRIC 23 and definitions used

The Interpretation clarifies how to apply the recognition and measurement requirements of IAS 12 when there is uncertainty over income tax treatments. Those requirements should be applied after determining the relevant taxable profit (tax loss), tax bases, unused tax losses, unused tax credits and tax rates for the entity. *[IFRIC 23.4]*.

The following issues are addressed by the Interpretation: *[IFRIC 23.5]*

a) whether an entity should consider uncertain tax treatments separately;

b) the assumptions an entity should make about the examination of tax treatments by taxation authorities;

c) how an entity should determine taxable profit (tax loss), tax bases, unused tax losses, unused tax credits and tax rates; and

d) how an entity should consider changes in facts and circumstances.

The Interpretation applies only to income taxes within the scope of IAS 12 and therefore does not apply to levies and other taxes not within the scope of that Standard. *[IFRIC 23.BC6]*.

Despite a request from a number of respondents to the Draft Interpretation to do so, IFRIC 23 does not include requirements relating to interest and penalties associated with uncertain tax treatments. Instead the Committee noted that an entity may or may not regard a particular amount for interest and penalties as an income tax within the scope of IAS 12 and apply the Interpretation only to those determined to be in scope. *[IFRIC 23.BC8, BC9]*. In September 2017, the Committee decided not to add a project on interest and penalties to its agenda, but nevertheless observed that the determination of whether interest and penalties are within the scope of IAS 12 is a judgement and not an accounting policy choice for entities.[49] We discuss at 4.4 above the attributes that might be relevant to determining whether interest and penalties fall within the scope of IAS 12.

The Interpretation uses the following terms in addition to those defined in IAS 12: *[IFRIC 23.3]*

- *tax treatments* refers to the treatments used or planned to be used by the entity in its income tax filings;
- *taxation authority* is the body or bodies that decide whether tax treatments are acceptable under the law. This might include a court;
- *uncertain tax treatment* is a tax treatment over which there is uncertainty concerning its acceptance under the law by the relevant taxation authority. For example, an entity's decision not to submit any tax filing in a particular tax jurisdiction or not to include specific income in taxable profit would be an uncertain tax treatment, if its acceptability is unclear under tax law.

In determining 'uncertainty', the entity only needs to consider whether a particular tax treatment is probable, rather than highly likely or certain, to be accepted by the taxation authorities. As explained at 9.4 below, if the entity determines it is probable that a tax treatment will be accepted, then it should measure its income taxes on that basis. Only if the entity believes the likelihood of acceptance is not probable, would there be an uncertain tax treatment to be addressed by IFRIC 23.

9.1.1 Business combinations

The Committee considered whether the Interpretation should address the accounting for tax assets and liabilities acquired or assumed in a business combination when there is uncertainty over income tax treatments. It noted that IFRS 3 applies to all assets acquired and liabilities assumed in a business combination and concluded that on this basis the Interpretation should not explicitly address tax assets and liabilities acquired or assumed in a business combination. *[IFRIC 23.BC23]*.

Nonetheless, IFRS 3 requires an entity to account for deferred tax assets and liabilities that arise as part of a business combination by applying IAS 12. *[IFRS 3.24]*. Accordingly, the Interpretation applies to such assets and liabilities when there is uncertainty over income tax treatments that affect deferred tax. *[IFRIC 23.BC24]*.

IFRS 3 suggests that current tax should be measured at fair value, which differs from the subsequent measurement required by IFRIC 23. Entities must consider whether the application of IFRS 3 fair value requirements to current tax assets and liabilities (which may result in possible Day 2 gains and losses) takes precedence over the requirements of IFRIC 23 for the measurement of uncertain current tax assets and liabilities.

We believe either approach is acceptable, provided that it is applied consistently (see also Chapter 9 at 5.6.2).

9.2 Whether to consider uncertain tax treatments separately (unit of account)

A key input to any estimation process is to determine the unit of account for uncertain tax treatments. In practice this might be an entire tax computation, individual uncertain treatments, or a group of related uncertain treatments (e.g. all positions in a particular tax jurisdiction, or all positions of a similar nature or relating to the same interpretation of tax legislation).

The Interpretation requires that entities determine whether to consider tax uncertainties separately or grouped together on the basis of which approach provides a better prediction of the resolution of the uncertainty. For example, if the entity prepares and supports tax treatments as a group or if the entity expects the taxation authority to assess items collectively during a tax examination, it would be appropriate to consider those uncertain tax treatments together. *[IFRIC 23.6]*. This implies that material tax uncertainties would be considered separately if there was no such inter-dependency as to the expected outcome.

9.3 Assumptions about the examination of tax treatments ('detection risk')

'Detection risk' is a term commonly used to refer to the likelihood that the taxation authority examines the amounts reported to it by the entity. The Committee concluded that in cases where the taxation authority has a right to examine amounts reported to it, the entity should assume that it will do so; and that when it performs those examinations, the taxation authority will have full knowledge of all related information. *[IFRIC 23.8]*.

The Committee noted that this position is consistent with the requirement in paragraphs 46 and 47 of IAS 12 to measure the amount of a tax liability or asset based on the tax laws that have been enacted or substantively enacted at the reporting date. *[IFRIC 23.BC11]*. The Committee also rejected a suggestion by a few respondents to the Draft Interpretation that the consideration of probability of examination should be taken into account and would be particularly important if there was no time limit on the right of the taxation authority to examine income tax filings. It determined that no exception would be appropriate and noted that the threshold for reflecting the effects of uncertainty is whether it is probable that the taxation authority will accept an uncertain tax treatment and not based on whether the taxation authority will examine a tax treatment. *[IFRIC 23.12, BC13]*. Indeed, in many jurisdictions, the tax law imposes a legal obligation on an entity operating in that jurisdiction to disclose its full liability to tax, or to assess its own liability to tax, and to make all relevant information available to the taxation authorities. In such a tax jurisdiction it might be difficult, as a matter of corporate governance, for an entity to argue that it can calculate its tax liability on the basis that the taxation authority will not become aware of information regarding a particular treatment which the entity has a legal obligation to disclose to that authority.

9.4 Determining the effect of an uncertain tax treatment or group of tax treatments

A variety of methodologies had been applied in the past for determining the effect of uncertain tax treatments on estimates of taxable profit (tax loss), tax bases, unused tax losses, unused tax credits and tax rates. These included a weighted average probability of outcomes, the most likely single outcome and an 'all or nothing approach' (i.e. no liability is recognised for an uncertain tax treatment with a probability of occurrence below the selected recognition threshold and a full liability for a position with a probability of occurrence above the threshold).

The Interpretations Committee decided that entities should first consider whether or not it is probable that a taxation authority will accept an uncertain tax treatment or group of uncertain tax treatments. *[IFRIC 23.9]*. The Interpretation does not define probable, but is generally referred to in other IFRSs as meaning more likely than not (see 7.1.2 above). If the entity concludes that it is probable that the taxation authority will accept the tax treatment used or planned to be used in its tax filings, the entity determines its tax position on that basis. *[IFRIC 23.10]*. This is consistent with the requirement that current tax is measured at the amount expected to be paid or recovered from the taxation authorities, *[IAS 12.46]*, and that deferred tax is measured using the rates and tax laws expected to apply when the related asset is realised or liability is settled. *[IAS 12.47]*. This means that all likelihoods beyond the probable threshold are treated in the same way. That is, any likelihood of acceptance by the taxation authority beyond probable is treated in the same way as 100 per cent likelihood of acceptance. Therefore it is not necessary to distinguish between outcomes that are probable, highly likely or virtually certain.

If the entity concludes that acceptance of the uncertain tax treatment by the taxation authorities is not probable, it should apply one of the following two methods for reflecting the effect of uncertainty in its estimate of the amount it expects to pay or recover from the tax authorities: *[IFRIC 23.11]*

(a) the most likely amount – the single most likely amount in a range of possible outcomes; or

(b) the expected value – the sum of the probability-weighted amounts in a range of possible outcomes.

The entity is required to use the method that it expects to better predict the resolution of the uncertainty. The Interpretation suggests that the most likely amount may be a better method if the outcomes are binary (for example where an item might be deductible or disallowed for tax purposes) or are concentrated on one value (that is clearly more likely than the alternative outcomes). The expected value method may be more appropriate if possible outcomes are widely dispersed with low individual probabilities (where a number of individual but related uncertainties have been combined into a single unit of account). *[IFRIC 23.11]*.

The Interpretation includes two examples to illustrate how an entity might apply its requirements for hypothetical situations and based on the limited facts presented, as follows:

- when multiple tax treatments are considered together and when the expected value is used to reflect the effect of uncertainty. *[IFRIC 23.IE2-IE6]*. (Example 33.39 below); and

- when current and deferred tax is recognised and measured based on the most likely amount for a tax base that reflects the effect of uncertainty. *[IFRIC 23.IE7-IE10]*. (Example 33.40 below).

In both of these examples, the entities have assumed that the taxation authority will examine the amounts reported to it and have full knowledge of all related information, as discussed at 9.3 above. *[IFRIC 23.IE1]*.

Example 33.39: Multiple treatments, expected value method

Entity A's tax filing included a number of deductions related to transfer pricing. The taxation authority in its jurisdiction may challenge those tax treatments. Entity A notes that the taxation authority's decision on one transfer pricing matter would affect, or be affected by, the other transfer pricing matters. Entity A determines that the tax treatments should be considered together, because this better predicts the resolution of the uncertainty. At the end of the reporting period, Entity A concludes, on the basis of an evaluation of all available evidence, that it is not probable that the taxation authority will accept all of the tax treatments.

Entity A estimates the probabilities of what would be added to its taxable profits (in Euros), as follows:

	Estimated additional amount	Probability	Expected value
Outcome 1	–	5%	–
Outcome 2	200	5%	10
Outcome 3	400	20%	80
Outcome 4	600	20%	120
Outcome 5	800	30%	240
Outcome 6	1,000	20%	200
		100%	650

Outcome 5 is the most likely outcome, with a probability of 30%. However, entity A observes that the possible outcomes are neither binary nor concentrated in one value. Entity A therefore concludes that the expected value (€650) better predicts the resolution of the uncertainty. Accordingly, Entity A adds €650 to its estimate of the taxable profit, in addition to the amount reported in its tax filing.

Example 33.40: Treatment relates to deferred tax asset, most likely amount is applied

Entity B acquired a separately identifiable intangible asset for £100 that has an indefinite life and is, therefore, not amortised in accordance with IAS 38. Tax law specifies that the full amount of the intangible asset is deductible for tax purposes, but the timing of deductibility (i.e. period of amortisation under the tax law) is uncertain. Entity B has no similar intangible assets and it therefore decides that this tax treatment should be considered separately.

Entity B deducted £100 (the cost of the intangible asset) in calculating its taxable profit for Year 1 in its income tax filing. At the end of Year 1, Entity B concludes, on the basis of an evaluation of all available evidence (e.g. information about disputes for other entities' similar transactions), that it is not probable that this tax treatment will be accepted. Entity B estimates that the most likely deduction that the tax authority will accept for Year 1 is £10, and that the most likely amount better predicts the resolution of the tax uncertainty. Accordingly, at the end of Year 1, Entity B recognises and measures a deferred tax liability based on the amount of the temporary difference between the carrying amount of the intangible asset in its financial statements and the most likely amount of the tax base (i.e. the difference between £100 and £90).

Entity B also concludes that it should make similar judgements in estimating the most likely amount for its current tax for Year 1, because this uncertain tax treatment also affects the taxable profit. Entity B recognises and measures its current tax liability, based on the taxable profit that includes £90, in addition to the amount in its tax filing. (This is because Entity B deducted £100 from taxable income for Year 1, whereas the most likely amount is now estimated to be £10. Entity B concluded that it is not probable that the tax treatment used in its filing will be accepted.)

Where the uncertain tax treatment affects both current tax and deferred tax, an entity is required to make estimates and judgements on a consistent basis. *[IFRIC 23.12]*.

9.5 Consideration of changes in facts and circumstances

An entity is required to reassess its judgements about the acceptability of tax treatments or its estimates of the effect of uncertainty, or both, if facts and circumstances change or if new information becomes available. *[IFRIC 23.13]*. In such a situation, the entity reflects the effect as a change in accounting estimate, applying the requirements of IAS 8 to its measure of the taxable profit (tax loss), tax bases, unused tax losses, unused tax credits and tax rates. Where circumstances change or new information becomes available after the end of the reporting period, the entity should apply the guidance in IAS 10 to determine whether the change is an adjusting or non-adjusting event. *[IFRIC 23.14]*.

The Application Guidance in Appendix A to the Interpretation provides some examples of changes that can result in the reassessment of judgements or estimates previously made by the entity. *[IFRIC 23.A2]*.

(a) The results of examinations or actions taken by a taxation authority. For example:
   (i) agreement or disagreement by the taxation authority with the tax treatment or a similar tax treatment used by the entity;
   (ii) information that the taxation authority has agreed or disagreed with a similar tax treatment used by another entity; and
   (iii) information about the amount received or paid to settle a similar tax treatment;
(b) changes in rules established by the taxation authority; and
(c) the expiry of a taxation authority's right to examine or re-examine a tax treatment.

An uncertain tax treatment is resolved when the treatment is accepted or rejected by the taxation authorities. The Interpretation does not discuss the manner of acceptance (i.e. implicit or explicit) of an uncertain tax treatment by the taxation authorities. In practice, a taxation authority might accept a tax return without commenting explicitly on any particular treatment in it. Alternatively, it might raise some questions in an examination of a tax return. Unless such clearance is provided explicitly, it is not always clear if a taxation authority has accepted an uncertain tax treatment.

An entity may consider the following to determine whether a taxation authority has implicitly or explicitly accepted an uncertain tax treatment:

- the tax treatment is explicitly mentioned in a report issued by the taxation authorities following an examination;
- the treatment was specifically discussed with the taxation authorities (e.g. during an on-site examination) and the taxation authorities verbally agreed with the approach; or
- the treatment was specifically highlighted in the income tax filings, but not subsequently queried by the taxation authorities in their examination.

The Application Guidance goes on to say that the absence of agreement or disagreement by a taxation authority with a tax treatment, in isolation, is unlikely to constitute a change in facts and circumstances or new information that affects the judgements and estimates required by the Interpretation. *[IFRIC 23.A3]*. In such situations, an entity has to consider other available facts and circumstances before concluding that a reassessment of the judgements and estimates is required.

9.5.1 The expiry of a taxation authority's right to examine or re-examine a tax treatment

As noted above, the expiry of a taxation authority's right to examine or re-examine a tax treatment is one example of a change in facts and circumstances cited in the guidance to IFRIC 23. Where this right expires between the end of the reporting period and the date when the financial statements are authorised for issue, the entity should apply the guidance in IAS 10 to determine whether the change is an adjusting or non-adjusting event. *[IFRIC 23.14]*.

IAS 10 defines adjusting events as 'those that provide evidence of conditions that existed at the end of the reporting period'. Non-adjusting events are 'those that are indicative of conditions that arose after the reporting period'. *[IAS 10.3]*.

If the right of the tax authority to examine or re-examine a tax treatment does not expire until a date falling after the end of the reporting period, it is clearly indicative of conditions that arose after the reporting period and would therefore be regarded as a non-adjusting event. In addition, because the Interpretation requires an entity to reflect the effect of a change in facts and circumstances or of new information as a change in accounting estimate applying IAS 8, *[IFRIC 23.14]*, the effect of such a change would be recognised prospectively in the period of the change, with no restatement of any estimates made as at the end of the (previous) reporting period. *[IAS 8.36]*.

9.6 Disclosures relating to uncertain tax treatments

IFRIC 23 does not propose any new disclosures. Instead the Application Guidance requires entities to consider whether the following existing disclosure requirements are relevant in these circumstances:

- to disclose judgements made in the process of applying the entity's accounting policies in accordance with paragraph 122 of IAS 1 *[IFRIC 23.A4(a)]* (see Chapter 3 at 5.1.1.B). Such judgements might include the decision to consider uncertain tax treatments separately or together (see 9.2 above); the determination as to whether acceptance by the taxation authorities is probable; or the decision to apply the 'most likely amount' or 'expected value' method to reflect uncertainty (see 9.4 above); and
- to disclose information about the assumptions and estimates made in determining taxable profit or loss, tax bases, unused tax losses, unused tax credits and tax rates in accordance with paragraphs 125 to 129 of IAS 1 regarding the sources of significant estimation uncertainty, *[IFRIC 23.A4(b)]*, (see Chapter 3 at 5.2.1).

As discussed at 9.4 above, if an entity determines that it is probable that a taxation authority will accept the tax treatment used or planned to be used in its tax filings, it determines its tax position on that basis. *[IFRIC 23.10]*. Nevertheless, the entity should still consider whether to disclose the potential effect of the uncertainty as a tax-related contingency applying paragraph 88 of IAS 12. *[IFRIC 23.A5]*.

As noted above, uncertain tax treatments generally relate to the estimate of the entity's liability for current tax. Any amount recognised for an uncertain current tax treatment should therefore normally be classified as current tax, and presented (or disclosed) as current or non-current in accordance with the general requirements of IAS 1 (see Chapter 3 at 3.1.1).

However, there are circumstances where an uncertain tax treatment affects the tax base of an asset or liability and therefore relates to deferred tax, as illustrated in Example 33.40 above. For example, there might be doubt as to the amount of tax depreciation that can be deducted in respect of a particular asset, which in turn would lead to doubt as to the tax base of the asset. There may sometimes be an equal and opposite uncertainty relating to current and deferred tax. For example, there might be uncertainty as to whether a particular item of income is taxable, but – if it is – any tax payable will be reduced to zero by a loss carried forward from a prior period. As discussed at 13.1.1.C below, it is not appropriate to offset current and deferred tax items.

9.7 Presentation of liabilities or assets for uncertain tax treatments

Neither IAS 12 nor IFRIC 23 contain requirements on the presentation of uncertain tax liabilities or assets in the statement of financial position. Before the Interpretation was issued, there was diversity in practice between entities that presented uncertain tax liabilities as current (or deferred) tax liabilities and those that included these balances within another line item such as provisions.

In response to a request for clarification on this matter, the Interpretations Committee issued an agenda decision in September 2019 that, applying IAS 1, an entity is required to present uncertain tax liabilities as current tax liabilities *[IAS 1.54(n)]* or deferred tax liabilities *[IAS 1.54(o)]* and that uncertain tax assets are presented as current tax assets *[IAS 1.54(n)]* or deferred tax assets. *[IAS 1.54(o)]*.

This conclusion had been reached based on the following considerations:[50]

- When there is uncertainty over income tax treatments, IFRIC 23 requires an entity to 'recognise and measure its current or deferred tax asset or liability applying the requirements in IAS 12 based on taxable profit (tax loss), tax bases, unused tax losses, unused tax credits and tax rates determined applying this Interpretation'. *[IFRIC 23.4]*.
- Current tax is defined as the amount of income taxes payable (recoverable) in respect of the taxable profit (tax loss) for a period; and deferred tax liabilities (or assets) are defined as the amounts of income taxes payable (recoverable) in future periods in respect of taxable (deductible) temporary differences and, in the case of deferred tax assets, the carry forward of unused tax losses and credits. *[IAS 12.5]*.
- Because no specific requirements are set out in IAS 12 or IFRIC 23, the presentation requirements in IAS 1 apply, which 'lists items that are sufficiently different in nature or function to warrant separate presentation in the statement of financial position'. *[IAS 1.57]*. This list includes line items for 'liabilities and assets for current tax, as defined in IAS 12' and for 'deferred tax liabilities and deferred tax assets, as defined in IAS 12'. *[IAS 1.54]*. In addition, IAS 1 requires an entity to 'present separately items of a dissimilar nature or function unless they are immaterial'. *[IAS 1.29]*.

On this basis, the Committee proposed not to add the matter to its standard-setting agenda.[51]

9.8 Recognition of an asset for payments on account

IAS 12 requires that the liability for current tax is recorded after deducting payments made, and states that if the amount already paid exceeds the tax liability for current and past periods, an asset is recognised for the excess. *[IAS 12.12]*.

In some jurisdictions, entities are required to make payments to the tax authorities before an uncertain tax treatment is resolved. If an entity considers its liability to be lower than the assessment made by the tax authorities, it would record an asset for a payment in excess of its estimated liability for current tax, but recovery of that excess would be contingent upon the successful resolution of the uncertainty.

In these circumstances, some had argued that the 'virtually certain' threshold in IAS 37 should be applied before allowing recognition of such a 'contingent' asset. *[IAS 37.35]*. Others argued that the requirement in IAS 12 to measure current tax assets at the amount expected to be recovered from the tax authorities requires only a 'probable' assessment of recovery to be sufficient for recognising an asset. *[IAS 12.46]*. As a result, there had been diversity in the approach used to determine whether an asset should be recognised for the amount potentially recoverable from the tax authority.

In 2014, the Interpretations Committee considered a request to clarify the criteria under which a tax asset would be recognised in these circumstances. In the situation described by the submitter, the entity expects, but is not certain, to recover some, or all, of the amount paid. The Interpretations Committee noted that:

a) paragraph 12 of IAS 12 provides guidance on the recognition of current tax assets and current tax liabilities. In particular, it states that:
   i) current tax for current and prior periods shall, to the extent unpaid, be recognised as a liability; and
   ii) if the amount already paid in respect of current and prior periods exceeds the amount due for those periods, the excess shall be recognised as an asset.

b) in the specific fact pattern described in the submission, an asset is recognised if the amount of cash paid (which is a certain amount) exceeds the amount of tax expected to be due (which is an uncertain amount); and

c) the timing of payment should not affect the amount of current tax expense recognised.

The Interpretations Committee acknowledged that the reference to IAS 37 in paragraph 88 of IAS 12 in respect of tax-related contingent liabilities and contingent assets may have been understood by some to mean that IAS 37 applied to the recognition of such items. However, the Interpretations Committee noted that this paragraph provides guidance only on disclosures required for such items. Accordingly, the Interpretations Committee determined that IAS 12, not IAS 37, provides the relevant guidance on recognition.[52] It was this determination that led to the development of IFRIC 23, discussed above. *[IFRIC 23.BC4]*.

In January 2019, the Committee confirmed a similar conclusion regarding the recoverability of payments relating to uncertain tax treatments that are outside the scope of IAS 12 (i.e. payments on account for taxes other than income tax). It concluded that, on making the payment, the entity has the right to receive future economic benefits either in the form of a cash refund or by using the payment to settle the tax liability. As such, an asset exists as defined in the Conceptual Framework, as opposed to a contingent asset as defined in IAS 37, and it is recognised when the payment is made to the tax authority.[53] This agenda decision is discussed in Chapter 26 at 6.8.4.

10 ALLOCATION OF TAX CHARGE OR CREDIT

Current and deferred tax is normally recognised as income or an expense in the profit or loss for the period, except to the extent that it arises from:

- an item that has been recognised directly outside profit or loss, whether in the same period or in a different period (see 10.1 to 10.7 below);
- a share-based payment transaction (see 10.8 below); or
- a business combination (see 12 below). *[IAS 12.57, 58, 68A-68C]*.

Where a deferred tax asset or liability is remeasured subsequent to its initial recognition, the change should be accounted for in profit or loss, unless it relates to an item originally recognised outside profit or loss, in which case the change should also be accounted for outside profit or loss. Such remeasurement might result from:

- a change in tax law;
- a re-assessment of the recoverability of deferred tax assets (see 7.4 above); or
- a change in the expected manner of recovery of an asset or settlement of a liability (see 8.4.11 above). *[IAS 12.60]*.

Whilst IAS 12 as drafted refers only to remeasurement of 'deferred' tax, it seems clear that these principles should also be applied to any remeasurement of current tax.

Any current tax or deferred tax on items recognised outside profit or loss, whether in the same period or a different period, is also recognised directly outside profit or loss. Such items include:

- revaluations of property, plant and equipment under IAS 16 (see 10.1 below);
- retrospective restatements or retrospective applications arising from corrections of errors and changes in accounting policy under IAS 8 (see 10.2 below);
- exchange differences arising on translation of the financial statements of a foreign operation under IAS 21 (see 7.5 above); and
- amounts taken to equity on initial recognition of a compound financial instrument by its issuer (so-called 'split accounting') under IAS 32 (see 7.2.8 above). *[IAS 12.61A, 62, 62A]*.

IAS 12 acknowledges that, in exceptional circumstances, it may be difficult to determine the amount of tax that relates to items recognised in other comprehensive income and/or equity. In these cases an entity may use a reasonable *pro rata* method, or another method that achieves a more appropriate allocation in the circumstances. IAS 12 gives the following examples of situations where such an approach may be appropriate:

- there are graduated rates of income tax and it is impossible to determine the rate at which a specific component of taxable profit (tax loss) has been taxed;
- a change in the tax rate or other tax rules affects a deferred tax asset or liability relating (in whole or in part) to an item that was previously recognised outside profit or loss; or
- an entity determines that a deferred tax asset should be recognised, or should no longer be recognised in full, and the deferred tax asset relates (in whole or in part) to an item that was previously recognised outside profit or loss. [IAS 12.63].

IAS 12 requires tax relating to items not accounted for in profit or loss, whether in the same period or a different period, to be recognised:

- in other comprehensive income, if it relates to an item accounted for in other comprehensive income; and
- directly in equity, if it relates to an item accounted for directly in equity. [IAS 12.61A].

This requirement to have regard to the previous history of a transaction in accounting for its tax effects is commonly referred to as 'backward tracing'.

10.1 Revalued and rebased assets

Where an entity depreciates a revalued item of PP&E, it may choose to transfer the depreciation in excess of the amount that would have arisen on a historical cost basis from revaluation surplus to retained earnings. In such cases, the relevant portion of any deferred tax liability recognised on the revaluation should also be transferred to retained earnings. A similar treatment should be adopted by an entity which has a policy of transferring revaluation gains to retained earnings on disposal of a previously revalued asset. [IAS 12.64].

When an asset is revalued for tax purposes and that revaluation is related to an accounting revaluation of an earlier period, or to one that is expected to be carried out in a future period, the tax effects of both the asset revaluation and the adjustment of the tax base are credited or charged to equity in the periods in which they occur.

However, if the revaluation for tax purposes is not related to an accounting revaluation of an earlier period, or to one that is expected to be carried out in a future period, the tax effects of the adjustment of the tax base are recognised in profit or loss. [IAS 12.65]. For example, when tax law gives additional deductions to reflect the indexation of assets for tax purposes (see 6.2.2.D above) the tax base of the asset changes without any corresponding change to the asset's carrying amount in the financial statements. Because the carrying amount has not changed, there is no gain or loss in relation to indexation in profit and loss or in other comprehensive income. Accordingly, the effect of the change in tax base is recorded in profit or loss. [IAS 12.65].

10.1.1 Non-monetary assets or liabilities with a tax base determined in a different currency

Another example arises when the tax base of a non-monetary asset or liability is determined in a different currency to the entity's functional currency for accounting purposes. This can be the case in oil and gas producing entities that have a functional currency of US dollars but operate (and are accountable for income taxes) in various local jurisdictions under different currencies (see Chapter 43 at 9.1).

IAS 12 notes that in this situation the entity measures its non-monetary asset or liability using its functional currency as at the date of initial recognition, as required by IAS 21. However, if the tax base of its non-monetary assets and liabilities is determined in a different currency, changes in the exchange rate will give rise to temporary differences that result in a recognised deferred tax liability or deferred tax asset (if recoverable). Because this retranslation has no effect on carrying values recognised in the financial statements, there is no corresponding gain or loss against which the tax can be allocated. As a result, the movement in deferred tax is recorded in profit or loss. *[IAS 12.41]*.

In 2015, the Interpretations Committee considered a submission that requested confirmation as to whether deferred taxes arising from the effect of exchange rate changes on the tax bases of such non-current assets are recognised through profit or loss. The Committee completed its deliberations in January 2016 and, in noting the requirement in paragraph 41 of IAS 12, determined that:[54]

- deferred tax does not arise from a transaction or event that is recognised outside profit or loss and is therefore charged or credited to profit or loss in accordance with paragraph 58 of IAS 12;
- such a deferred tax charge or credit would be presented with other deferred taxes, instead of with foreign exchange gains or losses, in the statement of profit or loss; and
- paragraph 79 of IAS 12 requires the disclosure of the major components of tax expense (income). When changes in the exchange rate are the cause of a major component of the deferred tax charge or credit, an explanation of this in accordance with paragraph 79 of IAS 12 would help explain the tax expense (income) to the users of the financial statements.

In the light of the existing IFRS requirements the Interpretations Committee determined that neither an Interpretation nor an amendment to a Standard was necessary.[55]

10.2 Retrospective restatements or applications

IAS 8 requires retrospective restatements or retrospective applications arising from corrections of errors and changes in accounting policy to be accounted for by adjusting the amounts presented in the financial statements of comparative periods and restating the opening balances of assets, liabilities and equity for the earliest prior period presented as if the new accounting policy had always been applied. *[IAS 8.23]*. IFRS 1 – *First-time Adoption of International Financial Reporting Standards* – requires first-time adopters to recognise the adjustments resulting from the application of IFRS to the opening IFRS statement of financial position directly in retained earnings (or, if appropriate, another category of equity), on the basis that those adjustments 'arise from events and transactions before the date of transition to IFRS'. *[IFRS 1.11]*.

Because IAS 12 requires tax relating to an item that has been recognised outside profit or loss to be treated in the same way, any tax effect of a retrospective restatement or retrospective application on the opening comparative statement of financial position is dealt with as an adjustment to equity also. *[IAS 12.58]*. The Standard identifies the adjustment to the opening balance of retained earnings under IAS 8 as an example where IFRS requires or permits particular items to be charged or credited directly to equity. *[IAS 12.62A(a)]*.

However, the fact that IAS 12 states that tax arising in a different period, but relating to a transaction or event arising outside profit or loss should also be recognised in other comprehensive income or equity (as applicable) is taken by some to mean that any subsequent remeasurement of tax originally recognised in equity as part of a prior year adjustment should be accounted for in equity also. In our view, such an assertion fails to reflect the true nature of retrospective application, which as noted above is defined in IAS 8 as the application of a new accounting policy 'to transactions, other events and conditions *as if that policy had always been applied'* (our emphasis), *[IAS 8.5]*, and under IFRS 1 'arise from events and transactions before the date of transition to IFRS'. This is illustrated by Example 33.41 below.

Example 33.41: Remeasurement of deferred tax liability recognised as the result of retrospective application

Entity A applied IAS 19 when it first became effective and recognised a pension asset of €3 million and a corresponding deferred tax liability, which was accounted for as a prior year adjustment in retained earnings under IAS 8. At that time, the effective tax rate applicable to Entity A was 40%, resulting in a deferred tax liability of €1,200,000.

Entity B's date of transition to IFRS was 1 January 2014. As a result of the adoption of IAS 37, its first IFRS financial statements (prepared for the year ended 31 December 2015) showed an additional liability for environmental rectification costs of €5 million as an adjustment to opening reserves, together with an associated deferred tax asset at 40% of €2 million.

The pension asset in Entity A and the environmental liability in Entity B do not change substantially over the following accounting periods, but during the year ended 31 December 2021 the tax rate falls to 30%. This requires Entity A to remeasure to €900,000 its deferred tax liability relating to the pension asset, giving rise to a tax benefit of €300,000. For Entity B, the deferred tax asset is remeasured to €1.5 million, giving rise to a tax expense of €500,000. Should this expense be recognised in profit or loss for the period or in equity?

When the carrying amount of deferred tax assets and liabilities change because of a change in tax rates, the resulting deferred tax is recorded in profit or loss, 'except to the extent that it relates to items previously recognised outside profit or loss'. *[IAS 12.60]*. Paragraph 61A of IAS 12 also requires an entity to recognise in other comprehensive income or directly in equity the tax effect of items that are recognised, in the same or a different period, outside profit or loss. If read in isolation, IAS 12 could be construed as requiring the amounts arising on the remeasurement of deferred tax in the examples above to be accounted for in equity, as being a remeasurement of amounts originally recognised in equity. However, as discussed above, this interpretation fails to reflect the true nature of what is meant by retrospective restatement.

IAS 8 defines retrospective application as the application of a new accounting policy 'to transactions, other events or conditions as if that policy had always been applied' and the treatment required by IFRS 1 is based on the fact that an entity is restating amounts that arise from events and transactions before the date of transition to IFRS.

Accordingly, if the item that gave rise to the deferred tax would have been recognised in profit or loss in the normal course of events had the new accounting policies (or IFRS) always been applied, the effect of subsequent re-measurement is also recognised in profit or loss. In the fact patterns for both entities A and B in Example 33.41 above, the changes in the tax rate relating to the pension asset and the environmental liability are recognised in profit or loss.

Where the retrospective restatement giving rise to a deferred tax asset or liability directly in equity represented the cumulative total of amounts that would have been recognised ordinarily in other comprehensive income or directly in equity in previous periods if the new accounting policy had always been applied (e.g. deferred tax relating to the revaluation of property, plant, or equipment), any subsequent re-measurement of the deferred tax is also accounted for in the same manner, i.e. in other comprehensive income or directly in equity.

10.3 Dividends and transaction costs of equity instruments

10.3.1 Dividend subject to differential tax rate

In some jurisdictions, the rate at which tax is paid depends on whether profits are distributed or retained. In other jurisdictions, distribution may lead to an additional liability to tax, or a refund of tax already paid. IAS 12 requires current and deferred taxes to be measured using the rate applicable to undistributed profits until a liability to pay a dividend is recognised, at which point the tax consequences of that dividend should also be recognised. This is discussed further at 8.5 above.

Where taxes are remeasured on recognition of a liability to pay a dividend, the difference should normally be recognised in profit or loss rather than directly in equity, even though the dividend itself is recognised directly in equity under IFRS. IAS 12 takes the view that any additional (or lower) tax liability relates to the original profit now being distributed rather than to the distribution itself. Where, however, the dividend is paid out of profit arising from a transaction that was originally recognised in other comprehensive income or equity, the adjustment to the tax liability should also be recognised in other comprehensive income or equity. *[IAS 12.57A]*.

10.3.2 Dividend subject to withholding tax

Where dividends are paid by the reporting entity subject to withholding tax, the withholding tax should be included as part of the dividend charged to equity. *[IAS 12.65A]*.

It is noteworthy that there may be little economic difference, from the paying entity's perspective, between a requirement to pay a 5% 'withholding tax' on all dividends and a requirement to pay an additional 5% 'income tax' on distributed profit. Yet, the accounting treatment varies significantly depending on the analysis. If the tax is considered a withholding tax, it is treated as a deduction from equity in all circumstances. If, however, it is considered as an additional income tax, it will generally be treated as a charge to profit or loss (see 10.3.1 above). This distinction therefore relies on a clear definition of withholding tax, which IAS 12 unfortunately does not provide.

IAS 12 describes a withholding tax as a 'portion of the dividends [paid] to taxation authorities on behalf of shareholders'. *[IAS 12.65A]*. However, it is not clear whether the determination of whether or not the tax is paid 'on behalf of shareholders' should be made by reference to the characterisation of the tax:

- in the paying entity's tax jurisdiction – in which case, there is the problem noted above that one jurisdiction's 'additional distribution tax' may be economically identical to another jurisdiction's 'withholding tax'; or
- in the receiving entity's tax jurisdiction – in which case there would be the problem that the tax on a dividend paid to one shareholder is a 'withholding tax' (because credit is given for it on the shareholder's tax return) but the tax on a dividend paid to another shareholder the same time is not (because no credit is given for it on that shareholder's tax return).

This distinction is also relevant in accounting for dividend income that has been subject to withholding tax, as discussed at 10.3.4 below.

10.3.3   Intragroup dividend subject to withholding tax

Where irrecoverable withholding tax is suffered on intragroup dividends, the withholding tax does not relate to an item recognised in equity in the consolidated financial statements (since the intragroup dividend to which it relates has been eliminated in those financial statements). The tax should therefore be accounted for in profit or loss for the period.

10.3.4   Incoming dividends

IAS 12 does not directly address the treatment of incoming dividends on which tax has been levied (i.e. whether they should be shown at the amount received, or gross of withholding tax together with a corresponding tax charge). As discussed at 4.2 above, we believe that judgement is required to determine whether a tax deducted from investment income at the source of the income is a withholding tax in the scope of IAS 12.

As well as the considerations discussed at 4.2 above, it is noted at 10.3.2 above that an entity paying dividends that are subject to withholding tax would record the gross value of the distribution in equity, on the basis that the withholding tax is regarded as an amount paid to the tax authorities 'on behalf of shareholders'. *[IAS 12.65A]*. If it is determined from the point of view of the recipient of the dividend that a particular withholding tax is an income tax in the scope of IAS 12, it would therefore be consistent with this treatment for the recipient to show dividends (and other income subject to withholding taxes) gross of withholding taxes and to recognise any non-refundable portion of such withholding taxes as a tax expense in the statement of comprehensive income.

Some jurisdictions also give tax deductions for the 'underlying' tax suffered on dividends received. This is based on the concept that the dividend has been paid out of profits already subject to tax, so that to tax the full amount received again would amount to a punitive double taxation of the underlying profits. In our view, such underlying tax (which would form part of the tax charge, not the dividend, of the paying company) is not directly paid on behalf of the shareholder, and accordingly incoming dividends should not be grossed up for underlying tax.

10.3.5 Tax benefits of distributions and transaction costs of equity instruments

IAS 32 as originally issued required distributions to shareholders and transaction costs of equity instruments to be accounted for in equity net of any related income tax benefit (see Chapter 47 at 8.2). However, as discussed below, the 'default' allocation for income tax on equity distributions is now to profit or loss, with the tax consequences of transaction costs relating to equity instruments still being taken to equity, provided that the related costs are also recognised in equity.

Annual Improvements to IFRSs 2009-2011 Cycle, issued in May 2012, amended IAS 32 so as to remove the reference to income tax benefit. This means that all tax effects of equity transactions are allocated in accordance with the general principles of IAS 12. Unfortunately, IAS 12 was not entirely clear as to how the tax effects of certain equity transactions should be dealt with, as illustrated by Example 33.42 below.

Example 33.42: Tax deductible distribution on equity instrument

An entity paying tax at 25% has issued €25 million 4% preference shares at par value that are treated as equity instruments for accounting purposes (because coupon payments are subject to an equity dividend blocker and are therefore discretionary). The preference shares are treated as debt for tax purposes (i.e. all coupon payments are deductible in determining taxable profit). The entity makes a payment of €1 million and is able to claim a tax deduction of €250,000. There are no restrictions on the recoverability of that deduction for tax purposes.

Some would have allocated the tax deduction to equity on the basis that it relates to the coupon payment, which was accounted for in equity. Others would have considered the distribution as being sourced from an accumulation of retained earnings originally accounted for in profit or loss and, therefore, have allocated the tax deduction for the dividend payment in profit or loss. The cause of this divergence was paragraph 52B of IAS 12, which stated the following:

'In the circumstances described in paragraph 52A, the income tax consequences of dividends are recognised when a liability to pay the dividend is recognised. The income tax consequences of dividends are more directly linked to past transactions or events than to distributions to owners. Therefore, the income tax consequences of dividends are recognised in profit or loss for the period as required by paragraph 58 except to the extent that the income tax consequences of dividends arise from the circumstances described in paragraph 58(a) and (b).' *[IAS 12(2018).52A].*

Those who believed that the tax deduction should be accounted for in equity argued that paragraph 52B of IAS 12 only applies 'in the circumstances described in paragraph 52A' and the example does not include differential tax rates for retained and distributed profits. Those who argued that the tax deduction should be credited to profit or loss considered that the reference in paragraph 52A of IAS 12 to taxes 'payable at a higher or lower rate', should be interpreted as including a higher or lower effective rate, as well as a higher or lower headline rate.

The Interpretations Committee observed that the circumstances to which the requirements in paragraph 52B of IAS 12 apply were unclear and decided that a limited amendment to IAS 12 was required to clarify that the requirements in paragraph 52B of IAS 12 apply to all payments on financial instruments classified as equity that are distributions of profits, and are not limited to the circumstances described in paragraph 52A of IAS 12.[56]

In December 2017, the IASB published – *Annual Improvements to IFRS Standards – 2015-2017 Cycle*, which moves the text in paragraph 52B to paragraph 57A, thereby relating it more closely to the general requirements for the allocation of tax set out at 10 above, and removes any reference to the specific circumstances when there are different tax rates for distributed and undistributed profits. Accordingly, the tax benefits of equity distributions will be recognised in profit or loss, unless it can be demonstrated that the profits being distributed were previously generated in transactions recognised in other comprehensive income or equity. These amendments are mandatory for annual periods beginning on or after 1 January 2019. When an entity first applies these amendments, it applies them to the income tax consequences of dividends recognised on or after the beginning of the earliest comparative period. *[IAS 12.98I].*

The Board concluded that entities would have sufficient information to apply the amendments in this way, which will enhance comparability of reporting periods. *[IAS 12.BC70].*

10.3.5.A Tax benefits of transaction costs of equity instruments

In its Basis of Conclusions, the Board noted that the amendments should not be interpreted to mean that an entity recognises in profit or loss the income tax consequences of all payments on financial instruments classified as equity. Rather, an entity would exercise judgement in determining whether payments on such instruments are distributions of profits (i.e. dividends). If they are, then the requirements in paragraph 57A apply. If they are not, then the requirements of paragraph 61A of IAS 12 apply to the income tax consequences of those payments, meaning the related tax is recognised in equity. *[IAS 12.BC67].*

The Board considered and rejected the suggestion that it should provide guidance on how to determine if payments on financial instruments classified as equity are distributions of profits on the basis that:

(a) any attempt by the Board to define or describe distributions of profits could affect other IFRS Standards and IFRIC Interpretations, and risks unintended consequences; and

(b) the amendments do not change what is and is not a distribution of profits. They simply clarify that the requirements in paragraph 57A apply to all income tax consequences of dividends.

Nevertheless, the Board concluded that finalising the amendments without adding specific guidance would eliminate the potential for inconsistent accounting that resulted from the ambiguity of the scope of the requirements that had existed previously. *[IAS 12.BC69]*. In our opinion, guidance will be needed ultimately on how to determine which payments on financial instruments classified as equity would not be regarded as distributions of profits.

Whilst some payments in relation to equity instruments, such as the issue costs of equity shares, can clearly be regarded as a transaction cost than a distribution of profits, entities will have to exercise judgement in determining the appropriate treatment of other items. In making such a judgement, the legal and regulatory requirements in the entity's jurisdiction would also be relevant, for example if those local requirements stipulate whether a particular payment is, in law, a distribution.

10.4 Gains and losses reclassified ('recycled') to profit or loss

Several IFRSs (notably IAS 21 and IFRS 9) require certain gains and losses that have been accounted for outside profit or loss to be reclassified ('recycled') to profit or loss at a later date when the assets or liabilities to which they relate are realised or settled. Whilst IAS 12 requires any tax consequences of the original recognition of the gains or losses outside profit or loss also to be accounted for outside profit or loss, it is silent on the treatment to be adopted when the gains or losses are reclassified. In our view, any tax consequences of reclassified gains or losses originally recognised outside profit or loss should also be reclassified through profit or loss in the same period as the gains or losses to which they relate. Indeed, such reclassification is often an automatic consequence of the reversal of previously recognised deferred tax income or expense and its 're-recognition' as current tax income or expense, as illustrated in Example 33.43.

Example 33.43: Tax on reclassified ('recycled') items

An entity has an annual reporting period ending 30 September. On 1 January 2021 an entity purchases for €2,000 a debt security that it classifies under IFRS 9 as fair value through other comprehensive income ('FVOCI') with recycling. At 30 September 2021 it restates the security to its fair value of €2,400, which was also its fair value on 1 May 2022. On 1 July 2022 it disposes of the investment for €2,100.

The entity's tax rate for the year ending 30 September 2021 is 40% and for 2022 35%. The change of rate was made in legislation enacted (without previous substantive enactment) on 1 May 2022. The entity is subject to tax on disposal of the investment (based on disposal proceeds less cost) in the period of disposal.

The accounting entries for this transaction would be as follows:

	€	€
1 January 2021		
Debt security	2,000	
Cash		2,000
30 September 2021		
Debt security [€2,400 – €2,000]	400	
Deferred tax (statement of financial position) [€400 @ 40%]		160
Other comprehensive income ('OCI')		240
Recognition of increase in value of asset, and related deferred tax		
1 May 2022		
Deferred tax (statement of financial position) [€400 @ (35% – 40%)]	20	
OCI		20
Remeasurement of deferred tax (no change in the fair value of the debt security since 30 September 2021)		
1 July 2022		
Debt security		300
OCI (revaluation of €300 less deferred tax of €105)	195	
Deferred tax (statement of financial position)	105	
Recognition of decrease in value of asset, and related deferred tax		
Cash	2,100	
OCI (reclassification of €100 (before tax) to income statement)	100	
Debt security		2,100
Profit on disposal of debt security [cash €2,100 less original cost €2,000]		100
Deferred tax (statement of financial position)	35	
Deferred tax income (OCI)		35
Current tax (profit or loss)	35	
Current tax (statement of financial position) [35% of €100 pre-tax profit]		35
To record the sale of the debt security and related taxation		

10.4.1 Debt instrument measured at fair value through OCI under IFRS 9

IFRS 9 requires an entity to recognise a loss allowance for expected credit losses (ECLs) on financial assets that are debt instruments measured at fair value through other comprehensive income (FVOCI). *[IFRS 9.5.5.1]*.

Under the general approach, at each reporting date, an entity recognises a loss allowance based on either 12-month expected credit losses or lifetime expected credit losses, depending on whether there has been a significant increase in credit risk on the financial instrument since initial recognition. *[IFRS 9.5.5.3, 5.5.5]*.

The Standard states that these expected credit losses do not reduce the carrying amount of the financial assets in the statement of financial position, which remains at fair value. Instead, an amount equal to the allowance that would arise if the asset was measured at amortised cost is recognised in other comprehensive income as the 'accumulated impairment amount'. *[IFRS 9.4.1.2A, 5.5.2, Appendix A]*.

The accounting treatment (ignoring the accounting for any tax) and journal entries for debt instruments measured at FVOCI are illustrated in Chapter 51 at 9.1 by the following example, based on Illustrative Example 3 in the Implementation Guidance for the standard. *[IFRS 9 IG Example 13, IE78-IE81].*

Example 33.44: Debt instrument measured at fair value through other comprehensive income

An entity purchases a debt instrument with a fair value of £1,000 on 15 December 2021 and measures the debt instrument at fair value through other comprehensive income (FVOCI). The instrument has an interest rate of 5 per cent over the contractual term of 10 years and has a 5 per cent effective interest rate. At initial recognition the entity determines that the asset is not purchased or originated credit-impaired.

	Debit	Credit
Financial asset – FVOCI	£1,000	
Cash		£1,000

To recognise the debt instrument measured at its fair value

On 31 December 2021 (the reporting date), the fair value of the debt instrument has decreased to £950 as a result of changes in market interest rates. The entity determines that there has not been a significant increase in credit risk since initial recognition and that ECLs should be measured at an amount equal to 12-month expected credit losses, which amounts to £30. For simplicity, journal entries for the receipt of interest revenue are not provided.

	Debit	Credit
Impairment loss (profit or loss)	£30	
Other comprehensive income[(a)]	£20	
Financial asset – FVOCI		£50

To recognise 12-month expected credit losses and other fair value changes on the debt instrument

(a) The cumulative loss in other comprehensive income at the reporting date was £20. That amount consists of the total fair value change of £50 (i.e. £1,000 – £950) offset by the change in the accumulated impairment amount representing 12-month ECLs that was recognised (£30).

On 1 January 2022, the entity decides to sell the debt instrument for £950, which is its fair value at that date.

	Debit	Credit
Cash	£950	
Financial asset – FVOCI		£950
Loss (profit or loss)	£20	
Other comprehensive income		£20

To derecognise the fair value through other comprehensive income asset and recycle amounts accumulated in other comprehensive income to profit or loss, i.e. £20.

As noted in Chapter 51 at 9.1, this means that in contrast to financial assets measured at amortised cost, there is no separate allowance for credit losses but, instead, impairment gains or losses are accounted for as an adjustment of the revaluation reserve accumulated in other comprehensive income, with a corresponding charge to profit or loss (which is then reflected in retained earnings).

Assume that, for tax purposes, current tax does not arise until the asset is recovered. In Example 33.44 above, the asset revaluation creates a temporary difference as the carrying value is now different to its original cost (being its tax base). The asset revaluation is first accounted for in OCI, therefore, the related tax is recorded in OCI. *[IAS 12.61A].*

As regards the recognition of the ECLs, and as noted above, there is no further change to the carrying value of the asset. Impairment gains or losses are accounted for as an adjustment of the revaluation reserve accumulated in other comprehensive income, with a corresponding charge to profit or loss. Under the general principal in IAS 12, the entity would transfer the related deferred tax out of OCI and into profit or loss in respect of the ECLs reallocated out of OCI. A similar transfer would be made in respect of any earlier revaluation entries that are recycled to profit or loss on derecognition of the debt instrument. *[IAS 12.61A]*. Accordingly, if the applicable rate of tax is 20%, the tax-effected journals in Example 33.44 above would be as follows:

Example 33.45: Debt instrument measured at fair value through other comprehensive income – tax effect

When the entity recognises the reduction in fair value of the instrument from £1,000 to £950 and the 12-month ECLs:

	Debit	Credit
Deferred tax asset (statement of financial position))[a]	£10	
Profit or loss – deferred tax		£6
Other comprehensive income – deferred tax		£4

(a) The deferred tax asset arising from the deductible temporary difference on revaluation is £10 (£50 @ 20%), with related deferred tax credits in profit or loss and OCI at a rate of 20% applied to the amounts recognised in each of those statements of £30 and £20 respectively.

On 1 January 2022, the entity decides to sell the debt instrument for £950, which is its fair value at that date. The tax rate on a disposal is also 20% in this example. The related tax journals are as follows.

	Debit	Credit
Deferred tax asset (statement of financial position)		£10
Profit or loss – deferred tax	£6	
Other comprehensive income – deferred tax	£4	
Current tax liability (statement of financial position)		£10
Profit or loss – current tax	£10	

Being the reversal of the deductible temporary differences on disposal of the debt instrument and the recognition of current tax deduction on the taxable loss on sale.

10.4.2 Recognition of expected credit losses with no change in fair value

Consider an example where there has been no change to the asset's fair value since its acquisition, but an expected credit loss has been determined. Current tax is charged on realisation of the asset only.

As discussed above, the ECLs are accounted for as an adjustment (credit) to the revaluation reserve accumulated in other comprehensive income, with a corresponding charge to profit or loss. However, in this case, there is no change to the carrying amount of the asset. *Prima facie*, therefore, there is no temporary difference associated with the asset. However, the treatment discussed at 7.2.4.D above would support a conclusion that this temporary difference of nil should in fact be analysed into:

- a deductible temporary difference arising on the ECLs that affect accounting profit; and
- a taxable temporary difference of an equal amount arising on the amount reflected in OCI, which is effectively an upward revaluation to restore the asset back to its fair value.

This analysis indicates it would be appropriate to recognise a deferred tax asset for amounts recognised for ECLs in profit or loss *[IAS 12.58]* and to recognise the tax effect of the 'item that is recognised outside profit or loss' (i.e. the credit to OCI) in other comprehensive income. *[IAS 12.61A]*.

This approach is illustrated in Example 33.46 below:

Example 33.46: Tax effect of expected credit losses with no change in fair value

An entity purchases a debt instrument with a fair value of £1,000 and measures the debt instrument at fair value through other comprehensive income (FVOCI). The instrument has an interest rate of 5 per cent over the contractual term of 10 years, and has a 5 per cent effective interest rate. At initial recognition the entity determines that the asset is not purchased or originated credit-impaired. Current tax is charged or credited on realisation of the asset, at an enacted rate of 20%.

	Debit	Credit
Financial asset – FVOCI	£1,000	
Cash		£1,000

To recognise the debt instrument measured at its initial fair value

The entity determines that expected credit losses (ECLs) should be measured at an amount equal to 12-month expected credit losses, which amounts to £30. However, the fair value of the debt instrument is still £1,000.

	Debit	Credit
Impairment loss (profit or loss)	£30	
Other comprehensive income		£30
Financial asset – FVOCI	Nil	

To recognise 12-month expected credit losses on the debt instrument and (in OCI) its increase in fair value

The entity determines that paragraphs 58 and 61A of IAS 12 require the tax effect of amounts recognised in profit and loss to be recognised in profit or loss and for the tax effect of amounts recognised in other comprehensive income to be recorded in the same place.

	Debit	Credit
Profit or loss – deferred tax		£6
Other comprehensive income – deferred tax	£6	
Deferred tax asset (statement of financial position)	Nil	

The entity in Example 33.46 above could have determined that the recognition of the expected credit loss does not generate a temporary difference because neither the carrying amount nor the tax base of the asset has changed. However, this determination can have unwanted consequences as the debt instrument is later revalued and realised, in particular with respect to variability in the effective tax rate reported in both profit or loss and in other comprehensive income.

10.5 Gain/loss in profit or loss and loss/gain outside profit or loss offset for tax purposes

It often happens that a gain or loss accounted for in profit or loss can be offset for tax purposes against a gain or loss accounted for in other comprehensive income (or an increase or decrease in equity). This raises the question of how the tax effects of such transactions should be accounted for, as illustrated by Example 33.47 below.

Example 33.47: **Loss in other comprehensive income and gain in profit or loss offset for tax purposes**

During the year ended 31 December 2021, an entity that pays tax at 35% makes a taxable profit of €50,000 comprising:

- €80,000 trading profit less finance costs accounted for in profit or loss; and
- €30,000 foreign exchange losses accounted for in other comprehensive income ('OCI').

Should the total tax liability of €17,500 (35% of €50,000) be presented as either:

(a) a charge of €17,500 in profit or loss; or
(b) a charge of €28,000 (35% of €80,000) in profit or loss and a credit of €10,500 (35% of €30,000) in OCI?

In our view, (b) is the appropriate treatment, since the amount accounted for in OCI represents the difference between the tax that would have been paid absent the exchange loss accounted for in OCI and the amount actually payable. This indicates that this is the amount that, in the words of paragraph 61A of IAS 12, 'relates to' items that are recognised outside profit or loss.

Similar issues may arise where a transaction accounted for outside profit or loss generates a suitable taxable profit that allows recognition of a previously unrecognised tax asset relating to a transaction previously accounted for in profit or loss, as illustrated by Example 33.48 below.

Example 33.48: **Recognition of deferred tax asset in profit or loss on the basis of tax liability accounted for outside profit or loss**

An entity that pays tax at 30% has brought forward unrecognised deferred tax assets (with an indefinite life) totalling £1 million, relating to trading losses accounted for in profit or loss in prior periods. On 1 January 2021 it invests £100,000 in government bonds, which it holds until they are redeemed for the same amount on maturity on 31 December 2024. For tax purposes, any gain made by the entity on disposal of the bonds can be offset against the brought forward tax losses. The tax base of the bonds remains £100,000 at all times.

The entity elects to account for the bonds as fair value through other comprehensive income and therefore carries them at fair value in the statement of financial position and amortised cost information is presented in profit or loss (see Chapter 50 at 2.3). Over the period to maturity the fair value of the bonds at the end of each reporting period (31 December) is as follows:

	Fair value	Amortised cost	Movement in OCI
	£000	£000	£000
2021	111	101	10
2022	117	102	15
2023	122	102	20
2024	100	100	–

Under IFRS 9 the movements in fair value in excess of the amounts recognised in profit or loss (excluding any amounts received in cash, e.g. the coupon on a bond) would be accounted for in other comprehensive income ('OCI') – see Chapter 50 at 2.3. Taken in isolation, the valuation gains recorded in OCI in 2021 to 2023 would give rise to a deferred tax liability (at 30%) of £3,000 (2021), £4,500 (2022) and £6,000 (2023). However, these liabilities arise from taxable temporary differences that can be offset against the losses brought forward (see 7.4 above), and accordingly the (equal and opposite) deferred tax liability and deferred tax asset are offset in the statement of financial position (see 13.1.1 below). This raises the question as to whether there should be either:

(a) no tax charge or credit in either profit or loss or OCI in any of the periods affected; or
(b) in each period, a deferred tax charge in OCI (in respect of the taxable temporary difference arising from valuation gains on the bonds) and deferred tax income in profit or loss (representing the recognition of the previously unrecognised deferred tax asset).

In our view, the treatment in (b) should be followed. The fact that no deferred tax is presented in the statement of financial position arises from the offset of a deferred tax asset and deferred tax liability – it does not imply that there is no deferred tax. Moreover, although the recognition of the deferred tax asset is possible only as the result of the recognition of a deferred tax liability arising from a transaction accounted for in OCI, the asset itself relates to a trading loss previously accounted for in profit or loss. Accordingly, the deferred tax credit arising from the recognition of the asset is properly accounted for in profit or loss.

10.6 Discontinued operations

IAS 12 does not explicitly address the allocation of income tax charges and credits between continuing and discontinued operations. However, that some allocation is required is implicit in the requirement of paragraph 33(b)(ii) of IFRS 5 to disclose how much of the single figure post-tax profit or loss of discontinued operations disclosed in the statement of comprehensive income is comprised of 'the related income tax expense' (see Chapter 4). *[IFRS 5.33(b)(ii)]*. In our view, the provisions of IAS 12 for the allocation of tax income and expense between profit or loss, other comprehensive income and equity also form a basis for allocating tax income and expense between continuing and discontinued operations, as illustrated by Examples 33.49 to 33.51 below.

Example 33.49: Profit in continuing operations and loss in discontinued operations offset for tax purposes

Entity A, which pays tax at 25%, has identified an operation as discontinued for the purposes of IFRS 5. During the period the discontinued operation incurred a loss of £2 million and the continuing operations made a profit of £10 million. The net £8 million profit is fully taxable in the period, and there is no deferred tax income or expense. In our view, the tax expense should be allocated as follows:

	£m	£m
Current tax expense (continuing operations)[1]	2.5	
Current tax income (discontinued operation)[2]		0.5
Current tax liability[3]		2.0

1 Continuing operations profit £10m @ 25% = £2.5m
2 Discontinued operations loss £2m @ 25% = £0.5m.
3 Net taxable profit £8m @ 25% = £2.0m

The tax allocated to the discontinued operation represents the difference between the tax that would have been paid absent the loss accounted for in discontinued operations and the amount actually payable.

Example 33.50: Taxable profit on disposal of discontinued operation reduced by previously unrecognised tax losses

Entity B disposes of a discontinued operation during the current accounting period. The disposal gives rise to a charge to tax of €4 million. However, this is reduced to zero by offset against brought forward tax losses, which relate to the continuing operations of the entity, and for which no deferred tax asset has previously been recognised.

In our view, even though there is no overall tax expense, this should be reflected for financial reporting purposes as follows:

	€m	€m
Current tax expense (discontinued operation)	4.0	
Current tax income (continuing operations)		4.0

This allocation reflects that fact that, although the transaction that allows recognition of the brought forward tax losses is accounted for as a discontinued operation, the losses themselves arose from continuing operations. This is essentially the same analysis as is used in Example 33.48 above (where a deferred tax liability recognised in other comprehensive income gives rise to an equal deferred tax asset recognised in profit or loss).

Example 33.51: **Taxable profit on disposal of discontinued operation reduced by previously recognised tax losses**

Entity B disposes of a discontinued operation during the current accounting period. The disposal gives rise to a charge to tax of €4 million. However, this is reduced to zero by offset against brought forward tax losses, which relate to the entity's continuing operations, and for which a deferred tax asset has previously been recognised.

In our view, even though there is no overall tax expense, this should be reflected for financial reporting purposes as follows:

	€m	€m
Current tax expense (discontinued operation)	4.0	
Deferred tax expense (continuing operations)	4.0	
Current tax income (continuing operations)		4.0
Deferred tax asset (statement of financial position)		4.0

This allocation reflects that fact that, although the transaction that allows realisation of the brought forward tax losses is accounted for as a discontinued operation, the losses themselves arose from continuing operations. This is essentially the same analysis as is used in Example 33.50 above.

10.7 Defined benefit pension plans

IAS 19 requires an entity, in accounting for a defined benefit post-employment benefit plan, to recognise actuarial gains and losses relating to the plan in full in other comprehensive income ('OCI'). At the same time, a calculated current (and, where applicable, past) service cost and net interest on the net defined benefit liability or asset are recognised in profit or loss – see Chapter 35 at 10.

In many jurisdictions, tax deductions for post-employment benefits are given on the basis of cash contributions paid to the plan fund (or benefits paid when a plan is unfunded).

This significant difference between the way in which defined plans are treated for tax and financial reporting purposes can make the allocation of tax deductions for them between profit or loss and OCI somewhat arbitrary, as illustrated by Example 33.52 below.

Example 33.52: **Tax deductions for defined benefit pension plans**

At 1 January 2021 an entity that pays tax at 40% has a fully-funded defined benefit pension scheme. During the year ended 31 December 2021 it records a total cost of €1 million, of which €800,000 is allocated to profit or loss and €200,000 to other comprehensive income ('OCI'). In January 2022 it makes a funding payment of €400,000, a tax deduction for which is received through the current tax charge for the year ended 31 December 2022.

Assuming that the entity is able to recognise a deferred tax asset for the entire €1 million charged in 2021, it will record the following entry for income taxes in 2021.

	€	€
Deferred tax asset [€1,000,000 @ 40%]	400,000	
Deferred tax income (profit or loss) [€800,000 @ 40%]		320,000
Deferred tax income (OCI) [€200,000 @ 40%]		80,000

When the funding payment is made in January 2022, the accounting deficit on the fund is reduced by €400,000. This gives rise to deferred tax expense of €160,000 (€400,000 @ 40%), as some of the deferred tax asset as at 31 December 2021 is released, and current tax income of €160,000 is recorded. The difficulty is how to allocate this movement in the deferred tax asset between profit or loss and OCI, as it is ultimately a matter of arbitrary allocation as to whether the funding payment is regarded as making good (for example):

- €400,000 of the €800,000 deficit previously accounted for in profit or loss;
- the whole of the €200,000 of the deficit previously accounted for in OCI and €200,000 of the €800,000 deficit previously accounted for in profit or loss; or
- a *pro rata* share of those parts of the total deficit accounted for in profit or loss and OCI.

In the example above, the split is of relatively minor significance, since the entity was able to recognise 100% of the potential deferred tax asset associated with the pension liability. This means that, as the scheme is funded, there will be an equal and opposite amount of current tax income and deferred tax expense. The only real issue is therefore one of presentation, namely whether the gross items comprising this net nil charge are disclosed within the tax charge in profit or loss or in OCI.

In other cases, however, there might be an amount of net tax income or expense that needs to be allocated. Suppose that, as above, the entity recorded a pension cost of €1 million in 2021 but determined that the related deferred tax asset did not meet the criteria for recognition under IAS 12. In 2022, the entity determines that an asset of €50,000 can be recognised in view of the funding payments and taxable profits anticipated in 2022 and later years. This results in a total tax credit of €210,000 (€160,000 current tax, €50,000 deferred tax) in 2022, raising the question of whether it should be allocated to profit or loss, to OCI, or allocated on a *pro rata* basis. This question might also arise if, as the result of newly enacted tax rates, the existing deferred tax balance were required to be remeasured.

In our view, these are instances of the exceptional circumstances envisaged by IAS 12 when a strict allocation of tax between profit or loss and OCI is not possible (see 10 above). Accordingly, any reasonable method of allocation may be used, provided that it is applied on a consistent basis.

One approach might be to compare the funding payments made to the scheme in the previous few years with the charges made to profit or loss under IAS 19 in those periods. If, for example, it is found that the payments were equal to or greater than the charges to profit or loss, it might reasonably be concluded that the funding payments have 'covered' the charge recognised in profit or loss, so that any surplus or deficit on the statement of financial position is broadly represented by items that have been accounted for in OCI.

However, a surplus may also arise from funding the scheme to an amount greater than the liability recognised under IAS 19 (for example under a minimum funding requirement imposed by local legislation or agreed with the pension fund trustees). In this case, the asset does not result from previously recognised income but from a reduction in another asset (i.e. cash). The entity should assess the expected manner of recovery of any asset implied by the accounting treatment of the surplus – i.e. whether it has been recognised on the basis that it will be 'consumed' (resulting in an accounting expense) or refunded to the entity in due course. The accounting treatment of refunds is discussed further in Chapter 35, and at 10.7.1 below.

The entity will account for the tax consequences of the expected manner of recovery implied by the accounting treatment. Where it is concluded that the asset will be 'consumed' (resulting in accounting expense), the entity will need to determine whether such an expense is likely to be recognised in profit or loss or in OCI in a future period.

10.7.1 Tax on refund of pension surplus

In some jurisdictions, a pension fund may be permitted or required to make a refund to the sponsoring employee of any surplus in the fund not required to settle the known or anticipated liabilities of the fund. It may be that such a refund is subject to tax. IFRIC 14 – *IAS 19 – The Limit on a Defined Benefit Asset, Minimum Funding Requirements and their Interaction* – requires any asset recorded in respect of such a refund to be shown net of any tax other than an income tax (see Chapter 35). In determining whether such a tax is an income tax of the entity, the general principles at 4.1 above should be applied. Relevant factors may include:

- whether tax is levied on the pension fund or the sponsoring entity; and
- whether tax is levied on the gross amount of the refund in all cases, or has regard to the sponsoring entity's other taxable income, or the amount of tax deductions received by the sponsoring entity in respect of contributions to the fund.

10.8 Share-based payment transactions

The accounting treatment of share-based payment transactions, some knowledge of which is required to understand the discussion below, is dealt with in Chapter 34.

In many tax jurisdictions, an entity receives a tax deduction in respect of remuneration paid in shares, share options or other equity instruments of the entity. The amount of any tax deduction may differ from the related remuneration expense, and may arise in a later accounting period. For example, in some jurisdictions, an entity may recognise an expense for employee services in accordance with IFRS 2 (based on the fair value of the award at the date of grant), but not receive a tax deduction until the share options are exercised (based on the intrinsic value of the award at the date of exercise).

As noted at 6.1.4 above, IAS 12 effectively considers the cumulative expense associated with share-based payment transactions as an asset that has been fully expensed in the financial statements in advance of being recognised for tax purposes, thus giving rise to a deductible temporary difference. *[IAS 12.68A, 68B]*.

If the tax deduction available in future periods is not known at the end of the period, it should be estimated based on information available at the end of the period. For example, if the tax deduction will be dependent upon the entity's share price at a future date, the measurement of the deductible temporary difference should be based on the entity's share price at the end of the period. *[IAS 12.68B]*.

10.8.1 Allocation of tax deduction between profit or loss and equity

Where the amount of any tax deduction (or estimated future tax deduction) exceeds the amount of the related cumulative remuneration expense, the current or deferred tax associated with the excess should be recognised directly in equity. *[IAS 12.68C]*. This treatment is illustrated by Example 33.53 below.

Example 33.53: Tax deductions for share-based payment transactions – allocation to profit or loss and equity

At the start of year 1, an entity with a tax rate of 40% grants options, which vest at the end of year 3 and are exercised at the end of year 5. Tax deductions are received at the date of exercise of the options, based on their intrinsic value at the date of exercise. Details of the expense recognised for employee services received and consumed in each accounting period, the number of options expected to vest by the entity at each year-end during the vesting period and outstanding after the end of the vesting period, and the intrinsic value of the options at each year-end, are as follows:

Year	IFRS 2 expense for period £	Cumulative IFRS 2 expense £	Number of options	Intrinsic value per option £	Total intrinsic value £
1	188,000	188,000	50,000	5	250,000
2	185,000	373,000	45,000	8	360,000
3	190,000	563,000	40,000	13	520,000
4		563,000	40,000	17	680,000
5		563,000	40,000	20	800,000

The tax base of, and the temporary difference and deferred tax asset associated with, the employee services is calculated as follows. Since the book value of the employee services is in all cases zero, the temporary difference associated with the services is at all times equal to their tax base as set out below.

Year	Intrinsic value (see table above) £	Expired portion of vesting period [1]	Tax base (and temporary difference) £	Tax asset [2] £	Tax income [3] £
	a	b	c = a × b	c @ 40%	
1	250,000	1/3	83,333	33,333	33,333
2	360,000	2/3	240,000	96,000	62,667
3	520,000	3/3	520,000	208,000	112,000
4	680,000	3/3	680,000	272,000	64,000
5	800,000	3/3	800,000	320,000	48,000

[1] The expired portion of the vesting period is consistent with that used to calculate the cumulative charge employee costs under IFRS 2 (see Chapter 34).

[2] Deferred tax asset in years 1 to 4 and current tax asset in year 5.

[3] Year-on-year increase in asset.

By comparing the 'Cumulative IFRS 2 expense' column in the first table with the 'Tax base (and temporary difference)' column in the second table it can be seen that in years 1 to 3 the expected tax deduction is lower than the cumulative expense charged, and is therefore dealt with entirely in profit or loss. However in years 4 and 5 the expected (and in year 5 the actual) tax deduction is higher than the cumulative expense charged. The tax relating to the cumulative expense charged is dealt with in profit or loss, and the tax relating to the excess of the tax-deductible amount over the amount charged in profit or loss is dealt with in equity as follows:

	Debit	Credit
Year 1		
Deferred tax (statement of financial position)	33,333	
Deferred tax (profit or loss)		33,333

	Debit	Credit
Year 2		
Deferred tax (statement of financial position)	62,667	
Deferred tax (profit or loss)		62,667
Year 3		
Deferred tax (statement of financial position)	112,000	
Deferred tax (profit or loss)		112,000
Year 4		
Deferred tax (statement of financial position)	64,000	
Deferred tax (profit or loss)[1]		17,200
Equity		46,800
Year 5		
Deferred tax (profit or loss)	225,200	
Deferred tax (equity)	46,800	
Deferred tax (statement of financial position)		272,000
Current tax (statement of financial position)	320,000	
Current tax (profit or loss)[2]		225,200
Current tax (equity)		94,800

[1] Cumulative tax credit to profit or loss restricted to 40% of cumulative expense of £563,000 = £225,200. Amount credited in years 1 to 3 is £(33,333 + 62,667 + 112,000) = £212,000. Therefore, the amount recognised in profit or loss is £(225,200 – 212,000) = £17,200.

[2] Current tax credit in profit or loss is restricted to £225,200 as explained in note 1 above. The £48,000 net increase in total cumulative tax income since year 4 (£320,000 – £272,000) is dealt with entirely in equity (current tax income €94,800 less deferred tax charge €46,800).

Example 33.53 above is based on Example 5 in the illustrative examples accompanying IAS 12 (as inserted by IFRS 2). However, the example included in IAS 12 states that the cumulative tax income is based on the number of options 'outstanding' at each period end. This would be inconsistent with the methodology in IFRS 2 (see Chapter 34), which requires the share-based payment expense during the vesting period to be based on the number of options expected to vest (as that term is defined in IFRS 2), not the total number of options outstanding, at the period end. It would only be once the vesting period is complete that the number of options outstanding becomes relevant. We assume that this is simply a drafting slip by the IASB.

IAS 12 asserts that the allocation of the tax deduction between profit or loss and equity illustrated in Example 33.53 is appropriate on the basis that the fact that the tax deduction (or estimated future tax deduction) exceeds the amount of the related cumulative remuneration expense 'indicates that the tax deduction relates not only to remuneration expense but also to an equity item.' *[IAS 12.68C]*.

The treatment required by IFRS 2 seems to have been adopted for consistency with US GAAP. However, as the IASB acknowledges, while the final cumulative allocation of tax between profit or loss and equity is broadly consistent with that required by US GAAP, the basis on which it is measured and reported at reporting dates before exercise date is quite different. *[IFRS 2.BC311-BC329]*.

10.8.2 Determining the tax base

IAS 12 does not specify exactly how the tax base of a share-based payment transaction is to be determined. However, Example 5 in the illustrative examples accompanying IAS 12 (the substance of which is reproduced at 10.8.1 above) calculates the tax base as:

- the amount that would be deductible for tax if the event triggering deduction occurred at the end of the reporting period; multiplied by
- the expired portion of the vesting period at the end of the reporting period.

IFRS 2 treats certain share-based payment awards as, in effect, a parcel of a number of discrete awards, each with a different vesting period. This may be the case where an award is subject to graded vesting, has been modified, or has separate equity and liability components (see Chapter 34). In order to determine the tax base for such an award, it is necessary to consider separately the part, or parts, of the award with the same vesting period, as illustrated in Example 33.54 below.

Example 33.54: Tax deductions for share-based payment transactions – 'multi-element' awards

An entity awards 550 free shares to an employee, with no conditions other than continuous service. 100 shares vest after one year, 150 shares after two years and 300 shares after three years. Any shares received at the end of years 1 and 2 have vested unconditionally.

At the date the award is granted, the fair value of a share delivered in one year's time is €3.00; in two years' time €2.80; and in three years' time €2.50.

Under IFRS 2, the analysis is that the employee has simultaneously received an award of 100 shares vesting over one year, an award of 150 shares vesting over two years and an award of 300 shares vesting over 3 years (see Chapter 34 at 6.2.2). This would be accounted for as follows (assuming that the award was expected to vest in full at each reporting date and did actually vest in full – see Chapter 34):

Year	Calculation of cumulative expense	Cumulative expense (€)	Expense for period (€)
1	[100 shares × €3.00] + [150 shares × €2.80 × 1/2] + [300 shares × €2.50 × 1/3]	760	760
2	[100 shares × €3.00] + [150 shares × €2.80 × 2/2] + [300 shares × €2.50 × 2/3]	1,220	460
3	[100 shares × €3.00] + [150 shares × €2.80 × 2/2] + [300 shares × €2.50 × 3/3]	1,470	250

The entity receives a tax deduction at 30% for the awards based on the fair value of the shares delivered. The fair value of a share at the end of years 1, 2 and 3 is, respectively, €3.60, €2.00 and €6.00.

At the end of year 1, a current tax deduction of €108 (100 shares × €3.60 @ 30%) is receivable in respect of the 100 shares that vest. The tax base of the shares expected to vest in years 2 and 3 is calculated by reference to the year-end share price of €3.60 as:

- in respect of the 150 shares expected to vest at the end of year 2, €270 (150 shares × €3.60 × 1/2). This will give rise to a deferred tax asset of €81 (€270 @ 30%); and
- in respect of the 300 shares expected to vest at the end of year 3, €360 (300 shares × €3.60 × 1/3). This will give rise to a deferred tax asset of €108 (€360 @ 30%).

The total deferred tax asset at the end of year is therefore €189 (€81 + €108).

At the end of year 2, a current tax deduction of €90 is receivable in respect of the 150 shares that vest (150 shares × €2.00 @ 30%). The tax base of the shares expected to vest in year 3 is calculated by reference to the year-end share price of €2.00 as €400 (300 shares × €2.00 × 2/3). This gives rise to a deferred tax asset of €120 (€400 @ 30%).

At the end of year 3, a current tax deduction of €540 (300 shares × €6.00 @ 30%) is receivable in respect of the 300 shares that vest.

When an award has multiple elements that vest at different times, the question arises as to whether the unit of account for applying the 'cap' on recognition of the tax benefit in profit or loss is the award as a whole or each element separately accounted for. In our view, the determination needs to be made for each element of the award separately. This is similar to our analysis at 10.7.3 below (multiple awards outstanding) and 10.7.4 below (awards for which a tax deduction is received on exercise which are exercised at different times).

Based on the information above, the total current and deferred tax income or expense (i.e. before allocation to profit or loss and equity) at the ends of years 1 to 3 would be as follows, assuming in each case that there is no restriction on the recognition of tax assets (see 7.4 above).

Year	Current tax asset and income €	Deferred tax asset €	Deferred tax income/(expense) €
1	108	189	189
2	90	120	(69)
3	540	–	(120)

The required accounting entries for income taxes are as follows:

	Debit	Credit
Year 1		
Current tax (statement of financial position)	108	
Current tax (profit or loss)		90
Current tax (equity)[1]		18
Deferred tax (statement of financial position)	189	
Deferred tax (profit or loss) (€63 + €75 – see below)		138
Deferred tax (equity)[2] (€18 + €33 – see below)		51

[1] The current tax deduction relates to the 100 shares vesting in year 1, for which the charge to profit or loss is €300 (100 shares × €3.00). The tax deduction accounted for in profit or loss is therefore restricted to 30% of €300 = €90. The balance of €18 is credited to equity and relates to the €0.60 difference between the grant date fair value of a 'Year 1' share at grant (€3.00) and at vesting (€3.60) – 100 shares × €0.60 = €60 @ 30% = €18.

[2] The total deferred tax income of €189 represents:

- €81 (see above) in respect of the 150 shares expected to vest in year 2, for which the charge to profit or loss is €210 (150 shares × €2.80 × 1/2). The tax deduction accounted for in profit or loss is restricted to 30% of €210 = €63, with the balance of €18 credited to equity; and

- €108 (see above) in respect of the 300 shares expected to vest in year 3, for which the expected charge to profit or loss is €250 (300 shares × €2.50 × 1/3). The tax deduction accounted for in profit or loss is therefore restricted to 30% of €250 = €75, with the balance of €33 credited to equity.

	Debit	Credit
Year 2		
Current tax (statement of financial position)	90	
Current tax (profit or loss)[3]		90
Deferred tax (profit or loss)[4]	18	
Deferred tax (equity)[4]	51	
Deferred tax (statement of financial position)[4]		69

[3] The current tax deduction relates to the 150 shares vesting in year 2, for which the cumulative charge to profit or loss is €420 (150 shares × €2.80). The cumulative tax deduction accounted for in profit or loss would therefore be restricted to 30% of €420 = €126. The entire amount of current tax deduction received (€90) is therefore credited to profit or loss.

[4] At the end of year 2, the deferred tax relates to the 300 shares expected to vest at the end of year 3, which has been measured based on the year end share price of €2.00. This is lower than the share price on which the IFRS 2 charge has been based. Therefore, there is no requirement to allocate any deferred tax to equity, and the balance of deferred tax in equity is reduced to nil. The balance of the total €69 movement in the deferred tax balance is allocated to profit or loss.

The net tax credit in profit or loss in year 2 of €72 (current tax credit €90, less deferred tax charge €18) can be seen as representing:

Credit relating to IFRS 2 expense recognised in the period[5]	105
Charge relating to remeasurement of prior year deferred tax[6]	(33)
Total	72

[5] In this case the tax credit recognised in profit or loss is not the 'expected' credit of €138 (IFRS 2 charge of €460 @ 30%). This is because the current tax deduction for the shares vesting in year 2 and the deferred tax deduction for the shares expected to vest in year 3 are based on the year-end share price of €2.00, which is lower than the share values used to calculate the IFRS 2 charge (€2.80 and €2.50). During the year, an IFRS 2 expense has been recognised for 75 'whole share equivalents' in respect of the shares vesting in year 2 (150 shares × 1/2) and 100 'whole share equivalents' in respect of the shares expected to vest in year 3 (300 shares × 1/3), a total of 175 'whole share equivalents'. Accordingly the credit for the year is €105 (175 × €2.00 × 30%).

[6] In year 1 the deferred tax credit (based on the year 1 year-end share price of €3.60) recognised in profit of loss in respect of the shares expected to vest in years 2 and 3 was €138. If this had been based on the year 2 year-end share price of €2.00 this would have been only €105. [150 × 1/2 × €2.00] + [300 × 1/3 × €2.00] = €350 × 30% = €105. €138 − €105 = €33.

	Debit	Credit
Year 3		
Current tax (statement of financial position)	540	
Current tax (profit or loss)		225
Current tax (equity)[7]		315
Deferred tax (profit or loss)	120	
Deferred tax (statement of financial position)[8]		120

[7] The current tax deduction relates to the 300 shares vesting in year 1, for which the cumulative charge to profit or loss is €750 (300 shares × €2.50). The tax deduction accounted for in profit or loss is therefore restricted to 30% of €750 = €225.

[8] The deferred tax asset, all of which was – on a cumulative basis – recognised in profit or loss, is derecognised in profit or loss.

The net tax credit in profit or loss in year 3 of €105 (current tax credit €225, less deferred tax charge €120) can be seen as representing:

Credit relating to IFRS 2 expense recognised in the period[9]	75
Credit relating to remeasurement of prior year deferred tax[10]	30
Total	105

[9] €250 @ 30%.
[10] The opening balance deferred tax asset of €120 is based on the year 2 share price of €2.00. If this had been based on the year 3 share price of €6.00 it would have been €360. However, the amount recognised in profit or loss would have been restricted to €150 – 30% of the cumulative expense at the end of year 2 of €500 (300 shares × €2.50 × 2/3). €150 – €120 = €30.

10.8.3 Allocation when more than one award is outstanding

As noted above, IAS 12 requires that, 'where the amount of any tax deduction ... exceeds the amount of the related cumulative remuneration expense, the current or deferred tax associated with the excess should be recognised directly in equity'. Some have therefore argued that, as drafted, IAS 12 requires the cumulative expense for all outstanding share schemes to be compared in aggregate with the aggregate tax deduction for all share schemes. Others argue that the comparison should be made for each scheme separately. The effect of each treatment is illustrated in Example 33.55 below.

Example 33.55: Tax deductions for share-based payment transactions – more than one award

An entity that pays tax at 30% has two outstanding share schemes, Scheme A and Scheme B. The entity receives tax deductions for share-based payment transactions based on their intrinsic value at the date of exercise.

At the end of the reporting period, the cumulative expense charged for each scheme is £1 million. Scheme A has a negative intrinsic value at the end of the reporting period and is not expected to recover its value to the extent that employees will exercise their options. Accordingly no deferred tax asset is recognised for Scheme A. Scheme B has an intrinsic value of £1.5 million. The entity will therefore record a deferred tax asset of £450,000 (30% of £1.5 million), subject to the recognition criteria for deferred tax assets being satisfied.

Those who argue that comparison of share-based payment expense to tax deduction should be made on an aggregated basis would conclude that, because the cumulative potential tax deduction of £1.5 million (which relates only to Scheme B) is lower than the cumulative aggregate expense for both Scheme A and Scheme B (£2 million), the deferred tax income should be recognised entirely in profit or loss.

However, those who argue that comparison of share-based payment expense to tax deduction should be made on a discrete basis for each scheme would conclude that, because the cumulative tax deduction for Scheme B (£1.5 million) is higher than the cumulative aggregate expense for Scheme B (£1 million), only £300,000 of the deferred tax income (30% of £1 million) should be recognised in profit or loss, with the remaining £150,000 recognised in equity.

In our view, the comparison must be made on a discrete scheme-by-scheme basis. As noted at 10.8.2 above, it is clear from IAS 12 and the Basis for Conclusions to IFRS 2 that the IASB's intention was to exclude from profit or loss any tax deduction that is effectively given for the growth in fair value of an award that accrues after grant date. *[IAS 12.68C, IFRS 2.BC311-BC329].* This can be determined only on an award-by-award basis. Moreover, IAS 12 requires the amount of any tax deduction to be accounted for in equity when it 'exceeds the amount of the *related* cumulative remuneration expense' (emphasis added). In Example 33.55 above, the tax deduction on Scheme B cannot, in our view, be said to be 'related' to the remuneration expense for Scheme A. Accordingly, the expense relating to Scheme A is not relevant for determining the amount of tax income relating to Scheme B that is required to be accounted for in equity.

It may also be that what is regarded as a single scheme may need to be further sub-divided for the purposes of the comparison for reasons such as the following:

- where the same award is made to regular employees and also to top management, the fair value of the options granted to each population may nevertheless be different for the purposes of IFRS 2 given different exercise behaviours (see Chapter 34 at 8.5.2.A);
- an award is made to employees which attracts tax deductions in more than one tax jurisdiction; or
- an award is made in the same tax jurisdiction to employees in different entities, not all of which are able to recognise a deferred tax asset.

10.8.4 Staggered exercise of awards

The example in IAS 12, the substance of which is included in Example 33.53 at 10.8.1 above, addresses a situation in which all vested awards are exercised simultaneously. In practice, however, vested awards are often exercised at different dates.

Once an award under a given scheme has vested, and different awards in that scheme are exercised at different times, the question arises as to whether the 'cap' on recognition of the tax benefit in profit or loss should be calculated by reference to the cumulative expense recognised in respect of the total number of awards vested, or in respect only of as yet unexercised vested awards. In our view, where a tax deduction is received on exercise, the calculation must be undertaken by reference to the cumulative expense recognised for outstanding unexercised options. This is illustrated by Example 33.56 below.

Example 33.56: Tax deductions for share-based payment transactions – staggered exercise of award

At the start of year 1, an entity with a tax rate of 40% grants 20 options each to 5 employees. The options have a fair value of €5 and vest at the end of year 2. The options vest in full. 25 are exercised at the end of year 3 and 75 at the end of year 6. The entity is able to support the view that any deferred tax asset arising before exercise will be recoverable, and may therefore be recognised in full.

Tax deductions are given in the year of exercise, based on the intrinsic value of the options at the date of exercise. The intrinsic value of options at the end of each reporting period is as follows:

Year	Intrinsic value per option €
1	3
2	8
3	8
4	1
5	7
6	6

On the basis of the information above:

- there would be an IFRS 2 charge of €250 in years 1 and 2 (20 options × 5 employees × €5 × 1/2 (portion of vesting period)
- current and deferred tax assets should be recognised at the end of each period as follows:

Current tax

Year	Number of options exercised	Intrinsic value per option €	Total intrinsic value €	Tax effect at 40% €
3	25	8	200	80
6	75	6	450	180

Deferred tax

Year	Number of options outstanding	Temporary difference per option €	Total temporary difference €	Tax effect at 40% €
1	100	1.5[1]	150	60
2	100	8	800	320
3	75	8	600	240
4	75	1	75	30
5	75	7	525	210
6	–	6	–	–

1 Intrinsic value €3 × 1/2 (expired portion of vesting period).

The required accounting entries for income taxes are as follows

	Debit €	Credit €
Year 1		
Deferred tax (statement of financial position)	60	
Deferred tax (profit or loss)[1]		60
Year 2		
Deferred tax (statement of financial position)[2]	260	
Deferred tax (profit or loss)[3]		140
Deferred tax (equity)		120
Year 3		
Deferred tax (profit or loss)[4]	50	
Deferred tax (equity)	30	
Deferred tax (statement of financial position)[5]		80
Current tax (statement of financial position)[6]	80	
Current tax (profit or loss)[4]		50
Current tax (equity)		30
Year 4		
Deferred tax (profit or loss)[7]	120	
Deferred tax (equity)	90	
Deferred tax (statement of financial position)[8]		210
Year 5		
Deferred tax (statement of financial position)[9]	180	
Deferred tax (profit or loss)[10]		120
Deferred tax (equity)		60
Year 6		
Deferred tax (profit or loss)[11]	150	
Deferred tax (equity)	60	
Deferred tax (statement of financial position)		210
Current tax (statement of financial position)[12]	180	
Current tax (profit or loss)[13]		150
Current tax (equity)		30

1. The cumulative tax income is based on expected deductions of €150, which is less than the cumulative IFRS 2 charge of €250 (see above).
2. Year 2 year-end balance of €320 (see table above), less €60 recognised at end of year 1 = €140.
3. Cumulative deferred tax recognised in profit or loss must not exceed 40% × €500 (cumulative IFRS 2 charge) = €200. This limits the credit for year 2 to €200 less the €60 credited in year 1 = €140.
4. Reversal of deferred tax income previously recognised in profit or loss for the 25 options exercised: 25 × €5 [IFRS 2 charge per option] × 40% = €50. This also represents the limit on the amount of current tax deduction that can be recognised in profit or loss.
5. Year 3 year-end balance of €240 (see table above), less €320 recognised at end of year 2 = €80.
6. 25 options × €8 intrinsic value × 40% = €80.

In years 4 to 6, the amount of tax recognised in profit or loss is restricted by the cumulative IFRS 2 expense of €375 for the 75 options left outstanding (75 options × €5).

7. Cumulative (maximum) tax deduction already recognised in profit or loss is €375 @ 40% = €150. This needs to be reduced to €30 (year end deferred tax balance), giving rise to a charge of €150 – €30 = €120. This can be seen as representing the fact that, at the start of the period a cumulative potential tax deduction of €5 per award had been recognised in profit or loss. At the end of the period it is expected that deductions of only €1 per award will be available. Therefore there is a loss to be recognised in profit or loss of 75 awards × (€5 – €1) × 40% = €120.
8. Year 4 year-end balance of €30 (see table above), less €240 recognised at end of year 3 = €(210).
9. Year 5 year-end balance of €210 (see table above), less €30 recognised at end of year 4 = €180.

10 Cumulative maximum tax deduction that can be recognised in profit or loss is €150 (see note 7). €30 cumulative deduction is brought forward, so that credit for period is limited to €150 – €30 = €120.
11 Reversal of deferred tax previously recognised. The amount previously taken to profit or loss was limited to €150 (see notes 7 and 9).
12 75 options × €6 × 40% = €180.
13 Deduction restricted to €375 [IFRS 2 charge] × 40% = €150.

It will be noted that the cumulative effect of the above entries in profit or loss is as follows (tax income in brackets):

Year	Deferred tax €	Current tax €	Total €
1	(60)		(60)
2	(140)		(140)
3	50	(50)	–
4	120		120
5	(120)		(120)
6	150	(150)	–
		Total	(200)

The cumulative effect of the above entries in equity is as follows (tax income in brackets):

Year	Deferred tax €	Current tax €	Total €
1			–
2	(120)		(120)
3	30	(30)	–
4	90		90
5	(60)		(60)
6	60	(30)	30
		Total	(60)

The overall effect is to take credit in profit or loss for the lower of total tax deductions actually received of €260 (€80 in year 3 and €180 in year 6) and the tax deductions on the IFRS 2 expense of €200 (40% of €500). The excess tax deductions of €60 are recognised in equity.

10.8.5 Replacement awards in a business combination

IFRS 3 contains some detailed provisions on the treatment of share-based payment awards issued by an acquirer to replace awards made by the acquired entity before the business combination occurred. These are discussed in Chapter 34 at 11.

IFRS 3 amended IAS 12 to include an illustrative example for the treatment of tax deductions on such replacement awards, the substance of which is reproduced as Example 33.57 below. *[IAS 12 IE Example 6]*.

Example 33.57: Deferred tax on replacement share-based awards in a business combination

On 1 January 2021 Entity A acquired Entity B. A paid cash consideration of €400 million to the former owners of B. At the acquisition date B had outstanding fully-vested employee share options with a fair value of €100 million. As part of the business combination B's outstanding share options are replaced by fully vested share options of A (replacement awards) with a market-based measure of €100 million and an intrinsic value of €80 million. In accordance with IFRS 3, the replacement awards are part of the consideration transferred for B (see Chapter 34 at 11).

A tax deduction will be given only when the options are exercised, based on the intrinsic value of the options at that date. A's tax rate is 40%.

A recognises a deferred tax asset of €32 million (intrinsic value of €80m × 40%) on the replacement awards at the acquisition date (see 10.8.1 above). IAS 12 does not indicate the calculation if only part of the fair value of the award were regarded as part of the consideration transferred. However, it would be consistent with the general approach indicated at 10.8.2 above to calculate the tax base of the award by adjusting the intrinsic value by the ratio of the expired vesting period at acquisition to the total vesting period of the award (as determined for the purposes of IFRS 3 – see Chapter 34 at 11).

A measures the identifiable net assets obtained in the business combination (excluding deferred tax assets and liabilities) at €450 million, with a combined tax base of €300 million, giving rise to a taxable temporary difference at the acquisition date of €150 million, on which deferred tax at 40% of €60 million is recognised. Goodwill is calculated as follows:

	€m
Cash consideration	400
Replacement options	100
Total consideration	500
Identifiable net assets (excluding deferred tax)	(450)
Deferred tax asset	(32)
Deferred tax liability	60
Goodwill	78

Reductions in the carrying amount of goodwill are not deductible for tax purposes. In accordance with the initial recognition exception in IAS 12 (see 7.2 above), A recognises no deferred tax liability for the taxable temporary difference associated with the goodwill recognised in the business combination. The accounting entry for the business combination is therefore as follows:

	Debit €m	Credit €m
Goodwill	78	
Identifiable net assets	450	
Deferred tax asset	32	
Cash		400
Equity		100
Deferred tax liability		60

On 31 December 2021 the intrinsic value of the replacement awards is €120 million, in respect of which A recognises a deferred tax asset of €48 million (€120 m at 40%). This gives rise to deferred tax income of €16 million (€48 million recognised at 31 December 2021 less €32 million arising on acquisition). IAS 12 notes, somewhat redundantly, that this amount is credited to 'deferred tax income', but with no indication as to whether the amount should be recognised in profit or loss or in equity. In our view, the general principles of IAS 12 regarding tax deductions on share-based payment transactions suggest that the entire amount is recognised in equity. This is because the consolidated financial statements of A have never recognised any expense for the award in profit or loss (since it is attributed fully to the consideration transferred). Therefore none of the tax deductions can be recognised in profit or loss either.

10.8.6 Share-based payment transactions subject to transitional provisions of IFRS 1 and IFRS 2

IFRS 1 and IFRS 2 provide, respectively, first-time adopters and existing IFRS preparers with some transitional exemptions from accounting for share-based payment transactions. The accounting treatment of the tax effects of transactions to which these exemptions have been applied is discussed in Chapter 5 at 7.3.2. Whilst that discussion specifically addresses the tax effects of transactions subject to the exemption for first-time adopters of IFRS, it is equally applicable to the tax effects of transactions subject to the exemptions in IFRS 2 for existing IFRS preparers.

10.9 Change in tax status of entity or shareholders

Sometimes there is a change in an entity's tax assets and liabilities as a result of a change in the tax status of the entity itself or that of its shareholders. SIC-25 clarifies that the effect of such a change should be recognised in profit or loss except to the extent that it involves a remeasurement of tax originally accounted for in other comprehensive income or in equity, in which case the change should also be dealt with in, respectively, other comprehensive income or equity. *[SIC-25.4]*.

10.10 Previous revaluation of PP&E treated as deemed cost on transition to IFRS

IFRS 1 requires full retrospective application of standards effective at the end of a first-time adopter's first IFRS reporting period, unless a specific exemption is provided therein. *[IFRS 1.7]*. In some cases IFRS 1 allows an entity, on transition to IFRS, to treat the carrying amount of property, plant, and equipment (PP&E) revalued under its pre-transition GAAP as a deemed cost for the purposes of IFRS (see Chapter 5 at 5.5).

Where an asset is carried at deemed cost on transition to IFRS, but the tax base of the asset remains at original cost (or an amount based on original cost), the pre-transition revaluation will give rise to a temporary difference (often, a taxable temporary difference) associated with the asset. While the deemed cost provisions in IFRS 1 establish an appropriate measurement base for the carrying amount of previously revalued assets in the financial statements at the date of transition, they have no impact on whether a temporary difference exists. IFRS 1 does not provide an exemption from applying IAS 12, which requires deferred tax to be recognised on any such temporary difference at transition.

If, after transition, the deferred tax is required to be remeasured (e.g. because of a change in tax rate, or a re-basing of the asset for tax purposes), and the asset concerned was revalued outside profit or loss under pre-transition GAAP, the question arises as to whether the resulting deferred tax income or expense should be recognised in, or outside, profit or loss. A literal interpretation of IAS 12 would require changes relating to the past revaluation of the PP&E to be reflected in other comprehensive income, because that is where such an earlier revaluation would have been recorded under IFRS (see 10.2 above). However, where an entity elects to apply the cost model of IAS 16, the subsequent accounting treatment of the asset is the same, regardless of whether the 'deemed cost' of the asset on transition to IFRS was an earlier valuation, a revaluation as at the date of transition or original cost less depreciation and impairment up to that date. In all cases, subsequent depreciation and impairments are charged to profit or loss. In these circumstances, it could be argued that the deemed cost exemption on transition requires the asset to be treated in all respects as if its original cost had been the carrying value as at the transition date. In this way, any backward tracing of deferred tax in relation to past revaluations of an asset carried at 'deemed cost' should also be ignored and the effect of subsequent measurement should also be recognised in profit or loss.

In our view, either approach is acceptable as long as it is applied consistently.

10.11 Disposal of an interest in a subsidiary that does not result in a loss of control

Under IFRS 10 – *Consolidated Financial Statements* – a decrease in a parent's ownership interest in a subsidiary that does not result in a loss of control is accounted for in the consolidated financial statements as an equity transaction, i.e. a transaction with owners in their capacity as owners. *[IFRS 10.23]*. In these circumstances, the carrying amounts of the controlling and non-controlling interests are adjusted to reflect the changes in their relative interests in the subsidiary. 'The entity shall recognise directly in equity any difference between the amount by which the non-controlling interests are adjusted and the fair value of the consideration paid or received, and attribute it to the owners of the parent.' *[IFRS 10.B96]*. In other words, no changes in a subsidiary's assets (including goodwill) and liabilities are recognised in a transaction in which a parent increases or decreases its ownership interest in a subsidiary that it already controls. *[IFRS 10.BCZ173]*. Increases or decreases in the ownership interest in a subsidiary do not result in the recognition of a gain or loss. Accounting for disposals of interests that do not result in a loss of control is discussed in Chapter 7 at 4.

As the transaction is accounted for as an equity transaction, which does not affect profit or loss in the consolidated financial statements, one might assume that the full amount of any tax effect should also be recognised in equity. *[IAS 12.58(a)]*. However, this is not the case to the extent that any adjustment to non-controlling interests relates to the post acquisition profit of the subsidiary, which was previously recognised in the consolidated income statement, as illustrated in Example 33.58 below.

Example 33.58: Tax effect of a disposal of an interest in a subsidiary that does not result in a loss of control

A parent owns 100% of the equity shares of a subsidiary and presents the investment at a cost of $1,000,000 in its separate financial statements. At the end of the reporting period, the subsidiary's post acquisition profit and net asset value recognised in the parent's consolidated financial statements are $500,000 and $1,500,000 respectively. Previously, the parent had not recognised deferred taxation, as it considered it probable that the temporary difference would not reverse in the foreseeable future. The parent disposes of a 20% interest in the subsidiary for a cash consideration of $1,400,000 (the 'Transaction').

It is assumed that the tax base of the investment in the subsidiary is the same as its original cost of $1,000,000. The taxable gain is calculated on the same basis as the gain recognised in the separate financial statements and the applicable tax rate is 25%.

The parent recognises a gain of $1,200,000 (i.e. $1,400,000 – [$1,000,000 × 20%]) in its separate financial statements and is liable for a current tax of $300,000 (i.e. $1,200,000 × 25%).

The Transaction does not result in the parent losing control of the subsidiary and it is accounted for in equity in the consolidated financial statements of the parent. The parent recognises non-controlling interests of $300,000 (i.e. $1,500,000 × 20%) and credits equity for $1,100,000, being the difference between the consideration of $1,400,000 and the non-controlling interests of $300,000, in the consolidated financial statements of the parent.

What are the current and deferred tax effects in the consolidated financial statements if:

(a) the transaction is not completed until after the end of the reporting period; or

(b) the transaction is completed at the end of the reporting period?

If the transaction is not completed until after the end of the reporting period, no current tax is recognised. However, as the parent intends to recover 20% of its investment in the subsidiary through sale, it must recognise a deferred tax liability in the consolidated financial statements for the temporary difference associated with its investment in the subsidiary that is expected to reverse in the foreseeable future. *[IAS 12.39]*. Its carrying value in the consolidated financial statements is $1,500,000 and its tax base is $1,000,000. Accordingly, deferred tax of $25,000 (i.e. [$1,500,000 − $1,000,000] × 20% × 25%) should be recognised in profit or loss in the consolidated financial statements. This deferred tax would reverse through profit or loss upon disposal, because it relates to the post acquisition profit recognised in an earlier period. *[IAS 12.58]*.

If the transaction is completed at the end of the reporting period, the consolidated financial statements would include a current tax charge of $300,000 on the taxable gain on sale recorded by the subsidiary. Whilst the transaction is recorded in equity in the consolidated financial statements, because there is no loss of control, only $1,100,000 out of the total taxable gain of $1,200,000 was taken to non-controlling interests in equity. *[IAS 12.58(a)]*. $275,000 (i.e. $1,100,000 × 25%) of the current tax charge relates to the amount that is recognised directly in equity ($1,100,000) and is, therefore, recognised directly in equity. *[IAS 12.61A(b)]*. The remaining $25,000 (i.e. [$1,500,000 − $1,000,000] × 20% × 25%) is recognised as a current tax expense in profit or loss in the consolidated financial statements, as it does not relate to an amount directly recognised in equity, but to the crystallisation of part of the outside basis temporary difference arising from the post-acquisition profits of the subsidiary.

11 CONSOLIDATED TAX RETURNS AND OFFSET OF TAXABLE PROFITS AND LOSSES WITHIN GROUPS

In some jurisdictions one member of a group of companies may file a single tax return on behalf of all, or some, members of the group. Sometimes this is a mandatory requirement for a parent entity and its eligible subsidiaries operating in the same tax jurisdiction; and sometimes adoption is elective. In other jurisdictions, it is possible for one member of a group to transfer its tax losses to one or more other members of the group in order to reduce their tax liabilities. In some groups a company whose tax liability is reduced by such an arrangement may be required to make a payment to the member of the group that pays tax on its behalf, or transfers losses to it, as the case may be. In other groups no such charge is made.

Such transactions raise the question of the appropriate accounting treatment in the separate financial statements of the group entities involved – in particular, whether the company benefiting from such an arrangement should reflect income (or more likely a capital contribution) from another member of the group equal to the tax expense mitigated as a result of the arrangement.

Some argue that the effects of such transactions should be reflected in the separate financial statements of the entities involved, as is required by some national standards (e.g. those of the US and Australia). Others argue that, except to the extent that a management charge is actually made (see 11.1 below), there is no need to reflect such transactions in the separate financial statements of the entities involved. Those that take this view point out that it is inconsistent to require companies to show a capital contribution for tax losses ceded to them without charge, unless all other intragroup transactions are also restated on arm's-length terms – which would be somewhat radical. Moreover, IAS 24 – *Related Party Disclosures* – merely requires disclosure of the actual terms of such transactions, not that they be remeasured, either for financial reporting or disclosure purposes, on the same basis as a similar notional arm's length transaction (see Chapter 39).

IAS 12 is silent on the issue and, in our view, no single approach can be said to either be prohibited or required. Accordingly, a properly considered approach may be adopted, provided that it is applied on a consistent basis and the related judgements are disclosed where their impact is believed to be material. In arriving at an appropriate judgement, the discussion at 4.1 and 4.4 above is relevant in considering whether entities should apply IAS 12 or another standard (such as IAS 37). Any judgement should be based on the particular facts and circumstances relating to the legislation giving rise to tax-consolidation, the nature of the obligations and rights of entities in the group and local company law. As noted at 4.4 above, where there is a predominant local consensus in evidence or specific guidance issued by regulators in the relevant tax jurisdiction, then we believe that the entity should apply this consensus or guidance.

11.1 Examples of accounting by entities in a tax-consolidated group

In a typical tax-consolidation arrangement, a single consolidated annual tax return is prepared for the tax-consolidated group as a whole. Transactions between the entities in the tax-consolidated group are eliminated, and therefore ignored for tax purposes. A single legal entity in the group (usually the parent) is primarily liable for the current income tax liabilities of that group. Each entity in the group would be jointly and severally liable for the current income tax liability of the group if the parent entity defaults. There might also be a legally binding agreement between the entities in the group which establishes how tax assets and liabilities are allocated within the group.

As noted above, IAS 12 is silent on the issue and there is diversity in practice where these arrangements exist. Some entities apply IAS 37 principles to the recognition, measurement and allocation of current tax assets and liabilities to individual entities in the group, on the basis that tax is determined on the basis of the taxable profits of the group as a whole and not on the profits of the individual entities themselves. In that case current tax assets and liabilities are allocated on the basis of each entity's legal or constructive obligations to the tax authorities (for example where joint and several liability is determined to exist) or to other entities in the tax-consolidated group (including where formal agreements are implemented for the funding and sharing or tax liabilities and assets). Deferred tax is not accounted for in separate financial statements in these circumstances. Other entities apply the recognition and measurement principles of IAS 12 on the basis that tax is still determined on the basis of the taxable profits of each entity in the group on the obligations of each entity to the tax authorities. When IAS 12 is deemed to apply, entities will account for both current and deferred tax in their separate financial statements. Various approaches may be acceptable under IFRS for the determination of how current and deferred tax is allocated between entities in the tax-consolidated group. In Australia, where entities apply a standard virtually identical to IAS 12 in separate financial statements, three alternative approaches are suggested as examples of acceptable allocation methods:[57]

- a 'stand-alone taxpayer' approach for each entity, as if it continued to be a taxable entity in its own right.
- a 'separate taxpayer within group' approach for each entity, on the basis that the entity is subject to tax as part of the tax-consolidated group. This method requires adjustments for transactions and events occurring within the tax-consolidated group that do not give rise to a tax consequence for the group or that have a different tax consequence at the level of the group; and
- a 'group allocation' approach, under which the income tax amounts for the tax-consolidated group are allocated among each entity in the group.

Nevertheless, there may be other methods that are also appropriate.

11.2 Payments for intragroup transfer of tax losses

Where one member of a group transfers tax losses to another member of the group, the entity whose tax liability is reduced may be required, as matter of group policy, to pay an amount of compensation to the member of the group that transfers the losses to it. Such payments are known by different terms in different jurisdictions, but are referred to in the discussion below as 'tax loss payments'.

Tax loss payments are generally made in an amount equal to the tax saved by the paying company. In some cases, however, payment may be made in an amount equal to the nominal amount of the tax loss, which will be greater than the amount of tax saved. This raises the question of how such payments should be accounted for.

The first issue is whether such payments should be recognised:

- in total comprehensive income; or
- as a distribution (in the case of a payment from a subsidiary to a parent) or a capital contribution (in the case of a payment from a parent to a subsidiary).

The second issue is, to the extent that the payments are accounted for in total comprehensive income, whether they should be classified as:

- income tax, allocated between profit or loss, other comprehensive income or equity (see 10 above). The argument for this treatment is that the payments made or received are amounts that would otherwise be paid to or received from (or offset against an amount paid to) a tax authority; or
- operating income or expense in profit or loss (on the grounds that, as a matter of fact, the payments are not made to or received from any tax authority).

IAS 12 is silent on these issues. However, there is a long-standing practice in many jurisdictions that such payments are treated as if they were income taxes. We believe that this practice is appropriate to the extent that the intragroup payment is for an amount up to the amount of tax that would otherwise have been paid by the paying company. Where a tax loss payment is made in excess of this amount, we consider that it is more appropriate to account for the excess not as an income tax but as either:

- a distribution or capital contribution (as applicable); or
- operating income or expense (as applicable).

In considering the applicable treatment, the legal and regulatory requirements in the entity's jurisdiction would also be relevant, for example if those local requirements stipulate whether the excess payment is, in law, a distribution. The chosen treatment should be applied consistently.

11.3 Recognition of deferred tax assets where tax losses are transferred in a group

The ability of one member of a group to transfer its tax losses to another member of the group that expects to have taxable profits against which those losses can be utilised is an example of a tax planning opportunity 'that will create taxable profit in appropriate periods'. *[IAS 12.29(b)]*. Accordingly, it would be appropriate to recognise in the entity's consolidated financial statements a deferred tax asset in respect of unused tax losses and unused tax credits that are expected to be utilised in this way. *[IAS 12.29]*.

In the separate financial statements of the member of the group that holds the unused losses and tax credits, it would only be appropriate to recognise an asset to the extent that this entity expects to benefit itself from any transfer. Such benefits might be in the form of payment for losses as discussed at 11.1 above, or as a result of taxable profits otherwise created in the surrendering entity as a result of the transfer. If the surrendering entity is not expected to receive any benefit in relation to the unused losses and tax credits given up, then no asset should be recognised in the separate financial statements of that entity.

12 BUSINESS COMBINATIONS

Additional deferred tax arises on business combinations as a result of items such as:

- the application of IAS 12 to the assets and liabilities of the acquired business in the consolidated financial statements, when it has not been applied in the separate financial statements of that business;
- where the acquired entity already applies IAS 12 in its own financial statements, the recognition in the fair value exercise of deferred tax in respect of assets and liabilities of the acquired entity where no deferred tax is provided in those financial statements. This may be the case where a temporary difference arose on initial recognition of an asset or liability in the acquired entity's own financial statements. Deferred tax would then be recognised in the acquirer's consolidated financial statements, because, in those statements, the difference arises on initial recognition in a business combination (see 7.2 above); and
- adjustments made to measure the assets and liabilities of the acquired business fair value, with consequential changes in the temporary differences associated with those assets and liabilities.

Any deferred tax assets or liabilities on temporary differences that arise on a business combination affect the amount of goodwill or bargain purchase gain. *[IAS 12.66]*. Example 33.26 at 7.5.1 above illustrates the application of this principle.

12.1 Measurement and recognition of deferred tax in a business combination

IFRS 3 generally requires assets acquired and liabilities assumed in a business combination to be:

- recognised only to the extent that they were assets or liabilities of the acquired entity at the date of acquisition; *[IFRS 3.10]* and
- measured at fair value. *[IFRS 3.18]*.

These provisions of IFRS 3 are discussed in more detail in Chapter 9 at 5. As exceptions to this general principle, IFRS 3 requires an acquirer to:

- recognise and measure a deferred tax asset or liability arising from the assets acquired and liabilities assumed in a business combination 'in accordance with IAS 12'; *[IFRS 3.24]* and
- account for the potential tax effects of temporary differences and carryforwards of an acquiree that exist at the acquisition date or arise as a result of the acquisition 'in accordance with IAS 12'. *[IFRS 3.25]*.

There are essentially two reasons underlying these exceptions. The first is that IAS 12 does not purport to measure future tax at fair value, but at an amount based on a prescribed model that takes no account of the time value of money. Secondly, and more subtly, IAS 12 requires a number of questions of both recognition and measurement to be resolved by reference to management's plans and expectations – in particular, the expected manner of recovery of assets (see 8.4 above) or the likelihood of recovering deferred tax assets (see 7.4 above). The expectations and plans of the acquirer may well differ from those of the acquired entity. For example, the acquired entity might have assessed, for the purposes of IAS 12, that an asset would be recovered through use, whereas the acquirer assesses it as recoverable through sale. The exceptions made by IFRS 3 allow the deferred tax recognised in a business combination to reflect the expectations of the acquirer rather than those of the acquiree.

Areas that give rise to particular difficulties of interpretation are:

- determining the manner of recovery of assets and settlement of liabilities at the date of the business combination (see 12.1.1 below); and
- deferred tax assets (see 12.1.2 below).

12.1.1 Determining the manner of recovery of assets and settlement of liabilities

As discussed at 8.4 above, IAS 12 requires deferred tax to be measured at an amount that reflects the tax consequences that would follow from the manner in which the entity expects to recover its assets or settle its liabilities. The expected manner of recovery or settlement may affect both the tax base of an asset or liability and the tax rate to be applied to any temporary difference arising.

As further noted above, the acquirer's assessment of the manner of recovery for the purposes of IAS 12 may well differ from that of the acquired entity. For example, the acquired entity might have intended to recover an asset through use, whereas the acquirer intends to sell it. In such a case, in our view, the requirement of IFRS 3 to recognise and measure deferred tax in accordance with IAS 12 has the effect that the expectations of the acquirer are used to determine the tax base of an item and the measurement of any deferred tax associated with the item.

12.1.1.A   Changes in tax base consequent on the business combination

In some jurisdictions, a business combination may provide the opportunity to revise the tax base of an asset to an amount equal to the fair value assigned to it in accounting for the business combination. Most significantly, this may include the ability to create a tax base for an intangible asset or goodwill which may have had no tax base at all for the acquiree.

In some cases, the increase (as it generally is) in tax base may be more or less automatic. In others, the taxpayer may be required to make a formal claim or election for the increase to the tax authority. Sometimes further restructuring may be required – for example, it may be necessary for the business of the acquired entity to be transferred to another entity in the acquirer's group in the same tax jurisdiction.

An increase in a tax base that requires action by the relevant entity after the acquisition (such as making a claim or election or undertaking a restructuring) occurs after the business combination. However, some hold the view that the ability to increase a tax base following a business combination is a benefit that is taken into account by an informed buyer in negotiating the purchase price. Accordingly, it is argued, the increase is most appropriately reflected by adjusting the tax base of assets acquired as at the date of the business combination as if the increase had occurred at that date. This reduces any deferred tax liability and, therefore, reduces any goodwill (or increases any 'bargain purchase' gain).

Those who support this view note that, if the increase in tax base is accounted for only when it legally occurs in the post-combination period, the net effect is to increase goodwill and reduce post-combination tax expense when in reality the entity may have done little more than fill in a form. It might also be difficult to sustain the higher carrying amount of goodwill arising from this treatment.

We believe that it is generally appropriate to anticipate an increase to a tax base that legally occurs following a business combination in accounting for the business combination where the increase:

- is automatic or requires only a notification to the tax authority;
- requires an application to the tax authority that is not normally refused for transactions of a comparable nature; or
- is contingent on some post-acquisition restructuring, where this can be done without substantial difficulty.

Conversely, we believe that it would not generally be appropriate to account for an increase in a tax base until it occurs where the increase:

- relies on 'bespoke' tax planning that may be challenged by the tax authority;
- requires an application to the tax authority that in practice is frequently and successfully challenged for transactions of a comparable nature; or
- is contingent on some post-acquisition restructuring, where this will involve a substantial process, such as obtaining approval from regulators, unions, pension fund trustees etc.

12.1.2 Deferred tax assets arising on a business combination

12.1.2.A Assets of the acquirer

If, as a result of a business combination, the acquiring entity is able to recognise a previously unrecognised tax asset of its own (e.g. unused tax losses), the recognition of the asset is accounted for as income, and not as part of the accounting for the business combination. *[IAS 12.67]*.

12.1.2.B Assets of the acquiree

It may be the case that deferred tax assets of an acquired entity do not meet the recognition criteria of IAS 12 from the perspective of the acquired entity, but do meet the criteria from the perspective of the acquirer. In such cases, the general principles of IAS 12 require the acquirer's perspective to be applied as at the date of the business combination.

The potential benefit of the acquiree's income tax loss carryforwards or other deferred tax assets may not satisfy the criteria for separate recognition when a business combination is initially accounted for but may be realised subsequently. Any changes in recognised deferred tax assets of an acquired entity are accounted for as follows:

- Acquired deferred tax benefits recognised within the measurement period (see Chapter 9 at 5.6.2) that result from new information about facts and circumstances that existed at the acquisition date are applied to reduce the carrying amount of any goodwill related to that acquisition. If the carrying amount of that goodwill is zero, any remaining deferred tax benefits are recognised in profit or loss.
- All other acquired deferred tax benefits realised are recognised in profit or loss (or outside profit or loss if IAS 12 so requires – see 10 above). *[IAS 12.68]*.

12.1.3 Deferred tax liabilities of acquired entity

IAS 12 contains no specific provisions regarding the recognition of a deferred tax liability of an acquired entity after the date of the original combination. The recognition of such liabilities should therefore be accounted for in accordance with the normal rules of IAS 12 (i.e. in the period in which the liability arises), unless either:

- the recognition of the liability occurs within the provisional measurement period for the business combination and reflects new information about facts and circumstances that existed at the acquisition date, in which case the acquisition date value of the liability is retrospectively adjusted – see Chapter 9 at 12; or
- the failure to recognise the liability at the time of the combination was an error, in which case the provisions of IAS 8 should be applied – see Chapter 3 at 4.6.

12.2 Tax deductions for replacement share-based payment awards in a business combination

IFRS 3 contains some guidance on the treatment of tax deductions for share-based payment transactions made by an acquirer as a replacement for awards made by the acquired entity before the business combination. This is discussed in more detail at 10.8.5 above.

12.3 Apparent immediate impairment of goodwill created by deferred tax

The requirement of IAS 12 to recognise deferred tax on all temporary differences arising on net assets acquired in a business combination leads to the creation of goodwill which, on a literal reading of IAS 36 may then be required to be immediately impaired, as illustrated by Example 33.59 below.

Example 33.59: *Apparent 'day one' impairment arising from recognition of deferred tax in a business combination*

Entity A, which is taxed at 40%, acquires Entity B for €100m in a transaction that is a business combination. The fair values and tax bases of the identifiable net assets of Entity B are as follows:

	Fair value €m	Tax base €m
Brand name	60	–
Other net assets	20	15

This will give rise to the following consolidation journal:

	€m	€m
Goodwill (balance)	46	
Brand name	60	
Other net assets	20	
Deferred tax[1]		26
Cost of investment		100

1 40% of (€[60m + 20m] – €15m)

The fair value of the consolidated assets of the subsidiary (excluding deferred tax) and goodwill is now €126m, but the cost of the subsidiary is only €100m. Clearly €26m of the goodwill arises solely from the recognition of deferred tax. However, IAS 36, paragraph 50, explicitly requires tax to be excluded from the estimate of future cash flows used to calculate any impairment. This raises the question of whether there should be an immediate impairment write-down of the assets to €100m. In our view, this cannot have been the intention of IAS 36 (see the further discussion in Chapter 20 at 8.3.1).

12.4 Tax deductions for acquisition costs

Under IFRS 3 transaction costs are required to be expensed. However, in a number of jurisdictions, transaction costs are regarded as forming part of the cost of the investment for tax purposes, with the effect that a tax deduction for them is given only when the investment is subsequently sold or otherwise disposed of, rather than at the time that the costs are charged to profit or loss.

In such jurisdictions, there will be a deductible 'outside' temporary difference (see 7.5 above) between the carrying value of the net assets and goodwill of the acquired entity in the consolidated financial statements (which will exclude transaction costs) and tax base of the investment in the entity (which will include transaction costs). Whether or not a deferred tax asset is recognised in respect of such a deductible temporary difference will be determined in accordance with the general provisions of IAS 12 for deductible temporary differences (see 7.5.3 above).

In the separate financial statements of the acquirer, there may be no temporary difference where the transaction costs are, under IAS 27, included in the cost of the investment.

12.5 Temporary differences arising from the acquisition of a group of assets that is not a business

Although the acquisition of an asset or a group of assets that do not constitute a business is not within the scope of IFRS 3, in such cases the acquirer has to identify and recognise the individual identifiable assets acquired (including intangible assets) and liabilities assumed. The cost of the group is allocated to the individual identifiable assets and liabilities on the basis of their relative fair values at the date of purchase. These transactions or events do not give rise to goodwill. *[IFRS 3.2(b)]*. Temporary differences may therefore arise because the new carrying value of each acquired asset and liability could be changed without any equivalent adjustment for tax purposes.

However, in these circumstances the acquirer cannot account for any deferred tax assets or deferred tax liabilities, resulting from temporary differences identified. Since the acquisition does not constitute a business combination, the initial recognition exception applies as discussed at 7.2 above. Indeed, the application of the IRE would mean that no deferred tax is recognised by an acquiring entity, either on initial recognition or subsequently, for any temporary differences related to the 'tax history' of the related assets and liabilities (i.e. in relation to differences between their carrying values before their transfer and their tax base). Furthermore, an entity does not recognise subsequent changes in the unrecognised deferred tax liability or asset as the asset is depreciated. *[IAS 12.22(c)]*.

The requirements of IFRS 3 in relation to the acquisition of an asset or a group of assets that does not constitute a business is discussed in Chapter 9 at 2.2.2.

13 PRESENTATION

13.1 Statement of financial position

Tax assets and liabilities should be shown separately from other assets and liabilities and current tax should be shown separately from deferred tax on the face of the statement of financial position. Where an entity presents current and non-current assets and liabilities separately, deferred tax should not be shown as part of current assets or liabilities. *[IAS 1.54-56]*.

13.1.1 Offset

13.1.1.A Current tax

Current tax assets and liabilities should be offset if, and only if, the entity:

- has a legally enforceable right to set off the recognised amounts; and
- intends either to settle them net or simultaneously. *[IAS 12.71]*.

These requirements are based on the offset criteria in IAS 32 for financial instruments. The phrase 'if and only if' means that offset is required if both the above conditions are met, but prohibited if they are not both met. Accordingly, while entities in many jurisdictions have a right to offset current tax assets and liabilities, and the tax authority permits the entity to make or receive a single net payment, IAS 12 permits offset in financial statements only where there is a positive intention for simultaneous net settlement. *[IAS 12.72]*.

The offset requirements in IAS 12 also have the effect that, in consolidated financial statements, a current tax asset of one member of the group is offset against a current tax liability of another, if and only if the two group members have a legally enforceable right to make or receive a single net payment and a positive intention to recover the asset or settle the liability simultaneously. *[IAS 12.73]*.

13.1.1.B Deferred tax

Deferred tax assets and liabilities should be offset if, and only if:

- the entity has a legally enforceable right to set off current tax assets against current liabilities; and
- the deferred tax assets and liabilities concerned relate to income taxes raised by the same taxation authority on either:
  - the same taxable entity; or
  - different taxable entities which intend, in each future period in which significant amounts of deferred tax are expected to be settled or recovered, to settle their current tax assets and liabilities either on a net basis or simultaneously. *[IAS 12.74]*.

The phrase 'if and only if' means that offset is required if both the above conditions are met, but prohibited if they are not both met.

The position is that where in a particular jurisdiction current tax assets and current tax liabilities relating to future periods will be offset under the requirements set out at 13.1.1.A above, deferred tax assets and liabilities relating to that jurisdiction and those periods must also be offset.

This requirement was adopted in order to avoid the need for detailed scheduling of the reversal of temporary differences that would otherwise have been necessary to determine whether taxable temporary differences and deductible temporary differences would reverse in the same periods (and therefore be eligible for offset in their own right). *[IAS 12.75].*

However, IAS 12 notes that, in rare circumstances, an entity may have a legally enforceable right of set-off, and an intention to settle net, for some periods but not for others. In such circumstances, detailed scheduling may be required to establish reliably whether the deferred tax liability of one taxable entity in the group will result in increased tax payments in the same period in which a deferred tax asset of a second taxable entity in the group will result in decreased payments by that second taxable entity. *[IAS 12.76].*

13.1.1.C No offset of current and deferred tax

IAS 12 contains no provisions allowing or requiring the offset of current tax and deferred tax. Also, as noted at 13.1 above, IAS 1 requires tax assets and liabilities to be shown separately from other assets and liabilities and current tax to be shown separately from deferred tax on the face of the statement of financial position. *[IAS 1.54(n), 54(o)].* Accordingly, in our view, current and deferred tax may not be offset against each other and should always be presented gross.

13.2 Statement of comprehensive income

The tax expense (or income) related to profit or loss from ordinary activities should be presented as a component of profit or loss in the statement of comprehensive income. *[IAS 12.77].*

The results of discontinued operations should be presented on a post-tax basis. *[IFRS 5.33].* This is discussed further in Chapter 4 at 3.2.

The results of equity-accounted entities should be presented on a post-tax basis. *[IAS 1.IG6].* Any income tax relating to a 'tax-transparent' equity-accounted entity (see 7.6 above) forms part of the investor's tax charge. It is therefore included in the income tax line in profit or loss and not shown as part of the investor's share of the results of the tax-transparent entity.

Entities are required to disclose the amount of income tax relating to each item of other comprehensive income, including reclassification adjustments, either in the statement of profit or loss and other comprehensive income or in the notes. *[IAS 1.90].* Components of other comprehensive income may be presented either:

- net of related tax effects; or
- before related tax effects with one amount shown for the total income tax effects relating to the items that might be reclassified subsequently to profit and loss and another amount shown for the total income tax effects relating to those items that will not be subsequently reclassified to profit and loss. *[IAS 1.91].*

IAS 12 notes that, whilst IAS 21 requires certain exchange differences to be recognised within income or expense, it does not specify where exactly in the statement of comprehensive income they should be presented. Accordingly, exchange differences relating to deferred tax assets and liabilities may be classified as deferred tax expense (or income), if that presentation is considered to be the most useful to users of the financial statements. *[IAS 12.78]*. IAS 12 makes no reference to the treatment of exchange differences on current tax assets and liabilities but, presumably, the same considerations apply.

13.3 Statement of cash flows

Cash flows arising from taxes on income are separately disclosed and classified as cash flows from operating activities, unless they can be specifically identified with financing and investing activities. *[IAS 7.35]*.

IAS 7 – *Statement of Cash Flows* – notes that, whilst it is relatively easy to identify the expense relating to investing or financing activities, the related tax cash flows are often impracticable to identify. Therefore, taxes paid are usually classified as cash flows from operating activities. However, when it is practicable to identify the tax cash flow with an individual transaction that gives rise to cash flows that are classified as investing or financing activities, the tax cash flow is classified as an investing or financing activity as appropriate. When tax cash flows are allocated over more than one class of activity, the total amount of taxes paid is disclosed. *[IAS 7.36]*.

14 DISCLOSURE

IAS 12 imposes extensive disclosure requirements as follows.

14.1 Components of tax expense

The major components of tax expense (or income) should be disclosed separately. These may include:

(a) current tax expense (or income);
(b) any adjustments recognised in the period for current tax of prior periods;
(c) the amount of deferred tax expense (or income) relating to the origination and reversal of temporary differences;
(d) the amount of deferred tax expense (or income) relating to changes in tax rates or the imposition of new taxes;
(e) the amount of the benefit arising from a previously unrecognised tax loss, tax credit or temporary difference of a prior period that is used to reduce current tax expense;
(f) the amount of the benefit from a previously unrecognised tax loss, tax credit or temporary difference of a prior period that is used to reduce deferred tax expense;
(g) deferred tax expense arising from the write-down, or reversal of a previous write-down, of a deferred tax asset; and

(h) the amount of tax expense (or income) relating to those changes in accounting policies and errors which are included in the profit or loss in accordance with IAS 8 because they cannot be accounted for retrospectively (see Chapter 3 at 4.7). [IAS 12.79-80].

14.2 Other disclosures

The following should also be disclosed separately: [IAS 12.81]

(a) the aggregate current and deferred tax relating to items that are charged or credited to equity;

(b) the amount of income tax relating to each component of other comprehensive income; The analysis in (b) can be provided either in the statement of profit or loss and other comprehensive income or in the notes; [IAS 1.90]

(c) an explanation of the relationship between tax expense (or income) and accounting profit in either or both of the following forms:
   (i) a numerical reconciliation between tax expense (or income) and the product of accounting profit multiplied by the applicable tax rate(s), disclosing also the basis on which the applicable tax rate(s) is (are) computed; or
   (ii) a numerical reconciliation between the average effective tax rate (i.e. tax expense (or income) divided by accounting profit), [IAS 12.86], and the applicable tax rate, disclosing also the basis on which the applicable tax rate is computed;

This requirement is discussed further at 14.2.1 below.

(d) an explanation of changes in the applicable tax rate(s) compared to the previous accounting period;

(e) the amount (and expiry date, if any) of deductible temporary differences, unused tax losses, and unused tax credits for which no deferred tax asset is recognised in the statement of financial position;

(f) the aggregate amount of temporary differences associated with investments in subsidiaries, branches and associates and interests in joint arrangements, for which deferred tax liabilities have not been recognised;

This is discussed further at 14.2.2 below.

(g) in respect of each type of temporary difference, and in respect of each type of unused tax losses and unused tax credits:
   (i) the amount of the deferred tax assets and liabilities recognised in the statement of financial position for each period presented; and
   (ii) the amount of the deferred tax income or expense recognised in profit or loss, if this is not apparent from the changes in the amounts recognised in the statement of financial position;

The analysis in (ii) will be required, for example, by any entity with acquisitions and disposals, or deferred tax accounted for in other comprehensive income or equity, since this will have the effect that the year-on-year movement in the statement of financial position is not solely due to items recognised in profit or loss;

(h) in respect of discontinued operations, the tax expense relating to:
  (i) the gain or loss on discontinuance; and
  (ii) the profit or loss from the ordinary activities of the discontinued operation for the period, together with the corresponding amounts for each prior period presented;
(i) the amount of income tax consequences of dividends to shareholders of the entity that were proposed or declared before the financial statements were authorised for issue, but are not recognised as a liability in the financial statements.

Further disclosures are required in respect of the tax consequences of distributing retained earnings, which are discussed at 14.4 below;

(j) if a business combination in which the entity is the acquirer causes a change in the amount of a pre-acquisition deferred tax asset of the entity (see 12.1.2 above), the amount of that change; and
(k) if the deferred tax benefits acquired in a business combination are not recognised at the acquisition date, but are recognised after the acquisition date (see 12.1.2 above), a description of the event or change in circumstances that caused the deferred tax benefits to be recognised.

Tax-related contingent liabilities and contingent assets (such as those arising from unresolved disputes with taxation authorities) are disclosed in accordance with IAS 37 (see 9.6 above and Chapter 26 at 7). *[IAS 12.88]*.

Significant effects of changes in tax rates or tax laws enacted or announced after the reporting period on current and deferred tax assets and liabilities are disclosed in accordance with IAS 10 (see Chapter 38 at 2). *[IAS 12.88]*.

14.2.1 Tax (or tax rate) reconciliation

IAS 12 explains that the purpose of the tax reconciliation required by (c) above is to enable users of financial statements to understand whether the relationship between tax expense (or income) and accounting profit is unusual and to understand the significant factors that could affect that relationship in the future. The relationship may be affected by the effects of such factors as:

- revenue and expenses that are outside the scope of taxation;
- tax losses; and
- foreign tax rates. *[IAS 12.84]*.

Accordingly, in explaining the relationship between tax expense (or income) and accounting profit, an entity should use an applicable tax rate that provides the most meaningful information to the users of its financial statements.

Often, the most meaningful rate is the domestic rate of tax in the country in which the entity is domiciled. In this case, the tax rate applied for national taxes should be aggregated with the rates applied for any local taxes which are computed on a substantially similar level of taxable profit (tax loss). However, for an entity operating in several jurisdictions, it may be more meaningful to aggregate separate reconciliations prepared using the domestic rate in each individual jurisdiction. *[IAS 12.85]*. Where this latter approach is adopted, the entity may need to discuss the effect of significant changes in either tax rates, or the mix of profits earned in different jurisdictions, in order to satisfy the requirement of IAS 12 to explain changes in the applicable tax rate(s) compared to the previous accounting period – see item (d) at 14.2 above.

Example 33.60 illustrates how the selection of the applicable tax rate affects the presentation of the numerical reconciliation.

Example 33.60:   Alternative presentations of tax reconciliation

In 2021 an entity has accounting profit of €3,000m (2020: €2,500m) comprising €1,500m (2020: €2,000m) in its own jurisdiction (country A) and €1,500m (2020: €500m) in country B. The tax rate is 30% in country A and 20% in country B. In country B, expenses of €200m (2020: €100m) are not deductible for tax purposes. There are no other differences between accounting profit and profit that is subject to current tax, or on which deferred tax has been provided for under IAS 12.

Thus the accounting tax charge in the financial statements for each period will be as follows:

	2021 €m	2020 €m
Country A		
€1,500m/€2,000m @ 30%	450	600
Country B		
€[1,500 + 200]m/€[500 + 100]m @ 20%	340	120
Total tax charge	790	720

Reconciliation based on A's domestic tax rate

If the entity presents a tax reconciliation based on its own (i.e. country A's) domestic tax rate, the following presentation would be adopted.

	2021 €m	2020 €m
Accounting profit	3,000	2,500
Tax at domestic rate of 30%	900	750
Effect of:		
Expenses not deductible for tax purposes[1]	60	30
Overseas tax rates[2]	(170)	(60)
Tax expense	790	720

[1]   €200m/€100m @ 30%
[2]   B's taxable profit €1,700m/€600m @ (20% – 30%)

Reconciliation based on each jurisdiction's tax rate

If the entity presents a tax reconciliation based on each jurisdiction's domestic tax rate, the following presentation would be adopted.

	2021 €m	2020 €m
Accounting profit	3,000	2,500
Tax at domestic rates applicable to individual group entities[1]	750	700
Effect of:		
Expenses not deductible for tax purposes[2]	40	20
Tax expense	790	720

[1] 2021: A = €450m [€1,500m @ 30%], B = €300m [€1,500m @ 20%], total €750m
2020: A = €600m [€2,000m @ 30%], B = €100m [€500m @ 20%], total €700m

[2] €200m/€100m @ 20%

14.2.2 Temporary differences relating to subsidiaries, associates, branches and joint arrangements

IAS 12 requires an entity to disclose the gross temporary differences associated with subsidiaries, associates, branches and joint arrangements for which a deferred tax liability is not recognised, as opposed to the unrecognised deferred tax on those temporary differences – see (f) under 14.2 above.

IAS 12 clarifies that this approach is adopted because it would often be impracticable to compute the amount of unrecognised deferred tax. Nevertheless, where practicable, entities are encouraged to disclose the amounts of the unrecognised deferred tax liabilities because financial statement users may find such information useful. *[IAS 12.87]*.

14.3 Reason for recognition of particular tax assets

Separate disclosure is required of the amount of any deferred tax asset that is recognised, and the nature of the evidence supporting its recognition, when:

(a) utilisation of the deferred tax asset is dependent on future profits in excess of those arising from the reversal of deferred tax liabilities; and

(b) the entity has suffered a loss in the current or preceding period in the tax jurisdiction to which the asset relates. *[IAS 12.82]*.

In effect these disclosures are required when the entity has rebutted the presumption inherent in the recognition rules of IAS 12 that tax assets should not normally be recognised in these circumstances (see 7.4 above).

14.4 Dividends

As discussed at 8.5 above, where there are different tax consequences for an entity depending on whether profits are retained or distributed, tax should be measured at the rates applicable to retained profits except to the extent that there is a liability to pay dividends at the end of the reporting period, where the rate applicable to distributed profits should be used.

Where such differential tax rates apply, the entity should disclose the nature of the potential income tax consequences that would arise from a payment of dividends to shareholders. It should quantify the amount of potential income tax consequences that is practicably determinable and disclose whether there are any potential income tax consequences that are not practicably determinable. *[IAS 12.82A]*. This will include disclosure of the important features of the income tax systems and the factors that will affect the amount of the potential income tax consequences of dividends. *[IAS 12.87A]*.

The reason for this rather complicated requirement is that, as IAS 12 acknowledges, it can often be very difficult to quantify the tax consequences of a full distribution of profits (e.g. where there are a large number of overseas subsidiaries). Moreover, IAS 12 concedes that there is a tension between, on the one hand, the exemption from disclosing the deferred tax associated with temporary differences associated with subsidiaries and other investments (see 14.2.2 above) and, on the other hand, this requirement to disclose the tax effect of distributing undistributed profits – in some cases they could effectively be the same number.

However, to the extent that any liability can be quantified, it should be disclosed. This may mean that consolidated financial statements will disclose the potential tax effect of distributing the earnings of some, but not all, subsidiaries, associates, branches and joint arrangements.

IAS 12 emphasises that, in an entity's separate financial statements, this requirement applies only to the undistributed earnings of the entity itself and not those of any of its subsidiaries, associates, branches and joint arrangements. *[IAS 12.87A-87C]*.

14.5 Examples of disclosures

In Extract 33.1 below, Royal Dutch Shell sets out the components of the tax expense and provides a reconciliation of the tax charge in the income statement. *[IAS 12.79-80, 81(c)]*.

Extract 33.1: Royal Dutch Shell plc (2019)

Notes to the Consolidated Financial Statements [extract]

16 – TAXATION [extract]

Taxation charge

			$ million
	2019	2018	2017
Current tax:			
Charge in respect of current period	7,597	10,415	7,204
Adjustments in respect of prior periods	(1)	60	(613)
Total	7,596	10,475	6,591
Deferred tax:			
Relating to the origination and reversal of temporary differences, tax losses and credits	1,377	1,438	(4,102)
Relating to changes in tax rates and legislation	(67)	(157)	2,004[A]
Adjustments in respect of prior periods	147	(41)	202
Total	1,457	1,240	(1,896)
Total taxation charge	9,053	11,715	4,695

[A] Mainly in respect of the US Tax Cuts and Jobs Act.

Adjustments in respect of prior periods relate to events in the current period and reflect the effects of changes in rules, facts or other factors compared with those used in establishing the current tax position or deferred tax balance in prior periods.

Reconciliation of applicable tax charge at statutory tax rates to taxation charge

			$ million
	2019	2018	2017
Income before taxation	25,485	35,621	18,130
Less: share of profit of joint ventures and associates	(3,604)	(4,106)	(4,225)
Income before taxation and share of profit of joint ventures and associates	21,881	31,515	13,905
Applicable tax charge at standard statutory tax rates [A]	7,214	11,641	4,709
Adjustments in respect of prior periods	146	19	(411)
Tax effects of: [B]			
Expenses not deductible for tax purposes	1,493	1,176	1,000
Derecognition/(recognition) of deferred tax assets	846	(381)	(957)
Incentives for investment and development [A]	(757)	(557)	(527)
Disposals	(235)	(524)	(910)
Income not subject to tax at standard statutory rates	159	(286)	(359)
Changes in tax rates and legislation	(67)	(157)	2,004
Exchange rate differences	(34)	623	320
Other reconciling items	288	161	(174)
Taxation charge	9,053	11,715	4,695

[A] Incentives for investment and development include conditional preferential tax rates to attract investment, uplift on carried forward losses and capital expenditure, investment tax allowances and credits for research and development. Up to and including 2018, preferential tax rates were reported within the applicable tax charge at standard statutory tax rates. Comparative numbers for 2018 and 2017 were reclassified to conform with the current year presentation.

[B] The tax effect categories have changed to provide better insights. Comparative numbers for 2018 and 2017 were reclassified to conform with the current year presentation.

The weighted average of statutory tax rates was 33% in 2019 (2018: 37% as revised; 2017: 34% as revised). Compared with 2018, the decrease in the rate reflects a higher proportion of earnings in the Downstream and Integrated Gas segments, subject to relatively lower tax rates than earnings in the Upstream segment. In addition, a higher proportion of Integrated Gas income was earned in countries with relatively lower statutory tax rates.

In Extract 33.2 below, BP p.l.c. provides an analysis of deferred tax income or expense recognised in profit or loss and the amount of the deferred tax assets and liabilities recognised in the statement of financial position. [IAS 12.81(g)].

Extract 33.2: BP p.l.c. (2018)
Notes on financial statements [extract]
9. Taxation [extract]
Deferred tax [extract]

The following table provides an analysis of deferred tax in the income statement and the balance sheet by category of temporary difference:

$ million

	Income statement[a,b]			Balance sheet[a,b]	
	2019	2018	2017	2019	2018
Deferred tax liability					
Depreciation	(1,436)	(1,297)	(3,971)	22,627	22,565
Pension plan surpluses	(31)	65	(12)	2,290	1,956
Derivative financial instruments	29	(36)	(27)	29	–
Other taxable temporary differences	159	(57)	(64)	1,496	1,224
	(1,279)	(1,325)	(4,074)	26,442	25,745
Deferred tax asset					
Lease liabilities	264	8	(16)	(1,380)	(90)
Pension plan and other post-retirement benefit plan deficits	62	(6)	340	(1,367)	(1,319)
Decommissioning, environmental and other provisions	(472)	1,505	3,503	(7,579)	(7,126)
Derivative financial instruments	63	(31)	(47)	(24)	(95)
Tax credits	(336)	123	1,476	(3,964)	(3,626)
Loss carry forward	12	559	(964)	(5,834)	(5,900)
Other deductible temporary differences	402	316	(772)	(1,104)	(1,483)
	(5)	2,474	3,520	(21,252)	(19,639)
Net deferred tax charge (credit) and net deferred tax liability[c]	(1,284)	1,149	(554)	5,190	6,106
Of which – deferred tax liabilities				9,750	9,812
– deferred tax assets				4,560	3,706

[a] The 2017 and 2018 income statement and 2018 balance sheet are impacted by the reduction in US federal corporate income tax rate from 35% to 21%, effective from 1 January 2018.

[b] The 2019 balance sheet is impacted by the adoption of IFRS 16 and minor amendments have been made to the balance sheet and income statement comparatives to align with current period presentation.

[c] Included within the net deferred tax liability is a deferred tax asset balance of $5,526 million (2018 $5,562 million) related to the Gulf of Mexico oil spill.

Of the $4,560 million of deferred tax assets recognised on the group balance sheet at 31 December 2019 (2018 $3,706 million), $2,421 million (2018 $2,758 million) relates to entities that have suffered a loss in either the current or preceding period. This amount is supported by forecasts that indicate sufficient future taxable profits will be available to utilize such assets. For 2019, $2,421 million relates to the US (2018 $1,563 million relates to the US and $1,108 million relates to India).

In Extract 33.3 below, Hochschild Mining describes the general nature of its tax-related contingent liabilities relating to fiscal periods that are still open to review by the tax authorities and quantifies its estimate of the possible total exposure to tax assessments. [IAS 12.88].

> **Extract 33.3: Hochschild Mining PLC (2019)**
> NOTES TO THE CONSOLIDATED FINANCIAL STATEMENTS [extract]
> 34   Contingencies [extract]
> (a)   **Taxation**
>
> Fiscal periods remain open to review by the tax authorities for four years in Peru, five years in Argentina and Mexico and three years in Chile, preceding the year of review. During this time the authorities have the right to raise additional tax assessments including penalties and interest. Under certain circumstances, reviews may cover longer periods.
>
> Because a number of fiscal periods remain open to review by the tax authorities, coupled with the complexity of the Group and the transactions undertaken by it, there remains a risk that significant additional tax liabilities may arise. As at 31 December 2019, the Group had exposures totalling US$29,334,000 (2018: US$26,345,000) which are assessed as 'possible', rather than 'probable'. No amounts have been provided in respect of these items. This predominantly relates to potential tax penalties and related interest on intercompany loans.
>
> Notwithstanding this risk, the Directors believe that management's interpretation of the relevant legislation and assessment of taxation is appropriate and that it is probable that the Group's tax and customs positions will be sustained in the event of a challenge by the tax authorities. Consequently, the Directors consider that they have made adequate provision for any future outflow of resources and no additional provision is required in respect of these claims or risks.

The disclosures in Extract 33.4 below include information about deductible temporary differences, unused tax losses and unused tax credits in respect of which no deferred tax asset has been recognised, together with details of the aggregate amount of temporary differences associated with its investments in subsidiaries and equity-accounted entities for which deferred tax liabilities have not been recognised. *[IAS 12.81(e), 81(f)].*

> **Extract 33.4: BP p.l.c. (2018)**
> Notes on financial statements [extract]
> 9.   Taxation [extract]
> **Deferred tax** [extract]
>
> A summary of temporary differences, unused tax credits and unused tax losses for which deferred tax has not been recognized is shown in the table below.
>
> | | | $ billion |
> |---|---|---|
> | At 31 December | 2019 | 2018 |
> | Unused US state tax losses[a] | 2.3 | 6.6 |
> | Unused tax losses – other jurisdictions[b] | 3.5 | 4.3 |
> | Unused tax credits | 25.4 | 22.5 |
> | of which   – arising in the UK[c] | 21.5 | 18.7 |
> | – arising in the US[d] | 3.9 | 3.8 |
> | Deductible temporary differences[e] | 40.4 | 37.3 |
> | Taxable temporary differences associated with investments in subsidiaries and equity-accounted entities | 1.5 | 1.5 |
>
> [a]   For 2019 these losses expire in the period 2020–2039 with applicable tax rates ranging from 3% to 12%.
> [b]   The majority of the unused tax losses have no fixed expiry date.
> [c]   The UK unused tax credits arise predominantly in overseas branches of UK entities based in jurisdictions with higher statutory corporate income tax rates than the UK. No deferred tax asset has been recognized on these tax credits as they are unlikely to have value in the future; UK taxes on these overseas branches are largely mitigated by double tax relief in respect of overseas tax. These tax credits have no fixed expiry date.
> [d]   For 2019 the US unused tax credits expire in the period 2020-2029.
> [e]   The majority comprises fixed asset temporary differences in the UK. Substantially all of the temporary differences have no expiry date.

	$ million		
Impact of previously unrecognized deferred tax or write-down of deferred tax assets on tax charge	2019	2018	2017
Current tax benefit relating to the utilization of previously unrecognized deferred tax assets	272	83	22
Deferred tax benefit arising from the reversal of a previous write-down of deferred tax assets	96	–	–
Deferred tax benefit relating to the recognition of previously unrecognized deferred tax assets	364	112	436
Deferred tax expense arising from the write-down of a previously recognized deferred tax asset	73	169	78

14.6 Discontinued operations – interaction with IFRS 5

IFRS 5 requires the post-tax results of discontinued operations to be shown separately on the face of the statement of comprehensive income (and any separate income statement presenting the components of profit or loss). This may be done by giving the results of discontinued operations after those of continuing operations. This is discussed further in Chapter 4.

The definitions of income tax, tax expense and taxable profit in IAS 12 (see 3 above) do not distinguish between the results of continuing and discontinued operations, or the tax on those results. Thus, as drafted, IAS 12 applies not only to the tax income or expense on continuing operations (i.e. the amount shown in the 'tax line' in the income statement) but also to any tax income or expense relating to the results of discontinued operations separately disclosed after those of continuing operations.

However, IFRS 5 clarifies that items accounted for under that standard are not subject to the disclosure requirements of other standards, other than:

- specific disclosures in respect of non-current assets (or disposal groups) classified as held for sale or discontinued operations; or
- disclosures about the measurement of assets and liabilities within a disposal group that are not within the scope of the measurement requirements of IFRS 5, where such disclosures are not already provided in the other notes to the financial statements. *[IFRS 5.5B]*.

References

1 Throughout this Chapter, the tax treatment described in examples is purely illustrative, and does not necessarily relate to a specific provision of tax law in a jurisdiction using the currency in the example.
2 SIC-25, *Income Taxes – Changes in the Tax Status of an Entity or its Shareholders*, SIC, July 2000.
3 *IFRIC Update*, March 2006.
4 *IFRIC Update*, May 2009.
5 *IFRIC Update*, September 2017.
6 Based on a summary in *IASB Update*, February 2005.
7 *IFRIC Update*, June 2004.
8 In some cases, research and share-based payment costs may be included as part of the cost of other assets, such as inventories or PP&E.
9 ED/2009/2 – *Income Tax*, IASB, March 2009, Appendix A, definition of 'tax basis'.
10 ED/2009/2, paras. 20 and 23.
11 *IFRIC Update*, June 2018.

12. ED/2019/5 – *Deferred Tax related to Assets and Liabilities arising from a Single Transaction: Proposed amendments to IAS 12*, IASB, July 2019, Introduction.
13. *IASB Update*, April 2020.
14. IASB work plan – maintenance projects, IASB website, https://www.ifrs.org/projects/work-plan/ (accessed on 27 August 2020).
15. *IFRIC Update*, April 2005.
16. *IFRIC Update*, June 2005.
17. ED/2019/5 – *Deferred Tax related to Assets and Liabilities arising from a Single Transaction: Proposed amendments to IAS 12*, IASB, July 2019, Introduction.
18. ED/2019/5, BC13(a).
19. ED/2019/5, BC15(a).
20. ED/2019/5, BC6.
21. ED/2019/5, BC5.
22. ED/2019/5, BC7(a).
23. ED/2019/5, BC10.
24. *IASB Update*, April 2020.
25. IASB work plan – maintenance projects, IASB website, https://www.ifrs.org/projects/work-plan/ (accessed on 27 August 2020).
26. IASB Staff Paper, IASB Agenda ref 12G – *Deferred Tax Related to Assets and Liabilities arising from a Single Transaction (Amendments to IAS 12)*, Feedback summary – Background and overview, April 2020, para. 17(b).
27. *IFRIC Update*, March 2017.
28. *IFRIC Update*, May 2014.
29. *IFRIC Update*, May 2014.
30. *IFRIC Update*, May 2014.
31. *IFRIC Update*, June 2020.
32. *IFRIC Update*, February 2003.
33. *IFRIC Update*, April 2020.
34. *IFRIC Update*, April 2020.
35. SIC-21, Income Taxes – *Recovery of Non-Depreciable Assets*, SIC, July 2000, para. 4.
36. *IFRIC Update*, July 2016.
37. *IFRIC Update*, November 2011.
38. *IFRIC Update*, March 2015.
39. *IFRIC Update*, June 2020.
40. *IFRIC Update*, June 2020.
41. *IFRIC Update*, May 2012.
42. *IFRIC Update*, May 2012.
43. *IFRIC Update*, July 2014.
44. *IFRIC Update*, July 2014.
45. ED/2009/2, paras. 27(d), B31-B32.
46. *IFRIC Update*, May 2014.
47. *IFRIC Update*, July 2014.
48. *IFRIC Update*, July 2014.
49. *IFRIC Update*, September 2017.
50. *IFRIC Update*, September 2019.
51. *IFRIC Update*, September 2019.
52. *IFRIC Update*, July 2014.
53. *IFRIC Update*, January 2019.
54. *IFRIC Update*, January 2016.
55. *IFRIC Update*, January 2016.
56. *IFRIC Update*, March 2016.
57. Urgent Issues Group Interpretation 1052 – *Tax Consolidation Accounting*, AASB, as amended June 2010.

Chapter 34 Share-based payment

1 INTRODUCTION 2637
  1.1 Background 2637
  1.2 Development of IFRS 2 and amendments to the standard 2637
      1.2.1 IFRS 2 research project... 2639
  1.3 Scope of the chapter and referencing convention 2640
  1.4 Overall approach of IFRS 2 2640
      1.4.1 Classification differences between IFRS 2 and IAS 32/IFRS 9 2641

2 THE OBJECTIVE AND SCOPE OF IFRS 2 2642
  2.1 Objective 2642
  2.2 Scope 2642
      2.2.1 Definitions 2642
      2.2.2 Transactions within the scope of IFRS 2 2643
            2.2.2.A Group schemes and transactions with group shareholders: scope issues 2644
            2.2.2.B Transactions with employee benefit trusts and similar vehicles 2651
            2.2.2.C Transactions where the identifiable consideration received appears to be less than the consideration given 2651
            2.2.2.D 'All employee' share plans 2652
            2.2.2.E Vested transactions 2653
      2.2.3 Transactions not within the scope of IFRS 2 2653
            2.2.3.A Transactions with shareholders in their capacity as such 2654
            2.2.3.B Transfer of assets in group restructuring arrangements 2654
            2.2.3.C Business combinations 2654

		2.2.3.D	Common control transactions and formation of joint arrangements.. 2655
		2.2.3.E	Transactions in the scope of IAS 32 and IFRS 9 2655
		2.2.3.F	Transactions in financial assets outside the scope of IAS 32 and IFRS 9 2655
	2.2.4	\multicolumn{2}{l}{Some practical applications of the scope requirements............ 2656}
		2.2.4.A	Remuneration in non-equity shares and arrangements with put rights over equity shares 2656
		2.2.4.B	Equity-settled award of subsidiary with put option against the parent – treatment in consolidated accounts of parent............................ 2657
		2.2.4.C	Increase in ownership interest with no change in number of shares held 2658
		2.2.4.D	Awards for which the counterparty has paid 'fair value' 2658
		2.2.4.E	Cash bonus dependent on share price performance 2659
		2.2.4.F	Cash-settled awards based on an entity's 'enterprise value' or other formula 2659
		2.2.4.G	Awards with a foreign currency strike price 2660
		2.2.4.H	Holding own shares to satisfy or 'hedge' awards 2660
		2.2.4.I	Shares or warrants issued in connection with a loan or other financial liability.............................. 2661
		2.2.4.J	Options over puttable instruments classified as equity under specific exception in IAS 32 2661
		2.2.4.K	Special discounts to certain categories of investor on a share issue 2662

3 GENERAL RECOGNITION PRINCIPLES... 2663
   3.1 Vesting conditions... 2664
       3.1.1 'Malus' clauses and clawback conditions 2665
       3.1.2 Vesting conditions based on an employee's performance rating.. 2666
   3.2 Non-vesting conditions (conditions that are neither service conditions nor performance conditions).. 2667
       3.2.1 Background 2667
       3.2.2 Defining a non-vesting condition 2668
       3.2.3 Non-compete agreements 2670
   3.3 Vesting period... 2671
   3.4 Vesting and non-vesting conditions: issues referred to the Interpretations Committee and the IASB 2672

4	EQUITY-SETTLED TRANSACTIONS – OVERVIEW		2672
	4.1	Summary of accounting treatment	2672
	4.2	The credit entry	2674
5	EQUITY-SETTLED TRANSACTIONS – COST OF AWARDS		2674
	5.1	Cost of awards – overview	2674
	5.2	Transactions with employees	2676
		5.2.1 Who is an 'employee'?	2676
		5.2.2 Basis of measurement	2677
	5.3	Grant date	2677
		5.3.1 Determination of grant date	2678
		5.3.2 Communication of awards to employees and services in advance of grant date	2679
		5.3.3 Exercise price or performance target dependent on a formula or future share price	2681
		5.3.4 Exercise price paid in shares (net settlement of award)	2681
		5.3.5 Award of equity instruments to a fixed monetary value	2681
		5.3.6 Awards over a fixed pool of shares (including 'last man standing' arrangements)	2682
		5.3.7 Awards with multiple service and performance periods	2684
		5.3.8 Awards subject to modification by entity after original grant date	2685
		5.3.8.A Significant equity restructuring or transactions	2685
		5.3.8.B Interpretation of general terms	2686
		5.3.8.C Discretion to make further awards	2686
		5.3.9 'Good leaver' arrangements	2687
		5.3.9.A Provision for 'good leavers' made in original terms of award	2687
		5.3.9.B Discretionary awards to 'good leavers'	2688
		5.3.9.C Automatic full or pro rata entitlement on leaving employment	2689
		5.3.10 Special purpose acquisition companies ('SPACs')	2690
	5.4	Transactions with non-employees	2691
		5.4.1 Effect of change of status from employee to non-employee (or vice versa)	2691
	5.5	Determining the fair value of equity instruments	2692
		5.5.1 Reload features	2693
6	EQUITY-SETTLED TRANSACTIONS – ALLOCATION OF EXPENSE		2693
	6.1	Overview	2693
		6.1.1 The continuous estimation process of IFRS 2	2694
		6.1.2 Vesting and forfeiture	2695
		6.1.3 Accounting after vesting	2696

6.2	Vesting conditions other than market conditions		2696
	6.2.1	Awards with service conditions	2696
	6.2.2	Equity instruments vesting in instalments ('graded' vesting)	2697
	6.2.3	Transactions with variable vesting periods due to non-market performance vesting conditions	2699
	6.2.4	Transactions with variable number of equity instruments awarded depending on non-market performance vesting conditions	2701
	6.2.5	Transactions with variable exercise price due to non-market performance vesting conditions	2702
6.3	Market conditions		2703
	6.3.1	What is a 'market condition'?	2703
	6.3.2	Summary of accounting treatment	2704
	6.3.3	Transactions with market conditions and known vesting periods	2707
	6.3.4	Transactions with variable vesting periods due to market conditions	2708
	6.3.5	Transactions with multiple outcomes depending on market conditions	2709
	6.3.6	Transactions with independent market conditions, non-market vesting conditions or non-vesting conditions	2710
		6.3.6.A Independent market and non-market vesting conditions	2710
		6.3.6.B Independent market conditions and non-vesting conditions	2711
	6.3.7	Transactions with hybrid or interdependent market conditions and non-market vesting conditions	2711
	6.3.8	Awards with a condition linked to flotation price	2712
6.4	Non-vesting conditions		2712
	6.4.1	Awards with no conditions other than non-vesting conditions	2712
	6.4.2	Awards with non-vesting conditions and variable vesting periods	2713
	6.4.3	Failure to meet non-vesting conditions	2713

7 EQUITY-SETTLED TRANSACTIONS – MODIFICATION, CANCELLATION AND SETTLEMENT 2714

7.1	Background		2714
7.2	Valuation requirements when an award is modified, cancelled or settled		2715
7.3	Modification		2716
	7.3.1	Modifications that increase the value of an award	2717
		7.3.1.A Increase in fair value of equity instruments granted	2717

		7.3.1.B	Increase in number of equity instruments granted 2718
		7.3.1.C	Removal or mitigation of non-market vesting conditions 2718
	7.3.2	Modifications that decrease the value of an award 2719	
		7.3.2.A	Decrease in fair value of equity instruments granted 2720
		7.3.2.B	Decrease in number of equity instruments granted 2721
		7.3.2.C	Additional or more onerous non-market vesting conditions 2721
	7.3.3	Modifications with altered vesting period 2722	
	7.3.4	Modifications that reduce the number of equity instruments granted but maintain or increase the value of an award ('value for value' exchanges and 'give and take' modifications) 2724	
	7.3.5	Modification of award from equity-settled to cash-settled (and vice versa) 2726	
7.4	Cancellation and settlement 2726		
	7.4.1	Distinction between cancellation and forfeiture 2727	
		7.4.1.A	Termination of employment by entity 2727
		7.4.1.B	Surrender of award by employee 2727
	7.4.2	Distinction between cancellation and modification 2728	
	7.4.3	Calculation of the expense on cancellation 2728	
	7.4.4	Replacement awards 2730	
		7.4.4.A	Designation of award as replacement award 2730
		7.4.4.B	Incremental fair value of replacement award 2731
		7.4.4.C	Replacement of vested awards 2734
7.5	Replacement and *ex gratia* awards on termination of employment 2734		
7.6	Entity's plans for future modification or replacement of award – impact on estimation process at reporting date 2736		
7.7	Two awards running 'in parallel' 2737		
7.8	Share splits and consolidations 2738		

8 EQUITY-SETTLED TRANSACTIONS – VALUATION 2739

8.1	Introduction 2739		
8.2	Options 2740		
	8.2.1	Call options – overview 2740	
	8.2.2	Call options – valuation 2741	
	8.2.3	Factors specific to employee share options 2742	
		8.2.3.A	Non-transferability 2743
		8.2.3.B	Continued employment requirement 2743

		8.2.3.C	Vesting and non-vesting conditions	2743
		8.2.3.D	Periods during which exercise is restricted	2743
		8.2.3.E	Limited ability to hedge option values	2743
		8.2.3.F	Dilution effects	2744
8.3	Selection of an option-pricing model			2744
	8.3.1	The Black-Scholes-Merton formula		2745
	8.3.2	The binomial model		2747
		8.3.2.A	Lattice models – number of time steps	2750
	8.3.3	Monte Carlo Simulation		2751
8.4	Adapting option-pricing models for share-based payment transactions			2753
	8.4.1	Non-transferability		2753
	8.4.2	Treatment of vesting and non-vesting conditions		2753
		8.4.2.A	Market-based performance conditions and non-vesting conditions	2754
		8.4.2.B	Non-market vesting conditions	2754
8.5	Selecting appropriate assumptions for option-pricing models			2754
	8.5.1	Expected term of the option		2755
		8.5.1.A	Expected term under the Black-Scholes-Merton formula	2756
	8.5.2	Exercise and termination behaviour		2757
		8.5.2.A	Grouping employees with homogeneous exercise behaviour	2758
		8.5.2.B	Post-vesting termination behaviour	2759
	8.5.3	Expected volatility of share price		2759
		8.5.3.A	Newly listed entities	2761
		8.5.3.B	Unlisted entities	2761
		8.5.3.C	Listed entities that have undergone significant restructuring	2761
		8.5.3.D	Expected volatility under the Black-Scholes-Merton formula	2761
		8.5.3.E	Expected volatility under lattice models	2762
	8.5.4	Expected dividends		2762
		8.5.4.A	Expected dividends under the Black-Scholes-Merton formula	2763
		8.5.4.B	Expected dividends under the binomial model and other lattice models	2763
	8.5.5	Risk-free interest rate		2763
		8.5.5.A	Risk-free interest rate under the Black-Scholes-Merton formula	2764
		8.5.5.B	Risk-free interest rate under binomial and other lattice models	2764

	8.6	Capital structure effects and dilution	2764
	8.7	Valuation of equity-settled awards other than options	2765
		8.7.1 Shares	2765
		8.7.2 Non-recourse loans	2765
		8.7.3 Share appreciation rights (SARs)	2766
		8.7.4 Performance rights	2766
	8.8	Awards whose fair value cannot be measured reliably	2766
		8.8.1 Intrinsic value method – the basic accounting treatment	2766
		8.8.2 Modification, cancellation and settlement	2768
	8.9	Awards with reload features	2768
	8.10	Awards of equity instruments to a fixed monetary value	2769
9	CASH-SETTLED TRANSACTIONS		2770
	9.1	Scope of requirements	2770
	9.2	What constitutes a cash-settled award?	2770
		9.2.1 Formal and informal arrangements for the entity to purchase illiquid shares or otherwise settle in cash (awards to be treated as cash-settled, including unlisted company schemes)	2771
		9.2.2 Market purchases of own equity used to satisfy awards	2772
		9.2.3 Market purchases of own equity following equity-settlement of award	2772
		9.2.4 Arrangements to sell employees' shares including 'broker settlement'	2773
	9.3	Cash-settled transactions: required accounting	2774
		9.3.1 Basic accounting treatment	2774
		9.3.2 Application of the accounting treatment	2775
		9.3.2.A Determining the vesting period	2777
		9.3.2.B Periodic allocation of cost	2777
		9.3.2.C Non-market vesting conditions	2777
		9.3.2.D Market conditions and non-vesting conditions	2779
		9.3.2.E Modification, cancellation and settlement	2779
	9.4	Modification of award from equity-settled to cash-settled or from cash-settled to equity-settled	2779
		9.4.1 Equity-settled award modified to cash-settled award	2780
		9.4.2 Cash-settled award modified to equity-settled award	2786
10	TRANSACTIONS WITH EQUITY AND CASH ALTERNATIVES		2788
	10.1	Transactions where the counterparty has choice of settlement in equity or in cash	2788
		10.1.1 Transactions in which the fair value is measured directly	2789
		10.1.2 Transactions in which the fair value is measured indirectly – including transactions with employees	2789

	10.1.3	Accounting treatment	2790
		10.1.3.A During vesting period	2790
		10.1.3.B Settlement	2792
	10.1.4	Transactions with cash-settlement alternative for employee introduced after grant date	2792
	10.1.5	'Backstop' cash settlement rights	2794
	10.1.6	Convertible bonds issued to acquire goods or services	2794
10.2	Transactions where the entity has choice of settlement in equity or in cash		2795
	10.2.1	Transactions treated as cash-settled	2795
		10.2.1.A Entity choice has no substance due to economic or other compulsion for cash settlement (including unlisted entity awards with a presumption of cash settlement)	2796
	10.2.2	Transactions treated as equity-settled	2796
	10.2.3	Change in entity's settlement policy or intention leading to change in classification of award after grant date	2797
10.3	Awards requiring cash or equity settlement in specific circumstances (awards with contingent cash or contingent equity settlement)		2798
	10.3.1	Approach 1 – Treat as cash-settled if contingency is outside entity's control	2798
	10.3.2	Approach 2 – Treat as cash-settled if contingency is outside entity's control and probable	2799
	10.3.3	Application of Approach 1 and Approach 2 to awards requiring cash settlement on a change of control	2800
	10.3.4	Accounting for change in manner of settlement where award is contingent on future events outside the control of the entity and the counterparty	2801
		10.3.4.A Distinction between re-assessment of settlement method and modification of terms of award	2801
	10.3.5	Manner of settlement contingent on future events: discussions by the IASB and the Interpretations Committee	2802
10.4	Cash settlement alternative where cash sum is not based on share price or value		2803

11 REPLACEMENT SHARE-BASED PAYMENT AWARDS ISSUED IN A BUSINESS COMBINATION ... 2803

11.1	Background		2803
11.2	Replacement awards in business combinations accounted for under IFRS 3		2804
	11.2.1	Awards that the acquirer is 'obliged' to replace	2805

		11.2.1.A	Illustrative examples of awards that the acquirer is 'obliged' to replace	2806
	11.2.2	Acquiree awards that the acquirer is not 'obliged' to replace		2808
	11.2.3	Accounting for changes in vesting assumptions after the acquisition date		2808
11.3	Acquiree award not replaced by acquirer			2810
11.4	Financial statements of the acquired entity			2811

12 GROUP SHARE SCHEMES 2812

12.1	Typical features of a group share scheme			2812
12.2	Accounting treatment of group share schemes – summary			2814
	12.2.1	Background		2814
	12.2.2	Scope of IFRS 2 for group share schemes		2814
	12.2.3	Entity receiving goods or services		2815
	12.2.4	Entity settling the transaction		2816
	12.2.5	Transactions settled in equity of the entity or its parent		2816
		12.2.5.A	Awards settled in equity of subsidiary	2816
		12.2.5.B	Awards settled in equity of the parent	2817
	12.2.6	Cash-settled transactions not settled by the entity receiving goods or services		2817
	12.2.7	Intragroup recharges and management charges		2818
		12.2.7.A	Timing of recognition of intercompany recharges: discussion by the IFRS Interpretations Committee	2820
12.3	Employee benefit trusts ('EBTs') and similar arrangements			2820
	12.3.1	Background		2820
	12.3.2	Accounting for EBTs		2821
	12.3.3	Illustrative Examples – awards satisfied by shares purchased by, or issued to, an EBT		2823
	12.3.4	Separate financial statements of sponsoring entity		2825
	12.3.5	Financial statements of the EBT		2827
12.4	Illustrative example of group share scheme – equity-settled award satisfied by market purchase of shares			2827
	12.4.1	Consolidated financial statements		2827
	12.4.2	Parent		2828
		12.4.2.A	Accounting by parent where subsidiary is the employing entity and EBT is treated as separate entity	2829
		12.4.2.B	Accounting by parent where subsidiary is the employing entity and EBT is treated as extension of the parent	2829
		12.4.2.C	Parent company as employing entity	2830

	12.4.3	Employing subsidiary		2831
12.5	Illustrative example of group share scheme – equity-settled award satisfied by fresh issue of shares			2832
	12.5.1	Consolidated financial statements		2832
	12.5.2	Parent		2833
		12.5.2.A	Accounting by parent where subsidiary is the employing entity and EBT is treated as separate entity	2834
		12.5.2.B	Accounting by parent where subsidiary is the employing entity and EBT is treated as extension of parent	2834
		12.5.2.C	Parent as employing entity	2835
	12.5.3	Employing subsidiary		2837
12.6	Illustrative example – cash-settled transaction not settled by the entity receiving goods or services			2838
	12.6.1	Consolidated financial statements		2838
	12.6.2	Parent		2839
	12.6.3	Employing subsidiary		2840
12.7	Employee transferring between group entities			2840
12.8	Group reorganisations			2841
12.9	Share-based payments to employees of joint ventures or associates			2842
	12.9.1	Financial statements of the associate or joint venture		2842
	12.9.2	Consolidated financial statements of the investor		2843
	12.9.3	Separate financial statements of the investor		2844

13 DISCLOSURES 2844

13.1	Nature and extent of share-based payment arrangements			2845
13.2	Valuation of share-based payment arrangements			2846
13.3	Impact of share-based payment transactions on financial statements			2848
13.4	Example of IFRS 2 disclosures			2849

14 TAXES RELATED TO SHARE-BASED PAYMENT TRANSACTIONS.............2853

14.1	Income tax deductions for the entity			2853
14.2	Employment taxes of the employer			2854
	14.2.1	Applicable standard		2854
		14.2.1.A	IAS 37	2854
		14.2.1.B	IFRS 2	2854
		14.2.1.C	IAS 19	2855
	14.2.2	Recovery of employer's taxes from employees		2855
	14.2.3	Holding of own shares to 'hedge' employment tax liabilities		2857

14.3	Sale or surrender of shares by employee to meet employee's tax liability ('sell to cover' and 'net settlement')		2857
	14.3.1	Share-based payments with a net settlement feature for withholding tax obligations (net settlement where IFRS 2 exception applies)	2860

15 OTHER PRACTICAL ISSUES 2862

15.1	Matching share awards (including deferred bonuses delivered in shares)		2862
15.2	Loans to employees to purchase shares (limited recourse and full recourse loans)		2868
15.3	Awards entitled to dividends or dividend equivalents during the vesting period		2870
15.4	Awards vesting or exercisable on an exit event or change of control (flotation, trade sale etc.)		2872
	15.4.1	Grant date	2873
	15.4.2	Vesting period	2873
	15.4.3	Is flotation or sale a vesting condition or a non-vesting condition?	2874
	15.4.4	Awards requiring achievement of a minimum price on flotation or sale	2875
	15.4.5	Awards 'purchased for fair value'	2876
	15.4.6	'Drag along' and 'tag along' rights	2877
15.5	South African black economic empowerment ('BEE') and similar arrangements		2878
	15.5.1	Nature of the trust	2879
	15.5.2	Measurement and timing of the accounting cost	2880
	15.5.3	Classification of awards as equity- or cash-settled	2882
15.6	Shares used as a currency of payment		2882
	15.6.1	Awards assessed on the market value of a subsidiary or business unit and settled by reference to the fair value of shares in the parent entity	2883

16 FIRST-TIME ADOPTION AND TRANSITIONAL PROVISIONS 2884

16.1	First-time adoption provisions	2884

List of examples

Example 34.1:	Meaning of 'vesting period' – award with vesting conditions only	2671
Example 34.2:	Meaning of 'vesting period' – award with vesting and non-vesting conditions	2671
Example 34.3:	Determination of grant date	2680
Example 34.4:	Awards with multiple service and performance periods	2684
Example 34.5:	Award with non-vesting condition only	2693
Example 34.6:	Award with service condition only	2694
Example 34.7:	Award with no change in the estimate of number of awards vesting	2697
Example 34.8:	Award with re-estimation of number of awards vesting due to staff turnover	2697
Example 34.9:	Award vesting in instalments ('graded' vesting)	2698
Example 34.10:	Award with non-market vesting condition and variable vesting period	2699
Example 34.11:	Award with non-market performance vesting condition and variable number of equity instruments	2701
Example 34.12:	Award with non-market performance vesting condition and variable exercise price	2703
Example 34.13:	Award with market condition	2705
Example 34.14:	Award with market condition and fixed vesting period	2707
Example 34.15:	Award with market condition and variable vesting period	2708
Example 34.16:	Award with market conditions and multiple outcomes	2709
Example 34.17:	Award with independent market conditions and non-market vesting conditions	2710
Example 34.18:	Does a modification increase or decrease the value of an award?	2716
Example 34.19:	Award modified by repricing	2717
Example 34.20:	Modification of non-market performance condition in employee's favour	2718
Example 34.21:	Increase in number of equity instruments or modification of vesting conditions?	2719
Example 34.22:	Award modified by replacing a non-market condition with a market condition	2720
Example 34.23:	Award modified by changing non-market performance conditions or service conditions	2721
Example 34.24:	Award modified by reducing the exercise price and extending the vesting period	2722
Example 34.25:	Modification where number of equity instruments is reduced but total fair value of award is unchanged	2724
Example 34.26:	Modification where number of equity instruments is reduced but total fair value of award is increased	2724

Share-based payment 2635

Example 34.27:	Cancellation and settlement – basic accounting treatment	2728
Example 34.28:	Cancellation and settlement – best estimate of cancellation expense	2729
Example 34.29:	Replacement awards – is there an accounting arbitrage between accounting for a modification and accounting for cancellation and a new grant?	2731
Example 34.30:	Replacement award on termination of employment	2735
Example 34.31:	Estimation of number of awards expected to vest – treatment of anticipated future events	2736
Example 34.32:	Two option awards running in parallel	2738
Example 34.33:	Binomial model	2748
Example 34.34:	Intrinsic value method	2767
Example 34.35:	Award of shares to a fixed monetary value	2769
Example 34.36:	Equity-settled award satisfied with market purchase of treasury shares	2771
Example 34.37:	Cash-settled transaction with service condition	2775
Example 34.38:	Cash-settled transaction with service condition and non-market performance condition	2778
Example 34.39:	Modification of equity-settled award to cash-settled award	2782
Example 34.40:	Modification of cash-settled award to equity-settled award	2787
Example 34.41:	Award with employee choice of settlement with different fair values for cash-settlement and equity-settlement	2790
Example 34.42:	Award with employee cash-settlement alternative introduced after grant	2793
Example 34.43:	Settlement of transaction treated as equity-settled where fair value of cash settlement exceeds fair value of equity settlement	2797
Example 34.44:	Settlement of transaction treated as equity-settled where fair value of equity settlement exceeds fair value of cash settlement	2797
Example 34.45:	Replacement award requiring no post-combination service replacing vested acquiree award	2807
Example 34.46:	Replacement award requiring no post-combination service replacing unvested acquiree award	2807
Example 34.47:	Replacement award requiring post-combination service replacing vested acquiree award	2807
Example 34.48:	Replacement award requiring post-combination service replacing unvested acquiree award	2808
Example 34.49:	Accounting for post-acquisition changes in estimates relating to replacement awards	2809
Example 34.50:	Interaction of IFRS 10, IAS 32 and IFRS 2 (market purchase)	2823

Example 34.51:	Interaction of IFRS 10, IAS 32 and IFRS 2 (fresh issue of shares)	2824
Example 34.52:	EBTs in separate financial statements of sponsoring entity	2826
Example 34.53:	Group share scheme (market purchase of shares)	2827
Example 34.54:	Group share scheme (fresh issue of shares)	2832
Example 34.55:	Cash-settled scheme not settled by receiving entity	2838
Example 34.56:	Share-based payment to employees of associate	2842
Example 34.57:	Recovery of employment tax on share-based payment from employee	2856
Example 34.58:	Surrendering of vested shares by employee to indemnify liability of entity to pay employee's tax liability (net settlement where IFRS 2 exception does not apply)	2858
Example 34.59:	Share-based payment transactions with a net settlement feature for withholding tax obligations (application of IFRS 2 exception)	2861
Example 34.60:	Mandatory investment by employee of cash bonus into shares with mandatory matching award by employer	2863
Example 34.61:	Mandatory investment by employee of cash bonus into shares with discretionary matching award by employer	2864
Example 34.62:	Discretionary investment by employee of cash bonus into shares with no matching award	2865
Example 34.63:	Discretionary investment by employee of cash bonus into shares with mandatory matching award by employer	2865
Example 34.64:	Discretionary investment by employee of cash bonus into shares with discretionary matching award by employer	2867
Example 34.65:	Award with rights to receive (and retain) dividends during vesting period	2871
Example 34.66:	Award vesting in instalments with a floatation or sale condition	2874
Example 34.67:	Receipt of BEE credentials with no service or performance condition	2881

Chapter 34 Share-based payment

1 INTRODUCTION

1.1 Background

Most share-based payment transactions undertaken by entities are awards of shares and options as remuneration to employees, in particular senior management and directors. In a number of countries, shares and options now comprise the greatest element of the total remuneration package of senior personnel, a trend encouraged by the consensus that it is a matter of good corporate governance to promote significant long-term shareholdings by senior management, so as to align their economic interests with those of shareholders.

One advantage of shares and options as remuneration is that they need not entail any cash cost to the entity. If an executive is entitled under a bonus scheme to a free share, the entity can satisfy this award simply by printing another share certificate, which the executive can sell, so that the cash cost of the award is effectively borne by shareholders rather than by the entity itself. However, this very advantage was the source of the controversy surrounding share-based remuneration.

Investors became increasingly concerned that share-based remuneration was resulting in a significant cost to them, through dilution of their existing shareholdings. As a result, there emerged an increasing consensus among investors that awards of shares and share options should be recognised as a cost in the financial statements.

The opposing view, held by most entities, was that the financial statements were simply reflecting the economic reality that such awards are ultimately a cost to other shareholders and not to the entity. Another powerful argument for those opposed to expensing options was to point out that some clearly successful companies, particularly in the new technology sector, would never have shown a profit if they had been required to book an accounting expense for options.

1.2 Development of IFRS 2 and amendments to the standard

In November 2002, the IASB issued an exposure draft ED 2 – *Share-based Payment* – proposing that share-based payments for goods and services should be expensed. The exposure draft proved highly controversial. Those who supported it in principle nevertheless had concerns on nearly every detail of the accounting treatment proposed, in particular the fact that it did not permit any 'truing up', i.e. reversing any expense previously charged for an award that never actually crystallises. More fundamentally, many questioned whether there yet existed a methodology sufficiently robust for valuing shares and share options subject to the restrictions and performance conditions typically associated with employee share awards. There also remained a significant minority who still questioned the whole principle of expensing options and other share awards.

Despite these comments, the IASB finalised its proposals with the publication of IFRS 2 – *Share-based Payment* – on 19 February 2004, although some significant changes had been necessary to the prohibition on 'truing up' in the ED. In particular, IFRS 2 requires an expense to be recognised only for awards that vest (or are considered by IFRS 2 to vest), but (in the case of awards settled in shares) based on their fair value at the date of grant. Nevertheless, IFRS 2 remains contentious: for example, there is still only limited provision for 'truing up', with the result that significant costs can potentially be recognised for awards that ultimately have no value to their recipients, and give rise to no dilution of the interests of other shareholders. Some commentators continue to question whether existing option valuation models can produce a reliable valuation of employee share awards.

The IASB has issued the following amendments to the original version of IFRS 2:

- *Vesting Conditions and Cancellations*,[1] issued in January 2008 ('the January 2008 amendment'). Entities are required to apply IFRS 2 as modified by this amendment for periods beginning on or after 1 January 2009; *[IFRS 2.62]*

- *Group Cash-settled Share-based Payment Transactions*,[2] issued in June 2009 ('the June 2009 amendment'). Entities are required to apply IFRS 2 as modified by this amendment for periods beginning on or after 1 January 2010; *[IFRS 2.63]*

- *Improvements to IFRSs*, issued in April 2009 ('the April 2009 amendment'). This made a minor amendment to the scope of IFRS 2;

- *Annual Improvements to IFRSs 2010-2012 Cycle*, issued in December 2013, which made amendments to the definitions in Appendix A of IFRS 2 relating to vesting conditions; and

- *Classification and Measurement of Share-based Payment Transactions*,[3] issued in June 2016 ('the June 2016 amendments'). Entities are required to apply these amendments for accounting periods beginning on or after 1 January 2018. *[IFRS 2.63D]*.

There have also been two interpretations of IFRS 2 by the IFRS Interpretations Committee, IFRIC 8 – *Scope of IFRS 2* – and IFRIC 11 – *IFRS 2 – Group and Treasury Share Transactions*, but these were incorporated into IFRS 2 as part of the June 2009 amendment and the separate interpretations withdrawn. *[IFRS 2.64]*.

Revision of, and amendments to, IFRS 3 – *Business Combinations* – in 2008 and 2010 respectively, led to consequential amendments to IFRS 2. The revised and amended IFRS 3 provides guidance on the replacement of share-based payment awards in a business combination (see 11 below).

A *cash-settled share-based payment transaction* is 'a share-based payment transaction in which the entity acquires goods or services by incurring a liability to transfer cash or other assets to the supplier of those goods or services for amounts that are based on the price (or value) of equity instruments (including shares or share options) of the entity or another group entity'.

A *group entity* in the four definitions above means any parent, subsidiary, or subsidiary of any parent, of the entity and is based on the definition of 'group' in Appendix A to IFRS 10 – *Consolidated Financial Statements* – as 'a parent and its subsidiaries'. *[IFRS 2.63A, BC22E]*.

An *equity instrument* is 'a contract that evidences a residual interest in the assets of an entity after deducting all of its liabilities'.

An *equity instrument granted* is 'the right (conditional or unconditional) to an equity instrument of the entity conferred by the entity on another party, under a share-based payment arrangement'.

A *share option* is 'a contract that gives the holder the right, but not the obligation, to subscribe to the entity's shares at a fixed or determinable price for a specified period of time'.

It will be seen from these definitions that IFRS 2 applies not only to awards of shares and share options but also to awards of cash (or other assets) of a value equivalent to the value, or a movement in the value, of a particular number of shares. Such cash awards may arise in a number of situations. For example:

- an entity may wish to extend its share scheme to the employees of overseas subsidiaries in jurisdictions where it may be difficult, or even illegal, to trade in the entity's shares, or where delivering shares would not give the same tax benefits to employees as would apply in the parent's own jurisdiction; or
- the entity may not wish to dilute existing shareholdings by significant share awards to employees.

In such cases, the employees may instead be offered cash equivalent to the value of the shares that they would otherwise have obtained.

2.2.2 Transactions within the scope of IFRS 2

Subject to the exceptions noted at 2.2.3 below, IFRS 2 must be applied to all share-based payment transactions, including:

(a) equity-settled share-based payment transactions (discussed at 4 to 8 below);

(b) cash-settled share-based payment transactions (discussed at 9 below); and

(c) transactions where either the entity or the supplier of goods or services can choose whether the transaction is to be equity-settled or cash-settled (discussed at 10 below). *[IFRS 2.2]*.

Whilst the boundaries between these types of transaction are reasonably self-explanatory, there may be transactions – as discussed in more detail at 9 and 10 below – that an entity may intuitively regard as equity-settled which are in fact required to be treated as cash-settled under IFRS 2.

Although IFRS 2 was primarily a response to concerns over share-based remuneration, its scope is not restricted to transactions with employees. For example, if an external supplier of goods or services, including another group entity, is paid in shares or share options, or cash (or other assets) of equivalent value, IFRS 2 must be applied. Goods include:

- inventories;
- consumables;
- property, plant and equipment;
- intangibles; and
- other non-financial assets. *[IFRS 2.5]*.

It will be seen that 'goods' do not include financial assets, which raises some further issues (see 2.2.3.F below).

The scope of IFRS 2 extends to:

- group share schemes and certain transactions with shareholders (see 2.2.2.A below);
- transactions with employee benefit trusts and similar vehicles (see 2.2.2.B below);
- transactions where the identifiable consideration received appears to be less than the consideration given (see 2.2.2.C below);
- 'all employee' share plans (see 2.2.2.D below); and
- vested transactions (see 2.2.2.E below).

2.2.2.A Group schemes and transactions with group shareholders: scope issues

The definitions of 'share-based payment arrangement' and 'share-based payment transaction' at 2.2.1 above have the effect that the scope of IFRS 2 is not restricted to transactions where the reporting entity acquires goods or services in exchange for its own equity instruments (or cash or other assets based on the cost or value of those equity instruments). Within a group of companies it is common for one member of the group (typically the parent) to have the obligation to settle a share-based payment transaction in which services are provided to another member of the group (typically a subsidiary). This transaction is within the scope of IFRS 2 for the entity receiving the services (even though it is not a direct party to the arrangement between its parent and its employee), the entity settling the transaction and the group as a whole.

Accordingly, IFRS 2 requires an entity to account for a transaction in which it either:

- receives goods or services when another entity in the same group (or a shareholder of any group entity) has the obligation to settle the share-based payment transaction, or
- has an obligation to settle a share-based payment transaction when another entity in the same group receives the goods or services

unless the transaction is clearly for a purpose other than payment for goods or services supplied to the entity receiving them. *[IFRS 2.3A]*.

Moreover, the definitions of 'equity-settled share-based payment transaction' and 'cash-settled share-based payment transaction' have the effect that the analysis of the transaction as equity-settled or cash-settled (and its accounting treatment) may differ when viewed from the perspective of the entity receiving the goods or services, the entity settling the transaction and the group as a whole. *[IFRS 2.43A]*.

We consider below seven scenarios, based on the simple structure in Figure 34.1 below. These scenarios are by no means exhaustive, but cover the situations most commonly seen in practice.

The scenarios considered in this section do not consider recharge arrangements between group entities. The accounting treatment of group share schemes, including those with recharge arrangements, is discussed in more detail at 12 below.

Figure 34.1:   Scope of IFRS 2

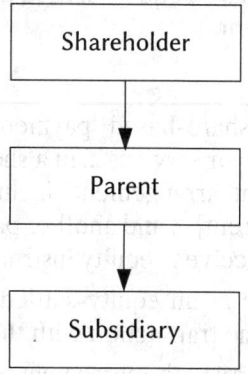

The scenarios assume that:
- the shareholder is not a group entity; and
- the subsidiary is directly owned by the parent company (see 12.2.1 below in relation to intermediate parent companies).

Scenario	Who grants the award?	Which entity receives the goods or services?	Who settles the award?	On which entity's shares is the award based?	Award settled in shares or cash?
1	Parent	Subsidiary	Parent	Parent	Shares
2	Shareholder	Subsidiary	Shareholder	Parent	Shares
3	Subsidiary	Subsidiary	Subsidiary	Parent	Shares
4	Subsidiary	Subsidiary	Subsidiary	Subsidiary	Shares
5	Parent	Subsidiary	Parent	Subsidiary	Shares
6	Parent	Subsidiary	Parent	Parent	Cash
7	Shareholder	Subsidiary	Shareholder	Parent	Cash

Scenario 1

Parent awards equity shares in Parent to employees of Subsidiary in exchange for services to Subsidiary. Parent settles the award with the employees of Subsidiary.
[IFRS 2.43B-43C, B52(a), B53-B54].

Consolidated financial statements of Parent

Under the definition of 'share-based payment transaction', 'the entity [i.e. the Parent group] ... receives goods or services ... in a share-based payment arrangement ...'. A share-based payment arrangement includes 'an agreement between the entity ... and another party (including an employee) that entitles the other party to receive ... equity instruments ... of the entity ...'.

The transaction is classified as an equity-settled transaction because it is settled in an equity instrument of the group.

Separate financial statements of Parent

Under the definition of 'share-based payment transaction', 'the entity [i.e. the Parent as a single entity] ... incurs an obligation to settle the transaction with the supplier in a share-based payment arrangement when another group entity receives those goods or services'.

The transaction is classified as an equity-settled transaction because it is settled in an equity instrument of Parent.

Subsidiary

Under the definition of 'share-based payment transaction', 'the entity [i.e. Subsidiary] ... receives goods or services ... in a share-based payment arrangement ...'. A 'share-based payment arrangement' includes 'an agreement between ... another group entity [i.e. Parent] ... and another party (including an employee) that entitles the other party to receive ... equity instruments of ... another group entity'.

The transaction is classified as an equity-settled transaction because Subsidiary 'has no obligation to settle the transaction with the supplier'.

Even if Subsidiary is not a party to the agreement with its employees, it nevertheless records a cost for this transaction. In effect, the accounting treatment is representing that Subsidiary has received a capital contribution from Parent, which Subsidiary has then 'spent' on employee remuneration. This treatment is often referred to as 'push-down' accounting – the idea being that a transaction undertaken by one group entity (in this case, Parent) for the benefit of another group entity (in this case, Subsidiary) is 'pushed down' into the financial statements of the beneficiary entity.

Scenario 2

Shareholder awards equity shares in Parent to employees of Subsidiary in exchange for services to Subsidiary. Shareholder settles the award with the employees of Subsidiary. *[IFRS 2.B48(b)].*

Consolidated financial statements of Parent

Under the definition of 'share-based payment transaction', 'the entity [i.e. the Parent group] ... receives goods or services ... in a share-based payment arrangement'. A 'share-based payment arrangement' includes 'an agreement between ... any shareholder ... and another party (including an employee) that entitles the other party to receive ... equity instruments (including shares or share options) of the entity...'.

The transaction is classified as an equity-settled transaction, because the Parent group 'has no obligation to settle the transaction with the supplier'.

Separate financial statements of Parent

Scenario 2 is not within the scope of IFRS 2 for the separate financial statements of Parent, because Parent (as a separate entity) receives no goods or services, nor does it settle the transaction.

Subsidiary

Under the definition of 'share-based payment transaction', 'the entity [i.e. Subsidiary] ... receives goods or services ... in a share-based payment arrangement'. A 'share-based payment arrangement' includes 'an agreement between ... any shareholder of any group entity [i.e. Shareholder] ... and another party (including an employee) that entitles the other party to receive equity instruments of ... another group entity [i.e. Parent]'.

The transaction is classified as an equity-settled transaction, because Subsidiary 'has no obligation to settle the transaction with the supplier'.

IFRS 2 does not explicity address the accounting treatment for such a transaction within the financial statements of a shareholder that is not a group entity. *[IFRS 2.BC22G].* We discuss at 12.9 below the accounting treatment of such transactions in the financial statements of a shareholder that is an investor in a joint venture or associate.

Scenario 3

Subsidiary awards equity shares in Parent to employees of Subsidiary in exchange for services to Subsidiary. Subsidiary settles the award with the employees of Subsidiary. *[IFRS 2.43B, B52(b), B55].*

Consolidated financial statements of Parent

Under the definition of 'share-based payment transaction', 'the entity [i.e. the Parent group] ... receives goods or services ... in a share-based payment arrangement'. A 'share-based payment arrangement' includes 'an agreement between the entity ... and another party (including an employee) that entitles the other party to receive ... equity instruments (including shares or share options) of the entity'.

The transaction is classified as an equity-settled transaction, because the Parent group 'receives goods or services as consideration for its own equity instruments (including shares or share options) ...'.

Separate financial statements of Parent

Scenario 3 is not within the scope of IFRS 2 for the separate financial statements of Parent, because Parent (as a separate entity) receives no goods or services, nor does it settle the transaction.

Subsidiary

Under the definition of 'share-based payment transaction', 'the entity [i.e. Subsidiary] ... receives goods or services ... in a share-based payment arrangement'. A 'share-based payment arrangement' includes 'an agreement between ... [a] group entity [i.e. Subsidiary] ... and another party (including an employee) that entitles the other party to receive equity instruments of ... another group entity [i.e. Parent]'.

The transaction is classified as a cash-settled transaction because Subsidiary has the obligation to settle the award with equity instruments issued by Parent – i.e. a financial asset in Subsidiary's separate financial statements – rather than with Subsidiary's own equity instruments.

However, for the approach in this Scenario to apply, it must be the case that Subsidiary grants the award as a principal rather than as agent for Parent and Subsidiary has the obligation to settle. If Subsidiary appears to be granting an award but is really doing so only on the instructions of Parent, as will generally be the case in certain jurisdictions, then the approach in Scenario 1 above is more likely to apply. This is discussed in more detail at 12.2.5.B below.

Scenario 4

Subsidiary awards equity shares in Subsidiary to employees of Subsidiary in exchange for services to Subsidiary. Subsidiary settles the award with the employees of Subsidiary. *[IFRS 2.43B, B49].*

Consolidated financial statements of Parent

Under the definition of 'share-based payment transaction', 'the entity [i.e. the Parent group] ... receives goods or services ... in a share-based payment arrangement'. A share-based payment arrangement includes 'an agreement between the entity ... and another party (including an employee) that entitles the other party to receive ... equity instruments ... of the entity ...'.

The transaction is classified as an equity-settled transaction, because it is settled in an equity instrument of the group. In the consolidated financial statements of Parent, shares of Subsidiary not held by Parent are a non-controlling interest, classified as equity (see Chapter 7 at 4).

Separate financial statements of Parent

Scenario 4 is not within the scope of IFRS 2 for the separate financial statements of Parent, because Parent (as a separate entity) receives no goods or services, nor does it settle the transaction.

Subsidiary

Under the definition of 'share-based payment transaction', 'the entity [i.e. Subsidiary] ... receives goods or services ... in a share-based payment arrangement'.

The transaction is classified as an equity-settled transaction, because it is settled in an equity instrument of Subsidiary.

Scenario 5

Parent awards equity shares in Subsidiary to employees of Subsidiary in exchange for services to Subsidiary. Parent settles the award with the employees of Subsidiary. *[IFRS 2.43B-43C, B50].*

Consolidated financial statements of Parent

Under the definition of 'share-based payment transaction', 'the entity [i.e. the Parent group] ... receives goods or services ... in a share-based payment arrangement'. A share-based payment arrangement includes 'an agreement between the entity ... and another party (including an employee) that entitles the other party to receive ... equity instruments of the entity ...'.

The transaction is classified as an equity-settled transaction, because it is settled in an equity instrument of the group. In the consolidated financial statements of Parent, shares of Subsidiary not held by Parent are a non-controlling interest, classified as equity (see Chapter 7 at 4).

Separate financial statements of Parent

Under the definition of 'share-based payment transaction', 'the entity [i.e. the Parent as a single entity] ... incurs an obligation to settle the transaction with the supplier in a share-based payment arrangement when another group entity [i.e. Subsidiary] receives those goods or services'. The transaction is a share-based payment arrangement for Subsidiary (see below) and the consolidated financial statements of Parent (see above).

For Parent, the transaction is classified as a cash-settled transaction, because it is settled not in an equity instrument issued by Parent, but in an equity instrument issued by a subsidiary and held by Parent – i.e. a financial asset in Parent's separate financial statements.

Subsidiary

Under the definition of 'share-based payment transaction', 'the entity [i.e. Subsidiary] ... receives goods or services ... in a share-based payment arrangement'. A 'share-based payment arrangement' includes 'an agreement between ... another group entity [i.e. Parent] ... and another party (including an employee) that entitles the other party to receive equity instruments of the entity...'.

The transaction is classified as an equity-settled transaction, because Subsidiary 'has no obligation to settle the transaction with the supplier'.

Scenario 6

Parent awards cash based on the value of shares in Parent to employees of Subsidiary in exchange for services to Subsidiary. Parent settles the award with the employees of Subsidiary. *[IFRS 2.43C, B56-B58]*.

Consolidated financial statements of Parent

Under the definition of 'share-based payment transaction', 'the entity [i.e. the Parent group] ... receives goods or services ... in a share-based payment arrangement'. A 'share-based payment arrangement' includes 'an agreement between the entity ... and another party (including an employee) that entitles the other party to receive ... cash ... of the entity ... based on the price (or value) of equity instruments ... of the entity ...'.

The transaction is classified as a cash-settled transaction, because it is settled in cash of the group.

Separate financial statements of Parent

Under the definition of 'share-based payment transaction', 'the entity [i.e. the Parent as a single entity] ... incurs an obligation to settle the transaction with the supplier in a share-based payment arrangement when another group entity [i.e. Subsidiary] receives those goods or services'.

The transaction is classified as a cash-settled transaction, because it is settled in cash of Parent.

Subsidiary

IFRS 2 contains detailed guidance for the accounting treatment of such transactions by the employing subsidiary (see 12 below), from which it may reasonably be inferred that the IASB intended them to be in the scope of IFRS 2 for the subsidiary.

However, this is strictly not the case when the drafting of IFRS 2 is examined closely. In order to be a share-based payment transaction (and therefore in the scope of IFRS 2) for the reporting entity, a transaction must also be a share-based payment arrangement. A share-based payment arrangement is defined as one in which the counterparty receives (our emphasis added):

- equity of the entity or any other group entity, or
- cash or other assets of the entity.

As drafted, the definition has the effect that a transaction settled in equity is in the scope of IFRS 2 for a reporting entity, whether the equity used to settle is the entity's own equity or that of another group entity. Where a transaction is settled in cash, however, the definition has the effect that a transaction is in the scope of IFRS 2 for a reporting entity only when that entity's own cash (or other assets) is used in settlement, and not when another group entity settles the transaction.

However, given the guidance referred to above in IFRS 2 for the accounting treatment for the reporting entity of transactions settled in cash by another group entity, we believe that the exclusion of such transactions from the definition of 'share-based payment arrangement' should be disregarded as a drafting slip.

The transaction is classified as an equity-settled transaction by Subsidiary, because Subsidiary 'has no obligation to settle the transaction with the supplier'.

Scenario 7

Shareholder awards cash based on the value of shares in Parent to employees of Subsidiary in exchange for services to Subsidiary. Shareholder settles the award with the employees of Subsidiary.

For the reasons set out in Scenario 6 above, this transaction is not strictly in the scope of IFRS 2 as drafted either for the consolidated or separate financial statements of Parent or for the individual financial statements of Subsidiary. As noted in Scenario 6 above, the definition of 'share-based payment arrangement' as drafted excludes any arrangement that is settled in cash by a party other than the reporting entity. Moreover, whilst IFRS 2 gives detailed guidance that effectively appears to 'over-ride' the definition in respect of a transaction settled by another group entity (see Scenario 6 above), there is no such over-riding guidance in respect of a transaction settled in cash by a non-group shareholder. The transaction is not within the scope of IFRS 2 for the separate financial statements of Parent, because Parent (as a separate entity) receives no goods or services, nor does it settle the transaction.

Nevertheless, we believe that the transaction should be treated as within the scope of IFRS 2 for the consolidated financial statements of Parent and the individual financial statements of Subsidiary. One of the original objectives of the project that led to the issue of the June 2009 amendment to IFRS 2 was to address a concern that, as originally issued, IFRS 2 did not require an entity to account for a cash-settled share-based payment transaction settled by an external shareholder.

In addition to the accounting treatment under IFRS 2, the group entities in this Scenario would need to consider the requirements of IAS 24 – *Related Party Disclosures* – as any payments by a shareholder would potentially need to be disclosed (see Chapter 39).

2.2.2.B Transactions with employee benefit trusts and similar vehicles

In some jurisdictions, it is common for an entity to establish a trust to hold shares in the entity for the purpose of satisfying, or 'hedging' the cost of, share-based awards to employees. In such cases, it is often the trust, rather than any entity within the legal group, that actually makes share-based awards to employees.

A sponsoring employer (or its wider group) will need to assess whether it controls the trust in accordance with the requirements of IFRS 10 and therefore whether the trust should be consolidated (see 12.3 below and Chapter 6).

Awards by employee benefit trusts and similar vehicles are within the scope of IFRS 2, irrespective of whether or not the trust is consolidated, since:

- where the trust is consolidated, it is an award by a group entity; and
- where the trust is not consolidated, it is an award by a shareholder.

2.2.2.C Transactions where the identifiable consideration received appears to be less than the consideration given

A share-based payment transaction as defined (see 2.2.1 above) involves the receipt of goods or services by the reporting entity or by another group entity. Nevertheless, IFRS 2 also applies to share-based payment transactions where no specifically identifiable goods or services have been (or will be) received. *[IFRS 2.2]*.

IFRS 2 asserts that, if the identifiable consideration received (if any) appears to be less than the fair value of consideration given, the implication is that, in addition to the identifiable goods and services acquired, the entity must also have received some unidentifiable consideration equal to the difference between the fair value of the share-based payment and the fair value of any identifiable consideration received. Accordingly, the cost of the unidentified consideration must be accounted for in accordance with IFRS 2. *[IFRS 2.13A]*.

For example, if an entity agrees to pay a supplier of services with a clearly identifiable market value of £1,000 by issuing shares with a value of £1,500, IFRS 2 requires the entity to recognise an expense of £1,500. This is notwithstanding the normal requirement of IFRS 2 that an equity-settled share-based payment transaction with a non-employee be recognised at the fair value of the goods or services received (see 5.1 and 5.4 below).

This requirement was introduced by IFRIC 8 (since incorporated into IFRS 2). The reason for the change is alluded to in an illustrative example. *[IFRS 2.IG5D, IG Example 1]*. As part of general economic reforms in South Africa, under arrangements generally referred to as black economic empowerment or 'BEE' (discussed further at 15.5 below), various entities issued or transferred significant numbers of shares to bodies representing historically disadvantaged communities. Some took the view that these transactions did not fall within the scope of IFRS 2 as originally drafted because the entities concerned were not purchasing goods or services. Rather, BEE arrangements were simply meant to replicate a transfer of shares from one group of shareholders to another. Accordingly, it was argued, such transactions did not fall within the scope of IFRS 2, since it is intrinsic to the definition of a 'share-based payment transaction' (see 2.2.1 above) that goods or services are received.

IFRS 2 rejects this argument. It effectively takes the view that, since the directors of an entity would not issue valuable consideration for nothing, something must have been received. *[IFRS 2.BC18C]*. IFRS 2 suggests that a transfer of equity under BEE and similar schemes is made 'as a means of enhancing [the entity's] image as a good corporate citizen'. *[IFRS 2 IG Example 1]*.

There seems little doubt that this aspect of IFRS 2 is in part an 'anti-avoidance' measure. As discussed in 4 to 8 below, the general measurement rule in IFRS 2 is that share-based payment transactions with employees are measured by reference to the fair value of the consideration given and those with non-employees by reference to the fair value of the consideration received. We argue at 5.2.2 below that the requirement to measure transactions with employees by reference to the consideration given is essentially an anti-avoidance provision. It prevents entities from recognising a low cost for employee share options on the grounds that little incremental service is provided for them beyond that already provided for cash-based remuneration. The changes introduced by IFRIC 8 removed the potential for a similar abuse in accounting for transactions with non-employees.

Nevertheless, the IASB acknowledges that there may be rare circumstances in which a transaction may occur in which no goods or services are received by the entity. For example, a principal shareholder of an entity, for reasons of estate planning, may transfer shares to a relative. In the absence of indications that the relative has provided, or is expected to provide, goods or services to the entity in exchange for the shares, such a transfer would be outside the scope of IFRS 2. *[IFRS 2.BC18D]*.

See also the discussions at 2.2.3.A below relating to transactions with shareholders in their capacity as such and at 2.2.4.K below relating to dual pricing on a share issue.

2.2.2.D 'All employee' share plans

Many countries encourage wider share-ownership by allowing companies to award a limited number of free or discounted shares to employees without either the employee or the employer incurring tax liabilities which would apply if other benefits in kind to an equivalent value were given to employees.

Some national accounting standards exempt some such plans from their scope, to some extent as the result of local political pressures. Prior to issuing IFRS 2, the IASB received some strong representations that IFRS should give a similar exemption, on the grounds that not to do so would discourage companies from continuing with such schemes.

The IASB concluded that such an exemption would be wrong in principle and difficult to draft in practice. By way of concession, the Basis for Conclusions hints that if the IFRS 2 charge for such schemes is (as asserted by some of the proponents of an exemption) *de minimis*, then there would be no charge under IFRS 2 anyway, since, like all IFRSs, it applies only to material items. *[IFRS 2.BC8-17]*. However, our experience is that, in many cases, the charge is material.

2.2.2.E   Vested transactions

Once a transaction accounted for under IFRS 2 has vested in the counterparty (see 3 below), it does not necessarily cease to be in the scope of IFRS 2 just because the entity has received the goods or services required for the award to vest. This is made clear by the numerous provisions of IFRS 2 referring to the accounting treatment of vested awards.

Once equity shares have been unconditionally delivered or beneficially transferred to the counterparty (e.g. as the result of the vesting of an award of ordinary shares, or the exercise of a vested option over ordinary shares), the holder of those shares will often be in exactly the same position as any other holder of ordinary shares and the shares will generally be accounted for under IAS 32 and IFRS 9 rather than IFRS 2.

If, however, the holder of a share or vested option enjoys rights not applicable to all holders of that class of share, such as a right to put the share or the option to the entity for cash, or holds a special class of share with rights that do not apply to other classes of equity, the share or option might still remain in the scope of IFRS 2 as long as any such rights continue to apply. The same is true of modifications made after vesting which add such rights to a vested share or option or otherwise alter the life of the share-based payment transaction. The special terms or rights will often be linked to the holder's employment with the entity but could also apply to an arrangement with a non-employee.

The significance of this is that issued equity instruments and financial liabilities not within the scope of IFRS 2 would typically fall within the scope of IAS 32 and IFRS 9, which might require a significantly different accounting treatment from that required by IFRS 2. See, for example:

- the discussion at 2.2.4.B below of the treatment in consolidated financial statements of an award with a right to put the share to the parent entity;
- the discussion at 2.2.4.G below which highlights that a share option with a foreign currency strike price is accounted for as an equity instrument under IFRS 2, but as a liability under IAS 32 and IFRS 9; and
- the discussion at 10.1.6 below of the treatment of convertible instruments issued in exchange for goods and services and accounted for under IFRS 2 rather than under IAS 32 and IFRS 9.

2.2.3   Transactions not within the scope of IFRS 2

The following transactions are outside the scope of IFRS 2:

- transactions with shareholders as a whole and with shareholders in their capacity as such (see 2.2.3.A below);
- transfers of assets in certain group restructuring arrangements (see 2.2.3.B below);
- business combinations (see 2.2.3.C below);
- combinations of businesses under common control and the contribution of a business to form a joint venture (see 2.2.3.D below); and
- transactions in the scope of IAS 32 and IFRS 9 (see 2.2.3.E below).

In addition, the scope exemptions in IFRS 2 combined with those in IAS 32 and IFRS 9 appear to have the effect that there is no specific guidance in IFRS for accounting for certain types of investment when acquired in return for shares (see 2.2.3.F below).

As noted at 2.2.2.D above, there is no exemption from IFRS 2 for share schemes aimed mainly at lower- and middle-ranking employees, referred to in different jurisdictions by terms such as 'all-employee share schemes', 'employee share purchase plans' and 'broad-based plans'.

2.2.3.A   Transactions with shareholders in their capacity as such

IFRS 2 does not apply to transactions with employees (and others) purely in their capacity as shareholders. For example, an employee may already hold shares in the entity as a result of previous share-based payment transactions. If the entity then raises funds through a rights issue, for example, whereby all shareholders (including the employee) can acquire additional shares for less than the current fair value of the shares, such a transaction is not a share-based payment transaction for the purposes of IFRS 2. *[IFRS 2.4].*

2.2.3.B   Transfer of assets in group restructuring arrangements

In some group restructuring arrangements, one entity will transfer a group of net assets, which does not meet the definition of a business, to another entity in return for shares. Careful consideration of the precise facts and circumstances is needed in order to determine whether, for the separate or individual financial statements of any entity affected by the transfer, such a transfer falls within the scope of IFRS 2. If the transfer is considered primarily to be a transfer of goods by their owner in return for payment in shares then, in our view, this should be accounted for under IFRS 2. However, if the transaction is for another purpose and is driven by the group shareholder in its capacity as such, the transaction may be outside the scope of IFRS 2 (see 2.2.3.A above). Accounting for intra-group asset transfers in return for shares is considered further in Chapter 8 at 4.4.1.

2.2.3.C   Business combinations

IFRS 2 does not apply to share-based payments to acquire goods (such as inventories or property, plant and equipment) as part of a business combination to which IFRS 3 applies.

However, the Interpretations Committee has clarified that in a reverse acquisition involving an entity that does not constitute a business (i.e. an asset acquisition or the provision of a service), IFRS 2 rather than IFRS 3 is likely to apply (see Chapter 9 at 14.8).[11]

Transactions in which equity instruments are issued to acquire goods as part of the net assets in a business combination are outside the scope of IFRS 2 but equity instruments granted to the employees of the acquiree in their capacity as employees (e.g. in return for continued service following the business combination) are within its scope, as are the cancellation, replacement or modification of a share-based payment transaction as a result of the business combination or other equity restructuring (see 11 and 12.8 below). *[IFRS 2.5].*

Thus, if a vendor of an acquired business remains as an employee of that business following the business combination and receives a share-based payment for transferring control of the entity and for remaining in continuing employment, it is necessary to determine how much of the share-based payment relates to the acquisition of control (which forms part of the cost of the combination, accounted for under IFRS 3) and how much relates to the provision of future services (which is a post-combination operating expense accounted for under IFRS 2). Guidance on this issue is given in IFRS 3 – see Chapter 9 at 11.2 – and there is discussion of related issues at 2.2.4.B below.

2.2.3.D Common control transactions and formation of joint arrangements

IFRS 2 also does not apply to a combination of entities or businesses under common control (see Chapter 10), or the contribution of a business on the formation of a joint venture as defined by IFRS 11 – *Joint Arrangements* (see Chapter 12). *[IFRS 2.5]*.

It should be noted that the contribution of non-financial assets (which do not constitute a business) to a joint venture in return for shares is within the scope of IFRS 2 and the assets should be accounted for at fair value in accordance with IFRS 2 (see 2.2.2 above).

IFRS 2 does not directly address other types of transactions involving joint ventures or transactions involving associates, particularly arrangements relating to the employees of associates or joint ventures. These are discussed further at 12.9 below.

2.2.3.E Transactions in the scope of IAS 32 and IFRS 9

IFRS 2 does not apply to transactions within the scope of IAS 32 and IFRS 9 (see Chapter 45). For example, if an entity enters into a share-based payment transaction to purchase a commodity surplus to its production requirements or with a view to short-term profit taking, the contract is treated as a financial instrument under IAS 32 and IFRS 9 rather than a share-based payment transaction under IFRS 2. *[IFRS 2.6]*.

Some practical examples of scope issues involving IFRS 2 and IAS 32/IFRS 9 are discussed at 2.2.4 below.

2.2.3.F Transactions in financial assets outside the scope of IAS 32 and IFRS 9

As noted at 2.2.2 above, IFRS 2 applies to share-based payment transactions involving goods or services, with 'goods' defined so as to exclude financial assets, presumably on the basis that these fall within IAS 32 and IFRS 9. However, investments in subsidiaries, associates and joint ventures in the separate financial statements of the investing entity are financial assets as defined in IAS 32 (and hence outside the scope of IFRS 2) but are outside the scope of IFRS 9 where the entity chooses to account for them at cost (see Chapter 8 at 2.1 and Chapter 45 at 3.1).

Moreover, IFRS has no general requirements for accounting for the issue of equity instruments. Rather, consistent with the position taken by the *Conceptual Framework* that equity is a residual rather than an item 'in its own right', the amount of an equity instrument is normally measured by reference to the item (expense or asset) in consideration for which the equity is issued, as determined in accordance with IFRS applicable to that other item.

This means that, when (as is commonly the case) an entity acquires an investment in a subsidiary, associate or joint venture in return for the issue of equity instruments, there is no explicit guidance in IFRS as to the required accounting in the separate financial statements of the investor, and in particular as to how the 'cost' of such an item is to be determined. This is discussed further in Chapter 8 at 2.1.1.A.

2.2.4 Some practical applications of the scope requirements

This section addresses the application of the scope requirements of IFRS 2 to a number of situations frequently encountered in practice:

- remuneration in non-equity shares and arrangements with put rights over equity shares (see 2.2.4.A below);
- the treatment in the consolidated accounts of the parent of an equity-settled award of a subsidiary with a put option against the parent (see 2.2.4.B below);
- an increase in the counterparty's ownership interest with no change in the number of shares held (see 2.2.4.C below);
- awards for which the counterparty has paid 'fair value' (see 2.2.4.D below);
- a cash bonus which depends on share price performance (see 2.2.4.E below);
- cash-settled awards based on an entity's 'enterprise value' or other formula (see 2.2.4.F below);
- awards with a foreign currency strike price (see 2.2.4.G below);
- holding own shares to satisfy or 'hedge' awards (see 2.2.4.H below);
- shares or warrants issued in connection with a loan or other financial liability (see 2.2.4.I below);
- options over puttable instruments classified as equity under the specific exception in IAS 32 in the absence of other equity instruments (see 2.2.4.J below); and
- special discounts to certain categories of investor on a share issue (see 2.2.4.K below).

The following aspects of the scope requirements are covered elsewhere in this chapter:

- employment taxes on share-based payment transactions (see 14 below); and
- instruments such as limited recourse loans and convertible bonds that sometimes fall within the scope of IFRS 2 rather than IAS 32/IFRS 9 because of the link both to the entity's equity instruments and to goods or services received in exchange. Convertible bonds are discussed at 10.1.6 below and limited recourse loans at 15.2 below.

2.2.4.A Remuneration in non-equity shares and arrangements with put rights over equity shares

A transaction is within the scope of IFRS 2 only where it involves the delivery of an equity instrument, or cash or other assets based on the price or value of an 'equity instrument', in return for goods or services (see 2.2.1 above).

In some jurisdictions, there can be fiscal advantages in giving an employee, in lieu of a cash payment, a share that carries a right to a 'one-off' dividend, or is mandatorily redeemable, at an amount equivalent to the intended cash payment. Such a share would almost certainly be classified as a liability under IAS 32 (see Chapter 47). Payment in such a share would not fall in the scope of IFRS 2 since the consideration paid by the entity for services received is a financial liability rather than meeting the definition of an equity instrument (see the definitions in 2.2.1 above).

If, however, the amount of remuneration delivered in this way were equivalent to the value of a particular number of equity instruments issued by the entity, then the transaction would be in scope of IFRS 2 as a cash-settled share-based payment transaction, since the entity would have incurred a liability (i.e. by issuing the redeemable shares) for an amount based on the price of its equity instruments.

Similarly, if an entity grants an award of equity instruments to an employee together with a put right whereby the employee can require the entity to purchase those shares for an amount based on their fair value, both elements of that transaction are in the scope of IFRS 2 as a single cash-settled transaction (see 9 below). This is notwithstanding the fact that, under IAS 32, the share and the put right might well be analysed as a single synthetic instrument and classified as a liability with no equity component (see Chapter 47).

Differences in the classification of instruments between IFRS 2 and IAS 32 are discussed further at 1.4.1 above.

Put options over instruments that are only classified as equity in limited circumstances (in accordance with paragraphs 16A to 16B of IAS 32) are discussed at 2.2.4.J below.

2.2.4.B Equity-settled award of subsidiary with put option against the parent – treatment in consolidated accounts of parent

It is sometimes the case that a subsidiary entity grants an award over its own equity instruments and, either on the same date or later, the parent entity separately grants the same counterparty a put option to sell the equity instruments of the subsidiary to the parent for a cash amount based on the fair value of the equity instruments. Accounting for such an arrangement in the separate financial statements of the subsidiary and the parent will be determined in accordance with the general principles of IFRS 2 (see 2.2.2.A above). However, IFRS 2 does not explicitly address the accounting treatment of all such arrangements in the parent's consolidated financial statements.

In our view, the analysis differs according to whether the put option is granted during or after the vesting period and whether it relates to ordinary shares or to share options.

If the put option is granted during the vesting period (whether at the same time as the grant of the equity instruments or later), the two transactions should be treated as linked and accounted for in the consolidated financial statements as a single cash-settled transaction from the date the put option is granted. This reflects the fact that this situation is similar in group terms to a modification of an award to add a cash-settlement alternative – see 10.1.4 below.

If the put option is only granted once the equity instruments have vested, the accounting will depend on whether the equity instruments in the original share-based payment transaction are unexercised options or whether they are ordinary shares.

If they are unexercised options, the vested options remain within the scope of IFRS 2 until they are exercised (see 2.2.2.E above) and, in this case, the put option should be treated as a linked transaction. Its effect in group terms is to modify the original award from an equity- to a cash-settled transaction until final settlement date.

However, if the equity instruments are fully vested ordinary shares (whether free shares or shares from the exercise of options), rather than unexercised options, they are generally no longer within the scope of IFRS 2 as they are no different from any other ordinary shares issued by the subsidiary. In such cases, the parent entity will need to evaluate whether or not the grant of the put option, as a separate transaction which modifies the terms of certain of the subsidiary's equity instruments, falls within the scope of IFRS 2. For example, the addition of a condition that relates to one (non-controlling) shareholder of a subsidiary might indicate that it continues to be appropriate to account for the arrangement in accordance with the requirements of IFRS 2. By contrast, a modification to an entire class of ordinary shares would generally not be within the scope of IFRS 2.

A similar analysis is required in a situation where an individual sells a controlling interest in an entity for fair value and put and call options are granted over the individual's remaining non-controlling interest or over shares in the acquirer which have been given to the individual in return for the business acquired. To the extent that the exercise price of the call option depends on the fulfilment of a service condition in the period following the acquisition of the controlling interest, it is likely that the arrangement will fall within the scope of IFRS 2 with any payments contingent on future services recognised as compensation costs.

Put options over non-controlling interests that do not fall within the scope of IFRS 2 are addressed in Chapter 7 at 6.2.

2.2.4.C   Increase in ownership interest with no change in number of shares held

An arrangement typically found in entities with venture capital investors is one where an employee (often part of the key management) subscribes initially for, say, 1% of the entity's equity with the venture capitalist holding the other 99%. The employee's equity interest will subsequently increase by a variable amount depending on the extent to which certain targets are met. This is achieved not by issuing new shares but by cancelling some of the venture capitalist's shares. In our view, such an arrangement falls within the scope of IFRS 2 as the employee is rewarded with an increased equity stake in the entity if certain targets are achieved. The increased equity stake is consistent with the definition in Appendix A of IFRS 2 of an equity instrument as 'a contract that evidences a residual interest ...' notwithstanding the fact that no additional shares are issued.

In such arrangements, it is often asserted that the employee has subscribed for a share of the equity at fair value. However, the subscription price paid must represent a fair value using an IFRS 2 valuation basis in order for there to be no additional IFRS 2 expense to recognise (see 2.2.4.D below).

2.2.4.D   Awards for which the counterparty has paid 'fair value'

In certain situations, such as where a special class of share is issued, the counterparty might be asked to subscribe a certain amount for the share which is agreed as being its 'fair value' for taxation or other purposes. This does not mean that such arrangements fall outside the scope of IFRS 2, either for measurement or disclosure purposes, if the arrangement meets the definition of a share-based payment transaction. In many cases, the agreed 'fair value' will be lower than a fair value measured in accordance with IFRS 2 because it will reflect the impact of service and non-market performance vesting conditions which are excluded from an IFRS 2 fair value. This is addressed in more detail at 15.4.5 below.

2.2.4.E Cash bonus dependent on share price performance

An entity might agree to pay its employees a €100 cash bonus if its share price remains at €10 or more over a given period. Intuitively, this appears to be within the scope of IAS 19 – *Employee Benefits* – rather than that of IFRS 2 because the employee is not being given cash of equivalent value to a particular number of shares. However, it could be argued that it does fall within the scope of IFRS 2 on the basis that the entity has incurred a liability, and the amount of that liability is 'based on' the share price (in accordance with the definition of a cash-settled share-based payment transaction) – it is nil if the share price is below €10 and €100 if the share price is €10 or more. In our view, either interpretation is acceptable.

2.2.4.F Cash-settled awards based on an entity's 'enterprise value' or other formula

As noted at 2.2.1 above, IFRS 2 includes within its scope transactions in which the entity acquires goods or services by incurring a liability 'based on the price (or value) of equity instruments (including shares or share options) of the entity or another group entity'. Employees of an unquoted entity may receive a cash award based on the value of the equity of that entity. Such awards are typically, but not exclusively, made by venture capital investors to the management of entities in which they have invested and which they aim to sell in the medium term. Further discussion of the accounting implications of awards made in connection with an exit event may be found at 15.4 below.

More generally, where employees of an unquoted entity receive a cash award based on the value of the equity, there is no quoted share price and an 'enterprise value' has therefore to be calculated as a surrogate for it. This begs the question of whether such awards are within the scope of IFRS 2 (because they are based on the value of the entity's equity) or that of IAS 19.

In order for an award to be within the scope of IFRS 2, any calculated 'enterprise value' must represent the fair value of the entity's equity. Where the calculation uses techniques recognised by IFRS 2 as yielding a fair value for equity instruments (as discussed at 8 below), we believe that the award should be regarded as within the scope of IFRS 2.

Appendix B of IFRS 2 notes that an unquoted entity may have calculated the value of its equity based on net assets or earnings (see 8.5.3.B below). *[IFRS 2.B30]*. In our view, this is not intended to imply that it is always appropriate to do so, but simply to note that it may be appropriate in some cases.

Where, for example, the enterprise value is based on a constant formula, such as a fixed multiple of earnings before interest, tax, depreciation and amortisation ('EBITDA'), in our view it is unlikely that this will represent a good surrogate for the fair value of the equity on an ongoing basis, even if it did so at the inception of the transaction. It is not difficult to imagine scenarios in which the fair value of the equity of an entity could be affected with no significant change in EBITDA, for example as a result of changes in interest rates and effective tax rates, or a significant impairment of assets. Alternatively, there might be a significant shift in the multiple of EBITDA equivalent to fair value, for example if the entity were to create or acquire a significant item of intellectual property.

For an award by an individual entity, there is unlikely to be any significant difference in the cost ultimately recorded under IFRS 2 or IAS 19. However, the disclosure requirements of IFRS 2 are more onerous than those of IAS 19. In a group situation where the parent entity grants the award to the employees of a subsidiary, the two standards could result in different levels of expense in the books of the subsidiary because IAS 19, unlike IFRS 2, does not require the employing subsidiary to recognise an expense for a transaction which it has no direct obligation to settle and for which the parent does not allocate the cost (see Chapter 35 at 2.2.2).

The accounting treatment of awards based on the 'market price' of an unquoted subsidiary or business unit – where there is no actual market for the shares – raises similar issues about whether an equity value is being used, as discussed more fully at 15.6 below.

2.2.4.G Awards with a foreign currency strike price

Many entities award their employees options with a foreign currency strike price. This will arise most commonly in a multinational group where employees of overseas subsidiaries are granted options on terms that they can pay the option strike price in their local currency. Such awards may also arise where an entity, which has a functional currency different from that of the country in which it operates (e.g. an oil company based in the United Kingdom with a functional currency of United States dollars), grants its UK-based employees options with a strike price in pounds sterling, which is a foreign currency from the perspective of the currency of the financial statements.

Under IAS 32, as currently interpreted, such an award could not be regarded as an equity instrument because the strike price to be tendered is not a fixed amount of the reporting entity's own currency (see Chapter 47 at 5.2.3). However, under IFRS 2, as discussed at 2.2.1 above, equity instruments include options, which are defined as the right to acquire shares for a 'fixed or determinable price'. Moreover, it is quite clear from the Basis for Conclusions in IFRS 2 that an award which ultimately results in an employee receiving equity is equity-settled under IFRS 2 whatever its status under IAS 32 might be (see 1.4.1 above). Thus, an option over equity with a foreign currency strike price is an equity instrument if accounted for under IFRS 2.

The fair value of such an award should be assessed at grant date and, where the award is treated as equity-settled, should not subsequently be revised for foreign exchange movements (on the basis that the equity instrument is a non-monetary item translated using the exchange rate at the date when the fair value was measured). This applies to the separate financial statements of a parent or subsidiary entity as well as to consolidated financial statements. Where the award is treated as cash-settled, however, the periodic reassessment through profit or loss of the fair value of the award required by IFRS 2 will also need to take into account any exchange difference arising from the requirements of IAS 21 – *The Effects of Changes in Foreign Exchange Rates*.

2.2.4.H Holding own shares to satisfy or 'hedge' awards

Entities often seek to hedge the cost of share-based payment transactions, most commonly by buying their own equity instruments in the market. For example, an entity could grant an employee options over 10,000 shares and buy 10,000 of its own shares into treasury at the date that the award is made. If the award is share-settled, the entity will deliver the shares to the counterparty. If it is cash-settled, it can sell the shares to raise the cash it is required to deliver to the counterparty. In either case, the cash cost of the award is capped at the market price of the shares at the date the award is made, less any amount paid by the employee on exercise. It could of course be argued that such an arrangement is not a true hedge at all. If the share price goes down so that the option is never exercised, the entity is left holding 10,000 of its own shares that cost more than they are now worth.

Whilst these strategies may cap the cash cost of share-based payment transactions that are eventually exercised, they will not have any effect on the charge to profit or loss required by IFRS 2 for such transactions. This is because purchases and sales of own shares are accounted for as movements in equity and are therefore never included in profit or loss (see 4.1 below).

The illustrative examples of group share schemes at 12.4 and 12.5 below show the interaction of the accounting required for a holding of own shares and the requirements of IFRS 2.

2.2.4.I   Shares or warrants issued in connection with a loan or other financial liability

As noted at 2.2.3.E above, IFRS 2 does not apply to transactions within the scope of IAS 32 and IFRS 9. However, if shares or warrants are granted by a borrower to a lender as part of a loan or other financing arrangement, the measurement of those shares or warrants might fall within the scope of IFRS 2. The determination of the relevant standard is likely to require significant judgement based on the precise terms of individual transactions. If the shares or warrants are considered to be granted by the borrower in lieu of a cash fee for services provided by the lender then IFRS 2 is likely to be the appropriate standard, but if the shares or warrants are considered instead to be part of the overall return to the lender on the financing arrangement then IAS 32 and IFRS 9 are more likely to apply.

2.2.4.J   Options over puttable instruments classified as equity under specific exception in IAS 32

Some entities, such as certain types of trust, issue tradeable puttable instruments that are classified as equity instruments rather than as a financial liability because the entity has no other equity instruments. This classification is based on a specific exception in IAS 32 that makes it clear that such instruments are not equity instruments for the purposes of IFRS 2. *[IAS 32.16A-16B, 96C]*. However, should options over such instruments granted to employees – and allowing them to obtain the instruments at a discount to the market price – be treated as cash-settled awards under IFRS 2 or are they outside the scope of IFRS 2 and within that of IAS 19?

The entity has no equity apart from the instruments classified as such under the narrow exception in IAS 32 and, in the absence of equity, the entity cannot logically issue equity instruments in satisfaction of an award to employees nor can it pay cash based on the price or value of its equity instruments. In our view, paragraph 96C of IAS 32 should be interpreted as meaning that, for the purposes of IFRS 2, such awards are not share-based payments and the appropriate standard is IAS 19 rather than IFRS 2.

Those who take the view that such options could be cash-settled share-based payments seem to rely more on the general IAS 32 definition of equity than on the more specific requirements of paragraph 96C of IAS 32 (that 'these instruments should not be considered as equity instruments under IFRS 2'). We believe that the more specific guidance should take precedence over the general definition.

2.2.4.K   Special discounts to certain categories of investor on a share issue

In the context of a flotation or other equity fundraising, an entity might offer identical shares at different prices to institutional investors and to individual (retail) investors. Should the additional discount given to one class of investor be accounted for under IFRS 2 as representing unidentified goods or services received or receivable?

The Interpretations Committee was asked to clarify the accounting treatment in this area. The request submitted to the Committee referred to the fact that the final retail price could differ from the institutional price because of:

- an unintentional difference arising from the book-building process; or
- an intentional difference arising from a retail discount given by the issuer of the equity instruments as indicated in the prospectus.

For example, a discount to the institutional investor price might need to be offered to encourage retail investors to buy shares in order to meet the requirements of a particular stock exchange for an entity to have a minimum number of shareholders.

The Interpretations Committee considered whether the discount offered to retail investors in the above example involves the receipt of identifiable or unidentifiable goods or services from the retail shareholder group and, therefore, whether the discount is a share-based payment transaction within the scope of IFRS 2.

IFRS 2 was specifically amended for situations where the identifiable consideration received by the entity appears to be less than the fair value of the equity instruments granted (see 2.2.2.C above). *[IFRS 2.2, 13A]*. The Interpretations Committee noted that the application of this guidance requires judgement and consideration of the specific facts and circumstances of each transaction.

In the circumstances underlying the submission to the Interpretations Committee, the Committee observed that the entity issues shares at two different prices to two different groups of investors for the purpose of raising funds. Any difference in price between the two groups appears to relate to the existence of different markets – one accessible only to retail investors and the other accessible only to institutional investors – rather than to the receipt of additional goods or services. The only relationships involved are those between the investors and the investee entity and the investors are acting in their capacity as shareholders.

The Interpretations Committee therefore observed that the guidance in IFRS 2 is not applicable because there is no share-based payment transaction.

A distinction was drawn between the example above and a situation considered by the Interpretations Committee in 2013 (accounting for reverse acquisitions that do not constitute a business – see 2.2.3.C above). In the latter situation, a stock exchange listing received by the accounting acquirer was considered to be a service received from the accounting acquiree and to represent the difference between the fair value of the equity instruments issued and the identifiable net assets acquired. Hence an IFRS 2 expense would be required in order to recognise this difference. In the situation relating to retail and institutional investors considered above, however, there is no service element and the difference in prices for the two different types of investor is due solely to an investor-investee relationship rather than to unidentifiable goods or services received from the investors.

At its July 2014 meeting the Interpretations Committee decided not to add this matter to its agenda on the basis that sufficient guidance exists without further interpretation or the need for an amendment to a standard.[12]

In other situations, an entity might voluntarily offer a discount to one class of investor, e.g. to an institution underwriting the share issue. In our view, this type of discount is likely to require an IFRS 2 expense to be recognised unless there is evidence that separate prices, and therefore different fair values, are required for each category of investor.

However, in some cases – such as the example above where an institution provides underwriting services – it might be possible to conclude that any additional cost under IFRS 2 is actually a cost of issuing the equity instruments and should therefore be debited to equity rather than to profit or loss.

Similar considerations to those discussed in this section apply when, in advance of an IPO, a private company issues convertible instruments at a discount to their fair value in order both to attract key investors and to boost working capital. There is further discussion on convertible instruments at 10.1.6 below.

3 GENERAL RECOGNITION PRINCIPLES

The recognition rules in IFRS 2 are based on a so-called 'service date model'. In other words, IFRS 2 requires the goods or services received or acquired in a share-based payment transaction to be recognised when the goods are acquired or the services rendered. *[IFRS 2.7]*. For awards to employees (or others providing similar services), this contrasts with the measurement rules, which normally require a share-based payment transaction to be measured as at the date on which the transaction was entered into, which may be some time before or after the related services are received – see 4 to 7 below.

Where the goods or services received or acquired in exchange for a share-based payment transaction do not qualify for recognition as assets they should be expensed. *[IFRS 2.8]*. The standard notes that typically services will not qualify as assets and should therefore be expensed immediately, whereas goods will generally be recognised initially as assets and expensed later as they are consumed. However, some payments for services may be capitalised (e.g. as part of the cost of PP&E, intangible assets or inventories) and some payments for goods may be expensed immediately (e.g. where they are for items included within development costs written off as incurred). *[IFRS 2.9]*.

The corresponding credit entry is, in the case of an equity-settled transaction, an increase in equity and, in the case of a cash-settled transaction, a liability (or decrease in cash or other assets). *[IFRS 2.7]*.

The primary focus of the discussion in the remainder of this chapter is the application of these rules to transactions with employees. The accounting treatment of transactions with non-employees is addressed further at 5.1 and 5.4 below.

3.1 Vesting conditions

Under IFRS 2, the point at which a cost is recognised for goods or services depends on the concept of 'vesting'. The following definitions in Appendix A to IFRS 2 are relevant.

A share-based payment to a counterparty is said to *vest* when it becomes an entitlement of the counterparty. Under IFRS 2, a share-based payment arrangement vests when the counterparty's entitlement is no longer conditional on the satisfaction of any vesting conditions. *[IFRS 2 Appendix A]*.

A *vesting condition* is a condition that determines whether the entity receives the services that entitle the counterparty to receive cash, other assets or equity instruments of the entity, under a share-based payment arrangement. A vesting condition is either a service condition or a performance condition. *[IFRS 2 Appendix A]*.

A *service condition* is a vesting condition that requires the counterparty to complete a specified period of service during which services are provided to the entity. If the counterparty, regardless of the reason, ceases to provide service during the vesting period, it has failed to satisfy the condition. A service condition does not require a performance target to be met. *[IFRS 2 Appendix A]*. For example, if an employee is granted a share option with a service condition of remaining in employment with an entity for three years, the award vests three years after the date of grant if the employee is still employed by the entity at that date.

A *performance condition* is a vesting condition that requires:

(a) the counterparty to complete a specified period of service (i.e. a service condition); the service requirement can be explicit or implicit; and

(b) specified performance target(s) to be met while the counterparty is rendering the service required in (a).

The period of achieving the performance target(s):

(a) shall not extend beyond the end of the service period; and

(b) may start before the service period on the condition that the commencement date of the performance target is not substantially before the commencement of the service period.

A performance target is defined by reference to:

(a) the entity's own operations (or activities) or the operations or activities of another entity in the same group (i.e. a non-market condition); or

(b) the price (or value) of the entity's equity instruments or the equity instruments of another entity in the same group (including shares and share options) (i.e. a market condition).

A performance target might relate either to the performance of the entity as a whole or to some part of the entity (or part of the group), such as a division or individual employee. *[IFRS 2 Appendix A]*.

The definition of a *market condition* is included at 6.3 below.

In order for a condition to be a vesting condition – rather than a 'non-vesting' condition (see 3.2 below) – there must be a service requirement and any additional performance target must relate to the entity or to some part of the entity or group. Thus a condition that an award vests if, in three years' time, earnings per share has increased by 10% and the employee is still in employment, is a performance condition. If, however, the award becomes unconditional in three years' time if earnings per share has increased by 10%, irrespective of whether the employee is still in employment, that condition is not a performance condition but a non-vesting condition because there is no associated service requirement.

The different types of performance condition and the related accounting requirements are discussed more fully at 6 below. The distinction between vesting and non-vesting conditions is discussed at 3.2 below.

The accounting treatment in a situation where the counterparty fails to meet a service condition – a situation now explicitly covered by the definition of a service condition above – is considered in more detail at 7.4.1.A below.

In addition to the general discussion throughout section 3, specific considerations relating to awards that vest on a flotation or change of control (or similar exit event) are addressed at 15.4 below.

The definitions of 'vesting condition', 'service condition' and 'performance condition' reproduced above reflect the amendments in the IASB's *Annual Improvements to IFRSs 2010-2012 Cycle* aimed at clarifying the distinction between different types of condition attached to a share-based payment (see 1.2 above).

3.1.1 'Malus' clauses and clawback conditions

Whether as a result of an entity's own decision or in response to regulatory requirements, an increasing number of share-based payment awards include conditions that mean that the awards will only vest if there is no breach of any 'malus' clause on the part of the employee and/or the entity. Often these or other provisions are put in place to allow an entity to claw back vested awards from employees should any wrongdoing or underperformance be identified.

The impact of such clauses on the accounting treatment required by IFRS 2 depends on the precise terms of a particular arrangement. Aspects of arrangements that entities will need to consider include the following:

- whether the terms are sufficiently clear at the inception of the arrangement that there can still be a grant in IFRS 2 terms (see 5.3 below for further discussion of the requirements relating to grant date);
- whether the malus clause relates only to the actions of the individual employee (so-called 'at fault' malus) and whether the relevant period for consideration of the condition is limited to the vesting period or extends over a longer period;
- whether the malus clause relates only to the overall performance of the entity (so-called 'not at fault' malus) and, again, the applicable period during which the clause may be invoked; and
- whether the associated clawback arrangements are clear or depend on further decisions by the entity at the time the relevant 'malus' clause is invoked.

Broadly, it is likely to be the case that there will be a grant at inception provided the terms of the malus and clawback arrangements are sufficiently clear for there to be a shared understanding of the arrangements by both parties.

If the employee's ultimate entitlement to an award depends on an 'at fault' malus clause not being invoked, this is generally likely to be taken into account as part of any service vesting condition. If the condition extends beyond the usual vesting date of the award and the employee breaches the condition after the end of the vesting period, the vested awards will be treated as a cancellation under IFRS 2 (but there would be no impact on the expense already recognised for a vested award).

Depending on the precise terms, the assessment of a 'not at fault' malus clause is likely to require greater judgement. To the extent that the entity's overall performance formed part of the conditions on which the award would vest, it seems appropriate to treat the condition as part of a performance vesting condition. To the extent that a 'not at fault' malus clause could result in the clawback of an award after the end of the vesting period, there would need to be an assessment of how the identified fault or wrongdoing interacted with the position of the entity as previously determined at the end of the vesting period. The fault might relate solely to a situation that should have prevented the original vesting of the award (for example, a restatement of accounts relating to the vesting period) or it might be a more general condition relating to the ongoing performance of the entity.

If the condition extended beyond the service period, the entity would need to consider whether the award had a non-vesting condition from inception (see 3.2 below). However, given the nature of the condition, in our view it would be unlikely that there would be a significant reduction, if any, in the fair value of the award as a consequence of the non-vesting condition.

3.1.2 Vesting conditions based on an employee's performance rating

An entity may grant awards to employees that vest based on conditions that include the employee's performance rating. A performance rating would appear to meet the definition of a non-market performance condition in that it is a vesting condition that requires an employee to render service for a period of time and to achieve a specified performance rating while providing the service in employment of the entity (see 3.1 above). Performance ratings can be influenced by the judgement of the individual(s) conducting an employee's evaluation, therefore, the question often arises whether the inherent subjectivity of a performance evaluation could delay the grant date for the award (see 5.3 below). The impact of such condition on the accounting treatment required by IFRS 2 depends on the framework that is established by the entity to facilitate an employee's understanding of how their performance will be measured. A framework that clearly articulates criteria and includes more objective measures is more likely to result in a more predictive outcome and, thus likely a non-market performance condition. On the contrary, a framework that contains more subjective measures that provide less clarity and is less predictive of the outcome, would not. The following are aspects of the framework that should be considered in making the determination:

- whether the criteria is sufficiently clear at the inception of the share-based payment arrangement such that there is a mutual understanding between the entity and the employee about how it will be measured;
- whether the criteria relates only to the performance of the individual employee or the employee's performance relative to their peers, over the relevant measurement period; and
- whether the employee is able to predict the outcome under the related performance rating framework, given the set criteria.

In certain cases, the number of instruments underlying the award might vary depending on the employee's performance relative to the criteria in the framework. The entity will be required to estimate the potential outcome during the performance period and to recognise the cost for the number of instruments that the employee is expected to be entitled based on their performance rating (see 6.2.4 below).

3.2 Non-vesting conditions (conditions that are neither service conditions nor performance conditions)

3.2.1 Background

Some share-based payment transactions, particularly those with employees, require the satisfaction of conditions that are neither service conditions nor performance conditions. For example, an employee might be given the right to 100 shares in three years' time, subject only to the employee not working in competition with the reporting entity during that time. An undertaking not to work for another entity does not 'determine whether the entity receives ... services' – the employee could sit on a beach for three years and still be entitled to collect the award. Accordingly, such a condition is not regarded as a vesting condition for the purposes of IFRS 2, but is instead referred to as a 'non-vesting condition'. The accounting treatment of non-vesting conditions is discussed in detail at 6.4 below.

IFRS 2 does not explicitly define a 'non-vesting condition' (see 3.2.2 below), but uses the term to describe a condition that is neither a service condition nor a performance condition. Sometimes the condition will be wholly within the control of the counterparty and unconnected with the delivery of services, such as a requirement to save (see below). However, the identification of such conditions is not always straightforward.

The concept of a 'non-vesting condition', like much of IFRS 2 itself, had its origins as an anti-avoidance measure. It arose from a debate on how to account for employee share option schemes linked to a savings contract. In some jurisdictions, options are awarded to an employee on condition that the employee works for a fixed minimum period and, during that period, makes regular contributions to a savings account, which is then used to exercise the option. The employee is entitled to withdraw from the savings contract before vesting, in which case the right to the award lapses.

Entities applying IFRS 2 as originally issued almost invariably treated an employee's obligation to save as a vesting condition. If the employee stopped saving this was treated as a failure to meet a vesting condition and accounted for as a forfeiture, with the reversal of any expense so far recorded (see 6.1 and 6.2 below).

Some saw in this a scope for abuse of the general principle of IFRS 2 that, if a share-based payment transaction is cancelled, any amount not yet expensed for it is immediately recognised in full (see 7.4 below). The concern was that, if such a plan were 'out of the money', the employer, rather than cancel the plan (and thereby trigger an acceleration of expense) would 'encourage' the employee to stop saving (and thereby create a reversal of any expense already charged).

The broad effect of the January 2008 amendment to IFRS 2 (see 1.2 above) was to remove this perceived anomaly from the standard.

However, following the publication of the January 2008 amendment, it became apparent that the concept of the 'non-vesting' condition was not clear. This resulted in differing views on the appropriate classification of certain types of condition depending on whether or not they were considered to be measures of the entity's performance or activities and hence performance vesting conditions.

The Interpretations Committee took a number of the above issues onto its agenda as part of a wider project on vesting and non-vesting conditions. Where the issues were not addressed through the IASB's *Annual Improvements to IFRSs 2010-2012 Cycle*, there is further discussion at 3.4 below.

3.2.2 Defining a non-vesting condition

As noted at 3.1 above, IFRS 2 defines a vesting condition as a condition that determines whether the entity receives the services that entitle the counterparty to receive payment in equity or cash. Performance conditions are those that require the counterparty to complete a specified period of service and specified performance targets to be met (such as a specified increase in the entity's profit over a specified period of time).

The Basis for Conclusions to IFRS 2 adds that the feature that distinguishes a performance condition from a non-vesting condition is that the former has an explicit or implicit service requirement and the latter does not. *[IFRS 2.BC171A]*.

In issuing its *Annual Improvements to IFRSs 2010-2012 Cycle* in December 2013 the IASB considered whether a definition of 'non-vesting condition' was needed. It decided that 'the creation of a stand-alone definition ... would not be the best alternative for providing clarity on this issue'. *[IFRS 2.BC364]*. Instead, it sought to provide further clarification in the Basis for Conclusions to IFRS 2, as follows:

'...the Board observed that the concept of a non-vesting condition can be inferred from paragraphs BC170-BC184 of IFRS 2, which clarify the definition of vesting conditions. In accordance with this guidance it can be inferred that a non-vesting condition is any condition that does not determine whether the entity receives the services that entitle the counterparty to receive cash, other assets or equity instruments of the entity under a share-based payment arrangement. In other words, a non-vesting condition is any condition that is not a vesting condition.' *[IFRS 2.BC364]*.

Although it is stated that the Basis for Conclusions does not form part of IFRS 2, the IASB nonetheless appears to rely on users of the standard referring to the Basis for Conclusions in order to 'infer' the definition of a non-vesting condition.

A performance metric may be a non-vesting condition rather than a vesting condition in certain circumstances. For a condition to be a performance vesting condition, it is not sufficient for the condition to be specific to the performance of the entity. There must also be an explicit or implied service condition that extends to the end of the performance period. For example, a condition that requires the entity's profit before tax or its share price to reach a minimum level, but without any requirement for the employee to remain in employment throughout the performance period, is not a performance condition but a non-vesting condition.

Specific examples of non-vesting conditions given by IFRS 2 include:
- a requirement to make monthly savings during the vesting period;
- a requirement for a commodity index to reach a minimum level;
- restrictions on the transfer of vested equity instruments; or
- an agreement not to work for a competitor after the award has vested – a 'non-compete' agreement (see 3.2.3 below). *[IFRS 2.BC171B, IG24].*

The IASB has also clarified in the Basis for Conclusions to IFRS 2 that a condition related to a share market index target (rather than to the specific performance of the entity's own shares) is a non-vesting condition because a share market index reflects not only the performance of an entity but also that of other entities outside the group. Even where an entity's share price makes up a substantial part of the share market index, the IASB confirmed that this would still be a non-vesting condition because it reflects the performance of other, non-group, entities. *[IFRS 2.BC353-BC358].*

Thus, whilst conditions that are not related to the performance of the entity are always, by their nature, non-vesting conditions, conditions that relate to the performance of the entity may or may not be non-vesting conditions depending on whether there is also a requirement for the counterparty to render service.

As noted at 3.1 above, the definition of a performance vesting condition was clarified and expanded in the IASB's *Annual Improvements*. The amended definition includes wording intended to clarify the extent to which the period of achieving the performance target(s) needs to coincide with the service period and states that this performance period:

(a) shall not extend beyond the end of the service period; and

(b) may start before the service period on the condition that the commencement date of the performance target is not substantially before the commencement of the service period.

During the process of finalising the amended definition, the IASB moved away from a requirement for the duration of the performance condition to fall wholly within the period of the related service requirement. In response to comments on the draft version of the *Annual Improvements*, the Board decided to make a late adjustment to clarify that the start of the performance period may be before the start of the service period, provided that the commencement date of the performance target is not substantially before the commencement of the service period. As stated in the definition above, however, the performance period may not extend beyond the end of the service period.

It is interesting to note that, in the US, the EITF also considered the question of non-coterminous service and performance conditions but, unlike the IASB, reached the conclusion that a performance target that affects the vesting of a share-based payment and that could be achieved after the requisite service period is a performance condition and does not need to be reflected in the fair value of the award at grant date.[13] This was on the premise that the original definition of a performance condition in ASC 718 – *Compensation – Stock Compensation* – requires only a specified period of service. Before finalising the amendments to IFRS 2, the IASB specifically reconfirmed its own decision against the background of the US decision.[14] This is therefore an area of difference between IFRS and US GAAP.

The late adjustment by the IASB goes some way towards removing an issue that is extremely common in practice, particularly with awards made to employees under a single scheme but at various times. The IASB gives the example of an earnings per share target as one of the areas in which respondents to the draft definitions observed that there could be a problem in practice, noting that the measure of earnings per share growth set as a performance target could often be that between the most recently published financial statements at grant date and those before the vesting date. *[IFRS 2.BC341]*. However, notwithstanding the amended definition, there clearly remains an element of judgement in the interpretation of 'substantially' as used in the definition.

There is further discussion of the accounting treatment of non-vesting conditions at 6.4 below.

3.2.3 Non-compete agreements

In some jurisdictions it is relatively common to have a non-compete clause in share-based payment arrangements so that if the counterparty starts to work for a competitor within a specified timescale, i.e. he breaches the non-compete provision, he is required to return the shares (or an equivalent amount of cash) to the entity. Generally, a non-compete provision is relevant once an individual has ceased employment with the entity and so no future service is expected to be provided to the entity. However, the non-compete provision is often found in share-based payment awards entered into while the individual is still an employee of the entity and when there is no current intention for employment to cease. There are two divergent views on how such non-compete arrangements should be accounted for under IFRS 2.

The Basis for Conclusions to IFRS 2 states that 'a share-based payment vests when the counterparty's entitlement to it is no longer conditional on future service or performance conditions. Therefore, conditions such as non-compete provisions and transfer restrictions, which apply after the counterparty has become entitled to the share-based payment, are not vesting conditions.' *[IFRS 2.BC171B]*.

One view is that, under the current definitions in the standard, this means that all non-compete agreements should be treated as non-vesting conditions with the condition reflected in the grant date fair value. Another reading of paragraph BC171B is that in some situations such arrangements meet the definition of a vesting condition and this allows any IFRS 2 expense to be reversed should the condition not be met. This view is explained further below. The lack of clarity in the standard as currently drafted means that there is diversity in practice.

Those who take the view that a non-compete arrangement is not always a non-vesting condition read paragraph BC171B as distinguishing between non-compete clauses which apply after the counterparty has become entitled to an award (a non-vesting condition) and those that, by implication, apply before the counterparty has become entitled to an award (a vesting condition). Broadly, therefore, if an employee has been given shares at the start of a non-compete period he is entitled to them (a non-vesting condition), but if the shares are retained by the entity or held in escrow, the employee is not entitled to the shares until the end of the non-compete period (a vesting condition).

This view may be difficult to reconcile with IFRS 2 as currently drafted because:

- it requires the reference to 'entitlement' to an award to be read as including a contingent obligation to forfeit the share, which is not in accordance with the general approach of IFRS 2; and
- it requires the words 'which apply after the counterparty has become entitled to the share-based payment' to be read with an implied emphasis on the word 'after', so as to distinguish it from an implied (unstated) alternative scenario in which the conditions apply before the counterparty becomes entitled to the share-based payment. A more natural reading is to consider these words as describing all non-compete agreements and transfer restrictions.

The classification of a non-compete provision is a matter that had been referred to the Interpretations Committee and to the IASB (see 3.4 below).

3.3 Vesting period

The *vesting period* is the period during which all the specified vesting conditions of a share-based payment arrangement are to be satisfied. *[IFRS 2 Appendix A]*. This is not the same as the exercise period or the life of the option, as illustrated by Example 34.1 below.

Example 34.1: Meaning of 'vesting period' – award with vesting conditions only

An employee is awarded options that can be exercised at any time between three and ten years from the date of the award, provided the employee remains in service for at least three years from the date of the award. For this award, the vesting period is three years; the exercise period is seven years; and the life of the option is ten years. However, as discussed further at 8 below, for the purposes of calculating the fair value of the award under IFRS 2, the life of the award is taken as the period ending with the date on which the counterparty is most likely actually to exercise the option, which may be some time before the full ten year life expires.

It is also important to distinguish between vesting conditions and other restrictions on the exercise of options and/or trading in shares, as illustrated by Example 34.2 below.

Example 34.2: Meaning of 'vesting period' – award with vesting and non-vesting conditions

An employee is awarded options that can be exercised at any time between five and ten years from the date of the award, provided the employee remains in service for at least three years from the date of the award. In this case, the vesting period remains three years as in Example 34.1 above, provided that the employee's entitlement to the award becomes absolute at the end of three years – in other words, the employee does not have to provide any services to the entity in years 4 and 5. The restriction on exercise of the award in the period after vesting is a non-vesting condition, which would be reflected in the original valuation of the award at the date of grant (see 4, 5 and 8 below).

The accounting implications of vesting conditions, non-vesting conditions and vesting periods for equity-settled transactions are discussed in 4 to 7 below and for cash-settled transactions in 9 below.

3.4 Vesting and non-vesting conditions: issues referred to the Interpretations Committee and the IASB

In January 2010 the Interpretations Committee added to its agenda a request for clarification of the following:

- the basis on which vesting conditions, especially performance conditions, can be distinguished from non-vesting conditions, especially the distinction between a service condition, a performance condition and a non-vesting condition; and
- the interaction of multiple conditions.

The amendments to IFRS 2 published in December 2013 as part of the IASB's *Annual Improvements to IFRSs 2010-2012 Cycle* were intended to address the first bullet point together with related application issues that had been raised with the Interpretations Committee (see 3.1 and 3.2 above).

In addition to considering matters subsequently addressed by the IASB in the *Annual Improvements*, the Interpretations Committee tentatively decided at its meetings in July and September 2010[15] that a non-compete provision should be presumed to be a 'contingent feature' – a term not defined in IFRS 2.[16]

The Interpretations Committee subsequently concluded that the classification of a non-compete provision and the question of how to account for the interaction of multiple vesting conditions should be referred to the IASB.[17] In September 2011 the IASB agreed that these issues should be considered as future agenda items.[18]

The IASB launched and concluded a research project into IFRS 2 (see 1.2.1 above). The IASB decided in May 2016 not to perform further research and published a summary of the research findings in October 2018 – even though the issues continue to result in some diversity in practice (see also 3.2.3 above and 6.3.6 to 6.3.7 below).[19]

4 EQUITY-SETTLED TRANSACTIONS – OVERVIEW

4.1 Summary of accounting treatment

The detailed provisions of IFRS 2 are complex, but their key points can be summarised as follows.

(a) All equity-settled transactions are measured at fair value. However, transactions with employees are normally measured using a 'grant date model' (i.e. the transaction is recorded at the fair value of the equity instrument at the date when it is originally granted), whereas transactions with non-employees are normally measured using a 'service date model' (i.e. the transaction is recorded at the fair value of the goods or services received at the date they are received). As noted in 3 above, all transactions, however measured, are recognised using a 'service date model' (see 5 below).

Share-based payment 2673

(b) Where an award is made subject to future fulfilment of conditions, a 'market condition' (i.e. one related to the market price (or value) of the entity's equity instruments) or a 'non-vesting condition' (i.e. one that is neither a service condition nor a performance condition) is taken into account in determining the fair value of the award. However, the effect of conditions other than market and non-vesting conditions is ignored in determining the fair value of the award (see 3 above and 6 below).

(c) Where an award is made subject to future fulfilment of vesting conditions, its cost is recognised over the period during which the service condition is fulfilled (see 3 above and 6 below). The corresponding credit entry is recorded within equity (see 4.2 below).

(d) Until an equity instrument has vested (i.e. the entitlement to it is no longer conditional on future service) any amounts recorded are in effect contingent and will be adjusted if more or fewer awards vest than were originally anticipated to do so. However, an equity instrument awarded subject to a market condition or a non-vesting condition is considered to vest irrespective of whether or not that market or non-vesting condition is fulfilled, provided that all other vesting conditions are satisfied (see 6 below).

(e) No adjustments are made, either before or after vesting, to reflect the fact that an award has no value to the employee or other counterparty e.g. in the case of a share option, because the option exercise price is above the current market price of the share (see 6.1.1 and 6.1.3 below).

(f) If an equity instrument is cancelled, whether by the entity or the counterparty (see (g) below) before vesting, any amount remaining to be expensed is charged in full at that point (see 7.4 below). If an equity instrument is modified before vesting (e.g. in the case of a share option, by changing the performance conditions or the exercise price), the financial statements must continue to show a cost for at least the fair value of the original instrument, as measured at the original grant date, together with any excess of the fair value of the modified instrument over that of the original instrument, as measured at the date of modification (see 7.3 below).

(g) Where an award lapses during the vesting period due to a failure by the counterparty to satisfy a non-vesting condition within the counterparty's control, or a failure by the entity to satisfy a non-vesting condition within the entity's control, the lapse of the award is accounted for as if it were a cancellation (see (f) above and 6.4.3 below).

(h) In determining the cost of an equity-settled transaction under IFRS 2, whether the entity satisfies its obligations under the transaction with a fresh issue of shares or by purchasing own shares in the financial markets is completely irrelevant to the charge in profit or loss, although there is clearly a difference in the cash flows. Where own shares are purchased, they are accounted for as treasury shares under IAS 32 (see 2.2.4.H above and Chapter 47 at 9). *[IFRS 2.BC330-333]*.

The requirements summarised in (d) to (g) above can have the effect that IFRS 2 requires a cost to be recorded for an award that ultimately has no value to the counterparty, because the award either does not vest or vests but is not exercised. These rather counter-intuitive requirements of IFRS 2 are in part 'anti-abuse' provisions to prevent entities from applying a 'selective' grant date model, whereby awards that increase in value after grant date remain measured at grant date while awards that decrease in value are remeasured. This is discussed further in the detailed analysis at 5 to 7 below.

4.2 The credit entry

As noted at (c) in the summary in 4.1 above, the basic accounting entry for an equity-settled share-based payment transaction is: debit profit or loss for the period (often classified as employee costs), credit equity (classified as a transaction with owners in their capacity as owners rather than as part of other comprehensive income).

IFRS 2 does not prescribe the component of equity to which the credit should be taken. The IASB presumably adopted this non-prescriptive approach so as to ensure there was no conflict between, on the one hand, the basic requirement of IFRS 2 that there should be a credit in equity and, on the other, the legal requirements of various jurisdictions as to exactly how that credit should be allocated within equity. Depending on the requirements of the particular jurisdiction, it might be appropriate to take the credit to retained earnings or to a separate component of equity or entities may be able to make a policy choice.

Occasionally there will be a credit to profit or loss (see for instance Example 34.11 at 6.2.4 below) and a corresponding reduction in equity.

In some arrangements the share-based payment transaction will be settled in equity instruments of a subsidiary of the reporting entity. This is most commonly the case where the subsidiary is partly-owned with traded shares held by external shareholders. In the consolidated financial statements, the question arises as to whether the credit entry for such transactions should be presented as a non-controlling interest (NCI) or as part of the equity attributable to the shareholders of the parent. This is discussed further in Chapter 7 at 5.6.

5 EQUITY-SETTLED TRANSACTIONS – COST OF AWARDS

5.1 Cost of awards – overview

The general measurement rule in IFRS 2 is that an entity must measure the goods or services received, and the corresponding increase in equity, directly, at the fair value of the goods or services received, unless that fair value cannot be estimated reliably. If the fair value of the goods or services received cannot be estimated reliably, the entity must measure their value, and the corresponding increase in equity, indirectly, by reference to the fair value of the equity instruments granted. *[IFRS 2.10]*. 'Fair value' is defined as the amount for which an asset could be exchanged, a liability settled, or an equity instrument granted could be exchanged, between knowledgeable, willing parties in an arm's length transaction. *[IFRS 2 Appendix A]*. IFRS 2 has its own specific rules in relation to determining the fair value of share-based payments which differ from the more general fair value measurement requirements in IFRS 13 – *Fair Value Measurement* (see 5.5 below). *[IFRS 2.6A]*.

On their own, the general measurement principles of IFRS 2 would suggest that the reporting entity must determine in each case whether the fair value of the equity

instruments granted or that of the goods or services received is more reliably determinable. However, IFRS 2 goes on to clarify that:
- in the case of transactions with employees, the fair value of the equity instruments must be used (see 5.2 below), except in those extremely rare cases where it is not possible to measure this fair value reliably, when the intrinsic value of the equity instruments may be used instead (see 5.5 below); but
- in the case of transactions with non-employees, there is a rebuttable presumption that the fair value of the goods or services provided is more reliably determinable (see 5.4 below).

Moreover, transactions with employees are measured at the date of grant (see 5.2 below), whereas those with non-employees are measured at the date when goods or services are received (see 5.4 below).

The overall position can be summarised by the following matrix.

Counterparty	Measurement basis	Measurement date	Recognition date
Employee	Fair value of equity instruments awarded	Grant date	Service date
Non-employee	Fair value of goods or services received	Service date	Service date

The Basis for Conclusions addresses the issue of why the accounting treatment for apparently identical transactions should, in effect, depend on the identity of the counterparty.

The main argument put forward to justify the approach adopted for transactions with employees is essentially that, once an award has been agreed, the value of the services provided pursuant to the transaction does not change significantly with the value of the award. *[IFRS 2.BC88-96]*. However, some might question this proposition, on the grounds that employees are more likely to work harder when the value of their options is rising than when it has sunk irretrievably.

As regards transactions with non-employees, the IASB offers two main arguments for the use of measurement at service date.

The first is that, if the counterparty is not firmly committed to delivering the goods or services, the counterparty would consider whether the fair value of the equity instruments at the delivery date is sufficient payment for the goods or services when deciding whether to deliver the goods or services. This suggests that there is a high correlation between the fair value of the equity instruments at the date the goods or services are received and the fair value of those goods or services. *[IFRS 2.BC126]*. This argument is clearly vulnerable to the challenge that it has no relevance where (as would more likely be the case) the counterparty is firmly committed to delivering the goods or services.

The second is that non-employees generally provide services over a short period commencing some time after grant date, whereas employees generally provide services over an extended period beginning on the grant date. This leads to a concern that transactions with non-employees could be entered into well in advance of the due date for delivery of goods or services. If an entity were able to measure the expense of such a transaction at the grant date fair value, the result, assuming that the entity's share price rises, would be to understate the cost of goods and services delivered. *[IFRS 2.BC126-127]*.

The true reason for the IASB's approach may have been political as much as theoretical. One effect of a grant date measurement model is that, applied to a grant of share options that is eventually exercised, it 'freezes' the accounting cost at the (typically) lower fair value at the date of grant. This excludes from the post-grant financial statements the increased cost and volatility that would be associated with a model that constantly remeasured the award to fair value until exercise date. The IASB might well have perceived it as a marginally easier task to persuade the corporate sector of the merits of a 'lower cost, zero volatility' approach as opposed to a 'fair value at exercise date' model (such as is used for cash-settled awards – see 9 below).

The price to be paid in accounting terms for the grant date model is that, when an award falls in value after grant date, it continues to be recognised at its higher grant date value. It is therefore quite possible that, during a period of general economic downturn, financial statements will show significant costs for options granted in previous years, but which are currently worthless. This could well lead to (in fact, sometimes groundless) accusations of rewarding management for failure.

5.2 Transactions with employees

These will comprise the great majority of transactions accounted for under IFRS 2, and include all remuneration in the form of shares, share options and any other form of reward settled in equity instruments of the entity or a member of its group.

5.2.1 Who is an 'employee'?

Given the difference between the accounting treatment of equity-settled transactions with employees and with non-employees, it is obviously important for IFRS 2 to define what is meant by employees. In fact IFRS 2 strictly refers to 'employees and others providing similar services' *[IFRS 2.11]* who are defined as individuals who render personal services to the entity and either:

(a) the individuals are regarded as employees for legal or tax purposes;

(b) the individuals work for the entity under its direction in the same way as individuals who are regarded as employees for legal or tax purposes; or

(c) the services rendered are similar to those rendered by employees.

The term encompasses all management personnel, i.e. those persons having authority and responsibility for planning, directing and controlling the activities of the entity, including non-executive directors. *[IFRS 2 Appendix A]*.

The implication of (a) and (b) above is that it is not open to an entity to argue that an individual who is not an employee as a matter of law is therefore automatically a non-employee for the purposes of IFRS 2.

The implication of (b) and (c) above is that, where a third party provides services pursuant to a share-based payment transaction that could be provided by an employee (e.g. where an external IT consultant works alongside an in-house IT team), that third party is treated as an employee rather than a non-employee for the purposes of IFRS 2.

Conversely, however, where an entity engages a consultant to undertake work for which there is not an existing in-house function, the implication is that such an individual is not regarded as an employee. In other words, in our view, the reference in (c) to 'services ... similar to those rendered by employees' is to services rendered by employees that the entity actually has, rather than to employees that the entity might have if it were to recruit them. Otherwise, the distinction in IFRS 2 between employees and non-employees would have no effect, since it would always be open to an entity to argue that it could employ someone to undertake any task instead of engaging a contractor.

Exceptionally there might be cases where the same individual is engaged in both capacities. For example, a director of the entity might also be a partner in a firm of lawyers and be engaged in that latter capacity to advise the entity on a particular issue. It might be more appropriate to regard payment for the legal services as made to a non-employee rather than to an employee.

Related questions of interpretation arise where an award is made to an employee of an associate or a joint venture (see 12.9 below).

The effect of a change of status from employee to non-employee (or *vice versa*) is addressed at 5.4.1 below.

5.2.2 Basis of measurement

As noted above, IFRS 2 requires equity-settled transactions with employees to be measured by reference to the fair value of the equity instruments granted at 'grant date' (see 5.3 below). *[IFRS 2.11]*. IFRS 2 asserts that this approach is necessary because shares, share options and other equity instruments are typically only part of a larger remuneration package, such that it would not be practicable to determine the value of the work performed in consideration for the cash element of the total package, the benefit-in-kind element, the share option element and so on. *[IFRS 2.12]*.

In essence, this is really an anti-avoidance provision. The underlying concern is that, if an entity were able to value options by reference to the services provided for them, it might assert that the value of those services was zero, on the argument that its personnel are already so handsomely rewarded by the non-equity elements of their remuneration package (such as cash and health benefits), that no additional services are (or indeed could be) obtained by granting options.

5.3 Grant date

As noted above, IFRS 2 requires equity-settled transactions with employees to be accounted for at fair value at grant date, defined as 'the date at which the entity and another party (including an employee) agree to a share-based payment arrangement, being when the entity and the counterparty have a shared understanding of the terms and conditions of the arrangement...'. *[IFRS 2 Appendix A]*.

The determination of grant date is critical to the measurement of equity-settled share-based transactions with employees, since grant date is the date at which such transactions must be measured (see 5.2.2 above).

In practice, it is not always clear when a mutual understanding of the award (and, therefore, grant date) has occurred. Issues of interpretation can arise as to:
- how precise the shared understanding of the terms of the award must be; and
- exactly what level of communication between the reporting entity and the counterparty is sufficient to ensure that there is the appropriate degree of agreement and 'shared understanding'.

As a consequence, the determination of the grant date is often difficult in practice. We discuss the following issues in more detail in the sections below:
- basic determination of grant date (see 5.3.1 below);
- the communication of awards to employees and the rendering of services in advance of grant date (see 5.3.2 below);
- awards where the exercise price or performance depends on a formula or on a future share price (see 5.3.3 below);
- awards where the exercise price is paid in shares (net settlement of award) (see 5.3.4 below);
- an award of equity instruments to a fixed monetary value (see 5.3.5 below);
- awards over a fixed pool of shares (including 'last man standing' arrangements) (see 5.3.6 below);
- awards with multiple service and performance periods (see 5.3.7 below);
- awards subject to modification or discretionary re-assessment by the entity after the original grant date (see 5.3.8 below);
- mandatory or discretionary awards to 'good leavers' (see 5.3.9 below); and
- shares issued by special purpose acquisition companies (see 5.3.10 below).

The grant date for 'matching' awards (i.e. arrangements where an additional award of shares is granted to match an initial cash bonus or award of shares) is discussed at 15.1 below.

5.3.1 Determination of grant date

IFRS 2 and the accompanying implementation guidance emphasise that a grant occurs only when all the conditions are understood and agreed by the parties to the arrangement and any required approval process has been completed. Thus, for example, if an entity makes an award 'in principle' to an employee of options whose terms are subject to review or approval by a remuneration committee or the shareholders, 'grant date' is the later date when the necessary formalities have been completed. *[IFRS 2 Appendix A, IG1-3].*

The implementation guidance to IFRS 2 emphasises that the word 'agree' is 'used in its usual sense, which means that there must be both an offer and an acceptance of that offer'. Therefore, there cannot be a grant unless an offer by one party has been accepted by the other party. The guidance notes that agreement will be explicit in some cases (e.g. if an agreement has to be signed), but in others it might be implicit, such as when an employee starts to deliver services for the award. *[IFRS 2.IG2].*

The counterparty's agreement to an offer might be particularly difficult to determine when it is implicit rather than explicit. For example, if an award required both the rendering of service and a subscription payment (other than a minimal one) by the employee, it is likely that the employee's agreement, and hence the grant date of the award, would coincide with the payment date – provided this occurs shortly after the offer date. If, however, the employee had the choice at the offer date of deferring payment until a much later date and could therefore decide whether the entity's subsequent performance justified his payment, then it is more likely that grant date would be the date on which the services commenced. Determination of when the counterparty has agreed to an offer will often be an area of judgement that depends on the precise facts and circumstances of a particular situation.

The implementation guidance to IFRS 2 further notes that employees may begin rendering services in consideration for an award before it has been formally ratified. For example, a new employee might join the entity on 1 January and be granted options relating to performance for a period beginning on that date, but subject to formal approval by the remuneration committee at its next quarterly meeting on 15 March. In that case, the entity would typically begin expensing the award from 1 January based on a best estimate of its fair value, but would subsequently adjust that estimate so that the ultimate cost of the award was its actual fair value at 15 March. *[IFRS 2.IG4]*. This reference to formal approval could be construed as indicating that, in fact, IFRS 2 requires not merely that there is a mutual understanding of the award (which might well have been in existence since 1 January), but also that the entity has completed all processes necessary to make the award a legally binding agreement.

In practice, many situations are much less clear-cut than the examples given in the implementation guidance. For example, if a remuneration committee has discretion over some aspects of an award and whether it vests, does that mean that there is not a shared understanding until the vesting date? Similarly, does the counterparty need to have full quantification of every aspect of an award (performance targets, exercise price, etc.) or would an understanding of the formula for calculating performance or price be sufficient?

Some of these practical interpretation issues are considered further in the sections below.

5.3.2 Communication of awards to employees and services in advance of grant date

As discussed at 5.3.1 above, the implementation guidance to IFRS 2 indicates that, in order for a grant to have been made, there must not merely be a mutual understanding of the terms – including the conditions attached to the award as discussed further in the sections that follow – but there must also be a legally enforceable arrangement. Thus, if an award requires board or shareholder approval for it to be legally binding on the reporting entity, for the purposes of IFRS 2 it has not been granted until such approval has been given, even if the terms of the award are fully understood at an earlier date. However, if services are effectively being rendered for an award from a date earlier than the grant date as defined in IFRS 2, the cost of the award should be recognised over a period starting with that earlier date. An estimate of the grant date fair value of the award is used (e.g. by estimating the fair value of the equity instruments at the end of the reporting period), for the purposes of recognising the services received during the period between service commencement date and grant date. *[IFRS 2.IG4]*.

In some situations the employee will have a valid expectation of an award, and the entity will have a corresponding obligation, based on an earlier commitment by the entity. However, it might be the case that not all of the precise terms and conditions have been finalised. In our view, provided it is possible to estimate the fair value of the arrangement, an estimated cost for services should be recognised in advance of grant date in such cases as well as in those situations where formal approval does not take place until a later date.

In situations where the entity estimates at the reporting date the grant date fair value of an award for services received in advance of grant date, the estimate is revised at subsequent reporting periods until the date of grant has been established. Once grant date has been established the entity revises the earlier estimate so that the amounts recognised for services received in respect of the grant are ultimately based on the grant date fair value of the equity instruments awarded.

The implications of the paragraph IG4 requirement are illustrated in Example 34.3 below for a situation where formal approval of an award is delayed. It is important, however, to retain a sense of proportion in considering the overall impact on the financial statements. For example, in cases where the share price is not particularly volatile, whether the grant date is, say, 1 January or 1 April may not make a great difference to the valuation of the award, particularly when set beside the range of acceptable valuations resulting from the use of estimates in the valuation model.

Example 34.3:   Determination of grant date

Scenario 1

On 1 January an entity advises employees of the terms of a share award designed to reward performance over the following three years. The award is subject to board approval, which is given two months later on 1 March. Grant date is 1 March. However, the cost of the award would be recognised over the three year period beginning on 1 January, since the employees would effectively been rendering service for the award from that date.

Scenario 2

On 1 January an entity's board resolves to implement a share scheme designed to reward performance over the following three years. The award is notified to employees two months later on 1 March. Grant date is again 1 March. *Prima facie*, in this case, the cost of the award would be recognised over the period of two years and ten months beginning on 1 March, since the employees could not be regarded as rendering service in January and February for an award of which they were not aware at that time.

However, if a similar award is made each year, and according to a similar timescale, there might be an argument that, during January and February of each year, the employees are rendering service for an award of which there is high expectation, and that the cost should therefore, as in Scenario 1, be recognised over the full three year period. The broader issue of the accounting treatment for awards of which there is a high expectation is addressed in the discussion of matching share awards at 15.1 below.

Scenario 3

On 1 January an entity advises employees of the terms of a share award designed to reward performance over the following three years. The award is subject to board approval, which is given two months later on 1 March. However, in giving such approval, the board makes some changes to the performance conditions as originally communicated to employees on 1 January. The revised terms of the award are communicated to employees a month later on 1 April. Grant date is 1 April. However, the cost of the award would be recognised over the three year period beginning on 1 January, since the employees would have effectively been rendering service for the award from that date.

Examples of situations where an employee might render service in advance of the IFRS 2 grant date because the precise conditions of an award are outstanding are considered at 5.3.3 to 5.3.7 and at 15.1 and 15.4.1 below.

5.3.3 Exercise price or performance target dependent on a formula or future share price

Some share plans define the exercise price not in absolute terms, but as a factor of the share price. For example, the price might be expressed as:
- a percentage of the share price at exercise date; or
- a percentage of the lower of the share price at grant date and at exercise date.

The effect of this is that, although the actual exercise price is not known until the date of exercise, both the entity and the counterparty already have a shared understanding of how the price will be calculated and it is possible to estimate the outcome on an ongoing basis without the need for additional approval or inputs.

A similar approach might be applied in the setting of performance targets i.e. they are set by reference to a formula rather than in absolute terms and so do not require further input by the entity or its remuneration committee, for example.

In order for there to be a shared understanding and a grant date, the formula or method of determining the outcome needs to be sufficiently clear and objective to allow both the entity and the counterparty to make an estimate of the outcome of the award during the vesting period. Accordingly, in our view, grant date is the date on which the terms and conditions (including the formula for calculating the exercise price or performance target) are determined sufficiently clearly and agreed by the entity and the counterparty, subject to the matters discussed at 5.3.2 above.

5.3.4 Exercise price paid in shares (net settlement of award)

Some share awards allow the exercise price to be paid in shares. In practical terms, this means that the number of shares delivered to the counterparty will be the total 'gross' number of shares awarded less as many shares as have, at the date of exercise, a fair value equal to the exercise price.

In our view, this situation is analogous to that in 5.3.3 above in that, whilst the absolute 'net' number of shares awarded will not be known until the date of exercise, the basis on which that 'net' number will be determined is established in advance. Accordingly, in our view, grant date is the date on which the terms and conditions (including the ability to surrender shares to a fair value equal to the exercise price) are determined and agreed by the entity and the counterparty, subject to the matters discussed at 5.3.2 above.

Such a scheme could be analysed as a share-settled share appreciation right (whereby the employee receives shares to the value of the excess of the value of the shares given over the exercise price), which is treated as an equity-settled award under IFRS 2.

Awards settled in shares net of a cash amount to meet an employee's tax obligation are considered further at 14.3 below.

5.3.5 Award of equity instruments to a fixed monetary value

Some entities may grant employees awards of shares to a fixed value. For example, an entity might award as many shares as are worth €100,000, with the number of shares being calculated by reference to the share price as at the vesting date. The number of shares ultimately received will not be known until the vesting date. This begs the question of whether such an award can be regarded as having been granted until that date, on the argument that it is only then that the number of shares to be delivered – a key term of the award – is known, and therefore there cannot be a 'shared understanding' of the terms of the award until that later date.

In our view, however, this situation is analogous to those in 5.3.3 and 5.3.4 above. Although the absolute number of shares awarded will not be known until the vesting date, the basis on which that number will be determined is established in advance in a manner sufficiently clear and objective to allow an ongoing estimate by the entity and by the counterparty of the number of awards expected to vest. Accordingly, in our view, grant date is the date on which the terms and conditions are determined sufficiently clearly and agreed by the entity and the counterparty, subject to the matters discussed at 5.3.2 above.

The measurement of such awards raises further issues of interpretation, which we discuss at 8.10 below.

5.3.6 Awards over a fixed pool of shares (including 'last man standing' arrangements)

An award over a fixed pool of shares is sometimes granted to a small group of, typically senior, employees. Such awards might involve an initial allocation of shares to each individual but also provide for the redistribution of each employee's shares to the other participants should any individual leave employment before the end of the vesting period. This is often referred to as a 'last man standing' arrangement.

The accounting requirements of IFRS 2 for such an arrangement are unclear. In the absence of specific guidance, several interpretations are possible and we believe that an entity may make an accounting policy choice, provided that choice is applied consistently to all such arrangements.

The first approach is based on the view that the unit of account is all potential shares to be earned by the individual employee and that, from the outset, each employee has a full understanding of the terms and conditions of both the initial award and the reallocation arrangements. This means that there is a grant on day one with each individual's award being valued on the basis of:

- that employee's initial allocation of shares; plus
- an additional award with a non-vesting condition relating to the potential reallocation of other participants' shares.

Under this approach, the departure of an employee will be accounted for as a forfeiture and any cost reversed as the service condition will not have been met (see 6.1.2 below), but the redistribution of that individual's shares to the other employees will have no accounting impact. This approach is likely to result in a total expense that is higher than the number of shares awarded multiplied by the grant date price per share.

The second approach, which we believe is consistent with US GAAP, also considers the individual employee's award to be the unit of account. Under this approach, there is an initial grant to all the employees and it is only these awards for which the fair value is measured at the date of the initial grant. Any subsequent reallocations of shares should be accounted for as a forfeiture of the original award and a completely new grant to the remaining employees, measured at the new grant date. This approach accounts only for the specific number of shares that have been allocated to the individual employee as at the end of each reporting period. No account is taken in this approach of shares that might be allocated to the individual employee in the future due to another employee's forfeiture, even though the reallocation formula is known to the individual employees at the initial grant date.

A third view, which takes a pragmatic approach in the light of the issues arising from the two approaches outlined above, is to account for the award on the basis of the total pool of shares granted rather than treating the individual employee as the unit of account. In our view this approach is likely to be materially acceptable for many arrangements where the pool of shares relates to the same small number of participants from the outset. Under this approach, the fair value of the total pool of shares is measured at the grant date (day one) with the non-vesting condition effectively ignored for valuation purposes. Subsequent forfeitures and reallocations would have no effect on the accounting.

There is a distinction between the 'last man standing' arrangement described above and a situation where an entity designates a fixed pool of shares to be used for awards to employees but where the allocation of leavers' shares is discretionary rather than pre-determined. In this situation, the valuation of the initial award would not take account of any potential future reallocations. If an employee left employment during the vesting period, that individual's award would be accounted for as a forfeiture and any reallocation of that individual's shares would be accounted for as a new grant with the fair value determined at the new grant date (i.e. a similar accounting treatment to that in approach two above).

A further type of award relating to a fixed pool of shares is one where an entity makes an award over a fixed number or percentage of its shares to a particular section of its workforce, the final allocation of the pool being made to those employed at the vesting date. In such an arrangement, some employees will typically join and leave the scheme during the original vesting period which will lead to changes in each employee's allocation of shares. Although employees are aware of the existence, and some of the terms, of the arrangement at the outset, the fact that there is no objective formula (see 5.3.3 to 5.3.5 above) for determining the number of shares that each individual will ultimately receive means that there is no grant under IFRS 2 until the date of final allocation. However, because the employees render service under the arrangement in advance of the grant date – either from day one or from a later joining date – the entity should estimate the fair value of the award to each individual from the date services commence and subsequently update it at each reporting period. The fair value estimated is expensed over the full service period of the award with a final truing up of the expense to the fair value of the award at the eventual grant date (see 5.3.2 above).

This has the effect that, where an entity decides to set aside a bonus pool of a fixed amount of cash, say £1 million, with the allocation to individual employees to be made at a later date, there is a known fixed cost of £1 million. However, where an entity decides to set aside a bonus pool of a fixed number of shares, with the allocation to individual employees to be made at a later date, the final cost is not determined until the eventual grant date.

5.3.7 Awards with multiple service and performance periods

Entities frequently make awards that cover more than one reporting period, but with different performance conditions for each period, rather than a single cumulative target for the whole vesting period. In such cases, the grant date may depend on the precision with which the terms of the award are communicated to employees, as illustrated by Example 34.4 below.

Example 34.4: Awards with multiple service and performance periods

Scenario 1

At the beginning of year 1, an entity enters into a share-based payment arrangement with an employee. The employee is informed that the maximum potential award is 40,000 shares, 10,000 of which will vest at the end of year 1, and 10,000 more at the end of each of years 2 to 4. Vesting of each of the four tranches of 10,000 shares is conditional on:

(a) the employee having been in continuous service until the end of each relevant year; and

(b) revenue targets for each of those four years, as communicated to the employee at the beginning of year 1, having been attained.

In this case, the terms of the award are clearly understood by both parties at the beginning of year 1, and this is therefore the grant date under IFRS 2 (subject to issues such as any requirement for later formal approval – see 5.3 to 5.3.2 above). The cost of the award would be recognised using a 'graded' vesting approach – see 6.2.2 below.

Scenario 2

At the beginning of year 1, an entity enters into a share-based payment arrangement with an employee. The employee is informed that the maximum potential award is 40,000 shares, 10,000 of which will vest at the end of year 1, and 10,000 more at the end of each of years 2 to 4. Vesting of each of the four tranches of 10,000 shares is conditional on:

(a) the employee having been in continuous service until the end of each relevant year; and

(b) revenue targets for each of those four years, to be communicated to the employee at the beginning of each relevant year in respect of that year only, having been attained.

In this case, in our view, at the beginning of year 1 there is a clear shared understanding only of the terms of the first tranche of 10,000 shares that will potentially vest at the end of year 1. There is no clear understanding of the terms of the tranches potentially vesting at the end of years 2 to 4 because their vesting depends on revenue targets for those years which have not yet been set.

Accordingly, each of the four tranches of 10,000 shares has a separate grant date (and, therefore, a separate measurement date) – i.e. the beginning of each of years 1, 2, 3 and 4, and a vesting period of one year from the relevant grant date.

In this type of situation, the entity would also need to consider whether, in the absence of a grant date, the employee was nonetheless rendering services in advance of the grant date. However, if targets are unquantified and do not depend on a formula, for example, then it is likely to be difficult to estimate an expense in advance of the grant date (see 5.3.2 above).

A variation on the above two scenarios which is seen quite frequently in practice is an award where the target is quantified for the first year and the targets for subsequent years depend on a formula-based increase in the year 1 target. The formula is set at the same time as the year 1 target. Whether the accounting treatment for scenario 1 above or scenario 2 above is the more appropriate in such a situation is, in our view, a matter of judgement depending on the precise terms of the arrangement (see 5.3.3 above).

5.3.8 Awards subject to modification by entity after original grant date

As noted at 5.3.1 above, some employee share awards are drafted in terms that give the entity discretion to modify the detailed terms of the scheme after grant date. Some have questioned whether this effectively means that the date originally determined as the 'grant date' is not in fact the grant date as defined in IFRS 2, on the grounds that the entity's right to modify means that the terms are not in fact understood by both parties in advance.

In our view, this is very often not an appropriate analysis. If it were, it could also mean that, in some jurisdictions, nearly all share-based awards to employees would be required to be measured at vesting date, which clearly was not the IASB's intention.

However, the assessment of whether or not an intervention by the entity after grant date constitutes a modification is often difficult. Some situations commonly encountered in practice are considered in the sections below. See also the discussion at 3.1.1 above relating to the clawback of awards.

5.3.8.A Significant equity restructuring or transactions

Many schemes contain provisions designed to ensure that the value of awards is maintained following a major capital restructuring (such as a share split or share consolidation – see 7.8 below) or a major transaction with shareholders as a whole (such as the insertion of a new holding company over an existing group (see 12.8 below), a major share buyback or the payment of a special dividend). These provisions will either specify the adjustments to be made in a particular situation or, alternatively, may allow the entity to make such discretionary adjustments as it sees fit in order to maintain the value of awards. In some cases the exercise of such discretionary powers may be relatively mechanistic (e.g. the adjustment of the number of shares subject to options following a share split). In other cases, more subjectivity will be involved (e.g. in determining whether a particular dividend is a 'special' dividend for the purposes of the scheme).

In our view, where the scheme rules specify the adjustments to be made or where there is a legal requirement to make adjustments in order to remedy any dilution that would otherwise arise, the implementation of such adjustments would not result in the recognition of any incremental IFRS 2 fair value. This assumes that the adjustment would simply operate on an automatic basis to put the holders of awards back to the position that they would have been in had there not been a restructuring and hence there would be no difference in the fair value of the awards before and after the restructuring (or other specified event).

However, where there is no such explicit requirement in the scheme rules or under relevant legislation, we believe that there should be a presumption that the exercise of the entity's discretionary right to modify is a 'modification' as defined in IFRS 2. In such a situation, the fair values before and after the modification may differ and any incremental fair value should be expensed over the remaining vesting period (see 7.3 below).

5.3.8.B Interpretation of general terms

More problematic might be the exercise of any discretion by the entity or its remuneration committee to interpret the more general terms of a scheme in deciding whether performance targets have been met and therefore whether, and to what extent, an award should vest. Suppose, for example, that an entity makes an award to its executives with a market performance condition based on total shareholder return (TSR) with a maximum payout if the entity is in the top quartile of a peer group of 100 entities (i.e. it is ranked between 1 and 25 in the peer group).

It might be that the entity is ranked 26 until shortly before the end of the performance period, at which point the entity ranked 25 suddenly announces that it is in financial difficulties and ceases trading shortly afterwards. This then means that the reporting entity moves up from 26 to 25 in the rankings. However, the entity might take the view that, in the circumstances, it could not be considered as having truly been ranked 25 in the peer group, so that a maximum payout is not justified.

In this case, the entity's intervention might be considered to be a modification. However, as the effect would be to reduce the fair value of the award, it would have no impact on the accounting treatment (see 7.3.2 below).

If such an intervention were not regarded as a modification, then the results might be different depending on the nature of the award. Where an award is subject to a market condition, as here, or to a non-vesting condition, an expense might well have to be recognised in any event, if all the non-market vesting conditions (e.g. service) were satisfied – see 6.3 and 6.4 below.

However, suppose that the award had been based on a non-market performance condition, such as an EPS target, which was met, but only due to a gain of an unusual, non-recurring nature, such as the revaluation of PP&E for tax purposes, giving rise to a deferred tax credit. The remuneration committee concludes that this should be ignored, with the effect that the award does not vest. If this is regarded as the exercise of a pre-existing right to ensure that the award vests only if 'normal' EPS reaches a given level, then there has been no modification. On this analysis, the award has not vested, and any expense previously recognised would be reversed. If, however, the committee's intervention is regarded as a modification, it would have no impact on the accounting treatment in this particular case, as the effect would not be beneficial to the employee and so the modification would be ignored under the general requirements of IFRS 2 relating to modifications (see 7.3.2 below).

5.3.8.C Discretion to make further awards

Some schemes may give the entity the power to increase an award in circumstances where the recipient is considered to have delivered exceptional performance, or some such similar wording. In our view, unless the criteria for judging such exceptional performance are so clear as to be, in effect, performance conditions under IFRS 2, the presumption should be that any award made pursuant to such a clause is granted, and therefore measured, when it is made. We note at 15.1 below that there may be circumstances where an award described as 'discretionary' may not truly be so, since the entity has created an expectation amounting to an obligation to make the award. However, we believe that it would be somewhat contradictory to argue that such expectations had been created in the case of an award stated to be for (undefined) exceptional performance only.

5.3.9 'Good leaver' arrangements

In some jurisdictions it is common for awards to contain a so-called 'good leaver' clause. A 'good leaver' clause is one which makes provision for an employee who leaves employment before the end of the full vesting period of the award to receive some or all of the award on leaving (see 5.3.9.A below).

In other cases, the original terms of an award will either make no reference to 'good leavers' or will not be sufficiently specific to allow the accounting treatment on cessation of employment to be an automatic outcome of the original terms of the scheme. In such cases, and in situations where awards are made to leavers on a fully discretionary basis, the approach required by IFRS 2 differs from that required where the original terms are clear about 'good leaver' classification and entitlement (see 5.3.9.B below).

In some jurisdictions awards are structured in a way which allows the majority of participants, rather than just a few specified categories of 'good leaver', to retain all or part of an award if they leave employment during the vesting period (see 5.3.9.C below).

We refer throughout this section on 'good leavers' to an employee leaving employment, but similar considerations apply when an individual automatically becomes entitled to an award before the end of the original vesting period due to other reasons specified in the terms of the agreement, e.g. attaining a certain age or achieving a specified length of service, even if the individual remains in employment after the relevant date. In these situations, the date of full entitlement is the date on which any services – and therefore expense recognition – cease for IFRS 2 purposes.

Arrangements for a good leaver to receive all, or part, of an award on leaving employment should be distinguished from a situation where an employee leaves with no award and where forfeiture accounting is likely to apply (see 7.4.1.A below).

5.3.9.A Provision for 'good leavers' made in original terms of award

In some cases the types of person who are 'good leavers' may be explicitly defined in the original terms of the arrangement (common examples being persons who die or reach normal retirement age before the end of the full vesting period, or who work for a business unit that is sold or closed during the vesting period). In other cases, the entity may have the discretion to determine on a case-by-case basis whether a person should be treated as a 'good leaver'.

In addition, some schemes may specify the entitlement of a 'good leaver' on leaving (e.g. that the leaver receive a portion of the award *pro rata* to the extent that the performance conditions have been met), whereas others leave the determination of the award to the entity at the time that the employee leaves.

Whichever situation applies, any expense relating to an award to a good leaver must be fully recognised by the leaving date because, at that point, the good leaver ceases to provide any services to the entity and any remaining conditions attached to the award will be treated as non-vesting rather than vesting conditions (see 3.2 above).

In our view, an award which vests before the end of the original vesting period due to the operation of a 'good leaver' clause is measured at the original grant date only where, under the rules of the scheme as understood by both parties at the original grant date, the award is made:

- to a person clearly identified as a 'good leaver'; and
- in an amount clearly quantified or quantifiable.

Where, as outlined above, the rules of the scheme make clear the categories of 'good leaver' and their entitlement, the entity should assess at grant date how many good leavers there are likely to be and to what extent the service period for these particular individuals is expected to be shorter than the full vesting period. The grant date fair value of the estimated awards to good leavers should be separately determined, where significant, and the expense relating to good leavers recognised over the expected reduced vesting period between grant date and leaving employment. In this situation the entity would re-estimate the number of good leavers and adjust the cumulative expense at each reporting date. This would be a change of estimate rather than a modification of the award as it would all be in accordance with the original terms and would require no discretionary decisions on the part of the entity. We would not generally expect an entity to have significant numbers of good leavers under such an arrangement.

It is important to draw a clear distinction between the IFRS 2 accounting on a straight-line basis over a reduced vesting period in the above case and that on a graded vesting basis in a situation of broader entitlement as outlined at 5.3.9.C below.

5.3.9.B   Discretionary awards to 'good leavers'

At 5.3.9.A above we discuss awards where the arrangements for leavers are clear as at the original grant date of the award. However, where – as is more usually the case – the entity determines only at the time that the employee leaves either that the employee is a 'good leaver' or the amount of the award, grant date or modification date (see further below) should be taken as the later of the date on which such determination is made or the date on which the award is notified to the employee. This is because the employee had no clear understanding at the original grant date of an automatic entitlement to equity instruments other than through full vesting of the award at the end of the full service period.

In our view, an entity should assess the appropriate accounting treatment based on the particular facts and circumstances and the extent to which the discretionary award is linked to the original award. The discretionary award at the time of leaving is considered to be either a modification of an original award in the employee's favour (for example, where vesting conditions are waived to allow an individual to keep an award) or the forfeiture of the original award and the granting of a completely new award on a discretionary basis (see 7.3 and 7.5 below).

In some cases, a good leaver will be allowed, on a discretionary basis, to keep existing awards that remain subject to performance conditions established at the original grant date. In this situation, any conditions that were previously treated as vesting conditions will become non-vesting conditions following the removal of the service requirement (see 3.1 and 3.2 above). This will be the case whether the discretionary arrangement is accounted for as the forfeiture of the old award plus a new grant or as a modification of the original award.

The non-vesting conditions will need to be reflected in the measurement of the fair value of the award as at the date of modification or new grant (although the non-vesting conditions alone will not result in any incremental fair value). Any fair value that is unrecognised as at the date of the good leaver ceasing employment will need to be expensed immediately as there is no further service period over which to recognise the expense.

There is further discussion of modifications at 7.3 below and of replacement and *ex gratia* awards granted on termination of employment at 7.5 below.

5.3.9.C   Automatic full or pro rata entitlement on leaving employment

In some jurisdictions entities establish schemes where a significant number of the participants will potentially leave employment before the end of the full vesting period and will be allowed to keep a *pro rata* share of the award. This gives rise to a much broader category of employee than the small number of good leavers that one would generally expect under a scheme where 'good leaver' refers only to employees who die, retire or work for a business unit that is sold or closed (see 5.3.9.A above).

The substance of an arrangement where significant numbers of employees are expected to leave with a *pro rata* entitlement is that the entire award to all participants vests on a graded basis over the vesting period as a whole. So, for example, an arrangement that gives employees 360 shares at the end of three years but, whether under the rules of the scheme or by precedent, allows the majority of leavers to take a *pro rata* share – based on the number of months that have elapsed – at their date of departure, should be treated as vesting at the rate of 10 shares per month for all employees. Such an arrangement should be accounted for using the graded vesting approach illustrated at 6.2.2 below.

Some take the view that the situation outlined in the previous paragraph does not require graded vesting and that a straight-line approach may be taken because the award only vests *pro rata* if an employee leaves employment. Supporters of this view argue that the requirement to leave employment in order to receive the award before the end of the full vesting period is itself a substantive condition over and above the requirement to provide ongoing service. If an employee remains in employment the award only vests on completion of three years' service and there is no earlier entitlement on a *pro rata* basis. Although this treatment has some appeal, in our view it is difficult to reconcile to the standard and is not therefore an appropriate alternative accounting treatment to the graded approach outlined above.

In other cases, rather than just a *pro rata* apportionment, any good leaver will be allowed to keep the entire award regardless of when they leave employment. If this is the case, and in substance there is no required minimum service period attached to the award, then the award should be treated as immediately vested in all employees and fully expensed at the grant date.

5.3.10 Special purpose acquisition companies ('SPACs')

IPOs and trade sales may be achieved through the medium of special purpose acquisition companies ('SPACs'). The detailed features of SPACs may vary, but common features tend to be:

- The SPAC is established by a small number of founders, typically with expertise in selecting attractive targets for flotation or sale. The founder shares contain a term to the effect that, if a target is eventually identified and floated or sold, the holders of the founder shares will receive a greater proportion of any proceeds than other shareholders at the time of flotation.
- At a later date, other (non-founder) shareholders invest. This is frequently achieved by an IPO of the SPAC. It is typically the case that, if a specific target is not identified and agreed by a required majority of non-founder shareholders, within a finite timescale, the other (non-founder) shareholders will have their funds returned.
- The SPAC seeks a target which is then approved (or not, as the case may be) by the required majority of non-founder shareholders.

The three stages outlined above have given rise to three interpretations as to the grant date for IFRS 2 purposes.

The first view is that there is no shared understanding until the specific target is identified and agreed (the third stage above). Holders of this view argue that the substance of the founder shareholders' interest is economically equivalent to an award of shares in any target finally approved. Therefore, until the target is finally approved, there is no clarity as to the nature and value of the award to the founder shareholders.

The second view is that a shared understanding occurs at the point at which the non-founder shareholders invest (i.e. the second stage above). Holders of this view argue that a share-based payment can only occur when there has been a transfer of value from the non-founder shareholders to the founder shareholders and this cannot occur until there are some non-founder shareholders in place. However, once those non-founder shareholders are in place, there is a shared understanding that – if a transaction is subsequently approved – there will be a benefit for founder shareholders.

The third view is that a shared understanding occurs on the issue of the founder shares (i.e. the first stage above). Holders of this view argue that at that point there is a shared understanding that there will be a benefit for founder shareholders if non-founder shareholders are subsequently introduced and a transaction is subsequently approved. The benefit for founder shareholders consists both in seeking further investors and in identifying a suitable target. The founder shareholders will be actively rendering service towards these goals from the outset.

The IFRS Interpretations Committee conducted some initial outreach research into how SPACs are treated in practice, but the question has not been formally discussed to date. Until such time as additional guidance is given, it seems that the diversity in practice outlined above will remain and entities should use judgement to determine an appropriate grant date based on the specific terms of the arrangement.

5.4 Transactions with non-employees

In accounting for equity-settled transactions with non-employees, the entity must adopt a rebuttable presumption that the value of the goods or services received provides the more reliable indication of the fair value of the transaction. The fair value to be used is that at the date on which the goods are obtained or the services rendered. *[IFRS 2.13]*. This implies that, where the goods or services are received on a number of dates over a period, the fair value at each date should be used, although in the case of a relatively short period there may be no great fluctuation in fair value.

If 'in rare cases' the presumption is rebutted, the entity may use as a surrogate measure the fair value of the equity instruments granted, but as at the date when the goods or services are received, not the original grant date. However, where the goods or services are received over a relatively short period where the share price does not change significantly, an average share price can be used in calculating the fair value of equity instruments granted. *[IFRS 2.13, IG5, IG6-7]*.

This contrasts with US GAAP[20] which requires the fair value of goods or services received from non-employees to be measured at grant date of the equity-instruments to be received, rather than based on the fair value at the date the goods are obtained or services are rendered.

5.4.1 Effect of change of status from employee to non-employee (or vice versa)

IFRS 2 does not give specific guidance on how to account for an award when the status of the counterparty changes from employee to non-employee (or *vice versa*) but, in all other respects, the award remains unchanged. In our view, the accounting following the change of status will depend on the entity's assessment of whether or not the counterparty is performing the same or similar services before and after the change of status.

If it is concluded that the counterparty is providing the same or similar services before and after the change of status, the measurement approach remains unchanged.

However, if the services provided are substantially different, the accounting following the change of status will be determined by the counterparty's new status, as follows:

- For a change from non-employee to employee status, the expense for periods following the change should be measured as if the award had been granted at the date of change of status. This revised measurement only applies to the expense for the portion of the award that vests after the change of status and there is no effect on the expense recognised in prior periods.

- For a change from employee to non-employee status, the expense for periods following the change should be measured on the basis of the fair value of the counterparty's services as they are received – if this is reliably determinable. Otherwise, the fair value used is that of the equity instruments granted but measured at the date the services are received (see 5.4 above). There is no effect on the expense recognised in prior periods.

If the status of the counterparty changes and the terms of the award are modified in order to allow the award to continue to vest, the modification and change of status should be assessed in accordance with the general principles in IFRS 2 relating to the modification of awards (see 7.3 below).

5.5 Determining the fair value of equity instruments

As discussed in 5.2 and 5.4 above, IFRS 2 requires the following equity-settled transactions to be measured by reference to the fair value of the equity instruments issued rather than that of the goods or services received:

- all transactions with employees (except where it is impossible to determine fair value – see below); and
- transactions with non-employees where, in rare cases, the entity rebuts the presumption that the fair value of goods or services provided is more reliably measurable.

There will also be situations where the identifiable consideration received (if any) from non-employees appears to be less than the fair value of consideration given. In such cases, the cost of the unidentifiable goods or services received, if any, must be accounted for in accordance with IFRS 2 by determining the fair value of the equity instruments. This requirement is discussed at 2.2.2.C above.

For all transactions measured by reference to the fair value of the equity instruments granted, IFRS 2 requires fair value to be measured at the 'measurement date' – i.e. grant date in the case of transactions with employees and service date in the case of transactions with non-employees. *[IFRS 2 Appendix A]*. Fair value should be based on market prices if available. *[IFRS 2.16]*. In the absence of market prices, a valuation technique should be used to estimate what the market price would have been on the measurement date in an arm's length transaction between informed and willing parties. The technique used should be a recognised technique and incorporate all factors that would be taken into account by knowledgeable and willing market participants. *[IFRS 2.17]*.

Appendix B to IFRS 2 contains more detailed guidance on valuation, which is discussed at 8 below. *[IFRS 2.18]*. IFRS 2 also deals with those 'rare' cases where it is not possible to value equity instruments reliably, where an intrinsic value approach may be used. This is more likely to apply to awards of options than to awards of shares and is discussed further at 8.8 below.

IFRS 2 rather confusingly states that the fair value of equity instruments granted must take into account the terms and conditions on which they were granted, but this requirement is said to be 'subject to the requirements of paragraphs 19-22'. *[IFRS 2.16]*. When those paragraphs are consulted, a somewhat different picture emerges, since they draw a distinction between:

- non-vesting conditions (i.e. those that are neither service conditions nor performance conditions);
- vesting conditions which are market conditions (i.e. those related to the entity's share price); and
- other vesting conditions (i.e. service and non-market performance conditions).

These are discussed in more detail at 6.2 to 6.4 and at 8 below, but the essential difference is that, while non-vesting conditions and market conditions must be taken into account in any valuation, other vesting conditions must be ignored. *[IFRS 2.19-21A]*. As we explain in the more detailed discussion later, these essentially arbitrary distinctions originated in part as anti-avoidance measures.

The 'fair value' of equity instruments under IFRS 2 therefore takes account of some, but not all, conditions attached to an award rather than being a 'true' fair value.

The approach to determining the fair value of share-based payments continues to be that specified in IFRS 2 and share-based payments fall outside the scope of IFRS 13 which applies more generally to the measurement of fair value under IFRSs (see Chapter 14). *[IFRS 2.6A]*.

5.5.1 Reload features

A 'reload feature' is a feature in a share option that provides for an automatic grant of additional share options (reload options) whenever the option holder exercises previously granted options using the entity's shares, rather than cash, to satisfy the exercise price. *[IFRS 2 Appendix A]*. IFRS 2 requires reload features to be ignored in the initial valuation of options that contain them. Instead any reload option should be treated as if it were a newly granted option when the reload conditions are satisfied. *[IFRS 2.22]*. This is discussed further at 8.9 below.

6 EQUITY-SETTLED TRANSACTIONS – ALLOCATION OF EXPENSE

6.1 Overview

Equity-settled transactions, particularly those with employees, raise particular accounting problems since they are often subject to vesting conditions (see 3.1 above) that can be satisfied only over an extended vesting period. This raises the issue of whether a share-based payment transaction should be recognised:

- when the relevant equity instrument is first granted;
- when it vests;
- during the vesting period; or
- during the life of the option.

An award of equity instruments that vests immediately is presumed, in the absence of evidence to the contrary, to relate to services that have already been rendered, and is therefore expensed in full at grant date. *[IFRS 2.14]*. This may lead to the immediate recognition of an expense for an award to which the employee may not be legally entitled for some time, as illustrated in Example 34.5.

Example 34.5: Award with non-vesting condition only

An entity grants a director share options, exercisable after three years provided the director does not compete with the reporting entity for a period of at least three years. The 'non-compete' clause is considered to be a non-vesting condition (see 3.2 above and 6.4 below). As this is the only condition to which the award is subject, the award has no vesting conditions and therefore vests immediately. The fair value of the award at the date of grant, including the effect of the 'non-compete' clause, is determined to be €150,000. Accordingly, the entity immediately recognises a cost of €150,000.

This cost can never be reversed, even if the director goes to work for a competitor and loses the award. This is discussed more fully at 3.2.3 above and at 6.1.2 and 6.4 below.

Where equity instruments are granted subject to vesting conditions (as in many cases they will be, particularly where payments to employees are concerned), IFRS 2 creates a presumption that they are a payment for services to be received in the future, during the 'vesting period', with the transaction being recognised during that period, as illustrated in Example 34.6. *[IFRS 2.15]*.

Example 34.6: Award with service condition only

An entity grants a director share options on condition that the director remain in employment for three years. The requirement to remain in employment is a service condition, and therefore a vesting condition, which will take three years to fulfil. The fair value of the award at the date of grant, ignoring the effect of the vesting condition, is determined to be €300,000. The entity will record a cost of €100,000 a year in profit or loss for three years, with a corresponding increase in equity.

In practice, the calculations required by IFRS 2 are unlikely to be as simple as that in Example 34.6. In particular:

- the final number of awards that vest cannot be known until the vesting date (because employees may leave before the vesting date, or because relevant performance conditions may not be met); and/or
- the length of the vesting period may not be known in advance (since vesting may depend on satisfaction of a performance condition with no, or a variable, time-limit on its attainment).

In order to deal with such issues, IFRS 2 requires a continuous re-estimation process as summarised in 6.1.1 below.

6.1.1 The continuous estimation process of IFRS 2

The overall objective of IFRS 2 is that, at the end of the vesting period, the cumulative cost recognised in profit or loss (or, where applicable, included in the carrying amount of an asset), should represent the product of:

- the number of equity instruments that have vested, or would have vested, but for the failure to satisfy a market condition (see 6.3 below) or a non-vesting condition (see 6.4 below); and
- the fair value (excluding the effect of any non-market vesting conditions, but including the effect of any market conditions or non-vesting conditions) of those equity instruments at the date of grant.

It is essential to appreciate that the 'grant date' measurement model in IFRS 2 seeks to capture the value of the contingent right to shares promised at grant date, to the extent that that promise becomes (or is deemed by IFRS 2 to become – see 6.1.2 below) an entitlement of the counterparty, rather than the value of any shares finally delivered. Therefore, if an option vests, but is not exercised because it would not be in the counterparty's economic interest to do so, IFRS 2 still recognises a cost for the award.

In order to achieve this outcome, IFRS 2 requires the following process to be applied:

(a) at grant date, the fair value of the award (excluding the effect of any service and non-market performance vesting conditions, but including the effect of any market performance conditions or non-vesting conditions) is determined;

(b) at each subsequent reporting date until vesting, the entity calculates a best estimate of the cumulative charge to profit or loss at that date, being the product of:
  (i) the grant date fair value of the award determined in (a) above;
  (ii) the current best estimate of the number of awards that will vest (see 6.1.2 below); and
  (iii) the expired portion of the vesting period;
(c) the charge (or credit) to profit or loss for the period is the cumulative amount calculated in (b) above less the amounts already charged in previous periods. There is a corresponding credit (or debit) to equity; *[IFRS 2.19-20]*
(d) once the awards have vested, no further accounting adjustments are made to the cost of the award, except in respect of certain modifications to the award – see 7 below; and
(e) if a vested award is not exercised, an entity may (but need not) make a transfer between components of equity – see 6.1.3 below.

The overall effect of this process is that a cost is recognised for every award that is granted, except when it is forfeited, as that term is defined in IFRS 2 (see 6.1.2 below). *[IFRS 2.19]*.

6.1.2 Vesting and forfeiture

In normal English usage, and in many share scheme documents, an award is described as 'vested' when all the conditions needed to earn it have been met, and as 'forfeited' where it lapses before vesting because one or more of the conditions has not been met.

IFRS 2 uses the term 'forfeiture' in a much more restricted sense to mean an award that does not vest in IFRS 2 terms. This is a particularly complex aspect of IFRS 2, which is discussed in more detail at 6.2 to 6.4 below. Essentially:

- where an award is subject only to vesting conditions other than market conditions, failure to satisfy any one of the conditions is treated as a forfeiture by IFRS 2;
- where an award is subject to both
  - vesting conditions other than market conditions, and
  - market conditions and/or non-vesting conditions,

  failure to satisfy any one of the vesting conditions other than market conditions is treated as a forfeiture by IFRS 2. Otherwise (i.e. where all the vesting conditions other than market conditions are satisfied), the award is deemed to vest by IFRS 2 even if the market conditions and/or non-vesting conditions have not been satisfied; and
- where an award is subject only to non-vesting conditions, it is always deemed to vest by IFRS 2.

Where an award has been modified (see 7.3 below) so that different vesting conditions apply to the original and modified elements of an award, forfeiture will not apply to the original award if the service and non-market performance conditions attached to that element have been met. This will be the case even if the service and non-market performance conditions attached to the modified award have not been met and so the modified award is considered to have been forfeited (resulting in the reversal of any incremental expense relating to the modification). Examples 34.23 and 34.24 at 7.3 below illustrate this point.

As a result of the interaction of the various types of condition, the reference in the summary at 6.1.1 above to the 'best estimate of the number of awards that will vest' really means the best estimate of the number of awards for which it is expected that all service and non-market vesting conditions will be met.

In practice, however, it is not always clear how that best estimate is to be determined, and in particular what future events may and may not be factored into the estimate. This is discussed further at 6.2 to 6.4 and at 7.6 below.

6.1.3 Accounting after vesting

Once an equity-settled transaction has vested (or, in the case of a transaction subject to one or more market or non-vesting conditions, has been treated as vested under IFRS 2 – see 6.1.2 above), no further accounting entries are made to reverse the cost already charged, even if the instruments that are the subject of the transaction are subsequently forfeited or, in the case of options, are not exercised. However, the entity may make a transfer between different components of equity. *[IFRS 2.23]*. For example, an entity's accounting policy might be to credit all amounts recorded for share-based transactions to a separate reserve such as 'Shares to be issued'. Where an award lapses after vesting, it would then be appropriate to transfer an amount equivalent to the cumulative cost for the lapsed award from 'Shares to be issued' to another component of equity.

This prohibition against 'truing up' (i.e. reversing the cost of vested awards that lapse) is controversial, since it has the effect that a cost is still recognised for options that are never exercised, typically because they are 'underwater' (i.e. the current share price is lower than the option exercise price), so that it is not in the holder's interest to exercise the option. Some commentators have observed that an accounting standard that can result in an accounting cost for non-dilutive options does not meet the needs of those shareholders whose concerns about dilution were the catalyst for the share-based payment project in the first place (see 1.1 above).

The IASB counters such objections by pointing out that the treatment in IFRS 2 is perfectly consistent with that for other 'contingent' equity instruments, such as warrants, that ultimately result in no share ownership. Where an entity issues warrants for valuable consideration such as cash and those warrants lapse unexercised, the entity recognises no gain under IFRS. *[IFRS 2.BC218-221]*.

6.2 Vesting conditions other than market conditions

6.2.1 Awards with service conditions

Most share-based payment transactions with employees are subject to explicit or implied service conditions. Examples 34.7 and 34.8 below illustrate the application of the allocation principles discussed in 6.1 above to awards subject only to service conditions. *[IFRS 2.IG11]*.

Example 34.7: **Award with no change in the estimate of number of awards vesting**

An entity grants 100 share options to each of its 500 employees. Vesting is conditional upon the employees working for the entity over the next three years. The entity estimates that the fair value of each share option is €15. The entity's best estimate at each reporting date is that 100 (i.e. 20%) of the original 500 employees will leave during the three year period and therefore forfeit their rights to the share options.

If everything turns out exactly as expected, the entity will recognise the following amounts during the vesting period for services received as consideration for the share options.

Year	Calculation of cumulative expense	Cumulative expense (€)	Expense for period‡ (€)
1	50,000 options × 80%* × €15 × 1/3†	200,000	200,000
2	50,000 options × 80% × €15 × 2/3	400,000	200,000
3	50,000 options × 80% × €15 × 3/3	600,000	200,000

* The entity expects 100 of its 500 employees to leave and therefore only 80% of the options to vest.
† The vesting period is 3 years, and 1 year of it has expired.
‡ In each case the expense for the period is the difference between the calculated cumulative expense at the beginning and end of the period.

Example 34.8: **Award with re-estimation of number of awards vesting due to staff turnover**

As in Example 34.7 above, an entity grants 100 share options to each of its 500 employees. Vesting is conditional upon the employee working for the entity over the next three years. The entity estimates that the fair value of each share option is €15.

In this case, however, 20 employees leave during the first year, and the entity's best estimate at the end of year 1 is that a total of 75 (15%) of the original 500 employees will have left before the end of the vesting period. During the second year, a further 22 employees leave, and the entity revises its estimate of total employee departures over the vesting period from 15% to 12% (i.e. 60 of the original 500 employees). During the third year, a further 15 employees leave. Hence, a total of 57 employees (20 + 22 + 15) forfeit their rights to the share options during the three year period, and a total of 44,300 share options (443 employees × 100 options per employee) finally vest.

The entity will recognise the following amounts during the vesting period for services received as consideration for the share options.

Year	Calculation of cumulative expense	Cumulative expense (€)	Expense for period (€)
1	50,000 options × 85% × €15 × 1/3	212,500	212,500
2	50,000 options × 88% × €15 × 2/3	440,000	227,500
3	44,300 options × €15 × 3/3	664,500	224,500

Note that in Example 34.8 above, the number of employees that leave during year 1 and year 2 is not directly relevant to the calculation of cumulative expense in those years, but would naturally be a factor taken into account by the entity in estimating the likely number of awards finally vesting.

6.2.2 Equity instruments vesting in instalments ('graded' vesting)

An entity may make share-based payments that vest in instalments (sometimes referred to as 'graded' vesting). For example, an entity might grant an employee 600 options, 100 of which vest if the employee remains in service for one year, a further 200 after two years and the final 300 after three years. In today's more mobile labour markets, such awards are often favoured over awards which vest only on an 'all or nothing' basis after an extended period.

IFRS 2 requires such an award to be treated as three separate awards, of 100, 200 and 300 options, on the grounds that the different vesting periods will mean that the three tranches of the award have different fair values. [IFRS 2.IG11]. This may well have the effect that compared to the expense for an award with a single 'cliff' vesting, the expense for an award vesting in instalments will be for a different amount in total and require accelerated recognition of the expense in earlier periods, as illustrated in Example 34.9 below.

Example 34.9:   Award vesting in instalments ('graded' vesting)

An entity is considering the implementation of a scheme that awards 600 free shares to each of its employees, with no conditions other than continuous service. Two alternatives are being considered:

- All 600 shares vest in full only at the end of three years.
- 100 shares vest after one year, 200 shares after two years and 300 shares after three years. Any shares received at the end of years 1 and 2 would have vested unconditionally.

The fair value of a share delivered in one year's time is €3; in two years' time €2.80; and in three years' time €2.50.

For an employee that remains with the entity for the full three year period, the first alternative would be accounted for as follows:

Year	Calculation of cumulative expense	Cumulative expense (€)	Expense for period (€)
1	600 shares × €2.50 × 1/3	500	500
2	600 shares × €2.50 × 2/3	1,000	500
3	600 shares × €2.50 × 3/3	1,500	500

For the second alternative, the analysis is that the employee has simultaneously received an award of 100 shares vesting over one year, an award of 200 shares vesting over two years and an award of 300 shares vesting over 3 years. This would be accounted for as follows:

Year	Calculation of cumulative expense	Cumulative expense (€)	Expense for period (€)
1	[100 shares × €3.00] + [200 shares × €2.80 × 1/2] + [300 shares × €2.50 × 1/3]	830	830
2	[100 shares × €3.00] + [200 shares × €2.80 × 2/2] + [300 shares × €2.50 × 2/3]	1,360	530
3	[100 shares × €3.00] + [200 shares × €2.80 × 2/2] + [300 shares × €2.50 × 3/3]	1,610	250

At first sight, such an approach seems to be taking account of vesting conditions other than market conditions in determining the fair value of an award, contrary to the basic principle of paragraph 19 of IFRS 2 (see 6.1.1 above). However, it is not the vesting conditions that are being taken into account *per se*, but the fact that the varying vesting periods will give rise to different lives for the award (which are required to be taken into account – see 7.2 and 8 below).

Provided all conditions are clearly understood at the outset, the accounting treatment illustrated in Example 34.9 would apply even if the vesting of shares in each year also depended on a performance condition unique to that year (e.g. that profit in that year must reach a given minimum level), as opposed to a cumulative performance condition (e.g. that profit must have grown by a minimum amount by the end of year 1, 2 or 3). This is because all tranches of the arrangement have the same service commencement date and so for the awards that have a performance condition relating to year 2 or year 3 there is a service condition covering a longer period than the performance condition. In other words, an award that vests at the end of year 3 conditional on profitability in year 3 is also conditional on the employee providing service for three years from the date of grant in order to be eligible to receive the award. This is discussed further at 5.3.7 above.

A variant of Example 34.9, is one where a share-based payment transaction vests with employees in instalments and the service period is not at least as long as the duration of the non-market performance condition, for example, a flotation or sale condition. The flotation or sale condition will be treated as a non-vesting condition and be incorporated into the determination of fair value (see 3.2 above). In contrast, when the service condition is the same duration as the flotation and sale condition, that condition will be treated as non-market performance condition, see Example 34.66 at 15.4.3 below.

The accounting treatment illustrated in Example 34.9 is the only treatment for graded vesting permitted under IFRS 2 whether an arrangement just has a service condition or whether it has both service and performance conditions. This contrasts with US GAAP[21] which permits, for awards with graded vesting where vesting depends solely on a service condition, a policy choice between the approach illustrated above and a straight-line recognition method.

6.2.3 Transactions with variable vesting periods due to non-market performance vesting conditions

An award may be made with a vesting period of variable length. For example, an award might be contingent upon achievement of a particular performance target (such as achieving a given level of cumulative earnings) within a given period, but vesting immediately once the target has been reached. Alternatively, an award might be contingent on levels of earnings growth over a period, but with vesting occurring more quickly if growth is achieved more quickly. Also some plans provide for 're-testing', whereby an original target is set for achievement within a given vesting period, but if that target is not met, a new target and/or a different vesting period are substituted.

In such cases, the entity needs to estimate the length of the vesting period at grant date, based on the most likely outcome of the performance condition. Subsequently, it is necessary continuously to re-estimate not only the number of awards that will finally vest, but also the date of vesting, as shown by Example 34.10. *[IFRS 2.15(b), IG12]*. This contrasts with the treatment of awards with market conditions and variable vesting periods, where the initial estimate of the vesting period may not be revised (see 6.3.4 below).

Example 34.10: Award with non-market vesting condition and variable vesting period

At the beginning of year 1, the entity grants 100 shares each to 500 employees, conditional upon the employees remaining in the entity's employment during the vesting period. The shares will vest:

- at the end of year 1 if the entity's earnings increase by more than 18%;
- at the end of year 2 if the entity's earnings increase by more than an average of 13% per year over the two year period; or
- at the end of year 3 if the entity's earnings increase by more than an average of 10% per year over the three year period.

The award is estimated to have a fair value of $30 per share at grant date. It is expected that no dividends will be paid during the whole three year period.

By the end of the first year, the entity's earnings have increased by 14%, and 30 employees have left. The entity expects that earnings will continue to increase at a similar rate in year 2, and therefore expects that the shares will vest at the end of year 2. The entity expects, on the basis of a weighted average probability, that a further 30 employees will leave during year 2, and therefore expects that an award of 100 shares each will vest for 440 (500 – 30 – 30) employees at the end of year 2.

By the end of the second year, the entity's earnings have increased by only 10% and therefore the shares do not vest at the end of that year. 28 employees have left during the year. The entity expects that a further 25 employees will leave during year 3, and that the entity's earnings will increase by at least 6%, thereby achieving the average growth of 10% per year necessary for an award after 3 years, so that an award of 100 shares each will vest for 417 (500 – 30 – 28 – 25) employees at the end of year 3.

By the end of the third year, a further 23 employees have left and the entity's earnings have increased by 8%, resulting in an average increase of 10.67% per year. Therefore, 419 (500 – 30 – 28 – 23) employees receive 100 shares at the end of year 3.

The entity will recognise the following amounts during the vesting period for services received as consideration for the shares:

Year	Calculation of cumulative expense	Cumulative expense ($)	Expense for period ($)
1	440 employees × 100 shares × $30 × 1/2*	660,000	660,000
2	417 employees × 100 shares × $30 × 2/3*	834,000	174,000
3	419 employees × 100 shares × $30	1,257,000	423,000

* The entity's best estimate at the end of year 1 is that it is one year through a two year vesting period and at the end of year 2 that it is two years through a three year vesting period.

It will be noted that in Example 34.10, which is based on IG Example 2 in the implementation guidance to IFRS 2, it is assumed that the entity will pay no dividends (to any shareholders) throughout the maximum possible three year vesting period. This has the effect that the fair value of the shares to be awarded is equivalent to their market value at the date of grant.

If dividends were expected to be paid during the vesting period, this would no longer be the case. Employees would be better off if they received shares after two years rather than three, since they would have a right to receive dividends from the end of year two. In practice, an entity is unlikely to suspend dividend payments in order to simplify the calculation of its share-based payment expense, and it is unfortunate that IG Example 2 is not more realistic. *[IFRS 2 IG Example 2].*

One solution might be to use the approach in IG Example 4 in the implementation guidance to IFRS 2 (the substance of which is reproduced as Example 34.12 at 6.2.5 below). That Example deals with an award whose exercise price is either CHF12 or CHF16, dependent upon various performance conditions. Because vesting conditions other than market conditions must be ignored in determining the value of an award, the approach is in effect to treat the award as the simultaneous grant of two awards, whose value, in that case, varies by reference to the different exercise prices. *[IFRS 2 IG Example 4].*

The same principle could be applied to an award of shares that vests at different times according to the performance conditions, by determining different fair values for the shares (in this case depending on whether they vest after one, two or three years). The cumulative charge during the vesting period would be based on a best estimate of which outcome will occur, and the final cumulative charge would be based on the grant date fair value of the actual outcome (which will require some acceleration of expense if the actual vesting period is shorter than the previously estimated vesting period).

Such an approach appears to be taking account of non-market vesting conditions in determining the fair value of an award, contrary to the basic principle of paragraph 19 of IFRS 2 (see 6.1.1 above). However, it is not the vesting conditions that are being taken into account *per se*, but the fact that the varying vesting periods will give rise to different lives for the award (which are required to be taken into account – see 7.2 and 8 below). That said, the impact of the time value of the different lives on the fair value of the award will, in many cases, be insignificant and it will therefore be a matter of judgement as to how precisely an entity switches from one fair value to another.

Economically speaking, the entity in Example 34.10 has made a single award, the true fair value of which must be a function of the weighted probabilities of the various outcomes occurring. However, under the accounting model for share-settled awards in IFRS 2, the probability of achieving non-market performance conditions is not taken into account in valuing an award. If this is required to be ignored, the only approach open is to proceed as in Example 34.10 above and treat the arrangement as if it consisted of the simultaneous grant of three awards.

Some might object that this methodology is not relevant to the award in Example 34.10 above, since it is an award of shares rather than, in the case of Example 34.12 (see 6.2.5 below), an award of options. However, an award of shares is no more than an award of options with an exercise price of zero. Moreover, the treatment outlined in the previous paragraph is broadly consistent with the rationale given by IFRS 2 for the treatment of an award vesting in instalments (see 6.2.2 above).

In Example 34.10 above, the vesting period, although not known, is at least one of a finite number of known possibilities. The vesting period for some awards, however, may be more open-ended, such as is frequently the case for an award that vests on a trade sale or flotation of the business. Such awards are discussed further at 15.4 below.

6.2.4 Transactions with variable number of equity instruments awarded depending on non-market performance vesting conditions

More common than awards with a variable vesting period are those where the number of equity instruments awarded varies, typically increasing to reflect the margin by which a particular minimum target is exceeded. In accounting for such awards, the entity must continuously revise its estimate of the number of shares to be awarded, as illustrated in Example 34.11 below (which is based on IG Example 3 in the implementation guidance to IFRS 2). *[IFRS 2 IG Example 3].*

Example 34.11: Award with non-market performance vesting condition and variable number of equity instruments

At the beginning of year 1, an entity grants an option over a variable number of shares (see below), estimated to have a fair value at grant date of £20 per share under option, to each of its 100 employees working in the sales department. The share options will vest at the end of year 3, provided that the employees remain in the entity's employment, and provided that the volume of sales of a particular product increases by at least an average of 5% per year. If the volume of sales of the product increases by an average of between 5% and 10% per year, each employee will be entitled to exercise 100 share options. If the volume of sales increases by an average of between 10% and 15% each year, each employee will be entitled to exercise 200 share options. If the volume of sales increases by an average of 15% or more, each employee will be entitled to exercise 300 share options.

By the end of the first year, seven employees have left and the entity expects that a total of 20 employees will leave by the end of year 3. Product sales have increased by 12% and the entity expects this rate of increase to continue over the next two years, so that 80 employees will be entitled to exercise 200 options each.

By the end of the second year, a further five employees have left. The entity now expects only three more employees to leave during year 3, and therefore expects a total of 15 employees to have left during the three year period. Product sales have increased by 18%, resulting in an average of 15% over the two years to date. The entity now expects that sales will average 15% or more over the three year period, so that 85 employees will be entitled to exercise 300 options each.

By the end of year 3, a further seven employees have left. Hence, 19 employees have left during the three year period, and 81 employees remain. However, due to trading conditions significantly poorer than expected, sales have increased by a 3 year average of only 12%, so that the 81 remaining employees are entitled to exercise only 200 share options.

The entity will recognise the following amounts during the vesting period for services received as consideration for the options.

Year	Calculation of cumulative expense	Cumulative expense (£)	Expense for period (£)
1	80 employees × 200 options × £20 × 1/3	106,667	106,667
2	85 employees × 300 options × £20 × 2/3	340,000	233,333
3	81 employees × 200 options × £20	324,000	(16,000)

This Example reinforces the point that, under the methodology in IFRS 2, it is quite possible for an equity-settled transaction to give rise to a credit to profit or loss for a particular period during the period to vesting.

Other types of awards seen where variable number of equity instruments are awarded depending on non-market conditions include an employee receiving awards dependent on an individual's performance rating, the higher the rating the more equity-instruments are awarded (see 3.1.2 above). When the vesting of a share-based payment arrangement is based on an individual's performance rating, for there to be a grant date of such an award the framework for determining the outcome needs to be sufficiently clear and objective to allow both the entity and the employee to make an estimate of the outcome of the award during the vesting period (see 5.3.3 above). Consistent with Example 34.11 above, the entity must continuously revise its estimate of the number of shares to be awarded, provided a grant date has been established for the award. However, if the framework for determining the performance rating outcome is not sufficiently clear and objective, the grant date may not occur until a later date, but the entity would need to consider if services are effectively being rendered for an award from a date earlier than the grant date as defined in IFRS 2 and the cost of the award recognised over a period starting with that earlier date (see 5.3.2 above).

6.2.5 Transactions with variable exercise price due to non-market performance vesting conditions

Another mechanism for delivering higher value to the recipient of a share award so as to reflect the margin by which a particular target is exceeded might be to vary the exercise price depending on performance. IFRS 2 requires such an award to be dealt with, in effect, as more than one award. The fair value of each award is determined, and the cost during the vesting period based on the best estimate of which award will actually vest, with the final cumulative charge being based on the actual outcome. *[IFRS 2.IG12, IG Example 4]*.

This is illustrated in Example 34.12 below.

Example 34.12: Award with non-market performance vesting condition and variable exercise price

An entity grants to a senior executive 10,000 share options, conditional upon the executive's remaining in the entity's employment for three years. The exercise price is CHF40. However, the exercise price drops to CHF30 if the entity's earnings increase by at least an average of 10% per year over the three year period.

On grant date, the entity estimates that the fair value of the share options, with an exercise price of CHF30, is CHF16 per option. If the exercise price is CHF40, the entity estimates that the share options have a fair value of CHF12 per option. During year 1, the entity's earnings increased by 12%, and the entity expects that earnings will continue to increase at this rate over the next two years. The entity therefore expects that the earnings target will be achieved, and hence the share options will have an exercise price of CHF30.

During year 2, the entity's earnings increased by 13%, and the entity continues to expect that the earnings target will be achieved. During year 3, the entity's earnings increased by only 3%, and therefore the earnings target was not achieved. The executive completes three years' service, and therefore satisfies the service condition. Because the earnings target was not achieved, the 10,000 vested share options have an exercise price of CHF40.

The entity will recognise the following amounts during the vesting period for services received as consideration for the options.

Year	Calculation of cumulative expense	Cumulative expense (CHF)	Expense for period (CHF)
1	10,000 options × CHF16 × 1/3	53,333	53,333
2	10,000 options × CHF16 × 2/3	106,667	53,334
3	10,000 options × CHF12	120,000	13,333

At first sight this may seem a rather surprising approach. In reality, is it not the case that the entity in Example 34.12 has made a single award, the fair value of which must lie between CHF12 and CHF16, as a function of the weighted probabilities of either outcome occurring? Economically speaking, this is indeed the case. However, under the accounting model for equity-settled share-based payments in IFRS 2, the probability of achieving non-market performance conditions is not taken into account in valuing an award. If this is required to be ignored, the only approach open is to proceed as above.

6.3 Market conditions

6.3.1 What is a 'market condition'?

IFRS 2 defines a market condition as follows:

'A performance condition upon which the exercise price, vesting or exercisability of an equity instrument depends that is related to the market price (or value) of the entity's equity instruments (or the equity instruments of another entity in the same group), such as:

(a) attaining a specified share price or a specified amount of intrinsic value of a share option; or

(b) achieving a specified target that is based on the market price (or value) of the entity's equity instruments (or the equity instruments of another entity in the same group) relative to an index of market prices of equity instruments of other entities.

A market condition requires the counterparty to complete a specified period of service (i.e. a service condition); the service requirement can be explicit or implicit.' *[IFRS 2 Appendix A].*

A market condition is a type of performance condition and the above definition should be read together with the definition of a performance condition (see 3.1 above). If there is no service requirement, the condition will be a non-vesting condition rather than a performance vesting condition (see 3.2 above).

The 'intrinsic value' of a share option means 'the difference between the fair value of the shares to which the counterparty has the (conditional or unconditional) right to subscribe or which it has the right to receive, and the price (if any) the counterparty is (or will be) required to pay for those shares'. *[IFRS 2 Appendix A].* In other words, an option to pay $8 for a share with a fair value of $10 has an intrinsic value of $2. A performance condition based on the share price and one based on the intrinsic value of the option are effectively the same, since the values of each will obviously move in parallel.

An example of a market condition is a condition based on total shareholder return (TSR). TSR is a measure of the increase or decrease in a given sum invested in an entity over a period on the assumption that all dividends received in the period had been used to purchase further shares in the entity. The market price of the entity's shares is an input to the calculation.

However, a condition linked to a purely internal financial performance measure such as profit or earnings per share is not a market condition. Such measures will affect the share price, but are not directly linked to it, and hence are not market conditions.

A condition linked to a general market index is a non-vesting condition rather than a market condition (see 3.2 above and 6.4 below). For example, suppose that an entity engaged in investment management and listed only in London grants options to an employee responsible for the Far East equities portfolio. The options have a condition linked to movements in a general index of shares of entities listed in Hong Kong, so as to compare the performance of the portfolio of investments for which the employee is responsible with that of the overall market in which they are traded. That condition would not be regarded as a market condition under IFRS 2, because even though it relates to the performance of a market, the reporting entity's own share price is not relevant to the satisfaction of the condition.

However, if the condition were that the entity's own share price had to outperform a general index of shares of entities listed in Hong Kong, that condition would be a market condition because the reporting entity's own share price is then relevant to the satisfaction of the condition.

6.3.2 Summary of accounting treatment

The key feature of the accounting treatment of an equity-settled transaction subject to a market condition is that the market condition is taken into account in valuing the award at the date of grant, but then subsequently ignored, so that an award is treated as vesting irrespective of whether the market condition is satisfied, provided that all service and non-market performance vesting conditions are satisfied. *[IFRS 2.21, IG13].* This can have rather controversial consequences, as illustrated by Example 34.13.

Example 34.13: Award with market condition

An entity grants an employee an option to buy a share on condition of remaining in employment for three years and the share price at the end of that period being at least €7. At the end of the vesting period, the share price is €6.80. The share price condition is factored into the initial valuation of the option, and the option is considered to vest provided that the employee remains for three years, irrespective of whether the share price does in fact reach €7.

Therefore, IFRS 2 sometimes treats as vesting (and recognises a cost for) awards that do not actually vest in the natural sense of the word. See also Example 34.15 at 6.3.4 below.

This treatment is clearly significantly different from that for transactions involving a non-market vesting condition, where no cost would be recognised where the conditions were not met. The Basis for Conclusions indicates that the IASB accepted this difference for two main reasons:

(a) it was consistent with the approach in the US standard FAS 123 – *Accounting for Stock-Based Compensation*; and

(b) in principle, the same approach should have been adopted for all performance conditions. However, whereas market conditions can be readily incorporated into the valuation of options, other conditions cannot. *[IFRS 2.BC183-184]*.

The methodology prescribed by IFRS 2 for transactions with a vesting condition other than a market condition is therefore to determine the fair value of the option ignoring the condition and then to multiply that fair value by the estimated (and ultimately the actual) number of awards expected to vest based on the likelihood of that non-market vesting condition being met (see 6.2 above). It is interesting to note, however, that the January 2008 amendment to IFRS 2 (see 1.2 above) had the effect that certain conditions previously regarded as non-market vesting conditions (and therefore 'impossible' to incorporate in the determination of fair value) became non-vesting conditions (and therefore required to be incorporated in the determination of fair value).

One of the reasons for adoption of this approach under US GAAP (not referred to in the Basis for Conclusions in IFRS 2) was as an 'anti-avoidance' measure. The concern was that the introduction of certain market conditions could effectively allow for the reversal of the expense for 'underwater' options (i.e. those whose exercise price is higher than the share price such that it is not in the holder's interest to exercise the option) for which all significant vesting conditions had been satisfied, contrary to the general principle in US GAAP (and IFRS 2) that no revisions should be made to the expense for an already vested option.

For example, when the share price is £10 an entity could grant an employee an option, exercisable at £10, provided that a certain sales target had been met within one year. If the target were achieved, IFRS 2 would require an expense to be recognised even if the share price at the end of the year were only £8, so that the employee would not rationally exercise the option. If, however, the performance conditions were that (a) the sales target was achieved and (b) the share price was at least £10.01, the effect would be (absent specific provision for market conditions) that the entity could reverse any expense for 'underwater' options.

It appears that it may be possible to soften the impact of IFRS 2's rules for market conditions relatively easily by introducing a non-market vesting condition closely correlated to the market condition. For instance, the option in Example 34.13 above could be modified so that exercise was dependent not only upon the €7 target share price and continuous employment, but also on a target growth in earnings per share. Whilst there would not be a perfect correlation between earnings per share and the share price, it would be expected that they would move roughly in parallel, particularly if the entity has historically had a fairly consistent price/earnings ratio. Thus, if the share price target were not met, it would be highly likely that the earnings per share target would not be met either. This would allow the entity to show no cumulative cost for the option, since only one (i.e. not all) of the non-market related vesting conditions would have been met.

Similarly, entities in sectors where the share price is closely related to net asset value (e.g. property companies and investment trusts) could incorporate a net asset value target as a non-market performance condition that would be highly likely to be satisfied only if the market condition was satisfied.

The matrices below illustrate the interaction of market conditions and vesting conditions other than market conditions. Matrix 1 summarises the possible outcomes for an award with the following two vesting conditions:

- the employee remaining in service for three years ('service condition'); and
- the entity's total shareholder return ('TSR') relative to that of a peer group being in the top 10% of its peer group at the end of the period ('TSR target (market condition)').

Matrix 1

	Service condition met?	TSR target (market condition) met?	IFRS 2 expense?
1	Yes	Yes	Yes
2	Yes	No	Yes
3	No	Yes	No
4	No	No	No

It will be seen that, to all intents and purposes, the 'TSR target (market condition) met?' column is redundant, as this market condition is not relevant to whether or not the award is treated as vesting by IFRS 2. The effect of this is that the entity would recognise an expense for outcome 2, even though no awards truly vest.

Matrix 2 summarises the possible outcomes for an award with the same conditions as in Matrix 1, plus a requirement for earnings per share to grow by a general inflation index plus 10% over the period ('EPS target').

Matrix 2

	Service condition met?	TSR target (market condition) met?	EPS target (non-market condition) met?	IFRS 2 expense?
1	Yes	Yes	Yes	Yes
2	Yes	No	Yes	Yes
3	Yes	Yes	No	No
4	Yes	No	No	No
5	No	Yes	Yes	No
6	No	No	Yes	No
7	No	Yes	No	No
8	No	No	No	No

Again it will be seen that, to all intents and purposes, the 'TSR target (market condition) met?' column is redundant, as this market condition is not relevant to whether or not the award is treated as vesting by IFRS 2. The effect of this is that the entity would recognise an expense for outcome 2, even though no awards truly vest. However, no expense would be recognised for outcome 4, which is, except for the introduction of the EPS target, equivalent to outcome 2 in Matrix 1, for which an expense is recognised. This illustrates that the introduction of a non-market vesting condition closely related to a market condition may mitigate the impact of IFRS 2.

Examples of the application of the accounting treatment for transactions involving market conditions are given in 6.3.3 to 6.3.5 below.

6.3.3 Transactions with market conditions and known vesting periods

The accounting for such transactions is essentially the same as that for transactions without market conditions but with a known vesting period (including 'graded' vesting – see 6.2.2 above), except that adjustments are made to reflect the changing probability of the achievement of the non-market vesting conditions only, as illustrated by Example 34.14 below. *[IFRS 2.19-21, IG13, IG Example 5].*

Example 34.14: Award with market condition and fixed vesting period

At the beginning of year 1, an entity grants to 100 employees 1,000 share options each, conditional upon the employees remaining in the entity's employment until the end of year 3. However, the share options cannot be exercised unless the share price has increased from €50 at the beginning of year 1 to more than €65 at the end of year 3.

If the share price is above €65 at the end of year 3, the share options can be exercised at any time during the next seven years, i.e. by the end of year 10. The entity applies a binomial option pricing model (see 8 below), which takes into account the possibility that the share price will exceed €65 at the end of year 3 (and hence the share options vest and become exercisable) and the possibility that the share price will not exceed €65 at the end of year 3 (and hence the options will be treated as having vested under IFRS 2 but will never be exercisable – as explained below). It estimates the fair value of the share options with this market condition to be €24 per option.

IFRS 2 requires the entity to recognise the services received from a counterparty who satisfies all other vesting conditions (e.g. services received from an employee who remains in service for the specified service period), irrespective of whether that market condition is satisfied. It makes no difference whether the share price target is achieved, since the possibility that the share price target might not be achieved has already been taken into account when estimating the fair value of the share options at grant date. However, the options are subject to another condition (i.e. continuous employment) and the cost recognised should be adjusted to reflect the ongoing best estimate of employee retention.

By the end of the first year, seven employees have left and the entity expects that a total of 20 employees will leave by the end of year 3, so that 80 employees will have satisfied all conditions other than the market condition (i.e. continuous employment).

By the end of the second year, a further five employees have left. The entity now expects only three more employees will leave during year 3, and therefore expects that a total of 15 employees will have left during the three year period, so that 85 employees will have satisfied all conditions other than the market condition.

By the end of year 3, a further seven employees have left. Hence, 19 employees have left during the three year period, and 81 employees remain. However, the share price is only €60, so that the options cannot be exercised. Nevertheless, as all conditions other than the market condition have been satisfied, a cumulative cost is recorded as if the options had fully vested in 81 employees.

The entity will recognise the following amounts during the vesting period for services received as consideration for the options (which in economic reality do not vest).

Year	Calculation of cumulative expense	Cumulative expense (€)	Expense for period (€)
1	80 employees × 1,000 options × €24 × 1/3	640,000	640,000
2	85 employees × 1,000 options × €24 × 2/3	1,360,000	720,000
3	81 employees × 1,000 options × €24	1,944,000	584,000

6.3.4 Transactions with variable vesting periods due to market conditions

Where a transaction has a variable vesting period due to a market condition, a best estimate of the most likely vesting period will have been used in determining the fair value of the transaction at the date of grant. IFRS 2 requires the expense for that transaction to be recognised over an estimated expected vesting period consistent with the assumptions used in the valuation, without any subsequent revision. *[IFRS 2.15(b), IG14]*.

This may mean, for example, that, if the actual vesting period for an employee share option award turns out to be longer than that anticipated for the purposes of the initial valuation, a cost is nevertheless recorded in respect of all employees who reach the end of the anticipated vesting period, even if they do not reach the end of the actual vesting period, as shown by Example 34.15 below, which is based on IG Example 6 in the implementation guidance in IFRS 2. *[IFRS 2 IG Example 6]*.

Example 34.15: Award with market condition and variable vesting period

At the beginning of year 1, an entity grants 10,000 share options with a ten year life to each of ten senior executives. The share options will vest and become exercisable immediately if and when the entity's share price increases from £50 to £70, provided that the executive remains in service until the share price target is achieved.

The entity applies a binomial option pricing model, which takes into account the possibility that the share price target will be achieved during the ten year life of the options, and the possibility that the target will not be achieved. The entity estimates that the fair value of the share options at grant date is £25 per option. From the option pricing model, the entity determines that the most likely vesting period is five years. The entity also estimates that two executives will have left by the end of year 5, and therefore expects that 80,000 share options (10,000 share options × 8 executives) will vest at the end of year 5.

Throughout years 1 to 4, the entity continues to estimate that a total of two executives will leave by the end of year 5. However, in total three executives leave, one in each of years 3, 4 and 5. The share price target is achieved at the end of year 6. Another executive leaves during year 6, before the share price target is achieved.

Paragraph 15 of IFRS 2 requires the entity to recognise the services received over the expected vesting period, as estimated at grant date, and also requires the entity not to revise that estimate. Therefore, the entity recognises the services received from the executives over years 1-5. Hence, the transaction amount is ultimately based on 70,000 share options (10,000 share options × 7 executives who remain in service at the end of year 5). Although another executive left during year 6, no adjustment is made, because the executive had already completed the expected vesting period of 5 years.

The entity will recognise the following amounts during the initial expected five year vesting period for services received as consideration for the options.

Year	Calculation of cumulative expense	Cumulative expense (£)	Expense for period (£)
1	8 employees × 10,000 options × £25 × 1/5	400,000	400,000
2	8 employees × 10,000 options × £25 × 2/5	800,000	400,000
3	8 employees × 10,000 options × £25 × 3/5	1,200,000	400,000
4	8 employees × 10,000 options × £25 × 4/5	1,600,000	400,000
5	7 employees × 10,000 options × £25	1,750,000	150,000

Share-based payment

IFRS 2 does not specifically address the converse situation, namely where the award actually vests before the end of the anticipated vesting period. In our view, where this occurs, any expense not yet recognised at the point of vesting should be immediately accelerated. We consider that this treatment is most consistent with the overall requirement of IFRS 2 to recognise an expense for share-based payment transactions 'as the services are received'. *[IFRS 2.7].* It is difficult to regard any services being received for an award after it has vested.

Moreover, the prohibition in IFRS 2 on adjusting the vesting period as originally determined refers to 'the estimate of the expected vesting period'. In our view, the acceleration of vesting that we propose is not the revision of an estimated period, but the substitution of a known vesting period for an estimate.

Suppose in Example 34.15 above, the award had in fact vested at the end of year 4. We believe that the expense for such an award should be allocated as follows:

Year	Calculation of cumulative expense	Cumulative expense (£)	Expense for period (£)
1	8 employees × 10,000 options × £25 × 1/5	400,000	400,000
2	8 employees × 10,000 options × £25 × 2/5	800,000	400,000
3	8 employees × 10,000 options × £25 × 3/5	1,200,000	400,000
4	8 employees × 10,000 options × £25 × 4/4	2,000,000	800,000

6.3.5 Transactions with multiple outcomes depending on market conditions

In practice, it is very common for an award subject to market conditions to give varying levels of reward that increase depending on the extent to which a 'base line' market performance target has been met. Such an award is illustrated in Example 34.16 below.

Example 34.16: Award with market conditions and multiple outcomes

At the beginning of year 1, the reporting entity grants an employee an award of shares that will vest on the third anniversary of grant if the employee is still in employment. The number of shares depends on the share price achieved at the end of the three-year period. The employee will receive:

- no shares if the share price is below €10.00
- 100 shares if the share price is in the range €10.00-€14.99
- 150 shares if the share price is in the range €15.00-€19.99
- 180 shares if the share price is €20.00 or above.

In effect the entity has made three awards, which need to be valued as follows:

(a) 100 shares if the employee remains in service for three years and the share price is in the range €10.00-€14.99
(b) 50 (150 – 100) shares if the employee remains in service for three years and the share price is in the range €15.00-€19.99; and
(c) 30 (180 – 150) shares if the employee remains in service for three years and the share price is €20.00 or more.

Each award would be valued, ignoring the impact of the three-year service condition but taking account of the share price target. This would result in each tranche of the award being subject to an increasing level of discount to reflect the relative probability of the share price target for each tranche of the award being met. All three awards would then be expensed over the three-year service period, and forfeited only if the awards lapsed as a result of the employee leaving during that period.

It can be seen that the (perhaps somewhat counterintuitive) impact of this is that an equity-settled share-based payment where the number of shares increases in line with increases in the entity's share price may nevertheless have a fixed grant date value irrespective of the number of shares finally awarded.

6.3.6 Transactions with independent market conditions, non-market vesting conditions or non-vesting conditions

6.3.6.A Independent market and non-market vesting conditions

The discussion at 6.3.2 above addressed the accounting treatment of awards with multiple conditions that must all be satisfied, i.e. a market condition and a non-market vesting condition. However, entities might also make awards with multiple conditions, only one of which need be satisfied, i.e. the awards vest on satisfaction of either a market condition *or* a non-market vesting condition. IFRS 2 provides no explicit guidance on the treatment of such awards, which is far from clear, as illustrated by Example 34.17 below.

Example 34.17: Award with independent market conditions and non-market vesting conditions

An entity grants an employee 100 share options that vest after three years if the employee is still in employment and the entity achieves either:

- cumulative total shareholder return (TSR) over three years of at least 15%; or
- cumulative profits over three years of at least £200 million.

The fair value of the award, ignoring vesting conditions, is £300,000. The fair value of the award, taking account of the TSR condition, but not the other conditions, is £210,000.

In our view, the entity has, in effect, simultaneously issued two awards – call them 'A' and 'B' – which vest as follows:

A   on achievement of three years' service plus minimum TSR; and
B   on achievement of three years' service plus minimum earnings growth.

If the conditions for both awards are simultaneously satisfied, one or other effectively lapses.

It is clear that award A, if issued separately, would require the entity to recognise an expense of £210,000 if the employee were still in service at the end of the three year period. It therefore seems clear that, if the employee does remain in service, there should be a charge of £210,000 irrespective of whether the award actually vests. It would be anomalous for the entity to avoid recording a charge that would have been recognised if the entity had made award A in isolation simply by packaging it with award B.

If in fact the award vested because the earnings condition, but not the market condition, had been satisfied, it would then be appropriate to recognise a total expense of £300,000.

During the vesting period, we believe that the entity should make an assessment at each reporting date of the basis on which the award is expected to vest. It should assess whether, as at that date, the award is expected to vest by virtue of the earnings condition, but not the TSR condition, being satisfied. Assume (for example) that the entity assesses at the end of year 1 that the award is likely to vest by virtue of the TSR condition, and at the end of year 2 that it is likely to vest by virtue of the earnings condition, and that the award actually does not vest, but the employee remains in service. This would give rise to annual expense as follows:

Year	Calculation of cumulative expense	Cumulative expense (£)	Expense for period (£)
1	210,000 × 1/3	70,000	70,000
2	300,000 × 2/3	200,000	130,000
3	210,000 × 3/3	210,000	10,000

We believe that ongoing reassessment during the vesting period is most consistent with the general approach of IFRS 2 to awards with a number of possible outcomes (see 10 below).

Of course, as for other awards, the accounting treatment would also require an assessment of whether or not the employee was actually going to remain in service.

A further question that arises is how the award should be accounted for if both conditions are satisfied. It would clearly be inappropriate to recognise an expense of £510,000 (the sum of the separate fair values of the award) – this would be double-counting, because the employee receives only one package of 100 options. However, should the total expense be taken as £210,000 or £300,000? In our view, it is appropriate to recognise a cost of £300,000 since the non-market vesting condition has been satisfied.

Ultimately, this is an issue which only the IASB can solve, since it arises from the inconsistent treatment by IFRS 2 of awards with market conditions and those with non-market conditions. As noted at 3.4 above, the IASB has concluded not to perform further research into IFRS 2.[22] Therefore we continue to believe that ongoing reassessment during the vesting period is most consistent with the general approach of IFRS 2 for awards with multiple possible outcomes.

6.3.6.B   Independent market conditions and non-vesting conditions

Arrangements are also seen where a share-based payment transaction vests on the satisfaction of either a market condition or a non-vesting condition.

In our view, an entity granting an award on the basis of a service condition (and any other non-market vesting conditions) plus either a market condition or a non-vesting condition should measure the fair value of the award at grant date taking into account the probability that either the market condition or the non-vesting condition will be met. The fact that there are two alternative conditions on which the award might vest means that, unless the two conditions are perfectly correlated, the grant date fair value of such an award will be higher than that of an award where there is only one possible basis on which the award might vest. Irrespective of whether the market condition and/or the non-vesting conditions are met, the entity will recognise the grant date fair value provided all other service and non-market vesting conditions are met (i.e. the expense recognition is consistent with that of any award with market and/or non-vesting conditions).

6.3.7   Transactions with hybrid or interdependent market conditions and non-market vesting conditions

Awards may sometimes have a performance condition which depends simultaneously on a market element and a non-market element, sometimes known as 'hybrid' conditions. Examples of such conditions include:

- a particular price-earnings (PE) ratio (calculated by reference to share price, a market condition, and earnings, a non-market vesting condition); and
- a maximum level of discount of market capitalisation (a market condition) below net asset value (a non-market vesting condition).

Such awards are rather curious, in the sense that these ratios may remain fairly constant irrespective of the underlying performance of the entity, so that a performance condition based on them is arguably of limited motivational value.

In our view, in contrast to our suggested treatment of awards with independent market and non-market vesting conditions discussed at 6.3.6.A above, awards with interdependent market and non-market vesting conditions must be accounted for entirely as awards with market conditions. These awards contain at least one element that meets the definition of a market condition but which cannot be completely split from the non-market element for separate assessment. An indicator such as the PE ratio, or discount of market capitalisation below net asset value, is a market condition as defined since it is 'related to the market price ... of the entity's equity instruments' (see 6.3.1 above).

6.3.8 Awards with a condition linked to flotation price

Awards in an unlisted entity may be granted with a condition linked to the achievement of a specific price when the entity floats. On flotation there is a market and a market price for the entity's equity instruments and the achievement of a specific price on flotation would, in our view, be a market condition when accompanied by a corresponding service requirement (see 15.4 below).

6.4 Non-vesting conditions

The accounting treatment for awards with non-vesting conditions has some similarities to that for awards with market conditions in that:
- the fair value of the award at grant date is reduced to reflect the impact of the condition; and
- an expense is recognised for the award irrespective of whether the non-vesting condition is met, provided that all vesting conditions (other than market conditions) are met. *[IFRS 2.21A]*.

However, in some situations the accounting for non-vesting conditions differs from that for market conditions as regards the timing of the recognition of expense if the non-vesting condition is not satisfied (see 6.4.3 below).

6.4.1 Awards with no conditions other than non-vesting conditions

The effect of the treatment required by IFRS 2 is that any award that has only non-vesting conditions (e.g. an option award to an employee that may be exercised on a trade sale or IPO of the entity, irrespective of whether the employee is still in employment at that time) must be expensed in full at grant date. This is discussed further at 3.2 above and at 15.4 below, and illustrated in Example 34.5 at 6.1 above.

6.4.2 Awards with non-vesting conditions and variable vesting periods

IFRS 2 does not explicitly address the determination of the vesting period for an award with a non-vesting condition but a variable vesting period (e.g. an award which delivers 100 shares when the price of gold reaches a given level, but without limit as to when that level must be achieved, so long as the employee is still in employment when the target is reached). However, given the close similarity between the required treatment for awards with non-vesting conditions and that for awards with market conditions, we believe that entities should follow the guidance in the standard for awards with market conditions and variable vesting periods (see 6.3.4 above).

6.4.3 Failure to meet non-vesting conditions

As noted above, the accounting for non-vesting conditions sometimes differs from that for market conditions as regards the timing of the recognition of expense if the non-vesting condition is not satisfied. The treatment depends on the nature of the non-vesting condition, as follows:

- if a non-vesting condition within the control of the counterparty (e.g. making monthly savings in an SAYE scheme or holding a specified number of shares in a matching share arrangement) is not satisfied during the vesting period, the failure to satisfy the condition is treated as a cancellation (see 7.4 below), with immediate recognition of any expense for the award not previously recognised; [IFRS 2.28A, IG24, IG Example 9A]

- if a non-vesting condition within the control of the entity (e.g. continuing to operate the scheme) is not satisfied during the vesting period, the failure to satisfy the condition is treated as a cancellation (see 7.4 below), with immediate recognition of any expense for the award not previously recognised; [IFRS 2.28A, IG24] but

- if a non-vesting condition within the control of neither the counterparty nor the entity (e.g. a financial market index reaching a minimum level) is not satisfied, there is no change to the accounting and the expense continues to be recognised over the vesting period, unless the award is otherwise treated as forfeited by IFRS 2. [IFRS 2.BC237A, IG24]. In our view, the reference to the vesting period would include any deemed vesting period calculated as described in 6.4.2 above.

If an award is forfeited due to a failure to satisfy a non-vesting condition after the end of the vesting period (e.g. a requirement for an employee not to work for a competitor for a two year period after vesting), no adjustment is made to the expense previously recognised, consistent with the general provisions of IFRS 2 for accounting for awards in the post-vesting period (see 6.1.3 above). This would be the case even if shares previously issued to the employee were required to be returned to the entity on forfeiture (see 3.1.1 and 3.2.3 above for further discussion of clawback arrangements and non-compete arrangements respectively).

7 EQUITY-SETTLED TRANSACTIONS – MODIFICATION, CANCELLATION AND SETTLEMENT

7.1 Background

It is quite common for equity instruments to be modified or cancelled before or after vesting. Typically this is done where the conditions for an award have become so onerous as to be virtually unachievable, or (in the case of an option) where the share price has fallen so far below the exercise price of an option that it is unlikely that the option will ever be 'in the money' to the holder during its life. In such cases, an entity may take the view that the equity awards are so unattainable as to have little or no motivational effect, and accordingly replace them with less onerous alternatives. Conversely, and more rarely, an entity may make the terms of a share award more onerous (possibly because of shareholder concern that targets are insufficiently demanding). In addition an entity may 'settle' an award, i.e. cancel it in return for cash or other consideration.

A target entity might modify existing share-based payment arrangements in the period leading up to a business combination. In this situation, it needs to be determined whether the guidance in IFRS 2 is applicable or whether the modification is being made for the benefit of the acquirer or the combined entity, in which case the guidance in IFRS 3 is likely to apply (see 11.2 below).

IFRS 2 contains detailed provisions for modification, cancellation and settlement. Whilst these provisions (like the summary of them below) are framed in terms of share-based payment transactions with employees, they apply to transactions with parties other than employees that are measured by reference to the fair value of the equity instruments granted (see 5.4 above). In that case, however, all references to 'grant date' should be taken as references to the date on which the third party supplied goods or rendered service. *[IFRS 2.26]*.

In the discussion below, any reference to a 'cancellation' is to any cancellation, whether instigated by the entity or the counterparty. As well as more obvious situations where an award is cancelled by either the entity or the counterparty, cancellations include:

- a failure by the entity to satisfy a non-vesting condition (see 6.4.3 above) within the control of the entity; and
- a failure by the counterparty to satisfy a non-vesting condition (see 6.4.3 above) within the control of the counterparty. *[IFRS 2.28A, IG24]*.

The discussion below is not relevant to cancellations and modifications of those equity-settled transactions that are (exceptionally) accounted for at intrinsic value (see 8.8 below).

The basic principles of the rules for modification, cancellation and settlement, which are discussed in more detail at 7.3 and 7.4 below, can be summarised as follows.

- As a minimum, the entity must recognise the amount that would have been recognised for the award if it remained in place on its original terms. *[IFRS 2.27]*.
- If the value of an award to an employee is reduced (e.g. by reducing the number of equity instruments subject to the award or, in the case of an option, by increasing the exercise price), there is no reduction in the cost recognised in profit or loss. *[IFRS 2.27, B42, B44]*.
- However, where the effect of the modification, cancellation or settlement is to increase the value of the award to an employee (e.g. by increasing the number of equity instruments subject to the award or, in the case of an option, by reducing the exercise price), the incremental fair value must be recognised as a cost. The incremental fair value is the difference between the fair value of the original award and that of the modified award, both measured at the date of modification. *[IFRS 2.27, B43]*.

It might be thought that, when an award has been modified, and certainly when it has been cancelled altogether, it no longer exists, and that it is therefore not appropriate to recognise any cost for it. However, such a view would be consistent with a vesting date measurement model rather than with the grant/service date measurement model of IFRS 2. Under the IFRS 2 model, the value of an award at grant date or service date cannot be changed by subsequent events.

Another reason given for the approach in IFRS 2 is that if entities were able not to recognise the cost of modified or cancelled options they would in effect be able to apply a selective form of 'truing up', whereby options that increased in value after grant would remain 'frozen' at their grant date valuation under the general principles of IFRS 2, whilst options that decreased in value could be modified or cancelled after grant date and credit taken for the fall in value. *[IFRS 2.BC222-237]*.

7.2 Valuation requirements when an award is modified, cancelled or settled

These provisions have the important practical consequence that, when an award is modified, cancelled or settled, the entity must obtain a fair value not only for the modified award, but also for the original award, updated to the date of modification. If the award had not been modified, there would have been no need to obtain a valuation for the original award after the date of grant.

Any modification of a performance condition clearly has an impact on the 'real' value of an award but it may have no direct effect on the value of the award for the purposes of IFRS 2. As discussed at 6.2 to 6.4 above, this is because market vesting conditions and non-vesting conditions are taken into account in valuing an award whereas non-market vesting conditions are not. Accordingly, by implication, a change to a non-market performance condition will not necessarily affect the expense recognised for the award under IFRS 2.

For example, if an award is contingent upon sales of a given number of units and the number of units required to be sold is decreased, the 'real' value of the award is clearly increased. However, as the performance condition is a non-market condition, and therefore not relevant to the original determination of the value of the award, there is no incremental fair value required to be accounted for by IFRS 2. If the change in the condition results in an increase in the estimated number of awards expected to vest, the change of estimate will however give rise to an accounting charge (see 6.1 to 6.4 above).

If an award is modified by changing the service period, the situation is more complex. A service condition does not of itself change the fair value of the award for the purposes of IFRS 2, but a change in service period may indirectly change the life of the award, which is relevant to its value (see 8 below). Similar considerations apply where performance conditions are modified in such a way as to alter the anticipated vesting date.

The valuation requirements relating to cancelled and settled awards are considered further at 7.4 below.

7.3 Modification

When an award is modified, the entity must as a minimum recognise the cost of the original award as if it had not been modified (i.e. at the original grant date fair value, spread over the original vesting period, and subject to the original vesting conditions). This applies unless the award does not vest because of failure to satisfy a vesting condition (other than a market condition) that was specified at grant date. *[IFRS 2.27, B42].*

In addition, a further cost must be recognised for any modifications that increase the fair value of the award. This additional cost is spread over the period from the date of modification until the vesting date of the modified award, which might not be the same as that of the original award. Where a modification is made after the original vesting period has expired, and is subject to no further vesting conditions, any incremental fair value should be recognised immediately. *[IFRS 2.27, B42-43].*

Whether a modification increases or decreases the fair value of an award is determined as at the date of modification, as illustrated by Example 34.18. *[IFRS 2.27, B42-44].*

Example 34.18: Does a modification increase or decrease the value of an award?

At the beginning of year 1, an entity granted two executives, A and B, a number of options worth $100 each.

At the beginning of year 2, A's options are modified such that they have a fair value of $85, their current fair value being $80. This is treated as an increase in fair value of $5 (even though the modified award is worth less than the original award when first granted). Therefore an additional $5 of expense would be recognised in respect of A's options.

At the beginning of year 3, B's options are modified such that they have a fair value of $120, their current fair value being $125. This is treated as a reduction in fair value of $5 (even though the modified award is worth more than the original award when first granted). However, there is no change to the expense recognised for B's options as IFRS 2 requires the entity to recognise, as a minimum, the original grant date fair value of the options (i.e. $100).

This treatment ensures that movements in the fair value of the original award are not reflected in the entity's profit or loss, consistent with the treatment of other equity instruments under IFRS.

Share-based payment

IFRS 2 provides further detailed guidance on this requirement as discussed below.

7.3.1 Modifications that increase the value of an award

7.3.1.A Increase in fair value of equity instruments granted

If the modification increases the fair value of the equity instruments granted, (e.g. by reducing the exercise price or changing the exercise period), the incremental fair value, measured at the date of modification, must be recognised over the period from the date of modification to the date of vesting for the modified instruments, as illustrated in Example 34.19 below. *[IFRS 2.B43(a), IG15, IG Example 7].*

Example 34.19: Award modified by repricing

At the beginning of year 1, an entity grants 100 share options to each of its 500 employees. Each grant is conditional upon the employee remaining in service over the next three years. The entity estimates that the fair value of each option is €15.

By the end of year 1, the entity's share price has dropped, and the entity reprices its share options. The repriced share options vest at the end of year 3. The entity estimates that, at the date of repricing, the fair value of each of the original share options granted (i.e. before taking into account the repricing) is €5 and that the fair value of each repriced share option is €8.

40 employees leave during year 1. The entity estimates that a further 70 employees will leave during years 2 and 3, so that there will be 390 employees at the end of year 3 (500 – 40 – 70).

During year 2, a further 35 employees leave, and the entity estimates that a further 30 employees will leave during year 3, so that there will be 395 employees at the end of year 3 (500 – 40 – 35 – 30).

During year 3, 28 employees leave, and hence a total of 103 employees ceased employment during the original three year vesting period, so that, for the remaining 397 employees, the original share options vest at the end of year 3.

IFRS 2 requires the entity to recognise:

- the cost of the original award at grant date (€15 per option) over a three year vesting period beginning at the start of year 1, plus

- the incremental fair value of the repriced options at repricing date (€3 per option, being the €8 fair value of each repriced option less the €5 fair value of the original option) over a two year vesting period beginning at the date of repricing (end of year 1).

This would be calculated as follows:

Year	Calculation of cumulative expense		Cumulative expense (€) (a+b)	Expense for period (€)
	Original award (a)	Modified award (b)		
1	390 employees × 100 options × €15 × 1/3		195,000	195,000
2	395 employees × 100 options × €15 × 2/3	395 employees × 100 options × €3 × 1/2	454,250	259,250
3	397 employees × 100 options × €15	397 employees × 100 options × €3	714,600	260,350

In effect, IFRS 2 treats the original award and the incremental value of the modified award as if they were two separate awards.

A similar treatment to that in Example 34.19 above is adopted where the fair value of an award subject to a market condition has its value increased by the removal or mitigation of the market condition. *[IFRS 2.B43(a), B43(c)].* Where a vesting condition other than a market condition is changed, the treatment set out in 7.3.1.C below is adopted. IFRS 2 does not specifically address the situation where the fair value of an award is increased by the removal or mitigation of a non-vesting condition. It seems appropriate, however, to account for this increase in the same way as for a modification caused by the removal or mitigation of a market condition – i.e. as in Example 34.19 above.

7.3.1.B   Increase in number of equity instruments granted

If the modification increases the number of equity instruments granted, the fair value of the additional instruments, measured at the date of modification, must be recognised over the period from the date of modification to the date of vesting for the modified instruments. If there is no further vesting period for the modified instruments, the incremental cost should be recognised immediately. *[IFRS 2.B43(b)].*

7.3.1.C   Removal or mitigation of non-market vesting conditions

Where a vesting condition, other than a market condition, is modified in a manner that is beneficial to the employee, the modified vesting condition should be taken into account when applying the general requirements of IFRS 2 as discussed in 6.1 to 6.4 above – in other words, the entity would continuously estimate the number of awards likely to vest and/or the vesting period. *[IFRS 2.B43(c)].* This is consistent with the general principle of IFRS 2 that vesting conditions, other than market conditions, are not taken into account in the valuation of awards, but are reflected by recognising a cost for those instruments that ultimately vest on achievement of those conditions. See also the discussion at 7.2 above.

IFRS 2 does not provide an example that addresses this point specifically, but we assume that the intended approach is as in Example 34.20 below. In this Example, the entity modifies an award in a way that is beneficial to the employee even though the modification does not result in any incremental fair value. The effect of the modification is therefore recognised by basing the expense on the original grant date fair value of the awards and an assessment of the extent to which the modified vesting conditions will be met.

Example 34.20:   Modification of non-market performance condition in employee's favour

At the beginning of year 1, the entity grants 1,000 share options to each member of its sales team, with exercise conditional upon the employee remaining in the entity's employment for three years, and the team selling more than 50,000 units of a particular product over the three year period. The fair value of the share options is £15 per option at the date of grant.

At the end of year 1, the entity estimates that a total of 48,000 units will be sold, and accordingly records no cost for the award in year 1.

During year 2, there is so severe a downturn in trading conditions that the entity believes that the sales target is too demanding to have any motivational effect, and reduces the target to 30,000 units, which it believes is achievable. It also expects 14 members of the sales team to remain in employment throughout the three year performance period. It therefore records an expense in year 2 of £140,000 (£15 × 14 employees × 1,000 options × 2/3). This cost is based on the originally assessed value of the award (i.e. £15) since the performance condition was never factored into the original valuation, such that any change in performance condition likewise has no effect on the valuation and does not result in any incremental fair value.

By the end of year 3, the entity has sold 35,000 units, and the share options vest as the modified performance condition has been met. Twelve members of the sales team have remained in service for the three year period. The entity would therefore recognise a total cost of £180,000 (12 employees × 1,000 options × £15), giving an additional cost in year 3 of £40,000 (total charge £180,000, less £140,000 charged in year 2).

The difference between the accounting consequences for different methods of enhancing an award could cause confusion in some cases. For example, it may sometimes not be clear whether an award has been modified by increasing the number of equity instruments or by lowering the performance targets, as illustrated in Example 34.21.

Example 34.21: Increase in number of equity instruments or modification of vesting conditions?

An entity grants a performance-related award which provides for different numbers of options to vest after 3 years, depending on different performance targets as follows:

Profit growth	Number of options
5%-10%	100
10%-15%	200
over 15%	300

During the vesting period, the entity concludes that the criteria are too demanding and modifies them as follows:

Profit growth	Number of options
5%-10%	200
over 10%	300

This raises the issue of whether the entity has changed:

(a) the performance conditions for the vesting of 200 or 300 options; or

(b) the number of equity instruments awarded for achieving growth of 5%-10% or growth of over 10%.

In our view, the reality is that the change is to the performance conditions for the vesting of 200 or 300 options, and should therefore be dealt with as in 7.3.1.C, rather than 7.3.1.B, above. Suppose, however, that the conditions had been modified as follows:

Profit growth	Number of options
5%-10%	200
10%-15%	300
over 15%	400

In that case, there has clearly been an increase in the number of equity instruments subject to an award for a growth increase of over 15%, which would have to be accounted for as such (i.e. under 7.3.1.B, rather than 7.3.1.C, above). In such a case, it seems more appropriate also to deal with the changes to the lower bands as changes to the number of shares awarded rather than as changes to the performance conditions.

7.3.2 Modifications that decrease the value of an award

This type of modification does not occur very often, as the effect would be somewhat demotivating and, in some cases, contrary to local labour regulations. However, there have been occasional examples of an award being made more onerous – usually in response to criticism by shareholders that the original terms were insufficiently demanding.

The general requirement of IFRS 2 (as outlined at 7.3 above) is that, where an award is made more onerous (and therefore less valuable), the financial statements must still recognise the cost of the original award. This rule is in part an anti-avoidance measure since, without it, an entity could reverse the cost of an out-of-the-money award by modifying it so that it was unlikely to vest (for example, by adding unattainable non-market performance conditions) rather than cancelling the award and triggering an acceleration of expense as in 7.1 above.

7.3.2.A Decrease in fair value of equity instruments granted

If the modification decreases the fair value of the equity instruments granted (e.g. by increasing the exercise price or reducing the exercise period), the decrease in value is effectively ignored and the entity continues to recognise a cost for services as if the awards had not been modified. *[IFRS 2.B44(a)]*. This approach also applies to reductions in the fair value of an award by the addition of a market condition or by making an existing market condition more onerous. *[IFRS 2.B44(a), B44(c)]*. Although IFRS 2 has no specific guidance on the point, we assume that reductions in the fair value resulting from the addition or amendment of a non-vesting condition are similarly ignored.

Example 34.22: Award modified by replacing a non-market condition with a market condition

At the beginning of year 1, an entity grants 1,000 share options to each of its 10 employees, with exercise conditional upon the employee remaining in the entity's employment for three years, and an earnings per share (EPS) target (non-market condition) being met over the three year period. The fair value of the share options is £15 per option at the date of grant.

At the end of year 1, the entity estimates that all the employees will remain in service until the end of year 3 and that the EPS target will be met. It therefore records a cost of £50,000 for the award in year 1 (£15 × 10 employees × 1,000 options × 1/3).

During year 2, the entity reassesses the arrangement and replaces the EPS target with a share price target (market condition) that must be achieved by the end of year 3. At the date of modification, the fair value of the option with the market condition is £12 and the fair value of the original option is £17. Therefore, the fair value of the awards has decreased as a result of the modification but, under IFRS 2, this decrease is not accounted for and the entity must continue to use the original grant date fair value. An expense must be recognised based on this grant date fair value unless the award does not vest due to failure to meet a service or non-market performance condition specified at the original grant date. At the original grant date the conditions were a service condition and a non-market performance condition. With the removal of the non-market performance condition, the only condition that has been in place since grant date is the service condition.

At the end of year 2 the entity estimates that nine employees will fulfil the service condition by the end of year 3. It therefore records a cumulative expense in year 2 of £90,000 (£15 × 9 employees × 1,000 options × 2/3) and an expense for the year of £40,000 (£90,000 – £50,000).

At the end of year 3 the share price target has not been met but eight employees have met the service condition. The entity therefore recognises a cumulative expense of £120,000 ((£15 × 8 employees × 1,000 options) and an expense for the year of £30,000 (£120,000 – £90,000).

It can be seen that the only expense reversal relates to those employees who have forfeited their options by failing to fulfil the employment condition. There is no reversal of expense for those employees who met the service condition but whose options did not vest (in real terms) because the market condition was not met. In IFRS 2 terms the options of those eight employees vested because all non-market conditions were met and so the entity has to recognise the grant date fair value for those awards. This is the case even though the original grant date fair value did not take account of the effect of the market condition (unlike an award with a market condition specified from grant date). This outcome is the result of the different treatment of market and non-market conditions under IFRS 2 and the requirement to recognise an expense for an award with a market condition provided all other conditions have been met (see further discussion at 6.3.2 above).

7.3.2.B Decrease in number of equity instruments granted

If the modification reduces the number of equity instruments granted, IFRS 2 requires the reduction to be treated as a cancellation of that portion of the award (see 7.4 below). *[IFRS 2.B44(b)]*. Essentially this has the effect that any previously unrecognised cost of the cancelled instruments is immediately recognised in full, whereas the cost of an award whose value is reduced by other means continues to be spread in full over the remaining vesting period.

In situations where a decrease in the number of equity instruments is combined with other modifications so that the total fair value of the award remains the same or increases, it is unclear whether IFRS 2 requires an approach based on the value of the award as a whole or, as in the previous paragraph, one based on each equity instrument as the unit of account. This is considered further at 7.3.4 below.

7.3.2.C Additional or more onerous non-market vesting conditions

Where a non-market vesting condition is modified in a manner that is not beneficial to the employee, again it is ignored and a cost recognised as if the original award had not been modified, as shown by Example 34.23 (which is based on IG Example 8 in the implementation guidance to IFRS 2). *[IFRS 2.B44(c), IG15, IG Example 8]*.

Example 34.23: Award modified by changing non-market performance conditions or service conditions

At the beginning of year 1, the entity grants 1,000 share options to each member of its sales team, conditional upon the employee remaining in the entity's employment for three years, and the team selling more than 50,000 units of a particular product over the three year period. The fair value of the share options is £15 per option at the date of grant. During year 2, the entity believes that the sales target is insufficiently demanding and increases it to 100,000 units. By the end of year 3, the entity has sold 55,000 units, and the modified share options are forfeited. Twelve members of the sales team have remained in service for the three year period.

On the basis that the original target would have been met, and twelve employees would have been eligible for awards, the entity would recognise a total cost of £180,000 (12 employees × 1,000 options × £15) in accordance with the minimum cost requirements of paragraph 27 of IFRS 2. The cumulative cost in years 1 and 2 would, as in the Examples above, reflect the entity's best estimate of the original 50,000 unit sales target being achieved at the end of year 3. If, conversely, sales of only 49,000 units had been achieved, any cost booked for the award in years 1 and 2 would have been reversed in year 3, since the original target of 50,000 units would not have been met.

It is noted in IG Example 8 that the same accounting result would have occurred if the entity had increased the service requirement rather than modifying the performance target. Because such a modification would make it less likely that the options would vest, which would not be beneficial to the employees, the entity would take no account of the modified service condition when recognising the services received. Instead, it would recognise the services received from the twelve employees who remained in service for the original three year vesting period. Other modifications to vesting periods are discussed below.

7.3.3 Modifications with altered vesting period

As noted at 7.3.1 above, where an award is modified so that its value increases, IFRS 2 requires the entity to continue to recognise an expense for the grant date fair value of the unmodified award over its original vesting period, even where the vesting period of the modified award is longer. This appears to have the effect that an expense may need to be recognised for awards that do not actually vest, as illustrated by Example 34.24 (which is based on Example 34.19 above).

Example 34.24: Award modified by reducing the exercise price and extending the vesting period

At the beginning of year 1, an entity grants 100 share options to each of its 500 employees, with vesting conditional upon the employee remaining in service over the next three years. The entity estimates that the fair value of each option is €15.

By the end of year 1, the entity's share price has dropped, and the entity reprices its share options. The repriced share options vest at the end of year 4. The entity estimates that, at the date of repricing, the fair value of each of the original share options granted (i.e. before taking into account the repricing) is €5 and that the fair value of each repriced share option is €7.

40 employees leave during year 1. The entity estimates that a further 70 employees will leave during years 2 and 3, and a further 25 employees during year 4, such that there will be 390 employees at the end of year 3 (500 – 40 – 70) and 365 (500 – 40 – 70 – 25) at the end of year 4.

During year 2, a further 35 employees leave, and the entity estimates that a further 30 employees will leave during year 3 and 30 more in year 4, such that there will be 395 employees at the end of year 3 (500 – 40 – 35 – 30) and 365 (500 – 40 – 35 – 30 – 30) at the end of year 4.

During year 3, 28 employees leave, and hence a total of 103 employees ceased employment during the original three year vesting period, so that, for the remaining 397 employees, the original share options would have vested at the end of year 3. The entity now estimates that only a further 20 employees will leave during year 4, leaving 377 at the end of year 4. In fact 25 employees leave, so that 372 satisfy the criteria for the modified options at the end of year 4.

In our view IFRS 2 requires the entity to recognise:

- the cost of the original award at grant date (€15 per option) over a three year vesting period beginning at the start of year 1, based on the ongoing best estimate of, and ultimately the actual, number of employees at the end of the original three-year vesting period;

- the incremental fair value of the repriced options at repricing date (€2 per option, being the €7 fair value of each repriced option less the €5 fair value of the original option) over a three year vesting period beginning at the date of repricing (end of year one), but based on the ongoing best estimate of, and ultimately the actual, number of employees at the end of the modified four-year vesting period.

This would be calculated as follows:

Year	Calculation of cumulative expense Original award	Modified award	Cumulative expense (€)	Expense for period (€)
1	390 employees × 100 options × €15 × 1/3		195,000	195,000
2	395 employees × 100 options × €15 × 2/3	365 employees × 100 options × €2 × 1/3	419,333	224,333
3	397 employees × 100 options × €15	377 employees × 100 options × €2 × 2/3	645,767	226,434
4	397 employees × 100 options × €15	372 employees × 100 options × €2	669,900	24,133

It may seem strange that a cost is being recognised for the original award in respect of the 25 employees who leave during year 4, who are never entitled to anything. However, in our view, this is consistent with:

- the overall requirement of IFRS 2 that the minimum cost of a modified award should be the cost that would have been recognised if the award had not been modified; and
- IG Example 8 in IFRS 2 (the substance of which is reproduced in Example 34.23 above) where an expense is clearly required to be recognised to the extent that the original performance conditions would have been met if the award had not been modified.

Moreover, as Examples 34.23 and 34.24 illustrate, the rule in IFRS 2 requiring recognition of a minimum expense for a modified award (i.e. as if the original award had remained in place) applies irrespective of whether the effect of the modification is that an award becomes less valuable to the employee (as in Example 34.23) or more valuable to the employee (as in Example 34.24).

Where a modified vesting period is shorter than the original vesting period, all of the expense relating to both the original and modified elements of the award should, in our view, be recognised by the end of the modified vesting period as no services will be rendered beyond that point. In this type of modification – as distinct from a change of estimate where there is a variable vesting period (see 6.2.3 above) – we believe that an entity has an accounting policy choice between retrospective and prospective adjustment of the vesting period as at the modification date. The overall expense recognised between grant date and vesting date will be the same in both cases, but there will be timing differences in the recognition of the expense, with retrospective accounting resulting in a higher expense as at the modification date itself.

7.3.4 Modifications that reduce the number of equity instruments granted but maintain or increase the value of an award ('value for value' exchanges and 'give and take' modifications)

As discussed at 7.3.2.B above, cancellation accounting has to be applied to a reduction in the number of equity instruments when a modification reduces both the number of equity instruments granted and the total fair value of the award. [IFRS 2.B44(b)]. This approach is consistent with the fact that part of the award has been removed without compensation to the employee. However, a modification of this kind is rarely seen in practice because of the demotivating effect and, in some jurisdictions, a requirement to pay compensation to the counterparty. An entity is more likely to modify an award so that the overall fair value remains the same, or increases, even if the number of equity instruments is reduced. These types of modification, sometimes known as 'value for value' exchanges or 'give and take' modifications, are considered below.

Where an entity reduces the number of equity instruments but also makes other changes so that the total fair value of the modified award remains the same as, or exceeds, that of the original award as at the modification date, it is unclear whether the unit of account for accounting purposes should be an individual equity instrument or the award as a whole. Examples 34.25 and 34.26 below illustrate the two situations and the two approaches.

Example 34.25: **Modification where number of equity instruments is reduced but total fair value of award is unchanged**

At the beginning of year 1, an entity granted an employee 200 share options with a grant date fair value of £9 and a vesting period of three years. During years 1 and 2, the entity recognises a cumulative expense of £1,200 (200 × £9 × 2/3). At the end of year 2 the exercise price of the options is significantly higher than the market price and the options have a fair value of £5 per option. On this date, the entity modifies the award and exchanges the 200 underwater options for 100 'at the money' options with a fair value of £10 each. The total fair value of the new awards of £1,000 (100 × £10) equals the total fair value of the awards exchanged (200 × £5), as measured at the modification date.

View 1 is that the unit of account is an individual option. Taking this approach, the decrease in the number of options from 200 to 100 will be accounted for as a cancellation with an acceleration at the modification date of any unexpensed element of the grant date fair value of 100 options (i.e. recognition of an additional amount of £300 (100 × £9 × 1/3)) The grant date fair value of the remaining 100 options continues to be recognised over the remainder of the vesting period together with their incremental fair value following the modification. Therefore, in year 3, there would be an expense of £300 (for the remaining grant date fair value) plus £500 (100 × (£10 – £5)) for the incremental fair value of 100 options. In total, therefore, an expense of £2,300 is recognised.

View 2 is that the total number of options exchanged is the more appropriate unit of account. In this case, the cancellation of the original options and the grant of replacement options are accounted for as one modification. There would therefore be no acceleration of expense in respect of the reduction in the number of options from 200 to 100 and the grant date fair value of the original award would continue to be recognised over the vesting period. In this case, the total expense recognised would be £1,800 (200 × £9).

Example 34.26: **Modification where number of equity instruments is reduced but total fair value of award is increased**

At the beginning of year 1, an entity granted to its employees 1,000 share options with an exercise price equal to the market price of the shares at grant date. There is a two year vesting period and the grant date fair value is £10 per option. The entity's share price has declined significantly so that the share price is currently significantly less than the exercise price. At the end of year 1, the entity decides to reduce the exercise price of the options and, as part of the modification, it also reduces the number of options from 1,000 to 800. At the date of modification, the fair value of the original options is £7 per option and that of the modified options £11 per option.

View 1 is that the unit of account is an individual option. Taking this approach, the decrease in the number of options from 1,000 to 800 will be accounted for as a cancellation of 200 options with an acceleration at the modification date of any remaining grant date fair value relating to those 200 options. The total expense recognised in year 1 is £6,000 ((800 × £10 × ½) + (200 × £10)). The grant date fair value of the remaining 800 options continues to be recognised over the remainder of the vesting period together with the incremental fair value of those options as measured at the modification date. In total the entity will recognise an expense of £13,200 (original grant date fair value of £10,000 (1,000 × £10) plus incremental fair value of £3,200 (800 × £(11 − 7)).

View 2 is that the unit of account is the total number of options as there are linked modifications forming one package. In this case, the incremental fair value is calculated as the difference between the total fair value before and after the modification. In total the entity will recognise an expense of £11,800 (original grant date fair value of £10,000 (1,000 × £10) plus incremental fair value on modification of £1,800 ((800 × £11) − (1,000 × £7))).

In both Examples above, the first view is based on paragraph B44(b) of IFRS 2 which states that 'if the modification reduces the number of equity instruments granted to an employee, that reduction shall be accounted for as a cancellation of that portion of the grant, in accordance with the requirements of paragraph 28'. This is perhaps further supported by paragraph B43(a) which, in providing guidance on accounting for a modification that increases the fair value of an equity instrument, appears only to refer to individual equity instruments when it states that 'the incremental fair value granted' in a modification is 'the difference between the fair value of the modified equity instrument and that of the original equity instrument, both estimated as at the date of modification'. *[IFRS 2.B43-44]*.

The second view is based on the overriding requirement in paragraph 27 of IFRS 2 for the grant date fair value of the equity instruments to be recognised unless the awards do not vest due to a failure to meet a vesting condition (other than a market condition) that was specified at grant date. This requirement is applicable even if the award is modified after the grant date. The same paragraph also requires an entity to recognise the effect of modifications 'that increase the total fair value of the share-based payment arrangement or are otherwise beneficial to the employee'. This reference to 'total fair value' supports the view that the total award is the unit of account and is reiterated in paragraphs B42 and B44 which provide guidance, respectively, for situations where the total fair value decreases or increases as a consequence of the modification of an award. Supporters of view 2 further consider that, in contrast to the cancellation accounting approach that is required in the very specific case where part of the award is, in effect, settled for no consideration (see 7.3.2.B above), a modification that reduces the number of equity instruments but maintains or increases the overall fair value of the award clearly provides the counterparty with a benefit. As a consequence, it is considered that no element of the grant date fair value should be accelerated as a cancellation expense. *[IFRS 2.27, B42, B44]*.

Given the lack of clarity in IFRS 2, we believe that an entity may make an accounting policy choice as to whether it considers the unit of account to be an individual equity instrument or an award as a whole. However, once made, that accounting policy choice should be applied consistently to all modifications that reduce the number of equity instruments but maintain or increase the overall fair value of an award. Whichever policy is chosen, the general requirements of IFRS 2 will still need to be applied in order to determine whether or not the amendments to the arrangement are such that it is appropriate to treat the changes as a modification (in IFRS 2 terms) rather than as a completely new award (see 7.4.2 and 7.4.4 below).

7.3.5 Modification of award from equity-settled to cash-settled (and vice versa)

Occasionally an award that was equity-settled when originally granted is modified so as to become cash-settled, or an originally cash-settled award is modified so as to become equity-settled. Such modifications are discussed at 9.4 below.

7.4 Cancellation and settlement

Where an award is cancelled or settled (i.e. cancelled with some form of compensation), other than by forfeiture for failure to satisfy the vesting conditions:

(a) if the cancellation or settlement occurs during the vesting period, it is treated as an acceleration of vesting, and the entity recognises immediately the amount that would otherwise have been recognised for services received over the remainder of the vesting period;

(b) where the entity pays compensation for a cancelled award:

   (i) any compensation paid up to the fair value of the award at cancellation or settlement date (whether before or after vesting) is accounted for as a deduction from equity, as being equivalent to the redemption of an equity instrument;

   (ii) any compensation paid in excess of the fair value of the award at cancellation or settlement date (whether before or after vesting) is accounted for as an expense in profit or loss; and

   (iii) if the share-based payment arrangement includes liability components, the fair value of the liability is remeasured at the date of cancellation or settlement. Any payment made to settle the liability component is accounted for as an extinguishment of the liability; and

(c) if the entity grants new equity instruments during the vesting period and, on the date that they are granted, identifies them as replacing the cancelled or settled instruments, the entity is required to account for the new equity instruments as if they were a modification of the cancelled or settled award. Otherwise it accounts for the new instruments as an entirely new award. *[IFRS 2.28, 29].*

The treatment of the cancelled or settled award in (a) above is similar, in its effect on profit or loss, to the result that would have occurred if:

- the fair value of the equity instruments issued had been recorded in full at grant date with a corresponding debit to a prepayment for 'services to be rendered';
- the prepayment were written off on a periodic basis until cancellation or settlement; and
- any remaining prepayment at the date of cancellation or settlement were written off in full.

It should be noted that the calculation of any additional expense in (b) above depends on the fair value of the award at the date of cancellation or settlement, not on the cumulative expense already charged. This has the important practical consequence that, when an entity pays compensation on cancellation or settlement of an award, it must obtain a fair value for the original award, updated to the date of cancellation or settlement. If the award had not been cancelled or settled, there would have been no need to obtain a valuation for the original award after the date of grant.

These requirements raise some further detailed issues of interpretation on a number of areas, as follows:
- the distinction between 'cancellation' and 'forfeiture' (see 7.4.1 below);
- the distinction between 'cancellation' and 'modification' (see 7.4.2 below);
- the calculation of the expense on cancellation (see 7.4.3 below); and
- replacement awards (see 7.4.4 and 7.5 below).

7.4.1 Distinction between cancellation and forfeiture

The provisions of IFRS 2 summarised at 7.4 above apply when an award of equity instruments is cancelled or settled 'other than a grant cancelled by forfeiture when the vesting conditions are not satisfied'. *[IFRS 2.28]*. The significance of this is that the terms of many share-based awards provide that they are, or can be, 'cancelled', in a legal sense, on forfeiture. IFRS 2 is clarifying that, where an award is forfeited (within the meaning of that term in IFRS 2 – see 6.1.2 above), the entity should apply the accounting treatment for a forfeiture (i.e. reversal of expense previously recognised), even if the award is legally cancelled as a consequence of the forfeiture.

7.4.1.A Termination of employment by entity

Based on the guidance in paragraph 28 of IFRS 2 referred to at 7.4.1 above, it might not always be immediately clear whether cancellation or forfeiture has occurred, particularly where options lapse as the result of a termination of employment by the entity. For example, an entity might grant options to an employee at the beginning of year 1 on condition of his remaining in employment until at least the end of year 3. During year 2, however, economic conditions require the entity to make a number of its personnel, including that employee, redundant, as a result of which his options lapse. Is this lapse a forfeiture or a cancellation for the purposes of IFRS 2?

The uncertainty arises because it could be argued either that the employee will be unable to deliver the services required in order for the options to vest (suggesting a forfeiture) or that the options lapse as a direct result of the employer's actions (suggesting a cancellation).

The IASB addressed this question by amending the definition of 'service condition' in IFRS 2 (see 3.1 above). The definition includes the following guidance:

'... If the counterparty, regardless of the reason, ceases to provide service during the vesting period, it has failed to satisfy the condition. ...' *[IFRS 2 Appendix A]*.

Therefore, IFRS 2 requires the failure to satisfy a service condition as the result of any termination of employment to be accounted for as a forfeiture rather than as a cancellation.

7.4.1.B Surrender of award by employee

It is sometimes the case that an employee, often a member of senior management, will decide – or be encouraged by the entity – to surrender awards during the vesting period. The question arises as to whether this should be treated as a cancellation or forfeiture for accounting purposes. IFRS 2 allows forfeiture accounting, and the consequent reversal of any cumulative expense, only in situations where vesting conditions are not satisfied. A situation where the counterparty voluntarily surrenders an award, and therefore the opportunity to meet the vesting conditions, is a decision within the control of the counterparty rather than a failure to satisfy a vesting condition and should be accounted for as a cancellation rather than as a forfeiture.

In its amendment of IFRS 2 (as discussed at 7.4.1.A above), we do not believe that the IASB's intention was to allow an employee to 'fail' to meet a service condition by voluntarily surrendering an award. Such an action should therefore continue to be treated as a cancellation rather than as a forfeiture.

7.4.2 Distinction between cancellation and modification

One general issue raised by IFRS 2 is where the boundary lies between 'modification' of an award in the entity's favour and outright cancellation of the award. As a matter of legal form, the difference is obvious. However, if an entity were to modify an award in such a way that there was no realistic chance of it ever vesting (for example, by introducing a requirement that the share price increase 1,000,000 times by vesting date), some might argue that this amounts to a *de facto* cancellation of the award. The significance of the distinction is that, whereas the cost of a 'modified' award continues to be recognised on a periodic basis over the vesting period (see 7.3 above), the remaining cost of a cancelled award is recognised immediately.

7.4.3 Calculation of the expense on cancellation

The basic accounting treatment for a cancellation and settlement is illustrated in Example 34.27 below.

Example 34.27: Cancellation and settlement – basic accounting treatment

At the start of year 1 an entity grants an executive 30,000 options on condition that she remain in employment for three years. Each option is determined to have a fair value of $10.

At the end of year 1, the executive is still in employment and the entity charges an IFRS 2 expense of $100,000 (30,000 × $10 × 1/3). At the end of year 2, the executive is still in employment. However, the entity's share price has suffered a decline which the entity does not expect to have reversed by the end of year 3, such that the options, while still 'in the money' now have a fair value of only $6. Moreover, the entity is under pressure from major shareholders to end option schemes with no performance criteria other than continuing employment.

Accordingly, the entity cancels the options at the end of year 2 and in compensation pays the executive $6.50 per option cancelled, a total payment of $195,000 (30,000 options × $6.50).

IFRS 2 first requires the entity to record a cost as if the options had vested immediately. The total cumulative cost for the award must be $300,000 (30,000 options × $10). $100,000 was recognised in year 1, so that an additional cost of $200,000 is recognised.

As regards the compensation payment, the fair value of the awards cancelled is $180,000 (30,000 options × $6.00). Accordingly, $180,000 of the payment is accounted for as a deduction from equity, with the remaining payment in excess of fair value, $15,000, charged to profit or loss.

The net effect of this is that an award that ultimately results in a cash payment to the executive of only $195,000 (i.e. $6.50 per option) has resulted in a total charge to profit or loss of $315,000 (i.e. $10.50 per option, representing $10 grant date fair value + $6.50 compensation payment – $6.00 cancellation date fair value).

Example 34.27 illustrates the basic calculation of the cancellation 'charge' required by IFRS 2. In more complex situations, however, the amount of the 'charge' may not be so clear-cut, due to an ambiguity in the drafting of paragraph 28(a) of the standard, which reads as follows:

'the entity shall account for the cancellation or settlement as an acceleration of vesting, and shall therefore recognise immediately the amount that would otherwise have been recognised for services received over the remainder of the vesting period.' *[IFRS 2.28(a)]*.

There is something of a contradiction within this requirement as illustrated by Example 34.28.

Example 34.28: Cancellation and settlement – best estimate of cancellation expense

At the beginning of year 1, entity A granted 150 employees an award of free shares, with a grant date fair value of £5, conditional upon continuous service and performance targets over a 3-year period from grant date. The number of shares awarded varies according to the extent to which targets (all non-market vesting conditions) have been met, and could result in each employee still in service at the end of year 3 receiving a minimum of 600, and a maximum of 1,000 shares.

Half way through year 2 (i.e. 18 months after grant date), A is acquired by B, following which A cancels all of its share awards. At the time of the cancellation, 130 of the original 150 employees were still in employment. At that time, it was A's best estimate that, had the award run to its full term, 120 employees would have received 900 shares each. Accordingly the cumulative expense recognised by A for the award as at the date of takeover would, under the normal estimation processes of IFRS 2 discussed at 6.1 to 6.4 above, be £270,000 (900 shares × 120 employees × £5 × 18/36).

How should A account for the cancellation of this award?

The opening phrase of paragraph 28(a) – 'the entity shall account for the cancellation ... as an acceleration of vesting' – suggests that A should recognise a cost for all 130 employees in service at the date of cancellation. However, the following phrase – '[the entity] shall therefore recognise immediately the amount that would otherwise have been recognised for services received over the remainder of the vesting period' – suggests that the charge should be based on only 120 employees, the best estimate, as at the date of cancellation of the number of employees in whom shares will finally vest. In our view, either reading of paragraph 28(a) is possible.

There is then the issue of the number of shares per employee that should be taken into account in the cancellation charge. Should this be 1,000 shares per employee (the maximum number that could vest) or 900 shares per employee (the number expected by the entity at the date of cancellation actually to vest)?

In our view, it is unclear from the standard whether the intention was that the cancellation charge should be based on the number of shares considered likely, as at the date of cancellation, to vest for each employee (900 shares in this example) or whether it should be based on the maximum number of shares (1,000 shares in this example). Given the lack of clarity, in our view an entity may make an accounting policy choice.

In extreme cases, the entity's best estimate, as at the date of cancellation, might be that no awards are likely to vest. In this situation, no cancellation expense would be recognised. However, there would need to be evidence that this was not just a rather convenient assessment made as at the date of cancellation. Typically, the previous accounting periods would also have reflected a cumulative IFRS 2 expense of zero on the assumption that the awards would never vest.

An effect of these requirements is that IFRS 2 creates an accounting arbitrage between an award that is 'out of the money' but not cancelled (the cost of which continues to be spread over the remaining period to vesting) and one which is formally cancelled (the cost of which is recognised immediately). Entities might well prefer to opt for cancellation so as to create a 'one-off' charge to earnings rather than continue to show, particularly during difficult trading periods, significant periodic costs for options that no longer have any real value. However, such early cancellation of an award precludes any chance of the cost of the award being reversed through forfeiture during, or at the end of, the vesting period if the original vesting conditions are not met.

7.4.4 Replacement awards

The required accounting treatment of replacement awards, whilst generally clear, nevertheless raises some issues of interpretation. Most of this sub-section addresses the replacement of unvested awards but the treatment of vested awards is addressed at 7.4.4.C below.

As set out at 7.4 above, a new award that meets the criteria in paragraph 28(c) of IFRS 2 to be treated as a replacement of a cancelled or settled award is accounted for as a modification of the original award and any incremental value arising from the granting of the replacement award is recognised over the vesting period of that replacement award. Where the criteria are not met, the new equity instruments are accounted for as a new grant (in addition to accounting for the cancellation or settlement of the original arrangement). The requirements are discussed in more detail below.

7.4.4.A Designation of award as replacement award

Whether or not an award is a 'replacement' award (and therefore recognised at only its incremental, rather than its full, fair value) is determined by whether or not the entity designates it as such on the date that it is granted. In other words, the accounting treatment effectively hinges on declared management intent, notwithstanding the IASB's systematic exclusion of management intent from many other areas of financial reporting. The Basis for Conclusions does not really explain the reason for this approach, which is also hard to reconcile with the fact that the value of an award is unaffected by whether, or when, the entity declares it to be a 'replacement' award for the purposes of IFRS 2. Presumably, the underlying reason is to prevent a retrospective, and possibly opportunistic, assertion that an award that has been in issue for some time is a replacement for an earlier award.

Entities need to ensure that designation occurs on grant date as defined by IFRS 2 (see 5.3 above). For example, if an entity cancels an award on 15 March and notifies an employee in writing on the same day of its intention to ask the remuneration committee to grant replacement options at its meeting two months later, on 15 May, such notification (although formal and in writing) may not strictly meet IFRS 2's requirement for designation on grant date (i.e. 15 May). However, in our view, what is important is that the entity establishes a clear link between the cancellation of the old award and the granting of a replacement award even if there is later formal approval of the replacement award following the communication of its terms to the counterparty at the same time as the cancellation of the old award.

As drafted, IFRS 2 gives entities an apparently free choice to designate any newly granted awards as replacement awards. In our view, however, such designation cannot credibly be made unless there is evidence of some connection between the cancelled and replacement awards. This might be that the cancelled and replacement awards involve the same counterparties, or that the cancellation and replacement are part of the same arrangement.

7.4.4.B Incremental fair value of replacement award

Where an award is designated as a replacement award, any incremental fair value must be recognised over the vesting period of the replacement award. The incremental fair value is the difference between the fair value of the replacement award and the 'net fair value' of the cancelled or settled award, both measured at the date on which the replacement award is granted. The net fair value of the cancelled or settled award is the fair value of the award, immediately before cancellation, less any compensation payment that is accounted for as a deduction from equity. *[IFRS 2.28(c)]*. Thus the 'net fair value' of the original award can never be less than zero (since any compensation payment in excess of the fair value of the cancelled award would be accounted for in profit or loss, not in equity – see Example 34.27 at 7.4.3 above).

There is some confusion within IFRS 2 as to whether a different accounting treatment is intended to result from, on the one hand, modifying an award and, on the other hand, cancelling it and replacing it with a new award on the same terms as the modified award. This is explored in the discussion of Example 34.29 below, which is based on the same fact pattern as Example 34.19 at 7.3.1.A above.

Example 34.29:   Replacement awards – is there an accounting arbitrage between accounting for a modification and accounting for cancellation and a new grant?

At the beginning of year 1, an entity grants 100 share options to each of its 500 employees. Each grant is conditional upon the employee remaining in service over the next three years. The entity estimates that the fair value of each option is €15.

By the end of year 1, the entity's share price has dropped. The entity cancels the existing options and issues options which it identifies as replacement options, which also vest at the end of year 3. The entity estimates that, at the date of cancellation, the fair value of each of the original share options granted is €5 and that the fair value of each replacement share option is €8.

40 employees leave during year 1. The entity estimates that a further 70 employees will leave during years 2 and 3, so that there will be 390 employees at the end of year 3 (500 – 40 – 70).

During year 2, a further 35 employees leave, and the entity estimates that a further 30 employees will leave during year 3, so that there will be 395 employees at the end of year 3 (500 – 40 – 35 – 30).

During year 3, 28 employees leave, and hence a total of 103 employees ceased employment during the original three year vesting period, so that, for the remaining 397 employees, the replacement share options vest at the end of year 3.

The intention of the IASB appears to have been that the arrangement should be accounted for in exactly the same way as the modification in Example 34.19 above, since the Basis for Conclusions to IFRS 2 notes:

> '...the Board saw no difference between a repricing of share options and a cancellation of share options followed by the granting of replacement share options at a lower exercise price, and therefore concluded that the accounting treatment should be the same.' *[IFRS 2.BC233]*.

However, it is not clear that this intention is actually reflected in the drafting of IFRS 2, paragraph 28 of which reads as follows:

> 'If a grant of equity instruments is cancelled or settled during the vesting period (other than a grant cancelled by forfeiture when the vesting conditions are not satisfied):
>
> (a) the entity shall account for the cancellation or settlement as an acceleration of vesting, and shall therefore recognise immediately the amount that otherwise would have been recognised for services received over the remainder of the vesting period.
>
> (b) any payment made to the employee on the cancellation or settlement of the grant shall be accounted for as the repurchase of an equity interest, i.e. as a deduction from equity, except to the extent that the payment exceeds the fair value of the equity instruments granted, measured at the repurchase date. Any such excess shall be recognised as an expense. ...
>
> (c) if new equity instruments are granted to the employee and, on the date when those new equity instruments are granted, the entity identifies the new equity instruments granted as replacement equity instruments for the cancelled equity instruments, the entity shall account for the granting of replacement equity instruments in the same way as a modification of the original grant of equity instruments, in accordance with paragraph 27 and the guidance in Appendix B...'. *[IFRS 2.28]*.

As a matter of natural construction, paragraph (a) requires the cancellation of the existing award to be treated as an acceleration of vesting – explicitly and without qualification. In particular there is no rider to the effect that the requirement of paragraph (a) is to be read as 'subject to paragraph (c) below'.

Paragraph (c) requires any 'new equity instruments' granted to be accounted for in the same way as a modification of the original grant of equity instruments. It does not require this treatment for the cancellation of the original instruments, because this has already been addressed in paragraph (a).

Moreover, in order to construe paragraphs (a) and (c) in a manner consistent with the Basis for Conclusions to the standard, it would be necessary to read paragraph (c) as effectively superseding paragraph (a). However, for this to be a valid reading, it would also be necessary to read paragraph (b) as also superseding paragraph (a), and this would produce a manifestly incorrect result, namely that, if an award is cancelled and settled, there is no need ever to expense any part of the cancelled award not yet expensed at the date of cancellation.

The application of, firstly, the main text of IFRS 2 and, secondly, the Basis for Conclusions to IFRS 2 to the entity in Example 34.29 is set out below.

The main text in IFRS 2 appears to require the entity to recognise:

- The entire cost of the original options at the end of year 1 (since cancellation has the effect that they are treated as vesting at that date), based on the 390 employees expected at that date to be in employment at the end of the vesting period. This is not the only possible interpretation of the requirement of paragraph 28(a) – see below and the broader discussion in Example 34.28 at 7.4.3 above.

- For the options replacing the 390 cancelled awards, the incremental fair value of the replacement options at repricing date (€3 per option, being the €8 fair value of each replacement option less the €5 fair value of each cancelled option) over a two year vesting period beginning at the date of cancellation (end of year 1), based on the (at first estimated and then actual) number of employees at the end of year 3 (i.e. the final number could be less than the estimate of 390).

- For any additional replacement options (i.e. replacement options awarded in excess of the 390 × 100 options that were expected to vest at cancellation date), the full incremental fair value at repricing date (being the €8 fair value of each replacement option) over a two year vesting period beginning at the repricing date (end of year 1). The expense is based on the (at first estimated and then actual) number of employees in excess of 390 at the end of year 3.

This would be calculated as follows:

Year	Calculation of cumulative expense Original award	Replacement award	Cumulative expense (€)	Expense for period (€)
1	390 employees × 100 options × €15	–	585,000	585,000
2	390 employees × 100 options × €15	390 employees × 100 options × €3 × 1/2 5 employees × 100 options × €8 × 1/2	645,500	60,500
3	390 employees × 100 options × €15	390 employees × 100 options × €3 7 employees × 100 options × €8	707,600	62,100

By contrast, the accounting treatment implied by the Basis for Conclusions is as follows (see Example 34.19 above):

Year	Calculation of cumulative expense Original award (a)	Modified award (b)	Cumulative expense (€) (a+b)	Expense for period (€)
1	390 employees × 100 options × €15 × 1/3	–	195,000	195,000
2	395 employees × 100 options × €15 × 2/3	395 employees × 100 options × €3 × 1/2	454,250	259,250
3	397 employees × 100 options × €15	397 employees × 100 options × €3	714,600	260,350

It will be seen that both the periodic allocation of expense and the total expense differ under each interpretation. This is because, under the first interpretation, the cost of the original award is accelerated at the end of year 1 for all 390 employees expected at that date to be in employment at the end of the vesting period, whereas under the second interpretation a cost is recognised for the 397 employees whose awards finally vest. The difference between the two total charges of €7,000 (€714,600 − €707,600) represents 397 − 390 = 7 employees @ €1,000 [100 options × €10[€15 + €3 − €8]] each = €7,000.

We believe that either interpretation is valid, and an entity should adopt one or other consistently as a matter of accounting policy.

In Example 34.29 above, we base the cancellation calculations on 390 employees (the number expected to be employed at the end of the vesting period as estimated at the cancellation date) rather than on 460 employees (the number in employment at the cancellation date). As discussed in Example 34.28 at 7.4.3 above, either approach may be adopted but the selected approach should be applied consistently.

The illustrative examples above involve a relatively straightforward fact pattern where, as at the date of cancellation and replacement, there was an amount to accelerate in respect of the cancelled awards and an incremental fair value associated with the replacement awards. In other scenarios, the two accounting outcomes might result in greater divergence. For example, if the cancelled awards were expected never to vest, because performance conditions had become unachievable and this had been the conclusion for some time (see 7.4.3 above), the cancelled awards might have a value of zero on a cancellation basis and the full value of the replacement awards would be recognised. If modification accounting were applied, however, the entity would have to recognise the grant date fair value of the cancelled awards plus any incremental value of the replacement awards over the fair value of the cancelled awards as at cancellation date. The latter approach might result in a significantly higher cost.

The discussion above relates to situations in which awards are cancelled and replaced for reasons other than expected, or actual, failure by the counterparty to meet a service condition. Changes to awards in contemplation, or as a consequence, of cessation of employment are considered at 5.3.9.B above and at 7.5 and 7.6 below.

7.4.4.C Replacement of vested awards

The rules for replacement awards summarised in paragraph (c) at 7.4 above apply 'if a grant of equity instruments is cancelled or settled during the vesting period ...'. *[IFRS 2.28]*. However, if the original award has already vested when a replacement award is granted, there is no question of accelerating the cost of the cancelled award, as it has already been recognised in full during the vesting period. The issue is rather the treatment of the new award itself. IFRS 2 does not explicitly address this point but it appears that such a replacement award should be treated in the same way as a completely new award. In other words, its full fair value should be recognised immediately or, if there are any vesting conditions for the replacement award, over its vesting period.

By contrast, the rules for modification of awards discussed in 7.3 above apply whether the award has vested or not. Paragraphs 26 and 27 of IFRS 2 (modifications) are not restricted to events 'during the vesting period' in contrast to paragraph 28 (cancellation and settlement, including replacement awards), which is restricted to events 'during the vesting period'. *[IFRS 2.26-28]*.

This has the effect that the accounting cost of modifying an already vested award (i.e. the incremental fair value of the modified award) may, at first sight, appear to be lower than the cost of cancelling and replacing it, which requires the full fair value of the new award to be expensed. However, the full fair value of the new replacement award will be reduced by the fair value of the cancelled award that the employee has surrendered as part of the consideration for the new award. This analysis will, in many cases, produce an accounting outcome similar to that of the modification of an unvested award.

7.5 Replacement and *ex gratia* awards on termination of employment

When an employee's employment is terminated during the vesting period of an award of shares or options, the award will typically lapse in consequence, in other words applying IFRS 2 the award is 'forfeited' (see 6.1.2 and 7.4 above). It is common in such situations, particularly where the employee was part of the senior management, for the entity to make an alternative award, or to allow the employee to retain existing awards, as part of the package of benefits agreed with the employee on termination of employment.

Generally, such an award is an *ex gratia* award – in other words, it is a discretionary award to which the outgoing employee had no legal entitlement under the terms of the original award. However, a number of plan rules set out, in a 'good leaver' clause (see 5.3.9 above), the terms on which any *ex gratia* award may be made, usually by applying a formula to determine, or limit, how much of the original award can be considered to have vested.

In many cases the award will be made on a fully vested basis, i.e. the employee has full entitlement without further conditions needing to be fulfilled. In other cases, however, an employee will be allowed to retain awards that remain subject to the fulfilment of the original conditions (other than future service). Whichever form the award takes, in IFRS 2 terms it will be treated as vesting at the date of termination of employment because any remaining conditions will be accounted for as non-vesting conditions in the absence of an explicit or implied service condition (see 3.2 above).

As discussed at 7.4.1.A above, IFRS 2 requires an entity to apply forfeiture (rather than cancellation) accounting to awards that lapse if an employee is unable to satisfy a service condition for any reason. In amending the standard to make clear that forfeiture accounting applied to the termination of employment, the IASB did not specifically address the accounting for any replacement or *ex gratia* awards on termination of employment.

If the original award is accounted for as a forfeiture and any previously recognised cost reversed in anticipation of the employee's expected departure, it perhaps follows that any replacement award will be treated as a completely new award and recognised and measured based on its own grant date. However, the standard is not clear and there might be situations where entities consider it more appropriate to apply modification accounting (recognising the original grant date fair value of the award that would otherwise be forfeited on its original terms (because the service condition would not be met) plus the incremental value of the modified terms). In the absence of clarity in IFRS 2, we believe that judgement will be required based on the specific facts and circumstances and the extent to which the changes to the arrangements are considered to be a waiver of existing conditions in connection with the cessation of employment rather than the introduction of a discretionary replacement arrangement on completely new terms.

Example 34.30: Replacement award on termination of employment

At the beginning of year 1, an executive is granted the right to 10,000 free shares on condition of remaining in service until the end of year 3. The fair value of the award at grant date is £2.00 per share.

At the end of year 2, the executive's employment is terminated and he therefore loses his right to any shares. However, as *ex gratia* (voluntary) compensation, the remuneration committee awards him 6,667 shares vesting immediately. As at the end of year 2 the share price was £4.00, and the fair value of the original award was £3.60 per share. (This is lower than the current share price because the holder of a share is entitled to receive any dividends paid during year 3 whereas the holder of an unvested right to a share is not – see 8.5.4 below.)

This raises the question of how the *ex gratia* award of 6,667 shares should be accounted for. The factors to be considered in determining the grant date in such cases are discussed further at 5.3.9 above. For the purposes of this Example, it is assumed that the replacement award is treated as having been granted, or the original award is treated as having been modified, at the end of year 2 rather than the terms being in place as at the beginning of year 1.

Where the lapse is treated as a forfeiture, the entity:

- reverses the cost already booked for the award of £13,333 (10,000 shares × £2 × 2/3); and
- recognises the cost of the *ex gratia* award (at the fair value at that award's grant date) of £26,668 (6,667 shares × £4).

This results in a net charge on termination of £13,335.

If the lapse is treated as a modification of the original award, the entity:

- accelerates the cost not yet booked for the original award of £6,667 (10,000 shares × £2 = £20,000, less £13,333 already recognised – see above) as there is no future service period; and
- treats the *ex gratia* award as a replacement award at incremental value. The fair value of the replacement award of £26,668 (6,667 shares × £4 – see above) is compared to the fair value of the original award of £36,000 (10,000 shares × £3.60). Since the fair value of the replacement award is less than that of the original award, there is no incremental cost required to be recorded under IFRS 2.

This results in a net charge on termination of £6,667.

Example 34.30 assumes that the entity treats the entire award as the unit of account. An entity that has instead made a policy choice to base its modification accounting on an individual share or option as the unit of account (see further discussion at 7.3.4 above) will have a different accounting outcome.

7.6 Entity's plans for future modification or replacement of award – impact on estimation process at reporting date

As discussed at 6.1.1 and 6.1.2 above, IFRS 2 requires an entity to determine a cumulative IFRS 2 charge at each reporting date by reference to the 'best available estimate' of the number of awards that will vest (within the special meaning of that term in IFRS 2).

In addition to the normal difficulties inherent in any estimation process, it is not entirely clear which anticipated future events should be taken into account in the IFRS 2 estimation process and which should not, as illustrated by Example 34.31 below.

Example 34.31:   Estimation of number of awards expected to vest – treatment of anticipated future events

At the beginning of year 1, an entity granted an award of 1,000 shares to each of its 600 employees at a particular manufacturing unit. The award vests on completion of three years' service. As at the end of year 1, the entity firmly intends to close the unit, and terminate the employment of employees, as part of a rationalisation programme. This closure would occur part way through year 2. The entity has not, however, announced its intentions or taken any other steps so as to allow provision for the closure under IAS 37 – *Provisions, Contingent Liabilities and Contingent Assets* (see Chapter 26 at 6.1).

Under the original terms of the award, the award would lapse on termination of employment. However, the entity intends to compensate employees made redundant by changing the terms of their award so as to allow full vesting on termination of employment.

What is the 'best estimate', as at the end of year 1, of the number of awards expected to vest? Specifically should the entity:

(a) ignore the intended closure altogether, on the grounds that there is no other recognition of it in the financial statements;

(b) take account of the impact of the intended closure on vesting of the current award, but ignore the intended future change to the terms of the award to allow vesting; or

(c) take account of both the intended closure and the intended change to the terms of the award?

In our view, there is no basis in IFRS 2 for accounting for an anticipated future change to the terms of an award. The entity must account for those awards in issue at the reporting date, not those that might be in issue in the future. Accordingly we do not consider approach (c) above to be appropriate if any change to the issued awards was simply an intention.

Equally, we struggle to support approach (a) above. IFRS 2 requires the entity to use its 'best available estimate' and its best available estimate as at the end of year 1 must be that the unit will be closed, and the employees' employment terminated, in year 2. This view is supported by the fact that, unlike IAS 36 – *Impairment of Assets* (see Chapter 20) and IAS 37 (see Chapter 26), IFRS 2 does not explicitly prohibit an entity from taking account of the consequences of reorganisations and similar transactions to which it is not yet committed.

Accordingly, we believe that approach (b) should be followed under IFRS 2.

The entity's best estimate at the end of year 1 must be that none of the awards currently in place will vest (because all the employees will be made redundant and so will not meet the service condition before the end of the vesting period). It therefore applies forfeiture accounting at the end of year 1 and reverses any cost previously recorded for the award.

When the terms of the award are changed at the time of the redundancy in year 2 to allow full vesting, the entity will either recognise the full cost of the new award (as all cost relating to the original award has been reversed) or will treat the revised arrangement as a modification of the original award that is beneficial to the employee. In effect, the modification approach is based on a view that the original award is not now going to lapse because it will be modified before employment ceases and the forfeiture crystallises. In our view, in the absence of clarity in IFRS 2, the entity should assess the more appropriate approach based on the particular facts and circumstances.

Either approach will have what many may see as the less than ideal result that the entity will recognise a credit in profit or loss in year 1 and an expense in year 2, even though there has been no change in management's best estimate of the overall outcome. This follows from the analysis, discussed above, that we do not believe that the entity can account in year 1 for the award on the basis of what its terms may be in year 2.

The best estimate is made as at each reporting date. A change in estimate made in a later period in response to subsequent events affects the accounting expense from that later period only (i.e. there is no restatement of earlier periods presented).

7.7 Two awards running 'in parallel'

In some jurisdictions, it is not straightforward to cancel or modify an award. This may be because cancellation or modification triggers either a legal requirement for the entity to pay compensation to the holder, or adverse tax consequences for the holder. In such cases, where an award has become unattractive (for example, because it is 'out-of-the-money'), the entity may issue a second award rather than cancel or modify the original award. The second award cannot be designated as a replacement award, because the original award is still in place. The entity therefore has two awards running 'in parallel'.

However, a mechanism is then put in place to ensure that the employee can receive only one award. For instance, if the original award were 1,000 options, it might be replaced with a second award of 1,000 options, but on condition that, if options under one award are exercised, the number of options exercisable under the other award is correspondingly reduced, so that no more than 1,000 options can be exercised in total.

The accounting for such arrangements is discussed in Example 34.32 below.

Example 34.32: Two option awards running in parallel

At the beginning of year 1, an entity granted 1,000 A options to an employee, subject to non-market vesting conditions. The grant date fair value of an A option was €50.

As at the beginning of year 2, the entity's share price is significantly below the exercise price of an A option, which now has a fair value of €5. Without modifying or cancelling the A options, the entity awards the employee 1,000 new B options. The B options are subject to non-market vesting conditions different in nature from, and more onerous than, those applicable to the A options, but have a lower exercise price. The terms of the B options include a provision that for every A option that is exercised, the number of B options that can be exercised is reduced by one, and *vice versa*. The fair value of a B option at the beginning of year 2 is €15.

Clearly, the employee will exercise whichever series of options, A or B, has the higher intrinsic value. There are four possible outcomes:

1. Neither the A options nor the B options vest.
2. Only the A options vest.
3. Only the B options vest.
4. Both the A options and B options vest and the employee must choose which to exercise. Rationally, the employee would exercise the B options as they have the lower exercise price.

In our view, the B options are most appropriately accounted for as if they were a modification of the A options. In substance the A options have been modified by adding alternative non-market vesting conditions with a different option exercise price.

On the date of the substantive modification, the entity estimates the fair value of both the original and modified options and calculates the incremental fair value of the modification. As only one series of options can be exercised, we believe that the most appropriate treatment is to account for whichever award the entity believes, at each reporting date, is more likely to be exercised. This is analogous to the accounting treatment we suggest in Example 34.12 at 6.2.5 above and in Example 34.17 at 6.3.6 above.

If the entity believes that neither award will vest, any expense previously recorded would be reversed.

If the entity believes that only the A options will vest, it will recognise expense based on the grant date fair value of the A options (€50 each).

If the entity believes that only the B options will vest, it will recognise expense based on:

(a) the grant date fair value of the A options (€50 each) over the original vesting period of the A options, plus

(b) the incremental fair value of the B options, as at their grant date (€10 each, being their €15 fair value less the €5 fair value of an A option), over the vesting period of the B options.

If the entity believes that both the A options and B options will vest, it follows the accounting treatment of outcome 3 above (i.e. vesting of the B options). This is because the employee will either choose the B options or, if the employee decides to choose the A options, the entity has to expense both the value of the A options and the incremental value of the B options because that incremental value relates to a vested award.

The entity revises the assessment at each reporting date and at the end of the vesting period when the actual outcome is known, so that the cumulative expense is based on the actual outcome.

Examples of other types of arrangement with multiple outcomes are illustrated at 6.2.5 above and at 10.3 and 15.4 below.

7.8 Share splits and consolidations

It is common for an entity to divide its existing equity share capital into a larger number of shares (share splits) or to consolidate its existing share capital into a smaller number of shares (share consolidations). The impact of such splits and consolidations is not specifically addressed in IFRS 2, and a literal application of IFRS 2 could lead to some rather anomalous results.

Suppose that an employee has options over 100 shares in the reporting entity, with an exercise price of £1. The entity undertakes a '1 for 2' share consolidation – i.e. the number of shares in issue is halved such that, all other things being equal, the value of one share in the entity after the consolidation is twice that of one share before the consolidation.

IFRS 2 is required to be applied to modifications to an award arising from equity restructurings. *[IFRS 2.BC24]*. In many cases, a share scheme will provide for automatic adjustment so that, following the consolidation, the employee holds options over only 50 shares with an exercise price of £2. As discussed at 5.3.8.A above, all things being equal, it would be expected that the modified award would have the same fair value as the original award and so there would be no incremental expense to be accounted for.

However, it may be that the scheme has no such provision for automatic adjustment, such that the employee still holds options over 100 shares. The clear economic effect is that the award has been modified, since its value has been doubled. It could be argued that, on a literal reading of IFRS 2, no modification has occurred, since the employee holds options over 100 shares at the same exercise price before and after the consolidation. The Interpretations Committee discussed this issue at its July and November 2006 meetings but decided not to take it onto its agenda because it 'was not a normal commercial occurrence and ... unlikely to have widespread significance'.[23] This decision was re-confirmed by the Interpretations Committee in March 2011.[24] In our view, whilst it seems appropriate to have regard to the substance of the transaction, and treat it as giving rise to a modification, it can be argued that IFRS 2 as drafted does not require such a treatment, particularly given the decision of the Interpretations Committee not to discuss the issue further.

Sometimes, the terms of an award give the entity discretion to make modifications at a future date in response to more complex changes to the share structure, such as those arising from bonus issues, share buybacks and rights issues where the effect on existing options may not be so clear-cut. These are discussed further at 5.3.8.A above.

8 EQUITY-SETTLED TRANSACTIONS – VALUATION

8.1 Introduction

The IASB provides some guidance on valuation in Appendix B to the standard, which we summarise and elaborate upon below. The guidance is framed in terms of awards to employees which are valued at grant date, but many of the general principles are equally applicable to awards to non-employees valued at service date. *[IFRS 2.B1]*.

As discussed in more detail at 4 to 7 above, IFRS 2 requires a 'modified grant-date' approach, under which the fair value of an equity award is estimated on the grant date without regard to the possibility that any service conditions or non-market performance vesting conditions will not be met. Although the broad intention of IFRS 2 is to recognise the cost of the goods or services to be received, the IASB believes that, in the case of services from employees, the fair value of the equity instruments awarded is more readily determinable than the fair value of the services received.

As noted at 5.1 above, IFRS 2 defines fair value as 'the amount for which an asset could be exchanged, a liability settled, or an equity instrument granted could be exchanged, between knowledgeable, willing parties in an arm's length transaction'.

IFRS 2 requires fair value to be based on the market price of the equity instruments, where available, or calculated using an option-pricing model. While fair value may be readily determinable for awards of shares, market quotations are not available for long-term, non-transferable share options because these instruments are not generally traded.

As discussed further at 8.2.2 below, the fair value of an option at any point in time is made up of two basic components – intrinsic value and time value. Intrinsic value is the greater of (a) the market value of the underlying share less the exercise price of the option and (b) zero.

Time value reflects the potential of the option for future gain to the holder, given the length of time during which the option will be outstanding, and possible changes in the share price during that period. Because market price information is not normally available for an employee share option, the IASB believes that, in the absence of such information, the fair value of a share option awarded to an employee generally must be estimated using an option-pricing model. *[IFRS 2.BC130]*. This is discussed further at 8.3 below.

The discussion below aims to provide guidance on the valuation of options and similar awards under IFRS 2; it is not intended to provide detailed instructions for constructing an option pricing model.

The approach to determining the fair value of share-based payments continues to be that specified in IFRS 2 as share-based payments fall outside the scope of IFRS 13 which applies more generally to the measurement of fair value under IFRSs (see Chapter 14). *[IFRS 2.6A]*.

8.2 Options

8.2.1 Call options – overview

Before considering the features of employee share options that make their valuation particularly difficult, a general overview of call options may be useful.

Call options give the holder the right, but not the obligation, to buy the underlying shares at a specified price (the 'exercise' or 'strike' price) on, or before, a specified date. Share-based payments take the form of call options over the underlying shares.

Options are often referred to as American or European. American options can be exercised at any time up to the expiry date, whereas European options can be exercised only on the expiry date itself.

The terms of employee options commonly have features of both American and European options, in that there is a period, generally two or three years, during which the option cannot be exercised (i.e. the vesting period). At the end of this period, if the options vest, they can be exercised at any time up until the expiry date. This type of option is known as a Window American option or Bermudan option.

A grant of shares is equivalent to an option with an exercise price of zero and will be exercised regardless of the share price on the vesting date. Throughout the discussion below, any reference to share options therefore includes, to the extent applicable, share grants or zero strike price options. There is further discussion of grants of free shares at 8.7.1 below.

8.2.2 Call options – valuation

As noted in 8.1 above, option value consists of intrinsic value and time value. For a call option, intrinsic value is the greater of:

- the share price less the exercise price, and
- zero.

Figure 34.2 below sets out the intrinsic value (or payoff) for a call option with an exercise price of $5.00.

Figure 34.2: Intrinsic value of a call option

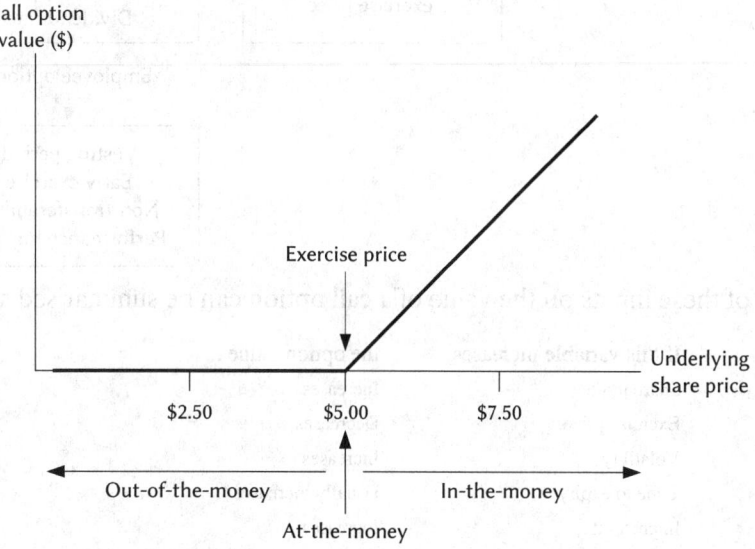

A call option is said to be 'in-the-money' when the share price is above the exercise price of the option and 'out-of-the-money' when the share price is less than the exercise price. An option is 'at-the-money' when the share price equals the exercise price of the option.

The time value of an option arises from the time remaining to expiry. As well as the share price and the exercise price, it is impacted by the volatility of the share price, time to expiry, dividend yield and the risk-free interest rate and the extent to which it is in- or out-of-the-money. For example, when the share price is significantly less than the exercise price, the option is said to be 'deeply' out-of-the-money. In this case, the fair value consists entirely of time value, which decreases the more the option is out-of-the-money.

The main inputs to the value of a simple option are:

- the exercise price of the option;
- the term of the option;
- the current market price of the underlying share;
- the expected future volatility of the price of the underlying share;
- the dividends expected to be paid on the shares during the life of the option (if any); and
- the risk-free interest rate(s) for the expected term of the option.

Their effect on each of the main components of the total value (intrinsic value and time value) is shown in Figure 34.3 below.

Figure 34.3: Determinants of the fair value of a call option

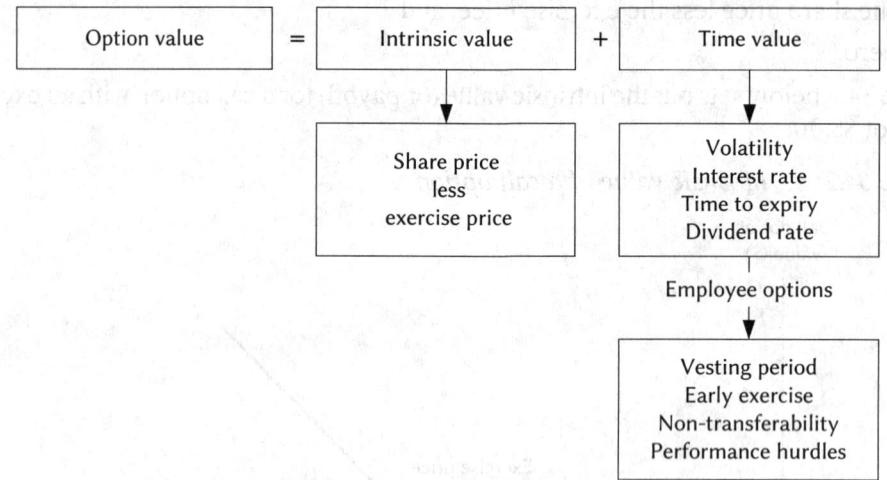

The effect of these inputs on the value of a call option can be summarised as follows:

If this variable increases,	the option value ...
Share price	Increases
Exercise price	Decreases
Volatility	Increases
Time to expiry	Usually increases*
Interest rate	Increases
Dividend yield/payout	Decreases

*   In most cases the time value of an option is positive. Whilst an American option always has positive or zero time value, a European option may have a zero or negative time value when there is a high dividend yield and the option is considerably in-the-money. In this case, as the time to expiry increases, a European call option will reduce in value (negative time value) and an American call option will stay constant in value (zero time value).

The factors to be considered in estimating the determinants of an option value in the context of IFRS 2 are considered in more detail at 8.5 below.

8.2.3   Factors specific to employee share options

In addition to the factors referred to in 8.2.2 above, employee share options are also affected by a number of specific factors that can affect their true economic value. These factors, not all of which are taken into account for IFRS 2 valuation purposes (see 8.4 and 8.5 below), include the following:

- non-transferability (see 8.2.3.A below);
- continued employment requirement (see 8.2.3.B below);
- vesting and non-vesting conditions (see 8.2.3.C below);
- periods during which holders cannot exercise their options – referred to in various jurisdictions as 'close', 'restricted' or 'blackout' periods (see 8.2.3.D below);

- limited ability to hedge option values (see 8.2.3.E below); and
- dilution effects (see 8.2.3.F below).

8.2.3.A Non-transferability

Holders of freely-traded share options (i.e. those outside a share-based payment transaction) can choose to 'sell' their options (typically by writing a call option on the same terms) rather than exercise them. By contrast, employee share options are generally non-transferable, leading to early (and sub-optimal) exercise of the option. This will lower the value of the options.

8.2.3.B Continued employment requirement

Holders of freely-traded share options can maintain their positions until they wish to exercise, regardless of other circumstances. In contrast, employee share options cannot normally be held once employment is terminated. If the options have not vested, they will be lost. If the options have vested, the employee will be forced to exercise the options immediately or within a short timescale, or forfeit them altogether, losing all time value. This will lower the value of the options.

8.2.3.C Vesting and non-vesting conditions

Holders of freely-traded share options have an unconditional right to exercise their options. In contrast, employee share options may have vesting and non-vesting conditions attached to them, which may not be met, reducing their value. This is discussed in more detail in 8.4 below.

Although a non-market vesting condition reduces the 'true' fair value of an award, it does not directly affect its valuation for the purposes of IFRS 2 (see 6.2 above). However, non-market vesting conditions may indirectly affect the value. For example, when an award vests on satisfaction of a particular target rather than at a specified time, its value may vary depending on the assessment of when that target will be met, since that may influence the expected life of the award, which is relevant to its fair value under IFRS 2 (see 6.2.3 and 8.2.2 above and 8.5.1 below).

8.2.3.D Periods during which exercise is restricted

Holders of freely-traded American or Bermudan share options can exercise at any time during the exercisable window. In contrast, employees may be subject to 'blackout' periods in which they cannot exercise their options, for example to prevent insider trading. While this could conceivably make a significant impact if the shares were significantly mis-priced in the market, in an efficient market blackout periods will only marginally decrease the value.

8.2.3.E Limited ability to hedge option values

In the case of freely-traded share options, it is reasonable to justify the theoretical valuation on the basis that, for any other value, arbitrage opportunities could arise through hedging. In contrast, employee share options are usually awarded only in relatively small amounts, and the employees are usually subject to restrictions on share trading (especially short selling the shares, as would be required to hedge an option). When considered in combination with the non-transferability of the options (see 8.2.3.A above), this means that exercising the options is the only way to remove exposure to fluctuations in value, which lowers the value of the options.

8.2.3.F   Dilution effects

When third parties write traded share options, the writer delivers shares to the option holder when the options are exercised, so that the exercise of the traded share options has no dilutive effect. By contrast, if an entity writes share options to employees and, when those share options are exercised, issues new shares (or uses shares previously repurchased and held in treasury) to settle the awards, there is a dilutive effect as a result of the equity-settled awards. As the shares will be issued at the exercise price rather than the current market price at the date of exercise, this actual or potential dilution may reduce the share price, so that the option holder does not make as large a gain as would arise on the exercise of similar traded options which do not dilute the share price.

8.3   Selection of an option-pricing model

Where, as will almost always be the case, there are no traded options over the entity's equity instruments that mirror the terms of share options granted to employees, IFRS 2 requires the fair value of options granted to be estimated using an option-pricing model. The entity must consider all factors that would be considered by knowledgeable, willing market participants in selecting a model. *[IFRS 2.B4-5]*.

The IASB decided that it was not necessary or appropriate to prescribe the precise formula or model to be used for option valuation. It notes that there is no particular option pricing model that is regarded as theoretically superior to the others, and there is the risk that any model specified might be superseded by improved methodologies in the future. *[IFRS 2.BC131]*.

The three most common option-pricing methodologies for valuing employee options are:

- the Black-Scholes-Merton formula (see 8.3.1 below);
- the binomial model (see 8.3.2 below); and
- the Monte Carlo Simulation (see 8.3.3 below).

It is important to understand all the terms and conditions of a share-based payment arrangement, as this will influence the choice of the most appropriate option pricing model.

IFRS 2 names the Black-Scholes-Merton formula and the binomial model as examples of acceptable models to use when estimating fair value, *[IFRS 2.BC152]*, while noting that there are certain circumstances in which the Black-Scholes-Merton formula may not be the most appropriate model (see 8.3.1 below). Moreover, there may be instances where, due to the particular terms and conditions of the share-based payment arrangement, neither of these models is appropriate, and another methodology is more appropriate to achieving the intentions of IFRS 2. A model commonly used for valuing more complex awards is Monte Carlo Simulation (often combined with the Black-Scholes-Merton formula or the binomial model). This can deal with the complexities of a plan such as one with a market condition based on relative total shareholder return (TSR), which compares the return on a fixed sum invested in the entity to the return on the same amount invested in a peer group of entities.

8.3.1 The Black-Scholes-Merton formula

The Black-Scholes-Merton methodology is commonly used for assessing the value of a freely-traded put or call option and allows for the incorporation of static dividends on shares. The assumptions underlying the Black-Scholes-Merton formula are as follows:

- the option can be exercised only on the expiry date (i.e. it is a European option);
- there are no taxes or transaction costs and no margin requirements;
- the volatility of the underlying asset is constant and is defined as the standard deviation of the continuously compounded rates of return on the share over a specified period;
- the risk-free interest rate is constant over time;
- short selling is permitted;
- there are no risk-free arbitrage opportunities;
- there are log normal returns (i.e. the continuously compounded rate of return is normally distributed); and
- security trading is continuous.

The main limitation of the Black-Scholes-Merton methodology is that it only calculates the option price at one point in time. It does not consider the steps along the way when there could be a possibility of early exercise of an American option (although as discussed at 8.4 below this can be partially mitigated by using an assumed expected term as an input to the calculation).

The Black-Scholes-Merton formula is an example of a closed-form model, which is a valuation model that uses an equation to produce an estimated fair value. The formula is as shown in Figure 34.4 below.

Figure 34.4:   The Black-Scholes-Merton formula

$$c = S_0 e^{-qT} N(d_1) - K e^{-rT} N(d_2)$$

Where:

$$d_1 = \frac{\ln(S_0/K) + (r - q + \sigma^2/2)T}{\sigma \sqrt{T}}$$

$$d_2 = d_1 - \sigma \sqrt{T}$$

- c = price of a written call
- S_0 = price of the underlying share
- N = the cumulative probability distribution function for a standardised normal distribution
- q = dividend yield (continuously compounded)
- K = call option exercise price
- r = the continuously compounded risk-free rate
- σ = annualised volatility of the underlying share
- T = time to expiry (in years)

Note: 'e' represents the mathematical constant, the base of the natural logarithm (2.718282...), and 'ln' is the natural logarithm of the indicated value

Whilst the Black-Scholes-Merton formula is complex, its application in practice is relatively easy. It can be programmed into a spreadsheet, and numerous programs and calculators exist that use it to calculate the fair value of an option. As a result, the formula is used widely by finance professionals to value a large variety of options. However, a number of the assumptions underlying the formula may be better suited to valuing short-term, exchange-traded share options rather than employee share options.

The attributes of employee share options that render the Black-Scholes-Merton formula less effective as a valuation technique include:

- *Long term to expiry*

    The formula assumes that volatility, interest rates and dividends are constant over the life of the option. While this may be appropriate when valuing short-term options, the assumption of constant values is less appropriate when valuing long-term options.

- *Non-transferability and early exercise*

    The formula assumes a fixed maturity/exercise date. While IFRS 2 provides for the use of an 'expected term' in place of the contractual life to reflect the possibility of early exercise resulting from the non-transferability of employee share options or other reasons (see 8.5 below), this may not adequately describe early exercise behaviour.

- *Vesting conditions and non-vesting conditions*

    The formula does not take into account any market-based vesting conditions or non-vesting conditions.

- *Blackout periods*

    As the formula assumes exercise on a fixed date, and does not allow earlier exercise, it does not take into consideration any blackout periods (see 8.2.3.D above).

In summary, application of the Black-Scholes-Merton formula is relatively simple, in part because many of the complicating factors associated with the valuation of employee share options cannot be incorporated into it directly and, therefore, must be derived outside of the formula (e.g. the input of an expected term).

IFRS 2 states that the Black-Scholes-Merton formula may not be appropriate for long-lived options which can be exercised before the end of their life and which are subject to variation in the various inputs to the model over the life of the option. However, IFRS 2 suggests that the Black-Scholes-Merton formula may give materially correct results for options with shorter lives and with a relatively short exercise period. *[IFRS 2.B5].*

The development of appropriate assumptions for use in the Black-Scholes-Merton formula is discussed at 8.5 below.

As noted above, the Black-Scholes-Merton formula is an example of a closed form model that is not generally appropriate for awards that include market performance conditions. However, in certain circumstances it may be possible to use closed form solutions other than the Black-Scholes-Merton formula to value options where, for example, the share price has to reach a specified level for the options to vest. These other solutions are beyond the scope of this chapter.

8.3.2 The binomial model

The binomial model is one of a subset of valuation models known as lattice models, which adopt a flexible, iterative approach to valuation that can capture the unique aspects of employee share options. A binomial model produces an estimated fair value based on the assumed changes in prices of a financial instrument over successive periods of time. In each time period, the model assumes that at least two price movements are possible. The lattice represents the evolution of the value of either a financial instrument or a market variable for the purpose of valuing a financial instrument.

The concepts that underpin lattice models and the Black-Scholes-Merton formula are the same, but the key difference between a lattice model and a closed-form model is that a lattice model is more flexible. The valuations obtained using the Black-Scholes-Merton formula and a lattice model will be very similar if the lattice model uses identical assumptions to the Black-Scholes-Merton calculation (e.g. constant volatility, constant dividend yields, constant risk-free rate, the same expected life). However, a lattice model can explicitly use dynamic assumptions regarding the term structure of volatility, dividend yields, and interest rates.

Further, a lattice model can incorporate assumptions about how the likelihood of early exercise of an employee share option may increase as the intrinsic value of that option increases, or how employees may have a high tendency to exercise options with significant intrinsic value shortly after vesting.

In addition, a lattice model can incorporate market conditions that may be part of the design of an option, such as a requirement that an option is only exercisable if the underlying share price reaches a certain level (sometimes referred to as 'target share price' awards). The Black-Scholes-Merton formula is not generally appropriate for awards that have a market-based performance condition because it cannot handle that additional complexity.

Most valuation specialists believe that lattice models, through their versatility, generally provide a more accurate estimate of the fair value of an employee share option with market performance conditions or with the possibility of early exercise than a value based on a closed-form Black-Scholes-Merton formula. As a general rule, the longer the term of the option and the higher the dividend yield, the larger the amount by which the binomial lattice model value may differ from the Black-Scholes-Merton formula value.

To implement the binomial model, a 'tree' is constructed the branches (or time steps) of which represent alternative future share price movements over the life of the option. In each time step over the life of the option, the share price has a certain probability of moving up or down by a certain percentage amount. It is important to emphasise the assumption, in these models, that the valuation occurs in a risk-neutral world, where investors are assumed to require no extra return on average for bearing risks and the expected return on all securities is the risk-free interest rate.

To illustrate how the binomial model is used, Example 34.33 below constructs a simple binomial lattice model with a few time steps. The valuation assumptions and principles will not differ in essence from those in a Black-Scholes-Merton valuation except that the binomial lattice model will allow for early exercise of the option. The relevant difference between the two models is the specification of a very small number of time steps, for illustrative purposes, in the binomial lattice model (see also 8.3.2.A below). We discuss below how the model can be augmented for a more complex set of assumptions.

Example 34.33: Binomial model

A share option is issued with an exercise price of $10, being the share price on the grant date. This Example assumes a constant volatility (50%) and risk-free rate (5% continuously compounded) although, as discussed later, those static assumptions may not be appropriate when valuing a long-term share option. It is also assumed that: the grantor pays dividends with a yield of 2% (continuously compounded) on its shares; the term of the option is five years; and each branch of the tree represents a length of time of one year.

At $t = 0$ (the grant date), the model is started at the grant date share price ($10 in this Example). At each node (the base of any price time step), two possible price changes (one increase and one decrease) are computed based on the volatility of the shares. The two new share prices are computed as follows:

The up-node price utilises the following formula:

$u = e^{\sigma\sqrt{dt}} = e^{0.5*\sqrt{1}} = 1.6487$

Where:

σ = annualised volatility of the underlying share

dt = period of time between nodes

The down-node is the inverse of the up-node:

$$d = \frac{1}{u} = \frac{1}{1.6487} = 0.6065$$

The probability of each upward and downward price movement occurring is calculated from:
- the probability of an upward movement in price:

$$p = \frac{e^{(r-q)dt} - d}{u - d} = \frac{e^{(.05-.02)*1} - 0.6065}{1.6487 - 0.6065} = 0.4068$$

Where:

e = represents the mathematical constant, the base of the natural logarithm (2.718282...)

r = continuously compounded risk-free rate

q = dividend yield (continuously compounded)

dt = period of time between nodes

- the probability of a downward movement in price:

$= 1 - p = 1 - 0.4068 = 0.5932$

Using the above price multiples, the price tree can then be constructed as shown diagrammatically below – each rising node is built by multiplying the previous price by 'u' and each falling node is similarly calculated by multiplying the previous price by 'd'.

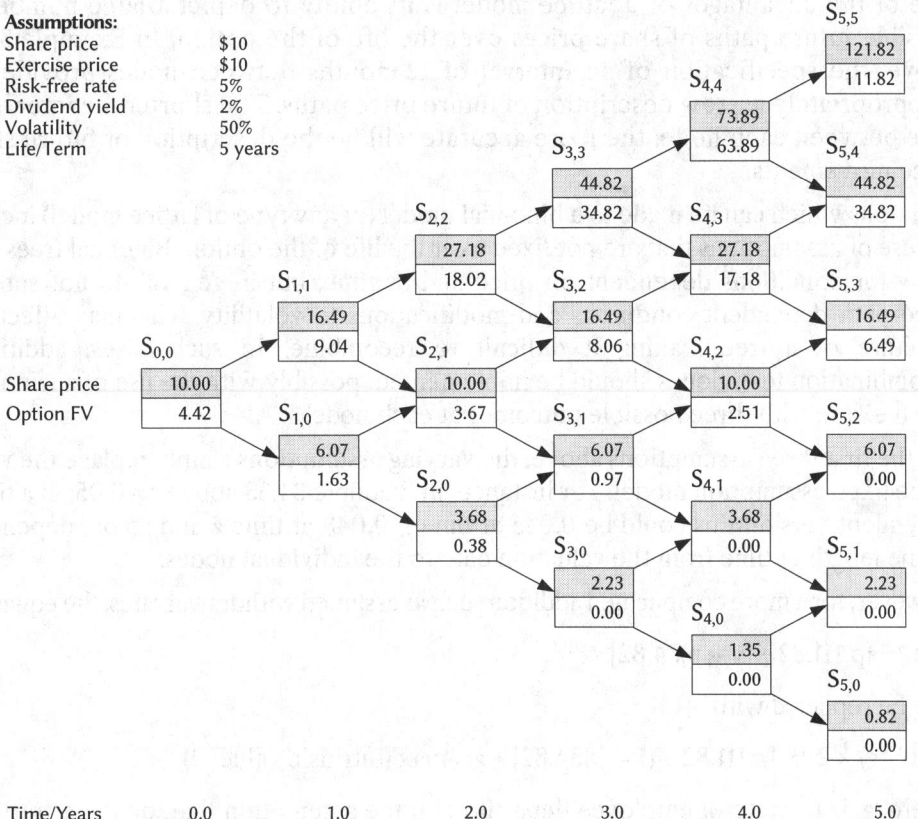

To calculate the option value:

- The option payoffs at the final time node (time 5 above) must be calculated. This is the share price less the exercise price, or zero if the payoff is negative.

- Then the option values must be calculated at the previous time point (time 4 above). This is done by calculating the expected value of the option for the branch paths available to the particular node being valued discounted at the risk-free rate. For example, for $S_{4,4}$ in the chart above the option value is the probability of going to node $S_{5,5}$ multiplied by the option value at that node plus the probability of going to node $S_{5,4}$ multiplied by the option value at that node, all discounted at the risk-free rate):

$$= e^{-r.dt}\{p.111.82 + (1-p)34.82\} = 0.95\{0.4068 \times 111.82 + 0.5932 \times 34.82\} = 62.92$$

This would be the value at node $S_{4,4}$ if the option were European and could not be exercised earlier. As the binomial model can allow for early exercise, the option value at node $S_{4,4}$ is the greater of the option value just calculated and the intrinsic value of the option which is calculated the same way as the end option payoff. In this case, as the intrinsic value is $63.89 ($73.89 – $10.00), the node takes the value of $63.89.

- The previous steps are then repeated throughout the entire lattice (i.e. for all nodes at time 4, then all nodes at time 3, etc.) until finally the option value is determined at time 0 – this being the binomial option value of $4.42.

- Additionally, if there is a vesting period during which the options cannot be exercised, the model can be adjusted so as not to incorporate the early exercise condition stipulated in the previous point and allow for this only after the option has vested and has the ability to be exercised before expiry.

One of the advantages of a lattice model is its ability to depict a large number of possible future paths of share prices over the life of the option. In Example 34.33 above, the specification of an interval of 12 months between nodes provides an inappropriately narrow description of future price paths. The shorter the interval of time between each node, the more accurate will be the description of future share price movements.

Additions which can be made to a binomial model (or any type of lattice model) include the use of assumptions that are not fixed over the life of the option. Binomial trees may allow for conditions dependent on price and/or time, but in general do not support price-path dependent conditions and modifications to volatility. This may affect the structure of a tree making it difficult to recombine. In such cases, additional recombination techniques should be implemented, possibly with the use of a trinomial tree (i.e. one with three possible outcomes at each node).

For the first three assumptions above, the varying assumptions simply replace the value in the fixed assumption model. For instance, in Example 34.33 above r = 0.05; in a time-dependent version this could be 0.045 at time 1, 0.048 at time 2 and so on, depending on the length of time from the valuation date to the individual nodes.

However, for a more complicated addition such as assumed withdrawal rates, the equation:

$$= e^{-r.dt} \{p.111.82 + (1 - p)34.82\}$$

may be replaced with

$$= (1 - g) \times e^{-r.dt} \{p.111.82 + (1 - p)34.82\} + g \times \max (\text{intrinsic value}, 0)$$

where 'g' is the rate of employee departure, on the assumption that, on departure, the option is either forfeited or exercised. As with the other time- and price-dependent assumptions, the rate of departure could also be made time- or price-dependent (i.e. the rate of departure could be assumed to increase as the share price increases, or increase as time passes, and so forth).

8.3.2.A Lattice models – number of time steps

When performing a lattice valuation, a decision must be taken as to how many time steps to use in the valuation (i.e. how much time passes between each node). Generally, the greater the number of time steps, the more accurate the final value. However, as more time steps are added, the incremental increase in accuracy declines. To illustrate the increases in accuracy, consider the diagram below, which values the option in Example 34.33 above as a European option. In this case, the binomial model has not been enhanced to allow for early exercise (i.e. the ability to exercise prior to expiry).

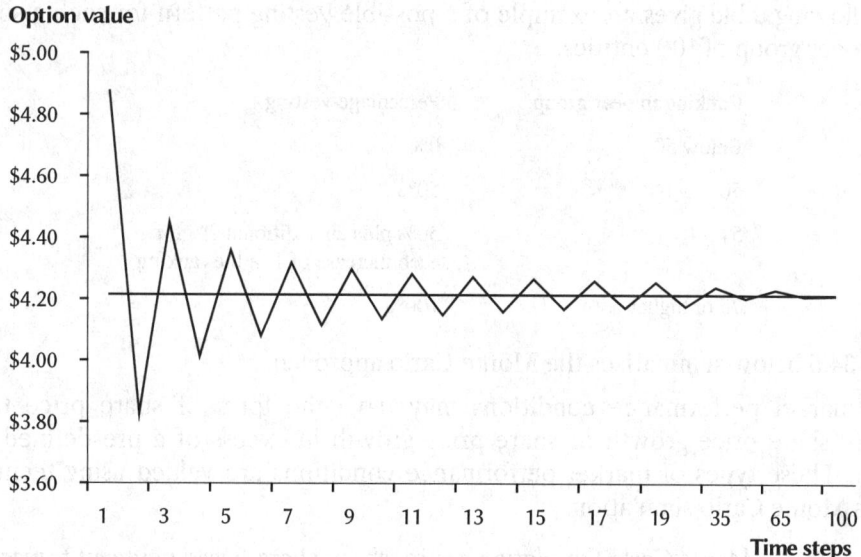

Whilst the binomial model is very flexible and can deal with much more complex assumptions than the Black-Scholes-Merton formula, there are certain complexities it cannot handle, which can best be accomplished by Monte Carlo Simulation – see 8.3.3 below.

The development of appropriate assumptions for use in a binomial model is discussed at 8.5 below.

In addition to the binomial model, other lattice models such as trinomial models or finite difference algorithms may be used. Discussion of these models is beyond the scope of this publication.

8.3.3 Monte Carlo Simulation

In order to value options with market-based performance targets where the market value of the entity's equity is an input to the determination of whether, or to what extent, an award has vested, the option methodology applied must be supplemented with techniques such as Monte Carlo Simulation.

A typical market performance condition is a TSR condition. TSR compares the return on a fixed sum invested in the entity to the return on the same amount invested in a peer group of entities. Typically, the entity is then ranked in the peer group and the number of share-based awards that vest depends on the ranking. For example, no award might vest for a low ranking, the full award might vest for a higher ranking, and a pro-rated level of award might vest for a median ranking.

The following table gives an example of a possible vesting pattern for such a scheme, with a peer group of 100 entities.

Ranking in peer group	Percentage vesting
Below 50	0%
50	50%
51-74	50% plus an additional 2% for each increase of 1 in the ranking
75 or higher	100%

Figure 34.5 below summarises the Monte Carlo approach.

Other market performance conditions may have the form of share price targets, absolute share price growth or share price growth in excess of a pre-defined index growth. These types of market performance conditions are valued using techniques such as Monte Carlo simulation.

Figure 34.5: Monte Carlo Simulation approach for share-based payment transactions

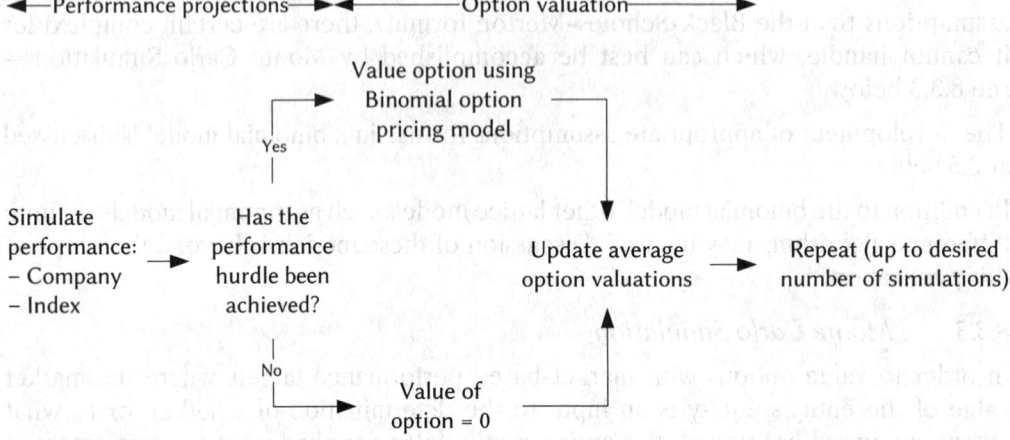

The valuation could be performed using either:

- a binomial valuation or the Black-Scholes-Merton formula, dependent on the results of the Monte Carlo Simulation; or
- the Monte Carlo Simulation on its own.

The framework for calculating future share prices uses essentially the same underlying assumptions as lie behind Black-Scholes-Merton and binomial models – namely a risk-neutral world and a log normal distribution of share prices.

For a given simulation, the risk-neutral returns of the entity and those of the peer group or index are projected until the performance target is achieved and the option vests. At this point, the option transforms into a 'vanilla' equity call option that may be valued using an option pricing model. This value is then discounted back to the grant date so as to give the value of the option for a single simulation.

When the performance target is not achieved and the option does not vest, a zero value is recorded. This process is repeated thousands or millions of times. The average option value obtained across all simulations provides an estimate of the value of the option, allowing for the impact of the performance target.

8.4 Adapting option-pricing models for share-based payment transactions

Since the option-pricing models discussed in 8.3 above were developed to value freely-traded options, a number of adjustments are required in order to account for the restrictions usually attached to share-based payment transactions, particularly those with employees. The restrictions not accounted for in these models include:

- non-transferability (see 8.4.1 below); and
- vesting conditions, including performance targets, and non-vesting conditions that affect the value for the purposes of IFRS 2 (see 8.4.2 below).

8.4.1 Non-transferability

As noted at 8.2.3.A above, employee options and other share-based awards are almost invariably non-transferable, except (in some cases) to the employee's estate in the event of death in service. Non-transferability often results in an option being exercised early (i.e. before the end of its contractual life), as this is the only way for the employee to realise its value in cash. Therefore, by imposing the restriction of non-transferability, the entity may cause the effective life of the option to be shorter than its contractual life, resulting in a loss of time value to the holder. *[IFRS 2.BC153-169]*.

One aspect of time value is the value of the right to defer payment of the exercise price until the end of the option term. When the option is exercised early because of non-transferability, the entity receives the exercise price much earlier than it otherwise would. Therefore, as noted by IFRS 2, the effective time value granted by the entity to the option holder is less than that indicated by the contractual life of the option.

IFRS 2 requires the effect of early exercise as a result of non-transferability and other factors to be reflected either by modelling early exercise in a binomial or similar model or by using expected life rather than contractual life as an input into the option-pricing model. This is discussed further at 8.5.1 below.

Reducing the time to expiry effectively reduces the value of the option. This is a simplified way of reducing the value of the employee stock option to reflect the fact that employees are unable to sell their vested options, rather than applying an arbitrary discount to take account of non-transferability.

8.4.2 Treatment of vesting and non-vesting conditions

Many share-based payment awards to employees have vesting and non-vesting conditions attached to them which must be satisfied before the award can be exercised. It must be remembered that a non-market vesting condition, while reducing the 'true' fair value of an award, does not directly affect its valuation for the purposes of IFRS 2 (see 6.2 above). However, non-market vesting conditions may indirectly affect the value. For example, when an award vests on satisfaction of achieving a particular operational target rather than at a specified time, its value may vary depending on the assessment of when that target will be met, since that may influence the expected life of the award, which is relevant to its fair value under IFRS 2 (see 6.2.3 and 8.2.2 above and 8.5 below).

8.4.2.A Market-based performance conditions and non-vesting conditions

As discussed at 6.3 and 6.4 above, IFRS 2 requires market-based vesting conditions and non-vesting conditions to be taken into account in estimating the fair value of the options granted. Moreover, the entity is required to recognise a cost for an award with a market condition or non-vesting condition if all the non-market vesting conditions attaching to the award are satisfied regardless of whether the market condition or non-vesting condition is satisfied. This means that a more sophisticated option pricing model may be required.

8.4.2.B Non-market vesting conditions

As discussed at 6.2 above, IFRS 2 requires non-market vesting conditions to be ignored when estimating the fair value of share-based payment transactions. Instead, such vesting conditions are taken into account by adjusting the number of equity instruments included in the measurement of the transaction (by estimating the extent of forfeiture based on failure to vest) so that, ultimately, the amount recognised is based on the number of equity instruments that eventually vest.

8.5 Selecting appropriate assumptions for option-pricing models

IFRS 2 notes that, as discussed at 8.2.2 above, option pricing models take into account, as a minimum:

- the exercise price of the option;
- the life of the option (see 8.5.1 and 8.5.2 below);
- the current price of the underlying shares;
- the expected volatility of the share price (see 8.5.3 below);
- the dividends expected on the shares (if appropriate – see 8.5.4 below); and
- the risk-free interest rate for the life of the option (see 8.5.5 below). *[IFRS 2.B6]*.

Of these inputs, only the exercise price and the current share price are objectively determinable. The others are subjective, and their development will generally require significant analysis. The discussion below addresses the development of assumptions for use both in a Black-Scholes-Merton formula and in a lattice model.

IFRS 2 requires other factors that knowledgeable, willing market participants would consider in setting the price to be taken into account, except for those vesting conditions and reload features that are excluded from the measurement of fair value – see 5 and 6 above and 8.9 below. Such factors include:

- restrictions on exercise during the vesting period or during periods where trading by those with inside knowledge is prohibited by securities regulators; or
- the possibility of the early exercise of options (see 8.5.1 below). *[IFRS 2.B7-9]*.

However, the entity should not consider factors that are relevant only to an individual employee and not to the market as a whole (such as the effect of an award of options on the personal motivation of an individual). *[IFRS 2.B10]*.

The objective of estimating the expected volatility of, and dividends on, the underlying shares is to approximate the expectations that would be reflected in a current market or negotiated exchange price for the option. Similarly, when estimating the effects of early exercise of employee share options, the objective is to approximate the expectations about employees' exercise behaviour that would be developed by an outside party with access to detailed information at grant date. Where (as is likely) there is a range of reasonable expectations about future volatility, dividends and exercise behaviour, an expected value should be calculated, by weighting each amount within the range by its associated probability of occurrence. *[IFRS 2.B11-12]*.

Such expectations are often based on past data. In some cases, however, such historical information may not be relevant (e.g. where the business of the entity has changed significantly) or even available (e.g. where the entity is unlisted or newly listed). An entity should not base estimates of future volatility, dividends or exercise behaviour on historical data without considering the extent to which they are likely to be reasonably predictive of future experience. *[IFRS 2.B13-15]*.

8.5.1 Expected term of the option

IFRS 2 allows the estimation of the fair value of an employee share award to be based on its expected life, rather than its maximum term, as this is a reasonable means of reducing the value of the award to reflect its non-transferability.

Option value is not a linear function of option term. Rather, value increases at a decreasing rate as the term lengthens. For example, a two year option is worth less than twice as much as a one year option, if all other assumptions are equal. This means that to calculate a value for an award of options with widely different individual lives based on a single weighted average life is likely to overstate the value of the entire award. Accordingly, assumptions need to be made as to what exercise or termination behaviour an option holder will exhibit. Considerations include:

- vesting period – the expected term of the option must be at least as long as its vesting period. The length of time employees hold options after they vest may vary inversely with the length of the vesting period;
- past history of employee exercise and termination patterns for similar grants (adjusted for current expectations) – see 8.5.2 below;
- expected volatility of the underlying share – on average, employees tend to exercise options on shares with higher volatility earlier;
- periods during which exercise may be precluded and related arrangements (e.g. agreements that allow for exercise to occur automatically during such periods if certain conditions are satisfied);
- employee demographics (age, tenure, sex, position etc.); and
- time from vesting date – the likelihood of exercise typically increases as time passes.

As discussed at 8.4 above, IFRS 2 notes that the effect of early exercise can be reflected:

- by treating the expected, rather than the contractual, life of the option as an input to a pricing model, such as the Black-Scholes-Merton formula (see 8.5.1.A below); or
- by using contractual life as an input to a binomial or similar model. *[IFRS 2.B16-17]*.

8.5.1.A Expected term under the Black-Scholes-Merton formula

An estimate of expected term based on the types of inputs described above can be used in the Black-Scholes-Merton formula as well as a lattice model. However, the formula requires only a single expected term to be used. This is one of the reasons why the Black-Scholes-Merton formula may provide a higher valuation for the same options than a lattice model.

The difference in value that arises from using only a single expected term results, in part, from the convex shape of a typical option valuation curve, as illustrated below.

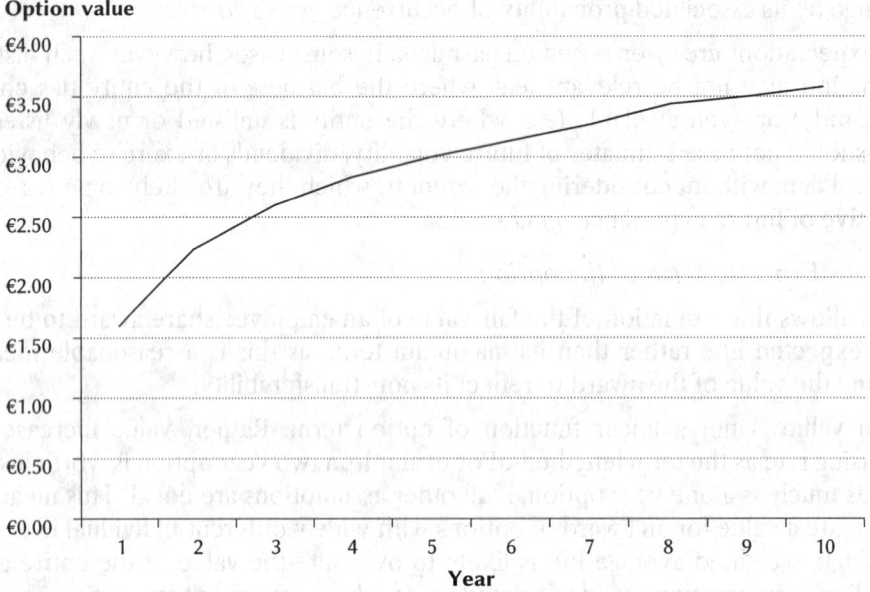

It is assumed, for the purposes of this illustration, that an at-the-money option on a €10 share with a 10-year contractual term is equally likely to be exercised at the end of each year beginning with year two. An average expected term of six years [(2+3+4+...10)/9] would be used in a Black-Scholes-Merton calculation giving a fair value of €3.10 for the option. If, instead, nine separate valuations were performed, each with a different expected term corresponding to each of the possible terms (from two to ten years), the average of those valuations (also calculated using the Black-Scholes-Merton formula) would be €2.9854. The latter amount is lower than €3.10 because of the convex shape of the valuation curve, reflecting the fact that the value increases at a decreasing rate as the term lengthens. Therefore, the value of the share option with an average expected term of six years will exceed the value derived from averaging the separate valuations for each potential term.

In a lattice model, exercise can occur at any time based on the rules specified in the model regarding exercise behaviour. The lattice model can therefore be thought of as analogous to the calculation in the above example in which the fair value was calculated as the average of the valuations from periods two to ten. In contrast, the Black-Scholes-Merton valuation allows only a single expected term to be specified. Therefore, it is analogous to the valuation described in the above example based on a single average expected term of six years.

Therefore, even if the expected term derived from a lattice model were used as an input in the Black-Scholes-Merton formula (and all other inputs were identical), the two models would give different values.

To mitigate the impact of the convex shape of the valuation curve, an entity with a broad-based share option plan might consider stratifying annual awards into different employee groups for the purposes of estimating the expected option lives (see 8.5.2 below).

Determining a single expected term can be quite challenging, particularly for an entity seeking to base its estimate on the periods for which previously granted options were outstanding, which would have been highly dependent on the circumstances during those periods. For example, if the entity's share price had increased significantly during the option period (as would be the case for share options granted by certain entities at the beginning of a bull market), it is likely that employees would have exercised options very soon after vesting. Alternatively, if options were granted at the end of a bull market and the share price declined significantly after the grant date, it is likely that the options would be exercised much later (if at all). These relationships would exist because, as discussed previously, the extent to which an option is in-the-money has a significant impact on exercise behaviour. Accordingly, deriving a single expected term in these situations involves considerable judgement.

8.5.2 Exercise and termination behaviour

IFRS 2 notes that employees often exercise options early for a number of reasons, most typically:

- restrictions on transferability mean that this is the only way of realising the value of the option in cash;
- aversion to the risk of not exercising 'in the money' options in the hope that they increase in value; or
- in the case of leavers, a requirement to exercise, or forfeit, all vested options on or shortly after leaving (see 8.5.2.B below).

Factors to consider in estimating early exercise include:

(a) the length of the vesting period, because the share option cannot be exercised until the end of the vesting period. Hence, determining the valuation implications of expected early exercise is based on the assumption that the options will vest;

(b) the average length of time similar options have remained outstanding in the past;

(c) the price of the underlying shares. Experience may indicate that employees tend to exercise options when the share price reaches a specified level above the exercise price;

(d) the employee's level within the organisation. For example, experience might indicate that higher-level employees tend to exercise options later than lower-level employees (see also 8.5.2.A below); and

(e) the expected volatility of the underlying shares. On average, employees might tend to exercise options on highly volatile shares earlier than on shares with low volatility. *[IFRS 2.B18]*.

In addition, the pattern of terminations of employment after vesting may be relevant (see 8.5.2.B below).

In our view, past exercise behaviour should generally serve as the starting point for determining expected exercise behaviour. That behaviour should be analysed, correlated to the factors above, and extrapolated into the future. However, significant changes in the underlying share price or in other salient characteristics of the entity, changes in option plans, tax laws, share price volatility and termination patterns may indicate that past exercise behaviour is not indicative of expected exercise behaviour. The expected life may also be estimated indirectly, by using a modified option pricing model to compute an option value, an input to which is an assumption that the options will be expected to be exercised when a particular share price is reached.

Some entities, including recently listed entities, or entities for which all outstanding grants have been out-of-the-money for a long period, may simply not be able to observe any exercise behaviour or may not possess enough history to perform a reasonable analysis of past exercise behaviour. In these cases, in our view, entities may have to look to the exercise history of employees of similar entities to develop expectations of employee exercise behaviour. At present there is only limited publicly-available information about employee exercise patterns, but valuation professionals and human resource consultants may have access to relevant data, based on which they may have articulated specific exercise patterns. In such circumstances, considerable judgement is required in assessing the comparability and appropriateness of the historic data used (including whether the data is current).

In the absence of extensive information regarding exercise behaviour, another solution could be to use a midpoint assumption – i.e. selecting as the expected date of exercise the midpoint between the first available exercise date (the end of the vesting period) and the last available exercise date (the contracted expiry date). However, this should be undertaken only when the entity is satisfied that this does not lead to a material misstatement. It is also plausible to assume exercise at the earliest possible time or to undertake a reasonable analysis of past behaviour and set up the amount of intrinsic value which, when exceeded, will trigger exercise of the option.

8.5.2.A Grouping employees with homogeneous exercise behaviour

IFRS 2 emphasises that the estimated life of an option is critical to its valuation. Therefore, where options are granted to a group of employees, it will generally be necessary to ensure that either:

(a) all the employees are expected to exercise their options within a relatively narrow time-frame; or

(b) if not, that the group is divided into sub-groups of employees who are expected to exercise their options within a similar relatively narrow time-frame.

IFRS 2 suggests that it may become apparent that middle and senior management tend to exercise options later than lower-level employees, either because they choose to do so, or because they are encouraged or compelled to do so as a result of required minimum levels of ownership of equity instruments (including options) among more senior employees. *[IFRS 2.B19-21]*.

8.5.2.B   Post-vesting termination behaviour

Most employee share options provide that, if employment is terminated, the former employee typically has only a short period (e.g. 90 days from the date of termination of employment) in which to exercise any vested options, the contractual expiry of which would otherwise be some years away. Accordingly, an entity should look at its prior termination patterns, adjust those patterns for future expectations and incorporate those expected terminations into a lattice model as expected early exercises.

Patterns of employee turnover are not necessarily linear and may be a non-linear function of a variety of factors, such as:

- employee demographics (age, sex, tenure, position, etc.);
- path of share price – for example, if options are deeply out-of-the-money, they may have little retention value and more employees may leave than if the options were at- or in-the-money; and
- economic conditions and other share prices.

8.5.3 Expected volatility of share price

Expected volatility is a measure of the amount by which a price is expected to fluctuate during a period. Share price volatility has a powerful influence on the estimation of the fair value of an option, much of the value of which is derived from its potential for appreciation. The more volatile the share price, the more valuable the option. It is therefore essential that the choice of volatility assumption can be properly supported.

IFRS 2 notes that the measure of volatility used in option pricing models is the annualised standard deviation of the continuously compounded rates of return on the share over a period of time. Volatility is typically expressed in annualised terms that are comparable regardless of the time period used in the calculation (for example, daily, weekly or monthly price observations).

The expected annualised volatility of a share is the range within which the continuously compounded annual rate of return is expected to fall approximately two-thirds of the time. For example, to say that a share with an expected continuously compounded rate of return of 12% has a volatility of 30% means that the probability that the rate of return on the share for one year will be between minus 18% (12% – 30%) and 42% (12% + 30%) is approximately two-thirds. If the share price is €100 at the beginning of the year, and no dividends are paid, the year-end share price would be expected to be between €83.53 (€100 × $e^{-0.18}$) and €152.20 (€100 × $e^{0.42}$) approximately two-thirds of the time.

The rate of return (which may be positive or negative) on a share for a period measures how much a shareholder has benefited from dividends and appreciation (or depreciation) of the share price. *[IFRS 2.B22-24].*

IFRS 2 gives examples of factors to consider in estimating expected volatility including the following: *[IFRS 2.B25]*

- *Implied volatility from traded share options*

  Implied volatility is the volatility derived by using an option pricing model with the traded option price (if available) as an input and solving for the volatility as the unknown on the entity's shares. It may also be derived from other traded instruments of the entity that include option features (such as convertible debt).

  Implied volatilities are often calculated by analysts and reflect market expectations for future volatility as well as imperfections in the assumptions in the valuation model. For this reason, the implied volatility of a share may be a better measure of prospective volatility than historical volatility (see below). However, traded options are usually short-term, ranging in general from one month to two years. If the expected lives are much longer than this, both the implied and historical volatilities will need to be considered.

- *Historical volatility*

  It may be relevant to consider the historical volatility of the share price over the most recent period that is generally commensurate with the expected term of the option (taking into account the remaining contractual life of the option and the effects of expected early exercise). However, this assumes that past share price behaviour is likely to be representative of future share price behaviour. Upon any restructuring of an entity, the question of whether or not past volatility will be likely to predict future volatility would need to be reassessed.

  The historical volatilities of similar entities may be relevant for newly listed entities, unlisted entities or entities that have undergone substantial restructuring (see 8.5.3.A to 8.5.3.C below).

- *The length of time the entity's shares have been publicly traded*

  A newly listed entity might have a high historical volatility, compared with similar entities that have been listed longer. Further guidance for newly listed entities is given in 8.5.3.A below.

- *'Mean-reverting tendency'*

  This refers to the tendency of volatility to revert to its long-term average level, and other factors indicating that expected future volatility might differ from past volatility. For example, if an entity's share price was extraordinarily volatile for some identifiable period of time because of a failed takeover bid or a major restructuring, that period could be disregarded in computing historical average annual volatility. However, an entity should not exclude general economic factors such as the effect of an economic downturn on share price volatility.

- *Appropriate and regular intervals for price observations*

  The price observations should be consistent from period to period. For example, an entity might use the closing price for each week or the opening price for the week, but it should not use the closing price for some weeks and the opening price for other weeks. Also, the price observations should be expressed in the same currency as the exercise price. In our view, at least thirty observations are generally required to calculate a statistically valid standard deviation. Our experience has been that, in general, it is more appropriate to make such observations daily or weekly rather than monthly.

8.5.3.A Newly listed entities

As noted under 'Historical volatility' at 8.5.3 above, an entity should consider the historical volatility of the share price over the most recent period that is generally commensurate with the expected option term. If a newly listed entity does not have sufficient information on historical volatility, it should compute historical volatility for the longest period for which trading activity is available. It should also consider the historical volatility of similar entities. For example, an entity that has been listed for only one year and grants options with an average expected life of five years might consider the historical volatility of entities in the same industry, which are of a similar size and operate similar businesses, for the first six years in which the shares of those entities were publicly traded. *[IFRS 2.B26]*.

8.5.3.B Unlisted entities

An unlisted entity will have neither historical nor current market information to consider when estimating expected volatility. IFRS 2 suggests that, in some cases, an unlisted entity that regularly issues options or shares might have set up an internal market for its shares. The volatility of those share prices could be considered when estimating expected volatility. Alternatively, if the entity has based the value of its shares on the share prices of similar listed entities, the entity could consider the historical or implied volatility of the shares of those similar listed entities. *[IFRS 2.B27-29]*.

If the entity has not used a valuation methodology based on the share prices of similar listed entities, the entity could derive an estimate of expected volatility consistent with the valuation methodology used. For example, the entity might consider it appropriate to value its shares on a net asset or earnings basis if this approximates to the fair value of the equity instruments, in which case it could consider the expected volatility of those net asset values or earnings. *[IFRS 2.B30]*.

8.5.3.C Listed entities that have undergone significant restructuring

An issue not specifically addressed by IFRS 2 is the approach required in the case of an entity that has been listed for some time but which has recently undergone significant restructuring or refocusing of the business (e.g. as a result of acquisitions, disposals or refinancing). In such cases, it may well be appropriate to adopt the approach advocated for newly listed entities in 8.5.3.A above.

8.5.3.D Expected volatility under the Black-Scholes-Merton formula

In calculating the fair value of a share option using the Black-Scholes-Merton formula, a single expected volatility assumption must be used. That amount should be based on the volatility expected over the expected term of the option. Frequently, expected volatility is based on observed historical share price volatility during the period of time equal to the expected term of the option and ending on the grant date. Implied volatilities (i.e. volatilities implied by actual option prices on the entity's shares observed in the market) also may be considered in determining the expected volatility assumption (see 8.5.3 above).

When developing an expected volatility assumption, current and historical implied volatilities for publicly traded options and historical realised share volatilities should be considered for shares of the grantor and shares of other entities in the grantor's industry and comparable entities.

The volatility of a market index will not generally provide an appropriate input as the diversified nature of the index tends to produce a lower volatility figure than that applicable to individual shares.

8.5.3.E Expected volatility under lattice models

Expected volatility is more accurately taken into account by lattice models than by the Black-Scholes-Merton formula, because lattice models can accommodate dynamic assumptions regarding the term structure and path-dependence of volatility. For example, there is evidence that volatility during the life of an option depends on the term of the option and, in particular, that short-term options often exhibit higher volatility than similar options with longer terms. Additionally, volatility is path-dependent, in that it is often lower (higher) after an increase (decrease) in share price.

An entity that can observe sufficiently extensive trading of options over its shares may decide, when developing a term structure of expected volatility, to place greater weight on current implied volatilities than on historical observed and implied volatilities. It is likely that current implied volatilities are better indicators of the expectations of market participants about future volatility.

8.5.4 Expected dividends

The valuation of an award of options depends on whether or not the holder is entitled to dividends or dividend equivalents (whether in the form of cash payments or reductions in the exercise price) before the award is ultimately exercised. *[IFRS 2.B31-32, B34]*. The accounting treatment of awards that entitle the holder to dividends before exercise is discussed further at 15.3 below.

Dividends paid on the underlying share will impact the share option value – the higher the expected dividend yield (i.e. dividend per share ÷ share price), the lower the option value. Option holders generally do not have dividend rights until they actually exercise the options and become shareholders. All other things being equal, a share option for a share yielding a high dividend is less valuable than one for a share yielding a low dividend.

Where employees are entitled to dividends or dividend equivalents, the options granted should be valued as if no dividends will be paid on the underlying shares, so that the input for expected dividends (which would otherwise reduce the valuation of an option) is zero. Conversely, where employees are not entitled to dividends or dividend equivalents, the expected dividends should be included in the application of the pricing model. *[IFRS 2.B31-32, B34]*.

While option pricing models generally call for an expected dividend yield, they may be modified to use an expected dividend amount rather than a yield. Where an entity uses expected payments rather than expected yields, it should consider its historical pattern of increases in dividends. For example, if an entity's policy has generally been to increase dividends, its estimated option value should not assume a fixed dividend amount throughout the life of the option unless there is evidence to support that assumption. *[IFRS 2.B35]*.

Determination of the expected dividends over the expected term of the option requires judgement. Generally, the expected dividend assumption should be based on current expectations about an entity's anticipated dividend policy. For example, an entity that has demonstrated a stable dividend yield in past years, and has indicated no foreseeable plans to change its dividend policy, may simply use its historical dividend yield to estimate the fair value of its options. If an entity has never paid a dividend, but has publicly announced that it will begin paying a dividend yielding 2% of the current share price, it is likely that an expected dividend yield of 2% would be assumed in estimating the fair value of its options.

Generally, assumptions about expected dividends should be based on publicly available information. Thus, an entity that does not pay dividends and has no plans to do so should assume an expected dividend yield of zero. However, an emerging entity with no history of paying dividends might expect to begin paying dividends during the expected lives of its employee share options. Such entities could use an average of their past dividend yield (zero) and the mean dividend yield of a comparable peer group of entities. [IFRS 2.B36].

8.5.4.A   Expected dividends under the Black-Scholes-Merton formula

Closed-form option-pricing models generally call for a single expected dividend yield as an input. That input should be determined based on the guidance at 8.5.4 above.

8.5.4.B   Expected dividends under the binomial model and other lattice models

Lattice models can be adapted to use an expected dividend amount rather than a dividend yield, and therefore can also take into account the impact of anticipated dividend changes. Such approaches might better reflect expected future dividends, since dividends do not always move in a fixed fashion with changes in the entity's share price. This may be a time- or price-dependent assumption, similar to those described in the discussion of the binomial model at 8.3.2 above. Expected dividend estimates in a lattice model should be determined based on the general guidance above. Additionally, when the present value of dividends becomes significant in relation to the share price, standard lattice models may need to be amended.

8.5.5   Risk-free interest rate

Typically, the risk-free interest rate is the implied yield currently available on zero-coupon government issues of the country in whose currency the exercise price is expressed, with a remaining term equal to the expected term of the option being valued (based on the remaining contractual life of the option and taking into account the effects of expected early exercise). It may be necessary to use an appropriate substitute, if no such government issues exist, or where the implied yield on zero-coupon government issues may not be representative of the risk-free interest rate (for example, in high inflation economies). An appropriate substitute should also be used if market participants would typically determine the risk-free interest rate by using that substitute. [IFRS 2.B37].

The risk-free interest rate will not have an impact on most free share grants unless the counterparty is not entitled to dividends during the vesting period and the fair value of the grant has been reduced by the present value of the dividends. Otherwise, grants of free shares have an exercise price of zero and therefore involve no cash outflow for the holder.

8.5.5.A   Risk-free interest rate under the Black-Scholes-Merton formula

The Black-Scholes-Merton formula expressed at 8.3.1 above uses a continuously compounded interest rate, which means that any interest rate calculated or obtained needs to be in this format. The continuously compounded interest rate is given by the formula:

continuously compounding rate = ln(1 + annual rate),

where ln represents a natural logarithm. For example, a 1.50% annual effective rate results in a continuously compounded rate of 1.49%:

1.49% = ln(1 + 0.0150)

8.5.5.B   Risk-free interest rate under binomial and other lattice models

At each node in the lattice, the option values in the lattice should be discounted using an appropriate forward rate as determined by a yield curve constructed from the implied yield on zero-coupon government bond issues. In stable economies this will have minimal impact and it is therefore likely that a flat risk-free rate that is consistent with the expected life assumption will be a reasonable estimate for this input.

8.6 Capital structure effects and dilution

Typically, traded share options are written by third parties, not the entity issuing the shares that are the subject of the option. When these share options are exercised, the writer delivers to the option holder shares acquired from existing shareholders. Hence the exercise of traded share options has no dilutive effect. By contrast, when equity-settled share options written by the entity are exercised, new shares may be issued (either in form or in substance, if shares previously repurchased and held in treasury are used), giving rise to dilution. This actual or potential dilution may reduce the share price, so that the option holder does not make as large a gain on exercise as would be the case on exercising an otherwise similar traded option that does not dilute the share price. *[IFRS 2.B38-39]*.

Whether or not this has a significant effect on the value of the share options granted depends on various factors, such as the number of new shares that will be issued on exercise of the options compared with the number of shares already issued. Also, if the market already expects that the option grant will take place, the market may have already factored the potential dilution into the share price at the date of grant. However, the entity should consider whether the possible dilutive effect of the future exercise of the share options granted might have an impact on their estimated fair value at grant date. Option pricing models can be adapted to take into account this potential dilutive effect. *[IFRS 2.B40-41]*.

In practice, in our view, it is unlikely that a listed entity would be required to make such an adjustment unless it makes a very large, unanticipated grant of share options. Indeed, even in that case, if the potential dilution is material and is not already incorporated into the share price, it would be expected that the announcement of the grant would cause the share price to decline by a material amount. Unlisted entities should consider whether the dilutive impact of a very large option grant is already incorporated into the estimated share price used in their option-pricing model. If that is not the case, some adjustment to the fair value may be appropriate.

8.7 Valuation of equity-settled awards other than options

As noted at 8.1 above, the discussion in 8.3 to 8.5 above may well be relevant to share-based payments other than options. These include, but are not restricted to:

- awards of shares (see 8.7.1 below);
- non-recourse loans (see 8.7.2 below);
- share appreciation rights (SARs) (see 8.7.3 below); and
- performance rights (see 8.7.4 below).

8.7.1 Shares

IFRS 2 requires shares granted to employees to be valued at their market price (where one exists) or an estimated market value (where the shares are not publicly traded), in either case adjusted to take account of the terms and conditions on which the shares were granted, other than those vesting conditions that IFRS 2 requires to be excluded in determining the grant date fair value (see 6.2 above). *[IFRS 2.B2]*.

For example, the valuation should take account of restrictions on the employee's right:

- to receive dividends in the vesting period (see below); or
- to transfer shares after vesting, but only to the extent that such restrictions would affect the price that a knowledgeable and willing market participant would pay for the shares. Where the shares are traded in a deep and liquid market, the effect may be negligible.

The valuation should not, however, take account of restrictions on transfer or other restrictions that exist during the vesting period and which stem from the existence of vesting conditions. *[IFRS 2.B3]*.

Whether dividends should be taken into account in measuring the fair value of shares depends on whether the counterparty is entitled to dividends or dividend equivalents (which might be paid in cash) during the vesting period. When the grant date fair value of shares granted to employees is estimated, no adjustment is required if the employees are entitled to receive dividends during the vesting period (as they are in no different a position in this respect than if they already held shares). However, where employees are not entitled to receive dividends during the vesting period, the valuation should be reduced by the present value of dividends expected to be paid during the vesting period. *[IFRS 2.B31, B33-34]*. The basis on which expected dividends during the vesting period might be determined is discussed in the context of the impact of expected dividends on the fair value of share options at 8.5.4 above.

The accounting treatment of awards which give the right to receive dividends or dividend equivalents during the vesting period is discussed further at 15.3 below.

8.7.2 Non-recourse loans

Non-recourse loans are loans granted by an entity to the employee to allow the employee to buy shares, and are discussed in more detail at 15.2 below. Generally, however, the loan is interest-free, with the dividends received on the purchased shares being used to repay the loan. The loan acts like an option, in that, at the point in time when the holder decides to sell the shares to repay the loan, if the shares are worth less than the loan, the remaining part of the loan is forgiven, with the effect that, just as in the case of an option, the holder bears no risk of ownership.

8.7.3 Share appreciation rights (SARs)

A share appreciation right (SAR) is a grant whereby the employee will become entitled either to shares or, more commonly, to a future cash payment based on the increase in the entity's share price from a specified level over a period of time (see further discussion at 9 below on cash-settled awards). This essentially has the same payoff as a call option, except the award is generally cash- rather than equity-settled.

8.7.4 Performance rights

A performance right is the right to acquire further shares after vesting, upon certain criteria being met. These criteria may include certain performance conditions which can usually be modelled with either a Black-Scholes-Merton formula or a binomial lattice model or a Monte Carlo Simulation depending on the nature of the conditions attached to the rights. Such awards may be structured as matching share awards, as discussed in more detail at 15.1 below.

8.8 Awards whose fair value cannot be measured reliably

IFRS 2 acknowledges that there may be rare cases where it is not possible to determine the fair value of equity instruments granted. In such cases, the entity is required to adopt a method of accounting based on the intrinsic value of the award (i.e. the price of the underlying share less the exercise price, if any, for the award). This is slightly puzzling in the sense that, for unlisted entities, a significant obstacle to determining a reliable fair value for equity instruments is the absence of a market share price, which is also a key input in determining intrinsic value. In fact, the intrinsic value model is arguably more onerous than the fair value model since, as discussed further in 8.8.1 and 8.8.2 below, it requires intrinsic value to be determined not just once, but at initial measurement date and each subsequent reporting date until exercise.

8.8.1 Intrinsic value method – the basic accounting treatment

Under the intrinsic value method:

(a) the entity measures the intrinsic value of the award at each reporting date between grant date and settlement (whether through exercise, forfeiture or lapse);

(b) at each reporting date during the vesting period the cumulative expense should be determined as the intrinsic value of the award at that date multiplied by the expired portion of the vesting period, with all changes in the cumulative expense recognised in profit or loss; and

(c) once options have vested, all changes in their intrinsic value until settlement should be recognised in profit or loss. *[IFRS 2.24(a)]*.

The cumulative expense during the vesting period, like that for awards measured at fair value, should always be based on the best estimate of the number of awards that will actually vest (see 6 above). However, the distinction between market vesting conditions, non-market vesting conditions and non-vesting conditions that would apply to equity-settled awards measured at fair value (see 6.1 to 6.4 above) does not apply in the case of awards measured at intrinsic value. *[IFRS 2.24(b)]*. In other words, where an award measured at intrinsic value is subject to a market condition or non-vesting condition that is not met, there is ultimately no accounting expense for that award. This is consistent with a model requiring constant remeasurement.

The cost of awards measured at intrinsic value is ultimately revised to reflect the number of awards that are actually exercised. However, during the vesting period the cost should be based on the number of awards estimated to vest and thereafter on the number of awards that have vested. In other words, any post-vesting forfeiture or lapse should not be anticipated, but should be accounted for as it occurs. *[IFRS 2.24(b)]*.

Example 34.34 is based on IG Example 10 in the implementation guidance to IFRS 2 and illustrates the intrinsic value method. *[IFRS 2 IG Example 10]*.

Example 34.34: Intrinsic value method

At the beginning of year 1, an entity grants 1,000 share options to 50 employees.

The share options will vest at the end of year 3, provided the employees remain in service until then. The options can be exercised at the end of year 4, and then at the end of each subsequent year up to and including year 10. The exercise price, and the entity's grant date share price, is €60. At the date of grant, the entity concludes that it cannot estimate reliably the fair value of the share options granted.

At the end of year 1, the entity estimates that 10 of the employees will have left employment by the end of the vesting period and so 80% of the share options will vest. At the end of year 2, the entity revises the number of leavers to 7 and its estimate of the number of share options that it expects will vest to 86%.

During the vesting period, a total of 7 employees leave, so that 43,000 share options vest.

The intrinsic value of the options, and the number of share options exercised during years 4-10, are as follows:

Year	Share price at year end €	Intrinsic value €	Number exercised at year end
1	63	3	
2	65	5	
3	75	15	
4	88	28	6,000
5	100	40	8,000
6	90	30	5,000
7	96	36	9,000
8	105	45	8,000
9	108	48	5,000
10	115	55	2,000

The expense recognised under IFRS 2 will be as follows. In the period up to vesting the 'cumulative expense' methodology used in the examples at 6.1 to 6.4 above can be adopted to derive the expense for each period:

Year	Calculation of cumulative expense	Cumulative expense (€)	Expense for period (€)
1	50,000 options × €3 × 80% × 1/3	40,000	40,000
2	50,000 options × €5 × 86% × 2/3	143,333	103,333
3	43,000 options × €15	645,000	501,677

In years 4 to 10 it is more straightforward to calculate the expense directly. Since all options exercised during each year are exercised at the end of that year, the annual expense can be calculated as the change in intrinsic value during each year of the options outstanding at the start of the year.

Year		Expense for period (€)
4	43,000 options × €(28 – 15)	559,000
5	43,000 – 6,000 = 37,000 options × €(40 – 28)	444,000
6	37,000 – 8,000 = 29,000 options × €(30 – 40)	(290,000)
7	29,000 – 5,000 = 24,000 options × €(36 – 30)	144,000
8	24,000 – 9,000 = 15,000 options × €(45 – 36)	135,000
9	15,000 – 8,000 = 7,000 options × €(48 – 45)	21,000
10	7,000 – 5,000 = 2,000 options × €(55 – 48)	14,000

If, more realistically, the options had been exercisable, and were exercised, at other dates, it would have been necessary to record as an expense for those options the movement in intrinsic value from the start of the year until exercise date. For example, if the 6,000 options in year 4 had been exercised during the year when the intrinsic value was €20, the expense for that period would have been €511,000 comprising €481,000 change in value for the options outstanding at the end of year [37,000 options × €(28 – 15)] and €30,000 change in value of options exercised during the period [6,000 options × €(20 – 15)].

Since the intrinsic value method will initially be applied at the date at which the entity obtains the goods or the counterparty renders service and continues to be applied at the end of each reporting period until the date of final settlement, in our view the entity should continue to apply this method of measurement throughout the life of such an award even if it becomes possible to measure the fair value of the award at some stage prior to its settlement.

8.8.2 Modification, cancellation and settlement

The methodology of the intrinsic value method has the effect that modification or cancellation is dealt with automatically, and the rules for modification and cancellation of awards measured at fair value (see 7 above) therefore do not apply. *[IFRS 2.25]*.

Where an award accounted for at intrinsic value is settled in cash, the following provisions apply, which are broadly similar to the rules for settlement of awards accounted for at fair value.

If settlement occurs before vesting, the entity must treat this as an acceleration of vesting and 'recognise immediately the amount that would otherwise have been recognised for services received over the remainder of the vesting period'. *[IFRS 2.25(a)]*. The wording here is the same as that applicable to settlement of awards accounted for at fair value, which we discuss in more detail at 7.4.3 above.

Any payment made on settlement must be deducted from equity, except to the extent that it is greater than the intrinsic value of the award at settlement date. Any such excess is accounted for as an expense. *[IFRS 2.25(b)]*.

8.9 Awards with reload features

Some share options contain a reload feature (see 5.5.1 above). Reloads commonly provide that, where an exercise price is satisfied in shares of the issuing entity rather than cash, there is a new grant of at-the-money options over as many shares as are equal to the exercise price of the exercised option. For example, if there were 100 options with an exercise price of $10, and the new share price were $15, 67 options (€1,000 ÷ €15) would be re-issued.

Even though the reload feature (i.e. the possibility that additional options would be issued in the future) is a feature of the original option, and can be readily incorporated into the valuation of the original option using a lattice model, the IASB concluded that the fair value of a reload feature should not be incorporated into the estimate of the fair value of the award at grant date. As a result, subsequent grants of reload awards under the reload feature would be accounted for as new awards and measured on their respective grant dates. *[IFRS 2.BC188-192].*

On the assumption that the exercise price of an award is at least the share price at grant date, the grant-date fair value of the reload award will generally be greater than the incremental value of the reload feature as at the date the original award was granted. This is because the reload award will only be granted if the original option is in-the-money and is exercised. As a result, the award would have increased in the period between the original grant date and the reload grant date, and the higher share price would be used to value the reload grant. However, from the perspective of the aggregate compensation cost, this result is mitigated by the fact that, as the value of the underlying share increases, fewer shares must be tendered to satisfy the exercise price requirement of the exercised option and, therefore, fewer reload options will be granted (as above when only 67 options are re-issued for the 100 originally issued).

If the reload feature were incorporated into the valuation of the original grant, then not only would a lower price be used, but the valuation would consider the possibility that the original option would never be exercised and, therefore, that the reload options would not be granted. Under the approach in IFRS 2, if the original award expires unexercised, no compensation cost results from the reload feature, so that the compensation cost is lower than would be the case if the value of the reload feature were incorporated into the measurement of the original award. Effectively, the approach in IFRS 2 incorporates subsequent share price changes into the valuation of a reload award.

8.10 Awards of equity instruments to a fixed monetary value

Entities may make an award of shares equivalent to a fixed monetary value (see 5.3.5 above). This is commonly found as part of a matching share award where an employee may be offered the choice of receiving cash or shares of an equivalent value, or a multiple of that value (see 15.1 below).

IFRS 2 does not address directly the valuation of such awards. Example 34.35 below illustrates how such awards are valued:

Example 34.35: Award of shares to a fixed monetary value

At the beginning of year 1 the reporting entity grants:
- to Employee A an award of 1,000 shares subject to remaining in employment for three years; and
- to Employee B €10,000 subject to remaining in employment for three years, to be paid in as many shares as are (at the end of year 3) worth €10,000.

Both awards vest, and the share price at the end of year 3 is €10, so that both employees receive 1,000 shares.

The IFRS 2 charge for A's award is clearly 1000 × the fair value as at the beginning of year 1 of a share deliverable in three years' time. What is the charge for B's award?

In our view, the fair value of the equity instruments granted for B's award would be the €10,000 adjusted for the time value of money, as the value employee B will receive is fixed at €10,000 and is independent of the share price. This amount, determined at grant date, would be recognised as an expense over the vesting period, which in this case is a three year service condition for employee B.

Although IFRS 2 does not directly address the valuation of awards of equity instruments equivalent to a fixed monetary value, IFRS 2 does require the grant date fair value of the equity instruments awarded to be recognised, which for a fixed monetary award would be the fixed monetary amount to be received adjusted for the time value of money.

9 CASH-SETTLED TRANSACTIONS

Throughout the discussion in this section, 'cash' should be read as including 'other assets' in accordance with the definition of a cash-settled share-based payment transaction (see 2.2.1 above).

9.1 Scope of requirements

Cash-settled share-based payment transactions include transactions such as:
- share appreciation rights (SARs), where employees are entitled to a cash payment equivalent to the gain that would have arisen from a holding of a particular number of shares from the date of grant to the date of exercise; or
- phantom options, where employees are entitled to a cash payment equivalent to the gain that would have been made by exercising options at a notional price over a notional number of shares and then selling the shares at the date of exercise. *[IFRS 2.31].*

However, IFRS 2 looks beyond the simple issue of whether an award entitles an employee to receive instruments that are in form shares or options to the terms of those instruments. For example, an award of shares or options over shares whose terms provide for their redemption either mandatorily according to their terms (e.g. on cessation of employment) or at the employee's option would be treated as a cash-settled, not an equity-settled, award under IFRS 2. *[IFRS 2.31].* This is consistent with the fact that IAS 32 would regard a share with these terms as a financial liability rather than an equity instrument of the issuer (see Chapter 47 at 4).

In some cases the boundary between equity-settled and cash-settled schemes may appear somewhat blurred, so that further analysis may be required to determine whether a particular arrangement is equity-settled or cash-settled. Some examples of such arrangements are discussed at 9.2 below.

9.2 What constitutes a cash-settled award?

There are a number of possible circumstances in which, on, or shortly after, settlement of an equity-settled award either:
- the entity incurs a cash outflow equivalent to that which would arise on cash-settlement (e.g. because it purchases shares in the market at fair value to deliver to counterparties); or

- the counterparty receives a cash inflow equivalent to that which would arise on cash-settlement (e.g. because the shares are sold in the market for cash on behalf of the counterparty).

Such situations raise the question of whether such schemes are in fact truly equity-settled or cash-settled.

Examples of relatively common mechanisms for delivering the cash-equivalent of an equity-settled award to employees are discussed below. It emerges from the analysis below that, in reality, IFRS 2 is driven by questions of form rather than substance. To put it rather crudely, what matters is often not so much whether the entity has made a cash payment for the fair value of the award, but rather the name of the payee.

The significance of this is that the analysis affects the profit or loss charge for the award, as illustrated by Example 34.36 below.

Example 34.36: Equity-settled award satisfied with market purchase of treasury shares

An entity awards an employee a free share with a fair value at grant date of £5 which has a fair value of £8 at vesting. At vesting the entity purchases a share in the market for £8 for delivery to the employee. If the scheme were treated as cash-settled, there would be a charge to profit or loss of £8 (the fair value at vesting date – see 9.3 below). If it were treated as equity-settled (as required in this case by IFRS 2), profit or loss would show a charge of only £5 (the fair value at grant date), with a further net charge of £3 in equity, comprising the £8 paid for the share accounted for as a treasury share (see Chapter 47 at 9) less the £5 credit to equity (being the credit entry corresponding to the £5 charge to profit or loss – see 4.2 above).

The analyses below all rely on a precise construction of the definition of a cash-settled share-based payment transaction, i.e. one 'in which the entity acquires goods or services *by incurring a liability to transfer cash or other assets to the supplier of those goods or services* for amounts that are based on the price (or value) of equity instruments (including shares or share options) of the entity or another group entity' (emphasis added). *[IFRS 2 Appendix A]*. Thus, if the entity is not actually required – legally or constructively – to pay cash to the counterparty, there is no cash-settled transaction under IFRS 2, even though the arrangement may give rise to an external cash flow and, possibly, a liability under another standard.

9.2.1 Formal and informal arrangements for the entity to purchase illiquid shares or otherwise settle in cash (awards to be treated as cash-settled, including unlisted company schemes)

Some share-based payment awards, particularly when made by unlisted entities, might appear to be equity-settled in form but, in our view, may need to be accounted for as cash-settled awards under IFRS 2. This reflects either specific arrangements put in place by the entity (or a shareholder) for the employees to sell their shares or, more generally, the illiquid market in the shares which, in the absence of compelling evidence to the contrary, is likely to result in a cash payment by the entity to the counterparty at some stage. Such awards need to be carefully analysed, in the light of their particular facts and circumstances.

This is similar to the assessment for awards where the agreement states that entities have a choice of settlement in equity or cash (see 10.2.1.A below).

9.2.2 Market purchases of own equity used to satisfy awards

It is common for an entity to choose to settle equity-settled transactions using shares previously purchased in the market rather than by issuing new shares. This does not mean that the transaction is cash-settled, since there is no obligation to deliver cash to the counterparty. *[IFRS 2.B48-49]*.

The purchase of own shares is accounted for in accordance with the provisions of IAS 32 relating to treasury shares and other transactions over own equity (see Chapter 47 at 9).

A question sometimes asked is whether the entity should recognise some form of liability to repurchase its own equity in situations where the entity has a stated policy of settling equity-settled transactions using previously purchased treasury shares. In our view, the normal provisions of IAS 32 apply. For example, a public commitment to settle equity-settled transactions by purchasing treasury shares is no different in substance to a commitment to a share buyback programme. There would be no question under IAS 32 of recognising a liability to repurchase own equity on the basis merely of a declared intention. It is only when the entity enters into a forward contract or a call option with a third party that some accounting recognition of a future share purchase may be required.

9.2.3 Market purchases of own equity following equity-settlement of award

An entity might sometimes make a market purchase of its own shares shortly after issuing a similar number of shares in settlement of an equity-settled transaction. This raises the question of whether such a scheme would be considered as in substance cash-settled.

In our view, further enquiry into the detailed circumstances of the market purchase is required in order to determine the appropriate analysis under IFRS 2.

Broadly speaking, so long as there is no obligation (explicit or implicit) for the entity to settle in cash with the counterparty, such market purchase arrangements will not require a scheme to be treated as cash-settled under IFRS 2. This will be the case even where the entity, as a means of managing the dilutive impact on earnings per share of equity-settlement, routinely buys back shares broadly equivalent to the number issued in settlement.

However, in our view, there might be situations in which post-settlement market share purchases are indicative of an obligation to the counterparty, such that treatment as a cash-settled scheme would be appropriate.

For example, the shares might be quoted in a market which is not very deep, or in which the entity itself is a major participant. If the entity were to create an expectation by employees that any shares awarded can always be liquidated immediately, because the entity will ensure that there is sufficient depth in the market to do so, it could well be appropriate to account for such a scheme as cash-settled. The treatment of schemes in which the entity has a choice of settlement, but has created an expectation of cash-settlement, provides a relevant analogy (see 10.2.1 below).

A more extreme example of such a situation would be where the entity has arranged for the shares delivered to the counterparty to be sold on the counterparty's behalf by a broker (see 9.2.4 below), but has at the same time entered into a contract to purchase those shares from the broker. In that situation, in our view, the substance is that:

- the entity has created an expectation by the counterparty of a right to receive cash; and

- the broker is no more than an agent paying that cash to the counterparty on behalf of the entity.

Accordingly, it would be appropriate to account for such an arrangement as a cash-settled award.

In a situation where the entity had pre-arranged to purchase some, but not all, the shares from the broker, in our view it would generally be appropriate to treat the award as cash-settled only to the extent of the shares subject to the purchase agreement.

9.2.4 Arrangements to sell employees' shares including 'broker settlement'

Many recipients of share awards, particularly employees in lower and middle ranking positions within an entity, do not wish to become long-term investors in the entity and prefer instead to realise any equity-settled awards in cash soon after receipt. In order to facilitate this, the entity may either sell the shares in the market on the employees' behalf or, more likely, arrange for a third party broker to do so.

Such an arrangement (sometimes referred to as 'broker settlement') does not of itself create a cash-settled award, provided that the entity has not created any obligation to provide cash to the employees. If, however, the entity has either created an expectation among employees that it will step in to make good any lack of depth in the market, or has indeed itself contracted to repurchase the shares in question, that may well mean that analysis as a cash-settled scheme is more appropriate (see also 9.2.3 above).

Broker settlement arrangements may raise a general concern that an entity may be masking what are really issues of shares to raise cash to pay its employees as sales of shares on behalf of employees. If an entity were simply to issue shares (or reissue treasury shares) for cash, and then use that cash to pay an employee's salary, the normal accounting treatment for such a transaction would be to credit equity with the proceeds of issue or reissue of shares, and to charge the payment to the employee to profit or loss.

By contrast, a sale of shares on behalf of an employee is undertaken by the entity as agent and does not give rise to an increase in equity and an expense, although an expense will be recognised for the award of shares under IFRS 2. However, the entity may enter into much the same transaction with a broker whether it is selling shares on its own behalf or on behalf of its employees. The challenge is therefore for the entity to be able to demonstrate the true economic nature of the transaction.

For this reason, some take the view that a sale of shares can be regarded as part of a broker settlement arrangement only if the shares are first legally registered in the name of the employee. Whilst we understand the concerns that lie behind this view, we nevertheless question whether legal registration is necessary to demonstrate the substance of a broker settlement arrangement. For example, suppose that 100 shares vest in each of 10 employees who all express a wish that the entity sell the shares on their behalf, and the entity then sells 1,000 treasury shares on behalf of the employees, but without first re-registering title to the shares to the employees. We do not believe that the entity should automatically be precluded from regarding this as a broker settlement arrangement, particularly where the treasury shares are held not by the entity directly but through an employee benefit trust or similar vehicle (see 12.3 below) that is permitted to hold or sell shares only for the benefit of employees.

By contrast, the entity might regularly purchase and sell treasury shares, but identify some of the sales as being undertaken on behalf of employees only after they have occurred. Such an arrangement, in our view, is more difficult to construe as a true broker-settlement arrangement.

Where shares are sold on behalf of an employee, they will typically attract transaction costs, such as brokerage fees or taxes. If such costs are borne by the entity, they should, in our view, be included within profit or loss as an additional component of employment costs, rather than deducted from equity as a cost of a transaction in own shares.

This highlights a commercial disadvantage of broker settlement arrangements. The entity may have to:

- purchase shares in the market (incurring transaction costs) on behalf of an employee who does not want them and then sell them back into the market on the employee's behalf (incurring more transaction costs); or
- sell shares in the market (incurring transaction costs) on behalf of an employee who does not want them and then buy them back in the market on behalf of another employee who does want them (incurring more transaction costs).

In order to avoid this, entities may try to structure arrangements with their brokers involving back-to-back sale and purchase contracts, under which shares are never physically delivered, but the entity makes a cash payment to the broker in purported settlement of the purchase by the broker of shares on behalf of the entity and the broker passes it on to the employee in purported settlement of the sale of the shares by the broker on behalf of the employee.

In our view, such arrangements cannot be seen as equity-settled transactions with broker settlement, but must be regarded as cash-settled share-based payment transactions, using the broker as paying agent.

Related issues are raised by the 'drag along' and 'tag along' rights that are often a feature of awards designed to reward employees for a successful flotation or other exit event (see 15.4.6 below).

9.3 Cash-settled transactions: required accounting

9.3.1 Basic accounting treatment

It is clear that the ultimate cost of a cash-settled transaction must be the actual cash paid to the counterparty, which will be the fair value at settlement date. Moreover, the cumulative cost recognised until settlement is clearly a liability, not a component of equity.

The liability is recognised and measured as follows:

- at each reporting date between grant and settlement the fair value of the award is determined in accordance with the specific requirements of IFRS 2;
- during the vesting period, the liability recognised at each reporting date is the IFRS 2 fair value of the award at that date multiplied by the expired portion of the vesting period; and
- from the end of the vesting period until settlement, the liability recognised is the full fair value of the liability at the reporting date.

All changes in the liability are recognised in profit or loss for the period. *[IFRS 2.30-33D, IG Example 12, IG Example 12A]*. Where the cost of services received in a cash-settled transaction is recognised in the carrying amount of an asset (e.g. inventory) in the entity's statement of financial position, the carrying amount of the asset is not adjusted for changes in the fair value of the liability. *[IFRS 2.IG19]*.

The fair value of the liability should be determined, initially and at each reporting date until it is settled, by applying an option pricing model, taking into account the terms and conditions on which the cash-settled transaction was granted, and the extent to which the employees have rendered service to date. *[IFRS 2.33]*. Determination of fair value is subject to the requirements of paragraphs 33A to 33D of IFRS 2, these paragraphs clarify the treatment of vesting and non-vesting conditions and are discussed further at 9.3.2 below. *[IFRS 2.33]*.

This has the effect that, although the liability will ultimately be settled at its then intrinsic value, its measurement at reporting dates before settlement is based on its fair value. Before the initial publication of IFRS 2, a number of respondents to the IASB's earlier exposure draft suggested that, for reasons of consistency and simplicity of calculation, cash-settled transactions should be measured at intrinsic value throughout their entire life. The IASB, while accepting these merits of the intrinsic value approach, rejected it on the basis that, since it does not include a time value, it is not an adequate measure of either the liability or the cost of services consumed. *[IFRS 2.BC246-251]*.

As noted at 5.5 above, the approach to determining the fair value of share-based payments continues to be that specified in IFRS 2 as share-based payments fall outside the scope of IFRS 13 which applies more generally to the measurement of fair value under IFRSs (see Chapter 14). *[IFRS 2.6A]*.

IFRS 2 uses the term 'share appreciation rights' when referring to measurement of the liability but makes clear that this should be read as including any cash-settled share-based payment transaction. *[IFRS 2.31]*.

9.3.2 Application of the accounting treatment

The treatment required by IFRS 2 for cash-settled transactions is illustrated by Example 34.37 below and by Example 34.38 at 9.3.2.C below. These examples are based, respectively, on IG Examples 12 and 12A in the implementation guidance accompanying IFRS 2. *[IFRS 2 IG Example 12, IG Example 12A]*.

Example 34.37: Cash-settled transaction with service condition

An entity grants 100 cash-settled share appreciation rights (SARs) to each of its 500 employees, on condition that the employees remain in its employment for the next three years. The SARs can be exercised on the third, fourth and fifth anniversary of the grant date.

During year 1, 35 employees leave. The entity estimates that a further 60 will leave during years 2 and 3 (i.e. the award will vest in 405 employees).

During year 2, 40 employees leave and the entity estimates that a further 25 will leave during year 3 (i.e. the award will vest in 400 employees).

During year 3, 22 employees leave, so that the award vests in 403 employees. At the end of year 3, 150 employees exercise their SARs (leaving 253 employees still to exercise).

Another 140 employees exercise their SARs at the end of year 4, leaving 113 employees still to exercise, who do so at the end of year 5.

The entity estimates the fair value of the SARs at the end of each year in which a liability exists as shown below. The intrinsic values of the SARs at the date of exercise (which equal the cash paid out) at the end of years 3, 4 and 5 are also shown below.

Year	Fair value £	Intrinsic value £
1	14.40	
2	15.50	
3	18.20	15.00
4	21.40	20.00
5		25.00

The entity will recognise the cost of this award as follows:

Year	Calculation of liability	Calculation of cash paid	Liability (£)	Cash paid (£)	Expense for period (£)*
1	405 employees × 100 SARs × £14.40 × 1/3		194,400	–	194,400
2	400 employees × 100 SARs × £15.50 × 2/3		413,333	–	218,933
3	253 employees × 100 SARs × £18.20	150 employees × 100 SARs × £15.00	460,460	225,000	272,127
4	113 employees × 100 SARs × £21.40	140 employees × 100 SARs × £20.00	241,820	280,000	61,360
5	–	113 employees × 100 SARs × £25.00	–	282,500	40,680

* Liability at end of period + cash paid in period – liability at start of period

The accounting treatment for cash-settled transactions is therefore (despite some similarities in the methodology) significantly different from that for equity-settled transactions. An important practical issue is that, for a cash-settled transaction, the entity must determine the fair value at each reporting date and not merely at grant date (and at the date of any subsequent modification or settlement) as would be the case for equity-settled transactions.

As Example 34.37 shows, it is not generally necessary, although arguably required by IFRS 2, to determine the fair value of a cash-settled transaction at grant date, at least to determine the expense under IFRS 2. However, for entities subject to IAS 33 – *Earnings per Share* – the grant date fair value may be required in order to make the disclosures required by that standard – see Chapter 37 at 6.4.2.

We discuss in more detail at 9.3.2.A to 9.3.2.E below the following aspects of the accounting treatment of cash-settled transactions:

- determining the vesting period (see 9.3.2.A below);
- periodic allocation of cost (see 9.3.2.B below);
- treatment of non-market vesting conditions (see 9.3.2.C below);
- treatment of market conditions and non-vesting conditions (see 9.3.2.D below); and
- treatment of modification, cancellation and settlement (see 9.3.2.E below).

9.3.2.A Determining the vesting period

The rules for determining vesting periods are the same as those applicable to equity-settled transactions, as discussed in 6.1 to 6.4 above. Where an award vests immediately, IFRS 2 creates a presumption that, in the absence of evidence to the contrary, the award is in respect of services that have already been rendered, and should therefore be expensed in full at grant date. *[IFRS 2.32]*.

Where cash-settled awards are made subject to vesting conditions (as in many cases they will be, particularly where payments to employees are concerned), IFRS 2 creates a presumption that they are a payment for services to be received in the future, during the 'vesting period', with the transaction being recognised during that period, as illustrated in Example 34.37 above. *[IFRS 2.32]*.

9.3.2.B Periodic allocation of cost

IFRS 2 states that the required treatment for cash-settled transactions is simply to measure the fair value of the liability at each reporting date, *[IFRS 2.30]*, which might suggest that the full fair value, and not just a time-apportioned part of it, should be recognised at each reporting date – as would be the case for any liability that is a financial instrument and measured at fair value under IFRS 9.

However, the standard goes on to clarify that the liability is to be measured at an amount that reflects 'the extent to which employees have rendered service to date', and the cost is to be recognised 'as the employees render service'. *[IFRS 2.32-33]*. This, together with IG Examples 12-12A in IFRS 2 (the substance of which is reproduced as Examples 34.37 above and 34.38 below), indicates that a spreading approach is to be adopted.

9.3.2.C Non-market vesting conditions

IFRS 2 clarifies how performance vesting conditions and non-vesting conditions should be treated in the measurement of cash-settled share-based payment transactions. In this section we consider non-market performance conditions; market performance conditions and non-vesting conditions are discussed at 9.3.2.D below.

The standard makes clear that:

- vesting conditions (other than market conditions) should not be taken into account in estimating the fair value of a cash-settled share-based payment. Instead, as for equity-settled share-based payment transactions, such conditions should be taken into account by adjusting the number of awards included in the measurement of the liability arising from the cash-settled share-based payment transaction;
- the amount recognised for the goods or services received during the vesting period should be based on the entity's best estimate of the number of awards expected to vest. This estimate should be revised, if necessary, if subsequent information indicates that the number of awards expected to vest differs from previous estimates. On the vesting date, the entity should revise the estimate to equal the number of awards that ultimately vested; and
- on a cumulative basis, the amount ultimately recognised for goods or services received as consideration for the cash-settled share-based payment will be equal to the cash that is paid. *[IFRS 2.33A-33B, 33D]*.

IG Example 12A of the implementation guidance accompanying IFRS 2 illustrates the accounting treatment of a cash-settled award with a non-market performance condition. *[IFRS 2 IG Example 12A]*. This example forms the basis of Example 34.38 below and supplements the illustration of a service condition in IG Example 12 (broadly reproduced as Example 34.37 above).

Example 34.38: Cash-settled transaction with service condition and non-market performance condition

An entity grants 100 cash-settled share appreciation rights (SARs) to each of its 500 employees, on condition that the employees remain in its employment for the next three years and the entity reaches a revenue target (£1 billion in sales) by the end of year 3. The entity expects all employees to remain in employment for the full three years.

At the end of year 1, the entity expects that the revenue target will not be achieved by the end of year 3. During year 2, the entity's revenue increased significantly and it is expected that the revenue will continue to grow. Consequently, at the end of year 2, the entity expects that the revenue target will be achieved by the end of year 3.

At the end of year 3, the revenue target is achieved and 150 employees exercise their SARs. Another 150 employees exercise their SARs at the end of year 4 and the remaining 200 exercise their SARs at the end of year 5.

Using an option pricing model, the entity estimates the fair value of the SARs, ignoring the revenue target performance condition and the employment service condition, at the end of each year until all of the cash-settled share-based payments are settled. At the end of year 3, all of the SARs vest. The following table shows the estimated fair value of the SARs at the end of each year and the intrinsic values of the SARs at the date of exercise (which equal the cash paid out).

Year	Fair value £	Intrinsic value £
1	14.40	
2	15.50	
3	18.20	15.00
4	21.40	20.00
5	25.00	25.00

The entity will recognise a total expense and cash payment of £1,025,000 as follows:

Year	Calculation of liability	Calculation of cash paid	Liability (£)	Cash paid (£)	Expense for period (£)*
1	SARs are not expected to vest: no expense is recognised.		–	–	–
2	SARs are expected to vest: 500 employees × 100 SARs × £15.50 × 2/3		516,667	–	516,667
3	((500 – 150) employees × 100 SARs × £18.20 × 3/3) – 516,667	150 employees × 100 SARs × £15.00	637,000	225,000	345,333
4	((350 – 150) employees × 100 SARs × £21.40) – 637,000	150 employees × 100 SARs × £20.00	428,000	300,000	91,000
5	((200 – 200) employees × 100 SARs × £25.00) – 428,000	200 employees × 100 SARs × £25.00	–	500,000	72,000

* Liability at end of period + cash paid in period – liability at start of period

9.3.2.D Market conditions and non-vesting conditions

IFRS 2 clarifies that market conditions and non-vesting conditions should be taken into account when estimating the fair value of a cash-settled share-based payment when it is initially measured and at each remeasurement date until settlement. *[IFRS 2.33C]*. There will be no ultimate cost for a cash-settled award where a market condition or non-vesting condition is not satisfied as any liability would be reversed. The cumulative amount recognised will be equal to the cash paid. *[IFRS 2.33D]*. This is different from the accounting model for equity-settled transactions with market conditions or non-vesting conditions, which can result in a cost being recognised for awards subject to a market or non-vesting condition that is not satisfied (see 6.3 and 6.4 above).

9.3.2.E Modification, cancellation and settlement

IFRS 2 includes guidance for modifications that change the classification of a share-based payment transaction from cash-settled to equity-settled (see 9.4 below). Apart from this, IFRS 2 provides no specific guidance on modification, cancellation and settlement of cash-settled awards. However, as cash-settled awards are accounted for using a full fair value model no such guidance is needed. It is clear that:

- where an award is modified, the liability recognised at and after the point of modification will be based on its new fair value, with the effect of any movement in the liability recognised immediately;
- where an award is cancelled the liability will be derecognised, with a credit immediately recognised in profit or loss; and
- where an award is settled, the liability will be derecognised, and any gain or loss on settlement immediately recognised in profit or loss.

9.4 Modification of award from equity-settled to cash-settled or from cash-settled to equity-settled

An entity will sometimes modify the terms of an award in order to change the manner of settlement. In other words, an award that at grant date was equity-settled is modified so as to become cash-settled, or *vice versa*.

IFRS 2 provides no explicit guidance for modifications that change an award from being equity-settled to being cash-settled. As part of the discussions relating to the June 2016 amended guidance for modifications from cash-settled to equity-settled, the IASB considered, but rejected, suggestions that additional examples be added to the implementation guidance to illustrate other types of modification, including equity-settled to cash-settled (see further discussion at 9.4.1 below).

In order to develop the suggested accounting approaches discussed at 9.4.1 below we have used the provisions of IFRS 2 in respect of:

- the modification of equity-settled awards during the vesting period (see 7.3 above);
- the addition of a cash-settlement alternative to an equity-settled award after grant date, as illustrated by IG Example 9 in the implementation guidance to IFRS 2 (see 10.1.4 below); and
- the settlement of equity-settled awards in cash (see 7.4 above).

As noted at 10.2.3 below, the accounting in this section also applies where an entity with a choice of settlement in equity or cash switches between settlement methods.

9.4.1 Equity-settled award modified to cash-settled award

This section focuses on accounting for a change of settlement method rather than on the accounting treatment of other modifications to an equity-settled award that might be made at the same time as the change of settlement method (see 7.3 above).

Drawing on the principles within the guidance referred to at 9.4 above, we suggest that entities generally select one of the two approaches discussed below to account for the modification of an award from equity-settled to cash-settled during the vesting period. The first approach is based more closely on the IFRS 2 treatment for the modification of an equity-settled award (see 7.3 above) and the second on that for the repurchase or settlement in cash of an equity instrument (see 7.4 above).

Both approaches take into account IG Example 9 in the implementation guidance to IFRS 2 (see 10.1.4 below) which shows the recognition of an expense when the cash-settlement alternative is remeasured in the period following modification, in addition to an expense for the full grant date fair value of the equity-settled arrangement. Although this Example reflects a choice of settlement by the counterparty, rather than the elimination of a method of settlement (as is the case in a modification from equity-settlement to cash-settlement), we believe that an analogy may be drawn between the two situations because the addition of a cash alternative for the counterparty effectively results in the award being treated as cash-settled from the date of modification.

The two approaches are discussed in more detail below and illustrated in Example 34.39. In our view, either approach is acceptable in the absence of clear guidance in IFRS 2 but the choice of approach should be applied consistently to all such modifications.

Both approaches require the recognition, as a minimum, of an IFRS 2 expense which comprises the following elements:

- the grant date fair value of the original equity-settled award (see 7.3 above); plus
- any incremental fair value arising from the modification of that award (see 7.1 above); plus
- any remeasurement of the liability between its fair value at the modification date and the amount finally settled (see 10.1.4 below).

Over the vesting period as a whole, both approaches result in the same total IFRS 2 expense and the same liability/cash settlement amount. Under both approaches, the net overall difference between the expense and the cash settlement amount is an adjustment to equity. However, the timing of recognition of any incremental fair value arising on modification will differ under the two approaches, as explained below.

Approach 1

- At the date of modification a liability is recognised based on the fair value of the cash-settled award as at that date and the extent to which the vesting period has expired.
- The entire corresponding debit is taken to equity. Any incremental fair value of the cash-settled award over that of the equity-settled award as at the modification date will

be expensed over the period from the date of modification to the date of settlement of the cash-settled award (i.e. no expense is recognised at the date of modification).
- The total fair value of the cash-settled award is remeasured through profit or loss on an ongoing basis between the date of modification and the date of settlement.

As Approach 1 is based on the accounting treatment for a modification of an equity-settled award, no incremental fair value is recognised as an expense at the modification date. This means that, in cases where the fair value of the modified award is higher at the date of modification than that of the original award, the reduction in equity at the date of modification will be higher than the proportionate fair value at that date of the original equity-settled award. This situation reverses over the remainder of the vesting period when an expense (and corresponding credit to equity) will be recognised for the incremental fair value of the modified award.

Approach 2
- As for Approach 1, at the date of modification a liability is recognised based on the fair value of the cash-settled award as at that date and the extent to which the vesting period has expired.
- Unlike Approach 1, the corresponding debit is taken to equity only to the extent of the fair value of the original equity-settled award as at the date of modification. Any incremental fair value of the cash-settled award over the equity-settled award as at the modification date is expensed immediately on modification to the extent that the vesting period has expired. The remainder of any incremental value is expensed over the period from the date of modification to the date of settlement.
- As for Approach 1, the total fair value of the cash-settled award is remeasured through profit or loss on an ongoing basis between the date of modification and the date of settlement.

Approach 2 is based on the accounting treatment for the repurchase of an equity instrument where a reduction in equity up to the fair value of the equity instrument is recognised as at the date of repurchase with any incremental fair value of the repurchase arrangement being treated as an expense. Whilst Approach 2 avoids the potential problem of an immediate reduction in equity in excess of the fair value of the equity-settled award, its settlement approach could be seen as diverging from the basic IFRS 2 treatment for the modification of an equity-settled award where none of the incremental fair value arising on a modification is expensed at the date of modification.

As noted at the start of this section, the two approaches outlined above are based on the specific principles referred to at 9.4 above. In the absence of clear guidance in the standard, other interpretations of the appropriate expense and equity adjustment are also possible, although these will sometimes result in a higher expense through profit or loss than the two approaches above. For example, in relation to the cash-settled award, the approaches outlined above expense only the difference between the final settlement amount and the full fair value of the liability at the modification date, with the remainder adjusted through equity. An alternative view follows the accounting treatment for cash-settled awards which would lead to the recognition of an expense for the entire remeasurement of the liability from the amount recognised for a part-vested award at modification date to the amount finally settled.

As noted at 9.4 above, the IASB decided that existing implementation guidance in IFRS 2 could be applied by analogy to other types of modification. As an example of this, it states that IG Example 9 illustrates a grant of shares to which a cash settlement alternative is subsequently added. *[IFRS 2.BC237K]*. The approach in IG Example 9 has been considered within our two suggested accounting approaches and is also discussed further in the context of Example 34.39 below.

Example 34.39: Modification of equity-settled award to cash-settled award

A Modified award with same fair value as original award

At the beginning of year 1 an entity granted an equity-settled award, with a fair value at that date of €500, and vesting if the employee is still in service at the end of year 4. At the beginning of year 3, the award is modified so as to become cash-settled, but its terms are otherwise unchanged. The fair value at that date of both alternatives is €150. The liability is actually settled for €180 at the end of year 4.

	Approach 1			Approach 2		
	Expense €	Equity €	Liability €	Expense €	Equity €	Liability €
Years 1-2	250	(250)	–	250	(250)	–
Modification date (beginning of year 3)	–	75	(75)	–	75	(75)
Years 3-4	280	(175)	(105)	280	(175)	(105)
Totals	530	(350)	(180)	530	(350)	(180)

During years 1 and 2 the entity recognises a cumulative expense of €250, being the proportion of the grant date fair value of the equity-settled award of €500 attributable to 2/4 of the vesting period.

At modification date (beginning of year 3), it is necessary to recognise a liability of €75 (€150 × 2/4 – see 9.3.2 above). The full amount of this liability is recognised as a reduction in equity under both approaches as there is no difference between the fair value of the original and modified awards as at the modification date.

As the award is continuing, there is no acceleration at the modification date of the as yet unrecognised amount of the grant date fair value of the original award (€250, being €500 × 2/4), as would occur in an immediate settlement (see 7.4 above).

During years 3 and 4 (the period from modification to settlement date), the entity recognises an increase of €105 in the fair value of the liability (€180 – €75). During this period it also recognises employee costs totalling €280, being the remaining grant date fair value of €250 (€500 total less €250 expensed prior to modification) plus the post-modification remeasurement of the liability of €30 (€180 – €150). The balance of €175 is credited to equity.

In total the entity recognises an expense of €530, being the original grant date fair value of the equity-settled award of €500 plus the post-modification remeasurement of the liability of €30. This adjustment of €30 is consistent with the approach taken in IG Example 9 in the implementation guidance to IFRS 2 (see 10.1.4 and Example 34.42 below).

In Scenario A the modification date fair value is lower than the grant date fair value. Scenario E below considers a situation where the awards have the same fair value as at the date of modification but this fair value is higher than the original grant date fair value of the equity-settled award.

B Modified award with greater fair value than original award

At the beginning of year 1 an entity granted an equity-settled award, with a fair value at that date of €500, and vesting if the employee is still in service at the end of year 4. At the beginning of year 3, the award is modified so as to become cash-settled, with other modifications meaning that the new award has a higher fair value than the original award. At that date, the fair value of the original award is €150, but that of the cash-settled replacement award is €170. The liability is actually settled for €200 at the end of year 4.

	Approach 1			Approach 2		
	Expense €	Equity €	Liability €	Expense €	Equity €	Liability €
Years 1-2	250	(250)	–	250	(250)	–
Modification date (beginning of year 3)	–	85	(85)	10	75	(85)
Years 3-4	300	(185)	(115)	290	(175)	(115)
Totals	550	(350)	(200)	550	(350)	(200)

During years 1 and 2 the entity recognises a cumulative expense of €250, being the proportion of the grant date fair value of the equity-settled award of €500 attributable to 2/4 of the vesting period.

At modification date (beginning of year 3), it is necessary to recognise a liability of €85 (€170 × 2/4 – see 9.3.2 above). Under Approach 1 the difference between the fair value of the original equity-settled award and the modified award (€20 in total) is not recognised immediately as an expense but is spread over the remainder of the vesting period (i.e. starting from the date of modification). The liability of €85 is therefore recognised as a reduction in equity. Under Approach 2, the difference between the fair value of the original equity-settled award and the modified award is expensed immediately to the extent that the vesting period has already expired (€20 × 2/4) with the remainder being expensed in the post-modification period.

As the award is continuing, there is no acceleration at the modification date of the as yet unrecognised amount of the grant date fair value of the original award (€250, being €500 × 2/4) as would occur in an immediate settlement (see 7.4 above).

During years 3 and 4 (the period from modification to settlement date), the entity recognises an increase of €115 in the fair value of the liability (€200 – €85). During this period, under Approach 1 it also recognises employee costs totalling €300, being the remaining grant date fair value of €250 (€500 total less €250 expensed prior to modification) plus the incremental modification fair value of €20 (€170 – €150) plus the remeasurement of the liability of €30 (€200 – €170) between modification date and settlement date. The balance of €185 is credited to equity. For Approach 2, the expense and the credit to equity during this period are €10 less than under Approach 1 because a proportionate amount of the incremental fair value was expensed immediately at the modification date.

In total the entity recognises an expense of €550, being the original grant date fair value of the equity-settled award of €500 plus the incremental fair value of €20 arising on modification of the award plus the post-modification remeasurement of the liability of €30. This remeasurement adjustment of €30 is consistent with the approach taken in IG Example 9 in the implementation guidance to IFRS 2 (see 10.1.4 and Example 34.42 below).

C Modified award with lower fair value than original award

At the beginning of year 1 an entity granted an equity-settled award, with a fair value at that date of €500, and vesting if the employee is still in service at the end of year 4. At the beginning of year 3, the award is modified so as to become cash-settled, with other modifications meaning that the new award has a lower fair value than the original award. At that date, the fair value of the original award is €150, but that of the cash-settled replacement award is €130. The liability is actually settled for €180 at the end of year 4.

	Approach 1			Approach 2		
	Expense €	Equity €	Liability €	Expense €	Equity €	Liability €
Years 1-2	250	(250)	–	250	(250)	–
Modification date (beginning of year 3)	–	65	(65)	–	65	(65)
Years 3-4	300	(185)	(115)	300	(185)	(115)
Totals	550	(370)	(180)	550	(370)	(180)

During years 1 and 2 the entity recognises a cumulative expense of €250, being the proportion of the grant date fair value of the equity-settled award of €500 attributable to 2/4 of the vesting period.

At modification date (beginning of year 3), it is necessary to recognise a liability of €65 (€130 × 2/4) (see 9.3.2 above). The full amount of this liability is recognised as a reduction in equity under both approaches as the fair value of the modified award is lower than that of the original award. No gain is recognised for the reduction in fair value consistent with the general principle in IFRS 2 that the cost recognised for an equity-settled award must be at least the grant date fair value of the award.

As the award is continuing, there is no acceleration at the modification date of the as yet unrecognised amount of the grant date fair value of the original award (€250, being €500 × 2/4) as would occur in an immediate settlement (see 7.4 above).

During years 3 and 4 (the period from modification to settlement date), the entity recognises an increase of €115 in the fair value of the liability (€180 – €65). During this period it also recognises employee costs totalling €300, being the remaining grant date fair value of €250 (€500 total less €250 expensed prior to modification) plus the remeasurement of the liability of €50 (€180 – €130) between modification date and settlement date. The balance of €185 is credited to equity.

In total the entity recognises an expense of €550, being the original grant date fair value of the equity-settled award of €500 plus the post-modification remeasurement of the liability of €50. This adjustment of €50 is consistent with the approach taken in IG Example 9 in the implementation guidance to IFRS 2 (see 10.1.4 and Example 34.42 below).

Whilst the overall liability in Scenario C is the same as that in Scenario A above, the total expense and overall net credit to equity are higher even though the cash-settled award had a lower fair value at the modification date than that in Scenario A. This might appear illogical but is consistent with the approach in IG Example 9 and the requirement to recognise, as a minimum, the grant date fair value of the original equity-settled award together with any post-modification change in the fair value of the liability.

D Modified award with greater fair value than original award but settled for less than modification date fair value

At the beginning of year 1 an entity granted an equity-settled award, with a fair value at that date of €500, and vesting if the employee is still in service at the end of year 4. At the beginning of year 3, the award is modified so as to become cash-settled, with other modifications meaning that the new award has a higher fair value than the original award. At that date, the fair value of the original award is €150, but that of the cash-settled replacement award is €170. The liability is actually settled for €125 at the end of year 4.

	Approach 1			Approach 2		
	Expense €	Equity €	Liability €	Expense €	Equity €	Liability €
Years 1-2	250	(250)	–	250	(250)	–
Modification date (beginning of year 3)	–	85	(85)	10	75	(85)
Years 3-4	225	(185)	(40)	215	(175)	(40)
Totals	475	(350)	(125)	475	(350)	(125)

During years 1 and 2 the entity recognises a cumulative expense of €250, being the proportion of the grant date fair value of the equity-settled award of €500 attributable to 2/4 of the vesting period.

At modification date (beginning of year 3), it is necessary to recognise a liability of €85 (€170 × 2/4) (see 9.3.2 above). Under Approach 1 the difference between the fair value of the original equity-settled award and the modified award (€20 in total) is not recognised immediately as an expense but is spread over the remainder of the vesting period (i.e. starting from the date of modification). The liability of €85 is therefore recognised as a reduction in equity. Under Approach 2, the difference between the fair value of the original equity-settled award and the modified award is expensed immediately to the extent that the vesting period has already expired (€20 × 2/4) with the remainder being expensed in the post-modification period.

As the award is continuing, there is no acceleration at the modification date of the as yet unrecognised amount of the grant date fair value of the original award (€250, being €500 × 2/4) as would occur in an immediate settlement (see 7.4 above).

During years 3 and 4 (the period from modification to settlement date), the entity recognises an increase of €40 in the fair value of the liability (€125 – €85). During this period, under Approach 1 it also recognises employee costs totalling €225, being the remaining grant date fair value of €250 (€500 total less €250 expensed prior to modification) plus the incremental modification fair value of €20 less a reduction of €45 (€170 – €125) in the fair value of the liability since modification date. The balance of €185 is credited to equity. For Approach 2, the expense and the credit to equity during this period are €10 less than under Approach 1 because a proportionate amount of the incremental fair value was expensed immediately at the modification date.

In total the entity recognises an expense of €475, being the original grant date fair value of the equity-settled award of €500 plus the incremental fair value of €20 arising on modification of the award less the post-modification remeasurement of the liability of €45. This remeasurement adjustment of €45 is consistent with the approach taken in IG Example 9 in the implementation guidance to IFRS 2 (see 10.1.4 and Example 34.42 below).

E   Modified award with same fair value as original award but where modification date fair value is higher than original grant date fair value

At the beginning of year 1 an entity granted an equity-settled award, with a fair value at that date of €500, and vesting if the employee is still in service at the end of year 4. At the beginning of year 3, the award is modified so as to become cash-settled, but its terms are otherwise unchanged. The fair value of the award at that date on both an equity-settled basis and a cash-settled basis is €800. The liability is actually settled for €700 at the end of year 4.

	Approach 1			Approach 2		
	Expense	Equity	Liability	Expense	Equity	Liability
	€	€	€	€	€	€
Years 1-2	250	(250)	–	250	(250)	–
Modification date (beginning of year 3)	–	400	(400)	–	400	(400)
Years 3-4	300	–	(300)	300	–	(300)
Totals	550	150	(700)	550	150	(700)

During years 1 and 2 the entity recognises a cumulative expense of €250, being the proportion of the grant date fair value of the equity-settled award of €500 attributable to 2/4 of the vesting period.

At modification date (beginning of year 3), it is necessary to recognise a liability of €400 (€800 × 2/4 – see 9.3.2 above). The full amount of this liability is recognised as a reduction in equity under both approaches as there is no difference between the fair value of the original and modified awards as at the modification date.

As the award is continuing, there is no acceleration at the modification date of the as yet unrecognised amount of the grant date fair value of the original award (€250, being €500 × 2/4), as would occur in an immediate settlement (see 7.4 above).

During years 3 and 4 (the period from modification to settlement date), the entity recognises a net increase of €300 in the fair value of the liability (€700 – €400). During this period it also recognises employee costs totalling €300, being the remaining modification date fair value of the cash-settled award (€800 × 2/4) plus the post-modification remeasurement of the liability of €(100) (€800 – €700).

In total the entity recognises an expense of €550. This expense reflects three components: firstly, half of the grant date fair value of the original equity-settled award and secondly, half of the modification date fair value of the cash-settled award. As the award had increased in value between grant date and modification date, the requirement of paragraph 27 of IFRS 2 to recognise, as a minimum, the original grant date fair value of the equity-settled award (€250 for the portion of the vesting period prior to modification) has been met. The third component of the overall expense, in accordance with the requirements for cash-settled share-based payments, is the €(100) remeasurement of the liability between modification and settlement. In our view, this is consistent with the approach taken in IG Example 9 in the implementation guidance to IFRS 2 (see 10.1.4 and Example 34.42 below).

Some take the view that the approach in IG Example 9 would lead to a total expense of €400 in the example above, rather than €550 (being the original grant date fair value of €500 plus the remeasurement of the liability of €(100) in the period following the modification). The difference of €150 would be debited to equity in the two years following modification. In other words, in recognising an expense for the cash-settled award during the vesting period after the modification date, no account is taken of the fact that the fair value of the arrangement increased between the original grant date and the modification date.

IG Example 9 illustrates a situation where there is a decrease in the fair value between original grant date and modification date. As a result, that Example expenses the grant date fair value of the original equity-settled award (plus the remeasurement of the liability) in order to meet the minimum expense requirements of paragraph 27 of IFRS 2. In a situation such as that outlined in Scenario E above, it does not seem appropriate, in our view, to limit the post-modification expense for the cash-settled award to an amount based on the original grant date fair value of the equity-settled award (€150) rather than applying cash-settled accounting to the element of the award for which services are delivered in years 3 and 4 and recognising a corresponding expense of €300.

9.4.2 Cash-settled award modified to equity-settled award

IFRS 2 provides guidance in situations where the terms and conditions of a cash-settled award are modified so that it becomes equity-settled. Appendix B to IFRS 2 states that if a cash-settled transaction is modified so that it becomes equity-settled, the transaction will be accounted for as such from the date of the modification and specifically:

- the equity-settled share-based payment transaction is measured by reference to the modification date fair value of the equity instruments granted at that date;
- the equity-settled share-based payment transaction is recognised in equity on the modification date to the extent to which goods or services have been received;
- the liability for the cash-settled share-based payment transaction as at the modification date is derecognised on that date; and
- any difference between the carrying amount of the liability derecognised and the amount recognised in equity on the modification date is recognised immediately in profit or loss. *[IFRS 2.B44A]*.

If the vesting period is extended or shortened as a result of the modification, the modified vesting period is reflected in applying the requirements above. The standard also clarifies that these requirements apply even if the modification takes place after the vesting period. [IFRS 2.B44B].

The standard further clarifies that the above requirements apply if a cash-settled share-based payment is cancelled or settled (other than by forfeiture when vesting conditions are not satisfied) and equity instruments are designated as a replacement for the cancelled or settled share-based payment. In order to qualify as a replacement, the equity instruments must be designated as such on the grant date. [IFRS 2.B44C].

The IASB notes in the Basis for Conclusions that the immediate recognition in profit or loss of any difference between the derecognised liability and the amount recognised in equity is consistent with how cash-settled share-based payments are measured in accordance with paragraph 30 of IFRS 2. It also observes that the approach is consistent with the requirements for the extinguishment of a financial liability (fully or partially by the issue of equity instruments) in IFRS 9 and in IFRIC 19 – *Extinguishing Financial Liabilities with Equity Instruments*. [IFRS 2.BC237H].

IG Example 12C in the implementation guidance of IFRS 2 illustrates the above guidance and forms the basis of Example 34.40 below. [IFRS 2 IG Example 12C].

Example 34.40: Modification of cash-settled award to equity-settled award

At the beginning of year 1 an entity grants 100 cash-settled share appreciation rights (SARs) to each of 100 employees on condition that they remain in the entity's service for four years.

At the end of year 1 each SAR has an estimated fair value of €10 and at the end of year 2 €12.

At the end of year 2 the entity cancels the SARs and, in their place, grants 100 share options to each employee on condition that each remains in service for the next two years, i.e. the original service period is unchanged. At the date of grant, the fair value of each share option is €13.20. All of the employees are expected to meet the service condition.

In years 1 and 2 the entity recognises a cash-settled share-based payment expense of €25,000 and €35,000 respectively, based on the fair value of the SARs at each reporting date and the extent to which the vesting period has been completed. At the modification date, the requirements of paragraph B44A are applied as follows:

		€	€
Modification date (end of year 2)	Equity		66,000
	Liability	60,000	
	Profit or loss	6,000	

The entity compares the fair value of the equity award, measured as at the date of modification, of €66,000 (€132,000 × 2/4) with the fair value of the liability for the cash-settled award of €60,000 (€120,000 × 2/4) at the same date. The difference of €6,000 is recognised immediately in profit or loss.

The remainder of the equity-settled share-based payment, as measured at the modification date, is recognised in profit or loss during years 3 and 4 i.e. an expense of €33,000 in each of the two years.

10 TRANSACTIONS WITH EQUITY AND CASH ALTERNATIVES

It is common for share-based payment transactions (particularly those with employees) to provide either the entity or the counterparty with the choice of settling the transaction either in shares (or other equity instruments) or in cash (or other assets). The general principle of IFRS 2 is that a transaction with a cash alternative, or the components of that transaction, should be accounted for:

(a) as a cash-settled transaction if, and to the extent that, the entity has incurred a liability to settle in cash or other assets; or

(b) as an equity-settled transaction if, and to the extent that, no such liability has been incurred. *[IFRS 2.34]*.

More detailed guidance is provided as to how that general principle should be applied to transactions:

- where the counterparty has choice of settlement (see 10.1 below); and
- where the entity has choice of settlement (see 10.2 below).

Some specific types of arrangement that include cash and equity alternatives, either as a matter of choice or depending on the outcome of certain events are covered elsewhere in this chapter, as outlined below.

A common type of arrangement seen in practice is the 'matching' award or deferred bonus arrangement where an employee is offered a share award or a cash alternative to 'match' a share award or a cash bonus earned during an initial period. This type of arrangement is addressed at 15.1 below.

Rather than providing either the entity or the counterparty with a choice between settlement in equity or in cash, some transactions offer no choice but instead require an arrangement that will generally be equity-settled to be settled in cash in certain specific and limited circumstances (awards with contingent cash settlement). There will also be situations where there is contingent settlement in equity of an award that is otherwise cash-settled. These types of arrangement are considered in more detail at 10.3 below.

Some awards offer an equity alternative and a cash alternative where the cash alternative is not based on the price or value of the equity instruments. These arrangements are considered at 10.4 below.

10.1 Transactions where the counterparty has choice of settlement in equity or in cash

Where the counterparty has the right to elect for settlement in either shares or cash, IFRS 2 regards the transaction as a compound transaction to which split accounting must be applied. The general principle is that the transaction must be analysed into a liability component (the counterparty's right to demand settlement in cash) and an equity component (the counterparty's right to demand settlement in shares). *[IFRS 2.35]*. Once split, the two components are accounted for separately. The methodology of split accounting required by IFRS 2 is somewhat different from that required by IAS 32 for issuers of other compound instruments (see Chapter 47 at 6).

A practical issue is that, where a transaction gives the counterparty a choice of settlement, it will be necessary to establish a fair value for the liability component both at grant date and at each subsequent reporting date until settlement. By contrast, in the case of transactions that can be settled in cash only, a fair value is not generally required at grant date for IFRS 2 accounting purposes, but a fair value is required at each subsequent reporting date until settlement (see 9 above). However, for entities subject to IAS 33, the grant date fair value is required in order to make the disclosures required by that standard – see Chapter 37 at 6.4.2.

We consider in more detail at 10.1.1 to 10.1.3 below the accounting treatment required by IFRS 2 for transactions where the counterparty has a settlement choice. In addition, the following specific situations are discussed:

- the addition of a cash-settlement alternative after the grant date (see 10.1.4 below);
- arrangements where the counterparty is given a choice to cover more or less remote contingencies e.g. restrictions or limits on the issue of shares in a particular jurisdiction (see 10.1.5 below); and
- the issue of convertible bonds in return for goods or services (see 10.1.6 below).

10.1.1 Transactions in which the fair value is measured directly

Transactions with non-employees are normally measured by reference to the fair value of goods and services supplied at service date (i.e. the date at which the goods or services are supplied) – see 4 and 5 above.

Accordingly where an entity enters into such a transaction where the counterparty has choice of settlement, it determines the fair value of the liability component at service date. The equity component is the difference between the fair value (at service date) of the goods or services received and the fair value of the liability component. *[IFRS 2.35]*.

10.1.2 Transactions in which the fair value is measured indirectly – including transactions with employees

All other transactions, including those with employees, are measured by reference to the fair value of the instruments issued at 'measurement date', being grant date in the case of transactions with employees and service date in the case of transactions with non-employees *[IFRS 2 Appendix A]* – see 4.1 and 5.1 above.

The fair value should take into account the terms and conditions on which the rights to cash or equity instruments were issued. *[IFRS 2.36]*. IFRS 2 does not elaborate further on this, but we assume that the IASB intends a reporting entity to apply:

- as regards the equity component of the transaction, the provisions of IFRS 2 relating to the impact of terms and conditions on the valuation of equity-settled transactions (see 4 to 6 above); and
- as regards the liability component of the transaction, the provisions of IFRS 2 relating to the impact of terms and conditions on the valuation of cash-settled transactions (see 9.3 above).

The entity should first measure the fair value of the liability component and then that of the equity component. The fair value of the equity component must be reduced to take into account the fact that the counterparty must forfeit the right to receive cash in order to receive shares. The sum of the two components is the fair value of the whole compound instrument. *[IFRS 2.37]*. IG Example 13 in IFRS 2 (the substance of which is reproduced as Example 34.41 below) suggests that this may be done by establishing the fair value of the equity alternative and subtracting from it the fair value of the liability component. This approach may be appropriate in a straightforward situation involving ordinary shares and cash, as illustrated in the Example in the implementation guidance, but will not necessarily be appropriate in more complex situations that include, for example, the likelihood of options being exercised.

In many share-based payment transactions with a choice of settlement, the value to the counterparty of the share and cash alternatives is equal. The counterparty will have the choice between (say) 1,000 shares or the cash value of 1,000 shares. This will mean that the fair value of the liability component is equal to that of the transaction as a whole, so that the fair value of the equity component is zero. In other words, the transaction is accounted for as if it were a cash-settled transaction.

However, in some jurisdictions it is not uncommon, particularly in transactions with employees, for the equity-settlement alternative to have more value (as in Example 34.41 below). For example, an employee might be able to choose at vesting between the cash value of 1,000 shares immediately or 2,000 shares (often subject to further conditions such as a minimum holding period, or a further service period). In such cases the equity component will have an independent value. *[IFRS 2.37]*. Such schemes are discussed in more detail in Examples 34.63 and 34.64 at 15.1 below.

10.1.3 Accounting treatment

10.1.3.A During vesting period

Having established a fair value for the liability and equity components as set out in 10.1.1 and 10.1.2 above, the entity accounts for the liability component according to the rules for cash-settled transactions (see 9 above) and for the equity component according to the rules for equity-settled transactions (see 4 to 8 above). *[IFRS 2.38]*.

Example 34.41 below illustrates the accounting treatment for a transaction with an employee (as summarised in 10.1.2 above) where the equity component has a fair value independent of the liability component.

Example 34.41: Award with employee choice of settlement with different fair values for cash-settlement and equity-settlement

An entity grants to an employee an award with the right to choose settlement in either:

- 1,000 phantom shares, i.e. a right to a cash payment equal to the value of 1,000 shares; or
- 1,200 shares.

Vesting is conditional upon the completion of three years' service. If the employee chooses the share alternative, the shares must be held for three years after vesting date.

At grant date, the entity estimates that the fair value of the share alternative, after taking into account the effects of the post-vesting transfer restrictions, is €48 per share. The fair value of the cash alternative is estimated as:

	€
Grant date	50
Year 1	52
Year 2	55
Year 3	60

The grant date fair value of the equity alternative is €57,600 (1,200 shares × €48). The grant date fair value of the cash alternative is €50,000 (1,000 phantom shares × €50). Therefore the fair value of the equity component excluding the right to receive cash is €7,600 (€57,600 – €50,000). The entity recognises a cost based on the following amounts.

	Equity component			Liability component		
Year	Calculation of cumulative expense	Cumulative expense (€)	Expense for year (€)	Calculation of cumulative expense	Cumulative expense (€)	Expense for year (€)
1	€7,600 × 1/3	2,533	2,533	1,000 phantoms × €52 × 1/3	17,333	17,333
2	€7,600 × 2/3	5,066	2,533	1,000 phantoms × €55 × 2/3	36,667	19,334
3	€7,600	7,600	2,534	1,000 phantoms × €60	60,000	23,333

This generates the following accounting entries.

	€	€
Year 1		
Profit or loss (employment costs)	19,866	
Liability		17,333
Equity		2,533

	€	€
Year 2		
Profit or loss (employment costs)	21,867	
Liability		19,334
Equity		2,533

Year 3		
Profit or loss (employment costs)	25,867	
Liability		23,333
Equity		2,534

The above Example is based on IG Example 13 in IFRS 2, in which the share price at each reporting date is treated as the fair value of the cash alternative. As discussed more fully at 9 above, the fair value of a cash award is not necessarily exactly the same as the share price as it will depend on the terms and conditions of the award (see 9.3.2 above). Accordingly, in adapting IG Example 13 as Example 34.41 above, we have deliberately described the numbers used in respect of the liability component as 'fair value' and not as the 'share price'. *[IFRS 2 IG Example 13].*

Example 34.41 also ignores the fact that transactions of this type often have different vesting periods for the two settlement alternatives. For instance, the employee might have been offered:

(a) the cash equivalent of 1,000 shares in three years' time subject to performance conditions; or

(b) subject to the performance criteria in (a) above being met over three years, 3,000 shares after a further two years' service.

IFRS 2 offers no guidance as to how such transactions are to be accounted for. Presumably, however, the equity component would be recognised over a five year period and the liability component over a three year period. This is considered further in the discussion of 'matching' share awards at 15.1 below.

10.1.3.B Settlement

At the date of settlement, the liability component is restated to fair value through profit or loss. If the counterparty elects for settlement in equity, the restated liability is transferred to equity as consideration for the equity instruments issued. If the liability is settled in cash, the cash is obviously applied to reduce the liability. *[IFRS 2.39-40]*. In other words, if the transaction in Example 34.41 above had been settled in shares the accounting entry would have been:

	€	€
Liability*	60,000	
Equity†		60,000

* There is no need to remeasure the liability in this case as it has already been stated at fair value at vesting date, which is the same as settlement date.

† The precise allocation of this amount within equity, and its impact on distributable reserves, will depend on a number of factors, including jurisdictional legal requirements, which are not discussed here.

If the transaction had been settled in cash the entry would simply have been:

	€	€
Liability	60,000	
Cash		60,000

If the transaction is settled in cash, any amount taken to equity during the vesting period (€7,600 in Example 34.41 above) is not adjusted. However, the entity may transfer it from one component of equity to another (see 4.2 above). *[IFRS 2.40]*.

10.1.4 Transactions with cash-settlement alternative for employee introduced after grant date

Such transactions are not specifically addressed in the main body of IFRS 2. However, IG Example 9 in the implementation guidance does address this issue, in the context of the rules for the modification of awards (discussed at 7.3 and 9.4 above). The substance of this example is reproduced as Example 34.42 below. *[IFRS 2 IG Example 9]*.

Example 34.42: **Award with employee cash-settlement alternative introduced after grant**

At the beginning of year 1, the entity grants 10,000 shares with a fair value of $33 per share to a senior executive, conditional upon the completion of three years' service. By the end of year 2, the fair value of the award has dropped to $25 per share. At that date, the entity adds a cash alternative to the grant, whereby the executive can choose whether to receive 10,000 shares or cash equal to the value of 10,000 shares on vesting date. The share price is $22 on vesting. The implementation guidance to IFRS 2 proposes the following approach.

For the first two years, the entity would recognise an expense of $110,000 per year, (representing 10,000 shares × $33 × 1/3), giving rise to the cumulative accounting entry by the end of year 2:

	$	$
Profit or loss (employee costs)	220,000	
Equity		220,000

The addition of a cash alternative at the end of year 2 constitutes a modification of the award, but does not increase the fair value of the award at the date of modification, which under either settlement alternative is $250,000 (10,000 shares × $25), excluding the effect of the non-market vesting condition as required by IFRS 2.

The fact that the employee now has the right to be paid in cash requires the 'split accounting' treatment set out in 10.1.2 above. Because of the requirement, under the rules for modification of awards (see 7.3 above), to recognise at least the grant date fair value of the original award, a minimum fair value of $330,000 has to be recognised over the vesting period.

At the modification date, a liability of $166,667 (representing 2/3 of the $250,000 fair value of the liability component at modification date) is recognised as a transfer from equity to liabilities, the entry being:

	$	$
Equity	166,667	
Liability		166,667

In year 3 an expense of $110,000 is recognised as the final portion of the original grant date fair value. In addition to this, the liability is remeasured from its modification date value of $250,000 ($25 × 10,000 shares) to its settlement date value of $220,000 ($22 × 10,000 shares) resulting in a credit of $30,000 to profit or loss. This results in the following accounting entry for the expense in year 3:

	$	$
Profit or loss	80,000*	
Liability		53,333†
Equity		26,667‡

*   ((10,000 shares × $33 × 3/3) – ($220,000 expensed to date)) less the remeasurement of $30,000.

†   Carried forward liability $220,000 (10,000 shares × year 3 fair value $22) less the brought forward liability $166,667.

‡   Balancing figure.

The implementation guidance to IFRS 2 analyses the $300,000 total expense over the three years as the grant date fair value of the award ($330,000) less the movement in the fair value of the liability alternative ($30,000, being the fair value of $250,000 at the end of year 2 less the fair value of $220,000 at vesting).

IG Example 9 only illustrates a situation where the grant date fair value of the equity-settled award exceeds the modification date fair value of both the equity and cash alternatives and the settlement date value of the cash alternative. In Example 34.39 at 9.4.1 above we consider alternative scenarios, including one where the modification date fair value exceeds the grant date fair value.

10.1.5 'Backstop' cash settlement rights

Some schemes may provide cash settlement rights to the holder so as to cover more or less remote contingencies. For example, an employee whose nationality and/or country of permanent residence is different from the jurisdiction of the reporting entity may be offered the option of cash settlement in case unforeseen future events make the transfer of equity from the entity's jurisdiction, or the holding or trading of it in the employee's country, inconvenient or impossible.

If the terms of the award provide the employee with a general right of cash-settlement, IFRS 2 requires the award to be treated as cash-settled. This is the case even if the right of cash settlement is extremely unlikely to be exercised (e.g. because it would give rise to adverse tax consequences for the employee as compared with equity settlement). If, however, the right to cash-settlement is exercisable only in specific circumstances, a more detailed analysis may be required (see 10.3 below).

10.1.6 Convertible bonds issued to acquire goods or services

In some jurisdictions entities issue convertible bonds to employees or other counterparties in exchange for goods or services. When this occurs, the bond will generally be accounted for under IFRS 2 rather than IAS 32 since it falls within the scope of IFRS 2 as a transaction 'in which the entity receives or acquires goods or services and the terms of the arrangement provide either the entity or the supplier of those goods or services with a choice of whether the entity settles the transaction in cash (or other assets) or by issuing equity instruments' (see 2.2.1 and 2.2.2 above). *[IFRS 2.2(c)]*.

As noted at 10.1 above, the methodology for splitting such an instrument into its liability and equity components under IFRS 2 differs from that under IAS 32. Moreover, under IAS 32 a convertible instrument is (broadly) recognised at fair value on the date of issue, whereas under IFRS 2 the fair value is accrued over time if the arrangement includes the rendering of services after the date of grant.

It is therefore possible that, if an entity has issued to employees convertible bonds that have also been issued in the market, the accounting treatment of the bonds issued to employees will differ significantly from that of the bonds issued in the market.

Where a convertible instrument is issued to an employee, the IFRS 2 expense will be based on the fair value of the instrument. However, if an entity issues a convertible instrument to a non-employee in return for an asset, for example a property, the entity will initially recognise a liability component at fair value and an equity component based on the difference between the fair value of the property and the fair value of the liability component. *[IFRS 2.35]*. If the fair value of the property were lower than the fair value of the instrument as a whole then, in our view, the entity should also recognise the shortfall in accordance with the requirements of IFRS 2 for unidentified goods or services. *[IFRS 2.13A]*. In the case of the acquisition of an asset, it is possible that this additional debit could be capitalised as part of the cost of the asset under IAS 16 – *Property, Plant and Equipment* – but in other cases it would be expensed.

After the initial IFRS 2 accounting outlined above, the question arises as to whether the subsequent accounting for the convertible instrument should be in accordance with IFRS 2 or IFRS 9. In our view, the instrument should generally continue to be accounted for under IFRS 2 until shares or cash are delivered to the counterparty. However, if the vested instrument were freely transferable or tradeable prior to conversion or settlement then a switch to IFRS 9 might be appropriate following transfer to a different counterparty (if considered practical to apply) – see also the discussion at 2.2.2.E above.

10.2 Transactions where the entity has choice of settlement in equity or in cash

The accounting treatment for transactions where the entity has choice of settlement is quite different from transactions where the counterparty has choice of settlement, in that:

- where the counterparty has choice of settlement, a liability component and an equity component are identified (see 10.1 above); whereas
- where the entity has choice of settlement, the accounting treatment is binary – in other words the whole transaction is treated either as cash-settled or as equity-settled, depending on whether or not the entity has a present obligation to settle in cash, *[IFRS 2.41]*, determined according to the criteria discussed in 10.2.1 below.

10.2.1 Transactions treated as cash-settled

IFRS 2 requires a transaction to be treated as a liability (and accounted for using the rules for cash-settled transactions discussed in 9 above) if:

(a) the choice of settlement has no commercial substance (for example, because the entity is legally prohibited from issuing shares);

(b) the entity has a past practice or stated policy of settling in cash; or

(c) the entity generally settles in cash whenever the counterparty asks for cash settlement. *[IFRS 2.41-42]*.

These criteria are fundamentally different from those in IAS 32 for derivatives over own shares (which is what cash-settled share-based payment transactions are) not within the scope of IFRS 2. IAS 32 rejects an approach based on past practice or intention and broadly requires all derivatives over own equity that could result in an exchange by the reporting entity of anything other than a fixed number of shares for a fixed amount of cash to be treated as giving rise to a financial instrument (see Chapter 47 at 4).

An important practical effect of the IFRS 2 criteria is that some schemes that may appear at first sight to be equity-settled may in fact have to be treated as cash-settled. For example, if an entity has consistently adopted a policy of granting *ex gratia* cash compensation to all those deemed to be 'good' leavers (or all 'good' leavers of certain seniority) in respect of partially vested share options, such a scheme may well be treated as cash-settled for the purposes of IFRS 2 to the extent to which there are expected to be such 'good' leavers during the vesting period. 'Good leaver' arrangements are also discussed at 5.3.9 above.

Another common example is that an entity may have a global share scheme with an entity option for cash settlement which it always exercises in respect of awards to employees in jurisdictions where it is difficult or illegal to hold shares in the parent. Such a scheme should be treated as a cash-settled scheme in respect of those jurisdictions. However, in our view, it would be appropriate to account for the scheme in other jurisdictions as equity-settled (provided of course that none of the criteria in (a) to (c) above applied in those jurisdictions).

Where an entity has accounted for a transaction as cash-settled, IFRS 2 gives no specific guidance as to the accounting treatment on settlement, but it is clear from other provisions of IFRS 2 that the liability should be remeasured to fair value at settlement date and:
- if cash-settlement occurs, the cash paid is applied to reduce the liability; and
- if equity-settlement occurs, the liability is transferred into equity (see 10.1.3.B above).

10.2.1.A   Entity choice has no substance due to economic or other compulsion for cash settlement (including unlisted entity awards with a presumption of cash settlement)

Some awards may nominally give the reporting entity the choice of settling in cash or equity, while in practice giving rise to an economic compulsion to settle only in cash. In addition to the examples mentioned at 10.2.1 above, this will often be the case where an entity that is a subsidiary or owned by a small number of individuals, such as members of the same family, grants options to employees. In such cases there will normally be a very strong presumption that the entity will settle in cash in order to avoid diluting the existing owners' interests. Similarly, where the entity is not listed, there is little real benefit for an employee in receiving a share that cannot be realised except when another shareholder wishes to buy it or there is a change in ownership of the business as a whole.

In our view, such schemes are generally most appropriately accounted for as cash-settled schemes from inception. In any event, once the scheme has been operating for a while, it is likely that there will be a past practice of cash settlement such that the scheme is required to be treated as a liability under the general provisions of IFRS 2 summarised above.

A similar conclusion is often reached even where the terms of the agreement do not appear to offer the entity a choice of settling the award in cash but it has established a constructive obligation or a past practice of so doing (see 9.2.1 above).

10.2.2   Transactions treated as equity-settled

A transaction not meeting the criteria in 10.2.1 above to be treated as cash-settled should be accounted for as an equity-settled transaction using the rules for such transactions discussed in 4 to 8 above. [IFRS 2.43].

However, when the transaction is settled the following approach is adopted:

(a) if the entity chooses to settle in cash, the cash payment is accounted for as the repurchase of an equity interest, i.e. as a deduction from equity, except as noted in (c) below;

(b) if the entity chooses to settle by issuing equity instruments, no further accounting is required (other than a transfer from one component of equity to another, if necessary), except as noted in (c) below;

(c) if the entity chooses the settlement alternative with the higher fair value, as at the date of settlement, the entity recognises an additional expense for the excess value given, i.e. the difference between the cash paid and the fair value of the equity instruments that would otherwise have been issued, or the difference between the fair value of the equity instruments issued and the amount of cash that would otherwise have been paid, whichever is applicable. [IFRS 2.43].

This is illustrated in Examples 34.43 and 34.44 below.

Example 34.43: **Settlement of transaction treated as equity-settled where fair value of cash settlement exceeds fair value of equity settlement**

An entity has accounted for a share-based payment transaction where it has the choice of settlement as an equity-settled transaction, and has recognised a cumulative expense of £1,000 based on the fair value at grant date.

At settlement date the fair value of the equity-settlement option is £1,700 and that of the cash-settlement option £2,000. If the entity settles in equity, no further accounting entry is required by IFRS 2. However, either at the entity's discretion or in compliance with local legal requirements, there may be a transfer within equity of the £1,000 credited to equity during the vesting period.

If the entity settles in cash, the entity must recognise an additional expense of £300, being the difference between the fair value of the equity-settlement option (£1,700) and that of the cash-settlement option (£2,000). The accounting entry is:

	£	£
Profit or loss (employee costs)	300	
Equity	1,700	
Cash		2,000

Example 34.44: **Settlement of transaction treated as equity-settled where fair value of equity settlement exceeds fair value of cash settlement**

As in Example 34.43, an entity has accounted for a share-based payment transaction where it has the choice of settlement as an equity-settled transaction, and has recognised a cumulative expense of £1,000 based on the fair value at grant date.

In this case, however, at settlement date the fair value of the equity-settlement option is £2,000 and that of the cash-settlement option £1,700. If the entity chooses to settle in equity, it must recognise an additional expense of £300, being the difference between fair value of the equity-settlement option (£2,000) and that of the cash-settlement option (£1,700). The accounting entry is:

	£	£
Profit or loss (employee costs)	300	
Equity		300

No further accounting entry is required by IFRS 2. However, either at the entity's discretion or in compliance with local legal requirements, there may be a transfer within equity of the £1,300 credited during the vesting period and on settlement.

If the entity settles in cash, no extra expense is recognised, and the accounting entry is:

	£	£
Equity	1,700	
Cash		1,700

It can be seen in this case that, if the transaction is settled in equity, an additional expense is recognised. If, however, the transaction had simply been an equity-settled transaction (i.e. with no cash alternative), there would have been no additional expense on settlement and the cumulative expense would have been only £1,000 based on the fair value at grant date.

10.2.3 Change in entity's settlement policy or intention leading to change in classification of award after grant date

IFRS 2 does not specify whether a transaction where the entity has a choice of settlement in equity or cash should be assessed as equity-settled or cash-settled only at the inception of the transaction or also at each reporting date until it is settled.

However, in describing the accounting treatment IFRS 2 states several times that the accounting depends on whether the entity '*has a present obligation* to settle in cash' (our emphasis added). In our view, this suggests that IFRS 2 intends the position to be reviewed at each reporting date and not just considered at the inception of the transaction.

IFRS 2 does not specify how to account for a change in classification resulting from a change in the entity's policy or intention. In our view, the most appropriate treatment is to account for such a change as if it were a modification of the manner of settlement of the award (see 9.4 above). Where the entity is able to choose the manner of settlement, the substance of the situation is the same as a decision to modify the manner of settlement of an award which does not already give the entity a choice. These situations are distinct from those where the manner of settlement depends on the outcome of a contingent event outside the entity's control (see 10.3 below).

10.3 Awards requiring cash or equity settlement in specific circumstances (awards with contingent cash or contingent equity settlement)

This section is written with a focus on awards with contingent cash settlement. However, similar considerations will apply in a situation where it is the settlement in equity that depends on the outcome of circumstances outside the control of the entity or both the entity and the counterparty.

Rather than giving either the entity or the counterparty a general right to choose between equity- or cash-settlement, some awards require cash settlement in certain specific and limited circumstances but otherwise will be equity-settled. These arrangements are referred to by IAS 32 as contingent settlement provisions and are driven by the occurrence or non-occurrence of specific outcomes rather than by choice (see Chapter 47 at 4.3). In the absence of specific guidance in IFRS 2, questions then arise as to whether such an award should be accounted for as equity-settled or cash-settled and whether this should be re-assessed on an ongoing basis during the vesting period. This is a subject that has been considered by both the Interpretations Committee and the IASB and their discussions are considered further at 10.3.5 below.

In the sections below we consider:

- two different approaches to the assessment of awards with contingent cash settlement (see 10.3.1 to 10.3.2 below);
- awards that require cash settlement on a change of control (see 10.3.3 below); and
- the accounting treatment for changes in the manner of settlement where the award is contingent on future events (see 10.3.4 and 10.3.5 below).

10.3.1 Approach 1 – Treat as cash-settled if contingency is outside entity's control

One approach might be to observe that the underlying principle that determines whether an award is accounted for as equity-settled or cash-settled under IFRS 2 appears to be whether the reporting entity can unilaterally avoid cash-settlement (see 10.1 and 10.2 above). Under this approach, any award where the counterparty has a right to cash-settlement is always treated as a liability, irrespective of the probability of cash-settlement, since there is nothing that the entity could do to prevent cash-settlement. By contrast, an award where the choice of settlement rests with the entity is accounted for as a liability only where the entity's own actions have effectively put it in a position where it has no real choice but to settle in cash.

Applying this approach, it is first of all necessary to consider whether the event that requires cash-settlement is one over which the entity has control. If the event, however unlikely, is outside the entity's control, then under this approach the award should be treated as cash-settled. However, if the event is within the entity's control, the award should be treated as cash-settled only if the entity has a liability by reference to the criteria summarised in 10.1 and 10.2 above.

Whilst, in our view, this is an acceptable accounting approach, it does not seem entirely satisfactory. For example, in a number of jurisdictions, it is common for an equity-settled share-based payment award to contain a provision to the effect that, if the employee dies in service, the entity will pay to the employee's estate the fair value of the award in cash. The analysis above would lead to the conclusion that the award must be classified as cash-settled, on the basis that it is beyond the entity's control whether or not an employee dies in service. This seems a somewhat far-fetched conclusion, and is moreover inconsistent with the accounting treatment that the entity would apply to any other death-in-service benefit under IAS 19. IAS 19 would generally require the entity to recognise a liability for such a benefit based on an actuarial estimate (see Chapter 35 at 3.6), rather than on a presumption that the entire workforce will die in service.

10.3.2 Approach 2 – Treat as cash-settled if contingency is outside entity's control and probable

It was presumably considerations such as those above that led the FASB staff to provide an interpretation[25] of the equivalent provisions of ASC 718 regarding awards that are cash-settled in certain circumstances. This interpretation states that a cash settlement feature that can be exercised only upon the occurrence of a contingent event that is outside the employee's control does not give rise to a liability until it becomes probable that that event will occur.[26]

In our view, an approach based on the probability of a contingent event that is outside the control of both the counterparty and the entity is also acceptable under IFRS and is frequently applied in practice. The implied rationale (by reference to IFRS literature) is that:

- IFRS 2 clearly notes a number of inconsistencies between IFRS 2 and IAS 32 (see 1.4.1 above) and so there is no requirement to follow IAS 32 in respect of contingent cash settlement arrangements; and
- it is therefore appropriate to have regard to the principles of IAS 37 in determining whether an uncertain future event gives rise to a liability. IAS 37 requires a liability to be recognised only when it is probable (i.e. more likely than not) to occur (see Chapter 26).

The impact of Approach 1 and Approach 2 can be illustrated by reference to an award that requires cash-settlement in the event of a change of control of the entity (see 10.3.3 below).

10.3.3 Application of Approach 1 and Approach 2 to awards requiring cash settlement on a change of control

It is not uncommon for the terms of an award to provide for compulsory cash-settlement by the entity if there is a change of control of the reporting entity. Such a provision ensures that there is no need for any separate negotiations to buy out all employee options, so as to avoid non-controlling interests arising in the acquired entity when equity-settled awards are settled after the change of control.

The question of whether or not a change of control is within the control of the entity is a matter that has been the subject of much discussion in the context of determining the classification of certain financial instruments by their issuer, and is considered more fully in Chapter 47 at 4.3.

If the facts and circumstances of a particular case indicate that a change of control is within the entity's control, the conclusion under either Approach 1 or Approach 2 above would be that the award should be treated as cash-settled only if the entity has a liability by reference to the criteria summarised in 10.2.1 above.

If, however, the change of control is not considered to be within the control of the reporting entity, the conclusion will vary depending on whether Approach 1 or Approach 2 is followed. Under Approach 1, an award requiring settlement in cash on a change of control outside the control of the entity would be treated as cash-settled, however unlikely the change of control may be. Under Approach 2 however, an award requiring settlement in cash on a change of control outside the control of the entity would be treated as cash-settled only if a change of control were probable.

A difficulty with Approach 2 is that it introduces rather bizarre inconsistencies in the accounting treatment for awards when the relative probability of their outcome is considered. As noted at 10.1.5 above, an award that gives the counterparty an absolute right to cash-settlement is accounted for as a liability, however unlikely it is that the counterparty will exercise that right. Thus, under this approach, the entity could find itself in the situation where it treats:

- as a liability: an award with an unrestricted right to cash-settlement for the counterparty, where the probability of the counterparty exercising that right is less than 1%; but
- as equity: an award that requires cash settlement in the event of a change of control which is assessed as having a 49% probability of occurring.

In our view, an entity may adopt either of these accounting treatments, but should do so consistently and state its policy for accounting for such transactions if material.

In selecting an accounting policy, an entity should however be aware of the IASB's discussions on whether an approach based on the 'probable' outcome should be applied or whether an approach based on the accounting treatment for a compound instrument should be used (see 10.3.5 below).

There is further discussion at 15.4 below of awards that vest or are exercisable on a flotation or change of control, including the question of whether a cash-settlement obligation rests with the entity itself or with other parties involved in the change of control (see 15.4.6 below).

10.3.4 Accounting for change in manner of settlement where award is contingent on future events outside the control of the entity and the counterparty

When, under Approach 2 above, the manner of settlement of an award changes solely as a consequence of a re-assessment of the probability of a contingent event, there is neither settlement of the award nor modification of its original terms (see 10.3.4.A below for discussion of awards that have also been modified). The terms of the award are such that there have been two potential outcomes, one equity-settled and one cash-settled, running in parallel since grant date. It is as if, in effect, the entity has simultaneously issued two awards, only one of which will vest.

At each reporting date the entity should assess which outcome is more likely and account for the award on an equity- or cash-settled basis accordingly. In our view, any adjustments arising from a switch between the cumulative amount for the cash-settled award and the cumulative amount for the equity-settled award should be taken to profit or loss in the current period. This is similar to the approach for an award with multiple independent vesting conditions (see 6.3.6 above).

When applying an approach where the two outcomes have both been part of the arrangement from grant date, an entity measures the fair value of the equity-settled award only at the original grant date and there is no remeasurement of the equity-settled award on reassessment of the settlement method. As the cash-settled award would be remeasured on an ongoing basis, a switch in the manner of settlement during the period until the shares vest or the award is settled in cash could give rise to significant volatility in the cumulative expense. At the date of vesting or settlement, however, the cumulative expense will equate to either the grant date fair value of the equity-settled approach or the settlement value of the cash-settled approach depending on whether or not the contingent event has happened.

The situation discussed in this section (i.e. an arrangement with two potential outcomes from grant date because the manner of settlement is not within the control of either the entity or the counterparty) is not the same as an award where the manner of settlement is entirely within the entity's control. Where the entity has such control and therefore a choice of settlement, a change in the manner of settlement is treated as a modification with a potential catch-up adjustment through equity (see 9.4 and 10.2.3 above).

As noted at 10.3.5 below, discussions by the Interpretations Committee indicated a preference for treating an award as equity-settled or cash-settled in its entirety, based on the probable outcome, rather than as a compound instrument, but subsequent discussions by the IASB were divided.

10.3.4.A Distinction between re-assessment of settlement method and modification of terms of award

Some awards include arrangements for contingent cash-settlement if an event outside the control of the entity and the counterparty, such as some forms of exit, has not happened within a certain timescale. During the initial period of such an arrangement there might be an expectation that the exit (or other event) will take place. In this case, the award would be treated as equity-settled using an approach based on the probability of this outcome, as outlined at 10.3.4 above. However, if it is decided, close to the end of the period during which equity-settlement would apply, to modify the terms of the award so that this period is extended, the entity needs to re-assess the arrangement on both its original and modified terms.

It might therefore be the case that cash-settlement under the original terms of the award becomes the more likely outcome for a short time and that the entity has to switch the award from an equity-settled to a cash-settled basis in line with the guidance at 10.3.4 above. If a modification is then made to extend the period during which the award can be equity-settled and hence the settlement in cash once again becomes less likely, the entity should then switch again to an equity-settled basis of accounting using modification accounting (see 9.4.2 above).

10.3.5 Manner of settlement contingent on future events: discussions by the IASB and the Interpretations Committee

Following an earlier request to the Interpretations Committee for clarification on how share-based payment transactions should be classified and measured if the manner of settlement is contingent on either:

- a future event that is outside the control of both the entity and the counterparty; or
- a future event that is within the control of the counterparty,

the IASB agreed that transactions in which the manner of settlement is contingent on future events should be considered together with other issues relating to IFRS 2 (see 3.4 above).[27]

Prior to discussion by the IASB, the Interpretations Committee discussed the matter again in May 2013, noting that paragraph 34 of IFRS 2 requires an entity to account on a cash-settled basis if, and to the extent that, the entity has incurred a liability to settle in cash or other assets. However, it was further noted that IFRS 2 only provides guidance where the entity or the counterparty has a choice of settlement and not where the manner of settlement is contingent on a future event that is outside the control of both parties. The Interpretations Committee also observed that it was unclear which other guidance within IFRS and the *Conceptual Framework* would provide the best analogy to this situation. It was concluded that there was significant diversity in practice.[28]

In September 2013, the Interpretations Committee noted that the results of additional outreach indicated that shared-based payment transactions in which the manner of settlement is contingent on a future event within the control of the counterparty (but not the entity) are not significantly widespread and so the Committee decided not to add this element of the original submission to its agenda.[29]

The Interpretations Committee also returned to the question of accounting when the manner of settlement is contingent on a future event that is outside the control of both the entity and the counterparty. It was noted that such arrangements are settled either in cash or in equity instruments in their entirety and that neither party to the arrangement has control over the manner of settlement. Accordingly, the Committee observed that the share-based payment should be classified as either equity-settled or cash-settled in its entirety depending on which outcome is probable.

The Interpretations Committee also discussed the accounting for a change in classification of the transaction arising from a change in the more likely settlement method. A majority of the Committee thought that there should be a cumulative adjustment recorded at the time of the change of classification, in such a way that the cumulative cost would be the same as if the change of classification had occurred at the inception of the arrangement (see 10.3.4 above). The Committee decided to recommend that the IASB make a narrow-scope amendment to IFRS 2 based on the approach above.[30]

The IASB discussed these recommendations in February 2014. Some IASB members expressed concern over use of a 'probable' approach for deciding the classification of a share-based payment. They took the view that such share-based payment transactions were similar to those in which the counterparty has a choice of settlement method because the entity does not have the unconditional right to avoid delivering cash or other assets. Therefore they considered that such arrangements should be accounted for, by analogy, in accordance with the compound instrument approach set out in paragraphs 35 to 40 of IFRS 2, noting that this would also be consistent with the requirements for contingent settlement provisions in IAS 32.[31]

The topic was discussed again by the IASB in April 2014 when, notwithstanding the diversity in practice, the Board decided not to propose an amendment to IFRS 2 for this issue. Some IASB members were concerned that the suggested amendment would introduce a principle for distinguishing between a liability and equity in IFRS 2 that would be inconsistent with the requirements of IAS 32 and also noted that the definition of a liability was being discussed as part of the Conceptual Framework project (see Chapter 2).[32]

The IASB revised the *Conceptual Framework* in 2018 without addressing the above mentioned issue; the boundary between liabilities and equity will be further explored by the IASB in its research project on *Financial Instruments with Characteristics of Equity* (see 1.4.1 above). Until such time as any revised guidance is issued, we expect Approach 1 or Approach 2, outlined at 10.3.1 and 10.3.2 above, to continue to be applied.

10.4 Cash settlement alternative where cash sum is not based on share price or value

Some awards may provide a cash-settlement alternative that is not based on the share price. For example, an employee might be offered a choice between 500 shares or €1,000,000 on the vesting of an award. Whilst an award of €1,000,000, if considered in isolation, would obviously not be a share-based payment transaction, it nevertheless falls within the scope of IFRS 2, rather than – say – IAS 19, if it is offered as an alternative to a transaction that is within the scope of IFRS 2. The Basis for Conclusions to IFRS 2 states that the cash alternative may be fixed or variable and, if variable, may be determinable in a manner that is related, or unrelated, to the price of the entity's shares. *[IFRS 2.BC256].*

11 REPLACEMENT SHARE-BASED PAYMENT AWARDS ISSUED IN A BUSINESS COMBINATION

11.1 Background

It is frequently the case that an entity (A) acquires another (B) which, at the time of the business combination, has outstanding employee share options or other share-based awards. If no action were taken by A, employees of B would be entitled, once any vesting conditions had been satisfied, to shares in B. This is not a very satisfactory outcome for either party: A now has non-controlling (minority) shareholders in subsidiary B, which was previously wholly-owned, and the employees of B are the owners of unmarketable shares in an effectively wholly-owned subsidiary.

The obvious solution, adopted in the majority of cases, is for some mechanism to be put in place such that the employees of B end up holding shares in the new parent A. This can be achieved, for example, by:

- A granting options over its own shares to the employees of B in exchange for the surrender of the employees' options over the shares of B; or
- changing the terms of the options so that they are over a special class of shares in B which are mandatorily convertible into shares of A.

This raises the question of how such a substitution transaction should be accounted for in the consolidated financial statements of A (the treatment in the single entity financial statements of B is discussed at 11.4 below).

IFRS 3 addresses the accounting treatment required in a business combination where an acquirer:

- replaces acquiree awards on a mandatory basis (see 11.2.1 below);
- replaces acquiree awards on a voluntary basis, even if the acquiree awards would not expire as a consequence of the business combination (see 11.2.2 below); or
- does not replace acquiree awards (see 11.3 below).

Section 11 relates only to business combinations. Share-based payment arrangements in the context of group reorganisations are addressed at 12.8 below.

11.2 Replacement awards in business combinations accounted for under IFRS 3

A more comprehensive discussion of the requirements of IFRS 3 may be found in Chapter 9.

IFRS 3 requires an acquirer to measure a liability or an equity instrument related to the replacement of an acquiree's share-based payment awards in accordance with IFRS 2, rather than in accordance with the general principles of IFRS 3. References to the 'fair value' of an award in the following discussion therefore mean the fair value determined under IFRS 2, for which IFRS 3 uses the term 'market-based measure'. The fair value measurement is to be made as at the acquisition date determined in accordance with IFRS 3. *[IFRS 3.30]*.

IFRS 3 notes that a transaction entered into by or on behalf of the acquirer or primarily for the benefit of the acquirer or the combined entity, rather than that of the acquiree (or its former owners) before the combination, is likely to be a transaction separate from the business combination itself. This includes a transaction that remunerates employees or former owners of the acquiree for future services. *[IFRS 3.52]*. Target entities will therefore need to consider carefully whether any modifications to existing share-based payment arrangements in the period leading up to the business combination are straightforward modifications by the target entity for its own benefit or that of its owners at the time (and hence fully within the scope of IFRS 2) or whether the changes need to be assessed under the guidance in IFRS 3 because they are for the benefit of the acquirer or the combined entity. The indicators in paragraph B50 of IFRS 3 should be used to determine when the modification should be measured and recognised. *[IFRS 3.B50]*.

The Application Guidance in Appendix B to IFRS 3 and the illustrative examples accompanying the standard explain how the general principle of paragraph 52 is to be applied to replacement share-based payment transactions. Essentially, however, IFRS 3 appears to view an exchange of share options or other share-based payment awards in conjunction with a business combination as a form of modification (see 7.3 above). *[IFRS 3.B56]*.

11.2.1 Awards that the acquirer is 'obliged' to replace

Where the acquirer is 'obliged' to replace the acquiree awards (see below), either all or a portion of the fair value of the acquirer's replacement awards forms part of the consideration transferred in the business combination. *[IFRS 3.B56]*.

IFRS 3 regards the acquirer as 'obliged' to replace the acquiree awards if the acquiree or its employees have the ability to enforce replacement, for example if replacement is required by:

- the terms of the acquisition agreement;
- the terms of the acquiree's awards; or
- applicable laws or regulations. *[IFRS 3.B56]*.

The required treatment of replacement awards may be summarised as follows:

(a) at the date of acquisition, the fair values of the replacement award and the original award are determined in accordance with IFRS 2;

(b) the amount of the replacement award attributable to pre-combination service (and therefore included as part of the consideration transferred for the business) is determined by multiplying the fair value of the original award by the ratio of the vesting period completed, as at the date of the business combination, to the greater of:

- the total vesting period, as determined at the date of the business combination (being the period required to satisfy all vesting conditions, including conditions added to, or removed from, the original award by the replacement award); and
- the original vesting period; and

(c) any excess of the fair value of the replacement award over the amount determined in (b) above is recognised as a post-combination remuneration expense, in accordance with the normal principles of IFRS 2 (see 3 to 7 above). *[IFRS 3.B57-59]*.

The requirements summarised in (a) to (c) above have the effect that any excess of the fair value of the replacement award over the original award is recognised as a post-combination remuneration expense. The requirement in (b) above has the effect that, if the replacement award requires service in the period after the business combination, an IFRS 2 cost is recognised in the post-combination period, even if the acquiree award being replaced had fully vested at the date of acquisition. It also has the effect that if a replacement award requires no service in the post-combination period, but the acquiree award being replaced would have done so, a cost must be recognised in the post-combination period. *[IFRS 3.B59]*.

There is no specific guidance in IFRS 3 on how and when to recognise the post-combination remuneration expense in the consolidated financial statements of the acquirer. In our view, the expense should be recognised over the post-combination vesting period of the replacement award in accordance with the general principles of IFRS 2 (see 6.2 to 6.4 above).

The portions of the replacement award attributable to pre- and post-combination service calculated in (b) and (c) above are calculated, under the normal principles of IFRS 2, based on the best estimate of the number of awards expected to vest (or to be treated as vesting by IFRS 2). Rather than being treated as adjustments to the consideration for the business combination, any changes in estimates or forfeitures occurring after the acquisition date are reflected in remuneration cost for the period in which the changes occur in accordance with the normal principles of IFRS 2. Similarly, the effects of other post-acquisition events, such as modifications or the outcome of performance conditions, are accounted for in accordance with IFRS 2 as part of the determination of the remuneration expense for the period in which such events occur. *[IFRS 3.B60]*. The application of these requirements is discussed in more detail at 11.2.3 below.

The requirements above to split an award into pre-combination and post-combination portions apply equally to equity-settled and cash-settled replacement awards. All changes after the acquisition date in the fair value of cash-settled replacements awards and their tax effects (recognised in accordance with IAS 12 – *Income Taxes*) are recognised in the post-combination financial statements when the changes occur. *[IFRS 3.B61-62]*. IFRS 3 does not specify where in the income statement any changes in the pre-combination element of a cash-settled award should be reflected and, in the absence of clear guidance, an entity will need to consider whether this is remuneration expense or whether it is closer to a change in a liability for contingent consideration.

The treatment of the income tax effects of replacement share-based payment transactions in a business combination is discussed further in Chapter 33 at 10.8.5.

11.2.1.A Illustrative examples of awards that the acquirer is 'obliged' to replace

IFRS 3 provides some examples in support of the written guidance summarised above, the substance of which is reproduced as Examples 34.45 to 34.48 below. *[IFRS 3.IE61-71]*. These deal with the following scenarios.

Is post-combination service required for the replacement award?	Has the acquiree award being replaced vested before the combination?	Example
Not required	Vested	34.45
Not required	Not vested	34.46
Required	Vested	34.47
Required	Not vested	34.48

In all the examples, it is assumed that the replacement award is equity-settled.

Example 34.45: **Replacement award requiring no post-combination service replacing vested acquiree award**

Entity A acquires Entity B and issues replacement awards with a fair value at the acquisition date of €1.1 million for awards of Entity B with a fair value at the acquisition date of €1.0 million. No post-combination services are required for the replacement awards and Entity B's employees had rendered all of the required service for the acquiree awards as of the acquisition date.

The amount attributable to pre-combination service, and therefore included in the consideration transferred in the business combination, is the fair value of Entity B's awards at the acquisition date (€1.0 million). The amount attributable to post-combination service is €0.1 million, the difference between the total value of the replacement awards (€1.1 million) and the portion attributable to pre-combination service (€1.0 million). Because no post-combination service is required for the replacement awards, Entity A immediately recognises €0.1 million as remuneration cost in its post-combination financial statements.

Example 34.46: **Replacement award requiring no post-combination service replacing unvested acquiree award**

Entity A acquires Entity B and issues replacement awards with a fair value at the acquisition date of €1.0 million for awards of Entity B also with a fair value at the acquisition date of €1.0 million. When originally granted, the awards of Entity B had a vesting period of four years and, as of the acquisition date, the employees of Entity B had rendered two years' service. The replacement award vests in full immediately.

The portion of the fair value of the replacement awards attributable to pre-combination services is the fair value of the award of Entity B being replaced (€1 million) multiplied by the ratio of the pre-combination vesting period (two years) to the greater of the total vesting period (now two years) and the original vesting period of Entity B's award (four years). Thus, €0.5 million (€1.0 million × 2/4 years) is attributable to pre-combination service and therefore included in the consideration transferred for the acquiree. The remaining €0.5 million is attributable to post-combination service, but, because no post-combination service is required for the replacement award to vest, Entity A recognises the entire €0.5 million immediately as remuneration cost in the post-combination financial statements.

Example 34.47: **Replacement award requiring post-combination service replacing vested acquiree award**

Entity A acquires Entity B and issues replacement awards with a fair value at the acquisition date of €1.0 million for awards of Entity B also with a fair value at the acquisition date of €1.0 million. The replacement awards require one year of post-combination service. The awards of Entity B being replaced had a vesting period of four years. As of the acquisition date, employees of Entity B holding unexercised vested awards had rendered a total of seven years of service since the grant date.

Even though the Entity B employees have already rendered all of the service for their original awards, Entity A attributes a portion of the replacement award to post-combination remuneration cost, because the replacement awards require one year of post-combination service. The total vesting period is five years – the vesting period for the original Entity B award completed before the acquisition date (four years) plus the vesting period for the replacement award (one year). The fact that the employees have rendered seven years of service in total in the pre-combination period is not relevant to the calculation because only four years of that service were necessary in order to earn the original award.

The portion attributable to pre-combination services equals the fair value of the award of Entity B being replaced (€1 million) multiplied by the ratio of the pre-combination vesting period (four years) to the total vesting period (five years). Thus, €0.8 million (€1.0 million × 4/5 years) is attributed to the pre-combination vesting period and therefore included in the consideration transferred in the business combination. The remaining €0.2 million is attributed to the post-combination vesting period and is recognised as remuneration cost in Entity A's post-combination financial statements in accordance with IFRS 2, over the remaining one year vesting period.

Example 34.48: *Replacement award requiring post-combination service replacing unvested acquiree award*

Entity A acquires Entity B and issues replacement awards with a fair value at the acquisition date of €1.0 million for awards of Entity B also with a fair value at the acquisition date of €1.0 million. The replacement awards require one year of post-combination service. When originally granted, the awards of Entity B being replaced had a vesting period of four years and, as of the acquisition date, the employees had rendered two years' service.

The replacement awards require one year of post-combination service. Because employees have already rendered two years of service, the total vesting period is three years. The portion attributable to pre-combination services equals the fair value of the award of Entity B being replaced (€1 million) multiplied by the ratio of the pre-combination vesting period (two years) to the greater of the total vesting period (three years) or the original vesting period of Entity B's award (four years). Thus, €0.5 million (€1.0 million × 2/4 years) is attributable to pre-combination service and therefore included in the consideration transferred for the acquiree. The remaining €0.5 million is attributable to post-combination service and therefore recognised as remuneration cost in Entity A's post-combination financial statements, over the remaining one year vesting period.

11.2.2 Acquiree awards that the acquirer is not 'obliged' to replace

IFRS 3 notes that, in some situations, acquiree awards may expire as a consequence of a business combination. In such a situation, the acquirer might decide to replace those awards even though it is not obliged to do so. It might also be the case that the acquirer decides voluntarily to replace awards that would not expire and which it is not otherwise obliged to replace.

Under IFRS 3 there is no difference in the basic approach to accounting for a replacement award that the acquirer is obliged to make and one that it makes on a voluntary basis (i.e. the approach is as set out at 11.2.1 above). In other words, the accounting is based on the fair value of the replacement award at the date of acquisition, with an apportionment of that amount between the cost of acquisition and post-acquisition employment expense.

However, in situations where the acquiree awards would expire as a consequence of the business combination if they were not voluntarily replaced by the acquirer, none of the fair value of the replacement awards is treated as part of the consideration transferred for the business (and therefore included in the computation of goodwill), but the full amount is instead recognised as a remuneration cost in the post-combination financial statements. The IASB explains that this is because the new award by the acquirer can only be for future services to be provided by the employee as the acquirer has no obligation to the employee in respect of past services. [IFRS 3.B56, BC311B].

11.2.3 Accounting for changes in vesting assumptions after the acquisition date

Whilst the requirements outlined at 11.2.1 above to reflect changes in assumptions relating to the post-acquisition portion of an award through post-combination remuneration appear consistent with the general principles of IFRS 2 and IFRS 3, the application of the requirements to the pre-combination portion is less straightforward.

Paragraph B60 of IFRS 3 appears to require all changes to both the pre- and post-combination portions of the award to be reflected in post-combination remuneration expense. *[IFRS 3.B60]*. This could lead to significant volatility in post-combination profit or loss as a consequence of forfeitures, or other changes in estimates, relating to awards accounted for as part of the consideration for the business combination.

A second approach relies on a combination of paragraphs B60 and B63(d). Whilst paragraph B60 is clear that no adjustment can be made to the purchase consideration, paragraph B63(d) refers to IFRS 2 providing 'guidance on subsequent measurement and accounting for *the portion of replacement share-based payment awards ... that is attributable to employees' future services'* (emphasis added). *[IFRS 3.B60, B63(d)]*. Supporters of this view therefore argue that the remeasurement requirements of paragraph B60 apply only to the portion of the replacement award that is attributed to future service and that the award should be split into two parts:

- a pre-combination element that is treated as if it were vested at the acquisition date and then accounted for in the same way as other contingent consideration settled in equity; and
- a post-combination portion that is treated as a new award and reflects only the employees' post-combination service.

A third approach is based on the guidance in paragraph B59 of IFRS 3 which states that 'the acquirer attributes any excess of the market-based measure of the replacement award over the market-based measure of the acquiree award to post-combination service and recognises that excess as remuneration cost in the post-combination financial statements'. *[IFRS 3.B59]*. As for the second approach above, the pre-combination element is considered to be fixed and cannot be reversed. However, any subsequent changes in assumptions that give rise to an incremental expense over the amount recognised as pre-combination service should be recognised as part of the post-combination remuneration expense.

Whilst the second and third approaches above are more consistent with the general requirement under IFRS 2 that vested awards should not be adjusted, the first approach, based on paragraph B60, is arguably the most obvious reading of IFRS 3. In the absence of clear guidance in the standard, we believe that an entity may make an accounting policy choice between the three approaches but, once chosen, the policy should be applied consistently.

The three approaches are illustrated in Example 34.49 below.

Example 34.49:   Accounting for post-acquisition changes in estimates relating to replacement awards

Entity A grants an award of 1,000 shares to each of two employees. The award will vest after three years provided the employees remain in service. At the end of year 2, Entity A is acquired by Entity B which replaces the award with one over its own shares but otherwise on the same terms. The fair value of each share at the date of acquisition is €1. At this date, Entity B estimates that one of the two employees will leave employment before the end of the remaining one year service period.

At the date of acquisition, Entity B recognises €667 (1 employee × 1,000 shares × €1 × 2/3) as part of the consideration for the business combination and expects to recognise a further €333 as an expense through post-acquisition profit or loss (1 × 1,000 × €1 × 1/3).

However, if the estimates made as at the date of the acquisition prove to be inaccurate and either both employees leave employment during year 3, or both remain in employment until the vesting date, there are three alternative approaches to the accounting as explained above:

- Approach 1 – all changes in estimates are reflected in post-acquisition profit or loss (drawing on paragraph B60 of IFRS 3);
- Approach 2 – changes to the estimates that affect the amount recognised as part of the purchase consideration are not adjusted for and changes affecting the post-acquisition assumptions are adjusted through post-acquisition profit or loss (drawing on paragraph B63(d) of IFRS 3); or
- Approach 3 – the amount attributable to pre-combination service, and treated as part of the business combination, is fixed and cannot be reversed. However, any changes in assumptions that give rise to an additional cumulative expense are reflected through post-acquisition profit or loss (drawing on paragraph B59 of IFRS 3).

Using the fact pattern above, and assuming that both employees leave employment in the post-acquisition period, the three alternative approaches would give rise to the following entries in accounting for the forfeitures:

- Approach 1 – a credit of €667 to post-acquisition profit or loss to reflect the reversal of the amount charged to the business combination. In addition to this, any additional expense that had been recognised in the post-acquisition period would be reversed.
- Approaches 2 and 3 – the reversal through post-acquisition profit or loss of any additional expense that had been recognised in the post-acquisition period.

If, instead, both employees remained in employment in the post-acquisition period and both awards vested, the three alternative approaches would give rise to the following entries:

- Approach 1 – an expense of €1,333 through post-acquisition profit or loss to reflect the remaining €333 fair value of the award to the employee who was expected to remain in service plus €1,000 for the award to the employee who was not expected to remain in service.
- Approach 2 – an expense of €666 (2 × €333) through post-acquisition profit or loss for the remaining 1/3 of the acquisition date fair value of the two awards. There is no adjustment to the business combination or to post-acquisition profit or loss for the €667 pre-acquisition element of the award that, as at the acquisition date, was not expected to vest.
- Approach 3 – an expense of €1,333 through post-acquisition profit or loss to reflect the remaining €333 fair value of the award to the employee who was expected to remain in service plus €1,000 for the award to the employee who was not expected to remain in service.

11.3 Acquiree award not replaced by acquirer

It may occasionally happen that the acquirer does not replace awards of the acquiree at the time of the acquisition. This might be the case where, for example, the acquired subsidiary is only partly-owned and is itself listed.

IFRS 3 distinguishes between vested and unvested share-based payment transactions of the acquiree that are outstanding at the date of the business combination but which the acquirer chooses not to replace.

If vested, the outstanding acquiree share-based payment transactions are treated by the acquirer as part of the non-controlling interest in the acquiree and measured at their IFRS 2 fair value at the date of acquisition.

If unvested, the outstanding share-based payment transactions are fair valued in accordance with IFRS 2 as if the acquisition date were the grant date. The fair value should be allocated to the non-controlling interest in the acquiree on the basis of the ratio of the portion of the vesting period completed to the greater of:

- the total vesting period; and
- the original vesting period of the share-based payment transactions.

The balance is treated as a post-combination remuneration expense in accordance with the general principles of IFRS 2. *[IFRS 3.B62A-B62B]*. Forfeitures in the post-combination period will need to be assessed in accordance with the approaches set out at 11.2.3 above.

11.4 Financial statements of the acquired entity

The replacement of an award based on the acquiree's equity with one based on the acquirer's equity is, from the perspective of the acquired entity, a cancellation and replacement, to be accounted for in accordance with the general principles of IFRS 2 for such transactions (see 7.4 above). However, in addition to considerations about whether this is accounted for as a separate cancellation and new grant or as a modification of the original terms, the acquiree needs to take into account its new status as a subsidiary of the acquirer.

If the acquirer is responsible for settling the award in its own equity with the acquiree's employees, the acquiree will continue to account for the award on an equity-settled basis. If, however, the acquiree is responsible for settling the award with shares of the acquirer, then the acquiree would have to switch from an equity-settled basis of accounting to a cash-settled basis of accounting (see 2.2.2.A and 9.4.1 above). *[IFRS 2.43B, B52(b), B55]*.

Even if the acquiree continues to account for the award on an equity-settled basis, the share-based payment expense recorded in the consolidated financial statements (based on fair value at the date of the business combination) will generally not be the same as that in the financial statements of the acquired entity (based on fair value at the date of original grant plus any incremental value granted at the date of acquisition, if modification accounting is applied). The exact timing of the recognition of the expense in the financial statements of the acquired entity after the date of cancellation and replacement will depend on its interpretation of the requirements of IFRS 2 for the cancellation and replacement of options (see Example 34.29 at 7.4.4.B above).

12 GROUP SHARE SCHEMES

In this section we consider various aspects of share-based payment arrangements operated within a group and involving several legal entities. The focus of the section is on the accounting by the various parties involved and includes several comprehensive illustrative examples. The main areas covered are as follows:

- typical features of a group share scheme (see 12.1 below);
- a summary of the accounting treatment of group share schemes (see 12.2 below);
- employee benefit trusts ('EBTs') and similar vehicles (see 12.3 below);
- an example of a group share scheme (based on an equity-settled award satisfied by a market purchase of shares) illustrating the accounting by the different entities involved (see 12.4 below);
- an example of a group share scheme (based on an equity-settled award satisfied by a fresh issue of shares) illustrating the accounting by the different entities involved (see 12.5 below);
- an example of a group cash-settled transaction where the award is settled by an entity other than the one receiving goods or services (see 12.6 below);
- the accounting treatment when an employee transfers between group entities (see 12.7 below); and
- group reorganisations (see 12.8 below).

Whilst associates and joint arrangements accounted for as joint ventures do not meet the definition of group entities, there will sometimes be share-based payment arrangements that involve the investor or venturer and the employees of its associate or joint venture. These arrangements are discussed at 12.9 below.

12.1 Typical features of a group share scheme

In this section we use the term 'share scheme' to encompass any transaction falling within the scope of IFRS 2, whether accounted for as equity-settled or cash-settled.

It is common practice for a group to operate a single share scheme covering several subsidiaries. Depending on the commercial needs of the entity, the scheme might cover all group entities, all group entities in a particular country or all employees of a particular grade throughout a number of subsidiaries.

The precise terms and structures of group share schemes are so varied that it is rare to find two completely identical arrangements. From an accounting perspective, however, group share schemes can generally be reduced to a basic prototype, as described below, which will serve as the basis of the discussion.

A group scheme typically involves transactions by several legal entities:

- the parent, over whose shares awards are granted;
- the subsidiary employing an employee who has been granted an award ('the employing subsidiary'); and
- the trust that administers the scheme. Such trusts are known by various names in different jurisdictions, but, for the sake of convenience, in this section we will use the term 'EBT' ('employee benefit trust') to cover all such vehicles by whatever

name they are actually known. The accounting treatment of transactions with EBTs is discussed at 12.3 below.

In practice, it might not always be a simple assessment to determine which entity is receiving an employee's services and which entity is responsible for settling the award. For example, the scheme may be directed by a group employee services entity or an individual might be a director of the parent as well as providing services to other operating entities within the group.

Where an employee services company is involved it will be necessary to evaluate the precise group arrangements in order to decide whether that entity is, in substance, the employer or whether the entity or entities to which it makes a recharge for an individual's services should be treated as the employer(s). It will also often be the case that the services company is simply administering the arrangements on behalf of the parent entity.

Where an individual provides services to more than one group entity, an assessment will need to be made as to which entity or entities are receiving the individual's services in return for the award. This will depend on the precise facts and circumstances of a particular situation.

A share-based award is often granted to an employee by the parent, or a group employee services entity, which will in turn have an option exercisable against the EBT for the shares that it may be required to deliver to the employee. Less commonly, the trustees of the EBT make awards to the employees and enter into reciprocal arrangements with the parent.

If the parent takes the view that it will satisfy any awards using existing shares it will often seek to fix the cash cost of the award by arranging for the EBT to purchase in the market, on the day that the award is made, sufficient shares to satisfy all or part of the award. This purchase will be funded by external borrowings, a loan from the parent, a contribution from the employing subsidiary, or some combination. The cash received from the employee on exercise of the option can be used by the EBT to repay any borrowings.

If the parent takes the view that it will satisfy the options with a fresh issue of shares, these will be issued to the EBT, either:

(a) at the date on which the employee exercises his option (in which case the EBT will subscribe for the new shares using the cash received from the employee together with any non-refundable contribution made by the employing subsidiary – see below). Such arrangements are generally referred to as 'simultaneous funding';

(b) at some earlier date (in which case the EBT will subscribe for the new shares using external borrowings, a loan from the parent or a contribution from the employing subsidiary, or some combination. The cash received from the employee on exercise of the option may then be used by the EBT to repay any borrowings). Such arrangements are generally referred to as 'pre-funding'; or

(c) some shares will be issued before the exercise date as in (b) above, and the balance on the exercise date as in (a) above.

As noted in (a) above, the employing subsidiary often makes a non-refundable contribution to the EBT in connection with the scheme, so as to ensure that employing subsidiaries bear an appropriate share of the overall cost of a group-wide share scheme.

12.2 Accounting treatment of group share schemes – summary

12.2.1 Background

From a financial reporting perspective, it is generally necessary to consider the accounting treatment in:

- the group's consolidated financial statements;
- the parent's separate financial statements; and
- the employing subsidiary's financial statements.

We make the assumption throughout section 12 that the subsidiary is directly owned by the parent company. In practice, there will often be one or more intermediate holding companies between the ultimate parent and the subsidiary. The intermediate parent company generally will not be the entity granting the award, receiving the goods or services or responsible for settling the award. Therefore, under IFRS 2, we believe that there is no requirement for the intermediate company to account for the award in its separate or individual financial statements (although it might choose to recognise an increase in its investment in the subsidiary and a corresponding capital contribution from the ultimate parent in order for the transaction to be reflected throughout the chain of companies).

The accounting entries to be made in the various financial statements will broadly vary according to:

- whether the award is satisfied using shares purchased in the market or a fresh issue of shares;
- whether any charge is made to the employing subsidiary for the cost of awards to its employees;
- whether an employee benefit trust (EBT) is involved. The accounting treatment of transactions undertaken with and by EBTs is discussed in more detail at 12.3 below; and
- the tax consequences of the award. However, for the purposes of the discussion and illustrative examples below, tax effects are ignored, since these will vary significantly by jurisdiction. A more general discussion of the tax effects of share-based payment transactions may be found at 14 below and in Chapter 33 at 10.8.

12.2.2 Scope of IFRS 2 for group share schemes

By virtue of the definition of 'share-based payment transaction' (see 2.2.1 and 2.2.2.A above), a group share-based payment transaction is in the scope of IFRS 2 for:

- the consolidated financial statements of the group (the accounting for which follows the general principles set out in 3 to 10 above);
- the separate or individual financial statements of the entity in the group that receives goods or services (see 12.2.3 below); and
- the separate or individual financial statements of the entity in the group (if different from that receiving the goods or services) that settles the transaction with the counterparty. This entity will typically, but not necessarily, be the parent (see 12.2.4 below).

IFRS 2 provides further guidance on the application of its general principles to:
- transactions settled in the equity of the entity, or in the equity of its parent (see 12.2.5 below); and
- cash-settled transactions settled by a group entity other than the entity receiving the goods or services (see 12.2.6 below).

At 2.2.2.A above we consider seven scenarios commonly found in practice and outline the approach required by IFRS 2 in the consolidated and separate or individual financial statements of group entities depending on whether the award is settled in cash or shares and which entity grants the award, has the obligation to settle the award and receives the goods or services.

It is common practice in a group share scheme to require each participating entity in the group to pay a charge, either to the parent or to an EBT, in respect of the cost of awards made under the scheme to employees of that entity. This is generally done either as part of the group's cash-management strategy, or in order to obtain tax relief under applicable local legislation. The amount charged could in principle be at the discretion of the group, but is often based on either the fair value of the award at grant date or the fair value at vesting, in the case of an award of free shares, or exercise, in the case of an award of options.

IFRS 2 does not directly address the accounting treatment of such intragroup management charges and other recharge arrangements, which is discussed further at 12.2.7 below. *[IFRS 2.B45-46]*.

Worked examples illustrating how these various principles translate into accounting entries are given at 12.4 to 12.6 below.

12.2.3 Entity receiving goods or services

The entity in a group receiving goods or services in a share-based payment transaction determines whether the transaction should be accounted for, in its separate or individual financial statements, as equity-settled or cash-settled. It does this by assessing the nature of the awards granted and its own rights and obligations. *[IFRS 2.43A]*.

The entity accounts for the transaction as equity-settled when either the awards granted are the entity's own equity instruments, or the entity has no obligation to settle the share-based payment transaction. Otherwise, the entity accounts for the transaction as cash-settled. Where the transaction is accounted for as equity-settled it is remeasured after grant date only to the extent permitted or required by IFRS 2 for equity-settled transactions generally, as discussed at 3 to 7 above. *[IFRS 2.43B]*.

IFRS 2 notes that a possible consequence of these requirements is that the amount recognised by the entity may differ from the amount recognised by the consolidated group or by another group entity settling the share-based payment transaction. *[IFRS 2.43A]*. This is discussed further at 12.6 below.

The cost recognised by the entity receiving goods or services is always calculated according to the principles set out above, regardless of any intragroup recharging arrangement. *[IFRS 2.43D, B45]*. The accounting for such arrangements is discussed at 12.2.7 below.

12.2.4 Entity settling the transaction

A group entity which settles a share-based payment transaction in which another group entity receives goods or services accounts for the transaction as an equity-settled share-based payment transaction only if it is settled in the settling entity's own equity instruments. Otherwise, the transaction is accounted for as cash-settled. *[IFRS 2.43C]*.

IFRS 2 specifies only the credit entry – the classification of the transaction as equity- or cash-settled, and its measurement. IFRS 2 does not specify the debit entry, which is therefore subject to the general requirement of IFRS 2 that a share-based payment transaction should normally be treated as an expense, unless there is the basis for another treatment under other IFRS (see 3 above).

In our view, the settling entity is not always required to treat the transaction as an expense:

- Where the settling entity is a parent (direct or indirect) of the entity receiving the goods or services and is accounting for the transaction as equity-settled, it will generally account for the settlement under IAS 27 – *Separate Financial Statements* – as an addition to the cost of its investment in the employing subsidiary (or of that holding company of the employing subsidiary which is the settling entity's directly-held subsidiary). *[IFRS 2.B45]*. It may then be necessary to review the carrying value of that investment to ensure that it is not impaired.

- Where the settling entity is a parent (direct or indirect) of the entity receiving the goods or services and is accounting for the transaction as cash-settled (whereas the subsidiary will be accounting for the transaction as equity-settled), in our view it has an accounting policy choice for the treatment of the remeasurement of the cash-settled liability. Either:

    - it accounts for the entire award as part of the contribution to the subsidiary and therefore as an addition to the cost of its investment in the employing subsidiary (or of that holding company of the employing subsidiary which is the settling entity's directly-held subsidiary); or
    - after the initial capitalisation of the grant date fair value of the liability, it remeasures the liability through profit or loss.

    Whichever policy is chosen, it may then be necessary to review the carrying value of the investment to ensure that it is not impaired.

- In other cases (i.e. where the settling entity is a subsidiary (direct or indirect) or fellow subsidiary of the entity receiving the goods or services), it should treat the settlement as a distribution, and charge it directly to equity. Whether or not such a settlement is a legal distribution is a matter of law in the jurisdiction concerned.

We adopt the approach of full capitalisation by the parent entity in the worked examples set out in 12.4 to 12.6 below.

12.2.5 Transactions settled in equity of the entity or its parent

12.2.5.A Awards settled in equity of subsidiary

Where a subsidiary grants an award to its employees and settles it in its own equity, the subsidiary accounts for the award as equity-settled.

The parent accounts for the award as equity-settled in its consolidated financial statements. In its separate financial statements, the parent is not required by IFRS 2 to account for the award. In both cases, the transaction may have implications for other aspects of the financial statements, since its settlement results in the partial disposal of the subsidiary (see Chapter 7).

Where the parent is responsible for settling the award, it accounts for the transaction as equity-settled in its consolidated financial statements. In its separate financial statements, however, it accounts for the award as cash-settled, since it is settled not in its own equity, but in the equity of the subsidiary. From the perspective of the parent's separate financial statements, the equity of a subsidiary is a financial asset. *[IFRS 2.B50]*.

12.2.5.B Awards settled in equity of the parent

Where the parent grants an award directly to the employees of a subsidiary and settles it in its own equity, the subsidiary accounts for the award as equity-settled, with a corresponding increase in equity as a contribution from the parent. *[IFRS 2.B53]*.

The parent accounts for the award as equity-settled in both its consolidated and separate financial statements. *[IFRS 2.B54]*.

Where a subsidiary grants an award of equity in its parent to its employees and settles the award itself, it accounts for the award as cash-settled, since it is settled not in its own equity, but in the equity of its parent. From the perspective of the subsidiary's separate or individual financial statements, the equity of the parent is a financial asset. *[IFRS 2.B55]*.

This requirement potentially represents something of a compliance burden. For the purposes of the parent's consolidated financial statements the fair value of the award needs to be calculated once, at grant date. For the purposes of the subsidiary's financial statements, however, IFRS 2 requires the award to be accounted for as cash-settled, with the fair value recalculated at each reporting date.

It is, however, important to note that IFRS 2 requires this accounting treatment only for a subsidiary that 'grants' such an award. *[IFRS 2.B52, B53, B55]*. In some jurisdictions it is normal for grants of share awards to be made by the parent, or an employee service company or EBT, rather than by the subsidiary, although the subsidiary may well make recommendations to the grantor of the award as to which of its employees should benefit.

In those cases, the fact that the subsidiary may communicate the award to the employee does not necessarily mean that the subsidiary itself has granted the award. It may simply be notifying the employee of an award granted by another group entity and which the other group company has the obligation to settle. In that case the subsidiary should apply the normal requirement of IFRS 2 to account for the award as equity-settled.

12.2.6 Cash-settled transactions not settled by the entity receiving goods or services

IFRS 2 considers arrangements in which the parent has an obligation to make cash payments to the employees of a subsidiary linked to the price of either:
- the subsidiary's equity instruments; or
- the parent's equity instruments.

In both cases, the subsidiary has no obligation to settle the transaction and therefore accounts for the transaction as equity-settled, recognising a corresponding credit in equity as a contribution from its parent.

The subsidiary then subsequently remeasures the cost of the transaction only for any changes resulting from non-market vesting conditions not being met in accordance with the normal provisions of IFRS 2 discussed at 3 to 6 above. IFRS 2 points out that this will differ from the measurement of the transaction as cash-settled in the consolidated financial statements of the group. *[IFRS 2.B56-57]*.

In both cases, the parent has an obligation to settle the transaction in cash. Accordingly, the parent accounts for the transaction as cash-settled in both its consolidated and separate financial statements. *[IFRS 2.B58]*.

The requirement for the subsidiary to measure the transaction as equity-settled is somewhat controversial. The essential rationale for requiring the subsidiary to record the cost of a share-based payment transaction settled by its parent is to reflect that the subsidiary is effectively receiving a capital contribution from its parent.

The IASB specifically considered whether it would be more appropriate to measure that contribution by reference to the cash actually paid by the parent, but concluded that the approach adopted in IFRS 2 better reflects the perspective of the subsidiary as a separate reporting entity. An accounting treatment based on the cash paid by the parent would, in the IASB's view, reflect the perspective of the parent rather than that of the subsidiary. *[IFRS 2.BC268H-268K]*.

12.2.7 Intragroup recharges and management charges

As noted at 12.2.2 above, IFRS 2 does not deal specifically with the accounting treatment of intragroup recharges and management charges that may be levied within the group on the subsidiary that receives goods or services, the consideration for which is equity instruments or cash provided by another group entity.

The timing of the recognition of intercompany recharges was considered by the Interpretations Committee in 2013 (see 12.2.7.A below).

The accounting requirements of IFRS 2 for group share schemes derive from IFRIC 11 (now incorporated within IFRS 2 – see 1.2 above), which was based on an exposure draft (D17) published in 2005.

D17 proposed that any such payment made by a subsidiary should be charged directly to equity, on the basis that it represents a return of the capital contribution recorded as the credit to equity required by IFRS 2 (see 12.2.3 and 12.2.6 above) up to the amount of that contribution, and a distribution thereafter.[33]

In our view, whilst IFRS 2 as currently drafted does not explicitly require this treatment, this is likely to be the more appropriate analysis for most cases where the amount of the recharge or management charge to a subsidiary is directly related to the value of the share-based payment transaction. Indeed, the only alternative, 'mechanically' speaking, would be to charge the relevant amount to profit or loss. This would result in a double charge (once for the IFRS 2 charge, and again for the management charge or recharge) which we consider not only less desirable for most entities, but also less appropriate in cases where the amounts are directly related. Accordingly, in the examples at 12.4 to 12.6 below, we apply the treatment originally proposed in D17 to any payments made by the subsidiary for participation in the group scheme.

Many intragroup recharge arrangements are based directly on the value of the underlying share-based payment – typically at grant date, vesting date or exercise date. In other cases, a more general management charge might be levied that reflects not just share-based payments but also a number of other arrangements or services provided to the subsidiary by the parent. Where there is a more general management charge of this kind, we believe that it is more appropriate for the subsidiary to recognise a double charge to profit or loss (once for the IFRS 2 charge, and again for the management charge) rather than debiting the management charge to equity as would be the case for a direct recharge.

IFRS 2 also does not address how the parent should account for a recharge or management charge received. In our view, to the extent that the receipt represents a return of a capital contribution made to the subsidiary, the parent may choose whether to credit:

- the carrying amount of its investment in the subsidiary; or
- profit or loss (with a corresponding impairment review of the investment).

Even if part of the recharge received is credited to the carrying amount of the investment, any amount received in excess of the capital contribution previously debited to the investment in subsidiary should be accounted for as a distribution from the subsidiary and credited to the income statement of the parent. Where applicable, the illustrative examples at 12.4 to 12.6 below show the entire amount as a credit to the income statement of the parent rather than part of the recharge being treated as a credit to the parent's investment in its subsidiary.

The treatment of a distribution from a subsidiary in the separate financial statements of a parent is more generally discussed in Chapter 8 at 2.4.

A further issue that arises in practice is the timing of recognition of the recharge by the parties to the arrangement. The treatment adopted might depend to some extent on the precise terms and whether there are contractual arrangements in place, but two approaches generally result in practice:

- to account for the recharge when it is actually levied or paid (which is consistent with accounting for a distribution); or
- to accrue the recharge over the life of the award or the recharge agreement even if, as is commonly the case, the actual recharge is only made at vesting or exercise date.

An entity should choose the more appropriate treatment for its particular circumstances. The first approach is often the more appropriate in a group context where recharge arrangements might be rather informal and therefore not binding until such time as a payment is made. It is also consistent with the overall recognition of the arrangement through equity. The second approach, which is likely to be the more appropriate approach when a liability is considered to exist in advance of the payment date, is closer in some respects to the accounting treatment of a provision or financial liability but, unlike the requirements of IAS 37 or IFRS 9, reflects changes in the recognised amount through equity rather than profit or loss and builds up the recharge liability over the life of the award rather than recognising the liability in full when a present obligation has been identified.

Whichever accounting treatment is adopted, any adjustments to the amount to be recognised as a recharge, whether arising from a change in the IFRS 2 expense or other changes, should be recognised in the current period and previous periods should not be restated.

Where applicable, the examples at 12.4 to 12.6 below illustrate the first of the two treatments outlined above and recognise the recharge only when it becomes payable at the date of exercise.

12.2.7.A Timing of recognition of intercompany recharges: discussion by the IFRS Interpretations Committee

In January 2013 the Interpretations Committee discussed whether a subsidiary's liability to pay to its parent the settlement value of share-based payments made by the parent to the subsidiary's employees should be recognised by the subsidiary from the grant date of the award or only at the date of settlement of the award.

While outreach conducted by the Interpretations Committee suggested that there is diversity in practice (as indicated at 12.2.7 above), the Interpretations Committee concluded in May 2013 that the topic could not be restricted to recharges relating to share-based payments and therefore decided not to add this issue to its agenda.[34]

12.3 Employee benefit trusts ('EBTs') and similar arrangements

12.3.1 Background

For some time entities have established trusts and similar arrangements for the benefit of employees. These are known by various names in different jurisdictions, but, for the sake of convenience, in this section we will use the term 'EBT' ('employee benefit trust') to cover all such vehicles by whatever name they are actually known.

The commercial purposes of using such vehicles vary from employer to employer, and from jurisdiction to jurisdiction, but may include the following:

- An EBT, in order to achieve its purpose, needs to hold shares that have either been issued to it by the entity or been bought by the EBT on the open market. In some jurisdictions, the direct holding of shares in an entity by the entity itself is unlawful.
- In the case of longer-term benefits the use of an EBT may 'ring fence' the assets set aside for the benefit of employees in case of the insolvency of the entity.
- The use of an EBT may be necessary in order to achieve a favourable tax treatment for the entity or the employees, or both.

The detailed features of an EBT will again vary from entity to entity, and from jurisdiction to jurisdiction, but typical features often include the following:

- The EBT provides a warehouse for the shares of the sponsoring entity, for example by acquiring and holding shares that are to be sold or transferred to employees in the future. The trustees may purchase the shares with finance provided by the sponsoring entity (by way of cash contributions or loans), or by a third-party bank loan, or by a combination of the two. Loans from the entity are usually interest-free. In other cases, the EBT may subscribe directly for shares issued by the sponsoring entity or acquire shares in the market.
- Where the EBT borrows from a third party, the sponsoring entity will usually guarantee the loan, i.e. it will be responsible for any shortfall if the EBT's assets are insufficient to meet its debt repayment obligations. The entity will also generally make regular contributions to the EBT to enable the EBT to meet its interest payments, i.e. to make good any shortfall between the dividend income of the EBT (if any) and the interest payable. As part of this arrangement the trustees may waive their right to dividends on the shares held by the EBT.
- Shares held by the EBT are distributed to employees through an employee share scheme. There are many different arrangements – these may include:
  - the purchase of shares by employees when exercising their share options under a share option scheme;
  - the purchase of shares by the trustees of an approved profit-sharing scheme for allocation to employees under the rules of the scheme; or
  - the transfer of shares to employees under some other incentive scheme.
- The trustees of an EBT may have a legal duty to act at all times in accordance with the interests of the beneficiaries under the EBT. However, most EBTs (particularly those established as a means of remunerating employees) are specifically designed so as to serve the purposes of the sponsoring entity, and to ensure that there will be minimal risk of any conflict arising between the duties of the trustees and the interest of the entity.

12.3.2 Accounting for EBTs

Historically, transactions involving EBTs were accounted for according to their legal form. In other words, any cash gifted or lent to the EBT was simply treated as, respectively, an expense or a loan in the financial statements of the employing entity.

However, this treatment gradually came to be challenged, not least by some tax authorities who began to question whether it was appropriate to allow a corporate tax deduction for the 'expense' of putting money into an EBT which in some cases might remain in the EBT for some considerable time (or even be lent back to the entity) before being actually passed on to employees. Thus, the issue came onto the agenda of the national standard setters.

The accounting solution proposed by some national standard setters, such as those in the United States and the United Kingdom, was to require a reporting entity to account for an EBT as an extension of the entity. The basis for this treatment was essentially that, as noted at 12.3.1 above, EBTs are specifically designed to serve the purposes of the sponsoring entity, and to ensure that there will be minimal risk of any conflict arising between the duties of the trustees and the interest of the entity, suggesting that they are under the *de facto* control of the entity.

Unlike the approach required by some national standard setters, IFRS does not mandate the treatment of an EBT as an extension of the sponsoring entity in that entity's separate financial statements and the accounting treatment in the separate entity is therefore less clear under IFRS (see 12.3.4 below). If an entity does not treat the EBT as an extension of itself in its own financial statements it will need to assess for its consolidated IFRS financial statements whether the EBT should be consolidated as a separate vehicle. This assessment will be based on the control criteria set out in IFRS 10, as discussed in more detail in Chapter 6. However, in summary, the entity will need to decide whether:

- it has power over the EBT;
- it has exposure, or rights, to variable returns from its involvement with the EBT; and
- it has the ability to use its power over the EBT to affect the amount of the sponsoring entity's returns.

Paragraphs BC70 to BC74 of the Basis for Conclusions to IFRS 2 are clearly written on the assumption that the trust referred to in paragraph BC70 is being included in the financial statements of the reporting entity. This suggests that the IASB regards the consolidation of such vehicles as normal practice. *[IFRS 2.BC70-74]*.

In addition to a decision as to whether it is appropriate to consolidate an EBT, reporting entities also need to make an assessment as to the level within a group at which the EBT should be consolidated i.e. whether the EBT is controlled by a sponsoring entity at a sub-group level or whether just by the ultimate parent entity. In many cases, an EBT holding shares in the ultimate parent entity will be considered to be under the control of that entity but there will be exceptions in some group scenarios. The discussion below generally assumes that the reporting entity is the sponsoring entity of the EBT and consolidates an EBT holding the reporting entity's own shares.

Consolidation of an EBT will have the following broad consequences for the consolidated financial statements of the reporting entity:

- Until such time as the entity's own shares held by the EBT vest unconditionally in employees (e.g. as the result of the vesting of an award of ordinary shares, or the exercise of a vested option over ordinary shares):
  - any consideration paid for the shares should be deducted in arriving at shareholders' equity in accordance with IAS 32 (see Chapter 47 at 9); and
  - the shares should be treated as if they were treasury shares when calculating earnings per share under IAS 33 (see Chapter 37 at 3.2).
- Other assets and liabilities (including borrowings) of the EBT should be recognised as assets and liabilities in the consolidated financial statements of the sponsoring entity.

- No gain or loss should be recognised in profit or loss on the purchase, sale, issue or cancellation of the entity's own shares, as required by IAS 32. Although not explicitly required by IFRS, we suggest that entities show consideration paid or received for the purchase or sale of the entity's own shares in an EBT separately from other purchases and sales of the entity's own shares in the reconciliation of movements in shareholders' equity. This may be particularly relevant for entities in jurisdictions that distinguish between 'true' treasury shares (i.e. those legally held by the issuing entity) and those accounted for as such under IFRS (such as those held by an EBT).
- Any dividend income arising on own shares should be excluded in arriving at profit before tax and deducted from the aggregate of dividends paid and proposed. In our view, the deduction should be disclosed if material.
- Finance costs and any administration expenses should be charged as they accrue and not as funding payments are made to the EBT.

The discussion above, and in the remainder of Section 12, focuses on arrangements where the EBT holds unallocated shares of the reporting entity and/or shares that have been allocated to employees in connection with share awards but where the awards have not yet vested unconditionally. There will also be situations in practice in which an EBT reaches the stage where, or is designed so that, it only holds shares to which employees have full entitlement (i.e. the shares are fully vested). In this situation the shares are beneficially owned and controlled by the individual employees but might remain in trust for tax or other reasons in the period following vesting. Where an EBT does not hold any unvested shares and there are no other assets or liabilities in the EBT over which the entity continues to exercise control, there will be nothing left in the EBT to be consolidated.

12.3.3 Illustrative Examples – awards satisfied by shares purchased by, or issued to, an EBT

The following Examples assume that the EBT is consolidated in accordance with IFRS 10 and show the interaction of the requirements of IFRS 10 with those of IFRS 2. Example 34.50 illustrates the treatment where an award is satisfied using shares previously purchased in the market. Example 34.51 illustrates the treatment where freshly issued shares are used.

Example 34.50: Interaction of IFRS 10, IAS 32 and IFRS 2 (market purchase)

On 1 January in year 1, the EBT of ABC plc made a market purchase of 100,000 shares of ABC plc at £2.50 per share. These were the only ABC shares held by the EBT at that date.

On 1 May in the same year, ABC granted executives options over between 300,000 and 500,000 shares at £2.70 per share, which will vest at the end of year 1, the number vesting depending on various performance criteria. It is determined that the cost to be recognised in respect of this award under IFRS 2 is £0.15 per share.

Four months later, on 1 September, the EBT made a further market purchase of 300,000 shares at £2.65 per share.

At the end of year 1, options vested over 350,000 shares and were exercised immediately.

The accounting entries for the above transaction required by IFRS 10, IAS 32 and IFRS 2 in the consolidated financial statements of ABC would be as set out below. It should be noted that all these pronouncements require various entries to be recorded in 'equity'. Thus, some variation may be found in practice as to the precise characterisation of the reserves, depending on local legal requirements and other 'traditions' in national GAAP which are retained to the extent that they do not conflict with IFRS.

	£	£
1 January		
Own shares (equity)	250,000	
Cash		250,000
To record purchase of 100,000 £1 shares at £2.50/share		
1 May – 31 December		
Profit or loss	52,500	
Equity†		52,500
To record cost of vested 350,000 options at £0.15/option		
1 September		
Own shares (equity)	795,000	
Cash		795,000
To record purchase of 300,000 £1 shares at £2.65/share		

	£	£
31 December		
Cash	945,000	
Equity†1		945,000
Receipt of proceeds on exercise of 350,000 options at £2.70/share		
Equity†	914,375	
Own shares (equity)2		914,375
Release of shares from EBT to employees		

1   This reflects the fact that the entity's resources have increased as a result of a transaction with an owner, which gives rise to no gain or loss and is therefore credited direct to equity.

2   It is necessary to transfer the cost of the shares 'reissued' by the EBT out of own shares, as the deduction for own shares would otherwise be overstated. The total cost of the pool of 400,000 shares immediately before vesting was £1,045,000 (£250,000 purchased on 1 January and £795,000 purchased on 1 September), representing an average cost per share of £2.6125. £2.6125 × 350,000 shares = £914,375.

†   We recommend that, subject to any local legal restrictions, these amounts should all be accounted for in the same component of equity.

Example 34.50 illustrates the importance of keeping the accounting treatment required by IAS 32 for the cost of the shares completely separate from that for the cost of the award required by IFRS 2. In cash terms, ABC has made a 'profit' of £30,625, since it purchased 350,000 shares with a weighted average cost of £914,375 and issued them to the executives for £945,000. However, this 'profit' is accounted for entirely within equity, whereas a calculated IFRS 2 cost of £52,500 is recognised in profit or loss.

Example 34.51:   Interaction of IFRS 10, IAS 32 and IFRS 2 (fresh issue of shares)

On 1 January in year 1, the EBT of ABC plc subscribed for 100,000 £1 shares of ABC plc at £2.50 per share, paid for in cash provided by ABC by way of loan to the EBT. Under local law, these proceeds must be credited to the share capital account up to the par value of the shares issued, with any excess taken to a share premium account (additional paid-in capital). These were the only ABC shares held by the EBT at that date.

On 1 May in the same year, ABC granted executives options over between 300,000 and 500,000 shares at £2.70 per share, which will vest at the end of year 1, the number vesting depending on various performance criteria. It is determined that the cost to be recognised in respect of this award is £0.15 per share.

Four months later, on 1 September, the EBT subscribed for a further 300,000 shares at £2.65 per share, again paid for in cash provided by ABC by way of loan to the EBT.

At the end of year 1, options vested over 350,000 shares and were exercised immediately.

The accounting entries for the above transaction required by IFRS 10, IAS 32 and IFRS 2 in the consolidated financial statements of ABC would be as set out below. It should be noted that all these pronouncements require various entries to be recorded in 'equity'. Thus, some variation may be found in practice as to the precise characterisation of the reserves, depending on local legal requirements and other 'traditions' in national GAAP which are retained to the extent that they do not conflict with IFRS.

	£	£
1 January		
Equity[†1]	250,000	
Share capital		100,000
Share premium		150,000
To record issue of 100,000 £1 shares to EBT at £2.50/share		
1 May – 31 December		
Profit or loss	52,500	
Equity[†]		52,500
To record cost of vested 350,000 options at £0.15/option		
	£	£
1 September		
Equity[†1]	795,000	
Share capital		300,000
Share premium		495,000
To record issue of 300,000 £1 shares at £2.65/share		
31 December		
Cash	945,000	
Equity[2†]		945,000
Receipt of proceeds on exercise of 350,000 options at £2.70/share		

1   This entry is required to reconcile the requirement of local law to record an issue of shares with the fact that, in reality, there has been no increase in the resources of the reporting entity. All that has happened is that one member of the reporting group (the EBT) has transferred cash to another (the parent entity). In our view, this amount should not necessarily be accounted for within any 'Own shares reserve' in equity if such a reserve is generally restricted to shares acquired from third parties.

2   This reflects the fact that the entity's resources have increased as a result of a transaction with an owner, which gives rise to no gain or loss and is therefore credited direct to equity.

†   We recommend that, subject to any local legal restrictions, these amounts should all be accounted for in the same component of equity.

12.3.4   Separate financial statements of sponsoring entity

As noted at 12.3.2 above, in contrast to some national GAAPs, where an EBT is treated as a direct extension of the parent or other sponsoring entity, such that the assets and liabilities of the EBT are included in both the separate financial statements of the sponsoring entity and the group consolidated financial statements, under IFRS the accounting model is *prima facie* to treat the EBT as a separate group entity.

This means that the separate financial statements of the sponsoring entity must show transactions and balances with the EBT rather than the transactions, assets and liabilities of the EBT. This raises some accounting problems, for some of which IFRS currently provides no real solution, as illustrated by Example 34.52 below. This has led the Interpretations Committee and others to discuss whether the 'separate entity' approach to accounting for EBTs is appropriate (see further discussion below).

Example 34.52: EBTs in separate financial statements of sponsoring entity

An entity lends its EBT €1 million which the EBT uses to make a market purchase of 200,000 shares in the entity. In the separate financial statements of the EBT the shares will be shown as an asset. In the consolidated financial statements, the shares will be accounted for as treasury shares, by deduction from equity.

In the separate financial statements of the entity, on the basis that the EBT is a separate entity, like any other subsidiary, the normal accounting entry would be:

	€	€
Loan to EBT	1,000,000	
Cash		1,000,000

The obvious issue with this approach is that it is, in economic substance, treating the shares held by the EBT (represented by the loan to the EBT) as an asset of the entity, whereas, if they were held directly by the entity, they would have to be accounted for as treasury shares, by deduction from equity. If the share price falls such that the EBT has no means of repaying the full €1,000,000, *prima facie* this gives rise to an impairment of the €1,000,000 loan. Again, however, this seems in effect to be recognising a loss on own equity.

Suppose now that employees are granted options over the shares. The options have an exercise price of zero and a value under IFRS 2 of €1,200,000. The entity will therefore book an expense of €1,200,000 under IFRS 2. When the options are exercised, the shares are delivered to employees. At that point the €1,000,000 loan to the EBT clearly becomes irrecoverable (as it has no assets), and must be written off. Normally, the write-off of an investment or loan is an expense required to be recognised in profit or loss. However, to recognise the €1,000,000 loan write-off as an expense as well as the €1,200,000 IFRS 2 charge would clearly be a form of double counting.

Some suggest that a solution to this problem is to say that the entity has effectively bought a gross-settled call option over its own shares from the EBT, whereby it can require the EBT to deliver 200,000 shares in return for a waiver of its €1,000,000 loan. Thus the accounting for the settlement of the call over the shares is as for any other gross-settled purchased call option over own equity under IAS 32 – see Chapter 47 at 11.2.1.

	€	€
Own shares (deduction from equity)	1,000,000	
Loan to EBT		1,000,000

When the shares are delivered to employees (some milliseconds later), the entry is:

	€	€
Other component of equity	1,000,000	
Own shares (deduction from equity)		1,000,000

At its meetings in May and July 2006, the Interpretations Committee discussed whether the EBT should be treated as an extension of the sponsoring entity, such as a branch, or as a separate entity. The Interpretations Committee decided to explore how specific transactions between the sponsor and the EBT should be treated in the sponsor's separate or individual financial statements and whether transactions between the EBT and the sponsor's employees should be attributed to the sponsor.

Interestingly, the Interpretations Committee fell short of dismissing the 'extension of the parent company' approach and has not since revisited this topic other than to re-confirm in March 2011 that it had not become aware of additional concerns or of diversity in practice and hence it did not think it necessary for this to be considered for the IASB's agenda. In our view, whilst any requirement to consolidate EBTs under

IFRS 10 could be argued to give a clear steer towards treating the EBT as a separate entity, until there is any final clarification of this issue, it appears acceptable to treat an EBT as an extension of the sponsoring entity in that entity's separate financial statements. This treatment would result in outcomes essentially the same as those in Examples 34.50 and 34.51 above, while avoiding the problems highlighted in Example 34.52 above.

12.3.5 Financial statements of the EBT

The EBT may be required to prepare financial statements in accordance with requirements imposed by local law or by its own trust deed. The form and content of such financial statements are beyond the scope of this chapter.

12.4 Illustrative example of group share scheme – equity-settled award satisfied by market purchase of shares

The discussion in 12.4.1 to 12.4.3 below is based on Example 34.53 and addresses the accounting treatment for three distinct aspects of a group share scheme – a share-based payment arrangement involving group entities (see 12.2 above), the use of an EBT (see 12.3 above) and a group recharge arrangement (see 12.2.7 above).

This illustrative example treats the recharge by the parent to the subsidiary as an income statement credit in the individual accounts of the parent and recognises the recharge when it is paid. In some situations, entities might consider it appropriate to apply alternative accounting treatments (see 12.2.7 above).

Example 34.53: Group share scheme (market purchase of shares)

On 1 July 20x1 an employee of S Limited, a subsidiary of the H plc group, is awarded options under the H group share scheme over 3,000 shares in H plc at £1.50 each, exercisable between 1 July 20x4 and 1 July 20x7, subject to a service condition and certain performance criteria being met in the three years ending 30 June 20x4.

H plc is the grantor of the award, and has the obligation to settle it. On 1 January 20x2, in connection with the award, the H plc group EBT purchases 3,000 shares at the then prevailing market price of £2.00 each, funded by a loan from H plc. On exercise of the option, S Limited is required to pay the differential between the purchase price of the shares and the exercise price of the option (£0.50 per share) to the EBT.

For the purposes of IFRS 2, the options are considered to have a fair value at grant date of £1 per option. Throughout the vesting period of the option, H takes the view that the award will vest in full.

The option is exercised on 1 September 20x6, at which point the EBT uses the option proceeds, together with the payment by S Limited, to repay the loan from H plc.

H plc and its subsidiaries have a 31 December year end.

12.4.1 Consolidated financial statements

So far as the consolidated financial statements are concerned, the transactions to be accounted for are:

- the purchase of the shares by the EBT and their eventual transfer to the employee; and
- the cost of the award.

Transactions between H plc or S Limited and the EBT are ignored since, in this Example, the EBT is consolidated (see 12.3 above). The accounting entries required are set out below. As in other examples in this chapter, where an entry is shown as being made to equity the precise allocation to a particular component of equity will be a matter for local legislation and, possibly, local accounting 'tradition', to the extent that this is not incompatible with IFRS.

		£	£
y/e 31.12.20x1	Profit or loss (employee costs)*	500	
	Equity		500
1.1.20x2	Own shares (equity)	6,000	
	Cash		6,000
y/e 31.12.20x2	Profit or loss (employee costs)*	1,000	
	Equity		1,000
y/e 31.12.20x3	Profit or loss (employee costs)*	1,000	
	Equity		1,000
y/e 31.12.20x4	Profit or loss (employee costs)*	500	
	Equity		500
1.9.20x6	Cash (option proceeds)†	4,500	
	Equity‡	1,500	
	Own shares (equity)**		6,000

* Total cost £3,000 (3000 options × £1) spread over 36 months. Charge for period to December 20x1 is 6/36 × £3,000 = £500, and so on. In practice, where options are granted to a group of individuals, or with variable performance criteria, the annual charge will be based on a continually revised cumulative charge (see further discussion at 6.1 to 6.4 above).

† 3,000 options at £1.50 each.

‡ This reflects the fact that the overall effect of the transaction for the group *in cash terms* has been a 'loss' of £1,500 (£6,000 original cost of shares less £4,500 option proceeds received). However, under IFRS this is an equity transaction, not an expense.

** £6,000 cost of own shares purchased on 1 January 20x2 now transferred to the employee. In practice, it is more likely that the appropriate amount to be transferred would be based on the weighted average price of shares held by the EBT at the date of exercise, as in Example 34.50 at 12.3.3 above. In such a case there would be a corresponding adjustment to the debit to equity marked with ‡ above.

12.4.2 Parent

The accounting by the parent will depend on how the EBT is treated (i.e. whether it is accounted for as a separate entity or as an extension of the parent – see 12.3 above for guidance). The parent should apply the accounting set out in the appropriate section below:

- EBT treated as separate entity (see 12.4.2.A below); and
- EBT treated as extension of parent (see 12.4.2.B below).

We also discuss, at 12.4.2.C below, the accounting implications if the parent, rather than – as in Example 34.53 – a subsidiary, is the employing entity.

12.4.2.A Accounting by parent where subsidiary is the employing entity and EBT is treated as separate entity

The parent accounts for the share-based payment transaction under IFRS 2 as an equity-settled transaction, since the parent settles the award by delivering its own equity instruments to the employees of the subsidiary (see 12.2.4 above). However, as discussed at 12.2.4 above, instead of recording a cost, as in its consolidated financial statements, the parent records an increase in the carrying value of its investment in subsidiary. It might then be necessary to consider whether the ever-increasing investment in subsidiary is supportable or is in fact impaired. As this is a matter to be determined in the light of specific facts and circumstances, it is not considered in this example. Any impairment charge would be recorded in profit or loss.

In addition to accounting for the share-based payment transaction, the parent records its transactions with the EBT and the purchase of shares.

This gives rise to the following entries:

		£	£
y/e 31.12.20x1	Investment in subsidiary*	500	
	Equity		500
1.1.20x2	Loan to EBT	6,000	
	Cash		6,000
y/e 31.12.20x2	Investment in subsidiary*	1,000	
	Equity		1,000
y/e 31.12.20x3	Investment in subsidiary*	1,000	
	Equity		1,000
y/e 31.12.20x4	Investment in subsidiary*	500	
	Equity		500
1.9.20x6	Cash	6,000	
	Loan to EBT		6,000

* Total increase in investment £3,000 (3000 shares × £1 fair value of each option) recognised over 36 months. Increase during period to December 20x1 is 6/36 × £3,000 = £500, and so on. In practice, where options were granted to a group of individuals, or with variable performance criteria, the annual adjustment would be based on a continually revised cumulative adjustment (see further discussion at 6.1 to 6.4 above).

12.4.2.B Accounting by parent where subsidiary is the employing entity and EBT is treated as extension of the parent

The parent accounts for the share-based payment transaction under IFRS 2 as an equity-settled transaction, since the parent settles the award by delivering its own equity instruments to the employees of the subsidiary (see 12.2.4 above). However, as discussed at 12.2.4 above, instead of recording a cost, as in its consolidated financial statements, the parent records an increase in the carrying value of its investment in subsidiary. It might then be necessary to consider whether the ever-increasing investment in subsidiary is supportable or is in fact impaired. As this is a matter to be determined in the light of specific facts and circumstances, it is not considered in this example. Any impairment charge would be recorded in profit or loss.

In addition to accounting for the share-based payment transaction, the parent records the transactions of the EBT and the purchase of shares.

This gives rise to the following entries:

		£	£
y/e 31.12.20x1	Investment in subsidiary*	500	
	Equity		500
1.1.20x2	Own shares (equity)	6,000	
	Cash		6,000
y/e 31.12.20x2	Investment in subsidiary*	1,000	
	Equity		1,000
y/e 31.12.20x3	Investment in subsidiary*	1,000	
	Equity		1,000
y/e 31.12.20x4	Investment in subsidiary*	500	
	Equity		500
1.9.20x6	Cash†	6,000	
	Equity‡	1,500	
	Profit or loss§		1,500
	Own shares** (equity)		6,000

* Total increase in investment £3,000 (3000 shares × £1 fair value of each option) spread over 36 months. Increase during period to December 20x1 is 6/36 × £3,000 = £500, and so on. In practice, where options were granted to a group of individuals, or with variable performance criteria, the annual adjustment would be based on a continually revised cumulative adjustment (see further discussion at 6.1 to 6.4 above).

† £4,500 option exercise proceeds from employee plus £1,500 contribution from S Limited.

‡ This is essentially a balancing figure representing the fact that the entity is distributing own shares with an original cost of £6,000, but has treated £1,500 of the £6,000 of the cash it has received as income (see § below) rather than as payment for the shares.

§ The £1,500 contribution by the subsidiary to the EBT has been treated as a distribution from the subsidiary (see 12.2.7 above) and recorded in profit or loss. It might then be necessary to consider whether, as a result of this payment, the investment in the subsidiary had become impaired (see Chapter 8 at 2.4). As this is a matter to be determined in the light of specific facts and circumstances, it is not considered in this example. Any impairment charge would be recorded in profit or loss.

** £6,000 cost of own shares purchased on 1 January 20x2 now transferred to employee. In practice, it is more likely that the appropriate amount to be transferred would be based on the weighted average price of shares held by the EBT at the date of exercise, as in Example 34.50 at 12.3.3 above.

12.4.2.C Parent company as employing entity

If, in Example 34.53, the employing entity were the parent rather than the subsidiary, it would record an expense under IFRS 2. It would also normally waive £1,500 of its £6,000 loan to the EBT (i.e. the shortfall between the original loan and the £4,500 option proceeds received from the employee).

If the EBT is treated as an extension of the parent, the accounting entries for the parent would be the same as those for the group, as set out in 12.4.1 above.

If the EBT is treated as a separate entity, the accounting entries might be as follows:

		£	£
y/e 31.12.20x1	Profit or loss*	500	
	Equity		500
1.1.20x2	Loan to EBT	6,000	
	Cash		6,000
y/e 31.12.20x2	Profit or loss*	1,000	
	Equity		1,000
y/e 31.12.20x3	Profit or loss*	1,000	
	Equity		1,000
y/e 31.12.20x4	Profit or loss*	500	
	Equity		500
1.9.20x6	Own shares (Equity)†	1,500	
	Cash	4,500	
	Loan to EBT		6,000
	Equity	1,500	
	Own shares (Equity)		1,500

* Total cost £3,000 (3000 options × £1) spread over 36 months. Charge for period to December 20x1 is 6/36 × £3,000 = £500, and so on. In practice, where options were granted to a group of individuals, or with variable performance criteria, the annual charge would be based on a continually revised cumulative charge (see further discussion at 6.1 to 6.4 above).

† This takes the approach of treating the parent as having a gross-settled purchased call option over its own equity (see Example 34.52 at 12.3.4 above), under which it can acquire 3,000 own shares from the EBT for the consideration of the waiver of £1,500 of the original £6,000 loan. The £4,500 cash inflow represents the £4,500 option exercise proceeds received by the EBT from the employee, which is then used to pay the balance of the original £6,000 loan.

12.4.3 Employing subsidiary

The employing subsidiary is required to account for the IFRS 2 expense and the contribution to the EBT on exercise of the award. This gives rise to the accounting entries set out below. The entries to reflect the IFRS 2 expense are required by IFRS 2 (see 12.2.3 above). The contribution to the EBT is treated as a distribution (see 12.2.7 above).

		£	£
y/e 31.12.20x1	Profit or loss*	500	
	Equity		500
y/e 31.12.20x2	Profit or loss*	1,000	
	Equity		1,000
y/e 31.12.20x3	Profit or loss*	1,000	
	Equity		1,000
y/e 31.12.20x4	Profit or loss*	500	
	Equity		500
1.9.20x6	Equity†	1,500	
	Cash		1,500

* Total cost £3,000 (3000 options × £1) spread over 36 months. Charge for period to December 20x1 is 6/36 × £3,000 = £500, and so on. In practice, where options were granted to a group of individuals, or with variable performance criteria, the annual charge would be based on a continually revised cumulative charge (see further discussion at 6.1 to 6.4 above).

† This should be treated as a reduction of whatever component of equity was credited with the £3,000 quasi-contribution from the parent in the accounting entries above.

12.5 Illustrative example of group share scheme – equity-settled award satisfied by fresh issue of shares

Such schemes raise slightly different accounting issues. Again, these are most easily illustrated by way of an example. The discussion in 12.5.1 to 12.5.3 below is based on Example 34.54. As with Example 34.53 at 12.4 above, this section addresses the accounting treatment for three distinct aspects of a group share scheme – a share-based payment arrangement involving group entities (see 12.2 above), the use of an EBT (see 12.3 above) and a group recharge arrangement (see 12.2.7 above).

This illustrative example treats the recharge by the parent to the subsidiary as an income statement credit in the individual accounts of the parent and recognises the recharge when it is paid. In some situations, entities might consider it appropriate to apply alternative accounting treatments (see 12.2.7 above).

Example 34.54:   Group share scheme (fresh issue of shares)

On 1 July 20x1 an employee of S Limited, a subsidiary of the H plc group, is awarded options under the H group share scheme over 3,000 shares in H plc at £1.50 each, exercisable between 1 July 20x4 and 1 July 20x7, subject to a service condition and certain performance criteria being met in the three years ending 30 June 20x4. The fair value of the options on 1 July 20x1 is £1 each.

H plc grants the award and has the obligation to settle it.

When preparing accounts during the vesting period H plc and its subsidiaries assume that the award will vest in full. The options are finally exercised on 1 September 20x6, at which point H plc issues 3,000 new shares to the EBT at the then current market price of £3.50 for £10,500. The EBT funds the purchase using the £4,500 option proceeds received from the employee together with £6,000 contributed by S Limited, effectively representing the fair value of the options at exercise date (3,000 × [£3.50 – £1.50]).

H plc and its subsidiaries have a 31 December year end.

12.5.1 Consolidated financial statements

The consolidated financial statements need to deal with:

- the charge required by IFRS 2 in respect of the award; and
- the issue of shares.

Transactions between H plc or S Limited and the EBT are ignored since, in this Example, the EBT is consolidated (see 12.3 above). The accounting entries required are set out below. As in other examples in this chapter, where an entry is shown as being made to equity, the precise allocation to a particular component of equity will be a matter for local legislation and, possibly, local accounting 'tradition', to the extent that this is not incompatible with IFRS.

		£	£
y/e 31.12.20x1	Profit or loss*	500	
	Equity		500
y/e 31.12.20x2	Profit or loss*	1,000	
	Equity		1,000
y/e 31.12.20x3	Profit or loss*	1,000	
	Equity		1,000
y/e 31.12.20x4	Profit or loss*	500	
	Equity		500
1.9.20x6	Cash	4,500	
	Equity†		4,500

* Total cost £3,000 (3000 options × £1) spread over 36 months. Charge for period to December 20x1 is 6/36 × £3,000 = £500, and so on. In practice, where options were granted to a group of individuals, or with variable performance criteria, the annual charge would be based on a continually revised cumulative charge (see further discussion at 6.1 to 6.4 above).

† From the point of view of the consolidated group, the issue of shares results in an increase in net assets of only £4,500 (i.e. the exercise price received from the employee), since the £6,000 contribution from the employing subsidiary to the EBT is an intragroup transaction. However, it may be that, in certain jurisdictions, the entity is required to increase its share capital and share premium (additional paid in capital) accounts by the £10,500 legal consideration for the issue of shares. In that case, this entry would be expanded as below, which effectively treats the £6,000 consideration provided from within the group as a bonus issue.

		£	£
1.9.20x6	Cash	4,500	
	Other equity	6,000	
	Share capital/premium		10,500

12.5.2 Parent

The accounting by the parent will depend on how the EBT is treated (i.e. whether it is accounted for as a separate entity or as an extension of the parent – see 12.3 above for guidance). The parent should apply the accounting set out in the appropriate section below:

- EBT treated as separate entity (see 12.5.2.A below); and
- EBT treated as extension of parent (see 12.5.2.B below).

We also discuss, at 12.5.2.C below, the accounting implications if the parent, rather than – as in Example 34.54 – a subsidiary, is the employing entity.

12.5.2.A Accounting by parent where subsidiary is the employing entity and EBT is treated as separate entity

The parent accounts for the share-based payment transaction under IFRS 2 as an equity-settled transaction, since the parent settles the award by delivering its own equity instruments, via its EBT, to the employees of the subsidiary (see 12.2.4 above). However, as discussed at 12.2.4 above, instead of recording a cost, as in its consolidated financial statements, the parent records an increase in the carrying value of its investment in subsidiary. It might then be necessary to consider whether the ever-increasing investment in subsidiary is supportable or is in fact impaired. As this is a matter to be determined in the light of specific facts and circumstances, it is not considered in this example. Any impairment charge would be recorded in profit or loss.

In addition to accounting for the share-based payment transaction, the parent records its transactions with the EBT and the issue of shares.

		£	£
y/e 31.12.20x1	Investment in subsidiary*	500	
	Equity		500
y/e 31.12.20x2	Investment in subsidiary*	1,000	
	Equity		1,000
y/e 31.12.20x3	Investment in subsidiary*	1,000	
	Equity		1,000
y/e 31.12.20x4	Investment in subsidiary*	500	
	Equity		500
1.9.20x6	Cash†	10,500	
	Share capital/premium		10,500

* Total increase in investment £3,000 (3000 shares × £1 fair value of each option), recognised over 36 months. Increase in period to December 20x1 is 6/36 × £3,000 = £500, and so on. In practice, where options were granted to a group of individuals, or with variable performance criteria, the annual adjustment would be based on a continually revised cumulative adjustment (see further discussion at 6.1 to 6.4 above).

† £10,500 from EBT (which has received £4,500 option exercise proceeds from employee plus £6,000 contribution from the subsidiary).

12.5.2.B Accounting by parent where subsidiary is the employing entity and EBT is treated as extension of parent

The parent accounts for the share-based payment transaction under IFRS 2 as an equity-settled transaction, since the parent settles the award by delivering its own equity instruments, via its EBT, to the employees of the subsidiary (see 12.2.4 above). However, as discussed at 12.2.4 above, instead of recording a cost, as in its consolidated financial statements, the parent records an increase in the carrying value of its investment in subsidiary. It might then be necessary to consider whether the ever-increasing investment in subsidiary is supportable or is in fact impaired. As this is a matter to be determined in the light of specific facts and circumstances, it is not considered in this example. Any impairment charge would be recorded in profit or loss.

In addition to accounting for the share-based payment transaction, the parent records the transactions of the EBT and the issue of shares.

		£	£
y/e 31.12.20x1	Investment in subsidiary*	500	
	Equity		500
y/e 31.12.20x2	Investment in subsidiary*	1,000	
	Equity		1,000
y/e 31.12.20x3	Investment in subsidiary*	1,000	
	Equity		1,000
y/e 31.12.20x4	Investment in subsidiary*	500	
	Equity		500
1.9.20x6	Cash†	10,500	
	Equity‡	6,000	
	Profit or loss**		6,000
	Share capital/premium		10,500

* Total increase in investment £3,000 (3000 shares × £1 fair value of each option) spread over 36 months. Increase during period to December 20x1 is 6/36 × £3,000 = £500, and so on. In practice, where options were granted to a group of individuals, or with variable performance criteria, the annual adjustment would be based on a continually revised cumulative adjustment (see further discussion at 6.1 to 6.4 above).

† £4,500 option exercise proceeds from employee plus £6,000 contribution from the subsidiary.

‡ This assumes that local law requires the entity to record share capital and share premium (additional paid-in capital) of £10,500, as in 12.5.2.A above. However, IFRS *prima facie* requires the £6,000 cash received by the EBT from the subsidiary to be treated as income (see ** below) rather than as part of the proceeds of the issue of shares. In order, in effect, to reconcile these conflicting analyses, £6,000 of the £10,500 required by law to be capitalised as share capital and share premium has been treated as an appropriation out of other equity.

** The £6,000 contribution by the subsidiary to the EBT has been treated as a distribution from the subsidiary (see 12.2.7 above) and recorded in profit or loss. It might then be necessary to consider whether, as a result of this payment, the investment in the subsidiary had become impaired (see Chapter 8 at 2.4). As this is a matter to be determined in the light of specific facts and circumstances, it is not considered in this Example. Any impairment charge would be recorded in profit or loss.

12.5.2.C   Parent as employing entity

If, in Example 34.54, the employing entity were the parent rather than the subsidiary, it would clearly have to record an expense under IFRS 2. It would also have to fund the £6,000 shortfall between the option exercise proceeds of £4,500 and the £10,500 issue proceeds of the shares.

If the EBT is treated as an extension of the parent, the accounting entries for the parent would be the same as those for the group, as set out in 12.5.1 above.

In our view, the treatment in 12.5.1 above may also be appropriate for this specific transaction, even where the EBT is treated as a separate entity. The issue of shares requires the parent company to fund the EBT with £6,000 which immediately returns it to the parent, along with the £4,500 received from the employee, in exchange for an issue of shares. Whilst this 'circulation' of the £6,000 might have some significance for legal purposes it is, economically speaking, a non-transaction that could be ignored for accounting purposes under IFRS. It might, however, be relevant, under local law, to the amount of equity shown as share capital and share premium (additional paid-in capital), in which case the expanded entry in 12.5.1 above would be appropriate.

Where, however, the EBT is treated as a separate entity, and the cash used to subscribe for the shares arises from a prior transaction, such as an earlier loan to the EBT, matters are more complicated. Suppose that, during the life of the award under discussion, the company were to advance £50,000 to the EBT for general funding purposes. At that point it would clearly record the entry:

	£	£
Loan to EBT	50,000	
Cash		50,000

Suppose that, on exercise of the option, the EBT were to use some of that cash to fund the parent's 'top up' for the share issue. This effectively impairs the loan by £6,000 and leaves a 'missing debit' indicated by '?' in the journal below:

	£	£
Cash	10,500	
?	6,000	
Loan to EBT		6,000
Share capital/premium		10,500

This looks very much like an impairment loss on the loan required to be reported in profit or loss. On the other hand, it does not resemble a loss in any conventional sense. This suggests that another analysis may be possible.

Example 34.52 at 12.3.4 above addresses the situation where an EBT is pre-funded to enable it to buy the reporting entity's own shares in the market, and those shares are finally delivered to the entity for distribution to employees. Example 34.52 suggests that this could be construed as the execution of a gross-settled purchased call option by the entity.

If that analogy is extended, the present situation could be construed as comprising a back-to-back:

- gross-settled purchased call option (whereby the entity can require the EBT to provide 3,000 shares in return for waiver of £6,000 of its outstanding loan to the EBT), which triggers the exercise of;
- a gross-settled written call option (whereby the EBT can require the entity to issue 3,000 fresh shares for £10,500 to the EBT, so that it can satisfy its obligations to the entity under the purchased call).

If these two call options are accounted for under IAS 32 (see Chapter 47 at 11.2), the write-off of the loan to the EBT can be effectively charged to equity, as follows:

	£	£
Cash	10,500	
Share capital/premium		10,500
Exercise by EBT of written call		
Own shares (Equity)	6,000	
Loan to EBT		6,000
Exercise by entity of purchased call		
Equity (other)	6,000	
Own shares (Equity)		6,000
Issue of shares to employee		

12.5.3 Employing subsidiary

The employing subsidiary is required to account for the IFRS 2 expense and the contribution to the EBT on exercise of the award. This gives rise to the accounting entries set out below. The entries to reflect the IFRS 2 expense are required by IFRS 2 (see 12.2.3 above). The contribution to the EBT is treated as a distribution (see 12.2.7 above).

		£	£
y/e 31.12.20x1	Profit or loss*	500	
	Equity		500
y/e 31.12.20x2	Profit or loss*	1,000	
	Equity		1,000
y/e 31.12.20x3	Profit or loss*	1,000	
	Equity		1,000
y/e 31.12.20x4	Profit or loss*	500	
	Equity		500
1.9.20x6	Equity†	6,000	
	Cash		6,000

* Total cost £3,000 (3000 options × £1) spread over 36 months. Charge for period to December 20x1 6/36 × £3,000 = £500, and so on. In practice, where options were granted to a group of individuals, or with variable performance criteria, the annual charge would be based on a continually revised cumulative charge (see further discussion at 6.1 to 6.4 above).

† £3,000 of this payment should be treated as a reduction of whatever component of equity was credited with the £3,000 quasi-contribution from the parent in the accounting entries above. The remaining £3,000 would be treated as a distribution and charged to any appropriate component of equity.

12.6 Illustrative example – cash-settled transaction not settled by the entity receiving goods or services

The discussion in 12.6.1 to 12.6.3 below is based on Example 34.55.

Example 34.55: *Cash-settled scheme not settled by receiving entity*

On 1 July 20x1 an employee of S Limited, a subsidiary of the H plc group, is awarded a right, exercisable between 1 July 20x4 and 1 July 20x7, to receive cash equivalent to the value of 3,000 shares in H plc at the date on which the right is exercised. Exercise of the right is subject to a service condition and certain performance criteria being met in the three years ending 30 June 20x4. The cash will be paid to the employee not by S, but by H. Throughout the vesting period of the award, H and S take the view that it will vest in full.

The award does in fact vest, and the right is exercised on 1 September 20x6.

The fair value of the award (per share-equivalent) at various relevant dates is as follows:

Date	Fair value
	£
1.7.20x1	1.50
31.12.20x1	1.80
31.12.20x2	2.70
31.12.20x3	2.40
31.12.20x4	2.90
31.12.20x5	3.30
1.9.20x6	3.50

If the award had been equity-settled (i.e. the employee had instead been granted a right to 3,000 free shares), the grant date fair value of the award would have been £1.50 per share.

H plc and its subsidiaries have a 31 December year end.

12.6.1 Consolidated financial statements

The group has entered into a cash-settled transaction which is accounted for using the methodology discussed at 9.3 above. This gives rise to the following accounting entries:

		£	£
y/e 31.12.20x1	Profit or loss*	900	
	Liability		900
y/e 31.12.20x2	Profit or loss*	3,150	
	Liability		3,150
y/e 31.12.20x3	Profit or loss*	1,950	
	Liability		1,950
y/e 31.12.20x4	Profit or loss*	2,700	
	Liability		2,700
y/e 31.12.20x5	Profit or loss*	1,200	
	Liability		1,200
y/e 31.12.20x6	Profit or loss*	600	
	Liability		600
1.9.20x6	Liability	10,500	
	Cash		10,500

*   Charge for period to 31 December 20x1 is 6/36 × 3000 × £1.80 [reporting date fair value] = £900. Charge for year ended 31 December 20x2 is 18/36 × 3000 × £2.70 = £4,050 less £900 charged in 20x1 = £3,150 and so on (refer to Example 34.37 at 9.3.2 above). In practice, where options were granted to a group of individuals, or with variable performance criteria, the annual charge would be based on a continually revised cumulative charge (see further discussion at 9 above).

12.6.2 Parent

The parent accounts for the share-based payment transaction under IFRS 2 as a cash-settled transaction, since the parent settles the award by delivering cash to the employees of the subsidiary (see 12.2.4 above). However, as discussed at 12.2.4 above, instead of recording a cost, as in its consolidated financial statements, the parent treats the debit entry (including, as a matter of accounting policy choice, any remeasurement of the liability) as an increase in the carrying value of its investment in subsidiary. It might then be necessary to consider whether the ever-increasing investment in subsidiary is supportable or is in fact impaired. As this is a matter to be determined in the light of specific facts and circumstances, it is not considered in this example. Any impairment charge would be recorded in profit or loss.

This would result in the following accounting entries.

		£	£
y/e 31.12.20x1	Investment in subsidiary*	900	
	Liability		900
y/e 31.12.20x2	Investment in subsidiary*	3,150	
	Liability		3,150
y/e 31.12.20x3	Investment in subsidiary*	1,950	
	Liability		1,950
y/e 31.12.20x4	Investment in subsidiary*	2,700	
	Liability		2,700
y/e 31.12.20x5	Investment in subsidiary*	1,200	
	Liability		1,200
y/e 31.12.20x6	Investment in subsidiary*	600	
	Liability		600
1.9.20x6	Liability	10,500	
	Cash		10,500

*   Increase in investment to 31 December 20x1 is 6/36 × 3000 × £1.80 [reporting date fair value] = £900. Increase for year ended 31 December 20x2 is 18/36 × 3000 × £2.70 = £4,050 less £900 charged in 20x1 = £3,150 and so on (refer to Example 34.37 at 9.3.2 above). In practice, where options were granted to a group of individuals, or with variable performance criteria, the annual charge would be based on a continually revised cumulative charge (see further discussion at 9 above).

Where the parent entity was also the employing entity (and therefore receiving goods or services), it would apply the same accounting treatment in its separate financial statements as in its consolidated financial statements (see 12.6.1 above).

12.6.3 Employing subsidiary

The employing subsidiary accounts for the transaction as equity-settled, since it receives services, but incurs no obligation to its employees (see 12.2.3 and 12.2.6 above). This gives rise to the following accounting entries.

		£	£
y/e 31.12.20x1	Profit or loss*	750	
	Equity		750
y/e 31.12.20x2	Profit or loss*	1,500	
	Equity		1,500
y/e 31.12.20x3	Profit or loss*	1,500	
	Equity		1,500
y/e 31.12.20x4	Profit or loss*	750	
	Equity		750

* Charge for period to 31 December 20x1 is 6/36 × 3000 × £1.50 [grant date fair value] = £750, and so on. In practice, where options were granted to a group of individuals, or with variable performance criteria, the annual charge would be based on a continually revised cumulative charge (see further discussion at 6.1 to 6.4 above).

The effect of this treatment is that, while the group ultimately records a cost of £10,500, the subsidiary records a cost of only £4,500.

However, there may be cases where the subsidiary records a higher cost than the group. This would happen if, for example:

- the award vests, but the share price has fallen since grant date, so that the value of the award at vesting (as reflected in the consolidated financial statements) is lower than the value at grant (as reflected in the subsidiary's financial statements); or
- the award does not actually vest because of a failure to meet a market condition and/or a non-vesting condition (so that the cost is nil in the consolidated financial statements) but is treated by IFRS 2 as vesting in the subsidiary's financial statements, because it is accounted for as equity-settled (see 6.3 and 6.4 above).

12.7 Employee transferring between group entities

It is not uncommon for an employee to be granted an equity-settled share-based payment award while in the employment of one subsidiary in the group, but to transfer to another subsidiary in the group before the award is vested, but with the entitlement to the award being unchanged.

In such cases, each subsidiary measures the services received from the employee by reference to the fair value of the equity instruments at the date those rights to equity instruments were originally granted, and the proportion of the vesting period served by the employee with each subsidiary. *[IFRS 2.B59]*. In other words, for an award with a three-year vesting period granted to an employee of subsidiary A, who transfers to subsidiary B at the end of year 2, subsidiary A will (cumulatively) record an expense of 2/3, and subsidiary B 1/3, of the fair value at grant date. However, any subsidiary required to account for the transaction as cash-settled in accordance with the general principles discussed at 12.2 above accounts for its portion of the grant date fair value and also for any changes in the fair value of the award during the period of employment with that subsidiary. *[IFRS 2.B60]*.

After transferring between group entities, an employee may fail to satisfy a vesting condition other than a market condition, for example by leaving the employment of the group. In this situation each subsidiary adjusts the amount previously recognised in respect of the services received from the employee in accordance with the general principles of IFRS 2 (see 6.1 to 6.4 above). *[IFRS 2.B61]*. This imposes upon the original employing entity the rather curious burden of tracking the service record of its former employees, where the accounting impact is expected to be significant.

12.8 Group reorganisations

Following a group reorganisation, such as the insertion of a new parent entity above an existing group, share-based payment arrangements with employees are often amended or replaced so that they relate to the shares of the new parent. Group reorganisations of entities under common control are not within the scope of IFRS 3 and so the requirements set out at 11 above are not directly applicable.

In some cases, the terms and conditions of a share-based payment arrangement will contain provisions relating to restructuring transactions (see 5.3.8.A above) so that the application of any changes is not necessarily considered to be a modification in IFRS 2 terms. Where no such provision is made, the situation is less clear-cut.

In our view, in the consolidated financial statements, such changes to share-based payments would generally be construed as a cancellation and replacement to which modification accounting could be applied (see 7.4.4 above). However, in most cases, the changes made to the share-based payment awards following a group reorganisation are likely to be such that there is no incremental fair value arising from the cancellation and replacement, the intention being simply to replace like with like.

A subsidiary receiving the services of employees but with no obligation to settle the amended award would continue to apply equity-settled accounting in its own financial statements and, as for the consolidated financial statements, would strictly account for the changes as a cancellation and replacement of the original award. The accounting consequences would be more complicated if the subsidiary itself had an obligation to settle the award in the shares of its new parent, when previously it had had to settle in its own shares, as this would mean a change from equity-settled to cash-settled accounting (see 9.4 above). However, we would expect this to be a rare occurrence in practice (see 12.2.5.B above in relation to the grantor of an award in a situation involving parent and subsidiary entities).

The new parent entity becomes a party to the share-based payment arrangements for the first time and, assuming it has no employees of its own but is considered to have granted and to have the obligation to settle the awards, needs to account for the awards to the employees of its subsidiaries (see 12.2.4 and 12.2.5 above). The requirements of IFRS 2 in this situation are unclear and one could argue:

- either that this is a new award by the parent and so should be valued as at the date of the new award; or
- in accordance with the general principle that there is no overall change as a consequence of a reorganisation of entities under common control, that the parent should use the same (original grant date) fair value as the subsidiary.

In our view, either approach is acceptable provided it is applied consistently.

12.9 Share-based payments to employees of joint ventures or associates

The majority of share-based payment transactions with employees involve payments to employees of the reporting entity or of another entity in the same group. Occasionally, however, share-based payments may be made to employees of significant investees of the reporting entity such as joint ventures or associates. For example, if one party to a joint venture is a quoted entity and the other not, it might be commercially appropriate for the quoted venturer to offer payments based on its quoted shares to employees of the joint venture, while the unquoted party contributes to the venture in other ways.

Such arrangements raise some questions of interpretation of IFRS 2, as illustrated by Example 34.56 below. References to an associate in the example and discussions below should be read as also referring to a joint venture.

Example 34.56: Share-based payment to employees of associate

At the beginning of year 1, an entity grants an award of free shares with a fair value at that date of €600,000 to employees of its 40% associate. The shares vest over a three-year period. It is assumed throughout the vesting period of the award that it will vest in full, which is in fact the case.

12.9.1 Financial statements of the associate or joint venture

For the financial statements of the associate, the transaction does not strictly fall within the scope of IFRS 2. In order for a transaction to be in the scope of IFRS 2 for a reporting entity, it must be settled in the equity of the entity itself, or that of another member of the same group. A group comprises a parent and its subsidiaries (see Chapter 6 at 2.2), and does not include associates.

Nevertheless, we believe that it would be appropriate for the associate to account for the transaction as if it did fall within the scope of IFRS 2 by applying the 'GAAP hierarchy' in IAS 8 – *Accounting Policies, Changes in Accounting Estimates and Errors* (see Chapter 3 at 4.3). The investor has effectively made a capital contribution to the associate (in the form of the investor's own equity), no less than if it made a capital contribution in cash which was then used to pay employees of the associate.

If the investor in the associate had instead granted an award settled in the equity of the associate, the transaction would have been in the scope of IFRS 2 for the associate, as being the grant of an award over the equity of the reporting entity by a shareholder of that entity (see 2.2.2.A above).

If the award is, or is treated as being, within the scope of IFRS 2 for the associate, the following entries are recorded:

		€000	€000
Year 1	Employee costs†	200	
	Equity		200
Year 2	Employee costs	200	
	Equity		200
Year 3	Employee costs	200	
	Equity		200

† Grant date fair value of award €600,000 × 1/3. The credit to equity represents a capital contribution from the investor.

12.9.2 Consolidated financial statements of the investor

The investor has entered into a share-based payment transaction since it has granted an award over its equity to third parties (the employees of the associates) in exchange for their services to a significant investee entity. However, employees of an associate are not employees of a group entity and are therefore not employees of the investor's group.

The issue for IFRS 2 purposes is, therefore, whether the award should be regarded as being made to persons providing similar services to employees (and therefore measured at grant date) or to persons other than employees or those providing similar services to employees (and therefore measured at service date) – see 5.2 to 5.4 above.

In our view, it is more appropriate to regard such awards as made to persons providing similar services to employees and therefore measured at grant date.

There are then, we believe, two possible approaches to the accounting. In our view, in the absence of clear guidance in the standard, an entity should choose the more appropriate approach based on the specific circumstances.

In any event, the investor's consolidated financial statements must show a credit to equity of €200,000 a year over the vesting period. The accounting issue is the analysis of the corresponding debit.

It seems clear that the investor must as a minimum recognise an annual cost of €80,000 (40% of €200,000), as part of its 'one-line' share of the result of the associate. The issue then is whether it should account for the remaining €120,000 as a further cost or as an increase in the cost of its investment in its associate.

The argument for treating the €120,000 as an expense is that the associate will either have recorded nothing or, as set out in 12.9.1 above, an entry that results in no net increase in the equity of the associate. Therefore there has been no increase in the investor's share of the net assets of the associate, and there is no basis for the investor to record an increase in its investment. This is broadly the approach required under US GAAP (although US GAAP requires the associate itself to recognise the expense and a corresponding capital contribution applying the grant date measurement model of ASC 718).

It may be possible to conclude in some situations that the €120,000 is an increase in the cost of the investment in associate. IAS 28 – *Investments in Associates and Joint Ventures* – defines the equity method of accounting as (emphasis added):

> 'a method of accounting whereby the investment is *initially recognised at cost and adjusted thereafter* for the post-acquisition change in the investor's share of the investee's net assets'. *[IAS 28.3]*.

For example, there may be cases where another shareholder has made, or undertaken to make, contributions to the associate that are not reflected in its recognised net assets (such as an undertaking to provide knowhow or undertake mineral exploration).

Where an entity takes the view that the €120,000 is an increase in the cost of its investment, it is essential to ensure that the resulting carrying value of the investment is sustainable. This may be the case if, for example:
- the fair value of the investment in the associate exceeds its carrying amount; or
- the investor has agreed to enter into the transaction while another major shareholder has agreed to bear equivalent costs.

In other circumstances, the carrying amount of the investment may not be sustainable, and the investor may need to recognise an impairment of its investment in accordance with IAS 36 (see Chapter 20).

12.9.3 Separate financial statements of the investor

The discussion below assumes that the investor accounts for its investment in the associate at cost in its separate financial statements (see Chapter 8).

The issues here are much the same as in 12.9.2 above. The investor has clearly entered into a share-based payment transaction since it has granted an award over its equity to third parties (the employees of the associates) in exchange for their services to a significant investee entity. As in 12.9.2 above, we believe that this is most appropriately characterised as a transaction with persons providing similar services to employees and therefore measured at its grant date fair value.

In any event, the investor's separate financial statements must show a credit to equity of €200,000 a year over the vesting period but, as in 12.9.2 above, the analysis of the debit entry is more complex.

13 DISCLOSURES

IFRS 2 requires three main groups of disclosures, explaining:
- the nature and extent of share-based payment arrangements (see 13.1 below);
- the valuation of share-based payment arrangements (see 13.2 below); and
- the impact on the financial statements of share-based payment transactions (see 13.3 below).

All of the disclosure requirements of IFRS 2 are subject to the overriding materiality considerations of IAS 1 (see Chapter 3 at 4.1.5). However, depending on the identity of the counterparty and whether, for example, the individual is a member of key management, it will be necessary to assess whether an arrangement is material by nature even if it is immaterial in monetary terms.

13.1 Nature and extent of share-based payment arrangements

IFRS 2 requires an entity to 'disclose information that enables users of the financial statements to understand the nature and extent of share-based payment arrangements that existed during the period'. *[IFRS 2.44].*

In order to satisfy this general principle, the entity must disclose at least:

(a) a description of each type of share-based payment arrangement that existed at any time during the period, including the general terms and conditions of each arrangement, such as vesting requirements, the maximum term of options granted, and the method of settlement (e.g. whether in cash or equity). An entity with substantially similar types of share-based payment arrangements may aggregate this information, unless separate disclosure of each arrangement is necessary to satisfy the general principle above;

(b) the number and weighted average exercise prices of share options for each of the following groups of options:
   (i) outstanding at the beginning of the period;
   (ii) granted during the period;
   (iii) forfeited during the period;
   (iv) exercised during the period;
   (v) expired during the period;
   (vi) outstanding at the end of the period; and
   (vii) exercisable at the end of the period;

(c) for share options exercised during the period, the weighted average share price at the date of exercise. If options were exercised on a regular basis throughout the period, the entity may instead disclose the weighted average share price during the period; and

(d) for share options outstanding at the end of the period, the range of exercise prices and weighted average remaining contractual life. If the range of exercise prices is wide, the outstanding options must be divided into ranges that are meaningful for assessing the number and timing of additional shares that may be issued and the cash that may be received upon exercise of those options. *[IFRS 2.45].*

The reconciliation in (b) above should, in our view, reflect all changes in the number of equity instruments outstanding. In addition to awards with a grant date during the period, the reconciliation should include subsequent additions to earlier grants e.g. options or shares added to the award in recognition of dividends declared during the period (where this is part of the original terms of the award), and changes to the number of equity instruments as a result of demergers, share splits or consolidations and other similar changes.

The following extract from the financial statements of Dairy Crest Group plc shows additional awards from the reinvestment of dividends within the reconciliation of outstanding awards.

Extract 34.1: Dairy Crest Group plc (2018)

Notes to the financial statements [extract]

27 Share-based payment plans [extract]

The number of share options and weighted average exercise price for each of the principal schemes is set out as follows:

	LTAP*	TIA*	DBP*	LTISP*	Sharesave Scheme	
	number	number	number	number	number	weighted average exercise price (pence)
Options outstanding at 1 April 2017	1,071,194	262,374	73,533	130,393	941,136	431.1
Options granted during the year	217,007	–	–	–	–	–
Reinvested dividends	71,116	10,495	2,782	5,186	–	–
Options exercised during the year	(86,465)	–	–	(6,959)	(344,027)	377.2
Options forfeited during the year	–	(9,017)	–	–	(70,241)	456.6
Options outstanding at 31 March 2018	1,272,852	263,852	76,315	128,620	526,868	462.8
Exercisable at 31 March 2018	73,188	263,852	76,315	128,620	957	–

[...]

*LTAP, TIA, DBP and LTISP options are nil cost options.

As drafted, the requirements in (b) to (d) above appear to apply only to share options. However, since there is little distinction in IFRS 2 between the treatment of an option with a zero exercise price and the award of a free share, in our view the disclosures should not be restricted to awards of options.

13.2 Valuation of share-based payment arrangements

IFRS 2 requires an entity to 'disclose information that enables users of the financial statements to understand how the fair value of the goods or services received, or the fair value of the equity instruments granted, during the period was determined'. *[IFRS 2.46].*

As drafted, this requirement, and some of the detailed disclosures below, appears to apply only to equity-settled transactions. However, it would be anomalous if detailed disclosures were required about the valuation of an award to be settled in shares, but not one to be settled in cash. In our view, therefore, the disclosures apply both to equity-settled and to cash-settled transactions.

If the entity has measured the fair value of goods or services received as consideration for equity instruments of the entity indirectly, by reference to the fair value of the equity instruments granted (i.e. transactions with employees and, in exceptional cases only, with non-employees), the entity must disclose at least the following:

(a) for share options granted during the period, the weighted average fair value of those options at the measurement date and information on how that fair value was measured, including:

  (i) the option pricing model used and the inputs to that model, including the weighted average share price, exercise price, expected volatility, option life, expected dividends, the risk-free interest rate and any other inputs to the model, including the method used and the assumptions made to incorporate the effects of expected early exercise;

  (ii) how expected volatility was determined, including an explanation of the extent to which expected volatility was based on historical volatility; and

  (iii) whether and how any other features of the option grant were incorporated into the measurement of fair value, such as a market condition;

(b) for other equity instruments granted during the period (i.e. other than share options), the number and weighted average fair value of those equity instruments at the measurement date, and information on how that fair value was measured, including:

  (i) if fair value was not measured on the basis of an observable market price, how it was determined;

  (ii) whether and how expected dividends were incorporated into the measurement of fair value; and

  (iii) whether and how any other features of the equity instruments granted were incorporated into the measurement of fair value;

(c) for share-based payment arrangements that were modified during the period:

  (i) an explanation of those modifications;

  (ii) the incremental fair value granted (as a result of those modifications); and

  (iii) information on how the incremental fair value granted was measured, consistently with the requirements set out in (a) and (b) above, where applicable. *[IFRS 2.47]*.

These requirements can be seen to some extent as an anti-avoidance measure. It would not be surprising if the IASB had concerns that entities might seek to minimise the impact of IFRS 2 by using unduly pessimistic assumptions that result in a low fair value for share-based payment transactions, and the disclosures above seem designed to deter entities from doing so. However, these disclosures give information about other commercially sensitive matters. For example, (a)(i) above effectively requires disclosure of future dividend policy for a longer period than is generally covered by such forecasts. Entities may need to consider the impact on investors and analysts of dividend yield assumptions disclosed under IFRS 2.

In our view, it is important for entities, in making these disclosures, to ensure that any assumptions disclosed, particularly those relating to future performance, are consistent with those used in other areas of financial reporting that rely on estimates of future events, such as the impairment of property, plant and equipment, intangible assets and goodwill, income taxes (recovery of deferred tax assets out of future profits) and pensions and other post-retirement benefits.

If the entity has measured a share-based payment transaction directly by reference to the fair value of goods or services received during the period, the entity must disclose how that fair value was determined (e.g. whether fair value was measured at a market price for those goods or services). *[IFRS 2.48]*.

As discussed at 5.4 above, IFRS 2 creates a rebuttable presumption that, for an equity-settled transaction with a counterparty other than an employee, the fair value of goods and services received provides the more reliable basis for assessing the fair value of the transaction. Where the entity has rebutted this presumption, and has valued the transaction by reference to the fair value of equity instruments issued, it must disclose this fact, and give an explanation of why the presumption was rebutted. *[IFRS 2.49]*.

13.3 Impact of share-based payment transactions on financial statements

IFRS 2 requires an entity to 'disclose information that enables users of the financial statements to understand the effect of share-based payment transactions on the entity's profit or loss for the period and on its financial position.' *[IFRS 2.50]*.

In order to do this, it must disclose at least:

(a) the total expense recognised for the period arising from share-based payment transactions in which the goods or services received did not qualify for recognition as assets and hence were recognised immediately as an expense, including separate disclosure of that portion of the total expense that arises from transactions accounted for as equity-settled share-based payment transactions;

(b) for liabilities arising from share-based payment transactions:

   (i) the total carrying amount at the end of the period; and

   (ii) the total intrinsic value at the end of the period of liabilities for which the counterparty's right to cash or other assets had vested by the end of the period (e.g. vested share appreciation rights). *[IFRS 2.51]*.

The disclosures section of IFRS 2 has a final paragraph requiring an entity to disclose additional information about its share-based payments should the information requirements set out above and at 13.1 and 13.2 above be insufficient to meet the general disclosure principles of the standard. *[IFRS 2.52]*.

As an example of such additional disclosure, IFRS 2 says that if an entity has classified any share-based payment transactions as equity-settled when there is a net settlement feature for withholding tax obligations (see 14.3.1 below), it should disclose the estimated future payment to the tax authority when it is necessary to inform users of the financial statements about the future cash flow effects of a share-based payment arrangement. *[IFRS 2.52]*.

13.4 Example of IFRS 2 disclosures

An example of many of the disclosures required by IFRS 2 may be found in the financial statements of Aviva plc for the year ended 31 December 2018.

> **Extract 34.2: Aviva plc (2018)**
>
> **Notes to the consolidated financial statements** [extract]
>
> **33 – Group's share plans**
>
> This note describes various equity compensation plans operated by the Group, and shows how the Group values the options and awards of shares in the Company.
>
> **(a) Description of the plans**
>
> The Group maintains a number of active share option and award plans and schemes (the Group's share plans). These are as follows:
>
> *(i) Savings-related options*
>
> These are options granted under the tax-advantaged Save As You Earn (SAYE) share option scheme in the UK and Irish revenue-approved SAYE share option scheme in Ireland. The SAYE allows eligible employees to acquire options over the Company's shares at a discount of up to 20% of their market value at the date of grant.
>
> Options are normally exercisable during the six month period following either the third or fifth anniversary of the start of the relevant savings contract. Seven year contracts were offered prior to 2012. Savings contracts are subject to the statutory savings limits of £500 per month in the UK and €500 per month in Ireland. A limit of £250 per month was applied to contracts in the UK prior to 2016.
>
> *(ii) Aviva long-term incentive plan awards*
>
> These awards have been made under the Aviva Long-Term Incentive Plan 2011 (LTIP), and are described in section (b) below and in the directors' remuneration report.
>
> *(iii) Aviva annual bonus plan awards*
>
> These awards have been made under the Aviva Annual Bonus Plan 2011 (ABP), and are described in section (b) below and in the directors' remuneration report.
>
> *(iv) Aviva recruitment and retention share plan awards*
>
> These are conditional awards granted under the Aviva Recruitment and Retention Share Award plan (RRSAP) in relation to the recruitment or retention of senior managers excluding executive directors. The awards vest in tranches on various dates and vesting is conditional upon the participant being employed by the Group on the vesting date and not having served notice of resignation. Some awards can be subject to performance conditions. If a participant's employment is terminated due to resignation or dismissal, any tranche of the award which has vested within the 12 months prior to the termination date will be subject to clawback and any unvested tranches of the award will lapse in full.
>
> *(v) Aviva Investors deferred share award plan awards*
>
> These awards have been made under the Aviva Investors Deferred Share Award Plan (AI DSAP), where employees can choose to have the deferred element of their bonus deferred into awards over Aviva shares. The awards vest in three equal tranches on the second, third and fourth year following the year of grant.
>
> *(vi) Aviva Investors long-term incentive plan awards*
>
> These awards have been made under the Aviva Investors Long-Term Incentive Plan (AI LTIP)
>
> *(vii) Various all employee share plans*
>
> The Company maintains a number of active stock option and share award voluntary schemes:
> a) The global matching share plan
> b) Aviva Group employee share ownership scheme
> c) Aviva France employee profit sharing scheme.
>
> No new Aviva plc ordinary shares will be issued to satisfy awards made under plans iv, v, vi b) or vii c).

(b) Outstanding options and awards

(i) Share options

At 31 December 2018, options to subscribe for ordinary shares of 25 pence each in the Company were outstanding as follows:

Aviva savings related share option scheme	Option price p	Number of shares	Normally exercisable	Option price p	Number of shares	Normally exercisable
	268	145,323	2018	351	10,508,734	2019 or 2021
	312	267,209	2018	409	4,694,393	2020 or 2022
	380	3,856,295	2018 or 2020	387	7,563,395	2021 or 2023
	419	400,885	2019			

Aviva Ireland savings related share option scheme (in euros)	Option price c	Number of shares	Normally exercisable	Option price c	Number of shares	Normally exercisable
	369	8,259	2018	418	436,262	2019 or 2021
	518	107,293	2018 or 2020	447	233,305	2020 or 2022
	527	11,489	2019	432	425,184	2021 or 2023

The following table summarises information about options outstanding at 31 December 2018:

Range of exercise prices	Outstanding options Number	Weighted average remaining contractual life Years	Weighted average exercise price p
£2.66 – £3.16	420,791	1	296.80
£3.17 – £3.67	10,944,996	2	351.00
£3.68 – £4.19	17,292,239	2	392.43

The comparative figures as at 31 December 2017 were:

Range of exercise prices	Outstanding options Number	Weighted average remaining contractual life Years	Weighted average exercise price p
£2.66 – £3.16	960,378	1	288.10
£3.17 – £3.67	12,227,442	3	351.00
£3.68 – £4.19	11,908,758	3	397.83

(ii) Share awards

At 31 December 2018, awards issued under the Company's executive incentive plans over ordinary shares of 25 pence each in the Company were outstanding as follows:

Aviva long-term incentive plan 2011	Number of shares	Year of vesting
	9,151,821	2019
	6,745,024	2020
	7,898,212	2021

Aviva annual bonus plan 2011	Number of shares	Year of vesting
	5,452,009	2019
	2,764,620	2020
	2,008,514	2021

Aviva recruitment and retention share award plan	Number of shares	Year of vesting
	706,643	2019
	268,812	2020
	83,855	2021
	17,269	2022

Aviva investors deferred share award plan	Number of shares	Year of vesting
	101,695	2019
	86,024	2020
	50,300	2021

Aviva Investors long-term incentive plan 2015	Number of shares	Year of vesting
	313,419	2020

The global matching share plan	Number of shares	Year of vesting
	20,421	2019
	682,944	2020
	629,422	2021

The vesting of awards under the LTIP is subject to the attainment of performance conditions as described in the directors' remuneration report.

No performance conditions are attached to the awards under the ABP, AI DSAP or some of the awards under the RRSAP except as outlined below. There are no performance conditions attached to LTIP awards granted since 2017, with the exception of grants made to the Group Executive.

Under the RRSAP, some shares are subject to the attainment of the same performance conditions that apply to the LTIP grants as follows.

- Shares which vest in 2019:
  - 102,602 are subject to the same performance conditions that apply to the 2016 LTIP grant
  - 144,980 are subject to the performance conditions relating to the performance of the participant's previous employer
- Shares which vest in 2020:
  - 53,246 are subject to the performance conditions relating to the performance of the participant's previous employer
- Shares which vest in 2021:
  - 5,305 are subject to the performance conditions relating to the performance of the participant's previous employer

These performance conditions are as outlined in the relevant year's directors' remuneration report. Shares which do not vest will lapse.

(iii) Shares to satisfy awards and options

New issue shares are now generally used to satisfy all awards and options granted under plans that have received shareholder approval and where local regulations permit. Further details are given in note 32.

(c) Movements in the year

A summary of the status of the option plans as at 31 December 2017 and 2018, and changes during the years ended on those dates, is shown below.

	2018		2017	
	Number of options	Weighted average exercise price p	Number of options	Weighted average exercise price p
Outstanding at 1 January	25,096,578	370.81	24,253,209	355.08
Granted during the year	8,139,367	387.00	5,998,098	409.00
Exercised during the year	(2,111,514)	361.96	(3,094,372)	327.04
Forfeited during the year	(1,855,638)	385.00	(944,431)	364.03
Cancelled during the year	(495,646)	364.93	(1,004,017)	361.90
Expired during the year	(115,121)	381.97	(111,909)	355.32
Outstanding at 31 December	28,658,026	375.20	25,096,578	370.81
Exercisable at 31 December	3,457,732	369.88	911,019	366.51

(d) Expense charged to the income statement

The total expense recognised for the year arising from equity compensation plans were as follows:

	2018 £m	2017 £m
Equity-settled expense	64	77
Cash-settled expense	–	–
Total (note 11(b))	64	77

(e) Fair value of options and awards granted after 7 November 2002

The weighted average fair values of options and awards granted during the year, estimated by using the Binomial option pricing model and Monte Carlo Simulation model, were £0.78 and £4.84 *(2017: £1.00 and £4.94)* respectively.

(i) Share options

The fair value of the options was estimated on the date of grant, based on the following weighted average assumptions:

Weighted average assumption	2018	2017
Share price	480p	506p
Exercise price	387p	409p
Expected volatility	24.85%	26.04%
Expected life	3.67 years	3.70 years
Expected dividend yield	5.88%	4.61%
Risk-free interest rate	1.05%	0.55%

The expected volatility used was based on the historical volatility of the share price over a period equivalent to the expected life of the option prior to its date of grant. The risk-free interest rate was based on the yields available on UK government bonds as at the date of grant. The bonds chosen were those with a similar remaining term to the expected life of the options. 2,111,514 options granted after 7 November 2002 were exercised during the year *(2017: 3,094,372)*.

(ii) Share awards

The fair value of the awards was estimated on the date of grant based on the following weighted average assumptions:

Weighted average assumption	2018	2017
Share price	500p	523p
Expected volatility[1]	25%	28%
Expected volatility of comparator companies' share price[1]	25%	26%
Correlation between Aviva and comparator competitors' share price[1]	64%	59%
Expected life[1]	2.64 years	2.76 years
Expected dividend yield[2]	0.00%	0.00%
Risk-free interest rate[1]	0.80%	0.59%

1 For awards with market-based performance conditions only.
2 Expected dividend yield assumption was only used to fair value LTIP awards issued in France. In 2017, LTIP awards with no market performance conditions were issued in France therefore this assumption was not used in the year.

The expected volatility used was based on the historical volatility of the share price over a period equivalent to the expected life of the share award prior to its date of grant. The risk-free interest rate was based on the yields available on UK government bonds as at the date of grant. The bonds chosen were those with a similar remaining term to the expected life of the share awards.

Depending on the precise regulatory requirements of a particular jurisdiction, it might be possible to meet some of the IFRS 2 disclosure requirements by means of a cross-reference between the financial statements and other parts of an annual report published together with the financial statements, such as a management commentary or statutory remuneration report (as in the case of Aviva plc above). However, even where such an approach is permissible, care needs to be taken to ensure that any such cross-reference is clear and specific and that all of the relevant IFRS 2 requirements have been addressed as these requirements vary depending on when an award was granted. For example, detailed fair value information for an equity-settled award is generally required only in the year of grant (and as comparative information in the following period(s)), whereas the conditions attached to an award are required to be disclosed in every period in which that award is outstanding.

14 TAXES RELATED TO SHARE-BASED PAYMENT TRANSACTIONS

14.1 Income tax deductions for the entity

In many jurisdictions entities are entitled to receive income tax deductions for share-based payment transactions. In many, if not most, cases the tax deduction is given for a cost different to that recorded under IFRS 2. For example, some jurisdictions give a tax deduction for the fair or intrinsic value of the award at the date of exercise; others may give a tax deduction for amounts charged to a subsidiary by its parent, or by a trust controlled by the parent, in respect of the cost of group awards to the employees of that subsidiary. In either case, both the amount and timing of the expense for tax purposes will be different from the amount and timing of the expense required by IFRS 2.

The particular issues raised by share-based payment transactions are addressed in IAS 12 and discussed further in Chapter 33 at 10.8.

14.2 Employment taxes of the employer

It is frequently the case that an employing entity is required to pay employment taxes or social security contributions on share options and other share-based payment transactions with employees, just as if the employees had received cash remuneration. This raises the question of how such taxes should be accounted for.

14.2.1 Applicable standard

The choice of accounting method does not affect the total expense ultimately recognised (which must always be the tax actually paid), but rather its allocation to different accounting periods. IFRS is unclear as to which standard should be applied in accounting for such employment taxes. Some consider that such taxes are most appropriately accounted for under IAS 37 (see 14.2.1.A below), others favour IFRS 2 (see 14.2.1.B below) or IAS 19 (see 14.2.1.C below). A reporting entity may therefore choose what it considers an appropriate policy for employment taxes in its particular circumstances.

Such taxes do not fall within the scope of IFRS 9 since, like income taxes, they are not contractual liabilities (see Chapter 45 at 2.2.1).

14.2.1.A IAS 37

Some consider that, for the reasons set out in 14.2.1.B and 14.2.1.C below, employment taxes of the employer do not fall within the scope of IFRS 2 or of IAS 19. Accordingly, since the amount ultimately payable is uncertain, the most appropriate standard to apply is IAS 37.

Where IAS 37 is applied, the entity will recognise a provision for the employment tax in accordance with IFRIC 21 – *Levies* – which requires identification of the activity that triggers the payment, as identified by the legislation (see Chapter 26 at 3.1 and 6.8). However, there is some room for discussion as to what constitutes the activity that triggers the payment. Is it:

- the granting of the award;
- the consumption of services received from employees;
- the event (typically exercise) that gives rise to a real tax liability; or
- the vesting of the award?

Entities applying IAS 37 need therefore to consider the appropriate treatment of employment taxes in the light of IFRIC 21.

14.2.1.B IFRS 2

Some argue that, since the employment taxes are a payment of an amount of cash typically directly linked to the share price, they should be accounted for as a cash-settled share-based payment transaction under IFRS 2. This would require the taxes to be measured at each reporting date at fair value, multiplied by the expired vesting period of the award to which they relate (see 9.3.1 above).

A difficulty with this analysis is that IFRS 2 defines a cash-settled share-based payment transaction as one in which the entity incurs a liability to the 'supplier of ... goods or services'. The liability for such employment taxes is clearly due to the tax authorities, not to the supplier of goods and services (i.e. the employee). Some who support the application of IFRS 2 accept that IFRS 2 is not directly applicable but argue that it is nevertheless the most appropriate standard to apply under the 'GAAP hierarchy' in IAS 8 (see Chapter 3 at 4.3). The objective of IFRS 2 (see 2.1 above) states that the standard is intended to apply to 'expenses associated with transactions in which share options are granted to employees'. *[IFRS 2.2]*. However, the standard contains no explicit provisions relevant to this objective.

14.2.1.C   IAS 19

Some argue that such payments are more appropriately accounted for under IAS 19 (see Chapter 35) especially when the taxes are social security contribution, as such contributions benefit the employee indirectly on retirement. Again the difficulty is that IAS 19 defines employee benefits as 'all forms of consideration given by an entity in exchange for service rendered by employees or for the termination of employment' *[IAS 19.8]* which would appear to rule out payments to the tax authority, but for the fact that IAS 19 refers to social security contributions as a component part of short-term employee benefits. *[IAS 19.9(a)]*. However, many share-based payment transactions would, if they were within the scope of IAS 19, be classified as long-term benefits. That brings the added complication that IAS 19 would require the employment taxes due on long-term benefits to be accounted for, like the benefits themselves, using the projected unit credit method, which seems an unduly complex approach in the circumstances.

In some situations the entity may require employees to discharge any liability for employment taxes. The accounting issues raised by such arrangements are discussed at 14.2.2 and 14.3 below.

14.2.2   Recovery of employer's taxes from employees

As discussed at 14.2 above, in some jurisdictions employers are required to pay employment taxes on share-based payment transactions. This detracts from one of the key attractions for an employer of a share-based payment transaction, namely that it entails no cash cost. This is particularly the case where the tax payable is based on the fair value of the award at vesting, meaning that the employer's liability is potentially unlimited.

Accordingly, employers liable to such taxes will sometimes make it a condition of receiving a share-based award that the employee bear all or some of the employer's cash cost of any related employment taxes. This may be done in a number of ways, including:

- direct payment to the entity;
- authorising the entity to deduct the relevant amount from the employee's salary; or
- surrendering as many shares to the entity as have a fair value equal to the tax liability.

The accounting treatment of arrangements where the recovery of the employer's tax cost from the employee is made through surrendering of a number of shares with an equivalent value is similar to that discussed at 14.3 below for the recovery of the employee's taxes.

Where the scheme requires direct cash reimbursement by employees of the cost of the employer's taxes, different considerations apply, as illustrated by Example 34.57 below.

Example 34.57: Recovery of employment tax on share-based payment from employee

At the beginning of year 1, an entity granted an executive an award of free shares with a fair value of €100,000 on condition that the executive remain in employment for three years. In the jurisdiction concerned, an employment tax at the rate of 12% is payable by the employer when the shares vest, based on their fair value at the date of vesting. As a condition of obtaining the shares on vesting, the executive is required to pay cash equal to the tax liability to the employer.

When the shares vest at the end of year 3, their fair value is €300,000, on which employment taxes of €36,000 are due. The executive pays this amount to the entity.

In our view, this arrangement can be construed in one of two ways, with somewhat different accounting outcomes:

- View 1: The executive's obligation to make whole the employer's tax liability means that this is, economically, not an award of free shares, but an option to acquire the shares for an exercise price equivalent to 12% of their market value at the date of exercise. The employer's tax liability is a separate transaction.
- View 2: The executive's obligation to make whole the employer's tax liability should be accounted for as such, separately from the share-based payment transaction.

In our view, either approach may be adopted, so long as it is applied consistently as a matter of accounting policy. The essential differences between View 1 and View 2, as illustrated below, are that:

- under View 1 the reimbursement received from the employee is credited to equity, whereas under View 2 it is credited to profit or loss; and
- under View 1, the IFRS 2 charge is lower than under View 2 reflecting the fact that under View 1 the award is construed as an option, not an award of free shares.

View 1   Reimbursement treated as exercise price

On this analysis, the award is construed as an option to acquire shares with an exercise price of 12% of the fair value, at vesting, of the shares. The grant date fair value of the award construed as an option is €88,000. The entity would process the following accounting entries (on a cumulative basis).

	€000	€000
Employee costs*	88	
Equity		88
Employee costs†	36	
Cash		36
Cash§	36	
Equity		36

*   IFRS 2 charge.
†   Employment taxes (12% of €300,000).
§   The receipt of cash from the employee to reimburse the tax is treated as the receipt of the exercise price for an option and credited to equity.

View 2   Reimbursement treated separately from the IFRS 2 charge

On this analysis, the award is construed as an award of free shares, with a grant date fair value of €100,000. The reimbursement is accounted for as such, giving rise to a credit to profit or loss. The entity would process the following accounting entries (on a cumulative basis).

	€000	€000
Employee costs*	100	
Equity		100
Employee costs†	36	
Cash		36
Cash§	36	
Employee costs		36

*   IFRS 2 charge.

†   Employment taxes (12% of €300,000).

§   The receipt of cash from the employee to reimburse the tax is treated as a reduction in employee costs.

It will be seen that View 1 results in a total employee expense of €124,000, while View 2 results in a total employee expense of €100,000.

14.2.3   Holding of own shares to 'hedge' employment tax liabilities

As noted at 14.2 above, an award of shares or options to an employee may also give rise to an employment tax liability for the employer, often related to the fair value of the award when it vests or, in the case of an option, is exercised. Employers may hold their own shares in order to hedge this liability (in an economic sense, if not under the criteria in IFRS 9 – see 2.2.4.H above), and later sell as many shares as are needed to raise proceeds equal to the tax liability.

These are two separate transactions. The purchase and sale of own shares are treasury share transactions accounted for in accordance with IAS 32 (see Chapter 47 at 9). The accounting treatment of the employment tax liability is discussed at 14.2.1 above.

14.3   Sale or surrender of shares by employee to meet employee's tax liability ('sell to cover' and 'net settlement')

In some jurisdictions, an award of shares or options to an employee gives rise to a personal tax liability for the employee, often related to the fair value of the award when it vests or, in the case of an option, is exercised. In order to meet this tax liability, employees may wish to sell or surrender as many shares as are needed to raise proceeds equal to the tax liability (sometimes described respectively as 'sell to cover' or 'net settlement').

This in itself does not, in our view, require the scheme to be considered as cash-settled, any more than if the employee wished to liquidate the shares in order to buy a car or undertake home improvements. However, if the manner in which the cash is passed to, or realised for, the employee gives rise to a legal or constructive obligation for the employer, then the scheme might well be cash-settled (see 9.2.2 to 9.2.4 above), to the extent of any such obligation.

In some jurisdictions where employees must pay income tax on share awards, the tax is initially collected from (and is a legal liability of) the employer, but with eventual recourse by the tax authorities to the employee for tax not collected from the employer. Such tax collection arrangements mean that even an equity-settled award results in a cash cost for the employer for the income tax.

In such a situation, the employer may require the employee, as a condition of taking delivery of any shares earned, to indemnify the entity against the tax liability, for example by:

- direct payment to the entity;
- authorising the entity to deduct the relevant amount from the employee's salary; or
- surrendering as many shares to the entity as have a fair value equal to the tax liability.

If the entity requires the employee to surrender the relevant number of shares, in our view it is appropriate to treat the scheme as cash-settled to the extent of the indemnified amount, unless the criteria to account for the arrangement as equity-settled under the limited exception in IFRS 2 are met (see further below). This view relating to the general requirements of IFRS 2 was confirmed by the IASB in its discussions relating to the introduction of the exception into the standard. [IFRS 2.BC255G].

IFRS 2 contains a limited exception to the general requirement to consider whether a net-settled arrangement needs to be split into equity-settled and cash-settled portions. An entity is required to account for net-settled arrangements meeting certain specified criteria as equity-settled in their entirety. However, the exception is narrow in scope and the requirement to assess whether an arrangement has an equity-settled element and a cash-settled element continues to be relevant in many cases. The exception is discussed and illustrated further at 14.3.1 below.

The following example illustrates the application of IFRS 2 to an arrangement where the exception does not apply and so the entity has to separate the transaction into two elements.

Example 34.58: Surrendering of vested shares by employee to indemnify liability of entity to pay employee's tax liability (net settlement where IFRS 2 exception does not apply)

An entity operates in a jurisdiction where the personal tax rate is 40%, and free shares are taxed at their fair value on vesting. The entity grants an award of 100 free shares with a grant date fair value of £3 each. The fair value at vesting date is £5, so that the employee's tax liability (required to be discharged in the first instance by the employer) is £200 (40% of £500). The award is to be satisfied using treasury shares with an original cost of £2.50 per share. Tax law or regulation does not require the entity to withhold an amount for the employee's tax obligation (see Example 34.59 below for an illustration of that situation).

The terms of the agreement between the entity and the employee specify that the employee must surrender the 40 shares needed to settle the tax liability. In our view the substance of the transaction is that, at grant date, the entity is making an award of only 60 shares (with a grant date fair value of £3 each) and is bearing the cost of the employment tax itself. On this analysis, the entity will have recorded the following entries by the end of the vesting period:

	£	£
Employee costs (based on 60 shares at grant date fair value)	180	
Equity		180
Employee costs (based on 40% of vesting date value)	200	
Employment tax liability		200

The award is then satisfied by delivery of 60 treasury shares (with a cost of £2.50 each) to the employee:

	£	£
Equity	150	
Treasury shares		150

The entity might well then sell the 40 shares 'surrendered' by the employee in order to raise the cash to pay the tax, but this would be accounted for as an increase in equity on the reissue of treasury shares, not as income (see 14.2.3 above).

If, instead of being required to surrender shares, the employee has a free choice as to how to indemnify the employer, the employer will have recorded the following entries by the end of the vesting period:

	£	£
Employee costs (based on 100 shares at grant date fair value)	300	
Equity		300
Receivable from employee (based on 40% of vesting date value)	200	
Employment tax liability		200

The award is then satisfied by delivery of shares to the employee, and the employee indicates that he wishes to surrender 40 shares to discharge his obligation to the employer under the indemnity arrangement. The entity then receives 40 shares from the employee in settlement of the £200 receivable from him.

In practice, this would almost certainly be effected as a net delivery of 60 shares, but in principle there are two transactions, a release of 100 treasury shares, with a cost of £2.50 each, to the employee:

	£	£
Equity	250	
Treasury shares		250

and the re-acquisition of 40 of those shares at £5 each from the employee:

	£	£
Treasury shares	200	
Receivable from employee		200

The entity then settles the tax liability:

	£	£
Employment tax liability	200	
Cash		200

Even in this case, however, some might take the view that the substance of the arrangement is that the employee has the right to put 40 shares to the employer, and accordingly 40% of the award should be accounted for as cash-settled, resulting in essentially the same accounting as when the employee is required to surrender 40 shares, as set out above. An entity should therefore make a careful assessment of the appropriate accounting treatment based on the terms of a particular arrangement.

14.3.1 Share-based payments with a net settlement feature for withholding tax obligations (net settlement where IFRS 2 exception applies)

IFRS 2 contains an exception for specific types of share-based payment transaction with a net settlement feature.

The exception was introduced as a result of discussions by the Interpretations Committee about the classification of a share-based payment transaction in which an entity withholds a specified portion of shares that would otherwise be issued to the counterparty at the date of exercise or vesting. The shares are withheld in return for the entity settling the counterparty's tax liability relating to the share-based payment. The question asked was whether the portion of the share-based payment that is withheld should be classified as cash-settled or equity-settled in a situation where, in the absence of the net settlement feature, the award would be treated in its entirety as equity-settled?

The exception to the usual requirements of the standard (which are set out at 14.3 above) is narrow in scope and applies only in situations where there is a statutory withholding obligation. The standard explains that 'tax laws or regulations may oblige an entity to withhold an amount for an employee's tax obligation associated with a share-based payment and transfer that amount, normally in cash, to the tax authority on the employee's behalf. To fulfil this obligation, the terms of the share-based payment arrangement may permit or require the entity to withhold the number of equity instruments equal to the monetary value of the employee's tax obligation from the total number of equity instruments that otherwise would have been issued to the employee upon exercise (or vesting) of the share-based payment (i.e. the share-based payment arrangement has a "net settlement feature")'. *[IFRS 2.33E]*.

If a transaction meeting the above criteria would have been classified entirely as equity-settled were it not for this net settlement feature, then the exception in IFRS 2 applies and the transaction is accounted for as equity-settled in its entirety (rather than being divided into an equity-settled portion and a cash-settled portion as discussed at 14.3 above). *[IFRS 2.33F, BC255G-I]*.

An entity applying the exception has to account for the withholding of shares to fund the payment to the tax authority as a deduction from equity (in accordance with paragraph 29 of IFRS 2). However, the deduction from equity may only be made up to the fair value at the net settlement date of the shares required to be withheld. *[IFRS 2.33G]*. If the payment exceeds this fair value, the excess is expensed through profit or loss.

Where the entity withholds any equity instruments in excess of the employee's tax obligation associated with the share-based payment (i.e. the entity withholds an amount of shares that exceeds the monetary value of the employee's tax obligation), then the excess shares should be accounted for as a cash-settled share-based payment when this amount is paid in cash (or other assets) to the employee. *[IFRS 2.33H(b)]*. In other words, such shares are treated as a separate cash-settled share-based payment and fully recognised as an expense (rather than as a deduction from equity) as at the date of settlement.

To illustrate the application of the exception, the IASB has added an example to the implementation guidance accompanying IFRS 2. *[IFRS 2 IG Example 12B]*. The substance of this example is reproduced as Example 34.59 below.

An entity applying the exception will also need to consider whether additional disclosures are needed in respect of the future cash payment to the tax authorities (see 13.3 above). *[IFRS 2.52]*.

The IASB notes in the Basis for Conclusions to IFRS 2 that the exception is designed to alleviate the operational difficulties, and any associated undue cost, encountered by entities when they are required, under the requirements of IFRS 2, to divide a share-based payment transaction into an equity-settled element and a cash-settled element (see 14.3 above). *[IFRS 2.BC255J]*.

The IASB made it very clear during its discussions that the exception only addresses the narrow situation where the net settlement arrangement is designed to meet an entity's obligation under tax laws or regulations to withhold a certain amount to meet the counterparty's tax obligation associated with the share-based payment and transfer that amount in cash to the taxation authorities. This point has been incorporated into IFRS 2 as follows:

'The exception in paragraph 33F does not apply to:
(a) a share-based payment arrangement with a net settlement feature for which there is no obligation on the entity under tax laws or regulations to withhold an amount for an employee's tax obligation associated with that share-based payment ...'. *[IFRS 2.33H(a)]*.

Other types of arrangement that are very frequently seen in practice might appear similar in substance to the legal or regulatory obligation covered by the exception. For example, as discussed and illustrated at 14.3 above, the terms of a share-based payment arrangement between an entity and an employee might require the employee to forfeit sufficient shares to meet the tax liability or the employee might have some choice over whether or not shares are withheld and/or directly sold in order to raise cash to settle the tax liability. However, unless the arrangements for net settlement are put in place to meet the entity's obligation under tax laws or regulations as described above, the exception will not apply. Therefore, careful analysis of such arrangements continues to be necessary to determine whether part of the award should be treated as cash-settled or whether the exception applies and the entire arrangement should therefore be treated as equity-settled.

Example 34.59: Share-based payment transactions with a net settlement feature for withholding tax obligations (application of IFRS 2 exception)

At the beginning of year 1 an entity grants an award of 100 shares to an employee. The award is conditional upon the completion of four years' service which the employee is expected to achieve.

The employee's tax obligation of 40% is based on the fair value of the shares at vesting date. Tax law in the entity's jurisdiction requires the entity to withhold an amount for an employee's tax obligation associated with a share-based payment and transfer that amount in cash to the tax authority on behalf of the employee.

The terms and conditions of the share-based payment arrangement require the entity to withhold shares from the settlement of the award to the employee in order to settle the employee's tax obligation. Accordingly, the entity settles the transaction on a net basis by withholding the number of shares with a fair value equal to the monetary value of the employee's tax obligation and issuing the remaining shares to the employee at the end of the vesting period.

The fair value at grant date is £2 per share and at the end of year 4 is £10 per share.

The fair value of the shares on the vesting date (end of year 4) is £1,000 (100 × £10) and therefore the employee's tax obligation is £400 (100 × £10 × 40%). Accordingly, on the vesting date, the entity issues 60 shares to the employee, withholds 40 shares from the employee and pays £400 (the fair value of the shares withheld) in cash to the tax authority on the employee's behalf. In effect, it is as if the entity issued 100 vested shares to the employee and then repurchased 40 of them at fair value.

Accounting during the vesting period and on recognition and settlement of the tax obligation

Over the four-year vesting period, the entity recognises a cumulative IFRS 2 expense of £200 (£50 per annum) with a corresponding credit to equity. This is calculated as 100 shares × £2 grant date fair value.

	£	£
Employee costs	200	
Equity		200

At the date of vesting the tax liability is recognised and subsequently paid:

	£	£
Equity	400	
Tax liability		400
Tax liability	400	
Cash		400

The example in the implementation guidance also notes that the entity should consider disclosing at each reporting date an estimate of the expected tax payment (see 13.3 above).

15 OTHER PRACTICAL ISSUES

We discuss below the following aspects of the practical application of IFRS 2:

- matching share awards (including deferred bonuses delivered in shares) (see 15.1 below);
- loans to employees to purchase shares (limited recourse and full recourse loans) (see 15.2 below);
- awards entitled to dividends or dividend equivalents during the vesting period (see 15.3 below);
- awards vesting or exercisable on an exit event or change of control (flotation, trade sale etc.) (see 15.4 below);
- arrangements under South African black economic empowerment ('BEE') legislation and similar arrangements (see 15.5 below); and
- shares used as a currency of payment (see 15.6 below).

15.1 Matching share awards (including deferred bonuses delivered in shares)

As noted in the discussion at 10.1.2 above, the rules in IFRS 2 for awards where there is a choice of equity- or cash-settlement do not fully address awards where the equity and cash alternatives may have significantly different fair values and vesting periods. In some jurisdictions, a popular type of scheme giving rise to such issues is a matching share award. This section will generally refer to matching share awards but arrangements to defer bonus payments for later settlement in shares (without a matching element) raise a number of similar issues.

Under a matching share award, the starting point is usually that an employee is awarded a bonus for a one year performance period. At the end of that period, the employee may then be either required or permitted to take all or part of that bonus in shares rather than cash. To the extent that the employee takes shares rather than cash, the employing entity may then be required or permitted to make a 'matching' award of an equal number of shares (or a multiple or fraction of that number). The matching award will typically vest over a longer period.

Whilst such schemes can appear superficially similar, the accounting analysis under IFRS 2 may vary significantly, according to whether:
- the employee has a choice, or is required, to take some of the 'base' bonus in shares and whether any such shares have to be retained by the employee in order for the matching shares to vest; and/or
- the employer has a choice, or is required, to match any shares taken by the employee.

Examples 34.60 to 34.64 below set out an analysis of the five basic variants of such schemes, as summarised in the following matrix.

Employee's taking shares required or discretionary?	Employer's matching required or discretionary?	Example
Required	Required	34.60
Required	Discretionary	34.61
Discretionary	No provision for matching award	34.62
Discretionary	Required	34.63
Discretionary	Discretionary	34.64

A requirement for the employee to retain a base shareholding for the duration of the matching arrangement is a non-vesting condition and this is considered at the end of this section (following Example 34.64).

Example 34.60: Mandatory investment by employee of cash bonus into shares with mandatory matching award by employer

At the beginning of year 1 an employee is told that he is to participate in a bonus scheme which will pay £1,000 if certain performance criteria are met by the end of year 1 and he remains in service. The bonus will be paid at the beginning of year 2. 50% will be paid in cash and the employee will be required to invest the remaining 50% in as many shares as are worth £500 at the beginning of year 2. Thus, if the share price were £2.50, the employee would receive £500 cash and 200 shares. These shares are fully vested.

If this first award is achieved, the entity is required to award an equal number of additional shares ('matching shares') – in this example 200 shares – conditional upon the employee remaining in service until the end of year 3. The award of any matching shares will be made at the beginning of year 2.

Annual bonus

The 50% of the bonus paid in cash is outside the scope of IFRS 2 and within that of IAS 19 (see Chapter 35). The 50% of the annual bonus settled in shares is an equity-settled share-based payment transaction within the scope of IFRS 2, since there is no discretion over the manner of settlement. The measurement date for this element of the bonus is 1 January in year 1 and the vesting period is year 1, since all vesting conditions have been met by the end of that year. Notwithstanding that the two legs of the award strictly fall within the scope of two different standards, the practical effect will be to charge an expense over the course of year 1.

Matching shares

The terms of the award of 200 matching shares have the effect that the entity has committed, as at the beginning of year 1, to award shares with a value of £500 as at the beginning of year 2, subject to satisfaction of:

- a performance condition relating to year 1; and
- a three year service condition (years 1 to 3).

Those terms are understood by all parties at the beginning of year 1, which is therefore the measurement date. The fact that the matching award is not formally made until the beginning of year 2 is not relevant, since there has been a binding commitment to make the award, on terms understood both by the entity and the employee, since the beginning of year 1 (see 5.3 above).

The vesting period is the three year period to the end of year 3. As at the end of year 1 only one of the vesting conditions (i.e. the performance condition) has been met. The further vesting condition (i.e. the service condition) is not met until the end of year 3.

The discussion in 8.10 above is relevant to the valuation of the equity elements of the award.

Example 34.61: Mandatory investment by employee of cash bonus into shares with discretionary matching award by employer

At the beginning of year 1 an employee is told that he is to participate in a bonus scheme which will pay £1,000 if certain performance criteria are met by the end of year 1 and he remains in service. The bonus will be paid at the beginning of year 2. 50% will be paid in cash and the employee will be required to invest the remaining 50% in as many shares as are worth £500 at the beginning of year 2. Thus, if the share price were £2.50, the employee would receive £500 cash and 200 shares. These shares are fully vested.

If this first award is achieved, the entity has the discretion, but not the obligation, to award an equal number of additional shares ('matching shares') – in this case 200 shares – conditional upon the employee remaining in service until the end of year 3. The award of any matching shares will be made at the beginning of year 2.

Annual bonus

The 50% of the bonus paid in cash is outside the scope of IFRS 2 and within that of IAS 19 (see Chapter 35). The 50% of the annual bonus settled in shares is an equity-settled share-based payment transaction within the scope of IFRS 2, since there is no discretion over the manner of settlement. The measurement date for this element of the bonus is 1 January in year 1 and the vesting period is year 1, since all vesting conditions have been met by the end of that year. Notwithstanding that the two legs of the award strictly fall within the scope of two different standards, the practical effect will be to charge an expense over the course of year 1.

Matching shares

In our view, it is necessary to consider whether the entity's discretion is real or not, this being a matter for judgement in the light of individual facts and circumstances.

In some cases the entity's discretion to make awards may have little real substance. For example, the awards may simply be documented as 'discretionary' for tax and other reasons. It may also be that the entity has consistently made matching awards to all eligible employees (or all members of a particular class of eligible employees), so that it has no realistic alternative but to make matching awards if it wants to maintain good staff relations. In such cases, it may be helpful to consider what the accounting for the 'matching' award would be if it were a pure cash award falling within the scope of IAS 19:

> 'An entity may have no legal obligation to pay a bonus. Nevertheless, in some cases, an entity has a practice of paying bonuses. In such cases, the entity has a constructive obligation because the entity has no realistic alternative but to pay the bonus. The measurement of the constructive obligation reflects the possibility that some employees may leave without receiving a bonus.' *[IAS 19.21].*

This is discussed further in Chapter 35 at 12.3.

In making the determination of whether a constructive obligation would exist under IAS 19, it would be necessary to consider past data (e.g. the number of employees who have received matching awards having received the original award).

If it is concluded that the entity does not have a constructive obligation to make a matching award, the accounting treatment would follow the legal form of the transaction. On this view, the grant date (and therefore measurement date) would be 1 January in year 2, and the vesting period the two years from the beginning of year 2 to the end of year 3.

If it is concluded that the entity does have a constructive obligation to make a matching award, the effect is that the matching award of shares is equivalent to the mandatory matching award in Example 34.60 above, and should therefore be accounted for in the same way – i.e. the measurement date is 1 January in year 1 and the vesting period is the three year period to the end of year 3.

The discussion in 8.10 above is relevant to the valuation of the matching equity award.

Example 34.62: Discretionary investment by employee of cash bonus into shares with no matching award

At the beginning of year 1 an employee is told that he is to participate in a bonus scheme which will pay £1,000 if certain performance criteria are met by the end of year 1 and he remains in service. The bonus will be paid at the beginning of year 2. 50% will be paid in cash and the employee will be permitted, but not required, to invest the remaining 50% in as many shares as are worth £500 at the beginning of year 2. Thus, if the share price were £2.50, the employee could choose to receive either (a) £1,000 or (b) £500 cash and 200 shares. Any shares received are fully vested.

The 50% of the bonus automatically paid in cash is outside the scope of IFRS 2 and within that of IAS 19 (see Chapter 35).

The 50% of the bonus that may be invested in shares falls within the scope of IFRS 2 as a share-based payment transaction in which the terms of the arrangement provide the counterparty with the choice of settlement. This is the case even though the value of the alternative award is always £500 and does not depend on the share price (see 10.4 above).

The measurement date of the award is 1 January in year 1 and the vesting period is year 1. The methodology set out in IFRS 2 for awards where the counterparty has a choice of settlement would lead to recognition over the vesting period of a liability component of £500 and an equity component of zero (see 10.1.2 above). If in fact the employee took shares at vesting, the £500 liability would be transferred to equity.

Example 34.63: Discretionary investment by employee of cash bonus into shares with mandatory matching award by employer

At the beginning of year 1 an employee is told that he is to participate in a bonus scheme which will pay £1,000 if certain performance criteria are met by the end of year 1 and he remains in service. The bonus will be paid at the beginning of year 2. 50% will be paid in cash and the employee will be permitted, but not required, to invest the remaining 50% in as many shares as are worth £500 at the beginning of year 2. Thus, if the share price were £2.50, the employee could choose to receive either (a) £1,000 or (b) £500 cash and 200 shares.

If the employee elects to reinvest the bonus in shares, the shares are not fully vested unless the employee remains in service until the end of year 3. However, if the employee elects to receive 50% of the bonus in shares, the entity is required to award an equal number of additional shares ('matching shares'), in this case 200 shares, also conditional upon the employee remaining in service until the end of year 3. The award of any matching shares will be made at the beginning of year 2.

The 50% of the bonus automatically paid in cash is outside the scope of IFRS 2 and within that of IAS 19 (see Chapter 35).

The 50% of the bonus that may be invested in shares falls within the scope of IFRS 2 as a share-based payment transaction in which the terms of the arrangement provide the counterparty with the choice of settlement. This is the case even though the value of the alternative award is always £500 and does not depend on the share price (see 10.4 above).

The mandatory nature of the matching shares means that the award is a share-based payment transaction, entered into at the beginning of year 1 (and therefore measured as at that date), in which the terms of the arrangement provide the counterparty with a choice of settlement between:

- at the beginning of year 2: cash of £500, subject to service and performance during year 1; or
- at the end of year 3: shares with a value of £1,000 as at the beginning of year 2, subject to:
    (i) performance in year 1; and
    (ii) service during years 1 to 3.

The equity component as calculated in accordance with IFRS 2 will have a value in excess of zero (see 10.1.2 above). The measurement date of the equity component is the beginning of year 1. However, as discussed at 10.1.3.A above, IFRS 2 does not specify how to deal with a transaction where the counterparty has the choice of equity- or cash-settlement but the liability and equity components have different vesting periods. In our view it is appropriate to recognise the liability and equity components independently over their different vesting periods, i.e. in this case:

- for the liability component (i.e. the fair value of the cash alternative), during year 1;
- for the equity component (i.e. the excess of the total fair value of the award over the fair value of the cash alternative), during the three year period to the end of year 3.

Thus, at the end of year 1, the entity will have recorded an IFRS 2 expense together with a corresponding:

- liability for the cost of the portion of the annual award that the employee may take in cash or equity (the liability component referred to above);
- credit to equity, for one-third of the cost of the matching award (the equity component referred to above).

If the employee decides to take shares, the entity would simply transfer the amount recorded as a liability to equity and recognise the remaining cost of the matching shares over the following two years.

If, however, the employee elects to take cash, the position is more complicated. Clearly, the main accounting entry is to reduce the liability, with a corresponding reduction in cash, when the liability is settled. However, this raises the question of what is to be done with the one-third cost of the matching award already recognised in equity and the remaining, as yet unrecognised, two-thirds cost.

An election by the employee for cash at the end of year 1 should be treated as a cancellation of the matching award, due to the employee's failure to fulfil a non-vesting condition (i.e. not taking the cash alternative) for the matching award – see 3.2 and 6.4 above. Therefore, the one-third cost that had already been expensed would not be reversed and the remaining two-thirds of the matching award not yet recognised would be recognised immediately, resulting in an expense for an award that does not actually crystallise.

The analysis above assumes that the equity award either vests or is cancelled because the employee decides to take the cash award. An alternative outcome would be that the employee chooses the equity-settled award but then fails to meet the three year service condition attached to that award. This would result in forfeiture of the equity-settled award and the reversal of any expense previously recognised for the equity component. However, this raises a question about the treatment of the amount for the cash component that was credited to equity when the employee chose the equity award rather than the cash award. In our view, there are two alternative approaches:

- The employee's decision to invest 50% of the bonus into the share award is similar to the employee making a non-refundable deposit for the shares and so it is appropriate to leave this amount in equity and not reverse it through profit or loss as part of the forfeiture accounting for the equity award.
- The reclassification of £500 from liability to equity is part of the consideration for the forfeited equity instruments and relates to past service rendered in connection with the equity component of the award and so it is appropriate to reverse this amount through profit or loss as part of the forfeiture.

In our view, either approach is acceptable but should be applied consistently.

Example 34.64: **Discretionary investment by employee of cash bonus into shares with discretionary matching award by employer**

At the beginning of year 1 an employee is told that he is to participate in a bonus scheme which will pay £1,000 if certain performance criteria are met by the end of year 1 and he remains in service. The bonus will be paid at the beginning of year 2. 50% will be paid in cash and the employee will be permitted, but not required, to invest the remaining 50% in as many shares as are worth £500 at the beginning of year 2. Thus, if the share price were £2.50, the employee could choose to receive either (a) £1,000 or (b) £500 cash and 200 shares. Any shares received under this part of the arrangement are fully vested.

If the employee elects to receive shares, the entity has the discretion, but not the obligation, to award additional shares ('matching shares') – in this case 200 shares – conditional upon the employee remaining in service until the end of year 3. The award of any matching shares will be made at the beginning of year 2.

The 50% of the bonus automatically paid in cash is outside the scope of IFRS 2 and within that of IAS 19 (see Chapter 35).

The 50% of the bonus that may be invested in shares falls within the scope of IFRS 2 as a share-based payment transaction in which the terms of the arrangement provide the counterparty with the choice of settlement. This is the case even though the value of the alternative award is always £500 and does not depend on the share price (see 10.4 above).

In our view, it is necessary, as discussed in Example 34.61 above, to consider whether the entity's discretion to make an award of matching shares is real or not, this being a matter for judgement in the light of individual facts and circumstances.

If it is determined that the entity is effectively obliged to match any share award taken by the employee, then the award should be analysed as giving the employee the choice of settlement between:

- At the beginning of year 2: cash of £500, subject to service and performance during year 1; or
- At the beginning of year 2 shares with a value of £500 as at that date, subject to service and performance during year 1; and, at the end of year 3: the same number of shares again subject to (i) performance during year 1 and (ii) service during the three year period to the end of year 3.

In this case the grant date (and therefore measurement date) of all the equity awards would be taken as the beginning of year 1. As regards the award due to vest at the beginning of year 2, this would be split into its equity and liability components, and in this case the equity component would have a value of zero (since the two components are essentially worth the same amount of £500). Thus, the entity would accrue a liability during year 1. The matching share award would be expensed over the three year period to the end of year 3.

Thus, at the end of year 1, the entity will have recorded an IFRS 2 expense together with a corresponding:

- liability for the cost of the portion of the annual award that the employee may take in cash or equity (the liability component); and
- credit to equity for one-third of the cost of the matching award (the equity component).

If the employee decides to take shares at the beginning of year 2, the entity would simply transfer the amount recorded as a liability to equity and recognise the remaining cost of the matching shares over the following two years.

If, however, the employee elects to take cash, the position is more complicated. Clearly, the main accounting entry is to reduce the liability, with a corresponding reduction in cash, when the liability is settled. However, this raises the question of what is to be done with the one-third cost of the matching award already recognised in equity and the remaining, as yet unrecognised, two-thirds cost.

As in Example 34.63 above, an election by the employee for cash at the end of year 1 should be treated as a cancellation of the matching award, due to the employee's failure to fulfil a non-vesting condition (i.e. not taking the cash alternative) for the matching award – see 3.2 and 6.4 above. Therefore, the one-third cost that had already been expensed would not be reversed and the remaining two-thirds of the matching award not yet recognised would be recognised immediately, resulting in an expense for an award that does not actually crystallise.

If it is concluded that the entity has genuine discretion to make a matching award, the analysis is somewhat different.

The portion of the annual award that may be taken in shares should be analysed as giving the employee the choice, at the beginning of year 2, between cash of £500 and shares worth £500 (the number of shares being determined by reference to the share price at that date). This would be split into its equity and liability components, and in this case the equity component would have a value of zero (since the two components are essentially worth the same). Thus, the entity would accrue a liability during year 1. If the employee elected to receive shares, this liability would be transferred to equity.

Any matching share award would be treated as being granted on, and measured as at, the beginning of year 2. The cost would be recognised over the two year period from the beginning of year 2 to the end of year 3.

The discussion in 8.10 above is relevant to the valuation of the matching equity award.

Example 34.63 above discusses the accounting treatment in a situation where the employee fails to meet the service condition.

If, as is often the case in practice, the employee had to retain his original holding of shares and complete a further period of service in order for the matching award to vest, the requirement to retain the original shares would be treated as a non-vesting condition and taken into account in the grant date fair value of the matching award (see 6.4 above). Failure to meet this non-vesting condition, by disposing of the shares whilst remaining in employment during the matching period, would be treated as a cancellation of the matching award as holding the shares is a condition within the employee's control (see 6.4.3 above).

15.2 Loans to employees to purchase shares (limited recourse and full recourse loans)

In some jurisdictions, share awards to employees are made by means of so-called 'limited recourse loan' schemes. The detailed terms of such schemes vary, but typical features include the following:

- the entity makes an interest-free loan to the employee which is immediately used to acquire shares to the value of the loan on behalf of the employee;
- the shares may be held by the entity, or a trust controlled by it (see 12.3 above), until the loan is repaid;
- the employee is entitled to dividends, except that these are treated as paying off some of the outstanding loan;
- within a given period (say, five years) the employee must either have paid off the outstanding balance of the loan, at which point the shares are delivered to the employee, or surrendered the shares. Surrender of the shares by the employee is treated as discharging any outstanding amount on the loan, irrespective of the value of the shares.

The effect of such an arrangement is equivalent to an option exercisable within five years with an exercise price per share equal to the share price at grant date less total dividends since grant date – a view reinforced by the Interpretations Committee.[35] There is no real loan at the initial stage. The entity has no right to receive cash or another financial asset, since the loan can be settled by the employee returning the (fixed) amount of equity 'purchased' at grant date.

Indeed, the only true cash flow in the entire transaction is any amount paid at the final stage if the employee chooses to acquire the shares at that point. The fact that the exercise price is a factor of the share price at grant date and dividends paid between grant date and the date of repayment of the 'loan' is simply an issue for the valuation of the option.

The arrangement is valued using an option-pricing model and the fair value is based on the employee's implicit right to buy the shares at a future date rather than being the share price at grant date (the face value of the loan).

The loan arrangement might have a defined period during which the employee must remain in service (five years in the example above) and during which there might also be performance conditions to be met. Where this is the case, the IFRS 2 expense will be recognised by the entity over this period. However, where, as is frequently the case, such an award is subject to no future service or performance condition, i.e. the 'option' is, in effect, immediately exercisable by the employee should he choose to settle the 'loan', IFRS 2 requires the cost to be recognised in full at grant date (see 6.1 above).

There are also some arrangements where the loan to the employee to acquire the shares is a full recourse loan (i.e. it cannot be discharged simply by surrendering the shares and there can be recourse to other assets of the employee). However, the amount repayable on the loan is reduced not only by dividends paid on the shares, but also by the achievement of performance targets, such as the achievement of a given level of earnings.

The appropriate analysis of such awards is more difficult, as they could be viewed in two ways:

- either the employer has made a loan (which the employee has chosen to use to buy a share), accounted for under IFRS 9, and has then entered into a performance-related cash bonus arrangement with the employee, accounted for under IAS 19; or
- the transaction is a share option where the exercise price varies according to the satisfaction of performance conditions and the amount of dividends on the shares, accounted for under IFRS 2.

The different analyses give rise to potentially significantly different expenses. This will particularly be the case where one of the conditions for mitigation of the amount repayable on the loan is linked to the price of the employer's equity. As this is a market condition, the effect of accounting for the arrangement under IFRS 2 may be that an expense is recognised in circumstances where no expense would be recognised under IAS 19.

Such awards need to be carefully analysed, in the light of their particular facts and circumstances, in order to determine the appropriate treatment. Factors that could suggest that IFRS 2 is the more relevant standard would, in our view, include:

- the employee can use the loan only to acquire shares;
- the employee cannot trade the shares until the loan is discharged; or
- the entity has a practice of accepting (e.g. from leavers) surrender of the shares as full discharge for the amount outstanding on the loan and does not pursue any shortfall between the fair value of the shares and the amount owed by the employee. This would tend to indicate that, in substance, the loan is not truly full recourse.

15.3 Awards entitled to dividends or dividend equivalents during the vesting period

Some awards entitle the holder to receive dividends on unvested shares (or dividend equivalents on options) during the vesting period.

For example, in some jurisdictions, entities make awards of shares that are regarded as fully vested for the purposes of tax legislation (typically because the employee enjoys the full voting and dividend rights of the shares), but not for accounting purposes (typically because the shares are subject to forfeiture if a certain minimum service period is not achieved). In practice, the shares concerned are often held by an EBT until the potential forfeiture period has expired.

Another variant of such an award that is sometimes seen is where an entity grants an employee an option to acquire shares in the entity which can be exercised immediately. However, if the employee exercises the option but leaves within a certain minimum period from the grant date, he is required to sell back the share to the entity (typically either at the original exercise price, or the lower of that price or the market value of the share at the time of the buy-back – see also the discussions at 15.4.5 below).

Such awards do not fully vest for the purposes of IFRS 2 until the potential forfeiture or buy-back period has expired. The cost of such awards should therefore be recognised over this period.

This raises the question of the accounting treatment of any dividends paid to employees during the vesting period, either as a charge to profit or loss as employee costs or a return on an equity instrument. Conceptually, it could be argued that such dividends cannot be dividends for financial reporting purposes since the equity instruments to which they relate are not yet regarded as issued for financial reporting purposes. One consequence of this, is that shares subject to such an award are excluded from the number of ordinary shares outstanding for the purposes of calculating EPS in accordance with IAS 33. These dividend entitlements would, however they are accounted for, constitute a reduction in earnings available to ordinary shareholders when applying IAS 33 (which is discussed in Chapter 37). As it is argued that equity instruments to which the dividends relate are not yet regarded as issued for financial reporting purposes, this would lead to the conclusion that dividends paid in the vesting period should be charged to profit or loss as an employment cost.

However, the charge to be made for the award under IFRS 2 will already take account of the fact that the recipient is entitled to receive dividends during the vesting period. If the recipient is not entitled to receive dividends during the vesting period a discount would be reflected in the fair value of the award; if the recipient is entitled to dividends, no such adjustment is made (see 8.5.4 above). Thus, it could be argued that also to charge profit or loss with the dividends paid is a form of double counting. Moreover, whilst the relevant shares may not have been fully issued for financial reporting purposes, the basic IFRS 2 accounting does build up an amount in equity over the vesting period. It could therefore be argued that – conceptually, if not legally – any dividend paid relates not to an issued share, but rather to the equity instrument represented by the cumulative amount that has been recorded for the award as a credit to equity, and can therefore appropriately be shown as a deduction from equity.

The argument above is valid only to the extent that the credit to equity represents awards that are expected to vest. It cannot apply to dividends paid to employees whose awards are either known not to have vested or treated as expected not to vest when applying IFRS 2 (since there is no credit to equity for these awards). Accordingly, we believe that the most appropriate approach is to analyse the dividends paid so that, by the date of vesting, cumulative dividends paid on awards treated by IFRS 2 as vested are deducted from equity and those paid on awards treated by IFRS 2 as unvested are charged to profit or loss. The allocation for periods prior to vesting should be based on a best estimate of the final outcome, as illustrated by Example 34.65 below.

Example 34.65: Award with rights to receive (and retain) dividends during vesting period

An entity grants 100 free shares to each of its 500 employees. The shares are treated as fully vested for legal and tax purposes, so that the employees are eligible to receive any dividends paid. However, the shares will be forfeited if the employee leaves within three years of the award being made. Accordingly, for the purposes of IFRS 2, vesting is conditional upon the employee working for the entity over the next three years. The entity estimates that the fair value of each share (including the right to receive dividends during the IFRS 2 vesting period) is €15. Employees are entitled to retain any dividend received even if the award does not vest.

20 employees leave during the first year, and the entity's best estimate at the end of year 1 is that 75 employees will have left before the end of the vesting period. During the second year, a further 22 employees leave, and the entity revises its estimate of total employee departures over the vesting period from 75 to 60. During the third year, a further 15 employees leave. Hence, a total of 57 employees (20 + 22 + 15) forfeit their rights to the shares during the three year period, and a total of 44,300 shares (443 employees × 100 shares per employee) finally vest.

The entity pays dividends of €1 per share in year 1, €1.20 per share in year 2, and €1.50 in year 3.

Under IFRS 2, the entity will recognise the following amounts during the vesting period for services received as consideration for the shares.

Year	Calculation of cumulative expense	Cumulative expense (€)	Expense for period (€)
1	100 shares × 425 employees × €15 × 1/3	212,500	212,500
2	100 shares × 440 employees × €15 × 2/3	440,000	227,500
3	100 shares × 443 × €15 × 3/3	664,500	224,500

On the assumption that all employees who leave during a period do so on the last day of that period (and thus receive dividends paid in that period), in our view the dividends paid on the shares should be accounted for as follows:

		€	€
Year 1	Profit or loss (employee costs)[1]	7,500	
	Equity[1]	42,500	
	Cash[2]		50,000
Year 2	Profit or loss (employee costs)[3]	3,300	
	Equity[3]	54,300	
	Cash[4]		57,600
Year 3	Profit or loss (employee costs)[5]	1,590	
	Equity[5]	67,110	
	Cash[6]		68,700

1   20 employees have left and a further 55 are anticipated to leave. Dividends paid to those employees (100 shares × 75 employees × €1 = €7,500) are therefore recognised as an expense. Dividends paid to other employees are recognised as a reduction in equity.

2   100 shares × 500 employees × €1.

3   22 further employees have left and a further 18 are anticipated to leave. The cumulative expense for dividends paid to leavers and anticipated leavers should therefore be €10,800 (100 shares × 20 employees × €1 = €2,000 for leavers in year 1 + 100 shares × 40 employees × [€1 + €1.20] for leavers and anticipated leavers in year 2 = €8,800). €7,500 was charged in year 1, so the charge for year 2 should be €10,800 – €7,500 = €3,300. This could also have been calculated as charge for leavers and expected leavers in current year €4,800 (100 shares × 40 [22 + 18] employees × €1.20) less reversal of expense in year 1 for reduction in anticipated final number of leavers €1,500 (100 shares × 15 [75 – 60] employees × €1.00). Dividends paid to other employees are recognised as a reduction in equity.

4   100 shares × 480 employees in employment at start of year × €1.20.

5   15 further employees have left. The cumulative expense for dividends paid to leavers should therefore be €12,390 (€2,000 for leavers in year 1 (see 3 above) + 100 shares × 22 employees × [€1 + €1.20] = €4,840 for leavers in year 2 + 100 shares × 15 employees × [€1 + €1.20 + €1.50] = €5,550 for leavers in year 3). A cumulative expense of €10,800 (see 3 above) was recognised by the end of year 2, so the charge for year 3 should be €12,390 – €10,800 = €1,590. This could also have been calculated as charge for leavers in current year €2,250 (100 shares × 15 employees × €1.50) less reversal of expense in years 1 and 2 for reduction in final number of leavers as against estimate at end of year 2 €660 (100 shares × 3 [60 – 57] employees × [€1.00 + €1.20]). Dividends paid to other employees are recognised as a reduction in equity.

6   100 shares × 458 employees in employment at start of year × €1.50.

15.4 Awards vesting or exercisable on an exit event or change of control (flotation, trade sale etc.)

Entities frequently issue awards connected to a significant event such as a flotation, trade sale or other change of control of the business. It may be that an award that would otherwise be equity-settled automatically becomes cash-settled if such an event crystallises and the entity has no choice as to the method of settlement (as discussed at 10.3 above).

However, it may also be the case that an award vests only on such an event, which raises various issues of interpretation, as discussed below.

The sections below should be read together with the more general discussions elsewhere in this chapter (as referred to in the narrative below) on topics such as grant date, vesting period, vesting and non-vesting conditions and classification as equity-settled or cash-settled. References to flotation should be read as also including other exit events.

15.4.1 Grant date

Sometimes such awards are structured so that they will vest on flotation or so that they will vest on flotation subject to further approval at that time. For awards in the first category, grant date as defined in IFRS 2 will be the date on which the award is first communicated to employees (subject to the normal requirements of IFRS 2 relating to a shared understanding, offer and acceptance, as discussed at 5.3 above). For awards in the second category, grant date will be at or around the date of flotation, when the required further approval is given.

This means that the IFRS 2 cost of awards subject to final approval at flotation will generally be significantly higher than that of awards that do not require such approval. Moreover, as discussed further at 5.3.2 above, it may well be the case that employees begin rendering service for such awards before grant date (e.g. from the date on which the entity communicates its intention to make the award in principle). In that case, the entity would need to make an initial estimate of the value of the award for the purpose of recognising an expense from the date services have been provided, and continually re-assess that value up until the actual IFRS 2 grant date. As with any award dependent on a non-market vesting condition, an expense would be recognised only to the extent that the award is considered likely to vest. The classification of a requirement to float as a non-market vesting condition is discussed further at 15.4.3 below.

15.4.2 Vesting period

Many awards that vest on flotation have a time limit – in other words, the award lapses if flotation has not occurred on or before a given future date. In principle, as discussed at 6.2.3 above, when an award has a variable vesting period due to a non-market performance condition, the reporting entity should make a best estimate of the likely vesting period at each reporting date and calculate the IFRS 2 charge on the basis of that best estimate.

In practice, the likely timing of a future flotation is notoriously difficult to assess months, let alone years, in advance. In such cases, it would generally be acceptable simply to recognise the cost over the full potential vesting period until there is real clarity that a shorter period may be more appropriate. However, in making the assessment of the likelihood of vesting, it is important to take the company's circumstances into account. The likelihood of an exit event in the short- to medium-term is perhaps greater for a company owned by private equity investors seeking a return on their investment than for a long-established family-owned company considering a flotation.

It is worth noting that once an exit event becomes likely, the IFRS 2 expense will in some cases need to be recognised over a shorter vesting period than was originally envisaged as the probability of the exit event occurring will form the basis at the reporting date of the estimate of the number of awards expected to vest (see also the discussion at 6.2.3 and 7.6 above).

This contrasts with the US GAAP approach where, in practice, an exit event that is a change in control or an initial public offering is only recognised when it occurs. In a situation where a change in control or an initial public offering occurs shortly after the reporting date, it is therefore possible that the expense will need to be recognised in an earlier period under IFRS than under US GAAP.

15.4.3 Is flotation or sale a vesting condition or a non-vesting condition?

There was debate in the past about whether a requirement for a flotation or sale to occur in order for an award to vest was a vesting condition or a non-vesting condition. The argument for it being a non-vesting condition was that flotation or sale may occur irrespective of the performance of the entity. The counter-argument was essentially that the price achieved on flotation or sale, which typically affects the ultimate value of the award (see 15.4.4 below), reflects the performance of the entity and is therefore a non-market performance condition (provided there is an associated service condition – see further below).

As part of its wider project on vesting and non-vesting conditions, the Interpretations Committee reached a tentative decision in July 2010 that a condition requiring an initial public offering (IPO) or a change of control should be deemed to be a performance vesting condition rather than a non-vesting condition. This was subsequently reflected in general terms through the IASB's amendments to the definition of a performance condition in the *Annual Improvements to IFRSs 2010-2012 Cycle* (see 3.1 and 3.2 above). The amendments were intended, *inter alia*, to make clear that a requirement for flotation or sale (with an associated service condition) is a performance condition rather than a non-vesting condition on the basis that the flotation or sale condition is by reference to the entity's own operations.

The amendments also made it clear that a performance target period cannot extend beyond the end of the associated service period in order for the definition of a performance vesting condition to be met (see 3.2.2 above). Therefore, the flotation or sale condition will be treated as a non-vesting condition, rather than as a vesting condition, if the service period is not at least as long as the duration of the flotation or sale condition.

It is possible that in a share-based payment transaction a flotation or sale condition can be both a performance vesting condition and a non-vesting condition in an award that vests in instalments, 'graded vesting' (see 6.2.2 above). Where the share-based payment transaction vests in instalments and the service period is not at least as long as the duration of the flotation or sale condition, that condition will be treated as a non-vesting condition (see 3.2 above). In contrast, when the service condition is the same duration as the flotation and sale condition, that condition will be treated as non-market performance condition (see 3.1 above), this is illustrated in Example 34.66 below:

Example 34.66: Award vesting in instalments with a floatation or sale condition

An entity issues an award to employees at the beginning of year 1 with gradual vesting over five years. The award will vest 20 per cent in each year of service over the five year period. In addition to the service condition there is a flotation or sale condition that must be met at the end of year 5. As discussed at 6.2.2 above, the award that vests in instalments will be treated as five different tranches because each tranche has a different vesting period with different fair values. The flotation or sale condition will be a non-vesting condition and factored in the grant date fair value of tranches 1 to 4 as the service period is not as long as the duration of the flotation or sale condition. However, for tranche 5, the service and performance conditions are for the same duration, therefore the flotation or sale condition will be treated as a non-market performance condition and not factored into the grant date fair value but factored into the number of awards that will vest for tranche 5.

The impact of treating the flotation or sale condition differently, results in an expense being recognised for the first four tranches regardless of the flotation or sale condition being met, so long as the service condition is met, as the likelihood of not meeting the flotation or sale condition is factored into the grant date fair value. In contrast for tranche 5 if the floatation or service condition is not met but the service condition is met, no expense will be recognised as the non-market performance condition has not been met.

The floatation or sale condition even though is deemed to relate to the entity's own operations and therefore generally classified as a performance condition, it will sometimes be concluded that fulfilment of the condition is outside the control of both the entity and the counterparty. The settlement of an award in equity or cash might depend on the outcome of the condition i.e. there might be either cash- or equity-settlement that is entirely contingent on the exit event. Such contingent arrangements are discussed at 10.3 above.

15.4.4 Awards requiring achievement of a minimum price on flotation or sale

Some awards with a condition dependent on flotation (or another similar event) vest only if a minimum price per share is achieved. For example, an entity might grant all its employees share options, the vesting of which is conditional upon a flotation or sale of the shares at a price of at least €5 per share within five years, and the employee still being in employment at the time of the flotation or sale.

Taken alone, the requirement for a flotation or sale to occur is a non-market performance condition (see further below and at 15.4.3 above). However, if a minimum market price has to be achieved, the question arises as to whether, in addition to the service requirement, such an award comprises:

- a single market performance condition (i.e. float or sell within five years at a share price of at least €5); or
- two conditions:
  - a market performance condition (share price at time of flotation or sale of at least €5); and
  - a non-market performance condition (flotation or sale achieved within five years).

The significance of this is the issue discussed at 6.3 above, namely that an expense must always be recognised for all awards with a market condition, if all the non-market vesting conditions are satisfied, even if the market condition is not. In either case, however, there is a market condition which needs to be factored into the valuation of the award.

If the view is that 'flotation or sale at €5 within five years' is a single market condition, the entity will recognise an expense for the award for all employees still in service at the end of the five year period, since the sole non-market vesting condition (i.e. service) will have been met. Note that this assumes that the full five-year period is considered the most likely vesting period at grant date (see 6.3.4 and 15.4.2 above).

If, on the other hand, the view is that 'flotation or sale within five years' and 'flotation or sale share price €5' are two separate conditions, and no flotation or sale occurs, no expense will be recognised since the performance element of the non-market vesting condition (i.e. 'flotation or sale within five years') has not been satisfied. However, even on this second analysis, if a sale or flotation is achieved at a price less than €5, an expense must be recognised, even though the award does not truly vest, since the non-market condition (i.e. 'flotation or sale within five years' with its associated service requirement) will have been met.

In our view, the appropriate analysis is to regard 'flotation or sale within five years' and 'flotation or sale share price €5' as two separate conditions.

The example above assumes that there is a service condition equal in duration to the other conditions attached to the award and hence the analysis above only considers vesting conditions. If the fact pattern were such that there was no service condition, or a service condition that was of a shorter duration than the other conditions, then those conditions would need to be treated as non-vesting conditions rather than as performance vesting conditions (see 3.1 and 3.2 above and Example 34.66 above).

15.4.5 Awards 'purchased for fair value'

As noted at 2.2.4.D above, entities that are contemplating a flotation or trade sale may invite employees to subscribe for shares (often a special class of share) for a relatively nominal amount. In the event of a flotation or trade sale occurring, these shares may be sold or will be redeemable at a substantial premium. It is often argued that the initial subscription price paid represents the fair value of the share at the time, given the inherent high uncertainty as to whether a flotation or trade sale will in fact occur.

The premium paid on the shares in the event of a flotation or trade sale will typically be calculated in part by reference to the price achieved. The question therefore arises as to whether such awards fall within the scope of IFRS 2. It might be argued for example that, as the employee paid full fair value for the award at issue, there has been no share-based payment and, accordingly, the instrument should be accounted for under IAS 32 and IFRS 9.

In our view, in order to determine whether the arrangement falls within the scope of IFRS 2, it is necessary to consider whether the award has features that would not be expected in 'normal' equity transactions – in particular, a requirement for the holder of the shares to remain in employment until flotation or sale and/or individual buyback arrangements. If this is the case, regardless of the amount subscribed, the terms suggest that the shares are being awarded in connection with, and in return for, employee services and hence that the award is within the scope of IFRS 2. This may mean that, even if the award has no material fair value once the subscription price has been taken into account (and therefore gives rise to no IFRS 2 expense), it may be necessary to make the disclosures required by IFRS 2.

Moreover, even if the amount paid by the employees can be demonstrated to be fair value for tax or other purposes, that amount would not necessarily constitute fair value under IFRS 2. Specifically, a 'true' fair value would take into account non-market vesting conditions (such as a requirement for the employee to remain in employment until flotation or a trade sale occurs). However, a valuation for IFRS 2 purposes would not take such conditions into account (see 5.5 and 6.2.1 above) and would therefore typically be higher than the 'true' fair value.

If the arrangement relates to a special class of share rather than ordinary equity shares, the underlying shares might well be classified as a liability rather than as equity under IAS 32. However, if the redemption amount is linked to the flotation price of the 'real' equity, the arrangement will be a cash-settled share-based payment transaction under IFRS 2 (see 2.2.4.A above).

It is common in such situations for the cost of satisfying any obligations to the special shareholders to be borne by shareholders rather than by the entity itself. This raises a number of further issues, which are discussed at 2.2.2.A above and at 15.4.6 below.

The approach outlined in this section, i.e. that there will generally be no additional IFRS 2 expense to recognise when the counterparty subscribes for a share at fair value, is the approach most commonly applied in practice by entities accounting under IFRS. In this type of arrangement, the subscription price, or market value if lower, is often refundable to employees who leave employment before the shares vest. In such cases, subscription amounts paid by the counterparty for the shares are generally classified as a liability by the entity until such time as the shares finally vest (at which point the cash paid will be treated as the proceeds of issuing shares).

However, this is not the only approach seen in practice. US GAAP, for example, requires in certain circumstances the recognition of an expense (representing the amount potentially at risk) in cases where an employee subscribes for a share at fair value but risks forfeiting some, or all, of the price paid for that share, together with any subsequent increases in value, should he fail to fulfil the service condition. In determining whether an expense must be recognised for the amount risked by the employee, an entity applying US GAAP must establish that there is a clear business purpose for the employee taking such a risk. In our view, in the absence of specific guidance, the recognition of such an expense is not a requirement based on IFRS 2 as currently drafted.

15.4.6 'Drag along' and 'tag along' rights

An award might be structured to allow management of an entity to acquire a special class of equity at fair value (as in 15.4.5 above), but (in contrast to 15.4.5 above) with no redemption right on an exit event. However, rights are given:

- to any buyer of the 'normal' equity also to buy the special shares (sometimes called a 'drag along' right);
- to a holder of the special shares to require any buyer of the 'normal' equity also to buy the special shares (sometimes called a 'tag along' right).

Such schemes are particularly found in entities where the 'normal' equity is held by a provider of venture capital, which will generally be looking for an exit in the medium term.

It may well be that, under the scheme, the entity itself is required to facilitate the operation of the drag along or tag along rights, which may involve the entity collecting the proceeds from the buyer and passing them on to the holder of the special shares.

This raises the issue of whether such an arrangement is equity-settled or cash-settled. The fact that, in certain circumstances, the entity is required to deliver cash to the holder of a share suggests that the arrangement is an award requiring cash settlement in specific circumstances, the treatment of which is discussed at 10.3 above.

However, if the terms of the award are such that the entity is obliged to pass on cash to the holder of the share only if, and to the extent that, proceeds are received from an external buyer, in our view, the arrangement may be economically no different to the broker settlement arrangements typically entered into by listed entities, as discussed at 9.2.4 above. This could allow the arrangement to be regarded as equity-settled because the entity's only involvement as a principal is in the initial delivery of shares to employees, provided that consideration is given to all the factors (discussed at 9.2.4 above) that could suggest that the scheme is more appropriately regarded as cash-settled.

In making such an assessment, care needs to be taken to ensure that the precise facts of the arrangement are considered. For example, a transaction where the entity has some discretion over the amount of proceeds attributable to each class of shareholder might indicate that it is inappropriate to treat the entity simply as an agent in the cash payment arrangement. It might also be relevant to consider the extent to which, under relevant local law, the proceeds received can be 'ring fenced' so as not to be available to settle other liabilities of the entity.

It is also the case that arrangements that result in employees obtaining similar amounts of cash can be interpreted very differently under IFRS 2 depending on how the arrangement is structured and whether, for example:

- the entity is required to pay its employees cash on an exit (having perhaps held shares itself via a trust and those shares having been subject to 'drag along' rights); or
- the employees themselves have held the right to equity shares on a restricted basis with vesting – and 'drag along' rights – taking effect on a change of control and the employees receiving cash for their shares.

The appropriate accounting treatment in such cases requires a significant amount of judgement based on the precise facts and circumstances.

15.5 South African black economic empowerment ('BEE') and similar arrangements

As part of general economic reforms in South Africa, arrangements – commonly referred to as black economic empowerment or 'BEE' deals – have been put in place to encourage the transfer of equity, or economic interests in equity, to historically disadvantaged individuals. Similar arrangements have also been put in place in other jurisdictions. These arrangements are intended to give disadvantaged individuals, or entities controlled by disadvantaged individuals, a means of meaningful participation in the economy.

An entity can enhance its BEE status in a number of ways (through employment equity, skills development or preferential procurement policies to name but a few). This section focuses on BEE deals involving transfers of equity instruments, or interests in equity instruments, to historically disadvantaged individuals at a discount to fair value.

Such transfers have generally been concluded at a discount to the fair value of the equity instruments concerned, even where the fair value takes into account any restrictions on these equity instruments. As a result of having empowered shareholders, the reporting entity is able to claim its 'BEE credentials', thus allowing the reporting entity greater business opportunities in the South African economy. These arrangements raise a number of practical issues of interpretation, and indeed led to the scope of IFRS 2 being extended to include transactions where the consideration received appears less than the consideration given, as discussed further at 2.2.2.C above.

The goods or services received from the disadvantaged people or entities controlled by them in return for the equity instruments may or may not be specifically identifiable. As explained in guidance issued by the South African Institute of Chartered Accountants (SAICA),[36] it is therefore the case that IFRS 2 applies to the accounting for BEE transactions where the fair value of cash and other assets received is less than the fair value of equity instruments granted to the BEE partner, i.e. to the BEE equity credentials.

BEE deals are typically complex and their specific structures and terms may vary considerably. However, they do exhibit certain features with some regularity, as discussed below.

Typically BEE arrangements have involved the transfer of equity instruments to:
- empowerment companies controlled by prominent BEE qualifying individuals;
- BEE qualifying employees of the reporting entity; or
- beneficiaries in the BEE qualifying communities in which the entity operates.

The arrangements generally lock the parties in for a minimum specified period and if they want to withdraw they are able to sell their interest only to others with qualifying BEE credentials, usually with the lock-in provision also transferred to the buyer.

Generally these individuals have not been able to raise sufficient finance in order to purchase the equity instruments. Accordingly, the reporting entity often facilitates the transaction and assists the BEE party in securing the necessary financing.

A BEE arrangement often involves the creation of a trust or corporate entity, with the BEE party holding beneficial rights in the trust which in turn holds equity instruments of the reporting entity (or a member of its group).

The awards made by the trust may be in the form of:
- the equity instruments originally transferred to the trust;
- units in the trust itself, usually with a value linked in some way to the value of the equity instruments of the reporting entity originally transferred to the trust; or
- payments made from the proceeds (dividends received, sale of equity instruments etc.) that the trust generates.

The accounting issues arising from such schemes include:
- the nature of the trust (specifically, whether it meets the criteria for consolidation by the reporting entity);
- whether any charge arises under IFRS 2 and, if so, the grant date and therefore, under a grant date model, the amount of the charge; and
- whether awards are equity-settled or cash-settled.

15.5.1 Nature of the trust

The first issue to consider in any accounting analysis is whether any trust to which the equity instruments of the reporting entity have been transferred meets the requirements for consolidation by the reporting entity under IFRS 10 (see Chapter 6). Factors that may indicate that the trust should be consolidated include:

- the reporting entity is involved in the design of the trust and the trust deed at inception, the intention being that the design is such that the desired BEE credentials are obtained;
- the potential beneficiaries of the trust are restricted to persons in the employment of, or otherwise providing services to, the reporting entity;
- the reporting entity has a commitment to ensure that the trust operates as designed in order to maintain its BEE credentials;
- the reporting entity has the right to control (on 'autopilot' or otherwise), or does in practice control, the management of the trust; or
- the relevant activities of the trust are to service the loan and to make distributions to the beneficiaries in line with the trust deed,

but all the IFRS 10 control criteria will need to be assessed.

The generic form of a BEE arrangement normally requires the reporting entity either to finance the acquisition of the shares by the trust or to provide cross guarantees to the financiers of the trust. Alternative methodologies that have been employed include capital enhancements created in the trust by the sale of equity instruments at a severely discounted amount.

When the reporting entity finances the arrangement, the finance is generally interest-free or at a lower than market interest rate. The debt is serviced with the dividends received and, at the end of the repayment period, any outstanding balance can be treated in various ways; refinanced or waived by the reporting entity, or settled by the return of a number of shares equal to the outstanding value.

In summary, the BEE party generally injects only a notional amount of capital into the trust, which obtains financing to acquire the shares in the reporting entity and uses the dividend cash flows to service the debt it has raised. In such generic schemes, the BEE party faces a typical option return profile: the maximum amount of capital at risk is notional and the potential upside increase in value of the shares of the reporting entity accrues to the BEE party through the party's beneficial rights in the trust.

15.5.2 Measurement and timing of the accounting cost

If the analysis under 15.5.1 above is that the trust should be consolidated, the transfer of equity instruments to that entity is essentially the same as a transfer of own equity to an employee benefit trust, as discussed at 12.3 above. Such a transfer, considered alone, is an intra-entity transaction and therefore does not give rise to a charge under IFRS 2. The equity instruments held by the trust are therefore treated as treasury shares, and no non-controlling interests are recognised.

It is only when the trust itself makes an award to a third party that a charge arises, which will be measured at the time at which the grant to the third party occurs. In a rising stock market this will lead to a higher charge than would have occurred had there been a grant, as defined in IFRS 2, on the date that the equity instruments were originally transferred to the trust. Generally, the value of the award is based on an option pricing model and the BEE party is treated as the holder of an option.

Where the trust is not consolidated, the presumption will be that the transfer of equity instruments to the trust crystallises an IFRS 2 charge at the date of transfer. However, it is important to consider the terms of the transaction in their totality. For example, if the entity has the right to buy back the equity instruments at some future date, the benefit transferred may in fact be an economic interest in the equity instruments for a limited period. This may, depending on the method used to determine the buy-back price, influence the measurement of any IFRS 2 charge (which would normally be based on the presumption that the benefits of a vested share had been passed in perpetuity).

Some have sought to argue that BEE credentials result in the recognition of an intangible asset rather than an expense. In order to be recognised as an asset, an entity must have control over the resource as a result of a past event. Paragraphs 13 and 16 of IAS 38 – *Intangible Assets* – indicate that control over an intangible asset may be evidenced in two ways:

- as legal rights that are enforceable by law; or
- as exchange transactions for the same or similar non-contractual customer relationships.

In BEE transactions, a contract is usually entered into with a BEE partner. The contract between the entity and the BEE partner may include a contractual lock-in period or a clause that only allows the transfer of such equity instruments to another BEE partner, usually with the lock-in provision also transferred to the buyer. However, the contract does not provide the entity with legal rights that give it the power to obtain the future economic benefits arising from the BEE transaction, nor the ability to restrict the access of others to those benefits. Therefore, BEE credentials do not qualify for recognition of intangible assets and the difference between the fair value of the award and the consideration received should be expensed. This is consistent with guidance issued by SAICA.[37]

An issue to be considered in determining the timing of the IFRS 2 expense is that many BEE transactions require the BEE party to be 'locked into' the transaction for a pre-determined period. During this period the BEE party or trust is generally prohibited from selling or transferring the equity instruments. As no specific performance is generally required during this period, it is not considered part of the vesting period (see 3.3 and 6.1 above). Rather, the post-vesting restrictions would be taken into account in calculating the fair value of the equity instruments (see 8.4.1 above). This is illustrated in the following example (based in part on Example 5 in the SAICA guidance).

Example 34.67: Receipt of BEE credentials with no service or performance condition

Entity A grants shares with a fair value of $1,000,000 to a BEE consortium for no consideration. As a result of the BEE ownership entity A obtains BEE credentials. The BEE consortium are entitled to the shares immediately and not required to perform any services to entity A nor are any performance conditions required to be met. However, in order to secure the BEE credentials, the consortium may not sell their shares for a period of 7 years from grant date.

In this transaction shares have been issued at a discount to fair value in return for BEE credentials and would fall into the scope of IFRS 2. As there is neither a service nor a performance condition, the fair value of the shares given should be expensed at grant date. The restriction on the transfer of the shares would be treated as a post-vesting restriction and taken into account when estimating the fair value of the equity instruments granted. If the shares in this example were listed, the listed price would not necessarily be the fair value as the fair value would need to be adjusted for the restriction of transfer.

15.5.3 Classification of awards as equity- or cash-settled

Certain schemes, particularly where the reporting entity is not listed, give the BEE party the right to put the shares back to the entity (or another group entity) after a certain date. This is often done to create liquidity for the BEE parties, should they decide to exit the scheme. Such a feature would require the scheme to be classified as cash-settled (see 9.1 above).

Similarly, where the BEE transaction is facilitated through a trust, the trust may have granted awards to beneficiaries in the form of units in the trust. The trustees may have the power to reacquire units from beneficiaries in certain circumstances (e.g. where the beneficiaries are employees, when they leave the employment of the entity). Where the trust does not have sufficient cash with which to make such payments, the reporting entity may be obliged, legally or constructively, to fund them.

Such arrangements may – in their totality – create a cash-settled scheme from the perspective of the reporting entity. In analysing a particular scheme, it should be remembered that, under IFRS 2, cash-settled schemes arise not only from legal liabilities, but also from constructive or commercial liabilities (e.g. to prevent a former employee having rights against what is essentially an employee trust) – see 10.2 above.

Finally, a transaction may be structured in such a way that the trust holds equity instruments of the reporting entity for an indefinite period. Dividends received by the trust may be used to fund certain expenses in a particular community in which the reporting entity operates (e.g. tuition fees for children of the reporting entity's employees or the costs of certain community projects). The scheme may even make provision for the shares to be sold after a certain period with the eventual proceeds being distributed amongst members of the community.

In such a case it is necessary to consider the nature of the distribution requirement and whether or not the reporting entity (through the trust) has a legal or constructive obligation under the scheme to make cash payments based on the price or value of the shares held by the trust. Where there is such an obligation, the arrangement would be classified as a cash-settled scheme. If however the trust merely acts as a conduit through which:

- dividend receipts by the trust are paid out to beneficiaries with the shares never leaving the trust; or
- proceeds from the sale of shares are distributed to beneficiaries,

the precise terms of the arrangement should be assessed to determine whether or not the arrangement meets the definition of a cash-settled share-based payment (see 15.4.6 above for a discussion of similar considerations in the context of 'drag along' and 'tag along' rights).

Any dividend payments by the Group for the period that the trust is consolidated should be treated as an equity distribution or as an expense, as appropriate, in accordance with the principles discussed at 15.3 above.

15.6 Shares used as a currency of payment

Settlement of share-based payment arrangements can take many forms, and in some instances the market value of shares is used as currency to settle the share-based payment transaction. IFRS 2 contains little guidance on how to measure such arrangements. Awards of equity instruments to a fixed monetary value, as discussed above at 8.10, is one example where the market value of the equity instrument at vesting date is used as a currency to settle an award to a fixed value. An award issued to employees of a subsidiary or business unit which is settled by reference to the fair value of shares in another group entity is another example where the market value of shares is used as a currency to settle the share-based payment transaction (see discussion below).

15.6.1 Awards assessed on the market value of a subsidiary or business unit and settled by reference to the fair value of shares in the parent entity

Some entities implement share-based remuneration schemes which aim to reward employees by reference to the 'market' value of the equity of the business unit for which they work as long as service conditions are met. This may arise where the Group might consider the parent's share price to be a somewhat blunt instrument for measuring the performance of the employees of a particular subsidiary or business unit. Indeed, it is not difficult to imagine situations in which a particular subsidiary might perform well but the parent's share price might be dragged down by other factors, or conversely where the parent's share price might rise notwithstanding poor results for that subsidiary. The detail of such schemes varies, but they generally take the form as follows:

- at grant date, the employee is awarded a (real or notional) holding in the equity of the employing subsidiary, the market value of which is measured at grant date and the listed parent will convert the market value of those subsidiary shares at vesting date, into equal value of parent shares to settle the award (scenario 1); or

- the employee is granted an award of as many shares of the listed parent as have a value, at a specified future date (often at, or shortly after, the end of the vesting period but sometimes at a later date), equal to the increase over the vesting period in the market value of the employee's (notional) holding in the equity of the employing subsidiary, otherwise known as share-settled share appreciation rights (akin to an option granted to the employee that is settled in the parent's shares) (scenario 2).

In the two scenarios above, the parent's shares are used as a currency to settle an arrangement with the subsidiary employees that is not dependent on the parent's share price. The share price of the parent's shares is used to determine the number of parent shares that will be issued on settlement. Put another away, the parent's share price (either at grant date or subsequently) should not affect measurement of the award (see 8.10 above).

After grant date, IFRS 2 requires remeasurement of an equity-settled share-based payment transaction only for changes in the service condition being met and other non-market vesting conditions. There is no remeasurement after grant date for market vesting conditions and non-vesting conditions. Therefore, an important feature in accounting for the awards in the scenarios outlined above is to assess, whether the basis on which the subsidiary equity is valued truly yields a market price (or value) to determine the type of performance conditions attached to the awards.

If the basis on which the subsidiary equity is valued yields a 'market value', the awards in the two scenarios are considered as containing only a service condition, and those awards would not be considered as containing a non-market vesting condition or market vesting condition (there is no specific target share price to be achieved). The awards are measured at grant date using valuation inputs related to the subsidiary's share price and are not remeasured. The fair value at vesting date is used as a conversion feature to determine the number of parent shares to be received as an exit mechanism, and the employee is receiving 'value for value'. The expense recognised is only adjusted for the failure to meet vesting conditions other than market conditions (e.g. service conditions).

If the 'market value' of the subsidiary is based on a constant formula (e.g. an EBITDA multiple), an assessment is required whether that formula provides a good surrogate for the market value of the subsidiary on an ongoing basis (see 2.2.4.F above). If deemed not to provide a good surrogate for the market value, the awards outlined in the scenarios above could then be considered as containing a non-market vesting condition and the expense recognised would be equal to the number of equity instruments that vest (see 3.1 above). If the formula used to determine the number of shares to be awarded can be determined sometime after the employee has satisfied the service vesting condition then the formula driven condition would be treated as a non-vesting condition (see 3.2 above). In contrast to the approach used to measure the non-market vesting condition, the non-vesting condition is taken into account in estimating the fair value of the award granted and not subsequently remeasured. The expense recognised is only adjusted for the failure to meet vesting conditions other than market conditions (e.g. service conditions).

16 FIRST-TIME ADOPTION AND TRANSITIONAL PROVISIONS

16.1 First-time adoption provisions

The requirements of IFRS 1 – *First-time Adoption of International Financial Reporting Standards* – in relation to share-based payment arrangements are discussed in Chapter 5 at 5.3. However, one provision may remain relevant for entities that have already adopted IFRS and would no longer generally be considered 'first-time adopters'.

IFRS 1 does not require an entity to account for equity-settled transactions:

- granted on or before 7 November 2002; or
- granted after 7 November 2002 but vested before the later of the date of transition to IFRS and 1 January 2005.

However, where such an award is modified, cancelled or settled, the rules regarding modification, cancellation and settlement (see 7 above) apply in full unless the modification occurred before the date of transition to IFRS. *[IFRS 1.D2]*. The intention of this provision is to prevent an entity from avoiding the recognition of a cost for a new award by structuring it as a modification to an earlier award not in the scope of IFRS 2.

There is slight ambiguity on this point in the wording of IFRS 1, paragraph D2 of which refers only to the modification of such awards. However, paragraph D2 also requires an entity to apply 'paragraphs 26-29' of IFRS 2 to 'modified' awards. Paragraphs 26-29 deal not only with modification but also with cancellation and settlement, and indeed paragraphs 28 and 29 are not relevant to modification at all. This makes it clear, in our view, that the IASB intended IFRS 1 to be applied not only to the modification but also to the cancellation and settlement of such awards.

References

1. *Amendment to International Financial Reporting Standards: IFRS 2 Share-based Payment – Vesting Conditions and Cancellations*, IASB, January 2008 ('January 2008 amendment').
2. *Group Cash-settled Share-based Payment Transactions, Amendments to IFRS 2*, IASB, June 2009 ('June 2009 amendment').
3. *Classification and Measurement of Share-based Payment Transactions, Amendments to IFRS 2*, IASB, June 2016 ('June 2016 amendments').
4. *Amendments to References to the Conceptual Framework in IFRS Standards*, IASB, March 2018.
5. *IASB Update*, May 2015.
6. *IASB Update*, November 2015.
7. Agenda Paper 16, IASB, November 2015.
8. *IASB Update*, May 2016.
9. Project Summary, Share-based payment – Research on sources of accounting complexity, IASB, 31 October 2018.
10. *Financial Instruments with Characteristics of Equity*, Discussion Paper, IASB, June 2018.
11. *IFRIC Update*, March 2013.
12. *IFRIC Update*, July 2014.
13. Accounting Standards Update 2014-12, FASB, *Accounting for Share-Based Payments When the Terms of an Award Provide That a Performance Target Could Be Achieved after the Requisite Service Period (Topic 718)*.
14. *IASB Update*, November 2013.
15. *IFRIC Update*, July 2010 and September 2010.
16. 'Contingent feature' is not a defined term in IFRS 2 but is used in the September 2011 IASB Agenda Paper 7D (para. 49) to refer to a condition not currently defined in IFRS 2.
17. *IFRIC Update*, November 2010 and March 2011.
18. *IASB Update*, September 2011.
19. *IASB Update*, May 2016.
20. FASB Accounting Standard Update 2018-07, *Improvements to Nonemployee Share-Based Payment Accounting (Topic 718)*.
21. FASB ASC 718 – *Compensation – Stock Compensation* (formerly FAS123(R), *Share-Based Payment*), FASB, December 2004.
22. Project Summary, Share-based payment – Research on sources of accounting complexity, IASB, 31 October 2018.
23. *IFRIC Update*, July 2006.
24. *IFRIC Update*, March 2011.
25. FASB Staff Position 123(R)-4, *Classification of Options and Similar Instruments Issued as Employee Compensation That Allow for Cash Settlement upon the Occurrence of a Contingent Event*.
26. FASB ASC 718 – *Compensation – Stock Compensation* (formerly FAS123(R), *Share-Based Payment*), FASB, December 2004, para. 32, footnote 18a.
27. *IASB Update*, September 2011.
28. *IFRIC Update*, May 2013.
29. *IFRIC Update*, September 2013.
30. *IFRIC Update*, September 2013.
31. *IASB Update*, February 2014.
32. *IASB Update*, April 2014.
33. D17 – *IFRS 2 – Group and Treasury Share Transactions*, IASB, 2005, para. IE5.
34. *IFRIC Update*, May 2013.
35. *IFRIC Update*, November 2005.
36. Financial Reporting Guide 2 – *Accounting for Black Economic Empowerment (BEE) Transactions*, Accounting Practices Committee (APC) of SAICA, December 2012.
37. Financial Reporting Guide 2 – *Accounting for Black Economic Empowerment (BEE) Transactions*, Accounting Practices Committee (APC) of SAICA, December 2012.

Chapter 35 — Employee benefits

1	INTRODUCTION		2891
2	OBJECTIVE AND SCOPE OF IAS 19		2891
	2.1	Objective	2891
	2.2	Scope	2892
		2.2.1 General scope requirements of IAS 19	2892
		2.2.2 Employee benefits settled by a shareholder or another group entity	2893
3	PENSIONS AND OTHER POST-EMPLOYMENT BENEFITS – DEFINED CONTRIBUTION AND DEFINED BENEFIT PLANS		2894
	3.1	The distinction between defined contribution plans and defined benefit plans	2894
	3.2	Insured benefits	2896
	3.3	Multi-employer plans	2898
		3.3.1 Multi-employer plans other than plans sharing risks between entities under common control	2898
		3.3.1.A The treatment of multi-employer plans	2898
		3.3.1.B What to do when 'sufficient information' becomes available	2899
		3.3.1.C Withdrawal from or winding up of a multi-employer scheme	2900
		3.3.2 Defined benefit plans sharing risks between entities under common control	2900
	3.4	State plans	2901
	3.5	Plans that would be defined contribution plans but for the existence of a minimum return guarantee	2902
	3.6	Death-in-service benefits	2903
4	DEFINED CONTRIBUTION PLANS		2906
	4.1	General accounting requirements	2906

		4.2	Defined contribution plans with vesting conditions	2907
5	**DEFINED BENEFIT PLANS – GENERAL**			2907
6	**DEFINED BENEFIT PLANS – PLAN ASSETS**			2908
	6.1	Definition of plan assets		2908
	6.2	Measurement of plan assets		2910
	6.3	Qualifying insurance policies		2910
	6.4	Reimbursement rights		2910
	6.5	Contributions to defined benefit funds		2910
	6.6	Longevity swaps		2911
7	**DEFINED BENEFIT PLANS – PLAN LIABILITIES**			2912
	7.1	Legal and constructive obligations		2912
	7.2	Contributions by employees and third parties		2913
	7.3	Actuarial methodology		2917
	7.4	Attributing benefit to years of service		2918
	7.5	Actuarial assumptions		2922
	7.6	Discount rate		2924
		7.6.1	High quality corporate bonds	2926
		7.6.2	No deep market	2927
	7.7	Frequency of valuations		2928
8	**DEFINED BENEFIT PLANS – TREATMENT OF THE PLAN SURPLUS OR DEFICIT IN THE STATEMENT OF FINANCIAL POSITION**			2929
	8.1	Net defined benefit liability (asset)		2929
	8.2	Restriction of assets to their recoverable amounts		2929
		8.2.1	IFRIC Interpretation 14 – general requirements concerning the limit on a defined benefit asset	2931
		8.2.2	Economic benefits available as reduced future contributions when there are no minimum funding requirements for future service	2932
		8.2.3	IFRIC Interpretation 14 – the effect of a minimum funding requirement on the economic benefit available as a reduction in future contributions	2933
		8.2.4	IFRIC Interpretation 14 – when a minimum funding requirement may give rise to a liability	2936
		8.2.5	Pension funding payments contingent on future events within the control of the entity	2938
9	**DEFINED BENEFIT PLANS – PRESENTATION OF THE NET DEFINED BENEFIT LIABILITY (ASSET)**			2939
10	**DEFINED BENEFIT PLANS – TREATMENT IN PROFIT OR LOSS AND OTHER COMPREHENSIVE INCOME**			2940

10.1	Service cost		2940
10.2	Changes in a defined benefit plan		2941
	10.2.1	Past service cost	2942
	10.2.2	Acquisition of a qualifying insurance policy	2943
	10.2.3	Settlements	2943
10.3	Net interest on the net defined benefit liability (asset)		2945
10.4	Remeasurements		2946
	10.4.1	Actuarial gains and losses	2946
	10.4.2	The return on plan assets, excluding amounts included in net interest on the net defined benefit liability (asset)	2946

11 DEFINED BENEFIT PLANS – COSTS OF ADMINISTERING EMPLOYEE BENEFIT PLANS 2946

12 SHORT-TERM EMPLOYEE BENEFITS 2947

12.1	General recognition criteria for short-term employee benefits		2948
12.2	Short-term paid absences		2948
	12.2.1	Accumulating absences	2948
	12.2.2	Non-accumulating paid absences	2949
12.3	Profit-sharing and bonus plans		2949
	12.3.1	Present legal or constructive obligation	2949
	12.3.2	Reliable estimate of provision	2950
	12.3.3	Statutory profit-sharing based on taxable profit	2950

13 LONG-TERM EMPLOYEE BENEFITS OTHER THAN POST-EMPLOYMENT BENEFITS 2951

13.1	Meaning of other long-term employee benefits		2951
13.2	Recognition and measurement		2951
	13.2.1	Attribution to years of service	2952
	13.2.2	Long-term disability benefit	2952
	13.2.3	Long-term benefits contingent on a future event	2953

14 TERMINATION BENEFITS 2953

14.1	Statutory termination indemnities	2955
14.2	Recognition	2955
14.3	Measurement	2956

15 DISCLOSURE REQUIREMENTS 2957

15.1	Defined contribution plans		2957
15.2	Defined benefit plans		2957
	15.2.1	Characteristics of defined benefit plans and risks associated with them	2958
	15.2.2	Explanation of amounts in the financial statements	2959
	15.2.3	Amount, timing and uncertainty of future cash flows	2962

	15.2.4	Multi-employer plans	2964
		15.2.4.A Plans accounted for as defined benefit plans	2964
		15.2.4.B Plans accounted for as defined contribution plans	2964
	15.2.5	Defined benefit plans that share risks between entities under common control	2965
		15.2.5.A Plans accounted for as defined benefit plans	2965
		15.2.5.B Plans accounted for as defined contribution plans	2965
	15.2.6	Disclosure requirements in other IFRSs	2967
15.3	Other employee benefits		2967
16	**POSSIBLE FUTURE DEVELOPMENTS**		**2968**
16.1	IASB activities		2968
16.2	Interpretations Committee activities		2968
	16.2.1	The availability of a refund from a defined benefit plan	2968

List of examples

Example 35.1:	Defined benefit plan with employee contributions, where the discount rate is higher than the salary growth rate	2915
Example 35.2:	The projected unit credit method	2917
Example 35.3:	Attributing benefits to years of service	2920
Example 35.4:	Deficit-clearing future minimum funding requirements when refunds are not available	2934
Example 35.5:	Effect of a prepayment when a minimum funding requirement exceeds the expected future service charge	2936
Example 35.6:	Effect of the minimum funding requirement when there is an IAS 19 surplus and the minimum funding contributions payable are fully refundable to the entity	2937
Example 35.7:	Effect of a minimum funding requirement when there is an IAS 19 deficit and the minimum funding contributions payable would not be fully available	2937
Example 35.8:	Accumulating paid absences	2949
Example 35.9:	Profit sharing and bonus plans	2950
Example 35.10:	Termination benefits	2956

Chapter 35   Employee benefits

1 INTRODUCTION

This Chapter deals with IAS 19 – *Employee Benefits* – as published in June 2011 and most recently amended in February 2018. Predecessors of this standard are discussed in earlier editions of International GAAP.

Employee benefits typically form a very significant part of any entity's costs, and can take many and varied forms. Accordingly, IFRS devotes considerable attention to them in two separate standards. IFRS 2 – *Share-based Payment* – is discussed in Chapter 34. All other employee benefits are dealt with in IAS 19.

Many issues raised in accounting for employee benefits can be straightforward, such as the allocation of wages paid to an accounting period, and are generally dealt with by IAS 19 accordingly. In contrast, accounting for the costs of retirement benefits in the financial statements of employers presents a more difficult challenge. The amounts involved are large, the timescale is long, the estimation process is complex and involves many areas of uncertainty which have to be made the subject of assumptions. Furthermore, the complexities for an International Standard are multiplied by the wide variety of arrangements found in different jurisdictions.

2 OBJECTIVE AND SCOPE OF IAS 19

2.1 Objective

IAS 19 sets out its objective as follows:

'The objective of this Standard is to prescribe the accounting and disclosure for employee benefits. The Standard requires an entity to recognise:

(a) a liability when an employee has provided service in exchange for employee benefits to be paid in the future; and

(b) an expense when the entity consumes the economic benefit arising from service provided by an employee in exchange for employee benefits.' *[IAS 19.1]*.

This provides the overarching principle of the standard. Driven by the focus on assets and liabilities in the IASB's *Conceptual Framework* (which is discussed in Chapter 2), it approaches the issues from the perspective of the statement of financial position of the entity.

2.2 Scope

The general scope of the standard is dealt with at 2.2.1 below. The issue of employee benefits settled not by the employing entity but by a shareholder or other member of a group is discussed at 2.2.2 below.

2.2.1 General scope requirements of IAS 19

As its name suggests, IAS 19 is not confined to pensions and other post-retirement benefits, but rather addresses all forms of consideration (apart from share-based payments which are dealt with by IFRS 2 and discussed in Chapter 34) given by an employer in exchange for service rendered by employees or for the termination of employment. *[IAS 19.2, 8]*. In particular, in addition to post-retirement benefits employee benefits it includes: *[IAS 19.5]*

(a) short-term benefits, including wages and salaries, paid annual leave, bonuses, benefits in kind, etc. The accounting treatment of these is discussed at 12 below;

(b) other long-term benefits, such as long-service leave, long-term disability benefits, long-term bonuses, etc. These are to be accounted for in a similar, but not identical, way to post-retirement benefits by using actuarial techniques and are discussed at 13 below; and

(c) termination benefits. These are to be provided for and expensed when the employer becomes committed to the redundancy plan, on a similar basis to that required by IAS 37 – *Provisions, Contingent Liabilities and Contingent Assets* – for provisions generally, and are discussed at 14 below.

The standard addresses only the accounting by employers, and excludes from its scope reporting by employee benefit plans themselves. These are dealt with in IAS 26 – *Accounting and Reporting by Retirement Benefit Plans*. *[IAS 19.3]*. The specialist nature of these requirements puts them beyond the scope of this book.

The standard makes clear it applies widely and in particular to benefits:

(a) provided to all employees (whether full-time, part-time, permanent, temporary or casual staff and specifically including directors and other management personnel); *[IAS 19.7]*

(b) however settled, including payments in cash or goods or services, whether paid directly to employees, their spouses, children or other dependants or any other party (such as insurance companies); *[IAS 19.6]* and

(c) however provided, including:

   (i) under formal plans or other formal agreements between an entity and individual employees, groups of employees or their representatives;

   (ii) under legislative requirements, or through industry arrangements, whereby entities are required to contribute to national, state, industry or other multi-employer plans; or

   (iii) by those informal practices that give rise to a constructive obligation, that is where the entity has no realistic alternative but to pay employee benefits. An example of a constructive obligation is where a change in the entity's informal practices would cause unacceptable damage to its relationship with employees. *[IAS 19.4]*.

The standard does not define the term 'employee'. However, it is clear from the reference in (a) above to 'full-time, part-time, permanent, casual or temporary' staff and specifically including directors and other management personnel that the term is intended to apply widely. In particular, it is not necessary for there to be a contract of employment in order for an individual to be considered an employee for IAS 19 purposes, other indicators should also be considered such as:

- the individual is considered an employee for tax purposes;
- services must be performed by a particular individual who has no discretion to arrange for someone else to perform them;
- services must be performed at a location specified by the entity;
- there is a large amount of oversight and direction by the entity;
- necessary tools, equipment and materials are provided by the entity;
- individuals are paid on a time basis, rather than a project/fixed price basis; and
- individuals receive benefits of a nature typical for employees (e.g. paid holidays, paid sick leave, post-retirement benefits, or death and disability benefits).

In our view, the standard applies to anyone who is in substance an employee, and that will be a matter of judgement in light of all the facts and circumstances.

An example of benefits which may be under the scope of either IAS 19 or IFRS 2 includes a cash bonus dependent on share performance (see Chapter 34 at 2.2.4.E). Cash settled awards based on an entity's enterprise value would be under the scope of IAS 19 if the enterprise value used in the calculation did not represent the fair value of the entity's equity instruments (see Chapter 34 at 2.2.4.F). Cash bonuses may also be within the scope of both IAS 19 and IFRS 2 if they require a mandatory investment of part of the bonus into shares (see Chapter 34 at 15.1). The cash element paid would fall within the scope of IAS 19, whereas any bonus which results in a required or discretionary investment in shares would come under the scope of IFRS 2. Each element of a bonus would be under the scope of one of these standards, but not both standards.

2.2.2 Employee benefits settled by a shareholder or another group entity

In some circumstances, employee benefits may be settled by a party other than the entity to which services were rendered by employees. Examples would include a shareholder or another entity in a group of entities under common control.

IAS 19 is silent on whether, and if so how, an entity receiving employee services in this way should account for them. IFRS 2, on the other hand, devotes quite some detail to this topic for employee services within its scope.

An entity could make reference to the hierarchy in IAS 8 – *Accounting Policies, Changes in Accounting Estimates and Errors* (discussed in Chapter 3 at 4.3) when deciding on an accounting policy under IAS 19. Accordingly, these provisions of IFRS 2 could be applied by analogy to transactions within the scope of IAS 19.

The relevant requirements of IFRS 2 are discussed in Chapter 34 at 2.2.2.A and at 12.

3 PENSIONS AND OTHER POST-EMPLOYMENT BENEFITS – DEFINED CONTRIBUTION AND DEFINED BENEFIT PLANS

3.1 The distinction between defined contribution plans and defined benefit plans

IAS 19 draws the important distinction between defined contribution plans and defined benefit plans. The determination is made based on the economic substance of the plan as derived from its principal terms and conditions. *[IAS 19.27]*. The approach it takes is to define defined contribution plans, with the defined benefit plans being the default category. The relevant terms defined by the standard are as follows: *[IAS 19.8]*

'*Post-employment benefits* are employee benefits (other than termination benefits and short-term employee benefits) that are payable after the completion of employment'.

'*Post-employment benefit plans* are formal or informal arrangements under which an entity provides post-employment benefits for one or more employees'.

'*Defined contribution plans* are post-employment benefit plans under which an entity pays fixed contributions into a separate entity (a fund) and will have no legal or constructive obligation to pay further contributions if the fund does not hold sufficient assets to pay all employee benefits relating to employee service in the current and prior periods'.

'*Defined benefit plans* are post-employment benefit plans other than defined contribution plans'.

IAS 19 applies to all post-employment benefits (whether or not they involve the establishment of a separate entity to receive contributions and pay benefits) which include, for example, retirement benefits such as pensions; and post-employment life assurance or medical care. *[IAS 19.26]*. A less common benefit is the provision of services.

Under defined benefit plans the employer's obligation is not limited to the amount that it agrees to contribute to the fund. Rather, the employer is obliged (legally or constructively) to provide the agreed benefits to current and former employees. Examples of defined benefit schemes given by IAS 19 are: *[IAS 19.29]*

(a) plans where the benefit formula is not linked solely to the amount of contributions and requires the entity to provide further contributions if assets are insufficient to meet the benefits in the plan formula;

(b) guarantees, either directly or indirectly through a plan, of a specified return on contributions; and

(c) those informal practices that give rise to a constructive obligation, such as a history of increasing benefits for former employees to keep pace with inflation even where there is no legal obligation to do so.

The most significant difference between defined contribution and defined benefit plans is that, under defined benefit plans, some actuarial risk or investment risk (or both) falls, in substance, on the employer. This means that if actuarial or investment experience is worse than expected, the employer's obligation may be increased. *[IAS 19.30]*. Consequently, because the employer is in substance underwriting the actuarial and investment risks associated with the plan, the expense recognised for a defined benefit plan is not necessarily the amount of the contribution due for the period. *[IAS 19.56]*. Conversely, under defined contribution plans the benefits received by the employee are determined by the amount of contributions paid (either by the employer, the employee or both) to the benefit plan or insurance company, together with investment returns, and hence actuarial and investment risk fall in substance on the employee. *[IAS 19.28]*.

In 2019 the Interpretations Committee received a request concerning the classification of a post-employment benefit plan that is administered by a third party. The only relevant terms and conditions in the request were that:

- the entity has an obligation to pay fixed annual contributions into the plan. The entity has determined that it will have no legal or constructive obligation to pay further contributions into the plan if it does not hold sufficient assets to pay all employee benefits relating to employee service in current and prior periods; and
- the entity is entitled to a potential discount on its annual contributions if the ratio of plan assets to plan liabilities exceeds a set level.

The Interpretations Committee was asked to consider whether the existence of a right to a potential discount would result in classification as a defined benefit plan under IAS 19. The Committee concluded that based on the fact pattern provided in the request the existence of a right to a potential discount would not in itself result in the classification as a defined benefit plan. However, they re-iterated the importance of assessing all the relevant terms and conditions of a plan, as well as any informal practices that might give rise to a constructive obligation, in the classification of a plan. The Committee also concluded that the requirements of IAS 19 provide an adequate basis for an entity to determine the classification of a post-employment benefit plan as a defined contribution plan or a defined benefit plan and decided not to add this matter to its standard-setting agenda.[1]

The committee reached this conclusion through consideration of the definition of a defined contribution plan, which requires:

- contributions to be fixed with no further legal or constructive obligation to pay further contributions if the fund does not hold sufficient assets to pay all employee benefits; *[IAS 19.8]*
- that this does not exclude the upside potential where the cost to the entity may be less than expected; *[IAS 19.BC29]* and
- the fact that in a defined contribution scheme the actuarial risk falls in substance on the employee. *[IAS 19.28, 30]*.

The classification of plans such as those described in the fact pattern submitted will require careful consideration of all the facts and circumstances to determine whether actuarial risk has remained with the employer and a defined benefit classification is appropriate. An entity should also consider whether any significant judgements made in this determination should be disclosed in accordance with IAS 1 – *Presentation of Financial Statements*. *[IAS 1.122]*.

3.2 Insured benefits

One factor that can complicate making the distinction between defined benefit and defined contribution plans is the use of external insurers. IAS 19 recognises that some employers may fund their post-employment benefit plans by paying insurance premiums and observes that the benefits insured need not have a direct or automatic relationship with the entity's obligation for employee benefits. However, it makes clear that post-employment benefit plans involving insurance contracts are subject to the same distinction between accounting and funding as other funded plans. *[IAS 19.47]*.

Where insurance premiums are paid to fund post-employment benefits, the employer should treat the plan as a defined contribution plan unless it has (either directly or indirectly through the plan) a legal or constructive obligation to:

(a) pay the employee benefits directly when they fall due; or

(b) pay further amounts if the insurer does not pay all future employee benefits relating to employee service in the current and prior periods.

If the employer has retained such a legal or constructive obligation it should treat the plan as a defined benefit plan. *[IAS 19.46]*. In setting out how to apply defined benefit accounting, however, the standard refers to slightly different criteria to determine whether a legal or constructive obligation is retained. Rather than referring to 'either directly or indirectly through the plan', paragraph 48 of IAS 19 refers to 'the entity (either directly, indirectly through the plan, *through the mechanism for setting future premiums or through a related party relationship with the insurer*) retains a legal or constructive obligation' (emphasis added). *[IAS 19.48]*. In our view the additional text included with paragraph 48 should also be applied in paragraph 46.

In cases where such obligations are retained by the employer, it recognises its rights under a 'qualifying insurance policy' as a plan asset and recognises other insurance policies as reimbursement rights. *[IAS 19.48]*. Plan assets are discussed at 6 below.

By way of final clarification, the standard notes that where an insurance policy is in the name of a specified plan participant or a group of plan participants and the employer does not have any legal or constructive obligation to cover any loss on the policy, the employer has no obligation to pay benefits to the employees and the insurer has sole responsibility for paying the benefits. In that case, the payment of fixed premiums under such contracts is, in substance, the settlement of the employee benefit obligation, rather than an investment to meet the obligation. Consequently, the employer no longer has an asset or a liability. Accordingly, it should treat the payments as contributions to a defined contribution plan. *[IAS 19.49]*. The important point here is that employee entitlements will be of a defined benefit nature unless the employer has no obligation whatsoever to pay them should the insurance fail or otherwise be insufficient.

The analysis of insured plans given in the standard, which is described above, along with the definition of defined benefit and defined contribution plans seems comprehensive at first glance. However, there will be circumstances where the distinction may not be so apparent and careful analysis may be required. For example, it is possible that an employer buys insurance on a regular basis (say annually), retaining no further obligation in respect of the benefits insured, but has an obligation (legal or constructive) to keep doing so in the future. In such a scenario, the employer may be exposed to future actuarial variances reflected in a variable cost of purchasing the required insurance in future years (for example, due to changing mortality estimates by the insurer).

Another scenario would be where each year the employee earns an entitlement to a pension of (say) 2% of that year's (i.e. current as opposed to final) salary and the employer purchases each year an annuity contract to commence on the date of retirement.

In our view, the standard is not entirely clear as to the nature of such an arrangement. On the one hand, it could be argued that it is a defined contribution plan because the definition of defined contribution plans is met when:

- 'fixed' payments are paid to a separate fund; and
- the employer is not obliged to pay further amounts if the fund has insufficient assets to pay the benefits relating to employee service in the current and prior periods.

Further, as noted above the standard considers the payment of 'fixed' premiums to purchase insurance specific to an employee (or group thereof) with no retention of risk in respect of the insured benefits to be a defined contribution arrangement.

On the other hand, it could be argued that this is a defined benefit plan on the grounds that:

- the premiums of future years are not 'fixed' in any meaningful sense (certainly not in the same way as an intention simply to pay a one-off contribution of a given % of salary);
- the standard acknowledges that one factor that can mean insured arrangements are defined benefit in nature is when the employer retains an obligation indirectly through the mechanism for setting future premiums; [IAS 19.48] and
- the standard observes that under defined benefit plans '... actuarial risk (that benefits will cost more than expected) and investment risk fall, in substance, on the entity. If actuarial or investment experience are worse than expected, the entity's obligation may be increased'. [IAS 19.30].

Much would seem to depend on just what 'fixed' means in such circumstances. Although not expressly addressed by the standard, in our view such arrangements will very likely be defined benefit in nature, albeit with regular (and perhaps only partial) settlement and, if so, should be accounted for as such. This is because the employer has retained actuarial risks by committing to pay whatever it takes in future years to secure the requisite insurance. See 3.1 above for further discussion on 'fixed' contributions. Naturally, for any schemes that are determined to be defined benefit plans, the next step would be to see whether the frequent settlement renders the output of the two accounting models materially the same. That would depend, *inter alia*, on the attribution of the benefit to years of service and the impact of an unwinding discount.

The wide variety of possible arrangements in practice mean that careful consideration of individual circumstances will be required to determine the true substance of such arrangements.

3.3 Multi-employer plans

3.3.1 Multi-employer plans other than plans sharing risks between entities under common control

3.3.1.A The treatment of multi-employer plans

Multi-employer plans, other than state plans (see 3.4 below), under IAS 19 are defined contribution plans or defined benefit plans that:

(a) pool assets contributed by various entities that are not under common control; and

(b) use those assets to provide benefits to employees of more than one entity, on the basis that contribution and benefit levels are determined without regard to the identity of the entity that employs the employees. *[IAS 19.8]*.

Accordingly, they exclude group administration plans, which simply pool the assets of more than one employer, for investment purposes and the reduction of administrative and investment costs, but keep the claims of different employers segregated for the sole benefit of their own employees. The standard observes that group administration plans pose no particular accounting problems because information is readily available to treat them in the same way as any other single employer plan and because they do not expose the participating employers to actuarial risks associated with the current and former employees of other entities. Accordingly, the standard requires group administration plans to be classified as defined contribution plans or defined benefit plans in accordance with the terms of the plan (including any constructive obligation that goes beyond the formal terms). *[IAS 19.38]*.

The standard gives a description of one example of a multi-employer scheme as follows:

(a) the plan is financed on a pay-as-you-go basis: contributions are set at a level that is expected to be sufficient to pay the benefits falling due in the same period; and future benefits earned during the current period will be paid out of future contributions; and

(b) employees' benefits are determined by the length of their service and the participating entities have no realistic means of withdrawing from the plan without paying a contribution for the benefits earned by employees up to the date of withdrawal. Such a plan creates actuarial risk for the entity: if the ultimate cost of benefits already earned at the end of the reporting period is more than expected, it will be necessary for the entity either to increase its contributions or persuade employees to accept a reduction in benefits. Therefore, such a plan is a defined benefit plan. *[IAS 19.35]*.

A multi-employer plan should be classified as either a defined contribution plan or a defined benefit plan in accordance with its terms in the normal way (see 3.1 above). *[IAS 19.32]*. If a multi-employer plan is classified as a defined benefit plan, IAS 19 requires that the employer should account for its proportionate share of the defined benefit obligation, plan assets and costs associated with the plan in the same way as for any other defined benefit plan (see 5-11 below). *[IAS 19.33, 36]*.

The standard does, however, contain a practical exemption if insufficient information is available to use defined benefit accounting. This could be the case, for example, where:

(a) the entity does not have access to information about the plan that satisfies the requirements of the standard; or

(b) the plan exposes the participating entities to actuarial risks associated with the current and former employees of other entities, with the result that there is no consistent and reliable basis for allocating the obligation, plan assets and cost to individual entities participating in the plan. *[IAS 19.36]*.

In such circumstances, an entity should account for the plan as if it were a defined contribution plan and make the disclosures set out at 15.2.4 below. *[IAS 19.34, 36]*.

The standard notes that there may be a contractual agreement between the multi-employer plan and its participants that determines how the surplus in the plan will be distributed to the participants (or the deficit funded). In these circumstances, an entity participating in such a plan, and accounting for it as a defined contribution plan (as described above), should recognise the asset or liability arising from the contractual agreement and the resulting income or expense in profit or loss. *[IAS 19.37]*. The standard illustrates this with an example of an entity participating in a multi-employer defined benefit plan which it accounts for as a defined contribution plan because no IAS 19 valuations are prepared. A non-IAS 19 funding valuation shows a deficit of CU100 million in the plan. A contractual schedule of contributions has been agreed with the participating employers in the plan that will eliminate the deficit over the next five years. The entity's total contributions to eliminate the deficit under the contract are CU8 million. IAS 19 requires the entity to recognise immediately a liability for the contributions adjusted for the time value of money and an equal expense in profit or loss. The important point here is that the standard makes clear that 'defined contribution accounting' is not the same as cash accounting. Extra payments to make good a deficit should be provided for immediately when they are contracted for.

3.3.1.B What to do when 'sufficient information' becomes available

As discussed above, IAS 19 requires a multi-employer defined benefit plan to be treated for accounting purposes as a defined contribution plan when insufficient information is available to use defined benefit accounting. The standard does not address the accounting treatment required when that situation changes because sufficient information becomes available in a period. Two possible approaches present themselves:

(a) an immediate charge/credit to profit or loss equal to the deficit/surplus; or

(b) an actuarial gain or loss recognised on other comprehensive income.

Arguments in favour of (a) would be that for accounting purposes the scheme was a defined contribution scheme. Accordingly, starting defined benefit accounting is akin to introducing a new scheme. The defined benefit obligation recognised is essentially a past service cost. In addition, as discussed at 3.3.1.A above, the standard clarifies that while defined contribution accounting is being applied an asset or liability should be recognised where there is a contractual arrangement to share a surplus or fund a deficit. The receipt of full information could be considered to represent such an arrangement and hence require full recognition in the statement of financial position with an equivalent entry in profit or loss.

Arguments for (b) would be that the scheme has not changed and that defined contribution accounting was a proxy (and best available estimate) for what the defined benefit accounting should have been. Accordingly, any change to that estimate due to the emergence of new information is an actuarial variance which is recognised in other comprehensive income.

Given the ambiguity of the standard either approach is acceptable if applied consistently.

3.3.1.C Withdrawal from or winding up of a multi-employer scheme

IAS 19 requires the application of IAS 37 to determine when to recognise and how to measure a liability relating to the withdrawal from, or winding-up of, a multi-employer scheme. *[IAS 19.39]*.

3.3.2 Defined benefit plans sharing risks between entities under common control

IAS 19 provides that defined benefit plans that share risks between various entities under common control, for example a parent and its subsidiaries, are not multi-employer plans. *[IAS 19.40]*.

The test, described earlier, for allowing a defined benefit multi-employer plan to be accounted for as a defined contribution plan is that insufficient information is available. By completely excluding entities that are under common control from the definition of multi-employer plans the standard is essentially saying that for these employers sufficient information is deemed always to be available – at least for the plan as a whole. The standard requires an entity participating in such a plan to obtain information about the plan as a whole measured in accordance with IAS 19 on the basis of assumptions that apply to the plan as a whole. *[IAS 19.41]*. Whilst a subsidiary may not be in a position to demand such information (any more than participants in schemes described at 3.3.1 above), the standard is essentially saying that the parent must make the information available if it wants the subsidiary to be able to comply with IAS 19.

The standard then goes on to specify the accounting treatment to be applied in the individual financial statements of the participating entities. The standard states: 'If there is a contractual agreement or stated policy for charging to individual group entities the net defined benefit cost for the plan as a whole measured in accordance with this Standard, the entity shall, in its separate or individual financial statements, recognise the net defined benefit cost so charged. If there is no such agreement or policy, the net defined benefit cost shall be recognised in the separate or individual financial statements of the group entity that is legally the sponsoring employer for the plan. The other group entities shall, in their separate or individual financial statements, recognise a cost equal to their contribution payable for the period'. *[IAS 19.41]*. This seems to raise more questions than it answers. For example, it provides no clarity on what is meant by:

- the 'net defined benefit cost ... measured in accordance with [IAS 19]'. In particular, are actuarial gains and losses part of this 'net cost'?
- an entity that 'is legally the sponsoring employer for the plan'. The pan-jurisdictional scope of IFRS makes such a determination particularly difficult. Furthermore, it suggests that there is only one such legal sponsor – which may not be the case in practice.

A further difficulty with these provisions of the standard is whether it is ever likely in practice that entities would be charged an amount based on the 'defined benefit cost measured in accordance with [IAS 19]'. Naturally, situations vary not just across, but also within, individual jurisdictions. However, it is typically the case that funding valuations will not be on an IAS 19 basis, so that any amounts 'charged' will not be measured in accordance with IAS 19. Indeed, as discussed at 3.3.1 above, the standard gives non-IAS 19 funding valuations in a multi-employer plan as a reason why sufficient information to allow defined benefit accounting is not available.

Some further insight as to the IASB's intentions can be found in the Basis for Conclusions to the standard.

'The Board noted that, if there were a contractual agreement or stated policy on charging the net defined benefit cost to group entities, that agreement or policy would determine the cost for each entity. If there is no such contractual agreement or stated policy, the entity that is the sponsoring employer bears the risk relating to the plan by default. The Board therefore concluded that a group plan should be allocated to the individual entities within a group in accordance with any contractual agreement or stated policy. If there is no such agreement or policy, the net defined benefit cost is allocated to the sponsoring employer. The other group entities recognise a cost equal to any contribution collected by the sponsoring employer. This approach has the advantages of (a) all group entities recognising the cost they have to bear for the defined benefit promise and (b) being simple to apply'. *[IAS 19.BC48-49]*.

This analysis is particularly noteworthy in these respects:

(a) there is no mention of amounts charged being measured in accordance with IAS 19. Indeed, the third sentence refers to any such agreement or stated policy;

(b) the focus is not on 'amounts charged' but rather an 'allocation' of the scheme across entities;

(c) references are to a 'sponsoring employer' crucially not a legally sponsoring employer. The term is slightly clarified by the explanation that a sponsoring employer is one that by default bears the 'risks relating to the plan'; and

(d) the discussion of employers other than the sponsoring employer is explicitly by reference to 'amounts collected'.

Given the ambiguities in the standard we expect that, for entities applying IFRS at an individual company level, there may well be divergent treatments in practice.

The standard makes clear that, for each individual group entity, participation in such a plan is a related party transaction. Accordingly, the disclosures set out at 15.2.5 below are required. *[IAS 19.42]*.

3.4 State plans

IAS 19 observes that state plans are established by legislation to cover all entities (or all entities in a particular category, for example a specific industry) and are operated by national or local government or by another body (for example an autonomous agency created specifically for this purpose) which is not subject to control or influence by the reporting entity. *[IAS 19.44]*. The standard requires that state plans be accounted for in the same way as for a multi-employer plan (see 3.3.1 above). *[IAS 19.43]*. It goes on to note that it is characteristic of many state plans that:

- they are funded on a pay-as-you-go basis with contributions set at a level that is expected to be sufficient to pay the required benefits falling due in the same period; and
- future benefits earned during the current period will be paid out of future contributions.

Nevertheless, in most state plans, the entity has no legal or constructive obligation to pay those future benefits: its only obligation is to pay the contributions as they fall due and if the entity ceases to employ members of the state plan, it will have no obligation to pay the benefits earned by its own employees in previous years. For this reason, the standard considers that state plans are normally defined contribution plans. However, in cases when a state plan is a defined benefit plan, IAS 19 requires it to be treated as such as a multi-employer plan. *[IAS 19.45]*.

Some plans established by an entity provide both compulsory benefits which substitute for benefits that would otherwise be covered under a state plan and additional voluntary benefits. IAS 19 clarifies that such plans are not state plans. *[IAS 19.44]*.

3.5 Plans that would be defined contribution plans but for the existence of a minimum return guarantee

It is common in some jurisdictions for the employer to make contributions to a defined contribution post-employment benefit plan and to guarantee a minimum level of return on the assets in which the contributions are invested. In other words, the employee enjoys upside risk on the investments but has some level of protection from downside risk.

The existence of such a guarantee means the arrangement fails to meet the definition of a defined contribution plan (see 3.1 above) and accordingly is a defined benefit plan. Indeed, the standard is explicit, as it uses plans which guarantee a specified return on contributions as an example of a defined benefit arrangement. *[IAS 19.29(b)]*. The somewhat more difficult issue is how exactly to apply defined benefit accounting to such an arrangement, as this would require projecting forward future salary increases and investment returns, and discounting these amounts at corporate bond rates. Although this approach is required by the standard, some consider it to be inappropriate in such circumstances. This issue was debated by the Interpretations Committee, which published a draft interpretation on 8 July 2004 entitled D9 – *Employee Benefit Plans with a Promised Return on Contributions or Notional Contributions*. The approach taken in D9 was to distinguish two different types of benefits:

(a) a benefit of contributions or notional contributions plus a guarantee of a fixed return (in other words, benefits which can be estimated without having to make an estimate of future asset returns); and

(b) a benefit that depends on future asset returns.

For benefits under (a) above, it was proposed that the defined benefit methodology in IAS 19 be applied as normal. In summary, that meant:

- calculating the benefit to be paid in the future by projecting forward the contributions or notional contributions at the guaranteed fixed rate of return;
- allocating the benefit to periods of service;
- discounting the benefits allocated to the current and prior periods at the rate specified in IAS 19 to arrive at the plan liability, current service cost and net interest; and
- recognising any remeasurements in accordance with the entity's accounting policy (note that there is no longer an accounting policy choice under IAS 19 and remeasurements must be recorded in other comprehensive income).

For benefits covered by (b) above, it was proposed that the plan liability should be measured at the fair value, at the end of the reporting period, of the assets upon which the benefit is specified (whether plan assets or notional assets). No projection forward of the benefits would be made, and discounting of the benefit would not therefore be required.

D9 suggested that plans with a combination of a guaranteed fixed return and a benefit that depends on future asset returns should be accounted for by analysing the benefits into a fixed component and a variable component. The defined benefit asset or liability that would arise from the fixed component alone would be measured and recognised as described above. The defined benefit asset (or liability) that would arise from the variable component alone would then be calculated as described above and compared to the fixed component. An additional plan liability would be recognised to the extent that the asset (or liability) calculated for the variable component is smaller (or greater) than the asset (or liability) recognised in respect of the fixed component.

In August 2005, the Interpretations Committee however announced the withdrawal of D9, observing the following: 'The staff found the fixed/variable and modified fixed/variable approaches inadequate to give a faithful representation of the entity's obligation for more complex benefit structures. They believed that some aspects of the fixed/variable approach in D9 were not fully consistent with IAS 19. ... The staff ... recommended that the correct treatment for D9 plans should be determined as part of an IASB project.'

The Interpretations Committee was asked in 2012 whether the revisions to IAS 19 in 2011 affect the accounting for these types of employee benefits and concluded they do not.[2]

The Interpretations Committee re-opened its examination of the subject and spent some time considering the issue. In May 2014, it decided not to proceed with the issue, stating the following: 'In the Interpretations Committee's view, developing accounting requirements for these plans would be better addressed by a broader consideration of accounting for employee benefits, potentially through the research agenda of the IASB. The Interpretations Committee acknowledged that reducing diversity in practice in the short term would be beneficial. However, because of the difficulties encountered in progressing the issues, the Interpretations Committee decided to remove the project from its agenda. The Interpretations Committee notes the importance of this issue because of the increasing use of these plans. Consequently, the Interpretations Committee would welcome progress on the IASB's research project on post-employment benefits'.[3]

In February 2018 the Board announced a research project on pension benefits that depend on asset returns, see 16.1 below for further details.

3.6 Death-in-service benefits

The provision of death-in-service benefits is a common part of employment packages (either as part of a defined benefit plan or on a standalone basis). We think it is regrettable that IAS 19 provides no guidance on how to account for such benefits, particularly as E54 (the exposure draft preceding an earlier version of IAS 19) devoted considerable attention to the issue.[4] IAS 19 explains the removal of the guidance as follows: 'E54 proposed guidance on cases where death-in-service benefits are not insured externally and are not provided through a post-employment benefit plan. IASC concluded that such cases will be rare. Accordingly, IASC deleted the guidance on death-in-service benefits.' *[IAS 19.BC253]*.

In our view, this misses the point – E54 also gave guidance on cases where the benefits are externally insured and where they are provided through a post-employment benefit plan. In our view, the proposals in E54 had merit, and it is worth reproducing them here.

'An enterprise should recognise the cost of death-in-service benefits ... as follows:

(a) in the case of benefits insured or re-insured with third parties, in the period in respect of which the related insurance premiums are payable; and

(b) in the case of benefits not insured or re-insured with third parties, to the extent that deaths have occurred before the end of the reporting period.

'However, in the case of death-in-service benefits provided through a post-employment benefit plan, an enterprise should recognise the cost of those benefits by including their present value in the post-employment benefit obligation.

'If an enterprise re-insures a commitment to provide death-in-service benefits, it acquires a right (to receive payments if an employee dies in service) in exchange for an obligation to pay the premiums.

'Where an enterprise provides death-in-service benefits directly, rather than through a post-employment benefit plan, the enterprise has a future commitment to provide death-in-service coverage in exchange for employee service in those same future periods (in the same way that the enterprise has a future commitment to pay salaries if the employee renders service in those periods). That future commitment is not a present obligation and does not justify recognition of a liability. Therefore, an obligation arises only to the extent that a death has already occurred by the end of the reporting period.

'If death-in-service benefits are provided through a pension plan (or other post-employment plan) which also provides post-employment benefits to the same employee(s), the measurement of the obligation reflects both the probability of a reduction in future pension payments through death in service and the present value of the death-in-service benefits (see [E-54's discussion of mutual compatibility of actuarial assumptions]).

'Death-in-service benefits differ from post-employment life insurance because post-employment life insurance creates an obligation as the employee renders services in exchange for that benefit; an enterprise accounts for that obligation in accordance with [the requirements for defined benefit plans]. Life insurance benefits that are payable regardless of whether the employee remains in service comprise two components: a death-in-service benefit and a post-employment benefit. An enterprise accounts for the two components separately.'

We suggest that the above may continue to represent valid guidance to the extent it does not conflict with extant IFRS. In particular, an appropriate approach could be that:

- death-in-service benefits provided as part of a defined benefit post-employment plan are factored into the actuarial valuation. In this case any insurance cover should be accounted for in accordance with the normal rules of IAS 19 (see 6 below).

An important point here is that insurance policies for death-in-service benefits typically cover only one year, and hence will have a low or negligible fair value. As a result, it will not be the case that the insurance asset is equal and opposite to the defined benefit obligation;

- other death-in-service benefits which are externally insured are accounted for by expensing the premiums as they become payable; and
- other death-in-service benefits which are not externally insured are provided for as deaths in service occur.

The first bullet is particularly important. The measure of the post-employment benefit (like a pension) will be reduced to take account of expected deaths in service. Accordingly, it would be inappropriate to ignore the death in service payments that would be made. The question that arises is how exactly to include those expected payments. This raises the same issue as disability benefits (discussed at 13.2.2 below), i.e. what to do with the debit entry. However, IAS 19 has no explicit special treatment for death-in-service benefits comparable to that for disability benefits. Given the absence of specific guidance, the requirement is to apply the projected unit credit method to death in service benefits. As the benefit is fully vested, an argument could be made that the expected benefit should be accrued fully (on a discounted basis). Another approach would be to build up the credit entry in the statement of financial position over the period to the expected date of death.

An alternative approach could be to view death-in-service benefits as being similar to disability benefits. Proponents of this view would argue that the recognition requirements for disability benefits (discussed at 13.2.2 below) could also be applied to death-in-service.

In January 2008, the Interpretations Committee published its agenda decision explaining why it decided not to put death-in-service benefits onto its agenda.[5] In the view of the Interpretations Committee, 'divergence in this area was unlikely to be significant. In addition, any further guidance that it could issue would be application guidance on the use of the Projected Unit Credit Method'. In our view, the second reason seems more credible than the first.

As part of its analysis, the 'rejection notice' sets out some of the Interpretations Committee's views on the subject. It observes the following:

(a) in some situations, IAS 19 requires these benefits to be attributed to periods of service using the Projected Unit Credit Method;

(b) IAS 19 requires attribution of the cost of the benefits until the date when further service by the employee will lead to no material amount of further benefits under the plan, other than from further salary increases;

(c) the anticipated date of death would be the date at which no material amount of further benefit would arise from the plan; and

(d) using different mortality assumptions for a defined benefit pension plan and an associated death-in-service benefit would not comply with the requirement of IAS 19 to use actuarial assumptions that are mutually compatible.

Points (a) to (c) above support the analysis that a provision should be built up gradually from the commencement of employment to the expected date of death. They also suggest that making an analogy to the specific rules in the standard on disability may not be appropriate. In addition, point (c) is simply re-iterating a clear requirement of the standard. The above agenda decision of the Interpretations Committee is not as helpful as we would have liked. The use of the phrase 'in some situations' in point (a) above leaves uncertain just what those circumstances may be. In September 2007, the Interpretations Committee published a tentative agenda decision which said '[i]f these benefits are provided as part of a defined benefit plan, IAS 19 requires them to be attributed to periods of service using the Projected Unit Credit Method'.[6] At the following meeting the Interpretations Committee discussed the comment letters received which noted that it could be argued that such attribution would be required only if the benefits were dependent on the period of service. No decision was reached on the final wording of the rejection notice because 'IFRIC ... was unable to agree on wording for its agenda decision'.[7]

Given the lack of explicit guidance on death-in-service benefits in IAS 19 itself, and given the Interpretations Committee's decision not to address the matter, it seems likely that practice will be mixed.

4 DEFINED CONTRIBUTION PLANS

4.1 General accounting requirements

Accounting for defined contribution plans (see 3 above) is straightforward under IAS 19 because, as the standard observes, the reporting entity's obligation for each period is determined by the amounts to be contributed for that period. Consequently, no actuarial assumptions are required to be made to measure the obligation or the expense and there is no possibility of any actuarial gain or loss to the reporting entity. Moreover, the obligations are measured on an undiscounted basis, except where they are not expected to be settled wholly before twelve months after the end of the period in which the employees render the related service. *[IAS 19.50]*. Where discounting is required, the discount rate should be determined in the same way as for defined benefit plans, which is discussed at 7.6 below. *[IAS 19.52]*. In general, though, it would seem unlikely for a defined contribution scheme to be structured with such a long delay between the employee service and the employer contribution.

IAS 19 requires that, when an employee has rendered service during a period, the employer should recognise the contribution payable to a defined contribution plan in exchange for that service:

(a) as a liability (accrued expense), after deducting any contribution already paid. If the contribution already paid exceeds the contribution due for service before the end of the reporting period, the excess should be recognised as an asset (prepaid expense) to the extent that the prepayment will lead to, for example, a reduction in future payments or a cash refund; and

(b) as an expense, unless another IFRS requires or permits its capitalisation. *[IAS 19.51]*.

As discussed at 3.3.1.A above, IAS 19 requires multi-employer defined benefit plans to be accounted for as defined contribution plans in certain circumstances. The standard makes clear that contractual arrangements to make contributions to fund a deficit should be fully provided for (on a discounted basis) even if they are to be paid over an extended period. *[IAS 19.37]*.

4.2 Defined contribution plans with vesting conditions

In February 2011, the Interpretations Committee received a request seeking clarification on the effect that vesting conditions have on the accounting for defined contribution plans. The Interpretations Committee was asked whether contributions to such plans should be recognised as an expense in the period for which they are paid or over the vesting period. In the examples given in the submission, the employee's failure to meet a vesting condition could result in the refund of contributions to, or reductions in future contributions by, the employer.

The Interpretations Committee decided not to add the issue to its agenda, noting that there is no significant diversity in practice in respect of the effect that vesting conditions have on the accounting for defined contribution post-employment benefit plans, nor does it expect significant diversity in practice to emerge in the future.

Explaining its decision, the Interpretations Committee observed that 'each contribution to a defined contribution plan is to be recognised as an expense or recognised as a liability (accrued expense) over the period of service that obliges the employer to pay this contribution to the defined contribution plan. This period of service is distinguished from the period of service that entitles an employee to receive the benefit from the defined contribution plan (i.e. the vesting period), although both periods may be coincident in some circumstances. Refunds are recognised as an asset and as income when the entity/employer becomes entitled to the refunds, e.g. when the employee fails to meet the vesting condition'.[8]

5 DEFINED BENEFIT PLANS – GENERAL

The standard notes that accounting for defined benefit plans is complex because actuarial assumptions are required to measure both the obligation and the expense, and there is a possibility of actuarial gains and losses. Moreover, the obligations are measured on a discounted basis because they may be settled many years after the employees render the related service. *[IAS 19.55]*. Also, IAS 19 makes clear that it applies not just to unfunded obligations of employers but also to funded plans. The details of pension scheme arrangements vary widely from jurisdiction to jurisdiction and, indeed, within them. Frequently though, they involve some entity or fund, separate from the employer, to which contributions are made by the employer (and sometimes employees) and from which benefits are paid. Typically, the employer (through either legal or constructive obligations) essentially underwrites the fund in the event that the assets in the fund are insufficient to pay the required benefits. This is the key feature which means such an arrangement is a defined benefit plan (see 3 above). *[IAS 19.56]*.

In addition to specifying accounting and disclosure requirements, IAS 19 summarises the steps necessary to apply its rules, to be applied separately to each separate plan, as follows:

(a) determining the deficit or surplus by:
  (i) using an actuarial technique, the projected unit credit method, to make a reliable estimate of the ultimate cost to the entity of the benefit that employees have earned in return for their service in the current and prior periods. This requires an entity to determine how much benefit is attributable to the current and prior periods and to make estimates (actuarial assumptions) about demographic variables (such as employee turnover and mortality) and financial variables (such as future increases in salaries and medical costs) that will affect the cost of the benefit;
  (ii) discounting that benefit in order to determine the present value of the defined benefit obligation and the current service cost; and
  (iii) deducting the fair value of any plan assets from the present value of the defined benefit obligation.
(b) determining the amount of the net defined benefit liability (asset) as the amount of the deficit or surplus determined in (a), adjusted for any effect of limiting a net defined benefit asset to the asset ceiling;
(c) determining amounts to be recognised in profit or loss:
  (i) current service cost;
  (ii) any past service cost and gain or loss on settlement;
  (iii) net interest on the net defined benefit liability (asset); and
(d) determining the remeasurements of the net defined benefit liability (asset), to be recognised in other comprehensive income, comprising:
  (i) actuarial gains and losses;
  (ii) return on plan assets, excluding amounts included in net interest on the net defined benefit liability (asset); and
  (iii) any change in the effect of the asset ceiling, excluding amounts included in net interest on the net defined benefit liability (asset). *[IAS 19.57]*.

Retirement benefits will often be very significant in the context of an employer's financial statements. Therefore, the standard encourages, but does not require involvement of a qualified actuary in the measurement of all material post-employment benefit obligations. *[IAS 19.59]*. However, the standard acknowledges that in some circumstances estimates, averages and computational shortcuts may provide a reliable approximation. *[IAS 19.60]*. These steps are discussed in further detail in the sections 7.5 and 7.6 below.

6 DEFINED BENEFIT PLANS – PLAN ASSETS

6.1 Definition of plan assets

IAS 19 provides the following definitions relating to plan assets:

'*Plan assets* comprise:
(a) assets held by a long-term employee benefit fund; and
(b) qualifying insurance policies.' *[IAS 19.8]*.

'Plan assets exclude unpaid contributions due from the reporting entity to the fund, as well as any non-transferable financial instruments issued by the entity and held by the fund. Plan assets are reduced by any liabilities of the fund that do not relate to employee benefits for example, trade and other payables and liabilities resulting from derivative financial instruments.' [IAS 19.114].

'*Assets held by a long-term employee benefit fund* are assets (other than non-transferable financial instruments issued by the reporting entity) that:

(a) are held by an entity (a fund) that is legally separate from the reporting entity and exists solely to pay or fund employee benefits; and

(b) are available to be used only to pay or fund employee benefits, are not available to the reporting entity's own creditors (even in bankruptcy), and cannot be returned to the reporting entity, unless either:

 (i) the remaining assets of the fund are sufficient to meet all the related employee benefit obligations of the plan or the reporting entity; or

 (ii) the assets are returned to the reporting entity to reimburse it for employee benefits already paid.'

Whilst non-transferable financial instruments issued by the employer are excluded from the definition of plan assets, plans can, and do, own transferrable instruments issued by the employer (such as listed shares and bonds) and these would qualify as plan assets.

'A *qualifying insurance policy* is an insurance policy issued by an insurer that is not a related party (as defined in IAS 24 – *Related Party Disclosures* – see Chapter 39) of the reporting entity, if the proceeds of the policy:

(a) can be used only to pay or fund employee benefits under a defined benefit plan; and

(b) are not available to the reporting entity's own creditors (even in bankruptcy) and cannot be paid to the reporting entity, unless either:

 (i) the proceeds represent surplus assets that are not needed for the policy to meet all the related employee benefit obligations; or

 (ii) the proceeds are returned to the reporting entity to reimburse it for employee benefits already paid.' [IAS 19.8].

A footnote to this definition clarifies that a qualifying insurance policy is not necessarily an insurance contract as defined in IFRS 4/IFRS 17 – *Insurance Contracts* – see Chapters 55 and 56.

IFRS 4 further mentions insurance contracts in the context of pensions. It discusses insurance policies issued by an insurer to a pension plan covering employees of the insurer or another entity consolidated in the same financial statements as the insurer. In such circumstances, IFRS 4 provides that the contract will generally be eliminated from the financial statements. The financial statements will:

- include the full amount of the pension obligation under IAS 19, with no deduction for the plan's rights under the contract;
- not include a liability to policyholders under the contract; and
- include the assets backing the contract. [IFRS 4.IG2 E 1.21].

The above has not been carried over into IFRS 17, although we would expect the same practice to continue under this standard.

6.2 Measurement of plan assets

IAS 19 requires plan assets to be measured at their fair value, *[IAS 19.113]*, which is defined as the price that would be received to sell an asset or paid to transfer a liability in an orderly transaction between market participants at the measurement date. *[IAS 19.8]*. This is the same definition as is used in IFRS 13 – *Fair Value Measurement* (see Chapter 14).

The fair value of any plan assets is deducted from the present value of the defined benefit obligation in determining the deficit or surplus – see 8 below. *[IAS 19.113]*.

6.3 Qualifying insurance policies

Where plan assets include qualifying insurance policies that exactly match the amount and timing of some or all of the benefits payable under the plan, the fair value of those insurance policies is deemed to be the present value of the related obligations, subject to any reductions required if the amounts receivable under the insurance policies are not recoverable in full. *[IAS 19.115]*.

6.4 Reimbursement rights

Some employers may have in place arrangements to fund defined benefit obligations which do not meet the definition of qualifying insurance policies above but which do provide for another party to reimburse some or all of the expenditure required to settle a defined benefit obligation. In such a case, the expected receipts under the arrangement are not classified as plan assets under IAS 19 (and hence they are not presented as part of a net pension asset/liability – see 8 below). Instead, the employer should recognise its right to reimbursement as a separate asset, but only when it is virtually certain that another party will reimburse some or all of the expenditure required to settle a defined benefit obligation. The asset should be measured at fair value and, in all other respects, it should be treated in the same way as a plan asset. In particular, changes in fair value are disaggregated and accounted for in the same way as plan assets – see 10.3 below. In profit or loss, the expense relating to a defined benefit plan may be presented net of the amount recognised for a reimbursement. *[IAS 19.116-118]*.

As is the case for qualifying insurance policies, for reimbursement rights that exactly match the amount and timing of some or all of the benefits payable fair value is determined as the present value of the related obligation, subject to any reduction required if the reimbursement is not recoverable in full. *[IAS 19.119]*.

6.5 Contributions to defined benefit funds

Contributions to defined benefit plans under IAS 19 are a movement between line items in the statement of financial position – the reduction in cash for the employer being reflected by an increase in the plan assets. Perhaps because of this straightforward accounting, the standard provides no guidance on contributions, which it implicitly deals with as always being in the form of cash.

Although contributions are very commonly in cash, there is no reason why an employer could not contribute any other assets to a defined benefit plan and that raises the question of how to account for the disposal – particularly so, since from the point of transfer the assets will be measured at fair value under IAS 19. In our view, such a transfer of a non-cash asset should be treated as a disposal, with proceeds equal to the fair value of the asset. That would give rise to gains and losses in profit or loss (unless the asset in question was already carried at fair value) and, for certain assets (such as debt instruments held at fair value through other comprehensive income), the reclassification into profit or loss of amounts previously recognised in other comprehensive income.

6.6 Longevity swaps

A longevity swap transfers, from a pension scheme to an external party, the risk of members living longer (or shorter) than expected.

The Interpretations Committee was asked in August 2014 to clarify the measurement of longevity swaps held by an entity's defined benefit plan, and in particular discussed whether an entity should:

(a) account for a longevity swap as a single instrument and measure its fair value as part of plan assets (discussed at 6.2 above) with changes in fair value being recorded in other comprehensive income; or

(b) split longevity swaps into two components.

The two components in (b) would be a 'fixed leg' and a 'variable leg'. As the variable leg exactly matches some or all of the defined benefit obligation it would represent a qualifying insurance policy and be measured at the present value of the related obligation (discussed at 6.3 above). The fixed leg comprises a series of fixed payments to be made in return for the receipt of the variable leg receipts. In other words, a longevity swap could be considered to be economically equivalent to the purchase of qualifying insurance (commonly called a 'buy-in') but with the premium paid over a period of time rather than at inception.

The likely effect of disaggregating a longevity swap in this way would be to recognise a remeasurement loss at inception very similar to that for a buy-in. Conversely, considering the swap as a single instrument measured at fair value would likely have no initial effect as typically its fair value would be zero (that is, a premium neither received nor paid).

If the two legs were to be considered separately, an appropriate accounting policy would need to be applied to the fixed leg. Two possibilities were discussed by the Interpretations Committee as follows. The fixed leg would initially be measured at fair value with subsequent accounting either:

- if treated as part of plan assets, at fair value with interest reported in profit or loss and other changes being included in other comprehensive income (discussed at 6.2 above); or
- if treated as a financial liability at amortised cost using the effective interest rate method with interest recognised in profit and loss and no other remeasurements.

The Interpretations Committee noted that when such transactions take place, the predominant practice is to account for a longevity swap as a single instrument and measure it at fair value as part of plan assets.

The Interpretations Committee decided not to add this issue to its agenda as it did not expect diversity to develop in the application of IAS 19.[9] Given that the Interpretations Committee decided not to add this to its agenda we believe that either of the subsequent accounting options detailed above would be acceptable.

7 DEFINED BENEFIT PLANS – PLAN LIABILITIES

7.1 Legal and constructive obligations

IAS 19 refers to the liabilities of defined benefit plans as the present value of defined benefit obligations, which it defines as '... the present value, without deducting any plan assets, of expected future payments required to settle the obligation resulting from employee service in the current and prior periods'. *[IAS 19.8]*.

The obligations should include not only the benefits set out in the plan, but also any constructive obligations that arise from the employer's informal practices which go beyond the formal plan terms, and should where relevant include an estimate of expected future salary increases (taking into account inflation, seniority, promotion and other relevant factors, such as supply and demand in the employment market). *[IAS 19.61, 87-90]*.

A constructive obligation exists where a change in the employer's informal practices would cause unacceptable damage to its relationship with employees and which therefore leaves the employer with no realistic alternative but to pay those employee benefits. *[IAS 19.61]*. The term constructive obligation is not defined by IAS 19; however, as can be seen from the above it is very similar to the meaning of the term as used in IAS 37 where it is defined as follows:

'A constructive obligation is an obligation that derives from an entity's actions where:

(a) by an established pattern of past practice, published policies or a sufficiently specific current statement, the entity has indicated to other parties that it will accept certain responsibilities; and

(b) as a result, the entity has created a valid expectation on the part of those other parties that it will discharge those responsibilities.' *[IAS 37.10]*.

However, IAS 19 goes on to add a further nuance. The standard observes that it is usually difficult to cancel a retirement benefit plan (without payment) whilst still retaining staff, and in light of this it requires that reporting entities assume (in the absence of evidence to the contrary) any currently promised benefits will continue for the remaining working lives of employees. *[IAS 19.62]*. In our view, this is a somewhat lower hurdle, and could bring into the scope of defined benefit accounting promises which are (strictly) legally unenforceable and which would not necessarily be considered constructive obligations under IAS 37.

An employer's obligations (legal or constructive) may also extend to making changes to benefits in the future. The standard requires all such effects to be built into the computation of the obligation and gives the following examples of what they might comprise:

(a) the entity has a history of increasing benefits, for example, to mitigate the effects of inflation, and no indication that this practice will change in the future;

(b) the entity is obliged, either by the formal terms of the plan (or a further constructive obligation) or by legislation to use any surplus in the plan for the benefit of plan participants; or

(c) benefits vary in response to a performance target or other criteria. For example, the terms of the plan may state that it will pay reduced benefits or require additional contributions from employees if the plan assets are insufficient. The measurement of the obligation reflects the best estimate of the effect of target or other criteria. *[IAS 19.88].*

By contrast, any other future changes in the obligation (i.e. where no legal or constructive obligation previously existed) will be reflected in future current service costs, future past service costs or both (discussed at 10.1 below). *[IAS 19.89].*

IAS 19 also deals with the situation where the level of defined benefits payable by a scheme varies with the level of state benefits. When this is the case a best estimate of any changes in state benefit should be factored into the actuarial computations only if they are enacted by the end of the reporting period or are predictable based on past history or other evidence. *[IAS 19.87, 95].*

Some defined benefit plans limit the contributions that an entity is required to pay. The ultimate cost of the benefits takes account of the effect of a limit on contributions. The effect of a limit on contributions is determined over the shorter of the estimated life of the entity and the estimated life of the plan. *[IAS 19.91].*

7.2 Contributions by employees and third parties

The standard notes that some defined benefit plans require employees or third parties to contribute to the cost of the plan. Contributions by employees reduce the cost of the benefits to the entity. The standard requires an entity to 'consider' whether third-party contributions reduce the cost of the benefits to the entity, or are a reimbursement right (discussed at 6.4 above). Contributions by employees or third parties are either set out in the formal terms of the plan (or arise from a constructive obligation that goes beyond those terms), or are discretionary. IAS 19 requires discretionary contributions by employees or third parties to be accounted for as a reduction in service cost when they are paid to the plan. *[IAS 19.92].*

The standard draws a distinction between non-discretionary contributions from employees or third parties set out in the formal terms of the plan which are 'linked to service' and those which are not. Such contributions not dependent upon years of service reduce remeasurements of the net defined benefit liability (asset). An example given by the standard is if the contributions are required to reduce a deficit arising from losses on plan assets or actuarial losses. *[IAS 19.93].*

For contributions which are linked to service, the standard states that they reduce the service cost as follows:

- if the amount of the contributions is dependent on the number of years of service (e.g. contributions that increase with years of service), they should be attributed to periods of service using the same attribution method required for the gross benefit (i.e. either using the plan's contribution formula or on a straight-line basis – see 7.3 below); or
- if the amount of the contributions is independent of the number of years of service (e.g. contributions that are a fixed percentage of salary), they are permitted to be recognised as a reduction of the service cost in the period in which the related service is rendered. Examples of contributions that are independent of the number of years of service include those that are a fixed percentage of the employee's salary, a fixed amount throughout the service period or dependent on the employee's age. *[IAS 19.93]*.

Application guidance is given in Appendix A to the standard in the form of the following flow chart.

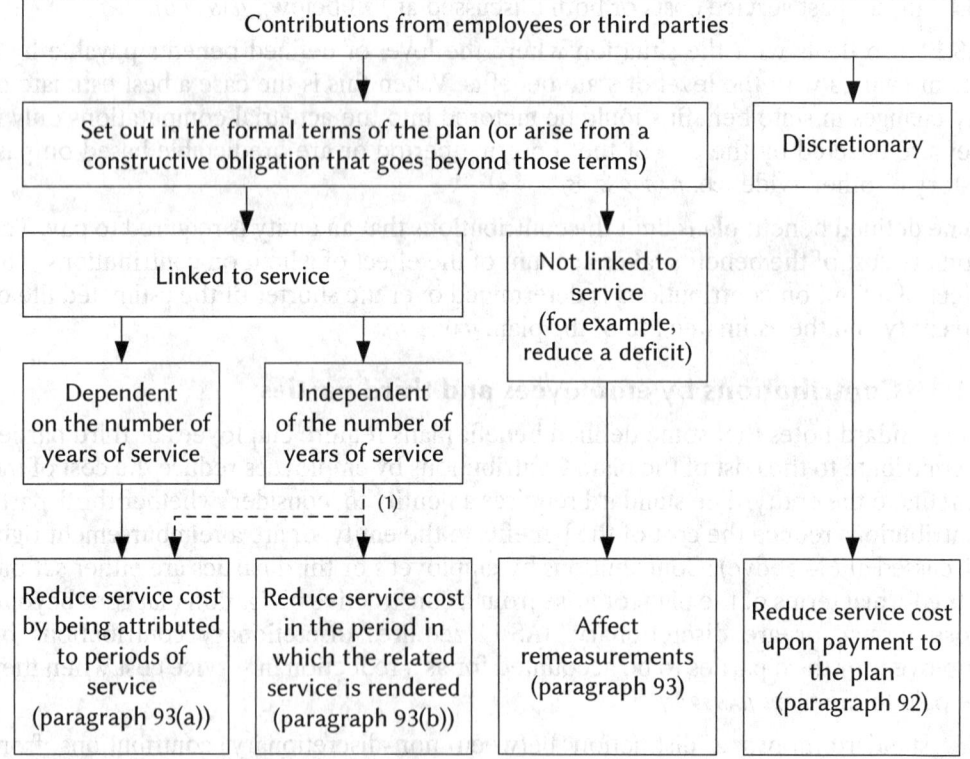

(1) This dotted arrow means that an entity is permitted to choose either accounting

Regrettably, the standard does not explain the 'mechanics' of an attribution which is required where contributions are linked to service.

In particular, it is unclear how to treat employee contributions made over the service period. As shown in Example 35.2 at 7.3 below, the projected unit credit method requires the net benefit to be expressed as a single net sum as at the date of retirement. Example 35.2 illustrates post-employment benefit payments being discounted to their present value as at the retirement date using the IAS 19 discount rate (discussed at 7.6 below). On the same principle, therefore, employee contributions made over the period of employment would logically need to be inflated to be expressed in the 'time value' as at retirement. However, IAS 19 does not indicate what rate should be used for this purpose.

We note, in this regard, that when the Interpretations Committee discussed the matter in November 2012, it considered a Staff Paper which touched on the matter. The numerical examples appended to the paper expressed the 'future value' of in-service employee contributions as at the date of retirement using the IAS 19 discount rate.[10] The content of the third example in this Staff Paper is reflected in the example set out below. This example pre-dates the amendments to IAS 19 in respect of employee contributions and therefore, we assume, that under the current standard that the entity has made an accounting policy choice to attribute contributions to periods of service, even though contributions are independent of the number of years of service.

Example 35.1:   Defined benefit plan with employee contributions, where the discount rate is higher than the salary growth rate

A lump sum benefit is payable on termination of service and equal to 1 per cent of final salary for each year of service.
The salary in year 1 is CU10,000 and is assumed to increase at 7 per cent (compound) each year. The discount rate used is 10 per cent per year.
Employees are required to contribute 0.5% of salary each year, on the last day of the year.

Year	1 CU	2 CU	3 CU	4 CU	5 CU	Total
Salary	10,000	10,700	11,449	12,250	13,108	
Benefit attributed to:						
– Prior years	–	131	262	393	524	
– Current year (1% of final salary) (a)	131	131	131	131	131	
	131	262	393	524	655	
Gross benefit						
Opening obligation	–	90	197	325	476	
Interest at 10%	–	9	20	32	48	109
Current service cost	90	98	108	119	131	546
Closing obligation	90	197	325	476	655	

Year	1 CU	2 CU	3 CU	4 CU	5 CU	Total
Employee contributions						
Actual contributions	(50)	(54)	(57)	(61)	(66)	(288)
Projected total contributions ('gross') (b)	(73)	(71)	(69)	(67)	(66)	(346)
Attributed contributions ('gross') (c)	(69)	(69)	(69)	(69)	(70)	(346)
Attributed contributions ('discounted')						
Opening	–	(47)	(104)	(172)	(251)	
Interest at 10%	–	(5)	(11)	(17)	(25)	(58)
Negative benefit (d)	(47)	(52)	(57)	(62)	(70)	(288)
Closing	(47)	(104)	(172)	(251)	(346)	
Benefit including effect of contributions						
Opening obligation	–	93	202	330	480	
Interest at 10% (e)	–	9	20	32	48	109
Net current service cost – current service cost less negative benefit (f)	43	46	51	57	61	258
Actual contributions	50	54	57	61	66	288
Closing	93	202	330	480	655	

Net benefit (gross benefit minus projected total contribution) is attributed to each year using the discount rate

Current service cost (f)	43	46	51	57	61	258

(a) Straight-lined (see 7.4 below)
(b) Future-valued contributions (e.g. for Year 1, value of contribution paid at end of year 1 at end of year 5 using discount rate of 10% will be $CU50 \times 1.1^4 = CU73$)
(c) Straight-lined to be on the same basis with the attributed benefit
(d) Present value of attributed contributions
(e) Includes rounding difference of (1) in Year 4
(f) Present value of gross benefit minus present value of projected total contributions

Journal entries (for Year 1)
To recognise net service cost
    Dr Service cost   43
        Cr Defined obligation   43
To reflect employee contributions
    Dr Plan asset   50
        Cr Defined benefit obligation   50

The standard notes that changes in employee or third-party contributions dependent on number of years of service result in:

(a) current and past service cost if the changes are not set out in the formal terms of the plan and do not arise from a constructive obligation; or

(b) actuarial gains and losses if the changes in contributions are set out in the formal terms of the plan or arise from a constructive obligation. *[IAS 19.94]*.

7.3 Actuarial methodology

IAS 19 notes that the ultimate cost of a defined benefit plan may be influenced by many variables, such as final salaries, employee turnover and mortality, employee contributions and medical cost trends. The ultimate cost of the plan is uncertain and this uncertainty is likely to persist over a long period of time. In order to measure the present value of the post-employment benefit obligations and the related current service cost, it is necessary:

- to apply an actuarial valuation method;
- to attribute benefit to periods of service; and
- to make actuarial assumptions. [IAS 19.66].

These steps are discussed in the following sections.

Plan obligations are to be measured using the projected unit credit method, [IAS 19.67], (sometimes known as the accrued benefit method pro-rated on service or as the benefit/years of service method). This method sees each period of service as giving rise to an additional unit of benefit entitlement and measures each unit separately to build up the final obligation. [IAS 19.68]. This actuarial method also determines the current service cost and any past service cost. [IAS 19.67]. IAS 19 provides a simple example of what this entails as follows: [IAS 19.68]

Example 35.2: The projected unit credit method

A lump sum benefit is payable on termination of service and equal to 1% of final salary for each year of service. The salary in year 1 is 10,000 and is assumed to increase at 7% (compound) each year. The discount rate used is 10% per year. The following table shows how the obligation builds up for an employee who is expected to leave at the end of year 5, assuming that there are no changes in actuarial assumptions. For simplicity, this example ignores the additional adjustment needed to reflect the probability that the employee may leave the entity at an earlier or later date.

Year	1	2	3	4	5
Benefit attributed to:					
– prior years	–	131	262	393	524
– current year (1% of final salary)	131	131	131	131	131
– current and prior years	131	262	393	524	655
Opening obligation	–	89	196	324	476
Interest at 10%	–	9	20	33	48
Current service cost	89	98	108	119	131
Closing obligation	89	196	324	476	655

Note:
– The opening obligation is the present value of benefit attributed to prior years.
– The current service cost is the present value of benefit attributed to the current year.
– The closing obligation is the present value of benefit attributed to current and prior years.

As can be seen in this simple example, the projected unit credit method produces a figure for current service cost and interest cost (and, although not illustrated here, would where appropriate produce a figure for past service cost). These cost components are discussed at 10 below.

This example from the standard contains no underlying workings or proofs. The most useful would be as follows:

Final salary at year 5 (10,000 compounded at 7%)	$10,000 \times (1 + 0.07)^4 = 13,100$
1% of final salary attributed to each year	131
Expected final benefit	5 years $\times$ 1% $\times$ 131,000 = 655

Current service cost, being present value of 131 discounted at 10%: e.g.

Year 1	$131 \times (1 + 0.1)^{-4} = 89$
Year 2	$131 \times (1 + 0.1)^{-3} = 98$

Closing obligation, being years served multiplied by present value of 131: e.g.

Year 3	3 years $\times$ 131 $\times (1 + 0.1)^{-2} = 324$

7.4 Attributing benefit to years of service

The projected unit credit method requires benefits to be attributed to the current period (in order to determine current service cost) and the current and prior periods (in order to determine the present value of defined benefit obligations).

IAS 19 requires benefits to be attributed to the periods in which the obligation to provide post-employment benefits arises. That is when employees render services in return for post-employment benefits which an entity expects to pay in future reporting periods. The standard takes the view that actuarial techniques allow an entity to measure that obligation with sufficient reliability to justify recognition of a liability. *[IAS 19.71]*.

The standard also explains that employee service gives rise to an obligation under a defined benefit plan even if the benefits are conditional on future employment (in other words they are not vested). *[IAS 19.70]*. Employee service before the vesting date is considered to give rise to a constructive obligation because, at each successive period end, the amount of future service that an employee will have to render before becoming entitled to the benefit is reduced. In measuring its defined benefit obligation, an entity should consider the probability that some employees may not satisfy any vesting requirements. Similarly, although certain post-employment benefits, such as post-employment medical benefits, become payable only if a specified event occurs when an employee is no longer employed, an obligation is considered to be created when the employee renders service that will provide entitlement to the benefit if the specified event occurs. The probability that the specified event will occur affects the measurement of the obligation but does not determine whether for accounting purposes the obligation exists. *[IAS 19.72]*.

In applying the projected unit credit method, IAS 19 normally requires benefits to be attributed to periods of service under the plan's 'benefit formula'. For example, in some schemes the benefit vests over time as service is provided, regardless of continued service in future periods. In these arrangements, an employee has some benefit vested whenever employment ceases, even if payment is made at a later date. Accordingly, the attribution of those benefits to periods of service is a straightforward matter and will match the period of employment (i.e. attribution commences on the hire date and ceases on the date that the participant leaves employment).

If, however, an employee's service in later years will lead to a materially higher level of benefit, the benefit should be attributed on a straight-line basis from:

(a) the date when service by the employee first leads to benefits under the plan; until

(b) the date when further service by the employee will lead to no material amount of further benefits under the plan, other than from further salary increases. *[IAS 19.70]*.

The requirements above apply the overarching principle of the standard, which is described as the 'objective' of IAS 19, i.e. that an entity recognises 'a liability when an employee has provided service in exchange for employee benefits to be paid in the future; and an expense when the entity consumes the economic benefits arising from service provided by an employee in exchange for employee benefits'.

As an example, some schemes have what some refer to as 'cliff vesting' where there is a requirement to be in employment at a certain age or on the occurrence of a certain future event in order for any entitlement to vest. For an arrangement like this it is necessary to determine the period over which the benefits should be recognised. The requirement to accrue benefits until 'further service by the employee will lead to no material amount of further benefits' effectively means that attribution should continue until the vesting date. Indeed, it would not be appropriate to have full provision for a benefit which has not yet vested – attribution must continue until the benefit has vested as this is the point at which 'further service by the employee will lead to no material amount of further benefits'.

The standard considers that this requirement is necessary because the employee's service throughout the entire period will ultimately lead to benefit at that higher level. *[IAS 19.73]*.

Once the date until when benefits should be attributed is determined, the next step is to determine the point from which 'service by the employees first leads to benefits under the plan'.

This is a factual matter to be determined in light of all the facts and circumstances.

For example, a scheme may require the participant to be in service at a certain age and also to have rendered a certain number of years of service to the employer. In this situation, some judgement may be required in determining when the period of attribution begins. This is illustrated by example 6 below where the benefit vests at the age of 55 provided 20 years' service have also been provided. The start of attribution is determined, in this example, by counting back 20 years from the vesting date.

IAS 19 illustrates the attribution of benefits to service periods with a number of worked examples as follows: *[IAS 19.71-74]*

Example 35.3: Attributing benefits to years of service

1. *A defined benefit plan provides a lump-sum benefit of 100 payable on retirement for each year of service.*

   A benefit of 100 is attributed to each year. The current service cost is the present value of 100. The present value of the defined benefit obligation is the present value of 100, multiplied by the number of years of service up to the end of the reporting period.

   If the benefit is payable immediately when the employee leaves the entity, the current service cost and the present value of the defined benefit obligation reflect the date at which the employee is expected to leave. Thus, because of the effect of discounting, they are less than the amounts that would be determined if the employee left at the end of the reporting period.

2. *A plan provides a monthly pension of 0.2% of final salary for each year of service. The pension is payable from the age of 65.*

   Benefit equal to the present value, at the expected retirement date, of a monthly pension of 0.2% of the estimated final salary payable from the expected retirement date until the expected date of death is attributed to each year of service. The current service cost is the present value of that benefit for the current year of service. The present value of the defined benefit obligation is the present value of monthly pension payments of 0.2% of final salary, multiplied by the number of years of service up to the end of the reporting period. The current service cost and the present value of the defined benefit obligation are discounted because pension payments begin at the age of 65.

3. *A plan pays a benefit of 100 for each year of service. The benefits vest after ten years of service.*

   A benefit of 100 is attributed to each year. In each of the first ten years, the current service cost and the present value of the obligation reflect the probability that the employee may not complete ten years of service.

4. *A plan pays a benefit of 100 for each year of service, excluding service before the age of 25. The benefits vest immediately.*

   No benefit is attributed to service before the age of 25 because service before that date does not lead to benefits (conditional or unconditional). A benefit of 100 is attributed to each subsequent year.

5. *A plan pays a lump-sum benefit of 1,000 that vests after ten years of service. The plan provides no further benefit for subsequent service.*

   A benefit of 100 (1,000 divided by ten) is attributed to each of the first ten years. The current service cost in each of the first ten years reflects the probability that the employee may not complete ten years of service. No benefit is attributed to subsequent years.

6. *A plan pays a lump-sum retirement benefit of 2,000 to all employees who are still employed at the age of 55 after twenty years of service, or who are still employed at the age of 65, regardless of their length of service.*

   For employees who join before the age of 35, service first leads to benefits under the plan at the age of 35 (an employee could leave at the age of 30 and return at the age of 33, with no effect on the amount or timing of benefits). Those benefits are conditional on further service. Also, service beyond the age of 55 will lead to no material amount of further benefits. For these employees, the entity attributes benefit of 100 (2,000 divided by twenty) to each year from the age of 35 to the age of 55.

   For employees who join between the ages of 35 and 45, service beyond twenty years will lead to no material amount of further benefits. For these employees, the entity attributes benefit of 100 (2,000 divided by twenty) to each of the first twenty years.

   For an employee who joins at the age of 55, service beyond ten years will lead to no material amount of further benefits. For this employee, the entity attributes benefit of 200 (2,000 divided by ten) to each of the first ten years.

   For all employees, the current service cost and the present value of the obligation reflect the probability that the employee may not complete the necessary period of service.

7. *A post-employment medical plan reimburses 40% of an employee's post-employment medical costs if the employee leaves after more than ten and less than twenty years of service and 50% of those costs if the employee leaves after twenty or more years of service.*

   Under the plan's benefit formula, the entity attributes 4% of the present value of the expected medical costs (40% divided by ten) to each of the first ten years and 1% (10% divided by ten) to each of the second ten years. The current service cost in each year reflects the probability that the employee may not complete the necessary period of service to earn part or all of the benefits. For employees expected to leave within ten years, no benefit is attributed.

8. *A post-employment medical plan reimburses 10% of an employee's post-employment medical costs if the employee leaves after more than ten and less than twenty years of service and 50% of those costs if the employee leaves after twenty or more years of service.*

   Service in later years will lead to a materially higher level of benefit than in earlier years. Therefore, for employees expected to leave after twenty or more years, the entity attributes benefit on a straight-line basis (see 7.3 above). Service beyond twenty years will lead to no material amount of further benefits. Therefore, the benefit attributed to each of the first twenty years is 2.5% of the present value of the expected medical costs (50% divided by twenty).

   For employees expected to leave between ten and twenty years, the benefit attributed to each of the first ten years is 1% of the present value of the expected medical costs. For these employees, no benefit is attributed to service between the end of the tenth year and the estimated date of leaving.

   For employees expected to leave within ten years, no benefit is attributed.

9. *Employees are entitled to a benefit of 3% of final salary for each year of service before the age of 55.*

   Benefit of 3% of estimated final salary is attributed to each year up to the age of 55. This is the date when further service by the employee will lead to no material amount of further benefits under the plan. No benefit is attributed to service after that age.

The following points of note are brought out in the above:

- The scenarios in 3 and 5 are economically identical and are attributed to years of service accordingly. In each case benefits only vest after ten years, however an obligation is to be built up over that period rather than at the end;

- Example 6 above illustrates a plan with two potential vesting outcomes: the employee is either in employment at the age of 65; or he or she has provided 20 years of service at the age of 55 or thereafter. We note that the initial fact pattern in example 6 does not include 'or thereafter' but we have assumed this is part of the fact pattern from the solution given in the example. This example highlights that the start and end of the period of attribution may be different from the dates of employment. While the example explains that the start date cannot be before the age of 35 on the grounds that an employee could leave and re-join the company before 35 without having any impact on the benefits received, a more realistic explanation perhaps is that an employee who is hired before the age of 35 would have no additional benefits compared to an employee who only joins at 35, regardless of how many years the former has worked for the company before the age of 35. This effectively means that any period before the age of 35 does not increase the employees' benefits under the plan formula and therefore no benefit should be attributed to service before the age of 35.

  As far as the end of the attribution period is concerned, the response provided in example 6 for employees who join between the ages of 35 and 45 assumes a fact that is not described in the initial fact pattern, i.e. that the benefits are earned by all employees who have provided 20 years of services and are 55 or above. Absent that fact, benefits would have to be straight-lined from the hiring date until the age of 65 for all employees joining after the age of 35. This illustrates how important it is to consider all facts and circumstances to work out an appropriate accounting treatment.

- Example 8 illustrates that accruing a 10% benefit over a period of 20 years of service which jumps to 50% once 20 years have been completed is an example of service in later years leading to a materially higher level of benefit. Accordingly, the obligation is to be built-up on a straight-line basis over 20 years.

- As regards example 9, the standard explains that where the amount of a benefit is a constant proportion of final salary for each year of service, future salary increases will affect the amount required to settle the obligation that exists for service before the end of the reporting period, but do not create an additional obligation. Therefore:
  (a) for the purpose of allocating benefits to years of service, salary increases are not considered to lead to further benefits, even though the amount of the benefits is dependent on final salary; and
  (b) the amount of benefit attributed to each period should be a constant proportion of the salary to which the benefit is linked. *[IAS 19.74]*.

7.5 Actuarial assumptions

The long timescales and numerous uncertainties involved in estimating obligations for post-employment benefits require many assumptions to be made when applying the projected unit credit method. These are termed actuarial assumptions and comprise:

(a) demographic assumptions about the future characteristics of current and former employees (and their dependants) who are eligible for benefits and deal with matters such as:
  (i) mortality, both during and after employment;
  (ii) rates of employee turnover, disability and early retirement;
  (iii) the proportion of plan members with dependants who will be eligible for benefits;
  (iv) the proportion of plan members who will select each form of payment option under the plan terms, (for example, a plan may offer participants a choice between a lump-sum cash payment, annuities and instalments over a defined period and these alternatives may have a significantly different impact on the measurement of the defined benefit obligation; and
  (v) claim rates under medical plans; and
(b) financial assumptions, dealing with items such as:
  (i) the discount rate;
  (ii) future salary and benefit levels, excluding the cost of benefits that will be met by the employees;
  (iii) in the case of medical benefits, future medical costs, including claim handling costs, which the standard describes as costs that will be incurred in processing and resolving claims, including legal and adjuster's fees; and
  (iv) taxes payable by the plan on contributions relating to service before the reporting date or on benefits resulting from that service. *[IAS 19.76]*.

The requirements of IAS 19 in this regard are set out below, with the exception of the discount rate which is discussed at 7.6 below.

The standard requires that actuarial assumptions be unbiased (that is, neither imprudent nor excessively conservative), mutually compatible and represent the employer's best estimates of the variables that will determine the ultimate cost of providing post-employment benefits. *[IAS 19.75-77]*. Actuarial assumptions are mutually compatible if they reflect the economic relationships between factors such as inflation, rates of salary increase and discount rates. For example, all assumptions which depend on a particular inflation level (such as assumptions about interest rates and salary and benefit increases) in any given future period should assume the same inflation level in that period. *[IAS 19.78]*.

The financial assumptions must be based on market expectations at the end of the reporting period, for the period over which the obligations are to be settled. *[IAS 19.80]*.

The standard requires that a defined benefit obligation be measured on a basis that reflects:

(a) the benefits set out in the terms of the plan (or resulting from any constructive obligation that goes beyond those terms) at the end of the reporting period;

(b) any estimated future salary increases that affect the benefits payable;

(c) the effect of any limit on the employer's share of the cost of the future benefits; and

(d) contributions from employees or third parties that reduce the ultimate cost to the entity of those benefits. *[IAS 19.87]*.

Regarding mortality, the standard requires assumptions to be a best estimate of the mortality of plan members both during and after employment. *[IAS 19.81]*. In particular, expected changes in mortality should be considered, for example by modifying standard mortality tables with estimates of mortality improvements. *[IAS 19.82]*.

Assumptions about medical costs should take account of inflation as well as specific changes in medical costs (including technological advances, changes in health care utilisation or delivery patterns, and changes in the health status of plan participants). *[IAS 19.96-97]*. The standard provides a quite detailed discussion of the factors that should be taken into account in making actuarial assumptions about medical costs, in particular:

(a) measuring post-employment medical benefits requires assumptions about the level and frequency of future claims, and the cost of meeting them. An employer should make such estimates based on its own experience, supplemented where necessary by historical data from other sources (such as other entities, insurance companies and medical providers); *[IAS 19.97]*

(b) the level and frequency of claims is particularly sensitive to the age, health status and sex of the claimants, and may also be sensitive to their geographical location. This means that any historical data used for estimating future claims need to be adjusted to the extent that the demographic mix of the plan participants differs from that of the population used as the basis for the historical data. Historical data should also be adjusted if there is reliable evidence that historical trends will not continue; *[IAS 19.98]* and

(c) estimates of future medical costs should take account of any contributions that claimants are required to make based on the terms (whether formal or constructive) of the plan at the end of the reporting period. The treatment of contributions by employees and third parties is discussed at 7.2 above.

Clearly, the application of actuarial techniques to compute plan obligations is a complex task, and it seems likely that few entities would seek to prepare valuations without the advice of qualified actuaries. However, IAS 19 only encourages, but does not require that an entity take actuarial advice. [IAS 19.59].

However sophisticated actuarial projections may be, reality will (apart from the most simple scenarios) always diverge from assumptions. This means that when a surplus or deficit is estimated, it will almost certainly be different from the predicted value based on the last valuation. These differences are termed actuarial gains and losses. The standard observes that actuarial gains and losses result from increases or decreases in the present value of a defined benefit obligation because of changes in actuarial assumptions and experience adjustments (see 10.4.1 below). Causes of actuarial gains and losses could include, for example:

(a) unexpectedly high or low rates of employee turnover, early retirement or mortality or of increases in salaries, benefits (if the formal or constructive terms of a plan provide for inflationary benefit increases) or medical costs;

(b) differences between the actual return on plan assets and amounts included as part of net interest in profit or loss;

(c) the effect of changes to assumptions concerning benefit payment options. Often an important example of this is the choice between an annuity and a lump sum payment as the various options are generally not actuarially equivalent (e.g. a lump sum payment will generally be less costly for the entity);

(d) the effect of changes in estimates of future employee turnover, early retirement or mortality or of increases in salaries, benefits (if the formal or constructive terms of a plan provide for inflationary benefit increases) or medical costs; and

(e) the effect of changes in the discount rate. [IAS 19.128, 111].

Actuarial gains and losses are discussed further at 10.4.1 below.

7.6 Discount rate

Due to the long timescales involved, post-employment benefit obligations are discounted. The whole obligation should be discounted, even if part of it is expected to be settled within twelve months of the end of the reporting period. [IAS 19.69]. The standard requires that the discount rate reflect the time value of money but not the actuarial or investment risk. Furthermore, the discount rate should not reflect the entity-specific credit risk borne by the entity's creditors, nor should it reflect the risk that future experience may differ from actuarial assumptions. [IAS 19.84]. The discount rate should reflect the estimated timing of benefit payments. For example, an appropriate rate may be quite different for a payment due in, say, ten years as opposed to one due in twenty. The standard observes that in practice, an acceptable answer can be obtained by applying a single weighted average discount rate that reflects the estimated timing and amount of benefit payments and the currency in which the benefits are to be paid. [IAS 19.85]. The standard does not preclude the use of a more granular approach in discounting cash flows at different periods along the yield curve. Nor does it preclude the use of different discount rates for different classes of participant in the interest of achieving a more precise measure of the defined benefit obligation than the computational shortcut which is allowed by the standard. An example of where discount rates may vary by class or participant is where there are both active and pensioner members, discount rates will vary by each of these classes purely as a result of their ages and the resultant timing of outflows associated to these classes. Whether it is acceptable to use the weighted average discount rate or a more granular approach is an entity's judgement which should be applied consistently. However, we would not expect an entity that elects to use the granular approach premised on it being a more precise measure to move back to the weighted average approach in subsequent periods.

The standard requires that actuarial assumptions, including discount rates be unbiased. [IAS 19.83]. A subpopulation of high quality corporate bonds (see 7.6.1 below) used to derive a discount rate would only result in an unbiased assumption if the selection from the population of bonds was not skewed. For example, the exclusion of bonds from a population outside two standard deviations of the mean (both at the higher end and the lower end) would not result in an unbiased selection of the discount rate. However, if the entity were to exclude say bonds with the lowest 40% and the highest 10% yields, or bonds with a yield below the median, these methods would produce biased results.

IAS 19 also stipulates that the discount rate (and other financial assumptions) should be determined in nominal (stated) terms, unless estimates in real (inflation-adjusted) terms are more reliable, for example, in a hyper-inflationary economy (see Chapter 16 for a discussion of IAS 29 – *Financial Reporting in Hyperinflationary Economies*), or where the benefit is index-linked and there is a deep market in index-linked bonds of the same currency and term. [IAS 19.79].

The basic part of this requirement – that a nominal rate be used – is consistent with the definition of the present value of a defined benefit obligation in that it should be ' ... the present value ... of expected future payments required to settle the obligation ...' (see 7.1 above). In other words, as the future cash flows are stated at the actual amounts expected to be paid, the rate used to discount them should reflect that and not be adjusted to remove the effects of expected inflation. In contrast, the reference to the use of index-linked bonds seems to allow taking account of inflation through the discount rate (which would require expressing cash flows in current prices). This approach seems to be in conflict with the definition of the obligation. However, in practice few index-linked corporate bonds exist (so it may be quite rare to have a deep market in them) and a more reliable approach may often be to take account of inflation via the projected cash flows.

The Interpretations Committee in July 2013 discussed whether the rate should be pre- or post-tax. It observed that the discount rate used to calculate a defined benefit obligation should be a pre-tax discount rate and decided not to add this issue to its agenda.[11]

Negative interest rates have been experienced in the past and at the time it was believed that these would be a temporary phenomenon, restricted to relatively short-term rates for certain government debt and deposits. This phenomenon has, however, not been short-lived with negative yields on government bonds seen in several countries and in some high quality corporate bonds. Discount rates are applied in various IFRS standards. In the context of IAS 19 specifically, the standard does not contain a zero percent floor and negative discount rates should be used.

7.6.1 High quality corporate bonds

The rate used should be determined 'by reference to' the yield (at the end of the reporting period) on high quality corporate bonds of currency and term consistent with the liabilities. For currencies in which there is no deep market in such bonds, the yields on government bonds should be used instead (see 7.6.2 below). *[IAS 19.83]*.

IAS 19 does not explain what is meant by the term 'high quality'. In practice it is considered, rightly in our view, to mean either: bonds rated AA, bonds rated AA or higher by Standard and Poor's, or an equivalent rating from another rating agency.

The requirement that the rate be determined 'by reference to' high quality bond rates is an important one.

The standard gives an example of this in the context of the availability of bonds with sufficiently long maturities. It notes that in some cases, there may be no deep market in bonds with a sufficiently long maturity to match the estimated maturity of all the benefit payments. In such cases, the standard requires the use of current market rates of the appropriate term to discount shorter-term payments, and estimation of the rate for longer maturities by extrapolating current market rates along the yield curve. In practice extrapolation is appropriate when longer maturities result in too few observable bonds for the rates derived from these to be meaningful. It goes on to observe that the total present value of a defined benefit obligation is unlikely to be particularly sensitive to the discount rate applied to the portion of benefits that is payable beyond the final maturity of the available corporate or government bonds. *[IAS 19.86]*.

In November 2013, the Interpretations Committee was asked whether corporate bonds with a rating lower than 'AA' can be considered to be 'high quality corporate bonds' ('HQCB').

The Interpretations Committee decided not to add the item to its agenda as issuing additional guidance or changing the requirements would be too broad for it to achieve in an efficient manner. The Interpretations Committee recommended that the IASB should address the issue as part of its research project on discount rates.[12] The Interpretations Committee reported this conclusion to the IASB at its December 2013 meeting. The IASB noted that no further work is currently planned on the issue of determining the discount rate for post-employment benefit obligations.[13]

The key observations of the Interpretations Committee were as follows.

- IAS 19 does not specify how to determine the market yields on HQCB, and in particular what grade of bonds should be designated as high quality;
- that 'high quality' as used in IAS 19 reflects an absolute concept of credit quality and not a concept of credit quality that is relative to a given population of corporate bonds, which would be the case, for example, if the paragraph used the term 'the highest quality'. Consequently, the concept of high quality should not change over time. Accordingly, a reduction in the number of HQCB should not result in a change to the concept of high quality. The Committee does not expect that an entity's methods and techniques used for determining the discount rate so as to reflect the yields on HQCB will change significantly from period to period;

- IAS 19 already contains requirements if the market in HQCB is no longer deep or if the market remains deep overall, but there is an insufficient number of HQCB beyond a certain maturity; and
- typically, the discount rate will be a significant actuarial assumption to be disclosed with sensitivity analyses under IAS 19.

As required by IAS 1 (see Chapter 3 at 5.1.1.B), disclosure is required of the judgements that management has made in the process of applying the entity's accounting policies and that have the most significant effect on the amounts recognised in the financial statements. Typically, the identification of the HQCB population used as a basis to determine the discount rate requires the use of judgement, which may often have a significant effect on the entity's financial statements.

In some countries ratings agencies may provide both a local rating and a global rating. As noted above the concept of 'high quality' is an absolute notion and therefore global ratings should be used to determine whether high quality corporate bonds exist in a currency.

7.6.2 No deep market

In currencies where there is no deep market in high quality corporate bonds, the market yields (at the end of the reporting period) on government bonds shall be used. *[IAS 19.83]*. This paragraph was amended by the Annual Improvements 2012-2014 Cycle replacing the reference to countries with a reference to currencies where there is no deep market in high quality corporate bonds. This amendment was issued to clarify, in particular, that for IAS 19 purposes the euro zone is considered in its entirety.

In June 2017, the Interpretations Committee considered a question on how an entity determines the rate to be used to discount post-employment benefit obligations in a country (in this case Ecuador) which has adopted another currency as its official or legal currency (in this case the US dollar). The entity's post-employment benefit obligation is denominated in US dollars. The submitter also confirmed that there was no deep market for high quality bonds denominated in US dollars in the country in which it operates (Ecuador).

The question asked by the submitter was whether in this situation the entity should consider the depth of the market in high quality corporate bonds denominated in US dollars in other markets or countries in which those bonds are issued. They also asked whether the entity can use market yields on bonds denominated in US dollars issued by the Ecuadorian government, or whether it is required to use market yields on bonds denominated in US dollars issued by a government in another market or country.

The Committee observed that applying paragraph 83 of IAS 19 (see 7.6.1 above) requires that:
- an entity with post-employment benefit obligations denominated in a particular currency assesses the depth of the market in high quality corporate bonds denominated in that currency, and does not limit this assessment to the market of country in which it operates;
- if there is a deep market in high quality corporate bonds denominated in that currency, the discount rate is determined by reference to market yields on high quality corporate bonds at the end of the reporting period;

- if there is no deep market in high quality corporate bonds in that currency, the entity determines the discount rate using market yields on government bonds denominated in that currency; and
- the entity applies judgement to determine the appropriate population of high quality corporate bonds or government bonds to reference when determining the discount rate. The currency and term of the bonds should be consistent with the currency and estimated term of the post-employment benefit obligations.

The Committee noted that the discount rate does not reflect the expected return on plan assets; the Basis of Conclusions IAS 19 confirms that the measurement of the obligation should be independent of the measurement of any plan assets held by the plan. *[IAS 19.BC130]*.

The Committee also considered the interaction between the matters discussed above and the requirement that actuarial assumptions be mutually compatible (see 7.5 above). *[IAS 19.75]*. The Committee concluded that it is not possible to assess whether, and to what extent, a discount rate derived by applying the specific requirements of IAS 19 is compatible with other actuarial assumptions and that the specific requirements of IAS 19 should be applied when determining the discount rate.

The overall conclusion of the Committee was that the requirements in IAS 19 provide an adequate basis for the determination of a discount rate in the circumstances described above. Consequently, the Committee decided not to add this matter to its agenda.

7.7 Frequency of valuations

When it addresses the frequency of valuations, IAS 19 does not give particularly prescriptive guidance. Rather, its starting point is simply to require that the present value of defined benefit obligations, and the fair value of plan assets, should be determined frequently enough to ensure that the amounts recognised in the financial statements do not differ materially from the amounts that would be determined at the end of the reporting period. *[IAS 19.58]*. An argument could be launched that, without a full valuation as at the end of the reporting period to compare with, it cannot be possible to know whether any less precise approach is materially different. However, it is reasonably clear that the intention of the standard is not necessarily to require full actuarial updates as at the reporting date. This is because the standard goes on to observe that for practical reasons a detailed valuation may be carried out before the end of the reporting period and that if such amounts determined before the end of the reporting period are used, they should be updated to take account of any material transactions or changes in circumstances up to the end of the reporting period. *[IAS 19.59]*. Much may depend on what is considered to be a 'material change', however it is expressly to include changes in market prices (hence requiring asset values to be those at the end of the reporting period) and interest rates, as well as financial actuarial assumptions. *[IAS 19.59, 80]*.

In this regard, it is also worth noting the observation in the standard that '[i]n some cases, estimates, averages and computational shortcuts may provide a reliable approximation of the detailed computations illustrated in this Standard'. *[IAS 19.60]*. It should be remembered, though, that it is the amounts in the financial statements which must not differ materially from what they would be based on a valuation at the end of the reporting period. For funded schemes, the net surplus or deficit is usually the difference between two very large figures – plan assets and plan liabilities. Such a net item is inevitably highly sensitive, in percentage terms, to a given percentage change in the gross amounts.

In summary, a detailed valuation will be required on an annual basis, but not necessarily as at the end of the reporting period. However, a valuation undertaken other than as at the end of the reporting period will need to be updated as at the end of the reporting period to reflect at least changes in observable market data, such as asset values and discount rates. The need for updates in respect of other elements of the valuation will depend on individual circumstances.

8 DEFINED BENEFIT PLANS – TREATMENT OF THE PLAN SURPLUS OR DEFICIT IN THE STATEMENT OF FINANCIAL POSITION

8.1 Net defined benefit liability (asset)

IAS 19 defines the net defined benefit liability or asset as the deficit or surplus in the plan adjusted for any effect of the asset ceiling (see 8.2 below).

The deficit or surplus is the present value of the defined benefit obligation (see 7 above) less the fair value of the plan assets (if any) (see 6 above).

The standard requires that the net defined benefit liability (asset) be recognised in the statement of financial position at each reporting period. *[IAS 19.63]*.

8.2 Restriction of assets to their recoverable amounts

The net defined benefit balance determined under IAS 19 may be an asset. The standard asserts that an asset may arise (that is, an asset measured on the basis of IAS 19) where a defined benefit plan has been 'over-funded' or when actuarial gains have arisen. The standard justifies the recognition of an asset in such cases because:

(a) the entity controls a resource, which is the ability to use the surplus to generate future benefits;

(b) that control is a result of past events (contributions paid by the entity and service rendered by the employee); and

(c) future economic benefits are available to the entity in the form of a reduction in future contributions or a cash refund, either directly to the entity or indirectly to another plan in deficit; the present value of those benefits is described as the asset ceiling. *[IAS 19.8, 65]*.

In practice, pension plans tend to be funded on a significantly more prudent basis than would be the case if a surplus or deficit was measured in accordance with IAS 19. In particular, the discount rate used for funding purposes is typically lower than the rate required by the standard. For this reason, an IAS 19 valuation may produce a surplus, when for funding purposes there is a deficit.

When there is a surplus in a defined benefit plan, the standard requires the net asset recognised to be restricted to the lower of the surplus in the plan and the asset ceiling discounted using the same discount rate used for determining the defined benefit obligation (see 7.6 above). *[IAS 19.8, 64, IFRIC 14.1]*.

Any adjustment required by the ceiling test is accounted for in other comprehensive income (see 10.4 below).

This limitation has proved quite problematic in practice and as a result was considered by the Interpretations Committee, initially in the context of statutory minimum funding requirements ('MFR'). This resulted in the publication, in July 2007, of IFRIC 14 – *IAS 19 – The Limit on a Defined Benefit Asset, Minimum Funding Requirements and their Interaction.* Whilst dealing with the interaction of the asset ceiling with MFR, IFRIC 14 also deals more generally with the restriction of an asset on recoverability grounds. *[IFRIC 14.1-3, 6]*. Subsequently, IFRIC 14 was amended to deal with pre-paid MFR – see 8.2.3 below. It should also be noted that the IASB has published an exposure draft of proposed amendments to IAS 19 and IFRIC 14 which addresses whether other parties' (for example pension trustees) power to enhance benefits for plan members or wind up a plan affects the availability of a refund (see 16.2.1 below). There is no current date for the finalisation of amendments to the interpretation and, at the date of writing, the current status of the project is described as follows: 'The Board decided not to finalise the proposed amendments to IFRIC 14. The Board will consider the project's direction at a future meeting. More specifically, the Board will consider whether to develop new proposals to address the matter.'

The Interpretations Committee notes that MFR exist in many countries and normally stipulate a minimum amount or level of contribution that must be made to a plan over a given period. Therefore, a minimum funding requirement may limit an entity's ability to reduce future contributions. *[IFRIC 14.2]*.

In addition, the limit on the measurement of a defined benefit asset may cause a minimum funding requirement to be onerous. Normally, a requirement to make contributions to a plan would not affect the measurement of the defined benefit asset or liability. This is because the contributions, once paid, will become plan assets and so the additional net liability is nil. However, a minimum funding requirement may give rise to a liability if the required contributions will not be available to the entity once they have been paid. *[IFRIC 14.3]*.

The issues addressed by IFRIC 14 are: *[IFRIC 14.6]*

- when refunds or reductions in future contributions should be regarded as available in accordance with the definition of the asset ceiling (discussed at 8.2.1 and 8.2.2 below);
- how a minimum funding requirement might affect the availability of reductions in future contributions (discussed at 8.2.3 below); and
- when a minimum funding requirement might give rise to a liability (discussed at 8.2.4 below).

8.2.1 IFRIC Interpretation 14 – general requirements concerning the limit on a defined benefit asset

IFRIC 14 clarifies that economic benefits, in the form of refunds or reduced future contributions, are available if they can be realised by the entity at some point during the life of the plan or when the plan liabilities are settled. In particular, such economic benefits may be available even if they are not realisable immediately at the end of the reporting period. *[IFRIC 14.8]*.

Furthermore, the benefit available does not depend on how the entity intends to use the surplus. The entity should determine the maximum economic benefit that is available from refunds, reductions in future contributions or a combination of both. However, economic benefits should not be recognised from a combination of refunds and reductions in future contributions based on assumptions that are mutually exclusive. *[IFRIC 14.9]*. Perhaps unnecessarily, the interpretation requires the availability of a refund or a reduction in future contributions to be determined in accordance with the terms and conditions of the plan and any statutory requirements in the jurisdiction of the plan. *[IFRIC 14.7]*.

The interpretation observes that an unconditional right to a refund can exist whatever the funding level of a plan at the end of the reporting period. The interpretation further states that benefits are available as a refund only if the entity has an unconditional right to a refund:

(a) during the life of the plan, without assuming that the plan liabilities must be settled in order to obtain the refund; or

(b) assuming the gradual settlement of the plan liabilities over time until all members have left the plan; or

(c) assuming the full settlement of the plan liabilities in a single event (i.e. as a plan wind-up).

However, if the right to a refund of a surplus depends on the occurrence or non-occurrence of one or more uncertain future events not wholly within an entity's control, the entity does not have an unconditional right and should not recognise an asset. *[IFRIC 14.11-12]*.

The economic benefit available as a refund should be measured as the amount of the surplus at the end of the reporting period (being the fair value of the plan assets less the present value of the defined benefit obligation) that the entity has a right to receive as a refund, less any associated costs. For example, if a refund would be subject to a tax other than income tax of the reporting entity, it should be measured net of the tax. *[IFRIC 14.13]*. Tax on defined benefit pension plans is discussed further in Chapter 33 at 10.7.

In measuring the amount of a refund available when the plan is wound up (point (c) above), the costs to the plan of settling the plan liabilities and making the refund should be included. For example, a deduction should be made for professional fees if these are paid by the plan rather than the entity, and the costs of any insurance premiums that may be required to secure the liability on wind-up. *[IFRIC 14.14]*.

It is usually the case that the trustees of a pension fund are independent of the entity. Trustees may have a variety of powers to influence a surplus in a plan. For example:
- setting the investment strategy whereby assets with lower risk and lower return would erode a surplus over time; or the purchase of assets in the form of insurance policies matching all or some of the cash outflows of the plan; or
- full or partial settlement of liabilities; or the improvement of benefits under the plan.

IFRIC 14 makes it clear that for future benefit improvements made by the employer and actuarial gains and losses, the existence of an asset at the end of the reporting period is not affected by possible future changes to the amount of the surplus. If future events occur that change the amount of the surplus, their effects are recognised when they occur. *[IFRIC 14.BC10]*.

The interpretation is also clear that if the right to a refund of a surplus depends on the occurrence or non-occurrence of one or more uncertain future events that are not wholly within an entity's control, the entity does not have an unconditional right and should not recognise a surplus. *[IFRIC 14.11-12]*.

However, neither IAS 19 nor IFRIC 14 address the question of whether the entity's right to a refund of a surplus which depends on the occurrence or non-occurrence of uncertain future events means that no surplus should be recognised in any scenario where trustees have the power to 'spend' a surplus.

As noted above, the IASB has published an exposure draft of proposed amendments to IFRIC 14 which addresses whether the power of other parties (for example pension trustees) to enhance benefits for plan members or wind up a plan affects the availability of a refund (see 16.2.1 below). This exposure draft was issued as a response to two requests to the Interpretations Committee, suggesting that there is diversity in practice in this area. In the Basis for Conclusions on the exposure draft the IASB noted that paragraph BC10 of IFRIC 14 had not specifically addressed the circumstances in which trustees have such unconditional powers. The exposure draft proposes that the amount of the surplus that the entity recognises as an asset on the basis of a future refund shall not include amounts that other parties can use for other purposes that affect the benefits for plan members, for example by enhancing those benefits without the entity's consent. Until the issue is clarified through the amendment to the standard and interpretation we expect diversity in practice to continue in this area.

If the amount of a refund is determined as the full amount or a proportion of the surplus, rather than a fixed amount, an entity should make no adjustment for the time value of money, even if the refund is realisable only at a future date. *[IFRIC 14.15]*.

8.2.2 Economic benefits available as reduced future contributions when there are no minimum funding requirements for future service

IFRIC 14 addresses separately cases where there are minimum funding requirements relating to benefits to be awarded in future periods in exchange for services to be rendered in those periods, and cases where there are no such funding requirements.

This section deals with the situation where there are no such funding requirements. The implications of future service minimum funding requirements are discussed at 8.2.3 below.

IFRIC 14 requires that the economic benefit available by way of reduced future contributions be determined as the future service cost to the entity for each period over the shorter of the expected life of the plan and the expected life of the entity. The future service cost to the entity excludes amounts that will be borne by employees. *[IFRIC 14.16]*.

Future service costs should be determined using assumptions consistent with those used to determine the defined benefit obligation and with the situation that exists at the end of the reporting period as determined by IAS 19. Accordingly, no future changes to the benefits to be provided by a plan should be assumed until the plan is amended, and a stable workforce in the future should be assumed unless the entity makes a reduction in the number of employees covered by the plan. In the latter case, the assumption about the future workforce should include the reduction. The present value of the future service cost should be determined using the same discount rate as that used in the calculation of the defined benefit obligation (discount rates are discussed at 7.6 above). *[IFRIC 14.17]*.

8.2.3 IFRIC Interpretation 14 – the effect of a minimum funding requirement on the economic benefit available as a reduction in future contributions

IFRIC 14 defines minimum funding requirements as 'any requirements to fund a post-employment or other long-term defined benefit plan'. *[IFRIC 14.5]*. This is clearly quite a wide definition encompassing more than just statutory regimes.

Some minimum funding arrangements require periodic reappraisal (for example, every three years). Should such an arrangement cover a longer period, all payments over this longer period constitute the minimum funding requirement, not just the three years until the next reappraisal. In its March 2015 meeting the Interpretations Committee, following a request for clarification, discussed whether an entity should assume that the minimum funding requirement for contributions to cover future services (see below) would continue over the estimated life of the pension plan. In its July 2015 meeting, the Interpretations Committee noted that the entity should assume a continuation of existing funding principles because:[14]

- For any factors not specified by the minimum funding basis (for example, the period to continue the plan is not specified by the existing funding principles), the assumptions for determining future service costs and those used to estimate the future minimum funding requirement contributions for future service must be consistent. This is because the Interpretation requires an entity to use assumptions that are consistent with those used to determine the defined benefit obligation and with the situation that exists at the end of the reporting period. *[IFRIC 14.17, 21]*.
- The estimate should not include changes to the funding principles to determine contributions for future service, if such changes require future negotiations with pension trustees. *[IFRIC 14.21, BC30]*.

The interpretation requires any minimum funding requirement at a given date to be analysed into contributions that are required to cover: *[IFRIC 14.18]*

(a) any existing shortfall for past service on the minimum funding basis. These contributions do not affect future contributions for future service. However, they may give rise to a liability under IFRIC 14 (see 8.2.4 below); *[IFRIC 14.19]* and

(b) future service.

If there is a minimum funding requirement for contributions relating to future service, the economic benefit available as a reduction in future contributions is the sum of: *[IFRIC 14.20]*

(a) any amount that reduces future minimum funding requirement contributions for future service because the entity made a pre-payment (that is, it paid the amount before being required to do so); and

(b) the estimated future service cost in each period (as discussed at 8.2.2 above) less the estimated minimum funding requirement contributions that would be required for future service in those periods if there were no pre-payment as described in (a).

The future minimum funding contributions required in respect of future service should be calculated:

- taking into account the effect of any existing surplus on the minimum funding requirement basis but excluding the pre-payment discussed in (a) immediately above;
- using assumptions consistent with the minimum funding requirement basis. For any factors not specified by the minimum funding requirement, the assumptions used should be consistent with those used to determine the defined benefit obligation and with the situation that exists at the end of the reporting period as determined by IAS 19;
- including any changes expected as a result of the entity paying the minimum contributions when they are due; and
- excluding the effect of expected changes in the terms and conditions of the minimum funding basis that are not substantively enacted or contractually agreed at the end of the reporting period. *[IFRIC 14.21]*.

If the future minimum funding contribution required in respect of future service exceeds the future IAS 19 service cost in any given period, the present value of that excess reduces the amount of the asset available as a reduction in future contributions. However, the amount of the asset available as a reduction in future contributions can never be less than zero. *[IFRIC 14.22]*.

The mechanics of the above requirements are illustrated in the following two examples based on the illustrative examples accompanying IFRIC 14. *[IFRIC 14.IE9-IE27]*. Example 35.4 also illustrates the requirement in certain circumstances to recognise an additional liability for future MFR payments in respect of past service (discussed at 8.2.4 below).

Example 35.4: Deficit-clearing future minimum funding requirements when refunds are not available

An entity has a funding level on the minimum funding requirement basis (which is measured on a different basis from that required under IAS 19) of 95% in Plan C. Under the minimum funding requirements, the entity is required to pay contributions to increase the funding level to 100% over the next three years. The contributions are required to make good the deficit on the minimum funding requirement basis (shortfall) and to cover future service.

Plan C also has an IAS 19 surplus at the end of the reporting period of €50m, which cannot be refunded to the entity under any circumstances. There are no unrecognised amounts.

The nominal amounts of the minimum funding contribution requirements in respect of the shortfall and the future IAS 19 service cost for the next three years are set out below.

Year	Total minimum funding contribution requirement €m	Minimum contributions required to make good the shortfall €m	Minimum contributions required to cover future accrual €m
1	135	120	15
2	125	112	13
3	115	104	11

The entity's present obligation in respect of services already received includes the contributions required to make good the shortfall but does not include the minimum contributions required to cover future service.

The present value of the entity's obligation, assuming a discount rate of 6% per year, is approximately 300, calculated as follows:

$$€120m \div (1.06) + €112m \div (1.06)^2 + €104m \div (1.06)^3$$

When these contributions are paid into the plan, the IAS 19 surplus (i.e. the fair value of assets less the present value of the defined benefit obligation) would, other things being equal, increase from €50m to €350m. However, the surplus is not refundable although an asset may be available as a future contribution reduction.

As noted above, the economic benefit available as a reduction in future contributions is the present value of:

- the future service cost in each year to the entity; less
- any minimum funding contribution requirements in respect of the future accrual of benefits in that year

over the expected life of the plan.

The amounts available as a future contribution reduction are set out below.

Year	IAS 19 service cost €m	Minimum contributions required to cover future accrual €m	Amount available as contribution reduction €m
1	13	15	(2)
2	13	13	0
3	13	11	2
4+	13	9	4

Assuming a discount rate of 6%, the economic benefit available as a future contribution reduction is therefore equal to:

$$€(2)m \div (1.06) + €0m \div (1.06)^2 + €2m \div (1.06)^3 + €4m \div (1.06)^4 + €4m \div (1.06)^5 + €4m \div (1.06)^6 \ldots = €56m.$$

The asset available from future contribution reductions is accordingly limited to €56m.

As discussed at 8.2.4 below, IFRIC 14 requires the entity to recognise a liability to the extent that the additional contributions payable will not be fully available. Therefore, the effect of the asset ceiling is to reduce the defined benefit asset by €294m (€50m + €300m – €56m).

As discussed at 10.4 below, the effect of the asset ceiling is part of remeasurements and the €294m is recognised immediately in other comprehensive income and the entity recognises a net liability of €244m. No other liability is recognised in respect of the obligation to make contributions to fund the minimum funding shortfall.

When the contributions of €300m are paid into the plan, the net asset will become €56m (€300m – €244m).

Example 35.5: Effect of a prepayment when a minimum funding requirement exceeds the expected future service charge

An entity is required to fund Plan D so that no deficit arises on the minimum funding basis. The entity is required to pay minimum funding requirement contributions to cover the service cost in each period determined on the minimum funding basis.

Plan D has an IAS 19 surplus of 35 at the beginning of 2017. This example assumes that the discount rate is 0%, and that the plan cannot refund the surplus to the entity under any circumstances but can use the surplus for reductions of future contributions.

The minimum contributions required to cover future service are €15 for each of the next five years. The expected IAS 19 service cost is €10 in each year.

The entity makes a prepayment of €30 at the beginning of 2017 in respect of years 2017 and 2018, increasing its surplus at the beginning of 2017 to €65. That prepayment reduces the future contributions it expects to make in the following two years, as follows:

Year	IAS 19 service cost (€)	Minimum funding requirement contribution: Before pre-payment (€)	After pre-payment (€)
2017	10	15	0
2018	10	15	0
2019	10	15	15
2020	10	15	15
2021	10	15	15
Total	50	75	45

At the beginning of 2017, the economic benefit available as a reduction in future contributions is the sum of:

- 30, being the prepayment of the minimum funding requirement contributions; and
- nil. The estimated minimum funding requirement contributions required for future service would be 75 if there was no prepayment. Those contributions exceed the estimated future service cost (50); therefore the entity cannot use any part of the surplus of 35.

Assuming a discount rate of 0%, the present value of the economic benefit available as a reduction in future contributions is equal to 30. Accordingly, the entity recognises an asset of 30 (because this is lower than the IAS 19 surplus of 65).

Two points worth noting in Example 35.5 above are as follows. The first is that, if IFRIC 14 did not allow the recognition of such prepayments, the full surplus of €65 would have been written off. The second is that, in the fact pattern of the question, it is unnecessary to know that the surplus before the prepayment was €35. This is because any surplus (other than the prepayment of MFR) would not be recognised because refunds are not available and future MFR exceeds future service costs.

8.2.4 IFRIC Interpretation 14 – when a minimum funding requirement may give rise to a liability

If there is an obligation under a minimum funding requirement to pay contributions to cover an existing shortfall on the minimum funding basis in respect of services already received, the entity should determine whether the contributions payable will be available as a refund or reduction in future contributions after they are paid into the plan. *[IFRIC 14.23]*. Recovery through reduced future contributions is discussed at 8.2.2 and 8.2.3 above.

If a surplus is recoverable by way of a refund (see 8.2.1 above), a minimum funding requirement to cover a shortfall in respect of past services will neither restrict an IAS 19 asset nor trigger the recognition of a liability as it will be recoverable with any refund. IFRIC 14 illustrates this by way of an example upon which the following is based. *[IFRIC 14.IE1-2]*.

Example 35.6: *Effect of the minimum funding requirement when there is an IAS 19 surplus and the minimum funding contributions payable are fully refundable to the entity*

An entity has a funding level on the minimum funding requirement basis (which is measured on a different basis from that required under IAS 19) of 82% in Plan A. Under the minimum funding requirements, the entity is required to increase the funding level to 95% immediately. As a result, the entity has a statutory obligation at the end of the reporting period to contribute €200m to Plan A immediately. The plan rules permit a full refund of any surplus to the entity at the end of the life of the plan. The year-end valuations for Plan A are set out below.

	€million
Fair value of assets	1,200
Present value of defined benefit obligation under IAS 19	(1,100)
Surplus	100
Defined benefit asset (before consideration of the minimum funding requirement)	100

Payment of the contributions of €200m will increase the IAS 19 surplus from €100m to €300m. Under the rules of the plan this amount will be fully refundable to the entity with no associated costs. Therefore, no liability is recognised for the obligation to pay the contributions and the net defined benefit asset will be recognised at €100m.

To the extent that the contributions payable will not be available after they are paid into the plan, a liability should be recognised when the obligation arises. The liability should reduce the net defined benefit asset or increase the net defined benefit liability so that no gain or loss is expected to result from the effect of the asset ceiling when the contributions are paid. *[IFRIC 14.24]*.

IFRIC 14 illustrates this by way of an example upon which the following is based. *[IFRIC 14.IE3-8]*.

Example 35.7: *Effect of a minimum funding requirement when there is an IAS 19 deficit and the minimum funding contributions payable would not be fully available*

An entity has a funding level on the minimum funding requirement basis (which is measured on a different basis from that required under IAS 19) of 77% in Plan B. Under the minimum funding requirements, the entity is required to increase the funding level to 100% immediately. As a result, the entity has a statutory obligation at the end of the reporting period to pay additional contributions of €300m to Plan B. The plan rules permit a maximum refund of 60% of the IAS 19 surplus to the entity and the entity is not permitted to reduce its contributions below a specified level which happens to equal the IAS 19 service cost. The year-end valuations for Plan B are set out below.

	€million
Fair value of assets	1,000
Present value of defined benefit obligation under IAS 19	(1,100)
Deficit	(100)

The payment of €300m would change the IAS 19 deficit of €100m to a surplus of €200m. Of this €200m, 60% (€120m) is refundable. Therefore, of the contributions of €300m,

€100m eliminates the IAS 19 deficit and €120m (60% of €200m) is available as an economic benefit. The remaining €80m (40% of €200m) of the contributions paid is not available to the entity. As discussed above, IFRIC 14 requires the entity to recognise a liability to the extent that the additional contributions payable are not available to it. Accordingly, the net defined benefit liability is €180m, comprising the deficit of €100m plus the additional liability of €80m with €80m also being recognised in other comprehensive income. No other liability is recognised in respect of the statutory obligation to pay contributions of €300m. When the contributions of €300m are paid, the net asset will be €120m. If the entity were required to achieve a 100% funding position at some point in the future, but not immediately, the present value of its contributions over this period would be used in the calculation above.

8.2.5 Pension funding payments contingent on future events within the control of the entity

As entities begin to consider moving away, in part at least, from deficit funding contributions which are fixed payments at fixed dates (which are clearly deficit clearing minimum funding requirements) to contributions contingent on future events, what constitutes a minimum funding requirement becomes more important, especially where it is concluded that an IAS 19 surplus is not recoverable. The definition of plan assets is discussed at 6.1 above and minimum funding requirements are discussed at 8.2.3 above. Where a surplus is not recoverable, under the asset ceiling:

- an instrument recognised as a plan asset would be written off; and
- an arrangement which, whilst not being a plan asset, is considered a minimum funding requirement, would be provided for under IFRIC 14.

However, an arrangement which is considered neither a plan asset nor a minimum funding requirement would not be accounted for until payments are made. An example of such a situation is a requirement to make a contribution to a plan at some multiple of any dividends paid within a specified period. Such a right to receive a contribution in these circumstances may or may not meet the definition of a plan asset depending on its precise terms (in particular, whether the right is a 'transferable' one).

In this situation, a funding payment only happens as a result of an action within the control of the entity. Accordingly, such an obligation on a stand-alone basis would not be considered a financial liability under IAS 32 – *Financial Instruments: Presentation*.

This leads to the key consideration of what accounting treatment to apply to a binding agreement requiring the making of payments to a plan only if the entity undertakes a separate transaction which is wholly within its control:

- if the corresponding entitlement of the plan does not meet the definition of a plan asset (for example, if it is non-transferable); and
- it is considered not to be a minimum funding requirement (as it is contingent on the actions of the entity).

Two possibilities present themselves, which would have quite different accounting consequences.

One view may be that these contingent contributions would meet the definition of a minimum funding requirement. IAS 19 is based on the best estimates of ultimate cashflows and it is unequivocal that cashflows used to calculate the defined benefit obligation include the effect of actions which are within the control of the entity. Most obviously, both continued employment and pay increases are within the control of the employer and are estimated to determine the defined benefit obligation and service cost (see 7.5 above). Therefore, if the defined benefit obligation reflects a best estimate of future actions within the control of the entity, an argument could be made that a similar approach could be taken to funding payments. If it is believed that contingent contributions meet the definition of a minimum funding requirement, any accounting consequences of them would be recognised at the inception of the agreement. Under this view the entity would need to make a best estimate of the amount and timing of any future contributions, and determine whether an additional liability arises under IFRIC 14 where these would not be recoverable (see 8.2.4 above).

An alternative view that contingent funding is not a minimum funding requirement could be formed by analogy to IAS 32 or IAS 37. A cash payment which the entity could avoid would not generally be accounted for as a financial liability under IAS 32. It could be argued that it would therefore not be encompassed within the phrase 'any requirement to fund'. Under this analysis the definition of a plan asset (see 6.1 above) becomes particularly important. A transferable instrument would be a plan asset, and would be written off under the asset ceiling mechanism if it is not considered recoverable under IFRIC 14. A non-transferable instrument would not meet the definition of a plan asset. If such an instrument was not considered a minimum funding requirement (because it could be avoided by the entity) it would not be accounted for until a payment were made.

If analogy were made to IAS 37, the presence of a constructive obligation could trigger recognition of a liability in respect of irrecoverable minimum funding payments at the moment it becomes probable that an outflow of resources will be required to settle the obligation and it can be estimated reliably.

The appropriate accounting treatment of any particular arrangement will require judgement to be made based on the individual facts and circumstances.

9 DEFINED BENEFIT PLANS – PRESENTATION OF THE NET DEFINED BENEFIT LIABILITY (ASSET)

Neither IAS 19 nor IAS 1 specifies where in the statement of financial position a net asset or net liability in respect of a defined benefit plan should be presented, nor whether such balances should be shown separately on the face of the statement of financial position or only in the notes – this is left to the discretion of the reporting entity subject to the general requirements of IAS 1 discussed in Chapter 3 at 3.1. If the format of the statement of financial position distinguishes current assets and liabilities from non-current ones, the question arises as to whether this split needs also to be made for pension balances. IAS 19 does not specify whether such a split should be made, on the grounds that it may sometimes be arbitrary. *[IAS 19.133, BC200]*.

Employers with more than one plan may find that some are in surplus while others are in deficit. IAS 19 contains offset criteria closely modelled on those in IAS 32. *[IAS 19.132]*. An asset relating to one plan may only be offset against a liability relating to another plan when there is a legally enforceable right to use a surplus in one plan to settle obligations under the other plan, and the employer intends to settle the obligations on a net basis or realise the surplus and settle the obligation simultaneously. *[IAS 19.131]*. We believe that these offset criteria are unlikely to be met in practice.

10 DEFINED BENEFIT PLANS – TREATMENT IN PROFIT OR LOSS AND OTHER COMPREHENSIVE INCOME

IAS 19 identifies three components of annual pension cost as follows:

(a) service cost (see 10.1 below);

(b) net interest on the net defined benefit liability (asset) (see 10.3 below); and

(c) remeasurements of the net defined benefit liability (see 10.4 below). *[IAS 19.120]*.

Of these, (a) and (b) are recognised in profit or loss and (c) is recognised in other comprehensive income. This is unless another standard requires or permits the costs to be included in the cost of an asset, for example IAS 2 – *Inventories* – and IAS 16 – *Property, Plant and Equipment*. Where the post-employment benefit costs are included in the cost of an asset the appropriate proportion of all the above items must be included. *[IAS 19.121]*. There is no guidance in the standard as to what an 'appropriate' proportion of these items might be, although both IAS 2 and IAS 16 are clear that only those costs which are directly attributable to the asset qualify for capitalisation. It is not necessarily the case that the appropriate proportion will be the same for all of the components and judgement will be required in deciding how much of each item can meaningfully be said to relate to the production of an asset.

Remeasurements recognised in other comprehensive income should not be reclassified to profit and loss in a subsequent period. The standard notes that those amounts may be transferred within equity. *[IAS 19.122]*.

The standard states that it does not specify how an entity should present service cost and net interest on the net defined benefit liability or asset. The presentation of these components in the profit and loss account are accounted for in accordance with IAS 1 (see Chapter 3 at 3.2) and could either be included in one line or split between lines in the income statement according to its nature. *[IAS 19.134]*. For example, the net interest could be presented in the income statement along with other finance items.

10.1 Service cost

Service cost comprises:

(a) current service cost – the increase in the present value of the defined benefit obligation resulting from employee service in the current period;

(b) past service cost – the change in the present value of the defined benefit obligation for employee service in prior periods, resulting from a plan amendment (the introduction or withdrawal of, or changes to, a defined benefit plan) or a curtailment (a significant reduction by the entity in the number of employees covered by a plan); and

(c) any gain or loss on settlement – the difference, at the date of settlement, between the present value of the defined benefit obligation being settled and the settlement price, including any plan assets transferred and any payments made directly by the entity in connection with the settlement. *[IAS 19.8, 109]*. The gain or loss is recognised when the settlement occurs. *[IAS 19.110]*.

The current service cost should be determined using the projected unit credit method. *[IAS 19.67]*. The basic computation is illustrated in Example 35.2 at 7.3 above.

There is no need to distinguish between past service cost resulting from a plan amendment, past service cost resulting from a curtailment and a gain or loss on settlement if these transactions occur together. In some cases, a plan amendment occurs before a settlement, such as when an entity changes the benefits under the plan and settles the amended benefits later. In those cases an entity recognises past service cost before any gain or loss on settlement. *[IAS 19.8, 100]*.

A settlement occurs together with a plan amendment and curtailment if a plan is terminated with the result that the obligation is settled and the plan ceases to exist. However, the termination of a plan is not a settlement if the plan is replaced by a new plan that offers benefits that are, in substance, the same. *[IAS 19.101]*.

10.2 Changes in a defined benefit plan

Accounting for past service costs (plan amendments or curtailments) and settlements are discussed in sections 10.2.1 and 10.2.3 below, respectively. The acquisition of a qualifying insurance policy not directly connected with a settlement is discussed at 10.2.2 below. Each of these sections detail where any gain or loss arising is recorded which will either be in the profit and loss account or other comprehensive income.

In summary, when determining the effect of such a transaction, the net defined benefit liability (asset) should be remeasured using up to date values for plan assets and actuarial assumptions before and after the event to determine the effect of it. *[IAS 19.99]*.

Any past service cost, or gain or loss on settlement should be recognised and measured without considering the effect of the asset ceiling (see 8.2 above). The effect of the asset ceiling should then be determined after the plan amendment, curtailment or settlement with any change in that effect, excluding amounts included in net interest, recognised in other comprehensive income. *[IAS 19.101A]*.

Current service cost should ordinarily be determined using actuarial assumptions as at the start of the reporting period. However, as discussed at 10.2.1 below, a plan amendment, curtailment or settlement during a reporting period will require remeasurement of the net defined benefit liability (asset). In such cases the current service cost for the remainder of the period, that is, after the plan amendment, curtailment or settlement, should be calculated using the actuarial assumptions used to for the remeasurement. *[IAS 19.122A]*.

The point in time at which a plan amendment occurs will often be a matter of fact based on the legal entitlements of plan members. Judgement may be required, based on individual facts and circumstances, if the benefits concerned constitute constructive, as opposed to legal, obligations (see 7.1 above).

Sometimes benefit plans are amended in such a way as to allow members a choice, for a limited period, between two or more benefit arrangements. In such cases a plan amendment occurs (and a positive or negative past service cost will be recognised) on the date at which the new arrangement comes into existence (legally or constructively) and not at the later date by which members are required to make their choice. This may mean that the initial accounting for the plan amendment will require estimates to be made of the choices which members will make. However, if it is known, at the time the relevant financial statements are prepared, what choices members have made (for example, because the 'window' for making selections closes before the financial statements are authorised for issue) this definitive data would remove the need for estimation. Any subsequent changes in estimates in the following years resulting from the confirmation process would be a change in estimate and recognised as a remeasurement gain or loss.

10.2.1 Past service cost

Past service cost is the change in the present value of the defined benefit obligation resulting from a plan amendment or curtailment. *[IAS 19.8, 102]*.

Past service costs should be recognised at the earlier of the date when:

(a) the plan amendment or curtailment occurs; and

(b) the entity recognises related restructuring costs in accordance with IAS 37 (discussed in Chapter 26 at 6.1). *[IAS 19.8, 103]*.

A plan amendment occurs when an entity introduces, or withdraws, a defined benefit plan or changes the benefits payable under an existing defined benefit plan. *[IAS 19.8, 104]*.

A curtailment occurs when an entity significantly reduces the number of employees covered by a plan. A curtailment may arise from an isolated event, such as the closing of a plant, discontinuance of an operation or termination or suspension of a plan. *[IAS 19.8, 105]*.

Past service cost may be either positive (when benefits are introduced or changed so that the present value of the defined benefit obligation increases) or negative (when benefits are withdrawn or changed so that the present value of the defined benefit obligation decreases). *[IAS 19.8, 106]*.

Where an entity reduces benefits payable under an existing defined benefit plan and, at the same time, increases other benefits payable under the plan for the same employees, the entity treats the change as a single net change. *[IAS 19.8, 107]*.

Past service cost excludes:

(a) the effect of differences between actual and previously assumed salary increases on the obligation to pay benefits for service in prior years (there is no past service cost because actuarial assumptions allow for projected salaries, accordingly the effect of any such difference is an actuarial gain or loss – see 7.5 above);

(b) under- and over-estimates of discretionary pension increases when an entity has a constructive obligation to grant such increases (there is no past service cost because actuarial assumptions allow for such increases, accordingly the effect of any such under- or over-estimate is an actuarial gain or loss – see 7.5 above);

(c) estimates of benefit improvements that result from actuarial gains or from the return on plan assets that have been recognised in the financial statements if the entity is obliged, by either the formal terms of a plan (or a constructive obligation that goes beyond those terms) or legislation, to use any surplus in the plan for the benefit of plan participants, even if the benefit increase has not yet been formally awarded (the resulting increase in the obligation is an actuarial loss and not past service cost, see 7.5 above); and

(d) the increase in vested benefits (that is, those not conditional on future employment) when, in the absence of new or improved benefits, employees complete vesting requirements (there is no past service cost because the estimated cost of benefits was recognised as current service cost as the service was rendered, accordingly the effect of any such increase is an actuarial gain or loss, see 7.5 above). *[IAS 19.108].*

10.2.2 Acquisition of a qualifying insurance policy

IAS 19 observes that an employer may acquire an insurance policy to fund some or all of the employee benefits relating to employee service in the current and prior periods. The acquisition of such a policy is not a settlement if the employer retains a legal or constructive obligation to pay further amounts if the insurer does not pay the employee benefits specified in the insurance policy (often referred to as a buy-in). *[IAS 19.112].* However, the acquisition of an insurance policy will mean an entity has an asset which needs to be measured at fair value. As discussed at 6.2 above, certain insurance policies are valued at an amount equal to the present value of the defined benefit obligation which they match. The cost of buying such a policy will typically greatly exceed its subsequent carrying amount. This loss is seen as an actuarial loss as it results from exchanging one plan asset for another, which is recognised in other comprehensive income, unless in substance the acquisition of the qualifying insurance policy is a settlement of the plan (see 10.2.3 below).

10.2.3 Settlements

IAS 19 defines a settlement as a transaction that eliminates all further legal or constructive obligations for part or all of the benefits provided under a defined benefit plan, other than a payment of benefits to, or on behalf of, employees that is set out in the terms of the plan and included in the actuarial assumptions. *[IAS 19.8].*

In other words, settlement occurs at the point of absolute risk extinguishment, for part or all of the employer obligations.

For example, a one-off transfer of significant employer obligations under the plan to an insurance company through the purchase of an insurance policy (often referred to as a buy-out) is a settlement; a lump sum cash payment, under the terms of the plan, to plan participants in exchange for their rights to receive specified post-employment benefits is not. *[IAS 19.111].*

The interaction between the asset ceiling and past service cost or a gain or loss on settlement is discussed further at 10.2.1 above.

Any transactions in advance of the legal date of a settlement would also need to be considered. For example, an entity may enter into a binding commitment to settle a defined benefit obligation in the future with an insurance company, which as at the year-end date is beyond recall, but legally risk only transfers to the insurer after the year end.

In this situation, the loss on settlement must be recognised at the point of commitment. However, the defined benefit obligation and related assets will remain on the statement of financial position until legal settlement occurs.

The following extract from IHG plc illustrates a buy-in which has occurred in one financial period and followed by a buy-out in the following financial period. As the policy was structured so as to enable the plan to move to a buy-out, and the intention was to proceed on that basis, the buy-in transaction was accounted for as a settlement with the loss arising recorded in the income statement.

Extract 35.1: InterContinental Hotels Group PLC (2014)

Notes to the Group Financial Statements [extract]

25. Retirement benefits [extract]

UK [extract]

Historically UK retirement and death in service benefits have been provided for eligible employees in the UK principally by the InterContinental Hotels UK Pension Plan, which has both defined benefit and defined contribution sections. The defined benefit section was subject to a buy-in transaction on 15 August 2013 whereby the assets of the plan were invested in a bulk purchase annuity policy with the insurer Rothesay Life under which the benefits payable to defined benefit members became fully insured. On 31 October 2014, the plan completed the move to a full buy-out of the defined benefit section, following which Rothesay Life has become fully and directly responsible for the pension obligations. On completion of the buy-out, the defined benefit assets (comprising the Rothesay Life insurance policy) and matching defined benefit liabilities were derecognised from the Group Statement of financial position.

US and other [extract]

In respect of the defined benefit plans, the amounts recognised in the Group income statement, in administrative expenses, are:

	Pension plans						Post-employment benefits			Total		
	UK			US and other								
	2014 $m	2013 $m	2012 $m	2014 $m	2013 $m	2012 $m	2014 $m	2013 $m	2012 $m	2014 $m	2013 $m	2012 $m
Current service cost	–	2	5	1	1	1	–	–	–	1	3	6
Past service cost	–	–	–	–	1	–	–	–	–	–	1	–
Net interest expense	2	–	1	3	3	3	1	1	1	6	4	5
Administration costs	3	1	1	–	1	1	–	–	–	3	2	2
Operating profit before exceptional items	5	3	7	4	6	5	1	1	1	10	10	13
Exceptional items: Settlement cost	6	147	–	–	–	–	–	–	–	6	147	–
	11	150	7	4	6	5	1	1	1	16	157	13

[...]

The settlement cost in 2013 resulted from the buy-in transaction described on the previous page and comprised a past service cost of $5m relating to additional benefits secured by the transaction, the $137m difference between the cost of the insurance policy and the accounting value of the liabilities secured and transaction costs of $5m. As the policy was structured to enable the plan to move to a buy-out and the intention was to proceed on that basis, the buy-in transaction was accounted for as a settlement with the loss arising recorded in the income statement. The full buy-out was completed on 31 October 2014.

10.3 Net interest on the net defined benefit liability (asset)

Net interest on the net defined benefit liability (asset) is the change during the period in the net defined benefit liability (asset) that arises from the passage of time. *[IAS 19.8]*. It is determined by multiplying the net defined benefit liability (asset) by the discount rate (see 7.6 above which also discusses the use of a more granular approach to determining the discount rate) taking into account any changes in the net defined benefit liability (asset) during the period resulting from contributions or benefit payments. *[IAS 19.123, 123A]*.

Unless there are certain plan changes in the period, the discount rate used for the whole period is that determined at the start of the reporting period. However, if the net defined benefit liability (asset) is remeasured to determine a past service cost, or a gain or loss on settlement the net interest for the remainder of the reporting period is determined using: *[IAS 19.123A]*

(a) the net defined benefit liability (asset) reflecting the benefits offered after the plan amendment, curtailment or settlement; and

(b) the discount rate used to remeasure the net defined benefit liability (asset).

Accounting for defined benefit schemes in interim financial statements is discussed in Chapter 41 at 9.3.3.

As the net item in the statement of financial position is comprised of up to three separate components (the defined benefit obligation, plan assets and the asset ceiling), the net interest is made up of interest unwinding on each of these components in the manner described above. *[IAS 19.124]*. Although, computationally, the net interest is so composed, for the purposes of presentation in profit or loss it is a single net amount.

Interest on plan assets calculated as described above will not, other than by coincidence, be the same as the actual return on plan assets. The difference is a remeasurement recognised in other comprehensive income (see 10.4.2 below). If the net plan liability (asset) is remeasured as a result of a plan amendment, curtailment or settlement the entity shall determine interest income for the remainder of the annual reporting period after the plan amendment, curtailment or settlement using the plan assets used to remeasure the net defined benefit liability (asset). In performing this calculation the entity shall also take into account any changes in the plan assets held during the period resulting from contributions or benefit payments. *[IAS 19.125]*.

Similarly, the difference in the asset ceiling between the start and end of the period is unlikely to equal the interest on this component described above. An entity shall determine the effect of the asset ceiling at the start of the annual reporting period. However, if an entity remeasures the net defined benefit liability (asset) as a result of a plan amendment, curtailment or settlement, the entity shall determine interest on the effect of the asset ceiling for the remainder of the annual reporting period after the plan amendment, curtailment or settlement taking into account any change in the effect of the asset ceiling as discussed in 10.2 above. The difference between the total change in the effect of the asset ceiling and the interest effect is accounted for as a remeasurement in other comprehensive income. *[IAS 19.126]*.

10.4 Remeasurements

Remeasurements of the net defined benefit liability (asset) comprise:

(a) actuarial gains and losses;

(b) the return on plan assets, excluding amounts included in net interest on the net defined benefit liability (asset); and

(c) any change in the effect of the asset ceiling (see 8.2 above), excluding amounts included in net interest on the net defined benefit liability (asset). *[IAS 19.8, 127].*

10.4.1 Actuarial gains and losses

Actuarial gains and losses are changes in the present value of the defined benefit obligation resulting from: experience adjustments (the effects of differences between the previous actuarial assumptions and what has actually occurred); and the effects of changes in actuarial assumptions. *[IAS 19.8].* These can result, for example, from:

(a) unexpectedly high or low rates of: employee turnover, early retirement, mortality, increases in salaries or benefits, or medical costs (if the formal or constructive terms of the plan provide for inflationary benefits);

(b) the effect of changes to assumptions concerning benefit payment options;

(c) the effect of changes in estimates of: future employee turnover, early retirement or mortality or of increases in salaries, benefits (if the formal or constructive terms of the plan provide for inflationary benefit increases) or medical costs; and

(d) the effect of changes in the discount rate. *[IAS 19.128].*

Actuarial gains and losses do not include changes in the present value of the defined benefit obligation because of the introduction, amendment, curtailment or settlement of the defined benefit plan, or changes to the benefits payable under the defined benefit plan. Such changes result in past service cost or gains or losses on settlement (see 10.2.1 and 10.2.3 above). *[IAS 19.129].*

10.4.2 The return on plan assets, excluding amounts included in net interest on the net defined benefit liability (asset)

The return on plan assets is interest, dividends and other income derived from the plan assets, together with realised and unrealised gains on the assets, less

- any costs of managing plan assets; and
- any tax payable by the plan itself, other than tax included in the actuarial assumptions used to measure the present value of the defined benefit obligation.

Other administration costs are not deducted from the return on plan assets, as discussed further at 11 below. *[IAS 19.130].*

11 DEFINED BENEFIT PLANS – COSTS OF ADMINISTERING EMPLOYEE BENEFIT PLANS

Some employee benefit plans incur costs as part of delivering employee benefits. The costs are generally more significant for post-retirement benefits such as pensions. Examples of costs include actuarial valuations, audits and the costs of managing any plan assets.

IAS 19 deals with some costs, as discussed below, but is silent on others.

The following costs are required to be factored into the measurement of the defined benefit obligation as part of the actuarial assumptions (see 7.5 above):

- in the case of medical benefits, future medical costs, including claim handling costs (i.e. the costs that will be incurred in processing and resolving claims, including legal and adjuster's fees); and
- taxes payable by the plan on contributions relating to service before the reporting date or on benefits resulting from that service. *[IAS 19.76(b)].*

The following costs (and no others) are deducted from the return on plan assets (see 10.4.2 above):

- the costs of managing the plan assets; and
- any tax payable by the plan itself, other than tax included in the actuarial assumptions used to measure the defined benefit obligation. *[IAS 19.130].*

As discussed at 10.3 above, net interest on the net liability or asset is reported in the income statement. This is a wholly computed amount which is uninfluenced by actual asset returns; the difference between actual asset returns and the credit element of the net interest amount forms part of remeasurements reported in other comprehensive income.

So, although not expressed in these terms, costs of administering plan assets and the tax mentioned above are reported in other comprehensive income.

The standard is silent on the treatment of any other costs of administering employee benefit plans. However, the Basis for Conclusions on IAS 19 contains the following: 'the Board decided that an entity should recognise administration costs when the administration services are provided. This practical expedient avoids the need to attribute costs between current and past service and future service'. *[IAS 19.BC127].* The Board may well have taken that decision, however it did not include such a requirement in the standard.

In our view, such an approach is certainly an acceptable way to account for costs not dealt with in the standard; however other approaches could be acceptable, for example, in relation to closed schemes as discussed below. Entities need, in compliance with IAS 8, to develop an accounting policy in light of the standard not dealing with these costs. However, IAS 1 is clear that such costs would not be reported in other comprehensive income. *[IAS 1.88].*

One alternative to simple accruals accounting as costs are incurred could be relevant to closed plans, where employees are no longer exchanging services for defined benefits. In this situation, it is clear that any and all future costs of administering the plan relate to past periods and no attribution is necessary. An entity with such an arrangement may select a policy of full provision of all costs of 'running-off' the plan (apart from those specifically dealt with by the standard).

12 SHORT-TERM EMPLOYEE BENEFITS

Short-term employee benefits are employee benefits (other than termination benefits) that are expected to be settled wholly before twelve months after the end of the annual reporting period in which the employees render the related service. *[IAS 19.8].*

The standard states that reclassification is not necessary if an entity's expectation of the timing of settlement changes temporarily. However, if the characteristics of the benefit change (such as a change from a non-accumulating benefit to an accumulating benefit) or if a change in expectations of the timing of settlement is not temporary, then the entity considers whether the benefit still meets the definition of short-term employee benefits. *[IAS 19.10]*.

They can include:

- wages, salaries and social security contributions;
- paid annual leave and paid sick leave;
- profit-sharing and bonuses; and
- non-monetary benefits (such as medical care, housing, cars and free or subsidised goods or services) for current employees. *[IAS 19.9]*.

12.1 General recognition criteria for short-term employee benefits

An entity should recognise the undiscounted amount of short-term benefits attributable to services that have been rendered in the period as an expense, unless another IFRS requires or permits the benefits to be included in the cost of an asset. This may particularly be the case under IAS 2 (see Chapter 22 at 3.1), IAS 16 (see Chapter 18 at 4) and IAS 38 – *Intangible Assets* (see Chapter 17 at 6.3.2). Any difference between the amount of cost recognised and cash payments made should be treated as a liability or prepayment as appropriate. *[IAS 19.11]*. There are further requirements in respect of short-term paid absences and profit-sharing and bonus plans as detailed below. Cost is not defined in IAS 19 and therefore the accounting for such benefits may vary depending on any other standards involved in the recognition of the transaction.

12.2 Short-term paid absences

These include absences for vacation (holiday), sickness and short-term disability, maternity or paternity leave, jury service and military service. These can either be accumulating or non-accumulating absences. *[IAS 19.14]*. Accumulating absences are those that can be carried forward and used in future periods if the entitlement in the current period is not used in full. They can be either vesting entitlements (which entitle employees to a cash payment in lieu of absences not taken on leaving the entity) or non-vesting entitlements (where no cash compensation is payable). Non-accumulating absences are those where there is no entitlement to carry forward unused days. An obligation arises as employees render service that increases their entitlement to future paid absences. *[IAS 19.15]*.

12.2.1 Accumulating absences

The cost of accumulating paid absences should be recognised when employees render the service that increases their entitlement to future paid absences. No distinction should be made between the recognition of vesting and non-vesting entitlements (see 12.2 above), on the basis that the liability arises as services are rendered in both cases. However, the measurement of non-vesting entitlements should take into account the possibility of employees leaving before receiving them. *[IAS 19.15]*.

The cost of accumulating paid absences should be measured as the additional amount that the entity expects to pay as a result of the unused entitlement that has accumulated at the end of the reporting period. *[IAS 19.16]*. In the case of unused paid sick leave, provision should be made only to the extent that it is expected that employees will use the sick leave in subsequent periods. The standard observes that in many cases, it may not be necessary to make detailed computations to estimate that there is no material obligation for unused paid absences. For example, IAS 19 considers it unlikely that a sick leave obligation will be material unless if there is a formal or informal understanding that unused paid sick leave may be taken as paid vacation. *[IAS 19.17]*.

The standard provides an example to illustrate the requirements for accumulating paid absences upon which the following is based: *[IAS 19.17]*

Example 35.8: Accumulating paid absences

An entity has 100 employees, who are each entitled to five working days of paid sick leave for each year. Unused sick leave may be carried forward for one calendar year. Sick leave is taken first out of the current year's entitlement and then out of any balance brought forward from the previous year (a LIFO basis). At 31 December 2019, the average unused entitlement is two days per employee. The entity expects, based on past experience which is expected to continue, that 92 employees will take no more than five days of paid sick leave in 2020 and that the remaining eight employees will take an average of six and a half days each.

The entity expects that it will pay an additional 12 days of sick pay as a result of the unused entitlement that has accumulated at 31 December 2019 (one and a half days each, for eight employees). Therefore, the entity recognises a liability equal to 12 days of sick pay.

12.2.2 Non-accumulating paid absences

The cost of non-accumulating absences should be recognised as and when they arise, on the basis that the entitlement is not directly linked to the service rendered by employees in the period. This is commonly the case for sick pay (to the extent that unused past entitlement cannot be carried forward), maternity or paternity leave, furlough periods and paid absences for jury service or military service. *[IAS 19.13(b), 18]*.

12.3 Profit-sharing and bonus plans

An entity should recognise the expected cost of profit-sharing and bonus payments when and only when:

- the entity has a present legal or constructive obligation to make such payments as a result of past events; and
- a reliable estimate of the obligation can be made. *[IAS 19.19]*.

The above are discussed in turn at 12.3.1 and 12.3.2 below. Statutory profit-sharing arrangements based on taxable profit are discussed at 12.3.3 below.

12.3.1 Present legal or constructive obligation

A present obligation exists when, and only when, the entity has no realistic alternative but to make the payments. *[IAS 19.19]*. IAS 19 clarifies that where a profit-sharing plan is subject to a loyalty period (i.e. a period during which employees must remain with the entity in order to receive their share), a constructive obligation is created as employees render service that increases the amount to be paid if they remain in service until the end of the specified period. However, the possibility of employees leaving during the loyalty period should be taken into account in measuring the cost of the plan. *[IAS 19.20]*. The standard illustrates the approach as follows:

Example 35.9:   Profit sharing and bonus plans

A profit-sharing plan requires an entity to pay a specified proportion of its net profit for the year to employees who serve throughout the year. If no employees leave during the year, the total profit-sharing payments for the year will be 3% of profit. The entity estimates that staff turnover will reduce the payments to 2.5% of profit.

The entity recognises a liability and an expense of 2.5% of net profit.

It is worth noting that in the scenario above, when an entity prepares its accounts for the year it will no longer be uncertain whether all eligible employees become entitled to the bonus, as that is determined at the year-end. That means the reduction in the accrual from 3% to 2.5% should be an observable fact not an 'estimate'.

The standard also states that where an entity has a practice of paying bonuses it has a constructive obligation to pay a bonus, even though there may be no legal obligation for it to do so. Again, however, in measuring the cost, the possibility of employees leaving before receiving a bonus should be taken into account. *[IAS 19.21]*.

12.3.2   Reliable estimate of provision

A reliable estimate of a legal or constructive obligation under a profit-sharing or bonus plan can be made when and only when:

- the formal terms of the plan contain a formula for determining the amount of the benefit;
- the entity determines the amounts to be paid before the financial statements are authorised for issue; or
- past practice gives clear evidence of the amount of the entity's constructive obligation. *[IAS 19.22]*.

It is worth noting that the paragraph above from IAS 19 deals only with the measurement of the provision and not the point of recognition which is discussed at 12.3.1 above. IAS 19 states that an obligation under a profit-sharing or bonus plan must be accounted for as an expense and not a distribution of profit, since it results from employee service and not from a transaction with owners. *[IAS 19.23]*. Where profit-sharing and bonus payments are not expected to be settled wholly before twelve months after the end of the annual reporting period in which the employees render the related service, they should be accounted for as other long-term employee benefits (see 13 below). *[IAS 19.24]*.

12.3.3   Statutory profit-sharing based on taxable profit

In November 2010, the Interpretations Committee was asked to clarify how to account for a particular statutory employee benefit whereby 10% of taxable profit is shared with employees. In particular, the request sought clarification as to whether analogy could be made to IAS 12 – *Income Taxes* – to account for temporary differences between accounting and taxable profit which would reverse in the future.

The Interpretations Committee thought that such an approach was not acceptable. It decided not to add the item to its agenda saying '[t]he Committee noted that the statutory employee profit-sharing arrangement described in the request should be accounted for in accordance with IAS 19, and that IAS 19 provides sufficient guidance on amounts that should be recognised and measured, with the result that significantly divergent interpretations are not expected in practice. Consequently, the Committee decided not to add this issue to its agenda'.[15]

13 LONG-TERM EMPLOYEE BENEFITS OTHER THAN POST-EMPLOYMENT BENEFITS

13.1 Meaning of other long-term employee benefits

These are all employee benefits other than post-employment benefits and termination benefits. *[IAS 19.8]*. They include the following if not expected to be settled wholly before twelve months after the end of the annual reporting period in which the employees rendered the related service:

- long-term paid absences such as long-service or sabbatical leave;
- jubilee or other long-service benefits;
- long-term disability benefits;
- profit-sharing and bonuses; and
- deferred remuneration. *[IAS 19.153]*.

13.2 Recognition and measurement

For such benefits IAS 19 requires a simplified version of the accounting treatment required in respect of defined benefit plans (which is discussed in detail at 5 above). The amount recognised as a liability for other long-term employee benefits should be the net total, at the end of the reporting period, of the present value of the defined benefit obligation and the fair value of plan assets (if any) out of which the obligations are to be settled directly. The net total of the following amounts should be recognised in profit or loss, except to the extent that another IFRS requires or permits their inclusion in the cost of an asset:

(a) service cost;

(b) net interest on the net defined benefit liability (asset); and

(c) remeasurements of the net defined benefit liability (asset).

In other words, all assets, liabilities, income and expenditure relating to such benefits should be accounted for in the same way, and subject to the same restrictions on the recognition of assets and income, as those relating to a defined benefit pension plan (see 8.1 and 8.2 above), except that remeasurements are recognised in profit or loss. *[IAS 19.155-156]*.

The standard explains the use of this simplified approach by asserting that the measurement of other long-term employee benefits is not usually subject to the same degree of uncertainty as that of post-employment benefits. *[IAS 19.154]*.

An illustration of the methodology to calculate the defined benefit obligation, service and interest costs is given in Example 35.2 at 7.3 above.

13.2.1 Attribution to years of service

Long-term employee benefit arrangements will typically have conditions attached to secure their vesting.

For example, employee bonuses are now commonly linked to vesting conditions which mean that they will not be settled wholly within 12 months after the period in which the employee renders the related service. In this case, the liability should be calculated using the projected unit credit method and spread on a straight-line basis over the full vesting period. For example, a bonus granted to an employee on 1 January 2021 which is based on the employees performance in 2021, but is not payable until February 2024 and is conditional on the employee remaining in service until 31 December 2023 will have a vesting period from 1 January 2021 to 31 December 2023 and the liability will be spread on a straight line basis over this three year period.

The Interpretations Committee also received questions concerning early retirement bonuses where bonus payments are given in exchange for a 50% reduction in working hours which are conditional on the employee completing a required service period when employment is terminated. The Interpretations Committee concluded that as the bonus payments were conditional upon the completion of service over a specified period this indicated that the benefits were provided in exchange for that service and should be attributed over this period of service (and were not a termination benefit).[16]

It is not always clear how the attribution of long-term benefits to the years of service over which they are earned should be performed.

Consider an award made at the start of the year for a fixed cash payment. A third of the payment vests on each of the first, second and third anniversaries of the grant for employees still employed at each vesting date.

One interpretation would be that the 'benefit formula' attributes a third of the award to each year and that each of the three income statements will bear one third of the expense.

An alternative view is that there are three distinct awards with the same grant date, but with durations of one, two and three years. This pattern of vesting is sometimes described as 'graded vesting' and is discussed, in relation to share-based payments, in Chapter 34 at 6.2.2 and illustrated in Example 34.9.

In our view, either approach is acceptable if applied consistently.

13.2.2 Long-term disability benefit

Where long-term disability benefit depends on the length of service of the employee, an obligation arises as the employee renders service, which is to be measured according to the probability that payment will be required and the length of time for which payment is expected to be made. If, however, the level of benefit is the same for all disabled employees regardless of years of service, the expected cost is recognised only when an event causing disability occurs. *[IAS 19.157]*.

It is not clear why this distinction is made, since in principle both types of benefit are equally susceptible to actuarial measurement. If anything the cost of benefits applicable to all employees regardless of service is probably easier to quantify actuarially. Given that an exposure to disability benefits which grows with years of service is fully provided for (actuarially) as it grows over time, it would seem logical for full provision to be made immediately for an exposure which comes into being (in full) on the day the employee commences employment. The problem with such an approach would be what to do with the debit entry. It would not represent an asset as envisaged in the *Conceptual Framework* (see Chapter 2), which would tend to imply an instant charge to profit or loss. This may have been the reason for the Board to make the exception and link the recognition to the actual disability event. These issues are similar to those surrounding death-in-service benefits discussed at 3.6 above.

13.2.3 Long-term benefits contingent on a future event

It may be the case that a long-term benefit becomes payable only on the occurrence of an uncertain future event, for example an initial public offering of an entity's shares (IPO) or an exit event. Such events are binary in nature and would result in payment either to no employees with entitlements under the plan or to all such employees.

As discussed at 13.2 above, the projected unit credit method is applied to long-term employee benefits, *[IAS 19.154]*, however the key question that arises is whether the accounting should reflect the single best estimate of the outcome; or, the expected value – that is, a weighted average of possible outcomes. Paragraph 72 of the standard states that 'the probability that the specified event will occur affects the measurement of the obligation, but does not determine whether the obligation exists'. This sets out the requirement that probability affects measurement. The manner in which probability affects measurement is dealt with in paragraph 76 which requires actuarial assumptions to be a best estimate of the ultimate cost of providing benefits. Accordingly, we believe that the best estimate of the outcome of the uncertain event should be used when accounting for long-term employee benefits where the outcome is binary. Therefore if an IPO (or exit event) is not probable the liability should be measured at nil. When the IPO (or exit event) is or becomes probable (that is, more likely than not) the actuarial assumption used in applying the projected unit credit method should reflect the full benefits which would be payable upon the occurrence of the event.

14 TERMINATION BENEFITS

Termination benefits are employee benefits payable as a result of either:
- an entity's decision to terminate an employee's employment before the normal retirement date; or
- an employee's decision to accept an offer of benefits in exchange for the termination of employment. *[IAS 19.8]*.

They are accounted for differently from other employee benefits because the event that gives rise to an obligation for them is the termination of employment rather than the rendering of service by the employee. *[IAS 19.159]*.

Termination benefits do not include employee benefits resulting from termination of employment at the request of the employee without an entity's offer, or as a result of mandatory retirement requirements, because those benefits are post-employment benefits. Some entities provide a lower level of benefit for termination of employment at the request of the employee (in substance, a post-employment benefit) than for termination of employment at the request of the entity. The difference between the benefit provided for termination of employment at the request of the employee and a higher benefit provided at the request of the entity is a termination benefit. *[IAS 19.160]*. Accordingly, employee benefits that are payable regardless of the reason for the employee's departure are accounted for as post-employment benefits. Any additional benefit payable as a result of termination at the request of the entity over the benefits payable as a result of termination at the request of the employee is accounted for as a termination benefit.

The form of the employee benefit does not determine whether it is provided in exchange for service or in exchange for termination of the employee's employment. Termination benefits are typically lump sum payments, but sometimes also include:

- enhancement of post-employment benefits, either indirectly through an employee benefit plan or directly; and
- salary until the end of a specified notice period if the employee renders no further service that provides economic benefits to the entity. *[IAS 19.161]*.

Indicators that an employee benefit is provided in exchange for services include the following:

- the benefit is conditional on future service being provided (including benefits that increase if further service is provided); and
- the benefit is provided in accordance with the terms of an employee benefit plan. *[IAS 19.162]*.

Some termination benefits are provided in accordance with the terms of an existing employee benefit plan. For example, they may be specified by statute, employment contract or union agreement, or may be implied as a result of the employer's past practice of providing similar benefits. As another example, if an entity makes an offer of benefits available for more than a short period, or there is more than a short period between the offer and the expected date of actual termination, an entity should consider whether it has established a new employee benefit plan and hence whether the benefits offered under that plan are termination benefits or post-employment benefits. Employee benefits provided in accordance with the terms of an employee benefit plan are termination benefits if they both result from an entity's decision to terminate an employee's employment and are not conditional on future service being provided. *[IAS 19.163]*. Benefits payable to incentivise employees to remain in service with the entity until the end of the termination period (referred to as stay bonuses) are not termination benefits because they are dependent on service being provided. These would be accounted for as either a short-term or long-term employee benefit as appropriate (see 12 and 13 above).

14.1 Statutory termination indemnities

Some employee benefits are provided regardless of the reason for the employee's departure. The payment of such benefits is certain (subject to any vesting or minimum service requirements) but the timing of their payment is uncertain. Although such benefits are described in some jurisdictions as termination indemnities or termination gratuities, they are post-employment benefits rather than termination benefits, and an entity accounts for them as post-employment benefits. *[IAS 19.164]*.

14.2 Recognition

An entity should recognise termination benefits as a liability and an expense at the earlier of the following dates:

- when it can no longer withdraw the offer of those benefits; and
- when it recognises costs for a restructuring that is within the scope of IAS 37 and involves the payment of termination benefits (discussed in Chapter 26 at 6.1). *[IAS 19.165]*.

For termination benefits payable as a result of an employee's decision to accept an offer of benefits in exchange for the termination of employment, the time when an entity can no longer withdraw the offer of termination benefits is the earlier of:

- when the employee accepts the offer; and
- when a restriction (e.g. a legal, regulatory or contractual requirement or other restriction) on the entity's ability to withdraw the offer takes effect. This would be when the offer is made, if the restriction existed at the time of the offer. *[IAS 19.166]*.

For termination benefits payable as a result of an entity's decision to terminate an employee's employment, the entity can no longer withdraw the offer when the entity has communicated to the affected employees a plan of termination meeting all of the following criteria:

- actions required to complete the plan indicate that it is unlikely that significant changes to the plan will be made;
- the plan identifies the number of employees whose employment is to be terminated, their job classifications or functions and their locations (but the plan need not identify each individual employee) and the expected completion date; and
- the plan establishes the termination benefits that employees will receive in sufficient detail that employees can determine the type and amount of benefits they will receive were their employment to be terminated. *[IAS 19.167]*.

The standard notes that when an entity recognises termination benefits, it may also have to account for a plan amendment or a curtailment of other employee benefits (discussed at 10.2 above). *[IAS 19.168]*.

14.3 Measurement

IAS 19 requires that on initial recognition and subsequent remeasurement, termination benefits should be measured in accordance with the nature of the employee benefit. If the termination benefits are an enhancement to post-employment benefits, the entity applies the requirements for post-employment benefits. Otherwise:

- if the termination benefits are expected to be settled wholly before twelve months after the end of the annual reporting period in which the termination benefit is recognised, the requirements for short-term employee benefits should be applied (discussed at 12 above); and

- if the termination benefits are not expected to be settled wholly before twelve months after the end of the annual reporting period, the requirements for other long-term employee benefits should be applied (discussed at 13 above). *[IAS 19.169].*

Because termination benefits are not provided in exchange for service, the standard notes that its rules relating to the attribution of the benefit to periods of service are not relevant (discussed at 7.4 above). *[IAS 19.170].*

IAS 19 illustrates the accounting for termination benefits with an example.

Example 35.10: Termination benefits

Background

As a result of a recent acquisition, an entity plans to close a factory in ten months and, at that time, terminate the employment of all of the remaining employees at the factory. Because the entity needs the expertise of the employees at the factory to complete some contracts, it announces a plan of termination as follows.

Each employee who stays and renders service until the closure of the factory will receive on the termination date a cash payment of $30,000. Employees leaving before closure of the factory will receive $10,000.

There are 120 employees at the factory. At the time of announcing the plan, the entity expects 20 of them to leave before closure. Therefore, the total expected cash outflows under the plan are $3,200,000 (i.e. 20 × $10,000 + 100 × $30,000). As required by the standard, the entity accounts for benefits provided in exchange for termination of employment as termination benefits and accounts for benefits provided in exchange for services as short-term employee benefits.

Termination benefits

The benefit provided in exchange for termination of employment is $10,000. This is the amount that an entity would have to pay for terminating the employment regardless of whether the employees stay and render service until closure of the factory or they leave before closure. Even though the employees can leave before closure, the termination of all employees' employment is a result of the entity's decision to close the factory and terminate their employment (i.e. all employees will leave employment when the factory closes). Therefore the entity recognises a liability of $1,200,000 (i.e. 120 × $10,000) for the termination benefits provided in accordance with the employee benefit plan at the earlier of when the plan of termination is announced and when the entity recognises the restructuring costs associated with the closure of the factory.

Benefits provided in exchange for service

The incremental benefits that employees will receive if they provide services for the full ten-month period are in exchange for services provided over that period. The entity accounts for them as short-term employee benefits because the entity expects to settle them before twelve months after the end of the annual reporting period. In this example, discounting is not required, so an expense of $200,000 (i.e. $2,000,000 ÷ 10) is recognised in each month during the service period of ten months, with a corresponding increase in the carrying amount of the liability.

15 DISCLOSURE REQUIREMENTS

15.1 Defined contribution plans

IAS 19 requires the disclosure of the expense recognised for defined contribution plans. It also notes that IAS 24 requires disclosure of the contributions in respect of key management personnel. *[IAS 19.53, 54]*.

15.2 Defined benefit plans

IAS 19 requires extensive disclosure in relation to defined benefit plans, as set out below.

The standard requires an entity to disclose information that:

(a) explains the characteristics of its defined benefit plans and risks associated with them;

(b) identifies and explains the amounts in its financial statements arising from its defined benefit plans; and

(c) describes how its defined benefit plans may affect the amount, timing and uncertainty of the entity's future cash flows. *[IAS 19.135]*.

To achieve the above, the standard sets out a long and detailed list of narrative and numerical disclosure requirements (considered further below).

The Board also noted that entities must comply with the general materiality requirements of IAS 1 (discussed in Chapter 3 at 4.1.5), including the requirement to disclose additional information if necessary, and that the financial statements need not contain disclosures that are not material. *[IAS 19.BC209]*.

One of the Board's objectives in regard to disclosure was to ensure that financial statements provide relevant information that is not obscured by excessive detail. *[IAS 19.BC207]*.

These references to excessive detail and non-disclosure of immaterial items confirm that entities should apply judgement to determine the appropriate level of detail to be provided rather than giving everything set out in the standard.

To meet the objectives above, the standard requires consideration of all the following:

(a) the level of detail necessary to satisfy the disclosure requirements;

(b) how much emphasis to place on each of the various requirements;

(c) how much aggregation or disaggregation to undertake; and

(d) whether users of financial statements need additional information to evaluate the quantitative information disclosed. *[IAS 19.136]*.

If the disclosures provided in accordance with the requirements of IAS 19 and other IFRSs are insufficient to meet the objectives above, an entity should disclose additional information necessary to meet those objectives. For example, an entity may present an analysis of the present value of the defined benefit obligation that distinguishes the nature, characteristics and risks of the obligation. Such a disclosure could distinguish:

(a) between amounts owing to active members, deferred members, and pensioners;
(b) between vested benefits and accrued but not vested benefits; and
(c) between conditional benefits, amounts attributable to future salary increases and other benefits. *[IAS 19.137]*.

An assessment should be made as to whether all or some disclosures should be disaggregated to distinguish plans or groups of plans with materially different risks. For example, an entity may disaggregate disclosure about plans showing one or more of the following features:

(a) different geographical locations;
(b) different characteristics such as flat salary pension plans, final salary pension plans or post-employment medical plans;
(c) different regulatory environments;
(d) different reporting segments; and
(e) different funding arrangements (e.g. wholly unfunded, wholly funded or partly funded). *[IAS 19.138]*.

15.2.1 Characteristics of defined benefit plans and risks associated with them

IAS 19 requires disclosure of:

(a) information about the characteristics of its defined benefit plans, including:
  (i) the nature of the benefits provided by the plan (e.g. final salary defined benefit plan or contribution-based plan with guarantee);
  (ii) a description of the regulatory framework in which the plan operates, for example the level of any minimum funding requirements, and any effect of the regulatory framework on the plan, such as the asset ceiling;
  (iii) a description of any other entity's responsibilities for the governance of the plan, for example responsibilities of trustees or of board members of the plan; and
(b) a description of the risks to which the plan exposes the entity, focused on any unusual, entity-specific or plan-specific risks, and of any significant concentrations of risk. For example, if plan assets are invested primarily in one class of investments, e.g. property, the plan may expose the entity to a concentration of property market risk; and
(c) a description of any plan amendments, curtailments and settlements. *[IAS 19.139]*.

15.2.2 Explanation of amounts in the financial statements

The disclosures should provide a reconciliation from the opening balance to the closing balance for each of the following, if applicable:

(a) the net defined benefit liability (asset), showing separate reconciliations for:
  (i) plan assets;
  (ii) the present value of the defined benefit obligation; and
  (iii) the effect of the asset ceiling; and
(b) any reimbursement rights. If there are reimbursement rights a description of the relationship between them and the related obligation should be given. *[IAS 19.140]*.

Each reconciliation listed in (a) and (b) above should show each of the following, if applicable:

(a) current service cost;
(b) interest income or expense (see 10.3 above);
(c) remeasurements of the net defined benefit liability (asset), showing separately:
  (i) the return on plan assets, excluding amounts included in interest in (b) above;
  (ii) actuarial gains and losses arising from changes in demographic assumptions;
  (iii) actuarial gains and losses arising from changes in financial assumptions; and
  (iv) changes in the effect of limiting a net defined benefit asset to the asset ceiling, excluding amounts included in interest in (b). There should also be disclosure of how the maximum economic benefit available was determined, i.e. whether those benefits would be in the form of refunds, reductions in future contributions or a combination of both;
(d) past service cost and gains and losses arising from settlements. Past service cost and gains and losses arising from settlements need not be distinguished if they occur together (see 10.2 above);
(e) the effect of changes in foreign exchange rates;
(f) contributions to the plan, showing separately those by the employer and by plan participants;
(g) payments from the plan, showing separately the amount paid in respect of any settlements; and
(h) the effects of business combinations and disposals. *[IAS 19.141]*.

The following extract from BT Group plc shows how they have presented the above reconciliations.

Extract 35.2: BT Group plc (2018)

Notes to the consolidated financial statements [extract]
20. Retirement benefit plans [extract]
Movements in defined benefit plan assets and liabilities

The table below shows the movements on the pension assets and liabilities and shows where they are reflected in the financial statements.

	Assets £m	Liabilities £m	Deficit £m
At 31 March 2016	43,968	(50,350)	(6,382)
Service cost (including administration expenses and PPF levy)	(44)	(237)	(281)
Interest on pension deficit	1,413	(1,622)	(209)
Included in the group income statement			**(490)**
Return on plan assets above the amount included in the group income statement	7,475	–	7,475
Actuarial loss arising from changes in financial assumptions[a]	–	(10,221)	(10,221)
Actuarial loss arising from changes in demographic assumptions[a]	–	(206)	(206)
Actuarial gain arising from experience adjustments[b]	–	163	163
Included in the group statement of comprehensive income			**(2,789)**
Regular contributions by employer	313	–	313
Deficit contributions by employer	274	–	274
Included in the group cash flow statement			**587**
Contributions by employees	8	(8)	–
Benefits paid	(2,315)	2,315	–
Foreign exchange	20	(34)	(14)
Other movements			**(14)**
At 31 March 2017	51,112	(60,200)	(9,088)
Service cost (including administration expenses and PPF levy)	(67)	(309)	(376)
Past service credit	–	17	17
Interest on pension deficit	1,201	(1,419)	(218)
Included in the group income statement			**(577)**
Return on plan assets above the amount included in the group income statement	10	–	10
Actuarial gain arising from changes in financial assumptions[a]	–	2,251	2,251
Actuarial loss arising from changes in demographic assumptions[a]	–	(221)	(221)
Actuarial gain arising from experience adjustments[b]	–	120	120
Included in the group statement of comprehensive income			**2,160**

Regular contributions by employer		264	–	264
Deficit contributions by employer		872	–	872
Included in the group cash flow statement				1,136
Contributions by employees		2	(2)	–
Benefits paid		(2,449)	2,449	–
Foreign exchange		11	(13)	(2)
Other movements				(2)
At 31 March 2018		50,956	(57,327)	(6,371)

a The actuarial gain or loss arises from changes in the assumptions used to value the defined benefit liabilities at the end of the year compared with the assumptions used at the start of the year. This includes both financial assumptions, which are based on market conditions at the year end, and demographic assumptions such as life expectancy.

b The actuarial loss or gain arising from experience adjustments on defined benefit liabilities represents the impact on the liabilities of differences between actual experience during the year compared with the assumptions made at the start of the year. Such differences might arise, for example, from members choosing different benefit options at retirement, actual salary increases being different from those assumed or actual benefit increases being different to the pension increase assumption.

The fair value of the plan assets should be disaggregated into classes that distinguish the nature and risks of those assets, subdividing each class of plan asset into those that have a quoted market price in an active market (as defined in IFRS 13, see Chapter 14) and those that do not. For example, and considering the level of detail of disclosure, aggregation and emphasis discussed at 15.2 above, an entity could distinguish between:

(a) cash and cash equivalents;
(b) equity instruments (segregated by industry type, company size, geography etc.);
(c) debt instruments (segregated by type of issuer, credit quality, geography etc.);
(d) real estate (segregated by geography etc.);
(e) derivatives (segregated by type of underlying risk in the contract, for example, interest rate contracts, foreign exchange contracts, equity contracts, credit contracts, longevity swaps etc.);
(f) investment funds (segregated by type of fund);
(g) asset-backed securities; and
(h) structured debt. *[IAS 19.142]*.

The fair value of an entity's own transferable financial instruments held as plan assets, and the fair value of plan assets that are property occupied by, or other assets used by, the entity should be disclosed. *[IAS 19.143]*.

The following extract from UBS Group AG illustrates how the plan assets may be disaggregated.

Extract 35.3: UBS Group AG (2018)

Notes to the UBS Group AG consolidated financial statements [extract]
Note 29 Pension and other post-employment benefit plans [extract]
Composition of fair value of plan assets [extract]
Swiss plan

	31.12.18				31.12.17			
	Fair value			Plan asset allocation %	Fair value			Plan asset allocation %
USD million	Quoted in an active market	Other	Total		Quoted in an active market	Other	Total	
Cash and cash equivalents	83	0	83	1	74	0	74	0
Real estate/property								
Domestic	0	1,808	1,808	11	0	1,758	1,758	11
Investment funds								
Equity								
Domestic	383	0	383	2	410	0	410	3
Foreign	3,492	925	4,417	28	4,615	818	5,433	33
Bonds								
Domestic, AAA to BBB–	1,569	0	1,569	10	1,401	0	1,401	9
Foreign, AAA to BBB–	3,781	0	3,781	24	3,919	0	3,919	24
Foreign, below BBB–	544	0	544	3	355	0	355	2
Real estate								
Foreign	0	7	7	0	0	14	14	0
Other	316	2,528	2,844	18	529	2,486	3,016	18
Other investments	324	11	335	2	0	8	8	0
Total fair value of assets	10,493	5,279	15,772	100	11,304	5,084	16,388	100

An entity should disclose the significant actuarial assumptions used to determine the present value of the defined benefit obligation. Such disclosure should be in absolute terms (e.g. as an absolute percentage, and not just as a margin between different percentages and other variables). When an entity provides disclosures in total for a grouping of plans, it should provide such disclosures in the form of weighted averages or relatively narrow ranges. [IAS 19.144].

15.2.3 Amount, timing and uncertainty of future cash flows

An entity should disclose:

(a) a sensitivity analysis for each significant actuarial assumption as of the end of the reporting period, showing how the defined benefit obligation would have been affected by changes in the relevant actuarial assumption that were reasonably possible at that date;

(b) the methods and assumptions used in preparing the sensitivity analyses required by (a) and the limitations of those methods; and

(c) changes from the previous period in the methods and assumptions used in preparing the sensitivity analyses, and the reasons for such changes. [IAS 19.145].

A description should be given of any asset-liability matching strategies used by the plan or the entity, including the use of annuities and other techniques, such as longevity swaps, to manage risk. [IAS 19.146].

To provide an indication of the effect of the defined benefit plan on the entity's future cash flows, an entity should disclose:

(a) a description of any funding arrangements and funding policies that affect future contributions;

(b) the expected contributions to the plan for the next annual reporting period; and

(c) information about the maturity profile of the defined benefit obligation. This will include the weighted average duration of the defined benefit obligation and may include other information about the distribution of the timing of benefit payments, such as a maturity analysis of the benefit payments. [IAS 19.147].

The following extract from BT Group plc illustrates the maturity profile of the defined benefit obligation.

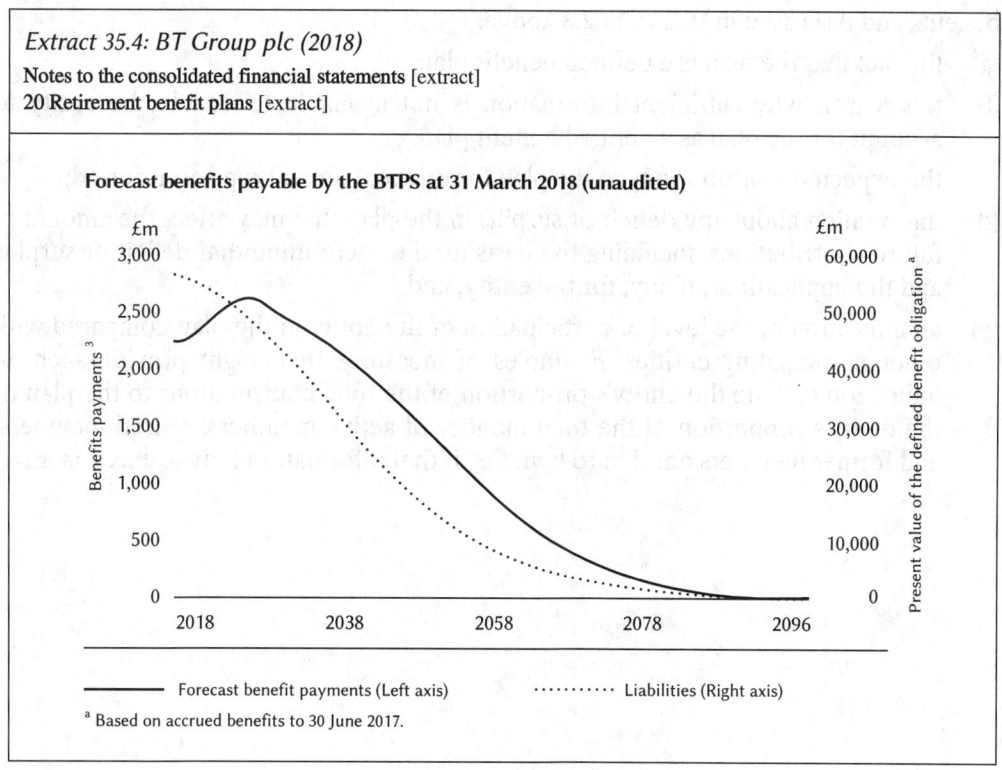

15.2.4 Multi-employer plans

If an entity participates in a multi-employer defined benefit plan, different disclosures are required depending upon how the arrangement is accounted for. These are discussed below.

15.2.4.A Plans accounted for as defined benefit plans

If an entity participates in a multi-employer defined benefit plan and accounts for it as such, it should make all the required disclosures discussed above. In addition, it should disclose:

(a) a description of the funding arrangements, including the method used to determine the entity's rate of contributions and any minimum funding requirements;

(b) a description of the extent to which the entity can be liable to the plan for other entities' obligations under the terms and conditions of the multi-employer plan;

(c) a description of any agreed allocation of a deficit or surplus on:
   (i) wind-up of the plan; or
   (ii) the entity's withdrawal from the plan. *[IAS 19.148]*.

15.2.4.B Plans accounted for as defined contribution plans

If an entity accounts for a multi-employer defined benefit plan as if it were a defined contribution plan, it should disclose the following, in addition to the information required by 15.2.4.A above and instead of the disclosures normally required for defined benefits and discussed in 15.2 to 15.2.3 above:

(a) the fact that the plan is a defined benefit plan;

(b) the reason why sufficient information is not available to enable the entity to account for the plan as a defined benefit plan;

(c) the expected contributions to the plan for the next annual reporting period;

(d) information about any deficit or surplus in the plan that may affect the amount of future contributions, including the basis used to determine that deficit or surplus and the implications, if any, for the entity; and

(e) an indication of the level of participation of the entity in the plan compared with other participating entities. Examples of measures that might provide such an indication include the entity's proportion of the total contributions to the plan or the entity's proportion of the total number of active members, retired members, and former members entitled to benefits, if that information is available. *[IAS 19.148]*.

15.2.5 Defined benefit plans that share risks between entities under common control

If an entity participates in a defined benefit plan that shares risks between entities under common control, the entity should disclose:

(a) the contractual agreement or stated policy for charging the net defined benefit cost or the fact that there is no such policy; and

(b) the policy for determining the contribution to be paid by the entity. *[IAS 19.149]*.

Further disclosures are required depending upon how the arrangement is accounted for. These are discussed below.

15.2.5.A Plans accounted for as defined benefit plans

If an entity participates in a defined benefit plan that shares risks between entities under common control and accounts for an allocation of the net defined benefit cost, it should also disclose all the information about the plan as a whole set out in 15.2 to 15.2.3 above. *[IAS 19.149]*.

15.2.5.B Plans accounted for as defined contribution plans

If an entity participates in a defined benefit plan that shares risks between entities under common control and accounts for the net contribution payable for the period, it should also disclose the information set out below. *[IAS 19.149]*.

The standard requires disclosure of information that:

(a) explains the characteristics of its defined benefit plans and risks associated with them;

(b) identifies and explains the amounts in its financial statements arising from its defined benefit plans; and

(c) describes how its defined benefit plans may affect the amount, timing and uncertainty of the entity's future cash flows.

To meet the objectives above, the standard requires consideration of all the following:

(a) the level of detail necessary to satisfy the disclosure requirements;

(b) how much emphasis to place on each of the various requirements;

(c) how much aggregation or disaggregation to undertake; and

(d) whether users of financial statements need additional information to evaluate the quantitative information disclosed. *[IAS 19.136]*.

If the disclosures provided in accordance with the requirements in IAS 19 and other IFRSs are insufficient to meet the objectives above, an entity should disclose additional information necessary to meet those objectives. For example, an entity may present an analysis of the present value of the defined benefit obligation that distinguishes the nature, characteristics and risks of the obligation. Such a disclosure could distinguish:

(a) between amounts owing to active members, deferred members, and pensioners;
(b) between vested benefits and accrued but not vested benefits; and
(c) between conditional benefits, amounts attributable to future salary increases and other benefits. [IAS 19.137].

IAS 19 requires disclosure of:

(a) information about the characteristics of its defined benefit plans, including:
   (i) the nature of the benefits provided by the plan (e.g. final salary defined benefit plan or contribution-based plan with guarantee);
   (ii) a description of the regulatory framework in which the plan operates, for example the level of any minimum funding requirements, and any effect of the regulatory framework on the plan, such as the asset ceiling; and
   (iii) a description of any other entity's responsibilities for the governance of the plan, for example responsibilities of trustees or of board members of the plan;
(b) a description of the risks to which the plan exposes the entity, focused on any unusual, entity-specific or plan-specific risks, and of any significant concentrations of risk. For example, if plan assets are invested primarily in one class of investments, e.g. property, the plan may expose the entity to a concentration of property market risk; and
(c) a description of any plan amendments, curtailments and settlements.

The fair value of the plan assets should be disaggregated into classes that distinguish the nature and risks of those assets, subdividing each class of plan asset into those that have a quoted market price in an active market (as defined in IFRS 13, discussed in Chapter 14) and those that do not. For example, and considering the level of detail of disclosure, aggregation and emphasis discussed at 15.2 above, an entity could distinguish between:

(a) cash and cash equivalents;
(b) equity instruments (segregated by industry type, company size, geography etc.);
(c) debt instruments (segregated by type of issuer, credit quality, geography etc.);
(d) real estate (segregated by geography etc.);
(e) derivatives (segregated by type of underlying risk in the contract, for example, interest rate contracts, foreign exchange contracts, equity contracts, credit contracts, longevity swaps etc.);
(f) investment funds (segregated by type of fund);
(g) asset-backed securities; and
(h) structured debt. [IAS 19.142].

The fair value of the entity's own transferable financial instruments held as plan assets, and the fair value of plan assets that are property occupied by, or other assets used by, the entity should be disclosed. *[IAS 19.143]*.

An entity should disclose the significant actuarial assumptions used to determine the present value of the defined benefit obligation. Such disclosure should be in absolute terms (e.g. as an absolute percentage, and not just as a margin between different percentages and other variables). When an entity provides disclosures in total for a grouping of plans, it shall provide such disclosures in the form of weighted averages or relatively narrow ranges.

To provide an indication of the effect of the defined benefit plan on the entity's future cash flows, an entity should disclose:

(a) a description of any funding arrangements and funding policy that affect future contributions; and

(b) the expected contributions to the plan for the next annual reporting period.

The information described above and in 15.2.5.A above must be presented in the entity's own accounts. The rest of the information discussed in this section may be disclosed by cross-reference to disclosures in another group entity's financial statements if:

(a) that group entity's financial statements separately identify and disclose the information required about the plan; and

(b) that group entity's financial statements are available to users of the financial statements on the same terms as the financial statements of the entity and at the same time as, or earlier than, the financial statements of the entity. *[IAS 19.150]*.

15.2.6 Disclosure requirements in other IFRSs

IFRIC 14 does not introduce any new disclosure requirements. However, it suggests that any restrictions on the current realisability of the surplus or a description of the basis used to determine the amount of the economic benefit available (see 8.2 above), may require disclosure under the provisions in IAS 1 about key sources of estimation uncertainty. *[IFRIC 14.10]*. These requirements are discussed in Chapter 3 at 5.2.1.

Where required by IAS 24 an entity discloses information about:

(a) related party transactions with post-employment benefit plans; and

(b) post-employment benefits for key management personnel. *[IAS 19.151]*.

Where required by IAS 37 an entity discloses information about contingent liabilities arising from post-employment benefit obligations. *[IAS 19.152]*.

15.3 Other employee benefits

IAS 19 has no specific disclosure requirements in respect of other types of employee benefits within its scope (i.e. short-term employee benefits, long-term employee benefits other than post-employment benefits and termination benefits) but contains reminders that:

- IAS 24 requires disclosure of employee benefits for key management personnel (see Chapter 39); and
- IAS 1 requires disclosure of employee benefits expense. *[IAS 19.25, 158, 171]*.

16 POSSIBLE FUTURE DEVELOPMENTS

16.1 IASB activities

As noted at 1 above, the IASB published the current version of IAS 19 in June 2011 (with the latest amendments in February 2018). In February 2018, the IASB reviewed its research pipeline and decided to start research on pension benefits that depend on asset returns.[17] Its objective is to assess whether it is feasible to place a cap on asset returns used in estimates of asset-dependent benefits to avoid what is perceived by some to be an anomaly (i.e. benefits being projected based on expected returns that exceed the discount rate, resulting in a liability even though employees will never be paid any amount above the fair value of the reference assets). If the research establishes that this approach would not be feasible the staff expect to recommend no further work on pensions. At the time of writing the staff are currently developing illustrative examples to compare the outcome under the existing model with that under the capped ultimate adjustment model.

The Board has completed a research project into why different standards require different discount rates to be used with the project summary 'Discount rates in IFRS Standards' published in February 2019. The Board intends to use the research findings in existing projects which includes the Primary Financial Statements project. The Exposure Draft *General Presentation and Disclosures* which was developed as part of the Primary financial Statements Project was published in December 2019, with comments due by 30 September 2020. The Exposure Draft includes a proposal to replace IAS 1 with a new standard which would require net interest to be presented in a single category (financing) after the subtotal of profit before financing and income tax. IAS 19 currently defers to the requirements of IAS 1 for the presentation of the components of defined benefit cost which allows entities to present net interest on a net defined benefit liability in a variety of ways such as an operating expense or a finance cost (see 10 above).

In March 2018, the Board added the Targeted Standards-level Review of Disclosures project to its agenda. The project includes a review of some disclosures relating to present value measures and will cover IAS 19 disclosures. The Board is expecting to issue an exposure draft with amendments to the disclosure requirements in IAS 19 in the first half of 2021.

16.2 Interpretations Committee activities

16.2.1 The availability of a refund from a defined benefit plan

At 8.2.1 above we discuss how certain powers of pension fund trustees (to set investment policy, for example) may influence the recognition of a net defined benefit asset by reference to refunds.

The Interpretations Committee received a similar question and, in May 2014, published a description of its initial discussion which is summarised below.

The Interpretations Committee discussed whether an employer has an unconditional right to a refund of a surplus in the following circumstances:

- the trustee acts on behalf of the plan's members and is independent from the employer; and

- the trustee has discretion in the event of a surplus arising in the plan to make alternative use of that surplus by augmenting the benefits payable to members or by winding up the plan through purchase of annuities, or both.

The question discussed related to a plan that is closed to accrual of future benefits, such that there will be no future service costs, and so no economic benefit is available through a reduction in future contributions. The Interpretations Committee also noted that:

- the fact that an existing surplus at the balance sheet date could be decreased or extinguished by uncertain future events that are beyond the control of the entity is not relevant to the existence of the right to a refund;
- if the trustee can use a surplus by augmenting the benefits in the future, pursuant to the formal terms of a plan (or a constructive obligation that goes beyond those terms), this fact should be considered when the entity measures its defined benefit obligation; and
- the amount of surplus to be recognised could be zero, as a consequence of the measurement of the defined benefit obligation.[18]

The Interpretations Committee discussed the matter again at its meeting in July 2014 and considered the informal feedback received from the IASB members.

The Interpretations Committee noted the difficulty associated with assessing the consequences of the trustee's future actions and its effect on the entity's ability to estimate reliably the amount to be received. Consequently, a majority of Interpretations Committee members observed that no asset should be recognised in this circumstance.

However, some Interpretations Committee members were concerned about the consequences that this conclusion could have on the accounting for a minimum funding requirement and the consistency of this conclusion with the recognition and measurement requirements of IAS 19.

Consequently, the Interpretations Committee requested the staff to perform further analysis on the interaction of this tentative decision with the requirement to recognise an additional liability when a minimum funding requirement applies and the relationship with the general requirements of IAS 19.

In its meeting in September 2014, as a result of its detailed analysis, the Interpretations Committee noted that it believed that there would be no conflicts between its conclusion at the July 2014 meeting and the recognition and measurement requirements of IAS 19, as the application of the asset ceiling requirements is separate from the determination of a surplus (deficit) under IAS 19. It also noted that the conclusion should lead to consistent results when a minimum funding requirement exists.[19] The Interpretations Committee thought that the trustees' powers to buy annuities or make other investment decisions are different from their ability to use a surplus to enhance benefits (a pension promise). It also thought that an entity's ability to realise an economic benefit through a 'gradual settlement' is restricted if a trustee can decide at any time to make a full settlement (i.e. a plan wind-up), even though IFRIC 14 allows the assumption of a gradual settlement over time until all members have left the plan. *[IFRIC 14.14]*. The Committee proposed amendments to IFRIC 14 which are detailed below.

As a result of the discussions in the September 2014 meeting, the IASB published an exposure draft setting out proposed amendments to IFRIC 14 to require that, when an entity determines the availability of a refund from a defined benefit plan:

- The amount of the surplus that an entity recognises as an asset on the basis of a future refund should not include amounts that other parties (for example, the plan trustees) can use for other purposes without the entity's consent.
- An entity should not assume gradual settlement of the plan as the justification for the recognition of an asset, if other parties can wind up the plan without the entity's consent.
- Other parties' power to buy annuities as plan assets or make other investment decisions without changing the benefits for plan members does not affect the availability of a refund.

The exposure draft also proposed amending IFRIC 14 to confirm that when an entity determines the availability of a refund and a reduction in future contributions, the entity should take into account the statutory requirements that are substantively enacted, as well as the terms and conditions that are contractually agreed and any constructive obligations.

In addition, the exposure draft addressed the interaction between the asset ceiling and a past service cost or a gain or loss on settlement. It proposed amending IAS 19 to clarify that:

- the past service cost or gain or loss on settlement is measured and recognised in profit and loss in accordance with IAS 19; and
- changes in the effect of the asset ceiling are recognised in other comprehensive income, and are determined after the recognition of the past service cost or the gain or loss on settlement.

A summary of the feedback on the exposure draft was discussed by the Interpretations Committee in their July 2016 meeting, but no decisions were made.[20] The Interpretations Committee deliberated the proposed amendments at their September 2016 meeting, taking into account the feedback received. Further, at its April 2017 meeting the Board tentatively decided to finalise the proposed amendments to IFRIC 14, subject to drafting changes.[21] However, some stakeholders subsequently communicated that they believed that the proposed amendments could have a significant effect on some defined benefit plans, particularly those in the United Kingdom. The original proposed amendments to IFRIC 14 included a new paragraph 12A which stated that 'An entity does not have an unconditional right to a refund of a surplus on the basis of assuming the gradual settlement described in paragraph 11(b) if other parties (for example, the plan trustees) can wind up the plan without the entity's consent. Other parties do not have the power to wind up the plan without the entity's consent, if the power is dependent on the occurrence or non-occurrence of one or more uncertain future events not wholly within the other parties' control.' In response to respondents' concerns over the inconsistencies between this new paragraph and paragraphs 11(c) and 14 of IFRIC 14, the Board tentatively decided to replace the reference to other parties' powers to 'wind up the plan' in this new paragraph with other parties powers to 'settle in full the plan liabilities in a single event (i.e. as a plan wind-up)'. In the United Kingdom although trustees do not generally have the right to legally wind up a defined benefit plan without the entity's consent, they do generally have the right to settle plan liabilities for individual plan members without an entity's consent if they are 'reasonable'. Although 'reasonable' is not defined in the applicable legislation it is generally understood that this type of partial settlement can be initiated by trustees if plan members would not be worse off as a result of the settlement. It is also understood that trustees do not generally need to obtain consent from plan members to initiate a settlement. Accordingly, trustees could exercise the right to settle liabilities for all plan members in a single event. Entities with defined benefit plans have generally measured the economic benefit available as a refund on a gradual settlement basis applying paragraph 13 of IFRIC 14. Applying the proposed paragraph 12A of IFRIC 14 to United Kingdom defined benefit plans could result in a significantly lower net defined benefit asset in some situations (due to measuring the asset on a wind-up basis in a single event) and may also require the recognition of an additional liability for any portion of any minimum funding requirement that would not be recoverable due to the lower asset ceiling.[22] At its meeting in July 2017 the Board agreed that during drafting further clarification would be sought on the possible impact the amendments would have on schemes with certain characteristics (such as those in the United Kingdom). The staff's next step was to explore if schemes with characteristics similar to those found in United Kingdom schemes exist in other jurisdictions. There were no plans to change the scope of the project.

In its June 2018 meeting the IASB received an update on the Interpretations Committee's work on how an entity might assess the availability of a refund of a surplus. The Interpretations Committee believe it would be possible to develop a principles-based approach focusing on the distinction between when an entity assumes a gradual settlement of plan liabilities over time and when it assumes full settlement of plan liabilities. The Committee believe that such an approach would however be broader in scope than that of the existing proposed amendments to IFRIC 14 and it is possible that any amendments may need to be exposed for further comments. It was proposed that all possible changes to accounting for employee benefits be considered at the same time and that the IASB would be better placed to consider the direction of the IFRIC 14 project when the outcome of the IAS 19 research project (see 16 above) is known. In its February 2020 meeting, the IASB decided not to finalise the proposed amendments to IFRIC 14. It was recommended that the Board should consider referring to a project on IFRIC 14 in its Request for Information (RFI) as part of its 2020 Agenda Consultation. At the time of writing the RFI is due to be published in the first half of 2021.

References

1 *IFRIC Update*, June 2019.
2 *IFRIC Update*, IFRS Interpretations Committee, September 2012.
3 *IFRIC Update*, May 2014.
4 E54 *Employee Benefits*, IASC, October 1996, paras. 17-21.

5 *IFRIC Update*, January 2008.
6 *IASB Update*, September 2007.
7 *IASB Update*, November 2007.
8 *IFRIC Update*, May 2011.
9 *IFRIC Update*, March 2015.
10 Staff paper for the February 2013 IASB meeting, Agenda ref 9B, Appendix C-Staff paper for the November 2012 IFRS IC meeting, Appendix A, Examples 3-5.
11 *IFRIC Update*, July 2013.
12 *IFRIC Update*, November 2013.
13 *IASB Update*, December 2013.
14 *IFRIC Update*, July 2015.
15 *IFRIC Update*, November 2010.
16 *IFRIC Update*, November 2011.
17 *IASB Update*, February 2018.
18 *IASB Update*, June 2019.
19 *IFRIC Update*, September 2014.
20 *IFRIC Update*, July 2016.
21 *IASB Update*, April 2017.
22 *IASB Agenda Paper 12C*, July 2017.

Chapter 36   Operating segments

1 INTRODUCTION 2977
   1.1   Background 2977
   1.2   The main features of IFRS 8 2978
   1.3   Disclosures required by IFRS 15 2980
   1.4   Terms used in IFRS 8 2980
   1.5   Transitional provisions 2981
2 OBJECTIVE AND SCOPE OF IFRS 8 2981
   2.1   Objective 2981
   2.2   Scope of IFRS 8 2982
          2.2.1   The meaning of 'traded in a public market' 2982
          2.2.2   Consolidated financial statements presented with those of the parent 2983
          2.2.3   Entities providing segment information on a voluntary basis 2983
3 IDENTIFYING A SINGLE SET OF OPERATING SEGMENTS 2983
   3.1   Definition of an operating segment 2984
          3.1.1   Revenue earning business activities 2984
          3.1.2   'Chief operating decision maker' and 'segment manager' 2984
          3.1.3   Availability of discrete financial information 2987
          3.1.4   When a single set of components is not immediately apparent 2988
          3.1.5   An equity accounted investment can be an operating segment 2989
   3.2   Identifying externally reportable segments 2990
          3.2.1   Aggregation criteria – aggregating internally reported operating segments into single reportable operating segments 2992
          3.2.2   Quantitative thresholds – operating segments which are reportable because of their size 2996

		3.2.3	Combining small operating segments into a larger reportable segment 2997
		3.2.4	'All other segments'..2997
		3.2.5	A 'practical limit' for the number of reported operating segments 2998
		3.2.6	Restatement of segments reported in comparative periods 2998
4	MEASUREMENT 2999
5	INFORMATION TO BE DISCLOSED ABOUT REPORTABLE SEGMENTS 3000
	5.1	General information about reportable segments... 3001
		5.1.1	Disclosure of how operating segments are aggregated 3001
	5.2	A measure of segment profit or loss, total assets and total liabilities 3002
		5.2.1	Other measures of segment performance 3002
	5.3	Disclosure of other elements of revenue, income and expense 3003
	5.4	Additional disclosures relating to segment assets..................................... 3005
	5.5	Explanation of the measurements used in segment reporting 3005
	5.6	Reconciliations 3007
	5.7	Restatement of previously reported information 3009
		5.7.1	Changes in organisation structure 3009
		5.7.2	Changes in segment measures... 3010
	5.8	Disclosure of commercially sensitive information 3011
6	ENTITY-WIDE DISCLOSURES FOR ALL ENTITIES 3012
	6.1	Information about products and services 3013
	6.2	Information about geographical areas 3013
	6.3	Information about major customers 3014
		6.3.1	Customers known to be under common control........................ 3015

List of examples

Example 36.1:	The meaning of 'public market' in the context of a fund 2982
Example 36.2:	Identifying operating segments – CODM and segment manager.. 2986
Example 36.3:	Similar products and services..2993
Example 36.4:	Similar production processes 2993
Example 36.5:	Type and class of customer 2994
Example 36.6:	Retail outlets and internet distribution 2994

Example 36.7:	Aggregating internally reported operating segments with similar characteristics into a single reportable operating segment	2994
Example 36.8:	Identifying reportable segments using the quantitative thresholds	2996
Example 36.9:	Reaching the threshold of 75% of external revenue	2998

Chapter 36 Operating segments

1 INTRODUCTION

1.1 Background

IFRS 8 – *Operating Segments* – was published in November 2006. The Standard has been mandatory since 2009. *[IFRS 8.35].*

In Europe, the introduction of IFRS 8 was controversial. Opponents shared concerns expressed in the dissenting opinions of two IASB members that the lack of a defined measure of segment profit or loss and the absence of any requirement for that measure to be consistent with the attribution of assets to reportable segments would encourage the proliferation of non-GAAP measures that could mislead users. *[IFRS 8.DO1-DO4].* These concerns were raised in the European Parliament together with questions about the governance of the IASB, as a result of which the process to endorse IFRS 8 in the European Union was not completed until November 2007, a year after the Standard had been published.

During this period, the IFRS Foundation announced enhancements to oversight and due process to include a requirement for the IASB to conduct 'a review of issues identified as contentious as part of the consultation process related to all new IFRSs (including IFRS 8), major amendments to IFRSs and major IFRIC interpretations'. Such a review would be performed after at least two full years of implementation and be completed within three years of the pronouncement's effective date.[1] IFRS 8 was the first standard subject to a post-implementation review, which was completed in 2013.

Based on the feedback to the post-implementation review, the IASB concluded that the benefits of applying the Standard were largely as expected and that overall the Standard achieved its objectives and has improved financial reporting. The IASB noted the concerns raised by some investors but concluded that they do not suggest significant failings in the Standard and therefore do not warrant a revision of the principles underlying IFRS 8.[2]

However, the IASB acknowledged that some issues could be considered for improvement and, in March 2017, issued an Exposure Draft proposing a limited number of improvements to the standard.[3]

In February 2019, the IASB issued a summary of the feedback received and the Board's response to it. Investors generally asked for more significant changes to IFRS 8 than those proposed in the ED. Preparers questioned whether all of the proposals would represent improvements to financial reporting. Other stakeholders were either asking for more clarification in some areas or questioned the benefits of the proposed amendments.

Based on the feedback received, the IASB decided not to proceed with these proposed amendments. Whilst it had initially decided proceeding with some of the proposals and to abandon the others, the Board concluded that, in aggregate, those remaining proposals would not result in sufficient improvements to justify the costs to stakeholders of implementing an amended standard.[4]

1.2 The main features of IFRS 8

IFRS 8 is a disclosure standard. It specifies the way an entity should report information about its operating segments in annual financial statements and, as a consequential amendment to IAS 34 – *Interim Financial Reporting*, requires an entity to report selected information about its operating segments in interim financial reports (see Chapter 41 at 4.4). It also sets out requirements for related disclosures about an entity's products and services, geographical areas and major customers. The disclosures required are discussed at 5 and 6 below and include:

- financial and descriptive information about the entity's reportable segments, which are operating segments above a certain size or (where specific criteria are met) aggregations of operating segments;
- segment revenues and a measure of profit or loss for each reportable segment, reconciled to the amounts disclosed in the entity's financial statements;
- a measure of segment assets, segment liabilities and particular income and expense items to the extent that such information is regularly provided to the chief operating decision maker of the entity, reconciled to the amounts disclosed in the entity's financial statements;
- unless the information is not available and the cost of its development would be excessive, information about the revenues derived from the entity's products and services (or groups of similar products and services), about the countries in which it earns revenues and holds assets, and about major customers, regardless of whether this information is used by management in making operating decisions; and
- descriptive information about the way that operating segments were determined, the products and services provided by the segments, differences between the measurements used in reporting segment information and those used in the entity's financial statements, and changes in the measurement of segment amounts from period to period.

The process of identifying operating segments for external reporting purposes begins with the information used by the entity's chief operating decision maker to assess performance and to make decisions about future allocations of resources. *[IFRS 8.5].*

Entities applying IFRS 8 report on a single set of components according to the way that the business is sub-divided for management reporting purposes. *[IFRS 8.10]*.

If a component of an entity is managed as a separate segment, IFRS 8 requires it to be treated as such even if it sells exclusively or primarily to other components of the same entity. *[IFRS 8.5(a)]*.

IFRS 8 does not go so far as to require an entity to report all the information that is reviewed by the chief operating decision maker, recognising that such detail may not be useful to users of financial statements and could be cumbersome in its presentation. Instead it allows entities to apply certain criteria for aggregating components and to disclose information only for those segments that exceed certain quantitative criteria. *[IFRS 8.BC Appendix A 72]*.

Under IFRS 8, the amounts reported about identified segments are prepared according to the manner in which information is presented to the entity's chief operating decision maker. This can be different to the way that the entity applies its accounting policies used in the preparation of the financial statements under IFRSs.

IFRS 8 requires an entity to describe the factors used to identify the entity's reportable segments, including a description of the basis of organisation. This description would explain whether the organisation is structured according to products and services, geographical areas, regulatory environments or other factors and state whether operating segments have been aggregated for reporting purposes. In addition, the entity must describe the types of products and services from which each reportable segment derives its revenues and disclose the judgements made by management in aggregating operating segments into reportable segments. *[IFRS 8.22]*.

IFRS 8 specifies amounts which should be disclosed about each reportable segment, but only if those measures are included in the measure of profit or loss used by, or otherwise regularly provided to, the chief operating decision maker (see 5.2 below). These specified amounts include a requirement to report separately interest revenue and interest expense by segment (but only if those measures are included in the measure of profit or loss used, or otherwise regularly provided to the chief operating decision maker) unless a majority of the segment's revenues is derived from interest and performance is assessed primarily on the basis of net interest revenue. *[IFRS 8.23]*.

Certain 'entity-wide disclosures' are also required to be provided under IFRS 8, even if the entity has only one reportable segment *[IFRS 8.31]* (see 6 below). Entity-wide information is disclosed for the entity as a whole about its products and services, geographical areas and major customers, regardless of the way the entity is organised and the information presented to the chief operating decision maker. The amounts reported for this entity-wide information is based on the financial information used to produce the entity's financial statements. *[IFRS 8.32-34]*.

There is no 'competitive harm' exemption in IFRS 8 from the requirement to disclose segment information, or components of such information, for example on the grounds of commercial sensitivity, confidentiality or being otherwise detrimental to the entity's competitive position. *[IFRS 8.BC43-45]*.

These features are discussed in more detail in this chapter.

1.3 Disclosures required by IFRS 15

IFRS 15 – *Revenue from Contracts with Customers*, requires entities to disclose disaggregated revenue information to illustrate how the nature, amount, timing and uncertainty about revenue and cash flows are affected by economic factors. *[IFRS 15.114]*. If an entity applies IFRS 8, it is also required to disclose 'sufficient information' to explain the relationship between the disaggregated revenue information and revenue information that is disclosed for each reportable segment. *[IFRS 15.115]*. IFRS 15 also acknowledges that information meeting its requirements might have already been provided under another standard, in which case it is not required to be duplicated. *[IFRS 15.112]*.

Accordingly, many entities choose to combine the IFRS 15 disclosures of disaggregated revenue with their segment information in the notes to the financial statements. However, the segment disclosures required by IFRS 8 are made by reference to the information provided to the entity's chief operating decision maker and may not be sufficiently disaggregated to achieve the disclosure objectives of IFRS 15. In addition, the information used for segment reporting may be based on non-GAAP information rather than measured in accordance with IFRS 15. *[IFRS 15.BC340]*. As a result, entities can choose to provide more disaggregated 'entity-wide' information about revenues (see 6 below) in order to meet the additional requirements of IFRS 15.

The requirements of IFRS 15 in this regard are discussed at in Chapter 32 at 3.2.1.A.

1.4 Terms used in IFRS 8

The following terms are used in IFRS 8 with the meanings specified:

Term	Meaning
Operating segment	A component of an entity: (a) that engages in business activities from which it may earn revenues and incur expenses (including revenues and expenses relating to transactions with other components of the same entity); (b) whose operating results are regularly reviewed by the entity's chief operating decision maker to make decisions about resources to be allocated to the segment and assess its performance; and (c) for which discrete financial information is available. *[IFRS 8.5, IFRS 8 Appendix A]*.
Chief operating decision maker	The function of allocating resources to and assessing the performance of the operating segments of an entity. This is not necessarily a manager with a specific title, but can be an entity's chief executive officer, chief operating officer, a group of executive directors or others. *[IFRS 8.7]*.
Segment manager	The function of being directly accountable to and maintaining regular contact with the chief operating decision maker to discuss operating activities, financial results, forecasts, or plans for the segment. *[IFRS 8.9]*.

Reportable segment	An operating segment or a group of two or more operating segments determined to be eligible for aggregation in accordance with IFRS 8.12; and which exceeds the quantitative thresholds in IFRS 8.13. *[IFRS 8.11]*.
Aggregation criteria	Two or more operating segments may be aggregated into a single operating segment if aggregation is consistent with the core principle of IFRS 8, they have similar economic characteristics, such as long-term average gross margins, and are similar in each of the following respects: (a) the nature of the products and services; (b) the nature of the production processes; (c) the type or class of customer for their products and services; (d) the methods used to distribute their products or provide their services; (e) if applicable, the nature of the regulatory environment, for example, banking, insurance or public utilities. *[IFRS 8.12]*.

Quantitative thresholds	Information about an operating segment that meets any of the following criteria:
	(a) its reported revenue, including both sales to external customers and intersegment sales or transfers, is 10% or more of combined revenue, internal and external, of all operating segments; or
	(b) its reported profit or loss is, in absolute terms, 10% or more of the greater of, in absolute amount:
	   (i) the combined profit of all operating segments that did not report a loss; and
	   (ii) the combined reported loss of all operating segments that reported a loss; or
	(c) its assets are 10% or more of the combined assets of all operating segments. *[IFRS 8.13]*.

1.5 Transitional provisions

There are no special arrangements for entities applying IFRS 8 for the first time, with the Standard requiring comparative information to be restated. Only where the necessary information is both unavailable and incapable of being developed without excessive cost is an entity exempt from full restatement. *[IFRS 8.36]*. Accordingly, an entity should ensure that internal reporting systems can provide the information needed to meet the disclosure requirements of IFRS 8 for all periods presented in its financial statements.

2 OBJECTIVE AND SCOPE OF IFRS 8

2.1 Objective

The objective of IFRS 8 is expressed as a 'core principle', being that an entity shall disclose information to enable users of its financial statements to evaluate the nature and financial effects of the business activities in which it engages and the economic environments in which it operates. *[IFRS 8.1]*.

2.2 Scope of IFRS 8

IFRS 8 applies to both the separate or individual financial statements of an entity and the consolidated financial statements of a group with a parent:

(a) whose debt or equity instruments are traded in a public market (a domestic or foreign stock exchange or an over-the-counter market, including local and regional markets); or

(b) that files, or is in the process of filing, its financial statements with a securities commission or other regulatory organisation for the purpose of issuing any class of instruments in a public market. *[IFRS 8.2]*.

The above test is applied to the parent entity alone. *[IFRS 8.2(b)]*. Therefore, IFRS 8 does not apply to a group headed by a parent that has no listed financial instruments, even if the group includes a subsidiary that has any of its equity or debt instruments traded in a public market. The scope of IAS 33 – *Earnings per Share* – is similarly defined. *[IFRS 8.BC23]*.

Of course, a subsidiary with publicly traded debt or equity instruments would be required to provide segment information under IFRS 8 in its own financial statements from its perspective as a reporting entity.

2.2.1 The meaning of 'traded in a public market'

The Standard describes a 'public market' as including a domestic or foreign stock exchange or an over-the-counter market, including local and regional markets, *[IFRS 8.2]*, but does not define what would make some markets 'public' and others not.

In our view, a market is 'public' when buyers and sellers (market participants) can transact with one another (directly; through agents; or in a secondary market) at a price determined in that market. A public market does not exist when the buyers and sellers can transact only with the entity itself (or an agent acting on its behalf). The requirement for an entity to list its securities on a stock exchange is not the sole factor determining whether the entity is in the scope of IFRS 8. Its securities must be traded in a public market meeting the criteria noted above.

Example 36.1: The meaning of 'public market' in the context of a fund

Many investment funds are listed on a public stock exchange for informational purposes, in particular to facilitate the valuation of portfolios by investors or because it is a requirement for the fund to be listed on a public stock exchange to make it eligible for investment by entities that are required to invest only in listed securities. However, in spite of such a listing, subscriptions and redemptions are handled by a fund administrator or a transfer agent (acting on behalf of the fund) and no transactions are undertaken on the public stock exchange. In addition, the prices for those transactions are determined by the fund agreement, such as on the basis of the fund's Net Asset Value, rather than the price quoted on the public stock exchange and determined by supply and demand.

In our view the debt or equity instruments of such entities are not traded in a public market and so the entity would not fall within the scope of IFRS 8. Nevertheless, regulators can mandate that funds provide segment information, or funds can voluntarily disclose segment information. In such cases, the funds need to comply with the requirements of IFRS 8.

Such 'public markets' would include exchange markets, dealer markets, brokered markets, and principal-to-principal markets as described in IFRS 13 – *Fair Value Measurement* – and listed in that Standard as examples of markets in which fair value inputs might be observable (see Chapter 14 at 15.1). *[IFRS 13.B34].*

2.2.2 Consolidated financial statements presented with those of the parent

When both the consolidated financial statements and the parent's separate or individual financial statements are contained in the same financial report, segment information is only required in the consolidated financial statements. *[IFRS 8.4].*

2.2.3 Entities providing segment information on a voluntary basis

Entities for which IFRS 8 is not mandatory might still want to provide information about their business activities, for example about sales by segment, without triggering the need to comply fully with the Standard. The Board concluded that this would be acceptable, provided that such disclosure is not referred to as 'segment information'. *[IFRS 8.BC22].* Consequently, entities giving information about segments on a voluntary basis cannot describe that information as 'segment information' unless it has been prepared in compliance with IFRS 8. *[IFRS 8.3].*

3 IDENTIFYING A SINGLE SET OF OPERATING SEGMENTS

IFRS 8 adopts a 'bottom up' approach to determining the level of detail required for segment reporting in the notes to the financial statements. It requires the entity's revenue earning activities to be divided into operating segments (based on the same components used by management to run the business) and only allows that information to be aggregated for reporting purposes if specific criteria are met. This process can involve considerable judgement, as it may not always be immediately clear what activities are operating segments for the purposes of the Standard or which layer of the entity's organisational structure represents the level at which those activities are managed. This is particularly the case when management information is presented in a number of different ways (for example by product, by geographical market and by legal entity) or where management structures distinguish operational, strategic and oversight responsibilities.

Notwithstanding such difficulties, the requirement is to identify a single set of components as constituting the entity's operating segments. *[IFRS 8.8].*

The process for determining operating segments is important not only to entities applying IFRS 8 for external reporting purposes, but also to entities implementing the requirements of IAS 36 – *Impairment of Assets* – for testing goodwill for impairment. As such, the way that operating segments are defined and determined under IFRS 8 can affect the financial statements of entities to which the disclosure requirements in IFRS 8 do not apply, such as those without traded equity or debt. This is because the Standard on impairment, applicable to all entities, states that goodwill cannot be allocated to a group of cash-generating units (CGUs) that is larger than an operating segment before aggregation (as determined below). *[IAS 36.80(b)].* See Chapter 20 at 8.1.4.

3.1 Definition of an operating segment

An operating segment is defined as a component of an entity:

(a) that engages in business activities from which it may earn revenues and incur expenses (including revenues and expenses relating to transactions with other components of the same entity);

(b) whose operating results are regularly reviewed by the entity's chief operating decision maker to make decisions about resources to be allocated to the segment and assess its performance; and

(c) for which discrete financial information is available. *[IFRS 8.5]*.

This means that the determination of an entity's operating segments starts with the smallest components of the business for which information about profit is presented for use by the entity's chief operating decision maker (sometimes referred to as 'CODM').

3.1.1 Revenue earning business activities

A significant feature of an operating segment is the potential for revenue generation rather than actually earning revenues in the reporting period. Accordingly, a start-up operation can be treated as an operating segment while it has yet to earn revenues. *[IFRS 8.5]*.

However, not every part of an entity is necessarily an operating segment. For example, a corporate headquarters or a functional department (such as a centralised data processing centre) that either does not earn revenues or for which revenues are only incidental to the activities of the entity would not be an operating segment for the purposes of IFRS 8. Similarly, an entity's post-employment benefit plans would not be regarded as operating segments. *[IFRS 8.6]*.

3.1.2 'Chief operating decision maker' and 'segment manager'

Arguably the most important judgements made in implementing IFRS 8 relate to the identification of the entity's chief operating decision maker. The nature of what is ultimately disclosed in the financial statements about operating segments and the level of detail (or segmentation) required is directly related to the information regularly provided to the chief operating decision maker.

References in the standard to 'chief operating decision maker' are to the function of allocating resources and assessing performance of the operating segments and not to a manager with a specific title. Often the chief operating decision maker of an entity is its chief executive officer or chief operating officer (i.e. an individual), but the term could refer equally to a group of executive directors or others charged with that role. *[IFRS 8.7]*.

In Extract 36.1 below, the Go-Ahead Group identifies its Group Chief Executive as the chief operating decision maker:

> Extract 36.1: The Go-Ahead Group plc (2019)
> **Notes to the consolidated financial statements** [extract]
> 3. Segmental analysis [extract]
> The information reported to the Group Chief Executive in his capacity as chief operating decision maker does not include an analysis of assets and liabilities and accordingly IFRS 8 does not require this information to be presented.

The determination of chief operating decision maker will not be the same for all entities applying IFRS 8 and will depend upon the particular facts and circumstances applying to each entity, including the entity's governance structure. However, in stating that the term could apply to a group of executive directors or others, [IFRS 8.7], the Standard is clear that the function of CODM is an executive role. The IFRS Interpretations Committee confirmed this view in 2011. While it observed that in practice the functions of CODM are sometimes carried out by multiple persons and that all such persons involved in those activities would be part of the CODM group, the Committee noted that the CODM would not normally include non-executive directors.[5] For example, an entity may have a single board of executive and non-executive directors which reviews the performance of individual business units, makes decisions about the operating budgets for those businesses and reviews significant applications for investment. In that case, the full board could be identified as the chief operating decision maker. However, if the entity also has a sub-committee of executive directors or another grouping of key management personnel (sometimes referred to as an 'operational board'), this smaller group of executives would be identified as the chief operating decision maker.

Essentially, the chief operating decision maker is found at the most senior executive decision-making level of an organisation and as such should be distinguished from higher levels of management fulfilling primarily an oversight or approval role and who, to reflect their non-executive function, are provided information at a more aggregated level as a matter of course. For example, in some jurisdictions, supervisory bodies may be part of an entity's governance structure and be entrusted with significant oversight responsibilities. This role may give the supervisory body significant veto rights and rights of approval. However, that supervision will not typically represent the level of decision-making implicit in the notion of the CODM.

In the extract below, Roche Group identifies as the CODM its Corporate Executive Committee, a group of senior executives which is headed by the Chief Executive Officer and is appointed by and reports to the Board of Directors.

> *Extract 36.2: Roche Holding Ltd (2019)*
>
> **Notes to the Roche Group Consolidated Financial Statements** [extract]
>
> **34. Significant accounting policies** [extract]
>
> **Segment reporting** [extract]
>
> For the purpose of segment reporting the Group's Corporate Executive Committee (CEC) is considered to be the Group's Chief Operating Decision Maker. The determination of the Group's operating segments is based on the organisation units for which information is reported to the CEC on a regular basis.

Another important distinction to be made is between chief operating decision maker and the function of 'segment manager'. The segment manager is accountable to and maintains regular contact with the chief operating decision maker to discuss operating activities, financial results, forecasts or plans for the segment. The chief operating decision maker may also fulfil the role of segment manager for some operating segments and a single segment manager may be responsible for more than one operating segment. [IFRS 8.9]. For example, if the CODM is a group of executives, members of that group may fulfil the role of segment manager for certain components of the entity.

Considerations of how components of the entity are managed are relevant to the identification of an entity's operating segments and not to how they might be reported in the financial statements. Accordingly, separate operating segments which otherwise meet the definition at 3.1 above are not aggregated into single reportable operating segments simply because they have a common segment manager. The Standard is clear that such segments are only aggregated into reportable operating segments if they exhibit similar long-term economic characteristics and are similar in respect of the qualitative criteria set out at 3.2.1 below. *[IFRS 8.12]*. In addition, because the oversight role of the CODM is separate from the operational role of the segment manager, it is possible that an entity could regard an investee accounted for by the equity method as an operating segment (see 3.1.5 below).

In practice, judgement is required to determine whether the component(s) for which a segment manager is held responsible represents one or more operating segments. For example, if targets are set by the CODM for the entire area of one segment manager's responsibility and the remuneration of that segment manager is based on the achievement of those targets, on an aggregated basis, this could support a determination that the area of responsibility is one operating segment in the absence of other evidence indicating that the CODM reviews the results of these components separately. Equally, whilst IFRS 8 states that segment managers will generally exist, their existence is an important indicator for identifying operating segments, but not a necessary condition. The key determinant is based on the activity of the CODM with respect to the internally reported results of that component.

A common situation in practice is that detailed financial information is provided or available to the chief operating decision maker on a regular basis about various levels of management and operational activity within an entity. In these circumstances, the interplay between the three criteria at 3.1 above becomes very important, as the existence of more detailed internal reporting could otherwise lead to a determination that there are more operating segments. If the three criteria apply to more than one set of components of an entity, but there is only one set that has segment managers, generally the set of components with segment managers constitutes the operating segments. *[IFRS 8.8]*.

Example 36.2: Identifying operating segments – CODM and segment manager

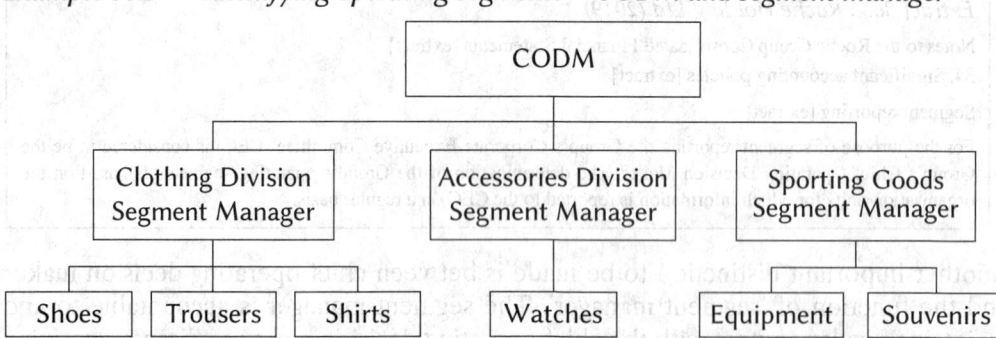

The diagram above sets out the internal reporting structure of Entity A. The CODM receives financial information about the entity's operations, the most detailed of which (including revenue and operating profit) relates to the six business units (Shoes, Trousers, Shirts, Watches, Equipment and Souvenirs). However, these units do not have their own segment manager. Instead, the six business units are grouped into three divisions (Clothing, Accessories and Sporting Goods), each of which has a divisional manager who reports directly to the CODM. The three divisions report financial information to the CODM who uses it to assess performance and allocate resources.

Marketing strategies are determined by the CODM for each division, and each divisional manager is responsible for their implementation at the business unit level. Also, quarterly financial information is presented to the Board of directors and investors at the division level, which is consistent with the level at which the CODM makes decisions. In addition, the company determines the following:

- Budgets and forecasts are prepared at the division level, and the CODM reviews budget-to-actual variances at that level on a monthly basis;
- The divisional managers are compensated in accordance with the company's bonus plan, which sets targets for each division.

In this case, the entity decides that the operating segments as defined in IFRS 8 comprise the three divisions as opposed to the six business units, because only the divisions have segment managers.

Proper application of the requirements of IFRS 8 requires a clear understanding of what information is given to the chief operating decision maker and how the CODM uses that information, in conjunction with the segment managers. In the above example, the fact that the CODM receives detailed financial information about activities below the divisional level could raise doubts about the determination that the divisions represent the entity's operating segments, rather than the business units. In these circumstances, entities would be required to demonstrate that:

- the more detailed information is not used by the CODM to assess performance and allocate resources;
- segment managers operate only at the divisional level and are not, in effect, managers for each of the business units in their division. As noted above, components otherwise meeting the characteristics of an operating segment under IFRS 8 are not combined simply because they share a segment manager.

It might be evident from the records of the discussions between segment managers and the CODM that results are monitored at divisional rather than at business unit level. It might equally be clear from the records of board meetings that more detailed information is not referred to by the CODM in its deliberations. However, there is evidence that when regulators and other enforcement agencies assess the quality of an entity's compliance with IFRS 8, they adopt the presumption that the CODM uses whatever detailed information is provided to him/her on a regular basis for decision-making and assessment purposes.

3.1.3 Availability of discrete financial information

As noted above, a component of an entity can only be regarded as an operating segment if discrete financial information is available about that component. *[IFRS 8.5(c)]*. This requirement relates solely to the existence of discrete information that allows the chief operating decision maker to make decisions about the allocation of resources and to assess the performance of that component.

Accordingly, a component of an entity is still regarded as an operating segment if the only information available relates to the profitability of that component. Such information would be sufficient for the chief operating decision maker to review its operating results, assess performance and make decisions about resource allocation. *[IFRS 8.5(b)]*. The financial information is not rendered useless by the lack of, for example, a separate statement of financial position or a separate statement of cash flows for that component.

However, it would be unlikely that a component of an entity could be regarded as an operating segment solely because the chief operating decision maker receives information about revenue from that component. Without a measure of the component's operating results it would be difficult to make meaningful assessments of the effect of allocating more or less resource to that activity. As such, information on revenue alone would have limited value in decision making. Therefore, the search for an entity's operating segments starts with the smallest components of the business for which a measure of profitability is provided to the entity's CODM.

3.1.4 When a single set of components is not immediately apparent

For many entities, the search for operating segments is concluded after applying the three criteria listed at 3.1 above.

However, in cases where a single set of operating segments cannot be identified clearly by applying the above criteria, for example in an entity where its business activities are reported internally and assessed in a variety of ways, IFRS 8 states that other factors should be considered, including the nature of the business activities of each component, the existence of a manager responsible for it, and the information presented to the board of directors. *[IFRS 8.8]*. Therefore, if an entity's activities are reported internally in a number of different ways, each with their own set of business components as defined above, but there is only one set to which segment managers are assigned, then that will comprise the operating segments to report in the financial statements for IFRS 8 purposes. *[IFRS 8.9]*. For example, if an entity's board of directors manages its business using information on revenues and costs analysed both by product grouping as well as by geographical market, but the management structure operates only on geographical lines, then the financial statements would include segmental information on a geographical basis.

A single set of operating segments must be identified, even where two or more sets of components of an entity are managed in a matrix structure, for example where financial information is available and performance is assessed and segment managers assigned not only on the basis of product and service lines worldwide but also by geographical area irrespective of products and service lines. In that situation the choice of a single set of components is a matter of judgement, made by reference to the core principle of the Standard as set out at 2.1 above. *[IFRS 8.10]*. This requirement is different to FASB ASC Topic 280 and ED 8, which proposed that in such circumstances operating segments be drawn up on product and service lines.[6] The IASB agreed with respondents to the exposure draft that a default position mandating the use of components based on products and services was inconsistent with a management approach founded on what is important to the chief operating decision maker. *[IFRS 8.BC27]*.

3.1.5 An equity accounted investment can be an operating segment

The definition of an operating segment focuses on the review of its operating results by the entity's chief operating decision maker and the assessment of its performance and the allocation of resources to it by the CODM. *[IFRS 8.5(b)]*. This raises the question of whether the reporting entity needs to have control over the activities conducted in what otherwise would meet the definition of an operating segment, or whether it is sufficient that the CODM reviews its results and this review influences decisions about investment in those activities. In our view, control over the activities in which the entity is investing is not a requirement.

The core principle of IFRS 8 requires the disclosure of information relating to the business activities in which an entity engages and the economic environments in which it operates. *[IFRS 8.1]*. No restriction is imposed according to the manner of that engagement, just the way in which the CODM makes decisions about allocating resources and assesses its performance.

For example, an equity method investee (i.e. associate or joint venture), could be considered an operating segment if it meets the criteria in IFRS 8. The CODM may regularly review the operating results and performance of an equity method investee for the purposes of making additional investments or advances, evaluating financial performance or evaluating whether to retain its investment. The CODM is not required to be responsible for making decisions at the investee operating level that affect the investee's operations and performance in order for it to be identified as an operating segment. Further, the definition of an operating segment does not require that the revenue generating activities of the investee are included in the entity's revenue as reported in the IFRS financial statements. Segment performance could be measured by reference to the amounts included in the entity's IFRS financial statements or equally by reference to the financial information prepared by the investee itself. Any difference between the measures used by the CODM and the accounting treatment under IFRS would be reported as a reconciling item in the entity's disclosures under IFRS 8 (see 5.6 below).

This view is consistent with the disclosure requirements of IFRS 8, which require the entity's share of the profits and losses of equity accounted associates and joint ventures and the amount of investment in equity accounted investees to be presented, if those amounts are included in the measures reviewed by the CODM of segment profit or loss and segment assets respectively (see 5.3 and 5.4 below). *[IFRS 8.23(g), IFRS 8.24(a)]*.

In 2019, HOCHTIEF Aktiengesellschaft changed its segment reporting to present a significant equity-method investee, which used to be presented in 'Corporate Headquarters' as a separate reportable segment:

> **Extract 36.3: HOCHTIEF Aktiengesellschaft (2019)**
>
> Notes to the Consolidated Financial Statements [extract]
>
> **36. Segment reporting [extract]**
>
> HOCHTIEF's structure reflects the operating focus of the business as well as the Group's presence in key national and international regions and markets. Segmental reporting in the HOCHTIEF Group is based on the Group's divisional operations. The breakdown mirrors the Group's internal reporting systems.
>
> The Group's reportable segments (divisions) are as follows:
>
> HOCHTIEF Americas encompasses the construction management and construction activities of operational units in the USA and Canada;
>
> HOCHTIEF Asia Pacific pools the construction activities, contract mining and services in the Asia-Pacific region;
>
> HOCHTIEF Europe brings together the core business in Europe as well as selected other regions and designs, develops, builds, operates, and manages real estate and infrastructure.
>
> Albertis Investment comprises the investment in Spanish toll road operator Albertis Infraestructuras S.A., which is accounted for as a separate segment from 2019. It was previously presented under Corporate and the prior-year segment information has been restated accordingly.
>
> Corporate comprises Corporate Headquarters, other activities not assignable to the separately listed divisions, including management of financial resources and insurance activities, plus consolidation effects. [...]
>
> | Divisions | EBITDA | | Ordinary depreciation/ amortization | | Share of profits and losses of equity-method associates and joint ventures | |
> |---|---|---|---|---|---|---|
> | | 2019 | 2018 (restated) | 2019 | 2018 (restated) | 2019 | 2018 |
> | (EUR thousand) | | | | | | |
> | HOCHTIEF Americas | 397,749 | 374,660 | 80,061 | 57,821 | 77,518 | 70,802 |
> | HOCHTIEF Asia Pacific | 1,334,204 | 1,209,490 | 570,715 | 457,597 | 41,514 | 36,990 |
> | HOCHTIEF Europe | 97,270 | 116,425 | 47,082 | 42,461 | 26,169 | 63,558 |
> | Albertis Investment | 122,355 | 84,284 | – | – | 122,355 | 84,284 |
> | Corporate | (58,732) | (98,622) | 2,900 | 2,481 | 14,730 | (23,792) |
> | **HOCHTIEF Group** | **1,892,846** | **1,686,237** | **700,758** | **560,360** | **282,286** | **231,842** |

3.2 Identifying externally reportable segments

Having identified a single set of internal operating segments, the Standard describes how reportable segments are determined. As a minimum an entity must separately disclose information on reportable segments above a certain size (see 3.2.2 below). In addition, a previously identified reportable segment continues to be disclosed separately in the current period if management judges it to be of continuing significance, even if it no longer satisfies the quantitative thresholds. *[IFRS 8.17]*.

Thereafter, an entity is only compelled to give information on other segments (either individually or in certain circumstances on a combined basis) if the unallocated element is too large (see 3.2.4 below).

The implementation guidance to IFRS 8 includes a diagram illustrating how to apply the main provisions of the Standard for identifying reportable segments, which is reproduced below:

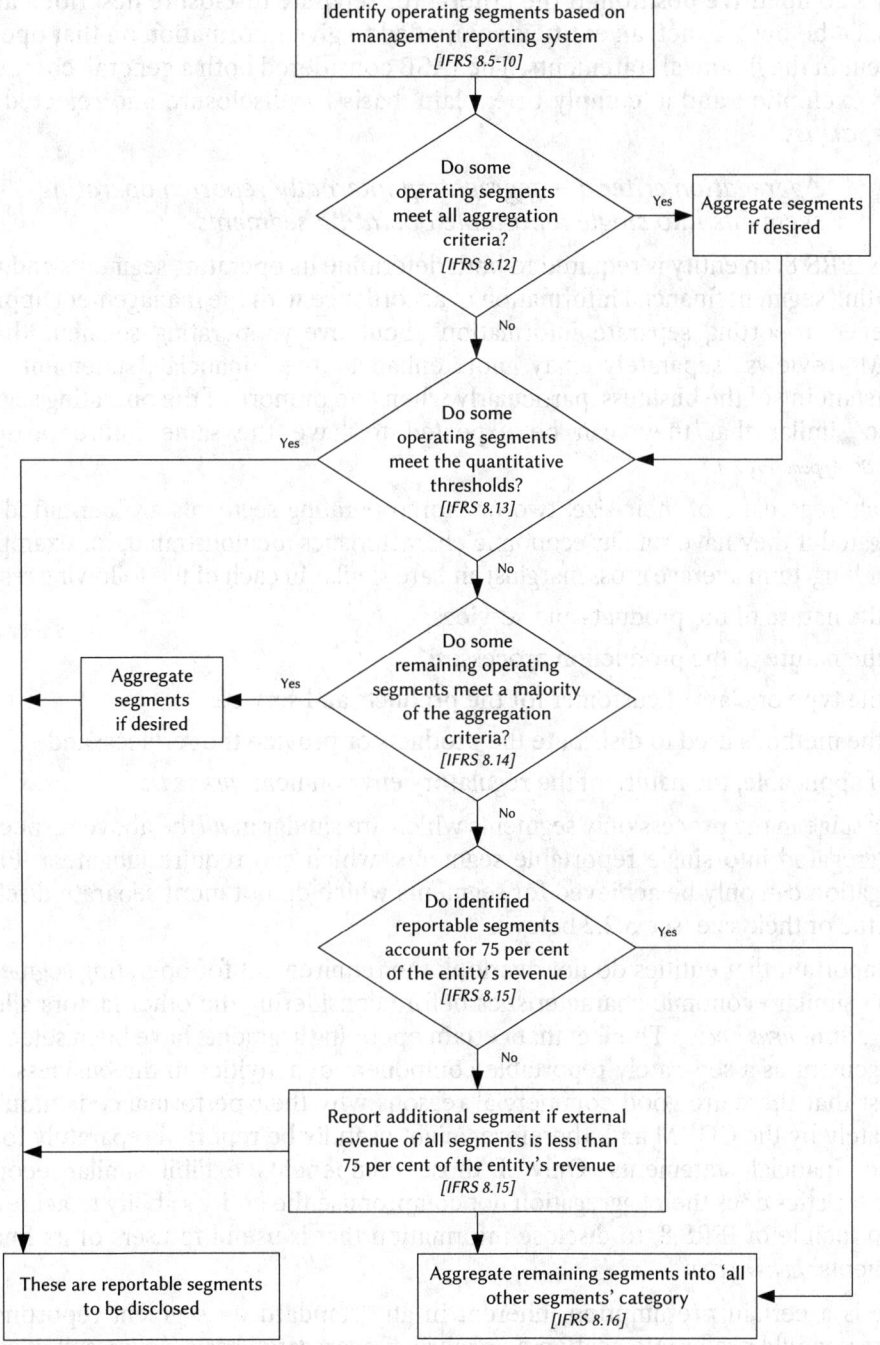

As indicated in the implementation guidance, the diagram is a visual supplement to the IFRS. It should not be interpreted as altering or adding to any requirements of the IFRS nor should it be regarded as a substitute for its requirements. *[IFRS 8.IG7]*.

IFRS 8 does not permit the omission of segment information when management believe that its disclosure is commercially sensitive or potentially detrimental to the entity's competitive position. If the criteria for separate disclosure described at 3.2.2 and 3.2.4 below are met, an entity is compelled to give information on that operating segment in the financial statements. The IASB considered both a general 'competitive harm' exemption and a 'comply or explain' basis for disclosure and rejected both. *[IFRS 8.BC43-45]*.

3.2.1 Aggregation criteria – aggregating internally reported operating segments into single reportable operating segments

Under IFRS 8, an entity is required to both determine its operating segments and report operating segment financial information in accordance with the management approach. However, reporting separate information about every operating segment that the CODM reviews separately may not enhance the financial statement user's understanding of the business, particularly when two or more of the operating segments are so similar that they 'can be expected to have the same future prospects.' *[IFRS 8.BC Appendix A 73]*.

As such, regardless of their size, two or more operating segments are permitted to be aggregated if they have similar economic characteristics (demonstrated, for example, by similar long-term average gross margins) and are similar in each of the following respects:

(a) the nature of the products and services;

(b) the nature of the production processes;

(c) the type or class of customer for the products and services;

(d) the methods used to distribute the products or provide the services; and

(e) if applicable, the nature of the regulatory environment. *[IFRS 8.12]*.

At this stage in the process only segments which are similar in *all* the above respects can be aggregated into single reportable segments, which can require judgment. Further aggregation can only be achieved for segments which do not merit separate disclosure by virtue of their size (see 3.2.2 below).

It is important that entities do not overlook the requirement for operating segments to exhibit similar economic characteristics before considering the other factors allowing aggregation. *[IFRS 8.BC30]*. The fact that certain operating segments have been selected by management as a separately reportable component of activities in the business would suggest that there are good commercial reasons why their performance is monitored separately by the CODM and, therefore, might usefully be reported separately to users of the financial statements. Only if those components exhibit similar economic characteristics does their aggregation not compromise the entity's ability to achieve the core principle of IFRS 8, to disclose information that is useful to users of its financial statements. *[IFRS 8.BC32]*.

There is a certain presumption inherent in any standard on segment reporting that investors would prefer information on a more disaggregated basis. As a result, it may be questioned whether it is consistent with the objective and basic principles of IFRS 8 for a company to report just one reportable segment or a limited number of reportable segments, especially if such reportable segments are inconsistent with an entity's basic organisational structure. Companies that choose to aggregate operating segments should be prepared to explain why an operating segment is important enough to be individually reported to the CODM, but similar enough to other segments to be aggregated when reported to investors.

In assessing whether the aggregation criteria are met, it is important to note that the aggregation criteria are tests, not indicators, of similarity between operating segments. The operating segments must be similar in each (i.e. all) of the following areas for aggregation to be permitted:

(a) *The nature of the products and services.* Similar products or services generally will have similar purposes or end uses. Thus, they may be subject to similar types and degrees of risk and similar opportunities for growth. We believe that it often will be appropriate to evaluate the similarity of products or services based on the range of activities of the organisation, as illustrated in the following example:

Example 36.3:   Similar products and services

Conglomerate Inc., a highly diversified company, manufactures a variety of consumer products, provides financial services and has a construction business. It determines that all of its consumer products activities are similar in the context of its business and aggregates them for reporting purposes, reporting its financial services and construction business results separately. By contrast, ConsumerPro Limited, an entity that only sells a variety of consumer products, determines that, in the context of its business activities, not all of its consumer products are similar in nature and report its results separately for each major product group.

(b) *The nature of the production processes.* A similar production process might be demonstrated by the sharing of common or interchangeable production facilities, equipment, labour force or service group and by using similar raw materials in the production process. Likewise, similarity in the nature and type of labour or amounts of capital required also may be indicative of a similar production process. The nature of the production process of two different products may be similar, even if the products do not function similarly. Consider the following example:

Example 36.4:   Similar production processes

Assume that Life Co., a life sciences company manufactures various pharmaceutical products for commercial sale. These products include cold medicines and diet pills. Each product is manufactured through the same production process, even though the products have different applications. Both products consist of various chemical compounds that are mixed together in batches to create the end product. Both products undergo quality control testing in order to confirm the efficacy of the product. Both products also use the same manufacturing equipment for parts of the production process. Thus, Life Co. concludes that for the purposes of the segment aggregation criteria, the production processes are similar, despite the differences in the applications of the end products.

(c) *The type or class of customer for their products and services.* Factors to consider in evaluating whether the type or class of customer are similar include: (1) the region or geography in which the products and services are marketed; (2) the methods used to market the products or services, including the use of a common or interchangeable sales force; and (3) the nature or type of customer including the industries in which the customers may operate. Entities should carefully consider whether this criterion has been met when the products or services of one operating segment are targeted to a different customer base or constitute a material revenue stream. Consider the following example:

Example 36.5:   Type and class of customer

Market Co., a diversified clothing manufacturer has two operating segments, Retail and Wholesale. Retail primarily markets its products to consumers through electronic and print advertising. In contrast, Wholesale principally markets its products through a network of sales representatives who call upon the distributors to purchase the products. In considering the type or class of customer, Market Co. concludes that the type and class of customer are not similar for the two operating segments based upon the distinction between retail and wholesale as well as the primary marketing methods for its products. As such, aggregation of the two operating segments would not be permitted.

(d) *The methods used to distribute their products or provide their services.* The determination of whether two methods of distribution are similar will depend on the structure of a particular company. Consider the following example:

Example 36.6:   Retail outlets and internet distribution

Software Co., a software retailer, has two operating segments: Retail, which distributes its products through retail outlets, and Internet, which distributes its products through a website on the internet. In evaluating whether these operating segments can be aggregated, Software Co., might conclude that the methods to distribute its products are not similar because Retail and Internet distribute products through different distribution channels.

(e) *If applicable, the nature of the regulatory environment,* for example, banking, insurance, or public utilities. Entities that operate within certain industries may be subject to regulatory requirements that are promulgated by a government agency. Sometimes two operating segments may produce the same product through the same production process, but because of differences in the class of customer and the regulatory environment, the operating segments should not be aggregated. For example, it may not be appropriate for an entity to aggregate an operating segment that produces a product under government contracts together with an operating segment that produces the same product for commercial purposes.

Some entities are comprised of operating segments that operate within different regulatory environments. We believe that the nature of the regulatory environments in which two or more operating segments operate can be regarded as similar, even if the regulatory bodies are not the same.

The following example illustrates how the management of an entity has interpreted these requirements. However, any judgments to be made will be specific to the entity and the environment in which it operates and in different circumstances some of the characteristics considered will be relatively more or less relevant than others.

Example 36.7:   Aggregating internally reported operating segments with similar characteristics into a single reportable operating segment

In the information presented to the executive directors, a single-product company has identified seven components of its business that are internally reported operating segments, Africa, Australia and Pacific, France, Germany, Italy, UK and Ireland and USA. The company dominates its markets in Australia and Pacific and in Germany and consequently enjoys superior operating profits. Its other markets are fragmented, competition is greater and therefore historic and expected margins are lower. Can any segments be aggregated for external reporting purposes?

Management has considered each of the criteria set out in paragraph 12 of IFRS 8 to determine whether the economic characteristics of these separate operating segments are similar, including competitive and operating risks, currency risks and political conditions, as well as current performance and future trading prospects. In these circumstances, management decided that it would not combine operating segments with different underlying currency risks and regulatory environments. That left only France, Germany and Italy as candidates for combination, since they all operate within the Euro zone. However, Germany has not been included in a larger reportable segment because, whilst similar in all other ways, its long-term financial performance is not expected to be comparable to France and Italy, as evidenced by its superior operating profits. On this basis, management decided to aggregate only its operations in France and Italy for external segment reporting purposes.

As can be seen in the above example, operating segments trading in clearly different economic environments (for example with unrelated functional currencies) should not be aggregated for segment reporting purposes (unless they are so small as to fall within the 'all other segments' category discussed at 3.2.4 below). The Standard states that the existence of similar long-term average gross margins would be a positive indicator. *[IFRS 8.12]*. This implies that operating segments should not be aggregated if their long-term average gross margins are significantly different, even if they are similar in all the other respects noted above. While IFRS 8 includes long-term gross margin as an example of similar economic characteristics, if the CODM uses a different measure of profit or loss (e.g. EBITDA) to assess performance and allocate resources to each operating segment, that measure of profit or loss should also be considered when assessing whether operating segments possess similar economic characteristics. In addition, if other economic measures are provided to the CODM, the similarities of those economic measures should also be considered. For example, if the CODM uses sales metrics, return on investment, or other standard industry measures, those metrics may also be relevant in determining economic similarity.

In assessing whether long-term average gross margins (or the appropriate measure of operating performance used by the CODM to assess performance and allocate resources, such as EBITDA) of operating segments are sufficiently similar, companies should look to past and present performance as indicators that segments are expected to have the same future prospects. In other words, if operating segments do not currently have similar gross margins and sales trends but are expected to have similar long-term average gross margins and sales trends, it may be appropriate to aggregate the two operating segments (provided all other criteria are met). Conversely, if operating segments happen to have similar gross margins or sales trends in a given year but it is not expected that the similar gross margins or sales trends will continue in the future, the operating segments should not be aggregated for the current-year segment disclosures just because current economic measures happen to be similar. It follows that operating segments that have been profitable over the longer term should not be combined with segments that over the longer term have been consistently loss-making.

IFRS 8 does not define the term 'similar' and does not provide guidance about what is similar for aggregation purposes. As the above discussion indicates, the determination of whether two or more operating segments are similar requires judgment and is dependent on the individual facts and circumstances.

In a response to a submission in 2011, the Interpretations Committee had acknowledged that IFRS 8 could usefully include further guidance on the meaning of 'similar economic characteristics' and the criteria for identifying similar segments listed in (a) to (e) above.[7] In a move to improve the Standard in this area, the IASB decided to enhance the disclosures on the aggregation of segments but not to add any further guidance at that time (see 5.1.1 below). More recently, the IASB intended to include further examples of similar economic characteristics a result of its Post-implementation Review. However, it has now decided not to amend IFRS 8 (see 1.1 above).

3.2.2 Quantitative thresholds – operating segments which are reportable because of their size

IFRS 8 includes a number of quantitative measures for determining whether information on the identified operating segments should be reported separately. Accordingly, an operating segment (or combination of segments meeting the qualitative criteria for aggregation described at 3.2.1 above) merits separate disclosure if it meets any of the following thresholds:

(a) its reported revenue (including both sales to external customers and intersegment sales or transfers) is 10% or more of the combined revenue (internal and external) of all operating segments; or

(b) its reported profit or loss is, in absolute terms, 10% or more of the greater of:
   (i) the combined profit of all operating segments that did not report a loss; or
   (ii) the combined loss of all operating segments that reported a loss; or

(c) its assets are 10% or more of the combined assets of all operating segments. [IFRS 8.13].

The definition of an operating segment includes a component of an entity earning revenues and incurring expenses relating to transactions with other components of the same entity. [IFRS 8.5]. Therefore an entity would have to report separately information on an operating segment that exceeds the above criteria, even if that segment earns a majority of its revenues from transactions with other components of the same entity.

Example 36.8: Identifying reportable segments using the quantitative thresholds

An entity divides its business into 9 operating units for internal reporting purposes and presents information to the Chief Operating Decision Maker as follows:

	Unit 1 £000	Unit 2 £000	Unit 3 £000	Unit 4 £000	Unit 5 £000	Unit 6 £000	Unit 7 £000	Unit 8 £000	Unit 9 £000	Total £000
Revenue:										
External	34,000	3,000	15,000	30,000	35,000	35,000	77,500	55,500	25,000	310,000
Internal	35,000	34,000	12,500	2,200	–	1,500	7,800	2,300	–	95,300
Total	69,000	37,000	27,500	32,200	35,000	36,500	85,300	57,800	25,000	405,300
Profit/(loss)	21,500	24,500	(4,500)	2,300	10,000	7,500	3,500	35,000	(21,250)	78,550
Assets	12,250	77,800	25,000	24,000	40,000	7,730	145,000	55,000	4,300	391,080

Assuming that none are eligible for aggregation under the qualitative aggregation criteria set out at 3.2.1 above, which units are required to be reported as operating segments in the entity's financial statements?

Applying the above quantitative thresholds, Units 1, 2, 5, 7, 8 and 9 should be identified as reportable segments, as follows:

- A Unit whose internal and external revenue is 10% or more of the total revenue of all segments is a reportable segment. On this criterion Unit 1 (17%), Unit 7 (21%) and Unit 8 (14%) are reportable segments.
- A Unit is a reportable segment if its profit or loss, in absolute terms, is 10% or more of the greater of the combined profits of all profitable segments or the combined losses of all segments in loss. The combined profit of all profitable segments is £104.3m, which is greater than the total of £25.75m for segments in loss. On this basis, Unit 1 (21%), Unit 2 (23%), Unit 8 (34%) and the loss-making Unit 9 (20%) are reportable segments.
- A Unit is also a reportable segment if the measure of assets reported to the chief operating decision maker is 10% or more of the total reported measure of assets of all segments. On this test, Unit 5 (10%) joins the list of reportable segments, with Unit 2 (20%), Unit 7 (37%) and Unit 8 (14%) having been already identified under other criteria.

In Example 36.8 above, units 1, 2, 5, 7, 8 and 9 are identified as reportable segments under IFRS 8 by virtue of their size. No further aggregation of large segments such as these would be possible unless all of the qualitative criteria set out at 3.2.1 above are met.

Even if an internally reported operating segment falls below all of the quantitative thresholds, it may still be considered as reportable, and separately disclosed, if management believes information about the segment would be useful to users of the financial statements. *[IFRS 8.13]*. Where information about segment assets is not disclosed under IFRS 8 because it is not provided regularly to the CODM, *[IFRS 8.23]*, it would be appropriate to ignore criterion (c) above for determining the reportable segments.

3.2.3 Combining small operating segments into a larger reportable segment

Operating segments which individually fall below the size criteria may be combined with other small operating segments into a single larger reporting segment provided that:

(a) the operating segments being combined have similar economic characteristics; and

(b) they share a majority (rather than all) of the criteria listed at 3.2.1 above. *[IFRS 8.14]*.

For the avoidance of doubt, if an entity proposes to combine a small operating segment with one that exceeds any of the quantitative thresholds, they must share all of the criteria described at 3.2.1 above. The requirement that combining segments must demonstrate similar economic characteristics applies to combinations of both larger and smaller operating segments into reportable segments, without exception.

3.2.4 'All other segments'

At this stage the entity has been divided into a single set of components, based on the elements reported to the chief operating decision maker. Components (operating segments) have been combined where permitted by the Standard and the entity has identified a number of individual operating segments or groups of operating segments that are required to be disclosed separately in the financial statements because each exceeds the quantitative thresholds for a reportable segment. The entity may then be left with a number of operating segments which have not been identified as being reportable, as well as other business activities that are not an operating segment or part of an operating segment.

Information about other business activities and operating segments that are not reportable should be combined and disclosed in a separate category for 'all other segments'. *[IFRS 8.16]*. However, this residual category cannot be too large. If total external revenue for the operating segments already reported separately is less than 75% of the entity's revenue, the entity should identify additional operating segments for external reporting until the 75% target is reached. In this situation segments would have to be reported separately even if they fall below the quantitative thresholds described at 3.2.2 above and are not otherwise regarded as being significant. *[IFRS 8.15]*.

There is no requirement to identify as a reportable segment the next largest internally reported operating segment. The choice of additional reporting segments is aimed simply to reach the 75% threshold, as illustrated below.

Example 36.9: Reaching the threshold of 75% of external revenue

In Example 36.8 above, Units 1, 2, 5, 7, 8 and 9 were identified as reportable segments. The total external revenue attributable to these reportable segments is £230m. This is only 74.2% of total external revenues and therefore less than the required 75% of total external revenue of £310m.

The entity is therefore required to identify additional segments as reportable segments, even if they do not meet the quantitative thresholds at 3.2.2 above. Entities that have numerous operating segments often will have latitude in selecting operating segments to meet the 75% test. In this case, Unit 3, with external revenue of £15m (4.8%), Unit 4's external revenue of £30m (9.7%) and Unit 6's external revenue of £35m (11.3%) would each take the total above the required 75%. The entity can choose to present any of these as a reportable segment, leaving the others to be combined to form the item for 'all other segments'.

The 'all other segments' category must be presented separately from other reconciling items. *[IFRS 8.16]*. This raises the question whether headquarters, treasury and similar central functions (sometimes referred to as 'corporate items') should be included in 'all other segments' or in the reconciliation. In practice, the headquarters activities and its related accounting effects will not always be allocated to the operating segments for internal reporting purposes. The description of 'all other segments' refers to 'other business activities and operating segments'. *[IFRS 8.16]*. It could be argued that central functions are not business activities, but support functions which should be part of the reconciliation. On the other hand, they could be regarded as incidental business activities. There is no guidance to suggest that either presentation is ruled out by the Standard.

3.2.5 A 'practical limit' for the number of reported operating segments

IFRS 8 states that there may be a practical limit to the number of separately reportable segments beyond which segment information may become too detailed. Without prescribing such a limit, it suggests that an entity expecting to disclose more than 10 separate reportable segments should consider whether the practical limit has been reached. *[IFRS 8.19]*.

3.2.6 Restatement of segments reported in comparative periods

When an operating segment is identified for the first time as a reportable segment in accordance with the thresholds at 3.2.2 above, the prior period segment data that is presented for comparative purposes should be restated to reflect the newly reportable segment regardless of whether it would have satisfied the quantitative thresholds in the prior period. Only if the necessary information is not available and the cost to develop it would be excessive would prior periods not be restated. *[IFRS 8.18]*.

4 MEASUREMENT

For an entity that does not present IFRS-compliant financial information to its chief operating decision maker, the measurement regime in IFRS 8 means that the values disclosed for segment revenue, profit or loss, and (when reported) assets or liabilities could be very different to those reported elsewhere in the financial statements. For example, management might include gains on sale of property, plant and equipment in its measure of segment revenue but not be permitted to do so in its financial statements. *[IAS 16.68]*.

There is no requirement in IFRS 8 for segment information to be prepared in conformity with the accounting policies used to present the financial statements of the consolidated group or entity. IFRS 8 requires amounts reported to be the same as those measures used by the chief operating decision maker for determining resource allocation and for assessing performance. *[IFRS 8.25]*. This requirement is interpreted strictly. For example, unless adjustments and eliminations made in preparing the financial statements are reflected in the information used by the chief operating decision maker, an entity is prohibited from restating reported segment profit or loss for those adjustments and eliminations. In addition, the Standard prohibits any further allocation of revenues, expenses and gains and losses in determining segment profit or loss unless that measure is used by the chief operating decision maker. *[IFRS 8.25]*. IFRS 8 does not require symmetry between the revenues and expenses included in segment result and the assets and liabilities allocated to segments; it simply requires disclosure of the nature and effect of any asymmetrical allocations to reportable segments, for example when depreciation expense is reflected in segment profit or loss, but the related depreciable assets are not allocated to that segment. *[IFRS 8.27(f)]*. Only those assets and liabilities taken into account by the chief operating decision maker will be included in assets and liabilities reported for that segment. *[IFRS 8.25]*.

The amounts presented for segment revenue, profit or loss, assets and liabilities need bear no relationship to the values reported elsewhere in the financial statements, if the only measure of each that is used by the chief operating decision maker is not prepared in accordance with the entity's accounting policies or even under IFRS. *[IFRS 8.26]*. However, there is a constraint on this otherwise 'free-for-all', since in those cases where a number of measures of segment profit or loss, assets or liabilities are used by the chief operating decision maker, an entity is required to select for its segment disclosures the measurements that are most consistent with those used in preparing the financial statements. *[IFRS 8.26]*. A key judgement that can significantly affect the segment disclosures reported in the financial statements arises when an entity seeks to distinguish information used by the chief operating decision maker for determining resource allocation and for assessing performance from other information and supporting detail which is regularly provided. Whether, for example, it is appropriate to ignore IFRS-compliant measures provided to the chief operating decision maker on the basis that they are not used for determining resource allocation and for assessing performance depends on the facts and circumstances supporting that assertion. Nevertheless, it might be appropriate to apply a rebuttable presumption that management effort is not normally wasted in providing the chief operating decision maker with information that is not used.

Instead of defining the elements of segment information to be disclosed and requiring that they be prepared under the same policies and principles applied in producing the financial statements, IFRS 8 requires an entity to explain how it has measured segment profit or loss and segment assets and liabilities for each reportable segment and to reconcile this to the information reported under IFRS. *[IFRS 8.27-28]*. These requirements are discussed at 5.5 and 5.6 below.

5 INFORMATION TO BE DISCLOSED ABOUT REPORTABLE SEGMENTS

IFRS 8 establishes a general principle for an entity to disclose information to enable users of its financial statements to evaluate the nature and financial effects of the types of business activities in which the entity engages and the economic environments in which it operates. *[IFRS 8.20]*. This principle is met by disclosing the following information for each period for which a statement of comprehensive income or separate income statement is presented:

(a) general information on segments identified for reporting;

(b) reported segment profit or loss, including information about specified revenues and expenses included in reported segment profit or loss, segment assets and segment liabilities (if reported to the CODM) and the basis of measurement; and

(c) reconciliations of the totals of segment revenues, reported segment profit or loss, segment assets, segment liabilities and other material segment items to the corresponding entity amounts in the financial statements. *[IFRS 8.21]*.

Reconciliations of amounts reported in the statement of financial position for reportable segments are required as at each date for which a statement of financial position is presented. *[IFRS 8.21]*.

These requirements are addressed in more detail below and the information described therein should be given separately for each segment determined to be reportable using the process set out at 3.2 above. *[IFRS 8.11]*.

As discussed at 3.1.2 above, the identification of the chief operating decision maker can be a critical judgment in applying IFRS 8 because of its potential impact on what information is considered for disclosure. However, there is no explicit requirement in the Standard to disclose the CODM. When in 2011, the Interpretations Committee and the IASB considered a request to amend the Standard to require disclosure, they decided to defer this issue until the completion of the Post-implementation Review of IFRS 8 rather than through an interpretation or annual improvement.[8] As noted at 1.1 above, the Board issued an Exposure Draft in March 2017. This ED proposed that entities disclose the title and description of the role of the individual or group which is identified as the CODM.[9] In our view, while the proposed disclosure requirement was not finally adopted, it would be good practice in any event to disclose the individual or group identified as CODM (see examples at 3.1.2 above).

5.1 General information about reportable segments

The factors used to identify reportable segments should be described. This would include an explanation of the entity's basis of organisation, for example whether management has chosen to organise the entity by different products and services, by geographical area, by regulatory environment or by applying a combination of factors.

The description would also indicate whether operating segments have been aggregated. The general information on reportable segments would include a description of the types of products and services from which each reportable segment derives its revenues. *[IFRS 8.22]*. The disclosures should also include a description of the sources of the revenue classified in the 'all other segments' category. *[IFRS 8.16]*.

In Extract 36.4 below, Daimler describes how its activities have been segmented into its principal business activities and specific product lines.

Extract 36.4: Daimler AG (2019)

NOTES TO THE CONSOLIDATED FINANCIAL STATEMENTS [extract]

34.   Segment reporting [extract]

Reportable segments

The reportable segments of the Group are Mercedes-Benz Cars, Daimler Trucks, Mercedes-Benz Vans, Daimler Buses and Daimler Mobility (formerly Daimler Financial Services). The segments are largely organized and managed separately, according to nature of products and services provided, brands, distribution channels and profile of customers.

The vehicle segments develop and manufacture passenger cars, trucks, vans and buses. The Mercedes-Benz Cars segment comprises premium vehicles of the Mercedes-Benz brand including the brands Mercedes-AMG and Mercedes-Maybach, and small cars under the smart brand, as well as the brand Mercedes me. Electric products are marketed under the EQ brand. Daimler Trucks distributes its trucks under the brand names Mercedes-Benz, Freightliner, Western Star, FUSO, Western Star and BharatBenz. Furthermore, buses under the brands Thomas Built Buses and FUSO are included in the Daimler Trucks range of products. The vans of the Mercedes-Benz Vans segment are primarily sold under the brand name Mercedes-Benz and also under the Freightliner brand. Daimler Buses sells completely built-up buses under the brand names Mercedes-Benz and Setra. In addition, Daimler Buses produces and sells bus chassis. The vehicle segments also sell related spare parts and accessories.

The Daimler Mobility segment supports the sales of the Group's vehicle segments worldwide. Its product portfolio primarily comprises tailored financing and leasing packages for end-customers and dealers, brokering of automotive insurance and banking services. The segment also provides services such as fleet management in Europe, which primarily takes place through the Athlon brand. Furthermore, Daimler Mobility is active in the area of innovative mobility services.

5.1.1 Disclosure of how operating segments are aggregated

IFRS 8 requires disclosure of the judgements made by management in applying the aggregation criteria in the Standard. This includes a brief description of the operating segments that have been aggregated in this way and the economic indicators that were considered in determining that the aggregated operating segments share similar economic characteristics. *[IFRS 8.22(aa)]*. The aggregation criteria are discussed at 3.2.1 above.

In Extract 36.5 below, Vodafone describes the composition of its two reportable segments, Europe and Rest of the World. The narrative explains the basis for aggregating countries into those reportable segments.

> Extract 36.5: Vodafone Group Plc (2020)
>
> Notes to the consolidated financial statements [extract]
>
> 2. Revenue disaggregation and segmental analysis [extract]
>
> Segmental analysis [extract]
>
> The Group's operating segments are established on the basis of those components of the Group that are evaluated regularly by the chief operating decision maker in deciding how to allocate resources and in assessing performance. The Group has determined the chief operating decision maker to be its Chief Executive Officer. The Group has a single group of similar services and products, being the supply of communications services and products. Revenue is attributed to a country or region based on the location of the Group company reporting the revenue. Transactions between operating segments are charged at arm's-length prices.
>
> Segment information is primarily provided on the basis of geographic areas, with the exception of Vodacom which encompasses South Africa and certain other smaller African markets, being the basis on which the Group manages its worldwide interests.
>
> The aggregation of operating segments into the Europe and Rest of the World regions reflects, in the opinion of management, the similar economic characteristics within each of those regions as well as the similar products and services offered and supplied, classes of customers and the regulatory environment. In the case of the Europe region this largely reflects membership of the European Union, while for the Rest of the World region this largely includes emerging and developing economies that are in the process of rapid growth and industrialisation.
>
> Certain financial information is provided separately within the Europe region for Germany, Italy, the UK and Spain, and within the Rest of the World region for Vodacom, as these operating segments are individually material for the Group. [...]

5.2 A measure of segment profit or loss, total assets and total liabilities

For each reportable segment, an entity is required to disclose a measure of profit or loss for each segment. An entity is also required to disclose a measure of total assets and total liabilities for each reportable segment, but only if such amounts are regularly provided to the chief operating decision maker. *[IFRS 8.23]*. This 'measure' means segment profit or loss and segment assets and liabilities as defined in the information used by the chief operating decision maker.

5.2.1 Other measures of segment performance

Entities typically use not only a measure of profit or loss, but also a combination of different financial and non-financial key performance indicators to assess performance of their operating segments and allocate resources to them. Examples include key measures based on capital invested like return on capital employed (ROCE), free cash flow or orders on hand. Since these are not measures of profit or loss, they would not need to be disclosed. However, the Standard does not prohibit their disclosure.

Siemens includes measures of new orders and free cash flow in its segment information as shown in Extract 36.6 below.

Extract 36.6: Siemens Aktiengesellschaft (2019)
B.6 Notes to Consolidated Financial Statements [extract]
NOTE 29 Segment information [extract]

	Orders		Free cash flow	
	Fiscal year		Fiscal year	
(in millions of €)	2019	2018	2019	2018
Digital Industries	15,944	16,287	2,635	2,610
Smart Infrastructure	16,244	15,198	1,572	1,128
Gas and Power	19,975	18,451	863	301
Mobility	12,894	11,025	903	998
Siemens Healthineers	15,853	14,506	1,618	1,673
Siemens Gamesa Renewable Energy	12,749	11,875	408	375
Industrial Businesses	**93,659**	**87,341**	**8,000**	**7,084**
Financial Services	832	825	621	553
Portfolio Companies	5,806	5,569	45	(14)
Reconciliation to Consolidated Financial Statements	(2,298)	(2,438)	(2,794)	(1,809)
Siemens (continuing operations)	**97,999**	**91,296**	**5,872**	**5,814**

5.3 Disclosure of other elements of revenue, income and expense

The following items should also be disclosed about each reportable segment if the specified amounts are included in the measure of segment profit or loss reviewed by the chief operating decision maker or are otherwise regularly provided in respect of those segments to the chief operating decision maker (even if not included in that measure of segment profit or loss):

(a) revenues from external customers;
(b) revenues from transactions with other operating segments of the same entity;
(c) interest revenue;
(d) interest expense;
(e) depreciation and amortisation;
(f) material items of income and expense disclosed in accordance with paragraph 97 of IAS 1 – *Presentation of Financial Statements*;
(g) the entity's interest in the profit or loss of associates and joint ventures accounted for by the equity method;
(h) income tax expense or income; and
(i) material non-cash items other than depreciation and amortisation. *[IFRS 8.23]*.

Interest revenue should be reported separately from interest expense for each reportable segment unless a majority of the segment's revenues are from interest and the chief operating decision maker relies primarily on net interest revenue to assess the performance of the segment and make decisions on the allocation of resources to it. In that case, the entity can report net interest revenue or expense for the segment provided that it discloses it has done so. *[IFRS 8.23]*.

Where the measure of segment profit or loss is determined after deducting depreciation and amortisation, these amounts will have to be disclosed separately for purposes of segment reporting, even if they are not separately reported to the CODM.

It can be seen that whilst IFRS 8 indicates the line items of income or expense or other information that might merit disclosure by segment, what an entity actually reports in its financial statements is determined by the line items used by the chief operating decision maker to define segment profit or loss and segment assets or liabilities, together with the other information otherwise regularly provided to the chief operating decision maker. [IFRS 8.23-24]. This means that different entities (even those with very similar activities) will make different disclosures, depending on what information is provided to the chief operating decision maker. Indeed, what is disclosed by one entity for each of its reportable segments might vary because, for example, the result of one segment is determined after deducting interest whilst that of other segments is drawn before interest; or because the information provided to the chief operating decision maker about one segment includes equity-accounted associates but for other segments does not. As such the disclosures made by an entity are tailored according to exactly what appears in the information presented to the chief operating decision maker.

Equinor ASA provides segment disclosures based on its internal management reporting, with reportable segments determined based on differences in the nature of their operations, products and services, as follows:

Extract 36.7: Equinor ASA (2019)

Consolidated financial statements and notes [extract]

3 Segments [extract]

Segment data for the years ended 31 December 2019, 2018 and 2017 are presented below [...]

(in USD million)	E&P Norway	E&P International	MMP	Other	Eliminations	Total
Full year 2019						
Revenues third party, other revenues and other income	1,048	2,127	60,491	527	0	64,194
Revenues inter-segment	17,769	8,168	439	4	(26,379)	0
Net income/(loss) from equity accounted investments	15	30	25	93	0	164
Total revenues and other income	18,832	10,325	60,955	624	(26,379)	64,357
Purchases [net of inventory variation]	(1)	(34)	(54,454)	(1)	24,958	(29,532)
Operating, selling, general and administrative expenses	(3,284)	(3,352)	(4,897)	272	793	(10,469)
Depreciation, amortisation and net impairment losses	(5,439)	(6,361)	(600)	(804)	0	(13,204)
Exploration expenses	(478)	(1,377)	0	0	0	(1,854)
Total operating expenses	(9,201)	(11,124)	(59,951)	(553)	25,750	(55,058)
Net operating income/(loss)	9,631	(800)	1,004	92	(629)	9,299
Additions to PP&E, intangibles and equity accounted investments	7,316	5,855	788	823	0	14,782

Balance sheet information						
Equity accounted investments	3	321	90	1,028	0	1,442
Non-current segment assets	33,795	37,558	5,124	4,214	0	80,691
Non-current assets, not allocated to segments						11,152
Total non-current assets						93,285

5.4 Additional disclosures relating to segment assets

If any of the following items are either included in the measure of segment assets reviewed by the chief operating decision maker or otherwise regularly provided in respect of those segments (whether included in segment assets or not), an entity should also disclose for each segment:

(a) the investment in equity-accounted associates and joint ventures; and

(b) total expenditures for additions to non-current assets other than financial instruments, deferred tax assets, post-employment benefit assets and rights arising under insurance contracts. *[IFRS 8.24]*.

5.5 Explanation of the measurements used in segment reporting

As noted at 4 above, instead of prescribing how an entity should calculate the amounts reported in its segmental disclosures, IFRS 8 requires an entity to explain how its measures of segment profit or loss, segment assets and segment liabilities have been determined. As a minimum, the following information is required:

(a) the basis of accounting for any transactions between reportable segments;

(b) if not apparent from the required reconciliations (see 5.6 below), the nature of any differences between the measurement of total reported segment profit or loss and the entity's profit or loss before income taxes and discontinued operations;

(c) the nature of any differences between the measurements of total reported segment assets and the entity's assets, if not apparent from the required reconciliations;

(d) the nature of any differences between the measurements of total reported segment liabilities and the entity's liabilities, if not apparent from the required reconciliations;

(e) the nature of any changes from prior periods in the measurement methods used to determine segment profit or loss, including the financial effect, if any, of those changes; and

(f) the nature and effect of any asymmetrical allocations to reportable segments, such as where depreciation is included in segment profit but the related property, plant and equipment is not included in segment assets. *[IFRS 8.27]*.

The kind of disclosures in (b), (c) and (d) above that are necessary for an understanding of the reported segment information could relate to the accounting policies used, including policies for the allocation of centrally incurred costs in arriving at segment profit or loss and for the allocation of jointly used assets and liabilities in determining segment assets and segment liabilities. [IFRS 8.27]. Other examples might include the use of previous local GAAP numbers, where internal reporting does not reflect the entity's move to IFRS, or the use of budgeted figures, for example when applying budgeted or constant foreign currency rates.

In Extract 36.8 below, Daimler confirms that segment information is prepared using the same accounting policies as the IFRS financial statements, describes how 'EBIT' is the measure of segment profit or loss and explains how segment assets and liabilities are determined.

> Extract 36.8: Daimler AG (2019)
> **NOTES TO THE CONSOLIDATED FINANCIAL STATEMENTS** [extract]
> 34. **Segment reporting** [extract]
>
> **Internal management and reporting structure** [extract]
>
> The internal management and reporting structure at the Daimler Group principally is based on the accounting policies that are described in ◊ Note 1 in the summary of significant accounting policies according to IFRS.
>
> The measure of the Group's profit or loss used by Daimler's management and reporting structure is referred to as "EBIT." EBIT comprises gross profit, selling and general administrative expenses, research and non-capitalized development costs, other operating income/expense, and the profit/loss on equity-method investments, net, as well as other financial income/expense, net. Although amortization of capitalized borrowing costs is included in cost of sales, it is not included in EBIT. The performance measure used by the Group's internal management and reporting structure for the automotive segments is return on sales.
>
> Intersegment revenue is generally recorded at values that approximate market terms.
>
> Segment assets principally comprise all assets. The vehicle segments' assets exclude income tax assets, assets from defined benefit pension plans and other post-employment benefit plans, and certain financial assets (including liquidity). Segment liabilities principally comprise all liabilities. The vehicle segments' liabilities exclude income tax liabilities, liabilities from defined benefit pension plans and other post-employment benefit plans, and certain financial liabilities (including financing liabilities).
>
> Daimler Mobility's performance is measured on the basis of return on equity, which is the usual procedure in the banking business.
>
> The residual value risks associated with the Group's operating leases and finance lease receivables are generally borne by the vehicle segments that manufactured the leased equipment. Risk sharing is based on agreements between the respective vehicle segments and Daimler Mobility; the terms vary by vehicle segment and geographic region.
>
> Non-current assets consist of intangible assets, property, plant and equipment and equipment on operating leases.
>
> [...]

In its 2019 financial statements, HOCHTIEF provided an explanation of the basis of accounting for transactions between reportable segments.

> **Extract 36.9: HOCHTIEF Aktiengesellschaft (2019)**
>
> **Notes to the Consolidated Financial Statements** [extract]
>
> **36. Segment reporting** [extract]
>
> HOCHTIEF's structure reflects the operating focus of the business as well as the Group's presence in key national and international regions and markets. Segmental reporting in the HOCHTIEF Group is based on the Group's divisional operations. The breakdown mirrors the Group's internal reporting systems.
>
> The Group's reportable segments (divisions) are as follows:
>
> [...]
>
> **Explanatory notes to the segmental data** [extract]
>
> Intersegment sales represent revenue generated between divisions. They are transacted on an arm's length basis. External sales mainly comprise performance obligations recognized under the percentage of completion method in the mainstream construction business, construction management, and contract mining. The sum of external sales and intersegment sales adds up to total sales revenue for each division.

5.6 Reconciliations

Reconciliations are required of all the following:

(a) the total of revenue from reportable segments to the entity's revenue;

(b) the total profit or loss for reportable segments to the entity's profit or loss before income taxes and discontinued operations. Where items such as income taxes have been allocated to arrive at segment profit or loss, the reconciliation can be made to the entity's profit or loss after those items;

(c) if segment assets are reported (see 5.2 above), the total of the reportable segments' assets to the entity's assets;

(d) if segment liabilities are reported (see 5.2 above), the total of reportable segments' liabilities to the entity's liabilities; and

(e) for every other material item of information the entity chooses to give in its segment information, the total of each item from all reportable segments to the corresponding amount for the entity. *[IFRS 8.28]*.

In each of the above reconciliations an entity must separately identify and describe all material reconciling items. For example, when reconciling segment profit or loss to the entity's profit or loss before income taxes and discontinued operations, each material adjustment arising from differences in accounting policies would have to be separately identified and described. *[IFRS 8.28]*. In addition, IFRS 8 requires information about the 'all other segments' category to be shown separately from other reconciling items. *[IFRS 8.16]*.

In its 2019 financial statements, National Australia Bank evaluated the performance of operating segments on the basis of cash earnings. This post-tax measure of the profit or loss of reportable segments is reconciled to the consolidated financial statements as follows:

Extract 36.10: National Australia Bank Limited (2019)
NOTES TO THE FINANCIAL STATEMENTS [extract]
NOTE 2 SEGMENT INFORMATION [extract]

	2019					
	Business and Private Banking	Consumer Banking and Wealth	Corporate and Institutional Banking	New Zealand Banking	Corporate Functions and Other[1]	Total
	$m	$m	$m	$m	$m	$m
Reportable segment information						
Net interest income	5,634	3,918	1,827	1,828	335	13,542
Other income	1,037	1,389	1,539	571	(857)	3,679
Net operating income	6,671	5,307	3,366	2,399	(522)	17,221
Operating expenses	(2,265)	(3,051)	(1,281)	(911)	(1,505)	(9,013)
Underlying profit/ (loss)	4,406	2,256	2,085	1,488	(2,027)	8,208
Credit impairment charge	(336)	(314)	(70)	(103)	(96)	(919)
Cash earnings/ (deficit) before tax and distributions	4,070	1,942	2,015	1,385	(2,123)	7,289
Income tax (expense) / benefit	(1,230)	(576)	(507)	(388)	592	(2,109)
Cash earnings/ (deficit) before distributions	2,840	1,366	1,508	997	(1,531)	5,180
Distributions	–	–	–	–	(83)	(83)
Cash earnings/ (deficit)	2,840	1,366	1,508	997	(1,614)	5,097
Fair value and hedge ineffectiveness	(3)	–	(23)	12	(9)	(23)
Other non-cash earnings items	–	(19)	–	–	32	13
Net profit/ (loss) for the year from continuing operations	2,837	1,347	1,485	1,009	(1,591)	5,087
Net (loss) after tax for the year from discontinued operations	–	–	–	–	(289)	(289)
Net profit/ (loss) attributable to the owners of NAB	2,837	1,347	1,485	1,009	(1,880)	4,798
Reportable segment assets	200,799	230,916	295,042	84,307	36,060	847,124

(1) Includes customer-related remediation and capitalised software change. Refer Note 3 Net interest income, Note 4 Other income and Note 5 Operating expenses for further details. It also includes Group eliminations

5.7 Restatement of previously reported information

Entities may need to change their organisation to respond to their business needs. This may have an impact on the entity's segment reporting. IFRS 8 provides explicit guidance if such a change in the organisation changes the composition of its reportable segments. However, it does not explicitly address any changes that impact reportable segments, such as a change in segment measures. This is discussed further below.

5.7.1 Changes in organisation structure

When an entity changes its organisational structure in a manner that causes a change in the composition of its reportable segments, corresponding amounts for earlier periods should be restated unless the information is not available and the cost to develop it would be excessive. This requirement also applies to the presentation of segment information in respect of interim periods. *[IFRS 8.29]*.

The exemption from restatement on grounds of excessive cost is applied to each individual item of disclosure. *[IFRS 8.29]*. This means that an entity should restate its comparative information for all the items it can, even if this results in some comparative information not being presented or restated, such as inter-segment revenues. When the composition of reportable segments has changed, an entity should disclose whether the corresponding items of segment information have been restated. *[IFRS 8.29]*.

Where corresponding information is not restated to reflect the new composition of reportable segments, the segment information for the current period should be presented on both the old and the new bases of segmentation. Only if the necessary information were unavailable and the cost of developing it excessive would an entity not have to show current information on the old basis of segmentation. *[IFRS 8.30]*. In our view, given the importance of comparable segment information in particular in years of changing segmentation, the 'excessive cost' criterion represents a high hurdle to overcome.

If an entity decides to change its organisational structure during the reporting period, the fact that this requirement applies equally to interim periods *[IFRS 8.29]* indicates that information presented at the reporting date is also restated to reflect the new basis of segmentation, even though for part of the annual reporting period the entity was managed and monitored on the old basis.

The following extract illustrates that changes in the composition of operating segments can often be combined with a review of other aspects of segment reporting, such as a review of performance measures:

> *Extract 36.11: Nestlé S.A. (2015)*
>
> Notes [extract]
>
> 1. **Accounting Policies** [extract]
>
> **Changes in presentation – Analyses by segment** [extract]
>
> The scope of the operating segments has been modified following the changes in management responsibilities as from 1 January 2015. Zone Europe has been renamed Zone Europe, Middle East and North Africa (EMENA) and now includes the Maghreb, the Middle East, the North East Africa region, Turkey and Israel, which were formerly included in Zone Asia, Oceania and Africa. Zone Asia, Oceania and Africa has been renamed Zone Asia, Oceania and sub-Saharan Africa (AOA). Nestlé Nutrition now includes Growing-Up Milks business formerly included in the geographic Zones. Finally, Other businesses now includes the Bübchen business, formerly included in Nestlé Nutrition.
>
> The amount of segment assets is no longer disclosed. Segment assets are not included in the measures used for allocating resources and assessing segment performance. The Group discloses on a voluntary basis invested capital (as defined in Note 3) as well as goodwill and intangible assets by segment for consistency with long-standing practice. Goodwill and intangible assets are not included in invested capital since the amounts recognised are not comparable between segments due to differences in the intensity of acquisition activity and changes in accounting standards which were applicable at various points in time when the Group undertook significant acquisitions.
>
> Information by product has been modified following the main transfer of Growing-Up Milks business in Milk products and Ice cream to Nutrition and Health Science.
>
> Sales and non-current assets in Switzerland and countries which individually represent at least 10% of the Group sales or 10% of the Group non-current assets are disclosed separately, instead of the top ten countries and Switzerland.
>
> In addition, intangible assets are attributed to the country of their legal owner rather than being allocated to the countries of the affiliated companies using these assets. Finally, goodwill items which were presented as part of unallocated items are attributed to the countries of the affiliated companies where the related acquired business is operated.
>
> 2014 comparative information has been restated.

Segment information may also change as a result of the disposal of an entire reportable segment or a component of it which qualifies under IFRS 5 – *Non-current Assets Held for Sale and Discontinued Operations* – as a discontinued operation. The presentation of discontinued operations is governed by IFRS 5. The requirements of other standards do not apply to discontinued operations, unless they specify disclosures applicable to them. *[IFRS 5.5B]*. Since IFRS 8 does not refer to discontinued operations, entities are not required to include them in their segment disclosures. This would be the case even if the CODM continued to monitor the discontinued operation until disposal. Nevertheless, an entity would not be prohibited from disclosing such information if it wished, on the basis that the requirements of IFRS 8 relate to the measures reported to the CODM without any adjustments being made in preparing the entity's IFRS financial statements. *[IFRS 8.25]*.

5.7.2 Changes in segment measures

When an entity changes any of its segment measures, including the definition of segment profit, or changes the allocation of income, expenses, assets or liabilities to segments, without a change to the composition of its reportable segments, the general principles of IAS 1 for changes in presentation or classification of items apply. Therefore, comparative information would be restated, unless this is impracticable. *[IAS 1.41]*.

In 2020, Vodafone Group Plc changed the segment information to reflect the adoption of IFRS 15 for purposes of internal decision making:

Extract 36.12: Vodafone Group Plc (2020)

Notes to the consolidated financial statements [extract]

2. Revenue disaggregation and segmental analysis [extract]

Segmental analysis [extract]

Segmental information used for internal decision making during the years ended 31 March 2018 and 2019 was on an IAS 18 (pre-IFRS 15) basis. In the year ended 31 March 2020 internal decisions were based upon IFRS 15 financial information and accordingly comparative information for the year ended 31 March 2019 was re-presented. Consequently, segmental information for the year ended 31 March 2018 is presented on an IAS 18 (pre-IFRS 15) basis and information for years ended 31 March 2020 and 2019 is presented on an IFRS 15 basis in accordance with the above revenue recognition policy. See note 32 "IAS 18 basis primary statements" for details of the IAS 18 revenue recognition policy.

The Group's measure of segment profit, adjusted EBITDA, excludes depreciation, amortisation, impairment loss, restructuring costs, loss on disposal of fixed assets, the Group's share of results in associates and joint ventures and other income and expense. A reconciliation of adjusted EBITDA to operating profit is shown below. For a reconciliation of operating profit to profit for the financial year, see the Consolidated income statement on page 141.

	2020	2019 (re-presented)[1]	2018
	€m	€m	€m
Adjusted EBITDA	14,881	13,918	14,737
Depreciation, amortisation and loss on disposal of fixed assets	(10,085)	(9,665)	(9,910)
Share of adjusted results in equity accounted associates and joint ventures[2]	(241)	(348)	389
Adjusted operating profit	**4,555**	**3,905**	**5,216**
Impairment losses	(1,685)	(3,525)	–
Restructuring costs[2]	(720)	(486)	(156)
Amortisation of acquired customer based and brand intangible assets[2]	(638)	(583)	(974)
Other income/(expense)[2]	2,257	(262)	213
Interest on lease liabilities	330	–	–
Operating profit/(loss)	4,099	(951)	4,299

Notes:

1. The results reflected in this table for the year ended 31 March 2019 were previously disclosed on an IAS 18 basis in the Annual Report for the year ended 31 March 2019 and have been re-presented in the table above on an IFRS 15 basis.
2. Share of results of equity accounted associates and joint ventures presented within the Consolidated income statement includes –€241m (2019: –€348 million, 2018 €389 million) included within Adjusted operating profit, –€25m (2019: –€26 million, 2018 –€9 million) included within Restructuring costs, –€215 million (2019: –€420 million, 2018 –€439 million) included within Amortisation of acquired customer based and brand intangible assets and –€2,024 million which is principally related to Vodafone Idea Limited (2019: –€114 million, 2018 €nil million) included within Other income/(expense).

5.8 Disclosure of commercially sensitive information

The criteria for determining the externally reportable segments, as discussed at 3.2 above, attempt to define which internally reported operating units can be combined, which must be reported separately and which are included in an unallocated reconciling item. The interaction between these criteria, in particular with the requirement that segments cannot be combined if they exhibit different long-term financial performance, leaves entities open to the risk of having to disclose information that management would be concerned about sharing with competitors, customers, suppliers or employees.

However, IFRS 8 does not permit the omission of segment information when management believes that its disclosure is commercially sensitive or potentially detrimental to the entity's competitive position. Indeed, IAS 1 requires an entity not only to present information in a manner that provides relevant, reliable, comparable and understandable information, but also to provide additional disclosures if compliance with an individual standard is insufficient to enable users to understand the entity's financial position and financial performance. *[IAS 1.17]*. The only justification for failing to meet these requirements is if disclosure would be so misleading that it would conflict with the objective of financial statements set out in the IASB's *Conceptual Framework*. *[IAS 1.19]*.

Given that the objective of IFRS 8 is to disclose information to help users of financial statements evaluate the nature and financial effects of the entity's business activities and the economic environments in which it operates, *[IFRS 8.1]*, this possibility would seem to be remote. The IASB rejected similar concerns raised by respondents to ED 8, noting that entities would be unlikely to suffer competitive harm from the required disclosures since most competitors have sources of detailed information about an entity other than its financial statements. *[IFRS 8.BC44]*. This concern was raised again by respondents to the post-implementation review. However, the IASB continues to reject such a limitation, because it would provide a means for broad-based non-compliance with the standard.[10]

6 ENTITY-WIDE DISCLOSURES FOR ALL ENTITIES

In addition to disclosing segment information derived from the formats and measurements presented to the chief operating decision maker, IFRS 8 requires certain entity-wide disclosures about products and services, geographical areas and major customers. The information described below is required even if the entity has only a single reportable segment, but need not be repeated if already provided as part of the disclosures on reportable segments set out above. *[IFRS 8.31]*. The amounts reported about products and services and about geographical areas in these entity-wide disclosures are measured using the same accounting policies and estimates as the entity's financial statements (i.e. IFRS amounts). *[IFRS 8.32-33]*. As such, the amounts disclosed in this part of the segment disclosures might well be different to the information already provided in other segment information, which might not be measured in accordance with IFRS (see 4 above).

Exemption from the requirements set out at 6.1 and 6.2 below is offered if the necessary information is unavailable and the cost to develop it would be excessive. If disclosure is not made on these grounds, that fact should be stated. *[IFRS 8.32-33]*. Some respondents to ED 8 expressed concern that the basis of this exemption was inconsistent with the test of impracticability in IAS 1, which makes no allowance for the cost of compliance. *[IAS 1.7]*. However, the IASB did not see any merit in divergence from FASB ASC Topic 280 in this respect and therefore retained the exemption from disclosure if the necessary information were unavailable and the cost of developing it excessive. *[IFRS 8.BC46-47]*.

This exemption is not available in respect of the disclosures about major customers set out at 6.3 below.

6.1 Information about products and services

An entity should report revenues from external customers for each product and service or for each group of similar products and services, measuring revenues on the same basis as the entity's financial statements. *[IFRS 8.32]*.

In Extract 36.7 above, Equinor ASA provides segment information based on its internal management reporting, with reportable segments relating to exploration and production activities in Norway and International; marketing, midstream and processing (MMP); and other activities. Accordingly, it also discloses external revenues by product group (and combines it with a geographical analysis of revenue), as follows:

Extract 36.13: Equinor ASA (2019)

Strategic report [extract]

Segment reporting [extract]

The following tables show total revenues and other income by country. [extract]

2019 Total revenues and other income by country (in USD million)	Crude oil	Natural gas	Natural gas liquids	Refined products	Other	Total
Norway	25,106	9,525	4,674	6,334	611	46,250
US	7,120	1,353	1,132	1,697	229	11,532
Denmark	0	12	0	2,580	191	2,783
Brazil	1,099	19	0	0	560	1,678
Other	180	372	0	41	1,358	1,951
Total revenues and other income[1]	33,505	11,281	5,807	10,652	2,949	64,194

1) Excluding net income (loss) from equity accounted investments

6.2 Information about geographical areas

IFRS 8 requires disclosure of the following geographical information:

(a) revenues from external customers, analysed between amounts attributed to the entity's country of domicile and the total of those attributed to all foreign countries; and

(b) non-current assets other than financial instruments, deferred tax assets, post-employment benefit assets and rights arising under insurance contracts, analysed between assets located in the entity's country of domicile and the total of those located in all foreign countries. *[IFRS 8.33]*.

In addition, if revenues from external customers or assets attributed to an individual foreign country are material, separate disclosure of that country's revenues or assets is required. *[IFRS 8.33]*. The Standard does not indicate what might be regarded as 'material', but given the criteria for a reportable segment and a major customer for reporting purposes (see 3.2.2 above and 6.3 below respectively) it would seem appropriate to consider the need for separate disclosure in respect of a foreign country accounting for more than 10% of total external revenues or more than 10% of total non-current assets.

Disclosure of the above information would be required even if the entity's segment reporting is already based on geography and it is determined that individual operating segments include a number of countries. Thus, an entity may need to provide additional information on revenue or non-current assets by country that is not disclosed in the segment information used by the chief operating decision maker.

The basis on which revenues from external customers are attributed to individual countries should be disclosed. An entity can elect to provide, in addition to the information required above, subtotals of geographical information about groups of countries. [IFRS 8.33]. In Extract 36.14 below, BAE Systems provides this more detailed level of disclosure and goes on to reconcile the measure of total segment assets to the amounts shown on the statement of financial position, even though such a reconciliation is not required for this entity-wide disclosure.

Extract 36.14: BAE Systems plc (2019)

Notes to the Group accounts [extract]

20. Geographical analysis of assets

Analysis of non-current assets by geographical location

Asset location	Notes	2019 £m	2018 £m
UK		4,119	3,610
Rest of Europe		935	909
US		8,830	8,466
Saudi Arabia		679	503
Australia		435	420
Rest of Asia and Pacific		10	7
Non-current segment assets		15,008	13,915
Post-employment benefit surpluses	23	302	308
Other financial assets	14	560	411
Tax	15,17	745	783
Inventories	16	835	774
Current trade, other and contract receivables	13	5,458	5,177
Cash and cash equivalents	18	2,587	3,232
Assets held for sale	19	135	146
Consolidated total assets		25,630	24,746

6.3 Information about major customers

IFRS 8 also requires an entity to give disclosures indicating the extent of its reliance on its major customers. If revenues from a single external customer account for 10% or more of the entity's total revenues, the entity should disclose:

(a) that fact;
(b) the total amount of revenues from each such customer; and
(c) the identity of the reportable segment or segments reporting the revenues. [IFRS 8.34].

Disclosure is not required of the name of each major customer, nor the amounts of revenue reported in each segment for that customer. [IFRS 8.34]. However, the disclosure must be provided if it relates only to one segment.

Roche elects to provide the customers' names in the following extract.

> **Extract 36.15: Roche Holding Ltd (2019)**
>
> Notes to the Roche Group Consolidated Financial Statements [extract]
> 2. Operating segment information [extract]
>
> **Major customers**
>
> In total three US national wholesale distributors represent approximately a third of the Group's revenues in 2019. The three US national wholesale distributors are McKesson Corp. with CHF 10 billion (2018: CHF 9 billion), AmerisourceBergen Corp. with CHF 8 billion (2018: CHF 7 billion) and Cardinal Health, Inc. with CHF 6 billion (2018: CHF 5 billion). Approximately 96% of these revenues were in the Roche Pharmaceuticals operating segment, with the residual in the Diagnostics operating segment.

6.3.1 Customers known to be under common control

For the purposes of the above disclosures, a group of entities known to a reporting entity to be under common control are to be considered a single customer. *[IFRS 8.34]*.

However, judgement is required to assess whether a government (including government agencies and similar bodies whether local, national or international), and entities known to the reporting entity to be under the control of that government are considered a single customer. The assessment of whether entities should be regarded as a single customer for these purposes should take into account the extent of economic integration between those entities. *[IFRS 8.34]*. The standard does not include any further guidance on the factors relevant to determining the extent of economic integration.

BAE Systems identifies revenues from three principal governments.

> **Extract 36.16: BAE Systems plc (2019)**
>
> Notes to the Group accounts [extract]
> 1. Segmental analysis [extract]
>
> **Revenue by major customer**
> Revenue from the Group's three principal customers, which individually represent over 10% of total revenue, is as follows:
>
> | | 2019 £m | 2018 £m |
> |---|---|---|
> | US Department of Defense | 6,547 | 5,148 |
> | UK Ministry of Defence[1] | 3,868 | 3,848 |
> | Kingdom of Saudi Arabia Ministry of Defence and Aviation | 2,541 | 2,366 |
>
> 1. Includes £0.6bn (2018 £0.7bn) generated under the Typhoon workshare agreement with Eurofighter Jagdflugzeug GmbH.
>
> Revenue from the UK Ministry of Defence and the US Department of Defense was generated by the five principal reporting segments. Revenue from the Kingdom of Saudi Arabia Ministry of Defence and Aviation was generated by Air and Maritime reporting segments.

References

1 Press Release, *Summary of the IASC Foundation Trustees meeting 2 and 3 July 2007, Madrid*, IFRS Foundation, 18 July 2007.
2 Report and Feedback Statement *Post-implementation Review: IFRS 8 Operating Segments*, July 2013, p.6.
3 ED/2017/2, *Improvements to IFRS 8 Operating Segments – Proposed amendments to IFRS 8 and IAS 34*, Introduction.
4 Project summary, *Responses to Exposure Draft, Improvements to IFRS 8 Operating Segments (ED/2017/02)*, February 2019.
5 *IFRIC Update*, July 2011.
6 ED 8, *Operating Segments*, IASB, January 2006.
7 *IFRIC Update*, September 2011.
8 *IASB Update*, September 2011.
9 *ED/2017/2*, para. 22(c).
10 Report and Feedback Statement *Post-implementation Review: IFRS 8 Operating Segments*, July 2013, p.19.

Chapter 37   Earnings per share

1 INTRODUCTION 3021
   1.1 Definitions 3021
2 OBJECTIVE AND SCOPE OF IAS 33 3021
   2.1 Objective 3021
   2.2 Scope 3022
3 THE BASIC EPS 3023
   3.1 Earnings 3023
   3.2 Number of shares 3023
4 CHANGES IN OUTSTANDING ORDINARY SHARES 3026
   4.1 Weighted average number of shares 3026
   4.2 Purchase and redemption of own shares 3027
   4.3 Changes in ordinary shares without corresponding changes in resources 3027
       4.3.1 Capitalisation, bonus issue, share split and share consolidation 3027
           4.3.1.A Capitalisation, bonus issues and share splits 3027
           4.3.1.B Stock dividends 3028
           4.3.1.C Share consolidations 3029
       4.3.2 Share consolidation with a special dividend 3029
       4.3.3 Rights issue 3029
       4.3.4 B share schemes 3031
       4.3.5 Put warrants priced above market value 3031
   4.4 Options exercised during the year 3032
   4.5 Post balance sheet changes in capital 3032
   4.6 Issue to acquire another business 3033
       4.6.1 Acquisitions 3033
       4.6.2 Reverse acquisitions 3033

		4.6.3	Establishment of a new parent undertaking	3033
	4.7	Adjustments to EPS in historical summaries		3034
5	MATTERS AFFECTING THE NUMERATOR			3035
	5.1	Earnings		3035
	5.2	Preference dividends		3035
	5.3	Retrospective adjustments		3036
	5.4	Participating equity instruments and two class shares		3036
		5.4.1	Tax deductible dividends on participating equity instruments	3038
	5.5	Other bases		3038
		5.5.1	Possible future changes	3039
6	DILUTED EARNINGS PER SHARE			3040
	6.1	The need for diluted EPS		3040
	6.2	Calculation of diluted EPS		3040
		6.2.1	Diluted earnings	3041
		6.2.2	Diluted number of shares	3042
	6.3	Dilutive potential ordinary shares		3042
		6.3.1	Dilution judged by effect on profits from continuing operations	3043
		6.3.2	Dilution judged by the cumulative impact of potential shares	3043
	6.4	Particular types of dilutive instruments		3045
		6.4.1	Convertible instruments	3045
			6.4.1.A Convertible debt	3046
			6.4.1.B Convertible preference shares	3047
			6.4.1.C Participating equity instruments and two class shares with conversion rights	3047
		6.4.2	Options, warrants and their equivalents	3048
			6.4.2.A The numerator	3048
			6.4.2.B Written call options	3050
			6.4.2.C Written put options and forward purchase agreements	3051
			6.4.2.D Options over convertible instruments	3052
			6.4.2.E Settlement of option exercise price with debt or other instruments of the entity	3052
			6.4.2.F Specified application of option proceeds	3052
		6.4.3	Purchased options and warrants	3053
		6.4.4	Partly paid shares	3053
		6.4.5	Share-based payments	3054
		6.4.6	Contingently issuable shares	3055

		6.4.6.A	Earnings-based contingencies	3056
		6.4.6.B	Share price-based contingencies	3058
		6.4.6.C	Other contingencies	3059
	6.4.7		Potential ordinary shares of investees	3059
	6.4.8		Contingently issuable potential ordinary shares	3061
7	PRESENTATION, RESTATEMENT AND DISCLOSURE			3061
	7.1		Presentation	3061
	7.2		Restatement	3062
	7.3		Disclosure	3063
8	APPENDIX			3064

List of examples

Example 37.1:	Calculation of weighted average number of shares	3026
Example 37.2:	A bonus issue	3028
Example 37.3:	Rights issue at less than full market price	3030
Example 37.4:	Put warrants priced above market value	3031
Example 37.5:	Calculation of EPS where a new holding company is established	3034
Example 37.6:	Increasing rate preference shares	3035
Example 37.7:	Participating equity instruments and two-class ordinary shares	3037
Example 37.8:	Calculation of weighted average number of shares: determining the order in which to include dilutive instruments	3044
Example 37.9:	Treatment of convertible bonds in diluted EPS calculations	3046
Example 37.10:	Convertible bonds settled in shares or cash at the issuer's option	3046
Example 37.11:	Effects of share options on diluted earnings per share	3050
Example 37.12:	Partly paid shares	3054
Example 37.13:	Determining the exercise price of employee share options	3055
Example 37.14:	Contingently issuable shares	3057
Example 37.15:	Warrants issued by a subsidiary	3060

Chapter 37   Earnings per share

1 INTRODUCTION

Earnings per share (EPS) is one of the most widely quoted statistics in financial analysis. It came into great prominence in the US during the late 1950s and early 1960s due to the widespread use of the price earnings ratio (PE) as a yardstick for investment decisions. As a result, standard setters in some jurisdictions (notably the US and the UK) have had rules on EPS for many years. However, it was not until 1997 that an international accounting standard on the subject was published.

IAS 33 – *Earnings per Share* – was introduced for accounting periods beginning on or after 1 January 1998. In December 2003, as part of the improvements project, the IASB updated IAS 33 to provide more detailed guidance in some complex areas. There have been no substantive changes since. The requirements of IAS 33 are discussed at 2 to 7 below. The standard includes illustrative examples of particular issues and one comprehensive worked example. The illustrative examples are included where relevant in the text of the chapter, whilst the comprehensive worked example is included as an appendix.

1.1 Definitions

IAS 33 defines a number of its terms and these are dealt with in the text of this chapter where appropriate. One term which is particularly pervasive is 'fair value'. This term is defined and explained in IFRS 13 – *Fair Value Measurement* – and is discussed in Chapter 14. *[IAS 33.8]*. However, in the context of share-based payments the term fair value has the meaning used in IFRS 2 – *Share-based Payment*. The relevance of share-based payment to EPS is discussed at 6.4.5 below; IFRS 2 is discussed in Chapter 34. *[IAS 33.47A]*.

2 OBJECTIVE AND SCOPE OF IAS 33

2.1 Objective

IAS 33 sets out its objective as follows: 'to prescribe principles for the determination and presentation of earnings per share, so as to improve performance comparisons between different entities in the same reporting period and between different reporting periods for the same entity. Even though earnings per share data have limitations because of the different accounting policies that may be used for determining "earnings", a consistently determined denominator enhances financial reporting. The focus of this Standard is on the denominator of the earnings per share calculation.' *[IAS 33.1]*.

The standard requires the computation of both basic and diluted EPS, explaining the objective of each as follows:

- the objective of basic earnings per share information is to provide a measure of the interests of each ordinary share of a parent entity in the performance of the entity over the reporting period; *[IAS 33.11]* and
- the objective of diluted earnings per share is consistent with that of basic earnings per share – to provide a measure of the interest of each ordinary share in the performance of an entity – while giving effect to all dilutive potential ordinary shares outstanding during the period. *[IAS 33.32]*.

The underlying logic here is that EPS, including diluted EPS, should be an historical performance measure. This impacts particularly on the reporting of diluted EPS, in steering it away from an alternative purpose: to warn of potential future dilution. Indeed the tension between these differing objectives is evident in the standard. As discussed more fully at 6.4.6 below, IAS 33 sets out a very restrictive regime for including certain potentially dilutive shares in the diluted EPS calculation. Yet diluted EPS is only to take account of those potential shares that would dilute earnings from continuing operations (see 6.3.1 below) which seems to have more of a forward looking 'warning signal' flavour. Discontinued operations are discussed in Chapter 4.

2.2 Scope

IAS 33 applies to:

(a) the separate or individual financial statements of an entity:
  (i) whose ordinary shares or potential ordinary shares are traded in a public market (a domestic or foreign stock exchange or an over-the-counter market, including local and regional markets); or
  (ii) that files, or is in the process of filing, its financial statements with a securities commission or other regulatory information for the purpose of issuing ordinary shares in a public market; and

(b) the consolidated financial statements of a group with a parent:
  (i) whose ordinary shares or potential ordinary shares are traded in a public market (a domestic or foreign stock exchange or an over-the-counter market, including local and regional markets); or
  (ii) that files, or is in the process of filing, its financial statements with a securities commission or other regulatory information for the purpose of issuing ordinary shares in a public market. *[IAS 33.2]*.

IAS 33 also applies to any other entity that discloses earnings per share. *[IAS 33.3]*. Where both the parent's consolidated and separate financial statements are presented, the standard only requires consolidated earnings per share to be given. If the parent chooses to present EPS data based on its separate financial statements the standard requires that the disclosures be restricted to the face of the parent-only statement of comprehensive income (or separate income statement) and not be included in the consolidated financial statements. *[IAS 33.4]*.

In January 2014, the IASB published IFRS 14 – *Regulatory Deferral Accounts*. This standard allows a first-time adopter within its scope to continue to account for regulatory deferral account balances in its first IFRS financial statements in accordance with its previous GAAP when it adopts IFRS. The standard introduces limited changes to some previous GAAP accounting practices for regulatory deferral account balances, which are primarily related to the presentation of these accounts. For entities applying IFRS 14 certain additional EPS disclosures are required. This is discussed in Chapter 5 at 5.20.6.B.

3 THE BASIC EPS

IAS 33 requires the computation of basic EPS for the profit or loss (and, if presented, the profit or loss from continuing operations) attributable to ordinary equity holders. *[IAS 33.9]*. It defines, or rather describes, basic earnings per share in the following manner: 'Basic earnings per share shall be calculated by dividing profit or loss attributable to ordinary equity holders of the parent entity (the numerator) by the weighted average number of ordinary shares outstanding (the denominator) during the period.' *[IAS 33.10]*.

3.1 Earnings

The starting point for determining the earnings figure to be used in the basic EPS calculation (both for total earnings and, if appropriate, earnings from continuing operations) is the net profit or loss for the period attributable to ordinary equity holders. *[IAS 33.12]*. This will, in accordance with IAS 1 – *Presentation of Financial Statements* – include all items of income and expense, including, dividends on preference shares classified as liabilities and tax and is stated after the deduction of non-controlling interests. *[IAS 33.13, A1]*. This is then adjusted for the after-tax amounts of preference dividends, differences arising on the settlement of preference shares, and other similar effects of preference shares classified as equity. *[IAS 33.12]*. These adjustments are discussed at 5.2 below.

3.2 Number of shares

An ordinary share is defined as 'an equity instrument that is subordinate to all other classes of equity instruments'. *[IAS 33.5]*. 'Equity instrument' has the same meaning as in IAS 32 – *Financial Instruments: Presentation* – that is 'any contract that evidences a residual interest in the assets of an entity after deducting all of its liabilities'. *[IAS 33.8, IAS 32.11]*. IAS 33 goes on to observe that ordinary shares participate in profit for the period only after other types of share such as preference shares have participated. *[IAS 33.6]*. The standard also clarifies that there may be more than one class of ordinary share and requires the computation and presentation of EPS for each class that has a different right to share in profit for the period. *[IAS 33.6, 66]*. In practice, it is usually straightforward to determine which instruments are ordinary shares for EPS purposes. The treatment of different classes of shares is discussed at 5.4 below.

The basic rule in IAS 33 is that all outstanding ordinary shares are brought into the basic EPS computation – time-weighted for changes in the period (changes in ordinary shares are discussed at 4 below). *[IAS 33.19]*. There are three exceptions to this:

- ordinary shares that are issued as partly paid are included in the weighted average as a fraction of a share based on their dividend participation relative to fully paid shares (so if although only partly paid, they ranked equally for dividends they would be included in full); *[IAS 33.A15]*
- treasury shares, which are presented in the financial statements as a deduction from equity, are not considered outstanding for EPS purposes for the period they are held in treasury. Although not stated explicitly in the standard itself, this requirement is clearly logical (as although the shares are still legally in issue, they are accounted for as if redeemed) and is illustrated in one of the examples appended to the standard (see Example 37.1 at 4.1 below); *[IAS 33.IE2]* and
- shares that are contingently returnable (that is, subject to recall) are not treated as outstanding until they cease to be subject to recall, and hence are excluded from basic EPS until that time. *[IAS 33.24]*.

The standard contains some specific guidance on when newly issued ordinary shares should be considered outstanding. In general, shares are to be included from the date consideration is receivable (considered by the standard generally to be the date of their issue), for example: *[IAS 33.21]*

- shares issued in exchange for cash are included when cash is receivable;
- shares issued on the voluntary reinvestment of dividends on ordinary or preference shares are included when the dividends are reinvested;
- shares issued as a result of the conversion of a debt instrument to ordinary shares are included as of the date interest ceases accruing;
- shares issued in place of interest or principal on other financial instruments are included as of the date interest ceases accruing;
- shares issued in exchange for the settlement of a liability of the entity are included as of the settlement date;
- shares issued as consideration for the acquisition of an asset other than cash are included as of the date on which the acquisition is recognised;
- shares issued in exchange for the rendering of services to the entity are included as the services are rendered; and
- shares that will be issued upon the conversion of a mandatorily convertible instrument are included in the calculation of basic earnings per share from the date the contract is entered into. *[IAS 33.23]*.

Most of these provisions are straightforward, however some are worthy of note.

Shares issued in exchange for services will be accounted for in accordance with IFRS 2, with a charge to income matched by a credit to equity. IAS 33 has some guidance on the inclusion of such potential shares in diluted EPS (see 6.4.5 below); however there is no further elaboration of the meaning of 'included as the services are rendered'. What seems to be implicit in the phrase is that the shares concerned vest unconditionally as services are rendered. On that basis, clearly it would be appropriate to include shares in basic EPS as entitlement to them vests, notwithstanding that the actual issue of shares may be at a different time. However, a very common form of share-based remuneration involves entitlement to shares vesting at the end of an extended period conditional on future events (typically continued employment and sometimes specific future performance). Such arrangements are clearly conditionally issuable shares and should be excluded from basic EPS until vesting. Indeed, when discussing employee share schemes in the context of diluted EPS the standard is explicit, as follows. 'Employee share options with fixed or determinable terms and non-vested ordinary shares are treated as options in the calculation of diluted earnings per share, even though they may be contingent on vesting. They are treated as outstanding on the grant date. Performance-based employee share options are treated as contingently issuable shares because their issue is contingent upon satisfying specified conditions in addition to the passage of time.' *[IAS 33.48]*. Contingently issuable shares are discussed at 6.4.6 below.

In respect of the final bullet point, the standard does not define what a mandatorily convertible instrument is. One view would be that the requirement to account for the shares in EPS from inception must mean it refers to instruments where the proceeds also are received at inception. On that basis, it would exclude a forward contract for the issue of shares which (as required by the first bullet above) would increase the denominator of basic EPS only from the time the cash is receivable. Similarly, in the reverse situation of a forward contract to redeem ordinary shares the shares would only be removed from basic EPS when the consideration becomes payable. Another view would be that all binding agreements to issue or redeem ordinary shares should be reflected in basic EPS when the entity becomes party to the arrangement. A further possible complexity is the question of whether or not a symmetrical treatment for the issue and redemption of shares should be applied for EPS purposes. Whilst that certainly seems logical, it is not beyond question in all circumstances particularly given the asymmetrical accounting treatment for certain derivatives over own shares required by IAS 32 (discussed in Chapter 47 at 5).

More generally, the standard goes on to say the timing of inclusion is determined by the attaching terms and conditions, and also that due consideration should be given to the substance of any contract associated with the issue. *[IAS 33.21]*. Ordinary shares that are issuable on the satisfaction of certain conditions (contingently issuable shares) are to be included in the calculation of basic EPS only from the date when all necessary conditions have been satisfied; in effect when they are no longer contingent. *[IAS 33.24]*. This provision is interpreted strictly, as illustrated in Example 7 appended to the standard (see Example 37.14 at 6.4.6.A below). In that example earnings in a year, by meeting certain thresholds, would trigger the issue of shares. Because it is not certain that the condition is met until the last day of the year (when earnings become known with certainty) the new shares are excluded from basic EPS until the following year. Where shares will be issued at some future date (that is, solely after the passage of time) they are not considered contingently issuable by IAS 33, as the passage of time is a certainty. *[IAS 33.24]*. In principle, this would seem to mean that they should be included in basic EPS from the agreement date. However, careful consideration of the individual facts and circumstances would be necessary.

The calculation of the basic EPS is often simple but a number of complications can arise; these may be considered under the following two headings:
(a) changes in ordinary shares outstanding; and
(b) matters affecting the numerator.

These are discussed in the next two sections.

4 CHANGES IN OUTSTANDING ORDINARY SHARES

Changes in ordinary shares outstanding can occur under a variety of circumstances, the most common of which are dealt with below. Whenever such a change occurs during the accounting period, an adjustment is required to the number of shares in the EPS calculation for that period; furthermore, in certain situations the EPS for previous periods will also have to be recalculated.

4.1 Weighted average number of shares

Implicit in the methodology of IAS 33 is a perceived correlation between the capital of an entity (or rather the income-generating assets it reflects) and earnings. Accordingly, to compute EPS as a performance measure requires adjusting the number of shares in the denominator to reflect any variations in the period to the capital available to generate that period's earnings. The standard observes that using the weighted average number of ordinary shares outstanding during the period reflects the possibility that the amount of shareholders' capital varied during the period as a result of a larger or smaller number of shares being outstanding at any time. The weighted average number of ordinary shares outstanding during the period is the number of ordinary shares outstanding at the beginning of the period, adjusted by the number of ordinary shares bought back or issued during the period multiplied by a time-weighting factor. The time-weighting factor is the number of days that the shares are outstanding as a proportion of the total number of days in the period; IAS 33 notes that a reasonable approximation of the weighted average is adequate in many circumstances. *[IAS 33.20]*. Computation of a weighted average number of shares is illustrated in the following example: *[IAS 33.IE2]*

Example 37.1: Calculation of weighted average number of shares

		Shares issued	Treasury shares*	Shares outstanding
1 January 2021	Balance at beginning of year	2,000	300	1,700
31 May 2021	Issue of new shares for cash	800	–	2,500
1 December 2021	Purchase of treasury shares for cash	–	250	2,250
31 December 2021	Balance at year end	2,800	550	2,250

Calculation of weighted average:

$(1{,}700 \times 5/12) + (2{,}500 \times 6/12) + (2{,}250 \times 1/12)$ = 2,146 shares *or*
$(1{,}700 \times 12/12) + (800 \times 7/12) - (250 \times 1/12)$ = 2,146 shares

* Treasury shares are equity instruments reacquired and held by the issuing entity itself or by its subsidiaries.

The use of a weighted average number of shares is necessary because the increase in the share capital would have affected earnings only for that portion of the year during which the issue proceeds were available to management for use in the business.

4.2 Purchase and redemption of own shares

An entity may, if it is authorised to do so by its constitution and it complies with any relevant legislation, purchase or otherwise redeem its own shares. Assuming this is done at fair value, then the earnings should be apportioned over the weighted average share capital in issue for the year. This was illustrated in Example 37.1 at 4.1 above in relation to the purchase of treasury shares. If, on the other hand, the repurchase is at significantly more than market value then IAS 33 requires adjustments to be made to EPS for periods before buy-back. This is discussed at 4.3.5 below.

4.3 Changes in ordinary shares without corresponding changes in resources

IAS 33 requires the number of shares used in the calculation to be adjusted (for all periods presented) for any transaction (other than the conversion of potential ordinary shares) that changes the number of shares outstanding without a corresponding change in resources. *[IAS 33.26]*. This is also to apply when some, but not all, such changes have happened after the year-end but before the approval of the financial statements.

The standard gives the following as examples of changes in the number of ordinary shares without a corresponding change in resources:

(a) a capitalisation or bonus issue (sometimes referred to as a stock dividend);
(b) a bonus element in any other issue, for example a bonus element in a rights issue to existing shareholders;
(c) a share split; and
(d) a reverse share split (share consolidation). *[IAS 33.27]*.

Another example not mentioned by the standard would be any bonus element in a buy-back, such as a put warrant involving the repurchase of shares at significantly more than their fair value. The adjustments required to EPS for each of these is discussed below.

As noted above, IAS 33 requires retrospective adjustment for all such events that happen in the reporting period. However, it only requires restatement for those in (a), (c) and (d) if they happen after the year-end but before the financial statements are authorised for issue. *[IAS 33.64]*.

4.3.1 Capitalisation, bonus issue, share split and share consolidation

4.3.1.A Capitalisation, bonus issues and share splits

A capitalisation or bonus issue or share split has the effect of increasing the number of shares in issue without any inflow of resources, as further ordinary shares are issued to existing shareholders for no consideration. Consequently, no additional earnings will be expected to accrue as a result of the issue. The additional shares should be treated as having been in issue for the whole period and also included in the EPS calculation of all earlier periods presented so as to give a comparable result. For example, on a two-for-one bonus issue, the number of ordinary shares outstanding before the issue is multiplied by three to obtain the new total number of ordinary shares, or by two to obtain the number of additional ordinary shares. *[IAS 33.28]*.

The EPS calculation involving a bonus issue is illustrated in the following example. [IAS 33.IE3].

Example 37.2:   A bonus issue

Profit attributable to ordinary equity holders of the parent entity 2020	£180
Profit attributable to ordinary equity holders of the parent entity 2021	£600
Ordinary shares outstanding until 30 September 2021	200
Bonus issue 1 October 2021	2 ordinary shares for each ordinary share outstanding at 30 September 2021
	200 × 2 = 400

$$\text{Basic earnings per share 2021} = \frac{£600}{(200 + 400)} = £1.00$$

$$\text{Basic earnings per share 2020} = \frac{£180}{(200 + 400)} = £0.30$$

Because the bonus issue was without consideration, it is treated as if it had occurred before the beginning of 2020, the earliest period presented.

Again, although the standard is silent on the matter, we believe that any financial ratios disclosed for earlier periods, which are based on the number of equity shares at a year-end (e.g. dividend per share) should also be adjusted in a similar manner.

4.3.1.B   Stock dividends

Stock or scrip dividends refer to the case where an entity offers its shareholders the choice of receiving further fully paid up shares in the company as an alternative to receiving a cash dividend. It could be argued that the dividend foregone represents payment for the shares, usually at fair value, and hence no restatement is appropriate. Alternatively, the shares could be viewed as being, in substance, bonus issues which require the EPS for the earlier period to be adjusted. IAS 33 seems to suggest the latter view, as it notes that capitalisation or bonus issues are sometimes referred to as stock dividends. However, entities often refer to these arrangements as dividend reinvestment plans which suggests the acquisition of new shares for valuable consideration.

In our view, this distinction should be a factual one. If an entity (say, through proposal and subsequent approval by shareholders) has a legal obligation to pay a dividend in cash or, at the shareholder's option, shares then the cash payment avoided if the stock dividend is taken up is consideration for the shares. This may be equivalent to an issue at fair value or it may contain some bonus element requiring retrospective adjustment of EPS. In practice the fair value of shares received as a stock dividend alternative may exceed the cash alternative; this is often referred to as an enhanced stock dividend. In these cases IAS 33 requires a bonus element to be identified, and prior EPS figures restated accordingly. This is essentially the same as adjustments for the bonus element in a rights issue, discussed at 4.3.3 below.

Furthermore, in this scenario, during the period between the obligation coming into existence and its settlement (in cash or shares) it could be argued to represent a written call option and hence potentially affect diluted EPS (see 6.4.2.B below). Given that the standard is silent on this aspect of some stock dividends we do not believe that such an approach was intended. In any event, we generally do not believe the effect on diluted EPS would be significant. Conversely, if the entity issues new shares instead of a dividend it would be a bonus issue requiring full retrospective adjustment to EPS.

4.3.1.C   Share consolidations

Occasionally, entities will consolidate their equity share capital into a smaller number of shares. Such a consolidation generally reduces the number of shares outstanding without a corresponding outflow of resources, and this would require an adjustment to the denominator for periods before the consolidation. *[IAS 33.29]*.

4.3.2   Share consolidation with a special dividend

Share consolidations as discussed at 4.3.1.C above normally do not involve any outflow of funds from the entity. However, entities may return surplus cash to their shareholders by paying special dividends accompanied by a share consolidation, the purpose of which is to maintain the value of each share following the payment of the dividend. This issue is specifically addressed by IAS 33. The normal rule of restating the outstanding number of shares for all periods for a share consolidation is not applied when the overall effect is a share repurchase at fair value because in such cases the reduction of shares is the result of a corresponding reduction in resources. In such cases the weighted average number of shares is adjusted for the consolidation from the date the special dividend is recognised. *[IAS 33.29]*.

4.3.3   Rights issue

A rights issue is a popular method through which entities are able to access the capital markets for further capital. Under the terms of such an issue, existing shareholders are given the opportunity to acquire further shares in the entity on a *pro rata* basis to their existing shareholdings.

The 'rights' shares will usually be offered either at the current market price or at a price below that. In the former case, the treatment of the issue for EPS purposes is as discussed at 4.1 above. However, where the rights price is at a discount to market it is not quite as straightforward, since the issue is equivalent to a bonus issue (see 4.3.1 above) combined with an issue at full market price. In such cases, IAS 33 requires an adjustment to the number of shares outstanding before the rights issue to reflect the bonus element inherent in it. *[IAS 33.26-27]*.

The bonus element of the rights issue available to all existing shareholders is given by the following adjustment factor, sometimes referred to as the bonus fraction: *[IAS 33.A2]*

$$\frac{\text{Fair value per share immediately before the exercise of rights}}{\text{Theoretical ex-rights fair value per share}}$$

The fair value per share immediately before the exercise of rights is the actual price at which the shares are quoted inclusive of the right to take up the future shares under the rights issue. Where the rights are to be traded separately from the shares the fair value used is the closing price on the last day on which the shares are traded inclusive of the right. *[IAS 33.A2]*.

The 'ex-rights fair value' is the theoretical price at which the shares would be expected to be quoted, other stock market factors apart, after the rights issue shares have been issued. It is calculated by adding the aggregate fair value of the shares immediately before the exercise of the rights to the proceeds from the exercise, and dividing by the number of shares outstanding after the exercise. [IAS 33.A2]. The EPS calculation involving a rights issue is illustrated in the following example. [IAS 33.IE4].

Example 37.3: Rights issue at less than full market price

	2019	2020	2021
Profit attributable to ordinary equity holders of the parent entity	$1,100	$1,500	$1,800

Shares outstanding before rights issue	500 shares
Rights issue	One new share for each five outstanding shares (100 new shares total)
	Exercise price: $5.00
	Date of rights issue: 1 January 2020
	Last date to exercise rights: 1 March 2020
Market price of one ordinary share immediately before exercise on 1 March 2020	$11.00
Reporting date	31 December

Calculation of theoretical ex-rights value per share

$$\frac{\text{Fair value of all outstanding shares before the exercise of rights} + \text{Total amount received from exercise of rights}}{\text{Number of shares outstanding before exercise} + \text{Number of shares issued in the exercise}} =$$

$$\frac{(\$11.00 \times 500 \text{ shares}) + (\$5.00 \times 100 \text{ shares})}{500 \text{ shares} + 100 \text{ shares}}$$

Theoretical ex-rights value per share = $10.00

Calculation of adjustment factor

$$\frac{\text{Fair value per share before exercise of rights}}{\text{Theoretical ex-rights value per share}} = \frac{\$11.00}{\$10.00} = 1.10$$

Calculation of basic earnings per share

	2019	2020	2021
2019 basic EPS as originally reported:			
$1,100 ÷ 500 shares =	$2.20		
2019 basic EPS restated for rights issue:			
$1,100 ÷ (500 shares × 1.1) =	$2.00		
2020 basic EPS including effects of rights issue:			
$\frac{\$1,500}{(500 \times 1.1 \times 2/12) + (600 \times 10/12)} =$		$2.54	
2021 basic EPS:			
$1,800 ÷ 600 shares =			$3.00

Rather than multiplying the denominator by 11/10ths, the previous year's EPS (and any EPS disclosures in a historical summary) could alternatively be arrived at by multiplying the original EPS by 10/11ths.

During the period that the rights are outstanding they represent, strictly speaking, a written call option over the entity's shares which could have implications for diluted EPS (see 6.4.2 below).

It is possible that shares could be issued as a result of open offers, placings and other offerings of equity shares not made to existing shareholders, at a discount to the market price. In such cases it would be necessary to consider whether the issue contained a bonus element, or rather simply reflected differing views on the fair value of the shares. In our opinion the latter is a more realistic alternative. Accordingly the shares should be dealt with on a weighted average basis without calculating any bonus element when computing the EPS.

4.3.4   B share schemes

One method by which some entities have returned capital to shareholders is the so-called 'B share scheme'. These schemes involve issuing 'B shares' (usually undated preference shares with low or zero coupons) to existing shareholders, either as a bonus issue or via a share split, following which the ordinary shares are consolidated. The 'B shares' are then repurchased or redeemed for cash and cancelled. The overall effect is intended to be the same as a repurchase of ordinary shares at fair value, and accordingly no retrospective adjustment to EPS is necessary, assuming that the intention is achieved. [IAS 33.29].

4.3.5   Put warrants priced above market value

As noted at 4.3 above, an example of a change in the number of shares outstanding without a corresponding change in resources not mentioned by the standard would be any bonus element in a buy-back, such as a put warrant involving the repurchase of shares at significantly more than their fair value. The accounting requirements for such instruments are discussed in Chapter 47 at 5.

IAS 33 does not give an illustrative calculation for a put warrant at significantly more than fair value, but it does for the more familiar rights issue (which are discussed at 4.3.3 above). In a rights issue new shares are issued at a discount to market value, whereas with put warrants shares are bought back at a premium to market value. In both cases the remaining shares are viewed as being devalued for the purposes of comparing EPS over time. Applying the logic of adjusting EPS when there is a change in the number of shares without a corresponding change in resources would seem to require that put warrants are treated as a reverse rights issue. This would mean calculating a similar 'adjustment factor', and applying it to the number of shares outstanding before the transaction. The difference in the calculation would be that the number of shares issued and the consideration received for them would be replaced by negative amounts representing the number of shares put back to the entity and the amount paid for them.

An illustration of what this might entail is as follows:

Example 37.4:   Put warrants priced above market value

The following example takes the same scenario as Example 37.3 above (a rights issue), altered to illustrate a put warrant scheme. In that example the shares are issued at a discount of $6.00 to the $11.00 market price on a one for five basis two months into the year. Reversing this would give a put warrant to sell shares back to the company at a $6 premium, again on a one for five basis. All other details have been left the same for comparability, although in reality the rising earnings following a rights issue may well become falling earnings after a buy-back. The calculation would then become:

Calculation of theoretical ex-warrant value per share

$$\frac{\text{Fair value of all outstanding shares before the exercise of warrants} - \text{Total amount paid on exercise of warrants}}{\text{Shares outstanding before exercise} - \text{Shares cancelled in the exercise}} =$$

$$\frac{(\$11 \times 500) - (\$17 \times 100)}{500 - 100} = \$9.50$$

Calculation of adjustment factor

$$\frac{\text{Fair value per share before exercise of warrants}}{\text{Theoretical ex-warrant value per share}} = \frac{\$11}{\$9.5} = 1.16$$

Calculation of basic earnings per share

	2019	2020	2021
2019 EPS as originally reported: $1,100 ÷ 500 shares =	$2.20		
2019 EPS restated for warrants: $1,100 ÷ (500 shares × 1.16) =	$1.90		
2020 EPS including effects of warrants: $\frac{\$1,500}{(500 \times 1.16 \times 2/12) + (400 \times 10/12)}$ =		$3.49	
2021 basic EPS: $1,800 ÷ 400 shares =			$3.49

Whilst the above seems a sensible interpretation of the requirements, as the procedure is not specified there may be scope for other interpretations.

4.4 Options exercised during the year

Shares issued as a result of options being exercised should be dealt with on a weighted average basis in the basic EPS. *[IAS 33.38]*. Furthermore, options that have been exercised during the year will also affect diluted EPS calculations. If the options in question would have had a diluting effect on the basic EPS had they been exercised at the beginning of the year, then they should be considered in the diluted EPS calculation as explained in 6.4.2 below, but on a weighted average basis for the period up to the date of exercise. The exercise of options is a 'conversion of potential ordinary shares'. The standard excludes such conversions from the general requirement (see 4.3 above) to adjust prior periods' EPS when a change in the number of shares happens without a corresponding change in resources. *[IAS 33.26]*.

4.5 Post balance sheet changes in capital

The EPS figure should not reflect any changes in the capital structure occurring after the reporting period, but before the financial statements are authorised for issue, which was effected for fair value. This is because any proceeds received from the issue were not available for use during the period. However, EPS for all periods presented should be adjusted for any bonus element in certain post year-end changes in the number of shares, as discussed at 4.3 above. When this is done that fact should be disclosed. *[IAS 33.64]*.

4.6 Issue to acquire another business

4.6.1 Acquisitions

As a result of a share issue to acquire another business, funds or other assets will flow into the reporting entity and extra profits will be expected to be generated. When calculating EPS, it should be assumed that the shares were issued on the acquisition date (even if the actual date of issue is later), since this will be the date from which the results of the newly acquired business are recognised. *[IAS 33.21(f), 22]*.

4.6.2 Reverse acquisitions

Reverse acquisition is the term used to describe a business combination whereby the legal parent entity after the combination is in substance the acquired and not the acquiring entity (discussed in Chapter 9 at 14). IAS 33 is silent on the subject; however, an appendix to IFRS 3 – *Business Combinations* – contains a discussion of the implications for EPS of such transactions. Following a reverse acquisition the equity structure appearing in the consolidated financial statements will reflect the equity of the legal parent, including the equity instruments issued by it to effect the business combination. *[IFRS 3.B25]*.

For the purposes of calculating the weighted average number of ordinary shares outstanding during the period in which the reverse acquisition occurs:

(a) the number of ordinary shares outstanding from the beginning of that period to the acquisition date shall be computed on the basis of the weighted average number of ordinary shares of the legal acquiree (accounting acquirer) outstanding during the period multiplied by the exchange ratio established in the merger agreement; and

(b) the number of ordinary shares outstanding from the acquisition date to the end of that period shall be the actual number of ordinary shares of the legal acquirer (the accounting acquiree) outstanding during that period. *[IFRS 3.B26]*.

The basic EPS disclosed for each comparative period before the acquisition date is calculated by dividing the profit or loss of the legal subsidiary attributable to ordinary shareholders in each of those periods by the legal acquiree's historical weighted average number of ordinary shares outstanding multiplied by the exchange ratio established in the acquisition agreement. *[IFRS 3.B27]*.

IFRS 3 presents an illustrative example of a reverse acquisition, including the EPS calculation, see Chapter 9 at 14.5.

4.6.3 Establishment of a new parent undertaking

Where a new parent entity is established by means of a share for share exchange and its consolidated financial statements have been presented as a continuation of the existing group (discussed in Chapter 10 at 4.2.1), the number of shares taken as being in issue for both the current and preceding periods would be the number of shares issued by the new parent entity. However, EPS calculations for previous periods in the new parent entity's financial statements would have to reflect any changes in the number of outstanding ordinary shares of the former parent entity that may have occurred in those periods, as illustrated in the example below:

Example 37.5:   Calculation of EPS where a new holding company is established

Entity A has been established as the newly formed parent entity of Entity B in a one for one share exchange on 30 June 2021. At that date, Entity B has 1,000,000 £1 ordinary shares in issue. Previously, on 30 June 2020 Entity B had issued 200,000 £1 ordinary shares for cash at full market price. Both entities have a 31 December year-end and the trading results of Entity B are as follows:

	2021 £	2020 £
Profit for equity shareholders after taxation	500,000	300,000

The earnings per share calculation of Entity A is shown below:

	2021		2020
Number of equity shares	$800,000 \times \dfrac{6}{12} =$	400,000	
	$1,000,000 \times \dfrac{6}{12} =$	500,000	
	1,000,000	900,000	
EPS	$\dfrac{500,000}{1,000,000} = £0.50$	$\dfrac{300,000}{900,000} = £0.33$	

If, in the above example, the share exchange did not take place on a one for one basis, but Entity A issued three shares for every one share held in Entity B, then the number of shares issued by Entity B in 2020 would have to be apportioned accordingly before carrying out the weighted average calculation. The earnings per share calculation would, therefore, have been as follows:

	2021		2020
Number of equity shares	$2,400,000 \times \dfrac{6}{12} =$	1,200,000	
	$3,000,000 \times \dfrac{6}{12} =$	1,500,000	
	3,000,000	2,700,000	
EPS	$\dfrac{500,000}{3,000,000} = £0.17$	$\dfrac{300,000}{2,700,000} = £0.11$	

4.7   Adjustments to EPS in historical summaries

In order to ensure comparability of EPS figures, the previously published EPS figures for all periods presented in IFRS financial statements should be adjusted for subsequent changes in capital not involving full consideration at fair value (apart from the conversion of potential ordinary shares) in the manner described at 4.3 above. Often entities will include EPS figures in historical summaries (typically five years) in the analyses and discussions accompanying (but not part of) the financial statements. We believe that all such analyses need similar adjustments in order to be meaningful. We also believe that the resultant figures should be described as restated.

5 MATTERS AFFECTING THE NUMERATOR

5.1 Earnings

The earnings figure on which the basic EPS calculation is based should be the consolidated net profit or loss for the year after tax, non-controlling interests and after adjusting for returns to preference shareholders that are not already included in net profit (as will be the case for preference shares classified as liabilities under IAS 32).

5.2 Preference dividends

The adjustments to net profit attributable to ordinary shareholders in relation to returns to preference shareholders should include:

- the after-tax amount of any preference dividends on non-cumulative preference shares declared in respect of the period; *[IAS 33.14(a)]*
- the after-tax amount of the preference dividends for cumulative preference shares required for the period, whether or not the dividends have been declared. This does not include the amount of any preference dividends for cumulative preference shares paid or declared during the current period in respect of previous periods; *[IAS 33.14(b)]*
- any original issue discount or premium on increasing rate preference shares which is amortised to retained earnings using the effective interest method. Increasing rate preference shares are those that provide: a low initial dividend to compensate an entity for selling them at a discount; or an above-market dividend in later periods to compensate investors for purchasing them at a premium (see Example 37.6 below); *[IAS 33.15]*
- the excess of the fair value of the consideration paid to shareholders over the carrying amount of the preference shares when the shares are repurchased under an entity's tender offer to the holders. As this represents a return to the holders of the shares (and a charge to retained earnings for the entity) it is deducted in calculating profit or loss attributable to ordinary equity holders of the parent entity; *[IAS 33.16]*
- the excess of the fair value of the ordinary shares or other consideration paid over the fair value of the ordinary shares issuable under the original conversion terms when early conversion of convertible preference shares is induced through favourable changes to the original conversion terms or the payment of additional consideration. This is a return to the preference shareholders, and accordingly is deducted in calculating profit or loss attributable to ordinary equity holders of the parent entity; *[IAS 33.17]* and
- any excess of the carrying amount of preference shares over the fair value of the consideration paid to settle them. This reflects a gain to the entity and is added in calculating profit or loss attributable to ordinary equity holders. *[IAS 33.18]*.

The computation of EPS involving increasing rate preference shares is illustrated in the following example. *[IAS 33.IE1]*.

Example 37.6: Increasing rate preference shares

Entity D issued non-convertible, non-redeemable class A cumulative preference shares of ¥100 par value on 1 January 2021. The class A preference shares are entitled to a cumulative annual dividend of ¥7 per share starting in 2024 At the time of issue, the market rate dividend yield on the class A preference shares was

7 per cent a year. Thus, Entity D could have expected to receive proceeds of approximately ¥100 per class A preference share if the dividend rate of ¥7 per share had been in effect at the date of issue.

In consideration of the dividend payment terms, however, the class A preference shares were issued at ¥81.63 per share, i.e. at a discount of ¥18.37 per share. The issue price can be calculated by taking the present value of ¥100, discounted at 7 per cent over a three-year period. Because the shares are classified as equity, the original issue discount is amortised to retained earnings using the effective interest method and treated as a preference dividend for earnings per share purposes. To calculate basic earnings per share, the following imputed dividend per class A preference share is deducted to determine the profit or loss attributable to ordinary equity holders of the parent entity:

Year paid	Carrying amount of class A preference shares 1 January ¥	Imputed dividend[1] ¥	Carrying amount of class A preference shares 31 December[2] ¥	Dividend ¥
2021	81.63	5.71	87.34	–
2022	87.34	6.12	93.46	–
2023	93.46	6.54	100.00	–
Thereafter:	100.00	7.00	107.00	(7.00)

[1] at 7% of the carrying amount.
[2] This is before dividend payment.

5.3 Retrospective adjustments

Where comparative figures have been restated (for example, to correct a material error or as a result of a change in accounting policy), earnings per share for all periods presented should also be restated. *[IAS 33.64]*.

5.4 Participating equity instruments and two class shares

As noted at 3.2 above, IAS 33 envisages entities having more than one class of ordinary shares and requires the calculation and presentation of EPS for each such class. *[IAS 33.66]*. Although perhaps not exactly obvious from the definition, some instruments that have a right to participate in profits are viewed by the standard as ordinary shares. The standard observes that the equity of some entities includes:

(a) instruments that participate in dividends with ordinary shares according to a predetermined formula (for example, two for one) with, at times, an upper limit on the extent of participation (for example, up to, but not beyond, a specified amount per share); and

(b) a class of ordinary shares with a different dividend rate from that of another class of ordinary shares but without prior or senior rights. *[IAS 33.A13]*.

Whilst category (a) could encompass some participating preference shares (as illustrated in Example 37.7 below), not all participating preference shares would necessarily be treated as ordinary shares for EPS purposes. This is because the participation features of some instruments could mean that they are not subordinate to all other classes of equity instrument. The meaning of ordinary shares for EPS purposes is discussed at 3.2 above.

To calculate basic (and diluted) earnings per share:

(a) profit or loss attributable to ordinary equity holders of the parent entity is adjusted (a profit reduced and a loss increased) by the amount of dividends declared in the period for each class of shares and by the contractual amount of dividends (or interest on participating bonds) that must be paid for the period (for example, unpaid cumulative dividends);

(b) the remaining profit or loss is allocated to ordinary shares and participating equity instruments to the extent that each instrument shares in earnings as if all of the profit or loss for the period had been distributed. The total profit or loss allocated to each class of equity instrument is determined by adding together the amount allocated for dividends and the amount allocated for a participation feature; and

(c) the total amount of profit or loss allocated to each class of equity instrument is divided by the number of outstanding instruments to which the earnings are allocated to determine the earnings per share for the instrument.

For the calculation of diluted earnings per share, all potential ordinary shares assumed to have been issued are included in outstanding ordinary shares. *[IAS 33.A14]*. This is discussed at 6.4 below.

Participating equity instruments and two-class ordinary shares are illustrated with the following example. *[IAS 33.IE11]*.

Example 37.7: Participating equity instruments and two-class ordinary shares

Profit attributable to equity holders of the parent entity	$100,000
Ordinary shares outstanding	10,000
Non-convertible preference shares	6,000
Non-cumulative annual dividend on preference shares (before any dividend is paid on ordinary shares)	$5.50 per share

After ordinary shares have been paid a dividend of $2.10 per share, the preference shares participate in any additional dividends on a 20:80 ratio with ordinary shares (i.e. after preference and ordinary shares have been paid dividends of $5.50 and $2.10 per share, respectively, preference shares participate in any additional dividends at a rate of one-fourth of the amount paid to ordinary shares on a per-share basis).

Dividends on preference shares paid	$33,000	($5.50 per share)
Dividends on ordinary shares paid	$21,000	($2.10 per share)

Basic earnings per share is calculated as follows:

	$	$
Profit attributable to equity holders of the parent entity		100,000
Less dividends paid:		
Preference	33,000	
Ordinary	21,000	
		(54,000)
Undistributed earnings		46,000

Allocation of undistributed earnings:
Allocation per ordinary share = A
Allocation per preference share = B; B = 1/4 A

(A × 10,000) + (1/4 A × 6,000) = $46,000
A = $46,000 ÷ (10,000 + 1,500)
A = $4.00
B = 1/4 A
B = $1.00

Basic per share amounts:

	Preference shares	Ordinary shares
Distributed earnings	$5.50	$2.10
Undistributed earnings	$1.00	$4.00
Totals	$6.50	$6.10

N.B. This example does not illustrate the classification of the components of convertible financial instruments as liabilities and equity or the classification of related interest and dividends as expenses and equity as required by IAS 32.

5.4.1 Tax deductible dividends on participating equity instruments

In June 2017 the Interpretations Committee published an agenda decision in response to a request to clarify the treatment for EPS purposes of tax deductible dividends on participating equity instruments.[1]

The question asked of the Committee was whether, in determining profit attributable to ordinary shareholders in the basic EPS calculation, an entity should reflect the tax benefit that would arise from the hypothetical distribution of profit to participating equity holders.

The Committee concluded that, when calculating basic EPS in the fact pattern described in the submission, an entity should adjust profit or loss attributable to ordinary shareholders for the portion of any tax benefit attributable to those ordinary shareholders. This is because the tax benefit is a direct consequence of the hypothetical distribution of profit to the participating equity holders required by IAS 33 (see 5.4 above). This accounting treatment should be applied regardless of whether an entity would have recognised the tax benefit in equity or in profit or loss.

Because, in its view, the principles and requirements in IAS 33 provide an adequate basis to calculate basic EPS in this scenario the Committee decided not to add this matter to its standard-setting agenda. In publishing this decision, the Committee indicated its decision to publish an illustrative example as educational material to accompany the agenda decision, although no indication of when it would do so was given.

5.5 Other bases

It is not uncommon for entities to supplement the EPS figures required by IAS 33 by voluntarily presenting additional amounts per share. For additional earnings per share amounts, the standard requires:

(a) that the denominator used should be that required by IAS 33;

(b) that basic and diluted amounts be disclosed with equal prominence and presented in the notes;

(c) an indication of the basis on which the numerator is determined, including whether amounts per share are before or after tax; and

(d) if the numerator is not reported as a line item in the statement of comprehensive income or separate statement of profit or loss, a reconciliation to be provided between it and a line item that is reported in the statement of comprehensive income. *[IAS 33.73, 73A]*.

In September 2007 the IASB indicated that it intended, as part of the annual improvements project, to modify IAS 33 to prohibit the presentation of alternative EPS figures on the face of the statement of comprehensive income. *[IAS 1.BC103]*. However, that project was ultimately finalised without addressing this issue. As a result, alternative EPS figures may be (and, in practice, are) presented on the face of the statement of comprehensive income (or separate income statement) as well as in the notes, provided that basic and diluted amounts are similarly disclosed with equal prominence. Possible future developments in this regard are discussed at 5.5.1 below.

The prevalence, within the European Union, of reporting alternative EPS measures on the face of the income statement was a matter considered by the European Securities and Markets Authority (ESMA). In April 2018 it published a report entitled *Enforcement and Regulatory Activities of Accounting Enforcers in 2017*.

The report includes (at paragraph 31) the following: 'Around 16% of issuers disclosed, in addition to basic and diluted earnings per share, amounts per share using a reported component of the statement of comprehensive income other than required by IAS 33.' The document goes on to observe that of these, 54% presented the information 'in the notes rather than on the face of the statement'.

From this we infer that, of the sample examined by ESMA, approximately half of entities disclosing alternative EPS presented the information on the face of the income statement.

5.5.1 Possible future changes

The IASB is in the process of developing what it describes as improvements in 'how information is communicated in the financial statements, with a focus on the statement(s) of financial performance'.[2] At its meeting in May 2019 the IASB decided the consultation document for this project would be an exposure draft which would not be preceded by a discussion paper. The exposure draft was published in December 2019; it contains a proposal to amend IAS 33 to include the following: 'If, ... an entity discloses an additional amount per share it shall ... be disclosed in the notes to financial statements, but not be presented in the primary financial statement(s).'[3] The deadline for comments on the draft was September 2020 and the Board will consider feedback on the Exposure Draft in developing its final requirements.

6 DILUTED EARNINGS PER SHARE

6.1 The need for diluted EPS

The presentation of basic EPS seeks to show a performance measure, by computing how much profit an entity has earned for each of the shares in issue for the period. Entities often enter into commitments to issue shares in the future which would result in a change in basic EPS. IAS 33 refers to such commitments as potential ordinary shares, which it defines as 'a financial instrument or other contract that may entitle its holder to ordinary shares'. *[IAS 33.5]*.

Examples of potential ordinary shares given by IAS 33 are:

(a) financial liabilities or equity instruments, including preference shares, that are convertible into ordinary shares;

(b) options and warrants (whether accounted for under IAS 32 or IFRS 2);

(c) shares that would be issued upon the satisfaction of conditions resulting from contractual arrangements, such as the purchase of a business or other assets. *[IAS 33.7]*.

When potential shares are actually issued, the impact on basic EPS will be two-fold. First, the number of shares in issue will change; second, profits could be affected, for example by lower interest charges or the return made on cash inflows. Scenarios whereby such an adjustment to basic EPS is unfavourable are described by the standard as dilution, defined as 'a reduction in earnings per share or an increase in loss per share resulting from the assumption that convertible instruments are converted, that options or warrants are exercised, or that ordinary shares are issued upon the satisfaction of specified conditions'. *[IAS 33.5]*. This potential fall in EPS is quantified by computing diluted EPS, and as a result:

(a) profit or loss attributable to equity holders is increased by the after-tax amount of dividends and interest recognised in the period in respect of the dilutive potential ordinary shares and is adjusted for any other changes in income or expense that would result from the conversion of the dilutive potential ordinary shares; and

(b) the weighted average number of ordinary shares outstanding is increased by the weighted average number of additional ordinary shares that would have been outstanding assuming the conversion of all dilutive potential ordinary shares. *[IAS 33.32]*.

6.2 Calculation of diluted EPS

IAS 33 requires a diluted EPS figure to be calculated for the profit or loss attributable to ordinary equity holders of the parent and, if presented, profit or loss from continuing operations attributable to them. *[IAS 33.30]*. For these purposes, the profit or loss attributable to ordinary equity holders and the weighted average number of shares outstanding should be adjusted for the effects of all potential ordinary shares. *[IAS 33.31]*. In calculating diluted EPS, the number of shares should be that used in calculating basic EPS, plus the weighted average number of shares that would be issued on the conversion of all the dilutive potential ordinary shares into ordinary shares. As is the case for outstanding shares in the basic EPS calculation, potential ordinary shares should be weighted for the period they are outstanding. *[IAS 33.36, 38]*. Accordingly, potential ordinary shares:

- should be deemed to have been converted into ordinary shares at the beginning of the period or, if not in existence at the beginning of the period, the date of their issue; *[IAS 33.36]*
- which are cancelled or allowed to lapse should be included only for the period they are outstanding; and
- which convert into ordinary shares during the period are included up until the date of conversion (from which point they will be included in the basic EPS). *[IAS 33.38]*.

The number of dilutive potential ordinary shares should be determined independently for each period presented, and not subsequently revisited. In particular, prior periods' EPS are not restated for changes in assumptions about the conversion of potential shares into shares. IAS 33 also stresses that the number of dilutive potential ordinary shares included in the year-to-date period is not a weighted average of the dilutive potential ordinary shares included in each interim computation. *[IAS 33.37, 65]*. This is illustrated in the comprehensive illustrative example accompanying IAS 33, the substance of which is reproduced in the appendix to this chapter.

6.2.1 Diluted earnings

The earnings figure should be that used for basic EPS adjusted to reflect any changes that would arise if the potential shares outstanding in the period were actually issued. Adjustment is to be made for the post-tax effects of:

(a) any dividends or other items related to dilutive potential ordinary shares deducted in arriving at the earnings figure used for basic EPS;

(b) any interest recognised in the period related to dilutive potential ordinary shares; and

(c) any other changes in income or expense that would result from the conversion of the dilutive potential ordinary shares. *[IAS 33.33]*.

These adjustments will also include any amounts charged in accordance with the effective interest method prescribed by IFRS 9 – *Financial Instruments* – as a result of allocating transaction costs, premiums or discounts over the term of the instrument. *[IAS 33.34]*. Instruments with a choice of settlement method may also require adjustments to the numerator as discussed at 6.2.2 below.

The standard notes that certain earnings adjustments directly attributable to the instrument could also affect other items of income or expense which will need to be accounted for. For example, the lower interest charge following conversion of convertible debt could lead to higher charges under profit sharing schemes. *[IAS 33.35]*.

No imputed earnings are taken into account in respect of the proceeds to be received on exercise of share options or warrants. The effect of such potential ordinary shares on the diluted EPS is reflected in the computation of the denominator. This is discussed at 6.4.2 below.

6.2.2 Diluted number of shares

IAS 33 discusses a number of specific types of potential ordinary shares and how they should be brought into the calculation; these are discussed at 6.4 below.

More generally, the standard also discusses scenarios where the method of conversion or settlement of potential ordinary shares is at the discretion of one of the parties, as follows:

(a) the number of shares that would be issued on conversion should be determined from the terms of the potential ordinary shares. When more than one basis of conversion exists, the calculation should assume the most advantageous conversion rate or exercise price from the standpoint of the holder of the potential ordinary shares; [IAS 33.39]

(b) when an entity has issued a contract that may be settled in shares or cash at its option, it should presume that the contract will be settled in shares. The resulting potential ordinary shares would be included in diluted earnings per share if the effect is dilutive. [IAS 33.58]. When such a contract is presented for accounting purposes as an asset or a liability, or has an equity component and a liability component, the numerator should be adjusted for any changes in profit or loss that would have resulted during the period if the contract had been classified wholly as an equity instrument. That adjustment is similar to the adjustments discussed at 6.2.1 above; [IAS 33.59] and

(c) for contracts that may be settled in ordinary shares or cash at the holder's option, the more dilutive of cash settlement and share settlement should be used in calculating diluted earnings per share. [IAS 33.60].

An example of an instrument covered by (b) above is a debt instrument that, on maturity, gives the issuer the unrestricted right to settle the principal amount in cash or in its own ordinary shares (see Example 37.10 at 6.4.1.A below). An example of an instrument covered by (c) is a written put option that gives the holder a choice of settling in ordinary shares or cash. [IAS 33.61].

In our view, the requirements of the standard in (b) and (c) above relating to settlement options are somewhat confused. In particular they seem to envisage a binary accounting model based on the strict legal form of settlement (cash or shares). However, IAS 32 sets out rules for three different settlement methods – net cash, net shares and gross physical settlement (discussed in Chapter 47 at 5). One consequence of the above is that, if taken literally, the numerator is only required to be adjusted to remove items of income or expense arising from a liability when there is a choice of settlement method. However, mandatory net share settlement also gives rise to a liability and income/expense under IAS 32. In our view any such income statement items should be removed for diluted EPS purposes.

6.3 Dilutive potential ordinary shares

Only those potential shares whose issue would have a dilutive effect on EPS are brought into the calculation. Potential ordinary shares are 'antidilutive' when their conversion to ordinary shares would increase earnings per share or decrease loss per share. [IAS 33.5, 43]. The calculation of diluted earnings per share should not assume conversion, exercise, or other issue of potential ordinary shares that would have an antidilutive effect on earnings per share. [IAS 33.43]. The standard gives detailed guidance for determining which potential shares are deemed to be dilutive, and hence brought into the diluted EPS calculation. This guidance covers the element of profit which needs to be diluted to trigger inclusion, and the sequence in which potential shares are tested to establish cumulative dilution. Each is discussed below.

6.3.1 Dilution judged by effect on profits from continuing operations

Potential ordinary shares are only to be treated as dilutive if their conversion to ordinary shares would decrease earnings per share or increase loss per share from continuing operations. The 'control number' that this focuses on is therefore the net result from continuing operations, which is the net profit or loss attributable to the parent entity, after deducting items relating to preference shares (see 5.2 above) and after excluding items relating to discontinued operations. *[IAS 33.42]*. The same denominator is required to be used to compute diluted EPS from continuing operations and total diluted EPS. Determining which potential shares are to be included by reference to their impact on continuing EPS can produce some slightly curious results for total EPS. For example, it is possible to exclude instruments which would dilute basic EPS (but not continuing EPS), and include items which are anti-dilutive as regards total profit. This latter point is acknowledged by the standard as follows.

> 'To illustrate the application of the control number notion ... assume that an entity has profit from continuing operations attributable to the parent entity of CU 4,800, a loss from discontinued operations attributable to the parent entity of (CU 7,200), a loss attributable to the parent entity of (CU 2,400), and 2,000 ordinary shares and 400 potential ordinary shares outstanding. The entity's basic earnings per share is CU 2.40 for continuing operations, (CU 3.60) for discontinued operations and (CU 1.20) for the loss. The 400 potential ordinary shares are included in the diluted earnings per share calculation because the resulting CU 2.00 earnings per share for continuing operations is dilutive, assuming no profit or loss impact of those 400 potential ordinary shares. Because profit from continuing operations attributable to the parent entity is the control number, the entity also includes those 400 potential ordinary shares in the calculation of the other earnings per share amounts, even though the resulting earnings per share amounts are antidilutive to their comparable basic earnings per share amounts, i.e. the loss per share is less [(CU 3.00) per share for the loss from discontinued operations and (CU 1.00) per share for the loss].'
> *[IAS 33.A3]*.

6.3.2 Dilution judged by the cumulative impact of potential shares

Where an entity has a number of different potential ordinary shares, in deciding whether they are dilutive (and hence reflected in the calculation), each issue or series of potential ordinary shares is to be considered in sequence from the most to the least dilutive. Only those potential shares which produce a cumulative dilution are to be included. This means that some potential shares which would dilute basic EPS if viewed on their own may need to be excluded. This results in a diluted EPS showing the maximum overall dilution of basic EPS. The standard observes that options and warrants should generally be included first as they do not affect the numerator in the diluted EPS calculation (but see the discussion at 6.4.2 below). *[IAS 33.44]*. The way this is to be done is illustrated in the following example. *[IAS 33.IE9]*.

Example 37.8: **Calculation of weighted average number of shares: determining the order in which to include dilutive instruments**

	$
Earnings	
Profit from continuing operations attributable to the parent entity	16,400,000
Less dividends on preference shares	(6,400,000)
Profit from continuing operations attributable to ordinary equity holders of the parent entity	10,000,000
Loss from discontinued operations attributable to the parent entity	(4,000,000)
Profit attributable to ordinary equity holders of the parent entity	6,000,000

Ordinary shares outstanding	2,000,000
Average market price of one ordinary share during year	$75.00

Potential Ordinary Shares

Options	100,000 with exercise price of $60
Convertible preference shares	800,000 shares with a par value of $100 entitled to a cumulative dividend of $8 per share. Each preference share is convertible to two ordinary shares.
5% convertible bonds	Nominal amount $100,000,000. Each $1,000 bond is convertible to 20 ordinary shares. There is no amortisation of premium or discount affecting the determination of interest expense.
Tax rate	40%

Increase in Earnings Attributable to Ordinary Equity Holders on Conversion of Potential Ordinary Shares

	Increase in earnings $	Increase in number of ordinary shares	Earnings per incremental share $
Options			
Increase in earnings	Nil		
Incremental shares issued for no consideration			
100,000 × ($75 − $60) ÷ $75 =		20,000	Nil
Convertible preference shares			
Increase in earnings			
$800,000 × 100 × 0.08 =	6,400,000		
Incremental shares			
2 × 800,000 =		1,600,000	4.00
5% convertible bonds			
Increase in earnings			
$100,000,000 × 0.05 × (1 − 0.40) =	3,000,000		
Incremental shares			
100,000 × 20 =		2,000,000	1.50

The order in which to include the dilutive instruments is therefore:
(1) Options
(2) 5% convertible bonds
(3) Convertible preference shares

Calculation of Diluted Earnings per Share

	Profit from continuing operations attributable to ordinary equity holders of the parent entity (control number) $	Ordinary shares	Per share $	
As reported	10,000,000	2,000,000	5.00	
Options	–	20,000		
	10,000,000	2,020,000	4.95	Dilutive
5% convertible bonds	3,000,000	2,000,000		
	13,000,000	4,020,000	3.23	Dilutive
Convertible preference shares	6,400,000	1,600,000		
	19,400,000	5,620,000	3.45	Antidilutive

Because diluted earnings per share is increased when taking the convertible preference shares into account (from $3.23 to $3.45), the convertible preference shares are antidilutive and are ignored in the calculation of diluted earnings per share. Therefore, diluted earnings per share for profit from continuing operations is $3.23.

	Basic EPS $		Diluted EPS $	
Profit from continuing operations attributable to ordinary equity holders of the parent entity	5.00		3.23	
Loss from discontinued operations attributable to ordinary equity holders of the parent entity	(2.00)	(a)	(0.99)	(b)
Profit attributable to ordinary equity holders of the parent entity	3.00	(c)	2.24	(d)

(a) ($4,000,000) ÷ 2,000,000 = ($2.00)
(b) ($4,000,000) ÷ 4,020,000 = ($0.99)
(c) $6,000,000 ÷ 2,000,000 = $3.00
(d) ($6,000,000 + $3,000,000) ÷ 4,020,000 = $2.24

This example does not illustrate the classification of the components of convertible financial instruments as liabilities and equity or the classification of related interest and dividends as expenses and equity as required by IAS 32.

6.4 Particular types of dilutive instruments

6.4.1 Convertible instruments

In order to secure a lower rate of interest, entities sometimes attach benefits to loan stock, debentures or preference shares in the form of conversion rights. These permit the holder to convert his holding in whole or part into equity capital. The right is normally exercisable between specified dates. The ultimate conversion of the instrument will have the following effects:

(a) there will be an increase in earnings by the amount of the interest (or items relating to preference shares) no longer payable. As interest is normally allowable for tax purposes, the effect on earnings may be net of a tax deduction relating to some or all of the items; and

(b) the number of ordinary shares in issue will increase. The diluted EPS should be calculated assuming that the instrument is converted into the maximum possible number of shares. *[IAS 33.49]*.

Convertible preference shares will be antidilutive whenever the amount of the dividend on such shares declared in or accumulated for the current period per ordinary share obtainable on conversion exceeds basic earnings per share. Similarly, convertible debt will be antidilutive whenever its interest (net of tax and other changes in income or expense) per ordinary share obtainable on conversion exceeds basic earnings per share. [IAS 33.50].

6.4.1.A Convertible debt

The EPS calculation for convertible bonds is illustrated in the following example: [IAS 33.IE6]

Example 37.9: Treatment of convertible bonds in diluted EPS calculations

Profit attributable to ordinary equity holders of the parent entity	$1,004
Ordinary shares outstanding	1,000
Basic earnings per share	$1.00
Convertible bonds	100
Each block of 10 bonds is convertible into three ordinary shares	
Interest expense for the current year relating to the liability component of the convertible bonds	$10
Current and deferred tax relating to that interest expense	$4

Note: the interest expense includes amortisation of the discount arising on initial recognition of the liability component (see IAS 32).

Adjusted profit attributable to ordinary equity holders of the parent entity	$1,004 + $10 – $4 = $1,010
Number of ordinary shares resulting from conversion of bonds	30
Number of ordinary shares used to calculate diluted earnings per share	1,000 + 30 = 1,030
Diluted earnings per share	$1,010 ÷ 1,030 = $0.98

This example does not illustrate the classification of the components of convertible financial instruments as liabilities and equity or the classification of related interest and dividends as expenses and equity as required by IAS 32.

As discussed at 6.2.2 above, the standard also discusses the impact on diluted EPS of different settlement options. As discussed earlier, we believe this should be taken to mean that for diluted EPS purposes earnings should be adjusted to remove any items that arose from an instrument being classified as an asset or liability rather than equity. The standard illustrates settlement options with the following example. [IAS 33.IE8].

Example 37.10: Convertible bonds settled in shares or cash at the issuer's option

An entity issues 2,000 convertible bonds at the beginning of Year 1. The bonds have a three-year term, and are issued at par with a face value of $1,000 per bond, giving total proceeds of $2,000,000. Interest is payable annually in arrears at a nominal annual interest rate of 6 per cent. Each bond is convertible at any time up to maturity into 250 common shares.

When the bonds are issued, the prevailing market interest rate for similar debt without a conversion option is 9 per cent. At the issue date, the market price of one common share is $3. Income tax is ignored.

Profit attributable to ordinary equity holders of the parent entity Year 1	$1,000,000
Ordinary shares outstanding	1,200,000
Convertible bonds outstanding	2,000
Allocation of proceeds of the bond issue:	
Liability component	* $1,848,122
Equity component	$151,878
	$2,000,000

The liability and equity components would be determined in accordance with IAS 32. These amounts are recognised as the initial carrying amounts of the liability and equity components. The amount assigned to the issuer conversion option equity element is an addition to equity and is not adjusted.

* This represents the present value of the principal and interest discounted at 9% – $2,000,000 payable at the end of three years; $120,000 payable annually in arrears for three years.

Basic earnings per share Year 1:

$$\frac{\$1,000,000}{1,200,000} = \$0.83 \text{ per ordinary share}$$

Diluted earnings per share Year 1:

It is presumed that the issuer will be required to settle the contract by the issue of ordinary shares. The dilutive effect is therefore calculated in accordance with paragraph 59 of the Standard.

$$\frac{\$1,000,000 + \$166,331^{(a)}}{1,200,000 + 500,000^{(b)}} = \$0.69 \text{ per ordinary share}$$

(a) Profit is adjusted for the accretion of $166,331 ($1,848,122 × 9%) of the liability because of the passage of time.

(b) 500,000 ordinary shares = 250 ordinary shares × 2,000 convertible bonds

6.4.1.B Convertible preference shares

The rules for convertible preference shares are very similar to those detailed above in the case of convertible debt, i.e. dividends and other returns to preference shareholders are added back to earnings used for basic EPS and the maximum number of ordinary shares that could be issued on conversion should be used in the calculation.

As discussed at 5.2 above, one possible return to preference shareholders is a premium payable on redemption or induced early conversion in excess of the original terms. IAS 33 notes that the redemption or induced conversion of convertible preference shares may affect only a portion of the previously outstanding convertible preference shares. In such cases, the standard makes clear that any excess consideration is attributed to those shares that are redeemed or converted for the purpose of determining whether the remaining outstanding preference shares are dilutive. In other words, the shares redeemed or converted are considered separately from those shares that are not redeemed or converted. [IAS 33.51].

6.4.1.C Participating equity instruments and two class shares with conversion rights

The treatment for basic EPS of participating equity instruments and two class shares is discussed at 5.4 above. When discussing these instruments the standard observes that when calculating diluted EPS:

- conversion is assumed for those instruments that are convertible into ordinary shares if the effect is dilutive;
- for those that are not convertible into a class of ordinary shares, profit or loss for the period is allocated to the different classes of shares and participating equity instruments in accordance with their dividend rights or other rights to participate in undistributed earnings. [IAS 33.A14].

What the standard seems to be hinting at here, without directly addressing, is how to present EPS for two or more classes of ordinary shares (say, class A and class B) when one class can convert into another (say, class B can convert into class A). In this scenario, in our view the basic EPS for each class should be calculated based on profit entitlement (see 5.4 above). For diluted EPS it would be necessary to attribute to class A the profits attributed to class B in the basic EPS – if the overall effect were dilutive to class A, conversion should be assumed.

6.4.2 Options, warrants and their equivalents

6.4.2.A The numerator

IAS 33 contains detailed guidance on the treatment for diluted EPS purposes of options, warrants and their equivalents which it defines as 'financial instruments that give the holder the right to purchase ordinary shares'. *[IAS 33.5]*. However, it was largely written before the significant developments in accounting for such instruments (IFRS 2 and IAS 32). As a result, individual facts and circumstances must be considered and judgment is required in some circumstances to address the dilutive effects on EPS.

IAS 33 clearly states that 'Options and warrants ... do not affect the numerator of the calculation' *[IAS 33.44]* and this text was added in 2003 as part of the improvements project, so clearly drafted against the back drop of the impending move to expensing share-based payments and also the (then) recent changes to IAS 32 regarding accounting for derivatives over an entity's own shares. As regards employee share options in particular, neither IAS 33 (as updated by IFRS 2) nor the worked example appended to it (see Example 37.13 at 6.4.5 below) make reference to removing either some or all the charge when computing diluted EPS. However, this seems to sit somewhat awkwardly (particularly for options outside the scope of IFRS 2) with the general requirement for calculating diluted EPS that earnings be adjusted for the effects of 'any other changes in income or expense that would result from the conversion of the dilutive potential ordinary shares'. *[IAS 33.33]*. Furthermore, IAS 33 explicitly requires an adjustment to the numerator in some circumstances:

(a) as discussed at 6.2.2 above, adjustment to the numerator may be required for a contract (which could include options and warrants) that may be settled in ordinary shares or cash at the entity's option when such a contract is presented for accounting purposes as an asset or a liability, or has an equity component and a liability component. In such a case, the standard requires that 'the entity shall adjust the numerator for any changes in profit or loss that would have resulted during the period if the contract had been classified wholly as an equity instrument'. For contracts that may be settled in ordinary shares or cash at the holder's option, 'the more dilutive of cash settlement and share settlement shall be used in calculating diluted earnings per share'; *[IAS 33.59-60]*

(b) where an option agreement requires or permits the tendering of debt in payment of the exercise price (and, if the holder could choose to pay cash, that tendering debt is more advantageous to him) the numerator should be adjusted for the after tax amount of any such debt assumed to be tendered (see 6.4.2.E below); *[IAS 33.A7]* and

(c) where option proceeds are required to be applied to redeem debt or other instruments of the entity (see 6.4.2.F below). *[IAS 33.A9]*.

For situations covered by (b) and (c) above the specific requirements of the standard for adjusting the numerator should be followed. In other circumstances, the interaction of these complex and conflicting requirements with each other and with IFRS 2 and IAS 32 lead to the following requirements when computing the numerator for diluted EPS:

(a) for instruments accounted for under IAS 32:
   (i) for a contract classified wholly as an equity instrument, no adjustment to the numerator will be necessary; and
   (ii) for a contract not classified wholly as an equity instrument, the numerator should be adjusted for any changes in profit or loss that would have resulted if it had been classified wholly as an equity instrument; and

(b) for instruments accounted for under IFRS 2:
   (i) for those treated as equity-settled, the IFRS 2 charge should not be adjusted for; and
   (ii) for those treated as cash-settled, the numerator should be adjusted for any changes in profit or loss that would have resulted if the instrument had been classified wholly as an equity instrument.

In respect of (b), part (i) is supported by the IASB's view regarding share-based payments as follows.

'Some argue that any cost arising from share-based payment transactions is already recognised in the dilution of earnings per share (EPS). If an expense were recognised in the income statement, EPS would be "hit twice".

'However, the Board noted that this result is appropriate. For example, if the entity paid the employees in cash for their services and the cash was then returned to the entity, as consideration for the issue of share options, the effect on EPS would be the same as issuing those options direct to the employees.

'The dual effect on EPS simply reflects the two economic events that have occurred: the entity has issued shares or share options, thereby increasing the number of shares included in the EPS calculation – although, in the case of options, only to the extent that the options are regarded as dilutive – and it has also consumed the resources it received for those options, thereby decreasing earnings. ...

'In summary, the Board concluded that the dual effect on diluted EPS is not double-counting the effects of a share or share option grant – the same effect is not counted twice. Rather, two different effects are each counted once.' *[IFRS 2.BC54-BC57]*.

As for part (ii) of (b) above, this is the explicit requirement of IAS 33 when the entity can choose cash or share settlement. It is also implicit in the requirement of the standard that for contracts that may be settled in ordinary shares or cash at the holder's option, the more dilutive of cash settlement and share settlement should be used in calculating diluted earnings per share. This would also explain why IFRS 2 requires the computation of grant date fair values for cash-settled share-based payments when that information is not actually required for accounting purposes (see Chapter 34 at 9.3.2).

6.4.2.B Written call options

Entities may issue options or warrants which give holders the right to subscribe for shares at fixed prices on specified future dates. If the options or warrants are exercised then:

(a) the number of shares in issue will be increased; and

(b) funds will flow into the company and these will produce income.

For calculating diluted EPS, IAS 33 requires the exercise of all dilutive options and warrants to be assumed. *[IAS 33.45]*. Options and warrants are considered dilutive when they would result in the issue of ordinary shares for less than the average market price of ordinary shares during the period. The amount of the dilution is taken to be the average market price of ordinary shares during the period minus the issue price. *[IAS 33.46]*.

Under IAS 33 the effects of such potential ordinary shares on the diluted EPS are reflected in the computation of the denominator using a method sometimes called the 'treasury stock method'.

For this purpose, the weighted average number of shares used in calculating the basic EPS is increased, but not by the full number of shares that would be issued on exercise of the instruments. To determine how many additional shares to include in the denominator, the assumed proceeds from these issues are to be treated as having been received in exchange for:

- a certain number of shares at their average market price for the period (i.e. no EPS impact); and
- the remainder for no consideration (i.e. full dilution). *[IAS 33.45-46]*.

This means that the excess of the total number of potential shares over the number that could be issued at their average market price for the period out of the issue proceeds is included within the denominator; the calculation is illustrated as follows: *[IAS 33.IE5]*

Example 37.11: Effects of share options on diluted earnings per share

Profit attributable to ordinary equity holders of the parent entity for year	₹1,200,000
Weighted average number of ordinary shares outstanding during year	500,000 shares
Average market price of one ordinary share during year	₹20.00
Weighted average number of shares under option during year	100,000 shares
Exercise price for shares under option during year	₹15.00

Calculation of earnings per share

	Earnings	Shares	Per share
Profit attributable to ordinary equity holders of the parent entity for year	₹1,200,000		
Weighted average shares outstanding during year		500,000	
Basic earnings per share			₹2.40
Weighted average number of shares under option		100,000	
Weighted average number of shares that would have been issued at average market price: (100,000 × ₹15.00) ÷ ₹20.00	*	(75,000)	
Diluted earnings per share	₹1,200,000	525,000	₹2.29

* Earnings have not increased because the total number of shares has increased only by the number of shares (25,000) deemed to have been issued for no consideration.

The number of shares viewed as fairly priced (and hence neither dilutive nor antidilutive) for this purpose is calculated on the basis of the average price of the ordinary shares during the reporting period. *[IAS 33.46]*. The standard observes that, in theory, calculating an average share price for the period could include every market transaction in the shares. However, it notes that as a practical matter an average (weekly or monthly) will usually be adequate. *[IAS 33.A4]*. The individual prices used should generally be the closing market price unless prices fluctuate widely, in which case the average of high and low prices may be more representative. Whatever method is adopted, it should be used consistently unless it ceases to yield a representative price. For example, closing prices may have been used consistently in a series of relatively stable periods then a change to high/low average could be appropriate when prices begin to fluctuate more widely. *[IAS 33.A5]*.

The shares would be deemed to have been issued at the beginning of the period or, if later, the date of issue of the warrants or options. Options which are exercised or lapse in the period are included for the portion of the period during which they were outstanding. *[IAS 33.36, 38]*.

Although the standard seems to require that the fair value used should be the average for the reporting period for all outstanding options or warrants, in our view, for instruments issued, lapsed or exercised during the period a credible case could be made for using an average price for that part of the reporting period that the instrument was outstanding. Indeed, this view is supported by the comprehensive example included in the standard (see the appendix to this chapter), where in computing the number of warrants to be included in calculating the diluted EPS for the full year, the average price used was not that for the full year, but only for the period that the warrants were outstanding.

One practical problem with this requirement is that the average market price of ordinary shares for the reporting period may not be available. Examples would include an entity only listed for part of the period, or an unlisted entity giving voluntary disclosures. In such cases estimates of the market price would need to be made.

6.4.2.C Written put options and forward purchase agreements

Contracts that require the entity to repurchase its own shares, such as written put options and forward purchase contracts, should be reflected in the calculation of diluted earnings per share if the effect is dilutive. If these contracts are 'in the money' during the period (i.e. the exercise or settlement price is above the average market price for that period), IAS 33 requires the potential dilutive effect on EPS to be calculated as follows:

- it should be assumed that at the beginning of the period sufficient ordinary shares are issued (at the average market price during the period) to raise proceeds to satisfy the contract;
- the proceeds from the issue are then assumed to be used to satisfy the contract (i.e. to buy back ordinary shares); and
- the incremental ordinary shares (the difference between the number of ordinary shares assumed issued and the number of ordinary shares received from satisfying the contract) should be included in the calculation of diluted earnings per share. *[IAS 33.63]*.

The standard illustrates this methodology as follows: '... assume that an entity has outstanding 120 written put options on its ordinary shares with an exercise price of CU 35. The average market price of its ordinary shares for the period is CU 28. In calculating diluted earnings per share, the entity assumes that it issued 150 shares at CU 28 per share at the beginning of the period to satisfy its put obligation of CU 4,200. The difference between the 150 ordinary shares issued and the 120 ordinary shares received from satisfying the put option (30 incremental ordinary shares) is added to the denominator in calculating diluted earnings per share.' *[IAS 33.A10]*.

6.4.2.D   Options over convertible instruments

Although not common, it is possible that an entity grants options or warrants to acquire not ordinary shares directly but other instruments convertible into them (such as convertible preference shares or debt). In this scenario, IAS 33 sets a dual test:

- exercise is assumed whenever the average prices of both the convertible instrument and the ordinary shares obtainable upon conversion are above the exercise price of the options or warrants; but
- exercise is not assumed unless conversion of similar outstanding convertible instruments, if any, is also assumed. *[IAS 33.A6]*.

6.4.2.E   Settlement of option exercise price with debt or other instruments of the entity

The standard notes that options or warrants may permit or require the tendering of debt or other instruments of the entity (or its parent or a subsidiary) in payment of all or a portion of the exercise price. In the calculation of diluted earnings per share, those options or warrants have a dilutive effect if (a) the average market price of the related ordinary shares for the period exceeds the exercise price or (b) the selling price of the instrument to be tendered is below that at which the instrument may be tendered under the option or warrant agreement and the resulting discount establishes an effective exercise price below the market price of the ordinary shares obtainable upon exercise. In the calculation of diluted EPS, those options or warrants should be assumed to be exercised and the debt or other instruments assumed to be tendered. If tendering cash is more advantageous to the option or warrant holder and the contract permits it, tendering of cash should be assumed. Interest (net of tax) on any debt assumed to be tendered is added back as an adjustment to the numerator. *[IAS 33.A7]*.

Similar treatment is given to preference shares that have similar provisions or to other instruments that have conversion options that permit the investor to pay cash for a more favourable conversion rate. *[IAS 33.A8]*.

6.4.2.F   Specified application of option proceeds

IAS 33 observes that the underlying terms of certain options or warrants may require the proceeds received from the exercise of those instruments to be applied to redeem debt or other instruments of the entity (or its parent or a subsidiary). In which case it requires that in 'the calculation of diluted earnings per share, those options or warrants are assumed to be exercised and the proceeds applied to purchase the debt at its average market price rather than to purchase ordinary shares. However, the excess proceeds received from the assumed exercise over the amount used for the assumed purchase of debt are considered (i.e. assumed to be used to buy back ordinary shares) in the diluted earnings per share calculation. Interest (net of tax) on any debt assumed to be purchased is added back as an adjustment to the numerator.' *[IAS 33.A9]*.

6.4.3 Purchased options and warrants

IAS 33 states that a holding by an entity of options over its own shares will always be antidilutive because:

- put options would only be exercised if the exercise price were higher than the market price; and
- call options would only be exercised if the exercise price were lower than the market price.

Accordingly, the standard requires that such instruments are not included in the calculation of diluted EPS. *[IAS 33.62]*.

However, depending upon the settlement mechanism and the share price at the beginning and end of the period, the option could have resulted in a gain being reported (see Chapter 47 at 5). It is therefore possible that the removal of any such gain from the numerator could have a greater dilutive effect than the reduction in the denominator and hence render the option dilutive. In that circumstance, the option should be included in the diluted EPS calculation.

6.4.4 Partly paid shares

As noted at 3.2 above, shares issued in partly paid form are to be included in the basic EPS as a fraction of a share, based on dividend participation. As regards diluted EPS they are to be treated, to the extent that they are not entitled to participate in dividends, as the equivalent of options or warrants. The unpaid balance is assumed to represent proceeds used to purchase ordinary shares. The number of shares included in diluted earnings per share is the difference between the number of shares subscribed and the number of shares assumed to be purchased. *[IAS 33.A16]*. The mechanics of this treatment are not further spelt out in the standard, but the phrase 'treated as a fraction of an ordinary share' is not repeated. Instead, it is 'the number of shares subscribed' which the standard says should be compared to the number assumed purchased to measure dilution. However, 'the number of shares subscribed' is not defined. Whilst this could be read to mean that the remaining unpaid consideration is to be treated as the exercise price for options over all of the shares issued in partly paid form, we believe the better interpretation is that the unpaid capital should be viewed as the exercise price for options over the proportion of the shares not reflected in the basic EPS. This would mean that if the average share price for the period were the same as the total issue price, then no dilution would be reported. Furthermore, an issue of partly paid shares, say 50% paid with 50% dividend entitlement is economically identical to an issue of half the quantity as fully paid (with full dividend entitlement) and a forward contract for the remaining half. In that scenario, the issued shares would be incorporated into the basic and diluted EPS in full from the date of issue. The forward contract would be included in diluted EPS calculation by comparing the contracted number of shares with the number of shares that could be bought out of proceeds based on the average share price for the period. In our view, these economically identical transactions should produce the same diluted EPS – that would be achieved by interpreting 'the number of shares subscribed' as the number economically subscribed, i.e. the proportion of part-paid shares not already included in basic EPS.

An illustration of what the calculation would look like is as follows:

Example 37.12: Partly paid shares

Capital structure

Issued share capital as at 31 December 2020:
2,000,000 ordinary shares of 10c each

Issued on 1 January 2021:
500,000 part paid ordinary shares of 10c each. Full consideration of 50c per share (being fair value at 1 January 2021) paid up 50% on issue. Dividend participation 50% until fully paid. New shares remain part paid at 31 December 2021.

Average fair value of one ordinary share for the period 60c.

Trading results

Net profit attributable to ordinary shareholders for the year ended 31 December 2021: $100,000.

Computation of basic and diluted EPS

	Net profit attributable to ordinary shareholders $	Ordinary shares No.	Per share
Fully paid shares		2,000,000	
Partly paid shares (1)		250,000	
Basic EPS	100,000	2,250,000	4.44c
Dilutive effect of partly paid shares (2)		41,667	
Diluted EPS	100,000	2,291,667	4.36c

(1) 50% dividend rights for 500,000 shares.

(2) Outstanding consideration of $125,000 (500,000 × 25c), using fair value of 60c this equates to 208,333 shares, hence the number of dilutive shares deemed issued for free is 41,667 (250,000 – 208,333).

The example assumes the fair value of the shares over the year is higher than the issue price, which explains why some extra shares are included in the diluted EPS. If the average fair value remained at the issue price of 50c then no additional shares would be included for diluted EPS.

6.4.5 Share-based payments

Share options and other incentive schemes are a common feature of employee remuneration, and can come in many forms. For diluted EPS purposes, IAS 33 identifies two categories and specifies the diluted EPS treatment for each. The categories are:

(a) performance-based employee share options; and
(b) employee share options with fixed or determinable terms and non-vested ordinary shares. *[IAS 33.48]*.

Before moving on to the diluted EPS treatment, it is worth noting an issue that arises from the way IAS 33 phrases this categorisation and subsequent guidance. Although not clearly stated in the standard, we believe all schemes should be treated as either category (a) or category (b). Any arrangements where entitlement is subject to future performance would fall into category (a) with category (b) being the default for all other arrangements.

Schemes in the first category are to be treated as contingently issuable shares (see 6.4.6 below) because their issue is contingent upon satisfying specified conditions in addition to the passage of time. *[IAS 33.48]*.

Those in the second category are to be treated as options (see 6.4.2 above). They should be regarded as outstanding from the grant date, even if they vest, and hence can be realised by the employees, at some later date. *[IAS 33.48]*. An example would be an unexpired loyalty period. This means that some shares may be included in diluted EPS which never, in fact, get issued to employees because they fail to remain with the company for this period. Furthermore, for share options and other share-based payment arrangements to which IFRS 2 applies, the proceeds figure to be used in calculating the dilution under such schemes should include the fair value (as determined in accordance with IFRS 2) of any goods or services to be supplied to the entity in the future under the arrangement. *[IAS 33.47A]*. An example illustrating the latter point is as follows: *[IAS 33.IE5A]*

Example 37.13: Determining the exercise price of employee share options

Weighted average number of unvested share options per employee	1,000
Weighted average amount per employee to be recognised over the remainder of the vesting period for employee services to be rendered as consideration for the share options, determined in accordance with IFRS 2	£1,200.00
Cash exercise price of unvested share options	£15.00
Calculation of adjusted exercise price	
Fair value of services yet to be rendered per employee:	£1,200.00
Fair value of services yet to be rendered per option: (£1,200 ÷ 1,000)	£1.20
Total exercise price of share options: (£15.00 + £1.20)	£16.20

Whilst the standard requires that the additional deemed proceeds is the fair value of goods or services yet to be received, the example clarifies that it is the IFRS 2 expense yet to be charged to income.

What this requirement seeks to reflect is that for such options the issuer will receive not just the cash proceeds (if any) under the option when it is exercised but also valuable goods and services over its life. This will result in the dilutive effect of the options increasing over time as the deemed proceeds on exercise of the options reduces.

6.4.6 Contingently issuable shares

IAS 33 contains considerable detailed guidance, including a numerical worked example, on contingently issuable shares. Contingently issuable ordinary shares are defined as 'ordinary shares issuable for little or no cash or other consideration upon satisfaction of specified conditions in a contingent share agreement.' A contingent share agreement is defined by the standard as 'an agreement to issue shares that is dependent on the satisfaction of specified conditions.' *[IAS 33.5]*. The basic rule is that the number of contingently issuable shares to be included in the diluted EPS calculation is 'based on the number of shares that would be issuable if the end of the period were the end of the contingency period'. *[IAS 33.52]*. This requirement to look at the status of the contingency at the end of the reporting period, rather than to consider the most likely outcome, seems to have the overall result of reducing the amount of dilution disclosed.

The discussions in the standard cover three broad categories: earnings-based contingencies, share price-based contingencies, and other contingencies. These are discussed in turn below.

The number of shares contingently issuable may depend on future earnings and future prices of the ordinary shares. In such cases, the standard makes clear that the number of shares included in the diluted EPS calculation is based on both conditions (i.e. earnings to date and the current market price at the end of the reporting period). In other words, contingently issuable shares are not included in the diluted EPS calculation unless both conditions are met. [IAS 33.55].

6.4.6.A Earnings-based contingencies

The standard discusses the scenario where shares would be issued contingent upon the attainment or maintenance of a specified amount of earnings for a period. In such a case the standard requires that 'if that amount has been attained at the end of the reporting period but must be maintained beyond the end of the reporting period for an additional period, then the additional ordinary shares are treated as outstanding, if the effect is dilutive, when calculating diluted earnings per share. In that case, the calculation of diluted earnings per share is based on the number of ordinary shares that would be issued if the amount of earnings at the end of the reporting period were the amount of earnings at the end of the contingency period'. [IAS 33.53]. As a result, earnings-based contingencies need to be viewed as an absolute cumulative hurdle which either is met or not met at the reporting date. Often, such contingencies may be contractually expressed in terms of annual performance over a number of years, say an average of $1million profit per year for three years. In our view, 'the attainment or maintenance of a specified amount of earnings for a period' in this scenario would mean generating a total of $3million of profits. If that is achieved by the end of a reporting period, the shares are outstanding for diluted EPS purposes and included in the computation if the effect is dilutive. It could, perhaps, be argued that the potential shares should be considered outstanding if profits of $1million were generated at the end of the first year. However, the requirement that the calculation be 'based on the number of ordinary shares that would be issued if the amount of earnings at the end of the reporting period were the amount of earnings at the end of the contingency period' means that the test must be: would shares be issued if the current earnings of $1million were all the profits earned by the end of the three year contingency period? In this example the answer is no, as that amount of earnings would fall short of averaging $1million per year. The standard then notes that, because earnings may change in a future period, the calculation of basic EPS does not include such contingently issuable shares until the end of the contingency period because not all necessary conditions have been satisfied. [IAS 33.53].

An earnings-based contingency is illustrated in the following example: [IAS 33.IE7]

Example 37.14: Contingently issuable shares

Ordinary shares outstanding during 2021:	1,000,000 (there were no options, warrants or convertible instruments outstanding during the period)
An agreement related to a recent business combination provides for the issue of additional ordinary shares based on the following conditions:	5,000 additional ordinary shares for each new retail site opened during 2021 1,000 additional ordinary shares for each $1,000 of consolidated profit in excess of $2,000,000 for the year ended 31 December 2021
Retail sites opened during the year:	one on 1 May 2021 one on 1 September 2021
Consolidated year-to-date profit attributable to ordinary equity holders of the parent entity:	$1,100,000 as of 31 March 2021 $2,300,000 as of 30 June 2021 $1,900,000 as of 30 September 2021 (including a $450,000 loss from a discontinued operation) $2,900,000 as of 31 December 2021

Basic earnings per share

	First quarter	Second quarter	Third quarter	Fourth quarter	Full year
Numerator ($)	1,100,000	1,200,000	(400,000)	1,000,000	2,900,000
Denominator:					
Ordinary shares outstanding	1,000,000	1,000,000	1,000,000	1,000,000	1,000,000
Retail site contingency	–	3,333 (a)	6,667 (b)	10,000	5,000 (c)
Earnings contingency (d)	–	–	–	–	–
Total shares	1,000,000	1,003,333	1,006,667	1,010,000	1,005,000
Basic earnings per share ($)	1.10	1.20	(0.40)	0.99	2.89

(a) 5,000 shares × 2/3
(b) 5,000 shares + (5,000 shares × 1/3)
(c) (5,000 shares × 8/12) + (5,000 shares × 4/12)
(d) The earnings contingency has no effect on basic earnings per share because it is not certain that the condition is satisfied until the end of the contingency period. The effect is negligible for the fourth-quarter and full-year calculations because it is not certain that the condition is met until the last day of the period.

Diluted earnings per share

	First quarter	Second quarter	Third quarter	Fourth quarter	Full year
Numerator ($)	1,100,000	1,200,000	(400,000)	1,000,000	2,900,000
Denominator:					
Ordinary shares outstanding	1,000,000	1,000,000	1,000,000	1,000,000	1,000,000
Retail site contingency	–	5,000	10,000	10,000	10,000
Earnings contingency	– (e)	300,000 (f)	– (g)	900,000 (h)	900,000 (h)
Total shares	1,000,000	1,305,000	1,010,000	1,910,000	1,910,000
Diluted earnings per share ($)	1.10	0.92	(0.40) (i)	0.52	1.52

(e) Year-to-date profits do not exceed $2,000,000 at 31 March 2021. The Standard does not permit projecting future earnings levels and including the related contingent shares.
(f) [($2,300,000 – $2,000,000) ÷ 1,000] × 1,000 shares = 300,000 shares.
(g) Year-to-date profit is less than $2,000,000.
(h) [($2,900,000 – $2,000,000) ÷ 1,000] × 1,000 shares = 900,000 shares.
(i) Because the loss during the third quarter is attributable to a loss from a discontinued operation, the antidilution rules do not apply. The control number (i.e. profit or loss from continuing operations attributable to the equity holders of the parent entity) is positive. Accordingly, the effect of potential ordinary shares is included in the calculation of diluted earnings per share.

This example from IAS 33 illustrates quarterly financial reporting. However, the principles are the same whether the reporting period is illustrated as three months or one year. The example does illustrate that the earnings target is a cumulative hurdle over the entire contingency period (four reporting periods in the example) rather than including potential shares based on the assumption that the level of quarterly profit would be maintained for the four quarters.

The standard only discusses earnings criteria based on absolute measures; in the example above a cumulative profit in excess of $2,000,000. In our experience such criteria are rare. In practice criteria are often phrased in terms of relative performance against an external benchmark. Examples would be earnings growth targets of inflation plus 2% or EPS growth being in the top quartile of a group of competitors. For contingencies such as these it is impossible to establish an absolute target in order to ask whether it is met at the period end. For example, consider the earnings contingency in IAS 33, discussed above, to achieve profits in excess of $2,000,000 over four quarters. If this instead required the profits to be $2,000,000 adjusted in line with inflation, it would be impossible to know how many shares would be issued if the cumulative profit at the end of the second quarter of $2,300,000 were the amount of earnings at the end of the contingency period. Until the end of the year the absolute level of profit required would be unknown; it would be more or less than $2,000,000 depending on the level of inflation or deflation over the period.

There would seem to be (at least) two different ways of interpreting the requirements of IAS 33 in such a scenario, each resulting in a different diluted EPS figure. One approach would be to consider such criteria as being based on 'a condition other than earnings or market price'. That would mean (as discussed at 6.4.6.C below) that the number of shares brought into diluted EPS would be based on the status of the condition at the end of the reporting period. *[IAS 33.56]*. If the target was earnings for the year in excess of $2,000,000 adjusted in line with inflation and at the end of the second quarter inflation had been 4%, then the target would become $2,080,000 and hence 220,000 shares would be included for diluted EPS for the second quarter. An alternative approach would be to regard it as an earnings-based contingency and make an assumption as to future inflation over the contingency period. This would allow a cumulative hurdle to be calculated and compared with actual earnings to date. If at the end of the second quarter it was estimated that the annual inflation for the year was 5%, then the target would become $2,100,000 and hence 200,000 shares would be included for diluted EPS for the second quarter. Given the lack of clarity in the standard, it seems likely that either of the above approaches may be selected in practice.

6.4.6.B Share price-based contingencies

The provisions here are more straightforward. In these cases, if the effect is dilutive, the calculation of diluted EPS is based on the number of shares that would be issued if the market price at the end of the reporting period were the market price at the end of the contingency period. If the condition is based on an average of market prices over a period of time that extends beyond the end of the reporting period, the average for the period of time that has lapsed should be used. Again the standard explains that, because the market price may change in a future period, the calculation of basic earnings per share does not include such contingently issuable ordinary shares until the end of the contingency period because not all necessary conditions have been satisfied. *[IAS 33.54]*.

6.4.6.C Other contingencies

The requirement regarding contingencies not driven by earnings or share price is as follows: 'assuming that the present status of the condition remains unchanged until the end of the contingency period, the contingently issuable ordinary shares are included in the calculation of diluted earnings per share according to the status at the end of the reporting period.' *[IAS 33.56]*.

The standard illustrates the 'other contingency' rules by the example of shares being issued depending upon the opening of a specified number of retail sites, and such a contingency is included in the numerical example in the standard (see Example 37.14 at 6.4.6.A above). As is the case for earnings-based contingencies discussed above, it would seem that such conditions are always deemed to be expressed as a cumulative hurdle which may or may not be met by the end of the reporting period. Accordingly, the required treatment would be the same if the condition had been expressed in terms of achieving a certain average annual level of shop openings.

6.4.7 Potential ordinary shares of investees

A subsidiary, joint venture or associate may issue to parties other than the parent or investors with joint control of, or significant influence over the investee potential ordinary shares that are convertible into either ordinary shares of the subsidiary, joint venture or associate, or ordinary shares of the parent or investors with joint control of, or significant influence over the investee (the reporting entity). If these potential ordinary shares of the subsidiary, joint venture or associate have a dilutive effect on the basic EPS of the reporting entity, they should be included in the calculation of diluted earnings per share. *[IAS 33.40]*.

The standard requires that such potential ordinary shares should be included in the calculation of diluted EPS as follows:

(a) instruments issued by a subsidiary, joint venture or associate that enable their holders to obtain ordinary shares of the subsidiary, joint venture or associate should be included in calculating the diluted EPS data of the subsidiary, joint venture or associate. Those EPS are then included in the reporting entity's EPS calculations based on the reporting entity's holding of the instruments of the subsidiary, joint venture or associate; and

(b) instruments of a subsidiary, joint venture or associate that are convertible into the reporting entity's ordinary shares should be considered among the potential ordinary shares of the reporting entity for the purpose of calculating diluted EPS. Similarly, options or warrants issued by a subsidiary, joint venture or associate to purchase ordinary shares of the reporting entity should be considered among the potential ordinary shares of the reporting entity in the calculation of consolidated diluted EPS. *[IAS 33.A11]*.

For the purpose of determining the EPS effect of instruments issued by a reporting entity that are convertible into ordinary shares of a subsidiary, joint venture or associate, the standard requires that the instruments are assumed to be converted and the numerator (profit or loss attributable to ordinary equity holders of the parent entity) adjusted as necessary in accordance with the normal rules (see 6.2.1 above). In addition to those adjustments, the numerator is adjusted for any change in the profit or loss recorded by the reporting entity (such as dividend income or equity method income) that is attributable to the increase in the number of ordinary shares of the subsidiary, joint venture or associate outstanding as a result of the assumed conversion. The denominator of the diluted EPS calculation is not affected because the number of ordinary shares of the reporting entity outstanding would not change upon assumed conversion. [IAS 33.A12].

The computation under (a) above is illustrated in the following example. [IAS 33.IE10].

Example 37.15: Warrants issued by a subsidiary

Parent:
Profit attributable to ordinary equity holders of the parent entity — $12,000 (excluding any earnings of, or dividends paid by, the subsidiary)
Ordinary shares outstanding — 10,000
Instruments of subsidiary owned by the parent — 800 ordinary shares
30 warrants exercisable to purchase ordinary shares of subsidiary
300 convertible preference shares

Subsidiary:
Profit — $5,400
Ordinary shares outstanding — 1,000
Warrants — 150, exercisable to purchase ordinary shares of the subsidiary
Exercise price — $10
Average market price of one ordinary share — $20
Convertible preference shares — 400, each convertible into one ordinary share
Dividends on preference shares — $1 per share

No inter-company eliminations or adjustments were necessary except for dividends. For the purposes of this illustration, income taxes have been ignored.

Subsidiary's earnings per share

Basic EPS $5.00 calculated: $\dfrac{\$5,400^{(a)} - \$400^{(b)}}{1,000^{(c)}}$

Diluted EPS $3.66 calculated: $\dfrac{\$5,400^{(d)}}{1,000 + 75^{(e)} + 400^{(f)}}$

(a) Subsidiary's profit.
(b) Dividends paid by subsidiary on convertible preference shares.
(c) Subsidiary's ordinary shares outstanding.
(d) Subsidiary's profit attributable to ordinary equity holders ($5,000) increased by $400 preference dividends for the purpose of calculating diluted earnings per share.
(e) Incremental shares from warrants, calculated: [($20 – $10) ÷ $20] × 150.
(f) Subsidiary's ordinary shares assumed outstanding from conversion of convertible preference shares, calculated: 400 convertible preference shares × conversion factor of 1.

Consolidated earnings per share

Basic EPS $1.63 calculated: $\dfrac{\$12,000^{(g)} - \$4,300^{(h)}}{10,000^{(i)}}$

Diluted EPS $1.61 calculated: $\dfrac{\$12,000 + \$2,928^{(j)} + \$55^{(k)} + \$1,098^{(l)}}{10,000}$

(g) Parent's profit attributable to ordinary equity holders of the parent entity.
(h) Portion of subsidiary's profit to be included in consolidated basic earnings per share, calculated: (800 × $5.00) + (300 × $1.00).
(i) Parent's ordinary shares outstanding.
(j) Parent's proportionate interest in subsidiary's earnings attributable to ordinary shares, calculated: (800 ÷ 1,000) × (1,000 shares × $3.66 per share)

(k) Parent's proportionate interest in subsidiary's earnings attributable to warrants, calculated: (30 ÷ 150) × (75 incremental shares × $3.66 per share)

(l) Parent's proportionate interest in subsidiary's earnings attributable to convertible preference shares, calculated: (300 ÷ 400) × (400 shares from conversion × $3.66 per share)

This example does not illustrate the classification of the components of convertible financial instruments as liabilities and equity or the classification of related interest and dividends as expenses and equity as required by IAS 32.

6.4.8 Contingently issuable potential ordinary shares

The standard requires that contingently issuable potential ordinary shares (other than those covered by a contingent share agreement, such as contingently issuable convertible instruments) to be included in the diluted EPS calculation as follows:

(a) determine whether the potential ordinary shares may be assumed to be issuable on the basis of the conditions specified for their issue in accordance with the provisions of the standard for contingent ordinary shares (see 6.4.6 above); and

(b) if those potential ordinary shares should be reflected in diluted EPS, determine their impact on the calculation of diluted earnings per share by following the provisions of the standard for that type of potential ordinary share.

However, exercise or conversion is not to be assumed for the purpose of calculating diluted earnings per share unless exercise or conversion of similar outstanding potential ordinary shares that are not contingently issuable is assumed. *[IAS 33.57]*.

7 PRESENTATION, RESTATEMENT AND DISCLOSURE

7.1 Presentation

As discussed in Chapter 3 at 3.2.1, IAS 1 requires that all items of income and expense be presented either:

(a) in a single statement of profit or loss and comprehensive income; or

(b) in two separate statements:
   (i) a statement of profit or loss; and
   (ii) a statement, beginning with profit or loss, presenting items of other comprehensive income. *[IAS 1.10A]*.

If the approach in (b) is followed, the separate statement of profit or loss must be displayed immediately before the statement of comprehensive income. *[IAS 1.10A]*.

If (a) is adopted, the EPS presentational requirements below apply to that single statement. If (b) is chosen, the requirements apply to the separate statement of profit or loss only and not the separate statement of comprehensive income. *[IAS 33.4A, 67A, 68A]*.

IAS 33 requires the presentation of basic and diluted EPS (with equal prominence and even if the amounts are negative – i.e. a loss per share) for each period for which a statement of comprehensive income (or separate income statement) is presented. *[IAS 33.66, 69]*. This is required for the profit or loss attributable to ordinary equity holders for:

(a) overall profit;

(b) profit or loss from continuing operations; and

(c) profit or loss from discontinued operations, if any. *[IAS 33.66, 68]*.

In the case of (a) and (b), separate figures are required for each class of ordinary shares with a different right to share in profits for the period. The figures for (a) and (b) must be displayed on the face of the statement. *[IAS 33.66]*. Those for (c) may be either on the face or in the notes. *[IAS 33.68]*. The standard states that if diluted EPS is given for at least one period it must be given for all periods presented. IAS 33 notes that if basic and diluted EPS are equal, dual presentation can be accomplished in one line in the statement. *[IAS 33.67]*.

Regarding (c), the wording of the standard is not very clear. In particular, if an entity has more than one discontinued operation it does not specify whether separate EPS disclosures are required for each or whether one aggregate figure is needed. The wording leans to the former, as it uses the singular – 'An entity that reports a discontinued operation shall disclose the basic and diluted amounts per share for the discontinued operation ...'. However, IFRS 5 – *Non-current Assets Held for Sale and Discontinued Operations* – only requires the statement of comprehensive income (or separate income statement) to identify the total result from all discontinued operations. *[IFRS 5.33]*. In light of this, we believe aggregate figures are acceptable.

The presentation of EPS data in addition to that required by IAS 33 is discussed at 5.5 above.

7.2 Restatement

IAS 33 contains requirements to restate prior periods' EPS for events that change the number of shares outstanding without a corresponding change in resources. Additionally it specifies circumstances when EPS should not be restated.

Basic and diluted EPS for all periods presented should be adjusted for:

- events (other than the conversion of potential ordinary shares) which change the number of ordinary shares without a corresponding change in resources (discussed at 4.3 above); *[IAS 33.26, 64]*
- the effects of errors and adjustments resulting from changes in accounting policies accounted for retrospectively (see 5.3 above); *[IAS 33.64]* and
- the effects of group reorganisations that are accounted for as a pooling of interests (discussed at 4.6 above).

No adjustment should be made:

- to basic or diluted EPS when a share consolidation is combined with a special dividend where the overall commercial effect is that of a share repurchase at fair value (discussed at 4.3.2 above); *[IAS 33.29]*
- to previously reported diluted EPS due to changes in the prices of ordinary shares which would have given a different dilutive effect for options and warrants; *[IAS 33.47]*
- to prior period diluted EPS as a result of a contingency period coming to an end without the conditions attaching to contingently issuable shares being met; *[IAS 33.52]* or
- to prior period diluted EPS for changes in the assumptions used in the calculations or for the conversion of potential ordinary shares into ordinary shares. *[IAS 33.65]*.

7.3 Disclosure

IAS 33 requires disclosure of the following:

(a) the amounts used as the numerators in calculating basic and diluted EPS, and a reconciliation of those amounts to profit or loss attributable to the parent entity for the period. The reconciliation should include the individual effect of each class of instruments that affects EPS;

(b) the weighted average number of ordinary shares used as the denominator in calculating basic and diluted earnings per share, and a reconciliation of these denominators to each other. The reconciliation should include the individual effect of each class of instruments that affects EPS;

(c) instruments (including contingently issuable shares) that could potentially dilute basic EPS in the future, but were not included in the calculation because they were antidilutive for the period(s) presented; and

(d) a description of ordinary share transactions or potential ordinary share transactions (other than those accounted for in EPS for the year – see 4.3 above – in which case that fact should be stated), that occur after the end of the reporting period and that would have changed significantly the number of ordinary shares or potential ordinary shares outstanding at the end of the period if those transactions had occurred before the end of the reporting period. *[IAS 33.70]*.

Examples of transactions in (d) include:

(a) an issue of shares for cash;

(b) an issue of shares when the proceeds are used to repay debt or preference shares outstanding at the end of the reporting period;

(c) the redemption of ordinary shares outstanding;

(d) the conversion or exercise of potential ordinary shares outstanding at the end of the reporting period into ordinary shares;

(e) an issue of options, warrants, or convertible instruments; and

(f) the achievement of conditions that would result in the issue of contingently issuable shares.

The standard observes that EPS amounts are not adjusted for such transactions occurring after the reporting period because such transactions do not affect the amount of capital used to produce profit or loss for the period. *[IAS 33.71]*. Changes in ordinary shares are discussed at 4 above.

The standard observes that financial instruments and other contracts generating potential ordinary shares may incorporate terms and conditions that affect the measurement of basic and diluted earnings per share. These terms and conditions may determine whether any potential ordinary shares are dilutive and, if so, the effect on the weighted average number of shares outstanding and any consequent adjustments to profit or loss attributable to ordinary equity holders. The disclosure of the terms and conditions of such financial instruments and other contracts is encouraged by IAS 33, if not otherwise required by IFRS 7 – *Financial Instruments: Disclosures* (discussed in Chapter 54). *[IAS 33.72]*.

8 APPENDIX

Reproduced below is the comprehensive worked example in IAS 33 of the computation and presentation of EPS. *[IAS 33.IE12]*. It illustrates four quarters and then the full year, but the principles and calculations would be the same whatever the length of the periods considered.

CALCULATION AND PRESENTATION OF BASIC AND DILUTED EARNINGS PER SHARE (COMPREHENSIVE EXAMPLE)

This example illustrates the quarterly and annual calculations of basic and diluted earnings per share in the year 20X1 for Company A, which has a complex capital structure. The control number is profit or loss from continuing operations attributable to the parent entity. Other facts assumed are as follows:

Average market price of ordinary shares: The average market prices of ordinary shares for the calendar year 20X1 were as follows:

First quarter	CU 49
Second quarter	CU 60
Third quarter	CU 67
Fourth quarter	CU 67

The average market price of ordinary shares from 1 July to 1 September 20X1 was CU 65.

Ordinary shares: The number of ordinary shares outstanding at the beginning of 20X1 was 5,000,000. On 1 March 20X1, 200,000 ordinary shares were issued for cash.

Convertible bonds: In the last quarter of 20X0, 5 per cent convertible bonds with a principal amount of CU 12,000,000 due in 20 years were sold for cash at CU 1,000 (par). Interest is payable twice a year, on 1 November and 1 May. Each CU 1,000 bond is convertible into 40 ordinary shares. No bonds were converted in 20X0. The entire issue was converted on 1 April 20X1 because the issue was called by Company A.

Convertible preference shares: In the second quarter of 20X0, 800,000 convertible preference shares were issued for assets in a purchase transaction. The quarterly dividend on each convertible preference share is CU 0.05, payable at the end of the quarter for shares outstanding at that date. Each share is convertible into one ordinary share. Holders of 600,000 convertible preference shares converted their preference shares into ordinary shares on 1 June 20X1.

Warrants: Warrants to buy 600,000 ordinary shares at CU 55 per share for a period of five years were issued on 1 January 20X1. All outstanding warrants were exercised on 1 September 20X1.

Options: Options to buy 1,500,000 ordinary shares at CU 75 per share for a period of 10 years were issued on 1 July 20X1. No options were exercised during 20X1 because the exercise price of the options exceeded the market price of the ordinary shares.

Tax rate: The tax rate was 40 per cent for 20X1.

20X1	Profit (loss) from continuing operations attributable to the parent entity (a)	Profit (loss) attributable to the parent entity	
	CU	CU	
First quarter	5,000,000	5,000,000	
Second quarter	6,500,000	6,500,000	
Third quarter	1,000,000	(1,000,000)	(b)
Fourth quarter	(700,000)	(700,000)	
Full year	11,800,000	9,800,000	

(a) This is the control number (before adjusting for preference dividends).
(b) Company A had a CU 2,000,000 loss (net of tax) from discontinued operations in the third quarter.

First Quarter 20X1

Basic EPS calculation

	CU	
Profit from continuing operations attributable to the parent entity	5,000,000	
Less: preference shares dividends	(40,000)	(c)
Profit attributable to ordinary equity holders of the parent entity	4,960,000	

Dates	Shares Outstanding	Fraction of period	Weighted-average shares
1 January 28 February	5,000,000	2/3	3,333,333
Issue of ordinary shares on 1 March	200,000		
1 March 31 March	5,200,000	1/3	1,733,333
Weighted-average shares			5,066,666

Basic EPS	CU 0.98

(c) 800,000 shares × CU 0.05

Diluted EPS calculation

Profit attributable to ordinary equity holders of the parent entity		CU 4,960,000
Plus: profit impact of assumed conversions		
Preference share dividends	CU 40,000	(d)
Interest on 5% convertible bonds	CU 90,000	(e)
Effect of assumed conversions		CU 130,000
Profit attributable to ordinary equity holders of the parent entity including assumed conversions		CU 5,090,000
Weighted-average shares		5,066,666
Plus: incremental shares from assumed conversions		
Warrants	0	(f)
Convertible preference shares	800,000	
5% convertible bonds	480,000	
Dilutive potential ordinary shares		1,280,000
Adjusted weighted-average shares		6,346,666

Diluted EPS	CU 0.80

(d) 800,000 shares × CU 0.05

(e) (CU 12,000,000 × 5%) ÷ 4; less taxes at 40%

(f) The warrants were not assumed to be exercised because they were antidilutive in the period (CU 55 [exercise price] > CU 49 [average price]).

Second Quarter 20X1

Basic EPS calculation

			CU	
Profit from continuing operations attributable to the parent entity			6,500,000	
Less: preference shares dividends			(10,000)	(g)
Profit attributable to ordinary equity holders of the parent entity			6,490,000	

Dates	Shares outstanding	Fraction of period	Weighted-average shares
1 April	5,200,000		
Conversion of 5% bonds on 1 April	480,000		
1 April–31 May	5,680,000	2/3	3,786,666
Conversion of preference shares on 1 June	600,000		
1 June–30 June	6,280,000	1/3	2,093,333
Weighted-average shares			5,880,000
Basic EPS			CU 1.10

(g) 200,000 shares × CU 0.05

Diluted EPS calculation

Profit attributable to ordinary equity holders of the parent entity			CU 6,490,000
Plus: profit impact of assumed conversions			
Preference share dividends	CU 10,000	(h)	
Effect of assumed conversions			CU 10,000
Profit attributable to ordinary equity holders of the parent entity including assumed conversions			CU 6,500,000
Weighted-average shares			5,880,000
Plus: incremental shares from assumed conversions			
Warrants	50,000	(i)	
Convertible preference shares	600,000	(j)	
Dilutive potential ordinary shares			650,000
Adjusted weighted-average shares			6,530,000
Diluted EPS			CU 1.00

(h) 200,000 shares × CU 0.05
(i) CU 55 × 600,000 = CU 33,000,000; CU 33,000,000 ÷ CU 60 = 550,000;
600,000 − 550,000 = 50,000 shares or
[(CU 60 − CU 55) ÷ CU 60] × 600,000 shares = 50,000 shares
(j) (800,000 shares × 2/3) + (200,000 shares × 1/3)

Third Quarter 20X1

Basic EPS calculation

	CU
Profit from continuing operations attributable to the parent entity	1,000,000
Less: preference shares dividends	(10,000)
Profit from continuing operations attributable to ordinary equity holders of the parent entity	990,000
Loss from discontinued operations attributable to the parent entity	(2,000,000)
Loss attributable to ordinary equity holders of the parent entity	(1,010,000)

Dates	Shares outstanding	Fraction of period	Weighted-average shares
1 July-31 August	6,280,000	2/3	4,186,666
Exercise of warrants on 1 September	600,000		
1 September-30 September	6,880,000	1/3	2,293,333
Weighted-average shares			6,480,000

Basic EPS

Profit from continuing operations	CU 0.15
Loss from discontinued operations	(CU 0.31)
Loss	(CU 0.16)

Diluted EPS calculation

Profit from continuing operations attributable to ordinary equity holders of the parent entity		CU 990,000
Plus: profit impact of assumed conversions		
Preference shares dividends	CU 10,000	
Effect of assumed conversions		CU 10,000
Profit from continuing operations attributable to ordinary equity holders of the parent entity including assumed conversions		CU 1,000,000
Loss from discontinued operations attributable to the parent entity		(CU 2,000,000)
Loss attributable to ordinary equity holders of the parent entity including assumed conversions		(CU 1,000,000)
Weighted-average shares		6,480,000
Plus: incremental shares from assumed conversions		
Warrants	61,538	(k)
Convertible preference shares	200,000	
Dilutive potential ordinary shares		261,538
Adjusted weighted-average shares		6,741,538

Diluted EPS

Profit from continuing operations	CU 0.15
Loss from discontinued operations	(CU 0.30)
Loss	(CU 0.15)

(k) [(CU 65 − CU 55) ÷ CU 65] × 600,000 = 92,308 shares; 92,308 × 2/3 = 61,538 shares

Note: The incremental shares from assumed conversions are included in calculating the diluted per-share amounts for the loss from discontinued operations and loss even though they are antidilutive. This is because the control number (profit from continuing operations attributable to ordinary equity holders of the parent entity, adjusted for preference dividends) was positive (i.e. profit, rather than loss).

Fourth Quarter 20X1

Basic and diluted EPS calculation	CU
Loss from continuing operations attributable to the parent entity	(700,000)
Add: preference shares dividends	(10,000)
Loss attributable to ordinary equity holders of the parent entity	(710,000)

Dates	Shares outstanding	Fraction of period	Weighted-average shares
1 October-31 December	6,880,000	3/3	6,880,000
Weighted-average shares			6,880,000

Basic and diluted EPS

Loss attributable to ordinary equity holders of the parent entity	(CU 0.10)

Note: The incremental shares from assumed conversions are not included in calculating the diluted per-share amounts because the control number (loss from continuing operations attributable to ordinary equity holders of the parent entity adjusted for preference dividends) was negative (i.e. a loss, rather than profit).

Full Year 20X1

Basic EPS calculation	CU
Profit from continuing operations attributable to the parent entity	11,800,000
Less: preference shares dividends	(70,000)
Profit from continuing operations attributable to ordinary equity holders of the parent entity	11,730,000
Loss from discontinued operations attributable to the parent entity	(2,000,000)
Profit attributable to ordinary equity holders of the parent entity	9,730,000

Dates	Shares Outstanding	Fraction of period	Weighted-average shares
1 January-28 February	5,000,000	2/12	833,333
Issue of ordinary shares on 1 March	200,000		
1 March-31 March	5,200,000	1/12	433,333
Conversion of 5% bonds on 1 April	480,000		
1 April-31 May	5,680,000	2/12	946,667
Conversion of preference shares on 1 June	600,000		
1 June-31 August	6,280,000	3/12	1,570,000
Exercise of warrants on 1 September	600,000		
1 September-31 December	6,880,000	4/12	2,293,333
Weighted-average shares			6,076,667

Basic EPS

Profit from continuing operations	CU 1.93
Loss from discontinued operations	(CU 0.33)
Profit	CU 1.60

Diluted EPS calculation

Profit from continuing operations attributable to ordinary equity holders of the parent entity			CU 11,730,000
Plus: profit impact of assumed conversions			
Preference share dividends	CU 70,000		
Interest on 5% convertible bonds	CU 90,000	(1)	
Effect of assumed conversions			CU 160,000
Profit from continuing operations attributable to ordinary equity holders of the parent entity including assumed conversions			CU 11,890,000
Loss from discontinued operations attributable to the parent entity			(CU 2,000,000)
Profit attributable to ordinary equity holders of the parent entity including assumed conversions			CU 9,890,000

Weighted-average shares	6,076,667
Plus: incremental shares from assumed conversions	

Warrants	14,880	(m)
Convertible preference shares	450,000	(n)
5% convertible bonds	120,000	(o)

Dilutive potential ordinary shares	584,880
Adjusted weighted-average shares	6,661,547

Diluted EPS

Profit from continuing operations	CU 1.78
Loss from discontinued operations	(CU 0.30)
Profit	CU 1.48

(l) (CU 12,000,000 × 5%) ÷ 4; less taxes at 40%
(m) [(CU 57.125† − CU 55) ÷ CU 57.125] × 600,000 = 22,320 shares; 22,320 × 8/12 = 14,880 shares
 †The average market price from 1 January 20X1 to 1 September 20X1
(n) (800,000 shares × 5/12) + (200,000 shares × 7/12)
(o) 480,000 shares × 3/12

The following illustrates how Company A might present its earnings per share data in its statement of comprehensive income. Note that the amounts per share for the loss from discontinued operations are not required to be presented on the face of the statement of comprehensive income.

	For the year ended 20X1 CU
Earnings per ordinary share	
Profit from continuing operations	1.93
Loss from discontinued operations	(0.33)
Profit	1.60
Diluted earnings per ordinary share	
Profit from continuing operations	1.78
Loss from discontinued operations	(0.30)
Profit	1.48

The following table includes the quarterly and annual earnings per share data for Company A. The purpose of this table is to illustrate that the sum of the four quarters' earnings per share data will not necessarily equal the annual earnings per share data. The Standard does not require disclosure of this information.

	First quarter CU	Second quarter CU	Third quarter CU	Fourth quarter CU	Full year CU
Basic EPS					
Profit (loss) from continuing operations	0.98	1.10	0.15	(0.10)	1.93
Loss from discontinued operations	–	–	(0.31)	–	(0.33)
Profit (loss)	0.98	1.10	(0.16)	(0.10)	1.60
Diluted EPS					
Profit (loss) from continuing operations	0.80	1.00	0.15	(0.10)	1.78
Loss from discontinued operations	–	–	(0.30)	–	(0.30)
Profit (loss)	0.80	1.00	(0.15)	(0.10)	1.48

This example does not illustrate the classification of the components of convertible financial instruments as liabilities and equity or the classification of related interest and dividends as expenses and equity as required by IAS 32.

References

1 *IFRIC Update*, June 2017.
2 ED/2019/7 *General Presentation and Disclosures*, Introduction, IASB, December 2019.
3 ED/2019/7 *General Presentation and Disclosures*, proposed new paras IAS 33.73B-73C.

Chapter 38

Events after the reporting period

1   INTRODUCTION 3073
2   REQUIREMENTS OF IAS 10 3074
    2.1   Objective, scope and definitions 3074
          2.1.1   Date when financial statements are authorised for issue 3074
                  2.1.1.A   Impact of preliminary reporting 3076
                  2.1.1.B   Re-issuing (dual dating) financial statements 3077
          2.1.2   Adjusting events 3078
          2.1.3   Non-adjusting events 3079
                  2.1.3.A   Dividend declaration 3081
    2.2   The treatment of adjusting events 3082
          2.2.1   Events requiring adjustment to the amounts recognised, or disclosures, in the financial statements 3082
          2.2.2   Events indicating that the going concern basis is not appropriate 3082
    2.3   The treatment of non-adjusting events 3083
          2.3.1   Declaration to distribute non-cash assets to owners 3085
          2.3.2   Breach of a long-term loan covenant and its subsequent rectification 3086
    2.4   Other disclosure requirements 3086
3   PRACTICAL ISSUES 3087
    3.1   Valuation of inventory 3087
    3.2   Percentage of completion estimates 3088
    3.3   Insolvency of a debtor and IFRS 9 expected credit losses 3088
    3.4   Valuation of investment property at fair value and tenant insolvency 3089

3.5 Discovery of fraud after the reporting period..3089
3.6 Changes to estimates of uncertain tax treatments....................................3090

List of examples

Example 38.1:   Financial statements required to be approved by
                 shareholders..3075
Example 38.2:   Financial statements required to be approved by
                 supervisory board..3075
Example 38.3:   Financial statements required to be approved by
                 supervisory board – changes are made by supervisory
                 board..3075
Example 38.4:   Release of financial information before date of
                 authorisation for issue...3076

Chapter 38   Events after the reporting period

1 INTRODUCTION

IAS 10 – *Events after the Reporting Period* – deals with accounting for, and disclosure of: 'those events, favourable and unfavourable, that occur between the end of the reporting period and the date when the financial statements are authorised for issue'. *[IAS 10.2, 3]*. This definition, therefore, includes all events occurring between those dates – irrespective of whether they relate to conditions that existed at the end of the reporting period. The principal issue is determining which events after the reporting period are required to be reflected in the financial statements as adjustments, which are material enough to require additional disclosure, and which require neither adjustment nor disclosure.

The following timeline illustrates events after the end of the reporting period that are within the scope of IAS 10 for an entity with a 31 December year-end:

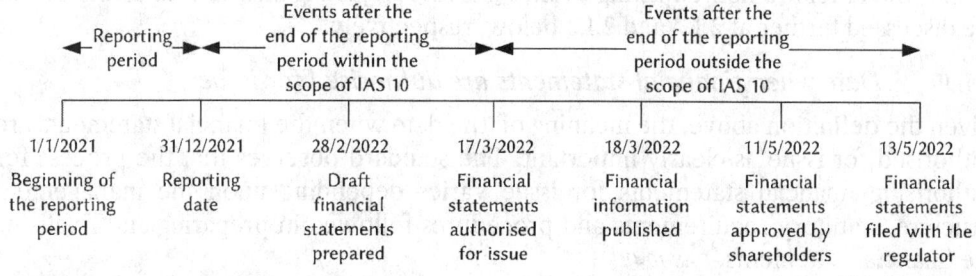

The financial statements of an entity present, among other things, its financial position at the end of the reporting period. Therefore, it is appropriate to adjust the financial statements for all events that offer greater clarity concerning the conditions that existed at the end of the reporting period, that occur prior to the date the financial statements are authorised for issue. The standard requires entities to adjust the amounts recognised in the financial statements for 'adjusting events' that provide evidence of conditions that existed at the end of the reporting period. *[IAS 10.3(a), 8]*. An entity does not recognise in the financial statements those events that relate to conditions that arose after the reporting period ('non-adjusting events'). However, if non-adjusting events are material (that is, non-disclosure of the event could reasonably be expected to influence decisions that the primary users of general purpose financial statements make on the basis of those financial statements), the standard requires certain disclosures about them. *[IAS 10.3(b), 10, 21]*.

One exception to the general rule of the standard for non-adjusting events is when the going concern basis becomes inappropriate. This is treated as an adjusting event. *[IAS 10.1, 14]*.

The requirements of IAS 10 and some practical issues resulting from these requirements are dealt with, respectively, at 2 and 3 below.

2 REQUIREMENTS OF IAS 10

2.1 Objective, scope and definitions

The objective of IAS 10 is to prescribe:

- when an entity should adjust its financial statements for events after the reporting period; and
- the disclosures that an entity should give about the date when the financial statements were authorised for issue and about events after the reporting period. *[IAS 10.1]*.

The standard does not permit an entity to prepare its financial statements on a going concern basis if events after the reporting period indicate that the going concern assumption is not appropriate. *[IAS 10.1]*. This requirement is discussed further at 2.2.2 below. The going concern basis is discussed in Chapter 3 at 4.1.2.

IAS 10 defines events after the reporting period as 'those events, favourable and unfavourable, that occur between the end of the reporting period and the date when the financial statements are authorised for issue'. *[IAS 10.3]*. This definition therefore includes events that provide additional evidence about conditions that existed at the end of the reporting period, as well as those that do not. The former are adjusting events, the latter are non-adjusting events. *[IAS 10.3]*. Adjusting and non-adjusting events are discussed further at 2.1.2 and 2.1.3 below, respectively.

2.1.1 Date when financial statements are authorised for issue

Given the definition above, the meaning of 'the date when the financial statements are authorised for issue' is clearly important. The standard observes that the process for authorising financial statements for issue varies depending upon the management structure, statutory requirements and procedures followed in preparing and finalising the financial statements. *[IAS 10.4]*.

The standard identifies two particular instances of the different meaning of 'authorised for issue' as follows:

(a) an entity may be required to submit its financial statements to its shareholders for approval after the financial statements have been issued. In such cases, the financial statements are authorised for issue on the date of issue, not the date when shareholders approve them; *[IAS 10.5]* and

(b) the management of an entity may be required to issue its financial statements to a supervisory board (made up solely of non-executives) for approval. Such financial statements are authorised for issue when management authorises them for issue to the supervisory board. *[IAS 10.6]*.

These two meanings are illustrated by the following two examples, which are based on the illustrative examples contained in IAS 10. *[IAS 10.5-6]*.

Example 38.1: Financial statements required to be approved by shareholders

The management of an entity completes draft financial statements for the year to 31 December 2021 on 28 February 2022. On 17 March 2022, the board of directors reviews the financial statements and authorises them for issue. The entity announces its profit and certain other financial information on 18 March 2022. The financial statements are made available to shareholders and others on 1 April 2022. The shareholders approve the financial statements at their annual meeting on 11 May 20221 and the approved financial statements are then filed with a regulatory body on 13 May 2022.

The financial statements are authorised for issue on 17 March 2022 (date of board authorisation for issue).

Example 38.2: Financial statements required to be approved by supervisory board

On 17 March 2022, the management of an entity authorises for issue to its supervisory board financial statements for the year ended 31 December 2021. The supervisory board consists solely of non-executives and may include representatives of employees and other outside interests. The supervisory board approves the financial statements on 25 March 2022. The financial statements are made available to shareholders and others on 1 April 2022. The shareholders approve the financial statements at their annual meeting on 11 May 2022 and the financial statements are filed with a regulatory body on 13 May 2022.

The financial statements are authorised for issue on 17 March 2022 (date of management authorisation for issue to the supervisory board).

An uncommon, but possible, situation that may occur is that the financial statements are changed after they are authorised for issue to the supervisory board. The following example illustrates such a situation.

Example 38.3: Financial statements required to be approved by supervisory board – changes are made by supervisory board

Same facts as in Example 38.2 above, except that the supervisory board reviews the financial statements on 25 March 2022 and proposes changes to certain note disclosures. The management of the entity incorporates the suggested changes and re-authorises those financial statements for issue to the supervisory board on 27 March 2022. The supervisory board then approves the financial statements on 30 March 2022.

The financial statements are authorised for issue on 27 March 2022 (date of management re-authorisation for issue to the supervisory board).

As governance structures vary by jurisdiction, entities may be allowed to organise their procedures differently and adjust the financial reporting process accordingly.

An example of a company which is required to submit its financial statements to its shareholders for approval is LafargeHolcim Ltd, as illustrated in the following extract:

> **Extract 38.1: LafargeHolcim Ltd (2019)**
>
> **Notes to the consolidated financial statements** [extract]
>
> **22.   Authorization of the financial statements for issuance**
>
> The consolidated financial statements were authorized for issuance by the Board of Directors of LafargeHolcim Ltd on 26 February 2020 and are subject to shareholder approval at the Annual General Meeting of shareholders scheduled for 12 May 2020.

As discussed above, an entity may be required to issue its financial statements to a supervisory board (made up solely of non-executives) for approval. For such instances, the phrase 'made up solely of non-executives' is not defined by the standard, although it contemplates that a supervisory board may include representatives of employees and other outside interests. However, it seems to draw a distinction between those responsible for the executive management of an entity (and the preparation of its financial statements) and those in a position of high-level oversight (including reviewing and approving the financial statements). This situation seems to describe the typical two-tier board system seen in some jurisdictions. An example of a company with this structure is Bayer AG, as illustrated in the following extract.

Extract 38.2: Bayer Aktiengesellschaft (2019)

Combined Management Report [extract]

4.   Corporate Governance Report [extract]

4.1   Declaration by Corporate Management Pursuant to Sections 289f and 315d of the German Commercial Code [extract]

Supervisory Board [extract]

Composition and objectives (diversity concept and expertise profile) [extract]

Under the German Codetermination Act, half of the Supervisory Board's 20 members are elected by the stockholders, and half by the company's employees.

[...]

Procedure and committees

The role of the Supervisory Board is to oversee and advise the Board of Management. The Supervisory Board is directly involved in decisions on matters of fundamental importance to the company, regularly conferring with the Board of Management on the company's strategic alignment and the implementation status of the business strategy. The Report of the Supervisory Board in this Annual Report provides details about the work of the Supervisory Board and its committees. In 2019, the Supervisory Board established a special committee to address the glyphosate litigations.

[...]

Report of the Supervisory Board [extract]

Financial statements and audits [extract]

We have approved the financial statements of Bayer AG and the consolidated financial statements of the Bayer Group prepared by the Board of Management. The financial statements of Bayer AG are thus confirmed.

2.1.1.A   Impact of preliminary reporting

The example below illustrates when the entity releases preliminary information, but not complete financial statements, before the date of the authorisation for issue.

Example 38.4:   Release of financial information before date of authorisation for issue

The management of an entity completes the primary financial statements for the year to 31 December 2021 on 21 January 2022, but has not yet completed the explanatory notes. On 26 January 2022, the board of directors (which includes management and non-executives) reviews the primary financial statements and authorises them for public media release. The entity announces its profit and certain other financial information on 28 January 2022. On 11 February 2022, management issues the financial statements (with full explanatory notes) to the board of directors, which approves the financial statements for filing on 18 February 2022. The entity files the financial statements with a regulatory body on 21 February 2022.

The financial statements are authorised for issue on 18 February 2022 (date the board of directors, approves the financial statements for filing).

Example 38.4 illustrates that events after the reporting period include all events up to the date when the financial statements are authorised for issue, even if those events occur after the public announcement of profit or of other selected financial information. *[IAS 10.7]*. Accordingly, the information in the financial statements might differ from the equivalent information in a preliminary announcement.

2.1.1.B   Re-issuing (dual dating) financial statements

IFRSs do not address whether and how an entity may amend its financial statements after they have been authorised for issue. Generally, such matters are dealt with in local laws or regulations.

If an entity re-issues financial statements (whether to correct an error or to include events that occurred after the financial statements were originally authorised for issue), there is a new date of authorisation for issue. The financial statements should then appropriately reflect all adjusting events, by updating the amounts recognised in the financial statements, and non-adjusting events, through additional disclosure, up to the new date of authorisation for issue.

However, in certain circumstances, the re-issuing of previously issued financial statements is required by local regulators particularly for inclusion in public offering and similar documents. Consequently, in November 2012, the Interpretations Committee was asked to clarify the accounting implications of applying IAS 10 when previously issued financial statements are re-issued in connection with an offering document.[1]

In May 2013, the Interpretations Committee responded that:

- the scope of IAS 10 is the accounting for, and disclosure of, events after the reporting period and that the objective of this Standard is to prescribe:
  (a)   when an entity should adjust its financial statements for events after the reporting period; and
  (b)   the disclosures that an entity should give about the date when the financial statements were authorised for issue and about events after the reporting period;
- financial statements prepared in accordance with IAS 10 should reflect all adjusting and non-adjusting events up to the date that the financial statements were authorised for issue; and
- IAS 10 does not address the presentation of re-issued financial statements in an offering document when the originally issued financial statements have not been withdrawn, but the re-issued financial statements are provided either as supplementary information or a re-presentation of the original financial statements in an offering document in accordance with regulatory requirements.

The Interpretations Committee decided not to add this issue to its agenda on the basis of the above and because the issue arises in multiple jurisdictions, each with particular securities laws and regulations which may dictate the form for re-presentations of financial statements.[2]

Accordingly, depending on the particular regulatory requirements in a given jurisdiction, there may be variations in how re-issued financial statements are presented.

2.1.2 Adjusting events

Adjusting events are 'those that provide evidence of conditions that existed at the end of the reporting period.' *[IAS 10.3(a)]*.

Examples of adjusting events are as follows:

(a) the settlement after the reporting period of a court case that confirms that the entity had a present obligation at the end of the reporting period. In this situation, an entity adjusts any previously recognised provision related to this court case in accordance with IAS 37 – *Provisions, Contingent Liabilities and Contingent Assets* – or recognises a new provision. Mere disclosure of a contingent liability is not sufficient because the settlement provides additional evidence of conditions that existed at the end of the reporting period that would give rise to a provision in accordance with IAS 37 (see Chapter 26 at 3.1.1 and 3.2.1);

(b) the receipt of information after the reporting period indicating that an asset was impaired at the end of the reporting period, or that the amount of a previously recognised impairment loss for that asset needs to be adjusted. For example:

   (i) the bankruptcy of a customer that occurs after the reporting period usually confirms that the customer was credit-impaired at the end of the reporting period (this is discussed further at 3.3 below); and

   (ii) the sale of inventories after the reporting period may give evidence about their net realisable value at the end of the reporting period;

(c) the determination after the reporting period of the cost of assets purchased, or the proceeds from assets sold, before the end of the reporting period;

(d) the determination after the reporting period of the amount of profit-sharing or bonus payments, if the entity had a present legal or constructive obligation at the end of the reporting period to make such payments as a result of events before that date (see Chapter 35 at 12.3); and

(e) the discovery of fraud or errors that show that the financial statements are incorrect (see 3.5 below). *[IAS 10.9]*.

In addition, IFRIC 23 – *Uncertainty over Income Tax Treatments* – requires entities to apply IAS 10 to determine whether changes in facts and circumstances or new information after the reporting period gives rise to an adjusting or non-adjusting event for reassessing a judgement or estimate of an uncertain tax position. *[IFRIC 23.14]*. An event would be considered adjusting if the change in facts and circumstances or new information after the reporting period provided evidence of conditions that existed at the end of the reporting period (see 3.6 below).

IAS 33 – *Earnings per Share* – is another standard that requires an adjustment for certain transactions after the reporting period. IAS 33 requires an adjustment to earnings per share for certain share transactions after the reporting period (such as bonus issues, share splits or reverse share splits (share consolidations) as discussed in

Chapter 37 at 4.3 and 4.5) even though the transactions themselves are non-adjusting events (see 2.1.3 below). *[IAS 10.22(f)]*.

2.1.3 Non-adjusting events

The standard states that non-adjusting events are 'those that are indicative of conditions that arose after the reporting period'. *[IAS 10.3(b)]*.

Examples of non-adjusting events after the reporting period are as follows:

(a) a major business combination (IFRS 3 – *Business Combinations* – requires specific disclosures in such cases, see Chapter 9 at 16.1.2) or disposing of a major subsidiary;

(b) announcing a plan to discontinue an operation;

(c) major purchases of assets, classification of assets as held for sale in accordance with IFRS 5 – *Non-current Assets Held for Sale and Discontinued Operations*, other disposals of assets, or expropriation of major assets by government (see Chapter 4 at 5.1 for certain disclosures that are required to be made);

(d) the destruction of a major production plant by a fire;

(e) announcing, or commencing the implementation of, a major restructuring (discussed in Chapter 26 at 6.1.2);

(f) major ordinary share transactions and potential ordinary share transactions (although as noted at 2.1.2 above, some transactions in ordinary shares are adjusting events for the purposes of computing earnings per share);

(g) abnormally large changes in asset prices or foreign exchange rates;[3]

(h) changes in tax rates or the enactment or announcement of tax laws that significantly affect current and deferred tax assets and liabilities (discussed in Chapter 33 at 5.1.3 and 8.1.2);

(i) entry into significant commitments or contingent liabilities, for example, by issuing significant guarantees;

(j) start of major litigation arising solely out of events that occurred after the reporting period;

(k) a decline in fair value of investments;

(l) a declaration of dividends to holders of equity instruments (as defined in IAS 32 – *Financial Instruments: Presentation* – discussed in Chapter 47 at 8);

(m) a subsequent rectification of a breach in a long debt term covenant; and

(n) a contingent asset becoming virtually certain after the end of the reporting period (discussed in Chapter 26 at 3.2.2). *[IAS 10.11, 12, 22, IAS 1.76, IAS 37.35]*.

The reference in (a) and (c) above to asset disposals as examples of non-adjusting events is not quite the whole story as these may indicate an impairment of assets, which may be an adjusting event. In addition, (b) and (e) above regarding announcements of plans to discontinue an operation or to restructure a business, respectively, may also lead to an impairment charge (see Chapter 20 at 5.1).

IFRS 5 makes it clear that the held for sale criteria must be met at the reporting date for a non-current asset (or disposal group) to be classified as held for sale in those financial statements. However, if those criteria are met after the reporting date but before the authorisation of the financial statements for issue, IFRS 5 requires certain additional disclosures (see Chapter 4 at 2.1.2 and 5.1). *[IFRS 5.12]*.

Information provided under (i) above, will be in addition to the disclosure of commitments that exist at the reporting date which other standards require. For example, IAS 16 – *Property, Plant and Equipment* – and IAS 38 – *Intangible Assets* – require commitments for the acquisition of property, plant and equipment and intangible assets to be disclosed (see Chapter 18 at 8.1 and Chapter 17 at 10.1). *[IAS 16.74(c), IAS 38.122(e)]*. IFRS 16 – *Leases* – requires a lessee to disclose the amount of its lease commitments for short-term leases if the portfolio of short-term leases to which it is committed at the end of the reporting period is dissimilar to the portfolio of short-term leases for which current period short-term lease expense disclosure was provided (see Chapter 23 at 5.8.2). *[IFRS 16.55]*.

For declines in fair value of investments, as in (k) above, the standard notes that the decline in fair value does not normally relate to the condition of the investments at the end of the reporting period, but reflects circumstances that arose subsequently. Therefore, in those circumstances the amounts recognised in financial statements for the investments are not adjusted. Similarly, the standard states that an entity does not update the amounts disclosed for the investments as at the end of the reporting period, although it may need to give additional disclosure, if material, as discussed at 2.3 below. *[IAS 10.11]*.

However, the assertion that a decline in fair value of investments does not normally relate to conditions at the end of the reporting period is similar wording to that used for bankruptcy and the sale of inventories (see 2.1.2(b) above). Therefore, it requires an assessment of the circumstances in order to determine which conditions actually existed at the end of the reporting period – although this can be difficult in practice, particularly when fraud is involved (see 3.5 below).

In addition to the examples of non-adjusting events the standard provides, IFRIC 23 requires entities to apply IAS 10 to determine whether changes in facts and circumstances or new information after the reporting period gives rise to an adjusting or non-adjusting event when reassessing a judgement or estimate of an uncertain tax position. *[IFRIC 23.14]*. An event would only be considered non-adjusting if the change in facts and circumstances or new information after the reporting period was indicative of conditions that arose after the reporting period (see 3.6 below).

The subsequent rectification of a breach in a long debt term covenant is not an adjusting event and therefore does not change the classification of the liability in the statement of financial position from current to non-current (see 2.3.2 below). *[IAS 1.76]*.

Another example of a non-adjusting event not mentioned by IAS 10 is where a contingent asset becomes virtually certain after the end of the reporting period. If the inflow of economic benefits from a contingent asset has become virtually certain, IAS 37 indicates that the asset and the related income should be recognised in the period in which the change occurs. The requirement to recognise the effect of changing circumstances in the period in which the change occurs extends to the analysis of information available after the end of the reporting period but before the date when the financial statements are authorised for issue. In contrast to contingent liabilities, no adjustment should be made to reflect the subsequent settlement of a legal claim in favour of the entity since the period in which the change occurs is after the end of the reporting period. An asset could only be recognised if, at the end of the reporting period, the entity could show that it was virtually certain that its claim would succeed (see Chapter 26 at 3.2.2). *[IAS 37.35]*.

2.1.3.A Dividend declaration

In respect of dividend declarations, as in (l) at 2.1.3 above, dividends are only recognised as a liability if declared on or by the end of the reporting period. If an entity declares dividends to holders of equity instruments (as defined in IAS 32) after the reporting period, the entity shall not recognise those dividends as a liability at the end of the reporting period. *[IAS 10.13]*. While an entity may have a past practice of paying dividends, such dividends are not declared and, therefore, not recognised as an obligation. *[IAS 10.BC4]*.

As a consequential amendment to IAS 10, the definition of 'declared' in this context was moved to IFRIC 17 – *Distributions of Non-cash Assets to Owners*. IFRIC 17 did not change the principle regarding the appropriate timing for the recognition of dividends payable. *[IFRIC 17.BC18-20]*. It states that an entity recognises a liability to pay a dividend when the dividend is appropriately authorised and is no longer at the discretion of the entity, which is the date:

- when declaration of the dividend, e.g. by management or the board of directors, is approved by the relevant authority, e.g. the shareholders, if the jurisdiction requires such approval; or
- when the dividend is declared, e.g. by management or the board of directors, if the jurisdiction does not require further approval. *[IFRIC 17.10]*.

In many jurisdictions, the directors may keep discretion to cancel an interim dividend until such time as it is paid. In this case, the interim dividend is not declared (within the meaning described above), and is, therefore, not recognised until paid. Final dividends proposed by directors, in many jurisdictions, are only binding when approved by shareholders in general meeting or by the members passing a written resolution. Therefore, such a final dividend is only recognised as a liability when declared, i.e. approved by the shareholders at the annual general meeting or through the passing of a resolution by the members of an entity.

IAS 10 contains a reminder that an entity discloses dividends, both proposed and declared after the reporting period but before the financial statements are authorised for issue, in the notes to the financial statements in accordance with IAS 1 – *Presentation of Financial Statements* (see Chapter 3 at 5.5). *[IAS 1.137, IAS 10.13]*.

Similar issues arise regarding the declaration of dividends by subsidiaries, associates and other equity investments. Although IAS 10 does not specifically address such items, IFRS 9 – *Financial Instruments* – requires a shareholder to recognise dividends when the shareholder's right to receive payment is established, it is probable that the economic benefits associated with the dividend will flow to the shareholder and the dividend can be measured reliably (see Chapter 50 at 2.5). *[IFRS 9.5.7.1A]*.

Similarly, IAS 27 – *Separate Financial Statements* – also contains this general principle in recognising in an entity's separate financial statements those dividends received from subsidiaries, joint ventures or associates when its right to receive the dividend is established (see Chapter 8 at 2.4.1). *[IAS 27.12]*. Accordingly, a shareholder does not recognise such dividend income until the period in which the dividend is declared.

2.2 The treatment of adjusting events

2.2.1 Events requiring adjustment to the amounts recognised, or disclosures, in the financial statements

IAS 10 requires that the amounts recognised in the financial statements be adjusted to take account of an adjusting event. *[IAS 10.8]*.

The standard also notes that an entity may receive information after the reporting period about conditions existing at the end of the reporting period relating to disclosures made in the financial statements but not affecting the amounts recognised in them. *[IAS 10.20]*. In such cases, the standard requires the entity to update the disclosures that relate to those conditions for the new information. *[IAS 10.19]*.

For example, evidence may become available after the reporting period about a contingent liability that existed at the end of the reporting period. In addition to considering whether to recognise or change a provision under IAS 37, IAS 10 requires an entity to update its disclosures about the contingent liability for that evidence. *[IAS 10.20]*.

2.2.2 Events indicating that the going concern basis is not appropriate

If management determines after the reporting period (but before the financial statements are authorised for issue) either that it intends to liquidate the entity or to cease trading, or that it has no realistic alternative but to do so, the financial statements should not be prepared on the going concern basis. *[IAS 10.14]*.

Deterioration in operating results and financial position after the reporting period may indicate a need to consider whether the going concern assumption is still appropriate. If the going concern assumption is no longer appropriate, the standard states that the effect is so pervasive that it results in a fundamental change in the basis of accounting, rather than an adjustment to the amounts recognised within the original basis of accounting. *[IAS 10.15]*. As discussed in Chapter 3 at 4.1.2, IFRS contains no guidance on this 'fundamental change in the basis of accounting'. Accordingly, entities will need to consider carefully their individual circumstances to arrive at an appropriate basis.

The standard also contains a reminder of the specific disclosure requirements under IAS 1:
(a) when the financial statements are not prepared on a going concern basis, that fact should be disclosed, together with the basis on which the financial statements have been prepared and the reason why the entity is not regarded as a going concern; or
(b) when management is aware of material uncertainties related to events or conditions that may cast significant doubt upon the entity's ability to continue as a going concern, disclosure of those uncertainties should be made. *[IAS 10.16(a), 16(b), IAS 1.25].*

While IFRSs are generally written from the perspective that an entity is a going concern, they are also applicable when another basis of accounting is used to prepare financial statements. Various IFRSs acknowledge that financial statements may be prepared on either a going concern basis or an alternative basis of accounting. *[IAS 1.25, IAS 10.14, CF 3.9].* Such IFRSs do not specifically exclude the application of IFRS when an alternative basis of accounting is used. As a result, financial statements prepared on a 'non-going concern' basis of accounting may be described as complying with IFRS as long as that other basis of preparation is sufficiently described in accordance with paragraph 25 of IAS 1. This is further discussed in Chapter 3 at 4.1.2.

Regarding the requirement in (b) above, the events or conditions requiring disclosure may arise after the reporting period. *[IAS 10.16(b)].*

2.3 The treatment of non-adjusting events

IAS 10 prohibits the adjustment of amounts recognised in financial statements to reflect non-adjusting events. *[IAS 10.10].* It indicates that if non-adjusting events are material, non-disclosure could reasonably be expected to influence decisions that the primary users of general purpose financial statements make on the basis of those financial statements. Accordingly, an entity should disclose the following for each material category of non-adjusting event:

(a) the nature of the event; and
(b) an estimate of its financial effect, or a statement that such an estimate cannot be made. *[IAS 10.21].*

To illustrate how these requirements have been applied in practice, two examples of disclosure for certain types of non-adjusting events are given below.

Possibly the non-adjusting events that appear most regularly in financial statements are the acquisition/disposal of a non-current asset, such as an investment in a subsidiary or a business, subsequent to the end of the reporting period.

Extract 38.3 contains an example of the disclosures required for 2.1.3(a) above related to a business combination:

Extract 38.3: Cranswick plc (2016)

Notes to the accounts [extract]

30. Events after the balance sheet date

On 8 April 2016, the Group acquired 100 per cent of the issued share capital of CCL Holdings Limited and its wholly owned subsidiary Crown Chicken Limited ('Crown') for net cash consideration of £39.3 million. The principal activities of Crown Chicken Limited are the breeding, rearing and processing of fresh chicken, as well as the milling of grain for the production of animal feed. The acquisition provides the Group with a fully integrated supply chain for its growing poultry business.

Fair values of the net assets at the date of acquisition were as follows:

	Provisional fair value £'000
Net assets acquired:	
Property, plant and equipment	17,501
Biological assets	4,805
Inventories	1,865
Trade and other receivables	9,845
Bank and cash balances	3,946
Trade and other payables	(7,900)
Corporation tax liability	(541)
Deferred tax liability	(1,815)
Finance lease obligations	(370)
	27,336
Goodwill arising on acquisition	15,878
Total consideration	43,214
Satisfied by:	
Cash	43,214
Net cash outflow arising on acquisition:	
Cash consideration paid	43,214
Cash and cash equivalents acquired	(3,946)
	39,268

The fair values on acquisition are provisional due to the timing of the transaction and will be finalised within twelve months of the acquisition date.

Included in the £15,878,000 of goodwill recognised above, are certain intangible assets that cannot be individually separated from the acquiree and reliably measured due to their nature. These items include the expected value of synergies and an assembled workforce and the strategic benefits of vertical integration including security of supply.

Transaction costs in relation to the acquisition are expected to total £0.4 million, expensed within administrative expenses.

All of the trade receivables acquired are expected to be collected in full.

Extract 38.4 contains an example of the disclosure of major ordinary share transactions after the reporting period as described at 2.1.3(f) above:

> **Extract 38.4: PGS ASA (2019)**
> Notes [extract]
> **31. SUBSEQUENT EVENTS** [extract]
> On February 13, 2020, an extraordinary general meeting of PGS ASA approved to increase the share capital in the Company by issuing new shares following a private placement of equity.

It is important to note that the list of examples of non-adjusting events in IAS 10, and summarised at 2.1.3 above, is not an exhaustive one; IAS 10 requires disclosure of any material non-adjusting event.

2.3.1 Declaration to distribute non-cash assets to owners

When an entity declares a dividend to distribute a *non-cash asset* to owners after the end of a reporting period but before the financial statements are authorised for issue, IFRIC 17 requires an entity to disclose: *[IFRIC 17.17]*

(a) the nature of the asset to be distributed;
(b) the carrying amount of the asset to be distributed as of the end of the reporting period; and
(c) the fair value of the asset to be distributed as of the end of the reporting period, if it is different from its carrying amount, and the following information about the method(s) used to measure that fair value:
   (i) the level of the fair value hierarchy within which the fair value measurement is categorised (Level 1, 2 or 3); *[IFRS 13.93(b)]*
   (ii) for fair value measurement categorised within Level 2 and Level 3 of the fair value hierarchy, a description of the valuation technique(s) and the inputs used in the fair value measurement. If there has been a change in valuation technique (e.g. changing from a market approach to an income approach or the use of an additional valuation technique), the entity should disclose that change and the reason(s) for making it. For fair value measurement categorised within Level 3 of the fair value hierarchy, quantitative information about the significant unobservable inputs used in the fair value measurement should be provided. An entity is not required to create quantitative information to comply with this disclosure requirement if quantitative unobservable inputs are not developed by the entity when measuring fair value (e.g. when an entity uses prices from prior transactions or third-party pricing information without adjustment). However, when providing this disclosure the quantitative unobservable inputs that are significant to the fair value measurement and are reasonably available to the entity should not be ignored; *[IFRS 13.93(d)]*
   (iii) for fair value measurement categorised within Level 3 of the fair value hierarchy, a description of the valuation processes used by the entity (including, for example, how an entity decides its valuation policies and

procedures and analyses changes in fair value measurements from period to period); [IFRS 13.93(g)] and

(iv) if the highest and best use of the non-financial asset differs from its current use, an entity should disclose that fact and why the non-financial asset is being used in a manner that differs from its highest and best use. [IFRS 13.93(i)].

In the case of (c) above, any quantitative disclosures are required to be presented in a tabular format, unless another format is more appropriate. [IFRS 13.99]. Fair value measurement is further discussed in Chapter 14.

2.3.2 Breach of a long-term loan covenant and its subsequent rectification

When an entity breaches a provision[4] of a long-term loan arrangement on or before the end of the reporting period with the effect that the liability becomes payable on demand, it classifies the liability as current in its statement of financial position (see Chapter 3 at 3.1.4.A and 3.1.4.B). [IAS 1.74]. This may also give rise to going concern uncertainties (see 2.2.2 above).

It is not uncommon that such covenant breaches are subsequently rectified; however, a subsequent rectification is not an adjusting event and therefore does not change the classification of the liability in the statement of financial position from current to non-current.

IAS 1 requires disclosure of the following[5] remedial arrangements if such events occur between the end of the reporting period and the date the financial statements are authorised for issue:

- refinancing on a long-term basis;
- rectification of a breach of a long-term loan arrangement; and
- the granting by the lender of a period of grace to rectify a breach of a long-term loan arrangement ending at least twelve months after the reporting period (see Chapter 3 at 5.5). [IAS 1.76].

2.4 Other disclosure requirements

The disclosures required in respect of non-adjusting events are discussed at 2.3 above. As IAS 10 only requires consideration to be given to events that occur up to the date when the financial statements are authorised for issue, it is important for users to know that date, since the financial statements do not reflect events after that date. [IAS 10.18]. Accordingly, IAS 10 requires disclosure of the date the financial statements were authorised for issue. Furthermore, it requires: disclosure of who authorised the financial statements for issue and, if the owners of the entity or others have the power to amend them after issue, disclosure of that fact. [IAS 10.17]. In practice, this information can be presented in a number of ways:

(a) on the face of a primary statement (for example, entities that are required to have the statement of financial position signed could include the information at that point);

(b) in the note dealing with other IAS 10 disclosures or another note (such as the summary of significant accounting policies); or

(c) in a separate statement such as a statement of directors' responsibilities for the financial statements (that is, outside of the financial statements as permitted in certain jurisdictions).

Strictly speaking, this information is required to be presented within the financial statements. So, if (c) above were chosen, either the whole report would need to be part of the financial statements or the information could be incorporated into them by way of a cross-reference.

In addition to the IAS 10 disclosure requirements, other standards may require disclosures to be provided about future events, for example, IAS 8 – *Accounting Policies, Changes in Accounting Estimates and Errors* – requires disclosure of the expected impact of new standards that are issued but are not yet effective at the reporting date (see Chapter 3 at 5.1.2.C). *[IAS 8.30]*.

3 PRACTICAL ISSUES

The standard alludes to practical issues such as those discussed below. It states that a decline in fair value of investments after the reporting period does not normally relate to conditions at the end of the reporting period and therefore would be a non-adjusting event (see 2.1.3 above). At the same time, the standard asserts that the bankruptcy of a customer that occurs after the reporting period would usually be an adjusting event (see 2.1.2 above). Judgement of the facts and circumstances is required to determine whether an event that occurs after the reporting period provides evidence about a condition that existed at the end of the reporting period, or whether the condition arose subsequent to the reporting period.

3.1 Valuation of inventory

The sale of inventories after the reporting period is normally a good indicator of their net realisable value (NRV) at that date. IAS 10 states that such sales 'may give evidence about their net realisable value at the end of the reporting period'. *[IAS 10.9(b)(ii)]*. However, in some cases, NRV decreases because of conditions that did not exist at the end of the reporting period.

Therefore, the problem is determining why NRV decreased. Did it decrease because of circumstances that existed at the end of the reporting period, which subsequently became known, or did it decrease because of circumstances that arose subsequently? A decrease in price is merely a response to changing conditions so it is important to assess the reasons for, and timing of, these changes.

Some examples of changing conditions are as follows:

(a) Price reductions caused by a sudden increase in cheap imports

Whilst it is arguable that the 'dumping' of cheap imports after the reporting period is a condition that arises subsequent to that date, it is more likely that this is a reaction to a condition that already existed such as overproduction in other parts of the world. Thus, it might be more appropriate in such a situation to adjust the value of inventories based on its subsequent NRV.

(b) Price reductions caused by increased competition

The reasons for price reductions and increased competition do not generally arise overnight but normally occur over a period. For example, a competitor may have built up a competitive advantage by investing in machinery that is more efficient. In these circumstances, it is appropriate for an entity to adjust the valuation of its inventories because its own investment in production machinery is inferior to its competitor's and this situation existed at the end of the reporting period.

(c) Price reductions caused by the introduction of an improved competitive product

It is unlikely that a competitor developed and introduced an improved product overnight. Therefore, it is correct to adjust the valuation of inventories held at the end of the reporting period to their NRV after that introduction because the entity's failure to maintain its competitive position in relation to product improvements existed at the end of the reporting period.

Competitive pressures that caused a decrease in NRV after the reporting period are generally additional evidence of conditions that developed over a period and existed at the end of the reporting period. Consequently, their effects normally require adjustment in the financial statements.

However, for certain types of inventory, there is clear evidence of a price at the end of the reporting period and it is inappropriate to adjust the price of that inventory to reflect a subsequent decline. An example is inventories for which there is a price on an appropriate commodities market. In addition, inventory may be physically damaged or destroyed after the reporting period (e.g. by fire, flood, or other disaster). In these cases, the entity does not adjust the financial statements. However, the entity may be required to disclose the subsequent decline in NRV of the inventories if the impact is material (see 2.3 above).

3.2 Percentage of completion estimates

Events after the reporting period frequently give evidence about the profitability of revenue from contracts with customers, where revenue is measured over time, that are in progress at the end of the reporting period.

IFRS 15 – *Revenue from Contracts with Customers* – requires an assessment to be made of the progress towards complete satisfaction of performance obligations satisfied over time (see Chapter 30 at 3). *[IFRS 15.40]*. In such an assessment, consideration should be given to events that occur after the reporting period and a determination should be made as to whether they are adjusting or non-adjusting events for which the financial effect is included in the method used to measure progress over time or the percentage of completion method.

3.3 Insolvency of a debtor and IFRS 9 expected credit losses

The insolvency of a debtor or inability to pay debts usually builds up over a period. Consequently, if a debtor has an amount outstanding at the end of the reporting period and this amount is written off because of information received after the reporting period, the event is normally adjusting. IAS 10 states that the bankruptcy of a customer that occurs after the reporting period usually confirms that the customer was credit-impaired (Stage 3 under the IFRS 9 general approach – refer to Chapter 51 at 3.1) at the end of the reporting period. *[IAS 10.9(b)(i)]*. If, however, there is evidence to show that the insolvency of the debtor resulted solely from an event occurring after the reporting period, then the event is a non-adjusting event. If the impact is material, the entity will be required to disclose the nature and effect of the debtor's default (see 2.3 above).

In April 2015 the IFRS Transition Resource Group for Impairment of Financial Instruments (ITG) discussed whether, and if so how, to incorporate events and forecasts that occur between the reporting date and the date the financial statements are authorised for issue, when applying the impairment requirements of IFRS 9 at the reporting date. The ITG noted that if new information becomes available between the reporting date and the date of signing the financial statements, an entity needs to apply judgement, based on the specific facts and circumstances, to determine whether it is an adjusting or non-adjusting event in accordance with IAS 10. This is further discussed in Chapter 51 at 5.9.4.

3.4 Valuation of investment property at fair value and tenant insolvency

The fair value of investment property reflects, among other things, the quality of tenants' covenants and the expected future rental income from the property. If a tenant ceases to be able to meet its lease obligations due to insolvency after the reporting period, an entity considers how this event is reflected in the financial statements at the end of the reporting period.

IAS 40 – *Investment Property* – requires the fair value of investment property, when measured in accordance with IFRS 13 – *Fair Value Measurement*, to reflect, among other things, rental income from current leases and other assumptions that market participants would use when pricing investment property under current market conditions. *[IAS 40.40]*. In addition, professional valuations generally reference the state of the market at the date of valuation without the use of hindsight. Consequently, the insolvency of a tenant is not normally an adjusting event to the fair value of the investment property because the investment property still holds value in the market. However, it would generally be indicative of an adjusting event for any rent receivable from that tenant. This conclusion is consistent with the treatment of investment property measured using the alternative cost model.

IAS 10 states that a decline in fair value of investments after the reporting period and before the date the financial statements are authorised for issue is a non-adjusting event, as the decline does not normally relate to a condition at the end of the reporting period (see 2.1.3 above). This decline in fair value, however, may be required to be disclosed if material (see 2.3 above). *[IAS 10.11]*.

3.5 Discovery of fraud after the reporting period

When fraud is discovered after the reporting date the implications on the financial statements should be considered. *[IAS 10.9(e)]*. In particular, it should be determined whether the fraud is indicative of a prior period error, and that financial information should be restated, or merely a change in estimate requiring prospective adjustment. Application of the IAS 8 definitions of a 'prior period error' and a 'change in accounting estimate' (see Chapter 3 at 4.5 and 4.6) in the case of a fraud requires the exercise of judgement. The facts and circumstances are evaluated to determine if the discovery of the fraud resulted from a previous failure to use, or misuse of, reliable information; or from new information. If the fraud meets the definition of a prior period error, the fraud would be an adjusting event as it relates to conditions that existed at the end of the reporting period. However, if the fraud meets the definition of a change in estimate, the facts and circumstances are evaluated to determine if the discovery of the fraud provides evidence of circumstances that existed at the end of the reporting period (i.e. an adjusting event) or circumstances that arose after that date (i.e. a non-adjusting event). Determining this is a complex task and requires judgement and careful consideration of the specifics to each case.

3.6 Changes to estimates of uncertain tax treatments

IFRIC 23 addresses how to reflect uncertainty in accounting for income taxes. It requires an entity to reassess any judgement or estimate relating to an uncertain tax treatment if the facts and circumstances on which the judgement or estimate was based change, or as a result of new information that affects the judgement or estimate. In cases where the change in facts and circumstances or new information occurs after the reporting period, the Interpretation requires an entity to apply IAS 10 to determine whether the change gives rise to an adjusting or non-adjusting event, as set out above at 2.1.2 and 2.1.3. *[IFRIC 23.13, 14].*

Examples of changes in facts and circumstances or new information that could result in the reassessment of a judgement or estimate required by IFRIC 23 include, but are not limited to, the following:

(a) examinations or actions by a taxation authority. For example:
 (i) agreement or disagreement by the taxation authority with the tax treatment or a similar tax treatment used by the entity;
 (ii) information that the taxation authority has agreed or disagreed with a similar tax treatment used by another entity; and
 (iii) information about the amount received or paid to settle a similar tax treatment;
(b) changes in rules established by a taxation authority; and
(c) the expiry of a taxation authority's right to examine or re-examine a tax treatment. *[IFRIC 23.A2].*

A change in rules established by a taxation authority after the reporting period constitutes a non-adjusting event. *[IAS 10.22(h)].* An entity should apply IAS 10 to determine whether any other change that occurs after a reporting period is an adjusting or non-adjusting event. The requirements of IFRIC 23 are further discussed in Chapter 33 at 9.

References

1 *IFRIC Update*, November 2012.
2 *IFRIC Update*, May 2013.
3 Abnormally large changes in exchange rates are not, in our experience, a common occurrence. An example of disclosure regarding abnormally large changes in foreign exchange rates after the reporting period can be found in the 2014 annual report of UBS AG.
4 Effective for financial periods beginning on or after 1 January 2023 (early application is permitted), the word 'provision' is replaced by 'condition'. [IAS 1(January 2023).74] (see Chapter 3 at 3.1.4.B).
5 After the amendments to IAS 1 issued in January 2020, the list of events in IAS 1.76 that require disclosure under IAS 10 now includes 'settlement of a liability classified as non-current'. [IAS 1(January 2023).76].

Chapter 39 Related party disclosures

1 INTRODUCTION 3097
  1.1 The related party issue 3097
  1.2 Possible solutions 3097
    1.2.1 Remeasurement of related party transactions at fair values 3097
2 REQUIREMENTS OF IAS 24 3098
  2.1 Objective and scope 3098
    2.1.1 Objective 3098
    2.1.2 Scope 3098
  2.2 Identification of a related party and related party transactions 3099
    2.2.1 Persons or close members of a person's family that are related parties 3100
      2.2.1.A Control 3102
      2.2.1.B Joint control 3102
      2.2.1.C Significant influence 3102
      2.2.1.D Key management personnel 3103
    2.2.2 Entities that are members of the same group 3104
    2.2.3 Entities that are associates or joint ventures 3105
      2.2.3.A Joint operations 3106
    2.2.4 Entities that are joint ventures of the same third party 3107
    2.2.5 Entities that are joint ventures of a third party and associates of the same third entity 3107
    2.2.6 Post-employment benefit plans 3108
    2.2.7 Entities under control or joint control of certain persons or close members of their family 3108
    2.2.8 Entities under significant influence of certain persons or close members of their family 3109
    2.2.9 Entities, or any member of the group of which they are a part, that provide key management personnel services 3110
    2.2.10 Government-related entities 3110

2.3	Parties that are not related parties		3111
2.4	Disclosure of controlling relationships		3112
2.5	Disclosable transactions		3114
	2.5.1	Materiality	3115
2.6	Disclosure of key management personnel compensation		3116
	2.6.1	Compensation	3116
	2.6.2	Short-term employee benefits	3117
	2.6.3	Post-employment benefits	3118
	2.6.4	Other long-term benefits	3118
	2.6.5	Termination benefits	3119
	2.6.6	Share-based payment transactions	3119
	2.6.7	Reporting entity part of a group	3119
	2.6.8	Key management personnel compensated by other entities	3120
	2.6.9	Illustrative disclosure of key management personnel compensation	3120
2.7	Disclosure of other related party transactions, including commitments		3120
	2.7.1	Related party transactions requiring disclosure	3120
		2.7.1.A Aggregation of items of a similar nature	3122
		2.7.1.B Commitments	3122
	2.7.2	Disclosures required for related party transactions, including commitments	3123
2.8	Disclosure of expense incurred with management entity		3127
2.9	Disclosures with government-related entities		3127

List of examples

Example 39.1:	Person as investor	3101
Example 39.2:	Close members of the family holding investments	3102
Example 39.3:	Entities that are members of the same group	3104
Example 39.4:	Associates of the reporting entity's group that are related parties	3106
Example 39.5:	Entities that are joint ventures of the same third party	3107
Example 39.6:	Entities that are joint ventures and associates of the same third entity	3108
Example 39.7:	Persons who control an entity and are a member of the key management personnel of another entity	3109
Example 39.8:	Entities that provide key management personnel services to a reporting entity	3110

Example 39.9:	Disclosure of parent, ultimate parent and ultimate controlling party	3113
Example 39.10:	Application of the disclosure exemption for government-related entities	3128
Example 39.11:	Individually significant transaction carried out on non-market terms	3130
Example 39.12:	Individually significant transaction because of size of transaction	3130
Example 39.13:	Collectively significant transactions	3130

Chapter 39 Related party disclosures

1 INTRODUCTION

Related party relationships and transactions between related parties are a normal feature of commerce and business. Many entities carry on their business activities through subsidiaries, joint ventures, and associates and there are inevitably transactions between these parties. The investor, in these circumstances, has the ability to affect the financial and operating policies of the investee. *[IAS 24.5]*. It is also common for entities under common control, which are not a group for financial reporting purposes, to transact with each other. The disclosures considered necessary in such circumstances are addressed by IAS 24 – *Related Party Disclosures*.

1.1 The related party issue

The problems posed by related party relationships and transactions are described in IAS 24 as follows:

> 'A related party relationship could have an effect on the profit or loss and financial position of an entity. Related parties may enter into transactions that unrelated parties would not. For example, an entity that sells goods to its parent at cost might not sell on those terms to another customer. Also, transactions between related parties may not be made at the same amounts as between unrelated parties.
>
> The profit or loss and financial position of an entity may be affected by a related party relationship even if related party transactions do not occur. The mere existence of the relationship may be sufficient to affect the transactions of the entity with other parties. For example, a subsidiary may terminate relations with a trading partner on acquisition by the parent of a fellow subsidiary engaged in the same activity as the former trading partner. Alternatively, one party may refrain from acting because of the significant influence of another – for example, a subsidiary may be instructed by its parent not to engage in research and development.' *[IAS 24.6-7]*.

1.2 Possible solutions

1.2.1 Remeasurement of related party transactions at fair values

In response to the problem posed by related party transactions, IAS 24 requires disclosure of those transactions, rather than an adjustment to the financial statements.

IAS 24 is purely a disclosure standard and does not establish any recognition or measurement requirements. Related party transactions are accounted for in accordance with the requirements of the IFRS applicable to the transaction. The disclosures required by IAS 24 are in addition to those required by other IFRSs. For example, a loan to a related party will also be subject to the disclosure requirements of IFRS 7 – *Financial Instruments: Disclosures*. This treatment of related party transactions and relationships using disclosure, rather than requiring adjustment, is in line with accounting standards internationally.

The purpose of disclosing information required by IAS 24 is to give users of the financial statements knowledge about transactions (for example, whether they are at fair value), outstanding balances, including commitments, and relationships with related parties that may affect their assessment of an entity's operations, including assessments of the risks and opportunities facing an entity. *[IAS 24.8]*.

An alternative solution to the problems posed by related party relationships and transactions would be to adjust the financial statements to value related party transactions as if they occurred with an independent third party and recognise any such transactions at an arm's length price (i.e. fair value). However, although it may be possible to do this, it is often not possible to establish what would have been the terms of any non-arm's length transaction, had it been negotiated on an arm's length basis. This is because no comparable transactions may have taken place and, in any event, the transaction might never have taken place at all if it had been negotiated at a different value.

2 REQUIREMENTS OF IAS 24

2.1 Objective and scope

2.1.1 Objective

IAS 24 states that its objective 'is to ensure that an entity's financial statements contain the disclosures necessary to draw attention to the possibility that its financial position and profit or loss may have been affected by the existence of related parties and by transactions and outstanding balances, including commitments, with such parties'. *[IAS 24.1]*.

Accordingly, IAS 24 requires disclosure of related party transactions and outstanding balances, including commitments, together with the names of any parties who control the reporting entity.

2.1.2 Scope

IAS 24 applies in:
(a) identifying related party relationships and transactions;
(b) identifying outstanding balances, including commitments, between an entity and its related parties;
(c) identifying the circumstances in which disclosure of the items in (a) and (b) is required; and
(d) determining the disclosures to be made about those items. *[IAS 24.2]*.

IAS 24 explicitly requires disclosure of related party relationships, transactions and outstanding balances, including commitments, in both the consolidated and separate financial statements of a parent or investors with joint control of, or significant influence over, an investee presented in accordance with IFRS 10 – *Consolidated Financial Statements* – or IAS 27 – *Separate Financial Statements*. The standard also applies to individual financial statements. *[IAS 24.3]*.

All entities within a group that prepare their financial statements under IFRS must disclose related party transactions and outstanding balances with other entities in the group in the entity's own financial statements. *[IAS 24.4]*. There are no disclosure exemptions for subsidiaries, or for parent companies that produce separate financial statements even where those separate financial statements are issued with the consolidated financial statements of the group of which they are a part. The IASB considers that the financial statements of an entity that is part of a consolidated group may include the effects of extensive intragroup transactions. Therefore, it concluded that the disclosures required by IAS 24 are essential to understanding the financial position and financial performance of such an entity and should be required for separate financial statements presented in accordance with IAS 27. The IASB also believes that disclosure of intragroup transactions is essential because external users of the financial statements need to be aware of the interrelationships between related parties, including the level of support provided by related parties, to assist in their economic decisions. *[IAS 24.BC16-17]*.

IAS 24 notes that 'intragroup related party transactions and outstanding balances are eliminated in the preparation of consolidated financial statements of the group'. *[IAS 24.4]*. This implies that disclosure of such transactions and balances is not required in the group's consolidated financial statements since, so far as those financial statements are concerned, such items do not exist. This would also apply to the parts of a transaction which have been eliminated when applying equity accounting. However, transactions and balances between an investment entity and those of its subsidiaries, held as part of an investment portfolio that are measured at fair value through profit or loss and not consolidated in accordance with IFRS 10 should be disclosed in the consolidated financial statements. *[IAS 24.4]*.

Some jurisdictions may have local laws and regulations which require specific information to be disclosed about particular related party transactions. These local requirements should be seen as a complement to, and not a substitute for, the disclosure requirements of IAS 24.

2.2 Identification of a related party and related party transactions

A related party is defined as 'a person or entity that is related to the entity that is preparing its financial statements (the "reporting entity")'. *[IAS 24.9]*. The definition of related parties is reciprocal. The use of the word 'party' means that the disclosure applies to both individuals and to entities. The factors considered in the identification of a related party is consistent whether the controlling party is a person or an entity.

With regard to entities, IAS 24 defines related parties more widely than simply the members of a group (as defined in Appendix A of IFRS 10, i.e. a parent and its subsidiaries). The definition includes joint ventures and associates of the parent (that are related to the subsidiaries of the parent), joint ventures and associates of a parent's subsidiary (that are related to the subsidiaries of the parent) and subsidiaries of an associate or a joint venture (that are related to the parent).

IAS 24 contains a multi-part definition of 'related party' and the following are considered to be related parties of the reporting entity:

- certain persons or a close member of that person's family (see 2.2.1 below);
- entities that are members of the same group (see 2.2.2 below);
- entities that are associates or joint ventures (see 2.2.3 below);
- entities that are joint ventures of the same third party (see 2.2.4 below);
- entities that are joint ventures of a third party and associates of the same third entity (see 2.2.5 below);
- post-employment benefit plans (see 2.2.6 below);
- entities under control or joint control of certain categories of persons or close members of such a person's family (see 2.2.7 below);
- entities under significant influence of certain categories of persons or close members of such a person's family (including a person who is a member of a key management personnel of the entity or of a parent of the entity) (see 2.2.8 below);
- entities, or any member of the group of which they are a part, that provide key management personnel services (see 2.2.9 below); and
- government-related entities (see 2.2.10 below).

The standard emphasises that attention should be directed to the substance of the relationship and not merely the legal form. *[IAS 24.10].*

A related party transaction is a transfer of resources, services or obligations between a reporting entity and a related party, regardless of whether a price is charged. *[IAS 24.9].*

2.2.1 Persons or close members of a person's family that are related parties

A person or close member of that person's family is related to a reporting entity if that person:

(i) has control or joint control over the reporting entity;

(ii) has significant influence over the reporting entity; or

(iii) is a member of the key management personnel of the reporting entity or of a parent of the reporting entity. *[IAS 24.9].*

Close members of a family of a person are defined as 'those family members who may be expected to influence, or be influenced by, that person in their dealings with the entity' and include:

(a) that person's children and spouse or domestic partner;

(b) children of that person's spouse or domestic partner; and

(c) dependants of that person or that person's spouse or domestic partner. *[IAS 24.9].*

The Interpretations Committee confirmed in May 2015 that the definition appears to provide no scope to argue that there are circumstances in which the specific family members described in (a) to (c) above are not related parties. Dependants are not limited to children and may include other relatives depending on the facts and circumstances.

The Interpretations Committee observed that the definition of close members of the family of a person:

- is expressed in a principle-based manner and involves the use of judgement to determine whether members of the family of a person (including that person's parents) are related parties or not; and
- includes a list of family members that are always considered close members of the family of a person.

The Interpretations Committee further noted that the list of family members that are always considered 'close members' is non-exhaustive and does not preclude other family members from being considered as close members of the family of a person. Consequently, other family members, including parents or grandparents, could qualify as close members of the family depending on the assessment of specific facts and circumstances. Therefore, the Interpretations Committee determined that neither an Interpretation nor an amendment to IAS 24 was necessary and therefore decided not to add this issue to its agenda.[1]

Relationships involving a person or close family members as investors are illustrated in the following examples, which are based on illustrative examples published by the IASB, which accompany, but are not part of IAS 24.

Example 39.1:   Person as investor

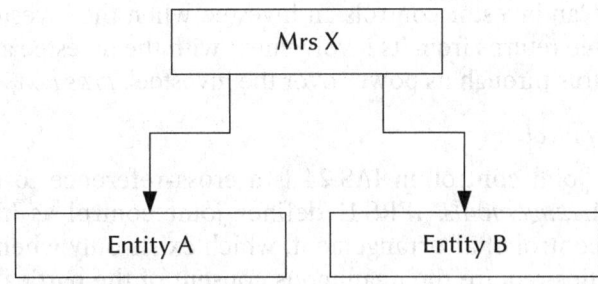

Mrs X has an investment in Entity A and Entity B.

For Entity A's financial statements, if Mrs X controls or jointly controls Entity A, Entity B is related to Entity A when Mrs X has control, joint control or significant influence over Entity B or is a member of Entity B's key management personnel.

For Entity B's financial statements, if Mrs X controls or jointly controls Entity A, Entity A is related to Entity B when Mrs X has control, joint control or significant influence over Entity B, or is a member of Entity's A key management personnel.

However, if Mrs X has significant influence over both Entity A and Entity B, Entities A and B are not related to each other.

If Mrs X is a member of the key management personnel of both Entity A and Entity B, Entities A and B are not, in the absence of any other indicator of a related party relationship, related to each other (see 2.3 below).

Example 39.2: **Close members of the family holding investments**

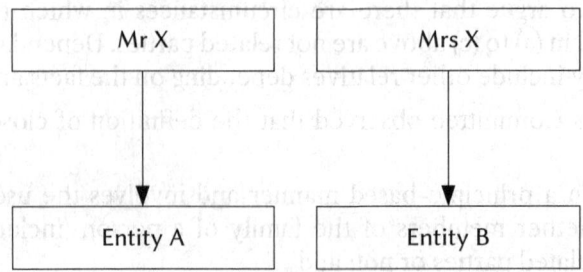

Mr X is the spouse of Mrs X. Mr X has an investment in Entity A and Mrs X has an investment in Entity B.

For Entity A's financial statements, if Mr X controls or jointly controls Entity A, Entity B is related to Entity A when Mrs X has control, joint control or significant influence over Entity B, or is a member of Entity B's management personnel.

For Entity B's financial statements, if Mr X controls or jointly controls Entity A, Entity A is related to Entity B when Mrs X has control, joint control or significant influence over Entity B, or is a member of Entity A's key management personnel.

If Mr X has significant influence (but not control or joint control) over Entity A and Mrs X has significant influence (but not control or joint control) over Entity B, Entities A and B are not related to each other (see 2.3 below).

If Mr X is a member of the key management personnel of Entity A and Mrs X is a member of the key management personnel of Entity B, Entities A and B are not, in the absence of any other indicator of a related party relationship, related to each other (see 2.3 below).

2.2.1.A   Control

The definition of 'control' in IAS 24 is a cross-reference to the definition in IFRS 10. IFRS 10 states that 'an investor controls an investee when the investor is exposed, or has rights, to variable returns from its involvement with the investee and has the ability to affect those returns through its power over the investee'. *[IFRS 10 Appendix A].*

2.2.1.B   Joint control

The definition of 'joint control' in IAS 24 is a cross-reference to the definition in IFRS 11 – *Joint Arrangements*. IFRS 11 defines joint control as 'the contractually agreed sharing of control of an arrangement, which exists only when decisions about the relevant activities require the unanimous consent of the parties sharing control'. *[IFRS 11 Appendix A].*

In the definition of a related party, a joint venture includes subsidiaries of the joint venture. *[IAS 24.12].* Therefore, for example, the subsidiary of a joint venture and the investor who has joint control are related to each other.

2.2.1.C   Significant influence

The definition of 'significant influence' in IAS 24 is a cross-reference to the definition in IAS 28 – *Investments in Associates and Joint Ventures*. IAS 28 defines significant influence as 'the power to participate in the financial and operating policy decisions of the investee but is not control or joint control of those policies'. *[IAS 28.3].*

In the definition of a related party, an associate includes subsidiaries of the associate. Therefore, for example, the subsidiary of an associate and the investor who has significant influence over the associate are related to each other. *[IAS 24.12].*

2.2.1.D Key management personnel

'Key management personnel' are those persons with authority and responsibility for planning, directing and controlling the activities of an entity, directly or indirectly, including any director (whether executive or otherwise) of that entity. *[IAS 24.9]*. A director of a reporting entity is normally automatically a member of key management personnel, even if they are not paid for their services by the reporting entity – thus a director of a subsidiary is still a member of key management personnel of the subsidiary, even if their services are paid for by the parent.

A related party includes all key management personnel of a reporting entity and of a parent of the reporting entity. This means that all key management personnel of all parents (i.e. the immediate parent, any intermediate parent and the ultimate parent) of a reporting entity are related parties of the reporting entity. When the reporting entity's financial statements represent a group, key management personnel of subsidiaries might not be key management personnel of the group if those persons do not participate in the management of the group.

Some entities may have more than one level of key management. For example, some entities may have a supervisory board, whose members have responsibilities similar to those of non-executive directors, as well as a board of directors that sets the overall operating strategy. All members of either board are therefore considered key management personnel.

The definition of key management personnel is not restricted to directors. It also includes other individuals with authority and responsibility for planning, directing and controlling the activities of an entity. The main intention of the definition is presumably to ensure that transactions with persons with responsibilities similar to those of directors, and the compensation paid to such persons, do not escape disclosure simply because they are not directors. Otherwise, there would be an obvious loophole in the standard. For example, in some jurisdictions, a chief financial officer or a chief operating officer may not be directors but could meet the definition of key management personnel. Other examples of the type of persons who are not directors but may meet the definition of key management personnel include a divisional chief executive or a director of a major trading subsidiary of the entity, but not of the entity itself, who nevertheless participates in the management of the reporting entity. A reference to individuals who are not directors in a reporting entity's business review or management discussion and analysis might indicate that those persons are considered to be key management personnel.

'Key management personnel' are normally employees of the reporting entity (or of another entity in the same group). However, the definition does not restrict itself to employees. Therefore, seconded staff and persons engaged under management or outsourcing contracts may also have a level of authority or responsibility such that they are 'key management personnel'.

The definition of key management personnel refers to 'persons'. In some jurisdictions, the term 'person' includes both a 'corporate person' and a 'natural person'. Additionally, in some jurisdictions, a corporate entity must by law have the authority and responsibility for planning, directing and controlling the activities of an investment fund for the benefit of the fund's investors in accordance with the fund's constitution and relevant statutes (i.e. the corporate entity is the body acting as key management personnel). IAS 24 clarifies that if a reporting entity receives key management personnel services from another entity (described as a 'management entity') the disclosure requirements for key management personnel compensation (see 2.2.9 below) do not apply to the compensation paid or payable by the management entity to the management entity's employees or directors. *[IAS 24.17A]*. Instead, amounts incurred for the service fee paid or payable by the reporting entity to the separate management entity for provision of key management personnel services are disclosed. *[IAS 24.18A]*. As a result of identifying the management entity as a related party of the reporting entity, other transactions with the management entity, such as loans, are also disclosed by the reporting entity.

2.2.2   Entities that are members of the same group

'An entity is related to a reporting entity if:

(i)   The entity and the reporting entity are members of the same group (which means that each parent, subsidiary and fellow subsidiary is related to the others).' *[IAS 24.9(b)]*.

The terms group, parent and subsidiary are defined in IFRS as follows:

- a group is 'a parent and its subsidiaries';
- a parent is 'an entity that controls one or more entities'; and
- a subsidiary as 'an entity that is controlled by another entity'. *[IFRS 10 Appendix A]*.

Therefore, all entities controlled by the same ultimate parent are related parties. This would include entities where the reporting entity holds less than a majority of the voting rights but which are subsidiaries as defined in IFRS 10. Conversely, a group would not include entities where the reporting entity holds a majority of the voting rights but which are not subsidiaries (e.g. because the group does not have control), though these are likely to be related parties of the reporting entity as they may fall into other categories of related party, such as associates.

Example 39.3:   Entities that are members of the same group

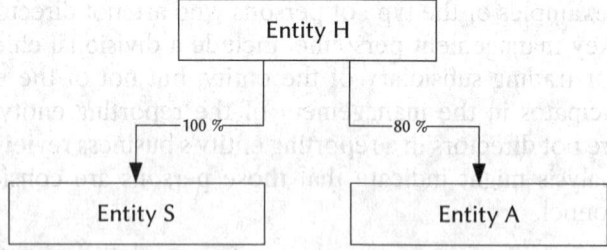

Entities H, S and A are all related parties to each other as they are members of the same group. Both Entity S and Entity A are subsidiaries of Entity H.

Related party disclosures will be required in the financial statements of Entity S in respect of transactions with Entities H and A, in the financial statements of Entity A in respect of transactions with Entities H and S and in the separate financial statements of Entity H in respect of transactions with Entities S and A.

2.2.3 Entities that are associates or joint ventures

'An entity is related to a reporting entity if:

...

(ii) One entity is an associate or joint venture of the other entity (or an associate or joint venture of a member of a group of which the other entity is a member).' *[IAS 24.9(b)]*.

The terms associate and joint venture are defined in IAS 28 and IFRS 11.

IAS 28 defines an associate as 'an entity over which the investor has significant influence'. *[IAS 28.3]*.

IFRS 11 defines a joint venture as 'a joint arrangement whereby the parties that have joint control of the arrangement have rights to the net assets of the arrangement'. *[IFRS 11 Appendix A]*.

Any entity that a reporting entity determines is an associate under IAS 28 or a joint venture under IFRS 11 is a related party. All associates and joint ventures are related parties regardless as to whether they are accounted for under the equity method or by another method. For example, investments in associates or joint ventures held by a venture capital organisation, mutual fund, unit trust or similar entity including unit-linked insurance funds are related parties, even where the investment is accounted for at fair value through profit or loss under IFRS 9 – *Financial Instruments* – rather than under the equity method. Likewise, any reporting entity that is an associate or joint venture of another entity must treat that investor entity as a related party.

As noted above, in the definition of a related party, an associate includes subsidiaries of the associate and a joint venture includes subsidiaries of the joint venture. Therefore, for example, an associate's subsidiary and the investor that has significant influence over the associate are related to one another. *[IAS 24.12]*.

The definition also means that an associate of a reporting entity's parent is also a related party of the reporting entity.

However, the definition does not cause investors in a joint venture or an associate to be related to each other (see 2.3 below). Investors in joint operations (as defined in IFRS 11) are also not related to each other. For the avoidance of doubt, two associates of the same third party are not related to one another (see 2.2.4 below).

The application of these requirements is illustrated in the example below, which is based on an illustrative example accompanying IAS 24. The example mainly focuses on the application of the requirements to associate entities.

Example 39.4:   Associates of the reporting entity's group that are related parties

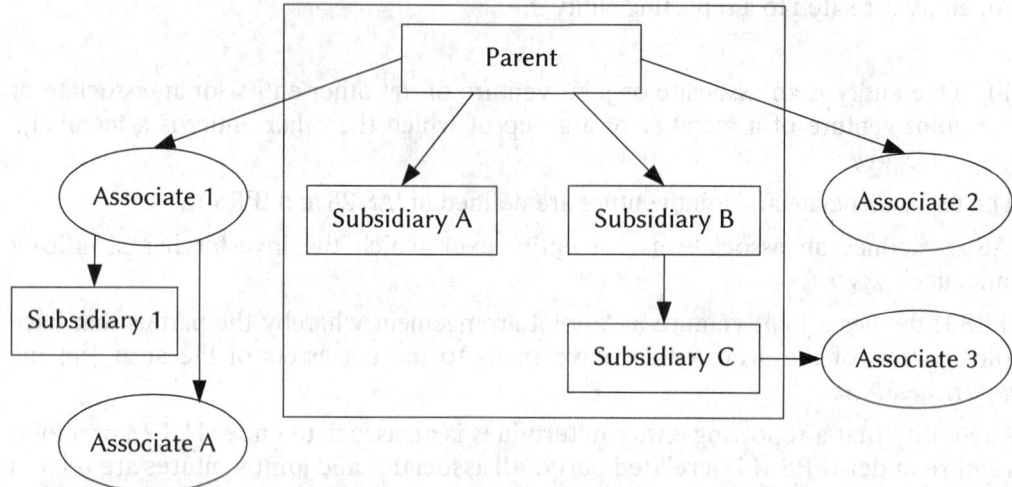

In Parent's separate financial statements, Associates 1 (including its subsidiary), 2 and 3 are related parties. For Parent's consolidated financial statements, Associates 1 (including its subsidiary), 2 and 3 are related to the group.

For Subsidiary A's financial statements, Associates 1 (including its subsidiary), 2 and 3 are related parties. For Subsidiary B's consolidated or separate financial statements, Associates 1 (including its subsidiary), 2 and 3 are related parties. For Subsidiary C's financial statements, Associates 1 (including its subsidiary), 2 and 3 are related parties.

For the financial statements of Associates 1 (consolidated or separate), 2 and 3, Parent and Subsidiaries A, B and C are related parties. Associates 1, 2 and 3 are not related to each other. In addition, for the separate financial statements of Associate 1, Subsidiary 1 and Associate A are also related and for the consolidated financial statements of Associate 1, Associate A is related.

For the financial statements of Subsidiary 1, Associate 1, Associate A, Parent and Subsidiaries A, B and C are related parties. For the financial statements of Associate A, Associate 1 and Subsidiary 1 are related.

2.2.3.A   Joint operations

IAS 24 defines 'joint ventures' of the reporting entity as related parties. The definition of a joint venture in IFRS 11 excludes joint operations, so that an investment in a joint operation is not a related party.

The exclusion of joint operations in is line with the IASB view that joint operations are part of the reporting entity and therefore a transaction with a joint operation is either a transaction by the reporting entity with itself or a transaction with the other joint operator which would not be a related party unless it otherwise met the related party definition in IAS 24 for some other reason (e.g. because it was an entity controlled by a member of key management personnel). *[IFRS 12.BC52]*.

2.2.4 Entities that are joint ventures of the same third party

'An entity is related to a reporting entity if:

...

(iii) Both entities are joint ventures of the same third party.' *[IAS 24.9(b)]*.

This is illustrated by the following example:

Example 39.5: Entities that are joint ventures of the same third party

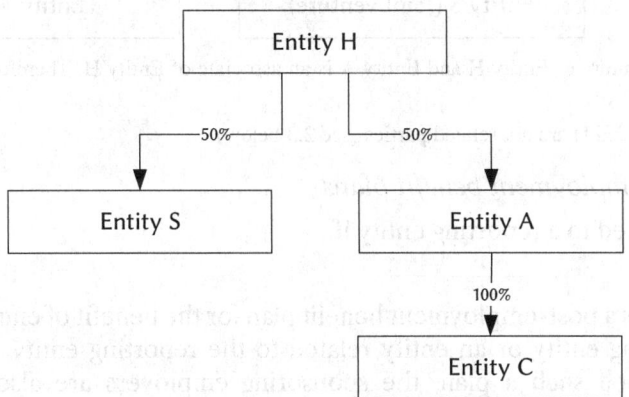

In this example, Entities S and A are joint ventures of Entity H and are therefore related parties. Entity C, as a subsidiary of Entity A, is also a related party of Entity H and Entity S.

If, however, Entities S and A were only associates (rather than joint ventures) of the same third party then they would not be related parties. In the Basis for Conclusions to IAS 24, it was explained that a distinction was made between joint ventures and associates because the IASB considered that 'significant influence' was not as close a relationship as control or joint control. *[IAS 24.BC19(a)]*.

As noted above, in the definition of a related party, a joint venture includes subsidiaries of the joint venture. Therefore a joint venture's subsidiary and the investor that has joint control over the joint venture are related to each other. *[IAS 24.12]*.

2.2.5 Entities that are joint ventures of a third party and associates of the same third entity

'An entity is related to a reporting entity if:

...

(iv) One entity is a joint venture of a third entity and the other entity is an associate of the third entity.' *[IAS 24.9(b)]*.

This definition treats joint ventures in a similar manner to subsidiaries as illustrated in Examples 39.3 and 39.5 above and therefore an associate and a joint venture are related parties where they share the same investor. This is illustrated in the example below:

Example 39.6: *Entities that are joint ventures and associates of the same third entity*

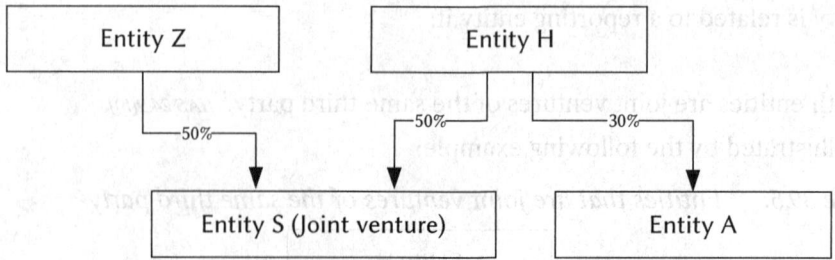

Entity S is a joint venture of Entity H and Entity A is an associate of Entity H. Therefore, Entities S and A are related parties.

However, Entities Z and H are not related parties (see 2.3 below).

2.2.6 Post-employment benefit plans

'An entity is related to a reporting entity if:

...

(v) The entity is a post-employment benefit plan for the benefit of employees of either the reporting entity or an entity related to the reporting entity. If the reporting entity is itself such a plan, the sponsoring employers are also related to the reporting entity.' *[IAS 24.9(b)]*.

The definition is quite wide-ranging and includes post-employment benefit plans of any entity related to the reporting entity. This includes, for example, post-employment benefit plans of an associate or joint venture of the reporting entity or a post-employment benefit plan of an associate of the reporting entity's parent.

The related party relationship would not extend to investment managers of the pension fund, provided that their acting for the fund was the only relationship. Any fees paid by the sponsoring employers (for example, to the investment manager) on behalf of the pension fund would be a related party transaction. 'Sponsoring employers' is not defined in IFRS, but is generally taken to mean the entity which has a legal duty to ensure that funds are available in the pension fund when the payment of pensions falls due.

Sponsoring employers are also related parties of a post-employment benefit plan.

2.2.7 Entities under control or joint control of certain persons or close members of their family

An entity is related to a reporting entity if:

...

(vi) The entity is controlled or jointly controlled by a person or close member of that person's family who has control or joint control over the reporting entity, has significant influence over the reporting entity or is a member of key management personnel of the reporting entity or of a parent of the reporting entity. *[IAS 24.9]*.

This is intended to cover situations in which an entity is controlled or jointly controlled by a person or close family member of that person and that person or close family member also controls, jointly controls, has significant influence over, or is a member of key management personnel of, the reporting entity or of a parent of the reporting entity. The situation whereby one company owns another is covered by Example 39.3 above. This is illustrated below:

Example 39.7: **Persons who control an entity and are a member of the key management personnel of another entity**

Mrs X has a 100% investment in Entity A and is a member of the key management personnel of Entity S. Entity M has a 100% investment in Entity S.

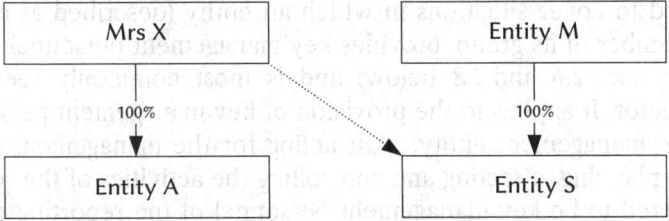

For Entity S's financial statements, Entity A is related to Entity S because Mrs X controls Entity A and is a member of the key management personnel of Entity S.

For Entity S's financial statements, Entity A is also related to Entity S if Mrs X is a member of the key management personnel of Entity M and not of Entity S.

This outcome would be the same if Mrs X has joint control over Entity A (if Mrs X only had significant influence over Entity A and not control or joint control then Entities A and S would not be related parties).

For Entity A's financial statements, Entity S is related to Entity A because Mrs X controls Entity A and is a member of Entity S's key management personnel. This outcome would be the same if Mrs X has joint control over Entity A and would further be the same if Mrs X is a member of the key management personnel of Entity M rather than Entity S (see 2.2.8 below). Note that Entity M would also be a related party of Entity A in this instance.

For Entity M's consolidated financial statements, Entity A is a related party of the Group if Mrs X is a member of the key management personnel of the Group.

For Entity M's separate financial statements, Entity S is a related party. Further, Entity A will be a related party if Mrs X is a member of the key management personnel of Entity M.

2.2.8 Entities under significant influence of certain persons or close members of their family

An entity is related to a reporting entity if:

...

(vii) A person or a close family member of that person who has control or joint control over the reporting entity has significant influence over the entity or is a member of the key management personnel of the entity (or of a parent of the entity). *[IAS 24.9(b)]*.

This is the reciprocal of 2.2.7 and is illustrated in Example 39.7 above.

Entities that are significantly influenced by the same person or close member of that person's family or who simply share the same key management personnel are not related parties in the absence of any control or joint control by those persons (see 2.3 below).

2.2.9 Entities, or any member of the group of which they are a part, that provide key management personnel services

'An entity is related to a reporting entity if:

...

(viii) The entity, or any member of a group of which it is a part, provides key management personnel services to the reporting entity or to the parent of the reporting entity.' [IAS 24.9(b)].

This is intended to cover situations in which an entity (described as a 'management entity'), or a member of its group, provides key management personnel services to the reporting entity (see 2.6 and 2.8 below) and is most commonly seen in the fund management sector. It applies to the provision of key management personnel services by the separate management entity. Staff acting for the management entity that are responsible for planning, directing and controlling the activities of the reporting entity are not considered to be key management personnel of the reporting entity. It is not necessary to look through the management entity to determine natural persons as key management personnel. [IAS 24.17A].

Example 39.8: Entities that provide key management personnel services to a reporting entity

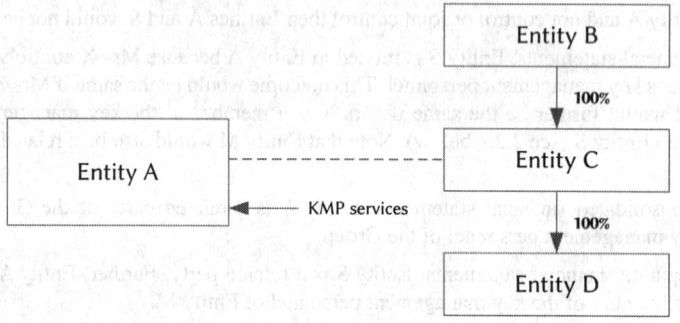

Entity C provides key management personnel services to Entity A. For Entity A's financial statements, Entities B, C and D are all related parties.

Entity A is not a related party of Entities B, C and D. The related party relationship between the management entity and the reporting entity is not symmetrical. In the absence of any other indicator of a related party relationship, the reporting entity (Entity A) cannot affect the management entity's (Entity C's) activities, financial position or profit or loss.

2.2.10 Government-related entities

A 'government-related entity' is an entity that is controlled, jointly controlled or significantly influenced by a government. [IAS 24.9].

'Government' in this context refers to government, government agencies and similar bodies whether local, national or international. [IAS 24.9]. This is the same as the definition used in IAS 20 – *Accounting for Government Grants and Disclosure of Government Assistance*. The Board decided that it would not provide a more comprehensive definition or additional guidance on how to determine what is meant by 'government'. In the Board's view, a more detailed definition could not capture every conceivable government structure across every jurisdiction. In addition, judgement is required by a reporting entity when applying the definition because every jurisdiction has its own way of organising government-related activities. *[IAS 24.BC41].* This implies that there may well be diversity in practice across different jurisdictions in defining what is meant by 'government'. For jurisdictions with multiple levels of government, judgement may be needed about whether parties controlled by different levels of government are related (for example, state versus federal), notwithstanding that both controlling parties are government bodies.

Where an entity is controlled, jointly controlled or significantly influenced by a government then relationships, transactions and outstanding balances, including commitments, with that government are related party transactions. Similarly, transactions and outstanding balances, including commitments, with other entities controlled, jointly controlled or significantly influenced by that government are related party transactions. However, not all such transactions should be disclosed, only those that are individually significant to an understanding of the financial statements of the reporting entity. The factors to consider when assessing whether a transaction is individually significant are discussed at 2.9 below. Additionally, transactions may be for significant amounts but still be immaterial from an IAS 1 – *Presentation of Financial Statements* – perspective (e.g. telecommunication costs with a government-controlled operator when these are at market conditions).

Related party transactions with government-related entities are subject to certain disclosure exemptions. These are discussed at 2.9 below.

2.3 Parties that are not related parties

Having included such a detailed definition of related parties, IAS 24 clarifies that the following are not related parties:

- two entities simply because they have a director or other member of key management personnel in common or because a member of key management personnel of one entity has significant influence over the other entity;
- two venturers simply because they share joint control over a joint venture;
- providers of finance, trade unions, public utilities and departments and agencies of a government that do not control, jointly control or significantly influence the reporting entity, simply by virtue of their normal dealings with the entity (even though they may affect the freedom of action of an entity or participate in its decision-making process); and
- a customer, supplier, franchisor, distributor or general agent with whom an entity transacts a significant volume of business, simply by virtue of the resulting economic dependence. *[IAS 24.11].*

The reason for these exclusions is that, without them, many entities that are not usually regarded as related parties could fall within the definition of related party. For example, a small clothing manufacturer selling 90% of its output to a single customer could be under the effective economic control of that customer.

These exclusions are effective only where these parties are 'related' to the reporting entity simply because of the relationship noted above. If there are other reasons why a party is a related party, the exclusions do not apply. Consider the following examples:

- A water company that supplies the reporting entity is not a related party if the only link between the two is the supply of water. If, however, the water company is also an associate of the reporting entity, the exclusion does not apply; the two are related parties, and the transactions relating to the supply of water are disclosed if material.

- Two investors in the same entity are not related parties simply because one holds a controlling interest and the other shareholder (not in the group) holds a non-controlling interest in a subsidiary of the group. Even if the investor holding the non-controlling interest exercises significant influence over the subsidiary, provided it is not otherwise related to the controlling investor, it is not normally a related party of the controlling investor. However, the non-controlling investor might have significant influence over the group if the subsidiary was significant to the group in which case the group, including the controlling investor and the non-controlling investor are related parties.

- Two entities are not related parties simply because they share common key management personnel. However, if the common member of key management personnel exerts control or joint control over one or more of the entities then they are related parties. See 2.2.7 or 2.2.8 above.

- An administrator, custodian, broker and fund manager of the same fund are not related parties, to each other or to the fund to which they provide services simply because they each provide services to the fund, even if any of the parties are economically dependent upon the income from such services. However, any such party could meet the definition of 'key management personnel' of the fund if it provides key management personnel services (see 2.2.9 above). In addition, any shared ownership (e.g. control, joint control, or significant influence) between such parties should be evaluated to determine if the parties are related.

An interest in an unconsolidated structured entity as defined by IFRS 12 – *Disclosure of Interests in Other Entities* – held by a reporting entity does not make the structured entity a related party to the reporting entity unless it would otherwise meet the definition of a related party (e.g. because the structured entity is an associate of the reporting entity).

2.4 Disclosure of controlling relationships

IAS 24 asserts that, in order to enable users of financial statements to form a view about the effects of related party relationships on an entity, it is appropriate to disclose the related party relationship when control exists, irrespective of whether there have been transactions between the related parties. *[IAS 24.14]*. Accordingly, IAS 24 requires an entity to disclose:

- the name of its parent; and, if different
- the ultimate controlling party.

If neither the entity's parent nor the ultimate controlling party produces consolidated financial statements available for public use, the name of the next most senior parent that does so must also be disclosed. *[IAS 24.13]*.

The 'next most senior parent' is the first parent in the group above the immediate parent that produces consolidated financial statements available for public use. *[IAS 24.16]*. Consequently, in some circumstances, an entity may need to disclose the names of three parents.

Disclosure must be made even if the parent or ultimate controlling party does not prepare financial statements. In the situation when the ultimate controlling party is an individual, rather than an entity, the reporting entity is likely to have to disclose the name of the next most senior parent in addition since the individual undoubtedly does not produce financial statements for public use. IAS 1 also requires disclosure of the 'ultimate parent' of the group. *[IAS 1.138(c)]*. This is not necessarily synonymous with the 'ultimate controlling party' where that party is an individual. This is illustrated in the example below.

Example 39.9:   Disclosure of parent, ultimate parent and ultimate controlling party

Entity S is controlled by Entity P which in turn is controlled by Entity H which in turn is controlled by Entity Y. The ultimate controlling party of Entity Y is Mr A. Entities P and Y do not produce consolidated financial statements available for public use.

The group structure is illustrated as follows:

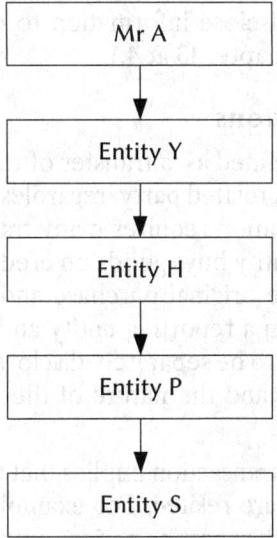

For Entity S's financial statements, IAS 24 requires disclosure of Entity P (the parent), Entity H (the next most senior parent that produces consolidated financial statements available for public use) and Mr A (the ultimate controlling party). In addition, IAS 1 requires disclosure of Entity Y (the ultimate parent of the group).

For Entity P's financial statements, IAS 24 requires disclosure of Entity H (the parent) and Mr A (the ultimate controlling party). In addition, IAS 1 requires disclosure of Entity Y (the ultimate parent of the group).

For Entity H's financial statements, IAS 24 requires disclosure of Entity Y (the parent) and Mr A (the ultimate controlling party). IAS 1 does not require any additional disclosure.

For Entity Y, IAS 24 requires disclosure of Mr A (ultimate controlling party).

The ultimate controlling party could be a group of individuals or entities acting together. IAS 24 is silent on the issue of individuals or entities acting together to exercise joint control. However, IFRS 3 – *Business Combinations* – states that a group of individuals can be regarded as a controlling party when, as a result of contractual arrangements, they collectively have the power to govern that entity's financial and operating policies so as to obtain benefits from its activities. *[IFRS 3.B2]*. In such circumstances, these entities or individuals should be identified as the controlling party. However, as discussed at 2.2 above, IAS 24 emphasises that attention should be directed to the substance of any related party relationship and not merely the legal form. It is likely that such an informal arrangement would at least give such individuals acting collectively significant influence over the reporting entity and as such, those individuals would be related parties to the reporting entity under IAS 24.

IAS 24 also clarifies that the requirement to disclose related party relationships between a parent and its subsidiaries is in addition to the disclosure requirements of IAS 27 and IFRS 12. *[IAS 24.15]*. IAS 27 requires a parent's separate financial statements to disclose:

- a list of the significant investments in subsidiaries, joint ventures and associates including the name, place of business (and, if different, country of incorporation);
- proportion of ownership interest (and if different, proportion of voting power held); and
- a description of the method used to account for such investments – see Chapter 8 at 3.1.

IFRS 12 requires an entity to disclose information to enable users to understand the composition of a group – see Chapter 13 at 4.1.

2.5 Disclosable transactions

A related party transaction is defined as 'a transfer of resources, services or obligations between a reporting entity and a related party, regardless of whether a price is charged.' *[IAS 24.9]*. Read literally, this definition requires many transactions to be disclosed more than once. For example, if an entity buys goods on credit from a related party and pays for them 30 days later, both the original purchase and the final payment represent a 'transfer of resources ... between a reporting entity and a related party' and, therefore on a literal reading, are required to be separately disclosed. However, we doubt that this reading is the IASB's intention, and the nature of the disclosures required by IAS 24 seems to support this view.

The definition of a related party transaction implies that transactions are disclosable only for the period in which parties are related. For example, where a reporting entity has disposed of a subsidiary during the reporting period, only transactions with the subsidiary up to the date of disposal are related party transactions in the financial statements of the reporting entity. Similarly, if a person became a member of key management personnel of a reporting entity during a reporting period, no disclosure is required of any remuneration paid to that person before that person's appointment as key management personnel. Likewise, transactions with a party in the comparative period are not disclosable as related party transactions if in the comparative period that party was not related to the reporting entity. Transactions with a party are not disclosable in the current year if the related party relationship had ceased before the beginning of the current period although, transactions in the comparative period are disclosed.

IAS 24 is unclear whether disclosure of outstanding balances at the reporting date is required in situations where an entity ceases to be a related party during the reporting period. In such situations, one view is that outstanding balances are not disclosable since the entity is not a related party as at the reporting date. A second view is that if the outstanding balances as at the reporting date comprise of amounts related to the transactions when the entities were related, such outstanding balances should be included in related party disclosures. In our view, either view is acceptable. However, if an entity becomes a related party during the year, outstanding balances as at the reporting date, that include amounts related to transactions entered into when the entities were unrelated, are disclosable.

In the case that entities become related after the reporting date, but before the financial statements were authorised for issue, it may be necessary to disclose the relationship, if it is considered by management to be a material non-adjusting event, in accordance with IAS 10 – *Events after the Reporting Period.* [IAS 10.21].

There is no requirement in IAS 24 to disclose information about related party transactions in one comprehensive note. However, it may be more useful to users of the financial statements to present information this way.

IAS 1 requires that, except where a standard permits otherwise (which IAS 24 does not), comparative information in respect of the previous period must be disclosed for all amounts reported in the current period's financial statements. [IAS 1.38]. This applies to all transactions for which a related party relationship existed in the prior period, but, as noted above, does not apply to transactions with a party which only became related in the current period.

2.5.1 Materiality

In determining whether an entity discloses related party transactions in financial statements, the general concept of materiality is applied. IAS 24 does not refer specifically to materiality since this requirement is in IAS 1, which states that 'an entity need not provide a specific disclosure required by an IFRS if the information resulting from that disclosure is not material.' [IAS 1.31]. Omissions, misstatements or obscuring of information are material within IAS 1 'if it could reasonably be expected to influence decisions that the primary users of general purpose financial statements make on the basis of those financial statements, which provide financial information about a specific reporting entity. Materiality depends on the nature or magnitude of information, or both. An entity assesses whether information, either individually or in combination with other information, is material in the context of its financial statements taken as a whole.' [IAS 1.7].

The nature of the qualitative aspect of materiality in respect of related party transactions is made explicit in the non-mandatory Practice Statement *Making Materiality Judgements,*[2] issued by the IASB Board in September 2017. The statement lists the involvement of a related party of the entity as an entity-specific qualitative materiality factor of an entity's transaction, other event or condition. It further explains that the presence of a qualitative factor lowers the thresholds for the quantitative assessment and that the more significant the qualitative factors, the lower the quantitative factors will be. *The Conceptual Framework for Financial Reporting,*[3] issued in March 2018, also emphasises that materiality is an entity-specific aspect of relevance, based on nature, magnitude or both and what could be material in a particular situation cannot be predetermined, nor can a uniform quantitative threshold be specified.

This qualitative aspect of materiality may have the effect that any related party transaction whose disclosure is considered sensitive (e.g. key management compensation or for tax reasons perhaps) is by definition material because it is expected by the reporting entity to influence a user of the financial statements. Therefore, it may not be possible to avoid disclosing such items on the grounds that they are quantitatively immaterial. In addition, a transaction conducted at advantageous terms to either the related party or the reporting entity is more likely to be material than one conducted at arm's length. Since IAS 24 requires disclosure of related party transactions irrespective of whether consideration is received, disclosure cannot be avoided on the argument that, since there is no consideration, the transaction must be immaterial.

2.6 Disclosure of key management personnel compensation

IAS 24 requires disclosure of key management personnel compensation including the amount of outstanding balances and commitments. Outstanding balances with key management personnel would include unpaid bonuses or liabilities under cash-settled share-based payment transactions.

There is no requirement in IAS 24 to disclose individual key management personnel compensation. Instead, entities are required to disclose key management personnel compensation in total and for each of the following categories:

- short-term employee benefits;
- post-employment benefits;
- other long-term benefits;
- termination benefits; and
- share-based payment. *[IAS 24.17]*.

These disclosures must be provided within the notes to the financial statements even when the same (or perhaps even more detailed) information is presented outside the financial statements. This is made clear by the Practice Statement *Making Materiality Judgements*, which emphasizes that publicly available information does not relieve an entity of the obligation to provide material information in its financial statements (paragraph 26 of the Practice Statement).

IAS 24 (see 2.2.9 above) clarifies that where an entity obtains key management personnel services from another entity ('management entity') it is not required to apply the requirements above to the compensation paid or payable by the management entity to the management entity's employees or directors. *[IAS 24.17A]*.

2.6.1 Compensation

'Compensation' includes all employee benefits (as defined in IAS 19 – *Employee Benefits*) including employee benefits to which IFRS 2 – *Share-based Payment* – applies. Employee benefits are all forms of consideration given by an entity, or on behalf of the entity, in exchange for services rendered to the entity. Employee benefits also include such consideration paid on behalf of a parent of the entity in respect of the entity. *[IAS 24.9]*. Therefore, the compensation disclosed by an entity in its financial statements is that which is for services to that entity, irrespective of whether it is paid by the reporting entity or by another entity or individual on behalf of the reporting entity. Further, the disclosures must include outstanding balances and commitments.

Compensation includes:

(a) short-term employee benefits, such as wages, salaries and social security contributions, paid annual leave and paid sick leave, profit-sharing and bonuses (if payable within twelve months of the end of the period) and non-monetary benefits (such as medical care, housing, cars and free or subsidised goods or services) for current employees;

(b) post-employment benefits such as pensions, other retirement benefits, post-employment life insurance and post-employment medical care;

(c) other long-term employee benefits, including long-service leave or sabbatical leave, jubilee or other long-service benefits, long-term disability benefits and, if they are not payable wholly within twelve months after the end of the reporting period, profit-sharing, bonuses and deferred compensation;

(d) termination benefits; and

(e) share-based payment. [IAS 24.9].

IAS 24 is not clear about the basis on which the amount for each of the categories above is determined. It is observed in the Basis for Conclusions that the IASB noted that the guidance on compensation in IAS 19 is sufficient to enable an entity to disclose the relevant information, which suggests that the IASB is expecting the compensation amounts to be based on the expense recognised under the relevant standards (IAS 19 or IFRS 2). [IAS 24.BC10]. This is indeed common observed practice. It is helpful to remember that the definition of compensation states that 'employee benefits are all forms of consideration paid, payable or provided by the entity, or on behalf of the entity in exchange for services rendered...' [IAS 24.9] and therefore compensation should be disclosed, even when provided by the parent or another group company.

Issues relating to each of the categories are discussed below.

For an illustrative example of the disclosure of key management personnel compensation, see Extract 39.1 at 2.6.9 below.

2.6.2 Short-term employee benefits

As indicated at 2.6.1 above, these include wages, salaries and social security contributions, paid annual leave and paid sick leave, profit-sharing and bonuses (if expected to be settled wholly before twelve months after the end of the reporting period). Most of these should not cause difficulty, since the expense for such items under IAS 19 is generally equivalent to the amount payable for the period. The disclosures would also include outstanding balances and commitments.

Non-monetary benefits (such as medical care, housing, cars and free or subsidised goods or services) must also be included within the amount disclosed for short-term employee benefits. [IAS 24.9]. In some cases, these might have been provided at no direct cost to the entity. In such circumstances it would appear reasonable to either attribute a value for non-monetary benefits (for example, the attributable tax benefit), so as to describe them quantitatively, or to describe such benefits qualitatively.

2.6.3 Post-employment benefits

As indicated at 2.6.1 above, these include pensions, other retirement benefits, post-employment life insurance and post-employment medical care. The inclusion of this category confirms that amounts are disclosed while members of key management are providing services. If amounts were only disclosed when the benefits are payable, then in many cases there would be no disclosure since the individuals would no longer be members of key management. The definition of related party transaction includes 'obligations between a reporting entity and a related party'. This implies that post-employment benefit obligations, including commitments, between the reporting entity and the members of the key management during the period covered by the financial statements are disclosed.

For defined contribution plans, it seems appropriate that the amount included is based on the total expense recognised under IAS 19, which is the equivalent of the contributions paid or payable to the plan for service rendered in the period.

The main issue related to defined benefit plans is to determine an appropriate calculation for the disclosable amount for the period. IAS 24 is silent on how the disclosable amount should be determined. Normally, for defined benefit plans, the expense recognised under IAS 19 differs from the contributions payable to the plan. Disclosing the contributions payable usually does not always reflect the benefits provided by the entity in exchange for the services rendered, particularly when the entity is benefitting from a contribution holiday. One approach to determine the disclosable amount would be to include an amount based on the total IAS 19 expense recognised in total comprehensive income. The total amounts recognised under IAS 19 for defined benefit plans includes items such as interest, actuarial remeasurement gains and losses and the effects of curtailments and settlements. This approach requires an apportionment of the total expense to the extent that it relates to the individuals concerned. Another approach would be to determine the disclosable amount based only on the current service cost and, when applicable, past service cost related to those individuals on the grounds that the other items relate more to the overall plan than to the individuals. An entity should adopt a consistent accounting policy for determining the amounts disclosed.

2.6.4 Other long-term benefits

As indicated at 2.6.1 above, these include long-service leave or sabbatical leave, jubilee or other long-service benefits, long-term disability benefits and, if they are not expected to be settled wholly before twelve months after the end of the reporting period, profit sharing, bonuses and deferred compensation. Since the accounting for such items under IAS 19 is on a similar basis to that for post-employment benefits similar issues to those discussed at 2.6.3 above are applicable.

2.6.5 Termination benefits

These should not cause difficulty, since an entity generally recognises such items, particularly for key management personnel, in line with the recognition criteria included in IAS 19.

2.6.6 Share-based payment transactions

This category includes share options, share awards or cash-settled awards granted in return for service by the members of key management. Such compensation is accounted for under IFRS 2. For equity-settled share-based payment transactions, such as share options or share awards, IFRS 2 broadly requires measurement of their fair value at grant date, and that expense is recognised over the period that employees render services. For cash-settled share-based payment transactions, IFRS 2 requires measurement and recognition based on the cash ultimately paid.

IAS 24 does not specify a basis on which the compensation disclosed should be determined. One basis would be to disclose an amount based on the expense under IFRS 2. This basis could lead to negative compensation being disclosed, for example, as a result of the reversal of a cumulative expense relating to share based options whose non-market vesting condition has not been satisfied. In this case, the reporting entity should consider whether additional disclosure is necessary to explain the amount and the change from the prior year. Another basis would be to disclose amounts based on the fair value that the individual received (based on the value of the shares at date of vesting, or at date of exercise of share options or the cash that is ultimately payable) rather than over the period of the service. An entity should adopt a consistent accounting policy for determining the amounts disclosed. In determining an appropriate accounting policy, the entity should also consider consistency with other disclosures related to key management personnel compensation made outside the financial statements.

2.6.7 Reporting entity part of a group

One additional practical difficulty for an entity in a group is that the disclosure of its key management personnel compensation is for the services rendered to the reporting entity. Accordingly, where key management personnel of the reporting entity also provide services to other entities within the group, an apportionment of the compensation is necessary. Likewise, where the reporting entity receives services from key management personnel that are also key management personnel of other entities within the group, the reporting entity may have to impute the compensation received. Such apportionments and allocations required judgement and an assessment of the time commitment involved.

2.6.8 Key management personnel compensated by other entities

A reporting entity also applies the principles set out at 2.6.7 above to situations in which the other entity is a third party, outside of the group, but is a related party.

2.6.9 Illustrative disclosure of key management personnel compensation

An example of the disclosure of key management personnel compensation can be found in the financial statements of BP p.l.c.

Extract 39.1: BP p.l.c. (2019)

Notes on financial statements [extract]

34. Remuneration of senior management and non-executive directors [extract]

Remuneration of directors and senior management

			$ million
	2019	2018	2017
Total for all senior management and non-executive directors			
Short-term employee benefits	30	25	29
Pensions and other post-retirement benefits	2	2	2
Share-based payments	32	32	29
Total	64	59	60

Senior management comprises members of the executive team, see pages 78-79 for further information.

Short-term employee benefits

These amounts comprise fees and benefits paid to the non-executive chairman and non-executive directors, as well as salary, benefits and cash bonuses for senior management. Deferred annual bonus awards, to be settled in shares, are included in share-based payments. Short-term employee benefits includes compensation for loss of office of $nil in 2019 (2018 $nil and 2017 $nil).

Pensions and other post-retirement benefits

The amounts represent the estimated cost to the group of providing pensions and other post-retirement benefits to senior management in respect of the current year of service measured in accordance with IAS 19 'Employee Benefits'.

Share-based payments

This is the cost to the group of senior management's participation in share-based payment plans, as measured by the fair value of options and shares granted, accounted for in accordance with IFRS 2 'Share-based Payments'.

2.7 Disclosure of other related party transactions, including commitments

IAS 24 requires an entity that has had related party transactions during the periods covered by its financial statements to disclose the nature of the related party relationship as well as information about those transactions and outstanding balances, including commitments, necessary for users to understand the potential effect of the relationship on the financial statements. *[IAS 24.18]*.

2.7.1 Related party transactions requiring disclosure

IAS 24 gives the following as examples of transactions to be disclosed, if they are with a related party. The list is not intended to be exhaustive:

- purchases or sales of goods (finished or unfinished);
- purchases or sales of property and other assets;
- rendering or receiving of services;
- leases;
- transfers of research and development;
- transfers under licence agreements;
- transfers under finance arrangements (including loans and equity contributions in cash or in kind);
- provisions of guarantees or collateral;
- commitments to do something if a particular event occurs or does not occur in the future, including executory contracts (recognised and unrecognised); and
- settlement of liabilities on behalf of the entity or by the entity on behalf of that related party. *[IAS 24.21]*.

IAS 24 does not contain any exemptions based on the nature of the transaction. Consequently, related party transactions include transactions such as dividend payments and the issue of shares under rights issues to major shareholders or key management personnel (i.e. those that fall within the definition of related parties), even where they participate on the same basis as other shareholders. However, for dividend payments, a preparer might conclude that no additional disclosures are necessary beyond those required by IAS 1, to explain the potential effect of the relationship on the financial statements. *[IAS 1.137]*. Further, not all transactions may need to be disclosed. Transactions with significant amounts may be immaterial from an IAS 1 perspective, giving due attention to the qualitative aspects of materiality, discussed at 2.5.1 above.

Related party transactions also include transactions with those individuals identified as related parties where their dealings with the entity are in a private capacity, rather than in a business capacity.

Participation by a parent or subsidiary in a defined benefit plan that shares risks between group entities is a transaction between related parties (see Chapter 35 at 3.3.2). *[IAS 24.22]*.

As indicated at 2.5 above, disclosure is required irrespective of whether or not consideration is received, which means that IAS 24 applies to gifts of assets or services and to asset swaps. Common examples of such transactions which may occur within a group include:

- administration by an entity of another entity within a group (or of its post-employment benefit plan) free of charge;
- transfer of tax assets from one member of a group to another without payment;
- rent-free accommodation or the loan of assets at no charge; or
- guarantees by directors of bank loans to the entity.

2.7.1.A Aggregation of items of a similar nature

Presumably in order to minimise the volume of disclosures, IAS 24 permits aggregation of items of a similar nature, except when separate disclosure is necessary for an understanding of the effects of the related party transactions on the financial statements of the entity. *[IAS 24.24]*. IAS 24 does not expand on this requirement, but it seems appropriate that, for example, purchases or sales of goods with other subsidiaries within a group can be aggregated, but any purchases or sales of property, plant, and equipment or of intangible assets with such entities are shown as a separate category. However, the level of aggregation is limited by the separate disclosure of transactions with particular categories of related parties (see 2.7.2 below).

2.7.1.B Commitments

IFRS provides the following definitions relating to commitments: IFRS 12 states that the commitments relating to joint ventures are those that may give rise to a future outflow of cash or other resources, *[IFRS 12.B18]*, and IFRS 9 defines a firm commitment as 'a binding agreement for the exchange of a specified quantity of resources at a specified price on a specified future date or dates'. *[IFRS 9 Appendix A]*. However, commitments should be considered more widely than these definitions: a typical example of a disclosable commitment might be the agreement to pay certain benefits to an employee on the termination of employment.

IAS 24 specifically mentions executory contracts (recognised and unrecognised) as commitments requiring disclosure. Executory contracts are excluded from the scope of IAS 37 – *Provisions, Contingent Liabilities and Contingent Assets* – unless they are onerous to the reporting entity. An executory contract is a contract under which neither party has performed any of its obligations or both parties have partially performed their obligations to an equal extent. *[IAS 37.3]*. An example of an executory contract would be a contract to buy an asset at a future date where neither the transfer of the asset nor the payment of consideration has occurred.

The words 'commitments to do something if a particular event occurs or does not occur in the future' can potentially have a wide application and is not limited to contractual commitments required to be disclosed by other standards. One obvious type of arrangement to which this applies would be some form of commitment by a subsidiary to its parent to undertake certain trading or research and development activities.

With respect to the type of transaction that the IASB is expecting to be disclosed, IFRS 12 provides a list of illustrative but not exhaustive examples of the type of unrecognised commitments that could relate to joint ventures. Some of these examples could apply equally to other related party arrangements. IFRS 12 clarifies that the commitments required to be disclosed under IAS 24 in respect of joint ventures include an entity's share of commitments made jointly with other investors with joint control of a joint venture. *[IFRS 12.B18]*.

IFRS 12 provides the following illustrations of commitments relating to joint ventures that would typically be disclosable under paragraph 18 of IAS 24 and could apply equally to other related party arrangements:

- unrecognised commitments to contribute funding or resources as a result of, for example:
  - the constitution or acquisition agreements of a joint venture (that, for example, require an entity to contribute funds over a specific period);
  - capital intensive projects undertaken by a joint venture;
  - unconditional purchase obligations, comprising procurement of equipment, inventory or services that an entity is committed to purchasing from, or on behalf of, a joint venture;
  - unrecognised commitments to provide loans or other financial support to a joint venture;
  - unrecognised commitments to contribute resources to a joint venture, such as assets or services; and
  - other non-cancellable unrecognised commitments relating to a joint venture;
- unrecognised commitments to acquire another party's ownership interest (or a portion of that ownership interest) in a joint venture if a particular event occurs or does not occur in the future. *[IFRS 12.B19-20]*.

Provisions of guarantees, which are a form of commitment, require separate disclosure. Disclosure of commitments to purchase property, plant and equipment and intangible assets in aggregate is required separately by IAS 16 – *Property, Plant and Equipment* – and IAS 38 – *Intangible Assets* – respectively. *[IAS 16.74(c), IAS 38.122(e)]*.

2.7.2 Disclosures required for related party transactions, including commitments

The standard states that, at a minimum, the disclosures must include:

(a) the amount of the transactions;

(b) the amount of outstanding balances, including commitments; and:
  (i) their terms and conditions, including whether they are secured, and the nature of the consideration to be provided in settlement; and
  (ii) details of any guarantees given or received;

(c) provisions for doubtful debts related to the amount of outstanding balances; and

(d) the expense recognised during the period in respect of bad or doubtful debts due from related parties. *[IAS 24.18]*.

The standard gives no exemption from disclosure on the grounds of sensitivity or confidentiality. However, since there is no requirement to disclose the name of a related party, this lack of exemption is likely to be less of a concern.

The requirement in (b) above could be read literally as requiring outstanding balances and commitments to be amalgamated into a single balance. However, commitments such as executory contracts do not give rise to outstanding balances. In practice, narrative disclosure of the terms and conditions of material commitments will be necessary.

There is no requirement to disclose individually significant transactions. However, as discussed at 2.9 below, there is such a requirement for transactions with government-related entities where a reporting entity has decided to apply the disclosure exemption.

The disclosures are made separately for each of the following categories:
(a) the parent;
(b) entities with joint control of, or significant influence over, the entity;
(c) subsidiaries;
(d) associates;
(e) joint ventures in which the entity is a joint venturer;
(f) key management personnel of the entity or its parent; and
(g) other related parties. *[IAS 24.19]*.

In our view the references in (a) and (f) above to 'the parent' should be read as including all parents of the entity, i.e. its immediate parent, any intermediate parent, and the ultimate parent. In the context of the financial statements of an entity within a group, it is insufficient to disclose related party transactions for a single category of 'group companies'. Separate categories are required for parent(s), subsidiaries and 'other related parties'.

IAS 24 does not identify the following relationships as a separate category of related party, and therefore we would normally expect to include information related to the following relationships within the category 'other related parties':

- fellow subsidiaries;
- subsidiaries of an investor with significant influence; and
- associates of the entity's controlling investor.

However, a preparer should consider separate disclosure of transactions with the above related parties if this would provide useful information to users of the entity's financial statements.

The classification of amounts payable to, and receivable from, related parties in the different categories is an extension of the disclosure requirement in IAS 1 for an entity to present information either in the statement of financial position or in the notes. *[IAS 1.77]*. The categories are extended to provide a more comprehensive analysis of related party balances and apply to related party transactions. *[IAS 24.20]*.

IAS 24 emphasises that an entity should not state that related party transactions are on an arm's length basis unless the reporting entity can demonstrate such terms and conditions. *[IAS 24.23]*. To substantiate that related party transactions are on an arm's length basis an entity would need to document that a transaction with similar terms and conditions could be obtained from an independent third party.

The company financial statements of Schroders plc provide the following disclosures of related party relationships with subsidiaries.

Extract 39.2: Schroders plc (2019)

Notes to the accounts [extract]

37. Related party transactions

The Company is not deemed to be controlled or jointly controlled by a party directly or through intermediaries under IFRS. As a result, the related parties of the Company comprise principally subsidiaries, joint ventures and associates, key management personnel, close family members of key management personnel and any entity controlled by those parties.

The Company has determined that key management personnel comprises only the Board of Directors.

Transactions between related parties

Details of transactions between the Company and its subsidiaries, which are related parties of the Company, and transactions between the Company and other related parties, excluding compensation (which is set out in note 31), are disclosed below:

	2019					
	Revenue £m	Expenses £m	Interest receivable £m	Interest payable £m	Amounts owed by related parties £m	Amounts owed to related parties £m
Subsidiaries of the Company	418.0	18.5	8.5	0.1	1,496.3	(14.7)
Key management personnel	0.3	–	–	(0.1)	–	(46.3)

	2018					
	Revenue £m	Expenses £m	Interest receivable £m	Interest payable £m	Amounts owed by related parties £m	Amounts owed to related parties £m
Subsidiaries of the Company	447.0	22.4	5.6	0.2	1,427.9	(7.5)
Key management personnel	0.4	–	–	0.1	3.8	(42.5)

Transactions with related parties were made at market rates. The amounts outstanding are unsecured and will be settled in cash.

The consolidated financial statements of J Sainsbury plc provide the following disclosures of related party relationships with joint ventures and associates.

> **Extract 39.3: J Sainsbury plc (2020)**
>
> Notes to the consolidated financial statements [extract]
> 40 Related party transactions [extract]
>
> b)   Joint ventures and associates [extract]
>
> Transactions with joint ventures and associates
>
> For the 52 weeks to 7 March 2020, the Group entered into various transactions with joint ventures and associates as set out below:
>
> | | 2020 £m | 2019 £m |
> |---|---|---|
> | Dividends and distributions received | 141 | 18 |
> | Repayment of loans from joint venture | – | (5) |
> | Disposals of joint ventures | (21) | – |
> | Rental expenses paid | (14) | (38) |
>
> Year-end balances arising from transactions with joint ventures and associates
>
> | | 2020 £m | 2019 £m |
> |---|---|---|
> | **Payables** | | |
> | Other payables | 18 | (5) |

The financial statements of British Sky Broadcasting Group plc illustrate the disclosure of transactions with a party controlled by a close family member of key management.

> **Extract 39.4: British Sky Broadcasting Group plc (2014)**
>
> Notes to the consolidated financial statements [extract]
> 28. Transactions with related parties and major shareholders [extract]
>
> c) Other transactions with related parties [extract]
>
> A close family member of one Director of the Company runs Freud Communications Limited ("Freud"), which has provided external support to the press and publicity activities of the Group. During the year the Group incurred expenditure amounting to £1 million (2013: £1 million) with Freud. At 30 June 2014 there was £1 million (2013: less than £1 million) due to Freud.

The financial statements of BP p.l.c. illustrate the disclosure of commitments to related parties:

> Extract 39.5: BP p.l.c. (2019)
> Notes on financial statements [extract]
> 13. Capital commitments
> Authorized future capital expenditure for property, plant and equipment (excluding right-of-use assets) by group companies for which contracts had been signed at 31 December 2019 amounted to $11,382 million (2018 $8,319 million, 2017 $11,340 million). BP has contracted capital commitments amounting to $787 million (2018 $1,227 million, 2017 $1,451 million) in relation to associates. BP's share of contracted capital commitments of joint ventures amounted to $1,024 million (2018 $619 million, 2017 $483 million).
>
> 17. Investments in associates [extract]
> BP has commitments amounting to $11,198 million (2018 $11,303 million), primarily in relation to contracts with its associates for the purchase of transportation capacity.

2.8 Disclosure of expense incurred with management entity

As discussed at 2.2.9 above disclosure of amounts incurred by the entity for the provision of key management personnel services by a separate management entity is required. *[IAS 24.18A]*.

2.9 Disclosures with government-related entities

IAS 24 provides an exemption from the disclosure requirements of paragraph 18, discussed at 2.7.2 above, in relation to related party transactions and outstanding balances, including commitments, with:

(a) a government that has control or joint control of, or significant influence over, the reporting entity; and

(b) another entity that is a related party because the same government has control or joint control of, or significant influence over, both the reporting entity and the other entity. *[IAS 24.25]*.

From the wording of (a) and (b) above, it would be possible to conclude that a reporting entity which is significantly influenced by a government is related to another entity also significantly influenced by the same government. This is not the case. The definition of a related party in IAS 24 does not include entities that are subject to significant influence from the same entity but are not otherwise related parties as defined in IAS 24 (see 2.2.3 above) and the definition in paragraph 25 cannot add to the definition of a related party.

The application of the disclosure exemption afforded by paragraph 18 is illustrated in the example below, which is based on an illustrative example accompanying IAS 24.

Example 39.10:   Application of the disclosure exemption for government-related entities

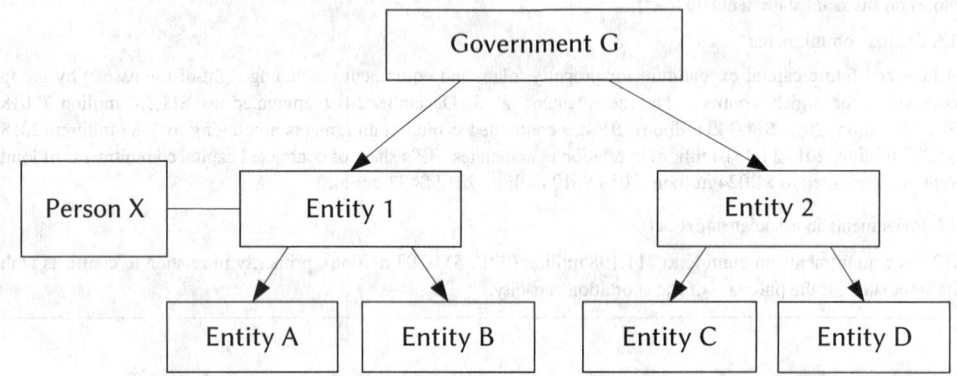

Government G directly or indirectly controls Entities 1 and 2 and Entities A, B, C and D. Person X is a member of the key management personnel of Entity 1.

For Entity A's financial statements the exemption applies to: (a) transactions with Government G which is the government that ultimately controls Entity A; and (b) transactions with Entities 1, 2, B, C and D which are related entities because they are controlled by the same government as A, i.e.: Government G.

The exemption does not apply to transactions with Person X because Person X is not controlled by Government G.

The use of the disclosure exemption is conditional on the reporting entity making the following disclosures about the transactions and related outstanding balances with the government-related entities:

(a) the name of the government and the nature of its relationship with the reporting entity (i.e. control, joint control or significant influence);

(b) the following information in sufficient detail to enable users of the entity's financial statements to understand the effect of related party transactions on its financial statements:

   (i) the nature and amount of each individually significant transaction; and

   (ii) for other transactions that are collectively, but not individually, significant, a qualitative or quantitative indication of their extent. Types of transactions include those discussed at 2.7.1 above. *[IAS 24.26]*.

The wording above does not explicitly mention 'commitments' when referring to transactions. However, given that IAS 24 describes a commitment as a form of transaction (see 2.7.1 above), disclosure of individually and collectively significant commitments with government-related entities is required.

In using its judgement to determine the level of detail to be disclosed in accordance with the requirements in (b) above, a reporting entity considers the closeness of the related party relationship and other factors, including materiality, relevant in establishing the level of significance of the transaction such as whether it is:

(a) significant in terms of size;
(b) carried out on non-market terms;
(c) outside normal day-to-day business operations, such as the purchase and sale of businesses;
(d) disclosed to regulatory or supervisory authorities;
(e) reported to senior management; and
(f) subject to shareholder approval. *[IAS 24.27]*.

Disclosure of the nature and amount of each individually significant transaction is not a requirement for other related party transactions (see 2.7.2 above). The Board considered that this requirement should not be too onerous for a reporting entity because:

(a) individually significant transactions should be a small subset, by number, of total related party transactions;
(b) the reporting entity should know what these transactions are; and
(c) reporting such items on an exceptional basis takes into account cost-benefit considerations. *[IAS 24.BC45]*.

The Board also considered that more disclosure of individually significant transactions would better meet the objective of IAS 24 because this approach focuses on transactions that, through their nature or size, are of more interest to users and are more likely to be affected by the related party relationship. *[IAS 24.BC46]*. In response to concerns about whether a reporting entity would be able to identify whether the counterparty to such transactions was a government-related entity, the Board concluded that 'management will know, or will apply more effort in establishing, who the counterparty to an individually significant transaction is and will have, or be able to obtain, background information on the counterparty'. *[IAS 24.BC47-48]*.

Extract 39.6 below from the financial statements of The Royal Bank of Scotland Group plc illustrates disclosure summarising the types of transactions with government-controlled entities that are related parties and details of an individually material transaction.

Extract 39.6: The Royal Bank of Scotland Group plc (2019)

Notes on the consolidated accounts [extract]

32   Related parties [extract]

UK Government

On 1 December 2008, the UK Government through HM Treasury became the ultimate controlling party of The Royal Bank of Scotland Group plc. The UK Government's shareholding is managed by UK Government Investments Limited, a company wholly owned by the UK Government. As a result, the UK Government and UK Government controlled bodies became related parties of RBS Group.

In 2015, HM Treasury sold 630 million of RBSG plc's ordinary shares and a further 925 million in June 2018. At 31 December 2019, HM Treasury's holding in the company's ordinary shares was 62.1%.

RBS Group enters into transactions with many of these bodies on an arm's length basis. Transactions include the payment of: taxes – principally UK corporation tax (Note 7) and value added tax; national insurance contributions; local authority rates; and regulatory fees and levies (including the bank levy (Note 3) and FSCS levies (Note 26) together with banking transactions such as loans and deposits undertaken in the normal course of banker-customer relationships.

The following are other illustrations of the type of disclosures required for transactions with government-related entities based on examples in the standard:

Example 39.11: Individually significant transaction carried out on non-market terms

On 15 January 2021 the company sold a 10-hectare piece of land to an entity controlled by Government G for €5,000,000. On 31 December 2021 a plot of land in a similar location, of similar size and with similar characteristics, was sold for €3,000,000. There had not been any appreciation or depreciation of the land in the intervening period. See Note X for disclosure of government assistance as required by IAS 20.

Example 39.12: Individually significant transaction because of size of transaction

In the year ended 31 December 2021 Government G provided the company with a loan equivalent to 50% of its funding requirement, repayable in quarterly instalments over the next five years. Interest is charged on the loan at a rate of 5%, which is comparable to that charged on the company's external bank loans.

Example 39.13: Collectively significant transactions

The company's significant transactions with Government G and other entities controlled, jointly controlled or significantly influenced by Government G are a large portion of its sales of goods and purchases of raw materials [alternatively – about 50% of its sales of goods and services and about 35% of its purchases of raw materials].

The company also benefits from guarantees by Government G of the company's bank borrowing. See Note X of the financial statements for disclosure of government assistance as required by IAS 20.

In Example 39.13 above, either a qualitative or a quantitative disclosure is permitted for transactions that are collectively but not individually significant.

References

1 *IFRIC Update*, May 2015, IASB.
2 *Making Materiality Judgements*, September 2017, IASB Practice Statement, para. 48 and examples I and J.
3 *The Conceptual Framework for Financial Reporting*, March 2018, para. 2.11.

Chapter 40 Statement of cash flows

1 INTRODUCTION 3135
    1.1   Background 3135
    1.2   The statement of cash flows as a primary financial statement 3135
    1.3   Transparency and consistency of cash flow presentation 3136
    1.4   Future developments 3137
    1.5   Terms used in IAS 7 3137

2 OBJECTIVE AND SCOPE OF IAS 7 3137
    2.1   Objective 3137
    2.2   Scope 3138

3 CASH AND CASH EQUIVALENTS 3138
    3.1   Components of cash equivalents and explanation of cash management policies 3139
    3.2   Components of cash and cash equivalents 3139
        3.2.1   Demand deposits and short-term investments 3139
        3.2.2   Money market funds...3140
        3.2.3   Investments with maturities greater than three months 3141
        3.2.4   Bank overdrafts 3142
        3.2.5   Cryptocurrencies.. 3142
        3.2.6   Client money.. 3143
    3.3   Reconciliation with items in the statement of financial position 3143
    3.4   Restrictions on the use of cash and cash equivalents 3143

4 CLASSIFICATION IN THE STATEMENT OF CASH FLOWS 3145
    4.1   Cash flows from operating activities..3147
        4.1.1   The direct method 3148
        4.1.2   The indirect method 3149
    4.2   Cash flows from investing activities.. 3151
    4.3   Cash flows from financing activities 3152

	4.4	Allocating items to operating, investing and financing activities	3153
		4.4.1 Interest and dividends	3153
		4.4.2 Taxes on income	3154
		4.4.3 Sales taxes and other non-income tax cash flows	3154
		4.4.4 Cash contributions to a long-term employee benefit fund	3155
		4.4.5 Cash flows from factoring of trade receivables	3155
		4.4.6 Cash flows from supply-chain financing and reverse factoring arrangements	3156
		4.4.7 Property, plant and equipment held for rental	3159
		4.4.8 Cash received as compensation for an insured loss	3159
		4.4.9 Cash flows for service concession arrangements	3160
		4.4.10 Treasury shares	3160
		4.4.11 Cash flows related to the costs of a share issue	3161
		4.4.12 Cash flows on derivative contracts	3161
		4.4.13 Debt instrument issued at a discount or redeemed at a premium	3162
		4.4.14 Early settlement of a debt instrument	3162
		4.4.15 Classification of cash flows – future developments	3163
5.	OTHER CASH FLOW PRESENTATION ISSUES		3163
	5.1	Material cash flows	3163
	5.2	Gross or net presentation of cash flows	3164
	5.3	Foreign currency cash flows	3165
		5.3.1 Entities applying the direct method	3165
		5.3.2 Entities applying the indirect method	3165
		5.3.2.A Treatment of operating cash flows	3166
		5.3.2.B Treatment of non-operating cash flows	3166
		5.3.2.C The indirect method and foreign subsidiaries	3166
	5.4	Non-cash transactions and transactions on deferred terms	3166
		5.4.1 Asset purchased on deferred terms from the supplier	3167
		5.4.2 Asset disposals on deferred terms	3167
		5.4.3 Revenue contracts with deferred payment terms	3168
	5.5	Cash flows from leasing transactions	3168
		5.5.1 Accounting as lessee	3168
		5.5.2 Payments made by the lessee before commencement date	3169
		5.5.3 Lease incentives	3169
		5.5.4 Sale and leaseback transactions	3169
		5.5.5 Accounting as lessor	3171
	5.6	Changes in liabilities arising from financing activities	3171
	5.7	Voluntary disclosures	3173
		5.7.1 Cash flows to increase and maintain operating capacity	3173

		5.7.2	Segment cash flow disclosures	3173
6	ADDITIONAL IAS 7 CONSIDERATIONS FOR GROUPS			3174
	6.1	Preparing a consolidated statement of cash flows		3175
	6.2	Transactions with non-controlling interests		3175
	6.3	Acquisitions and disposals		3176
		6.3.1	Acquisition-related costs	3177
		6.3.2	Deferred and other non-cash consideration	3178
		6.3.3	Contingent consideration	3178
			6.3.3.A Business combinations	3178
			6.3.3.B Asset acquisitions outside of business combinations	3178
			6.3.3.C Contingent consideration received on disposals	3179
		6.3.4	Settlement of amounts owed by the acquired entity	3179
		6.3.5	Settlement of intra-group balances on a demerger	3180
	6.4	Cash flows of associates, joint operations and investment entities		3180
		6.4.1	Investments in associates and joint ventures	3180
		6.4.2	Cash flows of joint operations	3180
		6.4.3	Cash flows in investment entities	3181
	6.5	Cash flows in separate financial statements		3181
		6.5.1	Cash flows of subsidiaries, associates and joint ventures	3181
		6.5.2	Group cash pooling and cash sharing arrangements	3181
		6.5.3	Group treasury arrangements	3182
		6.5.4	Cash pooling	3183
			6.5.4.A Notional cash pooling	3183
			6.5.4.B Physical cash pooling	3183
7	ADDITIONAL IAS 7 CONSIDERATIONS FOR FINANCIAL INSTITUTIONS			3184
	7.1	Operating cash flows		3184
	7.2	Reporting cash flows on a net basis		3185
8	REQUIREMENTS OF OTHER STANDARDS			3185
	8.1	Cash flows of discontinued operations		3185
	8.2	Cash flows arising from insurance contracts		3186
	8.3	Cash flows arising from the exploration of mineral resources		3187
	8.4	Cash flows arising from interests in subsidiaries, joint ventures and associates		3187

List of examples

Example 40.1:   Cash flows from derivatives not designated as hedges 3162
Example 40.2:   Sale and leaseback transaction: presentation of cash flows 3170
Example 40.3:   Reconciliation of liabilities arising from financing activities 3172

Chapter 40   Statement of cash flows

1   INTRODUCTION

1.1   Background

IAS 7 – *Statement of Cash Flows* – is one of the older standards in IFRS, having been issued in 1992.

The standard specifies how entities report information about the historical changes in cash and cash equivalents and applies to all entities regardless of their business activities, including financial institutions. Modifications to IAS 7 since it was originally published have been limited resulting in a standard that is much shorter and more succinct than many new and revised standards. It was last updated in 2016 to require entities to provide disclosures about changes in liabilities arising from financing activities.

IAS 7 requires that inflows and outflows of cash and cash equivalents are classified and reported under three different headings being:

- operating activities;
- investing activities; and
- financing activities. *[IAS 7.10]*.

The resulting information in the statement of cash flows should provide insight into an entity's ability to generate cash to fund operations, reinvest to maintain or expand operating capacity, repay debt and distribute dividends, and how it manages cash.

The definitions of operating, investing and financing activities in the standard, which are covered at 1.5 below, provide guidance on how to distinguish the cash flows by activity.

1.2   The statement of cash flows as a primary financial statement

The statement of cash flows is a primary financial statement and should be presented with equal prominence to the income statement, the statement of financial position and the statement of changes in equity. *[IAS 1.11]*. Arguably, it provides some of the most important information in the financial statements, as all entities need cash to run their day-to-day operations, pay their obligations and provide returns to investors, regardless of their particular line of business or geographical location.

This information, when combined with information in the rest of the financial statements, is useful in assessing factors that may affect the entity's liquidity, financial flexibility, profitability, and risk.

The importance of information on cash flows in the reporting period as a means to help users understand a reporting entity's operations, evaluate its financing and investing activities, assess its liquidity or solvency and interpret other information about financial performance is highlighted by the *Conceptual Framework for Financial Reporting* [CF 1.20] and was rightfully emphasized by the IFRS Interpretations Committee in its July 2014 agenda decision regarding the presentation and content of the condensed statement of cash flows in the interim financial statements according to IAS 34 – *Interim Financial Reporting*. It also helps users to assess management's stewardship of the entity's economic resources. The Framework guidance is further discussed in Chapter 2 at 4.2.2.

1.3 Transparency and consistency of cash flow presentation

In recent years, the statement of cash flows has become an area of scrutiny for investors as well as regulators from a number of different jurisdictions, with both misclassification errors and insufficient disclosures highlighted as areas of concern.

This is partly because the use of cashflows as a key performance metric in the entities' communication to the financial markets has become increasingly common along with, and sometimes even in replacement of, some other KPIs more focused on the generation of income.

Yet, this is also because the definitions of operating, investing and financing activities in IAS 7 are broad and only illustrated by lists of examples which are not exhaustive. Whilst it is tempting to think that cash flows should be a simple statement of fact and there is less need for judgement around recognition and measurement of cash flows compared to other areas of the financial statements, the lack of clarity in the standard as to how some cash flows from common transactions should be categorised has resulted in diversity amongst preparers. Some common areas where judgement may be required to classify investments in cash and flows are discussed at 3 and 4 below in reference to the definition of cash and cash equivalents and classification judgements.

In addition, the interaction of IAS 7 with new standards such as IFRS 9 – *Financial Instruments*, IFRS 15 – *Revenue from Contracts with Customers* – and IFRS 16 – *Leases* – has led to further difficulties in applying the standard.

The IFRS Interpretations Committee has received numerous requests for clarification on the requirements of the standard. However, clarifications have never been finalised, leaving preparers and users faced with ambiguity and inconsistency in the application of a standard in need of improvements.

Because the preparation of a cash flow statement is not merely a mechanical exercise, investors and regulators have focused on the adequacy of disclosures explaining how the requirements of IAS 7 have been applied. In our view, where the appropriate classification of cash flows in the cash flow statement is not clear from IAS 7 and an entity has therefore applied judgement to determine the appropriate presentation of material items based on the principals of IAS 7, these judgements should be clearly disclosed. This is further discussed at 5.7 below.

1.4 Future developments

Looking to the future, the IASB has proposed limited changes to the requirements of IAS 7 in the Exposure Draft 2019/7 – *General Presentation and Disclosures*, which was issued in December 2019. This is further discussed at 4.4.15 below. However, these proposed changes do not address many of the classification issues that are discussed in this chapter.

The Interpretations Committee has recently considered one specific area of judgement being the presentation and disclosure, including the presentation in the statement of cash flow, of the use of supply chain financing. Stakeholders have raised concerns about the transparency of these arrangements and the lack of consistency of treatment, particularly considering the attention that undisclosed supply chain financing arrangement have attracted in recent high-profile corporate failings. In June 2020 the committee published a tentative agenda decision outlining how IFRS, including IAS 7, should be applied to the different aspects of accounting for these arrangements.[1] The nature of supply chain financing and the committee's discussions are addressed at 4.4.5 below.

1.5 Terms used in IAS 7

The following terms are used in IAS 7 with the meanings specified: *[IAS 7.6]*

Cash comprises cash on hand and demand deposits.

Cash equivalents are short-term, highly liquid investments that are readily convertible to known amounts of cash and which are subject to an insignificant risk of changes in value.

Cash flows are inflows and outflows of cash and cash equivalents.

Operating activities are the principal revenue-producing activities of the entity and other activities that are not investing or financing activities.

Investing activities are the acquisition and disposal of long-term assets and other investments not included in cash equivalents.

Financing activities are activities that result in changes in the size and composition of the contributed equity and borrowings of the entity.

2 OBJECTIVE AND SCOPE OF IAS 7

2.1 Objective

The objective of IAS 7 is to require entities to provide information about changes in cash and cash equivalents in the reporting period in a statement which classifies cash flows from operating, investing and financing activities. The standard aims to give users of financial statements a basis to evaluate the entity's ability to generate cash and cash equivalents and its needs to utilise those cash flows. *[IAS 7 Objective]*.

A statement of cash flows, when used in conjunction with the rest of the financial statements, provides information that enables users to evaluate the changes in net assets of an entity, its financial structure (including its liquidity and solvency) and its ability to affect the amounts and timing of cash flows to adapt to changing circumstances and opportunities. *[IAS 7.4]*. The historical cash flow information is often used as an indicator of the amount, timing and certainty of future cash flows. It is also useful in examining the relationship between profitability and net cash flow and the impact of changing prices. *[IAS 7.5]*.

2.2 Scope

IAS 7 applies to all entities, regardless of size, operations, ownership structure or industry, and therefore includes wholly owned subsidiaries and banks, insurance entities and other financial institutions. There are no exemptions from the standard. The standard argues that users of an entity's financial statements are interested in how the entity generates and uses cash and cash equivalents regardless of the nature of the entity's activities and irrespective of whether cash can be viewed as the product of the entity, as may be the case with a financial institution. All entities need cash to conduct their operations, to pay their obligations, and to provide returns to their investors. Accordingly, all entities are required to present a statement of cash flows. *[IAS 7.3]*. A statement of cash flows is required to make up a complete set of any financial statements in accordance with IFRS. *[IAS 1.10]*. Therefore, the parent entity's cash flow statement should be presented even if the separate financial statements are presented together with consolidated financial statements which include a consolidated statement of cash flows.

3 CASH AND CASH EQUIVALENTS

Since the objective of a statement of cash flows is to provide an analysis of changes in cash and cash equivalents, the definitions of cash and of cash equivalents at 1.5 above are essential to its presentation. It is also important to understand the reporting entity's cash management policies, especially when considering whether balances that are not obviously cash on hand and demand deposits should be classified as cash equivalents, as the standard states that cash equivalents are held to meet short-term cash commitments rather than for investment or other purposes. *[IAS 7.7]*. Cash management includes the investment of cash in excess of immediate needs into cash equivalents, *[IAS 7.9]*, such as short-term investments. For investments to qualify as a cash equivalent, they must be:

- short term;
- highly liquid;
- readily convertible into known amounts of cash; and
- subject to insignificant risk of changes in value. *[IAS 7.6]*.

However, the purpose for which the investments are held must also be considered and this is a matter of facts and circumstances. Where investments meet the four criteria above but are not held by the entity to meet short term cash commitments, they should not be classified as cash equivalents.

A statement of cash flows under IAS 7 excludes movements between cash on hand and cash equivalents because these are components of an entity's cash management, rather than part of its operating, investing and financing activities. *[IAS 7.9]*. However, as shown below, the definition of cash equivalents can cause some difficulty in practice.

3.1 Components of cash equivalents and explanation of cash management policies

Regardless of an entity's cash management policies and practices, an investment can only be classified within cash equivalents if it is held by the entity to meet short term cash commitments and all other criteria in the definition are also satisfied (see 3.2 below).

In view of the variety of cash management practices and banking arrangements around the world, entities are required to disclose the composition of cash and cash equivalents *[IAS 7.45]* and explain their cash management policies. *[IAS 7.46]*.

For example, this is how VTech Holdings and Lufthansa satisfy these requirements:

Extract 40.1: VTech Holdings Limited (2020)

Notes to the Financial Statements [extract]

Principal Accounting Policies [extract]

R   Cash and Cash Equivalents

Cash and cash equivalents comprise cash at bank and on hand, demand deposits with banks and other financial institutions, short-term highly liquid investments that are readily convertible into known amounts of cash and which are subject to an insignificant risk of changes in value, having been within three months of maturity at acquisition. Bank overdrafts that are repayable on demand and form an integral part of the Group's cash management are also included as a component of cash and cash equivalents for the purpose of the statement of cash flows. Cash and cash equivalents are assessed for ECLs in accordance with the policy set out in note (N)(i).

Extract 40.2: Deutsche Lufthansa AG (2019)

CONSOLIDATED FINANCIAL STATEMENTS [extract]

Notes to the consolidated financial statements [extract]

NOTES TO THE CONSOLIDATED CASH FLOW STATEMENT [extract]

42 Notes to cash flow from operating, investing and financing activities [extract]

The cash flow statement shows how cash and cash equivalents have changed over the reporting period at the Lufthansa Group. In accordance with IAS 7, cash flows are divided into cash inflows and outflows from operating activities, from investing activities and from financing activities. The cash and cash equivalents shown in the cash flow statement comprise the statement of financial position items bank balances and cash-in-hand, without fixed-term deposits with terms of three to twelve months, amounting to EUR 0m (previous year: EUR 66m). The amount of liquidity in the broader sense is reached by adding securities that can be liquidated at short notice.

If an entity changes the purpose for which it holds certain investments, for example a deposit which was previously held for short term cash management is now held to generate an investment return, this would be considered a change in facts and circumstances, which would be accounted for prospectively. In these circumstances, the reclassification out of cash and cash equivalents would appear as a reconciling item in the cash flow statement.

3.2 Components of cash and cash equivalents

3.2.1 Demand deposits and short-term investments

In defining 'cash', IAS 7 does not explain what is meant by 'demand deposits', perhaps because the term is commonly understood as amounts that can be withdrawn on demand, without prior notice being required or a penalty being charged (for example, by an additional fee or forfeiture of interest). In any event, the distinction is largely irrelevant because amounts not classified as demand deposits may still qualify as cash equivalents and end up being treated in the same way. Thus, whether an amount meets the definition of a cash equivalent may become the more important determination.

Cash equivalents are held for the purpose of meeting short-term cash commitments rather than for investment or other purposes. For an investment to qualify as a cash equivalent it must be readily convertible to a known amount of cash and be subject to an insignificant risk of changes in value. Normally only an investment with a short maturity of, say, three months or less from the date of acquisition qualifies as a cash equivalent. Equity investments are excluded unless they are cash equivalents in substance. IAS 7 provides an example of such an instrument, being redeemable preference shares acquired within a short period of their maturity and with a specified redemption date. *[IAS 7.7]*. The Interpretations Committee considered, in July 2009,[2] what the standard means when it refers to a 'known amount of cash' and confirmed that the amount of cash that will be received must be known at the time of the initial investment. Accordingly, traded commodities, such as gold bullion, would not be eligible for inclusion in cash equivalents because the proceeds to be realised from such an investment is determined at the date of disposal rather than being known or determinable when the investment is made.

Cash held in a foreign currency or investments acquired in a currency other than the functional currency of the entity ('foreign currency') are not excluded from qualifying as cash and cash equivalents merely because they are denominated in a foreign currency, provided they meet the other criteria discussed above. *[IAS 7.28]*.

3.2.2 Money market funds

Entities commonly invest in money market-type funds such as an open-ended mutual fund that invests in money market instruments like certificates of deposit, commercial paper, treasury bills, bankers' acceptances and repurchase agreements. Although there are different types of money market funds, they generally aim to provide investors with low-risk, low-return investment while preserving the value of the assets and maintaining a high level of liquidity. The question then arises as to whether investments in such funds can be classified as cash equivalents. As discussed below, entities may consider the underlying investments of the fund when assessing the significance of the risk of changes in value, however when determining whether classification as a cash equivalent is appropriate, the unit of account is the investment in the money market fund itself.

To meet the definition of a cash equivalent, an investment must be: short term; highly liquid; readily convertible to a known amount of cash; and subject to insignificant risk of changes in value. IAS 7 considers a maturity date of three months or less from the date of acquisition to be short-term in the context of maturity, however money market funds generally do not have a legal maturity date. Instead, if the investments are puttable and can be sold back to the fund at any time, they may meet the short-term criterion.

Typically, investments in money market funds are redeemed directly with the fund, therefore in assessing liquidity of the investment, focus should be on the liquidity of the fund itself. In making this assessment, entities should consider the nature of any redemption restrictions in place as these may prevent the redemption of the investment in the short term. Alternatively, if a money market fund investment is quoted in an active market, it might be regarded as highly liquid on that basis.

The short-term and highly liquid investment must also be readily convertible into known amounts of cash which are subject to an insignificant risk of changes in value. [IAS 7.6]. As discussed at 3.2.1 above this means that the amount of cash that will be received must be known at the time of the initial investment. Accordingly, investments in shares or units of money market funds cannot be considered as cash equivalents simply because they are convertible at any time at the then market price in an active market.

The Interpretations Committee also confirmed that an entity would have to satisfy itself that any investment was subject to an insignificant risk of change in value for it to be classified as a cash equivalent.[3] In assessing whether the change in value of an investment in a money market fund can be regarded as insignificant, an entity must conclude that the range of possible returns is very small. This evaluation is first made at the time of acquiring the investment and reassessment is required if the facts and circumstances change. The evaluation will involve consideration of factors such as: the maturity of the underlying investments of the fund; the credit rating of the fund; the nature of the investments held by the fund (i.e. not subject to volatility); the extent of diversification in the portfolio (which is expected to be very high); the investment policy of the fund; and any mechanisms by the fund to guarantee returns (for example by reference to short-term money market interest rates).

Investments are often held for purposes other than to act as a ready store of value that can be quickly converted into cash when needed to meet short-term cash commitments. It is therefore important, even where the criteria above are met, to understand why the entity has invested in a particular money market fund. Where an investment otherwise satisfies the criteria in paragraph 6 of IAS 7, but is not held by the entity to satisfy short-term cash commitments, it should not be classified as a cash equivalent.

Substantial judgement may be required in assessing whether an investment in money market funds can be classified as a cash equivalent. Therefore, appropriate disclosure is essential. As discussed at 3.1 above, entities are required to disclose the composition of cash equivalents and, where relevant, this should include significant judgements made in classifying investments in money market funds.

3.2.3 Investments with maturities greater than three months

The longer the term of the investment, the greater the risk that a change in market conditions (such as interest rates) can significantly affect its value. For this reason, IAS 7 excludes most equity investments from cash equivalents and restricts the inclusion of other investments to those with a short maturity of, say, three months or less from the date of their acquisition by the entity. [IAS 7.7].

Similarly, an investment with a term on acquisition of, say, nine months is not reclassified as a cash equivalent from the date on which there is less than three months remaining to its maturity. If such reclassifications were permitted, the statement of cash flows would have to reflect movements between investments and cash equivalents. This would be misleading because no actual cash flows would have occurred.

The criteria explained above are guidelines, not rules, and a degree of common sense should be used in their application. In the final analysis, cash equivalents are held to meet short-term cash commitments and amounts should be included in cash equivalents only if they can be regarded as being nearly as accessible as cash and essentially as free from exposure to changes in value as cash.

For example, an entity might justify including in cash equivalents a fixed deposit with an original term longer than three months if it effectively functions like a demand deposit. Typically, a fixed deposit will carry a penalty charge for withdrawal prior to maturity. A penalty will usually indicate that the investment is held for investment purposes rather than the purpose of meeting short-term cash needs. However, some fixed deposits still offer interest at a prevailing demand deposit rate in the event of early withdrawal, with any penalty limited to the entity being required to forego the incremental higher interest that it would have received if the deposit were held to maturity. In this case, it may be arguable that there is effectively no significant penalty for early withdrawal, as the entity receives at least the same return that it otherwise would have in a demand deposit arrangement. Where an entity does assert that this type of investment is held for meeting short-term cash needs and classifies the investment as a cash equivalent, the calculation of the effective interest rate (EIR) in accordance with IFRS 9 should be on a consistent basis. IFRS 9 requires that, when calculating the EIR, all contractual terms of the financial instrument, for example prepayments, call and similar options, should be considered. See Chapter 50 at 3.4. *[IFRS 9 Appendix A]*. In this example, the entity is asserting that it is likely to withdraw the deposit should the need arise and, as a consequence, will only receive interest at the (lower) demand deposit rate. Therefore, the EIR should reflect this intention.

3.2.4 Bank overdrafts

Although bank borrowings are generally considered to be financing activities, there are circumstances in which bank overdrafts repayable on demand are included as a component of cash and cash equivalents. This is in cases where the use of short-term overdrafts forms an integral part of an entity's cash management practices. Evidence supporting such an assertion would be that the bank balance often fluctuates from being positive to overdrawn. *[IAS 7.8]*.

The Interpretations Committee confirmed that where overdrafts do not often fluctuate from being negative to positive, this is an indicator that the arrangement does not form part of an entity's cash management and, instead, represents a form of financing.[4]

3.2.5 Cryptocurrencies

The Interpretations Committee confirmed in its June 2019 meeting that a holding of cryptocurrency is not cash because cryptocurrencies do not currently have the characteristics of cash.[5] In particular, the Committee noted that, although some cryptocurrencies can be used in exchange for particular goods or services, the Committee is not aware of any cryptocurrency that is used as a medium of exchange or as the monetary unit in pricing goods or services to such an extent that it would be the basis on which all transactions are measured and recognised in financial statements.[6]

Cryptocurrencies are discussed in more detail in Chapter 17 at 11.5.

3.2.6 Client money

Some financial institutions and other entities hold money on behalf of clients. The terms on which such money is held can vary widely. This is discussed in more detail in Chapter 52 at 3.7.

There are numerous types of arrangements that result in an entity holding client money, so it is impossible to generalise as to the appropriate treatment. However, as explained in Chapter 52 at 3.7, where an entity enjoys sufficient use of the client money such that it is exposed to the credit risk associated with the cash and is entitled to all income accruing, the entity would include the client money as part of its cash balance and recognise a corresponding liability. Any restrictions on the use of the cash should be considered and disclosed as explained in 3.4 below.

3.3 Reconciliation with items in the statement of financial position

The amount shown alongside the caption in the statement of financial position for 'cash and cash equivalents' will not always be a reliable guide for IAS 7 purposes. Many entities present the components of cash and cash equivalents separately on the face of the statement of financial position, such as 'cash and bank balances' and 'short-term bank deposits'. Additionally, some entities may include bank overdrafts in cash and cash equivalents for cash flow purposes, but, if no legal right of set-off exists, will present bank overdrafts separate from cash in the statement of financial position as financial liabilities. [IAS 32.42].

The standard requires an entity to disclose the components of cash and cash equivalents and to present a reconciliation to the statement of financial position, [IAS 7.45], which means that any difference between 'cash and cash equivalents' for IAS 7 purposes and presentation in the statement of financial position will be evident in the notes to the financial statements.

Schiphol Group provides a reconciliation of the components of cash and cash equivalents, which includes cash held for sale.

> **Extract 40.3: Royal Schiphol Group N.V. (2017)**
> **Consolidated statement of cash flow for 2017** [extract]
> (in thousands of euros)
>
> | | 2017 | 2016 |
> |---|---|---|
> | Cash from continuing operations | 170,370 | 238,691 |
> | Cash held for sale | – | 12,076 |
> | | 170,370 | 250,767 |

3.4 Restrictions on the use of cash and cash equivalents

The amount of significant cash and cash equivalent balances that is not available for use by the group should be disclosed, together with a commentary by management to explain the circumstances of the restriction. [IAS 7.48]. Examples include cash and cash equivalents held by a subsidiary operating under exchange controls or other legal restrictions that prevent their general use by the parent or other subsidiaries. [IAS 7.49].

The nature of the restriction must also be assessed to determine if the balance is ineligible for inclusion in cash equivalents because the restriction results in the investment ceasing to be highly liquid or readily convertible. For example, where an entity covenants to maintain a minimum level of cash or deposits as security for certain short-term obligations, and provided that no amounts are required to be designated for that specific purpose, such balances could still be regarded as cash equivalents, albeit subject to restrictions, as part of a policy of managing resources to meet short-term commitments.

However, an entity may be required formally to set aside cash, for example as a result of a regulated minimum cash balance or by way of a deposit into an escrow account, as part of a specific project or transaction, such as the acquisition or construction of a property or as conditions of a bond issue. In such circumstances, it is necessary to consider the terms and conditions relating to the account and the conditions relating to both the entity's and the counterparty's access to the funds within it to determine whether it is appropriate for the deposit to be classified in cash equivalents.

In Extract 40.4 below, Lloyds Banking Group has various restricted cash balances. The Bank is required to exclude from cash and cash equivalents the mandatory reserve deposits held with local central banks because these amounts are not available to finance the entity's day-to-day operations. Conversely, certain balances held by its life fund subsidiaries do still meet the definition of cash and cash equivalents, and the Group is only required to disclose the restrictions thereon.

Extract 40.4: Lloyds Banking Group plc (2019)

Notes to the consolidated financial statements [extract]

Note 54: Consolidated cash flow statement [extract]

(D) Analysis of cash and cash equivalents as shown in the balance sheet

	2019 £m	2018 £m	2017 £m
Cash and balances at central banks	55,130	54,663	58,521
Less: mandatory reserve deposits[1]	(3,289)	(2,553)	(957)
	51,841	52,110	57,564
Loans and advances to banks	9,775	6,283	6,611
Less: amounts with a maturity of three months or more	(3,805)	(3,169)	(3,193)
	5,970	3,114	3,418
Total cash and cash equivalents	**57,811**	**55,224**	**60,982**

1   Mandatory reserve deposits are held with local central banks in accordance with statutory requirements; these deposits are not available to finance the Group's day-to-day operations.

Included within cash and cash equivalents at 31 December 2019 is £49 million (31 December 2018: £40 million; 1 January 2018 £48 million; 31 December 2017: £2,322 million) held within the Group's long-term insurance and investments businesses, which is not immediately available for use in the business.

Similarly, in the following extract, InterContinental Hotels Group has a number of restricted cash balances which it includes within 'Other financial assets' on the statement of financial position, rather than in cash and cash equivalents.

> Extract 40.5: InterContinental Hotels Group PLC (2019)
>
> **Notes to the Group Financial Statements** [extract]
>
> **17. Other financial assets** [extract]
>
> **Restricted funds**
>
> The shortfall reserve deposit is held for the specific purpose of funding shortfalls in owner returns relating to the Barclay associate. No amounts required release from the deposit during the current or prior year. Any shortfalls funded are subject to potential clawback in future years. The maximum length of time for which the restricted funds will be held is the life of the hotel management agreement.
>
> Amounts ring-fenced to satisfy insurance claims are principally held in the Group's Captive, which is a regulated entity. Further disclosures are included in note 21.
>
> The bank accounts pledged as security (£31m) are subject to a charge in favour of the members of the UK unfunded pension arrangement (see note 27). The amounts pledged as security may change in future years subject to the trustees' agreement and updated actuarial valuations. The bank accounts will continue to be pledged as security until the date at which the UK unfunded pension liabilities have been fully discharged, unless otherwise agreed with the trustees.

In the exposure draft ED/2014/6 – *Disclosure Initiative – Proposed amendments to IAS 7*, issued in December 2014, the IASB noted that additional restrictions, such as financial disincentives to utilising certain cash balances, or other considerations may be relevant to understanding the liquidity of the entity, as they affect the decision to utilise cash and cash equivalents. The example is given of tax liabilities that would arise on the repatriation of foreign cash and cash equivalent balances. The exposure draft proposed that where such matters exist, they should be disclosed. However, the IASB decided not to take these proposals forward and instead use the work done to date to inform the post implementation review of IFRS 12 – *Disclosure of Interests in Other Entities*.[7] Nevertheless, entities might want to consider making additional disclosures where such restrictions or disincentives exist.

4   CLASSIFICATION IN THE STATEMENT OF CASH FLOWS

The statement of cash flows reports inflows and outflows of cash and cash equivalents during the period classified under:

- operating activities;
- investing activities; and
- financing activities. *[IAS 7.10]*.

This classification is intended to allow users to assess the impact of these three types of activity on the financial position of the entity and the amount of its cash and cash equivalents. Whilst not stated explicitly in the standard, the presentation of operating, investing and financing cash flows usually follows this sequence in practice, and a total net cash flow for each standard heading should be shown. Comparative figures are required for all items in the statement of cash flows and the related notes. *[IAS 1.38]*.

The components of cash flows are classified as operating, investing or financing activities in a manner which is most appropriate to the business of the entity. *[IAS 7.11]*. For example, the purchase of investments is likely to be classified as an operating cash flow for a financial institution, but as an investing cash flow for a manufacturer. Additionally, a single transaction may comprise elements of differently classified cash flows. For example, when repayments on a loan include both interest and capital, the element reflecting the interest expense may be included in either operating activities or financing activities (see 4.4.1 below) whereas the capital repayment must be classified as a financing cash flow. [IAS 7.12].

The format of the statement of cash flows is illustrated in Extract 40.6. As permitted by the standard, AstraZeneca has included interest paid under operating activities, interest received under investing activities and dividends paid under financing activities.

Extract 40.6: AstraZeneca PLC (2019)

Financial Statements [extract]
Consolidated Statement of Cash Flows
for the year ended 31 December

	Notes	2019 $m	2018 $m	2017 $m
Cash flows from operating activities				
Profit before tax		1,548	1,993	2,227
Finance income and expense	3	1,260	1,281	1,395
Share of after tax losses of associates and joint ventures	11	116	113	55
Depreciation, amortisation and impairment		3,762	3,753	3,036
(Increase)/decrease in trade and other receivables		(898)	(523)	83
Increase in inventories		(316)	(13)	(548)
Increase/(decrease) in trade and other payables and provisions		868	(103)	415
Gains on disposal of intangible assets	2	(1,243)	(1,885)	(1,518)
Fair value movements on contingent consideration arising from business combinations	20	(614)	(495)	109
Non-cash and other movements	17	378	(290)	(524)
Cash generated from operations		4,861	3,831	4,730
Interest paid		(774)	(676)	(698)
Tax paid		(1,118)	(537)	(454)
Net cash inflow from operating activities		2,969	2,618	3,578
Cash flows from investing activities				
Non-contingent payments on business combinations		–	–	(1,450)
Payment of contingent consideration from business combinations	20	(709)	(349)	(434)
Purchase of property, plant and equipment		(979)	(1,043)	(1,326)
Disposal of property, plant and equipment		37	12	83
Purchase of intangible assets		(1,481)	(328)	(294)
Disposal of intangible assets		2,076	2,338	1,376
Movement in profit-participation liability		150	–	–
Purchase of non-current asset investments		(13)	(102)	(96)
Disposal of non-current asset investments		18	24	70
Movement in short-term investments, fixed deposits and other investing instruments		194	405	(345)
Payments to joint ventures	11	(74)	(187)	(76)
Interest received		124	193	164
Net cash (outflow)/ inflow from investing activities		(657)	963	(2,328)
Net cash inflow before financing activities		2,312	3,581	1,250

Cash flows from financing activities				
Proceeds from issue of share capital		3,525	34	43
Issue of loans		500	2,971	1,988
Repayment of loans		(1,500)	(1,400)	(1,750)
Dividends paid		(3,592)	(3,484)	(3,519)
Hedge contracts relating to dividend payments		4	(67)	(20)
Repayment of obligations under leases		(186)	–	(14)
Movement in short-term borrowings		(516)	(98)	336
Net cash outflow from financing activities		(1,765)	(2,044)	(2,936)
Net increase/(decrease) in Cash and cash equivalents in the period		547	1,537	(1,686)
Cash and cash equivalents at the beginning of the period		4,671	3,172	4,924
Exchange rate effects		5	(38)	(66)
Cash and cash equivalents at the end of the period	17	5,223	4,671	3,172

Having reviewed a variety of requests received from constituents for further guidance on the classification of cash flows, the Interpretations Committee and the IASB have reiterated the general requirement set out in paragraph 11 of IAS 7 that the primary principle for classification of cash flows should be in accordance with the nature of the activity in a manner that is most appropriate to the business of the entity.[8]

4.1 Cash flows from operating activities

Operating activities are defined as 'the principal revenue-producing activities of the entity and other activities that are not investing or financing activities'. *[IAS 7.6]*. The standard states that the value of information on operating cash flows is twofold. It provides a key indicator of the extent to which the entity has generated sufficient cash flows from its operations to repay debt, pay dividends and make investments to maintain and increase its operating capability, without recourse to external sources of financing. Also, information about the components of historical operating cash flows may assist in the process of forecasting future operating cash flows, when used in conjunction with other financial statement information. *[IAS 7.13]*.

Cash flows from operating activities generally result from transactions and other events that enter into the determination of profit or loss. Examples include: *[IAS 7.14]*

(a) cash receipts from the sale of goods and the rendering of services;
(b) cash receipts from royalties, fees, commissions and other revenue;
(c) cash payments to suppliers for goods and services;
(d) cash payments to and on behalf of employees;
(e) cash receipts and cash payments of an insurance entity for premiums and claims, annuities and other policy benefits;
(f) cash payments or refunds of income taxes unless they can be specifically identified with financing and investing activities; and
(g) cash receipts and payments from contracts held for dealing or trading purposes (see 4.4.12 below regarding the allocation of cash flows on derivative contracts).

Operating activities is also a 'default category' for any cash flows that do not meet the criteria of investing or financing cash flows. For example, as discussed at 6.3.1 below, acquisition-related costs in a business combination that must be recognised as an expense, *[IFRS 3.53]*, would also be classified as operating cash flows because there is no related asset that would justify classification as an investing cash flow. *[IAS 7.16]*.

When an entity holds securities and loans for dealing or trading purposes, they are similar to inventory acquired specifically for resale. Therefore, any related cash flows are classified as operating activities. Similarly, cash advances and loans made by financial institutions are usually classified as operating activities, since they relate to the main revenue-generating activity of that entity (see 7.1 below). *[IAS 7.15]*. IFRS 17 – *Insurance Contracts*, which is effective for periods beginning on or after 1 January 2023 (see Chapter 56 at 17.1), deletes the example in (e) above from IAS 7.

The proceeds from the sale of property, plant and equipment, which are usually included in cash flows from investing activities, are an example of an item that enters into the determination of profit or loss that is not usually an operating cash flow. *[IAS 7.14]*. However, the proceeds from sales of assets previously held for rental purposes are classified as cash flows from operating activities if the entity routinely sells such assets in its ordinary course of business. Similarly, cash payments to manufacture or acquire property, plant and equipment held for rental to others, and that are routinely sold in the ordinary course of business after rental, are also classified as cash flows from operating activities (see 4.4.7 below). *[IAS 7.14]*.

Cash flows from operating activities may be reported on a gross or net basis, also known as the direct and indirect methods. *[IAS 7.18]*. The use of the direct or indirect method is an accounting policy choice and should be applied consistently from period to period. Any change in method should be reported under IAS 8 – *Accounting Policies, Changes in Accounting Estimates and Errors*. This would require comparatives to be restated and additional disclosures given, including the reasons for the change in policy. *[IAS 8.29]*.

4.1.1 The direct method

Under the direct method, major classes of gross cash receipts and gross cash payments are disclosed. *[IAS 7.18]*. IAS 7 encourages entities to use the direct method, because it provides information which may be useful in estimating future cash flows and which is not available under the indirect method. *[IAS 7.19]*.

Under the direct method, information about major classes of gross cash receipts and payments may be obtained either:

(a) from the accounting records of the entity (essentially based on an analysis of the cash book); or

(b) by adjusting sales, cost of sales (interest and similar income and interest expenses and similar charges for a financial institution) and other items in the statement of comprehensive income for:

    (i) changes during the period in inventories and operating receivables and payables;

    (ii) other non-cash items; and

    (iii) other items for which the cash effects are investing or financing cash flows.

[IAS 7.19].

A statement of cash flows prepared under the direct method should include the same disclosures of gross cash receipts and gross cash payments irrespective of which approach has been used to determine their value. There is no requirement for entities using the approach described in (b) above to present a reconciliation showing the adjustments made between, for example, revenue in the statement of comprehensive income and cash receipts from customers.

African Rainbow Minerals Limited is an example of an entity using the direct method for presenting its cash flows from operating activities, as illustrated in Extract 40.7 below.

Extract 40.7: African Rainbow Minerals Limited (2019)

STATEMENTS OF CASH FLOWS [extract]

for the year ended 30 June 2019

	Notes	Group F2019 Rm	F2018 Rm
CASH FLOWS FROM OPERATING ACTIVITIES			
Cash receipts from customers		9 611	9 195
Cash paid to suppliers and employees		(7 488)	(7 261)
Cash generated from operations	33	2 123	1 934
Interest received		264	159
Interest paid		(80)	(100)
Taxation paid	34	(309)	(426)
		1 998	1 567
Dividends received from joint venture	8	3 315	3 000
Dividends received from other		8	–
Dividend paid to non-controlling interest – Impala Platinum		(241)	(253)
Dividend paid to shareholders	31	(2 206)	(1 714)
Net cash inflow from operating activities		2 874	2 600

4.1.2 The indirect method

The indirect method arrives at the same value for net cash flows from operating activities but does so by working back from amounts reported in the statement of comprehensive income. There are two approaches for presenting the net cash flows from operating activities when using the indirect method. The most common approach adjusts reported profit or loss for the effects of:

(a) changes in inventories and operating receivables and payables during the period;

(b) non-cash items such as depreciation, provisions, deferred taxes, unrealised foreign currency gains and losses, and undistributed profits of associates; and

(c) all other items for which the cash effects are investing or financing cash flows.
 [IAS 7.20].

Anheuser-Busch InBev has used this adjusted profit approach to present its indirect method statement of cash flows, as illustrated in Extract 40.8 below.

Extract 40.8: Anheuser-Busch InBev NV/SA (2019)
Consolidated statement of cash flows [extract]
For the year ended 31 December

Million US dollar	Notes	2019	2018 restated
OPERATING ACTIVITIES			
Profit from continuing operations		9 990	5 157
Depreciation, amortization and impairment	10	4 657	4 624
Impairment losses on receivables, inventories and other assets		112	107
Additions/(reversals) in provisions and employee benefits		216	504
Net finance cost/(income)	11	3 473	8 826
Loss/(gain) on sale of property, plant and equipment and intangible assets		(149)	(82)
Loss/(gain) on sale of subsidiaries, associates and assets held for sale		(34)	(20)
Equity-settled share-based payment expense	26	340	333
Income tax expense	12	2 786	2 585
Other non-cash items included in profit		(220)	(654)
Share of result of associates and joint ventures		(152)	(153)
Cash flow from operating activities before changes in working capital and use of provisions		21 019	21 227
Decrease/(increase) in trade and other receivables		(258)	(105)
Decrease/(increase) in inventories		(426)	(588)
Increase/(decrease) in trade and other payables		679	1 170
Pension contributions and use of provisions		(715)	(487)
Cash generated from operations		20 299	21 217
Interest paid		(4 450)	(4 559)
Interest received		523	429
Dividends received		160	141
Income tax paid		(3 136)	(3 047)
Cash flow from operating activities		13 396	14 181

Alternatively, the indirect method of presentation can show separately revenues and expenses, adjusted for non-cash, investing or financing items, making up operating profit before working capital changes. *[IAS 7.20]*. An example of this rarely used alternative is given at the end of Appendix A to IAS 7.

When an entity adopts the indirect method, the reconciliation should start either with profit or loss before tax (as in Extract 40.6 above) or profit or loss after tax (as in Extract 40.8 above). Any other basis, such as EBITDA, EBIT, or profit or loss excluding non-controlling interests, does not meet the requirement in IAS 7 for adjusting 'profit or loss', *[IAS 7.20]*, which includes 'all items of income and expense in a period'. *[IAS 1.88]*.

To obtain the information on working capital movements for the indirect method, the figures in the statement of financial position must be analysed according to the three standard headings of the statement of cash flows. Thus, the reconciliation of profit or loss to cash flow from operating activities will include, not the increase or decrease in all receivables or payables, but only in respect of those elements thereof that relate to operating activities. For example, amounts owed in respect of the acquisition of property, plant and equipment (other than assets held for rental and subsequent sale), intangible assets, or non-operational investments will be excluded from the movement in payables included in this reconciliation. Although this may not present practical difficulties in the preparation of a single-entity statement of cash flows, it is important that sufficient information is collected from subsidiaries for preparing the group statement of cash flows.

Furthermore, when a group has acquired a subsidiary during the year, the change in working capital items will have to be split between the increase due to the acquisition (to the extent that the purchase consideration was settled in cash, this will be shown under investing activities) and the element related to post-acquisition operating activities which will be shown in the reconciliation. In a similar way, if a group has disposed of a subsidiary during the year, the changes in the working capital items in the reconciliation will exclude the movements relating to the working capital of the subsidiary that has left the group. Further additional considerations needed when preparing a statement of cash flows for a group are explained at 6 below.

4.2 Cash flows from investing activities

Investing activities are defined as 'the acquisition and disposal of long-term assets and other investments not included in cash equivalents'. *[IAS 7.6]*. This separate category of cash flows allows users of the financial statements to understand the extent to which expenditures have been made for resources intended to generate future income and cash flows. Cash flows arising from investing activities include:

(a) payments to acquire, and receipts from the sale of, property, plant and equipment, intangibles and other long-term assets (including payments and receipts relating to capitalised development costs and self-constructed property, plant and equipment);

(b) payments to acquire, and receipts from the sale of, equity or debt instruments of other entities and interests in jointly controlled entities (other than payments and receipts for those instruments considered to be cash equivalents or those held for dealing or trading purposes);

(c) advances and loans made to, and repaid by, other parties (other than advances and loans made by a financial institution); and

(d) payments for, and receipts from, futures contracts, forward contracts, option contracts and swap contracts, except when the contracts are held for dealing or trading purposes, or the cash flows are classified as financing activities (see 4.4.12 below regarding allocation of cash flows on derivative contracts). *[IAS 7.16]*.

However, as part of its annual improvement project, the IASB added in 2008 that only expenditures that result in a recognised asset in the statement of financial position are eligible for classification as investing activities. *[IAS 7.16]*. Therefore, cash flows relating to costs recognised as an expense cannot be classified within investing activities. As a result, payments including those for exploration and evaluation activities and for research and development that are recognised as an asset are classified as investing cash flows, while entities that recognise such expenditures as an expense would classify the related payments as operating cash flows.

This requirement was added in response to submissions made to the Interpretations Committee about the classification of expenditure incurred with the aim of generating future revenues, but that may not always result in the recognition of an asset. Examples included exploration and evaluation expenditure, advertising and promotional activities, staff training, and research and development. *[IAS 7.BC3]*. The IASB believes this approach aligns the classification of investing cash flows with the presentation in the statement of financial position; reduces divergence in practice and, therefore, results in financial statements that are easier for users to understand. *[IAS 7.BC7]*. It does not seem unreasonable that recurrent expenditure on items such as research and expensed mining costs should be classified as operating cash flows. However, application to other items that do not give rise to an asset in the statement of financial position, such as acquisition-related costs (discussed at 6.3.1 below) and the settlement of contingent consideration in a business combination (discussed at 6.3.3 below) may prove to be more complicated.

The Interpretations Committee and the IASB have discussed the application of this requirement in practice, as some users appear to have given precedence to the classification of cash flows consistently with the classification of the related item in the statement of financial position, *[IAS 7.BC7]*, (sometime referred to as the 'cohesiveness principle') over the objective in the standard to classify cash flows in accordance with the nature of the activity giving rise to the cash flow. *[IAS 7.11]*. In its discussion, the IASB agreed that the primary principle for the classification of cash flows should be in accordance with the nature of the activity, and that the requirement for the recognition of an asset should be read as a constraint on the application of the primary principle, rather than as a competing principle.[9]

Major classes of gross receipts and gross payments arising from investing activities are reported separately, except for those items that IAS 7 permits to be reported on a net basis, as discussed at 5.2 below. *[IAS 7.21]*.

4.3 Cash flows from financing activities

Financing activities are defined as those 'activities that result in changes in the size and composition of the contributed equity and borrowings of the entity'. *[IAS 7.6]*. The standard states that this information is useful in predicting claims on future cash flows by providers of capital to the entity. *[IAS 7.17]*. However, it would seem more likely that information on financing cash flows would indicate the extent to which the entity has had recourse to external financing to meet its operating and investing needs in the period. The disclosure of the value and maturity of the entity's financial liabilities, as required by IFRS 7 – *Financial Instruments: Disclosures*, would contribute more to predicting future claims on cash flows. *[IFRS 7.39]*.

Cash flows arising from financing activities include:

(a) proceeds from issuing shares or other equity instruments;

(b) payments to owners to acquire or redeem the entity's shares;

(c) proceeds from issuing, and outflows to repay, debentures, loans, notes, bonds, mortgages and other short or long-term borrowings; and

(d) payments by a lessee for the reduction of the outstanding liability relating to a lease. *[IAS 7.17]*.

In consolidated financial statements, financing cash flows will include those arising from changes in ownership interests in a subsidiary that do not result in a loss of control (see 6.2 below). *[IAS 7.42A]*.

Major classes of gross receipts and gross payments arising from financing activities should be reported separately, except for those items that can be reported on a net basis, as discussed at 5.2 below. *[IAS 7.21]*.

Disclosure requirements in respect of changes in liabilities arising from financing activities are discussed at 5.6 below.

4.4 Allocating items to operating, investing and financing activities

Sometimes it is not clear how cash flows should be classified between operating, investing and financing activities. IAS 7 provides additional guidance on the classification of certain transactions, including interest, dividends and income taxes, while other questions are not addressed explicitly in the standard. These, as well as some common areas where judgement may be required to classify cash flows, are discussed below.

4.4.1 Interest and dividends

An entity is required to disclose separately cash flows from interest and dividends received and paid, and their classification as either operating, investing or financing activities should be applied in a consistent manner from period to period. *[IAS 7.31]*. For a financial institution, interest paid and interest and dividends received are usually classified as operating cash flows. However, IAS 7 notes that there is no consensus on the classification of these cash flows for other entities and suggests that:

- interest paid may be classified under either operating or financing activities; and
- interest received and dividends received may be included in either operating or investing cash flows. *[IAS 7.33]*.

The standard allows dividends paid to be classified as a financing cash flow (because they are a cost of obtaining financial resources) or as a component of cash flows from operating activities. *[IAS 7.34]*.

In Extract 40.6 at 4 above, AstraZeneca has included interest paid under operating activities, interest received under investing activities and dividends paid under financing activities, as permitted by the standard. A different treatment is adopted by Anheuser-Busch InBev in Extract 40.8 at 4.1.2 above, where interest paid, interest received and dividends received are all disclosed as operating cash flows.

All of these treatments are in compliance with the standard; however, the most appropriate treatment will depend on the nature of the entity and its activities. For example, if an entity does not include interest received or dividends received within revenue it may be more appropriate to include the interest or dividend cash inflows as investing cash flows rather than operating cash flows. This is because cash flows from operating activities are primarily derived from the principal revenue-producing activities of the entity, *[IAS 7.14]*, and the amount of cash flows arising from operating activities is intended to be a key indicator of the extent to which the operations of the entity have generated sufficient cash flows to repay loans, pay dividends and make new investments without recourse to external sources of financing. *[IAS 7.13]*. Similarly, an entity could treat interest and dividends paid as financing cash flows because they are a cost of obtaining financial resources. *[IAS 7.34]*. In addition, the standard requires the total amount of interest paid during the period to be disclosed in the statement of cash flows, whether it has been recognised as an expense or capitalised as part of the cost of an asset in accordance with IAS 23 – *Borrowing Costs*. *[IAS 7.32]*. A literal reading of this requirement might suggest that interest paid should be presented as a single figure under operating or financing activities. However, it would also seem appropriate to include the cash outflow relating to capitalised borrowing costs under investing activities, provided that when this is done, the total amount of interest paid is also disclosed, either on the face of the statement of cash flows or in the notes. This gives rise to an apparent inconsistency between paragraph 16 of IAS 7 and paragraphs 32 to 33 of IAS 7, but attempts to clarify the issue through an annual improvement[10] received negative feedback from respondents and ultimately no amendment was made.[11]

Where an entity has issued shares that are classified as financial liabilities in accordance with IAS 32 – *Financial Instruments: Presentation* (see Chapter 47), the dividends paid on those shares should be presented in the statement of cash flows as either operating or investing, in line with the entity's presentation of other interest paid.

4.4.2   Taxes on income

Cash flows arising from taxes on income should be separately disclosed within operating cash flows unless they can be specifically identified with investing or financing activities. *[IAS 7.35]*.

Whilst it is possible to match elements of tax expense to transactions for which the cash flows are classified under investing or financing activities; taxes paid are usually classified as cash flows from operating activities because it is often impracticable to match tax cash flows with specific elements of tax expense. Also, those tax cash flows may arise in a different period from the underlying transaction. *[IAS 7.36]*. This is the presentation adopted by Anheuser-Busch InBev in Extract 40.8 at 4.1.2 above. However, when it is practicable to make this determination, the tax cash flow is identified as an investing or financing activity in accordance with the individual transaction that gives rise to such cash flows. In cases where tax cash flows are allocated over more than one class of activity, the entity should disclose the total amount for taxes paid. *[IAS 7.36]*.

4.4.3   Sales taxes and other non-income tax cash flows

Although it provides guidance on the treatment of taxes on income, IAS 7 does not specifically address the treatment of cash flows relating to other taxes, such as value added tax (VAT) or other sales taxes and duty. The Interpretations Committee has considered whether it should add the question about VAT to its agenda and decided that it was not appropriate to develop an interpretation. Instead, it suggested that the issue of cash flows relating to VAT be considered by the IASB in its review of IAS 7 as part of the project on Financial Statement Presentation.

In explaining why, it would not add this question to its agenda, the Interpretations Committee noted that 'IAS 7 does not explicitly address the treatment of VAT' and added that 'while different practices may emerge, they are not expected to be widespread'.[12]

Therefore, it seems that entities can choose to disclose VAT receipts and VAT payments separately in the statement of cash flows or as part of the related cash inflows and outflows. Given the availability of alternative treatments, the Interpretations Committee noted that it would be appropriate in complying with IAS 1 – *Presentation of Financial Statements* – for entities to disclose whether cash flows are presented inclusive or exclusive of related VAT.[13] We believe that the same principles should be applied for other non-income taxes.

4.4.4 Cash contributions to a long-term employee benefit fund

As discussed at 4.1 above, the definition of operating activities in IAS 7 includes as one of its examples 'cash payments to and on behalf of employees'. *[IAS 7.14(d)]*. Such cash outflows would typically involve wages and salaries paid to employees, taxes paid on behalf of employees and any other employee benefit contributions made on behalf of employees. Where a company makes contributions to a long-term employee benefit fund on behalf of its employees, those cash outflows are part of the compensation for employment services and would be classified as operating cash flows as they are derived from the principal-revenue-producing activities of the entity.

4.4.5 Cash flows from factoring of trade receivables

Another question not explicitly addressed in the standard is the classification of cash receipts from the factoring of trade receivables.

In the case of debt factoring, an entity aims to provide cash flow from trade receivables more quickly than would arise from normal collection from customers, generally by transferring rights over those receivables to a financial institution. In our view, the classification of the cash receipt from the financial institution depends on whether the transfer results in derecognition of the trade receivables, or to the continued recognition of the trade receivables and the recognition of a financial liability for the funding received from the factoring entity. The characteristics determining which of these accounting treatments would be appropriate are discussed in Chapter 52 at 4.5 and 5.

Only to the extent that the factoring arrangement results in the derecognition of the original trade receivable would it be appropriate to regard the cash receipt in the same way as any other receipt from the sale of goods and rendering of services and classify it in operating activities. *[IAS 7.14(a)]*. In cases where the trade receivable is not derecognised and a liability is recorded, the nature of the arrangement is a borrowing secured against trade receivables and accordingly we believe that the cash receipt from factoring should be treated in the same way as any short-term borrowing and included in financing activities. *[IAS 7.17(c)]*. The later cash inflow from the customer for settlement of the trade receivable would be included in operating cash flows and the reduction in the liability to the financial institution would be a financing outflow. Following the principle in IFRS 9 for the disclosure of income and expenditure relating to a transferred asset that continues to be recognised, *[IFRS 9.3.2.22]*, these two amounts would not be offset in the statement of cash flows. However, it would be acceptable for the entity to disclose the net borrowing receipts from, and repayments to, the financial institution, if it was determined that these relate to advances made for and the repayment of short-term borrowings such as those which have a maturity period of three months or less. *[IAS 7.23A(c)]*. In some cases, the factoring arrangement requires customers to remit cash directly to the financial institution. When the transfer does not give rise to derecognition of the trade receivable by the reporting entity, we believe that it will usually be appropriate for the entity to reflect the later settlement of the debt by the customer as a non-cash transaction with no cash flows reported at the time of the ultimate derecognition of the trade receivable and the related factoring liability. However, the reporting entity may consider that the factoring entity is acting as its agent and is therefore collecting the cash on its behalf before drawing down amounts to settle the liability it is owed by the reporting entity. In this case the entity would report an operating cash inflow from the customer and a financing cash outflow to the financial institution.

4.4.6 Cash flows from supply-chain financing and reverse factoring arrangements

In the case of supply-chain financing or reverse factoring arrangements, typically, the entity aims to defer cash flows from the settlement of a trade payable for the supply of goods or services through an arrangement with a financial institution which will settle the liability to the supplier and will be repaid by the entity (see Chapter 54 at 7.4.3.A for further explanation).

Supply-chain finance arrangements can be varied and complex; however, the common link is simply that the financial institution pays the supplier before it is, in turn, paid by the purchaser. The primary accounting concern with these types of arrangements is therefore whether the liability to the financial institution should be presented as debt or as a trade or similar payable. However, such schemes also raise questions as to their presentation in the statement of cash flows.

The Interpretations Committee discussed the application of IFRS Standards to the reverse factoring arrangements in their June 2020 meeting. The committee described reverse factoring arrangements simply as ones in which a financial institution agrees to pay amounts an entity owes to the its suppliers and the entity agrees to pay the financial institution at a date later than suppliers are paid.

The committee issued a tentative agenda decision outlining how IFRS standards are applied to the different aspects of accounting for such arrangements, in particular on the classification of liabilities and disclosures about liquidity risks of such arrangements. Details of the tentative agenda decision and the impact on the statement of financial position can be found in Chapter 54 at 7.4.3.B and on the notes to the financial statements in Chapter 54 at 7.4.3.E.

An entity that has entered into a reverse factoring arrangement, would need to determine whether to classify cash flows under the arrangement as cash flows from operating activities or cash flows from financing activities.

This in turn poses the following challenges:
- Should the presentation of the liability to the financial institution in the statement of financial position impact the presentation of cash flows? For example, if the liability is presented outside of trade payables, should the ultimate payment to the financial institution be presented as a financing outflow? Or should it instead be presented as an operating cash flow based on the nature of the activities that initially led to the recognition of the trade payable that was settled through the supply-chain financing?
- Should the remittance of cash directly to the supplier by the financial institution be reflected at all in the statement of cash flow or is it a non-cash transaction?

With respect to the first question above, the committee observed in its tentative agenda decision, that an entity's assessment of the nature of the liabilities that are part of the arrangement may help in determining the nature of the related cash flows as arising from operating or financing activities. For example, if the entity considers the related liability to be a trade or other payable that is part of the working capital used in the entity's principal revenue-producing activities, the entity presents cash outflows to settle the liability as arising from operating activities in its statement of cash flows. In contrast, if the entity considers that the related liability is not a trade or other payable because the liability represents borrowings of the entity, the entity presents cash outflows to settle the liability as arising from financing activities in its statement of cash flows.

As regards the identification of cash flows and the second question above, the tentative agenda decision of the committee noted that transactions that do not require the use of cash shall be excluded from a statement of cash flows. *[IAS 7.43].* The committee went on to state 'consequently, if a cash inflow and cash outflow occur for an entity when an invoice is factored as part of a reverse factoring arrangement, the entity presents those cash flows in its statement of cash flows. If no cash flows are involved in a financing transaction of an entity, the entity discloses the transaction elsewhere in the financial statements in a way that provides all the relevant information about the financing activity'.

It is our view that this text may be interpreted differently by constituents and, as such may not resolve diversity in practice. In particular, the tentative agenda decision currently states the obvious, that is if no cash flows are involved, then no cash flows should be presented in the cash flow statement. However, it has been observed that certain entities consider that the relationship between themselves and the financial institution is, in substance, a principal/agent relationship. Such a conclusion would imply that the financial institution is acting as an agent of the entity and is, therefore, incurring cash flows on behalf of the entity when paying the supplier. It is unclear in the tentative agenda decision as to whether such an analysis would be appropriate.

As a result, we see different approaches being applied in practice:
- One approach is to treat the payment of the supplier by the financial institution as a non-cash transaction from the entity's perspective and the repayment of the financial institution as a financing or operating cashflow depending on whether the liability to the financial institution is shown, respectively, as a trade or similar payable or as debt.
- Another approach is to treat the payment of the supplier by the financial institution as a non-cash transaction from the entity's perspective and the repayment of the financial institution as an operating cashflow based on the nature of activities for which the trade payable was initially recognised, regardless of the classification of the liability in the statement of financial position.
- A third approach is to report an operating cash outflow and a financing cash inflow when the financial institution remits payment to the supplier in an arrangement that is deemed to be a financing arrangement, with the subsequent payment to the financial institution being reported as a financing cash outflow.

In its tentative agenda decision, the committee rightfully observed that assessing how to present liabilities and cash flows related to reverse factoring arrangements may involve judgement and emphasised the requirement in IAS 1 to disclose judgements that management has made in this respect if they are among the judgements made that have the most significant effect on the amounts recognised in the financial statements *[IAS 1.122]* as well as any information that is relevant to an understanding of any of the entity's financial statements. *[IAS 1.112]*.

Lastly, we would also point out that, currently, the tentative agenda decision suggests that the decision is whether to classify the associated cash flows as operating or financing activities. However, we note that if the cost of the goods or services is capitalised into a longer-term asset such as property, plant and equipment, or possibly an intangible asset, the classification decision would be between investing and financing activities. This may be particularly relevant in asset intense industries such as telecommunications or the extractive industries.

The committee noted that the effects of reverse factoring arrangements may also need to be included in the disclosure of:
- changes in liabilities arising from financing activities, as required by paragraph 44A of the standard (see 5.6 below). If an entity classifies the cash flows arising from a reverse factoring arrangement as financing, or will do so in the future, the related liabilities and cash and non-cash changes should be included in this disclosure; and
- liquidity risk, as required by IFRS 7 *[IFRS 7.33-35, 39, B11F]* because the entity has concentrated a portion of its liabilities with one financial institution rather than a diverse group of suppliers – see Chapter 54 at 7.4.3.E. Also, some suppliers may have become accustomed to, or reliant on, earlier payment of their trade receivables under the reverse factoring arrangement. If the financial institution were to withdraw the reverse factoring arrangement, those suppliers could demand shorter credit terms, which would affect the entity's liquidity, particularly if the entity were already in financial distress.

In practice, the appropriate level of disclosures for any reverse factoring arrangement is likely to involve a high degree of judgement. We believe that, whatever the presentation adopted, additional disclosure will be necessary whenever these arrangements have a material impact to explain the nature of the arrangements and amounts involved, the financial reporting judgements made and impacts thereof on the financial statements and, more specifically, the level of debt and the statement of cash flows.

At the time of writing, the IFRS interpretation committee has not yet revisited its tentative agenda decision based on comments received and is expected to do so at its December 2020 meeting. However, in accordance with the revised Due Process Handbook published in August 2020, the committee must formally involve the Board in the process of finalising its agenda decision and this could delay publication until the very last days of December 2020.

4.4.7 Property, plant and equipment held for rental

Payments to acquire and receipts from the sale of, property, plant and equipment are usually included in investing cash flows; however, this is not always the case.

A number of entities routinely sell assets that were previously held for rental, for example, car rental companies that acquire vehicles with the intention of holding them as rental cars for a limited period and then selling them. IAS 16 – *Property, Plant and Equipment* – requires an entity, that, in its ordinary course of business, routinely sells items of property, plant and equipment that it has held for rental to others, to classify gains on the sale of such property, plant and equipment as revenue. *[IAS 16.68A].* Accordingly, the proceeds from the sale of such assets are classified as cash flows from operating activities, as are cash payments to manufacture or acquire property, plant and equipment held for rental to others and routinely sold in the ordinary course of business. *[IAS 7.14].*

The requirement to classify payments for such property, plant and equipment held for rental under operating cash flows is intended to avoid initial expenditure on purchases of assets being classified as investing activities, while inflows from sales are recorded within operating activities. However, this means that management will need to determine, at the time of acquisition or manufacture, which of the assets that it intends to rent out will be ultimately held for sale in the ordinary course of business

4.4.8 Cash received as compensation for an insured loss

As noted in 4.2 above, cash flows arising from investing activities include receipts from the sale of property, plant and equipment and other long-term assets. *[IAS 7.16(b)].* This classification would also be appropriate if the receipt of cash came from insurance proceeds received to cover for the loss or damage of such assets. It would not be appropriate to present the cash inflow as an operating cash flow as the insurance proceeds are not derived from the principal-revenue-producing activities of the business. *[IAS 7.14].* However, the nature of the claim giving rise to the cash inflow should be carefully considered. If the claim relates only partially to the loss of damage of a long-term asset, it may be necessary for the cash inflows to be allocated between cash flows from operating activities (e.g., for the compensation for business interruption) and cash flows from investing activities.

4.4.9 Cash flows for service concession arrangements

Because a cash flow is only classified in investing activities if it results in a recognised asset in the statement of financial position, a question arises regarding the classification of the cash inflows and outflows of the operator of a service concession arrangement that is within the scope of IFRIC 12 – *Service Concession Arrangements*.

IFRIC 12 features two possible accounting models – the intangible asset model or the financial asset model. Under both models, the service element relating to the construction of the infrastructure asset is accounted for in accordance with IFRS 15 and the revenue recognised gives rise to an intangible or a financial asset, in the form of a receivable, respectively. It is unclear whether cash flows incurred in the construction or upgrade phase should always be regarded as operating cash flows because they relate to the provision of construction services; or whether they are more accurately classified as investing activities, as they reflect cash outflows that result in the recognition of an asset.

In the case of an arrangement under the intangible asset model, the cash flows incurred during construction or upgrading could be classified in investing activities as they relate to the acquisition of an intangible that will generate future income and cash flows. Once the operating phase is reached, the cash inflows received would be most appropriately classified in operating activities as most operating and maintenance costs are likely to be executory and will be accounted for as incurred.

On the other hand, when the financial asset model applies, cash outflows during the construction phase may considered to represent the provision of financing to the grantor and as such a financing outflow. In a corollary of the discussion on deferred payments at 5.4 below, where the time value of money is significant to the transaction, the transaction may be tantamount to providing a loan. In this case the repayment of such an instrument by the grantor during the operating phase could be considered an investing cash flow (or potentially split between investing and operating cash flows for the capital and interest components respectively, depending on the policy of the entity).

Since there is no specific guidance relating to the classification of cash flows for service concession arrangements, current practice is mixed. IFRIC 12 is discussed in more detail in Chapter 25.

4.4.10 Treasury shares

Treasury shares are an entity's own equity instruments that are acquired and held by the entity, a subsidiary, or other members of the consolidated group. The consideration paid or received for treasury shares is recognised directly in equity and not as a movement in investments. *[IAS 32.33]*. As such, it should be clear that payments and receipts to acquire or dispose of treasury shares should be classified within financing activities. *[IAS 7.17]*. Even where such treasury shares are acquired by the entity as part of an equity-settled share-based payment transaction, the cash outflow should be classified under financing activities. Whilst cash payments to and on behalf of employees are classified under operating activities, *[IAS 7.14]*, the acquisition of treasury shares does not settle a transaction between the entity and its employees. An equity-settled share-based payment transaction is completed when the entity transfers its equity instruments to employees in consideration for the services received.

When a cash payment is made by a subsidiary to its parent or a trust that holds treasury shares as part of an equity-settled share-based payment arrangement, the payment should be accounted for as a deduction from equity in the separate financial statements of the subsidiary, on the grounds that the payment does not settle the transaction with the employees, but is effectively a distribution to the parent or the trust (see Chapter 34 at 12.2.7). Having regarded this as a distribution, it follows that the cash flow should be classified as either operating or financing, according to the entity's policy on dividends as discussed at 4.4.1 above.

4.4.11 Cash flows related to the costs of a share issue

Costs directly related to the issue of shares are required to be deducted from equity. *[IAS 32.35]*. As the costs reduce the amount of the proceeds received from the share issue, they should be classified as a financing cash flow. *[IAS 7.17(a)]*. However, where a proposed share issue is cancelled, there would be no proceeds from the issue to record and the related expenses would be included in profit and loss rather than equity. As such, the definition of a financing cash flow would not be met, and the transaction costs would be classified in operating cash flows.

4.4.12 Cash flows on derivative contracts

Payments and receipts relating to derivative contracts can be classified within operating, investing or financing in different circumstances. Where the contract is held for dealing or trading purposes, the cash flows are classified under operating activities. *[IAS 7.14]*. IAS 7 requires that payments for, and receipts from, futures contracts, forward contracts, option contracts and swap contracts are classified as cash flows from investing activities, except when the contracts are held for dealing or trading purposes, or the cash flows are classified as financing activities. *[IAS 7.16]*.

The standard adds that when a contract is accounted for as a hedge of an identifiable position, the cash flows of the contract are classified under the same heading as the cash flows of the position being hedged. *[IAS 7.16]*. An example is an interest rate swap. An entity wishing to convert an existing fixed rate borrowing into a floating rate equivalent could enter into an interest rate swap under which it receives interest at fixed rates and pays at floating rates. All the cash flows under the swap should be reported under the same cash flow heading as interest paid (i.e. as financing activities or operating activities, in accordance with the entity's determined policy, as discussed at 4.4.1 above), because they are equivalent to interest or are hedges of interest payments.

More generally, IFRS 9 adds to the requirements of IAS 7 by clarifying that cash flows arising from hedging instruments are classified as operating, investing or financing activities, on the basis of the classification of the cash flows arising from the hedged item and that this should be consistent with the classification of these instruments as hedging instruments under IFRS 9. *[IFRS 9.IG.G.2]*.

This seems to leave an open question as to how an entity should classify the cash flows from a derivative contract that is considered by management as part of a hedging relationship, but for which the entity elects not to apply hedge accounting (taking all movements to profit or loss) or for which hedge accounting is not permitted under IFRS 9? Consider the following example.

Example 40.1: Cash flows from derivatives not designated as hedges

Company A has the euro as its functional currency. On 1 January 2020, it sells goods to a US customer for which it charges US$1,000,000. The spot exchange rate on this date is 1:1 and it recognises revenue of €1,000,000. Payment is due to be received on 30 June 2020. A enters into a forward contract to exchange US$1,000,000 for €1,095,000 on 30 June 2020. It does not designate it as a hedge because the effects of movements on the contract and those of retranslating the receivable will already offset in profit or loss. On 30 June 2020 the exchange rate is such that A receives the equivalent of €1,200,000 from its customer and pays €105,000 on the forward contract.

Taken literally, IAS 7 would suggest that the receipt from the customer of €1,200,000 is classified as an operating cash inflow; but, because the forward contract is not held for dealing or trading purposes and is not accounted for as a hedge of an identifiable position, the €105,000 cash outflow on the forward contract cannot be classified under operating activities. As such, the €105,000 would have to appear in investing or possibly financing cash flows. However, had the entity elected to apply hedge accounting, the standard would require the €105,000 to be included in operating cash flows.

In our opinion, since IAS 7 as not been updated to reflect IFRS 9, the requirements to classify cash flows arising from hedging instruments consistently with the classification of the cash flows arising from the hedged item are not restricted only to those hedging relationships that either are designated as hedges under IFRS 9, or would otherwise qualify for hedge accounting had they been so designated. Accordingly, in Example 40.1 above, entity A could include the payment on the forward contract in cash flows from operating activities.

4.4.13 Debt instrument issued at a discount or redeemed at a premium

Cash outflows that represent the repayment of the principal amount of a loan or other debt instrument are classified as financing activities. *[IAS 7.17]*. As noted in 4.4.1 above, interest paid may be classified under either operating or financing activities. Therefore, where an entity adopts a policy of classifying interest under operating activities, it may be necessary to carefully consider the nature of any payment to the lender to ensure the appropriate classification between operating and financing. This will be particularly relevant where the pattern of interest payments differs from the recognition of the interest expense in profit or loss.

For example, a company that issues a zero-coupon bond at nominal value, with a premium payable on redemption, will not make any interest payments over the life of the bond. However, in accounting for the financial liability at amortised cost under IFRS 9, the entity will recognise interest at the EIR, calculated to reflect the premium payable on redemption, as explained in Chapter 50 at 3.1. In our view, when the cash paid on redemption is presented in the statement of cash flows, a split should be made to appropriately show the amount that relates to the interest cost (within operating activities) and the amount that relates to the prepayment of the principle (within financing activities).

The same principles would be applied where a debt is issued at a discount or in any other situation where the pattern of cash flows relating to interest on a financial liability are not reflected in the pattern of recognition of the interest cost.

4.4.14 Early settlement of a debt instrument

A similar issue to that discussed in 4.4.13 above is how an entity should present the cash payments on early settlement of a loan or other borrowing. As already noted at 4.3 above, cash flows arising from financing activities include outflows to repay borrowings. However, in some situations an element of the cash paid on early settlement could be viewed as compensation to the lender for lost interest.

Lenders will often include a prepayment penalty provision in loan agreements that can be based on a number of factors, including an approximation of the interest that will not be paid as a result of early settlement. This would support a split presentation of the cash outflow between repayment of borrowings and cash outflow for interest. Alternatively, the nature of the entire cash outflow may also be viewed as relating to a financing activity, being the extinguishment of a liability, which should be presented as one amount in the financing activities section of the statement.

4.4.15 Classification of cash flows – future developments

In December 2019, the IASB issued Exposure Draft ED/2019/7 – *General Presentation and* Disclosures (the ED) in which the Board proposes to replace IAS 1 with a new standard and to make limited changes to the statement of financial position and the statement of cash flows.

The ED proposes to eliminate the current policy choice for classification of cash flows from interest and dividends in the statement of cash flows. For non-financial entities, dividends and interest paid should be classified as financing cash flows, whilst dividends and interest received should be classified as investing cash flows. Within the cash flows from investing activities section of the statement of cash flows, the cash flows from integral associates and joint ventures should be presented separately from non-integral associates and joint ventures based on the same classification as was applied in the statement of financial performance.

When applying the indirect approach, the ED clarifies that the starting point for the reconciliation is the operating profit subtotal.

For financial entities, cash flows from dividends received, interest paid and interest received should each be presented in a single category, that is, either as operating, investing or financing in a manner consistent with the presentation of the related income and expenses in the statement of financial performance.

The ED is discussed further in Chapter 3 at 6.1.2.

5. OTHER CASH FLOW PRESENTATION ISSUES

5.1 Material cash flows

IAS 1 requires the nature and amount of material items of income and expense to be disclosed separately. *[IAS 1.97]*. It also requires additional line items, headings and sub-totals to be presented on the face of the statement of financial position or of the statement(s) presenting profit or loss and other comprehensive income when this is relevant to an understanding of the entity's financial position. *[IAS 1.55, 85]*. In our view, although IAS 7 is silent on the matter, it would be similarly appropriate for material cash flows or cash flows relating to material items in the statements of financial position or of comprehensive income to be presented as separate line items on the face of the statement of cash flows, provided that they remain classified according to their nature as either operating, investing or financing cash flows.

5.2 Gross or net presentation of cash flows

In general, major classes of gross receipts and gross payments should be reported separately. [IAS 7.21]. Operating, investing or financing cash flows can be reported on a net basis if they arise from:

(a) cash flows that reflect the activities of customers rather than those of the entity and are thereby made on behalf of customers; or

(b) cash flows that relate to items in which the turnover is quick, the amounts are large, and the maturities are short. [IAS 7.22].

Examples of cash receipts and payments that reflect the activities of customers rather than those of the entity include the acceptance and repayment of demand deposits by a bank, funds held for customers by an investment company and rents collected on behalf of, and paid over to, the owners of properties. [IAS 7.23]. Other transactions where the entity is acting as an agent or collector for another party would be included in this category, such as the treatment of cash receipts and payments relating to concession sales.

Examples of cash receipts and payments in which turnover is quick, the amounts are large, and the maturities are short include advances made for and the repayment of:

(a) principal amounts relating to credit card customers;

(b) the purchase and sale of investments; and

(c) other short-term borrowings, such as those with a maturity on draw down of three months or less. [IAS 7.23A].

An example noted in IAS 20 – *Accounting for Government Grants and Disclosure of Government Assistance* – where gross presentation is deemed appropriate for major classes of cash flows is the receipt of government grants, which 'are often disclosed as separate items in the statement of cash flows regardless of whether or not the grant is deducted from the related asset for presentation purposes in the statement of financial position'. [IAS 20.28].

Neither IAS 20 nor IAS 7 provide guidance on where in the statement of cash flows to present the cash inflows from the receipt of government grants related to assets. The Interpretations Committee discussed the presentation of cash flows for several fact patterns including government grants in July 2012.[14] The issue was further discussed in March 2013 and no conclusion was reached.[15] As such there is likely to be diversity in practice. The presentation principles adopted should be applied consistently and clear disclosure of the principles and the impact thereof on the statement of cash flows presented should be provided in accordance with IAS 1.

Government grants are discussed in more detail in Chapter 24.

See 7.2 below for discussion of the gross or net presentation of cash flows for financial institutions.

5.3 Foreign currency cash flows

IAS 21 – *The Effects of Changes in Foreign Exchange Rates* – excludes from its scope the translation of cash flows of a foreign operation and the presentation of foreign currency cash flows in a statement of cash flows. *[IAS 21.7]*. Nevertheless, IAS 7 requires foreign currency cash flows to be reported in a manner consistent with IAS 21. *[IAS 7.27]*.

Accordingly, cash flows arising from transactions in a foreign currency should be reported in an entity's functional currency in the statement of cash flows by applying the exchange rate in effect at the date of the cash flow. *[IAS 7.25]*. Similarly, the cash flows of a foreign subsidiary should be translated using the exchange rates prevailing at the dates of the cash flows. *[IAS 7.26]*.

For practical reasons, an entity can apply a rate that approximates the actual rate on the date of the cash flow (such as a weighted average for a period) but, like the requirements of IAS 21 for income and expenses, translation using the exchange rate as at the end of the reporting period is not permitted. *[IAS 7.27]*. The requirements for entities falling within the scope of IAS 29 – *Financial Reporting in Hyperinflationary Economies* – are discussed in Chapter 16.

Unrealised gains and losses arising from exchange rate movements on foreign currency cash and cash equivalents are not cash flows. However, it is necessary to include these exchange differences in the statement of cash flows in order to reconcile the movement in cash and cash equivalents at the beginning and end of the period. The effect of exchange rate movements on cash and cash equivalents is presented as a single amount at the foot of the statement of cash flows, separately from operating, investing and financing cash flows and includes the differences, if any, had those cash flows been reported at end of period exchange rates. *[IAS 7.28]*. An example of this is illustrated in Extract 40.6 at 4 above.

5.3.1 Entities applying the direct method

When an entity enters into a transaction denominated in a foreign currency, there are no consequences for the statement of cash flows until payments are received or made. The receipts and payments will be recorded in the entity's accounting records at the exchange rate prevailing at the date of payment and these amounts should be reflected in the statement of cash flows. *[IAS 7.25]*.

The consolidated statement of cash flows prepared under the direct method uses the foreign currency financial statements of each foreign subsidiary as the starting point. This means that cash flows are measured first in the functional currency of the subsidiary and then retranslated into the currency in which the consolidated financial statements are presented.

5.3.2 Entities applying the indirect method

Under the indirect method, profit or loss is adjusted for the effects of transactions of a non-cash nature, any deferrals of operating cash receipts or payments and income or expenses associated with investing or financing cash flows. *[IAS 7.18]*. Exchange differences will be included in profit or loss when the settled amount differs from the amount recorded at the date of the transaction. Likewise, if the transaction remains unsettled at the reporting date, exchange differences will also be taken to profit or loss on the retranslation of the unsettled monetary items at closing rates. Entities must therefore determine what adjustments should be made to ensure that foreign currency items are only included in the statement of cash flows to the extent that cash flows have occurred.

5.3.2.A   Treatment of operating cash flows

Where the exchange differences relate to operating items such as sales or purchases of inventory by an entity, no adjustments need to be made when the indirect method of calculating the cash flow from operating activities is used. For example, if a sale transaction and cash settlement take place in the same period, the operating profit will include both the amount recorded at the date of sale and the amount of the exchange difference on settlement, the combination of which gives the amount of the actual cash flow. Even if settlement has not taken place until after the end of the period, no adjustment would be needed as the unrealised exchange gain or loss would already be reflected in the movement in the related receivable included in the reconciliation to operating profit.

5.3.2.B   Treatment of non-operating cash flows

Any exchange difference arising on a settled transaction relating to non-operating cash flows will give rise to an adjustment between reported profit and the cash flow from operating activities.

For example, the foreign currency purchase of property, plant and equipment would be recorded initially at the rate prevailing on the date of the transaction. The difference on payment of the foreign currency payable would be taken to the statement of comprehensive income as an exchange gain or loss. If left unadjusted in the statement of cash flows, the investing cash flow for the asset purchase would be recorded at the historical rate, rather than at the exchange rate prevailing at the date of settlement. This difference needs to be considered in calculating the cash flow to be shown under the relevant classification, in this case investing cash flows, which would otherwise be recorded at the amount shown in the note of the movements in property, plant and equipment.

5.3.2.C   The indirect method and foreign subsidiaries

Entities should exercise care when applying the indirect method at the 'more consolidated level' as described at 6.1 below when there are foreign subsidiaries. If the translated financial statements are used, exchange differences will be included in the movements between the opening and closing group balance sheets. For example, an increase in inventories held by a US subsidiary from $240 to $270 during the year will be reported as an unchanged amount of £150 if the opening exchange rate of £1=$1.60 becomes £1=$1.80 by the year-end. In these circumstances an entity should take the functional currency financial statements of the foreign subsidiary as the starting point.

5.4   Non-cash transactions and transactions on deferred terms

Non-cash transactions only ever appear in a statement of cash flows as adjustments to profit or loss for the period when using the indirect method of presenting cash flows from operating activities as discussed at 4.1.2 above. Investing and financing transactions that do not involve cash or cash equivalents are always excluded from the statement of cash flows. Disclosure is required elsewhere in the financial statements in order to provide all relevant information about these investing and financing activities. *[IAS 7.43]*.

Examples of such non-cash transactions include the conversion of debt to equity; acquiring assets by assuming directly related liabilities or by means of a lease; and issuing equity as consideration for the acquisition of another entity. *[IAS 7.44]*. Similarly, asset exchange transactions and the issue of bonus shares out of retained earnings are disclosed as non-cash transactions. Extract 40.9 below shows the disclosures made by China Mobile Limited.

> **Extract 40.9: China Mobile Limited (2019)**
> **Consolidated Statement of Cash Flows**
> for the year ended 31 December 2019 (Expressed in RMB) [extract]
> **Significant non-cash transactions**
>
> The Group recorded payables of RMB64,480 million (2018: RMB74,816 million) due to equipment suppliers as at 31 December 2019 for additions of construction in progress during the year then ended. In addition, the Group recorded lease liabilities of RMB13,219 million (2018: nil) as at 31 December 2019 for additions of right-of-use assets during the year then ended.

5.4.1 Asset purchased on deferred terms from the supplier

When an asset is purchased on deferred terms granted by the supplier directly, it may not be clear whether the associated cash flows should be classified under investing activities, as capital expenditure, or within financing activities, as the repayment of borrowings.

It could be argued that the payment of a deferred amount would not meet the definition of investing cash flows, because it does not result in recognition of an asset, but rather a reduction of a liability. However, as discussed above at 4, the Interpretations Committee and the IASB have affirmed in 2013 their position that in determining the classification of cash flows, the nature of the activity is still the primary principle to be considered.[16]

Accordingly, the classification of the payment comes down to a judgement as to whether its nature relates to the acquisition of an asset or the repayment of a liability. If the period between acquisition and payment is not significant, the existence of credit terms should not be interpreted as changing the nature of the cash payment from investing to financing. Therefore, the settlement of a short-term payable for the purchase of an asset is an investing cash flow. However, where the period between acquisition and payment is significant, the substance of the transaction might be that the seller is providing financing, so subsequent payments to the seller would then be included in financing cash flows. One method that may be used to determine whether the transaction involves a financing component is to look to the requirements in IFRS 15 in respect of whether a contract contains a significant financing component (see Chapter 29 at 2.5). *[IFRS 15.60-65]*.

Where an entity acquires a right-of-use asset under a lease, IAS 7 is clear that the transaction is a non-cash transaction. *[IAS 7.44]*. The cash flow presentation of leasing transactions is discussed at 5.5 below.

5.4.2 Asset disposals on deferred terms

The derecognition of property, plant and equipment by the lessor under a lease or another arrangement determined to be the provision of finance by the vendor would be disclosed as a non-cash transaction. Receipts to reduce the receivable from the purchaser would be investing cash flows, but appropriately described, for example as the receipt of deferred consideration rather than the proceeds on sale of property, plant and equipment. *[IAS 7.16]*.

5.4.3 Revenue contracts with deferred payment terms

As discussed in Chapter 29 at 2.5, a contract with a customer that has a significant financing component would be separated into a revenue component (for the notional cash sales price) and a loan component (for the effect of the deferred or advance payment terms). In the case of deferred payment terms this gives rise to two cash flow components i.e. the revenue component cash flows should be classified as cash flows from operating activities, and the cash flows related to the significant financing component should be classified consistently with the entity's choice to present cash flows from interests received. If the customer pays in advance, however, the sum of the cash amount and the accrued interest represent revenue, and thus there is only one cash flow component which should be classified as cash flows from operating activities.

5.5 Cash flows from leasing transactions

5.5.1 Accounting as lessee

As noted in 4.3 above, where an entity acquires a right-of-use asset under a lease, the acquisition of the asset is clearly a non-cash transaction. The requirements of IFRS 16 are covered in Chapter 23. The presentation and disclosure requirements of IFRS 16 are discussed in Chapter 23 at 5.7 and 5.8. In relation to the cash flow presentation, a lessee classifies:

(a) cash payments for the principal portion of the lease liability within financing activities;

(b) cash payments for the interest portion of the lease liability in a consistent manner to the presentation other interest paid (i.e. as operating or financing – see 4.4.1 above); and

(c) short-term lease payments, payments for leases of low-value assets and variable lease payments not included in the measurement of the lease liability within operating activities. *[IFRS 16.50]*.

IFRS 16 also requires disclosure of the total cash outflow for leases. *[IFRS 16.53(g)]*. It does not explicitly state that leases of low-value assets and short-term leases are excluded. Therefore, we believe the cash outflows related to those leases should be included in the disclosure.

A lessee would also include lease liabilities (and the related cash and non-cash movements) in the disclosures required by IAS 7.44A of changes in liabilities arising from financing activities – see 5.6 below.

However, care may be needed sometimes to distinguish a lease from a purchase of an asset based on the substance of that transaction and not its legal form. IFRS 16 applies to contracts that convey the right to use an underlying asset for a period of time and does not apply to transactions that transfer control of the underlying asset to an entity – such transactions are sales or purchases within the scope of other Standards *[IFRS 16.BC139-140]*. Consequently, if a contract grants rights that represent the in-substance purchase of an item of property, plant and equipment, such transaction may need to be presented as the purchase of the underlying asset (regardless of whether legal title transfers) either on deferred terms (see 5.4.1 above) if entered into directly with the manufacturer or dealer of the asset or together with the provision of financing if entered into with a financial institution which purchases the underlying asset on the entity's behalf from a designated supplier. In the latter case, this raises the question as to whether the payment of the supplier directly by the financial institution should be treated as a non-cash transaction or as a transaction in which the financial institution is acting as a paying agent for the entity. In this case the entity would report an investing cash outflow to the supplier and a financing cash inflow from the financial institution upon taking control of the underlying asset and subsequent financing cash outflows when the liability is settled in future periods.

5.5.2 Payments made by the lessee before commencement date

Where a lessee makes a lease payment at or before the commencement date, this payment is included in the initial measurement of the right-of-use asset. The nature of this cash outflow is consideration for the acquisition of the right-of-use asset and should therefore be classified as an investing activity.

5.5.3 Lease incentives

Lease incentives are defined in IFRS 16 as 'payments made by a lessor to a lessee associated with a lease, or the reimbursement or assumption by a lessor of costs of a lessee' and are dealt with in Chapter 23 at 4.5.2. *[IFRS 16 Appendix A]*.

Neither IFRS 16 nor IAS 7 provide specific guidance on the presentation of the cash inflows from lease incentives. It is however clear that IAS 7 considers a lease transaction to be essentially the provision of finance by the lessor to the lessee. *[IAS 7.17(e)]*. IFRS 16 defines lease payments as 'Payments made by a lessee to a lessor relating to the right to use an underlying asset during the lease term ... less any lease incentives'. *[IFRS 16 Appendix A]*. Considering this definition of lease payments in the context of IAS 7, in our view the most appropriate presentation of cash flows from lease incentives would be therefore to treat such incentives as part of financing activities in the statement of cash flows, regardless of whether they are received after the commencement date of the lease and are deducted from the lease liability or before the lease commencement date.

As with any judgements made as to the classification and disclosure of cash flows, additional disclosure may be necessary to ensure transparency of the treatment adopted.

5.5.4 Sale and leaseback transactions

A sale and leaseback transaction involves the transfer of an asset by an entity (the seller-lessee) to another entity (the buyer-lessor) and the leaseback of the same asset by the seller-lessee. Sale and leaseback transactions are discussed further in Chapter 23 at 8.

In terms of presentation in the statement of cash flows, IFRS 16 refers only to leases, requiring the cash payments for the principal portion of the lease liability to be presented in financing activities and cash payments for the interest portion to be presented in accordance with IAS 7. *[IFRS 16.50]*. Nothing is included in IFRS 16 or IAS 7 with respect to cash flow presentation in the case of a sale and lease-back transaction.

Presentation of the cash flows relating to the sale and leaseback transaction for a seller-lessee will depend on how the transaction is accounted for under IFRS 16, specifically whether the transfer of the asset is accounted for as a sale of the asset in accordance with the requirements of IFRS 15. *[IFRS 16.99]*.

If the transaction does satisfy the requirements of IFRS 15 to be accounted for as a sale, the cash received comprises an amount reflecting the fair value of the underlying asset plus the amount of any additional financing provided by the buyer-lessor to the seller-lessee. *[IFRS 16.101]*. This should be reflected in the statements of cash flows by splitting the proceeds between investing cash flows and financing cash flows. However, there are different approaches as to how this split could be determined. From an economic standpoint, the seller-lessee has sold only its interest in the value of the underlying asset at the end of the leaseback – it has retained its right to use the asset for the duration of the leaseback. *[IFRS 16.BC266]*. Therefore, in our view, the amount that should be shown as an investing cash inflow is the amount of the sale proceeds that reflects the proportion of the fair value of the underlying asset that is not retained by the seller-lessee. Any excess should be presented as part of cash flows from financing activities. This presentation in the statement of cash flows is consistent with the requirement in IFRS 16 to recognise only the amount of any gain or loss on the sale and leaseback relating to the rights that have been transferred to the buyer-lessor and also to measure the right-of-use asset as a proportion of the previous carrying amount of the underlying asset. *[IFRS 16.100]*. This can be seen in Example 40.2 below, which is based on Example 23.35 in Chapter 23.

If the transaction does not satisfy the requirements of IFRS 15 to be accounted for as a sale, the cash received is classified in the cash flow statement as a cash inflow from financing activities because the substance of the transaction is that the lessee has raised finance, with the asset provided as security. The resulting financial liability is accounted for under IFRS 9, *[IFRS 16.103]*, and the seller-lessee splits the cash outflows between repayment of the principal and payment of interest. Repayments of the principal are classified as financing cash flows, whereas interest should be presented in a manner consistent with the presentation of other interest paid in statement of cash flows (see 4.4.1 above).

Example 40.2: Sale and leaseback transaction: presentation of cash flows

An entity (Seller-lessee) sells a building to another entity (Buyer-lessor) for cash of CU2,000,000. Immediately before the transaction, the building is carried at a cost of CU1,000,000. At the same time, Seller-lessee enters into a contract with Buyer-lessor for the right to use the building for 18 years, with annual payments of CU120,000 payable at the end of each year. The terms and conditions of the transaction are such that the transfer of the building by Seller-lessee satisfies the requirements for determining when a performance obligation is satisfied in IFRS 15. Accordingly, Seller-lessee and Buyer-lessor account for the transaction as a sale and leaseback. This example ignores any initial direct costs.

The fair value of the building at the date of sale is CU1,800,000.

At the commencement date, Seller-lessee measures the right-of-use asset arising from the leaseback of the building at the proportion of the previous carrying amount of the building that relates to the right-of-use retained by Seller-lessee, which is CU699,555. This is calculated as: CU1,000,000 (the carrying amount of the building) ÷ CU1,800,000 (the fair value of the building) × CU1,259,200 (the discounted lease payments for the 18-year right-of-use asset) and represents 70% of the building's cost.

Seller-lessee has sold only 30% of the underlying asset as it has retained the use of 70% of the asset via the leaseback transaction. In its statement of cash flows Seller-lessee presents investing cash inflows of CU540,000 representing 30% of the fair value of the building (i.e. 30% × £1,800,000) and the remaining CU1,460,000 (i.e. CU2,000,000 – CU540,000) as financing cash flows.

An alternative approach in this example, could be to treat only the excess of any sale proceeds above the fair value of the underlying asset of CU200,000 (i.e. CU2,000,000 – CU1,800,000) as financing cash flows with CU1,800,000 presented within investing activities.

5.5.5 Accounting as lessor

For lessors, IFRS 16 is silent on the presentation of cash flows arising from their leasing activities. However, since lessor accounting under IFRS 16 is substantially unchanged from the accounting under the predecessor standard, IAS 17 – *Leases*, in practice the presentation of cash flows for lessors should be established and well understood. In summary, the cash inflows from operating leases will form part of the cash flows from operating activities, whether through use the direct or indirect method. The cash inflows from finance leases will follow the treatment set out above at 5.4.2 in relation to assets disposed of on deferred terms.

5.6 Changes in liabilities arising from financing activities

In January 2016, the IASB amended IAS 7 to require disclosures that enable users of financial statements to evaluate changes in liabilities arising from financing activities, including both changes arising from cash flows and non-cash changes. *[IAS 7.44A]*. This amendment was in response to feedback from users, who highlighted that understanding an entity's cash flows is critical to their analysis and that there is a need for improved disclosures about an entity's debt, including changes in debt during the reporting period. *[IAS 7.BC9]*. Liabilities arising from financing activities are liabilities for which cash flows were, or future cash flows will be, classified in the statement of cash flows as cash flows from financing activities (see 4.3 above). In addition, financial asset related cash flows which will be included in cash flows from financing activities (such as assets that hedge liabilities arising from financing activities), should also be included in the scope of this disclosure. *[IAS 7.44C]*.

The following changes should be disclosed to explain the movements in these instruments:

(a) changes from financing cash flows;

(b) changes arising from obtaining or losing control of subsidiaries or other businesses;

(c) the effect of changes in foreign exchange rates;

(d) changes in fair values; and

(e) other changes. *[IAS 7.44B]*.

The standard suggests that these disclosures could be presented in the form of a reconciliation of the opening and closing balances in the statement of financial position for liabilities arising from financing activities. Where such a reconciliation is presented, sufficient information should be provided to enable the link of items included in the reconciliation to the statement of financial position and the statement of cash flows. *[IAS 7.44D]*. If an entity provides the disclosure required by paragraph 44A in combination with disclosures of changes in other assets and liabilities, it should disclose the changes in liabilities arising from financing activities separately from changes in those other assets and liabilities. *[IAS 7.44E]*.

The Interpretations Committee provided further interpretation of these requirements in June 2019.[17] In providing the disclosures required by paragraph 44A of IAS 7. the Interpretations Committee noted that the requirements of IAS 1 on aggregation and disaggregation would apply (see Chapter 3 at 4.1.5). Therefore, an entity should disclose any individually material liability (or asset) and any material reconciling item (i.e. cash or non-cash changes) separately in the reconciliation. An entity should also consider whether additional explanation is needed in order to enable users of financial statements to evaluate changes in liabilities arising from financing activities. The disclosures should be structured and disaggregated appropriately to ensure that they:

- provide information about the entity's sources of finance;
- enables investors to check their understanding of the entity's cash flows; and
- enables investors to link items to the statement of financial position and the statement of cash flows, or related notes.

Example 40.3 below illustrates how an entity might satisfy the requirement to reconcile liabilities arising from financing activities. The cash flows shown in the example should reconcile to the net of the financing cash inflows and outflows in the statement of cash flows.

Example 40.3:   Reconciliation of liabilities arising from financing activities

	20X1	Cash flows	Non-cash changes			20X2
			Acquisition	New leases	Exchange differences	
Bank loans	1,040	250	200	–	25	1,515
Lease liabilities	–	(90)	–	900	10	820
Financing liabilities	1,040	160	200	900	35	2,335

In Extract 40.10 below, Inspired Energy also presents the disclosure in a tabular format, but with the categories of liabilities across the top of the table, which is equally acceptable.

Extract 40.10: Inspired Energy PLC (2018)

Notes to the Group financial statements [extract]

17.   Reconciliation of liabilities arising from financing activities [extract]

	Long-term borrowings £000	Short-term borrowings £000	Total £000
At 31 December 2017	17,809	2,037	19,846
Cash flows			
Repayment	–	(2,044)	(2,044)
Proceeds	4,562	2,838	7,400
Non-cash			
Foreign exchange differences	176	7	183
Debt issue costs releases	55	–	55
At 31 December 2018	22,602	2,838	25,440

5.7 Voluntary disclosures

IAS 7 encourages the disclosure of additional cash flow related information that may help users better understand the financial position of the entity, including a commentary by management, as follows:

(a) the amount of undrawn borrowing facilities that may be available for future operating activities and to settle capital commitments, indicating any restrictions on the use of these facilities;

(b) the aggregate amount of cash flows that represent increases in operating capacity separately from those cash flows that are required to maintain operating capacity (see 5.8.1 below); and

(c) the amount of the cash flows arising from the operating, investing and financing activities of each reportable segment (as defined in IFRS 8 – *Operating Segments*) (see 5.8.2 below). *[IAS 7.50].*

5.7.1 Cash flows to increase and maintain operating capacity

IAS 7 does not contain any guidance as to how to distinguish cash flows for expansion from cash flows for maintenance in relation to the voluntary disclosure referred to under (b) above. The standard merely states that this information is useful in helping the user to determine whether the entity is investing adequately in the maintenance of its operating capacity or whether it may be sacrificing future profitability for the sake of current liquidity and distributions to owners. *[IAS 7.51].*

Hongkong Land Holdings distinguishes renovations expenditure from developments capital expenditure in its analysis of investing cash flows.

Extract 40.11: Hongkong Land Holdings Limited (2019)

Consolidated Cash Flow Statement [extract]

for the year ended 31st December 2019	Note	2019 US$m	2018 US$m
Investing activities			
Major renovations expenditure		(116.4)	(93.0)
Developments capital expenditure		(27.3)	(57.4)
Investments in and advances to associates and joint ventures	20a	(646.0)	(978.4)
Acquisition of a subsidiary		(25.8)	–
Refund of deposit for a joint venture		–	72.9
Proceeds on disposal of other investments		157.5	–
Cash flows from investing activities		(658.0)	(1,055.9)

5.7.2 Segment cash flow disclosures

Disclosure of segmental cash flows is encouraged because it reveals the availability and variability of cash flows in each segment and allows users to better understand the relationship between the cash flows of the business as a whole and those of its component parts. *[IAS 7.52].*

IAS 7 contains an example of the segmental disclosure advocated at 5.7 above. [IAS 7 Appendix A part D]. However, this example simply reports the operating, investing and financing cash flows of its two segments with no reconciliation of the total to the statement of cash flows. In practice it might be difficult to allocate financing cash flows across the entity's reportable segments, given that this is not how treasury functions tend to operate.

A.P. Møller – Mærsk provided an analysis of operating cash flows and capital expenditure (part of its investing cash flows) by reportable segment. The entity did not disclose financing cash flows by reportable segment (comparative information is provided in the financial statements but is not reproduced here).

Extract 40.12: A.P. Møller – Mærsk A/S (2017)

Note 1 Segment information [extract]

	Maersk Line	APM Terminals	Damco	Svitzer	Maersk Container Industry	Total reportable segments
Cash flow from operating activities	2,389	827	–101	179	75	3.369
Cash flow used for capital expenditure	–6,142	–672	–4	–96	–20	–6,934

6 ADDITIONAL IAS 7 CONSIDERATIONS FOR GROUPS

IAS 7 does not distinguish between single entities and groups, and there are no specific requirements as to how an entity should prepare a consolidated statement of cash flows. In the absence of specific requirements, cash inflows and outflows would be treated in the same way as income and expenses under IFRS 10 – *Consolidated Financial Statements*. Applying these principles, the statement of cash flows presented in consolidated financial statements should reflect only the flows of cash and cash equivalents into and out of the group, i.e. consolidated cash flows are presented as those of a single economic entity. [IFRS 10 Appendix A]. On the same basis, the cash flows of a consolidated subsidiary should be included in the consolidated statement of cash flows for the same period as its results are reported in the consolidated statement of comprehensive income, i.e. from the date the group gains control until the date it loses control. [IFRS 10.B88].

Cash flows that are internal to the group (such as payments and receipts for intra-group sales, management charges, dividends, interest and financing arrangements) should be eliminated. [IFRS 10.B86]. However, transactions with non-controlling interests as well as with associates, joint ventures and unconsolidated subsidiaries would not be eliminated and are discussed in greater detail below.

6.1 Preparing a consolidated statement of cash flows

In principle, the group statement of cash flows should be built up from those prepared by individual subsidiaries with intra-group cash flows being eliminated as part of the aggregation process. This would generally be the case for entities presenting operating cash flows under the direct method, where information on gross cash receipts and payments has been obtained from each group entity's accounting records.

In practice, however, it may be possible to prepare a statement of cash flows at a more consolidated level, by starting with the disclosures in the consolidated statement of comprehensive income and statement of financial position and then applying the adjustments reflected as part of the financial statements consolidation process, together with information provided on external cash flows by individual subsidiaries. Thus, an entity adopting the direct method could use this information to derive the value of the major classes of gross cash receipts and gross cash payments. *[IAS 7.19]*. An entity presenting operating cash flows under the indirect method would use this information to calculate the values for movements in inventories, operating receivables and payables and other non-cash items that appear in the reconciliation of consolidated profit or loss to the group's cash flow from operating activities. *[IAS 7.20]*. As noted at 5.3.2.D above, groups with foreign subsidiaries will need to take extra care when using this method to ensure exchange differences are treated appropriately.

Cash flows from investing and financing activities could similarly be derived from a reconciliation of the relevant headings in the consolidated statement of comprehensive income to statement of financial position movements. However, for this to be possible, subsidiaries would have to provide supplementary information (as part of internal group reporting) to prevent gross cash flows from being netted off and to ensure that the cash flows are shown under the correct classifications. In particular, detailed information about receivables and payables would be essential to ensure that the movements in operating, investing and financing receivables and payables are identified.

6.2 Transactions with non-controlling interests

Dividends paid to non-controlling interest holders in subsidiaries are included under cash flows from financing activities or operating activities, in accordance with the entity's determined policy for dividends paid (see 4.4.1 above).

IFRS 10 requires entities to distinguish between transactions that give rise to a change in control and those that do not, because a transaction when there is no change in control is effectively one with the owners in their capacity as owners. *[IFRS 10.BCZ168]*. Changes in ownership interests in a subsidiary that do not result in a loss of control are therefore accounted for as equity transactions, and the resulting cash flows are classified in the same way as other transactions with owners. *[IAS 7.42B]*. Accordingly, IAS 7 requires that cash flows arising from changes in ownership interests in a subsidiary that occur after control is obtained, but do not give rise to a loss of control are classified as cash flows from financing activities. *[IAS 7.42A]*.

6.3 Acquisitions and disposals

An entity should present separately within investing activities the aggregate cash flows arising from obtaining or losing control of subsidiaries or other businesses. *[IAS 7.39]*. For transactions that involve obtaining or losing control of subsidiaries or other businesses during the period, disclosure is also required, in aggregate, of each of the following:

(a) the total consideration paid or received;
(b) the portion of the consideration consisting of cash and cash equivalents;
(c) the amount of cash and cash equivalents in the subsidiaries or other businesses over which control is obtained or lost; and
(d) the amount of the assets and liabilities, other than cash or cash equivalents, in the subsidiaries or other businesses over which control is obtained or lost, summarised by each major category. *[IAS 7.40]*.

Cash flows arising from changes in ownership interests in a subsidiary that do not result in a loss of control are classified as financing cash flows (see 6.2 above). *[IAS 7.42A]*.

The aggregate amount of cash paid or received as consideration is reported in the statement of cash flows net of cash and cash equivalents acquired or disposed of. *[IAS 7.42]*. The cash flow effects of losing control are not deducted from those of gaining control. *[IAS 7.41]*. This implies that entities should present one analysis for all acquisitions and another for all disposals, such as that presented by Naspers, shown in Extract 40.13 below.

Extract 40.13: Naspers Limited (2019)

Consolidated statement of cash flows [extract]
for the year ended 31 March 2019

	Notes	31 March 2019 US$'m	31 March 2018 US$'m
Cash flows from investing activities [extract]			
[...]			
Acquisitions of subsidiaries and businesses, net of cash acquired	36	(104)	(16)
Disposals of subsidiaries and businesses	37	(508)	40
[...]			

Notes to the consolidated annual financial statements [extract]
for the year ended 31 March 2019

36. ACQUISITIONS OF SUBSIDIARIES AND BUSINESSES

	31 March 2019 US$'m	31 March 2018 US$'m
Carrying values of assets and liabilities:		
property, plant and equipment	3	13
other intangible assets	58	142
net current assets	48	115
deferred taxation	(8)	(40)
long-term liabilities	(1)	(14)
contingent liability	–	(4)

	100	212
Non-controlling interests	(13)	(83)
Derecognition of equity-accounted investments	(15)	(102)
Remeasurement of previously held interest	(7)	(21)
Goodwill	105	124
Purchase consideration	170	130
Amount to be settled in future	–	(1)
Net cash in subsidiaries and businesses acquired	(66)	(113)
Net cash outflow from acquisitions of subsidiaries and businesses	104	16

37. DISPOSALS OF SUBSIDIARIES AND BUSINESSES

	31 March	
	2019 US$'m	2018 US$'m
Carrying values of assets and liabilities:		
property, plant and equipment	1	–
disposal groups classified as held for sale	874	225
goodwill	8	–
other intangible assets	4	–
net assets	28	10
deferred taxation	(1)	–
other liabilities	(9)	–
foreign currency translation reserve realised	594	110
	1 499	345
Distribution to owners [1]	(3 771)	(69)
Non-controlling interests	145	(94)
Existing control business combination reserve	(274)	–
Fair value of investments at fair value through other comprehensive income retained following distribution to owners [1]	(58)	(29)
Gain on disposal	2 513	(143)
Selling price	54	10
Net cash in subsidiaries and businesses disposed of	(562)	30
Net cash (outflow)/inflow from disposals of subsidiaries and businesses	(508)	40

(1) Relates to the group's video-entertainment business which was distributed to shareholders during the current year (refer to note 3 and note 11).

6.3.1 Acquisition-related costs

IFRS 3 – *Business Combinations* – requires acquisition-related costs (other than those costs relating to the issue of equity or debt securities) to be recognised as an expense in the period in which the costs are incurred and the services are received. *[IFRS 3.53]*. As discussed at 4.2 above, the definition of investing activities in IAS 7, states that 'only expenditures that result in a recognised asset in the statement of financial position' give rise to investing cash flows. *[IAS 7.16]*. As a result, cash flows relating to acquisition costs recognised as an expense would have to be classified within operating activities. This faithfully reflects the fact that these payments are for services received.

6.3.2 Deferred and other non-cash consideration

Not all acquisitions or disposals of businesses are satisfied in full by the exchange of cash. Any non-cash consideration, such as shares issued by either party or amounts to be paid or received by the entity at a later date, is not included in the amount presented under investing activities. *[IAS 7.43]*. Instead, the non-cash element of the acquisition or disposal is disclosed. As explained in more detail at 5.4 above, the purchase of assets on deferred terms can be a complicated area because it may not be clear whether the associated cash flows should be classified under investing activities, as capital expenditure, or within financing activities, as the repayment of borrowings. Hence judgement is required when determining the appropriate classification of the deferred payment in the statement of cash flows. These same principles apply on the acquisition of a business involving deferred consideration.

6.3.3 Contingent consideration

6.3.3.A Business combinations

When a business combination agreement allows for adjustments to the cost of the combination that are contingent on one or more future events, IFRS 3 requires the acquirer to recognise the acquisition-date fair value of the contingent consideration, *[IFRS 3.39]*, and classify an obligation to pay the contingent consideration as a liability or as equity in accordance with the provisions of IAS 32. *[IFRS 3.40]*. Changes resulting from events after the acquisition date, such as meeting a performance target, are not reflected by adjusting the recorded cost of the business combination. Instead, any payment or receipt in excess of the carrying amount of the related liability or asset is recognised in profit or loss. *[IFRS 3.58]*.

The primary principle for the classification of cash flows should be the nature of the activity giving rise to the cash flow, according to the definitions of operating, investing and financing activities in the Standard. This might imply that all payments relating to a business combination should be classified as investing cash flows. However, as discussed at 4.2 above, the Board added a requirement in IAS 7 that only expenditures that result in a recognised asset are eligible for classification as investing activities. *[IAS 7.16]*.

Accordingly, cash payments up to the amount recognised for the acquisition-date fair value of the contingent consideration (and thereby included in the carrying value of the acquired assets including goodwill) would be classified in investing activities. Since contingent consideration generally arises for reasons other than the provision of finance to the acquirer, any resulting payments would generally not seem to be eligible for classification as financing cash flows. As a result, any contingent consideration in excess of the amount that was recorded on the acquisition date, flows would need to be presented as operating cash flows by default.

6.3.3.B Asset acquisitions outside of business combinations

The purchase price of intangible assets or tangible assets acquired outside of a business combination commonly includes contingent consideration for example to resolve an uncertainty or a difference in views about the initial value of the asset transferred.

Accounting for the contingent consideration element of such asset purchases is discussed in Chapter 17 at 4.5 for intangible assets, and Chapter 18 at 4.1.9 for tangible assets. As explained in those chapters, such transactions are often very complex and payment can be dependent on a number of factors, with no specific guidance provided in IAS 38 – *Intangible Assets* – or IAS 16. Therefore, an entity should develop and consistently apply an accounting policy for the initial and subsequent measurement of such assets that results in information that is relevant and reliable in its particular circumstances.

Once such an accounting policy is developed, the presentation in the statement of cash flows should follow the accounting treatment adopted in the statement of financial position.

As discussed at 4.2 above, even though the reason for the cash flows in a genuine contingent consideration is to acquire a long-term asset, classifying the resulting cash flows as investing would only be appropriate if the cash flows are in settlement of an expenditure that results in a recognised asset in the statement of financial position. *[IAS 7.16]*. In other words, the IASB effectively required the classification of cash flows from investing activities in the statement of cash flows to be aligned with the presentation of recognised assets in the statement of financial position rather than to reflect an entity's judgment as to the most appropriate classification based the entity's business and the definitions of investing activities *[IAS 7.BC5-7]*.

Since contingent consideration generally arises for reasons other than the provision of finance to the purchaser, any resulting payments would generally not seem to be eligible for classification as financing cash flows. Therefore, payments not classified as investing cash flows would need to be presented as operating cash flows by default.

6.3.3.C Contingent consideration received on disposals

When an entity disposes of a subsidiary, it presents the cash flows separately within investing activities. This will be the case even for the receipt of contingent consideration because the cash inflow is still an investing cash flow being the receipt from the sale of equity or debt instruments of another entity (see 4.2 above).

6.3.4 Settlement of amounts owed by the acquired entity

A question that sometimes arises is how to treat a payment made by the acquirer to settle amounts owed by a new subsidiary, either to take over a loan that is owed to the vendor by that subsidiary or to extinguish an external borrowing.

Payments made to acquire debt instruments of other entities are normally included under investing activities. *[IAS 7.16]*. Therefore, a payment to the vendor to take over a loan that is owed to the vendor by the subsidiary is classified under the same cash flow heading irrespective of whether it is regarded as being part of the purchase consideration or the acquisition of a debt.

Payments made by the acquirer to the vendor before acquisition to extinguish an external borrowing of the subsidiary would similarly be classified as investing cash flows. This presentation can be contrasted with the repayment of an external borrowing by the new subsidiary after acquisition, using funds provided by the parent, which is a cash outflow from financing activities. *[IAS 7.17]*.

6.3.5 Settlement of intra-group balances on a demerger

A similarly fine distinction might apply on the demerger of subsidiaries. These sometimes involve the repayment of intra-group indebtedness out of the proceeds from external finance raised by the demerged subsidiary. If the external funding is raised immediately prior to the subsidiary leaving the group, it is strictly a financing inflow in the consolidated statement of cash flows, being cash proceeds from issuing short or long-term borrowings. *[IAS 7.17]*. If the subsidiary both raises the external funding and repays the intra-group debt after the demerger, the inflow is shown in the consolidated statement of cash flows under investing activities, being a cash receipt from the repayment of advances and loans made to other parties. *[IAS 7.16]*.

6.4 Cash flows of associates, joint operations and investment entities

6.4.1 Investments in associates and joint ventures

Changes in cash and cash equivalents relating to associates or joint ventures accounted for under the equity or cost method will impact the entity's statement of cash flows only to the extent of the cash flows between the group and the investee. *[IAS 7.37]*. The same concept would apply to associates or joint ventures carried at fair value as allowed by IAS 28 – *Investments in Associates and Joint Ventures* (discussed in Chapter 11). Examples include cash dividends received and loans advanced or repaid. *[IAS 7.37]*. Cash flows in respect of an entity's investment in an equity accounted associate or joint venture would also be presented. *[IAS 7.38]*.

Cash dividends received from equity accounted associates and joint ventures would be classified as operating or investing activities in accordance with the entity's determined policy for other dividends received (see 4.4.1 above). Where the net cash inflow from operating activities is determined using the indirect method, the group's share of profits or losses from equity-accounted investments will appear as a non-cash reconciling item in the cash flow statement (see 4.1.2 above).

The cash flows arising on the acquisition and disposal of an associate or joint venture would be classified as investing activities. In addition, the considerations set out at 6.3.2 and 6.3.3 above in respect of deferred and contingent consideration on acquisition and disposal of a subsidiary should also be applied when determining the appropriate classifications of cash flows relating to the acquisition and disposal of associates and joint ventures.

6.4.2 Cash flows of joint operations

IAS 7 does not specifically deal with the treatment of the cash flows of joint operations. However, following the guidance of IFRS 11 – *Joint Arrangements* – all transactions should be reflected in the accounts of the joint operator's financial results to the extent of its interests in those transactions. *[IFRS 11.20]*. Therefore, the cash flows of the joint arrangement are already included in the operator's financial statements and no additional adjustments are required to reflect the activities of the joint operation.

The treatment of cash flows for the acquisition and disposal of a joint operation is less clear as there is an argument for presentation either as a single net cash flow in investing activities (as is required for the cost of a business combination, discussed at 6.3 above); or as separate cash flows, classified according to the nature of the underlying assets and liabilities acquired. IFRS 11 requires an entity to determine whether the activity undertaken by a joint operation constitutes a business as defined in IFRS 3 and to apply business combination or asset acquisition accounting in accordance with that analysis. *[IFRS 11.21A]*. Therefore it would be appropriate to apply a similar approach to the presentation of the cash flows, with acquisitions and disposals of operations meeting the definition of a business giving rise to a single investing cash flow, and acquisitions and disposals of operations not regarded as a business giving rise to cash flows according to the nature of the assets and liabilities acquired or disposed.

6.4.3 Cash flows in investment entities

IAS 7 does not address the treatment of subsidiaries held at fair value in an investment entity. As these investments are accounted for at fair value through profit or loss in accordance with IFRS 9, the related cash flows would be treated consistently with cash flows from joint ventures and associates discussed at 6.4.1 above.

The disclosures required by an investment entity on the acquisition of subsidiaries are less than those required for other entities. Investment entities need only disclose the total consideration paid or received and the portion of the consideration consisting of cash and cash equivalents are required to be disclosed. *[IAS 7.40-40A]*.

6.5 Cash flows in separate financial statements

6.5.1 Cash flows of subsidiaries, associates and joint ventures

IAS 7 addresses the treatment of cash flows of associates, joint ventures and subsidiaries accounted for by use of the cost method, restricting its reporting in the statement of cash flows to the cash flows between investor and the investee, for example, to dividends and advances as discussed in 6.4.1 above. *[IAS 7.37]*. This treatment would also be applied to associates, joint ventures and subsidiaries either held at fair value through profit or loss, or using the equity accounted method in the separate financial statements, as allowed by IAS 27 – *Separate Financial Statements* – and discussed in Chapter 8 at 2.

6.5.2 Group cash pooling and cash sharing arrangements

Many groups use some form of cash pooling or cash sharing arrangement to manage the group's cash position on a consolidated basis, effectively concentrating the group's cash in one place. Such arrangements seek to maximise the return for the group as a whole on their cash, minimise the cost of funding and give visibility to the group's cash and currency position.

The terms and conditions of such arrangements vary, and it is important to understand the specific nature of the pooling or sharing arrangement in place in order to determine the appropriate accounting treatment.

At 6.5.3 and 6.5.4 below we discuss three of the most common types of arrangements.

6.5.3 Group treasury arrangements

Some groups adopt treasury arrangements under which cash resources are held centrally, either by the parent company or by a designated subsidiary company. Any excess cash is transferred to the central bank account which is in the name of the designated 'treasury entity'. In some cases, a subsidiary might not even have its own bank account, with all receipts and payments being made directly from the centrally controlled funds. Instead of presenting cash and bank deposits at each period end, the subsidiary should record an intercompany receivable for the amounts that have been transferred to the treasury entity. In extremely rare cases the intercompany balance may meet the definition of cash equivalents and be regarded as a short-term highly liquid investment that is readily convertible into known amounts of cash and are subject to insignificant risk of changes in value. However, in most cases such funds are transferred to the designated group entity for an indeterminate term and the subsidiary would not be able to withdraw on demand the amounts deposited without prior authorisation.

A further question that arises is whether or not a statement of cash flows should be presented when preparing the separate financial statements of the subsidiary given that there is no cash or cash equivalents balance held at each period end and, for some entities, at any time during the year. In our view, the preparation of the statement of cash flows should be based upon the actual cash flows during the period regardless of cash and cash equivalents balance held directly by the entity.

Where no cash flows through an entity, but rather all transactions flow through another group company acting on behalf of the entity, the entity should still record receipts from debtors and payments to suppliers, albeit with an associated deposit to or withdrawal from a balance with another group company. Just as a bank processes payments and receipts as agent for the account holder, so the group treasury function acts as agent for the entity, and these transactions should be reflected in a statement of cash flows. This approach is consistent with the requirements in IAS 7 that all entities should prepare a statement of cash flows which forms an integral part of the financial statements. *[IAS 7.1]*.

Where the subsidiary makes net deposits of funds to, or net withdrawals of funds from the designated group entity during the reporting period, a further question arises as to how movements should be presented in the subsidiary's statement of cash flows. As explained above, these transactions normally give rise to intercompany balances. Therefore, the deposits or withdrawals should be evaluated against the definitions of the categories of cash flows and presented as either operating activities or alternatively as investing or financing activities, as appropriate. Further consideration should be made as to whether these cash flows meet the criteria for net presentation as discussed at 5.2 above.

6.5.4 Cash pooling

Groups often use what are commonly known as cash pooling arrangements. Typically, these will involve a number of subsidiaries within a group each having a legally separate bank account with the same bank, but these accounts are managed, with the agreement of the bank, on a consolidated basis. For example, interest will normally be determined on a notional basis using the net balance of all accounts; similarly, any overdraft limit will normally apply to the net balance. Typical characteristics of notional cash pooling and physical cash pooling are discussed below however arrangements vary. Therefore, terms and conditions of each arrangement should be reviewed carefully to ensure that the accounting treatment adopted is appropriate for that specific arrangement.

6.5.4.A Notional cash pooling

Notional cash pooling arrangements allow the group to net off the balances of different accounts across jurisdictions, without physically moving the cash to a header or master account, but with each individual entity continuing to have access to the cash it has deposited in its individual account, sometimes called a 'memo' or 'mirror' account. This is, in essence, an interest rate adjustment, and the ownership of the cash does not change.

In such cases, therefore, each entity will continue to report their cash as 'cash and cash equivalents'.

6.5.4.B Physical cash pooling

Typically, in these arrangements, which are also known as zero balancing, cash concentration or physical cash sweeping, the group physically sweeps excess cash out of the individual bank accounts to a header account on a daily basis. In these arrangements, the ownership of the cash changes: the relationship moves from a deposit with a third-party bank to a loan to the group entity that is the cash pool header. As in the group treasury arrangements discussed above, the individual companies will need to consider how to present these balances at the period end.

When amounts from the individual bank accounts that have been pooled can be withdrawn upon demand by the individual companies without prior authorization or delay, presentation as cash and cash equivalents may be appropriate. In other circumstances, the balances may need to be presented as short-term intercompany receivables with appropriate disclosures about the terms of the cash-pooling arrangement.

The presentation of cash balances in cash pooling arrangements in the group accounts, in particular whether the individual balances should be presented net or gross, is discussed in Chapter 54 at 7.4.1.E.

7 ADDITIONAL IAS 7 CONSIDERATIONS FOR FINANCIAL INSTITUTIONS

IAS 7 applies to banks, insurance entities and other financial institutions. Nevertheless, there are some differences in its application as compared to entities that are not financial institutions. For example, in considering the components of cash and cash equivalents, banks would not usually have borrowings with the characteristics of an overdraft, and cash for their purposes should normally include cash and balances at central banks, together with loans and advances to other banks repayable on demand. Allianz discloses such items as components of its cash and cash equivalents, as shown in Extract 40.14 below.

Extract 40.14: Allianz SE (2019)
CONSOLIDATED STATEMENTS OF CASH FLOWS [extract]
Cash and cash equivalents
€ mn

As of 31 December	2019	2018
Balances with banks payable on demand	8,245	7,660
Balances with central banks	3,215	2,990
Cash on hand	64	57
Treasury bills, discounted treasury notes, similar treasury securities, bills of exchange and checks	6,952	6,526
Reverse repurchase agreements (due in three months or less)	2,598	–
Total	21,075	17,234

IAS 7 contains a number of additional provisions affecting the preparation of statements of cash flow by financial institutions. These are covered in broad outline below.

7.1 Operating cash flows

Cash advances and loans made by financial institutions are usually classified as operating activities (and not as investing activities, as they are for other entities) since they relate to a financial institution's main revenue-producing activity. *[IAS 7.15, 16(e)]*. Similarly, receipts from the repayment of loans and advances would be included in operating cash flows. *[IAS 7.16(f)]*.

Interest paid and interest and dividends received are usually classified as operating cash flows for a financial institution. *[IAS 7.33]*.

For an insurance entity, cash receipts and cash payments for premiums and claims, annuities and other policy benefits would be included in its operating cash flows as these relate to the principal activities of the entity.

Under the direct method of reporting operating cash flows, a financial institution that does not obtain information from its accounting records can derive the disclosures for major classes of gross cash receipts and payments by adjusting interest and similar income and interest expense and similar charges and other items recognised in profit or loss for:

(a) changes during the period in operating receivables and payables;

(b) other non-cash items; and

(c) other items for which the cash effects are investing or financing cash flows. *[IAS 7.19]*.

Where an insurance entity presents its operating cash flows using the direct method, it should separately disclose cash flows arising from insurance contracts. *[IFRS 4.37(b)]*. Comparative information is required. *[IFRS 4.42]*. When an entity adopts IFRS 17, which is effective from 1 January 2023 (see Chapter 56), the specific disclosure requirements under IFRS 4 – *Insurance Contracts* – will no longer apply.

Subject to the differences noted above, the principles for a financial institution presenting operating cash flows under the indirect method are the same as those discussed at 4.1.2 above for other entities.

7.2 Reporting cash flows on a net basis

Cash flows from each of the following activities of a financial institution may be reported on a net basis:

(a) cash receipts and payments for the acceptance and repayment of deposits with a fixed maturity date;

(b) the placement of deposits with and withdrawal of deposits from other financial institutions; and

(c) cash advances and loans made to customers and the repayment of those advances and loans. *[IAS 7.24]*.

8 REQUIREMENTS OF OTHER STANDARDS

8.1 Cash flows of discontinued operations

IFRS 5 – *Non-current Assets Held for Sale and Discontinued Operations* – requires an entity to disclose the net cash flows attributable to the operating, investing and financing activities of discontinued operations. These disclosures can be presented either on the face of the statement of cash flows or in the notes. Disclosure is not required for disposal groups that are newly acquired subsidiaries which are classified as held for sale on acquisition in accordance with IFRS 5. *[IFRS 5.33(c)]*. The general presentation requirements of IFRS 5 are dealt with in Chapter 4.

In the example below, Netcare Limited elected to show the cash flows of discontinued operations on the face of the statement of cash flows, as well as in the note. Over and above this, the entity has elected to include additional disclosures by splitting cash flows in respect of interest and tax paid into those relating to continuing and discontinued operations. In the notes to the financial statements, Netcare Limited further analyses these cash flows by separate major business line.

Extract 40.15: Netcare Limited (2012)

GROUP STATEMENT OF CASH FLOWS [extract]
for the year ended 30 September

Rm	2012	2011
Cash generated from operations	5 193	5 572
Interest paid	(1 976)	(1 836)
Continuing operations	(1 959)	(1 817)
Discontinued operations	(17)	(19)
Taxation paid	(740)	(674)
Continuing operations	(720)	(658)
Discontinued operations	(20)	(16)
Capital reductions paid		(83)
Ordinary dividends paid	(694)	(553)
Ordinary dividends paid by subsidiaries	(4)	(3)
Preference dividends paid	(46)	(47)
Distributions to beneficiaries of the HPFL trusts	(43)	(47)
Net cash from operating activities	1 690	2 329
Continuing operations	1 646	2 285
Discontinued operations	44	44

NOTES TO THE GROUP ANNUAL FINANCIAL STATEMENTS [extract]

12.1 Discontinued operations [extract]

Rm	Care	Transform	Total
2012			
Cash flows from operating activities	17	27	44
Cash flows from investing activities	(3)	(7)	(10)
2011			
Cash flows from operating activities	39	5	44
Cash flows from investing activities	(3)	(8)	(11)
Cash flows from financing activities	(14)	3	(11)

8.2 Cash flows arising from insurance contracts

IFRS 4 requires that where an insurance entity presents its operating cash flows using the direct method, it should separately disclose cash flows arising from insurance contracts. *[IFRS 4.37(b)]*. Comparative information is required. *[IFRS 4.42]*. When an entity adopts IFRS 17 the specific disclosure requirements under IFRS 4 will no longer apply (see 7.1 above).

8.3 Cash flows arising from the exploration of mineral resources

In a similar vein, IFRS 6 – *Exploration for and Evaluation of Mineral Resources* – requires that an entity discloses the amounts of operating and investing cash flows arising from the exploration for and evaluation of mineral resources. *[IFRS 6.24(b)]*. The requirements of IFRS 6 are discussed in Chapter 43. The requirement for investing cash flows to give rise to the recognition of an asset, discussed at 4.2 above, is particularly relevant to entities applying IFRS 6.

8.4 Cash flows arising from interests in subsidiaries, joint ventures and associates

IFRS 12 requires an entity to disclose in its consolidated financial statements summarised financial information about the cash flows for each subsidiary that has non-controlling interests that are material to the entity. *[IFRS 12.B10(b)]*. These amounts are stated before inter-company eliminations. *[IFRS 12.B11]*.

For each material joint venture and associate an entity is also required to disclose dividends received from the joint venture or associate *[IFRS 12.B12(a)]* and, for joint ventures, the amount of cash and cash equivalents. *[IFRS 12.B13(a)]*. In addition, the standard requires disclosure of any significant restrictions on the ability of joint ventures or associates to transfer funds to the entity in the form of cash dividends, or to repay loans or advances made by the entity. *[IFRS 12.22(a)]*.

IFRS 12 is discussed in more detail in Chapter 13.

References

1 *IFRIC Update*, July 2020.
2 *IFRIC Update*, July 2009.
3 *IFRIC Update*, July 2009.
4 *IFRIC Update*, June 2018.
5 *IFRIC Update*, June 2019.
6 *IFRIC Update*, June 2019.
7 *IASB Update*, December 2016.
8 *IASB Update*, April 2013.
9 *IASB Update*, April 2013.
10 ED 2012/1, *Annual Improvements to IFRSs 2010-2012 Cycle*, IASB, May 2012.
11 *IASB Update*, April 2013.
12 *IFRIC Update*, August 2005.
13 *IFRIC Update*, August 2005.
14 *IFRIC Update*, July 2012.
15 *IFRIC Update*, March 2013.
16 *IASB Update*, April 2013.
17 *IFRIC Update*, June 2019.

Chapter 41 Interim financial reporting

1 INTRODUCTION 3195
   1.1 Definitions 3196
2 OBJECTIVE AND SCOPE OF IAS 34 3196
   2.1 Objective 3196
   2.2 Scope 3197
3 COMPONENTS, FORM AND CONTENT OF AN INTERIM FINANCIAL REPORT UNDER IAS 34 3198
   3.1 Complete set of interim financial statements 3198
   3.2 Condensed interim financial statements 3199
   3.3 Requirements for both complete and condensed interim financial information 3203
   3.4 Management commentary 3203
4 DISCLOSURES IN CONDENSED FINANCIAL STATEMENTS 3204
   4.1 Significant events and transactions 3204
      4.1.1 Relevance of other standards in condensed financial statements 3205
   4.2 Other disclosures required by IAS 34 3206
      4.2.1 Location of the specified disclosures in an interim financial report 3208
   4.3 Illustrative examples of disclosures 3208
      4.3.1 Inventory write-down and reversals 3208
      4.3.2 Recognition and reversal of impairment losses 3209
      4.3.3 Acquisitions and disposals of property, plant and equipment 3210
      4.3.4 Capital commitments 3210
      4.3.5 Litigation settlements 3210

		4.3.6	Changes in circumstances affecting fair values	3211
		4.3.7	Default or breach of loan covenants not remedied before the end of interim period	3212
		4.3.8	Related party transactions	3212
		4.3.9	Transfers between different levels of fair value hierarchy	3214
		4.3.10	Contingent liabilities	3214
		4.3.11	Accounting policies and methods of computation	3215
		4.3.12	Seasonality or cyclicality of operations	3216
		4.3.13	Amounts that are unusual because of their nature, size or incidence	3216
		4.3.14	Issues, repurchases and repayments of debt and equity securities	3217
		4.3.15	Dividends paid	3218
		4.3.16	Events after the interim reporting date	3218
		4.3.17	Changes in the composition of the entity	3219
	4.4	Segment information		3221
	4.5	Fair value disclosures for financial instruments		3223
	4.6	Disclosure of compliance with IFRS		3224
	4.7	Disclosure in relation to the going concern assumption		3226
5	Periods for which interim financial statements are required to be presented			3227
	5.1	Other comparative information		3231
	5.2	Length of interim reporting period		3232
	5.3	Change in financial year-end		3232
	5.4	Comparatives following a financial period longer than a year		3234
	5.5	When the comparative period is shorter than the current period		3235
6	Materiality			3235
7	Disclosure in annual financial statements			3236
8	Recognition and measurement			3237
	8.1	Same accounting policies as in annual financial statements		3237
		8.1.1	Measurement on a year-to-date basis	3238
		8.1.2	New accounting pronouncements and other changes in accounting policies	3239
			8.1.2.A New pronouncements becoming mandatory during the current year	3240
			8.1.2.B Voluntary changes of accounting policy	3240
			8.1.2.C Transition disclosures in subsequent interim financial statements in the year of adoption	3241
			8.1.2.D New pronouncements becoming mandatory in future annual reporting periods	3241

	8.1.3	Voluntary changes in presentation	3242
8.2	Seasonal businesses		3242
	8.2.1	Revenues received seasonally, cyclically, or occasionally	3242
	8.2.2	Costs incurred unevenly during the year	3243

9 EXAMPLES OF THE RECOGNITION AND MEASUREMENT PRINCIPLES ... 3243

9.1	Property, plant and equipment and intangible assets			3244
	9.1.1	Depreciation and amortisation		3244
	9.1.2	Impairment of assets		3244
	9.1.3	Recognition of intangible assets		3244
	9.1.4	Capitalisation of borrowing costs		3245
9.2	Reversal of impairment losses recognised in a previous interim period (IFRIC 10)			3245
9.3	Employee benefits			3246
	9.3.1	Employer payroll taxes and insurance contributions		3246
	9.3.2	Year-end bonuses		3246
	9.3.3	Pensions		3247
	9.3.4	Vacations, holidays, and other short-term paid absences		3248
9.4	Inventories and cost of sales			3248
	9.4.1	Inventories		3248
	9.4.2	Contractual or anticipated purchase price changes		3249
	9.4.3	Interim period manufacturing cost variances		3249
9.5	Taxation			3249
	9.5.1	Measuring interim income tax expense		3249
	9.5.2	Changes in the effective tax rate during the year		3251
		9.5.2.A	Enacted changes for the current year that apply after the interim reporting date	3251
		9.5.2.B	Changes to previously reported estimated income tax rates for the current year	3252
		9.5.2.C	Enacted changes applying only to subsequent years	3253
	9.5.3	Difference in financial year and tax year		3254
	9.5.4	Tax loss and tax credit carrybacks and carryforwards		3254
	9.5.5	Tax credits		3257
9.6	Foreign currency translation			3257
	9.6.1	Foreign currency translation gains and losses		3257
	9.6.2	Interim financial reporting in hyperinflationary economies		3258
9.7	Provisions, contingencies and accruals for other costs			3259
	9.7.1	Provisions		3259
	9.7.2	Other planned but irregularly occurring costs		3260

	9.7.3	Major planned periodic maintenance or overhaul	3260
	9.7.4	Variable lease payments	3260
	9.7.5	Levies charged by public authorities	3261
9.8	Earnings per share		3264

10 USE OF ESTIMATES 3265

11 EFFECTIVE DATES AND TRANSITIONAL RULES 3266

11.1 First-time presentation of interim reports complying with IAS 34 3266

    11.1.1 Condensed financial statements in the year of incorporation or when an entity converts from its local GAAP to IFRS 3267

List of examples

Example 41.1:	Presenting the same headings and sub-totals in condensed interim financial statements	3200
Example 41.2:	Disclosure of default of loan covenant	3212
Example 41.3:	Going concern assessment under IAS 1	3226
Example 41.4:	Entity publishes interim financial reports half-yearly	3228
Example 41.5:	Entity publishes interim financial reports quarterly	3229
Example 41.6:	Disclosing movements on non-current assets in a complete set of interim financial statements	3232
Example 41.7:	Entity changes financial year-end	3232
Example 41.8:	Disclosing comparatives in interim financial statements when the preceding financial year covers a longer period	3234
Example 41.9:	Disclosing comparatives in interim financial statements when the preceding financial year covers a shorter period	3235
Example 41.10:	Measuring interim bonus expense	3246
Example 41.11:	Measuring interim income tax expense – progressive tax rates	3250
Example 41.12:	Measuring interim income tax expense – quarterly losses	3250
Example 41.13:	Measuring interim tax expense – many jurisdictions	3251
Example 41.14:	Changes in the effective tax rate during the year	3252
Example 41.15:	Enacted changes to tax rates applying after the current year	3253
Example 41.16:	Difference in financial year and tax year [IAS 34.B18]	3254
Example 41.17:	Tax loss carryforwards expected to be recovered in the current year [IAS 34.B22]	3254
Example 41.18:	Tax loss carryforwards in excess of current year expected profits	3255

Example 41.19:	Accounting by the parent when a hyperinflationary subsidiary first applies IAS 29 3259
Example 41.20:	A levy is triggered in full as soon as the entity generates revenue 3262
Example 41.21:	A levy is triggered in full as soon as the entity generates revenue from a certain activity above an annual threshold, which is reduced pro rata when the entity ceases participation in that activity during the year 3262
Example 41.22:	A levy is triggered in full as soon as the entity holds the property at a specified date 3263
Example 41.23:	A levy is triggered progressively as the entity holds the asset through a specified period of time 3263
Example 41.24:	Use of estimates 3265

Chapter 41 Interim financial reporting

1 INTRODUCTION

One of the major issues in interim financial reporting is whether the interim period is a discrete period, or whether an interim period is an instalment of the full year. Under the first approach, an entity uses the same accounting policies and principles for annual financial statements as for interim periods. Under the second approach, the purpose of the interim report is to give investors, analysts and other users a guide to the expected outcome for the full year, which requires modifications to the policies and principles used in annual financial reporting. The former approach is generally referred to as the 'discrete' approach, and the latter as the 'integral' approach.

The integral approach is not clearly defined but implies deferring or accruing items of income or expense in order to present measures of performance for that interim period that are more indicative of the expected outcome for the year as a whole. Critics say that this approach obscures the results of the interim period. Proponents say that such modifications prevent distortion; an interim period is a more artificial interval than a financial year, and that to report transactions outside of the context of the annual operating cycle for which they are incurred could potentially present a misleading picture.

In practice, the distinction between discrete and integral approaches is less clear-cut than the description above suggests. IAS 34 – *Interim Financial Reporting* – requires an entity to use a 'year-to-date' approach, *[IAS 34.28]*, which is largely based on the requirement to report the entity's financial position as at the interim reporting date, but for which certain estimates and measurements are based on the expected financial position of the entity at year-end. However, the standard does not allow such estimates and measurements to amount to the 'smoothing' of results (shifting revenue and expenses between different reporting periods in order to present the impression that a business has steady earnings) For example, the estimate of tax expense for an interim period is based on actual profits earned as at the interim reporting date and not the expected tax expense for the year divided by the number of interim reporting periods, as discussed at 9.5 below.

The extent of disclosures in interim reports raises similar questions as to the purpose. If interim reporting is simply a more frequently published version of annual reporting, then the form and content of the interim report should be the same. However, if interim reporting is only an instalment of a longer period, then a reporting package that highlights changes in circumstances during an interim period makes more sense than an update of all the disclosures in an entity's annual financial statements. IAS 34 allows an entity to include either a complete set of financial statements or a condensed version in the interim report. *[IAS 34.4]*. While some companies present a full set of financial statements in their interim reports, predominant practice under IFRS is to present the condensed version. The differences between full and condensed interim financial statements are discussed at 3 below.

There is no requirement for entities that prepare annual financial statements in conformity with IFRS to prepare interim financial statements in accordance with IAS 34. The fact that an entity may not have provided interim financial reports at all or may have provided interim financial reports that do not comply with this standard does not prevent the entity making an explicit and unreserved statement of compliance with IFRS in respect of its annual financial statements. *[IAS 34.2]*. Historically, interim reporting was the prerogative of capital markets and regulators and IAS 34 leaves governments, securities regulators, stock exchanges and others to determine which entities report interim information, how often and how soon after the reporting period. *[IAS 34.1]*. Accordingly, adherence to local regulatory or legal requirements in interim financial reports is required.

Nevertheless, governments and regulators often refer to compliance with IAS 34 as part of their own requirements for interim financial reporting.

1.1 Definitions

The standard defines an interim period as 'a financial reporting period shorter than a full financial year.' *[IAS 34.4]*.

The term 'interim financial report' means a financial report for an interim period that contains either a complete set of financial statements (as described in IAS 1 – *Presentation of Financial Statements*) or a set of condensed financial statements as described in IAS 34 (see 3.2 below). *[IAS 34.4]*.

2 OBJECTIVE AND SCOPE OF IAS 34

2.1 Objective

The stated objective of the standard is 'to prescribe the minimum content of an interim financial report and to prescribe the principles for recognition and measurement in complete or condensed financial statements for an interim period. Timely and reliable interim financial reporting improves the ability of investors, creditors, and others to understand an entity's capacity to generate earnings and cash flows and its financial condition and liquidity.' *[IAS 34 Objective]*.

2.2 Scope

IAS 34 does not prescribe which entities are required to publish interim financial reports, how often, or how soon after the end of an interim period. The standard notes that governments, securities regulators, stock exchanges, and accountancy bodies often require entities whose debt or equity securities are publicly traded to publish interim financial reports. Therefore, in the absence of any specific regulatory requirement (or obligation of the entity, for example, by covenant), entities are not required to publish interim financial information in a form that complies with IAS 34. Instead, IAS 34 only applies if an entity either elects or is required to publish an interim financial report in accordance with IFRS. *[IAS 34.1]*. Accordingly, if an entity's interim financial report states that it complies with IFRS, then the requirements of IAS 34 must be met in full. *[IAS 34.3]*.

The decision to present interim financial reports in accordance with IFRS operates independently of the annual financial statements. Hence, entities may still prepare annual financial statements conforming to IFRS even if their interim financial statements do not comply with IAS 34. *[IAS 34.2]*.

Nevertheless, the IASB encourages publicly traded entities to issue interim financial reports that conform to the recognition, measurement and disclosure principles set out in IAS 34. Those entities are specifically encouraged: *[IAS 34.1]*

(a) to provide interim financial reports at least as of the end of the first half of their financial year; and

(b) to make their interim financial reports available not later than 60 days after the end of the interim period.

However, an entity can only describe an interim financial report as complying with IFRS if it meets all of the requirements of IAS 34. *[IAS 34.3]*. Accordingly, an entity that applies all IFRS recognition and measurement requirements in its interim financial report, but does not include all the required disclosures in IAS 34 may not describe the interim financial report as complying with IFRS.

As shown in the Extract below, Proton Power Systems plc disclosed that its interim financial statements for the period ended 30 June 2019 were not prepared in accordance with IAS 34.

Extract 41.1: Proton Power Systems plc (Unaudited Interim Results for the six months to 30 June 2019)

Notes to the interim report [extract]

1. **Basis of preparation** [extract]

The 31 December 2018 consolidated financial statements of Proton Power Systems plc were prepared in accordance with International Financial Reporting Standards (IFRS) as issued by the International Accounting Standards Board (IASB) as adopted by the European Union and with those parts of the Companies Act 2006 applicable to those companies under IFRS. [...] The condensed consolidated interim financial statements have been prepared in accordance with the accounting policies adopted in the 31 December 2018 statutory audited financial statements. No new accounting standards have been adopted by the group since preparing its last annual report.

The Group has chosen not to adopt IAS 34 (Interim Financial Statements) in preparing these financial statements therefore the interim financial information is not in full compliance with IFRS.

3 COMPONENTS, FORM AND CONTENT OF AN INTERIM FINANCIAL REPORT UNDER IAS 34

The standard does not prohibit or discourage an entity from: *[IAS 34.7]*

- publishing a complete set of financial statements (as described in IAS 1) in its interim financial report, rather than condensed financial statements and selected explanatory notes; or
- including in condensed interim financial statements more than the minimum line items or selected explanatory notes as set out in IAS 34.

The recognition and measurement guidance in the standard, together with the note disclosures required by the standard, apply to both complete and condensed financial statements presented for an interim period. This means that a complete set of financial statements, prepared for an interim period, would include all of the disclosures required by IAS 34 as well as those required by other IFRSs. *[IAS 34.7]*.

3.1 Complete set of interim financial statements

An entity that publishes a complete set of financial statements in its interim financial report should include the following components, as required in IAS 1: *[IAS 34.5]*

(a) a statement of financial position as at the end of the interim period;
(b) a statement of profit or loss and other comprehensive income for the period;
(c) a statement of changes in equity for the period;
(d) a statement of cash flows for the period;
(e) notes, comprising significant accounting policies and other explanatory information;
(f) comparative information in respect of the preceding period for each of the statements listed at (a) to (d) above and related notes, and for all amounts reported in the current period's financial statements (unless specifically exempted by another IFRS); as well as (if relevant to understanding the current period's financial statements) comparative information for narrative and descriptive information; *[IAS 1.38, 38A]* and
(g) a statement of financial position as at the beginning of the preceding period (without a requirement for related notes) when: *[IAS 1.40A-40D]*

  (i) an accounting policy has been applied retrospectively; or
  (ii) a retrospective restatement has been made; or
  (iii) items have been reclassified,

  and the effect of such retrospective application on the information presented in that statement of financial position is material.

Entities may use alternative titles for the above statements other than those stated above. For example, an entity may use the title 'statement of comprehensive income' instead of 'statement of profit or loss and other comprehensive income'. *[IAS 34.5]*. Also, an entity can refer to the 'statement of financial position' as 'balance sheet'.

If an entity publishes a complete set of financial statements in its interim financial report, the form and content of those statements should conform to the requirements of IAS 1. *[IAS 34.9]*. These requirements are discussed in Chapter 3 at 3. In addition, the entity should disclose the information specifically required by IAS 34 for interim financial reports as well as those required by other IFRSs (particularly those discussed at 4 below). *[IAS 34.7]*.

3.2 Condensed interim financial statements

In the interest of timeliness, cost, and avoiding repetition of previously reported information, an entity might be required to or elect to give less information at interim dates as compared with its annual financial statements. *[IAS 34.6]*. The standard defines the minimum content of an interim report, as including condensed financial statements and selected notes, as follows: *[IAS 34.6, 8]*

(a) a condensed statement of financial position;
(b) a condensed statement or condensed statements of profit or loss and other comprehensive income;
(c) a condensed statement of changes in equity;
(d) a condensed statement of cash flows; and
(e) selected explanatory notes.

IAS 34 requires entities to confirm that the same accounting policies and methods of computation are followed in the interim financial statements as compared to their most recent annual financial statements or, if those policies or methods have changed, to describe the nature and effect of the change (see 4.2 below). *[IAS 34.16A(a)]*. Accordingly, an entity would only depart from the presentation as applied in its most recent annual financial statements if it had determined that the format will change in its next annual financial statements.

The condensed statement of profit or loss and other comprehensive income referred to at (b) above should be presented using the same format as the entity's annual financial statements. Accordingly, if an entity presents a separate statement of profit or loss in its annual financial statements, then it should present a separate statement in the interim financial report as well. Similarly, if a combined statement of profit or loss and other comprehensive income is presented in the annual financial statements, the same format must be adopted in the interim financial report. *[IAS 34.8A]*.

As a minimum, the condensed financial statements should include each of the headings and subtotals that were included in the entity's last annual financial statements. *[IAS 34.10]*. However, the condensed financial statements do not need to look exactly like the year-end financial statements. Whilst IAS 34 requires 'headings and subtotals' to be the same, there is no similar requirement for the 'line items' under those headings referred to in IAS 1. *[IAS 1.54, 82]*.

A literal reading could mean that an entity is only required to present non-current assets, current assets, etc. on an interim statement of financial position. However, one of the purposes of an interim report is to help the users of the financial statements to understand the changes in financial position and performance of the entity since the previous annual reporting period. *[IAS 34.15]*. To that end, IAS 34 also requires additional line items or notes to be included if their omission makes the condensed financial statements misleading. *[IAS 34.10]*. In addition, the overriding goal of IAS 34 is to ensure that the interim report includes all information necessary to understand the financial position and the performance during the interim period. *[IAS 34.25]*. Therefore, the aggregation of information to this extent would be inconsistent with the objectives of IAS 34 and judgement is required to determine which line items provide useful information for decision-makers, and are presented, accordingly.

Inclusion of most of the line items in the annual financial statements has the benefit of providing the most information to help users of the financial statements understand the changes since the previous year-end. Nonetheless, entities may aggregate line items used in the annual financial statements, if doing so does not render the information misleading or prevent users of the financial statements from performing meaningful trend analysis. In response to a submission relating to the presentation and content of the condensed statement of cash flows, the Interpretations Committee expressed a view that a three-line condensed statement of cash flows showing only a total for each of operating, investing and financing cash flows would generally not meet the requirements of IAS 34 as set out above.[1]

Consideration should also be given to regulatory requirements, for example, where a regulator requires an entity to present certain line items using some form of materiality criteria (e.g. in terms of amount, percentage relative to headings, or percentage change from prior periods).

Although it is not usual for an entity to use a presentation approach in its condensed interim financial statements that is different from its annual financial statements, the following example illustrates one possible way in which an entity might choose to combine line items presented separately in the annual financial statements when preparing a condensed set of interim financial statements. However, such presentation is at the discretion of management, based on facts and circumstances, including materiality (as noted above), regulatory environment, and the overarching goal of IAS 34 to provide relevant information. *[IAS 34.25]*. Accordingly, other presentations may be appropriate.

Example 41.1: Presenting the same headings and sub-totals in condensed interim financial statements

Statement of financial position	Annual financial statements	Condensed interim financial statements
Assets		
Non-current assets		
Intangible assets	●	●
Property, plant and equipment	●	●
Right-of-use assets	●	●
Deferred tax assets	●	●
Investments in associates and joint ventures	○	
Equity instruments at FVOCI	○	
Other non-current assets	○	○
Total non-current assets	●	●
Current assets		
Inventories	○	
Trade and other receivables	●	●
Customer contract assets	○	
Current income tax assets	○	
Other current assets	○	○
Cash and cash equivalents	●	●
Total current assets	●	●
Total assets	●	●

Liabilities
Current liabilities

	Annual	Interim
Trade and other payables	●	●
Customer contract liabilities	○	
Current income tax liabilities	○	
Borrowings	●	●
Provisions	○	
Other current liabilities	○	○
Total current liabilities	●	
Non-current liabilities		
Borrowings	●	●
Pension obligations	●	
Deferred tax liabilities	●	●
Other non-current liabilities	○	
Provisions	○	
Total non-current liabilities	●	●
Total liabilities	●	
Equity		
Share capital	●	●
Other reserves	●	●
Retained earnings	●	●
Total equity	●	●

● Presents the same line item in the annual and the interim financial statements
○ Presents line items that have been combined in the interim financial statements

Statement of profit or loss and other comprehensive income	Annual financial statements	Condensed interim financial statements
Revenue from contracts with customers	○	
Rental income	○	
Total revenue	○	○
Cost of sales	●	●
Gross profit	●	●
Selling and distribution expenses	○	
General and administrative costs	○	
Impairment losses on financial assets	○	
Other operating expenses	○	
Total operating expenses	○	○
Operating profit	●	●
Finance costs	●	●
Finance income	●	●
Share of profit of associates and joint ventures	●	●
Profit before tax	●	●
Income tax expense	●	●
Profit for the period	●	●

	Annual financial statements	Condensed interim financial statements
Other comprehensive income to be reclassified to profit or loss in subsequent periods		
Translation of foreign operations	○	
Net gain on hedge of net investment	○	
Related income tax expense	○	
Net other comprehensive income to be reclassified to profit or loss in subsequent periods	○	○
Other comprehensive income that will not be reclassified subsequently to profit or loss		
Actuarial losses on defined benefit plans	○	
Net gain / loss on equity instruments at FVOCI	○	
Related income tax credit	○	
Net other comprehensive income that will not be reclassified subsequently to profit or loss	○	○
Total other comprehensive income	●	●
Comprehensive income for the period	●	●

● Presents the same line item in the annual and the interim financial statements
○ Presents line items that have been combined in the interim financial statements

Statement of cash flows	Annual financial statements	Condensed interim financial statements
Operating activities		
Profit before tax	●	●
Non-cash adjustments:		
Depreciation and amortisation	○	
Gain on disposal of property	○	
Finance cost	○	
Impairment losses on financial assets	○	
Share of net profit of associate	○	
Movements in pensions	○	
Total non-cash adjustments	●	○
Working capital adjustments:		
Trade and other receivables	○	
Inventories	○	
Customer contract assets and liabilities	○	
Trade and other payables	○	
Total working capital adjustments	●	○
Net cash flows generated from operations	●	●
Income taxes paid	●	●
Acquisition expenses paid	●	●
Net cash flows from operating activities	●	●
Investing activities		
Interest received	●	●
Proceeds from sale of property	●	●
Purchases of property	●	●
Purchase of intangible assets	●	●
Proceeds from sale of equity instruments at FVOCI	●	●
Net cash flows from investing activities	●	●

Financing activities
Proceeds from borrowings • •
Repayment of borrowings • •
Payment of lease liabilities • •
Interest paid • •
Dividends paid • •
Net cash flows from financing activities • •

Net increase in cash and cash equivalents • •
Net foreign exchange difference • •
Cash and cash equivalents at beginning of year • •
Cash and cash equivalents at end of year • •

• Presents the same line item in the annual and the interim financial statements
○ Presents line items that have been combined in the interim financial statements

For reasons of space, a statement of changes in equity is not presented in this example.

3.3 Requirements for both complete and condensed interim financial information

The general principles for preparing annual financial statements are equally applicable to condensed interim financial statements. These principles include fair presentation, going concern, the accrual basis of accounting, materiality and aggregation, and offsetting. *[IAS 1.4, 15-35]*. (See Chapter 3 at 4.1).

Furthermore, the following requirements apply irrespective of whether an entity provides complete or condensed financial statements for an interim period:

- if applicable, basic and diluted earnings per share should be presented on the face of the statement that presents items of profit or loss for an interim period. *[IAS 34.11]*. If the entity presents items of profit or loss in a separate statement, it should present basic and diluted earnings per share in that statement; *[IAS 34.11A]* and

- if the last annual financial statements were consolidated financial statements, the interim financial report should also be prepared on a consolidated basis, if the entity continues to be a parent in the interim period. *[IAS 34.14]*.

If the entity's last annual financial report included the parent's separate financial statements and consolidated financial statements, IAS 34 neither requires nor prohibits the inclusion of the parent's separate financial statements in the interim financial report. *[IAS 34.14]*.

3.4 Management commentary

A management commentary is not required by IAS 34, but frequently included by entities in their interim financial reports along with the interim financial statements. In most cases the requirement for a narrative review comes from local stock market regulations and the entities should, therefore, follow the relevant guidance issued by those regulators.

IAS 34 allows information required under the standard to be presented outside the interim financial statements, i.e. in other parts of interim financial report (such as a management commentary or risk report). *[IAS 34.16A]*. The standard itself does not establish specific requirements for the content of a management commentary beyond what should be contained in (or cross-referred from) the interim financial statements (see 4.2.1 below).

4 DISCLOSURES IN CONDENSED FINANCIAL STATEMENTS

IAS 34 combines a number of disclosure principles:

- Entities should provide information about events and transactions in the interim period that are significant to an understanding of the changes in financial position and performance since the last annual reporting period. In this context it is not necessary to provide relatively insignificant updates to information reported in the last annual financial statements (see 4.1 below). *[IAS 34.15, 15A]*.
- In addition to information to explain significant changes since the last annual reporting period, a number of specific disclosures are required to be given, if not disclosed elsewhere in the interim financial report. *[IAS 34.16A]*.
- The materiality assessment for disclosure is based on the interim period by itself, to ensure all information is provided that is relevant to understanding the entity's financial position and its performance during the interim period (see 6 below). *[IAS 34.25]*.

Overall, applying those disclosure principles requires the exercise of judgement by the entity regarding what information is significant and relevant. The practice of interim reporting confirms that entities take advantage of that room for judgement, both for disclosures provided in the notes to the financial statements and outside.

4.1 Significant events and transactions

IAS 34 presumes that users of an entity's interim financial report also have access to its most recent annual financial report. *[IAS 34.15A]*. On that basis, an interim financial report should explain events and transactions that are significant to an understanding of the changes in financial position and performance of the entity since the previous annual reporting period and provide an update to the relevant information included in the financial statements of the previous year. *[IAS 34.15, 15C]*. The inclusion of only selected explanatory notes is consistent with the purpose of an interim financial report, to update the latest complete set of annual financial statements. Accordingly, condensed financial statements avoid duplicating previously reported information and focus on new activities, events, and circumstances. *[IAS 34.6]*.

The standard requires disclosure of the following events and transactions in interim financial reports, if they are significant: *[IAS 34.15B]*

(a) write-down of inventories to net realisable value and the reversal of such a write-down;

(b) recognition of a loss from the impairment of financial assets, property, plant, and equipment, intangible assets, assets arising from contracts with customers, or other assets, and the reversal of such an impairment loss;

(c) reversal of any provisions for the costs of restructuring;

(d) acquisitions and disposals of items of property, plant, and equipment;

(e) commitments for the purchase of property, plant, and equipment;

(f) litigation settlements;

(g) corrections of prior period errors;

(h) changes in the business or economic circumstances that affect the fair value of the entity's financial assets and financial liabilities, whether those assets or liabilities are recognised at fair value or amortised cost;

(i) any loan default or breach of a loan agreement that is not remedied on or before the end of the reporting period;
(j) related party transactions;
(k) transfers between levels of the fair value hierarchy used in measuring the fair value of financial instruments;
(l) changes in the classification of financial assets as a result of a change in the purpose or use of those assets; and
(m) changes in contingent liabilities or contingent assets.

The standard specifies that the above list of events and transactions is not exhaustive and the interim financial report should explain any additional events and transactions that are significant to an understanding of changes in the entity's financial position and performance. *[IAS 34.15, 15B]*. Therefore, when information relating to items not on the above list changes significantly, an entity should still provide disclosure in the interim financial statements in sufficient detail to explain the nature of the change and any changes in estimates. This would apply, for example, if:

- the range of reasonably possible changes in key assumptions has significantly changed since the end of the last annual reporting period, an update of relevant sensitivity disclosures may be required;
- the values of non-financial assets and liabilities that are measured at fair value change significantly.

4.1.1 Relevance of other standards in condensed financial statements

Whilst other standards specify disclosures required in a complete set of financial statements, if an entity's interim financial report includes only condensed financial statements as described in IAS 34, then the disclosures required by those other standards are not mandatory. However, if disclosure is considered to be necessary in the context of an interim report, those other standards provide guidance on the appropriate disclosures for many of these items. *[IAS 34.15C]*. For example, in meeting the requirements of (g) above to disclose the impact of corrections of prior period errors, the requirements of IAS 8 – *Accounting Policies, Changes in Accounting Estimates and Errors* – would be relevant to consider (see Chapter 3 at 5.3).

In practice, entities exercise judgement to determine whether including the disclosures required by other standards are material to an understanding of the entity and will provide a benefit to users of the interim financial statements. *[IAS 34.25]*. For example, the existence of acquisitions and disposal of items of property plant and equipment does not automatically require the interim report to include a reconciliation of the carrying amount at the beginning and end of the interim period. *[IAS 16.73(e)]*. In many cases, a narrative disclosure would be sufficient, and in some cases, the change may be immaterial, and therefore no disclosures are required. However, in an interim period with material changes, as for instance when assets are acquired by purchase, obtained in a business combination, and transferred to a disposal unit as well as sold in the normal course of business, such a reconciliation could be judged to be an appropriate way of presenting this information in the interim financial statements.

4.2 Other disclosures required by IAS 34

In addition to disclosing significant events and transactions as discussed at 4.1 above, IAS 34 requires an entity to include the following information in the notes to its interim financial statements if not disclosed elsewhere in the interim financial report: *[IAS 34.16A]*

(a) a statement that the same accounting policies and methods of computation are followed in the interim financial statements as in the most recent annual financial statements or, if those policies or methods have changed, a description of the nature and effect of the change;

(b) explanatory comments about the seasonality or cyclicality of interim operations;

(c) the nature and amount of items affecting assets, liabilities, equity, net income, or cash flows that are unusual because of their nature, size, or incidence;

(d) the nature and amount of changes in estimates of amounts reported in prior interim periods of the current year or changes in estimates of amounts reported in prior years;

(e) issues, repurchases, and repayments of debt and equity securities;

(f) dividends paid (aggregate or per share) separately for ordinary shares and other shares;

(g) certain segment disclosures required by IFRS 8 – *Operating Segments* – as discussed at 4.4 below;

(h) events after the interim period that are not reflected in the financial statements for the interim period;

(i) the effect of changes in the composition of the entity during the interim period, including business combinations, obtaining or losing control of subsidiaries and long-term investments, restructurings, and discontinued operations. For business combinations, the entity should disclose the information required under IFRS 3 – *Business Combinations* (see Chapter 9 at 16);

(j) for financial instruments, certain fair value disclosures required by IFRS 7 – *Financial Instruments: Disclosures* – and IFRS 13 – *Fair Value Measurement* – as discussed at 4.5 below;

(k) for entities becoming, or ceasing to be, investment entities, as defined in IFRS 10 – *Consolidated Financial Statements*, the disclosures in IFRS 12 – *Disclosure of Interests in Other Entities* – as required by paragraph 9B of that standard (see Chapter 13 at 4.6.2); and

(l) the disaggregation of revenue from contracts with customers required by paragraphs 114 and 115 of IFRS 15 – *Revenue from Contracts with Customers*. The requirement to disclose disaggregated revenue in interim financial statements is similar to the requirements applicable to annual financial statements. See Chapter 32 at 3.2.1.A for illustrative examples of disclosures.

This information is disclosed on a financial year-to-date basis. *[IAS 34.16A]*. However, the requirement in item (i) above for disclosures of business combinations applies not only for those effected during the current interim period, but also to business combinations after the reporting period but before the interim financial report is authorised for issue. *[IFRS 3.59(b), IFRS 3.B66]*. An entity is not required to provide all of the disclosures for business combinations after the reporting period, if the accounting for the business combination is incomplete as at the date on which the financial statements are authorised for issue. In this case, the entity should state which disclosures cannot be made and the reasons why they cannot be made. *[IFRS 3.B66]*.

IFRS 3 requires disclosures in aggregate for business combinations effected during the reporting period that are individually immaterial. *[IFRS 3.B65]*. However, materiality is assessed for the interim period financial data, *[IAS 34.23]*, which implies that IAS 34 may require detailed disclosures on business combinations that are material to an interim period, even if they could be aggregated for disclosure purposes in the annual financial statements.

The list above also requires disclosure of the effect of changes in the composition of the entity arising from disposals, discontinued operations and restructurings in the interim period. *[IAS 34.16A(i)]*.

If an entity has operations that are discontinued or disposed of during an interim period, these operations should be presented separately in the condensed interim statement of comprehensive income following the principles set out in IFRS 5 – *Non-current Assets Held for Sale and Discontinued Operations*. In addition, if an entity has non-current assets or a disposal group classified as held for sale or distribution at the end of the interim reporting period, then these should be measured in accordance with the requirements of IFRS 5 and presented separately from other assets and liabilities in the condensed interim statement of financial position.

An entity contemplating a significant restructuring that will have an impact on its composition should follow the guidance in IAS 37 – *Provisions, Contingent Liabilities and Contingent Assets* – for the recognition of any restructuring cost, *[IAS 37.71]*, and IAS 19 – *Employee Benefits* – for termination benefits. *[IAS 19.165(b)]*. In subsequent interim periods any significant changes to provisions will require disclosure. *[IAS 34.15B(c), 16A(d)]*.

The inclusion of the above disclosure requirements among the items required by the standard to be given 'in addition to disclosing significant events and transactions', *[IAS 34.16A]*, distinguishes them from the items listed at 4.1 above, which are disclosed to update information presented in the most recent annual financial report. *[IAS 34.15]*. Therefore, disclosure of the above information is required for each interim reporting period, subject only to a materiality assessment in relation to that interim report. *[IAS 34.25]*. In making that judgement care would need to be taken to ensure any omitted information would not make the interim financial report incomplete and therefore misleading.

4.2.1 Location of the specified disclosures in an interim financial report

IAS 34 defines an 'interim financial report' as 'a financial report containing either a complete set of financial statements... or a set of condensed financial statements... for an interim period.' *[IAS 34.4]*. Therefore, since an interim financial report contains the interim financial statements, it is clear that these are two different concepts. Accordingly, an entity is not required to disclose the information listed at 4.2 above in the interim financial statements themselves (but rather, might include the disclosures in the management commentary), as long as a cross-reference is provided from the financial statements to the location of the information included in another part of the interim financial report. *[IAS 34.16A]*.

Additionally, for a cross-reference to be acceptable, the information given 'elsewhere in the interim financial report' needs to both satisfy the disclosure requirements in IFRSs and be available on the same terms as the interim financial statements, i.e. users should have access to the referenced material (for example, the management commentary or a risk report) on the same basis and at the same time as they have for accessing the condensed financial statements from which the reference is made.

The cross-reference should identify the specific part that includes the required disclosure to allow the reader to easily navigate within the interim financial report.

4.3 Illustrative examples of disclosures

The extracts and examples below illustrate the disclosures required by IAS 34.

4.3.1 Inventory write-down and reversals

In the extract below, BP p.l.c. discloses write-downs of its inventories and reversals in the current and corresponding periods. *[IAS 34.15B(a)]*.

Extract 41.2: BP p.l.c. Group results (First quarter 2020)

Notes [extract]

Note 11.   Inventory valuation

A provision of $3,596 million was held against hydrocarbon inventories at 31 March 2020 ($290 million at 31 December 2019 and $124 million at 31 March 2019) to write them down to their net realizable value. The net movement charged to the income statement during the first quarter 2020 was $3,341 million as a result of significant decreases in prices for refined products, oil and gas during March (fourth quarter 2019 was a credit of $80 million and first quarter 2019 was a credit of $480 million).

In the Extract below, Equinor ASA discloses a reversal of an inventory write-down in the current period. *[IAS 34.15B(a)]*.

> **Extract 41.3: Equinor ASA (Second quarter 2020)**
>
> Condensed interim financial statement and notes [extract]
>
> Notes to the Condensed interim financial statements [extract]
> 2 Segments [extract]
>
> Due to the recovery in commodity prices, at the end of the second quarter as compared to the end of the first quarter, MMP has reversed USD 605 million in write-down of inventory included in the line item Purchases [net of inventory variation]. The impact is largely offset by loss on derivatives included in the line item Revenues third party, other revenue and other income.

4.3.2 Recognition and reversal of impairment losses

In the Extract below, as part of its note on segments, Equinor ASA explains the recognition and reversal of impairment losses during the reporting period. *[IAS 34.15B(b)]*.

> **Extract 41.4: Equinor ASA (First quarter 2020)**
>
> Condensed interim financial statement and notes [extract]
>
> Notes to the Condensed interim financial statements [extract]
> 2 Segments [extract]
>
> In the first quarter of 2020 Equinor recognised net impairment of USD 2,453 million of which USD 59 million was classified as exploration expenses.
>
> In the E&P Norway segment the net impairment was USD 862 million, hereof USD 3 million related to exploration assets. The impairments were triggered by decreased short-term oil price assumptions and construction delays mainly caused by the Covid-19 pandemic.
>
> In the E&P International segment the net impairment was USD 1,397 million of which USD 56 million was classified as exploration expenses. In the North America onshore unconventional area the impairments were USD 872 million, in the North America conventional Gulf of Mexico USD 142 million, in the North America offshore other areas USD 86 million. In Europe and Asia the impairment was USD 289 million and the impairment reversal was USD 47 million. The impairments were triggered mainly by the decreased short-term oil price assumptions, but also construction delays and re-phasing of the production in the North America – conventional other area and in the Europe and Asia area caused by the Covid-19 pandemic. In the Europe and Asia area the impairment reversal of USD 47 million was caused by increased reserves. Impairments classified as exploration were USD 16 million in the Sub Sahara area and USD 40 million in Australia.
>
> In the MMP segment the impairments were USD 194 million whereof USD 193 million related to a refinery due to increased asset retirement estimate and expected lower refinery margins in the short term.

4.3.3 Acquisitions and disposals of property, plant and equipment

In the Extract below, Hellenic Company for Telecommunications and Telematic Applications S.A. (Forthnet S.A.) gives a narrative description of its acquisitions of property, plant and equipment in the interim period. [IAS 34.15B(d)].

> **Extract 41.5: Forthnet S.A. (Interim financial report for the period 1 January 2019 to 30 June 2019)**
> **NOTES TO THE INTERIM CONDENSED FINANCIAL STATEMENTS** [extract]
> **13. Property, plant and equipment**
> During the period from January 1, 2019 until June 30, 2019, the Group's total investments in tangible assets amounted to € 2,446,283 and those of the Company's amounted to € 2,389,554 and mainly concern the expansion of Forthnet's private telecommunication network (June 30, 2018: € 1,697,843 for the Group and € 1,556,471 for the Company).
>
> It is noted that there are encumbrances on the privately owned building of the Company in Kallithea, Attica, in favour of Alpha Bank, National Bank of Greece SA and Piraeus Bank SA with a total value of € 6.5 million as collateral to the Banks claims' from corresponding open account credit agreements with Forthnet.
>
> It is noted that in the current period the "Right of use assets" that were included as at December 31, 2018 in the "Property, plant & equipment" and which amounted for the Group to € 30,203,693 and for the Company to € 2,015,561, were reclassified as part of the transition to IFRS 16 in the statement of financial position's line "Right-of-use assets". As of June 30, 2019 the amounts for the Group and the Company amounted to € 25,478,998 and 1,988,888 respectively (Note 5).

4.3.4 Capital commitments

In a brief descriptive note, Deutsche Lufthansa AG discloses its commitments for capital expenditure. [IAS 34.15B(e)].

> **Extract 41.6: Deutsche Lufthansa AG (1st interim report January – March 2020)**
> **Interim financial statements** [extract]
> **Notes** [extract]
> **4   Contingencies and events after the reporting period** [extract]
> At the end of March 2020 there were order commitments of EUR 15.6bn for capital expenditure on property, plant and equipment, including repairable spare parts, and for intangible assets. As of 31 December 2019, the order commitments came to EUR 14.6bn.

4.3.5 Litigation settlements

International Consolidated Airlines Group S.A provides details about significant litigation in its 2019 interim report. The extract below illustrates its disclosure about related settlements. [IAS 34.15B(f)].

> **Extract 41.7: International Consolidated Airlines Group, S.A. (Six months to June 30, 2019)**
>
> **NOTES TO THE ACCOUNTS** [extract]
>
> **15. EMPLOYEE BENEFIT OBLIGATIONS** [extract]
>
> The principal funded defined benefit pension schemes within the Group are the Airways Pension Scheme ('APS') and the New Airways Pension Scheme ('NAPS').
>
> [...]
>
> APS has been closed to new members since 1984. The benefits provided under APS are based on final average pensionable pay and, for the majority of members, are subject to inflationary increases in payment in line with the Government's Pension Increase (Review) Orders (PIRO), which are based on the CPI. The Trustee of APS proposed an additional discretionary increase above CPI for pensions in payment for the year ended March 31, 2014. British Airways challenged the decision and initiated legal proceedings to determine the legitimacy of the discretionary increase. The High Court issued a judgment in May 2017, which determined that the Trustee had the power to grant discretionary increases, whilst reiterating the Trustee must take into consideration all relevant factors and ignore irrelevant factors. British Airways appealed the judgment to the Court of Appeal. On July 5, 2018 the Court of Appeal released its judgment, upholding British Airways' appeal, concluding the Trustee did not have the power to introduce a discretionary increase rule. Following the judgment, the Trustee was allowed permission to appeal to the Supreme Court; and has appealed. In April 2019, subject to obtaining the approval of the High Court, the Trustee Directors of the Airways Pension Scheme unanimously agreed with British Airways terms for an out-of-court settlement ('the agreement'). This would bring to an end the litigation that commenced in 2013 and which is otherwise due to proceed to appeal at the Supreme Court later this year. Under the terms of the proposed settlement, the Trustee of APS will be permitted, subject to some affordability tests, to award Discretionary Increases so that APS pensions are increased up to the annual change in the Retail Prices Index (RPI) from 2021 with interim catch-up increases. British Airways will cease paying further deficit recovery contributions, including cash sweep payments, and the APS Trustee will withdraw its appeal to the Supreme Court. British Airways will provide a €45 million indemnity, payable in part or full as appropriate in late 2027/2028, in the event of adverse experience leading to the 2027 valuation showing the scheme is not able to pay pension increases at RPI for the remaining life of the scheme.

4.3.6   **Changes in circumstances affecting fair values**

In its interim report for 2019, Yorkshire Building Society describes the effect of volatility in financial markets during the period. *[IAS 34.15B(h)].*

> **Extract 41.8: Yorkshire Building Society (Six months ended 30 June 2019)**
>
> **Chief Executive's summary** [extract]
>
> **Strategic update:** [extract]
> - The current macroeconomic and market environment is very dynamic, with the impact of trade wars, the UK's exit from the EU and political uncertainty likely to continue into the foreseeable future, impacting business and consumer confidence and growth. Uncertainty around the future Bank Rate path is also leading to volatility in financial markets.
>
> **Business highlights** [extract]
> - A fair value volatility loss of £24.2m (30 June 2018: gain of £1.5m) is adverse to 2018 mainly due to a significant fall in swap rates since the beginning of the year. This is as a result of volatility in the financial markets, and is an accounting adjustment which will typically reverse in future periods.

4.3.7 Default or breach of loan covenants not remedied before the end of interim period

The Example below illustrates disclosure of a loan default that has not been remedied on or before the end of the reporting period, *[IAS 34.15B(i)]*, and the consequent impact on classification of the loans in the interim financial statements.

Example 41.2:   Disclosure of default of loan covenant

As at 30 June 2021, Entity A did not comply with certain financial covenants set out in its existing agreements for the ordinary bond loans issued by the Entity amounting to €100 million (hereinafter the Existing OBLs) and had not repaid matured loan instalments of €100 million from the Existing OBLs. Consequently, as of 30 June 2021, all Existing OBLs are classified as short-term liabilities. As a result of bond loans being presented as short-term liabilities as at 30 June 2021, total short-term liabilities of Entity A exceeded total short-term assets by €125 million.

4.3.8 Related party transactions

In Extract 41.9 below, Deutsche Bank Aktiengesellschaft discloses related party transactions. *[IAS 34.15B(j)]*.

> **Extract 41.9: Deutsche Bank Aktiengesellschaft (Interim report as of June 30, 2019)**
>
> **Other Financial Information** [extract]
> **Related Party Transactions**
>
> Parties are considered to be related if one party has the ability to directly or indirectly control the other party or exercise significant influence over the other party in making financial or operational decisions. The Group's related parties include:
> - key management personnel, close family members of key management personnel and entities which are controlled, significantly influenced by, or for which significant voting power is held by key management personnel or their close family members,
> - subsidiaries, joint ventures and associates and their respective subsidiaries, and
> - post-employment benefit plans for the benefit of Deutsche Bank employees.
>
> **Transactions with Key Management Personnel**
>
> Key management personnel are those persons having authority and responsibility for planning, directing and controlling the activities of Deutsche Bank Group, directly or indirectly. The Group considers the members of the Management Board as currently mandated and the Supervisory Board of the parent company to constitute key management personnel for purposes of IAS 24. Among the Group's transactions with key management personnel as of June 30, 2019, were loans and commitments of € 41 million and deposits of € 19 million. As of December 31, 2018, there were loans and commitments of € 45 million and deposits of € 34 million among the Group's transactions with key management personnel. In addition, the Group provides banking services, such as payment and account services as well as investment advice, to key management personnel and their close family members.

Transactions with Subsidiaries, Associates and Joint Ventures

Transactions between Deutsche Bank AG and its subsidiaries meet the definition of related party transactions. If these transactions are eliminated on consolidation, they are not disclosed as related party transactions. Transactions between the Group and its associated companies and joint ventures and their respective subsidiaries also qualify as related party transactions.

Transactions for subsidiaries, joint ventures and associates are presented combined in below table as these are not material individually.

Loans issued and guarantees granted

in € m.	Jun 30, 2019	Dec 31, 2018
Loans outstanding, beginning of period	228	256
Movement in loans during the period[1]	(2)	(21)
Changes in the group of consolidated companies	0	0
Exchange rate changes/other	0	(7)
Loans outstanding, end of period[2]	230	228
Other credit risk related transactions:		
Allowance for loan losses	0	0
Provision for loan losses	0	0
Guarantees and commitments	3	3

[1] Net impact of loans issued and loans repayment during the year is shown as "Movement in loans during the period".
[2] There were no past due loans as of June 30, 2019 and December 31, 2018. For the above loans, the Group held collateral of € 5 million and € 14 million as of June 30, 2019 and December 31, 2018, respectively.

Deposits received

in € m.	Jun 30, 2019	Dec 31, 2018
Deposits, beginning of period	68	67
Movement in deposits during the period[1]	(22)	2
Changes in the group of consolidated companies	0	0
Exchange rate changes/other	0	(0)
Deposits, end of period	47	68

[1] Net impact of deposits received and deposits repaid during the year is shown as "Movement in deposits during the period".

Other transactions

Trading assets and positive market values from derivative financial transactions with associated companies amounted to € 2 million as of June 30, 2019, and € 2 million as of December 31, 2018. Trading liabilities and negative market values from derivative financial transactions with associated companies were € 0 million as of June 30, 2019, and € 0 million as of December 31, 2018.

Transactions with Pension Plans

The Group has business relationships with a number of its pension plans pursuant to which it provides financial services to these plans, including investment management. Pension funds may hold or trade Deutsche Bank AG shares or securities. As of June 30, 2019, transactions with these plans were not material for the Group.

4.3.9 Transfers between different levels of fair value hierarchy

HSBC discloses in the extract below transfers of items between level 1 and level 2 of the fair value hierarchy. *[IAS 34.15B(k)]*. The disclosures in relation to transfers into and out of level 3 are included in a separate reconciliation of the movements from the opening balances to closing balances as required by paragraph 93(e) of IFRS 13 and paragraph 16A(j) of IAS 34 (see 4.5 below).

Extract 41.10: HSBC Holdings plc (Interim report 2019)

Notes on the Financial Statements [extract]
5 Fair values of financial instruments carried at fair value [extract]
Transfers between Level 1 and Level 2 fair values

	Assets				Liabilities		
	Financial investments $m	Trading assets $m	Designated and otherwise mandatorily measured at fair value $m	Derivatives $m	Trading liabilities $m	Designated at fair value $m	Derivatives $m
At 30 Jun 2019							
Transfers from Level 1 to Level 2	1,526	663	–	23	117	–	–
Transfers from Level 2 to Level 1	2,696	1,252	347	111	198	–	117
At 31 Dec 2018							
Transfers from Level 1 to Level 2	367	435	2	1	79	–	–
Transfers from Level 2 to Level 1	17,861	4,959	85	128	1,821	–	138

Transfers between levels of the fair value hierarchy are deemed to occur at the end of each quarterly reporting period. Transfers into and out of Levels of the fair value hierarchy are primarily attributable to observability of valuation inputs and price transparency.

4.3.10 Contingent liabilities

In the Extract below, Downer EDI Limited discloses changes in its contingent liabilities during the interim period in the notes to the condensed consolidated half-year financial report. *[IAS 34.15B(m)]*.

Extract 41.11: Downer EDI Limited (Half-year ended 31 December 2019)

Notes to the condensed consolidated financial report for the half-year ended 31 December 2019 [extract]

D9. Contingent liabilities [extract]

Other contingent liabilities [extract]

vi) On 16 September 2015, the Group announced that it had terminated a contract with Tecnicas Reunidas S.A. ("TR") following TR's failure to remedy a substantial breach of the contract and that the Group is pursuing a claim against TR in the order of $65 million. Downer has since demobilised from the site and has commenced a claim that will be determined via an arbitration process, with a hearing date currently expected to occur in April 2020. TR has initiated a counter-claim, which is being defended by Downer.

4.3.11 Accounting policies and methods of computation

In the Extract below, Daimler AG discloses changes to the accounting policies applied in its 2019 interim report. *[IAS 34.16A(a)]*. Using the guidance in IAS 8, Daimler AG provides information for the adoption of IFRS 16 – *Leases*.

Extract 41.12: Daimler AG (Interim report Q2 2019)

Notes to the Interim Consolidated Financial Statements [extract]

1. Presentation of the Interim Consolidated Financial Statements [extract]

IFRSs initially applied in the reporting period [extract]

In January 2016, the IASB published **IFRS 16 Leases**, replacing IAS 17 Leases and IFRIC 4 Determining Whether an Arrangement Contains a Lease and other interpretations. [...]

Daimler applies IFRS 16 for the first time at January 1, 2019. In compliance with the transition regulations, Daimler does not adjust the prior-year figures and presents the not significant accumulated transitional effects in retained earnings.

Daimler as lessee uses the following practical expedients of IFRS 16 at the date of initial application:

- With leases previously classified as operating leases according to IAS 17, the lease liability is measured at the present value of the outstanding lease payments, discounted by the incremental borrowing rate at January 1, 2019. The weighted average incremental borrowing rate was 2.27%. The respective right-of-use asset is generally recognized at an amount equal to the lease liability.
- An impairment review is not performed. Instead, a right-of-use asset is adjusted by the amount of any provision for onerous leases recognized in the Statement of Financial Position at December 31, 2018.
- Regardless of their original lease term, leases for which the lease term ends at the latest on December 31, 2019 are recognized as short-term leases.
- At the date of initial application, the measurement of a right-of-use asset excludes the initial direct costs.
- Current knowledge is given due consideration when determining the lease term if the contract contains options to extend or terminate the lease.

In the context of the transition to IFRS 16, right-of-use assets of €3,777 million (including finance leases of €335 million) and lease liabilities of €3,790 million were recognized at January 1, 2019. The following reconciliation (see ↗ E.08) to the opening balance for lease liabilities as at January 1, 2019 is based on the other financial obligations from rental agreements and operating leases at December 31, 2018.

E.08

Reconciliation to the lease liabilities in accordance with IFRS 16 In millions of euros	
Other financial obligations resulting from rental agreements and operating leases in accordance with IAS 17 at December 31, 2018	3,800
Exemptions for short-term leases	–226
Exemptions for leases of low-value assets	–36
Payments related to options to extend or terminate a lease	256
Payments related to non-lease components	77
Others	75
Obligations from operating lease arrangements (undiscounted)	**3,946**
Discounting	–503
Obligations from operating lease arrangements (discounted)	**3,443**
Carrying amount of liabilities from finance leases in accordance with IAS 17 as at December 31, 2018	347
Carrying amount of lease liability in accordance with IFRS 16 as at January 1, 2019	**3,790**

The right-of-use assets and lease liabilities include assets and liabilities, which were recognized until December 31, 2018 as finance leases in accordance with IAS 17.

4.3.12 Seasonality or cyclicality of operations

Extract 41.13 below shows how Ardagh Group S.A. discloses the effects of seasonality in its interim report. *[IAS 34.16A(b)]*.

> *Extract 41.13: Ardagh Group S.A. (Interim ended March 2020)*
> **NOTES TO THE UNAUDITED CONSOLIDATED INTERIM FINANCIAL STATEMENTS** [extract]
> **18. Seasonality of operations** [extract]
>
> The Group's revenue and cash flows are both subject to seasonal fluctuations with the Group generally building inventories in anticipation of these seasonal demands resulting in working capital requirements typically being the greatest at the end of the first quarter of the year.
>
> The demand for our metal beverage products is strongest during spells of warm weather and therefore demand typically peaks during the summer months, as well as in the period leading up to holidays in December. Demand for beverage products within our Glass Packaging business is similarly strongest during the summer and during periods of warm weather, as well as the period leading up to holidays in December.
>
> The Group manages the seasonality of working capital principally by supplementing operating cash flows with drawings under our Global Asset Based Loan facility.

4.3.13 Amounts that are unusual because of their nature, size or incidence

Sanofi discloses the nature and effects of unusual items in Extract 41.14 below by identifying 'restructuring costs' and similar items. *[IAS 34.16A(c)]*. The footnote provides further information on the nature of the costs. See Extract 41.20 for another example illustrating disclosures about restructuring activities.

> *Extract 41.14: Sanofi(2019 Half-Year Financial Report)*
> **B/ SIGNIFICANT INFORMATION FOR THE FIRST HALF OF 2019** [extract]
> **B.16. RESTRUCTURING COSTS AND SIMILAR ITEMS**
> **Restructuring costs and similar items** comprise the following:
>
> | (€ million) | June 30, 2019 (6 months) | June 30, 2018 (6 months) | December 31, 2018 (12 months) |
> |---|---|---|---|
> | Employee-related expenses | 667 | 206 | 517 |
> | Expenses related to property, plant and equipment and to inventories | 39 | 80 | 162 |
> | Compensation for early termination of contracts (other than contracts of employment) | 3 | 4 | 352 |
> | Decontamination costs | 1 | – | 5 |
> | Other restructuring costs | 37 | 317 | 444 |
> | Total | 747 | 607 | 1,480 |
>
> Restructuring costs in the first half of 2019 mainly reflect employee-related expenses associated with headcount adjustment plans, mainly in Europe and the United States.

4.3.14 Issues, repurchases and repayments of debt and equity securities

Extract 41.15 below illustrates the disclosure of material changes in borrowings. *[IAS 34.16A(e)]*.

Extract 41.15: Anheuser-Busch InBev NV/SA (30 June 2019)

Notes to the unaudited condensed consolidated interim financial statements [extract]

16. Interest-bearing loans and borrowings [extract]

On 11 February 2019, the company completed the tender offers of twelve notes issued by Anheuser-Busch InBev Finance, Anheuser-Busch Companies, LLC ("ABC") and Anheuser-Busch InBev Worldwide Inc and repurchased 16.3 billion US dollar aggregate principal amount of these notes. [...]

These tender offers were financed with cash.

On 25 April 2019, the company redeemed outstanding principal amount of certain notes due in 2020 and 2023. The principal amount of the notes that were retired is approximately 2.3 billion US dollar. [...]

AB InBev's net debt was restated to reflect the impact of the adoption of IFRS 16 and amounted to 104.2 billion US dollar as of 30 June 2019 and 31 December 2018. Apart from operating results net of capital expenditures, the net debt is mainly impacted by the payment of interests and taxes (4.2 billion US dollar), settlement of derivatives (0.8 billion US dollar increase of net debt) and dividend payments to shareholders of AB InBev (2.4 billion US dollar). Net debt to normalized EBITDA was 4.61× for the 12-month period ending 31 December 2018 on a Restated base and 4.58× for the 12-month period ending 30 June 2019 on a Reference base.

Extract 41.16 below illustrates the disclosure of changes in treasury stock resulting from disposal of treasury stock through third-party allotment. *[IAS 34.16A(e)]*.

Extract 41.16: Nippon Telegraph and Telephone Corporation
(Quarterly Securities Report – The First Quarter of the 36th Business Term – From April 1, 2020 to June 30, 2020)

Condensed Consolidated Financial Statement [extract]

Notes to Condensed Consolidated Financial Statement [extract]

11. Equity and Other Equity Items [extract]

(1) Issued Shares and Treasury Stock

Reconciliation of the number of issued shares and treasury stock

(shares)

	Issued Shares	Treasury Stock
April 1, 2019	1,950,394,470	32,997,746
Purchase of treasury stock under resolution of the board of directors	–	99,763,016
Repurchase of treasury stock based on less-than-one-unit share purchase demand	–	47,564
Disposal of treasury stock based on additional less-than-one-unit share purchase demand	–	(4,246)
Increase by stock split	1,950,394,470	132,788,632
March 31, 2020	3,900,788,940	265,592,712
Repurchase of shares based on less-than-one-unit share purchase demand	–	6,996
Disposal of treasury stock based on additional less-than-one-unit share purchase demand	–	(3,152)
Disposal of treasury stock through third-party allotment	–	(80,775,400)
June 30, 2020	3,900,788,940	184,821,156

Stock Split

NTT conducted a two-for-one stock split of its common stock, with a record date of December 31, 2019 and an effective date of January 1, 2020 based on the resolution at the meeting of board of directors on November 5, 2019.

Acquisition of Toyota Motor Corporation's Shares and Disposal of Treasury Stock by Way of Third-party Allotment

On March 24, 2020, the Board of Directors resolved that NTT would enter into a memorandum of understanding for a business and capital alliance (the "Alliance") with Toyota Motor Corporation ("Toyota") and entered into the Alliance on the same day. On April 9, 2020, Toyota and NTT mutually executed a comprehensive underwriting agreement for a third-party allotment of treasury stock of both parties based on the memorandum of understanding. NTT acquired Toyota's shares and conducted a disposition of shares of the NTT's treasury stock through the third-party allotment with Toyota as the subscriber for the shares on the same day.

Overview of a disposition of shares of the NTT's treasury stock through the third-party allotment, with Toyota as the subscriber for the shares

(1)	Disposition date	April 9, 2020
(2)	Type and number of shares disposed	80,775,400 shares of the NTT's common stock
(3)	Disposition price	¥2,476 per share
(4)	Amount of funds raised	¥199,999,890,400
(5)	Percentage to the total number of issued and outstanding shares held by Toyota	2.07% of the NTT's issued and outstanding common stock

4.3.15 Dividends paid

In the Extract below, Nestlé S.A. discloses dividends paid during the interim period. *[IAS 34.16A(f)]*.

> **Extract 41.17: Nestlé S.A. (Half-Year Report of the Nestlé Group 2019)**
>
> Notes [extract]
> **8. Equity** [extract]
> **8.2 Dividend**
>
> The dividend related to 2018 was paid on April 17, 2019 in accordance with the decision taken at the Annual General Meeting on April 11, 2019. Shareholders approved the proposed dividend of CHF 2.45 per share, resulting in a total dividend of CHF 7230 million.

4.3.16 Events after the interim reporting date

In the Extract below, thyssenkrupp AG reports a major restructuring and conclusion of a credit line after the end of the interim period. *[IAS 34.16A(h)]*.

> **Extract 41.18: thyssenkrupp, AG (Interim report 1st half 2019/2020)**
>
> **Condensed interim financial statements** [extract]
> Selected notes [extract]
> **14 Subsequent events**
>
> At the end of April 2020, thyssenkrupp decided on a major restructuring of the German sites of the Springs and Stabilizers business in the Automotive Technology business area. Under the restructuring plan, production of stabilizers at the Olpe site will be discontinued by the end of 2021. Production at the Hagen site is to be realigned. The restructuring will impact about 490 jobs, for which a reconciliation of interests and a social plan are to be agreed with the employee representatives in the coming weeks.
>
> On May 8, 2020 thyssenkrupp concluded a credit line of €1 billion from the KfW special program with a consortium of KfW and other banks. The credit line will additionally secure liquidity during the coronavirus pandemic until the cash inflow from the sale of the Elevator Technology business area before the end of this fiscal year.

Although not an explicit requirement under IAS 34, it is useful to disclose the date on which the interim financial statements are authorised for issue as it helps the users to understand the context of any disclosure of events after the interim reporting date. [IAS 10.17].

4.3.17 Changes in the composition of the entity

The notion of changes in the composition of the entity is broadly defined to include acquisitions, restructurings and discontinued operations. [IAS 34.16A(i)].

In the Extract below, Nine Entertainment Co. Holdings Limited discloses change in group structure resulting from acquisitions including additional interest during the interim period.

Extract 41.19: Nine Entertainment Co. Holdings Limited (Financial report for the half year ended 31 December 2019)

Notes to the Consolidated Financial Statements for the half year ended 31 December 2019 [extract]
5. GROUP STRUCTURE [extract]
5.1. Business combinations and acquisition of non-controlling interests [extract]
5.1 (a) Information on current year acquisitions and disposals

Acquisition of additional interest in Macquarie Media Limited

During the period, the Group acquired the remaining 45.6% stake in Macquarie Media Limited which it did not already own, for a total consideration of $113.9 million, with the acquisition completed on 21 November 2019. The Group acquired the remainder of Macquarie Media Limited to consolidate its position as a supplier of news and current affairs across all of the Group's key platforms. Macquarie Media Limited has previously been consolidated into the Group's results as a result of the Fairfax merger on 7 December 2018 and therefore there was no change to the net assets recorded in relation to this entity as a result of the acquisition of the remaining 45.6% stake.

Acquisition of Bidtracker Holdings Pty Limited

On 27 November 2019, Domain acquired 100% of the share capital in Bidtracker Holdings Pty Ltd and its subsidiaries ("Bidtracker Group") which operates the business Real Time Agent. The consideration for the acquisition is to be paid in three tranches with two of the three being contingent on the future financial performance of the Real Time Agent business.

The first tranche included payment of $19.4 million which was settled in cash on 27 November 2019 and $0.5 million cash effective settlement of the intercompany loan. Tranches two and three are due to be settled in September 2020 and 2021 based on the performance against defined targets in FY20 and FY21 respectively. An additional amount between nil and $15.6 million in cash is payable; the maximum consideration for the transaction across the three tranches is $35.5 million, the expected consideration for the transaction is $24.5 million.

The contingent consideration for tranches two and three is recognised as a financial liability on the balance sheet and is measured at fair value through the profit and loss. The contingent consideration is recognised in accordance with AASB 132 Financial Instruments: Presentation as a financial liability as there is an obligation to deliver cash consideration, based upon the post acquisition financial performance of the combined business.

Provisional goodwill of $23.9 million was recognised at the time of acquisition. The goodwill comprises expected synergies arising from the acquisition.

AASB 3 Business Combinations allows a measurement period after a business combination to provide the acquirer a reasonable time to obtain the information necessary to identify and measure all of the various components of the business combination as of the acquisition date. The period cannot exceed one year from the acquisition date.

In the Extract below, Roche Holding Ltd discloses information on its ongoing significant restructuring activities. In addition, comparative amounts and further break-down of additional costs incurred are provided (not reproduced here).

Extract 41.20: Roche Holding Ltd (Half-Year Report 2020)

Notes to the Roche Group Interim Consolidated Financial Statements [extract]

7 Global restructuring plans [extract]

During the six months ended 30 June 2020 the Group continued with the implementation of various global restructuring plans initiated in prior years.

Global restructuring plans: costs incurred in millions of CHF

	Diagnostics	Site consolidation	Other plans	Total
Six months ended 30 June 2020				
Global restructuring costs				
– Employee-related costs	36	3	103	142
– Site closure costs	17	3	20	40
– Divestment of products and businesses	0	0	0	0
– Other reorganisation expenses	30	4	37	71
Total global restructuring costs	83	10	160	253

[...]

Diagnostics Division. During the six months ended 30 June 2020 strategy plans in the Diagnostics Division incurred costs of CHF 45 million, mainly for employee-related costs.

Other global restructuring plans. During the six months ended 30 June 2020 initiatives for the outsourcing of IT and other functions to shared service centres and external providers incurred costs of CHF 66 million, mainly employee-related.

In the Extract below, Rolls-Royce Holdings plc describes the impact of its significant divestments.

Extract 41.21: Rolls-Royce Holdings plc (2019 Half Year Results)

Notes to the half-year financial statements [extract]

16 Acquisitions and disposals [extract]

Disposals

On the 1 April 2019, the Group completed the sale of its Commercial Marine business to KONGSBERG for £569m. The business was disclosed as held for sale from 30 June 2018. In our 2018 half year financial statements, we reported an impairment charge of £160m as a result of the decision to classify Commercial Marine as a business held for sale. Upon the disposal of Commercial Marine on 1 April 2019, and in accordance with IAS 21 *The Effects of Changes in Foreign Exchange Rates* we have recycled the cumulate currency translation reserve through the Income Statement in 2019. This has resulted in a cumulative currency translation gain of £98m. Under the Sale and Purchase Agreement, the cash consideration may be adjusted based upon finalisation of the net assets disposed of, expected to be concluded by 31 December 2019.

On the 15 April 2019, the Group sold its shareholding in Rolls-Royce Power Development Limited to Rockland Capital Partners for £29m. The principal activity of this company was to operate a fleet of six industrial Trent power stations in the UK.

	Total £m
Proceeds	
Cash consideration	598
Cash and cash equivalents disposed	(118)
Net cash consideration	480
Disposal costs paid	(22)
Cash inflow per cash flow statement	458
Assets and liabilities disposed	
Intangible assets	236
Property, plant and equipment	146
Right-of-use assets	40
Deferred tax assets	7
Inventory	210
Trade receivables and other assets	213
Current tax assets	1
Lease liabilities	(39)
Trade payables and other liabilities	(280)
Deposits (payments received on account)	(74)
Provisions for liabilities and charges	(28)
Post-retirement scheme deficits	(28)
Net assets disposed	404

The provisional gain of disposal of businesses (net of disposal costs) totalled £118m.

4.4 Segment information

If an entity is required to disclose segment information in its annual financial statements, certain segment disclosures are required in its interim financial report. IFRS 8 is discussed in more detail in Chapter 36.

An entity applying IFRS 8 in its annual financial statements should include the following information in its interim financial report about its reportable segments: [IAS 34.16A(g)]

(a) segment revenues from external customers (if included in the measure of segment profit or loss reviewed by or otherwise regularly provided to the chief operating decision maker);

(b) intersegment revenues (if included in the measure of segment profit or loss reviewed by or otherwise regularly provided to the chief operating decision maker);

(c) a measure of segment profit or loss;

(d) a measure of total assets and liabilities for a particular reportable segment if such amounts are regularly provided to the chief operating decision maker and if there has been a material change from the amount disclosed in the last annual financial statements for that reportable segment;

(e) a description of differences in the basis of segmentation or in the basis of measurement of segment profit or loss from the last annual financial statements; and

(f) a reconciliation of the total profit or loss for reportable segments to the entity's profit or loss before income taxes and discontinued operations. However, if an entity allocates such items as income taxes to arrive at segment profit or loss, the reconciliation can be to the entity's profit or loss after those items. The entity should separately identify and describe all material reconciling items.

In Extract 41.22 below, Daimler AG discloses segment revenues and segment profit or loss in its interim financial report for the second quarter of 2019. Presumably, information required by (d) above is not included because it is not applicable for the periods presented. In addition, the reconciliation to group figures is also provided for the full first half of 2018 (not reproduced here).

Extract 41.22: Daimler AG (Interim Report Q2 2019)

Notes to the Interim Consolidated Financial Statements [extract]

19.   Segment reporting [extract]

Segment information for the three-month periods ended June 30, 2019 and June 30, 2018 is as follows:

E.26

Segment reporting for the three-month periods ended June 30

	Mercedes-Benz Cars	Daimler Trucks	Mercedes-Benz Vans	Daimler Buses	Daimler Financial Services	Total segments	Recon-ciliation	Daimler Group
In millions of euros								
Q2 2019								
External revenue	21,437	9,998	3,435	1,237	6,543	42,650	–	42,650
Intersegment revenue	856	474	219	31	602	2,182	–2,182	–
Total revenue	22,293	10,472	3,654	1,268	7,145	44,832	–2,182	42,650
Segment profit/loss (EBIT)	–672	725	–2.050	106	431	–1,460	–95	–1,555
thereof share of gains/losses on equity-method investments	304	–6	12	–	–125	185	25	210
thereof gains/losses on compounding and effects from changes in discount rates of provisions for other risks	–60	–22	–5	–2	–	–89	–	–89

Reconciliation

Reconciliation of the total segments' profit (EBIT) to profit before income taxes is as shown in table ↗ E.28.

The reconciliation comprises corporate items for which headquarters is responsible. Transactions between the segments are eliminated in the context of consolidation.

E.28

Reconciliation to Group figures [extract]

In millions of euros	Q2 2019	Q2 2018
Total segments' profit (EBIT)	–1,460	2,731
Share of gains/losses on equity-method investments	25	26
Other corporate items	–139	–121
Eliminations	19	4
Group EBIT	1.555	2.640
Amortization of capitalized borrowing costs[1]	–3	–4
Interest income	121	70
Interest expense	–235	–176
Profit/loss before income taxes	–1,672	2,530

1 Amortization of capitalized borrowing costs is not considered in the internal performance measure "EBIT", but is included in cost of sales.

4.5 Fair value disclosures for financial instruments

IAS 34 requires that an entity should include the following in its interim financial report in relation to financial instruments: [IAS 34.16A(j)]

(a) disclosures to help users of the financial statements assess the valuation techniques and inputs used to develop the fair value measurements used for financial instruments in the statement of financial position and, for financial instruments measured using unobservable inputs, the effect of those measurements on profit or loss or other comprehensive income in the period, [IFRS 13.91], (see Chapter 14 at 20.1);

(b) certain disclosures for fair value measurements that are included in the statement of financial position after initial recognition, including the carrying amount, categorisation within the fair value hierarchy and additional disclosures for those not classified as level 1 (see Chapter 14 at 20.3); [IFRS 13.93]

(c) accounting policy disclosures relating to how the entity has determined appropriate classes of financial assets and liabilities for which information about fair value measurement is given; how it determined when transfers between levels of the fair value hierarchy have occurred; and how the entity has measured any groups of financial assets and liabilities managed on the basis of its net exposure (see Chapter 14 at 20.1.2.A and 20.2); [IFRS 13.94-96]

(d) disclosures regarding liabilities measured at fair value and issued with inseparable third-party credit enhancements (see Chapter 14 at 20.5); [IFRS 13.98] and

(e) disclosures about fair value required by IFRS 7, including for each class of financial asset and financial liability a comparison between fair value and carrying amount, unless the carrying amount is a reasonable approximation of the fair value, [IFRS 7.25, 26, 29(a)], and disclosures relating to the deferral and subsequent recognition of gains and losses arising when fair value is determined using unobservable inputs or when the fair value of a discretionary participation feature within a contract cannot be determined reliably (see Chapter 54 at 4.5). [IFRS 7.28, 29(c)].

Quantitative disclosures would normally be given in a tabular format unless another format is more appropriate. *[IFRS 13.99]*. The entity should assess whether the disclosures are sufficient to meet the disclosure objectives of IFRS 13. This requires judgements to be made about the level of detail; how much emphasis to place on each of the various requirements; and level of aggregation or disaggregation. If necessary, additional information should be given in order to meet those objectives (see Chapter 14 at 20.1). *[IFRS 13.92]*.

The Extract below from the half-year financial report of Nestlé S.A. illustrates disclosures related to the fair value hierarchy and valuation techniques used.

Extract 41.23: Nestlé S.A. (Half-Year Report of the Nestlé Group 2020)

Notes [extract]

9. Fair value of financial instruments [extract]

9.1 Fair value hierarchy [extract]

In millions of CHF	June 30, 2020	December 31, 2019
Derivative assets	33	135
Bonds and debt funds	1 774	573
Equity and equity funds	243	211
Other financial assets	12	3
Derivative liabilities	(92)	(22)
Prices quoted in active markets (Level 1)	**1 970**	**900**
Derivative assets	226	119
Bonds and debt funds	512	488
Equity and equity funds	203	248
Other financial assets	697	720
Derivative liabilities	(552)	(398)
Valuation techniques based on observable market data (Level 2)	**1 086**	**1 177**
Valuation techniques based on unobservable input (Level 3)	**104**	**91**
Total financial instruments at fair value	**3 160**	**2 168**

The fair values categorized in level 2 above were determined as follows:

- Derivatives are valued based on discounted contractual cash flows using risk adjusted discount rates and relying on observable market data for interest rates and foreign exchange rates; and
- The other level 2 investments are based on a valuation model derived from the most recently published observable financial prices for similar assets in active markets.

There have been no significant transfers between the different hierarchy levels in the 2020 and the 2019 interim periods.

4.6 Disclosure of compliance with IFRS

If an interim financial report complies with the requirements of IAS 34, this fact should be disclosed. Furthermore, an interim financial report should not be described as complying with IFRS unless it complies with all the requirements of International Financial Reporting Standards, *[IAS 34.19]*, a requirement similar to that found in IAS 1. *[IAS 1.16]*. Therefore, an entity would only provide a statement of compliance with IFRS (as opposed to IAS 34 alone) in its interim report if it prepared a complete set of interim financial statements.

> Extract 41.24: BMW Group (Quarterly Report 30 June 2019)
>
> Notes to the Group Financial Statements [extract]
> Accounting Principles and Policies [extract]
> 01 Basis of preparation [extract]
>
> The consolidated financial statements of Bayerische Motoren Werke Aktiengesellschaft (BMW Group Financial Statements or Group Financial Statements) at 31 December 2018 were drawn up in accordance with International Financial Reporting Standards (IFRS), as endorsed by the European Union (EU), and the supplementary requirements of § 315 e (1) of the German Commercial Code (HGB). The Interim Group Financial Statements (Interim Report) at 30 June 2019, which have been prepared in accordance with International Accounting Standard (IAS) 34 (Interim Financial Reporting), have been drawn up using, in all material respects, the same accounting methods as those utilised in the 2018 Group Financial Statements. Changes resulting from the first-time application of IFRS 16 are presented in →note 4. The BMW Group applies the option of publishing condensed group financial statements. All Interpretations issued by the International Financial Reporting Interpretations Committee (IFRIC) which were mandatory at 30 June 2019 have been applied. The Interim Report also complies with German Accounting Standard No. 16 (GAS 16) – *Interim Financial Reporting* – issued by the German Accounting Standards Committee e.V. (GASC).

When entities either choose or are required by local regulations to meet other requirements in addition to IAS 34, the statement of compliance can be more complicated. In Extract 41.24 above, BMW Group simply adds a statement confirming its compliance with the specific German Accounting Standard on interim reporting and the supplementary requirements of the German Commercial Code. Additional complexity can arise when the entity seeks to meet the requirements of its (IFRS-based) local GAAP as well as IFRS as issued by the IASB. Extract 41.25 below shows how the dual listed BHP Group disclosed compliance with IFRS, IFRS as endorsed by the EU, Australian Accounting Standards and the requirements of the Financial Conduct Authority in the UK.

> Extract 41.25: BHP (Financial Report – Half year ended 31 December 2019)
>
> Notes to the Financial Statements [extract]
> 1. Basis of preparation [extract]
>
> This general purpose financial report for the half year ended 31 December 2019 is unaudited and has been prepared in accordance with IAS 34 'Interim Financial Reporting' as issued by the International Accounting Standards Board (IASB) and as adopted by the European Union (EU), AASB 134 'Interim Financial Reporting' as issued by the Australian Accounting Standards Board (AASB) and the Disclosure and Transparency Rules of the Financial Conduct Authority in the United Kingdom and the Australian Corporations Act 2001 as applicable to interim financial reporting.

The extract above also highlights a compliance issue for adopters of IFRS-based standards, such as entities in Australia and the European Union. Because of the time taken to secure local endorsement of IFRS issued by the IASB, an entity may not be able to state at a particular reporting date that the financial statements comply with both IFRS as issued by the IASB and IFRS as endorsed locally.

For example, when the Interpretations Committee issues an interpretation that is effective for the annual period which includes the current interim reporting period, entities may choose not to comply with IAS 34 (as issued by the IASB) in their interim financial statements rather than risk applying an interpretation in their full year financial statements that is not yet locally endorsed. Alternatively, an entity may publish interim financial information prepared under locally endorsed IFRS, for example, IFRS as adopted by the European Union. In such cases, the basis of preparation should state that IAS 34 is being applied in this context.

4.7 Disclosure in relation to the going concern assumption

Although IAS 34 does not specifically address the issue of going concern, the general requirements of IAS 1 apply to both a complete set and to condensed interim financial statements. *[IAS 1.4]*. IAS 1 states that when preparing financial statements, management assesses an entity's ability to continue as a going concern, and that the financial statements are prepared on a going concern basis unless management either intends to liquidate the entity or cease trading or has no realistic alternative but to do so. *[IAS 1.25]*. The going concern assessment is discussed in more detail in Chapter 3 at 4.1.2.

Under IAS 1, the assessment is made based on all available information about the future, which at a minimum is twelve months from the end of the reporting period. *[IAS 1.26]*. Therefore, with respect to interim reporting under IAS 34, the minimum period for management's assessment is also at least twelve months from the interim reporting date; it is not limited, for example, to one year from the date of the most recent annual financial statements. In fact, local stock market requirements and other regulations might set a longer minimum period over which management are required to assess entity's ability to continue as a going concern, for example to consider a minimum period of twelve months after the date of approval of the interim financial statements.

Example 41.3:   Going concern assessment under IAS 1

An entity's financial year-end is 31 December (calendar year) and its annual financial statements as of 31 December 2020 are prepared on a going concern basis. In assessing the going concern assumption as at 31 December 2020, management considered all future available information through to 31 December 2021.

In preparing its quarterly interim financial statements (condensed or complete) as at 31 March 2021, management should evaluate all future available information to at least 31 March 2022.

If management becomes aware, in making its assessment, of material uncertainties related to events or conditions that may cast significant doubt upon the entity's ability to continue as a going concern, the entity should disclose those uncertainties in its interim financial statements. If the entity does not prepare financial statements on a going concern basis, it should disclose that fact, together with the basis on which it prepared the financial statements and the reason why the entity is not regarded as a going concern. *[IAS 1.25]*.

In its 2020 interim report, Vesuvius plc considers a period of at least twelve months after the date of approval of the interim financial statements, in accordance with local regulatory requirements.

> Extract 41.26: Vesuvius plc (Half Year Results for the six months ended 30 June 2020)
>
> Notes to the Condensed Group Financial Statements [extract]
> 1. Basis of preparation [extract]
> 1.3. Going concern [extract]
>
> [,,,] The Directors have prepared cash flow scenarios for the Group for a period at least 12 months from the date of approval of the 2020 Interim Condensed Financial Statements. These forecasts reflect an assessment of current and future end-market conditions and their impact on the Group's future trading performance. The analysis undertaken includes a severe but plausible downside scenario which assumes no improvement in sales from the current level of activity during the entire forecast period. This downside scenario assumes a continuation of weak markets in 2020 in line with Q2 and a further 5% decline in sales in 2021 due to a weaker first quarter relative to Q1 2020. Even in this downside scenario, the forecasts show that the Group has significant headroom in terms of both available committed liquidity and required compliance with financial covenants.
>
> On the basis of the exercise described above and the Group's available committed liquidity, the Directors consider that the Group and the Company have adequate resources to continue in operational existence for a period of at least 12 months from the date of signing of these Interim Condensed Financial Statements. Accordingly, they continue to adopt a going concern basis in preparing the Condensed Financial statements of the Group and the Company.

5 PERIODS FOR WHICH INTERIM FINANCIAL STATEMENTS ARE REQUIRED TO BE PRESENTED

Irrespective of whether an entity presents condensed or complete interim financial statements, the components of its interim reports should include information for the following periods: *[IAS 34.20]*

(a) statement of financial position as of the end of the current interim period and a comparative statement of financial position as of the end of the immediately preceding year;

(b) statements of profit or loss and other comprehensive income for the current interim period and cumulatively for the current year-to-date, with comparative statements of profit or loss and other comprehensive income for the comparable interim periods (current and year-to-date) of the immediately preceding year;

(c) statement of changes in equity cumulatively for the current year-to-date period, with a comparative statement for the comparable year-to-date period of the immediately preceding year; and

(d) statement of cash flows cumulatively for the current year-to-date, with a comparative statement for the comparable year-to-date period of the immediately preceding year.

An interim report may present for each period either a single statement of 'profit or loss and other comprehensive income', or separate statements of 'profit or loss' and 'comprehensive income'. *[IAS 1.10A, IAS 34.20(b)]*. The condensed statement of comprehensive income referred to at (b) above should be presented in a manner consistent with the entity's annual financial statements. Accordingly, if the entity presents a separate statement for items of profit or loss in its annual financial statements, it should present a separate condensed statement of profit or loss in the interim financial report. *[IAS 34.8A]*.

If an entity's business is highly seasonal, then the standard encourages reporting additional financial information for the twelve months up to the end of the interim period, and comparative information for the prior twelve-month period, in addition to the financial statements for the periods set out above. *[IAS 34.21]*.

The standard does not require an entity to present a statement of financial position as at the end of the comparable interim period. However, in practice many entities reporting under IFRS disclose this information, either on a voluntary basis, or due to local regulations. Similarly, many entities also present the income statement for the immediately preceding full year. Such presentation is allowed under IAS 34.

The examples below illustrate the periods that an entity is required to disclose under IAS 34. *[IAS 34.22, Illustrative examples part A]*. An entity is encouraged to present the periods illustrated below if the business is highly seasonal.

Example 41.4: Entity publishes interim financial reports half-yearly

If an entity's financial year ends on 31 December (calendar year), it should present the following financial statements (condensed or complete) in its half-yearly interim financial report as of 30 June 2021:

Half-yearly interim report	End of the current interim period 30/6/2021	End of the comparative interim period 30/6/2020	Immediately preceding year-end 31/12/2020
Statement of financial position	●		●
Statement(s) of profit or loss and other comprehensive income			
– Current period and year-to-date (6 months) ending	●	●	
– 12 months ending	○	○	
Statement of changes in equity			
– Year-to date (6 months) ending	●	●	
– 12 months ending	○	○	
Statement of cash flows			
– Year-to-date (6 months) ending	●	●	
– 12 months ending	○	○	

● Required   ○ Disclosure encouraged if the entity's business is highly seasonal

Interim financial reporting

If an entity publishes a separate interim financial report for the final interim period (i.e. second half of its financial year), it presents the following financial statements (condensed or complete) in its second half-yearly interim financial report as of 31 December 2021:

Second half-yearly interim report	End of the current interim period 31/12/2021	End of the comparative interim period 31/12/2020
Statement of financial position	●	●
Statement(s) of profit or loss and other comprehensive income		
– Current period (6 months) ending	●	●
– Year-to-date (12 months) ending	●	●
Statement of changes in equity		
– Year-to-date (12 months) ending	●	●
Statement of cash flows		
– Year-to-date (12 months) ending	●	●

● Required

Example 41.5:   Entity publishes interim financial reports quarterly

If an entity's financial year ends on 31 December (calendar year), it should present the following financial statements (condensed or complete) in its quarterly interim financial reports for 2021:

First quarter interim report	End of the current interim period 31/3/2021	End of the comparative interim period 31/3/2020	Immediately preceding year-end 31/12/2020
Statement of financial position	●		●
Statement(s) of profit or loss and other comprehensive income			
– Current period and year-to-date (3 months) ending	●	●	
– 12 months ending	○	○	
Statement of changes in equity			
– Year-to-date (3 months) ending	●	●	
– 12 months ending	○	○	
Statement of cash flows			
– Year-to-date (3 months) ending	●	●	
– 12 months ending	○	○	

● Required   ○ Disclosure encouraged if the entity's business is highly seasonal

Second quarter interim report	End of the current interim period	End of the comparative interim period	Immediately preceding year-end
	30/6/2021	30/6/2020	31/12/2020
Statement of financial position	●		●
Statement(s) of profit or loss and other comprehensive income			
– Current period (3 months) ending	●	●	
– Year-to-date (6 months) ending	●	●	
– 12 months ending	○	○	
Statement of changes in equity			
– Year-to-date (6 months) ending	●	●	
– 12 months ending	○	○	
Statement of cash flows			
– Year-to-date (6 months) ending	●	●	
– 12 months ending	○	○	

● Required   ○ Disclosure encouraged if the entity's business is highly seasonal

Third quarter interim report	End of the current interim period	End of the comparative interim period	Immediately preceding year-end
	30/9/2021	30/9/2020	31/12/2020
Statement of financial position	●		●
Statement(s) of profit or loss and other comprehensive income			
– Current period (3 months) ending	●	●	
– Year-to-date (9 months) ending	●	●	
– 12 months ending	○	○	
Statement of changes in equity			
– Year-to-date (9 months) ending	●	●	
– 12 months ending	○	○	
Statement of cash flows			
– Year-to-date (9 months) ending	●	●	
– 12 months ending	○	○	

● Required   ○ Disclosure encouraged if the entity's business is highly seasonal

If an entity publishes a separate interim financial report for the final interim period (i.e. fourth quarter of its financial year), it presents the following financial statements (condensed or complete) in its fourth quarter interim financial report as of 31 December 2021:

Fourth quarter interim report	End of the current interim period 31/12/2021	End of the comparative interim period 31/12/2020
Statement of financial position	●	●
Statement(s) of profit or loss and other comprehensive income		
– Current period (3 months) ending	●	●
– Year-to-date (12 months) ending	●	●
Statement of changes in equity		
– Year-to-date (12 months) ending	●	●
Statement of cash flows		
– Year-to-date (12 months) ending	●	●

● Required

5.1 Other comparative information

For entities presenting condensed financial statements under IAS 34, there is no explicit requirement that comparative information be presented in the explanatory notes. Nevertheless, where an explanatory note is required by the standard (such as for inventory write-downs, impairment provisions, segment revenues etc.) or otherwise determined to be needed to provide useful information about changes in the financial position and performance of the entity since the end of the last annual reporting period, *[IAS 34.15]*, it would be appropriate to provide information for each period presented. However, in certain cases it would be unnecessary to provide comparative information where this repeats information that was reported in the notes to the most recent annual financial statements. *[IAS 34.15A]*. For example, it would only be necessary to provide information about business combinations in a comparative period when there is a revision of previously disclosed fair values.

For entities presenting complete financial statements, whilst IAS 34 sets out the periods for which components of the interim report are included, it is less clear how these rules interact with IAS 1's requirement to report comparative information for all amounts in the financial statements. *[IAS 1.38]*. In our view, similar considerations discussed above in the case of condensed financial statements would also apply to complete set of interim financial statements.

Example 41.6: Disclosing movements on non-current assets in a complete set of interim financial statements

An entity preparing complete IFRS financial statements is required to reconcile the carrying amount at the beginning and end of the period showing movements during that period for both intangible assets and property, plant and equipment. *[IAS 38.118, IAS 16.73]*. Therefore, an entity presenting complete IFRS financial statements for the six months ended 30 June 2021 would disclose the movements in intangible assets and in property, plant and equipment between 1 January 2021 and 30 June 2021. In our view, the requirement for comparatives in IAS 1 requires the entity to reconcile movements during the comparative interim period, between 1 January 2020 and 30 June 2020, even though the entity is not required to present a statement of financial position as at 30 June 2020 (as shown in Example 41.4 above).

In addition to presenting comparative information for the corresponding interim period, it is suggested that entities preparing a complete set of interim financial statements also include information for the previous full year in the case of the statement of financial position, such as the required comparative information for the current interim period and reconciliations to the previous year-end statement of financial position. In Example 41.6 above, this requirement could be achieved by reconciling movements in non-current assets during the second six months of the previous year (between 1 July 2020 and 31 December 2020).

If an entity presents complete financial statements and restates comparative information (e.g. following a change in accounting policy, correction of an error, or reclassification) and this restatement is material, then the entity should present a third statement of financial position at the beginning of the earliest comparative period in its interim financial reporting accordance with IAS 1. *[IAS 1.10(f)]*. No such requirement applies in the case of an entity preparing a condensed set of interim financial statements, *[IAS 1.BC33]*, however, additional disclosures are required in the case of correction of prior period errors, *[IAS 34.15B(g)]*, or when accounting policies are changed, *[IAS 34.16A(a)]*, (see 4.3.11 above).

5.2 Length of interim reporting period

IAS 34 does not limit interim reporting to quarterly or half-yearly periods; an interim period may be any period shorter than a full year. *[IAS 34.4]*. Nevertheless, interim reporting for a period other than quarterly or half-yearly is not a common practice.

5.3 Change in financial year-end

The requirement in IAS 34 to present a comparative statement of profit or loss and other comprehensive income 'for the comparable interim periods (current and year-to-date) of the immediately preceding financial year', *[IAS 34.20]*, can give rise to diversity in practice in the case of an entity that changes its annual financial reporting date. For example, an entity changing its reporting date from 31 December to 31 March would change its half-yearly reporting date from 30 June to 30 September and therefore present its first half-yearly report after its new annual reporting date for the six-month period from 1 April to 30 September. A 'comparable' comparative interim period in this scenario could be taken to mean the six months ended 30 September in the prior year, as illustrated in Example 41.7 below.

Example 41.7: Entity changes financial year-end

An entity changes its financial year-end from 31 December (calendar year) to 31 March, and first reflects the change in its annual financial statements for the period ended 31 March 2021. It determines that the requirement for comparable comparative information in IAS 34 requires it to present the following financial statements (condensed or complete) in its half-yearly interim financial report for the six months ending 30 September 2021:

Half-yearly interim report	End of the current interim period 30/9/2021	End of the comparative interim period 30/9/2020	Immediately preceding year-end 31/03/2021
Statement of financial position	●		●
Statement(s) of profit or loss and other comprehensive income			
– Current period and year-to-date (6 months) ending	●	●	
– 12 months ending	○	○	
Statement of changes in equity			
– Year-to date (6 months) ending	●	●	
– 12 months ending	○	○	
Statement of cash flows			
– Year-to-date (6 months) ending	●	●	
– 12 months ending	○	○	

● Required   ○ Disclosure encouraged if the entity's business is highly seasonal

The entity in the example above did not show information for the half-year ended 30 June 2020 as the comparative period, notwithstanding the fact that this period would have been the reporting date for the last published half-yearly report.

Other interpretations of IAS 34 in this regard are also possible. As illustrated in the Extract below, Sirius Minerals changed its annual financial reporting period-end from March to December, which resulted in the company reporting on a shorter (nine-month) annual financial period ended 31 December 2015. For its next set of condensed interim financial statements (for the six months ended 30 June 2016), Sirius presented comparative information for the first six months of the previous annual financial period, being the six months ended 30 September 2015. The company have also included information for the previous annual reporting period (in this case the shortened nine-month period ended 31 December 2015), in common with many UK reporters who present comparative information for the previous annual reporting period in addition to the information required by IAS 34.

> Extract 41.27: Sirius Minerals Plc (Interim ended June 2016)
>
> **Basis of Preparation** [extract]
>
> The condensed interim unaudited consolidated financial statements for the six-month period ended 30 June 2016 have been prepared in accordance with the Disclosure and Transparency Rules of the Financial Conduct Authority and with IAS 34 'Interim Financial Reporting' as adopted by the European Union ("EU"). As a result of changing the accounting reference date, from 31 March to 31 December, these financial statements should be read in conjunction with the condensed financial statements for the six-month period ended 30 September 2015 which have been prepared in accordance with IFRSs as adopted by the EU. Comparability with the current period is maintained due to the low seasonality of the Group's operations.
>
> The accounting policies applied are consistent with those of the Group financial statements for the nine-month period ended 31 December 2015, which have also been voluntarily included in these financial statements for reference.

Given the lack of clarity in IAS 34 as to the meaning of 'comparable' in the case where the current financial year runs for a period that is different to 'the immediately preceding financial year', [IAS 34.20], there are arguments to support each of the interpretations illustrated in Example 41.7 and Extract 41.27 above.

In the Extract above, Sirius Minerals noted that it had considered seasonality of its operations in determining whether the information presented for a prior interim period is comparable. The implication is that had it determined that operations were seasonal, the entity might have reported a different comparative period (perhaps for the six months ended 30 June 2015). As noted at 5 above and illustrated in Example 41.3, in cases where the entity's business is highly seasonal, IAS 34 encourages the reporting of additional financial information for the twelve months up to the end of the interim period, and comparative information for the prior twelve-month period, in addition to the financial statements for the periods set out above. [IAS 34.21].

5.4 Comparatives following a financial period longer than a year

The discussion at 5.3 above demonstrates that when an entity changes its annual reporting date, the determination of comparative periods in the interim financial statements could be interpreted differently without definitive guidance in IAS 34.

Another situation where confusion may be caused by the requirement to present comparative information for 'the comparable interim periods (current and year-to-date) of the immediately preceding financial year', [IAS 34.20], arises when the previous annual financial statements related to a period other than twelve months. This situation is not uncommon for a newly incorporated entity, which might have either a shorter or a longer reporting period in its first financial year.

Consider an entity that has a long initial accounting period of eighteen months and that is required to prepare interim financial reports on a quarterly basis. Accordingly, it would have six 'quarters' in its first financial reporting period and in line with the requirements of IAS 34, the entity would present statements of profit or loss and other comprehensive income, changes in equity and cash flows for each three-month period and cumulatively for the year-to-date. In the next financial year, however, the previously published year-to-date amounts would no longer be comparable. The following example illustrates this situation.

Example 41.8:   Disclosing comparatives in interim financial statements when the preceding financial year covers a longer period

An entity's financial year-end is 31 December and it issues quarterly interim financial statements. It was incorporated on 1 July 2019 and prepared its first set of 'annual' financial statements for a period of eighteen months to 31 December 2020. In this period, the entity prepared interim financial statements under IAS 34 for each of the three-month periods ended 30 September 2019, 31 December 2019, 31 March 2020, 30 June 2020, 30 September 2020 and 31 December 2020. Each interim report contained information for the three-month period and the year-to-date, which started on 1 July 2019.

In the next year, a twelve-month annual reporting period, the entity is preparing its interim financial report for the three months (and half-year) ending 30 June 2021. Accordingly, it presents statements of profit or loss and other comprehensive income, changes in equity and cash flows for the three-month period from 1 April 2021 to 30 June 2021 and for the year-to-date (from 1 January 2021 to 30 June 2021). Under IAS 34, the entity is also required to present comparative statements of profit or loss and other comprehensive income, cash flows, and changes in equity for the comparable interim periods in the preceding financial year.

However, in its interim report for the three months ended 30 June 2020, i.e. in the prior financial year, the entity had presented information for the three month period from 1 April 2020 to 30 June 2020 as well as for the year-to-date period, from 1 July 2019 to 30 June 2020, which was then a period of twelve months.

The entity determines that the year-to-date comparative statements would cover the same period in the preceding year as the current year, which in this case would be for the three-month period from 1 April 2020 to 30 June 2020 and for the six-month period from 1 January 2020 to 30 June 2020.

It should be noted in the above example that none of the interim financial statements issued in the entity's first (eighteen month) reporting period would contain comparative information. In particular, no comparatives would be required for the three month periods ended 30 September 2020 and 31 December 2020 because the corresponding periods in the preceding calendar year (i.e. 30 September 2019 and 31 December 2019) actually form part of the same (eighteen month) financial period and therefore comparatives from a preceding financial reporting period did not exist.

5.5 When the comparative period is shorter than the current period

The same considerations apply when determining the comparable comparative period in the following circumstances when a newly incorporated entity's first financial year was less than twelve months.

Example 41.9: Disclosing comparatives in interim financial statements when the preceding financial year covers a shorter period

An entity was incorporated on 17 December 2020 and its equity shares were admitted to trading on a recognised stock market in April 2021. It determined that its annual reporting date will be 30 June each year and issued its first set of annual financial statements for the period ended 30 June 2021.

In compliance with the rules of the stock market, the entity issues its first half-yearly report for the six months ended 31 December 2021. This begs the question whether the comparative period for these interim financial statements would be the short period from 17 December 2020 (i.e. the date of incorporation) to 31 December 2020 or the first six months following the entity's incorporation, from 17 December 2020 to 16 June 2021.

As in Example 41.8 above, the entity could determine that the period-to-date comparative statements would cover the same period in the preceding annual reporting period as the current year, which in this case would be from 17 December 2020 to 31 December 2020. The entity should provide sufficient disclosure to explain the particular circumstances and the limited comparability with the current period.

6 MATERIALITY

In making judgements on recognition, measurement, classification, or disclosures in interim financial reports, the overriding goal in IAS 34 is to ensure that an interim financial report includes all information relevant to understanding an entity's financial position and performance during the interim period. *[IAS 34.25]*. The standard refers to IAS 1, which defines information as material if omitting, misstating or obscuring it could reasonably be expected to influence decisions that the primary users of general purpose financial statements make on the basis of those financial statements, which provide financial information about a specific reporting entity. *[IAS 1.7, IAS 34.24]*. However, IAS 34 notes that IAS 1 does not contain quantitative guidance on materiality. *[IAS 34.23]*. IAS 34 requires materiality to be assessed based on the interim period financial data. *[IAS 34.23]*.

Therefore, decisions on the recognition and disclosure of unusual items, changes in accounting policies or estimates, and errors are based on materiality in relation to the interim period figures to determine whether non-disclosure is misleading. [IAS 34.25].

Neither the previous year's annual financial statements nor any expectations of the financial position at the current year-end are relevant in assessing materiality for interim reporting. However, the standard acknowledges that interim measurements may rely on estimates to a greater extent than measurements of annual financial data. [IAS 34.23].

IFRS Practice Statement 2 – *Making Materiality Judgements* (Statement 2) is a non-mandatory statement and does not form part of IFRS. See Chapter 3 at 4.1.7 for a discussion on Statement 2.

Statement 2 includes guidance that specifically relates to materiality judgements for interim reporting. Whilst an entity considers the same materiality factors as in its annual assessment, it would also take into consideration the shorter time period and the different purpose of an interim financial report in the following respects:[2]

(a) assessing whether information in the interim financial report is material in relation to the interim period financial data, not annual data; [IAS 34.25]

(b) applying the materiality factors on the basis of both the current interim period data and also, whenever there is more than one interim period (e.g. in the case of quarterly reporting), the data for the current financial year to date; and

(c) considering whether to provide in the interim financial report information that is expected to be material to the annual financial statements. However, information that is expected to be material to the annual financial statements need not be provided in the interim financial report if it is not material to the interim financial report.

As regards purpose, the guidance suggests that entities should also have regard to the fact that an interim financial report is intended to provide an update on the latest complete set of annual financial statements. Information that is material to the interim period, but was already provided in the latest annual financial statements, does not need to be reproduced in the interim financial report, unless something new occurs or an update is needed. [IAS 34.15, 15A].[3]

When an entity concludes that information about estimation uncertainty is material, it needs to disclose that information. As discussed at 10 below, measurements included in interim financial reports often rely more on estimates than measurements included in the annual financial statements. [IAS 34.41]. That fact does not, in itself, make the estimated measurements material. Nevertheless, relying on estimates for interim financial data to a greater extent than for annual financial data might result in more disclosures about such uncertainties being material, and thus being provided in the interim financial report, compared with the annual financial statements.[4]

7 DISCLOSURE IN ANNUAL FINANCIAL STATEMENTS

An estimate of an amount reported in an interim period can change significantly during the remainder of the year. An entity that does not present a separate interim financial report for its final interim period should disclose the nature and amount of significant changes in estimates in a note to the annual financial statements for that year. *[IAS 34.26]*. This disclosure requirement is intended to be narrow in scope, relating only to the change in estimate, and does not create a requirement to include additional interim period financial information in the annual financial statements. *[IAS 34.27]*.

The requirement to disclose significant changes in estimates since the previous interim reporting date is consistent with IAS 8 and paragraph 16A(d) of IAS 34. These standards require disclosure of the nature and the amount of a change in estimate that has a material effect in the current reporting period or is expected to have a material effect in subsequent periods. IAS 34 cites changes in estimate in the final interim period relating to inventory write-downs, restructurings, or impairment losses recognised in an earlier interim period as examples of items that are required to be disclosed. *[IAS 34.27]*.

8 RECOGNITION AND MEASUREMENT

The recognition and measurement requirements in IAS 34 arise mainly from the requirement to report the entity's financial position as at the interim reporting date, but also requires certain estimates and measurements to take into account the expected financial position of the entity at year-end, where those measures are determined on an annual basis (as in the case of income taxes). Many preparers misinterpret this approach as representing some form of hybrid of the discrete and integral methods to interim financial reporting. This can cause confusion in application and can lead to the accusation that IAS 34 seems internally inconsistent.

In requiring the year-to-date to be treated as a discrete period, IAS 34 prohibits the recognition or deferral of revenues and costs for interim reporting purposes unless such recognition or deferral is appropriate at year-end. As with a set of annual financial statements complying with IAS 8, IAS 34 requires changes in estimates and judgements reported in previous interim periods to be revised prospectively, whereas changes in accounting policies and errors are required to be recognised by prior period adjustment. However, IAS 34 sometimes allows looking beyond the interim reporting period, for example in estimating the tax rate to be applied on earnings for the period, when a year-to-date approach does not.

The recognition and measurement requirements of IAS 34 apply regardless of whether an entity presents a complete or condensed set of financial statements for an interim period, *[IAS 34.7]*, and are discussed below.

8.1 Same accounting policies as in annual financial statements

The principles for recognising assets, liabilities, income and expenses for interim periods are the same as in the annual financial statements. *[IAS 34.29]*. Accordingly, an entity uses the same accounting policies in its interim financial statements as in its most recent annual financial statements, adjusted for accounting policy changes that will be reflected in the next annual financial statements. However, IAS 34 also states that the frequency of an entity's reporting (annual, half-yearly or quarterly) does not affect the measurement of its annual results. To achieve that objective, measurements for interim reporting purposes are on a year-to-date basis. *[IAS 34.28]*.

8.1.1 Measurement on a year-to-date basis

Measurement on a year-to-date basis acknowledges that an interim period is a part of a full year and allows adjustments to estimates of amounts reported in prior interim periods of the current year. *[IAS 34.29]*.

This does not override the requirement that the principles for recognition and the definitions of assets, liabilities, income, and expenses for interim periods are the same as in annual financial statements. *[IAS 34.29]*. Therefore, for assets, the same tests of future economic benefits apply at interim dates as at year-end. Costs that, by their nature, would not qualify as assets at year-end, do not qualify for recognition at interim dates either. Similarly, a liability at the end of an interim reporting period must represent an existing obligation at that date, just as it must at the end of an annual reporting period. *[IAS 34.32]*. Under IAS 34, as under the IASB's *Conceptual Framework*, an essential characteristic of income and expenses is that the related inflows and outflows of assets and liabilities have already occurred. If those inflows or outflows have occurred, the related income and expense are recognised; otherwise they are not recognised. *[IAS 34.33]*.

The standard lists several circumstances that illustrate these principles:

- inventory write-downs, impairments, or provisions for restructurings are recognised and measured on the same basis as at a year-end. Except for reversal of impairment losses recognised on goodwill (see 9.2 below), later changes in the original estimate are recognised in the subsequent interim period, either by recognising additional accruals or reversals of the previously recognised amount; *[IAS 34.30(a)]*

- costs that do not meet the definition of an asset at the end of an interim period are not deferred in the statement of financial position, either to await information on whether such costs meets the definition of an asset, or to smooth earnings over interim periods within a year. *[IAS 34.30(b)]*. For example, costs incurred in acquiring an intangible asset before the recognition criteria under IAS 38 – *Intangible Assets* – are met are expensed. Only those costs incurred after the recognition criteria are met can be recognised as an asset; there is no reinstatement as an asset in a later period of costs previously expensed because the recognition criteria were not met at that time; *[IAS 38.71]* and

- income tax expense is 'recognised in each interim period based on the best estimate of the weighted-average annual income tax rate expected for the full financial year. Amounts accrued for income tax expense in one interim period may have to be adjusted in a subsequent interim period of that financial year if the estimate of the annual income tax rate changes'. *[IAS 34.30(c)]*.

Another example would be acquisition costs (excluding debt or share issue costs) incurred in relation to a business combination, which are required to be accounted as expenses in the periods in which the costs are incurred and the services are received. *[IFRS 3.53]*. Such costs would not qualify for deferral at an interim reporting date, even if the business combination to which the costs relate had not been completed until after the interim reporting date.

The year-to-date approach differs from the discrete approach in that the financial position and performance at each reporting date are evaluated not as an isolated period but as part of a cumulative period that builds up to a full year, whose results should not be influenced by interim reporting practices. Amounts reported for previous interim periods are not retrospectively adjusted, and therefore year-to-date measurements may involve changes in estimates of amounts reported in previous interim periods of the current year. As discussed at 4.2 and 7 above, IAS 34 requires disclosure of the nature and amount of material changes in previously reported estimates in the interim financial report and when separate interim financial report is not presented for the final interim period, in the full year financial statements. *[IAS 34.16A(d), 26, 34-36]*. However, the principle that the results of the full year should not be influenced by interim reporting practices, has been challenged, as the IASB and Interpretations Committee have identified and tried to resolve certain conflicts between IAS 34 and other standards, as discussed at 9.2 below.

8.1.2 New accounting pronouncements and other changes in accounting policies

As noted above, under IAS 34, an entity uses the same accounting policies in its interim financial statements as in its most recent annual financial statements, adjusted for accounting policy changes that will be in the next annual financial statements, and to determine measurements for interim reporting purposes on a year-to-date basis. *[IAS 34.28]*.

Unless transition rules are specified by a new standard or interpretation, IAS 34 requires a change in accounting policy to be reflected by: *[IAS 34.43]*

(a) restating the financial statements of prior interim periods of the current year and the comparable interim periods of any prior financial years that will be restated in the annual financial statements under IAS 8; or

(b) when it is impracticable to determine the cumulative effect at the beginning of the year of applying a new accounting policy to all prior periods, adjusting the financial statements of prior interim periods of the current year and comparable interim periods of prior years to apply the new accounting policy prospectively from the earliest date practicable.

Therefore, regardless of when in a financial year an entity decides to adopt a new accounting policy, it has to be applied from no later than the beginning of the current financial year. *[IAS 34.44]*. For example, if an entity that reports on a quarterly basis decides in its third quarter to change an accounting policy, it must restate the information presented in earlier quarterly financial reports to reflect the new policy as if it had been applied from the start of the annual reporting period.

The only exception to the restatement of all comparative periods is when it is impracticable to determine the cumulative effect of applying a new accounting policy at the beginning of the year of application. IAS 1 states that application of a requirement is 'impracticable' when the entity cannot apply it after making every reasonable effort to do so. *[IAS 1.7]*.

Disclosures regarding the restatement can be presented on the face of the financial statements or disclosed in the notes to the financial statements. Only if an entity prepares a complete set of interim financial statements, is it required to present a third statement of financial position, as appropriate (see 3.1 above). *[IAS 34.5(f)]*.

8.1.2.A   New pronouncements becoming mandatory during the current year

One objective of the year-to-date approach is to ensure that a single accounting policy is applied to a particular class of transactions throughout a year. *[IAS 34.44]*. To allow accounting policy changes as of an interim date would mean applying different accounting policies to a particular class of transactions within a single year. This would make interim allocation difficult, obscure operating results, and complicate analysis and understandability of the interim period information. *[IAS 34.45]*.

Accordingly, when preparing interim financial information, consideration is given to which new standards and interpretations are mandatory in the next (current year) annual financial statements. The entity generally adopts these standards in all interim periods during that year.

For example, IFRS 16 was mandatory for annual periods beginning on or after 1 January 2019. *[IFRS 16.C1]*. Therefore, an entity with a 30 September year-end would have applied the standard in its half-yearly report for the six months ending 31 March 2020.

A change in accounting policy would require a restatement of prior comparative financial statements, except for new accounting standards that have specific application and transition requirements. *[IAS 34.43]*. For example, paragraph C5(b) of IFRS 16 allows an entity to apply the requirements in IFRS 16 without restating the prior comparative period (see Chapter 23 at 10.3.2).

8.1.2.B   Voluntary changes of accounting policy

An entity can also elect at any time during a year to apply a new standard or interpretation before it becomes mandatory through a voluntary change in accounting policy. However, IAS 1 and IAS 8 only permit an entity to change an accounting policy if the information results in information that is 'reliable and more relevant' to the users of the financial statements. *[IAS 8.14(b)]*.

After concluding that a voluntary change in accounting policy is permitted and appropriate, its effect is reflected in the first interim report the entity presents after the date on which the entity changed its policy and prior interim periods are restated. Under IAS 8, a change in accounting policy is reflected by retrospective application, with restatement of prior period financial data as far back as is practicable. However, if the cumulative amount of the adjustment relating to previous financial years is impracticable to determine, then under IAS 8, the new policy is applied prospectively from the earliest date practicable. *[IAS 34.44]*. Under IAS 34, an entity is not allowed to reflect the effect of such a voluntary change in accounting policy from a later date than the beginning of the current year, such as at the start of the most recent interim period in which the decision was made to change the policy. *[IAS 34.44]*. To allow two different accounting policies to be applied to a particular class of transactions within a single year would make interim allocations difficult, obscure operating results, and complicate analysis and understandability of the interim period information. *[IAS 34.45]*.

One exception to this principle of retrospective adjustment of earlier interim periods is when an entity changes from the cost model to the revaluation model under IAS 16 – *Property, Plant and Equipment* – or IAS 38. These are not changes in accounting policy that are covered by IAS 8 in the usual manner, but instead required to be treated as a revaluation in the period. *[IAS 8.17]*. Therefore, the general requirements of IAS 34 do not override the specific requirements of IAS 8 to treat such changes prospectively.

However, to avoid using two differing accounting policies for a particular class of assets in a single financial year, consideration should be given to changing from the cost model to the revaluation model at the beginning of the financial year. Otherwise, an entity will end up depreciating assets based on cost for some interim periods and based on the revalued amounts for later interim periods.

8.1.2.C   Transition disclosures in subsequent interim financial statements in the year of adoption

For an entity that prepares more than one set of interim financial statements during the year of adoption of a new standard (e.g. quarterly), it should provide information consistent with that which was disclosed in its first interim financial statements, but updated for the latest information. In some cases, the additional disclosures in a subsequent interim period only relate to the subsequent interim period as paragraph 16A of IAS 34 allows for cross-referencing to other documents available on the same terms. Entities should consider the views of local regulators when planning not to repeat in the current interim financial statements any disclosures already included in previous interim reports or other documents. That is because there are different views among regulators as to whether the policy and impact disclosures should be repeated in full in each set of interim financial statements issued during the year or whether cross-referencing to earlier interim financial statements or other documents outside the current interim report is acceptable. For example, in April 2018 the European Securities and Markets Authority (ESMA) published its report on the activities of accounting enforcers in 2017. In it, ESMA clarified that they expect issuers applying IFRS 15 for the first time and using a modified retrospective approach to provide the disclosures about transition required by paragraph C8 of IFRS 15 in all interim periods that include the date of initial application of IFRS 15.[5]

In any event, if an entity becomes aware of new information about the transitional impact of the new standards as at the date of initial application in a subsequent interim period, the previously reported disclosures will have to be updated in that later interim period to reflect the new information.

Local regulators may have additional requirements. For example, foreign private issuers reporting under IFRS that are required to file interim statements may be affected by the SEC's reporting requirement to provide both the annual and interim period disclosures prescribed by the new accounting standard, to the extent not duplicative, in each interim report in the year of adoption.[6]

8.1.2.D   New pronouncements becoming mandatory in future annual reporting periods

There is no explicit requirement in IAS 34 for a condensed set of financial statements to include disclosures about standards and interpretations that take effect in future annual reporting periods. However, if an entity has obtained new information about the impact of issued but not yet effective amendments of IFRS, it should consider whether to include updated information in the condensed interim financial statements. An entity that prepares a complete set of interim financial statements has not applied a new IFRS that has been issued but is not yet effective must disclose information as required in paragraph 30 of IAS 8 (see Chapter 3 at 5.1.2).

8.1.3 Voluntary changes in presentation

In some cases, the presentation of the interim financial statements might be changed from that used in prior interim reporting periods. However, before changing the presentation used in its interim report from that of previous periods, management should consider the interaction of the requirements of IAS 34 to include in a set of condensed financial statements the same headings and sub-totals as the most recent annual financial statements, *[IAS 34.10]*, and to apply the same accounting policies as the most recent or the next annual financial report, *[IAS 34.28]*, and the requirements of IAS 1 as they will relate to those next annual financial statements. IAS 1 states that an entity should retain the presentation and classification of items in the financial statements, unless it is apparent following a significant change in the nature of operations or a review of the financial statements that another presentation is more appropriate, or unless the change is required by IFRS. *[IAS 1.45]*.

If a presentation is changed, the entity should also reclassify comparative amounts for both earlier interim periods of the current financial year and comparable periods in prior years. *[IAS 34.43(a)]*. In such cases, an entity should disclose the nature of the reclassifications, the amount of each item (or class of items) that is reclassified, and the reason for the reclassification. *[IAS 1.41, IAS 8.29]*.

8.2 Seasonal businesses

Some entities do not earn revenues or incur expenses evenly throughout the year, for example, agricultural businesses, holiday companies, domestic fuel suppliers, or retailers who experience peak demand at Christmas. The financial year-end is often chosen to fit their annual operating cycle, which means that an individual interim period would give little indication of annual performance and financial position.

An extreme application of the integral approach would suggest that they should predict their annual results and contrive to report half of that in the half-year interim financial statements. However, this approach does not portray the reality of their business in individual interim periods, and is, therefore, not permitted under the year-to-date approach adopted in IAS 34. *[IAS 34.28]*.

8.2.1 Revenues received seasonally, cyclically, or occasionally

The standard prohibits the recognition or deferral of revenues that are received seasonally, cyclically, or occasionally at an interim date, if recognition or deferral would not be appropriate at year-end. *[IAS 34.37]*. Examples of such revenues include dividend revenue, royalties, government grants, and seasonal revenues of retailers; such revenues are recognised when they occur. *[IAS 34.38]*.

IAS 34 also requires an entity to explain the seasonality or cyclicality of its business and the effect on interim reporting (see 4.3.12 above). *[IAS 34.16A(b)]*. If businesses are highly seasonal, IAS 34 encourages reporting of additional information for the twelve months up to the end of the interim period and comparatives for the prior twelve-month period (see 5 above). *[IAS 34.21]*.

8.2.2 Costs incurred unevenly during the year

IAS 34 prohibits the recognition or deferral of costs for interim reporting purposes if recognition or deferral of that type of cost is inappropriate at year-end, *[IAS 34.39]*, which is based on the principle that assets and liabilities are recognised and measured using the same criteria as at year-end. *[IAS 34.29, 31]*. This principle prevents smoothing of costs in seasonal businesses. Furthermore, the recognition of assets or liabilities at the interim date would not be appropriate if they would not qualify for recognition at the end of an annual reporting period. *[IAS 34. 32]*.

For direct costs, this approach has limited consequences, as the timing of recognising these costs and the related revenues is usually similar. However, for indirect costs, the consequences may be greater, depending on which standard an entity follows.

For example, manufacturing entities that use fixed production overhead absorption rates recognise an asset in respect of attributable overheads based on the normal capacity of the production facilities in accordance with IAS 2 – *Inventories*. Any variances and unallocated overheads are expensed. *[IAS 2.13]*. Entities applying IFRS 15 can only capitalise allocations of costs incurred in fulfilling a contract with a customer that are not within the scope of another standard which meet all the following criteria: *[IFRS 15.95]*

- the costs relate directly to the contract or to an anticipated contract that can be specifically identified;
- the costs are expected to generate or enhance resources of the entity that will be used in satisfying (or in continuing to satisfy) performance obligations in the future; and
- the costs are expected to be recovered.

If these criteria are not met at the reporting date, the costs are expensed.

The circumstances in which IFRS 15 allows an asset to be recognised in relation to costs incurred to fulfil a contract are discussed in Chapter 31 at 5.2. What is clear is that an entity should not diverge from these requirements for recognising an expense or an asset just because information is being prepared for an interim period.

9 EXAMPLES OF THE RECOGNITION AND MEASUREMENT PRINCIPLES

Part B of the illustrative examples accompanying the standard provides several examples that illustrate the recognition and measurement principles in interim financial statements. *[IAS 34.40]*. In addition, IFRIC 10 – *Interim Financial Reporting and Impairment* – addresses the reversal of impairment losses recognised on goodwill in the interim periods. These examples are discussed below.

9.1 Property, plant and equipment and intangible assets

9.1.1 Depreciation and amortisation

Depreciation and amortisation for an interim period is based only on assets owned during that interim period and does not consider asset acquisitions or disposals planned for later in the year. *[IAS 34.B24]*.

An entity applying a straight-line method of depreciation (amortisation) does not allocate the depreciation (amortisation) charge between interim periods based on the level of activity. However, under IAS 16 and IAS 38 an entity may use a 'unit of production' method of depreciation, which results in a charge based on the expected use or output (see Chapter 18 at 5.6.2). An entity can only apply this method if it most closely reflects the expected pattern of consumption of the future economic benefits embodied in the asset. The chosen method should be applied consistently from period to period unless there is a change in the expected pattern of consumption of those future economic benefits. *[IAS 16.62, IAS 38.98]*. Therefore, an entity cannot apply a straight-line method of depreciation in its annual financial statements, while allocating the depreciation charge to interim periods using a 'unit of production' based approach.

9.1.2 Impairment of assets

IAS 36 – *Impairment of Assets* – requires an entity to recognise an impairment loss if the recoverable amount of an asset declines below its carrying amount. *[IAS 34.B35]*. An entity should apply the same impairment testing, recognition, and reversal criteria at an interim date as it would at year-end. *[IAS 34.B36]*.

However, IAS 34 states that an entity is not required to perform a detailed impairment calculation at the end of each interim period. Rather, an entity should perform a review for indications of significant impairment since the most recent year-end to determine whether such a calculation is needed. *[IAS 34.B36]*. Nevertheless, the standard does not exempt an entity from performing impairment tests at the end of its interim periods. For example, an entity that recognised an impairment charge in the immediately preceding year, may find that it needs to update its impairment calculations at the end of subsequent interim periods because impairment indicators remain. IFRIC 10 does not allow reversal of impairment loss recognised on goodwill in a previous interim period (see 9.2 below).

9.1.3 Recognition of intangible assets

An entity should apply the same IAS 38 definitions and recognition criteria for intangible assets in an interim period as in an annual period. Therefore, costs incurred before the recognition criteria are met should be recognised as an expense. *[IAS 34.B8]*. Expenditures on intangibles that are initially expensed under IAS 38 cannot be reinstated and recognised as part of the cost of an intangible asset subsequently (e.g. in a later interim period). *[IAS 38.71]*. Furthermore, 'deferring' costs as assets in an interim period in the hope that the recognition criteria will be met later in the year is not permitted. Only costs incurred after the specific point in time at which the criteria are met should be recognised as part of the cost of an intangible asset. *[IAS 34.B8]*.

9.1.4 Capitalisation of borrowing costs

An entity that recognises finance expenses in the cost of a qualifying asset under IAS 23 – *Borrowing Costs* – should determine the amount to be capitalised from the actual finance cost during the period (when funds are specifically borrowed) *[IAS 23.12]* or, when the asset is funded out of general borrowings, by applying a capitalisation rate equal to the weighted-average of the finance costs attributable to actual borrowings outstanding during the period *[IAS 23.14]* (see Chapter 21 at 5.2 and 5.3). For interim financial reporting, measurement should be made on a year-to-date basis, *[IAS 34.28]*, regardless of how often the entity issues interim reports during a year. For example, an entity that issues quarterly interim reports would have to revise its estimated capitalisation rate in successive quarters during the same year for changes in actual year-to-date borrowings and finance costs. As required in IAS 34, the cumulative effect of changes in the estimated capitalisation rate should be recognised in the current quarter (as a change in estimate) and not retrospectively. *[IAS 34.36]*.

9.2 Reversal of impairment losses recognised in a previous interim period (IFRIC 10)

The two requirements in IAS 34, to apply the same accounting policies in interim financial reports as are applied for the annual financial statements, and to use year-to-date measurements for interim reporting purposes, do not sit easily together when considering the reversal of certain impairments that IFRS does not allow to be reversed in a subsequent period. For example, IAS 36 prohibits the reversal in a subsequent period of an impairment loss recognised for goodwill. *[IAS 36.124]*.

As discussed at 9.1.2 above, the requirement to use the same accounting policies means that an entity should apply the same impairment testing, recognition, and reversal criteria at the end of an interim period as it would at year-end. *[IAS 34.B36]*.

However, the use of year-to-date measurements implies that the calculation of impairments as at interim reporting dates in the same annual reporting period should be based on conditions as at the end of each interim period and determined independently of assessments at earlier interim dates. Applying this requirement of IAS 34 would lead to reversals of previously reported impairments if conditions change and justify a higher carrying value for the related asset.

IFRIC 10 addresses the interaction between the requirements of IAS 34 and the recognition of impairment losses on goodwill in IAS 36, and the effect of that interaction on subsequent interim and annual financial statements. *[IFRIC 10.2]*.

Whilst it may be unlikely for the conditions causing an impairment of goodwill at an interim date to reverse before year-end, IFRIC 10 states that the specific requirements of IAS 36 take precedence over the more general statement in IAS 34. *[IFRIC 10.BC9]*. As such, IFRIC 10 prohibits the reversal of an impairment loss recognised in a previous interim period in respect of goodwill. *[IFRIC 10.8]*.

Thus, in the albeit unlikely event that the conditions giving rise to an impairment do reverse in successive interim periods, there can be situations where two entities facing an identical set of circumstances, yet with different frequency of interim reporting, could end up reporting different annual results.

IFRIC 10 should not be applied by analogy to derive a general principle that the specific requirements of a standard take precedence over the year-to-date approach in IAS 34. *[IFRIC 10.9]*.

9.3 Employee benefits

9.3.1 Employer payroll taxes and insurance contributions

If employer payroll taxes or contributions to government sponsored insurance funds are assessed on an annual basis, the employer's related expense should be recognised in interim periods using an estimated average annual effective rate, even if it does not reflect the timing of payments. A common example contained in Appendix B to IAS 34 is employer payroll tax or insurance contribution subject to a certain maximum level of earnings per employee. Higher income employees would reach the maximum income before year-end, and the employer would make no further payments for the remainder of the year. *[IAS 34.B1]*.

9.3.2 Year-end bonuses

The nature of year-end bonuses varies widely. Some bonus schemes only require continued employment whereas others require certain performance criteria to be attained on a monthly, quarterly, or annual basis. Payment of bonuses may be purely discretionary, contractual or based on years of historical precedent. *[IAS 34.B5]*. A bonus is recognised for interim reporting only if: *[IAS 34.B6]*

(a) the entity has a present legal or constructive obligation to make such payments as a result of past events; and

(b) a reliable estimate of the obligation can be made.

A present obligation exists only when an entity has no realistic alternative but to make the payments. *[IAS 19.19]*. IAS 19 gives guidance on accounting for profit sharing and bonus plans (see Chapter 35 at 12.3).

In recognising a bonus at an interim reporting date, an entity should consider the facts and circumstances under which the bonus is payable and determine an accounting policy that recognises an expense reflecting the obligation on the basis of the services received to date. Several possible accounting policies are illustrated in Example 41.10 below.

Example 41.10: Measuring interim bonus expense

An entity pays an annual performance bonus if earnings exceed £10 million, under which 5% of any earnings in excess over £10 million will be paid up to a maximum of £500,000. Earnings for the six months ended 30 June 2021 are £7 million, and the entity expects earnings for the full year ended 31 December 2021 to be £16 million.

The following table shows various accounting policies and the expense recognised thereunder in the interim financial statements for the six months ended 30 June 2021.

	Expense (£)
Method 1 – constructive obligation exists when earnings target is met	Nil
Method 2 – assume earnings for remainder of year will be same	200,000
Method 3 – proportionate recognition based on full-year estimate	131,250
Method 4 – one-half recognition based on full-year estimate	150,000

Method 1 is generally not appropriate, as this method disregards the fact that the entity has a present obligation under the performance bonus arrangement when the employees have provided services during the first six months towards earning the bonus.

Likewise, Method 2 is generally not appropriate, as the expense of £200,000 [(£14 million – £10 million) × 5%] assumes that the employees will continue to provide services in the latter half of the year to achieve the bonus target, but does not attribute any services to that period.

In contrast to Methods 1 and 2, Method 3 illustrates an accounting policy whereby an estimate is made of the full-year expense and attributed to the period based on the proportion of that bonus for which employees have provided services at 30 June 2021. The amount recognised is calculated as (£7 million ÷ £16 million) × [5% × (£16 million – £10 million)].

Similar to Method 3, Method 4 also takes the approach of recognising an expense based on the full year estimate, but allocates that full-year estimate equally to each period (which is similar to the approach used for share-based payment transactions). The amount recognised is calculated as [50% × 5% × (£16 million – £10 million)].

In addition to Methods 3 and 4, which might be appropriate, depending on the facts and circumstances, an entity might determine another basis on which to recognise bonus that considers both the constructive obligation that exists as of 30 June 2021, and the services performed to date, which is also appropriate.

9.3.3 Pensions

Pension costs for an interim period are calculated on a year-to-date basis using the actuarially determined pension cost rate at the end of the prior year, adjusted for significant market fluctuations and for significant one-off events, such as plan amendments, curtailments and settlements. *[IAS 34.B9]*.

In the absence of such significant market fluctuations and one-off events, the estimate of the actuarial liabilities is rolled forward in the scheme based on assumptions as at the beginning of the year and adjusted for significant changes in the membership of the scheme. If there are significant changes to pension arrangements during the interim period (such as changes resulting from a material business combination or from a major redundancy programme) consideration should be given to obtaining a new actuarial valuation of scheme liabilities. Similarly, if there are significant market fluctuations, such as those arising from changes in corporate bond markets, the validity of the assumptions in the last actuarial estimate, such as the discount rate applied to scheme liabilities, should be reviewed and revised as appropriate.

In Extract 41.28 below International Consolidated Airlines Group S.A. discloses changes in the discount rates used for pension obligations. In normal circumstances, companies would not necessarily go through the full process of measuring pension liabilities at interim reporting dates, but rather would look to establish a process to assess the impact of any changes in underlying parameters (e.g. through extrapolation). If, for example, the discount rate estimated based on circumstances prevalent at the half-year interim reporting date has changed, the following 'rule of thumb' may help assess the impact on the pension obligation:

- Estimated change in DBO (%) = [Change in the discount rate (basis points) × duration of the pension obligation (in years)] ÷ 100

(Note: Basis points = 0.01%)

As with all approximations, the appropriateness in the circumstances should be considered.

> *Extract 41.28: International Consolidated Airlines Group, S.A. (Six months to June 30, 2019)*
>
> **NOTES TO THE ACCOUNTS** [extract]
>
> **15. EMPLOYEE BENEFIT OBLIGATIONS** [extract]
>
> The principal funded defined benefit pension schemes within the Group are the Airways Pension Scheme ('APS') and the New Airways Pension Scheme ('NAPS').
>
> [...]
>
> At 30 June 2019, the assumptions used to determine the obligations under the APS and NAPS were reviewed and updated to the reflect market condition at that date. Key assumptions were as follows:
>
> | Per cent per annum | June 30, 2019 APS | June 30, 2019 NAPS | December 31, 2018 APS | December 31, 2018 NAPS |
> |---|---|---|---|---|
> | Inflation (CPI) | 2.25 | 2.15 | 2.10 | 2.05 |
> | Inflation (RPI) | 3.25 | 3.15 | 3.20 | 3.15 |
> | Salary increases (as RPI) | 3.25 | n/a | 3.20 | n/a |
> | Discount rate | 2.15 | 2.35 | 2.65 | 2.85 |
>
> Further information on the basis of the assumptions is included in note 30 of the Annual Report and Accounts for the year to December 31, 2018.

9.3.4 Vacations, holidays, and other short-term paid absences

IAS 19 distinguishes between accumulating and non-accumulating paid absences. *[IAS 19.13]*. Accumulating paid absences are those that are carried forward and can be used in future periods if the current period's entitlement is not used in full. IAS 19 requires an entity to measure the expected cost of and obligation for accumulating paid absences at the amount the entity expects to pay as a result of the unused entitlement that has accumulated at the end of the reporting period (see Chapter 35 at 12.2.1). IAS 34 requires the same principle to be applied at the end of interim reporting periods. Conversely, an entity should not recognise an expense or liability for non-accumulating paid absences at the end of an interim reporting period, just as it would not recognise any at the end of an annual reporting period. *[IAS 34.B10]*.

9.4 Inventories and cost of sales

9.4.1 Inventories

The recognition and measurement principles of IAS 2 are applied in the same way for interim financial reporting as for annual reporting purposes. At the end of a financial reporting period an entity would determine inventory quantities, costs, and net realisable values. However, IAS 34 does comment that to save cost and time, entities often use estimates to measure inventories at interim dates to a greater extent than at annual reporting dates. *[IAS 34.B25]*.

Net realisable values are determined using selling prices and costs to complete and dispose at the end of the interim period. A write-down should be reversed in a subsequent interim period only if it would be appropriate to do so at year-end (see Chapter 22 at 3.3). *[IAS 34.B26]*.

9.4.2 Contractual or anticipated purchase price changes

Both the payer and the recipient of volume rebates, or discounts and other contractual changes in the prices of raw materials, labour, or other purchased goods and services should anticipate these items in interim periods if it is probable that these have been earned or will take effect. However, discretionary rebates and discounts should not be recognised because the resulting asset or liability would not meet the recognition criteria in the IASB's *Conceptual Framework*. [IAS 34.B23].

9.4.3 Interim period manufacturing cost variances

Price, efficiency, spending, and volume variances of a manufacturing entity should be recognised in profit or loss at interim reporting dates to the same extent that those variances are recognised at year-end. It is not appropriate to defer variances expected to be absorbed by year-end, which could result in reporting inventory at the interim date at more or less than its actual cost. [IAS 34.B28].

9.5 Taxation

Taxation is one of the most difficult areas of interim financial reporting, primarily because IAS 34 does not clearly distinguish between current income tax and deferred tax, referring only to 'income tax expense'. This causes tension between the approach for determining the expense and the asset or liability in the statement of financial position. In addition, the standard's provisions combine terminology, suggesting an integral approach to measurement with guidance requiring a year-to-date basis to be applied in respect of recognition. The integral method appears to be the basis used in determining the effective income tax rate for the whole year, but that rate is applied to year-to-date profit in the interim financial statements. In addition, under a year-to-date basis, the estimated rate is based on tax rates and laws that are enacted or substantively enacted by the end of the interim period. Changes in legislation expected to occur before the end of the current year are not recognised in preparing the interim financial report. The assets and liabilities in the statement of financial position, at least for deferred taxes, are derived solely from a year-to-date approach, but sometimes the requirements of the standard are unclear, as discussed below.

9.5.1 Measuring interim income tax expense

IAS 34 states that income tax expense should be accrued using the 'best estimate of the weighted average annual income tax rate expected for the full financial year' and applying that rate to actual pre-tax income for the interim period. [IAS 34.30(c), B12]. Whilst the standard also describes this rate as 'the tax rate that would be applicable to expected total annual earnings', [IAS 34.B12], this is not the same as estimating the total tax expense for the year and allocating a proportion of that to the interim period (even though it might sometimes appear that way), as demonstrated in the discussion below.

Because taxes are assessed on an annual basis, using this approach to determine the annual effective income tax rate and applying it to year-to-date actual earnings is consistent with the basic concept in IAS 34, that the same recognition and measurement principles apply in interim financial reports as in annual financial statements. [IAS 34.B13].

In estimating the weighted-average annual income tax rate, an entity should reflect a blend of any progressive tax rate structure expected to be applicable to the full year's earnings, including changes in income tax rates scheduled to take effect later in the year that are enacted or substantively enacted as at the end of the interim period. *[IAS 34.B13]*. This situation is illustrated in Example 41.11 below. *[IAS 34.B15]*.

Example 41.11: Measuring interim income tax expense – progressive tax rates

An entity reporting quarterly expects to earn 10,000 pre-tax each quarter and operates in a jurisdiction with a tax rate of 20% on the first 20,000 of annual earnings and 30% on all additional earnings. Actual earnings match expectations. The following table shows the income tax expense reported each quarter:

	Pre-tax earnings	Effective tax rate	Tax expense
First quarter	10,000	25%	2,500
Second quarter	10,000	25%	2,500
Third quarter	10,000	25%	2,500
Fourth quarter	10,000	25%	2,500
Annual	40,000		10,000

10,000 of tax is expected to be payable for the full year on 40,000 of pre-tax income (20,000 @ 20% + 20,000 @ 30%), implying an average annual effective income tax rate of 25% (10,000 ÷ 40,000).

In the above example, it might look as if the interim income tax expense is calculated by dividing the total expected tax expense for the year (10,000) by the number of interim reporting periods (4). However, this is only the case in this example because profits are earned evenly over each quarter. The expense is actually calculated by determining the effective annual income tax rate and multiplying that rate to year-to-date earnings, as illustrated in Example 41.12 below. *[IAS 34.B16]*.

Example 41.12: Measuring interim income tax expense – quarterly losses

An entity reports quarterly, earns 15,000 pre-tax profit in the first quarter but expects to incur losses of 5,000 in each of the three remaining quarters (thus having zero income for the year), and operates in a jurisdiction in which its standard statutory annual income tax rate is 20%. The following table shows the income tax expense reported each quarter:

	Pre-tax earning	Effective tax rate	Tax expense
First quarter	15,000	20%	3,000
Second quarter	(5,000)	20%	(1,000)
Third quarter	(5,000)	20%	(1,000)
Fourth quarter	(5,000)	20%	(1,000)
Annual	0		0

The above example shows how an expense is recognised in periods reporting a profit and a credit is recognised when a loss is incurred. This result is very different from allocating a proportion of the expected total income tax expense for the year, which in this case is zero.

If an entity operates in a number of tax jurisdictions, or where different income tax rates apply to different categories of income (such as capital gains or income earned in particular industries), the standard requires that to the extent practicable, an entity: *[IAS 34.B14]*

- estimates the average annual effective income tax rate for each taxing jurisdiction separately and apply it individually to the interim period pre-tax income of each jurisdiction; and
- applies different income tax rates to each individual category of interim period pre-tax income.

This means that the entity should perform the analysis illustrated in Example 41.11 above for each tax jurisdiction and arrive at an interim tax charge by applying the tax rate for each jurisdiction to actual earnings from each jurisdiction in the interim period. However, the standard recognises that, whilst desirable, such a degree of precision may not be achievable in all cases and allows using a weighted-average rate across jurisdictions or across categories of income, if such rate approximates the effect of using rates that are more specific. *[IAS 34.B14]*.

Example 41.13: Measuring interim tax expense – many jurisdictions

An entity operates in 3 countries, each with its own tax rates and laws. In order to determine the interim tax expense, the entity determines the effective annual income tax rate for each jurisdiction and applies those rates to the actual earnings in each jurisdiction, as follows:

(All values in €)	Country A	Country B	Country C	Total
Expected annual tax rate	25%	40%	20%	
Expected annual earnings	300,000	250,000	200,000	750,000
Expected annual tax expense	75,000	100,000	40,000	215,000
Actual half-year earnings	140,000	80,000	150,000	370,000
Interim tax expense	35,000	32,000	30,000	97,000

By performing a separate analysis for each jurisdiction, the entity determines an interim tax expense of €97,000, giving an effective average tax rate of 26.2% (€97,000 ÷ €370,000). Had the entity used a weighted-average rate across jurisdictions, using the expected annual earnings, it would have determined an effective tax rate of 28.7% (€215,000 ÷ €750,000), resulting in a tax expense for the interim period of €106,190 (370,000 @ 28.7%). Whether the difference of nearly €9,000 lies within the range for a reasonable approximation is a matter of judgement.

9.5.2 Changes in the effective tax rate during the year

9.5.2.A Enacted changes for the current year that apply after the interim reporting date

As noted above, the estimated income tax rate applied in the interim financial report should reflect changes that are enacted or substantively enacted as at the end of the interim reporting period, but scheduled to take effect later in the year. *[IAS 34.B13]*. IAS 12 – *Income Taxes* – acknowledges that in some jurisdictions, announcements by government have substantively the same effect as enactment. *[IAS 12.48]*. Accordingly, an entity should determine the date on which a change in tax rate or tax law is substantively enacted based on the specific constitutional arrangements of the jurisdiction.

For example, assume that the 30% tax rate (on earnings above 20,000) in Example 41.11 was substantively enacted as at the second quarter reporting date and applicable before year-end. In that case, the estimated income tax rate for interim reporting would be the same as the estimated average annual effective income tax rate computed in that example (i.e. 25%) after considering the higher rate, even though the entity's earnings are not above the required threshold at the half-year.

If legislation is enacted only after the end of the interim reporting period but before the date of authorisation for issue of the interim financial report, its effect is disclosed as an event after the interim period that has not been reflected in the financial statements for the interim period. [IAS 34.16A(h)]. This is consistent with the requirement under IAS 10 – *Events after the Reporting Period* – where estimates of tax rates and related assets or liabilities are not revised in these circumstances. [IAS 10.22(h)].

9.5.2.B Changes to previously reported estimated income tax rates for the current year

IAS 34 requires an entity to re-estimate at the end of each interim reporting period the estimated average annual income tax rate on a year-to-date basis. [IAS 34.B13]. Accordingly, the amounts accrued for income tax expense in one interim period may have to be adjusted in a subsequent interim period if that estimate changes. [IAS 34.30(c)]. IAS 34 requires disclosure in interim financial statements of material changes in estimates of amounts reported in an earlier period or, in the annual financial statements, of material changes in estimates of amounts reported in the latest interim financial statements. [IAS 34.16A(d), 26].

Accordingly, just as the integral approach does not necessarily result in a constant tax charge in each interim reporting period, it also does not result in a constant effective tax rate when circumstances change. In 2019, Coca-Cola HBC AG described how its tax rate is estimated in their interim report.

Extract 41.29: Coca-Cola HBC AG
(Half-yearly financial report for the six months ended 28 June 2019)

Selected explanatory notes to the condensed consolidated interim financial statements (unaudited) [extract]

6. Tax [extract]

The Group's effective tax rate for 2019 may differ from the theoretical amount that would arise using the weighted average tax rate applicable to profits of the consolidated entities. This difference can be a consequence of a number of factors, the most significant of which are the application of statutory tax rates of the countries in which the Group operates, the non-deductibility of certain expenses, the non-taxable income and one off tax items.

Example 41.14: Changes in the effective tax rate during the year

Taking the fact pattern in Example 41.11 above, an entity reporting quarterly expects to earn 10,000 pre-tax each quarter; from the start of the third quarter the higher rate of tax on earnings over 20,000 increases from 30% to 40%. Actual earnings continue to match expectations. The following table shows the income tax expense reported in each quarter:

	Period pre-tax earnings	Pre-tax earnings: year to date	Effective tax rate	Tax expense: year to date	Period tax expense
First quarter †	10,000	10,000	25%	2,500	2,500
Second quarter †	10,000	20,000	25%	5,000	2,500
Third quarter	10,000	30,000	30%	9,000	4,000
Fourth quarter	10,000	40,000	30%	12,000	3,000
Annual	40,000				12,000

† As previously reported from Example 41.11 using an effective tax rate of 25%.

The increase in the tax rate means that 12,000 of tax is expected to be payable for the full year on 40,000 of pre-tax income (20,000 @ 20% + 20,000 @ 40%), implying an average annual effective income tax rate of 30% (12,000 / 40,000). With cumulative pre-tax earnings of 30,000 as at the end of the third quarter, the estimated tax liability is 9,000, requiring a tax expense of 4,000 (9,000 – 2,500 – 2,500) to be recognised during that quarter. In the final quarter, earnings of 10,000 results in a tax charge of 3,000 using the revised effective rate of 30%.

9.5.2.C   Enacted changes applying only to subsequent years

In many jurisdictions, tax legislation is enacted that takes effect not only after the interim reporting date but also after year-end. Such circumstances are not addressed explicitly in the standard. As IAS 34 does not clearly distinguish between current income tax and deferred tax, combined with the different approaches taken in determining the expense recognised in profit or loss compared to the statement of financial position, these issues can lead to confusion in this situation.

On the one hand, the standard states that the estimated income tax rate for the interim period includes enacted or substantively enacted changes scheduled to take effect later in the year. *[IAS 34.B13]*. This implies that the effect of changes that do not take effect in the current year is ignored in determining the appropriate rate for current tax. On the other hand, IAS 34 also requires that the principles for recognising assets, liabilities, income and expenses for interim periods are the same as in the annual financial statements. *[IAS 34.29]*. In annual financial statements, deferred tax is measured at the tax rates expected to apply to the period when the asset is realised or the liability is settled, based on tax rates (and tax laws) enacted or substantively enacted by the end of the reporting period, as required by IAS 12. *[IAS 12.47]*. Therefore, an entity should recognise the effect on deferred tax measurement of a change applying to future periods if enacted by the end of the interim reporting period.

These two requirements seem to be mutually incompatible. IAS 34 makes sense only in the context of calculating the effective current tax rate on income earned in the period. Once a deferred tax asset or liability is recognised, it should be measured under IAS 12. Therefore, an entity should recognise an enacted change applying to future years in measuring deferred tax assets and liabilities as at the end of the interim reporting period. One way to treat the cumulative effect to date of this remeasurement is to recognise it in full, by a credit to profit or loss or to other comprehensive income, depending on the nature of the temporary difference being remeasured, in the period during which the tax legislation is enacted, in a similar way to the treatment shown in Example 41.14 above, and as illustrated in Example 41.15 below.

Example 41.15:   Enacted changes to tax rates applying after the current year

An entity reporting half-yearly operates in a jurisdiction subject to a tax rate of 30%. Legislation is enacted during the first half of the current year, which reduces the tax rate to 28% on income earned from the beginning of the entity's next financial year. Based on a gross temporary difference of 1,000, the entity reported a deferred tax liability in its most recent annual financial statements of 300 (1,000 @ 30%). Of this temporary difference, 200 is expected to reverse in the second half of the current year and 800 in the next financial year. Assuming that no new temporary differences arise in the current period, what is the deferred tax balance at the interim reporting date?

Whilst the entity uses an effective tax rate of 30% to determine the tax expense relating to income earned in the period, it should use a rate of 28% to measure those temporary differences expected to reverse in the next financial year. Accordingly, the deferred tax liability at the half-year reporting date is 284 (200 @ 30% + 800 @ 28%).

Alternatively, if the effective current tax rate is not distinguished from the measurement of deferred tax, it could be argued that IAS 34 allows the reduction in the deferred tax liability of 16 (300 – 284) to be included in the estimate of the effective income tax rate for the year. Approach 2 in Example 41.17 below applies this argument. In our view, because IAS 34 does not distinguish between current and deferred taxes, either approach would be acceptable provided that is applied consistently.

9.5.3 Difference in financial year and tax year

If an entity's financial year and the income tax year differ, the income tax expense for the interim periods of that financial year should be measured using separate weighted-average estimated effective tax rates for each of the income tax years applied to the portion of pre-tax income earned in each of those income tax years. *[IAS 34.B17]*. In other words, an entity should compute a weighted-average estimated effective tax rate for each income tax year, rather than for its financial year.

Example 41.16: Difference in financial year and tax year *[IAS 34.B18]*

An entity's financial year ends 30 June and it reports quarterly. Its taxable year ends 31 December. For the financial year that begins 1 July 2020 and ends 30 June 2021, the entity earns 10,000 pre-tax each quarter.

The estimated average annual income tax rate is 30% in the income tax year to 31 December 2020 and 40% in the year to 31 December 2021.

Quarter ending	Pre-tax earnings	Effective tax rate	Tax expense
30 September 2020	10,000	30%	3,000
31 December 2020	10,000	30%	3,000
31 March 2021	10,000	40%	4,000
30 June 2021	10,000	40%	4,000
Annual	40,000		14,000

9.5.4 Tax loss and tax credit carrybacks and carryforwards

Appendix B to IAS 34 repeats the requirement in IAS 12 that for carryforwards of unused tax losses and tax credits, a deferred tax asset should be recognised to the extent that it is probable that future taxable profit will be available against which the unused tax losses and unused tax credits can be utilised. In assessing whether future taxable profit is available, the criteria in IAS 12 are applied at the interim date. If these criteria are met as at the end of the interim period, the effect of the tax loss carryforwards is included in the estimated average annual effective income tax rate. *[IAS 34.B21]*.

Example 41.17: Tax loss carryforwards expected to be recovered in the current year *[IAS 34.B22]*

An entity that reports quarterly has unutilised operating losses of 10,000 for income tax purposes at the start of the current financial year for which a deferred tax asset has not been recognised. The entity earns 10,000 in the first quarter of the current year and expects to earn 10,000 in each of the three remaining quarters. Excluding the effect of utilising losses carried forward, the estimated average annual income tax rate is 40%. Including the carryforward, the estimated average annual income tax rate is 30%. Accordingly, tax expense is determined by applying the 30% rate to earnings each quarter as follows:

	Pre-tax earnings	Effective tax rate	Tax expense
First quarter	10,000	30%	3,000
Second quarter	10,000	30%	3,000
Third quarter	10,000	30%	3,000
Fourth quarter	10,000	30%	3,000
Annual	40,000		12,000

This result is consistent with the general approach for measuring income tax expense in the interim report, in that any entitlement for relief from current tax due to carried forward losses is determined on an annual basis. Accordingly, its effect is included in the estimate of the average annual income tax rate and not, for example, by allocating all of the unutilised losses against the earnings of the first quarter to give an income tax expense of zero in the first quarter and 4,000 thereafter.

In contrast, the year-to-date approach of IAS 34 means that the benefits of a tax loss carryback are recognised in the interim period in which the related tax loss occurs, [IAS 34.B20], and are not included in the assessment of the estimated average annual tax rate, as shown in Example 41.12 above. This approach is consistent with IAS 12, which requires the benefit of a tax loss that can be carried back to recover current tax already incurred in a previous period to be recognised as an asset. [IAS 12.13]. Therefore, a corresponding reduction of tax expense or increase of tax income is also recognised. [IAS 34.B20].

Where previously unrecognised tax losses are expected to be utilised in full in the current year, it seems intuitive to recognise the recovery of those carried forward losses in the estimate of the average annual tax rate, as shown in Example 41.16 above. Where the level of previously unrecognised tax losses exceeds expected taxable profits for the current year, a deferred tax asset should be recognised for the carried forward losses that are now expected to be utilised, albeit in future years.

The examples in IAS 34 do not show how such a deferred tax asset is created in the interim financial report. In our view, two approaches are acceptable, as shown in Example 41.18 below.

Example 41.18: Tax loss carryforwards in excess of current year expected profits

An entity that reports half-yearly has unutilised operating losses of 75,000 for income tax purposes at the start of the current financial year for which no deferred tax asset has been recognised. At the end of its first interim period, the entity reports a profit before tax of 25,000 and expects to earn a profit of 20,000 before tax in the second half of the year. The entity reassesses the likelihood of generating sufficient profits to utilise its carried forward tax losses and determines that the IAS 12 recognition criteria for a deferred tax asset are satisfied for the full amount of 75,000. Excluding the effect of utilising losses carried forward, the estimated average annual income tax rate is the same as the enacted or substantially enacted rate of 40%.

As at the end of the current financial year the entity expects to have unutilised losses of 30,000 (75,000 carried forward less current year pre-tax profits of 45,000). Using the enacted rate of 40%, a deferred tax asset of 12,000 is recognised at year-end. How is this deferred tax asset recognised in the interim reporting periods?

Approach 1

Under the first approach, the estimate of the average annual effective tax rate includes only those carried forward losses expected to be utilised in the current financial year and a separate deferred tax asset is recognised for those carried forward losses now expected to be utilised in future annual reporting periods.

In the fact pattern above, using 45,000 of the carried forward tax losses gives an average effective annual tax rate of nil, as follows:

Estimation of the annual effective tax rate – Approach 1

Expected annual tax expense before utilising losses carried forward (45,000 @ 40%)	18,000
Tax benefit of utilising carried forward tax losses (45,000 @ 40%)	(18,000)
Expected annual tax expense before the effect of losses carried forward to future annual periods	0
Expected annual effective tax rate	0%
Effect of tax losses carried forward to future periods (75,000 – 45,000 @ 40%)	(12,000)
Tax income to be recognised in the interim period	(12,000)

The remaining tax losses give rise to a deferred tax asset of 12,000, which is recognised in full at the half-year, to give reported profits after tax as follows:

	First half-year	Second half-year	Annual
Profit before income tax	25,000	20,000	45,000
Income tax (expense)/credit			
– at expected annual effective rate	0	0	0
– recognition of deferred tax asset	12,000	0	12,000
Net profit after tax	37,000	20,000	57,000

Approach 2

Under the second approach, the estimate of the average annual effective tax rate reflects the expected recovery of all the previously unutilised tax losses from the beginning of the period in which the assessment of recoverability changed. In the fact pattern above, recognition of the unutilised tax losses gives an average effective annual tax rate of –26.67%, as follows:

Estimation of the annual effective tax rate – Approach 2

Expected annual tax expense before utilising losses carried forward (45,000 @ 40%)	18,000
Tax benefit of recognising unutilised tax losses (75,000 @ 40%)	(30,000)
Expected annual tax credit after recognising unutilised tax losses	(12,000)
Expected annual effective tax rate (–12,000 ÷ 45,000)	–26.67%

This approach results in reported profits after tax as follows:

	First half-year	Second half-year	Annual
Profit before income tax	25,000	20,000	45,000
Income tax (expense)/credit			
– at expected annual effective rate	6,667	5,333	12,000
Net profit after tax	31,667	25,333	57,000

Approach 1 is consistent with the requirements of IAS 12 as it results in recognising the full expected deferred tax asset as soon as it becomes 'probable that taxable profit will be available against which the deductible temporary difference can be utilised'. *[IAS 12.24]*. However, given that IAS 34 does not specifically address this situation, and is unclear about whether the effective tax rate reflects changes in the assessment of the recoverability of carried forward tax losses, we also believe that Approach 2 is acceptable.

9.5.5 Tax credits

IAS 34 also discusses in more detail the treatment of tax credits, which may for example be based on amounts of capital expenditures, exports, or research and development expenditures. Such benefits are often granted and calculated on an annual basis under tax laws and regulations and therefore are generally reflected in the estimated annual effective income tax rate used in the interim report. However, if tax benefits relate to a one-time event, they should be excluded from the estimate of the annual rate and deducted separately from income tax expense in that interim period, in the same way that special tax rates applicable to particular categories of income are not blended into a single effective annual tax rate. Occasionally, some tax credits are more akin to a government grant, which are recognised in the interim period in which they arise. *[IAS 34.B19]*. Similar considerations arise in determining the extent to which the existence of non-taxable income or non-deductible expenditure should be incorporated into the estimate of the weighted-average annual income tax rate expected for the full financial year. This requires the exercise of judgement.

In the Extract 41.30 below, Anheuser-Busch InBev NV/SA explains the reasons for an increase in the effective tax rate in the interim period and the effect of expenditure that is not deductible for tax purposes.

Extract 41.30: Anheuser-Busch InBev NV/SA (30 June 2019)

Notes to the unaudited condensed consolidated interim financial statements [extract]

9. Income taxes [extract]

The total income tax expense for the six-month period ended 30 June 2019 amounts to 1 666m US dollar compared to 1 420m US dollar in 2018. The effective tax rate decreased from 28.9% for the six-month period ended 30 June 2018 to 20.2% for the six-month period ended 30 June 2019. The 2019 effective tax rate was positively impacted by non-taxable gains from derivatives related to the hedging of share-based payment programs and the hedging of the shares issued in a transaction related to the combination with Grupo Modelo and SAB. The 2018 effective tax rate was negatively impacted by non-deductible losses from these derivatives.

9.6 Foreign currency translation

9.6.1 Foreign currency translation gains and losses

An entity measures foreign currency translation gains and losses for interim financial reporting using the same principles that IAS 21 – *The Effects of Changes in Foreign Exchange Rates* – requires at year-end (see Chapter 15). *[IAS 34.B29]*. An entity should use the actual average and closing foreign exchange rates for the interim period (i.e. it may not anticipate changes in foreign exchange rates for the remainder of the current year in translating at an interim date). *[IAS 34.B30]*. Where IAS 21 requires translation adjustments to be recognised as income or expense in the period in which they arise, the same approach should be used in the interim report. An entity should not defer some foreign currency translation adjustments at an interim date, even if it expects the adjustment to reverse before year-end. *[IAS 34.B31]*.

9.6.2 Interim financial reporting in hyperinflationary economies

Interim financial reports in hyperinflationary economies are prepared using the same principles as at year-end. *[IAS 34.B32]*. IAS 29 – *Financial Reporting in Hyperinflationary Economies* – requires that the financial statements of an entity that reports in the currency of a hyperinflationary economy be stated in terms of the measuring unit current at the end of the reporting period, and the gain or loss on the net monetary position be included in net income. In addition, comparative financial data reported for prior periods should be restated to the current measuring unit (see Chapter 16). *[IAS 34.B33]*. As shown in Examples 41.4 and 41.5 above, IAS 34 requires an interim report to contain many components, which are all restated at every interim reporting date.

The measuring unit used is the same as that as of the end of the interim period, with the resulting gain or loss on the net monetary position included in that period's net income. An entity may not annualise the recognition of gains or losses, nor may it estimate an annual inflation rate in preparing an interim financial report in a hyperinflationary economy. *[IAS 34.B34]*. See Chapter 16 at 10.1.

IAS 29 applies from the beginning of the reporting period in which an entity identifies the existence of hyperinflation in the country in whose currency it reports. *[IAS 29.4]*. Accordingly, for interim reporting purposes, IAS 29 should be applied from the beginning of the interim period in which the hyperinflation is identified. The Interpretations Committee has clarified that adoption of IAS 29 should be fully retrospective, by applying its requirements as if the economy had always been hyperinflationary (see Chapter 16 at 9). *[IFRIC 7.3]*.

It is less obvious how a parent, which does not operate in a hyperinflationary economy, should account for the restatement of a subsidiary that operates in an economy that becomes hyperinflationary in the current reporting period when incorporating it within its consolidated financial statements.

This issue has been clarified by paragraph 42(b) of IAS 21 which specifically prohibits restatement of comparative figures when the reporting currency is not hyperinflationary. This means that when the financial statements of a hyperinflationary subsidiary are translated into the non-hyperinflationary reporting currency of the parent, the comparative amounts are not adjusted.

Notwithstanding the above, some argue that in interim period reports of the subsequent year, the parent should adjust its comparative information for the corresponding interim periods which are part of the (first) full financial year affected by hyperinflation. This is because comparative interim information had been part of the full year financial statements, which were adjusted for hyperinflation.

In our view, the parent is allowed, but not required, to adjust the comparative interim information that relates to the first full financial year affected by hyperinflation, as illustrated in the example below:

Example 41.19: **Accounting by the parent when a hyperinflationary subsidiary first applies IAS 29**

A parent with 31 December year-end owns a subsidiary, whose functional currency is considered hyperinflationary from 31 July 2020 onwards. In preparing its interim consolidated financial statements for the quarter ended 31 March 2021, the parent consolidates this subsidiary in both the current and comparative interim periods.

In our view the parent is allowed, but not required, to adjust the comparative interim information (for the quarter ended 31 March 2020) in its 31 March 2021 interim financial report.

Whilst IAS 34 and IAS 29 are silent on the matter, a consequence of this approach suggests that when an economy stops being hyperinflationary, the entity should stop applying the requirements of IAS 29 during that interim period. However, in practice, it is difficult to determine when an economy stops being hyperinflationary. The characteristics indicating restored confidence in an economy (such as the population ceasing to store wealth in a more stable foreign currency) change gradually as sufficient time elapses to indicate that the three-year cumulative inflation rate is likely to stay below 100%. When the exit from hyperinflation can reasonably be identified, an entity should stop applying IAS 29 in that interim period. Prior interim periods should not be restated; instead, the entity should treat the amounts expressed in the measuring unit current as at the end of the previous reporting period as the basis for the carrying amounts in its subsequent interim reports. *[IAS 29.38]*, (see Chapter 16 at 10.2).

9.7 Provisions, contingencies and accruals for other costs

9.7.1 Provisions

IAS 34 requires an entity to apply the same criteria for recognising and measuring a provision at an interim date as it would at year-end. *[IAS 34.B4]*. Hence, an entity should recognise a provision when it has no realistic alternative but to transfer economic benefits because of an event that has created a legal or constructive obligation. *[IAS 34.B3]*. The standard emphasises that the existence or non-existence of an obligation to transfer benefits is a question of fact and does not depend on the length of the reporting period. *[IAS 34.B4]*. Also, as noted at 8.1.1 above, measurement on a year-to-date basis requires that a liability at the end of an interim reporting period must represent an existing obligation at that date, just as it must at the end of an annual reporting period. *[IAS 34.32]*. Entities should not anticipate obligations that are expected to arise later in the annual reporting period.

The obligation is adjusted upward or downward at each interim reporting date, if the entity's best estimate of the amount of the obligation changes. The standard states that any corresponding loss or gain should normally be recognised in profit or loss. *[IAS 34.B3]*. However, an entity applying IFRIC 1 – *Changes in Existing Decommissioning, Restoration and Similar Liabilities* – might instead need to adjust the carrying amount of the corresponding asset rather than recognise a gain or loss. *[IFRIC 1.4-6]*.

9.7.2 Other planned but irregularly occurring costs

Many entities budget for costs that they expect to incur irregularly during the year, such as advertising campaigns, employee training and charitable contributions. Even though these costs are planned and expected to recur annually, they tend to be discretionary in nature. Therefore, it is generally not appropriate to recognise an obligation at the end of an interim financial reporting period for such costs that are not yet incurred, as they do not meet the definition of a liability. *[IAS 34.B11]*.

As discussed at 8.2.2 above, IAS 34 prohibits the recognition or deferral of costs incurred unevenly throughout the year at the interim date if recognition or deferral would be inappropriate at year-end. *[IAS 34.39]*. Accordingly, such costs should be recognised as they are incurred and an entity should not recognise provisions or accruals in the interim report to adjust these costs to their budgeted amount.

In Extract 41.31 below, Coca-Cola HBC AG, in its June 2018 interim report, explains the reasons certain fixed costs are not significantly affected by business seasonality.

> *Extract 41.31: Coca-Cola HBC AG (Interim ended June 2018)*
>
> Selected explanatory notes to the condensed consolidated interim financial statements (unaudited) [extract]
>
> 1. Basis of preparation and accounting policies [extract]
>
> Basis of preparation [extract]
>
> Operating results for the first half of 2018 are not indicative of the results that may be expected for the year ending 31 December 2018 because of business seasonality. Business seasonality results from higher unit sales of the Group's products in the warmer months of the year. The Group's methods of accounting for fixed costs such as depreciation and interest expense are not significantly affected by business seasonality.

9.7.3 Major planned periodic maintenance or overhaul

The cost of periodic maintenance, a planned major overhaul, or other seasonal expenditures expected to occur after the interim reporting date should not be recognised for interim reporting purposes unless an event before the end of the interim period causes the entity to have a legal or constructive obligation. The mere intention or necessity to incur expenditures in the future is not sufficient to recognise an obligation as at the interim reporting date. *[IAS 34.B2]*. Similarly, an entity may not defer and amortise such costs if they are incurred early in the year, but do not satisfy the criteria for recognition as an asset as at the interim reporting date.

9.7.4 Variable lease payments

Variable lease payments can create legal or constructive obligations that are recognised as liabilities even though such amounts are not included in the lease liability in the period. If a lease includes variable payments based on achieving a certain level of annual sales (or annual use of the asset), an obligation can arise in an interim period before the required level of annual sales (or usage) is achieved. If the entity expects to achieve the required level of annual sales (or usage), it should recognise a liability as it has no realistic alternative but to make the future lease payment. *[IAS 34.B7]*.

9.7.5 Levies charged by public authorities

When governments or other public authorities impose levies on entities in relation to their activities, as opposed to income taxes, it is not always clear when the liability to pay a levy arises and a provision should be recognised. IFRIC 21 – *Levies* – addresses this issue. The scope of the Interpretation is limited to provisions within the scope of IAS 37 and specifically need not be applied to emissions trading schemes. *[IFRIC 21.2, 6]*.

The Interpretation requires that for an activity within its scope, an entity should recognise a liability for a levy only when the activity that triggers payment, as identified by the relevant legislation, occurs. *[IFRIC 21.8]*. The Interpretation states that neither a constructive nor a present obligation arises as a result of being economically compelled to continue operating; or from any implication of continuing operations in the future arising from the use of the going concern assumption in the preparation of financial statements (see Chapter 26 at 6.8). *[IFRIC 21.9-10]*.

The Interpretation states that the same recognition principles should be applied in the interim financial statements. Therefore, a liability for any levy expense should not be anticipated if there is no present obligation to pay the levy at the end of the interim reporting period. Similarly, a liability should not be deferred if a present obligation to pay the levy exists at the end of the interim period. *[IFRIC 21.31]*.

This is relatively simple when a levy is triggered on a specific day or when a specific event occurs. When a levy is triggered progressively, for example as the entity generates revenues, the levy is accrued over time. At any time in the year, the entity would have a present obligation to pay an amount of levy that would be based on revenues generated to that date and recognises a liability and an expense on that basis. *[IFRIC 21.11]*.

The following examples illustrate the above principles in a number of scenarios and demonstrate how the appropriate accounting treatment has to reflect the specific facts and circumstances that apply in determining an entity's obligation to pay the levy in line with the relevant legislation.

When the legislation provides that a levy is triggered by an entity operating in a market only at the end of the annual reporting period, no liability is recognised until the last day of the annual reporting period. No amount is recognised before that date in anticipation of the entity still operating in the market. This means that in the interim financial reports for that year, no liability for the levy expense is recognised. Only if the entity reports for the last quarter of that year would the expenditure appear in an interim report. *[IFRIC 21.IE1 Example 2]*.

If a levy is triggered in full as soon as the entity commences generating revenues, the liability is recognised in full on the first day that the entity commences generating revenue. In this case, the entity does not defer any expense and amortise this amount over the year or otherwise allocate it to subsequent interim periods. The example below illustrates this situation. *[IFRIC 21.IE1 Example 2]*.

Example 41.20: A levy is triggered in full as soon as the entity generates revenue

An entity has a calendar year end. In accordance with legislation, a levy is triggered in full as soon as the entity generates revenue in 2021. The amount of the levy is determined by reference to revenue generated by the entity in 2020. The entity generated revenue in 2020 and starts to generate revenue in 2021 on 3 January 2021.

In this example, the liability is recognised in full on 3 January 2021 because the obligating event, as identified by the legislation, is the first generation of revenue in 2021. The generation of revenue in 2020 is necessary, but not sufficient, to create a present obligation to pay a levy. Before 3 January 2021, the entity has no obligation. In other words, the activity that triggers the payment of the levy as identified by the legislation is the first generation of revenue at a point in time in 2021.

The generation of revenues in 2020 is not the activity that triggers the payment of the levy. The amount of revenue generated in 2020 only affects the measurement of the liability.

In the interim financial report, because the liability is recognised in full on 3 January 2021, the expense is recognised in full in the first interim period of 2021. The expense should not be deferred until subsequent interim periods and shall not be anticipated in previous interim periods.

Another situation is when a levy is triggered in full as soon as the entity generates revenue from an activity above a certain annual threshold is illustrated in the following example. *[IFRIC 21.IE1 Example 4].*

Example 41.21: A levy is triggered in full as soon as the entity generates revenue from a certain activity above an annual threshold, which is reduced pro rata *when the entity ceases participation in that activity during the year*

A bank has a calendar year end. In accordance with legislation, a bank levy is triggered only if the bank generated revenue above the annual threshold of CU10 million in 2021. The amount of the levy payable is calculated based on 0.1% of the annual threshold of CU10 million and is assessed as at 31 December every year. i.e. Annual revenue below CU10 million attracts no levy and revenue of at least CU10 million attracts a levy of CU10,000 (0.1% × CU10 million). However, if the bank ceases operations during the year, the annual threshold of CU10 million will then be reduced *pro rata*, based on the number of days the bank was in operation during the year and the levy payable will then be based on 0.1% of the pro-rated annual threshold.

The owners of the bank ceased operation with effect from 1 July 2021. As at 31 March 2021 and 30 June 2021, the revenue generated amounted to CU4 million and CU8 million, respectively.

In this example, the liability is recognised in the interim financial report as follows:

31 March 2021:	Nil
30 June 2021:	Nil
30 September 2021:	CU5,000 (CU10 million × (6/12 months) × 0.1%)
31 December 2021:	CU5,000 (CU10 million × (6/12 months) × 0.1%)

Based on discussions by the IFRS Interpretations Committee during their March 2015 meeting, the threshold for determining the entity's liability would only be reduced (or pro-rated) if, and only if, the entity stops the relevant activity before the end of the annual assessment period.[7] This means that the pro-rated annual threshold would only apply from the date the entity stops the relevant activity in the market.

At 31 March 2021 and 30 June 2021, the bank has not ceased operations and the annual threshold remains at CU10 million. Since the revenue generated as at 31 March 2021 and 30 June 2021 did not meet the annual threshold, no liability is recognised under IFRIC 21 on both dates.

In contrast, the bank ceased operation from 1 July 2021. Hence, the annual threshold would have been pro-rated and reduced to CU5 million at that date.

For the quarters as at 30 September and 31 December 2021 a liability of CU5,000 should thus be recognised accordingly.

In many countries, property taxes are levied by municipalities or other local government bodies on the owner of a property. Such taxes are relevant and may be material to entities in certain sectors (e.g. real estate). Even within a single jurisdiction, there could be several different property tax mechanisms. Generally, each property tax arrangement must be assessed on its own merits. To facilitate such assessments, we have explored some illustrative fact patterns of property tax mechanisms in the following examples:

Example 41.22: A levy is triggered in full as soon as the entity holds the property at a specified date

In accordance with the legislation, property tax is imposed on the registered owner of the property as at 1 April each year. The amount payable is calculated based on 0.1% of the appraised value estimated by the tax authorities as at 1 April each year. Payments are to be made in arrears in instalments on June, September, December and March month-end dates and any unpaid instalments remain as the liability of the registered owner of the property as at 1 April.

The law also states that if the property is sold during the year, there will be no refund from the government to the seller. The new property owner will only be liable to pay the property tax on 1 April of the coming year, subsequent to the date of purchase.

An entity has a calendar year-end and prepares quarterly interim financial reports. It holds a property as at 1 April 2021, which has an appraised value of CU50 million. On 30 June 2021, it sold the property to another entity.

In this example, the liability is recognised in the interim financial report as follows:

31 March 2021:	Nil, since the obligating event is not until 1 April, assuming that all previous year instalments have been paid on time
1 April 2021:	CU50,000 (CU50 million × 0.1%), i.e. the liability is recognised in full

For the subsequent interim period's reports as at 30 June, 30 September and 31 December, the liability recognised in the statement of financial position would be CU50,000 less the instalment payments made during the year.

If in a variation to the above fact pattern, the seller is able to obtain a refund of a proportionate share of the paid property tax (i.e. CU37,500) from the buyer of the property and this refund will form part of the sales price of the property based on the sales contract between the buyer and the seller, it would not change the accounting for the levy under IFRIC 21.

Yet another situation arises where a levy is triggered progressively.

Example 41.23: A levy is triggered progressively as the entity holds the asset through a specified period of time

In accordance with the legislation, property tax is imposed on the registered owner of the property as at 1 April each year. The amount payable is calculated based on 0.1% of the appraised value estimated by the tax authorities as at 1 April each year. Payments are to be made in instalments at every March, June, September and December month-end.

The law does not explicitly state that the property tax relates to a period of time. However, if the property is sold during the year, the amount of property tax will be pro-rated for the period from 1 April to the date of sale, and any excess will be refunded to the entity by the government. The new property owner will only be liable to pay the property tax upon the date of purchase, for the period from the date of purchase.

An entity has a calendar year-end and prepares quarterly interim financial reports. It holds a property as at 1 April 2021 to 31 March 2022, which has an appraised value of CU50 million as at 1 April 2021. Prior to 1 April 2021 the entity did not hold any property. For simplicity, assume that the appraised value does not change year on year.

In this example, although the law does not explicitly state that the property tax relates to the entity holding the property over a period of time, it is evident that the obligating event occurs rateably over the 12-month period from 1 April to 31 March. This is because the law allows for a pro-rated refund to be given to the entity for the period whereby the entity no longer holds the property. This implies that it is a time-based progressive levy.

As such, the levy is triggered over a 12-month period and the liability is recognised rateably over the 12-month period. In contrast with Example 41.21, it is not the ownership of the property at a specified date that is the obligating even. Rather, it is the continued holding of the property throughout the period that gives rise to the obligating event.

As such, the liability is recognised in the interim report as follows:

31 March 2021:	Nil
30 June 2021:	CU12,500 (CU50,000 divided by 4), less any instalment payments made
30 September 2021:	CU25,000 (cumulative portion of the prior quarter and current quarter), less any instalment payments made
31 December 2021:	CU37,500 (cumulative portion of the prior two quarters and current quarter), less any instalment payments made
31 March 2022:	CU50,000 (cumulative portion of the prior three quarter and current quarter), less any instalment payments made

The impact on interim reports for the various types of levies is summarised below:

Illustrative examples	Obligating event	Recognition of liability in interim reports
Levy triggered progressively as revenue is generated in specified period	Generation of revenue in the specified period	Recognise progressively based on revenue generated
Levy triggered in full as soon as revenue is generated in one period, based on revenues from a previous period	First generation of revenue in subsequent period	Recognise only if first revenue generated in interim period
Levy triggered in full if entity operates as a bank at the end of the annual reporting period	Operating as a bank at the end of the reporting period	Recognise only if interim period includes the last day of the annual reporting period specified in the legislation. Otherwise, a provision would not be permitted to be recognised in interim reports
Levy triggered if revenues are above a minimum specified threshold (e.g. when a certain level of revenue has been achieved)	Reaching the specified minimum threshold	Recognise only where the minimum threshold has been met or exceeded during the interim period. Otherwise, a provision would not be permitted to be recognised in interim reports

These requirements illustrate what is meant by the concept of the 'year-to-date' basis in IAS 34 and discussed at 8 above.

9.8 Earnings per share

Earnings per share (EPS) in an interim period is computed in the same way as for annual periods. However, IAS 33 – *Earnings per Share* – does not allow diluted EPS of a prior period to be restated for subsequent changes in the assumptions used in those EPS calculations. *[IAS 33.65]*. This approach might be perceived as inconsistent to the year-to-date approach which should be followed for computing EPS for an interim period. For example, if an entity, reporting quarterly, computes diluted EPS in its first quarter financial statements, it cannot restate the reported diluted EPS subsequently for any changes in the assumptions used. However, following a year-to-date approach, the entity should consider the revised assumptions to compute the diluted EPS for the six months in its second quarter financial statements, which, in this case would not be the sum of its diluted EPS for first quarter and the second quarter.

10 USE OF ESTIMATES

IAS 34 requires that the measurement procedures followed in an interim financial report should be designed to ensure that the resulting information is reliable and that all material financial information that is relevant to an understanding of the financial position or performance of the entity is appropriately disclosed. Whilst estimation is necessary in both interim and annual financial statements, the standard recognises that preparing interim financial reports generally requires greater use of estimates than at year-end. *[IAS 34.41]*. Because the standard accepts a higher degree of estimation by the entity, the measurement of assets and liabilities at an interim date may involve less use of outside experts in determining amounts for items such as provisions, contingencies, pensions or non-current assets revalued at fair values. Reliable measurement of such amounts may simply involve updating the previously reported year-end position. The procedures may be less rigorous than those at year-end. The example below is based on Appendix C to IAS 34. *[IAS 34.42]*.

Example 41.24: Use of estimates

Inventories	Full stock-taking and valuation procedures may not be required for inventories at interim dates, although it may be done at year-end. It may be sufficient to make estimates at interim dates based on sales margins.
Classifications of current and non-current assets and liabilities	Entities may do a more thorough investigation for classifying assets and liabilities as current or non-current at annual reporting dates than at interim dates.
Provisions	Determining the appropriate provision (such as a provision for warranties, environmental costs, and site restoration costs) may be complex and often costly and time-consuming. Entities sometimes engage outside experts to assist in the annual calculations. Making similar estimates at interim dates often entails updating of the prior annual provision rather than the engaging of outside experts to do a new calculation.
Pensions	IAS 19 requires an entity to determine the present value of defined benefit obligations and the fair value of plan assets at the end of each reporting period and encourages an entity to involve a professionally qualified actuary in measurement of the obligations. As discussed at 9.3.3 above, market values of plan assets as at the interim reporting date should be available without recourse to an actuary, and reliable measurement of defined benefit obligations for interim reporting purposes can often be extrapolated from the latest actuarial valuation.

Income taxes	Entities may calculate income tax expense and deferred income tax liability at annual dates by applying the tax rate for each individual jurisdiction to measures of income for each jurisdiction. Paragraph 14 of Appendix B (see 9.5.1 above) acknowledges that while that degree of precision is desirable at interim reporting dates as well, it may not be achievable in all cases, and a weighted-average of rates across jurisdictions or across categories of income is used if it is a reasonable approximation of the effect of using more specific rates.
Contingencies	The measurement of contingencies may involve the opinions of legal experts or other advisers. Formal reports from independent experts are sometimes obtained for contingencies. Such opinions about litigation, claims, assessments, and other contingencies and uncertainties may or may not also be needed at interim dates.
Revaluations and fair value accounting	IAS 16 allows an entity to choose as its accounting policy the revaluation model whereby items of property, plant and equipment are revalued to fair value. Similarly, IAS 40 – *Investment Property* – requires an entity to measure the fair value of investment property. An entity should revalue at the end of the interim reporting period, but may choose not to rely on professionally qualified valuers to the extent that is required at year-end.
Intercompany reconciliations	Some intercompany balances that are reconciled on a detailed level in preparing consolidated financial statements at year-end might be reconciled at a less detailed level in preparing consolidated financial statements at an interim date.
Specialised industries	Because of complexity, costliness, and time, interim period measurements in specialised industries might be less precise than at year-end. An example is calculation of insurance reserves by insurance companies.

Attention is given to items that are recognised at fair value. Although an entity is not required to use professionally qualified valuers at interim reporting dates, and may only update the previous year-end position, the entity is required to recognise impairments in the proper interim period.

11 EFFECTIVE DATES AND TRANSITIONAL RULES

11.1 First-time presentation of interim reports complying with IAS 34

IAS 34 does not contain any general transitional rules. Therefore, an existing IFRS reporting entity must apply the requirements of IAS 34 in full and without any transitional relief when it first chooses (or is required) to publish an interim financial report prepared under IFRS.

For example, an entity that has already published annual financial statements prepared under IFRS and either chooses (or is required) to prepare interim financial reports in compliance with IAS 34 must present all the information required by the standard for the current interim period, cumulatively for the current year-to-date, and for comparable periods (current and year-to-date) of the preceding year. *[IAS 34.20]*. The absence of any transitional provisions requires such entities to restate previously reported interim financial information to comply with IAS 34 and to present information relating to comparative interim periods, such as in respect of segment disclosures or in relation to asset write-downs and reversals thereof, which might not previously have been reported.

11.1.1 Condensed financial statements in the year of incorporation or when an entity converts from its local GAAP to IFRS

The standard defines 'interim period' as a financial reporting period shorter than a full financial year, [IAS 34.4], and requires the format of condensed financial statements for an interim period to include each of the headings and subtotals that were included in the entity's most recent annual financial statements. [IAS 34.10].

However, IAS 34 provides no guidance for an entity that either is required or chooses to issue interim financial statements before it has prepared a set of IFRS compliant annual financial statements. This situation might arise in the entity's first year of its existence or in the year in which the entity converts from its local GAAP to IFRS. Whilst the standard does not prohibit the entity from preparing a condensed set of interim financial statements, it does not specify how an entity would interpret the minimum disclosure requirements of IAS 34 when there are no annual financial statements to refer to.

The entity should consider making additional disclosures to recognise that a user of this first set of interim financial statements does not have the access otherwise assumed by the standard to the most recent annual financial report of the entity. Accordingly, the explanation of significant events and transactions and changes in financial position in the period should be more detailed than the update normally expected in IAS 34. [IAS 34.15]. In the absence of any specific regulatory requirements to which the entity is subject, the following are examples of additional considerations that would apply:

- since it is not possible to make a statement that the same accounting policies and methods of computation have been applied, [IAS 34.16A(a)], the entity should disclose all those accounting policies and methods of computation in the same level of detail as it would in a set of annual financial statements. When the entity issues interim reports on a quarterly basis, the first quarter interim report should provide the abovementioned details; subsequent quarterly reports could refer to the details included in the first quarter report;

- similarly, the disclosure of the nature and amount of changes in estimates of amounts reported in prior periods will have to go into more detail than just the changes normally required to be disclosed; [IAS 34.16A(d)]

- mere disclosure of transfers between levels of the fair value hierarchy used in measuring the fair value of financial instruments, [IAS 34.15B(k)], would not be meaningful unless put in the context of how those fair values are determined (e.g. methods used, any assumptions applied) and providing a detailed classification of all such financial instrument measurements using fair value hierarchy, based on the significance of the inputs used;

- rather than disclosing changes in the basis of segmentation or in the basis of measurement of segment profit and loss, [IAS 34.16A(g)(v)], a full description will be

- necessary, as will the disclosure of segment assets and liabilities, *[IAS 34.16A(g)(iv)]*, where such information is required to be disclosed in the annual financial statements; *[IAS 34.16A(g)]*
- more extensive disclosure than simply the changes since the last report date will be required for contingent liabilities and contingent assets; *[IAS 34.15B(m)]* and
- in the absence of a complete set of annual financial statements complying with IFRS, the entity should include each of the headings and subtotals in the condensed financial statements that it would expect to include in its first financial statements prepared under IFRS.

Entities that have converted from local GAAP to IFRS and have not yet presented IFRS annual financial statements are subject to additional requirements under IFRS 1 – *First-time Adoption of International Financial Reporting Standards* – when presenting interim reports in accordance with IAS 34. Such requirements are discussed in detail in Chapter 5 at 6.6.

References

1 *IFRIC Update*, March 2014.
2 IFRS Practice Statement 2 – *Making Materiality Judgements*, IASB, September 2017, para. 85.
3 IFRS Practice Statement 2, para. 87.
4 IFRS Practice Statement 2, para. 88.
5 Report – *Enforcement and Regulatory Activities of Accounting Enforcers in 2017*, ESMA, 03 April 2018, para. 63.
6 Division of Corporation Finance – Financial Reporting Manual, SEC, *1500: Interim Period Reporting Considerations (All Filings)*.
7 *IFRIC Update*, March 2014.

Chapter 42   Agriculture

1 INTRODUCTION 3273
2 OBJECTIVE, DEFINITIONS AND SCOPE 3273
    2.1 Objective 3273
    2.2 Definitions 3274
        2.2.1 Agriculture-related definitions 3274
            2.2.1.A Definition of bearer plants 3275
        2.2.2 General definitions 3277
    2.3 Scope 3277
        2.3.1 Biological assets outside the scope of IAS 41 3278
        2.3.2 Agricultural produce before and after harvest 3278
        2.3.3 Bearer plants and produce growing on a bearer plant 3279
        2.3.4 Products that are the result of processing after harvest 3279
        2.3.5 Leases of biological assets (excluding bearer plants) 3279
            2.3.5.A Leases of biological assets (excluding bearer plants) – lessee accounting 3280
            2.3.5.B Leases of biological assets (excluding bearer plants) – lessor accounting 3280
        2.3.6 Concessions 3281
3 RECOGNITION AND MEASUREMENT PRINCIPLES 3281
    3.1 Recognition 3281
        3.1.1 Control 3281
    3.2 Measurement 3282
        3.2.1 Biological assets within the scope of IAS 41 3282
            3.2.1.A Initial and subsequent measurement 3282
            3.2.1.B Subsequent expenditure 3282
        3.2.2 Agricultural produce 3283
        3.2.3 Requirements for produce growing on a bearer plant 3284
            3.2.3.A Requirements for bearer plants in the scope of IAS 16 3284

			3.2.3.B	Requirements for agricultural produce growing on bearer plants	3288
		3.2.4	Gains and losses		3289
		3.2.5	Inability to measure fair value reliably		3290
			3.2.5.A	Rebutting the presumption	3290
			3.2.5.B	The cost model	3292
	3.3	Government grants			3293
4	MEASURING FAIR VALUE LESS COSTS TO SELL				3294
	4.1	The interaction between IAS 41 and IFRS 13			3294
	4.2	Establishing what to measure			3295
		4.2.1	Unit of account		3295
		4.2.2	Grouping of assets		3295
	4.3	When to measure fair value			3295
	4.4	Determining costs to sell			3295
	4.5	Measuring fair value: IAS 41-specific requirements			3296
		4.5.1	Use of external independent valuers		3296
		4.5.2	Obligation to re-establish a biological asset after harvest		3296
		4.5.3	Forward sales contracts		3297
		4.5.4	Onerous contracts		3297
		4.5.5	Financing cash flows and taxation		3298
	4.6	Measuring fair value: overview of IFRS 13's requirements			3298
		4.6.1	The fair value measurement framework		3298
		4.6.2	Highest and best use and valuation premise		3299
			4.6.2.A	Biological assets attached to land	3300
		4.6.3	Selecting appropriate assumptions		3303
			4.6.3.A	Condition and location	3304
		4.6.4	Valuation techniques in IFRS 13		3305
			4.6.4.A	Cost as an approximation of fair value	3305
	4.7	The problem of measuring fair value for part-grown or immature biological assets			3306
5	DISCLOSURE				3308
	5.1	General			3308
		5.1.1	Statement of financial position		3308
			5.1.1.A	Current versus non-current classification	3309
			5.1.1.B	Bearer plants	3310
		5.1.2	Income statement		3313
		5.1.3	Groups of biological assets		3315
		5.1.4	Other disclosures		3316
	5.2	Fair value measurement disclosures			3320

| 5.3 | Additional disclosures if fair value cannot be measured reliably | 3322 |
| 5.4 | Government grants | 3323 |

List of examples

Example 42.1:	Conditional government grants	3294
Example 42.2:	Assets attached to land	3301
Example 42.3:	Presentation of biological assets in the statement of financial position	3308
Example 42.4:	Physical change and price change	3317

Chapter 42   Agriculture

1 INTRODUCTION

IAS 41 – *Agriculture* – prescribes the accounting treatment for most agricultural activity, from the initial recognition of a biological asset to the harvest of agricultural produce.

IAS 41 applies to some, but not all biological assets. In particular, IAS 41 excludes bearer plants, as defined, from its scope. Instead, they are within the scope of IAS 16 – *Property, Plant and Equipment* – and are subject to all of the requirements therein. However, agricultural produce growing on bearer plants (e.g. fruit growing on a tree) are within the scope of IAS 41 and are treated as biological assets.

Practical difficulties may arise when determining which assets are within the scope of the standard, particularly for arrangements that involve leases or concessions. Entities may also find it particularly challenging to apply two different measurement models under two different standards to bearer plants, as defined, and the produce growing thereon. However, it is IAS 41's application of the fair value model that can be the most challenging and contentious.

For assets that are in-scope, IAS 41 requires the application of the fair value model to animals and plant life alike, with limited relief. Under this approach, a market price for an animal or part-grown crop is presumed to exist (or is presumed to be reliably measurable if there is no such market price) and the animal or part-grown crop must be valued at this price in the entity's financial statements. The fair value model is applied to all biological assets that are in-scope, regardless of whether they are consumed as part of the agricultural activity (consumable biological assets) or not (bearer biological assets).

This chapter discusses the requirements of IAS 41, along with the requirements for bearer plants under IAS 16.

2 OBJECTIVE, DEFINITIONS AND SCOPE

2.1 Objective

The stated objective of IAS 41 is to 'prescribe the accounting treatment and disclosures related to agricultural activity'. *[IAS 41 Objective]*.

2.2 Definitions

2.2.1 Agriculture-related definitions

IAS 41 defines *agricultural activity* as 'the management by an entity of the biological transformation and harvest of biological assets for sale or for conversion into agricultural produce or into additional biological assets'. *[IAS 41.5]*.

The standard states that 'agricultural activity' covers a wide range of activities, e.g. 'raising livestock, forestry, annual or perennial cropping, cultivating orchards and plantations, floriculture, and aquaculture (including fish farming)'. *[IAS 41.6]*. Nevertheless, these agricultural activities have certain common features:

'(a) *Capability to change.* Living animals and plants are capable of biological transformation;

(b) *Management of change.* Management facilitates biological transformation by enhancing, or at least stabilising, conditions necessary for the process to take place (for example, nutrient levels, moisture, temperature, fertility, and light). Such management distinguishes agricultural activity from other activities. For example, harvesting from unmanaged sources (such as ocean fishing and deforestation) is not agricultural activity; and

(c) *Measurement of change.* The change in quality (for example, genetic merit, density, ripeness, fat cover, protein content, and fibre strength) or quantity (for example, progeny, weight, cubic metres, fibre length or diameter, and number of buds) brought about by biological transformation or harvest is measured and monitored as a routine management function.' *[IAS 41.6]*.

Biological transformation under IAS 41 'comprises the processes of growth, degeneration, production, and procreation that cause qualitative or quantitative changes in a biological asset'. *[IAS 41.5]*. The standard explains that biological transformation results in the following types of outcomes:

'(a) asset changes through (i) growth (an increase in quantity or improvement in quality of an animal or plant), (ii) degeneration (a decrease in the quantity or deterioration in quality of an animal or plant), or (iii) procreation (creation of additional living animals or plants); or

(b) production of agricultural produce such as latex, tea leaf, wool, and milk.' *[IAS 41.7]*.

IAS 41 defines the following additional terms that are used throughout the standard: *[IAS 41.5]*

- A *biological asset* is a living animal or plant.
- A *group of biological assets* is an aggregation of similar living animals or plants.
- *Agricultural produce* is the harvested product of the entity's biological assets.
- *Harvest* is the detachment of produce from a biological asset or the cessation of a biological asset's life processes.
- *Costs to sell* are the incremental costs directly attributable to the disposal of an asset excluding finance costs and income taxes.

The standard provides examples to illustrate the above definitions. In addition to providing these examples, the standard notes that some of the plants mentioned in the table may meet the definition of bearer plants and, therefore, be within the scope of IAS 16. However, the produce growing on such plants is within the scope of IAS 41 (see 2.2.1.A and 2.3.3 below) and is considered a biological asset. *[IAS 41.5C]*. Figure 42.1 below is based on those examples, but has been modified to provide examples of possible bearer plants and produce growing on those plants: *[IAS 41.4]*

Figure 42.1: Examples of biological assets (including possible bearer plants), agricultural produce and products that are the result of processing after harvest

Biological assets that may meet the definition of a bearer plant	Biological assets (including produce growing on a bearer plant)	Agricultural produce	Products that are the result of processing after harvest
	Sheep	Wool	Yarn, carpet
	Trees in a timber plantation	Felled trees	Logs, lumber
	Dairy cattle	Milk	Cheese
	Pigs	Carcass	Sausages, cured hams
Cotton plants	Growing cotton	Harvested cotton	Thread, clothing
Sugar-cane roots	Growing sugarcane	Harvested cane	Sugar
Tobacco plants	Leaves on the tobacco plants	Picked leaves	Cured tobacco
Tea bushes	Leaves on the tea bushes	Picked leaves	Tea
Grape vines	Grapes on the vines	Picked grapes	Wine
Fruit trees	Fruit on the trees	Picked fruit	Processed fruit
Oil palms	Growing fruit	Picked fruit	Palm oil
Rubber trees	Latex	Harvested latex	Rubber products

2.2.1.A   Definition of bearer plants

A bearer plant is defined as 'a living plant that:

(a) is used in the production or supply of agricultural produce;

(b) is expected to bear produce for more than one period; and

(c) has a remote likelihood of being sold as agricultural produce, except for incidental scrap sales'. *[IAS 41.5]*.

All of the above criteria need to be met for a plant to be considered a bearer plant.

The definition captures plants that would intuitively be considered to be bearers, for instance, grape vines. Some plants that may appear to be consumable, such as the root systems of perennial plants (e.g. sugar cane, bamboo or asparagus), but due to the perennial nature of their root systems, they are expected to meet the definition of a bearer plant.

Annual crops and other plants that are held solely to be harvested as agricultural produce (e.g. many traditional arable crops such as maize, wheat and soya, as well as trees grown for lumber), are explicitly excluded from the definition of a bearer plant. In addition, plants that have a dual use (i.e. plants cultivated to bear agricultural produce, but for which there is more than a remote likelihood that the plant itself will be harvested and sold as agricultural produce, beyond incidental scrap sales) are not bearer plants. *[IAS 41.5A]*. This may be the case when, for example, an entity holds rubber trees to sell both the latex as agricultural produce and the trees as lumber.

Bearer animals, like bearer plants, may be held solely for the produce that they bear. However, when IAS 41 was amended to exclude bearer plants from its scope, bearer animals were explicitly excluded from the amendments and continue to be accounted for under IAS 41 on the basis that the measurement model would become more complex if applied to such assets.

Determining whether an asset meets the definition of a bearer plant may not be entirely intuitive. Careful assessment is, therefore, important. We believe that judgement is needed in the following areas:

- *Used in the production or supply of agricultural produce*

    Judgement may be needed to determine whether a plant is used in the production or supply of agricultural produce, rather than consumed in the process. For example, some plants that are generally thought of as consumable are harvested twice, but with the first harvest having the principal purpose of improving the yield of the second harvest. It is not clear whether the fact that there are two harvests is sufficient to make these plants bearer assets.

    For certain plants, new produce may be capable of being grown from various parts of the plant (e.g. pineapples). For others, the plant itself may be cut back and re-grown. For example, after a harvest of bananas, the banana plant may be cut down to its base and re-grown the next year to produce more bananas. In such situations, judgement may be needed to determine which part of the plant might be the bearer plant (e.g. the banana palm or the base).

- *Expected to bear produce for more than one period*

    The definition of a bearer plant requires that a plant be expected to bear produce for more than one period. It would seem appropriate to think of an annual period in this context. However, the standard does not use this term, so an entity needs to consider if an interim period, a season or a production cycle (i.e. through to harvest) might also be appropriate.

- *Incidental scrap sales*

    Whether the likelihood of the plant being sold as agricultural produce is remote is also a matter of judgement. However, it is intended to be a high hurdle. The standard does allow for the fact that there may be some 'incidental scrap sales', but this term is not defined.

    The standard notes that bearer plants might be cut down and sold as scrap, (e.g. for firewood) at the end of their productive life and states that 'such incidental scrap sales would not prevent the plant from satisfying the definition of a bearer plant'. *[IAS 41.5B]*. However, in the example given in the standard (i.e. firewood), it is reasonably evident that such sales would be 'incidental'. Since no further guidance is given in the standard, entities need to apply judgement in determining what constitutes 'scrap sales' (e.g. would it include ad-hoc sales before the productive life has ended, such as selling trees removed while thinning?). Furthermore, the standard does not clarify at what level sales cease to be incidental and whether this is a qualitative or quantitative assessment. Therefore, judgement may be needed.

In addition to the considerations above, an entity may also need to reassess whether a plant meets the definition of a bearer plant after initial recognition. If a plant initially meets the definition of a bearer plant, but this subsequently changes, would IAS 41 then apply instead of IAS 16? Neither IAS 16 nor IAS 41 address this question or specify how to transfer such assets between IAS 16 and IAS 41 (or *vice versa*).

In the absence of guidance, management will need to apply judgement in developing an accounting policy in these situations. For example, entities might look to the requirements in IAS 40 – *Investment Property* – on transfers of property to, or from investment property for guidance on determining the threshold for when to account for a transfer of bearer plants to biological assets. Paragraph 57 of IAS 40 requires a transfer when there is 'a change in use' and states that '[a] change in use occurs when ... there is evidence of the change in use. In isolation, a change in management's intentions for the use of a property does not provide evidence of a change in use.' *[IAS 40.57]*.

Entities should, however, note that the Basis for Conclusions on IAS 16 states, 'The Board noted that it would be rare for transfers to take place between IAS 16 and IAS 41 for bearer plants, particularly in the light of the Board's decision to change criterion (c) of the definition of a bearer plant to "has a remote likelihood of being sold as agricultural produce, except for incidental scrap sales"'. *[IAS 16.BC83]*.

2.2.2 General definitions

IAS 41 defines the general terms it uses throughout the standard as follows: *[IAS 41.8]*

- *Carrying amount* is the amount at which an asset is recognised in the statement of financial position.
- Government grants are as defined in IAS 20 – *Accounting for Government Grants and Disclosure of Government Assistance* (see Chapter 24).

IFRS 13 – *Fair Value Measurement* – defines fair value as 'the price that would be received to sell an asset or paid to transfer a liability in an orderly transaction between market participants at the measurement date'. *[IAS 41.8, IFRS 13.9]*. Measuring fair value in accordance with IFRS 13 is discussed further at 4 below and in Chapter 14.

2.3 Scope

IAS 41 applies to most biological assets, agricultural produce at the point of harvest and government grants involving biological assets measured at fair value less costs to sell. However, to be within the scope of IAS 41, these items must relate to agricultural activity. *[IAS 41.1]*. As discussed at 2.2.1 above, agricultural activity refers to 'the management by an entity of the biological transformation and harvest of biological assets for sale or for conversion into agricultural produce or into additional biological assets'. *[IAS 41.5]*. It is important to note that this definition does not focus on the primary purpose of holding such assets or the number of sales that may result. In fact, the definition refers to 'sale or conversion'; therefore, an entity need not intend to sell the biological assets or agricultural produce in order for the entity to be undertaking agricultural activity. Furthermore, the standard contemplates an entity applying IAS 41 to assets that it will use itself; the Basis for Conclusions refers, as an example, to an entity accounting for trees as biological assets within IAS 41 when it intends to use the harvested logs in the construction of a building for its own use. *[IAS 41.B8]*.

IAS 41 explicitly excludes the following assets from its scope: *[IAS 41.2]*

- bearer plants (see 2.2.1.A above), which are within the scope of IAS 16 (see Chapter 18), however, produce growing on a bearer plant is still within the scope of IAS 41;
- government grants that relate to bearer plants, to which IAS 20 applies (see Chapter 24);
- land related to agricultural activity, which should be accounted for under either IAS 16 (see Chapter 18) or IAS 40 (see Chapter 19); *[IAS 41.B55-B57]*
- intangible assets related to agricultural activity, for instance the costs of developing new disease resistant crops, which should be accounted for under IAS 38 – *Intangible Assets* (see Chapter 17); *[IAS 41.B58-B60]* and
- right-of-use assets arising from a lease of land related to agricultural activity, which is accounted for under IFRS 16 – *Leases* (see Chapter 23).

2.3.1 Biological assets outside the scope of IAS 41

Biological assets may be outside the scope of IAS 41 when they are not used in agricultural activity. For example, animals in a zoo (or game park) that does not have an active breeding programme and rarely sells any animals or animal products would be outside the scope of the standard. Another example is activities in the pharmaceutical industry that involve the culture of bacteria. Such activity would not fall within the scope of IAS 41. While the bacteria may be considered a biological asset, the development of a culture by a pharmaceutical company would not constitute agricultural activity.

Biological assets outside the scope of IAS 41 will normally fall within the scope of either IAS 16 (see Chapter 18) or IAS 2 – *Inventories* (see Chapter 22).

2.3.2 Agricultural produce before and after harvest

IAS 41 applies to agricultural produce (i.e. harvested produce) at the point of harvest only; not prior or subsequent to harvest. Under IAS 41, unharvested agricultural produce is considered to be part of the biological asset from which it will be harvested. Therefore, before harvest, agricultural produce should not be accounted for separately from the biological asset from which it comes. For example, milk is accounted for as part of the dairy cow right up to the moment at which the cow is milked.

Subsequent to harvest, agricultural produce is accounted for under IAS 2 or another standard, if applicable. *[IAS 41.3]*. Under IAS 2, agricultural produce is initially recognised as inventory at its fair value less costs to sell (measured in accordance with IAS 41), which becomes its cost for IAS 2 purposes (see Chapter 22). *[IAS 41.B41, B45]*.

2.3.3 Bearer plants and produce growing on a bearer plant

IAS 41 explicitly excludes bearer plants (see 2.2.1.A above) from its scope; instead IAS 16 applies to these assets (see Chapter 18). However, the produce growing on a bearer plant remains within the scope of IAS 41. *[IAS 41.2(b)]*.

Entities will need to carefully assess which of its plants meet the definition of a bearer plant. This is because the scope exclusion, while focused on the definition of a bearer plant, also affects the accounting treatment for the produce growing on a bearer plant and any related government grants (see 3.3 below).

Bearer plants and their agricultural produce are considered to be two separate assets for accounting purposes (i.e. two units of account), with different measurement models being applied under different standards (see 3.2.3 below for further discussion).

In developing the requirements for bearer plants, the Board noted that bearer plants are held by an entity solely to grow produce over their productive life, similar to plant and equipment and, therefore, do not directly affect the entity's future cash flows. As a result, it decided that bearer plants should be treated as property, plant and equipment in accordance with IAS 16. However, the IASB believes that 'the same argument is not true for the produce growing on the bearer plants that is undergoing biological transformation until it is harvested (for example, grapes growing on a grape vine). The Board observed that the produce is a consumable biological asset growing on the bearer plant and the growth of the produce directly increases the expected revenue from the sale of the produce. Consequently, fair value measurement of the growing produce provides useful information to users of financial statements about future cash flows that an entity is expected to realise'. *[IAS 41.BC4B]*. The Board also indicated that such produce ultimately has a market value on its own, whereas the bearer plants on which it grows generally do not. As such, the Board decided that produce growing on a bearer plant should remain within the scope of IAS 41, which is expected to ensure consistency between produce growing in the ground and produce growing on a bearer plant. *[IAS 41.BC4A-BC4D]*.

2.3.4 Products that are the result of processing after harvest

IAS 41 does not deal with the processing of agricultural produce after harvest. The standard makes it clear that, even if the processing is considered 'a logical and natural extension of agricultural activity, and the events taking place ... bear some similarity to biological transformation, such processing is not included within the definition of agricultural activity'. *[IAS 41.3]*. For example, the process of brewing beer – in which yeast (a fungus) converts sugars into alcohol – would not meet the definition of agricultural activity in the standard. Similarly, cheese production would fall outside the definition of agricultural activity.

2.3.5 Leases of biological assets (excluding bearer plants)

Leases involving biological assets are common in some jurisdictions, for example, the leasing of a sheep farm, where the lessee rents the farm, including the land, sheep and other assets, tends the sheep and sells the wool. Other examples include leased dairy cows.

2.3.5.A Leases of biological assets (excluding bearer plants) – lessee accounting

IFRS 16 excludes from its scope the lessee accounting for leases of biological assets that are within the scope of IAS 41. *[IFRS 16.3(b)]*. The scope exemption in IFRS 16 does not specify whether the asset would be recognised in accordance with IAS 41; only that it is an asset that would be within the scope of IAS 41. Nor does it explain how an entity would account for its lease liability since it is outside the scope of IFRS 16. Entities affected by this scope exemption will need to use judgement to develop an appropriate accounting policy, considering the requirements of IAS 8 – *Accounting Policies, Changes in Accounting Estimates and Errors* (see Chapter 3), especially paragraphs 10-13.

It is important to note that leases of bearer plants that are within the scope of IAS 16 are not excluded from the scope of IFRS 16. 'Consequently, leases of bearer plants such as orchards and vineyards held by a lessee are within the scope of IFRS 16'. *[IFRS 16.BC68(b)]*.

2.3.5.B Leases of biological assets (excluding bearer plants) – lessor accounting

Chapter 23 contains a discussion of lessor accounting. For lessors, leases of biological assets, including those within the scope of IAS 41, are within the scope of IFRS 16. A lessor would account for its leases as either operating or finance leases in accordance with IFRS 16. *[IFRS 16.67-97]*.

For finance leases of biological assets the lessor would:

- Account for the net investment in the lease (i.e. the lease receivable, not the biological asset) in accordance with IFRS 16.

For operating leases of biological assets the lessor would:

- Account for the lease payments as income in accordance with IFRS 16.
- Present the leased biological asset in accordance with its nature, consistent with other assets in the scope of IAS 41.
- Account for other rights and obligations under the lease (e.g. lease income) in accordance with IFRS 16.
- Make disclosures both in accordance with IFRS 16, and for the asset subject to the operating lease, in accordance with IAS 41. *[IFRS 16.81-88]*.

Beyond discussing certain costs, depreciation and impairment, paragraphs 81-88 of IFRS 16 do not specifically discuss how to recognise and measure the asset subject to an operating lease if it is within the scope of IAS 41. *[IFRS 16.81-88]*. Paragraphs BC58-BC66 of IFRS 16 outline the IASB's rationale in retaining the requirements of the predecessor standard to IFRS 16, IAS 17 – *Leases*, for lessors, virtually unchanged. *[IFRS 16.BC58-BC66]*. Furthermore, paragraph B82(n) of the Basis for Conclusions on IAS 41, which outlined the interaction between IAS 41 and IAS 17, was not amended on the issuance of IFRS 16. *[IAS 41.B82(n)]*. Therefore, it is likely that lessors will continue to measure a biological asset in accordance with IAS 41.

Such lease arrangements may include the land to which the asset is attached. Any leased land would need to be separately accounted for under the relevant standard, for example IAS 16 or IAS 40, as it is explicitly excluded from the scope of IAS 41 (see 2.3 above). *[IAS 41.2(e)]*.

It is worth noting that, unless specifically excluded from its scope, IAS 41 applies to all biological assets when they relate to agricultural activity. *[IAS 41.1]*. In the example above, where the sheep are leased under an operating lease, the wool is the agricultural produce. The sheep are being managed to produce that wool, albeit by the lessee and not the lessor. Since IAS 41 does not specify who must do the managing, the definition of agricultural activity is met. Therefore, the leased sheep would be a lease of biological assets within the scope of IAS 41.

2.3.6 Concessions

A concession typically involves a government, or other controlling authority, granting land to an entity, but requiring that the land be used for a specific purpose, for example, growing certain crops for a minimum period of time.

The treatment of each concession will depend on the specific facts and circumstances. However, if the concession requires an entity to undertake agricultural activity, as defined in IAS 41 (see 2.2.1 above), the biological assets (other than bearer plants) and agriculture produce will be within the scope of IAS 41. The grant received may also be within the scope of the standard. However, the land granted would be within the scope of IAS 16 or IAS 40 (see Chapters 18 and 19, respectively). The discussion at 3.3 below addresses the treatment of government grants related to biological assets (other than bearer plants).

3 RECOGNITION AND MEASUREMENT PRINCIPLES

3.1 Recognition

An entity recognises a biological asset (including produce growing on a bearer plant) or agricultural produce that is within the scope of IAS 41 only when:

(a) it controls the asset as a result of past events;

(b) it is probable that future economic benefits associated with the asset will flow to the entity; and

(c) the fair value or cost of the asset can be measured reliably. *[IAS 41.10]*

Considerations for the recognition of produce growing on a bearer plant are discussed at 3.2.3.B below.

3.1.1 Control

In agricultural activity, an entity may evidence control by, for example, 'legal ownership of cattle and the branding or otherwise marking of the cattle on acquisition, birth, or weaning'. *[IAS 41.11]*.

3.2 Measurement

3.2.1 Biological assets within the scope of IAS 41

3.2.1.A Initial and subsequent measurement

A biological asset that is within the scope of IAS 41 (i.e. excluding bearer plants, but including produce growing on a bearer plant) is measured on initial recognition and at the end of each reporting period at its fair value less costs to sell, unless an entity can demonstrate at initial recognition that fair value cannot be measured reliably. *[IAS 41.12]*. In the latter case, the entity measures the biological asset at historic cost less any accumulated depreciation and any accumulated impairment losses (see 3.2.5 below), unless/until fair value becomes reliably measurable. *[IAS 41.30]*.

3.2.1.B Subsequent expenditure

IAS 41 does not prescribe how an entity should account for subsequent expenditure in relation to biological assets, because the (then) IASC believed this to be unnecessary with a fair-value-based measurement approach. *[IAS 41.B62]*.

Such expenditure may be expensed as incurred or capitalised as additions to the related biological asset. However, under the fair value model, the biological asset will be re-measured at the end of each reporting period. As such, any amounts capitalised will only result in a reallocation between expenses and the fair value gain or loss for the biological asset. Therefore, an entity's policy in relation to subsequent expenditure will have no effect on its equity or net profit or loss, although it will affect:

- the reconciliation of changes in the carrying amount of biological assets;
- the classification of the expenditure in the income statement as either an expense or as part of the net gain or loss on biological assets; and
- the presentation of subsequent expenditure on biological assets in the statement of cash flows as either operating or investing activities, as appropriate.

In our view, an entity should select an accounting policy for subsequent expenditure that is broadly consistent with the principles in other standards, such as IAS 16 and IAS 38. For example, in the case of livestock, an entity may expense maintenance costs, such as routine vaccinations, while treating costs that increase the originally expected yield of the asset as capital expenditure. In this case, an entity must consider whether it is appropriate to add costs that improve initially anticipated yields (such as additional vaccinations or feed supplements) to the carrying value of the asset. However, such additions would be adjusted at each period end when the biological asset concerned is revalued to its new fair value. Judgement may be required to determine whether costs that take place after maturity (e.g. vaccinations or feed supplements) would be maintenance costs or improvements. Furthermore, care will be needed when costs are related to both bearer plants and produce growing on a bearer plant or when it is not clear to which of those assets it relates. This is discussed further at 3.2.3 below.

In September 2019, the IFRS Interpretations Committee discussed a submission about the accounting for costs related to the biological transformation of biological assets (subsequent expenditure) applying IAS 41. The submitter asked whether an entity; (a) recognises subsequent expenditure as an expense when incurred; or (b) capitalises the subsequent expenditure (i.e. adds it to the carrying amount of the asset).

The Committee decided not to take the issue onto its standard setting agenda noting that IAS 41 does not specify requirements on the accounting for subsequent expenditure and an entity can either capitalise subsequent expenditure or recognise it as an expense when incurred. The Committee observed that capitalising subsequent expenditure or recognising it as an expense has no effect on the fair value measurement of biological assets nor does it have any effect on profit or loss; however, it affects the presentation of amounts in the statement of profit or loss.

The Committee drew attention to the requirements of:

- paragraph 13 of IAS 8, whereby an entity would apply its accounting policy for subsequent expenditure consistently to each group of biological assets; and
- paragraphs 117-124 of IAS 1 – *Presentation of Financial Statements* – whereby an entity would also disclose the selected accounting policy if that disclosure would assist users of financial statements in understanding how those transactions are reflected in reported financial performance. *[IAS 1.117-124; IAS 8.13]*.

The Committee also noted that when 'assessing how to present such subsequent expenditure in the statement of profit or loss, an entity would apply the requirements in paragraphs 81–105 of IAS 1'. In particular, an 'entity would:

- applying paragraph 85, "present additional line items (including by disaggregating the line items listed in paragraph 82), headings and subtotals in the statement(s) presenting profit or loss and other comprehensive income when such presentation is relevant to an understanding of the entity's financial performance"; and
- applying paragraph 99, present in the statement(s) presenting profit or loss and other comprehensive income or in the notes an analysis of expenses recognised in profit or loss using a classification based on either their nature or their function within the entity, whichever provides information that is reliable and more relevant'. *[IAS 1.85, 99]*.[1]

The presentation of items in the statement of profit or loss is further discussed In Chapter 3 at 3.2.

3.2.2 Agricultural produce

Agricultural produce harvested from an entity's biological assets should initially 'be measured at its fair value less costs to sell at the point of harvest'. *[IAS 41.13]*. The standard presumes that an entity can always reliably measure this amount and hence does not permit valuation at historical cost. *[IAS 41.32, B43]*.

The value resulting from initial measurement is subsequently used as cost in applying IAS 2 (if the agricultural produce is to be sold, see Chapter 22), IAS 16 (if harvested logs are used for the construction of a building, see Chapter 18) or other applicable IFRSs. *[IAS 41.13, B8]*.

An important reason for requiring agricultural produce at the point of harvest to be measured at fair value was to ensure that the basis of measurement would be consistent with that of biological assets and to avoid inconsistent and distorted reporting of current period performance upon harvest of agricultural produce. *[IAS 41.B42]*.

3.2.3 Requirements for produce growing on a bearer plant

3.2.3.A Requirements for bearer plants in the scope of IAS 16

Bearer plants are subject to all of the recognition and measurement requirements in IAS 16 (see Chapter 18), including the following (see Figure 42.2 below):

- before maturity, bearer plants must be measured at their accumulated cost, similar to the accounting treatment for a self-constructed item of plant and equipment before it is available for use; *[IAS 16.22A]* and
- after the bearer plant is mature, entities have a policy choice to measure the bearer plants using either the cost model or the revaluation model. *[IAS 16.29]*. It is important to note that:
  - if the revaluation model is selected, revaluations need to take place with sufficient regularity to ensure the carrying amount does not differ materially from the asset's fair value had it been measured at the end of the reporting period; *[IAS 16.22A]*
  - entities following either model need to determine the useful life of the bearer plant in order to depreciate it. The useful life needs to be re-evaluated each year; *[IAS 16.51]* and
  - unlike biological assets within the scope of IAS 41, items of property, plant and equipment within the scope of IAS 16 are not scoped out of IAS 36 – *Impairment of Assets*. Entities, therefore, need to assess whether there are indicators that a bearer plant is impaired at the end of each reporting period. If such indicators exist, the bearer plant will be subject to an impairment test in accordance with IAS 36. *[IAS 16.63, IAS 36.8-9]*. An impairment loss will be recognised if the carrying value is higher than the bearer asset's recoverable amount (being the higher of the asset's fair value less costs of disposal and its value in use). *[IAS 36.60]*. The requirements of IAS 36 are discussed in Chapter 20.

The requirements for bearer plants do not completely eliminate volatility in profit or loss, as entities still need to recognise any changes in the fair value of agricultural produce growing on the bearer plant, as discussed at 3.2.3.B below.

Figure 42.2: **Measurement requirements for bearer plants (assuming fair value can be reliably measured)**

At initial recognition	<ul><li>Measured separately from any related agricultural produce (i.e. two units of account).</li><li>Measured at cost, accumulated until maturity.</li></ul>
Subsequent measurement requirements	<ul><li>Measured separately from any related agricultural produce (i.e. two units of account).</li><li>Measured at:<ul><li>cost, less any subsequent accumulated depreciation and impairment, with changes recognised in profit or loss; or</li><li>fair value at each revaluation date, less any subsequent accumulated depreciation and impairment. Revaluation adjustments (and impairment, to the extent it reverses previous revaluation increases) recognised in other comprehensive income; all other changes recognised in profit or loss.</li></ul></li></ul>

IAS 16 is written with property, plant and equipment in mind. As such, entities may need to use judgement to apply its requirements to bearer plants and we note the following areas for consideration.

(a)   Unit of account for bearer plants

IAS 16 does not specify the unit of account for bearer plants. Therefore, entities need to use the general requirements of IAS 16 (see Chapter 18) and may need to consider that IAS 41 applies to each item of produce growing on a bearer plant.

The Basis for Conclusions to IAS 16 notes that 'IAS 16 does not prescribe the unit of measure, or the extent to which items can be aggregated and treated as a single item of property, plant and equipment. Consequently, applying the recognition criteria in IAS 16 to bearer plants will require judgement. This gives an entity flexibility, depending on its circumstances, to decide how to aggregate individual plants for the purpose of determining a measurable unit of bearer plants'. *[IAS 16.BC81]*.

(b)   Determining when a bearer plant is mature

IAS 16 requires an entity to determine when a bearer plant reaches maturity – that is, when it is in the 'location and condition necessary for it to be capable of operating in the manner intended by management'. *[IAS 16.16(b)]*. This determination is important because it is when an entity must cease capitalising costs as part of the initial cost of the asset. The requirements for bearer plants seem to assume that the point in time when a plant is capable of producing (which is referred to as 'maturity') marks a distinct end to all bearer plants' biological transformation. However, the life cycles of plants can vary widely and it may be difficult, in practice, to identify when maturity has been reached.

Determining at what stage during biological transformation a bearer plant would be considered mature could, therefore, be challenging. Alternatives could include:

- when the bearer plant is capable of producing its first crop;
- when the produce is expected to be of sufficient quality to be sold (e.g. macadamia trees start producing fruit after 3-4 years, but only reach commercial levels when the trees are 7 years old); or
- when the growth phase of biological transformation is complete for the bearer plant (and is thereafter expected to degenerate or for its productive capacity to decline).

The Board decided not to provide specific application guidance for bearer plants. As such, entities need to apply judgement to determine when a bearer plant is mature for accounting purposes. In reaching its decision not to provide additional guidance, the IASB noted that options, such as those listed above, would have needed further defining and could have led to interpretive issues. Furthermore, the Board noted that 'a similar scenario arises for a factory or retail outlet that is not yet capable of operating at full capacity and did not think that this was a major issue in practice'. *[IAS 16.BC82]*. Entities should, therefore, carefully consider the requirements of IAS 16, including those related to sales prior to an item of property, plant and equipment being available for use (see Chapter 18).

(c) Determining initial cost for bearer plants (prior to maturity)

IAS 16 requires that bearer plants be 'accounted for in the same way as self-constructed items of property, plant and equipment before they are in the location and condition necessary to be capable of operating in the manner intended by management. Consequently, references to "construction" should be read as covering activities that are necessary to cultivate the bearer plants before they are in the location and condition necessary to be capable of operating in the manner intended by management'. *[IAS 16.22A]*.

While IAS 16 provides guidance (see Chapter 18) that entities need to consider for bearer plants, there are differences between traditional plant and equipment and biological assets. As such, entities need to apply judgement in determining which costs can be capitalised. For example, as a plant is growing, an entity will incur costs related to water, fertiliser, greenhouses, etc. The entity needs to assess whether these costs are directly attributable to the bearer plant reaching maturity.

Another example is the cost of abnormal amounts of wasted material, labour and other resources. IAS 16 does not permit these costs to be included in the cost of a self-constructed asset. *[IAS 16.22]*. Entities need to determine what constitutes a normal level of wastage for bearer plants. For example, many bearer plants die before maturity (e.g. due to disease or adverse weather) and are subject to planned thinning. Whether either or both of these is normal wastage requires judgement.

(d) Costs incurred after maturity

A number of costs, such as fertilising, pruning and thinning are incurred after maturity and can improve the quality of the produce or extend the productive life of a bearer plant. Entities need to use judgement to determine whether these costs are maintenance costs or are considered to be improvements.

In addition, after maturity many costs are incurred to benefit both the bearer plant and the produce growing on the bearer plant. Entities need to carefully consider the basis on which to allocate costs between a bearer plant and the produce growing on a bearer plant when the costs are incurred in relation to both assets (e.g. fertilising costs).

(e) *Depreciation and impairment considerations*

Entities need to carefully consider an appropriate depreciation rate for their bearer plants. Similar considerations are discussed at 3.2.5.B below in relation to biological assets for which the cost model is used under IAS 41. The model in IAS 16 generally assumes that improvements in productivity and quality of produce do not occur after maturity without additional expenditure to improve the asset. However, many plants mature with age and cultivation. As discussed at 2.2.1 above, biological transformation continues after a bearer plant begins to produce and includes degeneration. *[IAS 41.5, 7].* A decline in productivity might, therefore, occur only at the end of a plant's productive life, which differs from wear and tear on an item of machinery.

Applying the requirements of IAS 36 to a bearer plant may also be challenging. For example, an individual bearer plant may not generate its own cash inflows and may, therefore, need to be tested for impairment as part of a cash generating unit. In addition, the produce growing on a bearer plant is treated as a separate asset from the bearer plant and, because it is measured at fair value less costs to sell on an ongoing basis under IAS 41, it is excluded from the scope of IAS 36. When testing the bearer plant for impairment, entities need to determine whether or not they can include the produce currently growing on the bearer plant in their impairment assessment.

(f) *Revaluation model in IAS 16*

IAS 16 permits an entity, after initial recognition to apply the revaluation model. However, this is not the same as applying the fair value model in IAS 41. The former is one that recognises valuation adjustments in other comprehensive income as a form of capital maintenance; the latter is a model that recognises valuation adjustments in the income statement as part of periodic performance. In addition, unlike the model in IAS 41, if the revaluation model is applied under IAS 16 entities are required to:

- depreciate bearer plants between revaluations, with the depreciation expense recognised in profit or loss;
- identify appropriate indicators of impairment for bearer plants in accordance with IAS 36, and assess annually whether indicators exist. If impairment indicators do exist, then those bearer plants are tested for impairment (as discussed above); and
- maintain cost records for each bearer plant so as to separately track those impairments that are recognised in profit or loss and those impairments that are recognised in other comprehensive income.

Furthermore, an entity is unable to recognise increases in fair value that arise from a bearer plant's biological transformation in profit or loss, during the periods in which it is held and used. Since bearer plants are considered property, plant and equipment, the sale of a bearer plant results in a gain or loss on disposal, while revenue is recognised only in relation to sales of agricultural produce.

Despite these challenges, entities may elect to measure their bearer plants using the revaluation model to ensure consistency with the produce growing on them or because the fair value information is useful. That is, a change in the productive capacity of a bearer plant, or a change in the prices for the future output of a bearer plant, can provide useful information.

3.2.3.B   Requirements for agricultural produce growing on bearer plants

As noted at 3.2.3.A above, IAS 16 and IAS 41 require an entity to recognise a bearer plant separately from produce growing on it from the time it exists until the point of harvest.

Produce growing on a bearer plant remains within the scope of IAS 41 and is measured at fair value less costs to sell, with changes recognised in profit or loss as the produce grows. In the IASB's view, this requirement ensures that produce growing in the ground as an annual crop (e.g. wheat) and produce growing on a bearer biological asset (e.g. grapes) are accounted for consistently. *[IAS 41.BC4D]*. As a result, changes in the fair value of such agricultural produce continue to be recognised in profit or loss at the end of each reporting period.

Figure 42.3:   Measurement requirements for produce growing on bearer plants

At the end of each reporting period prior to harvest (i.e. biological asset)	Measured separately from the bearer plant at fair value less costs to sell.
At the point of harvest (i.e. agricultural product)	Measured separately from the bearer plant at fair value less costs to sell.
After harvest	Measured separately from the bearer plant. Fair value less costs to sell at the point of harvest becomes initial cost for the purpose of applying IAS 2 or another applicable IFRS (see 2.3.2 above).

(a)   Determining when agricultural produce exists

As discussed at 3.1 above, paragraph 10 of IAS 41 provides criteria for recognising biological assets and agricultural produce. *[IAS 41.10]*. However, since produce growing on a plant is not acquired, but grown, it may be difficult to determine when that produce exists and can be recognised for accounting purposes. Would an entity, for example, wait for physical evidence, e.g. blossom on a tree? If so, how would this be done when the produce is within the bearer plant and not visible, such as with maple or rubber trees? Entities may also need to check their procedures for ensuring that sufficient information is gathered, i.e. identifying each item of produce growing on a bearer plant when it is at the right stage of development to be recognised. The key question when assessing the recognition criteria (see 3.1 above) may be whether it is probable that future economic benefits will flow to the entity. At such an early stage of development, this may be difficult to determine for each item of produce growing on the bearer plant. However, historical information about similar bearer plants and their produce may be of help.

Determining when produce on a bearer plant exists is important as it affects when an entity should recognise and initially measure fair value less costs to sell. This, in turn, determines when an entity should assess whether it is able to measure produce at fair value reliably (or otherwise apply the measurement exception discussed at 3.2.5 below).

(b) *Applying the requirements for biological assets to produce growing on a bearer plant*

IAS 41 does not explicitly address the accounting for produce growing on a bearer plant. Instead, the standard says that 'produce growing on bearer plants is a biological asset'. *[IAS 41.5C]*. Therefore, an entity is required to apply the accounting required for other biological assets to such produce. This has a number of consequences, including the following:

- The unit of account is each item of produce, not the produce growing on each plant as a group. However, while the unit of account is the individual item, an entity is permitted to group these together for measurement purposes (see 4.2.2 below).

- Each item of produce growing on a bearer plant must be measured at fair value less costs to sell from the time it is recognised until the point of harvest, unless the measurement exception for biological assets for which the fair value cannot be reliably measured at initial recognition is applicable. (See 3.2.5 below, including discussion by the Interpretations Committee in 2017 in relation to applying these requirements to produce growing on a bearer plant).

    The fair value less costs to sell may initially be negligible. That is, a market participant acquiring the bearer plant would only pay a negligible amount for the produce in the early stages of development because they would want to be compensated for the costs they would need to incur to continue growing the produce through to harvest and for the related risks, such as crop failure or price falls during the maturation period. Furthermore, cost to sell needs to be deducted from the fair value of the asset. As discussed at 3.2.3.A above, entities also need to carefully consider which costs relate to a bearer plant and which relate to the produce growing on the bearer plant.

    The different stages of maturity of the produce and the allocation of the costs related to both the bearer plants and to the produce may make valuing the produce on its own challenging. Measuring fair value for produce growing on a bearer plant also presents the same challenges as measuring part-grown biological assets and those that are physically attached to land (as discussed at 4.7 and 4.6.2.A below, respectively).

- The disclosure requirements that apply to biological assets also apply to produce growing on a bearer plant (see 5 below). Some of the required disclosures may be challenging for entities. For example, paragraph 46 of IAS 41 requires an entity to disclose non-financial measures or estimates of physical quantities for each group of biological assets. *[IAS 41.46]*. While entities may gather such information for management reporting purposes, they need to ensure that information is available for produce growing on bearer plants separately from the bearer plants on which they are growing.

3.2.4 Gains and losses

IAS 41 requires gains and losses arising on the initial recognition of a biological asset (including produce growing on a bearer plant) at fair value less costs to sell to be included in profit or loss for the period in which they arise. *[IAS 41.26]*. The standard warns that '[a] loss may arise on initial recognition of a biological asset, because costs to sell are deducted in determining fair value less costs to sell of a biological asset.' On the other hand, a gain may arise on the initial recognition of a biological asset (e.g. when a calf is born). *[IAS 41.27]*.

Subsequent to initial recognition, reported gains or losses essentially represent the difference between two fair values. As such, the standard effectively decouples profit recognition from a sales transaction. One consequence of this approach is to anticipate some of the profit that will be realised, often by a matter of years for long-term crops, such as trees.

The implications for initial recognition of agricultural produce are similar – an entity may need to recognise a gain or loss on agricultural produce upon harvesting, if the fair value of the harvested produce is different from the pre-harvest valuation. *[IAS 41.29]*. The standard requires that '[a] gain or loss arising on initial recognition of agricultural produce at fair value less costs to sell ... be included in profit or loss for the period in which it arises'. *[IAS 41.28]*.

3.2.5 Inability to measure fair value reliably

3.2.5.A Rebutting the presumption

Under IAS 41, there is a presumption that the fair value of all biological assets (including produce growing on a bearer plant) can be measured reliably. This presumption can only be rebutted on initial recognition for a biological asset (not agricultural produce). In our view, such a rebuttal will be rare, as to be able to do so, an entity must demonstrate both of the following:

(a) quoted market prices for the biological asset (including produce growing on a bearer plant) are not available; and

(b) alternative fair value measurements for the biological asset are determined to be clearly unreliable. *[IAS 41.30]*.

Since IAS 41 requires that the fair value of a biological asset (including produce growing on a bearer plant) be measured in accordance with IFRS 13 (see Chapter 14), an entity would need to consider the requirements of that standard in order to determine whether fair value can be reliably measured.

In relation to (a) above, it is important to note that IAS 41 does not restrict the criteria to quoted prices in an active market. Therefore, in order to rebut the presumption, an entity would need to determine that quoted prices in both active and inactive markets are unavailable for the asset.

If an entity is able to determine that quoted prices for the asset are unavailable, it would still need to determine that all other methods for measuring fair value are clearly unreliable before it can rebut the presumption. This is not the same identifying that a fair value measurement is complex and/or subjective. That is, measuring fair value often involves estimation and significant judgement, but this does not mean that it is automatically unreliable. Furthermore, the requirement is for the measurements to be 'clearly unreliable', which is arguably a higher hurdle than 'unreliable'.

Determining that alternative fair value measurements are clearly unreliable is likely to include, but not be limited to, considering the reliability of the following factors:

- Estimates of quantities on hand and the stage of development – while estimates are often required of quantities on hand (including current stage of biological transformation and anticipated yields for future agricultural produce), the mere fact that estimates are used is not sufficient to demonstrate that fair value is unreliable. Rather, an entity would need to demonstrate that their estimates of the quantity and current state of their biological assets are often incorrect. This may be challenging for entities to demonstrate if the underlying information is regularly used by management to make decisions about future operations of the business.
- Prices for the asset in a future state (e.g. for the mature biological asset or the agricultural produce that will ultimately be harvested).
- Price for similar assets that can be used as an input into the fair value measurement – this could include plants and animals that are similar to the asset held by the entity or the ultimate agricultural produce that will result from managing the biological transformation of the asset held by the entity.
- Cash flow projections for the asset.
- The replacement cost of the asset.

Entities may also need to consider whether other entities (within a country or globally) are able to demonstrate that fair value can be reliably measured for the same or similar assets.

In 2017, the IFRS Interpretations Committee received a request to consider whether fruit growing on oil palms is considered an example of a biological asset for which an entity might rebut the fair value presumption applying paragraph 30 of IAS 41. The Committee rejected this request observing that its role is not to conclude upon very specific application questions, particularly when they relate to the application of the judgements required in applying IFRS. In rejecting the request, 'the Committee concluded that the reference to "clearly unreliable" in paragraph 30 of IAS 41 indicates that, to rebut the presumption, an entity must demonstrate that any fair value measurement is clearly unreliable. Paragraph BC4C of IAS 41 suggests that, when developing the amendments to IAS 41 on bearer plants, the Board's expectation was that fair value measurements of produce growing on bearer plants might be clearly unreliable when an entity encounters significant practical difficulties. However, the Committee observed that the converse is not necessarily true – i.e. if an entity encounters significant practical difficulties, this does not necessarily mean that any fair value measurement of produce is clearly unreliable'.[2] *[IAS 41.30, BC4C]*. In addition to these observations, the Committee noted that possible differences in supportable assumptions, (which might give rise to significantly different measurements) do not constitute evidence of 'significant practical difficulties' as discussed in paragraph BC4C of IAS 41. This is because these would not, on their own, result in fair value measurements that are clearly unreliable.

The Committee's observations indicate that a rebuttal of the presumption that the fair value can be measured reliably will be rare. If they cannot rebut the presumption, entities will need to measure fair value and that fair value may be subject to significant estimation uncertainty. As a result, the Committee also emphasised that entities will need to comply with the disclosure requirements in paragraph 125 of IAS 1 (regarding significant assumptions and estimates) and those in paragraph 91 of IFRS 13 so as to assist users of financial statements understand the valuation techniques, inputs used and the effect of measurements that use Level 3 inputs.[3] *[IAS 1.125, IFRS 13.91].*

An entity that previously measured a biological asset at its fair value less costs to sell cannot revert to a cost-based measurement in a later period, even if a fair value can no longer be measured reliably. *[IAS 41.31].* The standard assumes that reliable estimates of fair value would rarely, if ever, cease to be available. *[IAS 41.B36].* This assumption holds during times of heightened market volatility or uncertainty. A more detailed discussion of some of the practical problems associated with determining fair value in the absence of a market price can be found at 4.7 below.

If it becomes possible at a later date to measure the fair value of a biological asset reliably, the entity is required to apply the fair value model to that asset from that date onwards. *[IAS 41.30].* In developing the standard, the (then) IASC noted in this respect that 'in agricultural activity, it is likely that fair value becomes measurable more reliably as biological transformation occurs and that fair value measurement is preferable to cost in those cases'. Therefore, the IASC 'decided to require fair value measurement once fair value becomes reliably measurable'. *[IAS 41.B35].*

IAS 41 presumes that the fair value of a non-current biological asset that 'meets the criteria to be classified as held for sale (or is included in a disposal group that is classified as held for sale) in accordance with IFRS 5 – *Non-current Assets Held for Sale and Discontinued Operations*' can always be measured reliably. *[IAS 41.30].*

In situations where the cost model is initially applied and then fair value becomes reliably measurable, a question that sometimes arises is whether acquisition-related transaction costs (i.e. those that have been incurred by the entity on purchasing the asset) that have been capitalised can be taken into account when subsequently measuring the fair value component of 'fair value less costs to sell'. Fair value is a market-based measure and is defined in IFRS 13 as an exit price. The objective is to measure the price that would be obtained in a transaction between market participants to sell an asset; not the costs each party would incur in order to transact – those costs reflect the characteristics of the transaction and not of the asset being hypothetically sold. It would, therefore, be inappropriate to include acquisition-related transaction costs, particularly since a seller would not incur such costs. In addition, as discussed at 4.6.4.A below, IFRS 13 specifically states that transaction costs that would be incurred in a transaction to sell an asset are not part of fair value (that is, they are not added to, or deducted from, the exit price used to measure fair value). *[IFRS 13.25].* However, IAS 41 requires 'costs to sell' to be deducted from fair value, measured in accordance with IFRS 13, before recognition in the financial statements leading to a lower valuation than a pure IFRS 13 valuation.

3.2.5.B The cost model

If on initial recognition an entity rebuts the presumption and demonstrates that fair value cannot be measured reliably, it applies the cost model to the biological asset (including produce growing on a bearer plant), i.e. the asset is measured at cost less any accumulated depreciation and any accumulated impairment losses. *[IAS 41.30].*

When determining cost, accumulated depreciation and accumulated impairment losses an entity needs to consider the requirements of IAS 2, IAS 16 and IAS 36. *[IAS 41.33].* Refer to

Chapter 22, Chapter 18 and Chapter 20, respectively, for discussion on each of these standards. IAS 41 provides no further guidance on the application of the cost model or the extent to which entities should consider the requirements of these standards.

Both IAS 2 and IAS 16 establish frameworks within which to determine cost. The nature of the biological asset may be helpful when determining which approach to use. Consumable biological assets that are to be harvested as agricultural produce or sold as biological assets, for example livestock to be slaughtered or held for sale, fish in farms or crops to be harvested, may be more consistent with inventories accounted for in accordance with IAS 2. Bearer biological assets, such as dairy cows may be more consistent with plant and equipment accounted for in accordance with IAS 16. When the IASB issued the bearer plants amendments, it noted that, although bearer plants are dissimilar in form to plant and machinery, similarities in how they are used supported accounting for them in the same way. *[IAS 16.BC67].*

The nature of the biological asset may also be helpful in determining when to commence depreciation and the useful life of the asset. Paragraph 53 of IAS 16 requires depreciation to commence when an asset is available for use. *[IAS 16.53].* Determining when a biological asset is available for use may be more obvious in relation to bearer biological assets. For example, a cow may be considered available for use as soon as it is sufficiently mature to produce milk. However, for consumable biological assets defining when an asset is available for use is less clear because the period between these assets reaching maturity and being sold or harvested is typically short.

The last component of the cost model is the assessment of impairment in accordance with IAS 36. That standard requires an entity to determine the recoverable amount of an asset or cash-generating unit (CGU) and compare it to its carrying amount in order to determine whether the asset or CGU is impaired. Recoverable amount is defined by IAS 36 as the higher of either the value in use or fair value less costs of disposal of the asset or CGU (IAS 36 is discussed in Chapter 20). Entities that have demonstrated that fair value cannot be reliably determined for a biological asset should be careful to apply a consistent approach when determining the recoverable amount of that asset. As such, using a value in use approach to determine recoverable amount will be required, possibly at the CGU level. Even in this situation, entities may need to carefully consider whether information used to measure value in use could be used to measure the fair value of the biological asset.

An entity that uses the reliability exception (and, therefore, applies the cost model) is required to disclose certain additional information in its financial statements. This is discussed further at 5.3 below. *[IAS 41.B37].*

3.3 Government grants

Government grants involving biological assets that are within the scope of IAS 41 (i.e. excluding bearer plants, which are specifically scoped out of IAS 41) are only accounted for under IAS 20 if the biological asset is 'measured at its cost less any accumulated depreciation and any accumulated impairment losses' as discussed at 3.2.5 above (see Chapter 24 for a discussion of government grants within the scope of IAS 20). *[IAS 41.37-38].* IAS 41 applies to government grants relating to all other biological assets (including produce growing on a bearer plant) accounted for at fair value less costs to sell.

What is not clear is whether government grants that relate to both a bearer plant and the produce growing on that bearer plant would be within the scope of either IAS 20 or IAS 41. It is also not clear how an entity should deal with a government grant if the related biological asset is initially measured in accordance with the cost model in IAS 41 (and so applies IAS 20 to the related government grant), but later is measured at fair value less costs to sell because fair value becomes reliably measurable. Entities will need to use judgement in relation to such grants.

Under IAS 20, government grants are either:

- recognised as deferred income and then recognised in profit or loss on a systematic basis over the useful life of the asset; or
- deducted in calculating the carrying amount of the asset and then recognised in profit or loss over the life of a depreciable asset as a reduced depreciation expense.

Under IAS 41, an unconditional government grant related to a biological asset that is 'measured at its fair value less costs to sell shall be recognised in profit or loss when, and only when, the government grant becomes receivable'. *[IAS 41.34]*. An entity is, therefore, not permitted under IAS 41 to deduct a government grant from the carrying amount of the related asset. This would be inconsistent with a 'fair value model in which an asset is measured and presented at its fair value' because the entity would recognise even conditional government grants in income immediately. *[IAS 41.B66]*.

Any conditional government grant related to a biological asset measured at its fair value less costs to sell – including government grants that require an entity not to engage in a specified agricultural activity – are only recognised when the conditions attaching to the grant are met. *[IAS 41.35]*. IAS 41 permits an entity to recognise a government grant as income only to the extent that it: (i) has met the terms and conditions of the grant; and (ii) has no obligation to return the grant. The following example, which is derived from IAS 41, illustrates how an entity should apply these requirements. *[IAS 41.36]*.

Example 42.1: Conditional government grants

A government grant requires an entity to farm in a particular location for five years and requires the entity to return the entire government grant if it farms for less than five years. The government grant is not recognised as income until the five years have passed.

Another government grant allows for part of the government grant to be retained based on the passage of time. The entity recognises this government grant as income on a time proportion basis.

4 MEASURING FAIR VALUE LESS COSTS TO SELL

4.1 The interaction between IAS 41 and IFRS 13

IFRS 13 specifies how to measure fair value. However, it does not specify what must be measured at fair value or when a fair value measurement must be performed. Therefore, an entity applies IAS 41 to determine what to measure at fair value less costs to sell and when to measure fair value (i.e. the measurement date). The entity then applies IFRS 13 to measure 'fair value', taking into consideration the specific requirements in IAS 41 (see 4.5 below). 'Costs to sell', measured in accordance with IAS 41, are then deducted.

As discussed at 5 below, disclosures in relation to the fair value measurement will need to be provided in accordance with IFRS 13 and also IAS 41, to the extent that it requires additional agriculture-specific disclosures.

The following sections consider further the interaction between IFRS 13 and IAS 41 and highlight some of the key requirements of IFRS 13 relating to biological assets and agricultural produce. See Chapter 14 for a discussion of the requirements in IFRS 13.

4.2 Establishing what to measure

4.2.1 Unit of account

The unit of account identifies what is being measured for financial reporting purposes, i.e. the level of aggregation (or disaggregation) for presentation and disclosure purposes. For example, whether the information presented and disclosed in the financial statements is for an individual asset or for a group of assets.

The unit of account in IAS 41 is the individual biological asset or agricultural produce. For example, the standard applies to the individual trees in a forest, not the forest as a whole. As discussed at 4.2.2 below, the standard does permit grouping of assets to facilitate measuring fair value, but this does not change the unit of account.

4.2.2 Grouping of assets

IAS 41 states that '[t]he fair value measurement of a biological asset or agricultural produce may be facilitated by grouping biological assets or agricultural produce according to significant attributes; for example, by age or quality. An entity selects the attributes corresponding to the attributes used in the market as a basis for pricing'. *[IAS 41.15]*.

For example, when undertaking a valuation of livestock, an entity may group each of the animals in the herd based on factors such as species, age, weight and the expected yield.

4.3 When to measure fair value

In order to apply the requirements of IFRS 13, an entity needs to determine when to measure fair value, i.e. the measurement date. IFRS 13 relies on the standard that requires, or permits, the fair value measurement to specify this date, i.e. IAS 41 for biological assets (including produce growing on a bearer plant) and agricultural produce.

As discussed at 3.2.1.A above, biological assets within the scope of IAS 41 are required to be measured at fair value less costs to sell at initial recognition and subsequently, on a recurring basis, at least at the end of each reporting period.

The fair value less costs to sell of agricultural produce is measured on the date that it is harvested (see 3.2.2 above).

4.4 Determining costs to sell

Costs to sell are defined in IAS 41 as 'the incremental costs directly attributable to the disposal of an asset, excluding finance costs and income taxes'. *[IAS 41.5]*.

Therefore, of all the costs that are necessary for a sale to occur, costs to sell only include those costs that would otherwise not arise. However, costs already included within the fair value measurement, such as transportation costs, should be excluded from costs to sell. Examples of costs to sell could include brokers' and dealers' commissions, levies by regulatory agencies and commodity exchanges, transfer taxes and duties. [IAS 41.BC3, B22].

4.5 Measuring fair value: IAS 41-specific requirements

4.5.1 Use of external independent valuers

IAS 41 does not require an entity to use an external independent valuer to determine the value of biological assets. In fact, the Board rejected a proposal to require external independent valuations because they are 'not commonly used for certain agricultural activity and it would be burdensome to require an external independent valuation. The Board believes that it is for entities to decide how to determine fair value reliably, including the extent to which independent valuers need to be involved'. [IAS 41.B33]. Furthermore, the Board also noted that requiring the disclosure of the extent to which the carrying amount of biological assets reflects a valuation by an external independent valuer would not be appropriate for the same reasons. [IAS 41.B81].

4.5.2 Obligation to re-establish a biological asset after harvest

It is common in certain industries, particularly where a biological asset is physically attached to land, for an entity to have an obligation to re-establish a biological asset after harvest. The standard gives the example of an entity that has an obligation to replant the trees in forest after harvest.

IAS 41 does not permit an entity to include the costs of re-establishing a biological asset after harvest when using estimated future cash flows to measure fair value. [IAS 41.22]. This is consistent with the unit of account being the individual biological asset (see 4.2.1 above). For example, an entity that owns a forest might consider its intention, or obligation, to replace its trees in the future if it were measuring the fair value of the forest as a whole. However, the entity is required by IAS 41 to measure the individual trees that are actually planted in the forest on the measurement date. It would be inconsistent to consider replanting, since removal of an existing tree (in order to plant a new tree) would be the end of that asset's useful life.

The Interpretations Committee considered such obligations in May 2004 and confirmed its previous decisions that if an entity has an obligation to re-establish a biological asset after harvest, that obligation is attached to the land and does not affect the fair value of the biological assets currently growing on the land.

The problem of how to account for an obligation to replant was considered by the Board in 2007. Circumstances can arise where an entity is legally obliged (whether by law or contract) to replant a biological asset after harvest. The interaction of the fair value measurement basis of IAS 41, the prohibition on including the replanting costs in determining that fair value in paragraph 22 of IAS 41 and the potential recognition of a provision for the cost of replanting in accordance with IAS 37 – *Provisions, Contingent Liabilities and Contingent Assets* (see Chapter 26) – when the biological asset is harvested, could lead to a net expense being recognised at the point of harvest.

Even in situations where there is a legal obligation to replant, an entity cannot consider replanting when measuring the fair value of a biological asset.

4.5.3 Forward sales contracts

When an entity enters into a contract to sell its biological assets (including produce growing on a bearer plant) or agricultural produce at a future date, the standard does not permit it to measure those assets at the contracted price, stating that 'the fair value ... is not adjusted because of the existence of a contract'. [IAS 41.16].

When IAS 41 was developed, the Board considered whether the standard should require sales contracts to be measured at fair value, but concluded that no solution would be practicable without a complete review of the accounting for commodity contracts that are not accounted for as financial instruments. [IAS 41.B50-B54].

It follows from this that if an entity engaged in agricultural activity enters into forward sales contracts for its produce it will need to consider whether such contracts are within the scope of IFRS 9 – *Financial Instruments*. Paragraph 2.4 of IFRS 9 states 'this standard shall be applied to those contracts to buy or sell a non-financial item that can be settled net in cash or another financial instrument, or by exchanging financial instruments, as if the contracts were financial instruments, with the exception of contracts that were entered into and continue to be held for the purpose of the receipt or delivery of a non-financial item in accordance with the entity's expected purchase, sale or usage requirements'. [IFRS 9.2.4]. Accordingly, an agricultural commodity sales contract will be accounted for under IFRS 9 by an entity that intends to net settle that contract even if it is also a producer of the underlying agricultural produce. Conversely, a farmer who intends to settle a forward sales contract for barley by physical delivery would not typically account for the contract under IFRS 9, but would treat it as an executory contract. However, IFRS 9 is applied to such contracts if an entity designates them as measured at fair value through profit or loss in accordance with paragraph 2.5 of IFRS 9. [IFRS 9.2.4]. This issue is discussed further in Chapter 45.

4.5.4 Onerous contracts

Although a forward sales contract scoped out of IFRS 9 is treated as an executory contract, IAS 41 notes that if the contracted price is lower than the fair value of the assets, the contract for the sale of a biological asset (including produce growing on a bearer plant) or agricultural produce may be an onerous contract, as defined in IAS 37. If it meets the definition of an onerous contract, it should be accounted for under IAS 37 [IAS 41.16] (the accounting for onerous contracts is dealt with in Chapter 26).

However, IAS 41 provides no further guidance on the subject of when such a contract becomes onerous. The standard is also silent on what this might mean, given the fact that IAS 37 defines an onerous contract as 'a contract in which the unavoidable costs of meeting the obligations under the contract exceed the economic benefits expected to be received under it'. [IAS 41.B50-B54]. In other words, a contract that is not loss-making, but that has a contract price lower than the fair value of the produce concerned, is not automatically defined as onerous by IAS 37, yet seems to be regarded as onerous under IAS 41.

Nevertheless, it is our view that a contract to sell a biological asset at an amount that is below its fair value less costs to sell (and, therefore, its carrying amount) should be regarded as onerous under IAS 37.

4.5.5 Financing cash flows and taxation

IAS 41 currently does not permit an entity to include any cash flows for financing an asset or tax cash flows when using estimated future cash flows to measure fair value. [IAS 41.22].

The exclusion of taxation is likely to be practically challenging if an entity uses an income approach to measure fair value. Valuers typically prepare post-tax calculations, discounting post-tax cash flows using a post-tax discount rate. If this approach is used to derive a pre-tax equivalent fair value, entities will need to ensure the assumptions related to tax are not entity-specific. As discussed at 4.6 below, IFRS 13 requires that assumptions used to measure fair value reflect what market participants would consider.

However, in May 2020 the Board issued an amendment to IAS 41 as part of its *Annual Improvements to IFRS Standards 2018–2020*[4] which removed the requirement in paragraph 22 of IAS 41 that entities exclude cash flows for taxation when measuring fair value in accordance with IAS 41. The amendment is effective for annual periods beginning on or after 1 January 2022 and applied prospectively. This amendment aligns the requirements in IAS 41 on fair value measurement with those in IFRS 13, which allows the use of post-tax cash flows and post-tax discount rates when measuring fair value.

4.6 Measuring fair value: overview of IFRS 13's requirements

4.6.1 The fair value measurement framework

The objective of a fair value measurement is 'to estimate the price at which an orderly transaction to sell the asset or to transfer the liability would take place between market participants at the measurement date under current market conditions'. [IFRS 13.B2]. In order to measure the fair value of a biological asset or agricultural produce, an entity needs to determine all of the following:

(a) the particular asset that is the subject of the measurement (consistent with its unit of account – see 4.2 above);

(b) the valuation premise that is appropriate for the measurement (consistent with its highest and best use – see 4.6.2 below);

(c) the principal market (or in the absence of a principal market, the most advantageous market) for the asset or liability (see 4.6.3 below); and

(d) the valuation technique(s) appropriate for the measurement, considering the availability of data with which to develop inputs that represent the assumptions that market participants would use when pricing the asset and the level of the fair value hierarchy within which the inputs are categorised (see 4.6.3 and 4.6.4 below).

[IFRS 13.B2].

When valuations are subject to significant measurement uncertainty due to market volatility and there is a wider range of possible estimates of fair value measurement, an entity is required to apply judgement to determine the point within that range that is most representative of fair value measurement in the circumstances.

4.6.2 Highest and best use and valuation premise

IFRS 13 requires that the fair value of non-financial assets, such as biological assets and agricultural produce, take into account 'a market participant's ability to generate economic benefits by using the asset in its *highest and best use* or by selling it to another market participant that would use the asset in its highest and best use' (emphasis added). *[IFRS 13.27]*.

The objective in determining highest and best use is to identify the use by market participants that would maximise the value of the asset, either on its own or with other assets and/or liabilities. Therefore, in order to determine the highest and best use of a non-financial asset, an entity needs to make the assessment from the perspective of market participants (see 4.6.3 below).

Importantly, IFRS 13 starts with the presumption that the highest and best use is an asset's current use. Alternative uses are not considered unless market or other factors suggest that market participants would use that asset differently to maximise the value of that asset. *[IFRS 13.29]*. If such factors exist, an entity would only consider those alternative uses that are physically possible, legally permissible and financially feasible. *[IFRS 13.28]*. Appropriately determining an asset's highest and best use is a critical step and can have significant implications on the measurement of fair value. Therefore, this assessment should be based on the weight of evidence available. Careful consideration is needed to ensure consistent assumptions regarding the principal market (or in the absence of a principal market, the most advantageous market) and the participants in that market, since highest and best use is determined from the market participants' perspective.

Determining highest and best use is discussed further in Chapter 14. As discussed in Chapter 14 and at 5.2 below, additional disclosures are required if an entity determines that the highest and best use of a non-financial asset is different from its current use.

Dependent on its highest and best use, the fair value of the non-financial asset will either be measured based on the value it would derive on a stand-alone basis or in combination with other assets or other assets and liabilities (known as the valuation premise). *[IFRS 13.31]*. For example, as discussed at 4.6.2.A below, the highest and best use of a biological asset might be in combination with the land to which it is physically attached. For produce growing on a bearer plant, it may also be in combination with the bearer plant on which it grows.

Even in situations where the valuation premise of a biological asset (including produce growing on a bearer plant) is 'in combination with other assets and/or liabilities', the objective of a fair value measurement is still to measure the price to sell the biological asset, not the combined group. IFRS 13 assumes that the market participants that would purchase the biological asset would use it in combination with those other assets and/or liabilities. That is, if the market participants already had those other assets and/or liabilities, what price would the market participants pay to acquire the biological asset? In reality, sales are unlikely to be structured in this way. Entities might need to sell the 'other assets and/or liabilities' in order to sell the biological asset (particularly if they are physically attached, as is discussed at 4.6.2.A below). However, regardless of how an entity might structure an actual sale, IFRS 13 contemplates a hypothetical sale and specifically states that, when the highest and best use is the use of the asset in combination with other assets and/or liabilities, a fair value measurement assumes that the market participant acquiring the asset already holds the complementary assets and/or the associated liabilities. *[IFRS 13.32]*.

In practice, an entity may need to measure the price to sell the biological asset by measuring the price for the combined assets and/or liabilities and then allocating that fair value to the various components. IFRS 13 does not specify which allocation approaches can or cannot be used. Therefore, an entity must use its judgement to select the most appropriate technique. Even if this approach is used, the objective is to measure the fair value of the biological asset assuming it is sold consistent with its unit of account, which for a biological asset is the individual asset. *[IFRS 13.32]*. This is discussed further at 4.6.2.A below.

4.6.2.A   Biological assets attached to land

IAS 41 observes that biological assets are often physically attached to land, for example, crops growing in a field. In many cases, there will be no separate market for biological assets in their current condition and location. The objective of a fair value measurement is to determine the price for the asset in its current form. However, as discussed at 4.7 below (see also Chapter 14 at 5.2), if no market exists for an biological asset in its current form, but there is a market for the converted or transformed asset, an entity would adjust the price that would be received for the converted or transformed asset for the costs a market participant would incur to re-condition the asset (after acquiring the asset in its current condition) and the compensation they would expect for the effort in order to measure fair value.

IFRS 13 does not require a market to be observable or active in order to measure fair value. However, it is clear that, if there is a principal market for the asset, the fair value measurement represents the price in that market at the measurement date (regardless of whether that price is directly observable or estimated using another valuation technique). This price must be used even if a price in a different market is potentially more advantageous. *[IFRS 13.18]*. While the price need not be observable to measure fair value, the standard does require an entity to prioritise observable inputs in the principal (or in the absence of a principal market, the most advantageous) market over unobservable inputs. *[IFRS 13.67]*.

If an income approach (such as a discounted cash flow approach) is used to measure the biological asset (excluding the land) and the land, to which the asset is physically attached, is owned by the entity, care is needed to ensure that fair value measurement is not overstated. This is because land owned by the entity would not derive any expected cash outflows. It is, therefore, common for entities to include a notional rental charge for the land, reflecting what would be paid to rent the land, using market participant assumptions.

IAS 41 suggests that where there is no separate market for biological assets in their current form and they are physically attached to land, an active market might exist for the combined assets, i.e. for the biological assets, land and land improvements. If this is the case, an entity could use the information regarding the combined assets to determine the fair value of the biological assets. *[IAS 41.25]*. Similar considerations will also be relevant for produce growing on a bearer plant, which is unlikely to have a separate market in its current form and is physically attached to the bearer plant and, in turn, to the land.

IFRS 13 defines an active market as 'a market in which transactions for the asset or liability take place with sufficient frequency and volume to provide pricing information on an ongoing basis'. *[IFRS 13 Appendix A]*. Whether such a market exists for the combined assets is a matter of judgement, taking into consideration all the relevant facts and circumstances. However, an entity should have sufficient evidence to support such an assumption.

Importantly, the unit of account established by IAS 41 is an individual asset (see 4.2.1 above). Therefore, if fair value is measured for the combined assets, the total fair value would need to be allocated to each component in order to derive the fair value for the biological asset or produce growing on a bearer plant (as is illustrated by Figure 42.4 below). As discussed at 4.6.2 above, IFRS 13 does not provide guidance on how to perform such an allocation. IAS 41 suggests the use of the residual method as one possible way to allocate the fair value between the biological assets and the land. However, this might be difficult to apply in practice, as illustrated in Example 42.2 below. Therefore, entities will need to apply judgement when determining the appropriate allocation.

Example 42.2:   Assets attached to land

Entity A acquired a 10-hectare vineyard on 1 January 2021 for $1,200. The purchase price of the vineyard was attributed as follows:

1 January 2021	$
Purchase price	1,200
Land	(780)
Vineyard improvements	(130)
Grape vines	(255)
Grapes growing on the vines	35

At the end of its financial year Entity A needs to determine the fair value of the grapes growing on the vines in accordance with IAS 41 and invites two equally skilled professional valuers to determine their value.

31 December 2021	Valuer 1 $	Valuer 2 $
Fair value of an average 10-hectare vineyard	1,105	1,100
Adjustment for soil and climatic conditions	135	150
Estimated fair value of Entity A's vineyard	1,240	1,250
Fair value of the land	(830)	(825)
Fair value of vineyard improvements	(135)	(125)
Fair value of grape vines	(245)	(250)
Grapes growing on the vines	30	50

Valuer 1 and Valuer 2 make a virtually identical assessment of the market values of the vineyard, the land, vineyard improvements and the grape vines. Nevertheless, because the value of grapes growing on the vines is calculated by subtracting all the other known elements from the total value of the vineyard, a noticeable difference arises in the valuation of the grapes growing on the vines. In a similar vein, entities that use only one valuer need to be aware that even small changes in assumptions from period-to-period could have a significant impact on the valuation of biological assets or plants growing on a bearer plant and, therefore, reported profits or losses. For this reason, IFRS 13 requires extensive disclosures about assumptions used in determining fair value.

In April 2012, the Interpretations Committee received a request to clarify the use of the residual approach, as discussed in paragraph 25 of IAS 41 (in light of the requirement in IFRS 13 to measure the fair value of non-financial assets based on their highest and best use).

Specifically, the Committee was asked to consider the situation where a biological asset was physically attached to land and no separate market for the biological asset existed in its current condition and location. The submitter of the request assumed entities would apply paragraph 25 of IAS 41, measure the biological asset and land on a combined basis and use the residual approach to derive a fair value for the biological asset. The submitter was concerned about situations where the highest and best use of the biological asset is in combination with the land, but the value of the land could be higher if measured assuming some alternative use (such as property development). In these circumstances, the allocated fair value of the biological asset might be nil or negligible. The fact pattern was further complicated because it was assumed the land to which the biological asset was attached was measured using the cost model in accordance with IAS 16.[5]

The Committee elected not to take the issue onto its agenda, but noted that, in the development of IFRS 13, the IASB had considered the situation where the highest and best use of an asset in a group of assets is different from its current use. However, 'IFRS 13 does not explicitly address the accounting implications if those circumstances arise and the fair value measurement of the asset based on its highest and best use assumes that other assets in the group need to be converted or destroyed'. The Committee also observed that this issue may affect non-financial assets within the scope of other standards, not just those within the scope of IAS 41.[6] The Committee asked the IASB to provide clarification of the accounting requirements for the issues it had considered. However, as outreach indicated the issue was not widespread, in May 2013, the IASB decided it could, instead, be considered for review in the Post-Implementation Review (PIR) of IFRS 13.[7] Most respondents to the IASB's requests for information as part of its PIR of IFRS 13 that had experience with biological assets said that fair value measurement of biological assets was challenging (highlighting specific aspects that are challenging) and asked for additional guidance (particularly in relation to measuring the fair value of growing produce) and/or changes to IAS 41. However, there were different views about how the Board could help.[8]

In considering all of the feedback on the RFI, the Board completed its review of findings and concluded in March 2018 that IFRS 13 is working as it intended. It also decided to:

'a. feed the PIR findings regarding the usefulness of disclosures into the Board's work on Better Communication in Financial Reporting, in particular, into the Targeted Standards-level Review of Disclosures and the Primary Financial Statements projects;

b. continue liaising with the valuation profession, monitor new developments in practice and promote knowledge development and sharing; and

c. conduct no other follow-up activities as a result of findings from the PIR.'[9]

In relation to education about measuring the fair value of biological assets, 'the Board concluded that, although there might be inconsistent application in fair value measurement of biological assets, detailed application questions are best addressed by the valuation profession, and not by accounting standard-setters.'[10] Determining the highest and best use of an asset requires judgement (see 4.6.2 above), but an entity should start with the presumption that the highest and best use is an asset's current use. As discussed above, paragraph 25 of IAS 41 is only relevant where there is no separate market for a biological asset or produce growing on a bearer plant in its current form and it (or the bearer plant on which it grows) is physically attached to land. In addition, that paragraph suggests an active market may exists for the combined assets (e.g. land and biological asset) and, therefore, that an observable price in that market for the assets (on a combined basis) could be used to derive fair value for the biological asset. [IAS 41.25]. Selecting appropriate valuation techniques with which to measure fair value in accordance with IFRS 13 requires judgement. Some might use the residual approach to do this, as indicated in the submission. However, paragraph 25 of IAS 41 does not require the use of the residual approach; it is only mentioned as an example. The IASB reaffirmed this when they considered this matter in May 2013. They also noted that IFRS 13 encourages the use of multiple valuation techniques, where appropriate.[11]

The outcome from a fact pattern such as the one the Committee discussed may be somewhat counterintuitive. However, the fact that the fair value of the land, in that situation, would not be recognised in the financial statements is, in our view, irrelevant to the measurement of fair value. The objective of a fair value measurement does not change regardless of whether it is recognised or unrecognised.

Figure 42.4:   Applying paragraph 25 of IAS 41 to measure the fair value of a biological asset

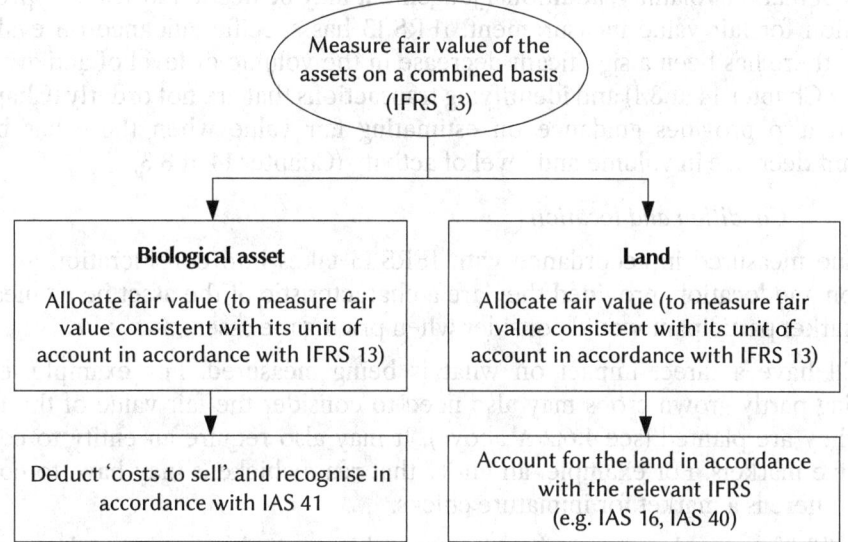

4.6.3   Selecting appropriate assumptions

Selecting the appropriate assumption with which to measure the fair value of biological assets and agricultural produce can often be difficult. According to IFRS 13, an entity should select assumptions that:

- market participants would use, i.e. they are not entity-specific;
- are consistent with the unit of account and characteristics of the asset, including an asset's condition and location and any restrictions on the use or sale of the asset;
- are consistent with an orderly transaction to sell the asset in the principal market, or in the absence of a principal market, the most advantageous market; and
- maximise the use of observable inputs and minimise the use of unobservable inputs (based on the fair value hierarchy, see Chapter 14).

IFRS 13 clarifies that the transaction to sell the asset would be between market participants, not between the entity and a market participant. In addition, assumptions should reflect those that market participants generally would assume, not those of a particular market participant. In order to select the appropriate assumptions, an entity would identify characteristics of market participants. At a minimum, IFRS 13 assumes that market participants will be independent of each other, knowledgeable about the asset, able and willing to enter into a transaction for the asset. *[IFRS 13 Appendix A]*. An entity need not identify specific market participants, but needs to identify the distinguishing characteristics of market participants. *[IFRS 13.23]*.

Identifying the appropriate market participants (or their characteristics) depends on the principal market for the asset or, in the absence of a principal market, the most advantageous market (see Chapter 14 for further discussion). *[IFRS 13.23]*. There is a general presumption in IFRS 13 that the principal market is the one in which the entity would normally enter into a transaction to sell the asset, unless there is evidence to the contrary. *[IFRS 13.17]*.

In times of market volatility, additional judgement may be needed to select appropriate assumption for fair value measurement. IFRS 13 has specific guidance on evaluating whether there has been a significant decrease in the volume or level of activity for an asset (see Chapter 14 at 8.1) and identifying transactions that are not orderly (Chapter 14 at 8.2). It also provides guidance on estimating fair value when there has been a significant decrease in volume and level of activity (Chapter 14 at 8.3).

4.6.3.A   Condition and location

Fair value measured in accordance with IFRS 13 takes into consideration an asset's condition and location, provided they are a characteristic of the asset being measured that a market participant would consider when pricing the asset. *[IFRS 13.11]*.

This will have a direct impact on what is being measured. For example, entities measuring partly grown crops may also need to consider the fair value of the land in which they are planted (see 4.6.2.A above). It may also require an entity to consider alternative markets. For example, an entity that rears chickens may have to consider whether there is a market for immature chicks.

It is possible for a market to exist in one geographical area, but not in another area. For example, transportation costs may limit the geographical size of the market for agricultural produce significantly, possibly to the point where a local cooperative or factory is the only buyer.

If no market exists for an asset in its current form, but there is a market for the converted or transformed asset, an entity adjusts the fair value for the costs a market participant would incur to re-condition the asset (after acquiring the asset in its current condition) and the compensation they would expect for the effort.

If the location of a biological asset or agricultural produce would require it to be transported to the market in order to sell it, transportation costs would be deducted from the market price in order to measure fair value. Given the logistical problems and generally high costs of transporting living animals and plants, there could be many different fair values for identical biological assets depending on their location.

4.6.4 Valuation techniques in IFRS 13

IFRS 13 does not limit the types of valuation techniques an entity might use to measure fair value. However, it does require the valuation techniques to be consistent with one of three approaches: the market approach; the income approach; or the cost approach. *[IFRS 13.62]*. According to IFRS 13, multiple techniques should be used, when applicable. Therefore, judgement is needed to select the techniques that are appropriate in the circumstances. *[IFRS 13.63]*. Selecting appropriate valuation techniques is discussed further in Chapter 14 at 14.

IFRS 13 does not prioritise the use of one valuation technique over another, or require the use of only one technique. Instead, IFRS 13 establishes a hierarchy for the inputs used in those valuation techniques, requiring an entity to maximise observable inputs and minimise the use of unobservable inputs (this is discussed further in Chapter 14 at 16). *[IFRS 13.74]*. The best indication of fair value is a quoted price in an active market for the identical asset. However, even when fair value needs to be estimated, an entity must maximise the use of observable inputs and minimise the use of unobservable inputs.

A significant decrease in volume or activity in a market can also influence which valuation techniques are used, how those techniques are applied and whether inputs are observable at the measurement date. This is discussed further in Chapter 14 at 8.3.

4.6.4.A Cost as an approximation of fair value

IFRS 13 defines fair value as a current exit price, not an entry price. Therefore, while exit and entry prices may be identical in many situations, the transaction price (an entry price) is not presumed to represent the fair value of an asset or liability measured in accordance with IFRS 13 on its initial recognition. *[IFRS 13.57-59]*.

IAS 41 indicates that cost may sometimes approximate fair value. The standard gives two situations where this might occur: *[IAS 41.24]*

- when little biological transformation has taken place since cost was initially incurred – seedlings planted immediately prior to the end of a reporting period and newly acquired livestock are given as examples; or
- when the impact of the biological transformation on price is not expected to be material – for example, during the initial phase of growth for a pine plantation with a 30-year production cycle.

Even in such situations, the objective is still to measure fair value in accordance with IFRS 13. Therefore, as with an entry price on initial recognition, an entity cannot presume that cost approximates fair value. Instead, it should ensure cost is materially consistent with a current exit price for the asset. For example, entities would need to carefully consider which costs could be included in the entry price. IFRS 13 specifically states that transaction costs are not part of fair value (that is, they are not added to or deducted from the exit price), *[IFRS 13.25]*, therefore, we would not expect an entity to deduct such costs from the entry price – particularly as 'costs to sell' are deducted from fair value before being recognised in the financial statements. Nor would we expect entities applying a fair value model to include acquisition-related transaction costs within an entry price used to approximate fair value.

4.7 The problem of measuring fair value for part-grown or immature biological assets

Entities may be required to measure their biological assets part way through the transformation process, particularly when the time to harvest is greater than 12 months. In these circumstances, there may not be an active market for the asset in its current condition and location. In the absence of an active market, preparers often use a discounted cash flow model to estimate fair value.

In these situations, a common question is whether an entity can take into consideration the future biological transformation when estimating the fair value of a biological asset.

As discussed at 4.6.3.A above, IFRS 13 makes it clear that the fair value of an asset considers characteristics of an asset, such as its current condition and location. An entity must consider this objective in determining an appropriate discount rate and estimating its future cash flows, which must be based on assumptions market participants would use. Therefore, if a market participant would consider the potential for future growth or maturation, the related cash flows and risks from that additional biological transformation should be included in determining the appropriate fair value.

IFRS 13 requires that, if there is a principal market for the asset or liability, the fair value measurement shall represent the price in that market at the measurement date (regardless of whether that price is directly observable or estimated using another valuation technique). The price in the principal market must be used even if the price in a different market is potentially more advantageous. *[IFRS 13.18]*. Since an entity can consider the expected cash flows the asset can generate in its principal market, the entity is not permitted to use available prices in other active markets for part-grown biological assets. Even in situations where there is no principal market, once the most advantageous market has been selected, an entity would not look to other markets for available prices or use prices in the most advantageous market if market participants would not consider them.

The original version of IAS 41 had caused confusion in this area, as it had required that the estimation of future cash flows 'exclude any increases in value from additional biological transformation and future activities of the entity'. *[IAS 41(2008).21]*. This seemed to suggest that the value of immature biological assets should be based on values in their current condition, rather than recognising that part of the value must logically lie in their potential, given appropriate husbandry, to grow to full size. The IASB amended IAS 41 to clarify that entities should consider the risks associated with cash flows from additional biological transformation in determining the cash flows, the discount rate or some combination of the two provided a market participant would take the additional biological transformation into consideration.

While paragraph 21 of IAS 41 was subsequently deleted by the introduction of IFRS 13, this clarification is consistent with the requirements in that standard and is helpful in understanding its requirements in situations where prices are available in an active market for part-grown biological assets, but that market is not the principal market (or in the absence of a principal market, the most advantageous market).

This issue is illustrated by an extract from (the former) CESR's database of enforcement decisions published in April 2007 (Decision ref. EECS/0407-11) in relation to the fair value measurement requirements in IAS 41 (prior to the issuance of IFRS 13). Norwegian fish farmers had developed a practice of recording live immature fish at cost on the basis that they were unable to value them reliably in accordance with paragraph 30 of IAS 41. The Norwegian regulator took the view that slaughtered fish sold whole and gutted should be considered the same as live salmon under paragraph 18(b) of the 2012 version of IAS 41 (IAS 41(2012)) and that it was possible to value the live immature fish based on the market price for slaughtered fish of the same size. Smaller fish are sold on the market because they are harvested with mature fish, however their value per kilo is significantly below that of mature fish and the Norwegian fish farming entities did not, therefore, believe that it was appropriate to use their market price as a basis for fair value. The regulator's decision was appealed to the Norwegian Ministry of Finance and the database reports the conclusion as follows:

> 'The Ministry of Finance upheld the decision of the enforcer, with some adjustments and additions. Most significantly, the final ruling upholds the enforcer's decision that slaughtered salmon which is sold whole and gutted is in an accounting sense to be considered as a similar asset of live salmon, according to IAS 41.18(b) and that this also applies to so-called immature farmed salmon. Hence, the observable prices of slaughtered salmon shall be used as a basis for determining the fair value of live immature salmon. The key amendment to the decision made by the Ministry of Finance is that it added certain comments relating to how the term "adjustments to reflect differences" in IAS 41.18(b) was to be applied. The adjustments should reflect the differences between the price of an immature salmon and the hypothetical market price in an active market for live immature salmon.'

As a result of this decision, the Norwegian entities were required to record immature salmon at fair value, rather than at cost, by making appropriate adjustments to available market prices for similar sized slaughtered fish.

While IFRS 13 has now replaced the requirements in paragraph 18(b) of IAS 41 (2012) to which this decision related, the same approach could be used when measuring fair value in accordance with that standard. IFRS 13 prioritises the use of observable inputs for identical or similar items when measuring fair value. Therefore, in situations where an active market does not exist for the asset in its current form, entities might use prices for similar assets, for which observable prices do exist, as an input into the fair value measurement.

As discussed in the Norwegian salmon example above and in Chapter 14 at 5.2.1, an entity would need to identify any differences between the asset being measured at fair value and similar asset (e.g. a converted or transformed asset), for which observable market prices are available. The entity would then adjust the similar asset's market price for the costs a market participant would incur (after acquiring the asset in its current condition) and the compensation they would expect for the effort. Such adjustments could affect the categorisation of the fair value measurement (as a whole) within the fair value hierarchy. Categorisation within the hierarchy is done for disclosure purposes and affects how much information must be disclosed about the fair value measurement (see 5.2 below). IFRS 13 requires that, '[i]f an observable input requires an adjustment using an unobservable input and that adjustment results in a significantly higher or lower fair value measurement, the resulting measurement would be categorised within Level 3 of the fair value hierarchy'. [IFRS 13.75]. Categorisation within IFRS 13's fair value hierarchy is discussed further in Chapter 14 at 16.

5 DISCLOSURE

5.1 General

5.1.1 Statement of financial position

IAS 1 requires biological assets (including produce growing on a bearer plant) to be presented separately on the face of an entity's statement of financial position (see Chapter 3). *[IAS 1.54]*. As discussed at 2.3.2 above, agricultural produce after the point of harvest is accounted for under IAS 2 or another applicable IFRS (e.g. IAS 16). IAS 2 does not require agricultural produce to be disclosed separately on the face of the statement of financial position (see Chapter 22). The following example, which is derived from the Illustrative Examples to IAS 41, illustrates the requirement to disclose biological assets in the statement of financial position. *[IAS 41.IE1]*.

Example 42.3: Presentation of biological assets in the statement of financial position

The statement of financial position below illustrates how a dairy farming business might present biological assets in its statement of financial position.

XYZ Dairy Ltd.
Statement of financial position

	31 December 20X1	31 December 20X0
ASSETS		
Non-current assets		
Dairy livestock – immature *	52,060	47,730
Dairy livestock – mature *	372,990	411,840
Subtotal – biological assets	425,050	459,570
Property, plant and equipment	1,462,650	1,409,800
Total non-current assets	1,887,700	1,869,370
Current assets		
Inventories	82,950	70,650
Trade and other receivables	88,000	65,000
Cash	10,000	10,000
Total current assets	180,950	145,650
Total assets	2,068,650	2,015,020
EQUITY AND LIABILITIES		
Equity		
Issued capital	1,000,000	1,000,000
Retained earnings	902,828	865,000
Total equity	1,902,828	1,865,000
Current liabilities		
Trade and other payables	165,822	150,020
Total current liabilities	165,822	150,020
Total equity and liabilities	2,068,650	2,015,020

* An entity is encouraged, but not required, to provide a quantified description of each group of biological assets, distinguishing between consumable and bearer biological assets or between mature and immature biological assets, as appropriate. An entity discloses the basis for making any such distinctions. (Bearer biological assets are those assets that self-regenerate, e.g. cows that bear calves).

5.1.1.A   Current versus non-current classification

IAS 1 requires an asset to be classified as current when: *[IAS 1.66]*

(a) the entity expects to sell, consume or realise the asset in its normal operating cycle;

(b) the asset is primarily for trading purposes;

(c) the entity expects to realise the asset within 12 months after the reporting period; or

(d) the asset is cash or a cash equivalent (as defined in IAS 7 – *Statement of Cash Flows*, see Chapter 40), unless it is restricted from being exchanged or used to settle a liability for at least twelve months after the reporting period.

If these criteria are not met, the asset is classified as non-current.

The classification of agricultural produce is usually consistent with an entity's assessment for its inventories, i.e. typically classified as a current asset because it will be sold, consumed or realised as part of the normal operating cycle.

The classification of biological assets (including produce growing on a bearer plant) typically varies based on the nature of the biological asset and the time it takes to mature.

For consumable biological assets that only have one harvest, classification will depend on when the asset will be harvested and sold. For example, livestock held for slaughter would likely be realised within 12 months after the end of the reporting period or as part of the normal operating cycle, and therefore would be classified as a current asset. Pine trees in a forest usually take more than 20 years to mature. Therefore, pine forests are usually classified as non-current.

Bearer biological assets, such as dairy cows or animals used for breeding, are often classified as non-current. Such assets usually provide multiple harvests, which may extend beyond one accounting period. Therefore, in order to classify the asset appropriately, an entity would need to consider the period over which it will derive future economic benefits from the asset, which is likely to be when the biological asset will be sold, replaced or removed. This is essentially consistent with determining the useful life of an item of property, plant and equipment in accordance with IAS 16.

In situations where biological assets are classified as non-current, there is some debate about whether a portion should be classified as current. Some believe that, particularly for bearer biological assets, the asset should be classified as non-current, consistent with the classification of property, plant and equipment under IAS 16. In this situation, an entity would probably only classify the asset as current when it is held for sale in accordance with IFRS 5 (see Chapter 4). Others argue that, since the unit of account in IAS 41 is the individual asset (see 4.2.1 above), a portion of a group of biological assets could be classified as current. The current portion would be comprised of biological assets that will be removed permanently (e.g. sold, up-rooted or otherwise removed) within 12 months after the end of the reporting period. Determining such a split may be more obvious for consumable biological assets with only one harvest, for example, the trees in a forest an entity expects to harvest within 12 months of the end of the reporting period. For other biological assets, care is needed to ensure that it is the final removal of the biological asset itself that is considered and not its agricultural produce. An example of the final removal of such biological assets include dairy cows in a herd that an entity sells for slaughter. Regardless of which approach is used, an entity should be consistent from period to period across all similar types of biological assets. An entity should also assess whether its policy for classifying, or not classifying, a portion of its biological assets as current should be disclosed (see Chapter 3 for further discussion).

Produce growing on a bearer plant (e.g. grapes on a vine) is accounted for in accordance with IAS 41, separately from the bearer plant (which is within the scope of IAS 16, see 3.2.3 above). As a result, entities need to consider the appropriate classification of any produce growing on a bearer plant. Produce growing on a bearer plant will likely be a current asset, unless it takes more than an operating cycle (e.g. a year) to mature.

5.1.1.B Bearer plants

The disclosure requirements of IAS 16 are applicable to bearer plants (see Chapter 18). Bearer plants are an example of a separate class of property, plant and equipment listed in paragraph 37 of IAS 16, therefore, the disclosure requirements of paragraph 73 of IAS 16 should be provided for bearer plants separately to those of other classes. *[IAS 16.37, 73].*

The extract below, from the consolidated financial statements of T&G Global Limited, is an example of disclosures provided of bearer plants (trees and vines) under IAS 16 and of the produce growing on the bearer plants (unharvested fruit) under IAS 41.

Extract 42.1: T&G Global Limited (2019)

NOTES TO THE FINANCIAL STATEMENTS [extract]

8. BIOLOGICAL ASSETS

Biological assets consists of unharvested fruit growing on bearer plants, and are stated at fair value based on their present location and condition less estimated point-of-sale costs. Any gain or loss from changes in the fair value of biological assets is recognised in the income statement.

Point-of-sale costs include all other costs that would be necessary to sell the assets.

The fair value of the Group's apples, grapes, berries, citrus fruit and tomatoes are determined by management using a discounted cash flow approach.

Costs are based on current average costs and referenced back to industry standard costs. The costs are variable depending on the location, planting and the variety of the biological asset. A suitable discount rate has been determined in order to calculate the present value of those cash flows. The fair value of biological assets at or before the point of harvest is based on the value of the estimated market price of the estimated volumes produced, net of harvesting and growing costs. Changes in the estimates and assumptions supporting the valuations could have a material impact on the carrying value of biological assets and reported profit.

The following significant assumptions and considerations have been taken into account in determining the fair value of the Group's biological assets:

- Forecasts for the following year based on management's view of projected cash flows, including sales and margins, adjusted for inflation, location and variety of crops.
- The Group has unhedged projected cash flows from sales in foreign currencies. These have been translated to the Group's functional currency at average exchange rates sourced from financial institutions based on forecasted sales profiles.
- Discount rates to adjust for risks inherent to the crop, including natural events, disease or any other adverse factors that may impact the quality, yield or price.
- Any significant changes to management of the crop in the current and following year.

Valuation process

Fair value assessments of the Group's biological assets are undertaken internally. Discussions of valuation processes and results of the assessment are held between the Chief Financial Officer and business division finance managers at least once every six months in line with the Group's reporting requirements.

The main level 3 inputs used by the Group are derived and evaluated as follows:

- Production yields, including tray carton equivalents per hectare and tonnes per hectare, are determined based on historical production trends for each orchard and forecasted expected yields based on the underlying age and health of the orchards.
- Annual gate prices represent management's assessment of expected future returns for the biological assets based on historical trends, current market pricing, and known market factors at reporting date.
- Discount rates are determined by reference to historical trends and loss events, and an assessment of the time value of money and any risks specific for the current crop being valued.

The fair value of biological assets and the level 3 inputs to the fair value model are analysed at the end of each reporting period as part of the half-yearly discussion held with the Chief Financial Officer.

As part of the analysis the level 3 inputs are reviewed and assessed for reasonableness with reference to current market conditions. The calculated fair value of biological assets is also reviewed to determine if it is a fair reflection of management's expected returns for each crop type.

The cash outflows used in the fair value calculation include notional cash flows for land and bearer plants owned by the Group. They are based on market rent payable for orchards of similar size.

	Apples $'000	Tomatoes $'000	Citrus $'000	Grapes $'000	Other $'000	Total $'000
2018						
Balance at 1 January	19,926	2,509	2,203	–	2,409	27,047
Capitalised costs	30,737	1,817	8,011	1,792	4,270	46,627
Change in fair value less costs to sell	6,137	4,014	468	–	(259)	10,360
Decrease due to harvest	(32,927)	(6,160)	(8,949)	(1,792)	(6,021)	(55,849)
Balance at 31 December	23,873	2,180	1,733	–	399	28,185
2019						
Balance at 1 January	23,873	2,180	1,733	–	399	28,185
Capitalised costs	28,505	1,655	5,661	7,313	902	44,036
Change in fair value less costs to sell	3,196	3,555	(59)	–	(253)	6,439
Decrease due to harvest	(37,214)	(5,536)	(5,358)	(6,702)	(1,217)	(56,027)
Balance at 31 December	18,360	1,854	1,977	611	(169)	22,633

In the prior year, kiwifruit and blueberries have been classified in the 'Other' category. In the current year, the 'Other' category only represents blueberries.

FAIR VALUE MEASUREMENT

Techniques applied by the Group which are used to value biological assets are considered to be level 3 in the fair value hierarchy. Inputs are not based on observable market data (that is, unobservable inputs). There have been no transfers between levels during the year.

The unobservable inputs used by the Group to fair value its biological assets are detailed below:

PRODUCE	UNOBSERVABLE INPUTS	RANGE OF UNOBSERVABLE INPUTS	
		2019	2018
Apples	Tray carton equivalent (TCE) per hectare per annum	1,400 to 6,500	1,400 to 6,500
	Weighted average TCE per hectare per annum	3,366	3,652
	Export prices per export TCE	$10 to $70	$10 to $65
	Weighted average export prices per export TCE per annum	$35.19	$29.22
	Risk-adjusted discount rate	25%	25%
Tomatoes	Tonnes per hectare per annum	171 to 628	180 to 605
	Weighted average tonnes per hectare per annum	431	420
	Annual price per kilogram (kg) per season	$1.49 to $18.78	$1.43 to $18.28
	Weighted average price per kg per season	$3.60	$4.10
	Risk-adjusted discount rate	25%	25%
Citrus	Tonnes per hectare per annum	29	29
	Weighted average tonnes per hectare per annum	29	29
	Annual gate price per tonne per season	$950 to $2,670	$950 to $2,670
	Weighted average gate price per tonne per season	$1,888	$2,070
	Risk-adjusted discount rate	14%	14%
Blueberries	Tonnes per hectare per annum	6.5	6.5
	Weighted average tonnes per hectare per annum	6.5	6.5
	Annual gate price per kg per season	$8.50 to $16.92	$8.50 to $28.00
	Weighted average gate price per kg per season	$16.50	$19.21
	Risk-adjusted discount rate	18%	18%

As the yield per hectare and gate price or export price per TCE increases, the fair value of biological assets increases. As the discount rate used increases, the fair value of biological assets decreases.

RISK

Being involved in agricultural activity, the Group is exposed to financial risks arising from adverse climatic or natural events. Financial risk also arises through adverse changes in market prices or volumes harvested, and adverse movements in foreign exchange rates.

Price risk is mitigated by close monitoring of commodity prices and factors that influence those commodity prices. The Group also takes reasonable measures to ensure that harvests are not affected by climatic and natural events, disease, or any other factors that may negatively impact on the quality and yield of crop. Foreign currency risk is mitigated by using derivative instruments such as foreign currency hedging contracts to hedge foreign currency exposure.

ACTIVITY ON PRODUCTIVE OWNED AND LEASED LAND

The productive owned and leased land growing different types of biological assets and by agricultural produce types are detailed in the table below:

	HECTARES		PRODUCTION UNITS		
	2019	2018	2019	2018	Unit Measure
Apples	779	710	1,622,308	1,610,435	TCE
Tomatoes	28	28	12,248,314	11,899,015	kg
Citrus	101	133	2,644,000	3,975,307	kg
Grapes	130	74	270,414	99,000	kg
Blueberries	11	11	73,182	50,839	kg
Kiwifruit	-	46	-	682,168	class 1 trays
Other	-	1	-	20,833	kg

9. PROPERTY, PLANT AND EQUIPMENT [extract]

Commercial land and improvements, orchard land and improvements, and buildings are stated at their fair value less accumulated depreciation and impairment losses. All other items of property, plant and equipment are stated at their cost less accumulated depreciation and impairment losses.

[…]

Depreciation

Depreciation of property, plant and equipment, other than commercial and orchard land which is not depreciated, is calculated on a straight-line basis so as to expense the cost of the assets, or the revalued amounts, to their expected residual values over their useful lives as follows:

- Commercial land improvements — 15 to 50 years
- Orchard land improvements — 15 to 50 years
- Buildings — 15 to 50 years
- Bearer plants — 7 to 40 years
- Glasshouses — 33 years
- Motor vehicles — 5 to 7 years
- Plant and equipment and hire containers — 3 to 15 years

Impairment

Items of property, plant and equipment are assessed for indicators of impairment at each reporting date. Impairment losses are recognised in profit or loss in the period in which they arise.

[...]

	Commercial land and improvements $'000	Orchard land and improvements $'000	Buildings $'000	Bearer plants $'000	
At 1 January 2019					
Cost or valuation	69,391	66,999	156,565	34,151	[...]
Accumulated depreciation and impairment	(1,768)	(1,439)	(12,846)	(6,649)	[...]
Net carrying amounts	67,623	65,560	143,719	27,502	[...]
Year ended 31 December 2019					
Opening net carrying amounts	67,623	65,560	143,719	27,502	[...]
Additions and transfers	502	140	835	5,523	[...]
Reclassifications	596	-	1,483	170	[...]
Depreciation	(1,376)	(669)	(5,915)	(1,597)	[...]
Disposals	(41,259)	(3,901)	(29,925)	(2,484)	[...]
Revaluations	18,503	18,502	11,913	–	[...]
Depreciation write back on revaluations	2,393	825	9,369	–	[...]
Foreign exchange movements	64	35	250	(376)	[...]
Closing net carrying amounts	47,046	80,492	131,729	28,468	[...]
At 31 December 2019					
Cost or valuation	47,394	81,705	140,883	36,547	[...]
Accumulated depreciation	(348)	(1,213)	(9,154)	(8,079)	[...]
Net carrying amounts	47,046	80,492	131,729	28,468	[...]

5.1.2 Income statement

IAS 1 is silent on the presentation of gains and losses on biological assets (including produce growing on a bearer plant) and agricultural produce in the income statement. IAS 41 requires that an entity disclose 'the aggregate gain or loss arising during the current period on initial recognition of biological assets and agricultural produce and from the change in fair value less costs to sell of biological assets'. *[IAS 41.40]*. The standard only requires disclosure of the aggregate gain or loss; it does not require or encourage disaggregating the gain or loss. *[IAS 41.B78-B79]*. Example 1 of the Illustrative Examples to

IAS 41 illustrates gains on biological assets and agricultural produce presented near the top of the income statement, although it is not entirely clear from the example whether losses on biological assets should be presented in the same position or elsewhere in the income statement. [IAS 41.IE1].

The extract below is from the combined and consolidated financial statements of Mondi Limited. The Mondi Limited group recognised changes in fair value less costs to sell in profit or loss, but did not separately disclose that amount on the face of the financial statements. Instead, as is illustrated below, the change in the fair value less costs to sell of biological assets was separately disclosed in the notes to the financial statements.

Extract 42.2: Mondi plc (2019)

Integrated report and financial statements 2019 [extract]

Notes to the consolidated financial statements [extracts]

31 Accounting policies [extract]

Non-current non-financial assets excluding goodwill, deferred tax and net retirement benefits assets [extract]

Agriculture – owned forestry assets (note 14)

Owned forestry assets are biological assets measured at fair value less costs to sell, calculated by applying the expected selling price, less costs to harvest and deliver, to the estimated volume of timber on hand at each reporting date. The fair value less costs to sell is determined using a market approach. The estimated volume of timber on hand is determined based on the maturity profile of the area under afforestation, the species, the geographic location and other environmental considerations and excludes future growth. The product of these is then adjusted for risks associated with forestry assets.

Changes in fair value are recognised in the consolidated income statement within other net operating expenses. At point of harvest, the carrying value of forestry assets is transferred to inventory and recorded as a felling cost reduction to the fair value of forestry assets.

Directly attributable costs incurred during the year of biological growth and investments in standing timber are capitalised and presented within cash flows from investing activities.

14 Forestry assets

€ million	2019	2018
At 1 January	340	325
Capitalised expenditure	46	46
Acquisition of assets	2	7
Acquired through business combinations	—	14
Fair value gains	71	43
Felling costs	(64)	(60)
Currency movements	16	(35)
At 31 December	**411**	**340**
Mature	251	197
Immature	160	143

The Group has 253,680 hectares (2018: 254,328 hectares) of owned and leased land available for forestry activities, all of which is in South Africa. 80,238 hectares (2018: 80,144 hectares) are set aside for conservation activities and infrastructure needs. 1,045 hectares (2018: 1,045 hectares) relate to non-core activities. The balance of 172,397 hectares (2018: 173,139 hectares) are under afforestation which forms the basis of the valuation set out above.

Mature forestry assets are those plantations that are harvestable, while immature forestry assets have not yet reached that stage of growth. Timber is harvested according to a rotation plan, once trees reach maturity. This period ranges from 6.5 to 16.5 years, depending on species, climate and location.

The fair value of forestry assets is a level 3 measure in terms of the fair value measurement hierarchy, consistent with prior years.

The following assumptions have a significant impact on the valuation of the Group's forestry assets:
- The net selling price, which is defined as the selling price less the costs of transport, harvesting, extraction and loading. The net selling price is based on third-party transactions and is influenced by the species, maturity profile and location of timber. In 2019, the net selling price used ranged from the South African rand equivalent of €17 per tonne to €48 per tonne (2018: €15 per tonne to €38 per tonne) with a weighted average of €31 per tonne (2018: €26 per tonne).
- The conversion factor, which is used to convert hectares of land under afforestation to tonnes of standing timber, is dependent on the species, the maturity profile of the timber, the geographic location, climate and a variety of other environmental factors. In 2019, the conversion factors ranged from 8.5 to 24.3 (2018: 8.4 to 24.5).
- The risk premium on immature timber of 13.9% (2018: 13.0%) is based on an assessment of the risks associated with forestry assets in South Africa and is applied for the years the immature timber has left to reach maturity. A risk premium on mature timber of 3.5% (2018: 0.0%) was applied from 2019. The increase in the proportion of mature timber and the risks associated with forestry assets in South Africa triggered a change in estimate.

The valuation of the Group's forestry assets is determined in South African rand and converted to euro at the closing exchange rate on 31 December of each year.

The Group has performed sensitivity analyses of reasonably possible changes in the significant assumptions and EUR/ZAR exchange rate, taking into account historical experience. The reported value of owned forestry assets would change as follows should there be a change in these underlying assumptions on the basis that all other factors remain unchanged:

€ million	2019
Effect of €5/tonne increase in net selling price	65
Effect of 1% increase in conversion factor (hectares to tonnes)	4
Effect of 1% increase in risk premium	(6)
Effect of 10% increase in EUR/ZAR exchange rate	(37)

IAS 41 is not clear about how gains should be presented in the income statement. IAS 1 prohibits offsetting of income and expenses in the income statement, unless required or permitted by another standard. *[IAS 1.32]*. Therefore, if the sale of biological assets or agricultural produce meets the definition of revenue under IFRS 15 – *Revenue from Contracts with Customers*, i.e. 'income arising from the ordinary activities of the entity', *[IFRS 15 Appendix A]*, it should be presented on a gross basis in the income statement. Furthermore, if the sale of biological assets results from a contract with a customer and is within the scope of IFRS 15, it would be presented as revenue from contracts with customers (see Chapters 27-32). However, for an entity's sales of non-current biological assets 'that do not generate revenue but are incidental to the main revenue-generating activities of the entity. An entity presents the results of such transactions, when this presentation reflects the substance of the transaction or other event, by netting any income with related expenses arising on the same transaction.' *[IAS 1.34]*. However, under IAS 41 the gross margin on agricultural produce sold shortly after harvest may be negligible, as the produce may have been previously carried at a valuation near to its sales price.

5.1.3 Groups of biological assets

The standard requires an entity to provide a narrative or quantitative description of each group of biological assets. *[IAS 41.41, 42]*. An entity is encouraged to provide 'a quantified description of each group of biological assets, distinguishing between consumable and bearer biological assets or between mature and immature biological assets, as appropriate'. *[IAS 41.43]*. The standard suggests that an entity may separately disclose the carrying amounts of: *[IAS 41.43, 44]*

- consumable biological assets (i.e. assets that are to be harvested as agricultural produce, sold as biological assets or produce growing on a bearer plant); and
- bearer biological assets (i.e. assets that are not consumable, but rather are self-regenerating).

The standard continues by suggesting that an entity 'may further divide those carrying amounts between mature and immature assets. These distinctions provide information that may be helpful in assessing the timing of future cash flows'. *[IAS 41.43]*. Mature biological assets are defined by the standard as those assets 'that have attained harvestable specifications (for consumable biological assets) or are able to sustain regular harvests (for bearer biological assets)'. *[IAS 41.45]*. If an entity makes such distinctions, it should disclose the basis for making those distinctions. *[IAS 41.43]*.

5.1.4 Other disclosures

If not disclosed elsewhere in information published with the financial statements, an entity is required to describe:

'(a) the nature of its activities involving each group of biological assets; and
(b) non-financial measures or estimates of the physical quantities of:
　(i) each group of the entity's biological assets at the end of the period; and
　(ii) output of agricultural produce during the period'. *[IAS 41.46]*.

In addition, an entity shall disclose the following information:

(a) the existence and carrying amounts of biological assets whose title is restricted, and the carrying amounts of biological assets pledged as security for liabilities; *[IAS 41.49]*
(b) the amount of commitments for the development or acquisition of biological assets; *[IAS 41.49]*
(c) financial risk management strategies related to agricultural activity; *[IAS 41.49]*
(d) a reconciliation of changes in the carrying amount of biological assets between the beginning and the end of the current period, which includes: *[IAS 41.50]*
　(i) the gain or loss arising from changes in fair value less costs to sell;
　(ii) increases due to purchases;
　(iii) decreases attributable to sales and biological assets classified as held for sale (or included in a disposal group that is classified as held for sale) in accordance with IFRS 5;
　(iv) decreases due to harvest;
　(v) increases resulting from business combinations;
　(vi) net exchange differences arising on the translation of financial statements into a different presentation currency, and on the translation of a foreign operation into the presentation currency of the reporting entity; and
　(vii) other changes.

Fair value measurement disclosures are discussed at 5.2 below and in Chapter 14.

The standard also encourages, but does not require, an entity 'to disclose, by group or otherwise, the amount of change in fair value less costs to sell included in profit or loss due to physical changes and due to price changes', because this information is 'useful in appraising current period performance and future prospects, particularly when there is a production cycle of more than one year'. *[IAS 41.51, B74-B77]*. IAS 41 notes that physical change itself can be broken down further into growth, degeneration, production and procreation, but the standard does not specifically encourage disclosure of this information. *[IAS 41.52]*. The following example, which is derived from the standard, explains how an entity should go about separating the effect of physical changes from those of price changes. *[IAS 41.IE2]*.

Example 42.4: Physical change and price change

A herd of ten 2-year-old animals was held at 1 January 2021. One animal aged 2½ years was purchased on 1 July 2021 for $108, and one animal was born on 1 July 2021. No animals were sold or disposed of during the period. Per-unit fair values less costs to sell were as follows:

	1/1/2021	1/7/2021	31/12/2021
Newborn animal	–	€70	€72
½ year old animal	–	–	€80
2 year old animal	€100	–	€105
2½ year old animal	–	€108	€111
3 year old animal	–	–	€120

Fair value less costs to sell of herd at 1 January 2021:

$(10 \times €100) =$ €1,000

Purchase on 1 July 2021:

$(1 \times €108) =$ €108

Increase in fair value less costs to sell due to price change:

$10 \times (€105 - €100) =$ €50
$1 \times (€111 - €108) =$ €3
$1 \times (€72 - €70) =$ €2

€55

Increase in fair value less costs to sell due to physical change:

$10 \times (€120 - €105) =$ €150
$1 \times (€120 - €111) =$ €9
$1 \times (€80 - €72) =$ €8
$1 \times €70 =$ €70

€237

Fair value less costs to sell of herd at 31 December 2021:

$11 \times €120 =$ €1,320
$1 \times €80 =$ €80

€1,400

In January 2012, the Interpretations Committee considered a request for clarification in relation to paragraph 51 of IAS 41. The submitter was concerned that this paragraph may be contributing to an unacceptable application of the market approach to valuing biological assets. To remedy this, the submitter suggested that the disclosure be amended as part of annual improvements so that it would only be encouraged when the entity's biological assets are at the same level of biological transformation as those quoted in an active market. However, the Committee did not believe an amendment was needed, noting that paragraph 51 of IAS 41 addresses disclosures, not measurement.

The Committee also pointed out that the requirements for measuring fair value are set out in IFRS 13, which is not affected by paragraph 51 of IAS 41.[12]

In addition to the above required and encouraged disclosures, the standard notes that agricultural activity is 'often exposed to climatic, disease and other natural risks. If an event occurs that gives rise to a material item of income or expense, the nature and amount of that item are disclosed in accordance with IAS 1' (see Chapter 3). For example, an entity may need to disclose events such as 'an outbreak of a virulent disease, a flood, a severe drought or frost, and a plague of insects'. *[IAS 41.53]*.

Many of the uncertainties and judgements inherent in the valuations that have to be made under IAS 41 are very clearly explained in the financial statements of T&G Global Limited, as shown above at 5.1.1.B, and Sappi Limited, as shown in the following extract.

Extract 42.3: Sappi Limited (2019)

NOTES TO THE GROUP ANNUAL FINANCIAL STATEMENTS [extract]

2. Accounting Policies [extract]
2.3 Critical accounting policies and key sources of estimation uncertainty [extract]
2.3.4 Plantations

Plantations are stated at fair value less costs to sell at the harvesting stage and is a Level 3 measure in terms of the fair value measurement hierarchy as established by IFRS 13 *Fair Value Measurement*. The group uses the income approach in determining fair value as it believes that this method yields the most appropriate valuation.

In arriving at plantation fair values, the key inputs are market prices, costs to sell, discount rates, and volume and growth estimations. Of these key inputs, discount rates and the volume and growth estimations are key assumptions that have significant estimation and judgement.

All changes in fair value are recognised in profit or loss in the period in which they arise.

The impact that changes in market prices, costs to sell, discount rates, and volume and growth assumptions may have on the calculated fair value on plantations is disclosed in note 11.

- *Market prices and costs to sell*

    The fair value is derived by using the prices explained below less costs to sell. Costs to sell includes all costs associated with getting the harvested agricultural produce to the market, including harvesting, loading, transport and allocated fixed overheads.

    The group uses a 12 quarter rolling historical average fair value to value all immature timber and mature timber which is to be felled more than 12 months from the reporting date. In total 12 quarters is considered a reasonable period of time after taking the length of the growth cycle of the plantations into account. Expected future price trends and recent market transactions involving comparable plantations are also considered for reasonability when estimating fair value.

    Mature timber that is expected to be felled within 12 months from the end of the reporting period is valued using unadjusted current market prices less costs to sell. Such timber is expected to be used in the short term and consequently, current market prices are considered an appropriate reflection of fair value.

- *Discount rate*

    The discount rate used is the applicable pre-tax discount rate.

- *Volume and growth estimations*

    The group focuses on good husbandry techniques which include ensuring that the rotation of plantations is met with adequate planting activities for future harvesting. The age threshold used for quantifying immature timber is dependent on the rotation period of the specific timber genus which varies between five and 18 years. In the Southern African region, softwood less than eight years and hardwood less than five years are classified as immature timber.

    Trees are generally felled at the optimum age when ready for intended use. At the time the tree is felled, it is taken out of plantations and accounted for under inventory and reported as a depletion cost (fellings).

Depletion costs includes harvesting (fellings) and damages. The fair value of timber felled is determined on the actual method while damages is calculated on the average method. Damages are written off against standing timber to record loss or damage caused by fire, storms, disease and stunted growth. Harvesting (fellings) depletion costs are accounted for as actual tonnes multiplied by the actual fair value. Damages depletion costs are accounted for as actual damaged tonnes multiplied by the actual 12 quarter rolling historical average price. Damaged tonnes are calculated using the projected growth to rotation age and are extrapolated to current age on a straight-line basis.

The group has projected growth estimation over a period of five to 18 years per rotation. In deriving this estimate, the group established a long-term sample plot network which is representative of the species and sites on which trees are grown and the measured data from these permanent sample plots were used as input into the group's growth estimation. Periodic adjustments are made to existing models for new genetic material.

Volume and growth assumptions are used in determining standing tons at valuation date.

The associated costs for managing plantations are recognised as silviculture costs in cost of sales (see note 4).

11. Plantations [extract]

Sappi manages the establishment, maintenance and harvesting of its plantations on a compartmentalised basis. These plantations are comprised of pulpwood and sawlogs and are managed to ensure that the optimum fibre balance is supplied to its paper and pulping operations in Southern Africa.

The group manages its plantations on a rotational basis. As such, increases by means of growth are negated by fellings, for the group's own use or for external sales, over the rotation period.

The group manages plantations on land that the group owns, as well as on land that the group leases. The group discloses both of these as directly managed plantations. With regard to indirectly managed plantations, the group has several different types of agreements with many independent farmers. The terms of the agreements depend on the type and specific needs of the farmer as well as the areas planted and range in duration from one to more than twenty years. In certain circumstances, the group provides loans to farmers that are disclosed as other non-current assets on the group balance sheet (these loans are considered, individually and in aggregate, immaterial to the group). If the group provides seedlings, silviculture and/or technical assistance, the costs are expensed when incurred by the group.

The group is exposed to financial risks arising from climatic changes, disease and other natural risks such as fire, flooding and storms as well as human-induced losses arising from strikes, civil commotion and malicious damage. These risks are covered by an appropriate level of insurance as determined by management. The plantations have an integrated management system that complies with Forest Stewardship Council™ standards.

Plantations are stated at fair value less costs to sell at the harvesting stage and is a Level 3 measure in terms of the fair value measurement hierarchy as established by IFRS 13 *Fair Value Measurement* which is consistent with the prior year.

The fair value of plantations has been calculated using a real pre-tax discount rate of 12.35% (2018: 11.04%). The group currently values approximately 28 million tons of timber (2018: 28 million tons) using selling prices and delivery costs that are benchmarked against industry norms. The average annual growth is measured at approximately 18 tons (2018: 16 tons) of timber per hectare while immature timber comprise approximately 107,000 hectares (2018: 107,000 hectares) of plantations. As changes to estimated prices, the discount rate, costs to sell, and volume and growth assumptions applied in the valuation of immature timber may impact the calculated fair value, the group has calculated the sensitivity of a change in each of these assumptions as tabled below:

(US$ million)	2019	2018
Market price changes		
1% increase in market prices	2	2
1% decrease in market prices	(2)	(2)
Discount rate (for immature timber)		
1% increase in rate	(2)	(3)
1% decrease in rate	2	3
Volume assumption		
1% increase in estimate of volume	4	4
1% decrease in estimate of volume	(4)	(4)

(US$ million)	2019	2018
Costs to sell		
1% increase in costs to sell	(2)	(2)
1% decrease in costs to sell	2	2
Growth assumptions		
1% increase in rate of growth	1	1
1% decrease in rate of growth	(1)	(1)

5.2 Fair value measurement disclosures

IFRS 13 specifies the disclosures that are required for fair value measurements of biological assets and agricultural produce.

IFRS 13 requires a substantial amount of information to be disclosed about fair value measurements, for example:

- the methods and assumptions used in measuring fair value;
- the categorisation of a fair value measurement (as a whole) within the fair value hierarchy, i.e. Level 1, 2 or 3, and, for recurring fair value measurements, any transfers between levels in the hierarchy;
- a detailed reconciliation of movements for fair value measurements classified within Level 3 of the hierarchy, along with narrative sensitivity analysis; and
- the highest and best use of a non-financial asset if it differs from its current use, including why the non-financial asset is being used in a manner that differs from its highest and best use. *[IFRS 13.93]*.

Chapter 14 at 20 discusses IFRS 13's disclosure requirements in more detail.

In times of heightened market volatility and uncertainty, entities should pay particular attention to the IFRS 13 disclosure requirements on the sensitivity of Level 3 measurements to changes in significant unobservable inputs. These are discussed in Chapter 14 at 20.3.8.

The following extract illustrates fair value disclosures for biological assets, as do the extracts at 5.1.1.B, 5.1.2 and 5.1.4 above.

Extract 42.4: Mowi ASA (2019)

Mowi Group Financial statements and notes [extract]

NOTE 6 – BIOLOGICAL ASSETS [extract]

VALUATION OF BIOLOGICAL ASSETS

Biological assets are, in accordance with IAS 41, measured at fair value less cost to sell. All fish at sea are subject to a fair value calculation, while broodstock and smolt are measured at cost less impairment losses. Cost is deemed a reasonable approximation for fair value for broodstock and smolt as there is little biological transformation (IAS 41.24).

Biomass measured at fair value, is categorized at Level 3 in the fair value hierarchy, as the input is mostly unobservable. In line with IFRS 13, the highest and best use of the biological assets is applied for the valuation. In accordance with the principle for highest and best use, we consider that the fish have optimal harvest weight when they have a live weight corresponding to 4 kg gutted weight. This corresponds to a live weight of 4.8 kg (there may be regional variances). Fish of this weight or above are classified as ready for harvest (mature fish), while fish that have still not achieved this weight are classified as not ready for harvest (immature fish). The valuations are carried out at business unit level based on a common model and basis for assumptions established at group level. All assumptions are subject to monthly quality assurance and analysis at the group level.

The valuations are based on an income approach and takes into consideration unobservable input based on biomass in the sea, the estimated growth rate and cost to completion at site level. Mortality, quality of the fish going forward and market price are considered at business unit level. A special assessment is performed for sites with high/low performance due to disease or other deviating factors. The market prices are derived from observable market prices where available.

ASSUMPTIONS USED FOR DETERMINING FAIR VALUE OF LIVE FISH

The estimated fair value of the biomass will always be based on uncertain assumptions, even though the group has built substantial expertise in assessing these factors. Estimates are applied to the following factors; biomass volume, the quality of the biomass, size distribution, cost, mortality and market prices.

Biomass volume: The biomass volume is in itself an estimate based on the number of smolt released into the sea, the estimated growth from the time of stocking, estimated mortality based on observed mortality in the period, etc. There is normally little uncertainty with regard to biomass volume.

The level of uncertainty will, however, be higher if an incident has resulted in mass mortality, especially early in the cycle, or if the fish's health status restricts handling. If the total biomass at sea was 1% lower than our estimates, this would result in an decrease in value of EUR 5.7 million.

The quality of the biomass: The quality of the biomass can be difficult to assess prior to harvesting, if the reason for downgrading is related to muscle quality (e.g. the effect of Kudoa in Canada). In Norway downgraded fish is normally priced according to standard rates of deduction compared to a Superior quality fish. For fish classified as Ordinary grade, the standard rate of reduction is EUR 0.15 to EUR 0.21 per kg gutted weight. For fish classified as Production grade, the standard rate of reduction is EUR 0.5 to EUR 1.5 per kg gutted weight, depending on the reason for downgrading. In our fair value model for salmon of Norwegian origin, we have used EUR 0.21 and EUR 0.61 as deductions from Superior grade for Ordinary and Production grade quality respectively. In other countries the price deductions related to quality are not as standardized. The quality of harvested fish has been good in 2019. For the Group as a whole, 91% of the fish were graded as Superior quality. A one percentage point change from Superior quality to Production grade quality would result in a change in value of EUR –0.9 million.

The size distribution: Fish in sea grow at different rates, and even in a situation with good estimates for the average weight of the fish there can be a considerable spread in the quality and weight of the fish. The size distribution affects the price achieved for the fish, as each size category of fish is priced separately in the market. When estimating the biomass value, a normal size distribution is applied.

Cost: For the estimation of future costs, there is uncertainty with regard to feed prices, other input costs and biological development. Mowi measures cost deviations vs. budget as part of the follow up of business units. Excluding special situations (incidents etc.), the deviations in costs vs budgets are normally limited for a group of sites, although individual sites might show deviations. The estimation of costs influences the biomass value through the recognised fair value adjustment in the statements of comprehensive income and financial position (calculated as fair value less accumulated biological costs).

Mortality: Normalized mortality will affect the fair value estimates both as a reduction of estimated harvesting volumes and because cost to completion includes cost incurred on fish that eventually will perish.

Market price: The market price assumption is very important for the valuation and even minor changes in the market price will result in significant changes in the valuation. The methodology used for establishing the market price is explained in Note 2. A EUR 0.1 decrease in the market price would result in a decrease in value of EUR 15.6 million.

The market price risk is reduced through fixed price/volume customer contracts and financial contracts, as well as our downstream integration as explained in Note 13.

WRITE-DOWN OF BIOMASS AND INCIDENT-BASED MORTALITY [extracts]

Incident-based mortality is accounted for when a site either experiences elevated mortality over time or substantial mortality due to an incident at the farm (outbreak of disease, lack of oxygen etc). The cost of incident based mortality is included in "cost of materials" in the statement of comprehensive income, see Note 33. The fair value element is adjusted through fair value adjustment on incident based mortality, and included in net fair value adjustment in the statement of comprehensive income.

RECONCILIATION OF CHANGES IN THE CARRYING AMOUNT OF BIOLOGICAL ASSETS (EUR MILLION)	2019	2018
Carrying amount as of 01.01	1 559.3	1 200.5
Cost to stock	1 685.0	1 471.0
Net fair value adjustment	–127.5	146.4
Mortality for fish in sea	–86.2	–42.8
Cost of harvested fish	–1 551.8	–1 290.7
Effects of business combinations	11.7	78.0
Currency translation differences	31.8	–3.0
Total carrying amount of biological assets as of 31.12	1 522.4	1 559.3

[...]

SENSITIVITY EFFECT ON FAIR VALUE (SALMON ONLY) AT YEAR-END (EUR MILLION)	PRICE –0.1 EUR	BIOMASS –1% LWT	QUALITY –1% SUP
Mowi Norway	–8.6	–3.6	–0.2
Mowi Chile	–2.2	–0.2	–0.1
Mowi Canada	–2.2	–0.7	–0.4
Mowi Scotland	–1.7	–0.4	–0.1
Mowi Faroe Islands	–0.6	–0.7	–0.1
Mowi Ireland	–0.3	–0.1	–
Mowi Fish Feed	–	–	–
Total sensitivity effect on fair value	–15.6	–5.7	–0.9

5.3 Additional disclosures if fair value cannot be measured reliably

If an entity rebuts the presumption that fair value can be reliably measured on initial recognition of a biological asset (including produce growing on a bearer plant) and measures the asset at its cost less any accumulated depreciation and any accumulated impairment losses it is required to disclose the following information:

(a) if the entity holds such assets at the end of the period: *[IAS 41.54]*

   (i) a description of the biological assets;

   (ii) an explanation of why fair value cannot be measured reliably;

   (iii) if possible, the range of estimates within which fair value is highly likely to lie;

   (iv) the depreciation method used;

   (v) the useful lives or the depreciation rates used; and

   (vi) the gross carrying amount and the accumulated depreciation (aggregated with accumulated impairment losses) at the beginning and end of the period;

(b) if the entity held such assets at any point during the current period: *[IAS 41.55]*

   (i) any gain or loss recognised on disposal of such biological assets;

   (ii) the reconciliation required by paragraph 50 of IAS 41 (see 5.1.4 above) shall disclose amounts related to such biological assets separately;

(iii) that reconciliation shall include the following amounts included in profit or loss related to those biological assets:
- impairment losses;
- reversals of impairment losses; and
- depreciation;

(c) if the entity held such assets and their fair value became reliably measurable during the current period: *[IAS 41.56]*

(i) a description of the biological assets;

(ii) an explanation of why fair value has become reliably measurable; and

(iii) the effect of the change.

5.4 Government grants

An entity that has received government grants related to agricultural activity covered by IAS 41 is required to disclose the following information:

'(a) the nature and extent of government grants recognised in the financial statements;

(b) unfulfilled conditions and other contingencies attaching to government grants; and

(c) significant decreases expected in the level of government grants.' *[IAS 41.57]*.

References

1 *IFRIC Update*, September 2019.
2 *IFRIC Update*, June 2017.
3 *IFRIC Update*, June 2017.
4 Annual Improvements to IFRS Standards 2018-2020, May 2020, pp.15-17.
5 Agenda Paper 13, *Valuation of biological assets using a residual method*, IFRS Interpretations Committee Meeting, May 2012.
6 *IFRIC Update*, March 2013.
7 *IASB Update*, May 2013.
8 Agenda Paper 7B, *Post-implementation Review of IFRS 13 Fair Value Measurement: Background-Detailed analysis of feedback received*, IASB meeting, March 2018.
9 IFRS Project Reporting and Feedback Statement: *Post-implementation Review of IFRS 13 Fair Value Measurement*, December 2018, p.8.
10 IFRS Project Reporting and Feedback Statement: *Post-implementation Review of IFRS 13 Fair Value Measurement*, December 2018, p.16.
11 *IASB Update*, May 2013.
12 *IFRIC Update*, January 2012.

Chapter 43   Extractive industries

1	INTRODUCTION AND BACKGROUND	3335
	1.1 Defining extractive industries	3335
	1.1.1 Definition of key terms	3338
	1.2 The development of IFRS 6 – *Exploration for and Evaluation of Mineral Resources*	3338
	1.3 April 2010 Discussion Paper: Extractive Activities	3339
	1.3.1 Definitions of reserves and resources	3340
	1.3.2 Asset recognition	3340
	1.3.3 Asset measurement	3340
	1.3.4 Disclosure	3341
	1.3.5 Publish What You Pay proposals	3341
	1.3.6 Status of Extractive Activities project	3342
	1.4 Status of the Statement of Recommended Practice, UK Oil Industry Accounting Committee, June 2001 (OIAC SORP)	3343
	1.5 Guidance under national accounting standards	3344
	1.6 Upstream versus downstream activities	3345
	1.6.1 Phases in upstream activities	3345
2	MINERAL RESERVES AND RESOURCES	3347
	2.1 International harmonisation of reserve reporting	3348
	2.2 Petroleum reserve estimation and reporting	3349
	2.2.1 Basic principles and definitions	3350
	2.2.2 Classification and categorisation guidelines	3352
	2.3 Mining resource and reserve reporting	3353
	2.3.1 CRIRSCO International Reporting Template (November 2019)	3354
	2.3.1.A Scope	3354
	2.3.1.B Reporting terminology	3355
	2.4 Disclosure of mineral reserves and resources	3356

		2.4.1	Oil and gas sector	3358
		2.4.2	Mining sector	3358
		2.4.3	Disclosure of the value of reserves	3359
			2.4.3.A ASC 932-235-50 – Disclosure of Standardised Measure of Oil and Gas	3360
3	IFRS 6 – *EXPLORATION FOR AND EVALUATION OF MINERAL RESOURCES*			3360
	3.1	Objective and scope		3360
		3.1.1	Scope exclusions in other standards relating to the extractive industries	3361
	3.2	Recognition of exploration and evaluation assets		3361
		3.2.1	Developing an accounting policy under IFRS 6	3361
		3.2.2	Options for an exploration and evaluation policy	3362
		3.2.3	Successful efforts method	3362
		3.2.4	Full cost method	3365
		3.2.5	Area-of-interest method	3366
		3.2.6	Changes in accounting policies	3367
	3.3	Measurement of exploration and evaluation assets		3367
		3.3.1	Types of expenditure in the exploration and evaluation phase	3368
		3.3.2	Capitalisation of borrowing costs in the exploration and evaluation phase	3370
	3.4	Presentation and classification		3370
		3.4.1	Reclassification of E&E assets	3371
	3.5	Impairment		3371
		3.5.1	Impairment testing 'triggers'	3372
		3.5.2	Specifying the level at which E&E assets are assessed for impairment	3372
		3.5.3	Cash-generating units comprising successful and unsuccessful E&E projects	3373
		3.5.4	Order of impairment testing	3373
		3.5.5	Additional considerations if E&E assets are impaired	3373
		3.5.6	Income statement treatment of E&E write downs – impairment or exploration expense	3374
		3.5.7	Reversal of impairment losses	3374
	3.6	Disclosure		3374
		3.6.1	Statement of cash flows	3376
4	UNIT OF ACCOUNT			3376
	4.1	Unit of account in the extractive industries		3377
5	LEGAL RIGHTS TO EXPLORE FOR, DEVELOP AND PRODUCE MINERAL PROPERTIES			3379

5.1	How does a mineral lease work?		3380
5.2	Concessionary agreements (concessions)		3381
5.3	Traditional production sharing contracts		3382
5.4	Pure-service contracts		3385
5.5	Evolving contractual arrangements		3385
	5.5.1	Risk service contracts	3386
5.6	Joint operating agreements		3387
5.7	Different types of royalty interests		3387
	5.7.1	Working interest and basic royalties	3387
	5.7.2	Overriding royalties	3388
	5.7.3	Production payment royalties	3388
	5.7.4	Net profits interests	3388
	5.7.5	Revenue and royalties: gross or net?	3389

6 RISK-SHARING ARRANGEMENTS ... 3390

6.1	Carried interests		3391
	6.1.1	Types of carried interest arrangements	3391
	6.1.2	Carried interest arrangements in the E&E phase	3393
	6.1.3	Financing-type carried interest arrangements in the development phase	3393
	6.1.4	Purchase/sale-type carried interest arrangements in the development phase	3394
6.2	Farm-ins and farm-outs		3396
	6.2.1	Farm-in arrangements in the E&E phase	3397
	6.2.2	Farm-in arrangements outside the E&E phase: accounting by the farmee	3397
		6.2.2.A Farming into an asset	3398
		6.2.2.B Farming into a business which is a joint operation or results in the formation of a joint operation	3399
	6.2.3	Farm-in arrangements outside the E&E phase: accounting by the farmor	3399
6.3	Asset swaps		3401
	6.3.1	E&E assets	3401
	6.3.2	PP&E, intangible assets and investment property	3402
	6.3.3	Exchanges of E&E assets for other types of assets	3402

7 INVESTMENTS IN THE EXTRACTIVE INDUSTRIES ... 3402

7.1	Joint arrangements		3403
	7.1.1	Assessing joint control	3404
		7.1.1.A Relevant activities	3404
		7.1.1.B Meaning of unanimous consent	3404

		7.1.2	Determination of whether a manager/lead operator of a joint arrangement has control 3405
			7.1.2.A Implications of controlling a joint operation 3406
			7.1.2.B Implications of controlling a joint venture 3407
		7.1.3	Parties to a joint arrangement without joint control or control 3407
			7.1.3.A Joint operations 3407
			7.1.3.B Joint ventures 3408
		7.1.4	Managers/lead operators of joint arrangements 3408
			7.1.4.A Reimbursements of costs 3408
			7.1.4.B Direct legal liability for costs incurred and contracts entered into 3409
			7.1.4.C Joint and several liability 3409
		7.1.5	Non-operators of joint arrangements 3410
	7.2	Undivided interests 3410
8	ACQUISITIONS 3411
	8.1	Business combinations versus asset acquisitions 3411
		8.1.1	Differences between asset purchase transactions and business combinations 3411
		8.1.2	Definition of a business 3411
	8.2	Business combinations 3412
		8.2.1	Goodwill in business combinations 3412
		8.2.2	Impairment of assets and goodwill recognised on acquisition 3413
		8.2.3	Value beyond proven and probable reserves (VBPP) 3414
	8.3	Acquisition of an interest in a joint operation that is a business 3417
	8.4	Asset acquisitions 3418
		8.4.1	Asset acquisitions and conditional purchase consideration 3418
		8.4.2	Accounting for land acquisitions 3421
9	FUNCTIONAL CURRENCY 3421
	9.1	Determining functional currency 3421
	9.2	Changes in functional currency 3423
10	DECOMMISSIONING AND RESTORATION/REHABILITATION 3426
	10.1	Recognition and measurement issues 3426
		10.1.1	Initial recognition 3426
		10.1.2	Measurement of the liability 3427
		10.1.3	Decommissioning or restoration costs incurred in the production phase 3428
	10.2	Treatment of foreign exchange differences 3428
	10.3	Indefinite life assets 3428

11	IMPAIRMENT OF ASSETS		3429
	11.1	Impairment indicators	3430
	11.2	Identifying cash-generating units (CGUs)	3431
		11.2.1 Markets for intermediate products	3432
		11.2.2 External users of processing assets	3432
		11.2.3 Shared infrastructure	3432
		11.2.4 Fields or mines operated on a portfolio basis	3433
	11.3	Basis of recoverable amount – value-in-use or fair value less costs of disposal	3434
	11.4	Calculation of VIU	3434
		11.4.1 Consistency in cash flows and book values attributed to the CGU	3434
		11.4.1.A Environmental provisions and similar provisions and liabilities	3435
		11.4.2 Projections of cash flows	3435
		11.4.2.A Cash flows from mineral reserves and resources and the appropriate discount rate	3436
		11.4.3 Commodity price assumptions	3436
		11.4.4 Future capital expenditure	3439
		11.4.5 Foreign currency cash flows	3440
	11.5	Calculation of FVLCD	3440
		11.5.1 Projections of cash flows	3441
		11.5.2 Commodity price assumptions	3441
		11.5.3 Future capital expenditure	3442
		11.5.4 Foreign currency cash flows	3442
	11.6	Low mine or field profitability near end of life	3442
12	REVENUE RECOGNITION		3443
	12.1	Revenue in the development phase	3443
		12.1.1 Incidental revenue	3444
		12.1.2 Integral to development	3444
		12.1.2.A Future developments	3446
	12.2	Sale of product with delayed shipment	3448
	12.3	Inventory exchanges with the same counterparty	3449
	12.4	Overlift and underlift (oil and gas)	3449
		12.4.1 Accounting for imbalances in revenue under IFRS 15	3450
		12.4.2 Consideration of cost of goods sold where revenue is recognised in accordance with IFRS 15	3451
		12.4.3 Facility imbalances	3452
	12.5	Production sharing contracts/arrangements (PSCs)	3452
	12.6	Forward-selling contracts to finance development	3453

	12.6.1	Accounting by the producer	3454
		12.6.1.A Sale of a mineral interest with a contract to provide services	3454
		12.6.1.B Commodity contract – forward sale of future production	3455
	12.6.2	Accounting by the investor	3456
12.7	Trading activities		3457
12.8	Embedded derivatives in commodity arrangements		3457
	12.8.1	Provisionally priced sales contracts	3458
12.9	Royalty income		3459
	12.9.1	Royalty arrangements with collaborative partners	3460
	12.9.2	Royalty arrangements with customers	3460
	12.9.3	Royalty arrangements and the sale of non-financial items	3461
12.10	Modifications to commodity-based contracts		3462
12.11	Principal versus agent considerations in commodity-based contracts		3462
	12.11.1	Relationships with joint arrangement partners	3462
	12.11.2	Royalty payments	3463
12.12	Shipping		3464
	12.12.1	Identification of performance obligations	3464
	12.12.2	Satisfaction of performance obligations – control assessment	3465
12.13	Gold bullion sales (mining only)		3466
12.14	Repurchase agreements		3466
12.15	Multi-period commodity-based sales contracts		3466
	12.15.1	Identify the contract	3467
	12.15.2	Identify the performance obligations	3467
	12.15.3	Determine the transaction price	3468
	12.15.4	Allocate the transaction price	3469
		12.15.4.A Variable consideration	3469
		12.15.4.B Fixed consideration	3469
	12.15.5	Recognise revenue	3470
12.16	Take-or-pay contracts		3470
	12.16.1	Volumes paid for, but not taken	3470
		12.16.1.A Payments cannot be applied to future volumes	3471
		12.16.1.B Payments can be applied to future volumes	3471
	12.16.2	Breakage (customers' unexercised rights)	3471
13 FINANCIAL INSTRUMENTS			3472
13.1	Normal purchase and sales exemption		3472
13.2	Embedded derivatives		3475

	13.2.1	Foreign currency embedded derivatives	3475
	13.2.2	Provisionally priced sales contracts	3476
	13.2.3	Long-term supply contracts	3476
	13.2.4	Development of gas markets	3477
13.3	Volume flexibility in supply contracts		3479
13.4	Hedging sales of metal concentrate (mining)		3479

14 INVENTORIES 3480

14.1	Recognition of work in progress		3481
14.2	Sale of by-products and joint products		3483
	14.2.1	By-products	3483
	14.2.2	Joint products	3484
14.3	Core inventories		3485
14.4	Inventory carried at fair value		3487
14.5	Stockpiles of low grade ore (mining)		3488
14.6	Heap leaching (mining)		3490

15 PROPERTY, PLANT AND EQUIPMENT 3492

15.1	Major maintenance and turnarounds/renewals and reconditioning costs		3492
15.2	Well workovers and recompletions (oil and gas)		3494
15.3	Care and maintenance		3494
15.4	Unitisations and redeterminations		3495
	15.4.1	Unitisations	3495
	15.4.2	Redeterminations	3497
		15.4.2.A Redeterminations as capital reimbursements	3498
		15.4.2.B 'Make-up' oil	3501
		15.4.2.C Decommissioning provisions	3501
15.5	Stripping costs in the production phase of a surface mine (mining)		3502
	15.5.1	Scope of IFRIC 20	3502
	15.5.2	Determining when production phase commences	3503
	15.5.3	Recognition criteria – stripping activity asset	3504
	15.5.4	Initial recognition	3505
		15.5.4.A Allocating costs between inventory and the stripping activity asset	3505
		15.5.4.B Identifying the component of the ore body	3509
	15.5.5	Subsequent measurement	3511
	15.5.6	Disclosures	3511

16 DEPRECIATION, DEPLETION AND AMORTISATION (DD&A) 3513

16.1	Requirements under IAS 16 and IAS 38		3513
	16.1.1	Mineral reserves	3514

	16.1.2	Assets depreciated using the straight-line method	3514
	16.1.3	Assets depreciated using the units of production method	3515
		16.1.3.A Units of production formula	3517
		16.1.3.B Reserves base	3518
		16.1.3.C Unit of measure	3524
		16.1.3.D Joint and by-products	3524
16.2	Block caving – depreciation, depletion and amortisation (mining)		3526

17 IFRS 16 – LEASES 3527

- 17.1 Scope and scope exclusions 3528
  - 17.1.1 Mineral rights 3528
  - 17.1.2 Land easements or rights of way 3529
  - 17.1.3 Subsurface rights 3529
- 17.2 Definition of a lease 3530
- 17.3 Substitution rights 3531
- 17.4 Identifying and separating lease and non-lease components 3531
- 17.5 Identifying lease payments included in the measurement of the lease liability 3532
- 17.6 Allocating contract consideration 3533
- 17.7 Interaction of leases with asset retirement obligations 3533

18 INTERACTION OF IFRS 16 AND IFRS 11 3534

- 18.1 Determining who has primary responsibility 3536
- 18.2 Identifying the customer when there is a JO 3537
- 18.3 Determining whether the contractual arrangement between the lead operator and the JO contains a sublease 3537
  - 18.3.1 Assessing the contractual arrangements between the lead operator and the non-operator parties to the JO 3539
    - 18.3.1.A Joint operating agreement 3539
    - 18.3.1.B Other enforceable contractual arrangements (written and verbal) 3539
  - 18.3.2 Determining if there is a sublease 3539
  - 18.3.3 Determining if there is an identified asset 3540
    - 18.3.3.A Specified asset – explicit or implicit 3540
    - 18.3.3.B Substantive substitution rights 3541
  - 18.3.4 Determining if the customer has the right to control the use of an identified asset 3542
    - 18.3.4.A Right to obtain substantially all of the economic benefits from the use of the identified asset 3542
    - 18.3.4.B The right to direct the use of the asset 3543
    - 18.3.4.C Right to direct the use is predetermined 3545

	18.4	Accounting by the lead operator		3545
		18.4.1	JOA and/or related contractual arrangements are, or contain, a sublease	3546
			18.4.1.A Classifying the sublease	3546
			18.4.1.B Accounting for the sublease – finance lease	3547
			18.4.1.C Accounting for the sublease – operating lease	3548
		18.4.2	JOA and/or related contractual arrangements are not, do not contain, a sublease	3549
		18.4.3	Other issues to consider	3550
	18.5	Accounting by the non-operator parties		3551
		18.5.1	JOA and/or related contractual arrangements contain a sublease	3551
		18.5.2	JOA and/or related contractual arrangements do not contain a sublease	3551
		18.5.3	Other factors to consider when evaluating the overall accounting	3552
	18.6	Other practical considerations		3552
		18.6.1	Access to information	3552
		18.6.2	Impact on systems and processes	3553
19	LONG-TERM CONTRACTS AND LEASES			3553
	19.1	Embedded leases		3553
	19.2	Take-or-pay contracts		3554
		19.2.1	Make-up product and undertake	3556
20	TOLLING ARRANGEMENTS			3556
21	TAXATION			3557
	21.1	Excise duties, production taxes and severance taxes		3558
		21.1.1	Production-based taxation	3558
		21.1.2	Petroleum revenue tax (or resource rent tax)	3559
	21.2	Grossing up of notional quantities withheld		3560
22	EVENTS AFTER THE REPORTING PERIOD			3561
	22.1	Reserves proven after the reporting period		3561
	22.2	Business combinations – application of the acquisition method		3562
	22.3	Completion of E&E activity after the reporting period		3563
23	GLOSSARY			3564

List of examples

Example 43.1:	Impairment losses on E&E assets	3373
Example 43.2:	Unit of account – dry well	3377
Example 43.3:	Production sharing contract	3384
Example 43.4:	Carried interests (1)	3391
Example 43.5:	Carried interests (2)	3395
Example 43.6:	Asset acquisitions with a conditional purchase price	3418
Example 43.7:	Single product entity	3433
Example 43.8:	Refurbishment costs – no legislative requirement	3492
Example 43.9:	Unitisation	3496
Example 43.10:	Reserves contributed in a unitisation	3497
Example 43.11:	Redetermination (1)	3499
Example 43.12:	Redetermination (2)	3501
Example 43.13:	Allocating costs between inventory and the stripping activity asset	3507
Example 43.14:	Exclusion of capitalised costs relating to undeveloped reserves	3519
Example 43.15:	Physical units of production method	3524
Example 43.16:	Identifying lease payments – inclement weather	3532
Example 43.17:	Identifying lease payments – major maintenance	3533
Example 43.18:	Identified asset – explicitly identified	3540
Example 43.19:	Identified asset – capacity portion of an asset	3541
Example 43.20:	Identified asset – explicitly identified but multiple assets available	3541
Example 43.21:	Assessing 'substantially all' when the customer's use of the asset is not 100% of the nominal operating capacity	3542
Example 43.22:	Right to direct the use – dedicated asset	3544
Example 43.23:	Right to direct the use – asset can be used on multiple locations for multiple JOs	3544
Example 43.24:	Right to direct the use – asset only used on one JO	3545
Example 43.25:	Classifying the sublease – finance lease	3547
Example 43.26:	Classifying the sublease – operating lease	3547
Example 43.27:	Accounting for the sublease – finance lease	3548
Example 43.28:	Petroleum revenue tax	3559
Example 43.29:	Grossing up of notional quantities withheld	3560
Example 43.30:	Acquisition of an entity that owns mineral reserves	3562

Chapter 43 Extractive industries

1 INTRODUCTION AND BACKGROUND

1.1 Defining extractive industries

'Extractive industries' were defined in the IASC's Issues Paper – *Extractive Industries* (IASC issues paper) published in November 2000 as 'those industries involved in finding and removing wasting natural resources located in or near the earth's crust'.[1] However, this chapter adopts a slightly narrower focus and concentrates on the accounting issues that affect mining companies and oil and gas companies. The IASC issues paper was prepared by the IASC as part of its original project on 'extractive industries' which was led by an IASC Steering Committee on Extractive Industries. This paper considered a broad range of issues including reserves and resources estimation, historical and valuation based concepts of measurement of resources related assets, treatment of removal and restoration costs, impairment, revenue, inventories and arrangements to share risks and costs. While it was non-authoritative this paper is referred to throughout this chapter where relevant as it provided a broad range of information on the common practices observed in the extractive industries and the common terms used.

IFRSs currently use the term 'minerals' and 'mineral assets' when referring to the extractive industries as a whole. This is used as a collective term to include both mining and oil and gas reserves and resources. In contrast, a distinction between the two industries was introduced in the Extractive Activities DP (discussed below at 1.3), where the term 'minerals' has been used to refer to the mining sector and the term 'oil and gas' has been used to refer to the oil and gas sector.

For the purposes of this chapter, consistency with the current wording in IFRSs will be maintained and therefore, unless stated otherwise, 'minerals' and 'mineral assets' will encompass both mining and oil and gas.

Historically the IASB and its predecessor, the IASC, have avoided dealing with specific accounting issues in the extractive industries by excluding minerals and mineral products/reserves from the scope of their accounting standards. Currently, minerals and mineral products/reserves are excluded at least in part from the scope of the following standards:

- IAS 2 – *Inventories*; [IAS 2.3(a), 4]
- IAS 16 – *Property, Plant and Equipment*; [IAS 16.3(d)]
- IFRS 16 – *Leases*; [IFRS 16.3(a)]
- IAS 38 – *Intangible Assets*; [IAS 38.2(c)] and
- IAS 40 – *Investment Property*. [IAS 40.4(b)].

While these standards exclude 'minerals' from their scope, the exact wording of the scope exclusions differ between standards – see 3.1.1 below for more information. In addition, although minerals and mineral products/reserves themselves are excluded from the scope of many standards, assets used for the exploration, development and extraction of minerals are covered by existing IFRSs.

Many of the financial reporting issues that affect entities that operate in the extractive industries are a result of the environment in which they operate. Specific accounting issues arise because of the uncertainties involved in mineral exploration and extraction, the wide range of risk sharing arrangements, and government involvement in the form of mandatory participations and special tax regimes. At the same time, however, some of the business arrangements that are aimed at mitigating certain risks give rise to financial reporting complications. The financial reports of these entities need to reflect the risks and rewards to which they are exposed. In many cases, there are legitimate differences of opinion about how an entity should account for these matters.

The IASC's Issues Paper identified the following characteristics of activities in the extractive industries, which are closely related to the financial reporting issues that are discussed in this chapter:

- *High risks* – In the extractive industries there is a high risk that the amounts spent in finding new mineral resources will not result in additional commercially recoverable reserves. In financial reporting terms this means that it can remain uncertain for a long period whether or not certain expenditures give rise to an asset. Further risks exist in relation to production (i.e. quantities actually produced may differ considerably from those previously estimated) and price (i.e. commodity prices are often volatile).
- *Little relationship between risks and rewards* – In the extractive industries a small expenditure may result in finding mineral deposits with a value of many times the amount of the expenditure. Conversely, large expenditures can frequently result in little or no future production. This has given rise to different approaches in financial reporting that can be broadly categorised as follows: (1) expense all expenditures as the future benefits are too uncertain; (2) capitalise some or all expenditures as the cumulative expenditures may be matched to the cumulative benefits, or (3) recognise the mineral assets found at fair value.
- *Long lag between expenditure and production* – Exploration and/or development may take years to complete. During this period it is often far from certain that economic benefits will be derived from the costs incurred.
- *High costs of individual projects* – The costs of individual projects can be very high (e.g. offshore oil and gas projects and deep mining projects). Exploration expenditures that are carried forward pending the outcome of mineral acquisition

and development projects may be highly significant in relation to the equity and the total assets of an entity.

- *Unique cost-sharing arrangements* – High costs and high risks, as discussed above, often lead entities in the extractive industries to enter into risk-sharing arrangements (e.g. joint arrangements, farm-out arrangements, carried interest arrangements, oilfield services arrangements and contract mining). These types of arrangements, which are much more common in the extractive industries than elsewhere, often give rise to their own financial reporting issues.

- *Intense government oversight and regulation* – The regulation of the extractive industries ranges from 'outright governmental ownership of some (especially petroleum) or all minerals to unusual tax benefits or penalties, price controls, restrictions on imports and exports, restrictions on production and distribution, environmental and health and safety regulations, and others'. Governments may also seek to charge an economic rent for resources extracted. These types of government involvement give rise to financial reporting issues, particularly when the precise nature of the government involvement is not obvious.

- *Scarce non-replaceable assets* – Mineral reserves are unique and scarce resources that an entity may not be able to replace in any location or in any form.

- *Economic, technological and political factors* – While these factors are not unique to the extractive industries, the IASC's Issues Paper argues that they tend to have a greater impact on the extractive industries because:

    '(a) fluctuating market prices for minerals (together with floating exchange rates) have a direct impact on the economic viability of reserves and mineral properties. A relatively small percentage change in long-term prices can change decisions on whether or when to explore for, develop, or produce minerals;

    (b) there is a sharp impact from cost changes and technological developments. Changes in costs and, probably more significantly, changes in technology can significantly change the economic viability of particular mineral projects; and

    (c) in almost every country, mineral rights are owned by the state. In those countries where some mineral rights are privately owned, public reliance on adequate sources of minerals for economic and defence purposes often leads to governmental regulations and control. At other times, governmental policies may be changed to levy special taxes or impose governmental controls on the extractive industries.'

While it may be the case that the above factors affect the extractive industries more than others, to the extent that they also arise in the pharmaceutical, bio-technology, agricultural and software industries some of these risks give rise to further financial reporting issues. However, those industries are not affected by the combination of these circumstances to the same extent as is the case with the extractive industries. It is a combination of these factors, a lack of specific guidance in IFRSs and a long history of industry practice and guidance from previous GAAPs that have given rise to a range of accounting practices in the extractive industries.

There is as yet no IFRS that addresses all of the specific issues of the extractive industries although attempts to devise such a standard commenced quite some time ago. Furthermore, these draft proposals to date would not have addressed many of these specific issues that affect the extractive industries.

1.1.1 Definition of key terms

The most important terms and abbreviations used are defined in this chapter when discussed or in the glossary at 23 below. However, alternative or more detailed definitions of financial reporting terms, and of mining and oil and gas technical terms and abbreviations, can be found in the following publications:

- *Issues Paper Extractive Industries*, IASC, November 2000;
- *Petroleum Resources Management System*, Society of Petroleum Engineers, 2007 (revised June 2018);
- *The Australasian Code for Reporting of Exploration Results, Mineral Resources and Ore Reserves* (the JORC Code), Australasian Joint Ore Reserves Committee (the JORC Committee); and
- The former UK Oil Industry Accounting Committee Statement of Recommended Practice (OIAC SORP) (see 1.4 below).

1.2 The development of IFRS 6 – *Exploration for and Evaluation of Mineral Resources*

In December 2004, the IASB issued IFRS 6 – *Exploration for and Evaluation of Mineral Resources* – which addresses the accounting for one particular aspect of the extractive industries – being exploration and evaluation ('E&E') activities. IFRS 6 was issued as a form of interim guidance to clarify the application of IFRSs and the IASB's *Conceptual Framework* to E&E activities and to provide temporary relief from existing IFRSs in some areas. The IASB decided to develop IFRS 6 because mineral rights and mineral resources are outside the scope of IAS 16 and IAS 38, E&E expenditures are significant to entities engaged in extractive activities, and there were different views on how these expenditures should be accounted for under IFRSs. Other standard-setting bodies have had diverse accounting practices for E&E assets which often differed from practices in other sectors with analogous expenditures. [IFRS 6(2010).IN1].

One of the IASB's goals in developing IFRS 6 was to avoid unnecessary disruption for both users and preparers. The Board therefore proposed to limit the need for entities to change their existing accounting policies for E&E assets. As a result, IFRS 6 defines what E&E expenditures are, makes limited improvements to existing accounting practices for E&E expenditures, such as specifying when entities need to assess E&E assets for impairment in accordance with IAS 36 – *Impairment of Assets,* and requires certain disclosures.

E&E expenditures are 'expenditures incurred by an entity in connection with the exploration for and evaluation of mineral resources before the technical feasibility and commercial viability of extracting a mineral resource are demonstrable'. E&E assets are 'exploration and evaluation expenditures recognised as assets in accordance with the entity's accounting policy'. [IFRS 6 Appendix A].

The IFRS Interpretations Committee ('the Interpretations Committee') has noted that the effect of the limited scope of IFRS 6 is to grant relief only to policies in respect of E&E activities, and that this relief did not extend to activities before or after the E&E phase. The Interpretations Committee confirmed that the scope of IFRS 6 limited the relief from the hierarchy to policies applied to E&E activities only and that there is no basis for interpreting IFRS 6 as granting any additional relief in areas outside its scope.

The detailed requirements of IFRS 6 are discussed at 3 below.

1.3 April 2010 Discussion Paper: Extractive Activities

In April 2010, as part of the long running project of trying to progress the issue of extractive industries accounting, the IASB published the staff Discussion Paper – *Extractive Activities* (the DP). The DP was developed by a research team comprising members of the Australian, Canadian, Norwegian and South African accounting standard-setters.[2] Although the IASB has discussed the project team's findings, the DP only reflects the views of the project team. The Board did not express any preliminary views or make any tentative decisions on the DP and, due to other standard-setting priorities, subsequently put the project on hold. In the past twelve months there has been some activity on the project. See 1.3.6 below for a status update.

The DP addressed some of the financial reporting issues associated with exploring for and finding minerals, oil and natural gas deposits, developing those deposits and extracting the minerals, oil and natural gas. These were collectively referred to as 'extractive activities' or, alternatively, as 'upstream activities'.[3] The aim of the project was to create a single accounting and disclosure model that would only apply to upstream extractive activities in both the minerals and oil and gas industries. This represented a change from IFRS 6, which currently includes exploration and evaluation activities relating to minerals, oil, natural gas and similar non-regenerative resources within its scope. The project team decided against a broader scope in the DP as this would result in the need to develop additional definitions, accounting models and disclosures.[4]

The DP concluded that there were similarities in the main business activities, and the geological and other risks and uncertainties of both the minerals and oil and gas industries.[5] There were also similarities in the definitions of reserves and resources used by the Committee for Mineral Reserves International Reporting Standards (CRIRSCO) and the Society of Petroleum Engineers Oil and Gas Reserves Committee (SPE OGRC).[6] The DP therefore proposed that there should be a single accounting and disclosure model that applies to all extractive activities (as defined, see 1.1 above).

While it has been generally acknowledged that the issues addressed in the DP are important, a significant number of respondents to the DP commented that the scope of the DP did not address many of the more complex accounting issues where practice is diverse and greater consistency is required.

These issues included:

- the lack of guidance on complex areas such as farm-out and farm-in transactions (see 6.2 below); and
- accounting for production sharing and royalty agreements (see 5.3 and 5.7 below).

The main proposals in the DP have been summarised briefly below.

1.3.1 Definitions of reserves and resources

The DP explored a number of alternatives for defining reserves and resources. The definition used is 'reserves and resources are either the most significant assets or amongst the most significant assets for most entities engaged in extractive activities. Assessing the financial position and performance of an entity engaged in extractive activities in order to make economic decisions therefore requires an understanding of the entity's minerals or oil and gas reserves and resources, which are the source of future cash flows'.[7]

This chapter considers the definitions of reserves and resources that should be used in financial reporting. See 2 below for further discussion.

1.3.2 Asset recognition

The DP proposed that legal rights (i.e. exploration rights and extraction rights) should form the basis of a mineral asset or oil and gas asset. An asset should be recognised when the legal rights are acquired. Associated with these legal rights is information about the (possible) existence of minerals or oil and gas, the extent and characteristics of the deposit, and the economics of their extraction. The project team believed that rights and information associated with minerals or oil and gas properties satisfy the asset recognition criteria. While such information does not represent a separate asset, the project team proposed that information obtained from subsequent exploration and evaluation activities and development works would be treated as enhancements of the asset represented by the legal rights.

When considering the appropriate unit of account (see 4 below), the DP proposed that the geographical boundary of the unit of account would be defined initially on the basis of the exploration rights held. As exploration, evaluation and development activities took place, the unit of account would contract progressively until it became no greater than a single area, or group of contiguous areas, for which the legal rights were held and which are managed separately and would be expected to generate largely independent cash flows.

1.3.3 Asset measurement

The DP considered both current value (e.g. fair value) and historical cost as potential measurement bases for minerals and oil and gas assets. Based on their findings, and taking the views of users and preparers into account, the project team concluded that minerals and oil and gas assets should be measured at historical cost and that detailed disclosures should be provided to enhance the relevance of the financial statements. The project team acknowledged that its choice of historical cost as the measurement basis was based to a large extent on doing the 'least harm'.

In relation to impairment, it was considered that the IAS 36 impairment testing model was not feasible for exploration properties given the early stage of such properties. Therefore, the DP concluded that exploration properties should only be tested for impairment whenever, in management's judgement, there is evidence that suggests that there is a high likelihood that the carrying amount of an exploration asset will not be recovered in full. This would require management to apply a separate set of indicators to such properties in order to assess whether their continued recognition as assets would be justified. In addition, further disclosures would be required in respect of the impairment of exploration properties due to the fact that management may take different views on the exploration properties.

These would include separate presentation of exploration properties, the factors that led to an impairment being recognised, and management's view as to why the remaining value of the asset or the other exploration assets is not impaired. This impairment assessment would need to be conducted separately for each exploration property.

1.3.4 Disclosure

The DP proposed extensive disclosures aimed at ensuring users of financial reports could evaluate:

- the value attributable to an entity's minerals or oil and gas assets;
- the contribution of those assets to current period financial performance; and
- the nature and extent of risks and uncertainties associated with those assets.

The DP proposed detailed disclosures about the quantities of reserves and resources, and production revenues and costs. If the assets are measured at historical cost then detailed information should be disclosed about their current value and how it was determined. If, instead, the assets are measured at fair value then detailed information should be disclosed about that fair value and how it was determined.

It is noted that a number of the proposed disclosures differ from US GAAP. These include disclosures of:

- key reserve estimate assumptions and sensitivity analysis (not required by US GAAP); and
- proved and probable reserves (US GAAP only requires proved reserves, with an option to disclose probable reserves).

1.3.5 Publish What You Pay proposals

A coalition of non-governmental organisations has promoted, and continues to promote, a campaign called Publish What You Pay (PWYP), proposing that entities undertaking extractive activities should be required to disclose, in their financial reports, the payments they make to each host government. Furthermore, PWYP recommended that its disclosure proposals should be incorporated into an eventual IFRS for extractive activities. Given this, a section in the DP was dedicated to the PWYP proposals. The DP acknowledged that the disclosure of payments made to governments provides information that would be of use to capital providers in making their investment and lending decisions, but noted that providing this information might be difficult and costly for some entities.

These proposals were partially in response to a perception that in certain countries some mining companies and oil and gas companies are not paying their 'fair share' in exchange for extracting scarce natural resources. In addition, there has been and continues to be increasing political pressure to expand the disclosure of payments to governments by entities within extractive industries as a means of reducing corruption by shining a light on these payments. As well as the proposals made in the DP, there are also increasing calls for transparency in the reporting of taxes and other payments to governments. This has led to a variety of transparency or publish what you pay types of initiatives being introduced in different jurisdictions around the world (e.g. US, Europe, UK, Canada, Australia, to name just a few), however these are outside the scope of IFRS and are governed by specific legislation.

1.3.6 Status of Extractive Activities project

After the 2011 Agenda Consultation, the Board adopted a more evidence-based approach to setting IFRS Standards, in that the Board would not start a standard-setting project before carrying out research to gather sufficient evidence that an accounting problem exists, that the problem is sufficiently important that standard-setting is required and that a feasible solution can be found.

Before the IASB's 2015 agenda consultation process, the IASB's research programme included a project on intangible assets, research and development and extractive activities. It was acknowledged that extractive activities are important globally and are particularly significant in some jurisdictions. IFRS 6 was originally intended to be a temporary Standard and provides a number of exemptions from other IFRS Standards that would otherwise apply. It was noted that a permanent solution would be required for reporting these activities.

After considering the feedback from the 2015 agenda consultation process, the Board created a pipeline of future research projects which included Extractive Activities. With respect to the latter, the IASB decided to narrow the scope to remove any reference to intangibles and research and development. The reason for this was primarily based on the amount of resources a combined project would require and a view that the Board could work more effectively and more efficiently on extractive activities if it did not try to address intangible assets and research and development at the same time.

The Board decided in February 2018 to start work on Extractive Activities by asking those national standard-setters whose staff contributed to the 2010 Discussion Paper *Extractive Activities* to make the Board aware of any developments since then.

At the March 2019, September 2019 and June 2020 IASB meetings, the Board discussed feedback from National Standard-setters and other stakeholders on changes in the extractives industry since the publication of the 2010 Extractive Activities Discussion Paper. The Board was not asked to make any decisions.

Overall, most National Standard-setters consulted identified that:

(a) the markets for minerals and oil and gas have become more volatile than they were in 2010;

(b) the risk profile of entities operating in the extractives industry has changed;

(c) entities operating in the extractives industry are engaging in new and more complex transactions whereby the current accounting requirements may not be clear;

(d) increasingly, entities operating in the extractives industry are engaging in unconventional extractives activities;

(e) the reporting of other information, such as payments to governments and sustainability reporting, is being mandated at a jurisdictional level; and

(f) there have been minor amendments to the relevant reserves and resource definitions within each jurisdiction.

Outreach performed with other stakeholders highlighted relatively consistent feedback with that identified by the National Standard-setters, noting that there are mixed views with respect to the appropriate scope and approach of the project going forward. Limited appetite seems to exist for a project with similar scope to that of the 2010 Extractive Activities Discussion Paper. However, the following two areas of focus were suggested by many of the other stakeholders with whom the IASB staff performed outreach:

- improving existing disclosures; and
- developing additional disclosures for IFRS and non-IFRS information.

Overall, the staff believe that the Discussion Paper and the feedback received on the Discussion Paper remain a valid starting point for the Board as it starts its new research project on Extractive Activities. However, the changes highlighted by the National Standard-setters summarised in this paper, in combination with the Discussion Paper, should also be considered by the Board.

Based on the analysis, staff propose further research into the effects of the following topics on the Discussion Paper and project proposals:

(a) 2018 *Conceptual Framework* for Financial Reporting;
(b) new standards and amendments, including other Board publications;
(c) changes to reserves and resources classifications and definitions; and
(d) changes to transparency and sustainability reporting, for example, payments to governments.

Staff analysis on each topic will be brought back at a future meeting to help the Board determine the scope of the Extractive Activities project.

Given this, it is unlikely that there will be any significant developments on this project in the near term.

1.4 Status of the Statement of Recommended Practice, UK Oil Industry Accounting Committee, June 2001 (OIAC SORP)

The Oil Industry Accounting Committee (OIAC), based in the United Kingdom, had previously developed a Statement of Recommended Practice (SORP) titled *Accounting for Oil and Gas Exploration, Development, Production and Decommissioning Activities*, which was updated and adopted by the UK Accounting Standards Board (ASB) in 2001.

The main function of the OIAC SORP had been to set out best practice in relation to activities in the oil and gas industry that were not covered directly by the main body of UK accounting standards. However, as much of the OIAC SORP has now been superseded by subsequent changes to accounting standards, the OIAC has concluded that the SORP is no longer applicable in directing best practice guidance. From 1 January 2015, non-listed UK GAAP reporting entities moved to new accounting standards – FRS 100 – *Application of Financial Reporting Requirements*, FRS 101 – *Reduced Disclosure Framework* – and FRS 102 – *The Financial Reporting Standard applicable in the UK and Republic of Ireland* – and were required by FRS 101 and FRS 102 to apply IFRS 6. As such, there is no intention to further update the SORP for future industry developments or changes in accounting standards. The ASB has indicated it will continue to provide the OIAC SORP as a reference document, but it will primarily be for educational purposes, it will not carry the authoritative accounting weight it did previously, and will not be reviewed or endorsed by the UK Financial Reporting Council (UK FRC). In the future, the OIAC may, when considered necessary, issue guidance notes addressing industry specific accounting matters under IFRS and UK GAAP but these will not be endorsed by the UK FRC.

Given the long history of companies in certain jurisdictions looking to the OIAC SORP for guidance for oil and gas accounting and reporting, and the lack of definitive guidance elsewhere, the SORP is likely to continue to be a valuable source of industry guidance e.g. reserves reporting (see 2.4.1 below). However, we highlight the importance of having to overlay IFRS pronouncements and guidance as and when they are available.

Throughout this chapter the OIAC SORP will be referred to as the 'former OIAC SORP' because it has been decommissioned.

1.5 Guidance under national accounting standards

Entities complying with IFRSs do not have a free hand in selecting accounting policies – indeed the very purpose of a body of accounting literature is to restrict such choices. IAS 8 – *Accounting Policies, Changes in Accounting Estimates and Errors* – makes it clear that when a standard or an interpretation specifically applies to a transaction, other event or condition, the accounting policy or policies applied to that item should be determined by applying the standard or interpretation and considering any relevant implementation guidance issued by the IASB. *[IAS 8.7]*.

However, in the extractive industries there are many circumstances where a particular event, transaction or other condition is not specifically addressed by IFRS. When this is the case, IAS 8 sets out a hierarchy of guidance to be considered in the selection of an accounting policy (see Chapter 3 at 4.3).

The primary requirement of the standard is that management should use its judgement in developing and applying an accounting policy that results in information that is both relevant and reliable. *[IAS 8.10]*.

In making the judgement, management should refer to, and consider the applicability of, the following sources in descending order:

(a) the requirements in standards and interpretations dealing with similar and related issues; and

(b) the definitions, recognition criteria and measurement concepts for assets, liabilities, income and expenses in the *Conceptual Framework*. *[IAS 8.11]*.

Management may also take into account the most recent pronouncements of other standard-setting bodies that use a similar conceptual framework to develop accounting standards, other accounting literature and accepted industry practices, to the extent that these do not conflict with the sources in (a) and (b) above. *[IAS 8.12]*.

The stock exchanges in Australia, Canada, South Africa, the United Kingdom and the United States have historically been home to the majority of the listed mining companies and oil and gas companies. Consequently, it is organisations from those countries that have been the most active in developing both reserves and resources measurement standards and accounting standards specifically for companies engaged in extractive activities. In developing an accounting policy for an issue that is not specifically dealt with in IFRSs, an entity operating in an extractive industry may find it useful to consider accounting standards developed in these countries. It should be noted, however, that the requirements in such guidance were developed under national accounting standards and may contradict specific requirements and guidance in IFRSs that deals with similar and related issues.

1.6 Upstream versus downstream activities

Upstream activities in the extractive industries are defined as 'exploring for, finding, acquiring, and developing mineral resources up to the point that the reserves are first capable of being sold or used, even if the enterprise intends to process them further'.[8]

Downstream activities are 'the refining, processing, marketing, and distributing of petroleum, natural gas, or mined mineral (other than refining or processing that is necessary to make the minerals that have been mined or extracted capable of being sold)'.[9]

Thus, activities that are required to make the product saleable or usable are generally considered to be upstream activities. For example, the removal of water to produce dry gas would be an upstream activity, because otherwise the gas cannot be sold at all. However, refining crude oil is considered to be a downstream activity, because crude oil can be sold.

This chapter focuses on upstream activities in the extractive industries as they are primarily affected by the issues discussed above. However, downstream activities are discussed to the extent that they give rise to issues that are unique to the extractive industries (e.g. provisional pricing clauses) or are subject to the same issues as upstream activities (e.g. production sharing contracts).

1.6.1 Phases in upstream activities

Although there is not a universally accepted classification of upstream activities in the extractive industries, the IASC Issues Paper identified the following eight phases which other authors also commonly identify:[10]

(a) *Prospecting* – Prospecting involves activities undertaken to search for an area of interest, a geologic anomaly or structure that may warrant detailed exploration.[11] Prospecting is undertaken typically before mineral rights in the area have been acquired, and if the prospecting results are negative the area of prospecting generally will be abandoned and no mineral rights acquired.[12] However, sometimes it will be necessary to acquire a prospecting permit as the prospecting activities require access to the land to carry out geological and geophysical tests.[13]

(b) *Acquisition of mineral rights* – The acquisition phase involves the activities related to obtaining legal rights to explore for, develop, and/or produce wasting resources on a mineral property.[14] Legal rights may be acquired in a number of ways as discussed at 5 below.

(c) *Exploration* – Exploration is the detailed examination of a geographical area of interest that has shown sufficient mineral-producing potential to merit further exploration, often using techniques that are similar to those used in the prospecting phase.[15] In the mining sector, exploration usually involves taking cores for analysis, sinking exploratory shafts, geological mapping, geochemical analysis, cutting drifts and crosscuts, opening shallow pits, and removing overburden in some areas.[16] In the oil and gas sector, exploration involves techniques such as shooting seismic, core drilling, and ultimately the drilling of an exploratory well to determine whether oil and gas reserves do exist.[17]

(d) *Appraisal or evaluation* – This involves determining the technical feasibility and commercial viability of mineral deposits that have been found through exploration.[18] This phase typically includes:[19]

   (i) detailed engineering studies and drilling of additional wells by oil and gas companies to determine how the reservoir can best be developed to obtain maximum recovery;

   (ii) determination by mining companies of the volume and grade of deposits through drilling of core samples, trenching, and sampling activities in an area known to contain mineral resources;

   (iii) examination and testing by mining companies of extraction methods and metallurgical or treatment processes;

   (iv) surveying transportation and infrastructure requirements;

   (v) conducting market and finance studies; and

   (vi) making detailed economic evaluations to determine whether development of the reserves is commercially justified.

(e) *Development* – Development is the establishment of access to the mineral reserve and other preparations for commercial production. In the mining sector, development includes sinking shafts and underground drifts, making permanent excavations, developing passageways and rooms or galleries, building roads and tunnels, and advance removal of overburden and waste rock.[20] In the oil and gas sector the development phase involves gaining access to, and preparing, well locations for drilling, constructing platforms or preparing drill sites, drilling wells, and installing equipment and facilities.[21]

(f) *Construction* – Construction involves installing facilities, such as buildings, machinery and equipment to extract, treat, and transport minerals.[22]

(g) *Production* – The production phase involves the extraction of the natural resources from the earth and the related processes necessary to make the produced resource marketable or transportable.[23]

(h) *Closure and decommissioning* – Closure means ceasing production, removing equipment and facilities, restoring the production site to appropriate conditions after operations have ceased and abandoning the site.[24]

The above phases are not necessarily discrete sequential steps. Instead, the phases often overlap or take place simultaneously. Nevertheless, they provide a useful framework for developing accounting policies in the extractive industries. Accounting for expenditures depends very much on the phase during which they are incurred; for example, as discussed further below, costs incurred in the prospecting phase cannot be recognised as assets, whereas most costs incurred in the construction phase should be capitalised.

2 MINERAL RESERVES AND RESOURCES

As noted in 1.1 above, IFRSs currently use the term 'minerals' and 'mineral assets' when referring to the extractive industries as a whole. This is used as a collective term to include both mining and oil and gas reserves and resources. For the purposes of this chapter, consistency with the current wording in IFRSs will be maintained and therefore, unless stated otherwise, 'minerals' and 'mineral assets' will encompass both mining and oil and gas.

This section discusses in some detail the underlying principles used by entities to estimate the quantity of recoverable mineral reserves and resources for both mining and oil and gas, that the entity owns or has a right to extract. At the commercial level, these estimates are considered of paramount importance by stakeholders in making investment decisions and are also fundamental in accounting for mining activities and oil and gas activities.

The importance of estimating reserves and resources is matched by the difficulty in doing so, both technically and methodologically. For example, there is no firm consensus amongst regulators and the industries on which commodity prices should be used in reserves and resources estimation (i.e. historical, spot or forward-looking). We therefore aim to provide an introduction to this subject, and to explain the main methods used to arrive at reserves and resources estimates, including the valuation methods used once quantities have been estimated. In our view, without a sound grasp of this aspect, it is difficult to make an informed judgement as to how to account for mineral extraction activities.

Mineral reserves and resources are often the most valuable assets of mining companies and oil and gas companies and mineral reserve estimates are a very important part of the way these companies report to their stakeholders. However, in an entity's financial statements, assets relating to extraction of mineral reserves and resources are generally measured under IFRSs at their historical cost which, other than by coincidence, will not be their market value. Currently, IFRSs do not require disclosure of reserves and resources, though certain national standards (e.g. US GAAP) and stock exchange regulators (e.g. US Securities and Exchange Commission (SEC), Australian Securities Exchange (ASX), Toronto Stock Exchange (TSX), Johannesburg Stock Exchange (JSE), Securities Commission Malaysia (SC) to name just a few) do. Having said this, there are variances in what is required and what categories are disclosed, including differences between mining and oil and gas.

Notwithstanding there are no specific disclosure requirements in IFRSs, reserves and resources estimates are required in order to apply historical cost accounting under IFRS in:

- deciding whether to capitalise E&E costs, based on an expectation of future commercial production from resource estimates (see 3.2 below);
- calculating the annual depreciation, depletion and amortisation charge under the units of production method (see 16.1.3 below);
- calculating deferred stripping cost adjustments (applicable to mining companies only – see 15.5 below);
- determining impairment charges and reversals under IAS 36 (see 11 below);

- determining whether a gain or loss should be recognised on transactions such as asset swaps, carried interest arrangements and farm-in or farm-out arrangements (see 6 below);
- determining the fair value of acquired mineral reserves and resources when applying the purchase method of accounting under IFRS 3 – *Business Combinations* (see 8 below); and
- estimating the timing of decommissioning or restoration activities (see 10 below).

Reserves and resources reporting in the mining sector and oil and gas sector have been under development since the beginning of the twentieth century. However, reserves and resources estimation techniques in the mining sector and oil and gas sector have developed largely independently as a result of the different nature of the reserves and resources involved. Therefore, the definitions and terminology used in the oil and gas sector and mining sector are discussed separately at 2.2 and 2.3 below respectively. Disclosure is discussed at 2.4 below.

The international efforts to harmonise reserve estimation and reporting are also discussed below.

2.1 International harmonisation of reserve reporting

The project team concluded in the Extractive Activities DP (see 1.3 above) that the nature and extent of the similarities between the CRIRSCO Template (mining) and the PRMS reserve and resource definitions (oil and gas) indicate that these definitions are capable of providing a platform for setting comparable accounting and disclosure requirements for both mining and oil and gas activities. Therefore, they recommended that the CRIRSCO template and the PRMS definitions of reserves and resources are suitable to use in a future IFRS for Extractive Activities. Nonetheless, there is some tension between the definition of an asset in the IASB's *Conceptual Framework* and the assumptions underlying the reserves and resources definitions.[25] The points of tension highlighted in the DP include:

- the CRIRSCO Template and the PRMS both make use of entity-specific assumptions that are applied to derive a reserve or resource estimate, whereas IFRS typically requires that estimates should make use of economic assumptions that reflect market-based evidence, where available; and
- the CRIRSCO Template and the PRMS require that certain conditions must exist before a resource can be converted into a reserve. In contrast, management's intentions are not a feature of the Conceptual Framework's definition of an asset.

While the DP recommended the use of the CRIRSCO Template and PRMS, it also recommended that the alternative option of using the *United Nations Framework Classification for Fossil Energy and Mineral Resources* (UNFC) should be reconsidered if an Extractive Activities project is added to the IASB's active agenda.[26]

In 2009, the SEC revised its oil and gas reserves and resources estimation and disclosure requirements. The primary objectives of the final rule – *Modernization of Oil and Gas Reporting (Release No. 33-8995)* – were to increase the transparency and information value of reserve disclosures and improve comparability among oil and gas companies, including comparability between domestic registrants and foreign private issuers.

Although the SEC has revised its oil and gas requirements, a similar revision process has not been undertaken for mineral reserves and resources. As a result, despite calls from both the CRIRSCO and the Society for Mining, Metallurgy and Exploration (SME) to consider the need for convergence given the increasing overlap between oil and gas and mining in such areas as tar sands and oil shales, no progress has been made in achieving convergence between the SEC requirements and the various other requirements. Key differences that still remain include:

- the SEC does not allow the term 'resources' to be used in reports;
- the SEC states that final or bankable feasibility studies need to be completed before new greenfield reserves and resources can be declared;
- the SEC requirement for oil and gas companies to use 12-month average prices under SEC Release No. 338995, to represent existing economic conditions to determine the economic producibility of oil and gas reserves for disclosure purposes; and
- the SEC requirement for mining companies to use three year trailing average rather than forward-looking commodity prices in reserve estimation under US Securities and Exchange Commission's Industry Guide 7 – *Description of Property by Issuers Engaged or to Be Engaged in Significant Mining Operations* (SEC Industry Guide 7).

2.2 Petroleum reserve estimation and reporting

The '*SPE/WPC/AAPG/SPEE Petroleum Resources Management System*' (SPE-PRMS), which was published in 2007, is the leading framework for the estimation and reporting of petroleum reserves and resources. It was prepared by the Oil and Gas Reserves Committee of the Society of Petroleum Engineers (SPE) and reviewed and sponsored by the World Petroleum Council (WPC), the American Association of Petroleum Geologists (AAPG) and the Society of Petroleum Evaluation Engineers (SPEE), and subsequently supported by the Society of Exploration Geophysicists (SEG), the Society of Petrophysicists and Well Log Analysts (SPWLA) and the European Association of Geoscientists & Engineers (EAGE).[27] The definitions and guidelines in the SPE-PRMS, which are internationally used within the oil and gas sector, deal with:[28]

- classification and categorisation of resources;
- evaluation and reporting; and
- estimation of recoverable quantities.

Most of the major regulatory agencies have developed disclosure guidelines that impose classification rules similar to, but not directly linked to, the SPE-PRMS, and most typically mandate disclosure of only a subset of the total reserves and resources defined in the SPE-PRMS. For example, the SEC specifies that only Proved Reserves should be disclosed,[29] but now allows for optional disclosure of Probable Reserves.

In June 2018 the SPE Board approved the revision of the Petroleum Resources Management System (PRMS) prepared by the Oil and Gas Reserves Committee of the SPE. The updated PRMS is a consensus of input collected from consulting and financial firms, government agencies, and exploration and production (E&P) companies. The process included a public comment period, and required input and approval by six sponsoring societies: the World Petroleum Council, the American Association of

Petroleum Geologists, the Society of Petroleum Evaluation Engineers, the Society of Exploration Geophysicists, the European Association of Geoscientists and Engineers, and the Society of Petrophysicists and Well Log Analysts.

2.2.1 Basic principles and definitions

The following graphically presents the SPE-PRMS resources classification system:[30]

Figure 43.1: Resources classification framework

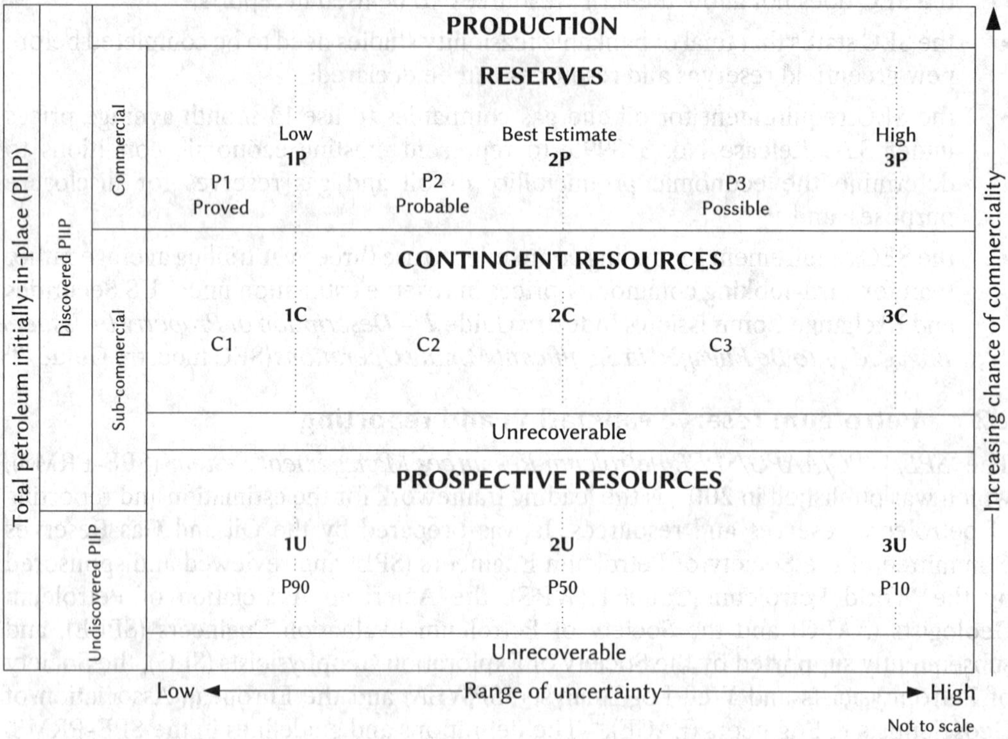

		Range of uncertainty		
		PRODUCTION		
		RESERVES		
	Low 1P / P1 Proved	Best Estimate 2P / P2 Probable	High 3P / P3 Possible	
		CONTINGENT RESOURCES		
	1C / C1	2C / C2	3C / C3	
		Unrecoverable		
		PROSPECTIVE RESOURCES		
	1U / P90	2U / P50	3U / P10	
		Unrecoverable		

(Vertical axis: Total petroleum initially-in-place (PIIP) — Discovered PIIP [Commercial, Sub-commercial], Undiscovered PIIP. Right axis: Increasing chance of commerciality. Horizontal axis: Range of uncertainty, Low to High. Not to scale.)

The horizontal axis reflects the *range of uncertainty* of estimated quantities potentially recoverable from an accumulation by a project, while the vertical axis represents the *chance of* commerciality, which is the chance that a project will be committed for development and reach commercial producing status.[31]

The SPE-PRMS defines proved, probable and possible reserves as follows:

- '*Reserves* are those quantities of petroleum anticipated to be commercially recoverable by application of development projects to known accumulations from a given date forward under defined conditions. Reserves must further satisfy four criteria: discovered, recoverable, commercial, and remaining (as of the evaluation's effective date) based on the development project(s) applied... Reserves are further categorized in accordance with the range of certainty associated with the estimates and may be sub-classified based on project maturity and/or characterized by development and production status.'[32]

- '*Proved Reserves* are those quantities of petroleum, that, by analysis of geoscience and engineering data, can be estimated with reasonable certainty to be commercially recoverable from known reservoirs and under defined technical and commercial conditions. If deterministic methods are used, the term "reasonable certainty" is intended to express a high degree of confidence that the quantities will be recovered. If probabilistic methods are used, there should be at least a 90% probability that the quantities actually recovered will equal or exceed the estimate.'[33]

- '*Probable Reserves* are those additional Reserves which analysis of geoscience and engineering data indicate are less likely to be recovered than Proved Reserves but more certain to be recovered than Possible Reserves. It is equally likely that actual remaining quantities recovered will be greater than or less than the sum of the estimated Proved plus Probable Reserves (2P). In this context, when probabilistic methods are used, there should be at least a 50% probability that the actual quantities recovered will equal or exceed the 2P estimate.'[34]

- '*Possible Reserves* are those additional reserves which analysis of geoscience and engineering data suggest are less likely to be recoverable than Probable Reserves. The total quantities ultimately recovered from the project have a low probability to exceed the sum of Proved plus Probable plus Possible (3P) Reserves, which is equivalent to the high estimate scenario. When probabilistic methods are used, there should be at least a 10% probability that the actual quantities recovered will equal or exceed the 3P estimate.'[35]

The SPE-PRMS distinguishes between Contingent and Prospective Resources:

- 'The term *Resources* as used herein is intended to encompass all quantities of petroleum naturally occurring on or within the Earth's crust, both discovered and undiscovered (whether recoverable or unrecoverable), plus those quantities already produced. Further, it includes all types of petroleum whether currently considered "conventional" or "unconventional" resources.'[36]

- '*Contingent Resources* are those quantities of petroleum estimated, as of a given date, to be potentially recoverable from known accumulations, by the application of development project(s) not currently deemed to be commercial owing to one or more contingencies. Contingent Resources have an associated chance of development. Contingent Resources may include, for example, projects for which there are currently no viable markets, or where commercial recovery is dependent on technology under development, or where evaluation of the accumulation is insufficient to clearly assess commerciality. Contingent Resources are further categorized in accordance with the range of uncertainty associated with the estimates and may be sub-classified based on project maturity and/or economic status.'[37]

- '*Prospective Resources* are those quantities of petroleum estimated, as of a given date, to be potentially recoverable from undiscovered accumulations by application of future development projects. Prospective Resources have both an associated chance of geologic discovery and a chance of development. Prospective Resources are further categorized in accordance with the range of uncertainty associated with recoverable estimates, assuming discovery and development, and may be sub-classified based on project maturity.'[38]

Total petroleum initially-in-place (PIIP) is all quantities of petroleum that are estimated to exist in naturally occurring accumulations, discovered and undiscovered, before production.

Discovered PIIP is the quantity of petroleum that is estimated, as of a given date, to be contained in known accumulations before production.[39] *Undiscovered PIIP* is that quantity of petroleum estimated, as of a given date, to be contained within accumulations yet to be discovered.[40]

Production is the cumulative quantities of petroleum that has been recovered at a given date.[41] *Unrecoverable Resources* are that portion of Discovered or Undiscovered PIIP evaluated, as of a given date, to be unrecoverable by the currently defined project(s). A portion of these quantities may become recoverable in the future as commercial circumstances change, technology is developed, or additional data are acquired. The remaining portion may never be recovered because of physical/chemical constraints represented by subsurface interaction of fluids and reservoir rocks.[42]

2.2.2 Classification and categorisation guidelines

The SPE-PRMS provides guidance on classifying resources depending on the relative maturity of the development projects being applied to yield the recoverable quantity estimates.[43]

Figure 43.2: Sub-classes based on project maturity

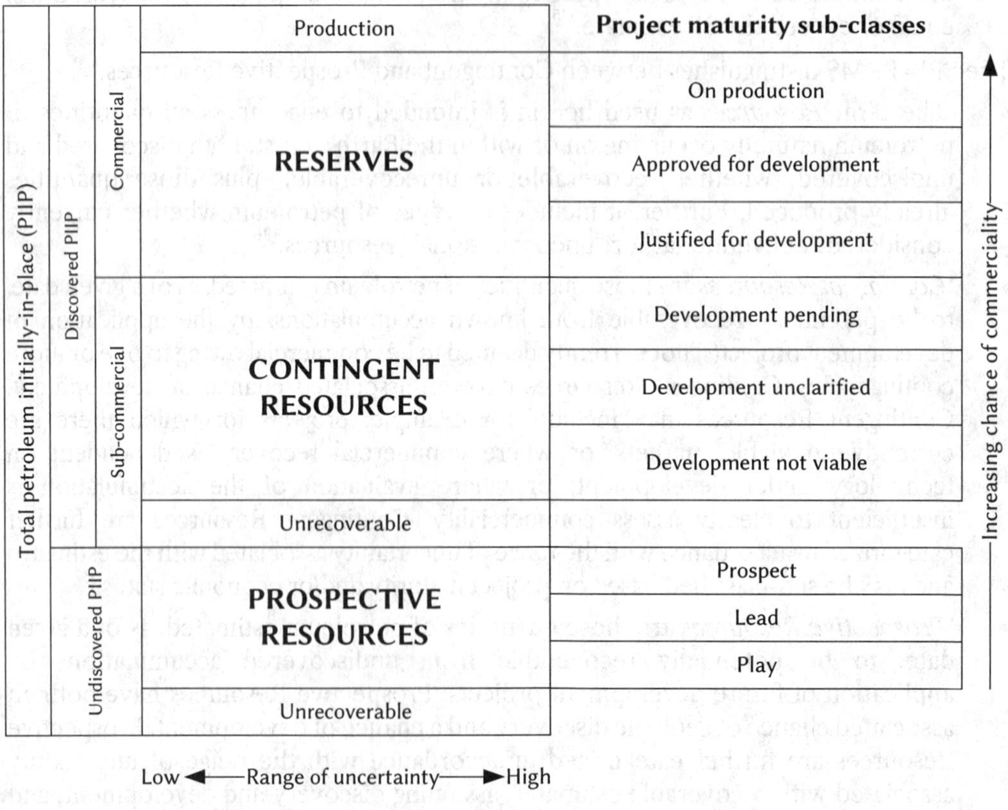

Total petroleum initially-in-place (PIIP)			Category	Project maturity sub-classes	Chance of commerciality
Discovered PIIP	Commercial		Production	On production	Increasing
			RESERVES	Approved for development	
				Justified for development	
	Sub-commercial		CONTINGENT RESOURCES	Development pending	
				Development unclarified	
				Development not viable	
			Unrecoverable		
Undiscovered PIIP			PROSPECTIVE RESOURCES	Prospect	
				Lead	
				Play	
			Unrecoverable		

Low ◄—— Range of uncertainty ——► High

As Figure 43.2[44] above illustrates, development projects and associated recoverable quantities may be sub-classified according to project maturity levels and the associated actions (i.e. business decisions) required to move a project forward to commercial production.[45]

The SPE-PRMS also provides guidance on categorising resources, depending on the associated degrees of uncertainty, into the following cumulative categories:[46]

- proved, probable and possible (1P, 2P and 3P) for reserves;
- low, best and high (1C, 2C and 3C) for contingent resources; and
- low estimate, best estimate and high estimate for prospective resources.

Additionally, guidance is provided on categorisation of reserves and resources related to incremental projects, such as workovers, infill drilling and improved recovery.[47]

To promote consistency in project evaluations and reporting, the SPE-PRMS provides guidelines on the economic assumptions that are to be used, measurement of production, and resources entitlement and recognition,[48] and also provides guidance on the analytical procedures, and on the deterministic and probabilistic methods to be used.

2.3 Mining resource and reserve reporting

The *Australasian Code for Reporting of Exploration Results, Mineral Resources and Ore Reserves* (JORC Code) is prepared by the Joint Ore Reserves Committee (JORC) of the Australasian Institute of Mining and Metallurgy, Australian Institute of Geoscientists and Minerals Council of Australia. The JORC was established in 1971, the first edition of the JORC Code was published in 1989,[49] with the most recent edition of the JORC Code issued in 2012. This version of the JORC code and associated ASX listing rules relating to the disclosure of reserves and resources by ASX listed mining and oil and gas exploration and production companies came into effect on 1 December 2013.

Subsequently, many jurisdictions have established similar national reporting standards. These include:

- Canada: *CIM Definition Standards on Mineral Resources and Mineral Reserves*, Canadian Institute of Mining, Metallurgy and Petroleum (CIM);
- Chile: *Code for the Certification of Exploration Prospects, Mineral Resources and Ore Reserves*, Instituto de Ingenieros de Minas de Chile (IIMCh);
- Pan European Reserves Reporting Committee (PERC) in the United Kingdom, Ireland and Western Europe;
- Peru: *Code for Reporting on Mineral Resources and Ore Reserves*, Joint Committee of the Venture Capital Segment of the Lima Stock Exchange;
- South Africa: *South African Code for Reporting of Mineral Resources and Mineral Reserves*, South African Mineral Resource Committee (SAMREC); and
- United States: *Guide for Reporting Exploration Information, Mineral Resources and Mineral Reserves*, Society for Mining, Metallurgy and Exploration (SME).

In July 2006, CRIRSCO first published a generic International Reporting Template for reporting mineral resources and mineral ore reserves, modelled on those of the JORC Code, and the latest update occurred in November 2019. This reflects best practice national reporting standards but excludes national regulatory requirements. The template serves as a guide to national standard-setters that do not have a reporting standard or who want to revise their existing standard to an internationally acceptable form.[50] 'The system is primarily targeted at establishing international best practice standards for regulatory and public disclosures and combines the basic components of a number of national reporting codes and guidelines that have been adopted in similar forms by all the major agencies [other than] the SEC. The classification is applied, with small modifications or extensions, by most mining companies for the purpose of internal resource management.'[51]

In the United States, public disclosures of mineral resources and mineral reserves are regulated by the SEC, which does not recognise the CRIRSCO guidelines. Unsurprisingly, some of the SEC requirements (Industry Guide 7) for public release of information are materially different from those applicable in other countries.[52] The SEC's Industry Guide 7 is discussed at 2.4.2 below.

2.3.1 CRIRSCO International Reporting Template (November 2019)

Set out below are the main requirements of the CRIRSCO International Reporting Template (CRIRSCO Template) to the extent that they are relevant to financial reporting by mining companies.

2.3.1.A Scope

The main principles governing the operation and application of the CRIRSCO Template are transparency, materiality and competence. These are aimed at ensuring that the reader of a public report is provided with:[53]

- sufficient information that is clear and unambiguous (transparency);
- a report that contains all relevant information which investors and their professional advisers would reasonably require and would reasonably expect to find, to be able to form a reasoned and balanced judgement about the Exploration Results, Mineral Resources or Mineral Reserves being reported (materiality); and
- information that is based on work that is the responsibility of suitably qualified and experienced persons who are subject to an enforceable professional code of ethics and rules of conduct (competence).

A *public report* is a report 'prepared for the purpose of informing investors or potential investors and their advisors on Exploration Targets, Exploration Results, Mineral Resources or Mineral Reserves. They include, but are not limited to, annual and quarterly company reports, media releases, information memoranda, technical papers, website postings and public presentations'.[54] The CRIRSCO Template is applicable to all solid minerals, including diamonds, other gemstones, industrial minerals, stone and aggregates, and coal.[55] The CRIRSCO Template provides supplementary rules on reporting related to coal, diamonds and industrial minerals, due to the special nature of those types of deposit.

A public report should be prepared by a *competent person*, defined in the CRIRSCO Template as '... a minerals industry professional, who is a NRO (to insert appropriate membership class and organisation including Recognised Professional Organisations) with enforceable disciplinary processes including the powers to suspend or expel a member'.[56] (Note that NRO stands for 'national representative organisations').

2.3.1.B Reporting terminology

The general relationship between Exploration Results, Mineral Resources and Mineral Reserves can be summarised in the following diagram:[57]

Figure 43.3:   The general relationship between results, resources and reserves

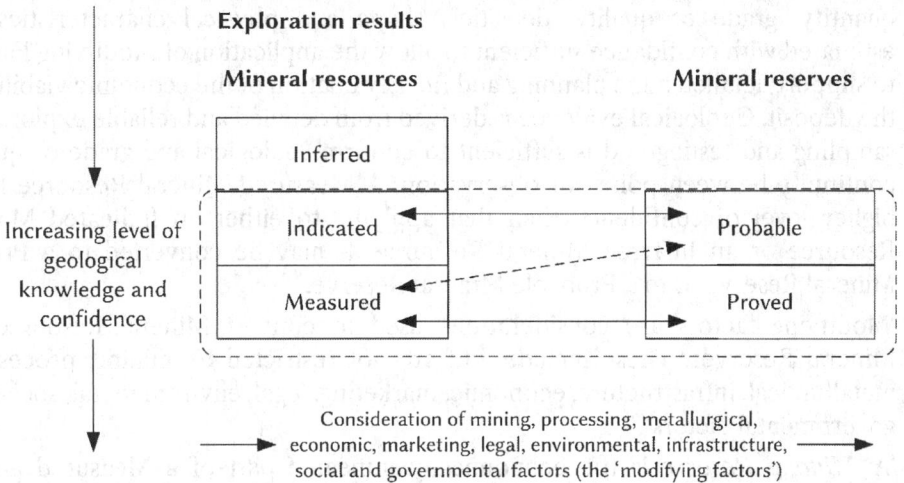

The terms in the above diagram are defined as follows:

Exploration Results include data and information generated by mineral exploration programmes that might be of use to investors but which do not form part of a declaration of Mineral Resources or Mineral Reserves.[58] The CRIRSCO Template specifically requires that any information relating to Exploration Results be expressed in such a way that it does not unreasonably imply that potentially economic mineralisation has been discovered.[59]

'A *Mineral Resource* is a concentration or occurrence of solid material of economic interest in or on the Earth's crust in such form, grade, quality and quantity that there are reasonable prospects for eventual economic extraction. The location, quantity, grade or quality, continuity and other geological characteristics of a Mineral Resource are known, estimated or interpreted from specific geological evidence and knowledge, including sampling. Mineral Resources are sub-divided, in order of increasing geological confidence, into Inferred, Indicated and Measured categories.'[60]

- 'An *Inferred Mineral Resource* is that part of a Mineral Resource for which quantity and grade or quality are estimated on the basis of limited geological evidence and sampling. Geological evidence is sufficient to imply but not verify geological and grade or quality continuity. An Inferred Resource has a lower level of confidence than that applying to an Indicated Mineral Resource and must not be converted to a Mineral Reserve. It is reasonably expected that the majority of Inferred Mineral Resources could be upgraded to Indicated Mineral Resources with continued exploration.'[61]

- 'An *Indicated Mineral Resource* is that part of a Mineral Resource for which quantity, grade or quality, densities, shape and physical characteristics are estimated with sufficient confidence to allow the application of Modifying Factors in sufficient detail to support mine planning and evaluation of the economic viability of the deposit. Geological evidence is derived from adequately detailed and reliable exploration, sampling and testing and is sufficient to assume geological and grade or quality continuity between points of observation. An Indicated Mineral Resource has a lower level of confidence than that applying to a Measured Mineral Resource and may only be converted to a Probable Mineral Reserve.'[62]

- 'A *Measured Mineral Resource* is that part of a Mineral Resource for which quantity, grade or quality, densities, shape and physical characteristics are estimated with confidence sufficient to allow the application of Modifying Factors to support detailed mine planning and final evaluation of the economic viability of the deposit. Geological evidence is derived from detailed and reliable exploration, sampling and testing and is sufficient to confirm geological and grade or quality continuity between points of observation. A Measured Mineral Resource has a higher level of confidence than that applying to either an Indicated Mineral Resource or an Inferred Mineral Resource. It may be converted to a Proved Mineral Reserve or to a Probable Mineral Reserve.'[63]

- 'Modifying factors are considerations used to convert Mineral Resources to Mineral Reserves. These include, but are not restricted to, mining, processing, metallurgical, infrastructure, economic, marketing, legal, environmental, social and governmental factors.'[64]

- 'A *Mineral Reserve* is the economically mineable part of a Measured and/or Indicated Mineral Resource. It includes diluting materials and allowances for losses, which may occur when the material is mined or extracted and is defined by studies at Pre-Feasibility or Feasibility level as appropriate that include application of Modifying Factors. Such studies demonstrate that, at the time of reporting, extraction could reasonably be justified.'[65]

- 'A *Probable Mineral Reserve* is the economically mineable part of an Indicated, and in some circumstances, a Measured Mineral Resource. The confidence in the Modifying Factors applying to a Probable Mineral Reserve is lower than that applying to a Proved Mineral Reserve. A Probable Mineral Reserve has a lower level of confidence than a Proved Mineral Reserve but is of sufficient quality to serve as the basis for a decision on the development of the deposit.'[66]

- 'A *Proved Mineral Reserve* is the economically mineable part of a Measured Mineral Resource. A Proved Mineral Reserve implies a high degree of confidence in the Modifying Factors. A Proved Mineral Reserve represents the highest confidence category of reserve estimate.'[67]

The CRIRSCO Template contains more detailed guidance on how a competent person should decide on mineral resource and mineral reserve classification and contains a checklist and guideline for the preparation of public reports.

2.4 Disclosure of mineral reserves and resources

Mineral reserves and resources, or subcategories thereof, are a significant element in communications by mining companies and oil and gas companies to their stakeholders. IFRS requires an entity to provide 'additional disclosures when compliance with the specific requirements in IFRSs is insufficient to enable users to understand the impact of particular transactions, other events and conditions on the entity's financial position and financial performance'. *[IAS 1.17(c)]*. Therefore, although IFRS does not specifically require it, disclosures regarding mineral resources and reserves will generally be necessary under IFRS to provide users with the information they need to understand the entity's financial position and performance.

As noted in 2 above, entities have to use reserves data and sometimes resources data for a number of accounting purposes and the methodology should be consistent with the definitions in the IFRS *Conceptual Framework* for asset recognition. We believe that users of the financial statements need to be able to identify the methodology used to estimate reserves and resources in order to understand an entity's financial statements. If management uses proved reserves for investment appraisal and uses these same reserves for depreciation and impairment calculations, this should be clearly identified in the reserves disclosure. Conversely, if management uses different reserves and/or resources definitions for different purposes, that should be made clear in the financial statements.

In the absence of guidance under IFRS, entities not subject to the requirements of a national regulator may wish to use the disclosure requirements of other standard-setters as a starting point in developing their own policies. The sections below discuss the disclosure requirements of several standard-setters for mineral reserve and resource quantities for oil and gas companies and mining companies (see 2.4.1 and 2.4.2 respectively below) and reserve values (see 2.4.3 below).

However, while disclosure of information about mineral reserves and resources is clearly very useful, users of financial statements should be aware that there are many variances between the requirements of different jurisdictions or even within those jurisdictions. Therefore, comparisons between entities may be difficult or even impossible. In particular, the following aspects are important:

- *Proven and probable reserves* – The definition of reserves can vary greatly, e.g. the former OIAC SORP permitted disclosure of either 'proven and probable' or 'proved developed and undeveloped' reserves, whereas Accounting Standards Codification (ASC) Topic 932-235-50 – *Extractive Activities – Oil and Gas – Notes to Financial Statements – Disclosure* – requires disclosure of 'proved reserves, proved developed reserves and proved undeveloped reserves';

- *Commodity price* – The quantity of economically recoverable reserves may depend to a large extent on the price assumptions that an entity uses. Differences often arise because the entity:
    - uses its own long-term price assumption which, for example, was permitted under the former OIAC SORP;
    - is required to use 12-month average prices, which is required by the SEC Release No. 33-8995 in the oil and gas sector; or
    - is required to use a three year trailing average, which is required to comply with the SEC's Industry Guide 7 in the mining sector;

- *Royalties* – Royalties payable in-kind to the government or legal owner of the mineral rights may or may not be included in reserves;

- *Non-controlling interests* – Generally 'reserves' include all reserves held by the parent and its consolidated subsidiaries. While in many jurisdictions mining companies and oil and gas companies are required to disclose the reserves attributable to significant non-controlling interests, this is not always required;

- *Associates, joint arrangements and other investments* – An entity may have economic ownership of reserves through investments in associates and joint arrangements, equity interests (see 7 below) or royalty yielding contracts (see 5.7 below). Such reserves are generally not included in consolidated reserves, but may need to be disclosed separately; and

- *Production sharing contracts and risk service contracts* (see 5.3 and 5.5.1 respectively below) – Frequently the mining company or oil and gas company does not legally own the mineral reserves and resources in the ground, i.e. the government retains legal ownership. A significant amount of judgement concerning the nature of the rights and economic interests of the entity may be required to determine whether the entity is the economic owner of any reserves or resources. Depending on the reserve reporting framework that the entity is subject to, such 'economic' reserves may or may not be included in reserves or resources.

In addition to those matters set out above, there may be other variances in the reserves definition and disclosure requirements in different jurisdictions of which users of IFRS financial statements should be aware. Such differences may affect IFRS financial reporting directly.

2.4.1 Oil and gas sector

Many oil and gas companies are required to disclose information about reserve quantities in accordance with the rules and requirements of the stock exchange on which they are listed. However, those oil and gas companies that are not subject to the specific disclosure requirements of a stock exchange or other local regulator should consider the need to disclose reserves and resources information to provide users with the information they need to understand the entity's financial position and performance.

Companies may continue to consider disclosing the information previously required under the former OIAC SORP or could look to the example disclosures contained in the 2010 DP at 1.3.4 above. Alternatively, companies could follow the disclosures required under US ASC 932-235-50 – *Disclosure of Standardised Measure of Oil and Gas* (US ASC 932-235-50), as required by SEC Regulation S-K.

2.4.2 Mining sector

Many mining companies are required to disclose information about reserve quantities in accordance with the rules and requirements of the stock exchange on which they are listed. However, those mining companies that are not subject to the specific disclosure requirements of a stock exchange or other local regulator may wish to consider disclosing the information required under SEC Industry Guide 7.

Mining companies that are subject to the SEC rules and regulations need to understand not only the content of Industry Guide 7, but also the current interpretation of this content by the SEC's staff. While many of the definitions may seem familiar, the SEC staff's interpretations may differ considerably from those of regulators in other countries.[68] Refer to SEC Industry Guide 7 sections I-III for details.

2.4.3 Disclosure of the value of reserves

As part of its work on the Extractive Activities DP (see 1.3.4 above) the IASB staff considered whether a disclosure-focused approach might be appropriate in an extractive industries financial reporting standard. It is in this context that the DP noted that, given the near unanimity of the feedback from users on the lack of relevance of either historical cost or current value accounting for reserves and resources, a disclosure-focused approach needed to be considered as one alternative in the discussion paper.[69]

One of the key issues to consider before developing a disclosure-focused approach is whether or not disclosure of the value of mineral reserves should be a requirement. A secondary issue is whether the mineral reserves should be disclosed at their fair value or at a standardised measure of value, similar to the requirement under ASC 932-235-50 which is based on discounted net cash flows.

This disclosure requirement is not uncontroversial, as the 'standardized measure of oil and gas' (often abbreviated to SMOG) does not represent the market value of an entity's proved reserves. However, the standardised measure of the value of oil and gas reserves greatly reduces the impact of management's opinion about future development on the value calculated, e.g. the method prescribes the discount rate and commodity price to be used. While this may not take into account relevant insights that management may have, the advantage is that comparability of the disclosures between entities is increased. As illustrated in Extract 43.1, some companies caution against over-reliance on these disclosures.

> *Extract 43.1: BP p.l.c. (2019)*
>
> **Supplementary information on oil and natural gas (unaudited)** [extract]
>
> **Standardized measure of discounted future net cash flows and changes therein relating to proved oil and gas reserves** [extract]
>
> The following tables set out the standardized measure of discounted future net cash flows, and changes therein, relating to crude oil and natural gas production from the group's estimated proved reserves. This information is prepared in compliance with FASB Oil and Gas Disclosures requirements.
>
> Future net cash flows have been prepared on the basis of certain assumptions which may or may not be realized. These include the timing of future production, the estimation of crude oil and natural gas reserves and the application of average crude oil and natural gas prices and exchange rates from the previous 12 months. Furthermore, both proved reserves estimates and production forecasts are subject to revision as further technical information becomes available and economic conditions change. BP cautions against relying on the information presented because of the highly arbitrary nature of the assumptions on which it is based and its lack of comparability with the historical cost information presented in the financial statements.

It is clear that reaching agreement as to what constitutes useful and relevant disclosures about the value of mineral reserves is not straightforward and will be controversial. Still, in September 2008, the Board indicated support for the Extractive Activities DP to propose the disclosure of 'a current value measurement, such as a standardised measure of discounted cash flows, and the key assumptions necessary for a user to make use of that measurement'. This would not be disclosed if the minerals or oil and gas assets are measured on the balance sheet at fair value or some other current value measurement. In that case, an entity would provide disclosures similar to those required in the US (by ASC 820-10-50-1, 2, 3 – *Fair Value Measurements and Disclosures*).[70] Accordingly, the DP concluded that:

- if the assets are measured at historical cost then detailed information should be disclosed about their current value (either fair value or standardised measure) and how it was determined; or
- if, instead, the assets are measured at fair value then detailed information should be disclosed about that fair value and how it was determined.

2.4.3.A ASC 932-235-50 – Disclosure of Standardised Measure of Oil and Gas

All entities engaged in significant oil and gas producing activities that report under US GAAP or are SEC IFRS filers are required by ASC 932-235-50 to disclose a standardised measure of discounted future net cash flows relating to proved oil and gas reserve quantities. There may also be non-US GAAP oil and gas companies who, while they are not subject to these specific disclosure requirements, still elect to refer to these when determining the reserves and resources information to provide to their users. ASC 932-235-50 is highly prescriptive and should be reviewed directly in full to ensure compliance with its requirements.

3 IFRS 6 – EXPLORATION FOR AND EVALUATION OF MINERAL RESOURCES

3.1 Objective and scope

The IASB's objective in developing IFRS 6, as noted at 1.2 above, was restricted to making limited improvements to existing accounting practices for exploration and evaluation (E&E) expenditures. E&E expenditures are 'expenditures incurred by an entity in connection with the exploration for and evaluation of mineral resources before the technical feasibility and commercial viability of extracting a mineral resource are demonstrable', while E&E assets are 'exploration and evaluation expenditures recognised as assets in accordance with the entity's accounting policy'. *[IFRS 6 Appendix A]*.

IFRS 6 is limited to specifying the financial reporting for the exploration for and evaluation of mineral resources, which the standard defines as 'the search for mineral resources, including minerals, oil, natural gas and similar non-regenerative resources after the entity has obtained legal rights to explore in a specific area, as well as the determination of the technical feasibility and commercial viability of extracting the mineral resource'. *[IFRS 6 Appendix A]*. The standard also specifies when entities need to assess E&E assets for impairment in accordance with IAS 36 and requires certain disclosures.

An entity may not apply IFRS 6 to expenditures incurred before the exploration for and evaluation of mineral resources (e.g. expenditures incurred before the entity has obtained the legal rights to explore a specific area such as prospecting and acquisition of mineral rights) or after the technical feasibility and commercial viability of extracting a mineral resource are demonstrable (e.g. development, construction, production and closure). *[IFRS 6.5]*. Furthermore, it deals only with E&E expenditures and does not provide guidance on other sector-specific issues that may arise during the E&E phase.

Equipment used in the E&E phase, e.g. property, plant and equipment and any other intangibles, such as software, are not in the scope of IFRS 6, instead, they are in the scope of IAS 16 or IAS 38.

3.1.1 Scope exclusions in other standards relating to the extractive industries

In the Basis for Conclusions on IFRS 6 the IASB confirmed that 'even though no IFRS has addressed extractive activities directly, all IFRSs (including International Accounting Standards and Interpretations) are applicable to entities engaged in the exploration for and evaluation of mineral resources that make an unreserved statement of compliance with IFRSs in accordance with IAS 1'. *[IFRS 6.BC6]*. However, certain aspects of activities that occur in the extractive industries that fall outside the scope of IFRS 6 are excluded from the scope of other standards.

Various standards exclude 'minerals' from their scope, but the exact wording of the scope exclusions differs from standard to standard. Therefore, it would be incorrect to conclude that the same aspects of the extractive industries' activities are excluded from the scope of these standards:

- IAS 2 – does not apply to the measurement of minerals and mineral products, 'to the extent that they are measured at net realisable value in accordance with well-established practices in those industries'. *[IAS 2.3(a), 4]*. The practice of measuring minerals and mineral products inventories at net realisable value is, in reality, relatively rare in many areas of the extractive industries.
- IAS 16 – does not apply to 'mineral rights and mineral reserves such as oil, natural gas and similar non-regenerative resources'. *[IAS 16.3(d)]*. In addition, the standard does not apply to 'the recognition and measurement of exploration and evaluation assets'. *[IAS 16.3(c)]*. Equipment used in extracting reserves is within the scope of IAS 16.
- IFRS 16 – does not apply to 'leases to explore for or use minerals, oil, natural gas and similar non-regenerative resources'. *[IFRS 16.3(a)]*. However, leases including leases of right-of-use assets in a sublease of assets used for exploration or evaluation activities are in the scope of IFRS 16.
- IAS 38 – does not apply to 'expenditure on the exploration for, or development and extraction of, minerals, oil, natural gas and similar non-regenerative resources' or to the recognition and measurement of E&E assets. *[IAS 38.2(c)-(d)]*.
- IAS 40 – does not apply to 'mineral rights and mineral reserves such as oil, natural gas and similar non-regenerative resources'. *[IAS 40.4(b)]*.

3.2 Recognition of exploration and evaluation assets

3.2.1 Developing an accounting policy under IFRS 6

When developing its accounting policy for E&E expenditures, IFRS 6 requires an entity recognising E&E assets to apply paragraph 10 of IAS 8. *[IFRS 6.6, BC19]*. Hence management should use its judgement in developing and applying an accounting policy that results in information that is relevant and reliable. *[IAS 8.10]*. However, IFRS 6 does provide an exemption from paragraphs 11 and 12 of IAS 8, *[IFRS 6.7, BC17]*, which 'specify sources of authoritative requirements and guidance that management is required to consider in developing an accounting policy for an item if no IFRS applies specifically to that item' (the so-called 'hierarchy', see Chapter 3 at 4.3). In developing such a policy, IFRS 6 imposes a number of significant constraints on an entity's choice of accounting policy because:

- an entity needs to specify which expenditures are recognised as E&E assets and apply that accounting policy consistently (see 3.3.1 below); *[IFRS 6.9]*
- expenditures related to the development of mineral resources should not be recognised as E&E assets (see 3.3.1 below); *[IFRS 6.10]* and
- the requirement to apply IAS 16, IAS 38 and IAS 36 after the E&E phase affects the choice of accounting policies during the E&E phase. In January 2006 the IFRIC clarified that 'it was clear that the scope of IFRS 6 consistently limited the relief from the hierarchy to policies applied to E&E activities and that there was no basis for interpreting IFRS 6 as granting any additional relief in areas outside its scope'.[71] For example, an entity may be able to apply the full cost method of accounting (see 3.2.4 below) during the E&E phase, but it will not be able to apply that policy after the E&E phase.

The IASB believed that waiving these requirements in IFRS 6 would 'detract from the relevance and reliability of an entity's financial statements to an unacceptable degree'. *[IFRS 6.BC23]*.

3.2.2 Options for an exploration and evaluation policy

Entities active in the extractive industries have followed, and continue to follow, a large variety of accounting practices for E&E expenditure, which range 'from deferring on the balance sheet nearly all exploration and evaluation expenditure to recognising all such expenditure in profit or loss as incurred'. *[IFRS 6.BC17]*. As mentioned earlier, IFRS 6 provides an exemption from paragraphs 11 and 12 of IAS 8. The inference from this is that the standard 'grandfathers' all existing practices by not requiring these to have any authoritative basis. The Basis for Conclusions states that 'the Board decided that an entity could continue to follow the accounting policies that it was using when it first applied the IFRS's requirements, provided they satisfy the requirements of paragraph 10 of IAS 8 ... with some exceptions ...'. *[IFRS 6.BC22]*. These exceptions in IFRS 6, described above, have a rather more profound impact than may be obvious at first sight and, in fact, instead of allowing previous national GAAP accounting policies, IFRS 6 effectively prohibits many of them.

There are several methods adopted by oil and gas companies (and modified by some mining companies) to account for E&E costs. These include successful efforts, full cost and area of interest accounting. These methods have evolved through the use of previous GAAPs and industry practice. While these terms and methods (or similar methods) are commonly used in the sector, none of these is specifically referred to in IFRS.

We explore below each of these methods and consider to what extent they are compliant with the requirements of IFRS.

3.2.3 Successful efforts method

The successful efforts methods that have been developed by different accounting standard-setters are generally based on the successful efforts concept as set out in US GAAP, under which generally only those costs that lead directly to the discovery, acquisition, or development of specific, discrete mineral resources and reserves are capitalised and become part of the capitalised costs of the cost centre. Costs that when incurred fail to meet this criterion are generally charged to expense in the period they are incurred. Some interpretations of the successful efforts concept allow entities to capitalise the cost of unsuccessful development wells.[72]

Under the successful efforts method an entity will generally consider each individual mineral lease, concession, or production sharing contract as a cost centre.

When an entity applies the successful efforts method under IFRS, it will need to account for prospecting costs incurred before the E&E phase under IAS 16 or IAS 38. As economic benefits are highly uncertain at this stage of a project, prospecting costs will typically be expensed as incurred. Costs incurred to acquire undeveloped mineral rights, however, should be capitalised under IFRS if an entity expects an inflow of future economic benefits.

To the extent that costs are incurred within the E&E phase of a project, IFRS 6 does not prescribe any recognition and measurement rules. Therefore, it would be acceptable for such costs to be recorded as assets and written off when it is determined that the costs will not lead to economic benefits or to be expensed as incurred if the outcome is uncertain. Deferred costs of an undeveloped mineral right may be depreciated over some determinable period, subject to an impairment test each period with the amount of impairment charged to expense, or an entity may choose to carry forward the deferred costs of the undeveloped mineral right until the entity determines whether the property contains mineral reserves.[73] However, E&E assets should no longer be classified as such when the technical feasibility and commercial viability of extracting mineral resources are demonstrable. *[IFRS 6.17]*. At that time the asset should be tested for impairment under IAS 36, reclassified in the statement of financial position and accounted for under IAS 16 or IAS 38. If it is determined that no commercial reserves are present, then the costs capitalised should be expensed. Costs incurred after the E&E phase should be accounted for in accordance with the applicable IFRSs (i.e. IAS 16 and IAS 38).

It is worth noting that with the emergence of unconventional resource E&E projects, such as shale, coal seam and tight oil or gas, the potential timeframe to determine the technical feasibility and commercial viability of a resource can be considerably longer than that of a conventional resource. This is primarily due to the scale of work required to determine the technical feasibility and commercial viability of these more complex and/or less accessible resources in a higher cost environment. Such feasibility determinations may include the drilling and analysing of a significant number of wells over an extended period of time. As such, the overall success of a drilling campaign targeting unconventional resources may not be determined until completion of the campaign – as opposed to the more common well by well basis that is often the case for conventional projects.

Therefore, the costs incurred on unconventional projects over an extended E&E campaign, may be carried forward under existing policies adopted, including capitalisation under a successful efforts policy that permits such treatment, until such time as the broader resource body is deemed to be either successful or unsuccessful.

The essence of most successful efforts approaches is that costs are capitalised pending evaluation, and this would be acceptable under IFRS.

The following extract from the financial statements of Premier Oil illustrates a typical successful efforts method accounting policy applied under IFRS.

> **Extract 43.2: Premier Oil plc (2019)**
> **ACCOUNTING POLICIES** [extract]
> **FOR THE YEAR ENDED 31 DECEMBER 2019**
> **OIL AND GAS ASSETS** [extract]
>
> The Company applies the successful efforts method of accounting for exploration and evaluation ('E&E') costs, having regard to the requirements of IFRS 6 Exploration for and Evaluation of Mineral Resources.
>
> **(a) Exploration and evaluation assets**
>
> Under the successful efforts method of accounting, all licence acquisition, exploration and appraisal costs are initially capitalised in well, field or specific exploration cost centres as appropriate, pending determination. Expenditure incurred during the various exploration and appraisal phases is then written off unless commercial reserves have been established or the determination process has not been completed.
>
> **Pre-licence costs**
>
> Costs incurred prior to having obtained the legal rights to explore an area are expensed as they are incurred.
>
> **Exploration and evaluation costs**
>
> Costs of E&E are initially capitalised as E&E assets. Payments to acquire the legal right to explore, costs of technical services and studies, seismic acquisition, exploratory drilling and testing are capitalised as intangible E&E assets.
>
> Tangible assets used in E&E activities (such as the Group's vehicles, drilling rigs, seismic equipment and other property, plant and equipment used by the Company's Exploration Function) are classified as property, plant and equipment. However, to the extent that such a tangible asset is consumed in developing an intangible E&E asset the amount reflecting that consumption is recorded as part of the cost of the intangible asset. Such intangible costs include directly attributable overhead, including the depreciation of property, plant and equipment utilised in E&E activities, together with the cost of other materials consumed during the exploration and evaluation phases. E&E costs are not amortised prior to the conclusion of appraisal activities.
>
> **Treatment of E&E assets at conclusion of appraisal activities**
>
> Intangible E&E assets related to each exploration licence/prospect are carried forward until the existence (or otherwise) of commercial reserves has been determined subject to certain limitations, including review for indications of impairment. If commercial reserves have been discovered, the carrying value, after any impairment loss, of the relevant E&E assets is then reclassified as development and production assets, once the project is deemed to be justified for development. If, however, commercial reserves have not been found, the capitalised costs are charged to expense after conclusion of appraisal activities.
>
> **(b) Oil and gas properties**
>
> Oil and gas properties are accumulated generally on a field-by-field basis and represent the cost of developing the commercial reserves discovered and bringing them into production, together with the E&E expenditures incurred in finding commercial reserves transferred from intangible E&E assets, as outlined in accounting policy (a) above.
>
> The cost of oil and gas properties also includes the cost of acquisitions and purchases of such assets, directly attributable overheads, finance costs capitalised, and the cost of recognising provision for future restoration and decommissioning.
>
> **Depreciation of producing assets**
>
> The net book values of producing assets (including pipelines) are depreciated generally on a field-by-field basis using the unit-of-production method by reference to the ratio of production in the year and the related commercial (proved and probable) reserves of the field, taking into account future development expenditures necessary to bring those reserves into production.
>
> Producing assets are generally grouped with other assets that are dedicated to serving the same reserves for depreciation purposes, but are depreciated separately from producing assets that serve other reserves.

3.2.4 Full cost method

The full cost method under most national GAAPs required all costs incurred in prospecting, acquiring mineral interests, exploration, appraisal, development, and construction to be accumulated in large cost centres, e.g. individual countries, groups of countries, or the entire world.[74] However, although an entity is permitted by IFRS 6 to develop an accounting policy without reference to other IFRSs or to the hierarchy, as described at 3.2.1 above, IFRS 6 cannot be extrapolated or applied by analogy to permit application of the full cost method outside the E&E phase. This was confirmed by the Interpretations Committee in January 2006.[75]

There are several other areas in which application of the full cost method under IFRS is restricted because:

- IFRS 6 requires E&E assets to be classified as tangible or intangible assets according to the nature of the assets. *[IFRS 6.15]*. In other words, even when an entity accounts for E&E costs in relatively large pools, it will still need to distinguish between tangible and intangible assets.
- While the full cost method under most national GAAPs requires the application of some form of 'ceiling test', IFRS 6 requires – when impairment indicators are present – an impairment test to be performed in accordance with IAS 36 (although in accordance with IFRS 6, E&E assets can be allocated to CGUs or groups of CGUs (which may include producing CGUs), provided certain criteria are met – see 3.5.2 below for further information).
- Once the technical feasibility and commercial viability of extracting mineral resources are demonstrable, IFRS 6 requires that E&E assets shall no longer be classified as such and need to be tested for impairment under IAS 36 and reclassified in the statement of financial position and accounted for under IAS 16 or IAS 38. *[IFRS 6.17]*. This means that it is not possible to account for successful and unsuccessful projects within one cost centre or pool.

For these reasons it is not possible to apply the full cost method of accounting under IFRS without making very significant modifications in the application of the method. An entity might want to use the full cost method as its starting point in developing its accounting policy for E&E assets under IFRS. However, it will rarely be appropriate to describe the resulting accounting policy as a 'full cost method' because key elements of the full cost method are not permitted under IFRS.

In July 2009, the IASB published an amendment to IFRS 1 – *Additional Exemptions for First-time Adopters (Amendments to IFRS 1)*, which introduced a first-time adoption exemption for first-time adopters that accounted under their previous GAAP for 'exploration and development costs for oil and gas properties in the development or production phases ... in cost centres that include all properties in a large geographical area' (i.e. the full cost method).[76] Under the exemption, a first-time adopter may elect to measure oil and gas assets at the date of transition to IFRSs on a deemed cost basis (see Chapter 5 at 5.5.3), but does not permit continued application of the previous GAAP accounting policy.

3.2.5 Area-of-interest method

The area-of-interest method is an accounting concept by which 'costs incurred for individual geological or geographical areas that have characteristics conducive to containing a mineral reserve are deferred as assets pending determination of whether commercial reserves are found. If the area of interest is found to contain commercial reserves, the accumulated costs are capitalised. If the area is found to contain no commercial reserves, the accumulated costs are charged to expense'.[77]

Some consider the area-of-interest method to be a version of the successful efforts method that uses an area-of-interest, rather than an individual licence, as its unit of account. Others believe that the area-of-interest method is more akin to the full cost method applied on an area-of-interest basis.[78] 'Under the area-of-interest concept, all costs identified with an area of interest would be deferred and capitalised if commercial reserves are later determined to exist in the area. However, costs incurred up to the point that an area of interest is identified (prospecting costs) are often charged to expense by those who consider that they are applying the area-of-interest concept. Costs of individual unsuccessful activities incurred on a specific area of interest, such as drilling an exploratory well that finds no reserves, are accumulated as part of the total cost of the area of interest.'[79]

While IFRS 6 will often not permit all aspects of an area-of-interest method defined by a national GAAP, an entity that uses relatively small areas of interest may be able to implement the method in a meaningful way under IFRS. The area-of-interest method is more common in the mining sector than in the oil and gas sector. Still, there are some entities that apply the method to oil and gas activities.

Extract 43.3: BHP Group Plc (2019)

Notes to the Financial Statements [extract]

11 Property, plant and equipment [extract]

Recognition and measurement [extract]

Exploration and evaluation

Exploration costs are incurred to discover mineral and petroleum resources. Evaluation costs are incurred to assess the technical feasibility and commercial viability of resources found.

Exploration and evaluation expenditure is charged to the income statement as incurred, except in the following circumstances in which case the expenditure may be capitalised:

In respect of minerals activities:

- the exploration and evaluation activity is within an area of interest that was previously acquired as an asset acquisition or in a business combination and measured at fair value on acquisition; or
- the existence of a commercially viable mineral deposit has been established.

In respect of petroleum activities:

- the exploration and evaluation activity is within an area of interest for which it is expected that the expenditure will be recouped by future exploitation or sale; or
- exploration and evaluation activity has not reached a stage that permits a reasonable assessment of the existence of commercially recoverable reserves.

A regular review of each area of interest is undertaken to determine the appropriateness of continuing to carry forward costs in relation to that area. Capitalised costs are only carried forward to the extent that they are expected to be recovered through the successful exploitation of the area of interest or alternatively by its sale. To the extent that capitalised expenditure is no longer expected to be recovered, it is charged to the income statement.

> **Key judgements and estimates** [extract]
>
> *Judgements*: Exploration and evaluation expenditure results in certain items of expenditure being capitalised for an area of interest where a judgement is made that it is likely to be recoverable by future exploitation or sale, or where the activities are judged not to have reached a stage that permits a reasonable assessment of the existence of reserves.
>
> *Estimates*: Management makes certain estimates and assumptions as to future events and circumstances, in particular when making quantitative assessment of whether an economically viable extraction operation can be established. These estimates and assumptions may change as new information becomes available. If, after having capitalised the expenditure under the policy, new information suggests that recovery of the expenditure is unlikely, the relevant capitalised amount is charged to the income statement.

3.2.6 Changes in accounting policies

The standard permits a change in an entity's accounting policies for E&E expenditures only if 'the change makes the financial statements more relevant to the economic decision-making needs of users and no less reliable, or more reliable and no less relevant to those needs'. *[IFRS 6.13]*. In making such a change, 'an entity should judge the relevance and reliability using the criteria in IAS 8'. *[IFRS 6.BC49]*. The entity should justify the change by demonstrating that the change 'brings its financial statements closer to meeting the criteria in IAS 8, but the change need not achieve full compliance with those criteria'. *[IFRS 6.14]*.

3.3 Measurement of exploration and evaluation assets

IFRS 6 draws a distinction between measurement at recognition (i.e. the initial recognition of an E&E asset on acquisition) and measurement after recognition (i.e. the subsequent treatment of the E&E asset).

The standard requires that upon initial recognition, E&E assets should be measured at cost, *[IFRS 6.8]*, which is the same as the initial recognition requirements found in IAS 16, *[IAS 16.15]*, and IAS 38. *[IAS 38.24]*. Therefore, the question arises as to what may be included in the cost of an item. The standard contains considerable guidance on this matter, under the heading 'Elements of cost of exploration and evaluation assets' (see also 3.3.1 below).

After initial recognition IFRS 6 allows one of two alternatives to be chosen as the accounting policy for E&E assets that it must apply consistently to all E&E assets, being either the cost model or the revaluation model. *[IFRS 6.12]*.

Under the cost model, the item is carried at cost less impairment. Entities that apply the cost model should therefore develop an accounting policy within the constraints of IFRS 6 (see 3.2.1 above). As a result, an entity will either develop an accounting policy based on the successful efforts type of method or area-of-interest type of method (see 3.2.3 and 3.2.5 above) – that requires capitalisation of E&E costs pending evaluation; or develop a policy similar to the full cost type of method, which capitalises all E&E costs (successful and unsuccessful), although it is not possible to continue using this method outside the E&E phase (see 3.2.4 above).

The alternative is the revaluation model, which is not defined in IFRS 6 itself. Instead, the standard requires an entity to classify E&E assets as tangible or intangible assets (see 3.4 below) and apply the IAS 16 revaluation model to the tangible assets and the IAS 38 revaluation model to the intangible assets (see Chapter 18 at 6 and Chapter 17 at 8.2). Practically what this means is that E&E classified as intangible assets may not be revalued, since the IAS 38 revaluation model may only be applied to intangible assets that are traded in an active market. [IAS 38.72, 75, IFRS 6.BC29-BC30].

3.3.1 Types of expenditure in the exploration and evaluation phase

The standard requires an entity to determine an accounting policy specifying which expenditures are recognised as E&E assets and apply the policy consistently. Such an accounting policy should take into account the degree to which the expenditure can be associated with finding specific mineral resources. Types of expenditure include:

(a) acquisition of rights to explore;
(b) topographical, geological, geochemical and geophysical studies;
(c) exploratory drilling;
(d) trenching;
(e) sampling; and
(f) activities in relation to evaluating the technical feasibility and commercial viability of extracting a mineral resource. [IFRS 6.9].

This list is not intended to be exhaustive.

In permitting geological and geophysical costs (G&G costs) to be included in the initial measurement of E&E assets, IFRS differs from US GAAP – ASC 932 – *Extractive Activities – Oil and Gas*, which does not permit capitalisation of G&G costs,[80] and may differ from the requirements under other national standards.

IFRS 6 allows an accounting policy choice as to how to treat expenditures on administration and other general overhead costs; however, the chosen policy should be consistent with one of the treatments available under other IFRSs, i.e. expense or capitalise. [IFRS 6.BC28]. This is because there are inconsistencies between IAS 16 (which does not allow such costs to be capitalised), IAS 2 (which requires capitalisation of production overheads but not general administration) and IAS 38 (which only allows capitalisation if directly attributable to bringing the asset into use, otherwise capitalisation is prohibited).

Expenditures related to the development of mineral resources should not be recognised as E&E assets. Instead, the IASB's *Conceptual Framework* and IAS 38 should be applied in developing guidance on accounting for such assets. [IFRS 6.10]. IFRS does not define 'development of mineral resources', but notes that 'development of a mineral resource once the technical feasibility and commercial viability of extracting the mineral resource had been determined was an example of the development phase of an internal project'. [IFRS 6.BC27]. While this is not a full definition, in practice this means that until a feasibility study is complete and a development is approved, accumulated costs are considered E&E assets and are accounted for under IFRS 6. The timing of transferring expenditure from the exploration phase to the development phase is discussed in further detail at 3.4.1 below.

The standard specifically requires the application of IAS 37 – *Provisions, Contingent Liabilities and Contingent Assets* – to any obligations for removal and restoration that are incurred during a particular period as a consequence of having undertaken the exploration for and evaluation of mineral resources. *[IFRS 6.11]*. Although IFRS 6 did not make a corresponding amendment to the scope of IFRIC 1 – *Changes in Existing Decommissioning, Restoration and Similar Liabilities* – which applies to such liabilities when they are recognised in property, plant and equipment under IAS 16, we believe that the interpretation should also be applied in relation to E&E assets. However, if the E&E costs were originally expensed, then the future costs of any related removal and restoration obligations should also be expensed.

The extract below from Glencore illustrates a typical accounting policy for E&E assets for a mining company.

Extract 43.4: Glencore plc (2019)

Notes to the financial statements [extract]

1. Accounting policies [extract]

Property, plant and equipment [extract]

(ii) Exploration and evaluation expenditure

Exploration and evaluation expenditure relates to costs incurred in the exploration and evaluation of potential mineral and petroleum resources and includes costs such as exploration and production licences, researching and analysing historical exploration data, exploratory drilling, trenching, sampling and the costs of pre-feasibility studies. Exploration and evaluation expenditure for each area of interest, other than that acquired from another entity, is charged to the consolidated statement of income as incurred except when the expenditure is expected to be recouped from future exploitation or sale of the area of interest and it is planned to continue with active and significant operations in relation to the area, or at the reporting period end, the activity has not reached a stage which permits a reasonable assessment of the existence of commercially recoverable reserves, in which case the expenditure is capitalised. As the intangible component (i.e. licences) represents an insignificant and indistinguishable portion of the overall expected tangible amount to be incurred and recouped from future exploitation, these costs along with other capitalised exploration and evaluation expenditure are recorded as a component of property, plant and equipment. Purchased exploration and evaluation assets are recognised at their fair value at acquisition.

As the capitalised exploration and evaluation expenditure asset is not available for use, it is not depreciated. All capitalised exploration and evaluation expenditure is monitored for indications of impairment. Where a potential impairment is indicated, an assessment is performed for each area of interest or at the CGU level. To the extent that capitalised expenditure is not expected to be recovered it is charged to the consolidated statement of income.

Administration costs that are not directly attributable to a specific exploration area are charged to the consolidated statement of income. Licence costs paid in connection with a right to explore in an existing exploration area are capitalised and amortised over the term of the permit.

The extract below from BP illustrates an accounting policy for E&E assets for an oil and gas company.

> *Extract 43.5: BP p.l.c. (2019)*
> **Notes on financial statements** [extract]
> **1. Significant accounting policies, judgements, estimates and assumptions** [extract]
> **Intangible assets** [extract]
> **Oil and natural gas exploration, appraisal and development expenditure**
> Oil and natural gas exploration, appraisal and development expenditure is accounted for using the principles of the successful efforts method of accounting as described below.
> **Licence and property acquisition costs**
> Exploration licence and leasehold property acquisition costs are capitalized within intangible assets and are reviewed at each reporting date to confirm that there is no indication that the carrying amount exceeds the recoverable amount. This review includes confirming that exploration drilling is still under way or planned or that it has been determined, or work is under way to determine, that the discovery is economically viable based on a range of technical and commercial considerations, and sufficient progress is being made on establishing development plans and timing. If no future activity is planned, the remaining balance of the licence and property acquisition costs is written off. Lower value licences are pooled and amortized on a straight-line basis over the estimated period of exploration. Upon internal approval for development and recognition of proved reserves of oil and natural gas, the relevant expenditure is transferred to property, plant and equipment.
> **Exploration and appraisal expenditure** [extract]
> Geological and geophysical exploration costs are recognized as an expense as incurred. Costs directly associated with an exploration well are initially capitalized as an intangible asset until the drilling of the well is complete and the results have been evaluated. These costs include employee remuneration, materials and fuel used, rig costs and payments made to contractors. If potentially commercial quantities of hydrocarbons are not found, the exploration well costs are written off. If hydrocarbons are found and, subject to further appraisal activity, are likely to be capable of commercial development, the costs continue to be carried as an asset. If it is determined that development will not occur then the costs are expensed.
> Costs directly associated with appraisal activity undertaken to determine the size, characteristics and commercial potential of a reservoir following the initial discovery of hydrocarbons, including the costs of appraisal wells where hydrocarbons were not found, are initially capitalized as an intangible asset. Upon internal approval for development and recognition of proved reserves, the relevant expenditure is transferred to property, plant and equipment.

3.3.2 Capitalisation of borrowing costs in the exploration and evaluation phase

IAS 23 – *Borrowing Costs* – requires capitalisation of borrowing costs that are directly attributable to the acquisition, construction or production of a 'qualifying asset' as part of the cost of that asset. *[IAS 23.8]*. An E&E asset will generally meet the definition of a qualifying asset as it 'necessarily takes a substantial period of time to get ready for its intended use or sale'. *[IAS 23.5]*. However, IAS 23 requires capitalisation of borrowing costs only when it is probable that they will result in future economic benefits to the entity and the costs can be measured reliably. *[IAS 23.9]*. Unlike IAS 23, IFRS 6 permits capitalisation of E&E assets even when it is not probable that they will result in future economic benefits. Unless an entity's E&E project has resulted in the classification of mineral resources as proven or probable, it is unlikely that future economic benefits from that project can be considered probable. In these circumstances, it is consistent with the requirements of IFRS 6 and IAS 23 to capitalise an E&E asset but not capitalise borrowing costs in respect of it.

3.4 Presentation and classification

E&E assets should be classified consistently as either tangible or intangible assets in accordance with the nature of the assets acquired. *[IFRS 6.15]*. For example, drilling rights may be presented as intangible assets, whereas vehicles and drilling rigs are tangible assets. A tangible asset that is used in developing an intangible asset should still be presented as a tangible asset. However, to the 'extent that a tangible asset is consumed in developing an intangible asset, the amount reflecting that consumption is part of the cost of the intangible asset'. For example, the depreciation of a drilling rig would be capitalised as part of the intangible E&E asset that represents the costs incurred on active exploration projects. *[IFRS 6.16, BC33]*. This assessment requires judgement and we observe different classification practices across the mining industry and the oil and gas industry.

3.4.1 Reclassification of E&E assets

E&E assets should no longer be classified as such when 'technical feasibility and commercial viability of extracting a mineral resource are demonstrable'. *[IFRS 6.17]*.

Determining when technical feasibility and commercial viability have been demonstrated may involve significant judgement, particularly in relation to complex assets or projects where feasibility assessment may be ongoing over an extended period of time: for example Liquefied Natural Gas (LNG) projects, unconventional assets, large scale, technically challenging projects, or where significant upfront investment in long lead items is required.

A final investment decision being approved is often a common signal that technical feasibility and commercial viability have been determined. However, absent this, other factors may also need to be considered, such as the booking of significant quantities of commercial reserves, approval of budgeted expenditure to commence commercial development activities or the actual commencement of expenditure on development activities. It should be noted that both technical feasibility and commercial viability must be demonstrated before an asset can be transferred out of E&E. Activities that occur prior to this point which are aimed at assessing the viability of a resource, may still be regarded as E&E in nature and must be accounted for accordingly.

Before reclassification, E&E assets should be assessed for impairment individually or as part of a cash-generating unit and any impairment loss should be recognised. *[IFRS 6.17]*.

3.5 Impairment

In some cases, and particularly in exploration-only entities, E&E assets do not generate cash inflows and there is insufficient information about the mineral resources in a specific area for an entity to make reasonable estimates of an E&E asset's recoverable amount. This is because the exploration for and evaluation of the mineral resources has not reached a stage at which information sufficient to estimate future cash flows is available to the entity. Without such information, it is not possible to estimate either fair value less costs of disposal ('FVLCD') or value in use ('VIU'), the two measures of recoverable amount in IAS 36. Therefore, without some sort of alternate impairment assessment approach, this would have led to immediate write-off of exploration expenditure.

Therefore, modifications were made to the impairment testing approach. Under IFRS 6, the assessment of impairment should be triggered by changes in facts and circumstances. However once an entity had determined that there is an impairment trigger for an E&E asset, IAS 36 should be used to measure, present and disclose that impairment in the financial statements. This is subject to the special requirements with respect to the level at which impairment is assessed. *[IFRS 6.BC37]*.

IFRS 6 makes two important modifications to IAS 36:
- it defines separate impairment testing 'triggers' for E&E assets; and
- it allows groups of cash-generating units to be used in impairment testing. *[IFRS 6.18-20]*.

3.5.1 Impairment testing 'triggers'

E&E assets should be assessed for impairment when facts and circumstances suggest that the carrying amount of an E&E asset may exceed its recoverable amount. *[IFRS 6.18]*. Under IFRS 6 one or more of the following facts and circumstances could indicate that an impairment test is required. The list is not intended to be exhaustive:

(a) the period for which the entity has the right to explore in the specific area has expired during the period or will expire in the near future, and is not expected to be renewed;

(b) substantive expenditure on further exploration for and evaluation of mineral resources in the specific area is neither budgeted nor planned;

(c) exploration for and evaluation of mineral resources in the specific area have not led to the discovery of commercially viable quantities of mineral resources and the entity has decided to discontinue such activities in the specific area; and

(d) sufficient data exist to indicate that, although a development in the specific area is likely to proceed, the carrying amount of the E&E asset is unlikely to be recovered in full from successful development or by sale. *[IFRS 6.20]*.

Finding that an exploratory or development well does not contain oil or gas in commercial quantities (i.e. finding a 'dry hole') is not listed in IFRS 6 as an impairment indicator. If finding a dry hole marks the end of budgeted or planned exploration activity, indicator (b) above would require impairment testing under IAS 36. Similarly, if the dry hole led to a decision that activities in the area would be discontinued, indicator (c) would require that an impairment test be performed, and indicator (d) requires an entity to do an impairment test if it is unlikely that it will recover the E&E costs from successful development or sale. However, absent one of these indicators being met, in isolation, drilling a dry hole would not necessarily trigger an impairment test. For example, if the first well in a three well campaign is a dry hole, but the entity still intends to drill the remaining two wells, an impairment trigger may not exist.

3.5.2 Specifying the level at which E&E assets are assessed for impairment

When deciding the level at which E&E assets should be assessed, rather than introduce a special CGU for E&E assets, IFRS 6 allows CGUs to be aggregated in a way consistent with the approach applied to goodwill in IAS 36. *[IFRS 6.BC40-BC47]*. Therefore, an entity should determine an accounting policy for allocating E&E assets to CGUs or to CGU groups for the purpose of assessing them for impairment. *[IFRS 6.21]*. Each CGU or group of CGUs to which an E&E asset is allocated should not be larger than an operating segment (which is smaller than a reportable segment) determined in accordance with IFRS 8 – *Operating Segments*. *[IFRS 6.21]*. See also Chapter 20 at 8.1.4.

Hence, the level identified by an entity for the purposes of testing E&E assets for impairment may be comprised of one or more CGUs. *[IFRS 6.22]*.

3.5.3 Cash-generating units comprising successful and unsuccessful E&E projects

IFRS 6 does not specifically address whether successful and unsuccessful E&E projects can be combined in a single CGU (which will occur under full cost accounting and may occur under area of interest accounting). There are some issues to consider before doing this:

- Regardless of whether there is an impairment trigger (see 3.5.1 above), IFRS 6 requires E&E assets to be tested for impairment before reclassification when the technical feasibility and commercial viability of extracting a mineral resource are demonstrable. *[IFRS 6.17]*. That means that the successful conclusion of a small E&E project and its reclassification out of E&E would result in an impairment test of a much larger CGU and possible recognition of an impairment loss on that larger CGU.

- Successful E&E projects should be reclassified as tangible or intangible assets under IAS 16 and IAS 38, respectively. *[IFRS 6.15]*. Therefore, a CGU comprising both successful and unsuccessful E&E projects would be subject to the impairment triggers in both IFRS 6 and IAS 36. This would significantly increase the frequency of impairment testing. *[IFRS 6.20, IAS 36.8-17]*.

- An entity should carefully consider the consequences of including several E&E projects in a CGU, because the unsuccessful conclusion of one project would usually trigger an impairment test of the entire CGU. *[IFRS 6.20]*.

3.5.4 Order of impairment testing

CGUs often contain other assets as well as E&E assets. When developing IFRS 6, Exposure Draft ED 6 – *Exploration for and Evaluation of Mineral Resources* – specifically stated that such other assets should be tested for impairment first, in accordance with IAS 36, before testing the CGU inclusive of the E&E assets.[81] However, IFRS 6 does not specifically address this topic. Despite this, we believe that as the impairment test is completed in accordance with IAS 36, and a similar approach is adopted as that applied to goodwill, the order of the impairment testing as set out in IAS 36 would apply. That is, an entity would test the underlying assets/CGU without the E&E assets first, recognise any write down (if applicable) and then test the CGU/CGU group with the E&E assets allocated.

3.5.5 Additional considerations if E&E assets are impaired

In some circumstances an entity that recognises an impairment of an E&E asset must also decide whether or not to derecognise the asset because no future economic benefits are expected, as illustrated in Example 43.1 below.

Example 43.1: Impairment losses on E&E assets

Entity A's exploration activity in a specific area does not discover oil and/or gas resources. Therefore, A recognises an impairment of the cash-generating unit and derecognises the related E&E assets.

Entity B's exploration activity in a specific area leads to the discovery of a significant quantity of resources, but these are located in a complex reservoir. Therefore, at present the costs of extraction of the discovered resources do not justify the construction of the required infrastructure. Nevertheless, B's management believes that the surrounding area has strong potential to yield other discoveries on other geological structures and it is considered possible that the required infrastructure will be constructed in the future, although at this stage management has no plans to undertake further exploration activity. Entity B recognises an impairment of the E&E assets, but since it expects future economic benefits the related E&E assets are not derecognised.

If an entity concludes that production is not technically feasible or commercially viable, that provides evidence that the related E&E asset needs to be tested for impairment. It is also possible that such evidence may indicate that no future economic benefits are expected from such assets and therefore any remaining assets should be derecognised. When considering the two examples above, in Entity A's situation, no oil and/or gas resources were discovered and based on current plans, no future economic benefits were expected from the related E&E assets so they were derecognised. Whereas in Entity B's situation, while oil and/or gas resources were discovered, extraction was not commercially viable at this stage. So while an impairment was recognised, the remaining assets were not derecognised as management did expect future economic benefits to flow from such assets.

Although IFRS 6 does not specifically deal with derecognition of E&E assets, the entity should derecognise the E&E asset because the asset is no longer in the exploration and evaluation phase and hence outside the scope of IFRS 6 and other asset standards such as IAS 16 and IAS 38 would require derecognition under those circumstances. Once derecognised, the costs of an E&E asset that have been written off cannot be re-recognised as part of a new E&E asset, so unlike an impairment, the write off is permanent.

3.5.6 Income statement treatment of E&E write downs – impairment or exploration expense

In some circumstances, it may be unclear whether an E&E asset is impaired, or whether a write off of unsuccessful exploration is required. In an unconventional project, or in circumstances where costs have been carried forward for some time pending determination of technical feasibility and commercial viability, judgement will be required in concluding on the most appropriate income statement presentation. Key considerations may include whether the objectives of drilling or other expenditure programs have been met, whether the indicative impairment triggers in IFRS 6 have been met, and management's future intentions for the asset.

3.5.7 Reversal of impairment losses

Any impairment loss on an E&E asset recognised in accordance with IFRS 6 needs to be reversed if there is evidence that the loss no longer exists or has decreased. The entity must apply the requirements specified in IAS 36 for reversing an impairment loss (see Chapter 20 at 11.4). *[IFRS 6.BC48, IAS 36.109-123].*

3.6 Disclosure

To identify and explain 'the amounts recognised in its financial statements arising from the exploration for and evaluation of mineral resources', *[IFRS 6.23],* an entity should disclose:

(a) its accounting policies for exploration and evaluation expenditures including the recognition of exploration and evaluation assets; and

(b) the amounts of assets, liabilities, income and expense and operating and investing cash flows arising from the exploration for and evaluation of mineral resources. *[IFRS 6.24].*

The extract below from Tullow Oil's 2019 financial statements illustrates the disclosures required by IFRS 6.

Extract 43.6: Tullow Oil plc (2019)

Group income statement [extract]
Year Ended 31 December 2019

	Notes	2019 $m	2018 $m
Continuing activities			
Sales revenue	2	1,682.6	1,859.2
Other operating income – lost production insurance proceeds	6	42.7	188.4
Cost of sales	4	(966.7)	(966.0)
Gross Profit		**758.6**	**1,081.6**
Administrative expenses	4	(111.5)	(90.3)
Gain on disposal	9	6.6	21.3
Exploration costs written off	10	(1,253.4)	(295.2)
Impairment of property, plant and equipment, net	11	(781.2)	(18.2)
Provisions for onerous contracts and restructuring	4,21	(4.2)	(170.8)

Group balance sheet [extract]
As at 31 December 2019

	Notes	2019 $m	2018 $m
ASSETS			
Non-current assets			
Intangible exploration and evaluation assets	10	1,764.4	1,898.6
Property, plant and equipment	11	3,891.7	4,916.4
Other non-current assets	12	623.2	696.4
Derivative financial instruments	19	3.1	51.2
Deferred tax assets	22	517.5	649.4
		6,799.9	**8,212.0**

Group cash flow statement [extract]
Year ended 31 December 2019

	Notes	2019 $m	2018 Restated $m
Cash flows from investing activities			
Proceeds from disposals	9	7.0	9.9
Purchase of intangible exploration and evaluation assets	29	(259.4)	(202.1)
Purchase of property, plant and equipment	29	(261.5)	(238.4)
Interest received		1.9	2.9
Net cash used in investing activities		(512.0)	(427.7)

Accounting policies [extract]
Year ended 31 December 2019
(k) **Exploration, evaluation and production assets**

The Group adopts the successful efforts method of accounting for exploration and evaluation costs. Pre-licence costs are expensed in the period in which they are incurred. All licence acquisition, exploration and evaluation costs and directly attributable administration costs are initially capitalised in cost centres by well, field or exploration area, as appropriate. Interest payable is capitalised insofar as it relates to specific development activities.

These costs are then written off as exploration costs in the income statement unless commercial reserves have been established or the determination process has not been completed and there are no indications of impairment.

All field development costs are capitalised as property, plant and equipment. Property, plant and equipment related to production activities is amortised in accordance with the Group's depletion and amortisation accounting policy.

Cash consideration received on farm-down of exploration and evaluation assets is credited against the carrying value of the asset.

Notes to the Group Financial Statements [extract]
Year ended 31 December 2019
Note 10. Intangible exploration and evaluation assets [extract]

	Notes	2019 $m	2018 $m
At 1 January		1,898.6	1,933.4
Additions	1	279.3	230.4
Disposals		(0.4)	(4.0)
Amounts written off		(1,253.4)	(295.2)
Net transfer from assets held for sale	16	840.2	32.2
Currency translation adjustments		0.1	1.8
At 31 December		1,764.4	1,898.6

An entity should treat E&E assets as a separate class of assets and make the disclosures required by IAS 16 and IAS 38 for tangible E&E assets and intangible E&E assets, respectively. *[IFRS 6.25, BC53]*.

3.6.1 Statement of cash flows

IAS 7 – *Statement of Cash Flows* – states that only expenditures that result in a recognised asset in the statement of financial position are eligible for classification as investing activities. *[IAS 7.16]*. The IASB specifically notes that 'the exemption in IFRS 6 applies only to recognition and measurement of exploration and evaluation assets, not to the classification of related expenditures in the statement of cash flows'. *[IFRS 6.BC23B]*. This means that an entity that expenses E&E expenditure will not be able to classify the associated cash flows as arising from investing activities.

4 UNIT OF ACCOUNT

One of the key issues in the development of accounting standards and in the selection of accounting policies by preparers, is deciding the level at which an entity should separately account for assets, i.e. what is the 'unit of account'? The definition of the unit of account has significant accounting consequences, as can be seen in the example below.

Example 43.2: Unit of account – dry well

An oil and gas company concludes, based on a number of exploration wells, that oil and gas reserves are present. However, it needs to drill a number of delineation wells to determine the amount of reserves present in the field. The first delineation well that is drilled is a dry hole, i.e. no reserves are found.

There are two ways of looking at the cost of drilling the dry hole:
- the dry hole provides important information about the extent of the oil and gas reserves present in the oil field and should therefore be capitalised as part of the larger oil field; or
- the dry hole will not produce oil in the future and in the absence of future economic benefits the costs should be expensed immediately.

This example suggests that assets or actions that have no value or meaning at one level may actually be valuable and necessary at another level.

The unit of account plays a significant role in:

(1) recognition and derecognition of assets;
(2) determining the rate of depreciation or amortisation;
(3) deciding whether or not certain costs should be capitalised;
(4) undertaking impairment testing;
(5) determining the substance of transactions;
(6) application of the measurement model subsequent to recognition of the asset; and
(7) determining the level of detail of the disclosures required.

The decisions about the unit of account will consider, *inter alia*, cost/benefits and materiality, whether the items are capable of being used separately, their useful economic lives, whether the economic benefits that the entity will derive are separable and the substance of the transaction. To some degree the choice of the unit of account will depend on industry practice, as discussed below.

In Example 43.2 above, an individual dry hole might not be considered a separate asset because individual wells are typically not capable of being used separately, their economic benefits are inseparable, the wells are similar in nature and the substance of the matter can only be understood at the level of the project as a whole. However, in concluding on whether to capitalise or expense the cost of the individual dry hole as set out in Example 43.2 above, an entity will consider its specific accounting policy and its definition of the unit of account. This is discussed further at 4.1 below.

4.1 Unit of account in the extractive industries

In the extractive industries the definition of the unit of account is particularly important in deciding whether or not certain costs may be capitalised, determining the rate of depreciation and in impairment testing. Historically entities in the extractive industries have accounted for preproduction costs using methods such as:

- successful efforts method;
- full cost method; and
- area-of-interest method.

These are discussed further at 3.2.3 to 3.2.5 above. A key issue under each of these methods is determining the appropriate unit of account, which is referred to in the industry as the 'cost centre' or 'pool'. In practice, entities would define their cost centres along geographical, political or legal boundaries or align them to the operating units in their organisation. The IASC's Issues Paper listed the following, commonly used, cost centres that have been used pre-IFRS:[82]

(a) the world;
(b) each country or group of countries in which the entity operates;
(c) each contractual or legal mineral acquisition unit, such as a lease or production sharing contract;
(d) each area of interest (geological feature, such as a mine or field, that lends itself to a unified exploration and development effort);
(e) geological units other than areas of interest (such as a basin or a geologic province); or
(f) the entity's organisational units.

IFRS does not provide industry specific guidance on determining appropriate units of account for the extractive industries. Nevertheless, we believe that in determining the unit of account an entity should take the legal rights (see (c) above) as its starting point and apply the criteria discussed above to assess whether the unit of account should be larger or smaller. The other cost centres listed above might result in a unit of account that is unjustifiably large when viewed in the light of the factors influenced by the unit of account as set out at 4 above.

The definition of 'unit of account' was considered in the Extractive Activities DP (see 1.3 above). While the DP would not need to be considered in the context of the IAS 8 hierarchy, it did draw attention to the fact that the selection of an appropriate unit of account might need to take into account the stage of the underlying activities. In particular, the DP proposed that '...the geographical boundary of the unit of account would be defined initially on the basis of the exploration rights held. As exploration, evaluation and development activities take place, the unit of account would contract progressively until it becomes no greater than a single area, or group of contiguous areas, for which the legal rights are held and which is managed separately and would be expected to generate largely independent cash flows'. The DP's view was that the components approach in IAS 16 would apply to determine the items that should be accounted for as a single asset. However, the DP suggested that an entity may decide to account for its assets using a smaller unit of account.

The thinking underlying the above proposal in the DP would be relevant in the following types of situations:

- Certain transactions in the extractive industries (e.g. carried interests arrangements) result in the creation of new legal rights out of existing legal rights. Whenever this is the case, an entity needs to assess whether such transactions give rise to new units of account. If so, the accounting policies should be applied to those new units of account rather than the previous unit/s of account.
- When an entity acquires a business that owns reserves and resources, it needs to consider whether it should define the unit of account at the level of the licence or separate ore zones or reservoirs within the licence.

Determining the unit of account is an area that requires a significant amount of judgement, which may need to be disclosed under IAS 1 – *Presentation of Financial Statements* –

together with other judgements that management has made in the process of applying the entity's accounting policies and that have the most significant effect on the amounts recognised in the financial statements. *[IAS 1.122]*.

As the prevalence of unconventional oil and gas projects increases, the determination of the unit of account is becoming an increasingly common topic. With unconventional programs, the objectives of individual wells or drilling campaigns may differ to those for a conventional drilling program. It may be that the drilling of each well provides important information about the extent of the oil and gas reserves present in the oil and gas field, but multiple wells need to be drilled before a decision can be made regarding success. So unlike conventional oil and gas projects, concluding whether a well cost should be capitalised may not be possible on an individual well basis immediately after each well is drilled. In these circumstances, an entity may determine that the costs of an individual well should be carried forward pending further analysis.

5 LEGAL RIGHTS TO EXPLORE FOR, DEVELOP AND PRODUCE MINERAL PROPERTIES

An entity can acquire legal rights to explore for, develop and produce wasting resources on a mineral property by:[83]

(a) purchasing of minerals (i.e. outright ownership);

(b) obtaining a lease or concession (see 5.2 below);

(c) entering into a production-sharing contract or production-sharing agreement (see 5.3 below);

(d) entering into a pure-service contract (see 5.4 below);

(e) entering into a service contract (also called a service agreement or risk service contract) (see 5.5.1 below);

(f) entering into a joint operating agreement (see 5.6 below); and

(g) retaining an overriding royalty or other royalty interest subsequent to sale of an interest (see 5.7 below).

Although many of these are more commonly encountered in the oil and gas sector, which is reflected in many of the examples and illustrations below, they are not restricted to this sector and mining companies can and do enter into similar arrangements.

The IASC Issues Paper noted that 'in the mining sector, rights to explore for, develop, and produce minerals are often acquired by purchase of either the mineral rights alone (which does not include ownership of the land surface) or by purchase of both mineral rights and surface rights. In other cases, they are acquired through a right to mine contract, which grants the enterprise the rights to develop and mine the property and may call for a payment at the time the contract becomes effective and subsequent periodic payments. In the mining sector, rights to explore, develop, and produce minerals may also be acquired by mineral leases from private owners or from the government'.[84]

In the oil and gas sector entities usually obtain the rights to explore for, develop, and produce oil and gas through mineral leases, concession agreements, production-sharing contracts, or service contracts.[85] Arrangements similar to production sharing contracts are also becoming more common in the mining sector. The type of legal arrangement used depends to a large extent on the legal framework of the country and market practice. The main features of each of these legal rights to access mineral reserves and resources, except for the outright ownership of minerals, are discussed below.

The extract below from the financial statements of TOTAL illustrates the different types of legal arrangements that an oil and gas company may enter into to secure access to mineral reserves and resources.

> *Extract 43.7: TOTAL S.A. (2019)*
>
> **2 Business overview for fiscal year 2019** [extract]
>
> **2.3.5 Contractual framework of Upstream hydrocarbons production activities**
>
> Licenses, permits and contracts governing the Group entities' ownership of oil and gas interests have terms that vary from country to country and are generally granted by or entered into with a government entity or a state-owned company or sometimes with private owners. These agreements usually take the form of concessions or production sharing contracts.
>
> In the framework of oil concession agreements, the oil company (or consortium) owns the assets and the facilities and is entitled to the entire production. In exchange, the operating risks, costs and investments are the oil company's or the consortium's responsibility and it agrees to remit to the relevant host country, usually the owner of the subsoil resources, a production-based royalty, income tax, and possibly other taxes that may apply under local tax legislation.
>
> The production sharing contract (PSC) involves a more complex legal framework than the concession agreement. It defines the terms and conditions of production sharing and sets the rules governing the cooperation between the company (the contractor) or consortium (the contracting group) in possession of the license and the host country, which is generally represented by a state-owned company. The latter can thus be involved in operating decisions, cost accounting and production allocation. The contractor (or contractor group) undertakes the execution and financing, at its own risk, of all exploration, development or operational activities. In exchange, it is entitled to a portion of the production, known as "cost oil", the sale of which is intended to cover its incurred expenses (capital and operating costs). The balance of production, known as "profit oil", is then shared in varying proportions, between the contractor (or the contracting group), on the one hand, and the host country or state-owned company, on the other hand.
>
> Today, concession agreements and PSCs can coexist, sometimes in the same country. Even though there are other contractual models, TOTAL's license portfolio is comprised mainly of concession agreements.
>
> On most licenses, the partners and authorities of the host country, often assisted by international accounting firms, perform joint- venture and PSC cost audits and ensure the observance of contractual obligations.
>
> In some countries, TOTAL has also signed contracts called "risked service contracts", which are similar to PSCs. However, the profit oil is replaced by a defined or determinable cash monetary remuneration, agreed by contract, which depends notably on field performance parameters such as the amount of barrels produced.
>
> Oil and gas exploration and production activities are subject to authorization granted by public authorities (licenses), which are granted for specific and limited periods of time and include an obligation to relinquish a large portion, or the entire portion in case of failure, of the area covered by the license at the end of the exploration period.
>
> TOTAL pays taxes on income generated from its oil and gas production and sales activities under its concessions, PSCs and risked service contracts, as provided for by local regulations. In addition, depending on the country, TOTAL's production and sales activities may be subject to a number of other taxes, fees and withholdings, including special petroleum taxes and fees. The taxes imposed on oil and gas production and sales activities are generally substantially higher than those imposed on other industrial or commercial businesses.

5.1 How does a mineral lease work?

In most countries the government owns all minerals and rights over those minerals, but in some other countries minerals and mineral rights can also be directly owned by individuals. While these contracts are negotiated individually, and therefore each may be different, they typically share a large number of common features, which are discussed below:

(a) the *owner/lessor* of the mineral rights retains a *royalty interest*, which entitles it to a specified percentage of the mineral produced. The lessor is normally only required to pay for its share of the severance taxes and the costs of getting the production into a marketable state, but not for any exploration and development costs. The *royalty* is either payable in cash or payable in kind. Although the lessor is normally not interested in receiving its royalty in kind, the option of receiving the royalty in kind is often included for tax purposes;

(b) the lessee obtains a *working interest* under the mineral lease, which entitles it to explore for, develop, and produce minerals from the property at its cost. The working interest can be held by more than one party, in which case a *joint operating agreement* needs to be executed (see 5.6 below);

(c) upon signing of the mineral lease agreement, the lessee typically pays the lessor a *lease bonus* or *signature bonus*, which is a one-off upfront payment in exchange for the lessor's signing of the mineral lease agreement;

(d) it is in the lessor's interest for the lessee to explore the property as quickly as possible. To ensure that the lessee does not delay exploration and development unnecessarily, the following terms are typically included:

- most mineral leases define a *primary term* during which the lessee is required to commence drilling;

- normally the lessee has a *drill or exploration obligation* that must be met within a certain period. However, by paying *delay rentals* the lessee can defer commencement of drilling or exploration; and

- the mineral lease will remain in force once the obligatory drilling/exploration programme has been completed successfully and production commences, but the lease will be cancelled if activities are suspended for a prolonged period;

(e) most mineral leases provide that the lessee and the lessor have the right to assign their interest to another party without approval from the owner/lessor. This means that both the lessee and the lessor can create new rights out of existing rights (see 5.7 below);

(f) under many oil and gas lease contracts the lessee can be required to pay *shut-in royalties* when a successful well capable of commercial production has been completed, but production has not commenced within a specified time; and

(g) the lessor is typically not entitled to royalties on any minerals consumed in producing further minerals from a property.

5.2 Concessionary agreements (concessions)

Concessionary agreements or concessions are mineral leases 'under which the government owning mineral rights grants the concessionaire the right to explore, develop, and produce the minerals'.[86] However, unlike a production sharing contract (see 5.3 below), under a concessionary agreement, the extractive industries company retains title to the assets constructed during the term of the concession. Furthermore, the company bears all the risks and there is no profit sharing arrangement with the government. Rather, the government is entitled to a royalty computed in much the same way as a royalty under lease contracts.[87] In addition, depending on the country's fiscal policies, the government will typically also collect taxes such as duties, severance or production taxes, and income taxes.

In some jurisdictions, the government may retain the option to participate in the project as a working interest owner in the property. In this case, the company initially holds 100% of the working interest. If the project is successful and reserves are found, the national oil company or entity representing the government becomes a working interest owner and will pay for its proportionate share of the investment.

5.3 Traditional production sharing contracts

A production sharing contract (PSC) or production sharing arrangement (PSA) is a contract between a national oil company (NOC) or the government of a host country and a contracting entity (contractor) to carry out oil and gas exploration and production activities in accordance with the terms of the contract, with the two parties sharing mineral output.[88] While these arrangements have historically been more commonly found in the oil and gas sector, similar types of arrangements do exist in the mining sector.

In such countries the ownership of the mineral reserves and resources in the ground does not pass to the contractor. Instead, the contractor is permitted to recover its costs and share in the profits from the exploration and production activities. Although the precise form and content of a PSC may vary, the following features are likely to be encountered in traditional oil and gas PSCs:[89]

(a) the government retains ownership of the reserves and resources and grants the contractor the right to explore for, develop, and produce the reserves;

(b) the government is often directly involved in the operation of the property, either by way of an *operating committee* that comprises representatives of the contractor and the government or NOC, or by requiring the contractor to submit its annual work programme and corresponding annual budget to the government or NOC for approval. The contractor is responsible to the NOC for carrying out operations in accordance with contract terms;

(c) upon signing of the PSC the contractor pays the government a *signature bonus*, which is a one-off upfront payment in exchange for the government's signing of the PSC;

(d) the contractor pays the government a *production bonus* upon commencement of production and when the average production over a given period first exceeds a threshold level;

(e) the government is entitled to a *royalty payment* that is calculated as a percentage of the net production (i.e. net of petroleum lost, flared or re-injected) and which is payable in kind or in cash at the option of the government. The royalty rate applicable is not necessarily a fixed percentage, but may depend on the production volume or destination of the production (e.g. different rates may apply to crude oil and gas that is exported);

(f) the contractor provides all financing and technology necessary to carry out operations and pays all of the costs specified;

(g) the contractor is typically required to bear all of the risks related to exploration and, perhaps, development (i.e. the government does not have a working interest during the exploration and development phases);

(h) the contractor is frequently required to provide infrastructure, such as streets, electricity, water systems, roads, hospitals, schools, and other items during various phases of activities. Additionally, the contract customarily requires the contractor to provide specified training of personnel. Infrastructure and training costs may or may not be recoverable from future production by the contractor;[90]

(i) the contractor may have a *domestic market obligation* that requires them to meet, as a priority, the needs of domestic oil and/or gas consumption in the host country. Alternatively, the contractor may be required to sell oil and/or gas to the NOC at the official oil or gas price;

(j) the contractor is normally committed to completing a *minimum work programme* in each of the phases of the project, which generally needs to be completed within a specified period. If the work is not performed, the contract may require the unspent amount to be paid in cash to the government;

(k) a PSC normally requires *relinquishment* of a certain percentage of the original contract area by the end of the initial term of the exploration period. A further reduction is typically required by the end of the exploration period. The government can negotiate a new contract with another party for the continued exploration of the surrendered acreage. Any data and information relating to the surrendered area often becomes the exclusive property of the government;

(l) equipment that is acquired for the development and production activities normally becomes the property of the government or NOC;

(m) operating costs and specified exploration and development costs are recoverable out of *cost recovery oil*, which is a specified percentage of production revenues after the royalty payment each year. The PSC specifies whether particular types of cost are recoverable or non-recoverable. Recoverable costs not recovered by the contractor in the current period can be carried forward to the following reporting period for recovery purposes;

(n) revenues remaining after royalty and cost recovery are called *profit oil*. Profit oil is split between the government and the contractor on a predetermined basis;

(o) many PSCs provide that the income tax to which the contractor is subject is deemed to have been paid to the government as part of the payment of profit oil (see 21.2 below); and

(p) some PSCs give the contractor the right to set up a decommissioning reserve fund which enables the contractor to recover the costs associated with future decommissioning and site restoration. In cases where the PSC terminates before the end of the life of the field, the government is typically responsible for decommissioning and site restoration.

Even in situations where the provisions of a PSC are fairly straightforward at first sight, it may be rather complicated to calculate the entitlement of each of the parties involved as is illustrated in the example below.

Example 43.3: Production sharing contract

An oil and gas company (contractor) entered into a PSC that includes the following terms:
- the oil and gas company pays for all exploration costs;
- the government is entitled to:
  - 15% royalty on the production;
  - severance tax of USD 2.50 per barrel;
  - USD 5 million production bonus when average production first exceeds 25,000 barrels per day; and
  - 10% of the profit oil;
- operating expenses are recoverable before exploration costs;
- development costs are recoverable after exploration costs;
- cost recovery oil is capped at 45% of the annual production; and
- the national oil company (NOC) and the contractor have a 51% and 49% working interest, respectively.

How should the production be allocated between parties, assuming the following for 2020?
- annual production in 2020 is 10 million barrels;
- recoverable operating costs in 2020 are USD 25 million;
- the average oil price in 2020 is USD 100/barrel (this amount is used to convert any amount calculated in monetary units i.e. USD, back into volumetric units i.e. barrels of oil);
- during 2020 average production exceeded 25,000 barrels per day for the first time;
- unrecovered exploration costs at the beginning of 2020 were USD 180 million; and
- unrecovered development costs at the beginning of 2020 were USD 275 million.

		Barrels	Contractor (49%)	NOC (51%)	Government
			bbls	bbls	bbls
Production in 2020	a	10,000,000			
Royalty 15% of 10,000,000 =	b	1,500,000			1,500,000
Severance tax 10,000,000 × $2.50 ÷ $100 =	c	250,000			250,000
Cost oil					
Operating costs $25,000,000 ÷ $100 =	d	250,000	122,500	127,500	
Exploration cost $180,000,000 ÷ $100 =	e	1,800,000	1,800,000		
Development cost $275,000,000 ÷ $100, but capped at 2,450,000	f	2,450,000	1,200,500	1,249,500	
Total cost oil 45% of 10,000,000 =	g	4,500,000			
Production bonus $5,000,000 ÷ $100 =	h	50,000			50,000
Profit oil: a – b – c – g – h =	i	3,700,000			
Government profit oil 10% of 3,700,000 =	j	370,000			370,000
Working interest in profit oil 3,700,000 – 370,000 =	k	3,330,000	1,631,700	1,698,300	
Total: (b + c + g + h + i)		10,000,000	4,754,700	3,075,300	2,170,000
Unrecovered development costs $275,000,000 – (2,450,000 × $100) =		$30,000,000	$14,700,000	$15,300,000	

The above example illustrates not only that calculating an entity's share in the production of the current period requires a detailed knowledge of the PSC's provisions, but also that calculating the contractor's share of the remaining reserves requires a number of assumptions.

The reserves and production that the parties are entitled to varies depending on the oil price. Had the average oil price in 2020 been $50/barrel the parties' entitlements would have been as follows: Contractor 5,540,400 barrels, NOC 2,019,600 barrels and Government 2,440,000 barrels. The quantity of reserves and production attributable to each of the parties often reacts to changes in oil prices in ways that, at first, might seem counterintuitive.

It is important to note that the type and nature of contracts emerging continue to evolve. New contracts have some attributes of PSCs, but do differ from the traditional PSC. We discuss these in more detail at 5.5 below.

5.4   Pure-service contracts

A pure-service contract is an agreement between a contractor and a host government that typically covers a defined technical service to be provided or completed during a specific period of time. The service company investment is typically limited to the value of equipment, tools, and personnel used to perform the service. In most cases, the service contractor's reimbursement is fixed by the terms of the contract with little exposure to either project performance or market factors. Payment for services is normally based on daily or hourly rates, a fixed turnkey rate, or some other specified amount. Payments may be made at specified intervals or at the completion of the service. Payments, in some cases, may be tied to the field performance, operating cost reductions, or other important metrics.

The risks of the service company under this type of contract are usually limited to non-recoverable cost overruns, losses owing to client breach of contract, default, or contractual dispute. Such a contract is generally considered to be a services contract that gives rise to revenue from the rendering of services and not income from the production of mineral. Therefore, the minerals produced are not included in the normal reserve disclosures of the contractor,[91] and the contractor bears no risk if reserves are not found. It is worth noting that such contracts do need to be assessed to determine whether the arrangement contains a lease in accordance with the requirements of IFRS 16. See 17.1 below for more information. As noted above with respect to PSCs, the type and nature of contracts continue to evolve. These new contracts also have some attributes of services contracts, but do differ from pure-service contracts. We discuss these in more detail at 5.5 below.

5.5   Evolving contractual arrangements

The type and nature of contracts emerging continues to evolve. New contracts have some attributes of PSCs, but do differ from the traditional PSC. As these contractual arrangements evolve, determining the accounting implications of these contracts is becoming increasingly complex. This not only has an impact on the accounting for such contracts but also on whether, and the extent to which, the contractor entity is able to recognise reserves in relation to its interests in mineral volumes arising from these contracts.

Each contractual arrangement needs to be analysed carefully to determine whether reserves recognition in relation to these contractual interests in mineral volumes is appropriate. Such an analysis would include, at a minimum:
- the extent of risk to which the contractor party is exposed, including exploration and/or development risk;
- the structure of the contractor's reimbursement arrangements and whether it is subject to performance/reservoir risk or price risk; and
- the ability for the contractor to take product in-kind, rather than a cash reimbursement only.

Other facts and circumstances may also be relevant in reaching the final assessment. Given the varying terms and conditions that exist within these contracts and the fact that they are continuing to change/evolve, each contract will need to be individually analysed and assessed in detail.

5.5.1 Risk service contracts

An example of a contractual arrangement that has continued to evolve is a risk service contract (RSC). Unlike pure-service contracts, under a RSC (also called risked service agreement or at-risk service contract), a fee is not certain: an entity (contractor) agrees to explore for, develop, and produce minerals on behalf of a host government, but the contractor is at risk for the amount spent on exploration and development costs. That is, if no minerals are found in commercial quantities, no fee is paid.[92] Although a RSC does not result in the contractor's ownership of the minerals in place, the contractor may be at risk for the costs of exploration and may have economic interest in those minerals. The IASC Issues Paper noted that in the case of RSCs:[93]
- the fee may be payable in cash or in minerals produced;
- the contract may call for the contractor to bear all or part of the costs of exploration that are usually recoverable, in whole or in part, from production. If there is no production, there is no recovery; and
- the contract may also give the contractor the right to purchase part of the minerals produced.

As noted in Extract 43.7 above from TOTAL's financial statements, RSCs are similar to PSCs in a number of respects. Although the precise form and content of a RSC may vary, the following features are common:

(a) the repayment of expenses and the compensation for services are established on a monetary basis;

(b) an RSC is for a limited period, after which the government or national oil company will take over operations;

(c) under an RSC the contractor does not obtain ownership of the mineral reserves or production;

(d) the contractor is normally required to carry out a minimum amount of work in providing the contracted services;

(e) the fee that is payable to the contractor covers its capital expenditure, operating costs and an agreed-upon profit margin; and

(f) ownership of the assets used under the contract passes to the government when the contractor has been reimbursed for its costs.

The SPE's *Guidelines for the Evaluation of Petroleum Reserves and Resources* notes in connection with RSCs that 'under the existing regulations, it may be more difficult for the contractor to justify reserves recognition, and special care must be taken in drafting the agreement. If regulations are satisfied, reserves equivalent to the value of the cost-recovery-plus-revenue-profit split are normally reported by the contractor'.[94]

The nature and terms and conditions of these RSCs continue to change over time. Therefore each contract will need to be analysed in detail to determine how it should be accounted for.

5.6 Joint operating agreements

When several entities are jointly involved in an arrangement (e.g. joint ownership of a property, production sharing contract or concession) they will need to enter into some form of joint operating agreement (JOA). A JOA is a contract between two or more parties to a joint arrangement that sets out the rights and obligations to operate the property. Typically, a JOA designates one of the working interest owners as the operator and it governs the operations and sharing of costs between parties. A JOA does not override, but instead builds upon, the contracts that are already in place (such as production sharing contracts). In fact, many production sharing contracts require the execution of a JOA between the parties.

A JOA may give rise to a joint arrangement under IFRS 11 – *Joint Arrangements* – if certain criteria are met. This is discussed in more detail at 7.1 below.

5.7 Different types of royalty interests

Mining companies and oil and gas companies frequently enter into royalty arrangements with owners of mineral rights (e.g. governments or private land owners). These royalties are often payable upon the extraction and/or sale of minerals. The royalty payments may be based on a specified rate per unit of the commodity (e.g. tonne or barrel) or the entity may be obliged to dispose of all of the relevant production and pay over a specified proportion of the aggregate proceeds of sale, often after deduction of certain extraction costs.

There are also other types of arrangements, which may be referred to as royalty payments/arrangements, but may potentially represent a different type of arrangement. Under these arrangements the royalty holder may have retained (or obtained) a more direct interest in the underlying production and may undertake mineral extraction and sale arrangements independently. We discuss these further below.

5.7.1 Working interest and basic royalties

As discussed at 5.1 above, under a mineral lease the owner/lessor of the mineral rights retains a *basic royalty* interest (or non-operating interest), which entitles it to a specified percentage of the mineral produced, while the lessee obtains a *working interest* (or operating interest) under the mineral lease, which entitles it to explore for, develop, and produce minerals from the property.

If the owner of a working interest cannot fund or does not wish to bear the risk of exploration, development or production from the property, it may be able to – if this is permitted by the underlying lease – sell the working interest or to create new types of interest out of its existing working interest. By creating new types of non-operating interests, the working interest owner is able to raise financing and spread the risk of the development. The original working interest holder may either:

- retain the new non-operating interest and transfer the working interest (i.e. the rights and obligations for exploring, developing and operating the property); or
- carve out and transfer a new non-operating interest to another party, while retaining the working interest.

The following non-operating interests are commonly created in practice:[95]

- overriding royalties (see 5.7.2 below);
- production payment royalties (see 5.7.3 below); and
- net profits interests (see 5.7.4 below).

5.7.2 Overriding royalties

An *overriding royalty* is very similar to a basic royalty, except that the former is created out of the operating interest and if the operating interest expires, the overriding royalty also expires.[96] An overriding royalty owner bears only its share of production taxes and sometimes of the costs incurred to get the product into a saleable condition.

5.7.3 Production payment royalties

A *production payment royalty* is the right to recover a specified amount of cash or a specified quantity of minerals, out of the working interest's share of gross production. For example, the working interest holder may assign a production payment royalty to another party for USD 12 million, in exchange for a repayment of USD 15 million plus 12% interest out of the first 65% of the working interest holder's share of production. Production payments that are specified as a quantity of minerals are often called volumetric production payments or VPPs.

5.7.4 Net profits interests

A *net profits interest* is similar to an overriding royalty. However, the amount to be received by the royalty owner is a share of the net proceeds from production (as defined in the contract) that is paid solely from the working interest owner's share. The owner of a net profits interest is not liable for any expenses.

5.7.5 Revenue and royalties: gross or net?

Many mineral leases, concession agreements and production sharing contracts require the payment of a royalty to the original owner of the mineral reserves or the government. The accounting treatment for government and other royalties payable has historically been diverse, as it has not been entirely clear whether revenue should be presented net of royalty payments or not. Historically, many companies have presented revenue net of those royalties that are paid in kind. This was on the basis that the entity had no legal right to the royalty product and, hence, never received any inflow of economic benefits from those volumes. However, when the entity is required to sell the physical product in the market and remit the net proceeds (after deduction of certain costs incurred) to the royalty holder, it may have been considered to have control of those volumes to such an extent that it was appropriate to present revenue on a gross basis and include the royalty payment within cost of sales or taxes (depending on how the royalty is calculated). See 12.11.2 below for further discussion.

Extracts 43.8 and 43.9 below, from the financial statements of Premier Oil and BHP respectively, illustrate typical accounting policies for royalties under IFRS.

Extract 43.8: Premier Oil plc (2019)

ACCOUNTING POLICIES [extract]

FOR THE YEAR ENDED 31 DECEMBER 2019

ROYALTIES

Royalties are charged as production costs to the income statement in the year in which the related production is recognised as income.

Extract 43.9: BHP Group Plc (2019)

Notes to the Financial Statements [extract]

6 Income tax expense [extract]

Recognition and measurement [extract]

Royalty-related taxation [extract]

Royalties and resource rent taxes are treated as taxation arrangements (impacting income tax expense/(benefit)) when they are imposed under government authority and the amount payable is calculated by reference to revenue derived (net of any allowable deductions) after adjustment for temporary differences. Obligations arising from royalty arrangements that do not satisfy these criteria are recognised as current provisions and included in expenses.

Extract 43.10 below, from the financial statements of Equinor, illustrates some of the complications that may arise in determining revenue when an entity sells product on behalf of the government.

> **Extract 43.10: Equinor ASA (2019)**
>
> **Notes to the Consolidated financial statements** [extract]
>
> **2 Significant accounting policies** [extract]
>
> **Transactions with the Norwegian State** [extract]
>
> Equinor markets and sells the Norwegian State's share of oil and gas production from the Norwegian continental shelf (NCS). The Norwegian State's participation in petroleum activities is organised through the SDFI. All purchases and sales of the SDFI's oil production are classified as purchases [net of inventory variation] and revenues from contracts with customers, respectively. Equinor sells, in its own name, but for the Norwegian State's account and risk, the State's production of natural gas. These sales and related expenditures refunded by the Norwegian State are presented net in the Consolidated financial statements. Natural gas sales made in the name of Equinor subsidiaries are also presented net of the SDFI's share in the Consolidated statement of income, but this activity is reflected gross in the Consolidated balance sheet.
>
> **Critical accounting judgements and key sources of estimation uncertainty** [extract]
>
> **Critical judgements in applying accounting policies** [extract]
>
> **Revenue recognition – gross versus net presentation of traded SDFI volumes of oil and gas production**
>
> As described under Transactions with the Norwegian State above, Equinor markets and sells the Norwegian State's share of oil and gas production from the NCS. Equinor includes the costs of purchase and proceeds from the sale of the SDFI oil production in purchases [net of inventory variation] and revenues from contracts with customers, respectively. In making the judgement, Equinor has considered whether it controls the State originated crude oil volumes prior to onwards sales to third party customers. Equinor directs the use of the volumes, and although certain benefits from the sales subsequently flow to the State, Equinor purchases the crude oil volumes from the State and obtains substantially all the remaining benefits. On that basis, Equinor has concluded that it acts as principal in these sales.
>
> Equinor sells, in its own name, but for the Norwegian State's account and risk, the State's production of natural gas. These gas sales, and related expenditures refunded by the State, are shown net in Equinor's Consolidated financial statements. In making the judgement, Equinor concluded that ownership of the gas had not been transferred from the SDFI to Equinor. Although Equinor has been granted the ability to direct the use of the volumes, all the benefits from the sales of these volumes flow to the State. On that basis, Equinor is not considered the principal in the sale of the SDFI's natural gas volumes.

The SPE-PRMS (see 2.2 above) notes that 'royalty quantities must be deducted from the lessee's entitlement to resources so that only the net revenue interest quantities are recognized'. In some agreements, production taxes imposed by the host government may be referred to as royalties. These payment obligations are expressed in monetary terms and are typically linked to production rates, quantities produced cost recovery, the value of production (price sensitive), or the profits derived from it. These payments are not associated with an interest retained by the lessor/host. Thus, such payment obligations are effectively a production tax instead of a royalty. In such cases, the production and underlying resources are controlled by the lessee/contractor who may (subject to contractual terms and/or regulatory guidance) elect to report these obligations as a tax without a corresponding reduction in lessor/contractor's entitlement.[97]

6 RISK-SHARING ARRANGEMENTS

As discussed at 1.1 above, the high costs and high risks in the extractive industries often lead entities to enter into risk-sharing arrangements. The following types of risk-sharing arrangements are discussed in this chapter:

- carried interests (see 6.1 below);

- farm-ins and farm-outs (see 6.2 below);
- asset swaps (see 6.3 below);
- unitisations (see 15.4 below);
- investments in subsidiaries, joint arrangements and associates (see 7 below);
- production sharing contracts (see 5.3 above), which result in a degree of risk sharing with local governments; and
- risk service contracts (see 5.5.1 above).

6.1 Carried interests

Carried interests often arise when a party in an arrangement is either unable or unwilling to bear the risk of exploration or is unable or unwilling to fund its share of the cost of exploration or development. A carried interest is an agreement under which one party (the carrying party) agrees to pay for a portion or all of the pre-production costs of another party (the carried party) on a licence in which both own a portion of the working interest.[98] In effect, commercially, the carried party is trading a share of any production to which it is entitled in the future in exchange for the carrying party funding one or more phases of the project. In other words, the parties create a new interest out of an existing working interest. If the project is unsuccessful then the carrying party will not be reimbursed for the costs that it has incurred on behalf of the carried party. If the project is successful then the carrying party will be reimbursed either in cash out of proceeds of the share of production attributable to the carried party, or by receiving a disproportionately high share of the production until the carried costs have been recovered.[99]

6.1.1 Types of carried interest arrangements

Carried interest arrangements tend to fall into one of the following two categories:

- *financing-type arrangements* – the carrying party provides funding to the carried party and receives a lender's return on the funds provided, while the right to additional production acts as a security that underpins the arrangement; or
- *purchase/sale-type arrangement* – the carried party effectively sells an interest or a partial interest in a project to the carrying party. The carrying party will be required to fund the project in exchange for an increased share of any proceeds if the project succeeds, while the carried party retains a reduced share of any proceeds.

In practice, however, it is not always easy to determine in which category a particular carried interest arrangement falls, as is illustrated in the example below.

Example 43.4:   Carried interests (1)

Scenario 1

The carrying party has proposed a $10 million project, which has a very high chance of succeeding. The carried party, which is unable to fund its share of the project, agrees that the carrying party is entitled to recover its cost plus 7% interest by giving it a disproportionately high share of the production. If the production from this project is insufficient to repay the initial investment, the carried party should reimburse the carrying party out of its share of production from other fields within the same licence.

Scenario 2

The carrying party has proposed a project that may cost up to $6 million, the outcome of which is uncertain. The carried party, which is unwilling to participate in the project, agrees that the carrying party is entitled to all production from the project until it has recovered three times its initial investment.

Scenario 3

The carrying party has proposed a project that may cost up to $5 million, which has a good chance of succeeding. The carrying party has a 60% interest in the licence and the carried party holds the remaining 40%. The carried party, which is unable to fund its share of the project, agrees that the carrying party is entitled to an additional 25% of the production until the carrying party has recovered its costs plus a 20% return.

When entering into a carried interest arrangement, an entity must assess whether the arrangement is a financing-type arrangement or purchase/sale-type arrangement. Some of the indicators that a carried interest arrangement should be accounted for as a financing-type arrangement are that:

- the carried party is unable to fund its share of the project;
- the risks associated with the development are not significant, i.e. financing-type arrangements will be more common in the development stage; and
- the carrying party receives a return that is comparable to a lender's rate of return.

Indicators that a carried interest arrangement should be treated as a purchase/sale-type arrangement include:

- the carrying party and carried party have genuinely different opinions about the chances of success of the project, and the carried party could fund its share of the project if it wanted to;
- there are significant uncertainties about the outcome of the project. Purchase/sale-type arrangements are therefore more common in the E&E phase;
- the arrangement gives the carrying party voting rights in the project;
- there are significant uncertainties about the costs of the project, perhaps because it involves use of a new technology or approach;
- the carrying party could lose all of its investment or possibly earn a return significantly in excess of a lender's rate of return; and
- the carrying party can only recover its investment from the project that is subject to the arrangement and there is no recourse to other assets or interests of the carried party.

In Example 43.4 above, scenario 1 has the characteristics of a financing-type arrangement, while scenario 2 has those of a purchase/sale-type arrangement. However, when an arrangement (such as scenario 3) has financing-type and purchase/sale-type characteristics (e.g. as a result of the relative bargaining strength of the parties), an entity will need to analyse the arrangement carefully and exercise judgement in developing an appropriate accounting policy.

The following types of carried interest arrangements are discussed below:

- carried interest arrangements in the E&E phase (see 6.1.2 below);
- financing-type carried interest arrangements in the development phase (see 6.1.3 below); and
- purchase/sale-type carried interest arrangements in the development phase (see 6.1.4 below).

6.1.2 Carried interest arrangements in the E&E phase

While IFRS 6 should be applied to accounting for E&E expenditures, the standard does not address other aspects of accounting by entities engaged in the exploration for and evaluation of mineral resources. *[IFRS 6.4]*. That leaves unanswered the question of whether carried interest arrangements can ever fall within the scope of IFRS 6. In the case of a purchase/sale-type carried interest arrangement the transaction, at least in economic terms, leads to the acquisition of an E&E asset by the carrying party and a disposal by the carried party. Therefore, we believe that purchase/sale-type carried interest arrangements in the E&E phase would fall within the scope of IFRS 6. Hence an entity has two options: either to develop an accounting policy under IAS 8 as discussed at 6.1.4 below, or, on transition to IFRS or first application under IFRS, to develop an accounting policy under IFRS 6 that is based on a previous national GAAP that contains such guidance. In practice this usually means that:

- the carrying party accounts for its expenditures under a carried interest arrangement in the same way as directly incurred E&E expenditure (see 3.2 and 3.3 above); and
- the carried party would not record expenditure incurred by the carrying party on its behalf subsequent to the arrangement commencing. However, the carried party may need to recognise a loss when the terms of the transaction indicate that the existing carrying value of the asset is impaired. Alternatively, to the extent that an arrangement is favourable, the carried party would – depending on its accounting policy – recognise the gain either in profit or loss or as a reduction in the carrying amount of the E&E asset.

On the other hand, a finance-type carried interest arrangement (which is generally not as common in the E&E phase) that has no significant impact on the risks and rewards that an entity derives from the underlying E&E working interest, may be more akin to a funding arrangement. As IFRS 6 deals only with accounting for E&E expenditures and assets, it is a matter of judgement whether or not the accounting for finance-type carried interest arrangements is considered to be outside the scope of IFRS 6. If an arrangement is considered to be outside the scope of IFRS 6, it might be appropriate to account for it in the same way as finance-type carried interest arrangements that relate to projects that are not in the E&E phase (see 6.1.3 below).

6.1.3 Financing-type carried interest arrangements in the development phase

As financing-type carried interest arrangements do not result in the transfer of the economic risks and rewards of the underlying working interest between parties, such arrangements are not accounted for as a sale (purchase) by the carried party (carrying party). Instead these arrangements are in effect secured borrowings in which the underlying asset is used as collateral that provides an identifiable stream of cash flows.

These arrangements are most appropriately accounted for as giving rise to a financial asset for the carrying party and a financial liability for the carried party.

The carried party will continue to recognise the expenditure incurred in relation to its full share of the working interest prior to the execution of the carried interest arrangement, and a corresponding financial liability for the amount that it is expected to reimburse to the carrying party as the pre-production costs being met by the carrying party are incurred, irrespective of whether it is a non-recourse arrangement or not. Under IFRS 9 – *Financial Instruments* – any financial liability would likely be measured at amortised cost unless it meets the definition of a derivative or is designated at fair value through profit or loss. See Chapter 48 at 3 for more information. As a financial liability measured at amortised cost, under IFRS 9 the carried party should accrete interest on the liability and reduce the loan to the extent the carrying party recovers its costs. It should be noted, however, that the application of the effective interest rate method under IFRS 9 requires adjustment of the carrying amount when the entity revises its estimates of the payments to be made. [IFRS 9.B5.4.6].

Conversely the carrying party should recognise a financial asset for the amount that it expects to recover as a reimbursement as the pre-production costs (which are being met by the carrying party) are incurred. Under IFRS 9 an entity would need to determine the classification of the financial asset based on an assessment of the entity's business model for managing financial assets and the contractual cash flow characteristics of the financial asset. See Chapter 48 at 2 for more information. Where the entity expects to recover all of its investment (so it is considered a debt instrument and not an equity instrument), the terms are solely payments of principal and interest and its business model is to hold the investment in order to collect contractual cash flows, the financial asset will be carried at amortised cost. This may be the case in financing-type carried interest arrangements. Where there is exposure to other factors, e.g. uncertainty about recovery and the exposure is through something other than principal and interest, the financial asset may have to be carried at fair value through profit or loss.

This approach to accounting for carried interest arrangements might not be appropriate if there were more than an insignificant transfer of risk (without necessarily resulting in a purchase/sale-type carried interest arrangement). The transfer of risk would suggest that:

- the carried party should recognise a provision under IAS 37 rather than a liability under IFRS 9; and
- the carrying party should account for its right to receive reimbursement as a financial asset at fair value through profit or loss under IFRS 9 or a reimbursement right under IAS 37.

Any financial liability would likely be measured at amortised cost unless it meets the definition of a derivative or was designated at fair value through profit or loss. See Chapter 48 at 3 for more information.

6.1.4 Purchase/sale-type carried interest arrangements in the development phase

The accounting suggested in this section for the carried party is the same as that set out in paragraph 155 of the former OIAC SORP, which stated that the disposal should be accounted for in accordance with the entity's normal accounting policy.

Historically, some entities have accounted for these types of transactions on a cash basis, i.e. the carried party does nothing and the carrying party accounts for its actual cash outlays. It is hard to see how this can be justified under IFRS.

In purchase/sale-type carried interest arrangements, the carried party effectively sells part of its interest in a project to the carrying party. For example, the carried party may sell part of its interest in the mineral reserves to the carrying party which, in exchange, is obliged to fund the remaining costs of developing the field. Consequently, the arrangement has two elements, the purchase/sale of mineral reserves and the funding of developments costs, which should be accounted for in accordance with their substance. Therefore, the carried party should:

- derecognise the part of the asset that it has sold to the carrying party, consistent with the derecognition principles of IAS 16 or IAS 38. *[IAS 16.67, IAS 38.112]*. Determining the amount to be derecognised may require a considerable amount of judgement depending on how the interest sold is defined;
- recognise the consideration received or receivable from the carrying party;
- recognise a gain or loss on the transaction for the difference between the net disposal proceeds and the carrying amount of the asset disposed of. Recognition of a gain would be appropriate only when the value of the consideration can be determined reliably. If not, then the carried party should account for the consideration received as a reduction in the carrying amount of the underlying assets. See 12.6.1.A below and Chapters 27 to 30 for discussion of how IFRS 15 – *Revenue from Contracts with Customers* – may impact such calculations; and
- test the retained interest for impairment if the terms of the arrangement indicate that the retained interest may be impaired.

In accounting for its purchase the carrying party should:

- recognise an asset that represents the underlying (partially) undeveloped interest acquired at cost in accordance with the principles of IAS 16 or IAS 38. *[IAS 16.15, IAS 38.21]*. Cost is defined in these standards as 'the amount of cash or cash equivalents paid or the fair value of the other consideration given to acquire an asset at the time of its acquisition or construction or, where applicable, the amount attributed to that asset when initially recognised in accordance with the specific requirements of other IFRSs'; *[IAS 16.6, IAS 38.8]* and
- recognise a liability for the obligation to make defined payments on behalf of the carried party, which relate to the carried party's share of future investments.

The application of this approach is illustrated in Example 43.5 below.

Example 43.5: Carried interests (2)

An oil and gas company is developing an oil field. Assume that the company did not capitalise any E&E costs in relation to the field, but that by 1 January 2020 it had capitalised $250 million of costs in relation to the construction of property, plant and equipment. To complete the development of the oil field and bring it to production a further investment in property, plant and equipment of $350 million is required in the first half of 2020.

At 1 January 2020, the oil and gas company (the carried party) enters into a purchase/sale-type carried interest arrangement with a carrying party, which will fund the entire $350 million required for the further development of the field. Upon entering into the carried interest arrangement the carried party's entitlement to oil is expected to be reduced from 15,000,000 barrels of oil to 9,000,000 barrels of oil, i.e. its interest in the oil field and the related property, plant and equipment has been reduced to 60% (9,000,000 ÷ 15,000,000). In practice, calculating the portion of the interest sold may require a considerable amount of judgement (e.g. in scenario 2 in Example 43.4 above it would not be straightforward to calculate the portion of the interest sold).

Both parties believe that the fair value of the oil field and related property, plant and equipment will be $1 billion once the remaining investment of $350 million has been made. Consequently, the fair value of the oil field and related property, plant and equipment at 1 January 2020 is $650 million ($1 billion – $350 million).

The fair value of the interest acquired (which comprises a portion of the oil field and a portion of the related property, plant and equipment) by the carrying party is $260 million (40% × $650 million). In exchange for its interest, the carrying party will pay $50 million in cash and undertakes to pay the remaining investments related to the carried party's interest.

The carried party accounts for the transaction as follows:

	$	$
Cash received from the carrying party	50	
Capital calls to be paid by the carrying party (60% × $350 million) †	210	
Property, plant and equipment (40% × $250 million)		100
Gain on sale (40% × ($650 million – $250 million))		160

† The carried party has obtained the commitment from the carrying party to make certain payments on its behalf.

If the carried party had recognised a loss on the interest sold, it would need to perform an impairment test on the interest retained.

The carrying party accounts for the transaction as follows:

	$	$
Assets acquired ($50 million + $210 million) †	260	
Cash paid to the carried party		50
Capital calls payable on behalf of the carried party (60% × $350 million) ‡		210

† As discussed above, the cost of property, plant and equipment is defined as the fair value of the consideration. In an arm's length transaction the fair value of property, plant and equipment acquired is normally equal to the fair value of the consideration paid. The fair value of the portion of the oil field and the portion of the related property, plant and equipment acquired is (40% × $650 million) $260 million.

‡ The carrying party has assumed a liability to make these payments on behalf of the carried party. The carrying party will also be required to pay (40% × $350 million) $140 million for its own share of the future investments, but that amount is only recognised as a liability upon recognition of the related property, plant and equipment.

The receivable recognised by the carried party and the corresponding liability recognised by the carrying party are reduced over the course of the construction of the assets to which they relate. The carrying party reduces the liability as it funds the carried party's share of the investment and the carried party recognises its share of the assets being constructed while reducing the balance of the receivable.

6.2 Farm-ins and farm-outs

A farm-out (from the viewpoint of the transferor) or a farm-in (from the viewpoint of the transferee) was defined in the former OIAC SORP as 'the transfer of part of an oil and gas interest in consideration for an agreement by the transferee (farmee) to meet, absolutely, certain expenditure which would otherwise have to be undertaken by the owner (farmor)'.[100] Farm-in transactions generally occur in the exploration or development phase and are characterised by the transferor (i.e. farmor) giving up future economic benefits, in the form of reserves, in exchange for a (generally) permanent reduction in future funding obligations.

Under a carried interest arrangement, the carried party transfers a portion of the risks and rewards of a property, in exchange for a funding commitment from the carrying party. Under a farm-in arrangement the farmor transfers all the risks and rewards of a proportion (i.e. a straight percentage) of a property, in exchange for a commitment from the farmee to fund certain expenditures. Therefore, a farm-out represents the complete disposal of a proportion of a property and is similar to purchase/sale-type carried interest arrangements as discussed at 6.1.4 above.

The following types of farm-in arrangements are separately discussed below:
- farm-in arrangements in the E&E phase (see 6.2.1 below); and
- farm-in arrangements outside the E&E phase (see 6.2.2 below).

6.2.1 Farm-in arrangements in the E&E phase

IFRS 6 deals only with accounting for E&E expenditures and does not address other aspects of accounting by entities engaged in the exploration for and evaluation of mineral resources. *[IFRS 6.4]*. That leaves open the question of whether farm-in arrangements can ever fall within the scope of IFRS 6. However, as a farm-in arrangement leads to the acquisition of an E&E asset by the farmee and a disposal by the farmor, we believe that a farm-in arrangement would fall within the scope of IFRS 6. Hence an entity has two options: either to develop an accounting policy under IAS 8 as discussed at 6.2.2 below; or to develop an accounting policy under IFRS 6. In practice many entities use the second option and apply an accounting policy to farm-in arrangements that is based on a previous national GAAP.

Accounting policies for farm-in arrangements in the E&E phase that are based on an entity's previous national GAAP will often require that:

- the farmee recognises its expenditure under the arrangement in respect of its own interest and that retained by the farmor, as and when the costs are incurred. The farmee accounts for its expenditures under a farm-in arrangement in the same way as directly incurred E&E expenditure; and
- the farmor accounts for the farm-out arrangement as follows:
  - the farmor does not record any expenditure made by the farmee on its behalf;
  - the farmor does not recognise a gain or loss on the farm-out arrangement, but rather redesignates any costs previously capitalised in relation to the whole interest as relating to the partial interest retained; and
  - any cash consideration received is credited against costs previously capitalised in relation to the whole interest with any excess accounted for by the farmor as a gain on disposal.

If an entity applies its previous GAAP accounting policy in respect of farm-in arrangements, we would expect the entity also to make the farm-in disclosures required by its previous GAAP.

6.2.2 Farm-in arrangements outside the E&E phase: accounting by the farmee

A farm-in represents the complete acquisition of a proportion of a property. The accounting for such an arrangement will depend on whether the entity is farming into an asset or into an arrangement that is considered a business (and which is a joint operation), or whether the farm-in results in the arrangement becoming a joint operation. See Chapter 9 at 3.2 for discussion of the new definition of a business which is applicable for annual reporting periods beginning on or after 1 January 2020.

6.2.2.A Farming into an asset

Where a farmee farms into an asset, regardless of whether it is a joint operation or results in the formation of a joint operation, it should recognise an asset that represents the underlying (partially) undeveloped interest acquired at cost in accordance with IAS 16 or IAS 38, *[IAS 16.15, IAS 38.21]*, and recognise a liability that reflects obligations to fund the farmor's share of the future investment from which the farmee itself will not derive any future economic benefits.

Farm-in arrangements can be structured in numerous ways, some requiring payment of a fixed monetary amount while others are more flexible and state, for example, that capital expenditures over the next five years will be paid for by the farmee regardless of what those amounts may be. Accounting for these arrangements is uncertain.

In some cases, the liability may meet the definition of a financial liability under IAS 32 – *Financial Instruments: Presentation* – and should be accounted for in accordance with IFRS 9. In other scenarios, such as the latter example above (i.e. where the farmee pays all capital expenditure incurred over a five year period, regardless of the amount), the liability may meet the definition of a provision under IAS 37 as the timing and amount of the liability are uncertain. *[IAS 37.10]*. If an entity concludes that IAS 37 applies, then there can be some debate as to when a provision should be recognised as that standard is not clear.

The issue of contingent consideration in the context of the acquisition of assets has been discussed by the Interpretations Committee but they were unable to reach consensus on whether IAS 37 or IFRS 9 applies. Hence, different treatments will continue to be encountered in practice. See 8.4.1 below for further discussion on this issue and an update on current status.

An arrangement involving a farm-in into an asset is illustrated below in the extract from Intrepid's 2018 financial statements.

Extract 43.11: Intrepid Mines Limited (2018)

CONSOLIDATED FINANCIAL STATEMENTS [extract]

27. FARM-IN AND JOINT VENTURE [extract]

Doolgunna Station Project

On 4 June 2018, Intrepid announced that it had entered into a Farm-in and Joint Venture Agreement ("Agreement") with Ausgold Limited (ASX:AUC) ("Ausgold") to earn up to an 80% interest of the Doolgunna Station Project ("Doolgunna"), located 150km north east of Meekatharra in West Australia's Bryah Basin.

Highlights of the Agreement are as follows:

- Intrepid to earn up to an 80% interest in Doolgunna by spending a minimum of $2,150,000 over two years;
- After the spending commitment is met, Ausgold will have right to retain a 30% contributing interest, or revert to a 20% free-carried interest to a decision to mine.

For further detail in relation to the Doolgunna deposit and the terms of the Agreement, please refer to the ASX announcement dated 4 June 2018.

Under the terms of the Agreement, a joint venture is not formed until the minimum spending requirement (the "Farm-in Period") is met by Intrepid. Therefore, joint venture accounting is not currently applicable. All expenditure throughout the Farm-in Period is recorded as exploration expenditure in the statement of comprehensive income, consistent with the accounting policy in relation to expenditure on mining properties outlined in note 2(f). In the period ended 31 December 2018, $564,000 of exploration expenditure was incurred in relation to Doolgunna.

6.2.2.B   Farming into a business which is a joint operation or results in the formation of a joint operation

Where a farmee farms into a project that is considered to be a business (as defined in IFRS 3) which is either a joint operation or results in the formation of a joint operation, historically there has been some diversity in how this was to be accounted for. Some have applied the business combination principles in IFRS 3 and other standards and some have applied the asset acquisition accounting principles (as discussed above at 6.2.2.A).

This issue was resolved by the IASB issuing an amendment to IFRS 11 which was effective for annual reporting periods commencing on or after 1 January 2016. This amendment requires that where an entity acquires an interest in a joint operation which constitutes a business, the business combination accounting principles of IFRS 3 and other standards must be applied. See Chapter 9 at 3.2 for discussion of the new definition of a business which is applicable for annual reporting periods beginning on or after 1 January 2020.

See Chapter 12 at 8.3.1 for further discussion on this issue. These requirements will include such interests acquired through a farm-in.

It is important to note that for the IFRS 11 amendment to mandatorily apply, the definition of a joint operation in accordance with IFRS 11 must be met, i.e. there must be joint control. Where there is joint control, the amendment applies to all entities party to the joint operation whether or not the entity is a party that has joint control. IFRS 11 specifies that 'a party that participates in, but does not have joint control of, a joint operation shall also account for its interest in the arrangement in accordance with paragraphs 20-22 if that party has rights to the assets, and obligations for the liabilities, relating to the joint operation. If a party that participates in, but does not have joint control of, a joint operation does not have rights to the assets, and obligations for the liabilities, relating to that joint operation, it shall account for its interest in the joint operation in accordance with the IFRSs applicable to that interest'. *[IFRS 11.23]*.

When it comes to accounting for the acquisition of an interest in an arrangement which does not meet the definition of a joint operation under IFRS 11, i.e. there is no joint control, there is no specific guidance as to how this should be accounted for. That is, it is not clear whether an entity can, or should, apply similar provisions to those applicable to acquiring an interest in a joint operation (discussed above). Given this, diversity may continue in practice.

6.2.3   Farm-in arrangements outside the E&E phase: accounting by the farmor

In accounting for a farm-in arrangement the farmor should:

- derecognise the proportion of the asset that it has sold to the farmee, consistent with the principles of IAS 16 or IAS 38; *[IAS 16.67, IAS 38.112]*
- recognise the consideration received or receivable from the farmee, which represents the farmee's obligation to fund the capital expenditure in relation to the interest retained by the farmor;
- recognise a gain or loss on the transaction for the difference between the net disposal proceeds and the carrying amount of the asset disposed of. *[IAS 16.71, IAS 38.113]*. Recognition of a gain would be appropriate only when the value of the consideration

can be determined reliably. If not, then the carried party should account for the consideration received as a reduction in the carrying amount of the underlying assets; and

- test the retained interest for impairment if the terms of the arrangement indicate that the retained interest may be impaired.

Under IAS 16, IAS 38 and IFRS 15, the amount of consideration to be included in the gain/loss arising from the derecognition of an item of property, plant and equipment or an intangible asset, and hence the receivable that is recognised, is determined in accordance with the requirements for determining the transaction price under IFRS 15. Subsequent changes to the estimated amount of the consideration included in the gain or loss calculation shall be accounted for in accordance with the requirements for changes in the transaction price in IFRS 15. *[IAS 16.72, IAS 38.116]*. See Chapter 27 at 4.3 and Chapter 29 at 2.9 for more information.

Any part of the consideration that is receivable in the form of cash will meet the definition of a financial asset under IAS 32, *[IAS 32.11]*, and should be accounted for in accordance with IFRS 9, either at amortised cost or fair value depending on the nature of the receivable or how the farmor designates the receivable. See Chapter 48 at 2 for more information on classifying a financial asset under IFRS 9.

The extract below describes the farm-in transactions of Harmony Gold.

Extract 43.12: Harmony Gold Mining Company Limited (2009)

Directors' report [extract]

Disposals [extract]

Sale of interest in PNG to Newcrest

During the year, the group sold 50% of its interest in its PNG assets in Morobe Province to Newcrest. This took place in three stages, with the disposal of 30.01% for US$229 million (stage one) being completed on 31 July 2008. Stages two and three were completed by the end of quarters three and four of the financial year respectively with Newcrest having earned in a further 10% and 9.99% respectively in each of these stages.

Notes to the group financial statements [extract]

6 Profit of sale of property, plant and equipment [extract]

Included in the total for 2009 is R931 million (US$111.9 million) profit on sale of 50% of Harmony's gold and copper assets in Morobe Province, Papua New Guinea, to Newcrest Mining Limited (Newcrest) in terms of the Master Purchase and Farm-in agreement. The sale was concluded in three stages. On 31 July 2008, stage 1, being the sale of an initial 30.1% participating interest in the assets, was concluded at a profit of R416 million (US$57.9 million). The remaining 19.99% interest was sold in two further stages, resulting in a profit of R439 million (US$44.6 million) for the 10% interest of stage 2 and a profit of R76 million (US$9.9 million) for the 9.99% interest of stage 3. These stages were completed on 27 February 2009 and 30 June 2009 respectively. Refer to note 23.

23 Investment in joint venture [extract]

a) Papua New Guinea (PNG) Partnership agreement (50%)

On 22 April 2008, Morobe Consolidated Goldfields Limited and Wafi Mining Limited, subsidiaries of Harmony Australia, entered into a Master Purchase and Farm-in Agreement with Newcrest. This agreement provided for Newcrest to purchase a 30.01% participating interest (stage 1) and a further farm-in of an additional 19.99% participating interest in Harmony's PNG gold and copper assets, giving them a 50% interest. The total value of the transaction was estimated at US$530 million.

On 16 July 2008, the conditions to the Master Purchase and Farm-in agreement were finalised, which included regulatory and statutory approvals by the PNG Government. Stage 1 completion took place on 31 July 2008, and a total consideration of R1 792 million (US$229.8 million) was received on 7 August 2008, of which R390 million (US$50 million) was placed in a jointly controlled escrow account. This amount was subsequently released to Harmony following confirmation of approval of an exploration licence during September 2008 by the PNG mining authorities.

> Harmony recognised a profit of R416 million (US$58 million) on the completion of stage 1, which represented a sale of a 30.01% undivided interest of Harmony's PNG gold and copper assets and liabilities comprising the joint venture.
>
> During the farm-in period, Harmony agreed to transfer a further 19.99% interest to Newcrest in consideration for an agreement by Newcrest to meet certain expenditure which would otherwise have to be undertaken by Harmony. The interest to be transferred were conditional on the level of capital expenditures funded by Newcrest at certain milestones, and by the end of February 2009, Newcrest acquired another 10% through the farm-in arrangement. The final 9.99% was acquired by 30 June 2009.
>
> At the date of completion of each party's obligations under the farm-in arrangement, Harmony derecognised the proportion of the mining assets and liabilities in the joint venture that it had sold to Newcrest, and recognised its interest in the capital expenditure at fair value. The difference between the net disposal proceeds and the carrying amounts of the asset disposed of during the farm-in arrangement amounted to a gain of R515 million (US$54 million), which has been included in the consolidated income statements for 2009.

6.3 Asset swaps

Asset exchanges are transactions that have challenged standard-setters for a number of years. For example, an entity might swap certain intangible assets that it does not require or is no longer allowed to use for those of a counterparty that has other surplus assets. It is not uncommon for entities to exchange assets as part of their portfolio and risk management activities or simply to meet demands of competition authorities.

The key accounting issues that need to be addressed are:

- whether such an exchange should give rise to a profit when the fair value of the asset received is greater than the carrying value of the asset given up; and
- whether the exchange of similar assets should be recognised.

In the extractive industries an exchange of assets could involve property, plant and equipment (PP&E), intangible assets, investment property or E&E assets, which are in the scope of IAS 16, IAS 38, IAS 40 and IFRS 6, respectively. Hence there are three possible types of exchanges (which will be discussed below), involving:

(a) only E&E assets;

(b) only PP&E, intangible assets and/or investment property; and

(c) a combination of E&E assets, PP&E, intangible assets and/or investment property.

6.3.1 E&E assets

Accounting for E&E assets, and therefore also accounting for swaps involving only E&E assets, falls within the scope of IFRS 6. *[IFRS 6.3]*. As that standard does not directly address accounting for asset swaps, it is necessary to consider its hierarchy of guidance in the selection of an accounting policy. IFRS 6 does not require an entity to look at other standards and interpretations that deal with similar issues, or the guidance in the IASB's *Conceptual Framework. [IFRS 6.7]*. Instead, it allows entities to develop their own accounting policies, or use the guidance issued by other standard-setters, thereby effectively allowing entities to continue using accounting policies that they applied under their previous national GAAP. Therefore, many entities, especially those which consider that they can never determine the fair value of E&E assets reliably, have selected an accounting policy under which they account for E&E assets obtained in a swap transaction at the carrying amount of the asset given up. An alternative approach, which is also permitted under IFRS 6, would be to apply an accounting policy that is based on the guidance in other standards as discussed below.

6.3.2 PP&E, intangible assets and investment property

Three separate international accounting standards contain virtually identical guidance on accounting for exchanges of assets: IAS 16, IAS 38 and IAS 40. These standards require the acquisition of PP&E, intangible assets or investment property, as the case may be, in exchange for non-monetary assets (or a combination of monetary and non-monetary assets) to be measured at fair value. The cost of the acquired asset is measured at fair value unless:

(a) the exchange transaction lacks 'commercial substance'; or

(b) the fair value of neither the asset received nor the asset given up is reliably measurable. *[IAS 16.24, IAS 38.45, IAS 40.27].*

For more information, see Chapter 18 at 4.4 (PP&E), Chapter 17 at 4.7 (intangible assets) and Chapter 19 at 4.6 (investment properties).

6.3.3 Exchanges of E&E assets for other types of assets

An entity that exchanges E&E assets for PP&E, intangible assets or investment property needs to apply an accounting treatment that meets the requirements of IFRS 6 and those of IAS 16, IAS 38 or IAS 40. As discussed above, exchanges involving PP&E, intangible assets and investment property that have commercial substance should be accounted for at fair value. Since this treatment is also allowed under IFRS 6, an entity that exchanges E&E assets for assets within the scope of IAS 16, IAS 38 or IAS 40 should apply an accounting policy that complies with the guidance in those standards.

7 INVESTMENTS IN THE EXTRACTIVE INDUSTRIES

Extractive industries are characterised by the high risks associated with the exploration for and development of mineral reserves and resources. To mitigate those risks, industry participants use a variety of ownership structures that are aimed at sharing risks, such as joint investments through subsidiaries, joint arrangements, associates or equity interests. IFRS defines each of these as follows:

- *subsidiaries* – entities controlled by the reporting entity. Sometimes entities in the extractive industries do not own 100% of these subsidiaries, and there can often be significant non-controlling shareholders that share in some of the risk and rewards. Accounting for non-controlling interests is discussed in detail in Chapter 7 at 5. Furthermore, the existence of put and/or call options over non-controlling interests may transfer some of the risks between the parent entity and the non-controlling shareholders. This issue is discussed in detail in Chapter 7 at 6;

- *joint arrangements* – contractual arrangements of which two or more parties have joint control (see 7.1 below);

- *undivided interests* – participations in projects which entitle the reporting entity only to a share of the production or use of an asset, and do not of themselves give the entity any form of control, joint control or significant influence (see 7.2 below);

- *associates* – entities that, while not controlled or jointly controlled by the reporting entity, are subject to significant influence by it (see Chapter 11 at 4); and

- *equity interests* – entities over which the reporting entity cannot exercise any control, joint control or significant influence (see Chapters 48 and 49).

7.1 Joint arrangements

Joint arrangements have always been, and continue to be, a common structure in the extractive industries. Such arrangements are used to bring in partners to source new projects, combine adjacent mineral licences, improve utilisation of expensive infrastructure, attract investors and help manage technical or political risk or comply with local regulations. The majority of entities operating in the extractive industries are party to at least one joint arrangement. However, not all arrangements that are casually described as 'joint arrangements' or 'joint ventures' meet the definition of a joint arrangement under IFRS.

Accounting for joint arrangements is governed by IFRS 11. Given the prevalence of joint arrangements in the extractive industries, careful analysis of IFRS 11, in conjunction with the requirements of IFRS 10 – *Consolidated Financial Statements* (see Chapter 6) and IFRS 12 – *Disclosure of Interests in Other Entities* (see Chapter 13) is required. Chapter 12 contains a full discussion on IFRS 11 and its requirements and therefore while some specific areas for extractives companies to consider are set out below, this section should be read in conjunction with that chapter.

We also discuss some issues relating to the acquisition of interests in joint operations (see 8.3 below).

A joint arrangement in the scope of IFRS 11 is an arrangement over which two or more parties have joint control. *[IFRS 11.4].* (See 7.1.1 below for further discussion on the definition of joint control). Under IFRS 11, there are two types of joint arrangements – 'joint operations' and 'joint ventures'.

Joint operation: a joint arrangement whereby the parties that have joint control of the arrangement have rights to the assets, and obligations for the liabilities, relating to the arrangement. *[IFRS 11 Appendix A].*

Joint venture: a joint arrangement whereby the parties that have joint control of the arrangement have rights to the net assets of the arrangement. *[IFRS 11 Appendix A].*

Classification between these two types of arrangements is based on the rights and obligations that arise from the contractual arrangement. An entity will need to have a detailed understanding of the specific rights and obligations of each of its arrangements to be able to determine the impact of this standard.

Subsequent to the issuance of IFRS 11, the Interpretations Committee discussed various implementation issues particularly when it came to classifying a joint arrangement that is structured through a separate vehicle. In March 2015, the Interpretations Committee issued an agenda decision dealing with a range of issues, including:

- how and why particular facts and circumstances create rights and obligations;
- implication of 'economic substance'; and
- application of 'other facts and circumstances' to specific fact patterns:
  - output sold at a market price;
  - financing from a third party;
  - nature of output (i.e. fungible or bespoke output); and
  - determining the basis for 'substantially all of the output'.

This agenda decision includes a number of fact patterns which may be relevant for extractive industries, including (for example) the impact on agreements to purchase a joint arrangement's output. See Chapter 12 at 5.4.3 for further discussion.

7.1.1 Assessing joint control

Joint control is defined as 'the contractually agreed sharing of control of an arrangement which exists only when the decisions about the relevant activities require the unanimous consent of the parties sharing control'. *[IFRS 11.7, Appendix A]*. IFRS 11 describes the key aspects of joint control as follows:

- *Contractually agreed* – contractual arrangements are usually, but not always, written, and set out the terms of the arrangements. *[IFRS 11.5(a), B2]*.
- *Control and relevant activities* – IFRS 10 describes how to assess whether a party has control, and how to identify the relevant activities, which are described in more detail in Chapter 6 at 3 and 4.1. Some of the aspects of 'relevant activities' and 'control' that are most relevant to extractives arrangements are discussed at 7.1.1.A and 7.1.2 below, respectively. *[IFRS 11.8, B5]*.
- *Unanimous consent* – means that any party (with joint control) can prevent any of the other parties, or a group of the parties, from making unilateral decisions about the relevant activities without its consent. *[IFRS 11.B9]*. Joint control requires sharing of control or collective control by two or more parties. Some of the aspects of 'unanimous consent' for extractives arrangements are discussed at 7.1.1.B below.

For more information on assessing joint control see Chapter 12 at 4.

7.1.1.A Relevant activities

Relevant activities are those activities of the arrangement which significantly affect the returns of the arrangement. Determining what these are for each arrangement may require significant judgement.

Examples of decisions about relevant activities include, but are not limited to:

- establishing operating and capital decisions of the arrangement including budgets – for an arrangement in the extractive industries, this may include approving the operating and/or capital expenditure programme for the next year; and
- appointing and remunerating a joint arrangement's key management personnel or service providers and terminating their services or employment – for example, appointing a contract miner or oil field services provider to undertake operations.

For more information on identifying relevant activities, see Chapter 6 at 4.1 and Chapter 12 at 4.1.

7.1.1.B Meaning of unanimous consent

Unanimous consent means that any party with joint control can prevent any of the other parties, or a group of parties, from making unilateral decisions about relevant activities.

For further discussion on unanimous consent, see Chapter 12 at 4.3.

In some extractive industries operations, decision-making may vary over the life of the project, e.g. during the exploration and evaluation phase, the development phase or the production phase. For example, it may be agreed at the time of initially entering the contractual arrangement that during the exploration and evaluation phase, one party to the arrangement may be able to make all of the decisions, whereas once the project enters the development phase, decisions may then require unanimous consent. To determine whether the arrangement is jointly controlled, it will be necessary to decide (at the point of initially entering the contractual arrangement, and subsequently, should facts and circumstances change) which of these activities, e.g. exploration and evaluation and/or development, most significantly affect the returns of the arrangement. This is because the arrangement will only be considered to be a joint arrangement if those activities which require unanimous consent are the ones that most significantly affect the returns. This will be a highly judgemental assessment.

For further information on the impact of different decision-making arrangements over various activities, see Chapter 12 at 4.1.

7.1.2 Determination of whether a manager/lead operator of a joint arrangement has control

It is common in the extractive industries for one of the parties to be appointed as the operator or manager of the joint arrangement. The manager is frequently referred to as the operator, but as IFRS 11 uses the terms 'joint operation' and 'joint operator' with specific meanings, to avoid confusion we refer to such a party as the manager/lead operator. The other parties to the arrangement may delegate some of the decision-making rights to this manager/lead operator. In many instances, it is considered that the manager/lead operator does not control the joint arrangement, but simply carries out the decisions of the parties under the joint venture (or operating) agreement (JOA), i.e. the manager/lead operator acts as an agent. This view is based on the way in which these roles are generally established and referred to, or perceived, in the industries. Under IFRS 11, consideration is given to whether the manager/lead operator actually controls the arrangement. This is because when decision-making rights have been delegated, IFRS 10 describes how to assess whether the decision-maker is acting as a principal or an agent, and therefore, which party (if any) has control.

Careful consideration of the following will be required:

- scope of the manager's/lead operator's decision-making authority;
- rights held by others (e.g. protective rights and removal rights);
- exposure to variability in returns through the remuneration of the manager/lead operator; and
- variable returns held through other interests (e.g. direct investments by the manager/lead operator in the joint arrangement).

Of these factors, rights held by others and variable returns held through other interests will be particularly relevant for mining companies and oil and gas companies. Each of the above is discussed in Chapter 6 at 6 in more detail.

It is important to note that assessing whether an entity is a principal or an agent will require consideration of all factors collectively. See Chapter 6 at 6.1 for more details regarding the principal versus agent requirements.

Where it is determined that a manager is acting as a principal and therefore controls an arrangement, the impact of this will depend upon the rights and obligations conveyed by the arrangement (see 7.1.2.A and 7.1.2.B below for further discussion on this issue). Where it is determined that the manager/lead operator is acting as an agent, the manager/lead operator would only recognise its own interests in the joint arrangement (the accounting for which will depend upon whether it is a joint operation or joint venture) and its operator/management fee.

7.1.2.A   Implications of controlling a joint operation

While the principal versus agent assessment may lead to a conclusion that a manager/lead operator has control, if the joint arrangement is a joint operation, and each party has specific rights to, and obligations for, the underlying assets and liabilities of the arrangement by virtue of the contract, then the manager/lead operator does not control anything over and above its own direct interest in those assets and liabilities. Therefore, it still only recognises its interest in those assets and liabilities conveyed to it by the contractual arrangement. This accounting applies regardless of whether the arrangement is in a separate vehicle or not, as the contractual terms are the primary determinant of the accounting. Note that IFRS 11 defines a separate vehicle as 'a separately identifiable financial structure, including separate legal entities or entities recognised by statute, regardless of whether those entities have a legal personality'. *[IFRS 11 Appendix A]*. To explain this further, it is worth considering the two types of joint arrangements contemplated by IFRS 11 – one that is not structured through a separate vehicle (e.g. a contract alone) and one that is structured through a separate vehicle.

No separate vehicle: Even if the manager/lead operator 'controlled' the arrangement, there is really nothing for it to control. This is because each party would continue to account for its rights and obligations arising from the contract, e.g. it would apply IAS 16 to account for its rights to any tangible assets, IAS 38 to account for its rights to any intangible assets or IFRS 9 to account for its obligations for any financial liabilities etc. Additionally, the consolidation requirements of IFRS 10 would not apply as they only apply to entities and, in most circumstances, a contract does not create an entity.

Separate vehicle: If a manager/lead operator controls an arrangement structured through a separate vehicle, e.g. a company or trust, one may consider that an entity would automatically look to IFRS 10 and consolidate the arrangement and account for the interests of the other parties as non-controlling interests. However, in such situations, a contract may exist which gives other parties to the arrangement direct rights to, and obligations for, the underlying assets and liabilities of that arrangement. Therefore, this requires consideration of the impact of such an arrangement on the separate financial statements of the joint operation.

Given this, the rights and obligations arising from the contractual arrangement should be accounted for first. That is, each party to the arrangement should recognise its respective share of the assets and liabilities (applying each IFRS as appropriate, e.g. IAS 16, IAS 38, IFRS 9 etc.).

To the extent that the parties to the arrangement have specific rights to the assets, or obligations for the liabilities, from the perspective of the separate vehicle, this means that the rights to, and obligations for, its assets and liabilities have been contracted out to other parties (i.e. the parties to the contractual arrangement) and therefore there may be no assets or liabilities remaining in the separate vehicle to recognise.

Consequently, from the perspective of the manager/lead operator of the joint arrangement, who may be considered to control the separate vehicle, it would initially account for its and other parties' rights and obligations arising from the contract, and then when it looks to consolidate the separate vehicle, there may be nothing left to consolidate, as the separate vehicle may effectively be empty. However, this would only apply where the separate vehicle was an entity as IFRS 10 only applies to entities.

The above analysis demonstrates that where parties to an arrangement genuinely have contractual rights to, and obligations for, the underlying assets and liabilities of the arrangement, concluding that a manager/lead operator controls the arrangement does not change the accounting for either the manager/lead operator or the non-operator parties. However, the disclosure requirements would likely differ, since IFRS 12 does not apply to joint arrangements in which a party does not have joint control, unless that party has significant influence. The disclosure requirements of IFRS 12 are discussed in Chapter 13.

7.1.2.B   Implications of controlling a joint venture

If a manager/lead operator has control of a joint venture which was structured through a separate vehicle which is considered to be an entity, the manager/lead operator would have to consolidate the separate vehicle and recognise any non-controlling interest(s). However, if the joint venture is structured through a separate vehicle that is not an entity, IFRS 10 would not apply, and the manager/lead operator would apply the relevant IFRSs.

7.1.3   Parties to a joint arrangement without joint control or control

The accounting treatment of an interest in a contractual arrangement that does not give rise to joint control or control depends on the rights and obligations of the party.

7.1.3.A   Joint operations

In some cases, a mining company or oil and gas company may be involved in a joint operation, but it does not have joint control or control of that arrangement. Similar to the situation discussed above at 7.1.2.A, effectively, if the joint arrangement is a joint operation (i.e. joint control exists between two or more parties), and the party has rights to the assets and obligations for the liabilities relating to that joint operation, it does not matter whether the party in question has control, joint control or not – the accounting is the same as that for a joint operation under IFRS 11, which is discussed in more detail in Chapter 12 at 6.4. *[IFRS 11.23]*. The critical aspect of this accounting is whether there is joint control by two or more parties within the arrangement (and therefore it is a joint operation in accordance with IFRS 11). However, the disclosure requirements would likely differ, since IFRS 12 does not apply to joint arrangements in which a party does not have joint control, unless that party has significant influence. The disclosure requirements of IFRS 12 are discussed in Chapter 13.

If the party does not have rights to the assets and obligations for the liabilities relating to the joint operation, it accounts for its interest in the joint operation in accordance with other applicable IFRSs. *[IFRS 11.23]*. For example, if it:

(a) has significant influence over a separate vehicle which is an entity – apply IAS 28 – *Investments in Associates and Joint Ventures*;

(b) has significant influence over a separate vehicle which is not an entity – apply other applicable IFRSs;

(c) does not have significant influence over a separate vehicle – account for that interest as a financial asset under IFRS 9; or

(d) has an interest in an arrangement without a separate vehicle – apply other applicable IFRSs.

7.1.3.B   Joint ventures

In some cases, a mining company or oil and gas company may be involved in a joint venture, but it does not have joint control or control of that arrangement. In this instance it would account for its interest as follows:

(a) significant influence over a separate vehicle which is an entity – still apply IAS 28, *[IFRS 11.25]*, however, the disclosure requirements differ for an associate versus a joint venture (see Chapter 13 at 5);

(b) significant influence over a separate vehicle which is not an entity – apply other applicable IFRSs; or

(c) does not have significant influence over a separate vehicle – account for that interest as a financial asset under IFRS 9 at fair value through profit or loss or other comprehensive income, unless the investment was held for trading. See Chapter 48 at 2.2 and 4 for further information on IFRS 9. *[IFRS 11.25, C14]*.

7.1.4   Managers/lead operators of joint arrangements

It is clear that a participant in a joint operation is required to recognise its rights to the assets, and its obligations for the liabilities (or share thereof), of the joint arrangement. Therefore, it is important that an entity fully understands what these rights and obligations are and how these may differ between the parties.

See 7.1.2 above for a discussion of the principal versus agent assessment that needs to be considered when an entity is appointed as manager/lead operator of a joint arrangement and what impact that assessment might have on the manager's/lead operator's accounting.

7.1.4.A   Reimbursements of costs

A manager/lead operator often carries out activities on behalf of the joint arrangement on a no gain, no loss basis. Generally, these activities can be identified separately and are carried out by the manager/lead operator in its capacity as an agent for the joint arrangement, which is effectively the principal in those transactions. The manager/lead operator receives reimbursement of direct costs recharged to the joint arrangement. Such recharges are reimbursements of costs that the manager/lead operator incurred as an agent for the joint arrangement and therefore have no effect on profit or loss in the statement of comprehensive income (or income statement) of the manager/lead operator.

In many cases, a manager/lead operator also incurs certain general overhead and other expenses in carrying out activities on behalf of the joint arrangement. As these costs can often not be specifically identified, many joint operating agreements allow the manager/lead operator to recover the general overhead expenses incurred by charging an overhead fee that is based on a fixed percentage of the total costs incurred for the year. Although the purpose of this recharge is very similar to the reimbursement of direct costs, the manager/lead operator is not acting as an agent in this case. Therefore, the manager/lead operator should recognise the general overhead expenses and the overhead fee in profit or loss in its statement of comprehensive income (or income statement) as an expense and income, respectively.

A specific example of this is where the manager/lead operator of a joint arrangement enters into a lease with a third party supplier, who then carries out activities on behalf of the joint arrangement with the leased asset and is entitled to reimbursement from the non-operator parties. This is discussed further at 18 below.

7.1.4.B Direct legal liability for costs incurred and contracts entered into

The manager/lead operator of a joint arrangement may have a direct legal liability to third party creditors in respect of the entire balance arising from transactions related to the joint arrangement, e.g. suppliers, lessors etc.[101] IFRS prohibits the offsetting of such liabilities against the amounts recoverable from the other joint arrangement participants. *[IAS 1.32, IAS 32.42]*. The manager/lead operator may therefore need to recognise and/or disclose, for example, some of the leases or supply arrangements that it has entered into on behalf of the joint arrangement, as if it had entered into these in its own name. This is discussed further at 18.1 below.

7.1.4.C Joint and several liability

It is also possible that there may be liabilities in the arrangement where the obligation is joint and several. That is, an entity is not only responsible for its proportionate share, but it is also liable for the other party's or parties' share(s) should it/they be unable or unwilling to pay. A common example of this in the extractives industries is restoration, rehabilitation and decommissioning obligations.

In these instances, each party not only takes up its proportionate share of the decommissioning/restoration obligation, it is also required to assess the likelihood that the other party(ies) will not be able or willing to meet their obligation for their share. The facts and circumstances would need to be assessed in each case, and any additional liability would be accounted for, and disclosed, in accordance with IAS 37.

Any increase in the provision would be accounted for under IFRIC 1, if it related to a restoration or decommissioning liability that had both been included as part of an asset measured in accordance with IAS 16 and measured as a liability in accordance with IAS 37 (see Chapter 26 at 6.3.1 and 6.3.2 for more details). Such an addition to the asset would also require an entity to consider whether this is an indication of impairment of the asset as a whole, and if so, would need to test for impairment in accordance with IAS 36. Increases that do not meet the requirements of IFRIC 1 would be recognised in profit or loss.

7.1.5 Non-operators of joint arrangements

For expenses and liabilities incurred by the manager/lead operator directly in its own name which it recharges to the non-operators, the non-operator entities would be required to recognise an amount payable to the operator for such amounts. Depending on the nature of these arrangements, these may need to be recognised as a financial instrument under IAS 32 and IFRS 9, as a lease (where a sublease exists between the lead operator and the joint arrangement), or potentially a provision under IAS 37, and not under the standard which relates to the type of cost being reimbursed. For example, the non-operator's share of employee entitlements relating to the manager's employees who work on the joint project would not be recognised as an employee benefit under IAS 19 – *Employee Benefits*. In addition, the related disclosure requirements of IAS 19 would not apply, instead the disclosure requirements of other standards, e.g. IFRS 7 – *Financial Instruments: Disclosures* – would apply.

Expenses and liabilities incurred by the manager/lead operator jointly on behalf of all of the parties to the arrangement would have to be recognised by each of the non-operator parties in proportion to their respective interests in the arrangement. Such amounts would be recognised for the costs incurred on an accruals basis for production costs, operating expenses etc. and associated 'joint venture payables' would be recognised. With respect to longer term arrangements, such as leases entered into by the lead operator on behalf of the joint arrangement, the non-operator parties would consider the broader contractual arrangements to determine whether or not there was a lease by the joint operation. This is discussed further at 18.5.1 below.

7.2 Undivided interests

Undivided interests are usually subject to joint control (see Chapter 12 at 4.4.1) and can, therefore, be accounted for as joint operations. However, some JOAs do not establish joint control but are, instead, based on some form of supermajority voting whereby a qualified majority (e.g. 75%) of the participants can approve decisions. This situation usually arises when the group of participants is too large for joint control to be practical or when the main investor wants to retain a certain level of influence.

Where joint control does not exist, such undivided interests cannot be accounted for as joint operations in the scope of IFRS 11. Instead, the appropriate accounting treatment by the investor depends on the nature of the arrangement:

- if the investor has rights to the underlying asset then the arrangement should be accounted for as a tangible or intangible asset under IAS 16 or IAS 38, respectively. The investor's proportionate share of the operating costs of the asset (e.g. repairs and maintenance) should be accounted for in the same way as the operating costs of wholly owned assets; or

- if the investor is entitled only to a proportion of the cash flows generated by the asset then its investment will generally meet the definition of a financial asset under IAS 32. As the investor is exposed to risks other than just credit risk, such investments are unlikely be considered debt instruments and instead would be considered equity investments under IFRS 9. Equity instruments are normally measured at fair value through profit or loss under IFRS 9. *[IFRS 9.4.1.4]*. However, on initial recognition, an entity may make an irrevocable election (on an instrument-by-instrument basis) to present in other comprehensive income subsequent changes in the fair value of an investment in an equity instrument within the scope of IFRS 9. See Chapter 48 at 2 for a detailed analysis of the impact of IFRS 9 on the classification of this investment.

With respect to such undivided interests, entities also enter into arrangements in which they buy and sell parts of undivided assets, e.g. carried interests (see 6.1 above) and farm-in arrangements outside the E&E phase (see 6.2.2 and 6.2.3 above). Although neither IAS 16 nor IAS 38 addresses part-disposals of undivided assets, it is industry practice to apply the principles in those standards when the vendor disposes of these interests in circumstances in which it can demonstrate that it neither controls nor jointly controls the whole of the original asset. In these circumstances, the principles of IAS 16 and IAS 38 are applied and the entity derecognises part of the asset, having calculated an appropriate carrying value for the part disposed of, and a gain or loss on disposal. See Chapter 17 at 9.5.1 and Chapter 18 at 7.3.

8 ACQUISITIONS

8.1 Business combinations versus asset acquisitions

When an entity acquires an asset or a group of assets, careful analysis is required to identify whether what is acquired constitutes a business or represents only an asset or group of assets. Accounting for business combinations is discussed in detail in Chapter 9.

8.1.1 Differences between asset purchase transactions and business combinations

The reason it is important to distinguish between an asset acquisition and a business combination is because the accounting consequences are significantly different. The main differences between accounting for an asset acquisition and a business combination can be summarised as follows:

- goodwill or a bargain purchase (also sometimes referred to as negative goodwill) only arise in business combinations;
- assets and liabilities are accounted for at fair value in a business combination, while they are assigned a carrying amount based on their relative fair values in an asset acquisition (see 8.4 below);
- transaction costs should be recognised as an expense under IFRS 3, but can be capitalised on an asset acquisition; and
- in an asset acquisition no deferred tax will arise in relation to acquired assets and assumed liabilities as the initial recognition exception for deferred tax under IAS 12 – *Income Taxes* – applies. See Chapter 33 at 7.2 for further details.

8.1.2 Definition of a business

In October 2018, the IASB issued amendments to the definition of a business in IFRS 3 that are effective for annual reporting periods beginning on or after 1 January 2020 (with early adoption permitted) and apply prospectively.

The revised definition of a business in IFRS 3 is 'an integrated set of activities and assets that is capable of being conducted and managed for the purpose of providing goods or services to customers, generating investment income (such as dividends or interest) or generating other income from ordinary activities'. *[IFRS 3 Appendix A]*. See Chapter 9 at 3.2.1 to 3.2.6 for further discussion on the definition of a business.

Major changes introduced by the amendments are:
- clarification on the minimum requirements for a business;
- removal of the assessment of whether market participants are capable of replacing any missing elements;
- narrowing of the definitions of a business and outputs;
- introduction of an optional fair value concentration test; and
- guidance added to help entities assess whether an acquired process is substantive.

For more detail on the revised definition of a business see Chapter 9 at 3.2.

Determining whether a particular set of integrated activities and assets is a business will often require a significant amount of judgement, particularly for oil and gas companies and mining companies depending on the stage of the asset in the asset life cycle. Examples are set out in Chapter 9 at 3.2.

8.2 Business combinations

8.2.1 Goodwill in business combinations

Prior to the adoption of IFRS, many mining companies and oil and gas companies assumed that the entire consideration paid for upstream assets should be allocated to the identifiable net assets acquired. That is, any excess of the consideration transferred over the fair value of the identifiable net assets (excluding mineral reserves and resources) acquired would then have been included within mineral reserves and resources acquired and goodwill would not generally be recognised. However, goodwill could arise as a result of synergies, overpayment by the acquirer, or when IFRS requires that acquired assets and/or liabilities are measured at an amount that is not fair value (e.g. deferred taxation). Therefore, it is unlikely to be appropriate for mining companies or oil and gas companies to simply assume that goodwill would never arise in a business combination and that any differential automatically goes to mineral reserves and resources. Mineral reserves and resources and any exploration potential (if relevant) acquired should be valued separately and any excess of the consideration transferred over and above the supportable fair value of the identifiable net assets (which include mineral reserves, resources and acquired exploration potential), should be allocated to goodwill.

By virtue of the way IFRS 3 operates, if an entity were simply to take any excess of the consideration transferred over the fair value of the identifiable net assets acquired to mineral reserves and resources, they may end up having to allocate significantly larger values to minerals reserves and resources than expected. This is because, under IFRS 3, an entity is required to provide for deferred taxation on the temporary differences relating to all identifiable net assets acquired (including mineral reserves and resources), but not on temporary differences related to goodwill. Therefore, if any excess was simply allocated to mineral reserves and resources, to the extent that this created a difference between the carrying amount and the tax base of the mineral reserves and resources, IAS 12 would give rise to a deferred tax liability on the temporary difference, which would create a further excess. This would then result in an iterative calculation in which the deferred tax liability recognised would increase the amount attributed to mineral reserves and resources, which would in turn give rise to an increase in the deferred tax liability (see Chapter 33 at 7.2.2). Given the very high marginal tax rates to which extractive activities are often subject (i.e. tax rates of 60 to 80% are not uncommon) the mineral reserves and resources might end up being grossed up by a factor of 2.5 to 5 (i.e. $1 \div (1 - 60\%) = 2.5$). Such an approach would only be acceptable if the final amount allocated to mineral reserves and resources remained in the range of fair values determined for those mineral reserves and resources. If not, such an approach would lead to excessive amounts being allocated to mineral reserves and resources which could not be supported by appropriate valuations.

In March 2020, the IASB published a comprehensive Discussion Paper – *Business Combinations – Disclosures, Goodwill and Impairment*.[102] The project arose as a result of the post-implementation review of IFRS 3. The IASB is proposing to retain the impairment-only approach for goodwill, simplification of the application of the impairment test, and that CGUs containing goodwill are only tested when there is an impairment trigger event, rather than an annual impairment test being required. For more detail on the IASB's preliminary views see Chapter 9 at 1.1.1.

The extract below from Glencore financial statements illustrates a typical accounting policy for business combinations in which excess consideration transferred is treated as goodwill.

Extract 43.13: Glencore plc (2019)

Notes to the financial statements [extract]

1. Accounting policies [extract]

Business combinations and goodwill [extract]

Acquisitions of subsidiaries and businesses are accounted for using the acquisition method of accounting. The cost of the acquisition is measured at fair value, which is calculated as the sum of the acquisition date fair values of the assets transferred, liabilities incurred to the former owners of the acquiree and the equity interests issued in exchange for control of the acquiree. The identifiable assets, liabilities and contingent liabilities ("identifiable net assets") are recognised at their fair value at the date of acquisition. Acquisition related costs are recognised in the consolidated statement of income as incurred.

Where a business combination is achieved in stages, Glencore's previously held interests in the acquired entity are remeasured to fair value at the acquisition date (i.e. the date Glencore attains control) and the resulting gain or loss, if any, is recognised in the consolidated statement of income.

Goodwill is measured as the excess of the sum of the consideration transferred, the amount of any non-controlling interests in the acquiree, and the fair value of the acquirer's previously held equity interest in the acquiree (if any) over the net of the acquisition-date amounts of the identifiable assets acquired and the liabilities assumed.

8.2.2 Impairment of assets and goodwill recognised on acquisition

There are a number of circumstances in which the carrying amount of assets and goodwill acquired as part of a business combination and as recorded in the consolidated accounts, may be measured at a higher amount through recognition of notional tax benefits, also known as tax amortisation benefits (i.e. the value has been grossed up on the assumption that its carrying value is deductible for tax) or deferred tax (which can increase goodwill as described above). Application of IAS 36 to goodwill which arises upon recognition of deferred tax liabilities in a business combination is discussed in Chapter 20 at 8.3.1.

8.2.3 Value beyond proven and probable reserves (VBPP)

In the mining sector specifically, the 'value beyond proven and probable reserves' (VBPP) is defined as the economic value of the estimated cash flows of a mining asset beyond that asset's proven and probable reserves.

While this term is specifically relevant to the mining sector by virtue of specific guidance in US GAAP, the concept may be equally relevant to the oil and gas sector, i.e. the economic value of an oil and gas licence/area beyond the proven and probable reserves.

For mining companies, there are various situations in which mineralisation and mineral resources might not be classified as proven or probable:

- prior to the quantification of a resource, a mining company may identify mineralisation following exploration activities. However, it may be too early to assess if the geology and grade is sufficiently expansive to meet the definition of a resource;
- Acquired Exploration Potential (AEP) represents the legal right to explore for minerals in a particular property, occurring in the same geological area of interest;
- carrying out the required assessments and studies to obtain classification of mineral reserves can be very costly. Consequently, these activities are often deferred until they become necessary for the planning of future operations. Significant mineral resources are often awaiting the initiation of this process; and
- if an entity acquires a mining company at a time when commodity prices are particularly low, the mineral resources owned by the acquiree may not meet the definition of proven or probable reserves because extraction might not be commercially viable.

While the above types of mineralisation and mineral resources cannot be classified as proven or probable, they will often be valuable because of the future potential that they represent (i.e. reserves may be proven in the future and commodity price increases may make extraction commercially feasible).

IFRS 3 requires that an acquirer recognises the identifiable assets acquired and liabilities assumed that meet the definitions of assets and liabilities at the acquisition date. *[IFRS 3.11].*

While the legal or contractual rights that allow an entity to extract minerals are not themselves tangible assets, the mineral reserves concerned clearly are. The legal or contractual rights – that allow an entity to extract mineral reserves and resources – acquired in business combinations should be recognised, without exception, at fair value.

An entity that acquires mineral reserves and resources that cannot be classified as proven or probable, should account for the VBPP as part of the value allocated to mining assets, to the extent that a market participant would include VBPP in determining the fair value of the asset, rather than as goodwill.[103] In practice, the majority of mining companies treat mining assets, the related mineral reserves and resources and licences as tangible assets on the basis that they relate to minerals in the ground, which are themselves tangible assets. However, some entities present the value associated with E&E assets as intangible assets.

AEP would often be indistinguishable from the value of the mineral licence to which it relates. Therefore, the classification of AEP may vary depending on how an entity presents its mining assets and licences. If an entity presents them as tangible assets, they may be likely to treat AEP (or its equivalent), where applicable, as forming part of mineral properties, and hence AEP would be classified as a tangible asset. For an entity that classifies some of its mineral assets as intangible assets, e.g. E&E assets, then they may classify AEP as an intangible also.

Determining the fair value of VBPP requires a considerable amount of expertise. An entity should not only take account of commodity spot prices but also consider the effects of anticipated fluctuations in the future price of minerals, in a manner that is consistent with the expectations of a market participant. An entity should consider all available information including current prices, historical averages, and forward pricing curves and maximise the use of observable inputs. Those market participant assumptions typically are consistent with the acquiring entity's operating plans for developing and producing minerals. However, entities need to undertake steps to demonstrate this is true (to ensure compliance with the requirements of IFRS 13 – *Fair Value Measurement*). The potential upside associated with mineral resources that are not classified as reserves can be much larger than the downward risk. A valuation model that only takes account of a single factor, such as the spot price, historical average or a single long-term price, without considering other information that a market participant would consider, would generally not be able to reflect the upward potential that determines much of the value of VBPP. Consequently, an entity may need to apply option valuation techniques in measuring VBPP.

There are commonly considered to be three categories of VBPP, including:
- mineral resources not yet tested for economic viability;
- early mineralisation; and
- acquired exploration potential.

The CRIRSCO reporting standards consider the geological definition of mineral resources that have not yet been tested for economic viability, which is the first category of VBPP. Valuation techniques used for this category include:
- probability weighted discounted-cash flows;
- resource reserve conversion adjustment;
- comparable transactions; and
- option valuation.

In relation to early mineralisation, the second category of VBPP, while it may represent a discovery, its true value will be determined by further appraisal/evaluation activities to confirm whether a resource exists. This category of VBPP is often grouped with the

next (and final) category, being AEP, even though it has a higher intrinsic value, and is valued using:
- cost based methods;
- budgeted expenditure methods;
- comparable sales;
- farm-in/out values; or
- sophisticated option pricing.

In relation to AEP, the basis for its valuation varies from studying historic cost to the use of sophisticated option valuation techniques.

As VBPP does not provide current economic benefits, there is no need to allocate its cost against current revenue and hence no need for amortisation or depreciation. However, as part of the process of completing the acquisition accounting, an entity should form a view about how that value will ultimately be ascribed to future discoveries and converted into proven and probable reserves and then ultimately depreciated. Such methodologies might include a per unit (e.g. tonnes/ounces) basis or possibly an area (e.g. acreage) basis. VBPP would need to be tested for impairment under IAS 36 if, depending on the classification of VBPP, there is an indicator of impairment under that standard or IFRS 6. The VBPP may ultimately be impaired because it may never be converted into proven or probable reserves, but impairment may not be confirmed until the entity is satisfied that the project will not continue.

An impairment of VBPP should be recognised if its book value exceeds the higher of fair value less costs of disposal and value in use. In practice, there may not be a convenient method to determine the value in use. Hence, impairment testing will often need to rely on an approach based on fair value less costs of disposal.

Extract 43.14 below illustrates that AngloGold Ashanti does not subsume the 'value beyond proven and probable reserves' in goodwill but instead recognises it as part of the value ascribed to mineral resources.

> **Extract 43.14: AngloGold Ashanti Limited (2019)**
> GROUP – NOTES TO THE FINANCIAL STATEMENTS [extract]
> For the year ended 31 December
> 1 ACCOUNTING POLICIES [extract]
> 1.2 SIGNIFICANT ACCOUNTING JUDGEMENTS AND ESTIMATES [extract]
> USE OF ESTIMATES [extract]
> Carrying value of goodwill and intangible assets [extract]
>
> Where an investment in a subsidiary, joint venture or an associate is made, any excess of the consideration transferred over the fair value of the attributable Mineral Resource including value beyond proved and probable Ore Reserve, exploration properties and net assets is recognised as goodwill.
>
> Intangible assets that have an indefinite useful life and separately recognised goodwill are not subject to amortisation and are tested annually for impairment and whenever events or changes in circumstance indicate that the carrying amount may not be recoverable. Assets that are subject to amortisation are tested for impairment whenever events or changes in circumstance indicate that the carrying amount may not be recoverable.

8.3 Acquisition of an interest in a joint operation that is a business

One area where there had historically been a lack of clarity was how to account for acquisitions of interests in joint operations (under IFRS 11) which constitute businesses. However, an amendment to IFRS 11 was made to clarify this, which applied prospectively to acquisitions that occurred on or after 1 January 2016. The amendment states that where an entity is acquiring an interest in a joint operation that is a business as defined in IFRS 3, it should apply, to the extent of its share in accordance with paragraph 20 of IFRS 11, all of the principles of business combinations accounting in IFRS 3, and in other IFRSs, that do not conflict with IFRS 11. In addition, the entity should disclose the information that is required in those IFRSs in relation to business combinations. However, if an entity acquires an interest in a (group of) asset(s) that is (are) not a business as defined in IFRS 3 then it should apply the guidance on asset acquisitions that IFRS already provides. *[IFRS 11.BC45I].*

The requirements apply to the acquisition of an initial interest in a joint operation or where the acquisition leads to the formation of a joint operation that constitute a business, and also to the acquisition of additional interests in a joint operation to the extent that joint control is maintained. The amendment also makes it clear that any previously held interest in the joint operation would not be remeasured if the joint operator acquires an additional interest while retaining joint control.

In addition to the matters outlined above, there are a number of additional issues which have been raised in relation to joint operations. These include:

- *A passive investor in a joint operation becomes a joint operator:* In this situation, the issue is whether a previously held interest in the assets and liabilities of a joint operation that is a business is remeasured to fair value when the investor's acquisition of an additional interest results in the investor becoming a joint operator (i.e. assumes joint control) in that joint operation.

  The Interpretations Committee considered this issue and tentatively decided that the previously held interest in this situation should not be remeasured. The IASB agreed with this decision and an amendment was issued as part of the 2015-2017 annual improvements cycle. This amendment clarifies that the previously held interests in a joint operation are not remeasured where a party that participates in, but does not have joint control of, a joint operation might obtain joint control of the joint operation in which the activity of the joint operation constitutes a business as defined in IFRS 3. *[IFRS 11.BC45A, BC45H].*

- *Obtaining control over a joint operation:* Where a party obtains control over a joint operation structured through a separate vehicle, over which it previously had joint control, it is required to apply the business combination achieved in stages accounting requirements in IFRS 3, if the acquiree meets the definition of a business. This includes remeasuring previously held interests in the assets and liabilities of the joint operation at fair value. In doing so, the acquirer remeasures its entire previously held interest in the joint operation (see Chapter 9 at 3.2 and 9).

See Chapter 12 at 8.3 for more information on the above matters.

8.4 Asset acquisitions

The acquisition of an asset, group of assets or an entity that does not constitute a business is not a business combination. In such cases the acquirer should identify and recognise the individual identifiable assets acquired and liabilities assumed. The cost of the acquisition should be allocated to the individual identifiable assets acquired and liabilities assumed on the basis of their relative fair values at the date of purchase. Such a transaction or event does not give rise to goodwill. *[IFRS 3.2(b)]*. Thus, existing book values or values in the acquisition agreement may not be appropriate.

As noted in 8.1 above, there are some key differences between an asset acquisition and a business combination. These are discussed in more detail in Chapter 9 at 2.2.2.

In November 2017, the Interpretations Committee issued an agenda decision that clarified how an entity accounts for the acquisition of a group of assets that does not constitute a business. This is also discussed in Chapter 9 at 2.2.2.

8.4.1 Asset acquisitions and conditional purchase consideration

When an asset or a group of assets/net assets that do not constitute a business are acquired, they are required to be accounted for at cost. There are various standards in which 'cost' is defined, with those of most relevance to the acquisition of an asset being IAS 16, IAS 38 and IAS 40. Cost is defined in those standards as 'the amount of cash or cash equivalents paid or the fair value of the other consideration given to acquire an asset at the time of its acquisition or construction or, where applicable, the amount attributed to that asset when initially recognised in accordance with the specific requirements of other IFRSs, e.g. IFRS 2 – *Share-based Payment*'. *[IAS 16.6, IAS 38.8, IAS 40.5]*. Amounts capitalised under IFRS 6 are also required to be measured initially at cost. *[IFRS 6.8]*.

These requirements sometimes give rise to issues in situations where the purchase price is conditional upon certain events or facts. Transactions involving contingent consideration are often very complex and payment is dependent on a number of factors. In the absence of specific guidance in IAS 16, entities trying to determine an appropriate accounting treatment are required not only to understand the commercial complexities of the transaction itself, but also to negotiate a variety of accounting principles and requirements. These issues can best be illustrated by an example.

Example 43.6: Asset acquisitions with a conditional purchase price

Scenario 1

Entity A agrees to buy a group of assets from Entity B which does not constitute a business for a total purchase price of $15 million. However, the purchase contract provides a formula for adjusting the purchase price upward or downward based on the report of a surveyor on the existence and quality of the assets listed in the contract.

Scenario 2

Entity C agrees to buy an exploration licence and several related assets from Entity D which do not constitute a business for a total purchase price of $35 million. However, Entity C would only be allowed to extract minerals in excess of 20 million barrels (or tonnes), upon payment of an additional consideration transferred of $12 million.

In scenario 1, we believe Entity A would be required to account for the fair value of the consideration transferred as determined at the date of acquisition. In contrast to the treatment under IFRS 3, there is no purchase price allocation or measurement period under IAS 16. However, suppose that three weeks after the initial accounting the surveyor reports that at the date of acquisition a number of assets listed in the contract were not present or were of inferior quality, the purchase price is therefore adjusted downwards to $14.5 million. Rather than recognising a profit arising from this adjustment, the entity should adjust the cost of the asset as the surveyor's report provides evidence of conditions that existed at the date of acquisition. *[IAS 10.3(a)]*.

In scenario 2 above, Entity C pays an additional $12 million in exchange for additional rights to extract minerals in excess of 20 million barrels (or tonnes) agreed upon in the initial transaction. At the date that Entity C purchases the additional rights it accounts for this as an additional asset acquisition. In more complicated scenarios, however, it might be necessary to assess whether the first and second acquisition should be accounted for together.

It is clear from the above two scenarios that changes in the facts and circumstances can have a significant effect on the accounting for conditional purchase consideration.

When considering asset acquisitions with contingent consideration, several issues need to be addressed. These include:

- how and when the contingent element should be accounted for, i.e. when a liability should be recognised and how it should be measured and this includes considering whether the purchaser can influence or control the crystallisation of the contingent payments or they are wholly dependent on its future activities;
- whether the initial cost of the asset acquired includes an amount relating to the contingent element; and
- how the remeasurement (if any) of any liability recognised in relation to the contingent element should be accounted for. Should it be recognised as an adjustment to the cost of the asset acquired, or should it be recognised in profit or loss?

Where the goods and services in question have been delivered, there is no doubt that there is a financial liability under IFRS 9. A contingent obligation to deliver cash meets the definition of a financial liability (see Chapter 47). Therefore, if the obligation to make the variable payment does not depend on the acquiring entity's future activity and the event that gives rise to the payment is outside its control then a financial liability would be recognised. *[IAS 32.25]*.

Further, because there is currently no exemption from applying IFRS 9 to such contracts, one might expect that such a liability would be accounted for in accordance with IFRS 9, i.e. any measurement changes to that liability would flow through profit or loss. This would be consistent with the accounting treatment for contingent consideration arising from a business combination under IFRS 3 (see Chapter 45 at 3.7.1.A). However, this is not necessarily clear and for this reason the issue of how to account for contingent consideration in the acquisition of an item of PP&E was taken to the Interpretations Committee. See below for further discussion of this issue.

The current definition of cost in IAS 16 and IAS 38 requires the cost of an asset on the date of purchase to include the fair value of the consideration given (if a reliable estimate can be made), such as an obligation to pay a contingent price. Based on our experience and the level of diversity of views identified as part of the Interpretations Committee's considerations of this, not all would agree that all contingent payments are for the original asset and, indeed, the circumstances of a particular contract might support this. In addition to this issue, there is the issue of how to account for the remeasurement of the liability and whether changes should be recognised in profit or loss, or included as an adjustment to the cost of the asset.

However, where the purchaser can influence or control the crystallisation of the contingent payments or they are wholly dependent on its future activities – such as those that take the form of production-based royalties, the circumstances are more difficult to interpret. Many consider that these arrangements contain executory contracts that are only accounted for when one of the contracting parties performs. Further complications arise when the terms of the agreement indicate that a future payment relates to the completion of a separate performance obligation, or the delivery of intangible rights in addition to those conferred by the exchange of the original asset.

These complexities can raise broader questions about the nature of the obligations and, as in the case of royalty-based contingent payments, the appropriate accounting standard to apply initially, as well as how to account for subsequent adjustments to any liability that may have been recognised. To date, these complexities and lack of clarity as to the appropriate accounting have led to various treatments where the purchaser can influence or control the crystallisation of the contingent payments (or they are wholly dependent on its future activities), or where the contingent payment relates to the completion of separate performance obligations or the delivery or additional intangible rights, including:

- the cost of the asset does not initially include any executory payments relating to the contingent element. Any subsequent payments made in relation to the contingent element are either adjusted against the cost of the asset (once paid) or recognised in profit or loss as incurred;
- the initial cost of the asset includes the fair value of all contingent consideration at the date of purchase. Subsequent changes in the liability relating to the contingent consideration are then recognised in profit or loss; or
- the initial cost of the asset includes the fair value of all the contingent consideration at the date of purchase. Subsequent changes in the liability relating to the contingent consideration that do not reflect the passage of time are adjusted against the cost of the asset.

The first approach (which is relatively common in the extractive industries) considers that the applicable standard is IAS 37, and applies the concepts of executory contract, obligating events, probability, contingencies and not providing for future operations. This means that nothing relating to the contingent payment is recognised at the date of purchase. The second approach applies the methodology in IFRS 3, while the third is based on the principles of IFRIC 1.[104]

Given this divergence in practice, this issue was referred to the Interpretations Committee. Between July 2013 and March 2016, the Interpretations Committee discussed accounting for contingent consideration but ultimately concluded that the issue was too broad for the Committee to address and referred it back to the Board.

In May 2016, the IASB tentatively agreed that this issue would be included in the research pipeline between 2017 and 2021.[105] In February 2018, the IASB decided that the IASB staff should carry out work to determine how broad the research project should be.[106] In February 2018, the IASB decided that the IASB staff should carry out work to determine how broad the research project should be.[107] At the time of writing, this is not listed as an active research project on the IASB's work plan.[108]

Until this matter is resolved, an entity should adopt and apply a consistent accounting policy to initial recognition and subsequent costs, in accordance with the hierarchy in IAS 8. An entity should exercise judgement in developing and consistently applying an accounting policy that results in information that is relevant and reliable in its particular circumstances. *[IAS 8.10]*. The accounting policy must be applied consistently.

While there is not an active research project on the IASB's work plan, those entities who have developed a policy under IAS 8 following the previous conceptual framework should be aware of any impacts arising from the revised conceptual framework, which is effective for periods commencing on or after 1 January 2020.

For further information on this issue see Chapter 17 at 4.5, Chapter 18 at 4.1.9 and Chapter 45 at 3.8.

8.4.2 Accounting for land acquisitions

Obtaining the legal rights to explore for, develop and produce minerals can be achieved in a number of ways, as outlined at 5 above. One of these ways is through the outright purchase of the minerals and the land on, or under, which the minerals are located. In undertaking such a transaction, it is not uncommon for an entity to pay an amount in excess of the intrinsic value of the land itself. In such a situation, an entity needs to ensure it appropriately allocates the purchase price between the fair value of the land and the fair value of the mineral or surface mining rights acquired. The amount allocated to land will be capitalised and not depreciated, whereas the amount allocated to the minerals or surface mining rights will form part of the total cost of mining assets and will ultimately be depreciated on a units of production basis over the economically recoverable reserves to which it relates.

9 FUNCTIONAL CURRENCY

9.1 Determining functional currency

Determining functional currency correctly is important because it will, for example, affect volatility of revenue and operating profit resulting from exchange rate movements, determine whether transactions can be hedged or not and influence the identification of embedded currency derivatives. The movements may give rise to temporary differences that affect profit or loss. *[IAS 12.41]*. While under IAS 21 – *The Effects of Changes in Foreign Exchange Rates* – an entity can select any presentation currency, it does not have a free choice in determining its functional currency. Choice of functional currency is discussed in detail in Chapter 15 at 4; below is a summary of the application of the requirements to the extractive industries.

IAS 21 requires an entity to determine separately the functional currency of each entity within a consolidated group. There is no concept of the functional currency of the group, only a presentation currency. Therefore, the functional currency of an operating subsidiary may differ from that of the group's parent and/or foreign sales company to which it sells its production. The factors taken into account in determining functional currency may differ for operating companies and for group entities that are financing or intermediate holding companies (see Chapter 15 at 4.2). IAS 21 requires an entity to consider the following factors in determining its functional currency:

(a) the currency that mainly influences sales prices for goods and services (this will often be the currency in which sales prices for its goods and services are denominated and settled);

(b) the currency of the country whose competitive forces and regulations mainly determine the sales prices of its goods and services; and

(c) the currency that mainly influences labour, material and other costs of providing goods or services (this will often be the currency in which such costs are denominated and settled). *[IAS 21.9]*.

While the currency referred to under (a) above will often be the currency in which sales prices for its goods and services are denominated and settled, this is not always the case. The US dollar is used for many commodities as the contract or settlement currency in transactions (e.g. iron ore, oil), but the pricing of transactions is often driven by factors completely unrelated to the US dollar or the US economy (e.g. it may be influenced more by demand from the local economy or other economies such as China).

As the extractive industries are international, it is often difficult to determine the currency of the country whose competitive forces and regulations mainly determine the sales prices of its goods and services. Therefore, factor (b) above will often prove to be inconclusive when a particular product is produced in many different countries.

It will generally be fairly straightforward to identify the currency that mainly influences an entity's key inputs (i.e. factor (c) above). In developing countries an entity will often need to import a significant proportion of its key inputs (e.g. fuel, equipment and expatriate workers) and even local inputs in an economy with a high inflation rate will often be linked to the US dollar. In such a case, the local currency is less likely to be the main currency that influences an entity's key inputs. In most developed countries, however, the inputs tend to be denominated in the local currency, although some inputs (e.g. major items of equipment) may be denominated in another currency. As the extractive industries are capital intensive, the cost of equipment often far exceeds the operating expenses incurred. Equipment is often purchased in US dollars.

When the factors (a) to (c) above are mixed, as they often are in practice, and the functional currency is not obvious, management should use 'its judgement to determine the functional currency that most faithfully represents the economic effects of the underlying transactions, events and conditions'. *[IAS 21.12]*. If the above factors are inconclusive then an entity should also consider the following secondary factors:

- the currency in which funds from financing activities (i.e. issuing debt and equity instruments) are generated;
- the currency in which receipts from operating activities are usually retained; and
- the functional currency of the reporting entity that has the foreign operation as its subsidiary, branch, associate or joint venture. *[IAS 21.10, 11]*.

After considering both the primary and secondary factors the functional currency may not be obvious because, for example, revenue is denominated in US dollars while virtually all expenses are denominated in the local currency. In that situation management may conclude that revenue, while denominated in US dollars, is in fact influenced by a basket of currencies. It is therefore possible that companies operating in a similar environment can reach different conclusions about their functional currency. Even in developed countries there is a general bias towards the US dollar as the functional currency.

Although local statutory and tax requirements should be ignored in determining the functional currency, there may be a requirement to keep two sets of accounting records when an entity concludes that its local currency is not its functional currency.

The extract below from Rio Tinto illustrates a typical currency translation accounting policy of a mining company.

> *Extract 43.15: Rio Tinto plc (2019)*
> Notes to the 2019 financial statements [extract]
> 1 Principal accounting policies [extract]
> **(d) Currency translation**
>
> The functional currency for each entity in the Group, and for joint arrangements and associates, is the currency of the primary economic environment in which that entity operates. For many of these entities, this is the currency of the country in which they are located. Transactions denominated in other currencies are converted to the functional currency at the exchange rate ruling at the date of the transaction. Monetary assets and liabilities denominated in foreign currencies are retranslated at period-end exchange rates.
>
> The Group's financial statements are presented in US dollars, as that presentation currency most reliably reflects the global business performance of the Group as a whole. On consolidation, income statement items for each entity are translated from the functional currency into US dollars at average rates of exchange, except for material one-off transactions, which are translated at the rate prevailing on the transaction date. Balance sheet items are translated into US dollars at period-end exchange rates.
>
> Exchange differences arising on the translation of the net assets of entities with functional currencies other than the US dollar are recognised directly in the currency translation reserve. These translation differences are shown in the statement of comprehensive income, with the exception of translation adjustments relating to Rio Tinto Limited's share capital which are shown in the statement of changes in equity.
>
> Where an intragroup balance is, in substance, part of the Group's net investment in an entity, exchange gains and losses on that balance are taken to the currency translation reserve.
>
> Except as noted above, or in note 1(q) relating to derivative contracts, all other exchange differences are charged or credited to the income statement in the year in which they arise.

9.2 Changes in functional currency

IAS 21 requires management to use its judgement to determine the entity's functional currency so that it most faithfully represents the economic effects of the underlying transactions, events and conditions that are relevant to the entity. Note that IAS 21 requires the functional currency to be determined by reference to factors that exist during the reporting period. Therefore, an entity should ignore future developments in its business, no matter how likely those developments are. For example, even if an entity is convinced that in three years' time it will have revenues that will be denominated in US dollars, this is not a factor to be considered in determining its functional currency today. This is particularly relevant for entities in the extractive industries given the nature of their operations. For example, a company may conclude that during the development phase of the project the local currency is its functional currency but that once production and sales commence the US dollar will become its functional currency. Alternatively, exposure to a particular currency may increase during a period.

This is illustrated in the extract below from Woodside Petroleum's 2010 financial statements.

> Extract 43.16: Woodside Petroleum Ltd (2010)
> Overview
> **CHIEF FINANCIAL OFFICER'S REPORT** [extract]
> Funding our growth plans and sustaining superior shareholder returns [extract]
>
> **US dollar functional currency implemented**
>
> With approximately 90% of revenue and more than 90% of debt denominated in US dollars, Woodside's directors adopted a US dollar functional currency and presentation currency for the purpose of all financial reporting, effective 1 January 2010. This change provides shareholders with a more accurate reflection of the company's underlying performance, while increasing comparability of our financial results with those of our industry peers.
>
> The one-off impacts of this change are highlighted in the Notes to the Financial Report.
>
> **Notes to and forming part of the Financial Report continued** [extract]
> For the year ended 31 December 2010
>
> **1. Summary of significant accounting policies (continued)** [extract]
>
> **(a) Basis of preparation (continued)** [extract]
>
> *Change in functional and presentation currency*
>
> An entity's functional currency is the currency of the primary economic environment in which the entity operates. Woodside Petroleum Ltd has experienced a period of sustained growth in US dollar revenue streams and in the period up to 31 December 2009 increased its US dollar debt levels significantly. Consequently, the company announced on 22 March 2010 that the directors had determined that the functional currency of the company and all its subsidiaries is US dollars. The change in functional currency has been applied prospectively with effect from 1 January 2010 in accordance with the requirements of the Accounting Standards.
>
> Following the change in functional currency, Woodside Petroleum Ltd has elected to change its presentation currency from Australian dollars to US dollars. The directors believe that changing the presentation currency to US dollars will enhance comparability with its industry peer group, the majority of which report in US dollars. The change in presentation currency represents a voluntary change in accounting policy, which has been applied retrospectively.
>
> To give effect to the change in functional currency, the assets and liabilities of entities with an Australian dollar functional currency at 31 December 2009 were converted into US dollars at a fixed exchange rate on 1 January 2010 of US$1:A$1.1193 and the contributed equity, reserves and retained earnings were converted at applicable historical rates. In order to derive US dollar comparatives (presentation currency), the Australian dollar functional currency assets and liabilities at 31 December 2009 were converted at the spot rate of US$1:A$1.1193 on the reporting date; revenue and expenses for the year ended 31 December 2009 were converted at the average exchange rate of US$1:A$1.261 for the reporting period, or at the exchange rates ruling at the date of the transaction to the extent practicable, and equity balances were converted at applicable historical rates.
>
> The above stated procedures resulted in a foreign currency translation reserve of US$594 million on 1 January 2009. Earnings per share for 2009 has also been restated in US dollars to reflect the change in the presentation currency (refer to Note 5).

Once the functional currency is determined, the standard allows it to be changed only if there is a change in those underlying transactions, events and conditions. For example, a change in the currency that mainly influences the sales prices of goods and services may lead to a change in an entity's functional currency. *[IAS 21.36]*.

The extract below, from Angel Mining plc's financial statements, provides an example of a change in conditions that resulted in a change in functional currency. Accounting for a change in functional currency is discussed in Chapter 15 at 5.5.

> *Extract 43.17: Angel Mining plc (2010)*
>
> **Notes to the financial statements**
> Year ended 28 February 2010 [extract]
>
> **1a. Basis of preparation – Change in functional currency**
>
> Previously, the directors considered the functional currency of the Company to be Sterling. In light of developments within the Company's operations and the nature of its funding, the directors have reassessed the functional currency of the Company and concluded that the currency of the primary economic environment in which Angel Mining operates is now the US dollar. The date of change from Sterling to US dollars has been taken as 1 March 2009. The key factors influencing this decision include the following:
>
> (i) During the year, the Company acquired the Nalunaq license and mining assets. This will be the first producing mine for the Company. The consideration for these assets was paid in US dollars;
>
> (ii) During the year, the Company sourced plant, machinery and employees with technical skills on a global basis. A significant proportion of these costs were based in US dollars. In prior years, the Company's costs had been incurred primarily in Sterling;
>
> (iii) The Company's primary form of finance during the period was the long term and short term debt facilities provided by FBC. These facilities are all based in US dollars. During prior periods, the Company had been more heavily dependent upon equity finance which was denominated in Sterling;
>
> (iv) The vast majority of the forms of finance which the Company has been pursuing and is likely to pursue going forward are US dollar based;
>
> (v) Commencing during the year, one of the largest consumables used by the Company in its operations in Greenland was diesel fuel. Although the Company pays for its diesel in Danish Kroner, the price of diesel is determined globally and priced in US dollars; and
>
> (vi) The resources that the Company is working to exploit are global commodities which are always priced in US dollars. When the Company begins producing, all its revenues will be dollar based.
>
> The change in the Company's functional currency has been accounted for prospectively from 1 March 2009 in accordance with IAS 21. This change constituted a prospective change in accounting policy. The financial statements for 2009 have been prepared using Sterling as the functional currency and US dollars as the presentational currency.
>
> The change in the presentational currency from Sterling to US dollar is and therefore is applied retrospectively in accordance with IAS 8 'Accounting Policies, Changes in Accounting Estimates and Errors' and therefore require comparative information to be restated and consequently, a third balance sheet is required to be presented in the financial statements.
>
> The impact of this change in presentational currency for 2009, is as follows:
>
> (i) The assets and liabilities for both the Group and the Company at 28 February 2009 have been translated using the closing rate for the same date of $1.426/£;
>
> (ii) The consolidated income statement for 2009 has been translated using the average rate for the year ended 28 February 2009 of $1.771/£ on the basis that this average rate approximates the exchange rates on the dates of transactions; and
>
> The resulting gain on retranslation from average to closing rate has been recognised in the consolidated statement of comprehensive income.

10 DECOMMISSIONING AND RESTORATION/REHABILITATION

The operations of entities engaged in extractive industries can have a significant impact on the environment. Decommissioning or restoration activities at the end of a mining or oil and gas operation may be required by law, the terms of mineral licences or an entity's stated policy and past practice. The associated costs of decommissioning, remediation or restoration can be significant. The accounting treatment for such costs is therefore critical. Different terms may be used, often interchangeably, to essentially refer to the same activity, e.g. restoration, remediation and rehabilitation. In this section we shall use the words decommissioning and restoration.

Accounting for decommissioning and restoration costs is governed by the requirements of IAS 37 and IFRIC 1. The discussion below should be read in conjunction with Chapter 18 (Property, Plant and Equipment) at 4.3, Chapter 26 (Provisions, Contingent Liabilities and Contingent Assets) at 6.3 and Chapter 33 (Income Taxes) at 7.2.7 and 7.2.7.A. Some of the specific issues to consider with respect to such provisions are listed below:

- initial recognition – see 10.1.1 below;
- initial measurement – see 10.1.2 below;
- discount rates – see Chapter 26 at 4.3;
- decommissioning or restoration costs incurred in the production phase – see 10.1.3 below;
- changes in decommissioning and restoration/rehabilitation costs – see Chapter 26 at 6.3.1 and 6.3.2;
- treatment of foreign exchange differences – see 10.2 below;
- accounting for deferred taxes – see Chapter 33 at 7.2.7;
- indefinite life assets – see 10.3 below; and
- funds established or put aside to meet a decommissioning or restoration obligation – see Chapter 26 at 6.3.3.

10.1 Recognition and measurement issues

10.1.1 Initial recognition

Initial recognition of a decommissioning or restoration provision only on commencement of commercial production is generally not appropriate under IFRS, because the obligation to remove facilities and to restore the environment typically arises during the development/construction of the facilities, with some further obligations arising during the production phase. Therefore, a decommissioning or restoration provision should be recognised during the development or construction phase (see 1.6.1 above) of the project, i.e. before any production takes place, and should form part of the cost of the assets acquired or constructed. It may also be necessary to recognise a further decommissioning or restoration provision during the production phase (see 10.1.3 below).

While the damage caused in the exploration phase may generally be immaterial, an entity should recognise a decommissioning or restoration provision where the damage is material and the entity will be required to carry out remediation. The accounting for such a provision will depend on how the related E&E costs have been accounted for. If the E&E costs are capitalised, the associated decommissioning costs should also be capitalised. However, if the E&E costs are expensed, any associated decommissioning or restoration costs should also be expensed.

Finally, even if decommissioning and restoration were not planned to take place in the foreseeable future (for example because the related assets are continually renewed and replaced), IAS 37 would still require a decommissioning or restoration provision to be recognised. However, in these cases the discounted value of the obligation may be comparatively insignificant.

10.1.2 Measurement of the liability

Measurement of a decommissioning or restoration provision requires a significant amount of judgement because:

- the amount of remedial work required will depend on the scale of the operations. In the extractives industries the environmental damage may vary considerably depending on the type and development of the project;
- the amount of remedial work further depends on environmental standards imposed by local regulators, which may vary over time;
- detailed decommissioning and remedial work plans will often not be developed until fairly shortly before closure of the operations;
- it may not always be clear which costs are directly attributable to decommissioning or restoration (e.g. security costs, maintenance cost, ongoing environmental monitoring and employee termination costs);
- the timing of the decommissioning or restoration depends on when the fields or mines cease to produce at economically viable rates, which depends upon future commodity prices and reserves; and
- the actual decommissioning or restoration work will often be carried out by specialised contractors, the cost of which will depend on future market prices for the necessary remedial work.

Many of the uncertainties above can only be finally resolved towards the end of the production phase, shortly before decommissioning and restoration are to take place. A significant increase in the decommissioning or restoration provision resulting from revised estimates would result in recognition of an additional asset. However, as IFRIC 1 specifically states that any addition to an asset as a result of an increase in a decommissioning or restoration provision is considered to be a trigger for impairment testing, a significant increase in a decommissioning or restoration provision close to the end of the production phase may lead to an immediate impairment of that additional asset. Conversely, a decrease in the decommissioning or restoration provision could exceed the carrying amount of the related asset, in which case the excess should be recognised as a gain in profit or loss.

10.1.3 Decommissioning or restoration costs incurred in the production phase

IAS 16 considers the initial estimate of the costs of dismantling and removing the item and restoring the site on which it is located to be part of the cost of an item of property, plant and equipment. *[IAS 16.16(c)]*. However, an entity should apply IAS 2 to the costs of obligations for dismantling, removing and restoring the site on which an item is located that are incurred during a particular period as a consequence of having used the item to produce inventories during that period. *[IAS 16.18]*. That means that such additional decommissioning or restoration costs resulting from production activities should be included in the cost of inventories, *[IAS 2.10]*, while decommissioning costs resulting from the construction of assets during the production phase should be accounted for as discussed above.

An entity that incurs abnormal amounts of costs (e.g. costs of remediation of soil contamination from oil spills or overflowing of a tailings pond) should not treat these as part of the cost of inventories under IAS 2, but expense them immediately. *[IAS 2.16]*.

10.2 Treatment of foreign exchange differences

In most cases it will be appropriate for the exchange differences arising on provisions to be taken to profit or loss in the period they arise. However, it may be that an entity has recognised a decommissioning provision under IAS 37 and capitalised it as part of the initial cost of an asset under IAS 16. One practical difficulty with decommissioning provisions recognised under IAS 37 is that due to the long period over which the actual cash outflows will arise, an entity may not know the currency in which the transaction will actually be settled. Nevertheless, if it is determined that it is expected to be settled in a foreign currency it will be a monetary item. The main issue then is what should happen to any exchange differences.

As discussed in Chapter 26 at 6.3.1, IFRIC 1 applies to any decommissioning or similar liability that has been both included as part of an asset and measured as a liability in accordance with IAS 37. IFRIC 1 requires, *inter alia*, that any adjustment to such a provision resulting from changes in the estimated outflow of resources embodying economic benefits (e.g. cash flows) required to settle the obligation should not be taken to profit or loss as it occurs, but should be added to or deducted from the cost of the asset to which it relates. Therefore, the requirement of IAS 21 to take the exchange differences arising on the provision to profit or loss in the period in which they arise conflicts with this requirement in IFRIC 1. It is our view that IFRIC 1 is the more relevant pronouncement for decommissioning purposes, therefore we consider that this type of exchange difference should not be taken to profit or loss, but dealt with in accordance with IFRIC 1.

10.3 Indefinite life assets

While the economic lives of oil fields and mines are finite, certain infrastructure assets (e.g. pipelines and refineries) are continually being repaired, replaced and upgraded. While individual parts of such assets may not have an indefinite economic life, these assets may occupy a particular site for an indefinite period.

Regardless of whether or not the related asset has an indefinite life, the decommissioning provision will normally meet the criteria relating to the recognition of a provision as set out in paragraphs 14(a) and (b) of IAS 37, in that an entity will have a present obligation and it will be probable that an outflow of resources will be required to settle the obligation. With respect to the final criterion in paragraph (c), while it might seem that a reliable estimate of the decommissioning provision cannot be made if the underlying asset has an indefinite life, 'indefinite' does not mean that the asset has an infinite life but that the life is long and has not yet been determined. IAS 37 presumes that:

> 'Except in extremely rare cases, an entity will be able to determine a range of possible outcomes and can therefore make an estimate of the obligation that is sufficiently reliable to use in recognising a provision.' [IAS 37.25].

Therefore, it should be extremely rare for an entity to conclude that it cannot make a reliable estimate of the amount of the obligation. Even if an entity did conclude in an extremely rare case that no reliable estimate could be made, there would still be a contingent liability and the following disclosures would be required:

- a brief description of the nature of the contingent liability; and
- where practicable:
  - an estimate of its financial effect, measured under paragraphs 36-52 of IAS 37;
  - an indication of the uncertainties relating to the amount or timing of any outflow; and
  - the possibility of any reimbursement. [IAS 37.26, 86].

Finally, it should be noted that the discounted value of decommissioning costs that will only be incurred far into the future may be relatively insignificant.

11 IMPAIRMENT OF ASSETS

The following issues require additional attention when a mining company or oil and gas company applies the impairment testing requirements under IFRS:

- impairment indicators (see 11.1 below);
- identifying cash-generating units (see 11.2 below);
- projections of cash flows (see 11.4.2 and 11.5.1 below);
- cash flows from mineral reserves and resources and the appropriate discount rate (see 11.4.2.A below);
- commodity price assumptions (see 11.4.3 and 11.5.2 below).
- future capital expenditure (see 11.4.4 and 11.5.3 below);
- foreign currency cash flows (see 11.4.5 and 11.5.4 below); and
- consistency in cash flows and the carrying amount of CGU (see 11.4.1 below).

The general requirements of IAS 36 are covered in Chapter 20.

11.1 Impairment indicators

Impairment indicators applicable to assets of mining companies and oil and gas companies are found in two places, IFRS 6 and IAS 36. IFRS 6 describes a number of situations in which an entity should test E&E assets for impairment, discussed at 3.5.1 above, while an entity should apply the impairment indicators in IAS 36 to assets other than E&E assets. The lists of impairment indicators in IFRS 6 and IAS 36 are not exhaustive. Entities operating in the extractive industries may also consider carrying out an impairment test in the following situations:[109]

- declines in prices of products or increases in production costs;
- governmental actions, such as new environmental regulations, imposition of price controls and tax increases;
- actual production levels from the cost centre or cost pool are below forecast and/or there is a downward revision in production forecasts;
- serious operational problems and accidents;
- capitalisation of large amounts of unsuccessful pre-production costs in the cost centre;
- decreases in reserve estimates;
- increases in the anticipated period over which reserves will be produced;
- substantial cost overruns during the development and construction phases of a field or mine; and
- adverse drilling results.

The extract below shows BHP's accounting policy for impairment testing.

> *Extract 43.18: BHP Group Plc (2019)*
> Notes to the Financial Statements [extract]
> 11 Property, plant and equipment [extract]
> Impairment of non-current assets
>
> Recognition and measurement
>
> Impairment tests for all assets are performed when there is an indication of impairment, although goodwill is tested at least annually. If the carrying amount of the asset exceeds its recoverable amount, the asset is impaired and an impairment loss is charged to the income statement so as to reduce the carrying amount in the balance sheet to its recoverable amount. Previously impaired assets (excluding goodwill) are reviewed for possible reversal of previous impairment at each reporting date. Impairment reversal cannot exceed the carrying amount that would have been determined (net of depreciation) had no impairment loss been recognised for the asset or cash generating units (CGUs). There were no reversals of impairment in the current or prior year.
>
> How recoverable amount is calculated
>
> The recoverable amount is the higher of an asset's fair value less cost of disposal (FVLCD) and its value in use (VIU). For the purposes of assessing impairment, assets are grouped at the lowest levels for which there are separately identifiable cash flows.
>
> Valuation methods
>
> *Fair value less cost of disposal*
>
> FVLCD is an estimate of the amount that a market participant would pay for an asset or CGU, less the cost of disposal. FVLCD for mineral and petroleum assets is generally determined using independent market assumptions to calculate the present value of the estimated future post-tax cash flows expected to arise from the continued use of the asset, including the anticipated cash flow effects of any capital expenditure to enhance production or reduce cost, and its eventual disposal where a market participant may take a consistent view. Cash flows are discounted using an appropriate post-tax market discount rate to arrive at a net present value of the asset, which is compared against the asset's carrying value. FVLCD may also take into consideration other market-based indicators of fair value.

Value in use

VIU is determined as the present value of the estimated future cash flows expected to arise from the continued use of the asset in its present form and its eventual disposal. VIU is determined by applying assumptions specific to the Group's continued use and cannot take into account future development. These assumptions are different to those used in calculating FVLCD and consequently the VIU calculation is likely to give a different result (usually lower) to a FVLCD calculation.

Key judgements and estimates

Judgements: Assessment of indicators of impairment or impairment reversal and the determination of CGUs for impairment purposes require significant management judgement.

Indicators of impairment may include changes in the Group's operating and economic assumptions, including those arising from changes in reserves or mine planning, updates to the Group's commodity supply, demand and price forecasts (which include carbon price forecasts), or the possible additional impacts from emerging risks such as those related to climate change and the transition to a lower carbon economy.

Additional impacts related to climate change and the transition to a lower carbon economy may include:

- a proportion of a CGU's reserves becoming incapable of extraction in an economically viable fashion;
- demand for the Group's commodities decreasing, due to policy, regulatory (including carbon pricing mechanisms), legal, technological, market or societal responses to climate change;
- physical impacts related to acute risks resulting from increased severity of extreme weather events, and those related to chronic risks resulting from longer-term changes in climate patterns.

Estimates: In determining the recoverable amount of assets, in the absence of quoted market prices, estimates are made regarding the present value of future post-tax cash flows. These estimates require significant management judgements and assumptions and are subject to risk and uncertainty that may be beyond the control of the Group; hence, there is a possibility that changes in circumstances will materially alter projections, which may impact the recoverable amount of assets at each reporting date. The estimates are made from the perspective of a market participant and include prices, future production volumes, operating costs, tax attributes and discount rates.

An indicator of impairment has been identified for the Jansen potash CGU at 30 June 2019 as the Group continues to assess project feasibility and the timing of project approval in accordance with the Group's Capital Allocation Framework. Accordingly, the Group has assessed the recoverable amount of the Jansen CGU using FVLCD methodology including a market participant's perspective of the net present value of future post-tax cash flows and other market-based indicators of fair value. The Jansen CGU carrying amount of US$3.0 billion as at 30 June 2019 is supported by the recoverable amount determination and as such, no impairment has been recognised.

The recoverable amount estimate is most sensitive to assumptions regarding the long-term forecasts of potash prices and discount rates:

- Potash price: prices are based on the latest internal forecasts taking into account expected demand and supply for potash globally (which includes, amongst a range of factors, carbon price forecasts), benchmarked with external sources of information;
- Discount rate: the discount rate is derived using the weighted average cost of capital methodology adjusted for any risks that are not reflected in the underlying cash flows, including where appropriate a country risk premium. A real post-tax discount rate of 7.5 per cent was applied to post-tax cash flows.

Changes in circumstances may affect the assumptions used to determine recoverable amount and could result in an impairment of non-current assets at future reporting dates.

11.2 Identifying cash-generating units (CGUs)

An entity is required under IAS 36 to test individual assets for impairment. However, if it is not possible to estimate the recoverable amount of an individual asset then an entity should determine the recoverable amount of the CGU to which the asset belongs. *[IAS 36.66]*. A CGU is defined by the standard as the smallest identifiable group of assets that generates cash inflows that are largely independent of the cash inflows from other assets or groups of assets. *[IAS 36.6]*. See Chapter 20 at 3 for further discussion about how an entity should determine its CGUs.

In determining appropriate CGUs, mining companies and oil and gas companies may need to consider some of the following issues:

(a) active markets for intermediate products (see 11.2.1 below);
(b) external users of the processing assets (see 11.2.2 below);
(c) fields or mines that are operated as one 'complex' through the use of shared infrastructure (see 11.2.3 below); and
(d) stand-alone fields or mines that operate on a portfolio basis (see 11.2.4 below).

These issues are discussed further below.

11.2.1 Markets for intermediate products

In vertically integrated operations, the successive stages of the extraction and production process are often considered to be one CGU as it is not possible to allocate net cash inflows to individual stages of the process. This is common in some mining operations. However, if there is an active market for intermediate commodities (e.g. bauxite, alumina and aluminium) then a vertically integrated mining company needs to consider whether its smelting and refining operations are part of the same CGU as its mining operations. If there is an active market for the output produced by an asset or group of assets, the assets concerned are identified as a separate CGU, even if some or all of the output is used internally. If extraction and smelting or refining are separate CGUs and the cash inflows generated by the asset or each CGU are based on internal transfer pricing, the best estimate of an external arm's length transaction price should be used in estimating the future cash flows to determine the asset's or CGU's VIU. *[IAS 36.70]*. See Chapter 20 at 3.

11.2.2 External users of processing assets

When an entity is able to derive cash inflows from its processing assets (e.g. smelting or refining facilities) under tolling arrangements (see 20 below), the question arises as to whether or not those processing assets are a separate CGU. If an entity's processing assets generate significant cash inflows from arrangements with third parties then those assets are likely to be a separate CGU.

11.2.3 Shared infrastructure

When several fields or mines share infrastructure (e.g. pipelines to transport gas or oil onshore, railways, ports or refining and smelting and other processing facilities) the question arises as to whether the fields or mines and the shared infrastructure should be treated as a single CGU. Treating the fields or mines and the shared infrastructure as part of the same CGU is not appropriate under the following circumstances:

(a) if the shared infrastructure is relatively insignificant;
(b) if the fields or mines are capable of selling their product without making use of the shared infrastructure;
(c) if the shared infrastructure generates substantial cash inflows from third parties as well as the entity's own fields or mines; or
(d) if the shared infrastructure is classified as a corporate asset, which is defined under IAS 36 as 'assets other than goodwill that contribute to the future cash flows of both the cash-generating unit under review and other cash-generating units'. *[IAS 36.6]*.

In that case, the entity should apply the requirements in IAS 36 regarding corporate assets, which are discussed in Chapter 20 at 4.2.

However, if none of the conditions under (a) to (d) above apply then it may be appropriate to treat the fields or mines and the shared infrastructure as one CGU.

Any shared infrastructure that does not belong to a single CGU but relates to more than one CGU still need to be considered for impairment purposes. It is considered that there are two ways to do this and an entity should use the method most appropriate. Shared infrastructure can be allocated to individual CGUs or the CGUs can be grouped together to test the shared assets (similar to the way corporate assets are tested – see commentary above).

Under the first approach, the shared assets should be allocated to each individual CGU or group of CGUs on a reasonable and consistent basis. The cash flows associated with the shared assets, such as fees from other users and expenditure, should be allocated similarly and should form part of the cash flows of the individual CGU. Under the second approach, the group of CGUs that benefit from the shared assets are grouped together with the shared assets to test the shared assets for impairment.

11.2.4 Fields or mines operated on a portfolio basis

Mining companies and oil and gas companies sometimes operate a 'portfolio' of similar mines or fields, which are completely independent from an operational point of view. However, IAS 36 includes the following illustrative example. *[IAS 36 IE Example 1C].*

Example 43.7: Single product entity

Entity M produces a single product and owns plants A, B and C. Each plant is located in a different continent. A produces a component that is assembled in either B or C. The combined capacity of B and C is not fully utilised. M's products are sold worldwide from either B or C. For example, B's production can be sold in C's continent if the products can be delivered faster from B than from C. Utilisation levels of B and C depend on the allocation of sales between the two sites.

Although there is an active market for the products assembled by B and C, cash inflows for B and C depend on the allocation of production across the two sites. It is unlikely that the future cash inflows for B and C can be determined individually. Therefore, it is likely that B and C together are the smallest identifiable group of assets that generates cash inflows that are largely independent.

The same rationale could also be applied by a mining company that, for example, operates two coal mines on a portfolio basis, or an oil and gas company that, for example, operates two fields within the one PSC and the entitlement to revenue is dependent on production of, the revenue earned and costs incurred across the PSC, not on a field by field basis. However, judgement needs to be exercised before concluding that it is appropriate to treat separate fields or mines as one CGU, particularly when the production costs of the output of fields or mines differ considerably. This is because there may be a desire to combine them into one CGU, so that the higher cost fields or mines are protected by the headroom of the lower cost fields or mine, thereby avoiding a recognition of an impairment charge. Therefore, to be able to combine on a portfolio basis, a mining company or oil and gas company would have to be able to demonstrate that the future cash inflows for the individual mines or fields cannot be determined individually and therefore, the combined group represents the smallest identifiable group of assets that generates cash inflows that are largely independent.

11.3 Basis of recoverable amount – value-in-use or fair value less costs of disposal

The standard requires the carrying amount of an asset or CGU to be compared with its recoverable amount, which is the higher of fair value less costs of disposal (FVLCD) and value-in-use (VIU). *[IAS 36.18]*. If either the FVLCD or the VIU is higher than the carrying amount, no further action is necessary as the asset is not impaired. *[IAS 36.19]*. Recoverable amount is calculated for an individual asset, unless that asset does not generate cash inflows that are largely independent of those from other assets or groups of assets. *[IAS 36.22]*.

At 11.4 and 11.5 below we further consider the practical and technical aspects associated with the calculation of VIU and FVLCD respectively for mining companies and oil and gas companies.

11.4 Calculation of VIU

IAS 36 defines VIU as the present value of the future cash flows expected to be derived from an asset or CGU. *[IAS 36.6]*. Estimating the VIU of an asset/CGU involves estimating the future cash inflows and outflows that will be derived from the use of the asset and from its ultimate disposal in its current condition, and discounting them at an appropriate rate. *[IAS 36.31]*. There are complex issues involved in determining the cash flows and choosing a discount rate and often there is no agreed methodology to follow. IAS 36 contains detailed and explicit requirements concerning the data to be assembled to calculate VIU that can best be explained and set out as a series of steps. The steps in the process are:

- Step 1: Dividing the entity into CGUs (see 11.2 above).
- Step 2: Allocating goodwill to CGUs or CGU groups (see Chapter 20 at 8.1).
- Step 3: Identifying the carrying amount of CGU assets (see 11.4.1 below).
- Step 4: Estimating the future pre-tax cash flows of the CGU under review (see 11.4.2 – 11.4.5 below).
- Step 5: Identifying an appropriate discount rate and discounting the future cash flows (see Chapter 20 at 7.2 and below at 11.4.2.A).
- Step 6: Comparing carrying value with VIU (assuming FVLCD is lower than carrying value) and recognising impairment losses (see Chapter 20 at 7.3 and 11).

11.4.1 Consistency in cash flows and book values attributed to the CGU

An essential requirement of impairment testing under IAS 36 is that the recoverable amount of a CGU must be determined in the same way as for an individual asset and its carrying amount must be determined on a basis that is consistent with the way in which its recoverable amount is determined. *[IAS 36.74, 75]*.

The carrying amount of a CGU includes only those assets that can be attributed directly, or allocated on a reasonable and consistent basis. These must be the assets that will generate the future cash inflows used in determining the CGU's VIU. It does not include the carrying amount of any recognised liability, unless the recoverable amount of the cash-generating unit cannot be determined without taking it into account.

For practical reasons the entity may determine the recoverable amount of a CGU after taking into account assets and liabilities such as receivables or other financial assets, trade payables, pensions and other provisions that are outside the scope of IAS 36 and not part of the CGU. *[IAS 36.79]*. If the cash flows of a CGU are determined taking into account these sorts of items, then it is essential that cash flows and assets and liabilities within CGUs are prepared on a consistent basis.

Specific issues mining companies and oil and gas companies will need to consider are:

- environmental provisions and similar provisions and liabilities (see 11.4.1.A below);
- the impact of cash flows associated with lease liabilities recognised in accordance with IFRS 16 (see Chapter 20 at 7.1.8.A); and
- working capital such as trade debtors, trade payables and inventories (see Chapter 20 at 4.1 and 4.1.3 for further discussion).

11.4.1.A   Environmental provisions and similar provisions and liabilities

IAS 36 requires the carrying amount of a liability to be excluded from the carrying amount of a CGU unless the recoverable amount of the CGU cannot be determined without consideration of that liability. *[IAS 36.76, 78]*. This typically applies when the asset/CGU cannot be separated from the associated liability. See Chapter 20 at 4.1.1 for further discussion of some of the practical challenges associated with this.

11.4.2   Projections of cash flows

IAS 36 requires that in calculating VIU an entity base its cash flow projection on the most recent financial budgets/forecasts approved by management, excluding any estimated future cash inflows or outflows expected to arise from future restructurings or from improving or enhancing the asset's performance. The assumptions used to prepare the cash flows should be reasonable and supportable, which can best be achieved by benchmarking against market data or performance against previous budgets. These projections cannot cover a period in excess of five years, unless a longer period can be justified. *[IAS 36.33(b)]*. Entities are permitted to use a longer period if they are confident that their projections are reliable, based on past experience. *[IAS 36.35]*.

In practice, most production or mining/field plans will cover a period of more than five years and hence management will typically make financial forecasts for a corresponding period. The use of such longer term forecasts may be appropriate where it is based on proved and probable reserves and expected annual production rates. Assumptions as to the level of reserves expected to be extracted should be consistent with the latest estimates prepared by reserve engineers; annual production rates should be consistent with those of preceding periods; and price and cost assumptions should be consistent with the final period of specific assumptions.

11.4.2.A Cash flows from mineral reserves and resources and the appropriate discount rate

As discussed at 2.2 and 2.3 above, a significant amount of work is required before an entity can conclude that its mineral resources should be classified as mineral reserves. In practice, an entity may not have formally completed all of the detailed work that is required in order to designate mineral resources as mineral reserves. IAS 36 requires the cash flow projection used in calculating the VIU of assets to be based on 'reasonable and supportable assumptions that represent management's best estimate of the range of economic conditions that will exist over the remaining useful life of the asset'. *[IAS 36.33(a)]*. Therefore, while ordinarily the starting point for the calculation of VIU would be based upon the mineral reserves recorded, it may sometimes be appropriate under IAS 36 to take into account mineral resources that have not formally been designated as mineral reserves. However an entity would need to adjust the discount rate it uses in its VIU calculation for the additional risks associated with mineral resources for which the future cash flow estimates have not been adjusted. *[IAS 36.55]*. If the risks have been factored into the future cash flow estimates modelled, an entity should be aware not to also adjust for this risk via the discount rate applied.

The requirements of IAS 36 for determining an appropriate discount rate are discussed in detail in Chapter 20 at 7.2.

11.4.3 Commodity price assumptions

Forecasting commodity prices is never straightforward, because it is not usually possible to know whether recent changes in commodity prices are a temporary aberration or the beginning of a longer-term trend. Management usually takes a longer term approach to estimates of commodity prices for internal management purposes but these are not always consistent with the VIU requirements. Given the long life of most mines and oil fields, an entity should not consider price levels only for the past three or four years. Instead, it should consider future pricing based on future supply and demand levels in a changing environment particularly with respect to climate risk. Historical price levels for longer periods, and how these prices were influenced by changes in underlying supply and demand levels, may provide some insight into pricing but must be considered in the context of future supply and demand.

For actively traded commodities, there are typically forward price curves available and in such situations, these provide another reference point for forecast price assumptions.

The commodity assumptions need to match the profile of the life of the mine or oil field. Spot prices and forward curve prices (where they are available as at the impairment testing date) are more relevant for shorter life mines and oil fields, or for pricing of volumes in the earlier years of a longer life mines or oil fields. Long-term price assumptions are more relevant for longer life mines and oil fields and are typically used beyond the initial 2-3-year period for which forward curve pricing may be used. Forecast prices (where available) should be used for the future periods covered by the VIU calculation. Where the forward price curve does not extend far enough into the future, the price at the end of the forward curve is generally held steady, or reverts to a longer term average price (in real terms), where appropriate.

The future cash flows relating to the purchase or sale of commodities might be known from forward purchase or long-term sales contracts for which prices are either fixed, or vary based on an index e.g. inflation. Use of these contracted prices in the VIU calculation in place of the spot price or forward curve price for the contracted volumes will generally be acceptable. However, it is possible that some of these forward contracts might be accounted for as derivatives contracts at fair value in accordance with IFRS 9, and therefore the related assets or liabilities will be recognised in the statement of financial position. It is important to ensure consistency between the carrying values included in the CGU and the cash flows included in the VIU calculation with respect to cash flow hedges, whether they qualify for hedge accounting or not. This is discussed further in Chapter 20 at 4.1.5.

The commodity price is a key assumption in calculating the VIU of any mine or oil field. Only in the context of impairment testing of goodwill and indefinite life intangible assets does IAS 36 specifically require disclosure of:

(i) a description of each key assumption on which management has based its cash flow projections for the period covered by the most recent budgets/forecasts. Key assumptions are those to which the unit's (group of units') recoverable amount is most sensitive; and

(ii) a description of management's approach to determining the value(s) assigned to each key assumption, whether those value(s) reflect past experience or, if appropriate, are consistent with external sources of information, and, if not, how and why they differ from past experience or external sources of information.

[IAS 36.134(d)(i)-(ii), 134(e)(i)-(ii)].

In practice, considerable differences may exist between entities in their estimates of future commodity prices. Therefore, we recommend disclosure of the actual commodity prices used in calculating the VIU of any mine or oil field that does not have any goodwill or indefinite life intangibles allocated to it, even though this is not specifically required by IAS 36 as these would generally be considered a significant judgement or estimate and hence would require disclosure under IAS 1. *[IAS 1.122, 125].* A possible approach to such disclosures is illustrated in the following extract from the financial statements of BP.

Extract 43.19: BP p.l.c. (2019)

Notes on financial statements [extract]

1. **Significant accounting policies, judgements, estimates and assumptions** [extract]

Significant judgements and estimates: recoverability of asset carrying values [extract]

Oil and natural gas properties [extract] *Oil and natural gas prices*

The long-term price assumptions used for investment appraisal are recommended by the group chief economist after considering a range of external price, and supply and demand forecasts under various energy transition scenarios. They are reviewed and approved by management. As a result of the current uncertainty over the pace of transition to lower-carbon supply and demand and the social, political and environmental actions that will be taken to meet the goals of the Paris climate change agreement, the forecasts and scenarios considered include those where those goals are met as well as those where they are not met. The assumptions below represent management's best estimate of future prices; they do not reflect a specific scenario and sit within the range of the external forecasts considered.

The long-term price assumptions used to determine recoverable amount based on value-in-use impairments tests are derived from the central case investment appraisal assumptions (see page 19) of $70 per barrel for Brent and $4 per mmBtu for Henry Hub gas, both in 2015 prices (2018 $75 per barrel and $4 per mmBtu respectively, in 2015 prices). These long-term prices are applied from 2025 and 2032 respectively (2018 both from 2024) and continue to be inflated for the remaining life of the asset.

The price assumptions used over the periods to 2025 and 2032 have been set such that there is a linear progression from our best estimate of 2020 prices, which were set by reference to 2019 average prices, to the long-term assumptions.

The majority of BP's reserves and resources that support the carrying value of the group's oil and gas properties are expected to be produced over the next 10 years. Average prices (in real 2015 terms) used to estimate cash flows over this period are $67 per barrel for Brent and $3.1 per mmBtu for Henry Hub gas.

Oil prices fell 10% in 2019 from 2018 due to trade tensions, a macroeconomic downturn, and a slight slowdown in oil demand. OPEC+ production restraint, unplanned outages, and sanctions on Venezuela and Iran kept prices from falling further. BP's long-term assumption for oil prices is higher than the 2019 price average, based on the judgement that current price levels would not encourage sufficient investment to meet global oil demand sustainably in the longer term, especially given the financial requirements of key low-cost oil producing economies.

US gas prices dropped by around 15% in 2019 compared to 2018. After an initial spike in January, they remained relatively low for much of the year due to a combination of strong associated gas production growth, and storage levels coming back to normal. US gas demand growth was much lower than the exceptional increase in 2018, while LNG exports continued to expand. BP's long-term price assumption for US gas is higher than recent market prices due to forecast rising domestic demand, rapidly increasing pipeline and LNG exports, and lowest cost resources being absorbed leading to production of more expensive gas, as well as requiring increased investment in infrastructure.

Management tested the impact of a reduction in prices of 15% against the best estimate for Brent oil and Henry Hub gas in all future years. These price reductions in isolation could indicatively lead to a reduction in the carrying amount of BP's oil and gas properties in the range of $2-3 billion, which is approximately 1-2% of the net book value of property, plant and equipment as at 31 December 2019.

Management also tested the impact of a scenario where Brent oil and Henry Hub gas prices start 15% lower than the best estimate and gradually reduce to 25% lower than the best estimate by 2040. Although this is not considered to be a reasonably possible change in the long-term assumptions within the next financial year, it reflects the inherent uncertainty in forecasting long-term prices. These price reductions in isolation could indicatively lead to a reduction in the carrying amount of BP's oil and gas properties in the range of $4-5 billion which is approximately 3-4% of the net book value of property, plant and equipment as at 31 December 2019. Additionally, such a price reduction does not indicate a reduction in the carrying amount of the Upstream goodwill balance.

These sensitivity analyses do not, however, represent management's best estimate of any impairments that might be recognized as they do not fully incorporate consequential changes that may arise, such as reductions in costs and changes to business plans, phasing of development, levels of reserves and resources, and production volumes. As the extent of a price reduction increases, the more likely it is that costs would decrease across the industry. The above sensitivity analyses therefore do not reflect a linear relationship between price and value that can be extrapolated. Past experience of performing impairment tests suggests that any impairment arising from such price reductions is likely to be lower once all these factors are taken into consideration. The interdependency of these inputs and risk factors plus the diverse characteristics of our oil and gas properties limits the practicability of estimating the probability or extent to which the overall recoverable amount is impacted by changes to the price assumptions.

The decline in oil and natural gas prices in the first quarter of 2020 is not expected to materially impact the recoverable amount of the group's oil and natural gas properties.

The extract below illustrates a similar type of disclosure by Newcrest Mining from its 30 June 2019 financial statements, in this case as part of the key assumption disclosures within its impairment disclosures.

Extract 43.20: Newcrest Mining Limited (2019)

Notes to the Consolidated Financial Statements [extract]
For the Year Ended 30 June 2019
12. Impairment of Non-Financial Assets [extract]
c) Key judgements, estimates and assumptions [extract]

The table below summarises the key assumptions used in the carrying value assessments as at 30 June 2019, and for comparison also provides the equivalent assumptions used in 2018:

	2019				2018			
Assumptions	2020	2021	2022	Long term (2023+)	2019	2020	2021	Long term (2022+)
Gold (US$ per ounce)	$1,250	$1,250	$1,250	$1,250	$1,250	$1,250	$1,250	$1,250
Copper (US$ per pound)	$2.80	$2.90	$3.00	$3.00	$3.00	$3.00	$3.00	$3.00

Commodity prices and exchange rates estimation approach

Commodity price and foreign exchange rates are estimated with reference to external market forecasts and reviewed at least annually. The rates applied have regard to observable market data including spot and forward values, and to market analysis including equity analyst estimates.

Metal prices

Newcrest has maintained the short-term and long-term US dollar gold and the long-term US dollar copper price estimates applied in 2018. Short-term copper prices assumptions have reduced from 2018 to align with observable market data, reflecting spot prices during the 2019 financial year and Newcrest's analysis of observable market forecasts for future periods.

11.4.4   Future capital expenditure

When determining VIU, although the standard permits an entity to take account of cash outflows required to make an asset ready for use, i.e. those relating to assets under construction, *[IAS 36.42]*, it does not allow inclusion of cash outflows relating to future restructuring to which an entity is not yet committed, or, improving or enhancing an asset's performance. *[IAS 36.44]*. This may have a significant impact on relatively new assets and on fields or mines that will be developed over time. Note that while enhancement capital expenditure may not be recognised, routine or replacement capital expenditure necessary to maintain the function or current performance of the asset or assets in the CGU has to be included. Entities must therefore distinguish between maintenance and enhancement expenditure. This distinction may not be easy to draw in practice but, for example, an anticipated increase in mineral reserves as a consequence of incurring future capital expenditure may be an indicator that the expenditure is enhancement expenditure.

11.4.5 Foreign currency cash flows

An entity in the extractive industries will often sell its product in a currency that is different from the one in which it incurs its production costs (e.g. silver production may be sold in US dollars while production costs may be incurred in pesos). In such situations, impairment testing and calculating VIU under IAS 36 require that the foreign currency cash flows should first be estimated in the currency in which they will be generated and then discounted using a discount rate appropriate for that currency. An entity should translate the present value calculated in the foreign currency using the spot exchange rate at the date of the VIU calculation. *[IAS 36.54]*. This is to avoid the problems inherent in using forward exchange rates, which are based on differential interest rates. Using such forward rates would result in double-counting the time value of money, first in the discount rate and then in the forward rate. *[IAS 36.BCZ49]*.

This requirement, however, is more complex than it may initially appear. Effectively, this method requires an entity to perform separate impairment tests for cash flows generated in different currencies, but make them consistent with one another so that the combined effect is meaningful. This can be a difficult exercise to undertake. Many different factors need to be considered, including relative inflation rates and relative interest rates, as well as appropriate discount rates for the currencies in question. Because of this, the possibility for error is significant, given this, it is important for entities to seek input from experienced valuers who will be able to assist them in dealing with these challenges.

11.5 Calculation of FVLCD

FVLCD is the price that would be received to sell an asset or paid to transfer a liability in an orderly transaction between market participants at the measurement date, less the costs of disposal. *[IAS 36.6]*. FVLCD is less restrictive in its application than VIU and can be easier to work with, which may be why some entities choose to use this approach for impairment testing purposes. While IAS 36 does not impose any restrictions on how an entity determines the FVLCD, there are specific requirements in IFRS 13 as to how to determine fair value. IFRS 13 is discussed in more detail in Chapter 14.

The concept of fair value in IFRS 13 is explicitly an exit price notion. FVLCD, like fair value, is not an entity-specific measurement, but is focused on market participants' assumptions for a particular asset or liability. Under IFRS 13, for non-financial assets, entities have to consider the highest and best use (from a market participant perspective) to which the asset could be put. However, it is generally presumed that an entity's current use of those mining or oil and gas assets or CGUs would be its highest and best use (unless market or other factors suggest that a different use by market participants would maximise the value of the asset).

IFRS 13 does not limit or prioritise the valuation technique(s) an entity might use to measure fair value. An entity may use any valuation technique, or multiple techniques, as long as it is consistent with one of three valuation approaches: market approach, income approach and cost approach and is appropriate for the type of asset/CGU being measured at fair value. However, IFRS 13 does focus on the type of inputs to be used and requires an entity to maximise the use of relevant observable inputs and minimise the use of the unobservable inputs.

Historically, many mining companies and oil and gas companies have calculated FVLCD using a discounted cash flow (DCF) valuation technique. This approach differs from VIU in a number of ways. One of the key differences is that FVLCD would require an entity to use assumptions that a market participant would be likely to take into account rather than entity-specific assumptions. For example, as mining sector and oil and gas sector market participants invest for the longer term, they would not restrict themselves to a limited project time horizon. Therefore, the cash flow forecasts included in a FVLCD calculation may cover a longer period than may be used in a VIU calculation. Moreover, market participants would also likely take into account future expansionary capital expenditure related to subsequent phases in the development of a mining property in a FVLCD calculation, whereas this is not permitted in a VIU calculation. Having said this, some of the issues discussed above for a VIU calculation also need to be considered for a FVLCD calculation which uses a DCF model (we discuss some of these further below). As illustrated in Extract 43.18 at 11.1 above, BHP uses this approach in determining the FVLCD for its mineral assets.

11.5.1 Projections of cash flows

As required by IFRS 13, the assumptions and other inputs used in a FVLCD DCF model are required to maximise the use of observable market inputs. These should be both realistic and consistent with what a typical market participant would assume.

11.5.2 Commodity price assumptions

Similar to a VIU calculation, commodity price is a key assumption in calculating the FVLCD of any mine or oil field when using a DCF model, and therefore similar issues as those discussed for a VIU calculation (see 11.4.3 above) apply. On the same basis, while the specific disclosure requirements relating to price assumptions in IAS 36 technically only apply in the context of impairment testing of CGUs to which goodwill and indefinite life intangible assets are allocated, because there can be considerable differences between entities in their estimates of future commodity prices, we recommend additional disclosures be provided. Regardless of the specific requirements of IAS 36, an entity is also required to consider the disclosure requirements relating to significant judgements or estimates and hence the requirements of IAS 1. *[IAS 1.122, 125]*. For example, an entity may wish to disclose the actual commodity prices used in calculating the FVLCD of any mine or oil field, as these would generally be considered a significant judgement or estimate and hence would require disclosure under IAS 1. *[IAS 1.122, 125]*.

11.5.3 Future capital expenditure

There are no restrictions similar to those applicable to a VIU calculation when determining FVLCD provided that it can be demonstrated that a market participant would be willing to attribute some value to the future enhancement and that the requirements of IFRS 13 have been complied with. IFRS 13 is discussed in more detail in Chapter 14.

The treatment of future capital expenditure in an impairment test is discussed in more detail in Chapter 20 at 7.1.2.

11.5.4 Foreign currency cash flows

For FVLCD calculations, the requirements relating to foreign currency cash flows are not specified other than they must reflect what a market participant would use when valuing the asset or CGU. In practice, entities that use a DCF analysis when calculating FVLCD will incorporate a forecast for exchange rates into their calculations rather than using the spot rate. A key issue in any forecast is the assumed timeframe over which the exchange rate may return to lower levels. This assumption is generally best analysed in conjunction with commodity prices in order to ensure consistency in the parameters used, i.e. a rise in prices will usually be accompanied by a rise in currency.

11.6 Low mine or field profitability near end of life

While mining companies and oil and gas companies would like to achieve steady profitability and returns over the life of a project, it is not uncommon to see profitability declining over the life of a mine or field. From an economic perspective, a mining company or oil and gas company will generally continue to extract minerals as long as the cash inflows from the sale of minerals exceed the cash cost of production.

From a mining perspective, most mine plans aim to maximise the net present value of mineral reserves by first extracting the highest grade ore with the lowest production costs. Consequently, in most mining operations, the grade of the ore mined steadily declines over the life of the mine which results in a declining annual production, while the production costs (including depreciation/amortisation) per volume of ore, e.g. tonne, gradually increases as it becomes more difficult to extract the ore. From an oil and gas perspective, both oil and gas may be produced from the same wells but ordinarily oil generates greater revenue per barrel of oil equivalent sold relative to gas. As the oil is often produced in greater quantities first, this means that the oil and gas operation is often more profitable in the earlier years relative to later years.

Consequently, where there is a positive net cash flow, a mining company or oil and gas company will continue to extract minerals even if it does not fully recover the depreciation of its property, plant and equipment and mineral reserves, as is likely to occur towards the end of the mine or field life. In part, this is the result of the depreciation methods applied:

- the straight-line method of depreciation allocates a relatively high depreciation charge to periods with a low annual production;
- a units of production method based on the quantity of ore extracted allocates a relatively high depreciation charge to production of lower grade ore compared to the price at which such ore is sold;

- a units of production method based upon the quantity of petroleum product produced in total terms allocates an even depreciation charge per barrel of oil equivalent, whereas the revenue earned varies; and
- a units of production method based on the quantity of minerals produced allocates a relatively high depreciation charge to production of minerals that are difficult to recover.

Each of these situations is most likely to occur towards the end of the life of a mine or field. It is possible the methods of depreciation most commonly used in each of the sectors do not allocate a sufficiently high depreciation charge to the early life of a project when production is generally most profitable. An entity should therefore be mindful of the fact that relatively small changes in facts and circumstances can lead to an impairment of assets.

Following on from this, the impairment tests in the early years of the life of a mine or field will often reveal that the project is cash flow positive and is able to produce a recoverable amount that is sufficient to recoup the carrying value of the project, i.e. the project is not impaired. However, when the impairment tests are conducted in later years, while the mine or field may still be cash flow positive, i.e. the expected cash proceeds from the future sale of minerals still exceed the expected future cash costs of production and hence management will continue with the mining or oil and gas operations, as margins generally reduce towards the end of mine or field life, the impairment tests may not produce a recoverable amount sufficient to recoup the remaining carrying value of the mine or field. Therefore, it will need to be impaired.

It is possible, when preparing the impairment models for a mine or field, for an entity to identify when (in the future) the remaining net cash inflows may no longer be sufficient to recoup the remaining carrying value, that is, when compared to the way in which the assets are expected to be depreciated over the remaining useful life. However, provided the recoverable amount as at the date of the impairment test exceeds the carrying amount of the mine or field, there is no requirement to recognise any possible future impairment. It is only when the recoverable amount actually falls below the carrying amount that an impairment must be recognised.

12 REVENUE RECOGNITION

The sub-sections below consider some of the specific revenue recognition issues faced by mining companies and oil and gas companies under the requirements as set out in IFRS 15 (see Chapters 27 to 32 for more details) or where they may earn other revenue (or other income) in the scope of other standards (see Chapter 27 at 4).

12.1 Revenue in the development phase

Under IAS 16, the cost of an item of property, plant and equipment includes any costs directly attributable to bringing the asset to the location and condition necessary for it to be capable of operating in the manner intended by management. *[IAS 16.16(b)]*. During the development/construction of an asset, an entity may generate some revenue. The current treatment of such revenue depends on whether it is considered incidental or integral to bringing the asset itself into the location and condition necessary for it to be capable of operating in the manner intended by management. However, for annual reporting periods beginning on or after 1 January 2022, amendments to IAS 16 will prohibit entities from deducting such sales proceeds from the cost of an item of property, plant and equipment. Instead, such proceeds must be recognised in profit or loss. This is discussed further at 12.1.2.A below. If the asset is already in the location and condition necessary for it to be capable of being used in the manner intended by management, then IAS 16 requires capitalisation to cease and depreciation to start. *[IAS 16.20]*. In these circumstances, all income earned from using the asset must be recognised as either revenue from contracts with customers or other income in profit or loss and the related costs of the activity should include an element of depreciation of the asset.

12.1.1 Incidental revenue

During the construction of an asset, an entity may enter into incidental operations that are not, in themselves, necessary to bring the asset itself into the location and condition necessary for it to be capable of operating in the manner intended by management. The standard gives the example of income earned by using a building site as a car park prior to starting construction. An extractives example may be income earned from leasing out the land surrounding the mine site or an onshore gas field to a local farmer to run his sheep on. Because incidental operations such as these are not necessary to bring an item to the location and condition necessary for it to be capable of operating in the manner intended by management, the income and related expenses of incidental operations are recognised in profit or loss and included in their respective classifications of income and expense. *[IAS 16.21]*. Such incidental income is not offset against the cost of the asset.

12.1.2 Integral to development

The directly attributable costs of an item of property, plant and equipment include the costs of testing whether the asset is functioning properly, after deducting the net proceeds from selling any items produced while bringing the asset to that location and condition. *[IAS 16.17(e)]*. The standard gives the example of samples produced when testing equipment.

There are other situations in which income may be generated wholly and necessarily as a result of the process of bringing the asset to the location and condition for its intended use. The extractive industries are highly capital intensive and there are many instances where income may be generated prior to the commencement of production.

Some mining examples include:

- During the evaluation phase, i.e. when the technical feasibility and commercial viability are being determined, an entity may 'trial mine', to determine which development method would be the most profitable and efficient in the circumstances, and which metallurgical process is the most efficient. Ore mined through trial mining may be processed and sold during the evaluation phase.
- As part of the process of constructing a deep underground mine, the mining operation may extract some saleable 'product' during the construction of the mine e.g. sinking shafts to the depth where the main ore-bearing rock is located.
- At the other end of the spectrum, income may be earned from the sale of product from 'ramping up' the mine to production at commercial levels.

Some oil and gas examples include:
- Onshore wells are frequently placed on long-term production test as part of the process of appraisal and formulation of a field development plan. Test production may be sold during this time.

Some interpret IAS 16's requirement quite narrowly as only applying to income earned from actually 'testing' the asset, while others interpret it more broadly to include other types of pre-commissioning or production testing revenue.

We have noted in practice that some income may be generated wholly and necessarily as a result of activities that are part of the process of bringing the asset into the location and condition for its intended use, i.e. the activities are integral to the construction or development of the mine or field. Some consider that as IAS 16 makes it clear that income generated from incidental operations is to be taken to revenue, *[IAS 16.21]*, but does not explicitly specify the treatment of integral revenue, it could be interpreted that income earned from activities that are integral to the development of the mine or field should be credited to the cost of the mine or field. This is because the main purpose of the activities is the development of the mine or field, not the production of ore or hydrocarbons. The income earned from production is an unintended benefit.

In our experience, practice in accounting for pre-commissioning or test production revenue varies. These various treatments have evolved as a result of the way in which the relatively limited guidance in IFRS has been interpreted and applied. In some instances, this has also been influenced by approaches that originated in previous and other GAAPs, where guidance was/is somewhat clearer.

The key challenge with this issue is usually not how to measure the revenue but how entities view this revenue and, more significantly, how to distinguish those costs that are directly attributable to developing the operating capability of the mine or field from those that represent the cost of producing saleable material. It can be extremely difficult to apportion these costs. Consequently, there is a risk of misstatement of gross profits if these amounts are recorded as revenue and the amount of costs included in profit or loss as cost of goods sold is too low or too high.

Other GAAPs have either previously provided or continue to provide further guidance that has influenced some of the approaches adopted under IFRS. For example, the now superseded Australian GAAP (AGAAP) standard on extractive industries[110] and the former OIAC SORP[111] provided more specific guidance. The former clearly required, and the latter recommended, that any proceeds earned from the sale of product obtained during the exploration, evaluation or development phases should be treated in the same manner as the proceeds from the sale of product in the production phase, i.e. recognised in profit or loss as part of income.

AGAAP required the estimated cost of producing the quantities concerned to be deducted from the accumulated costs of such activities and included as part of costs of goods sold.[112] By contrast, the former OIAC SORP was more specific and stated that an amount equivalent to the revenues should be both charged to cost of sales and credited against appraisal costs to record a zero net margin on such production.[113]

The various practices that are currently adopted and accepted include:
- all pre-commissioning/test production revenue is considered integral to the development of the mine or field and is therefore credited to the asset in its entirety;
- only revenue genuinely earned from the testing of assets, e.g. product processed as a result of testing the processing plant and associated facilities, is credited to the associated asset, with all other revenue being recognised in profit or loss; or
- all pre-commissioning or test production revenue is recognised in profit or loss.

For entities that recognise pre-commissioning or test production revenue in profit or loss, various approaches have been observed in practice to determine the amount to be included in cost of goods sold and include:
- an amount equivalent to the revenues is charged to cost of sales and credited against the asset to record a zero net margin on such production (similar to the guidance in the former OIAC SORP);
- a standard or expected cost of production is ascribed to the volumes produced, e.g. weighted average cost per tonne/barrel based on actual results over a historical period, e.g. the last two or three years; or for new mines or fields, the expected cost per tonne/bbl as set out in the business, mine or field plan, producing a standard margin;
- recognising only the incremental cost of processing the product; or
- recognising nothing in cost of goods sold.

The net effect of all of these approaches is that any excess of the total cost incurred over the amount recognised in profit or loss as cost of goods sold, is effectively capitalised as part of the asset. Note that the first approach, where cost of goods sold is recognised at the same amount as the revenue, produces the same net balance sheet and profit or loss result as if the revenue had been credited to the asset in its entirety.

While diverse treatments may have been adopted and accepted in practice to date, it is unlikely the third and fourth cost of goods sold approaches would be appropriate because they would not provide a fair reflection of the cost to produce the saleable product.

There is a significant degree of divergence as to how entities account for pre-commissioning revenue. Significant judgement will also be required to determine when the asset is in the location and condition to be capable of operating as intended by management, i.e. when it is ready for its intended use. In the absence of specific guidance this divergence will continue. However, capitalisation (including recognising income as a credit to the cost of the asset) is to cease when the asset is ready for its intended use, regardless of whether or not it is achieving its targeted levels of production or profitability, or even operating at all.

12.1.2.A Future developments

Accounting for revenue in the development phase was referred to the Interpretations Committee in July 2014 and was considered several times since this date. The Interpretations Committee received a request to clarify two specific aspects of IAS 16, including:
- whether the proceeds referred to in IAS 16 relate only to items produced from testing; and
- whether an entity deducts from the cost of an item of PP&E any proceeds that exceed the cost of testing.

After exploring different approaches to the issue, the Interpretations Committee recommended to the IASB to amend IAS 16. After the issuance of the exposure draft (ED) *Property, Plant and Equipment – Proceeds before Intended Use (Proposed amendments to IAS 16 (ED/2017/4)*, in May 2020, the Board issued amendments to IAS 16. These were based on those originally set out in the ED, with some modifications.

The amendments to IAS 16 will prohibit an entity from deducting from the cost of an item of PP&E any proceeds from selling items produced while bringing that asset to the location and condition necessary for it to be capable of operating in the manner intended by management (i.e. the point up until it is available for intended use). Instead, such proceeds would be recognised in profit or loss. The amendments state that the costs of producing items of inventory before an asset is ready for its intended use must be recognised in profit or loss in accordance with applicable standards, i.e. IAS 2. *[IAS 2.34]*.

The summary of the key decisions by the Board is as follows:

- to amend IAS 16 to require an entity to identify and measure the cost of items produced before an item of PPE is available for use applying the measurement requirements in IAS 2;
- to develop neither presentation nor disclosure requirements for the sale of items that are part of an entity's ordinary activities; and
- for the sale of items that are not part of an entity's ordinary activities (and to which an entity does not apply IFRS 15 and IAS 2), to require an entity to:
  - disclose separately the sales proceeds and their related production costs recognised in profit or loss;
  - specify the line item(s) in the statement of profit or loss and other comprehensive income that include(s) the sales proceeds and the production costs; and
- not to amend IFRS 6 or IFRIC 20 – *Stripping Costs in the Production Phase of a Surface Mine* – as a consequence of these proposed amendments.[114]

The Board agreed the amendments should apply to reporting periods beginning on or after 1 January 2022, with earlier application permitted. Entities will be required to apply the amendments retrospectively, but only to items of PP&E that are made available for use on or after the beginning of the earliest period present in the financial statements in which an entity first applies the amendments. Consequently, the cumulative effect of initially applying the amendments will be recognised as an adjustment to the opening balance of retained earnings (or other component of equity, as appropriate) on this date.

The amendments will provide consistency in how revenue earned before an asset is ready for its intended use would be treated (i.e. all revenue will be recognised in profit or loss regardless of when earned). The amendments will require an entity to separately identify the production costs associated with selling volumes before an asset is ready for its intended use. An entity will be required to identify and measure production costs applying the measurement requirements in IAS 2. This amendment is intended to address concerns about the lack of clarity regarding how such costs would be measured, reduce the practical challenges associated with identification of such costs, and reduce the need for judgement and consequential diversity in practice. The requirements in IAS 2 set out a framework to identify production costs without being overly prescriptive and the Board was not aware of significant difficulties in applying the existing cost allocation requirements in IAS 2.

In addition, while the amendments will lead to greater visibility of different revenue classes, should this revenue be so material that separate disclosures are required by IFRS 15 or other relevant standards, it would direct more attention to the date at which an asset is ready for its intended use, i.e. the commissioning date. This is a critical date as it impacts other aspects of the accounting for such assets, such as when costs (including borrowing costs) should cease to be capitalised, when accounting for stripping costs changes (mining companies only), and when depreciation commences.

The Basis for Conclusions indicate that, while the IASB observed that an entity would have to apply judgement in identifying the costs, the amendments would require little more judgement beyond that already required to apply current IFRS standards when allocating costs incurred. *[IAS 16(2022).BC16J]*.

The Basis for Conclusions acknowledge that such an approach would mean that the cost of such inventories would exclude depreciation of PP&E used in the production process. *[IAS 16(2022).BC16F-G]*.

While the amendments provide no specific guidance, for those entities that currently recognise pre-commissioning or test production revenue in profit or loss, the various approaches that have been observed in practice to determine the amount to be included in cost of goods sold are discussed at 12.1.2 above. Similar issues and considerations are likely to continue to arise and will require entities to exercise judgement. It is expected that entities will use their disclosures to clarify their approach to pre-commissioning/testing revenue and the determination of cost of goods sold.

12.2 Sale of product with delayed shipment

From time to time, an entity may enter into a sales arrangement where the purchaser pays a significant portion of the final estimated purchase price but then requests delayed shipment, for example, because of limited storage space. These sales can sometimes also be referred to as 'in store sales' or 'bill-and-hold' sales. These are commonly seen in the mining sector.

The application guidance in IFRS 15 specifically addresses bill-and-hold arrangements. IFRS 15 states that an entity will need to determine when it has satisfied its performance obligation to transfer a product by evaluating when a customer obtains control of that product (see Chapter 30 at 4 for more information on transfer of control). In addition to applying these general requirements, an entity must also meet the criteria to be able to demonstrate control has passed for a bill-and-hold arrangement. *[IFRS 15.B79-82]*. See Chapter 30 at 7 for more information.

IFRS 15 also states that even if an entity recognises revenue for the sale of a product on a bill-and-hold basis, it will also need to consider whether it has remaining performance obligations (e.g. for custodial services or security services) to which the entity will need to allocate a portion of the transaction price. *[IFRS 15.B82]*. See Chapter 30 at 7 for more information.

12.3 Inventory exchanges with the same counterparty

Mining companies and oil and gas companies may exchange inventory with other entities in the same line of business, which is often referred to as 'loans/borrows'. This can occur with commodities such as oil, uranium, coal or certain concentrates, for which suppliers exchange or swap inventories in various locations to supplement current production, to facilitate more efficient management of capacity and/or to help achieve lower transportation costs.

IFRS 15 scopes out certain non-monetary 'exchanges between entities in the same line of business to facilitate sales to customers or potential customers'. *[IFRS 15.5(d)]*. The legacy scope exclusion in IAS 18 – *Revenue* – was different. IAS 18 used the words 'similar in nature and value' and did not focus on the intention of the exchange. *[IAS 18.12]*. Therefore, some transactions that were treated as exchanges of dissimilar goods (and, hence, revenue-generating under IAS 18) may now not be considered to be revenue-generating if the entities are in the same line of business and the exchange is intended to facilitate sales to customers or potential customers. Conversely, some exchanges of similar items (and, therefore, excluded from IAS 18) may not be intended to facilitate sales to customers or potential customers and would, therefore, be within the scope of IFRS 15.

Accounting for exchanges of inventories requires a degree of judgement particularly:

- interpreting what 'same line of business' means and how broadly or narrowly this should be interpreted;
- whether the exchange is to facilitate sales to customers or potential customers; and
- whether the transaction is non-monetary and the impact of settling net in cash may have on this assessment.

Furthermore, while the scope section of IFRS 15 makes it clear that such inventory exchanges do not result in revenue generation, it does not provide application guidance on how these transactions between the two parties would be accounted for and no other specific requirements exist within IFRS. Despite this, any receivable or payable balance would not entirely meet the definition of inventory in IAS 2 but instead would likely be a non-monetary receivable or payable. The product receivable or payable would normally be recorded at cost within current assets or liabilities. However, given the lack of clarity, diversity in accounting practice may continue.

12.4 Overlift and underlift (oil and gas)

In jointly owned oil and gas operations, it is often not practical for each participant to take in kind or to sell its exact share of production during a period. In most periods, some participants in the jointly owned operations will be in an overlift position (i.e. they have taken more product than their proportionate entitlement) while other participants may be in an underlift position (i.e. they have taken less product than their proportionate entitlement).

Generally, costs are invoiced to the participants in a joint operation in proportion to their equity interest, creating a mismatch between the proportion of revenue lifted and sold and the proportion of costs borne.

Imbalances between volumes for which production costs are recognised and volumes sold (for which revenue is recognised in accordance with IFRS 15) may be settled between/among joint operation participants either in cash or by physical settlement.

The accounting may be different depending on the specific terms of the agreement. Such lifting imbalances are usually settled in one of three ways:[115]

- in future periods the owner in an underlift position may sell or take product in excess of their normal entitlement, while the owner in an overlift position will sell or take less product than the normal entitlement;
- cash balancing may be used, whereby the overlift party will make a cash payment to the underlift party for the value of the imbalance volume; or
- if the co-owners have joint ownership interests in other properties, they may agree to offset balances in the two properties to the extent possible.

12.4.1 Accounting for imbalances in revenue under IFRS 15

Revenue from contracts with customers that falls within the scope of IFRS 15 should be treated according to the requirements of IFRS 15. Sales of product by a participant in a joint operation to external customers are within the scope of IFRS 15 and should be recognised when the sales actually occur i.e. when the entity satisfies its performance obligation by transferring a promised good or service (i.e. an asset) to a customer. An asset is transferred when (or as) the customer obtains control of that asset. *[IFRS 15.31]*.

Transactions with other joint operation participants are unlikely to fall within the scope of IFRS 15 and, hence, may not form part of revenue from contracts with customers. *[IFRS 15.5(d), 6]*. This is consistent with paragraphs BC52-BC56 of IFRS 15, the March 2015 IFRIC agenda decision on IFRS 11 ('Recognition of revenue by a joint venture'), and IFRS 11 which states that 'A joint operator shall account for the assets, liabilities, revenues and expenses relating to its interest in a joint operation in accordance with the IFRSs applicable to the particular assets, liabilities, revenues and expenses'. *[IFRS 11.21, IFRS 15.BC52-BC56]*.

This was confirmed in the IFRIC agenda decision issued in March 2019 ('Sale of Output to an Operator'). The Committee concluded that 'in the fact pattern described in the request, the joint operator recognises revenue that depicts only the transfer of output to its customers in each reporting period, i.e. revenue recognised applying IFRS 15. This means, for example, the joint operator does not recognise revenue for the output to which it is entitled but which it has not received from the joint operation and sold. The Committee concluded that the principles and requirements in IFRS Standards provide an adequate basis for a joint operator to determine its revenue from the sale of its share of output arising from a joint operation as described in the request. Consequently, the Committee decided not to add this matter to its standard-setting agenda'.[116]

Accordingly, where a participant in a joint operation has contractual arrangements with customers which do fall within the scope of IFRS 15, it should record revenue from those contracts under IFRS 15, that is, based on its actual sales to customers in that period. No adjustments should be recorded in revenue to account for any variance between the actual share of production volumes sold to date and the share of production which the party has been entitled to sell to date.

Revenue from contracts with customers recognised in accordance with IFRS 15 is a subset of total revenue recognised by an entity, and should be presented separately as required by IFRS 15. *[IFRS 15.113(a)]*. However, recording adjustments through other revenue in order to align total revenue earned (i.e. revenue from contracts with customers under IFRS 15 plus other revenue) with the share of production the joint operation participant is entitled to in the period, would not be appropriate. Recording the amounts earned in one period in other revenue and, subsequently, recording them as revenue under IFRS 15 in a future period (or *vice versa*), would result in recycling of revenue earned between two line items in profit or loss. Furthermore, in periods where the adjustment being recorded through other revenue is to reduce total revenue recognised in the period, this would result in a debit entry or 'negative revenue' being disclosed in other revenue, which is not appropriate.

12.4.2 Consideration of cost of goods sold where revenue is recognised in accordance with IFRS 15

If revenue is recognised based on actual sales to customers in the period, and costs are based on invoiced costs to the participants in a joint operation in proportion to their equity interest, there will be a mismatch between the proportion of revenue lifted and sold and the proportion of costs borne.

Entities may determine that is it appropriate to adjust production costs to align volumes for which production costs are recognised with volumes sold (for which revenue has been recognised in accordance with IFRS 15). The accounting for the adjustments to cost of goods sold will depend on whether the imbalances are settled between/among joint operation participants in cash or by physical settlement, as well as whether the joint operation is in an overlift or underlift position.

In the case of physical settlement, an overlift participant would recognise a liability for future expenses by way of future production costs that are not matched by corresponding future revenues. This overlift liability meets the definition of a provision under IAS 37, as the timing and amount of the settlement are uncertain. In applying IAS 37, the amount recognised as a provision should be 'the best estimate of the expenditure required to settle the present obligation at the end of the reporting period', *[IAS 37.36]*, which is 'the amount that an entity would rationally pay to settle the obligation at the end of the reporting period or to transfer it to a third party at that time'. *[IAS 37.37]*.

The overlift liability is recorded at the market value or cost of the production imbalance, depending on whether the overlift liability is considered to represent: i) a provision for production costs attributable to the volumes sold in excess of currency entitlement (which would likely be recorded at cost); or, ii) an obligation for physical delivery of petroleum product (taken out of the entity's future entitlements) for which fair value measurement may be more appropriate.

Conversely, an underlift participant may recognise an underlift asset depending on whether the underlift participant considers they have: i) a right equivalent to a prepaid commodity purchase; or ii) a right to additional physical inventory, and therefore, applies IAS 2 by analogy. Consistent with IAS 2, an underlift asset would be measured at the lower of cost or net realisable value, *[IAS 2.9]*, or otherwise at net realisable value, if there is a well-established industry practice. *[IAS 2.3(a)]*.

If an overlift or underlift adjustment is recorded in cost of goods sold at fair value, this will result in the joint operator's gross margin reflecting the gross margin that would be earned based on its entitlement interest. If an adjustment were recorded through cost of goods sold at cost, the gross margin shown would reflect the gross margin attributed to the volumes actually sold to customers.

In some instances, not accounting for the effects of imbalances has been justified on the grounds that operating costs for the period should be expensed as incurred because they relate to the period's production activity and not to the revenues recognised.[117]

In the case of cash balancing, the underlift asset or overlift liability meets the definition of a financial asset or financial liability respectively, in accordance with IAS 32 and therefore, should be accounted for in accordance with IFRS 9. The initial recognition of that financial asset or financial liability would be at fair value. Depending on the designation of the financial asset or financial liability, subsequent measurement would be either at amortised cost or fair value.

Extract 43.21 below sets out Equinor ASA's disclosure of its accounting for revenues relating to oil and natural gas properties in which the group has an interest with other companies.

> **Extract 43.21: Equinor ASA (2019)**
> Notes to the Consolidated financial statements [extract]
> 2. Significant accounting policies [extract]
> **Revenue from contracts with customers** [extract]
> Revenues from the production of oil and gas properties in which Equinor shares an interest with other companies are recognized on the basis of volumes lifted and sold to customers during the period (the sales method). Where Equinor has lifted and sold more than the ownership interest, an accrual is recognized for the cost of the overlift. Where Equinor has lifted and sold less than the ownership interest, costs are deferred for the underlift.

12.4.3 Facility imbalances

Imbalances that are similar to overlifts and underlifts can also arise on facilities such as pipelines when a venturer delivers more or less product into a pipeline than it takes out in the same period. The resulting accounting issues arising are similar to those concerning overlifts and underlifts.

12.5 Production sharing contracts/arrangements (PSCs)

These arrangements are discussed more generally at 5.3 above. It is necessary to consider whether such contracts are within the scope of IFRS 15. That is, whether the relationship between the government entity and the contracting enterprise (i.e. the mining company or oil and gas company) represents one between a customer and a supplier. IFRS 15 defines a customer as 'a party that has contracted with an entity to obtain goods or services that are an output of the entity's ordinary activities in exchange for consideration'. See Chapter 27 at 3.3 and 3.4 for details. *[IFRS 15 Appendix A]*.

There are no specific requirements within IFRS governing the accounting for PSCs, which has resulted in accounting approaches that have evolved over time. These contracts are generally considered to be more akin to working interest relationships than pure services contracts. This is because the contracting enterprise assumes risks associated with performing the exploration, development and production activities and receives a share (and often a greater share) of future production as specified in the contract. When an entity determines it has an interest in the mineral rights themselves, revenue is recognised only when the mining company or oil and gas company receives its share of the extracted minerals under the PSC and sells those volumes to third-party customers. In other arrangements, the entity's share of production is considered a fee for services (e.g. construction, development and/or operating services) which is recognised as the services are rendered to the national government entity.

IFRS 15 notes that, in certain transactions, while there may be payments between parties in return for what appears to be goods or services of the entity, a counterparty may not always be a 'customer' of the entity. Instead, the counterparty may be a collaborator or partner that shares the results from the activity or process (such as developing an asset in a collaboration arrangement) rather than to obtain the output of the entity's ordinary activities. Generally, contracts with collaborators or partners are not within the scope of the standard, except as discussed below. *[IFRS 15.6].*

The IASB decided not to provide additional application guidance for determining whether certain revenue generating collaborative arrangements are in the scope of the standard. In the Basis for Conclusions to IFRS 15, it explains that it would not be possible to provide application guidance that applies to all collaborative arrangements. *[IFRS 15.BC54].*

In determining whether the contract between a government entity and a contracting enterprise is within the scope of the standard, an entity must look to the definition of a customer and what constitutes its 'ordinary activities' and there should also be a transfer of control of a good or service to the customer (if there is one). It may be that certain parts of the PSC relationship involve the contracting enterprise and the national government entity acting as collaborators (and, hence, that part of the arrangement would be outside the scope of IFRS 15), while for other parts of the arrangement the two parties may act as supplier and customer. The latter will be within the scope of IFRS 15 and an analysis of the impact of the requirements will be necessary. See Chapter 27 at 3.3.

12.6 Forward-selling contracts to finance development

Mineral and oil and gas exploration and development are highly capital intensive businesses and different financing methods have arisen. At times, obtaining financing for these major projects may be difficult, particularly if equity markets are tight and loan financing is difficult to obtain. Some increasingly common structured transactions continue to emerge which involve the owner of the mineral interests, or oil and gas interests, i.e. a mining entity or oil and gas entity (the producer), selling a specified volume of future production from a specified property/field to a third party 'investor' for cash. Such arrangements can be referred to as streaming arrangements.

A common example in the mining sector might be a precious metal streaming arrangement where a bulk commodity producer (e.g. a copper producer who has a mine that also produces precious metals as a by-product) enters into an arrangement with a streaming company (the investor). Here the producer receives an upfront cash payment and (usually) an ongoing predetermined per ounce payment for part or all of the by-product precious metal (the commodity) production – ordinarily gold and/or silver, which is traded on an active market. By entering into these contracts, the mining entity is able to access funding by monetising the non-core precious metal, while the investor receives the future production of precious metals without having to invest directly in, or operate, the mine.

We also note that similar types of arrangements are increasingly being used in the oil and gas sector as a source of funding.

These arrangements can take many forms and accounting for such arrangements can be highly complex. In many situations there is no specific guidance for accounting for these types of arrangements under IFRS.

12.6.1 Accounting by the producer

Generally, the accounting for these arrangements by the producer could be one of the following:

- *a financial liability* (i.e. debt) in accordance with IFRS 9. A key factor in determining whether the contract is a financial liability is whether the contract establishes an unavoidable contractual obligation for the producer to make payments in cash or another financial asset, *[IAS 32.11, IAS 32.16(a)]*, that is, whether the arrangement has more of the characteristics of debt;
- *a sale of a mineral interest* (under IAS 16 or IAS 38) *and a contract to provide services such as extraction, refining,* etc., in accordance with IFRS 15. This would occur when the arrangement effectively transfers control over a portion of the mine from the producer to the investor and there is an obligation to provide future extraction services; or
- *a commodity contract*, which is outside the scope of IFRS 9 and in the scope of IFRS 15. This would only occur when the arrangement is an executory contract to deliver an expected amount of the commodity in the future to the investor from the producer's own operation (i.e. it meets the 'own-use' exemption). If the commodity contract does not meet the own-use exemption, the arrangement will be in scope of IFRS 9.

Whether the arrangement constitutes debt, a sale of mineral interest and a contract to provide services or a forward sale of a commodity, is subject to significant judgement.

In each classification, the producer must assess and determine whether the arrangement contains separable embedded derivatives. That is, the producer would need to determine whether the arrangement contains a component or terms which had the effect that some of the cash flows of the combined instrument (being the arrangement) vary in a similar way to a stand-alone derivative (i.e. an embedded derivative).

For both the producer and the investor, each arrangement will have very specific facts and circumstances that will need to be understood and assessed, as different accounting treatments may apply in different circumstances. Understanding the economic motivations and outcomes for both the producer and the investor and the substance of the arrangement are necessary to ensure a robust and balanced accounting conclusion can be reached. In many cases, the route to determining the classification will be a non-linear and iterative process.

The potential implications of IFRS 15 need to be considered for transactions which are considered to be either a sale of a mineral interest with a contract to provide services or a commodity contract.

12.6.1.A Sale of a mineral interest with a contract to provide services

When the nature of the arrangement indicates that the investor's investment is more akin to an equity interest in the project (rather than debt), this may indicate that the producer has essentially sold an interest in a property to the investor in return for the advance. In such a situation, the arrangement would likely be considered (fully or partially) as a sale of a mineral interest. In some instances, some of the upfront payment may also relate to an extraction services contract representing the producer's obligation to extract the investor's share of the future production.

To apply this accounting, an entity would have to be able to demonstrate that the criteria in relation to the sale of an asset in IAS 16 and IAS 38 have been satisfied; that the investor bears the risks and economic benefits of ownership related to the output and control over a portion of the property (a mineral interest); and agrees to pay for a portion or all of the production costs of extracting and/or refining its new mineral interest to the producer. Some of the relevant risks include:

- production risk (which party bears the risk the project will be unable to produce output or will have a production outage);
- resource risk (which party bears the risk the project has insufficient reserves to repay the investor); and
- price risk (which party bears the risk the price of the output will fluctuate).

If this is possible, IFRS 15 would indicate that part of this arrangement is outside scope of IFRS 15 and will need to be accounted for in accordance with the applicable IFRS. Consequently, the amount paid by the investor will need to be allocated between the sale of the mineral interest and the provision of future extraction services.

For the portion allocated to the sale of the mineral interest, the issues discussed at 12.9.3 below will need to be considered.

For the portion allocated to the future extraction services, the following provisions of IFRS 15 will need to be considered:

- the identification of performance obligations, i.e. future extraction services (see Chapter 28 at 3);
- the determination of the transaction price and whether it contains a significant financing component (see Chapter 29 at 2 and 2.5);
- the allocation of the transaction price to those performance obligations and how subsequent changes to the transaction price should be allocated (see Chapter 29 at 3 and 3.5); and
- whether the performance obligations are satisfied over time or at a point in time (see Chapter 30 at 2 and 4).

Given the period over which these extraction services are to be provided may extend for quite some time into the future and/or may change (particularly if they relate to the remaining life of the mine or field), this may lead to some complexity in the accounting. A reasonable degree of uncertainty still exists as to how these issues should be addressed and how they will impact such arrangements.

12.6.1.B   Commodity contract – forward sale of future production

A producer and an investor may agree to enter such an arrangement where both parties have an expectation of the amount of the commodity to be delivered under the contract at inception (for example, based on the reserves) and that there may or may not be additional resources. On the basis that the reserves will be delivered under the contract (and the contract cannot be net settled in cash), the mining company or oil and gas company has effectively pre-sold its future production and the investor has made an upfront payment/advance which would be considered a deposit for some or all of the commodity volumes to be delivered at a future date.

In this case, the arrangement is a commodity contract that falls outside the scope of IFRS 9, but only if the contract will always be settled through the physical delivery of the commodity which has been extracted by the producer as part of its own operations (i.e. it meets the 'own-use exemption' discussed at 13.1 below). *[IAS 32.8, IFRS 9.2.4]*.

To determine if the own-use exemption applies and continues to apply, the key tests are whether the contract will always be settled through the physical delivery of a commodity (that is, not in cash and would not be considered to be capable of net settlement in cash), and that the commodity will always be extracted by the producer as part of its own operations. This means that there is no prospect of the producer settling part, or the entire advance, by delivering a different commodity or purchasing the commodity on the open market or from a third party.

The issues to be considered under IFRS 15 will be the same as those relating to the provision of future extraction services (see 12.6.1.A above).

Extract 43.22 below sets out Barrick's assessment of its streaming arrangements under IFRS 15.

Extract 43.22: Barrick Gold Corporation (2019)

Notes to Consolidated Financial Statements [extract]

2. Significant Accounting Policies [extract]

f) Revenue Recognition [extract]

Streaming Arrangements

As the deferred revenue on streaming arrangements is considered variable consideration, an adjustment is made to the transaction price per unit each time there is a change in the underlying production profile of a mine (typically in the fourth quarter of each year). The change in the transaction price per unit results in a cumulative catch-up adjustment to revenue in the period in which the change is made, reflecting the new production profile expected to be delivered under the streaming agreement. A corresponding cumulative catch-up adjustment is made to accretion expense, reflecting the impact of the change in the deferred revenue balance.

3. Critical Judgments, Estimates, Assumptions and Risks [extract]

Streaming Transactions [extract]

The upfront cash deposit received from Royal Gold on the gold and silver streaming transaction for production linked to Barrick's 60% interest in the Pueblo Viejo mine has been accounted for as deferred revenue since we have determined that it is not a derivative as it will be satisfied through the delivery of non-financial items (i.e., gold and silver) rather than cash or financial assets. It is our intention to settle the obligations under the streaming arrangement through our own production and if we were to fail to settle the obligations with Royal Gold through our own production, this would lead to the streaming arrangement becoming a derivative. This would cause a change to the accounting treatment, resulting in the revaluation of the fair value of the agreement through profit and loss on a recurring basis.

12.6.2 Accounting by the investor

From the investor's perspective, where the accounting becomes more complex is where the investor has acquired a right to receive cash, some quantity or value of a particular commodity, or the option to choose one or the other, or some combination of both.

From the investor's perspective, there are generally four common accounting outcomes that are frequently observed:

- acquisition of a mineral interest (under the principles of IAS 16 or IAS 38) and potentially a prepayment in relation to future services such as extraction, refining, etc., – this would occur when the arrangement effectively transfers control over a portion of the mine/field from the producer to the investor and there is a right to receive future extraction services;
- commodity contract, which is outside the scope of IFRS 9 and in the scope of IAS 38 – this would only occur when the arrangement is an executory contract to receive an expected amount of the commodity in the future from the producer and its meets the 'own-use' exemption for the investor. If the commodity contract does not meet the own-use exemption, the arrangement will be in scope of IFRS 9;
- a financial asset (i.e. a receivable or some sort of other financial asset) in accordance with IFRS 9 – this would occur when the arrangement establishes a contractual right to receive cash or another financial asset in the future; or
- a mix of all three.

The accounting implications of each for the investor, from a profit or loss perspective, can be significantly different.

12.7 Trading activities

Many mining and metals and oil and gas companies engage in trading activities (e.g. crude oil cargos or coal) and they may either take delivery of the product or resell it without taking delivery. Even when an entity takes physical delivery and becomes the legal owner of a commodity, it may still only be as part of its trading activities. Such transactions do not fall within the normal purchase and sales exemption (see 13.1 below) when 'for similar contracts, the entity has a practice of taking delivery of the underlying and selling it within a short period after delivery for the purpose of generating a profit from short-term fluctuations in price or dealer's margin'. *[IAS 32.9(c), IFRS 9.2.6(c)]*. Where the entity has a practice of settling similar physical commodity-based contracts net in cash, these contracts also do not fall within the normal purchase and sales exemption. *[IAS 32.9(b), IFRS 9.2.6(b)]*. In that case, the purchase and sales contracts should be accounted for as derivatives within the scope of IFRS 9.

12.8 Embedded derivatives in commodity arrangements

IFRS 15 states that if a contract is partially within scope of this standard and partially in the scope of another standard, entities will first apply the separation and measurement requirements of the other standard(s). *[IFRS 15.7]*. Therefore, to the extent that there is an embedded derivative contained within a revenue contract, e.g. provisional pricing mechanisms (discussed in more detail at 12.8.1 below), diesel price linkage in a crude oil contract, or oil price linkage in a gas sales contract, these will continue to be assessed and accounted for in accordance with IFRS 9.

Under IFRS 9, if a feature of a revenue contract is considered to be an embedded derivative that is not closely related to a non-financial host contract; the embedded derivative is required to be separated from the non-financial host contract. If it is closely related, it is not required to be separated. In the event that the embedded derivative is considered to be closely related to the non-financial host contract, once transfer of control of the product has occurred and the entity has an unconditional right to receive cash and the host contract becomes a financial asset (i.e. a receivable), the accounting changes.

Under IFRS 9, embedded derivatives are not separated from a host financial receivable. Instead, the receivable will fail the contractual cash flows test. As a consequence, the whole receivable will have to be subsequently measured at fair value through profit or loss from the date of recognition of that receivable. See Chapter 48 at 2 for more information on the classification of financial assets under IFRS 9.

IFRS 15 does not impact the treatment of embedded derivatives under IFRS 9. Revenue within the scope of IFRS 15 will be recognised when control passes to the customer and will be measured at the amount to which the entity expects to be entitled. Any subsequent fair value movements in the receivable would be recognised in profit or loss. However, as a result of the specific disclosure requirements of IFRS 15, these need to be presented separately from IFRS 15 revenue. This is discussed in relation to provisionally priced sales at 12.8.1 below.

12.8.1 Provisionally priced sales contracts

Sales contracts for certain commodities (e.g. copper and oil) often provide for provisional pricing at the time of shipment. The final sales price is often based on the average quoted market prices during a subsequent period (the 'quotational period' or 'QP'), the price on a fixed date after delivery or the amount subsequently realised by another party (e.g. the smelter or refiner, net of tolling charges).

As discussed at 13.2.2 below these QP pricing exposures may meet the definition of an embedded derivative under IFRS 9. The treatment of embedded derivatives in commodity contracts is discussed in more detail at 12.8 above.

From a revenue recognition perspective, under IFRS 15, revenue will be recognised when control passes to the customer and will be measured at the amount to which the entity expects to be entitled, being the estimate of the price expected to be received at the end of the QP, i.e. the forward price. *[IFRS 15.47]*.

If shipping is considered to be a separate performance obligation, some of the revenue may need to be allocated between the commodity and shipping services. See 12.12 below for further discussion.

With respect to the presentation of any fair value movements in the receivable from the date of sale, entities have often presented the QP movements as part of revenue. IFRS 15 does not address the presentation of fair value movements in receivables. Likewise, IFRS 9 does not specify where such movements should be presented in profit or loss.

IFRS 15 only addresses a subset of total revenue (i.e. revenue from contracts with customers). That is, transactions outside the scope of IFRS 15 might result in the recognition of revenue. However, while IFRS 15 does not specifically prohibit fair value movements of a receivable from being described as revenue, it does specifically require an entity to disclose revenue from contracts with customers separately from its other sources of revenue, either in the statement of comprehensive income or in the notes. *[IFRS 15.113]*. Therefore, entities will need to track these separately.

The extracts below set out the accounting policy for provisionally priced sales for Rio Tinto and Anglo American under IFRS 15.

> *Extract 43.23: Rio Tinto plc (2019)*
> **Notes to the 2019 financial statements** [extract]
> **1. Principal accounting policies** [extract]
> **(c) Sales revenue** [extract]
> *Recognition and measurement* [extract]
> Certain of the Group's products may be provisionally priced at the date revenue is recognised; however, substantially all iron ore and aluminium sales are reflected at final prices in the results for the period. The final selling price for all provisionally priced products is based on the price for the quotational period stipulated in the contract. Final prices for copper concentrate are normally determined between 30 - 180 days after delivery to the customer. The change in value of the provisionally priced receivable is based on relevant forward market prices and is included in sales revenue.
>
> *Presentation and disclosures* [extract]
> Consolidated sales revenue as reported in the income statement comprises sales to third parties. Certain of the Group's products may be provisionally priced at the date revenue is recognised. Sales revenue includes revenue from contracts with customers, which is accounted for under IFRS 15 "Revenue from Contracts with Customers" and subsequent movements in provisionally priced receivables which are accounted for under IFRS 9 "Financial Instruments". A breakdown of sales revenue between these two amounts is disclosed in the product analysis in note 3 and further detail on provisional pricing in note 3. Sales revenue includes revenue from movements in provisionally priced receivables, consistent with the treatment in prior periods.

> *Extract 43.24: Anglo American plc (2019)*
> **NOTES TO THE FINANCIAL STATEMENTS** [extract]
> **OTHER ITEMS** [extract]
> **38. ACCOUNTING POLICIES continued** [extract]
> **C. FINANCIAL PERFORMANCE** [extract]
> **Revenue recognition** [extract]
> Sales of metal concentrate are stated at their invoiced amount which is net of treatment and refining charges. Sales of certain commodities are provisionally priced such that the price is not settled until a predetermined future date and is based on the market price at that time. These sales are marked to market at each reporting date using the forward price for the period equivalent to that outlined in the contract. Revenue on provisionally priced sales is recognised at the forward market price when control passes to the customer and is classified as revenue from contracts with customers. Subsequent mark-to-market adjustments are recognised in revenue from other sources.

12.9 Royalty income

Entities in the extractive industries sometimes enter into arrangements whereby they may receive some form of royalty income. This may arise when they sell some or all their interest in a mining project or oil and gas project and in return agree to accept a future royalty amount which may be based on production and/or payable in cash or in kind. Alternatively, the acquiring entity may pay a net profit interest, that is, a percentage of the net profit (calculated using an agreed formula) generated by the interest sold. There may be other types of arrangements where the mining company or oil and gas company grants another entity a right in return for other types of payments – for example streaming arrangement (see 12.6 above for more detail).

Accounting for mineral rights and mineral reserves is scoped out of a number of standards including IAS 16, IAS 38 and IFRS 16. Consequently, diverse practice has emerged in the accounting for such transactions.

With respect to these royalty arrangements, these can take a number of different forms and different accounting approaches have emerged. These may include:

- *Future receipt is solely dependent on production:* For some arrangements, the future royalty stream is solely dependent on future production, such that, if there is no future production, no royalty income will be received.

  In some instances, the inflows (i.e. the royalty income) and the associated royalty receivable, are only recognised once the related mineral is extracted and the royalty is due, rather than when the interest in the project is originally sold. When such royalty receipts occur, they are often disclosed as either revenue or other income.

  An alternate approach observed is that the sale of the mineral interest is considered to create a contractual right to receive these royalty amounts (i.e. a contractual right to receive cash). Therefore, such royalty amounts (and, hence, the related receivable) would be recognised at the date of disposal and included in the calculation of the gain or loss on sale. Further divergence exists as to how subsequent movements in the receivable are recognised in profit or loss (i.e. as revenue or as other gains/losses).

  There is more specific guidance when the royalty receivable represents contingent consideration in the sale of a business (see Chapter 45 at 3.7.1.B).

- *Minimum additional amount due, but timing linked to production:* In other arrangements, the entity may be entitled to receive a certain additional (minimum) amount of cash regardless of the level of production, but the timing of receipt is linked to future production. This type of arrangement is considered to establish a contractual right to receive cash at the point when the disposal transaction occurs. Therefore, an entity recognises a receivable and the associated income when the arrangement is entered into and this will form part of the gain or loss on sale of the mineral interest.

The impact of IFRS 15 will depend on whether the royalty arrangement is considered to arise from a collaborative arrangement, in the context of a supplier-customer relationship, or from the sale of a non-financial asset.

12.9.1 Royalty arrangements with collaborative partners

As discussed at 12.5 above, IFRS 15 only addresses contracts with customers for goods or services provided in the ordinary course of an entity's business, it does not apply to arrangements between collaborative partners. *[IFRS 15.6]*. Where royalties are received by an entity as part of such an arrangement, they will generally not be in the scope of IFRS 15, unless the collaborator or partner meets the definition of a customer for some, or all, aspects of the arrangement. See 12.9.2 below.

12.9.2 Royalty arrangements with customers

IFRS 15 does not scope out revenue from the extraction of minerals. Therefore, regardless of the type of product being sold, if the counterparty to the contract is determined to be a customer, then the contract will be in scope of IFRS 15.

If a royalty arrangement is considered to be a supplier-customer relationship (and, hence, is in scope), mining companies and oil and gas companies may face a number of challenges in applying IFRS 15 to these arrangements. These may include identifying the performance obligations, determining the transaction price (e.g. if consideration is variable and dependent upon actions by the customer, which would be the case for the future extraction of minerals), applying the constraint on variable consideration, and reallocating the transaction price when and if there is a change in the transaction price. See Chapter 29 for more details on these requirements.

When considering the accounting for such royalties, IFRS 15 contains specific requirements that apply to licences of intellectual property, which may appear similar to some types of royalty arrangements in extractives industries. However, it is important to note that the IFRS 15 requirements only apply to licences of intellectual property and not all sales-based or usage-based royalties. So, the general requirements applicable to variable consideration, including those relating to the constraint, will need to be considered (see Chapter 29 at 2.2 for further discussion).

12.9.3 Royalty arrangements and the sale of non-financial items

If the royalty arrangement is not considered to relate to a contract with a customer nor to a collaborative arrangement, but instead, relates to the sale of a non-financial asset (e.g. an interest in a mining project or oil and gas project), IFRS 15 may still impact these arrangements. This is because the requirements for the recognition and measurement of a gain or loss on the transfer of some non-financial assets that are not the output of an entity's ordinary operations (e.g. property, plant and equipment in the scope of IAS 16), refer to the requirements of IFRS 15 (see Chapter 27 at 4.3 for more detail).

Specifically, an entity needs to:

- determine the date of disposal and, therefore, the date of derecognition (i.e. the date control transfers to the acquirer) (see Chapter 30 at 4 for more detail);
- measure the consideration to be included in the calculation of the gain or loss arising from disposal including any variable consideration requirements (see Chapter 29 at 2 for more detail); and
- recognise any subsequent changes to the estimated amount of consideration (see Chapter 29 at 2.9 for more detail).

Mineral rights and mineral reserves (and, hence, the associated capitalised costs) are outside the scope of both IAS 16 and IAS 38. However, in selecting an accounting policy for the disposal of these assets, in practice, most entities look to the principles of these two standards. Therefore, these requirements are likely to be applied by analogy to arrangements in which an entity sells all (or part) of its mining properties or oil and gas properties and some of the consideration comprises a royalty-based component.

There is also a lack of clarity as to how to apply the requirements of IFRS 15 to such arrangements where, by virtue of the royalty rights, the vendor is considered to have retained an interest in the mineral property. This may impact what is recognised or derecognised from the balance sheet in terms of mineral assets and/or financial assets, and also the gain/loss that is recognised in profit or loss.

There is more specific guidance on when the royalty receivable represents contingent consideration in the sale of a business (see Chapter 45 at 3.7.1.B).

12.10 Modifications to commodity-based contracts

Mining entities and oil and gas entities frequently enter into long-term arrangements for the sale, transportation or processing of commodities. Over time, these contractual arrangements may be amended to effect changes in tenure, volume, price, or delivery point, for example. This may take the form of amendments, new tranches under existing agreements, or, new contractual arrangements. IFRS 15 contains requirements on how to account for changes to a contract depending on whether the change is considered to be a contract modification, a new contract, or a combination of both. Further guidance on contract modifications is set out in Chapter 28 at 2.4.

12.11 Principal versus agent considerations in commodity-based contracts

When identifying performance obligations, there may be some arrangements for which an entity needs to determine whether it is acting as principal or agent. This will be important as it affects the amount of revenue the entity recognises. That is, when the entity is the principal in the arrangement, the revenue recognised is the gross amount to which the entity expects to be entitled. When the entity is the agent, the revenue recognised is the net amount the entity is entitled to retain in return for its services as the agent. The entity's fee or commission may be the net amount of consideration that the entity retains after paying the other party the consideration received in exchange for the goods or services to be provided by that party. The critical factor to consider here is whether the entity has control of the good or service before transferring on to its customer. See Chapter 28 at 3.4 for more information on the principal versus agent indicators.

12.11.1 Relationships with joint arrangement partners

It is not uncommon for valid vendor-customer relationships to exist alongside joint arrangement/collaborator contracts such as joint operating agreements or production sharing contracts. The manager/lead operator of a joint arrangement may have a vendor-customer contract to purchase volumes produced by the non-operating parties. The manager/lead operator would then on sell the product to third parties, and depending on the specific contract terms, could be acting as the principal in the onward sale, or as agent that is selling on behalf of the other joint arrangement partners.

Similarly, an entity with a gathering station or processing plant could purchase commodities from other parties with tenements or fields in the same region at the point of entry into the plant. Both the seller and purchaser would have to consider whether the purchaser is a principal or an agent in the onward sale to the third-party customer and account for the revenue accordingly.

> *Extract 43.25: Equinor ASA (2019)*
> Notes to the Consolidated financial statements [extract]
> 2 Significant accounting policies [extract]
> Critical accounting judgements and key sources of estimation uncertainty [extract]
> Critical judgements in applying accounting policies [extract]
> Revenue recognition – gross versus net presentation of traded SDFI volumes of oil and gas production
>
> As described under Transactions with the Norwegian State above, Equinor markets and sells the Norwegian State's share of oil and gas production from the NCS. Equinor includes the costs of purchase and proceeds from the sale of the SDFI oil production in purchases [net of inventory variation] and revenues from contracts with customers, respectively. In making the judgement, Equinor has considered whether it controls the State originated crude oil volumes prior to onwards sales to third party customers. Equinor directs the use of the volumes, and although certain benefits from the sales subsequently flow to the State, Equinor purchases the crude oil volumes from the State and obtains substantially all the remaining benefits. On that basis, Equinor has concluded that it acts as principal in these sales.
>
> Equinor sells, in its own name, but for the Norwegian State's account and risk, the State's production of natural gas. These gas sales, and related expenditures refunded by the State, are shown net in Equinor's Consolidated financial statements. In making the judgement, Equinor concluded that ownership of the gas had not been transferred from the SDFI to Equinor. Although Equinor has been granted the ability to direct the use of the volumes, all the benefits from the sales of these volumes flow to the State. On that basis, Equinor is not considered the principal in the sale of the SDFI's natural gas volumes.

12.11.2 Royalty payments

As discussed at 5.7.5 above, mining companies and oil and gas companies frequently enter into a range of different royalty arrangements with owners of mineral rights (e.g. governments or private land owners) and at times, the treatment is diverse. It is unclear whether, and how, such arrangements should be accounted for under IFRS 15.

In situations where the royalty holder retains or obtains a direct interest in the underlying production, it may be that the relationship between the mining company or oil and gas company and the royalty holder is more like a collaborative arrangement (and, hence, is not within the scope of IFRS 15). See 12.5 above for further discussion.

If these royalty payments are in scope, the requirements relating to principal versus agent in IFRS 15 will be helpful in assessing how these royalty payments should be presented. Specifically, an entity will need to determine whether it obtains control of all of the underlying minerals once extracted, sells the product to its customers and then remits the proceeds to the royalty holder. If so, the mining company or oil and gas company will be considered to be acting as the principal and, hence, would recognise the full amount as revenue with any payments to the royalty holder being recognised as part of cost of goods sold (or possibly as an income tax, depending on the nature of the royalty payment – see 21 below for further discussion on determining when an arrangement is an income tax). Where the entity does not obtain control over those volumes, it may be acting as the royalty holder's agent and extracting the minerals on its behalf.

The principal versus agent assessment under IFRS 15 is discussed in more detail in Chapter 28 at 3.4 and the issue of how sales (and other similar) taxes should be accounted for are discussed in Chapter 29 at 2.1.

12.12 Shipping

Given the location of the commodities produced in the mining sector and oil and gas sector, they generally have to be shipped to the customer. Such transportation may occur by road, rail or sea. The terms associated with shipping can vary depending on the method of shipping and the contract.

When applying IFRS 15, there are a number of factors to consider in relation to shipping terms linked to customer contracts which are set out below at 12.12.1 to 12.12.2.

12.12.1 Identification of performance obligations

Subsequent to the issuance of IFRS 15, there was some debate as to whether shipping represented a separate performance obligation. The issue was raised with the joint Transition Resources Group (TRG) and was also considered by the IASB and US FASB. The US FASB amended their standard to allow US GAAP entities to elect to account for shipping and handling activities performed after the control of a good has been transferred to the customer as a fulfilment cost (i.e. an expense). Without such an accounting policy choice, a US GAAP entity that has shipping arrangements after the customer has obtained control may determine that the act of shipping is a performance obligation under the standard. The IASB did not permit a similar policy choice under IFRS 15.

Given this, when assessing customer contracts, mining companies and oil and gas companies need to consider the requirements of IFRS 15 to determine whether shipping is a separate performance obligation. It is likely that any shipping services provided to a customer after the customer obtains control over a good will represent a separate performance obligation. If this is the case, where material, the transaction price for that contract will need to be allocated to the various performance obligations including shipping. Revenue will then be recognised when the goods are delivered and when the shipping services have been provided, either at a point in time or over time.

The extracts below illustrate how Rio Tinto and Anglo American have identified shipping services in certain types of arrangements to be separate performance obligations.

> *Extract 43.26: Rio Tinto plc (2019)*
>
> Notes to the 2019 financial statements [extract]
>
> 1. Principal accounting policies [extract]
>
> (c) Sales revenue [extract]
>
> *Recognition and measurement* [extract]
>
> The Group sells a significant proportion of its products on CFR or CIF Incoterms. This means that the Group is responsible (acts as principal) for providing shipping services and, in some instances, insurance after the date at which control of goods passes to the customer at the loading port.
>
> The Group therefore has separate performance obligations for freight and insurance services that are provided solely to facilitate sale of the commodities it produces. Other Incoterms commonly used by the Group are Free on Board (FOB), where the Group has no responsibility for freight or insurance once control of the goods has passed at the loading port, and Delivered at Place (DAP) where control of the goods passes when the product is delivered to the agreed destination. For these Incoterms there is only one performance obligation, being for provision of product at the point where control passes.

> **Extract 43.27: Anglo American plc (2018)**
> Notes to the financial statements [extract]
> OTHER ITEMS [extract]
> 38. ACCOUNTING POLICIES [extract]
> A. BASIS OF PREPARATION [extract]
> Changes in accounting policies and disclosures [extract]
> IFRS 15 *Revenue from Contracts with Customers* [extract]
>
> For the Incoterms Cost, Insurance and Freight (CIF) and Cost and Freight (CFR) the seller must contract for and pay the costs and freight necessary to bring the goods to the named port of destination. Consequently, the freight service on export commodity contracts with CIF/CFR Incoterms represents a separate performance obligation as defined under the new standard, and a portion of the revenue earned under these contracts, representing the obligation to perform the freight service, is deferred and recognised over time as this obligation is fulfilled, along with the associated costs.

12.12.2 Satisfaction of performance obligations – control assessment

Under IFRS 15, an entity recognises revenue only when it satisfies a performance obligation by transferring control of a promised good or service to the customer and control may be transferred over time or at a point in time. See Chapter 30 for more information.

When assessing contracts with customers, mining companies and oil and gas companies need to carefully examine the terms of their contracts, including shipping terms, in light of the indicators of control, to assess how shipping should be accounted for.

It is also worth noting that there may be some shipping arrangements where title to the goods must pass to the carrier during transportation, but the related contract includes a clause that requires the carrier to sell the goods back to the mining company or oil and gas company at the same or another specified price. The impact of repurchase clauses is discussed at 12.14 below.

The extract below illustrates how Anglo American recognises revenue from shipping services over time.

> **Extract 43.28: Anglo American plc (2019)**
> NOTES TO THE FINANCIAL STATEMENTS [extract]
> OTHER ITEMS [extract]
> 38. ACCOUNTING POLICIES [extract]
> C. FINANCIAL PERFORMANCE [extract]
>
> Revenue recognition [extract]
>
> Revenue from services is recognised over time in line with the policy above. For contracts which contain separate performance obligations for the sale of commodities and the provision of freight services, the portion of the revenue representing the obligation to perform the freight service is deferred and recognised over time as the obligation is fulfilled, along with the associated costs. In situations where the Group is acting as an agent, amounts billed to customers are offset against the relevant costs.

12.13 Gold bullion sales (mining only)

Under IFRS 15, revenue is recognised only when the identified performance obligation is satisfied by transferring the promised good or service to the customer. A good or service is transferred when the customer obtains control of that good or service.

When mining companies sell gold bullion, there is generally a period of time (usually a matter of days) between when the bullion leaves the mine site with the security shipper and when the gold (fine metal) is credited to the metal account of the customer. In the intervening period, the gold bullion is sent to the refinery where it is refined, 'out turned', and, finally, the fine metal is transferred or credited to the customer's metal account.

At the time when the gold bullion leaves the mine site, given the way these transactions are commonly structured, the customer may not control the bullion and the IFRS 15 indicators that control has transferred may not be present. That is, the customer may not have the ability to direct the use of, or receive the benefit from, the gold bullion. Instead, these indicators may only be present when the gold bullion is actually credited to the customer's metal account.

12.14 Repurchase agreements

Some agreements in the extractive industries include repurchase provisions, either as part of a sales contract or as a separate contract, that relate to the goods in the original agreement or similar goods (e.g. tolling, processing or shipping agreements). The application guidance to IFRS 15 clarifies the types of arrangements that qualify as repurchase agreements. The repurchased asset may be the asset that was originally sold to the customer, an asset that is substantially the same as that asset or another asset of which the asset that was originally sold is a component. *[IFRS 15.B64]*.

IFRS 15 specifically notes that repurchase agreements generally come in three forms:
- an entity's obligation to repurchase the asset (a forward);
- an entity's right to repurchase the asset (a call option); or
- an entity's obligation to repurchase the asset at the customer's request (a put option). *[IFRS 15.B65]*.

Where a repurchase agreement exists, this may change whether and when revenue is recognised. See Chapter 30 at 5 for more details on repurchase agreements. See 20 below for discussion on tolling arrangements.

12.15 Multi-period commodity-based sales contracts

In the extractive industries, entities commonly enter into long-term (multi-period) commodity-based sales contracts. There are a range of different issues to be considered when applying IFRS 15.

12.15.1 Identify the contract

Judgement will need to be applied when identifying the contract for these long-term arrangements. A contract is an agreement between two or more parties that creates enforceable rights and obligations. *[IFRS 15 Appendix A]*. Entities will need to determine what the enforceable part of the contract is. For example, whether there is a specified minimum the customer must buy (e.g. in take-or-pay contracts – see 12.16 below), whether it is the overall agreement, sometimes referred to as the master services agreement, or whether it is each purchase order. See Chapter 28 at 2 and 2.1 for more details.

12.15.2 Identify the performance obligations

The next step is to identify all the promised goods or services within the contract to determine which will be treated as separate performance obligations. Chapter 28 at 3 explores in detail the requirements for determining whether a good or service is distinct, whether the transfer of a good or service represents a separate performance obligation and/or whether (and when) they need to be bundled.

During the development of IFRS 15, some respondents thought it was unclear whether a three-year service or supply contract would be accounted for as a single performance obligation or a number of performance obligations covering smaller time periods (e.g. yearly, quarterly, monthly, daily) or individual units such as ounces, tonnes or barrels.

IFRS 15 clarifies that even if a good or service is determined to be distinct, if that good or service is part of a series of goods and services that are substantially the same and have the same pattern of transfer, that series of goods or services is treated as a single performance obligation. However, before such a treatment can be applied, specific criteria must be met. See Chapter 28 at 3.2.1 for further discussion and guidance.

Given the nature of these multi-period commodity-based sales arrangements, each unit (e.g. each metric tonne (mt) of coal or each barrel of oil), would likely be a distinct good and therefore, each unit would represent a separate performance obligation that is satisfied at a point in time. Because such goods are satisfied at a point in time, they would not meet the criteria to be considered a series of distinct goods that would have to be treated as a single performance obligation.

In addition, any option for additional goods or services will need to be evaluated to determine if those goods or services should be considered a separate performance obligation. See Chapter 28 at 3.6 for further discussion.

The extract below illustrates Rio Tinto's policy for identifying performance obligations in commodity sales contracts.

> **Extract 43.29: Rio Tinto plc (2019)**
> Notes to the 2019 financial statements [extract]
> 1. Principal accounting policies [extract]
> (c) Sales revenue [extract]
> *Recognition and measurement* [extract]
> Within each sales contract, each unit of product shipped is a separate performance obligation.

The extract below illustrates Equinor's policy for identifying performance obligations, and, whether they are recognised at a point in time or over time.

> **Extract 43.30: Equinor ASA (2019)**
> Notes to the Consolidated financial statements [extract]
> 2 Significant accounting policies [extract]
> **Revenue from contracts with customers**
> Revenue from contracts with customers is recognised upon satisfaction of the performance obligations for the transfer of goods and services in each such contract. The revenue amounts that are recognised reflect the consideration to which Equinor expects to be entitled in exchange for those goods and services. Revenue from the sale of crude oil, natural gas, petroleum products and other merchandise is recognised when a customer obtains control of those products, which normally is when title passes at point of delivery, based on the contractual terms of the agreements. Each such sale normally represents a single performance obligation. In the case of natural gas, sales are completed over time in line with the delivery of the physical actual quantities.

12.15.3 Determine the transaction price

The transaction price is the amount of consideration to which an entity expects to be entitled in exchange for transferring promised goods or services to a customer, excluding amounts collected on behalf of third parties (e.g. some sales taxes). When determining the transaction price, an entity should consider the effects of all of the following:

- variable consideration (including any related constraint);
- a significant financing component (i.e. the time value of money);
- non-cash consideration; and
- consideration payable to a customer.

In many cases, the transaction price is readily determinable because the entity will receive payment at or near the same time as it transfers the promised good or service and the price is fixed for the minimum committed purchases. However, determining the transaction price may be more challenging when it is variable in amount, when payment is received at a time that is different from when the entity provides the goods or services and the effect of the time value of money is significant to the contract, or when payment is in a form other than cash. See Chapter 29 at 2 for more information.

For a fixed price contract, this step will be relatively straightforward. For variable price contracts, determining the transaction price may appear to be significantly more complex than for a fixed price contract. Many commodity sales contracts contain market-based or index-based pricing terms that create variable consideration. After separating out any parts of the transaction price that are within the scope of another standard (e.g. IFRS 9 – see 12.8 above), an entity will need determine whether it should partially or fully constrain the portion of the variable transaction price. Chapter 29 at 2.2 discusses variable consideration and, in particular, the requirements relating to the constraint.

12.15.4 Allocate the transaction price

The next step is to allocate the transaction price to the performance obligations, generally in proportion to their stand-alone selling prices (i.e. on a relative stand-alone selling price basis), with two exceptions relating to the allocation of variable consideration and discounts. See Chapter 29 at 3 for detail. With commodity-based sales contracts, there are a number of things to consider depending on whether the transaction price is variable (or contains a variable component), fixed and/or whether there is a discount. Some factors to consider with variable and fixed consideration are discussed below, while the allocation of a discount is discussed in Chapter 29 at 3.4.

12.15.4.A Variable consideration

If certain criteria are met, an entity will need to allocate variable consideration (e.g. the market- or index-based price) to one or more, but not all, performance obligations (i.e. the distinct commodities transferred in that period) or distinct goods or services in a series (where relevant), instead of using the relative stand-alone selling price allocation approach to allocate variable consideration proportionately to all performance obligations. See Chapter 29 at 3 for detail on these criteria.

12.15.4.B Fixed consideration

Entities that have fixed-price commodity-based sales contracts that call for deliveries over multiple periods need to determine the stand-alone selling price of the performance obligations to allocate the transaction price if they do not qualify to be combined into a single performance obligation as a series of distinct goods (discussed further at 12.15.2 above). IFRS 15 states that the stand-alone selling price is the price at which an entity would sell a promised good or service separately to a customer. *[IFRS 15 Appendix A]*. This is best evidenced by the observable price of a good or service when the entity sells it separately in similar circumstances and to similar customers. In other cases, it must be estimated. Estimating the stand-alone selling price may require judgement in long-term fixed-price commodity-based sales contracts, particularly when forward prices are available for the commodity being sold in a location with an active market.

If stand-alone selling prices are not directly observable, entities should consider all information (including market conditions, entity-specific factors and information about the customer or class of customer) that is reasonably available to determine the stand-alone selling price for each performance obligation. An entity may consider a number of factors in making this estimate, such as the forward curve, spot prices, expectations of market supply and demand shifts that are not represented in the forward curve or spot prices and expected transportation and storage capacity constraints that lead to premiums or discounts. Entities should maximise the use of observable inputs and apply similar estimation methods consistently in similar circumstances. The standard sets out a number of different approaches for doing this. See Chapter 29 at 3 for further discussion.

12.15.5 Recognise revenue

Finally, an entity will recognise revenue once each performance obligation is satisfied which will occur when control of the good transfers to the customer. As discussed earlier, for long-term commodity-based sales arrangement, the performance obligations are likely to be satisfied at a point in time. See Chapter 30 for more information on how to determine when a performance obligation is satisfied. The precise timing of when control transfers to a customer may be impacted by the shipping terms associated with each contract. See 12.12 above and Chapter 30 at 4.1 for further discussion on shipping.

The extract below illustrates Rio Tinto's policy for determining when control of its commodity sales passes.

> **Extract 43.31: Rio Tinto plc (2019)**
> Notes to the 2019 financial statements [extract]
> 1. Principal accounting policies [extract]
> (c) Sales revenue [extract]
>
> *Recognition and measurement* [extract]
>
> Sales revenue is recognised on individual sales when control transfers to the customer. In most instances, control passes and sales revenue is recognised when the product is delivered to the vessel or vehicle on which it will be transported once loaded, the destination port or the customer's premises. There may be circumstances when judgment is required based on the five indicators of control below.
>
> – The customer has the significant risks and rewards of ownership and has the ability to direct the use of, and obtain substantially all of the remaining benefits from, the good or service.
>
> – The customer has a present obligation to pay in accordance with the terms of the sales contract. For shipments under the Incoterms Cost, Insurance and Freight (CIF)/Carriage Paid to (CPT)/Cost and Freight (CFR) this is generally when the ship is loaded, at which time the obligation for payment is for both product and freight.
>
> – The customer has accepted the asset. Sales revenue may be subject to adjustment if the product specification does not conform to the terms specified in the sales contract but this does not impact the passing of control. Assay and specification adjustments have been immaterial historically.
>
> – The customer has legal title to the asset. The Group usually retains legal title until payment is received for credit risk purposes only.
>
> – The customer has physical possession of the asset. This indicator may be less important as the customer may obtain control of an asset prior to obtaining physical possession, which may be the case for goods in transit.

12.16 Take-or-pay contracts

A take-or-pay contract is a specific type of long-term commodity-based sales agreement between a customer and a supplier in which the pricing terms are set for a specified minimum quantity of a particular good or service. The customer must pay the minimum amount as per the contract, even if it does not take the volumes. There may also be options for additional volumes in excess of the minimum.

We discuss some of the broader accounting considerations associated with these contracts further at 19.2 below. When applying IFRS 15, in addition to the issues outlined at 12.15 above, the matters outlined below may also need to be considered.

12.16.1 Volumes paid for, but not taken

A feature unique to take-or-pay contracts is the terms relating to payments made for volumes not taken, as explained further at 19.2.1 below. The requirements of IFRS 15 may result in different accounting considerations and possibly different conclusions depending on the specific facts and circumstances of each arrangement.

12.16.1.A Payments cannot be applied to future volumes

If payments received for unused volumes cannot be applied to future volumes, the seller has no obligation to deliver the unused volumes in the future. Such amounts can generally only be recognised as revenue once the seller's obligations no longer exist (i.e. once the customer's right to volumes has expired unused).

For most take-or-pay contracts, such an assessment may only be possible at the end of a pre-defined period (e.g. the end of each contract year). This is because the customer's rights have technically not expired and the entity is still obliged to deliver volumes if the customer requests them, until the end of the stated period. This treatment is consistent with current practice.

The standard does, however, consider whether it may be possible to recognise revenue in relation to a customer's unexercised rights earlier through the requirements relating to breakage. This is discussed in more detail at 12.16.2 below.

12.16.1.B Payments can be applied to future volumes

If payments received for unused volumes can be applied to future volumes, the seller has received consideration in advance for some future unsatisfied performance obligations (i.e. the delivery of the unused volumes at some point in the future). This amount represents a contract liability.

In this situation, an entity will need to determine how such future volumes can be taken. That is, whether the timing of the future transfer of those volumes is at the discretion of the customer or is determined by the entity itself. This determination will be important as it may require an assessment of the time value of money (i.e. the existence of a significant financing component). See Chapter 29 at 2.5 for further discussion.

It will also be necessary for an entity to understand whether the customer is likely to take its unused volumes as this may require an assessment of the requirements relating to unexercised customer rights or breakage (see 12.16.2 below for further information). This could impact the amount and timing of revenue recognised.

Such determinations will need to be made in light of the contract terms and an assessment of the expected customer behaviours. For example, such an assessment may involve considering whether the make-up volumes:

- will be the first volumes taken at the start of the following period;
- can only be taken after the minimum volumes have been satisfied in the following periods; or
- can only be taken after a certain amount of time or at the end of the contract period.

12.16.2 Breakage (customers' unexercised rights)

The standard requires that when an entity receives consideration that is attributable to a customer's unexercised rights, the entity is to recognise a contract liability equal to the amount prepaid by the customer (because the entity has not yet satisfied the performance obligations to which the payment relates). However, IFRS 15 discusses the situation where, in certain industries, customers may pay for goods or services in advance, but may not ultimately exercise all of their rights to these goods or services – either because they choose not to or are unable to. IFRS 15 refers to these unexercised rights as 'breakage'. *[IFRS 15.B44-47]*.

IFRS 15 states that when an entity expects to be entitled to a breakage amount, the expected breakage will be recognised as revenue in proportion to the pattern of rights exercised by the customer. Otherwise, breakage amounts will only be recognised when the likelihood of the customer exercising its right becomes remote. See Chapter 30 at 11 for more information.

This may apply to take-or-pay contracts, for which payments are received in relation to make-up volumes and the customer's rights remain unexercised. Such breakage provisions may be applicable if:

- a customer is unable to use the make-up volumes in other areas of its own operations;
- a customer is unable to store the make-up volumes and use them after the take-or-pay contract has expired;
- a customer is unable to take delivery of the make-up volumes and sell them into the market; or
- there are limitations (physical or contractual) that prevent the customer from taking all of the make-up volumes.

For take-or-pay contracts, this may mean that an entity may be able to recognise revenue in relation to breakage amounts in an earlier period, provided it can demonstrate it is not required to constrain its estimate of breakage. This could potentially occur in the following ways:

- At contract inception, the mining entity or oil and gas entity may be able to reliably estimate the amount of breakage and would include that amount in the transaction price and allocate that to expected actual usage.
- If the entity cannot estimate an amount of breakage, it will recognise the revenue associated with those unexercised rights when it becomes remote that they will be exercised. This could occur during a make-up period after the initial term of the contract or when the deficiency make-up period expires outright (which would be consistent with current accounting).

It is also possible that, given the nature of these arrangements and the inherent uncertainty in being able to predict a customer's behaviour, it may be difficult to satisfy the requirements relating to constraint because the entity's experience may not be predictive of the outcome at this level of certainty (i.e. highly probable).

13 FINANCIAL INSTRUMENTS

13.1 Normal purchase and sales exemption

Contracts to buy or sell non-financial items generally do not meet the definition of a financial instrument because the contractual right of one party to receive a non-financial asset or service and the corresponding obligation of the other party do not establish a present right or obligation of either party to receive, deliver or exchange a financial asset. For example, contracts that provide for settlement only by the receipt or delivery of non-financial items (e.g. forward purchase of oil or a forward purchase of copper) are not financial instruments. However, some of these contracts are traded in a standardised form on organised markets in the same way as derivative financial instruments. The parties buying and selling the contract are, in effect, trading the underlying commodity. The ability to buy or sell a commodity contract for cash does not alter the characteristics of the contract and make it into a financial instrument. Nevertheless, some contracts to buy or sell non-financial items that can be settled net or by exchanging financial instruments, or in which the non-financial item is readily convertible to cash, are within the scope of the IAS 32 and IFRS 9 as if they were financial instruments. *[IAS 32.8, IAS 32.AG20]*.

IAS 32 and IFRS 9 should generally be applied to those contracts to buy or sell a non-financial item that can be settled net as if the contracts were financial instruments, whether this be in cash, another financial instrument, or by exchanging financial instruments, unless the contracts were entered into and continue to be held for the purpose of the receipt or delivery of a non-financial item in accordance with the entity's expected purchase, sale or usage requirements. *[IAS 32.8, IFRS 9.2.4]*.

There are various ways in which a contract to buy or sell a non-financial item can be settled net, including:

(a) the terms of the contract permit either party to settle it net;

(b) the ability to settle the contract net is not explicit in its terms, but the entity has a practice of settling similar contracts net (whether with the counterparty, by entering into offsetting contracts or by selling the contract before its exercise or lapse);

(c) for similar contracts, the entity has a practice of taking delivery of the underlying and selling it within a short period after delivery for the purpose of generating a profit from short-term fluctuations in price or dealer's margin; and

(d) the non-financial item that is the subject of the contract is readily convertible to cash, e.g. precious metals or base metals quoted on the London Metal Exchange are considered to be readily convertible to cash. *[IAS 32.9, IFRS 9.2.6]*.

There is no further guidance in IFRS 9 explaining what is meant by 'readily convertible to cash'. Typically, a non-financial item would be considered readily convertible to cash if it consists of largely fungible units and quoted spot prices are available in an active market that can absorb the quantity held by the entity without significantly affecting the price. Further discussion on the net settlement criteria can be found in Chapter 45 at 4.1.

Commodity-based contracts that are excluded from IAS 32 and IFRS 9 are contracts that were entered into and continue to be held for the purpose of the receipt or delivery of a non-financial item in accordance with the entity's expected purchase, sale or usage requirements. Contracts that fall within this exemption, which is known as the 'normal purchase or sale exemption', 'executory contract exemption' or 'own-use exemption', are accounted for as executory contracts. An entity recognises such contracts in its statement of financial position only when one of the parties meets its obligation under the contract to deliver either cash or a non-financial asset. *[CF 4.46]*.

The IASB views the practice of settling net or taking delivery of the underlying and selling it within a short period after delivery as an indication that the contracts are not normal purchases or sales. Therefore, contracts to which (b) or (c) apply cannot be subject to the normal purchase or sale exception. Other contracts that can be settled net are evaluated to determine whether this exemption can actually apply. *[IAS 32.9, IFRS 9.2.6, BCZ2.18]*.

A written option to buy or sell a non-financial item that can be settled net in cash or another financial instrument, or by exchanging financial instruments, in accordance with (a) or (d) should be accounted for under IFRS 9 and does not qualify for use of the normal purchase or sale exemption. *[IFRS 9.2.7, BCZ2.18]*.

The conditions associated with the use of the normal purchase or sale exemption often pose problems for mining companies and oil and gas companies because, historically, they have settled many purchase and sales contracts on a net basis.

A further problem may arise when a mining company or oil and gas company holds a written option for the purpose of the receipt or delivery of a non-financial item in accordance with the entity's expected purchase, sale or usage requirements – because IFRS 9 would require such contracts to be accounted for as derivative financial instruments.

Finally, from time to time mining companies and oil and gas companies may need to settle contracts for the sale of commodities on a net basis because of operational problems. Such a situation may mean that the company would usually need to treat those contracts as derivative financial instruments under IFRS 9 as they may now have a practice of settling net under (b) or (c) above. Where this situation is caused by a unique event beyond management's control, a level of judgement will be required to determine whether that would prevent the company from applying the own use exemption to similar contracts. This should be assessed on a case by case basis.

Judgement will also be required as to what constitutes 'similar contracts'. The definition of similar contracts in IFRS 9, *[IFRS 9.2.6]*, considers the intended use for such contracts. This means that contracts identical in form may be dissimilar due to their intended use, e.g. own purchase requirements versus proprietary trading. If the intended use is for normal purchase or sale, such an intention must be documented at inception of the contract. A history of regular revisions of expected purchase or sale requirements could impair the ability of a company to distinguish identical contracts as being dissimilar.

IFRS 9 provides a fair value option for own use contracts which was not previously available under IAS 39 – *Financial Instruments: Recognition and Measurement*. At the inception of a contract, an entity may make an irrevocable designation to measure an own use contract at fair value through profit or loss (the 'fair value option') even if it was entered into for the purpose of the receipt or delivery of a non-financial item in accordance with the entity's expected purchase, sale or usage requirement. However, such designation is only allowed if it eliminates or significantly reduces an accounting mismatch that would otherwise arise from not recognising that contract because it is excluded from the scope of IFRS 9. *[IFRS 9.2.5]*.

See Chapter 45 at 4.2 for more information on the normal purchase and sales exemption.

The extract below from Alkane Resources 2019 financial statements illustrates how this could affect an entity's reported financial position.

> Extract 43.32: Alkane Resources Limited (2019)
> NOTES TO THE CONSOLIDATED FINANCIAL STATEMENTS [extract]
> Note 32. Commitments [extract]
> (c) Physical gold delivery commitments [extract]
>
> As part of its risk management policy, the Group enters into derivatives including gold forward contracts and gold put options to manage the gold price of a proportion of anticipated gold sales.
>
> The gold forward sales contracts disclosed below did not meet the criteria of financial instruments for accounting purposes on the basis that they met the normal purchase/sale exemption because physical gold would be delivered into the contract. Accordingly, the contracts were accounted for as sale contracts with revenue recognised in the period in which the gold commitment was met. The balances in the table below relate to the value of the contracts to be delivered into by transfer of physical gold.
>
> | | Gold for physical delivery Ounces | Contracted gold sale price per ounce ($) | Value of committed sales $'000 |
> |---|---|---|---|
> | **30 June 2019** | | | |
> | Fixed forward contracts | | | |
> | Within one year | 12,980 | 1,854 | 24,065 |
> | One to five years | 14,770 | 1,853 | 27,374 |
> | **30 June 2018** | | | |
> | Fixed forward contracts | | | |
> | Within one year | 4,000 | 1,750 | 6,999 |

13.2 Embedded derivatives

A contract that qualifies for the normal purchase and sale exemption still needs to be assessed for the existence of embedded derivatives. An embedded derivative is a component of a hybrid or combined instrument that also includes a non-derivative host contract; it has the effect that some of the cash flows of the combined instrument vary in a similar way to a stand-alone derivative. In other words, it causes some or all of the cash flows that otherwise would be required by the contract to be modified according to a specified interest rate, financial instrument price, commodity price, foreign exchange rate, index of prices or rates, credit rating or credit index, or other underlying variable (provided in the case of a non-financial variable that the variable is not specific to a party to the contract). *[IFRS 9.4.3.1]*.

The detailed requirements regarding the separation of embedded derivatives and the interpretation and application of those requirements under IFRS 9 are discussed in Chapter 46. A number of issues related to embedded derivatives that are of particular importance to the extractive industries are discussed at 13.2.1 to 13.2.4 below.

13.2.1 Foreign currency embedded derivatives

The most common embedded derivatives in the extractive industries are probably foreign currency embedded derivatives which arise when a producer of minerals sells these in a currency that is not the functional currency of any substantial party to the contract, the currency in which the price of the related commodity is routinely denominated in commercial transactions around the world or a currency that is commonly used in contracts to purchase or sell non-financial items in the economic environment in which the transaction takes place. *[IFRS 9.B4.3.8(d)]*. A more detailed analysis of these requirements can be found in Chapter 46 at 5.2.1.

13.2.2 Provisionally priced sales contracts

As discussed above at 12.8.1, sales contracts for certain commodities (e.g. copper and oil) often provide for provisional pricing at the time of shipment, with final pricing based on the average market price for a particular future period, i.e. the 'quotational period'.

If the contract is cancellable without penalty before delivery, the price adjustment feature does not meet the definition of a derivative because there is no contractual obligation until delivery takes place.

If the contract is non-cancellable, the price adjustment feature is considered to be an embedded derivative. The non-financial contract for the sale or purchase of the product, e.g. copper or oil, at a future date would be treated as the host contract.

For non–cancellable contracts, there will be a contractual obligation, but until control passes to the customer, the embedded derivative would be considered to be closely related to the non-financial host commodity contract and does not need to be recorded separately.

As discussed at 12.8.1 above, revenue is recognised when control passes to the customer. At this point, the non-financial host commodity contract is considered to be satisfied and a corresponding receivable is recognised. However, the receivable is still exposed to the price adjustment feature. As discussed at 12.8 above, under IFRS 9, embedded derivatives are not separated from financial assets, i.e. from the receivable. Instead, the receivable will need to be measured at fair value through profit or loss in its entirety. See Chapter 48 at 2 for more information on the classification of financial assets.

13.2.3 Long-term supply contracts

Long-term supply contracts sometimes contain embedded derivatives because of a desire to shift certain risks between contracting parties or as a consequence of existing market practices. The fair value of embedded derivatives in long-term supply contracts can be highly material to the entities involved. For example, in the mining sector electricity purchase contracts sometimes contain price conditions based on the commodity that is being sold, which provides an economic hedge for the mining company. While the electricity price component (if fixed) would meet the definition of an embedded derivative, it would be considered closely related to the host contract and hence would not have to be separated. However, the linkage to the commodity price would be unlikely to be considered closely related and would likely have to be separately accounted for as an embedded derivative. In the oil and gas sector the sales price of gas is at times based on that of electricity, which provides an economic hedge for the utility company that purchases the gas, and would also likely represent an embedded derivative that has to be separately accounted for. See Chapter 46 at 5.2.2 for further discussion.

As can be seen in the following extract from BHP Billiton's 2007 financial statements, the pricing terms of embedded derivatives in purchase (sales) contracts often match those of the product that the entity sells (purchases). (Note that while this disclosure is historical, it remains valid under IFRS 9).

> **Extract 43.33: BHP Billiton plc (2007)**
> **Notes to Financial Statements** [extract]
> **28 Financial instruments** [extract]
> **Embedded derivatives**
>
> Derivatives embedded in host contracts are accounted for as separate derivatives when their risks and characteristics are not closely related to those of the host contracts or have intrinsic value at inception and the host contracts are not carried at fair value. These embedded derivatives are measured at fair value with gains or losses arising from changes in fair value recognised in the income statement.
>
> Contracts are assessed for embedded derivatives when the Group becomes a party to them, including at the date of a business combination. Host contracts which incorporate embedded derivatives are entered into during the normal course of operations and are standard business practices in the industries in which the Group operate.
>
> The following table provides information about the principal embedded derivatives contracts:
>
> | | Maturity date | | Volume | | | Exposure |
> | --- | --- | --- | --- | --- | --- | --- |
> | | 2007 | 2006 | 2007 | 2006 | | price |
> | **Commodity Price Swaps** | | | | | | |
> | Electricity purchase arrangement (a) | 31 Dec 2024 | 31 Dec 2024 | 240,000 | 240,000 | MWh | Aluminium |
> | Electricity purchase arrangement (a) | 30 June 2020 | 30 June 2020 | 576,000 | 576,000 | MWh | Aluminium |
> | Gas sales (b) | 31 Dec 2013 | 31 Dec 2013 | 1,195,572 | 1,428,070 | '000 therms | Electricity |
> | **Commodity Price Options** | | | | | | |
> | Finance lease of plant and equipment (b) | 31 Dec 2018 | 30 Dec 2018 | 38.5 | 39.5 | mmboe | Crude Oil |
> | Copper concentrate purchases and sales (b) | 31 Dec 2007 | 31 Dec 2006 | 52 | 41 | '000 tonnes | Copper |
> | Lead concentrate purchases and sales (b) | 31 Dec 2007 | 1 January 2007 | 11 | 67 | '000 tonnes | Lead |
> | Zinc concentrate purchases and sales (b) | 31 Dec 2007 | 2 January 2007 | 51 | 6 | '000 tonnes | Zinc |
> | Silver concentrate sales (b) | 31 Dec 2007 | – | 4,604 | – | '000 ounces | Silver |
>
> (a) The volumes shown in these contracts indicate a megawatt volume per hour for each hour of the contract.
> (b) The volumes shown in these contracts indicate the total volumes for the contract.

13.2.4 Development of gas markets

Where there is no active local market in gas, market participants often enter into long-term contracts that are priced on the basis of a basket of underlying factors, such as oil prices, electricity prices and inflation indices. In the absence of an active market in gas, such price clauses are not considered to give rise to embedded derivatives because there is no accepted benchmark price for gas that could have been used instead.

An entity that applies IFRS 9 is required to assess whether an embedded derivative is required to be separated from the host contract (provided that host contract is not a financial asset (see 12.8 above for more information)) and accounted for as a derivative when the entity first becomes a party to the contract. *[IFRS 9.B4.3.11]*. Subsequent reassessment of embedded derivatives under IFRS 9 is generally prohibited. *[IFRS 9.B4.3.11]*. See Chapter 46 at 7 for more information. Therefore, in the case of gas, when an active market subsequently develops, an entity is not permitted to separate embedded derivatives from existing gas contracts, unless there is a change in the terms of the contract that significantly modifies the cash flows that otherwise would be required under the contract. However, if the entity enters into a new gas contract with exactly the same terms and conditions, it would be required to separate embedded derivatives from the new gas contract.

Judgement is required in determining whether there is an active market in a particular geographic region and the relevant geographic market for any type of commodity. Where no active market exists consideration should be given to the industry practice for pricing such commodity-based contracts. A pricing methodology that is consistent with industry practice would generally not be considered to contain embedded derivatives.

The extract below from BP shows the company's previous approach to embedded derivatives before and after the development of an active gas trading market in the UK, and demonstrates that the fair value of embedded derivatives in long-term gas contracts can be quite significant. (Note also that while this disclosure is historical, it remains valid under IFRS 9).

Extract 43.34: BP p.l.c. (2014)

Notes on financial statements [extract]

28. Derivative financial instruments [extract]

Embedded derivatives [extract]

The group is a party to certain natural gas contracts containing embedded derivatives. Prior to the development of an active gas trading market, UK gas contracts were priced using a basket of available price indices, primarily relating to oil products, power and inflation. After the development of an active UK gas market, certain contracts were entered into or renegotiated using pricing formulae not directly related to gas prices, for example, oil product and power prices. In these circumstances, pricing formulae have been determined to be derivatives, embedded within the overall contractual arrangements that are not clearly and closely related to the underlying commodity. The resulting fair value relating to these contracts is recognized on the balance sheet with gains or losses recognized in the income statement. [...]

The commodity price embedded derivatives relate to natural gas contracts and are categorized in level 2 and 3 of the fair value hierarchy. The contracts in level 2 are valued using inputs that include price curves for each of the different products that are built up from active market pricing data. Where necessary, the price curves are extrapolated to the expiry of the contracts (the last of which is in 2018) using all available external pricing information; additionally, where limited data exists for certain products, prices are interpolated using historic and long-term pricing relationships. [...]

The following table shows the changes during the year in the net fair value of embedded derivatives, within level 3 of the fair value hierarchy.

	$ million	
	2014	2013
	Commodity price	Commodity price
Net fair value of contracts at 1 January	(379)	(1,112)
Settlements	24	316
Gains recognized in the income statement	219	142
Transfers out of level 3	–	258
Exchange adjustments	10	17
Net fair value of contracts at 31 December	(126)	(379)

The amount recognized in the income statement for the year relating to level 3 embedded derivatives still held at 31 December 2014 was a $220 million gain (2013 $67 million gain related to derivatives still held at 31 December 2013).

13.3 Volume flexibility in supply contracts

It is not uncommon for other sales contracts, such as those with large industrial customers, to contain volume flexibility features. For example, a supplier might enter into a contract requiring it to deliver, say, 100,000 units at a given price as well as giving the counterparty the option to purchase a further 20,000 units at the same price. Often such a supply contract will be readily convertible to cash as parties to the contract can settle the contract on a net basis, as discussed at 13.1 above. For example, precious metals or base metals quoted on the London Metal Exchange or oil contracts are considered to be readily convertible to cash, whereas bulk materials without spot prices (e.g. coal and iron) are generally not considered to be readily convertible to cash. However, with increasing levels of liquidity in certain commodities, this view may need to be reconfirmed/re-challenged before concluding that this remains the case.

If the customer has access to markets for the non-financial item and, following the guidance of the Interpretations Committee the supplier might consider such a contract to be within the scope of IFRS 9 as it contains a written option (see Chapter 45 at 4.2.3). However, some would say that the supplier could split the contract into two separate components for accounting purposes: a forward contract to supply 100,000 units (which may qualify as a normal sale and so meet the recognition exemption) and a written option to supply 20,000 units (which would not). Arguments put forward include:

- the parties could easily have entered into two separate contracts, a forward contract and a written option; and
- it is appropriate to analogise to the requirements for embedded derivatives and separate a written option from the normal forward sale or purchase contract because it is not closely related.

Some contracts, however, contain operational volume tolerances such as, in the case of certain oil purchase and sale contracts, a volume that is plus or minus a certain (often quite small) percentage of the stated quantity. These tolerances relate to physical changes in the volume during transportation caused by, for example, evaporation. The optionality within the contract typically cannot be monetised by either party but, instead is a practical requirement of the contract. In such cases, the optionality would not be considered a separate derivative within the scope of IFRS 9. In other cases, however, the volume tolerance may be greater than that which is required for practical reasons. This optionality may give one party the ability to benefit from changing underlying prices and could be considered a separate derivative. Judgement is required in assessing the nature of these volume tolerances.

This issue is discussed in more detail in Chapter 45 at 4.2.4 and 4.2.5.

13.4 Hedging sales of metal concentrate (mining)

In the mining sector certain commodities are often sold in the form of a concentrate that comprises two or more metals and impurities. These concentrates are the output of mines and are sold and shipped to smelters for treatment and refining in order to extract the metals in their pure form from the concentrate (or, alternatively, the concentrate may be sold to traders who will subsequently sell and ship to smelters). The metal content of concentrate varies depending on the mine and grade of ore being mined. The sales proceeds of concentrate are typically determined as the total of the payments for the actual content of each of the metals contained in a given concentrate shipment and they reflect the condition in which the metal is sold (i.e. unrefined, still being dissolved in concentrate). Typical pricing formulas are based on the price for dissolved metal off the quoted price for refined metal (e.g. the London Metal Exchange (LME)), with deductions for amounts that reflect the fact that the metal sold is not treated and/or refined. Actual deductions may vary by contract but typically comprise treatment and refining charges, price participation clauses, transportation, impurity penalties, etc.

Under IFRS 9, an entity is permitted to designate a risk component of a non-financial item as the hedged item in a hedging relationship, provided the risk component is separately identifiable and reliably measurable. See Chapter 53 for IFRS 9 hedge accounting requirements and Chapter 53 at 2.2 for further information on hedging of risk components. These considerations also apply from the perspective of an entity that purchases metals in the form of a concentrate.

14 INVENTORIES

Inventories should be measured at the lower of cost and net realisable value under IAS 2. However, IAS 2 does not apply to the measurement of minerals and mineral products, to the extent that they are measured at net realisable value in accordance with well-established practices in those industries. *[IAS 2.3(a)]*. There is also an exception for commodity broker traders who measure their inventories at fair value less costs to sell. When such inventories are measured at fair value less costs to sell, changes in fair value less costs to sell are recognised in profit or loss in the period of the change. *[IAS 2.3(b)]*. This is discussed further at 14.4 below.

Where inventory is measured at cost, various cost methods are acceptable under IFRS and include specific identification, weighted average costs, or first-in first-out (FIFO). Last-in first-out (LIFO) is not permitted under IFRS.

Issues that mining companies and oil and gas companies commonly face in relation to inventory include:

- point of recognition (14.1 below);
- cost absorption in the measurement of inventory;
- method of allocating costs to inventory, e.g. FIFO or weighted average;
- determination of joint and by-products and measurement consequences (see 14.2 below);
- accounting for core inventories (see 14.3 below); and
- measuring inventory at fair value (see 14.4 below).

Additional issues relating to inventory for mining companies include:

- accounting for stockpiles of long-term, low grade ore (see 14.5 below); and
- heap leaching (see 14.6 below).

14.1 Recognition of work in progress

Determining when to start recognising inventory is more of an issue for mining companies than oil and gas companies. Inventory is recognised when it is probable that future economic benefits will flow to the entity and the asset has a cost or value than can be reliably measured.

Oil and gas companies often do not separately report work-in-progress inventories of either oil or gas. As is noted in the IASC Issues Paper 'the main reason is that, at the point of their removal from the earth, oil and gas frequently do not require processing and they may be sold or may be transferred to the enterprise's downstream operations in the form existing at the time of removal, that is, they are immediately recognised as finished goods. Even if the oil and gas removed from the earth require additional processing to make them saleable or transportable, the time required for processing is typically minimal and the amount of raw products involved in the processing at any one time is likely to be immaterial'.[118] However, if more than an insignificant quantity of product is undergoing processing at any given point in time then an entity may need to disclose work-in-progress under IAS 2. *[IAS 2.8, 37]*.

For mining companies, it has become accepted practice to recognise work-in-progress at the point at which ore is broken and the entity can make a reasonable assessment of quantity, recovery and cost.[119]

Extract 43.35 from the financial statements of Harmony Gold Mining illustrates the need for judgement in determining when work-in-progress can be recognised.

Extract 43.35: Harmony Gold Mining Company Limited (2019)
NOTES TO THE GROUP FINANCIAL STATEMENTS [extract]
for the years ended 30 June 2019
22 INVENTORIES [extract]
ACCOUNTING POLICY

Inventories, which include bullion on hand, gold-in-process, gold in lock-up, ore stockpiles and consumables, are measured at the lower of cost and net realisable value. Net realisable value is assessed at each reporting date and is determined with reference to relevant market prices.

The cost of bullion, gold-in-process and gold in lock-up is determined by reference to production cost, including amortisation and depreciation at the relevant stage of production. Ore stockpiles are valued at average production cost. Stockpiles and gold in lock-up are classified as non-current assets where the stockpile exceeds current processing capacity and where a portion of static gold in lock-up is expected to be recovered more than 12 months after balance sheet date.

Gold in-process inventories represent materials that are currently in the process of being converted to a saleable product. In-process material is measured based on assays of the material fed to process and the projected recoveries at the respective plants. In-process inventories are valued at the average cost of the material fed to process attributable to the source material coming from the mine or stockpile plus the in-process conversion costs, including the applicable depreciation relating to the process facility, incurred to that point in the process. Gold in-process includes gold in lock-up which is generally measured from the plants onwards. Gold in lock-up is expected to be extracted when plants are demolished at the end of their useful lives, which is largely dependent on the estimated useful life of the operations feeding the plants.

At the group's open pit operations, gold in-process represents production in broken ore form.

Consumables are valued at weighted average cost value after appropriate allowances for slow moving and redundant items.

Measurement issues can arise in relation to work-in-progress for concentrators, smelters and refineries, where significant volumes of product can be located in pipes or vessels, with no uniformity of grade. Work-in-progress inventories may also be in stockpiles, for example underground, where it is more difficult to measure quantities.

Processing varies in extent, duration and complexity depending on the type of mineral and different production and processing techniques that are used. Therefore, measuring work-in-progress, as it moves through the various stages of processing, is difficult and determining the quantities of work-in-progress may require a significant degree of estimation. Practice varies in this area, which is a reflection of the genuine differences mining companies face in their ability to assess mineral content and predict production and processing costs.

Extract 43.36 below from the financial statements of Anglo American Platinum illustrates the complexity involved in making such estimates.

> Extract 43.36: Anglo American Platinum Limited (2019)
> SIGNIFICANT ACCOUNTING PRINCIPLES [extract]
> for the year ended 31 December 2019
> CRITICAL ACCOUNTING ESTIMATES AND JUDGEMENTS [extract]
> Critical accounting estimates [extract]
> Metal inventory
> Work-in-progress metal inventory is valued at the lower of net realisable value (NRV) and the average cost of production or purchase less net revenue from sales of other metals, in the ratio of the contribution of these metals to gross sales revenue.
>
> Production costs are allocated to platinum, palladium, rhodium and nickel (joint products) by dividing the mine output into total mine production costs, determined on a 12-month rolling average basis. Concentrate purchased from third parties is determined on a 12-month rolling average basis. The quantity of ounces of joint products in work in progress is calculated based on the following factors:
> - The theoretical inventory at that point in time, which is calculated by adding the inputs to the previous physical inventory and then deducting the outputs for the inventory period.
> - The inputs and outputs include estimates due to the delay in finalising analytical values.
> - The estimates are subsequently trued up to the final metal accounting quantities when available.
> - The theoretical inventory is then converted to a refined equivalent inventory by applying appropriate recoveries depending on where the material is within the production pipeline. The recoveries are based on actual results as determined by the inventory count and are in line with industry standards.
> - Unrealised profits and losses are excluded from the inventory valuation before determining the lower of NRV and cost calculation.
>
> Other than at the precious metal refinery, an annual physical count of work in progress is done, usually around February of each year. The precious metal refinery is subject to a physical count usually every three years, but this could occur more frequently by exception. The most recent physical count of the precious metal refinery was in February 2019. The annual physical count is limited to once per annum due to the dislocation of production required to perform the physical inventory count and the in-process inventories being contained in tanks, pipes and other vessels. Once the results of the physical count are finalised, the variance between the theoretical count and actual count is investigated and recorded. Thereafter the physical quantity forms the opening balance for the theoretical inventory calculation. Consequently, the estimates are refined based on actual results over time. The nature of the production process inherently limits the ability to precisely measure recoverability levels. As a result, the metallurgical balancing process is constantly monitored and the variables used in the process are refined based on actual results over time.

Ore in circuit for a mining company at the end of a reporting period can be very difficult to measure as it is generally not easily accessible. The value of materials being processed should therefore be estimated based on inputs, throughput time and ore grade. The significance of the value of ore in circuit will depend on the type of commodity being processed. For example, precious metals producers may have a material value in process at reporting period end.

14.2 Sale of by-products and joint products

In the extractive industries it is common for more than one product to be extracted from the same reserves, e.g. copper is often found together with gold and silver and oil, gas and gas liquids are commonly found together. Products produced at the same time are classified as joint products or by-products and are usually driven by the importance of the different products to the viability of the mine or field. The same commodity may be treated differently based on differing grades and quantities of products. In most cases where more than one product is produced there is a clear distinction between the main product and the by-products. In other cases, the distinction may not be as clear.

The decision as to whether these are joint products or whether one is a by-product, is important, as it impacts the way in which costs are allocated. This decision may also affect the classification of sales of the various products.

14.2.1 By-products

A by-product is a secondary product obtained during the course of production or processing, having relatively small importance when compared with the principal product or products.

IAS 2 prescribes the following accounting for by-products:

> '...When the costs of conversion of each product are not separately identifiable, they are allocated between the products on a rational and consistent basis. The allocation may be based, for example, on the relative sales value of each product either at the stage in the production process when the products become separately identifiable, or at the completion of production. Most by-products, by their nature, are immaterial. When this is the case, they are often measured at net realisable value and this value is deducted from the cost of the main product. As a result, the carrying amount of the main product is not materially different from its cost.' *[IAS 2.14]*.

By-products that are significant in value should be accounted for as joint products as discussed at 14.2.2 below. However, there are some entities that treat such by-product sales as a negative cost, i.e. by crediting these against cost of goods sold of the main product. This treatment would likely only be acceptable on the basis of materiality. It is important to note that the negative cost approach discussed in IAS 2, *[IAS 2.14]*, only relates to the allocation of the costs of conversion between the main product and by-product and does not allow the revenue from a sale of by-products as a reduction of cost of goods sold (even if the sales are not significant).

If an entity determines the sale of by-products or scrap materials is in the course of its ordinary activities (even if they are not significant), the entity would recognise those sales as revenue from contracts with customers under IFRS 15. If an entity determines that such sales are not in its ordinary course of business, the entity would recognise those sales as either other income or other revenues (i.e. separate from revenue from contracts with customers) because they represent sales to non-customers.

Extracts 43.37 and 43.38 below illustrates how Rio Tinto and Anglo American respectively account for their by-product revenue under IFRS 15.

> *Extract 43.37: Rio Tinto plc (2019)*
> Notes to the 2019 financial statements [extract]
> 1. Principal accounting policies [extract]
> (c) Sales revenue [extract]
> *Presentation and disclosures* [extract]
> Revenues from the sale of significant by-products, such as gold, are included in sales revenue. Sundry revenue (eg sales of surplus power) incidental to the main revenue-generating activities of the operations, is treated as a credit to operating costs.

> *Extract 43.38: Anglo American plc (2019)*
> **NOTES TO THE FINANCIAL STATEMENTS** CONTINUED [extract]
> OTHER ITEMS [extract]
> 38. ACCOUNTING POLICIES [extract]
> **C. FINANCIAL PERFORMANCE** [extract]
> Revenue recognition [extract]
> Revenues from the sale of material by-products are recognised within revenue at the point control passes. Where a by-product is not regarded as significant, revenue may be credited against the cost of sales.

Although IAS 2 does not require extensive disclosures in respect of by-products, if amounts are material, disclosure of the following information, which many extractives companies provide on a voluntary basis, will greatly assist users:

- accounting policies applied to by-products;
- line items in the primary financial statements in which revenues and carried amounts have been disclosed;
- quantities of by-products sold; and
- average prices of by-products sold.

14.2.2 Joint products

Joint products are two or more products produced simultaneously from a common raw material source, with each product having a significant relative sales value. One joint product cannot be produced without the other and the products cannot be identified separately until a certain production stage, often called the 'split-off point', is reached. Joint products are very common in both the oil and gas sector (e.g. crude oil when run through a refinery produces a variety of products) and the mining sector.

Joint products, by definition, are all significant in value and require that an entity allocate on a rational and consistent basis the costs of conversion that are not separately identifiable for each product. The IASC Issues Paper outlined two approaches that have found acceptance in practice:[120]

(a) *allocation on the basis of physical characteristics* – In the oil and gas sector, entities often combine quantities of oil and gas based on their relative energy content (i.e. 6,000 cubic feet of gas is roughly equal in energy to one barrel of oil). This method, however, does not take account of the fact that, for example, gas is cheaper per unit of energy than oil because the latter is more difficult to transport; and

(b) *allocation on the basis of relative values* – This approach is more common in the mining sector where often it is not possible to identify a relevant physical characteristic that can be used to combine quantities of different products. The drawback of this method is that it results in very similar profit margins for each of the joint products, which may not be reflective of the underlying economic reality (i.e. one of the joint products, if mined in isolation, might have a completely different profit margin).

Although it should be kept in mind that neither method is perfect, both approaches are currently permitted under IFRS. It is true also that whichever method is selected, it is unlikely to have a material effect on reported profit overall. The extract below illustrates the application of approach (b) by Anglo American.

> Extract 43.39: Anglo American plc (2019)
> NOTES TO THE FINANCIAL STATEMENTS [extract]
> OTHER ITEMS [extract]
> 38. ACCOUNTING POLICIES [extract]
> E. WORKING CAPITAL
>
> Inventories [extract]
>
> Inventory and work in progress are measured at the lower of cost and net realisable value, except for inventory held by commodity broker-traders which is measured at fair value less costs to sell. The production cost of inventory includes an appropriate proportion of depreciation and production overheads. Cost is determined on the following basis:
> - Raw materials and consumables are measured at cost on a first in, first out (FIFO) basis or a weighted average cost basis.
> - Work in progress and finished products are measured at raw material cost, labour cost and a proportion of production overhead expenses.
> - Metal and coal stocks are included within finished products and are measured at average cost.
>
> At precious metals operations that produce 'joint products', cost is allocated among products according to the ratio of contribution of these metals to gross sales revenues.

14.3 Core inventories

In certain industries, for example the petrochemical sector, certain processes or storage arrangements require a core of inventory to be present in the system at all times in order for it to function properly. For example, in order for a crude oil refining process to take place, the plant must contain a certain minimum quantity of oil. This oil can only be taken out once the plant is abandoned and could then only be sold as sludge. Similarly, underground gas storage caves are filled with gas; but a substantial part (in some instances 25%) of that gas can never be sold as its function is to pressurise the cave, thereby allowing the remaining 75% to be extracted. Even though the gas will be turned around on a continuing basis, at any one time 25% of it will never be available to sell and cannot be recouped from the cave. Finally, long distance pipelines contain a significant volume of gas that keeps them operational.

Similar examples of core inventories exist in the mining sector where certain processes or processing facilities require a core or minimum amount of inventory to be present in the system at all times. These may include:

- potlines in the aluminium industry;
- blast furnaces in the steel industry;
- electrowinning plants; or
- carbon in leach processing in the gold industry.

The key issue with such minimum amounts of inventory is whether they should be accounted for as inventory in accordance with IAS 2 or as PP&E in accordance with IAS 16. It is our view that if an item of inventory is not held for sale or consumed in a production process, but is necessary to the operation of a facility during more than one operating cycle, and its cost cannot be recouped through sale (or is significantly impaired), this item of inventory should be accounted for as an item of property, plant and equipment under IAS 16 rather than as inventory under IAS 2. This applies even if the part of inventory that is deemed to be an item of PP&E cannot be separated physically from the rest of inventory.

These matters will always involve the exercise of judgement, however, in the above instances, we consider that:

- the deemed PP&E items do not meet the definition of inventories;
- although it is not possible to physically separate the chemicals involved into inventory and PP&E categories, there is no accounting reason why one cannot distinguish between identical assets with different uses and therefore account for them differently. Indeed, IAS 2 does envisage such a possibility when discussing different cost formulas; *[IAS 2.25]*
- the deemed PP&E items are necessary to bring another item of PP&E to the condition necessary for it to be capable of operating in the manner intended by management. This meets the definition of the costs of PP&E in IAS 16 upon initial recognition; *[IAS 16.16(b)]* and
- recognising these items as inventories would lead to an immediate loss because these items cannot be sold or consumed in a production process, or during the process of rendering services. This does not properly reflect the fact that the items are necessary to operate another asset over more than one operating cycle.

By contrast, core inventory that is not necessary to operate the asset and that is recoverable (e.g. gas in a pipeline) is considered to be held for sale or to be consumed in the production process or process of rendering services. Therefore, such gas is accounted for as inventory.

The issue of core inventories or 'minimum fill' was considered by the Interpretations Committee in March and July 2014. The staff paper considered by the Interpretations Committee proposed that base or cushion gas in storage facilities (required to maintain adequate cavern pressure) and pipeline fill (i.e. the minimum volume of oil or gas to be kept in a pipeline to ensure its operability) should be accounted for as property, plant and equipment under IAS 16 where the carrying amount was not considered recoverable through sale or consumption in the production process (which is consistent with our views above). After consideration of this issue, the Interpretations Committee noted that, although there was diversity in practice between industries, there was no, or only limited, diversity in practice within the industries for which the issue is significant (including extractive industries). Given there was not sufficient diversity within industry, they decided not to continue with the development of an interpretation, and to remove this item from its agenda.

The extract below from the financial statements of ENGIE SA shows how cushion gas is accounted for as a tangible asset that is depreciated over its economic life.

> Extract 43.40: ENGIE SA (2019)
> NOTES TO THE CONSOLIDATED FINANCIAL STATEMENTS [extract]
> NOTE 15 PROPERTY, PLANT AND EQUIPMENT [extract]
> **Cushion gas** [extract]
>
> "Cushion" gas injected into underground storage facilities is essential for ensuring that reservoirs can be operated effectively, and is therefore inseparable from these reservoirs. Unlike "working" gas which is included in inventories *(see Note 24.2 "Inventories")*, cushion gas is reported in property, plant and equipment.
>
> **24.2 Inventories** [extract]
> **Gas inventories** [extract]
>
> Gas injected into underground storage facilities includes working gas, which can be withdrawn without adversely affecting the operation of the reservoirs, and cushion gas, which is inseparable from the reservoirs and essential for their operation *(see Note 15 "Property, plant and equipment")*.
>
> Working gas is classified in inventories and measured at weighted average purchase cost upon entering the transportation network regardless of its source, including any regasification costs.
>
> Group inventory outflows are valued using the weighted average unit cost method.
>
> An impairment loss is recognized when the net realizable value of inventories is lower than their weighted average cost.

14.4 Inventory carried at fair value

As noted earlier, inventories should be measured at the lower of cost and net realisable value under IAS 2. However, IAS 2 does not apply to the measurement of minerals and mineral products, to the extent that they are measured at net realisable value in accordance with well-established practices in those industries. *[IAS 2.3(a)]*. There is also an exception for commodity broker traders who measure their inventories at fair value less costs to sell. When such inventories are measured at fair value less costs to sell, these changes in fair value are recognised in profit or loss in the period of the change. *[IAS 2.3(b)]*.

An extractives company that wishes to use the exemption relating to minerals and mineral products outlined above would need to demonstrate that valuation at net realisable value was a well-established practice in its industry, which may be difficult to do for base metals inventory.

The commodity broker trader exemption above is commonly used by companies that engage in commodity trading. The extract below from the financial statements of BP illustrates a typical accounting policy for an oil and gas company that makes use of this exemption.

An integrated oil company can include exploration, production, refinement and distribution along with a trading operation. In such cases, inventory held by the trading organisation may have originated from the entities own production. Where this has occurred it will be necessary to ensure the inventory that came from the entity's own production is valued at cost or net realisable value rather than fair value.

> *Extract 43.41: BP p.l.c. (2019)*
> Notes on financial statements [extract]
> 1. Significant accounting policies, judgements, estimates and assumptions [extract]
> Inventories [extract]
> Inventories held for short-term trading purposes are stated at fair value less costs to sell and any changes in fair value are recognized in the income statement.

14.5 Stockpiles of low grade ore (mining)

Mining companies often stockpile low grade ore that cannot be economically processed at current market prices or to give priority to the processing of higher grade ore. Low grade ore stockpiles may not be processed for many years until market prices or technology have improved or until no higher grade ore remains available. Extract 43.42 below from AngloGold Ashanti illustrates that stockpiles of low grade ore may be held for many years.

Mineralised waste that is stockpiled in the hope, but without the expectation, that it may become economical to process in the future should be accounted in the same way as overburden and other waste materials (see 15.5 below). Low grade ore that is stockpiled with the expectation that it will be processed in the future should be accounted for in the same way as high grade ore. However, if the cost of the low grade ore exceeds its net realisable value, an entity should recognise an impairment charge that it might need to reverse at some point in the future if (and when) commodity prices were to increase.

If and when processing of low grade ore becomes economically viable and management intends to process the stockpile in the future, the ore is often presented as non-current inventory under IAS 2. Such stockpiles should be measured at the lower of cost and net realisable value. *[IAS 2.9, 30]*. IAS 2 provides limited guidance in how to determine net realisable value. Therefore, in allocating production costs to the low grade ore stockpile and in subsequently assessing net realisable value, an entity should consider the following:

(1) timing of sale: what is a reasonable and supportable assumption about the time it takes to sell;

(2) commodity prices: whether to use those at the reporting date or future commodity prices. The commodity price at the reporting date may not be representative of the price that can realistically be expected to prevail when the ore is expected to be processed. The assumptions as to the long-term commodity prices used in the estimate of the sales proceeds and the expected timing of realisation, should generally be consistent with those used in the Life of Mine Plan and other models that would be used for valuation and impairment purposes;

(3) costs of processing: these may change in the future because of inflation, technological changes and new environmental regulations;

(4) storage costs: specifically how these should be factored in; and

(5) time value of money: depending on how net realisable value is determined and what inputs are used, the time value of money may impact the calculation of net realisable value. IAS 2 is silent as to how to address the time value of money and does not consider the degree to which the use of future commodity prices may already reflect the time value of money.

Given the above, significant judgement will be involved and key estimates and assumptions made should be disclosed where material.

The extract below shows how AngloGold Ashanti accounts for ore stockpiles.

> *Extract 43.42: AngloGold Ashanti Limited (2019)*
> GROUP – NOTES TO THE FINANCIAL STATEMENTS [extract]
> For the year ended 31 December
> 1 ACCOUNTING POLICIES [extract]
> 1.2 SIGNIFICANT ACCOUNTING JUDGEMENTS AND ESTIMATES
> USE OF ESTIMATES [extract]
>
> Stockpiles and metals in process
>
> Costs that are incurred in or benefit the production process are accumulated in stockpiles and metals in process values. Net realisable value tests are performed at least annually and represent the estimated future sales price of the product, based on prevailing and long-term metals prices, less estimated costs to complete production and bring the product to sale.
>
> Surface and underground stockpiles and metals in process are measured by estimating the number of tonnes added and removed from the stockpile, the number of contained ounces based on assay data, and the estimated recovery percentage based on the expected processing method. Stockpile ore tonnages are verified by periodic surveys.
>
> Although the quantities of recoverable metal are reconciled by comparing the grades of ore to the quantities of metals actually recovered (metallurgical balancing), the nature of the process inherently limits the ability to precisely monitor recoverability levels. As a result, the metallurgical balancing process is constantly monitored and engineering estimates are refined based on actual results over time.
>
> Variations between actual and estimated quantities resulting from changes in assumptions and estimates that do not result in write-downs to net realisable value are accounted for on a prospective basis.
>
> The carrying value of inventories (excluding finished goods and mine operating supplies) for the group at 31 December 2019 was $377m (2018: $404m; 2017: $424m).
>
> ANNEXURE A
> SUMMARY OF SIGNIFICANT ACCOUNTING POLICIES [extract]
> INVENTORIES [extract]
>
> Inventories are valued at the lower of cost and net realisable value after appropriate allowances for redundant and obsolete items. Cost is determined on the following bases:
> [...]
> - ore stockpiles are valued at the average moving cost of mining and stockpiling the ore. Stockpiles are classified as a non-current asset where the stockpile exceeds current processing capacity; [...]

The extract below illustrates the disclosure relating to the reversal of impairment of stockpiled ore.

> **Extract 43.43: IAMGOLD Corporation (2019)**
> NOTES TO CONSOLIDATED FINANCIAL STATEMENTS [extract]
> FOR THE YEAR ENDED DECEMBER 31, 2019 and 2018
>
> **10. INVENTORIES** [extract]
>
> | | December 31, 2019 | December 31, 2018 |
> |---|---:|---:|
> | Finished goods | $ 68.2 | $ 60.7 |
> | Ore stockpiles | 68.9 | 27.3 |
> | Mine supplies | 171.4 | 186.7 |
> | | 308.5 | 274.7 |
> | Non-current ore stockpiles | 223.2 | 202.9 |
> | | $ 531.7 | $ 477.6 |
>
> For the year ended December 31, 2019, the Company recognized a net realizable value reversal in ore stockpiles amounting to $15.8 million (December 31, 2018 – write-down of $1.0 million).
>
> For the year ended December 31, 2019, the Company recognized a write-down in mine supplies inventories amounting to $3.5 million (December 31, 2018 – $3.9 million).
>
> For the year ended December 31, 2019, the Company recognized $16.3 million and $13.2 million, respectively, in Cost of sales for costs related to operating below normal capacity at Westwood (December 31, 2018 – $nil) and Rosebel (December 31, 2018 – $nil).

14.6 Heap leaching (mining)

Heap leaching is a process which may be used for the recovery of metals from low grade ore. The crushed ore is laid on a slightly sloping, impermeable pad and leached by uniformly trickling a chemical solution through the heaps to be collected in ponds. The metals are subsequently extracted from the pregnant solution. Although heap leaching is one of the lowest cost methods of processing, recovery rates are relatively low.

Despite the estimation and measurement challenges associated with heap leaching, ore loaded on heap leach pads is usually recognised as inventory. An entity that develops an accounting policy for heap leaching needs to consider the following:

- the metal recovery factor is relatively low and will vary depending on the metallurgical characteristics of the material on the heap leach pad. The final (actual) recovery is therefore unknown until leaching is complete. Therefore, an entity will need to estimate the quantity of recoverable metal on each of its heap leach pads, based on laboratory test work or historical ore performance;
- the assayed head grade of ore added to the heap;
- the ore stockpiles on heap leach pads are accounted for as inventories that are measured at cost under IAS 2. As the valuable metal content is leached from these ore stockpiles, the cost basis is depleted based upon expected grades and recovery rates. The depletion charge should be accounted as the cost of production of work in progress or finished goods;

- the level at which the heap leach pads are measured – that is, whether they are measured separately, in groups or in total. The preferred approach is to consider each pad separately (where possible) because this reduces the expected volatility in ore type to more manageable levels; and
- ore stockpiles on heap leach pads from which metals are expected to be recovered in a period longer than 12 months are generally classified as non-current assets.

The extracts below from the financial statements of AngloGold Ashanti and Kinross Gold Corporation illustrate the issues that an entity will need to consider in developing an accounting policy for heap leaching.

> Extract 43.44: AngloGold Ashanti Limited (2019)
> GROUP – NOTES TO THE FINANCIAL STATEMENTS [extract]
> For the year ended 31 December
>
> ANNEXURE A
> SUMMARY OF SIGNIFICANT ACCOUNTING POLICIES [extract]
> INVENTORIES [extract]
>
> Inventories are valued at the lower of cost and net realisable value after appropriate allowances for redundant and obsolete items. Cost is determined on the following bases:
> [...]
> - heap leach pad materials are measured on an average total production cost basis.

> Extract 43.45: Kinross Gold Corporation (2019)
> NOTES TO THE CONSOLIDATED FINANCIAL STATEMENTS [extract]
> For the years ended December 31, 2019 and 2018
> 3. SUMMARY OF SIGNIFICANT ACCOUNTING POLICIES [extract]
> vi. Inventories [extract]
>
> Inventories consisting of metal in circuit ore, metal in-process and finished metal are valued at the lower of cost or net realizable value ("NRV"). NRV is calculated as the difference between the estimated gold prices based on prevailing and long-term metal prices and estimated costs to complete production into a saleable form and estimated costs to sell.
>
> Metal in circuit is comprised of ore in stockpiles and ore on heap leach pads. Ore in stockpiles is coarse ore that has been extracted from the mine and is available for further processing. Costs are added to stockpiles based on the current mining cost per tonne and removed at the average cost per tonne. Costs are added to ore on the heap leach pads based on current mining costs and removed from the heap leach pads as ounces are recovered, based on the average cost per recoverable ounce of gold on the leach pad. Ore in stockpiles not expected to be processed in the next twelve months is classified as long-term.
>
> The quantities of recoverable gold placed on the leach pads are reconciled by comparing the grades of ore placed on the leach pads to the quantities of gold actually recovered (metallurgical balancing); however, the nature of the leaching process inherently limits the ability to precisely monitor inventory levels. As a result, the metallurgical balancing process is constantly monitored and the engineering estimates are refined based on actual results over time. Variances between actual and estimated quantities resulting from changes in assumptions and estimates that do not result in write downs to NRV are accounted for on a prospective basis. The ultimate actual recovery of gold from a leach pad will not be known until the leaching process has concluded. In the event that the Company determines, based on engineering estimates, that a quantity of gold contained in ore on leach pads is to be recovered over a period exceeding twelve months, that portion is classified as long-term.
>
> In-process inventories represent materials that are in the process of being converted to a saleable product.
>
> Materials and supplies are valued at the lower of average cost and NRV.
>
> Write-downs of inventory are recognized in the consolidated statement of operations in the current period. The Company reverses inventory write downs in the event that there is a subsequent increase in NRV.

15 PROPERTY, PLANT AND EQUIPMENT

15.1 Major maintenance and turnarounds/renewals and reconditioning costs

Some assets (e.g. refineries, smelters and gas processing plants) require major maintenance at regular intervals, which is often described as an overhaul or turnaround in the oil and gas sector and renewal or reconditioning in the mining sector. When an entity incurs further costs in relation to an item of PP&E, IAS 16 requires it to determine the nature of the costs. Where such costs provide access to future economic benefits they should be capitalised. Costs of day-to-day servicing (e.g. costs of labour and consumables, and possibly the cost of small parts) should be expensed as incurred. *[IAS 16.12]*. If the costs relate to the replacement of a part of the entire asset then the entity derecognises the carrying amount of the part that is replaced and recognises the cost of the replacement part. *[IAS 16.13]*. However, the part need not represent a physical part of the asset.

When a major inspection, renewal or reconditioning project is performed, its cost should be recognised in the carrying amount of the item of property, plant and equipment and any remaining carrying amount of the cost of the previous inspection/renewal (which will be distinct from physical parts) is derecognised. This is not affected by whether the entity identified the cost of the previous inspection when the item was acquired or constructed. *[IAS 16.14]*. See Chapter 18 at 3.3.2.

Subsequent costs that meet the recognition criteria should therefore be capitalised even if the costs incurred merely restore the assets to their original standard of performance, and the remaining carrying amount of any cost previously capitalised should be expensed. However, under IAS 37 an entity cannot provide for the costs of planned future maintenance (e.g. turnarounds, renewals/reconditions) as is illustrated by Example 43.8, based on Example 11A in IAS 37. *[IAS 37 Appendix C]*.

Example 43.8: Refurbishment costs – no legislative requirement

A furnace has a lining that needs to be replaced every five years for technical reasons. At the end of the reporting period, the lining has been in use for three years.

Under IAS 37 no provision should be recognised as there is no present obligation. The cost of replacing the lining is not recognised because, at the end of the reporting period, no obligation to replace the lining exists independently of the company's future actions – even the intention to incur the expenditure depends on the company deciding to continue operating the furnace or to replace the lining. Instead of a provision being recognised, the depreciation of the lining takes account of its consumption, i.e. it is depreciated over five years. The re-lining costs then incurred are capitalised with the consumption of each new lining shown by depreciation over the subsequent five years.

Even a legal requirement to refurbish does not make the costs of a turnaround/renewal a liability under IAS 37, because no obligation exists independently of the entity's future actions – the entity could avoid the future overhaul expenditure by its future actions, for example by selling the refinery or the asset that is being renewed/reconditioned.

[IAS 37 IE Example 11B].

The extract below from BP illustrates a typical accounting policy for repairs, maintenance and inspection costs under IFRS.

> **Extract 43.46: BP p.l.c. (2019)**
> Notes on financial statements [extract]
> 1. Significant accounting policies, judgements, estimates and assumptions [extract]
> Property, plant and equipment [extract]
> Expenditure on major maintenance refits or repairs comprises the cost of replacement assets or parts of assets, inspection costs and overhaul costs. Where an asset or part of an asset that was separately depreciated is replaced and it is probable that future economic benefits associated with the item will flow to the group, the expenditure is capitalized and the carrying amount of the replaced asset is derecognized. Inspection costs associated with major maintenance programmes are capitalized and amortized over the period to the next inspection.
> Overhaul costs for major maintenance programmes, and all other maintenance costs are expensed as incurred.

Turnarounds/renewals can have a considerable impact on financial performance because of additional costs incurred and lower revenues. Therefore, fairly detailed information is generally disclosed about turnaround costs incurred in the past and turnarounds planned in the future.

> **Extract 43.47: BP p.l.c. (2012)**
> Business review: Group overview [extract]
> Our performance [extract]
> Safety [extract]
> We continued our programme of major upstream turnarounds, with 30 turnarounds completed in 2012. We expect to carry out up to 22 further turnarounds in 2013.
>
> Downstream [extract]
> Refinery operations were strong this year, with Solomon refining availability of 94.8%. (See refining availability on page 74.) Utilization rates were at 88% despite a relatively high level of turnaround activity in 2012.
>
> Business review: BP in more depth [extract]
> Profit or loss for the year [extract]
> Compared with 2010, in 2011 there were higher realizations, higher earnings from equity-accounted entities, a higher refining margin environment and a stronger supply and trading contribution, partly offset by lower production volumes, rig standby costs in the Gulf of Mexico, higher costs related to turnarounds, higher exploration write-offs, and negative impacts of increased relative sweet crude prices in Europe and Australia, primarily caused by the loss of Libya production and the weather-related power outages in the US.
>
> Risk factors [extract]
> Strategic and commercial risks [extract]
> Major project delivery – our group plan depends upon successful delivery of major projects, and failure to deliver major projects successfully could adversely affect our financial performance.
> Successful execution of our group plan depends critically on implementing the activities to deliver the major projects over the plan period. Poor delivery of any major project that underpins production or production growth and/or any other major programme designed to enhance shareholder value, including maintenance turnaround programmes, could adversely affect our financial performance. Successful project delivery requires, among other things, adequate engineering and other capabilities and therefore successful recruitment and development of staff is central to our plans.

15.2 Well workovers and recompletions (oil and gas)

Well workovers or recompletions are often required when the producing oil sands become clogged and production declines or other physical or mechanical problems arise.[121] Workover costs that relate to the day-to-day servicing of the wells (i.e. primarily the costs of labour and consumables, and possibly the cost of small parts) should be expensed as incurred. However, as discussed at 15.1 above, costs incurred to restore a well to its former level of production should be capitalised under IFRS, but an entity should derecognise any relevant previously capitalised well completion costs. However, to the extent that an entity can forecast future well workovers, it will need to depreciate the original well completion costs over a shorter economic life. Conversely, if an entity unexpectedly incurs well workover costs, it may need to consider whether those additional costs result in the need to perform an impairment test.

15.3 Care and maintenance

At certain times, a mining operation, gas plant or other substantial component of operations may be suspended because of a change in circumstances, which may include a weakening of global demand for the commodity, lower prices, higher costs, changes in demand for processing, changes in exchange rates, changes in government policy or other events of nature such as seismic events or cyclones. Such changes mean that continuing with production or further development becomes uneconomical. Instead of permanently shutting down and abandoning the mine or plant, the operations and development are curtailed and the mine, plant or operation is placed on 'care and maintenance'. This can happen either in the development phase or the production phase.

A decision to put an asset such as a mine or gas plant on care and maintenance would be an indicator of impairment (see 11.1 above). An impairment test would need to be conducted and if the recoverable amount of the CGU is less than the carrying amount, an impairment loss would need to be recognised.

While the asset remains in care and maintenance, expenditures are still incurred but usually at a lower rate than when the mine or gas plant is operating. A lower rate of depreciation for tangible non-current assets is also usually appropriate due to reduced wear and tear. Movable plant and machinery would generally be depreciated over its useful life. Management should consider depreciation to allow for deterioration. Where depreciation for movable plant and machinery had previously been determined on a units of production basis, this may no longer be appropriate.

Management should also ensure that any assets for which there are no longer any future economic benefits, i.e. which have become redundant, are written off.

The length of the closure and the associated care and maintenance expenditure may be estimated for depreciation and impairment purposes. However, it is not appropriate to recognise a provision for the entire estimated expenditure relating to the care and maintenance period. All care and maintenance costs are to be expensed as incurred.

Development costs amortised or depreciated using the units of production method would no longer be depreciated. Holding costs associated with such assets should be expensed in profit or loss in the period they are incurred. These may include costs such as security costs and site property maintenance costs.

The costs associated with restarting a mine or gas plant which had previously been on care and maintenance should only be capitalised if they improve the asset beyond its original operating capabilities. Entities will need to exercise significant judgement when performing this assessment.

15.4 Unitisations and redeterminations

15.4.1 Unitisations

A unitisation arrangement is 'an agreement between two parties each of which owns an interest in one or more mineral properties in an area to cross-assign to one another a share of the interest in the mineral properties that each owns in the area; from that point forward they share, as agreed, in further costs and revenues related to the properties'.[122] The parties pool their individual interests in return for an interest in the overall unit, which is then operated jointly to increase efficiency.[123] Once an area is subject to an unitisation arrangement, the parties share costs and production in accordance with their percentages established under the unitisation agreement. The unitisation agreement does not affect costs and production associated with non-unitised areas within the original licences, which continue to fall to the original licensees.[124]

IFRS does not specifically address accounting for a unitisation arrangement. Therefore, the accounting for such an arrangement depends on the type of asset that is subject to the arrangement. If the assets subject to the arrangement were E&E assets, then the transaction would fall within the scope of IFRS 6, which provides a temporary exemption from IAS 8 (see 3.2.1 above). An entity would be permitted to develop an accounting policy for unitisation arrangements involving E&E assets that is not based on IFRS. However, unitisations are unlikely to occur in the E&E phase when technical feasibility and commercial viability of extracting a mineral resource are not yet demonstrable.

For unitisations that occur outside the E&E phase, as there is no specific guidance in IFRS, an entity will need to develop an accounting policy in accordance with the IAS 8 hierarchy. The first step in developing an accounting policy for unitisations is setting criteria for determining which assets are included within the transaction. Particularly important is the assessment as to whether the unitisation includes the mineral reserves themselves or not. The main reason for not including the mineral reserves derives from the fact that they are subject to redetermination (see 15.4.2 below).

The example below, which is taken from the IASC's Issues Paper, illustrates how a unitisation transaction might work in practice.

Example 43.9: Unitisation[125]

Entities E and F have carried out exploration programs on separate properties owned by each in a remote area near the Antarctic Circle. Both entities have discovered petroleum reserves on their properties and have begun development of the properties. Because of the high operating costs and the need to construct support facilities, such as pipelines, dock facilities, transportation systems, and warehouses, the entities decide to unitise the properties, which mean that they have agreed to combine their properties into a single property. A joint operating agreement is signed and entity F is chosen as operator of the combined properties. Relevant data about each entity's properties and costs are given as follows:

Party E
Prospecting costs incurred prior to property acquisition	€8,000,000
Mineral acquisition costs	€42,000,000
Geological and geophysical exploration costs (G&G)	€12,000,000
Exploratory drilling costs:	
Successful	€16,000,000
Unsuccessful	€7,000,000
Development costs incurred	€23,000,000
Estimated reserves, agreed between parties (in barrels)	30,000,000

Party F
Prospecting costs incurred prior to property acquisition	€3,000,000
Mineral acquisition costs	€31,000,000
Geological and geophysical exploration costs (G&G)	€17,000,000
Exploratory drilling costs	
Successful	€24,000,000
Unsuccessful	€4,000,000
Development costs incurred	€36,000,000
Estimated reserves, agreed between parties (in barrels)	70,000,000

Ownership ratio in the venture is to be based on the relative quantity of agreed-upon reserves contributed by each party (30% to E and 70% to F). The parties agree that there should be an equalisation between them for the value of pre-unitisation exploration and development costs that directly benefit the unit, but not for other exploration and development costs. That is, there will be a cash settlement between the parties for the value of assets (other than mineral rights) or services that each party contributes to the unitisation. This is done so that the net value contributed by each party for the specified expenditures will equal that venturer's share of the total value of such expenditures at the time unitisation is consummated. Thus, the party contributing a value less than that party's share of ownership in the total value of those costs contributed by all the parties will make a cash payment to the other party so that each party's net contribution will equal that party's share of total value. The agreed amounts of costs to be equalised that are contributed by E and F are:

Expenditures made by:	E €	F €	Total €
Successful exploratory drilling	12,000,000	12,000,000	24,000,000
Development costs	18,000,000	30,000,000	48,000,000
Geological and geophysical exploration	4,000,000	14,000,000	18,000,000
Total expenditure	34,000,000	56,000,000	90,000,000

As a result of this agreement, F is obliged to pay E the net amount of €7,000,000 to equalise exploration and development costs. This is made up of the following components:

(a) €4,800,000 excess of value of exploratory drilling received by F (€16,800,000 = 70% × €24,000,000) in excess of value for successful exploratory drilling contributed (€12,000,000); plus

(b) €3,600,000 excess of value of development costs received by F in the unit (€33,600,000 = 70% × €48,000,000) in excess of the value of development costs contributed by F (€30,000,000); and less

(c) €1,400,000 excess of value of G&G costs contributed by F (€14,000,000) over the value of the share of G & G costs owned by F after unitisation (€12,600,000 = 70% × €18,000,000).

Although the reserves are unitised in the physical sense (i.e. each party will end up selling oil or gas that physically came out of the reserves of the other party), in volume terms the parties remain entitled to a quantity of reserves that is equal to that which they contributed. However, the timing of production and the costs to produce the reserves may be impacted by the unitisation agreement. The example below explains this in more detail.

Example 43.10: Reserves contributed in a unitisation

Entities A and B enter into a unitisation agreement and contribute Licences A and B, respectively. The table below shows the initial determination, redetermination and final determination of the reserves in each of the fields.

	Initial determination		Redetermination		Final determination	
	mboe		mboe		mboe	
Licence A	20	40.0%	19	37.3%	21	38.9%
Licence B	30	60.0%	32	62.7%	33	61.1%
	50	100.0%	51	100.0%	54	100.0%

Although Licences A and B were unitised, ultimately Entity A will be entitled to 21 mboe and Entity B will be entitled to 33 mboe, which is exactly the same quantity that they would have been entitled to had there been no unitisation.

To the extent that the unitisation of the mineral reserves themselves lacks commercial substance (see 6.3.2 above), it may be appropriate to exclude the mineral reserves in accounting for an unitisation. Where the unitisation significantly affects the risk and timing of the cash flows or the type of product (e.g. a unitisation could lead to an exchange of, say, gas reserves for oil reserves) there is likely to be substance to the unitisation of the reserves.

If the assets subject to the unitisation arrangement are not E&E assets, or not only E&E assets, then it is necessary to develop an accounting policy in accordance with the requirements of IAS 8. Unitisation arrangements generally give rise to joint control over the underlying assets or entities:

(a) if the unitisation arrangement results in joint control over a joint venture then the parties should apply IFRS 11 (see Chapter 12) and IAS 28 (see Chapter 11) and provide the relevant disclosures in accordance with the requirements contained in IFRS 12 (see Chapter 13); or

(b) if the unitisation arrangement gives rise to a joint operation or results in a swap of assets that are not jointly controlled, then each of the parties should account for the arrangement as an asset swap (see 6.3 above).

Under both (a) and (b) above, a party to a unitisation agreement would report a gain (or loss) depending on whether the fair value of the interest received is higher (or lower) than the carrying amount of the interest given up.

15.4.2 Redeterminations

The percentage interests in a unitisation arrangement are based on estimates of the relative quantities of reserves contributed by each of the parties. As field life progresses and production experience is gained, many unitisation agreements require the reserves to be redetermined, which often leads the parties to conclude that the recoverable reserves in one or perhaps both of the original properties are not as previously estimated. Unitisation agreements typically require one or more 'redeterminations' of percentage interests once better reservoir information becomes available. In most cases, the revised percentage interests are deemed to be effective from the date of the original unitisation agreement, which means that adjustments are required between the parties in respect of their relative entitlements to cumulative production and their shares of cumulative costs.[126]

Unitisation agreements normally set out when redeterminations need to take place and the way in which adjustments to the percentage interests should be effected. The former OIAC SORP described the process as follows:

'(a) Adjustments in respect of cumulative "capital" costs are usually made immediately following the redetermination by means of a lump sum reimbursement, sometimes including an "interest" or uplift element to reflect related financing costs.

(b) Adjustments to shares of cumulative production are generally effected prospectively. Participants with an increased share are entitled to additional "make-up" production until the cumulative liftings are rebalanced. During this period adjusted percentage interests are applied to both production entitlement and operating costs. Once equity is achieved the effective percentage interests revert to those established by the redetermination.'[127]

An adjustment to an entity's percentage interest due to a redetermination is not a prior period error under IFRS. *[IAS 8.5]*. Instead, the redetermination results from new information or new developments and therefore should be treated as a change in an accounting estimate. Accordingly, a redetermination should not result in a fully retrospective adjustment.

Redeterminations give rise to some further accounting issues which are discussed below.

15.4.2.A Redeterminations as capital reimbursements

Under many national GAAPs, redeterminations are accounted for as reimbursement of capital expenditure rather than as sales/purchases of a partial interest. Given that this second approach could result in the recognition of a gain upon redetermination, followed by a higher depreciation charge per barrel, it has become accepted industry practice that redeterminations should be accounted for as reimbursements of capital expenditure under IFRS. Both approaches are illustrated in Example 43.11 below.

In addition, a redetermination gives rise to a number of questions, for example, how should the entities account for:

- the adjustment of their share in the remaining reserves;
- the 'make-up' oil obligation; and
- their revised shares in the decommissioning liabilities.

The 'make-up' oil obligation and the revised shares in the decommissioning liabilities are discussed further following the example below.

Example 43.11: Redetermination (1)

Entities A and B have a 10% and 90% percentage interest in a unitised property, respectively. On 1 January 2020, after three years of operations, their interests in the property are redetermined. The relevant data about each entity's interest in the property are as follows:

	A	B	Total
Percentage interest after initial determination	10%	90%	100%
Percentage interest after redetermination	8%	92%	100%
Initial reserves at 1/1/2020 (million barrels of oil equivalent)	100 mboe	900 mboe	1000 mboe
Total production from 2017 to 2019	30 mboe	270 mboe	300 mboe
Remaining reserves at 31/12/2019 before redetermination	70 mboe	630 mboe	700 mboe
Reserves after redetermination at 1/1/2020	56 mboe	644 mboe	700 mboe
'Make-up' oil: 300 mboe × (10% – 8%) =	–6 mboe	6 mboe	–
Total entitlement at 1/1/2020	50 mboe	650 mboe	700 mboe
	$	$	$
Exploration and development asset at 1/1/2017	400	3,600	4,000
Units of production depreciation:			
$400 ÷ 100 mboe × 30 mboe =	120		120
$3,600 ÷ 900 mboe × 270 mboe =		1,080	1,080
Exploration and development asset at 31/12/2019 before redetermination	280	2,520	2,800

	A	B	Total
Total investment based on 'initial determination':			
A: 10% of $4,000 = $400 and B: 90% of $4,000 = $3,600	400	3,600	4,000
Total investment based on redetermination:			
A: 8% of $4,000 = $320 and B: 92% of $4,000 = $3,680	320	3,680	4,000
Reimbursement of exploration and development costs	80	–80	–
Decommissioning asset at 1/1/2017	100	900	1,000
Units of production depreciation:			
$100 ÷ 100 mboe × 30 mboe =	30		30
$900 ÷ 900 mboe × 270 mboe =		270	270
Decommissioning asset at 31/12/2019 before redetermination	70	630	700
Decommissioning provision at 1/1/2017	100	900	1,000
Accreted interest from 1/1/2017 to 31/12/2019	20	180	200
Decommissioning provision at 31/12/2019 before redetermination	120	1,080	1,200
Reduction in decommissioning provision	–24	24	–
Decommissioning provision at 1/1/2020:			
A: 8% of $1,200 = $96 and B: 92% of $1,200 = $1,104	96	1,104	1,200

There are different ways in which an entity might interpret the effect of a redetermination on the exploration and development asset:

(a) Reimbursement of capital expenditure; or
(b) Sale/purchase of a partial interest.

Reimbursement of capital expenditure

Under this approach, the redetermination is treated as a reimbursement of capital expenditure and the 'make-up' oil is accounted for prospectively. This would lead entity A to make the following journal entries:

		$	$
Dr	Cash	80	
Cr	Exploration and development asset		80

The reimbursement of exploration and development costs is accounted for as a reduction in the exploration and development asset.

The overall impact on the statement of financial position of both Entities A and B is summarised in the table below:

	A $	B $	Total $
Exploration and development asset at 31/12/2019 before redetermination	280	2,520	2,800
Reimbursement of exploration and development costs	–80	80	–
Exploration and development asset at 1/1/2020 after redetermination	200	2,600	2,800

Before the redetermination both A and B would record depreciation of the exploration and development asset of $4/barrel (i.e. A: $400 ÷ 100 mboe = $4/barrel and B: $3,600 ÷ 900 mboe = $4/barrel). After the redetermination the depreciation of the exploration and development asset is still $4/barrel for both A and B (i.e. A: $200 ÷ 50 mboe = $4/barrel and B: $2,600 ÷ 650 mboe = $4/barrel).

Sale/purchase of a partial interest

The second approach, which is sometimes advocated, is to treat the redetermination as the equivalent of a sale or purchase of part of an interest.

		$	$
Dr	Cash	80	
Cr	Exploration and development asset: (8% – 10%) ÷ 10% × $280 =		56
Cr	Gain on disposal of exploration and development asset		24

The reimbursement of exploration and development costs is accounted for as a partial disposal of the exploration and development asset.

However, Entity B will treat its entire payment of $80 to Entity A as the cost of the additional 2% interest that it 'acquired' in the redetermination. The overall impact on the statement of financial position of both Entities A and B is summarised in the table below:

	A $	B $	Total $
Exploration and development asset at 31/12/2019 before redetermination	280	2,520	2,800
Reimbursement of exploration and development costs	–56	80	–
Exploration and development asset at 1/1/2020 after redetermination	224	2,600	2,824

After the redetermination the depreciation of exploration and development asset for Entity A is ($224 ÷ 50 mboe =) $4.48/barrel and for Entity B is ($2,600 ÷ 650 mboe =) $4/barrel.

15.4.2.B 'Make-up' oil

As indicated in Example 43.11 above, Entity B would be entitled to 6 mboe of 'make-up' oil out of Entity A's share of the production. This raises the question whether Entity A should recognise a liability for the 'make-up' oil and whether Entity B should recognise an asset for the 'make-up' oil that it is entitled to.

'Make-up' oil is in many ways comparable to an overlift or underlift of oil, because after the redetermination it appears that Entity A is effectively in an overlift position (i.e. it has sold more product than its proportionate share of production) while Entity B is in an underlift position (i.e. it has sold less product than its proportionate share of production).

IFRS does not directly address accounting for underlifts and overlifts (as discussed at 12.4 above) or accounting for 'make-up' oil following a redetermination. Consequently, an entity that is entitled to receive or is obliged to pay 'make-up' oil will need to apply the hierarchy in IAS 8 to develop an accounting policy that is compliant with current IFRS. In doing so, the entity may look to the accounting standards of another standard-setter with a similar conceptual framework, such as US GAAP or UK GAAP, in which case the entity would not recognise an asset or liability and account for the 'make-up' oil prospectively.

Under many unitisation agreements, entities are required to give up oil only to the extent that there is production from the underlying field. Under these circumstances, Entity A would have no obligation to deliver oil or make another form of payment to the other parties under the unitisation agreement. In those cases, the 'make-up' oil obligation would not meet the definition of financial liability under IAS 32 or that of a provision under IAS 37. It may also be considered that Entity B cannot recognise an asset, because its right to 'make-up' oil only arises because of a future event (i.e. the future production of oil).

15.4.2.C Decommissioning provisions

Another effect of a redetermination is that it may increase or decrease an entity's share of the decommissioning liability in relation to the project, as illustrated in the example below.

Example 43.12: Redetermination (2)

Assuming the same facts as in Example 43.11 above, how should Entities A and B account for the change in the decommissioning provision?

Under IFRIC 1 the change in a decommissioning provision should be added to, or deducted from, the cost of the related asset in the current period. However, if a decrease in the liability exceeds the carrying amount of the asset, the excess should be recognised immediately in profit or loss. *[IFRIC 1.5].*

This would lead Entities A and B to make the following journal entries:

		$	$
Entity A			
Dr	Decommissioning provision	24	
Cr	Decommissioning asset		24
Entity B			
Dr	Decommissioning asset	24	
Cr	Decommissioning provision		24

The decommission asset is adjusted in accordance with IFRIC 1 for the change in the decommissioning provision.

If Entity A had recognised a gain of $24 upon the reduction of the decommissioning liability, this would have resulted in an increase in the depreciation of the decommissioning asset from ($100 ÷ 100 mboe =) $1/barrel to ($70 ÷ 50 mboe =) $1.40/barrel. The IFRIC 1 approach avoids this although it increases the depreciation of the decommissioning asset slightly to ($56 ÷ 50mboe =) $1.12/barrel, as the decommissioning provision is also affected by the accretion of interest. Nevertheless, the approach required by IFRIC 1 is largely consistent with the treatment of a redetermination as a reimbursement of capital expenditure in Example 43.11 above.

15.5 Stripping costs in the production phase of a surface mine (mining)

In surface mining operations it is necessary to remove overburden and other waste materials to gain access to ore from which minerals can be extracted – this is also referred to as stripping. IFRIC 20 specifies how stripping costs incurred during the production phase of a surface mine are to be accounted for. IFRIC 20 considers the different types of stripping costs encountered in a surface mining operation. These costs are separated into those incurred in the development phase of the mine (i.e. pre-production) and those that are incurred in the production phase. *[IFRIC 20.2, 3]*. For these purposes, the mine is considered to be an asset that is separate from the mineral rights and mineral reserves, which are outside the scope of IAS 16. *[IAS 16.3(d)]*.

15.5.1 Scope of IFRIC 20

Generally, those costs incurred in the development phase of a mine would be capitalised as part of the depreciable cost of building, developing and constructing the mine, under the principles of IAS 16. Ultimately, these capitalised costs are depreciated or amortised on a systematic basis, usually by using the units of production method, once production commences. The stripping costs incurred in the development phase of a mine are not considered by IFRIC 20.

Instead, the interpretation applies to all waste removal (stripping) costs incurred during the production phase of a surface mine (production stripping costs). *[IFRIC 20.2]*. It does not apply to oil and natural gas extraction and underground mining activities. Also, it does not address the question of whether oil sands extraction is considered to be a surface mining activity and therefore whether it is in scope or not. *[IFRIC 20.BC4]*.

Despite the importance of the term 'production phase', this is not defined in the Interpretation, or elsewhere in IFRS. See 15.5.2 below for further discussion of production phase.

Stripping activity undertaken during the production phase may create two benefits (1) the extraction of ore (inventory) in the current period and (2) improved access to the ore body to be mined in a future period. Where the benefits are realised in the form of inventory produced, the production stripping costs are to be accounted for in accordance with IAS 2. Where the benefits are improved access to ore to be mined in the future, these costs are to be recognised as a non-current asset, if the required criteria are met (see 15.5.2 below). The Interpretation refers to this non-current asset as the 'stripping activity asset'. *[IFRIC 20.8]*.

15.5.2 Determining when production phase commences

As noted above, there is no specific guidance or definition in IFRS relating to the concept of production phase. The production phase is considered to commence once the asset is in the location and condition necessary for it to be capable of operating in the manner intended by management. Given the nature of mining and metals projects, the key area of judgement is determining exactly when an asset is in the location and condition necessary for it to be capable of operating as intended by management.

The determination of the commencement of the production phase, which is also often referred to as the commissioning date, not only affects stripping costs, but also affects many other accounting issues in the extractive industries, described in more detail below. These include the cessation of the capitalisation of other costs, including borrowing costs, the commencement of depreciation or amortisation (see 16 below), and the treatment of certain pre-production revenues (see 12.1 above).

For some larger mining and metals entities, determining the production date may not be as critical as it may be for a smaller entity, particularly when that smaller entity only has one major mining project. In some instances, a difference of a week could have a material impact.

No specific guidance exists within IFRS, particularly as to what it means for an asset to be 'in the location and condition necessary for it to be capable of operating as intended by management'. Consequently, various approaches have evolved. It is common for many entities to simply refer to the achievement of 'commercial production' as the point at which the assets are commissioned, i.e. ready for their intended use, without providing any detail as to exactly what commercial production means. Having said this, some entities identify 'production start date' as a significant judgement and provide more detailed disclosures.

In our experience, many entities distinguish start-up/ commissioning from post-commissioning costs, which can also be referred as ramp-up or operating costs. Start-up/ commissioning costs are often capitalised when the asset is available for use, but is incapable of operating at normal levels without the necessary start-up/commissioning period. Generally, this allows costs associated with the physical capabilities of a mining and metals project to be capitalised, but not the costs incurred as a result of the need to build up demand. Deliberate or avoidable delays in achieving physical completion or obtaining necessary approvals to operate the mine are likely to be deemed abnormal and expensed as incurred.

While disclosures may sometimes be limited, as part of the process of assessing when a mining and metals project is ready for its intended use, a variety of factors are often considered with varying degrees of emphasis placed on each. The specific factors used are generally determined by the unique nature of each mine and is impacted by the complexity of the project and its location.

While not specifically contained in any IFRS guidance, some examples of the range of factors that are often considered include:
- the level of capital expenditure compared to the estimated construction cost;
- a majority of the assets making up the mining project are substantially complete and ready for use;
- completion of a reasonable period of testing of the mine plant and equipment;
- the project has been turned over to operations from the development team;
- a specified percentage of design capacity for the mine and/or mill, e.g. 50% to 70%, has been achieved over a continuous period, e.g. three months;
- the percentage grade (metal content) of ore being mined is sufficiently economic and consistent with the overall mine plan;
- the ability to produce the commodity in a saleable form (within specifications and the *de minimis* rule); and
- the ability to sustain ongoing production over a certain period, e.g. one to three months.

Generally, no single factor is considered more important than another. Entities must be cautious in how they apply these factors as they can sometimes be open to abuse. Each factor must be considered in context with the facts and circumstances of the specific project.

15.5.3 Recognition criteria – stripping activity asset

IFRIC 20 states that an entity must recognise a stripping activity asset if, and only if, all of the following criteria are satisfied:
(a) it is probable that the future economic benefit (improved access to the ore body) associated with the stripping activity will flow to the entity;
(b) the entity can identify the component of the ore body for which access has been improved; and
(c) the costs relating to the stripping activity associated with that component can be measured reliably. *[IFRIC 20.9]*.

Instead of being a separate asset, the stripping activity asset is to be accounted for as an addition to, or as an enhancement of, an existing asset. This means that the stripping activity asset will be accounted for as part of an existing asset. *[IFRIC 20.10]*. IFRIC 20 does not specify whether the stripping activity asset is a tangible or intangible asset. Instead, it simply states that it should be classified as tangible or intangible according to the nature of the existing asset of which it is part – so it will depend upon whether an entity classifies its mine assets as tangible or intangible.

The Interpretation considers that the stripping activity asset might add to or improve a variety of existing assets, such as, the mine property (land), the mineral deposit itself, an intangible right to extract the ore or an asset that originated in the mine development phase. *[IFRIC 20.BC10]*. In most instances, entities classify their producing mine assets as tangible assets; therefore, it is likely that the stripping activity assets will also be classified as tangible assets.

15.5.4 Initial recognition

The stripping activity asset is to be initially measured at cost. This will be the accumulation of costs directly incurred to perform the stripping activity that benefits the identified component of ore, plus an allocation of directly attributable overhead costs. *[IFRIC 20.12]*. Examples of the types of costs expected to be included as directly attributable overhead costs are items such as salary costs of the mine supervisor overseeing that component of the mine, and an allocation of rental costs of any equipment hired specifically to perform the stripping activity. *[IFRIC 20.BC12]*.

Some incidental operations may take place at the same time as the production stripping activity that are not necessary for the production stripping activity to continue as planned. The costs associated with these incidental operations are not to be included in the cost of the stripping activity asset. *[IFRIC 20.12]*. An example provided in the Interpretation is the building of an access ramp in the area in which the production stripping activity is taking place. These ancillary costs must be recognised as assets or expensed in accordance with other IFRSs.

15.5.4.A Allocating costs between inventory and the stripping activity asset

If the costs of waste removal can be directly allocated between inventory and the stripping activity asset, then the entity should allocate those costs accordingly. However, it may be difficult in practice to identify these costs separately, particularly if inventory is produced at the same time as access to the ore body is improved. This is likely to be very common in practice. Where this is the case, the Interpretation permits an entity to use an allocation approach that is based on a relevant production measure as this is considered to be a good indicator of the nature of benefits that are generated for the activity taking place in the mine. *[IFRIC 20.13]*.

The Interpretation provides a (non-exhaustive) list of some of the possible metrics that could be used to determine the appropriate allocation basis. These include:

- cost of inventory produced compared with expected cost;
- volume of waste extracted compared with expected volume, for a given volume of ore production; and
- mineral content of the ore extracted compared with expected mineral content to be extracted, for a given quantity of ore produced. *[IFRIC 20.13]*.

An allocation basis which uses sales value or relative sales value is not acceptable. *[IFRIC 20.BC15]*.

The production measure is calculated for each identified component of the ore body. Application of this allocation methodology effectively involves a comparison of the expected level of activity for that component with the actual level of activity for the same component, to identify when additional activity may have occurred and may be creating a future benefit. See 15.5.4.B below for further discussion about how to determine a component.

Where the actual level of activity exceeds the expected level of activity, the waste removal activity incurred at the expected level and its associated costs would then form part of the cost of inventory produced in that period. Any excess of actual activity over the expected level (and the associated costs of such excess activity) needs to be considered to determine whether it represents a stripping activity asset.

It is important to note that where actual stripping levels exceed those expected for the identified component, this will not automatically result in the recognition of a stripping activity asset. An entity will need to assess whether the removal of such additional waste has actually resulted in a future economic benefit, i.e. improved access to future ore. If not, such costs should not be capitalised as an asset, but instead should be recognised in profit or loss in the period incurred. For example, the mining of an unexpected fault or dyke should not be capitalised but instead expensed as incurred.

Where actual waste removal activity is less than the expected level of activity, only the actual waste removed and its associated costs, not the expected costs, will form part of the cost of inventory produced in that period. This is because continuing to recognise waste costs at the expected level would require an entity to recognise a deferred stripping liability. This is not permitted under IFRIC 20 or generally under IFRS because, in the absence of a legal or constructive obligation to continue to mine the deposit, such costs would not satisfy the criteria to be recognised as a liability.

It is worth noting that while some of the allocation approaches set out in the Interpretation are similar to the life-of-mine average strip ratio approach used by many entities prior to the introduction of IFRIC 20, there are differences.

The key difference is that the level at which the expected level of activity is to be determined when calculating the relevant production measure is likely to be lower than that was previously used for the life-of-mine average strip ratio approach. The life-of-mine average strip ratio approach used the entire ore body, whereas IFRIC 20 requires this to be determined for each component of the ore body, which is expected to be a subset of the ore body. See 15.5.4.B below for further discussion about how to determine a component.

The other difference relates to the way in which any stripping activity asset is recognised in profit or loss. Under the life-of-mine average stripping ratio approach, a portion of the deferred stripping asset was recognised in profit or loss when the actual stripping ratio fell below the expected average life-of-mine strip ratio. Under IFRIC 20 however, the stripping activity asset is to be depreciated or amortised over the useful life of the identified component of the ore body that becomes more accessible. The units of production (UOP) method is to be used unless another method is more appropriate. *[IFRIC 20.15]*.

It is important to note that the calculation of the expected production measure for each component will need to be reviewed and updated if there are material changes to the mine plan for that component (for example due to differences in actual versus budgeted performance or changes in future mining plans resulting from other factors, e.g. changes in commodity prices or increases in costs). Should these changes impact the expected production measure for the remaining life of the component, then the IFRIC 20 calculations will need to be updated and applied on a prospective basis. The calculation of the expected production measures will also be required if and when new components commence production.

Example 43.13: Allocating costs between inventory and the stripping activity asset

Scenario A – actual performance measure exceeds the expected performance measure

The following example illustrates how an entity would allocate costs between inventory and the stripping activity asset where the actual performance measure exceeds the expected performance measure for a component in a particular period.

Assume Entity A has a mine which comprises two separate pits which are accessing the one ore body. For the purposes of IFRIC 20, each pit is identified as a component. Pit 1 has a total life of three years and at reporting period end, has been in production for one year. Pit 2 has a total life of five years but production has not yet commenced.

At the commencement of production from pit 1, the company has forecast the following mining and stripping activity:

Expected ore to be extracted over the 3 years	1,000 tonnes
Expected volume of waste to be extracted over the 3 years	3,000 tonnes

During the current period, the following had occurred in relation to the production from pit 1:

Cost incurred for mining activity	$13,000,000 (a)
Actual tonnes of ore removed	100 tonnes (b)
Actual tonnes of waste removed	1,200 tonnes (c)
Average cost per tonne in year 1 = (a) / [(b)+(c)]	$10,000

The company determined that it is not practically possible to identify separately what portion of the waste removal costs leads to the extraction of inventory and what portion to improved access to future ore. This is because these two activities were occurring simultaneously as there were multiple shovels in operation in multiple parts of the component and a single haulage fleet was used.

Given this, the company has decided that it will allocate costs by comparing the actual volume of waste and ore extracted (the actual strip ratio) in the period with the expected volume of waste and ore (expected strip ratio) for the life of the component i.e. for pit 1.

The allocation of the actual waste removal costs incurred will involve the following steps:

Step 1: Calculate the expected strip ratio for pit 1

Expected volume of waste to be extracted / expected volume of ore to be extracted

= 3,000 tonnes / 1,000 tonnes

= 3.00 (expected strip ratio)

This means that for every 1 tonne of ore extracted over the life of pit 1, the company expects (on average) to remove 3 tonnes of waste.

Step 2: Calculate the additional waste extracted compared to the expected waste extracted for the actual volume of ore extracted

Actual volume of ore extracted × expected strip ratio

= 100 tonnes × 3 tonnes

= 300 tonnes

Actual volume of waste extracted in year 1 = 1,200 tonnes

Additional waste extracted in year 1 = actual waste extracted less expected waste to be extracted

= 1,200 tonnes – 300 tonnes

= 900 tonnes of additional waste was extracted

Step 3: Allocate mining costs between inventory and the stripping activity asset

Stripping activity asset

Additional waste tonnes removed × cost per tonne

= 900 tonnes × $10,000

= $9,000,000

Inventory

Total mining costs incurred less costs allocated to the stripping activity asset

= $13,000,000 – $9,000,000

= $4,000,000

This comprises:

(1) The cost of extracting the inventory tonnes

= 100 × $10,000

= $1,000,000

Plus:

(2) The cost of waste removal allocated directly to inventory (which was allocated at the expected level of 3:1)

= 300 tonnes × $10,000

= $3,000,000

Scenario B – actual strip ratio is less than the expected strip ratio

Assume the same basic fact pattern as per Scenario A above, but with different actual mining results for pit 1 in the current period:

Cost incurred for mining activity	$13,000,000 (a)
Actual tonnes of ore removed	1,200 tonnes (b)
Actual tonnes of waste removed	100 tonnes (c)
Average cost per tonne in year 1 = (a) / [(b) + (c)]	$10,000

The allocation of the actual waste removal costs incurred will involve the following steps:

Step 1: Calculate the expected strip ratio for pit 1

Expected volume of waste to be extracted / expected volume of ore to be extracted

= 3,000 tonnes / 1,000 tonnes

= 3.00 (expected strip ratio)

This means that for every 1 tonne of ore extracted over the life of pit 1, the company expects (on average) to remove 3 tonnes of waste.

Step 2: Calculate the additional waste extracted compared to the expected waste extracted for the actual volume of ore extracted

Actual volume of ore extracted × expected strip ratio

= 1,200 tonnes × 3 tonnes

= 3,600 tonnes

Actual volume of waste extracted in year 1 = 100 tonnes

During the current period the actual strip ratio was only 0.0833. As this is less than the expected strip ratio, as explained above, there is no additional waste removed during the period.

Step 3: Allocate mining costs between inventory and the stripping activity asset

Stripping activity asset

As the actual strip ratio was below the expected strip ratio, no additional waste was removed during the period; therefore there is no amount to be added to the stripping activity asset.

Inventory

As the actual amount of waste removed during the current period is less than the expected level of waste for the life of the component, and there is no amount to be allocated to the stripping activity asset, then the total mining costs for the period will be allocated to inventory.

= $13,000,000

This comprises:

(1) The cost of extracting the inventory tonnes

= 1,200 × $10,000

= $12,000,000

Plus:

(2) The cost of waste removal allocated directly to inventory (which is allocated based on the actual waste tonnes removed during the period)

= 100 tonnes × $10,000

= $1,000,000

15.5.4.B Identifying the component of the ore body

Identifying the various components of the ore body is one of the critical steps in applying IFRIC 20. This is necessary for several reasons:

(a) production stripping costs can only be capitalised as an asset if the component of the ore body for which access has been improved, can be identified;

(b) to allocate stripping activity costs between inventory and the stripping activity asset, an entity needs to determine the expected level of activity for each component of the mine; and

(c) the stripping activity asset is required to be depreciated or amortised on a systematic basis, over the expected useful life of the identified component of the ore body that becomes more accessible as a result of the stripping activity.

The Interpretation provides limited guidance on how to identify components, although it does appear a component is expected to be a subset of the whole ore body. This view is supported in several parts of IFRIC 20.

- A 'component' refers to the specific volume of the ore body that is made more accessible by the stripping activity; the identified component of the ore body would typically be a subset of the total ore body of the mine; and a mine may have several components, which are identified during the mine planning stage. [IFRIC 20.BC8].

- The depreciation or amortisation requirements state that the expected useful life of the identified component of the ore body that is used to depreciate or amortise the stripping activity asset will differ from the expected useful life that is used to depreciate or amortise the mine itself and the related life-of-mine assets, unless the stripping activity provides improved access to the whole of the ore body. [IFRIC 20.BC17].

In practice, the identification of components of an ore body is a complex process which requires a significant amount of management judgement. While it is considered that an entity's mine plan will provide the information required allowing these judgements to be made with reasonable consistency, this may not be a straightforward exercise, and it will be particularly challenging for the more complex mines. This is because ore bodies vary significantly in shape and size and are more haphazard than often illustrated in simple examples. Management may identify components in a number of different ways. These could include identifying discrete components in the mine plan, such as phases, sections, push backs, cutbacks, lay backs, blocks, etc.; examining annual production plans; or examining push back campaigns. Whatever approach is adopted, it is essential that the components are recognisable to those who are responsible for mine planning as they will be the ones who will need to track progress as ore is removed and will need to update the assessment of components should the mine plan change. Given this, practice has revealed that when identifying the components of an ore body, it is essential that input is obtained from those who best understand the mine plan, i.e. the mining engineers and operational personnel.

The identification of components will need to be reassessed and updated (if necessary) whenever there are material changes to the mine plan. Given this, an entity will need to establish systems, processes, procedures and controls to ensure it is able to identify when material changes to the mine plan have occurred that would require the IFRIC 20 calculations to be updated. Identification of components will also be required when an entity commences production on a new component of the ore body or in relation to a new ore body.

15.5.5 Subsequent measurement

After initial recognition, the stripping activity asset must be carried at its cost or revalued amount less depreciation or amortisation and less impairment losses, in the same way as the existing asset of which it is a part. *[IFRIC 20.14]*. The stripping activity asset is to be depreciated or amortised on a systematic basis, over the expected useful life of the identified component of the ore body that becomes more accessible as a result of the stripping activity. *[IFRIC 20.15]*.

The units of production method is effectively required to be applied unless another method is more appropriate. *[IFRIC 20.15]*. The expected useful life of the identified component that is used to depreciate or amortise the stripping activity asset will differ from the expected useful life that is used to depreciate or amortise the mine itself and the related life-of-mine assets, unless the stripping activity provides improved access to the whole of the ore body (this is expected to be rare). *[IFRIC 20.16]*.

Consistent with the units of production method used for other mining assets, the calculation of the units of production rate will be completed when a stripping activity asset is first recognised. It will then need to be reviewed (and if necessary, updated) at the end of each reporting period, or when the mine plan changes. The new units of production rate will be applied prospectively.

Given the depreciation or amortisation of the stripping activity asset represents the consumption of the benefits associated with the stripping activity asset, and those benefits are realised by the extraction of the ore to which the stripping activity asset relates (i.e. the ore for which access was improved by the removal of this waste in prior periods), this depreciation or amortisation effectively represents part of the cost of extracting that ore in future periods. In accordance with IAS 2, such costs should be included in the cost of that subsequent ore. This effectively means that the depreciation or amortisation of the stripping activity asset should be recapitalised as part of the cost of the inventory produced in those subsequent periods. Once the inventory is sold, those costs will be recognised in profit or loss as part of cost of goods sold.

15.5.6 Disclosures

IFRIC 20 has no specific disclosure requirements. However, the general disclosure requirements of IAS 1 are relevant, e.g. the requirements to disclose significant accounting policies, *[IAS 1.117]*, and significant judgements, estimates and assumptions. *[IAS 1.125]*. For many entities, it is likely that the accounting policy for stripping costs would be considered a significant accounting policy which would therefore warrant disclosure, as would the judgements, estimates and assumptions they make when applying this policy.

The extract below from Rio Tinto illustrates an IFRIC 20 accounting policy disclosure.

> **Extract 43.48: Rio Tinto plc (2019)**
> Notes to the 2019 financial statements [extract]
> 1 Principal accounting policies [extract]
> (h) Deferred stripping (note 14) [extract]
>
> In open pit mining operations, overburden and other waste materials must be removed to access ore from which minerals can be extracted economically. The process of removing overburden and waste materials is referred to as stripping. During the development of a mine (or, in some instances, pit; see below), before production commences, stripping costs related to a component of an orebody are capitalised as part of the cost of construction of the mine (or pit) and are subsequently amortised over the life of the mine (or pit) on a units of production basis.
>
> Where a mine operates several open pits that are regarded as separate operations for the purpose of mine planning, initial stripping costs are accounted for separately by reference to the ore from each separate pit. If, however, the pits are highly integrated for the purpose of mine planning, the second and subsequent pits are regarded as extensions of the first pit in accounting for stripping costs. In such cases, the initial stripping (i.e. overburden and other waste removal) of the second and subsequent pits is considered to be production phase stripping... The Group's judgment as to whether multiple pit mines are considered separate or integrated operations depends on each mine's specific circumstances.
>
> The following factors would point towards the initial stripping costs for the individual pits being accounted for separately:
> - If mining of the second and subsequent pits is conducted consecutively following that of the first pit, rather than concurrently;
> - If separate investment decisions are made to develop each pit, rather than a single investment decision being made at the outset;
> - If the pits are operated as separate units in terms of mine planning and the sequencing of overburden removal and ore mining, rather than as an integrated unit;
> - If expenditures for additional infrastructure to support the second and subsequent pits are relatively large; and
> - If the pits extract ore from separate and distinct orebodies, rather than from a single orebody.
>
> If the designs of the second and subsequent pits are significantly influenced by opportunities to optimise output from several pits combined, including the co-treatment or blending of the output from the pits, then this would point to treatment as an integrated operation for the purposes of accounting for initial stripping costs. The relative importance of each of the above factors is considered in each case.
>
> In order for production phase stripping costs to qualify for capitalisation as a stripping activity asset, three criteria must be met:
> - It must be probable that there will be an economic benefit in a future accounting period because the stripping activity has improved access to the orebody;
> - It must be possible to identify the "component" of the orebody for which access has been improved; and
> - It must be possible to reliably measure the costs that relate to the stripping activity.
>
> A "component" is a specific section of the orebody that is made more accessible by the stripping activity. It will typically be a subset of the larger orebody that is distinguished by a separate useful economic life (for example, a pushback).
>
> Production phase stripping can give rise to two benefits: the extraction of ore in the current period and improved access to ore which will be extracted in future periods. When the cost of stripping which has a future benefit is not distinguishable from the cost of producing current inventories, the stripping cost is allocated to each of these activities based on a relevant production measure using a life-of-component strip ratio. The ratio divides the tonnage of waste mined for the component for the period either by the quantity of ore mined for the component or by the quantity of minerals contained in the ore mined for the component. In some operations, the quantity of ore is a more appropriate basis for allocating costs, particularly where there are significant by-products. Stripping costs for the component are deferred to the extent that the current period ratio exceeds the life of component ratio. The stripping activity asset is depreciated on a "units of production" basis based on expected production of either ore or minerals contained in the ore over the life of the component unless another method is more appropriate.

The life-of-component ratios are based on the ore reserves of the mine (and for some mines, other mineral resources) and the annual mine plan; they are a function of the mine design and, therefore, changes to that design will generally result in changes to the ratios. Changes in other technical or economic parameters that impact the ore reserves (and for some mines, other mineral resources) may also have an impact on the life-of-component ratios even if they do not affect the mine design. Changes to the ratios are accounted for prospectively.

It may be the case that subsequent phases of stripping will access additional ore and that these subsequent phases are only possible after the first phase has taken place. Where applicable, the Group considers this on a mine-by-mine basis. Generally, the only ore attributed to the stripping activity asset for the purposes of calculating a life-of-component ratio, and for the purposes of amortisation, is the ore to be extracted from the originally identified component.

Deferred stripping costs are included in "Mining properties and leases" within "Property, plant and equipment" or within "Investments in equity accounted units", as appropriate. Amortisation of deferred stripping costs is included in "Depreciation of property, plant and equipment" within "Net operating costs" or in "Share of profit after tax of equity accounted units", as appropriate.

Critical accounting policies and estimates [extract]

(v) Deferral of stripping costs (note 14)

Stripping of waste materials takes place throughout the production phase of a surface mine or pit. The identification of components within a mine and of the life of component strip ratios requires judgment and is dependent on an individual mine's design and the estimates inherent within that. Changes to that design may introduce new components and/or change the life of component strip ratios. Changes in other technical or economic parameters that impact ore reserves may also have an impact on the life of component strip ratios, even if they do not affect the mine's design. Changes to the life of component strip ratios are accounted for prospectively.

The Group's judgment as to whether multiple pit mines are considered separate or integrated operations determines whether initial stripping of a pit is deemed to be pre-production or production phase stripping and, therefore, the amortisation base for those costs. The analysis depends on each mine's specific circumstances and requires judgment: another mining company could make a different judgment even when the fact pattern appears to be similar.

14 Property, plant and equipment [extract]

Property, plant and equipment – Owned [extract]

(a)   At 31 December 2019, the net book value of capitalised production phase stripping costs totalled US$2,276 million, with US$1,833 million within Property, plant and equipment and a further US$443 million within Investments in equity accounted units (2018: total of US$2,050 million, with US$1,572 million in Property, plant and equipment and a further US$478 million within Investments in equity accounted units). During the year capitalisation of US$536 million was partly offset by depreciation of US$316 million (including amounts recorded within equity accounted units). Depreciation of deferred stripping costs in respect of subsidiaries of US$139 million (2018: US$134 million; 2017: US$194 million) is included within "Depreciation for the year".

16   DEPRECIATION, DEPLETION AND AMORTISATION (DD&A)

16.1   Requirements under IAS 16 and IAS 38

The main types of depreciable assets of mining companies and oil and gas companies are property, plant and equipment, intangible assets and mineral reserves, although the exact titles given to these types of assets may vary.

While 'mineral rights and expenditure on the exploration for, or development and extraction of, minerals, oil, natural gas and similar non-regenerative resources' are outside the scope of IAS 16 and IAS 38, any items of property, plant and equipment (PP&E) and other intangible assets that are used in the extraction of mineral reserves should be accounted for under IAS 16 and IAS 38. *[IAS 16.2, 3, IAS 38.2]*.

For items of PP&E, various descriptions are used for such assets which can include producing mines, mine assets, oil and gas assets, producing properties. Whatever the description given, IAS 16 requires depreciation of an item of PP&E over its useful life. Depreciation is required to be calculated separately for each part (often referred to as a 'component'), of an item of PP&E with a cost that is significant in relation to the total cost of the item, unless the item can be grouped with other items of PP&E that have the same useful life and depreciation method. *[IAS 16.43, 45]*.

The guidance in IAS 16 relating to parts of an asset does not apply directly to intangible assets as IAS 38 does not apply a 'parts' approach, or to mineral rights, but we believe that entities should use the general principles for determining an appropriate unit of account that are outlined at 4 above. IAS 16's general requirements are described in Chapter 18 and IAS 38 is addressed in Chapter 17.

16.1.1 Mineral reserves

In the absence of a standard or an interpretation specifically applicable to mineral reserves and their related expenditures, which are technically outside the scope of IAS 16 and IAS 38, management needs to develop an accounting policy for the depreciation or amortisation of mineral reserves in accordance with the hierarchy in IAS 8, taking into account the requirements and guidance in Standards and Interpretations dealing with similar and related issues and the definitions, recognition criteria and measurement concepts for assets, liabilities, income and expenses in the *Conceptual Framework*. *[IAS 8.11]*. In practice, an entity will generally develop an accounting policy that is based on the depreciation and amortisation principles in IAS 16 and IAS 38, which deal with similar and related issues.

16.1.2 Assets depreciated using the straight-line method

The straight-line method of depreciation is generally preferred in accounting for the depreciation of property, plant and equipment. The main practical advantages of the straight-line method are considered to be its simplicity and the fact that its results are often not materially different from the units of production method if annual production is relatively constant.[128] In general, the straight-line method is considered to be preferable for:

- assets whose loss in value is more closely linked to the passage of time than to the quantities of minerals produced (e.g. front-end loaders that are used in stripping overburden and production of minerals);
- assets that are unrelated to production and that are separable from the field or mine (e.g. office buildings);
- assets with a useful life that is either much longer (e.g. offshore platforms) or much shorter (e.g. drill jumbos) than that of the field or mine in which they are used;
- assets used in fields or mines whose annual production is relatively constant. However, if assets are used in fields or mines that are expected to suffer extended outages, due to weather conditions or periodic repairs and maintenance, then the straight-line method may be less appropriate; and
- assets that are used in more than one field or mine (e.g. service trucks).

If the production of a field or mine drops significantly towards the end of its productive life, then the straight-line method may result in a relatively high depreciation charge per unit of production in these latter years. In those cases, an entity may need to perform an impairment test on the assets involved.

The extract below indicates the assets to which BHP applies the straight-line method.

> **Extract 43.49: BHP Group Plc (2019)**
>
> Notes to the Financial Statements [extract]
>
> 11 Property, plant and equipment [extract]
>
> Depreciation
>
> Depreciation of assets, other than land, assets under construction and capitalised exploration and evaluation that are not depreciated, is calculated using either the straight-line (SL) method or units of production (UoP) method, net of residual values, over the estimated useful lives of specific assets. The depreciation method and rates applied to specific assets reflect the pattern in which the asset's benefits are expected to be used by the Group. The Group's reported reserves are used to determine UoP depreciation unless doing so results in depreciation charges that do not reflect the asset's useful life. Where this occurs, alternative approaches to determining reserves are applied, such as using management's expectations of future oil and gas prices rather than yearly average prices, to provide a phasing of periodic depreciation charges that better reflects the asset's expected useful life.
>
> Where assets are dedicated to a mine or petroleum lease, the below useful lives are subject to the lesser of the asset category's useful life and the life of the mine or petroleum lease, unless those assets are readily transferable to another productive mine or lease.
>
> Key estimates
>
> The determination of useful lives, residual values and depreciation methods involves estimates and assumptions and is reviewed annually. Any changes to useful lives or any other estimates or assumptions may affect prospective depreciation rates and asset carrying values. The table below summarises the principal depreciation methods and rates applied to major asset categories by the Group.
>
> | Category | Buildings | Plant and equipment | Mineral rights and petroleum interests | Capitalised exploration, evaluation and development expenditure |
> |---|---|---|---|---|
> | Typical depreciation methodology | SL | SL | UoP | UoP |
> | Depreciation rate | 25-50 years | 3-30 years | Based on the rate of depletion of reserves | Based on the rate of depletion of reserves |

16.1.3 Assets depreciated using the units of production method

When it comes to assets relating to mineral reserves, the units of production method is the most common method applied. 'The underlying principle of the units of production method is that capitalised costs associated with a cost centre are incurred to find and develop the commercially producible reserves in that cost centre, so that each unit produced from the centre is assigned an equal amount of cost.'[129] The units of production method thereby effectively allocates an equal amount of depreciation to each unit produced, rather than an equal amount to each year as under the straight-line method.

When the level of production varies considerably over the life of a project (e.g. the production of oil fields is much higher in the periods just after the start of production than in the final periods of production), depreciation based on a units of production method will produce a more equal cost per unit from year to year than straight-line methods. Under the straight-line method the depreciation charge per unit in the early years of production could be much less than the depreciation per unit in later years. 'That factor, coupled with the fact that typically production costs per unit increase in later years, means that the profitability of operations would be distorted if the straight-line method is used, showing larger profits in early years and lower profits in later years of the mineral resource's life. The higher cost per unit in later years is, in part, due to fewer units being produced while many production costs remain fixed and, in part, a result of many variable costs per unit increasing over time because reserves may be harder to extract, there may be greater equipment repairs, and similar other factors.'[130] Nevertheless, even under the units of production method, profitability often drops significantly towards the end of the productive life of a field or mine. When this happens, an entity will need to carry out an impairment test and may need to recognise an impairment charge (see 11 above).

In general, the units of production method is considered to be preferable for:
- assets used in fields or mines whose annual production may vary considerably over their useful economic life;
- assets whose loss in value is more closely linked to the quantities of minerals produced than to the passage of time (e.g. draglines used in the extraction of mineral ore);
- assets that are used in production or that are inseparable from the field or mine (e.g. wells and well heads);
- assets with a useful life that is the same as that of the field or mine in which they are used; and
- assets that are used in only one field or mine (e.g. overland conveyor belts).

Extract 43.49 above and Extract 43.50 below indicate the classes of asset to which BHP and Lonmin, respectively, apply the units of production method.

Extract 43.50: Lonmin Plc (2018)

Notes to the Accounts [extract]

1 Statement on accounting policies [extract]

Intangible assets

Intangible assets, other than goodwill, acquired by the Group have finite useful lives and are measured at cost less accumulated amortisation and accumulated impairment losses. Where amortisation is charged on these assets, the expense is taken to the income statement through operating costs.

Amortisation of mineral rights is provided on a 'units of production' basis over the remaining life of mine to residual value (20 to 40 years).

All other intangible assets are amortised over their useful economic lives subject to a maximum of 20 years and are tested for impairment at each reporting date when there is an indication of a possible impairment.

Property, plant and equipment [extract]

Depreciation

Depreciation is provided on a straight-line or units of production basis as appropriate over their expected useful lives or the remaining life of mine, if shorter, to residual value. The life of mine is based on proven and probable reserves. The expected useful lives of the major categories of property, plant and equipment are as follows:

	Method	Rate	
Shafts and underground	Units of production	2.5%-5.0% per annum	20-40 years
Metallurgical	Straight line	2.5%-7.1% per annum	14-40 years
Infrastructure	Straight line	2.5%-2.9% per annum	35-40 years
Other plant and equipment	Straight line	2.5%-50.0% per annum	2-40 years

No depreciation is provided on surface mining land which has a continuing value and capital work in progress.

Residual values and useful lives are re-assessed annually and if necessary changes are accounted for prospectively.

The practical application of the units of production method gives rise to the following issues that require entities to exercise a considerable degree of judgement in determining the:

(a) units of production formula (see 16.1.3.A below);
(b) reserves base (see 16.1.3.B below);
(c) unit of measure (see 16.1.3.C below); and
(d) joint and by-products (see 16.1.3.D below).

As discussed at 16.1.3.B below, the asset base that is subject to depreciation should be consistent with the reserves base that is used, which may require an entity to exclude certain costs from (or include future investments in) the depreciation pool.

16.1.3.A Units of production formula

There are a number of different ways in which an entity could calculate a depreciation charge under the units of production method. The most obvious of these is probably the following formula:

$$\text{Depreciation charge for the period} = \text{Current period's production} \times \frac{\text{Cost of the asset at the beginning of the period} - \text{Cumulative depreciation and impairment at the beginning of the period}}{\text{Opening reserves estimated at the beginning of the period}}$$

The reserves estimate used in the above formula is the best estimate of the reserves at the beginning of the period, but by the end of the period a revised and more accurate estimate is often available. Therefore, it may be considered that in order to take into account the most recent information, the opening reserves should be calculated by adding the 'closing reserves estimated at the end of the period' to the 'current period's production'. However, reserves estimates might change for a number of reasons:

(a) more detailed knowledge about existing reserves (e.g. detailed engineering studies or drilling of additional wells which occurred after the commencement of the period);
(b) new events that affect the physical quantity of reserves (e.g. major fire in a mine); and
(c) changes in economic assumptions (e.g. higher commodity prices).

It is generally not appropriate to take account of these events retrospectively. For example, changes in reserves estimates that result from events that took place after the end of the reporting period (such as those under (b) and (c)) are non-adjusting events that should be accounted for prospectively in accordance with IFRS. *[IAS 8.32-38, IAS 10.3]*. Changes in reserves estimates that result from new information or new developments which do not offer greater clarity concerning the conditions that existed at the end of the reporting period (such as those under (a)) are not considered to be corrections of errors; instead they are changes in accounting estimates that should be accounted for prospectively under IFRS. *[IAS 8.5, 32-38]*.

Determining whether actual changes in reserves estimates should be treated as adjusting or non-adjusting events will depend upon the specific facts and circumstances and may require significant judgement.

Usually, an entity will continue to invest during the year in assets in the depreciation pool (see 16.1.3.B below for a discussion of 'depreciation pools') that are used to extract minerals. This raises the question as to whether or not assets that were used for only part of the production during the period should be depreciated on a different basis. Under the straight-line method, an entity will generally calculate the depreciation of asset additions during the period based on the assumption that they were added (1) at the beginning of the period, (2) in the middle of the period or (3) at the end of the period. While method (2) is often the best approximation, methods (1) and (3) are generally not materially different when the accounting period is rather short (e.g. monthly or quarterly reporting) or when the level of asset additions is relatively low compared to the asset base.

The above considerations explain why the units of production formula that is commonly used in the extractive industries is slightly more complicated than the formula given above:

$$\text{Depreciation charge for the period} = \text{Current period's production} \times \frac{\text{Cost of the asset at the end of the period} - \text{Cumulative depreciation and impairment at the beginning of the period}}{\text{Opening reserves estimated at the end of the period} + \text{Current period's production}}$$

This units of production formula is widely used in the oil and gas sector by entities that apply US GAAP or did apply the former OIAC SORP. In the mining sector, however, both the first and the second units of production formulae are used in practice.

16.1.3.B Reserves base

An important decision in applying the units of production method is selecting the reserves base that will be used. The following reserves bases could in theory be used:

(a) proved developed reserves (see (a) below);
(b) proved developed and undeveloped reserves (see (b) below);
(c) proved and probable reserves (see (c) below);
(d) proved and probable reserves and a portion of resources expected to be converted into reserves (see (d) below); and
(e) proved, probable and possible reserves.

The term 'possible reserves', which is used in the oil and gas sector, is associated with a probability of only 10% (see 2.2.1 above). Therefore, it is generally not considered acceptable to include possible reserves within the reserves base in applying the units of production method.

It is important that whatever reserves base is chosen the costs applicable to that category of reserves are included in the depreciable amount to achieve a proper matching of costs and production.[131] For example, 'if the cost centre is not fully developed ... there may be costs that do not apply, in total or in part, to proved developed reserves, which may create difficulties in matching costs and reserves. In addition, some reserve categories will require future costs to bring them to the point where production may begin'.[132]

IFRS does not provide any guidance on the selection of an appropriate reserves base or cost centre (i.e. unit of account) for the application of the units of production method. The relative merits for the use of each of the reserves bases listed under (a) to (c) above are discussed in detail below.

(a) *Proved developed reserves*

Under some national GAAPs that have accounting standards for the extractive industries, an entity is required to use proved developed reserves as its reserves base for the depreciation of certain types of assets. An entity would therefore calculate its depreciation charge on the basis of actual costs that have been incurred to date. However, the cost centre frequently includes capitalised costs that relate to undeveloped reserves. To calculate the depreciation charge correctly, it will be necessary to exclude a portion of the capitalised costs from the depreciation calculation. Example 43.14 below, which is taken from the IASC's Issues Paper, illustrates how this might work.

Example 43.14: Exclusion of capitalised costs relating to undeveloped reserves[133]

In an offshore oil and gas field a platform may be constructed from which 20 development wells will be drilled. The platform's cost has been capitalised as a part of the total cost of the cost centre. If only 5 of the 20 wells have been drilled, it would be inappropriate to depreciate that portion of platform costs, as well as that portion of all other capitalised costs, that are deemed to be applicable to the 15 wells not yet drilled. Only 5/20ths of the platform costs would be subject to depreciation in the current year, while 15/20ths of the platform costs (those applicable to the 15 undrilled wells) would be withheld from the depreciable amount. The costs withheld would be transferred to the depreciable amount as the additional wells are drilled. In lieu of basing the exclusion from depreciation on the number of wells, the exclusion (and subsequent transfer to depreciable amount) could be based on the quantity of reserves developed by individual wells compared with the estimated total quantity of reserves to be developed.

Similarly, an appropriate portion of prospecting costs, mineral acquisition costs, exploration costs, appraisal costs, and future dismantlement, removal, and restoration costs that have been capitalised should be withheld from the depreciation calculation if proved developed reserves are used as the reserves base and if there are undeveloped reserves in the cost pool.[134]

By withholding some of the costs from the depreciation pool, an entity is able to achieve a better matching of the costs incurred with the benefits of production. This is particularly important in respect of pre-development costs, which provide future economic benefits in relation to reserves that are not yet classified as 'proved developed'.

However, excluding costs from the depreciation pool may not be appropriate if it is not possible to determine reliably the portion of costs to be excluded or if the reserves that are not 'proved developed' are highly uncertain. It may not be necessary to exclude any costs at all from the depreciation pool if those costs are immaterial, which is sometimes the case in mining operations.

As illustrated in Extract 43.51, Royal Dutch Shell, in reporting under IFRS, applies the units of production method based on proved developed reserves.

> Extract 43.51: Royal Dutch Shell plc (2019)
> NOTES TO THE CONSOLIDATED FINANCIAL STATEMENTS [extract]
> 2A – SIGNIFICANT ACCOUNTING POLICIES, JUDGEMENTS AND ESTIMATES [extract]
> PROPERTY, PLANT AND EQUIPMENT AND INTANGIBLE ASSETS [extract]
>
> Depreciation, depletion and amortisation [extract]
>
> Property, plant and equipment related to hydrocarbon production activities are in principle depreciated on a unit-of-production basis over the proved developed reserves of the field concerned, other than assets whose useful lives differ from the lifetime of the field which are depreciated applying the straight-line method. However, for certain Upstream assets, the use for this purpose of proved developed reserves, which are determined using the SEC-mandated yearly average oil and gas prices, would result in depreciation charges for these assets which do not reflect the pattern in which their future economic benefits are expected to be consumed as, for example, it may result in assets with long-term expected lives being depreciated in full within one year. Therefore, in these instances, other approaches are applied to determine the reserves base for the purpose of calculating depreciation, such as using management's expectations of future oil and gas prices rather than yearly average prices, to provide a phasing of periodic depreciation charges that more appropriately reflects the expected utilisation of the assets concerned.
>
> Rights and concessions in respect of proved properties are depleted on the unit-of-production basis over the total proved reserves of the relevant area. Where individually insignificant, unproved properties may be grouped and depreciated based on factors such as the average concession term and past experience of recognising proved reserves.

(b) *Proved developed and undeveloped reserves*

Another approach that is common under IFRS is to use 'proved developed and undeveloped reserves' as the reserves base for the application of the units of production method. This approach reflects the fact that it is often difficult to allocate costs that have already been incurred between developed and undeveloped reserves and has the advantage that it effectively straight-lines the depreciation charge per unit of production across the different phases of a project. For example, if the depreciation cost in phase 1 of the development is $24/barrel and the depreciation cost in phase 2 of the development could be $18/barrel, an entity that uses proved developed and undeveloped reserves as its reserves base might recognise depreciation of, say, $22/barrel during phase 1 and phase 2.

Application of this approach is complicated by the fact that phase 1 of the project will start production before phase 2 is completed. To apply the units of production method on the basis of proved developed and undeveloped reserves, the entity would need to forecast the remaining investment related to phase 2. The approach does not appear unreasonable at first sight, given that the proved reserves are reasonably certain to exist and 'the costs of developing the proved undeveloped reserves will be incurred in the near future in most situations, the total depreciable costs can also be estimated with a high degree of reliability'.[135] Nevertheless, the entity would therefore define its cost pool (i.e. unit of account) as including both assets that it currently owns and certain future investments.

Although there is no specific precedent within IFRS for using such a widely defined unit of account, such an approach is not prohibited, while in practice it has gained a broad measure of acceptance within the extractive industries.

(c) *Proved and probable reserves*

The arguments in favour of using 'proved and probable reserves' as the reserves base in applying the units of production method are similar to those discussed at (b) above. The IASC's Issues Paper summarised the arguments in favour of this approach as follows:

> 'Proponents of [using "proved and probable reserves" as the reserve base] use the same arguments given for including proved undeveloped reserves and related future costs in calculating depreciation. They point out that in a cost centre in which development has only begun a large part of capitalised prospecting, mineral acquisition, exploration, and appraisal costs may apply to probable reserves. Often in this situation there are large quantities of probable reserves, lacking only relatively minor additional exploration and/or appraisal work to be reclassified as proved reserves. They argue that, in calculating depreciation, it would be possible to defer all costs relating to the probable reserves if either proved developed reserves only, or all proved reserves, were to be used as the quantity on which depreciation is based. They contend that using probable and proved reserves in the reserve base and including in the depreciable costs any additional costs anticipated to explore and develop those reserves provides more relevant and reliable information.'[136]

The main drawbacks of this approach are that estimates of probable reserves are almost certainly different from actual reserves that will ultimately be developed and estimates of the costs to complete the development are likely to be incorrect because of the potentially long time scales involved.[137] Nevertheless, this approach has also found a considerable degree of acceptance under IFRS among mining companies and oil and gas companies that were permitted to apply the approach under their national GAAP before (e.g. UK GAAP). Both Tullow Oil and Anglo American apply this approach, as illustrated in Extracts 43.52 and 43.53 respectively below.

Extract 43.52: Tullow Oil plc (2019)

Accounting Policies [extract]

Year ended 31 December 2019

(l) Commercial reserves

Commercial reserves are proven and probable oil and gas reserves, which are defined as the estimated quantities of crude oil, natural gas and natural gas liquids which geological, geophysical and engineering data demonstrate with a specified degree of certainty to be recoverable in future years from known reservoirs and which are considered commercially producible. There should be a 50 per cent statistical probability that the actual quantity of recoverable reserves will be more than the amount estimated as proven and probable reserves and a 50 per cent statistical probability that it will be less.

(m) Depletion and amortisation

All expenditure carried within each field is amortised from the commencement of production on a unit of production basis, which is the ratio of oil and gas production in the period to the estimated quantities of commercial reserves at the end of the period plus the production in the period, generally on a field-by-field basis or by a group of fields which are reliant on common infrastructure. Costs used in the unit of production calculation comprise the net book value of capitalised costs plus the estimated future field development costs required to recover the commercial reserves remaining. Changes in the estimates of commercial reserves or future field development costs are dealt with prospectively.

> **Extract 43.53: Anglo American plc (2019)**
> NOTES TO THE FINANCIAL STATEMENTS [extract]
> OTHER ITEMS [extract]
> 38. ACCOUNTING POLICIES [extract]
> D. CAPITAL BASE [extract]
> Property, plant and equipment [extract]
> Depreciation of property, plant and equipment [extract]
>
> Mining properties are depreciated to their residual values using the unit of production method based on Proved and Probable Ore Reserves and, in certain limited circumstances, other Mineral Resources included in the Life of Mine Plan. These other Mineral Resources are included in depreciation calculations where, taking into account historical rates of conversion to Ore Reserves, there is a high degree of confidence that they will be extracted in an economic manner. This is the case principally for diamond operations, where depreciation calculations are based on Diamond Reserves and Diamond Resources included in the Life of Mine Plan. This reflects the unique nature of diamond deposits where, due to the difficulty in estimating grade, Life of Mine Plans frequently include significant amounts of Indicated or Inferred Resources.

(d) *Proved and probable reserves and a portion of resources expected to be converted into reserves (mining entities only)*

We observe in practice that some mining entities adopt a slightly different approach when depreciating some of their mining assets. They use proven and probable reserves and a portion of resources expected to be converted into reserves. Such an approach tends to be limited to mining companies where the type of mineral and the characteristics of the ore body indicate that there is a high degree of confidence that those resources will be converted into reserves. For example, this is very common for underground operations that only perform infill drilling just prior to production commencing. This is done so that capital is not spent too early before it is really needed.

Such resources can comprise measured, indicated and inferred resources, and even exploration potential. Determining which of those have a high degree of confidence of being extracted in an economic manner will require judgement. Such an assessment will take into account the specific mineralisation and the 'reserves to resource' conversion that has previously been achieved for a mine.

Such an approach is generally justified on the basis that it helps to ensure the depreciation charges reflect management's best estimate of the useful life of the assets and provides greater accuracy in the calculation of the consumption of future economic benefits.

Anglo American applies this approach, as illustrated in Extract 43.53 above, as does Rio Tinto, as illustrated in Extract 43.54 below.

> **Extract 43.54: Rio Tinto plc (2019)**
> Notes to the 2019 financial statements [extract]
> 1 Principal accounting policies [extract]
> (i) Depreciation and impairment (notes 13 and 14) [extract]
> Depreciation of non-current assets [extract]
>
> *Units of production basis*
>
> For mining properties and leases and certain mining equipment, consumption of the economic benefits of the asset is linked to production. Except as noted below, these assets are depreciated on the units of production basis.
>
> In applying the units of production method, depreciation is normally calculated based on production in the period as a percentage of total expected production in current and future periods based on ore reserves and, for some mines, other mineral resources. Other mineral resources may be included in the calculations of total expected production in limited circumstances where there are very large areas of contiguous mineralisation, for which the economic viability is not sensitive to likely variations in grade, as may be the case for certain iron ore, bauxite and industrial minerals deposits and where there is a high degree of confidence that the other mineral resources can be extracted economically. This would be the case when the other mineral resources do not yet have the status of ore reserves merely because the necessary detailed evaluation work has not yet been performed and the responsible technical personnel agree that inclusion of a proportion of measured and indicated resources in the calculation of total expected production is appropriate based on historical reserve conversion rates.
>
> The required level of confidence is unlikely to exist for minerals that are typically found in low-grade ore (as compared with the above), such as copper or gold. In these cases, specific areas of mineralisation have to be evaluated in detail before their economic status can be predicted with confidence.
>
> Where measured and indicated resources are used in the calculation of depreciation for infrastructure, primarily rail and port, which will benefit current and future mines, then the measured and indicated resources may relate to mines which are currently in production or to mines where there is a high degree of confidence that they will be brought into production in the future. The quantum of mineral resources is determined taking into account future capital costs as required by the JORC code. The depreciation calculation, however, applies to current mines only and does not take into account future development costs for mines which are not yet in production. Measured and indicated resources are currently incorporated into depreciation calculations in the Group's Australian iron ore business.

An entity preparing its financial statements under IFRS will need to choose between using 'proved developed reserves', 'proved developed and undeveloped reserves', 'proved and probable reserves' and, for mining entities in relation to certain mines, 'proved and probable reserves and a portion of resources expected to be converted into reserves' as its reserves base. Each of these approaches is currently acceptable under IFRS. Preparers of financial statements should, however, be aware of the difficulties that exist in ensuring that the reserves base and the costs that are being depreciated correspond. Users of financial statements need to understand that comparability between entities reporting under IFRS may sometimes be limited and need to be aware of the impact that each of the approaches has on the depreciation charge that is reported. Given this, detailed disclosures are essential.

16.1.3.C Unit of measure

Under the units of production method, an entity assigns an equal amount of cost to each unit produced. Determining the appropriate unit by which to measure production requires a significant amount of judgement. An entity could measure the units of production by reference to physical units or, when different minerals are produced in a common process, cost could be allocated between the different minerals on the basis of their relative sales prices.

(a) Physical units of production method

If an entity uses the physical units of production method, each physical unit of reserves (such as barrels, tonnes, ounces, gallons, and cubic metres) produced is assigned a *pro rata* portion of undepreciated costs less residual value.

Example 43.15: Physical units of production method[138]

If an entity produces 100 units during the current period and the estimated remaining commercial reserves at the end of the period are 1,900 units, the units available would be 2,000. The fractional part of the depreciable basis to be charged to depreciation expense would be 100/2,000. Therefore, if the depreciable basis was 5,000 monetary units, the depreciation for the period would be 250 monetary units.

In applying the physical units of production method, a mining company needs to decide whether to use either the quantity of ore produced or the quantity of mineral contained in the ore as the unit of measure.[139] Similarly, an oil and gas company needs to decide whether to use either the volume of hydrocarbons or the volume of hydrocarbons plus gas, water and other materials. When mining different grades of ore, a mining company's gross margin on the subsequent sale of minerals will fluctuate far less when it uses the quantity of minerals as its unit of measure. While a large part of the wear and tear of equipment used in mining is closely related to the quantity of ore produced, the economic benefits are more closely related to the quantity of mineral contained in the ore. Therefore, both approaches are currently considered to be acceptable under IFRS.

(b) Revenue-based units of production method

Another possible approach in applying the units of production method that may have been used by some entities previously is to measure the units produced based on the gross selling price of mineral.[140] However, this approach is no longer permitted. This is because as part of the 2011-2013 cycle of annual improvements the IASB approved an amendment to IAS 16 and IAS 38 to clarify that a revenue-based depreciation or amortisation method would not be appropriate.

16.1.3.D Joint and by-products

In the extractive industries it is common for more than one product to be extracted from the same reserves (e.g. copper mines often produce gold and silver; lead and zinc are often found together; and many oil fields produce both oil and gas). When the ratio between the joint products or between the main product and the by-products is stable, this does not pose any complications. Also, if the value of the by-products is immaterial then it will often be acceptable to base the depreciation charge on the main product. In other cases, however, it will be necessary to define a unit of measure that takes into account all minerals produced. The IASC's Issues Paper listed the following approaches in defining conversion factors for calculating such a unit of measure:[141]

'(a) physical characteristics:
  (i) based on volume: such as barrels, litres, gallons, thousand cubic feet or cubic metres;
  (ii) based on weight: such as tonnes, pounds, and kilograms; or
  (iii) based on energy content (British thermal units) of oil and gas;
(b) gross revenues for the period in relation to estimated total gross revenues of the current period and future periods (more commonly seen in the mining sector); and
(c) net revenues for the period in relation to total net revenues of the current and future periods'.

Calculation of a conversion factor based on volume or weight has the benefit of being easy to apply and can lead to satisfactory results if the relative value of the products is fairly stable. For example, some mining companies that produce both gold and silver from the same mines express their production in millions of ounces of silver equivalent. This is calculated as the sum of the ounces of silver produced plus their ounces of gold produced multiplied by some ratio of the gold price divided by the silver price. For example, if the gold price was $900 and the silver price was $12, this would provide a ratio of 1/75 – so the quantity of gold would be multiplied by 75 to determine the equivalent ounces of silver. However, these ratios can change depending on the relationship between gold and silver.

Calculation of a conversion factor based on other physical characteristics is quite common in the oil and gas sector. Typically, production and reserves in oil fields are expressed in millions of barrels of oil equivalent (mmboe), which is calculated by dividing the quantity of gas expressed in thousands of cubic feet by 6 and adding that to the quantity of oil expressed in barrels. This conversion is based on the fact that one barrel of oil contains as much energy as 6,000 cubic feet of gas. While this approach is commonly used, it is important to recognise two limiting factors: the actual energy conversion factor will not always be 1:6 but may vary between 1:5½ to 1:6½ and the market price of gas per unit of energy (typically BTU) is often lower than that of oil because of government price controls and the need for expensive infrastructure to deliver gas to end users.

An approach that is commonly used (more so in the mining sector than the oil and gas sector) in calculating a conversion factor when joint products are extracted, is to base it on gross revenues. As discussed at 16.1.3.C above, the main drawback of this method is that it requires an entity to forecast future commodity prices. Despite this drawback, there will be situations where no other viable alternative exists for calculating an appropriate conversion factor.

Finally, it is possible to calculate a conversion factor based on net revenue after deducting certain direct processing costs. An argument in favour of this method is that gross revenues do not necessarily measure the economic benefits from an asset. However, taken to an extreme this argument would lead down a path where no depreciation is charged in unprofitable years, which is clearly not an acceptable practice.

Accounting for the sale of joint products and by-products is addressed at 14.2 above.

16.2 Block caving – depreciation, depletion and amortisation (mining)

Given the nature of mining operations, determining the appropriate unit of account has always been a matter requiring considerable judgement for mining entities. See 4 above for further discussion. This issue is particularly relevant when assessing how to account for new mining techniques. For example, block cave mining is one such mining technique that is being increasingly proposed or used for a number of deposits worldwide.

Block cave mining is a mass mining method that allows for the bulk mining of large, relatively lower grade, ore bodies for which the grade is consistently distributed throughout. The word 'block' refers to the layout of the mine – which effectively divides the ore body into large sections, with areas that can be several thousand square metres in size. This approach adopts a mine design and process which involves the creation of an undercut by fracturing the rock section underneath the block through the use of blasting. This blasting destroys the rock's ability to support the block above. Caving of the rock mass then occurs under the natural forces of gravity (which can be in the order of millions of tonnes), when a sufficient amount of rock has been removed underneath the block. The broken ore is then removed from the base of the block. This mine activity occurs without the need for drilling and blasting, as the ore above continues to fall while the broken ore beneath is removed. Broken ore is removed from the area at the extraction level through the use of a grid of draw points. These effectively funnel the broken ore down to a particular point so that it can be collected and removed for further processing.

Block caving has been applied to large scale extraction of various metals and minerals, sometimes in thick beds of ore but more usually in steep to vertical masses. Examples of block caving operations include Northparkes (Australia), Palabora (South Africa), Questa Mine (New Mexico) and Freeport (Indonesia).[142]

Block cave mining does require substantial upfront development costs, as initial underground access followed by large excavations (undercutting), must be completed to gain access and initially 'undermine' the block that is to cave. In addition, large underground and above ground haulage and milling infrastructure must be constructed to extract and then process the ore that a successful cave will generate.

One of the key issues to be addressed is how these substantial upfront development costs, in addition to the ongoing development costs associated with each block (i.e. to extend the undercutting beneath each new block and construct the draw points for each block) should be treated for depreciation or amortisation.

Generally, these costs are depreciated or amortised on a units of production basis – therefore in determining useful life, it is necessary to determine what the appropriate reserves base should be for each of these different types of costs. For example, in relation to the costs associated with initially going underground and constructing the main haulage tunnel which will be used to access and extract the reserves from the entire ore body, the useful life associated with such assets may be the reserves of the entire ore body.

In relation to the costs associated in constructing the milling infrastructure, it is possible that such assets may be used to process ore from multiple ore bodies. Therefore, the useful life of such assets may be the reserves of multiple ore bodies. However, this will depend upon the specific facts and circumstances of the particular development.

For those costs associated with each individual block, e.g. the undercutting costs directly attributable to each block and the costs associated in constructing the draw points for that block, the appropriate reserves base may potentially only be those to be extracted from that particular block, which may only be a component of the entire ore body.

The approach adopted by each entity will be determined by the specific facts and circumstances of each mine development, such as the nature of the block cave mining technique employed and how the associated assets will be used. Such an assessment will require entities to exercise considerable judgement. Appropriate disclosures are recommended where significant judgements and estimates are considered material.

17 IFRS 16 – *LEASES*

IFRS 16 governs the accounting for leases. IFRS 16 requires lessees to recognise most leases on their balance sheet as lease liabilities together with corresponding right-of-use assets. However, lessees can make accounting policy elections to apply accounting similar to operating lease accounting under IAS 17 – *Leases* – to short-term leases and leases of low-value assets.

Lessees will apply a single model for most leases. The profit or loss impact will largely comprise interest (on the lease liability) and depreciation (of the right-of-use asset). There may also be other lease expenses which continue to be recognised as an operating expense, e.g. variable payments not based on an index or rate, short-term lease payments and lease payments relating to low-value assets.

Lessor accounting is substantially unchanged from current accounting. Lessors are required to classify their leases into two types: finance leases and operating leases. Lease classification determines how and when a lessor recognises lease revenue and what assets a lessor records.

While the requirements of the IFRS 16 model are discussed in detail in Chapter 23, some of the key aspects of IFRS 16 that are particularly relevant to mining companies and oil and gas companies include:

- scope and exclusions (see 17.1 below and Chapter 23 at 2.2);
- definition of a lease (see 17.2 below and Chapter 23 at 2.4 and 3.1);
- leases of subsurface rights (see 17.1.3 below and Chapter 23 at 3.1.2);
- substitution rights (see 17.3 below and Chapter 23 at 3.1.3);
- identifying and separating lease and non-lease components and allocating contract consideration (see 17.4 below and Chapter 23 at 3.2);
- identifying lease payments (see 17.5 below and Chapter 23 at 4.5);
- allocating contract consideration (see 17.6 below and Chapter 23 at 3.2.3.B);
- interaction of leases and asset retirement obligations (see 17.7 below); and
- arrangements entered into by joint arrangements (see 18 below and Chapter 23 at 3.1.1).

17.1 Scope and scope exclusions

17.1.1 Mineral rights

Leases to explore for or use minerals, oil, natural gas and similar non-regenerative resources are excluded from the scope of IFRS 16, *[IFRS 16.3]*, (amongst other types of arrangements – see Chapter 23 at 2.2 for the full list of scope exclusions).

IFRS 16 does not specify whether the scope exclusion for leases to explore for or use minerals, oil, natural gas and similar non-regenerative resources applies broadly to other leases that relate to, or are part of, the process of exploring for, or using, those resources. For example, in some jurisdictions, the minerals are owned by the government, but the land within which the minerals are located is privately owned. In these jurisdictions, a mining and metals entity needs to enter into a mineral lease with the government as well as a surface lease (i.e. the right to use the land) with the private landowner. IFRS 16's Basis for Conclusions states that IFRS 6 specifies the accounting for rights to explore for, and evaluate, mineral resources. *[IFRS 16.BC68(a)]*.

The US GAAP leases standard (ASC 842 – *Leases*), includes more specific guidance on how this scope exclusion should be applied. It states that leases of minerals, oil, natural gas and similar non-regenerative resources, including the intangible rights to explore for those resources and the rights to use the land in which those natural resources are contained (unless those rights of use include more than the right to explore for natural resources) are outside the scope of ASC 842. However, equipment used to explore for the natural resources is within the scope of ASC 842.2.

Entities will need to apply judgement to determine how broadly to interpret and apply this scope exclusion under IFRS 16.

IFRS 16 is not specific as to whether the scope exclusion only applies to mineral rights in the E&E phase or whether it also applies to other rights (e.g. exploitation and/or extraction rights that arise in connection with development and production phases). The wording of the exclusion specifies that it applies to 'leases to *explore for or use* minerals' (emphasis added), which suggests that it applies more broadly (i.e. to the E&E, development and production phases). However, the reference to IFRS 6 in the Basis for Conclusions of IFRS 16 *[IFRS 16.BC68(a)]* may infer that the exclusion is limited to rights in the E&E phase.

Most mining companies and oil and gas companies generally apply the scope exclusion to the mineral rights in the E&E, development and production phases. We would expect that given the wording in the main body of the standard, the scope exclusion would apply to mineral rights in all phases. We would also expect that consistent with ASC 842, in the event that rights extend to more than the right to explore for or use natural resources, the scope exclusion would not apply. For example, in the event that there is also a corporate head office building on part of the land, an apportionment would be applied, and the scope exclusion would not apply to the portion of the land upon which the head office is built. Furthermore, we would not expect the scope exclusion to extend to equipment used to explore, develop or produce mineral rights.

17.1.2 Land easements or rights of way

Land easements or rights of way are rights to use, access or cross another entity's land for a specified purpose. For example, a land easement might be obtained for the right to construct and operate a pipeline or other assets (e.g. a railway line) over, under or through an existing area of land or body of water while allowing the landowner continued use of the land for other purposes (e.g. farming), as long as the landowner does not interfere with the rights conveyed in the land easement.

When determining whether a contract for a land easement or right of way is a lease, mining companies and oil and gas companies will need to assess whether there is an identified asset and whether the customer obtains substantially all of the economic benefits of the identified asset and has the right to direct the use of that asset(s) throughout the period of use.

This will require careful consideration of the rights and obligations in each arrangement and conclusions may vary given that the nature of these contracts can also vary by jurisdictions. The issue of accounting for land easements is discussed in Chapter 23 at 3.1.2.

17.1.3 Subsurface rights

In June 2019, the Interpretations Committee discussed a contract for subsurface rights.[143] In the contract described, a pipeline operator obtains the right to place an oil pipeline in underground space for 20 years in exchange for consideration. The contract specifies the exact location and dimensions (path, width and depth) of the underground space within which the pipeline will be placed. The landowner retains the right to use the surface of the land above the pipeline, but it has no right to access or otherwise change the use of the specified underground space throughout the 20-year period of use. The customer has the right to perform inspection, repairs and maintenance work (including replacing damaged sections of the pipeline when necessary).

During the discussion, the Interpretations Committee noted the following:

- Paragraph 3 of IFRS 16 requires an entity to apply IFRS 16 to all leases, with limited exceptions. In the contract described in the request, none of the exceptions in paragraphs 3 and 4 of IFRS 16 apply. In particular, the Interpretations Committee noted that the underground space is tangible. Accordingly, if the contract contains a lease, IFRS 16 applies to that lease. If the contract does not contain a lease, the entity would then consider which other IFRS standard applies.
- Applying paragraph B9 of IFRS 16, to meet the definition of a lease the customer must have both:
  - the right to obtain substantially all the economic benefits from use of an identified asset throughout the period of use; and
  - the right to direct the use of the identified asset throughout the period of use.
- The specified underground space is physically distinct from the remainder of the land. The contract's specifications include the path, width and depth of the pipeline, thereby defining a physically distinct underground space. The space being underground does not in itself affect whether it is an identified asset – the specified underground space is physically distinct in the same way that a specified area of space on the land's surface would be physically distinct. As the landowner

does not have the right to substitute the underground space throughout the period of use, the Committee concluded that the specified underground space is an identified asset as described in paragraphs B13–B20.

- The customer has the right to obtain substantially all the economic benefits from use of the specified underground space throughout the 20-year period of use. The customer has exclusive use of the specified underground space throughout that period of use.

- The customer has the right to direct the use of the specified underground space throughout the 20-year period of use because the customer has the right to operate the asset throughout the period of use without the supplier having the right to change those operating instructions. How and for what purpose the specified underground space will be used (i.e. to locate the pipeline with specified dimensions through which oil will be transported) is predetermined in the contract. The customer has the right to operate the specified underground space by having the right to perform inspection, repairs and maintenance work. The customer makes all the decisions about the use of the specified underground space that can be made during the 20-year period of use.

Consequently, the Interpretations Committee concluded that the contract described in the request contains a lease as defined in IFRS 16. The customer would therefore apply IFRS 16 in accounting for that lease.

17.2 Definition of a lease

A lease is a contract (i.e. an agreement between two or more parties that creates enforceable rights and obligations), or part of a contract, that conveys the right to use an asset (the underlying asset) for a period of time in exchange for consideration. *[IFRS 16 Appendix A]*. To be a lease, a contract must convey the right to control the use of an identified asset.

As discussed above, a wide variety of arrangements exist in the mining sector and oil and gas sector that may provide a right to control the use of an identified asset(s). Some examples include:

- mining or oil field services contracts (e.g. equipment used to deliver a service, including drilling contracts);
- shipping, freight and other transportation arrangements, including railway infrastructure and harbour loading services contracts;
- refining, processing and tolling arrangements; and
- storage arrangements (including certain capacity portions of such arrangements).

Also, while not specific to the mining sector or oil and gas sector, there are many other arrangements commonly entered into by mining companies and oil and gas companies that will also need to be considered. Such arrangements include outsourcing arrangements, such as IT, and utility supply arrangements; such as those for the purchase of gas, electricity, water or telecommunications.

All of these arrangements will need to be assessed to determine whether they represent, or contain, a lease.

17.3 Substitution rights

IFRS 16 states that even if an asset is specified in an arrangement, a customer does not have the right to use an identified asset if, at inception of the contract, a supplier has the substantive right to substitute the asset throughout the period of use. *[IFRS 16.B14]*. A substitution right is substantive if the supplier has both the practical ability to substitute alternative assets throughout the period of use and the supplier would benefit economically from exercising its right to substitute the asset. *[IFRS 16.B14(a)-(b)]*. If the customer cannot readily determine whether the supplier has a substantive substitution right, the customer presumes that any substitution right is not substantive. *[IFRS 16.B19]*.

Entities will need to carefully evaluate whether a supplier's substitution right is substantive based on facts and circumstances at inception of the contract. In many cases, it will be clear that the supplier will not benefit from the exercise of a substitution right because of the costs associated with substituting an asset. *[IFRS 16.BC113]*. For example, an asset is highly customised and/or significant costs have been incurred to ensure the asset meets the specifications required by the contract such that the supplier would not benefit economically from exercising its substitution right. In addition, the supplier's substitution rights may not be substantive if alternative assets are not readily available to the supplier or they could not be sourced by the supplier within a reasonable period of time and hence there is no practical ability to substitute them.

See Chapter 23 at 3.1.3 for further discussion.

17.4 Identifying and separating lease and non-lease components

Many contracts may contain a lease(s) coupled with an agreement to purchase or sell other goods or services (non-lease components). Examples of contracts in the mining sector and oil and gas sector that may contain a lease and significant non-lease components for services provided by the supplier include but are not limited to:

- transportation and storage contracts, which generally require the supplier to operate the facilities, and/or provide staff/crew;
- outsourced mining services contracts or oilfield services arrangements including closure arrangements; and
- exploration drilling contracts, which typically include operation services.

For these contracts, IFRS 16 requires an entity to account for each lease component within the contract as a lease separately from non-lease components of the contract, unless the entity applies the practical expedient to combine lease and associated non-lease components. *[IFRS 16.12]*. The non-lease components are identified and accounted for separately from the lease component(s), in accordance with other standards. For example, the non-lease components may be accounted for as executory arrangements by lessees (customers) or as contracts subject to IFRS 15 by lessors (suppliers).

See Chapter 23 at 3.2 for further information.

17.5 Identifying lease payments included in the measurement of the lease liability

Some lease agreements include payments that are described as variable or may appear to contain variability but are in-substance fixed payments because the contract terms require the payment of a fixed amount that is unavoidable. Such payments are lease payments included in the measurement of the lease liability and right-of-use assets at the commencement date.

For example, consideration paid for the use of equipment, such as drilling rigs, is typically expressed as a rate paid for each operating day, hour or fraction of an hour. The types of rates a lessee may be charged include:

- full operating rate – a rate charged when the rig is operating at full capacity with a full crew (in which case there could be a non-lease component of crew services);
- standby rate or cold-stack rate – a rate charged when the lessee unilaterally puts the rig on standby;
- major maintenance rate – a minimal rate, or in some cases a 'zero rate' charged when the lessor determines that maintenance needs to be performed and the rig is not available for use by the lessee; or
- inclement weather rate – a minimal rate, or in some cases a 'zero rate' charged when weather makes it dangerous to operate the rig and, therefore, it is not available for use by the lessee.

There will likely be variability in the pricing of a drilling contract, however typically there will be a minimum rate in these types of contracts. This amount would likely be the lowest rate that the lessee would pay while the asset is available for use by the lessee. Depending on the contract, this rate may be referred to using terms such as a standby or cold-stack rate. When identifying lease payments in an arrangement, mining companies and oil and gas companies should only consider rates that apply when the asset is available for use.

Example 43.16: Identifying lease payments – inclement weather

Upstream Entity A enters into a 3-year contract with Rig Owner for the right to use Drilling Rig 1 over a three year period. The contract is considered to contain a lease. The contract specifies the rates a lessee may be charged and these include:

- full operating rate of 100,000 CU per day – charged when the rig is operating at full capacity with a full crew;
- standby rate of 40,000 CU per day – charged when the lessee unilaterally puts the rig on standby; and
- inclement weather rate of zero CU per day – charged when weather makes it dangerous to operate the rig and, therefore, it is not available for use by the lessee.

Analysis

In calculating the lease liability, the standby rate of 40,000 CU per day for 3 years would be used. The inclement weather rate is not applicable in calculating the minimum lease payments as the rate only applies when the asset is not available for use.

Example 43.17: Identifying lease payments – major maintenance

Mining entity Z enters into an arrangement with Equipment Supplier T for the lease of a piece of processing equipment to be utilised at the mine site. The contract requires payment of 10,000 CU per day for the equipment, but stipulates Supplier T perform 10 days per annum of major maintenance that is required on the equipment. The day rate for those 10 major maintenance days is zero CU per day.

Analysis

In calculating the lease liability, the rate of 10,000 CU per day would be used. However, the rate would only be applied for 355 days each year on the basis that the contractual arrangement clearly sets out that there are 10 days per annum where the equipment will not be available for use to allow for major maintenance to be undertaken and that a zero day rate will apply on those days. Accordingly, contractually, the minimum lease payments are in fact lower, as the equipment will only be available for 355 days per annum.

This differs from the zero day rate that applies for inclement weather in Example 43.16 above because the period of time when the inclement weather rate will apply, is outside of the control of both parties.

See Chapter 23 at 4.5 for further discussion.

17.6 Allocating contract consideration

Lessees allocate the consideration in the contract to the lease and non-lease components on a relative stand-alone price basis. However, IFRS 16 provides a practical expedient that permits lessees to make an accounting policy election, by class of underlying asset, to account for each separate lease component of a contract and any associated non-lease components as a single lease component. Lessors are required to apply IFRS 15 to allocate the consideration in a contract between the lease and non-lease components, generally, on a relative stand-alone selling price basis. See Chapter 23 at 3.2.3.B for further information.

17.7 Interaction of leases with asset retirement obligations

When undertaking remediation and rehabilitation activities, it may be possible that a mining company or oil and gas company enters into an arrangement with a supplier that is, or contains, a lease. The costs associated with these activities form a significant component of the costs which make up the asset retirement obligation (ARO) that was recognised by the mining company or oil and gas company at commencement of the mine or field.

Assuming this lease is not a short-term lease and does not relate to the lease of a low-value asset, a right-of-use asset and lease liability will need to be recognised. One of the issues to consider is whether the mining company or oil and gas company's recognition of the lease liability results in the derecognition of the ARO liability recognised on the balance sheet. Given that prior to the commencement of any ARO-related activities, the mining company or oil and gas company still has an obligation to rehabilitate under IAS 37, it cannot derecognise the ARO liability. Instead, it now has a separate lease liability for the financing of the lease of the asset. Accordingly, acquiring the right-of-use asset does not result in the derecognition of the ARO liability, rather, it would be the activity undertaken or output of the asset which would ultimately settle the ARO liability. This approach would be consistent with a scenario where an asset, e.g. the leased asset, had been purchased, using bank finance, and the finance liability relating to the bank debt used to purchase the asset, is separately recognised on the balance sheet.

As such, at the point prior to any ARO activity (assuming this occurs at end of mine/field life), the mining company or oil and gas company has:
- no ARO asset (fully amortised);
- an ARO liability for the full ARO estimate;
- a right-of-use asset; and
- a lease liability.

See Chapter 23 at 5.2 and 5.3 for discussion on measurement of the right-of-use asset and lease liability.

The impacts of this will include:
- amortisation of the right-of-use asset across the period of use;
- interest expense on the lease liability;
- interest expense arising from the unwinding on the discount on the ARO liability, assuming interest continues to unwind over the remediation and rehabilitation activity period; and
- the use (reduction) of the ARO liability (as the leased asset is used to settle the obligation).

Consideration should be given to the requirements of IAS 37, *[IAS 37.61-62]*, which sets out that a provision shall be used only for expenditures for which the provision was originally recognised, i.e. that expenditures that relate to the original provision are set against it. See Chapter 26 at 4.9.

18 INTERACTION OF IFRS 16 AND IFRS 11

In the mining and metals sector and oil and gas sector, it is common for a group of entities to collaboratively perform exploration, development and/or production activities using a joint operation ('JO').[144] In such circumstances, a single party will often be appointed to be responsible for undertaking the operations on behalf of parties to the JO (i.e. the lead operator). The arrangement is often governed by a joint operating agreement ('JOA'). There may also be other contractual arrangements that govern the relationship and activities between the non-operator parties and the lead operator, some arrangements may involve specific agreements such as rig sharing agreements, and these may be verbal or written.

These agreements generally provide the lead operator with a right to recover the costs it incurs on behalf of the non-operator parties, including costs related to leasing assets to be used in the JO. Some stakeholders may have previously considered that the right to recover costs pursuant to a separately negotiated JOA meant that the lead operator was only required to recognise a lease liability incurred as part of a contract with a third party supplier (lessor) in proportion to its interest in the JO.

One issue highlighted during the implementation of IFRS 16, was how a lead operator should recognise lease-related assets and liabilities when it is the sole signatory to a contract that is or contains a lease. This issue was taken to the Interpretations Committee in 2019 and they discussed a question relating to lease arrangements in a JO under IFRS 16. The question asked was how a lead operator recognises a lease liability. The question specifically focused on situations where the JO is not structured through a separate vehicle and the lead operator, as the sole signatory, enters into a lease contract with a third party supplier (lessor) for an item of property, plant and equipment that will be operated jointly as part of the JO's activities. The lead operator has the right to recover a share of the lease costs from the other joint operators in accordance with the contractual and other arrangements governing the JO.

The Interpretations Committee concluded that in accordance with IFRS 11, a joint operator identifies and recognises both:

(a) liabilities it incurs in relation to its interest in the JO; and

(b) its share of any liabilities incurred jointly with other parties to the joint arrangement.

It observed that identifying the liabilities a joint operator incurs and those incurred jointly requires an assessment of the terms and conditions of all contractual agreements that relate to the JO, including consideration of the laws pertaining to those agreements.[145] It also acknowledged contractual agreements relating to each JO are likely to differ.

The Interpretations Committee further observed, in accordance with IFRS 11, the liabilities a joint operator recognises include those for which it has primary responsibility.[146] Also, in the fact pattern as it was presented, the conclusion was that the JOA and related contractual arrangements did not extinguish or transfer the lead operator's primary responsibility for the lease liability.[147] Therefore, as sole signatory and where a lead operator has primary responsibility for a lease, the lead operator recognises 100% of the lease liability.

The Interpretations Committee concluded that the principles and requirements in IFRS standards provide an adequate basis for the lead operator to identify and recognise its liabilities in relation to its interest in a JO and, consequently, the Interpretations Committee decided not to add this matter to its standard-setting agenda.[148]

Consequently, if the lead operator is the primary obligor in a lease arrangement, even when the underlying asset will be used to satisfy the activities of the JO, the lead operator should account for the lease by recognising the full lease liability measured in accordance with IFRS 16. In this circumstance, even though the lead operator has a right to recover costs from the non-operator parties, including their share of the lease obligation, it is not appropriate for the lead operator to only recognise its proportionate share of the lease liability by relying on the terms and conditions of the JOA or other arrangements with the non-operator parties to which the third party supplier is not a party. This is because the JOA and other arrangements are separately negotiated with the non-operators and do not extinguish the lead operator's obligation for the lease with the third party supplier.

As a direct consequence of this decision, the immediate issue is then to determine who has primary responsibility for the arrangement with the third party supplier. Determining whether a lead operator, each joint operator party, or the JO itself, has primary responsibility for obligations such as a lease liability, may require a detailed evaluation of all relevant terms and conditions and facts and circumstances, including the legal environment in which the arrangement(s) operate (see 18.1 below).

While the agenda decision addressed the accounting for lease liabilities in relation to a joint operator's interest in a JO, it did not address some of the related issues that often arise in these situations.

This section explores and discusses some of these related issues and the potential considerations for arrangements between lead operators and the other joint operators (referred to as non-operator parties) of a JO, particularly in relation to their respective rights and obligations. It explores a range of factors that may need to be considered when assessing how to account for these contractual arrangements, and acknowledges different conclusions could be reached for different joint arrangements and in different jurisdictions.

This section primarily considers situations where the lead operator has a lease with a third party supplier for which it has primary responsibility, and then specifically focuses on determining how the contractual arrangement(s) between the lead operator and the non-operator parties should be assessed and accounted for under IFRS.[149] However, similar issues may arise where the lead operator owns the asset used on a JO.

There may also be some similar concerns, i.e. identification of a lease and other consequential impacts, where the lead operator and the non-operator parties (together, the parties to the JO) enter into an arrangement directly with a third party supplier. However, this is not the primary focus of this section.

Some of the potential follow-on issues to consider include, but may not be limited to:

- who is the customer (see 18.2 below);
- whether the arrangement between the lead operator and the JO is, or contains, a sublease (see 18.3 below); and
- depending on the conclusion reached in determining whether the arrangement between the lead operator and the JO contains a sublease (see 18.3 below), determining the appropriate accounting by the lead operator (see 18.4 below) and the non-operator parties (see 18.5 below).

See Chapter 23 for a general discussion of the requirements of IFRS 16.

18.1 Determining who has primary responsibility

Determining whether a lead operator, each party to the JO or the JO itself, has primary responsibility for obligations, such as a lease liability, may require a careful evaluation of all relevant terms and conditions as well as facts and circumstances and the legal environment in which the arrangement(s) operate.

When assessing the fact pattern presented to the Interpretation Committee, the analysis in the March 2019 Agenda paper[150] specifically focused on the derecognition requirements of IFRS 9. The Agenda paper noted that an entity could only derecognise a liability when it was extinguished, i.e. when the entity discharges the liability or is legally released from primary responsibility for the liability either by process of laws or by the creditor.

It also referred to the considerations the IASB undertook when developing IFRS 16 and whether an intermediate lessor should be permitted to offset payments received under the sublease against the liability recognised on the head lease. The IASB decided not to permit this on the basis that each contract was negotiated separately, with the counterparty to the sublease being different to the counterparty to the head lease. As such, the obligations arising from the head lease were generally not extinguished by the terms and conditions of the sublease. This analysis indicated that the legal form of the arrangements is essential in determining who has primary responsibility. As noted above, the outcome may vary depending on the legal jurisdiction in which the arrangements operate.

Where it is established the lead operator has primary responsibility, the Interpretation Committee decision made it clear that the lead operator will initially recognise the entire lease liability and related right-of-use asset in accordance with IFRS 16.

Before undertaking the lease assessment, set out in 18.2 below, it is critical to first determine who the customer is. This is because a lease arises when a customer has a right to control the use of an identified asset for a period of time in exchange for consideration.

18.2 Identifying the customer when there is a JO

Once it has been established the lead operator has primary responsibility for the lease arrangement with the third party supplier, it is then necessary to assess the arrangement(s) between the lead operator and the JO. In undertaking this assessment, it is important to remember that where there is a joint arrangement, IFRS 16 makes it clear that for the purposes of identifying a lease, it is the JO that is the customer in the arrangement with the lead operator rather than each of the parties to the JO individually.[151]

However, the Interpretation Committee staff paper also noted paragraph B11 of IFRS 16 was developed to apply only when assessing whether a contract contains a lease and in determining who is the 'customer' as per the requirements of IFRS 16. It has no further effect on the required accounting for the lease or the joint arrangement, or when assessing who is the customer for the purposes of other standards.[152] See 18.4.2 below for further discussion of where the term customer is used in other standards.

18.3 Determining whether the contractual arrangement between the lead operator and the JO contains a sublease

When assessing the nature of the relationship between the lead operator and the JO and the potential consequential accounting outcomes, including whether there is a sublease, all relevant enforceable contracts, facts and circumstances and the relevant legal environment, need to be considered.

Some examples of potential contracts that may need to be considered when identifying relevant facts and circumstances and enforceable rights and obligations are set out at 18.3.1 below. Some of the factors that need to be assessed to determine whether there is a sublease arrangement in place are discussed at 18.3.2 below.

3538 Chapter 43

This overall assessment process is summarised in the following flow chart:

Figure 43.4: Determining whether the contractual arrangements between the lead operator (as the supplier) and the JO (as the customer) is, or contains, a sublease; and the subsequent accounting for the arrangement

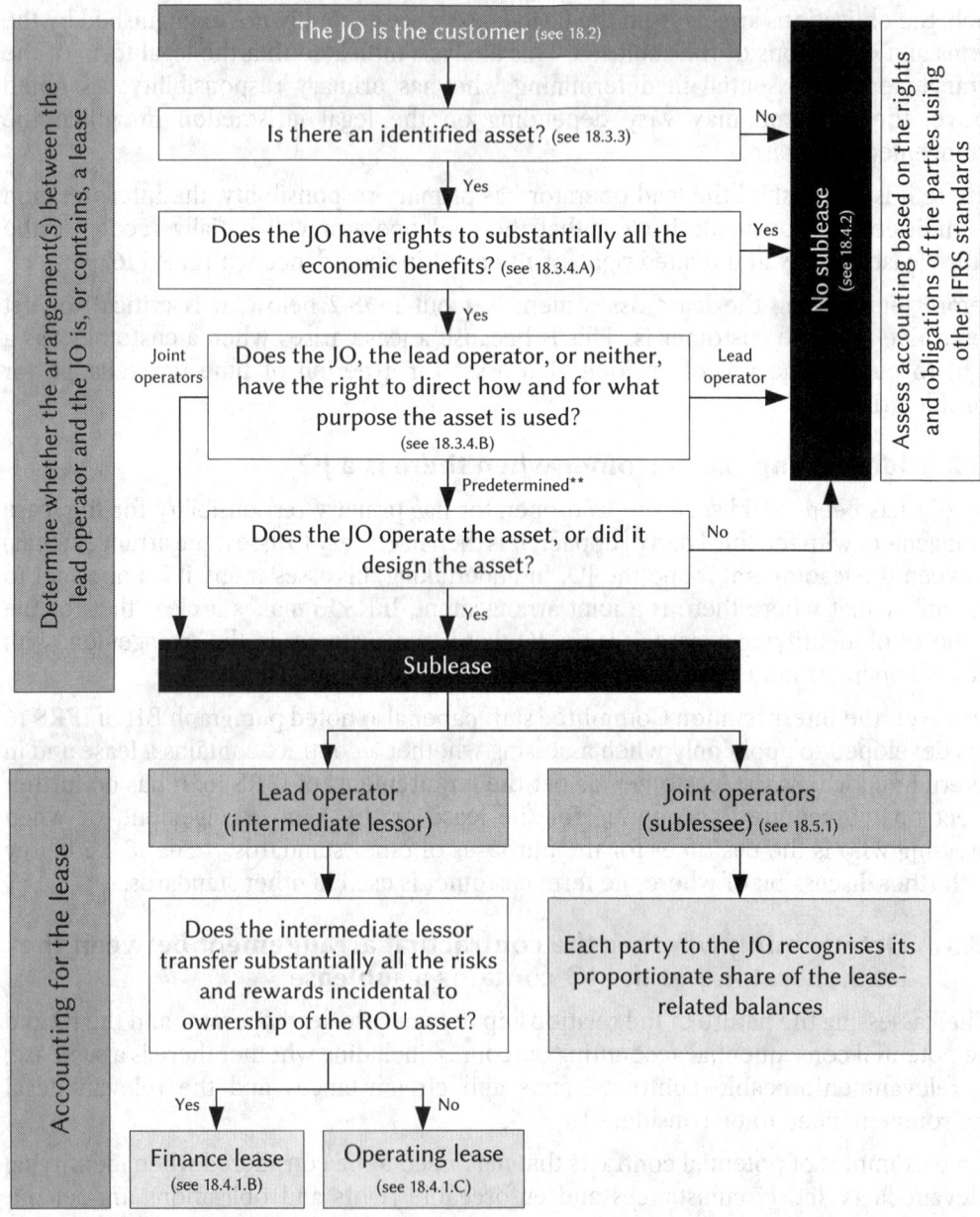

** In accordance with IFRS 16.B24, a customer has the right to direct the use of an identified asset throughout the period of use if the relevant decisions about how and for what purpose the asset is used are predetermined and: (i) the customer has the right to operate the asset (or to direct others to operate the asset in a manner that it determines) throughout the period of use, without the supplier having the right to change those operating instructions; or (ii) the customer designed the asset (or specific aspects of the asset) in a way that predetermines how and for what purpose the asset will be used throughout the period of use.

18.3.1 Assessing the contractual arrangements between the lead operator and the non-operator parties to the JO

18.3.1.A Joint operating agreement

It is common in the extractives industries for a JOA to exist between the parties to the JO. Depending on the terms of the JOA, the underlying activities may be determined and governed by the field/mine development plan and/or the annual operating plans and these may require the unanimous consent or a majority vote of the parties to the JO. In some instances, the JOA may not be explicit as to how all aspects of the JO will operate, particularly when it comes to determining which party (i.e. the lead operator or the JO) has the right to control the use of the assets used to perform the activities of the JO. In other instances, the JOA may give the lead operator primary authority over the development and operations plan for the field/mine and/or the right to determine the relevant decisions over certain assets (e.g. the right to determine when and whether specific assets will be used in the development and operations plan).

As JOAs can vary between JOs and across jurisdictions as they relate to control and responsibility for the activities pursuant to the development and operations plan, each arrangement needs to be carefully considered based on individual facts and circumstances to identify the enforceable rights and obligations.

18.3.1.B Other enforceable contractual arrangements (written and verbal)

Other enforceable contractual arrangements, written and/or verbal, may also affect the rights and obligations of the lead operator and the non-operator parties and thus need to be taken into consideration. For example, for significant assets such as a deepwater drilling rig that is integral to the activities of the JO, a separate contractual arrangement between the lead operator and non-operator parties may exist. This may have been required to evidence the non-operator parties' agreement to use of the specific drilling rig and specific contractual terms including the payment terms, prior to the lead operator entering into the lease arrangement with the third party lessor. This may take the form of a written agreement, or, for example, could be via enforceable verbal agreements reached through the operating committee meetings of the JO which are then minuted.

The extent and nature of contractual arrangements can vary between JOs and relevant legal environments in different jurisdictions. Given this, the specific facts and circumstances and enforceability of each contractual arrangement need to be considered to determine the rights and obligations of the lead operator and the JO.

18.3.2 Determining if there is a sublease

Once it has been established there is a customer-supplier relationship between the lead operator and the JO, the next step is to determine whether there is a lease.

IFRS 16 states that a contract is, or contains, a lease if the contract conveys the right to control the use of an identified asset for a period of time in exchange for consideration. *[IFRS 16.9]*. In assessing whether a contract conveys the right to control the use of an

identified asset for a period of time, an entity assesses whether, throughout the period of use, the customer has both:
- the right to obtain substantially all of the economic benefits from use of the identified asset; and
- the right to direct the use of the identified asset.

The key factor to determine whether there is a sublease is whether it is the lead operator (as the supplier) or the JO (as the customer) that has the right to control the use of the identified asset.

18.3.3 Determining if there is an identified asset

18.3.3.A Specified asset – explicit or implicit

The first step in a lease assessment is to determine if there is an identified asset. As noted in the introduction at 18 above, this assessment will be the same irrespective of whether the asset in question is owned or leased by the lead operator. However, the focus of this publication is on situations where the asset in question is leased by the lead operator from a third party supplier.

An asset is typically identified by being explicitly specified in a contract. However, an asset can also be identified by being implicitly specified at the time that it is made available for use by the customer. A capacity or other portion of an asset, that is not physically distinct, may be an identified asset if the customer's rights to use that asset represent substantially all of the capacity of the asset and thereby provide the customer with the right to obtain substantially all of the economic benefits from use of the asset. For example, a capacity portion of a pipeline or processing plant being used by the JO, could be an identified asset if the portion represents substantially all of the capacity, even if it is not physically distinct.

When analysing the contractual arrangement between the lead operator and the third party supplier, if a capacity or other portion of an asset has been appropriately evaluated, the right to use the asset still needs to be assessed to determine whether it is an identified asset for the purpose of evaluating the existence of a sublease between the lead operator and the JO. This assessment will be based not only on the enforceable terms and conditions of the contractual arrangement between the lead operator and the non-operator parties, but also other relevant facts and circumstances, *[IFRS 16.2]*, inclusive of supplier substitution rights (see 18.3.3.B below for a discussion on substantive substitution rights).

Example 43.18: Identified asset – explicitly identified

A lead operator enters into a lease with a third party supplier for the use of an identified drilling rig for a period of three years. This drilling rig is to be used on JO1 for the full three-year period and this has been discussed and agreed between all parties to the JO at its Operating Committee (OpComm) and has been documented in the OpComm meeting minutes, which are enforceable under this JOA and for this jurisdiction. The lead operator has no substantive substitution rights with respect to this drilling rig throughout the three-year term of the arrangement with JO1.

Analysis: The drilling rig is an identified asset. The drilling rig is explicitly specified in OpComm meeting minutes, and there are no substantive substitution rights.

Example 43.19: Identified asset – capacity portion of an asset

A lead operator enters into a lease with a third party supplier for the right to use an explicitly specified iron ore processing plant for three years. The lead operator then uses this processing plant to process iron ore received from multiple JO's, including JO1. The JOA between the lead operator and JO1 requires the lead operator to undertake all iron ore processing activities using the processing plant which the lead operator has leased. Given the quantity of JO1's iron ore which needs to be processed and the capacity of the processing plant, this arrangement provides JO1 with the right to substantially all of the processing plant's capacity. The lead operator has no substantive substitution rights with respect to this processing plant.

Analysis: The processing plant is an identified asset. While the capacity portion of the processing plant is not physically distinct, as JO1 has the right to substantially all of the processing plant's capacity, JO1 has the right to obtain substantially all of the economic benefits from use of the processing plant. Also, there are no substantive substitution rights.

18.3.3.B   Substantive substitution rights

IFRS 16 states that even if an asset is specified, a customer does not have the right to use an identified asset if the supplier has the substantive right to substitute the asset throughout the period of use. *[IFRS 16.B14]*. In determining whether the lead operator has the substantive right to substitute the asset throughout the period of use, it will be necessary to consider whether the lead operator has the practical ability to substitute (e.g. due to having a portfolio of similar underlying assets which it owns or leases and can easily substitute), and, whether it would benefit economically from doing so.

Demonstrating there is an economic benefit from substitution is a high hurdle, as the customer (i.e. the JO) has to be able to demonstrate the supplier has the practical ability to substitute the underlying asset and the supplier's economic benefits associated with substituting the asset, throughout the period of use, would exceed its costs. If the customer cannot readily determine whether the supplier has a substantive substitution right, the customer presumes the right is not substantive. *[IFRS 16.B19]*.

Example 43.20: Identified asset – explicitly identified but multiple assets available

A lead operator enters into a lease with a third party supplier for the use of helicopter XYZ for a period of three years. The lead operator plans to use helicopter XYZ for flights to and from JO1 (a remote mining operation) for the full three-year period. The use of helicopter XYZ has been agreed between the lead operator and the non-operator parties to JO1.

However, while all the parties to JO1 have agreed to use helicopter XYZ, the lead operator also leases two other helicopters of the same specifications, and all three helicopters are retained at the same nearby air base. The minutes from the same OpComm meeting also confirm that to maximise efficiency of operations, the lead operator is permitted to utilise helicopter XYZ on the lead operator's other unrelated nearby JOs and the similar helicopters can be used on JO1 provided each continues to meet specified safety requirements.

The lead operator's lease arrangements with its third party suppliers allows each of the three helicopters leased by the lead operator to be used for flights to and from each of its mining operations.

Analysis: The arrangement does not contain an identified asset. The lead operator has substantive substitution rights as it has access to two other helicopters that can fly to and from the JO1 mine site. Also, as the helicopters are of the same specification and are held at the same nearby air base, practically substitution can occur. The lead operator would substitute where it provides for efficiency of operations, and accordingly, an economic benefit would arise from substitution. Therefore, notwithstanding helicopter XYZ is explicitly specified in the minutes to the OpComm meeting for JO1, there is no identified asset as the lead operator has a substantive right of substitution.

The existence of a substantive substitution right should be considered on a lease-by-lease basis taking into consideration the specific facts and circumstances existing at lease inception. Given the nature of some assets used within these types of contractual arrangements and the location of the underlying assets, it will often be difficult to demonstrate that the lead operator has a substantive right to substitute the asset under these circumstances. This is because it is likely the lead operator may not have the practical ability to substitute the assets and, even so, costs of substitution would be high. Therefore, it may be difficult to demonstrate, throughout the period of use, that the benefits of substitution are greater than the costs.

18.3.4 Determining if the customer has the right to control the use of an identified asset

As discussed above at 18.2 above, when applying the requirements of IFRS 16 (as outlined below) and specifically when considering the concept of the customer, it is the JO that is the customer. The JO (as the customer) has the right to control the use of an identified asset if it has both the right to obtain substantially all of the economic benefits from use and the right to direct the use of the asset. It would be inappropriate to conclude that a contract does not contain a lease on the grounds that each of the parties to the JO either obtains only a portion of the economic benefits from use of the underlying asset or does not unilaterally direct the use of the underlying asset. *[IFRS 16.BC126]*.

18.3.4.A Right to obtain substantially all of the economic benefits from the use of the identified asset

To control the use of an identified asset, a customer is required to have the right to obtain substantially all of the economic benefits from use of the identified asset throughout the period of use (e.g. by having exclusive use of the asset throughout that period).

There may be some situations where there is a difference between an asset's nominal/expected capacity and the capacity expected to be used by the customer. This may impact the assessment of whether a customer has the right to substantially all of the economic benefits from the use of the identified asset.

Example 43.21: Assessing 'substantially all' when the customer's use of the asset is not 100% of the nominal operating capacity

A lead operator enters into a 30-year lease with Supplier A to transport gas through a pipeline. The lead operator has the right to use 100% of the pipeline. The lead operator will then use the pipeline to transport gas for JO1. At the commencement of the arrangement with JO1, JO1 has the right to use 70% of the pipeline's nominal capacity. The pipeline is located in a remote area where the probability of another customer using the excess capacity of the pipeline is remote.

Analysis: Where the likelihood of another customer using the excess capacity is not substantive, JO1 will be considered to have the right to obtain substantially all of the economic benefits from using the pipeline throughout the period of use.

Determining whether JO1 has the right to obtain substantially all of the economic benefits from using the pipeline throughout the period of use requires consideration of all facts and circumstances. This includes considering the reason for the unused excess capacity.

In this situation, the assessment should be performed based on JO1's right to use 70% of the capacity, combined with an assessment of the likelihood of another customer using the excess capacity.

There is a range of factors to take into consideration when determining whether the JO has the right to substantially all of the economic benefits from the use of an asset. These include (but are not limited to):
- the importance of these types of assets used in the activities of JOs in the mining sector/oil and gas sector and the location of the assets, e.g. in locations which are difficult to get to and/or are remote;
- whether they are located on the mining entity's/oil and gas entity's property; and
- the likelihood of another customer being able to access any excess capacity.

18.3.4.B The right to direct the use of the asset

IFRS 16 states that a customer can obtain the right to direct the use of an identified asset throughout the period of use if the customer has the right to direct how and for what purpose the asset is used throughout the period of use.

When assessing the range of service arrangements used in the mining sector/oil and gas sector, to determine if they are, or contain, leases, it is essential to understand what and who dictates how and for what purpose an identified asset is used. In undertaking this assessment, the decision-making rights most relevant to changing how and for what purpose an identified asset is used throughout the period of use are considered. Decision-making rights are relevant when they affect the economic benefits to be derived from use.

When assessing arrangements between a lead operator and a JO, it is critical to assess whether it is the lead operator or the JO as a whole, that has the right to direct the use of the asset. This involves obtaining an understanding of the JOA and other relevant enforceable arrangements to determine who has the right to make (and change) the key decisions with respect to the use of the asset throughout the period of use.

Under IFRS 11, a joint arrangement exists where:
- the contractual arrangement gives all the parties, or a group of the parties, control over the arrangement collectively; and
- the decisions about the relevant activities require the unanimous consent of the parties sharing control. *[IFRS 11.5, 7]*.

For arrangements in the extractives industries, under the terms of a JOA, approval of the mine plan or field plan and/or annual operating budget may be considered a relevant activity, and, for this to require unanimous consent of all parties to the JO for approval. Identification of relevant activities and determining which require unanimous consent, is a critical part of the rationale to support joint control such that the arrangement is a joint arrangement in scope of IFRS 11.

When assessing who has the right to direct the use of an asset in accordance with IFRS 16, in some arrangements, the lead operator may retain this right and therefore there will be no sublease between the lead operator and JO.

However, if the enforceable terms of the JOA and other arrangements in place and relevant facts and circumstances support this, it is possible the JO may have the right to direct the use of an identified asset(s) used as part of the activities of the JO.

For example, where it has been concluded that the mine plan or field plan is specific enough that it provides the JO the right to determine how and for what purpose an identified asset is used throughout the period of use and subsequent changes to that mine plan or field plan require unanimous consent, then the JO may direct the use of the identified asset. If the JO also has the right to substantially all of the economic benefits from use of the asset, the JO (as the customer) has the right to control the use of the asset.

Example 43.22: Right to direct the use – dedicated asset

Company A, in its role as lead operator, enters into a 10-year lease (head lease) for a Floating Production Storage Offloading (FPSO) vessel with a third party supplier, as sole signatory and has primary responsibility for the lease payments. It recognises the entire lease liability and related right-of-use asset in respect of the head lease. The FPSO is highly specialised to allow for production from a single specified field, owned by JO1, on which it is to be deployed. The FPSO will be used by JO1 for 10 years.

The enforceable terms of the JOA for JO1 specify that the lead operator is responsible for sourcing an appropriate FPSO to be used on JO1 for 10 years. Once identified, the lead operator will not have a substantive right to substitute the underlying FPSO during the 10-year period.

In addition, in this example, the field development and operations plans, which determine how and for what purpose the FPSO is used throughout the period of use, require the unanimous consent of the parties to JO1. Due to changing oil prices, costs, field performance, etc. the parties to JO1 also have the right to change these plans. Therefore, such decisions are the relevant decisions impacting the economic benefits derived from use of the FPSO.

The lead operator recovers its costs related to the lease of the FPSO payable to the third party supplier by billing all parties to JO1, pro rated based on their equity interests in JO1 throughout the 10-year right of use term.

Analysis: There is a sublease between the lead operator and the JO. In this instance, given the enforceable terms of the JOA and other relevant facts and circumstances, the FPSO is implicitly identified and JO1 has the right to substantially all of the economic benefits and has the right to direct the use of the identified FPSO throughout the period of use.

Example 43.23: Right to direct the use – asset can be used on multiple locations for multiple JOs

Company B is the lead operator for a range of different JOs, each of which have exploration licences in close proximity to each other. Exploration and appraisal drilling is expected to occur over the two year period. Company B's equity interest in each JO varies. Given expected upcoming drilling activity, Company B enters into a lease with a third party supplier for a drilling rig for a period of two years.

Under the terms of the JOAs governing each of the JOs, Company B is required to execute drilling activity over the coming two years over a number of the licences, but has flexibility in determining the exact timing of drilling to be performed on each respective licence.

Company B has the substantive right to determine when and where to drill for each licence and can change such decisions, throughout the period of use. The JOs have no right to make or change relevant decisions about the use of the asset, even when the drilling rig is currently in use on their respective licenses.

Throughout the period in which the rig is drilling on a licence, Company B has the right to recover costs incurred from the respective JOs relative to the equity interests of each of the non-operator parties. When the drilling rig is idle, Company B has no right to recover costs from any JO.

Analysis: The arrangements between the lead operator and the JOs do not contain a sublease. In this situation, the lead operator has the right to make the relevant decisions about the use of the drilling rig. Those decisions include determining when and where to use the drilling rig throughout the period of use. No single JO has the right to control the use of the drilling rig over the full two-year lease term; rather, Company B has the right to control the use of the drilling rig.

Example 43.24: Right to direct the use – asset only used on one JO

Company C is the lead operator for JO2, an onshore field in the development phase. Development drilling is planned for the next 15 months and the field development plan sets out that 30-60 wells will be drilled within a pre-approved budget. Company C has entered into a 15 month lease with a third party supplier to secure a drilling rig for the activity.

Under the terms of the JOA governing JO2, Company C is required to utilise its knowledge of the field to execute the drilling programme that maximises the economics of JO2's development plan. In this example, Company C has the right to determine whether, when and where each well will be drilled within the licence area and has the right to change such decisions, throughout the period of use. JO2 has no right to make or change relevant decisions about the use of the asset.

Throughout the period in which the rig is drilling on the licence, Company C has the right to recover costs incurred from the JO2 non-operator parties relative to their equity interests in the licence.

Analysis: The arrangement between the lead operator and the JO does not contain a sublease. In this situation, the lead operator has the right to make the relevant decisions about the use of the drilling rig. In this example, those decisions include determining whether, when and where to use the drilling rig throughout the period of use. In this example, Company C has the right to control the use of the drilling rig throughout the period of use.

18.3.4.C Right to direct the use is predetermined

IFRS 16 also considers circumstances whereby the right to direct the use of the asset is 'predetermined'. That is, a customer has the right to direct the use of an identified asset throughout the period of use if the relevant decisions about how and for what purpose the asset is used are predetermined and: (i) the customer has the right to operate the asset (or to direct others to operate the asset in a manner that it determines) throughout the period of use, without the supplier having the right to change those operating instructions; or (ii) the customer designed the asset (or specific aspects of the asset) in a way that predetermines how and for what purpose the asset will be used throughout the period of use. *[IFRS 16.B24]*. The concept of predetermined has not been considered in detail in this publication.

There are a range of factors entities will need to consider to determine whether a sublease exists between a lead operator and a JO. Entities need to ensure the evidence used to support conclusions about joint control for the purposes of applying IFRS 11 (in particular, the factors used to conclude that there is a joint arrangement and the lead operator is not controlling the arrangement itself, but instead is just carrying out the decisions of the parties to the joint arrangement), is taken into consideration when determining who has the right to control the use of an identified asset used as part of the JO activities in accordance with IFRS 16, i.e. the lead operator or the JO.

18.4 Accounting by the lead operator

Where the lead operator is the sole signatory to, and has primary responsibility for, the contract that is or contains a lease with the third party supplier, the lead operator is required to initially recognise 100% of the right-of-use asset and the related lease liability in accordance with IFRS 16. Regardless of whether the JOA and related arrangements are considered to contain a sublease, for as long as the lead operator remains a party to the lease arrangement with the third party supplier, the lead operator will continue to recognise 100% of the lease liability. This is on the basis that the JOA and related arrangements do not extinguish or transfer the lead operator's enforceable rights and obligations under the contract with the third party supplier and instead, the lead operator retains the primary responsibility for the lease liability. However, the subsequent accounting for the right-of-use asset and the accounting for the amounts received or receivable from the non-operator parties will depend on whether a sublease exists, and if there is a sublease, whether it is a finance lease or operating lease.

A summary of the potential outcomes is as follows:

Figure 43.5: Lead operator's accounting for the contractual arrangement with the JO – potential accounting outcomes

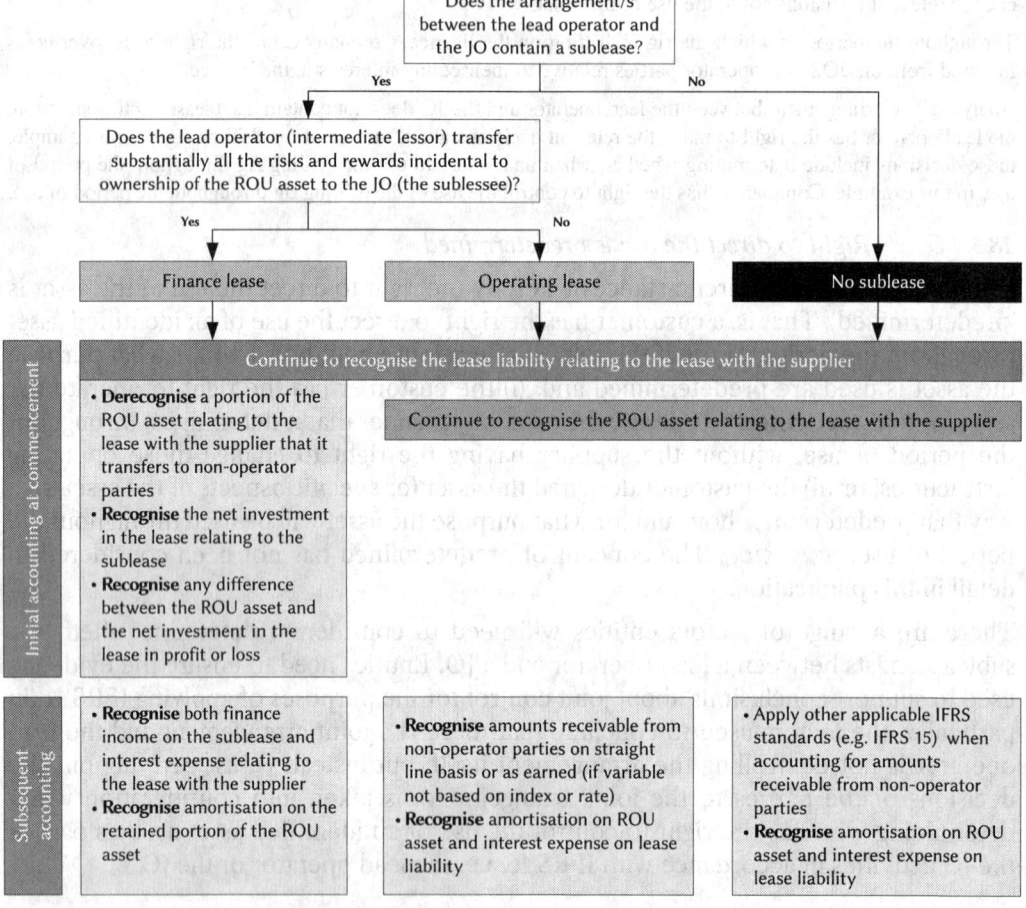

18.4.1 JOA and/or related contractual arrangements are, or contain, a sublease

18.4.1.A Classifying the sublease

Lessor accounting remains largely unchanged from that prescribed by the previous accounting standard, IAS 17. Therefore, the lessor needs to determine whether the arrangement transfers substantially all the risks and rewards incidental to ownership of the underlying asset and if so, it is a finance lease. When assessing the lease classification, this is undertaken by reference to the right-of-use asset arising from the head lease, not by reference to the underlying asset. If the head lease is a short-term lease that the lead operator, as a lessee, has accounted for applying the practical expedient, *[IFRS 16.6]*, the sublease is classified as an operating lease.

For more information on classifying leases by a lessor see Chapter 23 at 6.1.

Example 43.25: Classifying the sublease – finance lease

Company A, as lead operator of JO1, enters into a 10-year contract with a third party supplier that contains a lease (head lease) for a FPSO vessel as a sole signatory and has primary responsibility for the lease payments. Therefore, the lead operator recognises 100% of the lease liability and the related right-of-use asset.

The FPSO is used on JO1 and for the purposes of this illustration, it has been concluded that the arrangement contain a 10-year sublease.

The FPSO is highly specialised to allow for production from a single specified license, owned by JO1, on which it is to be deployed, and hence can only be used by JO1 (as the sublessee), without major modifications. The FPSO has an estimated useful life of 25 years.

Analysis: The sublease is classified as a finance lease. The sublease is classified by reference to the right-of-use asset in the head lease and not the underlying FPSO. The lease term for the sublease represents all (and hence a major part) of the life of the right-of-use asset, as the sublease is for 10 years and the tenure of the right-of-use asset is also 10 years. Furthermore, the asset is specialised in nature.

Example 43.26: Classifying the sublease – operating lease

Company A, as lead operator of JO1, enters into a contract with a third party supplier that contains a lease of an excavator for five years (head lease). The excavator is not specialised.

For the purposes of this illustration, it has been concluded the arrangement contains a 2-year sublease of the excavator.

Analysis: The sublease is classified as an operating lease. The sublease is classified with reference to the right-of-use asset in the head lease and not the underlying excavator. The lease period does not represent a major part of the life of the right-of-use asset, because the sublease is only for two years and the right-of-use asset is for five years. Also, there are no other factors in this example which would indicate there is a finance lease.

18.4.1.B Accounting for the sublease – finance lease

At commencement of the sublease: the lead operator, as intermediate lessor:

- derecognises a portion of the right-of-use asset which had been recognised in relation to the lease with the third party supplier – the portion derecognised represents the portion of the right-of-use asset transferred to the non-operator parties;
- the portion of the right-of-use asset retained represents the lead operator's share of the sublease as a participant in the JO recognised in accordance with IFRS 11;
- recognises a net investment in the lease – the net investment in the lease is measured as the sum of the discounted lease payments receivable from the non-operator parties in respect of the sublease and any unguaranteed residual value in the right-of-use asset accruing to the lead operator as intermediate lessor;
- recognises any difference between the portion of the right-of-use asset derecognised and the net investment in the lease recognised in profit or loss; and
- continues to recognise the existing lease liability relating to the lease with the third party supplier in its statement of financial position, which represents the lease payments it owes to the third party supplier as the head lessor.

During the term of the sublease: the lead operator, as the intermediate lessor, recognises finance income on the sublease (net investment in the lease), amortisation of its share of the right-of-use asset which is retained in its books and interest expense on the lease liability relating to the head lease. For more information on accounting for finance leases by a lessor see Chapter 23 at 6.2. Any variable lease payments that do not depend on an index or rate (e.g. performance- or usage-based payments) are recognised in profit or loss (unless they are included in the carrying amount of another asset in accordance with other IFRS) in the period in which the event that triggers the payment occurs.

Example 43.27: Accounting for the sublease – finance lease

Assume the lead operator recognises a right-of-use asset and lease liability of $100 on a head lease (assume there were no other adjustments required against either of these balances), and the arrangement between the lead operator and the JO contains a sublease classified as a finance lease.

The lease term for the head lease and sublease are both 10 years, have the same commencement dates, and the timing and amounts of the lease payments are identical.

The lead operator remains primarily obligated for the lease, including the lease payments under the head lease.

The lead operator (as a participant in the JO) has a 40% interest in the JO. The entries recognised by the lead operator will be, as follows:

Commencement of the head lease

		$	$
Dr	Right-of-use asset	100	
Cr	Lease liability (head lease)		100

Journal entry to recognise the head lease determined using the sum of the discounted lease payments.

Commencement of the sublease

		$	$
Dr	Net investment in the lease	60	
Cr	Right-of-use asset		60

Journal entry to derecognise a portion of the ROU asset relating to the head lease equal to the non-operators' interests in the lease between the lead operator and the JO and recognise the discounted value of the sum of the related amounts receivable from the non-operator parties.

Net impact for lead operator

		$	$
Dr	Right-of-use asset#	40	
Dr	Net investment in the lease	60	
Cr	Lease liability (head lease)		100

\# The right-of-use asset retained by the lead operator represents the lead operator's 40% share of the lease between itself and the JO which it recognises because it is also a participant in the JO.

18.4.1.C   Accounting for the sublease – operating lease

At lease commencement: the lead operator, as intermediate lessor:

- continues to recognise the right-of-use asset relating to the lease with the third party supplier; and
- continues to recognise the lease liability relating to the lease with the third party supplier in its statement of financial position, which represents the lease payments it owes to the third party supplier as the head lessor.

During the term of the sublease: the lead operator, as the intermediate lessor, recognises amortisation of the right-of-use asset and interest expense on the lease liability relating to the lease with the third party supplier. It also recognises payments received from the non-operator parties as income, on either a straight-line basis or another systematic basis if that better represents the pattern in which benefit is expected to be derived from the use of the asset. Any variable lease payments that do not depend on an index or rate (e.g. performance- or usage-based payments) are recognised in profit or loss (unless they are included in the carrying amount of another asset in accordance with other IFRS) in the period in which the event that triggers the payment occurs.

18.4.2 JOA and/or related contractual arrangements are not, do not contain, a sublease

When the contractual arrangements between the lead operator and the JO do not contain a sublease, the lead operator continues to recognise the right-of-use asset and related lease liability in relation to the lease with the third party supplier at lease commencement and will recognise amortisation of the right-of-use asset and interest on the lease liability across the term of the lease.

The arrangement with the JO will then likely represent an executory contract and the accounting by the lead operator for amounts receivable from the non-operator parties will depend on the nature of this arrangement. Some of the potential accounting considerations may include the matters listed below. When undertaking these assessments, as discussed at 18.2 above, it is important to note that the determination of the customer for the purposes of applying IFRS 16 does not necessarily impact the determination of a customer for the purposes of other standards. For example, a customer, for the purposes of IFRS 15, is determined by applying the specific requirements and guidance of IFRS 15.

- Provision of JO management services whereby the JO is considered to be a customer: the arrangement will be in the scope, and the lead operator will apply the provisions, of IFRS 15. Revenue will be recognised at the amount the lead operator expects to be entitled to in exchange for providing the JO management services to the JO as the relevant performance obligations are satisfied. See Chapters 27 to 31 for more information on factors to consider when applying IFRS 15.

- JO does not represent a customer: where the lead operator does not consider it is providing JO management services to the non-operator parties within the scope of IFRS 15, the lead operator will need to apply other relevant IFRS standards, or when no specific IFRS standards are applicable, use judgement to determine the appropriate accounting treatment for the arrangement. The lead operator will need to apply IAS 8 to determine the nature of the relationship and whether and when it should recognise amounts receivable from the non-operator parties. Specifically, the lead operator will need to assess whether the provisions of IFRS 9 relating to financial assets apply or whether the reimbursement requirements of IAS 37 apply. The lead operator will also need to assess whether these amounts represent a form of income or a direct reimbursement of expenditure.

18.4.3 Other issues to consider

In addition to the above, there are a number of other potential issues that a lead operator may need to consider when evaluating the overall accounting implications, which include but are not limited to:

- Capitalisation of costs: where the activities of the JO are being undertaken in relation to a project that is in the exploration and evaluation (E&E) phase or the development phase, depending on the lead operator's accounting policies, it may need to consider whether some of the costs incurred, e.g. a portion of the amortisation of the right-of-use asset and/or interest expense on the lease liability, should be capitalised. The lead operator will need to assess whether such costs meet the requirements for capitalisation under the relevant standards (including IAS 23 which explicitly scopes in interest in respect of leases under IFRS 16), and if so, determine the amount that should be capitalised versus the amount that should be expensed.

- Mismatch between the lead operator's costs and the amounts receivable from the non-operator parties: in each period, the lead operator's accounting for the expenses relating to the lease with a third party which are to effectively be reimbursed by the non-operator parties, will not necessarily be equivalent to the amounts receivable from the non-operator parties. This is because the IFRS 16 accounting for the lease with the third party supplier will generally be more front ended and will comprise amortisation of the right-of-use asset and interest on the lease liability. This will differ from the income a lead operator will recognise under sublease operating accounting or executory contract accounting. This will lead to timing mismatches for the lead operator in its profit or loss.

- Presentation of amounts receivable from the non-operator parties (where the arrangement is not a 'sublease which is a finance lease', i.e. it is either an operating lease or not a sublease): in this situation, a question that may be asked is whether any amounts receivable from the non-operator parties can be offset against the amounts recognised by the lead operator. This question is generally raised because from an economic perspective, the non-operator parties are effectively paying their respective share of the cash costs incurred by the lead operator on the lease with the third party supplier. Hence, some lead operators may prefer to present the effects of this on a net basis, if / where possible.

    When assessing this offsetting issue, the following needs to be considered:

    - Ability to offset: IAS 1, *[IFRS 1.32]*, and the Conceptual Framework, *[CF 7.10]*, provide the requirements and guidance with respect to offsetting of assets and liabilities and income and expenses. IAS 1 states offsetting is not allowed unless required/permitted by another standard and the Conceptual Framework notes it is generally not permitted as offsetting classifies dissimilar items together. Given this, it is expected the ability to achieve offsetting will be rare.

- Lead operator capitalises its costs as part of an E&E or development asset: in such a situation, the lead operator would only be able to capitalise the portion of the costs incurred on the head lease relating to its ownership in the JO assets. This is on the basis that it would not receive the future economic benefits associated with the costs attributable to the non-operator parties. These costs would therefore need to be recognised in profit or loss (P&L). See below for further discussion on the issues this would present.
- Lead operator recognises its costs in P&L: in this situation, the question is whether the lead operator can offset the amounts receivable from non-operator parties directly against the line items within P&L in which it has recognised the costs relating to the lease with the third party supplier. The challenges here may include:
  - mismatches in amounts (as discussed above);
  - whether such amounts received can be offset and if so, upon what basis; and
  - if a valid argument could be mounted to support offsetting, which is considered difficult to achieve, given the lead operator will be recognising amortisation and interest, it is unclear how the amounts received would be allocated between the two line items.

18.5 Accounting by the non-operator parties

As discussed at 18.4 above, where the lead operator is the sole signatory to, and has primary responsibility for, the contract that is or contains a lease with the third party supplier, the lead operator is required to initially recognise 100% of the lease-related balances. The accounting by the non-operator parties will then depend on whether the JOA and/or related contractual arrangements contain a sublease or not.

18.5.1 *JOA and/or related contractual arrangements contain a sublease*

When the JO is the sublessee, under IFRS 16, there is no longer any differentiation between operating or finance leases. As a result, there will be a right-of-use asset and lease liability in relation to the lease with the lead operator, for which each participant in the JO will, in accordance with IFRS 11, need to:

- recognise its proportionate share of the right-of-use asset and lease liability based on its respective interest in the JO; and
- during the term of the sublease:
  - recognise amortisation of its share of the right-of-use asset; and
  - recognise interest expense in relation to its share of the lease liability.

18.5.2 *JOA and/or related contractual arrangements do not contain a sublease*

Where the JOA and/or related contractual arrangements do not contain a sublease, IFRS 16 does not apply to the JO. Therefore, the non-operator parties will likely continue to recognise amounts payable to the lead operator consistently based on their existing accounting policies.

18.5.3 Other factors to consider when evaluating the overall accounting

In addition to the above, there are a number of other potential factors which non-operator parties will need to consider when evaluating the overall accounting, which include but are not limited to:

- Capitalisation of costs: where the activities of the JO are being undertaken in relation to a project that is in the E&E phase or the development phase, depending on the non-operator's accounting policies, it may need to consider whether the costs incurred, e.g. amortisation of the right-of-use asset and/or interest expense on the lease liability, should be capitalised. Each non-operator party will need to assess whether such costs meet the eligibility requirements for capitalisation in accordance with the relevant standard (including IAS 23), their own policies and appropriate industry practice. If so, the amount that will need to be capitalised versus the amount that will be expensed will need to be identified.

- Cash flow impact: the profile over which right-of-use amortisation and interest expense will be recognised will vary depending on the nature of the particular asset and could vary significantly from the pattern in which cash costs are incurred. This is because it is expected that most lead operators will seek to align cost recovery with the pattern in which their cash costs are incurred. This is likely to lead to timing and potentially overall measurement differences between amounts incurred and cash outflows recognised.

18.6 Other practical considerations

In addition to the issues discussed above, there are other factors requiring consideration which are relevant to both the lead operator and non-operator parties.

18.6.1 Access to information

If the contractual arrangement between the lead operator and the JO are concluded to contain a sublease, or the JO itself is considered to have entered into a lease directly with a third party supplier, the parties to the JO will need to recognise their respective share of the lease liability, right-of-use asset, amortisation expense, interest expense and variable lease payments, if any. To do this, the lead operator will need to provide non-operator parties with the required information. Therefore, parties to the JO will need to discuss and agree what information is required, who will prepare and provide such information and when such information will be made available.

Where lead operators agree to prepare, or are required to prepare, such information on behalf of the non-operator parties, the non-operator parties will need to consider whether there are any material differences in accounting policies which need to be adjusted for before recognising such amounts in their own financial statements. Also, on transition to IFRS 16, it will be necessary to consider the impact of different transition options taken by each of the parties. For example, if the JO exists at transition date and the lead operator prepares this information on a full retrospective basis, but one of the non-operator parties adopts IFRS 16 using the modified retrospective approach, adjustments will be required to align to their transition approach (if material).

18.6.2 Impact on systems and processes

Where leases are concluded to exist, this may require significant alterations to systems and processes. Lead operators will be required to consider the ability of existing systems and processes to execute joint interest billing going forward in light of these changes. Non-operator parties will need to consider whether their systems and processes are capable of accounting for leases.

Entities are encouraged to liaise closely with parties to each of their JOs, sharing sufficient information so that each member of the JO is able to determine their appropriate accounting.

19 LONG-TERM CONTRACTS AND LEASES

Given the nature of the extractive industries, mining companies and oil and gas companies regularly enter into a wide range of long-term contracts. These may relate to the provision of services or the sale of goods. There are a number of potential issues to be addressed when considering the accounting for these arrangements, these are discussed below. This should be read in conjunction with the general discussion set out in Chapter 23.

19.1 Embedded leases

IFRS 16 requires an entity to determine whether a contract is, or contains, a lease at the inception of the contract. *[IFRS 16.9]*. The assessment of whether a contract is or contains a lease will be straightforward in most arrangements. However, judgement may be required in applying the definition of a lease to certain arrangements. For example, in contracts that include significant services, determining whether the contract conveys the right to direct the use of an identified asset may be challenging.

There are a range of arrangements commonly found in the extractive industries which may convey the right to control the use of an identified asset to the customer, as well as provide the customer with related services or outputs. This may include:

- outsourcing arrangements;
- take-or-pay and similar contracts (see 19.2 below);
- service arrangements – such as contract mining services arrangements or oilfield services arrangements;
- throughput arrangements (which may take the form of a take-or-pay arrangement);
- tolling contracts (see 20 below);
- contractor facilities located on the mining company's or oil and gas company's property;
- storage facility arrangements;
- energy-related or utility contracts, e.g. gas, electricity, telecommunications, water; or
- transportation/freight/shipping/handling services contracts.

IFRS 16 makes it clear that one of these types of arrangements (or part thereof) could be within the scope of IFRS 16 if it meets the definition of a lease, e.g. if it conveys to the lessee the right to use an asset (the underlying asset) for a period of time in in exchange for consideration. *[IFRS 16 Appendix A]*. This is regardless of the fact that the arrangement is not described as a lease and is likely to grant rights that are significantly different from those in a formal lease agreement. IFRS 16 is to be applied to each lease component within the contract as a lease separately from non-lease components of the contract, unless the entity applies the practical expedient to combine the lease and associated non-lease components. *[IFRS 16.12]*. The detailed requirements of IFRS 16 and the definition of a lease are discussed in Chapter 23 at 2.

See 17 and 18 above for a discussion of the impact of the IFRS 16 on mining companies and oil and gas companies and Chapter 23 for a general discussion on IFRS 16.

Barrick's acknowledgement that non-lease contracts need to be assessed for the existence of embedded leases under IFRS 16 is provided in Extract 43.55 below.

> *Extract 43.55: Barrick Gold Corporation (2018)*
> NOTES TO THE CONSOLIDATED FINANCIAL STATEMENTS [extract]
> 2. Significant Accounting Policies [extract]
> z) New Accounting Standards Issued But Not Yet Effective [extract]
>
> IFRS 16 Leases [extract]
>
> We have developed a full implementation plan to determine the impact on our financial statements and internal controls. In the fourth quarter of 2017, we formed an IFRS 16 working group and began the process of compiling all of our existing operating leases and service contracts. In the first quarter of 2018, we began reviewing the relevant agreements to identify which of the operating leases and service contracts are in scope for IFRS 16. In the second quarter of 2018, we had largely completed our review of existing service contracts for embedded leases and had identified all operating leases. In the third quarter of 2018, we continued our review of existing service contracts for embedded leases.

19.2 Take-or-pay contracts

A 'take-or-pay' contract is a specific type of long-term commodity-based sales agreement between a customer and a supplier in which the pricing terms are set for a specified minimum quantity of a particular good or service. The customer must pay the minimum amount as per the contract, even if it does not take the volumes. There may also be options for additional volumes in excess of the minimum. Take-or-pay contracts for the supply of gas are particularly common, because entities developing gas fields need to make very significant investments in infrastructure such as pipelines, liquefaction plants and shipping terminals, to make transport of gas to the end-consumer economically viable. In order to raise the funds to finance such investments, it is crucial to know that there is a profitable market for the gas, as it cannot easily be diverted and sold in an alternative market or to an alternative customer.

While take-or-pay contracts perhaps most commonly involve the supply of gas, they can also include other arrangements such as contracts for pipeline capacity or LNG regasification facilities. Take-or-pay contracts also are used in the mining sector, e.g. with some coal contracts, though less frequently than in the oil and gas sector. Often take-or-pay contracts permit the purchaser to recover payments for quantities not taken, by allowing the purchaser to take more than the minimum in later years and to apply the previously paid-for undertake amount towards the cost of product taken in the later years.[153]

The following issues need to be considered in accounting for take-or-pay contracts:

- *Structured entities* – If a take-or-pay contract transfers the majority of the risks and rewards from the development of a mine or gas field to the customer, it is necessary to consider whether the entity developing the gas field has, in effect, become a structured entity of that customer and therefore, the customer needs to consider the level of influence it has over that mining entity or oil and gas entity (see Chapter 6 at 4.4.1).

- *Embedded leases* – Take-or-pay contracts are often for a very significant portion of the output of the gas field that it relates to. Therefore, as illustrated in Extract 43.55 above, the operator and customer need to consider whether the take-or-pay contract contains a lease of the related assets (see 19.1 above for further discussion).
- *Embedded derivatives* – As illustrated in Extract 43.56 below, the price of gas sold under take-or-pay contracts is often based on a 'basket' of fuel prices and/or inflation price indices. If there is an active market for gas then this often means that an embedded derivative needs to be separated from the underlying host take-or-pay contract (see 13.2 above).
- *Guarantees* – Lenders are often willing to provide funding for the development of a gas field only if the operator can present a solid business case, which includes a 'guaranteed' stream of revenue from a reputable customer. In such cases, the take-or-pay contract acts as a form of credit enhancement or possibly as a guarantee. The operator and customer may need to consider whether the take-or-pay arrangement includes a guarantee that should be accounted for such under IFRS 9 (see Chapter 45 at 3.4).
- *Make-up product and undertake* – A customer that fails to take the specified volume during the period specified must nevertheless pay for the agreed-volume. However, a take-or-pay contract sometimes permits the customer to take an equivalent amount of production (makeup product) at a later date after the payment for the guaranteed amount has been made (see 12.16 above and 19.2.1 below).

Extract 43.56 below from the financial statements of ENGIE SA gives an overview of some of these important terms and conditions that exist in take-or-pay contracts.

Extract 43.56: ENGIE SA (2017)

2017 Registration Document
2 Risk factors [extract]
2.3 Operational risks[extract]
2.3.1 Purchases and sales [extract]
2.3.1.1 Purchase and sale of natural gas

The Group has established a procurement portfolio composed in part of long-term contracts, including some with a take-or-pay clause which, under certain conditions, stipulates that minimum quantities will be taken during a period.

In case of major gas supply interruption (for example, due to an interruption of Russian deliveries or an interruption of transit in Ukraine) or an interruption of LNG supply (for example, from Yemen or Egypt), or difficulty in renewing certain contracts under favorable economic conditions, the replacement cost for gas, including transportation, could be higher and affect the Group's margins. To mitigate this risk, the Group has a number of tools for flexibility and modulation (flexibility in long-term contracts, storage and regasification capacity, and purchasing in the marketplaces) as well as a diversified portfolio.

Prices of long-term purchase contracts (partially indexed to the price indices of oil products) may be decorrelated from selling prices or prices in the gas markets. This spread might have a significant impact on the Group's results. Long-term contracts include price adjustment clauses, so that the economic balance between producer and buyer can be altered. The Group's buy/sell margin may therefore change according to price adjustments in LNG or gaseous gas contracts and the state of the gas market in general.

Negotiations in recent years have led to the integration of market indices in long-term contracts and/or to the reduction of the difference between the contract price and market price. They have also led to increased frequency of price revisions.

19.2.1 Make-up product and undertake

Under some take-or-pay arrangements, a customer who is required to pay for the product not taken will often have no right of future recovery. The customer should recognise an expense equal to the payment made, while the operator recognises the same amount as revenue. However, if the substance of the relationship between the operator and customer is such that a renegotiation of the arrangement is probable then it may be more appropriate for the operator to recognise the penalty payment as a contract liability, i.e. deferred revenue. The customer, however, should still recognise an expense in this case as it does not have a legal right to receive reimbursement or makeup product.[154]

The accounting is different when a customer that is required to pay for product not taken has a right to take makeup product in the future.

In this case, the operator would recognise a contract liability, i.e. unearned revenue, in relation to the 'undertake' measured in accordance with IFRS 15, as it represents an obligation for the operator to have to provide the product in the future. The operator only recognises revenue in accordance with IFRS 15 once the make-up product has been taken by the customer, i.e. the performance obligation is satisfied. Only once the make-up period has expired or it is clear that the purchaser has become unable to take the product, would the liability be eliminated and revenue recognised.[155] For a discussion of the IFRS 15 considerations for these types of arrangements, see 12.16 above.

From the customer's perspective, it would normally recognise a prepaid amount representing the make-up product that it is entitled to receive in the future. However, if the customer is entitled to more make-up product than it can sell, it may need to recognise an impairment charge.

20 TOLLING ARRANGEMENTS

In the mining sector it is common for entities to provide raw material to a smelter or refiner for further processing. If the raw material is sold to the smelter or refiner and the relevant criteria are satisfied, the mining company recognises revenue in accordance with IFRS 15. However, under a 'tolling' arrangement a mining company generally supplies, without transferring ownership, raw material to a smelter or refiner which processes it for a fee and then returns the finished product to the customer. Alternatively, the mining company may sell the raw material to the smelter or refiner, but is required to repurchase the finished product. In the latter two situations, no revenue should be recognised under IFRS 15 when the raw material is shipped to the smelter or refiner as the customer, i.e. the smelter or refiner, has not obtained control of the raw materials. An entity should carefully assess the terms and conditions of its tolling arrangements to determine:

- when and if it is appropriate to recognise revenue;
- whether those arrangements contain embedded leases that require separation under IFRS 16 (see 19.1 above);
- whether the tolling arrangement is part of a series of transactions with a joint arrangement; and
- whether the toll processing entity is a structured entity that requires consolidation under IFRS 10 (see Chapter 6 at 4.4.1 for more information).

Extract 43.57 below describes a tolling arrangement between Norsk Hydro and one of its joint arrangements.

> **Extract 43.57: Norsk Hydro ASA (2013)**
> Notes to the consolidated financial statements [extract]
> Note 26 – Investments in jointly controlled entities [extract]
> **Aluminium Norf GmbH (Alunorf)** located in Germany is the world's largest rolling mill and is owned by Hydro and Hindalco Industries (50 percent each). Alunorf produces flat rolled products from raw material from the partners based on a tolling arrangement. Sales from Alunorf to Hydro amounted to NOK 1,499 million in 2013 and NOK 1,423 million in 2012. Hydro's capital and financing commitments are regulated in the Joint Venture agreement. Alunorf has investment commitments amounting to NOK 444 million as of December 31, 2013. Hydro's financing commitment based on its interest is NOK 189 million as of December 31, 2013. Alunorf is part of Rolled Products.

For a discussion on the impacts of IFRS 15 on repurchase agreements, see 12.14 above.

21 TAXATION

As mentioned at 1.1 above, one of the characteristics of the extractive industries is the intense government involvement in their activities, which ranges from 'outright governmental ownership of some (especially petroleum) or all minerals to unusual tax benefits or penalties, price controls, restrictions on imports and exports, restrictions on production and distribution, environmental and health and safety regulations, and others'.[156]

Mining companies and oil and gas companies typically need to make payments to governments in their capacity as:

- owner of the mineral resources;
- co-owner or joint arrangement partner in the projects;
- regulator of, among other things, environmental matters and health and safety matters; and
- tax authority.

The total payment to a government is often described as the 'government take'. This includes fixed payments or variable payments that are based on production, revenue, or a net profit figure; and which may take the form of fees, bonuses, royalties or taxes. Determining whether a payment to government meets the definition of income tax is not straightforward.

IAS 12 should be applied in accounting for income taxes, defined as including:

(a) all domestic and foreign taxes which are based on taxable profits; and

(b) taxes, such as withholding taxes, which are payable by a subsidiary, associate or joint arrangements on distributions to the reporting entity. *[IAS 12.1-2]*.

As discussed in Chapter 33 at 4.1, it is not altogether clear what an income tax actually is. In the extractive industries the main problem with the definition in IAS 12 occurs when:

(a) a government raises 'taxes' on sub-components of net profit (e.g. net profit before financing costs or revenue minus allowed costs); or

(b) there is a mandatory government participation in certain projects that entitle the government to a share of profits as defined in a joint operating agreement.

A considerable amount of judgement is required to determine whether a particular arrangement falls within the definition of 'income tax' under IAS 12 or whether it is another form of government take. From a commercial perspective the overall share of the economic benefits that the government takes is much more important than the distinction between its different forms. In practice, most governments receive benefits from extractive activities in several different ways, as discussed below. Governments can choose any of these methods to increase or decrease their share of the benefits.

However, the distinction is crucial given the considerable differences in the accounting treatments and disclosures that apply to income taxes, other taxes, fees and government participations. For example, it will affect where these amounts are presented in the profit or loss, e.g. in operating costs or income tax expense; and it will determine whether deferred tax balances are required to be recognised and the related disclosures provided.

21.1 Excise duties, production taxes and severance taxes

Excise duties, production taxes and severance taxes result in payments that are due on production (or severance) of minerals from the earth. Depending on the jurisdiction and the type of mineral involved, they are calculated:

(a) as a fixed amount per unit produced;

(b) as a percentage of the value of the minerals produced; or

(c) based on revenue minus certain allowable costs.

21.1.1 Production-based taxation

If the tax is based on a fixed amount per unit produced or as a percentage of the value of the minerals produced, then it will not meet the definition of an income tax under IAS 12. In these cases the normal principles of liability recognition under IAS 37 apply in recognising the tax charge.

Another issue that arises is whether these taxes are, in effect, collected by the entity from customers on behalf of the taxing authority, as an agent. In other cases, the taxpayer's role is more in the nature of principal than agent. The regulations differ significantly from one country to another. The practical accounting issue that arises concerns the interpretation of the requirements of IFRS 15 which states that the 'transaction price is the amount of consideration to which an entity expects to be entitled in exchange for transferring promised goods or services to a customer, excluding amounts collected on behalf of third parties (for example, some sales taxes)'. *[IFRS 15.47]*. Specifically, should excise duties, production taxes and severance taxes be deducted from revenue (net presentation) or included in the production costs and, therefore, revenue (gross presentation)? See 12.11.2 above for further discussion on the impact of IFRS 15 on the presentation of royalty payments.

The appropriate accounting treatment will depend on the particular circumstances. In determining whether gross or net presentation is appropriate, the entity needs to consider whether it is acting in a manner similar to that of an agent or principal. For further discussion of principal versus agent under IFRS 15 see 12.11 above and Chapter 28 at 3.4 and presentation of royalties at 5.7.5 above.

Given that excise duties, production taxes and severance taxes are aimed at taxing the production of minerals rather than the sale of minerals, they are considered to be a tax on extractive activities rather than a tax collected by a mining company or oil and gas company on behalf of the government. Based on this, the tax should be presented as a production cost.

However, it may be considered that when the excise duty, production tax or severance tax is payable in kind, that the mining company or oil and gas company never receives any of the benefits associated with the production of the associated minerals. Hence, it would be more appropriate to present revenue net of the production or severance tax as it is in substance the same as a royalty payment.

21.1.2 Petroleum revenue tax (or resource rent tax)

Determining whether a petroleum revenue tax (or resource rent tax) is a production- or profit-based tax is often not straightforward. Example 43.28 below describes the petroleum revenue tax in the United Kingdom.

Example 43.28: Petroleum revenue tax[157]

Petroleum revenue tax (PRT) is a special tax that seeks to tax a high proportion of the economic rent (super-profits) from the exploitation of the UK's oil and gas. PRT is a cash-based tax that is levied on a field-by-field basis: in general, the costs of developing and running a field can only be set against the profits generated by that field. Any losses, e.g. arising from unused expenditure relief, can be carried back or forward within the field indefinitely. There is also a range of reliefs, including:

- oil allowance – a PRT-free slice of production;
- supplement – a proxy for interest and other financing costs;
- Tariff Receipts Allowance (TRA) – participators owning assets, for example pipelines, relating to one field will sometimes allow participators from other fields to share the use of the asset in return for the payment of tariffs, and TRA relieves some of the tariffs received from PRT;
- exemption from PRT for gas sold to British Gas under a pre-July 1975 contract; and
- cross-field relief for research expenditure.

PRT is currently charged at 50% on profits after these allowances. For a limited period, safeguard relief then applies to ensure that PRT does not reduce the annual return in the early years of production of a field to below 15% of the historic capital expenditure on the field.

PRT was abolished on 16 March 1993 for all fields given development consent on or after that date. This was part of a package of PRT reforms which also included the reduction of the rate of PRT from 75 per cent to 50 per cent and the abolition of PRT relief for Exploration and Appraisal (E&A) expenditure.

The UK PRT is similar to an income tax in that the tax is a percentage of revenue minus certain costs. However, there are also a number of other features that are not commonly found in income taxes or in some other resource rent taxes:

- the oil allowance is a physical quantity of oil that is PRT exempt in each field, subject to a cumulative maximum over the life of the field; and
- the tax is levied on individual oil fields rather than the entity owning the oil field as a whole.

There are many different types of petroleum revenue taxes (or resource rent taxes) around the world, some of which are clearly not income taxes, while others have some of the characteristics of an income tax. In determining whether a particular production tax meets the definition of an income tax under IAS 12, an entity will need to assess whether or not the tax is based on (or closely enough linked to) net profit for the period. If it does not meet the definition of an income tax, an entity should develop an accounting policy under the hierarchy in IAS 8.

Practice is mixed, which means that while some entities may treat a particular petroleum revenue tax (or resource rent tax) as an income tax under IAS 12 and hence provide for current and deferred taxes (see Extract 43.58 below), others may consider the same tax to be outside the scope of IAS 12.

> Extract 43.58: Woodside Petroleum Ltd (2019)
> NOTES TO THE FINANCIAL STATEMENTS [extract]
> A. EARNINGS FOR THE YEAR [extract]
> A.5 Taxes [extract]
> Key estimates and judgements [extract]
> (a) Income tax classification [extract]
> PRRT is considered, for accounting purposes, to be an income tax.

As illustrated in Extract 43.59 below, BHP assesses resource rent taxes and royalties individually to determine whether they meet the definition of an income tax or not.

> Extract 43.59: BHP Group Plc (2019)
> Notes to the Financial Statements [extract]
> 6 Income tax expense [extract]
> Recognition and measurement [extract]
> Royalty-related taxation [extract]
> Royalties and resource rent taxes are treated as taxation arrangements (impacting income tax expense/(benefit)) when they are imposed under government authority and the amount payable is calculated by reference to revenue derived (net of any allowable deductions) after adjustment for temporary differences. Obligations arising from royalty arrangements that do not satisfy these criteria are recognised as current provisions and included in expenses.

21.2 Grossing up of notional quantities withheld

Many production sharing contracts provide that the income tax to which the contractor is subject is deemed to have been paid to the government as part of the payment of profit oil to the government or its representative (e.g. the designated national oil company) (see 5.3 above). This raises the question as to whether an entity should be presenting current and deferred taxation arising from such 'notional' income tax, which is only deemed to have been paid, on a net or a gross basis.

Example 43.29: Grossing up of notional quantities withheld

Entity A is the operator of an oil field that produces 10 million barrels of oil per year. Under the production sharing contract between entity A and the national government, entity A and the government are entitled to 4,000,000 and 6,000,000 barrels of oil, respectively. The production sharing contract includes the following clause:

> 'The share of the profit petroleum to which the government is entitled in any calendar year in accordance with the production sharing contract shall be deemed to include a portion representing the corporate income tax imposed upon and due by entity A, and which will be paid directly by the government on behalf of entity A to the appropriate tax authorities.'

Assuming the following facts, how should entity A account for the income tax that it is deemed to have paid in 2019:
- the normal corporate income tax rate in the country in which entity A operates is 40%;
- entity A made a net profit of USD 30 million in 2018; and
- the average oil price during the year was USD 50/barrel.

Gross presentation

Entity A's profit after 40% corporate income tax was USD 30 million. Therefore, its profit before tax would have been USD 50 million (i.e. USD 30 million ÷ (100% – 40%)). In other words, the government is deemed to have paid corporate income tax of USD 20 million on behalf of entity A. Therefore, the government is deemed to have taken 400,000 barrels (i.e. USD 20 million ÷ USD 50/barrel) out of entity A's share of the production. Hence, entity A's share of production before corporate income tax was 4,400,000 barrels (i.e. 4,000,000 barrels + 400,000 barrels).

Net presentation

Under the net presentation approach, entity A ignores the corporate income tax that was deemed to have been paid by the government because it is not a transaction that entity A was party to *or* because the deemed transaction did not actually take place.

The disadvantage of presenting such tax on a gross basis is that the combined production attributed to the entity and that attributable to the government exceeds the total quantity of oil that is actually produced (i.e. in the above example the government and entity A would report a combined production of 10.4 million barrels whereas actual production was only 10 million barrels). Similarly, if the reserves were to be expressed on the same basis as revenues, the reserves reported by the entity would include oil reserves that it would not actually be entitled to.

On the other hand, if the host country has a well-established income tax regime that falls under the authority of the ministry of finance and the production sharing contract requires an income tax return to be filed, then the entity would have a legal liability to pay the tax until the date on which the national oil company or the ministry responsible for extractive activities (e.g. the ministry of mines, industry and energy) pays the tax on its behalf. In such cases it may be appropriate to present revenue and income tax on a gross basis.

22 EVENTS AFTER THE REPORTING PERIOD

22.1 Reserves proven after the reporting period

IAS 10 – *Events after the Reporting Period* – distinguishes between two types of events:
- adjusting events after the reporting period being those that provide evidence of conditions that existed at the end of the reporting period; and
- non-adjusting events after the reporting period being those that are indicative of conditions that arose after the reporting period. *[IAS 10.3]*.

This raises the question as to how an entity should deal with information regarding mineral reserves that it obtains after the end of its reporting period, but before its financial statements are authorised for issue i.e. finalised. For example, suppose that an entity concludes after the year-end that its remaining mineral reserves at that date were not 10 million barrels (or tonnes) but only 8 million barrels (or tonnes). As discussed at 16.1.3.A above, a company needs to assess whether such a change in mineral reserves should be treated as an adjusting event in accordance with IAS 10 (i.e. the new estimate provides evidence of conditions that existed previously) or as a change in estimate in accordance with IAS 8 (i.e. the new estimate resulted from new information or new developments).

22.2 Business combinations – application of the acquisition method

If the initial accounting for a business combination can be determined only provisionally by the end of the period in which the combination is effected – because either the fair values to be assigned to the acquiree's identifiable assets, liabilities or contingent liabilities or the fair value of the combination can be determined only provisionally – the acquirer should account for the combination using those provisional values. Where, as a result of completing the initial accounting within 12 months from the acquisition date, adjustments to the provisional values have been found to be necessary, IFRS 3 requires them to be recognised from the acquisition date. *[IFRS 3.45]*. Specifically, IFRS 3 states that the provisional values are to be retrospectively adjusted to reflect new information obtained about facts and circumstances that existed as at the acquisition date and, if known, would have affected the measurement of the amounts recognised as at that date. This raises the question of how an entity should account for new information that it receives regarding an acquiree's reserves before it has finalised its acquisition accounting.

Example 43.30: Acquisition of an entity that owns mineral reserves

Entity A acquires Entity B for €27 million at 31 October 2019. At the time it assigned the following fair values to the acquired net assets:

	€ million
Mineral reserves (assuming reserves of 10 million barrels)	10
Other net assets acquired	5
Goodwill	12
Consideration transferred	27

At 30 June 2020, after conducting a drilling programme which commenced in March 2020, Entity A obtains information about the reserves (as at 30 June 2020), which when added to the production for the period (i.e. from 31 October 2019 to 30 June 2020) reveals that the mineral reserves at the date of acquisition were not 10 million barrels, as previously thought, but were only 8 million barrels.

Can Entity A revise its initial acquisition accounting to reflect the fact that the mineral reserves are only 8 million barrels, rather than 10 million?

The answer to this question is not straightforward and it is a matter of significant judgement which needs to be made based on the facts and circumstances of each individual situation.

IFRS 3 requires assets acquired and liabilities assumed to be measured at fair value as at the acquisition date. It then defines fair value as: the amount for which an asset could be exchanged, or a liability settled, between knowledgeable, willing parties in an arm's length transaction. The challenge with the new information obtained about the mineral reserves in Example 43.30 above is determining whether it provided new information about facts and circumstances that existed as at the acquisition date or whether it resulted from events that occurred after the acquisition date. As discussed at 16.1.3.A above, it is difficult to determine exactly what causes a reserve estimate to change, i.e. whether the facts and circumstances existed at acquisition date or whether it was due to new events.

In Example 43.30 above, the new reserves information arose as a result of a drilling programme that commenced five months after the acquisition date and it is not entirely clear why the reserves estimate changed. One may therefore conclude that as entity A should be valuing the mineral reserves acquired on the basis of information that a knowledgeable, willing party would and could reasonably have been expected to use in an arm's length transaction at 31 October 2019, that this new information should not have an impact on the provisional accounting. This is on the basis that this new information was not available at acquisition date and could not reasonably have been expected to be considered as part of the acquisition.

Similarly, if entity A had concluded at 30 June 2020 that its internal long-term oil price assumption was $60/barrel instead of $70/barrel that would not have any effect on the acquisition accounting. Entity A should be valuing the mineral reserves on the basis of information that a knowledgeable, willing party would have used in an arm's length transaction at 31 October 2019; this may, of course, have been neither $60/bbl nor $70/bbl.

The conclusion may differ however, if the drilling programme had been completed and the information was available at acquisition date, but due to the pressures of completing the transaction, entity A had not been able to assess fully or take into account all of this information e.g. it had not had time to properly analyse all of the information available in the data room. In this instance, it would be appropriate to adjust the provisional accounting.

22.3 Completion of E&E activity after the reporting period

As discussed at 3.5.1 above, IFRS 6 requires E&E assets to be tested for impairment when exploration for and evaluation of mineral resources in the specific area have not led to the discovery of commercially viable quantities of mineral resources and the entity has decided to discontinue its activities in the specific area. *[IFRS 6.20]*. An entity that concludes, after its reporting period, that an exploration and evaluation project is unsuccessful, should account for this conclusion as:

- a *non-adjusting event* if the conclusion is indicative of conditions that arose after the reporting period, for example new information or new developments that did not offer greater clarity concerning the conditions that existed at the end of the reporting period (one possible example may be drilling that only commenced after reporting date). The new information or new developments are considered to be changes in accounting estimates under IAS 8. Also, based on the information that existed at the reporting period, the fair value less costs of disposal of the underlying E&E asset might well have been in excess of its carrying amount; *[IAS 8.5]*

- an *adjusting event* if the decision not to sanction the project for development was based on information that existed at the reporting date. Failure to use, or misuse of, reliable information that was available when financial statements for those periods were authorised for issue and could reasonably be expected to have been obtained and taken into account in the preparation and presentation of those financial statements, would constitute an error under IAS 8. *[IAS 8.5]*.

Evaluating whether information obtained subsequent to the reporting period but before the financial statements are authorised for issue is an adjusting or non-adjusting event may require significant judgement. The conditions should be carefully evaluated based on the facts and circumstances of each individual situation.

23 GLOSSARY

The glossary below defines some of the terms and abbreviations commonly used in the extractive industries.[158]

Abandon	To discontinue attempts to produce oil or gas from a well or lease, plug the reservoir in accordance with regulatory requirements and recover equipment.
Area-of-interest method	An accounting concept by which costs incurred for individual geological or geographical areas that have characteristics conducive to containing a mineral reserve are deferred as assets pending determination of whether commercial reserves are found. If the area of interest is found to contain commercial reserves, the accumulated costs are capitalised. If the area is found to contain no commercial reserves, the accumulated costs are charged to expense.
Barrels of oil equivalent (BOE)	Using prices or heating content, units of sulphur, condensate, natural gas and by products are converted to and expressed in equivalent barrels of oil for standard measurement purposes.
British Thermal Unit (BTU)	A measure of the amount of heat required to raise the temperature of one pound of water one degree Fahrenheit at the temperature at which water has its greatest density (39 degrees Fahrenheit).
Bullion	Metal in bars, ingots or other uncoined form.
Carried interest	An agreement by which an entity that contracts to operate a mineral property and, therefore, agrees to incur exploration or development costs (the carrying party) is entitled to recover the costs incurred (and usually an amount in addition to actual costs incurred) before the entity that originally owned the mineral interest (the carried party) is entitled to share in revenues from production.
Carried party	The party for whom funds are advances in a carried interest arrangement.
Carrying party	The party advancing funds in a carried interest agreement.
Concession	A contract, similar to a mineral lease, under which the government owning mineral rights grants the concessionaire the right to explore, develop, and produce the minerals.

Cost recovery oil	Oil revenue paid to an operating entity to enable that entity to recover its operating costs and specified exploration and development costs from a specified percentage of oil revenues remaining after the royalty payment to the property owner.
Customer smelter	A smelter which processes concentrates from independent mines. Concentrates may be purchased or the smelter may be contracted to do the processing for the independent company.
Delay rental	Annual payments by the lessee of a mineral property to the lessor until drilling has begun.
Delineation well	A well to define, or delineate, the boundaries of a reservoir.
Development well	A well drilled to gain access to oil or gas classified as proved reserves.
Downstream activities	The refining, processing, marketing, and distributing of petroleum, natural gas, or mined mineral (other than refining or processing that is necessary to make the minerals that have been mined or extracted capable of being sold).
Dry gas	Natural gas composed of vapours without liquids and which tends not to liquefy.
Dry hole	An exploratory or development well that does not contain oil or gas in commercial quantities.
Entitlements method	A method of revenue recognition by which a joint venturer records revenue based on the share of production for the period to which that venturer is entitled.
Exploratory well	A well drilled to find and produce oil or gas in an unproved area, to find a new reservoir in a field previously found to be productive of oil or gas in another reservoir, or to extend a known reservoir.
Farm out and farm in	An agreement by which the owner of operating rights in a mineral property (the farmor) transfers a part of that interest to a second party (the farmee) in return for the latter's paying all of the costs, or only specified costs, to explore the property and perhaps to carry out part or all of the development of the property if reserves are found.
Full cost method	An accounting concept by which all costs incurred in searching for, acquiring, and developing mineral reserves in a cost centre are capitalised, even though a specific cost clearly resulted from an effort that was a failure.
Geological and geophysical costs (G&G)	Costs of topographical, geological, geochemical, and geophysical studies.

Infill drilling	Technical and commercial analyses may support drilling additional producing wells to reduce the spacing beyond that utilised within the initial development plan. Infill drilling may have the combined effect of increasing recovery efficiency and accelerating production.
Joint operating agreement (JOA)	A contract between two parties to a sharing arrangement that sets out the rights and obligations to operate the property, if operating interests are owned by both parties after a sharing arrangement.
Overlift or underlift	Overlift is the excess of the amount of production that a participant in a joint venture has taken as compared to that participant's proportionate share of ownership in total production. Underlift is the shortfall in the amount of production that a participant in a joint venture has taken as compared to that participant's proportionate share of ownership in total production.
Production sharing contract (PSC)	A contract between a national oil company or the government of a host country and a contracting entity (contractor) to carry out oil and gas exploration and production activities in accordance with the terms of the contract, with the two parties sharing mineral output.
Profit oil	Revenue in excess of cost recovery oil and royalties.
Recompletion	The process of re-entering a previously completed well to install new equipment or to perform such services necessary to restore production.
Redetermination	A retroactive adjustment to the relative percentage interests of the participants in a field that is subject to an unitisation agreement.
Risk service contract	A contract by which an entity agrees to explore for, develop, and produce minerals on behalf of a host government in return for a fee paid by the host government.
Royalty	A portion of the proceeds from production, usually before deducting operating expenses, payable to a party having an interest in a lease.
Sales method	A method of revenue recognition by which a joint venturer records revenue based on the actual amount of product it has sold (or transferred downstream) during the period. No receivable or other asset is recorded for undertaken production (underlift) and no liability is recorded for overtaken production (overlift).

Stripping ratio	The ratio of tonnes removed as waste relative to the number of tonnes of ore removed from an open pit mine.
Successful efforts method	An accounting concept that capitalises only those upstream costs that lead directly to finding, acquiring and developing mineral reserves, while those costs that do not lead directly to finding, acquiring and developing mineral reserves are charged to expense.
Take-or-pay contracts	An agreement between a buyer and seller in which the buyer will still pay some amount even if the product or service is not provided. If the purchaser does not take the minimum quantity, payment is required for that minimum quantity at the contract price. Normally, deficiency amounts can be made up in future years if purchases are in excess of minimum amounts.
Unitisation	An agreement between two parties, each of which owns an interest in one or more mineral properties in an area, to cross-assign to one another a share of the interest in the mineral properties that each owns in the area; from that point forward they share, as agreed, in further costs and revenues related to the properties.
Upstream activities	Exploring for, finding, acquiring, and developing mineral reserves up to the point that the reserves are first capable of being sold or used, even if the entity intends to process them further.
Workovers	Major repairs, generally of oil and gas wells.

References

1 IASC Issues Paper, *Issues Paper Extractive Industries*, IASC, November 2000, 1.5.
2 Discussion Paper DP/2010/1, *Extractive Activities*, IASB, April 2010, p.7.
3 DP/2010/1, 1.1.
4 DP/2010/1, 1.4-1.5.
5 DP/2010/1, 1.9.
6 DP/2010/1, 1.10.
7 DP/2010/2.1.
8 IASC Issues Paper, 1.16.
9 IASC Issues Paper, 1.18.
10 IASC Issues Paper, 2.3.
11 IASC Issues Paper, 2.5.
12 IASC Issues Paper, 2.6.
13 IASC Issues Paper, 2.10.
14 IASC Issues Paper, 2.12.
15 IASC Issues Paper, 2.24.
16 IASC Issues Paper, 2.26.
17 IASC Issues Paper, 2.27.
18 IASC Issues Paper, 2.29.
19 IASC Issues Papers, 2.29, 2.30.
20 IASC Issues Paper, 2.32.
21 IASC Issues Paper, 2.34.
22 IASC Issues Paper, 2.36.
23 IASC Issues Paper, 2.38.
24 IASC Issues Paper, 2.42.

25 Discussion Paper DP/2010/1, para. 2.48.
26 Discussion Paper DP/2010/1, para. 2.23.
27 SPE-PRMS, *Petroleum Resources Management Systems*, Society of Petroleum Engineers, 2007 (revised June 2018).
28 SPE-PRMS, *Petroleum Resources Management Systems*, Society of Petroleum Engineers, 2007 (revised June 2018).
29 IASB Agenda Paper 13A, *Comparison of Petroleum and Minerals Reserves and Resource Classification Systems*, IASB, 22 June 2007, pp.3-4.
30 IASB Agenda Paper 13A, p.8 and SPE PRMS, Figure 1-1.
31 SPE-PRMS, p.2.
32 SPE-PRMS, p.3.
33 SPE-PRMS, p.13.
34 SPE-PRMS, p.13.
35 SPE-PRMS, p.13.
36 SPE-PRMS, p.1.
37 SPE-PRMS, p.3.
38 SPE-PRMS, p.3.
39 SPE-PRMS, p.2
40 SPE-PRMS, p.3.
41 SPE-PRMS, p.2
42 SPE-PRMS, p.3.
43 SPE-PRMS, p.8.
44 SPE-PRMS, Figure 2.1.
45 SPE-PRMS, p.8.
46 SPE-PRMS, pp.10-14.
47 SPE-PRMS, pp.14-15.
48 SPE-PRMS, pp.17-24.
49 JORC Code, Australasian Code for Reporting of Exploration Results, Mineral Resources and Ore Reserves, Joint Ore Reserves Committee of the Australasian Institute of Mining and Metallurgy, Australian Institute of Geoscientists and Minerals Council of Australia (JORC), 2004, para. 1.
50 Stephenson and Weatherstone, *Developments in International Mineral Resource and Reserve Reporting*, p.5.
51 IASB Agenda Paper 13A, p.3.
52 J. M. Rendu, *Reporting Mineral Resources and Mineral Reserves in the United States of America – Technical and Regulatory Issues*, 20-25 August 2006, p.2.
53 CRIRSCO Template, *International Reporting Template for the public reporting of exploration results, mineral resources and mineral reserves*, CRIRSCO, November 2019, 2.6-2.8.
54 CRIRSCO Template, 2.3.
55 CRIRSCO Template, 2.3.
56 CRIRSCO Template, 3.6.
57 CRIRSCO Template, Figure 1.
58 CRIRSCO Template, 6.1.
59 CRIRSCO Template, 6.3.
60 CRIRSCO Template, 7.1.
61 CRIRSCO Template, 7.4.
62 CRIRSCO Template, 7.8.
63 CRIRSCO Template, 7.10.
64 CRIRSCO Template, 4.7.
65 CRIRSCO Template, 8.1.
66 CRIRSCO Template, 8.7-8.8.
67 CRIRSCO Template, 8.9-8.10.
68 J. M. Rendu, *Reporting Mineral Resources and Mineral Reserves in the United States of America – Technical and Regulatory Issues*, 20-25 August 2006, pp.9 and 10.
69 IASB Agenda Paper 15C, *Possible principles for a historical cost accounting model that accompanies decision-useful disclosures of minerals and oil & gas reserves and resources*, IASB, 22 June 2007, para. 6.
70 *IASB Update*, September 2008, p.3.
71 *IFRIC Update*, January 2006, p.3.
72 IASC Issues Paper 4.18.
73 IASC Issues Paper 4.20.
74 IASC Issues Paper 4.45.
75 *IFRIC Update*, January 2006, p.3.
76 Amendments to IFRS 1, *Additional Exemptions for First-time Adopters*, IASB, July 2009, D8A.
77 IASC Issues Paper 4.16(b).
78 IASC Issues Paper 4.36.
79 IASC Issues Paper 4.39.
80 ASC 932-720-25-1, *Extractive Activities – Oil and Gas – Other Expenses – Recognition*.
81 ED 6, *Exploration for and Evaluation of Mineral Resources*, IASB, January 2004, 14.
82 IASC Issues Paper, 6.3.
83 IASC Issues Paper, 2.12.
84 IASC Issues Paper, 2.13.
85 IASC Issues Paper, 2.14.
86 IASC Issues Paper, 2.21.
87 IASC Issues Paper, 2.21.
88 IASC Issues Paper, Glossary.
89 IASC Issues Paper, 2.19.
90 IASC Issues Paper, 12.12(b).
91 IASC Issues Paper, 12.68.
92 IASC Issues Paper, 12.69.
93 IASC Issues Paper, 2.23.
94 *Guidelines for the Evaluation of Petroleum Reserves and Resources – A Supplement to the SPE/WPC Petroleum Reserves Definitions and the SPE/WPC/AAPG Petroleum Resources Definitions*, Society of Petroleum Engineers, 2001, p.120.
95 D. R. Jennings, J. B. Feiten and H. R. Brock, *Petroleum Accounting, Principles, Procedures, & Issues*, 5th edition, Professional Development Institute, Denton (Texas), pp.165-169.
96 IASC Issues Paper, 12.9.
97 SPE-PRMS, pp.23-24.

98 Former Oil Industry Association Committee Statement of Recommended Practice *Accounting for Oil and Gas Exploration, Development, Production and Decommissioning Activities* (July 2001) 'Former OIAC SORP' 149.
99 Former OIAC SORP 150.
100 Former OIAC SORP 16.
101 Former OIAC SORP 144.
102 Discussion Paper (DP/2020/1), Business Combinations – Disclosures, Goodwill and Impairment, IASB, March 2020
103 ASC 930-805-30-1 *Extractive Activities – Mining – Business Combinations – Initial Measurement (pre-codification EITF 04-3, Mining Assets: Impairment and Business Combinations*, EITF, March 2004).
104 *IFRIC Update*, January 2011.
105 *IASB Update*, May 2016.
106 *IASB Update*, February 2018.
107 *IASB Update*, February 2018.
108 *IASB Work plan – research projects*, IASB website (accessed on 4 September 2020) https://www.ifrs.org/projects/work-plan/
109 IASC Issues Paper, 9.26.
110 AASB 1022 *Accounting for the Extractive Industries* (now superseded).
111 Former OIAC SORP.
112 AASB 1022 Accounting for the Extractive Industries (now superseded) para. 62.
113 Former OIAC SORP 127.
114 *IASB update*, June 2019.
115 IASC Issues Paper 10.27.
116 *IFRIC Update*, March 2019.
117 IASC Issues Paper 10.29.
118 IASC Issues Paper 11.17.
119 IASC Issues Paper 11.9-11.16.
120 IASC Issues Paper 7.61-7.68.
121 IASC Issues Paper 6.64.
122 IASC Issues Paper, 12.14.
123 Former OIAC SORP 175.
124 Former OIAC SORP 176.
125 IASC Issues Paper, 12.14.
126 Former OIAC SORP 177-178.
127 Former OIAC SORP 179-180.
128 IASC Issues Paper, 7.13.
129 IASC Issues Paper, 7.19.
130 IASC Issues Paper, 7.20.
131 IASC Issues Paper, 7.36.
132 IASC Issues Paper, 7.39.
133 IASC Issues Paper, 7.41.
134 IASC Issues Paper, 7.42.
135 IASC Issues Paper, 7.46.
136 IASC Issues Paper, 7.49.
137 IASC Issues Paper, 7.50.
138 IASC Issues Paper, 7.23.
139 IASC Issues Paper, 7.24.
140 IASC Issues Paper, 7.25.
141 IASC Issues Paper, 7.61.
142 Global infomine www.technology.infomine.com/reviews/Blockcaving (accessed 09/10/2015).
143 *IFRS Update* June 2019.
144 Appendix A of IFRS 11 defines a joint operation as a joint arrangement whereby the parties that have joint control of the arrangement have rights to the assets and obligations for the liabilities, relating to the arrangement.
145 IFRS IC March 2019 agenda paper 9 'Liabilities in relation to a joint operator's interest in a joint operation (IFRS 11)' para. 30(a).
146 IFRS IC March 2019 agenda paper 9 'Liabilities in relation to a joint operator's interest in a joint operation (IFRS 11)' para. 30(b).
147 IFRS IC March 2019 agenda paper 9 'Liabilities in relation to a joint operator's interest in a joint operation (IFRS 11)' para. 28.
148 *IFRIC Update*, March 2019.
149 When considering the implications of these issues from a US GAAP perspective, while the IFRS and US GAAP lease standards are aligned with respect to the definition of a lease, there is no equivalent US standard to IFRS 11 when accounting for joint arrangements. Also, as noted above, contractual arrangements can and will differ between JO's and legal jurisdictions. Given this, it cannot be assumed the issues identified in this publication and the analysis that would be required to determine the accounting under IFRS would be the same under US GAAP.
150 IFRS IC March 2019 Agenda paper 9: 'Liabilities in relation to a joint operator's interest in a joint operation (IFRS 11)' paras. 35-39.
151 IFRS 16.B11 specifically states that when a contract to receive goods or services is entered into by a joint arrangement [as defined in IFRS 11], or, on behalf of a joint arrangement, for the purpose of a lease assessment, the joint operators to the joint arrangement, collectively, are considered to be the customer in the contract
152 IFRS IC March 2019 Agenda paper 9: 'Liabilities in relation to a joint operator's interest in a joint operation (IFRS 11)' para. 17; and IFRS IC Agenda September 2018 paper 3: 'IFRS 11 Joint Arrangements – joint operations' paras. 40-44
153 IASC Issues Paper, 10.26.
154 IASC Issues Paper, 10.23.
155 IASC Issues Paper, 10.24.
156 IASC Issues Paper, 1.27.
157 HM Revenue & Customs website, https://www.hmrc.gov.uk, *International – Taxation of UK oil production.*
158 IASC Issues Paper, Glossary of Terms.

Index of extracts from financial statements

3i Group plc	956
A.P. Møller – Mærsk A/S	1530, 3174
Accelerate Property Fund Ltd	1487
adidas AG	683
AEGON N.V.	4631
African Rainbow Minerals Limited	3149
AGF Mutual Funds	233
Airbus SE	2419
Akzo Nobel N.V.	1395, 1840, 1992
Alkane Resources Limited	3475
Allianz SE	3184, 4576, 4580, 4626
Allied Electronics Corporation	684
AMP Limited	4572, 4636, 4646
Angel Mining plc	3425
Anglo American Platinum Limited	3482
Anglo American plc	3459, 3465, 3484, 3485, 3522
AngloGold Ashanti Limited	1683, 1980, 3416, 3489, 3491
Anheuser-Busch InBev NV/SA	1314, 1841, 3150, 3217, 3257
ArcelorMittal	1413
Ardagh Group S.A.	3216
ARINSO International SA	383
ASML Holding N.V.	2421, 2426
ASOS Plc	1328
Assicurazioni Generali S.p.A.	4598
AstraZeneca PLC	3146, 4514
Aveng Limited	816
Aviva plc	986, 2849, 3681, 4624, 4638, 4642, 4656, 4665

Index of extracts from financial statements

AXA SA 4573, 4590
BAE Systems plc 3014, 3015
Barclays PLC 981
Barrick Gold Corporation 3456, 3554
Bayer Aktiengesellschaft 976, 1326, 3076
BBA Aviation plc 1241
Beazley plc 4646
Belarusian National Reinsurance Organisation 1276
Berendsen plc 4456
BHP Billiton plc 3477
BHP Group Plc 3366, 3389, 3430, 3515, 3560
BMW Group 3225
Bombardier Inc. 344, 348, 364, 2393, 2429
BP p.l.c. 955, 977, 1154, 2619, 2620, 3120, 3127, 3208, 3359,
  .... 3370, 3438, 3478, 3488, 3493, 3647, 4470, 4508
Brit Limited 4653
British Airways Plc 1396
British Sky Broadcasting Group plc 3126
BT Group plc 2960, 2963
Canadian Imperial Bank of Commerce 362
Capita plc 2413, 2438
Capital & Counties Properties PLC 1506
Centrais Elétricas Brasileiras S.A. – Eletrobras 320
Centrica plc 1940, 4031
China Mobile Limited 3167
CNP Assurances 4629, 4640
Coca-Cola FEMSA S.A.B. de C.V. 305
Coca-Cola HBC AG 3260
Cranswick plc 3084
CRH plc 1693
Daimler AG 3001, 3006, 3215, 3222
Dairy Crest Group plc 2846
Deutsche Bank Aktiengesellschaft 962, 3212
Deutsche Lufthansa AG 3139, 3210
Deutsche Post AG 1777, 1816

Downer EDI Limited	3214
E.ON SE	1398
Enersource Corporation	300
ENGIE SA	428, 1883, 3487, 3555
Eni S.p.A.	1431
Equinor ASA	3004, 3013, 3209, 3390, 3452, 3463, 3468
Eskom Holdings SOC Ltd	1844
Fédération Internationale de Football Association	2398, 2416
Ferrovial, S.A.	2406
Forthnet S.A.	3210
Fortum Oyj	1989
Glencore plc	3369, 3413
Greencore Group plc	1840
Groupe Renault	3624
Harmony Gold Mining Company Limited	3400, 3481
Heineken N.V.	1389
Hochschild Mining PLC	2620
HOCHTIEF Aktiengesellschaft	2990, 3007
Hongkong Land Holdings Limited	3173
HSBC Holdings plc	964, 983, 1942, 3214, 3709, 4028
Hunting PLC	4436, 4468
Husky Energy Inc.	269
IAMGOLD Corporation	3490
Icade	1488
Infosys Technologies Limited	235
ING Groep N.V.	1082, 1137, 1196
Inspired Energy PLC	3172
InterContinental Hotels Group PLC	2944, 3145
International Consolidated Airlines Group, S.A.	1354, 3211, 3248
Intrepid Mines Limited	3398
ITV plc	1300
J Sainsbury plc	3126
KAZ Minerals PLC	1666, 1671
Kendrion N.V.	1401
Kinross Gold Corporation	3491

Klépierre..1484, 1485
Koninklijke Philips N.V...2004, 2424
LafargeHolcim Ltd...3075
Land Securities Group PLC..1481, 1489, 1492
Legal & General Group plc..4649
Liverpool Victoria Friendly Society Limited..4546
Lloyds Banking Group plc...1208, 3144
Lonmin Plc..3516
Lucas Bols N.V..1432
Manulife Financial Corporation..289
MERCK Kommanditgesellschaft auf Aktien..1310, 1325
MOL Hungarian Oil and Gas Plc..1363
Mondi plc..3314
Mowi ASA...3320
MS Amlin plc..4650
Münchener Rückversicherungs – Gesellschaft Aktiengesellschaft.......................4628
Naspers Limited...3176
National Australia Bank Limited..3008
Nestlé S.A. 884, 1357, 1779, 3010, 3218, 3224, 4460
Netcare Limited...3186
Newcrest Mining Limited...3439
Nexen Inc..293
Nine Entertainment Co. Holdings Limited..3219
Nokia Corporation..883
Norsk Hydro ASA..3557
Old Mutual plc..4589, 4594
Pearson plc..1228
PGS ASA..3085
Ping An Insurance...4634, 4666
Poste Italiane SpA...1812, 1817
Premier Oil plc...3364, 3389
Priorbank JSC...1282
ProSiebenSat.1 Media SE...2420
Proton Power Systems plc...3197
Prudential plc...4576, 4630, 4637, 4662

PSA Peugeot Citroën 1833
QBE Insurance Group 4651
Quilter plc 980
RAI – Radiotelevisione italiana SpA 1344
RELX PLC 1298
Repsol, S.A. 1364
Rio Tinto plc 1155, 3423, 3459, 3464, 3468, 3470, 3484, 3512, 3523
Robert Bosch Gesellschaft mit beschränkter Haftung 961
Roche Holding Ltd 2010, 2985, 3015, 3220
Rolls-Royce Holdings plc 3220, 3599
Royal Dutch Shell plc 2618, 3520
Royal Schiphol Group N.V. 3143
RSA Insurance Group plc 4586, 4631
RWE Aktiengesellschaft 883
Sanofi 1324
SAP SE 2430, 2434
Sappi Limited 3318
Sberbank of Russia 1211
Schroders plc 3125
Siemens Aktiengesellschaft 3003
Sirius Minerals Plc 3233
Skanska AB 1388, 1409
Slater and Gordon Limited 2405, 2436
Société nationale SNCF 2415
Spotify Technology S.A. 2423
Stagecoach Group plc 1845
Stora Enso Oyj 1699
Suncor Energy Inc 293
T&G Global Limited 3310
Telefónica, S.A. 1283
Telenor ASA 1901
The British Land Company PLC 1464, 1477
The Crown Estate 1479
The Go-Ahead Group plc 2984
The Rank Group Plc 678

The Royal Bank of Scotland Group plc 3129, 4461
The Toronto-Dominion Bank 270
The Village Building Co. Limited 2405
thyssenkrupp, AG 3218
TOTAL S.A. 975, 3380
Tullow Oil plc 3375, 3521
UBS Group AG 958, 985, 988, 1151, 1240, 2962, 3805, 4432
Unibail-Rodamco-Westfield SE 1470, 1499, 1507
Unilever PLC and Unilever N.V. 1698, 4459
Vivendi SE 1304, 1345
Vodafone Group Plc 1636, 3002, 3011, 4421
Volkswagen Aktiengesellschaft 4452, 4460
VTech Holdings Limited 3139
Woodside Petroleum Ltd. 3424, 3560
Yorkshire Building Society 3211
Zargon Oil & Gas Ltd. 299
Zurich Insurance Group, Zurich 4660

Index of standards

SP 1

SP 1.1	Ch.2, p.48
SP 1.2	Ch.2, p.48
SP 1.3	Ch.2, p.48
SP 1.4	Ch.2, p.48
SP 1.5	Ch.2, p.48

Conceptual Framework (2001)

CF(2001) 4.4	Ch.9, p.667

Conceptual Framework (2010)

CF(2010) 4.29	Ch.27, p.2018
CF(2010) 4.29	Ch.27, p.2027
CF(2010) 4.29	Ch.32, p.2406
CF(2010) 4.31	Ch.27, p.2018
CF(2010) 4.55(b)	Ch.16, p.1260
CF(2010) 4.59(a)	Ch.16, p.1251
CF(2010) BC3.28	Ch.26, p.1949
CF(2018) BC4.96	Ch.32, p.2406
CF(2010) QC12	Ch.26, p.1949
CF(2010) QC14	Ch.26, p.1949

Conceptual Framework

CF 1.1	Ch.2, p.49
CF 1.1-1.2	Ch.2, p.59
CF 1.2	Ch.2, p.49
CF 1.2	Ch.5, p.231
CF 1.3	Ch.2, p.50
CF 1.4	Ch.2, p.50
CF 1.5	Ch.2, p.49
CF 1.6	Ch.2, p.50
CF 1.7	Ch.2, p.50
CF 1.8	Ch.2, p.50
CF 1.9	Ch.2, p.50
CF 1.9	Ch.5, p.231
CF 1.10	Ch.2, p.49
CF 1.11	Ch.2, p.50
CF 1.12	Ch.2, p.50
CF 1.13	Ch.2, p.51
CF 1.14	Ch.2, p.51
CF 1.15	Ch.2, p.51
CF 1.16	Ch.2, p.51
CF 1.17	Ch.2, p.52
CF 1.17	Ch.3, p.156
CF 1.18	Ch.2, p.51
CF 1.19	Ch.2, p.52
CF 1.20	Ch.2, p.52
CF 1.20	Ch.40, p.3136
CF 1.21	Ch.2, p.51
CF 1.22	Ch.2, p.52
CF 1.23	Ch.2, p.52
CF 2.1	Ch.2, p.52
CF 2.2	Ch.2, p.53
CF 2.3	Ch.2, p.53
CF 2.4	Ch.2, p.53
CF 2.4	Ch.2, p.56
CF 2.4	Ch.2, p.92
CF 2.5	Ch.2, p.52
CF 2.6	Ch.2, p.54
CF 2.7	Ch.2, p.54
CF 2.8	Ch.2, p.54
CF 2.9	Ch.2, p.54
CF 2.10	Ch.2, p.54
CF 2.11	Ch.2, p.54
CF 2.12	Ch.2, p.54
CF 2.12	Ch.46, p.3654
CF 2.13	Ch.2, p.54
CF 2.13	Ch.26, p.1949
CF 2.14	Ch.2, p.55
CF 2.15	Ch.2, p.55
CF 2.15	Ch.3, p.165
CF 2.15	Ch.26, p.1949
CF 2.16	Ch.2, p.55
CF 2.16	Ch.3, p.165
CF 2.17	Ch.2, p.55
CF 2.18	Ch.2, p.55
CF 2.19	Ch.2, p.53
CF 2.20	Ch.2, p.56
CF 2.21	Ch.2, p.56
CF 2.22	Ch.2, p.56
CF 2.23	Ch.2, p.52
CF 2.23	Ch.2, p.56
CF 2.24	Ch.2, p.57
CF 2.25-2.27	Ch.2, p.57
CF 2.26-2.28	Ch.2, p.57
CF 2.29	Ch.2, p.57
CF 2.30	Ch.2, p.57
CF 2.31	Ch.2, p.57
CF 2.32	Ch.2, p.57
CF 2.33	Ch.2, p.57
CF 2.34	Ch.2, p.58

Index of standards

CF 2.35	Ch.2, p.58	CF 4.21	Ch.2, p.69
CF 2.36	Ch.2, p.49	CF 4.22	Ch.2, p.69
CF 2.36	Ch.2, p.58	CF 4.23	Ch.2, p.69
CF 2.37	Ch.2, p.58	CF 4.24	Ch.2, p.69
CF 2.38	Ch.2, p.58	CF 4.25	Ch.2, p.69
CF 2.39	Ch.2, p.52	CF 4.26	Ch.2, p.62
CF 2.39	Ch.2, p.58	CF 4.26	Ch.2, p.70
CF 2.40	Ch.2, p.58	CF 4.26	Ch.26, p.1932
CF 2.41	Ch.2, p.58	CF 4.26	Ch.55, p.4569
CF 2.42	Ch.2, p.58	CF 4.27	Ch.2, p.70
CF 2.42	Ch.2, p.59	CF 4.27	Ch.26, p.1932
CF 2.43	Ch.2, p.59	CF 4.28	Ch.2, p.70
CF 3.1	Ch.2, p.59	CF 4.28	Ch.55, p.4569
CF 3.2	Ch.2, p.59	CF 4.29	Ch.2, p.70
CF 3.3	Ch.2, p.59	CF 4.29	Ch.55, p.4569
CF 3.4	Ch.2, p.60	CF 4.30	Ch.2, p.70
CF 3.5	Ch.2, p.60	CF 4.31	Ch.2, p.70
CF 3.6	Ch.2, p.60	CF 4.32	Ch.2, p.70
CF 3.7	Ch.2, p.60	CF 4.33	Ch.2, p.70
CF 3.8	Ch.2, p.60	CF 4.34	Ch.2, p.71
CF 3.9	Ch.2, p.60	CF 4.35	Ch.2, p.71
CF 3.9	Ch.38, p.3083	CF 4.36	Ch.2, p.71
CF 3.10	Ch.2, p.59	CF 4.37	Ch.2, p.71
CF 3.10	Ch.2, p.60	CF 4.38	Ch.2, p.71
CF 3.10	Ch.6, p.391	CF 4.39	Ch.2, p.71
CF 3.10	Ch.6, p.402	CF 4.40	Ch.2, p.71
CF 3.10	Ch.9, p.752	CF 4.41	Ch.2, p.71
CF 3.10	Ch.10, p.774	CF 4.42	Ch.2, p.72
CF 3.11	Ch.2, p.61	CF 4.43	Ch.2, p.72
CF 3.12	Ch.2, p.61	CF 4.44	Ch.2, p.72
CF 3.12	Ch.6, p.401	CF 4.45	Ch.2, p.72
CF 3.13	Ch.2, p.61	CF 4.46	Ch.2, p.72
CF 3.13-14	Ch.6, p.403	CF 4.46	Ch.43, p.3473
CF 3.14	Ch.2, p.61	CF 4.47	Ch.2, p.72
CF 3.15	Ch.2, p.62	CF 4.48	Ch.2, p.63
CF 3.16	Ch.2, p.62	CF 4.49	Ch.2, p.63
CF 3.17	Ch.2, p.62	CF 4.49	Ch.3, p.160
CF 3.18	Ch.2, p.62	CF 4.50	Ch.2, p.63
CF 4.1-4.4	Ch.2, p.62	CF 4.51	Ch.2, p.64
CF 4.2	Ch.2, p.70	CF 4.52	Ch.2, p.64
CF 4.2	Ch.55, p.4569	CF 4.53	Ch.2, p.64
CF 4.3	Ch.25, p.1862	CF 4.54	Ch.2, p.64
CF 4.5	Ch.2, p.66	CF 4.55	Ch.2, p.65
CF 4.6	Ch.2, p.66	CF 4.56	Ch.2, p.65
CF 4.7	Ch.2, p.67	CF 4.56	Ch.17, p.1302
CF 4.8	Ch.2, p.67	CF 4.57	Ch.2, p.65
CF 4.9	Ch.2, p.67	CF 4.57	Ch.17, p.1302
CF 4.10	Ch.2, p.67	CF 4.58	Ch.2, p.65
CF 4.11	Ch.2, p.67	CF 4.58	Ch.17, p.1302
CF 4.12	Ch.2, p.67	CF 4.59	Ch.2, p.65
CF 4.13	Ch.2, p.68	CF 4.60	Ch.2, p.66
CF 4.14	Ch.2, p.68	CF 4.61	Ch.2, p.66
CF 4.15	Ch.2, p.68	CF 4.62	Ch.2, p.66
CF 4.16	Ch.2, p.68	CF 4.63	Ch.2, p.62
CF 4.17	Ch.2, p.68	CF 4.63	Ch.2, p.72
CF 4.18	Ch.2, p.68	CF 4.63-4.64	Ch.7, p.540
CF 4.19	Ch.2, p.69	CF 4.64	Ch.2, p.72
CF 4.20	Ch.2, p.69	CF 4.65	Ch.2, p.73

Index of standards

CF 4.66	Ch.2, p.73
CF 4.67	Ch.2, p.73
CF 4.68	Ch.2, p.62
CF 4.68	Ch.3, p.160
CF 4.68	Ch.27, p.2018
CF 4.68-70	Ch.2, p.73
CF 4.69	Ch.2, p.62
CF 4.71	Ch.2, p.73
CF 4.72	Ch.2, p.73
CF 5.1	Ch.2, p.74
CF 5.2	Ch.2, p.74
CF 5.2	Ch.2, p.101
CF 5.3	Ch.2, p.74
CF 5.3	Ch.2, p.103
CF 5.4	Ch.2, p.75
CF 5.5	Ch.2, p.75
CF 5.6	Ch.2, p.75
CF 5.7	Ch.2, p.75
CF 5.8	Ch.2, p.76
CF 5.9	Ch.2, p.76
CF 5.10	Ch.2, p.76
CF 5.11	Ch.2, p.76
CF 5.12	Ch.2, p.76
CF 5.13	Ch.2, p.76
CF 5.14	Ch.2, p.77
CF 5.15	Ch.2, p.77
CF 5.16	Ch.2, p.77
CF 5.17	Ch.2, p.77
CF 5.18	Ch.2, p.77
CF 5.19	Ch.2, p.77
CF 5.20	Ch.2, p.78
CF 5.21	Ch.2, p.78
CF 5.22	Ch.2, p.78
CF 5.23	Ch.2, p.78
CF 5.24	Ch.2, p.79
CF 5.25	Ch.2, p.79
CF 5.26	Ch.2, p.79
CF 5.27	Ch.2, p.79
CF 5.27	Ch.2, p.80
CF 5.28	Ch.2, p.80
CF 5.29	Ch.2, p.80
CF 5.30	Ch.2, p.80
CF 5.31	Ch.2, p.81
CF 5.32	Ch.2, p.81
CF 5.33	Ch.2, p.81
CF 6.1	Ch.2, p.81
CF 6.2	Ch.2, p.82
CF 6.3	Ch.2, p.82
CF 6.4	Ch.2, p.82
CF 6.5	Ch.2, p.82
CF 6.6	Ch.2, p.83
CF 6.7	Ch.2, p.83
CF 6.8	Ch.2, p.83
CF 6.9	Ch.2, p.83
CF 6.10	Ch.2, p.83
CF 6.11	Ch.2, p.83
CF 6.12	Ch.2, p.84
CF 6.13	Ch.2, p.84
CF 6.14	Ch.2, p.84
CF 6.15	Ch.2, p.84
CF 6.16	Ch.2, p.84
CF 6.17	Ch.2, p.85
CF 6.18	Ch.2, p.85
CF 6.19	Ch.2, p.85
CF 6.20	Ch.2, p.85
CF 6.21	Ch.2, p.85
CF 6.22	Ch.2, p.85
CF 6.23	Ch.2, p.86
CF 6.24	Ch.2, p.90
CF 6.25	Ch.2, p.90
CF 6.26	Ch.2, p.90
CF 6.27	Ch.2, p.90
CF 6.28	Ch.2, p.90
CF 6.29	Ch.2, p.90
CF 6.30	Ch.2, p.91
CF 6.31	Ch.2, p.91
CF 6.32	Ch.2, p.91
CF 6.33	Ch.2, p.91
CF 6.34	Ch.2, p.91
CF 6.35	Ch.2, p.91
CF 6.36	Ch.2, p.91
CF 6.37	Ch.2, p.91
CF 6.38	Ch.2, p.91
CF 6.39	Ch.2, p.92
CF 6.40	Ch.2, p.92
CF 6.41	Ch.2, p.92
CF 6.42	Ch.2, p.92
CF 6.43	Ch.2, p.92
CF 6.44	Ch.2, p.92
CF 6.45	Ch.2, p.92
CF 6.46	Ch.2, p.93
CF 6.47	Ch.2, p.92
CF 6.48	Ch.2, p.93
CF 6.49	Ch.2, p.93
CF 6.50	Ch.2, p.93
CF 6.51	Ch.2, p.93
CF 6.52	Ch.2, p.93
CF 6.53	Ch.2, p.94
CF 6.54	Ch.2, p.94
CF 6.55	Ch.2, p.94
CF 6.56	Ch.2, p.94
CF 6.57	Ch.2, p.94
CF 6.58	Ch.2, p.95
CF 6.59	Ch.2, p.95
CF 6.60	Ch.2, p.95
CF 6.61	Ch.2, p.95
CF 6.62	Ch.2, p.95
CF 6.63	Ch.2, p.95
CF 6.64	Ch.2, p.95
CF 6.65	Ch.2, p.95
CF 6.66	Ch.2, p.96
CF 6.67	Ch.2, p.96
CF 6.68	Ch.2, p.96
CF 6.69	Ch.2, p.96
CF 6.70	Ch.2, p.96
CF 6.71	Ch.2, p.96

CF 6.72	Ch.2, p.96	CF 8.7	Ch.2, p.106
CF 6.73	Ch.2, p.96	CF 8.8	Ch.2, p.106
CF 6.74	Ch.2, p.97	CF 8.9	Ch.2, p.105
CF 6.75	Ch.2, p.97	CF 8.10	Ch.2, p.105
CF 6.76	Ch.2, p.97	CF Appendix	Ch.6, p.391
CF 6.77	Ch.2, p.93	CF Appendix	Ch.6, p.400
CF 6.78	Ch.2, p.98	CF Appendix	Ch.6, p.402
CF 6.79	Ch.2, p.98	CF BC0.27	Ch.2, p.46
CF 6.80	Ch.2, p.98	CF BC0.28	Ch.2, p.47
CF 6.81	Ch.2, p.98	CF BC3.21	Ch.2, p.61
CF 6.82	Ch.2, p.98	CF BC3.21	Ch.6, p.401
CF 6.83	Ch.2, p.98	CF BC4.96	Ch.27, p.2018
CF 6.84	Ch.2, p.98	CF BC6.1	Ch.2, p.82
CF 6.85	Ch.2, p.99	CF BC6.10	Ch.2, p.82
CF 6.86	Ch.2, p.99	CF BC7.29	Ch.2, p.104
CF 6.87	Ch.2, p.99	CF BC7.24	Ch.2, p.103
CF 6.88	Ch.2, p.99		
CF 6.89	Ch.2, p.99		

IFRS 1

CF 6.90	Ch.2, p.100
CF 6.91	Ch.2, p.100
CF 6.92	Ch.2, p.100
CF 6.93	Ch.2, p.100
CF 6.94	Ch.2, p.100
CF 6.95	Ch.2, p.100
CF 7.1	Ch.2, p.101
CF 7.2	Ch.2, p.101
CF 7.3	Ch.2, p.101
CF 7.4	Ch.2, p.101
CF 7.5	Ch.2, p.102
CF 7.6	Ch.2, p.102
CF 7.7	Ch.2, p.102
CF 7.8	Ch.2, p.102
CF 7.9	Ch.2, p.102
CF 7.10	Ch.2, p.102
CF 7.10(a)	Ch.43, p.3550
CF 7.11	Ch.2, p.102
CF 7.12	Ch.2, p.102
CF 7.13	Ch.2, p.103
CF 7.14	Ch.2, p.103
CF 7.15	Ch.2, p.103
CF 7.16	Ch.2, p.103
CF 7.17	Ch.2, p.103
CF 7.18	Ch.2, p.104
CF 7.19	Ch.2, p.104
CF 7.20	Ch.2, p.104
CF 7.21	Ch.2, p.104
CF 7.22	Ch.2, p.101
CF 7.22	Ch.2, p.104
CF 8.1	Ch.2, p.105
CF 8.2	Ch.2, p.105
CF 8.3(a)	Ch.2, p.105
CF 8.3(b)	Ch.2, p.106
CF 8.4	Ch.2, p.104
CF 8.5	Ch.2, p.105
CF 8.5	Ch.2, p.106
CF 8.6	Ch.2, p.104
CF 8.6	Ch.2, p.105
CF 8.7	Ch.2, p.105

IFRS 1.1	Ch.5, p.227
IFRS 1.2-3	Ch.5, p.233
IFRS 1.2(a)	Ch.5, p.232
IFRS 1.2(b)	Ch.5, p.232
IFRS 1.3	Ch.5, p.229
IFRS 1.3(a)	Ch.5, p.229
IFRS 1.3(b)	Ch.5, p.232
IFRS 1.3(b)-(c)	Ch.5, p.231
IFRS 1.3(d)	Ch.5, p.232
IFRS 1.4	Ch.5, p.230
IFRS 1.5	Ch.5, p.232
IFRS 1.6	Ch.5, p.236
IFRS 1.7	Ch.5, p.238
IFRS 1.7	Ch.5, p.266
IFRS 1.7	Ch.5, p.268
IFRS 1.7	Ch.5, p.291
IFRS 1.7	Ch.5, p.302
IFRS 1.7	Ch.5, p.364
IFRS 1.7	Ch.33, p.2599
IFRS 1.8	Ch.5, p.238
IFRS 1.9	Ch.5, p.240
IFRS 1.9	Ch.5, p.249
IFRS 1.10	Ch.5, p.239
IFRS 1.10	Ch.5, p.281
IFRS 1.10	Ch.5, p.296
IFRS 1.11	Ch.5, p.239
IFRS 1.11	Ch.5, p.367
IFRS 1.11	Ch.5, p.368
IFRS 1.11	Ch.33, p.2572
IFRS 1.12	Ch.5, p.241
IFRS 1.12(b)	Ch.5, p.266
IFRS 1.13	Ch.5, p.238
IFRS 1.13	Ch.5, p.240
IFRS 1.13-17	Ch.5, p.241
IFRS 1.14	Ch.5, p.244
IFRS 1.14	Ch.5, p.377
IFRS 1.14	Ch.5, p.379
IFRS 1.14-15	Ch.5, p.369

Index of standards

IFRS 1.14-17	Ch.5, p.365	IFRS 1.32(b)	Ch.5, p.358
IFRS 1.14-17	Ch.5, p.377	IFRS 1.32(c)	Ch.5, p.365
IFRS 1.4(a)	Ch.5, p.235	IFRS 1.32-33	Ch.5, p.356
IFRS 1.4A	Ch.5, p.233	IFRS 1 Appendix A	Ch.5, p.228
IFRS 1.4B	Ch.5, p.233	IFRS 1 Appendix A	Ch.5, p.229
IFRS 1.15	Ch.5, p.244	IFRS 1 Appendix A	Ch.5, p.232
IFRS 1.16	Ch.5, p.244	IFRS 1 Appendix A	Ch.5, p.234
IFRS 1.17	Ch.5, p.245	IFRS 1 Appendix A	Ch.5, p.236
IFRS 1.18	Ch.5, p.238	IFRS 1 Appendix A	Ch.5, p.240
IFRS 1.18	Ch.5, p.240	IFRS 1 Appendix B	Ch.5, p.241
IFRS 1.18	Ch.5, p.243	IFRS 1 Appendix C	Ch.5, p.242
IFRS 1.20	Ch.5, p.342	IFRS 1 Appendix C	Ch.5, p.266
IFRS 1.21	Ch.5, p.237	IFRS 1 Appendix C	Ch.5, p.267
IFRS 1.21	Ch.5, p.342	IFRS 1 Appendix C	Ch.5, p.307
IFRS 1.21-30	Ch.5, p.290	IFRS 1 Appendix D	Ch.5, p.242
IFRS 1.22	Ch.5, p.343	IFRS 1.B2	Ch.5, p.247
IFRS 1.23	Ch.5, p.343	IFRS 1.B2	Ch.5, p.271
IFRS 1.23	Ch.5, p.347	IFRS 1.B3	Ch.5, p.247
IFRS 1.23	Ch.5, p.360	IFRS 1.B4(a)	Ch.5, p.250
IFRS 1.23	Ch.5, p.365	IFRS 1.B4(b)	Ch.5, p.250
IFRS 1.23-28	Ch.5, p.322	IFRS 1.B5	Ch.5, p.248
IFRS 1.23A	Ch.5, p.233	IFRS 1.B5	Ch.5, p.252
IFRS 1.23B	Ch.5, p.233	IFRS 1.B6	Ch.5, p.248
IFRS 1.24(a)	Ch.5, p.345	IFRS 1.B6	Ch.5, p.252
IFRS 1.24(a)	Ch.5, p.358	IFRS 1.B6	Ch.5, p.253
IFRS 1.24(a)-(b)	Ch.5, p.365	IFRS 1.B6	Ch.5, p.256
IFRS 1.24(b)	Ch.5, p.345	IFRS 1.B7	Ch.5, p.262
IFRS 1.24(b)	Ch.5, p.358	IFRS 1.B7	Ch.5, p.268
IFRS 1.24(c)	Ch.5, p.356	IFRS 1.B8	Ch.5, p.262
IFRS 1.24(c)	Ch.5, p.376	IFRS 1.B8A	Ch.5, p.262
IFRS 1.25	Ch.5, p.345	IFRS 1.B8A	Ch.5, p.356
IFRS 1.25	Ch.5, p.358	IFRS 1.B8B	Ch.5, p.263
IFRS 1.25	Ch.5, p.364	IFRS 1.B8B	Ch.5, p.357
IFRS 1.26	Ch.5, p.245	IFRS 1.B8C	Ch.5, p.263
IFRS 1.26	Ch.5, p.345	IFRS 1.B8D	Ch.5, p.264
IFRS 1.26	Ch.5, p.358	IFRS 1.B8E	Ch.5, p.264
IFRS 1.26	Ch.5, p.365	IFRS 1.B8F	Ch.5, p.264
IFRS 1.27	Ch.5, p.346	IFRS 1.B8F(a)	Ch.5, p.264
IFRS 1.27	Ch.5, p.365	IFRS 1.B8G	Ch.5, p.264
IFRS 1.27A	Ch.5, p.347	IFRS 1.B9	Ch.5, p.265
IFRS 1.27A	Ch.5, p.365	IFRS 1.B10	Ch.5, p.265
IFRS 1.28	Ch.5, p.345	IFRS 1.B11	Ch.5, p.265
IFRS 1.29	Ch.5, p.314	IFRS 1.B12	Ch.5, p.265
IFRS 1.29-29A	Ch.5, p.356	IFRS 1.B13	Ch.5, p.266
IFRS 1.29A	Ch.5, p.315	IFRS 1.C1	Ch.5, p.262
IFRS 1.30	Ch.5, p.295	IFRS 1.C1	Ch.5, p.268
IFRS 1.30	Ch.5, p.296	IFRS 1.C1	Ch.5, p.271
IFRS 1.31	Ch.5, p.357	IFRS 1.C1	Ch.5, p.283
IFRS 1.32	Ch.5, p.360	IFRS 1.C2	Ch.5, p.282
IFRS 1.32	Ch.43, p.3550	IFRS 1.C2	Ch.5, p.283
IFRS 1.33	Ch.5, p.361	IFRS 1.C3	Ch.5, p.283
IFRS 1.30. D5	Ch.5, p.357	IFRS 1.C4(a)	Ch.5, p.271
IFRS 1.31A	Ch.5, p.298	IFRS 1.C4(a)	Ch.5, p.276
IFRS 1.31A	Ch.5, p.357	IFRS 1.C4(b)	Ch.5, p.271
IFRS 1.31B	Ch.5, p.300	IFRS 1.C4(b)	Ch.5, p.273
IFRS 1.31B	Ch.5, p.357	IFRS 1.C4(b)	Ch.5, p.277
IFRS 1.31C	Ch.5, p.358	IFRS 1.C4(b)	Ch.5, p.281
IFRS 1.32(a)	Ch.5, p.358	IFRS 1.C4(b)	Ch.5, p.286

IFRS 1.C4(b)(ii)	Ch.5, p.278	IFRS 1.D5	Ch.5, p.292
IFRS 1.C4(b)(ii)	Ch.5, p.280	IFRS 1.D5	Ch.5, p.293
IFRS 1.C4(b)(ii)	Ch.5, p.281	IFRS 1.D5	Ch.5, p.375
IFRS 1.C4(b)(ii)	Ch.5, p.378	IFRS 1.D5-D7	Ch.5, p.295
IFRS 1.C4(c)	Ch.5, p.272	IFRS 1.D5-D8	Ch.5, p.294
IFRS 1.C4(c)	Ch.5, p.281	IFRS 1.D5-D8	Ch.5, p.296
IFRS 1.C4(c)(i)	Ch.5, p.277	IFRS 1.D6	Ch.5, p.292
IFRS 1.C4(c)(i)	Ch.5, p.278	IFRS 1.D6	Ch.5, p.293
IFRS 1.C4(c)(ii)	Ch.5, p.281	IFRS 1.D7	Ch.5, p.292
IFRS 1.C4(d)	Ch.5, p.276	IFRS 1.D7	Ch.5, p.294
IFRS 1.C4(d)	Ch.5, p.277	IFRS 1.D7	Ch.5, p.296
IFRS 1.C4(e)	Ch.5, p.263	IFRS 1.D7	Ch.5, p.357
IFRS 1.C4(e)	Ch.5, p.274	IFRS 1.D7	Ch.5, p.375
IFRS 1.C4(e)	Ch.5, p.277	IFRS 1.D8	Ch.5, p.295
IFRS 1.C4(f)	Ch.5, p.272	IFRS 1.D8	Ch.5, p.296
IFRS 1.C4(f)	Ch.5, p.273	IFRS 1.D8	Ch.5, p.297
IFRS 1.C4(f)	Ch.5, p.277	IFRS 1.D9	Ch.5, p.273
IFRS 1.C4(f)	Ch.5, p.278	IFRS 1.D9	Ch.5, p.302
IFRS 1.C4(f)	Ch.5, p.280	IFRS 1.D12	Ch.5, p.304
IFRS 1.C4(f)	Ch.5, p.281	IFRS 1.D12	Ch.5, p.305
IFRS 1.C4(f)	Ch.5, p.286	IFRS 1.D12	Ch.5, p.310
IFRS 1.C4(f)	Ch.5, p.378	IFRS 1.D13	Ch.5, p.304
IFRS 1.C4(g)	Ch.5, p.272	IFRS 1.D13	Ch.5, p.305
IFRS 1.C4(g)	Ch.5, p.276	IFRS 1.D13	Ch.5, p.310
IFRS 1.C4(g)	Ch.5, p.277	IFRS 1.D13	Ch.5, p.311
IFRS 1.C4(g)	Ch.5, p.279	IFRS 1.D13	Ch.5, p.312
IFRS 1.C4(g)(i)	Ch.5, p.273	IFRS 1.D13A	Ch.5, p.304
IFRS 1.C4(g)(i)	Ch.5, p.278	IFRS 1.D13A	Ch.5, p.310
IFRS 1.C4(g)(i)	Ch.5, p.281	IFRS 1.D13A	Ch.5, p.312
IFRS 1.C4(g)(i)	Ch.5, p.286	IFRS 1.D14	Ch.5, p.306
IFRS 1.C4(g)(ii)	Ch.5, p.375	IFRS 1.D15	Ch.5, p.284
IFRS 1.C4(g)(ii)	Ch.5, p.376	IFRS 1.D15	Ch.5, p.306
IFRS 1.C4(h)	Ch.5, p.279	IFRS 1.D15	Ch.5, p.307
IFRS 1.C4(h)	Ch.5, p.280	IFRS 1.D15	Ch.5, p.357
IFRS 1.C4(h)	Ch.5, p.281	IFRS 1.D15	Ch.8, p.597
IFRS 1.C4(h)(i)	Ch.5, p.275	IFRS 1.D15A	Ch.5, p.307
IFRS 1.C4(i)	Ch.5, p.281	IFRS 1.D15A	Ch.8, p.598
IFRS 1.C4(i)(i)	Ch.5, p.281	IFRS 1.D16	Ch.5, p.307
IFRS 1.C4(i)(i)	Ch.5, p.282	IFRS 1.D16	Ch.5, p.308
IFRS 1.C4(i)(ii)	Ch.5, p.282	IFRS 1.D16-D17	Ch.5, p.307
IFRS 1.C4(j)	Ch.5, p.283	IFRS 1.D16(a)	Ch.5, p.304
IFRS 1.C4(j)	Ch.5, p.284	IFRS 1.D16(a)	Ch.5, p.313
IFRS 1.C4(j)	Ch.5, p.306	IFRS 1.D17	Ch.5, p.277
IFRS 1.C4(k)	Ch.5, p.273	IFRS 1.D17	Ch.5, p.283
IFRS 1.C4(k)	Ch.5, p.277	IFRS 1.D17	Ch.5, p.306
IFRS 1.C4(k)	Ch.5, p.278	IFRS 1.D17	Ch.5, p.307
IFRS 1.C4(k)	Ch.5, p.281	IFRS 1.D17	Ch.5, p.311
IFRS 1.C4(k)	Ch.5, p.285	IFRS 1.D17	Ch.5, p.313
IFRS 1.C4(k)	Ch.5, p.286	IFRS 1.D17	Ch.5, p.314
IFRS 1.C5	Ch.5, p.271	IFRS 1.D18	Ch.5, p.314
IFRS 1.C5	Ch.5, p.279	IFRS 1.D19	Ch.5, p.315
IFRS 1.C5	Ch.5, p.285	IFRS 1.D19	Ch.5, p.356
IFRS 1.C5	Ch.5, p.375	IFRS 1.D19-D19C	Ch.5, p.265
IFRS 1.D2	Ch.5, p.287	IFRS 1.D19A	Ch.5, p.314
IFRS 1.D2	Ch.5, p.289	IFRS 1.D19A	Ch.5, p.356
IFRS 1.D2	Ch.34, p.2884	IFRS 1.D19B	Ch.5, p.315
IFRS 1.D3	Ch.5, p.287	IFRS 1.D19C	Ch.5, p.315
IFRS 1.D4	Ch.5, p.290	IFRS 1.D20	Ch.5, p.316

IFRS 1.D21	Ch.5, p.316	IFRS 1.IG27(a)	Ch.5, p.306
IFRS 1.D21A	Ch.5, p.298	IFRS 1.IG27(b)	Ch.5, p.306
IFRS 1.D21A	Ch.5, p.319	IFRS 1.IG27(c)	Ch.5, p.284
IFRS 1.D22	Ch.5, p.319	IFRS 1.IG27(c)	Ch.5, p.306
IFRS 1.D23	Ch.5, p.320	IFRS 1.IG28	Ch.5, p.306
IFRS 1.D25	Ch.5, p.321	IFRS 1.IG30	Ch.5, p.312
IFRS 1.D26	Ch.5, p.321	IFRS 1.IG31	Ch.5, p.309
IFRS 1.D26-D30	Ch.5, p.358	IFRS 1.IG32	Ch.5, p.375
IFRS 1.D27	Ch.5, p.321	IFRS 1.IG33	Ch.5, p.375
IFRS 1.D27	Ch.16, p.1276	IFRS 1.IG34	Ch.5, p.375
IFRS 1.D28	Ch.5, p.321	IFRS 1.IG35	Ch.47, p.3699
IFRS 1.D29	Ch.5, p.321	IFRS 1.IG35-IG36	Ch.5, p.314
IFRS 1.D30	Ch.5, p.322	IFRS 1.IG36	Ch.47, p.3699
IFRS 1.D31	Ch.5, p.285	IFRS 1.IG37	Ch.5, p.358
IFRS 1.D31	Ch.5, p.322	IFRS 1.IG39	Ch.5, p.376
IFRS 1.D32	Ch.5, p.322	IFRS 1.IG40	Ch.5, p.376
IFRS 1.D33	Ch.5, p.342	IFRS 1.IG40	Ch.5, p.377
IFRS 1.D34	Ch.5, p.335	IFRS 1.IG41	Ch.5, p.376
IFRS 1.D34	Ch.5, p.336	IFRS 1.IG41	Ch.5, p.377
IFRS 1.D34	Ch.5, p.371	IFRS 1.IG43	Ch.5, p.376
IFRS 1.D35	Ch.5, p.335	IFRS 1.IG44	Ch.5, p.378
IFRS 1.D35	Ch.5, p.336	IFRS 1.IG46	Ch.5, p.378
IFRS 1.D35	Ch.5, p.337	IFRS 1.IG47	Ch.5, p.378
IFRS 1.D35	Ch.5, p.371	IFRS 1.IG48	Ch.5, p.378
IFRS 1.D36	Ch.5, p.342	IFRS 1.IG49	Ch.5, p.378
IFRS 1.D8(b)	Ch.5, p.297	IFRS 1.IG51	Ch.5, p.379
IFRS 1.D8A	Ch.5, p.298	IFRS 1.IG53	Ch.5, p.247
IFRS 1.D8A(b)	Ch.5, p.357	IFRS 1.IG53	Ch.5, p.248
IFRS 1.D8B	Ch.5, p.299	IFRS 1.IG54	Ch.5, p.247
IFRS 1.D8B	Ch.5, p.300	IFRS 1.IG55	Ch.5, p.264
IFRS 1.D8B	Ch.5, p.357	IFRS 1.IG56	Ch.5, p.262
IFRS 1.D9B	Ch.5, p.302	IFRS 1.IG57	Ch.5, p.263
IFRS 1.D9B	Ch.5, p.303	IFRS 1.IG58A	Ch.5, p.250
IFRS 1.D9B-D9E	Ch.5, p.273	IFRS 1.IG58A	Ch.5, p.263
IFRS 1.D9C	Ch.5, p.303	IFRS 1.IG58B	Ch.5, p.245
IFRS 1.D9D	Ch.5, p.303	IFRS 1.IG58B	Ch.5, p.250
IFRS 1.D9E	Ch.5, p.303	IFRS 1.IG59	Ch.5, p.263
IFRS 1.IG3	Ch.5, p.244	IFRS 1.IG60	Ch.5, p.248
IFRS 1.IG4	Ch.5, p.245	IFRS 1.IG60	Ch.5, p.256
IFRS 1.IG7	Ch.5, p.277	IFRS 1.IG60	Ch.5, p.257
IFRS 1.IG7	Ch.5, p.369	IFRS 1.IG60	Ch.5, p.258
IFRS 1.IG9	Ch.5, p.295	IFRS 1.IG60A	Ch.5, p.254
IFRS 1.IG10	Ch.5, p.370	IFRS 1.IG60B	Ch.5, p.253
IFRS 1.IG11	Ch.5, p.294	IFRS 1.IG60B	Ch.5, p.254
IFRS 1.IG11	Ch.5, p.296	IFRS 1.IG60B	Ch.5, p.255
IFRS 1.IG12	Ch.5, p.292	IFRS 1.IG60B	Ch.5, p.256
IFRS 1.IG12	Ch.5, p.371	IFRS 1.IG62	Ch.5, p.369
IFRS 1.IG13	Ch.5, p.316	IFRS 1.IG201	Ch.5, p.316
IFRS 1.IG14	Ch.5, p.371	IFRS 1.IG201-IG203	Ch.5, p.316
IFRS 1.IG17	Ch.5, p.372	IFRS 1.IG Example 1	Ch.5, p.246
IFRS 1.IG19	Ch.5, p.372	IFRS 1.IG Example 10	Ch.5, p.359
IFRS 1.IG20	Ch.5, p.373	IFRS 1.IG Example 11	Ch.5, p.345
IFRS 1.IG21	Ch.5, p.372	IFRS 1.IG Example 12	Ch.5, p.265
IFRS 1.IG21A	Ch.5, p.282	IFRS 1.IG Example 2	Ch.5, p.276
IFRS 1.IG23	Ch.5, p.320	IFRS 1.IG Example 3	Ch.5, p.272
IFRS 1.IG24	Ch.5, p.320	IFRS 1.IG Example 4	Ch.5, p.285
IFRS 1.IG26	Ch.5, p.305	IFRS 1.IG Example 4	Ch.5, p.286
IFRS 1.IG27(a)	Ch.5, p.283	IFRS 1.IG Example 5	Ch.5, p.281

IFRS 1.IG Example 6	Ch.5, p.284	IFRS 2.5	Ch.34, p.2644
IFRS 1.IG Example 7	Ch.5, p.273	IFRS 2.5	Ch.34, p.2654
IFRS 1.IG Example 8	Ch.5, p.308	IFRS 2.5	Ch.34, p.2655
IFRS 1.IG Example 9	Ch.5, p.277	IFRS 2.6	Ch.34, p.2655
IFRS 1.IG Example 9	Ch.5, p.311	IFRS 2.6A	Ch.34, p.2674
IFRS 1.IG5-IG6	Ch.5, p.365	IFRS 2.6A	Ch.34, p.2693
IFRS 1.BC3	Ch.5, p.227	IFRS 2.6A	Ch.34, p.2740
IFRS 1.BC5	Ch.5, p.230	IFRS 2.6A	Ch.34, p.2775
IFRS 1.BC6	Ch.5, p.230	IFRS 2.7	Ch.34, p.2663
IFRS 1.BC9	Ch.5, p.228	IFRS 2.7	Ch.34, p.2709
IFRS 1.BC10	Ch.5, p.228	IFRS 2.8	Ch.34, p.2663
IFRS 1.BC11	Ch.5, p.238	IFRS 2.9	Ch.34, p.2663
IFRS 1.BC14	Ch.5, p.240	IFRS 2.10	Ch.8, p.615
IFRS 1.BC36	Ch.5, p.274	IFRS 2.10	Ch.9, p.750
IFRS 1.BC39	Ch.5, p.279	IFRS 2.10	Ch.34, p.2674
IFRS 1.BC43	Ch.5, p.302	IFRS 2.11	Ch.34, p.2676
IFRS 1.BC45	Ch.5, p.292	IFRS 2.11	Ch.34, p.2677
IFRS 1.BC45	Ch.5, p.376	IFRS 2.12	Ch.34, p.2677
IFRS 1.BC47	Ch.5, p.294	IFRS 2.13	Ch.9, p.750
IFRS 1.BC62	Ch.5, p.309	IFRS 2.13	Ch.34, p.2691
IFRS 1.BC63	Ch.5, p.311	IFRS 2.13A	Ch.9, p.750
IFRS 1.BC67	Ch.5, p.375	IFRS 2.13A	Ch.34, p.2651
IFRS 1.BC75	Ch.5, p.252	IFRS 2.13A	Ch.34, p.2662
IFRS 1.BC84	Ch.5, p.244	IFRS 2.13A	Ch.34, p.2794
IFRS 1.BC91	Ch.5, p.343	IFRS 2.14	Ch.34, p.2693
IFRS 1.BC94	Ch.5, p.356	IFRS 2.15	Ch.34, p.2694
IFRS 1.BC97	Ch.5, p.347	IFRS 2.15(b)	Ch.34, p.2699
IFRS 1.BC11A	Ch.5, p.238	IFRS 2.15(b)	Ch.34, p.2708
IFRS 1.BC12(a)	Ch.5, p.242	IFRS 2.16	Ch.34, p.2692
IFRS 1.BC12(b)	Ch.5, p.241	IFRS 2.17	Ch.34, p.2692
IFRS 1.BC3B	Ch.5, p.228	IFRS 2.18	Ch.34, p.2692
IFRS 1.BC46B	Ch.5, p.297	IFRS 2.19	Ch.34, p.2695
IFRS 1.BC47A	Ch.5, p.298	IFRS 2.19-20	Ch.34, p.2695
IFRS 1.BC47B	Ch.5, p.298	IFRS 2.19-21	Ch.34, p.2707
IFRS 1.BC47D	Ch.5, p.298	IFRS 2.19-21A	Ch.34, p.2693
IFRS 1.BC47F	Ch.5, p.299	IFRS 2.21	Ch.34, p.2704
IFRS 1.BC47G	Ch.5, p.300	IFRS 2.21A	Ch.34, p.2712
IFRS 1.BC47H	Ch.5, p.300	IFRS 2.22	Ch.34, p.2693
IFRS 1.BC47I	Ch.5, p.299	IFRS 2.23	Ch.34, p.2696
IFRS 1.BC55C	Ch.5, p.310	IFRS 2.24(a)	Ch.34, p.2766
IFRS 1.BC63CA	Ch.5, p.319	IFRS 2.24(b)	Ch.34, p.2767
IFRS 1.BC63J	Ch.5, p.322	IFRS 2.25	Ch.34, p.2768
IFRS 1.BC6C	Ch.5, p.233	IFRS 2.25(a)	Ch.34, p.2768
IFRS 1.BC83A	Ch.5, p.316	IFRS 2.25(b)	Ch.34, p.2768
IFRS 1.BC89B	Ch.5, p.342	IFRS 2.26	Ch.34, p.2714
		IFRS 2.26-28	Ch.34, p.2734
		IFRS 2.26-29	Ch.5, p.287
		IFRS 2.26-29	Ch.5, p.289
		IFRS 2.27	Ch.34, p.2715

IFRS 2

IFRS 2.1	Ch.34, p.2642	IFRS 2.27	Ch.34, p.2716
IFRS 2.2	Ch.34, p.2643	IFRS 2.27	Ch.34, p.2725
IFRS 2.2	Ch.34, p.2651	IFRS 2.28	Ch.34, p.2726
IFRS 2.2	Ch.34, p.2662	IFRS 2.28	Ch.34, p.2727
IFRS 2.2	Ch.34, p.2855	IFRS 2.28	Ch.34, p.2732
IFRS 2.2(c)	Ch.34, p.2794	IFRS 2.28	Ch.34, p.2734
IFRS 2.3A	Ch.34, p.2644	IFRS 2.28(a)	Ch.34, p.2729
IFRS 2.4	Ch.34, p.2654	IFRS 2.28(b)	Ch.47, p.3743
IFRS 2.5	Ch.8, p.619	IFRS 2.28(c)	Ch.34, p.2731

IFRS 2.28A	Ch.34, p.2713	IFRS 2.63D	Ch.34, p.2638
IFRS 2.28A	Ch.34, p.2714	IFRS 2 Appendix A	Ch.34, p.2642
IFRS 2.29	Ch.34, p.2726	IFRS 2 Appendix A	Ch.34, p.2664
IFRS 2.30	Ch.34, p.2777	IFRS 2 Appendix A	Ch.34, p.2671
IFRS 2.30-33D	Ch.34, p.2775	IFRS 2 Appendix A	Ch.34, p.2674
IFRS 2.31	Ch.34, p.2770	IFRS 2 Appendix A	Ch.34, p.2676
IFRS 2.31	Ch.34, p.2775	IFRS 2 Appendix A	Ch.34, p.2677
IFRS 2.32	Ch.34, p.2777	IFRS 2 Appendix A	Ch.34, p.2678
IFRS 2.32-33	Ch.34, p.2777	IFRS 2 Appendix A	Ch.34, p.2692
IFRS 2.33	Ch.34, p.2775	IFRS 2 Appendix A	Ch.34, p.2693
IFRS 2.33A-33B	Ch.34, p.2777	IFRS 2 Appendix A	Ch.34, p.2704
IFRS 2.33C	Ch.34, p.2779	IFRS 2 Appendix A	Ch.34, p.2727
IFRS 2.33D	Ch.34, p.2777	IFRS 2 Appendix A	Ch.34, p.2771
IFRS 2.33D	Ch.34, p.2779	IFRS 2 Appendix A	Ch.34, p.2789
IFRS 2.33E	Ch.34, p.2860	IFRS 2.B1	Ch.34, p.2739
IFRS 2.33F	Ch.34, p.2860	IFRS 2.B2	Ch.34, p.2765
IFRS 2.33G	Ch.34, p.2860	IFRS 2.B3	Ch.34, p.2765
IFRS 2.33H(a)	Ch.34, p.2861	IFRS 2.B4-5	Ch.34, p.2744
IFRS 2.33H(b)	Ch.34, p.2860	IFRS 2.B5	Ch.34, p.2746
IFRS 2.34	Ch.34, p.2788	IFRS 2.B6	Ch.34, p.2754
IFRS 2.35	Ch.34, p.2788	IFRS 2.B7-9	Ch.34, p.2754
IFRS 2.35	Ch.34, p.2789	IFRS 2.B10	Ch.34, p.2754
IFRS 2.35	Ch.34, p.2794	IFRS 2.B11-12	Ch.34, p.2755
IFRS 2.36	Ch.34, p.2789	IFRS 2.B13-15	Ch.34, p.2755
IFRS 2.37	Ch.34, p.2790	IFRS 2.B16-17	Ch.34, p.2755
IFRS 2.38	Ch.34, p.2790	IFRS 2.B18	Ch.34, p.2757
IFRS 2.39-40	Ch.34, p.2792	IFRS 2.B19-21	Ch.34, p.2758
IFRS 2.40	Ch.34, p.2792	IFRS 2.B22-24	Ch.34, p.2759
IFRS 2.41	Ch.34, p.2795	IFRS 2.B25	Ch.34, p.2760
IFRS 2.41-42	Ch.34, p.2795	IFRS 2.B26	Ch.34, p.2761
IFRS 2.43	Ch.34, p.2796	IFRS 2.B27-29	Ch.34, p.2761
IFRS 2.43A	Ch.34, p.2644	IFRS 2.B30	Ch.34, p.2659
IFRS 2.43A	Ch.34, p.2815	IFRS 2.B30	Ch.34, p.2761
IFRS 2.43B	Ch.34, p.2647	IFRS 2.B31	Ch.34, p.2765
IFRS 2.43B	Ch.34, p.2648	IFRS 2.B31-32	Ch.34, p.2762
IFRS 2.43B	Ch.34, p.2811	IFRS 2.B33-34	Ch.34, p.2765
IFRS 2.43B	Ch.34, p.2815	IFRS 2.B34	Ch.34, p.2762
IFRS 2.43B-43C	Ch.34, p.2645	IFRS 2.B35	Ch.34, p.2762
IFRS 2.43B-43C	Ch.34, p.2648	IFRS 2.B36	Ch.34, p.2763
IFRS 2.43C	Ch.34, p.2649	IFRS 2.B37	Ch.34, p.2763
IFRS 2.43C	Ch.34, p.2816	IFRS 2.B38-39	Ch.34, p.2764
IFRS 2.43D	Ch.34, p.2815	IFRS 2.B40-41	Ch.34, p.2764
IFRS 2.44	Ch.5, p.287	IFRS 2.B42	Ch.34, p.2715
IFRS 2.44	Ch.34, p.2845	IFRS 2.B42	Ch.34, p.2716
IFRS 2.45	Ch.5, p.287	IFRS 2.B42	Ch.34, p.2725
IFRS 2.45	Ch.34, p.2845	IFRS 2.B42-43	Ch.34, p.2716
IFRS 2.46	Ch.34, p.2846	IFRS 2.B42-44	Ch.34, p.2716
IFRS 2.47	Ch.34, p.2847	IFRS 2.B43	Ch.34, p.2715
IFRS 2.48	Ch.34, p.2848	IFRS 2.B43(a)	Ch.34, p.2717
IFRS 2.49	Ch.34, p.2848	IFRS 2.B43(a)	Ch.34, p.2718
IFRS 2.50	Ch.34, p.2848	IFRS 2.B43(b)	Ch.34, p.2718
IFRS 2.51	Ch.34, p.2848	IFRS 2.B43(c)	Ch.34, p.2718
IFRS 2.52	Ch.34, p.2848	IFRS 2.B43-44	Ch.34, p.2725
IFRS 2.52	Ch.34, p.2861	IFRS 2.B44	Ch.34, p.2715
IFRS 2.62	Ch.34, p.2638	IFRS 2.B44	Ch.34, p.2725
IFRS 2.63	Ch.34, p.2638	IFRS 2.B44(a)	Ch.34, p.2720
IFRS 2.64	Ch.34, p.2638	IFRS 2.B44(b)	Ch.34, p.2721
IFRS 2.63A	Ch.34, p.2643	IFRS 2.B44(b)	Ch.34, p.2724

IFRS 2.B44(c)	Ch.34, p.2720	IFRS 2.IG Example 9	Ch.34, p.2792
IFRS 2.B44(c)	Ch.34, p.2721	IFRS 2.IG Example 9A	Ch.34, p.2713
IFRS 2.B44A	Ch.34, p.2786	IFRS 2.IG Example 10	Ch.34, p.2767
IFRS 2.B44B	Ch.34, p.2787	IFRS 2.IG Example 12	Ch.34, p.2775
IFRS 2.B44C	Ch.34, p.2787	IFRS 2.IG Example 12A	Ch.34, p.2775
IFRS 2.B45	Ch.34, p.2815	IFRS 2.IG Example 12A	Ch.34, p.2778
IFRS 2.B45	Ch.34, p.2816	IFRS 2.IG Example 12B	Ch.34, p.2860
IFRS 2.B45-46	Ch.34, p.2815	IFRS 2.IG Example 12C	Ch.34, p.2787
IFRS 2.B48-49	Ch.34, p.2772	IFRS 2.IG Example 13	Ch.34, p.2791
IFRS 2.B48(b)	Ch.34, p.2646	IFRS 2.BC8-17	Ch.34, p.2653
IFRS 2.B49	Ch.34, p.2648	IFRS 2.BC18C	Ch.34, p.2652
IFRS 2.B50	Ch.34, p.2648	IFRS 2.BC18D	Ch.34, p.2652
IFRS 2.B50	Ch.34, p.2817	IFRS 2.BC22E	Ch.34, p.2643
IFRS 2.B52	Ch.34, p.2817	IFRS 2.BC22G	Ch.34, p.2647
IFRS 2.B52(a)	Ch.34, p.2645	IFRS 2.BC24	Ch.34, p.2739
IFRS 2.B52(b)	Ch.34, p.2647	IFRS 2.BC54-BC57	Ch.37, p.3049
IFRS 2.B52(b)	Ch.34, p.2811	IFRS 2.BC70-74	Ch.34, p.2822
IFRS 2.B53	Ch.34, p.2817	IFRS 2.BC88-96	Ch.34, p.2675
IFRS 2.B53-B54	Ch.34, p.2645	IFRS 2.BC109	Ch.34, p.2641
IFRS 2.B54	Ch.34, p.2817	IFRS 2.BC109	Ch.47, p.3704
IFRS 2.B55	Ch.34, p.2647	IFRS 2.BC110	Ch.34, p.2641
IFRS 2.B55	Ch.34, p.2811	IFRS 2.BC110	Ch.47, p.3704
IFRS 2.B55	Ch.34, p.2817	IFRS 2.BC126	Ch.34, p.2675
IFRS 2.B56-B57	Ch.34, p.2818	IFRS 2.BC126-127	Ch.34, p.2676
IFRS 2.B56-B58	Ch.34, p.2649	IFRS 2.BC130	Ch.34, p.2740
IFRS 2.B58	Ch.34, p.2818	IFRS 2.BC131	Ch.34, p.2744
IFRS 2.B59(c)	Ch.34, p.2840	IFRS 2.BC152	Ch.34, p.2744
IFRS 2.B60	Ch.34, p.2840	IFRS 2.BC153-169	Ch.34, p.2753
IFRS 2.B61	Ch.34, p.2841	IFRS 2.BC171A	Ch.34, p.2668
IFRS 2.IG1-3	Ch.34, p.2678	IFRS 2.BC171B	Ch.34, p.2669
IFRS 2.IG2	Ch.34, p.2678	IFRS 2.BC171B	Ch.34, p.2670
IFRS 2.IG4	Ch.34, p.2679	IFRS 2.BC183-184	Ch.34, p.2705
IFRS 2.IG5	Ch.34, p.2691	IFRS 2.BC188-192	Ch.34, p.2769
IFRS 2.IG5D	Ch.34, p.2651	IFRS 2.BC218-221	Ch.34, p.2696
IFRS 2.IG6-7	Ch.34, p.2691	IFRS 2.BC222-237	Ch.34, p.2715
IFRS 2.IG11	Ch.34, p.2696	IFRS 2.BC233	Ch.34, p.2732
IFRS 2.IG11	Ch.34, p.2698	IFRS 2.BC237A	Ch.34, p.2713
IFRS 2.IG12	Ch.34, p.2699	IFRS 2.BC237H	Ch.34, p.2787
IFRS 2.IG12	Ch.34, p.2702	IFRS 2.BC237K	Ch.34, p.2782
IFRS 2.IG13	Ch.34, p.2704	IFRS 2.BC246-251	Ch.34, p.2775
IFRS 2.IG13	Ch.34, p.2707	IFRS 2.BC255G	Ch.34, p.2858
IFRS 2.IG14	Ch.34, p.2708	IFRS 2.BC255G-I	Ch.34, p.2860
IFRS 2.IG15	Ch.34, p.2717	IFRS 2.BC255J	Ch.34, p.2861
IFRS 2.IG15	Ch.34, p.2721	IFRS 2.BC256	Ch.34, p.2803
IFRS 2.IG19	Ch.34, p.2775	IFRS 2.BC268H-268K	Ch.34, p.2818
IFRS 2.IG24	Ch.34, p.2669	IFRS 2.BC311-BC329	Ch.33, p.2589
IFRS 2.IG24	Ch.34, p.2713	IFRS 2.BC311-BC329	Ch.33, p.2593
IFRS 2.IG24	Ch.34, p.2714	IFRS 2.BC330-333	Ch.34, p.2673
IFRS 2.IG Example 1	Ch.34, p.2651	IFRS 2.BC341	Ch.34, p.2670
IFRS 2.IG Example 1	Ch.34, p.2652	IFRS 2.BC353-BC358	Ch.34, p.2669
IFRS 2.IG Example 2	Ch.34, p.2700	IFRS 2.BC364	Ch.34, p.2668
IFRS 2.IG Example 3	Ch.34, p.2701		
IFRS 2.IG Example 4	Ch.34, p.2700		
IFRS 2.IG Example 4	Ch.34, p.2702		
IFRS 2.IG Example 5	Ch.34, p.2707		
IFRS 2.IG Example 6	Ch.34, p.2708		
IFRS 2.IG Example 7	Ch.34, p.2717		
IFRS 2.IG Example 8	Ch.34, p.2721		

IFRS 3 (2000)

IFRS 3(2000).21B	Ch.9, p.669

IFRS 3 (2007)

IFRS 3(2007).B8 .... Ch.8, p.595
IFRS 3(2007).B8 .... Ch.9, p.744
IFRS 3(2007).BC28 .... Ch.10, p.771

IFRS 3 (2022)

IFRS 3(2022).11 .... Ch.9, p.668
IFRS 3(2022).11 .... Ch.9, p.686
IFRS 3(2022).23A Ch.9, p.686
IFRS 3(2022).BC114D Ch.9, p.686

IFRS 3

IFRS 3.1 .... Ch.10, p.768
IFRS 3.2 .... Ch.9, p.647
IFRS 3.2 .... Ch.9, p.648
IFRS 3.2 .... Ch.10, p.766
IFRS 3.2 .... Ch.12, p.932
IFRS 3.2 .... Ch.46, p.3652
IFRS 3.2(a) Ch.11, p.856
IFRS 3.2(a) Ch.12, p.893
IFRS 3.2(b) Ch.6, p.393
IFRS 3.2(b) Ch.7, p.504
IFRS 3.2(b) Ch.8, p.620
IFRS 3.2(b) Ch.18, p.1397
IFRS 3.2(b) Ch.19, p.1457
IFRS 3.2(b) Ch.33, p.2516
IFRS 3.2(b) Ch.33, p.2609
IFRS 3.2(b) Ch.43, p.3418
IFRS 3.2(b) Ch.49, p.3857
IFRS 3.2(b) Ch.56, p.4864
IFRS 3.2(c) Ch.6, p.393
IFRS 3.2(c) Ch.10, p.768
IFRS 3.2(c) Ch.56, p.4870
IFRS 3.2A Ch.5, p.267
IFRS 3.2A Ch.9, p.647
IFRS 3.3 .... Ch.5, p.267
IFRS 3.3 .... Ch.7, p.504
IFRS 3.3 .... Ch.7, p.514
IFRS 3.3 .... Ch.9, p.650
IFRS 3.3 .... Ch.10, p.768
IFRS 3.4 .... Ch.5, p.271
IFRS 3.4 .... Ch.9, p.659
IFRS 3.5 .... Ch.5, p.271
IFRS 3.5 .... Ch.9, p.659
IFRS 3.5 .... Ch.10, p.777
IFRS 3.6 .... Ch.9, p.659
IFRS 3.7 .... Ch.9, p.659
IFRS 3.7 .... Ch.9, p.752
IFRS 3.8 .... Ch.6, p.393
IFRS 3.8 .... Ch.7, p.503
IFRS 3.8 .... Ch.9, p.665
IFRS 3.9 .... Ch.9, p.665
IFRS 3.10 .... Ch.7, p.541
IFRS 3.10 .... Ch.9, p.666
IFRS 3.10 .... Ch.9, p.710
IFRS 3.10 .... Ch.33, p.2605
IFRS 3.11 .... Ch.2, p.47
IFRS 3.11 .... Ch.9, p.667
IFRS 3.11 .... Ch.43, p.3414
IFRS 3.12 .... Ch.9, p.667
IFRS 3.12 .... Ch.9, p.726
IFRS 3.13 .... Ch.9, p.667
IFRS 3.14 .... Ch.9, p.666
IFRS 3.15 .... Ch.9, p.670
IFRS 3.15 .... Ch.46, p.3652
IFRS 3.15 .... Ch.53, p.4277
IFRS 3.15 .... Ch.56, p.4863
IFRS 3.16 .... Ch.9, p.670
IFRS 3.16(b) Ch.53, p.4277
IFRS 3.16(c) Ch.46, p.3652
IFRS 3.17 .... Ch.9, p.670
IFRS 3.17(b) Ch.55, p.4549
IFRS 3.18 .... Ch.9, p.666
IFRS 3.18 .... Ch.17, p.1365
IFRS 3.18 .... Ch.33, p.2605
IFRS 3.18 .... Ch.49, p.3857
IFRS 3.18 .... Ch.51, p.4016
IFRS 3.19 .... Ch.7, p.504
IFRS 3.19 .... Ch.7, p.541
IFRS 3.19 .... Ch.7, p.554
IFRS 3.19 .... Ch.9, p.666
IFRS 3.19 .... Ch.9, p.710
IFRS 3.19 .... Ch.9, p.714
IFRS 3.19 .... Ch.20, p.1602
IFRS 3.20 .... Ch.9, p.666
IFRS 3.20 .... Ch.9, p.669
IFRS 3.21 .... Ch.9, p.690
IFRS 3.22 .... Ch.9, p.690
IFRS 3.23 .... Ch.9, p.691
IFRS 3.23 .... Ch.26, p.1935
IFRS 3.23 .... Ch.26, p.1942
IFRS 3.23 .... Ch.26, p.1961
IFRS 3.24 .... Ch.9, p.692
IFRS 3.24 .... Ch.33, p.2562
IFRS 3.24 .... Ch.33, p.2605
IFRS 3.25 .... Ch.9, p.692
IFRS 3.25 .... Ch.33, p.2605
IFRS 3.26 .... Ch.9, p.692
IFRS 3.26 .... Ch.20, p.1584
IFRS 3.27 .... Ch.9, p.693
IFRS 3.27 .... Ch.45, p.3606
IFRS 3.27-28 .... Ch.9, p.693
IFRS 3.28 .... Ch.9, p.693
IFRS 3.29 .... Ch.9, p.695
IFRS 3.30 .... Ch.7, p.541
IFRS 3.30 .... Ch.9, p.695
IFRS 3.30 .... Ch.20, p.1584
IFRS 3.30 .... Ch.34, p.2804
IFRS 3.31 .... Ch.9, p.695
IFRS 3.31A Ch.56, p.4863
IFRS 3.32 .... Ch.9, p.697

IFRS 3.32	Ch.9, p.708
IFRS 3.32	Ch.10, p.777
IFRS 3.33	Ch.9, p.699
IFRS 3.33	Ch.9, p.709
IFRS 3.33	Ch.9, p.741
IFRS 3.33	Ch.10, p.779
IFRS 3.34	Ch.9, p.697
IFRS 3.34	Ch.9, p.724
IFRS 3.34	Ch.10, p.777
IFRS 3.35	Ch.9, p.724
IFRS 3.36	Ch.9, p.724
IFRS 3.36	Ch.51, p.4016
IFRS 3.37	Ch.8, p.584
IFRS 3.37	Ch.9, p.698
IFRS 3.37	Ch.10, p.779
IFRS 3.37	Ch.11, p.828
IFRS 3.38	Ch.9, p.698
IFRS 3.39	Ch.7, p.539
IFRS 3.39	Ch.9, p.700
IFRS 3.39	Ch.40, p.3178
IFRS 3.39-40	Ch.9, p.703
IFRS 3.40	Ch.5, p.287
IFRS 3.40	Ch.7, p.539
IFRS 3.40	Ch.9, p.704
IFRS 3.40	Ch.9, p.706
IFRS 3.40	Ch.40, p.3178
IFRS 3.41	Ch.9, p.717
IFRS 3.41-42	Ch.11, p.836
IFRS 3.41-42	Ch.11, p.870
IFRS 3.42	Ch.9, p.717
IFRS 3.42A	Ch.9, p.723
IFRS 3.42A	Ch.12, p.937
IFRS 3.43	Ch.9, p.708
IFRS 3.44	Ch.9, p.709
IFRS 3.45	Ch.9, p.736
IFRS 3.45	Ch.9, p.737
IFRS 3.45	Ch.20, p.1589
IFRS 3.45	Ch.43, p.3562
IFRS 3.46	Ch.9, p.736
IFRS 3.46	Ch.20, p.1589
IFRS 3.47	Ch.9, p.737
IFRS 3.48	Ch.9, p.738
IFRS 3.49	Ch.9, p.737
IFRS 3.50	Ch.9, p.738
IFRS 3.51	Ch.9, p.726
IFRS 3.51-53	Ch.9, p.708
IFRS 3.52	Ch.9, p.727
IFRS 3.52	Ch.9, p.731
IFRS 3.52	Ch.34, p.2804
IFRS 3.53	Ch.9, p.707
IFRS 3.53	Ch.14, p.1051
IFRS 3.53	Ch.40, p.3148
IFRS 3.53	Ch.40, p.3177
IFRS 3.53	Ch.41, p.3238
IFRS 3.53	Ch.47, p.3739
IFRS 3.54	Ch.9, p.690
IFRS 3.54	Ch.9, p.739
IFRS 3.55	Ch.9, p.695
IFRS 3.56	Ch.9, p.691
IFRS 3.56	Ch.26, p.1942
IFRS 3.56	Ch.26, p.1962
IFRS 3.57	Ch.9, p.693
IFRS 3.57	Ch.51, p.3959
IFRS 3.58	Ch.5, p.287
IFRS 3.58	Ch.7, p.539
IFRS 3.58	Ch.9, p.707
IFRS 3.58	Ch.40, p.3178
IFRS 3.58	Ch.55, p.4542
IFRS 3.58	Ch.56, p.4691
IFRS 3.58(b)(i)	Ch.45, p.3602
IFRS 3.59	Ch.9, p.753
IFRS 3.59(b)	Ch.41, p.3207
IFRS 3.60	Ch.9, p.753
IFRS 3.61	Ch.9, p.756
IFRS 3.62	Ch.9, p.756
IFRS 3.63	Ch.9, p.757
IFRS 3.64	Ch.20, p.1602
IFRS 3.64N	Ch.56, p.4863
IFRS 3.64N	Ch.56, p.4922
IFRS 3.67	Ch.20, p.1597
IFRS 3 Appendix A	Ch.5, p.267
IFRS 3 Appendix A	Ch.6, p.393
IFRS 3 Appendix A	Ch.7, p.503
IFRS 3 Appendix A	Ch.7, p.504
IFRS 3 Appendix A	Ch.7, p.514
IFRS 3 Appendix A	Ch.8, p.619
IFRS 3 Appendix A	Ch.9, p.639
IFRS 3 Appendix A	Ch.9, p.650
IFRS 3 Appendix A	Ch.9, p.665
IFRS 3 Appendix A	Ch.9, p.672
IFRS 3 Appendix A	Ch.9, p.694
IFRS 3 Appendix A	Ch.9, p.697
IFRS 3 Appendix A	Ch.9, p.699
IFRS 3 Appendix A	Ch.9, p.703
IFRS 3 Appendix A	Ch.9, p.709
IFRS 3 Appendix A	Ch.9, p.710
IFRS 3 Appendix A	Ch.9, p.752
IFRS 3 Appendix A	Ch.10, p.768
IFRS 3 Appendix A	Ch.10, p.789
IFRS 3 Appendix A	Ch.17, p.1296
IFRS 3 Appendix A	Ch.43, p.3412
IFRS 3 Appendix A	Ch.55, p.4598
IFRS 3 Appendix A	Ch.56, p.4870
IFRS 3.B1	Ch.10, p.768
IFRS 3.B1	Ch.20, p.1623
IFRS 3.B1-B4	Ch.9, p.649
IFRS 3.B1-B4	Ch.10, p.768
IFRS 3.B2	Ch.10, p.769
IFRS 3.B2	Ch.39, p.3114
IFRS 3.B3	Ch.10, p.769
IFRS 3.B4	Ch.10, p.769
IFRS 3.B4	Ch.10, p.787
IFRS 3.B5	Ch.9, p.650
IFRS 3.B6	Ch.9, p.650
IFRS 3.B7	Ch.9, p.651
IFRS 3.B7	Ch.55, p.4598

IFRS 3.B7-B12D	Ch.7, p.514	IFRS 3.B37	Ch.9, p.685
IFRS 3.B7A	Ch.9, p.651	IFRS 3.B37	Ch.20, p.1584
IFRS 3.B7A	Ch.19, p.1454	IFRS 3.B38	Ch.9, p.686
IFRS 3.B7A	Ch.19, p.1456	IFRS 3.B38	Ch.20, p.1584
IFRS 3.B7B	Ch.9, p.652	IFRS 3.B39	Ch.9, p.739
IFRS 3.B7B	Ch.19, p.1455	IFRS 3.B40	Ch.9, p.686
IFRS 3.B7C	Ch.9, p.653	IFRS 3.B41	Ch.9, p.687
IFRS 3.B7-B8	Ch.56, p.4870	IFRS 3.B41	Ch.49, p.3857
IFRS 3.B7-B12D	Ch.7, p.504	IFRS 3.B41	Ch.51, p.4017
IFRS 3.B8	Ch.9, p.651	IFRS 3.B42	Ch.9, p.671
IFRS 3.B8	Ch.9, p.654	IFRS 3.B43	Ch.9, p.687
IFRS 3.B8	Ch.9, p.655	IFRS 3.B44	Ch.9, p.711
IFRS 3.B8A	Ch.9, p.654	IFRS 3.B45	Ch.9, p.711
IFRS 3.B9	Ch.9, p.651	IFRS 3.B46	Ch.9, p.709
IFRS 3.B11	Ch.9, p.655	IFRS 3.B47	Ch.9, p.709
IFRS 3.B11	Ch.19, p.1454	IFRS 3.B47	Ch.9, p.710
IFRS 3.B12B	Ch.9, p.654	IFRS 3.B48	Ch.9, p.710
IFRS 3.B12B	Ch.9, p.658	IFRS 3.B49	Ch.9, p.710
IFRS 3.B12C	Ch.9, p.655	IFRS 3.B50	Ch.9, p.727
IFRS 3.B12D(a)	Ch.9, p.654	IFRS 3.B50	Ch.34, p.2805
IFRS 3.B12D(b)	Ch.9, p.655	IFRS 3.B51	Ch.9, p.728
IFRS 3.B12D(c)	Ch.9, p.655	IFRS 3.B52	Ch.9, p.728
IFRS 3.B13	Ch.9, p.659	IFRS 3.B53	Ch.9, p.730
IFRS 3.B14	Ch.9, p.660	IFRS 3.B54	Ch.9, p.731
IFRS 3.B14	Ch.9, p.748	IFRS 3.B55	Ch.9, p.732
IFRS 3.B15	Ch.9, p.660	IFRS 3.B55(a)	Ch.9, p.732
IFRS 3.B16	Ch.9, p.660	IFRS 3.B55(a)	Ch.9, p.733
IFRS 3.B17	Ch.9, p.660	IFRS 3.B55(e)	Ch.9, p.733
IFRS 3.B18	Ch.9, p.661	IFRS 3.B56	Ch.9, p.707
IFRS 3.B18	Ch.10, p.789	IFRS 3.B56	Ch.34, p.2805
IFRS 3.B19	Ch.5, p.271	IFRS 3.B56	Ch.34, p.2808
IFRS 3.B19	Ch.9, p.740	IFRS 3.B56-B62	Ch.9, p.707
IFRS 3.B19	Ch.9, p.750	IFRS 3.B56-B62	Ch.9, p.734
IFRS 3.B19	Ch.9, p.752	IFRS 3.B56-B62	Ch.9, p.749
IFRS 3.B19	Ch.10, p.789	IFRS 3.B57-59	Ch.34, p.2805
IFRS 3.B20	Ch.9, p.740	IFRS 3.B59	Ch.34, p.2805
IFRS 3.B21	Ch.9, p.742	IFRS 3.B59	Ch.34, p.2809
IFRS 3.B22	Ch.9, p.743	IFRS 3.B60	Ch.34, p.2806
IFRS 3.B23	Ch.9, p.745	IFRS 3.B60	Ch.34, p.2809
IFRS 3.B24	Ch.9, p.745	IFRS 3.B61-62	Ch.34, p.2806
IFRS 3.B25	Ch.9, p.746	IFRS 3.B62A	Ch.7, p.541
IFRS 3.B25	Ch.37, p.3033	IFRS 3.B62A	Ch.9, p.707
IFRS 3.B26	Ch.9, p.747	IFRS 3.B62A	Ch.9, p.714
IFRS 3.B26	Ch.37, p.3033	IFRS 3.B62A-B62B	Ch.34, p.2811
IFRS 3.B27	Ch.9, p.747	IFRS 3.B62B	Ch.7, p.541
IFRS 3.B27	Ch.37, p.3033	IFRS 3.B62B	Ch.9, p.707
IFRS 3.B31	Ch.9, p.672	IFRS 3.B62B	Ch.9, p.714
IFRS 3.B31	Ch.9, p.673	IFRS 3.B63	Ch.9, p.698
IFRS 3.B32	Ch.9, p.673	IFRS 3.B63	Ch.9, p.739
IFRS 3.B32	Ch.17, p.1315	IFRS 3.B63(a)	Ch.7, p.498
IFRS 3.B32(b)	Ch.17, p.1299	IFRS 3.B63(a)	Ch.20, p.1582
IFRS 3.B33	Ch.9, p.672	IFRS 3.B63(d)	Ch.34, p.2809
IFRS 3.B33	Ch.17, p.1315	IFRS 3.B64	Ch.9, p.753
IFRS 3.B34	Ch.9, p.672	IFRS 3.B64(g)	Ch.54, p.4433
IFRS 3.B34	Ch.17, p.1315	IFRS 3.B64(h)	Ch.54, p.4433
IFRS 3.B35	Ch.9, p.684	IFRS 3.B64(o)(i)	Ch.9, p.753
IFRS 3.B36	Ch.9, p.685	IFRS 3.B65	Ch.9, p.755
IFRS 3.B36	Ch.9, p.695	IFRS 3.B65	Ch.41, p.3207

IFRS 3.B66	Ch.9, p.756
IFRS 3.B66	Ch.41, p.3207
IFRS 3.B67	Ch.9, p.756
IFRS 3.B69(e)	Ch.5, p.281
IFRS 3.IE1-IE5	Ch.9, p.740
IFRS 3.IE9	Ch.9, p.747
IFRS 3.10	Ch.9, p.747
IFRS 3.IE11-IE15	Ch.9, p.745
IFRS 3.IE16	Ch.17, p.1315
IFRS 3.IE16-IE44	Ch.9, p.673
IFRS 3.IE16-44	Ch.17, p.1315
IFRS 3.IE23-31	Ch.17, p.1297
IFRS 3.IE28	Ch.9, p.676
IFRS 3.IE30	Ch.9, p.675
IFRS 3.IE30	Ch.17, p.1317
IFRS 3.IE30(d)	Ch.55, p.4600
IFRS 3.IE30(d)	Ch.56, p.4871
IFRS 3.IE34	Ch.9, p.675
IFRS 3.IE45-IE49	Ch.9, p.725
IFRS 3.IE50-IE53	Ch.9, p.737
IFRS 3.IE54-IE57	Ch.9, p.729
IFRS 3.IE57	Ch.9, p.729
IFRS 3.IE58-IE60	Ch.9, p.733
IFRS 3.IE61-IE71	Ch.9, p.734
IFRS 3.IE61-71	Ch.34, p.2806
IFRS 3.IE72	Ch.9, p.758
IFRS 3.IE73-123	Ch.9, p.653
IFRS 3.IE74	Ch.19, p.1456
IFRS 3.IE75-76	Ch.19, p.1456
IFRS 3.IE77	Ch.19, p.1456
IFRS 3.IE78	Ch.19, p.1457
IFRS 3.BC21F	Ch.9, p.655
IFRS 3.BC21G	Ch.19, p.1454
IFRS 3.BC21H-21I	Ch.9, p.655
IFRS 3.BC21M	Ch.9, p.654
IFRS 3.BC21Q	Ch.9, p.658
IFRS 3.BC21V	Ch.19, p.1455
IFRS 3.BC21W	Ch.19, p.1455
IFRS 3.BC21Y	Ch.19, p.1456
IFRS 3.BC23	Ch.10, p.773
IFRS 3.BC58	Ch.9, p.647
IFRS 3.BC60	Ch.9, p.647
IFRS 3.BC61B-BC61D	Ch.9, p.647
IFRS 3.BC71-BC72	Ch.9, p.647
IFRS 3.BC79	Ch.9, p.647
IFRS 3.BC110	Ch.9, p.665
IFRS 3.BC112	Ch.9, p.667
IFRS 3.BC120	Ch.9, p.734
IFRS 3.BC122	Ch.9, p.728
IFRS 3.BC125-BC130	Ch.9, p.667
IFRS 3.BC132	Ch.9, p.667
IFRS 3.BC132	Ch.9, p.734
IFRS 3.BC137	Ch.9, p.667
IFRS 3.BC137	Ch.9, p.734
IFRS 3.BC146	Ch.9, p.671
IFRS 3.BC148	Ch.9, p.671
IFRS 3.BC148	Ch.19, p.1461
IFRS 3.BC149-BC156	Ch.9, p.673
IFRS 3.BC149-BC156	Ch.9, p.679
IFRS 3.BC178	Ch.9, p.685
IFRS 3.BC180	Ch.9, p.685
IFRS 3.BC182-BC184	Ch.9, p.685
IFRS 3.BC217	Ch.9, p.712
IFRS 3.BC218	Ch.9, p.713
IFRS 3.BC245	Ch.9, p.691
IFRS 3.BC258	Ch.54, p.4432
IFRS 3.BC260	Ch.54, p.4433
IFRS 3.BC275	Ch.9, p.691
IFRS 3.BC276	Ch.9, p.686
IFRS 3.BC276	Ch.20, p.1584
IFRS 3.BC296-BC300	Ch.9, p.692
IFRS 3.BC298	Ch.9, p.696
IFRS 3.BC302-BC303	Ch.9, p.693
IFRS 3.BC 303	Ch.9, p.694
IFRS 3.BC308	Ch.9, p.695
IFRS 3.BC310	Ch.9, p.695
IFRS 3.BC311	Ch.9, p.696
IFRS 3.BC311B	Ch.34, p.2808
IFRS 3.BC313	Ch.9, p.697
IFRS 3.BC313	Ch.20, p.1584
IFRS 3.BC316	Ch.9, p.697
IFRS 3.BC317	Ch.20, p.1584
IFRS 3.BC323	Ch.20, p.1583
IFRS 3.BC328	Ch.9, p.697
IFRS 3.BC337-342	Ch.9, p.699
IFRS 3.BC338-BC342	Ch.9, p.699
IFRS 3.BC342	Ch.9, p.699
IFRS 3.BC347	Ch.9, p.701
IFRS 3.BC348	Ch.9, p.701
IFRS 3.BC349	Ch.9, p.701
IFRS 3.BC357	Ch.9, p.706
IFRS 3.BC360I	Ch.9, p.707
IFRS 3.BC370	Ch.9, p.708
IFRS 3.BC370	Ch.9, p.734
IFRS 3.BC371	Ch.9, p.724
IFRS 3.BC372-BC375	Ch.9, p.724
IFRS 3.BC376-BC377	Ch.9, p.724
IFRS 3.BC379	Ch.9, p.724
IFRS 3.BC384	Ch.8, p.589
IFRS 3.BC384	Ch.9, p.717
IFRS 3.BC384	Ch.11, p.836
IFRS 3.BC392	Ch.9, p.736
IFRS 3.BC393	Ch.9, p.736

IFRS 4

IFRS 4.1	Ch.55, p.4537
IFRS 4.1	Ch.55, p.4621
IFRS 4.2	Ch.55, p.4538
IFRS 4.2(b)	Ch.45, p.3594
IFRS 4.2(b)	Ch.55, p.4539
IFRS 4.2(b)	Ch.55, p.4574
IFRS 4.3	Ch.55, p.4540
IFRS 4.4(a)	Ch.55, p.4540
IFRS 4.4(b)	Ch.55, p.4541

IFRS 4.4(c)	Ch.55, p.4541
IFRS 4.4(d)	Ch.45, p.3598
IFRS 4.4(d)	Ch.55, p.4541
IFRS 4.4(e)	Ch.55, p.4542
IFRS 4.4(f)	Ch.45, p.3599
IFRS 4.4(f)	Ch.51, p.3958
IFRS 4.4(f)	Ch.55, p.4542
IFRS 4.5	Ch.55, p.4538
IFRS 4.5	Ch.55, p.4600
IFRS 4.6	Ch.55, p.4539
IFRS 4.7	Ch.55, p.4560
IFRS 4.7	Ch.56, p.4713
IFRS 4.8	Ch.55, p.4561
IFRS 4.8	Ch.55, p.4562
IFRS 4.8	Ch.56, p.4713
IFRS 4.9	Ch.55, p.4561
IFRS 4.10	Ch.55, p.4563
IFRS 4.10-12	Ch.56, p.4715
IFRS 4.10(a)	Ch.55, p.4564
IFRS 4.10(b)	Ch.55, p.4564
IFRS 4.10(c)	Ch.55, p.4564
IFRS 4.11	Ch.55, p.4564
IFRS 4.12	Ch.55, p.4564
IFRS 4.13	Ch.55, p.4576
IFRS 4.14	Ch.55, p.4577
IFRS 4.14(a)	Ch.55, p.4577
IFRS 4.14(c)	Ch.55, p.4582
IFRS 4.14(d)	Ch.55, p.4583
IFRS 4.15	Ch.55, p.4578
IFRS 4.16	Ch.55, p.4579
IFRS 4.17	Ch.55, p.4580
IFRS 4.18	Ch.55, p.4579
IFRS 4.18	Ch.55, p.4580
IFRS 4.19	Ch.55, p.4580
IFRS 4.20	Ch.55, p.4584
IFRS 4.20A	Ch.26, p.1935
IFRS 4.20A	Ch.55, p.4601
IFRS 4.20A	Ch.55, p.4616
IFRS 4.20B	Ch.26, p.1935
IFRS 4.20B	Ch.55, p.4601
IFRS 4.20B	Ch.55, p.4603
IFRS 4.20C	Ch.55, p.4603
IFRS 4.20D	Ch.55, p.4603
IFRS 4.20E	Ch.55, p.4604
IFRS 4.20F	Ch.55, p.4604
IFRS 4.20G	Ch.55, p.4606
IFRS 4.20H	Ch.55, p.4607
IFRS 4.20I	Ch.55, p.4607
IFRS 4.20J	Ch.55, p.4607
IFRS 4.20K	Ch.55, p.4608
IFRS 4.20L	Ch.55, p.4608
IFRS 4.20L-20N	Ch.5, p.291
IFRS 4.20M	Ch.55, p.4608
IFRS 4.20N	Ch.55, p.4608
IFRS 4.20O	Ch.11, p.861
IFRS 4.20O	Ch.55, p.4609
IFRS 4.20P	Ch.11, p.861
IFRS 4.20P	Ch.55, p.4609
IFRS 4.20Q	Ch.11, p.861
IFRS 4.20Q	Ch.55, p.4609
IFRS 4.20R	Ch.55, p.4617
IFRS 4.20S	Ch.55, p.4617
IFRS 4.21	Ch.55, p.4587
IFRS 4.22	Ch.55, p.4587
IFRS 4.23	Ch.55, p.4588
IFRS 4.24	Ch.55, p.4590
IFRS 4.25	Ch.55, p.4588
IFRS 4.25(a)	Ch.55, p.4588
IFRS 4.25(b)	Ch.55, p.4589
IFRS 4.25(c)	Ch.7, p.503
IFRS 4.25(c)	Ch.55, p.4589
IFRS 4.26	Ch.55, p.4590
IFRS 4.27	Ch.55, p.4591
IFRS 4.28	Ch.55, p.4592
IFRS 4.29	Ch.55, p.4592
IFRS 4.30	Ch.55, p.4593
IFRS 4.31	Ch.55, p.4596
IFRS 4.31	Ch.56, p.4924
IFRS 4.31(a)	Ch.55, p.4596
IFRS 4.31(b)	Ch.55, p.4596
IFRS 4.32	Ch.55, p.4597
IFRS 4.33	Ch.55, p.4597
IFRS 4.33	Ch.55, p.4599
IFRS 4.34(a)-(b)	Ch.55, p.4571
IFRS 4.34(b)	Ch.56, p.4839
IFRS 4.34(c)	Ch.55, p.4571
IFRS 4.34(c)	Ch.55, p.4572
IFRS 4.34(d)-(e)	Ch.55, p.4572
IFRS 4.35(b)	Ch.55, p.4581
IFRS 4.35(d)	Ch.54, p.4411
IFRS 4.35(d)	Ch.55, p.4574
IFRS 4.35A	Ch.55, p.4600
IFRS 4.35B	Ch.55, p.4617
IFRS 4.35B	Ch.55, p.4618
IFRS 4.35C	Ch.55, p.4600
IFRS 4.35C	Ch.55, p.4617
IFRS 4.35C(b)	Ch.55, p.4601
IFRS 4.35D	Ch.55, p.4618
IFRS 4.35E	Ch.55, p.4619
IFRS 4.35F	Ch.55, p.4619
IFRS 4.35G	Ch.55, p.4619
IFRS 4.35H	Ch.55, p.4619
IFRS 4.35I	Ch.55, p.4620
IFRS 4.35J	Ch.55, p.4620
IFRS 4.35K	Ch.55, p.4620
IFRS 4.35L	Ch.55, p.4618
IFRS 4.35M	Ch.55, p.4619
IFRS 4.35N	Ch.5, p.291
IFRS 4.35N	Ch.55, p.4620
IFRS 4.36	Ch.55, p.4623
IFRS 4.37	Ch.55, p.4623
IFRS 4.37(a)	Ch.55, p.4623
IFRS 4.37(b)	Ch.40, p.3185
IFRS 4.37(b)	Ch.40, p.3186
IFRS 4.37(b)	Ch.55, p.4626
IFRS 4.37(b)(i)-(ii)	Ch.55, p.4633

IFRS 4.37(c)	Ch.55, p.4633	IFRS 4.B10	Ch.55, p.4552
IFRS 4.37(d)	Ch.55, p.4637	IFRS 4.B11	Ch.55, p.4552
IFRS 4.37(e)	Ch.55, p.4639	IFRS 4.B12	Ch.55, p.4548
IFRS 4.38	Ch.55, p.4643	IFRS 4.B13	Ch.55, p.4552
IFRS 4.39	Ch.55, p.4643	IFRS 4.B14	Ch.55, p.4553
IFRS 4.39(a)	Ch.55, p.4645	IFRS 4.B15	Ch.55, p.4553
IFRS 4.39(c)	Ch.55, p.4648	IFRS 4.B16	Ch.55, p.4553
IFRS 4.39(c)(i)	Ch.55, p.4650	IFRS 4.B17	Ch.55, p.4547
IFRS 4.39(c)(ii)	Ch.55, p.4652	IFRS 4.B18	Ch.55, p.4555
IFRS 4.39(c)(iii)	Ch.55, p.4654	IFRS 4.B18(l)	Ch.45, p.3594
IFRS 4.39(d)	Ch.55, p.4658	IFRS 4.B19	Ch.55, p.4557
IFRS 4.39(d)(i)	Ch.55, p.4661	IFRS 4.B19(a)	Ch.45, p.3594
IFRS 4.39(d)(ii)	Ch.55, p.4663	IFRS 4.B19(f)	Ch.45, p.3596
IFRS 4.39(e)	Ch.55, p.4664	IFRS 4.B19(g)	Ch.45, p.3594
IFRS 4.39D	Ch.55, p.4612	IFRS 4.B20	Ch.55, p.4554
IFRS 4.39A	Ch.55, p.4651	IFRS 4.B21	Ch.55, p.4554
IFRS 4.39B	Ch.55, p.4609	IFRS 4.B22	Ch.55, p.4544
IFRS 4.39C	Ch.55, p.4610	IFRS 4.B23	Ch.55, p.4544
IFRS 4.39E	Ch.55, p.4613	IFRS 4.B24	Ch.55, p.4548
IFRS 4.39F	Ch.55, p.4613	IFRS 4.B25	Ch.55, p.4546
IFRS 4.39G	Ch.55, p.4613	IFRS 4.B25 fn7	Ch.55, p.4547
IFRS 4.39H	Ch.55, p.4615	IFRS 4.B26	Ch.55, p.4548
IFRS 4.39I	Ch.55, p.4615	IFRS 4.B27	Ch.55, p.4549
IFRS 4.39J	Ch.55, p.4615	IFRS 4.B28	Ch.55, p.4547
IFRS 4.39K	Ch.55, p.4620	IFRS 4.B29	Ch.55, p.4549
IFRS 4.39L	Ch.55, p.4620	IFRS 4.B30	Ch.55, p.4549
IFRS 4.39M	Ch.55, p.4621	IFRS 4.IG2 E 1.3	Ch.55, p.4545
IFRS 4.40-45	Ch.5, p.290	IFRS 4.IG2 E 1.3	Ch.56, p.4702
IFRS 4.41	Ch.55, p.4535	IFRS 4.IG2 E 1.6	Ch.55, p.4556
IFRS 4.42	Ch.40, p.3185	IFRS 4.IG2 E 1.7	Ch.55, p.4549
IFRS 4.42	Ch.40, p.3186	IFRS 4.IG2 E 1.10	Ch.55, p.4557
IFRS 4.44	Ch.5, p.290	IFRS 4.IG2 E 1.11	Ch.45, p.3599
IFRS 4.45	Ch.55, p.4595	IFRS 4.IG2 E 1.12	Ch.55, p.4557
IFRS 4.46	Ch.55, p.4600	IFRS 4.IG2 E 1.13	Ch.55, p.4556
IFRS 4.46-49	Ch.5, p.291	IFRS 4.IG2 E 1.14	Ch.55, p.4558
IFRS 4.47	Ch.55, p.4610	IFRS 4.IG2 E 1.15	Ch.55, p.4551
IFRS 4.48	Ch.55, p.4600	IFRS 4.IG2 E 1.18	Ch.55, p.4558
IFRS 4.49	Ch.55, p.4618	IFRS 4.IG2 E 1.19	Ch.55, p.4558
IFRS 4.50	Ch.55, p.4616	IFRS 4.IG2 E 1.20	Ch.55, p.4552
IFRS 4.50	Ch.55, p.4617	IFRS 4.IG2 E 1.21	Ch.35, p.2909
IFRS 4.51	Ch.55, p.4617	IFRS 4.IG2 E 1.21	Ch.55, p.4558
IFRS 4 Appendix A	Ch.45, p.3593	IFRS 4.IG2 E 1.22	Ch.55, p.4556
IFRS 4 Appendix A	Ch.45, p.3594	IFRS 4.IG2 E 1.23	Ch.55, p.4548
IFRS 4 Appendix A	Ch.45, p.3596	IFRS 4.IG2 E 1.25	Ch.55, p.4556
IFRS 4 Appendix A	Ch.55, p.4537	IFRS 4.IG2 E 1.26	Ch.55, p.4556
IFRS 4 Appendix A	Ch.55, p.4543	IFRS 4.IG2 E 1.29	Ch.55, p.4553
IFRS 4 Appendix A	Ch.55, p.4551	IFRS 4.IG2 E 1.27	Ch.55, p.4559
IFRS 4 Appendix A	Ch.55, p.4563	IFRS 4.IG4 E 2.1	Ch.55, p.4561
IFRS 4 Appendix A	Ch.55, p.4568	IFRS 4.IG4 E 2.3	Ch.55, p.4562
IFRS 4 Appendix B	Ch.45, p.3593	IFRS 4.IG4 E 2.12	Ch.55, p.4562
IFRS 4.B2	Ch.55, p.4550	IFRS 4.IG4 E 2.14	Ch.55, p.4562
IFRS 4.B3	Ch.55, p.4550	IFRS 4.IG4 E 2.17	Ch.55, p.4562
IFRS 4.B4	Ch.55, p.4550	IFRS 4.IG4 E 2.18	Ch.55, p.4562
IFRS 4.B5	Ch.55, p.4550	IFRS 4.IG5	Ch.55, p.4567
IFRS 4.B6	Ch.55, p.4550	IFRS 4.IG5 E 3	Ch.55, p.4567
IFRS 4.B7	Ch.55, p.4551	IFRS 4.IG8	Ch.55, p.4593
IFRS 4.B8	Ch.55, p.4551	IFRS 4.IG9	Ch.55, p.4594
IFRS 4.B9	Ch.55, p.4551	IFRS 4.IG10	Ch.55, p.4593

IFRS 4.IG10	Ch.55, p.4594	IFRS 4.IG65B	Ch.55, p.4661
IFRS 4.IG10 E 4	Ch.55, p.4594	IFRS 4.IG65C	Ch.55, p.4661
IFRS 4.IG12	Ch.55, p.4622	IFRS 4.IG65D	Ch.55, p.4663
IFRS 4.IG13	Ch.55, p.4622	IFRS 4.IG65E	Ch.55, p.4663
IFRS 4.IG15-16	Ch.55, p.4622	IFRS 4.IG65F	Ch.55, p.4664
IFRS 4.IG17	Ch.55, p.4624	IFRS 4.IG65G	Ch.55, p.4663
IFRS 4.IG18	Ch.55, p.4626	IFRS 4.IG65G	Ch.55, p.4664
IFRS 4.IG19	Ch.55, p.4633	IFRS 4.IG66	Ch.55, p.4664
IFRS 4.IG20	Ch.55, p.4627	IFRS 4.IG67	Ch.55, p.4664
IFRS 4.IG21	Ch.55, p.4627	IFRS 4.IG68	Ch.55, p.4664
IFRS 4.IG22	Ch.55, p.4627	IFRS 4.IG69	Ch.55, p.4665
IFRS 4.IG23	Ch.55, p.4627	IFRS 4.IG70	Ch.55, p.4665
IFRS 4.IG23A	Ch.55, p.4629	IFRS 4.IG71	Ch.55, p.4667
IFRS 4.IG24	Ch.55, p.4630	IFRS 4.BC2	Ch.55, p.4533
IFRS 4.IG25	Ch.55, p.4632	IFRS 4.BC3	Ch.55, p.4533
IFRS 4.IG26	Ch.55, p.4632	IFRS 4.BC3	Ch.55, p.4534
IFRS 4.IG27	Ch.55, p.4632	IFRS 4.BC10(c)	Ch.55, p.4540
IFRS 4.IG28	Ch.55, p.4632	IFRS 4.BC12	Ch.55, p.4544
IFRS 4.IG29	Ch.55, p.4633	IFRS 4.BC13	Ch.55, p.4544
IFRS 4.IG30	Ch.55, p.4628	IFRS 4.BC26-28	Ch.55, p.4552
IFRS 4.IG30	Ch.55, p.4632	IFRS 4.BC29	Ch.55, p.4552
IFRS 4.IG31	Ch.55, p.4633	IFRS 4.BC32	Ch.55, p.4545
IFRS 4.IG32	Ch.55, p.4634	IFRS 4.BC33	Ch.55, p.4545
IFRS 4.IG33	Ch.55, p.4633	IFRS 4.BC34	Ch.55, p.4545
IFRS 4.IG34	Ch.55, p.4637	IFRS 4.BC34	Ch.55, p.4546
IFRS 4.IG35	Ch.55, p.4637	IFRS 4.BC35	Ch.55, p.4545
IFRS 4.IG36	Ch.55, p.4638	IFRS 4.BC38	Ch.55, p.4549
IFRS 4.IG37	Ch.55, p.4639	IFRS 4.BC39	Ch.55, p.4549
IFRS 4.IG38	Ch.55, p.4639	IFRS 4.BC40	Ch.55, p.4563
IFRS 4.IG39	Ch.55, p.4642	IFRS 4.BC41	Ch.55, p.4564
IFRS 4.IG40	Ch.55, p.4643	IFRS 4.BC44-46	Ch.55, p.4564
IFRS 4.IG41	Ch.55, p.4644	IFRS 4.BC54	Ch.55, p.4567
IFRS 4.IG42	Ch.55, p.4644	IFRS 4.BC69	Ch.55, p.4541
IFRS 4.IG43	Ch.55, p.4644	IFRS 4.BC71	Ch.55, p.4541
IFRS 4.IG45	Ch.55, p.4644	IFRS 4.BC73	Ch.55, p.4542
IFRS 4.IG46	Ch.55, p.4644	IFRS 4.BC77	Ch.55, p.4575
IFRS 4.IG47	Ch.55, p.4645	IFRS 4.BC79	Ch.55, p.4577
IFRS 4.IG48	Ch.55, p.4645	IFRS 4.BC81	Ch.55, p.4575
IFRS 4.IG51	Ch.55, p.4648	IFRS 4.BC82	Ch.55, p.4575
IFRS 4.IG51A	Ch.55, p.4649	IFRS 4.BC83	Ch.55, p.4575
IFRS 4.IG52	Ch.55, p.4651	IFRS 4.BC87	Ch.55, p.4577
IFRS 4.IG52A	Ch.55, p.4651	IFRS 4.BC89(d)	Ch.55, p.4578
IFRS 4.IG53	Ch.55, p.4651	IFRS 4.BC90	Ch.55, p.4578
IFRS 4.IG53A	Ch.55, p.4651	IFRS 4.BC92(a)	Ch.55, p.4578
IFRS 4.IG54A	Ch.55, p.4651	IFRS 4.BC93	Ch.55, p.4578
IFRS 4.IG55	Ch.55, p.4652	IFRS 4.BC94	Ch.55, p.4578
IFRS 4.IG56	Ch.55, p.4653	IFRS 4.BC95	Ch.55, p.4580
IFRS 4.IG57	Ch.55, p.4653	IFRS 4.BC101	Ch.55, p.4579
IFRS 4.IG58	Ch.55, p.4666	IFRS 4.BC104	Ch.55, p.4580
IFRS 4.IG59	Ch.55, p.4654	IFRS 4.BC105	Ch.55, p.4582
IFRS 4.IG60	Ch.55, p.4654	IFRS 4.BC105	Ch.55, p.4584
IFRS 4.IG61	Ch.55, p.4654	IFRS 4.BC106	Ch.55, p.4583
IFRS 4.IG61 IE 5	Ch.55, p.4654	IFRS 4.BC107-108	Ch.55, p.4583
IFRS 4.IG62	Ch.55, p.4658	IFRS 4.BC110	Ch.55, p.4585
IFRS 4.IG64	Ch.55, p.4658	IFRS 4.BC111	Ch.55, p.4585
IFRS 4.IG64A	Ch.55, p.4658	IFRS 4.BC113	Ch.55, p.4585
IFRS 4.IG64B	Ch.55, p.4666	IFRS 4.BC116	Ch.55, p.4586
IFRS 4.IG65A	Ch.55, p.4667	IFRS 4.BC120	Ch.55, p.4586

IFRS 4.BC122	Ch.55, p.4586
IFRS 4.BC123	Ch.55, p.4587
IFRS 4.BC125	Ch.55, p.4587
IFRS 4.BC126	Ch.55, p.4588
IFRS 4.BC128	Ch.55, p.4588
IFRS 4.BC129	Ch.55, p.4589
IFRS 4.BC131	Ch.55, p.4589
IFRS 4.BC132	Ch.7, p.503
IFRS 4.BC132	Ch.55, p.4589
IFRS 4.BC133	Ch.55, p.4590
IFRS 4.BC138	Ch.55, p.4591
IFRS 4.BC140	Ch.55, p.4537
IFRS 4.BC141	Ch.55, p.4592
IFRS 4.BC142	Ch.55, p.4591
IFRS 4.BC144	Ch.55, p.4592
IFRS 4.BC145	Ch.55, p.4595
IFRS 4.BC147	Ch.55, p.4596
IFRS 4.BC148	Ch.55, p.4597
IFRS 4.BC149	Ch.55, p.4597
IFRS 4.BC153	Ch.55, p.4596
IFRS 4.BC154	Ch.55, p.4569
IFRS 4.BC155	Ch.55, p.4569
IFRS 4.BC157	Ch.55, p.4571
IFRS 4.BC158	Ch.55, p.4571
IFRS 4.BC160	Ch.55, p.4570
IFRS 4.BC161	Ch.55, p.4570
IFRS 4.BC162	Ch.55, p.4569
IFRS 4.BC163	Ch.55, p.4573
IFRS 4.BC164	Ch.55, p.4571
IFRS 4.BC183	Ch.55, p.4593
IFRS 4.BC190	Ch.55, p.4560
IFRS 4.BC193	Ch.55, p.4561
IFRS 4.BC212	Ch.55, p.4633
IFRS 4.BC217	Ch.55, p.4648
IFRS 4.BC220	Ch.55, p.4654
IFRS 4.BC222	Ch.55, p.4653
IFRS 4.BC229	Ch.55, p.4600
IFRS 4.BC240	Ch.55, p.4617
IFRS 4.BC240(b)(i)	Ch.55, p.4619
IFRS 4.BC240(b)(ii)	Ch.55, p.4619
IFRS 4.BC241	Ch.55, p.4617
IFRS 4.BC252	Ch.55, p.4602
IFRS 4.BC255(a)	Ch.55, p.4604
IFRS 4.BC255(b)	Ch.55, p.4604
IFRS 4.BC256	Ch.55, p.4605
IFRS 4.BC258	Ch.55, p.4603
IFRS 4.BC264	Ch.55, p.4606
IFRS 4.BC265	Ch.55, p.4606
IFRS 4.BC266	Ch.55, p.4607
IFRS 4.BC273	Ch.55, p.4601
IFRS 4.BC277D	Ch.55, p.4616
IFRS 4.BC277E-F	Ch.55, p.4616
IFRS 4.BC277F	Ch.55, p.4616
IFRS 4.BC279	Ch.55, p.4609
IFRS 4.BC282	Ch.55, p.4608

IFRS 5

IFRS 5.1	Ch.4, p.189
IFRS 5.2	Ch.4, p.189
IFRS 5.2	Ch.4, p.191
IFRS 5.2	Ch.4, p.198
IFRS 5.3	Ch.3, p.122
IFRS 5.3	Ch.4, p.205
IFRS 5.4	Ch.4, p.190
IFRS 5.4	Ch.4, p.198
IFRS 5.5	Ch.4, p.189
IFRS 5.5	Ch.4, p.198
IFRS 5.5	Ch.7, p.532
IFRS 5.5	Ch.8, p.602
IFRS 5.5A	Ch.4, p.189
IFRS 5.5A	Ch.4, p.191
IFRS 5.5A	Ch.4, p.193
IFRS 5.5A	Ch.7, p.532
IFRS 5.5A	Ch.7, p.533
IFRS 5.5A	Ch.8, p.602
IFRS 5.5B	Ch.4, p.214
IFRS 5.5B	Ch.33, p.2621
IFRS 5.5B	Ch.36, p.3010
IFRS 5.5B	Ch.45, p.3606
IFRS 5.6	Ch.4, p.190
IFRS 5.6	Ch.4, p.191
IFRS 5.6	Ch.18, p.1427
IFRS 5.7	Ch.4, p.191
IFRS 5.7	Ch.18, p.1427
IFRS 5.8	Ch.4, p.193
IFRS 5.8	Ch.18, p.1427
IFRS 5.8A	Ch.4, p.196
IFRS 5.8A	Ch.5, p.262
IFRS 5.9	Ch.4, p.194
IFRS 5.10	Ch.4, p.191
IFRS 5.11	Ch.4, p.191
IFRS 5.12	Ch.4, p.191
IFRS 5.12	Ch.4, p.213
IFRS 5.12	Ch.38, p.3080
IFRS 5.12A	Ch.4, p.193
IFRS 5.12A	Ch.7, p.532
IFRS 5.12A	Ch.8, p.602
IFRS 5.13	Ch.4, p.191
IFRS 5.13	Ch.4, p.196
IFRS 5.13	Ch.4, p.207
IFRS 5.14	Ch.4, p.196
IFRS 5.14	Ch.4, p.207
IFRS 5.15	Ch.4, p.198
IFRS 5.15	Ch.11, p.824
IFRS 5.15	Ch.19, p.1486
IFRS 5.15A	Ch.4, p.199
IFRS 5.15A	Ch.7, p.532
IFRS 5.15A	Ch.8, p.602
IFRS 5.16	Ch.4, p.199
IFRS 5.17	Ch.4, p.198
IFRS 5.18	Ch.4, p.198
IFRS 5.18	Ch.20, p.1545
IFRS 5.19	Ch.4, p.200

IFRS 5.20	Ch.4, p.200
IFRS 5.21	Ch.4, p.200
IFRS 5.22	Ch.4, p.200
IFRS 5.23	Ch.4, p.200
IFRS 5.24	Ch.4, p.202
IFRS 5.25	Ch.4, p.199
IFRS 5.25	Ch.19, p.1486
IFRS 5.26	Ch.4, p.191
IFRS 5.26	Ch.4, p.205
IFRS 5.26A	Ch.4, p.206
IFRS 5.27	Ch.4, p.205
IFRS 5.28	Ch.4, p.206
IFRS 5.28	Ch.4, p.212
IFRS 5.28	Ch.12, p.938
IFRS 5.29	Ch.4, p.205
IFRS 5.30	Ch.3, p.123
IFRS 5.30	Ch.4, p.202
IFRS 5.31	Ch.4, p.207
IFRS 5.32	Ch.4, p.207
IFRS 5.33	Ch.5, p.327
IFRS 5.33	Ch.33, p.2611
IFRS 5.33	Ch.37, p.3062
IFRS 5.33(a)	Ch.4, p.208
IFRS 5.33(a)(ii)	Ch.3, p.136
IFRS 5.33(b)	Ch.4, p.208
IFRS 5.33(b)(ii)	Ch.33, p.2584
IFRS 5.33(c)	Ch.4, p.210
IFRS 5.33(c)	Ch.40, p.3185
IFRS 5.33(d)	Ch.4, p.208
IFRS 5.33A	Ch.4, p.208
IFRS 5.34	Ch.4, p.208
IFRS 5.34	Ch.4, p.211
IFRS 5.35	Ch.4, p.210
IFRS 5.36	Ch.4, p.213
IFRS 5.36A	Ch.4, p.196
IFRS 5.37	Ch.4, p.206
IFRS 5.37	Ch.4, p.208
IFRS 5.37	Ch.4, p.212
IFRS 5.38	Ch.4, p.203
IFRS 5.38-39	Ch.3, p.124
IFRS 5.39	Ch.4, p.203
IFRS 5.40	Ch.4, p.211
IFRS 5.41	Ch.4, p.213
IFRS 5.42	Ch.4, p.214
IFRS 5 Appendix A	Ch.4, p.190
IFRS 5 Appendix A	Ch.4, p.193
IFRS 5 Appendix A	Ch.4, p.195
IFRS 5 Appendix A	Ch.4, p.198
IFRS 5 Appendix A	Ch.4, p.205
IFRS 5 Appendix A	Ch.4, p.207
IFRS 5 Appendix A	Ch.17, p.1301
IFRS 5 Appendix A	Ch.26, p.1944
IFRS 5 Appendix A	Ch.29, p.2180
IFRS 5 Appendix A	Ch.33, p.2491
IFRS 5 Appendix B	Ch.4, p.194
IFRS 5.IG1-3	Ch.4, p.192
IFRS 5.IG4	Ch.4, p.194
IFRS 5.IG5-7	Ch.4, p.195
IFRS 5.IG8	Ch.4, p.196
IFRS 5.IG9	Ch.4, p.207
IFRS 5.IG10	Ch.4, p.200
IFRS 5.IG11	Ch.4, p.209
IFRS 5.IG12	Ch.4, p.203
IFRS 5.IG13	Ch.4, p.199
IFRS 5.BC24B-24C	Ch.4, p.197
IFRS 5.BC58	Ch.4, p.203

IFRS 6 (2010)

IFRS 6(2010).IN1	Ch.43, p.3338

IFRS 6

IFRS 6.2(b)	Ch.20, p.1521
IFRS 6.3	Ch.43, p.3401
IFRS 6.4	Ch.43, p.3393
IFRS 6.4	Ch.43, p.3397
IFRS 6.5	Ch.43, p.3360
IFRS 6.6	Ch.43, p.3361
IFRS 6.7	Ch.43, p.3361
IFRS 6.7	Ch.43, p.3401
IFRS 6.8	Ch.43, p.3367
IFRS 6.8	Ch.43, p.3418
IFRS 6.9	Ch.43, p.3362
IFRS 6.9	Ch.43, p.3368
IFRS 6.10	Ch.43, p.3362
IFRS 6.10	Ch.43, p.3368
IFRS 6.11	Ch.43, p.3369
IFRS 6.12	Ch.43, p.3367
IFRS 6.13	Ch.43, p.3367
IFRS 6.14	Ch.43, p.3367
IFRS 6.15	Ch.43, p.3365
IFRS 6.15	Ch.43, p.3370
IFRS 6.15	Ch.43, p.3373
IFRS 6.16	Ch.43, p.3371
IFRS 6.17	Ch.43, p.3363
IFRS 6.17	Ch.43, p.3365
IFRS 6.17	Ch.43, p.3371
IFRS 6.17	Ch.43, p.3373
IFRS 6.18	Ch.43, p.3372
IFRS 6.18-20	Ch.43, p.3372
IFRS 6.20	Ch.43, p.3372
IFRS 6.20	Ch.43, p.3373
IFRS 6.20	Ch.43, p.3563
IFRS 6.21	Ch.43, p.3372
IFRS 6.22	Ch.43, p.3372
IFRS 6.23	Ch.43, p.3374
IFRS 6.24	Ch.43, p.3374
IFRS 6.24(b)	Ch.40, p.3187
IFRS 6.25	Ch.43, p.3376
IFRS 6 Appendix A	Ch.43, p.3338
IFRS 6 Appendix A	Ch.43, p.3360
IFRS 6.BC6	Ch.43, p.3361
IFRS 6.BC17	Ch.43, p.3361

IFRS 6.BC17	Ch.43, p.3362	IFRS 7.11A	Ch.54, p.4426
IFRS 6.BC19	Ch.43, p.3361	IFRS 7.11A(d)	Ch.54, p.4486
IFRS 6.BC22	Ch.43, p.3362	IFRS 7.11B	Ch.54, p.4427
IFRS 6.BC23	Ch.43, p.3362	IFRS 7.12B	Ch.54, p.4427
IFRS 6.BC23B	Ch.43, p.3376	IFRS 7.12C	Ch.54, p.4427
IFRS 6.BC27	Ch.43, p.3368	IFRS 7.12D	Ch.54, p.4427
IFRS 6.BC28	Ch.43, p.3368	IFRS 7.13A	Ch.54, p.4500
IFRS 6.BC29-BC30	Ch.43, p.3368	IFRS 7.13B	Ch.54, p.4500
IFRS 6.BC33	Ch.43, p.3371	IFRS 7.13C	Ch.54, p.4501
IFRS 6.BC37	Ch.43, p.3371	IFRS 7.13D	Ch.54, p.4502
IFRS 6.BC40-BC47	Ch.43, p.3372	IFRS 7.13E	Ch.54, p.4503
IFRS 6.BC48	Ch.43, p.3374	IFRS 7.13F	Ch.54, p.4503
IFRS 6.BC49	Ch.43, p.3367	IFRS 7.14	Ch.54, p.4428
IFRS 6.BC53	Ch.43, p.3376	IFRS 7.14-15	Ch.55, p.4629
		IFRS 7.15	Ch.54, p.4428
		IFRS 7.16A	Ch.54, p.4424

IFRS 7 (2010)

IFRS 7(2010).IG3	Ch.54, p.4408

IFRS 7

IFRS 7.1	Ch.44, p.3577	IFRS 7.17	Ch.54, p.4428
IFRS 7.1	Ch.54, p.4406	IFRS 7.18	Ch.54, p.4428
IFRS 7.2	Ch.54, p.4406	IFRS 7.19	Ch.54, p.4429
IFRS 7.3	Ch.14, p.1010	IFRS 7.20	Ch.54, p.4410
IFRS 7.3	Ch.45, p.3591	IFRS 7.20(a)(i)	Ch.54, p.4489
IFRS 7.3	Ch.45, p.3594	IFRS 7.20(a)(vii)	Ch.54, p.4489
IFRS 7.3(a)	Ch.45, p.3592	IFRS 7.20(a)(viii)	Ch.54, p.4489
IFRS 7.3(a)	Ch.45, p.3593	IFRS 7.20(b)	Ch.54, p.4411
IFRS 7.3(a)	Ch.45, p.3602	IFRS 7.20(c)	Ch.54, p.4411
IFRS 7.3(b)	Ch.45, p.3605	IFRS 7.20A	Ch.54, p.4410
IFRS 7.3(d)	Ch.45, p.3593	IFRS 7.21	Ch.54, p.4409
IFRS 7.3(d)	Ch.45, p.3595	IFRS 7.21A	Ch.54, p.4412
IFRS 7.3(d)	Ch.45, p.3598	IFRS 7.21A(a)	Ch.53, p.4273
IFRS 7.3(d)	Ch.56, p.4918	IFRS 7.21B	Ch.54, p.4413
IFRS 7.3(e)	Ch.45, p.3605	IFRS 7.21C	Ch.54, p.4413
IFRS 7.4	Ch.45, p.3600	IFRS 7.21D	Ch.54, p.4412
IFRS 7.4	Ch.54, p.4406	IFRS 7.22A	Ch.54, p.4413
IFRS 7.5	Ch.45, p.3607	IFRS 7.22B	Ch.54, p.4413
IFRS 7.5	Ch.45, p.3608	IFRS 7.22C	Ch.54, p.4414
IFRS 7.5A	Ch.45, p.3607	IFRS 7.23A	Ch.54, p.4415
IFRS 7.6	Ch.54, p.4408	IFRS 7.23B	Ch.54, p.4415
IFRS 7.6	Ch.54, p.4409	IFRS 7.23C	Ch.53, p.4277
IFRS 7.7	Ch.54, p.4409	IFRS 7.23C	Ch.53, p.4278
IFRS 7.8	Ch.54, p.4424	IFRS 7.23C	Ch.54, p.4415
IFRS 7.9	Ch.54, p.4426	IFRS 7.23D	Ch.54, p.4416
IFRS 7.10(a)	Ch.54, p.4425	IFRS 7.23E	Ch.54, p.4416
IFRS 7.10(b)	Ch.54, p.4425	IFRS 7.23F	Ch.54, p.4416
IFRS 7.10(c)	Ch.54, p.4425	IFRS 7.24A	Ch.54, p.4416
IFRS 7.10(d)	Ch.54, p.4425	IFRS 7.24B	Ch.54, p.4417
IFRS 7.10A(a)	Ch.54, p.4425	IFRS 7.24C	Ch.54, p.4418
IFRS 7.10A(b)	Ch.54, p.4425	IFRS 7.24D	Ch.54, p.4415
IFRS 7.11	Ch.54, p.4426	IFRS 7.24E	Ch.54, p.4420
IFRS 7.11(a)	Ch.54, p.4425	IFRS 7.24F	Ch.54, p.4421
IFRS 7.11(b)	Ch.54, p.4425	IFRS 7.24G	Ch.53, p.4388
IFRS 7.11(c)	Ch.54, p.4425	IFRS 7.24G	Ch.54, p.4423
		IFRS 7.24H	Ch.54, p.4423
		IFRS 7.24I	Ch.54, p.4473
		IFRS 7.24J	Ch.54, p.4473
		IFRS 7.25	Ch.14, p.1009
		IFRS 7.25	Ch.14, p.1010
		IFRS 7.25	Ch.41, p.3223
		IFRS 7.25	Ch.54, p.4429

IFRS 7.26	Ch.41, p.3223	IFRS 7.35H(c)	Ch.51, p.3931
IFRS 7.26	Ch.54, p.4429	IFRS 7.35I	Ch.51, p.4074
IFRS 7.28	Ch.41, p.3223	IFRS 7.35I	Ch.54, p.4442
IFRS 7.28	Ch.54, p.4430	IFRS 7.35J	Ch.54, p.4442
IFRS 7.29	Ch.14, p.1009	IFRS 7.35K	Ch.51, p.4074
IFRS 7.29(a)	Ch.14, p.1010	IFRS 7.35K	Ch.54, p.4444
IFRS 7.29(a)	Ch.41, p.3223	IFRS 7.35K(a)	Ch.56, p.4917
IFRS 7.29(a)	Ch.54, p.4430	IFRS 7.35K(c)	Ch.51, p.3928
IFRS 7.29(c)	Ch.41, p.3223	IFRS 7.35L	Ch.51, p.4070
IFRS 7.29(c)	Ch.54, p.4430	IFRS 7.35L	Ch.51, p.4075
IFRS 7.29(c)	Ch.55, p.4574	IFRS 7.35L	Ch.54, p.4446
IFRS 7.29(c)	Ch.55, p.4667	IFRS 7.35M	Ch.51, p.4075
IFRS 7.29(d)	Ch.14, p.1010	IFRS 7.35M	Ch.54, p.4446
IFRS 7.29(d)	Ch.54, p.4430	IFRS 7.35N	Ch.54, p.4446
IFRS 7.30	Ch.54, p.4430	IFRS 7.36	Ch.13, p.987
IFRS 7.30	Ch.55, p.4667	IFRS 7.36-38	Ch.55, p.4659
IFRS 7.31	Ch.54, p.4433	IFRS 7.36(a)	Ch.51, p.4050
IFRS 7.31-42	Ch.15, p.1244	IFRS 7.36(a)	Ch.54, p.4449
IFRS 7.32	Ch.54, p.4433	IFRS 7.36(b)	Ch.54, p.4449
IFRS 7.32A	Ch.54, p.4433	IFRS 7.38	Ch.54, p.4449
IFRS 7.33(a)	Ch.54, p.4435	IFRS 7.39	Ch.40, p.3152
IFRS 7.33(b)	Ch.54, p.4435	IFRS 7.39	Ch.40, p.3158
IFRS 7.33(c)	Ch.54, p.4436	IFRS 7.39	Ch.55, p.4661
IFRS 7.33-35	Ch.40, p.3158	IFRS 7.39(a)	Ch.54, p.4454
IFRS 7.34(a)	Ch.54, p.4438	IFRS 7.39(b)	Ch.54, p.4454
IFRS 7.34(b)	Ch.54, p.4438	IFRS 7.39(c)	Ch.54, p.4462
IFRS 7.34(c)	Ch.54, p.4471	IFRS 7.40	Ch.54, p.4463
IFRS 7.35	Ch.54, p.4438	IFRS 7.40	Ch.55, p.4663
IFRS 7.35A	Ch.54, p.4439	IFRS 7.41	Ch.54, p.4469
IFRS 7.35A(a)	Ch.32, p.2399	IFRS 7.41	Ch.55, p.4663
IFRS 7.35A(a)	Ch.54, p.4444	IFRS 7.42	Ch.54, p.4470
IFRS 7.35A(b)	Ch.54, p.4445	IFRS 7.42	Ch.55, p.4663
IFRS 7.35B	Ch.51, p.4074	IFRS 7.42A	Ch.54, p.4474
IFRS 7.35B	Ch.54, p.4439	IFRS 7.42B	Ch.54, p.4474
IFRS 7.35C	Ch.54, p.4439	IFRS 7.42C	Ch.54, p.4477
IFRS 7.35D	Ch.54, p.4439	IFRS 7.42D	Ch.54, p.4475
IFRS 7.35E	Ch.54, p.4439	IFRS 7.42E	Ch.54, p.4478
IFRS 7.35F	Ch.54, p.4440	IFRS 7.42F	Ch.54, p.4480
IFRS 7.35F(a)	Ch.51, p.3969	IFRS 7.42G	Ch.54, p.4480
IFRS 7.35F(a)	Ch.51, p.4074	IFRS 7.42G	Ch.54, p.4481
IFRS 7.35F(b)	Ch.51, p.4074	IFRS 7.42H	Ch.54, p.4474
IFRS 7.35F(c)	Ch.51, p.4074	IFRS 7.42R	Ch.5, p.262
IFRS 7.35F(d)	Ch.51, p.4074	IFRS 7.42R	Ch.5, p.356
IFRS 7.35F(e)	Ch.51, p.4070	IFRS 7.42S	Ch.5, p.263
IFRS 7.35F(e)	Ch.51, p.4075	IFRS 7.42S	Ch.5, p.357
IFRS 7.35F(f)	Ch.51, p.4034	IFRS 7.44DE	Ch.54, p.4520
IFRS 7.35F(f)	Ch.51, p.4075	IFRS 7.44DF	Ch.54, p.4520
IFRS 7.35G	Ch.51, p.4050	IFRS 7.44GG	Ch.54, p.4520
IFRS 7.35G	Ch.54, p.4440	IFRS 7.44HH	Ch.54, p.4520
IFRS 7.35G(a)(i)	Ch.51, p.4074	IFRS 7 Appendix A	Ch.50, p.3872
IFRS 7.35G(a)(ii)	Ch.51, p.3969	IFRS 7 Appendix A	Ch.53, p.4285
IFRS 7.35G(a)(ii)	Ch.51, p.4074	IFRS 7 Appendix A	Ch.54, p.4428
IFRS 7.35G(a)(iii)	Ch.51, p.4074	IFRS 7 Appendix A	Ch.54, p.4434
IFRS 7.35G(b)	Ch.51, p.4074	IFRS 7 Appendix A	Ch.54, p.4448
IFRS 7.35G(c)	Ch.51, p.3969	IFRS 7 Appendix A	Ch.56, p.4915
IFRS 7.35G(c)	Ch.51, p.4074	IFRS 7.B1	Ch.54, p.4408
IFRS 7.35H	Ch.51, p.4074	IFRS 7.B2	Ch.54, p.4409
IFRS 7.35H	Ch.54, p.4441	IFRS 7.B3	Ch.54, p.4408

Index of standards

IFRS 7.B5	Ch.54, p.4410
IFRS 7.B5(a)	Ch.54, p.4409
IFRS 7.B5(c)	Ch.54, p.4409
IFRS 7.B5(e)	Ch.54, p.4409
IFRS 7.B5(f)	Ch.54, p.4409
IFRS 7.B5(g)	Ch.54, p.4409
IFRS 7.B5(aa)	Ch.54, p.4409
IFRS 7.B6	Ch.54, p.4435
IFRS 7.B6-B24	Ch.15, p.1244
IFRS 7.B7	Ch.54, p.4438
IFRS 7.B8	Ch.54, p.4472
IFRS 7.B8A	Ch.51, p.4074
IFRS 7.B8A	Ch.54, p.4440
IFRS 7.B8B	Ch.51, p.4034
IFRS 7.B8B	Ch.51, p.4075
IFRS 7.B8B	Ch.54, p.4440
IFRS 7.B8C	Ch.54, p.4441
IFRS 7.B8D	Ch.54, p.4442
IFRS 7.B8E	Ch.51, p.4073
IFRS 7.B8E	Ch.54, p.4442
IFRS 7.B8F	Ch.51, p.4074
IFRS 7.B8F	Ch.54, p.4445
IFRS 7.B8G	Ch.51, p.4074
IFRS 7.B8G	Ch.54, p.4445
IFRS 7.B8H	Ch.51, p.4075
IFRS 7.B8H	Ch.54, p.4448
IFRS 7.B8I	Ch.51, p.4075
IFRS 7.B8I	Ch.54, p.4448
IFRS 7.B8J	Ch.54, p.4448
IFRS 7.B9	Ch.54, p.4445
IFRS 7.B10	Ch.54, p.4445
IFRS 7.B10A	Ch.54, p.4454
IFRS 7.B11	Ch.54, p.4454
IFRS 7.B11A	Ch.54, p.4458
IFRS 7.B11B	Ch.54, p.4454
IFRS 7.B11C(a)	Ch.54, p.4455
IFRS 7.B11C(b)	Ch.54, p.4456
IFRS 7.B11C(c)	Ch.54, p.4456
IFRS 7.B11C(c)	Ch.54, p.4458
IFRS 7.B11D	Ch.54, p.4456
IFRS 7.B11D	Ch.55, p.4661
IFRS 7.B11E	Ch.54, p.4462
IFRS 7.B11E	Ch.55, p.4661
IFRS 7.B11F	Ch.40, p.3158
IFRS 7.B11F	Ch.54, p.4462
IFRS 7.B17	Ch.54, p.4464
IFRS 7.B18	Ch.54, p.4465
IFRS 7.B19	Ch.54, p.4467
IFRS 7.B20	Ch.54, p.4469
IFRS 7.B21	Ch.54, p.4463
IFRS 7.B22	Ch.54, p.4434
IFRS 7.B23	Ch.54, p.4434
IFRS 7.B24	Ch.54, p.4464
IFRS 7.B25	Ch.54, p.4434
IFRS 7.B25	Ch.54, p.4467
IFRS 7.B26	Ch.54, p.4434
IFRS 7.B27	Ch.54, p.4464
IFRS 7.B28	Ch.54, p.4463
IFRS 7.B29	Ch.54, p.4478
IFRS 7.B30	Ch.54, p.4478
IFRS 7.B30A	Ch.54, p.4478
IFRS 7.B31	Ch.54, p.4478
IFRS 7.B32	Ch.54, p.4475
IFRS 7.B33	Ch.54, p.4480
IFRS 7.B34	Ch.54, p.4479
IFRS 7.B35	Ch.54, p.4479
IFRS 7.35J	Ch.51, p.4034
IFRS 7.35J	Ch.51, p.4075
IFRS 7.B36	Ch.54, p.4479
IFRS 7.B37	Ch.54, p.4479
IFRS 7.B38	Ch.54, p.4481
IFRS 7.B39	Ch.54, p.4474
IFRS 7.B40	Ch.54, p.4500
IFRS 7.B41	Ch.54, p.4501
IFRS 7.B42	Ch.54, p.4503
IFRS 7.B43	Ch.54, p.4501
IFRS 7.B44	Ch.54, p.4502
IFRS 7.B45	Ch.54, p.4502
IFRS 7.B46	Ch.54, p.4502
IFRS 7.B47	Ch.54, p.4502
IFRS 7.B48	Ch.54, p.4502
IFRS 7.B49	Ch.54, p.4503
IFRS 7.B50	Ch.54, p.4503
IFRS 7.B51	Ch.54, p.4503
IFRS 7.B52	Ch.54, p.4503
IFRS 7.B53	Ch.54, p.4500
IFRS 7.IG1	Ch.54, p.4407
IFRS 7.IG2	Ch.54, p.4407
IFRS 7.IG5	Ch.54, p.4408
IFRS 7.IG6	Ch.54, p.4408
IFRS 7.IG12	Ch.54, p.4429
IFRS 7.IG13	Ch.54, p.4483
IFRS 7.IG13C	Ch.54, p.4416
IFRS 7.IG13D	Ch.54, p.4417
IFRS 7.IG13E	Ch.54, p.4418
IFRS 7.IG14	Ch.54, p.4430
IFRS 7.IG14	Ch.54, p.4431
IFRS 7.IG15	Ch.54, p.4436
IFRS 7.IG16	Ch.54, p.4436
IFRS 7.IG17	Ch.54, p.4436
IFRS 7.IG18	Ch.54, p.4472
IFRS 7.IG19	Ch.54, p.4471
IFRS 7.IG20	Ch.54, p.4438
IFRS 7.IG20B	Ch.54, p.4443
IFRS 7.IG20C	Ch.54, p.4446
IFRS 7.IG20D	Ch.54, p.4446
IFRS 7.IG21	Ch.54, p.4439
IFRS 7.IG22	Ch.54, p.4449
IFRS 7.IG31A	Ch.54, p.4455
IFRS 7.IG32	Ch.54, p.4434
IFRS 7.IG32	Ch.54, p.4464
IFRS 7.IG33	Ch.54, p.4466
IFRS 7.IG34	Ch.54, p.4466
IFRS 7.IG35	Ch.54, p.4467
IFRS 7.IG36	Ch.54, p.4467
IFRS 7.IG37(a)	Ch.54, p.4470

IFRS 7.IG37(b)	Ch.54, p.4471	IFRS 8.2	Ch.36, p.2982
IFRS 7.IG37(c)	Ch.54, p.4471	IFRS 8.2(b)	Ch.36, p.2982
IFRS 7.IG38	Ch.54, p.4471	IFRS 8.3	Ch.36, p.2983
IFRS 7.IG39	Ch.54, p.4471	IFRS 8.4	Ch.36, p.2983
IFRS 7.IG40	Ch.54, p.4471	IFRS 8.5	Ch.20, p.1587
IFRS 7.IG40C	Ch.54, p.4476	IFRS 8.5	Ch.20, p.1588
IFRS 7.IG40C	Ch.54, p.4480	IFRS 8.5	Ch.36, p.2978
IFRS 7.IG40D	Ch.54, p.4503	IFRS 8.5	Ch.36, p.2980
IFRS 7.BC6	Ch.54, p.4406	IFRS 8.5	Ch.36, p.2984
IFRS 7.BC8	Ch.45, p.3602	IFRS 8.5	Ch.36, p.2996
IFRS 7.BC9	Ch.54, p.4406	IFRS 8.5(a)	Ch.36, p.2979
IFRS 7.BC10	Ch.54, p.4406	IFRS 8.5(b)	Ch.32, p.2411
IFRS 7.BC10	Ch.54, p.4408	IFRS 8.5(b)	Ch.36, p.2987
IFRS 7.BC11	Ch.54, p.4406	IFRS 8.5(b)	Ch.36, p.2989
IFRS 7.BC13	Ch.54, p.4409	IFRS 8.5(c)	Ch.36, p.2987
IFRS 7.BC14	Ch.54, p.4424	IFRS 8.6	Ch.36, p.2984
IFRS 7.BC15	Ch.54, p.4424	IFRS 8.7	Ch.36, p.2980
IFRS 7.BC22	Ch.54, p.4425	IFRS 8.7	Ch.36, p.2984
IFRS 7.BC25	Ch.54, p.4428	IFRS 8.7	Ch.36, p.2985
IFRS 7.BC31	Ch.54, p.4428	IFRS 8.8	Ch.36, p.2983
IFRS 7.BC32	Ch.54, p.4428	IFRS 8.8	Ch.36, p.2986
IFRS 7.BC33	Ch.54, p.4411	IFRS 8.8	Ch.36, p.2988
IFRS 7.BC34	Ch.54, p.4411	IFRS 8.9	Ch.36, p.2980
IFRS 7.BC35	Ch.54, p.4412	IFRS 8.9	Ch.36, p.2985
IFRS 7.BC35C	Ch.54, p.4412	IFRS 8.9	Ch.36, p.2988
IFRS 7.BC35O	Ch.54, p.4520	IFRS 8.10	Ch.20, p.1587
IFRS 7.BC35P	Ch.54, p.4412	IFRS 8.10	Ch.36, p.2979
IFRS 7.BC35U	Ch.54, p.4416	IFRS 8.10	Ch.36, p.2988
IFRS 7.BC35W	Ch.54, p.4416	IFRS 8.11	Ch.36, p.2981
IFRS 7.BC35X	Ch.54, p.4416	IFRS 8.11	Ch.36, p.3000
IFRS 7.BC36	Ch.54, p.4429	IFRS 8.11-12	Ch.20, p.1587
IFRS 7.BC40(b)	Ch.54, p.4435	IFRS 8.12	Ch.20, p.1588
IFRS 7.BC41	Ch.54, p.4435	IFRS 8.12	Ch.36, p.2981
IFRS 7.BC42	Ch.54, p.4435	IFRS 8.12	Ch.36, p.2986
IFRS 7.BC43	Ch.54, p.4435	IFRS 8.12	Ch.36, p.2992
IFRS 7.BC44	Ch.54, p.4435	IFRS 8.12	Ch.36, p.2995
IFRS 7.BC45	Ch.54, p.4435	IFRS 8.13	Ch.36, p.2981
IFRS 7.BC46	Ch.54, p.4435	IFRS 8.13	Ch.36, p.2996
IFRS 7.BC47	Ch.54, p.4438	IFRS 8.13	Ch.36, p.2997
IFRS 7.BC47A	Ch.54, p.4408	IFRS 8.14	Ch.36, p.2997
IFRS 7.BC48	Ch.54, p.4438	IFRS 8.15	Ch.36, p.2998
IFRS 7.BC56	Ch.54, p.4449	IFRS 8.16	Ch.36, p.2997
IFRS 7.BC57	Ch.54, p.4455	IFRS 8.16	Ch.36, p.2998
IFRS 7.BC58A(a)	Ch.54, p.4457	IFRS 8.16	Ch.36, p.3001
IFRS 7.BC58A(b)	Ch.54, p.4454	IFRS 8.16	Ch.36, p.3007
IFRS 7.BC58D	Ch.54, p.4462	IFRS 8.17	Ch.36, p.2990
IFRS 7.BC59	Ch.54, p.4463	IFRS 8.18	Ch.36, p.2998
IFRS 7.BC61	Ch.54, p.4469	IFRS 8.19	Ch.36, p.2998
IFRS 7.BC65	Ch.54, p.4472	IFRS 8.20	Ch.32, p.2411
IFRS 7.BC72B	Ch.54, p.4407	IFRS 8.20	Ch.36, p.3000
IFRS 7.BC72C	Ch.54, p.4407	IFRS 8.21	Ch.36, p.3000
		IFRS 8.22	Ch.36, p.2979

IFRS 8

		IFRS 8.22	Ch.36, p.3001
		IFRS 8.22(aa)	Ch.36, p.3001
IFRS 8.1	Ch.36, p.2981	IFRS 8.23	Ch.36, p.2979
IFRS 8.1	Ch.36, p.2989	IFRS 8.23	Ch.36, p.2997
IFRS 8.1	Ch.36, p.3012	IFRS 8.23	Ch.36, p.3002

IFRS 8.23	Ch.36, p.3003	IFRS 9.2.1	Ch.45, p.3591
IFRS 8.23-24	Ch.36, p.3004	IFRS 9.2.1	Ch.51, p.4046
IFRS 8.23(g)	Ch.36, p.2989	IFRS 9.2.1(a)	Ch.7, p.499
IFRS 8.24	Ch.36, p.3005	IFRS 9.2.1(a)	Ch.7, p.550
IFRS 8.24(a)	Ch.36, p.2989	IFRS 9.2.1(a)	Ch.11, p.876
IFRS 8.25	Ch.36, p.2999	IFRS 9.2.1(a)	Ch.11, p.877
IFRS 8.25	Ch.36, p.3010	IFRS 9.2.1(a)	Ch.45, p.3592
IFRS 8.26	Ch.36, p.2999	IFRS 9.2.1(a)	Ch.45, p.3593
IFRS 8.27	Ch.36, p.3005	IFRS 9.2.1(b)	Ch.45, p.3593
IFRS 8.27	Ch.36, p.3006	IFRS 9.2.1(b)	Ch.51, p.4046
IFRS 8.27-28	Ch.36, p.3000	IFRS 9.2.1(b)(i)	Ch.52, p.4088
IFRS 8.27(f)	Ch.36, p.2999	IFRS 9.2.1(b)(ii)	Ch.52, p.4088
IFRS 8.28	Ch.36, p.3007	IFRS 9.2.1(c)	Ch.45, p.3605
IFRS 8.29	Ch.36, p.3009	IFRS 9.2.1(d)	Ch.45, p.3602
IFRS 8.30	Ch.36, p.3009	IFRS 9.2.1(e)	Ch.26, p.1935
IFRS 8.31	Ch.36, p.2979	IFRS 9.2.1(e)	Ch.45, p.3593
IFRS 8.31	Ch.36, p.3012	IFRS 9.2.1(e)	Ch.45, p.3594
IFRS 8.32	Ch.36, p.3013	IFRS 9.2.1(e)	Ch.45, p.3595
IFRS 8.32-34	Ch.36, p.2979	IFRS 9.2.1(e)(iv)	Ch.45, p.3595
IFRS 8.32-33	Ch.36, p.3012	IFRS 9.2.1(e)	Ch.45, p.3598
IFRS 8.33	Ch.36, p.3013	IFRS 9.2.1(e)	Ch.45, p.3599
IFRS 8.33	Ch.36, p.3014	IFRS 9.2.1(e)(iv)	Ch.48, p.3837
IFRS 8.34	Ch.36, p.3014	IFRS 9.2.1(e)	Ch.51, p.3958
IFRS 8.34	Ch.36, p.3015	IFRS 9.2.1(e)	Ch.55, p.4539
IFRS 8.35	Ch.36, p.2977	IFRS 9.2.1(e)(iv)	Ch.56, p.4692
IFRS 8.36	Ch.36, p.2981	IFRS 9.2.1(f)	Ch.45, p.3603
IFRS 8 Appendix A	Ch.36, p.2980	IFRS 9.2.1(g)	Ch.45, p.3600
IFRS 8.D01-D04	Ch.36, p.2977	IFRS 9.2.1(g)	Ch.49, p.3861
IFRS 8.IG7	Ch.36, p.2991	IFRS 9.2.1(g)	Ch.50, p.3879
IFRS 8.BC22	Ch.36, p.2983	IFRS 9.2.1(g)	Ch.51, p.3924
IFRS 8.BC23	Ch.36, p.2982	IFRS 9.2.1(g)	Ch.51, p.4049
IFRS 8.BC27	Ch.36, p.2988	IFRS 9.2.1(g)	Ch.52, p.4088
IFRS 8.BC30	Ch.36, p.2992	IFRS 9.2.1(h)	Ch.45, p.3605
IFRS 8.BC32	Ch.36, p.2992	IFRS 9.2.1(i)	Ch.45, p.3606
IFRS 8.BC43-45	Ch.36, p.2979	IFRS 9.2.1(j)	Ch.45, p.3606
IFRS 8.BC43-45	Ch.36, p.2992	IFRS 9.2.1(j)	Ch.52, p.4089
IFRS 8.BC44	Ch.36, p.3012	IFRS 9.2.3	Ch.50, p.3879
IFRS 8.BC46-47	Ch.36, p.3012	IFRS 9.2.3	Ch.51, p.3924
IFRS 8.BC Appendix A 72	Ch.36, p.2979	IFRS 9.2.3	Ch.51, p.4049
IFRS 8.BC Appendix A 73	Ch.36, p.2992	IFRS 9.2.3(a)	Ch.45, p.3600
		IFRS 9.2.3(b)	Ch.45, p.3600
		IFRS 9.2.3(b)	Ch.45, p.3601
		IFRS 9.2.3(c)	Ch.45, p.3600
IFRS 9 (2012)		IFRS 9.2.3(c)	Ch.50, p.3879
IFRS 9(2012).B5.4.12	Ch.14, p.1009	IFRS 9.2.3(c)	Ch.51, p.4049
		IFRS 9.2.4	Ch.17, p.1366
		IFRS 9.2.4	Ch.42, p.3297
IFRS 9 (2022)		IFRS 9.2.4	Ch.43, p.3456
IFRS 9(2022).7.1.9	Ch.52, p.4158	IFRS 9.2.4	Ch.43, p.3473
IFRS 9(2022).7.2.35	Ch.52, p.4158	IFRS 9.2.4	Ch.45, p.3607
IFRS 9(2022).B3.3.6	Ch.52, p.4158	IFRS 9.2.4	Ch.45, p.3608
IFRS 9(2022).B3.3.6A	Ch.52, p.4161	IFRS 9.2.4	Ch.45, p.3609
		IFRS 9.2.4	Ch.53, p.4388
		IFRS 9.2.5	Ch.5, p.342
IFRS 9		IFRS 9.2.5	Ch.43, p.3474
IFRS 9.1.1	Ch.44, p.3577	IFRS 9.2.5	Ch.45, p.3613
		IFRS 9.2.5	Ch.53, p.4389
		IFRS 9.2.6	Ch.43, p.3473

IFRS 9.2.6	Ch.43, p.3474
IFRS 9.2.6	Ch.45, p.3608
IFRS 9.2.6	Ch.45, p.3609
IFRS 9.2.6(b)	Ch.43, p.3457
IFRS 9.2.6(c)	Ch.43, p.3457
IFRS 9.2.7	Ch.43, p.3474
IFRS 9.2.7	Ch.45, p.3610
IFRS 9.3.1.1	Ch.15, p.1188
IFRS 9.3.1.1	Ch.48, p.3812
IFRS 9.3.1.1	Ch.49, p.3841
IFRS 9.3.1.1	Ch.49, p.3845
IFRS 9.3.1.1	Ch.50, p.3880
IFRS 9.3.1.2	Ch.50, p.3880
IFRS 9.3.2.1	Ch.53, p.4364
IFRS 9.3.2.2	Ch.52, p.4093
IFRS 9.3.2.2	Ch.52, p.4098
IFRS 9.3.2.2(b)	Ch.52, p.4105
IFRS 9.3.2.3	Ch.50, p.3880
IFRS 9.3.2.3	Ch.52, p.4099
IFRS 9.3.2.4	Ch.52, p.4103
IFRS 9.3.2.5	Ch.52, p.4108
IFRS 9.3.2.6	Ch.52, p.4114
IFRS 9.3.2.6(a)	Ch.52, p.4114
IFRS 9.3.2.6(b)	Ch.52, p.4114
IFRS 9.3.2.6(c)	Ch.52, p.4114
IFRS 9.3.2.6(c)	Ch.52, p.4119
IFRS 9.3.2.7	Ch.52, p.4114
IFRS 9.3.2.7	Ch.52, p.4115
IFRS 9.3.2.8	Ch.52, p.4114
IFRS 9.3.2.9	Ch.52, p.4119
IFRS 9.3.2.10	Ch.52, p.4132
IFRS 9.3.2.11	Ch.52, p.4129
IFRS 9.3.2.12	Ch.51, p.4015
IFRS 9.3.2.12	Ch.52, p.4129
IFRS 9.3.2.13	Ch.52, p.4130
IFRS 9.3.2.13	Ch.52, p.4140
IFRS 9.3.2.14	Ch.52, p.4131
IFRS 9.3.2.15	Ch.52, p.4134
IFRS 9.3.2.16	Ch.52, p.4138
IFRS 9.3.2.16(a)	Ch.52, p.4138
IFRS 9.3.2.16(b)-(c)	Ch.52, p.4139
IFRS 9.3.2.17	Ch.52, p.4139
IFRS 9.3.2.18	Ch.52, p.4139
IFRS 9.3.2.19	Ch.52, p.4139
IFRS 9.3.2.21	Ch.52, p.4140
IFRS 9.3.2.22	Ch.40, p.3155
IFRS 9.3.2.22	Ch.52, p.4151
IFRS 9.3.2.23	Ch.52, p.4152
IFRS 9.3.3.1	Ch.47, p.3671
IFRS 9.3.3.1	Ch.49, p.3847
IFRS 9.3.3.1	Ch.52, p.4099
IFRS 9.3.3.1	Ch.52, p.4154
IFRS 9.3.3.1	Ch.55, p.4582
IFRS 9.3.3.2	Ch.52, p.4099
IFRS 9.3.3.2	Ch.52, p.4157
IFRS 9.3.3.3	Ch.52, p.4166
IFRS 9.3.3.4	Ch.52, p.4166
IFRS 9.3.3.5	Ch.52, p.4171
IFRS 9.3.3.5	Ch.56, p.4695
IFRS 9.4.1.1	Ch.48, p.3771
IFRS 9.4.1.1	Ch.50, p.3869
IFRS 9.4.1.2	Ch.5, p.262
IFRS 9.4.1.2	Ch.48, p.3774
IFRS 9.4.1.2	Ch.48, p.3780
IFRS 9.4.1.2	Ch.51, p.3924
IFRS 9.4.1.2-2A	Ch.51, p.3974
IFRS 9.4.1.2(b)	Ch.50, p.3889
IFRS 9.4.1.2(b)	Ch.53, p.4289
IFRS 9.4.1.2A	Ch.5, p.262
IFRS 9.4.1.2A	Ch.5, p.263
IFRS 9.4.1.2A	Ch.33, p.2579
IFRS 9.4.1.2A	Ch.48, p.3774
IFRS 9.4.1.2A	Ch.48, p.3783
IFRS 9.4.1.2A	Ch.51, p.3924
IFRS 9.4.1.2A	Ch.51, p.4036
IFRS 9.4.1.2A	Ch.51, p.4074
IFRS 9.4.1.2A	Ch.53, p.4220
IFRS 9.4.1.2A(b)	Ch.53, p.4289
IFRS 9.4.1.3(a)	Ch.48, p.3791
IFRS 9.4.1.3(b)	Ch.48, p.3792
IFRS 9.4.1.4	Ch.43, p.3410
IFRS 9.4.1.4	Ch.48, p.3774
IFRS 9.4.1.4	Ch.53, p.4289
IFRS 9.4.1.5	Ch.5, p.314
IFRS 9.4.1.5	Ch.48, p.3774
IFRS 9.4.1.5	Ch.48, p.3826
IFRS 9.4.2.1	Ch.7, p.555
IFRS 9.4.2.1	Ch.48, p.3777
IFRS 9.4.2.1	Ch.50, p.3869
IFRS 9.4.2.1-2	Ch.7, p.539
IFRS 9.4.2.1(a)	Ch.51, p.3924
IFRS 9.4.2.1(a)	Ch.50, p.3879
IFRS 9.4.2.1(b)	Ch.50, p.3881
IFRS 9.4.2.1(c)	Ch.50, p.3879
IFRS 9.4.2.1(c)	Ch.51, p.4048
IFRS 9.4.2.1(c)-(d)	Ch.53, p.4388
IFRS 9.4.2.1(d)	Ch.51, p.3924
IFRS 9.4.2.1(d)	Ch.50, p.3879
IFRS 9.4.2.1(d)	Ch.51, p.4049
IFRS 9.4.2.1(d)	Ch.45, p.3600
IFRS 9.4.2.1(d)	Ch.51, p.4048
IFRS 9.4.2.1(d)	Ch.51, p.4050
IFRS 9.4.2.1(e)	Ch.7, p.539
IFRS 9.4.2.2	Ch.5, p.315
IFRS 9.4.2.2	Ch.7, p.555
IFRS 9.4.2.2	Ch.48, p.3776
IFRS 9.4.2.2(a)	Ch.48, p.3826
IFRS 9.4.2.2(b)	Ch.48, p.3784
IFRS 9.4.2.2(b)	Ch.48, p.3826
IFRS 9.4.2.2(b)	Ch.48, p.3828
IFRS 9.4.3.1	Ch.43, p.3475
IFRS 9.4.3.1	Ch.46, p.3629
IFRS 9.4.3.1	Ch.46, p.3630
IFRS 9.4.3.1	Ch.46, p.3653
IFRS 9.4.3.1	Ch.55, p.4559
IFRS 9.4.3.1	Ch.56, p.4713

Index of standards

IFRS 9.4.3.2	Ch.46, p.3629
IFRS 9.4.3.2	Ch.46, p.3631
IFRS 9.4.3.2	Ch.46, p.3641
IFRS 9.4.3.2	Ch.48, p.3774
IFRS 9.4.3.3	Ch.5, p.264
IFRS 9.4.3.3	Ch.46, p.3629
IFRS 9.4.3.3	Ch.46, p.3630
IFRS 9.4.3.3	Ch.50, p.3889
IFRS 9.4.3.3	Ch.55, p.4560
IFRS 9.4.3.3	Ch.56, p.4712
IFRS 9.4.3.4	Ch.54, p.4488
IFRS 9.4.3.4	Ch.54, p.4509
IFRS 9.4.3.5	Ch.48, p.3776
IFRS 9.4.3.5	Ch.48, p.3826
IFRS 9.4.3.5	Ch.48, p.3829
IFRS 9.4.3.6	Ch.5, p.264
IFRS 9.4.3.6	Ch.46, p.3630
IFRS 9.4.3.7	Ch.46, p.3630
IFRS 9.4.4.1	Ch.48, p.3832
IFRS 9.4.4.1	Ch.55, p.4595
IFRS 9.5.1.1	Ch.7, p.509
IFRS 9.5.1.1	Ch.8, p.627
IFRS 9.5.1.1	Ch.8, p.629
IFRS 9.5.1.1	Ch.14, p.1052
IFRS 9.5.1.1	Ch.24, p.1832
IFRS 9.5.1.1	Ch.25, p.1875
IFRS 9.5.1.1	Ch.25, p.1909
IFRS 9.5.1.1	Ch.25, p.1910
IFRS 9.5.1.1	Ch.25, p.1913
IFRS 9.5.1.1	Ch.26, p.2007
IFRS 9.5.1.1	Ch.32, p.2399
IFRS 9.5.1.1	Ch.49, p.3854
IFRS 9.5.1.1	Ch.49, p.3859
IFRS 9.5.1.1	Ch.51, p.4015
IFRS 9.5.1.1A	Ch.7, p.509
IFRS 9.5.1.1A	Ch.49, p.3855
IFRS 9.5.1.2	Ch.7, p.509
IFRS 9.5.1.2	Ch.49, p.3860
IFRS 9.5.1.3	Ch.7, p.509
IFRS 9.5.1.3	Ch.32, p.2399
IFRS 9.5.1.3	Ch.49, p.3854
IFRS 9.5.2.1	Ch.11, p.835
IFRS 9.5.2.1	Ch.50, p.3870
IFRS 9.5.2.1	Ch.50, p.3872
IFRS 9.5.2.1	Ch.50, p.3877
IFRS 9.5.2.1	Ch.51, p.4017
IFRS 9.5.2.2	Ch.50, p.3870
IFRS 9.5.2.2	Ch.50, p.3871
IFRS 9.5.2.2	Ch.51, p.4017
IFRS 9.5.2.3	Ch.50, p.3880
IFRS 9.5.3.1	Ch.50, p.3871
IFRS 9.5.3.1	Ch.50, p.3872
IFRS 9.5.3.2	Ch.50, p.3880
IFRS 9.5.4.1	Ch.5, p.338
IFRS 9.5.4.1	Ch.27, p.2039
IFRS 9.5.4.1	Ch.50, p.3871
IFRS 9.5.4.1	Ch.50, p.3882
IFRS 9.5.4.1	Ch.51, p.3916
IFRS 9.5.4.1	Ch.51, p.3927
IFRS 9.5.4.1(b)	Ch.51, p.4070
IFRS 9.5.4.2	Ch.51, p.3928
IFRS 9.5.4.3	Ch.50, p.3871
IFRS 9.5.4.3	Ch.50, p.3894
IFRS 9.5.4.3	Ch.50, p.3897
IFRS 9.5.4.3	Ch.51, p.4034
IFRS 9.5.4.3	Ch.51, p.4035
IFRS 9.5.4.3	Ch.52, p.4100
IFRS 9.5.4.4	Ch.51, p.3928
IFRS 9.5.4.4	Ch.51, p.4036
IFRS 9.5.4.4	Ch.51, p.4068
IFRS 9.5.4.4	Ch.52, p.4103
IFRS 9.5.4.4	Ch.54, p.4440
IFRS 9.5.4.5	Ch.52, p.4101
IFRS 9.5.4.5	Ch.52, p.4159
IFRS 9.5.4.5-7	Ch.53, p.4370
IFRS 9.5.4.7	Ch.50, p.3899
IFRS 9.5.4.7	Ch.52, p.4101
IFRS 9.5.4.7	Ch.52, p.4159
IFRS 9.5.4.8(a)	Ch.50, p.3899
IFRS 9.5.4.8	Ch.52, p.4102
IFRS 9.5.4.8	Ch.52, p.4159
IFRS 9.5.4.8	Ch.53, p.4370
IFRS 9.5.4.9	Ch.52, p.4102
IFRS 9.5.4.9	Ch.52, p.4159
IFRS 9.5.4.9	Ch.52, p.4160
IFRS 9.5.5	Ch.51, p.4017
IFRS 9.5.5.1	Ch.33, p.2579
IFRS 9.5.5.1	Ch.51, p.3924
IFRS 9.5.5.2	Ch.33, p.2579
IFRS 9.5.5.2	Ch.50, p.3871
IFRS 9.5.5.2	Ch.51, p.4036
IFRS 9.5.5.2	Ch.51, p.4074
IFRS 9.5.5.3	Ch.33, p.2579
IFRS 9.5.5.3	Ch.51, p.3925
IFRS 9.5.5.3	Ch.51, p.3926
IFRS 9.5.5.3	Ch.51, p.3929
IFRS 9.5.5.3	Ch.51, p.4015
IFRS 9.5.5.3	Ch.51, p.4017
IFRS 9.5.5.4	Ch.51, p.3926
IFRS 9.5.5.5	Ch.33, p.2579
IFRS 9.5.5.5	Ch.51, p.3925
IFRS 9.5.5.5	Ch.51, p.3926
IFRS 9.5.5.5	Ch.51, p.3929
IFRS 9.5.5.5	Ch.51, p.4015
IFRS 9.5.5.5	Ch.51, p.4017
IFRS 9.5.5.6	Ch.5, p.264
IFRS 9.5.5.6	Ch.51, p.4047
IFRS 9.5.5.7	Ch.51, p.3926
IFRS 9.5.5.8	Ch.51, p.3925
IFRS 9.5.5.8	Ch.51, p.4017
IFRS 9.5.5.8	Ch.51, p.4068
IFRS 9.5.5.9	Ch.51, p.3944
IFRS 9.5.5.9	Ch.51, p.3970
IFRS 9.5.5.9	Ch.51, p.3972
IFRS 9.5.5.9	Ch.51, p.3973
IFRS 9.5.5.9	Ch.51, p.4047

IFRS 9.5.5.10	Ch.5, p.264
IFRS 9.5.5.10	Ch.51, p.3990
IFRS 9.5.5.11	Ch.5, p.264
IFRS 9.5.5.11	Ch.51, p.3979
IFRS 9.5.5.11	Ch.51, p.3980
IFRS 9.5.5.11	Ch.51, p.3994
IFRS 9.5.5.12	Ch.51, p.4034
IFRS 9.5.5.12	Ch.51, p.4036
IFRS 9.5.5.13	Ch.51, p.3929
IFRS 9.5.5.13	Ch.51, p.3930
IFRS 9.5.5.13	Ch.51, p.4015
IFRS 9.5.5.14	Ch.51, p.3930
IFRS 9.5.5.15	Ch.51, p.3928
IFRS 9.5.5.15	Ch.51, p.3932
IFRS 9.5.5.15(a)	Ch.51, p.4043
IFRS 9.5.5.15(a)(i)	Ch.51, p.3928
IFRS 9.5.5.15(a)(i)	Ch.51, p.3932
IFRS 9.5.5.15(a)(ii)	Ch.51, p.3929
IFRS 9.5.5.15(b)	Ch.51, p.3929
IFRS 9.5.5.15(b)	Ch.51, p.4044
IFRS 9.5.5.16	Ch.51, p.3929
IFRS 9.5.5.17	Ch.51, p.3934
IFRS 9.5.5.17	Ch.51, p.3952
IFRS 9.5.5.17	Ch.51, p.4043
IFRS 9.5.5.17(a)	Ch.51, p.3947
IFRS 9.5.5.17(b)	Ch.51, p.3943
IFRS 9.5.5.17(c)	Ch.51, p.3962
IFRS 9.5.5.18	Ch.51, p.3947
IFRS 9.5.5.18	Ch.51, p.4036
IFRS 9.5.5.19	Ch.51, p.3944
IFRS 9.5.5.19	Ch.51, p.3946
IFRS 9.5.5.19	Ch.51, p.4047
IFRS 9.5.5.20	Ch.51, p.3945
IFRS 9.5.5.20	Ch.51, p.3946
IFRS 9.5.5.20	Ch.51, p.4047
IFRS 9.5.5.20	Ch.51, p.4051
IFRS 9.5.5.20	Ch.51, p.4054
IFRS 9.5.6.1	Ch.48, p.3835
IFRS 9.5.6.1	Ch.50, p.3878
IFRS 9.5.6.2	Ch.50, p.3879
IFRS 9.5.6.3	Ch.50, p.3879
IFRS 9.5.7.1	Ch.48, p.3775
IFRS 9.5.7.1	Ch.50, p.3872
IFRS 9.5.7.1(b)	Ch.48, p.3775
IFRS 9.5.7.1(d)	Ch.50, p.3871
IFRS 9.5.7.1A	Ch.5, p.338
IFRS 9.5.7.1A	Ch.27, p.2039
IFRS 9.5.7.1A	Ch.38, p.3081
IFRS 9.5.7.1A	Ch.50, p.3877
IFRS 9.5.7.2	Ch.50, p.3870
IFRS 9.5.7.2	Ch.50, p.3871
IFRS 9.5.7.3	Ch.50, p.3880
IFRS 9.5.7.4	Ch.49, p.3848
IFRS 9.5.7.4	Ch.50, p.3880
IFRS 9.5.7.4	Ch.51, p.4016
IFRS 9.5.7.4	Ch.51, p.4047
IFRS 9.5.7.5	Ch.5, p.263
IFRS 9.5.7.5	Ch.5, p.315
IFRS 9.5.7.5	Ch.11, p.835
IFRS 9.5.7.5	Ch.48, p.3775
IFRS 9.5.7.5	Ch.48, p.3830
IFRS 9.5.7.5	Ch.50, p.3877
IFRS 9.5.7.5	Ch.50, p.3900
IFRS 9.5.7.6	Ch.5, p.338
IFRS 9.5.7.6	Ch.48, p.3831
IFRS 9.5.7.6	Ch.50, p.3877
IFRS 9.5.7.7	Ch.14, p.1076
IFRS 9.5.7.7	Ch.48, p.3776
IFRS 9.5.7.7	Ch.50, p.3872
IFRS 9.5.7.7-8	Ch.5, p.315
IFRS 9.5.7.8	Ch.48, p.3776
IFRS 9.5.7.8	Ch.50, p.3872
IFRS 9.5.7.9	Ch.50, p.3872
IFRS 9.5.7.10	Ch.50, p.3871
IFRS 9.5.7.10	Ch.52, p.4129
IFRS 9.5.7.11	Ch.50, p.3871
IFRS 9.5.7.11	Ch.53, p.4388
IFRS 9.5.7.11	Ch.54, p.4482
IFRS 9.6.1.1	Ch.53, p.4185
IFRS 9.6.1.1	Ch.53, p.4187
IFRS 9.6.1.1	Ch.53, p.4191
IFRS 9.6.1.1	Ch.53, p.4274
IFRS 9.6.1.1	Ch.53, p.4280
IFRS 9.6.1.1	Ch.53, p.4394
IFRS 9.6.1.1	Ch.53, p.4395
IFRS 9.6.1.2	Ch.53, p.4188
IFRS 9.6.1.2	Ch.53, p.4275
IFRS 9.6.1.2	Ch.53, p.4289
IFRS 9.6.1.3	Ch.53, p.4186
IFRS 9.6.1.3	Ch.53, p.4382
IFRS 9.6.1.3	Ch.53, p.4385
IFRS 9.6.1.3	Ch.53, p.4386
IFRS 9.6.2.1	Ch.53, p.4234
IFRS 9.6.2.1	Ch.53, p.4238
IFRS 9.6.2.2	Ch.53, p.4234
IFRS 9.6.2.2	Ch.53, p.4240
IFRS 9.6.2.2	Ch.53, p.4241
IFRS 9.6.2.2	Ch.53, p.4396
IFRS 9.6.2.3	Ch.53, p.4234
IFRS 9.6.2.3	Ch.53, p.4248
IFRS 9.6.2.3	Ch.53, p.4249
IFRS 9.6.2.4	Ch.53, p.4235
IFRS 9.6.2.4	Ch.53, p.4243
IFRS 9.6.2.4	Ch.53, p.4247
IFRS 9.6.2.4	Ch.53, p.4330
IFRS 9.6.2.4(a)	Ch.53, p.4246
IFRS 9.6.2.4(a)	Ch.53, p.4278
IFRS 9.6.2.4(a)	Ch.53, p.4330
IFRS 9.6.2.4(b)	Ch.53, p.4247
IFRS 9.6.2.4(c)	Ch.53, p.4243
IFRS 9.6.2.5	Ch.53, p.4234
IFRS 9.6.2.5	Ch.53, p.4242
IFRS 9.6.2.5	Ch.53, p.4306
IFRS 9.6.2.6	Ch.53, p.4235
IFRS 9.6.3.1	Ch.53, p.4189
IFRS 9.6.3.2	Ch.53, p.4189

IFRS 9.6.3.3	Ch.53, p.4189	IFRS 9.6.5.8	Ch.53, p.4221
IFRS 9.6.3.3	Ch.53, p.4216	IFRS 9.6.5.8	Ch.53, p.4290
IFRS 9.6.3.4	Ch.53, p.4189	IFRS 9.6.5.8	Ch.53, p.4344
IFRS 9.6.3.4	Ch.53, p.4224	IFRS 9.6.5.8	Ch.53, p.4345
IFRS 9.6.3.4	Ch.53, p.4226	IFRS 9.6.5.8	Ch.53, p.4380
IFRS 9.6.3.4	Ch.53, p.4233	IFRS 9.6.5.8(b)	Ch.53, p.4292
IFRS 9.6.3.5	Ch.53, p.4189	IFRS 9.6.5.8(b)	Ch.53, p.4355
IFRS 9.6.3.5	Ch.53, p.4248	IFRS 9.6.5.8(b)	Ch.53, p.4380
IFRS 9.6.3.5	Ch.53, p.4259	IFRS 9.6.5.9	Ch.53, p.4293
IFRS 9.6.3.6	Ch.53, p.4189	IFRS 9.6.5.10	Ch.5, p.258
IFRS 9.6.3.6	Ch.53, p.4259	IFRS 9.6.5.10	Ch.51, p.4019
IFRS 9.6.3.6	Ch.53, p.4260	IFRS 9.6.5.10	Ch.53, p.4292
IFRS 9.6.3.7	Ch.53, p.4190	IFRS 9.6.5.10	Ch.53, p.4355
IFRS 9.6.3.7(a)	Ch.53, p.4190	IFRS 9.6.5.11	Ch.53, p.4295
IFRS 9.6.3.7(c)	Ch.53, p.4201	IFRS 9.6.5.11	Ch.53, p.4344
IFRS 9.6.4.1	Ch.5, p.248	IFRS 9.6.5.11(a)	Ch.53, p.4232
IFRS 9.6.4.1	Ch.5, p.252	IFRS 9.6.5.11(a)	Ch.53, p.4288
IFRS 9.6.4.1	Ch.5, p.256	IFRS 9.6.5.11(a)	Ch.53, p.4352
IFRS 9.6.4.1	Ch.53, p.4271	IFRS 9.6.5.11(a)(ii)	Ch.53, p.4228
IFRS 9.6.4.1	Ch.53, p.4275	IFRS 9.6.5.11(a)(ii)	Ch.53, p.4329
IFRS 9.6.4.1(a)	Ch.5, p.248	IFRS 9.6.5.11(d)	Ch.53, p.4297
IFRS 9.6.4.1(a)	Ch.5, p.252	IFRS 9.6.5.11(d)	Ch.53, p.4379
IFRS 9.6.4.1(b)	Ch.5, p.248	IFRS 9.6.5.11(d)(i)	Ch.53, p.4298
IFRS 9.6.4.1(b)	Ch.5, p.252	IFRS 9.6.5.11(d)(i)	Ch.53, p.4343
IFRS 9.6.4.1(b)	Ch.53, p.4272	IFRS 9.6.5.11(d)(i)	Ch.53, p.4379
IFRS 9.6.4.1(b)	Ch.53, p.4275	IFRS 9.6.5.11(d)(ii)	Ch.53, p.4379
IFRS 9.6.4.1(b)	Ch.53, p.4306	IFRS 9.6.5.12	Ch.5, p.253
IFRS 9.6.4.1(b)	Ch.53, p.4308	IFRS 9.6.5.12	Ch.53, p.4298
IFRS 9.6.4.1(c)	Ch.5, p.248	IFRS 9.6.5.12	Ch.53, p.4355
IFRS 9.6.4.1(c)	Ch.5, p.252	IFRS 9.6.5.12(b)	Ch.5, p.253
IFRS 9.6.4.1(c)	Ch.53, p.4279	IFRS 9.6.5.13	Ch.5, p.255
IFRS 9.6.4.1(c)(ii)	Ch.53, p.4325	IFRS 9.6.5.13	Ch.53, p.4300
IFRS 9.6.4.1(c)(iii)	Ch.53, p.4288	IFRS 9.6.5.13	Ch.53, p.4301
IFRS 9.6.5.1	Ch.5, p.256	IFRS 9.6.5.13	Ch.53, p.4303
IFRS 9.6.5.1	Ch.53, p.4289	IFRS 9.6.5.13	Ch.53, p.4305
IFRS 9.6.5.2	Ch.53, p.4187	IFRS 9.6.5.14	Ch.53, p.4300
IFRS 9.6.5.2	Ch.53, p.4220	IFRS 9.6.5.14	Ch.53, p.4364
IFRS 9.6.5.2	Ch.53, p.4221	IFRS 9.6.5.15	Ch.5, p.259
IFRS 9.6.5.2	Ch.53, p.4222	IFRS 9.6.5.15	Ch.53, p.4246
IFRS 9.6.5.2	Ch.53, p.4262	IFRS 9.6.5.15	Ch.53, p.4330
IFRS 9.6.5.2(b)	Ch.53, p.4329	IFRS 9.6.5.15	Ch.53, p.4331
IFRS 9.6.5.2(c)	Ch.53, p.4307	IFRS 9.6.5.15	Ch.53, p.4332
IFRS 9.6.5.3	Ch.53, p.4220	IFRS 9.6.5.15	Ch.53, p.4338
IFRS 9.6.5.3	Ch.53, p.4221	IFRS 9.6.5.15(b)	Ch.53, p.4381
IFRS 9.6.5.3	Ch.53, p.4345	IFRS 9.6.5.15(c)	Ch.53, p.4333
IFRS 9.6.5.3	Ch.53, p.4396	IFRS 9.6.5.15(c)	Ch.53, p.4341
IFRS 9.6.5.5	Ch.53, p.4349	IFRS 9.6.5.15(c)	Ch.53, p.4342
IFRS 9.6.5.6	Ch.5, p.248	IFRS 9.6.5.15(c)	Ch.53, p.4382
IFRS 9.6.5.6-7	Ch.5, p.253	IFRS 9.6.5.16	Ch.5, p.259
IFRS 9.6.5.6-7	Ch.5, p.256	IFRS 9.6.5.16	Ch.53, p.4247
IFRS 9.6.5.6	Ch.53, p.4344	IFRS 9.6.5.16	Ch.53, p.4299
IFRS 9.6.5.6	Ch.53, p.4347	IFRS 9.6.5.16	Ch.53, p.4304
IFRS 9.6.5.6	Ch.53, p.4353	IFRS 9.6.5.16	Ch.53, p.4336
IFRS 9.6.5.6	Ch.53, p.4359	IFRS 9.6.5.16	Ch.53, p.4338
IFRS 9.6.5.6	Ch.53, p.4362	IFRS 9.6.5.16	Ch.53, p.4339
IFRS 9.6.5.7	Ch.5, p.248	IFRS 9.6.6.1	Ch.5, p.252
IFRS 9.6.5.8	Ch.5, p.258	IFRS 9.6.6.1	Ch.53, p.4211
IFRS 9.6.5.8	Ch.51, p.4019	IFRS 9.6.6.1(c)	Ch.53, p.4213

IFRS 9.6.6.1(c)(ii)	Ch.53, p.4215	IFRS 9.7.2.25	Ch.53, p.4391
IFRS 9.6.6.2	Ch.53, p.4211	IFRS 9.7.2.26(a)	Ch.53, p.4391
IFRS 9.6.6.3	Ch.53, p.4212	IFRS 9.7.2.26(b)	Ch.53, p.4392
IFRS 9.6.6.3(c)	Ch.53, p.4287	IFRS 9.7.2.26(b)	Ch.53, p.4393
IFRS 9.6.6.4	Ch.53, p.4213	IFRS 9.7.2.26(d)	Ch.53, p.4367
IFRS 9.6.6.4	Ch.53, p.4381	IFRS 9.7.2.36	Ch.53, p.4377
IFRS 9.6.6.4	Ch.54, p.4487	IFRS 9.7.2.37(b)	Ch.53, p.4377
IFRS 9.6.6.5	Ch.53, p.4381	IFRS 9.7.2.37	Ch.53, p.4377
IFRS 9.6.6.6	Ch.53, p.4216	IFRS 9.7.2.39	Ch.56, p.4941
IFRS 9.6.7.1	Ch.53, p.4387	IFRS 9.7.2.40	Ch.56, p.4941
IFRS 9.6.7.2	Ch.53, p.4387	IFRS 9.7.2.43	Ch.52, p.4102
IFRS 9.6.7.3	Ch.53, p.4387	IFRS 9.7.2.43	Ch.52, p.4160
IFRS 9.6.7.4	Ch.53, p.4387	IFRS 9.7.2.46	Ch.52, p.4102
IFRS 9.6.8.1	Ch.53, p.4366	IFRS 9.7.2.46	Ch.52, p.4160
IFRS 9.6.8.4	Ch.53, p.4366	IFRS 9 Appendix A	Ch.5, p.338
IFRS 9.6.8.5	Ch.53, p.4366	IFRS 9 Appendix A	Ch.27, p.2039
IFRS 9.6.8.6	Ch.53, p.4366	IFRS 9 Appendix A	Ch.33, p.2579
IFRS 9.6.8.7	Ch.53, p.4367	IFRS 9 Appendix A	Ch.39, p.3122
IFRS 9.6.8.8	Ch.53, p.4367	IFRS 9 Appendix A	Ch.40, p.3142
IFRS 9.6.8.9	Ch.53, p.4368	IFRS 9 Appendix A	Ch.45, p.3596
IFRS 9.6.8.10	Ch.53, p.4368	IFRS 9 Appendix A	Ch.46, p.3620
IFRS 9.6.8.11	Ch.53, p.4368	IFRS 9 Appendix A	Ch.46, p.3624
IFRS 9.6.8.12	Ch.53, p.4368	IFRS 9 Appendix A	Ch.46, p.3628
IFRS 9.6.8.13	Ch.53, p.4368	IFRS 9 Appendix A	Ch.47, p.3667
IFRS 9.6.9.1	Ch.53, p.4370	IFRS 9 Appendix A	Ch.47, p.3740
IFRS 9.6.9.2	Ch.53, p.4371	IFRS 9 Appendix A	Ch.48, p.3776
IFRS 9.6.9.3	Ch.53, p.4371	IFRS 9 Appendix A	Ch.48, p.3777
IFRS 9.6.9.3-4	Ch.53, p.4370	IFRS 9 Appendix A	Ch.48, p.3835
IFRS 9.6.9.5	Ch.53, p.4371	IFRS 9 Appendix A	Ch.49, p.3845
IFRS 9.6.9.6	Ch.53, p.4372	IFRS 9 Appendix A	Ch.49, p.3860
IFRS 9.6.9.7	Ch.53, p.4372	IFRS 9 Appendix A	Ch.50, p.3878
IFRS 9.6.9.8	Ch.53, p.4372	IFRS 9 Appendix A	Ch.50, p.3881
IFRS 9.6.9.9	Ch.53, p.4372	IFRS 9 Appendix A	Ch.50, p.3882
IFRS 9.6.9.10	Ch.53, p.4372	IFRS 9 Appendix A	Ch.50, p.3883
IFRS 9.6.9.11	Ch.53, p.4372	IFRS 9 Appendix A	Ch.50, p.3887
IFRS 9.6.9.12	Ch.53, p.4372	IFRS 9 Appendix A	Ch.51, p.3916
IFRS 9.7.1.8	Ch.53, p.4366	IFRS 9 Appendix A	Ch.51, p.3924
IFRS 9.7.1.9	Ch.52, p.4102	IFRS 9 Appendix A	Ch.51, p.3925
IFRS 9.7.1.9	Ch.52, p.4160	IFRS 9 Appendix A	Ch.51, p.3926
IFRS 9.7.1.9	Ch.53, p.4377	IFRS 9 Appendix A	Ch.51, p.3927
IFRS 9.7.2.1	Ch.53, p.4391	IFRS 9 Appendix A	Ch.51, p.3930
IFRS 9.7.2.1	Ch.56, p.4941	IFRS 9 Appendix A	Ch.51, p.3934
IFRS 9.7.2.2	Ch.53, p.4390	IFRS 9 Appendix A	Ch.51, p.3935
IFRS 9.7.2.2	Ch.53, p.4391	IFRS 9 Appendix A	Ch.51, p.3936
IFRS 9.7.2.14A	Ch.45, p.3613	IFRS 9 Appendix A	Ch.51, p.3937
IFRS 9.7.2.15	Ch.53, p.4390	IFRS 9 Appendix A	Ch.51, p.3944
IFRS 9.7.2.15	Ch.56, p.4941	IFRS 9 Appendix A	Ch.51, p.3947
IFRS 9.7.2.19(a)	Ch.5, p.264	IFRS 9 Appendix A	Ch.51, p.3956
IFRS 9.7.2.20	Ch.5, p.264	IFRS 9 Appendix A	Ch.51, p.4034
IFRS 9.7.2.21	Ch.5, p.249	IFRS 9 Appendix A	Ch.51, p.4035
IFRS 9.7.2.21	Ch.50, p.3880	IFRS 9 Appendix A	Ch.51, p.4036
IFRS 9.7.2.21	Ch.53, p.4186	IFRS 9 Appendix A	Ch.51, p.4045
IFRS 9.7.2.21	Ch.53, p.4386	IFRS 9 Appendix A	Ch.51, p.4067
IFRS 9.7.2.21	Ch.53, p.4389	IFRS 9 Appendix A	Ch.51, p.4068
IFRS 9.7.2.21-26	Ch.53, p.4390	IFRS 9 Appendix A	Ch.51, p.4070
IFRS 9.7.2.22	Ch.53, p.4390	IFRS 9 Appendix A	Ch.51, p.4073
IFRS 9.7.2.23	Ch.53, p.4391	IFRS 9 Appendix A	Ch.51, p.4074
IFRS 9.7.2.24	Ch.53, p.4391	IFRS 9 Appendix A	Ch.52, p.4088

IFRS 9 Appendix A	Ch.53, p.4285	IFRS 9.B3.2.13(c)	Ch.52, p.4144
IFRS 9 Appendix A	Ch.54, p.4515	IFRS 9.B3.2.13(d)	Ch.52, p.4145
IFRS 9 Appendix A	Ch.55, p.4559	IFRS 9.B3.2.13(e)	Ch.52, p.4147
IFRS 9 Appendix A	Ch.56, p.4690	IFRS 9.B3.2.13(a)	Ch.52, p.4150
IFRS 9 Appendix A	Ch.56, p.4713	IFRS 9.B3.2.14	Ch.49, p.3843
IFRS 9.B1	Ch.45, p.3587	IFRS 9.B3.2.14	Ch.52, p.4152
IFRS 9.B2	Ch.46, p.3628	IFRS 9.B3.2.15	Ch.48, p.3825
IFRS 9.B2.1	Ch.45, p.3594	IFRS 9.B3.2.15	Ch.49, p.3843
IFRS 9.B2.1	Ch.46, p.3622	IFRS 9.B3.2.16(r)	Ch.51, p.4068
IFRS 9.B2.3	Ch.45, p.3593	IFRS 9.B3.2.16(r)	Ch.52, p.4103
IFRS 9.B2.4	Ch.45, p.3594	IFRS 9.B3.2.16(h)-(i)	Ch.52, p.4116
IFRS 9.B2.5	Ch.45, p.3598	IFRS 9.B3.2.16(a)	Ch.52, p.4121
IFRS 9.B2.5(a)	Ch.45, p.3594	IFRS 9.B3.2.16(b)	Ch.52, p.4121
IFRS 9.B2.5(a)	Ch.45, p.3598	IFRS 9.B3.2.16(c)	Ch.52, p.4122
IFRS 9.B2.5(a)	Ch.49, p.3857	IFRS 9.B3.2.16(d)	Ch.52, p.4122
IFRS 9.B2.5(b)	Ch.45, p.3596	IFRS 9.B3.2.16(e)	Ch.52, p.4122
IFRS 9.B2.5(c)	Ch.45, p.3599	IFRS 9.B3.2.16(j)	Ch.52, p.4122
IFRS 9.B2.6	Ch.45, p.3599	IFRS 9.B3.2.16(k)	Ch.52, p.4122
IFRS 9.B2.6	Ch.55, p.4542	IFRS 9.B3.2.16(f)	Ch.52, p.4123
IFRS 9.B2.6	Ch.56, p.4690	IFRS 9.B3.2.16(g)	Ch.52, p.4123
IFRS 9.B3.1.1	Ch.49, p.3843	IFRS 9.B3.2.16(h)	Ch.52, p.4124
IFRS 9.B3.1.2(b)	Ch.15, p.1188	IFRS 9.B3.2.16(h)-(i)	Ch.52, p.4124
IFRS 9.B3.1.2(a)	Ch.49, p.3842	IFRS 9.B3.2.16(i)	Ch.52, p.4124
IFRS 9.B3.1.2(b)	Ch.49, p.3842	IFRS 9.B3.2.16(j)	Ch.52, p.4125
IFRS 9.B3.1.2(c)	Ch.49, p.3842	IFRS 9.B3.2.16(k)	Ch.52, p.4125
IFRS 9.B3.1.2(d)	Ch.49, p.3842	IFRS 9.B3.2.16(l)	Ch.52, p.4125
IFRS 9.B3.1.2(e)	Ch.49, p.3842	IFRS 9.B3.2.16(m)	Ch.52, p.4125
IFRS 9.B3.1.2(d)	Ch.52, p.4123	IFRS 9.B3.2.16(n)	Ch.52, p.4127
IFRS 9.B3.1.2(e)	Ch.53, p.4235	IFRS 9.B3.2.16(o)	Ch.52, p.4128
IFRS 9.B3.1.3	Ch.49, p.3845	IFRS 9.B3.2.16(p)	Ch.52, p.4128
IFRS 9.B3.1.3	Ch.50, p.3880	IFRS 9.B3.2.16(q)	Ch.52, p.4128
IFRS 9.B3.1.4	Ch.49, p.3845	IFRS 9.B3.2.16(g)	Ch.54, p.4477
IFRS 9.B3.1.5	Ch.49, p.3845	IFRS 9.B3.2.16(h)	Ch.54, p.4477
IFRS 9.B3.1.5	Ch.49, p.3848	IFRS 9.B3.2.17	Ch.52, p.4116
IFRS 9.B3.1.5	Ch.50, p.3880	IFRS 9.B3.2.17	Ch.52, p.4142
IFRS 9.B3.1.6	Ch.49, p.3845	IFRS 9.B3.2.17	Ch.52, p.4149
IFRS 9.B3.1.6	Ch.49, p.3848	IFRS 9.B3.3.1	Ch.52, p.4154
IFRS 9.B3.1.6	Ch.50, p.3880	IFRS 9.B3.3.1(b)	Ch.52, p.4154
IFRS 9.B3.2.1	Ch.52, p.4090	IFRS 9.B3.3.2	Ch.52, p.4154
IFRS 9.B3.2.1	Ch.52, p.4091	IFRS 9.B3.3.3	Ch.52, p.4156
IFRS 9.B3.2.2	Ch.52, p.4103	IFRS 9.B3.3.4	Ch.52, p.4154
IFRS 9.B3.2.3	Ch.52, p.4108	IFRS 9.B3.3.4	Ch.52, p.4155
IFRS 9.B3.2.4	Ch.52, p.4115	IFRS 9.B3.3.5	Ch.52, p.4156
IFRS 9.B3.2.4(c)	Ch.52, p.4123	IFRS 9.B3.3.6	Ch.50, p.3897
IFRS 9.B3.2.5	Ch.52, p.4115	IFRS 9.B3.3.6	Ch.52, p.4099
IFRS 9.B3.2.5(d)	Ch.52, p.4123	IFRS 9.B3.3.6	Ch.52, p.4157
IFRS 9.B3.2.6	Ch.52, p.4114	IFRS 9.B3.3.6	Ch.52, p.4162
IFRS 9.B3.2.6	Ch.52, p.4126	IFRS 9.B3.3.7	Ch.52, p.4167
IFRS 9.B3.2.6	Ch.52, p.4152	IFRS 9.B4.1.1	Ch.48, p.3779
IFRS 9.B3.2.7	Ch.52, p.4120	IFRS 9.B4.1.2	Ch.48, p.3779
IFRS 9.B3.2.8(a)	Ch.52, p.4120	IFRS 9.B4.1.2	Ch.48, p.3780
IFRS 9.B3.2.8(b)	Ch.52, p.4120	IFRS 9.B4.1.2A	Ch.48, p.3778
IFRS 9.B3.2.9	Ch.52, p.4120	IFRS 9.B4.1.2A	Ch.48, p.3779
IFRS 9.B3.2.10	Ch.52, p.4132	IFRS 9.B4.1.2B	Ch.48, p.3779
IFRS 9.B3.2.11	Ch.52, p.4131	IFRS 9.B4.1.2C	Ch.48, p.3780
IFRS 9.B3.2.12	Ch.52, p.4134	IFRS 9.B4.1.3	Ch.48, p.3781
IFRS 9.B3.2.13(a)	Ch.52, p.4141	IFRS 9.B4.1.3A	Ch.48, p.3781
IFRS 9.B3.2.13(b)	Ch.52, p.4142	IFRS 9.B4.1.3B	Ch.48, p.3781

Index of standards

IFRS 9.B4.1.3B	Ch.48, p.3782
IFRS 9.B4.1.3B	Ch.48, p.3787
IFRS 9.B4.1.4A	Ch.48, p.3784
IFRS 9.B4.1.4B	Ch.48, p.3784
IFRS 9.B4.1.4 Example 1	Ch.48, p.3786
IFRS 9.B4.1.4 Example 2	Ch.48, p.3787
IFRS 9.B4.1.4 Example 3	Ch.48, p.3787
IFRS 9.B4.1.4 Example 4	Ch.48, p.3788
IFRS 9.B4.1.4C Example 5	Ch.48, p.3788
IFRS 9.B4.1.4C Example 6	Ch.48, p.3788
IFRS 9.B4.1.4C Example 7	Ch.48, p.3789
IFRS 9.B4.1.5	Ch.48, p.3785
IFRS 9.B4.1.5	Ch.48, p.3790
IFRS 9.B4.1.6	Ch.48, p.3784
IFRS 9.B4.1.6	Ch.48, p.3785
IFRS 9.B4.1.6	Ch.53, p.4219
IFRS 9.B4.1.7A	Ch.25, p.1876
IFRS 9.B4.1.7A	Ch.48, p.3791
IFRS 9.B4.1.7A	Ch.48, p.3792
IFRS 9.B4.1.7B	Ch.48, p.3791
IFRS 9.B4.1.8	Ch.48, p.3809
IFRS 9.B4.1.9	Ch.48, p.3809
IFRS 9.B4.1.9	Ch.48, p.3811
IFRS 9.B4.1.9A	Ch.48, p.3792
IFRS 9.B4.1.9B	Ch.48, p.3799
IFRS 9.B4.1.9B-9D	Ch.5, p.262
IFRS 9.B4.1.9B-9D	Ch.5, p.356
IFRS 9.B4.1.9C	Ch.48, p.3799
IFRS 9.B4.1.9C	Ch.48, p.3801
IFRS 9.B4.1.9D	Ch.48, p.3801
IFRS 9.B4.1.9D	Ch.48, p.3802
IFRS 9.B4.1.9E	Ch.48, p.3795
IFRS 9.B4.1.9E	Ch.48, p.3802
IFRS 9.B4.1.10	Ch.48, p.3803
IFRS 9.B4.1.11	Ch.48, p.3803
IFRS 9.B4.1.11(b)	Ch.48, p.3807
IFRS 9.B4.1.12	Ch.5, p.263
IFRS 9.B4.1.12	Ch.5, p.357
IFRS 9.B4.1.12	Ch.48, p.3806
IFRS 9.B4.1.12	Ch.50, p.3889
IFRS 9.B4.1.12(c)	Ch.48, p.3807
IFRS 9.B4.1.12A	Ch.48, p.3804
IFRS 9.B4.1.12A	Ch.48, p.3806
IFRS 9.B4.1.13 Instrument C	Ch.48, p.3794
IFRS 9.B4.1.13 Instrument D	Ch.48, p.3794
IFRS 9.B4.1.13 Instrument A	Ch.48, p.3796
IFRS 9.B4.1.13 Instrument B	Ch.48, p.3801
IFRS 9.B4.1.13 Instrument E	Ch.48, p.3811
IFRS 9.B4.1.13 Instrument A	Ch.48, p.3812
IFRS 9.B4.1.14	Ch.48, p.3808
IFRS 9.B4.1.14 Instrument F	Ch.48, p.3810
IFRS 9.B4.1.14 Instrument G	Ch.48, p.3810
IFRS 9.B4.1.14 Instrument H	Ch.48, p.3810
IFRS 9.B4.1.15	Ch.48, p.3814
IFRS 9.B4.1.16	Ch.48, p.3814
IFRS 9.B4.1.17	Ch.48, p.3794
IFRS 9.B4.1.17	Ch.48, p.3814
IFRS 9.B4.1.18	Ch.25, p.1876
IFRS 9.B4.1.18	Ch.48, p.3791
IFRS 9.B4.1.18	Ch.48, p.3797
IFRS 9.B4.1.18	Ch.48, p.3804
IFRS 9.B4.1.18	Ch.48, p.3808
IFRS 9.B4.1.18	Ch.48, p.3814
IFRS 9.B4.1.19	Ch.48, p.3794
IFRS 9.B4.1.20	Ch.48, p.3816
IFRS 9.B4.1.20	Ch.48, p.3817
IFRS 9.B4.1.20	Ch.48, p.3820
IFRS 9.B4.1.20-26	Ch.51, p.3974
IFRS 9.B4.1.21	Ch.48, p.3816
IFRS 9.B4.1.21	Ch.48, p.3817
IFRS 9.B4.1.21(b)	Ch.48, p.3820
IFRS 9.B4.1.21(b)-(c)	Ch.48, p.3819
IFRS 9.B4.1.22	Ch.48, p.3816
IFRS 9.B4.1.22	Ch.48, p.3819
IFRS 9.B4.1.23-25	Ch.48, p.3816
IFRS 9.B4.1.25	Ch.48, p.3817
IFRS 9.B4.1.26	Ch.48, p.3817
IFRS 9.B4.1.26	Ch.48, p.3821
IFRS 9.B4.1.27	Ch.48, p.3826
IFRS 9.B4.1.28	Ch.48, p.3826
IFRS 9.B4.1.29	Ch.48, p.3827
IFRS 9.B4.1.30	Ch.48, p.3827
IFRS 9.B4.1.31	Ch.48, p.3828
IFRS 9.B4.1.32	Ch.48, p.3828
IFRS 9.B4.1.33	Ch.48, p.3784
IFRS 9.B4.1.33	Ch.48, p.3828
IFRS 9.B4.1.34	Ch.48, p.3828
IFRS 9.B4.1.35	Ch.48, p.3826
IFRS 9.B4.1.35	Ch.48, p.3828
IFRS 9.B4.1.36	Ch.48, p.3784
IFRS 9.B4.1.36	Ch.48, p.3829
IFRS 9.B4.3.1	Ch.47, p.3699
IFRS 9.B4.3.2	Ch.46, p.3630
IFRS 9.B4.3.3	Ch.46, p.3649
IFRS 9.B4.3.3	Ch.46, p.3650
IFRS 9.B4.3.3	Ch.49, p.3860
IFRS 9.B4.3.4	Ch.46, p.3651
IFRS 9.B4.3.5(a)	Ch.46, p.3641
IFRS 9.B4.3.5(b)	Ch.46, p.3635
IFRS 9.B4.3.5(b)	Ch.46, p.3637
IFRS 9.B4.3.5(c)-(d)	Ch.46, p.3639
IFRS 9.B4.3.5(c)-(d)	Ch.56, p.4714
IFRS 9.B4.3.5(e)	Ch.46, p.3633
IFRS 9.B4.3.5(e)	Ch.46, p.3637
IFRS 9.B4.3.5(e)	Ch.47, p.3727
IFRS 9.B4.3.5(e)	Ch.47, p.3734
IFRS 9.B4.3.5(e)	Ch.55, p.4561
IFRS 9.B4.3.5(e)(ii)	Ch.46, p.3636
IFRS 9.B4.3.5(f)	Ch.46, p.3640
IFRS 9.B4.3.5(f)	Ch.51, p.4022
IFRS 9.B4.3.6	Ch.46, p.3641
IFRS 9.B4.3.7	Ch.46, p.3641
IFRS 9.B4.3.7	Ch.55, p.4563
IFRS 9.B4.3.7	Ch.56, p.4715
IFRS 9.B4.3.8	Ch.46, p.3630
IFRS 9.B4.3.8(a)	Ch.46, p.3631

IFRS 9.B4.3.8(a)	Ch.46, p.3633	IFRS 9.B5.4.6	Ch.47, p.3724
IFRS 9.B4.3.8(b)	Ch.46, p.3637	IFRS 9.B5.4.6	Ch.50, p.3887
IFRS 9.B4.3.8(b)	Ch.46, p.3647	IFRS 9.B5.4.6	Ch.50, p.3894
IFRS 9.B4.3.8(c)	Ch.46, p.3631	IFRS 9.B5.4.6	Ch.51, p.3931
IFRS 9.B4.3.8(d)	Ch.43, p.3476	IFRS 9.B5.4.7	Ch.50, p.3882
IFRS 9.B4.3.8(d)	Ch.46, p.3642	IFRS 9.B5.4.7	Ch.51, p.3929
IFRS 9.B4.3.8(d)	Ch.46, p.3651	IFRS 9.B5.4.7	Ch.51, p.3930
IFRS 9.B4.3.8(e)	Ch.46, p.3637	IFRS 9.B5.4.8	Ch.47, p.3740
IFRS 9.B4.3.8(f)(i)	Ch.46, p.3648	IFRS 9.B5.4.8	Ch.49, p.3860
IFRS 9.B4.3.8(f)(ii)	Ch.46, p.3648	IFRS 9.B5.4.9	Ch.51, p.4036
IFRS 9.B4.3.8(f)(iii)	Ch.46, p.3648	IFRS 9.B5.4.9	Ch.51, p.4069
IFRS 9.B4.3.8(g)	Ch.46, p.3648	IFRS 9.B5.4.9	Ch.52, p.4103
IFRS 9.B4.3.8(g)	Ch.55, p.4563	IFRS 9.B5.5.1	Ch.51, p.3926
IFRS 9.B4.3.8(g)	Ch.56, p.4715	IFRS 9.B5.5.1-6	Ch.5, p.264
IFRS 9.B4.3.8(h)	Ch.46, p.3648	IFRS 9.B5.5.2	Ch.51, p.3979
IFRS 9.B4.3.8(h)	Ch.56, p.4712	IFRS 9.B5.5.4	Ch.51, p.4000
IFRS 9.B4.3.8(h)	Ch.56, p.4714	IFRS 9.B5.5.5	Ch.51, p.4002
IFRS 9.B4.3.9	Ch.48, p.3829	IFRS 9.B5.5.6	Ch.51, p.4002
IFRS 9.B4.3.10	Ch.48, p.3829	IFRS 9.B5.5.7	Ch.51, p.3969
IFRS 9.B4.3.11	Ch.5, p.265	IFRS 9.B5.5.8	Ch.51, p.3970
IFRS 9.B4.3.11	Ch.43, p.3477	IFRS 9.B5.5.8	Ch.51, p.4047
IFRS 9.B4.3.11	Ch.46, p.3630	IFRS 9.B5.5.9	Ch.51, p.3988
IFRS 9.B4.3.11	Ch.46, p.3652	IFRS 9.B5.5.10	Ch.51, p.3988
IFRS 9.B4.3.12	Ch.46, p.3652	IFRS 9.B5.5.11	Ch.51, p.3972
IFRS 9.B4.4.1	Ch.48, p.3832	IFRS 9.B5.5.11	Ch.51, p.3988
IFRS 9.B4.4.2	Ch.48, p.3835	IFRS 9.B5.5.12	Ch.51, p.3971
IFRS 9.B4.4.3	Ch.48, p.3833	IFRS 9.B5.5.12	Ch.51, p.3975
IFRS 9.B4.4.3(a)	Ch.48, p.3833	IFRS 9.B5.5.13	Ch.51, p.3995
IFRS 9.B5.1.1	Ch.8, p.627	IFRS 9.B5.5.14	Ch.51, p.3995
IFRS 9.B5.1.1	Ch.24, p.1832	IFRS 9.B5.5.15	Ch.51, p.3975
IFRS 9.B5.1.1	Ch.46, p.3638	IFRS 9.B5.5.16	Ch.51, p.3967
IFRS 9.B5.1.1	Ch.49, p.3854	IFRS 9.B5.5.16	Ch.51, p.3975
IFRS 9.B5.1.1	Ch.49, p.3855	IFRS 9.B5.5.17	Ch.51, p.3973
IFRS 9.B5.1.1	Ch.50, p.3883	IFRS 9.B5.5.17	Ch.51, p.3976
IFRS 9.B5.1.2	Ch.49, p.3856	IFRS 9.B5.5.17(f)	Ch.51, p.4067
IFRS 9.B5.1.2A	Ch.49, p.3854	IFRS 9.B5.5.17(g)	Ch.51, p.4067
IFRS 9.B5.1.2A	Ch.49, p.3855	IFRS 9.B5.5.17(i)	Ch.51, p.4067
IFRS 9.B5.1.2A(b)	Ch.5, p.316	IFRS 9.B5.5.17(j)	Ch.51, p.3973
IFRS 9.B5.2.1	Ch.50, p.3872	IFRS 9.B5.5.17(k)	Ch.51, p.3973
IFRS 9.B5.2.2	Ch.49, p.3859	IFRS 9.B5.5.17(l)	Ch.51, p.3973
IFRS 9.B5.2.2	Ch.49, p.3860	IFRS 9.B5.5.18	Ch.51, p.3975
IFRS 9.B5.2.2A	Ch.49, p.3855	IFRS 9.B5.5.19	Ch.51, p.3980
IFRS 9.B5.2.3	Ch.50, p.3877	IFRS 9.B5.5.19	Ch.51, p.4006
IFRS 9.B5.2.4	Ch.50, p.3878	IFRS 9.B5.5.20	Ch.51, p.3980
IFRS 9.B5.2.5	Ch.50, p.3878	IFRS 9.B5.5.21	Ch.51, p.3969
IFRS 9.B5.2.6	Ch.50, p.3878	IFRS 9.B5.5.21	Ch.51, p.3980
IFRS 9.B5.4.1	Ch.50, p.3882	IFRS 9.B5.5.22	Ch.51, p.3990
IFRS 9.B5.4.1-3	Ch.5, p.338	IFRS 9.B5.5.22-24	Ch.5, p.264
IFRS 9.B5.4.1-7	Ch.5, p.338	IFRS 9.B5.5.23	Ch.51, p.3990
IFRS 9.B5.4.1-7	Ch.27, p.2039	IFRS 9.B5.5.24	Ch.51, p.3990
IFRS 9.B5.4.2	Ch.50, p.3882	IFRS 9.B5.5.25	Ch.51, p.4033
IFRS 9.B5.4.3	Ch.50, p.3882	IFRS 9.B5.5.26	Ch.51, p.3930
IFRS 9.B5.4.4	Ch.50, p.3886	IFRS 9.B5.5.26	Ch.51, p.4033
IFRS 9.B5.4.4	Ch.50, p.3891	IFRS 9.B5.5.27	Ch.51, p.4034
IFRS 9.B5.4.4	Ch.51, p.4070	IFRS 9.B5.5.28	Ch.51, p.3935
IFRS 9.B5.4.5	Ch.50, p.3883	IFRS 9.B5.5.28	Ch.51, p.3952
IFRS 9.B5.4.5	Ch.50, p.3885	IFRS 9.B5.5.28	Ch.51, p.4047
IFRS 9.B5.4.6	Ch.43, p.3394	IFRS 9.B5.5.28	Ch.51, p.3947

IFRS 9.B5.5.29	Ch.32, p.2399	IFRS 9.B5.7.1	Ch.48, p.3830
IFRS 9.B5.5.29	Ch.51, p.3935	IFRS 9.B5.7.1	Ch.49, p.3859
IFRS 9.B5.5.30	Ch.51, p.3936	IFRS 9.B5.7.1	Ch.50, p.3877
IFRS 9.B5.5.30	Ch.51, p.4047	IFRS 9.B5.7.1A	Ch.50, p.3871
IFRS 9.B5.5.31	Ch.51, p.3936	IFRS 9.B5.7.2	Ch.50, p.3871
IFRS 9.B5.5.31	Ch.51, p.3944	IFRS 9.B5.7.2	Ch.50, p.3880
IFRS 9.B5.5.32	Ch.51, p.3936	IFRS 9.B5.7.2	Ch.50, p.3900
IFRS 9.B5.5.32	Ch.51, p.4047	IFRS 9.B5.7.2-2A	Ch.50, p.3900
IFRS 9.B5.5.32	Ch.51, p.4048	IFRS 9.B5.7.2A	Ch.50, p.3871
IFRS 9.B5.5.33	Ch.51, p.4019	IFRS 9.B5.7.2A	Ch.50, p.3900
IFRS 9.B5.5.34	Ch.51, p.4044	IFRS 9.B5.7.3	Ch.11, p.835
IFRS 9.B5.5.35	Ch.51, p.3932	IFRS 9.B5.7.3	Ch.15, p.1197
IFRS 9.B5.5.35	Ch.51, p.4043	IFRS 9.B5.7.3	Ch.15, p.1198
IFRS 9.B5.5.37	Ch.51, p.3935	IFRS 9.B5.7.3	Ch.16, p.1258
IFRS 9.B5.5.37	Ch.51, p.3938	IFRS 9.B5.7.3	Ch.50, p.3877
IFRS 9.B5.5.38	Ch.51, p.3945	IFRS 9.B5.7.3	Ch.50, p.3900
IFRS 9.B5.5.38	Ch.51, p.4047	IFRS 9.B5.7.5	Ch.50, p.3875
IFRS 9.B5.5.39	Ch.51, p.3945	IFRS 9.B5.7.6	Ch.50, p.3875
IFRS 9.B5.5.39	Ch.51, p.4047	IFRS 9.B5.7.7	Ch.50, p.3875
IFRS 9.B5.5.39	Ch.51, p.4051	IFRS 9.B5.7.8	Ch.50, p.3872
IFRS 9.B5.5.39	Ch.51, p.4052	IFRS 9.B5.7.8	Ch.50, p.3876
IFRS 9.B5.5.40	Ch.51, p.3945	IFRS 9.B5.7.9	Ch.50, p.3872
IFRS 9.B5.5.40	Ch.51, p.4047	IFRS 9.B5.7.10	Ch.48, p.3776
IFRS 9.B5.5.40	Ch.51, p.4055	IFRS 9.B5.7.10	Ch.50, p.3876
IFRS 9.B5.5.41	Ch.51, p.3947	IFRS 9.B5.7.11	Ch.50, p.3876
IFRS 9.B5.5.42	Ch.51, p.3947	IFRS 9.B5.7.12	Ch.50, p.3876
IFRS 9.B5.5.43	Ch.51, p.3936	IFRS 9.B5.7.13	Ch.50, p.3872
IFRS 9.B5.5.43	Ch.51, p.3935	IFRS 9.B5.7.14	Ch.50, p.3873
IFRS 9.B5.5.44	Ch.51, p.3952	IFRS 9.B5.7.15	Ch.50, p.3873
IFRS 9.B5.5.44	Ch.51, p.3953	IFRS 9.B5.7.16	Ch.50, p.3873
IFRS 9.B5.5.44	Ch.51, p.4047	IFRS 9.B5.7.16(b)	Ch.50, p.3875
IFRS 9.B5.5.44	Ch.51, p.4064	IFRS 9.B5.7.17	Ch.50, p.3873
IFRS 9.B5.5.45	Ch.51, p.3930	IFRS 9.B5.7.18	Ch.50, p.3873
IFRS 9.B5.5.45	Ch.51, p.3953	IFRS 9.B5.7.19	Ch.50, p.3875
IFRS 9.B5.5.46	Ch.51, p.3953	IFRS 9.B5.7.20	Ch.50, p.3875
IFRS 9.B5.5.46	Ch.51, p.4044	IFRS 9.B6.2.1	Ch.53, p.4238
IFRS 9.B5.5.47	Ch.48, p.3813	IFRS 9.B6.2.2	Ch.53, p.4242
IFRS 9.B5.5.47	Ch.51, p.3953	IFRS 9.B6.2.3	Ch.53, p.4241
IFRS 9.B5.5.47	Ch.51, p.4047	IFRS 9.B6.2.3	Ch.53, p.4303
IFRS 9.B5.5.47	Ch.51, p.4063	IFRS 9.B6.2.3	Ch.53, p.4306
IFRS 9.B5.5.48	Ch.51, p.3953	IFRS 9.B6.2.4	Ch.53, p.4235
IFRS 9.B5.5.48	Ch.51, p.4047	IFRS 9.B6.2.4	Ch.53, p.4236
IFRS 9.B5.5.49	Ch.51, p.3962	IFRS 9.B6.2.5	Ch.53, p.4241
IFRS 9.B5.5.49-54	Ch.51, p.3967	IFRS 9.B6.2.6	Ch.53, p.4243
IFRS 9.B5.5.50	Ch.51, p.3964	IFRS 9.B6.3.1	Ch.9, p.698
IFRS 9.B5.5.51	Ch.51, p.3962	IFRS 9.B6.3.1	Ch.53, p.4221
IFRS 9.B5.5.51	Ch.51, p.3963	IFRS 9.B6.3.1	Ch.53, p.4343
IFRS 9.B5.5.51	Ch.51, p.3967	IFRS 9.B6.3.2	Ch.53, p.4263
IFRS 9.B5.5.51	Ch.51, p.3944	IFRS 9.B6.3.2	Ch.53, p.4267
IFRS 9.B5.5.52	Ch.51, p.3964	IFRS 9.B6.3.3	Ch.53, p.4234
IFRS 9.B5.5.52	Ch.51, p.3965	IFRS 9.B6.3.4	Ch.53, p.4226
IFRS 9.B5.5.53	Ch.51, p.3965	IFRS 9.B6.3.4	Ch.53, p.4227
IFRS 9.B5.5.54	Ch.51, p.3964	IFRS 9.B6.3.5	Ch.53, p.4260
IFRS 9.B5.5.55	Ch.45, p.3599	IFRS 9.B6.3.6	Ch.53, p.4298
IFRS 9.B5.5.55	Ch.51, p.3955	IFRS 9.B6.3.7	Ch.53, p.4191
IFRS 9.B5.5.55	Ch.51, p.3973	IFRS 9.B6.3.7	Ch.53, p.4193
IFRS 9.B5.6.2	Ch.50, p.3879	IFRS 9.B6.3.7	Ch.53, p.4202
IFRS 9.B5.7.1	Ch.11, p.835	IFRS 9.B6.3.8	Ch.53, p.4190

IFRS 9.B6.3.8	Ch.53, p.4191	IFRS 9.B6.4.8	Ch.53, p.4284
IFRS 9.B6.3.8	Ch.53, p.4197	IFRS 9.B6.4.10	Ch.53, p.4288
IFRS 9.B6.3.8	Ch.53, p.4201	IFRS 9.B6.4.11(a)	Ch.53, p.4288
IFRS 9.B6.3.9	Ch.53, p.4191	IFRS 9.B6.4.11(a)	Ch.53, p.4296
IFRS 9.B6.3.9	Ch.53, p.4194	IFRS 9.B6.4.11(b)	Ch.53, p.4289
IFRS 9.B6.3.9	Ch.53, p.4197	IFRS 9.B6.4.12	Ch.53, p.4280
IFRS 9.B6.3.9	Ch.53, p.4201	IFRS 9.B6.4.12	Ch.53, p.4283
IFRS 9.B6.3.9	Ch.53, p.4373	IFRS 9.B6.4.12	Ch.53, p.4346
IFRS 9.B6.3.10	Ch.53, p.4191	IFRS 9.B6.4.13	Ch.53, p.4280
IFRS 9.B6.3.10	Ch.53, p.4192	IFRS 9.B6.4.14	Ch.53, p.4281
IFRS 9.B6.3.10(b)	Ch.53, p.4195	IFRS 9.B6.4.15	Ch.53, p.4277
IFRS 9.B6.3.10(c)	Ch.53, p.4196	IFRS 9.B6.4.15	Ch.53, p.4282
IFRS 9.B6.3.10(c)(i)	Ch.53, p.4208	IFRS 9.B6.4.15	Ch.53, p.4310
IFRS 9.B6.3.10(d)	Ch.53, p.4194	IFRS 9.B6.4.16	Ch.53, p.4280
IFRS 9.B6.3.10(d)	Ch.53, p.4373	IFRS 9.B6.4.16	Ch.53, p.4282
IFRS 9.B6.3.11	Ch.53, p.4191	IFRS 9.B6.4.17	Ch.53, p.4276
IFRS 9.B6.3.11	Ch.53, p.4198	IFRS 9.B6.4.17	Ch.53, p.4280
IFRS 9.B6.3.11	Ch.53, p.4290	IFRS 9.B6.4.18	Ch.53, p.4280
IFRS 9.B6.3.11	Ch.53, p.4308	IFRS 9.B6.4.18	Ch.53, p.4282
IFRS 9.B6.3.12	Ch.53, p.4246	IFRS 9.B6.4.18	Ch.53, p.4283
IFRS 9.B6.3.12	Ch.53, p.4306	IFRS 9.B6.4.18	Ch.53, p.4344
IFRS 9.B6.3.12	Ch.53, p.4327	IFRS 9.B6.4.19	Ch.53, p.4276
IFRS 9.B6.3.12	Ch.53, p.4328	IFRS 9.B6.4.19	Ch.53, p.4280
IFRS 9.B6.3.12	Ch.53, p.4329	IFRS 9.B6.5.1	Ch.53, p.4262
IFRS 9.B6.3.13	Ch.53, p.4200	IFRS 9.B6.5.2	Ch.53, p.4218
IFRS 9.B6.3.14	Ch.53, p.4200	IFRS 9.B6.5.2	Ch.53, p.4264
IFRS 9.B6.3.15	Ch.53, p.4200	IFRS 9.B6.5.3	Ch.53, p.4263
IFRS 9.B6.3.16	Ch.53, p.4201	IFRS 9.B6.5.3	Ch.53, p.4266
IFRS 9.B6.3.17	Ch.53, p.4201	IFRS 9.B6.5.3	Ch.53, p.4343
IFRS 9.B6.3.18	Ch.53, p.4202	IFRS 9.B6.5.4	Ch.53, p.4241
IFRS 9.B6.3.18	Ch.53, p.4203	IFRS 9.B6.5.4	Ch.53, p.4309
IFRS 9.B6.3.19	Ch.53, p.4202	IFRS 9.B6.5.4	Ch.53, p.4312
IFRS 9.B6.3.20	Ch.53, p.4203	IFRS 9.B6.5.4	Ch.53, p.4329
IFRS 9.B6.3.21	Ch.53, p.4206	IFRS 9.B6.5.5	Ch.53, p.4304
IFRS 9.B6.3.21	Ch.53, p.4210	IFRS 9.B6.5.5	Ch.53, p.4305
IFRS 9.B6.3.21-22	Ch.53, p.4206	IFRS 9.B6.5.5	Ch.53, p.4310
IFRS 9.B6.3.23	Ch.53, p.4209	IFRS 9.B6.5.5	Ch.53, p.4312
IFRS 9.B6.3.23	Ch.53, p.4210	IFRS 9.B6.5.5	Ch.53, p.4313
IFRS 9.B6.3.24	Ch.53, p.4206	IFRS 9.B6.5.5	Ch.53, p.4325
IFRS 9.B6.3.25	Ch.53, p.4207	IFRS 9.B6.5.5	Ch.53, p.4326
IFRS 9.B6.4.1	Ch.53, p.4191	IFRS 9.B6.5.5	Ch.53, p.4328
IFRS 9.B6.4.1	Ch.53, p.4198	IFRS 9.B6.5.5	Ch.53, p.4339
IFRS 9.B6.4.1	Ch.53, p.4276	IFRS 9.B6.5.7	Ch.53, p.4347
IFRS 9.B6.4.1	Ch.53, p.4280	IFRS 9.B6.5.7	Ch.53, p.4348
IFRS 9.B6.4.1	Ch.53, p.4290	IFRS 9.B6.5.8	Ch.53, p.4350
IFRS 9.B6.4.1	Ch.53, p.4307	IFRS 9.B6.5.9	Ch.53, p.4347
IFRS 9.B6.4.1	Ch.53, p.4308	IFRS 9.B6.5.10	Ch.53, p.4347
IFRS 9.B6.4.1	Ch.53, p.4325	IFRS 9.B6.5.11	Ch.53, p.4295
IFRS 9.B6.4.2	Ch.53, p.4276	IFRS 9.B6.5.11	Ch.53, p.4350
IFRS 9.B6.4.3	Ch.53, p.4362	IFRS 9.B6.5.12	Ch.53, p.4350
IFRS 9.B6.4.4	Ch.53, p.4200	IFRS 9.B6.5.13	Ch.53, p.4349
IFRS 9.B6.4.4	Ch.53, p.4281	IFRS 9.B6.5.14	Ch.53, p.4349
IFRS 9.B6.4.5	Ch.53, p.4281	IFRS 9.B6.5.16	Ch.53, p.4350
IFRS 9.B6.4.6	Ch.53, p.4281	IFRS 9.B6.5.16-20	Ch.53, p.4352
IFRS 9.B6.4.6	Ch.53, p.4283	IFRS 9.B6.5.21	Ch.53, p.4353
IFRS 9.B6.4.6	Ch.53, p.4344	IFRS 9.B6.5.24	Ch.53, p.4273
IFRS 9.B6.4.7	Ch.53, p.4284	IFRS 9.B6.5.24	Ch.53, p.4356
IFRS 9.B6.4.7	Ch.53, p.4286	IFRS 9.B6.5.24(a)	Ch.53, p.4357

IFRS 9.B6.5.26(a)	Ch.53, p.4393	IFRS 9.IE66-IE73 Example 11	Ch.51, p.4034
IFRS 9.B6.5.27(a)	Ch.53, p.4352	IFRS 9.IE74-IE77 Example 12	Ch.51, p.4043
IFRS 9.B6.5.24(b)	Ch.53, p.4277	IFRS 9.IE78-IE81 Example 13	Ch.33, p.2580
IFRS 9.B6.5.24(b)	Ch.53, p.4359	IFRS 9.IE78-IE81 Example 13	Ch.51, p.4036
IFRS 9.B6.5.28	Ch.53, p.4190	IFRS 9.IE82-IE102	Ch.51, p.4037
IFRS 9.B6.5.28	Ch.53, p.4209	IFRS 9.IE115-147	Ch.53, p.4225
IFRS 9.B6.5.28	Ch.53, p.4234	IFRS 9.IE116-127	Ch.53, p.4231
IFRS 9.B6.5.28	Ch.53, p.4276	IFRS 9.IE119(b)	Ch.53, p.4231
IFRS 9.B6.5.28	Ch.53, p.4310	IFRS 9.IE119(b)	Ch.53, p.4232
IFRS 9.B6.5.29	Ch.53, p.4331	IFRS 9.IE122	Ch.53, p.4232
IFRS 9.B6.5.29-39	Ch.5, p.259	IFRS 9.IE123	Ch.53, p.4232
IFRS 9.B6.5.29(b)	Ch.53, p.4303	IFRS 9.IE128-137	Ch.53, p.4227
IFRS 9.B6.5.29(b)	Ch.53, p.4338	IFRS 9.IE131(b)	Ch.53, p.4227
IFRS 9.B6.5.30	Ch.53, p.4331	IFRS 9.IE134	Ch.53, p.4229
IFRS 9.B6.5.31	Ch.53, p.4334	IFRS 9.IE134(a)	Ch.53, p.4228
IFRS 9.B6.5.32	Ch.53, p.4334	IFRS 9.IE138-147	Ch.53, p.4229
IFRS 9.B6.5.33	Ch.53, p.4334	IFRS 9.IE139(b)	Ch.53, p.4230
IFRS 9.B6.5.34-36	Ch.53, p.4336	IFRS 9.IE143	Ch.53, p.4230
IFRS 9.B6.5.37	Ch.53, p.4337	IFRS 9.IG A.1	Ch.45, p.3609
IFRS 9.B6.5.37	Ch.53, p.4338	IFRS 9.IG A.2	Ch.45, p.3611
IFRS 9.B6.5.37	Ch.53, p.4343	IFRS 9.IG B.3	Ch.46, p.3627
IFRS 9.B6.5.38	Ch.53, p.4343	IFRS 9.IG B.4	Ch.46, p.3625
IFRS 9.B6.6.1	Ch.53, p.4211	IFRS 9.IG B.5	Ch.46, p.3626
IFRS 9.B6.6.7	Ch.53, p.4213	IFRS 9.IG B.6	Ch.46, p.3628
IFRS 9.B6.6.7	Ch.53, p.4215	IFRS 9.IG B.6	Ch.53, p.4235
IFRS 9.B6.6.8	Ch.53, p.4215	IFRS 9.IG B.7	Ch.46, p.3627
IFRS 9.B6.6.12	Ch.53, p.4212	IFRS 9.IG B.8	Ch.46, p.3621
IFRS 9.B6.6.13	Ch.54, p.4487	IFRS 9.IG B.9	Ch.46, p.3625
IFRS 9.B6.6.13-15	Ch.53, p.4380	IFRS 9.IG B.9	Ch.46, p.3626
IFRS 9.B6.6.14	Ch.54, p.4487	IFRS 9.IG B.10	Ch.46, p.3626
IFRS 9.B6.6.15	Ch.53, p.4215	IFRS 9.IG B.11	Ch.48, p.3778
IFRS 9.B6.6.15	Ch.54, p.4487	IFRS 9.IG B.24	Ch.50, p.3889
IFRS 9.B6.6.16	Ch.53, p.4381	IFRS 9.IG B.25	Ch.50, p.3889
IFRS 9.B6.6.16	Ch.54, p.4487	IFRS 9.IG B.26	Ch.50, p.3884
IFRS 9.B7.2.2	Ch.5, p.264	IFRS 9.IG B.26	Ch.50, p.3888
IFRS 9.B7.2.2-3	Ch.5, p.264	IFRS 9.IG B.27	Ch.50, p.3884
IFRS 9.B7.2.3	Ch.5, p.264	IFRS 9.IG B.28	Ch.49, p.3846
IFRS 9.BA.1	Ch.46, p.3621	IFRS 9.IG B.29	Ch.49, p.3846
IFRS 9.BA.2	Ch.46, p.3627	IFRS 9.IG B.30	Ch.49, p.3846
IFRS 9.BA.3	Ch.46, p.3624	IFRS 9.IG B.31	Ch.49, p.3847
IFRS 9.BA.3	Ch.46, p.3625	IFRS 9.IG C.1	Ch.46, p.3649
IFRS 9.BA.4	Ch.46, p.3629	IFRS 9.IG C.2	Ch.46, p.3650
IFRS 9.BA.4	Ch.49, p.3860	IFRS 9.IG C.2	Ch.46, p.3651
IFRS 9.BA.5	Ch.46, p.3622	IFRS 9.IG C.4	Ch.46, p.3641
IFRS 9.BA.6	Ch.48, p.3778	IFRS 9.IG C.6	Ch.46, p.3653
IFRS 9.BA.7	Ch.48, p.3778	IFRS 9.IG C.6	Ch.46, p.3654
IFRS 9.BA.7(d)	Ch.48, p.3778	IFRS 9.IG C.7	Ch.46, p.3645
IFRS 9.BA.8	Ch.48, p.3778	IFRS 9.IG C.8	Ch.46, p.3645
IFRS 9.IE1-IE5	Ch.50, p.3874	IFRS 9.IG C.9	Ch.46, p.3643
IFRS 9.IE7-11 Example 1	Ch.51, p.3982	IFRS 9.IG C.10	Ch.46, p.3631
IFRS 9.IE12-17 Example 2	Ch.51, p.3982	IFRS 9.IG D.1.1	Ch.49, p.3844
IFRS 9.IE18-IE23 Example 3	Ch.51, p.3972	IFRS 9.IG D.2.1	Ch.49, p.3848
IFRS 9.IE24-IE28 Example 4	Ch.51, p.3992	IFRS 9.IG D.2.2	Ch.49, p.3848
IFRS 9.IE29-IE39 Example 5	Ch.51, p.4004	IFRS 9.IG D.2.2	Ch.50, p.3881
IFRS 9.IE40-IE42 Example 6	Ch.51, p.3998	IFRS 9.IG D.2.3	Ch.49, p.3853
IFRS 9.IE43-IE47 Example 7	Ch.51, p.3997	IFRS 9.IG E.1.1	Ch.49, p.3859
IFRS 9.IE53-IE57 Example 9	Ch.51, p.3942	IFRS 9.IG E.3.2	Ch.50, p.3900
IFRS 9.IE58-IE65 Example 10	Ch.51, p.4055	IFRS 9.IG E.3.3	Ch.50, p.3902

IFRS 9.IG E.3.4	Ch.50, p.3900	IFRS 9.BC4.193	Ch.48, p.3806
IFRS 9.IG G.2	Ch.40, p.3161	IFRS 9.BC4.194	Ch.48, p.3807
IFRS 9.IG G.2	Ch.54, p.4520	IFRS 9.BC4.206(a)	Ch.48, p.3821
IFRS 9.BCZ2.2	Ch.45, p.3600	IFRS 9.BC4.225	Ch.48, p.3805
IFRS 9.BCZ2.2	Ch.45, p.3601	IFRS 9.BC4.232	Ch.48, p.3805
IFRS 9.BCZ2.2	Ch.51, p.4045	IFRS 9.BC4.252	Ch.52, p.4163
IFRS 9.BCZ2.2	Ch.51, p.4046	IFRS 9.BC4.252-253	Ch.50, p.3894
IFRS 9.BCZ2.3	Ch.45, p.3600	IFRS 9.BC4.253	Ch.52, p.4163
IFRS 9.BCZ2.3	Ch.49, p.3862	IFRS 9.BC5.13	Ch.50, p.3878
IFRS 9.BCZ2.6	Ch.45, p.3601	IFRS 9.BC5.16	Ch.50, p.3878
IFRS 9.BCZ2.7	Ch.45, p.3601	IFRS 9.BC5.18	Ch.50, p.3878
IFRS 9.BCZ2.12	Ch.45, p.3598	IFRS 9.BC5.21	Ch.48, p.3830
IFRS 9.BCZ2.14	Ch.45, p.3600	IFRS 9.BC5.25(a)	Ch.48, p.3832
IFRS 9.BCZ2.18	Ch.43, p.3474	IFRS 9.BC5.25(c)	Ch.48, p.3831
IFRS 9.BCZ2.18	Ch.45, p.3608	IFRS 9.BC5.40	Ch.48, p.3776
IFRS 9.BCZ2.18	Ch.45, p.3609	IFRS 9.BC5.41	Ch.48, p.3776
IFRS 9.BCZ2.18	Ch.45, p.3610	IFRS 9.BCZ5.67	Ch.50, p.3881
IFRS 9.BCZ2.24	Ch.45, p.3613	IFRS 9.BC5.75	Ch.51, p.4070
IFRS 9.BCZ2.39	Ch.45, p.3603	IFRS 9.BC5.78	Ch.51, p.4071
IFRS 9.BCZ2.40	Ch.45, p.3603	IFRS 9.BC5.87	Ch.51, p.3912
IFRS 9.BCZ2.41	Ch.45, p.3603	IFRS 9.BC5.89	Ch.51, p.3912
IFRS 9.BCZ2.42	Ch.11, p.827	IFRS 9.BC5.92	Ch.51, p.3912
IFRS 9.BCZ2.42	Ch.45, p.3604	IFRS 9.BC5.93	Ch.51, p.3913
IFRS 9.BCZ3.4-12	Ch.52, p.4138	IFRS 9.BC5.95	Ch.51, p.3913
IFRS 9.BC4.23	Ch.48, p.3790	IFRS 9.BC5.96	Ch.51, p.3913
IFRS 9.BC4.26	Ch.48, p.3817	IFRS 9.BC5.104	Ch.51, p.3929
IFRS 9.BC4.28	Ch.48, p.3818	IFRS 9.BC5.111	Ch.51, p.3913
IFRS 9.BC4.29	Ch.48, p.3818	IFRS 9.BC5.112	Ch.51, p.3913
IFRS 9.BC4.33	Ch.48, p.3818	IFRS 9.BC5.114	Ch.51, p.3915
IFRS 9.BC4.34	Ch.48, p.3818	IFRS 9.BC5.116	Ch.51, p.3915
IFRS 9.BC4.35(d)	Ch.48, p.3822	IFRS 9.BC5.123	Ch.51, p.3976
IFRS 9.BCZ4.61	Ch.48, p.3827	IFRS 9.BC5.135	Ch.51, p.3937
IFRS 9.BCZ4.66	Ch.48, p.3829	IFRS 9.BC5.141	Ch.51, p.3926
IFRS 9.BCZ4.68-70	Ch.48, p.3830	IFRS 9.BC5.154	Ch.32, p.2398
IFRS 9.BCZ4.70	Ch.48, p.3830	IFRS 9.BC5.157	Ch.51, p.3970
IFRS 9.BCZ4.74-76	Ch.48, p.3826	IFRS 9.BC5.157	Ch.51, p.3975
IFRS 9.BCZ4.92	Ch.46, p.3629	IFRS 9.BC5.160	Ch.51, p.3971
IFRS 9.BCZ4.92	Ch.46, p.3619	IFRS 9.BC5.161	Ch.51, p.3971
IFRS 9.BCZ4.94	Ch.46, p.3643	IFRS 9.BC5.162	Ch.51, p.3971
IFRS 9.BCZ4.97	Ch.46, p.3636	IFRS 9.BC5.163	Ch.51, p.3971
IFRS 9.BCZ4.99	Ch.46, p.3651	IFRS 9.BC5.164	Ch.51, p.3971
IFRS 9.BCZ4.100	Ch.46, p.3651	IFRS 9.BC5.165	Ch.51, p.3971
IFRS 9.BCZ4.100-101	Ch.46, p.3652	IFRS 9.BC5.168	Ch.51, p.3997
IFRS 9.BCZ4.105	Ch.46, p.3653	IFRS 9.BC5.171	Ch.51, p.3987
IFRS 9.BCZ4.106	Ch.46, p.3652	IFRS 9.BC5.172	Ch.51, p.3987
IFRS 9.BC4.117	Ch.48, p.3834	IFRS 9.BC5.178	Ch.51, p.3995
IFRS 9.BC4.150	Ch.48, p.3774	IFRS 9.BC5.181	Ch.51, p.3989
IFRS 9.BC4.150	Ch.50, p.3871	IFRS 9.BC5.182	Ch.51, p.3989
IFRS 9.BC4.158	Ch.48, p.3790	IFRS 9.BC5.183	Ch.51, p.3989
IFRS 9.BC4.171	Ch.48, p.3790	IFRS 9.BC5.184	Ch.51, p.3989
IFRS 9.BC4.172	Ch.48, p.3790	IFRS 9.BC5.188	Ch.51, p.3990
IFRS 9.BC4.178	Ch.48, p.3793	IFRS 9.BC5.190	Ch.51, p.3980
IFRS 9.BC4.180	Ch.48, p.3791	IFRS 9.BC5.192	Ch.51, p.3980
IFRS 9.BC4.180	Ch.48, p.3802	IFRS 9.BC5.199	Ch.51, p.3937
IFRS 9.BC4.182(a)	Ch.48, p.3791	IFRS 9.BC5.214	Ch.51, p.3930
IFRS 9.BC4.182(b)	Ch.48, p.3791	IFRS 9.BC5.216	Ch.52, p.4099
IFRS 9.BC4.182(b)	Ch.48, p.3792	IFRS 9.BC5.217	Ch.51, p.3930
IFRS 9.BC4.182(b)	Ch.48, p.3793	IFRS 9.BC5.225	Ch.51, p.3929

IFRS 9.BC5.227	Ch.52, p.4099	IFRS 9.BC6.380	Ch.54, p.4490
IFRS 9.BC5.248	Ch.51, p.3935	IFRS 9.BC6.387	Ch.53, p.4329
IFRS 9.BC5.249	Ch.51, p.3935	IFRS 9.BC6.398	Ch.53, p.4335
IFRS 9.BC5.252	Ch.51, p.3935	IFRS 9.BC6.399	Ch.53, p.4333
IFRS 9.BC5.252	Ch.51, p.3938	IFRS 9.BC6.416	Ch.53, p.4337
IFRS 9.BC5.254-261	Ch.51, p.4053	IFRS 9.BC6.422	Ch.53, p.4336
IFRS 9.BC5.259	Ch.51, p.4054	IFRS 9.BC6.435	Ch.53, p.4211
IFRS 9.BC5.260	Ch.51, p.4064	IFRS 9.BC6.436	Ch.53, p.4211
IFRS 9.BC5.260	Ch.51, p.4061	IFRS 9.BC6.438	Ch.53, p.4212
IFRS 9.BC5.260	Ch.51, p.3944	IFRS 9.BC6.439	Ch.53, p.4212
IFRS 9.BC5.265	Ch.51, p.3938	IFRS 9.BC6.455	Ch.53, p.4213
IFRS 9.BC5.281	Ch.51, p.3964	IFRS 9.BC6.457	Ch.53, p.4380
IFRS 9.BC5.306	Ch.50, p.3898	IFRS 9.BC6.461	Ch.53, p.4380
IFRS 9.BC5.309	Ch.50, p.3899	IFRS 9.BC6.470	Ch.53, p.4387
IFRS 9.BC5.311	Ch.50, p.3899	IFRS 9.BC6.470	Ch.53, p.4192
IFRS 9.BC5.312	Ch.50, p.3899	IFRS 9.BC6.491	Ch.53, p.4387
IFRS 9.BC5.318	Ch.50, p.3899	IFRS 9.BC6.504	Ch.53, p.4387
IFRS 9.BC6.327	Ch.53, p.4354	IFRS 9.BC6.517	Ch.53, p.4192
IFRS 9.BC6.330	Ch.53, p.4354	IFRS 9.BC6.560	Ch.53, p.4367
IFRS 9.BC6.82	Ch.53, p.4187	IFRS 9.BC6.567	Ch.53, p.4367
IFRS 9.BC6.91-95	Ch.53, p.4385	IFRS 9.BC6.568	Ch.53, p.4367
IFRS 9.BC6.93-95	Ch.53, p.4394	IFRS 9.BC6.575	Ch.53, p.4367
IFRS 9.BC6.93-95	Ch.53, p.4187	IFRS 9.BC6.594	Ch.53, p.4368
IFRS 9.BC6.94-95	Ch.53, p.4265	IFRS 9.BC6.619	Ch.53, p.4375
IFRS 9.BC6.97	Ch.53, p.4394	IFRS 9.BC6.647	Ch.53, p.4374
IFRS 9.BC6.97-101	Ch.53, p.4274	IFRS 9.BC6.587-593	Ch.53, p.4368
IFRS 9.BC6.98	Ch.53, p.4275	IFRS 9.BC6.616-619	Ch.53, p.4371
IFRS 9.BC6.98	Ch.53, p.4381	IFRS 9.BC7.44-51	Ch.53, p.4393
IFRS 9.BC6.98	Ch.53, p.4394	IFRS 9.BC7.49	Ch.53, p.4393
IFRS 9.BC6.100(a)	Ch.53, p.4381	IFRS 9.BC7.49	Ch.53, p.4392
IFRS 9.BC6.100(a)	Ch.53, p.4275	IFRS 9.BC7.52	Ch.5, p.249
IFRS 9.BC6.100(b)	Ch.53, p.4394	IFRS 9.BC7.52	Ch.5, p.252
IFRS 9.BC6.100(b)	Ch.53, p.4275	IFRS 9.BC7.88	Ch.53, p.4377
IFRS 9.BC6.104	Ch.54, p.4412		
IFRS 9.BC6.104	Ch.53, p.4386		
IFRS 9.BC6.104	Ch.53, p.4390	**IFRS 10**	
IFRS 9.BC6.117-122	Ch.53, p.4238		
IFRS 9.BC6.142-150	Ch.53, p.4250	IFRS 10.1	Ch.6, p.394
IFRS 9.BC6.151	Ch.53, p.4236	IFRS 10.2	Ch.6, p.394
IFRS 9.BC6.153	Ch.53, p.4236	IFRS 10.2	Ch.27, p.2035
IFRS 9.BC6.167	Ch.53, p.4233	IFRS 10.3	Ch.6, p.394
IFRS 9.BC6.174	Ch.53, p.4193	IFRS 10.4	Ch.5, p.313
IFRS 9.BC6.331	Ch.53, p.4354	IFRS 10.4	Ch.6, p.394
IFRS 9.BC6.176	Ch.53, p.4198	IFRS 10.4	Ch.8, p.577
IFRS 9.BC6.176	Ch.53, p.4191	IFRS 10.4-4B	Ch.27, p.2035
IFRS 9.BC6.200	Ch.53, p.4361	IFRS 10.4(a)	Ch.6, p.395
IFRS 9.BC6.226-228	Ch.53, p.4206	IFRS 10.4(a)	Ch.8, p.577
IFRS 9.BC6.238	Ch.53, p.4281	IFRS 10.4A	Ch.6, p.398
IFRS 9.BC6.269	Ch.53, p.4282	IFRS 10.4B	Ch.6, p.399
IFRS 9.BC6.297	Ch.53, p.4330	IFRS 10.5	Ch.6, p.405
IFRS 9.BC6.301	Ch.53, p.4350	IFRS 10.6	Ch.6, p.405
IFRS 9.BC6.303	Ch.53, p.4347	IFRS 10.6	Ch.9, p.659
IFRS 9.BC6.310	Ch.53, p.4350	IFRS 10.7	Ch.6, p.405
IFRS 9.BC6.324	Ch.53, p.4354	IFRS 10.7	Ch.6, p.410
IFRS 9.BC6.332-337	Ch.52, p.4102	IFRS 10.7	Ch.6, p.436
IFRS 9.BC6.333	Ch.52, p.4167	IFRS 10.7	Ch.6, p.439
IFRS 9.BC6.335	Ch.52, p.4155	IFRS 10.7	Ch.6, p.445
IFRS 9.BC6.380	Ch.54, p.4421	IFRS 10.7	Ch.7, p.508

IFRS 10.8	Ch.6, p.406	IFRS 10.24	Ch.7, p.546
IFRS 10.8	Ch.6, p.410	IFRS 10.24	Ch.7, p.547
IFRS 10.8	Ch.6, p.467	IFRS 10.24	Ch.7, p.548
IFRS 10.8	Ch.7, p.508	IFRS 10.24	Ch.7, p.549
IFRS 10.8	Ch.52, p.4153	IFRS 10.25	Ch.6, p.405
IFRS 10.9	Ch.6, p.406	IFRS 10.25	Ch.6, p.488
IFRS 10.10	Ch.6, p.408	IFRS 10.25	Ch.7, p.509
IFRS 10.10	Ch.6, p.409	IFRS 10.25	Ch.7, p.514
IFRS 10.10	Ch.6, p.432	IFRS 10.25	Ch.7, p.518
IFRS 10.11	Ch.6, p.413	IFRS 10.25	Ch.7, p.519
IFRS 10.11	Ch.6, p.434	IFRS 10.25	Ch.7, p.520
IFRS 10.12	Ch.6, p.415	IFRS 10.25	Ch.7, p.565
IFRS 10.13	Ch.6, p.409	IFRS 10.25	Ch.11, p.857
IFRS 10.14	Ch.6, p.409	IFRS 10.25	Ch.12, p.933
IFRS 10.14	Ch.6, p.414	IFRS 10.26	Ch.7, p.509
IFRS 10.14	Ch.6, p.416	IFRS 10.26	Ch.7, p.514
IFRS 10.15	Ch.6, p.439	IFRS 10.26	Ch.7, p.518
IFRS 10.16	Ch.6, p.439	IFRS 10.26	Ch.7, p.519
IFRS 10.17	Ch.6, p.445	IFRS 10.26	Ch.7, p.520
IFRS 10.18	Ch.6, p.445	IFRS 10.26	Ch.7, p.524
IFRS 10.18	Ch.6, p.446	IFRS 10.26	Ch.7, p.525
IFRS 10.19	Ch.5, p.335	IFRS 10.26	Ch.7, p.526
IFRS 10.19	Ch.7, p.497	IFRS 10.26	Ch.7, p.527
IFRS 10.19	Ch.55, p.4589	IFRS 10.26	Ch.7, p.531
IFRS 10.20	Ch.6, p.399	IFRS 10.26	Ch.7, p.565
IFRS 10.20	Ch.6, p.405	IFRS 10.27	Ch.6, p.473
IFRS 10.20	Ch.7, p.497	IFRS 10.28	Ch.6, p.473
IFRS 10.20	Ch.7, p.503	IFRS 10.29	Ch.6, p.473
IFRS 10.20	Ch.8, p.578	IFRS 10.30	Ch.6, p.474
IFRS 10.20	Ch.27, p.2035	IFRS 10.30	Ch.6, p.488
IFRS 10.21	Ch.7, p.497	IFRS 10.31	Ch.5, p.313
IFRS 10.21	Ch.7, p.498	IFRS 10.31	Ch.6, p.485
IFRS 10.21	Ch.7, p.499	IFRS 10.31	Ch.8, p.583
IFRS 10.21	Ch.7, p.501	IFRS 10.31	Ch.45, p.3592
IFRS 10.21	Ch.7, p.502	IFRS 10.31-33	Ch.7, p.497
IFRS 10.21	Ch.7, p.503	IFRS 10.31-33	Ch.7, p.540
IFRS 10.21	Ch.7, p.523	IFRS 10.32	Ch.5, p.313
IFRS 10.21	Ch.7, p.547	IFRS 10.32	Ch.6, p.475
IFRS 10.21	Ch.7, p.549	IFRS 10.32	Ch.6, p.485
IFRS 10.21	Ch.7, p.550	IFRS 10.33	Ch.5, p.313
IFRS 10.22	Ch.7, p.498	IFRS 10.33	Ch.6, p.489
IFRS 10.22	Ch.7, p.545	IFRS 10 Appendix A	Ch.5, p.285
IFRS 10.22	Ch.11, p.840	IFRS 10 Appendix A	Ch.5, p.313
IFRS 10.22	Ch.11, p.867	IFRS 10 Appendix A	Ch.6, p.394
IFRS 10.23	Ch.5, p.262	IFRS 10 Appendix A	Ch.6, p.405
IFRS 10.23	Ch.7, p.498	IFRS 10 Appendix A	Ch.6, p.416
IFRS 10.23	Ch.7, p.533	IFRS 10 Appendix A	Ch.7, p.497
IFRS 10.23	Ch.7, p.538	IFRS 10 Appendix A	Ch.7, p.498
IFRS 10.23	Ch.8, p.623	IFRS 10 Appendix A	Ch.7, p.540
IFRS 10.23	Ch.10, p.788	IFRS 10 Appendix A	Ch.7, p.544
IFRS 10.23	Ch.11, p.868	IFRS 10 Appendix A	Ch.8, p.577
IFRS 10.23	Ch.20, p.1606	IFRS 10 Appendix A	Ch.12, p.898
IFRS 10.23	Ch.33, p.2600	IFRS 10 Appendix A	Ch.13, p.951
IFRS 10.23	Ch.47, p.3741	IFRS 10 Appendix A	Ch.13, p.959
IFRS 10.24	Ch.7, p.498	IFRS 10 Appendix A	Ch.27, p.2035
IFRS 10.24	Ch.7, p.499	IFRS 10 Appendix A	Ch.39, p.3102
IFRS 10.24	Ch.7, p.533	IFRS 10 Appendix A	Ch.39, p.3104
IFRS 10.24	Ch.7, p.538	IFRS 10 Appendix A	Ch.40, p.3174

IFRS 10.B1	Ch.6, p.457	IFRS 10.B35	Ch.6, p.421
IFRS 10.B2	Ch.6, p.406	IFRS 10.B36	Ch.6, p.421
IFRS 10.B2	Ch.6, p.410	IFRS 10.B37	Ch.6, p.421
IFRS 10.B2	Ch.6, p.436	IFRS 10.B38	Ch.6, p.421
IFRS 10.B3	Ch.6, p.406	IFRS 10.B39	Ch.6, p.433
IFRS 10.B3	Ch.12, p.897	IFRS 10.B40	Ch.6, p.433
IFRS 10.B4	Ch.6, p.406	IFRS 10.B41	Ch.6, p.423
IFRS 10.B5	Ch.6, p.407	IFRS 10.B42	Ch.6, p.423
IFRS 10.B6	Ch.6, p.406	IFRS 10.B42	Ch.6, p.429
IFRS 10.B6	Ch.6, p.408	IFRS 10.B43	Ch.6, p.424
IFRS 10.B6	Ch.6, p.409	IFRS 10.B43 Example 4	Ch.6, p.424
IFRS 10.B6	Ch.6, p.420	IFRS 10.B43 Example 5	Ch.6, p.433
IFRS 10.B7	Ch.6, p.408	IFRS 10.B44	Ch.6, p.424
IFRS 10.B8	Ch.6, p.408	IFRS 10.B44 Example 6	Ch.6, p.424
IFRS 10.B8	Ch.6, p.441	IFRS 10.B45	Ch.6, p.425
IFRS 10.B9	Ch.6, p.408	IFRS 10.B45 Example 7	Ch.6, p.425
IFRS 10.B10	Ch.6, p.409	IFRS 10.B45 Example 8	Ch.6, p.426
IFRS 10.B11-B12	Ch.6, p.409	IFRS 10.B46	Ch.6, p.423
IFRS 10.B13	Ch.6, p.409	IFRS 10.B47	Ch.6, p.428
IFRS 10.B13 Example 1	Ch.6, p.409	IFRS 10.B47	Ch.6, p.430
IFRS 10.B13 Example 1	Ch.12, p.898	IFRS 10.B48	Ch.6, p.428
IFRS 10.B13 Example 2	Ch.6, p.410	IFRS 10.B49	Ch.6, p.429
IFRS 10.B14	Ch.6, p.413	IFRS 10.B50	Ch.6, p.429
IFRS 10.B14	Ch.6, p.430	IFRS 10.B50 Example 9	Ch.6, p.431
IFRS 10.B15	Ch.6, p.414	IFRS 10.B50 Example 10	Ch.6, p.429
IFRS 10.B16	Ch.6, p.414	IFRS 10.B51	Ch.6, p.438
IFRS 10.B17	Ch.6, p.434	IFRS 10.B52	Ch.6, p.434
IFRS 10.B18	Ch.6, p.437	IFRS 10.B53	Ch.6, p.435
IFRS 10.B19	Ch.6, p.437	IFRS 10.B53 Example 11	Ch.6, p.436
IFRS 10.B19	Ch.6, p.440	IFRS 10.B53 Example 12	Ch.6, p.436
IFRS 10.B20	Ch.6, p.420	IFRS 10.B54	Ch.6, p.420
IFRS 10.B20	Ch.6, p.438	IFRS 10.B54	Ch.6, p.436
IFRS 10.B20	Ch.6, p.440	IFRS 10.B55	Ch.6, p.439
IFRS 10.B21	Ch.6, p.437	IFRS 10.B56	Ch.6, p.439
IFRS 10.B22	Ch.6, p.414	IFRS 10.B56	Ch.6, p.440
IFRS 10.B22	Ch.6, p.430	IFRS 10.B56	Ch.13, p.947
IFRS 10.B23	Ch.6, p.414	IFRS 10.B56	Ch.13, p.948
IFRS 10.B23	Ch.6, p.451	IFRS 10.B57	Ch.6, p.439
IFRS 10.B23(a)	Ch.6, p.431	IFRS 10.B57	Ch.6, p.444
IFRS 10.B23(a)(ii)	Ch.6, p.430	IFRS 10.B57(c)	Ch.6, p.444
IFRS 10.B23(a)(vi)	Ch.6, p.451	IFRS 10.B58	Ch.6, p.446
IFRS 10.B23(b)	Ch.6, p.450	IFRS 10.B58	Ch.6, p.447
IFRS 10.B24	Ch.6, p.415	IFRS 10.B59	Ch.6, p.447
IFRS 10.B24	Ch.6, p.430	IFRS 10.B59	Ch.6, p.454
IFRS 10.B24	Ch.6, p.432	IFRS 10.B60	Ch.6, p.447
IFRS 10.B24 Example 3-3D	Ch.6, p.415	IFRS 10.B60	Ch.6, p.457
IFRS 10.B25	Ch.6, p.416	IFRS 10.B61	Ch.6, p.447
IFRS 10.B26	Ch.6, p.416	IFRS 10.B62	Ch.6, p.448
IFRS 10.B26-27	Ch.12, p.898	IFRS 10.B63	Ch.6, p.448
IFRS 10.B27	Ch.6, p.416	IFRS 10.B64	Ch.6, p.449
IFRS 10.B28	Ch.6, p.416	IFRS 10.B64	Ch.6, p.451
IFRS 10.B29	Ch.6, p.417	IFRS 10.B65	Ch.6, p.450
IFRS 10.B30	Ch.6, p.418	IFRS 10.B66	Ch.6, p.449
IFRS 10.B31	Ch.6, p.418	IFRS 10.B67	Ch.6, p.450
IFRS 10.B32	Ch.6, p.418	IFRS 10.B68	Ch.6, p.452
IFRS 10.B33	Ch.6, p.418	IFRS 10.B69	Ch.6, p.453
IFRS 10.B34	Ch.6, p.420	IFRS 10.B70	Ch.6, p.453
IFRS 10.B34	Ch.6, p.421	IFRS 10.B71	Ch.6, p.454

Index of standards

IFRS 10.B72	Ch.6, p.455
IFRS 10.B72 Example 13	Ch.6, p.449
IFRS 10.B72 Example 13	Ch.6, p.453
IFRS 10.B72 Example 13	Ch.6, p.457
IFRS 10.B72 Example 14	Ch.6, p.453
IFRS 10.B72 Example 14	Ch.6, p.457
IFRS 10.B72 Example 14-14A	Ch.6, p.449
IFRS 10.B72 Example 14A	Ch.6, p.458
IFRS 10.B72 Example 14B	Ch.6, p.458
IFRS 10.B72 Example 14C	Ch.6, p.458
IFRS 10.B72 Example 15	Ch.6, p.450
IFRS 10.B72 Example 15	Ch.6, p.453
IFRS 10.B72 Example 15	Ch.6, p.459
IFRS 10.B72 Example 16	Ch.6, p.460
IFRS 10.B72 Example 16	Ch.13, p.982
IFRS 10.B73	Ch.6, p.462
IFRS 10.B73	Ch.6, p.463
IFRS 10.B74	Ch.6, p.462
IFRS 10.B74	Ch.6, p.463
IFRS 10.B75	Ch.6, p.462
IFRS 10.B75(f)	Ch.6, p.463
IFRS 10.B76	Ch.6, p.464
IFRS 10.B77	Ch.6, p.464
IFRS 10.B78	Ch.6, p.467
IFRS 10.B79	Ch.6, p.467
IFRS 10.B80	Ch.6, p.467
IFRS 10.B80	Ch.7, p.508
IFRS 10.B81	Ch.6, p.467
IFRS 10.B82	Ch.6, p.467
IFRS 10.B82	Ch.6, p.471
IFRS 10.B83	Ch.6, p.467
IFRS 10.B84	Ch.6, p.467
IFRS 10.B85	Ch.6, p.468
IFRS 10.B85A	Ch.6, p.473
IFRS 10.B85A	Ch.6, p.485
IFRS 10.B85B	Ch.6, p.474
IFRS 10.B85C	Ch.6, p.475
IFRS 10.B85D	Ch.6, p.475
IFRS 10.B85E	Ch.6, p.475
IFRS 10.B85F	Ch.6, p.477
IFRS 10.B85G	Ch.6, p.477
IFRS 10.B85H	Ch.6, p.477
IFRS 10.B85H	Ch.6, p.485
IFRS 10.B85I	Ch.6, p.478
IFRS 10.B85J	Ch.6, p.479
IFRS 10.B85K	Ch.6, p.479
IFRS 10.B85L	Ch.6, p.479
IFRS 10.B85L	Ch.12, p.892
IFRS 10.B85L	Ch.12, p.929
IFRS 10.B85L(b)	Ch.11, p.820
IFRS 10.B85M	Ch.6, p.479
IFRS 10.B85N	Ch.6, p.473
IFRS 10.B85O	Ch.6, p.480
IFRS 10.B85P	Ch.6, p.480
IFRS 10.B85Q	Ch.6, p.480
IFRS 10.B85R	Ch.6, p.480
IFRS 10.B85S	Ch.6, p.480
IFRS 10.B85T	Ch.6, p.481
IFRS 10.B85U	Ch.6, p.481
IFRS 10.B85V	Ch.6, p.481
IFRS 10.B85W	Ch.6, p.482
IFRS 10.B86	Ch.7, p.498
IFRS 10.B86	Ch.11, p.846
IFRS 10.B86	Ch.11, p.847
IFRS 10.B86	Ch.40, p.3174
IFRS 10.B86	Ch.53, p.4248
IFRS 10.B86(c)	Ch.7, p.501
IFRS 10.B86(c)	Ch.7, p.502
IFRS 10.B87	Ch.7, p.497
IFRS 10.B87	Ch.7, p.503
IFRS 10.B87	Ch.10, p.780
IFRS 10.B88	Ch.7, p.497
IFRS 10.B88	Ch.7, p.498
IFRS 10.B88	Ch.7, p.503
IFRS 10.B88	Ch.7, p.523
IFRS 10.B88	Ch.10, p.783
IFRS 10.B88	Ch.40, p.3174
IFRS 10.B89	Ch.7, p.499
IFRS 10.B89	Ch.7, p.547
IFRS 10.B89	Ch.7, p.549
IFRS 10.B90	Ch.7, p.499
IFRS 10.B90	Ch.7, p.547
IFRS 10.B90	Ch.7, p.549
IFRS 10.B91	Ch.7, p.499
IFRS 10.B91	Ch.7, p.550
IFRS 10.B91	Ch.45, p.3592
IFRS 10.B92	Ch.7, p.502
IFRS 10.B93	Ch.7, p.503
IFRS 10.B94	Ch.5, p.262
IFRS 10.B94	Ch.7, p.498
IFRS 10.B94	Ch.7, p.499
IFRS 10.B94	Ch.7, p.546
IFRS 10.B94	Ch.7, p.547
IFRS 10.B94	Ch.7, p.548
IFRS 10.B94	Ch.7, p.549
IFRS 10.B94	Ch.11, p.840
IFRS 10.B94	Ch.11, p.867
IFRS 10.B95	Ch.7, p.547
IFRS 10.B96	Ch.5, p.262
IFRS 10.B96	Ch.7, p.533
IFRS 10.B96	Ch.7, p.538
IFRS 10.B96U	Ch.7, p.548
IFRS 10.B96V	Ch.10, p.788
IFRS 10.B96	Ch.11, p.868
IFRS 10.B96	Ch.33, p.2600
IFRS 10.B97	Ch.7, p.524
IFRS 10.B97	Ch.7, p.525
IFRS 10.B97	Ch.9, p.715
IFRS 10.B97-B99	Ch.5, p.262
IFRS 10.B98	Ch.7, p.509
IFRS 10.B98	Ch.7, p.514
IFRS 10.B98	Ch.7, p.518
IFRS 10.B98	Ch.7, p.565
IFRS 10.B98(a)	Ch.7, p.527
IFRS 10.B98(b)	Ch.7, p.531
IFRS 10.B98(b)(i)	Ch.45, p.3605

IFRS 10.B98(d)	Ch.7, p.527	IFRS 10.BC240F	Ch.6, p.475
IFRS 10.B99	Ch.7, p.509	IFRS 10.BC240H	Ch.6, p.476
IFRS 10.B99	Ch.7, p.518	IFRS 10.BC242	Ch.6, p.478
IFRS 10.B99	Ch.7, p.526	IFRS 10.BC243	Ch.6, p.479
IFRS 10.B99	Ch.7, p.527	IFRS 10.BC248	Ch.6, p.477
IFRS 10.B99	Ch.7, p.565	IFRS 10.BC250	Ch.6, p.479
IFRS 10.B99A	Ch.7, p.514	IFRS 10.BC251	Ch.6, p.479
IFRS 10.B99A	Ch.7, p.519	IFRS 10.BC252	Ch.6, p.478
IFRS 10.B99A	Ch.7, p.520	IFRS 10.BC260	Ch.6, p.480
IFRS 10.B99A	Ch.7, p.565	IFRS 10.BC261	Ch.6, p.481
IFRS 10.B100	Ch.6, p.489	IFRS 10.BC263	Ch.6, p.481
IFRS 10.B101	Ch.6, p.488	IFRS 10.BC264	Ch.6, p.481
IFRS 10.C1A	Ch.6, p.393	IFRS 10.BC266	Ch.6, p.481
IFRS 10.C1B	Ch.6, p.393	IFRS 10.BC271	Ch.8, p.589
IFRS 10.C1B	Ch.6, p.472	IFRS 10.BC272	Ch.6, p.476
IFRS 10.C1C	Ch.7, p.514	IFRS 10.BC276-278	Ch.6, p.489
IFRS 10.C1C	Ch.7, p.565	IFRS 10.BC280	Ch.6, p.489
IFRS 10.C1D	Ch.6, p.393	IFRS 10.BC281	Ch.6, p.489
IFRS 10.C1D	Ch.6, p.397	IFRS 10.BC282	Ch.6, p.489
IFRS 10.C1D	Ch.6, p.473	IFRS 10.BC283	Ch.6, p.489
IFRS 10.IE1-IE6	Ch.6, p.483	IFRS 10.BC298-BC300	Ch.6, p.472
IFRS 10.IE7-IE8	Ch.6, p.483		
IFRS 10.IE12-IE15	Ch.6, p.485		

IFRS 11

IFRS 10.BCZ18	Ch.6, p.396
IFRS 10.BCZ21	Ch.6, p.471
IFRS 10.BC28A-B	Ch.6, p.397
IFRS 10.BC28A-28B	Ch.8, p.578
IFRS 10.BC28D	Ch.6, p.398
IFRS 10.BC37-BC39	Ch.6, p.445
IFRS 10.BC63	Ch.6, p.456
IFRS 10.BC66	Ch.6, p.442
IFRS 10.BC69	Ch.6, p.406
IFRS 10.BC124	Ch.6, p.431
IFRS 10.BC124	Ch.6, p.469
IFRS 10.BC130	Ch.6, p.455
IFRS 10.BC132	Ch.6, p.454
IFRS 10.BC152	Ch.6, p.468
IFRS 10.BCZ162-164	Ch.7, p.548
IFRS 10.BCZ165	Ch.7, p.548
IFRS 10.BCZ168	Ch.40, p.3175
IFRS 10.BCZ173	Ch.7, p.533
IFRS 10.BCZ173	Ch.33, p.2600
IFRS 10.BCZ175	Ch.7, p.500
IFRS 10.BCZ180	Ch.7, p.509
IFRS 10.BCZ182	Ch.7, p.512
IFRS 10.BCZ185	Ch.7, p.524
IFRS 10.BCZ186	Ch.7, p.525
IFRS 10.BC190I	Ch.7, p.518
IFRS 10.BC190I	Ch.7, p.565
IFRS 10.BC190J	Ch.7, p.520
IFRS 10.BC190L-190O	Ch.7, p.565
IFRS 10.BC190M-190N	Ch.7, p.565
IFRS 10.BC190N	Ch.18, p.1429
IFRS 10.BC190O	Ch.7, p.514
IFRS 10.BC190O	Ch.18, p.1429
IFRS 10.BC239	Ch.6, p.475
IFRS 10.BC240B	Ch.6, p.476
IFRS 10.BC240E	Ch.6, p.475

IFRS 11.1	Ch.12, p.892
IFRS 11.2	Ch.12, p.892
IFRS 11.3	Ch.12, p.892
IFRS 11.4	Ch.12, p.891
IFRS 11.4	Ch.43, p.3403
IFRS 11.5	Ch.12, p.891
IFRS 11.5	Ch.43, p.3543
IFRS 11.5(a)	Ch.43, p.3404
IFRS 11.6	Ch.12, p.891
IFRS 11.6	Ch.12, p.904
IFRS 11.7	Ch.12, p.895
IFRS 11.7	Ch.43, p.3404
IFRS 11.7	Ch.43, p.3543
IFRS 11.8	Ch.12, p.898
IFRS 11.8	Ch.43, p.3404
IFRS 11.9	Ch.12, p.901
IFRS 11.10	Ch.12, p.897
IFRS 11.10	Ch.12, p.901
IFRS 11.11	Ch.12, p.895
IFRS 11.11	Ch.13, p.953
IFRS 11.12	Ch.12, p.896
IFRS 11.13	Ch.12, p.897
IFRS 11.13	Ch.12, p.931
IFRS 11.14	Ch.12, p.904
IFRS 11.15	Ch.12, p.904
IFRS 11.16	Ch.12, p.904
IFRS 11.17	Ch.12, p.906
IFRS 11.18	Ch.12, p.894
IFRS 11.19	Ch.12, p.931
IFRS 11.20	Ch.8, p.580
IFRS 11.20	Ch.12, p.923
IFRS 11.20	Ch.27, p.2037
IFRS 11.20	Ch.40, p.3180

IFRS 11.20-23	Ch.5, p.375	IFRS 11.B15	Ch.12, p.906
IFRS 11.20-23	Ch.12, p.929	IFRS 11.B16	Ch.12, p.923
IFRS 11.21	Ch.12, p.923	IFRS 11.B17	Ch.12, p.923
IFRS 11.21	Ch.27, p.2037	IFRS 11.B18	Ch.12, p.923
IFRS 11.21	Ch.43, p.3450	IFRS 11.B19	Ch.12, p.906
IFRS 11.21A	Ch.12, p.936	IFRS 11.B20	Ch.12, p.906
IFRS 11.21A	Ch.40, p.3181	IFRS 11.B21	Ch.12, p.907
IFRS 11.22	Ch.7, p.523	IFRS 11.B22	Ch.12, p.908
IFRS 11.22	Ch.12, p.928	IFRS 11.B23	Ch.12, p.908
IFRS 11.23	Ch.8, p.580	IFRS 11.B24	Ch.12, p.907
IFRS 11.23	Ch.12, p.927	IFRS 11.B25	Ch.12, p.909
IFRS 11.23	Ch.18, p.1430	IFRS 11.B26	Ch.12, p.909
IFRS 11.23	Ch.43, p.3399	IFRS 11.B27	Ch.12, p.908
IFRS 11.23	Ch.43, p.3407	IFRS 11.B27	Ch.12, p.910
IFRS 11.23	Ch.43, p.3408	IFRS 11.B27	Ch.12, p.913
IFRS 11.24	Ch.12, p.929	IFRS 11.B28	Ch.12, p.910
IFRS 11.25	Ch.12, p.929	IFRS 11.B29	Ch.12, p.911
IFRS 11.25	Ch.43, p.3408	IFRS 11.B30	Ch.12, p.911
IFRS 11.26	Ch.8, p.580	IFRS 11.B31	Ch.12, p.911
IFRS 11.26(a)	Ch.12, p.929	IFRS 11.B31-B32	Ch.12, p.914
IFRS 11.26(b)	Ch.12, p.930	IFRS 11.B31-B32	Ch.12, p.916
IFRS 11.27(a)	Ch.12, p.929	IFRS 11.B32	Ch.12, p.912
IFRS 11.27(b)	Ch.12, p.930	IFRS 11.B32	Ch.12, p.916
IFRS 11 Appendix A	Ch.6, p.410	IFRS 11.B32-B33	Ch.12, p.914
IFRS 11 Appendix A	Ch.6, p.433	IFRS 11.B32 Example 5	Ch.12, p.911
IFRS 11 Appendix A	Ch.12, p.891	IFRS 11.B33A	Ch.12, p.936
IFRS 11 Appendix A	Ch.12, p.892	IFRS 11.B33B	Ch.12, p.936
IFRS 11 Appendix A	Ch.12, p.893	IFRS 11.B33C	Ch.12, p.936
IFRS 11 Appendix A	Ch.12, p.895	IFRS 11.B33CA	Ch.12, p.937
IFRS 11 Appendix A	Ch.12, p.906	IFRS 11.B33D	Ch.12, p.936
IFRS 11 Appendix A	Ch.13, p.951	IFRS 11.B34	Ch.7, p.523
IFRS 11 Appendix A	Ch.39, p.3102	IFRS 11.B34	Ch.12, p.928
IFRS 11 Appendix A	Ch.39, p.3105	IFRS 11.B34	Ch.18, p.1429
IFRS 11 Appendix A	Ch.43, p.3403	IFRS 11.B35	Ch.7, p.523
IFRS 11 Appendix A	Ch.43, p.3404	IFRS 11.B35	Ch.12, p.928
IFRS 11 Appendix A	Ch.43, p.3406	IFRS 11.B36	Ch.12, p.928
IFRS 11 Appendix C	Ch.5, p.322	IFRS 11.B37	Ch.12, p.928
IFRS 11.B2	Ch.10, p.769	IFRS 11.C14	Ch.12, p.897
IFRS 11.B2	Ch.12, p.893	IFRS 11.C14	Ch.12, p.929
IFRS 11.B2	Ch.43, p.3404	IFRS 11.C14	Ch.43, p.3408
IFRS 11.B3	Ch.12, p.893	IFRS 11.IE1	Ch.12, p.917
IFRS 11.B4	Ch.12, p.893	IFRS 11.IE2-IE52	Ch.12, p.917
IFRS 11.B5	Ch.12, p.897	IFRS 11 Examples 1-6	Ch.12, p.917
IFRS 11.B5	Ch.12, p.898	IFRS 11 Example 4	Ch.12, p.909
IFRS 11.B5	Ch.43, p.3404	IFRS 11 Example 5	Ch.12, p.916
IFRS 11.B6	Ch.12, p.901	IFRS 11.BC14	Ch.12, p.897
IFRS 11.B7	Ch.12, p.901	IFRS 11.BC15-18	Ch.12, p.892
IFRS 11.B8	Ch.12, p.902	IFRS 11.BC20	Ch.12, p.894
IFRS 11.B8 Example 1	Ch.12, p.902	IFRS 11.BC24	Ch.12, p.891
IFRS 11.B8 Example 2	Ch.12, p.902	IFRS 11.BC25	Ch.12, p.891
IFRS 11.B8 Example 3	Ch.12, p.902	IFRS 11.BC27	Ch.12, p.907
IFRS 11.B9	Ch.12, p.901	IFRS 11.BC28	Ch.12, p.891
IFRS 11.B9	Ch.43, p.3404	IFRS 11.BC29	Ch.12, p.906
IFRS 11.B10	Ch.12, p.896	IFRS 11.BC31	Ch.12, p.907
IFRS 11.B10	Ch.12, p.903	IFRS 11.BC32	Ch.12, p.907
IFRS 11.B11	Ch.12, p.897	IFRS 11.BC35	Ch.12, p.894
IFRS 11.B14	Ch.12, p.906	IFRS 11.BC36	Ch.12, p.894
IFRS 11.B14	Ch.12, p.914	IFRS 11.BC38	Ch.12, p.923

IFRS 11.BC43	Ch.12, p.908	IFRS 12.21	Ch.13, p.971
IFRS 11.BC43	Ch.12, p.915	IFRS 12.21A	Ch.13, p.971
IFRS 11.BC45A	Ch.43, p.3417	IFRS 12.22	Ch.13, p.971
IFRS 11.BC45E	Ch.12, p.936	IFRS 12.22	Ch.15, p.1244
IFRS 11.BC45F	Ch.12, p.936	IFRS 12.22(a)	Ch.40, p.3187
IFRS 11.BC45H	Ch.43, p.3417	IFRS 12.24	Ch.13, p.978
IFRS 11.BC45I	Ch.43, p.3417	IFRS 12.25	Ch.13, p.979
		IFRS 12.25A	Ch.13, p.978
		IFRS 12.26	Ch.13, p.979

IFRS 12

IFRS 12.27			Ch.13, p.982
IFRS 12.28			Ch.13, p.982
IFRS 12.1	Ch.13, p.945	IFRS 12.29	Ch.13, p.987
IFRS 12.2	Ch.13, p.945	IFRS 12.30	Ch.13, p.989
IFRS 12.3	Ch.13, p.946	IFRS 12.31	Ch.13, p.989
IFRS 12.4	Ch.13, p.951	IFRS 12 Appendix A	Ch.6, p.407
IFRS 12.5	Ch.13, p.946	IFRS 12 Appendix A	Ch.6, p.435
IFRS 12.5A	Ch.4, p.214	IFRS 12 Appendix A	Ch.13, p.983
IFRS 12.5A	Ch.13, p.950	IFRS 12 Appendix A	Ch.13, p.992
IFRS 12.6(a)	Ch.13, p.953	IFRS 12.B3	Ch.13, p.951
IFRS 12.6(b)	Ch.8, p.604	IFRS 12.B4	Ch.13, p.950
IFRS 12.6(b)	Ch.13, p.953	IFRS 12.B5	Ch.13, p.951
IFRS 12.6(c)	Ch.13, p.953	IFRS 12.B6	Ch.13, p.951
IFRS 12.6(d)	Ch.13, p.954	IFRS 12.B7	Ch.13, p.947
IFRS 12.7	Ch.12, p.896	IFRS 12.B8	Ch.13, p.947
IFRS 12.7	Ch.12, p.906	IFRS 12.B8	Ch.13, p.948
IFRS 12.7	Ch.13, p.954	IFRS 12.B9	Ch.6, p.442
IFRS 12.8	Ch.13, p.954	IFRS 12.B9	Ch.13, p.948
IFRS 12.9	Ch.13, p.954	IFRS 12.B10	Ch.5, p.333
IFRS 12.9A	Ch.6, p.473	IFRS 12.B10	Ch.13, p.959
IFRS 12.9A	Ch.13, p.956	IFRS 12.B10(b)	Ch.40, p.3187
IFRS 12.9B	Ch.13, p.968	IFRS 12.B11	Ch.13, p.959
IFRS 12.9(d)	Ch.11, p.816	IFRS 12.B11	Ch.40, p.3187
IFRS 12.9(e)	Ch.11, p.816	IFRS 12.B12	Ch.13, p.972
IFRS 12.10	Ch.13, p.957	IFRS 12.B12(a)	Ch.40, p.3187
IFRS 12.10	Ch.15, p.1244	IFRS 12.B12-13	Ch.5, p.333
IFRS 12.11	Ch.13, p.957	IFRS 12.B13	Ch.13, p.973
IFRS 12.12	Ch.5, p.333	IFRS 12.B13(a)	Ch.40, p.3187
IFRS 12.12	Ch.13, p.959	IFRS 12.B14	Ch.13, p.973
IFRS 12.12(e)	Ch.5, p.332	IFRS 12.B15	Ch.13, p.974
IFRS 12.13	Ch.13, p.962	IFRS 12.B16	Ch.5, p.333
IFRS 12.13	Ch.15, p.1244	IFRS 12.B16	Ch.13, p.976
IFRS 12.14	Ch.13, p.964	IFRS 12.B17	Ch.4, p.214
IFRS 12.15	Ch.13, p.965	IFRS 12.B17	Ch.13, p.950
IFRS 12.16	Ch.13, p.966	IFRS 12.B17	Ch.13, p.976
IFRS 12.17	Ch.13, p.966	IFRS 12.B18	Ch.13, p.977
IFRS 12.18	Ch.13, p.966	IFRS 12.B18	Ch.39, p.3122
IFRS 12.19	Ch.5, p.333	IFRS 12.B19	Ch.13, p.977
IFRS 12.19	Ch.13, p.967	IFRS 12.B19-20	Ch.39, p.3123
IFRS 12.19A	Ch.13, p.968	IFRS 12.B22	Ch.6, p.435
IFRS 12.19B	Ch.13, p.968	IFRS 12.B22	Ch.13, p.949
IFRS 12.19C	Ch.13, p.968	IFRS 12.B23	Ch.6, p.435
IFRS 12.19D	Ch.13, p.969	IFRS 12.B23	Ch.13, p.949
IFRS 12.19E	Ch.13, p.969	IFRS 12.B24	Ch.6, p.435
IFRS 12.19F	Ch.13, p.969	IFRS 12.B24	Ch.13, p.950
IFRS 12.19G	Ch.13, p.969	IFRS 12.B25-26	Ch.13, p.990
IFRS 12.20	Ch.13, p.970	IFRS 12.BC16	Ch.13, p.956
IFRS 12.20	Ch.15, p.1244	IFRS 12.BC19	Ch.13, p.956
IFRS 12.21	Ch.5, p.333	IFRS 12.BC27	Ch.13, p.959

IFRS 12.BC28	Ch.13, p.959
IFRS 12.BC29	Ch.13, p.959
IFRS 12.BC31	Ch.13, p.962
IFRS 12.BC32	Ch.13, p.962
IFRS 12.BC33	Ch.13, p.962
IFRS 12.BC34	Ch.13, p.963
IFRS 12.BC35	Ch.13, p.963
IFRS 12.BC38-39	Ch.13, p.967
IFRS 12.BC49	Ch.13, p.974
IFRS 12.BC50-51	Ch.13, p.974
IFRS 12.BC52	Ch.13, p.974
IFRS 12.BC52	Ch.39, p.3106
IFRS 12.BC60	Ch.13, p.974
IFRS 12.BC61C	Ch.13, p.969
IFRS 12.BC61I	Ch.13, p.968
IFRS 12.BC69	Ch.13, p.952
IFRS 12.BC72	Ch.13, p.979
IFRS 12.BC77	Ch.13, p.952
IFRS 12.BC82	Ch.13, p.949
IFRS 12.BC83	Ch.13, p.950
IFRS 12.BC83-85	Ch.13, p.950
IFRS 12.BC87	Ch.13, p.982
IFRS 12.BC90	Ch.13, p.983
IFRS 12.BC94	Ch.13, p.986
IFRS 12.BC96	Ch.13, p.979
IFRS 12.BC96	Ch.13, p.980
IFRS 12.BC97	Ch.13, p.987
IFRS 12.BC98-99	Ch.13, p.987
IFRS 12.BC100	Ch.13, p.987
IFRS 12.BC104	Ch.13, p.966
IFRS 12.BC105-106	Ch.13, p.965
IFRS 12.BC113-114	Ch.13, p.990

IFRS 13

IFRS 13.1	Ch.14, p.1003
IFRS 13.1	Ch.24, p.1838
IFRS 13.2	Ch.9, p.669
IFRS 13.2	Ch.9, p.682
IFRS 13.2	Ch.14, p.1006
IFRS 13.2	Ch.14, p.1007
IFRS 13.2	Ch.14, p.1017
IFRS 13.2	Ch.18, p.1419
IFRS 13.2	Ch.19, p.1469
IFRS 13.2	Ch.20, p.1546
IFRS 13.3	Ch.14, p.1007
IFRS 13.3	Ch.14, p.1045
IFRS 13.4	Ch.14, p.1008
IFRS 13.5	Ch.10, p.779
IFRS 13.5	Ch.14, p.1007
IFRS 13.5	Ch.24, p.1830
IFRS 13.6	Ch.9, p.695
IFRS 13.6	Ch.14, p.1007
IFRS 13.6	Ch.20, p.1546
IFRS 13.6(c)	Ch.19, p.1473
IFRS 13.6(c)	Ch.20, p.1581
IFRS 13.7	Ch.14, p.1008
IFRS 13.7(c)	Ch.20, p.1546
IFRS 13.8	Ch.14, p.1008
IFRS 13.9	Ch.4, p.198
IFRS 13.9	Ch.10, p.779
IFRS 13.9	Ch.14, p.1016
IFRS 13.9	Ch.19, p.1468
IFRS 13.9	Ch.24, p.1830
IFRS 13.9	Ch.42, p.3277
IFRS 13.9	Ch.52, p.4088
IFRS 13.11	Ch.14, p.1025
IFRS 13.11	Ch.14, p.1110
IFRS 13.11	Ch.20, p.1546
IFRS 13.11	Ch.42, p.3304
IFRS 13.12	Ch.14, p.1025
IFRS 13.13	Ch.14, p.1019
IFRS 13.14	Ch.14, p.1019
IFRS 13.15	Ch.14, p.1017
IFRS 13.15	Ch.14, p.1038
IFRS 13.16	Ch.14, p.1029
IFRS 13.16	Ch.14, p.1033
IFRS 13.17	Ch.14, p.1030
IFRS 13.17	Ch.42, p.3304
IFRS 13.18	Ch.14, p.1029
IFRS 13.18	Ch.42, p.3300
IFRS 13.18	Ch.42, p.3306
IFRS 13.19	Ch.14, p.1031
IFRS 13.20	Ch.14, p.1031
IFRS 13.20	Ch.14, p.1038
IFRS 13.21	Ch.14, p.1030
IFRS 13.22	Ch.14, p.1034
IFRS 13.22	Ch.14, p.1035
IFRS 13.22	Ch.19, p.1469
IFRS 13.23	Ch.14, p.1034
IFRS 13.23	Ch.42, p.3304
IFRS 13.24	Ch.14, p.1050
IFRS 13.25	Ch.14, p.1017
IFRS 13.25	Ch.14, p.1050
IFRS 13.25	Ch.19, p.1469
IFRS 13.25	Ch.19, p.1476
IFRS 13.25	Ch.42, p.3292
IFRS 13.25	Ch.42, p.3305
IFRS 13.26	Ch.14, p.1050
IFRS 13.27	Ch.14, p.1053
IFRS 13.27(c)	Ch.18, p.1419
IFRS 13.27	Ch.19, p.1460
IFRS 13.27	Ch.20, p.1546
IFRS 13.27	Ch.42, p.3299
IFRS 13.27-28	Ch.19, p.1482
IFRS 13.28	Ch.14, p.1053
IFRS 13.28	Ch.18, p.1419
IFRS 13.28	Ch.42, p.3299
IFRS 13.29	Ch.14, p.1056
IFRS 13.29	Ch.14, p.1057
IFRS 13.29	Ch.18, p.1419
IFRS 13.29	Ch.19, p.1481
IFRS 13.29	Ch.20, p.1546
IFRS 13.29	Ch.42, p.3299
IFRS 13.30	Ch.14, p.1057

IFRS 13.31	Ch.42, p.3299
IFRS 13.31(a)-(b)	Ch.18, p.1420
IFRS 13.31(a)(i)	Ch.14, p.1059
IFRS 13.31(a)(ii)	Ch.14, p.1062
IFRS 13.31(a)(iii)	Ch.14, p.1060
IFRS 13.31(b)	Ch.14, p.1059
IFRS 13.32	Ch.14, p.1062
IFRS 13.32	Ch.42, p.3300
IFRS 13.34	Ch.9, p.699
IFRS 13.34	Ch.14, p.1064
IFRS 13.34(a)	Ch.9, p.700
IFRS 13.36	Ch.10, p.779
IFRS 13.36	Ch.14, p.1066
IFRS 13.37	Ch.9, p.701
IFRS 13.37	Ch.14, p.1066
IFRS 13.38	Ch.14, p.1066
IFRS 13.39	Ch.14, p.1067
IFRS 13.40	Ch.14, p.1066
IFRS 13.40	Ch.14, p.1069
IFRS 13.41	Ch.14, p.1070
IFRS 13.42	Ch.9, p.704
IFRS 13.42-44	Ch.14, p.1073
IFRS 13.44	Ch.14, p.1078
IFRS 13.45	Ch.14, p.1087
IFRS 13.46	Ch.14, p.1087
IFRS 13.47	Ch.7, p.552
IFRS 13.47	Ch.14, p.1088
IFRS 13.47	Ch.47, p.3712
IFRS 13.47	Ch.53, p.4222
IFRS 13.48	Ch.14, p.1085
IFRS 13.48	Ch.14, p.1088
IFRS 13.48	Ch.14, p.1092
IFRS 13.48	Ch.14, p.1094
IFRS 13.49	Ch.14, p.1089
IFRS 13.50	Ch.14, p.1090
IFRS 13.51	Ch.14, p.1090
IFRS 13.52	Ch.14, p.1089
IFRS 13.53	Ch.14, p.1096
IFRS 13.54	Ch.14, p.1091
IFRS 13.54	Ch.14, p.1095
IFRS 13.55	Ch.14, p.1095
IFRS 13.56	Ch.14, p.1096
IFRS 13.57	Ch.14, p.1096
IFRS 13.57-59	Ch.42, p.3305
IFRS 13.58	Ch.14, p.1096
IFRS 13.58	Ch.49, p.3854
IFRS 13.59	Ch.14, p.1096
IFRS 13.60	Ch.14, p.1097
IFRS 13.60	Ch.49, p.3854
IFRS 13.60	Ch.49, p.3855
IFRS 13.61	Ch.9, p.682
IFRS 13.61	Ch.14, p.1100
IFRS 13.61	Ch.18, p.1420
IFRS 13.61	Ch.20, p.1546
IFRS 13.62	Ch.9, p.681
IFRS 13.62	Ch.14, p.1100
IFRS 13.62	Ch.18, p.1420
IFRS 13.62	Ch.19, p.1471
IFRS 13.62	Ch.20, p.1546
IFRS 13.62	Ch.42, p.3305
IFRS 13.63	Ch.14, p.1101
IFRS 13.63	Ch.42, p.3305
IFRS 13.64	Ch.14, p.1105
IFRS 13.65	Ch.14, p.1105
IFRS 13.65	Ch.14, p.1106
IFRS 13.65	Ch.14, p.1114
IFRS 13.66	Ch.14, p.1106
IFRS 13.66	Ch.18, p.1421
IFRS 13.66	Ch.20, p.1547
IFRS 13.67	Ch.14, p.1109
IFRS 13.67	Ch.19, p.1472
IFRS 13.67	Ch.42, p.3300
IFRS 13.68	Ch.14, p.1109
IFRS 13.69	Ch.14, p.1109
IFRS 13.69	Ch.14, p.1111
IFRS 13.69	Ch.14, p.1112
IFRS 13.69	Ch.14, p.1113
IFRS 13.70	Ch.14, p.1114
IFRS 13.71	Ch.14, p.1114
IFRS 13.72	Ch.14, p.1117
IFRS 13.72	Ch.18, p.1421
IFRS 13.72	Ch.20, p.1547
IFRS 13.73	Ch.14, p.1119
IFRS 13.73	Ch.14, p.1120
IFRS 13.74	Ch.14, p.1100
IFRS 13.74	Ch.14, p.1118
IFRS 13.74	Ch.42, p.3305
IFRS 13.75	Ch.14, p.1119
IFRS 13.75	Ch.14, p.1121
IFRS 13.75	Ch.14, p.1126
IFRS 13.75	Ch.42, p.3307
IFRS 13.76	Ch.14, p.1125
IFRS 13.76	Ch.18, p.1421
IFRS 13.77	Ch.14, p.1125
IFRS 13.78	Ch.14, p.1126
IFRS 13.79	Ch.14, p.1125
IFRS 13.79(a)	Ch.14, p.1126
IFRS 13.79(b)	Ch.14, p.1127
IFRS 13.79(c)	Ch.14, p.1126
IFRS 13.80	Ch.14, p.1112
IFRS 13.80	Ch.14, p.1127
IFRS 13.81	Ch.14, p.1127
IFRS 13.82	Ch.14, p.1127
IFRS 13.83	Ch.14, p.1130
IFRS 13.84	Ch.14, p.1130
IFRS 13.86	Ch.14, p.1131
IFRS 13.87	Ch.14, p.1131
IFRS 13.87	Ch.14, p.1132
IFRS 13.87-89	Ch.20, p.1547
IFRS 13.88	Ch.14, p.1132
IFRS 13.89	Ch.14, p.1049
IFRS 13.89	Ch.14, p.1131
IFRS 13.89	Ch.14, p.1132
IFRS 13.89	Ch.20, p.1548
IFRS 13.91	Ch.9, p.669
IFRS 13.91	Ch.14, p.1134

IFRS 13.91	Ch.41, p.3223
IFRS 13.91	Ch.42, p.3292
IFRS 13.91(a)	Ch.9, p.753
IFRS 13.92	Ch.14, p.1134
IFRS 13.92	Ch.19, p.1505
IFRS 13.92	Ch.41, p.3224
IFRS 13.93	Ch.7, p.533
IFRS 13.93	Ch.14, p.1138
IFRS 13.93	Ch.14, p.1139
IFRS 13.93	Ch.14, p.1140
IFRS 13.93	Ch.14, p.1146
IFRS 13.93	Ch.18, p.1434
IFRS 13.93	Ch.18, p.1435
IFRS 13.93	Ch.41, p.3223
IFRS 13.93	Ch.42, p.3320
IFRS 13.93	Ch.55, p.4667
IFRS 13.93(a)	Ch.14, p.1136
IFRS 13.93(b)	Ch.19, p.1498
IFRS 13.93(b)	Ch.38, p.3085
IFRS 13.93(c)	Ch.14, p.1122
IFRS 13.93(c)	Ch.14, p.1144
IFRS 13.93(c)	Ch.19, p.1498
IFRS 13.93(d)	Ch.14, p.1137
IFRS 13.93(d)	Ch.14, p.1146
IFRS 13.93(d)	Ch.19, p.1498
IFRS 13.93(d)	Ch.38, p.3085
IFRS 13.93(e)	Ch.19, p.1498
IFRS 13.93(e)(iv)	Ch.14, p.1122
IFRS 13.93(e)(iv)	Ch.14, p.1144
IFRS 13.93(f)	Ch.19, p.1499
IFRS 13.93(g)	Ch.19, p.1499
IFRS 13.93(g)	Ch.38, p.3086
IFRS 13.93(h)	Ch.19, p.1499
IFRS 13.93(i)	Ch.14, p.1056
IFRS 13.93(i)	Ch.14, p.1156
IFRS 13.93(i)	Ch.19, p.1498
IFRS 13.93(i)	Ch.38, p.3086
IFRS 13.94	Ch.14, p.1135
IFRS 13.94	Ch.19, p.1504
IFRS 13.94	Ch.19, p.1505
IFRS 13.94-96	Ch.41, p.3223
IFRS 13.95	Ch.14, p.1122
IFRS 13.95	Ch.14, p.1137
IFRS 13.95	Ch.14, p.1144
IFRS 13.96	Ch.14, p.1137
IFRS 13.97	Ch.14, p.1156
IFRS 13.97	Ch.55, p.4667
IFRS 13.98	Ch.14, p.1156
IFRS 13.98	Ch.41, p.3223
IFRS 13.99	Ch.7, p.533
IFRS 13.99	Ch.14, p.1135
IFRS 13.99	Ch.38, p.3086
IFRS 13.99	Ch.41, p.3224
IFRS 13 Appendix A	Ch.5, p.292
IFRS 13 Appendix A	Ch.14, p.1014
IFRS 13 Appendix A	Ch.14, p.1030
IFRS 13 Appendix A	Ch.14, p.1033
IFRS 13 Appendix A	Ch.14, p.1034
IFRS 13 Appendix A	Ch.14, p.1043
IFRS 13 Appendix A	Ch.14, p.1050
IFRS 13 Appendix A	Ch.14, p.1053
IFRS 13 Appendix A	Ch.14, p.1115
IFRS 13 Appendix A	Ch.14, p.1118
IFRS 13 Appendix A	Ch.17, p.1293
IFRS 13 Appendix A	Ch.17, p.1335
IFRS 13 Appendix A	Ch.18, p.1419
IFRS 13 Appendix A	Ch.19, p.1497
IFRS 13 Appendix A	Ch.20, p.1534
IFRS 13 Appendix A	Ch.20, p.1547
IFRS 13 Appendix A	Ch.24, p.1825
IFRS 13 Appendix A	Ch.42, p.3301
IFRS 13 Appendix A	Ch.42, p.3304
IFRS 13 Appendix A	Ch.52, p.4088
IFRS 13.B2	Ch.14, p.1017
IFRS 13.B2	Ch.42, p.3298
IFRS 13.B3	Ch.14, p.1061
IFRS 13.B4(a)-(b)	Ch.14, p.1097
IFRS 13.B4(c)	Ch.14, p.1096
IFRS 13.B4(c)	Ch.14, p.1099
IFRS 13.B4(d)	Ch.14, p.1097
IFRS 13.B5	Ch.14, p.1106
IFRS 13.B5	Ch.18, p.1420
IFRS 13.B5	Ch.20, p.1547
IFRS 13.B6	Ch.14, p.1106
IFRS 13.B6	Ch.18, p.1420
IFRS 13.B6	Ch.20, p.1547
IFRS 13.B7	Ch.14, p.1106
IFRS 13.B8	Ch.9, p.682
IFRS 13.B8	Ch.14, p.1107
IFRS 13.B8	Ch.18, p.1421
IFRS 13.B8	Ch.20, p.1547
IFRS 13.B9	Ch.9, p.682
IFRS 13.B9	Ch.14, p.1107
IFRS 13.B9	Ch.18, p.1421
IFRS 13.B9	Ch.20, p.1547
IFRS 13.B10	Ch.14, p.1108
IFRS 13.B10	Ch.18, p.1421
IFRS 13.B10	Ch.20, p.1547
IFRS 13.B11	Ch.14, p.1108
IFRS 13.B11	Ch.18, p.1421
IFRS 13.B11	Ch.20, p.1547
IFRS 13.B12	Ch.14, p.1160
IFRS 13.B13	Ch.14, p.1161
IFRS 13.B13(c)	Ch.14, p.1162
IFRS 13.B14	Ch.14, p.1162
IFRS 13.B15	Ch.14, p.1162
IFRS 13.B16	Ch.9, p.703
IFRS 13.B16	Ch.14, p.1115
IFRS 13.B16	Ch.14, p.1162
IFRS 13.B17	Ch.14, p.1163
IFRS 13.B18	Ch.14, p.1163
IFRS 13.B19	Ch.14, p.1163
IFRS 13.B19	Ch.14, p.1164
IFRS 13.B20-21	Ch.14, p.1165
IFRS 13.B22	Ch.14, p.1164
IFRS 13.B23	Ch.14, p.1166

IFRS 13.B24	Ch.14, p.1166	IFRS 13.IE66	Ch.14, p.1153
IFRS 13.B25	Ch.14, p.1167	IFRS 13.BC6	Ch.14, p.1170
IFRS 13.B25-B29	Ch.14, p.1115	IFRS 13.BC8	Ch.14, p.1011
IFRS 13.B26	Ch.14, p.1167	IFRS 13.BC21	Ch.14, p.1010
IFRS 13.B27-B29	Ch.14, p.1168	IFRS 13.BC22	Ch.14, p.1010
IFRS 13.B30	Ch.14, p.1168	IFRS 13.BC24	Ch.19, p.1473
IFRS 13.B31	Ch.14, p.1070	IFRS 13.BC29	Ch.14, p.1016
IFRS 13.B32	Ch.14, p.1070	IFRS 13.BC31	Ch.14, p.1017
IFRS 13.B33	Ch.14, p.1070	IFRS 13.BC36	Ch.14, p.1016
IFRS 13.B34	Ch.14, p.1109	IFRS 13.BC39	Ch.14, p.1017
IFRS 13.B34	Ch.36, p.2983	IFRS 13.BC40	Ch.14, p.1017
IFRS 13.B35	Ch.14, p.1128	IFRS 13.BC46	Ch.14, p.1025
IFRS 13.B35(g)	Ch.19, p.1497	IFRS 13.BC52	Ch.14, p.1030
IFRS 13.B36	Ch.14, p.1132	IFRS 13.BC52	Ch.14, p.1033
IFRS 13.B37	Ch.14, p.1040	IFRS 13.BC55-BC59	Ch.14, p.1034
IFRS 13.B38	Ch.14, p.1046	IFRS 13.BC57	Ch.14, p.1035
IFRS 13.B39	Ch.14, p.1115	IFRS 13.BC63	Ch.14, p.1053
IFRS 13.B40	Ch.14, p.1045	IFRS 13.BC69	Ch.14, p.1055
IFRS 13.B40	Ch.14, p.1102	IFRS 13.BC81	Ch.14, p.1065
IFRS 13.B41	Ch.14, p.1017	IFRS 13.BC82	Ch.14, p.1065
IFRS 13.B42	Ch.14, p.1045	IFRS 13.BC88	Ch.14, p.1067
IFRS 13.B43	Ch.14, p.1039	IFRS 13.BC89	Ch.9, p.702
IFRS 13.B43	Ch.14, p.1043	IFRS 13.BC89	Ch.14, p.1067
IFRS 13.B43	Ch.14, p.1044	IFRS 13.BC91	Ch.14, p.1116
IFRS 13.B43	Ch.19, p.1472	IFRS 13.BC92	Ch.14, p.1075
IFRS 13.B43	Ch.20, p.1548	IFRS 13.BC93	Ch.14, p.1075
IFRS 13.B44	Ch.14, p.1043	IFRS 13.BC94	Ch.14, p.1075
IFRS 13.B44	Ch.14, p.1044	IFRS 13.BC95	Ch.14, p.1076
IFRS 13.B44	Ch.14, p.1046	IFRS 13.BC96-BC98	Ch.14, p.1076
IFRS 13.B44(c)	Ch.14, p.1044	IFRS 13.BC99	Ch.14, p.1028
IFRS 13.B45	Ch.14, p.1122	IFRS 13.BC99	Ch.14, p.1087
IFRS 13.B46	Ch.14, p.1116	IFRS 13.BC100	Ch.14, p.1028
IFRS 13.B47	Ch.14, p.1123	IFRS 13.BC100	Ch.14, p.1087
IFRS 13.C1	Ch.14, p.1003	IFRS 13.BCZ102-BCZ103	Ch.14, p.1088
IFRS 13.IE3-IE6	Ch.14, p.1036	IFRS 13.BC106	Ch.14, p.1063
IFRS 13.IE7-IE8	Ch.14, p.1056	IFRS 13.BC119A	Ch.14, p.1089
IFRS 13.IE7-IE8	Ch.18, p.1420	IFRS 13.BC119B	Ch.14, p.1089
IFRS 13.IE9	Ch.14, p.1057	IFRS 13.BC121	Ch.14, p.1090
IFRS 13.IE11-IE14	Ch.14, p.1103	IFRS 13.BC138	Ch.14, p.1097
IFRS 13.IE11-IE14	Ch.14, p.1108	IFRS 13.BC138	Ch.49, p.3854
IFRS 13.IE15-IE17	Ch.14, p.1102	IFRS 13.BC138A	Ch.14, p.1010
IFRS 13.IE19-IE20	Ch.14, p.1029	IFRS 13.BC138A	Ch.49, p.3854
IFRS 13.IE19.21-IE22	Ch.14, p.1033	IFRS 13.BC145	Ch.14, p.1105
IFRS 13.IE24-IE26	Ch.14, p.1098	IFRS 13.BC157	Ch.14, p.1113
IFRS 13.IE28-IE29	Ch.14, p.1026	IFRS 13.BC164	Ch.14, p.1114
IFRS 13.IE31	Ch.14, p.1073	IFRS 13.BC165	Ch.14, p.1099
IFRS 13.IE32	Ch.14, p.1074	IFRS 13.BC184	Ch.14, p.1133
IFRS 13.IE34	Ch.14, p.1074	IFRS 13.BC208	Ch.14, p.1170
IFRS 13.IE35-IE39	Ch.14, p.1070	IFRS 13.BC238(a)	Ch.14, p.1172
IFRS 13.IE40-IE42	Ch.14, p.1067	IFRS 13.BC238(b)	Ch.14, p.1172
IFRS 13.IE43-IE47	Ch.14, p.1068	IFRS 13.BC238(c)	Ch.14, p.1172
IFRS 13.IE49-IE58	Ch.14, p.1047		
IFRS 13.IE60	Ch.14, p.1142		
IFRS 13.IE61	Ch.14, p.1150		

IFRS 14

IFRS 14.5	Ch.5, p.323
IFRS 14.5	Ch.26, p.1966
IFRS 14.6	Ch.5, p.323

IFRS 13.IE62	Ch.14, p.1151
IFRS 13.IE63	Ch.14, p.1147
IFRS 13.IE64(a)	Ch.14, p.1134
IFRS 13.IE65	Ch.14, p.1152

IFRS 14.6	Ch.26, p.1966
IFRS 14.7	Ch.5, p.325
IFRS 14.8	Ch.5, p.323
IFRS 14.8	Ch.5, p.335
IFRS 14.9	Ch.5, p.324
IFRS 14.9	Ch.5, p.325
IFRS 14.9-10	Ch.5, p.324
IFRS 14.11	Ch.5, p.324
IFRS 14.11	Ch.5, p.326
IFRS 14.11	Ch.5, p.334
IFRS 14.12	Ch.5, p.334
IFRS 14.12-15	Ch.5, p.324
IFRS 14.13	Ch.2, p.47
IFRS 14.13	Ch.5, p.325
IFRS 14.13	Ch.5, p.326
IFRS 14.13	Ch.26, p.1966
IFRS 14.13-15	Ch.5, p.324
IFRS 14.14	Ch.5, p.325
IFRS 14.15	Ch.5, p.325
IFRS 14.16	Ch.5, p.333
IFRS 14.17	Ch.5, p.333
IFRS 14.18-19	Ch.5, p.324
IFRS 14.20	Ch.5, p.326
IFRS 14.20-24	Ch.5, p.328
IFRS 14.21	Ch.5, p.326
IFRS 14.22	Ch.5, p.326
IFRS 14.23	Ch.5, p.326
IFRS 14.24	Ch.5, p.326
IFRS 14.24	Ch.5, p.327
IFRS 14.24	Ch.5, p.331
IFRS 14.25	Ch.5, p.327
IFRS 14.26	Ch.5, p.327
IFRS 14.26	Ch.5, p.328
IFRS 14.27	Ch.5, p.331
IFRS 14.28	Ch.5, p.331
IFRS 14.29	Ch.5, p.331
IFRS 14.29(a)	Ch.5, p.332
IFRS 14.30	Ch.5, p.331
IFRS 14.31	Ch.5, p.332
IFRS 14.32	Ch.5, p.332
IFRS 14.33	Ch.5, p.327
IFRS 14.33	Ch.5, p.332
IFRS 14.34	Ch.5, p.332
IFRS 14.35	Ch.5, p.332
IFRS 14.35	Ch.5, p.333
IFRS 14.36	Ch.5, p.333
IFRS 14 Appendix A	Ch.5, p.299
IFRS 14 Appendix A	Ch.5, p.322
IFRS 14.B1	Ch.5, p.323
IFRS 14.B2	Ch.5, p.323
IFRS 14.B3	Ch.5, p.325
IFRS 14.B4	Ch.5, p.324
IFRS 14.B5	Ch.5, p.325
IFRS 14.B6	Ch.5, p.326
IFRS 14.B7-B28	Ch.5, p.333
IFRS 14.B8	Ch.5, p.333
IFRS 14.B9	Ch.5, p.334
IFRS 14.B10	Ch.5, p.334
IFRS 14.B11	Ch.5, p.326
IFRS 14.B12	Ch.5, p.327
IFRS 14.B12	Ch.5, p.331
IFRS 14.B14	Ch.5, p.327
IFRS 14.B15	Ch.5, p.334
IFRS 14.B15-B16	Ch.5, p.334
IFRS 14.B16	Ch.5, p.334
IFRS 14.B17-B18	Ch.5, p.334
IFRS 14.B19	Ch.5, p.334
IFRS 14.B20	Ch.5, p.327
IFRS 14.B21	Ch.5, p.327
IFRS 14.B22	Ch.5, p.327
IFRS 14.B23	Ch.5, p.335
IFRS 14.B24	Ch.5, p.335
IFRS 14.B25	Ch.5, p.332
IFRS 14.B26-B27	Ch.5, p.333
IFRS 14.B28	Ch.5, p.333
IFRS 14.C1	Ch.26, p.1966
IFRS 14.IE1	Ch.5, p.326
IFRS 14.IE1	Ch.5, p.328
IFRS 14.IE1	Ch.5, p.329
IFRS 14.IE1	Ch.5, p.333
IFRS 14.IE2	Ch.5, p.328
IFRS 14.BC10	Ch.2, p.47
IFRS 14.BC10	Ch.26, p.1966
IFRS 14.BC22	Ch.5, p.323
IFRS 14.BC23	Ch.5, p.323
IFRS 14.BC32	Ch.5, p.324
IFRS 14.BC33	Ch.5, p.325

IFRS 15 (2016)

IFRS 15(2016).IN5	Ch.27, p.2020

IFRS 15

IFRS 15.1	Ch.27, p.2021
IFRS 15.2	Ch.27, p.2021
IFRS 15.2	Ch.31, p.2345
IFRS 15.3	Ch.27, p.2022
IFRS 15.4	Ch.28, p.2068
IFRS 15.5	Ch.27, p.2024
IFRS 15.5(c)	Ch.27, p.2035
IFRS 15.5(d)	Ch.18, p.1406
IFRS 15.5(d)	Ch.43, p.3449
IFRS 15.5(d)	Ch.43, p.3450
IFRS 15.6	Ch.27, p.2028
IFRS 15.6	Ch.43, p.3450
IFRS 15.6	Ch.43, p.3453
IFRS 15.6	Ch.43, p.3460
IFRS 15.7	Ch.27, p.2029
IFRS 15.7	Ch.29, p.2249
IFRS 15.7	Ch.31, p.2327
IFRS 15.7	Ch.43, p.3457
IFRS 15.8	Ch.25, p.1896
IFRS 15.8	Ch.27, p.2026

IFRS 15.8	Ch.31, p.2358	IFRS 15.31	Ch.19, p.1492
IFRS 15.9	Ch.28, p.2053	IFRS 15.31	Ch.25, p.1908
IFRS 15.9	Ch.28, p.2054	IFRS 15.31	Ch.30, p.2257
IFRS 15.9(e)	Ch.28, p.2058	IFRS 15.31	Ch.43, p.3450
IFRS 15.10	Ch.25, p.1869	IFRS 15.32	Ch.19, p.1492
IFRS 15.10	Ch.25, p.1914	IFRS 15.32	Ch.25, p.1908
IFRS 15.10	Ch.28, p.2052	IFRS 15.32	Ch.30, p.2258
IFRS 15.10	Ch.28, p.2055	IFRS 15.32	Ch.30, p.2259
IFRS 15.11	Ch.28, p.2052	IFRS 15.33	Ch.28, p.2125
IFRS 15.11	Ch.28, p.2061	IFRS 15.33	Ch.30, p.2257
IFRS 15.12	Ch.28, p.2061	IFRS 15.33	Ch.30, p.2258
IFRS 15.13	Ch.28, p.2053	IFRS 15.34	Ch.30, p.2298
IFRS 15.14	Ch.28, p.2083	IFRS 15.35	Ch.30, p.2259
IFRS 15.15	Ch.28, p.2066	IFRS 15.35(a)	Ch.25, p.1908
IFRS 15.15	Ch.28, p.2082	IFRS 15.35(a)	Ch.25, p.1916
IFRS 15.16	Ch.28, p.2082	IFRS 15.35(a)	Ch.28, p.2092
IFRS 15.18	Ch.28, p.2065	IFRS 15.35(b)	Ch.25, p.1908
IFRS 15.18	Ch.28, p.2069	IFRS 15.35(b)	Ch.25, p.1915
IFRS 15.18	Ch.28, p.2077	IFRS 15.35(c)	Ch.5, p.337
IFRS 15.18	Ch.29, p.2172	IFRS 15.35(c)	Ch.30, p.2264
IFRS 15.19	Ch.28, p.2069	IFRS 15.36	Ch.30, p.2264
IFRS 15.20	Ch.28, p.2071	IFRS 15.36	Ch.30, p.2266
IFRS 15.20(a)	Ch.28, p.2072	IFRS 15.36	Ch.30, p.2276
IFRS 15.20(b)	Ch.28, p.2072	IFRS 15.37	Ch.30, p.2267
IFRS 15.20-21	Ch.5, p.335	IFRS 15.37	Ch.30, p.2276
IFRS 15.21	Ch.28, p.2073	IFRS 15.38	Ch.23, p.1802
IFRS 15.21(a)	Ch.29, p.2248	IFRS 15.38	Ch.28, p.2126
IFRS 15.22	Ch.25, p.1870	IFRS 15.38	Ch.30, p.2291
IFRS 15.22	Ch.25, p.1906	IFRS 15.39	Ch.25, p.1898
IFRS 15.22	Ch.28, p.2084	IFRS 15.39	Ch.30, p.2278
IFRS 15.22(b)	Ch.28, p.2109	IFRS 15.40	Ch.30, p.2278
IFRS 15.22(b)	Ch.28, p.2116	IFRS 15.40	Ch.38, p.3088
IFRS 15.23	Ch.28, p.2084	IFRS 15.41	Ch.30, p.2279
IFRS 15.23	Ch.28, p.2109	IFRS 15.41	Ch.30, p.2280
IFRS 15.23	Ch.28, p.2116	IFRS 15.42	Ch.30, p.2278
IFRS 15.24	Ch.28, p.2085	IFRS 15.43	Ch.30, p.2278
IFRS 15.24	Ch.28, p.2089	IFRS 15.44	Ch.30, p.2279
IFRS 15.25	Ch.28, p.2085	IFRS 15.45	Ch.25, p.1908
IFRS 15.25	Ch.28, p.2086	IFRS 15.45	Ch.30, p.2279
IFRS 15.25	Ch.28, p.2089	IFRS 15.46	Ch.29, p.2164
IFRS 15.26	Ch.25, p.1870	IFRS 15.47	Ch.19, p.1493
IFRS 15.26	Ch.25, p.1906	IFRS 15.47	Ch.25, p.1871
IFRS 15.26	Ch.28, p.2085	IFRS 15.47	Ch.25, p.1907
IFRS 15.26(e)	Ch.28, p.2087	IFRS 15.47	Ch.29, p.2164
IFRS 15.26(g)	Ch.28, p.2087	IFRS 15.47	Ch.29, p.2166
IFRS 15.27	Ch.25, p.1870	IFRS 15.47	Ch.33, p.2459
IFRS 15.27	Ch.25, p.1906	IFRS 15.47	Ch.43, p.3458
IFRS 15.28	Ch.28, p.2097	IFRS 15.47	Ch.43, p.3558
IFRS 15.29	Ch.28, p.2098	IFRS 15.48	Ch.29, p.2164
IFRS 15.29	Ch.28, p.2099	IFRS 15.49	Ch.29, p.2164
IFRS 15.29	Ch.28, p.2104	IFRS 15.49	Ch.31, p.2384
IFRS 15.29(a)	Ch.28, p.2100	IFRS 15.50	Ch.25, p.1871
IFRS 15.29(b)	Ch.28, p.2102	IFRS 15.50	Ch.25, p.1907
IFRS 15.29(c)	Ch.28, p.2102	IFRS 15.50	Ch.29, p.2175
IFRS 15.30	Ch.25, p.1870	IFRS 15.50-51	Ch.29, p.2167
IFRS 15.30	Ch.25, p.1906	IFRS 15.51	Ch.25, p.1871
IFRS 15.30	Ch.28, p.2095	IFRS 15.51	Ch.25, p.1907
IFRS 15.30	Ch.28, p.2120	IFRS 15.51	Ch.29, p.2167

IFRS 15.51	Ch.29, p.2172
IFRS 15.51	Ch.29, p.2174
IFRS 15.52	Ch.29, p.2167
IFRS 15.53	Ch.25, p.1871
IFRS 15.53	Ch.25, p.1907
IFRS 15.53	Ch.29, p.2176
IFRS 15.54	Ch.29, p.2176
IFRS 15.55	Ch.9, p.689
IFRS 15.55	Ch.26, p.2006
IFRS 15.55	Ch.29, p.2188
IFRS 15.56	Ch.25, p.1871
IFRS 15.56	Ch.25, p.1907
IFRS 15.56	Ch.29, p.2179
IFRS 15.57	Ch.29, p.2179
IFRS 15.58	Ch.29, p.2180
IFRS 15.59	Ch.29, p.2187
IFRS 15.60	Ch.29, p.2192
IFRS 15.60	Ch.51, p.3928
IFRS 15.60-65	Ch.40, p.3167
IFRS 15.61	Ch.29, p.2192
IFRS 15.61(a)	Ch.29, p.2201
IFRS 15.62	Ch.25, p.1871
IFRS 15.62	Ch.25, p.1915
IFRS 15.62	Ch.29, p.2193
IFRS 15.62(a)	Ch.28, p.2154
IFRS 15.62(c)	Ch.29, p.2201
IFRS 15.63	Ch.25, p.1909
IFRS 15.63	Ch.29, p.2193
IFRS 15.63	Ch.29, p.2202
IFRS 15.63	Ch.51, p.3928
IFRS 15.64	Ch.25, p.1872
IFRS 15.64	Ch.25, p.1876
IFRS 15.64	Ch.25, p.1907
IFRS 15.64	Ch.25, p.1909
IFRS 15.64	Ch.25, p.1911
IFRS 15.64	Ch.25, p.1913
IFRS 15.64	Ch.29, p.2193
IFRS 15.64	Ch.29, p.2196
IFRS 15.65	Ch.29, p.2205
IFRS 15.66	Ch.18, p.1402
IFRS 15.66	Ch.25, p.1880
IFRS 15.66	Ch.29, p.2206
IFRS 15.67	Ch.25, p.1880
IFRS 15.67	Ch.25, p.1915
IFRS 15.67	Ch.29, p.2206
IFRS 15.68	Ch.29, p.2207
IFRS 15.69	Ch.29, p.2207
IFRS 15.70	Ch.29, p.2210
IFRS 15.70	Ch.29, p.2214
IFRS 15.70	Ch.29, p.2215
IFRS 15.70-72	Ch.25, p.1864
IFRS 15.71	Ch.29, p.2210
IFRS 15.71	Ch.29, p.2214
IFRS 15.72	Ch.29, p.2211
IFRS 15.72	Ch.29, p.2212
IFRS 15.72	Ch.29, p.2215
IFRS 15.73	Ch.29, p.2222
IFRS 15.74	Ch.25, p.1872
IFRS 15.74	Ch.25, p.1908
IFRS 15.74	Ch.25, p.1915
IFRS 15.74	Ch.29, p.2222
IFRS 15.75	Ch.29, p.2222
IFRS 15.76	Ch.29, p.2222
IFRS 15.76	Ch.29, p.2235
IFRS 15.77	Ch.29, p.2222
IFRS 15.77	Ch.29, p.2223
IFRS 15.77	Ch.29, p.2224
IFRS 15.77	Ch.29, p.2225
IFRS 15.78	Ch.29, p.2223
IFRS 15.78	Ch.29, p.2224
IFRS 15.78	Ch.29, p.2225
IFRS 15.78	Ch.29, p.2228
IFRS 15.79	Ch.25, p.1872
IFRS 15.79	Ch.25, p.1908
IFRS 15.79	Ch.25, p.1915
IFRS 15.79	Ch.29, p.2224
IFRS 15.79	Ch.29, p.2225
IFRS 15.79(c)	Ch.29, p.2226
IFRS 15.80	Ch.29, p.2225
IFRS 15.80	Ch.29, p.2227
IFRS 15.81	Ch.29, p.2244
IFRS 15.82	Ch.29, p.2244
IFRS 15.82(b)	Ch.29, p.2215
IFRS 15.83	Ch.29, p.2244
IFRS 15.84	Ch.29, p.2237
IFRS 15.85	Ch.28, p.2153
IFRS 15.85	Ch.29, p.2237
IFRS 15.85	Ch.29, p.2238
IFRS 15.85	Ch.31, p.2347
IFRS 15.86	Ch.29, p.2237
IFRS 15.86	Ch.29, p.2246
IFRS 15.87	Ch.29, p.2222
IFRS 15.88	Ch.29, p.2223
IFRS 15.88-89	Ch.28, p.2079
IFRS 15.88-89	Ch.29, p.2247
IFRS 15.89	Ch.28, p.2152
IFRS 15.90	Ch.29, p.2248
IFRS 15.90(a)	Ch.29, p.2248
IFRS 15.90(b)	Ch.29, p.2249
IFRS 15.91	Ch.25, p.1896
IFRS 15.91-93	Ch.31, p.2359
IFRS 15.91-93	Ch.55, p.4586
IFRS 15.92	Ch.25, p.1896
IFRS 15.92	Ch.31, p.2359
IFRS 15.93	Ch.25, p.1896
IFRS 15.94	Ch.31, p.2363
IFRS 15.95	Ch.25, p.1897
IFRS 15.95	Ch.31, p.2365
IFRS 15.95	Ch.41, p.3243
IFRS 15.95-96	Ch.22, p.1687
IFRS 15.95-96	Ch.31, p.2365
IFRS 15.97	Ch.26, p.1974
IFRS 15.97	Ch.31, p.2367
IFRS 15.98	Ch.26, p.1974
IFRS 15.98	Ch.31, p.2368
IFRS 15.99	Ch.31, p.2375

IFRS 15.99	Ch.31, p.2376	IFRS 15.117	Ch.32, p.2417
IFRS 15.99	Ch.31, p.2380	IFRS 15.118	Ch.32, p.2417
IFRS 15.99	Ch.31, p.2384	IFRS 15.119	Ch.29, p.2168
IFRS 15.100	Ch.31, p.2376	IFRS 15.119-120	Ch.32, p.2422
IFRS 15.101	Ch.31, p.2384	IFRS 15.119(a)	Ch.30, p.2260
IFRS 15.101(a)	Ch.31, p.2384	IFRS 15.120	Ch.5, p.335
IFRS 15.102	Ch.31, p.2384	IFRS 15.120	Ch.32, p.2432
IFRS 15.102	Ch.31, p.2385	IFRS 15.121	Ch.32, p.2430
IFRS 15.103	Ch.31, p.2385	IFRS 15.121	Ch.32, p.2432
IFRS 15.104	Ch.31, p.2385	IFRS 15.122	Ch.32, p.2430
IFRS 15.105	Ch.9, p.689	IFRS 15.123	Ch.3, p.175
IFRS 15.105	Ch.32, p.2393	IFRS 15.123	Ch.29, p.2168
IFRS 15.105	Ch.32, p.2395	IFRS 15.123	Ch.32, p.2433
IFRS 15.105	Ch.52, p.4089	IFRS 15.123(a)	Ch.30, p.2260
IFRS 15.106	Ch.9, p.688	IFRS 15.124	Ch.30, p.2260
IFRS 15.106-107	Ch.32, p.2394	IFRS 15.124	Ch.32, p.2433
IFRS 15.107	Ch.9, p.689	IFRS 15.125	Ch.32, p.2433
IFRS 15.107	Ch.25, p.1876	IFRS 15.126	Ch.29, p.2168
IFRS 15.107	Ch.25, p.1883	IFRS 15.126	Ch.32, p.2435
IFRS 15.107	Ch.25, p.1910	IFRS 15.127-128	Ch.32, p.2437
IFRS 15.107	Ch.25, p.1912	IFRS 15.129	Ch.32, p.2439
IFRS 15.107	Ch.25, p.1913	IFRS 15 Appendix A	Ch.8, p.627
IFRS 15.107	Ch.25, p.1916	IFRS 15 Appendix A	Ch.9, p.689
IFRS 15.107	Ch.32, p.2395	IFRS 15 Appendix A	Ch.25, p.1869
IFRS 15.107	Ch.32, p.2398	IFRS 15 Appendix A	Ch.25, p.1905
IFRS 15.107	Ch.45, p.3607	IFRS 15 Appendix A	Ch.25, p.1906
IFRS 15.107	Ch.52, p.4089	IFRS 15 Appendix A	Ch.25, p.1914
IFRS 15.108	Ch.25, p.1875	IFRS 15 Appendix A	Ch.27, p.2018
IFRS 15.108	Ch.25, p.1876	IFRS 15 Appendix A	Ch.27, p.2023
IFRS 15.108	Ch.25, p.1877	IFRS 15 Appendix A	Ch.27, p.2027
IFRS 15.108	Ch.25, p.1885	IFRS 15 Appendix A	Ch.27, p.2033
IFRS 15.108	Ch.25, p.1909	IFRS 15 Appendix A	Ch.28, p.2057
IFRS 15.108	Ch.25, p.1910	IFRS 15 Appendix A	Ch.42, p.3315
IFRS 15.108	Ch.25, p.1911	IFRS 15 Appendix A	Ch.43, p.3452
IFRS 15.108	Ch.25, p.1912	IFRS 15 Appendix A	Ch.43, p.3467
IFRS 15.108	Ch.32, p.2395	IFRS 15 Appendix A	Ch.43, p.3469
IFRS 15.108	Ch.32, p.2399	IFRS 15 Appendix A	Ch.51, p.3924
IFRS 15.108	Ch.32, p.2404	IFRS 15 Appendix A	Ch.51, p.3928
IFRS 15.108	Ch.45, p.3606	IFRS 15.B3	Ch.30, p.2261
IFRS 15.108	Ch.49, p.3854	IFRS 15.B4	Ch.25, p.1908
IFRS 15.108	Ch.52, p.4089	IFRS 15.B4	Ch.30, p.2261
IFRS 15.109	Ch.32, p.2396	IFRS 15.B5	Ch.30, p.2263
IFRS 15.110	Ch.32, p.2408	IFRS 15.B6	Ch.30, p.2264
IFRS 15.111	Ch.32, p.2408	IFRS 15.B7	Ch.30, p.2264
IFRS 15.112	Ch.32, p.2408	IFRS 15.B7	Ch.30, p.2265
IFRS 15.112	Ch.32, p.2410	IFRS 15.B8	Ch.30, p.2265
IFRS 15.112	Ch.36, p.2980	IFRS 15.B9	Ch.30, p.2267
IFRS 15.113	Ch.32, p.2404	IFRS 15.B10	Ch.30, p.2268
IFRS 15.113	Ch.43, p.3458	IFRS 15.B11	Ch.30, p.2268
IFRS 15.113(a)	Ch.43, p.3450	IFRS 15.B12	Ch.30, p.2267
IFRS 15.113(b)	Ch.29, p.2206	IFRS 15.B12	Ch.30, p.2269
IFRS 15.113(b)	Ch.32, p.2399	IFRS 15.B13	Ch.30, p.2269
IFRS 15.113(b)	Ch.32, p.2400	IFRS 15.B14	Ch.30, p.2279
IFRS 15.114	Ch.32, p.2409	IFRS 15.B15	Ch.30, p.2279
IFRS 15.114	Ch.36, p.2980	IFRS 15.B16	Ch.30, p.2280
IFRS 15.115	Ch.32, p.2411	IFRS 15.B16	Ch.30, p.2281
IFRS 15.115	Ch.36, p.2980	IFRS 15.B17	Ch.30, p.2280
IFRS 15.116	Ch.32, p.2417	IFRS 15.B18	Ch.25, p.1908

IFRS 15.B18	Ch.25, p.1915	IFRS 15.B41	Ch.28, p.2150
IFRS 15.B18	Ch.30, p.2280	IFRS 15.B42	Ch.29, p.2231
IFRS 15.B19	Ch.25, p.1898	IFRS 15.B43	Ch.29, p.2231
IFRS 15.B19	Ch.30, p.2283	IFRS 15.B43	Ch.29, p.2232
IFRS 15.B19	Ch.30, p.2284	IFRS 15.B44-B47	Ch.28, p.2154
IFRS 15.B19(a)	Ch.30, p.2284	IFRS 15.B44-B47	Ch.43, p.3472
IFRS 15.B20	Ch.28, p.2154	IFRS 15.B45	Ch.30, p.2309
IFRS 15.B20	Ch.29, p.2188	IFRS 15.B46	Ch.28, p.2066
IFRS 15.B21	Ch.29, p.2188	IFRS 15.B46	Ch.30, p.2309
IFRS 15.B21	Ch.29, p.2189	IFRS 15.B46	Ch.30, p.2311
IFRS 15.B22	Ch.28, p.2154	IFRS 15.B46	Ch.31, p.2348
IFRS 15.B22	Ch.29, p.2188	IFRS 15.B48	Ch.29, p.2218
IFRS 15.B23	Ch.29, p.2189	IFRS 15.B49	Ch.28, p.2089
IFRS 15.B24	Ch.29, p.2189	IFRS 15.B49	Ch.29, p.2218
IFRS 15.B25	Ch.29, p.2189	IFRS 15.B50	Ch.29, p.2218
IFRS 15.B25	Ch.32, p.2402	IFRS 15.B51	Ch.29, p.2218
IFRS 15.B26	Ch.28, p.2154	IFRS 15.B52	Ch.31, p.2320
IFRS 15.B26	Ch.29, p.2188	IFRS 15.B53	Ch.31, p.2321
IFRS 15.B27	Ch.28, p.2154	IFRS 15.B54	Ch.28, p.2096
IFRS 15.B27	Ch.29, p.2188	IFRS 15.B54	Ch.31, p.2324
IFRS 15.B28	Ch.31, p.2350	IFRS 15.B56	Ch.31, p.2320
IFRS 15.B28-B33	Ch.28, p.2096	IFRS 15.B58	Ch.31, p.2328
IFRS 15.B29	Ch.31, p.2350	IFRS 15.B59	Ch.31, p.2328
IFRS 15.B29	Ch.31, p.2353	IFRS 15.B59A	Ch.31, p.2329
IFRS 15.B30	Ch.25, p.1906	IFRS 15.B60	Ch.31, p.2333
IFRS 15.B30	Ch.25, p.1914	IFRS 15.B61	Ch.31, p.2333
IFRS 15.B30	Ch.26, p.1936	IFRS 15.B61	Ch.31, p.2335
IFRS 15.B30	Ch.26, p.2003	IFRS 15.B61	Ch.31, p.2336
IFRS 15.B30	Ch.31, p.2350	IFRS 15.B62(a)	Ch.31, p.2324
IFRS 15.B30	Ch.31, p.2354	IFRS 15.B62(b)	Ch.31, p.2326
IFRS 15.B31	Ch.31, p.2350	IFRS 15.B63	Ch.31, p.2337
IFRS 15.B32	Ch.31, p.2353	IFRS 15.B63	Ch.31, p.2348
IFRS 15.B32	Ch.31, p.2355	IFRS 15.B63A	Ch.31, p.2338
IFRS 15.B33	Ch.26, p.1936	IFRS 15.B63B	Ch.31, p.2340
IFRS 15.B33	Ch.31, p.2350	IFRS 15.B64	Ch.30, p.2298
IFRS 15.B33	Ch.31, p.2351	IFRS 15.B64	Ch.43, p.3466
IFRS 15.B34	Ch.28, p.2121	IFRS 15.B65	Ch.30, p.2298
IFRS 15.B34	Ch.28, p.2123	IFRS 15.B65	Ch.43, p.3466
IFRS 15.B34	Ch.28, p.2124	IFRS 15.B66-B67	Ch.30, p.2299
IFRS 15.B34A(a)	Ch.28, p.2123	IFRS 15.B68-B69	Ch.30, p.2300
IFRS 15.B34A(b)	Ch.28, p.2125	IFRS 15.B70	Ch.30, p.2301
IFRS 15.B34A	Ch.28, p.2121	IFRS 15.B70	Ch.30, p.2302
IFRS 15.B35	Ch.28, p.2121	IFRS 15.B70-B71	Ch.30, p.2301
IFRS 15.B35	Ch.28, p.2122	IFRS 15.B72	Ch.30, p.2302
IFRS 15.B35A	Ch.28, p.2126	IFRS 15.B73	Ch.30, p.2302
IFRS 15.B35B	Ch.28, p.2131	IFRS 15.B74	Ch.30, p.2302
IFRS 15.B36	Ch.28, p.2121	IFRS 15.B75	Ch.30, p.2301
IFRS 15.B36	Ch.28, p.2131	IFRS 15.B76	Ch.30, p.2302
IFRS 15.B37	Ch.28, p.2129	IFRS 15.B77	Ch.30, p.2304
IFRS 15.B37A	Ch.28, p.2129	IFRS 15.B77	Ch.30, p.2305
IFRS 15.B38	Ch.28, p.2132	IFRS 15.B78	Ch.30, p.2304
IFRS 15.B39	Ch.28, p.2140	IFRS 15.B79	Ch.30, p.2305
IFRS 15.B39-B43	Ch.28, p.2096	IFRS 15.B79-B82	Ch.43, p.3448
IFRS 15.B40	Ch.28, p.2140	IFRS 15.B80	Ch.30, p.2305
IFRS 15.B40	Ch.28, p.2148	IFRS 15.B81	Ch.30, p.2306
IFRS 15.B40	Ch.28, p.2154	IFRS 15.B82	Ch.30, p.2306
IFRS 15.B41	Ch.28, p.2141	IFRS 15.B82	Ch.43, p.3448
IFRS 15.B41	Ch.28, p.2148	IFRS 15.B83	Ch.30, p.2295

IFRS 15.B84	Ch.30, p.2296	IFRS 15.IE238A-IE238G	Ch.28, p.2133
IFRS 15.B85	Ch.30, p.2296	IFRS 15.IE239-IE243	Ch.28, p.2134
IFRS 15.B86	Ch.30, p.2296	IFRS 15.IE244-IE248	Ch.28, p.2134
IFRS 15.B87	Ch.32, p.2410	IFRS 15.IE248A-IE248F	Ch.28, p.2135
IFRS 15.B87-B89	Ch.32, p.2410	IFRS 15.IE250-IE253	Ch.28, p.2141
IFRS 15.C1	Ch.27, p.2020	IFRS 15.IE257-IE266	Ch.28, p.2151
IFRS 15.C5	Ch.5, p.335	IFRS 15.IE267-IE270	Ch.30, p.2310
IFRS 15.C5(a)(ii)	Ch.5, p.339	IFRS 15.IE281	Ch.31, p.2322
IFRS 15.C5(a)(ii)	Ch.5, p.341	IFRS 15.IE281-IE284	Ch.31, p.2331
IFRS 15.C5(c)	Ch.5, p.336	IFRS 15.IE285-IE288	Ch.31, p.2322
IFRS 15.C6	Ch.5, p.336	IFRS 15.IE297-IE302	Ch.31, p.2334
IFRS 15.C10	Ch.27, p.2020	IFRS 15.IE303-IE306	Ch.31, p.2335
IFRS 15.IE3-IE6	Ch.28, p.2059	IFRS 15.IE307-IE308	Ch.31, p.2340
IFRS 15.IE7-IE9	Ch.29, p.2169	IFRS 15.IE309-IE313	Ch.31, p.2342
IFRS 15.IE14-IE17	Ch.28, p.2061	IFRS 15.IE315	Ch.30, p.2303
IFRS 15.IE17	Ch.28, p.2061	IFRS 15.IE315-IE318	Ch.30, p.2300
IFRS 15.IE19	Ch.28, p.2074	IFRS 15.IE319-IE321	Ch.30, p.2303
IFRS 15.IE19-IE21	Ch.28, p.2073	IFRS 15.IE323-IE327	Ch.30, p.2307
IFRS 15.IE22-IE24	Ch.28, p.2074	IFRS 15.BC32	Ch.28, p.2052
IFRS 15.IE33-IE36	Ch.28, p.2074	IFRS 15.BC32	Ch.28, p.2086
IFRS 15.IE37-IE41	Ch.28, p.2076	IFRS 15.BC33	Ch.28, p.2053
IFRS 15.IE42-IE43	Ch.28, p.2069	IFRS 15.BC34	Ch.28, p.2053
IFRS 15.IE45-IE48C	Ch.28, p.2116	IFRS 15.BC35	Ch.28, p.2055
IFRS 15.IE49-IE58	Ch.28, p.2117	IFRS 15.BC36	Ch.28, p.2056
IFRS 15.IE58A-IE58K	Ch.28, p.2118	IFRS 15.BC37	Ch.28, p.2056
IFRS 15.IE59-IE65A	Ch.28, p.2087	IFRS 15.BC40	Ch.28, p.2056
IFRS 15.IE67-IE68	Ch.28, p.2114	IFRS 15.BC43	Ch.28, p.2057
IFRS 15.IE67-IE68	Ch.30, p.2262	IFRS 15.BC45	Ch.28, p.2057
IFRS 15.IE69-IE72	Ch.30, p.2269	IFRS 15.BC46	Ch.28, p.2058
IFRS 15.IE73-IE76	Ch.30, p.2265	IFRS 15.BC46C	Ch.28, p.2058
IFRS 15.IE77-IE80	Ch.30, p.2270	IFRS 15.BC46E	Ch.28, p.2057
IFRS 15.IE81-IE90	Ch.30, p.2270	IFRS 15.BC46E	Ch.28, p.2058
IFRS 15.IE92-IE94	Ch.30, p.2286	IFRS 15.BC46H	Ch.28, p.2083
IFRS 15.IE95-IE100	Ch.30, p.2284	IFRS 15.BC46H	Ch.28, p.2084
IFRS 15.IE98	Ch.30, p.2286	IFRS 15.BC47	Ch.28, p.2083
IFRS 15.IE102-IE104	Ch.29, p.2173	IFRS 15.BC48	Ch.28, p.2066
IFRS 15.IE110-IE115	Ch.29, p.2190	IFRS 15.BC48	Ch.28, p.2083
IFRS 15.IE116-IE123	Ch.29, p.2182	IFRS 15.BC52-BC56	Ch.43, p.3450
IFRS 15.IE124-IE128	Ch.29, p.2167	IFRS 15.BC54	Ch.27, p.2028
IFRS 15.IE129-IE133	Ch.29, p.2184	IFRS 15.BC54	Ch.43, p.3453
IFRS 15.IE135-IE140	Ch.29, p.2197	IFRS 15.BC56	Ch.27, p.2028
IFRS 15.IE141-IE142	Ch.29, p.2198	IFRS 15.BC58	Ch.27, p.2026
IFRS 15.IE143-IE147	Ch.29, p.2199	IFRS 15.BC69	Ch.28, p.2068
IFRS 15.IE148-IE151	Ch.29, p.2199	IFRS 15.BC71	Ch.28, p.2067
IFRS 15.IE152-IE154	Ch.29, p.2200	IFRS 15.BC73	Ch.28, p.2068
IFRS 15.IE156-IE158	Ch.29, p.2207	IFRS 15.BC74	Ch.28, p.2067
IFRS 15.IE160-IE162	Ch.29, p.2216	IFRS 15.BC75	Ch.28, p.2067
IFRS 15.IE164-IE166	Ch.29, p.2227	IFRS 15.BC76	Ch.28, p.2070
IFRS 15.IE167-IE177	Ch.29, p.2244	IFRS 15.BC79	Ch.27, p.2024
IFRS 15.IE178-IE187	Ch.29, p.2242	IFRS 15.BC79	Ch.28, p.2071
IFRS 15.IE178-IE187	Ch.31, p.2340	IFRS 15.BC83	Ch.29, p.2248
IFRS 15.IE189-IE191	Ch.31, p.2362	IFRS 15.BC85	Ch.28, p.2084
IFRS 15.IE192-IE196	Ch.31, p.2368	IFRS 15.BC87	Ch.28, p.2086
IFRS 15.IE198-IE200	Ch.32, p.2396	IFRS 15.BC87	Ch.28, p.2088
IFRS 15.IE201-IE204	Ch.32, p.2397	IFRS 15.BC88	Ch.28, p.2086
IFRS 15.IE210-IE211	Ch.32, p.2412	IFRS 15.BC89	Ch.28, p.2086
IFRS 15.IE212-IE219	Ch.32, p.2430	IFRS 15.BC90	Ch.28, p.2090
IFRS 15.IE220-IE221	Ch.32, p.2432	IFRS 15.BC92	Ch.28, p.2087

IFRS 15.BC100	Ch.28, p.2097
IFRS 15.BC100	Ch.28, p.2104
IFRS 15.BC101	Ch.28, p.2097
IFRS 15.BC102	Ch.28, p.2096
IFRS 15.BC102	Ch.28, p.2099
IFRS 15.BC105	Ch.28, p.2104
IFRS 15.BC107	Ch.28, p.2101
IFRS 15.BC108	Ch.28, p.2101
IFRS 15.BC109	Ch.28, p.2102
IFRS 15.BC110	Ch.28, p.2102
IFRS 15.BC112	Ch.28, p.2103
IFRS 15.BC113	Ch.28, p.2109
IFRS 15.BC113	Ch.28, p.2112
IFRS 15.BC114	Ch.28, p.2109
IFRS 15.BC115	Ch.28, p.2111
IFRS 15.BC116	Ch.28, p.2112
IFRS 15.BC116D	Ch.28, p.2090
IFRS 15.BC116J	Ch.28, p.2099
IFRS 15.BC116J	Ch.28, p.2104
IFRS 15.BC116J-BC116L	Ch.28, p.2100
IFRS 15.BC116K	Ch.28, p.2099
IFRS 15.BC116K	Ch.28, p.2104
IFRS 15.BC116L	Ch.28, p.2099
IFRS 15.BC116N	Ch.28, p.2100
IFRS 15.BC116N	Ch.28, p.2104
IFRS 15.BC116U	Ch.28, p.2090
IFRS 15.BC118	Ch.30, p.2257
IFRS 15.BC120	Ch.30, p.2257
IFRS 15.BC121	Ch.30, p.2258
IFRS 15.BC125	Ch.30, p.2260
IFRS 15.BC126	Ch.30, p.2261
IFRS 15.BC127	Ch.30, p.2262
IFRS 15.BC129	Ch.30, p.2263
IFRS 15.BC130	Ch.30, p.2263
IFRS 15.BC135	Ch.30, p.2265
IFRS 15.BC136	Ch.30, p.2266
IFRS 15.BC137	Ch.30, p.2265
IFRS 15.BC138	Ch.30, p.2265
IFRS 15.BC138-BC139	Ch.27, p.2025
IFRS 15.BC139	Ch.30, p.2266
IFRS 15.BC141	Ch.30, p.2266
IFRS 15.BC142	Ch.30, p.2267
IFRS 15.BC142	Ch.30, p.2268
IFRS 15.BC144	Ch.30, p.2268
IFRS 15.BC145	Ch.30, p.2269
IFRS 15.BC145	Ch.30, p.2273
IFRS 15.BC146	Ch.30, p.2273
IFRS 15.BC148	Ch.30, p.2293
IFRS 15.BC154	Ch.30, p.2293
IFRS 15.BC155	Ch.30, p.2292
IFRS 15.BC160	Ch.30, p.2280
IFRS 15.BC161	Ch.30, p.2278
IFRS 15.BC161	Ch.30, p.2288
IFRS 15.BC163	Ch.30, p.2281
IFRS 15.BC165	Ch.30, p.2280
IFRS 15.BC166	Ch.30, p.2281
IFRS 15.BC171	Ch.30, p.2284
IFRS 15.BC171	Ch.30, p.2285
IFRS 15.BC171	Ch.30, p.2286
IFRS 15.BC172	Ch.30, p.2284
IFRS 15.BC172	Ch.30, p.2285
IFRS 15.BC172	Ch.30, p.2286
IFRS 15.BC174	Ch.30, p.2284
IFRS 15.BC174	Ch.30, p.2285
IFRS 15.BC179	Ch.30, p.2279
IFRS 15.BC180	Ch.30, p.2279
IFRS 15.BC185	Ch.29, p.2164
IFRS 15.BC187	Ch.29, p.2164
IFRS 15.BC188D	Ch.28, p.2136
IFRS 15.BC188D	Ch.29, p.2166
IFRS 15.BC191	Ch.29, p.2167
IFRS 15.BC194	Ch.28, p.2059
IFRS 15.BC194	Ch.29, p.2170
IFRS 15.BC200	Ch.29, p.2176
IFRS 15.BC200	Ch.29, p.2177
IFRS 15.BC201	Ch.29, p.2177
IFRS 15.BC202	Ch.29, p.2176
IFRS 15.BC203	Ch.29, p.2179
IFRS 15.BC204	Ch.29, p.2179
IFRS 15.BC211	Ch.29, p.2180
IFRS 15.BC212	Ch.29, p.2180
IFRS 15.BC215	Ch.29, p.2185
IFRS 15.BC219	Ch.31, p.2337
IFRS 15.BC228	Ch.29, p.2187
IFRS 15.BC228	Ch.29, p.2249
IFRS 15.BC229	Ch.29, p.2193
IFRS 15.BC230	Ch.29, p.2193
IFRS 15.BC232	Ch.29, p.2194
IFRS 15.BC233	Ch.29, p.2194
IFRS 15.BC233	Ch.29, p.2195
IFRS 15.BC234	Ch.29, p.2196
IFRS 15.BC235	Ch.29, p.2194
IFRS 15.BC236	Ch.29, p.2194
IFRS 15.BC238	Ch.29, p.2195
IFRS 15.BC239	Ch.29, p.2196
IFRS 15.BC244	Ch.29, p.2205
IFRS 15.BC247	Ch.29, p.2206
IFRS 15.BC252	Ch.29, p.2209
IFRS 15.BC254C	Ch.29, p.2208
IFRS 15.BC254E	Ch.29, p.2208
IFRS 15.BC254H	Ch.29, p.2209
IFRS 15.BC257	Ch.29, p.2213
IFRS 15.BC266	Ch.29, p.2222
IFRS 15.BC272	Ch.29, p.2226
IFRS 15.BC273	Ch.29, p.2226
IFRS 15.BC278	Ch.29, p.2237
IFRS 15.BC279-BC280	Ch.29, p.2243
IFRS 15.BC280	Ch.29, p.2237
IFRS 15.BC283	Ch.29, p.2244
IFRS 15.BC296	Ch.31, p.2356
IFRS 15.BC307	Ch.31, p.2365
IFRS 15.BC307	Ch.31, p.2367
IFRS 15.BC308	Ch.25, p.1897
IFRS 15.BC308	Ch.31, p.2367
IFRS 15.BC309	Ch.31, p.2377
IFRS 15.BC312	Ch.31, p.2370

IFRS 15.BC313	Ch.31, p.2371	IFRS 15.BC414P	Ch.31, p.2326
IFRS 15.BC315	Ch.31, p.2371	IFRS 15.BC414Q	Ch.31, p.2325
IFRS 15.BC317	Ch.32, p.2400	IFRS 15.BC414S	Ch.31, p.2336
IFRS 15.BC323	Ch.32, p.2396	IFRS 15.BC414T	Ch.31, p.2337
IFRS 15.BC323-BC324	Ch.32, p.2395	IFRS 15.BC414U	Ch.31, p.2337
IFRS 15.BC325	Ch.32, p.2395	IFRS 15.BC414X	Ch.31, p.2321
IFRS 15.BC327	Ch.32, p.2408	IFRS 15.BC414X	Ch.31, p.2331
IFRS 15.BC331	Ch.32, p.2408	IFRS 15.BC414Y	Ch.31, p.2332
IFRS 15.BC332	Ch.32, p.2404	IFRS 15.BC415	Ch.31, p.2338
IFRS 15.BC334	Ch.32, p.2404	IFRS 15.BC416	Ch.31, p.2338
IFRS 15.BC336	Ch.32, p.2410	IFRS 15.BC421	Ch.31, p.2343
IFRS 15.BC340	Ch.32, p.2411	IFRS 15.BC421E	Ch.31, p.2338
IFRS 15.BC340	Ch.36, p.2980	IFRS 15.BC421F	Ch.31, p.2343
IFRS 15.BC341	Ch.32, p.2417	IFRS 15.BC421G	Ch.31, p.2338
IFRS 15.BC346	Ch.32, p.2417	IFRS 15.BC421I	Ch.31, p.2337
IFRS 15.BC347	Ch.32, p.2418	IFRS 15.BC421I	Ch.31, p.2341
IFRS 15.BC348	Ch.32, p.2428	IFRS 15.BC421J	Ch.31, p.2340
IFRS 15.BC350	Ch.32, p.2428	IFRS 15.BC423	Ch.30, p.2299
IFRS 15.BC354	Ch.32, p.2421	IFRS 15.BC425	Ch.30, p.2300
IFRS 15.BC355	Ch.32, p.2433	IFRS 15.BC427	Ch.30, p.2299
IFRS 15.BC355	Ch.32, p.2435	IFRS 15.BC427	Ch.30, p.2303
IFRS 15.BC364	Ch.28, p.2154	IFRS 15.BC431	Ch.30, p.2304
IFRS 15.BC371	Ch.31, p.2353	IFRS 15.BC441	Ch.5, p.338
IFRS 15.BC376	Ch.31, p.2353	IFRS 15.BC445D	Ch.5, p.338
IFRS 15.BC376	Ch.31, p.2354		
IFRS 15.BC383-BC385	Ch.28, p.2132	**IFRS 16**	
IFRS 15.BC385B	Ch.28, p.2123		
IFRS 15.BC385D	Ch.28, p.2121	IFRS 16.1	Ch.23, p.1710
IFRS 15.BC385E	Ch.28, p.2121	IFRS 16.2	Ch.23, p.1710
IFRS 15.BC385H	Ch.28, p.2129	IFRS 16.2	Ch.43, p.3540
IFRS 15.BC385O	Ch.28, p.2123	IFRS 16.3	Ch.17, p.1294
IFRS 15.BC385O	Ch.28, p.2127	IFRS 16.3	Ch.23, p.1710
IFRS 15.BC385Q	Ch.28, p.2123	IFRS 16.3	Ch.43, p.3528
IFRS 15.BC385R	Ch.28, p.2128	IFRS 16.3(a)	Ch.43, p.3336
IFRS 15.BC385S	Ch.28, p.2125	IFRS 16.3(a)	Ch.43, p.3361
IFRS 15.BC385U	Ch.28, p.2126	IFRS 16.3(b)	Ch.42, p.3280
IFRS 15.BC385V	Ch.28, p.2127	IFRS 16.3(c)	Ch.25, p.1857
IFRS 15.BC385Z	Ch.28, p.2136	IFRS 16.4	Ch.23, p.1710
IFRS 15.BC386	Ch.28, p.2140	IFRS 16.5	Ch.23, p.1710
IFRS 15.BC390	Ch.29, p.2231	IFRS 16.6	Ch.5, p.303
IFRS 15.BC391	Ch.28, p.2064	IFRS 16.6	Ch.23, p.1752
IFRS 15.BC394	Ch.29, p.2231	IFRS 16.6	Ch.23, p.1753
IFRS 15.BC 394	Ch.29, p.2232	IFRS 16.6	Ch.43, p.3547
IFRS 15.BC395	Ch.29, p.2232	IFRS 16.7	Ch.23, p.1752
IFRS 15.BC398	Ch.30, p.2309	IFRS 16.8	Ch.23, p.1752
IFRS 15.BC400	Ch.30, p.2309	IFRS 16.8	Ch.23, p.1753
IFRS 15.BC405-BC406	Ch.31, p.2325	IFRS 16.9	Ch.17, p.1373
IFRS 15.BC407	Ch.31, p.2320	IFRS 16.9	Ch.23, p.1713
IFRS 15.BC407	Ch.31, p.2330	IFRS 16.9	Ch.23, p.1714
IFRS 15.BC412(b)	Ch.28, p.2094	IFRS 16.9	Ch.25, p.1857
IFRS 15.BC413	Ch.31, p.2329	IFRS 16.9	Ch.43, p.3539
IFRS 15.BC414	Ch.31, p.2333	IFRS 16.9	Ch.43, p.3553
IFRS 15.BC414	Ch.31, p.2336	IFRS 16.9-11	Ch.5, p.302
IFRS 15.BC414I	Ch.31, p.2329	IFRS 16.10	Ch.23, p.1714
IFRS 15.BC414K	Ch.31, p.2330	IFRS 16.11	Ch.5, p.302
IFRS 15.BC414N	Ch.31, p.2330	IFRS 16.11	Ch.23, p.1728
IFRS 15.BC414O	Ch.31, p.2325	IFRS 16.12	Ch.23, p.1728
IFRS 15.BC414P	Ch.31, p.2325		

IFRS 16.12	Ch.27, p.2030
IFRS 16.12	Ch.43, p.3531
IFRS 16.12	Ch.43, p.3554
IFRS 16.13	Ch.23, p.1731
IFRS 16.14	Ch.23, p.1731
IFRS 16.15	Ch.23, p.1730
IFRS 16.15-16	Ch.26, p.1977
IFRS 16.16	Ch.23, p.1729
IFRS 16.17	Ch.23, p.1734
IFRS 16.17	Ch.27, p.2030
IFRS 16.18	Ch.23, p.1736
IFRS 16.19	Ch.23, p.1736
IFRS 16.20	Ch.23, p.1741
IFRS 16.21	Ch.23, p.1742
IFRS 16.22	Ch.23, p.1751
IFRS 16.22	Ch.45, p.3587
IFRS 16.23	Ch.23, p.1754
IFRS 16.24	Ch.19, p.1463
IFRS 16.24	Ch.23, p.1754
IFRS 16.24(b)	Ch.19, p.1462
IFRS 16.24(b)	Ch.23, p.1743
IFRS 16.24(d)	Ch.26, p.1986
IFRS 16.25	Ch.23, p.1754
IFRS 16.25	Ch.26, p.1986
IFRS 16.26	Ch.23, p.1749
IFRS 16.26	Ch.23, p.1754
IFRS 16.26	Ch.45, p.3587
IFRS 16.27	Ch.23, p.1755
IFRS 16.27(a)	Ch.19, p.1462
IFRS 16.27(a)	Ch.23, p.1743
IFRS 16.28	Ch.23, p.1744
IFRS 16.29	Ch.23, p.1755
IFRS 16.29-35	Ch.18, p.1426
IFRS 16.30	Ch.23, p.1755
IFRS 16.31	Ch.23, p.1755
IFRS 16.31	Ch.26, p.2003
IFRS 16.32	Ch.23, p.1755
IFRS 16.33	Ch.20, p.1521
IFRS 16.33	Ch.23, p.1756
IFRS 16.33	Ch.23, p.1773
IFRS 16.34	Ch.19, p.1444
IFRS 16.34	Ch.23, p.1756
IFRS 16.35	Ch.23, p.1756
IFRS 16.36	Ch.23, p.1756
IFRS 16.37	Ch.23, p.1756
IFRS 16.38	Ch.23, p.1756
IFRS 16.38(b)	Ch.23, p.1746
IFRS 16.39	Ch.23, p.1748
IFRS 16.39	Ch.23, p.1758
IFRS 16.40	Ch.23, p.1758
IFRS 16.41	Ch.23, p.1758
IFRS 16.42	Ch.23, p.1758
IFRS 16.42(a)	Ch.23, p.1745
IFRS 16.42(b)	Ch.23, p.1744
IFRS 16.43	Ch.23, p.1758
IFRS 16.44	Ch.23, p.1759
IFRS 16.45	Ch.23, p.1760
IFRS 16.46	Ch.23, p.1760
IFRS 16.47	Ch.18, p.1388
IFRS 16.47	Ch.23, p.1774
IFRS 16.48	Ch.18, p.1388
IFRS 16.48	Ch.19, p.1445
IFRS 16.48	Ch.23, p.1774
IFRS 16.49	Ch.23, p.1774
IFRS 16.50	Ch.23, p.1775
IFRS 16.50	Ch.40, p.3168
IFRS 16.50	Ch.40, p.3169
IFRS 16.51	Ch.23, p.1776
IFRS 16.52	Ch.23, p.1776
IFRS 16.53	Ch.23, p.1776
IFRS 16.53(i)	Ch.23, p.1807
IFRS 16.53(g)	Ch.23, p.1778
IFRS 16.53(g)	Ch.40, p.3168
IFRS 16.54	Ch.23, p.1776
IFRS 16.55	Ch.23, p.1778
IFRS 16.55	Ch.38, p.3080
IFRS 16.56	Ch.19, p.1445
IFRS 16.56	Ch.23, p.1778
IFRS 16.57	Ch.23, p.1778
IFRS 16.58	Ch.23, p.1778
IFRS 16.58	Ch.54, p.4455
IFRS 16.59	Ch.23, p.1779
IFRS 16.60	Ch.23, p.1751
IFRS 16.61	Ch.23, p.1781
IFRS 16.62	Ch.23, p.1781
IFRS 16.63	Ch.23, p.1782
IFRS 16.64	Ch.23, p.1782
IFRS 16.65	Ch.23, p.1782
IFRS 16.66	Ch.5, p.371
IFRS 16.66	Ch.23, p.1783
IFRS 16.67	Ch.23, p.1784
IFRS 16.67	Ch.23, p.1796
IFRS 16.67	Ch.25, p.1856
IFRS 16.67-97	Ch.42, p.3280
IFRS 16.68	Ch.23, p.1785
IFRS 16.68	Ch.23, p.1799
IFRS 16.69	Ch.23, p.1751
IFRS 16.69	Ch.23, p.1785
IFRS 16.70	Ch.23, p.1785
IFRS 16.70(a)	Ch.23, p.1743
IFRS 16.70(c)	Ch.23, p.1745
IFRS 16.71	Ch.23, p.1785
IFRS 16.72	Ch.23, p.1786
IFRS 16.73	Ch.23, p.1786
IFRS 16.74	Ch.23, p.1786
IFRS 16.75	Ch.23, p.1787
IFRS 16.76	Ch.23, p.1787
IFRS 16.77	Ch.23, p.1787
IFRS 16.77	Ch.23, p.1789
IFRS 16.77	Ch.51, p.4045
IFRS 16.78	Ch.23, p.1788
IFRS 16.79	Ch.23, p.1793
IFRS 16.80	Ch.23, p.1793
IFRS 16.81	Ch.19, p.1462
IFRS 16.81	Ch.23, p.1791
IFRS 16.81-88	Ch.42, p.3280

IFRS 16.82	Ch.23, p.1791	IFRS 16.B7	Ch.23, p.1753
IFRS 16.83	Ch.19, p.1463	IFRS 16.B7	Ch.23, p.1799
IFRS 16.83	Ch.23, p.1791	IFRS 16.B8	Ch.23, p.1753
IFRS 16.84	Ch.23, p.1791	IFRS 16.B9	Ch.17, p.1373
IFRS 16.85	Ch.23, p.1791	IFRS 16.B9	Ch.23, p.1714
IFRS 16.86	Ch.23, p.1791	IFRS 16.B9	Ch.25, p.1857
IFRS 16.87	Ch.23, p.1793	IFRS 16.B10	Ch.23, p.1714
IFRS 16.88	Ch.23, p.1796	IFRS 16.B11	Ch.23, p.1714
IFRS 16.89	Ch.23, p.1797	IFRS 16.B12	Ch.23, p.1714
IFRS 16.90	Ch.23, p.1797	IFRS 16.B13	Ch.23, p.1716
IFRS 16.91	Ch.23, p.1797	IFRS 16.B14	Ch.23, p.1720
IFRS 16.92	Ch.23, p.1797	IFRS 16.B14	Ch.43, p.3531
IFRS 16.93	Ch.23, p.1797	IFRS 16.B14	Ch.43, p.3541
IFRS 16.94	Ch.23, p.1797	IFRS 16.B14(a)-(b)	Ch.43, p.3531
IFRS 16.95	Ch.23, p.1798	IFRS 16.B15	Ch.23, p.1720
IFRS 16.96	Ch.23, p.1798	IFRS 16.B16	Ch.23, p.1720
IFRS 16.97	Ch.23, p.1798	IFRS 16.B17	Ch.23, p.1720
IFRS 16.98	Ch.23, p.1801	IFRS 16.B18	Ch.23, p.1721
IFRS 16.99	Ch.23, p.1801	IFRS 16.B19	Ch.23, p.1721
IFRS 16.99	Ch.40, p.3170	IFRS 16.B19	Ch.43, p.3531
IFRS 16.100	Ch.23, p.1803	IFRS 16.B19	Ch.43, p.3541
IFRS 16.100	Ch.40, p.3170	IFRS 16.B20	Ch.23, p.1717
IFRS 16.101	Ch.23, p.1805	IFRS 16.B21	Ch.23, p.1722
IFRS 16.101	Ch.40, p.3170	IFRS 16.B22	Ch.23, p.1722
IFRS 16.102	Ch.23, p.1805	IFRS 16.B23	Ch.23, p.1722
IFRS 16.103	Ch.23, p.1807	IFRS 16.B24	Ch.23, p.1722
IFRS 16.103	Ch.40, p.3170	IFRS 16.B24	Ch.23, p.1724
IFRS 16 Appendix A	Ch.5, p.303	IFRS 16.B24	Ch.43, p.3545
IFRS 16 Appendix A	Ch.17, p.1373	IFRS 16.B25	Ch.23, p.1723
IFRS 16 Appendix A	Ch.19, p.1462	IFRS 16.B26	Ch.23, p.1723
IFRS 16 Appendix A	Ch.19, p.1463	IFRS 16.B27	Ch.23, p.1724
IFRS 16 Appendix A	Ch.23, p.1711	IFRS 16.B28	Ch.23, p.1725
IFRS 16 Appendix A	Ch.23, p.1713	IFRS 16.B29	Ch.23, p.1726
IFRS 16 Appendix A	Ch.23, p.1720	IFRS 16.B30	Ch.23, p.1726
IFRS 16 Appendix A	Ch.23, p.1735	IFRS 16.B31	Ch.23, p.1726
IFRS 16 Appendix A	Ch.23, p.1742	IFRS 16.B32	Ch.23, p.1728
IFRS 16 Appendix A	Ch.23, p.1743	IFRS 16.B32	Ch.27, p.2030
IFRS 16 Appendix A	Ch.23, p.1749	IFRS 16.B33	Ch.23, p.1728
IFRS 16 Appendix A	Ch.23, p.1750	IFRS 16.B33	Ch.23, p.1729
IFRS 16 Appendix A	Ch.23, p.1751	IFRS 16.B33	Ch.27, p.2030
IFRS 16 Appendix A	Ch.23, p.1752	IFRS 16.B34	Ch.23, p.1739
IFRS 16 Appendix A	Ch.23, p.1759	IFRS 16.B35	Ch.23, p.1739
IFRS 16 Appendix A	Ch.23, p.1780	IFRS 16.B36	Ch.23, p.1736
IFRS 16 Appendix A	Ch.23, p.1784	IFRS 16.B37	Ch.23, p.1736
IFRS 16 Appendix A	Ch.23, p.1792	IFRS 16.B37	Ch.23, p.1737
IFRS 16 Appendix A	Ch.23, p.1798	IFRS 16.B38	Ch.23, p.1737
IFRS 16 Appendix A	Ch.23, p.1806	IFRS 16.B39	Ch.23, p.1738
IFRS 16 Appendix A	Ch.40, p.3169	IFRS 16.B40	Ch.23, p.1738
IFRS 16 Appendix A	Ch.43, p.3530	IFRS 16.B41	Ch.23, p.1741
IFRS 16 Appendix A	Ch.43, p.3553	IFRS 16.B42	Ch.23, p.1743
IFRS 16.B1	Ch.23, p.1773	IFRS 16.B43	Ch.23, p.1735
IFRS 16.B1	Ch.23, p.1796	IFRS 16.B44	Ch.23, p.1735
IFRS 16.B2	Ch.23, p.1734	IFRS 16.B45	Ch.23, p.1735
IFRS 16.B3	Ch.23, p.1753	IFRS 16.B46	Ch.23, p.1735
IFRS 16.B3-B8	Ch.5, p.303	IFRS 16.B47	Ch.23, p.1736
IFRS 16.B4	Ch.23, p.1753	IFRS 16.B48	Ch.23, p.1779
IFRS 16.B5	Ch.23, p.1753	IFRS 16.B49	Ch.23, p.1780
IFRS 16.B6	Ch.23, p.1753	IFRS 16.B50	Ch.23, p.1780

IFRS 16.B51	Ch.23, p.1780
IFRS 16.B52	Ch.23, p.1807
IFRS 16.B53	Ch.23, p.1781
IFRS 16.B54	Ch.23, p.1783
IFRS 16.B55	Ch.23, p.1783
IFRS 16.B56	Ch.23, p.1729
IFRS 16.B56	Ch.23, p.1783
IFRS 16.B57	Ch.23, p.1729
IFRS 16.B57	Ch.23, p.1783
IFRS 16.B58	Ch.23, p.1799
IFRS 16.C1	Ch.23, p.1808
IFRS 16.C1	Ch.41, p.3240
IFRS 16.C2	Ch.23, p.1809
IFRS 16.C3	Ch.23, p.1809
IFRS 16.C4	Ch.23, p.1809
IFRS 16.C4	Ch.25, p.1857
IFRS 16.C5	Ch.23, p.1809
IFRS 16.C6	Ch.23, p.1809
IFRS 16.C7	Ch.23, p.1810
IFRS 16.C8	Ch.23, p.1810
IFRS 16.C9	Ch.23, p.1811
IFRS 16.C10	Ch.23, p.1811
IFRS 16.C11	Ch.23, p.1816
IFRS 16.C12	Ch.23, p.1819
IFRS 16.C13	Ch.23, p.1819
IFRS 16.C14	Ch.23, p.1818
IFRS 16.C15	Ch.23, p.1818
IFRS 16.C16	Ch.23, p.1818
IFRS 16.C17	Ch.23, p.1818
IFRS 16.C18	Ch.23, p.1818
IFRS 16.C19	Ch.23, p.1819
IFRS 16.C20	Ch.23, p.1819
IFRS 16.IE4	Ch.23, p.1732
IFRS 16.IE7	Ch.23, p.1760
IFRS 16.IE8	Ch.23, p.1800
IFRS 16.IE11	Ch.23, p.1807
IFRS 16.BC58-BC66	Ch.42, p.3280
IFRS 16.BC68(a)	Ch.43, p.3528
IFRS 16.BC68(b)	Ch.42, p.3280
IFRS 16.BC69	Ch.25, p.1857
IFRS 16.BC100	Ch.23, p.1753
IFRS 16.BC113	Ch.23, p.1720
IFRS 16.BC113	Ch.43, p.3531
IFRS 16.BC120	Ch.23, p.1723
IFRS 16.BC121	Ch.23, p.1724
IFRS 16.BC126	Ch.43, p.3542
IFRS 16.BC130-BC132	Ch.23, p.1734
IFRS 16.BC135 (b)	Ch.23, p.1730
IFRS 16.BC139-BC140	Ch.40, p.3168
IFRS 16.BC165	Ch.23, p.1744
IFRS 16.BC170	Ch.23, p.1745
IFRS 16.BC173	Ch.23, p.1736
IFRS 16.BC178	Ch.19, p.1444
IFRS 16.BC178	Ch.19, p.1467
IFRS 16.BC179	Ch.19, p.1471
IFRS 16.BC179(b)	Ch.19, p.1443
IFRS 16.BC180	Ch.19, p.1471
IFRS 16.BC181	Ch.19, p.1471
IFRS 16.BC182	Ch.19, p.1445
IFRS 16.BC199	Ch.23, p.1773
IFRS 16.BC222	Ch.23, p.1778
IFRS 16.BC235	Ch.23, p.1800
IFRS 16.BC236	Ch.23, p.1800
IFRS 16.BC262	Ch.23, p.1802
IFRS 16.BC266	Ch.40, p.3170
IFRS 16.BC287	Ch.23, p.1811
IFRS 16.BC298	Ch.23, p.1808

IFRS 17

IFRS 17.IN4	Ch.56, p.4681
IFRS 17.IN5	Ch.56, p.4681
IFRS 17.IN7	Ch.56, p.4682
IFRS 17.IN8	Ch.56, p.4682
IFRS 17.1	Ch.56, p.4683
IFRS 17.1	Ch.56, p.4898
IFRS 17.2	Ch.56, p.4696
IFRS 17.3	Ch.56, p.4686
IFRS 17.3(c)	Ch.45, p.3594
IFRS 17.3(c)	Ch.56, p.4855
IFRS 17.4	Ch.56, p.4687
IFRS 17.5	Ch.56, p.4687
IFRS 17.7	Ch.56, p.4688
IFRS 17.7(a)	Ch.56, p.4689
IFRS 17.7(b)	Ch.56, p.4689
IFRS 17.7(c)	Ch.56, p.4689
IFRS 17.7(d)	Ch.56, p.4689
IFRS 17.7(e)	Ch.26, p.1935
IFRS 17.7(e)	Ch.45, p.3598
IFRS 17.7(e)	Ch.56, p.4690
IFRS 17.7(f)	Ch.56, p.4691
IFRS 17.7(g)	Ch.45, p.3599
IFRS 17.7(g)	Ch.51, p.3958
IFRS 17.7(g)	Ch.56, p.4691
IFRS 17.7(h)	Ch.45, p.3595
IFRS 17.7(h)	Ch.48, p.3837
IFRS 17.7(h)	Ch.56, p.4692
IFRS 17.8	Ch.27, p.2025
IFRS 17.8	Ch.56, p.4693
IFRS 17.8A	Ch.45, p.3596
IFRS 17.8A	Ch.48, p.3835
IFRS 17.8A	Ch.56, p.4694
IFRS 17.9	Ch.56, p.4703
IFRS 17.9	Ch.56, p.4710
IFRS 17.9	Ch.56, p.4718
IFRS 17.10	Ch.56, p.4710
IFRS 17.11	Ch.56, p.4710
IFRS 17.11(a)	Ch.45, p.3595
IFRS 17.11(b)	Ch.45, p.3595
IFRS 17.11(b)	Ch.56, p.4716
IFRS 17.12	Ch.56, p.4710
IFRS 17.12	Ch.56, p.4720
IFRS 17.13	Ch.56, p.4703
IFRS 17.13	Ch.56, p.4710
IFRS 17.14	Ch.56, p.4722

Index of standards

IFRS 17.14	Ch.56, p.4723	IFRS 17.54	Ch.56, p.4809
IFRS 17.14	Ch.56, p.4872	IFRS 17.55	Ch.56, p.4812
IFRS 17.16	Ch.56, p.4722	IFRS 17.55(b)	Ch.56, p.4814
IFRS 17.17	Ch.56, p.4726	IFRS 17.56	Ch.56, p.4809
IFRS 17.18	Ch.56, p.4732	IFRS 17.57	Ch.56, p.4813
IFRS 17.18	Ch.56, p.4813	IFRS 17.58	Ch.56, p.4813
IFRS 17.19	Ch.56, p.4726	IFRS 17.59(a)	Ch.56, p.4809
IFRS 17.20	Ch.56, p.4727	IFRS 17.59(b)	Ch.56, p.4816
IFRS 17.20	Ch.56, p.4728	IFRS 17.61	Ch.56, p.4819
IFRS 17.21	Ch.56, p.4722	IFRS 17.62	Ch.56, p.4733
IFRS 17.21	Ch.56, p.4727	IFRS 17.62A	Ch.56, p.4734
IFRS 17.22	Ch.56, p.4728	IFRS 17.63	Ch.56, p.4822
IFRS 17.23	Ch.56, p.4725	IFRS 17.63	Ch.56, p.4828
IFRS 17.24	Ch.56, p.4723	IFRS 17.64	Ch.56, p.4828
IFRS 17.24	Ch.56, p.4725	IFRS 17.65	Ch.56, p.4823
IFRS 17.24	Ch.56, p.4730	IFRS 17.65A	Ch.56, p.4823
IFRS 17.25	Ch.56, p.4732	IFRS 17.66	Ch.56, p.4829
IFRS 17.26	Ch.56, p.4732	IFRS 17.66A	Ch.56, p.4824
IFRS 17.28	Ch.56, p.4732	IFRS 17.66B	Ch.56, p.4825
IFRS 17.28	Ch.56, p.4733	IFRS 17.66(bb)	Ch.56, p.4833
IFRS 17.28	Ch.56, p.4764	IFRS 17.67	Ch.56, p.4832
IFRS 17.28A	Ch.56, p.4735	IFRS 17.68	Ch.56, p.4819
IFRS 17.28A	Ch.56, p.4749	IFRS 17.69	Ch.56, p.4836
IFRS 17.28B	Ch.56, p.4735	IFRS 17.70	Ch.56, p.4837
IFRS 17.28C	Ch.56, p.4862	IFRS 17.70A	Ch.56, p.4837
IFRS 17.28D	Ch.56, p.4735	IFRS 17.71	Ch.56, p.4737
IFRS 17.28E-F	Ch.56, p.4801	IFRS 17.71	Ch.56, p.4856
IFRS 17.28F	Ch.56, p.4802	IFRS 17.72	Ch.56, p.4858
IFRS 17.29	Ch.56, p.4738	IFRS 17.72	Ch.56, p.4859
IFRS 17.30	Ch.15, p.1190	IFRS 17.73	Ch.56, p.4858
IFRS 17.30	Ch.56, p.4739	IFRS 17.74	Ch.56, p.4859
IFRS 17.31	Ch.56, p.4749	IFRS 17.75	Ch.56, p.4859
IFRS 17.31	Ch.56, p.4765	IFRS 17.76	Ch.56, p.4860
IFRS 17.32	Ch.56, p.4737	IFRS 17.77	Ch.56, p.4860
IFRS 17.32	Ch.56, p.4740	IFRS 17.77	Ch.56, p.4861
IFRS 17.33	Ch.56, p.4749	IFRS 17.78	Ch.56, p.4872
IFRS 17.33	Ch.56, p.4750	IFRS 17.79	Ch.56, p.4872
IFRS 17.34	Ch.56, p.4740	IFRS 17.80	Ch.56, p.4874
IFRS 17.35	Ch.56, p.4741	IFRS 17.81	Ch.56, p.4775
IFRS 17.36	Ch.56, p.4762	IFRS 17.81	Ch.56, p.4881
IFRS 17.37	Ch.56, p.4770	IFRS 17.82	Ch.56, p.4874
IFRS 17.38	Ch.56, p.4776	IFRS 17.83	Ch.56, p.4876
IFRS 17.39	Ch.56, p.4776	IFRS 17.84	Ch.56, p.4880
IFRS 17.40	Ch.56, p.4777	IFRS 17.85	Ch.56, p.4715
IFRS 17.41	Ch.56, p.4779	IFRS 17.85	Ch.56, p.4719
IFRS 17.42	Ch.56, p.4780	IFRS 17.85	Ch.56, p.4878
IFRS 17.43	Ch.56, p.4780	IFRS 17.86	Ch.56, p.4874
IFRS 17.44	Ch.56, p.4780	IFRS 17.86	Ch.56, p.4880
IFRS 17.45	Ch.56, p.4849	IFRS 17.86(c)	Ch.56, p.4874
IFRS 17.46	Ch.56, p.4784	IFRS 17.87	Ch.56, p.4881
IFRS 17.47	Ch.56, p.4794	IFRS 17.88	Ch.56, p.4883
IFRS 17.48	Ch.56, p.4794	IFRS 17.88	Ch.56, p.4886
IFRS 17.49	Ch.56, p.4794	IFRS 17.89	Ch.56, p.4892
IFRS 17.50	Ch.56, p.4794	IFRS 17.90	Ch.56, p.4886
IFRS 17.51	Ch.56, p.4795	IFRS 17.91	Ch.56, p.4862
IFRS 17.52	Ch.56, p.4795	IFRS 17.91(a)	Ch.56, p.4887
IFRS 17.53	Ch.56, p.4808	IFRS 17.91(b)	Ch.56, p.4895
IFRS 17.53	Ch.56, p.4812	IFRS 17.92	Ch.56, p.4882

IFRS 17.93	Ch.56, p.4898
IFRS 17.93	Ch.56, p.4900
IFRS 17.93	Ch.56, p.4912
IFRS 17.93(b)	Ch.56, p.4909
IFRS 17.94	Ch.56, p.4899
IFRS 17.95	Ch.56, p.4872
IFRS 17.95	Ch.56, p.4899
IFRS 17.96	Ch.56, p.4899
IFRS 17.97	Ch.56, p.4906
IFRS 17.98	Ch.56, p.4872
IFRS 17.98	Ch.56, p.4900
IFRS 17.99	Ch.56, p.4900
IFRS 17.99	Ch.56, p.4906
IFRS 17.100	Ch.56, p.4900
IFRS 17.100	Ch.56, p.4906
IFRS 17.100	Ch.56, p.4915
IFRS 17.101	Ch.56, p.4902
IFRS 17.102	Ch.56, p.4900
IFRS 17.103	Ch.56, p.4900
IFRS 17.103	Ch.56, p.4907
IFRS 17.104	Ch.56, p.4902
IFRS 17.105	Ch.56, p.4904
IFRS 17.105	Ch.56, p.4907
IFRS 17.105A	Ch.56, p.4904
IFRS 17.105B	Ch.56, p.4904
IFRS 17.106	Ch.56, p.4904
IFRS 17.107	Ch.56, p.4905
IFRS 17.108	Ch.56, p.4905
IFRS 17.109	Ch.56, p.4906
IFRS 17.109A	Ch.56, p.4906
IFRS 17.110	Ch.56, p.4907
IFRS 17.111	Ch.56, p.4908
IFRS 17.112	Ch.56, p.4908
IFRS 17.113	Ch.56, p.4908
IFRS 17.114	Ch.56, p.4908
IFRS 17.115	Ch.56, p.4908
IFRS 17.116	Ch.56, p.4909
IFRS 17.117	Ch.56, p.4909
IFRS 17.118	Ch.56, p.4909
IFRS 17.119	Ch.56, p.4910
IFRS 17.120	Ch.56, p.4910
IFRS 17.121	Ch.56, p.4912
IFRS 17.122	Ch.56, p.4912
IFRS 17.123	Ch.56, p.4912
IFRS 17.124	Ch.56, p.4912
IFRS 17.125	Ch.56, p.4912
IFRS 17.126	Ch.56, p.4918
IFRS 17.127	Ch.56, p.4913
IFRS 17.128	Ch.56, p.4914
IFRS 17.129	Ch.56, p.4915
IFRS 17.130	Ch.56, p.4915
IFRS 17.131	Ch.56, p.4917
IFRS 17.132	Ch.56, p.4917
IFRS 17 Appendix A	Ch.45, p.3593
IFRS 17 Appendix A	Ch.56, p.4684
IFRS 17 Appendix A	Ch.56, p.4695
IFRS 17 Appendix A	Ch.56, p.4698
IFRS 17 Appendix A	Ch.56, p.4715
IFRS 17 Appendix A	Ch.56, p.4735
IFRS 17 Appendix A	Ch.56, p.4758
IFRS 17 Appendix A	Ch.56, p.4778
IFRS 17 Appendix A	Ch.56, p.4779
IFRS 17 Appendix A	Ch.56, p.4791
IFRS 17 Appendix A	Ch.56, p.4796
IFRS 17 Appendix A	Ch.56, p.4817
IFRS 17 Appendix A	Ch.56, p.4851
IFRS 17 Appendix A	Ch.56, p.4855
IFRS 17.B2	Ch.56, p.4697
IFRS 17.B2-B30	Ch.45, p.3593
IFRS 17.B3	Ch.56, p.4697
IFRS 17.B4	Ch.56, p.4697
IFRS 17.B5	Ch.56, p.4697
IFRS 17.B5	Ch.56, p.4797
IFRS 17.B5	Ch.56, p.4835
IFRS 17.B5	Ch.56, p.4868
IFRS 17.B6	Ch.56, p.4698
IFRS 17.B7	Ch.56, p.4698
IFRS 17.B8	Ch.56, p.4698
IFRS 17.B9	Ch.56, p.4698
IFRS 17.B10	Ch.56, p.4699
IFRS 17.B11	Ch.56, p.4699
IFRS 17.B12	Ch.56, p.4699
IFRS 17.B13	Ch.56, p.4700
IFRS 17.B14	Ch.56, p.4700
IFRS 17.B15	Ch.56, p.4700
IFRS 17.B16	Ch.56, p.4703
IFRS 17.B17	Ch.56, p.4701
IFRS 17.B18	Ch.56, p.4701
IFRS 17.B19	Ch.56, p.4701
IFRS 17.B20	Ch.56, p.4701
IFRS 17.B21	Ch.56, p.4704
IFRS 17.B22	Ch.56, p.4703
IFRS 17.B23	Ch.56, p.4704
IFRS 17.B24	Ch.56, p.4706
IFRS 17.B25	Ch.56, p.4705
IFRS 17.B25	Ch.56, p.4857
IFRS 17.B26	Ch.56, p.4706
IFRS 17.B26(k)	Ch.45, p.3594
IFRS 17.B27	Ch.56, p.4708
IFRS 17.B27(a)	Ch.45, p.3594
IFRS 17.B27(c)	Ch.56, p.4703
IFRS 17.B27(f)	Ch.45, p.3596
IFRS 17.B27(g)	Ch.45, p.3594
IFRS 17.B28	Ch.56, p.4709
IFRS 17.B29	Ch.56, p.4709
IFRS 17.B30	Ch.45, p.3596
IFRS 17.B30	Ch.56, p.4709
IFRS 17.B31	Ch.56, p.4717
IFRS 17.B32	Ch.56, p.4717
IFRS 17.B33	Ch.56, p.4721
IFRS 17.B34	Ch.56, p.4721
IFRS 17.B35	Ch.56, p.4721
IFRS 17.B35A	Ch.56, p.4736
IFRS 17.B35A	Ch.56, p.4749
IFRS 17.B35B	Ch.56, p.4749
IFRS 17.B35C	Ch.56, p.4737

IFRS 17.B35D	Ch.56, p.4802
IFRS 17.B37	Ch.56, p.4750
IFRS 17.B38	Ch.56, p.4750
IFRS 17.B39	Ch.56, p.4751
IFRS 17.B40	Ch.56, p.4751
IFRS 17.B41	Ch.56, p.4751
IFRS 17.B42	Ch.56, p.4752
IFRS 17.B43	Ch.56, p.4752
IFRS 17.B44	Ch.56, p.4752
IFRS 17.B45	Ch.56, p.4752
IFRS 17.B46	Ch.56, p.4752
IFRS 17.B47	Ch.56, p.4752
IFRS 17.B48	Ch.56, p.4753
IFRS 17.B49	Ch.56, p.4753
IFRS 17.B50	Ch.56, p.4753
IFRS 17.B51	Ch.56, p.4754
IFRS 17.B52	Ch.56, p.4754
IFRS 17.B53	Ch.56, p.4754
IFRS 17.B54	Ch.56, p.4754
IFRS 17.B55	Ch.56, p.4755
IFRS 17.B56	Ch.56, p.4755
IFRS 17.B57	Ch.56, p.4755
IFRS 17.B58	Ch.56, p.4755
IFRS 17.B59	Ch.56, p.4755
IFRS 17.B60	Ch.56, p.4755
IFRS 17.B61	Ch.56, p.4740
IFRS 17.B62	Ch.56, p.4756
IFRS 17.B63	Ch.56, p.4741
IFRS 17.B64	Ch.56, p.4741
IFRS 17.B65	Ch.56, p.4757
IFRS 17.B65(c)	Ch.56, p.4804
IFRS 17.B66	Ch.56, p.4762
IFRS 17.B66A	Ch.56, p.4776
IFRS 17.B67	Ch.56, p.4840
IFRS 17.B68	Ch.56, p.4840
IFRS 17.B69	Ch.56, p.4841
IFRS 17.B70	Ch.56, p.4841
IFRS 17.B71	Ch.56, p.4841
IFRS 17.B72-B73	Ch.56, p.4763
IFRS 17.B73	Ch.56, p.4764
IFRS 17.B74	Ch.56, p.4765
IFRS 17.B75	Ch.56, p.4765
IFRS 17.B76	Ch.56, p.4765
IFRS 17.B77	Ch.56, p.4766
IFRS 17.B78	Ch.56, p.4766
IFRS 17.B79	Ch.56, p.4766
IFRS 17.B80	Ch.56, p.4767
IFRS 17.B81	Ch.56, p.4767
IFRS 17.B82	Ch.56, p.4768
IFRS 17.B83	Ch.56, p.4768
IFRS 17.B84	Ch.56, p.4768
IFRS 17.B85	Ch.56, p.4769
IFRS 17.B86	Ch.56, p.4770
IFRS 17.B87	Ch.56, p.4770
IFRS 17.B87	Ch.56, p.4771
IFRS 17.B88	Ch.56, p.4771
IFRS 17.B89	Ch.56, p.4771
IFRS 17.B90	Ch.56, p.4771
IFRS 17.B91	Ch.56, p.4772
IFRS 17.B92	Ch.56, p.4773
IFRS 17.B93	Ch.56, p.4864
IFRS 17.B94	Ch.56, p.4865
IFRS 17.B95	Ch.56, p.4865
IFRS 17.B95A	Ch.56, p.4865
IFRS 17.B95B	Ch.56, p.4865
IFRS 17.B95C	Ch.56, p.4866
IFRS 17.B95D	Ch.56, p.4866
IFRS 17.B95E	Ch.56, p.4867
IFRS 17.B95F	Ch.56, p.4867
IFRS 17.B96	Ch.56, p.4720
IFRS 17.B96	Ch.56, p.4781
IFRS 17.B97	Ch.56, p.4783
IFRS 17.B98	Ch.56, p.4784
IFRS 17.B99	Ch.56, p.4785
IFRS 17.B100	Ch.56, p.4785
IFRS 17.B101	Ch.56, p.4844
IFRS 17.B102	Ch.56, p.4844
IFRS 17.B103	Ch.56, p.4846
IFRS 17.B104	Ch.56, p.4843
IFRS 17.B105	Ch.56, p.4844
IFRS 17.B106	Ch.56, p.4844
IFRS 17.B107	Ch.56, p.4845
IFRS 17.B107(b)(i)	Ch.56, p.4842
IFRS 17.B108	Ch.56, p.4846
IFRS 17.B109	Ch.56, p.4837
IFRS 17.B109	Ch.56, p.4839
IFRS 17.B111	Ch.56, p.4849
IFRS 17.B112	Ch.56, p.4849
IFRS 17.B113	Ch.56, p.4850
IFRS 17.B113(a)	Ch.56, p.4849
IFRS 17.B114	Ch.56, p.4850
IFRS 17.B115	Ch.56, p.4852
IFRS 17.B116	Ch.56, p.4853
IFRS 17.B117	Ch.56, p.4852
IFRS 17.B117A	Ch.56, p.4853
IFRS 17.B117A	Ch.56, p.4883
IFRS 17.B118	Ch.56, p.4853
IFRS 17.B119	Ch.56, p.4785
IFRS 17.B119A	Ch.56, p.4792
IFRS 17.B119A	Ch.56, p.4851
IFRS 17.B119B	Ch.56, p.4792
IFRS 17.B119D	Ch.56, p.4825
IFRS 17.B119E	Ch.56, p.4825
IFRS 17.B119E	Ch.56, p.4835
IFRS 17.B119F	Ch.56, p.4833
IFRS 17.B120	Ch.56, p.4876
IFRS 17.B121	Ch.56, p.4877
IFRS 17.B123	Ch.56, p.4759
IFRS 17.B123	Ch.56, p.4760
IFRS 17.B123	Ch.56, p.4877
IFRS 17.B123A	Ch.56, p.4878
IFRS 17.B124	Ch.56, p.4878
IFRS 17.B125	Ch.56, p.4759
IFRS 17.B125	Ch.56, p.4878
IFRS 17.B126	Ch.56, p.4815
IFRS 17.B126	Ch.56, p.4880

IFRS 17.B127	Ch.56, p.4815	IFRS 17.C25	Ch.56, p.4924
IFRS 17.B127	Ch.56, p.4880	IFRS 17.C26	Ch.56, p.4924
IFRS 17.B128	Ch.56, p.4881	IFRS 17.C27	Ch.56, p.4924
IFRS 17.B129	Ch.56, p.4883	IFRS 17.C28	Ch.56, p.4921
IFRS 17.B130	Ch.56, p.4887	IFRS 17.C29	Ch.56, p.4938
IFRS 17.B131	Ch.56, p.4887	IFRS 17.C30	Ch.56, p.4939
IFRS 17.B132(a)	Ch.56, p.4888	IFRS 17.C31	Ch.56, p.4939
IFRS 17.B132(b)	Ch.56, p.4889	IFRS 17.C32	Ch.56, p.4939
IFRS 17.B132(c)	Ch.56, p.4889	IFRS 17.C33	Ch.56, p.4939
IFRS 17.B133	Ch.56, p.4892	IFRS 17.C34	Ch.56, p.4919
IFRS 17.B134	Ch.56, p.4893	IFRS 17.IE43-51	Ch.56, p.4718
IFRS 17.B135	Ch.56, p.4895	IFRS 17.IE51-55	Ch.56, p.4721
IFRS 17.B136	Ch.56, p.4895	IFRS 17.IE95(c)	Ch.56, p.4795
IFRS 17.B137	Ch.56, p.4896	IFRS 17.IE124-129	Ch.56, p.4823
IFRS 17.B137	Ch.56, p.4924	IFRS 17.IE130-138	Ch.56, p.4830
IFRS 17.C1	Ch.56, p.4919	IFRS 17.IE138A-138K	Ch.56, p.4826
IFRS 17.C2	Ch.56, p.4919	IFRS 17.IE138L-138M	Ch.56, p.4833
IFRS 17.C3	Ch.56, p.4919	IFRS 17.IE139-151	Ch.56, p.4866
IFRS 17.C3(a)	Ch.56, p.4921	IFRS 17.IE155-IE172	Ch.56, p.4889
IFRS 17.C3(b)	Ch.56, p.4922	IFRS 17.IE173-IE185	Ch.56, p.4893
IFRS 17.C4	Ch.56, p.4923	IFRS 17.IE186-IE191	Ch.56, p.4930
IFRS 17.C5	Ch.56, p.4919	IFRS 17.IE192-IE199	Ch.56, p.4932
IFRS 17.C5A	Ch.56, p.4919	IFRS 17.BC34	Ch.56, p.4719
IFRS 17.C5B	Ch.56, p.4920	IFRS 17.BC63	Ch.56, p.4687
IFRS 17.C6	Ch.56, p.4925	IFRS 17.BC64	Ch.56, p.4687
IFRS 17.C6(a)	Ch.56, p.4920	IFRS 17.BC65(a)	Ch.45, p.3594
IFRS 17.C7	Ch.56, p.4925	IFRS 17.BC65(c)	Ch.18, p.1408
IFRS 17.C8	Ch.56, p.4925	IFRS 17.BC66	Ch.45, p.3599
IFRS 17.C9	Ch.56, p.4927	IFRS 17.BC66	Ch.56, p.4691
IFRS 17.C9A	Ch.56, p.4927	IFRS 17.BC67	Ch.56, p.4696
IFRS 17.C10	Ch.56, p.4927	IFRS 17.BC69	Ch.56, p.4696
IFRS 17.C11	Ch.56, p.4927	IFRS 17.BC73	Ch.56, p.4699
IFRS 17.C12	Ch.56, p.4928	IFRS 17.BC74	Ch.56, p.4699
IFRS 17.C13	Ch.56, p.4928	IFRS 17.BC75	Ch.56, p.4699
IFRS 17.C14	Ch.56, p.4928	IFRS 17.BC77	Ch.56, p.4702
IFRS 17.C14A	Ch.56, p.4929	IFRS 17.BC78	Ch.56, p.4701
IFRS 17.C14B	Ch.56, p.4928	IFRS 17.BC79	Ch.56, p.4702
IFRS 17.C14C	Ch.56, p.4929	IFRS 17.BC79	Ch.56, p.4703
IFRS 17.C14D	Ch.56, p.4929	IFRS 17.BC80	Ch.56, p.4702
IFRS 17.C15	Ch.56, p.4929	IFRS 17.BC80	Ch.56, p.4705
IFRS 17.C16	Ch.56, p.4929	IFRS 17.BC80	Ch.56, p.4706
IFRS 17.C16A	Ch.56, p.4930	IFRS 17.BC81	Ch.56, p.4706
IFRS 17.C16B	Ch.56, p.4930	IFRS 17.BC83	Ch.56, p.4855
IFRS 17.C16C	Ch.56, p.4930	IFRS 17.BC87(d)	Ch.56, p.4690
IFRS 17.C17	Ch.56, p.4931	IFRS 17.BC89	Ch.56, p.4689
IFRS 17.C17A	Ch.56, p.4930	IFRS 17.BC90	Ch.56, p.4689
IFRS 17.C18	Ch.56, p.4933	IFRS 17.BC91	Ch.56, p.4690
IFRS 17.C19	Ch.56, p.4934	IFRS 17.BC93	Ch.56, p.4690
IFRS 17.C20	Ch.56, p.4935	IFRS 17.BC94	Ch.56, p.4691
IFRS 17.C20A	Ch.56, p.4936	IFRS 17.BC94B	Ch.45, p.3595
IFRS 17.C20B	Ch.56, p.4936	IFRS 17.BC94B	Ch.48, p.3836
IFRS 17.C21-C22	Ch.56, p.4936	IFRS 17.BC94B	Ch.56, p.4692
IFRS 17.C22A	Ch.56, p.4936	IFRS 17.BC94C	Ch.45, p.3595
IFRS 17.C23	Ch.56, p.4936	IFRS 17.BC94C	Ch.56, p.4692
IFRS 17.C23	Ch.56, p.4937	IFRS 17.BC94E	Ch.56, p.4694
IFRS 17.C24	Ch.56, p.4937	IFRS 17.BC94F	Ch.56, p.4694
IFRS 17.C24A	Ch.56, p.4937	IFRS 17.BC95	Ch.56, p.4693
IFRS 17.C24B	Ch.56, p.4937	IFRS 17.BC96-97	Ch.56, p.4693

IFRS 17.BC99	Ch.56, p.4710
IFRS 17.BC104	Ch.56, p.4712
IFRS 17.BC105(a)	Ch.56, p.4713
IFRS 17.BC105(b)	Ch.56, p.4713
IFRS 17.BC108	Ch.45, p.3595
IFRS 17.BC108	Ch.56, p.4716
IFRS 17.BC108(b)	Ch.56, p.4719
IFRS 17.BC109	Ch.56, p.4716
IFRS 17.BC111	Ch.56, p.4720
IFRS 17.BC112	Ch.56, p.4720
IFRS 17.BC113	Ch.56, p.4721
IFRS 17.BC114	Ch.56, p.4717
IFRS 17.BC114	Ch.56, p.4721
IFRS 17.BC114	Ch.56, p.4806
IFRS 17.BC119	Ch.56, p.4725
IFRS 17.BC129	Ch.56, p.4726
IFRS 17.BC132	Ch.56, p.4727
IFRS 17.BC133	Ch.56, p.4728
IFRS 17.BC136	Ch.56, p.4728
IFRS 17.BC137	Ch.56, p.4728
IFRS 17.BC138	Ch.56, p.4728
IFRS 17.BC138	Ch.56, p.4841
IFRS 17.BC139	Ch.56, p.4725
IFRS 17.BC139J	Ch.56, p.4730
IFRS 17.BC139K	Ch.56, p.4730
IFRS 17.BC139L	Ch.56, p.4731
IFRS 17.BC139M	Ch.56, p.4731
IFRS 17.BC139N	Ch.56, p.4731
IFRS 17.BC139O	Ch.56, p.4731
IFRS 17.BC139P	Ch.56, p.4731
IFRS 17.BC139T	Ch.56, p.4729
IFRS 17.BC162	Ch.56, p.4742
IFRS 17.BC163	Ch.56, p.4742
IFRS 17.BC164	Ch.56, p.4743
IFRS 17.BC166	Ch.56, p.4756
IFRS 17.BC168	Ch.56, p.4756
IFRS 17.BC169	Ch.56, p.4756
IFRS 17.BC170	Ch.56, p.4841
IFRS 17.BC170A	Ch.56, p.4762
IFRS 17.BC172	Ch.56, p.4840
IFRS 17.BC182(a)	Ch.56, p.4757
IFRS 17.BC183	Ch.56, p.4759
IFRS 17.BC184B	Ch.56, p.4736
IFRS 17.BC184C-D	Ch.56, p.4736
IFRS 17.BC184E	Ch.56, p.4736
IFRS 17.BC184F	Ch.56, p.4736
IFRS 17.BC184H	Ch.56, p.4764
IFRS 17.BC184J	Ch.56, p.4802
IFRS 17.BC184K	Ch.56, p.4802
IFRS 17.BC184N	Ch.56, p.4776
IFRS 17.BC209	Ch.56, p.4770
IFRS 17.BC213	Ch.56, p.4772
IFRS 17.BC214	Ch.56, p.4772
IFRS 17.BC217	Ch.56, p.4773
IFRS 17.BC228	Ch.56, p.4764
IFRS 17.BC235	Ch.56, p.4783
IFRS 17.BC235fn	Ch.56, p.4783
IFRS 17.BC236	Ch.56, p.4896
IFRS 17.BC236B-C	Ch.56, p.4898
IFRS 17.BC240	Ch.56, p.4843
IFRS 17.BC241	Ch.56, p.4843
IFRS 17.BC244	Ch.56, p.4843
IFRS 17.BC245(a)	Ch.56, p.4845
IFRS 17.BC245(b)	Ch.56, p.4845
IFRS 17.BC245(b)(ii)	Ch.56, p.4848
IFRS 17.BC248	Ch.56, p.4837
IFRS 17.BC256B	Ch.56, p.4853
IFRS 17.BC256C	Ch.56, p.4854
IFRS 17.BC256D-F	Ch.56, p.4854
IFRS 17.BC265	Ch.56, p.4804
IFRS 17.BC265fn27	Ch.56, p.4804
IFRS 17.BC269B	Ch.56, p.4805
IFRS 17.BC277	Ch.56, p.4739
IFRS 17.BC278	Ch.56, p.4739
IFRS 17.BC279	Ch.56, p.4786
IFRS 17.BC280	Ch.56, p.4786
IFRS 17.BC282	Ch.56, p.4786
IFRS 17.BC283	Ch.56, p.4787
IFRS 17.BC283B	Ch.56, p.4791
IFRS 17.BC283C	Ch.56, p.4792
IFRS 17.BC283D-E	Ch.56, p.4792
IFRS 17.BC283I	Ch.56, p.4761
IFRS 17.BC287	Ch.56, p.4795
IFRS 17.BC298	Ch.56, p.4818
IFRS 17.BC302	Ch.56, p.4818
IFRS 17.BC304	Ch.56, p.4734
IFRS 17.BC305(a)	Ch.56, p.4734
IFRS 17.BC305(b)	Ch.56, p.4734
IFRS 17.BC308	Ch.56, p.4828
IFRS 17.BC309	Ch.56, p.4832
IFRS 17.BC309E	Ch.56, p.4820
IFRS 17.BC309F	Ch.56, p.4820
IFRS 17.BC312	Ch.56, p.4823
IFRS 17.BC314	Ch.56, p.4829
IFRS 17.BC315	Ch.56, p.4830
IFRS 17.BC315C	Ch.56, p.4825
IFRS 17.BC315E	Ch.56, p.4825
IFRS 17.BC315F	Ch.56, p.4826
IFRS 17.BC315G	Ch.56, p.4826
IFRS 17.BC315H	Ch.56, p.4825
IFRS 17.BC322	Ch.56, p.4860
IFRS 17.BC327A	Ch.56, p.4870
IFRS 17.BC327B-C	Ch.56, p.4864
IFRS 17.BC327E	Ch.56, p.4869
IFRS 17.BC327G	Ch.56, p.4869
IFRS 17.BC327I	Ch.56, p.4868
IFRS 17.BC330B	Ch.56, p.4874
IFRS 17.BC330C	Ch.56, p.4873
IFRS 17.BC330D	Ch.56, p.4873
IFRS 17.BC342A	Ch.56, p.4882
IFRS 17.BC347	Ch.56, p.4898
IFRS 17.BC348	Ch.56, p.4899
IFRS 17.BC349	Ch.56, p.4899
IFRS 17.BC369-371	Ch.56, p.4918
IFRS 17.BC373	Ch.56, p.4920
IFRS 17.BC374	Ch.56, p.4923

IFRS 17.BC377 .... Ch.56, p.4920
IFRS 17.BC378 .... Ch.56, p.4920
IFRS 17.BC380A Ch.56, p.4926
IFRS 17.BC380B Ch.56, p.4926
IFRS 17.BC380C Ch.56, p.4925
IFRS 17.BC380C Ch.56, p.4926
IFRS 17.BC380D Ch.56, p.4925
IFRS 17.BC382A Ch.56, p.4927
IFRS 17.BC384A-B Ch.56, p.4935
IFRS 17.BC390 .... Ch.56, p.4921
IFRS 17.BC391 .... Ch.56, p.4927
IFRS 17.BC392 .... Ch.56, p.4927
IFRS 17.BC393C Ch.56, p.4922
IFRS 17.BC393D-E Ch.56, p.4922
IFRS 17.BC398A-B Ch.56, p.4941
IFRS 17.BC407 .... Ch.5, p.266

IAS 1 (2023)

IAS 1(2023).74 .... Ch.38, p.3086
IAS 1(2023).76 .... Ch.38, p.3086
IAS 1(2023).76A Ch.15, p.1219
IAS 1(2023).76A Ch.54, p.4516
IAS 1(2023).76B Ch.54, p.4516
IAS 1(2023).136U Ch.54, p.4520
IAS 1(2023).139U Ch.3, p.126

IAS 1

IAS 1.1 .... Ch.3, p.114
IAS 1.2 .... Ch.3, p.114
IAS 1.2 .... Ch.5, p.231
IAS 1.3 .... Ch.3, p.114
IAS 1.4 .... Ch.3, p.114
IAS 1.4 .... Ch.41, p.3203
IAS 1.4 .... Ch.41, p.3226
IAS 1.5 .... Ch.3, p.114
IAS 1.6 .... Ch.3, p.114
IAS 1.7 .... Ch.3, p.114
IAS 1.7 .... Ch.3, p.115
IAS 1.7 .... Ch.3, p.117
IAS 1.7 .... Ch.3, p.119
IAS 1.7 .... Ch.3, p.133
IAS 1.7 .... Ch.3, p.134
IAS 1.7 .... Ch.3, p.140
IAS 1.7 .... Ch.3, p.144
IAS 1.7 .... Ch.3, p.157
IAS 1.7 .... Ch.3, p.158
IAS 1.7 .... Ch.5, p.231
IAS 1.7 .... Ch.7, p.502
IAS 1.7 .... Ch.8, p.600
IAS 1.7 .... Ch.16, p.1278
IAS 1.7 .... Ch.36, p.3012
IAS 1.7 .... Ch.39, p.3115
IAS 1.7 .... Ch.41, p.3235
IAS 1.7 .... Ch.41, p.3239

IAS 1.7(i)-(j) Ch.56, p.4874
IAS 1.8 .... Ch.3, p.133
IAS 1.9 .... Ch.3, p.116
IAS 1.10 .... Ch.3, p.134
IAS 1.10 .... Ch.40, p.3138
IAS 1.10(f) Ch.41, p.3232
IAS 1.10-10A Ch.3, p.121
IAS 1.10-11 .... Ch.3, p.116
IAS 1.10-11 .... Ch.3, p.121
IAS 1.10A Ch.3, p.134
IAS 1.10A Ch.37, p.3061
IAS 1.10A Ch.41, p.3228
IAS 1.11 .... Ch.40, p.3135
IAS 1.13 .... Ch.3, p.117
IAS 1.14 .... Ch.3, p.117
IAS 1.15 .... Ch.3, p.152
IAS 1.15 .... Ch.45, p.3606
IAS 1.15-35 .... Ch.41, p.3203
IAS 1.16 .... Ch.1, p.22
IAS 1.16 .... Ch.3, p.120
IAS 1.16 .... Ch.41, p.3224
IAS 1.17 .... Ch.3, p.153
IAS 1.17 .... Ch.36, p.3012
IAS 1.17(c) Ch.43, p.3357
IAS 1.18 .... Ch.3, p.153
IAS 1.19 .... Ch.3, p.154
IAS 1.19 .... Ch.36, p.3012
IAS 1.20-21 .... Ch.3, p.154
IAS 1.22 .... Ch.3, p.154
IAS 1.23 .... Ch.3, p.155
IAS 1.24 .... Ch.3, p.153
IAS 1.25 .... Ch.3, p.155
IAS 1.25 .... Ch.38, p.3083
IAS 1.25 .... Ch.41, p.3226
IAS 1.26 .... Ch.3, p.155
IAS 1.26 .... Ch.41, p.3226
IAS 1.27 .... Ch.3, p.156
IAS 1.28 .... Ch.3, p.156
IAS 1.29 .... Ch.3, p.157
IAS 1.29 .... Ch.33, p.2568
IAS 1.29 .... Ch.54, p.4511
IAS 1.30 .... Ch.3, p.157
IAS 1.30 .... Ch.3, p.158
IAS 1.30A Ch.2, p.50
IAS 1.30A Ch.3, p.157
IAS 1.30A Ch.3, p.161
IAS 1.31 .... Ch.3, p.158
IAS 1.31 .... Ch.39, p.3115
IAS 1.32 .... Ch.3, p.159
IAS 1.32 .... Ch.23, p.1800
IAS 1.32 .... Ch.24, p.1841
IAS 1.32 .... Ch.32, p.2406
IAS 1.32 .... Ch.42, p.3315
IAS 1.32 .... Ch.43, p.3409
IAS 1.32 .... Ch.54, p.4487
IAS 1.32 .... Ch.54, p.4491
IAS 1.32-33 .... Ch.24, p.1841
IAS 1.33 .... Ch.3, p.159

IAS 1.33	Ch.54, p.4487	IAS 1.54(ma)	Ch.56, p.4872
IAS 1.33	Ch.54, p.4508	IAS 1.54(n)	Ch.33, p.2568
IAS 1.34	Ch.3, p.159	IAS 1.54(n)	Ch.33, p.2611
IAS 1.34	Ch.27, p.2018	IAS 1.54(o)	Ch.33, p.2568
IAS 1.34	Ch.32, p.2406	IAS 1.54(o)	Ch.33, p.2611
IAS 1.34	Ch.42, p.3315	IAS 1.54(q)	Ch.54, p.4517
IAS 1.34	Ch.54, p.4487	IAS 1.54(r)	Ch.54, p.4517
IAS 1.34(a)	Ch.32, p.2406	IAS 1.55	Ch.3, p.128
IAS 1.35	Ch.3, p.159	IAS 1.55	Ch.17, p.1356
IAS 1.35	Ch.54, p.4487	IAS 1.55	Ch.40, p.3163
IAS 1.36	Ch.3, p.116	IAS 1.55	Ch.54, p.4508
IAS 1.36	Ch.5, p.237	IAS 1.55	Ch.54, p.4511
IAS 1.37	Ch.3, p.116	IAS 1.55	Ch.54, p.4517
IAS 1.37	Ch.5, p.238	IAS 1.55	Ch.56, p.4873
IAS 1.38	Ch.3, p.117	IAS 1.55A	Ch.3, p.130
IAS 1.38	Ch.3, p.118	IAS 1.55A	Ch.54, p.4509
IAS 1.38	Ch.5, p.237	IAS 1.56	Ch.3, p.124
IAS 1.38	Ch.5, p.343	IAS 1.56	Ch.3, p.125
IAS 1.38	Ch.39, p.3115	IAS 1.57	Ch.3, p.128
IAS 1.38	Ch.40, p.3145	IAS 1.57	Ch.3, p.129
IAS 1.38	Ch.41, p.3198	IAS 1.57	Ch.33, p.2568
IAS 1.38	Ch.41, p.3231	IAS 1.57	Ch.54, p.4508
IAS 1.38A	Ch.3, p.118	IAS 1.57	Ch.54, p.4511
IAS 1.38A	Ch.41, p.3198	IAS 1.57(a)	Ch.54, p.4508
IAS 1.38B	Ch.3, p.119	IAS 1.57(b)	Ch.54, p.4509
IAS 1.38C	Ch.3, p.118	IAS 1.58	Ch.3, p.128
IAS 1.38D	Ch.3, p.118	IAS 1.58	Ch.3, p.130
IAS 1.40A	Ch.3, p.118	IAS 1.58	Ch.54, p.4509
IAS 1.40A-40D	Ch.41, p.3198	IAS 1.58	Ch.54, p.4511
IAS 1.40C	Ch.3, p.118	IAS 1.59	Ch.3, p.128
IAS 1.41	Ch.3, p.119	IAS 1.59	Ch.54, p.4509
IAS 1.41	Ch.36, p.3010	IAS 1.60	Ch.3, p.122
IAS 1.41	Ch.41, p.3242	IAS 1.60	Ch.3, p.123
IAS 1.42	Ch.3, p.119	IAS 1.60	Ch.17, p.1356
IAS 1.43	Ch.3, p.119	IAS 1.60	Ch.55, p.4627
IAS 1.45	Ch.3, p.156	IAS 1.61	Ch.3, p.123
IAS 1.45	Ch.41, p.3242	IAS 1.62	Ch.3, p.122
IAS 1.46	Ch.3, p.156	IAS 1.63	Ch.3, p.123
IAS 1.48	Ch.3, p.121	IAS 1.64	Ch.3, p.123
IAS 1.49-50	Ch.3, p.120	IAS 1.65	Ch.3, p.123
IAS 1.51	Ch.3, p.120	IAS 1.66	Ch.3, p.122
IAS 1.52	Ch.3, p.120	IAS 1.66	Ch.3, p.124
IAS 1.53	Ch.3, p.120	IAS 1.66	Ch.42, p.3309
IAS 1.54	Ch.3, p.128	IAS 1.66	Ch.54, p.4515
IAS 1.54	Ch.3, p.129	IAS 1.67	Ch.3, p.122
IAS 1.54	Ch.7, p.546	IAS 1.67	Ch.17, p.1356
IAS 1.54	Ch.13, p.961	IAS 1.68	Ch.3, p.122
IAS 1.54	Ch.13, p.970	IAS 1.68	Ch.3, p.124
IAS 1.54	Ch.17, p.1356	IAS 1.68	Ch.22, p.1678
IAS 1.54	Ch.33, p.2568	IAS 1.69	Ch.3, p.122
IAS 1.54	Ch.41, p.3199	IAS 1.69	Ch.3, p.125
IAS 1.54	Ch.42, p.3308	IAS 1.69	Ch.32, p.2398
IAS 1.54	Ch.54, p.4508	IAS 1.69	Ch.54, p.4515
IAS 1.54	Ch.54, p.4511	IAS 1.69(d)	Ch.54, p.4516
IAS 1.54	Ch.55, p.4626	IAS 1.69(d)	Ch.54, p.4517
IAS 1.54-56	Ch.33, p.2609	IAS 1.70	Ch.3, p.122
IAS 1.54(da)	Ch.56, p.4872	IAS 1.70	Ch.3, p.125
IAS 1.54(e)	Ch.11, p.882	IAS 1.70	Ch.54, p.4511

IAS 1.71	Ch.3, p.125	IAS 1.85	Ch.40, p.3163
IAS 1.72	Ch.3, p.126	IAS 1.85	Ch.42, p.3283
IAS 1.73	Ch.3, p.126	IAS 1.85	Ch.54, p.4485
IAS 1.73	Ch.54, p.4516	IAS 1.85	Ch.56, p.4875
IAS 1.73	Ch.54, p.4517	IAS 1.85-86	Ch.3, p.134
IAS 1.74	Ch.3, p.126	IAS 1.85A	Ch.3, p.135
IAS 1.74	Ch.38, p.3086	IAS 1.85A	Ch.54, p.4485
IAS 1.75	Ch.3, p.126	IAS 1.85B	Ch.3, p.135
IAS 1.76	Ch.3, p.126	IAS 1.86	Ch.3, p.134
IAS 1.76	Ch.3, p.183	IAS 1.86	Ch.3, p.135
IAS 1.76	Ch.38, p.3079	IAS 1.86	Ch.54, p.4481
IAS 1.76	Ch.38, p.3080	IAS 1.86	Ch.54, p.4485
IAS 1.76	Ch.38, p.3086	IAS 1.87	Ch.3, p.148
IAS 1.77	Ch.3, p.130	IAS 1.87	Ch.54, p.4486
IAS 1.77	Ch.39, p.3124	IAS 1.88	Ch.3, p.133
IAS 1.77	Ch.54, p.4509	IAS 1.88	Ch.3, p.160
IAS 1.77	Ch.54, p.4517	IAS 1.88	Ch.35, p.2947
IAS 1.78	Ch.3, p.130	IAS 1.88	Ch.40, p.3150
IAS 1.78(b)	Ch.54, p.4509	IAS 1.89	Ch.3, p.160
IAS 1.78(e)	Ch.54, p.4517	IAS 1.90	Ch.3, p.145
IAS 1.79	Ch.3, p.131	IAS 1.90	Ch.33, p.2611
IAS 1.79(a)	Ch.54, p.4518	IAS 1.90	Ch.33, p.2613
IAS 1.79(a)(vi)	Ch.47, p.3742	IAS 1.91	Ch.3, p.140
IAS 1.79(b)	Ch.54, p.4517	IAS 1.91	Ch.3, p.145
IAS 1.80	Ch.3, p.131	IAS 1.91	Ch.33, p.2611
IAS 1.80	Ch.54, p.4518	IAS 1.92-93	Ch.3, p.144
IAS 1.80A	Ch.3, p.131	IAS 1.92	Ch.53, p.4295
IAS 1.80A	Ch.54, p.4518	IAS 1.92	Ch.53, p.4297
IAS 1.81A	Ch.3, p.136	IAS 1.92	Ch.53, p.4379
IAS 1.81A	Ch.3, p.140	IAS 1.94	Ch.3, p.141
IAS 1.81B	Ch.3, p.136	IAS 1.94	Ch.3, p.144
IAS 1.81B	Ch.3, p.141	IAS 1.95	Ch.3, p.144
IAS 1.81B	Ch.7, p.546	IAS 1.96	Ch.3, p.145
IAS 1.81B	Ch.13, p.961	IAS 1.96	Ch.54, p.4490
IAS 1.81B(a)	Ch.54, p.4485	IAS 1.97	Ch.3, p.119
IAS 1.81B(b)	Ch.54, p.4490	IAS 1.97	Ch.3, p.148
IAS 1.82	Ch.3, p.135	IAS 1.97	Ch.19, p.1509
IAS 1.82	Ch.13, p.970	IAS 1.97	Ch.21, p.1671
IAS 1.82	Ch.41, p.3199	IAS 1.97	Ch.40, p.3163
IAS 1.82(a)	Ch.51, p.4034	IAS 1.97	Ch.54, p.4486
IAS 1.82(a)	Ch.53, p.4379	IAS 1.98	Ch.3, p.148
IAS 1.82(a)	Ch.54, p.4482	IAS 1.98	Ch.54, p.4486
IAS 1.82(a)(ii)	Ch.56, p.4874	IAS 1.99	Ch.3, p.137
IAS 1.82(aa)	Ch.54, p.4410	IAS 1.99	Ch.42, p.3283
IAS 1.82(aa)	Ch.54, p.4482	IAS 1.99-100	Ch.3, p.136
IAS 1.82(ab)-(ac)	Ch.56, p.4874	IAS 1.100	Ch.3, p.137
IAS 1.82(b)	Ch.54, p.4483	IAS 1.101	Ch.3, p.137
IAS 1.82(ba)	Ch.51, p.4068	IAS 1.102	Ch.3, p.138
IAS 1.82(ba)	Ch.51, p.4069	IAS 1.103	Ch.3, p.140
IAS 1.82(ba)	Ch.54, p.4482	IAS 1.104	Ch.3, p.140
IAS 1.82(bb)-(bc)	Ch.56, p.4874	IAS 1.105	Ch.3, p.137
IAS 1.82(c)	Ch.11, p.883	IAS 1.105	Ch.3, p.138
IAS 1.82(ca)	Ch.54, p.4483	IAS 1.106	Ch.3, p.148
IAS 1.82(cb)	Ch.54, p.4483	IAS 1.106	Ch.7, p.546
IAS 1.82A	Ch.3, p.140	IAS 1.106	Ch.13, p.961
IAS 1.82A	Ch.11, p.884	IAS 1.106	Ch.47, p.3741
IAS 1.82A	Ch.54, p.4489	IAS 1.106	Ch.54, p.4490
IAS 1.85	Ch.20, p.1612	IAS 1.106(d)	Ch.13, p.967

Standard	Reference	Standard	Reference
IAS 1.106A	Ch.3, p.149	IAS 1.125-129	Ch.33, p.2473
IAS 1.106A	Ch.54, p.4490	IAS 1.125-129	Ch.33, p.2540
IAS 1.107	Ch.3, p.149	IAS 1.125-133	Ch.15, p.1244
IAS 1.107	Ch.54, p.4490	IAS 1.126	Ch.3, p.177
IAS 1.108	Ch.3, p.149	IAS 1.127	Ch.3, p.178
IAS 1.109	Ch.3, p.149	IAS 1.128	Ch.3, p.178
IAS 1.109	Ch.7, p.538	IAS 1.129	Ch.3, p.178
IAS 1.109	Ch.47, p.3741	IAS 1.130	Ch.3, p.178
IAS 1.110	Ch.3, p.149	IAS 1.131	Ch.3, p.179
IAS 1.111	Ch.3, p.121	IAS 1.132	Ch.3, p.178
IAS 1.112	Ch.3, p.151	IAS 1.133	Ch.3, p.178
IAS 1.112	Ch.40, p.3158	IAS 1.134	Ch.3, p.180
IAS 1.112	Ch.54, p.4513	IAS 1.135	Ch.3, p.180
IAS 1.113	Ch.3, p.151	IAS 1.135	Ch.55, p.4665
IAS 1.114	Ch.3, p.151	IAS 1.135	Ch.56, p.4918
IAS 1.116	Ch.3, p.151	IAS 1.136	Ch.3, p.180
IAS 1.117	Ch.3, p.174	IAS 1.136	Ch.55, p.4666
IAS 1.117	Ch.17, p.1361	IAS 1.136	Ch.56, p.4918
IAS 1.117	Ch.21, p.1671	IAS 1.136A	Ch.3, p.182
IAS 1.117	Ch.23, p.1780	IAS 1.136A	Ch.54, p.4463
IAS 1.117	Ch.32, p.2391	IAS 1.137	Ch.3, p.182
IAS 1.117	Ch.43, p.3511	IAS 1.137	Ch.38, p.3081
IAS 1.117	Ch.56, p.4910	IAS 1.137	Ch.39, p.3121
IAS 1.117-121	Ch.15, p.1244	IAS 1.138	Ch.3, p.183
IAS 1.117-124	Ch.42, p.3283	IAS 1.138(b)	Ch.13, p.957
IAS 1.118	Ch.3, p.163	IAS 1.138(c)	Ch.39, p.3113
IAS 1.118	Ch.3, p.174	IAS 1.IG3	Ch.3, p.131
IAS 1.119	Ch.3, p.174	IAS 1.IG6	Ch.33, p.2611
IAS 1.121	Ch.3, p.174	IAS 1.IG10-11	Ch.3, p.180
IAS 1.121	Ch.17, p.1361	IAS 1.IG Part I	Ch.3, p.131
IAS 1.122	Ch.3, p.175	IAS 1.IG Part I	Ch.3, p.138
IAS 1.122	Ch.13, p.956	IAS 1.IG Part I	Ch.3, p.141
IAS 1.122	Ch.15, p.1244	IAS 1.IG Part I	Ch.3, p.144
IAS 1.122	Ch.16, p.1267	IAS 1.IG Part I	Ch.3, p.146
IAS 1.122	Ch.19, p.1453	IAS 1.IG Part I	Ch.3, p.150
IAS 1.122	Ch.21, p.1672	IAS 1.BC13L	Ch.3, p.161
IAS 1.122	Ch.23, p.1781	IAS 1.BC13Q	Ch.3, p.157
IAS 1.122	Ch.26, p.1936	IAS 1.BC30F	Ch.3, p.161
IAS 1.122	Ch.33, p.2475	IAS 1.BC32C	Ch.3, p.118
IAS 1.122	Ch.35, p.2895	IAS 1.BC33	Ch.41, p.3232
IAS 1.122	Ch.40, p.3158	IAS 1.BC38G	Ch.3, p.130
IAS 1.122	Ch.43, p.3379	IAS 1.BC38I	Ch.54, p.4515
IAS 1.122	Ch.43, p.3438	IAS 1.BC38J	Ch.54, p.4515
IAS 1.122	Ch.43, p.3441	IAS 1.BC38L-P	Ch.3, p.125
IAS 1.122	Ch.54, p.4513	IAS 1.BC55	Ch.3, p.137
IAS 1.122	Ch.56, p.4909	IAS 1.BC56	Ch.3, p.137
IAS 1.122-133	Ch.32, p.2433	IAS 1.BC64	Ch.3, p.148
IAS 1.123	Ch.3, p.175	IAS 1.BC76D	Ch.3, p.151
IAS 1.124	Ch.3, p.175	IAS 1.BC84	Ch.3, p.179
IAS 1.125	Ch.3, p.177	IAS 1.BC86	Ch.3, p.180
IAS 1.125	Ch.23, p.1781	IAS 1.BC86	Ch.54, p.4472
IAS 1.125	Ch.26, p.2009	IAS 1.BC88	Ch.54, p.4473
IAS 1.125	Ch.33, p.2475	IAS 1.BC100B	Ch.3, p.182
IAS 1.125	Ch.42, p.3292	IAS 1.BC103	Ch.37, p.3039
IAS 1.125	Ch.43, p.3438		
IAS 1.125	Ch.43, p.3441		
IAS 1.125	Ch.43, p.3511		
IAS 1.125	Ch.45, p.3606		

IAS 2

IAS 2.1	Ch.22, p.1675
IAS 2.2	Ch.22, p.1676
IAS 2.3	Ch.17, p.1366
IAS 2.3	Ch.22, p.1676
IAS 2.3(a)	Ch.43, p.3336
IAS 2.3(a)	Ch.43, p.3361
IAS 2.3(a)	Ch.43, p.3451
IAS 2.3(a)	Ch.43, p.3480
IAS 2.3(a)	Ch.43, p.3487
IAS 2.3(b)	Ch.22, p.1688
IAS 2.3(b)	Ch.22, p.1694
IAS 2.3(b)	Ch.43, p.3480
IAS 2.3(b)	Ch.43, p.3487
IAS 2.4	Ch.22, p.1676
IAS 2.4	Ch.43, p.3336
IAS 2.4	Ch.43, p.3361
IAS 2.5	Ch.22, p.1676
IAS 2.6	Ch.17, p.1299
IAS 2.6	Ch.17, p.1366
IAS 2.6	Ch.22, p.1676
IAS 2.6	Ch.22, p.1678
IAS 2.6	Ch.22, p.1682
IAS 2.6	Ch.32, p.2407
IAS 2.7	Ch.22, p.1683
IAS 2.8	Ch.22, p.1677
IAS 2.8	Ch.43, p.3481
IAS 2.9	Ch.17, p.1344
IAS 2.9	Ch.22, p.1682
IAS 2.9	Ch.29, p.2215
IAS 2.9	Ch.43, p.3451
IAS 2.9	Ch.43, p.3488
IAS 2.10	Ch.22, p.1683
IAS 2.10	Ch.43, p.3428
IAS 2.11	Ch.22, p.1683
IAS 2.12	Ch.22, p.1684
IAS 2.12	Ch.22, p.1696
IAS 2.12	Ch.22, p.1697
IAS 2.12	Ch.26, p.1974
IAS 2.13	Ch.22, p.1684
IAS 2.13	Ch.41, p.3243
IAS 2.14	Ch.22, p.1685
IAS 2.14	Ch.22, p.1696
IAS 2.14	Ch.43, p.3483
IAS 2.15	Ch.22, p.1685
IAS 2.15	Ch.22, p.1686
IAS 2.16	Ch.22, p.1685
IAS 2.16	Ch.22, p.1694
IAS 2.16	Ch.43, p.3428
IAS 2.16(b)	Ch.22, p.1685
IAS 2.16(c)	Ch.22, p.1686
IAS 2.16(c)	Ch.26, p.1974
IAS 2.17	Ch.22, p.1686
IAS 2.18	Ch.22, p.1687
IAS 2.20	Ch.22, p.1676
IAS 2.21	Ch.22, p.1689
IAS 2.22	Ch.22, p.1689
IAS 2.23	Ch.22, p.1690
IAS 2.24	Ch.22, p.1690
IAS 2.25	Ch.22, p.1690
IAS 2.25	Ch.43, p.3486
IAS 2.26	Ch.22, p.1690
IAS 2.27	Ch.22, p.1691
IAS 2.28	Ch.22, p.1692
IAS 2.28	Ch.29, p.2215
IAS 2.29	Ch.22, p.1692
IAS 2.30	Ch.22, p.1692
IAS 2.30	Ch.43, p.3488
IAS 2.31	Ch.22, p.1692
IAS 2.32	Ch.22, p.1692
IAS 2.32	Ch.22, p.1693
IAS 2.33	Ch.22, p.1693
IAS 2.34	Ch.22, p.1697
IAS 2.34	Ch.43, p.3447
IAS 2.35	Ch.22, p.1697
IAS 2.36	Ch.22, p.1697
IAS 2.37	Ch.22, p.1698
IAS 2.37	Ch.43, p.3481
IAS 2.38	Ch.22, p.1685
IAS 2.38	Ch.22, p.1698
IAS 2.39	Ch.22, p.1699
IAS 2.BC9	Ch.22, p.1691

IAS 7

IAS 7 Objective	Ch.40, p.3137
IAS 7.1	Ch.40, p.3182
IAS 7.3	Ch.40, p.3138
IAS 7.4	Ch.40, p.3137
IAS 7.5	Ch.40, p.3138
IAS 7.6	Ch.16, p.1272
IAS 7.6	Ch.40, p.3137
IAS 7.6	Ch.40, p.3138
IAS 7.6	Ch.40, p.3141
IAS 7.6	Ch.40, p.3147
IAS 7.6	Ch.40, p.3151
IAS 7.6	Ch.40, p.3152
IAS 7.6-8	Ch.5, p.363
IAS 7.7	Ch.40, p.3138
IAS 7.7	Ch.40, p.3140
IAS 7.7	Ch.40, p.3141
IAS 7.8	Ch.5, p.363
IAS 7.8	Ch.40, p.3142
IAS 7.9	Ch.40, p.3138
IAS 7.10	Ch.16, p.1272
IAS 7.10	Ch.40, p.3135
IAS 7.10	Ch.40, p.3145
IAS 7.11	Ch.40, p.3145
IAS 7.11	Ch.40, p.3152
IAS 7.12	Ch.40, p.3146
IAS 7.13	Ch.40, p.3147
IAS 7.13	Ch.40, p.3154
IAS 7.14	Ch.18, p.1427
IAS 7.14	Ch.27, p.2041

IAS 7.14	Ch.40, p.3147
IAS 7.14	Ch.40, p.3148
IAS 7.14	Ch.40, p.3153
IAS 7.14	Ch.40, p.3159
IAS 7.14	Ch.40, p.3160
IAS 7.14	Ch.40, p.3161
IAS 7.14(a)	Ch.40, p.3155
IAS 7.14(d)	Ch.40, p.3155
IAS 7.15	Ch.40, p.3148
IAS 7.15	Ch.40, p.3184
IAS 7.16	Ch.40, p.3148
IAS 7.16	Ch.40, p.3151
IAS 7.16	Ch.40, p.3161
IAS 7.16	Ch.40, p.3168
IAS 7.16	Ch.40, p.3177
IAS 7.16	Ch.40, p.3178
IAS 7.16	Ch.40, p.3179
IAS 7.16	Ch.40, p.3180
IAS 7.16	Ch.43, p.3376
IAS 7.16(b)	Ch.40, p.3159
IAS 7.16(e)	Ch.40, p.3184
IAS 7.16(f)	Ch.40, p.3184
IAS 7.17	Ch.40, p.3152
IAS 7.17	Ch.40, p.3160
IAS 7.17	Ch.40, p.3162
IAS 7.17	Ch.40, p.3179
IAS 7.17	Ch.40, p.3180
IAS 7.17(a)	Ch.40, p.3161
IAS 7.17(c)	Ch.40, p.3155
IAS 7.17(e)	Ch.40, p.3169
IAS 7.18	Ch.40, p.3148
IAS 7.18	Ch.40, p.3165
IAS 7.19	Ch.40, p.3148
IAS 7.19	Ch.40, p.3175
IAS 7.19	Ch.40, p.3185
IAS 7.20	Ch.40, p.3149
IAS 7.20	Ch.40, p.3150
IAS 7.20	Ch.40, p.3175
IAS 7.21	Ch.40, p.3152
IAS 7.21	Ch.40, p.3153
IAS 7.21	Ch.40, p.3164
IAS 7.22	Ch.40, p.3164
IAS 7.23	Ch.40, p.3164
IAS 7.23A	Ch.40, p.3164
IAS 7.23A(c)	Ch.40, p.3155
IAS 7.24	Ch.40, p.3185
IAS 7.25	Ch.40, p.3165
IAS 7.26	Ch.40, p.3165
IAS 7.27	Ch.40, p.3165
IAS 7.28	Ch.40, p.3140
IAS 7.28	Ch.40, p.3165
IAS 7.31	Ch.40, p.3153
IAS 7.32	Ch.40, p.3154
IAS 7.33	Ch.40, p.3153
IAS 7.33	Ch.40, p.3184
IAS 7.34	Ch.40, p.3153
IAS 7.34	Ch.40, p.3154
IAS 7.35	Ch.33, p.2612
IAS 7.35	Ch.40, p.3154
IAS 7.36	Ch.33, p.2612
IAS 7.36	Ch.40, p.3154
IAS 7.37	Ch.40, p.3180
IAS 7.37	Ch.40, p.3181
IAS 7.38	Ch.40, p.3180
IAS 7.39	Ch.40, p.3176
IAS 7.39-42	Ch.9, p.757
IAS 7.40	Ch.40, p.3176
IAS 7.40-40A	Ch.40, p.3181
IAS 7.41	Ch.40, p.3176
IAS 7.42	Ch.40, p.3176
IAS 7.42A	Ch.40, p.3153
IAS 7.42A	Ch.40, p.3175
IAS 7.42A	Ch.40, p.3176
IAS 7.42B	Ch.40, p.3175
IAS 7.43	Ch.40, p.3157
IAS 7.43	Ch.40, p.3166
IAS 7.43	Ch.40, p.3178
IAS 7.43	Ch.54, p.4512
IAS 7.44	Ch.40, p.3167
IAS 7.44A	Ch.40, p.3171
IAS 7.44A	Ch.54, p.4513
IAS 7.44B	Ch.40, p.3171
IAS 7.44C	Ch.40, p.3171
IAS 7.44D	Ch.40, p.3171
IAS 7.44E	Ch.40, p.3172
IAS 7.45	Ch.40, p.3139
IAS 7.45	Ch.40, p.3143
IAS 7.46	Ch.40, p.3139
IAS 7.48	Ch.15, p.1244
IAS 7.48	Ch.40, p.3143
IAS 7.49	Ch.15, p.1244
IAS 7.49	Ch.40, p.3143
IAS 7.50	Ch.40, p.3173
IAS 7.51	Ch.40, p.3173
IAS 7.52	Ch.40, p.3173
IAS 7 Appendix A part D	Ch.40, p.3174
IAS 7.IE Example A	Ch.3, p.138
IAS 7.BC3	Ch.40, p.3152
IAS 7.BC5-7	Ch.40, p.3179
IAS 7.BC7	Ch.40, p.3152
IAS 7.BC9	Ch.40, p.3171
IAS 7.BC11	Ch.54, p.4510

IAS 8

IAS 8.1	Ch.3, p.115
IAS 8.2	Ch.3, p.115
IAS 8.3	Ch.3, p.114
IAS 8.4	Ch.3, p.115
IAS 8.5	Ch.3, p.114
IAS 8.5	Ch.3, p.157
IAS 8.5	Ch.3, p.163
IAS 8.5	Ch.3, p.166
IAS 8.5	Ch.3, p.168
IAS 8.5	Ch.3, p.169

IAS 8.5	Ch.3, p.171	IAS 8.16	Ch.3, p.167
IAS 8.5	Ch.3, p.172	IAS 8.17	Ch.18, p.1425
IAS 8.5	Ch.5, p.244	IAS 8.17	Ch.41, p.3241
IAS 8.5	Ch.5, p.365	IAS 8.17-18	Ch.3, p.167
IAS 8.5	Ch.5, p.368	IAS 8.19	Ch.55, p.4588
IAS 8.5	Ch.30, p.2279	IAS 8.19-20	Ch.3, p.166
IAS 8.5	Ch.33, p.2473	IAS 8.21	Ch.3, p.167
IAS 8.5	Ch.33, p.2540	IAS 8.22	Ch.3, p.166
IAS 8.5	Ch.33, p.2573	IAS 8.23	Ch.3, p.166
IAS 8.5	Ch.43, p.3498	IAS 8.23	Ch.3, p.172
IAS 8.5	Ch.43, p.3518	IAS 8.23	Ch.33, p.2572
IAS 8.5	Ch.43, p.3563	IAS 8.24	Ch.3, p.172
IAS 8.5	Ch.51, p.4020	IAS 8.25	Ch.3, p.172
IAS 8.5	Ch.56, p.4920	IAS 8.26	Ch.3, p.166
IAS 8.7	Ch.3, p.164	IAS 8.26	Ch.3, p.172
IAS 8.7	Ch.10, p.765	IAS 8.27	Ch.3, p.172
IAS 8.7	Ch.43, p.3344	IAS 8.28	Ch.3, p.176
IAS 8.8	Ch.3, p.153	IAS 8.28	Ch.56, p.4923
IAS 8.8	Ch.3, p.164	IAS 8.29	Ch.3, p.176
IAS 8.8	Ch.5, p.239	IAS 8.29	Ch.40, p.3148
IAS 8.8	Ch.14, p.1010	IAS 8.29	Ch.41, p.3242
IAS 8.8	Ch.49, p.3854	IAS 8.30	Ch.3, p.177
IAS 8.9	Ch.3, p.114	IAS 8.30	Ch.38, p.3087
IAS 8.10	Ch.3, p.164	IAS 8.30	Ch.55, p.4601
IAS 8.10	Ch.5, p.324	IAS 8.31	Ch.3, p.177
IAS 8.10	Ch.5, p.325	IAS 8.32-33	Ch.3, p.167
IAS 8.10	Ch.8, p.586	IAS 8.32-38	Ch.43, p.3518
IAS 8.10	Ch.17, p.1309	IAS 8.32-40	Ch.5, p.245
IAS 8.10	Ch.18, p.1403	IAS 8.32-40	Ch.5, p.250
IAS 8.10	Ch.19, p.1465	IAS 8.32(d)	Ch.18, p.1415
IAS 8.10	Ch.43, p.3344	IAS 8.34	Ch.3, p.167
IAS 8.10	Ch.43, p.3361	IAS 8.34	Ch.20, p.1588
IAS 8.10	Ch.43, p.3421	IAS 8.34	Ch.30, p.2279
IAS 8.10	Ch.53, p.4295	IAS 8.35	Ch.3, p.163
IAS 8.10	Ch.55, p.4587	IAS 8.35	Ch.3, p.164
IAS 8.10-11	Ch.51, p.3958	IAS 8.35	Ch.3, p.167
IAS 8.10-12	Ch.5, p.239	IAS 8.36	Ch.3, p.168
IAS 8.10-12	Ch.7, p.517	IAS 8.36	Ch.17, p.1347
IAS 8.10-12	Ch.31, p.2383	IAS 8.36	Ch.17, p.1349
IAS 8.11	Ch.3, p.165	IAS 8.36	Ch.18, p.1415
IAS 8.11	Ch.5, p.324	IAS 8.36	Ch.26, p.1957
IAS 8.11	Ch.17, p.1308	IAS 8.36	Ch.33, p.2476
IAS 8.11	Ch.43, p.3344	IAS 8.36	Ch.33, p.2567
IAS 8.11	Ch.43, p.3514	IAS 8.36-37	Ch.30, p.2279
IAS 8.11-12	Ch.55, p.4587	IAS 8.36-38	Ch.3, p.168
IAS 8.11(a)	Ch.7, p.504	IAS 8.38	Ch.3, p.163
IAS 8.12	Ch.3, p.165	IAS 8.38	Ch.17, p.1347
IAS 8.13	Ch.42, p.3283	IAS 8.39	Ch.3, p.179
IAS 8.12	Ch.5, p.324	IAS 8.40	Ch.3, p.179
IAS 8.12	Ch.5, p.325	IAS 8.41	Ch.3, p.168
IAS 8.12	Ch.43, p.3344	IAS 8.42	Ch.3, p.169
IAS 8.13	Ch.3, p.157	IAS 8.42	Ch.33, p.2476
IAS 8.13	Ch.24, p.1831	IAS 8.43	Ch.3, p.170
IAS 8.14	Ch.3, p.166	IAS 8.43	Ch.3, p.173
IAS 8.14	Ch.22, p.1690	IAS 8.44	Ch.3, p.173
IAS 8.14-15	Ch.5, p.325	IAS 8.45	Ch.3, p.173
IAS 8.14(b)	Ch.41, p.3240	IAS 8.46	Ch.3, p.169
IAS 8.15	Ch.3, p.157	IAS 8.47	Ch.3, p.174

IAS 8.48	Ch.3, p.164	IAS 10.17	Ch.38, p.3086
IAS 8.48	Ch.3, p.168	IAS 10.17	Ch.41, p.3219
IAS 8.49	Ch.3, p.179	IAS 10.18	Ch.38, p.3086
IAS 8.50	Ch.3, p.171	IAS 10.19	Ch.38, p.3082
IAS 8.51	Ch.3, p.171	IAS 10.20	Ch.38, p.3082
IAS 8.52	Ch.3, p.172	IAS 10.21	Ch.33, p.2474
IAS 8.53	Ch.3, p.171	IAS 10.21	Ch.33, p.2476
IAS 8.IG1	Ch.3, p.169	IAS 10.21	Ch.33, p.2542
IAS 8.IG3	Ch.3, p.172	IAS 10.21	Ch.38, p.3074
		IAS 10.21	Ch.38, p.3083
		IAS 10.21	Ch.39, p.3115

IAS 10

		IAS 10.22	Ch.38, p.3079
		IAS 10.22(e)	Ch.26, p.1968
IAS 10.1	Ch.38, p.3074	IAS 10.22(f)	Ch.38, p.3079
IAS 10.2	Ch.38, p.3073	IAS 10.22(h)	Ch.33, p.2474
IAS 10.3	Ch.33, p.2473	IAS 10.22(h)	Ch.33, p.2475
IAS 10.3	Ch.33, p.2541	IAS 10.22(h)	Ch.33, p.2541
IAS 10.3	Ch.33, p.2567	IAS 10.22(h)	Ch.38, p.3090
IAS 10.3	Ch.38, p.3073	IAS 10.22(h)	Ch.41, p.3252
IAS 10.3	Ch.38, p.3074	IAS 10.BC4	Ch.38, p.3081
IAS 10.3	Ch.43, p.3518		
IAS 10.3	Ch.43, p.3561		

IAS 12 (2018)

IAS 12(2018).52A	Ch.33, p.2577

IAS 10.3(a)	Ch.38, p.3073
IAS 10.3(a)	Ch.38, p.3078
IAS 10.3(a)	Ch.43, p.3419
IAS 10.3(b)	Ch.38, p.3074
IAS 10.3(b)	Ch.38, p.3079

IAS 12

IAS 10.4	Ch.38, p.3074	IAS 12 Objective	Ch.33, p.2455
IAS 10.5	Ch.38, p.3074	IAS 12 Objective	Ch.33, p.2456
IAS 10.5-6	Ch.38, p.3075	IAS 12.1-2	Ch.33, p.2458
IAS 10.6	Ch.38, p.3074	IAS 12.1-2	Ch.43, p.3557
IAS 10.7	Ch.38, p.3077	IAS 12.2	Ch.33, p.2457
IAS 10.8	Ch.38, p.3073	IAS 12.2	Ch.33, p.2461
IAS 10.8	Ch.38, p.3082	IAS 12.4	Ch.24, p.1828
IAS 10.9	Ch.26, p.1939	IAS 12.4	Ch.33, p.2458
IAS 10.9	Ch.26, p.1945	IAS 12.4	Ch.33, p.2462
IAS 10.9	Ch.38, p.3078	IAS 12.5	Ch.33, p.2457
IAS 10.9(b)(i)	Ch.38, p.3088	IAS 12.5	Ch.33, p.2471
IAS 10.9(b)(ii)	Ch.22, p.1692	IAS 12.5	Ch.33, p.2478
IAS 10.9(b)(ii)	Ch.38, p.3087	IAS 12.5	Ch.33, p.2482
IAS 10.9(e)	Ch.38, p.3089	IAS 12.5	Ch.33, p.2494
IAS 10.10	Ch.5, p.244	IAS 12.5	Ch.33, p.2519
IAS 10.10	Ch.38, p.3074	IAS 12.5	Ch.33, p.2522
IAS 10.10	Ch.38, p.3083	IAS 12.5	Ch.33, p.2523
IAS 10.11	Ch.38, p.3079	IAS 12.5	Ch.33, p.2568
IAS 10.11	Ch.38, p.3080	IAS 12.7	Ch.33, p.2479
IAS 10.11	Ch.38, p.3089	IAS 12.7	Ch.33, p.2530
IAS 10.11	Ch.51, p.3966	IAS 12.8	Ch.33, p.2480
IAS 10.12	Ch.33, p.2535	IAS 12.9	Ch.33, p.2481
IAS 10.12	Ch.38, p.3079	IAS 12.10	Ch.33, p.2456
IAS 10.13	Ch.8, p.599	IAS 12.10	Ch.33, p.2481
IAS 10.13	Ch.38, p.3081	IAS 12.10	Ch.33, p.2546
IAS 10.14	Ch.38, p.3074	IAS 12.11	Ch.33, p.2478
IAS 10.14	Ch.38, p.3082	IAS 12.11	Ch.33, p.2560
IAS 10.14	Ch.38, p.3083	IAS 12.12	Ch.33, p.2471
IAS 10.15	Ch.38, p.3082	IAS 12.12	Ch.33, p.2569
IAS 10.16(a)	Ch.38, p.3083		
IAS 10.16(b)	Ch.38, p.3083		

IAS 12.13	Ch.41, p.3255	IAS 12.29(b)	Ch.33, p.2604
IAS 12.13-14	Ch.33, p.2471	IAS 12.29A	Ch.33, p.2522
IAS 12.15	Ch.5, p.365	IAS 12.30	Ch.33, p.2520
IAS 12.15	Ch.33, p.2491	IAS 12.31	Ch.33, p.2518
IAS 12.15	Ch.33, p.2516	IAS 12.32A	Ch.9, p.692
IAS 12.15	Ch.33, p.2531	IAS 12.32A	Ch.33, p.2495
IAS 12.15(a)	Ch.5, p.277	IAS 12.33	Ch.33, p.2488
IAS 12.15(b)	Ch.33, p.2515	IAS 12.33	Ch.33, p.2498
IAS 12.15(b)	Ch.33, p.2516	IAS 12.34	Ch.33, p.2464
IAS 12.16	Ch.33, p.2453	IAS 12.34	Ch.33, p.2526
IAS 12.16	Ch.33, p.2456	IAS 12.35	Ch.33, p.2526
IAS 12.17-20	Ch.33, p.2482	IAS 12.35	Ch.33, p.2527
IAS 12.19	Ch.55, p.4599	IAS 12.36	Ch.33, p.2527
IAS 12.20	Ch.33, p.2516	IAS 12.37	Ch.33, p.2528
IAS 12.20	Ch.33, p.2517	IAS 12.38	Ch.33, p.2531
IAS 12.20	Ch.33, p.2522	IAS 12.39	Ch.33, p.2534
IAS 12.20	Ch.33, p.2528	IAS 12.39	Ch.33, p.2535
IAS 12.21	Ch.33, p.2495	IAS 12.39	Ch.33, p.2537
IAS 12.21A	Ch.33, p.2495	IAS 12.39	Ch.33, p.2601
IAS 12.21A	Ch.33, p.2499	IAS 12.39(b)	Ch.33, p.2536
IAS 12.21A	Ch.33, p.2503	IAS 12.40	Ch.33, p.2534
IAS 12.21B	Ch.33, p.2496	IAS 12.41	Ch.15, p.1242
IAS 12.22	Ch.33, p.2497	IAS 12.41	Ch.33, p.2572
IAS 12.22(a)	Ch.20, p.1593	IAS 12.41	Ch.43, p.3421
IAS 12.22(c)	Ch.33, p.2493	IAS 12.42	Ch.33, p.2534
IAS 12.22(c)	Ch.33, p.2499	IAS 12.43	Ch.33, p.2534
IAS 12.22(c)	Ch.33, p.2508	IAS 12.44	Ch.33, p.2535
IAS 12.22(c)	Ch.33, p.2609	IAS 12.45	Ch.33, p.2535
IAS 12.23	Ch.33, p.2515	IAS 12.46	Ch.33, p.2471
IAS 12.24	Ch.5, p.365	IAS 12.46	Ch.33, p.2473
IAS 12.24	Ch.33, p.2488	IAS 12.46	Ch.33, p.2475
IAS 12.24	Ch.33, p.2491	IAS 12.46	Ch.33, p.2561
IAS 12.24	Ch.33, p.2492	IAS 12.46	Ch.33, p.2564
IAS 12.24	Ch.33, p.2516	IAS 12.46	Ch.33, p.2569
IAS 12.24	Ch.33, p.2531	IAS 12.47	Ch.33, p.2475
IAS 12.24	Ch.41, p.3256	IAS 12.47	Ch.33, p.2539
IAS 12.24-31	Ch.5, p.367	IAS 12.47	Ch.33, p.2540
IAS 12.25	Ch.33, p.2456	IAS 12.47	Ch.33, p.2561
IAS 12.26	Ch.33, p.2482	IAS 12.47	Ch.33, p.2564
IAS 12.26(d)	Ch.33, p.2522	IAS 12.47	Ch.41, p.3253
IAS 12.27	Ch.33, p.2492	IAS 12.48	Ch.33, p.2471
IAS 12.27	Ch.33, p.2517	IAS 12.48	Ch.33, p.2539
IAS 12.27	Ch.33, p.2523	IAS 12.48	Ch.41, p.3251
IAS 12.27A	Ch.33, p.2518	IAS 12.49	Ch.33, p.2539
IAS 12.27A	Ch.33, p.2524	IAS 12.51	Ch.33, p.2542
IAS 12.28	Ch.33, p.2518	IAS 12.51A	Ch.33, p.2544
IAS 12.28	Ch.33, p.2525	IAS 12.51A	Ch.33, p.2551
IAS 12.28	Ch.33, p.2526	IAS 12.51B	Ch.33, p.2547
IAS 12.28	Ch.33, p.2528	IAS 12.51C	Ch.33, p.2549
IAS 12.29	Ch.33, p.2512	IAS 12.51C	Ch.33, p.2550
IAS 12.29	Ch.33, p.2518	IAS 12.51D	Ch.33, p.2550
IAS 12.29	Ch.33, p.2525	IAS 12.51E	Ch.33, p.2547
IAS 12.29	Ch.33, p.2604	IAS 12.51E	Ch.33, p.2550
IAS 12.29(a)(i)	Ch.33, p.2519	IAS 12.52A	Ch.33, p.2536
IAS 12.29(a)(i)	Ch.33, p.2523	IAS 12.52A	Ch.33, p.2554
IAS 12.29(a)(ii)	Ch.33, p.2519	IAS 12.53	Ch.33, p.2477
IAS 12.29(b)	Ch.33, p.2542	IAS 12.53	Ch.33, p.2556
IAS 12.29(b)	Ch.33, p.2543	IAS 12.54	Ch.33, p.2556

IAS 12.55	Ch.33, p.2556
IAS 12.56	Ch.33, p.2528
IAS 12.57	Ch.33, p.2570
IAS 12.57A	Ch.33, p.2536
IAS 12.57A	Ch.33, p.2554
IAS 12.57A	Ch.33, p.2574
IAS 12.58	Ch.15, p.1242
IAS 12.58	Ch.33, p.2570
IAS 12.58	Ch.33, p.2573
IAS 12.58	Ch.33, p.2582
IAS 12.58	Ch.33, p.2601
IAS 12.58(a)	Ch.33, p.2600
IAS 12.58(a)	Ch.33, p.2601
IAS 12.60	Ch.33, p.2570
IAS 12.60	Ch.33, p.2573
IAS 12.61A	Ch.5, p.365
IAS 12.61A	Ch.5, p.366
IAS 12.61A	Ch.5, p.368
IAS 12.61A	Ch.33, p.2528
IAS 12.61A	Ch.33, p.2541
IAS 12.61A	Ch.33, p.2570
IAS 12.61A	Ch.33, p.2571
IAS 12.61A	Ch.33, p.2580
IAS 12.61A	Ch.33, p.2581
IAS 12.61A	Ch.33, p.2582
IAS 12.61A(b)	Ch.33, p.2601
IAS 12.62	Ch.33, p.2570
IAS 12.62A	Ch.33, p.2570
IAS 12.62A(a)	Ch.33, p.2573
IAS 12.63	Ch.33, p.2571
IAS 12.64	Ch.33, p.2571
IAS 12.65	Ch.33, p.2571
IAS 12.65A	Ch.33, p.2574
IAS 12.65A	Ch.33, p.2575
IAS 12.65A	Ch.33, p.2576
IAS 12.66	Ch.33, p.2604
IAS 12.67	Ch.33, p.2607
IAS 12.68	Ch.9, p.692
IAS 12.68	Ch.20, p.1597
IAS 12.68	Ch.33, p.2607
IAS 12.68A	Ch.33, p.2587
IAS 12.68A-68C	Ch.5, p.367
IAS 12.68A-68C	Ch.33, p.2570
IAS 12.68B	Ch.33, p.2587
IAS 12.68C	Ch.5, p.367
IAS 12.68C	Ch.33, p.2587
IAS 12.68C	Ch.33, p.2589
IAS 12.68C	Ch.33, p.2593
IAS 12.71	Ch.33, p.2610
IAS 12.72	Ch.33, p.2610
IAS 12.73	Ch.33, p.2610
IAS 12.74	Ch.33, p.2610
IAS 12.75	Ch.33, p.2611
IAS 12.76	Ch.33, p.2611
IAS 12.77	Ch.33, p.2611
IAS 12.78	Ch.33, p.2612
IAS 12.79-80	Ch.33, p.2613
IAS 12.79-80	Ch.33, p.2617
IAS 12.80(d)	Ch.33, p.2541
IAS 12.81	Ch.33, p.2613
IAS 12.81(c)	Ch.33, p.2460
IAS 12.81(c)	Ch.33, p.2617
IAS 12.81(d)	Ch.33, p.2474
IAS 12.81(d)	Ch.33, p.2541
IAS 12.81(e)	Ch.33, p.2620
IAS 12.81(f)	Ch.33, p.2620
IAS 12.81(g)	Ch.33, p.2619
IAS 12.82	Ch.33, p.2616
IAS 12.82A	Ch.33, p.2617
IAS 12.84	Ch.33, p.2614
IAS 12.85	Ch.33, p.2615
IAS 12.86	Ch.33, p.2613
IAS 12.87	Ch.33, p.2616
IAS 12.87A	Ch.33, p.2617
IAS 12.87A-87C	Ch.33, p.2617
IAS 12.88	Ch.26, p.1935
IAS 12.88	Ch.33, p.2541
IAS 12.88	Ch.33, p.2614
IAS 12.88	Ch.33, p.2619
IAS 12.98I	Ch.33, p.2455
IAS 12.98I	Ch.33, p.2577
IAS 12.IE.A-C	Ch.33, p.2482
IAS 12.IE.A.18	Ch.16, p.1266
IAS 12 IE Example 4	Ch.33, p.2515
IAS 12 IE Example 6	Ch.33, p.2597
IAS 12 IE Example 7	Ch.33, p.2524
IAS 12.BC1A	Ch.33, p.2520
IAS 12.BC6	Ch.33, p.2545
IAS 12.BC6	Ch.33, p.2547
IAS 12.BC37	Ch.33, p.2520
IAS 12.BC38	Ch.33, p.2521
IAS 12.BC39	Ch.33, p.2521
IAS 12.BC40	Ch.33, p.2522
IAS 12.BC42-44	Ch.33, p.2522
IAS 12.BC47	Ch.33, p.2521
IAS 12.BC49	Ch.33, p.2523
IAS 12.BC50	Ch.33, p.2523
IAS 12.BC52	Ch.33, p.2521
IAS 12.BC53	Ch.33, p.2521
IAS 12.BC53	Ch.33, p.2523
IAS 12.BC55	Ch.33, p.2521
IAS 12.BC55	Ch.33, p.2523
IAS 12.BC56	Ch.33, p.2519
IAS 12.BC56	Ch.33, p.2523
IAS 12.BC57	Ch.33, p.2521
IAS 12.BC58	Ch.33, p.2523
IAS 12.BC59	Ch.33, p.2524
IAS 12.BC67	Ch.33, p.2577
IAS 12.BC69	Ch.33, p.2578
IAS 12.BC70	Ch.33, p.2577

IAS 16 (2022)

IAS 16(2022).17(e)	Ch.18, p.1405
IAS 16(2022).BC16F-G	Ch.43, p.3448

IAS 16

IAS 16(2022).BC16J	Ch.43, p.3448

IAS 16

IAS 16.1	Ch.18, p.1385
IAS 16.2	Ch.43, p.3513
IAS 16.2-3	Ch.18, p.1386
IAS 16.3	Ch.18, p.1386
IAS 16.3	Ch.43, p.3513
IAS 16.3(b)	Ch.18, p.1393
IAS 16.3(c)	Ch.43, p.3361
IAS 16.3(d)	Ch.43, p.3336
IAS 16.3(d)	Ch.43, p.3361
IAS 16.3(d)	Ch.43, p.3502
IAS 16.5	Ch.18, p.1386
IAS 16.5	Ch.18, p.1418
IAS 16.6	Ch.8, p.585
IAS 16.6	Ch.18, p.1387
IAS 16.6	Ch.18, p.1393
IAS 16.6	Ch.18, p.1410
IAS 16.6	Ch.18, p.1419
IAS 16.6	Ch.32, p.2407
IAS 16.6	Ch.33, p.2545
IAS 16.6	Ch.43, p.3395
IAS 16.6	Ch.43, p.3418
IAS 16.7	Ch.18, p.1388
IAS 16.7	Ch.18, p.1428
IAS 16.8	Ch.18, p.1389
IAS 16.9	Ch.5, p.292
IAS 16.9	Ch.5, p.371
IAS 16.9	Ch.18, p.1389
IAS 16.9	Ch.18, p.1428
IAS 16.10	Ch.18, p.1394
IAS 16.11	Ch.18, p.1390
IAS 16.12	Ch.5, p.371
IAS 16.12	Ch.18, p.1395
IAS 16.12	Ch.43, p.3492
IAS 16.13	Ch.5, p.371
IAS 16.13	Ch.18, p.1395
IAS 16.13	Ch.43, p.3492
IAS 16.14	Ch.18, p.1396
IAS 16.14	Ch.18, p.1397
IAS 16.14	Ch.43, p.3492
IAS 16.15	Ch.18, p.1397
IAS 16.15	Ch.21, p.1647
IAS 16.15	Ch.43, p.3367
IAS 16.15	Ch.43, p.3395
IAS 16.15	Ch.43, p.3398
IAS 16.16	Ch.18, p.1397
IAS 16.16	Ch.18, p.1399
IAS 16.16	Ch.18, p.1405
IAS 16.16	Ch.18, p.1414
IAS 16.16	Ch.26, p.1941
IAS 16.16	Ch.26, p.1979
IAS 16.16(a)	Ch.26, p.2001
IAS 16.16(b)	Ch.18, p.1403
IAS 16.16(b)	Ch.19, p.1457
IAS 16.16(b)	Ch.21, p.1647
IAS 16.16(b)	Ch.42, p.3285
IAS 16.16(b)	Ch.43, p.3443
IAS 16.16(b)	Ch.43, p.3486
IAS 16.16(c)	Ch.5, p.316
IAS 16.16(c)	Ch.26, p.1947
IAS 16.16(c)	Ch.26, p.1985
IAS 16.16(c)	Ch.33, p.2509
IAS 16.16(c)	Ch.43, p.3428
IAS 16.17	Ch.18, p.1399
IAS 16.17	Ch.18, p.1404
IAS 16.17(e)	Ch.43, p.3444
IAS 16.18	Ch.18, p.1398
IAS 16.18	Ch.26, p.1947
IAS 16.18	Ch.26, p.1986
IAS 16.18	Ch.43, p.3428
IAS 16.19	Ch.18, p.1400
IAS 16.20	Ch.18, p.1400
IAS 16.20	Ch.18, p.1404
IAS 16.20	Ch.43, p.3444
IAS 16.20A	Ch.17, p.1308
IAS 16.20A	Ch.18, p.1404
IAS 16.21	Ch.18, p.1403
IAS 16.21	Ch.18, p.1404
IAS 16.21	Ch.19, p.1466
IAS 16.21	Ch.43, p.3444
IAS 16.21	Ch.43, p.3445
IAS 16.22	Ch.18, p.1399
IAS 16.22	Ch.18, p.1400
IAS 16.22	Ch.42, p.3286
IAS 16.22A	Ch.18, p.1393
IAS 16.22A	Ch.42, p.3284
IAS 16.22A	Ch.42, p.3286
IAS 16.23	Ch.16, p.1261
IAS 16.23	Ch.18, p.1401
IAS 16.24	Ch.8, p.613
IAS 16.24	Ch.8, p.616
IAS 16.24	Ch.18, p.1406
IAS 16.24	Ch.18, p.1408
IAS 16.24	Ch.43, p.3402
IAS 16.25	Ch.11, p.852
IAS 16.25	Ch.18, p.1407
IAS 16.26	Ch.8, p.613
IAS 16.26	Ch.8, p.615
IAS 16.26	Ch.18, p.1408
IAS 16.28	Ch.18, p.1408
IAS 16.29	Ch.18, p.1408
IAS 16.29	Ch.18, p.1417
IAS 16.29	Ch.18, p.1418
IAS 16.29	Ch.42, p.3284
IAS 16.29A-29B	Ch.18, p.1409
IAS 16.30	Ch.18, p.1408
IAS 16.30	Ch.19, p.1483
IAS 16.31	Ch.14, p.1136
IAS 16.31	Ch.18, p.1417
IAS 16.31	Ch.21, p.1647
IAS 16.34	Ch.14, p.1136
IAS 16.34	Ch.18, p.1418

IAS 16.35	Ch.18, p.1423	IAS 16.62A	Ch.18, p.1415
IAS 16.36	Ch.18, p.1418	IAS 16.63	Ch.18, p.1417
IAS 16.37	Ch.18, p.1418	IAS 16.63	Ch.42, p.3284
IAS 16.37	Ch.42, p.3310	IAS 16.65	Ch.18, p.1417
IAS 16.38	Ch.18, p.1418	IAS 16.65	Ch.18, p.1431
IAS 16.39	Ch.18, p.1422	IAS 16.66	Ch.18, p.1417
IAS 16.39	Ch.18, p.1424	IAS 16.66	Ch.18, p.1431
IAS 16.40	Ch.18, p.1422	IAS 16.66(c)	Ch.55, p.4542
IAS 16.41	Ch.18, p.1422	IAS 16.67	Ch.18, p.1426
IAS 16.41	Ch.18, p.1426	IAS 16.67	Ch.18, p.1428
IAS 16.41	Ch.27, p.2040	IAS 16.67	Ch.43, p.3395
IAS 16.42	Ch.18, p.1423	IAS 16.67	Ch.43, p.3399
IAS 16.43	Ch.5, p.371	IAS 16.68	Ch.18, p.1406
IAS 16.43	Ch.18, p.1394	IAS 16.68	Ch.18, p.1426
IAS 16.43	Ch.18, p.1409	IAS 16.68	Ch.27, p.2018
IAS 16.43	Ch.26, p.1963	IAS 16.68	Ch.27, p.2040
IAS 16.43	Ch.43, p.3514	IAS 16.68	Ch.36, p.2999
IAS 16.44	Ch.17, p.1299	IAS 16.68A	Ch.3, p.122
IAS 16.44	Ch.18, p.1394	IAS 16.68A	Ch.18, p.1406
IAS 16.44	Ch.18, p.1409	IAS 16.68A	Ch.18, p.1427
IAS 16.44	Ch.19, p.1485	IAS 16.68A	Ch.19, p.1509
IAS 16.44	Ch.26, p.1964	IAS 16.68A	Ch.22, p.1677
IAS 16.44	Ch.26, p.2003	IAS 16.68A	Ch.22, p.1681
IAS 16.45	Ch.18, p.1392	IAS 16.68A	Ch.27, p.2040
IAS 16.45	Ch.18, p.1410	IAS 16.68A	Ch.27, p.2041
IAS 16.45	Ch.43, p.3514	IAS 16.68A	Ch.40, p.3159
IAS 16.46	Ch.18, p.1410	IAS 16.69	Ch.18, p.1426
IAS 16.47	Ch.18, p.1410	IAS 16.69	Ch.27, p.2040
IAS 16.48	Ch.18, p.1410	IAS 16.70	Ch.18, p.1394
IAS 16.49	Ch.18, p.1410	IAS 16.70	Ch.18, p.1426
IAS 16.50	Ch.18, p.1411	IAS 16.71	Ch.18, p.1426
IAS 16.51	Ch.5, p.369	IAS 16.71	Ch.25, p.1865
IAS 16.51	Ch.5, p.370	IAS 16.71	Ch.27, p.2040
IAS 16.51	Ch.18, p.1410	IAS 16.71	Ch.43, p.3399
IAS 16.51	Ch.18, p.1411	IAS 16.72	Ch.18, p.1427
IAS 16.51	Ch.19, p.1483	IAS 16.72	Ch.25, p.1865
IAS 16.51	Ch.42, p.3284	IAS 16.72	Ch.27, p.2040
IAS 16.52	Ch.18, p.1411	IAS 16.72	Ch.43, p.3400
IAS 16.53	Ch.18, p.1411	IAS 16.72	Ch.45, p.3605
IAS 16.53	Ch.42, p.3293	IAS 16.73	Ch.41, p.3232
IAS 16.54	Ch.18, p.1411	IAS 16.73	Ch.42, p.3310
IAS 16.55	Ch.18, p.1414	IAS 16.73(a)	Ch.18, p.1431
IAS 16.55	Ch.18, p.1415	IAS 16.73(b)	Ch.18, p.1431
IAS 16.56	Ch.18, p.1412	IAS 16.73(c)	Ch.18, p.1432
IAS 16.56	Ch.18, p.1414	IAS 16.73(d)	Ch.18, p.1432
IAS 16.56(c)	Ch.18, p.1414	IAS 16.73(d)	Ch.20, p.1612
IAS 16.57	Ch.18, p.1411	IAS 16.73(e)	Ch.18, p.1432
IAS 16.57	Ch.18, p.1412	IAS 16.73(e)	Ch.41, p.3205
IAS 16.57	Ch.18, p.1414	IAS 16.73(e)(iv)	Ch.20, p.1612
IAS 16.58	Ch.18, p.1413	IAS 16.74	Ch.18, p.1433
IAS 16.59	Ch.18, p.1413	IAS 16.74(c)	Ch.38, p.3080
IAS 16.59	Ch.18, p.1414	IAS 16.74(c)	Ch.39, p.3123
IAS 16.60-62	Ch.18, p.1415	IAS 16.74A	Ch.18, p.1434
IAS 16.61	Ch.5, p.369	IAS 16.75	Ch.18, p.1431
IAS 16.61	Ch.18, p.1414	IAS 16.75	Ch.18, p.1432
IAS 16.61	Ch.18, p.1415	IAS 16.76	Ch.18, p.1434
IAS 16.62	Ch.18, p.1416	IAS 16.77	Ch.18, p.1434
IAS 16.62	Ch.41, p.3244	IAS 16.78	Ch.18, p.1436

IAS 16.79	Ch.18, p.1436	IAS 19.11	Ch.35, p.2948
IAS 16.80D	Ch.18, p.1405	IAS 19.13	Ch.41, p.3248
IAS 16.81N	Ch.18, p.1405	IAS 19.13(b)	Ch.35, p.2949
IAS 16.BC19	Ch.18, p.1406	IAS 19.14	Ch.35, p.2948
IAS 16.BC21	Ch.17, p.1311	IAS 19.15	Ch.35, p.2948
IAS 16.BC21	Ch.18, p.1407	IAS 19.16	Ch.35, p.2949
IAS 16.BC22	Ch.11, p.852	IAS 19.17	Ch.35, p.2949
IAS 16.BC23	Ch.18, p.1408	IAS 19.18	Ch.35, p.2949
IAS 16.BC29	Ch.18, p.1410	IAS 19.19	Ch.35, p.2949
IAS 16.BC35C	Ch.27, p.2041	IAS 19.19	Ch.41, p.3246
IAS 16.BC67	Ch.42, p.3293	IAS 19.20	Ch.35, p.2950
IAS 16.BC81	Ch.42, p.3285	IAS 19.21	Ch.34, p.2864
IAS 16.BC82	Ch.42, p.3286	IAS 19.21	Ch.35, p.2950
IAS 16.BC83	Ch.42, p.3277	IAS 19.22	Ch.35, p.2950
		IAS 19.23	Ch.35, p.2950
		IAS 19.24	Ch.35, p.2950

IAS 17

IAS 17.4	Ch.51, p.4044	IAS 19.25	Ch.35, p.2967
		IAS 19.26	Ch.35, p.2894
		IAS 19.27	Ch.35, p.2894
		IAS 19.28	Ch.35, p.2895
		IAS 19.29	Ch.35, p.2894
		IAS 19.29(b)	Ch.35, p.2902

IAS 18

IAS 18.12	Ch.43, p.3449	IAS 19.30	Ch.35, p.2894
IAS 18.16	Ch.5, p.341	IAS 19.30	Ch.35, p.2895
		IAS 19.30	Ch.35, p.2897
		IAS 19.32	Ch.35, p.2898
		IAS 19.33	Ch.35, p.2898

IAS 19

IAS 19.1	Ch.35, p.2891	IAS 19.34	Ch.35, p.2899
IAS 19.2	Ch.35, p.2892	IAS 19.35	Ch.35, p.2898
IAS 19.3	Ch.35, p.2892	IAS 19.36	Ch.35, p.2898
IAS 19.4	Ch.35, p.2892	IAS 19.36	Ch.35, p.2899
IAS 19.5	Ch.35, p.2892	IAS 19.37	Ch.35, p.2899
IAS 19.6	Ch.35, p.2892	IAS 19.37	Ch.35, p.2907
IAS 19.7	Ch.35, p.2892	IAS 19.38	Ch.35, p.2898
IAS 19.8	Ch.34, p.2855	IAS 19.39	Ch.35, p.2900
IAS 19.8	Ch.35, p.2892	IAS 19.40	Ch.35, p.2900
IAS 19.8	Ch.35, p.2894	IAS 19.41	Ch.35, p.2900
IAS 19.8	Ch.35, p.2895	IAS 19.42	Ch.35, p.2901
IAS 19.8	Ch.35, p.2898	IAS 19.43	Ch.35, p.2901
IAS 19.8	Ch.35, p.2908	IAS 19.44	Ch.35, p.2901
IAS 19.8	Ch.35, p.2909	IAS 19.44	Ch.35, p.2902
IAS 19.8	Ch.35, p.2910	IAS 19.45	Ch.35, p.2902
IAS 19.8	Ch.35, p.2912	IAS 19.46	Ch.35, p.2896
IAS 19.8	Ch.35, p.2929	IAS 19.47	Ch.35, p.2896
IAS 19.8	Ch.35, p.2930	IAS 19.48	Ch.35, p.2896
IAS 19.8	Ch.35, p.2941	IAS 19.48	Ch.35, p.2897
IAS 19.8	Ch.35, p.2942	IAS 19.49	Ch.35, p.2896
IAS 19.8	Ch.35, p.2943	IAS 19.50	Ch.35, p.2906
IAS 19.8	Ch.35, p.2945	IAS 19.51	Ch.35, p.2906
IAS 19.8	Ch.35, p.2946	IAS 19.52	Ch.35, p.2906
IAS 19.8	Ch.35, p.2947	IAS 19.53	Ch.35, p.2957
IAS 19.8	Ch.35, p.2951	IAS 19.54	Ch.35, p.2957
IAS 19.8	Ch.35, p.2953	IAS 19.55	Ch.35, p.2907
IAS 19.9	Ch.35, p.2948	IAS 19.56	Ch.35, p.2895
IAS 19.9(a)	Ch.34, p.2855	IAS 19.56	Ch.35, p.2907
IAS 19.10	Ch.35, p.2948	IAS 19.57	Ch.35, p.2908
		IAS 19.58	Ch.35, p.2928
		IAS 19.59	Ch.5, p.372

Standard	Reference	Standard	Reference
IAS 19.59	Ch.35, p.2908	IAS 19.100	Ch.35, p.2941
IAS 19.59	Ch.35, p.2924	IAS 19.101	Ch.35, p.2941
IAS 19.59	Ch.35, p.2928	IAS 19.101A	Ch.35, p.2941
IAS 19.60	Ch.35, p.2908	IAS 19.102	Ch.35, p.2942
IAS 19.60	Ch.35, p.2928	IAS 19.103	Ch.5, p.373
IAS 19.61	Ch.35, p.2912	IAS 19.103	Ch.35, p.2942
IAS 19.62	Ch.35, p.2912	IAS 19.104	Ch.35, p.2942
IAS 19.63	Ch.35, p.2929	IAS 19.105	Ch.35, p.2942
IAS 19.64	Ch.35, p.2930	IAS 19.106	Ch.35, p.2942
IAS 19.65	Ch.35, p.2929	IAS 19.107	Ch.35, p.2942
IAS 19.66	Ch.35, p.2917	IAS 19.108	Ch.35, p.2943
IAS 19.67	Ch.35, p.2917	IAS 19.109	Ch.35, p.2941
IAS 19.67	Ch.35, p.2941	IAS 19.110	Ch.35, p.2941
IAS 19.68	Ch.35, p.2917	IAS 19.111	Ch.35, p.2924
IAS 19.69	Ch.35, p.2924	IAS 19.111	Ch.35, p.2943
IAS 19.70	Ch.35, p.2918	IAS 19.112	Ch.35, p.2943
IAS 19.70	Ch.35, p.2919	IAS 19.113	Ch.35, p.2910
IAS 19.71	Ch.35, p.2918	IAS 19.114	Ch.35, p.2909
IAS 19.71-74	Ch.35, p.2920	IAS 19.115	Ch.35, p.2910
IAS 19.72	Ch.35, p.2918	IAS 19.116-118	Ch.35, p.2910
IAS 19.73	Ch.35, p.2919	IAS 19.119	Ch.35, p.2910
IAS 19.74	Ch.35, p.2922	IAS 19.120	Ch.15, p.1200
IAS 19.75	Ch.35, p.2928	IAS 19.120	Ch.35, p.2940
IAS 19.75-77	Ch.35, p.2923	IAS 19.121	Ch.35, p.2940
IAS 19.76	Ch.15, p.1201	IAS 19.122	Ch.7, p.526
IAS 19.76	Ch.35, p.2922	IAS 19.122	Ch.35, p.2940
IAS 19.76(b)	Ch.35, p.2947	IAS 19.122A	Ch.35, p.2941
IAS 19.78	Ch.35, p.2923	IAS 19.123	Ch.35, p.2945
IAS 19.79	Ch.35, p.2925	IAS 19.123A	Ch.35, p.2945
IAS 19.80	Ch.35, p.2923	IAS 19.124	Ch.35, p.2945
IAS 19.80	Ch.35, p.2928	IAS 19.125	Ch.35, p.2945
IAS 19.81	Ch.35, p.2923	IAS 19.126	Ch.35, p.2945
IAS 19.82	Ch.35, p.2923	IAS 19.127	Ch.35, p.2946
IAS 19.83	Ch.15, p.1201	IAS 19.127(b)	Ch.15, p.1200
IAS 19.83	Ch.26, p.1952	IAS 19.128	Ch.35, p.2924
IAS 19.83	Ch.35, p.2925	IAS 19.128	Ch.35, p.2946
IAS 19.83	Ch.35, p.2926	IAS 19.129	Ch.35, p.2946
IAS 19.83	Ch.35, p.2927	IAS 19.130	Ch.35, p.2946
IAS 19.84	Ch.26, p.1952	IAS 19.130	Ch.35, p.2947
IAS 19.84	Ch.35, p.2924	IAS 19.131	Ch.35, p.2940
IAS 19.85	Ch.35, p.2924	IAS 19.132	Ch.35, p.2939
IAS 19.86	Ch.26, p.1953	IAS 19.133	Ch.3, p.125
IAS 19.86	Ch.35, p.2926	IAS 19.133	Ch.35, p.2939
IAS 19.87	Ch.35, p.2913	IAS 19.134	Ch.35, p.2940
IAS 19.87	Ch.35, p.2923	IAS 19.135	Ch.35, p.2957
IAS 19.87-90	Ch.35, p.2912	IAS 19.136	Ch.35, p.2957
IAS 19.88	Ch.35, p.2913	IAS 19.136	Ch.35, p.2965
IAS 19.89	Ch.35, p.2913	IAS 19.137	Ch.35, p.2958
IAS 19.91	Ch.35, p.2913	IAS 19.137	Ch.35, p.2966
IAS 19.92	Ch.35, p.2913	IAS 19.138	Ch.35, p.2958
IAS 19.93	Ch.35, p.2913	IAS 19.139	Ch.35, p.2958
IAS 19.93	Ch.35, p.2914	IAS 19.140	Ch.35, p.2959
IAS 19.94	Ch.35, p.2916	IAS 19.141	Ch.35, p.2959
IAS 19.95	Ch.35, p.2913	IAS 19.142	Ch.35, p.2961
IAS 19.96-97	Ch.35, p.2923	IAS 19.142	Ch.35, p.2966
IAS 19.97	Ch.35, p.2923	IAS 19.143	Ch.35, p.2961
IAS 19.98	Ch.35, p.2923	IAS 19.143	Ch.35, p.2967
IAS 19.99	Ch.35, p.2941	IAS 19.143	Ch.47, p.3742

IAS 19.144 ... Ch.35, p.2962
IAS 19.145 ... Ch.5, p.372
IAS 19.145 ... Ch.35, p.2963
IAS 19.146 ... Ch.35, p.2963
IAS 19.147 ... Ch.35, p.2963
IAS 19.148 ... Ch.35, p.2964
IAS 19.149 ... Ch.35, p.2965
IAS 19.150 ... Ch.35, p.2967
IAS 19.151 ... Ch.35, p.2967
IAS 19.152 ... Ch.35, p.2967
IAS 19.153 ... Ch.35, p.2951
IAS 19.154 ... Ch.35, p.2951
IAS 19.154 ... Ch.35, p.2953
IAS 19.155-156 ... Ch.35, p.2951
IAS 19.157 ... Ch.35, p.2952
IAS 19.158 ... Ch.35, p.2967
IAS 19.159 ... Ch.35, p.2954
IAS 19.160 ... Ch.35, p.2954
IAS 19.161 ... Ch.35, p.2954
IAS 19.162 ... Ch.35, p.2954
IAS 19.163 ... Ch.35, p.2954
IAS 19.164 ... Ch.35, p.2955
IAS 19.165 ... Ch.35, p.2955
IAS 19.165(b) ... Ch.41, p.3207
IAS 19.166 ... Ch.35, p.2955
IAS 19.167 ... Ch.35, p.2955
IAS 19.168 ... Ch.35, p.2955
IAS 19.169 ... Ch.35, p.2956
IAS 19.170 ... Ch.35, p.2956
IAS 19.171 ... Ch.35, p.2967
IAS 19.BC29 ... Ch.35, p.2895
IAS 19.BC48-49 ... Ch.35, p.2901
IAS 19.BC127 ... Ch.35, p.2947
IAS 19.BC130 ... Ch.35, p.2928
IAS 19.BC200 ... Ch.3, p.125
IAS 19.BC200 ... Ch.35, p.2939
IAS 19.BC207 ... Ch.35, p.2957
IAS 19.BC209 ... Ch.35, p.2957
IAS 19.BC253 ... Ch.35, p.2904

IAS 20

IAS 20.1 ... Ch.24, p.1826
IAS 20.2 ... Ch.24, p.1827
IAS 20.2 ... Ch.33, p.2462
IAS 20.2(b) ... Ch.24, p.1828
IAS 20.2(d) ... Ch.24, p.1823
IAS 20.3 ... Ch.24, p.1823
IAS 20.3 ... Ch.24, p.1825
IAS 20.3 ... Ch.24, p.1826
IAS 20.3 ... Ch.24, p.1830
IAS 20.3 ... Ch.24, p.1831
IAS 20.3 ... Ch.25, p.1854
IAS 20.4 ... Ch.24, p.1824
IAS 20.4 ... Ch.24, p.1826
IAS 20.5 ... Ch.24, p.1824
IAS 20.6 ... Ch.24, p.1823
IAS 20.6 ... Ch.24, p.1825
IAS 20.7 ... Ch.24, p.1830
IAS 20.7 ... Ch.24, p.1843
IAS 20.8 ... Ch.24, p.1830
IAS 20.9 ... Ch.24, p.1824
IAS 20.9 ... Ch.24, p.1830
IAS 20.10 ... Ch.24, p.1831
IAS 20.10A ... Ch.5, p.265
IAS 20.10A ... Ch.24, p.1823
IAS 20.10A ... Ch.24, p.1827
IAS 20.10A ... Ch.24, p.1832
IAS 20.10A ... Ch.24, p.1833
IAS 20.10A ... Ch.24, p.1836
IAS 20.10A ... Ch.49, p.3855
IAS 20.11 ... Ch.24, p.1830
IAS 20.12 ... Ch.24, p.1824
IAS 20.12 ... Ch.24, p.1832
IAS 20.12 ... Ch.24, p.1834
IAS 20.12 ... Ch.24, p.1836
IAS 20.13 ... Ch.24, p.1834
IAS 20.15 ... Ch.24, p.1834
IAS 20.16 ... Ch.24, p.1834
IAS 20.16 ... Ch.24, p.1835
IAS 20.16 ... Ch.24, p.1836
IAS 20.17 ... Ch.24, p.1824
IAS 20.17 ... Ch.24, p.1834
IAS 20.17 ... Ch.24, p.1835
IAS 20.18 ... Ch.24, p.1835
IAS 20.19 ... Ch.24, p.1835
IAS 20.19 ... Ch.24, p.1837
IAS 20.20 ... Ch.24, p.1837
IAS 20.20-22 ... Ch.24, p.1835
IAS 20.23 ... Ch.17, p.1310
IAS 20.23 ... Ch.17, p.1361
IAS 20.23 ... Ch.17, p.1367
IAS 20.23 ... Ch.24, p.1825
IAS 20.23 ... Ch.24, p.1830
IAS 20.24 ... Ch.24, p.1840
IAS 20.25 ... Ch.24, p.1840
IAS 20.26 ... Ch.24, p.1840
IAS 20.27 ... Ch.24, p.1840
IAS 20.28 ... Ch.24, p.1842
IAS 20.28 ... Ch.40, p.3164
IAS 20.29 ... Ch.17, p.1367
IAS 20.29 ... Ch.24, p.1840
IAS 20.30 ... Ch.24, p.1841
IAS 20.31 ... Ch.24, p.1841
IAS 20.32 ... Ch.24, p.1838
IAS 20.33 ... Ch.24, p.1838
IAS 20.34 ... Ch.24, p.1824
IAS 20.34 ... Ch.24, p.1826
IAS 20.34 ... Ch.24, p.1838
IAS 20.35 ... Ch.24, p.1824
IAS 20.35 ... Ch.24, p.1826
IAS 20.35 ... Ch.24, p.1834
IAS 20.35 ... Ch.24, p.1839
IAS 20.36 ... Ch.24, p.1824
IAS 20.36 ... Ch.24, p.1839

Index of standards   85

IAS 20.38	Ch.24, p.1826
IAS 20.38	Ch.24, p.1839
IAS 20.39	Ch.24, p.1843
IAS 20.39(b)	Ch.24, p.1834
IAS 20.39(b)	Ch.24, p.1839
IAS 20.39(b)	Ch.24, p.1845
IAS 20.41	Ch.24, p.1823
IAS 20.41	Ch.24, p.1838
IAS 20.43	Ch.24, p.1823
IAS 20.45	Ch.24, p.1830

IAS 21

IAS 21.1	Ch.15, p.1180
IAS 21.2	Ch.15, p.1180
IAS 21.3	Ch.15, p.1180
IAS 21.4	Ch.15, p.1181
IAS 21.5	Ch.15, p.1181
IAS 21.6	Ch.15, p.1181
IAS 21.7	Ch.15, p.1181
IAS 21.7	Ch.40, p.3165
IAS 21.8	Ch.15, p.1181
IAS 21.8	Ch.15, p.1196
IAS 21.8	Ch.15, p.1217
IAS 21.8	Ch.16, p.1258
IAS 21.8	Ch.26, p.1959
IAS 21.8	Ch.53, p.4307
IAS 21.8-14	Ch.5, p.373
IAS 21.9	Ch.15, p.1182
IAS 21.9	Ch.15, p.1183
IAS 21.9	Ch.43, p.3422
IAS 21.10	Ch.15, p.1183
IAS 21.10	Ch.43, p.3422
IAS 21.11	Ch.5, p.373
IAS 21.11	Ch.15, p.1183
IAS 21.11	Ch.43, p.3422
IAS 21.12	Ch.15, p.1183
IAS 21.12	Ch.43, p.3422
IAS 21.13	Ch.15, p.1184
IAS 21.14	Ch.16, p.1254
IAS 21.14	Ch.16, p.1277
IAS 21.15	Ch.15, p.1217
IAS 21.15	Ch.53, p.4269
IAS 21.15A	Ch.15, p.1220
IAS 21.16	Ch.15, p.1196
IAS 21.16	Ch.15, p.1197
IAS 21.16	Ch.16, p.1258
IAS 21.17	Ch.15, p.1182
IAS 21.18	Ch.15, p.1182
IAS 21.18	Ch.15, p.1204
IAS 21.19	Ch.15, p.1182
IAS 21.20	Ch.15, p.1187
IAS 21.21	Ch.5, p.333
IAS 21.21	Ch.5, p.373
IAS 21.21	Ch.15, p.1188
IAS 21.21	Ch.26, p.1959
IAS 21.21	Ch.53, p.4261
IAS 21.22	Ch.15, p.1188
IAS 21.22	Ch.15, p.1190
IAS 21.23	Ch.5, p.333
IAS 21.23	Ch.5, p.373
IAS 21.23	Ch.15, p.1193
IAS 21.23	Ch.26, p.1959
IAS 21.23	Ch.50, p.3899
IAS 21.23	Ch.53, p.4325
IAS 21.23(a)	Ch.53, p.4322
IAS 21.24	Ch.15, p.1193
IAS 21.25	Ch.15, p.1193
IAS 21.25	Ch.20, p.1558
IAS 21.26	Ch.15, p.1191
IAS 21.26	Ch.15, p.1192
IAS 21.27	Ch.15, p.1181
IAS 21.28	Ch.15, p.1194
IAS 21.28	Ch.26, p.1959
IAS 21.29	Ch.15, p.1194
IAS 21.30	Ch.15, p.1195
IAS 21.30	Ch.15, p.1196
IAS 21.31	Ch.15, p.1195
IAS 21.32	Ch.5, p.304
IAS 21.32	Ch.15, p.1194
IAS 21.32	Ch.15, p.1217
IAS 21.32	Ch.15, p.1219
IAS 21.33	Ch.15, p.1219
IAS 21.33	Ch.15, p.1220
IAS 21.34	Ch.15, p.1204
IAS 21.35	Ch.15, p.1202
IAS 21.36	Ch.15, p.1202
IAS 21.36	Ch.43, p.3425
IAS 21.37	Ch.15, p.1202
IAS 21.38	Ch.7, p.500
IAS 21.38	Ch.15, p.1204
IAS 21.38	Ch.16, p.1277
IAS 21.39	Ch.5, p.304
IAS 21.39	Ch.15, p.1205
IAS 21.39	Ch.16, p.1264
IAS 21.39	Ch.16, p.1278
IAS 21.39(b)	Ch.15, p.1216
IAS 21.39(b)	Ch.53, p.4261
IAS 21.40	Ch.15, p.1206
IAS 21.40	Ch.15, p.1212
IAS 21.41	Ch.15, p.1206
IAS 21.41	Ch.15, p.1208
IAS 21.41	Ch.15, p.1216
IAS 21.41	Ch.16, p.1278
IAS 21.41	Ch.16, p.1279
IAS 21.42	Ch.15, p.1209
IAS 21.42	Ch.16, p.1264
IAS 21.42	Ch.16, p.1277
IAS 21.42	Ch.16, p.1278
IAS 21.42(b)	Ch.16, p.1280
IAS 21.42(b)	Ch.16, p.1281
IAS 21.43	Ch.15, p.1209
IAS 21.43	Ch.15, p.1210
IAS 21.43	Ch.16, p.1277
IAS 21.43	Ch.16, p.1279

IAS 21.44	Ch.15, p.1204	IAS 23.4	Ch.22, p.1686
IAS 21.44	Ch.53, p.4307	IAS 23.4(a)	Ch.21, p.1647
IAS 21.45	Ch.15, p.1216	IAS 23.4(b)	Ch.21, p.1646
IAS 21.45	Ch.15, p.1217	IAS 23.4(b)	Ch.29, p.2204
IAS 21.45	Ch.15, p.1223	IAS 23.5	Ch.21, p.1646
IAS 21.46	Ch.7, p.503	IAS 23.5	Ch.21, p.1649
IAS 21.46	Ch.15, p.1225	IAS 23.5	Ch.43, p.3370
IAS 21.47	Ch.5, p.282	IAS 23.5-6	Ch.29, p.2204
IAS 21.47	Ch.15, p.1226	IAS 23.6	Ch.15, p.1195
IAS 21.48	Ch.5, p.304	IAS 23.6	Ch.21, p.1649
IAS 21.48	Ch.11, p.873	IAS 23.6(e)	Ch.21, p.1650
IAS 21.48	Ch.15, p.1227	IAS 23.6(e)	Ch.21, p.1657
IAS 21.48	Ch.53, p.4364	IAS 23.7	Ch.21, p.1646
IAS 21.48-48B	Ch.7, p.527	IAS 23.7	Ch.21, p.1648
IAS 21.48A	Ch.11, p.871	IAS 23.7	Ch.22, p.1686
IAS 21.48A	Ch.15, p.1229	IAS 23.7	Ch.29, p.2204
IAS 21.48B	Ch.7, p.534	IAS 23.7	Ch.29, p.2205
IAS 21.48B	Ch.15, p.1229	IAS 23.8	Ch.21, p.1645
IAS 21.48C	Ch.7, p.534	IAS 23.8	Ch.21, p.1650
IAS 21.48C	Ch.11, p.872	IAS 23.8	Ch.21, p.1651
IAS 21.48C	Ch.15, p.1230	IAS 23.8	Ch.22, p.1686
IAS 21.48C	Ch.15, p.1231	IAS 23.8	Ch.29, p.2204
IAS 21.48D	Ch.15, p.1230	IAS 23.8	Ch.43, p.3370
IAS 21.49	Ch.15, p.1228	IAS 23.9	Ch.21, p.1650
IAS 21.49	Ch.15, p.1230	IAS 23.9	Ch.21, p.1651
IAS 21.50	Ch.15, p.1242	IAS 23.9	Ch.21, p.1663
IAS 21.51	Ch.15, p.1243	IAS 23.9	Ch.21, p.1665
IAS 21.52	Ch.15, p.1242	IAS 23.9	Ch.43, p.3370
IAS 21.52	Ch.15, p.1243	IAS 23.10	Ch.21, p.1651
IAS 21.52	Ch.15, p.1244	IAS 23.10	Ch.21, p.1661
IAS 21.52(a)	Ch.54, p.4486	IAS 23.11	Ch.21, p.1651
IAS 21.53	Ch.15, p.1243	IAS 23.12	Ch.21, p.1651
IAS 21.54	Ch.15, p.1243	IAS 23.12	Ch.41, p.3245
IAS 21.55	Ch.15, p.1243	IAS 23.13	Ch.21, p.1651
IAS 21.56	Ch.15, p.1243	IAS 23.14	Ch.21, p.1652
IAS 21.57	Ch.15, p.1243	IAS 23.14	Ch.41, p.3245
IAS 21.BC6	Ch.15, p.1183	IAS 23.15	Ch.21, p.1652
IAS 21.BC17	Ch.15, p.1208	IAS 23.16	Ch.5, p.320
IAS 21.BC18	Ch.7, p.500	IAS 23.16	Ch.21, p.1669
IAS 21.BC18	Ch.15, p.1209	IAS 23.17	Ch.21, p.1664
IAS 21.BC18	Ch.15, p.1214	IAS 23.18	Ch.21, p.1652
IAS 21.BC19	Ch.15, p.1209	IAS 23.18	Ch.21, p.1656
IAS 21.BC20	Ch.15, p.1208	IAS 23.18	Ch.21, p.1665
IAS 21.BC27	Ch.15, p.1225	IAS 23.19	Ch.21, p.1665
IAS 21.BC30	Ch.15, p.1226	IAS 23.20	Ch.21, p.1668
IAS 21.BC31	Ch.15, p.1226	IAS 23.21	Ch.21, p.1668
IAS 21.BC32	Ch.15, p.1226	IAS 23.22	Ch.21, p.1669
IAS 21.BC33-34	Ch.11, p.872	IAS 23.23	Ch.21, p.1669
IAS 21.BC35	Ch.15, p.1230	IAS 23.24	Ch.21, p.1669
		IAS 23.25	Ch.21, p.1669
		IAS 23.25	Ch.21, p.1670
		IAS 23.26	Ch.5, p.320

IAS 23

		IAS 23.26	Ch.21, p.1671
IAS 23.1	Ch.21, p.1645	IAS 23.29	Ch.21, p.1645
IAS 23.2	Ch.21, p.1646	IAS 23.BC2	Ch.21, p.1645
IAS 23.3	Ch.21, p.1646	IAS 23.BC6	Ch.21, p.1646
IAS 23.3	Ch.21, p.1663	IAS 23.BC6	Ch.21, p.1647
IAS 23.4	Ch.21, p.1646	IAS 23.BC14B	Ch.21, p.1653

IAS 23.BC14C	Ch.21, p.1653
IAS 23.BC14D	Ch.21, p.1653
IAS 23.BC14E	Ch.21, p.1654
IAS 23.BC21	Ch.21, p.1661
IAS 23.BC22	Ch.11, p.828

IAS 24

IAS 24.1	Ch.39, p.3098
IAS 24.2	Ch.39, p.3098
IAS 24.3	Ch.39, p.3099
IAS 24.4	Ch.39, p.3099
IAS 24.5	Ch.39, p.3097
IAS 24.6-7	Ch.39, p.3097
IAS 24.8	Ch.39, p.3098
IAS 24.9	Ch.10, p.769
IAS 24.9	Ch.39, p.3099
IAS 24.9	Ch.39, p.3100
IAS 24.9	Ch.39, p.3103
IAS 24.9	Ch.39, p.3108
IAS 24.9	Ch.39, p.3110
IAS 24.9	Ch.39, p.3114
IAS 24.9	Ch.39, p.3116
IAS 24.9	Ch.39, p.3117
IAS 24.9(b)	Ch.39, p.3104
IAS 24.9(b)	Ch.39, p.3105
IAS 24.9(b)	Ch.39, p.3107
IAS 24.9(b)	Ch.39, p.3108
IAS 24.9(b)	Ch.39, p.3109
IAS 24.9(b)	Ch.39, p.3110
IAS 24.10	Ch.39, p.3100
IAS 24.11	Ch.39, p.3111
IAS 24.12	Ch.39, p.3102
IAS 24.12	Ch.39, p.3105
IAS 24.12	Ch.39, p.3107
IAS 24.13	Ch.39, p.3112
IAS 24.14	Ch.39, p.3112
IAS 24.15	Ch.39, p.3114
IAS 24.16	Ch.39, p.3113
IAS 24.17	Ch.39, p.3116
IAS 24.17A	Ch.39, p.3104
IAS 24.17A	Ch.39, p.3110
IAS 24.17A	Ch.39, p.3116
IAS 24.18	Ch.13, p.977
IAS 24.18	Ch.39, p.3120
IAS 24.18	Ch.39, p.3123
IAS 24.18	Ch.51, p.4050
IAS 24.18A	Ch.39, p.3104
IAS 24.18A	Ch.39, p.3127
IAS 24.18-19	Ch.13, p.977
IAS 24.19	Ch.39, p.3124
IAS 24.20	Ch.39, p.3124
IAS 24.21	Ch.39, p.3121
IAS 24.21	Ch.51, p.4050
IAS 24.22	Ch.39, p.3121
IAS 24.23	Ch.39, p.3124
IAS 24.24	Ch.39, p.3122
IAS 24.25	Ch.39, p.3127
IAS 24.26	Ch.39, p.3128
IAS 24.27	Ch.39, p.3129
IAS 24.BC10	Ch.39, p.3117
IAS 24.BC16-17	Ch.39, p.3099
IAS 24.BC19(a)	Ch.39, p.3107
IAS 24.BC41	Ch.39, p.3111
IAS 24.BC45	Ch.39, p.3129
IAS 24.BC46	Ch.39, p.3129
IAS 24.BC47-48	Ch.39, p.3129

IAS 27

IAS 27.2	Ch.6, p.395
IAS 27.2	Ch.8, p.575
IAS 27.3	Ch.8, p.575
IAS 27.4	Ch.8, p.575
IAS 27.7	Ch.8, p.575
IAS 27.7	Ch.8, p.577
IAS 27.7	Ch.13, p.953
IAS 27.8	Ch.6, p.395
IAS 27.8	Ch.6, p.400
IAS 27.8	Ch.8, p.578
IAS 27.8A	Ch.6, p.487
IAS 27.8A	Ch.8, p.576
IAS 27.8A	Ch.8, p.578
IAS 27.10	Ch.8, p.583
IAS 27.10	Ch.11, p.813
IAS 27.10	Ch.11, p.881
IAS 27.10	Ch.12, p.930
IAS 27.10	Ch.20, p.1625
IAS 27.10	Ch.45, p.3592
IAS 27.10	Ch.53, p.4307
IAS 27.10(a)	Ch.20, p.1625
IAS 27.10(c)	Ch.33, p.2533
IAS 27.11	Ch.8, p.583
IAS 27.11	Ch.11, p.881
IAS 27.11	Ch.12, p.930
IAS 27.11	Ch.45, p.3592
IAS 27.11A	Ch.6, p.487
IAS 27.11A	Ch.8, p.578
IAS 27.11A	Ch.8, p.583
IAS 27.11B	Ch.8, p.584
IAS 27.11B(a)	Ch.6, p.489
IAS 27.11B(b)	Ch.6, p.488
IAS 27.12	Ch.8, p.584
IAS 27.12	Ch.8, p.599
IAS 27.12	Ch.11, p.882
IAS 27.12	Ch.33, p.2533
IAS 27.12	Ch.38, p.3082
IAS 27.13	Ch.8, p.591
IAS 27.13	Ch.8, p.594
IAS 27.13(b)	Ch.8, p.593
IAS 27.13(c)	Ch.8, p.592
IAS 27.14	Ch.8, p.591
IAS 27.15	Ch.8, p.604
IAS 27.16	Ch.8, p.604

IAS 27.16(a)	Ch.6, p.397	IAS 28.19	Ch.11, p.821
IAS 27.16A	Ch.8, p.578	IAS 28.19	Ch.45, p.3592
IAS 27.16A	Ch.8, p.605	IAS 28.20	Ch.4, p.197
IAS 27.17	Ch.8, p.581	IAS 28.20	Ch.11, p.824
IAS 27.17	Ch.8, p.582	IAS 28.20	Ch.11, p.870
IAS 27.17	Ch.8, p.605	IAS 28.20	Ch.12, p.892
IAS 27.17	Ch.8, p.606	IAS 28.20	Ch.12, p.935
IAS 27.BC10D	Ch.8, p.579	IAS 28.21	Ch.4, p.197
IAS 27.BC24(a)	Ch.8, p.592	IAS 28.21	Ch.4, p.212
IAS 27.BC24(b)	Ch.8, p.592	IAS 28.21	Ch.11, p.824
IAS 27.BC25	Ch.8, p.594	IAS 28.21	Ch.12, p.935
IAS 27.BC27	Ch.8, p.591	IAS 28.22	Ch.11, p.870
		IAS 28.22	Ch.11, p.871
		IAS 28.22	Ch.12, p.935

IAS 28

		IAS 28.23	Ch.11, p.871
		IAS 28.23	Ch.12, p.935
IAS 28.1	Ch.11, p.813	IAS 28.24	Ch.11, p.837
IAS 28.2	Ch.8, p.579	IAS 28.24	Ch.11, p.870
IAS 28.2	Ch.9, p.722	IAS 28.24	Ch.11, p.872
IAS 28.2	Ch.11, p.814	IAS 28.24	Ch.12, p.934
IAS 28.3	Ch.6, p.409	IAS 28.25	Ch.11, p.872
IAS 28.3	Ch.11, p.814	IAS 28.25	Ch.12, p.934
IAS 28.3	Ch.11, p.824	IAS 28.25	Ch.15, p.1231
IAS 28.3	Ch.11, p.828	IAS 28.26	Ch.10, p.797
IAS 28.3	Ch.11, p.868	IAS 28.26	Ch.11, p.827
IAS 28.3	Ch.11, p.874	IAS 28.26	Ch.11, p.830
IAS 28.3	Ch.13, p.952	IAS 28.26	Ch.11, p.846
IAS 28.3	Ch.34, p.2843	IAS 28.26	Ch.11, p.847
IAS 28.3	Ch.39, p.3102	IAS 28.26	Ch.11, p.885
IAS 28.3	Ch.39, p.3105	IAS 28.27	Ch.11, p.839
IAS 28.4	Ch.11, p.814	IAS 28.27	Ch.11, p.840
IAS 28.4	Ch.11, p.881	IAS 28.27	Ch.11, p.868
IAS 28.5	Ch.11, p.815	IAS 28.28	Ch.7, p.514
IAS 28.5	Ch.11, p.816	IAS 28.28	Ch.7, p.515
IAS 28.5	Ch.55, p.4604	IAS 28.28	Ch.11, p.841
IAS 28.6	Ch.11, p.815	IAS 28.28-31	Ch.7, p.515
IAS 28.7	Ch.11, p.817	IAS 28.29	Ch.7, p.515
IAS 28.8	Ch.11, p.817	IAS 28.29	Ch.11, p.843
IAS 28.9	Ch.11, p.815	IAS 28.29	Ch.11, p.846
IAS 28.10	Ch.11, p.825	IAS 28.30	Ch.7, p.514
IAS 28.10	Ch.11, p.828	IAS 28.30	Ch.11, p.851
IAS 28.10	Ch.11, p.863	IAS 28.30	Ch.11, p.854
IAS 28.10	Ch.11, p.865	IAS 28.31	Ch.11, p.851
IAS 28.10	Ch.11, p.884	IAS 28.31A	Ch.11, p.857
IAS 28.11	Ch.11, p.826	IAS 28.31B	Ch.11, p.858
IAS 28.12	Ch.11, p.838	IAS 28.32	Ch.10, p.798
IAS 28.13	Ch.11, p.838	IAS 28.32	Ch.11, p.825
IAS 28.14	Ch.11, p.838	IAS 28.32	Ch.11, p.830
IAS 28.14A	Ch.11, p.878	IAS 28.32	Ch.11, p.854
IAS 28.14A	Ch.45, p.3592	IAS 28.32	Ch.11, p.883
IAS 28.15	Ch.11, p.882	IAS 28.32	Ch.20, p.1629
IAS 28.16	Ch.11, p.818	IAS 28.33	Ch.11, p.859
IAS 28.17	Ch.11, p.818	IAS 28.34	Ch.11, p.860
IAS 28.17	Ch.11, p.819	IAS 28.35	Ch.11, p.860
IAS 28.18	Ch.8, p.577	IAS 28.35-36	Ch.5, p.335
IAS 28.18	Ch.11, p.819	IAS 28.36	Ch.11, p.860
IAS 28.18	Ch.11, p.821	IAS 28.36A	Ch.11, p.820
IAS 28.18	Ch.45, p.3592	IAS 28.36A	Ch.11, p.861

IAS 28.37	Ch.11, p.838
IAS 28.37	Ch.11, p.865
IAS 28.38	Ch.11, p.846
IAS 28.38	Ch.11, p.862
IAS 28.38	Ch.11, p.882
IAS 28.39	Ch.11, p.862
IAS 28.40	Ch.11, p.876
IAS 28.40	Ch.11, p.877
IAS 28.40	Ch.11, p.884
IAS 28.40-41A	Ch.20, p.1627
IAS 28.40-43	Ch.20, p.1629
IAS 28.41A	Ch.11, p.877
IAS 28.41A	Ch.20, p.1627
IAS 28.41A	Ch.20, p.1628
IAS 28.41B	Ch.11, p.877
IAS 28.41C	Ch.11, p.878
IAS 28.42	Ch.11, p.874
IAS 28.42	Ch.11, p.878
IAS 28.42	Ch.20, p.1521
IAS 28.42	Ch.20, p.1626
IAS 28.42	Ch.20, p.1629
IAS 28.43	Ch.11, p.877
IAS 28.43	Ch.20, p.1628
IAS 28.44	Ch.8, p.579
IAS 28.44	Ch.11, p.881
IAS 28.44	Ch.45, p.3592
IAS 28.45C	Ch.7, p.514
IAS 28.45C	Ch.7, p.565
IAS 28.45G	Ch.11, p.878
IAS 28.45G	Ch.45, p.3592
IAS 28.45I	Ch.45, p.3592
IAS 28.BC12	Ch.11, p.820
IAS 28.BC13	Ch.11, p.820
IAS 28.BC16	Ch.11, p.817
IAS 28.BCZ18	Ch.11, p.815
IAS 28.BCZ19	Ch.11, p.860
IAS 28.BC22	Ch.11, p.822
IAS 28.BC23-27	Ch.11, p.824
IAS 28.BC30	Ch.12, p.934
IAS 28.BC37J	Ch.7, p.514
IAS 28.BC37J	Ch.7, p.565
IAS 28.BCZ39-40	Ch.11, p.862

IAS 29

IAS 29.1	Ch.16, p.1254
IAS 29.2	Ch.16, p.1253
IAS 29.3	Ch.16, p.1255
IAS 29.4	Ch.16, p.1255
IAS 29.4	Ch.41, p.3258
IAS 29.7	Ch.16, p.1282
IAS 29.8	Ch.16, p.1274
IAS 29.8-9	Ch.16, p.1253
IAS 29.10	Ch.16, p.1254
IAS 29.10	Ch.16, p.1260
IAS 29.11	Ch.16, p.1253
IAS 29.12	Ch.16, p.1258

IAS 29.13	Ch.16, p.1259
IAS 29.14	Ch.16, p.1260
IAS 29.15	Ch.16, p.1260
IAS 29.15	Ch.16, p.1263
IAS 29.16	Ch.16, p.1261
IAS 29.17	Ch.16, p.1256
IAS 29.18	Ch.16, p.1260
IAS 29.19	Ch.16, p.1257
IAS 29.19	Ch.16, p.1261
IAS 29.19	Ch.16, p.1262
IAS 29.19	Ch.16, p.1263
IAS 29.20	Ch.16, p.1263
IAS 29.20	Ch.16, p.1264
IAS 29.21	Ch.16, p.1261
IAS 29.21	Ch.16, p.1262
IAS 29.21	Ch.21, p.1663
IAS 29.22	Ch.16, p.1261
IAS 29.24	Ch.16, p.1266
IAS 29.25	Ch.16, p.1266
IAS 29.25	Ch.16, p.1279
IAS 29.26	Ch.16, p.1268
IAS 29.26	Ch.16, p.1269
IAS 29.27	Ch.16, p.1270
IAS 29.28	Ch.16, p.1259
IAS 29.28	Ch.16, p.1269
IAS 29.28	Ch.16, p.1270
IAS 29.29	Ch.16, p.1260
IAS 29.30	Ch.16, p.1268
IAS 29.31	Ch.16, p.1270
IAS 29.32	Ch.16, p.1266
IAS 29.33	Ch.16, p.1272
IAS 29.34	Ch.16, p.1273
IAS 29.35	Ch.16, p.1264
IAS 29.36	Ch.16, p.1264
IAS 29.37	Ch.16, p.1256
IAS 29.38	Ch.16, p.1275
IAS 29.38	Ch.41, p.3259
IAS 29.39	Ch.16, p.1281

IAS 32

IAS 32.2	Ch.44, p.3577
IAS 32.2	Ch.47, p.3665
IAS 32.3	Ch.47, p.3665
IAS 32.4	Ch.45, p.3591
IAS 32.4(a)	Ch.45, p.3592
IAS 32.4(a)	Ch.45, p.3593
IAS 32.4(b)	Ch.45, p.3605
IAS 32.4(d)	Ch.45, p.3593
IAS 32.4(d)	Ch.45, p.3598
IAS 32.4(e)	Ch.45, p.3594
IAS 32.4(f)(i)	Ch.45, p.3605
IAS 32.4(f)(ii)	Ch.45, p.3605
IAS 32.8	Ch.43, p.3456
IAS 32.8	Ch.43, p.3473
IAS 32.8	Ch.45, p.3607
IAS 32.8	Ch.45, p.3608

IAS 32.9	Ch.43, p.3473
IAS 32.9	Ch.43, p.3474
IAS 32.9	Ch.45, p.3608
IAS 32.9	Ch.45, p.3609
IAS 32.9(b)	Ch.43, p.3457
IAS 32.9(c)	Ch.43, p.3457
IAS 32.10	Ch.45, p.3610
IAS 32.11	Ch.7, p.540
IAS 32.11	Ch.9, p.705
IAS 32.11	Ch.26, p.2007
IAS 32.11	Ch.37, p.3023
IAS 32.11	Ch.43, p.3400
IAS 32.11	Ch.43, p.3454
IAS 32.11	Ch.45, p.3585
IAS 32.11	Ch.47, p.3665
IAS 32.11	Ch.47, p.3666
IAS 32.11	Ch.47, p.3667
IAS 32.11	Ch.47, p.3709
IAS 32.11	Ch.51, p.4046
IAS 32.11	Ch.52, p.4087
IAS 32.11	Ch.52, p.4088
IAS 32.11	Ch.55, p.4569
IAS 32.11(b)(i)	Ch.47, p.3731
IAS 32.11(b)(i)	Ch.47, p.3733
IAS 32.11(b)(ii)	Ch.47, p.3705
IAS 32.13	Ch.45, p.3585
IAS 32.13	Ch.47, p.3667
IAS 32.14	Ch.45, p.3585
IAS 32.14	Ch.47, p.3667
IAS 32.15	Ch.5, p.314
IAS 32.15	Ch.47, p.3668
IAS 32.15	Ch.47, p.3731
IAS 32.16	Ch.47, p.3668
IAS 32.16	Ch.47, p.3669
IAS 32.16(a)	Ch.43, p.3454
IAS 32.16b(i)	Ch.47, p.3737
IAS 32.16b(ii)	Ch.47, p.3737
IAS 32.16A	Ch.7, p.546
IAS 32.16A	Ch.47, p.3687
IAS 32.16A-16B	Ch.34, p.2661
IAS 32.16A-16B	Ch.47, p.3686
IAS 32.16B	Ch.7, p.546
IAS 32.16B	Ch.47, p.3687
IAS 32.16C	Ch.7, p.546
IAS 32.16C	Ch.47, p.3688
IAS 32.16C-16D	Ch.47, p.3688
IAS 32.16D	Ch.7, p.546
IAS 32.16D	Ch.47, p.3688
IAS 32.16E	Ch.47, p.3693
IAS 32.16F(a)	Ch.47, p.3693
IAS 32.16F(b)	Ch.47, p.3693
IAS 32.17	Ch.47, p.3669
IAS 32.18	Ch.47, p.3670
IAS 32.18(a)	Ch.47, p.3679
IAS 32.18(b)	Ch.47, p.3686
IAS 32.19	Ch.47, p.3670
IAS 32.20	Ch.47, p.3672
IAS 32.20	Ch.47, p.3709
IAS 32.20(a)	Ch.24, p.1831
IAS 32.21	Ch.47, p.3678
IAS 32.21	Ch.47, p.3707
IAS 32.22	Ch.47, p.3677
IAS 32.22	Ch.47, p.3678
IAS 32.22	Ch.47, p.3703
IAS 32.22	Ch.47, p.3720
IAS 32.22A	Ch.47, p.3677
IAS 32.22A	Ch.47, p.3703
IAS 32.22A	Ch.47, p.3711
IAS 32.22A	Ch.47, p.3714
IAS 32.23	Ch.7, p.552
IAS 32.23	Ch.7, p.555
IAS 32.23	Ch.47, p.3678
IAS 32.23	Ch.47, p.3711
IAS 32.23	Ch.47, p.3712
IAS 32.24	Ch.47, p.3678
IAS 32.24	Ch.47, p.3707
IAS 32.25	Ch.17, p.1308
IAS 32.25	Ch.18, p.1403
IAS 32.25	Ch.43, p.3419
IAS 32.25	Ch.47, p.3673
IAS 32.26	Ch.47, p.3705
IAS 32.26	Ch.47, p.3710
IAS 32.27	Ch.47, p.3710
IAS 32.28	Ch.5, p.314
IAS 32.28	Ch.47, p.3715
IAS 32.28	Ch.47, p.3716
IAS 32.29	Ch.47, p.3715
IAS 32.29	Ch.47, p.3716
IAS 32.30	Ch.47, p.3719
IAS 32.31	Ch.47, p.3717
IAS 32.31	Ch.47, p.3726
IAS 32.31-32	Ch.47, p.3717
IAS 32.33	Ch.40, p.3160
IAS 32.33	Ch.47, p.3742
IAS 32.33	Ch.47, p.3743
IAS 32.33A	Ch.47, p.3744
IAS 32.34	Ch.47, p.3743
IAS 32.34	Ch.54, p.4491
IAS 32.34	Ch.54, p.4518
IAS 32.35	Ch.7, p.538
IAS 32.35	Ch.40, p.3161
IAS 32.35	Ch.47, p.3739
IAS 32.35A	Ch.47, p.3742
IAS 32.36	Ch.47, p.3664
IAS 32.36	Ch.47, p.3740
IAS 32.37	Ch.7, p.538
IAS 32.37	Ch.47, p.3740
IAS 32.38	Ch.47, p.3741
IAS 32.38	Ch.49, p.3859
IAS 32.39	Ch.54, p.4491
IAS 32.40	Ch.47, p.3740
IAS 32.40	Ch.54, p.4486
IAS 32.41	Ch.47, p.3740
IAS 32.41	Ch.54, p.4488
IAS 32.42	Ch.14, p.1090
IAS 32.42	Ch.26, p.1991

IAS 32.42	Ch.40, p.3143	IAS 32.AG22	Ch.45, p.3588
IAS 32.42	Ch.43, p.3409	IAS 32.AG23	Ch.45, p.3589
IAS 32.42	Ch.52, p.4151	IAS 32.AG25	Ch.47, p.3670
IAS 32.42	Ch.54, p.4491	IAS 32.AG25	Ch.47, p.3678
IAS 32.42	Ch.55, p.4583	IAS 32.AG25	Ch.47, p.3679
IAS 32.43	Ch.54, p.4492	IAS 32.AG26	Ch.47, p.3680
IAS 32.44	Ch.54, p.4492	IAS 32.AG27	Ch.47, p.3711
IAS 32.45	Ch.54, p.4492	IAS 32.AG27	Ch.47, p.3714
IAS 32.46	Ch.54, p.4492	IAS 32.AG27(a)	Ch.47, p.3703
IAS 32.47	Ch.54, p.4495	IAS 32.AG27(a)-(b)	Ch.47, p.3711
IAS 32.48	Ch.54, p.4495	IAS 32.AG27(b)	Ch.7, p.552
IAS 32.48	Ch.54, p.4496	IAS 32.AG27(b)	Ch.47, p.3712
IAS 32.49(a)	Ch.54, p.4497	IAS 32.AG27(c)	Ch.47, p.3711
IAS 32.49(b)	Ch.54, p.4497	IAS 32.AG27(c)	Ch.47, p.3714
IAS 32.49(c)	Ch.54, p.4497	IAS 32.AG27(d)	Ch.47, p.3707
IAS 32.49(d)	Ch.54, p.4497	IAS 32.AG27(d)	Ch.47, p.3710
IAS 32.49(e)	Ch.54, p.4497	IAS 32.AG28	Ch.47, p.3674
IAS 32.50	Ch.54, p.4495	IAS 32.AG29	Ch.7, p.546
IAS 32.96C	Ch.34, p.2661	IAS 32.AG29	Ch.7, p.555
IAS 32.AG3	Ch.45, p.3586	IAS 32.AG29	Ch.47, p.3695
IAS 32.AG4	Ch.45, p.3586	IAS 32.AG29A	Ch.7, p.546
IAS 32.AG5	Ch.45, p.3586	IAS 32.AG29A	Ch.47, p.3689
IAS 32.AG6	Ch.45, p.3586	IAS 32.AG30	Ch.47, p.3715
IAS 32.AG6	Ch.47, p.3695	IAS 32.AG30	Ch.47, p.3716
IAS 32.AG7	Ch.45, p.3585	IAS 32.AG31(b)	Ch.47, p.3717
IAS 32.AG8	Ch.45, p.3587	IAS 32.AG32	Ch.47, p.3720
IAS 32.AG9	Ch.14, p.1010	IAS 32.AG33	Ch.47, p.3722
IAS 32.AG9	Ch.45, p.3587	IAS 32.AG34	Ch.47, p.3722
IAS 32.AG10	Ch.45, p.3587	IAS 32.AG35	Ch.47, p.3725
IAS 32.AG11	Ch.45, p.3588	IAS 32.AG36	Ch.47, p.3742
IAS 32.AG12	Ch.45, p.3585	IAS 32.AG36	Ch.47, p.3743
IAS 32.AG12	Ch.45, p.3586	IAS 32.AG37	Ch.47, p.3679
IAS 32.AG13	Ch.45, p.3589	IAS 32.AG37	Ch.47, p.3715
IAS 32.AG13	Ch.45, p.3591	IAS 32.AG37	Ch.47, p.3739
IAS 32.AG13	Ch.47, p.3677	IAS 32.AG38A	Ch.54, p.4493
IAS 32.AG13	Ch.47, p.3678	IAS 32.AG38B	Ch.54, p.4493
IAS 32.AG13	Ch.47, p.3703	IAS 32.AG38C	Ch.54, p.4493
IAS 32.AG14	Ch.47, p.3678	IAS 32.AG38D	Ch.54, p.4493
IAS 32.AG14B	Ch.47, p.3690	IAS 32.AG38E	Ch.54, p.4492
IAS 32.AG14C	Ch.47, p.3690	IAS 32.AG38F	Ch.54, p.4496
IAS 32.AG14D	Ch.47, p.3690	IAS 32.AG39	Ch.54, p.4497
IAS 32.AG14E	Ch.47, p.3687	IAS 32.IE2-6	Ch.47, p.3746
IAS 32.AG14F	Ch.47, p.3692	IAS 32.IE7-11	Ch.47, p.3748
IAS 32.AG14G	Ch.47, p.3692	IAS 32.IE12-16	Ch.47, p.3752
IAS 32.AG14H	Ch.47, p.3693	IAS 32.IE17-21	Ch.47, p.3754
IAS 32.AG14I	Ch.47, p.3693	IAS 32.IE22-26	Ch.47, p.3756
IAS 32.AG14J	Ch.47, p.3692	IAS 32.IE27-31	Ch.47, p.3758
IAS 32.AG15	Ch.45, p.3589	IAS 32.IE31	Ch.47, p.3761
IAS 32.AG16	Ch.45, p.3589	IAS 32.IE32	Ch.54, p.4488
IAS 32.AG16	Ch.45, p.3590	IAS 32.IE32	Ch.54, p.4518
IAS 32.AG17	Ch.45, p.3590	IAS 32.IE33	Ch.54, p.4489
IAS 32.AG18	Ch.45, p.3590	IAS 32.IE33	Ch.54, p.4519
IAS 32.AG19	Ch.45, p.3591	IAS 32.IE34-36	Ch.47, p.3717
IAS 32.AG20	Ch.43, p.3473	IAS 32.IE37-38	Ch.47, p.3727
IAS 32.AG20	Ch.45, p.3588	IAS 32.IE39-46	Ch.47, p.3722
IAS 32.AG20	Ch.45, p.3607	IAS 32.IE47-50	Ch.47, p.3725
IAS 32.AG20	Ch.51, p.4046	IAS 32.BC4I	Ch.47, p.3709
IAS 32.AG21	Ch.45, p.3589	IAS 32.BC4K	Ch.47, p.3709

Index of standards

IAS 32.BC7-BC8 .... Ch.47, p.3686
IAS 32.BC9 .... Ch.47, p.3682
IAS 32.BC12 .... Ch.47, p.3711
IAS 32.BC17 .... Ch.47, p.3674
IAS 32.BC21(a) Ch.47, p.3701
IAS 32.BC67 .... Ch.47, p.3689
IAS 32.BC68 .... Ch.47, p.3689
IAS 32.BC77 .... Ch.54, p.4500
IAS 32.BC80 .... Ch.54, p.4493
IAS 32.BC83 .... Ch.54, p.4494
IAS 32.BC84 .... Ch.54, p.4494
IAS 32.BC94 .... Ch.54, p.4492
IAS 32.BC94-BC100 .... Ch.54, p.4496
IAS 32.BC101 .... Ch.54, p.4497
IAS 32.BC103 .... Ch.54, p.4499
IAS 32.BC105-BC111 .... Ch.54, p.4500

IAS 33

IAS 33.1 .... Ch.37, p.3022
IAS 33.2 .... Ch.37, p.3022
IAS 33.3 .... Ch.37, p.3022
IAS 33.4 .... Ch.37, p.3023
IAS 33.4A Ch.37, p.3061
IAS 33.5 .... Ch.37, p.3023
IAS 33.5 .... Ch.37, p.3040
IAS 33.5 .... Ch.37, p.3042
IAS 33.5 .... Ch.37, p.3048
IAS 33.5 .... Ch.37, p.3055
IAS 33.6 .... Ch.37, p.3023
IAS 33.7 .... Ch.37, p.3040
IAS 33.8 .... Ch.37, p.3021
IAS 33.8 .... Ch.37, p.3023
IAS 33.9 .... Ch.37, p.3023
IAS 33.10 .... Ch.37, p.3023
IAS 33.11 .... Ch.37, p.3022
IAS 33.12 .... Ch.37, p.3023
IAS 33.13 .... Ch.37, p.3023
IAS 33.14(a) Ch.37, p.3035
IAS 33.14(b) Ch.37, p.3035
IAS 33.15 .... Ch.37, p.3035
IAS 33.16 .... Ch.37, p.3035
IAS 33.17 .... Ch.37, p.3035
IAS 33.18 .... Ch.37, p.3035
IAS 33.19 .... Ch.37, p.3024
IAS 33.20 .... Ch.37, p.3026
IAS 33.21 .... Ch.37, p.3024
IAS 33.21 .... Ch.37, p.3025
IAS 33.21(f) Ch.37, p.3033
IAS 33.22 .... Ch.37, p.3033
IAS 33.23 .... Ch.37, p.3024
IAS 33.24 .... Ch.37, p.3024
IAS 33.24 .... Ch.37, p.3025
IAS 33.26 .... Ch.37, p.3027
IAS 33.26 .... Ch.37, p.3032
IAS 33.26 .... Ch.37, p.3062
IAS 33.26-27 .... Ch.37, p.3029

IAS 33.27 .... Ch.37, p.3027
IAS 33.28 .... Ch.37, p.3027
IAS 33.29 .... Ch.37, p.3029
IAS 33.29 .... Ch.37, p.3031
IAS 33.29 .... Ch.37, p.3062
IAS 33.30 .... Ch.37, p.3040
IAS 33.31 .... Ch.37, p.3040
IAS 33.32 .... Ch.37, p.3022
IAS 33.32 .... Ch.37, p.3040
IAS 33.33 .... Ch.37, p.3041
IAS 33.33 .... Ch.37, p.3048
IAS 33.34 .... Ch.37, p.3041
IAS 33.35 .... Ch.37, p.3041
IAS 33.36 .... Ch.37, p.3041
IAS 33.36 .... Ch.37, p.3051
IAS 33.37 .... Ch.37, p.3041
IAS 33.38 .... Ch.37, p.3032
IAS 33.38 .... Ch.37, p.3041
IAS 33.38 .... Ch.37, p.3051
IAS 33.39 .... Ch.37, p.3042
IAS 33.40 .... Ch.37, p.3059
IAS 33.42 .... Ch.37, p.3043
IAS 33.43 .... Ch.37, p.3042
IAS 33.44 .... Ch.37, p.3043
IAS 33.44 .... Ch.37, p.3048
IAS 33.45 .... Ch.37, p.3050
IAS 33.45-46 .... Ch.37, p.3050
IAS 33.46 .... Ch.37, p.3050
IAS 33.46 .... Ch.37, p.3051
IAS 33.47 .... Ch.37, p.3062
IAS 33.47A Ch.37, p.3021
IAS 33.47A Ch.37, p.3055
IAS 33.48 .... Ch.37, p.3025
IAS 33.48 .... Ch.37, p.3054
IAS 33.48 .... Ch.37, p.3055
IAS 33.49 .... Ch.37, p.3045
IAS 33.50 .... Ch.37, p.3046
IAS 33.51 .... Ch.37, p.3047
IAS 33.52 .... Ch.37, p.3055
IAS 33.52 .... Ch.37, p.3062
IAS 33.53 .... Ch.37, p.3056
IAS 33.54 .... Ch.37, p.3058
IAS 33.55 .... Ch.37, p.3056
IAS 33.56 .... Ch.37, p.3058
IAS 33.56 .... Ch.37, p.3059
IAS 33.57 .... Ch.37, p.3061
IAS 33.58 .... Ch.37, p.3042
IAS 33.59 .... Ch.37, p.3042
IAS 33.59-60 .... Ch.37, p.3048
IAS 33.60 .... Ch.37, p.3042
IAS 33.61 .... Ch.37, p.3042
IAS 33.62 .... Ch.37, p.3053
IAS 33.63 .... Ch.37, p.3051
IAS 33.64 .... Ch.37, p.3027
IAS 33.64 .... Ch.37, p.3033
IAS 33.64 .... Ch.37, p.3036
IAS 33.64 .... Ch.37, p.3062
IAS 33.65 .... Ch.37, p.3041

Index of standards

IAS 33.65	Ch.37, p.3062
IAS 33.65	Ch.41, p.3265
IAS 33.66	Ch.37, p.3023
IAS 33.66	Ch.37, p.3036
IAS 33.66	Ch.37, p.3061
IAS 33.66	Ch.37, p.3062
IAS 33.67	Ch.37, p.3062
IAS 33.67A	Ch.3, p.141
IAS 33.67A	Ch.37, p.3061
IAS 33.68	Ch.37, p.3061
IAS 33.68	Ch.37, p.3062
IAS 33.68A	Ch.37, p.3061
IAS 33.69	Ch.37, p.3061
IAS 33.70	Ch.37, p.3063
IAS 33.71	Ch.37, p.3063
IAS 33.72	Ch.37, p.3063
IAS 33.73	Ch.37, p.3039
IAS 33.73A	Ch.37, p.3039
IAS 33.A1	Ch.37, p.3023
IAS 33.A2	Ch.37, p.3029
IAS 33.A2	Ch.37, p.3030
IAS 33.A3	Ch.37, p.3043
IAS 33.A4	Ch.37, p.3051
IAS 33.A5	Ch.37, p.3051
IAS 33.A6	Ch.37, p.3052
IAS 33.A7	Ch.37, p.3048
IAS 33.A7	Ch.37, p.3052
IAS 33.A8	Ch.37, p.3052
IAS 33.A9	Ch.37, p.3048
IAS 33.A9	Ch.37, p.3053
IAS 33.A10	Ch.37, p.3052
IAS 33.A11	Ch.37, p.3059
IAS 33.A12	Ch.37, p.3060
IAS 33.A13	Ch.37, p.3036
IAS 33.A14	Ch.37, p.3037
IAS 33.A14	Ch.37, p.3047
IAS 33.A15	Ch.37, p.3024
IAS 33.A16	Ch.37, p.3053
IAS 33.IE1	Ch.37, p.3035
IAS 33.IE2	Ch.37, p.3024
IAS 33.IE2	Ch.37, p.3026
IAS 33.IE3	Ch.37, p.3028
IAS 33.IE4	Ch.37, p.3030
IAS 33.IE5	Ch.37, p.3050
IAS 33.IE5A	Ch.37, p.3055
IAS 33.IE6	Ch.37, p.3046
IAS 33.IE7	Ch.37, p.3057
IAS 33.IE8	Ch.37, p.3046
IAS 33.IE9	Ch.37, p.3043
IAS 33.IE10	Ch.37, p.3060
IAS 33.IE11	Ch.37, p.3037
IAS 33.IE12	Ch.37, p.3064

IAS 34

IAS 34 Objective	Ch.19, p.1495
IAS 34 Objective	Ch.41, p.3196
IAS 34.1	Ch.41, p.3196
IAS 34.1	Ch.41, p.3197
IAS 34.2	Ch.41, p.3196
IAS 34.2	Ch.41, p.3197
IAS 34.3	Ch.41, p.3197
IAS 34.4	Ch.41, p.3196
IAS 34.4	Ch.41, p.3208
IAS 34.4	Ch.41, p.3232
IAS 34.4	Ch.41, p.3267
IAS 34.5	Ch.41, p.3198
IAS 34.5(f)	Ch.41, p.3240
IAS 34.6	Ch.41, p.3199
IAS 34.6	Ch.41, p.3204
IAS 34.7	Ch.41, p.3198
IAS 34.7	Ch.41, p.3199
IAS 34.7	Ch.41, p.3237
IAS 34.8	Ch.41, p.3199
IAS 34.8A	Ch.41, p.3199
IAS 34.8A	Ch.41, p.3228
IAS 34.9	Ch.41, p.3198
IAS 34.10	Ch.41, p.3199
IAS 34.10	Ch.41, p.3242
IAS 34.10	Ch.41, p.3267
IAS 34.11	Ch.41, p.3203
IAS 34.11A	Ch.41, p.3203
IAS 34.14	Ch.41, p.3203
IAS 34.15	Ch.32, p.2440
IAS 34.15	Ch.41, p.3199
IAS 34.15	Ch.41, p.3204
IAS 34.15	Ch.41, p.3205
IAS 34.15	Ch.41, p.3207
IAS 34.15	Ch.41, p.3231
IAS 34.15	Ch.41, p.3236
IAS 34.15	Ch.41, p.3267
IAS 34.15	Ch.54, p.4407
IAS 34.15-15A	Ch.5, p.361
IAS 34.15A	Ch.41, p.3204
IAS 34.15A	Ch.41, p.3231
IAS 34.15A	Ch.41, p.3236
IAS 34.15A	Ch.54, p.4407
IAS 34.15B	Ch.32, p.2440
IAS 34.15B	Ch.41, p.3204
IAS 34.15B	Ch.41, p.3205
IAS 34.15B	Ch.54, p.4407
IAS 34.15B(a)	Ch.41, p.3208
IAS 34.15B(a)	Ch.41, p.3209
IAS 34.15B(b)	Ch.41, p.3209
IAS 34.15B(c)	Ch.41, p.3207
IAS 34.15B(d)	Ch.41, p.3210
IAS 34.15B(e)	Ch.41, p.3210
IAS 34.15B(f)	Ch.41, p.3210
IAS 34.15B(g)	Ch.41, p.3232
IAS 34.15B(h)	Ch.41, p.3211
IAS 34.15B(i)	Ch.41, p.3212
IAS 34.15B(j)	Ch.41, p.3212
IAS 34.15B(k)	Ch.41, p.3214
IAS 34.15B(k)	Ch.41, p.3267
IAS 34.15B(m)	Ch.41, p.3214

IAS 34.15B(m)	Ch.41, p.3268	IAS 34.26	Ch.41, p.3239
IAS 34.15C	Ch.41, p.3204	IAS 34.26	Ch.41, p.3252
IAS 34.15C	Ch.41, p.3205	IAS 34.27	Ch.41, p.3237
IAS 34.15C	Ch.54, p.4407	IAS 34.28	Ch.41, p.3195
IAS 34.16A	Ch.41, p.3203	IAS 34.28	Ch.41, p.3237
IAS 34.16A	Ch.41, p.3204	IAS 34.28	Ch.41, p.3239
IAS 34.16A	Ch.41, p.3206	IAS 34.28	Ch.41, p.3242
IAS 34.16A	Ch.41, p.3207	IAS 34.28	Ch.41, p.3245
IAS 34.16A	Ch.41, p.3208	IAS 34.29	Ch.41, p.3237
IAS 34.16A(a)	Ch.41, p.3199	IAS 34.29	Ch.41, p.3238
IAS 34.16A(a)	Ch.41, p.3215	IAS 34.29	Ch.41, p.3243
IAS 34.16A(a)	Ch.41, p.3232	IAS 34.29	Ch.41, p.3253
IAS 34.16A(a)	Ch.41, p.3267	IAS 34.30(a)	Ch.41, p.3238
IAS 34.16A(b)	Ch.41, p.3216	IAS 34.30(b)	Ch.41, p.3238
IAS 34.16A(b)	Ch.41, p.3243	IAS 34.30(c)	Ch.41, p.3238
IAS 34.16A(c)	Ch.41, p.3216	IAS 34.30(c)	Ch.41, p.3249
IAS 34.16A(d)	Ch.41, p.3207	IAS 34.30(c)	Ch.41, p.3252
IAS 34.16A(d)	Ch.41, p.3239	IAS 34.31	Ch.41, p.3243
IAS 34.16A(d)	Ch.41, p.3252	IAS 34.32	Ch.41, p.3238
IAS 34.16A(d)	Ch.41, p.3267	IAS 34.32	Ch.41, p.3243
IAS 34.16A(e)	Ch.41, p.3217	IAS 34.32	Ch.41, p.3259
IAS 34.16A(f)	Ch.41, p.3218	IAS 34.33	Ch.41, p.3238
IAS 34.16A(g)	Ch.41, p.3221	IAS 34.34-36	Ch.41, p.3239
IAS 34.16A(g)	Ch.41, p.3268	IAS 34.36	Ch.41, p.3245
IAS 34.16A(g)(iv)	Ch.41, p.3268	IAS 34.37	Ch.41, p.3242
IAS 34.16A(g)(v)	Ch.41, p.3267	IAS 34.38	Ch.41, p.3242
IAS 34.16A(h)	Ch.41, p.3218	IAS 34.39	Ch.41, p.3243
IAS 34.16A(h)	Ch.41, p.3252	IAS 34.39	Ch.41, p.3260
IAS 34.16A(i)	Ch.9, p.753	IAS 34.40	Ch.41, p.3243
IAS 34.16A(i)	Ch.13, p.946	IAS 34.41	Ch.41, p.3236
IAS 34.16A(i)	Ch.41, p.3207	IAS 34.41	Ch.41, p.3265
IAS 34.16A(i)	Ch.41, p.3219	IAS 34.42	Ch.41, p.3265
IAS 34.16A(j)	Ch.41, p.3223	IAS 34.43	Ch.41, p.3239
IAS 34.16A(j)	Ch.54, p.4407	IAS 34.43	Ch.41, p.3240
IAS 34.16A(k)	Ch.13, p.946	IAS 34.43(a)	Ch.41, p.3242
IAS 34.16A(l)	Ch.32, p.2439	IAS 34.44	Ch.41, p.3239
IAS 34.19	Ch.41, p.3224	IAS 34.44	Ch.41, p.3240
IAS 34.20	Ch.41, p.3227	IAS 34.45	Ch.41, p.3240
IAS 34.20	Ch.41, p.3232	IAS 34.B1	Ch.41, p.3246
IAS 34.20	Ch.41, p.3234	IAS 34.B2	Ch.41, p.3260
IAS 34.20	Ch.41, p.3266	IAS 34.B3	Ch.41, p.3259
IAS 34.20(b)	Ch.41, p.3228	IAS 34.B4	Ch.41, p.3259
IAS 34.21	Ch.41, p.3228	IAS 34.B5	Ch.41, p.3246
IAS 34.21	Ch.41, p.3234	IAS 34.B6	Ch.41, p.3246
IAS 34.21	Ch.41, p.3243	IAS 34.B7	Ch.41, p.3260
IAS 34.22	Ch.41, p.3228	IAS 34.B8	Ch.41, p.3244
IAS 34.23	Ch.41, p.3207	IAS 34.B9	Ch.41, p.3247
IAS 34.23	Ch.41, p.3235	IAS 34.B10	Ch.41, p.3248
IAS 34.23	Ch.41, p.3236	IAS 34.B11	Ch.41, p.3260
IAS 34.24	Ch.41, p.3235	IAS 34.B12	Ch.41, p.3249
IAS 34.25	Ch.41, p.3199	IAS 34.B13	Ch.41, p.3249
IAS 34.25	Ch.41, p.3200	IAS 34.B13	Ch.41, p.3250
IAS 34.25	Ch.41, p.3204	IAS 34.B13	Ch.41, p.3251
IAS 34.25	Ch.41, p.3205	IAS 34.B13	Ch.41, p.3252
IAS 34.25	Ch.41, p.3207	IAS 34.B13	Ch.41, p.3253
IAS 34.25	Ch.41, p.3235	IAS 34.B14	Ch.41, p.3250
IAS 34.25	Ch.41, p.3236	IAS 34.B14	Ch.41, p.3251
IAS 34.26	Ch.41, p.3237	IAS 34.B15	Ch.41, p.3250

IAS 34.B16	Ch.41, p.3250	IAS 36.10-11	Ch.20, p.1610
IAS 34.B17	Ch.41, p.3254	IAS 36.11	Ch.20, p.1522
IAS 34.B18	Ch.41, p.3254	IAS 36.11	Ch.20, p.1610
IAS 34.B19	Ch.41, p.3257	IAS 36.12	Ch.20, p.1523
IAS 34.B20	Ch.41, p.3255	IAS 36.12-13	Ch.20, p.1522
IAS 34.B21	Ch.41, p.3254	IAS 36.12(f)	Ch.18, p.1415
IAS 34.B22	Ch.41, p.3254	IAS 36.12(h)	Ch.8, p.599
IAS 34.B23	Ch.41, p.3249	IAS 36.13	Ch.8, p.600
IAS 34.B24	Ch.41, p.3244	IAS 36.13	Ch.20, p.1518
IAS 34.B25	Ch.41, p.3248	IAS 36.13	Ch.20, p.1628
IAS 34.B26	Ch.41, p.3248	IAS 36.14	Ch.20, p.1523
IAS 34.B28	Ch.41, p.3249	IAS 36.15	Ch.20, p.1522
IAS 34.B29	Ch.41, p.3257	IAS 36.15	Ch.20, p.1523
IAS 34.B30	Ch.41, p.3257	IAS 36.16	Ch.20, p.1525
IAS 34.B31	Ch.41, p.3257	IAS 36.16	Ch.20, p.1565
IAS 34.B32	Ch.16, p.1273	IAS 36.17	Ch.20, p.1523
IAS 34.B32	Ch.41, p.3258	IAS 36.18	Ch.19, p.1486
IAS 34.B33	Ch.16, p.1273	IAS 36.18	Ch.20, p.1544
IAS 34.B33	Ch.41, p.3258	IAS 36.18	Ch.43, p.3434
IAS 34.B34	Ch.16, p.1274	IAS 36.19	Ch.20, p.1544
IAS 34.B34	Ch.41, p.3258	IAS 36.19	Ch.43, p.3434
IAS 34.B35	Ch.41, p.3244	IAS 36.20	Ch.20, p.1544
IAS 34.B36	Ch.41, p.3244	IAS 36.20	Ch.20, p.1548
IAS 34.B36	Ch.41, p.3245	IAS 36.21	Ch.20, p.1545
IAS 34.IE A	Ch.41, p.3228	IAS 36.22	Ch.17, p.1350
IAS 34.IE C7	Ch.19, p.1495	IAS 36.22	Ch.20, p.1544
		IAS 36.22	Ch.43, p.3434
		IAS 36.23	Ch.20, p.1544

IAS 36

IAS 36.2	Ch.20, p.1521	IAS 36.24	Ch.20, p.1610
IAS 36.3	Ch.20, p.1521	IAS 36.24	Ch.20, p.1611
IAS 36.4	Ch.20, p.1521	IAS 36.28	Ch.20, p.1546
IAS 36.4	Ch.20, p.1625	IAS 36.29	Ch.20, p.1546
IAS 36.6	Ch.14, p.1051	IAS 36.30	Ch.20, p.1551
IAS 36.6	Ch.20, p.1525	IAS 36.30	Ch.20, p.1552
IAS 36.6	Ch.20, p.1544	IAS 36.30	Ch.20, p.1563
IAS 36.6	Ch.43, p.3431	IAS 36.31	Ch.20, p.1544
IAS 36.6	Ch.43, p.3432	IAS 36.31	Ch.20, p.1551
IAS 36.6	Ch.43, p.3434	IAS 36.31	Ch.43, p.3434
IAS 36.6	Ch.43, p.3440	IAS 36.32	Ch.20, p.1551
IAS 36.8-9	Ch.8, p.599	IAS 36.33	Ch.20, p.1552
IAS 36.8-9	Ch.20, p.1522	IAS 36.33	Ch.20, p.1557
IAS 36.8-9	Ch.42, p.3284	IAS 36.33(a)	Ch.43, p.3436
IAS 36.8-17	Ch.43, p.3373	IAS 36.33(b)	Ch.43, p.3435
IAS 36.9	Ch.17, p.1339	IAS 36.34	Ch.20, p.1552
IAS 36.9	Ch.20, p.1522	IAS 36.35	Ch.20, p.1553
IAS 36.9	Ch.20, p.1591	IAS 36.35	Ch.43, p.3435
IAS 36.9	Ch.20, p.1610	IAS 36.36	Ch.20, p.1553
IAS 36.10	Ch.9, p.680	IAS 36.37	Ch.20, p.1553
IAS 36.10	Ch.17, p.1319	IAS 36.38	Ch.20, p.1553
IAS 36.10	Ch.17, p.1339	IAS 36.39	Ch.20, p.1553
IAS 36.10	Ch.17, p.1347	IAS 36.39(b)	Ch.20, p.1526
IAS 36.10	Ch.17, p.1350	IAS 36.39(b)	Ch.20, p.1558
IAS 36.10	Ch.20, p.1522	IAS 36.40	Ch.20, p.1553
IAS 36.10	Ch.20, p.1595	IAS 36.41	Ch.20, p.1554
IAS 36.10	Ch.20, p.1610	IAS 36.41	Ch.20, p.1559
IAS 36.10-11	Ch.20, p.1531	IAS 36.42	Ch.20, p.1554
		IAS 36.42	Ch.43, p.3439
		IAS 36.43	Ch.20, p.1553

IAS 36.44	Ch.20, p.1554	IAS 36.78	Ch.20, p.1561
IAS 36.44	Ch.20, p.1556	IAS 36.78	Ch.43, p.3435
IAS 36.44	Ch.20, p.1559	IAS 36.79	Ch.20, p.1536
IAS 36.44	Ch.43, p.3439	IAS 36.79	Ch.20, p.1540
IAS 36.45	Ch.20, p.1556	IAS 36.79	Ch.20, p.1554
IAS 36.46	Ch.20, p.1556	IAS 36.79	Ch.43, p.3435
IAS 36.47	Ch.20, p.1556	IAS 36.80	Ch.20, p.1582
IAS 36.48	Ch.20, p.1554	IAS 36.80	Ch.20, p.1585
IAS 36.49	Ch.20, p.1555	IAS 36.80	Ch.20, p.1587
IAS 36.50	Ch.20, p.1554	IAS 36.80	Ch.20, p.1621
IAS 36.50	Ch.20, p.1584	IAS 36.80(b)	Ch.20, p.1588
IAS 36.51	Ch.20, p.1554	IAS 36.80(b)	Ch.36, p.2983
IAS 36.51	Ch.20, p.1584	IAS 36.81	Ch.20, p.1582
IAS 36.52	Ch.20, p.1556	IAS 36.81	Ch.20, p.1587
IAS 36.53	Ch.20, p.1556	IAS 36.82	Ch.20, p.1583
IAS 36.53A	Ch.20, p.1581	IAS 36.83	Ch.20, p.1583
IAS 36.53A	Ch.20, p.1582	IAS 36.84	Ch.20, p.1589
IAS 36.54	Ch.20, p.1557	IAS 36.84	Ch.20, p.1590
IAS 36.54	Ch.26, p.1959	IAS 36.84	Ch.20, p.1591
IAS 36.54	Ch.43, p.3440	IAS 36.85	Ch.20, p.1589
IAS 36.55	Ch.20, p.1564	IAS 36.86	Ch.20, p.1598
IAS 36.55	Ch.20, p.1567	IAS 36.87	Ch.20, p.1588
IAS 36.55	Ch.20, p.1577	IAS 36.87	Ch.20, p.1599
IAS 36.55	Ch.20, p.1578	IAS 36.88	Ch.20, p.1613
IAS 36.55	Ch.43, p.3436	IAS 36.89	Ch.20, p.1610
IAS 36.56	Ch.20, p.1564	IAS 36.89	Ch.20, p.1611
IAS 36.56	Ch.20, p.1568	IAS 36.90	Ch.20, p.1590
IAS 36.59	Ch.20, p.1612	IAS 36.90	Ch.20, p.1591
IAS 36.60	Ch.20, p.1612	IAS 36.96	Ch.20, p.1591
IAS 36.60	Ch.42, p.3284	IAS 36.97-98	Ch.20, p.1592
IAS 36.61	Ch.18, p.1422	IAS 36.99	Ch.20, p.1592
IAS 36.62	Ch.20, p.1612	IAS 36.100	Ch.20, p.1542
IAS 36.63	Ch.20, p.1612	IAS 36.101	Ch.20, p.1542
IAS 36.64	Ch.20, p.1613	IAS 36.102	Ch.20, p.1542
IAS 36.66	Ch.20, p.1551	IAS 36.104	Ch.17, p.1350
IAS 36.66	Ch.43, p.3431	IAS 36.104	Ch.20, p.1531
IAS 36.67	Ch.20, p.1551	IAS 36.104	Ch.20, p.1604
IAS 36.68	Ch.20, p.1525	IAS 36.104	Ch.20, p.1613
IAS 36.68-69	Ch.20, p.1528	IAS 36.105	Ch.20, p.1545
IAS 36.69	Ch.20, p.1525	IAS 36.105	Ch.20, p.1613
IAS 36.70	Ch.20, p.1534	IAS 36.105	Ch.20, p.1614
IAS 36.70	Ch.20, p.1558	IAS 36.106	Ch.20, p.1614
IAS 36.70	Ch.20, p.1620	IAS 36.107	Ch.20, p.1615
IAS 36.70	Ch.43, p.3432	IAS 36.108	Ch.20, p.1614
IAS 36.71	Ch.20, p.1534	IAS 36.108	Ch.26, p.1976
IAS 36.72	Ch.20, p.1531	IAS 36.109-123	Ch.43, p.3374
IAS 36.73	Ch.20, p.1531	IAS 36.109-125	Ch.31, p.2385
IAS 36.74	Ch.43, p.3434	IAS 36.110	Ch.20, p.1616
IAS 36.74-79	Ch.5, p.334	IAS 36.111	Ch.20, p.1616
IAS 36.75	Ch.20, p.1535	IAS 36.112	Ch.20, p.1616
IAS 36.75	Ch.43, p.3434	IAS 36.113	Ch.20, p.1616
IAS 36.76	Ch.20, p.1535	IAS 36.114-116	Ch.20, p.1617
IAS 36.76	Ch.43, p.3435	IAS 36.117	Ch.18, p.1424
IAS 36.77	Ch.20, p.1535	IAS 36.117	Ch.20, p.1617
IAS 36.78	Ch.20, p.1536	IAS 36.118	Ch.20, p.1617
IAS 36.78	Ch.20, p.1537	IAS 36.119	Ch.5, p.376
IAS 36.78	Ch.20, p.1538	IAS 36.119	Ch.20, p.1618
IAS 36.78	Ch.20, p.1546	IAS 36.119	Ch.20, p.1619

IAS 36.120	Ch.20, p.1619	IAS 36.BCZ85	Ch.20, p.1567
IAS 36.121	Ch.20, p.1618	IAS 36.BCZ85	Ch.20, p.1569
IAS 36.121	Ch.20, p.1619	IAS 36.BCZ85	Ch.20, p.1576
IAS 36.122	Ch.20, p.1618	IAS 36.BCZ88	Ch.20, p.1568
IAS 36.123	Ch.20, p.1618	IAS 36.BC139	Ch.20, p.1585
IAS 36.124	Ch.20, p.1593	IAS 36.BC156	Ch.20, p.1598
IAS 36.124	Ch.20, p.1615	IAS 36.BC162	Ch.20, p.1591
IAS 36.124	Ch.20, p.1629	IAS 36.BC173	Ch.20, p.1591
IAS 36.124	Ch.41, p.3245	IAS 36.BC177	Ch.20, p.1593
IAS 36.125	Ch.20, p.1593		
IAS 36.125	Ch.20, p.1615		

IAS 37 (2022)

IAS 37(2022).68A	Ch.31, p.2357

IAS 1

IAS 36.126	Ch.20, p.1630	IAS 37 Objective	Ch.26, p.1932
IAS 36.127	Ch.20, p.1630	IAS 37.1	Ch.26, p.1929
IAS 36.128	Ch.20, p.1630	IAS 37.1	Ch.26, p.1932
IAS 36.129	Ch.20, p.1630	IAS 37.2	Ch.26, p.1935
IAS 36.130	Ch.20, p.1631	IAS 37.3	Ch.26, p.1932
IAS 36.131	Ch.20, p.1632	IAS 37.3	Ch.26, p.1934
IAS 36.132	Ch.20, p.1632	IAS 37.3	Ch.26, p.1945
IAS 36.133	Ch.20, p.1632	IAS 37.3	Ch.39, p.3122
IAS 36.134	Ch.20, p.1634	IAS 37.5	Ch.26, p.1934
IAS 36.134(d)(i)-(ii)	Ch.43, p.3437	IAS 37.5	Ch.26, p.2006
IAS 36.134(d)(v)	Ch.20, p.1575	IAS 37.5	Ch.33, p.2561
IAS 36.134(e)(i)-(ii)	Ch.43, p.3437	IAS 37.5(c)	Ch.26, p.1934
IAS 36.134(f)	Ch.20, p.1524	IAS 37.5(c)	Ch.26, p.1975
IAS 36.134(f)(ii)	Ch.20, p.1635	IAS 37.5(g)	Ch.26, p.1936
IAS 36.135	Ch.20, p.1634	IAS 37.5(g)	Ch.26, p.1977
IAS 36.135	Ch.20, p.1635	IAS 37.7	Ch.26, p.1936
IAS 36.A2	Ch.20, p.1563	IAS 37.8	Ch.26, p.1946
IAS 36.A4	Ch.20, p.1563	IAS 37.9	Ch.26, p.1935
IAS 36.A6	Ch.20, p.1563	IAS 37.9	Ch.26, p.1967
IAS 36.A7	Ch.20, p.1563	IAS 37.9	Ch.26, p.2012
IAS 36.A10	Ch.20, p.1563	IAS 37.10	Ch.9, p.690
IAS 36.A10-13	Ch.20, p.1564	IAS 37.10	Ch.13, p.978
IAS 36.A15	Ch.20, p.1578	IAS 37.10	Ch.26, p.1931
IAS 36.A16	Ch.20, p.1564	IAS 37.10	Ch.26, p.1932
IAS 36.A17	Ch.20, p.1564	IAS 37.10	Ch.26, p.1936
IAS 36.A17	Ch.20, p.1580	IAS 37.10	Ch.26, p.1938
IAS 36.A18	Ch.20, p.1565	IAS 37.10	Ch.26, p.1939
IAS 36.A19	Ch.20, p.1565	IAS 37.10	Ch.26, p.1943
IAS 36.A19	Ch.20, p.1579	IAS 37.10	Ch.26, p.1944
IAS 36.A20	Ch.20, p.1565	IAS 37.10	Ch.26, p.1965
IAS 36.A21	Ch.20, p.1565	IAS 37.10	Ch.26, p.1966
IAS 36.C1	Ch.20, p.1602	IAS 37.10	Ch.26, p.1972
IAS 36.C2	Ch.20, p.1602	IAS 37.10	Ch.26, p.1974
IAS 36.C3	Ch.20, p.1604	IAS 37.10	Ch.26, p.1979
IAS 36.C4	Ch.20, p.1604	IAS 37.10	Ch.35, p.2912
IAS 36.C6	Ch.20, p.1602	IAS 37.10	Ch.43, p.3398
IAS 36.C7	Ch.20, p.1602	IAS 37.10	Ch.55, p.4569
IAS 36.C8	Ch.20, p.1604	IAS 37.11	Ch.26, p.1936
IAS 36.IE5-10	Ch.20, p.1535	IAS 37.11(a)	Ch.54, p.4511
IAS 36.IE62-68	Ch.20, p.1604	IAS 37.12	Ch.26, p.1937
IAS 36.IE69-IE79	Ch.20, p.1543		
IAS 36.IE Example 1C	Ch.43, p.3433		
IAS 36.BCZ28-BCZ29	Ch.20, p.1550		
IAS 36.BCZ49	Ch.20, p.1557		
IAS 36.BCZ49	Ch.43, p.3440		
IAS 36.BCZ81	Ch.20, p.1568		
IAS 36.BCZ84	Ch.20, p.1569		

IAS 37.13	Ch.26, p.1937	IAS 37.34	Ch.26, p.1942
IAS 37.13	Ch.26, p.1943	IAS 37.34	Ch.26, p.1945
IAS 37.14	Ch.17, p.1361	IAS 37.35	Ch.26, p.1945
IAS 37.14	Ch.26, p.1937	IAS 37.35	Ch.33, p.2569
IAS 37.14	Ch.26, p.1943	IAS 37.35	Ch.38, p.3079
IAS 37.14	Ch.26, p.1992	IAS 37.35	Ch.38, p.3081
IAS 37.14	Ch.26, p.2005	IAS 37.36	Ch.17, p.1361
IAS 37.14	Ch.26, p.2006	IAS 37.36	Ch.26, p.1947
IAS 37.14	Ch.55, p.4547	IAS 37.36	Ch.26, p.1952
IAS 37.14	Ch.56, p.4703	IAS 37.36	Ch.26, p.1958
IAS 37.15	Ch.24, p.1830	IAS 37.36	Ch.43, p.3451
IAS 37.15	Ch.26, p.1938	IAS 37.36-37	Ch.26, p.1947
IAS 37.15	Ch.26, p.2005	IAS 37.36-47	Ch.55, p.4580
IAS 37.16	Ch.26, p.1938	IAS 37.37	Ch.17, p.1364
IAS 37.16	Ch.26, p.1939	IAS 37.37	Ch.26, p.1947
IAS 37.16	Ch.26, p.2005	IAS 37.37	Ch.43, p.3451
IAS 37.16(a)	Ch.26, p.1943	IAS 37.38	Ch.26, p.1948
IAS 37.16(b)	Ch.26, p.1943	IAS 37.39	Ch.26, p.1942
IAS 37.17	Ch.26, p.1939	IAS 37.39	Ch.26, p.1948
IAS 37.17	Ch.26, p.1963	IAS 37.39	Ch.26, p.2004
IAS 37.17	Ch.26, p.2002	IAS 37.40	Ch.26, p.1942
IAS 37.18	Ch.26, p.1939	IAS 37.40	Ch.26, p.1949
IAS 37.18	Ch.26, p.1963	IAS 37.41	Ch.26, p.1947
IAS 37.18	Ch.26, p.1964	IAS 37.42	Ch.26, p.1949
IAS 37.18	Ch.26, p.2002	IAS 37.43	Ch.26, p.1949
IAS 37.19	Ch.26, p.1940	IAS 37.43	Ch.26, p.1950
IAS 37.19	Ch.26, p.1962	IAS 37.43	Ch.26, p.1951
IAS 37.19	Ch.26, p.1963	IAS 37.44	Ch.26, p.1950
IAS 37.19	Ch.26, p.1964	IAS 37.45	Ch.26, p.1950
IAS 37.19	Ch.26, p.1966	IAS 37.46	Ch.26, p.1950
IAS 37.19	Ch.26, p.1969	IAS 37.47	Ch.26, p.1950
IAS 37.19	Ch.26, p.1975	IAS 37.47	Ch.26, p.1951
IAS 37.19	Ch.26, p.2002	IAS 37.47	Ch.26, p.1952
IAS 37.20	Ch.26, p.1941	IAS 37.47	Ch.26, p.1954
IAS 37.21	Ch.26, p.1941	IAS 37.47	Ch.26, p.1957
IAS 37.22	Ch.26, p.1941	IAS 37.48	Ch.26, p.1958
IAS 37.22	Ch.26, p.1992	IAS 37.49	Ch.26, p.1959
IAS 37.23	Ch.17, p.1301	IAS 37.50	Ch.26, p.1959
IAS 37.23	Ch.26, p.1941	IAS 37.51	Ch.26, p.1972
IAS 37.23	Ch.26, p.1943	IAS 37.51-52	Ch.26, p.1961
IAS 37.23	Ch.26, p.1945	IAS 37.53	Ch.17, p.1363
IAS 37.23	Ch.33, p.2491	IAS 37.53	Ch.26, p.1959
IAS 37.24	Ch.26, p.1941	IAS 37.53	Ch.51, p.3958
IAS 37.24	Ch.26, p.2004	IAS 37.53	Ch.51, p.3959
IAS 37.25	Ch.26, p.1942	IAS 37.54	Ch.26, p.1959
IAS 37.25	Ch.26, p.2005	IAS 37.55	Ch.26, p.1959
IAS 37.25	Ch.43, p.3429	IAS 37.56	Ch.26, p.1960
IAS 37.26	Ch.26, p.1942	IAS 37.56	Ch.55, p.4542
IAS 37.26	Ch.26, p.1943	IAS 37.57	Ch.26, p.1960
IAS 37.26	Ch.43, p.3429	IAS 37.58	Ch.26, p.1960
IAS 37.27-28	Ch.26, p.1942	IAS 37.59	Ch.26, p.1955
IAS 37.29	Ch.26, p.1960	IAS 37.59	Ch.26, p.1961
IAS 37.30	Ch.26, p.1944	IAS 37.59	Ch.26, p.1981
IAS 37.31	Ch.26, p.1942	IAS 37.60	Ch.26, p.1954
IAS 37.32	Ch.26, p.1944	IAS 37.60	Ch.26, p.1956
IAS 37.33	Ch.9, p.686	IAS 37.60	Ch.26, p.1961
IAS 37.33	Ch.26, p.1944	IAS 37.61	Ch.26, p.1961
IAS 37.33	Ch.55, p.4542	IAS 37.61	Ch.26, p.2009

IAS 37.61-62	Ch.43, p.3534
IAS 37.62	Ch.26, p.1961
IAS 37.63	Ch.26, p.1962
IAS 37.63	Ch.26, p.1966
IAS 37.63	Ch.26, p.1970
IAS 37.63	Ch.26, p.1972
IAS 37.64	Ch.26, p.1962
IAS 37.65	Ch.26, p.1963
IAS 37.66	Ch.26, p.1972
IAS 37.66	Ch.31, p.2356
IAS 37.67	Ch.26, p.1972
IAS 37.67-68	Ch.31, p.2357
IAS 37.68	Ch.26, p.1960
IAS 37.68	Ch.26, p.1972
IAS 37.68	Ch.26, p.1977
IAS 37.68A	Ch.26, p.1973
IAS 37.69	Ch.26, p.1975
IAS 37.69	Ch.31, p.2356
IAS 37.70	Ch.26, p.1967
IAS 37.71	Ch.26, p.1967
IAS 37.71	Ch.41, p.3207
IAS 37.72	Ch.26, p.1967
IAS 37.72	Ch.26, p.1969
IAS 37.73	Ch.26, p.1968
IAS 37.74	Ch.26, p.1968
IAS 37.75	Ch.26, p.1968
IAS 37.76	Ch.26, p.1969
IAS 37.77	Ch.26, p.1969
IAS 37.78	Ch.26, p.1969
IAS 37.79	Ch.26, p.1970
IAS 37.80	Ch.26, p.1970
IAS 37.80	Ch.26, p.1971
IAS 37.81	Ch.26, p.1964
IAS 37.81	Ch.26, p.1970
IAS 37.82	Ch.26, p.1972
IAS 37.83	Ch.26, p.1972
IAS 37.84	Ch.26, p.2009
IAS 37.84(e)	Ch.26, p.1957
IAS 37.85	Ch.26, p.2009
IAS 37.86	Ch.13, p.978
IAS 37.86	Ch.26, p.2012
IAS 37.86	Ch.43, p.3429
IAS 37.87	Ch.26, p.2012
IAS 37.88	Ch.26, p.2012
IAS 37.89	Ch.26, p.2013
IAS 37.90	Ch.26, p.2013
IAS 37.91	Ch.26, p.2012
IAS 37.91	Ch.26, p.2013
IAS 37.92	Ch.26, p.2013
IAS 37.94A	Ch.26, p.1973
IAS 37.105	Ch.26, p.1973
IAS 37 Appendix C	Ch.43, p.3492
IAS 37.IE Example 1	Ch.26, p.2004
IAS 37.IE Example 2A	Ch.26, p.1992
IAS 37.IE Example 2B	Ch.26, p.1938
IAS 37.IE Example 2B	Ch.26, p.1992
IAS 37.IE Example 3	Ch.26, p.1946
IAS 37.IE Example 3	Ch.26, p.1979
IAS 37.IE Example 4	Ch.26, p.1938
IAS 37.IE Example 4	Ch.26, p.2005
IAS 37.IE Example 5A	Ch.26, p.1968
IAS 37.IE Example 5B	Ch.26, p.1969
IAS 37.IE Example 6	Ch.26, p.1940
IAS 37.IE Example 7	Ch.26, p.1939
IAS 37.IE Example 10	Ch.26, p.1944
IAS 37.IE Example 11A	Ch.18, p.1396
IAS 37.IE Example 11A	Ch.26, p.1963
IAS 37.IE Example 11B	Ch.18, p.1396
IAS 37.IE Example 11B	Ch.26, p.1940
IAS 37.IE Example 11B	Ch.26, p.1963
IAS 37.IE Example 11B	Ch.43, p.3492
IAS 37.IE D Examples: disclosures Example 3	Ch.26, p.2013
IAS 37.BC7	Ch.26, p.1973

IAS 38

IAS 38.1	Ch.17, p.1294
IAS 38.2	Ch.17, p.1294
IAS 38.2	Ch.43, p.3513
IAS 38.2(c)	Ch.43, p.3336
IAS 38.2(c)-(d)	Ch.43, p.3361
IAS 38.3	Ch.17, p.1292
IAS 38.3	Ch.17, p.1294
IAS 38.3	Ch.17, p.1295
IAS 38.3	Ch.17, p.1299
IAS 38.3(a)	Ch.22, p.1677
IAS 38.3(a)	Ch.22, p.1680
IAS 38.3(a)	Ch.32, p.2407
IAS 38.3(e)	Ch.22, p.1680
IAS 38.3(g)	Ch.56, p.4868
IAS 38.3(i)	Ch.31, p.2383
IAS 38.4	Ch.17, p.1298
IAS 38.4	Ch.18, p.1391
IAS 38.5	Ch.17, p.1295
IAS 38.5	Ch.17, p.1299
IAS 38.6	Ch.17, p.1294
IAS 38.6	Ch.17, p.1299
IAS 38.7	Ch.17, p.1295
IAS 38.8	Ch.9, p.672
IAS 38.8	Ch.9, p.681
IAS 38.8	Ch.17, p.1292
IAS 38.8	Ch.17, p.1293
IAS 38.8	Ch.17, p.1295
IAS 38.8	Ch.17, p.1298
IAS 38.8	Ch.17, p.1305
IAS 38.8	Ch.17, p.1312
IAS 38.8	Ch.17, p.1320
IAS 38.8	Ch.17, p.1329
IAS 38.8	Ch.17, p.1338
IAS 38.8	Ch.17, p.1341
IAS 38.8	Ch.17, p.1347
IAS 38.8	Ch.17, p.1350
IAS 38.8	Ch.17, p.1368
IAS 38.8	Ch.17, p.1369

IAS 38.8	Ch.17, p.1374	IAS 38.33	Ch.17, p.1313
IAS 38.8	Ch.33, p.2545	IAS 38.33-35	Ch.9, p.679
IAS 38.8	Ch.43, p.3395	IAS 38.34	Ch.9, p.673
IAS 38.8	Ch.43, p.3418	IAS 38.34	Ch.9, p.679
IAS 38.9	Ch.17, p.1295	IAS 38.34	Ch.17, p.1318
IAS 38.10	Ch.17, p.1295	IAS 38.35	Ch.17, p.1314
IAS 38.11	Ch.9, p.672	IAS 38.36	Ch.9, p.678
IAS 38.11	Ch.17, p.1296	IAS 38.36	Ch.17, p.1314
IAS 38.12	Ch.9, p.672	IAS 38.37	Ch.9, p.678
IAS 38.12	Ch.17, p.1293	IAS 38.37	Ch.17, p.1314
IAS 38.12	Ch.17, p.1296	IAS 38.42	Ch.9, p.680
IAS 38.12	Ch.17, p.1313	IAS 38.42	Ch.17, p.1319
IAS 38.12(b)	Ch.17, p.1299	IAS 38.43	Ch.9, p.680
IAS 38.12(b)	Ch.17, p.1368	IAS 38.43	Ch.17, p.1319
IAS 38.13	Ch.17, p.1293	IAS 38.44	Ch.17, p.1310
IAS 38.13	Ch.17, p.1296	IAS 38.45	Ch.17, p.1311
IAS 38.13	Ch.17, p.1297	IAS 38.45	Ch.25, p.1881
IAS 38.13	Ch.17, p.1299	IAS 38.45	Ch.43, p.3402
IAS 38.13	Ch.17, p.1352	IAS 38.46	Ch.17, p.1311
IAS 38.13	Ch.17, p.1368	IAS 38.46	Ch.17, p.1312
IAS 38.13	Ch.17, p.1374	IAS 38.47	Ch.17, p.1311
IAS 38.13-14	Ch.17, p.1296	IAS 38.48	Ch.17, p.1295
IAS 38.15	Ch.17, p.1297	IAS 38.48	Ch.17, p.1319
IAS 38.15	Ch.31, p.2367	IAS 38.49	Ch.17, p.1319
IAS 38.16	Ch.17, p.1296	IAS 38.50	Ch.17, p.1319
IAS 38.16	Ch.17, p.1297	IAS 38.51	Ch.17, p.1320
IAS 38.17	Ch.17, p.1298	IAS 38.52	Ch.17, p.1320
IAS 38.17	Ch.17, p.1368	IAS 38.52	Ch.17, p.1322
IAS 38.18	Ch.17, p.1297	IAS 38.53	Ch.17, p.1320
IAS 38.18	Ch.17, p.1301	IAS 38.53	Ch.17, p.1321
IAS 38.19	Ch.17, p.1301	IAS 38.53	Ch.17, p.1322
IAS 38.20	Ch.17, p.1305	IAS 38.54	Ch.9, p.679
IAS 38.20	Ch.17, p.1326	IAS 38.54	Ch.17, p.1320
IAS 38.20	Ch.17, p.1352	IAS 38.54-55	Ch.17, p.1321
IAS 38.20	Ch.17, p.1369	IAS 38.55	Ch.17, p.1322
IAS 38.21	Ch.5, p.281	IAS 38.56	Ch.17, p.1320
IAS 38.21	Ch.9, p.679	IAS 38.56	Ch.17, p.1369
IAS 38.21	Ch.17, p.1301	IAS 38.57	Ch.9, p.679
IAS 38.21	Ch.17, p.1313	IAS 38.57	Ch.17, p.1321
IAS 38.21	Ch.17, p.1376	IAS 38.57	Ch.17, p.1369
IAS 38.21	Ch.43, p.3395	IAS 38.57(d)	Ch.24, p.1832
IAS 38.21	Ch.43, p.3398	IAS 38.58	Ch.17, p.1321
IAS 38.22	Ch.17, p.1301	IAS 38.59	Ch.17, p.1320
IAS 38.23	Ch.17, p.1301	IAS 38.60	Ch.9, p.679
IAS 38.24	Ch.17, p.1304	IAS 38.60	Ch.17, p.1321
IAS 38.24	Ch.17, p.1329	IAS 38.61	Ch.17, p.1322
IAS 38.24	Ch.43, p.3367	IAS 38.62	Ch.17, p.1322
IAS 38.25	Ch.17, p.1305	IAS 38.63	Ch.17, p.1292
IAS 38.26	Ch.17, p.1305	IAS 38.63	Ch.17, p.1305
IAS 38.27	Ch.17, p.1306	IAS 38.63-64	Ch.17, p.1326
IAS 38.28	Ch.17, p.1306	IAS 38.64	Ch.17, p.1292
IAS 38.29-30	Ch.17, p.1307	IAS 38.65	Ch.17, p.1329
IAS 38.30	Ch.17, p.1306	IAS 38.66	Ch.17, p.1330
IAS 38.31	Ch.17, p.1307	IAS 38.67	Ch.17, p.1328
IAS 38.31	Ch.17, p.1324	IAS 38.67	Ch.17, p.1330
IAS 38.32	Ch.17, p.1306	IAS 38.67(a)	Ch.26, p.1974
IAS 38.32	Ch.25, p.1892	IAS 38.68	Ch.17, p.1301
IAS 38.33	Ch.9, p.681	IAS 38.68	Ch.17, p.1329

IAS 38.68	Ch.17, p.1330
IAS 38.68-69	Ch.31, p.2367
IAS 38.69	Ch.17, p.1330
IAS 38.69	Ch.17, p.1332
IAS 38.69	Ch.25, p.1898
IAS 38.69A	Ch.17, p.1331
IAS 38.69A	Ch.17, p.1332
IAS 38.70	Ch.17, p.1331
IAS 38.71	Ch.5, p.378
IAS 38.71	Ch.17, p.1301
IAS 38.71	Ch.17, p.1329
IAS 38.71	Ch.17, p.1334
IAS 38.71	Ch.41, p.3238
IAS 38.71	Ch.41, p.3244
IAS 38.72	Ch.17, p.1333
IAS 38.72	Ch.43, p.3368
IAS 38.73	Ch.17, p.1333
IAS 38.73	Ch.17, p.1335
IAS 38.74	Ch.17, p.1333
IAS 38.75	Ch.17, p.1333
IAS 38.75	Ch.17, p.1334
IAS 38.75	Ch.17, p.1335
IAS 38.75	Ch.43, p.3368
IAS 38.76	Ch.17, p.1334
IAS 38.77	Ch.17, p.1334
IAS 38.78	Ch.17, p.1334
IAS 38.78	Ch.17, p.1335
IAS 38.79	Ch.17, p.1335
IAS 38.80	Ch.17, p.1337
IAS 38.81-82	Ch.17, p.1333
IAS 38.81-82	Ch.17, p.1334
IAS 38.82	Ch.17, p.1335
IAS 38.83	Ch.17, p.1335
IAS 38.84	Ch.17, p.1335
IAS 38.85	Ch.17, p.1335
IAS 38.86	Ch.17, p.1336
IAS 38.87	Ch.17, p.1337
IAS 38.87	Ch.27, p.2040
IAS 38.88	Ch.17, p.1338
IAS 38.88	Ch.33, p.2548
IAS 38.88	Ch.33, p.2549
IAS 38.89	Ch.17, p.1338
IAS 38.90	Ch.17, p.1339
IAS 38.91	Ch.17, p.1338
IAS 38.91	Ch.20, p.1610
IAS 38.91	Ch.33, p.2548
IAS 38.92	Ch.17, p.1338
IAS 38.92	Ch.17, p.1339
IAS 38.93	Ch.17, p.1339
IAS 38.94	Ch.17, p.1340
IAS 38.94-95	Ch.17, p.1340
IAS 38.96	Ch.17, p.1340
IAS 38.97	Ch.17, p.1341
IAS 38.97	Ch.17, p.1342
IAS 38.97	Ch.17, p.1344
IAS 38.97	Ch.25, p.1880
IAS 38.97	Ch.25, p.1881
IAS 38.97-98	Ch.17, p.1344
IAS 38.98	Ch.17, p.1342
IAS 38.98	Ch.25, p.1881
IAS 38.98	Ch.41, p.3244
IAS 38.98A	Ch.17, p.1345
IAS 38.98A	Ch.17, p.1346
IAS 38.98A	Ch.25, p.1882
IAS 38.98B	Ch.17, p.1346
IAS 38.98B	Ch.25, p.1883
IAS 38.98C	Ch.17, p.1346
IAS 38.98C	Ch.25, p.1883
IAS 38.99	Ch.17, p.1342
IAS 38.100	Ch.17, p.1348
IAS 38.101	Ch.17, p.1348
IAS 38.102	Ch.17, p.1348
IAS 38.103	Ch.17, p.1348
IAS 38.104	Ch.5, p.379
IAS 38.104	Ch.17, p.1347
IAS 38.105	Ch.17, p.1347
IAS 38.106	Ch.17, p.1347
IAS 38.107	Ch.17, p.1349
IAS 38.108	Ch.17, p.1349
IAS 38.109	Ch.17, p.1349
IAS 38.109	Ch.33, p.2549
IAS 38.110	Ch.17, p.1349
IAS 38.111	Ch.17, p.1350
IAS 38.112	Ch.17, p.1350
IAS 38.112	Ch.17, p.1365
IAS 38.112	Ch.43, p.3395
IAS 38.112	Ch.43, p.3399
IAS 38.113	Ch.17, p.1351
IAS 38.113	Ch.17, p.1357
IAS 38.113	Ch.17, p.1365
IAS 38.113	Ch.27, p.2040
IAS 38.113	Ch.43, p.3399
IAS 38.114	Ch.17, p.1350
IAS 38.114	Ch.27, p.2040
IAS 38.115	Ch.17, p.1352
IAS 38.115A	Ch.17, p.1351
IAS 38.116	Ch.17, p.1351
IAS 38.116	Ch.27, p.2040
IAS 38.116	Ch.43, p.3400
IAS 38.116	Ch.45, p.3605
IAS 38.117	Ch.17, p.1342
IAS 38.118	Ch.17, p.1353
IAS 38.118	Ch.41, p.3232
IAS 38.118(d)	Ch.17, p.1357
IAS 38.119	Ch.17, p.1333
IAS 38.119	Ch.17, p.1353
IAS 38.120	Ch.17, p.1355
IAS 38.121	Ch.17, p.1355
IAS 38.122	Ch.17, p.1356
IAS 38.122(e)	Ch.38, p.3080
IAS 38.122(e)	Ch.39, p.3123
IAS 38.123	Ch.17, p.1356
IAS 38.124	Ch.17, p.1357
IAS 38.125	Ch.17, p.1358
IAS 38.126-127	Ch.17, p.1358
IAS 38.128	Ch.17, p.1356

IAS 38.BC5	Ch.17, p.1295	IAS 39.91(b)	Ch.53, p.4397
IAS 38.BC7	Ch.17, p.1295	IAS 39.91(c)	Ch.53, p.4397
IAS 38.BC8	Ch.17, p.1295	IAS 39.96	Ch.53, p.4397
IAS 38.BC10	Ch.17, p.1296	IAS 39.101(b)	Ch.53, p.4397
IAS 38.BC13	Ch.17, p.1296	IAS 39.101(d)	Ch.53, p.4397
IAS 38.BC19A	Ch.17, p.1313	IAS 39.102A-102N	Ch.53, p.4369
IAS 38.BC19B	Ch.17, p.1313	IAS 39.102B	Ch.55, p.4616
IAS 38.BCZ40	Ch.17, p.1302	IAS 39.102F	Ch.53, p.4369
IAS 38.BCZ41	Ch.17, p.1302	IAS 39.102G	Ch.53, p.4369
IAS 38.BC46B	Ch.17, p.1331	IAS 39.102H	Ch.53, p.4369
IAS 38.BC46D	Ch.17, p.1331	IAS 39.102M	Ch.53, p.4378
IAS 38.BC46E	Ch.17, p.1331	IAS 39.102P(d)	Ch.53, p.4378
IAS 38.BC46G	Ch.17, p.1332	IAS 39.102V	Ch.53, p.4378
IAS 38.BC59	Ch.17, p.1348	IAS 39.108G	Ch.53, p.4369
IAS 38.BC62	Ch.17, p.1338	IAS 39.AG4A	Ch.55, p.4542
IAS 38.BC72H-72I	Ch.17, p.1346	IAS 39.AG5	Ch.51, p.3930
IAS 38.BC74	Ch.33, p.2548	IAS 39.AG30(g)	Ch.55, p.4561
IAS 38.BC82	Ch.9, p.679	IAS 39.AG32	Ch.55, p.4563
IAS 38.BC82	Ch.17, p.1319	IAS 39.AG33(g)	Ch.55, p.4563
		IAS 39.AG87	Ch.55, p.4584
		IAS 39.AG88	Ch.55, p.4584

IAS 39 (2006)

IAS 39(2006).BC222(v)(ii)	Ch.49, p.3855	IAS 39.AG94	Ch.53, p.4236
		IAS 39.AG94	Ch.53, p.4396
		IAS 39.AG98	Ch.9, p.698

IAS 39 (2010)

		IAS 39.AG99F	Ch.53, p.4395
		IAS 39.AG99F(a)	Ch.53, p.4194
IAS 39(2010).AG70	Ch.14, p.1114	IAS 39.AG99F(a)	Ch.53, p.4378
		IAS 39.AG100	Ch.53, p.4395
		IAS 39.AG105(b)	Ch.53, p.4396
		IAS 39.AG107	Ch.53, p.4283
		IAS 39.AG110	Ch.53, p.4221

IAS 39 (2017)

		IAS 39.AG114-132	Ch.53, p.4382
IAS 39(2017).AG84	Ch.14, p.1012	IAS 39.IG B.9	Ch.46, p.3625
		IAS 39.IG E.4.4	Ch.51, p.4018
		IAS 39.IG F.1.2	Ch.53, p.4238
		IAS 39.IG F.1.3(b)	Ch.53, p.4236

IAS 39

		IAS 39.IG F.1.4	Ch.53, p.4248
		IAS 39.IG F.1.4	Ch.53, p.4249
IAS 39.2(e)	Ch.55, p.4539	IAS 39.IG F.1.5	Ch.53, p.4251
IAS 39.9	Ch.51, p.4045	IAS 39.IG F.1.6	Ch.53, p.4252
IAS 39.9	Ch.55, p.4559	IAS 39.IG F.1.7	Ch.53, p.4252
IAS 39.10	Ch.55, p.4559	IAS 39.IG F.1.9	Ch.53, p.4283
IAS 39.11	Ch.55, p.4560	IAS 39.IG F.1.13	Ch.53, p.4243
IAS 39.39	Ch.55, p.4582	IAS 39.IG F.1.14	Ch.53, p.4235
IAS 39.50	Ch.55, p.4595	IAS 39.IG F.2.1	Ch.53, p.4220
IAS 39.50A(c)	Ch.55, p.4595	IAS 39.IG F.2.2	Ch.53, p.4264
IAS 39.72	Ch.53, p.4396	IAS 39.IG F.2.3	Ch.53, p.4223
IAS 39.74	Ch.53, p.4397	IAS 39.IG F.2.3	Ch.53, p.4382
IAS 39.81A	Ch.53, p.4382	IAS 39.IG F.2.5	Ch.53, p.4265
IAS 39.82	Ch.53, p.4395	IAS 39.IG F.2.5	Ch.53, p.4266
IAS 39.83	Ch.53, p.4395	IAS 39.IG F.2.6	Ch.53, p.4274
IAS 39.84	Ch.53, p.4395	IAS 39.IG F.2.8	Ch.53, p.4221
IAS 39.86	Ch.53, p.4390	IAS 39.IG F.2.12	Ch.53, p.4218
IAS 39.86	Ch.53, p.4396	IAS 39.IG F.2.14	Ch.53, p.4261
IAS 39.88	Ch.53, p.4396	IAS 39.IG F.2.15	Ch.53, p.4252
IAS 39.88(a)	Ch.53, p.4395	IAS 39.IG F.2.17	Ch.53, p.4197
IAS 39.89	Ch.53, p.4397	IAS 39.IG F.3.5	Ch.53, p.4262
IAS 39.89A	Ch.53, p.4382	IAS 39.IG F.3.6	Ch.53, p.4263

IAS 39.IG F.3.6	Ch.53, p.4264	IAS 40.19A	Ch.19, p.1444
IAS 39.IG F.3.6	Ch.53, p.4292	IAS 40.19A	Ch.19, p.1451
IAS 39.IG F.3.7	Ch.52, p.4123	IAS 40.20	Ch.14, p.1052
IAS 39.IG F.3.7	Ch.53, p.4217	IAS 40.20	Ch.19, p.1457
IAS 39.IG F.3.10	Ch.53, p.4202	IAS 40.20	Ch.19, p.1460
IAS 39.IG F.3.10	Ch.53, p.4361	IAS 40.21	Ch.19, p.1457
IAS 39.IG F.3.11	Ch.53, p.4360	IAS 40.21	Ch.19, p.1476
IAS 39.IG F.5.2	Ch.53, p.4296	IAS 40.23(a)	Ch.19, p.1459
IAS 39.IG F.5.5	Ch.53, p.4319	IAS 40.23(b)	Ch.19, p.1459
IAS 39.IG F.5.6	Ch.53, p.4324	IAS 40.23(c)	Ch.19, p.1459
IAS 39.IG F.5.6	Ch.53, p.4336	IAS 40.24	Ch.19, p.1460
IAS 39.IG F.6.1-3	Ch.53, p.4382	IAS 40.27	Ch.43, p.3402
IAS 39.IG F.6.1-3	Ch.53, p.4385	IAS 40.27-29	Ch.19, p.1461
IAS 39.BC15	Ch.51, p.4045	IAS 40.29A	Ch.19, p.1461
IAS 39.BC220O-Q	Ch.53, p.4362	IAS 40.30	Ch.19, p.1467
IAS 39.BC220R	Ch.53, p.4362	IAS 40.31	Ch.19, p.1467
IAS 39.BC220S	Ch.53, p.4362	IAS 40.32	Ch.19, p.1467
IAS 39.BC222(d)	Ch.49, p.3860	IAS 40.32	Ch.19, p.1469
		IAS 40.32A	Ch.19, p.1467
		IAS 40.32A	Ch.55, p.4540
IAS 40		IAS 40.32A	Ch.56, p.4695
		IAS 40.32B	Ch.19, p.1467
IAS 40.1	Ch.19, p.1441	IAS 40.32C	Ch.19, p.1468
IAS 40.2	Ch.19, p.1441	IAS 40.33	Ch.14, p.1020
IAS 40.4	Ch.19, p.1443	IAS 40.33	Ch.19, p.1468
IAS 40.4(a)	Ch.19, p.1451	IAS 40.33	Ch.19, p.1474
IAS 40.4(b)	Ch.43, p.3336	IAS 40.35	Ch.19, p.1468
IAS 40.4(b)	Ch.43, p.3361	IAS 40.40	Ch.19, p.1469
IAS 40.5	Ch.19, p.1442	IAS 40.40	Ch.38, p.3089
IAS 40.5	Ch.19, p.1468	IAS 40.40A	Ch.19, p.1444
IAS 40.5	Ch.22, p.1695	IAS 40.40A	Ch.19, p.1472
IAS 40.5	Ch.43, p.3418	IAS 40.41	Ch.19, p.1472
IAS 40.7	Ch.19, p.1443	IAS 40.48	Ch.19, p.1472
IAS 40.7	Ch.19, p.1445	IAS 40.50	Ch.19, p.1473
IAS 40.7	Ch.19, p.1446	IAS 40.50(a)	Ch.19, p.1450
IAS 40.8	Ch.19, p.1445	IAS 40.50(a)	Ch.19, p.1477
IAS 40.8	Ch.19, p.1446	IAS 40.50(b)	Ch.19, p.1450
IAS 40.9	Ch.19, p.1445	IAS 40.50(b)	Ch.19, p.1477
IAS 40.9	Ch.19, p.1446	IAS 40.50(c)	Ch.19, p.1477
IAS 40.10	Ch.19, p.1447	IAS 40.50(d)	Ch.19, p.1479
IAS 40.10	Ch.19, p.1448	IAS 40.52	Ch.19, p.1482
IAS 40.11	Ch.9, p.657	IAS 40.53	Ch.19, p.1473
IAS 40.11	Ch.19, p.1448	IAS 40.53	Ch.19, p.1474
IAS 40.11-14	Ch.9, p.641	IAS 40.53	Ch.19, p.1475
IAS 40.11-14	Ch.9, p.657	IAS 40.53A	Ch.19, p.1475
IAS 40.12-13	Ch.19, p.1449	IAS 40.53B	Ch.19, p.1475
IAS 40.13	Ch.19, p.1449	IAS 40.54	Ch.19, p.1474
IAS 40.14	Ch.19, p.1443	IAS 40.55	Ch.19, p.1474
IAS 40.14	Ch.19, p.1447	IAS 40.56	Ch.19, p.1444
IAS 40.14	Ch.19, p.1448	IAS 40.56	Ch.19, p.1483
IAS 40.14	Ch.19, p.1449	IAS 40.56	Ch.19, p.1486
IAS 40.14A	Ch.9, p.657	IAS 40.57	Ch.19, p.1488
IAS 40.14A	Ch.19, p.1453	IAS 40.57	Ch.19, p.1490
IAS 40.15	Ch.19, p.1446	IAS 40.57	Ch.42, p.3277
IAS 40.16	Ch.19, p.1451	IAS 40.57(d)	Ch.19, p.1490
IAS 40.17	Ch.19, p.1451	IAS 40.58	Ch.19, p.1490
IAS 40.18	Ch.19, p.1452	IAS 40.59	Ch.19, p.1461
IAS 40.19	Ch.19, p.1452	IAS 40.59	Ch.19, p.1490

IAS 40.60	Ch.19, p.1491	IAS 41.5A	Ch.18, p.1393
IAS 40.61	Ch.19, p.1491	IAS 41.5A	Ch.42, p.3276
IAS 40.62	Ch.19, p.1491	IAS 41.5B	Ch.18, p.1393
IAS 40.63	Ch.19, p.1491	IAS 41.5B	Ch.42, p.3276
IAS 40.64	Ch.19, p.1491	IAS 41.5C	Ch.18, p.1393
IAS 40.65	Ch.19, p.1492	IAS 41.5C	Ch.42, p.3275
IAS 40.66	Ch.19, p.1492	IAS 41.5C	Ch.42, p.3289
IAS 40.67	Ch.19, p.1492	IAS 41.6	Ch.42, p.3274
IAS 40.67	Ch.27, p.2040	IAS 41.7	Ch.42, p.3274
IAS 40.68	Ch.19, p.1494	IAS 41.7	Ch.42, p.3287
IAS 40.69	Ch.19, p.1493	IAS 41.8	Ch.42, p.3277
IAS 40.69	Ch.27, p.2040	IAS 41.10	Ch.42, p.3281
IAS 40.70	Ch.19, p.1493	IAS 41.10	Ch.42, p.3288
IAS 40.70	Ch.27, p.2040	IAS 41.11	Ch.42, p.3281
IAS 40.71	Ch.19, p.1493	IAS 41.12	Ch.19, p.1443
IAS 40.72	Ch.19, p.1495	IAS 41.12	Ch.42, p.3282
IAS 40.73	Ch.19, p.1495	IAS 41.13	Ch.42, p.3283
IAS 40.74	Ch.19, p.1496	IAS 41.13	Ch.42, p.3284
IAS 40.75	Ch.19, p.1497	IAS 41.15	Ch.42, p.3295
IAS 40.76	Ch.19, p.1505	IAS 41.16	Ch.42, p.3297
IAS 40.77	Ch.19, p.1506	IAS 41.22	Ch.42, p.3296
IAS 40.78	Ch.19, p.1508	IAS 41.22	Ch.42, p.3298
IAS 40.79	Ch.19, p.1509	IAS 41.24	Ch.42, p.3305
IAS 40.79(e)	Ch.14, p.1008	IAS 41.25	Ch.42, p.3300
IAS 40.79(e)	Ch.19, p.1467	IAS 41.25	Ch.42, p.3303
IAS 40.79(e)(iii)	Ch.14, p.1012	IAS 41.26	Ch.42, p.3289
IAS 40.BC19-20	Ch.19, p.1453	IAS 41.27	Ch.42, p.3290
IAS 40.BC25	Ch.19, p.1489	IAS 41.28	Ch.42, p.3290
IAS 40.BC26	Ch.19, p.1489	IAS 41.29	Ch.42, p.3290
IAS 40.BC27	Ch.19, p.1489	IAS 41.30	Ch.14, p.1012
IAS 40.BC28	Ch.19, p.1489	IAS 41.30	Ch.42, p.3282
		IAS 41.30	Ch.42, p.3290
		IAS 41.30	Ch.42, p.3291

IAS 41 (2008)

IAS 41(2008).21	Ch.42, p.3306

IAS 41.30	Ch.42, p.3292
IAS 41.31	Ch.42, p.3292
IAS 41.32	Ch.42, p.3283
IAS 41.33	Ch.42, p.3292
IAS 41.34	Ch.24, p.1843
IAS 41.34	Ch.42, p.3294
IAS 41.35	Ch.24, p.1843
IAS 41.35	Ch.42, p.3294
IAS 41.36	Ch.24, p.1843
IAS 41.36	Ch.42, p.3294
IAS 41.37-38	Ch.24, p.1842
IAS 41.37-38	Ch.42, p.3293
IAS 41.38	Ch.24, p.1842
IAS 41.40	Ch.42, p.3313
IAS 41.41	Ch.42, p.3315
IAS 41.42	Ch.42, p.3315
IAS 41.43	Ch.42, p.3316
IAS 41.44	Ch.42, p.3316
IAS 41.45	Ch.42, p.3316
IAS 41.46	Ch.42, p.3289
IAS 41.46	Ch.42, p.3316
IAS 41.49	Ch.42, p.3316
IAS 41.50	Ch.42, p.3316
IAS 41.51	Ch.42, p.3317
IAS 41.52	Ch.42, p.3317

IAS 41

IAS 41 Objective	Ch.42, p.3273
IAS 41.1	Ch.42, p.3277
IAS 41.1	Ch.42, p.3281
IAS 41.1(a)	Ch.24, p.1842
IAS 41.2	Ch.19, p.1443
IAS 41.2	Ch.42, p.3278
IAS 41.2(b)	Ch.42, p.3279
IAS 41.2(e)	Ch.42, p.3281
IAS 41.3	Ch.42, p.3278
IAS 41.3	Ch.42, p.3279
IAS 41.4	Ch.42, p.3275
IAS 41.5	Ch.24, p.1825
IAS 41.5	Ch.24, p.1842
IAS 41.5	Ch.42, p.3274
IAS 41.5	Ch.42, p.3275
IAS 41.5	Ch.42, p.3277
IAS 41.5	Ch.42, p.3287
IAS 41.5	Ch.42, p.3295

IAS 41.53	Ch.42, p.3318
IAS 41.54	Ch.42, p.3322
IAS 41.55	Ch.42, p.3322
IAS 41.56	Ch.42, p.3323
IAS 41.57	Ch.42, p.3323
IAS 41.B8	Ch.42, p.3278
IAS 41.B8	Ch.42, p.3284
IAS 41.B22	Ch.42, p.3296
IAS 41.B33	Ch.42, p.3296
IAS 41.B35	Ch.42, p.3292
IAS 41.B36	Ch.42, p.3292
IAS 41.B37	Ch.42, p.3293
IAS 41.B41	Ch.42, p.3278
IAS 41.B42	Ch.42, p.3284
IAS 41.B43	Ch.42, p.3283
IAS 41.B45	Ch.42, p.3278
IAS 41.B50-B54	Ch.42, p.3297
IAS 41.B55-B57	Ch.42, p.3278
IAS 41.B58-B60	Ch.42, p.3278
IAS 41.B62	Ch.42, p.3282
IAS 41.B66	Ch.24, p.1827
IAS 41.B66	Ch.24, p.1843
IAS 41.B66	Ch.42, p.3294
IAS 41.B67	Ch.24, p.1827
IAS 41.B69	Ch.24, p.1830
IAS 41.B74-B77	Ch.42, p.3317
IAS 41.B78-B79	Ch.42, p.3313
IAS 41.B81	Ch.42, p.3296
IAS 41.B82(n)	Ch.42, p.3280
IAS 41.IE1	Ch.42, p.3308
IAS 41.IE1	Ch.42, p.3314
IAS 41.IE2	Ch.42, p.3317
IAS 41.BC3	Ch.42, p.3296
IAS 41.BC4A-D	Ch.42, p.3279
IAS 41.BC4B	Ch.42, p.3279
IAS 41.BC4C	Ch.42, p.3291
IAS 41.BC4D	Ch.42, p.3288

IFRIC 1

IFRIC 1.1	Ch.25, p.1900
IFRIC 1.1	Ch.26, p.1981
IFRIC 1.2	Ch.18, p.1406
IFRIC 1.2	Ch.26, p.1982
IFRIC 1.2	Ch.26, p.1985
IFRIC 1.3	Ch.18, p.1406
IFRIC 1.3	Ch.26, p.1982
IFRIC 1.4-6	Ch.41, p.3259
IFRIC 1.4-7	Ch.26, p.1982
IFRIC 1.5	Ch.25, p.1900
IFRIC 1.5	Ch.26, p.1957
IFRIC 1.5	Ch.26, p.1982
IFRIC 1.5	Ch.33, p.2509
IFRIC 1.5	Ch.43, p.3501
IFRIC 1.6	Ch.26, p.1983
IFRIC 1.6	Ch.26, p.1984
IFRIC 1.7	Ch.18, p.1414
IFRIC 1.7	Ch.26, p.1957
IFRIC 1.7	Ch.26, p.1982
IFRIC 1.8	Ch.25, p.1900
IFRIC 1.8	Ch.26, p.1954
IFRIC 1.8	Ch.26, p.1961
IFRIC 1.8	Ch.26, p.1982
IFRIC 1.IE1-4	Ch.26, p.1983
IFRIC 1.IE5	Ch.26, p.1957
IFRIC 1.IE5	Ch.26, p.1985
IFRIC 1.IE6-10	Ch.26, p.1984
IFRIC 1.IE7	Ch.26, p.1985
IFRIC 1.IE11-12	Ch.26, p.1984
IFRIC 1.BC23	Ch.26, p.1985
IFRIC 1.BC26	Ch.26, p.1954
IFRIC 1.BC26-27	Ch.26, p.1982

IFRIC 2

IFRIC 2.1-4	Ch.47, p.3693
IFRIC 2.5	Ch.47, p.3694
IFRIC 2.6	Ch.47, p.3694
IFRIC 2.6-8	Ch.47, p.3694
IFRIC 2.8	Ch.47, p.3694
IFRIC 2.9	Ch.47, p.3694
IFRIC 2.10	Ch.47, p.3694
IFRIC 2.11	Ch.47, p.3694
IFRIC 2.BC10	Ch.47, p.3734

IFRIC 5

IFRIC 5.1	Ch.26, p.1986
IFRIC 5.2	Ch.26, p.1987
IFRIC 5.3	Ch.26, p.1987
IFRIC 5.4	Ch.26, p.1987
IFRIC 5.5	Ch.26, p.1987
IFRIC 5.5	Ch.45, p.3606
IFRIC 5.6	Ch.26, p.1988
IFRIC 5.7	Ch.26, p.1988
IFRIC 5.7	Ch.26, p.1990
IFRIC 5.8	Ch.26, p.1988
IFRIC 5.9	Ch.26, p.1988
IFRIC 5.10	Ch.26, p.1990
IFRIC 5.11	Ch.26, p.1991
IFRIC 5.12	Ch.26, p.1991
IFRIC 5.13	Ch.26, p.1991
IFRIC 5.BC7	Ch.26, p.1990
IFRIC 5.BC8	Ch.26, p.1991
IFRIC 5.BC14	Ch.26, p.1988
IFRIC 5.BC19-20	Ch.26, p.1988
IFRIC 5.BC19-20	Ch.26, p.1989

IFRIC 6

IFRIC 6.3	Ch.26, p.1995
IFRIC 6.4	Ch.26, p.1995

IFRIC 6.5	Ch.26, p.1996	IFRIC 12.10	Ch.25, p.1917
IFRIC 6.6	Ch.26, p.1995	IFRIC 12.11	Ch.25, p.1853
IFRIC 6.7	Ch.26, p.1996	IFRIC 12.11	Ch.25, p.1858
IFRIC 6.8	Ch.26, p.1995	IFRIC 12.11	Ch.25, p.1867
IFRIC 6.9	Ch.26, p.1996	IFRIC 12.11	Ch.25, p.1879
IFRIC 6.BC5	Ch.26, p.1996	IFRIC 12.11	Ch.25, p.1890
IFRIC 6.BC6	Ch.26, p.1996	IFRIC 12.12	Ch.25, p.1868
IFRIC 6.BC7	Ch.26, p.1996	IFRIC 12.12	Ch.25, p.1884
		IFRIC 12.13	Ch.25, p.1868
		IFRIC 12.13	Ch.25, p.1869

IFRIC 7

		IFRIC 12.13	Ch.25, p.1884
		IFRIC 12.14	Ch.25, p.1853
IFRIC 7.3	Ch.16, p.1263	IFRIC 12.14	Ch.25, p.1857
IFRIC 7.3	Ch.16, p.1274	IFRIC 12.14	Ch.25, p.1867
IFRIC 7.3	Ch.41, p.3258	IFRIC 12.14	Ch.25, p.1869
IFRIC 7.4	Ch.16, p.1265	IFRIC 12.14	Ch.25, p.1875
IFRIC 7.5	Ch.16, p.1265	IFRIC 12.14	Ch.25, p.1879
IFRIC 7.IE1-IE6	Ch.16, p.1265	IFRIC 12.14	Ch.25, p.1890
IFRIC 7.BC21-BC22	Ch.16, p.1264	IFRIC 12.14	Ch.25, p.1899
		IFRIC 12.15	Ch.25, p.1853
		IFRIC 12.15	Ch.25, p.1873

IFRIC 10

		IFRIC 12.15	Ch.25, p.1879
		IFRIC 12.16	Ch.25, p.1873
IFRIC 10.2	Ch.41, p.3245	IFRIC 12.16	Ch.25, p.1875
IFRIC 10.8	Ch.41, p.3245	IFRIC 12.16	Ch.45, p.3589
IFRIC 10.9	Ch.41, p.3246	IFRIC 12.17	Ch.25, p.1873
IFRIC 10.BC9	Ch.41, p.3245	IFRIC 12.17	Ch.25, p.1879
		IFRIC 12.18	Ch.25, p.1873
		IFRIC 12.18	Ch.25, p.1885

IFRIC 12

		IFRIC 12.19	Ch.25, p.1853
		IFRIC 12.19	Ch.25, p.1868
IFRIC 12 references	Ch.2, p.47	IFRIC 12.19	Ch.25, p.1873
IFRIC 12.1	Ch.5, p.319	IFRIC 12.19	Ch.25, p.1875
IFRIC 12.1	Ch.25, p.1854	IFRIC 12.19	Ch.25, p.1879
IFRIC 12.1	Ch.25, p.1855	IFRIC 12.19	Ch.25, p.1883
IFRIC 12.1	Ch.25, p.1862	IFRIC 12.19	Ch.25, p.1899
IFRIC 12.2	Ch.5, p.319	IFRIC 12.19	Ch.25, p.1909
IFRIC 12.2	Ch.25, p.1853	IFRIC 12.19	Ch.25, p.1910
IFRIC 12.3	Ch.25, p.1853	IFRIC 12.19	Ch.25, p.1912
IFRIC 12.3	Ch.25, p.1854	IFRIC 12.19	Ch.25, p.1916
IFRIC 12.3	Ch.25, p.1892	IFRIC 12.20	Ch.25, p.1853
IFRIC 12.4	Ch.25, p.1854	IFRIC 12.20	Ch.25, p.1869
IFRIC 12.4	Ch.25, p.1858	IFRIC 12.20	Ch.25, p.1899
IFRIC 12.5	Ch.25, p.1854	IFRIC 12.20	Ch.25, p.1901
IFRIC 12.5	Ch.25, p.1857	IFRIC 12.21	Ch.25, p.1899
IFRIC 12.5	Ch.25, p.1858	IFRIC 12.21	Ch.25, p.1901
IFRIC 12.5	Ch.25, p.1869	IFRIC 12.21	Ch.25, p.1906
IFRIC 12.5(b)	Ch.25, p.1859	IFRIC 12.21	Ch.25, p.1914
IFRIC 12.6	Ch.25, p.1854	IFRIC 12.22	Ch.25, p.1876
IFRIC 12.6	Ch.25, p.1861	IFRIC 12.22	Ch.25, p.1879
IFRIC 12.7	Ch.25, p.1853	IFRIC 12.22	Ch.25, p.1916
IFRIC 12.7	Ch.25, p.1854	IFRIC 12.23	Ch.25, p.1916
IFRIC 12.7	Ch.25, p.1862	IFRIC 12.24	Ch.25, p.1876
IFRIC 12.7	Ch.25, p.1864	IFRIC 12.25	Ch.25, p.1876
IFRIC 12.8	Ch.25, p.1862	IFRIC 12.26	Ch.25, p.1881
IFRIC 12.8	Ch.25, p.1865	IFRIC 12.27	Ch.25, p.1904
IFRIC 12.9	Ch.25, p.1854	IFRIC 12.29	Ch.5, p.319
IFRIC 12.9	Ch.25, p.1858	IFRIC 12.30	Ch.5, p.319

IFRIC 12.AG2	Ch.25, p.1859
IFRIC 12.AG3	Ch.25, p.1859
IFRIC 12.AG5	Ch.25, p.1858
IFRIC 12.AG6	Ch.25, p.1858
IFRIC 12.AG6	Ch.25, p.1860
IFRIC 12.AG7	Ch.25, p.1855
IFRIC 12.AG7	Ch.25, p.1866
IFRIC 12.AG8	Ch.25, p.1866
IFRIC 12.IE15	Ch.25, p.1879
IFRIC 12.IE15	Ch.25, p.1916
IFRIC 12.IE19	Ch.25, p.1902
IFRIC 12.IE20	Ch.25, p.1902
IFRIC 12.BC7	Ch.2, p.47
IFRIC 12.BC11-13	Ch.25, p.1852
IFRIC 12.BC11-13	Ch.25, p.1854
IFRIC 12.BC13	Ch.25, p.1855
IFRIC 12.BC14	Ch.25, p.1858
IFRIC 12.BC15	Ch.25, p.1858
IFRIC 12.BC16	Ch.25, p.1865
IFRIC 12.BC20	Ch.2, p.47
IFRIC 12.BC21	Ch.25, p.1858
IFRIC 12.BC22	Ch.25, p.1858
IFRIC 12.BC31	Ch.25, p.1867
IFRIC 12.BC31	Ch.25, p.1869
IFRIC 12.BC32	Ch.25, p.1880
IFRIC 12.BC35	Ch.25, p.1884
IFRIC 12.BC44	Ch.25, p.1873
IFRIC 12.BC52	Ch.25, p.1874
IFRIC 12.BC53	Ch.25, p.1885
IFRIC 12.BC65	Ch.25, p.1881
IFRIC 12.BC66	Ch.25, p.1900
IFRIC 12.BC68	Ch.25, p.1900

IFRIC 14

IFRIC 14.1	Ch.35, p.2930
IFRIC 14.1-3	Ch.35, p.2930
IFRIC 14.2	Ch.35, p.2930
IFRIC 14.3	Ch.35, p.2930
IFRIC 14.5	Ch.35, p.2933
IFRIC 14.6	Ch.35, p.2930
IFRIC 14.7	Ch.35, p.2931
IFRIC 14.8	Ch.35, p.2931
IFRIC 14.9	Ch.35, p.2931
IFRIC 14.10	Ch.35, p.2967
IFRIC 14.11-12	Ch.35, p.2931
IFRIC 14.11-12	Ch.35, p.2932
IFRIC 14.13	Ch.35, p.2931
IFRIC 14.14	Ch.35, p.2931
IFRIC 14.14	Ch.35, p.2969
IFRIC 14.15	Ch.35, p.2932
IFRIC 14.16	Ch.35, p.2933
IFRIC 14.17	Ch.35, p.2933
IFRIC 14.18	Ch.35, p.2934
IFRIC 14.19	Ch.35, p.2934
IFRIC 14.20	Ch.35, p.2934
IFRIC 14.21	Ch.35, p.2933
IFRIC 14.21	Ch.35, p.2934
IFRIC 14.22	Ch.35, p.2934
IFRIC 14.23	Ch.35, p.2936
IFRIC 14.24	Ch.35, p.2937
IFRIC 14.IE1-2	Ch.35, p.2937
IFRIC 14.IE3-8	Ch.35, p.2937
IFRIC 14.IE9-27	Ch.35, p.2934
IFRIC 14.BC10	Ch.35, p.2932
IFRIC 14.BC30	Ch.35, p.2933

IFRIC 16

IFRIC 16.1	Ch.53, p.4266
IFRIC 16.2	Ch.53, p.4267
IFRIC 16.2	Ch.53, p.4306
IFRIC 16.3	Ch.53, p.4300
IFRIC 16.4	Ch.53, p.4266
IFRIC 16.7	Ch.53, p.4267
IFRIC 16.7	Ch.53, p.4306
IFRIC 16.8	Ch.53, p.4267
IFRIC 16.10	Ch.53, p.4267
IFRIC 16.11	Ch.53, p.4268
IFRIC 16.11	Ch.53, p.4269
IFRIC 16.12	Ch.53, p.4267
IFRIC 16.13	Ch.53, p.4269
IFRIC 16.13	Ch.53, p.4270
IFRIC 16.14	Ch.53, p.4270
IFRIC 16.14	Ch.53, p.4302
IFRIC 16.14	Ch.53, p.4303
IFRIC 16.15	Ch.53, p.4301
IFRIC 16.15	Ch.53, p.4302
IFRIC 16.16	Ch.53, p.4364
IFRIC 16.17	Ch.7, p.500
IFRIC 16.17	Ch.7, p.501
IFRIC 16.17	Ch.15, p.1214
IFRIC 16.17	Ch.53, p.4364
IFRIC 16.17	Ch.53, p.4365
IFRIC 16.AG1-3	Ch.53, p.4268
IFRIC 16.AG2	Ch.53, p.4268
IFRIC 16.AG2	Ch.53, p.4303
IFRIC 16.AG2	Ch.53, p.4304
IFRIC 16.AG4	Ch.53, p.4268
IFRIC 16.AG4	Ch.53, p.4301
IFRIC 16.AG5	Ch.53, p.4301
IFRIC 16.AG5	Ch.53, p.4302
IFRIC 16.AG6	Ch.53, p.4269
IFRIC 16.AG6	Ch.53, p.4271
IFRIC 16.AG7	Ch.53, p.4301
IFRIC 16.AG8	Ch.53, p.4365
IFRIC 16.AG10	Ch.53, p.4269
IFRIC 16.AG11	Ch.53, p.4270
IFRIC 16.AG12	Ch.53, p.4270
IFRIC 16.AG12	Ch.53, p.4302
IFRIC 16.AG13	Ch.53, p.4270
IFRIC 16.AG14	Ch.53, p.4269
IFRIC 16.AG15	Ch.53, p.4270
IFRIC 16.BC24A	Ch.53, p.4270

IFRIC 16.BC24B Ch.53, p.4270
IFRIC 16.BC36 .... Ch.7, p.501

IFRIC 17

IFRIC 17.3 .... Ch.7, p.531
IFRIC 17.3 .... Ch.8, p.601
IFRIC 17.4 .... Ch.7, p.531

IFRIC 17.4 .... Ch.8, p.602
IFRIC 17.5 .... Ch.7, p.531
IFRIC 17.5 .... Ch.8, p.602
IFRIC 17.5 .... Ch.8, p.617
IFRIC 17.6 .... Ch.7, p.531
IFRIC 17.6 .... Ch.8, p.602
IFRIC 17.7 .... Ch.7, p.531
IFRIC 17.7 .... Ch.8, p.602
IFRIC 17.8 .... Ch.7, p.531
IFRIC 17.10 .... Ch.7, p.531
IFRIC 17.10 .... Ch.8, p.599
IFRIC 17.10 .... Ch.8, p.602
IFRIC 17.10 .... Ch.38, p.3081
IFRIC 17.11 .... Ch.7, p.532
IFRIC 17.11 .... Ch.8, p.602
IFRIC 17.12 .... Ch.7, p.532
IFRIC 17.12 .... Ch.8, p.602
IFRIC 17.13 .... Ch.7, p.532
IFRIC 17.13 .... Ch.8, p.602
IFRIC 17.14-15 .... Ch.7, p.532
IFRIC 17.14-15 .... Ch.8, p.603
IFRIC 17.16 .... Ch.7, p.533
IFRIC 17.16 .... Ch.8, p.603
IFRIC 17.17 .... Ch.7, p.533
IFRIC 17.17 .... Ch.8, p.604
IFRIC 17.17 .... Ch.38, p.3085
IFRIC 17.BC5 .... Ch.8, p.602
IFRIC 17.BC18-20 .... Ch.38, p.3081
IFRIC 17.BC22 .... Ch.45, p.3591
IFRIC 17.BC27 .... Ch.45, p.3591
IFRIC 17.BC55 .... Ch.7, p.532
IFRIC 17.BC56 .... Ch.7, p.532

IFRIC 19

IFRIC 19 references Ch.2, p.47
IFRIC 19.1 .... Ch.47, p.3737
IFRIC 19.2 .... Ch.5, p.321
IFRIC 19.2 .... Ch.47, p.3737
IFRIC 19.3 .... Ch.5, p.321
IFRIC 19.3 .... Ch.47, p.3738
IFRIC 19.5-7 .... Ch.47, p.3738
IFRIC 19.7 .... Ch.47, p.3738
IFRIC 19.8 .... Ch.47, p.3738
IFRIC 19.9 .... Ch.47, p.3738

IFRIC 19.10 .... Ch.47, p.3739
IFRIC 19.11 .... Ch.47, p.3738
IFRIC 19.13 .... Ch.5, p.321
IFRIC 19.BC16 .... Ch.2, p.47
IFRIC 19.BC22 .... Ch.47, p.3738
IFRIC 19.BC33 .... Ch.5, p.321

IFRIC 20

IFRIC 20 references Ch.2, p.47
IFRIC 20.1 .... Ch.5, p.322
IFRIC 20.2 .... Ch.43, p.3502
IFRIC 20.3 .... Ch.5, p.322
IFRIC 20.3 .... Ch.43, p.3502
IFRIC 20.5 .... Ch.5, p.322
IFRIC 20.8 .... Ch.43, p.3502
IFRIC 20.9 .... Ch.43, p.3504
IFRIC 20.10 .... Ch.43, p.3504
IFRIC 20.12 .... Ch.43, p.3505
IFRIC 20.13 .... Ch.43, p.3505
IFRIC 20.14 .... Ch.43, p.3511
IFRIC 20.15 .... Ch.43, p.3506
IFRIC 20.15 .... Ch.43, p.3511
IFRIC 20.16 .... Ch.43, p.3511
IFRIC 20 Appendix A Ch.5, p.322
IFRIC 20.BC4 .... Ch.43, p.3502
IFRIC 20.BC8 .... Ch.43, p.3510
IFRIC 20.BC10 .... Ch.43, p.3504
IFRIC 20.BC12 .... Ch.43, p.3505
IFRIC 20.BC15 .... Ch.43, p.3505
IFRIC 20.BC17 .... Ch.43, p.3510

IFRIC 21

IFRIC 21.2 .... Ch.26, p.1997
IFRIC 21.2 .... Ch.41, p.3261
IFRIC 21.3 .... Ch.26, p.1997
IFRIC 21.3 .... Ch.26, p.2000
IFRIC 21.4 .... Ch.26, p.1932
IFRIC 21.4 .... Ch.26, p.1997
IFRIC 21.4 .... Ch.26, p.1998
IFRIC 21.5 .... Ch.26, p.1997
IFRIC 21.5 .... Ch.26, p.2001
IFRIC 21.6 .... Ch.26, p.1997
IFRIC 21.6 .... Ch.41, p.3261
IFRIC 21.7 .... Ch.26, p.1997
IFRIC 21.8 .... Ch.26, p.1997
IFRIC 21.8 .... Ch.26, p.1998
IFRIC 21.8 .... Ch.41, p.3261
IFRIC 21.9 .... Ch.26, p.1998
IFRIC 21.9-10 .... Ch.41, p.3261
IFRIC 21.10 .... Ch.26, p.1998
IFRIC 21.11 .... Ch.26, p.1998
IFRIC 21.11 .... Ch.41, p.3261
IFRIC 21.12 .... Ch.26, p.1998
IFRIC 21.14 .... Ch.26, p.1998

IFRIC 21.14 .... Ch.26, p.2000
IFRIC 21.14 .... Ch.26, p.2001
IFRIC 21.31 .... Ch.41, p.3261
IFRIC 21.A1 .... Ch.26, p.1997
IFRIC 21.IE1 .... Ch.26, p.1999
IFRIC 21.IE1 Example 2 .... Ch.26, p.1998
IFRIC 21.IE1 Example 2 .... Ch.41, p.3261
IFRIC 21.IE1 Example 3 .... Ch.26, p.2000
IFRIC 21.IE1 Example 4 .... Ch.41, p.3262
IFRIC 21.BC4 .... Ch.26, p.1997
IFRIC 21.BC4 .... Ch.26, p.2001

IFRIC 22

IFRIC 22 references Ch.2, p.47
IFRIC 22.4 .... Ch.5, p.341
IFRIC 22.4 .... Ch.15, p.1189
IFRIC 22.5 .... Ch.15, p.1189
IFRIC 22.6 .... Ch.15, p.1190
IFRIC 22.7 .... Ch.5, p.342
IFRIC 22.8 .... Ch.15, p.1189
IFRIC 22.8-9 .... Ch.5, p.342
IFRIC 22.9 .... Ch.15, p.1189
IFRIC 22.BC8 .... Ch.15, p.1190
IFRIC 22.BC17 .... Ch.2, p.47
IFRIC 22.BC17 .... Ch.15, p.1197

IFRIC 23

IFRIC 23.3 .... Ch.33, p.2458
IFRIC 23.3 .... Ch.33, p.2476
IFRIC 23.3 .... Ch.33, p.2542
IFRIC 23.3 .... Ch.33, p.2562
IFRIC 23.4 .... Ch.26, p.1935
IFRIC 23.4 .... Ch.33, p.2561
IFRIC 23.4 .... Ch.33, p.2568
IFRIC 23.5 .... Ch.33, p.2561
IFRIC 23.6 .... Ch.33, p.2563
IFRIC 23.8 .... Ch.33, p.2563
IFRIC 23.9 .... Ch.33, p.2564
IFRIC 23.10 .... Ch.33, p.2564
IFRIC 23.10 .... Ch.33, p.2567
IFRIC 23.11 .... Ch.33, p.2564
IFRIC 23.12 .... Ch.33, p.2563
IFRIC 23.12 .... Ch.33, p.2566
IFRIC 23.13 .... Ch.33, p.2477
IFRIC 23.13 .... Ch.33, p.2566
IFRIC 23.13 .... Ch.38, p.3090
IFRIC 23.14 .... Ch.33, p.2477
IFRIC 23.14 .... Ch.33, p.2566
IFRIC 23.14 .... Ch.33, p.2567
IFRIC 23.14 .... Ch.38, p.3078
IFRIC 23.14 .... Ch.38, p.3080
IFRIC 23.14 .... Ch.38, p.3090
IFRIC 23.A2 .... Ch.33, p.2566
IFRIC 23.A2 .... Ch.38, p.3090

IFRIC 23.A3 .... Ch.33, p.2567
IFRIC 23.A4(a) Ch.33, p.2567
IFRIC 23.A4(b) Ch.33, p.2567
IFRIC 23.A5 .... Ch.33, p.2567
IFRIC 23.B1 .... Ch.33, p.2455
IFRIC 23.B1 .... Ch.33, p.2561
IFRIC 23.B2 .... Ch.33, p.2561
IFRIC 23.IE1 .... Ch.33, p.2565
IFRIC 23.IE2-6 .... Ch.33, p.2564
IFRIC 23.IE7-10 .... Ch.33, p.2565
IFRIC 23.BC4 .... Ch.33, p.2569
IFRIC 23.BC6 .... Ch.33, p.2561
IFRIC 23.BC8 .... Ch.33, p.2562
IFRIC 23.BC9 .... Ch.33, p.2562
IFRIC 23.BC11 .... Ch.33, p.2563
IFRIC 23.BC13 .... Ch.33, p.2563
IFRIC 23.BC23 .... Ch.9, p.691
IFRIC 23.BC23 .... Ch.33, p.2562
IFRIC 23.BC24 .... Ch.9, p.692
IFRIC 23.BC24 .... Ch.33, p.2562

SIC-7

SIC-7.3 .... Ch.15, p.1241
SIC-7.4 .... Ch.15, p.1242
SIC-7.5 .... Ch.15, p.1241
SIC-7.6 .... Ch.15, p.1242
SIC-7.7 .... Ch.15, p.1242

SIC-10

SIC-10.3 .... Ch.24, p.1827

SIC-25

SIC-25.4 .... Ch.33, p.2475
SIC-25.4 .... Ch.33, p.2599

SIC-29

SIC-29.1 .... Ch.25, p.1855
SIC-29.1 .... Ch.25, p.1856
SIC-29.1 .... Ch.25, p.1917
SIC-29.2 .... Ch.25, p.1917
SIC-29.2(a) Ch.25, p.1855
SIC-29.3 .... Ch.25, p.1917
SIC-29.4 .... Ch.25, p.1852
SIC-29.5 .... Ch.25, p.1917
SIC-29.6 .... Ch.25, p.1917
SIC-29.6 .... Ch.25, p.1918
SIC-29.6A Ch.25, p.1918
SIC-29.7 .... Ch.25, p.1918

SIC-32

SIC-32.1	Ch.17, p.1326
SIC-32.2	Ch.17, p.1327
SIC-32.3	Ch.17, p.1327
SIC-32.5-6	Ch.17, p.1327
SIC-32.7	Ch.17, p.1326
SIC-32.8	Ch.17, p.1327
SIC-32.9	Ch.17, p.1327
SIC-32.10	Ch.17, p.1328

Management Commentary

MC.12	Ch.2, p.107
MC.13	Ch.2, p.107
MC.24	Ch.2, p.107
MC Appendix	Ch.2, p.106
MC.IN2	Ch.2, p.106
MC.IN3	Ch.2, p.106
MC.IN4	Ch.2, p.106
MC.IN5	Ch.2, p.107

PS 2

PS 2.2	Ch.3, p.160
PS 2.5-7	Ch.3, p.161
PS 2.8-10	Ch.3, p.161
PS 2.11-12	Ch.3, p.161
PS 2.13-23	Ch.3, p.161
PS 2.24-26	Ch.3, p.161
PS 2.28	Ch.3, p.161
PS 2.29-32	Ch.3, p.162
PS 2.35-39	Ch.3, p.162
PS 2.40-55	Ch.3, p.162
PS 2.56-59	Ch.3, p.162
PS 2.60-65	Ch.3, p.162
PS 2.66-71	Ch.3, p.162
PS 2.72-80	Ch.3, p.163
PS 2.81-83	Ch.3, p.163
PS 2.84-88	Ch.3, p.163

Index

Note: This index uses chapter number followed by section number for locators. A section number includes all its sub-sections. For example the locator Ch. 37, 2.7 will include subsections 2.7.1 and 2.7.2 in chapter 37. The locator Ch. 21, 5.3.1 will include subsections and 5.3.1.B. Where a range is indicated, for example, Ch. 3, 2–3, this means the topic starts from the beginning of section 2 to the end of section 3.

Accounting estimates
  vs. accounting policies, Ch. 3, 4.2
  changes in, Ch. 3, 4.5
  disclosures of, Ch. 3, 5.2
Accounting policies, Ch. 3, 4. *See also* IAS 1; IAS 8
  vs. accounting estimates, Ch. 3, 4.2
  accrual basis of accounting, Ch. 3, 4.1.3
  aggregation, Ch. 3, 4.1.5.A
  application of, Ch. 3, 4.3
  changes in, Ch. 3, 4.4
  consistency, Ch. 3, 4.1.4; Ch. 7, 2.6
  correction of errors, Ch. 3, 4.6
  definition of, Ch. 3, 4.2
  disclosures relating to, Ch. 3, 5.1
    changes in accounting policies, Ch. 3, 5.1.2
    changes pursuant to the initial application of an IFRS, Ch. 3, 5.1.2.A
    judgements made in applying accounting policies, Ch. 3, 5.1.1.B
    new IFRS, future impact of, Ch. 3, 5.1.2.C
    summary of significant accounting policies, Ch. 3, 5.1.1.A
    voluntary changes in accounting policy, Ch. 3, 5.1.2.B
  fair presentation, Ch. 3, 4.1.1
  general principles, Ch. 3, 4.1
  going concern, Ch. 3, 4.1.2
  interim financial reports, Ch. 41, 8.1
    measurement on a year-to-date basis, Ch. 41, 8.1.1
    new accounting pronouncements and other changes in accounting policies, Ch. 41, 8.1.2
    voluntary changes in presentation, Ch. 41, 8.1.3
  materiality, Ch. 3, 4.1.5.A
  offset, Ch. 3, 4.1.5.B
  Practice Statement 2, Ch. 3, 4.1.7
  profit or loss for the period, Ch. 3, 4.1.6
  selection of, Ch. 3, 4.3
Accounting Standards Advisory Forum (ASAF), Ch. 1, 2.8
Accounting Standards Board (AcSB), Ch. 1, 4.3.2
Accounting Standards Board of Japan (ASBJ), Ch. 1, 4.4.2
Accounting Standards Codification (ASC). *See under* ASC
Accounting Standards for Business Enterprises (ASBE), Ch. 1, 4.4.1.A
Accrual basis of accounting, Ch. 3, 4.1.3

Accrued operating lease income, Ch. 19, 6.6
  rental income and lease incentives, Ch. 19, 6.6.1
Acquired receivables, Ch. 49, 3.3.4; Ch. 54, 4.6.1
Acquirer's obligation to transfer proceeds from realisation of acquired contingent asset, Ch. 9, 5.6.4.A
Acquisition method of accounting, Ch. 9, 4. *See also* Business combinations; IFRS 3
  acquisition date determination, Ch. 9, 4.2
  business combinations under common control, application to, Ch. 10, 3.1–3.2
  identifying the acquirer, Ch. 9, 4.1
  'reverse acquisitions', Ch. 9, 4.1
Acquisition of cash flows, insurance contracts, Ch. 56, 8.2.3.E
Acquisition of insurance contracts, Ch. 56, 13
Acquisition-related costs, Ch. 9, 7.3; Ch. 40, 6.3.1
Active market, Ch. 14, 3, 8.1.1, 17; Ch. 20, 3.3
Active market identifying CGUs, Ch. 20, 3.3
Actuarial assumptions, Ch. 35, 7.5
Actuarial gains and losses, Ch. 35, 7.5
Actuarial methodology, Ch. 35, 7.3
Adjusting events, Ch. 38, 2.1.2
  determining value in use, Ch. 20, 7
  treatment of, Ch. 38, 2.2
Advisory bodies, Ch. 1, 2.9
  Accounting Standards Advisory Forum (ASAF), Ch. 1, 2.8
  Advisory Council, IFRS, Ch. 1, 2.7
  Capital Markets Advisory Committee, Ch. 1, 2.9
  Consultative Group for Rate Regulation, Ch. 1, 2.9
  Emerging Economies Group, Ch. 1, 2.9
  Global Preparers Forum, Ch. 1, 2.9
  IFRS Taxonomy Consultative Group, Ch. 1, 2.9
  Islamic Finance Consultative Group, Ch. 1, 2.9
  Management Commentary Consultative Group, Ch. 1, 2.9
  SME Implementation Group, Ch. 1, 2.9
  Transition Resource Group for IFRS 17 Insurance Contracts, Ch. 1, 2.9
  World Standard-setters Conferences, Ch. 1, 2.9
Agenda consultation 2011, Ch. 10, 6.1
Agenda consultation 2015, Ch. 10, 6.1; Ch. 43, 1.3.6, 8.4.1
Aggregated exposures, hedge accounting, Ch. 53, 2.7
Aggregation criteria, operating segments, Ch. 36, 1.3, 3.2.1

Agriculture, Ch. 42, 1–5. *See also* IAS 41
'All employee' share plans, Ch. 34, 2.2.2.D
All-in-one hedges, hedge accounting, Ch. 53, 5.2.1
Americas, IFRS adoption in, Ch. 1, 4.3
Amortisation of intangible assets, Ch. 17, 9
    assessing the useful life of an intangible asset as finite/indefinite, Ch. 17, 9.1
    factors affecting the useful life, Ch. 17, 9.1.1
    useful life of contractual/other legal rights, Ch. 17, 9.1.2
    impairment losses, Ch. 17, 9.4; Ch. 20, 11
    intangible assets with a finite useful life, Ch. 17, 9.2
        amortisation period and method, Ch. 17, 9.2.1
            amortisation of programme and other broadcast rights, Ch. 17, 9.2.1.B
            amortising customer relationships and similar intangible assets, Ch. 17, 9.2.1.A
        residual value, Ch. 17, 9.2.4
        revenue-based amortisation, Ch. 17, 9.2.2
        review of amortisation period and amortisation method, Ch. 17, 9.2.3
    intangible assets with an indefinite useful life, Ch. 17, 9.3; Ch. 20, 10
    retirements and disposals, Ch. 17, 9.5
        derecognition of parts of intangible assets, Ch. 17, 9.5.1
Amortised cost, Ch. 50, 3; Ch. 51, 14.1
    financial assets measured at, Ch. 50, 2.1; Ch. 51, 14.1
    financial liabilities measured at, Ch. 50, 2.2
    transfers of assets measured at, Ch. 52, 5.4.2
Area-of-interest method, E&E expenditure, Ch. 43, 3.2.5
ASC 310–*Receivables*, Ch. 27, 3.5.1.C
ASC 405–*Liabilities*, Ch. 27, 3.5.1.B
ASC 460–*Guarantees*, Ch. 27, 3.5.1.B
ASC 718–*Compensation Stock Compensation*, Ch. 34, 1.1
ASC 815–*Derivatives and Hedging*, Ch. 27, 3.5.1.B
ASC 860–*Transfers and Servicing*, Ch. 27, 3.5.1.B
ASC 924–*Entertainment–Casinos*, Ch. 27, 3.5.1.F
ASC 958–605–*Not-for-Profit Entities–Revenue Recognition*, Ch. 27, 3.5.1.E
Asia, IFRS adoption in, Ch. 1, 4.4
Asset swap accounts, Ch. 43, 6.3
Associates. *See also* Equity method/accounting, IAS 28; Investments in associates and joint ventures
    cash flows of, Ch. 40, 6.4
    definition, Ch. 11, 3
    disclosure, Ch. 13, 5
        nature, extent and financial effects of interests in associates, Ch. 13, 5.1
        risks associated with interests in associates, Ch. 13, 5.2
    dividends from, Ch. 8, 2.4.1
    equity accounted associate or joint venture that is not a business becomes a subsidiary in an acquisition in stages, Ch. 7,3.1.2
    first-time adoption
        assets and liabilities of, Ch. 5, 5.9
        investments in, Ch. 5, 5.8
    investments in, Ch. 11, 5.3; Ch. 20, 12.4
    loss of control – interest retained in former subsidiary is an associate, Ch. 7, 3.3.2, 7.1; Ch. 11, 7.4.1
    separate financial statements and interests in, Ch. 8, 1.1.1
    share-based payments to employee of, Ch. 34, 12.9
    significant influence, Ch. 11, 4
        fund managers, Ch. 11, 4.6
        holdings of less than 20% of the voting power, Ch. 11, 4.3
        lack of, Ch. 11, 4.2
        potential voting rights, Ch. 11, 4.4
        severe long-term restrictions impairing ability to transfer funds to the investor, Ch. 11, 4.1
        voting rights held in a fiduciary capacity, Ch. 11, 4.5
Assurance-type warranty, Ch. 31, 3.3
Australia, IFRS adoption in, Ch. 1, 4.5
Australian Accounting Standards (AAS), Ch. 1, 4.5
'Back-to-back' forward contracts, Ch. 47, 11.1.3
Balance sheet. *See* Statement of financial position
Bank overdrafts, Ch. 40, 3.2.4
Barter transactions, Ch. 29, 2.6.2
Basel Committee on Banking Supervision, Ch. 1, 2.5
'Basic' sensitivity analysis, Ch. 54, 5.5.1
Bearer plants, Ch. 18, 3.1.7; Ch. 42, 2.3.3
    definition, Ch. 18, 2.2; Ch. 42, 2.2.1.A
    requirements for produce growing on, Ch. 42, 3.2.3
    in scope of IAS 16, Ch. 18, 2.1; Ch. 42, 3.2.3.A
Bid-ask spread, Ch. 14, 15.3.2
Binomial model, Ch. 34, 8.3.2
Biological assets, Ch. 42, 2.3.1. *See also* IAS 41–*Agriculture*
    definition of, Ch. 42, 2.2.1
    disclosure of groups of, Ch. 42, 5.1.3
    fair value measurement, Ch. 42, 4.5.2, 4.6.2.A
    leases of, Ch. 42, 2.3.5
    measurement, Ch. 42, 3.2.1
Black economic empowerment (BEE) and share-based payment, Ch. 34, 15.5
Black-Scholes-Merton formula, Ch. 34, 8.3.1
Block caving, depreciation, depletion and amortisation (mining), Ch. 43, 16.2
Bonds. *See* Convertible bonds
Borrowing costs, Ch. 21. *See also* Capitalisation of borrowing costs; IAS 23
    definition of, Ch. 21, 4
    eligible for capitalisation, Ch. 17, 6.3.2; Ch. 21, 5
        accrued costs and trade payables, Ch. 21, 5.3.3
        calculation of capitalisation rate, Ch. 21, 5.3.2
        directly attributable, Ch. 21, 5.1
        exchange differences as, Ch. 21, 5.4
        general borrowings, Ch. 21, 5.3
            completed qualifying assets, related to, Ch. 21, 5.3.1.A
            specific non-qualifying assets, related to, Ch. 21, 5.3.1.B
        group considerations, Ch. 21, 5.7
        hyperinflationary economies, Ch. 21, 5.6
        specific borrowings, Ch. 21, 5.2
    intangible assets, Ch. 17, 4.2
    interim reporting, Ch. 41, 9.1.4
    inventory, Ch. 22, 3.1.3C
    investment property, Ch. 19, 4.8
    on 'land expenditures', Ch. 21, 6.3.1
    other finance costs as, Ch. 21, 4.2, 5.5
    property, plant and equipment, Ch. 18, 4.1.2

Branches, foreign exchange, Ch. 15, 4.4
Brazil, IFRS adoption in, Ch. 1, 4.3.3
Broadcast rights, intangible assets amortisation of, Ch. 17, 9.2.1.B
Business Advisory Council (BAC), Ch. 1, 4.4.2
Business combination exemption (first-time adoption), Ch. 5, 5.2
   associates and joint arrangements, Ch. 5, 5.2, 5.2.2.A
   classification of business combinations, Ch. 5, 5.2.3
   currency adjustments to goodwill, Ch. 5, 5.2.6
   goodwill previously deducted from equity, Ch. 5, 5.2.5.C
   goodwill, restatement of, Ch. 5, 5.2.5
   measurement of deferred taxes and non-controlling interests, Ch. 5, 5.2.9
   option to restate business combinations retrospectively, Ch. 5, 5.2.2
   previously consolidated entities that are not subsidiaries, Ch. 5, 5.2.8
   previously unconsolidated subsidiaries, Ch. 5, 5.2.7
   recognition of assets and liabilities, Ch. 5, 5.2.4
   subsequent measurement under IFRSs not based on cost, Ch. 5, 5.2.4.E
Business combinations, Ch. 9, 1–16. *See also* Common control business combinations; IFRS 3; Income taxes
   achieved in stages (step acquisitions), Ch. 9, 9
   accounting for previously held interests in a joint operation, Ch. 9, 9.1
   achieved without the transfer of consideration, Ch. 9, 7.4
   acquired receivables, Ch. 54, 4.6
   acquirer and a vendor in, contracts between, Ch. 44, 3.7.2
   acquirer, identifying the, Ch. 9, 4.1
   acquirer, new entity formed to effect business combination, Ch. 9, 4.1.1
   acquirer that is not a legal entity, Ch. 9, 4.1
   acquisition method of accounting, Ch. 9, 4
      determining the acquisition date, Ch. 9, 4.2
      identifying the acquirer, Ch. 9, 4.1
   acquisition of intangible assets in, Ch. 17, 5
      customer relationship intangible assets, Ch. 17, 5.4
      in-process research and development, Ch. 17, 5.5
      intangible assets acquired, examples, Ch. 17, 5.2
      measuring the fair value of intangible assets, Ch. 17, 5.3
      recognition of intangible assets, Ch. 17, 5.1
   acquisition related costs, Ch. 9, 7.3
      presentation in statement of cash flows, Ch. 40, 6.3.1
   acquisitions of investment property in or a, Ch. 19, 3.3
   apparent immediate impairment of goodwill created by deferred tax, Ch. 33, 12.3
   assessing whether acquired process is substantive, Ch. 9, 3.2.4
      bargain purchase transactions, Ch. 9, 10
      recognising and measuring goodwill or a gain in, Ch. 9, 6
   'business' under IFRSs, definition of, Ch. 9, 3.2; Ch. 19, 3.3.1
      assessment whether acquired set of activities and assets constitutes a, Ch. 9, 3.2.2
   'capable of' from the viewpoint of a market participant, Ch. 9, 3.2.5
   common control, Ch. 10, 1–6; Ch. 56, 13.3
   concentration test, Ch. 9, 3.2.3
   consideration transferred, Ch. 9, 7
   contingent consideration, Ch. 9, 7.1

      cash flows, Ch. 40. 6.3.3
      and indemnification assets, Ch. 54, 4.6.2
      payable by an acquirer, Ch. 45, 3.7.1.A
      receivable by a vendor, Ch. 45, 3.7.1.B
   contingent liabilities recognised in a business combination, Ch. 9, 5.6.1
      changes in, Ch. 26, 4.10
   by contract alone, Ch. 9, 7.4.1
   contracts between acquirer and vendor, Ch. 45, 3.7.2
   customer relationship intangible assets acquired in, Ch. 17, 5.4
   deferred taxes, Ch. 33, 6.2.1.E, 6.2.2.E,
      arising on a business combination, Ch. 33, 12.1.2
         assets of the acquiree, Ch. 33, 12.1.2.B
         assets of the acquirer, Ch. 33, 12.1.2.A
   development stage entities, Ch. 9, 3.2.7
   disclosures, Ch. 9, 16
      combinations during current reporting period, Ch. 9, 16.1.1
      combinations effected after the end of reporting period, Ch. 9, 16.1.2
      financial effects of adjustments, Ch. 9, 16.2
      nature and financial effect, Ch. 9, 16.1
   exceptions to recognition and/or measurement principles, Ch. 9, 5.6
      assets held for sale, Ch. 9, 5.6.6
      contingent liabilities, Ch. 9, 5.6.1
      employee benefits, Ch. 9, 5.6.3
      income taxes, Ch. 9, 5.6.2
      indemnification assets, Ch. 9, 5.6.4
      insurance contracts within the scope of IFRS 17, Ch. 9, 5.6.9
      leases in which the acquiree is a lessee, Ch. 9, 5.6.8
      reacquired rights, Ch. 9, 5.6.5
      share-based payment transactions, Ch. 9, 5.6.7
   fair value of intangible assets acquired in, measuring, Ch. 17, 5.3
   goodwill, Ch. 9, 6
   identifying a, Ch. 9, 3.1
   identifying the acquirer, Ch. 9, 4.1
   in-process research and development (IPR&D) acquired in, Ch. 17, 5.5
   insurance contracts acquired in, Ch. 55, 9
   intangible assets acquired in, recognition of
      identifiability in relation to an intangible asset, Ch. 17, 5.1.3
         contractual-legal rights, Ch. 17, 5.1.3.A
         separability, Ch. 17, 5.1.3.B
      probable inflow of benefits, Ch. 17, 5.1.1
      reliability of measurement, Ch. 17, 5.1.2
   involving a Newco, Ch. 9, 4.1.1; Ch. 10, 4
   involving mutual entities, Ch. 9, 7.5
   leases, Ch. 23, 9
   loans and receivables acquired in, Ch. 49, 3.3.4
   measurement and recognition of deferred tax in, Ch. 33, 12.1
      deferred tax assets arising on a business combination, Ch. 33, 12.1.2
      deferred tax liabilities of acquired entity, Ch. 33, 12.1.3
      manner of recovery of assets and settlement of liabilities, determining, Ch. 33, 12.1.1
         changes in tax base consequent on the business combination, Ch. 33, 12.1.1.A

Business combinations—*contd*
  measurement period, Ch. 9, 12
  non-controlling interest as part of a business combination under common control, Ch. 10, 3.3.5
  non-controlling interests, measurement in, Ch. 7, 3.2, 3.1.1, 3.1.2, 5.2, 5.3
  pre-existing relationships, Ch. 9, 11.1
  process, Ch. 9, 3.2.1
  push down accounting, Ch. 9, 15
  recognition and measurement of assets acquired, liabilities assumed and non-controlling interests, Ch. 9, 5
    assembled workforce, Ch. 9, 5.5.4.A
    assets and liabilities related to contacts with customers, Ch. 9, 5.5.8
    assets with uncertain cash flows, Ch. 9, 5.5.5
    equity-accounted entities, investments in, Ch. 9, 5.5.7
    future contract renewals, Ch. 9, 5.5.4.B
    items not qualifying as assets, Ch. 9, 5.5.4.B
    liabilities assumed, Ch. 9, 5
    non-controlling interests, Ch. 9, 5.1, 7.2, 7.4.1
    reacquired rights, Ch. 9, 5.5.3
  replacement share-based payment awards in, Ch. 9, 7.2; Ch. 34, 11
  reverse acquisitions, Ch. 9, 14, 14.8, 14.9
  spin-off transaction, Ch. 9, 4.1.1
  stapling arrangements, Ch. 9, 4.1.2
  subsequent measurement and accounting, Ch. 9, 13
  tax deductions for acquisition costs, Ch. 33, 12.4
  tax deductions for replacement share-based payment awards in a business combination, Ch. 33, 12.2
  temporary differences arising from the acquisition of a group of assets that is not a business, Ch. 33, 12.5

Business combinations under common control' (BCUCC) research project
  accounting methods and disclosures, Ch. 10, 6.2
  background and scope, Ch. 10, 6.1
  next steps, Ch. 10, 6.3

'Business model' assessment, financial assets, Ch. 48, 5
  anticipated capital expenditure, Ch. 48, 5.6
  applying in practice, Ch. 48, 5.6
  credit-impaired financial assets in a hold to collect business model, Ch. 48, 5.6
  credit risk management activities, Ch. 48, 5.6
  hedging activities in a hold to collect business model, Ch. 48, 5.6
  hold to collect contractual cash flows, Ch. 48, 5.2
  hold to collect contractual cash flows and selling financial assets, Ch. 48, 5.3
  impact of sales on the assessment, Ch. 48, 5.2.1
  level at which the business model assessment should be applied, Ch. 48, 5.1
  liquidity portfolio for every day liquidity needs, Ch. 48, 5.6
  liquidity portfolio for stress case scenarios, Ch. 48, 5.6
  loans that are to be sub-participated, Ch. 48, 5.6
  opportunistic portfolio management, Ch. 48, 5.6
  other business models, Ch. 48, 5.4
  portfolio managed on a fair value basis, Ch. 48, 5.6
  replication portfolios, Ch. 48, 5.6
  sales to manage concentration risk, Ch. 48, 5.6
  securitisation, Ch. 48, 5.6
  splitting portfolios, Ch. 48, 5.6
  subsidiary that is held for sale, Ch. 48, 5.5
  transferred financial assets that are not derecognised, Ch. 48, 5.2.2

Buying reinsurance, gains/losses on, Ch. 55, 7.2.6.C

By-products, extractive industries, Ch. 43, 12.6, 14.2.1, 16.1.3.D

Call options, Ch. 7, 6.1, 6.3, 6.4, 6.5; Ch. 34, 8.2.1; Ch. 47, 11.2
  over non-controlling interests, Ch. 7, 6.1, 6.3, 6.4, 6.5; Ch. 9, 8.5
    call and put options entered into in relation to existing non-controlling interests, Ch. 7, 6.4
    call options only, Ch. 7, 6.1
    combination of call and put options, Ch. 7, 6.3
    separate financial statements, Ch. 7, 6.5
  purchased call option, Ch. 47, 11.2.1
  share-based payment, Ch. 34, 8.2.1
    intrinsic value and time value, Ch. 34, 8.2.2
  written call option, Ch. 47, 11.2.2

Canada, IFRS adoption in, Ch. 1, 4.3.2

Capital commitments, Ch. 41, 4.3.4

Capital, disclosures about, Ch. 3, 5.4; Ch. 54, 5.6.3
  general capital disclosures, Ch. 3, 5.4.1
  puttable financial instruments classified as equity, Ch. 3, 5.4.2

Capital Markets Advisory Committee, Ch. 1, 2.9

Capitalisation of borrowing costs, Ch. 21, 1–7. *See also* IAS 23
  cessation of capitalisation, Ch. 21, 6.3
    borrowing costs on 'land expenditures', Ch. 21, 6.3.1
  commencement, Ch. 21, 6.1
    expenditures on a qualifying asset, Ch. 21, 6.1.1
  disclosure requirements, Ch. 21, 7
  group considerations, Ch. 21, 5.7
    borrowings in one company and development in another, Ch. 21, 5.7.1
    qualifying assets held by joint arrangements, Ch. 21, 5.7.2
  in hyperinflationary economies, Ch. 21, 5.6
  interim financial reporting, Ch. 41, 9.1.4
  suspension of, Ch. 21, 6.2
    impairment considerations, Ch. 21, 6.2.1

Carried interests/party, extractive industries, Ch. 43, 6.1
  in E&E phase, Ch. 43, 6.1.2
  financing-type, Ch. 43, 6.1.3
  purchase/sale-type, Ch. 43, 6.1.4

Carve-out financial statements. *See* Combined financial statements

Cash and cash equivalents, Ch. 40, 3. *See also* IAS 7
  components of, Ch. 40, 3.2
    bank overdrafts, Ch. 40, 3.2.4
    client money, Ch. 40, 3.2.6
    cryptocurrencies, Ch. 40, 3.2.5
    demand deposits, Ch. 40, 3.2.1
    investments with maturities greater than three months, Ch. 40, 3.2.3
    money market funds (MMF), Ch. 40, 3.2.2
    short-term investments, Ch. 40, 3.2.1
  restrictions on the use of, Ch. 40, 3.4
  statement of financial position items, reconciliation with, Ch. 40, 3.3

Cash flow hedges, Ch. 53, 1.5, 5.2, 7.2; Ch. 54, 4.3.3
  acquisition or disposal of subsidiaries, Ch. 53, 7.2.4

acquisitions, Ch. 53, 7.2.4
all-in-one hedges, Ch. 53, 5.2.1
discontinuation, Ch. 53, 8.3
of firm commitments, Ch. 53, 5.2.2
of foreign currency monetary items, Ch. 53, 5.2.3
hypothetical derivatives, Ch. 53, 7.4.4
leased assets, CGU identification, Ch. 20, 3.2
measuring ineffectiveness, Ch. 53, 7.4.6
of a net position, Ch. 53, 2.5.3
presentation, Ch. 53, 10.1
reclassification of gains and losses, Ch. 53, 7.2.2

Cash-generating units (CGUs). *See also* Impairment of assets; Value in use (VIU)
active markets, identifying, Ch. 20, 3.2
carrying amount of, identifying, Ch. 20, 4
dividing the entity into, Ch. 20, 3
estimating the future pre-tax cash flows of, Ch. 20, 7.1
and goodwill impairment, Ch. 20, 8
impairment losses, Ch. 20, 11.2
leased assets and CGUs, Ch. 20, 3.2
reversal of impairments, Ch. 20, 11.4

Cash-settled share-based payment transaction, Ch. 34, 9; Ch. 36, 2.2.1. *See also* Equity-settled share-based payment transaction; IFRS 2; Share-based payment transactions
accounting treatment, Ch. 34, 9.3
application of the accounting treatment, Ch. 34, 9.3.2
market conditions and non-vesting conditions, Ch. 34, 9.3.2.D
modification, cancellation and settlement, Ch. 34, 9.3.2.E
non-market vesting conditions, Ch. 34, 9.3.2.C
periodic allocation of cost, Ch. 34, 9.3.2.B
vesting period determination, Ch. 34, 9.3.2.A
basic accounting treatment, Ch. 34, 9.3.1
modification to or from equity-settlement, Ch. 34, 9.4
cash-settled award modified to equity-settled award, Ch. 34, 9.4.2
equity-settled award modified to cash-settled award, Ch. 34, 9.4.1
scope of requirements, Ch. 34, 9.1
transactions with equity and cash alternatives, Ch. 34, 10.1, 10.2, 10.3
what constitutes a cash-settled award?, Ch. 34, 9.2
arrangements to sell employees' shares including 'broker settlement,' Ch. 34, 9.2.4
economic compulsion for cash settlement (including unlisted company schemes), Ch. 34, 10.2.1.A
formal and informal arrangements for the entity to purchase illiquid shares or otherwise settle in cash, Ch. 34, 9.2.1
market purchases of own equity following equity-settlement of award, Ch. 34, 9.2.3
market purchases of own equity to satisfy awards, Ch. 34, 9.2.2

Catastrophe provisions, Ch. 55, 7.2.1
CCIRS. *See* Cross-currency interest rate swaps (CCIRS)
CCP. *See* Central clearing party (CCP)
Cedant, Ch. 55, 2.2.1
Chief operating decision maker (CODM), Ch. 36, 1.3, 3.1
China Accounting Standards Committee (CASC), Ch. 1, 4.4.1.A

China, IFRS adoption in, Ch. 1, 4.4.1
Clawback conditions, share-based payment, Ch. 34, 3.1.1
Clean-up call options, Ch. 52, 4.2.7
Client money, Ch. 40, 3.2.6; Ch. 52, 3.7
'Closely related,' meaning of, Ch. 46, 5
Cloud computing, Ch. 17, 11.6
implementation costs, Ch. 17, 11.6.2
'software as a service' cloud computing arrangements, Ch. 17, 11.6.1
'Collar' put and call options, Ch. 52, 5.4.3.C
Collateral, Ch. 51, 5.8.1; Ch. 52, 5.5.2
Collectability, revenue IFRS 15, Ch. 28, 2.1.6
assessing for a portfolio of contracts, Ch. 28, 2.1.6.A
determining when to reassess, Ch. 28, 2.1.6.B
Combined financial statements, Ch. 6, 2.2.6
common control, Ch. 6, 2.2.6.A
preparation of, Ch. 6, 2.2.6.C
purpose and users, Ch. 6, 2.2.6.B
reporting entity in, Ch. 6, 1.1; Ch. 6, 2.2.6.B; Ch. 6, 2.2.6.C; Ch. 6, 2.2.6.E
'special- purpose' vs 'general- purpose', Ch. 6, 2.2.6.D
Comissão de Valores Mobiliários (CVM), Ch. 1, 2.3, 4.3.3
Commencement of lease, Ch. 23, 4.2
Committee for Mineral Reserves International Reporting Standards (CRIRSCO), Ch. 43, 1.3
International Reporting Template, Ch. 43, 2.3.1
reporting terminology, Ch. 43, 2.3.1.B
scope, Ch. 43, 2.3.1.A
Commodity-based contracts, extractive industries
allocate the transaction price, Ch. 43, 12.15.4
definition of commodity contract, Ch. 43, 12.6.1
fixed consideration, Ch. 43, 12.15.4.B
forward-selling to finance development, Ch. 43, 12.6
modifications to, Ch. 43, 12.10
multi-period, Ch. 43, 12.15
normal purchase and sales exemption, Ch. 43, 13.1
principal *vs.* agent considerations in, Ch. 43, 12.11
revenue recognition, Ch. 43, 12.15.5
take-or-pay contracts, Ch. 43, 12.16, 17.2
trading activities, Ch. 43, 12.7
Commodity broker-traders, Ch. 45, 4.2.2
Commodity, equity-linked interest and principal payments, Ch. 46, 5.1.7
Commodity price assumptions, Ch. 43, 11.4.3, 11.5.2
Common control business combinations, Ch. 10, 1–6
accounting for, Ch. 10, 3
application of the acquisition method under IFRS 3, Ch. 10, 3.2
application of the pooling of interests method, Ch. 10, 3.3
acquisition of non-controlling interest as part of a business combination under common control, Ch. 10, 3.3.5
carrying amounts of assets and liabilities, Ch. 10, 3.3.2
equity reserves and history of assets and liabilities carried over, Ch. 10, 3.3.4
general requirements, Ch. 10, 3.3.1
restatement of financial information for periods prior to the date of the combination, Ch. 10, 3.3.3

Common control business combinations—*contd*
  accounting for—*contd*
    pooling of interests method versus acquisition method, Ch. 10, 3.1
    accounting for transactions under common control (or ownership) involving a Newco, Ch. 10, 4
      inserting a new intermediate parent within an existing group, Ch. 10, 4.3
      setting up a new top holding company, Ch. 10, 4.2
        transactions effected through issuing equity interests, Ch. 10, 4.2.1
        transactions involving consideration other than equity interests, Ch. 10, 4.2.2
      transferring businesses outside an existing group using a Newco, Ch. 10, 4.4
    accounting for transfers of associates/joint ventures under common control, Ch. 10, 5
    future developments, Ch. 10, 6
      BCUCC research project
        accounting methods and disclosures, Ch. 10, 6.2
        background and scope, Ch. 10, 6.1
        next steps, Ch. 10, 6.3
  group reorganisations, Ch. 10, 1.2
  IFRS 3 scope exclusion, Ch. 10, 2
    common control by an individual/group of individuals, Ch. 10, 2.1.1
    transitory control, Ch. 10, 2.1.2
  scope of chapter, Ch. 10, 1.3

Common control/group transactions, individual financial statements, Ch. 8, 4. *See also* Group reorganisations
  application of the principles in practice, Ch. 8, 4.4
    acquiring and selling businesses–transfers between subsidiaries, Ch. 8, 4.4.2
      accounting for a business that has been acquired, Ch. 8, 4.4.2.B
      accounting for transactions if net assets are not a business, Ch. 8, 4.4.2.D
      purchase and sale of a business for cash/equity not representative of fair value of business, Ch. 8, 4.4.2.C
    financial instruments within the scope of IFRS 9 (or IAS 39), Ch. 8, 4.4.5
      financial guarantee contracts, parent guarantee issued on behalf of subsidiary, Ch. 8, 4.4.5.B
      interest-free or non-market interest rate loans, Ch. 8, 4.4.5.A
    incurring expenses and settling liabilities without recharges, Ch. 8, 4.4.4
    transactions involving non-monetary assets, Ch. 8, 4.4.1
      acquisition of assets for shares, Ch. 8, 4.4.1.C
      contribution and distribution of assets, Ch. 8, 4.4.1.D
      parent exchanges PP&E for a non-monetary asset of the subsidiary, Ch. 8, 4.4.1.B
      sale of PP&E from parent to subsidiary for an amount of cash not representative of fair value of asset, Ch. 8, 4.4.1.A
      transfers between subsidiaries, Ch. 8, 4.4.1.E
    transfers of businesses between parent and subsidiary, Ch. 8, 4.4.3
      distributions of businesses without consideration, Ch. 8, 4.4.3.A
      legal merger of parent and subsidiary, Ch. 8, 4.4.3.B
      subsidiary as a surviving entity, Ch. 8, 4.4.3.B
  cost of investments acquired in, Ch. 8, 2.1.1.B
  disclosures, Ch. 8, 4.5
  measurement, Ch. 8, 4.3
    fair value in intra-group transactions, Ch. 8, 4.3.1
  recognition, Ch. 8, 4.2

Comparative information, Ch. 3, 2.4; Ch. 4, 4; Ch. 5, 6.1
  interim financial statements, Ch. 41, 5.1
  treatment on cessation of classification as held for sale, Ch. 4, 4.2
  treatment on initial classification as held for sale statement of comprehensive income, Ch. 4, 4.1.1

Compensation, related-party disclosures, Ch. 39. 2.6.1

Compound financial instruments, Ch. 47, 6
  background, Ch. 47, 6.1
  common forms of convertible bonds, Ch. 47, 6.6
    bond convertible into fixed percentage of equity, Ch. 47, 6.6.6
    contingent convertible bond, Ch. 47, 6.6.2
    convertible bonds with down round or ratchet features, Ch. 47, 6.6.7
    convertibles with cash settlement at the option of the issuer, Ch. 47, 6.6.5
    foreign currency convertible bond, Ch. 47, 6.6.4
    functional currency bond convertible into a fixed number of shares, Ch. 47, 6.6.1
    mandatorily convertible bond, Ch. 47, 6.6.3
  components of a compound instrument, Ch. 47, 6.4
    compound instruments with embedded derivatives, Ch. 47, 6.4.2
      issuer call option-'closely related' embedded derivatives, Ch. 47, 6.4.2.A
    determining, Ch. 47, 6.4.1
  conversion at maturity, Ch. 47, 6.3.1
    before maturity, Ch. 47, 6.3.2
      accounting treatment, Ch. 47, 6.3.2.B
      embedded derivatives, Ch. 47, 6.3.2.C
      'fixed stated principal' of a bond, Ch. 47, 6.3.2.A
  deferred tax, initial recognition exception, Ch. 33, 7.2.8
  early redemption/repurchase, Ch. 47, 6.3.3
    through exercising an embedded call option, Ch. 47, 6.3.3.B
    through negotiation with bondholders, Ch. 47, 6.3.3.A
  modification, Ch. 47, 6.3.4
  with multiple embedded derivatives, statement of financial position, Ch. 54, 4.4.7
  'split accounting', Ch. 47, 6.2
    initial recognition of a compound instrument, Ch. 47, 6.2
      accounting for the equity component, Ch. 47, 6.2.1
      temporary differences arising from, Ch. 47, 6.2.2
  treatment by holder and issuer contrasted, Ch. 47, 6.1.1

Comprehensive income, Ch. 3, 3.2

Comprehensive income statement. *See* Statement of comprehensive income

Concentration test, Ch. 9, 3.2.3

Concentrations of risk, Ch. 54, 5.6.1; Ch. 55, 11.2.4

Conceptual Framework for Financial Reporting 2010, Ch. 2, 2

Conceptual framework, IASB's, Ch. 1, 2.5; Ch. 2, 1–12. *See also* General purpose financial reporting
- contents, Ch. 2, 3.1
- derecognition, Ch. 2, 8.3
- development, Ch. 2, 2
- discussion paper on, Ch. 2, 1
- effective date, Ch. 2, 2
- enhancing qualitative characteristics, Ch. 2, 5.2
    - applying, Ch. 2, 5.2.5
    - comparability, Ch. 2, 5.2.1
    - timeliness, Ch. 2, 5.2.3
    - understandability, Ch. 2, 5.2.4
    - verifiability, Ch. 2, 5.2.2
- financial capital maintenance, Ch. 2.11.1
- financial statements, Ch. 2.6.1
    - assets, Ch. 2.7.2
    - consolidated and unconsolidated, Ch. 2.6.2.1
    - elements, Ch. 2.7
    - equity, Ch. 2.7.4
    - executory contracts, Ch. 2.7.1.2
    - going concern assumption, Ch. 2.6.1.4
    - income and expenses, Ch. 2.7.5
    - liabilities, Ch. 2.7.3
    - objective and scope, Ch. 2.6.1.1
    - perspective adopted in financial statements, Ch. 2.6.1.3
    - reporting period and comparative information, Ch. 2.6.1.2
    - substance of contractual rights and contractual obligations, Ch. 2.7.1.3
    - unit of account, Ch. 2.7.1.1
- fundamental qualitative characteristics, Ch. 2, 5.1
    - applying, Ch. 2, 5.1.3
    - cost constraint, Ch. 2, 5.3
    - faithful representation, Ch. 2, 5.1.2
    - relevance (including materiality), Ch. 2, 5.1.1
- general purpose financial reporting, Ch. 2, 4
    - economic resources, Ch. 2, 4.2.1
    - limitations, Ch. 2, 4.1.2
    - objective and usefulness, Ch. 2, 4.1.1
- management commentary, Ch. 2, 12
- measurement, Ch. 2, 9
    - bases, Ch. 2, 9.1
    - cash-flow-based measurement techniques, Ch. 2, 9.5
    - equity, Ch. 2, 9.4
    - factors to consider in selecting measurement bases, Ch. 2, 9.3
    - information provided by different measurement bases, Ch. 2, 9.2
- physical capital maintenance, Ch. 2, 11.2
- political and economic environment influences, Ch. 2, 1.2
- presentation and disclosure, Ch. 2, 10
    - aggregation, Ch. 2, 10.3
    - classification, Ch. 2, 10.2
    - objectives and principles, Ch. 2, 10.1
- purpose, Ch. 2, 3.2
- recognition criteria, Ch. 2, 8.2
    - faithful representation, Ch. 2, 8.2.2
    - relevance, Ch. 2, 8.2.1
- recognition process, Ch. 2, 8.1
- reporting entity, Ch. 2, 6.2
- scope, Ch. 2, 3
- standard settings, Ch. 2, 1.2
- status, Ch. 2, 3.2
- useful financial information, qualitative characteristics of, Ch. 2, 5

Concession agreements. *See* Service concession arrangements (SCA)
- mineral reserves and resources, Ch. 43, 2

Concessionary agreements (concessions), extractive industries, Ch. 43, 5.2

Condensed interim financial statements, Ch. 41, 3.2. *See also under* IAS 34
- disclosures in, Ch. 41, 4
    - accounting policies and methods of computation, Ch. 41, 4.3.11
    - amounts that are unusual because of their nature, size or incidence, Ch. 41, 4.3.13
    - capital commitments, Ch. 41, 4.3.4
    - changes in circumstances affecting fair values, Ch. 41, 4.3.6
    - changes in composition of the entity, Ch. 41, 4.3.17
    - compliance with IFRS, Ch. 41, 4.6
    - contingent liabilities, Ch. 41, 4.3.10
    - debt and equity securities, Ch. 41, 4.3.14
    - default or breach of loan covenants not remedied before end of interim period, Ch. 41, 4.3.7
    - dividends paid Ch. 41, 4.3.15
    - events after the interim reporting date, Ch. 41, 4.3.16
    - fair value disclosures, Ch. 41, 4.5
    - fair value hierarchy levels, transfers between, Ch. 41, 4.3.9
    - inventory write-down and reversals, Ch. 41, 4.3.1
    - litigation settlements, Ch. 41, 4.3.5
    - PP&E, acquisition and disposal of, Ch. 41, 4.3.3
    - recognition and reversal of impairment losses, Ch. 41, 4.3.2
    - related party transactions, Ch. 41, 4.3.8
    - seasonality or cyclicality of operations, Ch. 41, 4.3.12
    - segment information, Ch. 41, 4.4
    - significant events and transactions, Ch. 41, 4.1
    - transfers between different levels of fair value hierarchy, , Ch. 41, 4.3.9
- first-time presentation, Ch. 41, 11.1
- requirements for interim financial information, Ch. 41, 3.3

Consideration transferred, Ch. 9, 7. *See also* Contingent consideration
- acquisition-related costs, Ch. 9, 7.3

Consignment stock and sale and repurchase agreements, Ch. 22, 2.3.1F

Consistency in application of IFRS, Ch. 1, 5

Consistent accounting policies, Ch. 7, 2.6; Ch. 11, 7.8. *See also* Financial statements, presentation of; IAS 1

Consolidated financial statements, Ch. 6, 1–11; Ch. 8, 1.1. *See also* consolidation procedures, IFRS 10
- continuous assessment, Ch. 6, 9
- control, Ch. 6, 3
- control of specified assets, Ch. 6, 8
- employee benefit trusts, Ch. 6, 2.2.2; Ch. 34, 12.3, 12.4.1, 12.5.1
- entity no longer a parent at the end of reporting period, Ch. 6, 2.2.4
- exemption from preparing
    - consent of non-controlling shareholders, Ch. 6, 2.2.1.A

Consolidated financial statements—*contd*
　exemption from preparing—*contd*
　　not filing financial statements for listing securities, Ch. 6, 2.2.1.C
　　parent's IFRS financial statements are publicly available, Ch. 6, 2.2.1.D
　　securities not traded in a public market, Ch. 6, 2.2.1.B
　exposure to variable returns, Ch. 6, 5
　future developments, Ch. 6, 11
　investment entities, Ch. 6, 10
　power over an investee, Ch. 6, 4
　principal-agency situations, Ch. 6, 6
　related parties and *de facto* agents, Ch. 6, 7

Consolidated statement of cash flows, preparing, Ch. 40, 6.1

Consolidation procedures, Ch. 7. *See also* non-controlling interests
　basic principles, Ch. 7, 2.1
　changes in control, Ch. 7, 3
　　accounting for a loss of control Ch. 7, 3.2
　　deemed disposal, Ch. 7, 3.6
　　demergers and distributions of non-cash assets to owners, Ch. 7, 3.7, Ch. 8, 2.4.2. *See also* IFRIC 17
　　interest retained in the former subsidiary, Ch. 7, 3.3
　　　associate or joint venture, Ch. 7, 3.3.2, 7.1
　　　financial asset, Ch. 7, 3.3.1
　　　joint operation, Ch. 7, 3.3.3, 7.2
　　Interpretations Committee and IASB discussions about the sale of a single asset entity containing real estate, Ch. 7.3.2.1
　　loss of control in multiple arrangements, Ch. 7, 3.4
　　other comprehensive income, Ch. 7, 3.5
　changes in ownership interest without a loss of control, Ch. 7, 4
　　contingent consideration on purchase of a noncontrolling interest, Ch. 7, 4.5
　　goodwill attributable to non-controlling interests, Ch. 7, 4.2; Ch. 20, 9
　　non-cash acquisition of non-controlling interests, Ch. 7, 4.3
　　reattribution of other comprehensive income, Ch. 7, 4.1
　　transaction costs, Ch. 7, 4.4
　commencement and cessation of consolidation, Ch. 7, 3.1
　　acquisition in stages: associate or joint venture that is not a business becomes a subsidiary, Ch. 7, 3.1.2
　　acquisition of a subsidiary that is not a business, Ch. 7, 3.1.1
　　demergers and distributions of non-cash assets to owners, Ch. 7, 3.7
　　　presentation and disclosure, Ch. 7, 3.7.3
　　　recognition and measurement in IFRIC 17, Ch. 7, 3.7.2
　　　scope of IFRIC 17, Ch. 7, 3.7.1
　consistent accounting policies, Ch. 7, 2.6
　consolidating foreign operations, Ch. 7, 2.3
　intragroup eliminations, Ch. 7, 2.4
　non-coterminous accounting periods, Ch. 7, 2.5
　proportion consolidated, Ch. 7, 2.2, 5.6

Constructive obligation, Ch. 26, 3.1
　employee benefits, Ch. 37, 7.1
　provisions, Ch. 26, 3.1

Consultative Group for Rate Regulation, Ch. 1, 2.9

Contingent assets, Ch. 26, 3.2.2
　definition, Ch. 26, 3.2.2
　disclosure of, Ch. 26, 7.3
　relating to business combinations, Ch. 9, 5.5.4.B

Contingent consideration, Ch. 7, 4.5; Ch. 9, 7.1
　cash flows in business combinations, Ch. 40, 6.3.3.A
　　payable by an acquirer, Ch. 45, 3.7.1.A
　　receivable by a vendor, Ch. 45, 3.7.1.B
　initial recognition and measurement, Ch. 9, 7.1.1
　intangible assets acquired for, Ch. 17, 4.5
　on loss of control of a subsidiary, Ch. 7.3.2
　obligation, classification, Ch. 9, 7.1.2
　on purchase of non-controlling interest, Ch. 7, 4.5
　subsequent measurement and accounting, Ch. 9, 7.1.3

Contingent convertible bond, Ch. 47, 6.6.2

Contingent costs, investment property, Ch. 19, 4.10

Contingent liabilities, Ch. 26, 3.2.1
　business combinations, Ch. 9, 5.6.1
　definition, Ch. 26, 3.2.1
　disclosure of, Ch. 26, 7.2
　joint ventures and associates, Ch. 13, 5.2.2

Contingent resources, extractive industries, Ch. 43, 2.2.1

Contingent settlement provisions, Ch. 47, 4.3
　contingencies that are 'not genuine,' Ch. 47, 4.3.1
　liabilities that arise only on a change of control, Ch. 47, 4.3.3
　liabilities that arise only on liquidation, Ch. 47, 4.3.2
　some typical contingent settlement provisions, Ch. 47, 4.3.4

Contingently issuable shares (EPS), Ch. 37, 6.4.6
　earnings-based contingencies, Ch. 37, 6.4.6.A
　share-price-based contingencies, Ch. 37, 6.4.6.B

Continuous assessment of control, Ch. 6, 9; Ch. 12, 8
　bankruptcy filings, Ch. 6, 9.2
　changes in market conditions, Ch. 6, 9.1
　control re-assessment, Ch. 6, 9.3
　joint arrangements, Ch. 12, 8
　troubled debt restructurings, Ch. 6, 9.2

Contract asset, Ch. 32, 2.1
　presentation requirements for, Ch. 32, 2.1

Contract costs, Ch. 31, 5
　amortisation of capitalised costs, Ch. 31, 5.3
　　classification and presentation of capitalised contract costs and related amortisation, Ch. 31, 5.3.6
　costs to fulfil a contract, Ch. 31, 5.2
　　assets recognised from, Ch. 32, 3.2.3
　costs to obtain a contract, Ch. 31, 5.1
　impairment of capitalised costs, Ch. 31, 5.4

Contract liability, Ch. 32, 2.1
　presentation requirements for, Ch. 32, 2.1

Contract modifications, Ch. 28, 2.4
　not a separate contract, Ch. 28, 2.4.2
　represents a separate contract, Ch. 28, 2.4.1

Contractual arrangement, business combinations, Ch. 6, 4.4
　additional rights from, Ch. 6, 4.3.6
　with other vote holders, Ch. 6, 4.3.5
　structured entities, Ch. 6, 4.4.1

Contractual cash flows, financial instruments IFRS 9, Ch. 48, 6
　auction rate securities, Ch. 48, 6.4.4.B

bonds with a capped or floored interest rate, Ch. 48, 6.3.3
contractual features that may affect the classification, Ch. 48, 6.4
   de minimis and non-genuine features, Ch. 48, 6.4.1
   features that change the timing or amount of contractual cash flows, Ch. 48, 6.4.4
      prepayment – assets originated at a premium or discount, Ch. 48, 6.4.4.B
      prepayment – negative compensation, Ch. 48, 6.4.4.A
   features that modify the consideration for the time value of money, Ch. 48, 6.4.2
   features that normally do not represent payment of principal and interest, Ch. 48, 6.4.5
   regulated interest rates, Ch. 48, 6.4.3
contractual features that normally pass the test, Ch. 48, 6.3
   bonds with a capped or floored interest rate, Ch. 48, 6.3.3
   conventional subordination features, Ch. 48, 6.3.1
   features which compensate the lender for changes in tax or other related costs, Ch. 48, 6.3.6
   full recourse loans secured by collateral, Ch. 48, 6.3.2
   lender has discretion to change the interest rate, Ch. 48, 6.3.4
   unleveraged inflation-linked bonds, Ch. 48, 6.3.5
contractually linked instruments, Ch. 48, 6.6
   assessing the characteristics of the underlying pool, Ch. 48, 6.6.1
   assessing the exposure to credit risk in the tranche held, Ch. 48, 6.6.2
conventional subordination features, Ch. 48, 6.3.1
convertible debt, Ch. 48, 6.4.5
de minimis features, Ch. 48, 6.4.1.A
debt covenants, Ch. 48, 6.4.4.B
dual currency instruments, Ch. 48, 6.4.5
five-year constant maturity bond, Ch. 48, 6.4.2
fixed rate bond prepayable by the issuer at fair value, Ch. 48, 6.4.5
full recourse loans secured by collateral, Ch. 48, 6.3.2
interest rate period, Ch. 48, 6.4.2
inverse floater, Ch. 48, 6.4.5
investment in open-ended money market or debt funds, Ch. 48, 6.4.5
lender has discretion to change the interest rate, Ch. 48, 6.3.4
loan commitments, Ch. 48, 6.4.6
meaning of 'interest,' Ch. 48, 6.2
meaning of 'principal', Ch. 48, 6.1
modified time value of money component, Ch. 48, 6.4.2
multiple of a benchmark interest rate, Ch. 48, 6.4.5
non-genuine features, Ch. 48, 6.4.1.B
non-recourse assets, Ch. 48, 6.5
non-recourse loans, Ch. 48, 6.5
perpetual instruments with potentially deferrable coupons, Ch. 48, 6.4.5
prepayment, assets originated at a premium or discount, Ch. 48, 6.4.4.B
prepayment, negative compensation, Ch. 48, 6.4.4.A
prepayment options, Ch. 48, 6.4.4
regulated interest rates, Ch. 48, 6.4.3
unleveraged inflation-linked bonds, Ch. 48, 6.3.5
Contractual-legal criterion (intangible assets), Ch. 9, 5.5.2

Contractual service margin (CSM), insurance contracts, Ch. 56, 8.5
   measurement of, using the variable fee approach, Ch. 56, 11.2.2
   recognition of in profit or loss, Ch. 56, 11.2.4
   release of, Ch. 56, 10.4.1
   subsequent measurement, Ch. 56, 8.6.2
Contractually linked instruments, Ch. 48, 6.6
   assessing the characteristics of the underlying pool, Ch. 48, 6.6.1
   assessing the exposure to credit risk in the tranche held, Ch. 48, 6.6.2
Control, Ch. 6, 3; Ch. 12, 4, Ch 30
   assessing control, Ch. 6, 3.1
   changes in control (*see* Consolidation procedures)
   common control, Ch. 6, 2.2.6.A
   de facto control, Ch. 6, 4.3.3
   joint, Ch. 12, 4
   potential voting rights, Ch. 6, 4.3.4
   purpose and design of investee, Ch. 6, 3.2
   of specified assets, Ch. 6, 8
      of silo, evaluating, Ch. 6, 8.2
   transfer of, Ch 30
Controlling relationships, disclosure of, Ch. 39, 2.4
Convergence, IFRS/US GAAP, Ch. 1, 3.2
Convertible bonds, Ch. 47, 6.6
   bond convertible into fixed percentage of equity, Ch. 47, 6.6.6
   with cash settlement at the option of the issuer, Ch. 47, 6.6.5
   contingent convertible bond, Ch. 47, 6.6.2
   with down round or ratchet features, Ch. 47, 6.6.7
   foreign currency convertible bond, Ch. 47, 6.6.4
   functional currency bond convertible into a fixed number of shares, Ch. 47, 6.6.1
   issued to acquire goods/services, Ch. 34, 10.1.6
   mandatorily convertible bond, Ch. 47, 6.6.3
Convertible debt instruments, Ch. 46, 5.1.9
Convertible instruments (EPS), Ch. 37, 6.4.1
   convertible debt, Ch. 37, 6.4.1.A
   convertible preference shares, Ch. 37, 6.4.1.B
   participating equity instruments, Ch. 37, 6.4.1.C
Convertible loans, Ch. 54, 7.4.4.B
Core deposits, Ch. 43, 2.6.7
Core inventories, extractive industries, Ch. 43, 14.3
Corporate assets, Ch. 20, 4.2, Ch. 20, 3.1.1
   leased corporate assets, Ch. 20, 4.2.1
Cost approach, Ch. 18, 6.1.1.C
Cost of investment, Ch. 8, 2.1.1
   acquired for own shares or other equity instruments, Ch. 8, 2.1.1.A
   acquired in a common control transactions, Ch. 8, 2.1.1.B
   formation of a new parent, Ch. 8, 2.1.1.E–F
   reverse acquisitions in the separate financial statements, Ch. 8, 2.1.1.G
   subsidiary accounted for at cost: partial disposal, Ch. 8, 2.1.1.D
   subsidiary, associate or joint venture acquired in stages, Ch. 8, 2.1.1.C

Cost model
  investment property, Ch. 19, 7
    impairment, Ch. 19, 7.3
    incidence of use of the cost model, Ch. 19, 7.2
    initial recognition, Ch. 19, 7.1
      non-physical parts, identification of, Ch. 19, 7.1.2
      physical parts, identification of, Ch. 19, 7.1.1
  property, plant and equipment, Ch. 18, 5
    depreciable amount, Ch. 18, 5.2
    depreciation charge, Ch. 18, 5.3
    depreciation methods, Ch. 18, 5.6
    impairment, Ch. 18, 5.7
    land, Ch. 18, 5.4.2
    repairs and maintenance, Ch. 18, 5.4.1
    residual values, Ch. 18, 5.2
    significant parts of assets, Ch. 18, 5.1
    technological change, Ch. 18, 5.4.3
    useful lives, Ch. 18, 5.4
    when depreciation starts, Ch. 18, 5.5

Costs of hedging, accounting for, Ch. 53, 7.5
  foreign currency basis spreads in financial instruments, Ch. 53, 7.5.3
    measurement of the costs of hedging for, Ch. 53, 7.5.3.A
    transition, Ch. 53, 13.3.3
  forward element of forward contracts, Ch. 53, 7.5.2
    forward element in net investment hedge, Ch. 53, 7.5.2.A
    transition, Ch. 53, 13.3.2
  time value of options, Ch. 53, 7.5.1
    aligned time value, Ch. 53, 7.5.1.A
    transition, Ch. 53, 13.3.1

Council of European Securities Regulators (CESR), Ch. 1, 5
Credit break clauses, Ch. 53, 3.2.4
Credit card arrangements, Ch. 27, 3.5.1.C
  and similar arrangements which give rise to insurance risk, Ch. 45, 3.3.4
Credit card-holder rewards programmes, Ch. 27, 3.5.1.D
Credit enhancements, Ch. 51, 6.1.1; Ch. 52, 3.3.1
Credit guarantees, Ch. 52, 4.3
Credit-linked notes, Ch. 46, 5.1.8
Credit losses. *See* Expected credit losses (ECLs)
Credit risk, Ch. 54, 5.3
  changes in, calculating gain/loss attributable to, Ch. 51, 6.2.1
  counterparty
    fair value measurement, Ch. 14, 12.2.2
    valuation of derivative transactions, Ch. 14, 11.3.2
  disclosures, Ch. 55, 11.2.6.A
  exposure, Ch. 54, 5.3.4
  of financial instrument, Ch. 54, 5.3
  hedging, Ch. 53, 12.1
  illustrative disclosures, Ch. 54, 5.3.6
  impact on hedged item, Ch. 53, 6.4.2.A
  impact on hedging instrument, Ch. 53, 6.4.2.B, 7.4.9
  incorporation into valuation of derivative contracts, Ch. 14, 11.3.3
  management practices, Ch. 54, 5.3.2
  significant increases in, determining, Ch. 51, 6
    change in the risk of a default occurring, Ch. 51, 6.1
      contractually linked instruments (CLIs) and subordinated interests, Ch. 51, 6.1.2
      determining change in risk of a default under loss rate approach, Ch. 51, 6.1.3
      impact of collateral, credit enhancements and financial guarantee contracts, Ch. 51, 6.1.1
    collective assessment, Ch. 51, 6.5
      basis of aggregation for collective assessment, Ch. 51, 6.5.2
      example of collective assessment ('bottom up' and 'top down' approach), Ch. 51, 6.5.3
      example of individual assessment of changes in credit risk, Ch. 51, 6.5.1
    determining the credit risk at initial recognition of an identical group of financial assets, Ch. 51, 6.6
    factors/indicators of changes in credit risk, Ch. 51, 6.2
      concessions granted to a wide range of customers, Ch. 51, 6.2.3
      examples, Ch. 51, 6.2.1
      illustrative examples when assessing significant increases in credit risk, Ch. 51, 6.2.4
      past due status and more than 30 days past due presumption, Ch. 51, 6.2.2
      use of behavioural factors, Ch. 51, 6.2.5
    operational simplifications, Ch. 51, 6.4
      assessment at the counterparty level, Ch. 51, 6.4.4
      delinquency, Ch. 51, 6.4.2
      determining maximum initial credit risk for a portfolio, Ch. 51, 6.4.5
      low credit risk, Ch. 51, 6.4.1
      12-month risk as an approximation for change in lifetime risk, Ch. 51, 6.4.3
    revolving credit facilities, Ch. 51, 12
  in the tranche held, Ch. 48, 6.6.2

Cross-currency interest rate swaps (CCIRS), Ch. 53, 3.2.4.A, 7.3.3.B, 7.5.3
Crypto-assets
  additional disclosure requirements for, Ch. 22, 6.2
  cost model, Ch. 17, 11.5.2.A
  Cryptocurrencies as cash, Ch. 40, 3.2.5
  In scope of IAS 2, Ch. 22, 2.3.1.D
  recognition and initial measurement, Ch. 17, 11.5.1
  revaluation model, Ch. 17, 11.5.2.B
  standard setter activity, Ch. 17, 11.5.3
  subsequent measurement, Ch. 17, 11.5.2
Cryptocurrencies, Ch. 40, 3.2.5
CSM. *See* Contractual service margin
Cumulative preference shares, Ch. 11, 7.5.2
Cumulative translation differences, foreign operations, Ch. 5, 5.7
Current assets, Ch. 3, 3.1.3
Current liabilities, Ch. 3, 3.1.4
  Subsequent rectification of a covenant breach, Ch. 38, 2.3.2
Current service cost, employee benefits, Ch. 35, 5, 10.1
Current tax, Ch. 33, 5. *See also* IAS 12
  definition, Ch. 33, 3
Customer, Ch. 28, 3.6
  definition, Ch. 27, 3.3
Customer relationship intangible assets, Ch. 9, 5.5.2.B
Customer-supplier relationship, Ch. 6, 7.1
DAC. *See* Deferred acquisition costs

Date of transition to IFRSs, Ch. 5, 1.3
'Day 1' profits, Ch. 49, 3.3
De facto **agents**, Ch. 12, 4.2.5
De facto **control**, Ch. 6, 4.3.3
Death-in-service benefits, Ch. 35, 3.6
Death waivers, loans with, Ch. 45, 3.3.5
Debt, extinguishment of, Ch. 52, 6.1
    gains and losses on, Ch. 52, 6.3
Debt instruments, Ch. 45, 3.4.1.B; Ch. 48, 2.1
    convertible and exchangeable, Ch. 37, 6.4.1.A; Ch. 46, 5.1.9
    measured at fair value through other comprehensive income, Ch. 51, 9
    term extension and similar call, put and prepayment options in, Ch. 46, 5.1.4
Debt investments, foreign currency, Ch. 51, 9.2
Decommissioning, Ch. 26, 6.3; Ch. 43, 10
    accounting for changes in costs, Ch. 18, 4.3
    in extractive industries, Ch. 43, 10
        foreign exchange differences, treatment of, Ch. 43, 10.2
        indefinite life assets, Ch. 43, 10.3
        recognition and measurement issues, Ch. 43, 10.1
    provisions, Ch. 26, 6.3
Deductible temporary differences, Ch. 33, 6.2.2. *See also* Temporary differences, Deferred tax assets
    business combinations and consolidation, Ch. 33, 6.2.2.E
    definition, Ch. 33, 3
    foreign currency differences, Ch. 33, 6.2.2.F
    recognition, Ch. 33, 7.1.2
        initial recognition of goodwill, Ch. 33, 7.2.2.B
        restrictions on recognition, Ch. 33, 7.4
            and future and 'probable' taxable profit, Ch. 33, 7.4.3
            and unrealised losses, Ch. 33, 7.4.5
    revaluations, Ch. 33, 6.2.2.C
    tax re-basing, Ch. 33, 6.2.2.D
    transactions that affect, Ch. 33, 6.2.2.A
        profit/loss, Ch. 33, 6.2.2.A
        statement of financial position, Ch. 33, 6.2.2.B
Deemed cost on first-time adoption, Ch. 5, 5.5
    for assets used in operations subject to rate regulation, Ch. 5, 5.5.4
    disclosures regarding, Ch. 5, 6.5
    event-driven fair value measurement as, Ch. 5, 5.5.2
        exemption for event-driven revaluations after the date of transition, Ch. 5, 5.5.2.C
        'fresh start' accounting, Ch. 5, 5.5.2.B
        'push down' accounting, Ch. 5, 5.5.2.A
    fair value or revaluation as, Ch. 5, 5.5.1
        determining deemed cost, Ch. 5, 5.5.1.A
            before the date of transition to IFRSs, Ch. 5, 5.5.1.B
    for oil and gas assets, Ch. 5, 5.5.3
    of subsidiary, on transition to IFRS, Ch. 8, 2.1.2
    use of
        after severe hyperinflation, Ch. 5, 6.5.5
        for assets used in operations subject to rate regulation, Ch. 5, 6.5.4
        fair value as, Ch. 5, 6.5.1
        for investments in subsidiaries, joint ventures and associates, Ch. 5, 6.5.2
        for oil and gas assets, Ch. 5, 6.5.3

Deemed disposals, Ch. 7, 3.6; Ch. 11, 7.12.6
Default
    change in the risk of a default occurring, Ch. 51, 6.1
        contractually linked instruments (CLIs) and subordinated interests, Ch. 51, 6.1.2
        determining change in risk of a default under loss rate approach, Ch. 51, 6.1.3
        impact of collateral, credit enhancements and financial guarantee contracts, Ch. 51, 6.1.1
    definition of, Ch. 51, 5.1
    exposure at default, revolving facilities, Ch. 51, 12.3
    losses expected in the event of default, Ch. 51, 5.8
        cash flows from the sale of a defaulted loan, Ch. 51, 5.8.2
        credit enhancements: collateral and financial guarantees, Ch. 51, 5.8.1
        treatment of collection costs paid to an external debt collection agency, Ch. 51, 5.8.3
    probability of default (PD) and loss rate approaches, Ch. 51, 5.4
        loss rate approach, Ch. 51, 5.4.2
        probability of default approach, Ch. 51, 5.4.1
Deferred acquisition costs (DAC), Ch. 55, 9.1.1.B
Deferred tax, Ch. 33, 6–8. *See also* IAS 12; Income taxes; Tax bases; Temporary differences
    assets, Ch. 33, 6.1.1; Ch. 33, 7.1.2
    investment property held by a 'single asset' entity, Ch. 19, 6.10
    liabilities, Ch. 33, 6.1.2, 7.1.1
    measurement, Ch. 33, 8
        different tax rates applicable to retained and distributed profits, Ch. 33, 8.5
            effectively tax-free entities, Ch. 33, 8.5.1
            withholding tax/distribution tax?, Ch. 33, 8.5.2
        discounting, Ch. 33, 8.6
        expected manner of recovery of assets/settlement of liabilities, Ch. 33, 8.4
            assets and liabilities with more than one tax base, Ch. 33, 8.4.3
            carrying amount, Ch. 33, 8.4.2
            change in expected manner of recovery of an asset/settlement of a liability, Ch. 33, 8.4.11
            depreciable PP&E and intangible assets, Ch. 33, 8.4.5
            determining the expected manner of recovery of assets, Ch. 33, 8.4.4
            investment properties, Ch. 19, 6.10; Ch. 33, 8.4.7
            non-depreciable PP&E and intangible assets, Ch. 33, 8.4.6
            non-amortised or indefinite life intangible assets, Ch. 33, 8.4.6.B
            PP&E accounted for using the revaluation model, Ch. 33, 8.4.6.A
            other assets and liabilities, Ch. 33, 8.4.8
            'outside' temporary differences relating to subsidiaries, branches, associates and joint arrangements, Ch. 33, 8.4.9
            'single asset' entities, Ch. 19, 4.1.2, 6.10; Ch. 33, 8.4.10
            tax planning strategies, Ch. 33, 8.4.1
        legislation at the end of the reporting period, Ch. 33, 8.1

Deferred tax—*contd*
  measurement—*contd*
    'prior year adjustments' of previously presented tax balances and expense (income), Ch. 33, 8.3
    uncertain tax treatments, Ch. 33, 8.2, 9
    unrealised intragroup profits and losses in consolidated financial, Ch. 33, 8.7
      intragroup transfers of goodwill and intangible assets, Ch. 33, 8.7.1
        consolidated financial statements, Ch. 7, 2.4, Ch. 33, 8.7.1.C
        individual financial statements of buyer, Ch. 33, 8.7.1.A
        individual financial statements of seller, Ch. 33, 8.7.1.B
        when the tax base of goodwill is retained by the transferor entity, Ch. 33, 8.7.1.D
  recognition, Ch. 33, 7
    assets carried at fair value/revalued amount, Ch. 33, 7.3
    basic principles, Ch. 33, 7.1
      deductible temporary differences (deferred tax assets), Ch. 33, 7.1.2
      taxable temporary differences (deferred tax liabilities), Ch. 33, 7.1.1
    deferred taxable gains, Ch. 33, 7.7
    initial recognition exception, Ch. 33, 7.2
      acquisition of an investment in a subsidiary, associate, branch or joint arrangement, Ch. 33, 7.2.10
      acquisition of subsidiary that does not constitute a business, Ch. 33, 7.2.9
      changes to temporary differences after initial recognition, Ch. 33, 7.2.4
        change in carrying value due to revaluation, Ch. 33, 7.2.4.B
        change in tax base due to deductions in tax return, Ch. 33, 7.2.4.C
        depreciation, amortisation/impairment of initial carrying value, Ch. 33, 7.2.4.A
        temporary difference altered by legislative change, Ch. 33, 7.2.4.D
      initial recognition of compound financial instruments by the issuer, Ch. 33, 7.2.8
      initial recognition of goodwill, Ch. 33, 7.2.2
      initial recognition of other assets and liabilities, Ch. 33, 7.2.3
      intragroup transfers of assets with no change in tax base, Ch. 33, 7.2.5
      partially deductible and super-deductible assets, Ch. 33, 7.2.6
      tax losses, acquisition of, Ch. 33, 7.2.1
      transactions involving the initial recognition of an asset and liability, Ch. 33, 7.2.7
        decommissioning costs, Ch. 33, 7.2.7.A
        finance leases under IFRS 16 taxed as operating leases, Ch. 33, 7.2.7.B
    interpretation issues, Ch. 33, 7.1.3
      accounting profit, Ch. 33, 7.1.3.A
      taxable profit 'at the time of the transaction,' Ch. 33, 7.1.3.B
    'outside' temporary differences relating to subsidiaries, branches, associates and joint arrangements, Ch. 33, 7.5
      calculation of, Ch. 33, 7.5.1
        consolidated financial statements, Ch. 33, 7.5.1.A
        separate financial statements of investor, Ch. 33, 7.5.1.B
      deductible temporary differences, Ch. 33, 7.5.3
      foreseeable future – anticipated intragroup dividend, Ch. 33, 7.5.4
        consolidated financial statements of receiving entity, Ch. 33, 7.5.4.A
        separate financial statements of paying entity, Ch. 33, 7.5.4.B
      taxable temporary differences, Ch. 33, 7.5.2
      unpaid intragroup interest, royalties, management charges etc., Ch. 33, 7.5.5
    restrictions on recognition of deferred tax assets, Ch. 33, 7.4
      effect of disposals on recoverability of tax losses, Ch. 33, 7.4.8
        tax losses of retained entity recoverable against profits of subsidiary disposed of, Ch. 33, 7.4.8.B
        tax losses of subsidiary disposed of recoverable against profits of retained entity, Ch. 33, 7.4.8.C
        tax losses of subsidiary disposed of recoverable against profits of that subsidiary, Ch. 33, 7.4.8.A
      re-assessment of deferred tax assets, Ch. 33, 7.4.7
      restrictions imposed by relevant tax laws, Ch. 33, 7.4.1
      sources of 'probable' taxable profit, estimates of future taxable profits, Ch. 33, 7.4.3
        ignore origination of new future deductible temporary differences, Ch. 33, 7.4.3.A
        ignore reversal of existing deductible temporary differences, Ch. 33, 7.4.3.B
      sources of 'probable' taxable profit, taxable temporary differences, Ch. 33, 7.4.2
      tax planning opportunities, Ch. 33, 7.4.4
      unrealised losses on debt securities measured at fair value, Ch. 33, 7.4.5
      unused tax losses and unused tax credits, Ch. 33, 7.4.6
    'tax-transparent' ('flow-through') entities, Ch. 33, 7.6
  tax bases and temporary differences, Ch. 33, 6

Deferred tax assets, Ch. 33, 3, 7.4

Deferred tax liabilities, Ch. 33, 3

Defined benefit plans, Ch. 35, 5–11. *See also* IAS 19; IFRIC 14
  costs of administering, Ch. 35, 11
  vs. defined contribution plans, Ch. 35, 3.1
  disclosure requirements, Ch. 35, 15.2
    amounts in financial statements, Ch. 35, 15.2.2
    characteristics and risks associated with, Ch. 35, 15.2.1
    future cash flows, amount, timing and uncertainty of, Ch. 35, 15.2.3
    multi-employer plans, Ch. 35, 15.2.4
    in other IFRSs, Ch. 35, 15.2.6
    sharing risks between entities under common control, Ch. 35, 15.2.5
  and insured benefits, Ch. 35, 3.2
  and multi-employer plans, Ch. 35, 3.3
  net defined benefit liability (asset), presentation of, Ch. 35, 9

plan assets, Ch. 35, 6
    contributions to defined benefit funds, Ch. 35, 6.5
    definition of, Ch. 35, 6.1
    longevity swaps, Ch. 35, 6.6
    measurement of, Ch. 35, 6.2
    qualifying insurance policies, Ch. 35, 6.3
    reimbursement rights, Ch. 35, 6.4
plan liabilities, Ch. 35, 7
    actuarial assumptions, Ch. 35, 7.5
    actuarial methodology, Ch. 35, 7.3
    attributing benefit to years of service, Ch. 35, 7.4
    contributions by employees and third parties, Ch. 35, 7.2
    discount rate, Ch. 35, 7.6
    frequency of valuations, Ch. 35, 7.7
    legal and constructive obligations, Ch. 35, 7.1
refund from, Ch. 35, 16.2.1
sharing risks between entities under common control, Ch. 35, 3.3.2
treatment in profit/loss and other comprehensive income, Ch. 35, 10
    acquisition of a qualifying insurance policy, Ch. 35, 10.2.2
    net interest on the net defined benefit liability (asset), Ch. 35, 10.2
    past service cost, Ch. 35, 10.1.1
    remeasurements, Ch. 35, 10.3
    service cost, Ch. 35, 10.1
    settlements, Ch. 35, 10.2.3
treatment of the plan surplus/deficit in the statement of financial position, Ch. 35, 8
    assets restriction to their recoverable amounts, Ch. 35, 8.2
        economic benefits available as reduced future contributions when no minimum funding requirements for future service, Ch. 35, 8.2.2
        IFRIC 14 requirements concerning limit on defined benefit asset, Ch. 35, 8.2.1
        minimum funding requirements, IFRIC interpretation effect on economic benefit available as a reduction in future contributions, Ch. 35, 8.2.3
        when the requirement may give rise to a liability, Ch. 35, 8.2.4
        pension funding payments contingent on future events within the control of the entity, Ch. 35, 8.2.5
    net defined benefit liability (asset), Ch. 35, 8.1

Defined contribution plans, Ch. 35, 4
    accounting requirements, Ch. 35, 4.1
    vs. defined benefit plans, Ch. 35, 3.1
    disclosure requirements, Ch. 35, 15
    with vesting conditions, Ch. 35, 4.1.2

Delegated decision making, Ch. 12, 4.2.4

Delegated power, Ch. 6, 6.1

Demand deposits, Ch. 40, 3.2.1

Deposit components unbundling, Ch. 55, 5
    illustration, Ch. 55, 5.2
    practical difficulties, Ch. 55, 5.3
    requirements, Ch. 55, 5.1

Depreciation, depletion and amortisation (DD&A), extractive industries, Ch. 43, 16
    block caving, Ch. 43, 16.2
    determining when production phase commences, Ch. 43, 15.5.2
    requirements under IAS 16 and IAS 38, Ch. 43, 16.1
        assets depreciated using the straight-line method, Ch. 43, 16.1.2
        assets depreciated using the units of production method, Ch. 43, 16.1.3
        joint and by-products, Ch. 43, 16.1.3.D
        reserves base, Ch. 43, 16.1.3.B
        unit of measure, Ch. 43, 16.1.3.C
        units of production formula, Ch. 43, 16.1.3.A
    mineral reserves, Ch. 43, 16.1.1

Depreciation, property, plant and equipment (PP&E), Ch. 18, 5
    charge, Ch. 18, 5.3
    depreciable amount and residual values, Ch. 18, 5.2
    methods, Ch. 18, 5.6
        diminishing balance methods, Ch. 18, 5.6.1
        sum of the digits method, Ch. 18, 5.6.1
        unit-of-production method, Ch. 18, 5.6.2
    and useful life of asset, Ch. 18, 5.4

Derecognition, financial instruments, Ch. 52, 1–8
    accounting treatment, Ch. 52, 5
        collateral, Ch. 52, 5.5.2
        offset, Ch. 52, 5.5.1
        reassessing derecognition, Ch. 52, 5.6
        reassessment of consolidation of subsidiaries and SPEs, Ch. 52, 5.6.1
        rights/obligations over transferred assets that continue to be recognised, Ch. 52, 5.5.3
        transfers that do not qualifying for derecognition, through retention of risks and rewards, Ch. 52, 5.2
        transfers that qualify for derecognition, Ch. 52, 5.1
        servicing assets and liabilities, Ch. 52, 5.1.2
        transferred asset part of larger asset, Ch. 52, 5.1.1
        transfers with continuing involvement, Ch. 52, 5.3
        associated liability, Ch. 52, 5.3.3
        continuing involvement in part only of a larger asset, Ch. 52, 5.3.5
        guarantees, Ch. 52, 5.3.1
        options, Ch. 52, 5.3.2
        subsequent measurement of assets and liabilities, Ch. 52, 5.3.4
        transfers with continuing involvement–accounting examples, Ch. 52, 5.4
        continuing involvement in part only of a financial asset, Ch. 52, 5.4.4
        transfers of assets measured at amortised cost, Ch. 52, 5.4.2
        transfers of assets measured at fair value, Ch. 52, 5.4.3
            'collar' put and call options, Ch. 52, 5.4.3.C
            transferor's call option, Ch. 52, 5.4.3.A
            transferee's put option, Ch. 52, 5.4.3.B
        transfers with guarantees, Ch. 52, 5.4.1
    CUSIP 'netting', Ch. 52, 7
    definitions, Ch. 52, 2.1
    development of IFRS, Ch. 52, 2
    financial assets, Ch. 52, 3
        background, Ch. 52, 3.1
        client money, Ch. 52, 3.7
        contractual rights to receive cash flows from the asset, expiration of, Ch. 52, 3.4

Derecognition, financial instruments—*contd*
  financial assets—*contd*
    contractual rights to receive cash flows from the asset, expiration of—*contd*
      asset restructuring in the context of Greek government debt, Ch. 52, 3.4.2
      IBOR reform, Ch. 52, 3.4.3
      novation of contracts to intermediary counterparties, Ch. 52, 3.4.4
      renegotiation of the terms of an asset, Ch. 52, 3.4.1
      write-offs, Ch. 52, 3.4.5
    retention of rights subject to obligation to pay over to others (pass-through arrangement), Ch. 52, 3.5.2
    transfers of, Ch. 52, 3.5.1
    decision tree, Ch. 52, 3.2
      importance of applying tests in sequence, Ch. 52, 3.2.1
    groups of financial assets, Ch. 52, 3.3.2
      IASB's view and the Interpretations Committee's tentative conclusions, Ch. 52, 3.3.2.A
      similar assets, Ch. 52, 3.3.2.B
    principles, parts of assets and groups of assets, Ch. 52, 3.3
      credit enhancement through, Ch. 52, 3.3.1
      transfer of asset (or part of asset) for only part of its life, Ch. 52, 3.3.3
    securitisations, Ch. 52, 3.6
      'empty' subsidiaries or SPEs, Ch. 52, 3.6.6
      insurance protection, Ch. 52, 3.6.3
      non-optional derivatives along with a group of financial assets transfers, Ch. 52, 3.6.5
      recourse to originator, Ch. 52, 3.6.1
      short-term loan facilities, Ch. 52, 3.6.2
      treatment of collection proceeds, Ch. 52, 3.6.4
    transfer/retention of substantially all the risks and rewards of ownership, Ch. 52, 3.8
      evaluating extent to which risks and rewards are transferred, Ch. 52, 3.8.4
    transferee's 'practical ability' to sell the asset, Ch. 52, 3.9.1
      transfers, cumulative basis, Ch. 52, 3.8.5
      transfers, resulting in neither transfer nor retention of substantially all risks and rewards, Ch. 52, 3.8.3
      transfers, resulting in retention of substantially all risks and rewards, Ch. 52, 3.8.2
      transfers, resulting in transfer of substantially all risks and rewards, Ch. 52, 3.8.1
  financial liabilities, Ch. 52, 6
    derivatives that can be financial assets or financial liabilities, Ch. 52, 6.4
    exchange or modification of debt by original lender, Ch. 52, 6.2
      costs and fees, Ch. 52, 6.2.5
      examples, Ch. 52, 6.2.4
      IBOR reform, Ch. 52, 6.2.2
      loan syndications, Ch. 52, 6.2.3
      modification gains and losses, Ch. 52, 6.2.6
      settlement of financial liability with issue of new equity instrument, Ch. 52, 6.2.8
      'substantially' different, Ch. 52, 6.2.1
      through intermediary, Ch. 52, 6.2.4
    extinguishment of debt
      in exchange for transfer of assets not meeting the derecognition criteria, Ch. 52, 6.1.4
      'in-substance defeasance' arrangements, Ch. 52, 6.1.3
      legal release by creditor, Ch. 52, 6.1.2
      what constitutes 'part' of a liability, Ch. 52, 6.1.1
    gains and losses on extinguishment of debt, Ch. 52, 6.3
    supply-chain finance, Ch. 52, 6.5
  future developments, Ch. 52, 8
  off-balance sheet finance, Ch. 52, 1.1
  practical application factoring of trade receivables, Ch. 52, 4.5
  repurchase agreements ('repos') and securities lending, Ch. 52, 4.1
    agreement to repurchase at fair value, Ch. 52, 4.1.5
    agreements to return the same asset, Ch. 52, 4.1.1
    agreements with right of substitution, Ch. 52, 4.1.3
    agreements with right to return the same or substantially the same asset, Ch. 52, 4.1.2
    net cash-settled forward repurchase, Ch. 52, 4.1.4
    right of first refusal to repurchase at fair value, Ch. 52, 4.1.6
    wash sale, Ch. 52, 4.1.7
  scope, Ch. 52, 2.2
  subordinated retained interests and credit guarantees, Ch. 52, 4.3
  transfers by way of swaps, Ch. 52, 4.4
    interest rate swaps, Ch. 52, 4.4.2
    total return swaps, Ch. 52, 4.4.1
  transfers subject to put and call options, Ch. 52, 4.2
    changes in probability of exercise of options after initial transfer of asset, Ch. 52, 4.2.9
    clean-up call options, Ch. 52, 4.2.7
    deeply in the money put and call options, Ch. 52, 4.2.1
    deeply out of the money put and call options, Ch. 52, 4.2.2
    net cash-settled options, Ch. 52, 4.2.5
    option to put or call at fair value, Ch. 52, 4.2.4
    options that are neither deeply out of the money nor deeply in the money, Ch. 52, 4.2.3
    removal of accounts provision, Ch. 52, 4.2.6
    same (or nearly the same) price put and call options, Ch. 52, 4.2.8

Derivative(s), Ch. 46, 1–3. *See also* Embedded derivatives
  call and put options over non-controlling interest. Ch. 7, 6. *See also* 'Non-controlling interest'
  changes in value in response to changes in underlying, Ch. 46, 2.1
    non-financial variables specific to one party to the contract, Ch. 46, 2.1.3
    notional amounts, Ch. 46, 2.1.1
    underlying variables, Ch. 46, 2.1.2
  common derivatives, Ch. 46, 3.1
  contracts, cash flows on, Ch. 40, 4.4.12
  defining characteristics, Ch. 46, 2
    changes in value in response to changes in underlying, Ch. 46, 2.1
    future settlement, Ch. 46, 2.3
    initial net investment, Ch. 46, 2.2
  discount rates for calculating fair value of, Ch. 53, 7.4.5
  in-substance derivatives, Ch. 46, 3.2
  linked and separate transactions, Ch. 46, 8
  regular way contracts, Ch. 46, 3.3

restructuring of, Ch. 53, 3.6.3
'synthetic' instruments, Ch. 46, 8
Derivative financial instruments, Ch. 45, 2.2.8; Ch. 53, 3.2
   basis swaps, Ch. 53, 3.2.5
   credit break clauses, Ch. 53, 3.2.4
      principal resetting cross currency swaps, Ch. 53, 3.2.4.A
   embedded derivatives, Ch. 53, 3.2.3
   net written options, Ch. 53, 3.2.2
   offsetting external derivatives, Ch. 53, 3.2.1
Designation at fair value through profit or loss, Ch. 48, 7
Dilapidation provision, Ch. 26, 6.9
Diluted EPS, Ch. 37, 6. *See also* Earnings per share (EPS); IAS 33
   calculation of, Ch. 37, 6.2; Ch. 37, 8
      diluted earnings, Ch. 37, 6.2.1
      diluted number of shares, Ch. 37, 6.2.2
   contingently issuable potential ordinary shares, Ch. 37, 6.4.8
   contingently issuable shares, Ch. 37, 6.4.6
      earnings-based contingencies, Ch. 37, 6.4.6.A
      not driven by earnings or share price, Ch. 37, 6.4.6.C
      share-price-based contingencies, Ch. 37, 6.4.6.B
   convertible instruments, Ch. 37, 6.4.1
      convertible debt, Ch. 37, 6.4.1.A
      convertible preference shares, Ch. 37, 6.4.1.B
      participating equity instruments, Ch. 37, 6.4.1.C
   dilutive instruments, types, Ch. 37, 6.4
   dilutive potential ordinary shares, Ch. 37, 6.3
      judged by effect on profits from continuing operations, Ch. 37, 6.3.1
      judged by the cumulative impact of potential shares, Ch. 37, 6.3.2
   need for, Ch. 37, 6.1
   options, warrants and their equivalents, Ch. 37, 6.4.2
      forward purchase agreements, Ch. 37, 6.4.2.C
      numerator, Ch. 37, 6.4.2.A
      options over convertible instruments, Ch. 37, 6.4.2.D
      settlement of option exercise price, Ch. 37, 6.4.2.E
      specified application of option proceeds, Ch. 37, 6.4.2.F
      written call options, Ch. 37, 6.4.2.B
      written put options, Ch. 37, 6.4.2.C
   partly paid shares, Ch. 37, 6.4.4
   potentially ordinary shares of investees, Ch. 37, 6.4.7
   presentation, restatement and disclosure, Ch. 37, 7
   purchased options and warrants, Ch. 37, 6.4.3
   share-based payments, Ch. 37, 6.4.5
Diminishing balance methods, depreciation, Ch. 18, 5.6.1
Direct method of consolidation, foreign operations, Ch. 7, 2.3; Ch. 15, 6.6.3
Directly attributable borrowing costs, Ch. 21, 5.1
'Directly attributable' costs, Ch. 18, 4.1.1
'Dirty' fair values, Ch. 53, 7.4.10
Disclosure(s). *See also* individual entries for standards
   in annual financial statements, Ch. 32, 3
   business combinations, Ch. 9, 16
   capital disclosures, Ch. 3, 5.4; Ch. 54, 5.6.3
   capitalisation of borrowing costs, Ch. 21, 7
   of changes in ownership interests in subsidiaries, Ch. 13, 4.5
   common control transactions, Ch. 8, 4.3.1
   in condensed interim financial statements, Ch. 41, 4
   earnings per share (EPS), Ch. 37, 7.3
   employee benefits, Ch. 35, 15
   first-time adoption, Ch. 5, 6
   financial instruments
      qualitative disclosures, Ch. 54, 5.1
      quantitative disclosures, Ch. 54, 5.2, 5.6
   foreign exchange, Ch. 15, 10
   government assistance, Ch. 24, 6
   government grants, Ch. 24, 6
   of IFRS information before adoption of IFRSs, Ch. 5, 6.7
   of IFRS information in financial statements, Ch. 5, 6.3.1
   impairment of fixed assets and goodwill, Ch. 20, 13.3
   income taxes, Ch. 33, 14
   insurance contracts, Ch. 55, 11; Ch. 56, 16
   intangible assets, Ch. 17, 11
      additional disclosures when the revaluation model is applied, Ch. 17, 10.4
      general disclosures, Ch. 17, 10.1
      profit/loss presentation, Ch. 17, 10.3
      of research and development expenditure, Ch. 17, 10.5
      statement of financial position presentation, Ch. 17, 10.2
   inventories, Ch. 22, 6
      additional disclosure requirements for crypto-assets, Ch. 22, 6.2
      general disclosure requirements, Ch. 22, 6.1
   investment property, Ch. 19, 12
   investments in associates and joint ventures, Ch. 11, 10; Ch. 13, 5
   joint arrangements, Ch. 13, 5
   leases (IFRS 16), Ch. 23, 10.6
   of mineral reserves and resources, Ch. 43, 2.4
   objective and general requirements, Ch. 32, 3.1
   offsetting, Ch. 2, 10.2.1.A; Ch. 54, 7.4.2.D
   property, plant and equipment (PP&E), Ch. 18, 8–8.3
   provisions, contingent liabilities and contingent assets, Ch. 26, 7
   related party disclosures, Ch. 39, 1–2
   relating to accounting policies, Ch. 3, 5
      changes in accounting estimates, Ch. 3, 5.2.2
      changes in accounting policies, Ch. 3, 5.1.2
      changes pursuant to the initial application of an IFRS, Ch. 3, 5.1.2.A
      estimation uncertainty, Ch. 3, 5.2.1
      judgements made in applying accounting policies, Ch. 3, 5.1.1.B
      new IFRS, future impact of, Ch. 3, 5.1.2.C
      prior period errors, Ch. 3, 5.3
      significant accounting policies, Ch. 3, 5.1.1.A
      voluntary changes in accounting policy, Ch. 3, 5.1.2.B
   reportable segments, Ch. 36, 5
   revenue and contract cost disclosure requirements, Ch. 32, 3.2
   separate financial statements, Ch. 8, 3
   service concession arrangements (SCA), Ch. 25, 7
   share-based payment, Ch. 34, 13
Disclosure of interests in other entities, Ch. 13, 1–6. *See also* IFRS 12; Interests in joint arrangements and associates
   definitions, Ch. 13, 2.2.1
      interaction of IFRS 12 and IFRS 5, Ch. 13, 2.2.1.C
      interests in other entities, Ch. 13, 2.2.1.A
      structured entities, Ch. 13, 2.2.1.B
   interests disclosed under IFRS 12, Ch. 13, 2.2.2
   interests not within the scope of IFRS 12, Ch. 13, 2.2.3

Disclosure of interests in other entities—*contd*
   joint arrangements and associates, Ch. 13, 5
      nature, extent and financial effects, Ch. 13, 5.1
      risks associated, Ch. 13, 5.2
         commitments relating to joint ventures, Ch. 13, 5.2.1
         contingent liabilities relating to joint ventures and associates, Ch. 13, 5.2.2
   objective, Ch. 13, 2.1
   scope, Ch. 13, 2.2
   significant judgements and assumptions, Ch. 13, 3
   subsidiaries, Ch. 13, 4
      changes in ownership interests in subsidiaries, Ch. 13, 4.5
      composition of the group, Ch. 13, 4.1
      consolidated structured entities, nature of risks, Ch. 13, 4.4
         current intentions to provide financial or other support, Ch. 13, 4.4.4
         financial or other support to with no contractual obligation, Ch. 13, 4.4.2
         terms of contractual arrangements, Ch. 13, 4.4.1
      nature and extent of significant restrictions, Ch. 13, 4.3
      non-controlling interests, Ch. 13, 4.2
   unconsolidated structured entities, Ch. 13, 6
      nature of interests, Ch. 13, 6.1
      nature of risks, Ch. 13, 6.2
         actual and intended financial and other support to structured entities, Ch. 13, 6.2.2
         disclosure of funding difficulties, Ch. 13, 6.3.6
         disclosure of liquidity arrangements, Ch. 13, 6.3.5
         disclosure of losses, Ch. 13, 6.3.2
         disclosure of ranking and amounts of potential losses, Ch. 13, 6.3.4
         disclosure of support, Ch. 13, 6.3.1
         disclosure of the forms of funding of an unconsolidated structured entity, Ch. 13, 6.3.7
         disclosure of types of income received, Ch. 13, 6.3.3
         maximum exposure to loss from those interests, Ch. 13, 6.2.1

Discontinued operation, Ch. 3, 3.2.5; Ch. 4, 3.2. *See also* IFRS 5
   cash flows of, Ch. 40, 8.1
   definition of, Ch. 4, 3.1
   presentation of, Ch. 4, 3.2
   property, plant and equipment, derecognition and disposal, Ch. 18, 7.1
   trading with continuing operations, Ch. 4, 3.3

Discount rate
   for calculating fair value of derivatives, Ch. 53, 7.4.5
   employee benefits, Ch. 35, 7.6
      high quality corporate bonds, Ch. 35, 7.6.1
      no deep market, Ch. 35, 7.6.2
   estimated cash flows to a present value (provisions), Ch. 26, 4.3
      adjusting for risk and using a government bond rate, Ch. 26, 4.3.2
      effect of changes in interest rates on the discount rate applied, Ch. 26, 4.3.6
      own credit risk is not taken into account, Ch. 26, 4.3.3
      pre-tax discount rate, Ch. 26, 4.3.4
      real *vs.* nominal rate, Ch. 26, 4.3.1
      unwinding of the discount, Ch. 26, 4.3.5
   impairment of fixed assets and goodwill, Ch. 20, 7.2
      approximations and short cuts, Ch. 20, 7.2.4
      discount rates other than WACC, Ch. 20, 7.2.9
      entity-specific WACCs and capital structure, Ch. 20, 7.2.8
      entity-specific WACCs and different project risks within the entity, Ch. 20, 7.2.7
      pre-tax discount rate, calculating, Ch. 20, 7.2.2
      pre-tax discount rates disclosing when using a post-tax methodology, Ch. 20, 7.2.5
      pre-tax rates determination taking account of tax losses, Ch. 20, 7.2.6
      VIU calculation using post-tax cash flows, Ch. 20, 7.2.3
      WACC, Ch. 20, 7.2.1
   insurance contracts, Ch. 56, 8.3
   leases, Ch. 23, 4.6
   significant financing components, Ch. 29, 2.5

Discretionary participation feature (DPF), Ch. 55, 2.2.1, 6
   definition, Ch. 55, 2.2.1
   in financial instruments, Ch. 55, 6.2
   guaranteed benefits, Ch. 55, 6
   in insurance contracts, Ch. 55, 6.1
   investment contracts with, Ch. 55, 2.2.2, 6.1, 6.2, 7.2.2.C
   practical issues, Ch. 55, 6.3
      contracts with switching features, Ch. 55, 6.3.2
      negative DPF, Ch. 55, 6.3.1

Discussion Paper (DP)–*Accounting for Dynamic Risk Management*, Ch. 53, 11.1

Discussion Paper (DP)–*Extractive Activities*, Ch. 43, 1.3

Discussion Paper (DP)–*Preliminary Views on Insurance Contracts*, Ch. 55, 1.1

Discussion Paper (DP)–*A Review of the Conceptual Framework for Financial Reporting*, Ch. 2, 1

Disposal groups held for sale/distribution, Ch. 3, 3.1.2; Ch. 4, 1–6. *See also* IFRS 5
   changes to a plan of sale/plan of distribution, Ch. 4, 2.2.5
   classification as held for sale/held for distribution to owners, Ch. 4, 2.1.2
      abandonment, Ch. 4, 2.1.2.C
      available for immediate sale, meaning of, Ch. 4, 2.1.2.A
      criteria met after the reporting period, Ch. 38, 2.1.3
      highly probable, meaning of, Ch. 4, 2.1.2.B
   comparative information, Ch. 4, 4
   concept of disposal group, Ch. 4, 2.1.1
   disclosure requirements, Ch. 4, 5
   discontinued operations, Ch. 4, 3
   future developments, Ch. 4, 6
   measurement, Ch. 4, 2.2
      impairments and reversals of impairment, Ch. 4, 2.2.3
      presentation in statement of financial position, Ch. 4, 2.2.4
   partial disposals of operations, Ch. 4, 2.1.3
      of an associate or joint venture, Ch. 4, 2.1.3.B
      loss of control of a subsidiary, Ch. 4, 2.1.3.A; Ch. 7, 3.2, 3.4, 3.5, 3.7

'Dividend blocker' clause, Ch. 47, 4.5.3.A

Dividend discount model (DDM), Ch. 20, 12.2, 12.4.2.A

'Dividend pusher' clause, Ch. 47, 4.5.3.B

Dividends, Ch. 8, 2.4; Ch. 11, 7.11.1
   declared after the reporting period, Ch. 38, 2.1.3.A

and other distributions, Ch. 8, 2.4
    distributions of noncash assets to owners (IFRIC 17), Ch. 7, 3.7; Ch. 8, 2.4.2
    dividend exceeding total comprehensive income, Ch. 8, 2.4.1
    resulting in carrying amount of an investment exceeding consolidated net assets, Ch. 8, 2.4.1.B
    returns of capital, Ch. 8, 2.4.1.C
    from subsidiaries, joint ventures or associates, Ch. 8, 2.4.1
    payable on shares classified as financial liabilities, Ch. 21, 5.5.4

Divisions, foreign exchange, Ch. 15, 4.4

Downstream activities, extractive industries, Ch. 43, 1.6

'Downstream' transactions elimination, equity accounted investments, Ch. 11, 7.6.1

Downward valuations of property, plant and equipment, reversals of, Ch. 18, 6.3

DP. *See under* Discussion Paper

DPF. *See* Discretionary participation feature (DPF)

Due Process Handbook, Ch. 1, 2.6

Dynamic hedging strategies, Ch. 53, 6.3.2

Earnings-based contingencies (EPS), Ch. 37, 6.4.6.A

Earnings per share (EPS), Ch. 37, 1–8. *See also* Diluted EPS; IAS 33
    basic EPS, Ch. 37, 3
        earnings, Ch. 37, 3.1
        number of shares, Ch. 37, 3.2
    definitions, Ch. 37, 1.1
    disclosure, Ch. 37, 7.3
    interim financial reporting, Ch. 41, 9.8
    numerator, matters affecting, Ch. 37, 5
        earnings, Ch. 37, 5.1
        other bases, Ch. 37, 5.5
        participating equity instruments, Ch. 37, 5.4
        preference dividends, Ch. 37, 5.2
        retrospective adjustments, Ch. 37, 5.3
        tax deductible dividends on, Ch. 37, 5.4.1
    outstanding ordinary shares, changes in, Ch. 37, 4
    presentation, Ch. 37, 7.1
    restatement, Ch. 37, 7.2
    reverse acquisitions, business combinations, Ch. 9, 14.5; Ch. 37, 4.6.2

EBTs. *See* Employee benefit trusts (EBTs)

Economic relationship, hedge accounting, Ch. 53, 6.4.1

EDs. *See* Exposure Drafts (EDs)

Effective interest method, Ch. 50, 3

Effective interest rate (EIR), Ch. 50, 3.1

Effective tax rate, Ch. 33, 14.2
    changes in during the year, Ch. 41, 9.5.2

Embedded derivatives, Ch. 46, 4–7; Ch. 55, 4
    cash flows, Ch. 54, 5.4.2.E
    characteristics, Ch. 55, 4
    in commodity arrangements, Ch. 43, 12.8
    compound financial instruments with multiple, Ch. 54, 4.4.7
    compound instruments with, Ch. 47, 6.4.2
    contracts for the sale of goods or services, Ch. 46, 5.2
        floors and caps, Ch. 46, 5.2.4
            foreign currency derivatives, Ch. 46, 5.2.1
            fund performance fees, Ch. 46, 5.2.5
            inflation-linked features, Ch. 46, 5.2.3
            inputs, ingredients, substitutes and other proxy pricing mechanisms, Ch. 46, 5.2.2
    decision tree, Ch. 55, 4
    derivative and, Ch. 46, 4
    exposures to market risk from, Ch. 55, 11.2.7
    extractive industries, Ch. 43, 13.2
    financial instrument hosts, Ch. 46, 5.1
        commodity-and equity-linked interest and principal payments, Ch. 46, 5.1.7
        convertible and exchangeable debt instruments, Ch. 46, 5.1.9
        credit-linked notes, Ch. 46, 5.1.8
        fallback provisions relating to interest rate benchmark reform, Ch. 46, 5.1.3
        foreign currency monetary items, Ch. 46, 5.1.1
        inflation-linked debt instruments, Ch. 46, 5.1.6
        interest rate floors and caps, Ch. 46, 5.1.5
        interest rate indices, Ch. 46, 5.1.2
        puttable instruments, Ch. 46, 5.1.10
        term extension and similar call, put and prepayment options in debt instruments, Ch. 46, 5.1.4
    foreign currency embedded derivatives, Ch. 43, 13.2.1
    gains and losses recognised in profit/loss, Ch. 54, 7.1.4
    gas markets, development of, Ch. 43, 13.2.4
    hedging instruments, Ch. 53, 3.2.3
    and host contracts, identifying the terms, Ch. 46, 6
        embedded non-option derivatives, Ch. 46, 6.1
        embedded option-based derivative, Ch. 46, 6.2
        multiple embedded derivatives, Ch. 46, 6.3
    initial measurement, Ch. 49, 3.5
    insurance contracts, Ch. 46, 5.4
    leases, Ch. 46, 5.3
        contingent rentals based on related sales, Ch. 46, 5.3.3
        contingent rentals based on variable interest rates, Ch. 46, 5.3.4
        foreign currency derivatives, Ch. 46, 5.3.1
        inflation-linked features, Ch. 46, 5.3.2
    long-term supply contracts, Ch. 43, 13.2.3
    provisionally priced contracts, Ch. 43, 13.2.2
    reassessment, Ch. 46, 7
        acquisition of contracts, Ch. 46, 7.1
        business combinations, Ch. 46, 7.2
        remeasurement issues arising from, Ch. 46, 7.3
    unit-linked features, Ch. 55, 4.1

Embedded leases, extractive industries, Ch. 43, 17.1

Embedded value (EV) of insurance contract, Ch. 55, 1.4.3

Emerging Economies Group, Ch. 1, 2.9

Emission rights, Ch. 9, 5.5.2.E; Ch. 17, 11.2
    acquired in a business combination, Ch. 9, 5.5.2.E; Ch. 17, 11.2.5
    amortisation, Ch. 17, 11.2.4
    by brokers and traders, accounting for, Ch. 17, 11.2.7
    impairment testing, Ch. 17, 11.2.4
    sale of, Ch. 17, 11.2.6

Emissions trading schemes, intangible assets, Ch. 17, 11.2
    accounting for emission rights by brokers and traders, Ch. 17, 11.2.7
    amortisation and impairment testing of emission rights, Ch. 17, 11.2.4

Emissions trading schemes, intangible assets—*contd*
   emission rights acquired in a business combination, Ch. 17, 11.2.5
   government grant approach, Ch. 17, 11.2.3
   green certificates compared to, Ch. 26, 6.6 IFRIC 3, Ch. 17, 11.2.1
   liabilities associated with, Ch. 26, 6.5
   net liability approaches, Ch. 17, 11.2.2
   sale of emission rights, Ch. 17, 11.2.6

Employee benefit(s), Ch. 35, 1–16. *See also* Defined benefit plans; Defined contribution plans; IAS 19; Long-term employee benefits, Multi-employer plans; Short-term employee benefits
   costs of administering, Ch. 35, 11
   death-in-service benefits, Ch. 35, 3.6
   defined benefit plans, Ch. 35, 5–11
   defined contribution plans, Ch. 35, 4
   disclosure requirements, Ch. 35, 15
      defined benefit plans, Ch. 35, 15.2
      defined contribution plans, Ch. 35, 15.1
      multi-employer plans, Ch. 35, 15.2.4
   future developments, Ch. 35, 16
   insured benefits, Ch. 35, 3.2
   interim financial reporting, Ch. 41, 9.3
      employer payroll taxes and insurance contributions, Ch. 41, 9.3.1
      pensions, Ch. 41, 9.3.3
      vacations, holidays and other short-term paid absences, Ch. 41, 9.3.4
      year-end bonuses, Ch. 41, 9.3.2
   long-term employee benefits, Ch. 35, 13
   multi-employer plans, Ch. 35, 3.3
   objective of IAS 19, Ch. 35, 2.1
   pensions, Ch. 35, 3
   plans that would be defined contribution plans, Ch. 35, 3.5
   post-employment benefits, Ch. 35, 3
   scope of IAS 19, Ch. 35, 2.2
   short-term employee benefits, Ch. 35, 12
   state plans, Ch. 35, 3.4
   termination benefits, Ch. 35, 14

Employee benefit plans, Ch. 6, 2.2.2; Ch. 13, 2.2.3.A

Employee benefit trusts (EBTs) and similar arrangements, Ch. 34, 12.3
   accounting for, Ch. 34, 12.3.2
   awards satisfied by shares purchased by, or issued to, an EBT, Ch. 34, 12.3.3
   background, Ch. 34, 12.3.1
   EBT as extension of parent, Ch. 34, 12.4.2.B, 12.5.2.B
   financial statements of the EBT, Ch. 34, 12.3.5
   financial statements of the parent, Ch. 34, 12.4.2, 12.5.2
   group share scheme illustrative examples
      equity-settled award satisfied by fresh issue of shares, Ch. 34, 12.5
      equity-settled award satisfied by market purchase of shares, Ch. 34, 12.4
   separate financial statements of sponsoring entity, Ch. 34, 12.3.4

Employee, definition, Ch. 34, 5.2.1

'Empty' subsidiaries, Ch. 52, 3.6.6

'End-user' contracts, Ch. 45, 4.2.4

Enhanced Disclosure Task Force (EDTF), Ch. 54, 9.2

Entity's functional currency determination, Ch. 15, 4
   branches and divisions, Ch. 15, 4.4
   documentation of judgements made, Ch. 15, 4.5
   intermediate holding companies/finance subsidiaries, Ch. 15, 4.2
   investment holding companies, Ch. 15, 4.3

EPS. *See* Earnings per share

Equalisation provisions, Ch. 55, 7.2.1

Equity instruments, Ch. 8, 2.1.1.A; Ch. 45, 2.2.7, 3.6
   classification, Ch. 48, 2.2
   contracts to issue equity instruments, Ch. 47, 4.4.2
   contracts settled by delivery of the entity's own equity instruments, Ch. 47, 5
      contracts accounted for as equity instruments, Ch. 47, 5.1
         comparison with IFRS 2–share-based payment, Ch. 47, 5.1.1
         contracts to acquire non-controlling interests, Ch. 47, 5.3.2
         contracts to purchase own equity during 'closed' or 'prohibited' periods, Ch. 47, 5.3.1
         exchange of fixed amounts of equity (equity for equity), Ch. 47, 5.1.4
         number of equity instruments issued adjusted for capital restructuring or other event, Ch. 47, 5.1.2
         stepped up exercise price, Ch. 47, 5.1.3
      contracts accounted for as financial assets/liabilities, Ch. 47, 5.2
         derivative financial instruments with settlement options, Ch. 47, 5.2.8
         fixed amount of cash denominated in a currency other than entity's functional currency, Ch. 47, 5.2.3
            rights issues with a price fixed in a currency other than entity's functional currency, Ch. 47, 5.2.3.A
         fixed amount of cash determined by reference to share price Ch. 47, 5.2.6
         fixed number of equity instruments for variable consideration, Ch. 47, 5.2.2
         fixed number of equity instruments with variable value, Ch. 47, 5.2.5
         instrument with equity settlement alternative of significantly higher value than cash settlement alternative, Ch. 47, 5.2.4
         net-settled contracts over own equity, Ch. 47, 5.2.7
         variable number of equity instruments, Ch. 47, 5.2.1
      gross-settled contracts for the sale or issue of the entity's own equity instruments, Ch. 47, 5.4
      liabilities arising from gross-settled contracts for the purchase of the entity's own equity instruments, Ch. 47, 5.3
         contracts to acquire non-controlling interests, Ch. 47, 5.3.2
         contracts to purchase own equity during 'closed' or 'prohibited' periods, Ch. 47, 5.3.1
   definition, Ch. 34, 2.2.1; Ch. 45, 2.1; Ch. 47, 3
   determining fair value of, Ch. 14, 11.2; Ch. 34, 5.5
   holder, Ch. 45, 3.6.2
   investments in, designated at fair value through OCI, Ch. 51, 9
   issued instruments, Ch. 45, 3.6.1; Ch. 47, 4.4.1

Equity method/accounting, Ch. 11, 7
- application of the equity method, Ch. 11, 7
  - consistent accounting policies, Ch. 11, 7.8
  - date of commencement of equity accounting, Ch. 11, 7.3
  - discontinuing the use of the equity method, Ch. 11, 7.12
    - deemed disposals, Ch. 11, 7.12.6
    - investment in associate becomes a joint venture (or vice versa), Ch. 11, 7.12.4
    - investment in associate/joint venture that is a business becoming a subsidiary, Ch. 11, 7.12.1
    - investment in associate or joint venture that is not a business becoming a subsidiary, Ch. 11, 7.12.2
    - partial disposals of interests in associate/joint venture, Ch. 11, 7.12.4
    - retained investment in the former associate or joint venture is a financial asset, Ch. 11, 7.12.3
  - distributions received in excess of the carrying amount, Ch. 11, 7.10
  - equity accounting and consolidation, comparison between, Ch. 11, 7.2
  - equity transactions in an associate's/joint venture's financial statements, Ch. 11, 7.11
    - dividends/other forms of distributions, Ch. 11, 7.11.1
    - effects of changes in parent/non-controlling interests in subsidiaries, Ch. 11, 7.11.4
    - equity-settled share-based payment transactions, Ch. 11, 7.11.3
    - issues of equity instruments, Ch. 11, 7.11, 7.11.2
  - impairment losses, Ch. 11, 8
    - general, Ch. 11, 8.1
    - investment in the associate or joint venture, Ch. 11, 8.2
    - other interests that are not part of the net investment in the associate or joint venture, Ch. 11, 8.3
  - impairment of investments in subsidiaries, associates and joint ventures, Ch. 20, 12.4
    - equity accounted investments and CGU's, Ch. 20, 12.4.5
    - equity accounted investments and goodwill for impairment, Ch. 20, 12.4.6
    - indicators of impairment, Ch. 20, 12.4.3, 12.4.4
  - initial carrying amount of an associate/joint venture, Ch. 11, 7.4
    - cost-based approach, Ch. 11, 7.4.2.A
    - fair value (IFRS 3) approach, Ch. 11, 7.4.2.A
    - following loss of control of an entity, Ch. 7, 3.3.2, 7.1, 3.2; Ch. 11, 7.4.1, 7.6.5
    - piecemeal acquisition, Ch. 11, 7.4.2
      - common control transactions involving sales of associates, Ch. 11, 7.4.2.D
      - existing associate that becomes a joint venture, or vice versa, Ch. 11, 7.4.2.C
      - financial instrument becoming an associate/joint venture, Ch. 11, 7.4.2.A
      - step increase in an existing associate/joint venture without a change in status of the investee, Ch. 11, 7.4.2.B
  - loss-making associates/joint ventures, Ch. 11, 7.9
  - non-coterminous accounting periods, Ch. 11, 7.7
  - overview, Ch. 11, 7.1
  - share of the investee, Ch. 11, 7.5
    - accounting for potential voting rights, Ch. 11, 7.5.1
    - cumulative preference shares held by parties other than the investor, Ch. 11, 7.5.2
    - several classes of equity, Ch. 11, 7.5.3
    - where the investee is a group, Ch. 11, 7.5.5
    - where the reporting entity is a group, Ch. 11, 7.5.4
  - transactions between the reporting entity and its associates/joint ventures, Ch. 11, 7.6
    - contributions of non-monetary assets to an associate/a joint venture, Ch. 11, 7.6.5
    - commercial substance, Ch. 11, 7.6.5.A
    - conflict between IAS 28 and IFRS 10, Ch. 11, 7.6.5.C
    - practical application, Ch. 11, 7.6.5.B
    - elimination of 'upstream' and 'downstream' transactions, Ch. 11, 7.6.1
    - loans and borrowings between the reporting entity, Ch. 11, 7.6.3
    - reciprocal interests, Ch. 11, 7.6.2
    - statement of cash flows, Ch. 11, 7.6.4
- exemptions from applying the equity method, Ch. 11, 5.3
  - investments held in associates/joint ventures held by venture capital organisations, Ch. 11, 5.3
    - application of IFRS 9 (or IAS 39) to exempt, Ch. 11, 5.3.2
    - entities with a mixture of activities, Ch. 11, 5.3.2.A
  - investment entities exception, Ch. 11, 5.3.1
- former subsidiary that becomes an equity-accounted investee, Ch. 7, 3.3.2, 7.1
  - application of partial gain recognition where the gain exceeds the carrying amount of the investment in the associate or joint venture accounted using the equity method, Ch. 7, 3.3.2.D
  - conflict between IFRS 10 and IAS 28 (September 2014 amendments applied), Ch. 7, 3.3.2.B, 3.3.2.E, 7.1
  - conflict between IFRS 10 and IAS 28 (September 2014 amendments not applied), Ch. 7, 3.3.2.A, 3.3.2.E
  - determination of the fair value of the retained interest in a former subsidiary that is an associate or joint venture, Ch. 7, 3.3.2.F
  - examples of accounting for sales or contributions to an existing associate, Ch. 7, 3.3.2.E
  - presentation of comparative information for a former subsidiary that becomes an investee for using the equity method, Ch. 7, 3.3.2.G
  - reclassification of items of other comprehensive income where the interest retained in the former subsidiary is an associate or joint venture accounted using the equity method, Ch. 7, 3.3.2.C
- parents exempt from preparing consolidated financial statements, Ch. 11, 5.1
- partial use of fair value measurement of associates, Ch. 11, 5.4
- subsidiaries meeting certain criteria, Ch. 11, 5.2
- transfers of associates/joint ventures between entities under common control, Ch. 10, 5

Equity-settled share-based payment transactions, Ch. 34, 2.2.1, 4–8. *See also* Cash-settled share-based payment transactions; IFRS 2*;* Share-based payment/transactions; Vesting, share-based payment
- accounting treatment, summary, Ch. 34, 4.1

Equity-settled share-based payment transactions—*contd*
- allocation of expense, Ch. 34, 6
  - market conditions, Ch. 34, 6.3
  - non-vesting conditions, Ch. 34, 6.4
  - overview, Ch. 34, 6.1
    - accounting after vesting, Ch. 34, 6.1.3
    - continuous estimation process of IFRS 2, Ch. 34, 6.1.1
    - vesting and forfeiture, Ch. 34, 6.1.2
  - vesting conditions other than market conditions, Ch. 34, 6.2
    - 'graded' vesting, Ch. 34, 6.2.2
    - service conditions, Ch. 34, 6.2.1
    - variable exercise price, Ch. 34, 6.2.5
    - variable number of equity instruments, Ch. 34, 6.2.4
    - variable vesting periods, Ch. 34, 6.2.3
- award modified to, or from, cash-settled, Ch. 34, 9.4
- cancellation, replacement and settlement, Ch. 34, 7.4
  - calculation of the expense on cancellation, Ch. 34, 7.4.3
  - cancellation and forfeiture, distinction between, Ch. 34, 7.4.1
    - surrender of award by employee, Ch. 34, 7.4.1.B
    - termination of employment by entity, Ch. 34, 7.4.1.A
  - cancellation and modification, distinction between, Ch. 34, 7.4.2
  - replacement awards, Ch. 34, 7.4.4
    - designation, Ch. 34, 7.4.4.A
    - incremental fair value of, Ch. 34, 7.4.4.B
    - replacement of vested awards, Ch. 34, 7.4.4.C
  - valuation requirements when an award is cancelled or settled, Ch. 34, 7.2
- cost of awards, Ch. 34, 5
  - determining the fair value of equity instruments, Ch. 34, 5.5, 8
    - reload features, Ch. 34, 5.5.1, 8.9
  - grant date, Ch. 34, 5.3
  - overview, Ch. 34, 5.1
  - transactions with employees, Ch. 34, 5.2
  - transactions with non-employees, Ch. 34, 5.4
- credit entry, Ch. 34, 4.2
- entity's plans for future modification/replacement of award, Ch. 34, 7.6
- grant date, Ch. 34, 5.3
- market conditions, Ch. 34, 6.3
  - accounting treatment summary, Ch. 34, 6.3.2
  - awards with a condition linked to flotation price, Ch. 34, 6.3.8
  - definition, Ch. 34, 6.3.1
  - hybrid/interdependent market conditions and non-market vesting conditions, Ch. 34, 6.3.7
  - independent market conditions and non-market vesting conditions, Ch. 34, 6.3.6
  - market conditions and known vesting periods, Ch. 34, 6.3.3
  - multiple outcomes depending on market conditions, Ch. 34, 6.3.5
  - transactions with variable vesting periods due to market conditions, Ch. 34, 6.3.4
- market purchases of own equity, Ch. 34, 9.2.2, 9.2.3
- modification, Ch. 34, 7.3
  - altering vesting period, Ch. 34, 7.3.3
  - decreasing the value of an award, Ch. 34, 7.3.2
    - additional/more onerous non-market vesting conditions, Ch. 34, 7.3.2.C
    - decrease in fair value of equity instruments granted, Ch. 34, 7.3.2.A
    - decrease in number of equity instruments granted, Ch. 34, 7.3.2.B
  - from equity-settled to cash-settled, Ch. 34, 7.3.5
  - increasing the value of an award, Ch. 34, 7.3.1
    - increase in fair value of equity instruments granted, Ch. 34, 7.3.1.A
    - increase in number of equity instruments granted, Ch. 34, 7.3.1.B
    - removal/mitigation of non-market vesting conditions, Ch. 34, 7.3.1.C
  - that reduces the number of equity instruments granted but maintains or increases the value of an award, Ch. 34, 7.3.4
  - share splits and consolidations, Ch. 34, 7.8
  - two awards running 'in parallel', Ch. 34, 7.7
  - valuation requirements when an award is modified, Ch. 34, 7.2
- non-vesting conditions, Ch. 34, 6.4
  - awards with no conditions other than non-vesting conditions, Ch. 34, 6.4.1
  - awards with non-vesting conditions and variable vesting periods, Ch. 34, 6.4.2
  - failure to meet non-vesting conditions, Ch. 34, 6.4.3
- reload features, Ch. 34, 5.5.1, 8.9
- termination of employment by entity, Ch. 34, 7.4.1.A
- replacement and *ex gratia* awards, Ch. 34, 7.5
- transactions with employees, Ch. 34, 5.2
  - basis of measurement, Ch. 34, 5.2.2
  - employee definition, Ch. 34, 5.2.1
- transactions with non-employees, Ch. 34, 5.4
  - effect of change of status from employee to non-employee (or vice versa), Ch. 34, 5.4.1
- transactions with equity and cash alternatives, Ch. 34, 10.1, 10.2, 10.3
  - awards requiring cash settlement in specific circumstances (awards with contingent cash settlement), Ch. 34, 10.3
    - change in manner of settlement where award is contingent on future events outside the control of the entity and the counterparty, Ch. 34, 10.3.4
    - cash settlement on a change of control, Ch. 34, 10.3.3
    - IASB discussion, Ch. 34, 10.3.5
    - treat as cash-settled if contingency is outside entity's control, Ch. 34, 10.3.1
    - contingency outside entity's control and probable, Ch. 34, 10.3.2
  - cash settlement alternative not based on share price/value, Ch. 34, 10.4
- transactions where the counterparty has choice of settlement, Ch. 34, 10.1
  - accounting treatment, during vesting period, Ch. 34, 10.1.3.A
  - accounting treatment, settlement, Ch. 34, 10.1.3.B
  - 'backstop' cash settlement rights, Ch. 34, 10.1.5
  - cash-settlement alternative for employee introduced after grant date, Ch. 34, 10.1.4

convertible bonds issued to acquire goods/services, Ch. 34, 10.1.6
    transactions in which the fair value is measured directly, Ch. 34, 10.1.1
    transactions in which the fair value is measured indirectly, Ch. 34, 10.1.2
transactions where the entity has choice of settlement, Ch. 34, 10.2
    change in entity's settlement policy/intention leading to change in classification of award after grant date, Ch. 34, 10.2.3
    transactions treated as cash-settled, Ch. 34, 10.2.1
        economic compulsion for cash settlement, Ch. 34, 10.2.1.A
    transactions treated as equity-settled, Ch. 34, 10.2.2
valuation, Ch. 34, 8
    awards of equity instruments to a fixed monetary value, Ch. 34, 8.10
    awards other than options, Ch. 34, 8.7
        non-recourse loans, Ch. 34, 8.7.2
        performance rights, Ch. 34, 8.7.4
        share appreciation rights (SAR), Ch. 34, 8.7.3
        shares, Ch. 34, 8.7.1
    awards whose fair value cannot be measured reliably, Ch. 34, 8.8
        intrinsic value method, Ch. 34, 8.8.1
        modification, cancellation and settlement, Ch. 34, 8.8.2
    awards with reload features, Ch. 34, 8.9
    capital structure effects and dilution, Ch. 34, 8.6
    option-pricing model, selection of, Ch. 34, 8.3
        binomial model, Ch. 34, 8.3.2
        Black-Scholes-Merton formula, Ch. 34, 8.3.1
        Monte Carlo Simulation, Ch. 34, 8.3.3
    option-pricing model, selecting appropriate assumptions, Ch. 34, 8.5
        exercise and termination behaviour, Ch. 34, 8.5.2
        expected dividends, Ch. 34, 8.5.4
        expected term of the option, Ch. 34, 8.5.1
        expected volatility of share price, Ch. 34, 8.5.3
        risk-free interest rate, Ch. 34, 8.5.5
    option-pricing models, adapting for share-based payment, Ch. 34, 8.4
        non-transferability, Ch. 34, 8.4.1
        vesting and non-vesting conditions, treatment of, Ch. 34, 8.4.2
    options, Ch. 34, 8.2
        call options, overview, Ch. 34, 8.2.1
        call options, valuation, Ch. 34, 8.2.2
        factors specific to employee share options, Ch. 34, 8.2.3
    vesting conditions other than market conditions, Ch. 34, 6.2
    'graded' vesting, Ch. 34, 6.2.2
    service conditions, Ch. 34, 6.2.1
    variable exercise price, Ch. 34, 6.2.5
    variable number of equity instruments, Ch. 34, 6.2.4
    variable vesting periods, Ch. 34, 6.2.3

Equity transactions
    in an associate's/joint venture's financial statements, Ch. 11, 7.11
        dividends/other forms of distributions, Ch. 11, 7.11.1

        effects of changes in parent/non-controlling interests in subsidiaries, Ch. 11, 7.11.4
        equity-settled share-based payment transactions, Ch. 11, 7.11.3
        issues of equity instruments, Ch. 11, 7.11.2
    tax effects of, Ch. 47, 8.2
    transaction costs of, Ch. 47, 8.1

Errors, prior period
    correction of, Ch. 3, 4.6
    disclosure of, Ch. 3, 5.3
    discovery of fraud after the reporting period, Ch. 38, 3.5
    impracticability of restatement, Ch. 3, 4.7.2

Estimates. *See* Accounting Estimates

Estimation uncertainty, Ch. 3, 5.2
    disclosures of, Ch. 3, 5.2
    sources of, Ch. 3, 5.2.1

Euro, introduction of, Ch. 15, 8

European Commission, Ch. 1, 1, 2.2–2.3, 2.5, 4.2.1

European Embedded Values (EEV), Ch. 55, 1.4.3

European Financial Reporting Advisory Group (EFRAG), Ch. 1, 4.2.1

European Securities and Markets Authority (ESMA), Ch. 1, 5

European Union
    adoption of IRFS in the EU, Ch. 1, 4.2.1
    EU directive on WE&EE (IFRIC 6), Ch. 26, 6.7
    EU 'top up' for financial conglomerates, Ch. 1, 4.2.1
    introduction of the euro, Ch. 15, 8
    tax implications of UK withdrawal from the (EU), Ch. 33, 5.1.4

Events after the reporting period, Ch. 38, 1–3. *See also* IAS 10
    adjusting events, Ch. 38, 2.1.2
        treatment of, Ch. 38, 2.2
    extractive industries, Ch. 43, 20
        business combinations-application of the acquisition method, Ch. 43, 20.2
        completion of E&E activity after, Ch. 43, 20.3
        reserves proven after the reporting period, Ch. 43, 20.1
    impairment, Ch. 20, 7.1.9
    non-adjusting events, Ch. 38, 2.1.3
        dividend declaration, Ch. 38, 2.1.3.A
        treatment of, Ch. 38, 2.3
    practical issues, Ch. 38, 3
        changes to estimates of uncertain tax treatments, Ch. 38, 3.6
        discovery of fraud after the reporting period, Ch. 38, 3.5
        insolvency of a debtor and IFRS 9 expected credit losses, Ch. 38, 3.3
        percentage of completion estimates, Ch. 38, 3.2
        valuation of inventory, Ch. 38, 3.1
        valuation of investment property at fair value and tenant insolvency, Ch. 38, 3.4

Evidence of power over an investee, Ch. 6, 4.5

Ex gratia **share-based payment award**, Ch. 34, 7.5

Exchanges of assets, Ch. 17, 4.7; Ch. 18, 4.4
    commercial substance, Ch. 17, 4.7.2; Ch. 18, 4.4.1
    measurement of assets exchanged, Ch. 17, 4.7.1
    reliably measurable, Ch. 18, 4.4.2

Executory contract, Ch. 26, 2.2.1.A

Existing rights, investee
  budget approval rights, Ch. 6, 4.2.2.C
  evaluation whether rights are protective, Ch. 6, 4.2.2
  evaluation whether rights are substantive, Ch. 6, 4.2.1
  franchises, Ch. 6, 4.2.2.B
  incentives to obtain power, Ch. 6, 4.2.3
  independent directors, Ch. 6, 4.2.2.D
  veto rights, Ch. 6, 4.2.2.A

Expected credit losses (ECLs), Ch. 51, 14. *See also* Credit risk
  approaches, Ch. 51, 3
    general approach, Ch. 51, 3.1
      purchased/originated credit-impaired financial assets, Ch. 51, 3.3
    simplified approach, Ch. 51, 3.2
  background and history of impairment project, Ch. 51, 1.1
  calculations, Ch. 51, 7
    Basel guidance on accounting for ECLs, Ch. 51, 7.1
    date of derecognition and date of initial recognition, Ch. 51, 7.3.1
    Global Public Policy Committee (GPPC) guidance, Ch. 51, 7.2
    interaction between expected credit losses calculations and fair value hedge accounting, Ch. 51, 7.5; Ch. 53, 6.4.2.B
    interaction between the initial measurement of debt instruments acquired in a business combination and the impairment model of IFRS 9, Ch. 51, 7.4
    measurement dates of ECLs, Ch. 51, 7.3
    trade date and settlement date accounting, Ch. 51, 7.3.2
  derecognition of contract assets, Ch. 32, 2.1.4
  disclosures, Ch. 51, 15
  financial assets measured at fair value through other comprehensive income, Ch. 51, 9; Ch. 53, 2.6.3
    accounting treatment for debt instruments measured at fair value through other comprehensive income, Ch. 51, 9.1
      interaction between foreign currency translation, fair value hedge accounting and impairment, Ch. 51, 9.2
  financial guarantee contracts, Ch. 51, 11
  Global Public Policy Committee guidance, Ch. 51, 7.2
  IFRS Transition Resource Group for Impairment of Financial Instruments (ITG) and IASB webcasts, Ch. 51, 1.5
  impairment of contract assets, Ch. 32, 2.1.3
  impairment requirements (IFRS 9), Ch. 51, 1.2
  initial measurement of receivables, Ch. 32, 2.1.5
  intercompany loans, Ch. 51, 13
  key changes from the IAS 39 requirements and the main implications of these changes, Ch. 51, 1.3
  key differences from the FASB's requirements, Ch. 51, 1.4
  loan commitments, Ch. 51, 11
  measurement, Ch. 51, 5
    definition of default, Ch. 51, 5.1
    expected life *vs.* contractual period, Ch. 51, 5.5
    lifetime expected credit losses, Ch. 51, 5.2
    losses expected in the event of default, Ch. 51, 5.8
      cash flows from the sale of a defaulted loan, Ch. 51, 5.8.2
      credit enhancements: collateral and financial guarantees, Ch. 51, 5.8.1
      treatment of collection costs paid to an external debt collection agency, Ch. 51 5.8.3
    12-month expected credit losses, Ch. 51, 5.3
    probability of default (PD) and loss rate approaches, Ch. 51, 5.4
      loss rate approach, Ch. 51, 5.4.2
      probability of default approach, Ch. 51, 5.4.1
    probability-weighted outcome, Ch. 51, 5.6
    reasonable and supportable information, Ch. 51, 5.9
      information about past events, current conditions and forecasts of future economic conditions, Ch. 51, 5.9.3
      sources of information, Ch. 51, 5.9.2
      undue cost/effort, Ch. 51, 5.9.1
    time value of money, Ch. 51, 12.4
  modified financial assets, accounting treatment, Ch. 51, 8
    if assets are derecognised, Ch. 51, 8.1
    if assets are not derecognised, Ch. 51, 8.2
  other guidance on ECLs, Ch. 51, 1.6
  presentation of ECLs in the statement of financial position, Ch. 51, 14
    accumulated impairment amount for debt instruments measured at fair value through other comprehensive income, Ch. 51, 14.3
    allowance for financial assets measured at amortised cost, contract assets and lease receivables, Ch. 51, 14.1
      presentation of the gross carrying amount and ECL allowance for credit-impaired assets, Ch. 51, 14.1.2
      write-off, Ch. 51, 14.1.1
    provisions for loan commitments and financial guarantee contracts, Ch. 51, 14.2
  revolving credit facilities, Ch. 51, 12
    determining a significant increase in credit risk, Ch. 51, 12.5
    exposure at default, Ch. 51, 12.3
    period over which to measure ECLs, Ch. 51, 12.2
    scope of the exception, Ch. 51, 12.1
    time value of money, Ch. 51, 12.4
  scope of IFRS 9 impairment requirements, Ch. 51, 2
  trade receivables, contract assets and lease receivables, Ch. 51, 10
    lease receivables, Ch. 51, 10.2
    trade receivables and contract assets, Ch. 51, 10.1

Expenses analysis, Ch. 3, 3.2.3
  by function, Ch. 3, 3.2.3.B
  by nature, Ch. 3, 3.2.3.A

Exploration and evaluation (E&E) assets. *See also* IFRS 6
  asset swaps, Ch. 43, 6.3.1
  carried interest in E&E phase, Ch. 43, 6.1.2
  exchanges of E&E assets for other types of assets, Ch. 43, 6.3.3
  farm-in arrangements, Ch. 43, 6.2
  impairment of, Ch. 43, 3.5
    additional considerations if E&E assets are impaired, Ch. 43, 3.5.5
    cash-generating units comprising successful and unsuccessful E&E projects, Ch. 43, 3.5.3
    impairment testing 'triggers,' Ch. 43, 3.5.1

income statement treatment of E&E write downs, Ch. 43, 3.5.6
order of impairment testing, Ch. 43, 3.5.4
reversal of impairment losses, Ch. 43, 3.5.7
specifying the level at which E&E assets are assessed for impairment, Ch. 43, 3.5.2
measurement of, Ch. 43, 3.3
capitalisation of borrowing costs in the E&E phase, Ch. 43, 3.3.2
types of expenditure in the E&E phase, Ch. 43, 3.3.1
reclassification of, Ch. 43, 3.4.1
recognition of, Ch. 43, 3.2
area-of-interest method, Ch. 43, 3.2.5
changes in accounting policies, Ch. 43, 3.2.6
developing an accounting policy under IFRS 6, Ch. 43, 3.2.1
full cost method, Ch. 43, 3.2.4
options for an exploration and evaluation policy, Ch. 43, 3.2.2
successful efforts method, Ch. 43, 3.2.3

Exposure Drafts (EDs)
ED 5–*Insurance Contracts*, Ch. 55, 1.2
ED/2009/2–*Income Tax*, Ch. 33, 1.3, 8.5.1
ED/2014/4 – *Measuring Quoted Investments in Subsidiaries, Joint Ventures and Associates at Fair Value (Proposed amendments to IFRS 10, IFRS 12, IAS 27, IAS 28 and IAS 36 and Illustrative Examples for IFRS 13)*, Ch. 7, 3.3.2.F; Ch. 14, 5.1.1
ED/2017/5 – *Accounting Policies and Accounting Estimates – Proposed amendments to IAS 8*, Ch. 3, 6.2.1; Ch. 22, 3.2.2
ED/2019/5 – *Deferred Tax related to Assets and Liabilities arising from a Single Transaction: Proposed amendments to IAS 12*, Ch. 33, 7.2.7
ED/2019/6 – *Disclosure of Accounting Policies, Proposed amendments to IAS 1 and IFRS Practice Statement 2*, Ch. 3, 6.2.2
ED/2019/7 – *General Presentation and Disclosure*, Ch. 3, 6.1.2

External hedging instruments, offsetting, Ch. 53, 3.2.1
Extractive industries, Ch. 43, 1–20. *See also* IFRS 6; Mineral reserves and resources; Reserves
acquisitions, Ch. 43, 8
accounting for land acquisitions, Ch. 43, 8.4.2
acquisition of an interest in a joint operation that is a business, Ch. 43, 8.3
asset acquisitions and conditional purchase consideration, Ch. 43, 8.4.1
business combinations, Ch. 43, 8.2
events after the reporting period, Ch. 43, 22.2
goodwill in business combinations, Ch. 43, 8.2.1
impairment of assets and goodwill recognised on acquisition, Ch. 43, 8.2.2
value beyond proven and probable reserves (VBPP), Ch. 43, 8.2.3
business combinations *vs.* asset acquisitions, Ch. 43, 8.1
definition of a business, Ch. 43, 8.1.2
differences between asset purchase transactions and, Ch. 43, 8.1.1
April 2010 discussion paper, extractive activities, Ch. 43, 1.3
asset measurement, Ch. 43, 1.3.3
asset recognition, Ch. 43, 1.3.2

disclosure, Ch. 43, 1.3.4
Extractive Activities project, status of, Ch. 43, 1.3.6
project status, Ch. 43, 1.3.6
publish what you pay proposals, Ch. 43, 1.3.5
reserves and resources, definitions of, Ch. 43, 1.3.1
decommissioning and restoration/rehabilitation, Ch. 43, 10
indefinite life assets, Ch. 43, 10.3
recognition and measurement issues, Ch. 43, 10.1
treatment of foreign exchange differences, Ch. 43, 10.2
definitions, Ch. 43, 1.1, 21
depreciation, depletion and amortisation (DD&A), Ch. 43, 16
block caving, Ch. 43, 16.2
determining when production phase commences, Ch. 43, 15.5.2
requirements under IAS 16 and IAS 38, Ch. 43, 16.1
assets depreciated using the straight-line method, Ch. 43, 16.1.2
assets depreciated using the units of production method, Ch. 43, 16.1.3
mineral reserves, Ch. 43, 16.1.1
events after the reporting period, Ch. 43, 22
business combinations-application of the acquisition method, Ch. 43, 22.2
completion of E&E activity after, Ch. 43, 22.3
reserves proven after the reporting period, Ch. 43, 22.1
financial instruments, Ch. 43, 13
embedded derivatives, Ch. 43, 13.2
development of gas markets, Ch. 43, 13.2.4
foreign currency embedded derivatives, Ch. 43, 13.2.1
long-term supply contracts, Ch. 43, 13.2.3
provisionally priced sales contracts, Ch. 43, 13.2.2
hedging sales of metal concentrate (mining), Ch. 43, 13.4
normal purchase and sales exemption, Ch. 43, 13.1
volume flexibility in supply contracts, Ch. 43, 13.3
functional currency, Ch. 43, 9
changes in, Ch. 43, 9.2
determining, Ch. 43, 9.1
guidance under national accounting standards, Ch. 43, 1.5
impact of IFRS 15, Ch. 43, 12
commodity-based contracts, modifications to, Ch. 43, 12.10
embedded derivatives in commodity arrangements, Ch. 43, 12.8
forward-selling contracts to finance development, Ch. 43, 12.6
gold bullion sales (mining only), Ch. 43, 12.13
inventory exchanges with the same counterparty, Ch. 43, 12.3
multi-period commodity-based sales contracts, Ch. 43, 12.15
overlift and underlift (oil and gas), Ch. 43, 12.4
principal *vs.* agent considerations in commodity-based contracts, Ch. 43, 12.11
production sharing contracts/arrangements (PSCs), Ch. 43, 12.5
repurchase agreements, Ch. 43, 12.14
royalty income, Ch. 43, 12.9
sale of product with delayed shipment, Ch. 43, 12.2
shipping, Ch. 43, 12.12
take-or-pay contracts, Ch. 43, 12.16
trading activities, Ch. 43, 12.7

Extractive industries—contd
- impact of IFRS 16, Ch. 43, 17, 18
    - allocating contract consideration, Ch. 43, 17.6
    - definition of a lease, Ch. 43, 17.2
    - identifying and separating lease and non-lease components, Ch. 43, 17.
    - identifying lease payments included in the measurement of the lease liability, Ch. 43, 17.5
    - interaction of IFRS 16 and IFRS 11, Ch. 43, 18
    - interaction of leases with asset retirement obligations, Ch. 43, 17.7
    - joint arrangements, Ch. 43, 18
    - land easements or rights of way, Ch. 43, 17.1.2
    - scope and scope exclusions, Ch. 43, 17.1
    - substitution rights, Ch. 43, 17.3
    - subsurface rights, Ch. 43, 17.1.3
- impairment of assets, Ch. 43, 11
    - basis of recoverable amount – value-in-use (VIU) or fair value less costs of disposal (FVLCD), Ch. 43, 11.3
    - calculation of FVLCD, Ch. 43, 11.5
    - calculation of VIU, Ch. 43, 11.4
    - cash flows from mineral reserves and resources and the appropriate discount rate, Ch. 43, 11.4.2.A
    - commodity price assumptions, Ch. 43, 11.4.3, 11.5.2
    - foreign currency cash flows, Ch. 43, 11.4.5, 11.5.4
    - future capital expenditure, Ch. 43, 11.4.4, 11.5.3
    - identifying cash-generating units (CGUs), Ch. 43, 11.2
    - impairment indicators, Ch. 43, 11.1
    - low mine or field profitability near end of life, Ch. 43, 11.6
    - projections of cash flows, Ch. 43, 11.4.2, 11.5.1
- inventories, Ch. 43, 14
    - carried at fair value, Ch. 43, 14.4
    - core inventories, Ch. 43, 14.3
    - heap leaching (mining), Ch. 43, 14.6
    - recognition of work in progress, Ch. 43, 14.1
    - sale of by-products and joint products, Ch. 43, 14.2
        - by-products, Ch. 43, 14.2.1
        - joint products, Ch. 43, 14.2.2
    - stockpiles of low grade ore (mining), Ch. 43, 14.5
- investments in the extractive industries, Ch. 43, 7
    - joint arrangements, Ch. 43, 7.1
        - assessing joint control, Ch. 43, 7.1.1
        - determining whether a manager has control, Ch. 43, 7.1.2
        - managers of joint arrangements, Ch. 43, 7.1.4
        - non-operators, Ch. 43, 7.1.5
        - parties without joint control/control, Ch. 43, 7.1.3
    - undivided interests, Ch. 43, 7.2
- legal rights to explore for, develop and produce mineral properties, Ch. 43, 5
    - concessionary agreements (concessions), Ch. 43, 5.2
    - different types of royalty interests, Ch. 43, 5.7
        - net profits interests, Ch. 43, 5.7.4
        - overriding royalties, Ch. 43, 5.7.2
        - production payment royalties, Ch. 43, 5.7.3
        - revenue and royalties: gross or net?, Ch. 43, 5.7.5
        - working interest and basic royalties, Ch. 43, 5.7.1
    - evolving contractual arrangements, Ch. 43, 5.5
    - how a mineral lease works, Ch. 43, 5.1
    - joint operating agreements, Ch. 43, 5.6
    - pure-service contract, Ch. 43, 5.4
    - traditional production sharing contracts, Ch. 43, 5.3
- long-term contracts and leases, Ch. 43, 19
    - embedded leases, Ch. 43, 19.1
    - impact of IFRS 16, Ch. 43, 19.3
    - take-or-pay contracts, Ch. 43, 19.2
        - make-up product and undertake, Ch. 43, 19.2.1
- mineral reserves and resources, Ch. 43, 2
    - disclosure of mineral reserves and resources, Ch. 43, 2.4
        - mining sector, Ch. 43, 2.4.2
        - oil and gas sector, Ch. 43, 2.4.1
        - value of reserves, Ch. 43, 2.4.3
    - international harmonisation of reserve reporting, Ch. 43, 2.1
    - mining resource and reserve reporting, Ch. 43, 2.3
        - CIRSCO International reporting template, Ch. 43, 2.3.1
    - petroleum reserve estimation and reporting, Ch. 43, 2.2
        - basic principles and definitions, Ch. 43, 2.2.1
        - classification and categorisation guidelines, Ch. 43, 2.2.2
- property, plant and equipment, Ch. 43, 15
    - care and maintenance, Ch. 43, 15.3
    - major maintenance and turnarounds/renewals and reconditioning costs, Ch. 43, 15.1
    - redeterminations, Ch. 43, 15.4.2
        - as capital reimbursements, Ch. 43, 15.4.2.A
        - decommissioning provisions, Ch. 43, 15.4.2.C
        - 'make-up' oil, Ch. 43, 15.4.2.B
    - stripping costs in the production phase of a surface mine (mining), Ch. 43, 15.5
        - determining when production phase commences, Ch. 43, 15.5.2
        - disclosures, Ch. 43, 15.5.6
        - initial recognition, Ch. 43, 15.5.4
        - recognition criteria-stripping activity asset, Ch. 43, 15.5.3
        - scope of IFRIC 20, Ch. 43, 15.5.1
        - subsequent measurement, Ch. 43, 15.5.5
    - unitisations, Ch. 43, 15.4
    - well workovers and recompletions (oil and gas), Ch. 43, 15.2
- revenue recognition, Ch. 43, 12
    - forward-selling contracts to finance development, Ch. 43, 12.6
    - inventory exchanges with the same counterparty, Ch. 43, 12.3
    - overlift and underlift (oil and gas), Ch. 43, 12.4
        - accounting for imbalances in revenue under IFRS 15, Ch. 43, 12.4.1
        - consideration of cost of goods sold where revenue is recognised in accordance with IFRS 15, Ch. 43, 12.4.2
        - facility imbalances, Ch. 43, 12.4.3
    - revenue in the development phase, Ch. 43, 12.1
        - incidental revenue, Ch. 43, 12.1.1
        - integral to development, Ch. 43, 12.1.2
    - sale of product with delayed shipment, Ch. 43, 12.2
    - trading activities, Ch. 43, 12.7
- risk-sharing arrangements, Ch. 43, 6
    - asset swaps, Ch. 43, 6.3

E&E assets, Ch. 43, 6.3.1
  Exchanges of E&E assets for other types of assets, Ch. 43, 6.3.3
  PP&E, intangible assets and investment property, Ch. 43, 6.3.2
carried interests, Ch. 43, 6.1
  arrangements in E&E phase, Ch. 43, 6.1.2
  financing-type carried interest arrangements in the development phase, Ch. 43, 6.1.3
  purchase/sale-type carried interest arrangements in the development phase, Ch. 43, 6.1.4
  types of carried interests, Ch. 43, 6.1.1
    farm-ins and farm-outs, Ch. 43, 6.2
    farm-in arrangements in E&E phase, Ch. 43, 6.2.1
    farm-in arrangements outside the E&E phase: accounting by the farmee, Ch. 43, 6.2.2
    farm-in arrangements outside the E&E phase: accounting by the farmor, Ch. 43, 6.2.3
  status of the statement of recommended practice, UK Oil Industry Accounting Committee, June 2001 (OIAC SORP), Ch. 43, 1.4
taxation, Ch. 43, 21
  excise duties, production taxes and severance taxes, Ch. 43, 21.1
    petroleum revenue tax (or resource rent tax), Ch. 43, 21.1.2
    production-based taxation, Ch. 43, 21.1.1
  grossing up of notional quantities withheld, Ch. 43, 21.2
  tolling arrangements, Ch. 43, 20
unit of account, Ch. 43, 4
upstream versus downstream activities, Ch. 43, 1.6

Fair presentation, Ch. 3, 4.1.1
  and compliance with IFRS, Ch. 3, 4.1.1.A
  override, Ch. 3, 4.1.1.B

Fair value. *See also* Fair value hedges; Fair value hierarchy; Fair value less costs of disposal (FVLCD);

Fair value measurement *under* **IFRS 13**. *See also* Fair value measurement and IFRS 13 below
  'clean' *vs.* 'dirty' values, Ch. 53, 7.4.10
  definition, Ch. 14, 3
  derivatives, discount rates for calculating, Ch. 53, 7.4.5
  designation of own use contracts at fair value through profit or loss, Ch. 53, 12.2
  financial assets and financial liabilities at, Ch. 50, 2.4
  financial assets designated at fair value through profit/loss, Ch. 54, 4.4.3
  financial liabilities designated at fair value through profit/loss, Ch. 54, 4.4.2
  first-time adoption, Ch. 5, 3.3
  future investment management fees in, Ch. 55, 8.2.1.B
  hedged items held at fair value through profit/loss, Ch. 53, 2.6.2
  hedging using instruments with non-zero fair value, Ch. 53, 7.4.3
  on initial recognition of financial instrument, measurement of, Ch. 49, 3.3.2
  of insurer's liabilities, Ch. 55, 9.1.1.B
  of intangible assets, determining, Ch. 9, 5.5.2.F
  in intra-group transactions, Ch. 8, 4.3.1
  investment property, fair value model, Ch. 19, 6
    deferred taxation for property held by a 'single asset' entity, Ch. 19, 6.10
    estimating fair value, Ch. 19, 6.1
      comparison with value in use, Ch. 19, 6.1.3
      'double counting,' Ch. 19, 6.1.4
      methods of estimation, Ch. 19, 6.1.1
      observable data, Ch. 19, 6.1.2
    fair value of investment property under construction, Ch. 19, 6.3
    fair value of properties held under a lease, valuation adjustments to the, Ch. 19, 6.7
    fixtures and fittings subsumed within fair value, Ch. 19, 6.5
    future capital expenditure and development value ('highest and best use'), Ch. 19, 6.8
    inability to determine fair value of completed investment property, Ch. 19, 6.2
    negative present value, Ch. 19, 6.9
    prepaid and accrued operating lease income, Ch. 19, 6.6
      accrued rental income and lease incentives, Ch. 19, 6.6.1
      prepaid rental income, Ch. 19, 6.6.2
    transaction costs incurred by the reporting entity on acquisition, Ch. 19, 6.4
  property, plant and equipment, revaluation model, Ch. 18, 6
    meaning of fair value, Ch. 18, 6.1
      cost approach, Ch. 18, 6.1.1.C
      highest and best use, Ch. 18, 6.1.1.A
      revaluing assets under IFRS 13, Ch. 18, 6.1.1
      valuation approaches, Ch. 18, 6.1.1.B
  and value in use (VIU), differences between, Ch. 20, 7.3

Fair value hedges, Ch. 53, 1.5, 5.1, 7.1; Ch. 54, 4.3.3
  adjustments to the hedged item, Ch. 53, 7.1.2
  discontinuing, Ch. 53, 8.3
  firm commitments, Ch. 53, 5.1.1
  foreign currency monetary items, Ch. 53, 5.1.2
  layer components for, Ch. 53, 2.3.2
  presentation, Ch. 53, 9.2

Fair value hierarchy, Ch. 14, 16
  categorisation within, Ch. 14, 16.2
    over-the-counter derivative instruments, Ch. 14, 16.2.4
    significance of inputs, assessing, Ch. 14, 16.2.1
    third-party pricing services/brokers, Ch. 14, 16.2.3
    transfers between levels within, Ch. 14, 16.2.2

Fair value less costs of disposal (FVLCD), Ch. 20, 6
  calculation of (extractive industries), Ch. 43, 11.5
  depreciated replacement cost/current replacement cost as, Ch. 20, 6.1.2
  estimating, Ch. 20, 6.1
  investments in subsidiaries, associates and joint ventures, Ch. 20, 12.4.1
  and unit of account, Ch. 20, 6.1.1

Fair value measurement, Ch. 14, 1–23. *See also* Fair value; Fair value hierarchy; IFRS 13; Offsetting positions; Valuation techniques
  agriculture, Ch. 42, 4
    establishing what to measure, Ch. 42, 4.2
    determining costs to sell, Ch. 42, 4.4
    disclosures, Ch. 42, 5.2
      additional disclosures if fair value cannot be measured reliably, Ch. 42, 5.3

Fair value measurement—*contd*
  agriculture—*contd*
    IAS 41-specific requirements, Ch. 42, 4.5
    interaction between IAS 41 and IFRS 13, Ch. 42, 4.1
    overview of IFRS 13 requirements, Ch. 42, 4.6
    problem of measuring fair value for part-grown or immature biological assets, Ch. 42, 4.7
    when to measure fair value, Ch. 42, 4.3
  asset/liability, Ch. 14, 5
    characteristics
      condition and location, Ch. 14, 5.2.1
      restrictions on assets/liabilities, Ch. 14, 5.2.2
    unit of account
      asset's (or liability's) components, Ch. 14, 5.1.4
      and portfolio exception, Ch. 14, 5.1.2
      and PxQ, Ch. 7, 3.3.2.F; Ch. 14, 5.1.1
      vs. valuation premise, Ch. 14, 5.1.3
  of associates, partial use of, Ch. 11, 5.4
  convergence with US GAAP, Ch. 14, 22
    disclosures, Ch. 14, 22.2.4
    fair value of liabilities with demand feature, Ch. 14, 22.2.2
    IFRS 13, development of, Ch. 14, 22.1
    practical expedient for alternative investments, Ch. 14, 22.2.1
    recognition of day-one gains and losses, Ch. 14, 22.2.3
  day 1 profits, financial instruments, Ch. 54, 4.5.2
  definitions, Ch. 14, 3
  disclosures, Ch. 14, 20
    accounting policy, Ch. 14, 20.2
    objectives
      format of, Ch. 14, 20.1.1
      level of disaggregation, Ch. 14, 20.1.2
      'recurring' *vs.* 'non-recurring, Ch. 14, 20.1.3
    for recognised fair value measurements, Ch. 14, 20.3
      fair value hierarchy categorisation, Ch. 14, 20.3.3
      highest and best use, Ch. 14, 20.3.9
      level 3 reconciliation, Ch. 14, 20.3.6
      non-recurring fair value measurements, Ch. 14, 20.3.2
      recurring fair value measurements, Ch. 14, 20.3.1
      sensitivity of level 3 measurements to changes in significant unobservable inputs, Ch. 14, 20.3.8
      transfers between hierarchy levels for recurring fair value measurements, Ch. 14, 20.3.4
      of valuation processes for level 3 measurements, Ch. 14, 20.3.7
      valuation techniques and inputs, Ch. 14, 20.3.5
    regarding liabilities issued with an inseparable third-party credit enhancement, Ch. 14, 20.5
    for unrecognised fair value measurements, Ch. 14, 20.4
  effective date and transition, Ch. 14, 22
  fair value framework, Ch. 14, 4
    definition, Ch. 14, 4.1
    measurement, Ch. 14, 4.2
  financial assets and liabilities with offsetting positions, Ch. 14, 12
    criteria for using the portfolio approach for offsetting positions, Ch. 14, 12.1
      accounting policy considerations, Ch. 14, 12.1.1
      level 1 instruments in, Ch. 14, 12.1.4
      minimum level of offset, to use portfolio approach, Ch. 14, 12.1.3
      presentation considerations, Ch. 14, 12.1.2
    measuring fair value for offsetting positions, Ch. 14, 12.2
      exposure to market risks, Ch. 14, 12.2.1
      exposure to the credit risk of a particular counterparty, Ch. 14, 12.2.2
  hierarchy, Ch. 14, 16
    categorisation within, Ch. 14, 16.2
      over-the-counter derivative instruments, Ch. 14, 16.2.4
      significance of inputs, assessing, Ch. 14, 16.2.1
      third-party pricing services/brokers, Ch. 14, 16.2.3
      transfers between levels within, Ch. 14, 16.2.2
  IFRS 13, objective of, Ch. 14, 1.3
  IFRS 13, overview, Ch. 14, 1.2
  at initial recognition, Ch. 14, 13
    day 1 gains and losses, Ch. 14, 13.2
    exit price *vs.* entry price, Ch. 14, 13.1
    related party transactions, Ch. 14, 13.3
  inputs to valuation techniques, Ch. 14, 15
    broker quotes and pricing services, Ch. 14, 15.5
    general principles, Ch. 14, 15.1
    premiums and discounts, Ch. 14, 15.2
      blockage factors (or block discounts), Ch. 14, 15.2.1
    pricing within the bid-ask spread, Ch. 14, 15.3
      bid-ask spread, Ch. 14, 15.3.2
      mid-market pricing, Ch. 14, 15.3.1
    risk premiums, Ch. 14, 15.4
  of intangible assets, determining, Ch. 9, 5.5.2.F
  level 1 inputs, Ch. 14, 17
    alternative pricing methods, Ch. 14, 17.2
    quoted prices in active markets Ch. 14, 17.3
    unit of account, Ch. 14, 17.4
    use of, Ch. 14, 17.1
  level 2 inputs, Ch. 14, 18
    examples of, Ch. 14, 18.2
    making adjustments to, Ch. 14, 18.4
    market corroborated inputs, Ch. 14, 18.3
    recently observed prices in an inactive market, Ch. 14, 18.5
  level 3 inputs, Ch. 14, 19
    examples of, Ch. 14, 19.2
    use of, Ch. 14, 19.1
  liabilities and an entity's own equity, application to, Ch. 14, 11
    financial liability with demand feature, Ch. 14, 11.5
    general principles
      fair value of an entity's own equity, Ch. 14, 11.1.2
      fair value of liability, Ch. 14, 11.1.1
      settlement value *vs.* transfer value, Ch. 14, 11.1.3
    non-performance risk, Ch. 14, 11.1
      counterparty credit risk and its own credit risk, Ch. 14, 11.3.2
      derivative liabilities, Ch. 14, 11.3.4
      entity incorporate credit risk into the valuation of its derivative contracts, Ch. 14, 11.3.3
      with third-party credit enhancements, Ch. 14, 11.3.1
    not held by other parties as assets, Ch. 14, 11.2.2
    restrictions preventing the transfer of, Ch. 14, 11.4
    that are held by other parties as assets, Ch. 14, 11.2.1
  market participants, Ch. 14, 7
    assumptions, Ch. 14, 7.2
    characteristics, Ch. 14, 7.1

non-financial assets, application to, Ch. 14, 10
   highest and best use, Ch. 14, 10.1
      vs. current use, Ch. 14, 10.1.2
      vs. intended use, Ch. 14, 10.1.3
      legally permissible, Ch. 14, 10.1.1
   valuation premise, Ch. 14, 10.2
      in combination with other assets and/or liabilities, Ch. 14, 10.2.2
      liabilities association, Ch. 14, 10.2.3
      stand-alone basis, Ch. 14, 10.2.1
      unit of account *vs.*, Ch. 14, 10.2.4
for part-grown or immature biological assets, Ch. 42, 4.7
present value techniques, Ch. 14, 21
   components of, Ch. 14, 21.2
      risk and uncertainty in, Ch. 14, 21.2.2
      time value of money, Ch. 14, 21.2.1
   discount rate adjustment technique, Ch. 14, 21.3
   expected present value technique, Ch. 14, 21.4
   general principles for use of, Ch. 14, 21.1
price, Ch. 14, 9
   transaction costs, Ch. 14, 9.1
   transportation costs, Ch. 14, 9.2
principal (or most advantageous) market, Ch. 14, 6
scope, Ch. 14, 2
   exclusions, Ch. 14, 2.2
      exemptions from the disclosure requirements of IFRS 13, Ch. 14, 2.2.4
      fair value, measurements similar to, Ch. 14, 2.2.3
      lease transactions, Ch. 14, 2.2.2
      share-based payments, Ch. 14, 2.2.1
   fair value measurement exceptions, Ch. 14, 2.4
   IFRS 13, items in scope of, Ch. 14, 2.1
      fair value disclosures, Ch. 14, 2.1.1
      fair value measurements, Ch. 14, 2.1.2
      short-term receivables and payables, Ch. 14, 2.1.3
   practical expedient for impaired financial assets carried at amortised cost, Ch. 14, 2.4.2
   present value techniques, Ch. 14, 2.3
transaction, Ch. 14, 8
   estimation, Ch. 14, 8.3
   identification, Ch. 14, 8.2
   volume and level of activity for an asset/liability, Ch. 14, 8.1
unit of account, Ch. 14, 5.1
   asset's (or liability's) components, Ch. 14, 5.1.4
   level 1 assets and liabilities, Ch. 14, 17.4
   and portfolio exception, Ch. 14, 5.1.2
   and PxQ, Ch. 7, 3.3.2.F; Ch. 14, 5.1.1
   vs. valuation premise, Ch. 14, 5.1.3
valuation techniques, Ch. 14, 14
   cost approach, Ch. 14, 14.3
   income approach, Ch. 14, 14.4
   market approach, Ch. 14, 14.2
   selecting appropriate, Ch. 14, 14.1
      making changes to valuation techniques, Ch. 14, 14.1.4
      single *vs.* multiple valuation techniques, Ch. 14, 14.1.1
      using multiple valuation techniques to measure fair value, Ch. 14, 14.1.2
      valuation adjustments, Ch. 14, 14.1.3

Fair value model, investment property, Ch. 19, 6. *See also* Fair value; Investment property
   completed investment property, inability to determine fair value, Ch. 19, 6.2
   deferred taxation for property held by a 'single asset' entity, Ch. 19, 6.10
   estimating fair value, Ch. 19, 6.1
   fixtures and fittings subsumed, Ch. 19, 6.5
   future capital expenditure and development value ('highest and best use'), Ch. 19, 6.8
   negative present value, Ch. 19, 6.9
   prepaid and accrued operating lease income, Ch. 19, 6.6
   properties held under a lease, valuation adjustment to the, Ch. 19, 6.7
   property under construction, Ch. 19, 6.3
   transaction costs incurred on acquisition, Ch. 19, 6.4

Fair value through other comprehensive income (FVTOCI), Ch. 48, 8; Ch. 54, 7.2
   debt instruments, subsequent measurement accumulated impairment amount for, Ch. 51, 14.3
   financial assets measured at, Ch. 51, 9
   hedges of exposures classified as, Ch. 53, 2.6.3
   non-derivative equity investments designation at, Ch. 48, 8

Faithful representation, Ch. 2, 5.1.2

Farm-ins and farm outs, extractive industries, Ch. 43, 6.2
   farm-in arrangements in the E&E phase, Ch. 43, 6.2.1
   farm-in arrangements outside the E&E phase: accounting by the farmee, Ch. 43, 6.2.2
      farming into an asset, Ch. 43, 6.2.2.A
      farming into a business which is a joint operation or results in the formation of a joint operation, Ch. 43, 6.2.2.B
   farm-in arrangements outside the E&E phase: accounting by the farmor, Ch. 43, 6.2.3

Finance costs as a borrowing cost, Ch. 21, 5.5
   derecognition of borrowings, gains and losses on, Ch. 21, 5.5.2
   derivative financial instruments, Ch. 21, 5.5.1
   derivative financial instruments, gains or losses on termination of, Ch. 21, 5.5.3
   dividends payable on shares classified as financial liabilities, Ch. 21, 5.5.4
   unwinding discounts, Ch. 21, 4.2

Finance leases, accounting for, Ch. 23, 6.2
   accounting by lessors, Ch. 23, 6.2–6.2.4
      initial measurement, Ch. 23, 6.2.1
      presentation in the statement of cash flows, Ch. 40, 5.5.5
      remeasurement, Ch. 23, 6.2.4
      subsequent measurement, Ch. 23, 6.2.3
         unguaranteed residual values, Ch. 23, 6.2.3.A
   manufacturer/dealer lessors, Ch. 23, 6.2.2

Financial Accounting Standards Board (FASB), Ch. 1, 2.9, 3.2; Ch. 14, 22.2

Financial assets
   accounting for loss of control, interest retained in the former subsidiary is a financial asset, Ch. 7, 3.3.1
   call options over non-controlling interest, Ch. 7, 6.1, 6.3, 6.4, 6.5

Financial assets—contd
  classification and measurement on first-time adoption, Ch. 5, 4.9
  classifying, Ch. 48, 2
    debt instruments, Ch. 48, 2.1
    equity instruments and derivatives, Ch. 48, 2.2
  contractual obligation to deliver, Ch. 47, 4.2
  definition, Ch. 45, 2.1; Ch. 47, 3; Ch. 52, 2.1
  derecognition, Ch. 52, 3
  designated as measured at fair value through profit/loss, Ch. 54, 4.4.3
  at fair value through profit/loss, Ch. 50, 2.4
  held for trading, Ch. 48, 4
  and liabilities with offsetting positions, Ch. 14, 12
    criteria for using the portfolio approach for offsetting positions, Ch. 14, 12.1
    measuring fair value for offsetting positions, Ch. 14, 12.2
  measured at amortised cost, Ch. 51, 14.1
  measured at fair value through other comprehensive income, Ch. 51, 14.3
  measured at fair value through profit/loss, Ch. 51, 9.1
  modified financial assets, Ch. 51, 8.2
  offsetting, Ch. 54, 7.4.1
    cash pooling arrangements, Ch. 54, 7.4.1.E
    disclosure, Ch. 54, 7.4.2
    enforceable legal right of set-off, Ch. 54, 7.4.1.A
    intention to settle net, Ch. 54, 7.4.1.C
    master netting agreements, Ch. 54, 7.4.1.B
    offsetting collateral amounts, Ch. 54, 7.4.1.F
    situations where offset is not normally appropriate, Ch. 54, 7.4.1.D
    unit of account, Ch. 54, 7.4.1.G
  reclassifications of, Ch. 48, 9; Ch. 50, 2.7
  redesignation of, Ch. 55, 8.4
  that are either past due or impaired, Ch. 54, 5.3.3
  transfers of, Ch. 54, 6
    assets that are derecognised in their entirety, Ch. 54, 6.3
      disclosure requirements, Ch. 54, 6.3.2
      meaning of continuing involvement, Ch. 54, 6.3.1
    assets that are not derecognised in their entirety, Ch. 54, 6.2
    meaning of 'transfer,' Ch. 54, 6.1
Financial capital maintenance (framework), Ch. 2, 11.1
Financial guarantee(s), Ch. 51, 5.8.1
  to provide a loan at a below-market interest rate, Ch. 50, 2.8
Financial guarantee contracts, Ch. 45, 3.4; Ch. 49, 3.3.3; Ch. 55, 2.2.3.D
  between entities under common control, Ch. 45, 3.4.4
  definition, Ch. 45, 3.4.1; Ch. 51, 11.1
    debt instrument, Ch. 45, 3.4.1.B
    form and existence of contract, Ch. 45, 3.4.1.C
    reimbursement for loss incurred, Ch. 45, 3.4.1.A
  holders of, Ch. 45, 3.4.3
  IFRS 9 impairment requirements, Ch. 51, 1.2
  issuers of, Ch. 45, 3.4.2
  maturity analysis, Ch. 54, 5.4.2.F
Financial instrument(s). *See also* IAS 32, IAS 39, IFRS 7; IFRS 9
  contracts to buy or sell commodities and other non-financial items, Ch. 45, 4
  contracts that may be settled net, Ch. 45, 4.1
  definitions, Ch. 45, 2.1
    applying, Ch. 45, 2.2
    contingent rights and obligations, Ch. 45, 2.2.3
    derivative financial instruments, Ch. 45, 2.2.8
    dividends payable, Ch. 45, 2.2.9
    equity instruments, Ch. 45, 2.1; Ch. 45, 2.2.7
    financial asset, Ch. 45, 2.1
    financial instrument, Ch. 45, 2.1
    financial liability, Ch. 45, 2.1
    leases, Ch. 45, 2.2.4
    need for a contract, Ch. 45, 2.2.1
    non-financial assets and liabilities and contracts thereon, Ch. 45, 2.2.5
    payments for goods and services, Ch. 45, 2.2.6
    simple financial instruments, Ch. 45, 2.2.2
  discretionary participation feature in, Ch. 55, 6.2
  normal sales and purchases (or own use contracts), Ch. 45, 4.2
    commodity broker-traders and similar entities, Ch. 45, 4.2.2
    contracts containing volume flexibility, Ch. 45, 4.2.5
    electricity and similar 'end-user' contracts, Ch. 45, 4.2.4
    fair value option in IFRS 9, Ch. 45, 4.2.6
    net settlement of similar contracts, Ch. 45, 4.2.1
    written options that can be settled net, Ch. 45, 4.2.3
  scope, Ch. 45, 3
    business combinations, Ch. 45, 3.7
    contingent pricing of property, plant and equipment and intangible assets, Ch. 45, 3.8
    disposal groups classified as held for sale and discontinued operations, Ch. 45, 3.11
    employee benefit plans and share-based payment, Ch. 45, 3.9
    equity instruments, Ch. 45, 3.6
    financial guarantee contracts, Ch. 45, 3.4
    indemnification assets, Ch. 45, 3.12
    insurance and similar contracts, Ch. 45, 3.3
      contracts with discretionary participation features, Ch. 45, 3.3.2
      separating financial instrument components including embedded derivatives from insurance contracts, Ch. 45, 3.3.3
      weather derivatives, Ch. 45, 3.3.1
    leases, Ch. 45, 3.2
    loan commitments, Ch. 45, 3.5
    reimbursement rights in respect of provisions, Ch. 45, 3.10
    rights and obligations within the scope of IFRS 15, Ch. 45, 3.13
    subsidiaries, associates, joint ventures and similar investments, Ch. 45, 3.1
Financial instrument hosts, Ch. 49, 3.5
Financial instruments, classification, Ch. 48, 1–9
  'business model' assessment, Ch. 48, 5
    applying in practice, Ch. 48, 5.6
    consolidated and subsidiary accounts, Ch. 48, 5.5
    hold to collect contractual cash flows, Ch. 48, 5.2
    hold to collect contractual cash flows and selling financial assets, Ch. 48, 5.3
    impact of sales on the assessment, Ch. 48, 5.2.1
    level at which the business model assessment is applied, Ch. 48, 5.1

transferred financial assets that are not derecognised, Ch. 48, 5.2.2
contractual cash flows, Ch. 48, 6
    auction rate securities, Ch. 48, 6.4.4
    bonds with a capped or floored interest rate, Ch. 48, 6.3.3
    contractual features that change the timing or amount, Ch. 48, 6.4.4
    contractually linked instruments, Ch. 48, 6.6
    conventional subordination features, Ch. 48, 6.3.1
    convertible debt, Ch. 48, 6.4.5
    de minimis features, Ch. 48, 6.4.1.A
    debt covenants, Ch. 48, 6.4.4
    dual currency instruments, Ch. 48, 6.4.5
    five-year constant maturity bond, Ch. 48, 6.4.2
    fixed rate bond prepayable by the issuer at fair value, Ch. 48, 6.4.5
    full recourse loans secured by collateral, Ch. 48, 6.3.2
    interest rate period, Ch. 48, 6.4.2
    inverse floater, Ch. 48, 6.4.5
    investment in open-ended money market or debt funds, Ch. 48, 6.4.5
    lender has discretion to change the interest rate, Ch. 48, 6.3.4
    meaning of 'interest', Ch. 48, 6.2
    meaning of 'principal,' Ch. 48, 6.1
    modified time value of money component, Ch. 48, 6.4.2
    multiple of a benchmark interest rate, Ch. 48, 6.4.5
    non-genuine features, Ch. 48, 6.4.1.B
    non-recourse loans, Ch. 48, 6.5
    perpetual instruments with potentially deferrable coupons, Ch. 48, 6.4.5
    prepayment, assets originated at a premium or discount, Ch. 48, 6.4.4.B
    prepayment options, Ch. 48, 6.4.4
    prepayment, negative compensation, Ch. 48, 6.4.4.A
    regulated interest rates, Ch. 48, 6.4.3
    term extension options, Ch. 48, 6.4.4
    unleveraged inflation-linked bonds, Ch. 48, 6.3.5
    variable interest rate, Ch. 48, 6.4.4
designation at fair value through profit or loss, Ch. 48, 7
financial assets and liabilities held for trading, Ch. 48, 4
financial assets classification, Ch. 48, 2
    debt instruments, Ch. 48, 2.1
    equity instruments and derivatives, Ch. 48, 2.2
financial liabilities classification, Ch. 48, 3
reclassification of financial assets, Ch. 48, 9

Financial instruments, derecognition, Ch. 52, 1–8. *See also* Derecognition

Financial instruments, derivatives and embedded derivatives, Ch. 46, 1–8
call and put options over noncontrolling interests, Ch. 7, 6. *See also* Non-controlling interests
changes in value in response to changes in underlying, Ch. 46, 2.1
    non-financial variables specific to one party to the contract, Ch. 46, 2.1.3
    notional amounts, Ch. 46, 2.1.1
    underlying variables, Ch. 46, 2.1.2
common derivatives, Ch. 46, 3.1
embedded derivatives, Ch. 46, 4
    contracts for the sale of goods or services, Ch. 46, 5.2
        floors and caps, Ch. 46, 5.2.4
        foreign currency derivatives, Ch. 46, 5.2.1
        fund performance fees, Ch. 46, 5.2.5
        inflation-linked features, Ch. 46, 5.2.3
        inputs, ingredients, substitutes and other proxy pricing mechanisms, Ch. 46, 5.2.2
    financial instrument hosts, Ch. 46, 5.1
        commodity-and equity-linked interest and principal payments, Ch. 46, 5.1.7
        convertible and exchangeable debt instruments, Ch. 46, 5.1.9
        credit-linked notes, Ch. 46, 5.1.8
        foreign currency monetary items, Ch. 46, 5.1.1
        inflation-linked debt instruments, Ch. 46, 5.1.6
        interest rate floors and caps, Ch. 46, 5.1.5
        interest rate indices, Ch. 46, 5.1.2
        puttable instruments, Ch. 46, 5.1.10
        term extension and similar call, put and prepayment options in debt instruments, Ch. 46, 5.1.14
    identifying the terms of embedded derivatives and host contracts, Ch. 46, 6
        embedded non-option derivatives, Ch. 46, 6.1
        embedded option-based derivative, Ch. 46, 6.2
        multiple embedded derivatives, Ch. 46, 6.3
    insurance contracts, Ch. 46, 5.4
    leases, Ch. 46, 5.3
    reassessment, Ch. 46, 7
        acquisition of contracts, Ch. 46, 7.1
        business combinations, Ch. 46, 7.2
        remeasurement issues arising from reassessment, Ch. 46, 7.3
future settlement, Ch. 46, 2.3
initial net investment, Ch. 46, 2.2
in-substance derivatives, Ch. 46, 3.2
linked and separate transactions and 'synthetic' instruments, Ch. 46, 8
prepaid forward purchase of shares, Ch. 46, 2.2
prepaid interest rate swap, Ch. 46, 2.2
regular way contracts, Ch. 46, 3.3

Financial Instruments: disclosures (IFRS 7), Ch. 54, 1–9

Financial instruments, extractive industries, Ch. 43, 13
embedded derivatives, Ch. 43, 13.2
    development of gas markets, Ch. 43, 13.2.4
    foreign currency embedded derivatives, Ch. 43, 13.2.1
    long-term supply contracts, Ch. 43, 13.2.3
    provisionally priced sales contracts, Ch. 43, 13.2.2
hedging sales of metal concentrate (mining), Ch. 43, 13.4
normal purchase and sales exemption, Ch. 43, 13.1
volume flexibility in supply contracts, Ch. 43, 13.3

Financial instruments: financial liabilities and equity, Ch. 47, 1–12
background, Ch. 47, 1.1
classification of instruments, Ch. 47, 4
    consolidated financial statements, Ch. 47, 4.8.1
    contingent settlement provisions, Ch. 47, 4.3
    contractual obligation to deliver cash or other financial assets, Ch. 47, 4.2
    definition of equity instrument, Ch. 47, 4.1
    examples of equity instruments, Ch. 47, 4.4

Financial instruments: financial liabilities and equity—*contd*
  classification of instruments—*contd*
    examples of equity instruments—*contd*
      contracts to issue equity instruments, Ch. 47, 4.4.2
      issued instruments, Ch. 47, 4.4.1
      instruments redeemable
        with a 'dividend blocker,' Ch. 47, 4.5.3.A
        with a 'dividend pusher,' Ch. 47, 4.5.3.B
        mandatorily or at the holder's option, Ch. 47, 4.5.1
        only at the issuer's option or not redeemable, Ch. 47, 4.5.2
      perpetual debt, Ch. 47, 4.7
      preference shares and similar instruments, Ch. 47, 4.5
      puttable instruments and instruments repayable only on liquidation, Ch. 47, 4.6.5
    reclassification of instruments
      change of circumstances, Ch. 47, 4.9.2
      change of terms, Ch. 47, 4.9.1
    single entity financial statements, Ch. 47, 4.8.2
  compound financial instruments, Ch. 47, 6
    background, Ch. 47, 6.1
    common forms of convertible bonds, Ch. 47, 6.6
      bond convertible into fixed percentage of equity, Ch. 47, 6.6.6
      contingent convertible bond, Ch. 47, 6.6.2
      convertible bonds with down round or ratchet features, Ch. 47, 6.6.7
      convertibles with cash settlement at the option of the issuer, Ch. 47, 6.6.5
      foreign currency convertible bond, Ch. 47, 6.6.4
      functional currency bond convertible into a fixed number of shares, Ch. 47, 6.6.1
      mandatorily convertible bond, Ch. 47, 6.6.3
    components, Ch. 47, 6.4
      compound instruments with embedded derivatives, Ch. 47, 6.4.2
      determining the components of a compound instrument, Ch. 47, 6.4.1
    conversion
      at maturity, Ch. 47, 6.3.1
      before maturity, Ch. 47, 6.3.2
    early redemption/repurchase, Ch. 47, 6.3.3
      exercising an embedded call option, Ch. 47, 6.3.3.B
      through negotiation with bondholders, Ch. 47, 6.3.3.A
    initial recognition–'split accounting,' Ch. 47, 6.2
      accounting for the equity component, Ch. 47, 6.2.1
      temporary differences arising from split accounting, Ch. 47, 6.2.2
    modification, Ch. 47, 6.3.4
    treatment by holder and issuer contrasted, Ch. 47, 6.1.1
  contracts accounted for as equity instruments, Ch. 47, 5.1
  contracts accounted for as financial assets or financial liabilities, Ch. 47, 5.2
  definitions, Ch. 47, 3
  derivatives over own equity instruments, Ch. 47, 11
    call options, Ch. 47, 11.2
      purchased call option, Ch. 47, 11.2.1
      written call option, Ch. 47, 11.2.2
    forward contracts, Ch. 47, 11.1
      'back-to-back' forward contracts, Ch. 47, 11.1.3
      forward purchase, Ch. 47, 11.1.1
      forward sale, Ch. 47, 11.1.2
    put options
      purchased put option, Ch. 47, 11.3.1
      written put option, Ch. 47, 11.3.2
  future developments, Ch. 47, 12

Financial Instruments with Characteristics of Equity Research Project (FICE), Ch. 7, 7.3, 7.4, 7.5; Ch. 47, 1, 4.6.6, 5.1.2, 5.3.2A, 6.6.3B, 12
  gross-settled contracts for the sale or issue of the entity's own equity instruments, Ch. 47, 5.4
  'hedging' of instruments classified as equity, Ch. 47, 10
  interest, dividends, gains and losses, Ch. 47, 8
    tax effects, Ch. 47, 8.2
    transaction costs, Ch. 47, 8.1
  liabilities arising from gross-settled contracts for the purchase of the entity's own equity instruments, Ch. 47, 5.3
    contracts to acquire non-controlling interests, Ch. 47, 5.3.2
    contracts to purchase own equity during 'closed' or 'prohibited' periods, Ch. 47, 5.3.1
  objective, Ch. 47, 2.1
  scope, Ch. 47, 2.2
  settlement of financial liability with equity instrument, Ch. 47, 7
    debt for equity swaps with shareholders, Ch. 47, 7.3
    requirements of IFRIC 19, Ch. 47, 7.2
    scope and effective date of IFRIC 19, Ch. 47, 7.1
  treasury shares, Ch. 47, 9
    IFRS 17 Treasury share election, Ch. 47, 9.2
    transactions in own shares not at fair value, Ch. 47, 9.1

Financial instruments: hedge accounting, Ch. 53, 1–14
  accounting for the costs of hedging, Ch. 53, 7.5
    foreign currency basis spreads in financial instruments, Ch. 53, 7.5.3
    forward element of forward contracts, Ch. 53, 7.5.2
    time value of options, Ch. 53, 7.5.1
  aggregated exposures, Ch. 53, 2.7
    accounting for, Ch. 53, 2.7.3
  alternatives to hedge accounting, Ch. 53, 12
    credit risk exposures, Ch. 53, 12.1
    own use contracts, Ch. 53, 12.2
  background, Ch. 53, 1.1
  development of, Ch. 53, 1.3
  discontinuation, Ch. 53, 8.3, 14.5
    of cash flow hedges, Ch. 53, 8.3.2
    of fair value hedges, Ch. 53, 8.3.1
    hedging counterparty within the same consolidated group, Ch. 53, 8.3.7
    hedged net investment, disposal of, Ch. 53, 8.3.8
    novation to central clearing parties, Ch. 53, 8.3.5
    settle to market derivatives, Ch. 53, 8.3.6
  economic relationship, Ch. 53, 6.4.1
  effective hedges, accounting for, Ch. 53, 7
    cash flow hedges, Ch. 53, 7.2
      acquisition or disposal of subsidiaries, Ch. 53, 7.2.4
      all-in-one hedges, Ch. 53, 5.2.1
      discontinuing, Ch. 53, 8.3.2
      firm commitments, hedges of, Ch. 53, 5.2.2
      foreign currency monetary items, Ch. 53, 5.2.3

hypothetical derivatives, Ch. 53, 7.4.4
measuring ineffectiveness of, Ch. 53, 7.4.6
of a net position, Ch. 53, 2.5.3
novation of, due to central clearing regulations, Ch. 53, 8.3.5
ongoing accounting, Ch. 53, 7.2.1
presentation, Ch. 53, 10.1
reclassification of gains and losses, Ch. 53, 7.2.2
documented rollover hedging strategy, Ch. 53, 7.7
equity instrument designated at fair value through OCI, Ch. 53, 7.8
fair value hedges, Ch. 53, 1.5, 5.1, 7.1
adjustments to the hedged item, Ch. 53,7.1.2
discontinuing, Ch. 53, 8.3.1
firm commitments, Ch. 53, 5.1.1
foreign currency monetary items, Ch. 53, 5.1.2
layer components for, Ch. 53, 2.3.2
ongoing accounting, Ch. 53, 7.1.1
presentation, Ch. 53, 10.2
hedges of a firm commitment to acquire a business, Ch. 53, 7.6
hedges of a net investment in a foreign operation, accounting for, Ch. 7, 2.3; Ch. 53, 1.5, 5.3, 7.3, 8.3.7
effective date and transition, Ch. 53, 13
limited retrospective application, Ch. 53, 13.3
prospective application in general, Ch. 53, 13.2
effectiveness assessment, Ch. 53, 8.1, 6.4
credit risk dominance, Ch. 53, 6.4.2
economic relationship, Ch. 53, 6.4.1
hedge ratio, Ch. 53, 6.4.3
effectiveness measurement, Ch. 53, 7.4
calculation of, Ch. 53, 7.4.6
'clean' vs. 'dirty' values, Ch. 53, 7.4.10
comparison of spot rate and forward rate methods, Ch. 53, 7.4.7
discount rates for calculating the change in value of the hedged item, Ch. 53, 7.4.5
effectiveness of options, Ch. 53, 7.4.11
foreign currency basis spreads, Ch. 53, 7.4.8
hedged items with embedded optionality, Ch. 53, 7.4.12
hedging instrument's impact on credit quality, Ch. 53, 7.4.9
hedging using instruments with a non-zero fair value, Ch. 53, 7.4.3
hypothetical derivatives, Ch. 53, 7.4.4
time value of money, Ch. 53, 7.4.2
hedged items, Ch. 53, 2
core deposits, Ch. 53, 2.6.7
held at fair value through profit or loss, Ch. 53, 2.6.2
held at fair value through OCI, Ch. 53, 2.6.3
firm commitment to acquire a business, Ch. 53, 7.6
forecast acquisition/issuance of foreign currency monetary items, Ch. 53, 2.6.5
general requirements, Ch. 53, 2.1
groups of items, Ch. 53, 2.5
cash flow hedge of a net position, Ch. 53, 2.5.3
general requirements, Ch. 53, 2.5.1
hedging a component of a group, Ch. 53, 2.5.2
nil net positions, Ch. 53, 2.5.4
highly probable, Ch. 53, 2.6.1
internal, Ch. 53, 4.3

nominal components. Ch. 53, 2.3
general requirement, Ch. 53, 2.3.1
layer component for fair value hedge, Ch. 53, 2.3.2
own equity instruments, Ch. 53, 2.6.6
risk components, Ch. 53, 2.2
contractually specified, Ch. 53, 2.2.2
foreign currency as, Ch. 53, 2.2.5
general requirements, Ch. 53, 2.2.1
inflation as, Ch. 53, 2.2.6
interest rate, Ch. 53, 2.2.7
non-contractually specified, Ch. 53, 2.2.3
partial term hedging, Ch. 53, 2.2.4
sub-LIBOR issue, Ch. 53, 2.4
negative interest rates, Ch. 53, 2.4.2
hedge ratio, Ch. 53, 6.4.3
hedging instruments, Ch. 53, 3
combinations of instruments, Ch. 53, 3.5
derivatives, Ch. 53, 3.2
basis swaps, Ch. 53, 3.2.5
credit break clauses, Ch. 53, 3.2.4
principal resetting cross currency swaps, Ch. 53, 3.2.4.A
embedded derivatives, Ch. 53, 3.2.3
net written options, Ch. 53, 3.2.2
offsetting external derivatives, Ch. 53, 3.2.1
embedded derivatives, Ch. 53, 3.2.3
general requirements, Ch. 53, 3.1
hedging different risks with one instrument, Ch. 53, 3.6.2
non-derivative financial instruments, Ch. 53, 3.3
of foreign currency risk, Ch. 53, 3.3.1
non-derivative liabilities, Ch. 53, 3.3
own equity instruments, Ch. 53, 3.4
portions and proportions of, Ch. 53, 3.6
different risks with one instrument, Ch. 53, 3.6.2
foreign currency basis spread, Ch. 53, 3.6.5
interest elements of forwards, Ch. 53, 3.6.5
portion of a time period, Ch. 53, 3.6.6
proportions of instruments, Ch. 53, 3.6.1
restructuring of derivatives, Ch. 53, 3.6.3
time value of options, Ch. 53, 3.6.4
hedging relationships, types of, Ch. 53, 5
cash flow hedges, Ch. 53, 5.2
all-in-one hedges, Ch. 53, 5.2.1
firm commitments hedges, Ch. 53, 5.2.2
foreign currency monetary items, Ch. 53, 5.2.3
fair value hedges, Ch. 53, 5.1
firm commitments, hedges of, Ch. 53, 5.1.1
foreign currency monetary items, hedges of, Ch. 53, 5.1.2
hedges of net investments in foreign operations, Ch. 53, 5.3
amount of the hedged item for which a hedging relationship may be designated, Ch. 53, 5.3.2
nature of the hedged risk, Ch. 53, 5.3.1
where the hedging instrument can be held, Ch. 53, 5.3.3
ineffectiveness, measuring, Ch. 53, 7.4
interbank Offered Rate Reform (IBOR), Ch. 53, 9
internal hedges and other group accounting issues, Ch. 53, 4
central clearing parties, Ch. 53, 4.1.1
external hedging instruments, offsetting, Ch. 53, 4.2

Financial instruments: hedge accounting—*contd*
   internal hedges and other group accounting issues—*contd*
      hedged item and hedging instrument held by different group entities, Ch. 53, 4.4
      internal hedged items, Ch. 53, 4.3
      internal hedging instruments, Ch. 53, 4.1
      offsetting internal hedges instruments, Ch. 53, 4.2
   macro hedging, Ch. 53, 11
      accounting for dynamic risk management, Ch. 53, 11.1
      macro hedging strategies under IFRS 9, Ch. 53, 11.2
   main differences between IFRS 9 and IAS 39 hedge accounting requirements, Ch. 53, 14
      discontinuation, Ch. 53, 14.5
      effectiveness criteria, Ch. 53, 14.4
      eligible hedged items, Ch. 53, 14.2
      eligible hedging instruments, Ch. 53, 14.3
      hedge accounting mechanisms, Ch. 53, 14.6
      objective of hedge accounting, Ch. 53, 14.1
   portfolio/macro hedging, Ch. 53, 11
   objective of, Ch. 53, 1.4
   overview, Ch. 53, 1.5
   own use contracts, Ch. 53, 12.2
   presentation, Ch. 53, 10
      cash flow hedges, Ch. 53, 10.1
      cost of hedging, Ch. 53, 10.4
      fair value hedges, Ch. 53, 10.2
      hedges of groups of items, Ch. 53, 10.3
   proxy hedges, Ch. 53, 6.2.1
   qualifying criteria, Ch. 53, 6
      credit risk dominance, Ch. 53, 6.4.2
         on the hedged item, Ch. 53, 6.4.2.B
         on the hedging instrument, Ch. 53, 6.4.2.A
      designating 'proxy hedges', Ch. 53, 6.2.1
      documentation and designation, Ch. 53, 6.3
         business combinations, Ch. 53, 6.3.1
         dynamic hedging strategies, Ch. 53, 6.3.2
         forecast transactions, Ch. 53, 6.3.3
      economic relationship, Ch. 53, 6.4.1
      general requirements, Ch. 53, 6.1
      hedge effectiveness requirements, Ch. 53, 6.4
         credit risk dominance, Ch. 53, 6.4.2
         economic relationship, Ch. 53, 6.4.1
         hedge ratio, Ch. 53, 6.4.3
      proxy hedging, Ch. 53, 6.2.1
      risk management strategy, Ch. 53, 6.2
      risk management objective, Ch. 53, 6.2
      setting the hedge ratio, Ch. 53, 6.4.3
   rebalancing, Ch. 53, 8.2
      definition, Ch. 53, 8.2.1
      mechanics of, Ch. 53, 8.2.3
      requirement to rebalance, Ch. 53, 8.2.2
   risk management, Ch. 53, 6.2, 6.3
      proxy hedges, Ch. 53, 6.2.1
      risk management objective, Ch. 53, 6.2
         change in, Ch. 53, 8.3
      risk management strategy, Ch. 53, 6.2
   standards, development of, Ch. 53, 1.3

Financial instruments: presentation and disclosure, Ch. 54, 1–9
   disclosures, structuring, Ch. 54, 3
      classes of financial instrument, Ch. 54, 3.3
      level of detail, Ch. 54, 3.1
      materiality, Ch. 54, 3.2
   effective date and transitional provisions, Ch. 54, 8
   future developments, Ch. 54, 9
   interim reports, Ch. 54, 2.3
   nature and extent of risks arising from financial instruments, Ch. 54, 5
      credit risk, Ch. 54, 5.3
         collateral and other credit enhancements obtained, Ch. 54, 5.3.5
         credit risk exposure, Ch. 54, 5.3.4
         credit risk management practices, Ch. 54, 5.3.2
         illustrative disclosures, Ch. 54, 5.3.6
         quantitative and qualitative information about amounts arising from expected credit losses, Ch. 54, 5.3.3
         scope and objectives, Ch. 54, 5.3.1
      liquidity risk, Ch. 54, 5.4
         information provided to key management, Ch. 54, 5.4.1
         management of associated liquidity risk, Ch. 54, 5.4.3
         maturity analyses, Ch. 54, 5.4.2
         puttable financial instruments classified as equity, Ch. 54, 5.4.4
      market risk, Ch. 54, 5.5
         'basic' sensitivity analysis, Ch. 54, 5.5.1
         other market risk disclosures, Ch. 54, 5.5.3
         value-at-risk and similar analyses, Ch. 54, 5.5.2
      qualitative disclosures, Ch. 54, 5.1
      quantitative disclosures, Ch. 54, 5.2, 5.6
         capital disclosures, Ch. 54, 5.6.3
         concentrations of risk, Ch. 54, 5.6.1
         operational risk, Ch. 54, 5.6.2
   presentation on the face of the financial statements and related disclosures, Ch. 54, 7
      gains and losses recognised in other comprehensive income, Ch. 54, 7.2
      gains and losses recognised in profit/loss, Ch. 54, 7.1
         embedded derivatives, Ch. 54, 7.1.4
         entities whose share capital is not equity, Ch. 54, 7.1.5
         further analysis of gains and losses recognised in profit/loss, Ch. 54, 7.1.2
         offsetting and hedges, Ch. 54, 7.1.3
         presentation on the face of the statement of comprehensive income (or income statement), Ch. 54, 7.1.1
   significance of financial instruments for an entity's financial position/performance, Ch. 54, 4
      accounting policies, Ch. 54, 4.1
      business combinations, Ch. 54, 4.6
         acquired receivables, Ch. 54, 4.6.1
         contingent consideration and indemnification assets, Ch. 54, 4.6.2
      day 1 profits, Ch. 54, 4.5.2
      fair values, Ch. 54, 4.5
      general disclosure requirements, Ch. 54, 4.5.1
      hedge accounting, Ch. 54, 4.3
         amount, timing and uncertainty of future cash flows, Ch. 54, 4.3.2
         effects of hedge accounting on financial position and performance, Ch. 54, 4.3.3

option to designate a credit exposure as measured at fair value through profit/loss, Ch. 54, 4.3.4
risk management strategy, Ch. 54, 4.3.1
uncertainty arising from interest rate benchmark (or IBOR) reform, Ch. 54, 4.3.5
income, expenses, gains and losses, Ch. 54, 4.2
fee income and expense, Ch. 54, 4.2.3
gains and losses by measurement category, Ch. 54, 4.2.1
interest income and expense, Ch. 54, 4.2.2
statement of cash flows, Ch. 54, 7.5
statement of changes in equity, Ch. 54, 7.3
statement of financial position, Ch. 54, 7.4, , Ch. 54, 4.4
assets and liabilities, Ch. 54, 7.4.3
categories of financial assets and financial liabilities, Ch. 54, 4.4.1
collateral, Ch. 54, 4.4.6
compound financial instruments with multiple embedded derivatives, Ch. 54, 4.4.7
current and non-current assets and liabilities, distinction between, Ch. 54, 7.4.4
convertible loans, Ch. 54, 7.4.4.B
debt with refinancing or roll over agreements, Ch. 54, 7.4.4.D
derivatives, Ch. 54, 7.4.4.A
A loan covenants, Ch. 54, 7.4.4.E
long-term loans with repayment on demand terms, Ch. 54, 7.4.4.C
defaults and breaches of loans payable, Ch. 54, 4.4.8
disclosure requirements, Ch. 54, 7.4.2.C
enforceable legal right of set-off, Ch. 54, 7.4.1.A
entities whose share capital is not equity, Ch. 54, 7.4.6
equity, Ch. 54, 7.4.5
financial assets designated as measured at fair value through profit/loss, Ch. 54, 4.4.3
financial liabilities designated at fair value through profit/loss, Ch. 54, 4.4.2
intention to settle net, Ch. 54, 7.4.1.C
interests in associates and joint ventures accounted for in accordance with IFRS 9, Ch. 54, 4.4.9
investments in equity instruments designated at fair value through other comprehensive income (IFRS 9), Ch. 54, 4.4.4
master netting agreements, Ch. 54, 7.4.1.B
objective, Ch. 54, 7.4.2.A
offsetting collateral amounts, Ch. 54, 7.4.1.F
offsetting financial assets and financial liabilities, Ch. 54, 7.4.1
offsetting financial assets and financial liabilities: disclosure, Ch. 54, 7.4.2
reclassification, Ch. 54, 4.4.5
scope, Ch. 54, 7.4.2.B
situations where offset is not normally appropriate, Ch. 54, 7.4.1.D
unit of account, Ch. 54, 7.4.1.G
transfers of financial assets, Ch. 54, 6
meaning of 'transfer,' Ch. 54, 6.1
transferred financial assets that are derecognised in their entirety, Ch. 54, 6.3
disclosure requirements, Ch. 54, 6.3.2
meaning of continuing involvement, Ch. 54, 6.3.1
transferred financial assets that are not derecognised in their entirety, Ch. 54, 6.2
transitional provisions, Ch. 54, 8

Financial instruments: recognition and initial measurement, Ch. 49, 1–3
initial measurement (IFRS 9), Ch. 49, 3
assets and liabilities arising from loan commitments, Ch. 49, 3.7
embedded derivatives and financial instrument hosts, Ch. 49, 3.5
general requirements, Ch. 49, 3.1
initial fair value and 'day 1' profits, Ch. 49, 3.3
financial guarantee contracts and off-market loan commitments, Ch. 49, 3.3.3
interest-free and low-interest long-term loans, Ch. 49, 3.3.1
loans and receivables acquired in a business combination, Ch. 49, 3.3.4
measurement of financial instruments following modification of contractual terms, Ch. 49, 3.3.2
regular way transactions, Ch. 49, 3.6
transaction costs, Ch. 49, 3.4
recognition (IFRS 9), Ch. 49, 2
general requirements, Ch. 49, 2.1
cash collateral, Ch. 49, 2.1.7
firm commitments to purchase/sell goods/services, Ch. 49, 2.1.2
forward contracts, Ch. 49, 2.1.3
option contracts, Ch. 49, 2.1.4
planned future/forecast transactions, Ch. 49, 2.1.5
principal versus agent, Ch. 49, 2.1.8
receivables and payables, Ch. 49, 2.1.1
transfers of financial assets not qualifying for derecognition by transferor, Ch. 49, 2.1.6
'regular way' transactions, Ch. 49, 2.2
exchanges of non-cash financial assets, Ch. 49, 2.2.5.A
financial liabilities, Ch. 49, 2.2.2
general requirements, Ch. 49, 2.2.1
settlement date accounting, Ch. 49, 2.2.4
trade date accounting, Ch. 49, 2.2.3

Financial instruments: subsequent measurement
amortised cost and the effective interest method, Ch. 50, 3
fixed interest rate instruments, Ch. 50, 3.2
floating rate instruments, Ch. 50, 3.3
inflation-linked debt, Ch. 50, 3.6
more complex financial liabilities, Ch. 50, 3.7
perpetual debt instruments, Ch. 50, 3.5
prepayment, call and similar options, Ch. 50, 3.4
revisions to estimated cash flows, Ch. 50, 3.4.1
foreign currencies, Ch. 50, 4
foreign entities, Ch. 50, 4.2
instruments, Ch. 50, 4.1
and recognition of gains and losses, Ch. 50, 2
financial assets and financial liabilities at fair value through profit/loss, Ch. 50, 2.4
financial guarantees and commitments to provide a loan at a below-market interest rate, Ch. 50, 2.8
reclassification of financial assets, Ch. 50, 2.7

Financial liabilities and equity, Ch. 47, 1–12. *See also* Equity instruments; Financial assets; IAS 32

Financial liabilities and equity—*contd*
- background, Ch. 47, 1.1
- classification, Ch. 48, 3
- classification of instruments
  - consolidated financial statements, Ch. 47, 4.8.1
  - contingent settlement provisions, Ch. 47, 4.3
    - contingencies that are 'not genuine,' Ch. 47, 4.3.1
    - liabilities that arise only on a change of control, Ch. 47, 4.3.3
    - liabilities that arise only on liquidation, Ch. 47, 4.3.2
    - some typical contingent settlement provisions, Ch. 47, 4.3.4
  - contractual obligation to deliver cash or other financial assets, Ch. 47, 4.2
    - implied contractual obligation to deliver cash or other financial assets, Ch. 47, 4.2.2
    - relationship between an entity and its members, Ch. 47, 4.2.1
  - definition of equity instrument, Ch. 47, 4.1
  - examples of equity instruments
    - contracts to issue equity instruments, Ch. 47, 4.4.2
    - issued instruments, Ch. 47, 4.4.1
  - IFRS development on, Ch. 47, 12
  - instruments redeemable
    - with a 'dividend blocker,' Ch. 47, 4.5.3.A
    - with a 'dividend pusher,' Ch. 47, 4.5.3.B
    - mandatorily or at the holder's option, Ch. 47, 4.5.1
    - only at the issuer's option or not redeemable, Ch. 47, 4.5.2
  - perpetual debt, Ch. 47, 4.7
  - preference shares and similar instruments, Ch. 47, 4.5
    - 'change of control,' 'taxation change' and 'regulatory change' clauses, Ch. 47, 4.5.8
    - economic compulsion, Ch. 47, 4.5.6
    - instruments redeemable mandatorily or at the holder's option, Ch. 47, 4.5.1
    - 'linked' instruments, Ch. 47, 4.5.7
    - perpetual instruments with a 'step-up' clause, Ch. 47, 4.5.4
    - relative subordination, Ch. 47, 4.5.5
  - puttable instruments and instruments repayable only on liquidation IFRIC 2, Ch. 47, 4.6.6
    - instruments entitling the holder to a pro rata share of net assets only on liquidation, Ch. 47, 4.6.3
    - instruments issued by a subsidiary, Ch. 47, 4.6.4.A
    - instruments that substantially fix or restrict the residual return to the holder of an instrument, Ch. 47, 4.6.4.E
    - issue, Ch. 47, 4.6.1
    - meaning of 'identical features,' Ch. 47, 4.6.4.C
    - no obligation to deliver cash or another financial asset, Ch. 47, 4.6.4.D
    - puttable instruments, Ch. 47, 4.6.2
    - reclassification, Ch. 47, 4.6.5
    - relative subordination of the instrument, Ch. 47, 4.6.4.B
    - transactions entered into by an instrument holder other than as owner of the entity, Ch. 47, 4.6.4.F
  - reclassification of instruments
    - change of circumstances, Ch. 47, 4.9.2
    - change of terms, Ch. 47, 4.9.1
  - single entity financial statements, Ch. 47, 4.8.2
- compound financial instruments, Ch. 47, 6
  - background, Ch. 47, 6.1
  - common forms of convertible bonds, Ch. 47, 6.6
    - bond convertible into fixed percentage of equity, Ch. 47, 6.6.6
    - contingent convertible bond, Ch. 47, 6.6.2
    - convertible bonds with down round or ratchet features, Ch. 47, 6.6.7
    - convertibles with cash settlement at the option of the issuer, Ch. 47, 6.6.5
    - foreign currency convertible bond, Ch. 47, 6.6.4
    - functional currency bond convertible into a fixed number of shares, Ch. 47, 6.6.1
    - mandatorily convertible bond, Ch. 47, 6.6.3
  - components, Ch. 47, 6.4
    - compound instruments with embedded derivatives, Ch. 47, 6.4.2
    - determining the components of a compound instrument, Ch. 47, 6.4.1
  - conversion
    - at maturity, Ch. 47, 6.3.1
    - before maturity, Ch. 47, 6.3.2
  - early redemption/repurchase, Ch. 47, 6.3.3
    - exercising an embedded call option, Ch. 47, 6.3.3.B
    - through negotiation with bondholders, Ch. 47, 6.3.3.A
  - initial recognition–'split accounting,' Ch. 47, 6.2
    - accounting for the equity component, Ch. 47, 6.2.1
    - temporary differences arising from split accounting, Ch. 47, 6.2.2
  - modification, Ch. 47, 6.3.4
  - treatment by holder and issuer contrasted, Ch. 47, 6.1.1
- contracts accounted for as equity instruments, Ch. 47, 5.1
  - comparison with IFRS 2–share-based payment, Ch. 47, 5.1.1
  - exchange of fixed amounts of equity (equity for equity), Ch. 47, 5.1.4
  - number of equity instruments issued adjusted for capital, Ch. 47, 5.1.2
  - restructuring or other event, Ch. 47, 5.1.2
  - stepped up exercise price, Ch. 47, 5.1.3
- contracts accounted for as financial assets or financial liabilities, Ch. 47, 5.2
  - derivative financial instruments with settlement options, Ch. 47, 5.2.8
  - fixed amount of cash (or other financial assets) denominated in a currency other than the entity's functional currency, Ch. 47, 5.2.3
  - fixed amount of cash determined by reference to share price, Ch. 47, 5.2.6
  - fixed number of equity instruments for variable consideration, Ch. 47, 5.2.2
  - fixed number of equity instruments with variable value, Ch. 47, 5.2.5
  - instrument with equity settlement alternative of significantly higher value than cash settlement alternative, Ch. 47, 5.2.4
  - net-settled contracts over own equity, Ch. 47, 5.2.7
  - variable number of equity instruments, Ch. 47, 5.2.1
- definitions, Ch. 45, 2.1; Ch. 47, 3; Ch. 52, 2.1

derecognition, Ch. 52, 6. *See also* Derecognition
   derivatives that can be financial assets or financial liabilities, Ch. 52, 6.4
   exchange or modification of debt by original lender, Ch. 52, 6.2
      costs and fees, Ch. 52, 6.2.5
      examples, Ch. 52, 6.2.7
      exchange of debt through an intermediary, Ch. 52, 6.2.4
      Interbank Offered Rate (IBOR) Reform, Ch. 52, 6.2.2
      loan syndications, Ch. 52, 6.2.3
      modification gains and losses, Ch. 52, 6.2.6
      settlement of financial liability with issue of new equity instrument, Ch. 52, 6.2.8
   extinguishment of debt, Ch. 52, 6.1
      extinguishment in exchange for transfer of assets not meeting the derecognition criteria, Ch. 52, 6.1.4
      'in-substance defeasance' arrangements, Ch. 52, 6.1.3
      legal release by creditor, Ch. 52, 6.1.2
      what constitutes 'part' of a liability?, Ch. 52, 6.1.1
   gains and losses on extinguishment of debt, Ch. 52, 6.3
   supply-chain finance, Ch. 52, 6.5
derivatives over own equity instruments, Ch. 47, 11
   call options, Ch. 47, 11.2
      call options over non-controlling interest, Ch. 7, 6.1, 6.3, 6.4, 6.5
      purchased call option, Ch. 47, 11.2.1
      written call option, Ch. 47, 11.2.2
   forward contracts, Ch. 47, 11.1
      'back-to-back' forward contracts, Ch. 47, 11.1.3
      forward purchase, Ch. 47, 11.1.1
      forward sale, Ch. 47, 11.2
   put options, Ch. 47, 11.3
      purchased put option, Ch. 47, 11.3.1
      put options over noncontrolling interest, Ch. 7, 6.2, 6.3, 6.4, 6.5
      written put option, Ch. 47, 11.3.2
designated at fair value through profit/loss, Ch. 54, 4.4.2; Ch. 50, 2.4
dividends payable on shares classified as, Ch. 21, 5.5.4
Financial Instruments with Characteristics of Equity Research Project (FICE), Ch. 7, 7.3, 7.4, 7.5; Ch. 47, 1, 4.6.6, 5.1.2, 5.3.2A, 6.6.3B, 12
future developments, Ch. 47, 12
gross-settled contracts for the sale or issue of the entity's own equity instruments, Ch. 47, 5.4
'hedging' of instruments classified as equity, Ch. 47, 10
held for trading, Ch. 48, 4
interest, dividends, gains and losses, Ch. 47, 8
   tax effects, Ch. 47, 8.2
   transaction costs, Ch. 47, 8.1
liabilities arising from gross-settled contracts for the purchase of the entity's own equity instruments, Ch. 47, 5.3
   contracts to acquire non-controlling interests, Ch. 47, 5.3.2
   contracts to purchase own equity during 'closed' or 'prohibited' periods, Ch. 47, 5.3.1
non-controlling interests classified as, Ch. 7, 5.5, 6.2, 6.3, 6.4
objective, Ch. 47, 2.1
offsetting, Ch. 54, 7.4.1
   cash pooling arrangements, Ch. 54, 7.4.1.E
   disclosure, Ch. 54, 7.4.2
   enforceable legal right of set-off, Ch. 54, 7.4.1.A
   intention to settle net, Ch. 54, 7.4.1.C
   master netting agreements, Ch. 54, 7.4.1.B
   offsetting collateral amounts, Ch. 54, 7.4.1.F
   situations where offset is not normally appropriate, Ch. 54, 7.4.1.D
   unit of account, Ch. 54, 7.4.1.G
recognition, Ch. 49, 2.2.2
scope, Ch. 47, 2.2
settlement of financial liability with equity instrument, Ch. 47, 7
   debt for equity swaps with shareholders, Ch. 47, 7.3
   requirements of IFRIC 19, Ch. 47, 7.2
   scope and effective date of IFRIC 19, Ch. 47, 7.1
   shares/warrants issued in connection with, Ch. 34, 2.2.4.I
treasury shares, Ch. 47, 9
   IFRS 17 Treasury share election, Ch. 47, 9.2
   transactions in own shares not at fair value, Ch. 47, 9.1
Financial reporting in hyperinflationary economies, Ch. 16, 1–12. *See also* Hyperinflation
Financial Service Agency, Japan, Ch. 1, 2.3
Financial Service Commission, Republic of Korea, Ch. 1, 2.3
Financial statements, Ch. 3, 2–3.4. *See also* IAS 1; IAS 8; IAS 10; Income statement; Statement of comprehensive income; Statement of financial position comparative information, Ch. 3, 2.4
   components of, Ch. 3, 2.3
   conceptual framework, IASB's, Ch. 2.6.1
      assets, Ch. 2.7.2
      consolidated and unconsolidated, Ch. 2.6.2.1
      elements, Ch. 2.7
      equity, Ch. 2.7.4
      executory contracts, Ch. 2.7.1.2
      going concern assumption, Ch. 2.6.1.4
      income and expenses, Ch. 2.7.5
      liabilities, Ch. 2.7.3
      objective and scope, Ch. 2.6.1.1
      perspective adopted in financial statements, Ch. 2.6.1.3
      reporting period and comparative information, Ch. 2.6.1.2
      substance of contractual rights and contractual obligations, Ch. 2.7.1.3
      unit of account, Ch. 2.7.1.1
   date when financial statements are authorised for issue, Ch. 38, 2.1.1
   events requiring adjustment to the amounts recognised/disclosures in, Ch. 38, 2.2.1
   first IFRS financial statements in scope of IFRS 1, Ch. 5, 2.1
   frequency of reporting and period covered, Ch. 3, 2.2
   identification of, Ch. 3, 2.5.1
   notes to, Ch. 3, 3.4
   purpose of, Ch. 3, 2.1
   re-issuing (dual dating), Ch. 38, 2.1.1.B
   statement of changes in equity, Ch. 3, 3.3
   statement of compliance with IFRS, Ch. 3, 2.5.2
   statement of comprehensive income and income statement, Ch. 3, 3.2
   statement of financial position, Ch. 3, 3.1
   structure of, Ch. 3, 3
Financial statements, presentation of, Ch. 3, 2–3. *See also* IAS 1

Financial statements, presentation of—*contd*
    comparative information, Ch. 3, 2.4
    components of a complete set of financial statements, Ch. 3, 2.3
    frequency of reporting and period covered, Ch. 3, 2.2 IAS 1, Ch. 3, 1.1
    IAS 8, Ch. 3, 1.2
    identification of, Ch. 3, 2.5.1
    purpose of, Ch. 3, 2.1
    statement of compliance with IFRS, Ch. 3, 2.5.2
    structure of financial statements, Ch. 3, 3
        notes to the financial statements, Ch. 3, 3.4
        statement of changes in equity, Ch. 3, 3.3
        statement of comprehensive income and the statement of profit or loss, Ch. 3, 3.2
            classification of expenses recognised in profit or loss by nature or function, Ch. 3, 3.2.3
            discontinued operations, Ch. 3, 3.2.5
            information required on the face of the statement of profit or loss, Ch. 3, 3.2.2
            material and extraordinary items, Ch. 3, 3.2.6
            operating profit, Ch. 3, 3.2.2.A
            profit and loss and comprehensive income, Ch. 3, 3.2.1
        statement of comprehensive income, Ch. 3, 3.2.4
        statement of financial position, Ch. 3, 3.1
            current assets, Ch. 3, 3.1.3
            current liabilities, Ch. 3, 3.1.4
            current/non-current assets and liabilities, distinction between, Ch. 3, 3.1.1
            information required either on the face of the statement of financial position or in the notes, Ch. 3, 3.1.6
            information required on the face of statement of financial position, Ch. 3, 3.1.5
            non-current assets and disposal groups held for sale/distribution, Ch. 3, 3.1.2

Financing activities, cash flows from, Ch. 40, 4.3

Firm commitments
    to acquire a business, hedges of, Ch. 53, 7.6
    hedges of, Ch. 53, 5.1.1, 5.2.2
    to purchase or sell goods or services, Ch. 49, 2.1.2

First-time adoption, Ch. 5, 1–8. *See also* IFRS 1
    actuarial assumptions, Ch. 5, 7.7.3
    authoritative literature, Ch. 5, 1.2
    business combinations, Ch. 5, 5.2
    classification and measurement of financial instruments, Ch. 5, 4.9
    compound financial instruments, Ch. 5, 5.10
    consolidated financial statements, Ch. 5, 5.8.1
    cumulative translation differences, Ch. 5, 5.7
    date of transition to IFRSs, Ch. 5, 5.5.1.B
    deemed cost, Ch. 5, 5.5
    defined terms, Ch. 5, 1.3
    derecognition of financial assets and financial liabilities, Ch. 5, 4.3
    embedded derivatives, Ch. 5, 4.11
    employee benefits, Ch. 5, 7.7
    estimates, Ch. 5, 4.2
    fair value, Ch. 5, 3.3, 5.5.1
    first IFRS financial statements, Ch. 5, 2.1
    first IFRS reporting period, Ch. 5, 7.2.1
    first-time adopter, identifying, Ch. 5, 2
        application of IFRS 1, Ch. 5, 2.2
        dual reporting entity, Ch. 5, 2.3
        first IFRS financial statements in scope of IFRS 1, Ch. 5, 2.1
        previous GAAP, determining, Ch. 5, 2.3
    full actuarial valuations, Ch. 5, 7.7.2
    full retrospective application, Ch. 5, 3.5
    government loans, Ch. 5, 4.12
    hedge accounting, Ch. 5, 4.4, 4.5, 4.6, 4.7
    insurance contracts, Ch. 5, 4.13, 5.4
    interim financial reports, Ch. 5, 6.6
    leases, Ch. 5, 5.6
    line-by-line reconciliations, Ch. 5, 6.3.2
    mandatory exceptions, Ch. 5, 3.5, 4.1
    measurement, Ch. 5, 4.9
    non-controlling interests, Ch. 5, 4.8
    objectives of, Ch. 5, 1.1
    opening IFRS statement of financial position, Ch. 5, 3
        accounting policies, applying, Ch. 5, 3.2
        timeline, Ch. 5, 3.1
    optional exemptions, Ch. 5, 5
    regulatory issues
        foreign private issuers that are SEC registrants, Ch. 5, 8.1
        International Practices Task Force (IPTF) guidance, Ch. 5, 8.1.2
    related hedges, gains and losses arising on, Ch. 5, 5.7.1
    restatement of goodwill, Ch. 5, 5.2.5
    revenue from contracts with customers, Ch. 5, 5.21
    separate financial statements, Ch. 5, 5.8.2
    timeline, Ch. 5, 3.1
    unrecognised past service costs, Ch. 5, 7.7.4

First-time presentation of interim reports, Ch. 41, 11.1

Fixed fee service contracts, Ch. 55, 3.5.1

Fixed interest rate instruments, Ch. 50, 3.2

'Fixed stated principal' of a bond, Ch. 47, 6.3.2.A

Floating interest rate instruments, Ch. 50, 3.3

Foreign currency basis spreads, Ch. 53, 3.6.5, 7.4.8, 7.5.3
    retrospective application, Ch. 53, 13.3.3

Foreign currency cash flows
    impairment, Ch. 20, 7.1.5
    statement of cash flows, Ch. 40, 5.3

Foreign currency convertible bond, Ch. 47, 6.6.4
    instrument issued by foreign subsidiary convertible into equity of parent, Ch. 47, 6.6.4.A

Foreign currency derivatives, Ch. 46, 5.2.1
    commonly used currencies, Ch. 46, 5.2.1.C
    functional currency of counterparty, Ch. 46, 5.2.1.A
    oil contract, Ch. 46, 5.2.1.D
    routinely denominated in commercial transactions, Ch. 46, 5.2.1.B

Foreign currency instruments, Ch. 50, 4.1
    debt security measured at fair value through other comprehensive income, Ch. 51, 14.3

Foreign currency translation, interim financial reporting, Ch. 41, 9.6

Foreign entities, subsequent measurement of financial instruments, Ch. 50, 4
   IFRS 9, Ch. 51, 1.2
Foreign exchange, Ch. 15, 1–11. *See also* IAS 21
   background, Ch. 15, 1.1
   change in functional currency, Ch. 15, 5.5
   change of presentation currency, Ch. 15, 7
   disclosure requirements, Ch. 15, 10
      convenience translations of financial statements/other financial information, Ch. 15, 10.3
      exchange differences, Ch. 15, 10.1
      judgements made in applying IAS 21 and related disclosures, Ch. 15, 10.4
      presentation and functional currency, Ch. 15, 10.2
   entity's functional currency determination, Ch. 15, 4
      branches and divisions, Ch. 15, 4.4
      documentation of judgements made, Ch. 15, 4.5
      general, Ch. 15, 4.1
      intermediate holding companies/finance subsidiaries, Ch. 15, 4.2
      investment holding companies, Ch. 15, 4.3
   future developments, Ch. 15, 11
   introduction of euro, Ch. 15, 8
   monetary/non-monetary determination, Ch. 15, 5.4
      deferred tax, Ch. 15, 5.4.5
      deposits and advance payments for actively traded commodities, Ch. 15, 5.4.2
      deposits/progress payments, Ch. 15, 5.4.1
      foreign currency share capital, Ch. 15, 5.4.4
      investments in preference shares, Ch. 15, 5.4.3
      post-employment benefit plans-foreign currency assets, Ch. 15, 5.4.6
      post-employment benefit plans-foreign currency plans, Ch. 15, 5.4.7
   presentation currency other than the functional currency, Ch. 15, 6
      average rate calculation, Ch. 15, 6.1.4
      disposal of a foreign operation, Ch. 15, 6.6; Ch. 7, 2.3, 3.5
         partial disposal, Ch. 15, 6.6.2; Ch. 7, 2.3, 4.1
         step-by-step and direct methods of consolidation, Ch. 15, 6.6.3; Ch. 7, 2.3
      exchange differences on intragroup balances, Ch. 15, 6.3
         becoming part of the net investment in a foreign operation, Ch. 15, 6.3.1.F
         ceasing to be part of the net investment in a foreign operation, Ch. 15, 6.3.61.G
         currency of monetary item, Ch. 15, 6.3.1.C dividends, Ch. 15, 6.3.2
         monetary items included as part of the net investment in a foreign operation, Ch. 15, 6.3.1
         transacted by other members of the group, Ch. 15, 6.3.1.E
         treatment in individual financial statements, Ch. 15, 6.3.1.D
         unrealised profits on intragroup transactions, Ch. 15, 6.3.3
      foreign operations where sub-groups exist, accounting for, Ch. 15, 6.1.5
      goodwill and fair value adjustments, Ch. 15, 6.5
      non-coterminous period ends, Ch. 15, 6.4
      partial disposal of a foreign operation, Ch. 15, 6.6.2

      translation of equity items, Ch. 15, 6.2
         equity balances resulting from income and expenses being recognised in other comprehensive income, Ch. 15, 6.2.3
         equity balances resulting from transactions with equity holders, Ch. 15, 6.2.2
         share capital, Ch. 15, 6.2.1
      translation to the presentation currency, Ch. 15, 6.1
         accounting for foreign operations where sub-groups exist, Ch. 15, 6.1.5
         calculation of average rate, Ch. 15, 6.1.4
         dual rates, suspension of rates and lack of exchangeability, Ch. 15, 6.1.3
         functional currency is not that of a hyperinflationary economy, Ch. 15, 6.1.1
         functional currency is that of a hyperinflationary economy, Ch. 15, 6.1.2; Ch. 16. 11
   reporting foreign currency transactions in the functional currency of an entity, Ch. 15, 5
      books and records not kept in functional currency, Ch. 15, 5.6
      change in functional currency, Ch. 15, 5.5
      at ends of subsequent reporting periods, Ch. 15, 5.2
      exchange differences, treatment of, Ch. 15, 5.3
         monetary items, Ch. 15, 5.3.1
         non-monetary items, Ch. 15, 5.3.2
      initial recognition, Ch. 15, 5.1
         deposits and other consideration received or paid in advance, Ch. 15, 5.1.2
         dual rates, Ch. 15, 5.1.4.A
         identifying the date of transaction, Ch. 15, 5.1.1
         suspension of rates: longer term lack of exchangeability, Ch. 15, 5.1.4.C
         practical difficulties in determining exchange rates, Ch. 15, 5.1.4
         suspension of rates: temporary lack of exchangeability, Ch. 15, 5.1.4.B
         using average rates, Ch. 15, 5.1.3
   tax effects of all exchange differences, Ch. 15, 9
Forfeiture, share-based payments, Ch. 34, 6.1.2, 7.4.1
Forward contracts, Ch. 47, 11.1; Ch. 49, 2.1.3
   'back-to-back' forward contracts, Ch. 47, 11.1.3
   forward purchase, Ch. 47, 11.1.1
   forward sale, Ch. 47, 11.1.2
Forward currency contracts, Ch. 53, 3.6.5, 7.3.3.A, 7.5.2, 13.3.2
Forward purchase agreements (EPS), Ch. 37, 6.4.2.C
Forward rate method, Ch. 53, 7.4.7
'Fresh start' accounting, Ch. 5, 5.5.2.B
Full cost method, extractive industries, Ch. 43, 3.2.4
Functional currency, Ch. 5, 7.8.1; Ch. 15, 3–6; Ch. 43, 9. *See also* Foreign exchange
   books and records not kept in, Ch. 15, 5.6
   change in, Ch. 15, 5.5; Ch. 43, 9.2
   definition of, Ch. 15, 2.3
   determining, Ch. 15, 4; Ch. 43, 9.1
   at ends of subsequent reporting periods, Ch. 15, 5.2
   exchange differences, treatment of, Ch. 15, 5.3
      monetary items, Ch. 15, 5.3.1
      non-monetary items, Ch. 15, 5.3.2
   initial recognition, Ch. 15, 5.1

Functional currency—*contd*
  initial recognition—*contd*
    deposits and other consideration received or paid in advance, Ch. 15, 5.1.2
    dual rates, Ch. 15, 5.1.4.A
    identifying the date of transaction, Ch. 15, 5.1.1
    suspension of rates: longer term lack of exchangeability, Ch. 15, 5.1.4.C
    practical difficulties in determining exchange rates, Ch. 15, 5.1.4
    suspension of rates: temporary lack of exchangeability, Ch. 15, 5.1.4.B
    using average rates, Ch. 15, 5.1.3
  monetary/non-monetary determination, Ch. 15, 5.4
    deferred tax, Ch. 15, 5.4.4
    deposits/progress payments, Ch. 15, 5.4.1
    foreign currency share capital, Ch. 15, 5.4.3
    investments in preference shares, Ch. 15, 5.4.2
    post-employment benefit plans-foreign currency assets, Ch. 15, 5.4.5
    post-employment benefit plans-foreign currency plans, Ch. 15, 5.4.6

Fund performance fees, Ch. 46, 5.2.5
FVTOCI. *See* Fair value through other comprehensive income
General price index, Ch. 16, 3
  not available for all periods, Ch. 16, 3.2
  selection of, Ch. 16, 3.1
General purpose financial reporting, Ch. 2, 4
  changes in economic resources and claims, Ch. 2, 4.2.2
  economic resources and claims, Ch. 2, 4.2.1
  information about the use of economic resources (stewardship), Ch. 2, 4.2.3
  objective and usefulness, Ch. 2, 4.1.1
  limitations, Ch. 2, 4.1.2
Global Preparers Forum, Ch. 1, 2.9
Global Public Policy Committee (GPPC) guidance, Ch. 51, 7.2
Going concern, Ch. 2, 6.1.4; Ch. 3, 4.1.2; Ch. 38, 2.2.2
  disclosure in relation to the going concern assumption, Ch. 41, 4.7
Gold bullion sales (mining), Ch. 43, 12.13
'Good leaver' arrangements, share-based payments, Ch. 34, 5.3.9
Goodwill, Ch. 9, 6
  and allocation to cash-generating units (CGUs), Ch. 20, 8.1
  attributable to non-controlling interests, changes in ownership interest without loss of control, Ch. 7, 4.2; Ch. 20, 9
  in business combinations, Ch. 9, 6;
  and fair value adjustments, foreign operations, Ch. 15, 6.5
  impairment of goodwill, Ch. 20, 8
    acquisitions by subsidiaries and determining the level at which the group tests goodwill for impairment, Ch. 20, 12.2.3
      effect of IFRS 8 – Operating Segments – on impairment tests, Ch. 20, 8.1.4
      goodwill initially unallocated to CGUs, Ch. 20, 8.1.5
      identifying synergies and CGUs/CGU groups for allocating goodwill, Ch. 20, 8.1.2, 12.2
      measuring the goodwill allocated to CGUs/GCU groups, Ch. 20, 8.1.3
      disposal of operation within a CGU to which goodwill has been allocated, Ch. 20, 8.5
      changes in composition of CGUs, Ch. 20, 8.5.1
      effect of IFRS 8 (operating segments) when allocating goodwill to CGU's in individual financial statements, Ch. 20, 12.2.2
    goodwill synergies arising outside of the reporting entity/subgroup, Ch. 20, 12.2.1
    impairment of assets and goodwill recognised on acquisition, Ch. 20, 8.3
      deferred tax assets and losses of acquired businesses, Ch. 20, 8.3.2
      testing goodwill 'created' by deferred tax for impairment, Ch. 20, 8.3.1; Ch. 33, 12.3
    impairment testing when a CGU crosses more than one operating segment, Ch. 20, 8.4
    in individual (or subgroup) financial statements and the interaction with the group financial statements, Ch. 20, 12.2
    when to test CGUs with goodwill for impairment, Ch. 20, 8.2
  internally generated, Ch. 17, 6.2
  measuring, Ch. 9, 6
  non-controlling interests (NCIs)
    goodwill attributable to, Ch. 7, 4.2, 5.2.1
    impact of impairment testing on, Ch. 20, 9
  recognising and measuring, Ch. 9, 6
  subsequent accounting for goodwill, Ch. 9, 6.1
  restatement of goodwill on first-time adoption, Ch. 5, 5.2.5
    derecognition of negative goodwill, Ch. 5, 5.2.5.B
    goodwill previously deducted from equity, Ch. 5, 5.2.5.C
    prohibition of other adjustments of goodwill, Ch. 5, 5.2.5.A
  tax deductible, Ch. 33, 7.2.2.C
  tax on initial recognition of, Ch. 33, 7.2.2
Government grants, Ch. 24, 1–6. *See also* IAS 20
  acquisition of intangible assets by way of, Ch. 17, 4.6
  acquisition of property, plant and equipment by way of, Ch. 18, 4.6
  agriculture, Ch. 42, 3.3
  definition, Ch. 24, 1.2
  disclosures, Ch. 24, 6
  presentation of grants, Ch. 24, 4
    cash flows, Ch. 24, 4.1.1
    related to assets, Ch. 24, 4.1
    related to income, Ch. 24, 4.2
  recognition and measurement, Ch. 24, 3
    forgivable loans, Ch. 24, 3.3
    general requirements of IAS 20, Ch. 24, 3.1
    government assistance, Ch. 24, 3.8
    in the income statement, Ch. 24, 3.6
    loans at lower than market rates of interest, Ch. 24, 3.4
    non-monetary grants, Ch. 24, 3.2
    repayment of government grants, Ch. 24, 3.7
  related to biological assets, IAS 41, Ch. 24, 5, Ch. 42, 3.3
  scope of IAS 20, Ch. 24, 2
Government-related entities, Ch. 39, 2.2.10
'Graded' vesting, Ch. 34, 6.2.2. *See also* Share-based payment transactions
Grant date, share-based payment, Ch. 34, 5.3

award of equity instruments to a fixed monetary value, Ch. 34, 5.3.5
awards over a fixed pool of shares (including 'last man standing' arrangements), Ch. 34, 5.3.6
awards subject to modification by entity after original grant date, Ch. 34, 5.3.8
  discretion to make further awards, Ch. 34, 5.3.8.C
  interpretation of general terms, Ch. 34, 5.3.8.B
  significant equity restructuring or transactions, Ch. 34, 5.3.8.A
awards with multiple service and performance periods, Ch. 34, 5.3.7
awards vesting or exercisable on an exit event or change of control, Ch. 34, 15.4.1
communication of awards to employees and services in advance of, Ch. 34, 5.3.2
determination of, Ch. 34, 5.3.1
exercise price paid in shares (net settlement of award), Ch. 34, 5.3.4
exercise price/performance target dependent on a formula/future share price, Ch. 34, 5.3.3
'good leaver' arrangements, Ch. 34, 5.3.9
  automatic full/pro rata entitlement on leaving employment, Ch. 34, 5.3.9.C
  discretionary awards to, Ch. 34, 5.3.9.B
  provision for 'good leavers' made in original terms of award, Ch. 34, 5.3.9.A
special purpose acquisition companies ('SPACs'), Ch. 34, 5.3.10

Gross/net presentation of cash flows, Ch. 40, 5.2
Gross-settled contracts for entity's own equity instruments, Ch. 47, 5.4
Group reorganisations, Ch. 10, 1.2
and the carrying value of investments in subsidiaries, Ch. 20, 12.3

Group share schemes, Ch. 34, 12. *See also* Employee benefit trusts (EBTs) and similar arrangements; Share-based payment transactions
accounting treatment of group share schemes, summary, Ch. 34, 12.2
  awards settled in equity of the subsidiary, Ch. 34, 12.2.5.A
  awards settled in equity of the parent, Ch. 34, 12.2.5.B
  cash-settled transactions not settled by the entity receiving goods/services, Ch. 34, 12.2.6, 12.6
  entity receiving goods or services, Ch. 34, 12.2.3
  entity settling the transaction, Ch. 34, 12.2.4
  intragroup recharges and management charges, Ch. 34, 12.2.7
  scope of IFRS 2 for group share schemes, Ch. 34, 12.2.2
cash-settled transactions not settled by the entity receiving goods/services, illustrative example, Ch. 34, 12.6
consolidated financial statements, Ch. 34, 12.6.1
employee benefit trusts ('EBTs') and similar arrangements, Ch. 34, 12.3
employee transferring between group entities, Ch. 34, 12.7
equity-settled award satisfied by fresh issue of shares, illustrative example, Ch. 34, 12.5
equity-settled award satisfied by market purchase of shares, illustrative example, Ch. 34, 12.4
features of a group share scheme, Ch. 34, 12.1
group reorganisations, Ch. 34, 12.8
joint ventures or associates, share-based payments to employees of, Ch. 34, 12.9
scope of IFRS 2 for group share schemes, Ch. 34, 12.2.2
timing of recognition of intercompany recharges, Ch. 34, 12.2.7.A

Group transactions. *See* Common control/group transactions
Group treasury arrangements, Ch. 40, 6.5.2
Groups of items, hedge accounting, Ch. 53, 2.5
cash flow hedge of a net position, Ch. 53, 2.5.3
general requirements, Ch. 53, 2.5.1
hedging a component of a group, Ch. 53, 2.5.2
layer component designation, Ch. 53, 2.3.2
macro hedging, Ch. 53, 11
  accounting for dynamic risk management, Ch. 53, 11.1
  applying hedge accounting for macro hedging strategies under IFRS 9, Ch. 53, 11.2
nil net positions, Ch. 53, 2.5.4

Guarantees, transferred assets, Ch. 52, 5.3.1, 5.4.1
parent guarantees issued on behalf of subsidiary, Ch. 8, 4.4.5.B

Heap leaching, mining, Ch. 43, 14.6
Hedge accounting
accounting for the costs of hedging, Ch. 53, 7.5
  foreign currency basis spreads in financial instruments, Ch. 53, 7.5.3
  forward element of forward contracts, Ch. 53, 7.5.2
  time value of options, Ch. 53, 7.5.1
aggregated exposures, Ch. 53, 2.7
  accounting for, Ch. 53, 2.7.3
alternatives to hedge accounting, Ch. 53, 12
  credit risk exposures, Ch. 53, 12.1
  own use contracts, Ch. 53, 12.2
background, Ch. 53, 1.1
development of, Ch. 53, 1.3
discontinuation, Ch. 53, 8.3, 14.5
  of cash flow hedges, Ch. 53, 8.3.2
  Documented hedged item no longer exists, Ch. 53, 8.3.4
  of fair value hedges, Ch. 53, 8.3.1
  hedged net investment, disposal of, Ch. 53, 8.3.8
  hedging counterparty within the same consolidated group, Ch. 53, 8.3.7
  novation to central clearing parties, Ch. 53, 8.3.5
  risk management objective, change in, Ch. 53, 8.3.3
  settle to market derivatives, Ch. 53, 8.3.6
economic relationship, Ch. 53, 6.4.1
effective hedges, accounting for, Ch. 53, 7
  cash flow hedges, Ch. 53, 7.2
    acquisition or disposal of subsidiaries, Ch. 53, 7.2.4
    all-in-one hedges, Ch. 53, 5.2.1
    discontinuing, Ch. 53, 8.3
    documented rollover hedging strategy, Ch. 53, 7.7
    equity instrument designated at fair value through OCI, Ch. 53, 7.8
    fair value hedges, Ch. 53, 1.5, 5.1, 7.1
      adjustments to the hedged item, Ch. 53, 7.1.2
      discontinuing, Ch. 53, 8.3.1
      firm commitments, Ch. 53, 5.1.1
      foreign currency monetary items, Ch. 53, 5.1.2
      layer components with prepayment risk for, Ch. 53, 2.3.2

Hedge accounting—*contd*
  effective hedges, accounting for—*contd*
    cash flow hedges—*contd*
      fair value hedges—*contd*
        ongoing accounting, Ch. 53, 7.1.1
        presentation, Ch. 53, 10.2
      firm commitments, hedges of, Ch. 53, 5.2.2
      foreign currency monetary items, Ch. 53, 5.2.3
      hedges of a firm commitment to acquire a business, Ch. 53, 7.6
      hedges of a net investment in a foreign operation, accounting for, Ch. 7, 2.3; Ch. 53, 1.5, 5.3, 7.3, 8.3.7
      hypothetical derivatives, Ch. 53, 7.4.4
      measuring ineffectiveness of, Ch. 53, 7.4
      of a net position, Ch. 53, 2.5.3
      novation of, due to central clearing regulations, Ch. 53, 8.3.5
      ongoing accounting, Ch. 53, 7.2.1
      presentation, Ch. 53, 10.1
      reclassification of gains and losses, Ch. 53, 7.2.2
  effective date and transition, Ch. 53, 13
    limited retrospective application, Ch. 53, 13.3
    prospective application in general, Ch. 53, 13.2
  effectiveness assessment, Ch. 53, 8.1, 6.4
    credit risk dominance, Ch. 53, 6.4.2
    economic relationship, Ch. 53, 6.4.1
    hedge ratio, Ch. 53, 6.4.3
  effectiveness measurement, Ch. 53, 7.4
    calculation of, Ch. 53, 7.4.6
    'clean' *vs.* 'dirty' values, Ch. 53, 7.4.10
    comparison of spot rate and forward rate methods, Ch. 53, 7.4.7
    detailed example of calculation of ineffectiveness for a cash flow hedge, Ch. 53, 7.4.6
    discount rates for calculating fair value of hypothetical derivatives, Ch. 53, 7.4.5
    effectiveness of options, Ch. 53, 7.4.11
    foreign currency basis spreads, Ch. 53, 7.4.8
    hedged items with embedded optionality, Ch. 53, 7.4.12
    hedging instrument's impact on credit quality, Ch. 53, 7.4.9
    hedging using instruments with a non-zero fair value, Ch. 53, 7.4.3
    hypothetical derivative, Ch. 53, 7.4.4
    time value of money, Ch. 53, 7.4.2
  hedge ratio, Ch. 53, 6.4.3
  hedged items, Ch. 53, 2
    core deposits, Ch. 53, 2.6.7
    firm commitment to acquire a business, Ch. 53, 7.64
    forecast acquisition/issuance of foreign currency monetary items, Ch. 53, 2.6.5
    general requirements, Ch. 53, 2.1
    groups of items, Ch. 53, 2.5
      cash flow hedge of a net position, Ch. 53, 2.5.3
      general requirements, Ch. 53, 2.5.1
      hedging a component of a group, Ch. 53, 2.5.2
      nil net positions, Ch. 53, 2.5.4
    held at fair value through profit or loss, Ch. 53, 2.6.2
    held at fair value through OCI, Ch. 53, 2.6.3
    highly probable, Ch. 53, 2.6.1
    internal, Ch. 53, 4.3
    nominal components, Ch. 53, 2.3
      general requirement, Ch. 53, 2.3.1
      layer component for fair value hedge with prepayment risk, Ch. 53, 2.3.2
      own equity instruments, Ch. 53, 2.6.6
    risk components, Ch. 53, 2.2
      contractually specified, Ch. 53, 2.2.2
      foreign currency as, Ch. 53, 2.2.5
      general requirements, Ch. 53, 2.2.1
      inflation as, Ch. 53, 2.2.6
      non-contractually specified, Ch. 53, 2.2.3
      partial term hedging, Ch. 53, 2.2.4
    sub-LIBOR issue, Ch. 53, 2.4
      negative interest rates, Ch. 53, 2.4.2
  hedging instruments, Ch. 53, 3
    combinations of instruments, Ch. 53, 3.5
    derivatives, Ch. 53, 3.2
      basis swaps, Ch. 53, 3.2.5
      credit break clauses, Ch. 53, 3.2.4
      embedded derivatives, Ch. 53, 3.2.3
      net written options, Ch. 53, 3.2.2
      offsetting external derivatives, Ch. 53, 3.2.1
    embedded derivatives, Ch. 53, 3.2.3
    general requirements, Ch. 53, 3.1
    hedging different risks with one instrument, Ch. 53, 3.7
    non-derivative financial instruments, Ch. 53, 3.3
      of foreign currency risk, Ch. 53, 3.3.1
    non-derivative liabilities, Ch. 53, 3.3
    own equity instruments, Ch. 53, 3.4
    portions and proportions of, Ch. 53, 3.6
      foreign currency basis spread, Ch. 53, 3.6.5
      interest elements of forwards, Ch. 53, 3.6.5
      notional decomposition, Ch. 53, 3.6.2
      portion of a time period, Ch. 53, 3.6.6
      proportions of instruments, Ch. 53, 3.6.1
      restructuring of derivatives, Ch. 53, 3.6.3
      time value of options, Ch. 53, 3.6.4
  hedging relationships, types of, Ch. 53, 5
    cash flow hedges, Ch. 53, 5.2
      all-in-one hedges, Ch. 53, 5.2.1
      firm commitments hedges, Ch. 53, 5.2.2
      foreign currency monetary items, Ch. 53, 5.2.3
    fair value hedges, Ch. 53, 5.1
      firm commitments, hedges of, Ch. 53, 5.1.1
      foreign currency monetary items, hedges of, Ch. 53, 5.1.2
    hedges of net investments in foreign operations, Ch. 53, 5.3
      amount of the hedged item for which a hedging relationship may be designated, Ch. 53, 5.3.2
      nature of the hedged risk, Ch. 53, 5.3.1
      where the hedging instrument can be held, Ch. 53, 5.3.3
  ineffectiveness, measuring, Ch. 53, 7.4
  internal hedges and other group accounting issues, Ch. 53, 4
    central clearing parties, Ch. 53, 4.1.1
    external hedging instruments, offsetting, Ch. 53, 4.2
    hedged item and hedging instrument held by different group entities, Ch. 53, 4.4
    internal hedged items, Ch. 53, 4.3

internal hedging instruments, Ch. 53, 4.1
offsetting internal hedges instruments, Ch. 53, 4.2
macro hedging, Ch. 53, 11
accounting for dynamic risk management, Ch. 53, 11.1
macro hedging strategies under IFRS 9, Ch. 53, 11.2
main differences between IFRS 9 and IAS 39 hedge accounting requirements, Ch. 53, 14
discontinuation, Ch. 53, 14.5
effectiveness criteria, Ch. 53, 14.4
eligible hedged items, Ch. 53, 14.2
eligible hedging instruments, Ch. 53, 14.3
hedge accounting mechanisms, Ch. 53, 14.5
objective of hedge accounting, Ch. 53, 14.1
negative interest rates, Ch. 53, 2.4.2
portfolio/macro hedging, Ch. 53, 11
presentation, Ch. 53, 10
cash flow hedges, Ch. 53, 10.1
cost of hedging, Ch. 53, 10.4
fair value hedges, Ch. 53, 10.2
hedges of groups of items, Ch. 53, 10.3
proxy hedges, Ch. 53, 6.2.1
objective of, Ch. 53, 1.4
overview, Ch. 53, 1.5
own use contracts, Ch. 53, 12.2
qualifying criteria, Ch. 53, 6
credit risk dominance, Ch. 53, 6.4.2
on the hedged item, Ch. 53, 6.4.2.B
on the hedging instrument, Ch. 53, 6.4.2.A
designating 'proxy hedges', Ch. 53, 6.2.1
documentation and designation, Ch. 53, 6.3
business combinations, Ch. 53, 6.3.1
dynamic hedging strategies, Ch. 53, 6.3.2
forecast transactions, Ch. 53, 6.3.3
economic relationship, Ch. 53, 6.4.1
general requirements, Ch. 53, 6.1
hedge effectiveness requirements, Ch. 53, 6.4
credit risk dominance, Ch. 53, 6.4.2
economic relationship, Ch. 53, 6.4.1
hedge ratio, Ch. 53, 6.4.3
proxy hedging, Ch. 53, 6.2.1
risk management strategy, Ch. 53, 6.2
risk management objective, Ch. 53, 6.2
setting the hedge ratio, Ch. 53, 6.4.3
rebalancing, Ch. 53, 8.2
definition, Ch. 53, 8.2.1
mechanics of, Ch. 53, 8.2.3
requirement to rebalance, Ch. 53, 8.2.2
risk management, Ch. 53, 6.2, 6.3
proxy hedges, Ch. 53, 6.2.1
risk management objective, Ch. 53, 6.2
change in, Ch. 53, 8.3
risk management strategy, Ch. 53, 6.2
standards, development of, Ch. 53, 1.3
Hedge ratio, setting, Ch. 53, 6.4.3
'Hedging' of instruments classified as equity, Ch. 47, 10
Hedging sales of metal concentrate (mining sector), Ch. 43, 13.4
High-Level Expert Group (HLEG), Ch. 1, 4.2.1.B
Hong Kong Accounting Standards (HKAS), Ch. 1, 4.4.1.B
Hong Kong Financial Reporting Standards (HKFRS), Ch. 1, 4.4.1.B

Hong Kong, IFRS adoption in, Ch. 1, 4.4.1.B
Hong Kong Institute of Certified Public Accountants (HKICPA), Ch. 1, 4.4.1.B
Hybrid taxes, Ch. 33, 4.1.2, 4.5
minimum based on a measure other than taxable profits, Ch. 33, 4.5.1
tax based on revenues, unless a profit measure gives a lower result, Ch. 33, 4.5.3
tax is the higher of measures based on taxable profits and revenues, Ch. 33. 4.5.2
Hyperinflation, Ch. 16, 1–12. *See also* IAS 29–*Financial Reporting in Hyperinflationary Economies*
background, Ch. 16, 1.1
capitalisation of borrowing costs, Ch. 21, 5.6
definition of, Ch. 16, 2.3
disclosures, Ch. 16, 12
general price index, selection of, Ch. 16, 3.1
hyperinflationary economies, Ch. 16, 1.2
capitalisation of borrowing costs in, Ch. 16, 4.1.4; Ch. 21, 5.6
interim financial reporting in, Ch. 16.9; Ch. 41, 9.6.2
restatement approach, Ch. 16, 1.3
restatement of comparative figures, Ch. 16, 8
restatement of the statement of cash flows, Ch. 16, 7
restatement of the statement of changes in equity, Ch. 16, 5
restatement of the statement of profit and loss and other comprehensive income, Ch. 16, 6
restatement of the statement of financial position, Ch. 16, 4
transition, Ch. 16, 10
translation to a different presentation currency, Ch. 16, 11
comparative information, Ch. 16, 11.2
Hypothetical derivative, hedge accounting, Ch. 53, 7.4.4
IAS 1–*Presentation of Financial Statements*, Ch. 3. *See also* Financial Statements, presentation of
accrual basis of accounting, Ch. 3, 4.1.3
capital disclosures, Ch. 3, 5.4.1
consistency, Ch. 3, 4.1.4
current assets criteria, Ch. 3, 3.1.3
current liabilities criteria, Ch. 3, 3.1.4
current *versus* non-current classification, Ch. 3, 3.1.1
disclosures, Ch. 3, 5.1, 5.5; Ch. 54, 5.2
capital disclosures, Ch. 3, 5.4.1; Ch. 54, 5.6.3
going concern basis, Ch. 3, 4.1.2
sources of estimation uncertainty, Ch. 3, 5.2.1
fair presentation and compliance with IFRS, Ch. 3, 4.1.1.A
fair presentation override, Ch. 3, 4.1.1.B
future developments, Ch. 3, 6
general principles, Ch. 3, 4.1
going concern basis, Ch. 3, 4.1.2
materiality concept, Ch. 3, 4.1.5; Ch. 54, 3.2
objective of, Ch. 3, 1.1 offset, Ch. 3, 4.1.5.B
profit or loss for the period, Ch. 3, 4.1.6 purpose of, Ch. 3, 2, Ch. 3, 2.1
scope of, Ch. 3, 1.1
statement of comprehensive income, Ch. 3, 3.2
IAS 2–*Inventories*, Ch. 22, 1–6
definitions, Ch. 22, 2.2
disclosure requirements of IAS 2, Ch. 22, 6
crypto-assets, Ch. 22, 6.2
measurement, Ch. 22, 3

IAS 2–*Inventories*—contd
  measurement—*contd*
    cost criteria, Ch. 22, 3.1
      borrowing costs and purchases on deferred terms, Ch. 22, 3.1.3.C
      costs of purchase, Ch. 22, 3.1.1
      costs of conversion, Ch. 22, 3.1.2
      drug production costs within the pharmaceutical industry, Ch. 22, 3.1.3.F
      forward contracts to purchase inventory, Ch. 22, 3.1.3.E
      general and administrative overheads, Ch. 22, 3.1.3.B
      other cost, Ch. 22, 3.1.3
      service providers, Ch. 22, 3.1.3.D
      storage and distribution costs, Ch. 22, 3.1.3.A
    cost formulas, Ch. 22, 3.2.2
      first-in, first-out (FIFO), Ch. 22, 3.2.2.A
      last-in, first-out (LIFO), Ch. 22, 3.2.2.C
      weighted average cost, Ch. 22, 3.2.2.B
    crypto-assets, Ch. 22, 3.4
      cost or lower net realisable value, Ch. 22, 3.4.1
      fair value less costs to sell, Ch. 22, 3.4.2
    net realisable value, Ch. 22, 3.4.1
      sale after the reporting period, Ch. 38, 3.3
      transfers of rental assets to inventory, Ch. 22, 2.3.1.E
  objective of, Ch. 22, 2
  real estate inventory, Ch. 22, 4
    classification, Ch. 22, 4.1
    costs of, Ch. 22, 4.2
      allocation to individual units in multi-unit developments, Ch. 22, 4.2.1
      property demolition and operating lease, Ch. 22, 4.2.2
  recognition in profit/loss, Ch. 22, 5
  scope and recognition issues, IAS 2/another IFRS, Ch. 22, 2.3
    crypto-assets, Ch. 22, 2.3.1.D
    broadcast rights - IAS 2/IAS 38, Ch. 22, 2.3.1.B
    consignment stock and sale and repurchase agreements, Ch. 22, 2.3.1.F
    core inventories and spare parts, Ch. 22, 2.3.1.A
    emission rights, Ch. 22, 2.3.1.C
    sales with a right of return, Ch. 22, 2.3.1.G
    transfers of rental assets to inventory, Ch. 22, 2.3.1.E
  techniques for the measurement of cost, Ch. 22, 3.2.1
    retail method, Ch. 22, 3.2.1.B
    standard cost, Ch. 22, 3.2.1.A

IAS 7–*Statement of Cash Flows*, Ch. 40, 1–8. *See also* Statement of cash flows
  additional IAS 7 considerations for financial institutions, Ch. 40, 7
    operating cash flows, Ch. 40, 7.1
    reporting cash flows on a net basis, Ch. 40, 7.2
  additional IAS 7 considerations for groups, Ch. 40, 6
    acquisitions and disposals, Ch. 40, 6.3
      acquisition-related costs, Ch. 40, 6.3.1
      contingent consideration, Ch. 40, 6.3.3
      deferred and other non-cash consideration, Ch. 40, 6.3.2
      settlement of amounts owed by the acquired entity, Ch. 40, 6.3.4
      settlement of intra-group balances on a demerger, Ch. 40, 6.3.5
    cash flows in separate financial statements, Ch. 40, 6.5
      cash flows of subsidiaries, associates and joint ventures, Ch. 40, 6.5.1
      cash pooling, Ch. 40, 6.5.4
        and cash sharing arrangements, Ch. 40, 6.5.2
        notional cash pooling, Ch. 40, 6.5.4.A
        physical cash pooling, Ch. 40, 6.5.4.B
      group treasury arrangements, Ch. 40, 6.5.3
    cash flows of subsidiaries, associates and joint ventures, Ch. 40, 6.4
      cash flows in investment entities, Ch. 40, 6.4.3
      cash flows of joint operations, Ch. 40, 6.4.2
      investments in associates and joint ventures, Ch. 40, 6.4.1
    preparing a consolidated statement of cash flows, Ch. 40, 6.1
    transactions with non-controlling interests, Ch. 40, 6.2
  background, Ch. 40, 1.1
  cash and cash equivalents, Ch. 40, 3
    cash management policies, Ch. 40, 3.1
    components of cash and cash equivalents, Ch. 40, 3.2
      bank overdrafts, Ch. 40, 3.2.4
      client money, Ch. 40, 3.2.6
      cryptocurrencies, Ch. 40, 3.2.5
      demand deposits and short-term investments, Ch. 40, 3.2.1
      investments with maturities greater than three months, Ch. 40, 3.2.3
      money market funds, Ch. 40, 3.2.2
    reconciliation with items in the statement of financial position, Ch. 40, 3.3
    restrictions on the use of cash and cash equivalents, Ch. 40, 3.4
  cash flow presentation issues, Ch. 40, 5
    exceptional and other material cash flows, Ch. 40, 5.1
    disclosure of accounting policies, Ch. 40, 5.7
    foreign currency cash flows, Ch. 40, 5.3
      entities applying the direct method, Ch. 40, 5.3.1
      entities applying the indirect method, Ch. 40, 5.3.2
      indirect method and foreign subsidiaries, Ch. 40, 5.3.2.C
      treatment of non-operating cash flows, Ch. 40, 5.3.2.B
      treatment of operating cash flows, Ch. 40, 5.3.2.A
    gross/net presentation of cash flows, Ch. 40, 5.2
    non-cash transactions and transactions on deferred terms, Ch. 40, 5.4
      asset disposals on deferred terms, Ch. 40, 5.4.2
      asset purchased on deferred terms from the supplier, Ch. 40, 5.4.1
      revenue contracts with deferred payment terms, Ch. 40, 5.4.3
      sale and leaseback transactions, Ch. 40, 5.5.4
    voluntary disclosures, Ch. 40, 5.7
      cash flows to increase and maintain operating capacity, Ch. 40, 5.7.1
      segment cash flow disclosures, Ch. 40, 5.7.2
  future developments, Ch. 40, 1.3
  liabilities arising from financing activities, changes in, Ch. 40, 5.6
  objective, Ch. 40, 2.1
  primary financial statement, Ch. 40, 1.2
  requirements of other standards, Ch. 40, 8

cash flows arising from insurance contracts, Ch. 40, 8.2
cash flows arising from interests in subsidiaries, joint ventures and associates, Ch. 40, 8.4
cash flows arising from the exploration of mineral resources, Ch. 40, 8.3
cash flows of discontinued operations, Ch. 40, 8.1
scope, Ch. 40, 2.2
terms used in IAS 7, Ch. 40, 1.5
transparency and consistency of cash flow presentation, Ch. 40, 1.3

IAS 8–*Accounting Policies, Changes in Accounting Estimates and Errors*, Ch. 3, 4; Ch. 5, 7.2. *See also* Accounting policies; Financial Statements
accounting policies defined by, Ch. 3, 4.2
changes in accounting estimates, Ch. 3, 4.5, 5.2.2, 6.2.2.6..C
changes in accounting policies, Ch. 3, 4.4, 6.2.2.6..C
changes in estimates, Ch. 3, 5.2.2
consistency of accounting policies, Ch. 3, 4.1.4
correction of errors, Ch. 3, 4.6
disclosure of prior period errors, Ch. 3, 5.3
during the first IFRS reporting period, Ch. 5, 7.2.1
materiality defined by, Ch. 3, 4.1.5.A
objective of, Ch. 3, 1.2
scope of, Ch. 3, 1.2

IAS 10–*Events after the Reporting Period*, Ch. 38, 1–3. *See also* Events after the reporting period
adjusting events, Ch. 38, 2.1.2
treatment of, Ch. 38, 2.2
date when financial statements are authorised for issue, Ch. 38, 2.1.1
impact of preliminary reporting, Ch. 38, 2.1.1.A
re-issuing (dual dating) financial statements, Ch. 38, 2.1.1.B
definitions, Ch. 38, 2.1
non-adjusting events, Ch. 38, 2.1.3
dividend declaration, Ch. 38, 2.1.3.A
treatment of, Ch. 38, 2.3
objective, Ch. 38, 2.1
other disclosures, Ch. 38, 2.4
practical issues, Ch. 38, 3
changes to estimates of uncertain tax treatments, Ch. 38, 3.6
discovery of fraud after the reporting period, Ch. 38, 3.5
insolvency of a debtor and IFRS 9 expected credit losses, Ch. 38, 3.3
percentage of completion estimates, Ch. 38, 3.2
valuation of inventory, Ch. 38, 3.1
valuation of investment property at fair value and tenant insolvency, Ch. 38, 3.4
scope, Ch. 38, 2.1
treatment of adjusting events, Ch. 38, 2.2
events indicating that the going concern basis is not appropriate, Ch. 38, 2.2.2
events requiring adjustment to the amounts recognised, or disclosures, in the financial statements, Ch. 38, 2.2.1
treatment of non-adjusting events, Ch. 38, 2.3
breach of a long-term loan covenant and its subsequent rectification, Ch. 38, 2.3.2
declaration to distribute non-cash assets to owners, Ch. 38, 2.3.1

IAS 12–*Income Taxes*, Ch. 33, 1–14. *See also* Deferred tax; Income taxes
allocation of tax charge or credit, Ch. 33, 10
business combinations, Ch. 33, 12
current tax, Ch. 33, 5
deferred tax
measurement, Ch. 33, 8
discounting, Ch. 33, 8.6
expected manner of recovery, Ch. 33, 8.4
recognition, Ch. 33, 7
assets carried at fair value or revalued amount, Ch. 33, 7.3
basic principles, Ch. 33, 7.1
initial recognition exception, Ch. 33, 7.2
'outside' temporary differences, Ch. 33, 7.5
restriction on recognition of deferred tax assets, Ch. 33, 7.4
'tax transparent' entities, Ch. 33, 7.6
tax bases and temporary differences, Ch. 33, 6
definitions, Ch. 33, 3
development of IAS 12, Ch. 33, 1.3
disclosure, Ch. 33, 14
first-time adoption, Ch. 5, 7.3
objective, Ch. 33, 2.1
overview, Ch. 33, 2.2
presentation, Ch. 33, 13
scope, Ch. 33, 4
uncertain tax treatments, Ch. 33, 9

IAS 16–*Property, Plant and Equipment*, Ch. 18, 1–8. *See also* Property, plant and equipment (PP&E)
definitions used in IAS 16, Ch. 18, 2.2
depreciation, Ch. 18, 5
derecognition and disposal, Ch. 18, 7
partial disposals and undivided interests, Ch. 18, 7.3
joint control, Ch. 18, 7.3.1
subsidiary that is a single asset entity, Ch. 19, 6.10
vendor retains control, Ch. 18, 7.3.2
and replacement of insured assets, Ch. 18, 7.4
sale of assets held for rental, Ch. 18, 7.2
disclosure requirements, Ch. 18, 8–8.3
additional disclosures for revalued assets, Ch. 18, 8.2
first-time adopter, Ch. 5, 7.4
general disclosures, Ch. 18, 8.1
other disclosures, Ch. 18, 8.3
measurement after recognition, cost model, Ch. 18, 5
depreciable amount and residual values, Ch. 18, 5.2
depreciation charge, Ch. 18, 5.3
depreciation methods, Ch. 18, 5.6
diminishing balance methods, Ch. 18, 5.6.1
unit-of-production method, Ch. 18, 5.6.2
impairment, Ch. 18, 5.7
significant parts of assets, Ch. 18, 5.1
useful lives, Ch. 18, 5.4
land, Ch. 18, 5.4.2
repairs and maintenance, Ch. 18, 5.4.1
technological change, Ch. 18, 5.4.3
when depreciation starts, Ch. 18, 5.5
measurement after recognition, revaluation model, Ch. 18, 6–6.5
accounting for valuation surpluses and deficits, Ch. 18, 6.2
adopting a policy of revaluation, Ch. 18, 6.4
assets held under finance leases, Ch. 18, 6.5

IAS 16–*Property, Plant and Equipment*—*contd*
   measurement after recognition, cost model—*contd*
      when depreciation starts—*contd*
         measurement after recognition, revaluation model—*contd*
            meaning of fair value, Ch. 18, 6.1
            reversals of downward valuations, Ch. 18, 6.3
   measurement at recognition, Ch. 18, 4
      accounting for changes in decommissioning and restoration costs, Ch. 18, 4.3
      assets acquired with the assistance of government grants, Ch. 18, 4.6
      assets held under finance leases, Ch. 18, 4.5
      elements of cost and cost measurement, Ch. 18, 4.1
         administration and other general overheads, Ch. 18, 4.1.3
         borrowing costs, Ch. 18, 4.1.2
         cessation of capitalisation, Ch. 18, 4.1.4
         deferred payment, Ch. 18, 4.1.6
         'directly attributable' costs, Ch. 18, 4.1.1
         land and buildings to be redeveloped, Ch. 18, 4.1.7
         self-built assets, Ch. 18, 4.1.5
         transfers of assets from customers (IFRIC 18), Ch. 18, 4.1.8
         variable and contingent consideration, Ch. 18, 4.1.9
      exchanges of assets, Ch. 18, 4.4
         commercial substance, Ch. 18, 4.4.1
         reliably measurable, Ch. 18, 4.4.2
      incidental and non-incidental income, Ch. 18, 4.2
         income earned while bringing the asset to the intended location and condition, Ch. 18, 4.2.1
         income received during the construction of property, Ch. 18, 4.2.2
         liquidated damages during construction, Ch. 18, 4.2.3
   and presentation of right-of-use assets, Ch. 18, 2.3
   recognition, Ch. 18, 3
      accounting for parts ('components') of assets, Ch. 18, 3.2
      aspects of recognition, Ch. 18, 3.1
         bearer plants, Ch. 18, 3.1.7, Ch. 42, 3.2.3.A
         classification of items as inventory or PP&E when minimum levels are maintained, Ch. 18, 3.1.5
         classification as PP&E/intangible asset, Ch. 18, 3.1.4
         environmental and safety equipment, Ch. 18, 3.1.2
         production stripping costs of surface mines, Ch. 18, 3.1.6
         property economic benefits and property developments, Ch. 18, 3.1.3
         spare parts and minor items, Ch. 18, 3.1.1
      initial and subsequent expenditure, Ch. 18, 3.3
         major inspections, Ch. 18, 3.3.2
         types of parts, Ch. 18, 3.3.1
   requirements of IAS 16, Ch. 18, 2
   scope, Ch. 18, 2.1

IAS 19–*Employee Benefits*, Ch. 35, 1–16. *See also* Defined benefit plans; Defined contribution plans; Employee benefits; Long-term employee benefits; short-term employee benefits
   defined contribution plans, Ch. 35, 4
      general accounting requirements, Ch. 35, 4.1
      with minimum return guarantee, Ch. 35, 3.5
      with vesting conditions, Ch. 35, 4.2
   disclosure requirements, Ch. 35, 15
   defined benefit plans, Ch. 35, 15.2
      amount, timing and uncertainty of future cash flows, Ch. 35, 15.2.3
      characteristics and risks associated with, Ch. 35, 15.2.1
      defined benefit plans that share risks between entities under common control, Ch. 35, 15.2.5
      disclosure requirements in other IFRSs, Ch. 35, 15.2.6
      explanation of amounts in financial statements, Ch. 35, 15.2.2
      multi-employer plans, Ch. 35, 15.2.4
      plans accounted for as defined benefit plans, Ch. 35, 15.2.5.A
      plans accounted for as defined contribution plans, Ch. 35, 15.2.5.B
   defined contribution plans, Ch. 35, 15.1
   first-time adopter, Ch. 5, 7.7
   future developments, Ch. 35, 16
   interpretations committee activities, Ch. 35, 16.2
      availability of refund from defined benefit plan, Ch. 35, 16.2.2
   long-term employee benefits other than post-employment benefits, Ch. 35, 13
      meaning of other long-term employee benefits, Ch. 35, 13.1
      recognition and measurement, Ch. 35, 13.2
         attribution to years of service, Ch. 35, 13.2.1
         long-term disability benefit, Ch. 35, 13.2.2
         long-term benefits contingent on a future event, Ch. 35, 13.2.3
   objective, Ch. 35, 2.1
   pensions and other post-employment benefits, defined contribution and defined benefit plans, Ch. 35, 3
      death-in-service benefits, Ch. 35, 3.6
      distinction between, Ch. 35, 3.1
      insured benefits, Ch. 35, 3.2
      multi-employer plans, Ch. 35, 3.3
      plans that would be defined contribution plans but for existence of minimum return guarantee, Ch. 35, 3.5
      state plans, Ch. 35, 3.4
   scope, Ch. 35, 2.2
      employee benefits settled by a shareholder or another group entity, Ch. 36, 2.2.2
      scope requirements of IAS 19, Ch. 35, 2.2.1
   short-term employee benefits, Ch. 35, 12
      general recognition criteria for, Ch. 35, 12.1
      profit-sharing and bonus plans, Ch. 35, 12.3
      short-term paid absences, Ch. 35, 12.2
   termination benefits, Ch. 35, 14

IAS 20–*Accounting for Government Grants and Disclosure of Government Assistance*, Ch. 24, 1–6
   definitions, Ch. 24, 1.2
   disclosures, Ch. 24, 6
      government assistance, Ch. 24, 6.2
      government grants, Ch. 24, 6.1
   government grants related to biological assets in the scope of IAS 41, Ch. 24, 5, Ch. 42, 3.3
   overview of IAS 20, Ch. 24, 1.1
   presentation of grants, Ch. 24, 4
      related to assets, Ch. 24, 4.1
         cash flows, Ch. 24, 4.1.1

impairment testing of assets that qualified for government grants, Ch. 24, 4.1.2
related to income, Ch. 24, 4.2
recognition and measurement, Ch. 24, 3
    forgivable loans, Ch. 24, 3.3
    general requirements of IAS 20, Ch. 24, 3.1
    government assistance, Ch. 24, 3.7
    loans at lower than market rates of interest, Ch. 24, 3
    non-monetary grants, Ch. 24, 3.2
    recognition in the income statement, Ch. 24, 3.6
        achieving the most appropriate matching, Ch. 24, 3.6.1
        loans at lower than market rates of interest, Ch. 24, 3.6.2
        period to be benefited by the grant, Ch. 24, 3.6.3
        separating grants into elements, Ch. 24, 3.6.4
    repayment of government grants, Ch. 24, 3.7
scope, Ch. 24, 2
    government assistance, Ch. 24, 2.1
    government grants, Ch. 24, 2.2
        definition, Ch. 24, 2.2.1
    scope exclusion, Ch. 24, 2.3
        general considerations, Ch. 24, 2.3.1
        investment tax credits, Ch. 24, 2.3.2

IAS 21–*The Effects of Changes in Foreign Exchange Rates*, Ch. 15, 1–11. *See also* Foreign exchange, Functional currency
background, Ch. 15, 1.1
change in functional currency, Ch. 15, 5.5
change of presentation currency, Ch. 15, 7
definitions of terms, Ch. 15, 2.3
disclosure requirements, Ch. 15, 10
    entity's functional currency determination, Ch. 15, 4
    branches and divisions, Ch. 15, 4.4
    documentation of judgements made, Ch. 15, 4.5
    general, Ch. 15, 4.1
    intermediate holding companies/finance subsidiaries, Ch. 15, 4.2
    investment holding companies, Ch. 15, 4.3
first-time adopter, Ch. 5, 7.8
future developments, Ch. 15, 11
introduction of euro, Ch. 15, 8
objective of the standard, Ch. 15, 2.1
presentation currency use other than the functional currency, Ch. 15, 6
    disposal or partial disposal of a foreign operation, Ch. 7, 2.3, 3.5, 4.1; Ch. 15, 6.6
        step-by-step and direct methods of consolidation, Ch. 7, 2.3; Ch. 15, 6.6.3
    exchange differences on intragroup balances, Ch. 15, 6.3
        monetary items included as part of the net investment in a foreign operation, Ch. 15, 6.3.1
            becoming part of the net investment in a foreign operation, Ch. 15, 6.3.1.F
            ceasing to be part of the net investment in a foreign operation, Ch. 15, 6.3.1.G
            currency of monetary item, Ch. 15, 6.3.1.C
            dividends, Ch. 15, 6.3.2
            manner of settlement of monetary, Ch. 15, 6.3.1.B
            trade receivables or payables included as part of the net investment in a foreign operation, Ch. 15, 6.3.1.A
            transacted by other members of the group, Ch. 15, 6.3.1.E
            treatment in individual financial statements, Ch. 15, 6.3.1.D
        unrealised profits on intragroup transactions, Ch. 15, 6.3.3
    goodwill and fair value adjustments, Ch. 15, 6.5
    non-coterminous period ends, Ch. 15, 6.4
    translation of equity items, Ch. 15, 6.2
        equity balances from income and expenses in OCI, Ch. 15, 6.2.3
        equity balances from transactions with equity holders, Ch. 15, 6.2.2
        share capital, Ch. 15, 6.2.1
    translation to the presentation currency, Ch. 15, 6.1
        accounting for foreign operations where sub-groups exist, Ch. 7, 2.3; Ch. 15, 6.1.5
        calculation of average rate, Ch. 15, 6.1.4
        dual rates, suspension of rates and lack of exchangeability, Ch. 15, 6.1.3
        functional currency is not that of a hyperinflationary economy, Ch. 15, 6.1.1
        functional currency is that of a hyperinflationary economy, Ch. 15, 6.1.2
relevant pronouncements, Ch. 15, 1.2
reporting foreign currency transactions in the functional currency of an entity, Ch. 15, 5
    books and records not kept in functional currency, Ch. 15, 5.6
    change in functional currency, Ch. 15, 5.5
    at ends of subsequent reporting periods, Ch. 15, 5.2
    exchange differences, treatment of, Ch. 15, 5.3
        monetary items, Ch. 15, 5.3.1
        non-monetary items, Ch. 15, 5.3.2
    initial recognition, Ch. 15, 5.1
        deposits and other consideration received or paid in advance, Ch. 15, 5.1.2
        dual rates, Ch. 15, 5.1.4.A
        identifying the date of transaction, Ch. 15, 5.1.1
        practical difficulties in determining exchange rates, Ch. 15, 5.1.4
        suspension of rates: longer term lack of exchangeability, Ch. 15, 5.1.4.C
        suspension of rates: temporary lack of exchangeability, Ch. 15, 5.1.4.B
        using average rates, Ch. 15, 5.1.3
    monetary/non-monetary determination, Ch. 15, 5.4
        deferred tax, Ch. 15, 5.4.5
        deposits and advance payments for actively traded commodities, Ch. 15, 5.4.2
        deposits or progress payments, Ch. 15, 5.4.1
        foreign currency share-capital, Ch. 15, 5.4.4
        investments in preference shares, Ch. 15, 5.4.3
        post-employment benefit plans-foreign currency assets, Ch. 15, 5.4.5
        post-employment benefit plans-foreign currency plans, Ch. 15, 5.4.6
summary of approach required by IAS 21, Ch. 15, 3
scope of IAS 21, Ch. 15, 2.2
tax effects of all exchange differences, Ch. 15, 9

IAS 23–*Borrowing Costs*, Ch. 21, 1–7. *See also* Borrowing costs

IAS 23–*Borrowing Costs*—contd
  borrowing costs eligible for capitalisation, Ch. 21, 5
    capitalisation of borrowing costs in hyperinflationary economies, Ch. 21, 5.6
    derivative financial instruments, Ch. 21, 5.5.1
    directly attributable borrowing costs, Ch. 21, 5.1
    dividends payable on shares classified as financial liabilities, Ch. 21, 5.5.4
    exchange differences as a borrowing cost, Ch. 21, 5.4
    gains and losses on derecognition of borrowings, Ch. 21, 5.5.2
    gains/losses on termination of derivative financial instruments, Ch. 21, 5.5.3
    general borrowings, Ch. 21, 5.3
      accrued costs and trade payables, Ch. 21, 5.3.3
      assets carried below cost in the statement of financial position, Ch. 21, 5.3.4
      calculation of capitalisation rate, Ch. 21, 5.3.2
      completed qualifying assets, related to, Ch. 21, 5.3.1.A
      definition of general borrowings, Ch. 21, 5.3.1
      specific non-qualifying assets, related to, Ch. 21, 5.3.1.B
    group considerations, Ch. 21, 5.7
      borrowings in one company and development in another, Ch. 21, 5.7.1
      qualifying assets held by joint arrangements, Ch. 21, 5.7.2
    specific borrowings, Ch. 21, 5.2
  commencement, suspension and cessation of capitalisation, Ch. 21, 6
    cessation, Ch. 21, 6.3
      borrowing costs on 'land expenditures', Ch. 21, 6.3.1
    commencement, Ch. 21, 6.1
      expenditures on a qualifying asset, Ch. 21, 6.1.1
    suspension, Ch. 21, 6.2
      impairment considerations, Ch. 21, 6.2.1
  definition of borrowing costs, Ch. 21, 4
    in IAS 23, Ch. 21, 4.1
    other finance costs, Ch. 21, 4.2
  disclosure requirements, Ch. 21, 7
  qualifying assets, Ch. 21, 3
    assets measured at fair value, Ch. 21, 3.2
    constructed good, over time transfer of, Ch. 21, 3.1
    financial assets, Ch. 21, 3.3
    inventories, Ch. 21, 3.1
  requirements of, Ch. 21, 2
    core principle, Ch. 21, 2.1
    scope, Ch. 21, 2.2

IAS 24–*Related Party Disclosures*, Ch. 39, 1–2. *See also* Key management personnel; Related party
  disclosable transactions, Ch. 39, 2.5
    materiality, Ch. 39, 2.5.1
  disclosure of controlling relationships, Ch. 39, 2.4
  disclosure of expense incurred with management entity, Ch. 39, 2.8
  disclosure of key management personnel compensation, Ch. 39, 2.6
    compensation, Ch. 39, 2.6.1
    key management personnel compensated by other entities, Ch. 39, 2.6.8
    post-employment benefits, Ch. 39, 2.6.3
    reporting entity part of a group, Ch. 39, 2.6.7
    share-based payment transactions, Ch. 39, 2.6.6
    short-term employee benefits, Ch. 39, 2.6.2
    termination benefits, Ch. 39, 2.6.5
  disclosure of other related party transactions, including commitments, Ch. 39, 2.7
    disclosures required for related party transactions, including commitments, Ch. 39, 2.7.2
    related party transactions requiring disclosure, Ch. 39, 2.7.1
      aggregation of items of a similar nature, Ch. 39, 2.7.1.A
      commitments, Ch. 39, 2.7.1.B
  disclosures with government-related entities, Ch. 39, 2.9
  objective, Ch. 39, 2.1.1
  parties that are not related parties, Ch. 39, 2.3
  possible solutions, Ch. 39, 1.2
    remeasurement of related party transactions at fair values, Ch. 39, 1.2.1
  related party and related party transactions, identification of, Ch. 39, 2.2
    entities that are associates/joint ventures, Ch. 39, 2.2.3
      joint operations, Ch. 39, 2.2.3.A
    entities that are joint ventures and associates of the same third entity, Ch. 39, 2.2.5
    entities that are joint ventures of the same third party, Ch. 39, 2.2.5
    entities that are members of the same group, Ch. 39, 2.2.2
    entities under control or joint control of certain persons/close members of their family, Ch. 39, 2.2.7
    entities under significant influence of certain persons/close members of their family, Ch. 39, 2.2.8
    government-related entities, Ch. 39, 2.2.10
    key management personnel services provided by a management entity, Ch. 39, 2.2.9
    persons/close members of a person's family that are related parties, Ch. 39, 2.2.1
      control, Ch. 39, 2.2.1.A
      joint control, Ch. 39, 2.2.1.B
      key management personnel, Ch. 39, 2.2.1.D
      significant influence, Ch. 39, 2.2.1.C
    post-employment benefit plans, Ch. 39, 2.2.6
  related party issue, Ch. 39, 1.1
  scope, Ch. 39, 2.1.2

IAS 27–*Separate Financial Statements*, Ch. 8, 1–3. *See also* Separate financial statements
  definitions, Ch. 8, 1
  disclosure, Ch. 8, 3
  requirements of separate financial statements, Ch. 8, 2
  scope, Ch. 8, 1

IAS 28–*Investments in Associates and Joint Ventures*, Ch. 11, 1–11. *See also* Investments in associates and joint ventures
  application of the equity method, Ch. 11, 7
  definitions, Ch. 11, 3
  entities with no subsidiaries but exempt from applying IAS 28, Ch. 8, 3.3.1
  exemptions from applying the equity method, Ch. 11, 5
    investments held in associates/joint ventures held by venture capital organisations, Ch. 11, 5.3
      application of IFRS 9 (or IAS 39) to exempt, Ch. 11, 5.3.2

designation of investments as 'at fair value through profit or loss', Ch. 11, 5.3.2.B
entities with a mixture of activities, Ch. 11, 5.3.2.A
investment entities exception, Ch. 11, 5.3.1
parents exempt from preparing consolidated financial statements, Ch. 11, 5.1
partial use of fair value measurement of associates, Ch. 11, 5.4
subsidiaries meeting certain criteria, Ch. 11, 5.2
first-time adoption, Ch. 5, 7.9
and IFRS 10, conflict between, Ch. 7, 3.3.2, 7.1; Ch. 11, 7.6.5.C; Ch. 12, 8.2.3
impairment losses, Ch. 11, 8, 9.1, 10.1.2
objective, Ch. 11, 2.1
scope, Ch. 11, 2.2
significant influence, Ch. 11, 4
fund managers, Ch. 11, 4.6
holdings of less than 20% of the voting power, Ch. 11, 4.3
lack of, Ch. 11, 4.2
potential voting rights, Ch. 11, 4.4
severe long-term restrictions impairing ability to transfer funds to the investor, Ch. 11, 4.1
voting rights held in a fiduciary capacity, Ch. 11, 4.5

IAS 29–*Financial Reporting in Hyperinflationary Economies,* Ch. 16, 1–12. *See also* Hyperinflation
context of, Ch. 16, 2.1
definition of hyperinflation, Ch. 16, 2.3
disclosures, Ch. 16, 12
restatement of comparative figures, Ch. 16, 8
restatement of the statement of cash flows, Ch. 16, 7
restatement of the statement of changes in equity, Ch. 16, 5
restatement of the statement of profit and loss and other comprehensive income, Ch. 16, 6
calculation of gain or loss on net monetary position, Ch. 16, 6.2
interest and exchange differences, Ch. 16, 6.1
measurement of reclassification adjustments within equity, Ch. 16, 6.3
restatement process, Ch. 16, 2.4
scope, Ch. 16, 2.2
selection of general price index, Ch. 16, 3.1
statement of financial position, analysis and restatement of, Ch. 16, 4
deferred taxation, calculation of, Ch. 16, 4.4
inventories, Ch. 16, 4.2
monetary and non-monetary items, Ch. 16, 4.1
distinguishing between, Ch. 16, 4.1.1
monetary items, Ch. 16, 4.1.2
non-monetary items carried at current cost, Ch. 16, 4.1.3
non-monetary items carried at historic cost, Ch. 16, 4.1.4
restatement of associates, joint ventures and subsidiaries, Ch. 16, 4.3
transition
economies becoming hyperinflationary, Ch. 16, 10.1
economies ceasing to be hyperinflationary, Ch. 16, 10.2
economies exiting severe hyperinflation, Ch. 16, 10.3
translation to a different presentation currency, Ch. 16, 11
comparative information, Ch. 16, 11.2
initial application and ceasing application of IAS 29, Ch. 16, 11.1

IAS 32–*Financial Instruments: Presentation*, Ch. 44, 2; Ch. 54, *See also* Financial instruments, financial liabilities and equity; Presentation and disclosure, financial instruments
definitions, Ch. 47, 3
objective, Ch. 47, 2.1
options over puttable instruments classified as equity, Ch. 34, 2.2.4.J
presentation
compound financial instruments, Ch. 47, 6
interest, dividends, losses and gains, Ch. 47, 8
liabilities and equity
contingent settlement provisions, Ch. 47, 4.3
contracts to issue equity instruments, Ch. 47, 4.4.2
contractual obligation to deliver cash or other financial assets, Ch. 47, 4.2
implied contractual obligation to deliver cash or other financial assets, Ch. 47, 4.2.2
perpetual debt, Ch. 47, 4.7
preference shares, Ch. 47, 4.5
puttable instruments, Ch. 47, 4.6
offsetting a financial asset and a financial liability, Ch. 54, 7.4.1
treasury shares, Ch. 47, 9
scope, Ch. 47, 2.2
transactions in financial assets outside the scope of, Ch. 34, 2.2.3.F
transactions not in the scope of (compared with IFRS 2), Ch. 34, 2.2.3.E

IAS 33–*Earnings per Share*, Ch. 37, 1–8. *See also* Diluted EPS
basic EPS, Ch. 37, 3
earnings, Ch. 37, 3.1
number of shares, Ch. 37, 3.2
changes in outstanding ordinary shares, Ch. 37, 4
adjustments to EPS in historical summaries, Ch. 37, 4.7
changes in ordinary shares without corresponding changes in resources, Ch. 37, 4.3
B share schemes, Ch. 37, 4.3.4
capitalisation, bonus issues and share splits, Ch. 37, 4.3.1.A
put warrants priced above market value, Ch. 37, 4.3.5
rights issue, Ch. 37, 4.3.3
share consolidation with a special dividend, Ch. 37, 4.3.2
share consolidations, Ch. 37, 4.3.1.C
stock dividends, Ch. 37, 4.3.1.B
issue to acquire another business, Ch. 37, 4.6
acquisitions, Ch. 37, 4.6.1
establishment of a new parent undertaking, Ch. 37, 4.6.3
reverse acquisitions, Ch. 37, 4.6.2
options exercised during the year, Ch. 37, 4.4
post balance sheet changes in capital, Ch. 37, 4.5
purchase and redemption of own shares, Ch. 37, 4.2
weighted average number of shares, Ch. 37, 4.1
contingently issuable potential ordinary shares, Ch. 37, 6.4.8
contingently issuable shares, Ch. 37, 6.4.6
earnings-based contingencies, Ch. 37, 6.4.6.A
share-price-based contingencies, Ch. 37, 6.4.6.B

IAS 33—*Earnings per Share*—contd
- convertible instruments, Ch. 37, 6.4.1
  - convertible debt, Ch. 37, 6.4.1.A
  - convertible preference shares, Ch. 37, 6.4.1.B
  - participating equity instruments, Ch. 37, 6.4.1.C
- definitions, Ch. 37, 1.1
- disclosure, Ch. 37, 7.3
- matters affecting the numerator, Ch. 37, 5
  - earnings, Ch. 37, 5.1
  - participating equity instruments and two class shares, Ch. 37, 5.4
  - preference dividends, Ch. 37, 5.2
  - retrospective adjustments, Ch. 37, 5.3
- objective, Ch. 37, 2.1
- options, warrants and their equivalents, Ch. 37, 6.4.2
  - forward purchase agreements, Ch. 37, 6.4.2.C
  - numerator, Ch. 37, 6.4.2.A
  - options over convertible instruments, Ch. 37, 6.4.2.D
  - settlement of option exercise price, Ch. 37, 6.4.2.E
  - specified application of option proceeds, Ch. 37, 6.4.2.F
  - written call options, Ch. 37, 6.4.2.B
  - written put options, Ch. 37, 6.4.2.C
- ordinary shares of investees, Ch. 37, 6.4.7
- partly paid shares, Ch. 37, 6.4.4
- presentation, Ch. 37, 7.1
- purchased options and warrants, Ch. 37, 6.4.3
- restatement, Ch. 37, 7.2
- scope, Ch. 37, 2.2
- share based payments, Ch. 37, 6.4.5

IAS 34—*Interim Financial Reporting*, Ch. 41, 1–11; Ch. 54, 2.3
- components, form and content, Ch. 41, 3
  - complete set of interim financial statements, Ch. 41, 3.1
  - condensed interim financial statements, Ch. 41, 3.2
  - management commentary, Ch. 41, 3.4
  - requirements for both complete and condensed interim financial information, Ch. 41, 3.3
- definitions, Ch. 41, 1.1
- disclosure in annual financial statements, Ch. 41, 7
- disclosures in condensed financial statements, Ch. 41, 4
  - disclosure of compliance with IFRS, Ch. 41, 4.6
  - examples of disclosures, Ch. 41, 4.3
    - accounting policies and methods of computation, Ch. 41, 4.3.11
    - acquisition and disposal of property, plant and equipment, Ch. 41, 4.3.3
    - amounts that are unusual because of their nature, size or incidence, Ch. 41, 4.3.14
    - capital commitments, Ch. 41, 4.3.4
    - changes in circumstances affecting fair values, Ch. 41, 4.3.6
    - changes in the composition of the entity, Ch. 41, 4.3.17
    - contingent liabilities, Ch. 41, 4.3.10
    - default/breach of loan covenants not remedied before the end of interim period, Ch. 41, 4.3.7
    - dividends paid, Ch. 41, 4.3.15
    - events after the interim reporting date, Ch. 41, 4.3.16
    - inventory write-down and reversals, Ch. 41, 4.3.1
    - issues, repurchases and repayments of debt and equity securities, Ch. 41, 4.3.14
    - litigation settlements, Ch. 41, 4.3.5
    - recognition and reversal of impairment losses, Ch. 41, 4.3.3
    - related party transactions, Ch. 41, 4.3.8
    - seasonality/cyclicality of operations, Ch. 41, 4.3.12
    - transfers between different levels of fair value hierarchy, Ch. 41, 4.3.9
  - fair value disclosures for financial instruments, Ch. 41, 4.5
  - going concern assumption, disclosure in relation to, Ch. 41, 4.7
  - other disclosures required by IAS 34, Ch. 41, 4.2
  - segment information, Ch. 41, 4.4
  - significant events and transactions, Ch. 41, 4.1
  - specified disclosures, location of, Ch. 41, 4.2.1
- effective dates and transitional rules, Ch. 41, 11
  - first-time presentation of interim reports complying with IAS 34, Ch. 41, 11.1
- estimates, use of, Ch. 41, 10
- materiality, Ch. 41, 6
- objective, Ch. 41, 2.1
- periods for which interim financial statements are required to be presented, Ch. 41, 5
  - change in financial year-end, Ch. 41, 5.3
  - comparatives following a financial period longer than a year, Ch. 41, 5.4
  - length of interim reporting period, Ch. 41, 5.2
  - other comparative information, Ch. 41, 5.1
  - when the comparative period is shorter than the current period, Ch. 41, 5.5
- recognition and measurement, Ch. 41, 8
  - examples of, Ch. 41, 9
    - contingent lease payments, Ch. 41, 9.7.4
    - contractual/anticipated purchase price changes, Ch. 41, 9.4.2
    - cost of sales, Ch. 41, 9.4
    - earnings per share, Ch. 41, 9.8
    - employee benefits, Ch. 41, 9.3
    - foreign currency translation, Ch. 41, 9.6
    - interim period manufacturing cost variances, Ch. 41, 9.4.3
    - inventories, Ch. 41, 9.4.1
    - levies charged by public authorities, Ch. 41, 9.7.5
    - periodic maintenance/overhaul, Ch. 41, 9.7.3
    - property, plant and equipment and intangible assets, Ch. 41, 9.1
    - provisions, contingencies and accruals for other costs, Ch. 41, 9.7
    - reversal of impairment losses recognised in a previous interim period (IFRIC 10), Ch. 41, 9.2
    - taxation, Ch. 41, 9.5
  - same accounting policies as in annual financial statements, Ch. 41, 8.1
    - measurement on a year-to-date basis, Ch. 41, 8.1.1
    - new accounting pronouncements and other changes in accounting policies, Ch. 41, 8.1.2
    - voluntary changes in presentation, Ch. 41, 8.1.3
  - seasonal businesses, Ch. 41, 8.2
    - costs incurred unevenly during the year, Ch. 41, 8.2.2
    - revenues received seasonally, cyclically, or occasionally, Ch. 41, 8.2.1
- scope, Ch. 41, 2.2
- use of estimates, Ch. 41, 10

IAS 36–*Impairment of Assets*, Ch. 20, 1–14. *See also* Goodwill; Impairment of assets; Value in use (VIU)
- carrying amount of CGU assets, identifying, Ch. 20, 4
  - consistency and the impairment test, Ch. 20, 4.1
  - corporate assets, Ch. 20, 4.2
    - leased corporate assets, Ch. 20, 4.2.1
- developments, Ch. 20, 14
- disclosures required by IAS 36, Ch. 20, 13.3
  - annual impairment disclosures for goodwill and intangible assets with an indefinite useful life, Ch. 20, 13.3
  - for impairment losses or reversals, Ch. 20, 13.2.1
  - material impairments, Ch. 20, 13.2.2
- dividing the entity into cash-generating units (CGUs), Ch. 20, 3
  - active markets and identifying CGUs, Ch. 20, 3.3
  - CGUs and intangible assets, Ch. 20, 3.1
- fair value less costs of disposal, Ch. 20, 6
  - estimating, Ch. 20, 6.1
    - Depreciated replacement costs or current replacement cost as FVLCD, Ch. 20, 6.1.2
    - FVLCD and the unit of account, Ch. 20, 6.1.1
- first-time adopters of IAS 36, Ch. 5, 7.12
- goodwill and its allocation to CGUs, Ch. 20, 8.1
  - composition of goodwill, Ch. 20, 8.1.1
  - effect of IFRS 8 on impairment tests, Ch. 20, 8.1.4
    - aggregation of operating segments for disclosure purposes, Ch. 20, 8.1.4.B
    - changes to operating segments, Ch. 20, 8.1.4.A
  - goodwill initially unallocated to CGUs, Ch. 20, 8.1.5
  - identifying synergies and identifying CGUs/CGU groups for allocating goodwill, Ch. 20, 8.1.2
  - measuring the goodwill allocated to CGUs/CGU groups, Ch. 20, 8.1.3
- group and separate financial statement issues, Ch. 20, 12
  - goodwill in individual (or subgroup) financial statements and the interaction with the group financial statements, Ch. 20, 12.2
  - group reorganisations and the carrying value of investments in subsidiaries, Ch. 20, 12.3
  - VIU: relevant cash flows and non-arm's length prices, Ch. 20, 12.1
- investments in subsidiaries, associates and joint ventures, Ch. 20, 12.4
- impairment of intangible assets with an indefinite useful life, Ch. 20, 10
- impairment losses, recognising and reversing, Ch. 20, 11
  - impairment losses and CGUs, Ch. 20, 11.2
  - on individual assets, Ch. 20, 11.1
  - reversal of impairment losses recognised in a previous interim period, Ch. 41, 9.2
    - relating to goodwill prohibited, Ch. 20, 11.3
    - relating to assets other than goodwill, Ch. 20, 11.4
- impairment of goodwill, Ch. 20, 8
  - disposal of operation within a CGU to which goodwill has been allocated, Ch. 20, 8.5
    - changes in composition of CGUs, Ch. 20, 8.5.1
  - impairment of assets and goodwill recognised on acquisition, Ch. 20, 8.3
    - deferred tax assets and losses of acquired businesses, Ch. 20, 8.3.2
    - testing goodwill 'created' by deferred tax for impairment, Ch. 20, 8.3.1
  - impairment testing when a CGU crosses more than one operating segment, Ch. 20, 8.4
  - when to test CGUs with goodwill for impairment, Ch. 20, 8.2
    - carry forward of a previous impairment test calculation, Ch. 20, 8.2.3
    - reversal of impairment loss for goodwill prohibited, Ch. 20, 8.2.4
    - sequence of impairment tests for goodwill and other assets, Ch. 20, 8.2.2
    - timing of impairment tests, Ch. 20, 8.2.1
- impairment review, features of, Ch. 20, 1.2
- impairment testing requirements, Ch. 20, 2
  - indicators of impairment, Ch. 20, 2.1
    - (future) performance, Ch. 20, 2.1.2
    - individual assets/part of CGU?, Ch. 20, 2.1.3
    - interest rates, Ch. 20, 2.1.4
    - market capitalisation, Ch. 20, 2.1.1
- non-controlling interests, impact on goodwill impairment testing, Ch. 7, 4.2, Ch. 20, 9
- recoverable amount, Ch. 20, 5
  - impairment of assets held for sale, Ch. 20, 5.1
- scope of IAS 36, Ch. 20, 1.3
- theory behind, Ch. 20, 1.1
- value in use (VIU), determining, Ch. 20, 7
  - appropriate discount rate and discounting the future cash flows, Ch. 20, 7.2
    - approximations and short cuts, Ch. 20, 7.2.4
    - calculating VIU using post-tax cash flows, Ch. 20, 7.2.3
    - determining pre-tax rates taking account of tax losses, Ch. 20, 7.2.6
    - disclosing pre-tax discount rates when using a post-tax methodology, Ch. 20, 7.2.5
    - discount rates and the weighted average cost of capital, Ch. 20, 7.2.1
    - entity-specific WACCs and capital structure, Ch. 20, 7.2.8
    - entity-specific WACCs and different project risks within the entity, Ch. 20, 7.2.7
    - pre-tax discount rate, calculating, Ch. 20, 7.2.2
    - use of discount rates other than the WACC, Ch. 20, 7.2.9
  - fair value and value in use, differences between, Ch. 20, 7.3
  - future pre-tax cash flows of the CGU under review, estimating, Ch. 20, 7.1
    - budgets and cash flows, Ch. 20, 7.1.1
    - cash inflows and outflows from improvements and enhancements, Ch. 20, 7.1.2
    - events after the reporting period, Ch. 20, 7.1.9
    - foreign currency cash flows, Ch. 20, 7.1.5
    - internal transfer pricing, Ch. 20, 7.1.6
    - lease payments, Ch. 20, 7.1.8
    - overheads and share-based payments, Ch. 20, 7.1.7
    - restructuring, Ch. 20, 7.1.3
    - terminal values, Ch. 20, 7.1.4

IAS 37–*Provisions, Contingent Liabilities and Contingent Assets*,
Ch. 26, 1–7. *See also* Provisions, contingent liabilities and
contingent assets
  cases in which no provision should be recognised, Ch. 26, 5
    future operating losses, Ch. 26, 5.1
    rate-regulated activities, Ch. 26, 5.4
    repairs and maintenance of owned assets, Ch. 26, 5.2
    staff training costs, Ch. 26, 5.3
  definitions, Ch. 26, 1.3
  disclosure requirements, Ch. 26, 7
    contingent assets, Ch. 26, 7.3
    contingent liabilities, Ch. 26, 7.2
    provisions, Ch. 26, 7.1
    reduced disclosure when information is seriously
      prejudicial, Ch. 26, 7.4
  first-time adopters, Ch. 5, 7.13
  interpretations related to the application of IAS 37,
    Ch. 26, 1.2
  measurement, Ch. 26, 4
    anticipating future events that may affect the estimate of
      cash flows, Ch. 26, 4.4
    best estimate of provision, Ch. 26, 4.1
    changes and uses of provisions, Ch. 26, 4.9
      changes in contingent liabilities recognised in a
        business combination, Ch. 26, 4.10
    dealing with risk and uncertainty in measuring a provision,
      Ch. 26, 4.2
    discounting the estimated cash flows to a present value,
      Ch. 26, 4.3
      adjusting for risk and using a government bond rate,
        Ch. 26, 4.3.2
      effect of changes in interest rates on the discount rate
        applied, Ch. 26, 4.3.6
      own credit risk is not taken into account,
        Ch. 26, 4.3.3
      pre-tax discount rate, Ch. 26, 4.3.4
      real *vs.* nominal rate, Ch. 26, 4.3.1
      unwinding of the discount, Ch. 26, 4.3.5
    joint and several liability, Ch. 26, 4.7
    provisions are not reduced for gains on disposal of related
      assets, Ch. 26, 4.8
    provisions that will be settled in a currency other than the
      entity's functional currency, Ch. 26, 4.5
    reimbursements, insurance and other recoveries from third
      parties, Ch. 26, 4.6
  objective of IAS 37, Ch. 26, 2.1
  recognition, Ch. 26, 3
    contingencies, Ch. 26, 3.2
      contingent assets, Ch. 26, 3.2.2
        obligations contingent on the successful recovery
          of, Ch. 26, 3.2.2.A
      contingent liabilities, Ch. 26, 3.2.1
      how probability determines whether to recognise or
        disclose, Ch. 26, 3.2.3
    determining when a provision should be recognised,
      Ch. 26, 3.1
      an entity has a present obligation as a result of a past
        event, Ch. 26, 3.1.1
      it is probable that an outflow of resources embodying
        economic benefits will be required to settle the
        obligation, Ch. 26, 3.1.2
      a reliable estimate can be made of the amount of the
        obligation, Ch. 26, 3.1.3
    recognising an asset when recognising a provision, Ch. 26,
      3.3
  scope of IAS 37, Ch. 26, 2.2
    distinction between provisions and contingent liabilities,
      Ch. 26, 2.2.3
    items outside the scope of IAS 37, Ch. 26, 2.2.1
      executory contracts, except where the contract is
        onerous, Ch. 26, 2.2.1.A
      items covered by another standard, Ch. 26, 2.2.1.B
    provisions compared to other liabilities, Ch. 26, 2.2.2
  specific examples of provisions and contingencies, Ch. 26, 6
    decommissioning provisions, Ch. 26, 6.3
      changes in estimated decommissioning costs
        (IFRIC 1), Ch. 26, 6.3.1
      changes in legislation after construction of the asset,
        Ch. 26, 6.3.2
      funds established to meet an obligation (IFRIC 5),
        Ch. 26, 6.3.3
      interaction of leases with asset retirement obligations,
        Ch. 26.6.3.4
    dilapidation and other provisions relating to leased assets,
      Ch. 26, 6.9
    environmental provisions, general guidance in IAS 37,
      Ch. 26, 6.4
    EU Directive on 'Waste Electrical and Electronic
      Equipment' (IFRIC 6), Ch. 26, 6.7
    green certificates compared to emissions trading schemes,
      Ch. 26, 6.6
    levies imposed by governments, Ch. 26, 6.8
      payments relating to taxes other than income tax,
        Ch. 26, 6.8.4
      recognition and measurement of levy liabilities,
        Ch. 26, 6.8.2
      recognition of an asset/expense when a levy is
        recorded, Ch. 26, 6.8.3
      scope of IFRIC 21, Ch. 26, 6.8.1
    liabilities associated with emissions trading schemes,
      Ch. 26, 6.5
    litigation and other legal claims, Ch. 26, 6.11
    obligations to make donations to non-profit organisations,
      Ch. 26, 6.14
    onerous contracts, Ch. 26, 6.2
      contracts with customers that are, or have become,
        onerous, Ch. 26, 6.2.2
      onerous leases, Ch. 26, 6.2.1
    refunds policy, Ch. 26, 6.12
    restructuring provisions, Ch. 26, 6.1
      costs that can (and cannot) be included in a
        restructuring provision, Ch. 26, 6.1.4
      definition, Ch. 26, 6.1.1
      recognition of a restructuring provision, Ch. 26, 6.1.2
      recognition of obligations arising from the sale of an
        operation, Ch. 26, 6.1.3
    self insurance, Ch. 26, 6.13
    settlement payments, Ch. 26, 6.15
    warranty provisions, Ch. 26, 6.10
IAS 38–*Intangible Assets*, Ch. 17, 1–11. *See also* Intangible assets
  acquisition as part of a business combination, Ch. 17, 5
    customer relationship intangible assets, Ch. 17, 5.4

in-process research and development, Ch. 17, 5.5
intangible assets acquired, Ch. 17, 5.2
measuring the fair value of intangible assets, Ch. 17, 5.3
recognition of intangible assets acquired in a business combination, Ch. 17, 5.1
agile software development, Ch. 17, 6.2.6
amortisation of intangible assets, Ch. 17, 9
    assessing the useful life of an intangible asset as finite/indefinite, Ch. 17, 9.1
        factors affecting the useful life, Ch. 17, 9.1.1
        useful life of contractual/other legal rights, Ch. 17, 9.1.2
    impairment losses, Ch. 17, 9.4
    intangible assets with a finite useful life, Ch. 17, 9.2
        amortisation period and method, Ch. 17, 9.2.1
            amortisation of programme and other broadcast rights, Ch. 17, 9.2.1.B
            amortising customer relationships and similar intangible assets, Ch. 17, 9.2.1.A
        residual value, Ch. 17, 9.2.4
        revenue-based amortisation, Ch. 17, 9.2.2
        review of amortisation period and amortisation method, Ch. 17, 9.2.3
    intangible assets with an indefinite useful life, Ch. 17, 9.3
    retirements and disposals, Ch. 17, 9.5
        derecognition of parts of intangible assets, Ch. 17, 9.5.1
background, Ch. 17, 1.1
cloud computing, Ch. 17, 11.6
    implementation costs, Ch. 17, 11.6.2
    'software as a service' cloud computing arrangements, Ch. 17, 11.6.1
development phase, Ch. 17, 6.2.2
disclosure, Ch. 17, 10
    additional disclosures when the revaluation model is applied, Ch. 17, 10.4
    general disclosures, Ch. 17, 10.1
    profit/loss presentation, Ch. 17, 10.3
    of research and development expenditure, Ch. 17, 10.5
    statement of financial position presentation, Ch. 17, 10.2
first-time adoption, Ch. 5, 7.14
identifiability, Ch. 17, 2.1.1
    in relation to asset acquired in a business combination, Ch. 17, 5.1.3
impairment losses, Ch. 17, 9.4
intangible asset, definition, Ch. 17, 2.1–2.1.3
    control, Ch. 17, 2.1.2
    future economic benefits, Ch. 17, 2.1.3
    identifiability, Ch. 17, 2.1.1
internally generated intangible assets, Ch. 17, 6
    cost of an internally generated intangible asset, Ch. 17, 6.3
        determining the costs eligible for capitalisation, Ch. 17, 6.3.2
        establishing the time from which costs can be capitalised, Ch. 17, 6.3.1
    development phase, Ch. 17, 6.2.2
    internally generated brands, mastheads, publishing titles and customer lists, Ch. 17, 6.2.4
    internally generated goodwill, Ch. 17, 6.1
    pharmaceutical industry, research and development in, Ch. 17, 6.2.3

research phase, Ch. 17, 6.2.1
website costs (SIC-32), Ch. 17, 6.2.5
measurement, Ch. 17, 3.2
    asset exchanges, Ch. 17, 4.7.1
    assets acquired for contingent consideration, Ch. 17, 4.5
measurement after initial recognition, Ch. 17, 8
    cost model for measurement of intangible assets, Ch. 17, 8.1
    revaluation model for measurement of intangible assets, Ch. 17, 8.2
        accounting for revaluations, Ch. 17, 8.2.3
        frequency of revaluations, Ch. 17, 8.2.2
        revaluation is only allowed if there is an active market, Ch. 17, 8.2.1
objective, Ch. 17, 2
recognition, Ch. 17, 3.1
    assets acquired in a business combination, Ch. 17, 5.1
    of expense, Ch. 17, 7
        catalogues and other advertising costs, Ch. 17, 7.1
    programme and other broadcast rights, Ch. 17, 3.1.1
    separately acquired intangible assets, Ch. 17, 4.1
research and development in pharmaceutical industry, Ch. 17, 6.2.3
retirements and disposals, Ch. 17, 9.5
scope of, Ch. 17, 2
separate acquisition, Ch. 17, 4
    by way of government grant, Ch. 17, 4.6
    components of cost, Ch. 17, 4.2
    costs to be expensed, Ch. 17, 4.3
    exchanges of assets
        commercial substance, Ch. 17, 4.7.2
        measurement of assets exchanged, Ch. 17, 4.7.1
    income from incidental operations, Ch. 17, 4.4
    measurement of intangible assets acquired for contingent consideration, Ch. 17, 4.5
    recognition, Ch. 17, 4.1
specific regulatory and environmental issues regarding intangible assets, Ch. 17, 11
    accounting for green certificates/renewable energy certificates, Ch. 17, 11.3
    accounting for REACH costs, Ch. 17, 11.4
    crypto-assets, Ch. 17, 11.5
    emissions trading schemes, Ch. 17, 11.2
    rate-regulated activities, Ch. 17, 11.1
subsequent expenditure, Ch. 17, 3.3
terms used in, Ch. 17, 1.2

IAS 39–*Financial Instruments: Recognition and Measurement*, Ch. 44, 3. *See also* Financial instruments, recognition and initial measurement
    hedge accounting, Ch. 53, 1.3, 14
        requirements in IAS 39, Ch. 53, 14

IAS 40–*Investment Property*, Ch. 13, 4.3; Ch. 19, 1–12. *See also* Investment property
    cost model, Ch. 19, 7
    definitions, Ch. 19, 2
    disclosure requirements of, Ch. 19, 12
        for cost model, Ch. 19, 12.3
        direct operating expenses, Ch. 19, 12.1.3
        for fair value model, Ch. 19, 12.2
        level of aggregation for IFRS 13 disclosures, Ch. 19, 12.1.2

IAS 40–*Investment Property*—*contd*
  disclosure requirements of—*contd*
    methods and assumptions in fair value estimates, Ch. 19, 12.1.1
    presentation of changes in fair value, Ch. 19, 12.2.1
    presentation of sales proceeds, Ch. 19, 12.4
    under both fair value and cost models, Ch. 19, 12.1
    where fair value cannot be determined reliably, Ch. 19, 12.2.2
  disposal of, Ch. 19, 10
  fair value model, Ch. 19, 6
  held for sale, Ch. 19, 8
  initial measurement, Ch. 19, 4
  interim reporting, Ch. 19, 11
  measurement after initial recognition, Ch. 19, 5
  recognition, Ch. 19, 3
    business combination, Ch. 19, 3.3
      definition of business, Ch. 19, 3.3.1
    cost recognition, Ch. 19, 3.2
      allocation into parts, Ch. 19, 3.2.2
      repairs and maintenance, Ch. 19, 3.2.1
    expenditure prior to planning permissions/zoning consents, Ch. 19, 3.1
  scope, Ch. 19, 2
    group of assets leased out under a single operating lease, Ch. 19, 2.10
    investment property under construction, Ch. 19, 2.5
    land, Ch. 19, 2.2
    property held for own use ('owner-occupied'), Ch. 19, 2.4
    property held/under construction for sale in the ordinary course of business, Ch. 19, 2.6
    property interests held under a lease, Ch. 19, 2.1
    property leased to others, Ch. 19, 2.3
    property where rentals are determined by reference to the operations in the property, Ch. 19, 2.9
    property with dual uses, Ch. 19, 2.7
    property with the provision of ancillary services, Ch. 19, 2.8
  transfer of assets to/from investment property, Ch. 19, 9

IAS 41–*Agriculture*, Ch. 42, 1–5
  control, Ch. 42, 3.1.1
  definitions, Ch. 42, 2.2
    agriculture-related definitions, Ch. 42, 2.2.1
      bearer plants, Ch. 42, 2.2.1.A
    general definitions, Ch. 42, 2.2.2
  disclosure, Ch. 42, 5
    additional disclosures if fair value cannot be measured reliably, Ch. 42, 5.3
    fair value measurement disclosures, Ch. 42, 5.2
    government grants, Ch. 42, 5.4
    groups of biological assets, Ch. 42, 5.1.3
    income statement, Ch. 42, 5.1.2
    statement of financial position, Ch. 42, 5.1.1
      current *vs.* non-current classification, Ch. 42, 5.1.1.A
  government grants, Ch. 42, 3.3
  measurement, Ch. 42, 3.2
    agricultural produce, Ch. 42, 3.2.2
    biological assets within the scope of IAS 41, Ch. 42, 3.2.1
      initial and subsequent measurement, Ch. 42, 3.2.1.A
      subsequent expenditure, Ch. 42, 3.2.1.B
    gains and losses, Ch. 42, 3.2.4
    inability to measure fair value reliably, Ch. 42, 3.2.5
      cost model, Ch. 42, 3.2.5.B
      rebutting the presumption, Ch. 42, 3.2.5.A
    requirements for produce growing on a bearer plant, Ch. 42, 3.2.3
      agricultural produce growing on bearer plants, Ch. 42, 3.2.3.B
      requirements for bearer plants in the scope of IAS 16, Ch. 42, 3.2.3.A
  measurement of change, Ch. 42, 2.2.1
  measuring fair value less costs to sell, Ch. 42, 4
    determining costs to sell, Ch. 42, 4.4
    establishing what to measure, Ch. 42, 4.2
      grouping of assets, Ch. 42, 4.2.2
      unit of account, Ch. 42, 4.2.1
    interaction between IAS 41 and IFRS 13, Ch. 42, 4.1
    measuring fair value: IAS 41-specific requirements, Ch. 42, 4.5
      financing cash flows and taxation, Ch. 42, 4.5.5
      forward sales contracts, Ch. 42, 4.5.3
      obligation to re-establish a biological asset after harvest, Ch. 42, 4.5.2
      onerous contracts, Ch. 42, 4.5.4
      use of external independent valuers, Ch. 42, 4.5.1
    measuring fair value: overview of IFRS 13's requirements, Ch. 42, 4.6
      fair value measurement framework, Ch. 42, 4.6.1
      highest and best use and valuation premise, Ch. 42, 4.6.2
        biological assets attached to land, Ch. 42, 4.6.2.A
      selecting appropriate assumptions, Ch. 42, 4.6.3
        condition and location, Ch. 42, 4.6.3.A
      valuation techniques in IFRS 13, Ch. 42, 4.6.4
        cost as an approximation of fair value, Ch. 42, 4.6.4.A
    problem of measuring fair value for part-grown or immature biological assets, Ch. 42, 4.7
    when to measure fair value, Ch. 42, 4.3
  objective, Ch. 42, 2.1
  recognition, Ch. 42, 3.1
  scope, Ch. 42, 2.3
    agricultural produce before and after harvest, Ch. 42, 2.3.2
    bearer plants and produce growing on a bearer plant, Ch. 42, 2.3.3
    biological assets outside the scope of IAS 41, Ch. 42, 2.3.1
    concessions, Ch. 42, 2.3.6
    leases of biological assets (excluding bearer plants), Ch. 42, 2.3.5
    products that are the result of processing after harvest, Ch. 42, 2.3.4

Identifiable assets acquired in a business combination, Ch. 9, 5.2
  acquisition-date fair values of, Ch. 9, 5.3
  classifying, Ch. 9, 5.4
  intangible assets, Ch. 9, 5.5.2
  operating leases, recognising and measuring, Ch. 9, 5.5
  recognising, Ch. 9, 5

IFRIC 1–*Changes in Existing Decommissioning, Restoration and Similar Liabilities*, Ch. 26, 1.2.1, 6.3
  changes in estimated decommissioning costs, Ch. 26, 6.3.1

IFRIC 12–*Service Concession Arrangements*, Ch. 25, 1–7. *See also* Service concession arrangements
   accounting by the concession operator, financial asset and intangible asset models, Ch. 25, 4
      accounting for contractual payments to be made by an operator to a grantor, Ch. 25, 4.7
         under the financial asset model, Ch. 25, 4.7.2
         under the intangible asset model, Ch. 25, 4.7.3
         variable payments in a service concession, Ch. 25, 4.7.1
      accounting for residual interests, Ch. 25, 4.6
      allocating the consideration, Ch. 25, 4.1.1
         allocating the transaction price to the performance obligations in the contract, Ch. 25, 4.1.1.D
         determining the transaction price under the contract, Ch. 25, 4.1.1.C
         identifying the contract(s) with a customer, Ch. 25, 4.1.1.A
         identifying the performance obligations in the contract, Ch. 25, 4.1.1.B
      'bifurcation,' single arrangements that contain both financial and intangible assets, Ch. 25, 4.5
      determining the accounting model after the construction phase, Ch. 25, 4.1.2
      financial asset model, Ch. 25, 4.2
      intangible asset model, Ch. 25, 4.3
         amortisation of the intangible asset, Ch. 25, 4.3.1
         impairment during the construction phase, Ch. 25, 4.3.2
      revenue recognition implications of the two models, Ch. 25, 4.4
   application of IFRIC 12 and interactions with IFRS 15 and IFRS 9, Ch. 26, 6
   control model, Ch. 25, 3
      assets within scope, Ch. 25, 3.3
      control of the residual interest, Ch. 25, 3.2
      partially regulated assets, Ch. 25, 3.4
      regulation of services, Ch. 25, 3.1
   definitions, Ch. 25, 1.2
   disclosure requirements, SIC-29, Ch. 25, 7
   revenue and expenditure during the operations phase, Ch. 25, 5
      accounting for the operations phase, Ch. 25, 5.2
      additional construction and upgrade services, Ch. 25, 5.1
         subsequent construction services that are part of the initial infrastructure asset, Ch. 25, 5.1.1
         subsequent construction services that comprise additions to the initial infrastructure, Ch. 25, 5.1.2
      items provided to the operator by the grantor, Ch. 25, 5.3
   scope of IFRIC 12, Ch. 25, 2
      accounting by grantors, Ch. 25, 2.5
      arrangements that are not in the scope of IFRIC 12, Ch. 25, 2.2
         outsourcing arrangements, Ch. 25, 2.2.1
      interaction of IFRS 16 and IFRIC 12, Ch. 25, 2.3
      private-to-private arrangements, Ch. 25, 2.4
      public service nature of the obligation, Ch. 25, 2.1

IFRIC 14–IAS 19–*The Limit on a Defined Benefit Asset Minimum Funding Requirements and their Interaction*, Ch. 35, 8.2

IFRIC 16–*Hedges of a Net Investment in a Foreign Operation*, Ch. 7, 2.3; Ch. 15, 6.1.5. *See also* Net investment hedges

IFRIC 17–*Distributions of Non-cash Assets to Owners*, Ch. 7, 3.7; Ch. 8, 2.4.2
   demerger and, Ch. 7, 3.7
   measurement in, Ch. 7, 3.7.2; Ch. 8, 2.4.2.B
   recognition in, Ch. 7, 3.7.2; Ch. 8, 2.4.2.B
   scope of, Ch. 7, 3.7.1; Ch. 8, 2.4.2.A

IFRIC 19–*Extinguishing Financial Liabilities with Equity Instruments*, Ch. 5, 5.16; Ch. 47, 7
   effective date, Ch. 47, 7.1
   requirements, Ch. 47, 7.2
   scope, Ch. 47, 7.1

IFRIC 20–*Stripping Costs in the Production Phase of a Surface Mine*, Ch. 5, 5.19; Ch. 18, 3.1.6; Ch. 43, 15.5
   determining when production phase commences, Ch. 43, 15.5.2
   disclosures, Ch. 43, 15.5.6
   initial recognition, Ch. 43, 15.5.4
      allocating costs between inventory and the stripping activity asset, Ch. 43, 15.5.4.A
      identifying the component of the ore body, Ch. 43, 15.5.4.B
   recognition criteria-stripping activity asset, Ch. 43, 15.5.3
   scope of IFRIC 20, Ch. 43, 15.5.1
   subsequent measurement, Ch. 43, 15.5.5

IFRIC 21–*Levies*, Ch. 26, 6.8

IFRIC 22–*Foreign Currency Transactions and Advance Consideration*, Ch. 5, 5.22

IFRIC 23–*Uncertainty over Income Tax Treatments*, Ch. 33, 9
   changes to estimates of uncertain tax treatments, Ch. 38, 3.6
   events after the reporting period
      adjusting events, Ch. 38, 2.1.2
      non-adjusting events, Ch. 38, 2.1.3

IFRS 1–*First-time Adoption of International Financial Reporting Standards*, Ch. 5, 1–8. *See also* First-time adoption accounting policies and practical application issues, Ch. 5, 7
   authoritative literature, Ch. 5, 1.2
   borrowing costs, Ch. 5, 5.15
   compound financial instruments, Ch. 5, 5.10
   cumulative translation differences, Ch. 5, 5.7
   decommissioning liabilities included in the cost of property, plant and equipment, Ch. 5, 5.13
   deemed cost, Ch. 5, 5.5
   designation of contracts to buy or sell a non-financial item, Ch. 5, 5.23
   designation of previously recognised financial instruments, Ch. 5, 5.11
   disclosures, Ch. 5, 5.20.6.B, 6
   embedded derivatives, Ch. 5, 4.11
   employee benefits, Ch. 5, 7.7
   exceptions to retrospective application of other IFRSs, Ch. 5, 4
   estimates, Ch. 5, 4.2
   extinguishing financial liabilities with equity instruments, Ch. 5, 5.16
   fair value measurement of financial assets and liabilities at initial recognition, Ch. 5, 5.12
   financial assets or intangible assets accounted for in accordance with IFRIC 12, Ch. 5, 5.14

IFRS 1–*First-time Adoption of International Financial Reporting Standards*—contd
financial instruments under IFRS 9, classification and measurement of, Ch. 5, 4.9
first-time adopter, Ch. 5, 2
foreign currency transactions and advance consideration, Ch. 5, 5.22
future developments, Ch. 5, 1.4
government loans, Ch. 5, 4.12
hedge accounting, Ch. 5, 4.4–4.7
    in opening IFRS statement of financial position, Ch. 5, 4.5
    subsequent treatment, Ch. 5, 4.6
impairment of financial instruments, Ch. 5, 4.10
insurance contracts, Ch. 5, 4.13, 5.4
investment entities, Ch. 5, 5.9.5
investments in subsidiaries, joint ventures and associates, Ch. 5, 6.5.2
joint arrangements, Ch. 5, 5.18
leases, Ch. 5, 5.6, 7.5
non-controlling interests, Ch. 5, 4.8
objectives of, Ch. 5, 1.1
opening IFRS statement of financial position, Ch. 5, 3
    and accounting policies, Ch. 5, 3.2
    defined terms, Ch. 5, 1.3
    departures from full retrospective application, Ch. 5, 3.5
    fair value and deemed cost, Ch. 5, 3.3
    first-time adoption timeline, Ch. 5, 3.1
    hedge accounting in, Ch. 5, 4.5
    transitional provisions in other standards, Ch. 5, 3.4
optional exemptions from the requirements of certain IFRSs, Ch. 5, 5
    business combinations and acquisitions of associates and joint arrangements, Ch. 5, 5.2
        associates and joint arrangements, Ch. 5, 5.2.2.A
    business combinations and acquisitions of associates and joint ventures asset acquisitions, Ch. 5, 5.2.1.A
        assets and liabilities excluded, Ch. 5, 5.2.4.B
        assets and liabilities to be recognised in the opening IFRS statement of financial position, Ch. 5, 5.2.4
        classification of business combinations, Ch. 5, 5.2.3
        currency adjustments to goodwill, Ch. 5, 5.2.6
        deferred taxes and non-controlling interests, measurement of, Ch. 5, 5.2.9
        definition of a 'business' under IFRS 3, Ch. 5, 5.2.1
        derecognition of negative goodwill, Ch. 5, 5.2.5.B
        goodwill previously deducted from equity, Ch. 5, 5.2.5.C
        in-process research and development, Ch. 5, 5.2.4.D
        option to restate business combinations retrospectively, Ch. 5, 5.2.2
        previous GAAP carrying amount as deemed cost, Ch. 5, 5.2.4.C
        previously consolidated entities that are not subsidiaries, Ch. 5, 5.2.8
        previously unconsolidated subsidiaries, Ch. 5, 5.2.7
        prohibition of other adjustments of goodwill, Ch. 5, 5.2.5.A
        recognition and measurement requirements, Ch. 5, 5.2.4.F
        recognition of assets and liabilities, Ch. 5, 5.2.4.B
        restatement of goodwill, Ch. 5, 5.2.5
        subsequent measurement under IFRSs not based on cost, Ch. 5, 5.2.4.E
        transition accounting for contingent consideration, Ch. 5, 5.2.10
presentation and disclosure, Ch. 5, 6
    comparative information, Ch. 5, 6.1 designation of financial instruments, Ch. 5, 6.4
    disclosure of IFRS information before adoption of IFRSs, Ch. 5, 6.7
    disclosures regarding deemed cost use, Ch. 5, 6.5
        after severe hyperinflation, Ch. 5, 6.5.5
        for assets used in operations subject to rate regulation, Ch. 5, 6.5.4
        for investments in subsidiaries, joint ventures and associates, Ch. 5, 6.5.2
        for oil and gas assets, Ch. 5, 6.5.3
        use of fair value as deemed cost, Ch. 5, 6.5.1
    explanation of transition to IFRSs, Ch. 5, 6.3
        disclosure of reconciliations, Ch. 5, 6.3.1
        inclusion of IFRS 1 reconciliations by cross reference, Ch. 5, 6.3.4
        line-by-line reconciliations and detailed explanations, Ch. 5, 6.3.2
        recognition and reversal of impairments, Ch. 5, 6.3.3
        reconciliation by a first-time adopter that continues to publish previous GAAP financial statements, Ch. 5, 6.3.1.A
    interim financial reports, Ch. 5, 6.6
        disclosures in, Ch. 5, 6.6.2
        reconciliations in, Ch. 5, 6.6.1
regulatory deferral accounts, Ch. 5, 5.20
regulatory issues, Ch. 5, 8
revenue from contracts with customers (IFRS 15), Ch. 5, 5.21; Ch. 5, 7.6
severe hyperinflation, Ch. 5, 5.17
share-based payment transactions, Ch. 5, 5.3
stripping costs in the production phase of a surface mine, Ch. 5, 5.19

IFRS 2 – *Share-based payment*, Ch. 34, 1–16. *See also* Cash-settled share based payment transactions; Equity-settled share-based payment transactions; Share-based payment transactions; Vesting
awards entitled to dividends during the vesting period, Ch. 34, 15.3
awards vesting/exercisable on an exit event/change of control, Ch. 34, 15.4
    awards 'purchased for fair value', Ch. 34, 15.4.5
    awards requiring achievement of a minimum price on flotation/sale, Ch. 34, 15.4.4
    'drag along' and 'tag along' rights, Ch. 34, 15.4.6
    is flotation/sale a vesting condition or a non-vesting condition?, Ch. 34, 15.4.3
    grant date, Ch. 34, 15.4.1
    vesting period, Ch. 34, 15.4.2
business combination, replacement share-based payment awards issued, Ch. 34, 11
    acquiree award not replaced by acquirer, Ch. 34, 11.3
    background, Ch. 34, 11.1
    financial statements of the acquired entity, Ch. 34, 11.4
    replacement award, Ch. 34, 11.2

accounting for changes in vesting assumptions after the acquisition date, Ch. 34, 11.2.3
    acquiree awards that the acquirer is not 'obliged' to replace, Ch. 34, 11.2.2
    awards that the acquirer is 'obliged' to replace, Ch. 34, 11.2.1
cash-settled transactions, Ch. 34, 9
cost of awards, equity-settled transactions, Ch. 34, 5
development of IFRS 2, Ch. 34, 1.2
definitions, Ch. 34, 2.2.1
disclosures, Ch. 34, 13
equity-settled transactions
    allocation of expense, Ch. 34, 6
    cost of awards, Ch. 34, 5
    modification, cancellation and settlement, Ch. 34, 7
    overview, Ch. 34, 4
    valuation, Ch. 34, 8
first-time adoption, Ch. 34, 16.1
general recognition principles, Ch. 34, 3
grant date, Ch. 34, 5.3. *See also* Grant date
group share schemes, Ch. 34, 12. *See also* Group share schemes
loans to employees to purchase shares, Ch. 34, 15.2
market conditions, Ch. 34, 6.3
matching share awards, Ch. 34, 15.1
modification, cancellation and settlement of equity-settled transactions, Ch. 34, 7
non-compete agreements, Ch. 34, 3.2.3
Non-controlling interests in share-based payment transactions, Ch. 7, 5.1, 5.2, 5.6
objective of IFRS 2, Ch. 34, 2.1
overall approach of IFRS 2, Ch. 34, 1.4
    classification differences between IFRS 2 and IAS 32/IFRS 9, Ch. 34, 1.4.1
research project, Ch. 34, 1.2.1
scope, Ch. 34, 2.2
    definitions, Ch. 34, 2.2.1
    practical applications of scope requirements, Ch. 34, 2.2.4
        awards for which the counterparty has paid 'fair value', Ch. 34, 2.2.4.D
        awards with a foreign currency strike price, Ch. 34, 2.2.4.G
        cash bonus dependent on share price performance, Ch. 34, 2.2.4.E
        cash-settled awards based on an entity's 'enterprise value' or other formula, Ch. 34, 2.2.4.F
        equity-settled award of subsidiary with put option against the parent, Ch. 34, 2.2.4.B
        holding own shares to satisfy or 'hedge' awards, Ch. 34, 2.2.4.H
        increase in ownership interest with no change in number of shares held, Ch. 34, 2.2.4.C
        options over puttable instruments classified as equity under specific exception in IAS 32, Ch. 34, 2.2.4.J
        remuneration in non-equity shares and arrangements with put rights over equity shares, Ch. 34, 2.2.4.A
        shares/warrants issued in connection with a financial liability, Ch. 34, 2.2.4.I
        special discounts to certain categories of investor on a share issue, Ch. 34, 2.2.4.K
    transactions not within the scope of IFRS 2, Ch. 34, 2.2.3
        business combinations, Ch. 34, 2.2.3.C
        common control transactions and formation of joint arrangements, Ch. 34, 2.2.3.D
        transactions in financial assets outside the scope of IAS 32 and IFRS 9, Ch. 34, 2.2.3.F
        transactions in the scope of IAS 32 and IFRS 9, Ch. 34, 2.2.3.E
        transactions with shareholders in their capacity as such, Ch. 34, 2.2.3.A
        transfer of assets in group restructuring arrangements, Ch. 34, 2.2.3.B
    transactions within the scope of IFRS 2, Ch. 34, 2.2.2
        'all employee' share plans, Ch. 34, 2.2.2.D
        group schemes and transactions with group shareholders, Ch. 34, 2.2.2.A
        transactions where the identifiable consideration received appears to be less than the consideration given, Ch. 34, 2.2.2.C
        transactions with employee benefit trusts and similar vehicles, Ch. 34, 2.2.2.B
        vested transactions, Ch. 34, 2.2.2.E
South African black economic empowerment ('BEE') and similar arrangements, Ch. 34, 15.5
taxes related to share-based payment transactions, Ch. 34, 14
transactions with equity and cash alternatives, Ch. 34, 10
    awards requiring cash settlement in specific circumstances (awards with contingent cash settlement), Ch. 34, 10.3
        accounting for change in manner of settlement where award is contingent on future events outside the control of the entity and the counterparty, Ch. 34, 10.3.4
        cash settlement on a change of control, Ch. 34, 10.3.3
        cash-settled if contingency is outside entity's control, Ch. 34, 10.3.1
        cash-settled if contingency is outside entity's control and probable, Ch. 34, 10.3.2
        manner of settlement contingent on future events, Ch. 34, 10.3.5
    cash settlement alternative not based on share price/value, Ch. 34, 10.4
    transactions where the counterparty has choice of settlement, Ch. 34, 10.1
        accounting treatment, Ch. 34, 10.1.3
        'backstop' cash settlement rights, Ch. 34, 10.1.5
        cash-settlement alternative for employee introduced after grant date, Ch. 34, 10.1.4
        convertible bonds issued to acquire goods/services, Ch. 34, 10.1.6
        transactions in which the fair value is measured directly, Ch. 34, 10.1.1
        transactions in which the fair value is measured indirectly, Ch. 34, 10.1.2
    transactions where the entity has choice of settlement, Ch. 34, 10.2
        change in entity's settlement policy/intention leading to change in classification of award after grant date, Ch. 34, 10.2.3
        transactions treated as cash-settled, Ch. 34, 10.2.1
        transactions treated as equity-settled, Ch. 34, 10.2.2
valuation of equity-settled transactions, Ch. 34, 8
vesting conditions, Ch. 34, 3.1

IFRS 2 – *Share-based payment—contd*
   vesting conditions other than market conditions, Ch. 34, 6.2
   vesting period, Ch. 34, 3.3
IFRS 3–*Business Combinations*, Ch. 9, 1–16. *See also* Business combinations
   acquisition method of accounting, Ch. 9, 4
      acquisition date determination, Ch. 9, 4.2
      identifying the acquirer, Ch. 9, 4.1
         new entity formed to effect a business combination, Ch. 9, 4.1.1
         stapling arrangements, Ch. 9, 4.1.2
   assessing what is part of the exchange for the acquiree, Ch. 9, 11
      effective settlement of pre-existing relationships, Ch. 9, 11.1
      reimbursement for paying the acquirer's acquisition-related costs, Ch. 9, 11.3
      remuneration for future services of employees or former owners of the acquire, Ch. 9, 11.2
      restructuring plans, Ch. 9, 11.4
   bargain purchase transactions, Ch. 9, 10
   business combinations achieved in stages ('step acquisitions'), Ch. 9, 9
   consideration transferred, Ch. 9, 7
      acquisition-related costs, Ch. 9, 7.3
      business combinations achieved without the transfer of consideration, Ch. 9, 7.4
         business combinations by contract alone, Ch. 9, 7.4.1
      combinations involving mutual entities, Ch. 9, 7.5
      contingent consideration, Ch. 9, 7.1
         classification of a contingent consideration obligation, Ch. 9, 7.1.2
         initial recognition and measurement, Ch. 9, 7.1.1
         subsequent measurement and accounting, Ch. 9, 7.1.3
      replacement share-based payment awards, Ch. 9, 7; Ch. 34, 11.2, 11.3
   disclosures, Ch. 9, 16
      financial effects of adjustments recognised in the current reporting period, Ch. 9, 16.2
      illustrative example, Ch. 9, 16.4
      nature and financial effect of business combinations, Ch. 9, 16.1
         business combinations during the current reporting period, Ch. 9, 16.1.1
         business combinations effected after the end of the reporting period, Ch. 9, 16.1.2
   identifying a business combination, Ch. 9, 3.2.3
      definition of a business, Ch. 9, 3.2; Ch. 19, 3.3.1
         assessing whether an acquired process is substantive, Ch. 9, 3.2.4
         assessment whether acquired set of activities and assets constitutes a business, Ch. 9, 3.2.2
         'capable of' from the viewpoint of a market participant, Ch. 9, 3.2.5
         concentration test, Ch. 9, 3.2.3
         development stage entities, Ch. 9, 3.2.7
         identifying business combinations, Ch. 9, 3.2.6
         inputs, processes and outputs, Ch. 9, 3.2.1
   IFRS 3 (as revised in 2008) and subsequent amendments, Ch. 9, 1.1
      post-implementation review, Ch. 9, 1.1.1

   measurement period, Ch. 9, 12
      adjustments made after end of measurement period, Ch. 9, 12.2
      adjustments made during measurement period to provisional amounts, Ch. 9, 12.1
   push down accounting, Ch. 9, 15
   recognising and measuring goodwill or a gain in a bargain purchase, Ch. 9, 6
      subsequent accounting for goodwill, Ch. 9, 6.1
   recognising and measuring non-controlling interests, Ch. 7, 3.1.1, 3.1.2, 5, 6; Ch. 9, 8
      call and put options over non-controlling interests, Ch. 7, 6; Ch. 9, 8.5
      implications of method chosen for measuring non-controlling interests, Ch. 9, 8.3
      measuring qualifying non-controlling interests at acquisition-date fair value, Ch. 9, 8.1
      measuring qualifying non-controlling interests at the proportionate share of the value of net identifiable assets acquired, Ch. 9, 8.2
      measuring share-based payment and other components of non-controlling interests, Ch. 7, 5.1, 5.2, 5.6; Ch. 9, 8.4
   recognition and measurement of assets acquired, liabilities assumed and non-controlling interests, Ch. 9, 5, 5.5
      acquisition-date fair values of identifiable assets acquired and liabilities assumed, Ch. 9, 5.3
      classifying or designating identifiable assets acquired and liabilities assumed, Ch. 9, 5.4
      exceptions to recognition and/or measurement principles, Ch. 9, 5.6
         assets held for sale, Ch. 9, 5.6.6
         contingent liabilities, Ch. 9, 5.6.1; 9, 5.6.1.B
         employee benefits, Ch. 9, 5.6.3
         income taxes, Ch. 9, 5.6.2
         indemnification assets, Ch. 9, 5.6.4
         initial recognition and measurement, Ch. 9, 5.6.1.A
         insurance contracts within the scope of IFRS 17, Ch. 9, 5.6.9
         leases in which the acquiree is the lessee, Ch. 9, 5.6.8
         reacquired rights, Ch. 9, 5.6.5
         share-based payment transactions, Ch. 9, 5.6.7
      recognising and measuring particular assets acquired and liabilities assumed, Ch. 9, 5.5
         assembled workforce and other items that are not identifiable, Ch. 9, 5.5.4
         assets and liabilities related to contacts with customers, Ch. 9, 5.5.8
         assets that the acquirer does not intend to use or intends to use in a way that is different from other market participants, Ch. 9, 5.5.6
         assets with uncertain cash flows (valuation allowances), Ch. 9, 5.5.5
         combining an intangible asset with a related contract, identifiable asset or liability, Ch. 9, 5.5.2.C
         customer relationship intangible assets, Ch. 9, 5.5.2.B
         determining the fair values of intangible assets, Ch. 9, 5.5.2.F
         emission rights, Ch. 9, 5.5.2.E
         in-process research or development project expenditure, Ch. 9, 5.5.2.D

intangible assets, Ch. 9, 5.5.2.
investments in equity-accounted entities, Ch. 9, 5.5.7
items not qualifying as assets, Ch. 9, 5.5.4.B
operating leases in which the acquiree is the lessor, Ch. 9, 5.5.1
reacquired rights, Ch. 9, 5.5.3
recognising identifiable assets acquired and liabilities assumed, Ch. 9, 5.2
replacement awards in business combinations, Ch. 34, 11; Ch. 7, 5.2
reverse acquisitions, Ch. 9, 14
cash consideration, Ch. 9, 14.6
earnings per share, Ch. 9, 14.5
measuring goodwill, Ch. 9, 14.2
measuring the consideration transferred, Ch. 9, 14.1
non-controlling interest, Ch. 9, 14.4
preparation and presentation of consolidated financial statements, Ch. 9, 14.3
reverse acquisitions and acquirers that are not legal entities, Ch. 9, 14.9
reverse acquisitions involving a non-trading shell company, Ch. 9, 14.8
share-based payments, Ch. 9, 14.7
scope of IFRS 3, Ch. 9, 2
acquisition by an investment entity, Ch. 9, 2.3
arrangements out of scope of IFRS 3, Ch. 9, 2.2
acquisition of an asset or a group of assets that does not constitute a business, Ch. 9, 2.2.2, Ch. 19, 4.1.1
arrangements under common control, Ch. 9, 2.2.3
formation of a joint arrangement, Ch. 9, 2.2.1
mutual entities, Ch. 9, 2.1
subsequent measurement and accounting, Ch. 9, 13
IFRS 4–*Insurance Contracts*, Ch. 55, 1–12. *See also* Insurance contracts, IFRS 17
development of, Ch. 55, 1.2
objectives of, Ch. 55, 2
scope of, Ch. 55, 2.2
definitions, Ch. 55, 2.2.1
product classification process, Ch. 55, 2.2.4
transactions not within the scope of IFRS 4, Ch. 55, 2.2.3
assets and liabilities arising from employment benefit plans, Ch. 55, 2.2.3.B
contingent consideration payable/receivable in a business combination, Ch. 55, 2.2.3.E
contingent rights and obligations related to non-financial items, Ch. 55, 2.2.3.C
direct insurance contracts in which the entity is the policyholder, Ch. 55, 2.2.3.F
financial guarantee contracts, Ch. 55, 2.2.3.D
product warranties, Ch. 55, 2.2.3.A
transactions within the scope of IFRS 4, Ch. 55, 2.2.2
IFRS 5–*Non-current Assets Held for Sale and Discontinued Operations*, Ch. 4, 1–6. *See also* Discontinued operation
comparative information, Ch. 4, 4
treatment on cessation of classification as held for sale, Ch. 4, 4.2
treatment on initial classification as held for sale
statement of comprehensive income, Ch. 4, 4.1.1
statement of financial position, Ch. 4, 4.1.2
disclosure requirements, Ch. 4, 5
discontinued operation, Ch. 4, 3.2
definition of, Ch. 4, 3.1
presentation of, Ch. 4, 3.2
trading with continuing operations, Ch. 4, 3.3
future developments, Ch. 4, 6
interaction with IFRS 9, Ch. 51, 7.4
interaction of IFRS 12 and, Ch. 13, 2.2.1.C
non-current assets (and disposal groups) held for sale/distribution, Ch. 4, 2
classification, Ch. 4, 2.1, 2.1.1–2.1.3B
abandonment, Ch. 4, 2.1.2.C
classification as held for sale or as held for distribution to owners, Ch. 4, 2.1.2–2.1.2.C
concept of a disposal group, Ch. 4, 2.1.1
loss of control of a subsidiary, Ch. 4, 2.1.3.A; Ch. 7, 3.2, 3.7
meaning of available for immediate sale, Ch. 4, 2.1.2.A
meaning of highly probable, Ch. 4, 2.1.2.B
partial disposal of an associate or joint venture, Ch. 4, 2.1.3.B
partial disposals of operations, Ch. 4, 2.1.3
measurement, Ch. 4, 2.2
changes to a plan of sale/distribution, Ch. 4, 2.2.5
impairments and reversals of impairment, Ch. 4, 2.2.3
on initial classification as held for sale, Ch. 4, 2.2.2.A
presentation in the statement of financial position of, Ch. 4, 2.2.4
scope of the measurement requirements, Ch. 4, 2.2.1
subsequent remeasurement, Ch. 4, 2.2.2.B
objective and scope, Ch. 4, 1
IFRS 6–*Exploration for and Evaluation of Mineral Resources*, Ch. 43, 3. *See also* Extractive industries
disclosure, Ch. 43, 3.6
impairment, Ch. 43, 3.5
additional considerations if E&E assets are impaired, Ch. 43, 3.5.5
cash-generating units comprising successful and unsuccessful E&E projects, Ch. 43, 3.5.3
impairment testing 'triggers,' Ch. 43, 3.5.1
income statement treatment of E&E, Ch. 43, 3.5.6
order of impairment testing, Ch. 43, 3.5.4
reversal of impairment losses, Ch. 43, 3.5.7
specifying the level at which E&E assets are assessed for impairment, Ch. 43, 3.5.2
measurement of exploration and evaluation assets, Ch. 43, 3.3
capitalisation of borrowing costs, Ch. 43, 3.3.2
types of expenditure in, Ch. 43, 3.3.1
objective, Ch. 43, 3.1
presentation and classification, Ch. 43, 3.4
reclassification of E&E assets, Ch. 43, 3.4.1
recognition of exploration and evaluation assets, Ch. 43, 3.2
area-of-interest method, Ch. 43, 3.2.5
changes in accounting policies, Ch. 43, 3.2.6
developing an accounting policy under IFRS 6, Ch. 43, 3.2.1
full cost method, Ch. 43, 3.2.4
options for an exploration and evaluation policy, Ch. 43, 3.2.2
successful efforts method, Ch. 43, 3.2.3
scope, Ch. 43, 3.1
scope exclusions in other standards relating to the extractive industries, Ch. 43, 3.1.1

Index

IFRS 7–*Financial Instruments: Disclosures*, Ch. 44, 4, Ch. 54, 1–9
- disclosures, structuring, Ch. 54, 3
  - classes of financial instrument, Ch. 54, 3.3
  - level of detail, Ch. 54, 3.1
  - materiality, Ch. 54, 3.2
- future developments, Ch. 54, 9
- interim reports, Ch. 54, 2.3
- nature and extent of risks arising from financial instruments, Ch. 54, 5
  - credit risk, Ch. 54, 5.3
    - collateral and other credit enhancements obtained, Ch. 54, 5.3.5
    - credit risk exposure, Ch. 54, 5.3.4
    - credit risk management practices, Ch. 54, 5.3.2
    - illustrative disclosures, Ch. 54, 5.3.6
    - quantitative and qualitative information about amounts arising from expected credit losses, Ch. 54, 5.3.3
    - scope and objectives, Ch. 54, 5.3.1
  - liquidity risk, Ch. 54, 5.4
    - information provided to key management, Ch. 54, 5.4.1
    - management of associated liquidity risk, Ch. 54, 5.4.3
    - maturity analyses, Ch. 54, 5.4.2
    - puttable financial instruments classified as equity, Ch. 54, 5.4.4
  - market risk, Ch. 54, 5.5
    - 'basic' sensitivity analysis, Ch. 54, 5.5.1
    - other market risk disclosures, Ch. 54, 5.5.3
    - value-at-risk and similar analyses, Ch. 54, 5.5.2
  - qualitative disclosures, Ch. 54, 5.1
  - quantitative disclosures, Ch. 54, 5.2, 5.6
    - capital disclosures, Ch. 54, 5.6.3
    - concentrations of risk, Ch. 54, 5.6.1
    - operational risk, Ch. 54, 5.6.2
- presentation on the face of the financial statements and related disclosures, Ch. 54, 7
  - gains and losses recognised in other comprehensive income, Ch. 54, 7.2
  - gains and losses recognised in profit/loss embedded derivatives, Ch. 54, 7.1.4
    - entities whose share capital is not equity, Ch. 54, 7.1.5
    - further analysis of gains and losses recognised in profit/loss, Ch. 54, 7.1.2
    - offsetting and hedges, Ch. 54, 7.1.3
    - presentation on the face of the statement of comprehensive income (or income statement), Ch. 54, 7
  - statement of cash flows, Ch. 54, 7.5
  - statement of changes in equity, Ch. 54, 7.3
  - statement of financial position, Ch. 54, 7.4
    - assets and liabilities, Ch. 54, 7.4.3
    - convertible loans, Ch. 54, 7.4.4.B
    - current and non-current assets and liabilities, distinction between, Ch. 54, 7.4.4
    - debt with refinancing or roll over agreements, Ch. 54, 7.4.4.D
    - derivatives, Ch. 54, 7.4.4.A
    - disclosure requirements, Ch. 54, 7.4.2.C
    - enforceable legal right of set-off, Ch. 54, 7.4.1.A
    - entities whose share capital is not equity, Ch. 54, 7.4.6
    - equity, Ch. 54, 7.4.5
    - intention to settle net, Ch. 54, 7.4.1.C
    - loan covenants, Ch. 54, 7.4.4.E
    - long-term loans with repayment on demand terms, Ch. 54, 7.4.4.C
    - master netting agreements, Ch. 54, 7.4.1.B
    - objective, Ch. 54, 7.4.2.A
    - offsetting collateral amounts, Ch. 54, 7.4.1.F
    - offsetting financial assets and financial liabilities, Ch. 54, 7.4.1
    - offsetting financial assets and financial liabilities: disclosure, Ch. 54, 7.4.2
    - scope, Ch. 54, 7.4.2.B
    - situations where offset is not normally appropriate, Ch. 54, 7.4.1.D
    - unit of account, Ch. 54, 7.4.1.G
- significance of financial instruments for an entity's financial position/performance, Ch. 54, 4
  - accounting policies, Ch. 54, 4.1
  - business combinations, Ch. 54, 4.6
    - acquired receivables, Ch. 54, 4.6.1
    - contingent consideration and indemnification assets, Ch. 54, 4.6.2
  - fair values, Ch. 54, 4.5
    - day 1 profits, Ch. 54, 4.5.2
    - general disclosure requirements, Ch. 54, 4.5.1
  - hedge accounting, Ch. 54, 4.3
    - amount, timing and uncertainty of future cash flows, Ch. 54, 4.3.2
    - effects of hedge accounting on financial position and performance, Ch. 54, 4.3.3
    - option to designate a credit exposure as measured at fair value through profit/loss, Ch. 54, 4.3.4
    - risk management strategy, Ch. 54, 4.3.1
    - uncertainty arising from interest rate benchmark (or IBOR) reform, Ch. 54, 4.3.5
  - income, expenses, gains and losses, Ch. 54, 4.2
    - fee income and expense, Ch. 54, 4.2.3
    - gains and losses by measurement category, Ch. 54, 4.2.1
    - interest income and expense, Ch. 54, 4.2.2
  - statement of financial position, Ch. 54, 4.4
    - categories of financial assets and financial liabilities, Ch. 54, 4.4.1
    - collateral, Ch. 54, 4.4.6
    - compound financial instruments with multiple embedded derivatives, Ch. 54, 4.4.7
    - defaults and breaches of loans payable, Ch. 54, 4.4.8
    - financial assets designated as measured at fair value through profit/loss, Ch. 54, 4.4.3
    - financial liabilities designated at fair value through profit/loss, Ch. 54, 4.4.2
    - interests in associates and joint ventures accounted for in accordance with IFRS 9, Ch. 54, 4.4.9
    - investments in equity instruments designated at fair value through other comprehensive income (IFRS 9), Ch. 54, 4.4.4
    - reclassification, Ch. 54, 4.4.5
- transfers of financial assets, Ch. 54, 6
  - meaning of 'transfer,' Ch. 54, 6.1

transferred financial assets that are derecognised in their entirety, Ch. 54, 6.3
    disclosure requirements, Ch. 54, 6.3.2
    meaning of continuing involvement, Ch. 54, 6.3.1
transferred financial assets that are not derecognised in their entirety, Ch. 54, 6.2
transitional provisions, Ch. 54, 8

IFRS 8–*Operating Segments*, Ch. 36, 1–6. *See also* Operating segments; Reportable segments
  definition of an operating segment, Ch. 36, 3.1.3
    availability of discrete financial information, Ch. 36, 1.3
    'chief operating decision maker' and 'segment manager,' Ch. 36, 3.1.2
    equity accounted investment can be an operating segment, Ch. 36, 3.1.5
    revenue earning business activities, Ch. 36, 3.1.1
    when a single set of components is not immediately apparent, Ch. 36, 3.1.4
  entity-wide disclosures for all entities, Ch. 36, 6
    information about geographical areas, Ch. 36, 6.2
    information about major customers, Ch. 36, 6.3
      customers known to be under common control, Ch. 36, 6.3.1
    information about products and services, Ch. 36, 6.1
  externally reportable segments, identifying, Ch. 36, 3.2
    aggregation criteria, Ch. 36, 3.2.1
    'all other segments,' Ch. 36, 3.2.4
    combining small operating segments into a larger reportable segment, Ch. 36, 3.2.3
    'practical limit' for the number of reported operating segments, Ch. 36, 3.2.5
    restatement of segments reported in comparative periods, Ch. 36, 3.2.6
    quantitative thresholds, operating segments which are reportable because of their size, Ch. 36, 3.2.2
  features of IFRS 8, Ch. 36, 1.2
  measurement, Ch. 36, 4
  objective of IFRS 8, Ch. 36, 2.1
  reportable segments, information to be disclosed, Ch. 36, 5
    additional disclosures relating to segment assets, Ch. 36, 5.4
    disclosures required by IFRS 15, Ch. 36, 1.3
    disclosure of commercially sensitive information, Ch. 36, 5.8
    disclosure of other elements of revenue, income and expense, Ch. 36, 5.3
    explanation of the measurements used in segment reporting, Ch. 36, 5.5
    general information about reportable segments, Ch. 36, 5.1
      disclosure of how operating segments are aggregated, Ch. 36, 5.1.1
    measure of segment profit or loss, total assets and total liabilities, Ch. 36, 5.2
    reconciliations, Ch. 36, 5.6
    restatement of previously reported information, Ch. 36, 5.7
      changes in organisation structure, Ch. 36, 5.7.1
      changes in segment measures, Ch. 36, 5.7.2
  scope of IFRS 8, Ch. 36, 2.2

    consolidated financial statements presented with those of the parent, Ch. 36, 2.2.2
    entities providing segment information on a voluntary basis, Ch. 36, 2.2.3
    meaning of 'traded in a public market', Ch. 36, 2.2.1
  single set of operating segments, identifying, Ch. 36, 3
  terms used in IFRS 8, Ch. 36, 1.4
  transitional provisions, Ch. 36, 1.5

IFRS 9–*Financial Instruments*, Ch. 44, 5; Ch. 48, 1–9; Ch. 49, 1–3. *See also* Financial instruments, classification (IFRS 9); Financial instruments, hedge accounting (IFRS 9); Financial instruments, subsequent measurement (IFRS 9)
  amortised cost and the effective interest method, Ch. 50, 3
    fixed interest, fixed term instruments, Ch. 50, 3.2
    floating rate instruments, Ch. 50, 3.3
    inflation-linked debt, Ch. 50, 3.6
    modified financial assets and liabilities, Ch. 50, 3.8
    more complex financial liabilities, Ch. 50, 3.7
    perpetual debt instruments, Ch. 50, 3.5
    prepayment, call and similar options, Ch. 50, 3.4
      estimated cash flows, revisions to, Ch. 50, 3.4.1
  'business model' assessment, Ch. 48, 5
    applying in practice, Ch. 48, 5.6
    consolidated and subsidiary accounts, Ch. 48, 5.5
    hold to collect contractual cash flows, Ch. 48, 5.2
      impact of sales on the assessment, Ch. 48, 5.2.1
    hold to collect contractual cash flows and selling financial assets, Ch. 48, 5.3
    level at which the business model assessment is applied, Ch. 48, 5.1
    transferred financial assets that are not derecognised, Ch. 48, 5.2.2
  classification, Ch. 48, 2
  contractual cash flows, Ch. 48, 6
    auction rate securities, Ch. 48, 6.4.4
    bonds with a capped or floored interest rate, Ch. 48, 6.3.3
    contractual features that change the timing or amount, Ch. 48, 6.4.4
    contractually linked instruments, Ch. 48, 6.6
      assessing the characteristics of the underlying pool, Ch. 48, 6.6.1
      assessing the exposure to credit risk in the tranche held, Ch. 48, 6.6.2
      characteristics of underlying pool, assessing, Ch. 48, 6.6.1
      exposure to credit risk in the tranche held, assessing, Ch. 48, 6.6.2
    conventional subordination features, Ch. 48, 6.3.1
    convertible debt, Ch. 48, 6.4.5
    de minimis features, Ch. 48, 6.4.1.A
    debt covenants, Ch. 48, 6.4.4
    dual currency instruments, Ch. 48, 6.4.5
    five-year constant maturity bond, Ch. 48, 6.4.2
    fixed rate bond prepayable by the issuer at fair value, Ch. 48, 6.4.5
    full recourse loans secured by collateral, Ch. 48, 6.3.2
    interest rate period, Ch. 48, 6.4.2
    inverse floater, Ch. 48, 6.4.5
    investment in open-ended money market or debt funds, Ch. 48, 6.4.5

IFRS 9–*Financial Instruments*—contd
  contractual cash flows—*contd*
    lender has discretion to change the interest rate, Ch. 48, 6.3.4
    loan commitments, Ch. 48, 6.4.6
    meaning of 'interest,' Ch. 48, 6.2
    meaning of 'principal,' Ch. 48, 6.1
    modified time value of money component, Ch. 48, 6.4.2
    multiple of a benchmark interest rate, Ch. 48, 6.4.5
    non-genuine features, Ch. 48, 6.4.1.B
    non-recourse loans, Ch. 48, 6.5
    perpetual instruments with potentially deferrable coupons, Ch. 48, 6.4.5
    prepayment, asset originated at a premium of discount, Ch. 48, 6.4.4.B
    prepayment, negative compensation, Ch. 48, 6.4.4.A
    prepayment options, Ch. 48, 6.4.4
    regulated interest rates, Ch. 48, 6.4.3
    term extension options, Ch. 48, 6.4.4
    unleveraged inflation-linked bonds, Ch. 48, 6.3.5
    variable interest rate, Ch. 48, 6.4.4
  designation at fair value through profit or loss, Ch. 48, 7
  designation of contracts to buy or sell a non-financial item, Ch. 5, 5.23
  designation of non-derivative equity investments at fair value through other comprehensive income, Ch. 48, 8
  fair value option for own use contracts, Ch. 45, 4.2.6
  financial assets and liabilities held for trading, Ch. 48, 4
  financial assets classification, Ch. 48, 2
    debt instruments, Ch. 48, 2.1
    equity instruments and derivatives, Ch. 48, 2.2
  financial instruments within the scope of, Ch. 8, 4.4.5
  financial liabilities classification, Ch. 48, 3
  IFRS 4 applying IFRS 9 with, Ch. 55, 10
    interest rate benchmark reform Ch. 55, 10.1.6
    overlay approach, Ch. 55, 10.2
    temporary exemption from IFRS 9, Ch. 55, 10.1
  impairment
    approaches, Ch. 51, 3
      general approach, Ch. 51, 3.1
      purchased/originated credit-impaired financial assets, Ch. 51, 3.3
      simplified approach, Ch. 51, 3.2
    calculation of expected credit losses (ECLs), other matters, Ch. 51, 7
      Basel guidance on accounting for ECLs, Ch. 51, 7.1
      changes in ECL methodologies – errors, changes in estimates or changes in accounting policies, Ch. 51, 7.6
      Global Public Policy Committee (GPPC) guidance, Ch. 51, 7.2
      interaction between expected credit losses calculations and fair value hedge accounting, Ch. 51, 7.5
      interaction between the initial and subsequent measurement of debt instruments acquired in a business combination and the impairment model of IFRS 9, Ch. 51, 7.4
      measurement dates of ECLs, Ch. 51, 7.3
        date of derecognition and date of initial recognition, Ch. 51, 7.3.1
        trade date and settlement date accounting, Ch. 51, 7.3.2
    determining significant increases in credit risk, Ch. 51, 6
      change in the risk of a default occurring, Ch. 51, 6.1
      collective assessment, Ch. 51, 6.5
      definition of significant, Ch. 51, 6.3
      factors/indicators of changes in credit risk, Ch. 51, 6.2
      at initial recognition of an identical group of financial assets, Ch. 51, 6.6
      multiple scenarios for 'staging' assessment, Ch. 51, 6.7
      operational simplifications, Ch. 51, 6.4
    disclosures, Ch. 51, 15
    expected credit losses measurement
      credit enhancements: collateral and financial guarantees, Ch. 51, 5.8.1
      definition of default, Ch. 51, 5.1
      expected life *vs.* contractual period, Ch. 51, 5.5
      information about past events, current conditions and forecasts of future economic conditions, Ch. 51, 5.9.3
      lifetime expected credit losses, Ch. 51, 5.2
      12-month expected credit losses, Ch. 51, 6.4.3
      probability-weighted outcome, Ch. 51, 5.6
      reasonable and supportable information, Ch. 51, 5.9
      sources of information, Ch. 51, 5.9.2
      time value of money, Ch. 51, 5.7
      undue cost/effort, Ch. 51, 5.9.1
    financial assets measured at fair value through other comprehensive income, Ch. 51, 9
      debt instruments measured at fair value through other comprehensive income, Ch. 51, 9.1
    financial guarantee contracts, Ch. 51, 11
    Global Public Policy Committee guidance, Ch. 51, 7.2
    history and background, Ch. 51, 1.1
    IFRS Transition Resource Group for Impairment of Financial Instruments (ITG), Ch. 51, 1.5
    intercompany loans, Ch. 51, 13
      determining the ECLs, Ch. 51, 13.3
      repayable on demand, Ch. 51, 13.2
      scope, Ch. 51, 13.1
    key changes from the IAS 39 impairment requirements and the main implications of these changes, Ch. 51, 1.3
    key differences from the FASB's standard, Ch. 51, 1.4 lease receivables, Ch. 51, 10.2
    lease receivables, Ch. 51, 10.2
    loan commitments and financial guarantee contracts, Ch. 51, 11
    measurement dates of expected credit losses, Ch. 51, 7.3
      date of derecognition and date of initial recognition, Ch. 51, 7.3.1
      trade date and settlement date accounting, Ch. 51, 7.3.2
    modified financial assets, Ch. 51, 8
    other guidance on expected credit losses, Ch. 51, 1.6
    presentation of expected credit losses in the statement of financial position, Ch. 51, 14
      accumulated impairment amount for debt instruments measured at fair value through other comprehensive income, Ch. 51, 14.3

allowance for financial assets measured at amortised cost, contract assets and lease receivables, Ch. 51, 14.1
provisions for loan commitments and financial guarantee contracts, Ch. 51, 14.2
requirements, Ch. 51, 1.2
revolving credit facilities, Ch. 51, 12
scope, Ch. 51, 2
trade receivables, contract assets and lease receivables, Ch. 51, 10
lease receivables, Ch. 51, 10.2
trade receivables and contract assets, Ch. 51, 10.1
initial measurement, Ch. 49, 3
acquisition of a group of assets that does not constitute a business, Ch. 49, 3.3.5
assets and liabilities arising from loan commitments, Ch. 49, 3.7
loan commitments outside the scope of IFRS 9, Ch. 49, 3.7.1
loan commitments within the scope of IFRS 9, Ch. 49, 3.7.2
embedded derivatives and financial instrument hosts, Ch. 49, 3.5
general requirements, Ch. 49, 3.1
initial fair value and 'day 1' profits, Ch. 49, 3.3
financial guarantee contracts and off-market loan commitments, Ch. 49, 3.3.3
interest-free and low-interest long-term loans, Ch. 49, 3.3.1
loans and receivables acquired in a business combination, Ch. 49, 3.3.4
measurement of financial instruments following modification of contractual terms that leads to initial recognition of a new instrument, Ch. 49, 3.3.2
regular way transactions, Ch. 49, 3.6
trade receivables without a significant financing component, Ch. 49, 3.2
transaction costs, Ch. 49, 3.4
interests in associates and joint ventures accounted for in accordance with IFRS 9, Ch. 54, 4.4.9
reclassification of financial assets, Ch. 48, 9
recognition, Ch. 49, 2
general requirements, Ch. 49, 2.1
cash collateral, Ch. 49, 2.1.7
firm commitments to purchase/sell goods/services, Ch. 49, 2.1.2
forward contracts, Ch. 49, 2.1.3
option contracts, Ch. 49, 2.1.4
planned future/forecast transactions, Ch. 49, 2.1.5
principal *vs.* agent, Ch. 49, 2.1.8
receivables and payables, Ch. 49, 2.1.1
transfers of financial assets not qualifying for derecognition by transferor, Ch. 49, 2.1.6
'regular way' transactions, Ch. 49, 2.2
financial assets: general requirements, Ch. 49, 2.2.1
contracts not settled according to marketplace convention: derivatives, Ch. 49, 2.2.1.B
exercise of a derivative, Ch. 49, 2.2.1.D
multiple active markets: settlement provisions, Ch. 49, 2.2.1.C
no established market, Ch. 49, 2.2.1.A
financial liabilities, Ch. 49, 2.2.2
illustrative examples, Ch. 49, 2.2.5
settlement date accounting, Ch. 49, 2.2.4
trade date accounting, Ch. 49, 2.2.3

IFRS 10–*Consolidated Financial Statements*, Ch. 6, 1–11. *See also* Consolidated financial statements, consolidation procedures
continuous assessment, Ch. 6, 9
control, Ch. 6, 3
control of specified assets, Ch. 6, 8
development of IFRS 10, Ch. 6, 1.2
disclosure requirements, Ch. 6, 1.4
exposure to variable returns, Ch. 6, 5
future developments, Ch. 6, 11
investment entities, Ch. 6, 10
accounting by a parent of an investment entity, Ch. 6, 10.4
accounting by an investment entity, Ch. 6, 10.3
definition, Ch. 6, 10.1
determining whether an entity is an investment entity, Ch. 6, 10.2
earnings from investments, Ch. 6, 10.2.3
exit strategies, Ch. 6, 10.2.2
fair value measurement, Ch. 6, 10.2.4
having more than one investor, Ch. 6, 10.2.6
holding more than one investment, Ch. 6, 10.2.5
intermediate holding companies established for tax optimisation purposes, Ch. 6, 10.2.1.B
investment entity illustrative examples, Ch. 6, 10.2.9
investment-related services, Ch. 6, 10.2.1.A
multi-layered fund structures, Ch. 6, 10.2.10
ownership interests, Ch. 6, 10.2.8
unrelated investors, Ch. 6, 10.2.7
objective of, Ch. 6, 2.1
power and returns, principal-agency situations, Ch. 6, 6
application examples, Ch. 6, 6.6–6.7
delegated power: principals and agents, Ch. 6, 6.1
exposure to variability of returns from other interests, Ch. 6, 6.5
remuneration, Ch. 6, 6.4
rights held by other parties, Ch. 6, 6.3
scope of decision-making, Ch. 6, 6.2
power over an investee, Ch. 6, 4
contractual arrangements, Ch. 6, 4.4
determining whether sponsoring (designing) a structured entity gives power, Ch. 6, 4.6
existing rights, Ch. 6, 4.2
relevant activities, Ch. 6, 4.1
voting rights, Ch. 6, 4.3
related parties and de facto agents, Ch. 6, 7
scope, Ch. 6, 2.2
combined and carve-out financial statements, Ch. 6, 2.2.6
employee benefit plans and employee share trusts, Ch. 6, 2.2.2
entity no longer a parent at the end of the reporting period, Ch. 6, 2.2.4
exemption from preparing consolidated financial statements by an intermediate parent, Ch. 6, 2.2.1
interaction of IFRS 10 and EU law, Ch. 6, 2.2.5
investment entity exception, Ch. 6, 2.2.3

62 Index

IFRS 11–*Joint Arrangements*, Ch. 12, 1–10. *See also* Joint arrangements
  accounting for joint operations, Ch. 12, 6
    accounting for rights and obligations, Ch. 12, 6.2
    determining the relevant IFRS, Ch. 12, 6.3
    interest in a joint operation without joint control, Ch. 12, 6.4
    not structured through a separate vehicle, Ch. 12, 6.1
    in separate financial statements, Ch. 12, 6.7
    transactions between a joint operator and a joint operation, Ch. 12, 6.6
  accounting for joint ventures, Ch. 12, 7
    contributions of non-monetary assets to a joint venture, Ch. 12, 7.2
    interest in a joint venture without joint control, Ch. 12, 7.1
    in separate financial statements, Ch. 12, 7.3
  classification of, Ch. 12, 5
    accompanying IFRS 11, illustrative examples, Ch. 12, 5.5
    contractual terms, Ch. 12, 5.3
    facts and circumstances, Ch. 12, 5.4
    legal form of the separate vehicle, Ch. 12, 5.2
    separate vehicle or not, Ch. 12, 5.1
  continuous assessment, Ch. 12, 8
    changes in ownership of a joint arrangement that does not constitute a business, Ch. 12, 8.4
    changes in ownership of a joint operation, Ch. 12, 8.3
      acquisition of an interest in a joint operation, Ch. 12, 8.3.1
      disposal of interest in a joint operation, Ch. 12, 8.3.5
      former subsidiary becomes a joint operation, Ch. 7, 3.3.3, 7.2; Ch. 12, 8.3.3
      obtaining control or joint control over a joint operation that is a business, Ch. 12, 8.3.2
      other changes in ownership of a joint operation, Ch. 12, 8.3.4
    changes in ownership of a joint venture, Ch. 12, 8.2
      acquisition of an interest, Ch. 12, 8.2.1
      becomes a financial asset (or vice versa), Ch. 12, 8.2.5
      becomes an associate (or vice versa), Ch. 12, 8.2.4
      control over a joint venture, Ch. 12, 8.3.2
      disposal of interest in, Ch. 12, 8.2.6
      former subsidiary becomes a joint venture, Ch. 7, 3.3.2, 7.1; Ch. 12, 8.3.3
      interest in a joint venture held for sale, Ch. 12, 8.2.7
    when to reassess under IFRS 11, Ch. 12, 8.1
  disclosures, Ch. 12, 9
  future developments, Ch. 12, 10
  joint control, Ch. 12, 4
    practical issues with assessing, Ch. 12, 4.4
      evaluate multiple agreements together, Ch. 12, 4.4.2
      lease/joint arrangement, Ch. 12, 4.4.1
    relevant activities in sequential activities, Ch. 12, 4.1.1
    rights to control collectively, Ch. 12, 4.2
      delegated decision-making, Ch. 12, 4.2.4
      evidence of, Ch. 12, 4.2.3
      government, role of, Ch. 12, 4.2.6
      potential voting rights and joint control, Ch. 12, 4.2.2
      protective rights, including some veto rights, Ch. 12, 4.2.1
      related parties and de facto agents, Ch. 12, 4.2.5
    sequential activities in, Ch. 12, 4.1.1
    unanimous consent, Ch. 12, 4.3
      arbitration, Ch. 12, 4.3.3
      arrangements involving passive investors, Ch. 12, 4.3.1
      statutory mechanisms, Ch. 12, 4.3.4
      ultimate voting authority, Ch. 12, 4.3.2
  nature of joint arrangements, Ch. 12, 1.1
  objective, Ch. 12, 2.1
  scope, Ch. 12, 2.2
    accounting by a joint operation, Ch. 12, 2.2.3
    application by venture capital organisations and similar entities, Ch. 12, 2.2.1
    application to joint arrangements held for sale, Ch. 12, 2.2.2

IFRS 12–*Disclosure of Interests in Other Entities*, Ch. 13, 1–6. *See also* Disclosure of interests in other entities
  definitions, Ch. 13, 2.2.1
    interaction of IFRS 12 and IFRS 5, Ch. 13, 2.2.1.C
    interests in other entities, Ch. 13, 2.2.1.A
    structured entities, Ch. 13, 2.2.1, 2.2.1.B
  interests disclosed under, Ch. 13, 2.2.2
  interests not within the scope of, Ch. 13, 2.2.3
  joint arrangements and associates, Ch. 13, 5
    nature, extent and financial effects, Ch. 13, 5.1
    risks associated with, Ch. 13, 5.2
      commitments relating to joint ventures, Ch. 13, 5.2.1
      contingent liabilities relating to joint ventures and associates, Ch. 13, 5.2.2
    significant judgements and assumptions, Ch. 13, 3
  objective, Ch. 13, 2.1
  scope, Ch. 13, 2.2
  subsidiaries, Ch. 13, 4
    changes in ownership interests in subsidiaries, Ch. 13, 4.5
    composition of the group, Ch. 13, 4.1
    consolidated structured entities, nature of risks, Ch. 13, 4.4
      current intentions to provide financial or other support, Ch. 13, 4.4.4
      financial or other support to, with no contractual obligation, Ch. 13, 4.4.2
      terms of contractual arrangements, Ch. 13, 4.4.1
    nature and extent of significant restrictions, Ch. 13, 4.3
    non-controlling interests, Ch. 13, 4.2
  unconsolidated structured entities, Ch. 13, 6
    nature of interests, Ch. 13, 6.1
      nature, purpose, size, activities and financing of structured entities, Ch. 13, 6.1.1
      sponsored structured entities for which no interest is held at the reporting date, Ch. 13, 6.1.2
    nature of risks, Ch. 13, 6.2–6.3
      actual and intended financial and other support to structured entities, Ch. 13, 6.2.2
      disclosure of funding difficulties, Ch. 13, 6.3.6
      disclosure of liquidity arrangements, Ch. 13, 6.3.5
      disclosure of losses, Ch. 13, 6.3.2
      disclosure of ranking and amounts of potential losses, Ch. 13, 6.3.4
      disclosure of support, Ch. 13, 6.3.1
      disclosure of the forms of funding of an unconsolidated structured entity, Ch. 13, 6.3.7

disclosure of types of income received, Ch. 13, 6.3.3
maximum exposure to loss from those interests, Ch. 13, 6.2.1
IFRS 13–*Fair Value Measurement*, Ch. 14, 1–23. *See also* Fair value; Fair value measurement; Valuation techniques
asset/liability, Ch. 14, 5
  characteristics, Ch. 14, 5.2
    condition and location, Ch. 14, 5.2.1
    restrictions on assets or liabilities, Ch. 14, 5.2.2
  unit of account, Ch. 14, 5.1
    asset's (or liability's) components, Ch. 14, 5.1.4
    and portfolio exception, Ch. 14, 5.1.2
    and PxQ, Ch. 7, 3.3.2.F; Ch. 14, 5.1.1
    vs. valuation premise, Ch. 14, 5.1.3
convergence with US GAAP, Ch. 14, 22
  disclosures, Ch. 14, 22.2.4
    fair value of liabilities with demand feature, Ch. 14, 22.2.2
    practical expedient for alternative investments, Ch. 14, 22.2.1
    recognition of day-one gains and losses, Ch. 14, 22.2.3
definitions, Ch. 14, 3
development of, Ch. 14, 22.1
disclosures, Ch. 14, 20
  accounting policy, Ch. 14, 20.2
  objectives, Ch. 14, 20.1
    format of, Ch. 14, 20.1.1
    level of disaggregation, Ch. 14, 20.1.2
    'recurring' *vs.* 'non-recurring', Ch. 14, 20.1.3
  proposed amendments resulting from the Targeted Standards-level, Ch. 14, 20.6
  for recognised fair value measurements, Ch. 14, 20.3
    fair value hierarchy categorisation, Ch. 14, 20.3.3
    highest and best use, Ch. 14, 20.3.9
    level 3 reconciliation, Ch. 14, 20.3.6
    non-recurring fair value measurements, Ch. 14, 20.3.2
    recurring fair value measurements, Ch. 14, 20.3.1
    sensitivity of level 3 measurements to changes in significant unobservable inputs, Ch. 14, 20.3.8
    transfers between hierarchy levels for recurring fair value measurements, Ch. 14, 20.3.4
    of valuation processes for level 3 measurements, Ch. 14, 20.3.7
    valuation techniques and inputs, Ch. 14, 20.3.5
  regarding liabilities issued with an inseparable third-party credit enhancement, Ch. 14, 20.5
  for unrecognised fair value measurements, Ch. 14, 20.4
fair value framework, Ch. 14, 4
  definition, Ch. 14, 4.1
  measurement, Ch. 14, 4.2
financial assets and liabilities with offsetting positions, Ch. 14, 12
  criteria for using the portfolio approach for offsetting positions
    accounting policy considerations, Ch. 14, 12.1.1
    level 1 instruments in, Ch. 14, 12.1.4
    minimum level of offset, to use portfolio approach, Ch. 14, 12.1.3
    presentation considerations, Ch. 14, 12.1.2
  measuring fair value for offsetting positions
    exposure to market risks, Ch. 14, 12.2.1
    exposure to the credit risk of a particular counterparty, Ch. 14, 12.2.2
hierarchy, Ch. 14, 16
  categorisation within, Ch. 14, 16.2
    over-the-counter derivative instruments, Ch. 14, 16.2.4
    significance of inputs, assessing, Ch. 14, 16.2.1
    third-party pricing services/brokers, Ch. 14, 16.2.3
    transfers between levels within, Ch. 14, 16.2.2
IFRS 13, objective of, Ch. 14, 1.3
IFRS 13, overview, Ch. 14, 1.2
at initial recognition, Ch. 14, 13
  day one gains and losses, Ch. 14, 13.2
    losses for over-the-counter derivative transactions, Ch. 14, 13.2.1
    when entry and exit markets are the same, Ch. 14, 13.2.2
  exit price *vs.* entry price, Ch. 14, 13.1
  related party transactions, Ch. 14, 13.3
inputs to valuation techniques, Ch. 14, 15
  broker quotes and pricing services, Ch. 14, 15.5
  general principles, Ch. 14, 15.1
  premiums and discounts, Ch. 14, 15.2
    blockage factors (or block discounts), Ch. 14, 15.2.1
  pricing within the bid-ask spread bid-ask spread, Ch. 14, 15.3
    mid-market pricing, Ch. 14, 15.3.1
  risk premiums, Ch. 14, 15.4
level 1 inputs, Ch. 14, 17
  alternative pricing methods, Ch. 14, 17.2
  quoted prices in active markets that are not representative of, Ch. 14, 17.3
  unit of account, Ch. 14, 17.4
  use of, Ch. 14, 17.1
level 2 inputs, Ch. 14, 18
  examples of, Ch. 14, 18.2
  making adjustments to, Ch. 14, 18.4
  market corroborated inputs, Ch. 14, 18.3
  recently observed prices in an inactive market, Ch. 14, 18.5
level 3 inputs, Ch. 14, 19
  examples of, Ch. 14, 19.2
  use of, Ch. 14, 19.1
liabilities and an entity's own equity, application to, Ch. 14, 11
  financial liability with demand feature, Ch. 14, 11.5
  non-performance risk, Ch. 14, 11.3
    counterparty credit risk and its own credit risk, Ch. 14, 11.3.2
    derivative liabilities, Ch. 14, 11.3.4
    entity incorporate credit risk into the valuation of its derivative contracts, Ch. 14, 11.3.3
    with third-party credit enhancements, Ch. 14, 11.3.1
  not held by other parties as assets, Ch. 14, 11.2.2
  principles, Ch. 14, 11.1
    fair value of an entity's own equity, Ch. 14, 11.1.2
    fair value of a liability, Ch. 14, 11.1.1
    settlement value *vs.* transfer value, Ch. 14, 11.1.3
  restrictions preventing the transfer of, Ch. 14, 11.1
  that are held by other parties as assets, Ch. 14, 11.2.1
market participants, Ch. 14, 7

IFRS 13–*Fair Value Measurement*—*contd*
  market participants—*contd*
    assumptions, Ch. 14, 7.2
    characteristics, Ch. 14, 7.1
  measurement exception to the fair value principles for financial instruments, Ch. 14, 2.5.2
  non-financial assets, application to, Ch. 14, 10
    highest and best use, Ch. 14, 10.1
      vs. current use, Ch. 14, 10.1.2
      vs. intended use, Ch. 14, 10.1.3
      legally permissible, Ch. 14, 10.1.1
    valuation premise, Ch. 14, 10.2
      in combination with other assets and/or liabilities, Ch. 14, 10.2.2
      liabilities association, Ch. 14, 10.2.3
      stand-alone basis, Ch. 14, 10.2.1 unit of account *vs.*, Ch. 14, 10.2.4
  practical expedient in, Ch. 14, 2.5.1
  present value technique, Ch. 14, 21
    components of, Ch. 14, 21.2
      risk and uncertainty in, Ch. 14, 21.2.2
      time value of money, Ch. 14, 21.2.1
    discount rate adjustment technique, Ch. 14, 21.3
    expected present value technique, Ch. 14, 21.4
    general principles for use of, Ch. 14, 21.1
  price, Ch. 14, 9
    transaction costs, Ch. 14, 9.1
    transportation costs, Ch. 14, 9.2
  principal (or most advantageous) market, Ch. 14, 6
  scope, Ch. 14, 2
    exclusions, Ch. 14, 2.2
      disclosure requirements of IFRS 13, exemptions from, Ch. 14, 2.2.4
      lease transactions, Ch. 14, 2.2.2
      measurements similar to fair value, Ch. 14, 2.2.3
      share-based payments, Ch. 14, 2.2.1
    fair value measurement exceptions, Ch. 14, 2.4
    IFRS 13, items in, Ch. 14, 2.1
      fair value disclosures, Ch. 14, 2.1.1
      fair value measurements, Ch. 14, 2.1.2
      short-term receivables and payables, Ch. 14, 2.1.3
    practical expedient for impaired financial assets carried at amortised cost, Ch. 14, 2.4.2
    present value techniques, Ch. 14, 2.3
  transaction, Ch. 14, 8
    estimation, Ch. 14, 8.3
    identification, Ch. 14, 8.2
    volume and level of activity for an asset/liability, Ch. 14, 8.1
  unit of account, Ch. 14, 5
    asset's (or liability's) components, Ch. 14, 5.1.4
    level 1 assets and liabilities, Ch. 14, 17.4
    and portfolio exception, Ch. 14, 5.1.2
    and PxQ, Ch. 7, 3.3.2.F; Ch. 14, 5.1.1
    vs. valuation premise, Ch. 14, 5.1.3
  valuation techniques, Ch. 14, 14
    cost approach, Ch. 14, 14.3
    income approach, Ch. 14, 14.4
    market approach, Ch. 14, 14.2
    selecting appropriate, Ch. 14, 14.1
    making changes to valuation techniques, Ch. 14, 14.1.4
    single *vs.* multiple valuation techniques, Ch. 14, 14.1.1
    using multiple valuation techniques to measure fair value, Ch. 14, 14.1.2
    valuation adjustments, Ch. 14, 14.1.3

IFRS 14–*Regulatory Deferral Accounts*, Ch. 5, 5.20; Ch. 26, 5.4
  changes in accounting policies, Ch. 5, 5.20.5
  continuation of previous GAAP accounting policies, Ch. 5, 5.20.3
  defined terms, Ch. 5, 5.20.1
  disclosures, Ch. 5, 5.20.7
  interaction with other standards, Ch. 5, 5.20.8
  presentation, Ch. 5, 5.20.6
  recognition of regulatory deferral account balances, Ch. 5, 5.20.4
  scope, Ch. 5, 5.20.2

IFRS 15–*Revenue recognition*, Ch. 27, 1–4; Ch. 28, 1–3; Ch. 29, 1–3; Ch. 30, 1–11; Ch. 31, 1–5; Ch. 32, 1–4. *See also* Revenue recognition
  allocate the transaction price to the performance obligations, Ch. 29, 3
    allocating a discount, Ch. 29, 3.4
    allocating variable consideration, Ch. 29, 3.3
    allocation of transaction price to components outside the scope of IFRS 15, Ch. 29, 3.6
    applying the relative stand-alone selling price method, Ch. 29, 3.2
    changes in transaction price after contract inception, Ch. 29, 3.5
    determining stand-alone selling prices, Ch. 29, 3.1
      additional considerations for determining, Ch. 29, 3.1.4
      factors to consider when estimating, Ch. 29, 3.1.1
      measurement of options that are separate performance obligations, Ch. 29, 3.1.5
      possible estimation approaches, Ch. 29, 3.1.2
      updating estimated, Ch. 29, 3.1.3
    relative stand-alone selling price method, Ch. 29, 3.2
    variable consideration allocation, Ch. 29, 3.3
  definitions, Ch. 27, 2.2
  determine the transaction price, Ch. 29, 2
    changes in the transaction price, Ch. 29, 2.9
    consideration paid/payable to a customer, Ch. 29, 2.7
      classification of different types and measurement of, Ch. 29, 2.7.3
      determining who is an entity's customer when applying the requirements for consideration payable to a customer, Ch. 29, 2.7.1
      forms of, Ch. 29, 2.7.2
      timing of recognition of, Ch. 29, 2.7.4
    non-cash consideration, Ch. 29, 2.6
    non-refundable upfront fees, Ch. 29, 2.8
    refund liabilities, Ch. 29, 2.3
    rights of return, Ch. 29, 2.4
    significant financing component, Ch. 29, 2.5
      application questions on identifying and accounting for, Ch. 29, 2.5.2
      examples of, Ch. 29, 2.5.1

financial statement presentation of financing component, Ch. 29, 2.5.3
implementation questions on identifying and accounting for, Ch. 29, 2.5.2
variable consideration, Ch. 29, 2.2
constraining estimates of, Ch. 29, 2.2.3
estimating, Ch. 29, 2.2.2
forms, Ch. 29, 2.2.1
reassessment of, Ch. 29, 2.2.4
disposal of non-financial assets not in the ordinary course of business, Ch. 27, 4.3
sale of assets held for rental, Ch. 27, 4.3.1
extractive industries, Ch. 43, 12
income and distributable profits, Ch. 27, 4.1
interest and dividends, Ch. 27, 4.2
identify the contract with the customer, Ch. 28, 2
arrangements not meeting the definition of a contract under the standard, Ch. 28, 2.5
attributes of a contract, Ch. 28, 2.1
collectability, Ch. 28, 2.1.6
commercial substance, Ch. 28, 2.1.5
consideration of side agreements, Ch. 28, 2.1.1.C
each party's rights regarding the goods/services to be transferred can be identified, Ch. 28, 2.1.3
free trial period, Ch. 28, 2.1.1.B
master supply arrangements (MSA), Ch. 28, 2.1.1.A
parties have approved the contract and are committed to perform their respective obligations, Ch. 28, 2.1.2
payment terms can be identified, Ch. 28, 2.1.4
combining contracts, Ch. 28, 2.3
portfolio approach practical expedient, Ch. 28, 2.3.1
contract enforceability and termination clauses, Ch. 28, 2.2
consideration that was received from a customer, but not recognised as revenue, when contract is cancelled, accounting for, Ch. 28, 2.2.1 E
evaluating termination clauses, Ch. 28, 2.2.1.A
evaluating the contract term when an entity has a past practice of not enforcing termination payments, Ch. 28, 2.2.1.C
partial termination of a contract, accounting for, Ch. 28, 2.2.1.D
termination payments in determining the contract term, Ch. 28, 2.2.1.A
contract modifications, Ch. 28, 2.4
blend-and-extend, accounting for, Ch. 28, 2.4.3.F
decrease scope of the contract, Ch. 28, 2.4.3.E
marketing offer, Ch. 28, 2.4.3. D
not a separate contract, Ch. 28, 2.4.2
reassessing criteria if contract modified, Ch. 28, 2.4.3.B
represents a separate contract, Ch. 28, 2.4.1
identify the performance obligations in the contract, Ch. 28, 3
consignment arrangements, Ch. 28, 3.5
customer options for additional goods/services, Ch. 28, 3.6
accounting for the exercise of a material right, Ch. 28, 3.6.1.J
considering whether prospective volume discounts determined to be customer options are material rights, Ch. 28, 3.6.1.G
customer option as a separate performance obligation when there are no contractual penalties, Ch. 28, 3.6.1.D
customer options that provide a material right: evaluating whether there is a significant financing component, Ch. 28, 3.6.1.K
customer options that provide a material right: recognising revenue when there is no expiration date, Ch. 28, 3.6.1.L
Considering the class of customer when evaluating whether a customer option is a material right, Ch. 28, 3.6.1.F
Considering whether a loyalty or reward programme is a material right, Ch. 28, 3.6.1 I
Considering whether a renewal option is a material right, Ch. 28, 3.6.1.H
distinguishing between a customer option and variable consideration, Ch. 28, 3.6.1.C
nature of evaluation of customer options: quantitative *versus* qualitative, Ch. 28, 3.6.1.B
prospective volume discounts determined to be customer options are material rights, Ch. 28, 3.6.1.F
transactions to consider when assessing customer options for additional goods/services, Ch. 28, 3.6.1.A
volume rebates and/or discounts on goods or services: customer options *versus* variable consideration, Ch. 28, 3.6.1.E
determining when promises are performance obligations, Ch. 28, 3.2
determination of 'distinct,' Ch. 28, 3.2.1
examples, Ch. 28, 3.2.3
series of distinct goods and services that are substantially the same and have the same pattern of transfer, Ch. 28, 3.2.2
identifying the promised goods and services in the contract, Ch. 28, 3.1
principal *versus* agent considerations, Ch. 28, 3.4
control of the specified good/service, Ch. 28, 3.4.2
examples, Ch. 28, 3.4.4
identifying the specified good/service, Ch. 28, 3.4.1
recognising revenue as principal/agent, Ch. 28, 3.4.3
promised goods and services that are not distinct, Ch. 28, 3.3
sale of products with a right of return, Ch. 28, 3.7
interaction with IFRIC 12, Ch. 25, 6
licences of intellectual property, Ch. 31, 2
identifying performance obligations in a licensing arrangement, Ch. 31, 2.1
application questions on, Ch. 31, 2.1.5
contracts that grant both permission for past use of intellectual property and a licence to use the intellectual property in the future, Ch. 31, 2.1.5.B
contractual restrictions, Ch. 31, 2.1.3
guarantees to defend or maintain a patent, Ch. 31, 2.1.4

IFRS 15—*Revenue recognition—contd*
  licences of intellectual property—*contd*
    identifying performance obligations in a licensing arrangement—*contd*
      licences of intellectual property that are distinct, Ch. 31, 2.1.1
      licences of intellectual property that are not distinct, Ch. 31, 2.1.2
    licence renewals, Ch. 31, 2.4
    nature of the entity's promise in granting a licence, determining, Ch. 31, 2.2
      applying the licensing application guidance to a single (bundled) performance obligation that includes a licence of intellectual property, Ch. 31, 2.2.1
      sales-based/usage-based royalties on, Ch. 31, 2.5
        application questions on the sales-based or usage-based royalty recognition constraint, Ch. 31, 2.5.2
        transfer of control of licensed intellectual property, Ch. 31, 2.3
        recognition of royalties for a licence that provides a right to access intellectual property, Ch. 31, 2.5.1
        right to access, Ch. 31, 2.3.1
        right to use, Ch. 31, 2.3.2
        use and benefit requirement, Ch. 31, 2.3.3
  objective, Ch. 27, 2
    contract costs, Ch. 31, 5
      amortisation of capitalised costs, Ch. 31, 5.3
      costs to obtain a contract, Ch. 31, 5.1
      costs to fulfil a contract, Ch. 31, 5.2
      impairment of capitalised costs, Ch. 31, 5.4
    onerous contracts, Ch. 31, 4
    warranties, Ch. 31, 3
      assurance-type warranty, Ch. 31, 3.3
      contracts that contain both assurance and service-type warranties, Ch. 31, 3.4
      service-type warranties, Ch. 31, 3.2
  overview, Ch. 27, 2.1
  presentation and disclosure
    disclosure objective and general requirements, Ch. 32, 3.1
    disclosures in interim financial statements, Ch. 32, 4
    presentation requirements for, Ch. 32, 2.2
      presentation of income outside the scope of IFRS 15, Ch. 32, 2.2.1
    presentation requirements for contract assets and contract liabilities, Ch. 32, 2.1
      application questions on presentation of contract assets and liabilities, Ch. 32, 2.1.6
    specific disclosure requirements, Ch. 32, 3.2
      assets recognised from the costs to obtain or fulfil a contract, Ch. 32, 3.2.3
      contracts with customers, Ch. 32, 3.2.1
        contract balances, Ch. 32, 3.2.1.B
        disaggregation of revenue, Ch. 32, 3.2.1.A
        performance obligations, Ch. 32, 3.2.1.C
        use of 'backlog' practical expedient when criteria to use 'right to invoice' expedient are not met, Ch. 32, 3.2.1.D
      practical expedients, Ch. 32, 3.2.4
      significant judgements, Ch. 32, 3.2.2
        timing of satisfaction of performance obligations, Ch. 32, 3.2.2.A
        transaction price and the amounts allocated to performance obligations, Ch. 32, 3.2.2.B
  satisfaction of performance obligations, Ch. 30, 1-11
    bill-and-hold arrangements, Ch. 30, 7
    breakage and prepayments for future goods/services, Ch. 30, 11
    consignment arrangements, Ch. 30, 6
    control transferred at a point in time, Ch. 30, 4
      customer acceptance, Ch. 30, 4.2
      effect of shipping terms when an entity has transferred control of a good to a customer, Ch. 30, 4.1
    over time, Ch. 30, 2
      asset with no alternative use and right to payment, Ch. 30, 2.3
        enforceable right to payment for performance completed to date, Ch. 30, 2.3.2
        considerations when assessing the over-time criteria for the sale of a real estate unit, Ch. 30, 2.3.2.F
        determining whether an entity has an enforceable right to payment, Ch. 30, 2.3.2.A
        determining whether an entity has an enforceable right to payment for a contract priced at a loss, Ch. 30, 2.3.2.D
        enforceable right to payment: contemplating consideration an entity might receive from the potential resale of the asset, Ch. 30, 2.3.2.G
        enforceable right to payment determination when not entitled to a reasonable profit margin on standard inventory materials purchased, but not yet used, Ch. 30, 2.3.2.E
        enforceable right to payment: does an entity need a present unconditional right to payment, Ch. 30, 2.3.2.B
        enforceable right to payment: non-refundable upfront payments that represent the full transaction price, Ch. 30, 2.3.2.C
      no alternative use, Ch. 30, 2.3.1
      customer controls asset as it is created/enhanced, Ch. 30, 2.2
      customer simultaneously receives and consumes benefits as the entity performs, Ch. 30, 2.1
      measuring progress over time, Ch. 30, 3
        application questions, Ch. 30, 3.4
        examples, Ch. 30, 3.3
        input methods, Ch. 30, 3.2
        output methods, Ch. 30, 3.1
  recognising revenue for customer options for additional goods and services, Ch. 30, 10
  recognising revenue for licences of intellectual property, Ch. 30, 8
  recognising revenue when a right of return exists, Ch. 30, 9
  repurchase agreements, Ch. 30, 5
    forward/call option held by the entity, Ch. 30, 5.1
    put option held by the customer, Ch. 30, 5.2
    sales with residual value guarantees, Ch. 30, 5.3
  regulatory assets and liabilities, Ch. 27, 4.4
  scope, Ch. 27, 3

collaborative arrangements, Ch. 27, 3.4
definition of customer, Ch. 27, 3.3
interaction with other standards, Ch. 27, 3.5
    certain fee-generating activities of financial institutions, Ch. 27, 3.5.1.B
    contributions, Ch. 27, 3.5.1.E
    credit card arrangements, Ch. 27, 3.5.1.C
    credit card-holder rewards programmes, Ch. 27, 3.5.1.D
    determining whether IFRS 10 or IFRS 15 applies to the sale of a corporate wrapper to a customer, Ch. 7, 3.2.1; Ch. 27, 3.5.1.J
    equity instruments issued by an entity to a customer in connection with a revenue arrangement, Ch. 27, 3.5.1.L
    fixed-odds wagering contracts, Ch. 27, 3.5.1.F
    Islamic financing transactions, Ch. 27, 3.5.1.A
    prepaid gift cards, Ch. 27, 3.5.1.I
    pre-production activities related to long-term supply arrangements, Ch. 27, 3.5.1.G
    revenue arising from an interest in a joint operation, Ch. 27, 3.5.1.K
    sales of by-products or scrap materials, Ch. 27, 3.5.1.H
rights and obligations within, Ch. 45, 3.13

IFRS 16–Leases, Ch. 23, 1–10. *See also* Leases (IFRS 16)
business combinations, Ch. 23, 9, 10.5.2
    acquiree in a business combination is a lessee, Ch. 23, 9.1
    acquiree in a business combination is a lessor, Ch. 23, 9.2
commencement date of the lease, Ch. 23, 4.2
definition, Ch. 23, 3
    contract combinations, Ch. 23, 3.3
    determining whether an arrangement contains a lease, Ch. 23, 3.1
    identifying and separating lease and non-lease components of a contract, Ch. 23, 3.2
discount rates, Ch. 23, 4.6
    determination of the incremental borrowing rate by a subsidiary with centralised treasury functions, Ch. 23, 4.6.1
economic life, Ch. 23, 4.8
effective date and transition, Ch. 23, 10
    amounts previously recognised in a business combination, Ch. 23, 10.5.2
    disclosure, Ch. 23, 10.6
    effective date, Ch. 23, 10.1; Ch. 54, 8.4
    lessee transition, Ch. 23, 10.3
        full retrospective approach, Ch. 23, 10.3.1
        modified retrospective approach, Ch. 23, 10.3.2
            leases previously classified as operating leases, Ch. 23, 10.3.2.A
            leases previously classified as finance leases, Ch. 23, 10.3.2.C
            separating and allocating lease and non-lease components of a contract upon transition, Ch. 23, 10.3.2.B
        lessor transition, Ch. 23, 10.4
            subleases, Ch. 23, 10.4.1
    references to IFRS 9, Ch. 23, 10.5.3
    sale and leaseback transactions, Ch. 23, 10.5.1
    transition, Ch. 23, 10.2
fair value, Ch. 23, 4.9
inception of the lease (inception date), Ch. 23, 4.1
initial direct costs, Ch. 23, 4.7; Ch. 19, 4.9.2
    directly attributable costs other than initial direct costs incurred by lessees, Ch. 23, 4.7.1
lease liabilities under IFRS 16, Ch. 20, 4.1.2
lease payments, Ch. 23, 4.5
    amounts expected to be payable under residual value guarantees– lessees only, Ch. 23, 4.5.6
    amounts payable under residual value guarantees–lessors only, Ch. 23, 4.5.7
    exercise price of a purchase option, Ch. 23, 4.5.4 in-substance fixed lease payments, Ch. 23, 4.5.1
    lease incentives, Ch. 23, 4.5.2; Ch. 19, 4.9.1
        presentation in the statement of cash flows, Ch. 40, 5.5.3
    payments for penalties for terminating a lease, Ch. 23, 4.5.5
    reassessment of the lease liability, Ch. 23, 4.5.9
    remeasurement by lessors, Ch. 23, 4.5.13
    security deposits, Ch. 23, 4.5.9
    value added tax and property taxes, Ch. 23, 4.5.10
    variable lease payments that depend on an index/rate, Ch. 23, 4.5.3
    variable lease payments which do not depend on an index or rate, Ch. 23, 4.5.8
lease term and purchase options, Ch. 23, 4.4
    cancellable leases, Ch. 23, 4.4.1
    reassessment of lease term and purchase options–lessees, Ch. 23, 4.4.2
    reassessment of lease term and purchase options–lessors, Ch. 23, 4.4.3
lessee accounting, Ch. 23, 5
    disclosure, Ch. 23, 5.8
        additional, Ch. 23, 5.8.3
        of assets, liabilities, expenses and cash flows, Ch. 23, 5.8.2
        objective, Ch. 23, 5.8.1
    initial measurement, Ch. 23, 5.2
        lease liabilities, Ch. 23, 5.2.2
        right-of-use assets, Ch. 23, 5.2.1
    initial recognition, Ch. 23, 5.1
        leases of low-value assets, Ch. 23, 5.1.2
        short-term leases, Ch. 23, 5.1.1
    lease modifications, Ch. 23, 5.5
        amendment to IFRS 16 for covid-19 related rent concessions, Ch. 23, 5.5.4
        application of lease modification guidance to rent concessions, Ch. 23, 5.5.3
        determining whether a lease modification results in a separate lease, Ch. 23, 5.5.1
        lessee accounting for a modification that does not result in a separate lease, Ch. 23, 5.5.2
    lessee matters, Ch. 23, 5.6
        impairment of right-of-use assets, Ch. 23, 5.6.1
        income tax accounting, Ch. 23, 5.6.4
        leases denominated in a foreign currency, Ch. 23, 5.6.2
        portfolio approach, Ch. 23, 5.6.3
    presentation, Ch. 23, 5.7
    remeasurement of lease liabilities and right-of-use assets, Ch. 23, 5.4

IFRS 16–*Leases*—*contd*
- lessee accounting—*contd*
  - subsequent measurement, Ch. 23, 5.3
    - expense recognition, Ch. 23, 5.3.3
    - lease liabilities, Ch. 23, 5.3.2
    - right-of-use assets, Ch. 23, 5.3.1
- lessee involvement with the underlying asset before the commencement date, Ch. 23, 4.3
- lessor accounting, Ch. 23, 6
  - cash flows, Ch. 40, 5.5.5
  - disclosure, Ch. 23, 6.7
    - for all lessors, Ch. 23, 6.7.2
    - for finance leases, Ch. 23, 6.7.3
    - objective, Ch. 23, 6.7.1
    - for operating leases, Ch. 23, 6.7.4
  - finance leases, Ch. 23, 6.2
    - initial measurement, Ch. 23, 6.2.1
    - manufacturer/dealer lessors, Ch. 23, 6.2.2
    - remeasurement of the net investment in the lease, Ch. 23, 6.2.4
    - subsequent measurement, Ch. 23, 6.2.3
    - unguaranteed residual values, Ch. 23, 6.2.3.A
  - lease classification, Ch. 23, 6.1
    - criteria, Ch. 23, 6.1.1
    - reassessment of, Ch. 23, 6.1.4
    - residual value guarantees included in the lease classification test, Ch. 23, 6.1.3
    - test for land and buildings, Ch. 23, 6.1.2
  - lease modifications, Ch. 23, 6.4
    - determining whether a modification to a finance lease results in a separate lease, Ch. 23, 6.4.1
    - lessor accounting for a modification to a finance lease that does not result in a separate lease, Ch. 23, 6.4.2
    - modification to an operating lease, Ch. 23, 6.4.3
  - lessor matters, Ch. 23, 6.5
    - portfolio approach, Ch. 23, 6.5
  - operating leases, Ch. 23, 6.3
    - income, Ch. 23, 6.3.1
  - presentation, Ch. 23, 6.6
- objective, Ch. 23, 2.1
- recognition exemptions, Ch. 23, 2.3
- sale and leaseback transactions, Ch. 23, 8
  - determining whether the transfer of an asset is a sale, Ch. 23, 8.1
  - disclosures, Ch. 23, 8.4
  - transactions in which the transfer of an asset is a sale, Ch. 23, 8.2
    - accounting for the leaseback, Ch. 23, 8.2.2
    - accounting for the sale, Ch. 23, 8.2.1
    - adjustment for off-market terms, Ch. 23, 8.2.3
  - transactions in which the transfer of an asset is not a sale, Ch. 23, 8.3
- scope, Ch. 23, 2.2
- service concession arrangements, Ch. 25, 2.3
- subleases, Ch. 23, 7
  - definition, Ch. 23, 7.1
  - disclosure, Ch. 23, 7.5
  - intermediate lessor accounting, Ch. 23, 7.2
  - presentation, Ch. 23, 7.4
  - sublessee accounting, Ch. 23, 7.3

IFRS 17-**Insurance contracts**, Ch. 56. *See also* Insurance contracts
- acquisitions of insurance contracts, Ch. 56, 13
  - cash flows acquired in a business combination within the scope of IFRS 3, Ch. 56, 13.1
  - common control business combinations, Ch. 56, 13.3
  - practical issues, Ch. 56, 13.4
  - subsequent treatment of contracts acquired in their settlement period, Ch. 56, 13.2
- definitions in IFRS 17, Ch. 56, 2.2
- derecognition, Ch. 56, 12.2
  - accounting for, Ch. 56, 12.3
- disclosure, Ch. 56, 16
  - accounting policies, Ch. 56, 16.4
  - explanation of recognised amounts, Ch. 56, 16.1
  - nature and extent of risks arising from contracts within the scope of IFRS 17, Ch. 56, 16.5
  - significant judgements in applying IFRS 17, Ch. 56, 16.3
  - transition amounts, Ch. 56, 16.2
- effective date and transition, Ch. 56, 17
  - effective date, Ch. 56, 17.1
  - entities that have not previously applied IFRS 9, Ch. 56, 17.7
  - fair value approach, Ch. 56, 17.5
  - modified retrospective approach, Ch. 56, 17.4
  - redesignation of financial assets – IFRS 9 previously applied, Ch. 56, 17.6
  - retrospective application of transition, Ch. 56, 17.3
  - transition, Ch. 56, 17.2
    - disclosures about the effect of, Ch. 56, 17.2.2
- impairment of insurance acquisition cash flows, Ch. 56, 8.10
- insurance contract definition, Ch. 56, 3
  - changes in the level of insurance risk, Ch. 56, 3.6
  - the definition, Ch. 56, 3.1
  - insurance and non-insurance contracts, Ch. 56, 3.7
  - insurance risk *vs.* financial risk, Ch. 56, 3.4
  - payments in kind, Ch. 56, 3.3
  - significant insurance risk, Ch. 56, 3.5
  - uncertain future events, Ch. 56, 3.2
- initial recognition, Ch. 56, 6
  - insurance acquisition cash flows as assets, Ch. 56, 6.3
- investment components, Ch. 56, 4.2
  - definition, Ch. 56, 4.2.1
  - separability of, Ch. 56, 4.2.2
  - measurement, Ch. 56, 4.2.3
  - investment-return service, Ch. 56, 8.7.2
- level of aggregation, Ch. 56, 5
  - identifying groups according to expected profitability, Ch. 56, 5.2
  - identifying groups for contracts applying the premium allocation approach, Ch. 56, 5.3
  - identifying portfolios, Ch. 56, 5.1
- measurement
  - contracts with participation features, Ch. 56, 11
    - cash flows that affect or are affected by cash flows to policyholders of other contracts (mutualisation), Ch. 56, 11.1
    - direct participation features, Ch. 56, 11.2
      - allocation of the contractual service margin to profit or loss, Ch. 56, 11.2.4
      - definition, Ch. 56, 11.2.1
      - disaggregation of finance income or expense between profit or loss and other comprehensive income, Ch. 56, 11.2.6

measurement of CSM using variable fee approach, Ch. 56, 11.2.3
risk adjustment for non-financial risk using the variable fee approach, Ch. 56, 11.2.2
risk mitigation, Ch. 56, 11.2.5
general model, Ch. 56, 8
allocation of the contractual service margin to profit or loss, Ch. 56, 8.7
contract boundary, Ch. 56, 8.1
acquisition cash flows paid on an initially written contract, Ch. 56, 8.1.4
constraints or limitations relevant in assessing repricing, Ch. 56, 8.1.2
contracts between an entity and customers of an association or bank, Ch. 56, 8.1.3
issues related to reinsurance contracts held, Ch. 56, 8.1.5
options to add insurance coverage, Ch. 56, 8.1.1
contractual service margin (CSM), Ch. 56, 8.5
allocation to profit or loss, Ch. 56, 8.7
discount rates, Ch. 56, 8.3
estimates of expected future cash flows, Ch. 56, 8.2
contract boundary, Ch. 56, 8.2.4
excluded from the contract boundary, Ch. 56, 8.2.4
market and non-market variables, Ch. 56, 8.2.1
using current estimates, Ch. 56, 8.2.2
within the contract boundary, Ch. 56, 8.2.3
impairment of assets recognised for insurance acquisition cash flows, Ch. 56, 8.10
insurance contracts issued by mutual entities, Ch. 56, 8.11
onerous contracts, Ch. 56, 8.8
other matters, Ch. 56, 8.12
impairment of insurance receivables, Ch. 56, 8.12.1
policyholder loans, Ch. 56, 8.12.2
reinsurance contracts issued, Ch. 56, 8.9
accounting for ceding commissions and reinstatement premiums, Ch. 56, 8.9.3
boundary of, Ch. 56, 8.9.1
determining the quantity of benefits for identifying coverage units, Ch. 56, 8.9.4
issued adverse loss development covers, Ch. 56, 8.9.2
risk adjustment for non-financial risk, Ch. 56, 8.4
consideration of reinsurance held, Ch. 56, 8.4.3
level, Ch. 56, 8.4.2
statement of comprehensive income, Ch. 56, 8.4.4
techniques, Ch. 56, 8.4.1
subsequent measurement, Ch. 56, 8.6
of CSM (for contracts without direct participation features), Ch. 56, 8.6.3
liability for incurred claims, Ch. 56, 8.6.2
liability for remaining coverage, Ch. 56, 8.6.1
investment contracts with discretionary participation features, Ch. 56, 11.3
contracts with switching features, Ch. 56, 11.3.1
overview of measurement, Ch. 56, 7

insurance contracts in a foreign currency, Ch. 56, 7.3
modifications to the general model, Ch. 56, 7.2
overview of general model, Ch. 56, 7.1
premium allocation approach, Ch. 56, 9
criteria for use of, Ch. 56, 9.1
applying materiality for the premium allocation approach eligibility assessment, Ch. 56, 9.1.1
main sources of difference between the premium allocation approach and the general approach, Ch. 56, 9.1.2
initial measurement, Ch. 56, 9.2
subsequent measurement, liability for incurred claims, Ch. 56, 9.4
remaining coverage, Ch. 56, 9.3
reinsurance contracts held, Ch. 56, 10
aggregation level, Ch. 56, 10.1
allocation of the CSM to profit or loss, Ch. 56, 10.5
boundary of, Ch. 56, 10.2
initial recognition, Ch. 56, 10.3
premium allocation approach for, Ch. 56, 10.6
subsequent measurement, Ch. 56, 10.4
and the variable fee approach, Ch. 56, 10.7
modification and derecognition, Ch. 56, 12
accounting for derecognition, Ch. 56, 12.3
derecognition, Ch. 56, 12.2
modification, Ch. 56, 12.1
mutual entities, Ch. 56, 3.2.2.B, 8.11
objective of IFRS 17, Ch. 56, 2.1
presentation in the statement of financial performance, Ch. 56, 15
insurance finance income or expenses, Ch. 56, 15.3
insurance revenue, Ch. 56, 15.1
and expense from reinsurance contracts held, Ch. 56, 15.1.3
related to the provision of services in a period, Ch. 56, 15.1.1
under the premium allocation approach, Ch. 56, 15.1.2
insurance service expenses, Ch. 56, 15.2
reporting the CSM in interim financial statements, Ch. 56, 15.4
presentation in the statement of financial position, Ch. 56, 14
scope of IFRS 17, Ch. 56, 2
separating components from an insurance contract, Ch. 56, 4
embedded derivatives from an insurance contract, Ch. 56, 4.1
investment components from an insurance contract, Ch. 56, 4.2
definition, Ch. 56, 4.2.1
measurement of the non-distinct, Ch. 56, 4.2.3
separable, Ch. 56, 4.2.2
a promise to provide distinct goods and non-insurance services from insurance contracts, Ch. 56, 4.3

IFRS Taxonomy, Ch. 1, 2.6, 2.9

IFRS Taxonomy Consultative Group, Ch. 1, 2.9

IFRS Transition Resource Group for Impairment of Financial Instruments (ITG), Ch. 51, 1.5

Impairment of assets, Ch. 20. *See also* IAS 36; Impairment of goodwill; Value in use (VIU)

Impairment of assets—contd
- basis of recoverable amount–value-in-use (VIU) or fair value less costs of disposal (FVLCD), Ch. 43, 11.3
- calculation of FVLCD, Ch. 20, 6.1, Ch. 43, 11.5
- calculation of VIU, Ch. 20, 7, Ch. 43, 11.4
- held for sale, Ch. 20, 5.1
- identifying cash-generating units (CGUs), Ch. 20, 3, Ch. 43, 11.2
  - external users of processing assets, Ch. 43, 11.2.2
  - fields/mines operated on a portfolio basis, Ch. 43, 11.2.4
  - markets for intermediate products, Ch. 43, 11.2.1
  - shared infrastructure, Ch. 43, 11.2.3
- impairment indicators, Ch. 20, 2.1, Ch. 43, 11.1
- intangible assets with an indefinite useful life, Ch. 20, 10
- low mine/field profitability near end of life, Ch. 43, 11.6

Impairment of goodwill, Ch. 20, 8 created by deferred tax, Ch. 33, 12.3
- disposal of operation within a cash-generating unit (CGU) to which goodwill has been allocated, Ch. 20, 8.5
  - changes in composition of cash-generating units CGUs, Ch. 20, 8.5.1
- goodwill and its allocation to cash-generating unites, Ch. 20, 8.1
- recognised on acquisition, Ch. 20, 8.3
  - deferred tax assets and losses of acquired businesses, Ch. 20, 8.3.2
  - testing goodwill 'created' by deferred tax for impairment, Ch. 20, 8.3.1
- impairment testing when a CGU crosses more than one operating segment, Ch. 20, 8.4
- when to test CGUs with goodwill for impairment, Ch. 20, 8.2
  - carry forward of a previous impairment test calculation, Ch. 20, 8.2.3
  - reversal of impairment loss, Ch. 20, 5, 8.2.4
  - sequence of tests, Ch. 20, 8.2.2
  - timing of tests, Ch. 20, 8.2.1

Impairments. *See also* IAS 36; Impairment of assets; Impairment of goodwill
- associates or joint ventures, Ch. 11, 8
  - in separate financial statements, Ch. 11, 9.1
- cost model, Ch. 18, 5; Ch. 19, 7.3
- of fixed assets and goodwill, Ch. 20, 1–14
  - intangible assets, Ch. 17, 9.4
- of insurance assets, hierarchy exemption, Ch. 55, 7.2.6.B
- of reinsurance assets, hierarchy exemption, Ch. 55, 7.2.5
- suspension of capitalisation of borrowing costs, Ch. 21, 6.2

Income approach (fair value), Ch. 14, 14.4
- property, plant and equipment, Ch. 18, 6.1.1.B

Income, definition of, Ch. 27, 4.1

Income statement (statement of profit or loss), Ch. 3, 3.2.1. *See also* Statement of comprehensive income
- classification of expenses recognised in profit/loss, Ch. 3, 3.2.3
  - analysis of expenses by function, Ch. 3, 3.2.3.B
  - analysis of expenses by nature, Ch. 3, 3.2.3.A
- face of, information required on, Ch. 3, 3.2.2

Income taxes, Ch. 33, 1–14. *See also* IAS 12
- allocation between periods, Ch. 33, 1.2
  - no provision for deferred tax ('flow through'), Ch. 33, 1.2.1
  - provision for deferred tax (the temporary difference approach), Ch. 33, 1.2.2
- allocation of tax charge/credit, Ch. 33, 10
  - change in tax status of entity/shareholders, Ch. 33, 10.9
  - defined benefit pension plans, Ch. 33, 10.7
    - tax on refund of pension surplus, Ch. 33, 10.7.1
  - discontinued operations, Ch. 33, 10.6
  - disposal of an interest in a subsidiary that does not result in a loss of control, Ch. 33, 10.11
  - dividends and transaction costs of equity instruments, Ch. 33, 10.3
    - dividend subject to differential tax rate, Ch. 33, 10.3.1
    - dividend subject to withholding tax, Ch. 33, 10.3.2
    - incoming dividends, Ch. 33, 10.3.4
    - intragroup dividend subject to withholding tax, Ch. 33, 10.3.3
    - tax benefits of distributions and transaction costs of equity instruments, Ch. 33, 10.3.5
  - gain/loss in profit/loss and loss/gain outside profit/loss offset for tax purposes, Ch. 33, 10.5
  - gains and losses reclassified ('recycled') to profit/loss, Ch. 33, 10.4
    - debt instrument measured at fair value through OCI under IFRS 9, Ch. 33, 10.4.1
    - recognition of expected credit losses with no change in fair value, Ch. 33, 10.4.2
  - previous revaluation of PP&E treated as deemed cost on transition to IFRS, Ch. 33, 10.10
  - retrospective restatements/applications, Ch. 33, 10.2
  - revalued and rebased assets, Ch. 33, 10.1
    - non-monetary assets with a tax base determined in a foreign currency, Ch. 33, 10.1.1
  - share-based payment transactions, Ch. 33, 10.8
    - allocation of tax deduction between profit/loss and equity, Ch. 33, 10.8.1
    - allocation when more than one award is outstanding, Ch. 33, 10.8.3
    - replacement awards in a business combination, Ch. 33, 10.8.5
    - share-based payment transactions subject to transitional provisions of IFRS 1 and IFRS 2, Ch. 33, 10.8.6
    - staggered exercise of awards, Ch. 33, 10.8.4
    - tax base, determining, Ch. 33, 10.8.2
- business combinations, Ch. 33, 12
  - apparent immediate impairment of goodwill created by deferred tax, Ch. 33, 12.3
  - measurement and recognition of deferred tax in, Ch. 33, 12.1
    - deferred tax assets rising on a business combination, Ch. 33, 12.1.2
    - deferred tax liabilities of acquired entity, Ch. 33, 12.1.3
    - manner of recovery of assets and settlement of liabilities, determining, Ch. 33, 12.1.1
  - tax deductions for acquisition costs, Ch. 33, 12.4
  - tax deductions for replacement share-based payment awards in a business combination, Ch. 33, 12.2
  - temporary differences arising from the acquisition of a group of assets that is not a business, Ch. 33, 12.5

consolidated tax returns and offset of taxable profits and losses within groups, Ch. 33, 11
   examples of accounting by entities in a tax-consolidated group, Ch. 33, 11.1
   payments for intragroup transfer of tax losses, Ch. 33, 11.2
   recognition of deferred tax assets where tax losses are transferred in a group, Ch. 33, 11.3
current tax, Ch. 33, 5
   discounting of current tax assets and liabilities, Ch. 33, 5.4
   enacted/substantively enacted tax legislation, Ch. 33, 5.1
      changes to tax rates and laws enacted after the reporting date, Ch. 33, 5.1.3
      changes to tax rates and laws enacted before the reporting date, Ch. 33, 5.1.2
      implications of the decision by the UK's to withdrawal from the EU, Ch. 33, 5.1.4
      substantive enactment meaning, Ch. 33, 5.1.1
   intra-period allocation, presentation and disclosure, Ch. 33, 5.5
   'prior year adjustments' of previously presented tax balances and expense, Ch. 33, 5.3
   uncertain tax treatments, Ch. 33, 5.2
deferred tax, measurement, Ch. 33, 8
   different tax rates applicable to retained and distributed profits, Ch. 33, 8.5
      effectively tax-free entities, Ch. 33, 8.5.1
      withholding tax/distribution tax, Ch. 33, 8.5.2
   discounting, Ch. 33, 8.6
   expected manner of recovery of assets/settlement of liabilities, Ch. 33, 8.4
      assets and liabilities with more than one tax base, Ch. 33, 8.4.3
      carrying amount, Ch. 33, 8.4.2
      change in expected manner of recovery of an asset/settlement of a liability, Ch. 33, 8.4.11
      depreciable PP&E and intangible assets, Ch. 33, 8.4.5
      determining the expected manner of recovery of assets, Ch. 33, 8.4.4
      investment properties, Ch. 33, 8.4.7
      non-depreciable PP&E and intangible assets, Ch. 33, 8.4.6
         non-amortised or indefinite life intangible assets, Ch. 33, 8.4.6.B
         PP&E accounted for using the revaluation model, Ch. 33, 8.4.6.A
      other assets and liabilities, Ch. 33, 8.4.8
      'outside' temporary differences relating to subsidiaries, branches, associates and joint arrangements, Ch. 33, 8.4.9
      'single asset' entities, Ch. 33, 8.4.10
      tax planning strategies to reduce liabilities are not anticipated, Ch. 33, 8.4.1
   legislation at the end of the reporting period, Ch. 33, 8.1
      changes to tax rates and laws enacted after the reporting date, Ch. 33, 8.1.2
      changes to tax rates and laws enacted before the reporting date, Ch. 33, 8.1.1
         backward tracing of changes in deferred taxation, Ch. 33, 8.1.1.B
         disclosures relating to changes, Ch. 33, 8.1.1.C
         managing uncertainty in determining the effect of new tax legislation, Ch. 33, 8.1.1.A
   'prior year adjustments' of previously presented tax balances and expense (income), Ch. 33, 8.3
   uncertain tax treatments, Ch. 33, 8.2, 9
   unrealised intragroup profits and losses in consolidated financial, Ch. 33, 8.7
      intragroup transfers of goodwill and intangible assets, Ch. 33, 8.7.1
         consolidated financial statements, Ch. 33, 8.7.1.C
         individual financial statements of buyer, Ch. 33, 8.7.1.A
         individual financial statements of seller, Ch. 33, 8.7.1.B
         when the tax base of goodwill is retained by the transferor entity, Ch. 33, 8.7.1.D
deferred tax, recognition, Ch. 33, 7
   assets carried at fair value/revalued amount, Ch. 33, 7.3
   basic principles, Ch. 33, 7.1
      deductible temporary differences (deferred tax assets), Ch. 33, 7.1.2
      interpretation issues, Ch. 33, 7.1.3
         accounting profit, Ch. 33, 7.1.3.A
         taxable profit 'at the time of the transaction,' Ch. 33, 7.1.3.B
      taxable temporary differences (deferred tax liabilities), Ch. 33, 7.1.1
   gains, Ch. 33, 7.7
   initial recognition exception, Ch. 33, 7.2
      acquisition of an investment in a subsidiary, associate, branch or joint arrangement, Ch. 33, 7.2.10
      acquisition of subsidiary that does not constitute a business, Ch. 33, 7.2.9
      acquisition of tax losses, Ch. 33, 7.2.1
      changes to temporary differences after initial recognition, Ch. 33, 7.2.4
         change in carrying value due to revaluation, Ch. 33, 7.2.4.B
         change in tax base due to deductions in tax return, Ch. 33, 7.2.4.C
         depreciation, amortisation/impairment of initial carrying value, Ch. 33, 7.2.4.A
         temporary difference altered by legislative change, Ch. 33, 7.2.4.D
      initial recognition of compound financial instruments by the issuer, Ch. 33, 7.2.8
      initial recognition of goodwill, Ch. 33, 7.2.2
         deductible temporary differences, Ch. 33, 7.2.2.B
         taxable temporary differences, Ch. 33, 7.2.2.A
         tax deductible goodwill, Ch. 33, 7.2.2.C
      initial recognition of other assets and liabilities, Ch. 33, 7.2.3
      intragroup transfers of assets with no change in tax base, Ch. 33, 7.2.5
      partially deductible and super-deductible assets, Ch. 33, 7.2.6
      transactions involving the initial recognition of an asset and liability, Ch. 33, 7.2.7
         decommissioning costs, Ch. 33, 7.2.7.A
         leases under IFRS 16 taxed as operating leases, Ch. 33, 7.2.7.B

Income taxes—*contd*
  deferred tax, recognition—*contd*
    'outside' temporary differences relating to subsidiaries, branches, associates and joint arrangements, Ch. 33, 7.5
      calculation of, Ch. 33, 7.5.1
        consolidated financial statements, Ch. 33, 7.5.1.A
        separate financial statements of the investor, Ch. 33, 7.5.1.B
      deductible temporary differences, Ch. 33, 7.5.3
      foreseeable future – anticipated intragroup dividend, Ch. 33, 7.5.4
        consolidated financial statements of receiving entity, Ch. 33, 7.5.4.A
        separate financial statements of paying entity, Ch. 33, 7.5.4.B
      taxable temporary differences, Ch. 33, 7.5.2
      unpaid intragroup interest, royalties, management charges etc., Ch. 33, 7.5.5
    restrictions on recognition of deferred tax assets, Ch. 33, 7.4
      effect of disposals on recoverability of tax losses, Ch. 33, 7.4.8
        tax losses of retained entity recoverable against profits of subsidiary disposed of, Ch. 33, 7.4.8.B
        tax losses of subsidiary disposed of recoverable against profits of retained entity, Ch. 33, 7.4.8.C
        tax losses of subsidiary disposed of recoverable against profits of that subsidiary, Ch. 33, 7.4.8.A
      re-assessment of deferred tax assets, Ch. 33, 7.4.7
      restrictions imposed by relevant tax laws, Ch. 33, 7.4.1
      sources of 'probable' taxable profit, estimates of future taxable profits, Ch. 33, 7.4.3
        ignore the origination of new future deductible temporary differences, Ch. 33, 7.4.3.B
        ignore the reversal of existing deductible temporary differences, Ch. 33, 7.4.3.A
      sources of 'probable' taxable profit, taxable temporary differences, Ch. 33, 7.4.2
      tax planning opportunities, Ch. 33, 7.4.4
      unrealised losses on debt securities measured at fair value, Ch. 33, 7.4.5
      unused tax losses and unused tax credits, Ch. 33, 7.4.6
    'tax-transparent' ('flow-through') entities, Ch. 33, 7.6
  deferred tax–tax bases and temporary differences, Ch. 33, 6
    tax base, Ch. 33, 6.1
      of assets, Ch. 33, 6.1.1
        assets and liabilities whose tax base is not immediately apparent, Ch. 33, 6.1.3
        disclaimed/with no economic value, Ch. 33, 6.1.7
        equity items with a tax base, Ch. 33, 6.1.5
        of items not recognised as assets/liabilities in financial statements, Ch. 33, 6.1.4
        items with more than one tax base, Ch. 33, 6.1.6
      of liabilities, Ch. 33, 6.1.2
    temporary differences, examples, Ch. 33, 6.2
      assets and liabilities with no temporary difference, Ch. 33, 6.2.3
      business combinations and consolidation, Ch. 33, 6.2.1.E, 6.2.2.E
      deductible, Ch. 33, 6.2.2
        business combinations and consolidation, Ch. 33, 6.2.2.E
        foreign currency differences, Ch. 33, 6.2.1.F, 6.2.2.F
        hyperinflation, Ch. 33, 6.2.1.G
        revaluations, Ch. 33, 6.2.1.C, 6.2.2.C
        tax re-basing, Ch. 33, 6.2.1.D, 6.2.2.D
        transactions that affect profit of loss, Ch. 33, 6.2.2.A
        transactions that affect statement of financial position, Ch. 33, 6.2.2.B
      taxable, Ch. 33, 6.2.1
        business combinations and consolidation, Ch. 33, 6.2.1.E
        foreign currency differences, Ch. 33, 6.2.1.F
        hyperinflation, Ch. 33, 6.2.1.G
        revaluations, Ch. 33, 6.2.1.C
        tax re-basing, Ch. 33, 6.2.1.D
      transactions that affect profit of loss, Ch. 33, 6.2.1.A, 6.2.2.A
      transactions that affect statement of financial position, Ch. 33, 6.2.1.B, 6.2.2.B
  definitions, Ch. 33, 3, 4.1
    effectively tax-free entities, Ch. 33, 4.56
    hybrid taxes (including minimum taxes), Ch. 33, 4.1.2, 4.5
      minimum based on a measure other than taxable profits, Ch. 33, 4.5.1
      tax based on revenues, unless a profit measure gives a lower result, Ch. 33, 4.5.3
      tax is the higher of measures based on taxable profits and revenues, Ch. 33, 4.5.2
    interest and penalties, Ch. 33, 4.4
    investment tax credits, Ch. 33, 4.3
    levies, Ch. 33, 4.1.1, Ch. 26, 6.8
    withholding and similar taxes, Ch. 33, 4.2
  development of IAS 12, Ch. 33, 1.3
  disclosure, Ch. 33, 14
    components of tax expense, Ch. 33, 14.1
    discontinued operations–interaction with IFRS 5, Ch. 33, 14.6
    dividends, Ch. 33, 14.4
    examples, Ch. 33, 14.5
    other disclosures, Ch. 33, 14.2
      tax (or tax rate) reconciliation, Ch. 33, 14.2.1
      temporary differences relating to subsidiaries, associates, branches and joint arrangements, Ch. 33, 14.2.2
    reason for recognition of certain tax assets, Ch. 33, 14.3
  nature of taxation, Ch. 33, 1.1
  presentation, Ch. 33, 13
    statement of cash flows, Ch. 33, 13.3
    statement of comprehensive income, Ch. 33, 13.2
    statement of financial position, Ch. 33, 13.1
      offset current tax, Ch. 33, 13.1.1.A
      offset deferred tax, Ch. 33, 13.1.1.B
      no offset of current and deferred tax, Ch. 33, 13.1.1.C
  uncertain tax treatments, Ch. 33, 9

assumptions about the examination of tax treatments ('detection risk'), Ch. 33, 9.3
consideration of changes in facts and circumstances, Ch. 33, 9.5
  the expiry of a taxation authority's right to examine or re-examine a tax treatment, Ch. 33, 9.5.1
considered separately (unit of account), Ch. 33, 9.2
determining effects of, Ch. 33, 9.4
disclosures relating to, Ch. 33, 9.6
IFRIC 23, scope and definitions used, Ch. 33, 9.1
presentation of liabilities or assets for uncertain tax treatments, Ch. 33, 9.7
recognition of an asset for payments on account, Ch. 33, 9.8
transition to IFRIC 23, Ch. 33,9.9

Indemnification assets, Ch. 9, 5.6.4; Ch. 45, 3.12
India, IFRS adoption in, Ch. 1, 4.4.3
Indian Accounting Standards (Ind AS), Ch. 1, 4.4.3
Individual financial statements, Ch. 8, 1–4. *See also* Separate and individual financial statements; Separate financial statements
common control or group transactions in, Ch. 8, 4
  application of the principles in practice, Ch. 8, 4.4
    acquiring and selling businesses, transfers between subsidiaries, Ch. 8, 4.4.2
    acquisition and sale of assets for shares, Ch. 8, 4.4.1.C
    contribution and distribution of assets, Ch. 8, 4.4.1.D
    financial guarantee contracts, Ch. 8, 4.4.5.B
    financial instruments within the scope of IFRS 9, Ch. 8, 4.4.5
    incurring expenses and settling liabilities without recharges, Ch. 8, 4.4.4
    interest-free or non-market interest rate loans, Ch. 8, 4.4.5.A
    legal merger of parent and subsidiary, Ch. 8, 4.4.3.B
    parent exchanges PP&E for a non-monetary asset of the subsidiary, Ch. 8, 4.4.1.B
    sale of PP&E from the parent to the subsidiary for an amount of cash not representative of the fair value of the asset, Ch. 8, 4.4.1.A
    subsidiary transferring business to the parent, Ch. 8, 4.4.3.A
    transactions involving non-monetary assets, Ch. 8, 4.4.1
    transfers between subsidiaries, Ch. 8, 4.4.1.E
    transfers of businesses between parent and subsidiary, Ch. 8, 4.4.3
  disclosures, Ch. 8, 4.5
  fair value in intra-group transactions, Ch. 8, 4.3.1
  measurement, Ch. 8, 4.3
  put and call options in separate financial statements, Ch. 7, 6.5
  recognition, Ch. 8, 4.2
Inflation-linked debt, Ch. 50, 3.6; Ch. 53, 2.2.6
Inflation risk, hedges of, Ch. 53, 2.2.6
Infrastructure assets. *See* Service concession arrangements (SCA)
Initial measurement of financial instruments, Ch. 49, 3
acquisition of a group of assets that does not constitute a business, Ch. 49, 3.3.5
business combination, loans and receivables acquired in, Ch. 49, 3.3.4

'day 1' profits, Ch. 49, 3.3
embedded derivatives, Ch. 49, 3.5
financial guarantee contracts, Ch. 49, 3.3.3
financial instrument hosts, Ch. 49, 3.5
general requirements, Ch. 49, 3.1
initial fair value, transaction price and 'day 1' profits, Ch. 49, 3.3
  interest-free and low-interest long-term loans, Ch. 49, 3.3.1
  measurement of financial instruments following modification of contractual terms that leads to initial recognition of a new instrument, Ch. 49, 3.3.2
loan commitments, assets and liabilities arising from, Ch. 49, 3.7
off-market loan commitments, Ch. 49, 3.3.3
regular way transactions, Ch. 49, 3.6
trade receivables without a significant financing component, Ch. 49, 3.2
transaction costs, Ch. 49, 3.4
transaction price, Ch. 49, 3.3

In-process research and development (IPR&D), Ch. 9, 5.5.2.D; Ch. 17, 5.5
Institute of Chartered Accountants of India (ICAI), Ch. 1, 4.4.3
In-substance defeasance arrangements, Ch. 52, 6.1.3
In-substance derivatives, Ch. 46, 3.2
Insurance acquisition cash flows, Ch. 56, 8.2.3.E
Insurance assets, Ch. 55, 2.2.2
derecognition of, Ch. 55, 7.2.6.A
impairment of, Ch. 55, 7.2.6.B
reconciliations of changes in, Ch. 55, 11.1.6
Insurance contracts, Ch. 45, 3.3; Ch. 55, 1–12; Ch. 56, 1–18. *See also* IFRS 4–*Insurance Contracts*; IFRS 17–*Insurance Contracts*
acquired in business combinations and portfolio transfers, Ch. 55, 9; Ch. 56, 13
  customer lists and relationships not connected to contractual insurance rights and obligations, Ch. 55, 9.2
  expanded presentation of insurance contracts, Ch. 55, 9.1
  practical issues, Ch. 55, 9.1.1; Ch. 56, 13.4
applying IFRS 9 with IFRS 4, Ch. 55, 1.3, 10
  overlay approach, Ch. 55, 10.2
    designation and de-designation of eligible financial assets, Ch. 55, 10.2.1
    disclosures required for entities using the overlay approach, Ch. 55, 10.2.3
    first-time adopters, Ch. 55, 10.2.2
  temporary exemption from IFRS 9, Ch. 55, 10.1
    activities that are predominantly connected with insurance, Ch. 55, 10.1.1
    disclosures required for entities using the temporary exemption, Ch. 55, 10.1.5
    first-time adopters, Ch. 55, 10.1.3
    initial assessment and reassessment of the temporary exemption, Ch. 55, 10.1.2
    interest rate benchmark reform, Ch. 55, 10.1.6
    relief from investors in associates and joint ventures, Ch. 55, 10.1.4
cash flows excluded from the contract boundary, Ch. 56, 8.2.4
cash flows within the contract boundary, Ch. 56, 8.2.3

Insurance contracts—*contd*
   changes in accounting policies, Ch. 55, 8
      criteria for, Ch. 55, 8.1
      practical issues, Ch. 55, 8.5
         changes to local GAAP, Ch. 55, 8.5.1
      redesignation of financial assets, Ch. 55, 8.4; Ch. 56, 17.6
      shadow accounting, Ch. 55, 8.3
      specific issues, Ch. 55, 8.2
         continuation of existing practices, Ch. 55, 8.2.1
         current market interest rates, Ch. 55, 8.2.2
         future investment margins, Ch. 55, 8.2.4
         prudence, Ch. 55, 8.2.3
   contract boundary, Ch. 56, 8.2.3
   contractual service margin (CSM), Ch. 56, 8.5
      measurement of using the variable fee approach, Ch. 56, 11.2.2
      recognition of in profit or loss, Ch. 56, 11.2.5
      release of, Ch. 56, 10.4.1
      subsequent measurement, Ch. 56, 8.6.2
   definition of, Ch. 55, 3; Ch. 56, 3
      accounting differences between insurance and non insurance contracts, Ch. 55, 3.7
      adverse effect on the policyholder, Ch. 55, 3.7
         insurance of non-insurance risks, Ch. 55, 3.7.2; Ch. 56, 3.4.3
         lapse, persistency and expense risk, Ch. 55, 3.7.1; Ch. 56, 3.4.2
      changes in the level of insurance risk, Ch. 55, 3.3; Ch. 56, 3.6
      examples of insurance and non-insurance contracts, Ch. 55, 3.9; Ch. 56, 3.7
      insurable interest, Ch. 56, 3.4.1
      insurance risk and financial risk, distinction between, Ch. 55, 3.6; Ch. 56, 3.4
      payments in kind, Ch. 55, 3.5; Ch. 56, 3.3
      service contracts, Ch. 55, 3.5.1
      significant insurance risk, Ch. 55, 3.2; Ch. 56, 3.5
      uncertain future events, Ch. 55, 3.4; Ch. 56, 3.2
   derecognition of, Ch. 56, 12
   with direct participating features, Ch. 56, 11.2
   direct participation features, Ch. 56, 11.2
      coverage period for insurance contracts with, Ch. 56, 11.2
      definition, Ch. 56, 11.2.1
      disaggregation of finance income or expense between profit/loss and OCI, Ch. 56, 11.2.6
      measurement of contractual service margin using variable fee approach, Ch. 56, 11.2.3
      risk mitigation, Ch. 56, 11.2.5
   disclosure, Ch. 55, 11; Ch. 56, 16
      nature and extent of risks arising from insurance contracts, Ch. 55, 11.2; Ch. 56, 16.5
         credit risk, liquidity risk and market risk disclosures, Ch. 55, 11.2.6; Ch. 56, 16.5.2, 16.5.4-16.5.5
         exposures to market risk from embedded derivatives, Ch. 55, 11.2.7
         insurance risk
            claims development information, Ch. 55, 11.2.5; Ch. 56, 16.5.3
            concentrations of risk, Ch. 55, 11.2.4; Ch. 56, 16.5.1
            insurance risk–general matters, Ch. 55, 11.2.2
         sensitivity information, Ch. 55, 11.2.3; Ch. 56, 16.5.2
         objectives, policies and processes for managing insurance contract risks, Ch. 55, 11.2.1
      other disclosure matters, Ch. 55, 11.2.8
         fair value disclosures, Ch. 55, 11.2.8.C
         financial guarantee contracts, Ch. 55, 11.2.8.B
         IAS 1 capital disclosures, Ch. 55, 11.2.8.A
         key performance indicators, Ch. 55, 11.2.8.D
      recognised amounts, explanation of, Ch. 55, 11.1; Ch. 56, 16.1
         disclosure of accounting policies, Ch. 55, 11.1.1; Ch. 56, 16.4
         effects of changes in assumptions, Ch. 55, 11.1.5
         gains/losses on buying reinsurance, Ch. 55, 11.1.3
         insurance finance income or expenses, Ch. 56, 16.1.3
         premium allocation approach, accounting policies adopted for, Ch. 56, 16.1.2
         process used to determine significant assumptions, Ch. 55, 11.1.4
         recognised assets, liabilities, income and expense, Ch. 55, 11.1.2
         reconciliations of changes in insurance assets and liabilities, Ch. 55, 11.1.6
         reconciliations required for contracts applying the general model, Ch. 56, 16.1.1
         reconciliations required for contracts applying the premium allocation approach, Ch. 56, 16.1.2
      regulatory, Ch. 56, 16.5.6
      significant judgements in applying IFRS 17, Ch. 56, 16.3
      transition amounts, Ch. 56, 16.2
   discount rates, Ch. 56, 8.3
   discretionary participation feature, Ch. 55, 6; Ch. 56, 11.3
      in financial instruments, Ch. 55, 6.2; Ch. 56, 11.2
      in insurance contracts, Ch. 55, 6.1
      investment contracts with, Ch. 56, 11.3
      practical issues, Ch. 55, 6.3
         contracts with switching features, Ch. 55, 6.3.2
         negative DPF, Ch. 55, 6.3.1
   embedded derivatives, Ch. 55, 4
      unit-linked features, Ch. 55, 4.1
   estimates of expected future cash flows, Ch. 56, 8.2
   existing accounting practices for, Ch. 55, 1.4
      embedded value, Ch. 55, 1.4.3
      life insurance, Ch. 55, 1.4.2
      non-life insurance, Ch. 55, 1.4.1
   first-time adoption, Ch. 5, 5.4
   foreign currency, Ch. 56, 7.3
   history of the IASB's insurance project, Ch. 55, 1.1
   liability for incurred claims, Ch. 56, 8.6.2
   liability for remaining coverage, Ch. 56, 8.6.1
   modification of, Ch. 56, 12.1
   with participating features, Ch. 56, 11
   premium allocation approach, criteria and measurement, Ch. 56, 9
   risk adjustment for non-financial risk, Ch. 56, 8.4
   selection of accounting policies, Ch. 55, 7
      hierarchy exemption, Ch. 55, 7.1
      limits on the hierarchy exemption, Ch. 55, 7.2

accounting policy matters not addressed by IFRS 4, Ch. 55, 7.2.6
catastrophe and equalisation provisions, Ch. 55, 7.2.1
impairment of reinsurance assets, Ch. 55, 7.2.5
insurance liability derecognition, Ch. 55, 7.2.3
liability adequacy testing, Ch. 55, 7.2.2
offsetting of insurance and related reinsurance contracts, Ch. 55, 7.2.4
unbundling of deposit components, Ch. 55, 5
illustration, Ch. 55, 5.2
practical difficulties, Ch. 55, 5.3
requirements, Ch. 55, 5.1
without direct participating features, Ch. 56, 8.6.3, 17.4.2

Insurance finance income or expense, Ch. 56, 15.3, 16.1.3, 17.5.1

Insurance liability, Ch. 55, 2.2.1
derecognition, Ch. 55, 7.2.3
reconciliations of changes in, Ch. 55, 11.1.6
on undiscounted basis, measuring, Ch. 55, 8.2.1.A

Insurance mutuals, Ch. 55, 3.2.2.B; Ch. 56, 3.5.2.B

Insurance protection, Ch. 52, 3.6.3

Insurance revenue, Ch. 56, 15.1

Insurance risk
changes in the level of, Ch. 55, 3.3; Ch. 56, 3.6
claims development information, Ch. 55, 11.2.5; Ch. 56, 16.5.3
concentrations of risk, Ch. 55, 11.2.4; Ch. 56, 16.5.1
financial risk, distinction from, Ch. 55, 3.6; Ch. 56, 3.4
general matters, Ch. 55, 11.2.2
sensitivity information, Ch. 55, 11.2.3
significant insurance risk, Ch. 55, 3.2; Ch. 56, 3.5
level of assessment, Ch. 55, 3.2.2
insurance mutuals, Ch. 55, 3.2.2.B
intragroup insurance contracts, Ch. 55, 3.2.2.C
self insurance, Ch. 55, 3.2.2.A
meaning of 'significant,' Ch. 55, 3.2.1
quantity of insurance risk, Ch. 56, 3.5.1
significant additional benefits, Ch. 55, 3.2.3

Insurance service expenses, Ch. 56, 15.2

Insured benefits, employee benefits, Ch. 35, 3.2

Insured event, Ch. 55, 2.2.1

Insurer, Ch. 55, 2, 2.2.1; Ch. 56, 2

Insurer's liabilities, fair value of, Ch. 55, 9.1.1.B

Intangible asset model, service concession arrangements, Ch. 25, 4.3

Intangible assets, Ch. 9, 5.5.2; Ch. 17, 1–11. *See also* Amortisation of intangible assets; IAS 38; Internally generated intangible assets
acquisition by way of government grant, Ch. 17, 4.6
agile software development, Ch. 17, 6.2.6
as corporate assets, Ch. 20, 3.1.1
cloud computing, Ch. 17, 11.6
accounting, intangible asset, Ch. 17, 11.6.4; Ch. 17, 11.6.5
arrangement contains a lease, Ch. 17, 11.6.2
arrangement contains an intangible asset, , Ch. 17, 11.6.3
arrangements that contain an intangible asset, accounting for, Ch. 17, 11.6.4
fees in the arrangement, Ch. 17, 11.6.4.A; Ch. 17, 11.6.4.B
implementation costs, Ch. 17, 11.6.4.B; Ch. 17, 11.6.5.B
types of cloud computing arrangements and determination of applicable IFRSs, Ch. 17, 11.6.1
definition, Ch. 17, 2.1
classification of programme and other broadcast rights as inventory/intangible assets, Ch. 17, 2.2.2
control, Ch. 17, 2.1.2
future economic benefits, Ch. 17, 2.1.3
identifiability, Ch. 17, 2.1.1
whether to record a tangible/intangible asset, Ch. 17, 2.2.1
disclosure, Ch. 17, 10
additional disclosures when the revaluation model is applied, Ch. 17, 10.4
general disclosures, Ch. 17, 10.1
profit/loss presentation, Ch. 17, 10.3
of research and development expenditure, Ch. 17, 10.5
statement of financial position presentation, Ch. 17, 10.2
exchanges of assets
commercial substance, Ch. 17, 4.7.2
measurement of assets exchanged, Ch. 17, 4.7.1
impairment losses, Ch. 17, 9.4
impairment of intangibles with an indefinite useful life, Ch. 20, 10
interim financial reporting, depreciation and amortisation, Ch. 41, 9.1
issues regarding, Ch. 17, 11
accounting for green certificates/renewable energy certificates, Ch. 17, 11.3
accounting for REACH costs, Ch. 17, 11.4
crypto-assets, Ch. 17, 11.5
emissions trading schemes, Ch. 17, 11.2
accounting for emission rights by brokers and traders, Ch. 17, 11.2.7
amortisation and impairment testing of emission rights, Ch. 17, 11.2.4
emission rights acquired in a business combination, Ch. 17, 11.2.5
government grant approach, Ch. 17, 11.2.3
IFRIC 3, Ch. 17, 11.2.1
net liability approaches, Ch. 17, 11.2.2
sale of emission rights, Ch. 17, 11.2.6
rate-regulated activities, Ch. 17, 11.1
measurement, Ch. 17, 3.2
acquired for contingent consideration, Ch. 17, 4.5
after initial recognition, Ch. 17, 8
cost model for measurement of intangible assets, Ch. 17, 8.1
revaluation model for measurement of intangible assets, Ch. 17, 8.2
accounting for revaluations, Ch. 17, 8.2.3
frequency of revaluations, Ch. 17, 8.2.2
revaluation is only allowed if there is an active market, Ch. 17, 8.2.1
recognising and measuring assets acquired and liabilities assumed in a business combination, Ch. 9, 5.5
combining an intangible asset with a related contract, Ch. 9, 5.5.2.C
contractual-legal, Ch. 9, 5.5.2

Intangible assets—*contd*
   recognising and measuring assets acquired and liabilities assumed in a business combination—*contd*
      customer relationship intangible assets, Ch. 9, 5.5.2.B
      emission rights, Ch. 9, 5.5.2.E
      fair values of intangible assets, determining, Ch. 9, 5.5.2.F
      in-process research or development project expenditure, Ch. 9, 5.5.2.D
      Multi Period Excess Earnings Method (MEEM), Ch. 9, 5.5.2.F
      Relief from Royalty method, Ch. 9, 5.5.2.F
      separability, Ch. 9, 5.5.2; Ch. 17, 5.1.3.B
   recognition, Ch. 17, 3.1
      PP&E components classified as, Ch. 18, 3.1.4
   separate acquisition, Ch. 17, 4
      acquisition by way of government grant, Ch. 17, 4.6
      components of cost, Ch. 17, 4.2
      costs to be expensed, Ch. 17, 4.3
      exchanges of assets, Ch. 17, 4.7
         commercial substance, Ch. 17, 4.7.2
         measurement of assets exchanged, Ch. 17, 4.7.1
      income from incidental operations, Ch. 17, 4.4
      measurement of intangible assets acquired for contingent consideration, Ch. 17, 4.5
      recognition, Ch. 17, 4.1
   subsequent expenditure, Ch. 17, 3.3
   useful life of, assessing, Ch. 17, 9.1
      with an indefinite useful life, Ch. 17, 9.3
      contractual/other legal rights, Ch. 17, 9.1.2
      factors affecting, Ch. 17, 9.1.1
      with a finite useful life, Ch. 17, 9.2

Intellectual property licences, Ch. 31, 2
   identifying performance obligations in a licensing arrangement, Ch. 31, 2.1
      application questions, Ch. 31, 2.1.5
      contracts that grant both permission for past use of intellectual property and a licence to use the intellectual property in the future, Ch. 31, 2.1.5.B
      contractual restrictions, Ch. 31, 2.1.3
      guarantees to defend or maintain a patent, Ch. 31, 2.1.4
      licences of intellectual property that are distinct, Ch. 31, 2.1.1
      licences of intellectual property that are not distinct, Ch. 31, 2.1.2
   licence renewals, Ch. 31, 2.4
   nature of the entity's promise in granting a licence, determining, Ch. 31, 2.2
      applying the licensing application guidance to a single (bundled) performance obligation that includes a licence of intellectual property, Ch. 31, 2.2.1
   recognising revenue for, Ch. 30, 8
   sales-based/usage-based royalties on, Ch. 31, 2.5
      application questions on the sales-based or usage-based royalty recognition constraint, Ch. 31, 2.5.2
      recognition of royalties for a licence that provides a right to access intellectual property, Ch. 31, 2.5.1
   transfer of control of licensed intellectual property, Ch. 31, 2.3
      right to access, Ch. 31, 2.3.1
      right to use, Ch. 31, 2.3.2
      use and benefit requirement, Ch. 31, 2.3.3

Interbank Offered Rate Reform (IBOR), Ch. 50, 3.8.3; Ch. 53,9; Ch. 54, 4.3.5, 5.7; Ch. 55, 10.1.6
Intercompany. *See* Intragroup
Interest-free long-term loans, Ch. 49, 3.3.1
Interest rate
   floors and caps, Ch. 46, 5.1.5
   indices, Ch. 46, 5.1.2
   negative, Ch. 53, 2.4.2
Interest rate risk, Ch. 54, 5
   contractually specified portions of, Ch. 53, 2.2.2
   offsetting internal hedging instruments, Ch. 53, 4.2
   sensitivity analysis, Ch. 54, 5.5.1
Interest rate swaps (IRS), Ch. 6, 5.3.1; Ch. 21, 5.5.1; Ch. 52, 4.4.2
   future settlement, Ch. 46, 2.3
   initial net investment, Ch. 46, 2.2
   at initial recognition, Ch. 14, 13.2.1
Interests in consolidated structured entities
   disclosure of risks associated with, Ch. 13, 4.4
Interests in joint arrangements and associates, disclosure of, Ch. 13, 5. *See also* IFRS 12
   extent, Ch. 13, 5.1
   financial effects, Ch. 13, 5.1
   individually immaterial joint ventures and associates, Ch. 13, 5.1.2
   joint ventures, Ch. 13, 5.2
   nature, Ch. 13, 5.1
   risks associated, Ch. 13, 5.2
   summarised financial information, Ch. 13, 5.1.1
Interests in other entities, Ch. 13, 2.2.1.A, 2.2.3.D
Interests in subsidiaries, disclosure of, Ch. 13, 4
   changes in ownership interests in subsidiaries, Ch. 13, 4.5
   composition of the group, Ch. 13, 4.1
   interests of non-controlling interests, Ch. 13, 4.2
   of nature and extent of significant restrictions, Ch. 13, 4.3
   required by investment entities, Ch. 13, 4.6
   risks associated with interests in consolidated structured entities, Ch. 13, 4.4
   terms of contractual arrangements, Ch. 13, 4.4.1
Interests in unconsolidated structured entities, disclosure of, Ch. 13, 6. *See also* IFRS 12
   nature of interests, Ch. 13, 6.1
      nature, purpose, size, activities and financing of structured entities, Ch. 13, 6.1.1
      sponsored structured entities for which no interest is held at the reporting date, Ch. 13, 6.1.2
   nature of risks, Ch. 13, 6.2–6.3
Interim financial reporting, Ch. 41, 1–11. *See also* IAS 34
Interim income tax expense, measuring, Ch. 41, 9.5.1
Internal hedges
   held by other group entities, Ch. 53, 4
   internal hedged items, Ch. 53, 4.3
      forecast intragroup transactions, Ch. 53, 4.3.2
      intragroup monetary items, Ch. 53, 4.3.1
   internal hedging instruments, Ch. 53, 4.1
      central clearing parties and ring fencing, Ch. 53, 4.1.1
   offsetting instruments, Ch. 53, 4.2
      foreign exchange risk, Ch. 53, 4.2.2
      interest rate risk, Ch. 53, 4.2.1

Internally generated intangible assets, Ch. 17, 6
  brands, Ch. 17, 6.2.4
  cost of
    eligible for capitalisation, Ch. 17, 6.3.2
    establishing the time from, Ch. 17, 6.3.1
  customer lists, Ch. 17, 6.2.4
  development phase, Ch. 17, 6.2.2
  goodwill, Ch. 17, 6.1
  mastheads, Ch. 17, 6.2.4
  pharmaceutical industry, research and development in, Ch. 17, 6.2.3
  publishing titles, Ch. 17, 6.2.4
  research phase, Ch. 17, 6.2.1
  website costs (SIC-32), Ch. 17, 6.2.5
    application and infrastructure, Ch. 17, 6.2.5
    content development, Ch. 17, 6.2.5
    graphical design development, Ch. 17, 6.2.5
    operating stage, Ch. 17, 6.2.5
    planning, Ch. 17, 6.2.5
International Accounting Standards (IAS), Ch. 1, 2.1. *See also individual* IAS *entries*
International Accounting Standards Board (IASB), Ch. 1, 2.4. *See also* Conceptual framework, IASB's
  agenda consultation, Ch. 1, 2.2, 2.4, 3.1,3.2
  annual improvements , Ch. 1, 2.5
  convergence, Ch. 1, 3.2
  current priorities, Ch. 1, 3.1
  Due Process Handbook, Ch. 1, 2.5, 2.6
  future agenda, Ch. 1, 3.1
  maintenance projects, Ch. 3, 6.2
  primary financial statements, Ch. 3, 6.1.2
  Monitoring Board, Ch. 1, 2.3
  standard-setting projects, Ch. 3, 6.1
  standard setting structure, Ch. 1, 2.1
    advisory bodies, Ch. 1, 2.9
    IFRS Advisory Council, Ch. 1, 2.7
    IFRS Foundation, Ch. 1, 2.2
    IFRS Interpretations Committee, Ch. 1, 2,1-2.2, 2.5–2.7
International Financial Reporting Standards (IFRS), Ch. 1, 2.1. *See also individual* IFRS *entries*
  adoption, worldwide, Ch. 1, 4.1
    Americas, Ch. 1, 4.3
    Asia, Ch. 1, 4.4
    Australia, Ch. 1, 4.5
    Europe, Ch. 1, 4.2
    South Africa, Ch. 1, 4.6
  consistency in application of, Ch. 1, 5
International Organisation of Securities Commissions (IOSCO), Ch. 1, 1, 2.3, 5
Interpretations Committee, Ch. 1, 2.5
  agenda decisions Ch. 1, 2.5.1
Intragroup (Intercompany)
  deferred tax on foreseeable future – anticipated intragroup dividend, Ch. 33, 7.5.4
  dividend subject to withholding tax, Ch. 33, 10.3.3
  eliminations, Ch. 7, 2.4
  insurance contracts, Ch. 56, 3.5.2.C
  transactions, Ch. 8, 4.3.1
  transfer of assets with no change in tax base, Ch. 33, 7.2.5
  transfer of tax losses, payments for, Ch. 33, 11.2
  unpaid interest, royalties, management charges etc., Ch. 33, 7.5.5
  unrealised profits and losses in consolidated financial statements, Ch. 33, 8.7
Intrinsic value method, share-based payments Ch. 34, 8.8.1
Inventories, Ch. 22, 1–6. *See also* IAS 2–*Inventories*
  disclosure requirements, Ch. 22, 6
  interim financial reporting, Ch. 41, 9.4
  measurement, Ch. 22, 3
  real estate inventory, Ch. 22, 4
  recognition in profit/loss, Ch. 22, 5
Inventories, extractive industries, Ch. 43, 14
  carried at fair value, Ch. 43, 14.4
  core inventories, Ch. 43, 14.3
  heap leaching (mining), Ch. 43, 14.6
  recognition of work in progress, Ch. 43, 14.1
  sale of by-products and joint products, Ch. 43, 14.2
    by-products, Ch. 43, 14.2.1
    joint products, Ch. 43, 14.2.2
  stockpiles of low grade ore (mining), Ch. 43, 14.5
Investing activities, cash flows, Ch. 40, 4.2
Investment contracts, Ch. 55, 2.2.2, 3.9.2
Investment contracts with discretionary participation features, Ch. 55, 6.1–6.2, 7.2.2.C; Ch. 56, 11.3
Investment entity, Ch. 6, 10
  accounting by a parent of an investment entity, Ch. 6, 10.4
  accounting by an investment entity, Ch. 6, 10.3
  cash flows in, Ch. 40, 6.4.3
  definition, Ch. 6, 10.1
  determining whether an entity is an investment entity, Ch. 6, 10.2
    earnings from investments, Ch. 6, 10.2.3
    exit strategies, Ch. 6, 10.2.2
    fair value measurement, Ch. 6, 10.2.4
    having more than one investor, Ch. 6, 10.2.6
    holding more than one investment, Ch. 6, 10.2.5
    intermediate holding companies established for tax optimization purposes, Ch. 6, 10.2.1.B
    investment entity illustrative examples, Ch. 6, 10.2.9
    investment-related services, Ch. 6, 10.2.1.A
    multi-layered fund structures, Ch. 6, 10.2.10
    ownership interests, Ch. 6, 10.2.8
    unrelated investors, Ch. 6, 10.2.7
  disclosures required by, Ch. 13, 4.6
Investment property, Ch. 19, 1–12. *See also* IAS 40
  cost model, Ch. 19, 7
    impairment, Ch. 19, 7.3
    incidence of use of the cost model, Ch. 19, 7.2
    initial recognition, Ch. 19, 7.1
      identification of non-physical parts, Ch. 19, 7.1.2
      identification of physical parts, Ch. 19, 7.1.1
  definitions, Ch. 19, 2
  disclosure requirements of IAS 40, Ch. 19, 12
    additional disclosures for the cost model, Ch. 19, 12.3
    additional disclosures for the fair value model, Ch. 19, 12.2
      extra disclosures where fair value cannot be determined reliably, Ch. 19, 12.2.2
      presentation of changes in fair value, Ch. 19, 12.2.1

Investment property—*contd*
  disclosure requirements of IAS 4—*contd*
    disclosures under both fair value and cost models, Ch. 19, 12.1
      disclosure of direct operating expenses, Ch. 19, 12.1.3
      level of aggregation for IFRS 13 disclosures, Ch. 19, 12.1.2
      methods and assumptions in fair value estimates, Ch. 19, 12.1.1
    presentation of sales proceeds, Ch. 19, 12.4
  disposal of investment property, Ch. 19, 10
    calculation of gain/loss on disposal, Ch. 19, 10.1
    compensation from third parties, Ch. 19, 10.4
    replacement of parts of investment property, Ch. 19, 10.3
    sale prior to completion of construction, Ch. 19, 10.2
  fair value model, Ch. 19, 6
    deferred taxation for property held by a 'single asset' entity, Ch. 19, 6.10
    estimating fair value, Ch. 19, 6.1
      comparison with value in use, Ch. 19, 6.1.3
      'double counting,' Ch. 19, 6.1.4
      methods of estimation, Ch. 19, 6.1.1
      observable data, Ch. 19, 6.1.2
    fair value of investment property under construction, Ch. 19, 6.3
    fixtures and fittings subsumed within fair value, Ch. 19, 6.5
    future capital expenditure and development value ('highest and best use'), Ch. 19, 6.8
    inability to determine fair value of completed investment property, Ch. 19, 6.2
    negative present value, Ch. 19, 6.9
    prepaid and accrued operating lease income, Ch. 19, 6.6
      accrued rental income and lease incentives, Ch. 19, 6.6.1
      prepaid rental income, Ch. 19, 6.6.2
    transaction costs incurred by the reporting entity on acquisition, Ch. 19, 6.4
    valuation adjustment to the fair value of properties held under a lease, Ch. 19, 6.7
  IFRS 5 and investment property, Ch. 19, 8
  initial measurement, Ch. 19, 4
    assets acquired in exchange transactions, Ch. 19, 4.6
    attributable costs, Ch. 19, 4.1
      acquisition of a group of assets that does not constitute a business, Ch. 19, 4.1.1
      deferred taxes when acquiring a 'single asset' entity that is not a business, Ch. 19, 4.1.2
    borrowing costs, Ch. 19, 4.8
    contingent costs, Ch. 19, 4.10
    deferred payments, Ch. 19, 4.3
    income from tenanted property during development, Ch. 19, 4.11
    initial recognition of tenanted investment property subsequently measured using the cost model, Ch. 19, 4.7
    lease incentives and initial costs of leasing a property, Ch. 19, 4.9
      initial direct costs of obtaining a lease, Ch. 19, 4.9.2
      lease incentives, Ch. 19, 4.9.1
    payments by the vendor to the purchaser, Ch. 19, 4.12
    property held under a lease, Ch. 19, 4.5
    reclassifications from property, plant and equipment ('PP&E'/from inventory, Ch. 19, 4.4
    start-up costs and self-built property, Ch. 19, 4.2
      cost of a building to be demolished in connection with the construction of a new building, Ch. 19, 4.2.1
  interim reporting and IAS 40, Ch. 19, 11
  measurement after initial recognition, Ch. 19, 5
    by insurers and similar entities, Ch. 19, 5.1
  recognition, Ch. 19, 3
  scope, Ch. 19, 2
  transfer of assets to/from investment property, Ch. 19, 9
    accounting treatment of transfers, Ch. 19, 9.2
    transfers from investment property to inventory, Ch. 19, 9.1
Investment tax credits, Ch. 24, 2.3.2; Ch. 33, 4.3
Investments in associates and joint ventures, Ch. 11, 1–11. *See also* Equity method/accounting; IAS 28; Reciprocal interests in equity accounted entities
  application of the equity method, Ch. 11, 7
    consistent accounting policies, Ch. 11, 7.8
    date of commencement of equity accounting, Ch. 11, 7.3
    discontinuing the use of the equity method, Ch. 11, 7.12
      deemed disposals, Ch. 11, 7.12.6
      investment in associate becomes a joint venture (or vice versa), Ch. 11, 7.12.4
      investment in associate/joint venture that is a business becoming a subsidiary, Ch. 11, 7.12.1
      partial disposals of interests in associate/joint venture, Ch. 11, 7.12.5
      retained investment in associate or joint venture that is not a business becoming a subsidiary, Ch. 11, 7.12.2
      retained investment in the former associate or joint venture is a financial asset, Ch. 11, 7.12.3
    distributions received in excess of the carrying amount, Ch. 11, 7.10
    equity accounting and consolidation, comparison between, Ch. 11, 7.2
    equity transactions in an associate's/joint venture's financial statements, Ch. 11, 7.11
      dividends/other forms of distributions, Ch. 11, 7.11.1
      effects of changes in parent/non-controlling interests in subsidiaries, Ch. 11, 7.11.4
      equity-settled share-based payment transactions, Ch. 11, 7.11.3
      issues of equity instruments, Ch. 11, 7.11.2
    initial carrying amount of an associate/joint venture, Ch. 11, 7.4
      applying a cost-based approach, Ch. 11, 7.4.2.A
      applying a fair value (IFRS 3) approach, Ch. 11, 7.4.2.A
      following loss of control of an entity, Ch. 7, 3.3.2, 7.1; Ch. 11, 7.4.1
      piecemeal acquisition, Ch. 11, 7.4.2
        common control transactions involving sales of associates, Ch. 11, 7.4.2.D
        existing associate that becomes a joint venture, or vice versa, Ch. 11, 7.4.2.C
        financial instrument becoming an associate/joint venture, Ch. 11, 7.4.2.A

step increase in an existing associate/joint venture without a change in status of the investee, Ch. 11, 7.4.2.B
loss-making associates/joint ventures, Ch. 11, 7.9
non-coterminous accounting periods, Ch. 11, 7.7
overview, Ch. 11, 7.1
share of the investee, Ch. 11, 7.5
    accounting for potential voting rights, Ch. 11, 7.5.1
    cumulative preference shares held by parties other than the investor, Ch. 11, 7.5.2
    several classes of equity, Ch. 11, 7.5.3
    where the investee is a group, Ch. 11, 7.5.5
    where the reporting entity is a group, Ch. 11, 7.5.4
transactions between the reporting entity and its associates/joint ventures, Ch. 11, 7.6
    contributions of non-monetary assets to an associate/joint venture, Ch. 11, 7.6.5
    commercial substance, Ch. 11, 7.6.5.A
    conflict between IAS 28 and IFRS 10, Ch. 7, 3.3.2, 7.1; Ch. 11, 7.6.5.C
    practical application, Ch. 11, 7.6.5.B
    elimination of 'upstream' and 'downstream' transactions, Ch. 11, 7.6.1
    loans and borrowings between the reporting entity, Ch. 11, 7.6.3
    reciprocal interests, Ch. 11, 7.6.2
    statement of cash flows, Ch. 11, 7.6.4
classification as held for sale (IFRS 5), Ch. 11, 6
definitions, Ch. 11, 3
disclosures, Ch. 11, 10.2
exemptions from applying the equity method, Ch. 11, 5.3
    investments held in associates/joint ventures held by venture capital organisations, Ch. 11, 5.3
    application of IFRS 9 to exempt, Ch. 11, 5.3.2
    entities with a mixture of activities, Ch. 11, 5.3.2.A
    application of IFRS 9 to exempt investments in associates or joint ventures, Ch. 11, 5.3.2
    investment entities exception, Ch. 11, 5.3.1
future developments, Ch. 11, 11
impairment losses, Ch. 11, 8
objective, Ch. 11, 2.1
parents exempt from preparing consolidated financial statements, Ch. 11, 5.1
partial use of fair value measurement of associates, Ch. 11, 5.4
presentation, Ch. 11, 10.1
    other items of comprehensive income, Ch. 11, 10.1.3
    profit/loss, Ch. 11, 10.1.2
    statement of cash flows, Ch. 11, 10.1.4
    statement of financial position, Ch. 11, 10.1.1
scope, Ch. 11, 2.2
separate financial statements, Ch. 11, 9
significant influence, Ch. 11, 4
    fund managers, Ch. 11, 4.6
    holdings of less than 20% of the voting power, Ch. 11, 4.3
    lack of, Ch. 11, 4.2
    potential voting rights, Ch. 11, 4.4
    severe long-term restrictions impairing ability to transfer funds to the investor, Ch. 11, 4.1
    voting rights held in a fiduciary capacity, Ch. 11, 4.5
subsidiaries meeting certain criteria, Ch. 11, 5.2
transfers of associates/joint ventures between entities under common control, Ch. 10, 5

Investments in subsidiaries, associates and joint ventures, Ch. 8.2.1, Ch. 20, 12.4
equity accounted investment and indicators of impairment, Ch. 20, 12.4.3
equity accounted investments and CGUs, Ch. 20, 12.4.5
equity accounted investments and long term loans, Ch. 20, 12.4.4
equity accounted investments and testing goodwill for impairment, Ch. 20,12.4.6
exemptions from applying the equity method, Ch. 11, 5
fair value less costs of disposal (FVLCD), Ch. 20, 12.4.1
value in use (VIU) for, Ch. 20, 12.4.2

Islamic Finance Consultative Group, Ch. 1, 2.9
Islamic financial institutions (IFIs), Ch. 27, 3.5.1.A
Japan, IFRS adoption in, Ch. 1, 4.4.2
Joint arrangements, Ch. 12, 1–910. *See also* IFRS 11; Joint control; Joint operations
accounting for joint operations, Ch. 12, 6
    accounting for rights and obligations, Ch. 12, 6.2
    determining the relevant IFRS, Ch. 12, 6.3
    interest in a joint operation without joint control, Ch. 12, 6.4
    not structured through a separate vehicle, Ch. 12, 6.1
    with a party that participates in a joint arrangement but does not have joint control, Ch. 12, 6.5
    in separate financial statements, Ch. 12, 6.7
    transactions between a joint operator and a joint operation, Ch. 12, 6.6
accounting for joint ventures, Ch. 12, 7
    contributions of non-monetary assets to a joint venture, Ch. 12, 7.2
    interest in a joint venture without joint control, Ch. 12, 7.1
    in separate financial statements, Ch. 12, 7.3
applications to joint arrangements held for sale, Ch. 12, 2.2.2
cash flows of, Ch. 40, 6.4.2
classification of, Ch. 12, 5
    contractual terms, Ch. 12, 5.3
    facts and circumstances, Ch. 12, 5.4
    illustrative examples, Ch. 12, 5.5
    legal form of the separate vehicle, Ch. 12, 5.2
    separate vehicle or not, Ch. 12, 5.1
continuous assessment, Ch. 12, 8
    changes in ownership of a joint arrangement that is not a business, Ch. 12, 8.4
        joint operator obtains control, Ch. 7, 3.1.2; Ch. 12, 8.4.1
        parties that participate in a joint arrangement but do not have joint control obtain joint control, Ch. 12, 8.4.1
    changes in ownership of a joint operation that is a business, Ch. 12, 8.3
        acquisition of an interest in, Ch. 12, 8.3.1
        disposal of interest in, Ch. 12, 8.3.5
        former subsidiary becomes, Ch. 7, 3.3.3, 7.2; Ch. 12, 8.3.3
        obtaining control or joint control over a joint operation that is a business, Ch. 12, 8.3.2
        other changes in ownership of, Ch. 12, 8.3.4

Joint arrangements—*contd*
  continuous assessment—*contd*
    changes in ownership of a joint venture that is a business, Ch. 12, 8.2
      acquisition of an interest, Ch. 12, 8.2.1
      becomes a financial asset (or vice versa), Ch. 12, 8.2.5
      becomes an associate (or vice versa), Ch. 12, 8.2.4
      control over a former joint venture, Ch. 12, 8.2.2
      disposal of interest in, Ch. 12, 8.2.6
      former subsidiary becomes a joint venture, Ch. 7, 3.3.2, 7.1; Ch. 12, 8.2.3
      interest in a joint venture held for sale, Ch. 12, 8.2.7
      when to reassess under IFRS 11, Ch. 12, 8.1
  definition of, Ch. 12, 3; Ch. 13, 2.2.2.B
  disclosures, Ch. 12, 9
  guarantees, Ch. 12, 5.3.1
  nature of, Ch. 12, 1.1
  objective, Ch. 12, 2.1
  scope, Ch. 12, 2.2
    accounting by a joint operation, Ch. 12, 2.2.3
    application by venture capital organisations and similar entities, Ch. 12, 2.2.1
    application to joint arrangements held for sale, Ch. 12, 2.2.2
  unit of account, Ch. 12, 3.1

Joint control, Ch. 12, 4
  assessing in extractive industries, Ch. 43, 7.1.1
    meaning of unanimous consent, Ch. 43, 7.1.1.B
    relevant activities, Ch. 43, 7.1.1.A
  practical issues with assessing, Ch. 12, 4.4
    evaluate multiple agreements together, Ch. 12, 4.4.2
    undivided share/lease/joint arrangement, Ch. 12, 4.4.1
  rights to control collectively, Ch. 12, 4.2
    de facto agents, Ch. 12, 4.2.5
    delegated decision-making, Ch. 12, 4.2.4
    evidence of, Ch. 12, 4.2.3
    government, role of, Ch. 12, 4.2.6
    potential voting rights and joint control, Ch. 12, 4.2.2
    protective rights, including some veto rights, Ch. 12, 4.2.1
  sequential activities in, Ch. 12, 4.1.1
  unanimous consent, Ch. 12, 4.3
    arbitration, Ch. 12, 4.3.3
    arrangements involving passive investors, Ch. 12, 4.3.1
    ultimate voting authority, Ch. 12, 4.3.2

Joint operating agreement (JOA), Ch. 43, 5.6, 17.3.3

Joint operations
  accounting for, Ch. 12, 6
    accounting for rights and obligations, Ch. 12, 6.2
    determining the relevant IFRS, Ch. 12, 6.3
    interest in a joint operation without joint control, Ch. 12, 6.4
    not structured through a separate vehicle, Ch. 12, 6.1
    with a party that participates in a joint arrangement but does not have joint control, Ch. 12, 6.5
    in separate financial statements, Ch. 12, 6.7
    transactions between a joint operator and a joint operation, Ch. 12, 6.6
  changes in ownership of, Ch. 12, 8.3 acquisition of an interest in, Ch. 12, 8.3.1
    disposal of interest in, Ch. 12, 8.3.5
    former subsidiary becomes, Ch. 7, 3.3.3, 7.2; Ch. 12, 8.3.3
    obtaining control or joint control over a joint operation that is a business, Ch. 12, 8.3.2
  implications of controlling, Ch. 43, 7.1.2.A
  in separate financial statements, Ch. 8, 1.1.2

Joint products, extractive industries, Ch. 43, 14.2, 16.1.3.D

Joint ventures. *See also* IAS 28–*Investments in associates and joint ventures*
  accounting for, Ch. 12, 7
    contributions of non-monetary assets to a joint venture, Ch. 12, 7.2
    interest in a joint venture without joint control, Ch. 12, 7.1
    in separate financial statements, Ch. 8, 1.1.1; Ch. 12, 7.3
  cash flows, Ch. 40, 6.4
    arising from interests in, Ch. 40, 8.4
    cash flows of joint operations, Ch. 40, 6.4.2
    investments in associates and joint ventures, Ch. 40, 6.4.1
  changes in ownership, Ch. 12, 8.2
  disclosure of commitments relating to, Ch. 13, 5.2.1
  disclosure of contingent liabilities relating to, Ch. 13, 5.2.2
  equity transactions in, Ch. 11, 7.11
  FVLCD for investments in, Ch. 20, 12.4.1
  implications of controlling, Ch. 43, 7.1.2.B
  initial carrying amount of an associate/joint venture, Ch. 11, 7.4
    following loss of control of an entity, Ch. 7, 3.3.2, 7.1; Ch. 11, 7.4.1
    piecemeal acquisition, Ch. 11, 7.4.2
      common control transactions involving sales of associates, Ch. 11, 7.4.2.D
      existing associate that becomes a joint venture, or vice versa, Ch. 11, 7.4.2.C
      financial instrument becoming an associate/joint venture, Ch. 11, 7.4.2.A
      step increase in an existing associate/joint venture without a change in status of the investee, Ch. 11, 7.4.2.B
  investments held in, Ch. 11, 5.3
  loans and borrowings between the reporting entity and, Ch. 11, 7.6.3
  risks associated with interests in, Ch. 13, 5.2
  separate financial statements and interests in, Ch. 8, 1.1.1
  share-based payments to employees of, Ch. 34, 12.9
  transactions between the reporting entity and, Ch. 11, 7.6
  VIU for investments in, calculating, Ch. 20, 12.4.2
    based on cash flows generated by underlying assets, Ch. 20, 12.4.2.B
    using dividend discount models, Ch. 20, 12.4.2.A

Key management personnel, related party, Ch. 39, 2.2.1.D

Leases (IFRS 16), Ch. 23, 1–10. *See also* IFRS 16
  acquiree in a business combination is a lessee, Ch. 23, 9.1
  acquiree in a business combination is a lessor, Ch. 23, 9.2
  business combinations, Ch. 23, 9–9.2
  commencement date of the lease, Ch. 23, 4.2
  contract combinations, Ch. 23, 3.3
  definition, Ch. 23, 3–3.3
    determining whether an arrangement contains a lease, Ch. 23, 3.1

flowchart of the decision making process, Ch. 23, 3.1.6
identified asset, Ch. 23, 3.1.2
joint arrangements, Ch. 23, 3.1.1
reassessment of the contract, Ch. 23, 3.1.7
right to direct the use of the identified asset, Ch. 23, 3.1.5
   how and for what purpose the asset is used, Ch. 23, 3.1.5.A
   protective rights, Ch. 23, 3.1.5.D
   relevant decisions about how and for what purpose the asset is used are predetermined, Ch. 23, 3.1.5.B
   specifying the output of an asset before the period of use, Ch. 23, 3.1.5.C
right to obtain substantially all of the economic benefits from use of the identified asset, Ch. 23, 3.1.4
substantive substitution rights, Ch. 23, 3.1.3
identifying and separating lease and non-lease components of a contract, Ch. 23, 3.2
   determining and allocating the consideration in the contract– lessees, Ch. 23, 3.2.3
   determining and allocating the consideration in the contract– lessors, Ch. 23, 3.2.4
   identifying and separating lease components of a contract, Ch. 23, 3.2.1
   identifying and separating lease from non-lease components of a contract, Ch. 23, 3.2.2
      lessee reimbursements, Ch. 23, 3.2.2.A
      practical expedient–lessees, Ch. 23, 3.2.2.B
discount rates, Ch. 23, 4.6
   determination of the incremental borrowing rate by a subsidiary with centralised treasury functions, Ch. 23, 4.6.1
economic life, Ch. 23, 4.8
effective date and transition, Ch. 23, 10
   amounts previously recognised in a business combination, Ch. 23, 10.5.2
   disclosure, Ch. 23, 10.6
   effective date, Ch. 23, 10.1
   lessee transition, Ch. 23, 10.3
      full retrospective approach, Ch. 23, 10.3.1
      modified retrospective approach, Ch. 23, 10.3.2
   lessor transition, Ch. 23, 10.4
      subleases, Ch. 23, 10.4.1
   sale and leaseback transactions, Ch. 23, 10.5.1
   transition, Ch. 23, 10.2
extractive industries, impact of IFRS 16 on, Ch. 43, 17, 18
   allocating contract consideration, Ch. 43, 17.6
   definition of a lease, Ch. 43, 17.2
   identifying and separating lease and non-lease components, Ch. 43, 17.
   identifying lease payments included in the measurement of the lease liability, Ch. 43, 17.5
   interaction of IFRS 16 and IFRS 11, Ch. 43, 18
   interaction of leases with asset retirement obligations, Ch. 43, 17.7
   joint arrangements, Ch. 43, 18
   scope and scope exclusions, Ch. 43, 17.1
   substitution rights, Ch. 43, 17.3

fair value, Ch. 23, 4.9
inception of a contract, Ch. 23, 4.1
initial direct costs, Ch. 23, 4.7; Ch. 19, 4.9.2
lease liabilities under IFRS 16, Ch. 20, 4.1.2
lease payments, Ch. 23, 4.5
   amounts expected to be payable under residual value guarantees lessees only, Ch. 23, 4.5.6
   co-tenancy clauses, Ch. 23, 4.5.11
   exercise price of a purchase option, Ch. 23, 4.5.4
   in-substance fixed lease payments, Ch. 23, 4.5.1
   lease incentives, Ch. 23, 4.5.2; Ch. 19, 4.9.1
   lessors only, Ch. 23, 4.5.7
   payments for penalties for terminating a lease, Ch. 23, 4.5.5
   reassessment of the lease liability, Ch. 23, 4.5.12
   remeasurement by lessors, Ch. 23, 4.5.13
   security deposits, Ch. 23, 4.5.9
   value added tax and property taxes, Ch. 23, 4.5.10
   variable lease payments that depend on an index/rate, Ch. 23, 4.5.3
   variable lease payments which do not depend on an index or rate, Ch. 23, 4.5.8
lease term and purchase options, Ch. 23, 4.4 cancellable leases, Ch. 23, 4.4.1
   reassessment of lease term and purchase options, lessees, Ch. 23, 4.4.2
   lessors, Ch. 23, 4.4.3
lessee accounting, Ch. 23, 5
   disclosure, Ch. 23, 5.8
      additional, Ch. 23, 5.8.3
      of assets, liabilities, expenses and cash flows, Ch. 23, 5.8.2 objective, Ch. 23, 5.8.1
   initial measurement, Ch. 23, 5.2
      lease liabilities, Ch. 23, 5.2.2
      right-of-use assets, Ch. 23, 5.2.1
   initial recognition, Ch. 23, 5.1
      leases of low-value assets, Ch. 23, 5.1.2
      short-term leases, Ch. 23, 5.1.1
   lease modifications, Ch. 23, 5.5
      amendment to IFRS 16 for covid-19 related rent concessions, Ch. 23, 5.5.4
         accounting for a concession in the form of a deferral of lease payments as if the lease is unchanged (Approach 3), Ch. 23, 5.5.4.C
         accounting for a concession, in the form of forgiveness or deferral of lease payments, as a negative variable lease payment (Approach 1), Ch. 23, 5.5.4.A
         accounting for a concession in the form of forgiveness or deferral of lease payments as a resolution of a contingency that fixes previously variable lease payments (Approach 2), Ch. 23, 5.5..B
         disclosure, Ch. 23, 5.5.4.D
         transition and effective date, Ch. 23, 5.5.4.E
      application of lease modification guidance to rent concessions, Ch. 23, 5.5.3
         lessee accounting for rent concessions as lease modifications, Ch. 23, 5.5.3.B
         rent concessions that change the consideration in the contract, Ch. 23, 5.5.3.A

Leases (IFRS 16)—*contd*
  lessee accounting—*contd*
    lease modifications—*contd*
      lessee accounting for a modification that does not result in a separate lease, Ch. 23, 5.5.2
      resulting in a separate lease, Ch. 23, 5.5.1
    lessee matters, Ch. 23, 5.6
      impairment of right-of-use assets, Ch. 23, 5.6.1
      income tax accounting, Ch. 23, 5.6.4
      leases denominated in a foreign currency, Ch. 23, 5.6.2
      portfolio approach, Ch. 23, 5.6.3
    presentation, Ch. 23, 5.7
    presentation in the statement of cash flows, Ch. 40, 5.5.1
    remeasurement of lease liabilities and right-of-use assets, Ch. 23, 5.4
    subsequent measurement, Ch. 23, 5.3
      expense recognition, Ch. 23, 5.3.3
      lease liabilities, Ch. 23, 5.3.2
      right-of-use assets, Ch. 23, 5.3.1
  lessee involvement with the underlying asset before the commencement date, Ch. 23, 4.3
  lessor accounting, Ch. 23, 6
    disclosure, Ch. 23, 6.7
      for all lessors, Ch. 23, 6.7.2
      for finance leases, Ch. 23, 6.7.3
      objective, Ch. 23, 6.7.1
      for operating leases, Ch. 23, 6.7.4
    finance leases, Ch. 23, 6.2
      initial measurement, Ch. 23, 6.2.1
      manufacturer/dealer lessors, Ch. 23, 6.2.2
      remeasurement of the net investment in the lease, Ch. 23, 6.2.4
      subsequent measurement, Ch. 23, 6.2.3
    lease classification, Ch. 23, 6.1
      criteria, Ch. 23, 6.1.1
      reassessment of, Ch. 23, 6.1.4
      residual value guarantees included in the lease classification test, Ch. 23, 6.1.3
      test for land and buildings, Ch. 23, 6.1.2
    lease modifications, Ch. 23, 6.4
      determining whether a modification to a finance lease results in a separate lease, Ch. 23, 6.4.1
      lessor accounting for a modification to a finance lease that does not result in a separate lease, Ch. 23, 6.4.2
      modification to an operating lease, Ch. 23, 6.4.3
    lessor matters, Ch. 23, 6.5
      portfolio approach, Ch. 23, 6.5.1
    operating leases, Ch. 23, 6.3
      income, Ch. 23, 6.3.1
    presentation, Ch. 23, 6.6
    presentation in the statement of cash flows, Ch. 40, 5.5.5
  sale and leaseback transactions, Ch. 23, 8
    determining whether the transfer of an asset is a sale, Ch. 23, 8.1
    disclosures, Ch. 23, 8.4
    transactions in which the transfer of an asset is a sale, Ch. 23, 8.2
      accounting for the leaseback, Ch. 23, 8.2.2
      accounting for the sale, Ch. 23, 8.2.1
      adjustment for off-market terms, Ch. 23, 8.2.3
    transactions in which the transfer of an asset is not a sale, Ch. 23, 8.3
  subleases, Ch. 23, 7
    definition, Ch. 23, 7.1
    disclosure, Ch. 23, 7.5
    intermediate lessor accounting, Ch. 23, 7.2
    presentation, Ch. 23, 7.4
    sublessee accounting, Ch. 23, 7.3
Leases of land, Ch. 23, 3.2
  separating land and buildings, Ch. 23, 6.1.2
Legal obligation, Ch. 26, 1.3, 3.1.1; Ch. 35, 7.1, 12.3.1
Legal right of set-off, enforceable, Ch. 54, 7.4.1.A
Lessee accounting (IFRS 16), Ch. 23, 5
  disclosure, Ch. 23, 5.8
    additional, Ch. 23, 5.8.3
    of assets, liabilities, expenses and cash flows, Ch. 23, 5.8.2
    objective, Ch. 23, 5.8.1
  initial measurement, Ch. 23, 5.2
    lease liabilities, Ch. 23, 5.2.2
    right-of-use assets, Ch. 23, 5.2.1
  initial recognition, Ch. 23, 5.1
    leases of low-value assets, Ch. 23, 5.1.2
    short-term leases, Ch. 23, 5.1.1
  lease liabilities under IFRS 16, Ch. 20, 4.1.2
  lease modifications, Ch. 23, 5.5
    determining whether a lease modification results in a separate lease, Ch. 23, 5.5.1
    lessee accounting for a modification that does not result in a separate lease, Ch. 23, 5.5.2
  lessee matters, Ch. 23, 5.6
    impairment of right-of-use assets, Ch. 23, 5.6.1
    income tax accounting, Ch. 23, 5.6.4
    leases denominated in a foreign currency, Ch. 23, 5.6.2
    portfolio approach, Ch. 23, 5.6.3
  presentation, Ch. 23, 5.7
  remeasurement of lease liabilities and right-of-use assets, Ch. 23, 5.4
  subsequent measurement, Ch. 23, 5.3
    expense recognition, Ch. 23, 5.3.3
    lease liabilities, Ch. 23, 5.3.2
    right-of-use assets, Ch. 23, 5.3.1
Lessor accounting (IFRS 16), Ch. 23, 6
  disclosure, Ch. 23, 6.7
    for all lessors, Ch. 23, 6.7.2
    for finance leases, Ch. 23, 6.7.3
    objective, Ch. 23, 6.7.1
    for operating leases, Ch. 23, 6.4.3
  finance leases, Ch. 23, 6.2
    initial measurement, Ch. 23, 6.2.1
    manufacturer/dealer lessors, Ch. 23, 6.2.2
    remeasurement of the net investment in the lease, Ch. 23, 6.2.4
    subsequent measurement, Ch. 23, 6.2.3
  lease classification, Ch. 23, 6.1
    criteria, Ch. 23, 6.1.1
    reassessment of, Ch. 23, 6.1.4
    residual value guarantees included in the lease classification test, Ch. 23, 6.1.3
    test for land and buildings, Ch. 23, 6.1.2

lease modifications, Ch. 23, 6.4
  determining whether a modification to a finance lease results in a separate lease, Ch. 23, 6.4.1
  lessor accounting for a modification to a finance lease that does not result in a separate lease, Ch. 23, 6.4.2
  modification to an operating lease, Ch. 23, 6.4.3
lessor matters, Ch. 23, 6.5
  portfolio approach, Ch. 23, 6.5.1
operating leases, Ch. 23, 6.3
presentation, Ch. 23, 6.6
Level 1, 2 and 3 inputs, fair value measurement, Ch. 14, 17, 18, 19; Ch. 19, 12.1.1
Levies, Ch. 33, 4.1.1, Ch. 26, 6.8
  charged by public authorities, interim reports, Ch. 41, 9.7.5
Liability adequacy testing, Ch. 55, 7.2.2
  investment contracts with a discretionary participation feature. Ch. 55, 7.2.2.C
  and shadow accounting, interaction between, Ch. 55, 7.2.2.D
  specified in IFRS Ch. 55, 7.2.2.B
  under existing accounting policies, Ch. 55, 7.2.2.A
LIBOR
  LIBOR replacement, Ch. 53, 8.3.5
  'sub-LIBOR issue', Ch. 53, 2.4
Life insurance, Ch. 55, 1.4.2
'Linked' instruments, Ch. 47, 4.5.7
Liquidity risk, Ch. 54, 5.4
  associated liquidity risk, management of, Ch. 54, 5.4.3
  information provided to key management, Ch. 54, 5.4.1
  maturity analyses, Ch. 54, 5.4.2
    cash flows: borrowings, Ch. 54, 5.4.2.C
    cash flows: derivatives, Ch. 54, 5.4.2.D
    cash flows: embedded derivatives, Ch. 54, 5.4.2.E
    cash flows: financial guarantee contracts and written options, Ch. 54, 5.4.2.F
    cash flows: general requirements, Ch. 54, 5.4.2.B
    examples of disclosures in practice, Ch. 54, 5.4.2.G
    time bands, Ch. 54, 5.4.2.A
  puttable financial instruments classified as equity, Ch. 54, 5.4.4
Litigation, provisions and contingencies, Ch. 26, 6.11
Loan commitments, Ch. 48, 6.4.6
  assets and liabilities from, Ch. 49, 3.7
  IFRS 9 impairment requirements, Ch. 51, 11
  off-market, Ch. 49, 3.3.3
  outside the scope of and IFRS 9, Ch. 49, 3.7.1
  within the scope of and IFRS 9, Ch. 49, 3.7.2
Loans
  acquired in business combination, Ch. 49, 3.3.4
  at a below-market interest rate, Ch. 50, 2.8
  commitment, Ch. 45, 3.5
  intercompany loans, Ch. 51, 13
  low-interest long-term, Ch. 49, 3.3.1
  payable, defaults and breaches of, Ch. 54, 4.4.8
Longevity swaps, Ch. 35, 6.6
Long-term contracts and leases, extractive industries Ch. 43, 19
  embedded leases, Ch. 43, 19.1
  impact of IFRS 16, Ch. 43, 19.3
  take-or-pay contracts, Ch. 43, 19.2
    make-up product and undertake, Ch. 43, 19.2.1

Long-term employee benefits, Ch. 35, 13
  meaning of, Ch. 35, 13.1
  other than post-employment benefits, Ch. 35, 13.1
  recognition and measurement, Ch. 35, 13.2
    attribution to years of service, Ch. 35, 13.2.1
    long-term disability benefit, Ch. 35, 13.2.2
    long-term benefits contingent on a future event, Ch. 35, 13.2.3
Long-term loans with repayment on demand terms, Ch. 54, 7.4.4.C
Loss-making associates/joint ventures, Ch. 11, 7.9
Loss-making subsidiaries, Ch. 7, 5.6.1
Low-interest long-term loans, Ch. 49, 3.3.1
Macro hedge accounting, Ch. 53, 11
'Make-up' oil, Ch. 43, 15.4.2.B
Make-up product and undertake, Ch. 43, 17.2.1
'Malus' clauses, share-based payments, Ch. 34, 3.1.1
Management commentary, Ch. 2, 12
Management Commentary Consultative Group, Ch. 1, 2.9
Mandatorily convertible bond, Ch. 47, 6.6.3
  convertible into a variable number of shares upon a contingent 'non-viability' event, Ch. 47, 6.6.3.B
  with option for issuer to settle early for a maximum number of shares, Ch. 47, 6.6.3.A
Mandatory tender offers, Ch. 7, 6.2.4, 7.4
Market and non-market variables, insurance contracts, Ch. 56, 8.2.1
Market approach, valuation technique, Ch. 14, 14.2
Market Consistent Embedded Value Principles (MCEV), Ch. 55, 1.4.3
Market participants, Ch. 14, 7
  assumptions, Ch. 14, 7.2
  characteristics, Ch. 14, 7.1
Market risk, Ch. 54, 5.5
  'basic' sensitivity analysis, Ch. 54, 5.5.1
  other market risk disclosures, Ch. 54, 5.5.3
  value-at-risk and similar analyses, Ch. 54, 5.5.2
Market vesting conditions, share-based payments, Ch. 34, 6.3. *See also* Cash-settled share-based payment transactions; Equity-settled share-based payment transactions; IFRS 2; Share-based payment transactions
Master netting agreements, Ch. 54, 7.4.1.B
  and non-performance risk, Ch. 14, 11.3.4
Material cash flows, Ch. 40, 5.1
Materiality, Ch. 3, 4.1.5.A; Ch. 54, 3.2
  interim financial reporting, Ch. 41, 6
Maturity analyses, liquidity risk, Ch. 54, 5.4.2
  cash flows
    borrowings, Ch. 54, 5.4.2.C
    derivatives, Ch. 54, 5.4.2.D
    embedded derivatives, Ch. 54, 5.4.2.E
    examples of disclosures in practice, Ch. 54, 5.4.2.G
    financial guarantee contracts and written options, Ch. 54, 5.4.2.F
    general requirements, Ch. 54, 5.4.2.B
    time bands, Ch. 54, 5.4.2.A
Measurement period, business combinations, Ch. 9, 12

Measurement period, business combinations—*contd*
   adjustments made during, Ch. 9, 12.1
      to provisional amounts, Ch. 9, 12.1
   after end of measurement period, Ch. 9, 12.2

Measurements based on fair value. *See* Fair value measurements

Measuring ECLs during the coronavirus (covid-19) pandemic, Ch. 51, 7.8
   calculation of ECLs, Ch. 51, 7.8.3
   determining whether there has been a significant increase in credit risk, Ch. 51, 7.8.4
   disclosures, Ch. 51, 7.8.5
   guidance, Ch. 51, 7.8.2
   introduction, Ch. 51, 7.8.1

Mineral reserves and resources, extractive industries
   disclosure of mineral reserves and resources, Ch. 43, 2.4
      associates, joint arrangements and other investments, Ch. 43, 2.4
      commodity price, Ch. 43, 2.4
      mining sector, Ch. 43, 2.4.2
      non-controlling interests, Ch. 43, 2.4
      oil and gas sector, Ch. 43, 2.4.1
      production sharing contracts and risk service contracts, Ch. 43, 2.4
      proven and probable reserves, Ch. 43, 2.4 royalties, Ch. 43, 2.4
      standardised measure of oil and gas, Ch. 43, 2.4.3.A
      value of reserves, Ch. 43, 2.4.3
   international harmonisation of reserve reporting, Ch. 43, 2.1
   legal rights to explore for, develop and produce mineral properties, Ch. 43, 5
      concessionary agreements (concessions), Ch. 43, 5.2
      different types of royalty interests, Ch. 43, 5.7
      evolving contractual arrangements, Ch. 43, 5.5
      joint operating agreements, Ch. 43, 5.6
   mineral lease agreements, Ch. 43, 5.1
   pure-service contract, Ch. 43, 5.4
      basic principles and definitions, Ch. 43, 2.2.1
      classification and categorisation guidelines, Ch. 43, 2.2.2
      mining resource and reserve reporting, Ch. 43, 2.3
      petroleum reserve estimation and reporting, Ch. 43, 2.2
      traditional production sharing contracts, Ch. 43, 5.3

Mining sector disclosures, Ch. 43, 2.4.2. *See also* Extractive industries

Ministry of Finance, People's Republic of China, Ch. 1, 2.3, 4.4.1.A

Modifications in share-based payment, Ch. 34, 7.3
   cash-settled modified to equity-settled, Ch. 34, 9.4.2
   decrease the value of an award, Ch. 34, 7.3.2
      additional/more onerous non-market vesting conditions, Ch. 34, 7.3.2.C
      decrease in fair value of equity instruments granted, Ch. 34, 7.3.2.A
      decrease in number of equity instruments granted, Ch. 34, 7.3.2.B
   distinction between cancellation and modification, Ch. 34, 7.4.2
   entity's plans for future, Ch. 34, 7.6
   equity-settled modified to cash-settled, Ch. 34, 7.3.5, 9.4.1
   'give and take', Ch. 34, 7.3.4
   increase the value of an award, Ch. 34, 7.3.1
      increase in fair value of equity instruments granted, Ch. 34, 7.3.1.A
      increase in number of equity instruments granted, Ch. 34, 7.3.1.B
      removal/mitigation of non-market vesting conditions, Ch. 34, 7.3.1.C
   reduce the number of equity instruments granted but maintain or increase the value of an award, Ch. 34, 7.3.4
   share splits and consolidations, Ch. 34, 7.8
   two awards running 'in parallel', Ch. 34, 7.7
   valuation requirements, Ch. 34, 7.2
   'value for value', Ch. 34, 7.3.4
   of vesting period, Ch. 34, 7.3.3

Modified International Standards (JMIS), Japan, Ch. 1, 4.4.2

Monetary/non-monetary determination, foreign exchange, Ch. 15, 5.4
   deferred tax, Ch. 15, 5.4.5
   deposits and advance payments for actively traded commodities, Ch. 15, 5.4.2
   deposits/progress payments, Ch. 15, 5.4.1
   foreign currency share capital, Ch. 15, 5.4.4
   insurance contracts, Ch. 56, 7.3
   investments in preference shares, Ch. 15, 5.4.3
   post-employment benefit plans-foreign currency assets, Ch. 15, 5.4.6
   post-employment benefit plans-foreign currency plans, Ch. 15, 5.4.7

Monetary/non-monetary distinction
   hyperinflationary economies, Ch. 16, 4.1.1

Money market funds (MMF), Ch. 40, 3.2.2

Monitoring Board, Ch. 1, 2.3

Monte Carlo Simulation, Ch. 34, 8.3.3

Most advantageous market, Ch. 14, 6.2

Multi-employer plans, employee benefits, Ch. 35, 3.3
   defined benefit plans sharing risks between entities under common control, Ch. 35, 3.3.2
   disclosure requirements
      other than plans sharing risks between entities under common control, Ch. 35, 3.3.1
      plans accounted for as defined benefit plans, Ch. 35, 15.2.4.A
      plans accounted for as defined contribution plans, Ch. 35, 15.2.4.B

Multi-layered fund structures, Ch. 6, 10.2.10

Multi Period Excess Earnings Method (MEEM), Ch. 9, 5.5.2.F

Multiple valuation techniques, fair value measurement, Ch. 14, 14.1.2
   vs. single valuation techniques, Ch. 14, 14.1.1

Mutual entities, Ch. 9, 2.1, 7.5

Negative compensation, Ch. 48, 6.4.4.A

Negative discretionary participation feature, Ch. 55, 6.3.1

Negative intangible assets, Ch. 55, 9.1.1.D

Net cash-settled forward repurchase, Ch. 52, 4.1.4

Net defined benefit liability (asset), employee benefits, Ch. 35, 8.1
   net interest on, Ch. 35, 10.3.2
   presentation of, Ch. 35, 9

Net finance costs, Ch. 54, 7.1.1

Net investment hedges
    combination of derivatives and non-derivatives, Ch. 53, 7.3.4
    in foreign operations, Ch. 53, 1.5, 5.3, 7.3; Ch. 54, 4.3.3
        amount of the hedged item for which a hedging relationship may be designated, Ch. 53, 5.3.2
        nature of the hedged risk, Ch. 53, 5.3.1
        where the hedging instrument can be held, Ch. 53, 5.3.3
    identifying the effective portion, Ch. 53, 7.3.1
        cross-currency interest rate swaps, Ch. 53, 7.3.3.B
        derivatives used as the hedging instrument, Ch. 53, 7.3.3
        forward currency contracts, Ch. 53, 7.3.3.A
    individual/separate financial statements, Ch. 53, 7.3.5
        non-derivative liabilities used as the hedging instrument, Ch. 53, 7.3.2
        purchased options, Ch. 53, 7.3.3.C

Net realisable value, inventories, Ch. 22, 3.3

Net-settled contracts over own equity, Ch. 47, 5.2.7

Nominal amount components, Ch. 53, 2.3
    general requirement, Ch. 53, 2.3.1
    layer components for fair value hedges with prepayment risk, Ch. 53, 2.3.2

Non-adjusting events, Ch. 38, 2.1.3, 2.3

Non-cash assets to owners, Ch. 7, 3.7; Ch. 8, 2.4.2
    declaration to distribute, Ch. 38, 2.3.1.A
    distributions of, Ch. 7, 3.7; Ch. 8, 2.4.2

Non-cash transactions and transactions on deferred terms, Ch. 40, 5.4

Non-contractually specified risk components, Ch. 53, 2.2.3

Non-controlling interests (NCI), Ch. 7, 2.1, 3.1.1, 3.1.2, 4, 5, 6; Ch. 43, 2.4
    acquisition of, as part of a business combination under common control, Ch. 10, 3.3.5
    associate holds an interest in a subsidiary, Ch. 7, 5.3
    business combinations, recognising and measuring NCIs, Ch. 7, 5.2.1; Ch. 9, 8
        call and put options over NCIs, Ch. 7, 6; Ch. 9, 8.5
        implications of method chosen for measuring NCIs, Ch. 9, 8.3
        measuring qualifying NCIs at acquisition-date fair value, Ch. 7, 5.2.1; Ch. 9, 8.1
        measuring qualifying NCIs at the proportionate share of the value of net identifiable assets acquired, Ch. 7, 5.2.1; Ch. 9, 8.2
        measuring share-based payment and other components of NCIs, Ch. 7, 5.2.1, 5.6; Ch. 9, 8.4
    call and put options over, Ch. 7, 6.5
        call and put options, combination, Ch. 7, 6.3
        call and put options entered into in relation to existing NCIs, Ch. 7, 6.4
        call options only, Ch. 7, 6.1
            options giving the acquirer present access to returns associated with that ownership interest, Ch. 7, 6.1.1
            options not giving the acquirer present access to returns associated with that ownership interest, Ch. 7, 6.1.2
        exercisable in cash or shares, Ch. 7, 6.2
        put options only, Ch. 7, 6.2
            assessing whether multiple transactions should be accounted for as a single arrangement, Ch. 7, 6.2.4
            financial liability for the NCI put, Ch. 7, 6.2.1
            full recognition of NCI, Ch. 7, 6.2.3.B
            mandatory tender offers, Ch. 7, 6.2.4
            NCI is subsequently derecognized, Ch. 7, 6.2.3.D
            NCI put does not provide a present ownership interest, Ch. 7, 6.2.3
            NCI put provides a present ownership interest, Ch. 7, 6.2.2, 6.2.3.A
            partial recognition of NCI, Ch. 7, 6.2.3.C
            separate financial statements, Ch. 7, 6.5
    changes in ownership interest without loss of control (*see* Consolidation procedures)
    classified as financial liabilities, Ch. 7, 5.5
    definition of NCI, Ch. 7, 5.1
    disclosure of interests held by, Ch. 13, 4.2
    exceptions to retrospective application of other IFRSs, Ch. 5, 4.8
    future developments, Ch. 7, 7
        financial instruments with characteristics of equity project, Ch. 7, 7.3
        mandatory purchase of NCIs, Ch. 7, 7.4
        Post-implementation Reviews of IFRS 10, IFRS 11 and IFRS 12, Ch. 7, 7.5
    goodwill impairment testing, Ch. 7, 4.2; Ch. 20, 9
        acquisitions of NCIs measured at the proportionate share of net identifiable assets, Ch. 20, 9.1.1
        testing for impairment in entities with NCIs, alternative allocation methodologies, Ch. 20, 9.3
        testing for impairment in entities with NCIs initially measured at fair value, Ch. 20, 9.2
        testing for impairment in entities with NCIs measured at the proportionate share of net identifiable assets, Ch. 20, 9.1
    initial measurement of NCIs in a business combination, Ch. 7, 5.2.1, 5.2.2
    initial measurement of NCIs in a subsidiary that is not a business combination, Ch. 7, 3.1.1, 5.2.2
    mandatory tender offers in a business combination, Ch. 7, 6.2.4
    measurement in, Ch. 7, 2.1, 2.2, 3.1.1, 3.1.2, 5
    measurement of NCI where an associate holds an interest in a subsidiary, Ch. 7, 5.3
    non-cash acquisition of, Ch. 7, 4
    not recognized, Ch. 7, 6.2.3.A
    presentation of NCIs, Ch. 7, 5.4
    reverse acquisitions, business combinations, Ch. 9, 14.4
    subsequent measurement of, Ch. 7, 5.6
        loss-making subsidiaries, Ch. 7, 5.6.1
    transactions with, IAS 7, Ch. 40, 6.2

Non-coterminous accounting periods, Ch. 7, 2.5; Ch. 11, 7.7; Ch. 15, 6.4

Non-current assets (and disposal groups) held for sale/distribution, Ch. 4, 2
    classification, Ch. 4, 2.1
        abandonment, Ch. 4, 2.1.2.C
        classification as held for sale or as held for distribution to owners, Ch. 4, 2.1.2
        concept of a disposal group, Ch. 4, 2.1.1
        loss of control of a subsidiary, Ch. 4, 2.1.3.A
        meaning of available for immediate sale, Ch. 4, 2.1.2.A

Non-current assets (and disposal groups) held for sale/distribution—*contd*
  classification—*contd*
    meaning of highly probable, Ch. 4, 2.1.2.B
    partial disposal of an associate or joint venture, Ch. 4, 2.1.3.B
    partial disposals of operations, Ch. 4, 2.1.3
  comparative information, Ch. 4, 4
  disclosure requirements, Ch. 4, 5
  discontinued operation, Ch. 4, 3.2
  future developments, Ch. 4, 6
  measurement, Ch. 4, 2.2
    changes to a plan of sale/distribution, Ch. 4, 2.2.5
    impairments and reversals of impairment, Ch. 4, 2.2.3
    on initial classification as held for sale, Ch. 4, 2.2.2.A
    presentation in the statement of financial position of, Ch. 4, 2.2.4
    scope of the measurement requirements, Ch. 4, 2.2.1
    subsequent remeasurement, Ch. 4, 2.2.2.B
  property, plant and equipment, Ch. 18, 7.1
  statement of financial position presentation, Ch. 4, 4.1.2

Non-employees, share-based payment transactions with, Ch. 34, 5.4.1

Non-financial assets
  financial instruments definition, Ch. 45, 2.2.5
  hedged item, Ch. 53, 2.2.3.A; Ch. 53, 2.2.1
  non-contractual risk components, Ch. 53, 2.2.3.A

Non-financial risk, risk adjustment for, Ch. 56, 8.4

Non insurance contracts, Ch. 55, 3.8; Ch. 56, 3.7.2

Non-life insurance, Ch. 55, 1.4.1

Non-market interest rate loans, Ch. 8, 4.4.5.A

Non-monetary assets
  to an associate/a joint venture, contributions of, Ch. 7, 3.3.2, 7.1; Ch. 11, 7.6.5.B
  transactions involving, Ch. 8, 4.4.1

Non-performance risk
  counterparty credit risk and its own credit risk, Ch. 14, 11.3.2
  derivative liabilities, Ch. 14, 11.3.4
  entity incorporate credit risk into the valuation of its derivative contracts, Ch. 14, 11.3.3
  with third-party credit enhancements, Ch. 14, 11.3.1

Non-recourse loans, Ch. 34, 8.7.2; Ch. 48, 6.5

Non-vesting conditions, share-based payment, Ch. 34, 3.2
  background, Ch. 34, 3.2.1
  cash-settled transactions, Ch. 34, 9.3.2.D
  defining non-vesting condition, Ch. 34, 3.2.2
  equity-settled transactions, Ch. 34, 6.4
  non-compete agreements, Ch. 34, 3.2.3
  option pricing models, treatment of non-vesting condition, Ch. 34, 8.4.2

Notional decomposition, hedging instruments, Ch. 53, 3.6.2

Novation of contracts to intermediary counterparties, Ch. 52, 3.4.4

Numerator (EPS), Ch. 37, 6.4.2.A

Obligating event, Ch. 26, 1.3, 3.1

Observable inputs, Ch. 14, 8.3.2

OCI. *See* Other Comprehensive Income (OCI)

Off-balance sheet finance, Ch. 52, 1.1

Off-market loan commitments, Ch. 49, 3.3.3

Offsetting and hedges, Ch. 54, 7.1.3
  external instruments, Ch. 53, 3.2.1
  internal hedging instruments, Ch. 53, 4.2
    foreign exchange risk, Ch. 53, 4.2.2
    interest rate risk, Ch. 53, 4.2.1

Offsetting financial assets and financial liabilities, Ch. 54, 7.4.1
  cash pooling arrangements, Ch. 54, 7.4.1.E
    presentation in the statement of cash flows, Ch. 40, 6.5
  collateral amounts, Ch. 54, 7.4.1.F
  disclosures, Ch. 54, 7.4.2
    examples, Ch. 54, 7.4.2.D
    objective, Ch. 54, 7.4.2.A
    requirements, Ch. 54, 7.4.2.C
    scope, Ch. 54, 7.4.2.B
  enforceable legal right of set-off criterion, Ch. 54, 7.4.1.A
  master netting agreements, Ch. 54, 7.4.1.B
  net settlement criterion, Ch. 54, 7.4.1.C
  situations where offset is not normally appropriate, Ch. 54, 7.4.1.D
  unit of account, Ch. 54, 7.4.1.G

Oil and gas sector. *See also* Extractive industries
  disclosures by, Ch. 43, 2.4.1
  IFRIC 1 exemption for oil and gas assets at deemed cost, Ch. 5, 5.13.2

Oil Industry Accounting Committee (OIAC), Statement of Recommended Practice (SORP), Ch. 43, 1.4

Onerous contracts, Ch. 26, 6.2
  onerous leases, Ch. 23, 10.3.2.A

Operating activities, cash flows from, Ch. 40, 4.1

Operating segments, Ch. 36, 1–7. *See also* IFRS 8; Reportable segments
  aggregation criteria, Ch. 36, 3.2.1
  'chief operating decision maker' and 'segment manager', Ch. 36, 3.1.2
  combining small operating segments into a larger reportable segment, Ch. 36, 3.2.3
  entity-wide disclosures for all entities, Ch. 36, 6
    information about geographical areas, Ch. 36, 6.2
    information about major customers, Ch. 36, 6.3
    information about products and services, Ch. 36, 6.1
  equity accounted investment can be an operating segment, Ch. 36, 3.1.5
  identifying externally reportable segments, Ch. 36, 3.2
  measurement, Ch. 36, 4
  operating segments which are reportable because of their size, Ch. 36, 3.2.2
    proposed amendments to IFRS 8 and IAS 34 (ED/2017/2), Ch. 36, 7.1
  reportable segments, information to be disclosed, Ch. 36, 5
    additional disclosures relating to segment assets, Ch. 36, 5.4
    disclosure of commercially sensitive information, Ch. 36, 5.8
    disclosure of other elements of revenue, income and expense, Ch. 36, 5.3
    explanation of the measurements used in segment reporting, Ch. 36, 5.5
    general information about reportable segments, Ch. 36, 5.1

disclosure of how operating segments are aggregated, Ch. 36, 5.1.1
measure of segment profit or loss, total assets and total liabilities, Ch. 36, 5.2
reconciliations, Ch. 36, 5.6
restatement of previously reported information, Ch. 36, 5.7
changes in organisation structure, Ch. 36, 5.7.1
changes in segment measures, Ch. 36, 5.7.2
restatement of segments reported in comparative periods, Ch. 36, 3.2.6
revenue earning business activities, Ch. 36, 3.1.1
scope, Ch. 36, 2.2
consolidated financial statements presented with those of the parent, Ch. 36, 2.2.2
entities providing segment information on a voluntary basis, Ch. 36, 2.2.3
meaning of 'traded in a public market,' Ch. 36, 2.2.1
single set of operating segments, identifying, Ch. 36, 3
definition of an operating segment, Ch. 36, 3.1
terms used in IFRS 8, Ch. 36, 1.3
transitional provisions, Ch. 36, 1.4

Operational risk, Ch. 54, 5.6.2

Option contracts, Ch. 49, 2.1.4

Option-pricing models. *See also* Share-based payment transactions
accounting for share-based payment, Ch. 34, 8.4
market-based performance measures and non-vesting conditions, Ch. 34, 8.4.2.A
non-market vesting conditions, Ch. 34, 8.4.2.B
non-transferability, Ch. 34, 8.4.1
vesting and non-vesting conditions, treatment of, Ch. 34, 8.4.2
selecting appropriate assumptions for, Ch. 34, 8.5
binomial model and other lattice models, Ch. 34, 8.5.4.B
Black-Scholes-Merton formula, Ch. 34, 8.5.4.A
exercise and termination behaviour, Ch. 34, 8.5.2
expected dividends, Ch. 34, 8.5.4
expected term of the option, Ch. 34, 8.5.1
expected volatility of share price, Ch. 34, 8.5.3
risk-free interest rate, Ch. 34, 8.5.5
selection of model, Ch. 34, 8.3
binomial model, Ch. 34, 8.3.2
Black-Scholes-Merton formula, Ch. 34, 8.3.1
lattice models-number of time steps, Ch. 34, 8.3.2.A
Monte Carlo Simulation, Ch. 34, 8.3.3

Orderly transaction, Ch. 14, 8.2.2

Other Comprehensive Income (OCI), Ch. 3, 3.2.1
accounting for loss of control, Ch. 7, 2.3, 3.5
cash flow hedge accounting, Ch. 53, 7.2, 7.3
debt instrument measured at fair value through OCI under IFRS 9, Ch. 33, 10.4.1
defined benefit plans, Ch. 33, 10.7; Ch. 35, 9
remeasurements, Ch. 35, 10.4
actuarial gains and losses, Ch. 35, 10.4.1
return on plan assets, excluding amounts included in net interest on the net defined benefit liability (asset), Ch. 35, 10.4.2
gains and losses recognised in, Ch. 54, 7.2
hedges of exposures affecting, Ch. 53, 2.6.3

insurance contracts, allocating finance income or expenses on, Ch. 56, 15.3
non-derivative equity investments designation at, Ch. 48, 8
reattribution of, changes in ownership interest without a loss of control, Ch. 7, 4.1
tax on items of, Ch. 3, 3.2.4.C

Outside temporary differences, deferred tax recognition, Ch. 33, 7.5
anticipated intragroup dividends in future foreseeable future, Ch. 33, 7.5.4
consolidated financial statements of receiving entity, Ch. 33, 7.5.4.A
separate financial statements of paying entity, Ch. 33, 7.5.4.B
calculation of, Ch. 33, 7.5.1
consolidated financial statements, Ch. 33, 7.5.1.A
separate financial statements, Ch. 33, 7.5.1.B
deductible temporary differences, Ch. 33, 7.5.3
other overseas income taxed only on remittance, Ch. 33, 7.5.6
taxable temporary differences, Ch. 33, 7.5.2
'tax transparent' entities, Ch. 33, 7.6
unpaid intragroup interest, royalties, management charges etc., Ch. 33, 7.5.5

Outstanding ordinary shares, changes in, Ch. 37, 4
adjustments to EPS in historical summaries, Ch. 37, 4.7
issue to acquire another business, Ch. 37, 4.6
acquisitions, Ch. 37, 4.6.1
establishment of a new parent undertaking, Ch. 37, 4.6.3
reverse acquisitions, Ch. 37, 4.6.2
new parent undertaking, establishment of, Ch. 37, 4.6.3
options exercised during the year, Ch. 37, 4.4
ordinary shares without corresponding changes in resources, changes in, Ch. 37, 4.3
B share schemes, Ch. 37, 4.3.4
bonus issue, Ch. 37, 4.3.1.A
capitalisation, Ch. 37, 4.3.1.A
put warrants priced above market value, Ch. 37, 4.3.5
rights issue, Ch. 37, 4.3.3
share consolidation, Ch. 37, 4.3.1.C
share consolidation with a special dividend, Ch. 37, 4.3.2
share consolidations, Ch. 37, 4.3.1.C
share split, Ch. 37, 4.3.1.A
stock dividends, Ch. 37, 4.3.1.B
post balance sheet changes in capital, Ch. 37, 4.5
purchase and redemption of own shares, Ch. 37, 4.2
weighted average number of shares, Ch. 37, 4.1

Overlift and underlift (oil and gas), Ch. 43, 12.4

Over-the-counter (OTC) derivatives
categorisation, Ch. 14, 16.2.4

Own equity instruments, Ch. 53, 3.4

Own use contracts, Ch. 53, 12.2

Owner-occupied property, Ch. 19, 2.4. *See also* IAS 16; Property, plant and equipment

Ownership changes in a joint venture, Ch. 12, 8.2
acquisition of an interest in a joint venture, Ch. 12, 8.2.1
control over a joint venture, Ch. 12, 8.3.2
demergers and distributions of non-cash assets to owners, Ch. 7, 3.7
disposal of interest in a joint venture, Ch. 12, 8.2.6

Ownership changes in a joint venture—*contd*
   former subsidiary becomes a joint venture, Ch. 7, 3.3.2, 7.1; Ch. 12, 8.3.3
   interest in a joint venture held for sale, Ch. 12, 8.2.7
   joint venture becomes a financial asset (or vice versa), Ch. 12, 8.2.5
   joint venture becomes an associate (or vice versa), Ch. 12, 8.2.4

Ownership interests, changes in, Ch. 7, 3, 4, 5.2, 6
   accounting for a loss of control, Ch. 7 3.2, 3.3, 3.4, 3.5, 3.6, 3.7, 7.1, 7.2
   acquisition of a subsidiary that is not a business, Ch. 7, 3.1.1, 3.1.2
   deemed disposal, Ch. 7, 3.6. *See also* IFRIC 17
   interest retained in the former subsidiary, Ch. 7, 3.3
      interest retained in the former subsidiary-associate or joint venture, Ch. 7, 3.3.2, 7.1
      interest retained in the former subsidiary–financial asset, Ch. 7, 3.3.1
      interest retained in the former subsidiary–joint operation, Ch. 7, 3.3.3, 7.2
   loss of control in multiple arrangements Ch. 7, 3.4
   mandatory tender offers in a business combination, Ch. 7, 6.2.4, 7.4
   multiple arrangements, loss of control in, Ch. 7, 3.4
   non-cash assets to owners, Ch. 7, 3.5
   other comprehensive income, Ch. 7, 2.3, 3.5, 4.1
   without a loss of control, Ch. 7, 4.1, 4.2, 4.3, 4.4, 4.5

Partial disposals. *See also* Ownership interests, changes in
   of an associate or joint venture, Ch. 4, 2.1.3.B; Ch. 11, 7.12.5
   of foreign operation, Ch. 15, 2.3, 4.1, 6.6.2.
   of interests in associate/joint venture, Ch. 11, 7.12.5
   of operations, Ch. 4, 2.1.3
   of property, plant and equipment, Ch. 18, 7.3

Partial term hedging, Ch. 53, 2.2.4
Parts (components) approach, assets, accounting for, Ch. 18, 3.2
Past service cost, employee benefits, Ch. 35, 10.2.1
Payables, Ch. 49, 2.1.1
Pension, Ch. 35, 3. *See also* Defined benefit plans; Defined contribution plans; IAS 19; IFRIC 14
   defined benefit plans, Ch. 35, 3.1, 5
   funding payments contingent on future events within the control of the entity, Ch. 35, 8.2.5
   insured benefits, Ch. 35, 3.2

Performance condition, share-based payment, Ch. 34, 3.1, 6.2, 6.3
Performance obligation, IFRS 15, Ch. 28, 3
Performance rating, share-based payment, Ch. 34, 3.1.2
Performance target, share-based payment, Ch. 34, 3.1, 5.3.3
Perpetual debt, Ch. 47, 4.7; Ch. 50, 3.5
Perpetual instruments with a 'step-up' clause, Ch. 47, 4.5.4
Persistency risk, insurance contracts, Ch. 55, 3.7.1
Petroleum reserve estimation and reporting, Ch. 43, 2.2
   basic principles and definitions, Ch. 43, 2.2.1
   classification and categorisation guidelines, Ch. 43, 2.2.2

Phantom options, share-based payment, Ch. 34, 9.1
Physical capital maintenance (framework), Ch. 2, 11.2
Piecemeal acquisition of an associate/joint venture, Ch. 11, 7.4.2

   common control transactions involving sales of associates, Ch. 11, 7.4.2.D
   cost-based approach, Ch. 11, 7.4.2.A
   existing associate that becomes a joint venture, or vice versa, Ch. 11, 7.4.2.C
   fair value (IFRS 3) approach, Ch. 11, 7.4.2.A
   financial instrument becoming an associate/joint venture, Ch. 11, 7.4.2.A
   step increase in an existing associate/joint venture without a change in status of the investee, Ch. 11, 7.4.2.B

Plan assets, employee benefits, Ch. 35, 6
   contributions to defined benefit funds, Ch. 35, 6.5
   definition of, Ch. 35, 6.1
   longevity swaps, Ch. 35, 6.6
   measurement of, Ch. 35, 6.2
   qualifying insurance policies, Ch. 35, 6.3
   reimbursement rights, Ch. 35, 6.4

Plan liabilities, employee benefits, Ch. 35, 7
   actuarial assumptions, Ch. 35, 7.5
   actuarial methodology, Ch. 35, 7.3
   attributing benefit to years of service, Ch. 35, 7.4
   contributions by employees and third parties, Ch. 35, 7.2
   discount rate, Ch. 35, 7.6
   frequency of valuations, Ch. 35, 7.7
   legal and constructive obligations, Ch. 35, 7.1

Policy administration and maintenance costs (insurance contracts), Ch. 56, 8.2.3.H
Policyholder, Ch. 55, 2.2.1
   adverse effect on, Ch. 55, 3.7
      insurance of non-insurance risks, Ch. 55, 3.7.2
      lapse, persistency and expense risk, Ch. 55, 3.7.1
   of direct insurance contracts, Ch. 55, 2.2.3.F

Policyholder loans, Ch. 55, 7.2.6.F; Ch. 56, 8.12.2
Pooling of interests method, Ch. 10, 3.1, 3.3
Post-employment benefits, Ch. 35, 3. *See also* Pension
   defined benefit plans, Ch. 35, 3.1
   defined contribution plans, Ch. 35, 3.1
   disclosure of key management personnel compensation, Ch. 39, 2.6.3
   insured benefits, Ch. 35, 3.2
   multi-employer plans, Ch. 35, 3.3
   related parties, Ch. 39, 2.2.6
   state plans, Ch. 35, 3.4

Post-tax cash flows, VIU calculation using, Ch. 20, 7.2.3
Power and returns, principal-agency situations, Ch. 6, 6
   application examples in IFRS 10, Ch. 6, 6.6–6.7
   available replacements, Ch. 6, 6.3.1.A
   decision-making, scope of, Ch. 6, 6.2
   delegated power: principals and agents, Ch. 6, 6.1
   exercise period, Ch. 6, 6.3.1.B
   exposure to variability of returns from other interests, Ch. 6, 6.5
   liquidation rights and redemption rights, Ch. 6, 6.3.2
   remuneration, Ch. 6, 6.4
   rights held by other parties, Ch. 6, 6.3

Power over an investee, Ch. 6, 4. *See also* Existing rights, investee; Voting rights, investee
   contractual arrangements, Ch. 6, 4.4
   determining whether sponsoring (designing) a structured entity gives power, Ch. 6, 4.6

existing rights, Ch. 6, 4.2
management of defaults on assets, Ch. 6, 4.1.4
more than one relevant activity, Ch. 6, 4.1.1
no relevant activities, Ch. 6, 4.1.2
relevant activities, Ch. 6, 4.1
single asset, single lessee vehicles, Ch. 6, 4.1.3
voting rights, Ch. 6, 4.3

PP&E. *See* Property, Plant and Equipment

Pre-existing relationships, business combination, Ch. 9, 11.1
assessing part of exchange for the acquiree, Ch. 9, 11
contingent payments, arrangements for, Ch. 9, 11.2.1
effective settlement of, Ch. 9, 11.1
reimbursement for paying acquirer's acquisition-related costs, Ch. 9, 11.3
remuneration for future services, Ch. 9, 11.2
restructuring plans, Ch. 9, 11.4
share-based payment awards, Ch. 9, 7.2

Preference dividends (EPS), Ch. 37, 5.2

Preference shares, Ch. 47, 4.5
'change of control,' 'taxation change' and 'regulatory change' clauses, Ch. 47, 4.5.8
economic compulsion, Ch. 47, 4.5.6
instruments redeemable
with a 'dividend blocker,' Ch. 47, 4.5.3.A
with a 'dividend pusher,' Ch. 47, 4.5.3.B
mandatorily or at the holder's option, Ch. 47, 4.5.1
only at the issuer's option or not redeemable, Ch. 47, 4.5.2
'linked' instruments, Ch. 47, 4.5.7
perpetual instruments with a 'step-up' clause, Ch. 47, 4.5.4
relative subordination, Ch. 47, 4.5.5

Premium allocation approach, insurance contracts, Ch. 56, 9
accounting policies adopted for contracts applying, Ch. 56, 16.1.2.A
aggregation for contracts applying, Ch. 56, 5.3
allocating insurance finance income/expenses for incurred claims when applying, Ch. 56, 15.3.2
criteria for use of, Ch. 56, 9.1
derecognition contracts, Ch. 56, 12.3.4
initial measurement, Ch. 56, 9.2
insurance revenue under, Ch. 56, 15.1.2
reconciliations required for contracts applying, Ch. 56, 16.1.1
for reinsurance contracts held, Ch. 56, 10.7
subsequent measurement
liability for incurred claims, Ch. 56, 9.4
liability for remaining coverage, Ch. 56, 9.3

Premium cash flows, Ch. 56, 8.2.3.A

Prepaid and accrued operating lease income, Ch. 19, 6.6

Prepayment, negative compensation, Ch. 48, 6.4.4.A

Present value of future profits (PVFP), Ch. 55, 9.1

Present value of in-force business (PVIF), Ch. 55, 9.1

Presentation and disclosure, financial instruments, Ch. 54, 1–9
disclosures, structuring, Ch. 54, 3
classes of financial instrument, Ch. 54, 3.3
level of detail, Ch. 54, 3.1
materiality, Ch. 54, 3.2
effective date and transitional provisions, Ch. 54, 8
future developments, Ch. 54, 9
interim reports, Ch. 54, 2.3

nature and extent of risks arising from financial instruments, Ch. 54, 5
qualitative disclosures, Ch. 54, 5.1
quantitative disclosures, Ch. 54, 5.2
'basic' sensitivity analysis, Ch. 54, 5.5.1
capital disclosures, Ch. 54, 5.6.3
cash flows, Ch. 54, 5.4.2
concentrations of risk, Ch. 54, 5.6.1
credit risk, Ch. 54, 5.3
credit risk exposure, Ch. 54, 5.3.4
credit risk management practices, Ch. 54, 5.3.2
illustrative disclosures, Ch. 54, 5.3.6
information provided to key management, Ch. 54, 5.4.1
liquidity risk, Ch. 54, 5.4
management of associated liquidity risk, Ch. 54, 5.4.3
market risk, Ch. 54, 5.5
maturity analyses, Ch. 54, 5.4.2
operational risk, Ch. 54, 5.6.2
puttable financial instruments classified as equity, Ch. 54, 5.4.4
quantitative and qualitative information about amounts arising from expected credit losses, Ch. 54, 5.3.3
scope and objectives, Ch. 54, 5.3.1
time bands, Ch. 54, 5.4.2.A
value-at-risk and similar analyses, Ch. 54, 5.5.2
presentation on the face of the financial statements and related disclosures, Ch. 54, 7
gains and losses recognised in other comprehensive income, Ch. 54, 7.2
gains and losses recognised in profit/loss embedded derivatives, Ch. 54, 7.1.4
entities whose share capital is not equity, Ch. 54, 7.1.4
further analysis of gains and losses recognised in profit/loss, Ch. 54, 7.1.2
offsetting and hedges, Ch. 54, 7.1.3
presentation on the face of the statement of comprehensive income (or income statement), Ch. 54, 7.1.1
statement of cash flows, Ch. 54, 7.5
statement of changes in equity, Ch. 54, 7.3
statement of financial position, Ch. 54, 7.4
assets and liabilities, Ch. 54, 7.4.3
convertible loans, Ch. 54, 7.4.4.B
current and non-current assets and liabilities, distinction between, Ch. 54, 7.4.4
debt with refinancing or roll over agreements, Ch. 54, 7.4.4.D
derivatives, Ch. 54, 7.4.4.A
disclosure requirements, Ch. 54, 7.4.2.C
enforceable legal right of set-off, Ch. 54, 7.4.1.A
entities whose share capital is not equity, Ch. 54, 7.4.6
equity, Ch. 54, 7.4.5
intention to settle net, Ch. 54, 7.4.1.C
loan covenants, Ch. 54, 7.4.4.E
long-term loans with repayment on demand terms, Ch. 54, 7.4.4.C
master netting agreements, Ch. 54, 7.4.1.B
objective, Ch. 54, 7.4.2.A
offsetting collateral amounts, Ch. 54, 7.4.1.F

Presentation and disclosure, financial instruments—*contd*
  presentation on the face of the financial statements and related disclosures—*contd*
    statement of financial position—*contd*
      offsetting financial assets and financial liabilities, Ch. 54, 7.4.1
      offsetting financial assets and financial liabilities: disclosure, Ch. 54, 7.4.2
      scope, Ch. 54, 7.4.2.B
      situations where offset is not normally appropriate, Ch. 54, 7.4.1.D
      unit of account, Ch. 54, 7.4.1.G
  significance of financial instruments for an entity's financial position/performance, Ch. 54, 4
    accounting policies, Ch. 54, 4.1
    business combinations, Ch. 54, 4.6
      acquired receivables, Ch. 54, 4.6.1
      contingent consideration and indemnification assets, Ch. 54, 4.6.2
    fair values, Ch. 54, 4.5
      day 1 profits, Ch. 54, 4.5.2
      general disclosure requirements, Ch. 54, 4.5.1
    hedge accounting, Ch. 54, 4.3
      amount, timing and uncertainty of future cash flows, Ch. 54, 4.3.2
      effects of hedge accounting on financial position and performance, Ch. 54, 4.3.3
      option to designate a credit exposure as measured at fair value through profit/loss, Ch. 54, 4.3.4
      risk management strategy, Ch. 54, 4.3.1
      uncertainty arising from interest rate benchmark (or IBOR) reform, Ch. 54, 4.3.5
    income, expenses, gains and losses, Ch. 54, 4.2
      fee income and expense, Ch. 54, 4.2.3
      gains and losses by measurement category, Ch. 54, 4.2.1
      interest income and expense, Ch. 54, 4.2.2
    statement of financial position, Ch. 54, 4.4
      categories of financial assets and financial liabilities, Ch. 54, 4.4.1
      collateral, Ch. 54, 4.4.6
      compound financial instruments with multiple embedded derivatives, Ch. 54, 4.4.7
      defaults and breaches of loans payable, Ch. 54, 4.4.8
      financial assets designated as measured at fair value through profit/loss, Ch. 54, 4.4.3
      financial liabilities designated at fair value through profit/loss, Ch. 54, 4.4.2
      interests in associates and joint ventures accounted for in accordance with IFRS 9, Ch. 54, 4.4.9
      investments in equity instruments designated at fair value through other comprehensive income (IFRS 9), Ch. 54, 4.4.4
      reclassification, Ch. 54, 4.4.5
  transfers of financial assets, Ch. 54, 6
    meaning of 'transfer,' Ch. 54, 6.1
    transferred financial assets that are derecognised in their entirety, Ch. 54, 6.3
      disclosure requirements, Ch. 54, 6.3.2
      meaning of continuing involvement, Ch. 54, 6.3.1
    transferred financial assets that are not derecognised in their entirety, Ch. 54, 6.2
  transitional provisions, Ch. 54, 8

Presentation currency. *See also* IAS 21
  average rate calculation, Ch. 15, 6.1.4
  change of, Ch. 15, 7
  disposal of a foreign operation, Ch. 15, 6.6
    step-by-step and direct methods of consolidation, Ch. 7, 2.3; Ch. 15, 6.6.3
  exchange differences on intragroup balances, Ch. 15, 6.3
    becoming part of the net investment in a foreign operation, Ch. 15, 6.3.1.F
    ceasing to be part of the net investment in a foreign operation, Ch. 15, 6.3.1.G
    currency of monetary item, Ch. 15, 6.3.1.C
    dividends, Ch. 15, 6.3.2
    manner of settlement of monetary, Ch. 15, 6.3.1.B
    monetary items included as part of the net investment in a foreign operation, Ch. 15, 6.3.1
    net investment in a foreign operation, Ch. 15, 6.3.1.F
    transacted by other members of the group, Ch. 15, 6.3.1.E
    treatment in individual financial statements, Ch. 15, 6.3.1.D
    unrealised profits on intragroup transactions, Ch. 15, 6.3.3
  foreign operations where sub-groups exist, accounting for, Ch. 15, 6.1.5
  goodwill and fair value adjustments, Ch. 15, 6.5
  non-coterminous period ends, Ch. 15, 6.4
  partial disposal of foreign operation, Ch. 7, 4.1 Ch. 15, 6.6.2
  translation of equity items, Ch. 15, 6.2
    equity balances resulting from income and expenses being recognised in other comprehensive income, Ch. 15, 6.2.3
    equity balances resulting from transactions with equity holders, Ch. 15, 6.2.2
    share capital, Ch. 15, 6.2.1
  translation to, Ch. 15, 6.1
    accounting for foreign operations where sub-groups exist, Ch. 15, 6.1.5
    calculation of average rate, Ch. 15, 6.1.4
    dual rates, suspension of rates and lack of exchangeability, Ch. 15, 6.1.3
    where functional currency is not that of a hyperinflationary economy, Ch. 15, 6.1.1
    where functional currency is that of a hyperinflationary economy, Ch. 15, 6.1.2
  use other than the functional currency, Ch. 15, 6

Presentation of financial statements and accounting policies, Ch. 3, 1–6. *See also* IAS 1; IAS 8

Previous GAAP, Ch. 5, 2.3
  carrying amount as deemed cost, Ch. 5, 5.2.4.C
  definition of, Ch. 5, 1.3
  determining, Ch. 5, 2.3
    transition to IFRSs from a similar GAAP, Ch. 5, 2.3.1
  restatement of costs recognised under, Ch. 5, 5.3.2

Price, fair value measurement, Ch. 14, 9
  transaction costs, Ch. 14, 9.1
  transportation costs, Ch. 14, 9.2

Price risk, Ch. 54, 5

Principal-agency situations, IFRS 10, Ch. 6, 6, IFRS 15, Ch. 28, 3.4
  application examples in IFRS 10, Ch. 6, 6.6–6.7
  delegated power: principals and agents, Ch. 6, 6.1
  exposure to variability of returns from other interests, Ch. 6, 6.5
  liquidation rights, Ch. 6, 6.3.2
  redemption rights, Ch. 6, 6.3.2
  remuneration, Ch. 6, 6.4
  rights held by other parties, Ch. 6, 6.3.
  scope of decision-making, Ch. 6, 6.2
Principal market, Ch. 14, 6
  entity-specific volume, Ch. 14, 6.1.2
  market-based volume and activity, Ch. 14, 6.1.2
  most advantageous market, Ch. 14, 6.2
Prior period errors
  correction of, Ch. 3, 4.6
  disclosure of, Ch. 3, 5.3
Probability-weighted outcome, Ch. 51, 5.6
Production sharing contracts (PSCs), Ch. 43, 5.3; Ch. 43, 12.5
Property, plant and equipment (PP&E), Ch. 18, 1–8. *See also* IAS 16; Investment property
  administration and other general overheads, Ch. 18, 4.1.3
  borrowing costs, Ch. 18, 4.1.2
  decommissioning and restoration costs, Ch. 18, 4.3
  deferred payment, Ch. 18, 4.1.6
  definitions, Ch. 18, 2.2
  depreciation, cost model, Ch. 18, 5
    charge, Ch. 18, 5.3
    depreciable amount, Ch. 18, 5.2
    methods, Ch. 18, 5.6
    significant 'parts' of asset, Ch. 18, 5.1
    start and finish, Ch. 18, 5.5
    and useful life of asset, Ch. 18, 5.4
  derecognition and disposal, Ch. 18, 7
    held for sale and discontinued operations (IFRS 5), Ch. 18, 7.1
    partial disposals and undivided interests, Ch. 18, 7.3
    of parts ('components') of an asset, Ch. 18, 3.2
    sale of assets held for rental, Ch. 18, 7.2
  disclosure, Ch. 18, 8
  environmental and safety equipment, Ch. 18, 3.1.2
  exchanges of assets, Ch. 18, 4.4
  extractive industries, Ch. 43, 15
    care and maintenance, Ch. 43, 15.3
    major maintenance and turnarounds/renewals and reconditioning costs, Ch. 43, 15.1
    redeterminations, Ch. 43, 15.4.2
      as capital reimbursements, Ch. 43, 15.4.2.A
      decommissioning provisions, Ch. 43, 15.4.2.C
      'make-up' oil, Ch. 43, 15.4.2.B
    stripping costs in the production phase of a surface mine (mining), Ch. 43, 15.5
      determining when production phase commences, Ch. 43, 15.5.2
      disclosures, Ch. 43, 15.5.6
      initial recognition, Ch. 43, 15.5.4
      recognition criteria-stripping activity asset, Ch. 43, 15.5.3
      scope of IFRIC 20, Ch. 43, 15.5.1
      subsequent measurement, Ch. 43, 15.5.5

  unitisations, Ch. 43, 15.4
  well workovers and recompletions (oil and gas), Ch. 43, 15.2
fair value, Ch. 18, 6.1
finance leases, assets held under, Ch. 18, 6.5
first-time adoption, Ch. 5, 7.4
  depreciation method and rate, Ch. 5, 7.4.1
  IFRIC 1 exemptions, Ch. 5, 5.13.1
  parts approach, Ch. 5, 7.4.4
  residual value and useful life estimation, Ch. 5, 7.4.2
  revaluation model, Ch. 5, 7.4.3
government grants, assets acquired with, Ch. 18, 4.6
impairment, Ch. 18, 5.7
income, Ch. 18, 4
  earned while bringing the asset to the intended location and condition, Ch. 18, 4.2.1
  received during the construction of property, Ch. 18, 4.2.2
interim financial reporting, Ch. 41, 9.1
inventory, classification as, Ch. 18, 3.1.5
land, Ch. 18, 5.4.2
measurement after recognition
  cost model, Ch. 18, 5
  revaluation model, Ch. 18, 6
residual values, Ch. 18, 5.2
revaluation
  assets held under finance leases, Ch. 18, 4.5
  revaluation policy, adopting, Ch. 18, 6.4
  reversals of downward valuations, Ch. 18, 6.3
  valuation surpluses and deficits, accounting for, Ch. 18, 6.2
sale of assets held for rental, Ch. 18, 7.2 scope, Ch. 18, 2.1
significant parts of assets, Ch. 18, 5.1
spare parts and minor items, Ch. 18, 3.1.1
technological change, Ch. 18, 5.4.3
unit of production method, Ch. 18, 5.6.2
useful lives, Ch. 18, 5.4
Prospective resources, Ch. 43, 2.2.1
Provisions, Contingent Liabilities and Contingent Assets, Ch. 26, 1–7. *See also* IAS 37; Restructuring provisions
  cases in which no provision should be recognised, Ch. 26, 5
    future operating losses, Ch. 26, 5.1
    rate-regulated activities, Ch. 26, 5.4
    repairs and maintenance of owned assets, Ch. 26, 5.2
    staff training costs, Ch. 26, 5.3
  disclosure requirements, Ch. 26, 7
    contingent assets, Ch. 26, 7.3
    contingent liabilities, Ch. 26, 7.2
    provisions, Ch. 26, 7.1
    reduced disclosure when information is seriously prejudicial, Ch. 26, 7.4
  examples of provisions and contingencies, Ch. 26, 6
    decommissioning provisions, Ch. 26, 6.3
      changes in estimated decommissioning costs (IFRIC 1), Ch. 26, 6.3.1
      changes in legislation after construction of the asset, Ch. 26, 6.3.2
      funds established to meet an obligation (IFRIC 5), Ch. 26, 6.3.3
    dilapidation and other provisions relating to leased assets, Ch. 26, 6.9

Provisions, Contingent Liabilities and Contingent Assets—*contd*
  examples of provisions and contingencies—*contd*
    environmental provisions–general guidance in IAS 37, Ch. 26, 6.4
    EU Directive on 'Waste Electrical and Electronic Equipment' (IFRIC 6), Ch. 26, 6.7
    green certificates compared to emissions trading schemes, Ch. 26, 6.6
    levies imposed by governments, Ch. 26, 6.8
      payments relating to taxes other than income tax, Ch. 26.6.8.4
      recognition and measurement of levy liabilities, Ch. 26, 6.8.2
      recognition of an asset/expense when a levy is recorded, Ch. 26, 6.8.3
      scope of IFRIC 21, Ch. 26, 6.8.1
    liabilities associated with emissions trading schemes, Ch. 26, 6.5
    litigation and other legal claims, Ch. 26, 6.11
    obligations to make donations to non-profit organisations, Ch. 26, 6.14
    onerous contracts, Ch. 26, 6.2
    refunds policy, Ch. 26, 6.12
    restructuring provisions, Ch. 26, 6.1
    self insurance, Ch. 26, 6.13
    settlement payments, Ch. 26.6.15
    warranty provisions, Ch. 26, 6.10
  measurement, Ch. 26, 4
    anticipating future events that may affect the estimate of cash flows, Ch. 26, 4.4
    best estimate of provision, Ch. 26, 4.1
    changes and uses of provisions, Ch. 26, 4.9
    changes in contingent liabilities recognised in a business combination, Ch. 26, 4.10
    dealing with risk and uncertainty in measuring a provision, Ch. 26, 4.2
    discounting the estimated cash flows to a present value, Ch. 26, 4.3
      adjusting for risk and using a government bond rate, Ch. 26, 4.3.2
      effect of changes in interest rates on the discount rate applied, Ch. 26, 4.3.6
      own credit risk is not taken into account, Ch. 26, 4.3.3
      pre-tax discount rate, Ch. 26, 4.3.4
      real *vs.* nominal rate, Ch. 26, 4.3.1
      unwinding of the discount, Ch. 26, 4.3.5
    disposal of related assets, Ch. 26, 4.8
    joint and several liability, Ch. 26, 4.7
    provisions are not reduced for gains on disposal of related assets, Ch. 26, 4.8
    provisions that will be settled in a currency other than the entity's functional currency, Ch. 26, 4.5
    reimbursements, insurance and other recoveries from third parties, Ch. 26, 4.6
    settlement in a foreign currency, Ch. 26, 4.5
  recognition, Ch. 26, 3
    contingencies, Ch. 26, 3.2
      contingent assets, Ch. 26, 3.2.2
        obligations contingent on the successful recovery of, Ch. 26, 3.2.2.A
      contingent liabilities, Ch. 26, 3.2.1
      how probability determines whether to recognise or disclose, Ch. 26, 3.2.3
    determining when a provision should be recognised, Ch. 26, 3.1
      an entity has a present obligation as a result of a past event, Ch. 26, 3.1.1
      it is probable that an outflow of resources embodying economic benefits will be required to settle the obligation, Ch. 26, 3.1.2
      a reliable estimate can be made of the amount of the obligation, Ch. 26, 3.1.3
    recognising an asset when recognising a provision, Ch. 26, 3.3

'Proxy hedges,' designating, Ch. 53, 6.2.1
Prudence, Ch. 55, 8.2.3
Public Company Accounting Oversight Board, Ch. 2, 1.2
Publicly accountable enterprises, Ch. 1, 4.3.2
Purchased options
  call option (EPS), Ch. 37, 6.4.3
  hedge accounting, Ch. 53, 3.2.2, 7.3.3.C
  put option (EPS), Ch. 37, 6.4.3
  and warrants (EPS), Ch. 37, 6.4.3
Pure-service contract, Ch. 43, 5.4
Push down accounting, Ch. 5, 5.5.2.A; Ch. 9, 15
Put option(s)
  held by the customer, Ch. 30, 5.2
  over non-controlling interests, Ch. 7, 6.2, 6.3, 6.4, 6.5, 6.6, 7.3, 7.4, 7.5;; Ch. 9, 8.5 (*see also* Noncontrolling interests, call and put options over)
  purchased put option, Ch. 47, 11.3.1
  written put option, Ch. 47, 11.3.2
Puttable instruments, Ch. 47, 4.6.2
  classified as equity, Ch. 3, 5.4.2; Ch. 47, 4.6; Ch. 54, 5.4.4
  options over, IAS 32 specific exception, Ch. 34, 2.2.4.J
  definitions, Ch. 47, 3
  embedded derivatives, Ch. 46, 5.1.10
  entitling the holder to a pro rata share of net assets only on liquidation, Ch. 47, 4.6.3
  IFRIC 2, Ch. 47, 4.6.6
  issue, Ch. 47, 4.6.1
  issued by a subsidiary, Ch. 47, 4.6.4.A
  meaning of 'identical features,' Ch. 47, 4.6.4.C
  no obligation to deliver cash or another financial asset, Ch. 47, 4.6.4.D
  reclassification, Ch. 47, 4.6.5
  relative subordination of the instrument, Ch. 47, 4.6.4.B
  substantially fix or restrict the residual return to the holder of an instrument, Ch. 47, 4.6.4.E
  transactions entered into by an instrument holder other than as owner of the entity, Ch. 47, 4.6.4.F
Qualifying assets, Ch. 21, 3. *See also* IAS 23
  assets measured at fair value, Ch. 21, 3.2
  constructed good, over time transfer of, Ch. 21, 3.4
  financial assets, Ch. 21, 3.3
  inventories, Ch. 21, 3.1
Qualitative disclosures, financial instruments, Ch. 54, 5.1
Quantitative disclosures, financial instruments, Ch. 54, 5.2, 5.6
  capital disclosures, Ch. 54, 5.6.3
  concentrations of risk, Ch. 54, 5.6.1
  operational risk, Ch. 54, 5.6.2

Quantitative thresholds, operating segments, Ch. 36, 1.3, 3.2.2
Quoted prices in active markets, Ch. 14, 17.3
    consideration of an entry price in measuring a liability or entity's own equity not held as an asset, Ch. 14, 11.2.2.B
    fair value of a liability or an entity's own equity, measuring when quoted prices for the liability or equity instruments are not available, Ch. 14, 11.2
    liabilities or an entity's own equity not held by other parties as assets, Ch. 14, 11.2.2
    liabilities or an entity's own equity that are held by other parties as assets, Ch. 14, 11.2.1
    use of present value techniques to measure fair value for liabilities and an entity's own equity instruments not held by other parties as asset, Ch. 14, 11.2.2.A
Rate-regulated activities, intangible assets, Ch. 17, 11.1
Reacquired rights, Ch. 9, 5.5.3
Real estate inventory, Ch. 22, 4
    classification of, Ch. 22, 4.1
    costs of, Ch. 22, 4.2
        individual units in multi-unit developments, Ch. 22, 4.2.1
        property demolition and operating lease costs, Ch. 22, 4.2.2
Real Estate Investment Trusts (REITs), Ch. 55, 6
Rebalancing, hedge accounting, Ch. 53, 8.2
    definition, Ch. 53, 8.2.1
    mechanics of, Ch. 53, 8.2.3
    requirement to rebalance, Ch. 53, 8.2.2
Receivables
    acquired in business combination, Ch. 49, 3.3.4; Ch. 54, 4.6.1
    distinction between contract assets and, Ch. 32, 2.1.1
    initial measurement of, Ch. 32, 2.1.5
    lease receivables, measurement of expected credit losses, Ch. 51, 10.2
    recognition, Ch. 49, 2.1.1
    trade receivables, measurement of expected credit losses, Ch. 51, 10.1
    trade receivables with no significant financing component initial measurement, Ch. 49, 3.2
Reciprocal interests in equity accounted entities, Ch. 11, 7.6.2
    measurement of noncontrolling interests where an associate holds and interest in a subsidiary, Ch. 7, 5.3
    in reporting entity accounted for, Ch. 11, 7.6.2.A
    in reporting entity not accounted for, Ch. 11, 7.6.2.B
Reclassification adjustments, financial statements, Ch. 3, 3.2.4.B
Recognition of financial instruments, Ch. 49, 2
    general requirements, Ch. 49, 2.1
        cash collateral, Ch. 49, 2.1.7
        firm commitments to purchase/sell goods/services, Ch. 49, 2.1.2
        forward contracts, Ch. 49, 2.1.3
        option contracts, Ch. 49, 2.1.4
        planned future/forecast transactions, Ch. 49, 2.1.5
        principal vs. agent, Ch. 49, 2.1.8
        receivables and payables, Ch. 49, 2.1.1
        transfers of financial assets not qualifying for derecognition by transferor, Ch. 49, 2.1.6
    'regular way' transactions, Ch. 49, 2.2
        exchanges of non-cash financial assets, Ch. 49, 2.2.5.A
        financial assets: general requirements, Ch. 49, 2.2.1
            contracts not settled according to marketplace convention: derivatives, Ch. 49, 2.2.1.B
            exercise of a derivative, Ch. 49, 2.2.1.D
            multiple active markets: settlement provisions, Ch. 49, 2.2.1.C
            no established market, Ch. 49, 2.2.1.A
        financial liabilities, Ch. 49, 2.2.2
        illustrative examples, Ch. 49, 2.2.5
        settlement date accounting, Ch. 49, 2.2.4
        trade date accounting, Ch. 49, 2.2.3
Recompletions, oil and gas wells, Ch. 43, 15.2
Reconciliation on first-time adoption, Ch. 5, 6.3.1.A
    inclusion of IFRS 1 reconciliations by cross reference, Ch. 5, 6.3.4
    line-by-line reconciliations, Ch. 5, 6.3.2
Recoverable amount, Ch. 20, 5. See also IAS 36.
Redesignation of financial assets, Ch. 55, 8.4; Ch. 56, 17.6
Redeterminations, Ch. 43, 15.4.2
Reduced Disclosure Requirements (RDRs), Ch. 1, 4.5
Registration, Evaluation, Authorisation and Restriction of Chemicals (REACH), Ch. 17, 11.4
Regression analysis, Ch. 53, 6.4.1
Regular way contracts, derivatives, Ch. 46, 3.3
'Regular way' transactions, Ch. 49, 2.2
    financial assets: general requirements, Ch. 49, 2.2.1
        contracts not settled according to marketplace convention: derivatives, Ch. 49, 2.2.1.B
        exercise of a derivative, Ch. 49, 2.2.1.D
        multiple active markets: settlement provisions, Ch. 49, 2.2.1.C
        no established market, Ch. 49, 2.2.1.A
    financial liabilities, Ch. 49, 2.2.2
    illustrative examples, Ch. 49, 2.2.5
    initial measurement, Ch. 49, 3.6
    settlement date accounting, Ch. 49, 2.2.4
    subsequent measurement exceptions, Ch. 50, 2.9.2
    trade date accounting, Ch. 49, 2.2.3
Reimbursement rights, Ch. 45, 3.10
Reinsurance assets
    definition, Ch. 55, 2.2.1
    impairments of, Ch. 55, 7.2.5; Ch. 56, 10.3
Reinsurance contract, Ch. 55, 2.2.1, 2.2.2, 3.7.2, 7.2.4; Ch. 56, 2.2, 2.3, 8.9
Reinsurance contracts held, Ch. 56, 10
    aggregation level, Ch. 56, 10.1
    allocation of the CSM to profit or loss, Ch. 56, 10.5
    boundary of, Ch. 56, 10.2
    measurement - initial recognition, Ch. 56, 10.3, 10.4
    premium allocation approach for, Ch. 56, 10.6
    subsequent measurement, Ch. 56, 10.4
    and the variable fee approach, Ch. 56, 10.7
Reinsurance contracts issued, Ch. 56, 8.9
    accounting for ceding commissions and reinstatement premiums, Ch. 56, 8.9.3
    boundary of, Ch. 56, 8.9.1
    determining the quantity of benefits for identifying coverage units, Ch. 56, 8.9.4
    issued adverse loss development covers, Ch. 56, 8.9.2

Reinsurer, Ch. 55, 2.2.1
Reissuing (dual dating) financial statements, Ch. 38, 2.1.1.B
Related party disclosures, Ch. 39. *See also* IAS 24
   compensation, defined, Ch. 39, 2.6.1
   disclosure
      of controlling relationships, Ch. 39, 2.4
      expense incurred with management entity, Ch. 39, 2.8
      with government-related entities, Ch. 39, 2.9
      key management personnel compensation, Ch. 39, 2.6
      other related party transactions, including commitments, Ch. 39, 2.7
      transactions, Ch. 39, 2.5
   identification of a related party and related party transactions, Ch. 39, 2.2
      entities that are associates/joint ventures, Ch. 39, 2.2.3
      entities that are joint ventures and associates of the same third entity, Ch. 39, 2.2.5
      entities that are joint ventures of the same third party, Ch. 39, 2.2.4
         joint operations (IFRS 11), Ch. 39, 2.2.3.A
      entities that are members of same group, Ch. 39, 2.2.2
      entities under control/joint control of certain persons/close members of their family, Ch. 39, 2.2.7
      entities under significant influence of certain persons/close members of their family, Ch. 39, 2.2.8
      government-related entities, Ch. 39, 2.2.10
      persons/close members of a person's family that are related parties, Ch. 39, 2.2.1
         control, Ch. 39, 2.2.1.A
         joint control, Ch. 39, 2.2.1.B
         key management personnel, Ch. 39, 2.2.1.D
         significant influence, Ch. 39, 2.2.1.C
      post-employment benefit plans, Ch. 39, 2.2.6
   parties that are not related parties, Ch. 39, 2.3
   post-employment benefits, Ch. 39, 2.6.3
   related party issue, Ch. 39, 1.1
   reporting entity part of a group, Ch. 39, 2.6.7
   share-based payment transactions, Ch. 39, 2.6.6
   short-term employee benefits, Ch. 39, 2.6.2
   termination benefits, Ch. 39, 2.6.5
   transactions requiring disclosure, Ch. 39, 2.7.1
Relative subordination, Ch. 47, 4.5.5, 4.6.4.B
   preference shares, Ch. 47, 4.5.5
   of puttable instrument, Ch. 47, 4.6.4.B
Relevant activities, investee
   management of defaults on assets, Ch. 6, 4.1.4
   more than one relevant activity, Ch. 6, 4.1.1
   no relevant activities, Ch. 6, 4.1.2
   single asset, single lessee vehicles, Ch. 6, 4.1.3
Renewable energy certificates (RECs), Ch. 17, 11.3
Rental assets transferred to inventory, Ch. 22, 2.3.1.E
Rental income, Ch. 19, 6.6.1. *See also* IFRS 16
Replacement share-based payment awards, Ch. 34, 7.4.4, 11.
   See also Equity-settled share-based payment transactions
   in a business combination, Ch. 7, 5.2.1; Ch. 9, 7.2; Ch. 34, 11
      accounted for under IFRS 3, Ch. 34, 11.2
         accounting for changes in vesting assumptions after the acquisition date, Ch. 34, 11.2.3
         acquiree awards the acquirer is not 'obliged' to replace, Ch. 34, 11.2.2
         awards that the acquirer is 'obliged' to replace, Ch. 34, 11.2.1
      acquiree award not replaced by acquirer, Ch. 34, 11.3
      background, Ch. 34, 11.1
      financial statements of the acquired entity, Ch. 34, 11.4
   designation of award as, Ch. 34, 7.4.4.A
   incremental fair value of, Ch. 34, 7.4.4.B
   replacement of vested awards, Ch. 34, 7.4.4.C
   tax deductions for, Ch. 33, 12.2
   on termination of employment, Ch. 34, 7.5
Reportable segments. *See also* IFRS 8; Operating segments
   externally reportable segments, identifying, Ch. 36, 3.2
      aggregation criteria, Ch. 36, 3.2.1
      'all other segments,' Ch. 36, 3.2.4
      combining small operating segments into a larger reportable segment, Ch. 36, 3.2.3
      'practical limit' for the number of reported operating segments, Ch. 36, 3.2.5
      restatement of segments reported in comparative periods, Ch. 36, 3.2.6
      quantitative thresholds, operating segments which are reportable because of their size, Ch. 36, 3.2.2
   information to be disclosed about, Ch. 36, 5
      commercially sensitive information, Ch. 36, 5.8
      explanation of measurements used in segment reporting, Ch. 36, 5.5
      general information, Ch. 36, 5.1
      other elements of revenue, income and expense, Ch. 36, 5.3
      reconciliations, Ch. 36, 5.6
      restatement of previously reported information, Ch. 36, 5.7
         organisation structure, changes in, Ch. 36, 5.7.1
         segment measures, changes in, Ch. 36, 5.7.2
      segment profit or loss, measure of, Ch. 36, 5.2
      total assets and total liabilities, measure of, Ch. 36, 5.2
Repurchase agreements ('repos')
   agreement to repurchase at fair value, Ch. 52, 4.1.5
   agreements to return the same asset, Ch. 52, 4.1.1
   agreements with right of substitution, Ch. 52, 4.1.3
   agreements with right to return the same or substantially the same asset, Ch. 52, 4.1.2
   derecognition criteria, securities lending, Ch. 52, 4.1
   inventory, Ch. 22, 2.3.1.F
   net cash-settled forward repurchase, Ch. 52, 4.1.4
   revenue from contracts with customers (IFRS 15)
      forward/call option held by the entity, Ch. 30, 5.1
      put option held by the customer, Ch. 30, 5.2
      sales with residual value guarantees, Ch. 30, 5.3
   right of first refusal to repurchase at fair value, Ch. 52, 4.1.6
   sale and leaseback transactions, Ch. 23, 7.3
   wash sale, Ch. 52, 4.1.7
Reserves and resources. *See also* Extractive industries
   definitions, Ch. 43, 1.3.1
   disclosure, Ch. 43, 2.4
      mining sector, Ch. 43, 2.4.2
      oil and gas sector, Ch. 43, 2.4.1
      standardised measure of oil and gas, Ch. 43, 2.4.3.A
      value of reserves, Ch. 43, 2.4.3
   reporting, Ch. 43, 2.1–2.3

Residual values
    definition, Ch. 23, 6.1.3
    finance lease accounting, Ch. 23, 6.2.3
    property, plant and equipment, Ch. 18, 5.2

Restatement
    hyperinflation, Ch. 16, 8
    of prior periods, impracticability of, Ch. 3, 4.7
        for change in accounting policy, Ch. 3, 4.7.1
        for a material error, Ch. 3, 4.7.2

Restatement of goodwill on first-time adoption, Ch. 5, 5.2.5
    derecognition of negative goodwill, Ch. 5, 5.2.5.B
    previously deducted from equity, Ch. 5, 5.2.5.C
    prohibition of other adjustments of goodwill, Ch. 5, 5.2.5.A

Restructuring of derivatives, hedging instruments, Ch. 53, 3.6.3

Restructuring provisions, Ch. 26, 6.1
    costs that can (and cannot) be included in, Ch. 26, 6.1.4
    definition, Ch. 26, 6.1.1
    recognition of, Ch. 26, 6.1.2
    recognition of obligations arising from the sale of an operation, Ch. 26, 6.1.3

Retrospective application, first-time adoption
    departures from, Ch. 5, 3.5
    estimates, Ch. 5, 4.2
    exceptions to, Ch. 5, 4
    financial assets and liabilities, derecognition of, Ch. 5, 4.3

Returns of capital, Ch. 8, 2.4.1.C

Revaluation model
    assets held under finance leases, Ch. 18, 6.5
    downward valuations, reversals of, Ch. 18, 6.3
    fair value before the adoption of IFRS 13, Ch. 18, 6.1.1.A
    first-time adopter, Ch. 5, 7.4.3
    for intangible assets measurement, Ch. 17, 8.2
        accounting for revaluations, Ch. 17, 8.2.3
        frequency of revaluations, Ch. 17, 8.2.2
        revaluation is only allowed if there is an active market, Ch. 17, 8.2.1
    meaning of fair value, Ch. 18, 6.1
    policy of revaluation, adopting, Ch. 18, 6.4
    revalued assets, disclosures for, Ch. 18, 8.2
    revaluing assets under IFRS 13, Ch. 18, 6.1.1
        cost approach, Ch. 18, 6.1.1.C
        highest and best use, Ch. 18, 6.1.1.A
        income approach, Ch. 18, 6.1.1.B
        market approach, Ch. 18, 6.1.1.B
        valuation approaches, Ch. 18, 6.1.1.B
    valuation surpluses and deficits, accounting for, Ch. 18, 6.2

Revenue from contracts with customers. *See* IFRS 15

Revenue recognition, Ch. 28, 1–3, Ch. 30, 1–11. *See also* IFRS 15; IFRS 17
    and agency relationships, Ch. 28, 3.4
    disclosure, Ch. 32
    extractive industries, Ch. 43, 12
        accounting for imbalances in revenue under IFRS 15, Ch. 43, 12.4.2
            consideration of cost of goods sold where revenue is recognised in accordance with IFRS 15, Ch. 43, 12.4.3
            facility imbalances, Ch. 43, 12.4.4
            future developments, Ch. 43, 12.1.2.A
            historical industry practice, Ch. 43, 12.4.1
            incidental revenue, Ch. 43, 12.1.1
            integral to development, Ch. 43, 12.1.2
            revenue in the development phase, Ch. 43, 12.1
        forward-selling contracts to finance development, Ch. 43, 12.6
            accounting by the investor, Ch. 43, 12.6.2
            accounting by the producer, Ch. 43, 12.6.1
        impact of IFRS 15, Ch. 43, 12
        inventory exchanges with the same counterparty, Ch. 43, 12.3
        overlift and underlift (oil and gas), Ch. 43, 12.4
        sale of product with delayed shipment, Ch. 43, 12.2
        trading activities, Ch. 43, 12.7
    insurance revenue, Ch. 56, 15.1

Reversal of impairment losses, Ch. 20, 11

Reverse acquisitions, Ch. 9, 14
    cash consideration, Ch. 9, 14.6
    earnings per share, Ch. 9, 14.5
    measuring goodwill, Ch. 9, 14.2
    measuring the consideration transferred, Ch. 9, 14.1
    non-controlling interest, Ch. 9, 14.4
    preparation and presentation of consolidated financial statements, Ch. 9, 14.3
    reverse acquisitions and acquirers that are not legal entities, Ch. 9, 14.9
    reverse acquisitions involving a non-trading shell company, Ch. 9, 14.8
    share-based payments, Ch. 9, 14.7

Reverse factoring, *See* Supply-chain finance

Reverse indemnification liabilities, Ch. 9, 5.6.4.A

Rights issue, Ch. 37, 4.3.3

Risk components, hedge accounting, Ch. 53, 2.2

Risk, concentrations of, Ch. 54, 5.6.1; Ch. 55, 11.2.4

Risk management objective, hedge accounting, Ch. 53, 6.2

Risk management strategy, hedge accounting, Ch. 53, 6.2; Ch. 54, 4.3.1

Risk service contracts, Ch. 43, 5.5.1

Risk-sharing arrangements, extractive industries, Ch. 43, 6
    asset swaps, Ch. 43, 6.3
    carried interests, Ch. 43, 6.1
    E&E assets, Ch. 43, 6.3.1
    exchanges of E&E assets for other types of assets, Ch. 43, 6.3.3
    farm-ins and farm-outs, Ch. 43, 6.2
    PP&E, intangible assets and investment property, Ch. 43, 6.3.2

Rollover hedging strategy, Ch. 53, 7.7

Royalties
    extractive industries, Ch. 43, 5.7, 12.9

Russia, IFRS adoption in, Ch. 1, 4.2.2

Russian Accounting Principles (RAP), Ch. 1, 4.2.2

Sale and leaseback transactions, Ch. 23, 7; Ch. 23, 8–8.4
    determining whether the transfer of an asset is a sale, Ch. 23, 8.1
    disclosures, Ch. 23, 8.4
    finance leaseback, Ch. 23, 7.2
    operating leaseback, Ch. 23, 7.2

Sale and leaseback transactions—*contd*
   presentation in the statement of cash flows, Ch. 40, 5.4.3
   repurchase agreements and options, Ch. 23, 8.1
   transactions in which the transfer of an asset is a sale, Ch. 23, 8.2
     accounting for the leaseback, Ch. 23, 8.2.2
     accounting for the sale, Ch. 23, 8.2.1
     adjustment for off-market terms, Ch. 23, 8.2.3
   transactions in which the transfer of an asset is not a sale, Ch. 23, 8.3

Sale of goods
   sale and repurchase agreements, Ch. 30, 5.3

Sale of a mineral interest and a contract to provide extraction services, Ch. 43, 12.1.2

SARs. *See* Share appreciation rights

Seasonal businesses, Ch. 41, 8.2
   costs incurred, Ch. 41, 8.2.2
   revenues received, Ch. 41, 8.2.1

Seasonality or cyclicality of operations, Ch. 41, 4.3.12

Securities and Exchange Board of India (SEBI), Ch. 1, 4.4.3

Securities and Exchange Commission (SEC), US, Ch. 1, 2.3, 3.2
   first-time adoption by foreign private issuers, Ch. 5, 8.1

Securities lending, Ch. 52, 4.1

Securitisations, Ch. 52, 3.6
   'business model' assessment, Ch. 48, 5.6
   'empty' subsidiaries or SPEs, Ch. 52, 3.6.6
   group of assets transfer, Ch. 52, 3.6.5
   insurance protection, Ch. 52, 3.6.3
   recourse to originator, Ch. 52, 3.6.1
   short-term loan facilities, Ch. 52, 3.6.2
   treatment of collection, Ch. 52, 3.6.4
   vehicles, Ch. 13, 2.2.1.B

Securitisations and special purpose entities (SPEs), Ch. 51, 7.7
   accounting for a financial liability issued, Ch. 51, 7.7.2
   ECL requirements for the SPE, Ch. 51, 7.7.1

Segment cash flow disclosures, Ch. 40, 5.6.2

Segment manager, Ch. 36, 3.1.2

Self-built assets, Ch. 18, 4.1.5

Self insurance, Ch. 26, 6.13; Ch. 55, 3.2.2.A; Ch. 56, 3.5.2.A

Separability criterion
   intangible assets, Ch. 9, 5.5.2; Ch. 17, 5.1.3.B

Separate and individual financial statements, Ch. 8, 1
   consolidated financial statements and, Ch. 8, 1.1
     associates and joint ventures, separate financial statements and interests in, Ch. 8, 1.1.1
     joint operation, separate financial statements and interests in, Ch. 8, 1.1.2
     publishing without consolidated financial statements or financial statements in which investments in associates or joint ventures are equity accounted, Ch. 8, 1.1.3
   disclosure, Ch. 8, 3
   entities incorporated in EU and consolidated and separate financial statements, Ch. 8, 1.2
   entities with no subsidiaries but exempt from applying IAS 28, Ch. 8, 3.3.1
   prepared by an entity other than a parent electing not to prepare consolidated financial statements, Ch. 8, 1.2
   prepared by parent electing not to prepare consolidated financial statements, Ch. 8, 3.1
   put and call options in separate financial statements, Ch. 7, 6.5

Separate financial statements, Ch. 8, 1–3; Ch. 13, 2.2.3.B. *See also* Separate and individual financial statements; Individual financial statements
   disclosure, Ch. 8, 3
   requirements of, Ch. 8, 2
     cost method, Ch. 8, 2.1
       cost of investment, Ch. 8, 2.1.1
       cost of investment in subsidiary, associate or joint venture acquired in stages, Ch. 8, 2.1.1.C
       deemed cost on transition to IFRS, Ch. 8, 2.1.2
       formation of a new parent, Ch. 8, 2.1.1.E formation of a new parent: calculating the cost and measuring equity, Ch. 8, 2.1.1.F
       investment in a subsidiary accounted for at cost: partial disposal, Ch. 8, 2.1.1.D
       investments acquired for own shares or other equity instruments, Ch. 8, 2.1.1.A
       investments acquired in common control transactions, Ch. 8, 2.1.1.B
       reverse acquisitions in the separate financial statements, Ch. 8, 2.1.1.G
     dividends and other distributions, Ch. 8, 2.4
       carrying amount of investment exceeds the consolidated net assets, Ch. 8, 2.4.1.B
       distributions of non-cash assets to owners (IFRIC 17), Ch. 8, 2.4.2
         recognition, measurement and presentation, Ch. 8, 2.4.2.B
         scope, Ch. 8, 2.4.2.A
       dividend exceeds the total comprehensive income, Ch. 8, 2.4.1.A
       dividends from subsidiaries, joint ventures or associates, Ch. 8, 2.4.1
       returns of capital, Ch. 8, 2.4.1.C
     equity method, Ch. 8, 2.3
     IFRS 9 method, Ch. 8, 2.2

Service concession arrangements (SCA), Ch. 25, 1–7. *See also* IFRIC 12
   accounting by grantors, Ch. 25, 2.5
   additional construction and upgrade services, Ch. 25, 5.1
     that comprise a new infrastructure asset, Ch. 25, 5.1.2
     that are part of the initial infrastructure asset, Ch. 25, 5.1.1
   bifurcation, Ch. 25, 4.5
   cash flows for, Ch. 40, 4.4.9
   consideration for services provided, Ch. 25, 4.1
     allocating, Ch. 25, 4.1.1
     determining accounting model, Ch. 25, 4.1.2
   construction phase, impairment during, Ch. 25, 4.3.2
   contract acquisition and mobilisation costs, Ch. 25, 4.8
   contractual payments made by an operator to a grantor, Ch. 25, 4.7
     under financial asset model, Ch. 25, 4.7.2
     under intangible asset model, Ch. 25, 4.7.3
     variable payments, Ch. 25, 4.7.1
   control model, Ch. 25, 3
     assets within scope, control model, Ch. 25, 3.3
     partially regulated assets, Ch. 25, 3.4
     residual interest, control of, Ch. 25, 3.2
     regulation of services, Ch. 25, 3.1
   disclosure requirements, Ch. 25, 7
   expenditure during operations phase, Ch. 25, 5

financial asset model, Ch. 25, 4.2
grantor, Ch. 25, 5.3
intangible asset model, Ch. 25, 4.3
    amortisation of, Ch. 25, 4.3.1
    impairment during construction phase, Ch. 25, 4.3.2
interaction of IFRS 16 and IFRIC 12, Ch. 25, 2.3
Interpretations Committee's approach to, Ch. 25, 1.1
operations phase, accounting for, Ch. 25, 5.2
operations services, Ch. 25, 4.1.1
outsourcing arrangements and, Ch. 25, 2.2.1
previously held assets, Ch. 25, 3.3.3
private-to-private arrangements, Ch. 25, 2.4
public service nature of the obligation, Ch. 25, 2.1
residual interests
    accounting for, Ch. 25, 4.6
    control of, Ch. 25, 3.2
revenue recognition, Ch. 25, 4.4
upgrade services, Ch. 25, 5.1

Service condition, share-based payment, Ch. 34, 3.1

Service cost, defined benefit pension plans, Ch. 35, 10.1
    current service cost, Ch. 35, 10.1
    past service cost, Ch. 35, 10.2.1
    settlements, Ch. 35, 10.2.3

Service-type warranties, Ch. 31, 3.2

Set-off, enforceable legal right of, financial assets and liabilities, Ch. 54, 7.4.1.A

Settlement date accounting, Ch. 49, 2.2.4; Ch. 51, 7.3.2
    exchange of non-cash financial assets, Ch. 49, 2.2.5.A

Shadow accounting, insurance contracts, Ch. 55, 7.2.2.D, 8.3

Share appreciation rights (SARs), Ch. 34, 8.7.3, 9.1

Share-based payment arrangement, Ch. 34, 2.2.1

Share-based payment transactions, Ch. 34, 2.2.1. *See also* Cash-settled share-based payment transactions; Equity-settled share-based payment transactions; IFRS 2; Vesting, share-based payment
    allocation of expense for equity-settled transactions, overview, Ch. 34, 6.1
    awards entitled to dividends or dividend equivalents during the vesting period, Ch. 34, 15.3
    awards exchanged for awards held by acquiree's employees, Ch. 9, 11.2.2
    awards vesting/exercisable on an exit event/change of control, Ch. 34, 15.4
    cash-settled transactions, Ch. 34, 9
        accounting, Ch. 34, 9.3
        modification of award from equity-settled to cash-settled (or vice versa), Ch. 34, 9.4
    cost of awards, equity-settled, Ch. 34, 5
        determining the fair value of equity instruments, Ch. 34, 5.5
        grant date, Ch. 34, 5.3
        transactions with employees, Ch. 34, 5.2
        transactions with non-employees, Ch. 34, 5.4
    disclosures, Ch. 34, 13
        impact of share-based payment transactions on financial statements, Ch. 34, 13.3
        of key management personnel compensation, Ch. 39, 2.6.6
        nature and extent of share-based payment arrangements, Ch. 34, 13.1
        valuation of share-based payment arrangements, Ch. 34, 13.2
    equity-settled transactions, allocation of expense, Ch. 34, 6
        cost of awards, Ch. 34, 5
        modification, cancellation and settlement, Ch. 34, 7
        overview, Ch. 34, 4
        valuation, Ch. 34, 8
    first-time adoption, Ch. 34, 16.1
    group share schemes, Ch. 34, 12
    loans to employees to purchase shares (limited recourse and full recourse loans), Ch. 34, 15.2
    matching share awards, Ch. 34, 15.1
        cancellation and settlement, Ch. 34, 7.4
        future modification or replacement of award, Ch. 34, 7.6
        modification, cancellation and settlement of equity-settled transactions, Ch. 34, 7
    modifications, Ch. 34, 7.3
        replacement and ex-gratia awards on termination of employment, Ch. 34, 7.5
        share splits and consolidations, Ch. 34, 7.8
        two awards running 'in parallel', Ch. 34, 7.7
        valuation requirements, Ch. 34, 7.2
    recognition, general principles of, Ch. 34, 3
        non-vesting conditions, Ch. 34, 3.2
        vesting conditions, Ch. 34, 3.1
            market conditions, Ch. 34, 6.3
            non-vesting conditions, Ch. 34, 6.4
        vesting conditions other than market conditions, Ch. 34, 6.2
        vesting period, Ch. 34, 3.3
    replacement awards in business combination, Ch. 34, 11; Ch. 7, 5.2.1; Ch. 9, 7.2
        accounted for under IFRS 3, Ch. 34, 11.2
        acquiree award not replaced by acquirer, Ch. 34, 11.3
        financial statements of the acquired entity, Ch. 34, 11.4
    South African black economic empowerment ('BEE') and similar arrangements, Ch. 34, 15.5
    tax base, determining, Ch. 33, 10.8.2
    taxes related to, Ch. 33, 10.8; Ch. 34, 14
        employment taxes of the employer, Ch. 34, 14.2
        income tax deductions for the entity, Ch. 34, 14.1
        sale or surrender of shares by employee to meet employee's tax liability ('sell to cover' and net settlement), Ch. 34, 14.3
    transactions with equity and cash alternatives, Ch. 34, 10
        awards requiring cash or equity settlement in specific circumstances (awards with contingent cash or contingent equity settlement), Ch. 34, 10.3
        cash settlement alternative not based on share price or value, Ch. 34, 10.4
        transactions where counterparty has choice of settlement, Ch. 34, 10.1
        transactions where entity has choice of settlement, Ch. 34, 10.2
    valuation of equity-settled transactions, Ch. 34, 8
        adapting option-pricing models, Ch. 34, 8.4
        appropriate assumptions for option-pricing models, Ch. 34, 8.5
        awards to a fixed monetary value, Ch. 34, 8.10
        awards whose fair value cannot be measured reliably, Ch. 34, 8.8

Share-based payment transactions—*contd*
   valuation of equity-settled transactions—*contd*
      awards with reload features, Ch. 34, 8.9
      option-pricing model selection, Ch. 34, 8.3
      other awards requiring the use of option valuation models, Ch. 34, 8.7
Share option, Ch. 34, 2.2
Share price-based contingencies, Ch. 37, 6.4.6.B
Share splits and consolidations, Ch. 37, 4.3.1
Shipping of commodities, Ch. 43, 12.12
   identification of performance obligations, Ch. 43, 12.12.1
   sale of product with delayed shipment, Ch. 43, 12.2
   satisfaction of performance obligations – control assessment, Ch. 43, 12.12.2
Short-term employee benefits, Ch. 35, 12
   disclosure of key management personnel compensation, Ch. 39, 2.6.2
   general recognition criteria for, Ch. 35, 12.1
   profit-sharing and bonus plans, Ch. 35, 12.3
      present legal or constructive obligation, Ch. 35, 12.3.1
      reliable estimate of provision, Ch. 35, 12.3.2
      statutory profit-sharing based on taxable profit, Ch. 35, 12.3.3
     short-term paid absences, Ch. 35, 12.2
      accumulating absences, Ch. 35, 12.2.1
      non-accumulating absences, Ch. 35, 12.2.2
Short-term loan facilities, Ch. 52, 3.6.2
Short-term receivables and payables, Ch. 14, 2.1.3
SIC-5—*Classification of Financial Instruments–Contingent Settlement Provisions*, Ch. 47, 4.3.1
SIC-7—*Introduction of the Euro*, Ch. 15, 1.2, 8
SIC-10—*Government Assistance-No Specific Relation to Operating Activities*, Ch. 24, 2.2.2
SIC-12—*Consolidation–Special Purpose Entities*, Ch. 6,
SIC-16—*Share Capital – Reacquired Own Equity Instruments (Treasury Shares)*, Ch. 47, 9.1
SIC-21—*Income Taxes–Recovery of Revalued Non-Depreciable Assets*, Ch. 33, 8.4.6
SIC-25—*Income Taxes– Changes in the Tax Status of an Entity or its Shareholders*, Ch. 33, 10.9
SIC-29—*Service Concession Arrangements: Disclosures*, Ch. 25.1–7
SIC-32—*Intangible Assets-Web Site Costs*, Ch. 17, 6.2.5
Significant estimates and judgements, disclosure of, Ch. 13, 3
Significant influence, Ch. 11, 4
   fund managers, Ch. 11, 4.6
   holdings of less than 20% of the voting power, Ch. 11, 4.3
   lack of, Ch. 11, 4.2
   potential voting rights, Ch. 11, 4.4
   severe long-term restrictions impairing ability to transfer funds to the investor, Ch. 11, 4.1
   voting rights held in a fiduciary capacity, Ch. 11, 4.5
Significant insurance risk, Ch. 55, 3.2; Ch. 56, 3.5
   changes in level of, Ch. 56, 3.6
   level of assessment, Ch. 55, 3.2.2; Ch. 56, 3.5.2
      insurance mutuals, Ch. 55, 3.2.2.B; Ch. 56, 3.5.2.B
      intragroup insurance contracts, Ch. 55, 3.2.2.C; Ch. 56, 3.5.2.C
      self insurance, Ch. 55, 3.2.2.A; Ch. 56, 3.5.2.A
   meaning of 'significant', Ch. 55, 3.5.1
   quantity of insurance risk, Ch. 56, 3.5.1
   significant additional amounts, Ch. 56, 3.5.3
   significant additional benefits, Ch. 55, 3.5.3
Silo, Ch. 6, 8
   consolidation of, Ch. 6, 8.3
   evaluating control of, Ch. 6, 8.2
   identifying, Ch. 6, 8.1
      in insurance industry, Ch. 6, 8.1.1
      in investment funds industry, Ch. 6, 8.1.2
Simplified Disclosure Standard (SDS), Ch. 1, 4.5
SME Implementation Group, Ch. 1, 2.9
South Africa, IFRS adoption in, Ch. 1, 4.6
SPACs. *See* Special purpose acquisition companies (SPACs)
Special purpose acquisition companies (SPACs), Ch. 34, 5.3.10
Special purpose entities (SPEs), Ch. 52, 3.6.6, 5.6.1
Split accounting, compound financial instruments, Ch. 47, 6.2
   accounting for the equity component, Ch. 47, 6.2.1
   temporary differences arising from split accounting, Ch. 47, 6.2.2
Standing Interpretations Committee (SIC), Ch. 1, 2.1
Start-up costs, investment properties, Ch. 19, 4.2
   intangible assets, Ch. 17, 7
Statement of cash flows, Ch. 40, 1–8. *See also* IAS 7
   acquisition-related costs, Ch. 40, 6.3.1
   acquisitions, Ch. 40, 6.3
   classification, Ch. 40, 4
      allocating items to operating, investing and financing activities, Ch. 40, 4.4
         cash flows for service concession arrangements, Ch. 40, 4.4.9
         cash flows from factoring of trade receivables, Ch. 40, 4.4.5
         cash flows from supply-chain financing (reverse factoring), Ch. 40, 4.4.6
         cash flows on derivative contracts, Ch. 40, 4.4.12
         cash flows related to the costs of a share issue, Ch. 40, 4.4.11
         classification of cash flows-future developments, Ch. 40, 4.4.11
         compensation for an insured loss, Ch. 40, 4.4.8
         contributions to a log-term employee benefit fund, Ch. 40, 4.4.4
         debt instrument issued at a discount or redeemed at a premium, Ch. 40, 4.4.13
         early settlement of a debt instrument, Ch. 40, 4.4.14
         interest and dividends, Ch. 40, 4.4.1
         property, plant and equipment held for rental, Ch. 40, 4.4.7
         sales taxes and other non-income tax cash flows, Ch. 40, 4.4.3
         taxes on income, Ch. 40, 4.4.2
         treasury shares, Ch. 40, 4.4.10
   cash flows from financing activities, Ch. 40, 4.3
   cash flows from investing activities, Ch. 40, 4.2
   cash flows from operating activities, Ch. 40, 4.1
      direct method, Ch. 40, 4.1.1
      indirect method, Ch. 40, 4.1.2
   consolidated statement of cash flows, preparing, Ch. 40, 6.1

contingent consideration, Ch. 40, 6.3.3
deferred and other non-cash consideration, Ch. 40, 6.3.2
disposals, Ch. 40, 6.3
first-time adopter, Ch. 5, 7.1
foreign currency cash flows, Ch. 40, 5.3
    entities applying the direct method, Ch. 40, 5.3.1
    entities applying the indirect method, Ch. 40, 5.3.2
gross/net presentation of cash flows, Ch. 40, 5.2
group treasury arrangements, Ch. 40, 6.5.2
non-cash transactions and transactions on deferred terms, Ch. 40, 5.4
    asset disposals on deferred terms, Ch. 40, 5,4,2
    asset purchased on deferred terms from the supplier, Ch. 40, 5.4.1
    revenue contracts with deferred payment terms, Ch. 40, 5.4.3
    sale and leaseback transactions, Ch. 40, 5.5.4
operating, investing and financing activities, allocating items to, Ch. 40, 4.4
    accounting as lessee, Ch. 40, 5.5.1
    accounting as lessor, Ch. 40, 5.5.5
    cash flows for service concession arrangements, Ch. 40, 4.4.9
    cash flows from factoring of trade receivables, Ch. 40, 4.4.5
    cash flows from leasing transactions, Ch. 40, 5.5
    cash flows from supply-chain financing (reverse factoring), Ch. 40, 4.4.6
    cash flows on derivative contracts, Ch. 40, 4.4.12
    cash flows related to the costs of a share issue, Ch. 40, 4.4.11
    contributions to a log-term employee benefit fund, Ch. 40, 4.4.4
    debt instrument issued at a discount or redeemed at a premium, Ch. 40, 4.4.13
    interest and dividends, Ch. 40, 4.4.1
    lease incentives, Ch. 40, 5.5.3
    payments made by the lessee before commencement date, Ch. 40, 5.5.2
    property, plant and equipment held for rental, Ch. 40, 4.4.7
    received as compensation for an insured loss, Ch. 40, 4.4.9
    sales taxes, Ch. 40, 4.4.3
    taxes on income, Ch. 40, 4.4.2
    treasury shares, Ch. 40, 4.4.10
settlement of amounts owed by the acquired entity, Ch. 40, 6.3.4
settlement of intra-group balances on a demerger, Ch. 40, 6.3.5
in subsidiaries, associates and joint ventures, Ch. 40, 6.5.1
transactions with non-controlling interests, Ch. 40, 6.2
voluntary disclosures, Ch. 40, 5.7
    cash flows to increase and maintain operating capacity, Ch. 40, 5.7.1
    segment cash flow disclosures, Ch. 40, 5.7.2

Statement of changes in equity, Ch. 3, 3.3

Statement of comprehensive income, Ch. 3, 3.2
    cash flow hedges, Ch. 54, 4.3.3
    comparative information, Ch. 4, 4
    for co-operative, Ch. 54, 7.1.5
    discontinued operations, Ch. 3, 3.2.5
    expenses analysis, Ch. 3, 3.2.3
        by function, Ch. 3, 3.2.3.B
        by nature, Ch. 3, 3.2.3.A
    extraordinary items, Ch. 3, 3.2.6.B
    face of, information required on, Ch. 3, 3.2.2
    fair value hedges, Ch. 54, 4.3.3
    material items, Ch. 3, 3.2.6.A
    for mutual fund, Ch. 54, 7.1.5
    operating profit, Ch. 3, 3.2.2.A
    ordinary activities, Ch. 3, 3.2.6.B
    presentation on face of, Ch. 54, 7
    reclassification adjustments, Ch. 3, 3.2.4.B
    tax on items of other comprehensive income, Ch. 3, 3.2.4.C

Statement of financial position, Ch. 3, 3.1. *See also* IAS 1
    comparative information, Ch. 3, 2.4; Ch. 4, 4.2
    current assets, Ch. 3, 3.1.3
    current liabilities, Ch. 3, 3.1.4
    current/non-current assets and liabilities, distinction between, Ch. 3, 3.1.1
    hyperinflation, Ch. 16, 4
    IFRS statement of financial position, opening, Ch. 5, 3
        and accounting policies, Ch. 5, 3.2
        assets and liabilities to be recognised in, Ch. 5, 5.2.4
        defined terms, Ch. 5, 1.3
        departures from full retrospective application, Ch. 5, 3.5
        fair value and deemed cost, Ch. 5, 3.3
        first-time adoption timeline, Ch. 5, 3.1
        hedge accounting in, Ch. 5, 4.5
        transitional provisions in other standards, Ch. 5, 3.4
    information required either on the face of the statement of financial position or in the notes, Ch. 3, 3.1.6
    information required on the face of statement of financial position, Ch. 3, 3.1.5
    non-current assets and disposal groups held for sale, Ch. 3, 3.1.2
    plan surplus or deficit in, treatment of, Ch. 35, 8
        assets restriction to their recoverable amounts, Ch. 35, 8.2
        net defined benefit liability (asset), Ch. 35, 8.1

Step acquisitions, Ch. 9, 9

Step-by-step method, Ch. 7, 2.3; Ch. 15, 6.6.3
    in consolidating foreign operations, Ch. 7, 2.3

Step-disposal of a subsidiary, Ch. 7, 3.4
    advance payment, Ch. 7, 3.4
    immediate disposal, Ch. 7, 3.4

'Step-up' clause, perpetual instruments, Ch. 47, 4.5.4

Stepped up exercise price, Ch. 47, 5.1.3

Stewardship, Ch. 2, 4.2.3

Straight-line method, assets depreciated using, Ch. 43, 16.1.2

Streaming arrangements, forward-selling contracts to finance development, Ch. 43, 12.6

Stripping costs in the production phase of a surface mine, Ch. 43, 15.5
    determining when production phase commences, Ch. 43, 15.5.2
    disclosures, Ch. 43, 15.5.6
    initial recognition, Ch. 43, 15.5.4
        allocating costs between inventory and the stripping activity asset, Ch. 43, 15.5.4.A
        identifying components of the ore body, Ch. 43, 15.5.4.B

Stripping costs in the production phase of a surface mine—*contd*
   recognition criteria-stripping activity asset, Ch. 43, 15.5.3
   scope of IFRIC 20, Ch. 43, 15.5.1
   subsequent measurement, Ch. 43, 15.5.5
Structured entities, Ch. 13, 2.2.1, 2.2.1.B
   disclosure of interests in unconsolidated, Ch. 13, 6
   disclosure of the nature of the risks associated with
      consolidated, Ch. 13, 4.4
   unconsolidated, Ch. 13, 2.2.2.D
Subleases, Ch. 23, 7
   definition, Ch. 23, 7.1
   disclosure, Ch. 23, 7.5
   intermediate lessor accounting, Ch. 23, 7.2
   presentation, Ch. 23, 7.4
   sublessee accounting, Ch. 23, 7.3
Sub-LIBOR issue, Ch. 53, 2.4
Subordinated financial support, Ch. 13, 2.2.1.B
Subordinated retained interests, Ch. 52, 4.3
Subrogation, Ch. 55, 7.2.6.E
Subsequent measurement, financial instruments, Ch. 50, 1–4.
   See also Impairments
   amortised cost and the effective interest method, Ch. 50, 3
      effective interest rate, Ch. 50, 3.1
      fixed interest rate instruments, Ch. 50, 3.2
      floating interest rate instruments, Ch. 50, 3.3
      inflation-linked debt instruments, Ch. 50, 3.6
      modified financial assets and liabilities, Ch. 50, 3.8
         accounting for modifications that do not result in
            derecognition, Ch. 50, 3.8.1, 5.1.1
         treatment of modification fees, Ch. 50, 3.8.2
      more complex financial liabilities, Ch. 50, 3.7
      perpetual debt instruments, Ch. 50, 3.5
      prepayment, call and similar options, Ch. 50, 3.4
         revisions to estimated cash flows, Ch. 50, 3.4.1
   estimated cash flows, revisions to, Ch. 50, 3.4.1
   exceptions to the general principles, Ch. 50, 2.9
      hedging relationships, Ch. 50, 2.9.1
      liabilities arising from 'failed derecognition' transactions,
         Ch. 50, 2.9.3
      regular way transactions, Ch. 50, 2.9.2
   financial assets and financial liabilities at fair value through
      profit/loss, Ch. 50, 2.4
   financial guarantees and commitments to provide a loan at a
      below-market interest rate, Ch. 50, 2.8
   floating interest rate instruments, Ch. 50, 3.3
   foreign currencies
      foreign entities, Ch. 50, 4.2
      instruments, Ch. 50, 4.1
   impairment, Ch. 51, 1-15
      approaches, Ch. 51, 3
      for corporates, Ch. 51, 4
      disclosures, Ch. 51, 15
      financial assets measured at fair value through other
         comprehensive income, Ch. 51, 9
      general approach, Ch. 51, 6
      intercompany loans, Ch. 51, 13
      introduction, Ch. 51, 1
      loan commitments and financial guarantee contracts,
         Ch. 51, 11
      measurement of ECL's, Ch. 51, 5
      modified financial assets, Ch. 51, 8
      presentation of credit losses, Ch. 51, 14
      revolving credit facilities, Ch. 51, 12
      scope, Ch. 51, 2
      trade receivables, contract assets and lease receivables,
         Ch. 51, 10
   reclassification of financial assets, Ch. 50, 2.7
   and recognition of gains and losses, Ch. 50, 2
      debt financial assets measured at amortised cost, Ch. 50,
         2.1
      debt financial assets measured at fair value through other
         comprehensive income, Ch. 50, 2.3
      exceptions to the general principles, Ch. 50, 2.9
         hedging relationships, Ch. 50, 2.9.1
         liabilities arising from 'failed derecognition'
            transactions, Ch. 50, 2.9.3
         regular way transactions, Ch. 50, 2.9.2
      financial assets and financial liabilities at fair value through
         profit/loss, Ch. 50, 2.4
      financial guarantees and commitments to provide a loan at
         a below-market interest rate, Ch. 50, 2.8
      financial liabilities measured at amortised cost, Ch. 50, 2.2
      reclassification of financial assets, Ch. 50, 2.7
      unquoted equity instruments and related derivatives,
         Ch. 50, 2.6
   unquoted equity instruments and related derivatives, Ch. 50, 2.6
Subsidiaries, Ch. 7; Ch. 13, 2.2.2.A. *See also* Ownership interests,
   changes in
   acquired in stages, cost of, Ch. 7, 3.1.1, 3.1.2; Ch. 8, 2.1.1.C
   acquisition, Ch. 8, 4.4.2
      deferred tax exemption, Ch. 33, 7.2.9
   becoming a first-time adopter later than its parent, Ch. 5,
      5.9.1
   dividends from, Ch. 8, 2.4.1
   former subsidiary
      comparative information for, Ch. 7, 3.3.2.G
      interest retained in, Ch. 7, 3.3.1
   investments in, Ch. 5, 5.8; Ch. 20, 12.4
   parent becoming a first-time adopter later than, Ch. 5, 5.9.2
Substantive rights, Ch. 6, 4.2.1
Substantively enacted tax legislation, Ch. 33, 5.1
Successful efforts method, E&E expenditure, Ch. 43, 3.2.3
Super-deductible assets (tax), Ch. 33, 7.2.6
Supply-chain finance, Ch. 52, 6.5; Ch. 40, 4.4.6
'Synthetic' instruments, Ch. 46, 8
Take-or-pay contracts, Ch. 43, 12.7.14, 17.2
Tax bases, Ch. 33, 6.1
   of assets, Ch. 33, 6.1.1
   assets and liabilities whose tax base is not immediately
      apparent, Ch. 33, 6.1.3
   disclaimed or with no economic value, Ch. 33, 6.1.7
   equity items with, Ch. 33, 6.1.5
   of items not recognised as assets/liabilities in financial
      statements, Ch. 33, 6.1.4
   items with more than one tax base, Ch. 33, 6.1.6
   of liabilities, Ch. 33, 6.1.2
Tax expense (tax income)
   definition, Ch. 33, 3
Tax planning opportunities, Ch. 33, 7.4.4, 8.4.1

Index

Taxable profit (tax loss)
   definition, Ch. 33, 3
Taxable temporary differences
   definition, Ch. 33, 3
Taxation, Ch. 33. *See also* Deferred tax; IAS 12–*Income taxes*; Income taxes
   extractive industries, Ch. 43, 19
   interim financial reporting, Ch. 41, 9.5
      changes in the effective tax rate during the year, Ch. 41, 9.5.2
      difference in financial year and tax year, Ch. 41, 9.5.3
      measuring interim income tax expense, Ch. 41, 9.5.1
      tax credits, Ch. 41, 9.5.5
      tax loss and tax credit carrybacks and carryforwards, Ch. 41, 9.5.4
Taxes related to share-based payment transactions, Ch. 34, 14
   employment taxes of the employer, Ch. 34, 14.2
      applicable standards, Ch. 34, 14.2.1
      holding of own shares to 'hedge' employment tax liabilities, Ch. 34, 14.2.3
      recovery of employer's taxes from employees, Ch. 34, 14.2.2
   income tax deductions for the entity, Ch. 34, 14.1
   sale or surrender of shares by employee to meet employee's tax liability ('sell to cover' and net settlement), Ch. 34, 14.3
      net settlement feature for withholding tax obligations, Ch. 34, 14.3.1
Temporal method, Ch. 15, 1.1
Temporary differences, Ch. 33, 6, 6.2, 7. *See also* Deferred tax
   changes after initial recognition Ch. 33, 7.42.4
      altered by legislative change, Ch. 33, 7.2.4.D
      amortisation, Ch. 33, 7.2.4.A
      in carrying value due to revaluation, Ch. 33, 7.2.4.B
      depreciation, Ch. 33, 7.2.4.A
      in tax base due to deductions in tax return, Ch. 33, 7.2.4.C
   deductible, Ch. 33, 3, 6, 6.1, 6.2.2, 7.2.2.B, 7.5.3
      business combinations and consolidation, Ch. 33, 6.2.2.E
      foreign currency differences, Ch. 33, 6.2.2.F
      revaluations, Ch. 33, 6.2.2.C
      tax re-basing, Ch. 33, 6.2.2.D
      transactions that affect profit of loss, Ch. 33, 6.2.2.A
      transactions that affect statement of financial position, Ch. 33, 6.2.2.B
   definition, Ch. 33, 3
   taxable, Ch. 33, 6.2.1
      business combinations and consolidation, Ch. 33, 6.2.1.E
      foreign currency differences, Ch. 33, 6.2.1.F
      hyperinflation, Ch. 33, 6.2.1.G
      revaluations, Ch. 33, 6.2.1.C
      tax re-basing, Ch. 33, 6.2.1.D
      transactions that affect profit of loss, Ch. 33, 6.2.1.A
      transactions that affect statement of financial position, Ch. 33, 6.2.1.B
Termination benefits, employee benefits, Ch. 35, 14
   measurement, Ch. 35, 14.3
   recognition, Ch. 35, 14.2
   statutory termination indemnities, Ch. 35, 14.1
Third-party credit enhancement, liabilities issued with
   by the issuer, Ch. 14, 11.3.1
   by a third-party, Ch. 14, 11.3.1.A

Time-period related hedged item, Ch. 53, 7.5.1
Time value of money, Ch. 51, 5.7
   hedge effectiveness, measurement of, Ch. 53, 7.4.2
Time value of options, Ch. 53, 3.6.4, 7.5.1
   aligned time value, Ch. 53, 7.5.1.A
   and effectiveness of options, Ch. 53, 7.4.12
   hedged items with embedded optionality, Ch. 53, 3.6.4
   retrospective application, Ch. 53, 12.3.1
Tolling arrangements, mining sector, Ch. 43, 20
Total Distributable Income (TDI), Ch. 55, 6
Total return swaps, Ch. 52, 4.4.1
Trade date accounting, Ch. 49, 2.2.3; Ch. 51, 7.3.2
   exchange of non-cash financial assets, Ch. 49, 2.2.5.A
Trade receivables. *See* Receivables
'**Traded in a public market,' meaning of**, Ch. 6, 2.2.1.B; Ch. 36, 2.2.1
Transaction-based taxes, Ch. 56, 8.2.3.I
Transaction costs
   changes in ownership interest without loss of control, Ch. 7, 4.4
   equity instruments, tax benefits, Ch. 33, 10.3.5
   equity transactions, Ch. 47, 8.1
   fair value measurement, Ch. 14, 9.1
   financial instruments, Ch. 49, 3.4
      accounting treatment, Ch. 49, 3.4.1
   identifying, Ch. 49, 3.4.2
   incurred by the reporting entity on acquisition of investment property, Ch. 19, 6.4
Transaction price, IFRS 15
   allocation of, Ch. 29, 3
   determination of, Ch. 29, 2
   initial measurement, Ch. 49, 3.3
Transaction related hedged item, Ch. 53, 7.5.1
Transfer of control, Ch 30. 2-4
Transferee's put option, Ch. 52, 5.4.3.B
Transferor's call option, Ch. 52, 5.4.3.A
Transfers of financial assets, Ch. 54, 6
   disclosure requirements, Ch. 54, 6.3.2
   meaning of continuing involvement, Ch. 54, 6.3.1
   meaning of 'transfer,' Ch. 54, 6.1
   transferred financial assets
      that are derecognised in their entirety, Ch. 54, 6.3
      that are not derecognised in their entirety, Ch. 54, 6.2
Transition Resource Group for Impairment of Financial Instruments, IFRS, Ch. 1, 2.9
Transition Resource Group for Insurance Contracts, Ch. 1, 2.9
Transition Resource Group for Revenue Recognition, Ch. 1, 2.9, 27, 28, 29, 30, 31, 32
Transportation costs, Ch. 14, 9.2
Treasury shares, Ch. 47, 9
   cash flow statement, Ch. 40, 4.4.10
   IFRS 17 Treasury share election, Ch. 47, 9.2
   transactions in own shares not at fair value, Ch. 47, 9.1
Trustees, IFRS Foundation, Ch. 1, 2,2–2.8, 3.2, 5
Unanimous consent, joint control, Ch. 12,4.3; Ch. 43, 7.1.1.B
Unbundling of deposit components, Ch. 55, 5
   illustration, Ch. 55, 5.2

Unbundling of deposit components—*contd*
   practical difficulties, Ch. 55, 5.3
   requirements, Ch. 55, 5.1
Uncertain future events, insurance contracts, Ch. 55, 3.4; Ch. 56, 3.2
Uncertain tax treatments, Ch. 33, 5.2, 8.2, 9
   assumptions about the examination of tax treatments ('detection risk'), Ch. 33, 9.3
   consideration of changes in facts and circumstances, Ch. 33, 9.5
   considered separately (unit of account), Ch. 33, 9.2
   determining effects of, Ch. 33, 9.4
   disclosures relating to, Ch. 33, 9.6
   IFRIC 23
      changes in estimates, Ch. 38, 3.6
      scope and definitions used, Ch. 33, 9.1
   presentation of liabilities or assets for, Ch. 33, 9.7
   recognition of an asset for payments on account, Ch. 33, 9.8
Unconsolidated structured entities, Ch. 13, 2.2.2.D
   disclosure of interests, Ch. 13, 6
   financial or other support to, Ch. 13, 4.4.3
Undivided interests, Ch. 18, 7.3; Ch. 43, 7.2
Unit of account, Ch. 14, 5.1
   extractive industries, Ch. 43, 4
   fair value measurement
      asset's (or liability's) components, Ch. 14, 5.1.4
      and portfolio exception, Ch. 14, 5.1.2
      and PxQ, Ch. 7, 3.3.2.F; Ch. 14, 5.1.1
      vs. valuation premise, Ch. 14, 5.1.3
      and FVLCD estimation, Ch. 20, 6.1.1
Unit of production method, Ch. 18, 5.6.2
United Kingdom (UK) adopted- IAS, Ch. 1, 4,.2.3
United Kingdom (UK), IFRS adoption in, Ch. 1, 4.2.3
United States of America (US), IFRS adoption in, Ch. 1, 3.2, 4.3.1
Unitisations, mineral properties, Ch. 43, 15.4.1
Unit-linked features, Ch. 55, 4.1
Units of production method, assets depreciated using, Ch. 43, 16.1.3
   joint and by-products, Ch. 43, 16.1.3.D
   reserves base, Ch. 43, 16.1.3.B
   unit of measure, Ch. 43, 16.1.3.C
   units of production formula, Ch. 43, 16.1.3.A
Unquoted equity instruments
   and related derivatives, Ch. 50, 2.6
Upstream activity phases, extractive industries, Ch. 43, 1.6.1
   acquisition of mineral rights, Ch. 43, 1.6.1
   appraisal/evaluation, Ch. 41, 1.6.1
   closure and decommissioning, Ch. 43, 1.6.1
   construction, Ch. 43, 1.6.1
   development, Ch. 43, 1.6.1
   exploration, Ch. 43, 1.6.1
   production, Ch. 43, 1.6.1
   prospecting, Ch. 43, 1.6.1
'Upstream' transactions elimination, equity accounted entities, Ch. 11, 7.6.1
US GAAP, convergence with IFRS, Ch. 1, 3.2
US, IFRS adoption in, Ch. 1, 3.2
Useful life, intangible assets, Ch. 17, 9.1.1
   contractual/other legal rights, Ch. 17, 9.1.2
   with a finite useful life, Ch. 17, 9.2
   with an indefinite useful life, Ch. 17, 9.3
Valuation techniques, fair value measurement, Ch. 14, 14
   cost approach, Ch. 14, 14.3
      use of depreciated replacement cost to measure fair value, Ch. 14, 14.3.1
   disclosure of, Ch. 14, 20.3.5
   income approach, Ch. 14, 14.4
   inputs to, Ch. 14, 15
      broker quotes and pricing services, Ch. 14, 15.5
      central clearing organisations, values from, Ch. 14, 15.5.1
      general principles, Ch. 14, 15.1
      premiums and discounts, Ch. 14, 15.2
         blockage factors (or block discounts), Ch. 14, 15.2.1
      pricing within the bid-ask spread, Ch. 14, 15.3
         bid-ask spread, Ch. 14, 15.3.2
         mid-market pricing, Ch. 14, 15.3.1
      risk premiums, Ch. 14, 15.4
   market approach, Ch. 14, 14.2
   property, plant and equipment, Ch. 18, 6.1.1.B
   selecting appropriate, Ch. 14, 14.1
      making changes to valuation techniques, Ch. 14, 14.1.4
      single *vs.* multiple valuation techniques, Ch. 14, 14.1.1
      using multiple valuation techniques to measure fair value, Ch. 14, 14.1.2
      valuation adjustments, Ch. 14, 14.1.3
Value-at-risk and similar analyses, Ch. 54, 5.5.2
Value beyond proven and probable reserves (VBPP), Ch. 43, 8.2.3
Value in use (VIU). *See also* IAS 36
   calculation of (extractive industries), Ch. 43, 11.4
      commodity price assumptions, Ch. 43, 11.4.3
      consistency in cash flows and book values attributed to the CGU, Ch. 43, 11.4.1
         environmental provisions and similar provisions and liabilities, Ch. 43, 11.4.1.A
      foreign currency cash flows, Ch. 43, 11.4.5
      future capital expenditure, Ch. 43, 11.4.4
      projections of cash flows, Ch. 43, 11.4.2
         cash flows from mineral reserves and resources and the appropriate discount rate, Ch. 43, 11.4.2.A
   differences between fair value and VIU, Ch. 20, 7.3
   estimating the future pre-tax cash flows of the CGU under review, Ch. 20, 7.1
      budgets and cash flows, Ch. 20, 7.1.1
      cash inflows and outflows from improvements and enhancements, Ch. 20, 7.1.2
      events after the reporting period, Ch. 20, 7.1.9
      foreign currency cash flows, Ch. 20, 7.1.5
      internal transfer pricing, Ch. 20, 7.1.6
      lease payments, Ch. 20, 7.1.8
      overheads and share-based payments, Ch. 20, 7.1.7
      restructuring, Ch. 20, 7.1.3
      terminal values, Ch. 20, 7.1.4
   identifying appropriate discount rate and discounting future cash flows, Ch. 20, 7.2
      approximations and short cuts, Ch. 20, 7.2.4
      calculating VIU using post-tax cash flows, Ch. 20, 7.2.3
      determining pre-tax rates taking account of tax losses, Ch. 20, 7.2.6

disclosing pre-tax discount rates when using a post-tax methodology, Ch. 20, 7.2.5
discount rates and the weighted average cost of capital, Ch. 20, 7.2.1
entity-specific WACCs and capital structure, Ch. 20, 7.2.8
entity-specific WACCs and different project risks within the entity, Ch. 20, 7.2.7
pre-tax discount rate, calculating, Ch. 20, 7.2.2
use of discount rates other than the WACC, Ch. 20, 7.2.9
for investment in subsidiaries, associates and joint ventures, Ch. 20, 12.4.2
based on cash flows generated by underlying assets, Ch. 20, 12.4.2.B
using dividend discount models, Ch. 20, 12.4.2.A
relevant cash flows and non-arm's length prices (transfer pricing), Ch. 20, 12.1

Value of business acquired (VOBA), Ch. 55, 9.1

Variable interest entity (VIE), Ch. 13, 2.2.1.B

Variable returns, exposure to
evaluating derivatives, Ch. 6, 5.3
as indicator of power, Ch. 6, 5.1
interest rate swaps, Ch. 6, 5.3.1
plain vanilla foreign exchange swaps, Ch. 6, 5.3.1
returns, Ch. 6, 5.2
total return swaps, Ch. 6, 5.3.2

Vested transactions, share-based payment, Ch. 34, 2.2.2.E

Vesting, share-based payment, Ch. 34, 3.1, 6.1, 9.3.2. *See also* Cash-settled share-based payment transactions; Equity-settled share-based payment transactions
market conditions, Ch. 34, 6.3
non-vesting conditions, Ch. 34, 3.2, 3.4, 6.4
background, Ch. 34, 3.2.1
defining, Ch. 34, 3.2.2
non-compete agreements Ch. 34, 3.2.3
treatment of, option-pricing models, Ch. 34, 8.4.2
overview, Ch. 34, 6.1
accounting after vesting, Ch. 34, 6.1.3
continuous estimation process of IFRS 2, Ch. 34, 6.1.1
vesting and forfeiture, Ch. 34, 6.1.2
shares used as a currency of payment, Ch. 34, 15.6
awards assessed on the market value of a subsidiary or business unit and settled by reference to the fair value of shares in the parent entity, Ch. 34, 15.6.1
vesting conditions, Ch. 34, 3.1, 3.4
employee's performance rating, Ch. 34, 3.1.2
'malus' clauses and clawback conditions, Ch. 34, 3.1.1
other than market conditions, Ch. 34, 6.2
service condition, Ch. 34, 6.2.1
vesting period, Ch. 34, 3.3
awards entitled to dividends during, Ch. 34, 15.3
determining, Ch. 34, 9.3.2.A
market conditions and known vesting periods, Ch. 34, 6.3.3
modifications with altered vesting period, Ch. 34, 7.3.3
non-vesting conditions and, Ch. 34, 6.4.2
variable vesting periods due to market conditions, Ch. 34, 6.3.4
variable vesting periods due to non-market vesting conditions, Ch. 34, 6.2.3
vesting in instalments ('graded vesting'), Ch. 34, 6.2.2

Veto rights, Ch. 6, 4.2.2.A

Voluntary changes of accounting policy, Ch. 3, 4.4; Ch. 41, 8.1.2.B
disclosures relating to, Ch. 3, 5.1.2

Voting power, Ch. 11, 4.3

Voting rights
held in fiduciary capacity, Ch. 11, 4.5
significant influence, potential, Ch. 11, 4.4

Voting rights, investee
additional rights from other contractual arrangements, Ch. 6, 4.3.6
contractual arrangement with other vote holders, Ch. 6, 4.3.5
de facto control, Ch. 6, 4.3.3
majority without power, Ch. 6, 4.3.3
potential voting rights, Ch. 6, 4.3.4
power with a majority, Ch. 6, 4.3.1

Warranties, Ch. 31, 3
assurance-type warranties, Ch. 31, 3.3
contracts that contain both assurance and service-type warranties, Ch. 31, 3.4
determining whether warranty is an assurance-type or service-type warranty, Ch. 31, 3.1
customer's return of defective item in exchange for compensation: right of return *vs.* assurance type warranty, Ch. 31, 3.1.3
evaluating whether a product warranty is a service-type warranty (i.e. a performance obligation) when it is not separately priced, Ch. 31, 3.1.1
how would an entity account for repairs provided outside the warranty period?, Ch. 31, 3.1.2
service-type warranties, Ch. 31, 3.2

Warranty provisions (IAS 37), Ch. 26, 6.10

Waste electrical and electronic equipment (WE&EE), EU directive, Ch. 26, 6.7

Weather derivatives, Ch. 45, 3.3.1

Website costs, Ch. 17, 6.2.5
application and infrastructure, Ch. 17, 6.2.5
content development, Ch. 17, 6.2.5
graphical design development, Ch. 17, 6.2.5
operating stage, Ch. 17, 6.2.5
planning, Ch. 17, 6.2.5

Weighted average cost of capital (WACC), Ch. 20, 7.2
discount rates and, Ch. 20, 7.2.1
entity-specific WACCs
and capital structure, Ch. 20, 7.2.8
and different project risks, Ch. 20, 7.2.7

Weighted average number of shares, Ch. 37, 4.1

Work in progress, recognition of, Ch. 43, 14.1

Workovers, oil and gas wells, Ch. 43, 15.2

World Standard-setters Conferences, Ch. 1, 2.9

Worldwide adoption of IFRS, Ch. 1, 4.1

Written options
call option, Ch. 37, 6.4.2.B; Ch. 47, 11.2.2
maturity analysis, Ch. 54, 5.4.2.F
net settlement, Ch. 45, 4.2.3
net written options, Ch. 53, 3.2.2
put option, Ch. 7, 6.2, 6.3, 6.4, 6.5, 7.3, 7.4; Ch. 37, 6.4.2.C; Ch. 47, 11.3.2

Notes

Notes

Notes

International GAAP®
Keeping you on course

Are you interested to see IGAAP in print and e-book formats?

Visit us at www.wileyigaap.com to find out more.

© 2020 EYGM Limited. All Rights Reserved. EYG No. 007351-20Gbl ED None.

International GAAP 2021

Generally Accepted Accounting Practice
under International Financial Reporting Standards

Cullum Allen	Lennart Hoogerwaard	Tina Patel
Jeremy Barnes	Jane Hurworth	Claire Patra
Anne-Cathrine Bernhoft	Ted Jones	Michael Pratt
Martin Beyersdorff	Heather de Jongh	Matthew Richardson
Mike Bonham	Parbin Khatun	Tim Rogerson
David Bradbery	Maria Kingston	Vadim Shelaginov
Rob Carrington	Bernd Kremp	Yuta Shimomura
Jessica Cayadi	Dean Lockhart	Anna Sirocka
Victor Chan	Sharon MacIntyre	Kirsty Smith
Wei Li Chan	Anna Malcolm	Sharanya Sreedaran
Larissa Connor	Amanda Marrion	David Stolker
Pieter Dekker	Emily Moll	Michael Varila
Tim Denton	Richard Moore	Aikaterini Vatzaki
Alicia Edelstein	Ayesha Moosa	Jane Watson
Prahalad Halgeri	Tom Mullins	
Andrea Holmes	Mqondisi Ndlovu	

EY
Building a better working world

WILEY

This edition first published in 2021 by John Wiley & Sons Ltd.
Cover, cover design and content copyright © 2021 Ernst & Young LLP.
The United Kingdom firm of Ernst & Young LLP is a member of Ernst & Young Global Limited.
International GAAP® is a registered trademark of Ernst & Young LLP.

This publication contains copyright © material and trademarks of the IFRS Foundation®. All rights reserved. Reproduced by Ernst & Young LLP with the permission of the IFRS Foundation. Reproduction and use rights are strictly limited. For more information about the IFRS Foundation and rights to use its material please visit www.ifrs.org.

Disclaimer: To the extent permitted by applicable law the Board and the IFRS Foundation expressly disclaims all liability howsoever arising from this publication or any translation thereof whether in contract, tort or otherwise (including, but not limited to, liability for any negligent act or omission) to any person in respect of any claims or losses of any nature including direct, indirect, incidental or consequential loss, punitive damages, penalties or costs.

Registered office
John Wiley & Sons Ltd, The Atrium, Southern Gate, Chichester, West Sussex, PO19 8SQ, United Kingdom

For details of our global editorial offices, for customer services and for information about how to apply for permission to reuse the copyright material in this book please see our website at www.wiley.com

The right of the author to be identified as the author of this work has been asserted in accordance with the Copyright, Designs and Patents Act 1988.

All rights reserved. No part of this publication may be reproduced, stored in a retrieval system, or transmitted, in any form or by any means, electronic, mechanical, photocopying, recording or otherwise, except as permitted by the UK Copyright, Designs and Patents Act 1988, without the prior permission of the publisher.

Wiley publishes in a variety of print and electronic formats and by print-on-demand. Some material included with standard print versions of this book may not be included in e-books or in print-on-demand. If this book refers to media such as a CD or DVD that is not included in the version you purchased, you may download this material at http://booksupport.wiley.com. For more information about Wiley products, visit www.wiley.com.

Designations used by companies to distinguish their products are often claimed as trademarks. All brand names and product names used in this book are trade names, service marks, trademarks or registered trademarks of their respective owners. The publisher is not associated with any product or vendor mentioned in this book.

Limit of Liability/Disclaimer of Warranty: While the publisher and author have used their best efforts in preparing this book, they make no representations or warranties with respect to the accuracy or completeness of the contents of this book and specifically disclaim any implied warranties of merchantability or fitness for a particular purpose. It is sold on the understanding that the publisher is not engaged in rendering professional services and neither the publisher nor the author shall be liable for damages arising herefrom. If professional advice or other expert assistance is required, the services of a competent professional should be sought.

This publication has been carefully prepared, but it necessarily contains information in summary form and is therefore intended for general guidance only, and is not intended to be a substitute for detailed research or the exercise of professional judgement. The publishers, Ernst & Young LLP, Ernst & Young Global Limited or any of its Member Firms or partners or staff can accept no responsibility for loss occasioned to any person acting or refraining from action as a result of any material in this publication. On any specific matter, reference should be made to the appropriate adviser.

ISBN 978-1-119-77243-9 (paperback)
[EY personnel only ISBN 978-1-119-77244-6]
ISBN 978-1-119-77245-3 (ebk)
ISBN 978-1-119-77266-8 (ebk)

A catalogue record for this book is available from the British Library.

Printed and bound by CPI Group (UK) Ltd, Croydon, CR0 4YY.

This book is printed on acid-free paper, responsibly manufactured from well-managed FSC®-certified forests and other controlled sources.

About this book

The 2021 edition of International GAAP® has been fully revised and updated in order to:
- Provide expanded discussion and practical illustrations on the many implementation issues arising as entities continue to apply IFRS 16 – *Leases*, including those related to recent rent concessions and the associated narrow scope amendment issued by the International Accounting Standards Board (IASB).
- Include an updated chapter on the new insurance contracts standard IFRS 17 – *Insurance Contracts*, which reflects the IASB's recently issued *Amendments to IFRS 17*, resulting in a number of significant changes as well as many other editorial alterations. The chapter also discusses implementation issues and explores other matters arising as insurers prepare for the adoption of the standard.
- Continue to investigate the many application issues arising as entities apply IFRS 9 – *Financial Instruments* – and IFRS 15 – *Revenue from Contracts with Customers*.
- Discuss the IASB's amendments to IFRS 9 and related standards to address the effects of the Interbank Offered Rates (IBOR) reform on financial reporting.
- Illustrate the application of IFRS to the accounting for natural disasters highlighted by the accounting issues related to the recent coronavirus pandemic.
- Discuss the new agenda decisions issued by the IFRS Interpretations Committee since the preparation of the 2020 edition.
- Address the amendments to standards and the many other initiatives that are currently being discussed by the IASB and the potential consequential changes to accounting requirements.
- Provide further insight on the many issues relating to the practical application of IFRS, based on the extensive experience of the book's authors in dealing with current issues.

The book is published in three volumes. The 56 chapters – listed on pages xi to xiii – are split between the three volumes as follows:
- Volume 1 - Chapters 1 to 22,
- Volume 2 - Chapters 23 to 43,
- Volume 3 - Chapters 44 to 56.

Each chapter includes a detailed list of contents and list of illustrative examples.

Each of the three volumes contains the following indexes covering all three volumes:
- an index of extracts from financial statements,
- an index of references to standards and interpretations,
- a general index.

Preface

The IASB noted in its 2018 analysis of the use of IFRS around the world that, other than China, India, Japan and the United States, the vast majority of the 166 jurisdictions they have researched require the use of IFRS for all or most domestic publicly accountable entities (listed companies and financial institutions) in their capital markets. Maintaining the current international alignment of accounting standards requires an ongoing commitment on the part of all jurisdictions involved, but the benefits of IFRS are clear when looking at the way in which the IASB was able to consider the impact of the coronavirus pandemic on financial reporting.

The coronavirus outbreak was first reported near the end of 2019, with the virus subsequently spreading worldwide. On 11 March 2020, the World Health Organisation classified the outbreak as a pandemic. While the coronavirus outbreak is first and foremost a public health concern, it has significantly impacted the world economy and, indirectly, financial reporting and the work of the IASB itself.

In response to the development, the IASB issued Amendments to IFRS 16 – *Leases: Covid-19-Related Rent Concessions*, deferred the effective date of Amendments to IAS 1 – *Presentation of Financial Statements: Classification of Liabilities as Current or Non-current*, decided to extend the consultation period of several consultation documents by three months, and decided to monitor the situation with a view to making further changes to its timelines, if necessary. As a result, the next milestones of many of the IASB's projects have been pushed out to accommodate the exceptional circumstances.

The economic impacts of the coronavirus outbreak can also be seen in the financial reports of companies where it has affected the accounting for and disclosure of going concern issues, impairment testing, government grants, leases, onerous contracts, income taxes and fair value measurement. While the economic uncertainty increased the need for the careful exercise of judgement, IFRS has offered an accounting framework that provides the necessary guidance to deal even with these unusual circumstances.

New standards

IFRS 16 became effective in 2019 and its interactions with other standards has given rise to a number of challenging implementation questions that continue to be addressed. The Interpretations Committee has published agenda decisions on the treatment of subsurface rights, determining the incremental borrowing rate, the definition of a lease and the interaction between the lease term and useful life of leasehold improvements. The IASB continues to work on its project that deals with the application of IAS 12 – *Income Taxes* – to right-of-use assets and lease liabilities, while the Interpretations

Committee is currently considering the accounting for the sale and leaseback of an asset in a single-asset entity.

IFRS 17 – *Insurance Contracts* – was amended in June 2020 and has an effective date of 1 January 2023. The IASB amended IFRS 17 in response to matters of concern raised primarily in Europe regarding the concepts and practical implementation of the standard that were raised by stakeholders. IFRS 17, together with IFRS 9 – *Financial Instruments*, will result in profound changes to the accounting in IFRS financial statements for insurance companies. This will also have a significant impact on data, systems and processes used to produce information for financial reporting purposes. The new model is likely to have a significant impact on the profit and total equity of some insurance entities, but IFRS 17 has been welcomed by the user community as it is expected to improve comparability between insurers and increase the transparency around the drivers of performance and source of earnings.

Current work plan

The IASB has deferred its agenda consultation until 2021 and is currently still working on the projects in its work plan for the period from 2017 until 2021. The work plan can be divided into three elements: the standard-setting and maintenance projects, the research projects, and the Better Communication in Financial Reporting initiative.

The IASB's standard-setting and maintenance agenda focuses almost exclusively on narrow scope projects that address certain aspects of existing standards. The exposure draft on the rate-regulated activities project – a more comprehensive project but limited in impact as it is industry-specific – was delayed by almost a year and is now expected to be published in early 2021.

As part of its active research agenda, the IASB's core model for dynamic risk management and discussion paper on business combinations under common control are expected in late 2020, while the comment period on the discussion paper on goodwill and impairment was extended to December 2020. The IASB is currently considering the direction on the projects on financial instruments with characteristics of equity and extractive activities. Although these technically complex but important projects are taking longer than expected, we encourage the IASB to continue its work as they deal with issues that have been the source of many accounting questions.

The IASB expects to publish, in late 2020, its request for information on the Post-Implementation Review of IFRS 10 – *Consolidated Financial Statements*, IFRS 11 – *Joint Arrangements* – and IFRS 12 – *Disclosure of Interests in Other Entities*. The Interpretations Committee has often discussed requests regarding the interpretation of IFRS 11 and it seems likely that the Post-Implementation Review will similarly give rise to questions from constituents.

Better communication and sustainability reporting

The IASB continues to work on the various aspects of its Better Communication in Financial Reporting initiative, such as the primary financial statements, management commentary and the taxonomy. The project to update the Management Commentary Practice Statement, for which an exposure draft is expected early in 2021, is seen by the

IASB as the cornerstone of the notion of 'broader financial information'. That said, there is an ongoing debate as to how 'broad' annual reporting, and by extension the IASB's own remit, should be.

In November 2019, Hans Hoogervorst, the Chairman of the IASB, noted in a speech that 'The popularity of non-GAAP has risen sharply and there is growing interest in broader reporting, particularly in the area of sustainability. [...] In the light of these developments, the IASB constantly asks itself how it can strengthen the relevance of IFRS Standards in this changing world.'[1] Sue Lloyd, the Vice-Chair of the IASB, noted in December 2019 that '[...] the IASB exists to write Standards that result in investors getting the information they need to make their investment decisions. We know that in order to make informed investment decisions, investors need information that goes beyond the boundaries of that captured within the traditional financial statements. Investors need information about items that are not recognised and measured for accounting purposes, but that can affect the company's future cash flows and the value of its equity.'[2]

Many of the non-financial issues that interest investors can be characterised as externalities, which are commonly defined as consequences of an industrial or commercial activity that affect other parties without being reflected in market prices. Traditional financial reporting has focused on how companies are affected by externalities that are inflicted upon them (i.e. the investor perspective), but far less on how their actions affect others (i.e. the societal perspective). In addressing these considerations, the IASB faces the challenge that it does not have the breadth of expertise that would allow it to cover the entire field of non-financial reporting and that its resources are limited.

In September 2020, Erik Thedéen, the Chair of IOSCO's Task Force on Sustainable Finance, noted in a speech that IOSCO is engaging with two initiatives that 'are both very interesting and very promising'.[3] Firstly, an alliance of five framework- and standard-setting institutions of international significance – CDP, the Climate Disclosure Standards Board (CDSB), the Global Reporting Initiative (GRI), the International Integrated Reporting Council (IIRC) and the Sustainability Accounting Standards Board (SASB) – announced a commitment to working towards a comprehensive corporate reporting system. Secondly, a working group of IFRS trustees is considering what role the IFRS Foundation can play in setting standards for sustainability reporting. The Trustees of the IFRS Foundation published a consultation paper on sustainability reporting to assess if there is sufficient demand for global sustainability standards and, if so, whether the development of a sustainability standards board under the governance structure of the IFRS Foundation would be an appropriate approach to achieving further consistency and global comparability in sustainability reporting.

---

1 Speech by Hans Hoogervorst, 5 November 2019 (IASB Chair delivers keynote at Eumedion Annual Symposium, Netherlands). IFRS Foundation website: http://www.ifrs.org/news-and-events/2019/11/the-iasb-from-financial-to-integrated-standard-setter/
2 Speech by Sue Lloyd, 9 December 2019 (Enhancing relevance in 2020 and beyond). IFRS Foundation website: http://www.ifrs.org/news-and-events/2019/12/enhancing-relevance-in-2020-and-beyond/
3 Speech by Erik Thedéen, 1 October 2020 (speech at the conference Driving Global Standards on Sustainable Finance). Swedish Finansinspektionen website: https://www.fi.se/en/published/presentations/2020/erik-thedeens-speech-at-driving-global-standards-on-sustainable-finance/

We commend the initiative of the Trustees of the IFRS Foundation in taking an active role in the efforts to improve the broader financial report, as non-financial reporting provides important information that allows users to put the financial statements in context and helps them in assessing future risks and opportunities. In addition to IOSCO, the International Federation of Accountants (IFAC) has also expressed support for the creation of a new sustainability standards board that would exist alongside the IASB under the IFRS Foundation. However, as legislators in some jurisdictions have already taken steps to ensure a minimum level of communication about sustainability issues, we believe it is crucial in the interest of broad acceptance to build as broad a base of support as possible.

This edition of *International GAAP®* covers the many interpretations, practices and solutions that have now been developed based on our work with clients, and discussions with regulators, standard-setters and other professionals. In particular, the edition has been revised to consider the many financial reporting issues that have arisen in the context of the coronavirus pandemic. We believe that *International GAAP®*, now in its sixteenth edition, plays an important role in ensuring consistent application of IFRS and helping companies as they address emerging issues (e.g. interest rate benchmark reform, application of IFRS 16 and implementation of IFRS 17). These issues are complex and give rise to many practical questions about the recognition, measurement, presentation and disclosure requirements.

Our team of authors and reviewers hails from all parts of the world and includes not only our global technical experts but also senior client-facing professionals. This gives us an in-depth knowledge of practice in many different countries and industry sectors, enabling us to go beyond mere recitation of the requirements of standards to explaining their application in many varied situations.

We are deeply indebted to many of our colleagues within the global organisation of EY for their selfless assistance and support in the publication of this book. It has been a truly international effort, with valuable contributions from EY people around the globe.

Our thanks go particularly to those who reviewed and edited the drafts, most notably: Elisa Alfieri, Mark Barton, Christian Baur, Paul Beswick, Silke Blaschke, Linzi Carr, Patrick Cavanagh, Larissa Clark, Tony Clifford, Angela Covic, Josh Forgione, Peter Gittens, Archibald Groenewald, Paul Hebditch, Lara Iob, Guy Jones, Steinar Kvifte, Michiel van der Lof, James Luke, Kerri Madden, Mark Mahar, Fernando Marticorena, John Offenbacher, John O'Grady, Christiana Panayidou, Pierre Phan Van Phi, Christoph Piesbergen, George Prieksaitis, Takeshi Saida, Gerard van Santen, Nicola Sawaki, Rachel Simons, Alison Spivey, Leo van der Tas, Daniel Trotman, Hans van der Veen, Tracey Waring, Arne Weber, Clare Wong and Luci Wright.

Our thanks also go to everyone who directly or indirectly contributed to the book's creation, including the following members of EY's IFRS desks: Thato Lengana, Steve Mwereria, Teresia Ng'ang'a, Anna Pickup and Tanay Rai.

We also thank Jeremy Gugenheim for his assistance with the production technology throughout the period of writing.

London,	Cullum Allen	Lennart Hoogerwaard	Tina Patel
October 2020	Jeremy Barnes	Jane Hurworth	Claire Patra
	Anne-Cathrine Bernhoft	Ted Jones	Michael Pratt
	Martin Beyersdorff	Heather de Jongh	Matthew Richardson
	Mike Bonham	Parbin Khatun	Tim Rogerson
	David Bradbery	Maria Kingston	Vadim Shelaginov
	Rob Carrington	Bernd Kremp	Yuta Shimomura
	Jessica Cayadi	Dean Lockhart	Anna Sirocka
	Victor Chan	Sharon MacIntyre	Kirsty Smith
	Wei Li Chan	Anna Malcolm	Sharanya Sreedaran
	Larissa Connor	Amanda Marrion	David Stolker
	Pieter Dekker	Emily Moll	Michael Varila
	Tim Denton	Richard Moore	Aikaterini Vatzaki
	Alicia Edelstein	Ayesha Moosa	Jane Watson
	Prahalad Halgeri	Tom Mullins	
	Andrea Holmes	Mqondisi Ndlovu	

Lists of chapters

Volume 1

 1 International GAAP 1
 2 The IASB's Conceptual Framework 39
 3 Presentation of financial statements and accounting policies 109
 4 Non-current assets held for sale and discontinued operations 187
 5 First-time adoption 217
 6 Consolidated financial statements 385
 7 Consolidation procedures and non-controlling interests 491
 8 Separate and individual financial statements 571
 9 Business combinations 633
10 Business combinations under common control 761
11 Investments in associates and joint ventures 807
12 Joint arrangements 887
13 Disclosure of interests in other entities 941
14 Fair value measurement 995
15 Foreign exchange 1175
16 Hyperinflation 1249
17 Intangible assets 1285
18 Property, plant and equipment 1381
19 Investment property 1437
20 Impairment of fixed assets and goodwill 1511
21 Capitalisation of borrowing costs 1643
22 Inventories 1673

Index of extracts from financial statements .... *index* 1
Index of standards .... *index* 7
Index .... *index* 111

The lists of chapters in volumes 2 and 3 follow overleaf.

Volume 2

23	Leases	1701
24	Government grants	1821
25	Service concession arrangements	1847
26	Provisions, contingent liabilities and contingent assets	1923
27	Revenue: Introduction and scope	2015
28	Revenue: Identify the contract and performance obligations	2045
29	Revenue: Determine and allocate the transaction price	2157
30	Revenue: Recognition	2253
31	Revenue: Licences, warranties and contract costs	2313
32	Revenue: Presentation and disclosure	2387
33	Income taxes	2441
34	Share-based payment	2623
35	Employee benefits	2887
36	Operating segments	2973
37	Earnings per share	3017
38	Events after the reporting period	3071
39	Related party disclosures	3093
40	Statement of cash flows	3131
41	Interim financial reporting	3189
42	Agriculture	3269
43	Extractive industries	3325

Index of extracts from financial statements .... *index* 1
Index of standards .... *index* 7
Index .... *index* 111

The list of chapters in volume 3 follows overleaf.

Volume 3

44	Financial instruments: Introduction	3571
45	Financial instruments: Definitions and scope	3579
46	Financial instruments: Derivatives and embedded derivatives	3615
47	Financial instruments: Financial liabilities and equity	3657
48	Financial instruments: Classification	3767
49	Financial instruments: Recognition and initial measurement	3839
50	Financial instruments: Subsequent measurement	3865
51	Financial instruments: Impairment	3905
52	Financial instruments: Derecognition	4079
53	Financial instruments: Hedge accounting	4173
54	Financial instruments: Presentation and disclosure	4399
55	Insurance contracts (IFRS 4)	4525
56	Insurance contracts (IFRS 17)	4669

Index of extracts from financial statements	*index* 1
Index of standards	*index* 7
Index	*index* 111

Abbreviations

The following abbreviations are used in this book:

Professional and regulatory bodies:

AASB	Australian Accounting Standards Board
AcSB	Accounting Standards Board of Canada
AICPA	American Institute of Certified Public Accountants
AOSSG	Asian-Oceanian Standard-Setters Group
APB	Accounting Principles Board (of the AICPA, predecessor of the FASB)
ARC	Accounting Regulatory Committee of representatives of EU Member States
ASAF	Accounting Standards Advisory Forum
ASB	Accounting Standards Board in the UK
ASBJ	Accounting Standards Board of Japan
ASU	Accounting Standards Update
CASC	China Accounting Standards Committee
CESR	Committee of European Securities Regulators, an independent committee whose members comprised senior representatives from EU securities regulators (replaced by ESMA)
CICA	Canadian Institute of Chartered Accountants
EC	European Commission
ECB	European Central Bank
ECOFIN	The Economic and Financial Affairs Council
EDTF	Enhanced Disclosure Task Force of the (FSB)
EFRAG	European Financial Reporting Advisory Group
EITF	Emerging Issues Task Force in the US
EPRA	European Public Real Estate Association
ESMA	European Securities and Markets Authority (see CESR)
EU	European Union
FAF	Financial Accounting Foundation
FASB	Financial Accounting Standards Board in the US
FCAG	Financial Crisis Advisory Group
FEE	Federation of European Accountants

FSB	Financial Stability Board (successor to the FSF)	
FSF	Financial Stability Forum	
G4+1	The (now disbanded) group of four plus 1, actually with six members, that comprised an informal 'think tank' of staff from the standard setters from Australia, Canada, New Zealand, UK, and USA, plus the IASC	
G7	The Group of Seven Finance Ministers (successor to G8)	
G8	The Group of Eight Finance Ministers	
G20	The Group of Twenty Finance Ministers and Central Bank Governors	
GPPC	Global Public Policy Committee of the six largest accounting networks	
HKICPA	Hong Kong Institute of Certified Public Accountants	
IASB	International Accounting Standards Board, or the Board	
IASC	International Accounting Standards Committee. The former Board of the IASC was the predecessor of the IASB	
IASCF	International Accounting Standards Committee Foundation (predecessor of the IFRS Foundation)	
ICAEW	Institute of Chartered Accountants in England and Wales	
ICAI	Institute of Chartered Accountants of India	
ICAS	Institute of Chartered Accountants of Scotland	
IFAC	International Federation of Accountants	
IFASS	International Forum of Accounting Standard Setters	
IFRIC	The IFRS Interpretations Committee (formerly the International Financial Reporting Interpretations Committee) of the IASB	
IGC	Implementation Guidance Committee on IAS 39 (now disbanded)	
IOSCO	International Organisation of Securities Commissions	
IPSASB	International Public Sector Accounting Standards Board	
IPTF	International Practices Task Force (a task force of the SEC Regulations Committee)	
ISDA	International Swaps and Derivatives Association	
IVSC	International Valuation Standards Council	
KASB	Korea Accounting Standards Board	
RICS	Royal Institution of Chartered Surveyors	
SAC	Standards Advisory Council, predecessor of the IFRS Advisory Council which provides advice to the IASB on a wide range of issues	
SEC	Securities and Exchange Commission (the US securities regulator)	
SIC	Standing Interpretations Committee of the IASC (replaced by IFRIC)	
TEG	Technical Expert Group, an advisor to the European Commission	
TRG	Joint Transition Resource Group for Revenue Recognition	

Accounting related terms:

ADS	American Depositary Shares
AFS	Available-for-sale investment
ARB	Accounting Research Bulletins (issued by the AICPA)
ARS	Accounting Research Studies (issued by the APB)
ASC	Accounting Standards Codification®. The single source of authoritative US GAAP recognised by the FASB, to be applied to non-governmental entities for interim and accounting periods ending after 15 September 2009
ASU	Accounting Standards Update
BCUCC	Business Combinations Under Common Control
CCIRS	Cross Currency Interest Rate Swap
CDO	Collateralised Debt Obligation
CLO	Collateralized Loan Obligation
CF	Conceptual Framework
CGU	Cash-generating Unit
CU	Currency Unit
DD&A	Depreciation, Depletion and Amortisation
DPF	Discretionary Participation Feature
E&E	Exploration and Evaluation
EBIT	Earnings Before Interest and Taxes
EBITDA	Earnings Before Interest, Taxes, Depreciation and Amortisation
EIR	Effective Interest Rate
EPS	Earnings per Share
FAS	Financial Accounting Standards (issued by the FASB). Superseded by Accounting Standards Codification® (ASC)
FC	Foreign currency
FICE	Financial Instruments with the Characteristics of Equity
FIFO	First-In, First-Out basis of valuation
FRS	Financial Reporting Standard (issued by the ASB)
FTA	First-time Adoption
FVLCD	Fair value less costs of disposal
FVLCS	Fair value less costs to sell (following the issue of IFRS 13, generally replaced by FVLCD)
FVPL	Fair value through profit and loss
FVOCI	Fair value through other comprehensive income

GAAP		Generally accepted accounting practice (as it applies under IFRS), or generally accepted accounting principles (as it applies to the US)
HTM		Held-to-maturity investment
IAS		International Accounting Standard (issued by the former board of the IASC)
IBOR		Interbank Offered Rate
IBNR		Incurred but not reported claims
IFRS		International Financial Reporting Standard (issued by the IASB)
IFRS for SMEs		International Financial Reporting Standard for Small and Medium-sized Entities
IGC Q&A		Implementation guidance to the original version of IAS 39 (issued by the IGC)
IPO		Initial Public Offering
IPR&D		In-process Research and Development
IPSAS		International Public Sector Accounting Standard
IRR		Internal Rate of Return
IRS		Interest Rate Swap
JA		Joint Arrangement
JCA		Jointly Controlled Asset
JCE		Jointly Controlled Entity
JCO		Jointly Controlled Operation
JO		Joint Operation
JV		Joint Venture
LAT		Liability Adequacy Test
LC		Local Currency
LIBOR		London Inter Bank Offered Rate
LIFO		Last-In, First-Out basis of valuation
NBV		Net Book Value
NCI		Non-controlling Interest
NPV		Net Present Value
NRV		Net Realisable Value
OCI		Other Comprehensive Income
PP&E		Property, Plant and Equipment
R&D		Research and Development
SCA		Service Concession Arrangement
SE		Structured Entity
SFAC		Statement of Financial Accounting Concepts (issued by the FASB as part of its conceptual framework project)

SFAS	Statement of Financial Accounting Standards (issued by the FASB). Superseded by Accounting Standards Codification® (ASC)
SME	Small or medium-sized entity
SPE	Special Purpose Entity
SPE-PRMS	Society of Petroleum Engineers – Petroleum Resources Management System
SV	Separate Vehicle
TSR	Total Shareholder Return
VIU	Value In Use
WACC	Weighted Average Cost of Capital

References to IFRSs, IASs, Interpretations and supporting documentation:

AG	Application Guidance
AV	Alternative View
BCZ	Basis for Conclusions on IASs
BC	Basis for Conclusions on IFRSs and IASs
DI	Draft Interpretation
DO	Dissenting Opinion
DP	Discussion Paper
ED	Exposure Draft
IE	Illustrative Examples on IFRSs and IASs
IG	Implementation Guidance
IN	Introduction to IFRSs and IASs
PIR	Post-implementation Review

Authoritative literature

The content of this book takes into account all accounting standards and other relevant rules issued up to September 2020. Consequently, it covers the IASB's *Conceptual Framework for Financial Reporting* and authoritative literature listed below.

References in the main text of each chapter to the pronouncements below are generally to the versions of those pronouncements as approved and expected to be included in the Blue Book edition of the Bound Volume 2021 International Financial Reporting Standards – IFRS – Consolidated without early application – Official pronouncements applicable on 1 January 2021, to be published by the IASB.

References to those pronouncements below which have an effective date after 1 January 2021 (such as IFRS 17 – *Insurance contracts*) are to the versions of those pronouncements that are expected to be included in the Red Book edition of the Bound Volume 2021 International Financial Reporting Standards – IFRS – Official pronouncements issued at 1 January 2021, to be published by the IASB.

US GAAP accounting standards are organised within a comprehensive FASB Accounting Standards Codification©, which is now the single source of authoritative US GAAP recognised by the FASB to be applied to non-governmental entities and has been applied in this publication.

† The standards and interpretations marked with a dagger have been withdrawn or superseded.

		IASB Framework
		The Conceptual Framework for Financial Reporting
		International Financial Reporting Standards (2021 Bound Volume)
	IFRS 1	First-time Adoption of International Financial Reporting Standards
	IFRS 2	Share-based Payment
	IFRS 3	Business Combinations
†	IFRS 4	Insurance Contracts
	IFRS 5	Non-current Assets Held for Sale and Discontinued Operations
	IFRS 6	Exploration for and Evaluation of Mineral Resources
	IFRS 7	Financial Instruments: Disclosures
	IFRS 8	Operating Segments
	IFRS 9	Financial Instruments
	IFRS 10	Consolidated Financial Statements

IFRS 11	Joint Arrangements
IFRS 12	Disclosure of Interests in Other Entities
IFRS 13	Fair Value Measurement
IFRS 14	Regulatory Deferral Accounts
IFRS 15	Revenue from Contracts with Customers
IFRS 16	Leases

International Financial Reporting Standards (mandatory after 1 January 2023)

| IFRS 17 | Insurance Contracts |

International Accounting Standards (2021 Bound Volume)

IAS 1	Presentation of Financial Statements
IAS 2	Inventories
IAS 7	Statement of Cash Flows
IAS 8	Accounting Policies, Changes in Accounting Estimates and Errors
IAS 10	Events after the Reporting Period
IAS 12	Income Taxes
IAS 16	Property, Plant and Equipment
IAS 19	Employee Benefits
IAS 20	Accounting for Government Grants and Disclosure of Government Assistance
IAS 21	The Effects of Changes in Foreign Exchange Rates
IAS 23	Borrowing Costs
IAS 24	Related Party Disclosures
IAS 26	Accounting and Reporting by Retirement Benefit Plans
IAS 27	Separate Financial Statements
IAS 28	Investments in Associates and Joint Ventures
IAS 29	Financial Reporting in Hyperinflationary Economies
IAS 32	Financial Instruments: Presentation
IAS 33	Earnings per Share
IAS 34	Interim Financial Reporting
IAS 36	Impairment of Assets
IAS 37	Provisions, Contingent Liabilities and Contingent Assets
IAS 38	Intangible Assets
IAS 39	Financial Instruments: Recognition and Measurement
IAS 40	Investment Property
IAS 41	Agriculture

IFRS Interpretations Committee Interpretations

IFRIC 1	Changes in Existing Decommissioning, Restoration and Similar Liabilities
IFRIC 2	Members' Shares in Co-operative Entities and Similar Instruments
IFRIC 5	Rights to Interests arising from Decommissioning, Restoration and Environmental Rehabilitation Funds
IFRIC 6	Liabilities arising from Participating in a Specific Market – Waste Electrical and Electronic Equipment
IFRIC 7	Applying the Restatement Approach under IAS 29 Financial Reporting in Hyperinflationary Economies
IFRIC 10	Interim Financial Reporting and Impairment
IFRIC 12	Service Concession Arrangements
IFRIC 14	IAS 19 – The Limit on a Defined Benefit Asset, Minimum Funding Requirements and their Interaction
IFRIC 16	Hedges of a Net Investment in a Foreign Operation
IFRIC 17	Distributions of Non-cash Assets to Owners
IFRIC 19	Extinguishing Financial Liabilities with Equity Instruments
IFRIC 20	Stripping Costs in the Production Phase of a Surface Mine
IFRIC 21	Levies
IFRIC 22	Foreign Currency Transactions and Advance Consideration
IFRIC 23	Uncertainty over Income Tax Treatments

Standing Interpretations Committee Interpretations

SIC-7	Introduction of the Euro
SIC-10	Government Assistance – No Specific Relation to Operating Activities
SIC-25	Income Taxes – Changes in the Tax Status of an Entity or its Shareholders
SIC-29	Service Concession Arrangements: Disclosures
SIC-32	Intangible Assets – Web Site Costs

IASB Exposure Drafts

ED/2015/5	Remeasurement on a Plan Amendment, Curtailment or Settlement/Availability of a Refund from a Defined Benefit Plan (Proposed amendments to IAS 19 and IFRIC 14)
ED/2017/5	Accounting Policies and Accounting Estimates (Proposed amendments to IAS 8)
ED/2019/5	Deferred Tax related to Assets and Liabilities arising from a Single Transaction (Proposed amendments to IAS 12)
ED/2019/6	Disclosure of Accounting Policies (Proposed amendments to IAS 1 and IFRS Practice Statement 2)
ED/2019/7	General Presentation and Disclosure

IASB Discussion Papers

DP/2014/1	Accounting for Dynamic Risk Management: a Portfolio Revaluation Approach to Macro Hedging
DP/2014/2	Reporting the Financial Effects of Rate Regulation
DP/2017/1	Disclosure Initiative – Principles of Disclosure
DP/2018/1	Financial Instruments with Characteristics of Equity
DP/2020/1	Business Combinations – Disclosures, Goodwill and Impairment

Other IASB publications

IFRS for SMEs	International Financial Reporting Standard (IFRS) for Small and Medium-sized Entities (SMEs)
Practice Statement 1	Management Commentary
Practice Statement 2	Making Materiality Judgements

Chapter 44 Financial instruments: Introduction

1 STANDARDS APPLYING TO FINANCIAL INSTRUMENTS 3573
2 IAS 32 3573
3 IAS 39 3574
4 IFRS 7 3575
5 IFRS 9 3575
6 STRUCTURE AND OBJECTIVES OF THE STANDARDS 3577

Chapter 44   Financial instruments: Introduction

1   STANDARDS APPLYING TO FINANCIAL INSTRUMENTS

The subject matter of this and the next ten chapters is the recognition, measurement, presentation and disclosure of financial instruments, the IASB's accounting requirements for which are regarded by many as some of the more difficult to understand. There are many likely reasons for this, including the fact that it is such a broad topic encompassing some of the more complex contracts entities enter into. In addition, the requirements have been subject to a process of almost continual change over the last twenty years or so and are dealt with in a number of different standards and other pronouncements.

The following are the standards which deal primarily with the accounting for financial instruments:

- IAS 32 – *Financial Instruments: Presentation*;
- IAS 39 – *Financial Instruments: Recognition and Measurement*;
- IFRS 7 – *Financial Instruments: Disclosures*; and
- IFRS 9 – *Financial Instruments*.

In addition a number of interpretations address the requirements of these standards, including:

- IFRIC 2 – *Members' Shares in Co-operative Entities and Similar Instruments*;
- IFRIC 16 – *Hedges of a Net Investment in a Foreign Operation*; and
- IFRIC 19 – *Extinguishing Financial Liabilities with Equity Instruments*.

Information about the development of the standards is set out at 2 to 5 below.

2   IAS 32

The original version of IAS 32 – *Financial Instruments: Disclosure and Presentation* – was published in March 1995. The presentation requirements of the standard were subject to significant review during 2002 and 2003 and a revised standard was published in December 2003. IFRS 7, which was published in August 2005, superseded the disclosure requirements in IAS 32 and the title of the latter standard was changed to reflect this. In February 2008, the IASB amended IAS 32 to change the classification of certain puttable financial instruments and instruments of limited life entities from liabilities to equity. Further amendments to IAS 32, designed to clarify its requirements for offsetting (or netting) of financial instruments, were issued in December 2011 and numerous other amendments have been made throughout the life of the standard.

The IASB recognises that the classification of financial instruments as liabilities or equity in accordance with IAS 32 presents many challenges and is working on a research project exploring what improvements could be made to the presentation and disclosure requirements for financial instruments with characteristics of equity. In June 2018 this resulted in the IASB publishing *Financial Instruments with Characteristics of Equity*, a discussion paper setting out its preliminary views on the subject. However, at the time of writing, the Board had tentatively decided to narrow the project's scope and address practice issues by clarifying some of principles in IAS 32, with a more formal decision expected by the end of 2020.

3 IAS 39

IAS 39 was originally published in March 1999. Its origins could be found in US GAAP and at a high level there were only limited differences between the two systems. In particular, both adopted a similar 'mixed attribute' model whereby some financial instruments were measured by reference to their historical cost and some by reference to their fair value.

By dealing with most aspects of virtually all financial instruments, it was the longest, and by far the most complex, standard issued by the IASC which also established a process to develop and publish guidance in the form of Questions and Answers (Q&As). IAS 39, like IAS 32, was subject to significant review during 2002 and 2003 and a revised standard, incorporating most of the Q&As as implementation guidance, was published in December 2003.

Many other changes have been made to IAS 39 since its original publication, including amendments in March 2004 allowing the use of hedge accounting for certain portfolio (or macro) fair value hedges of interest rate risk. However, subject to limited exceptions, most of the requirements of IAS 39 are now superseded by or carried forward into IFRS 9. Those exceptions are:

- any entity may continue applying the hedge accounting requirements of IAS 39 instead of those in IFRS 9 even after applying the rest of IFRS 9;
- any entity may apply the macro fair value hedge accounting requirements of IAS 39 for hedges of interest rate risk in addition to the hedge accounting requirements of IFRS 9; and
- certain insurers may delay their application of IFRS 9 (see 5 below).

This publication reflects the reduced applicability of IAS 39 by covering its requirements only at a high level, although there are explanations in Chapter 53 at 14 of the more important differences between hedge accounting under IAS 39 and IFRS 9.

4 IFRS 7

A project principally focused on revising the then IAS 30 – *Disclosures in the Financial Statements of Banks and Similar Financial Institutions* – evolved into a comprehensive review of all disclosure requirements related to financial instruments. This resulted in the publication of IFRS 7 in August 2005, superseding IAS 30 and the disclosure requirements in IAS 32.

IFRS 7 has been subject to a number of amendments since publication. The requirements relating to liquidity risk were improved in the light of experience gained in the financial crisis; disclosures about transfers of financial assets were enhanced following an aborted attempt to revise the requirements addressing derecognition of financial assets; and disclosure requirements about offsetting and netting agreements were added. More recently, to complement the requirements in IFRS 9 addressing the classification and measurement of financial instruments, a significant number of amendments and additions were made to IFRS 7 setting out extensive disclosure requirements for impairments and hedge accounting.

5 IFRS 9

In April 2009, during the financial crisis, the IASB committed itself to a comprehensive review of IAS 39. The IASB's plan split this project into the following three phases, each of which would result in the publication of requirements replacing the corresponding parts of IAS 39:

- classification of financial assets and financial liabilities;
- impairment and the effective interest method; and
- hedge accounting.

Originally, the IASB had proposed a simplified accounting model under which all financial instruments would be measured either at amortised cost or at fair value through profit or loss. Subsequently, additional categories of financial asset were introduced allowing certain investments in debt and equity instruments to be measured at fair value with most changes in value recognised in other comprehensive income. For debt instruments, those gains and losses are subsequently recycled to profit or loss on derecognition. In addition, the accounting for financial liabilities was eventually left much the same as in IAS 39, although the IASB introduced a requirement to recognise in other comprehensive income (rather than profit or loss) gains or losses on most financial liabilities designated at fair value through profit or loss to the extent they represent changes in the instrument's credit risk. The requirements of these parts of IFRS 9 are primarily covered in Chapters 48, and 50.

During the financial crisis, a number of commentators criticised the requirements of IAS 39 for unnecessarily delaying the recognition of impairments. IAS 39 uses a so called 'incurred loss' approach whereby impairments are not recognised until there is objective evidence of the impairment having occurred. The requirements in IFRS 9 are better described as an 'expected loss' approach. In almost all circumstances, applying IFRS 9 will result in the recognition of an impairment expense sooner than would have been the case under IAS 39. Consequently, at any point in time, an entity will have accumulated a higher impairment provision (and report a lower amount of equity) than would have arisen from applying IAS 39. This part of IFRS 9 is covered in Chapter 51.

The hedge accounting phase of the project was designed to simplify hedge accounting, expand the relationships for which hedge accounting could be applied and align the accounting requirements more closely with entities' risk management practices. IFRS 9 does not itself address portfolio hedge accounting and, viewed in isolation, is less accommodating than IAS 39 in this respect. However, IFRS 9 does allow for the continued application of the portfolio fair value hedge accounting requirements of IAS 39 alongside its more general hedge accounting requirements. In addition, entities wishing to use the portfolio cash flow hedge accounting guidance in IAS 39 can continue applying the entirety of IAS 39's hedge accounting requirements, although none of the benefits of applying the hedge accounting requirements of IFRS 9 would then be available.

The IASB has a separate research project which aims to eliminate any need for this continued application of IAS 39 (and also the so-called EU 'carve-out' – see Chapter 1 at 4.2.1.A). A discussion paper, *Accounting for Dynamic Risk Management: a Portfolio Revaluation Approach to Macro Hedging*, was published in April 2014, but the IASB later concluded it was not in a position to develop its proposals into an exposure draft. The IASB has subsequently developed a 'core model' addressing the most important issues and has been planning to perform outreach with various banks, although at the time of writing this had been delayed by the coronavirus pandemic until the later part of 2020. The hedge accounting requirements of IFRS 9 are covered in Chapter 53 which also highlights important differences between those requirements and those of IAS 39.

The first version of IFRS 9 was published in November 2009 with significant amendments following in October 2010 and November 2013 before it was substantially completed in July 2014. In October 2017, the IASB published limited amendments to the standard designed to address concerns about the classification of financial assets containing certain prepayment features.

Most entities were required to adopt IFRS 9 for periods commencing on or after 1 January 2018. However, a number of constituents identified adverse accounting consequences that might arise from insurers applying IFRS 9 before IFRS 17 – *Insurance Contracts* – adoption of which is not now mandatory for periods commencing before 1 January 2023, this having been delayed by two years in June 2020. The IASB responded by amending IFRS 4 – *Insurance Contracts* – to allow certain insurers to adopt IFRS 9 at a later date as well as offering other reliefs to those insurers that adopt IFRS 9 in a period before they adopt IFRS 17. Further information about these changes is included in Chapter 55 at 10.

During the development of IFRS 9, the IASB worked closely with its counterparts at the FASB with the aim of aligning as far as possible the financial reporting requirements for financial instruments in accordance with IFRS and US GAAP. The measurement of fair values under the two bodies of GAAP is to a large extent the same and in June 2016 the FASB published a new standard requiring impairment of financial assets to be based on expected losses, although it is somewhat different to the approach in IFRS 9. The FASB has made various other amendments to US GAAP in recent years, but important differences remain in the areas of classifying and measuring financial instruments and hedge accounting and there are significant differences in other areas including the approach to offsetting financial assets and financial liabilities.

One of the recommendations following the financial crisis was the reform of interbank offered rates (IBORs) which index trillions of dollars in a wide variety of financial products but whose long-term viability has been brought into question. Some jurisdictions have made clear progress towards replacing IBOR with alternative rates and the IASB responded to these developments in two phases. The first was designed to mitigate the effects of these reforms on hedge accounting in the period before financial instruments are issued or modified to reference these alternative rates and amendments to IAS 39 and IFRS 9 were published in September 2019. The second phase addressed changes made to contractual cash flows, including modifications of financial assets and financial liabilities, and to hedging relationships that arise when interest rate benchmarks are replaced with alternative benchmarks. As a result IAS 39 and IFRS 9 (as well as IFRS 4 and IFRS 16 – *Leases*) were amended in August 2020. These amendments are addressed primarily in Chapter 50 at 3.8.3, in Chapter 52 at 3.4.3 and at 6.2.2 and in Chapter 53 at 9.

At the time of writing the world was coming to terms with the effects of the coronavirus pandemic and companies were addressing the associated financial reporting effects such as the determination of expected credit loss provisions. In March 2020 the IASB issued '*IFRS 9 and covid-19 – Accounting for expected credit losses applying IFRS 9 Financial Instruments in the light of current uncertainty resulting from the covid-19 pandemic*', a short document intended to support the consistent application of IFRS 9. This document and the effects of the pandemic on expected credit losses more generally, including regulatory and other responses, are considered further in Chapter 51 at 7.8.

6 STRUCTURE AND OBJECTIVES OF THE STANDARDS

The main text of the standards is supplemented by application guidance (which is an integral part of each standard).[1] IAS 32 and IFRS 9 are each supplemented by illustrative examples and IFRS 7 and IFRS 9 by implementation guidance. These examples and implementation guidance accompany, but are not part of, the standards.[2]

The objective of IAS 32 is to establish principles for presenting financial instruments as liabilities or equity and for offsetting financial assets and financial liabilities. *[IAS 32.2]*. For IFRS 9 it is to establish principles for the financial reporting of financial assets and financial liabilities that present relevant and useful information to users of financial statements for their assessment of the amounts, timing and uncertainty of the entity's future cash flows. *[IFRS 9.1.1]*. Finally, the objective of IFRS 7 is to require entities to provide disclosures in their financial statements that enable users to evaluate:

(a) the significance of financial instruments for the entity's financial position and performance; and

(b) the nature and extent of risks arising from financial instruments to which the entity is exposed during the period and at the reporting date, and how the entity manages those risks. *[IFRS 7.1]*.

References

1 IAS 32, Application Guidance, para. before para. AG1, IFRS 7, *Financial Instruments: Disclosure,* Appendix B, Application guidance, para. after main heading, IFRS 9, *Financial Instruments,* Appendix B, Application guidance, para. after main heading.

2 IAS 32, Illustrative Examples, para. after main heading, IFRS 7, Guidance on implementing, para. after main heading and IFRS 9, Illustrative Examples, para. after main heading and Guidance on Implementing, para. before main heading Section A.

Chapter 45 Financial instruments: Definitions and scope

1 INTRODUCTION 3583
2 WHAT IS A FINANCIAL INSTRUMENT? 3584
    2.1 Definitions 3584
    2.2 Applying the definitions 3585
        2.2.1 The need for a contract 3585
        2.2.2 Simple financial instruments 3586
        2.2.3 Contingent rights and obligations 3586
        2.2.4 Leases 3587
        2.2.5 Non-financial assets and liabilities and contracts thereon 3587
        2.2.6 Payments for goods and services 3589
        2.2.7 Equity instruments 3589
        2.2.8 Derivative financial instruments 3589
        2.2.9 Dividends payable 3591
3 SCOPE 3591
    3.1 Subsidiaries, associates, joint ventures and similar investments 3591
    3.2 Leases 3593
    3.3 Insurance and similar contracts 3593
        3.3.1 Weather derivatives 3594
        3.3.2 Contracts with discretionary participation features 3594
        3.3.3 Separating financial instrument components including
              embedded derivatives from insurance contracts 3595
        3.3.4 Credit card contracts and similar arrangements which
              give rise to insurance risk 3595
        3.3.5 Loan contracts that transfer significant insurance risk only
              on settlement of the policyholder's obligation created by
              the contract 3595
    3.4 Financial guarantee contracts 3596

		3.4.1	Definition of a financial guarantee contract	3596
			3.4.1.A Reimbursement for loss incurred	3596
			3.4.1.B Debt instrument	3597
			3.4.1.C Form and existence of contract	3598
		3.4.2	Issuers of financial guarantee contracts	3598
		3.4.3	Holders of financial guarantee contracts	3599
		3.4.4	Financial guarantee contracts between entities under common control	3600
	3.5	Loan commitments		3600
	3.6	Equity instruments		3602
		3.6.1	Equity instruments issued	3602
		3.6.2	Equity instruments held	3602
	3.7	Business combinations		3602
		3.7.1	Contingent consideration in a business combination	3602
			3.7.1.A Payable by an acquirer	3602
			3.7.1.B Receivable by a vendor	3603
		3.7.2	Contracts between an acquirer and a vendor in a business combination	3603
	3.8	Contingent pricing of property, plant and equipment and intangible assets		3604
	3.9	Employee benefit plans and share-based payment		3605
	3.10	Reimbursement rights in respect of provisions		3605
	3.11	Disposal groups classified as held for sale and discontinued operations		3606
	3.12	Indemnification assets		3606
	3.13	Rights and obligations within the scope of IFRS 15		3606
4	CONTRACTS TO BUY OR SELL COMMODITIES AND OTHER NON-FINANCIAL ITEMS			3607
	4.1	Contracts that may be settled net		3608
	4.2	Normal sales and purchases (or own use contracts)		3608
		4.2.1	Net settlement of similar contracts	3609
		4.2.2	Commodity broker-traders and similar entities	3610
		4.2.3	Written options that can be settled net	3610
		4.2.4	Electricity and similar 'end-user' contracts	3611
		4.2.5	Other contracts containing volume flexibility	3612
		4.2.6	Fair value option	3613

List of examples

Example 45.1:	Rainfall contract – derivative financial instrument or insurance contract?	3594
Example 45.2:	Identifying classes of loan commitment	3601
Example 45.3:	Determining whether a copper forward is within the scope of IFRS 9	3609
Example 45.4:	Determining whether a put option on an office building is within the scope of IFRS 9	3611

Chapter 45 Financial instruments: Definitions and scope

1 INTRODUCTION

The standards which address financial instruments are IAS 32 – *Financial Instruments: Presentation*, IFRS 7 – *Financial Instruments: Disclosures* – and IFRS 9 – *Financial Instruments*, which for most entities became effective for periods beginning on or after 1 January 2018 and replaced substantially all of the requirements relating to the recognition and measurement of financial instruments in IAS 39 – *Financial Instruments: Recognition and Measurement.* As set out in Chapter 55 at 10.1, insurers that meet specified criteria are permitted to continue applying IAS 39 until accounting periods commencing on or after 1 January 2023.

In many cases it will be clear whether an asset, liability, equity share, or other similar instrument should be accounted for in accordance with one or more of these standards. However, at the margins, determining whether these standards should be applied is not so easy.

Firstly, one needs to determine whether the definition of a financial instrument is met; secondly, not all financial instruments are within the scope of each of these standards – some are within the scope of other standards and some are not within the scope of any standard; and finally, certain contracts that do not meet the definition of a financial instrument are within the scope of some of these standards.

This chapter addresses these issues in three main sections covering the following broad areas:

- application of the definitions used in IFRS, i.e. determining what a financial instrument actually is (see 2 below);
- determining which financial instruments are within the scope of which standards (see 3 below); and
- assessing whether a non-financial contract is to be accounted for as if it were a financial instrument (see 4 below).

2 WHAT IS A FINANCIAL INSTRUMENT?

2.1 Definitions

The main terms used in the standards that apply to financial instruments are defined in IAS 32 as follows:

A *financial instrument* is any contract that gives rise to a financial asset of one entity and a financial liability or equity instrument of another entity.

A *financial asset* is any asset that is:

(a) cash;

(b) an equity instrument of another entity;

(c) a contractual right:

    (i) to receive cash or another financial asset from another entity; or

    (ii) to exchange financial assets or financial liabilities with another entity under conditions that are potentially favourable to the entity; or

(d) a contract that will or may be settled in the entity's own equity instruments and is:

    (i) a non-derivative for which the entity is or may be obliged to receive a variable number of the entity's own equity instruments; or

    (ii) a derivative that will or may be settled other than by the exchange of a fixed amount of cash or another financial asset for a fixed number of the entity's own equity instruments. For this purpose, the entity's own equity instruments do not include certain puttable and similar financial instruments classified by exception as equity instruments (see Chapter 47 at 4.6) or instruments that are themselves contracts for the future receipt or delivery of the entity's own equity instruments.

A *financial liability* is any liability that is:

(a) a contractual obligation:

    (i) to deliver cash or another financial asset to another entity; or

    (ii) to exchange financial assets or financial liabilities with another entity under conditions that are potentially unfavourable to the entity; or

(b) a contract that will or may be settled in the entity's own equity instruments and is:

    (i) a non-derivative for which the entity is or may be obliged to deliver a variable number of the entity's own equity instruments; or

    (ii) a derivative that will or may be settled other than by the exchange of a fixed amount of cash or another financial asset for a fixed number of the entity's own equity instruments. For this purpose, rights, options or warrants to acquire a fixed number of the entity's own equity instruments for a fixed amount of any currency are equity instruments if the entity offers the rights, options or warrants *pro rata* to all of its existing owners of the same class of its own non-derivative equity instruments. Also, for this purpose the entity's own equity instruments do not include certain puttable and similar financial instruments classified by exception as equity instruments, or instruments that are themselves contracts for the future receipt or delivery of the entity's own equity instruments.

An *equity instrument* is any contract that evidences a residual interest in the assets of an entity after deducting all of its liabilities. *[IAS 32.11]*.

For the purpose of these definitions, 'entity' includes individuals, partnerships, incorporated bodies, trusts and government agencies. *[IAS 32.14]*.

2.2 Applying the definitions

2.2.1 The need for a contract

The terms 'contract' and 'contractual' are important to the definitions and refer to 'an agreement between two or more parties that has clear economic consequences that the parties have little, if any, discretion to avoid, usually because the agreement is enforceable by law'. Such contracts may take a variety of forms and need not be in writing. *[IAS 32.13]*.

The Interpretations Committee examined the question of what constitutes a contract in the context of gaming transactions. This is because, in some jurisdictions, a wager does not give rise to a contract that is enforceable under local contract law. The Interpretations Committee staff noted that a gaming transaction constitutes an agreement between two or more parties that has clear economic consequences for both. Furthermore, in most countries, gambling is heavily regulated and only parties acting within a regulated framework are licensed to operate gaming institutions, so that such entities cannot realistically fail to pay out on a good wager and therefore the gaming institution will have little or no discretion as to whether it pays out on the bet. Consequently, the Interpretations Committee agreed that a wager should be treated as a contract.[1]

Whilst this seems an entirely plausible analysis in context, it is a little difficult to reconcile with the conclusions of the Interpretations Committee and the IASB concerning the existence (or otherwise) of a contractual obligation to make payments on certain preference shares and similar securities. In those cases, terms of an instrument that effectively force the issuer to transfer cash or other financial assets to the holder although not legally required to do so (often referred to as 'economic compulsion'), are not taken into account (see Chapter 47 at 4.5.6).

A contractual right or contractual obligation to receive, deliver or exchange financial instruments is itself a financial instrument. A chain of contractual rights or contractual obligations meets the definition of a financial instrument if it will ultimately lead to the receipt or payment of cash or to the acquisition or issue of an equity instrument. *[IAS 32.AG7]*.

Assets and liabilities relating to non-contractual arrangements that arise as a result of statutory requirements imposed by governments, such as income taxes or levies are not financial liabilities or financial assets because they are not contractual. *[IAS 32.AG12]*. Accounting for income taxes is dealt with in more detail in another standard, IAS 12 – *Income Taxes* (see Chapter 33), while levies are covered by IFRIC 21 – *Levies* (see Chapter 26 at 6.8).

Similarly, constructive obligations as defined in IAS 37 – *Provisions, Contingent Liabilities and Contingent Assets* (see Chapter 26 at 3.1.1) do not arise from contracts and are therefore not financial liabilities. *[IAS 32.AG12]*.

2.2.2 Simple financial instruments

Currency (or cash) is a financial asset because it represents the medium of exchange and is therefore the basis on which all transactions are measured and recognised in financial statements. A deposit of cash with a bank or similar financial institution is a financial asset because it represents the contractual right of the depositor to obtain cash from the institution or to draw a cheque or similar instrument against the balance in favour of a creditor in payment of a financial liability. *[IAS 32.AG3]*.

The following common financial instruments give rise to financial assets representing a contractual right to receive cash in the future and corresponding financial liabilities representing a contractual obligation to deliver cash in the future:

(a) trade accounts receivable and payable;
(b) notes receivable and payable;
(c) loans receivable and payable; and
(d) bonds receivable and payable.

In each case, one party's contractual right to receive (or obligation to pay) cash is matched by the other party's corresponding obligation to pay (or right to receive). *[IAS 32.AG4]*.

Another type of financial instrument is one for which the economic benefit to be received or given up is a financial asset other than cash. For example, a note payable in government bonds gives the holder the contractual right to receive, and the issuer the contractual obligation to deliver, government bonds, not cash. The bonds are financial assets because they represent obligations of the issuing government to pay cash. The note is, therefore, a financial asset of the note holder and a financial liability of the note issuer. *[IAS 32.AG5]*.

Perpetual debt instruments (such as perpetual bonds, debentures and capital notes) normally provide the holder with the contractual right to receive payments on account of interest at fixed dates extending indefinitely, either with no right to receive a return of principal or a right to a return of principal under terms that make it very unlikely or very far in the future. For example, an entity may issue a financial instrument requiring it to make annual payments in perpetuity equal to a stated interest rate of 8% applied to a stated par or principal amount of $1,000. Assuming 8% is the market rate of interest for the instrument when issued, the issuer assumes a contractual obligation to make a stream of future interest payments having a net present value (or fair value) of $1,000 on initial recognition. The holder and issuer of the instrument have a financial asset and a financial liability, respectively. *[IAS 32.AG6]*.

2.2.3 Contingent rights and obligations

The ability to exercise a contractual right or the requirement to satisfy a contractual obligation may be absolute (as in the examples at 2.2.2 above), or it may be contingent on the occurrence of a future event. A contingent right or obligation, e.g. to receive or deliver cash, meets the definition of a financial asset or a financial liability. *[IAS 32.AG8]*.

For example, a financial guarantee is a contractual right of the lender to receive cash from the guarantor, and a corresponding contractual obligation of the guarantor to pay the lender, if the borrower defaults. The contractual right and obligation exist because of a past transaction or event (the assumption of the guarantee), even though the lender's ability to exercise its right and the requirement for the guarantor to perform under its obligation are both contingent on a future act of default by the borrower. *[IAS 32.AG8]*.

However, even though contingent rights and obligations can meet the definition of a financial instrument, they are not always recognised in the financial statements as such. For example, contingent rights and obligations may be insurance contracts within the scope of IFRS 4 – *Insurance Contracts* (see Chapter 55 at 3.3) or IFRS 17 – *Insurance Contracts* (see Chapter 56 at 3.6) or may otherwise be excluded from the scope of IFRS 9 (see 3 below). *[IAS 32.AG8]*.

2.2.4 Leases

A lease typically creates an entitlement of the lessor to receive, and an obligation of the lessee to make, a stream of payments that are substantially the same as blended payments of principal and interest under a loan agreement. The lessor accounts for its investment in the amount receivable under a finance lease rather than the underlying asset itself. Accordingly, a lessor regards a finance lease as a financial instrument. In contrast, a lessor does not recognise its entitlement to receive lease payments under an operating lease. The lessor continues to account for the underlying asset itself rather than any amount receivable in the future under the contract. Accordingly, a lessor does not regard an operating lease as a financial instrument, except as regards individual payments currently due and payable by the lessee. *[IAS 32.AG9]*.

IFRS 16 – *Leases* – requires a lessee to recognise a lease liability (with corresponding right-of-use asset) at the commencement date at the present value of the lease payments that are not paid at that date. *[IFRS 16.22, 26]*. Accordingly, under IFRS 16, a lessee regards a lease as giving rise to a financial liability.

Nevertheless, as discussed in more detail at 3.2 below, whilst leases can give rise to financial instruments for lessors and for lessees, those financial instruments are not always accounted for under IFRS 9.

2.2.5 Non-financial assets and liabilities and contracts thereon

Physical assets (such as inventories, property, plant and equipment), right-of-use assets and intangible assets (such as patents and trademarks) are not financial assets. Control of such physical assets, right-of-use assets and intangible assets creates an opportunity to generate an inflow of cash or another financial asset, but it does not give rise to a present right to receive cash or another financial asset. *[IAS 32.AG10]*. For example, whilst gold bullion is highly liquid (and perhaps more liquid than many financial instruments), it gives no contractual right to receive cash or another financial asset, and so is therefore a commodity, not a financial asset. *[IFRS 9.B.1]*.

Assets such as prepaid expenses, for which the future economic benefit is the receipt of goods or services rather than the right to receive cash or another financial asset, are not financial assets. Similarly, items such as deferred revenue and most warranty obligations are not financial liabilities because the outflow of economic benefits associated with them is the delivery of goods and services rather than a contractual obligation to pay cash or another financial asset. *[IAS 32.AG11]*.

Contracts to buy or sell non-financial items do not meet the definition of a financial instrument because the contractual right of one party to receive a non-financial asset or service and the corresponding obligation of the other party do not establish a present right or obligation of either party to receive, deliver or exchange a financial asset. For example, contracts that provide for settlement only by the receipt or delivery of a non-financial item (e.g. an option, future or forward contract on silver and many similar commodity contracts) are not financial instruments. However, as set out at 4 below, certain contracts to buy or sell non-financial items that can be settled net or by exchanging financial instruments, or in which the non-financial item is readily convertible into cash are included within the scope of IAS 32 and IFRS 9, essentially because they exhibit similar characteristics to financial instruments. *[IAS 32.AG20]*.

In some industries, e.g. brewing and heating gas, entities distribute their products in returnable containers. Often, these entities will collect a cash deposit for each container delivered which they have an obligation to refund on return of the container. The Interpretations Committee found itself in November 2007 addressing the classification of these obligations, in particular whether they met the definition of a financial instrument.[2] It is easy to jump to the conclusion (as the Interpretations Committee did initially)[3] that such an arrangement represents a contract to exchange a non-financial item (the container) for cash and is therefore outside the scope of IFRS 9. However, the Interpretations Committee recognised that this analysis holds true only if, in accounting terms, the container ceases to be an asset of the entity when the sale is made, i.e. it is derecognised. If the container is not derecognised, the entity cannot be regarded as receiving the non-financial asset because the accounting treatment regards the entity as retaining the asset. Instead, the deposit simply represents an obligation to transfer cash and is therefore a financial liability.[4]

Some contracts are commodity-linked, but do not involve settlement through the physical receipt or delivery of a commodity. Instead they specify settlement through cash payments that are determined according to a formula in the contract. For example, the principal amount of a bond may be calculated by applying the market price of oil prevailing at the maturity of the bond to a fixed quantity of oil, but is settled only in cash. Such a contract constitutes a financial instrument. *[IAS 32.AG22]*.

Financial instruments also include contracts that give rise to a non-financial asset or non-financial liability in addition to a financial asset or financial liability. Such arrangements often give one party an option to exchange a financial asset for a non-financial asset. For example, an oil-linked bond may give the holder the right to receive a stream of fixed periodic interest payments and a fixed amount of cash on maturity, with the option to exchange the principal amount for a fixed quantity of oil. The desirability of exercising this option will vary over time depending on the fair value of oil relative to the exchange ratio of cash for oil (the exchange price) inherent in the bond, but the intentions of the bondholder do not affect the substance of the component assets. The financial asset of the holder and the financial liability of the issuer make the bond a financial instrument, regardless of the other types of assets and liabilities also created. *[IAS 32.AG23]*.

2.2.6 Payments for goods and services

Where payment on a contract involving the receipt or delivery of physical assets is deferred past the date of transfer of the asset, a financial instrument arises at the date of delivery. In other words, the sale or purchase of goods on trade credit gives rise to a financial asset (a trade receivable) and a financial liability (a trade payable) when the goods are transferred. *[IAS 32.AG21]*. This is the case even if an invoice is not issued at the time of delivery.

IAS 32 does not explain whether the same logic should apply to the delivery of other, less tangible, non-financial items, e.g. construction or other services. IFRIC 12 – *Service Concession Arrangements* – provides guidance on how operators of service concessions over public infrastructure assets should account for these arrangements. Where an operator obtains an unconditional contractual right to receive cash from the grantor in exchange for construction or other services, the accrued revenue represents a financial asset. This is the case even if payment is not due immediately and even if it is contingent on the operator ensuring that the underlying infrastructure meets specified quality or efficiency requirements (see Chapter 25 at 4.2). *[IFRIC 12.16]*.

2.2.7 Equity instruments

Equity instruments include non-puttable ordinary shares, some puttable and similar instruments, some types of preference shares and warrants or written call options that allow the holder to subscribe for or purchase a fixed number of non-puttable ordinary shares in the issuing entity, in exchange for a fixed amount of cash or another financial asset. *[IAS 32.AG13]*. The definition of equity instruments is considered in more detail in Chapter 47 at 3.

2.2.8 Derivative financial instruments

In addition to primary instruments such as receivables, payables and equity instruments, financial instruments also include derivatives such as financial options, futures and forwards, interest rate swaps and currency swaps. Derivatives normally transfer one or more of the financial risks inherent in an underlying primary instrument between the contracting parties without any need to transfer the underlying instruments themselves (either at inception of the contract or even, where cash settled, on termination). *[IAS 32.AG15, AG16]*.

There are important accounting consequences for financial instruments that are considered to be derivatives, and the defining characteristics of derivatives are covered in more detail in Chapter 46 at 2.

As noted at 2.2.5 above, certain derivative contracts on non-financial items are included within the scope of IAS 32 and IFRS 9, even though they are not, strictly, financial instruments as defined. These contracts are covered in more detail at 4 below.

On inception, the terms of a derivative financial instrument generally give one party a contractual right (or obligation) to exchange financial assets or financial liabilities with another party under conditions that are potentially favourable (or unfavourable). Some instruments embody both a right and an obligation to make an exchange and, as prices in financial markets change, those terms may become either favourable or unfavourable. *[IAS 32.AG16]*.

A put or call option to exchange financial assets or financial liabilities gives the holder a right to obtain potential future economic benefits associated with changes in the fair value of the underlying instrument. Conversely, the writer of an option assumes an obligation to forgo such potential future economic benefits or bear potential losses associated with the underlying instrument. The contractual right (or obligation) of the holder (or writer) meets the definition of a financial asset (or liability). The financial instrument underlying an option contract may be any financial asset, including shares in other entities and interest-bearing instruments. An option may require the writer to issue a debt instrument, rather than transfer a financial asset, but the instrument underlying the option would constitute a financial asset of the holder if the option were exercised. The option-holder's right (or writer's obligation) to exchange the financial asset under potentially favourable (or unfavourable) conditions is distinct from the underlying financial asset to be exchanged upon exercise of the option. The nature of the holder's right and of the writer's obligation (which characterises such contracts as a financial instrument) are not affected by the likelihood that the option will be exercised. *[IAS 32.AG17]*.

Another common type of derivative is a forward contract. For example, consider a contract in which two parties (the seller and the purchaser) promise in six months' time to exchange $1,000 cash (the purchaser will pay cash) for $1,000 face amount of fixed rate government bonds (the seller will deliver the bonds). During those six months, both parties have a contractual right and a contractual obligation to exchange financial instruments (cash in exchange for bonds). If the market price of the government bonds rises above $1,000, the conditions will be favourable to the purchaser and unfavourable to the seller, and *vice versa* if the market price falls below $1,000. The purchaser has a contractual right (a financial asset) similar to the right under a call option held and a contractual obligation (a financial liability) similar to the obligation under a put option written. The seller has a contractual right (a financial asset) similar to the right under a put option held and a contractual obligation (a financial liability) similar to the obligation under a call option written. As with options, these contractual rights and obligations constitute financial assets and financial liabilities separate and distinct from the underlying financial instruments (the bonds and cash to be exchanged). Both parties to a forward contract have an obligation to perform at the agreed time, whereas performance under an option contract occurs only if and when the holder of the option chooses to exercise it. *[IAS 32.AG18]*.

Many other types of derivative also embody a right or obligation to make a future exchange, including interest rate and currency swaps, interest rate caps, collars and floors, loan commitments, note issuance facilities and letters of credit. An interest rate swap contract may be viewed as a variation of a forward contract in which the parties agree to make a series of future exchanges of cash amounts, one amount calculated with reference to a floating interest rate and the other with reference to a fixed interest rate. Futures contracts are another variation of forward contracts, differing primarily in that the contracts are standardised and traded on an exchange. *[IAS 32.AG19]*.

2.2.9 Dividends payable

As part of its project to provide authoritative accounting guidance for non-cash distributions (see Chapter 8 at 2.4.2), the Interpretations Committee found itself debating the seemingly simple question of how to account for a declared but unpaid cash dividend (or, more accurately, which standard applies to such a liability). Although there are clear indicators within IFRS that an obligation to pay a cash dividend is a financial liability, *[IAS 32.AG13]*, the Interpretations Committee originally proposed that IAS 37 should be applied to all dividend obligations,[5] a decision that appeared to have been made more on the grounds of expediency rather than using any robust technical analysis. By the time IFRIC 17 – *Distributions of Non-cash Assets to Owners* – was published in November 2008, the Interpretations Committee had modified its position slightly. Aside from those standards dealing with the measurement of liabilities that are clearly not relevant (e.g. IAS 12), they considered that others, except IAS 37 or IFRS 9, were simply not applicable because they addressed liabilities arising only from exchange transactions, whereas IFRIC 17 was developed to deal with non-reciprocal distributions. *[IFRIC 17.BC22]*. Finally, IFRIC 17 simply specifies the accounting treatment to be applied to distributions without linking to any individual standard. *[IFRIC 17.BC27]*. The Interpretations Committee concluded that it was not appropriate to conclude that all dividends payable are to be regarded as financial liabilities.

3 SCOPE

IAS 32, IFRS 7 and IFRS 9 apply to the financial statements of all entities that are prepared in accordance with International Financial Reporting Standards. *[IAS 32.4, IFRS 7.3, IFRS 9.2.1]*. In other words, there are no exclusions from the presentation, recognition, measurement, or even the disclosure requirements of these standards, even for entities that do not have publicly traded securities or those that are subsidiaries of other entities.

The standards do not, however, apply to all of an entity's financial instruments, some of which are excluded from their scope, for example, insurance contracts (see Chapters 55 and 56). These exceptions are considered in more detail below. Conversely, certain contracts over non-financial items that behave in a similar way to financial instruments but do not actually fall within the definition – essentially some commodity contracts – are included within the scope of the standards and these are considered at 4 below.

3.1 Subsidiaries, associates, joint ventures and similar investments

Most interests in subsidiaries, associates, and joint ventures that are consolidated or equity accounted in consolidated financial statements are outside the scope of IAS 32,

IFRS 7 and IFRS 9. However, such instruments should be accounted for in accordance with IFRS 9 and disclosed in accordance with IFRS 7 in the following situations: [IAS 32.4(a), IFRS 7.3(a), IFRS 9.2.1(a)]

- in separate financial statements of the parent or investor if the entity chooses not to account for those investments at cost or using the equity method as described in IAS 28 – *Investments in Associates and Joint Ventures* (see Chapter 8 at 2); [IAS 27.10, IAS 27.11, IAS 28.44]

- when investments in an associate or a joint venture held by a venture capital organisation, mutual fund, unit trust or similar entity are classified as financial instruments at fair value through profit or loss on initial recognition (see Chapter 11 at 5.3). [IAS 28.18]. When an entity has an investment in an associate, a portion of which is held indirectly through a venture capital organisation, mutual fund, unit trust or similar entity including an investment-linked insurance fund, the entity may elect to measure that portion of the investment in the associate at fair value through profit or loss regardless of whether the venture capital organisation, mutual fund, unit trust or similar entity has significant influence over that portion of the investment. If the election is made, the equity method should be applied to any remaining portion of the investment; [IAS 28.19] and

- an investment in a subsidiary by an investment entity that is measured at fair value through profit or loss using the investment entity exception (see Chapter 6 at 2.2.3). [IFRS 10.31].

In January 2013, the Interpretations Committee concluded that impairments of investments in subsidiaries, associates and joint ventures accounted for at cost in the separate financial statements of the investor are dealt with by IAS 36 – *Impairment of Assets* – not IFRS 9.[6]

Whilst the scope of IFRS 9 excludes interests in associates and joint ventures accounted for using the equity method, [IFRS 9.2.1(a)], it was initially unclear whether the scope also excludes long-term interests in an associate or joint venture that, in substance, form part of the net investment in the associate or joint venture (see Chapter 11 at 8.3). However, in October 2017, the IASB issued an amendment to IAS 28 clarifying that IFRS 9, including its impairment requirements, applies to the measurement of long-term interests in an associate or a joint venture that form part of the net investment in the associate or joint venture, but to which the equity method is not applied. [IAS 28.14A]. The amendment had an effective date of 1 January 2019. [IAS 28.45G]. When the amendment was adopted after the adoption of IFRS 9 the transitional requirements in IAS 28, which are similar to those in IFRS 9, were applied (see Chapter 11 at 8.3). [IAS 28.45I].

IAS 32, IFRS 7 and IFRS 9 apply to most derivatives on interests in subsidiaries, associates and joint ventures, irrespective of how the investment is otherwise accounted for. However, IFRS 9 does not apply to instruments containing potential voting rights that, in substance, give access to the economic benefits arising from an ownership interest which is consolidated or equity accounted (see Chapter 7 at 2.2, Chapter 11 at 4.4 and Chapter 12 at 4.2.2). [IFRS 10.B91].

From the perspective of an entity issuing derivatives, the requirements of IFRS 9 and IFRS 7 do not apply if such derivatives meet the definition of an equity instrument of the entity. *[IAS 32.4(a), IFRS 7.3(a), IFRS 9.2.1(a)].* For example, a written call option allowing the holder to acquire a subsidiary's shares that can be settled only by delivering a fixed number of those shares in exchange for a fixed amount of cash might meet the definition of equity in the group's consolidated financial statements (see 3.6 below and Chapter 47 at 5.1).

Sometimes an entity will make a strategic investment in the equity of another party. These are often made with the intention of establishing or maintaining a long-term operating relationship with the investee. Unless they are equity accounted as associates or joint ventures, these investments are within the scope of IFRS 9. *[IFRS 9.B2.3].*

3.2 Leases

Whilst all financial assets and liabilities arising from leases are within the scope of IAS 32 and IFRS 7, they are only within the scope of IFRS 9 to the following extent:

- lease receivables and lease liabilities are subject to the derecognition provisions (see Chapter 52);
- lease receivables are subject to the 'expected credit loss' requirements (see Chapter 51 at 5); and
- the relevant provisions that apply to derivatives embedded within leases (see Chapter 46 at 5.3).

Otherwise the applicable standard is IFRS 16 (see Chapter 23), not IFRS 9. *[IFRS 9.2.1(b)].*

3.3 Insurance and similar contracts

Although insurance contracts as defined in IFRS 4 or IFRS 17 often satisfy the definition of a financial instrument, for the most part they are excluded from the scope of IAS 32, IFRS 7 and IFRS 9. *[IAS 32.4(d), IFRS 7.3(d), IFRS 9.2.1(e)].* IFRS 4 is discussed in Chapter 55. IFRS 17, which was published in May 2017 and amended in June 2020, replaces IFRS 4 and is applicable for accounting periods beginning on or after 1 January 2023. IFRS 17 is discussed in Chapter 56.

An insurance contract is defined as one under which one party (the insurer or issuer) accepts significant insurance risk from another party (the policyholder) by agreeing to compensate the policyholder if a specified uncertain future event (the insured event) adversely affects the policyholder. Insurance risk is defined as risk, other than financial risk, transferred from the holder of a contract to the issuer. Financial risk is defined as the risk of a possible future change in one or more of a specified interest rate, financial instrument price, commodity price, foreign exchange rate, index of prices or rates, credit rating or credit index or other variable, provided in the case of a non-financial variable that the variable is not specific to a party to the contract. *[IFRS 4 Appendix A, IFRS 17 Appendix A].* In many cases it will be quite clear whether a contract is an insurance contract or not, although this will not always be the case and IFRS 4 and IFRS 17 contain several pages of guidance on this definition (see Chapter 55 at 3 and Chapter 56 at 3). *[IFRS 4 Appendix B, IFRS 17.B2-B30].*

Financial guarantee contracts, which meet the definition of an insurance contract if the risk transferred is significant, are normally accounted for by the issuer under IFRS 9 and disclosed in accordance with IFRS 7 (see 3.4 below). *[IFRS 9.B2.5(a)]*.

The application guidance makes it clear that insurers' financial instruments that are not within the scope of IFRS 4 or IFRS 17 (when applied) should be accounted for under IFRS 9. *[IFRS 9.B2.4]*.

3.3.1 Weather derivatives

Contracts which require a payment based on climatic variables (often referred to as 'weather derivatives') or on geological or other physical variables are within the scope of IFRS 9 unless they fall within the scope of IFRS 4 or IFRS 17. *[IFRS 9.B2.1]*. Generic or standardised contracts will rarely meet the definition of insurance contracts because the variable is unlikely to be specific to either party to the contract. *[IFRS 4.B18(l), B19(g), IFRS 17.B26(k), B27(g)]*. This is illustrated in the following example.

Example 45.1:   Rainfall contract – derivative financial instrument or insurance contract?

Company E has contracted to lease a stall at an open-air event from which it plans to sell goods to people attending the event. The event will be held at a village approximately 100 km from Capital City.

Because E is concerned that poor weather may deter people from attending the event, it enters into a contract with Financial Institution K, the terms of which are that, in return for a premium paid by E on inception of the contract, K will pay a fixed amount of money to E if, during the day of the event, it rains for more than three hours at the meteorological station in the centre of Capital City.

The non-financial variable in the contract, i.e. rainfall at the meteorological station, is not specific to E. Particularly, E will only suffer loss as a result of rainfall at the village, not at Capital City. Also, because the potential payment to be received is for a fixed amount, it might not be possible to demonstrate that E has suffered a loss for which it has been compensated. Therefore, E should account for the contract as a financial instrument under IFRS 9.

3.3.2 Contracts with discretionary participation features

IFRS 4 and IFRS 17 are clear that investment contracts that have the legal form of an insurance contract but do not expose the insurer to significant insurance risk (see Chapters 55 and 56) are financial instruments and not insurance contracts. *[IFRS 4.B19(a), IFRS 17.B27(a)]*. Investment contracts (normally taking the form of life insurance policies) which contain what are called discretionary participation features, essentially rights of the holder to receive additional benefits whose amount or timing is, contractually, at the discretion of the issuer, are accounted for under IFRS 4. *[IFRS 4 Appendix A]*. Accordingly, IFRS 9 and the parts of IAS 32 dealing with the distinction between financial liabilities and equity instruments (see Chapter 47 at 4) do not apply to such contracts, although the disclosure requirements of IFRS 7 do apply. *[IAS 32.4(e), IFRS 9.2.1(e), IFRS 4.2(b), IFRS 7.3]*. When IFRS 17 is applied, such contracts would fall within its scope if (and only if) the entity also issues insurance contracts as the IASB believes that applying IFRS 17 to these contracts in these circumstances would provide more relevant information about the contracts than would be provided by applying other standards. *[IFRS 17.3(c), BC65(a)]*. In rare cases where an entity issues contracts with a discretionary participation feature but does not issue any insurance contracts, those contracts would fall within the scope of IAS 32 and IFRS 9.

3.3.3 Separating financial instrument components including embedded derivatives from insurance contracts

IFRS 9 applies to derivatives that are embedded in insurance contracts or contracts containing discretionary participation features (see 3.3.2 above) if the derivative itself is not within the scope of IFRS 4. *[IFRS 9.2.1(e)]*. When IFRS 17 is applied, entities will use IFRS 9 to determine whether a contract contains an embedded derivative to be separated and apply IFRS 9 to those components that are separated. *[IFRS 17.11(a)]*. IFRS 7 applies to all embedded derivatives that are separately accounted for. *[IFRS 7.3(d)]*.

IFRS 17 requires an entity to separate an investment component (the amount an insurance contract requires the entity to repay to the policyholder even if an insured event does not occur *[IFRS 17.BC108]*) from a host insurance contract if the component is 'distinct' (see Chapter 56 at 4.2). The separated component is accounted for in accordance with IFRS 9. *[IFRS 17.11(b)]*.

3.3.4 Credit card contracts and similar arrangements which give rise to insurance risk

Credit card contracts or similar arrangements can in some circumstances meet the definition of an insurance contract. For example, some credit cards, charge cards, consumer financing and bank account contracts involve the lender providing guarantees to its customer in respect of products purchased using the arrangement. When IFRS 17 is applied, such contracts will be excluded from the scope of IFRS 17 if, and only if, the entity does not reflect an assessment of the insurance risk associated with an individual customer in setting the price of the contract with that customer. If excluded from IFRS 17, these contracts would be within the scope of IFRS 9. However, if, and only if, the insurance coverage is a contractual term of such a financial instrument, the entity shall separate that component and apply IFRS 17 to it (see Chapter 56 at 2.3.1.H). *[IFRS 17.7(b), IFRS 9.2.1(e)(iv)]*. Other IFRS Standards, such as IFRS 15 – *Revenue from Contracts with Customers* – or IAS 37, might apply to other components of the contract, such as other service components or insurance components required by law or regulation. *[IFRS 17.BC94C]*. Under IFRS 4, which has different criteria for separating components of an insurance contract when compared to IFRS 17, most entities separate the components of such contracts. For example, an entity applying IFRS 4 might account for the credit card component applying IFRS 9, the insurance component applying IFRS 4 and any other service component applying IFRS 15. *[IFRS 17.BC94B]*.

3.3.5 Loan contracts that transfer significant insurance risk only on settlement of the policyholder's obligation created by the contract

Some contracts meet the definition of an insurance contract but limit the compensation for insured events to the amount otherwise required to settle the policyholder's obligation created by the contract. These might include loans with death waivers such as lifetime or equity release mortgages in which the borrower's obligation on death or incapacitation is limited to the value of the property on which the loan is secured. When IFRS 17 is applied, if such contracts are not otherwise excluded from the scope of IFRS 17 an entity can elect to apply either IFRS 17 or IFRS 9 to such contracts that it issues. The choice should be made for each portfolio of insurance contracts and the choice for such portfolio is irrevocable (see Chapter 56 at 2.3.3). *[IFRS 17.8A]*.

Under IFRS 4, which has different criteria for separating components of an insurance contract when compared to IFRS 17, it is possible for an entity to separate the loan and insurance components. The entity would then account for the loan component under IFRS 9 and the insurance component under IFRS 4.

3.4 Financial guarantee contracts

Where a contract meets the definition of a financial guarantee contract (see 3.4.1 below) the issuer is normally required to apply specific accounting requirements within IFRS 9, which are different from those applying to other financial liabilities. Usually the contract is measured at fair value on initial recognition and subsequently at the higher of the amount of the loss allowance determined in accordance with the impairment requirements of IFRS 9 (see Chapter 51 at 11.2) and the amount initially recognised less, when appropriate, the cumulative amount of income recognised in accordance with the principles of IFRS 15 (see Chapter 50 at 2.8). There are exceptions to this general requirement and these are dealt with at 3.4.2 below.

3.4.1 Definition of a financial guarantee contract

A financial guarantee contract is defined as a contract that requires the issuer to make specified payments to reimburse the holder for a loss it incurs because a specified debtor fails to make payment when due in accordance with the original or modified terms of a debt instrument. *[IFRS 4 Appendix A, IFRS 9 Appendix A]*.

3.4.1.A Reimbursement for loss incurred

Some credit-related guarantees (or letters of credit, credit derivative default contracts or credit insurance contracts) do not, as a precondition for payment, require that the holder is exposed to, and has incurred a loss on, the failure of the debtor to make payments on the guaranteed asset when due. An example of such a guarantee is one that requires payments in response to changes in a specified credit rating or credit index. Such guarantees are not financial guarantee contracts, as defined in IFRS 9, nor are they insurance contracts, as defined in IFRS 4, or contracts within the scope of IFRS 17. Rather, they are derivatives and accordingly fall within the scope of IFRS 9. *[IFRS 9.B2.5(b), IFRS 4.B19(f), IFRS 17.B27(f), B30]*.

When a debtor defaults on a guaranteed loan a significant time period may elapse prior to full and final legal settlement of the loss. Because of this, certain credit protection contracts provide for the guarantor to make a payment at a fixed point after the default event using the best estimate of loss at the time. Such payments typically terminate the credit protection contract with no party having any further claim under it whilst ownership of the loan remains with the guaranteed party. In situations like this, if the final loss on the debtor exceeds the amount estimated on payment of the guarantee, the guaranteed party will suffer an overall financial loss; conversely, the guaranteed party may receive a payment under the guarantee but eventually suffer a smaller loss on the loan. Therefore such a contract will often not meet the essence of the definition of a financial guarantee. However, if the payment is designed to be a reasonable estimate of the loss actually incurred, such a feature (which is common in many conventional insurance contracts) will sometimes allow the contract to be classified as a financial guarantee contract. This will particularly be the case if such payments are agreed by both parties in order to settle the financial guarantee, as opposed to being specified as part of the original contract.

Also, such a contract should meet the definition of a guarantee if it was structured in either of the following ways:

- the contract requires the guarantor to purchase the defaulted loan for its nominal amount; or
- on settlement of the final loss, the contract provides for a further payment between the guarantor and guaranteed party for any difference between that amount and the initial loss estimate that was paid.

However, if there are circumstances in which the holder of the guarantee could be reimbursed for a loss that it has not incurred, for example where the guarantee is traded separately from the underlying debt and the holder could have acquired it without owning the underlying debt instrument, the guarantee does not meet the definition of a financial guarantee contract.

3.4.1.B   Debt instrument

Although the term 'debt instrument' is used extensively as a fundamental part of the definition of a 'financial guarantee contract', it is not defined within the financial instruments or insurance standards. The term will typically be considered to include trade debts, overdrafts and other borrowings including mortgage loans and certain debt securities.

However, entities often provide guarantees of other items and analysing these in the context of IFRS 9, IFRS 4 and IFRS 17 is not always straightforward. Consider, for example, a guarantee of a lessor's receipts under a lease. In substance, a finance lease gives rise to a loan agreement (see 2.2.4 above) and it therefore seems clear that a guarantee of payments on such a lease should be considered a financial guarantee contract.

From the perspective of the guarantor, a guarantee of a non-cancellable operating lease will give rise to a substantially similar exposure, i.e. credit risk of the lessee. Moreover, individual payments currently due and payable are recognised as financial (debt) instruments. Therefore, such guarantees would seem to meet the definition of a financial guarantee at least insofar as they relate to payments currently due and payable. It may be argued that the remainder of the contract (normally the majority) fails to meet the definition because it provides a guarantee of future debt instruments. However, the standard does not explicitly require the debt instrument to be accounted for as a financial instrument that is currently due and we believe a guarantee of a lessor's receipts under an operating lease could also be argued to meet the definition of a financial guarantee contract.

Where it is accepted that such a guarantee is not a financial guarantee contract, one must still examine how the related obligations should be accounted for – the contract is, after all, a financial instrument. The possibilities are a derivative financial instrument (accounted for at fair value through profit or loss under IFRS 9) or an insurance contract (accounted for under IFRS 4 – commonly resulting only in disclosure of a contingent liability, assuming payment is not considered probable – or under IFRS 17). The analysis depends on whether the risk transferred by the guarantee is considered financial risk or insurance risk (see 3.3 above). Credit risk sits on the cusp of the relevant definitions making the judgement a marginal one, although we believe that in many situations the arguments for treatment as an insurance contract will be credible. Of course, for this to be the case the guarantee must only compensate the holder for loss in the event of default.

Other types of guarantee can add further complications – for example guarantees of pension plan contributions to funded defined benefit schemes. Where such a guarantee is in respect of discrete identifiable payments, the analysis above for operating leases seems equally applicable. However, the terms of such a guarantee might have the effect that the guaranteed amount depends on the performance of the assets within the scheme. In these cases, the guarantee seems to give rise to a transfer of financial risk (i.e. the value of the asset) in addition to credit risk, which might lend support for its treatment as a derivative.

3.4.1.C   Form and existence of contract

The application guidance to IFRS 9 emphasises that, whilst financial guarantee contracts may have various legal forms (such as guarantees, some types of letters of credit, credit default contracts or insurance contracts), their accounting treatment does not depend on their legal form. *[IFRS 9.B2.5]*.

In some cases guarantees arise, directly or indirectly, as a result of the operation of statute or regulation. In such situations, it is necessary to examine whether the arrangement gives rise to a contract as that term is used in IAS 32. For example, in some jurisdictions, a subsidiary may avoid filing its financial statements or having them audited if its parent and fellow subsidiaries guarantee its liabilities by entering into a deed of cross guarantee. In other jurisdictions similar relief is granted if group companies elect to make a statutory declaration of guarantee. In the first situation it would seem appropriate for the issuer to regard the deed as a contract and hence any guarantee made under it would be within the scope of IFRS 9. The statutory nature of the declaration in the second situation makes the analysis more difficult. Although the substance of the arrangement is little different from the first situation, statutory obligations are not financial liabilities and are therefore outside the scope of IFRS 9.

3.4.2   Issuers of financial guarantee contracts

In general, issuers of financial guarantees contracts should apply IAS 32, IFRS 9 and IFRS 7 to those contracts even though they meet the definition of an insurance contract in IFRS 4 (or IFRS 17) if the risk transferred is significant. *[IFRS 9.B2.5(a)]*. However, if an entity has previously asserted explicitly that it regards such contracts as insurance contracts and has used accounting applicable to insurance contracts, the issuer may elect to apply either IFRS 9 or IFRS 4 (see Chapter 55 at 2.2.3.D) or IFRS 17 when applicable (see Chapter 56 at 2.3.1.E). That election may be made contract by contract, but the election for each contract is irrevocable. *[IAS 32.4(d), IFRS 4.4(d), IFRS 7.3(d), IFRS 9.2.1(e), IFRS 17.7(e)]*. This concession does not extend to contracts that are similar to financial guarantee contracts but are actually derivative financial instruments (see 3.4.1.A above).

The IASB was concerned that entities other than credit insurers could elect to apply IFRS 4 to financial guarantee contracts and consequently (if their accounting policies permitted) recognise no liability on inception. Therefore, it imposed the restrictions outlined in the previous paragraph. *[IFRS 9.BCZ2.12]*. The application guidance to IFRS 9 states that assertions that an issuer regards contracts as insurance contracts are typically found throughout the issuer's communications with customers and regulators, contracts, business documentation as well as in their financial statements. Furthermore, insurance contracts are often subject to accounting requirements that are distinct from the requirements for other types of transaction, such as contracts issued by banks or commercial companies. In such cases, an issuer's financial statements would typically include a statement that the issuer had used those accounting requirements, i.e. ones normally applied to insurance contracts. [IFRS 9.B2.6]. Nevertheless, other companies do consider it appropriate to apply IFRS 4 rather than IFRS 9 to these contracts. Rolls Royce disclosed the following accounting policy in respect of guarantees that it provides.

> Extract 45.1: Rolls-Royce Holdings plc (2019)
> NOTES TO THE CONSOLIDATED FINANCIAL STATEMENTS [extract]
> 1. Accounting policies [extract]
>   Customer financing support [extract]
>
> In connection with the sale of its products, the Group will, on occasion, provide financing support for its customers. These arrangements fall into two categories: credit-based guarantees and asset-value guarantees. In accordance with the requirements of IFRS 9 and IFRS 4 *Insurance Contracts*, credit-based guarantees are treated as insurance contracts. The Group considers asset-value guarantees to be non-financial liabilities and accordingly these are also treated as insurance contracts.

Accounting for the revenue associated with financial guarantee contracts issued in connection with the sale of goods is dealt with under IFRS 15 (see Chapters 27 to 32). [IFRS 9.B2.5(c)].

3.4.3 Holders of financial guarantee contracts

Financial guarantee contracts held are not within the scope of IFRS 9 because they are insurance contracts (see 3.3 above). [IFRS 9.2.1(e)]. However, IFRS 4 and IFRS 17 do not apply to insurance contracts that an entity holds (other than reinsurance contracts) either. [IFRS 4.4(f), IFRS 17.7(g)]. Therefore, financial guarantee contracts held by an entity are not required to be recognised separately by IFRS 9, IFRS 4 or IFRS 17.

For the purposes of measuring ECL, IFRS 9 requires the estimate of expected cash shortfalls to reflect the cash flows expected from collateral and other credit enhancements that are part of the contractual terms and are not recognised separately by the entity. [IFRS 9.B5.5.55]. This means that a financial guarantee contract held which is considered to be an integral component of the guaranteed debt instrument will be accounted for as part of the ECL on that debt instrument (see Chapter 51 at 5.8.1).

However, the holder of a financial guarantee contract which is not considered to be integral to the underlying debt instrument will need to develop an accounting policy in accordance with the 'hierarchy' in IAS 8 – *Accounting Policies, Changes in Accounting Estimates and Errors*. The IAS 8 hierarchy specifies criteria to use if no IFRS applies specifically (see Chapter 3 at 4). [IFRS 4.IG2 Example 1.11, IFRS 17.BC66].

In developing a policy, entities may look to the requirements of IAS 37 dealing with contingent assets (see Chapter 26 at 3.2.2) or reimbursement assets (see Chapter 51 at 5.8.1.B), at least as far as recoveries under the contract are concerned. In certain situations, it may also be appropriate for the holder of a financial guarantee contract to account for it as an asset at fair value through profit or loss. This might be the case if the guaranteed asset has itself been classified as at fair value through profit or loss.

3.4.4 Financial guarantee contracts between entities under common control

There is no exemption from the measurement requirements of IFRS 9 for guarantees issued between parents and their subsidiaries, between entities under common control nor by a parent or subsidiary on behalf of a subsidiary or a parent (unlike an exemption under US GAAP). *[IFRS 9.BCZ2.14]*.

Therefore, for example, where a parent guarantees the borrowings of a subsidiary, the guarantee should be accounted for as a standalone instrument in the parent's separate financial statements. However, for the purposes of the parent's consolidated financial statements, such guarantees are normally considered an integral part of the terms of the borrowing (see Chapter 47 at 4.8) and therefore should not be accounted for independently of the borrowing.

3.5 Loan commitments

Loan commitments are firm commitments to provide credit under pre-specified terms and conditions. *[IFRS 9.BCZ2.2]*. The term can include arrangements such as offers to individuals in respect of residential mortgage loans as well as committed borrowing facilities granted to a corporate entity.

Although they meet the definition of a derivative financial instrument (see 2.2.8 above and Chapter 46 at 2), a pragmatic decision has been taken by the IASB to simplify the accounting for holders and issuers of many loan commitments. *[IFRS 9.BCZ2.3]*. Accordingly, loan commitments that cannot be settled net – in practice, most loan commitments – may be excluded from the scope of IFRS 9, with the exception of the impairment requirements and derecognition provisions (see Chapters 51 and 52), but are included within the scope of IFRS 7. *[IFRS 9.2.1(g), IFRS 7.4]*. Some loan commitments, however, are within the scope of IFRS 9, namely: *[IFRS 9.2.1(g)]*

- those that are designated as financial liabilities at fair value through profit or loss (this may be appropriate if the associated risk exposures are managed on a fair value basis or because designation eliminates an accounting mismatch); *[IFRS 9.2.3(a)]*
- commitments that can be settled net in cash or by delivering or issuing another financial instrument; *[IFRS 9.2.3(b)]* and
- all those within the same class where the entity has a past practice of selling the assets resulting from its loan commitments shortly after origination. The IASB sees this as achieving net settlement. *[IFRS 9.2.3(a)]*.

In addition, commitments to provide a loan at a below-market interest rate are also within the scope of IFRS 9. *[IFRS 9.2.3(c)]*. For these loan commitments, IFRS 9 contains specific measurement requirements which are different from those applying to other financial liabilities. IFRS 9 requires the commitments to be measured at fair value on initial recognition and subsequently amortised to profit or loss using the principles of IFRS 15 (see Chapters 27 to 32) but requires the expected credit loss allowance to be used, if higher. *[IFRS 9.4.2.1(d)]*. The reason for this accounting treatment is that the IASB was concerned that liabilities resulting from such commitments might not be recognised in the statement of financial position because, often, no cash consideration is received. *[IFRS 9.BCZ2.7]*.

In respect of commitments that can be settled net in cash IFRS 9 contains only limited guidance on what 'net settlement' means. Clearly a fixed interest rate loan commitment that gives the lender and/or the borrower an explicit right to settle the value of the contract (taking into account changes in interest rates etc.) in cash or by delivery or issuing another financial instrument would be considered a form of net settlement and therefore a derivative. However, paying out a loan in instalments (for example, a mortgage construction loan where instalments are paid out in line with the progress of construction) is not regarded as net settlement. *[IFRS 9.2.3(b)]*.

As a matter of fact, most loan commitments could be settled net if both parties agreed, essentially by renegotiating the terms of the contract. Of more relevance is the question of whether one party has the practical ability to settle net, e.g. because the terms of the contract allow net settlement or by the use of some market mechanism.

Where the entity has a past practice of selling the assets shortly after origination, no guidance is given on what is meant by a class (although the Basis for Conclusions makes it clear that an entity can have more than one). *[IFRS 9.BCZ2.6]*. Therefore, an assessment will need to be made based on individual circumstances.

Example 45.2:   Identifying classes of loan commitment

A banking group has two main operating subsidiaries, one in country A and the other in country B. Although they share common functions (e.g. information systems) the two subsidiaries' operations are clearly distinct.

Both subsidiaries originate similar loans under loan commitments. In country A there is an active and liquid market for the assets resulting from loan commitments issued in that country. The subsidiary operating in that country has a past practice of disposing of such assets in this market shortly after origination. There is no such market in country B.

The fact that one subsidiary has a past practice of settling its loan commitments net (as the term is used in the standard) would not normally mean that the loan commitments issued in country B are required to be classified as at fair value through profit or loss.

The above example is relatively straightforward – in some circumstances it may be more difficult to define the class. However, there is no reason why an individual entity (say a subsidiary of a group) cannot have two or more classes of loan commitment, e.g. where they result in the origination of different types of asset that are clearly managed separately. Any associated entitlement to fees should be accounted for in accordance with IFRS 15 or IFRS 9 (see Chapters 27 to 32 and Chapter 50 at 3 respectively). No accounting requirements are specified for holders of loan commitments, but they will normally be accounted for as executory contracts – essentially, this means that fees payable will be recognised as an expense in a manner that is appropriate to the terms of the commitment. Any resulting borrowing will obviously be accounted for as a financial liability under IFRS 9.

Although much of the discussion has focused on loan commitments as options to provide credit, *[IFRS 9.BCZ2.2]*, we believe it can be appropriate to apply the exclusion from IFRS 9 to non-optional commitments to provide credit, provided the necessary conditions above are met.

The exclusion is available only for contracts to provide credit. Normally, therefore, it will be applicable only where there is a commitment to lend funds, and certainly not for all contracts that may result in the subsequent recognition of an asset or liability that is accounted for at amortised cost. Consider, for example, a contract between entities A and B that gives B the right to sell to A a transferable (but unquoted) debt security issued by entity C that B currently owns. Even if, on subsequent acquisition, A will measure the debt security at amortised cost or fair value through other comprehensive income, the contract would not generally be considered a loan commitment as it does not involve A providing credit to B.

3.6 Equity instruments

3.6.1 Equity instruments issued

Financial instruments (including options and warrants) that are issued by the reporting entity and meet the definition of equity instruments in IAS 32 (see 2.1 above and Chapter 47 at 3 and 4) are outside the scope of IFRS 9. *[IFRS 9.2.1(d)]*.

In principle, IFRS 7 applies to issued equity instruments except for those that are derivatives based on interests in subsidiaries, associates or joint ventures (see 3.1 above). *[IFRS 7.3(a)]*. However, this is of largely academic interest because IFRS 7 specifies no disclosure requirements for issued equity instruments.

In fact, the scope of IFRS 7 for these types of instrument is even more curious. Firstly, it is explained that derivatives over subsidiaries, associates and joint ventures that are equity instruments from the point of view of the issuer are excluded from the scope of IFRS 7 because equity instruments are not remeasured and hence do not expose the issuer to statement of financial position and income statement risk. Also, the disclosures about the significance of financial instruments for financial position and performance are not considered relevant for equity instruments. *[IFRS 7.BC8]*. Given the reasons quoted, it is not entirely clear why the IASB did not exclude all instruments meeting the definition of equity in IAS 32 from the scope of IFRS 7, e.g. non-puttable ordinary shares issued by the reporting entity. Secondly, it is very difficult to see how a derivative over a reporting entity's associate or joint venture could ever meet the definition of equity from the perspective of the reporting entity.

3.6.2 Equity instruments held

From the point of view of the holder, equity instruments are within the scope of IFRS 7 and IFRS 9 (unless they meet the exception at 3.1 above). *[IFRS 9.2.1(d)]*.

3.7 Business combinations

3.7.1 Contingent consideration in a business combination

3.7.1.A Payable by an acquirer

For business combinations accounted for under IFRS 3 – *Business Combinations*, contingent consideration that meets the definition of a financial asset or liability will be measured at fair value, with any resulting gain or loss recognised in profit or loss in accordance with IFRS 9 (see Chapter 9 at 7.1). *[IFRS 3.58(b)(i)]*.

Further, contingent consideration arising from an acquiree's prior business combination that an acquirer assumes in its subsequent acquisition of the acquiree does not meet the definition of contingent consideration in the acquirer's business combination. Rather, it is one of the identifiable liabilities assumed in the subsequent acquisition. Therefore, to the extent that such arrangements are financial instruments, they are within the scope of IAS 32, IFRS 9 and IFRS 7.[7]

3.7.1.B Receivable by a vendor

IFRS 9 does not go on to explain whether the vendor should be accounting for the contingent consideration in accordance with its provisions.

In most cases the vendor will have a contractual right to receive cash or another financial asset from the purchaser and, therefore, it is hard to avoid the conclusion that the contingent consideration meets the definition of a financial asset and hence is within the scope of IFRS 9, not IAS 37. IFRS 10 – *Consolidated Financial Statements* – requires consideration received on the loss of control of an entity or business to be measured at fair value, which is consistent with the treatment required by IFRS 9 for financial assets.

3.7.2 Contracts between an acquirer and a vendor in a business combination

IFRS 9 does not apply to forward contracts between an acquirer and a selling shareholder to buy or sell an acquiree that will result in a business combination at a future acquisition date. In order to qualify for this scope exclusion, the term of the forward contract should not exceed a reasonable period normally necessary to obtain any required approvals and to complete the transaction, for example to accommodate the completion of necessary regulatory and legal processes. *[IFRS 9.2.1(f), BCZ2.39].*

It applies only when completion of the business combination is not dependent on further actions of either party. Option contracts allow one party to control the occurrence or non-occurrence of future events depending on whether the option is exercised. Consequently, option contracts that on exercise will result in the reporting entity obtaining control of another entity are within the scope of IFRS 9, whether they are currently exercisable or not. *[IFRS 9.BCZ2.40, BCZ2.41].*

It was suggested that 'in-substance' or 'synthetic' forward contracts, e.g. the combination of a written put and purchased call where the strike prices, exercise dates and notional amounts are equal, or a deeply in- or out-of-the-money option, should be excluded from the scope of IFRS 9. However, the IASB staff did not agree with the notion that synthetic forward contracts (which do provide optionality to one or both parties) are substantially identical to forward contracts (which commit both parties). The IASB staff accepted that in normal financial instrument transactions, the economics of a synthetic forward will be favourable to one party to the contract and should therefore result in its exercise, but a similar assumption does not necessarily hold true in business combination transactions because one party may choose not to exercise the option due to other factors. Therefore, it is not possible to assert that the contracts will always result in a business combination.[8]

The acquisition of an interest in an associate represents the acquisition of a financial instrument, not an acquisition of a business. Therefore, the scope exclusion should not be applied by analogy to contracts to acquire investments in associates and similar transactions. *[IFRS 9.BCZ2.42]*.

Another related issue is the treatment of contracts, whether options or forwards, to purchase an entity that owns a single asset such as a ship or building which does not constitute a business. The reason a contract for a business combination is normally considered to be a financial instrument seems to be because it is a contract to purchase equity instruments. Consequently, a contract to purchase all of the shares in a single asset company would also meet the definition of a financial instrument, yet on the face of it such a contract would not be excluded from the scope of IFRS 9 if the asset did not represent a business. The IASB staff disagreed with this analysis and argued that such a contract should be analysed as a contract to purchase the underlying asset which would normally be outside the scope of IFRS 9.[9] Although forward contracts between an acquirer and a vendor in a business combination are scoped out of IFRS 9 and hence are not accounted for as derivatives, they are still within the scope of IFRS 7.

3.8 Contingent pricing of property, plant and equipment and intangible assets

IAS 32 (as currently worded) is clear that the purchase of goods on credit gives rise to a financial liability when the goods are delivered (see 2.2.6 above) and that a contingent obligation to deliver cash meets the definition of a financial liability (see 2.2.3 above). Consequently, it would seem that a financial liability arises on the outright purchase of an item of property, plant and equipment or an intangible asset, where the purchase contract requires the subsequent payment of contingent consideration, for example amounts based on the performance of the asset. Further, because there is no exemption from applying IFRS 9 to such contracts, one might expect that such a liability would be accounted for in accordance with IFRS 9, i.e. any measurement changes to that liability would flow through the statement of profit or loss. This would be consistent with the accounting treatment for contingent consideration arising from a business combination under IFRS 3 (see 3.7.1.A above).

However, in practice, contracts can be more complex than suggested in the previous paragraph and often give rise to situations where the purchaser can influence or control the crystallisation of the contingent payments, e.g. where the contingent payments take the form of sales-based royalties. These complexities can raise broader questions about the nature of the obligations and the appropriate accounting standard to apply. In March 2016, the Interpretations Committee determined that this issue is too broad for it to address within the confines of existing IFRS. Consequently, the Interpretations Committee decided not to add this issue to its agenda.

The Interpretations Committee had discussed this issue a number of times. Initially the discussions focused on purchases of individual assets, but they were later widened to cover contingent payments made under service concessions. The Interpretations Committee could not reach a consensus on whether the purchaser should recognise a liability at the date of purchasing the asset for variable payments that depend on its future activity or, instead, should recognise such a liability only when the related activity occurs. It was also unable to reach a consensus on how the purchaser should measure a liability for such variable payments. Accordingly, it concluded that the Board should address the accounting for variable payments comprehensively.[10] This issue is discussed in more detail in Chapter 17 at 4.5, Chapter 18 at 4.1.9 and Chapter 43 at 8.4.1.

Where contingent consideration arises on the sale of an asset that is within the scope of IAS 16 – *Property, Plant and Equipment* – or IAS 38 – *Intangible Assets* – then the requirements of IFRS 15 apply in determining the amount of consideration to be included in the gain or loss on derecognition of the asset (see Chapter 27 at 4.3). *[IAS 16.72, IAS 38.116]*. IFRS 15 requires that variable consideration (which includes contingent consideration) be estimated, using one of two methods, but requires that the amount of the estimate included within the transaction price be constrained to avoid significant reversals in future periods (see Chapter 29 at 2.2). During 2019 and 2020, the Interpretations Committee and the IASB discussed whether IFRS 10 or IFRS 15 applies when an entity loses control of a single asset entity containing real estate as part of its ordinary activities. As noted at 3.7.1.B above, IFRS 10 requires consideration received on the loss of control of a subsidiary to be measured at fair value. *[IFRS 10.B98(b)(i)]*. The outcome of these discussions may impact the determination of whether IFRS 10 (rather than IAS 16 or IAS 38) should apply to the transaction. Therefore, depending on which standard is applied to the disposal, the accounting outcome could be very different when contingent consideration is involved. This issue is discussed in more detail in Chapter 7 at 3.2 and Chapter 27 at 3.5.1.J

3.9 Employee benefit plans and share-based payment

Employers' rights and obligations under employee benefit plans, which are dealt with under IAS 19 – *Employee Benefits* – are excluded from the scope of IAS 32, IFRS 7 and IFRS 9. *[IAS 32.4(b), IFRS 7.3(b), IFRS 9.2.1(c)]*. The Interpretations Committee noted that IAS 19 indicates that employee benefit plans include a wide range of formal and informal arrangements and concluded it was clear that the exclusion of employee benefit plans from IAS 32 (and by implication IFRS 7 and IFRS 9) includes all employee benefits covered by IAS 19, for example a liability for long service leave.[11]

Similarly, most financial instruments, contracts and obligations arising from share-based payment transactions, which are dealt with under IFRS 2 – *Share-based Payment* – are also excluded. However, IAS 32, IFRS 7 and IFRS 9 do apply to contracts to buy or sell non-financial items in share-based transactions that can be settled net (as that term is used in this context) unless they are considered to be 'normal' sales and purchases (see 4 below). *[IAS 32.4(f)(i), IFRS 7.3(e), IFRS 9.2.1(h)]*. For example, a contract to purchase a fixed quantity of oil in exchange for issuing of a fixed number of shares that could be settled net would be excluded from the scope of IAS 32, IFRS 7 and IFRS 9 only if it qualified as a 'normal' purchase (which would be unlikely).

In addition, IAS 32 applies to treasury shares (see Chapter 47 at 9) that are purchased, sold, issued or cancelled in connection with employee share option plans, employee share purchase plans, and all other share-based payment arrangements. *[IAS 32.4(f)(ii)]*.

3.10 Reimbursement rights in respect of provisions

Most reimbursement rights in respect of provisions arise from insurance contracts and are therefore outside the scope of IFRS 9 as set out at 3.3 above. The scope of IFRS 9 is also restricted so as not to apply to other financial instruments that are rights to payments to reimburse the entity for expenditure it is required to make to settle a liability that it has recognised as a provision in accordance with IAS 37 in the current or an earlier period. *[IFRS 9.2.1(i)]*.

However, a residual interest in a decommissioning or similar fund that extends beyond a right to reimbursement, such as a contractual right to distributions once all the decommissioning has been completed or on winding up the fund, may be an equity instrument within the scope of IFRS 9. *[IFRIC 5.5]*.

3.11 Disposal groups classified as held for sale and discontinued operations

The disclosure requirements in IFRS 7 will not apply to financial instruments within a disposal group classified as held for sale or within a discontinued operation, except for disclosures about the measurement of those assets and liabilities (see Chapter 54 at 4) if such disclosures are not already provided in other notes to the financial statements. *[IFRS 5.5B]*. However, additional disclosures about such assets (or disposal groups) may be necessary to comply with the general requirements of IAS 1 – *Presentation of Financial Statements* – particularly for financial statements to achieve a fair presentation and to disclose information about assumptions made and the sources of estimation uncertainty (see Chapter 3 at 4.1.1.A and 5.2.1 respectively). *[IAS 1.15, 125, IFRS 5.5B]*.

3.12 Indemnification assets

IFRS 3 specifies the accounting treatment for 'indemnification assets', a term that is not defined but is described as follows:

> 'The seller in a business combination may contractually indemnify the acquirer for the outcome of a contingency or uncertainty related to all or part of a specific asset or liability. For example, the seller may indemnify the acquirer against losses above a specified amount on a liability arising from a particular contingency; in other words, the seller will guarantee that the acquirer's liability will not exceed a specified amount. As a result, the acquirer obtains an indemnification asset.' *[IFRS 3.27]*.

An indemnification asset will normally meet the definition of a financial asset within IAS 32. In some situations, the asset might be considered a right under an insurance contract (see 3.3 above) and in others it could be seen as similar to a reimbursement right (see 3.10 above). However, there will be cases where these assets are, strictly, within the scope of IFRS 9, creating something of a tension with IFRS 3. This appears to be nothing more than an oversight and, in our view, entities should apply the more specific requirements of IFRS 3 when accounting for these assets which are covered in more detail in Chapter 9 at 5.6.4.

3.13 Rights and obligations within the scope of IFRS 15

An unconditional right to consideration (i.e. only the passage of time is required before the payment of that consideration is due) in exchange for goods and services transferred to the customer (a receivable) is accounted for in accordance with IFRS 9. *[IFRS 9.2.1(j), IFRS 15.108]*. A conditional right to consideration in exchange for goods or services transferred to a customer (a contract asset) is accounted for in accordance with IFRS 15, which requires an entity to assess contract assets for impairment in accordance with IFRS 9. *[IFRS 15.107]*. Other rights and obligations within the scope of IFRS 15 are generally not accounted for as financial instruments.

The credit risk disclosure requirements within IFRS 7.35A-35N apply to those rights that IFRS 15 specifies are accounted for in accordance with IFRS 9 for the purposes of measurement of impairment gains and losses (i.e. contract assets). *[IFRS 7.5A]*.

4 CONTRACTS TO BUY OR SELL COMMODITIES AND OTHER NON-FINANCIAL ITEMS

Contracts to buy or sell non-financial items do not generally meet the definition of a financial instrument (see 2.2.5 above). However, many such contracts are standardised in form and traded on organised markets in much the same way as some derivative financial instruments. The application guidance explains that a commodity futures contract, for example, may be bought and sold readily for cash because it is listed for trading on an exchange and may change hands many times. *[IAS 32.AG20]*. In fact, this is not strictly true because such contracts are bilateral agreements that cannot be transferred in this way. Rather, the contract would normally be 'closed out' (rather than sold) by entering into an offsetting agreement with the original counterparty or with the exchange on which it is traded.

The ability to buy or sell such a contract for cash, the ease with which it may be bought or sold (or, more correctly, closed out), and the possibility of negotiating a cash settlement of the obligation to receive or deliver the commodity, do not alter the fundamental character of the contract in a way that creates a financial instrument. The buying and selling parties are, in effect, trading the underlying commodity or other asset. However, the IASB is of the view that there are many circumstances where they should be accounted for as if they were financial instruments. *[IAS 32.AG20]*.

Accordingly, the provisions of IAS 32, IFRS 7 and IFRS 9 are normally applied to those contracts to buy or sell non-financial items that can be settled net in cash or another financial instrument or by exchanging financial instruments or in which the non-financial instrument is readily convertible to cash, effectively as if the contracts were financial instruments (see 4.1 below). However, there is one exception for what are commonly termed 'normal' purchases and sales or 'own use' contracts (these are considered in more detail at 4.2 below). *[IAS 32.8, IFRS 9.2.4, IFRS 7.5]*.

Typically, the non-financial item will be a commodity, but this is not necessarily the case. For example, an emission right, which is an intangible asset (see Chapter 17 at 11.2), is a non-financial item. Therefore, these requirements would apply equally to contracts for the purchase or sale of emission rights if they could be settled net. These requirements will also be appropriate for determining whether certain commodity leases are within the scope of IFRS 9. Commodity leases generally do not fall within the scope of IFRS 16 as they do not relate to a specific or identified asset.

4.1 Contracts that may be settled net

IFRS 9 explains that there are various ways in which a contract to buy or sell a non-financial item can be settled net, including when: *[IAS 32.9, IFRS 9.2.6, BCZ2.18]*

(a) the terms of the contract permit either party to settle it net;

(b) the ability to settle the contract net is not explicit in its terms, but the entity has a practice of settling similar contracts (see 4.2.1 below) net (whether with the counterparty, by entering into offsetting contracts or by selling the contract before its exercise or lapse);

(c) for similar contracts (see 4.2.2 below), the entity has a practice of taking delivery of the underlying and selling it within a short period after delivery for the purpose of generating a profit from short-term fluctuations in price or dealer's margin; and

(d) the non-financial item that is the subject of the contract is readily convertible to cash (see below).

There is no further guidance in IFRS 9 explaining what is meant by 'readily convertible to cash'. Typically, a non-financial item would be considered readily convertible to cash if it consists of largely fungible units and quoted spot prices are available in an active market that can absorb the quantity held by the entity without significantly affecting the price.

Whether there exists an active market for a non-financial item, particularly a physical one such as a commodity, will depend on its quality, location or other characteristics such as size or weight. For example, if a commodity is actively traded in London, this may have the effect that the same commodity located in, say, Rotterdam is considered readily convertible to cash as well as if it was located in London. However, if it were located in Siberia it might not be considered readily convertible to cash if more than a little effort were required (often because of transportation needs) for it to be readily sold.

Like loan commitments, most contracts could as a matter of fact be settled net if both parties agreed to renegotiate terms. Again, we do not believe the IASB intended the possibility of such renegotiations to be considered in determining whether or not such contracts may be settled net. Of more relevance is the question of whether one party has the practical ability to settle net, e.g. in accordance with the terms of the contract or by the use of some market mechanism.

4.2 Normal sales and purchases (or own use contracts)

As indicated at 4 above, the provisions of IAS 32, IFRS 9 and IFRS 7 are not normally applied to those contracts to buy or sell non-financial items that can be settled net if they were entered into and continue to be held for the purpose of the receipt or delivery of the non-financial item in accordance with the entity's expected purchase, sale or usage requirements (a 'normal' purchase or sale). *[IAS 32.8, IFRS 7.5, IFRS 9.2.4]*. However, an entity may in certain circumstances be able to designate such a contract at fair value through profit or loss (see 4.2.6 below). It should be noted that this is a two-part test, i.e. in order to qualify as a normal purchase or sale, the contract needs to both (a) have been entered into, and (b) continue to be held, for that purpose. Consequently, a reclassification of an instrument can be only one way. For example, if a contract that was originally entered into for the purpose of delivery ceases to be held for that purpose at a later date, it should subsequently be accounted for as a financial instrument under IFRS 9. Conversely, where an entity holds a contract that was not originally held for the purpose of delivery and was accounted for under IFRS 9, but subsequently its intentions change such that it is expected to be settled by delivery, the contract remains within the scope of IFRS 9. The IASB views the practice of settling net or taking delivery of the underlying and selling it within a short period after delivery as an indication that the contracts are not normal purchases or sales. Therefore, contracts to which (b) or (c) at 4.1 above apply cannot be subject to the normal purchase or sale exception. Other contracts that can be settled net are evaluated to determine whether this exception can actually apply. *[IAS 32.9, IFRS 9.2.6, BCZ2.18]*.

The implications of this requirement are considered further at 4.2.1 and 4.2.2 below.

The implementation guidance illustrates the application of the exception as follows: *[IFRS 9.A.1]*

Example 45.3: Determining whether a copper forward is within the scope of IFRS 9

Company XYZ enters into a fixed-price forward contract to purchase 1,000 kg of copper in accordance with its expected usage requirements. The contract permits XYZ to take physical delivery of the copper at the end of twelve months, or to pay or receive a net settlement in cash, based on the change in fair value of copper.

The contract is a derivative instrument because there is no initial net investment, the contract is based on the price of copper, and it is to be settled at a future date. However, if XYZ intends to settle the contract by taking delivery and has no history of settling similar contracts net in cash, or of taking delivery of the copper and selling it within a short period after delivery for the purpose of generating a profit from short-term fluctuations in price or dealer's margin, the contract is accounted for as an executory contract rather than as a derivative.

Sometimes a market design or process imposes a structure or intermediary that prevents the producer of a non-financial item from physically delivering it to the customer. For example, a gold miner may produce gold bars (dore) that are physically delivered to a mint for refining and, whilst remaining at the mint, the gold could be credited to either the producer's or a counterparty's 'gold account'. Where the producer enters into a contract for the sale of gold which is settled by allocating gold to the counterparty's gold account, this may constitute 'delivery' as that term is used in the standard. Accordingly, a contract that is expected to be settled in this way could potentially be considered a normal sale (although of course it would need to meet all the other requirements). However, if the gold is credited to the producer's account and the sale contract was settled net in cash, this would not constitute delivery. In these circumstances, treating the contract as a normal sale would, in effect, link a non-deliverable contract entered into with a customer with a transaction to buy or sell through an intermediary as a single synthetic arrangement, contrary to the general requirements on linking contracts discussed in Chapter 46 at 8.[12]

4.2.1 Net settlement of similar contracts

If the terms of a contract do not explicitly provide for net settlement but an entity has a practice of settling similar contracts net, that contract should be considered as capable of being settled net (see 4.1 above). Net settlement could be achieved either by entering into offsetting contracts with the original counterparty or by selling the contract before its maturity. In these circumstances the contract cannot be considered a normal sale or purchase and is accounted for in accordance with IFRS 9 (see 4.1 above). *[IAS 32.9, IFRS 9.2.4, BCZ2.18]*.

The standard contains no further guidance on what degree of past practice would be necessary to prevent an entity from treating similar contracts as own use. We do not believe that any net settlement automatically taints an entity's ability to apply the own use exception, for example where an entity is required to close out a number of contracts as a result of an exceptional disruption arising from external events at a production facility. However, judgement will always need to be applied based on the facts and circumstances of each individual case.

Read literally, the reference to 'similar contracts' could be particularly troublesome. For example, it is common for entities in, say, the energy sector to have a trading arm that is managed completely separately from their other operations. These trading operations commonly trade in contracts on non-financial assets, the terms of which are similar, if not identical, to those used by the entity's other operations for the purpose of physical supply. Accordingly, the standard might suggest that the normal purchase or sale exemption is unavailable to any entity that has a trading operation. However, we believe that a more appropriate interpretation is that contracts should be 'similar' as to their purpose within the business (e.g. for trading or for physical supply) not just as to their contractual terms.

4.2.2 Commodity broker-traders and similar entities

IFRS 9 contains no further guidance on what degree of net settlement (or trading) is necessary to make the normal sale or purchase exemption inapplicable, but in many cases it will be reasonably clear. For example, in our view, the presumption must be that contracts entered into by a commodity broker-trader that measures its inventories at fair value less costs to sell in accordance with IAS 2 – *Inventories* (see Chapter 22 at 2.3) falls within the scope of IFRS 9. However, there will be situations that are much less clear-cut, and the application of judgement will be necessary. Factors to consider in making this assessment might include:

- how the entity manages the business and intends to profit from the contract;
- whether value is added by linking parties which are normal buyers and sellers in the value chain;
- whether the entity takes price risk;
- how the contract is settled; and
- the entity's customer base.

Again, the reference in the standard to 'similar contracts' in this context may be troublesome for certain entities. However, as noted at 4.2.1 above, we believe contracts should be 'similar' as to their purpose within the business (e.g. for trading or for physical supply) not just as to their contractual terms.

4.2.3 Written options that can be settled net

The IASB does not believe that a written option to buy or sell a non-financial item that can be settled net can be regarded as being for the purpose of receipt or delivery in accordance with the entity's expected sale or usage requirements. Essentially, this is because the entity cannot control whether or not the purchase or sale will take place. Accordingly, IAS 32, IFRS 7 and IFRS 9 apply to written options that can be settled net according to the terms of the contract or where the underlying non-financial item is readily convertible to cash (see (a) and (d) at 4.1 above). *[IAS 32.10, IFRS 9.2.7, BCZ2.18]*.

Example 45.4: **Determining whether a put option on an office building is within the scope of IFRS 9**

Company XYZ owns an office building. It enters into a put option with an investor, which expires in five years and permits it to put the building to the investor for £150 million. The current value of the building is £175 million. The option, if exercised, may be settled through physical delivery or net cash, at XYZ's option.

XYZ's accounting depends on its intention and past practice for settlement. Although the contract meets the definition of a derivative, XYZ does not account for it as a derivative if it intends to settle the contract by delivering the building in the event of exercise and there is no past practice of settling net.

The investor, however, cannot conclude that the option was entered into to meet its expected purchase, sale, or usage requirements because it does not have the ability to require delivery. The contract may be settled net and is a written option. Regardless of past practices, its intention does not affect whether settlement is by delivery or in cash. Accordingly, the investor accounts for the contract as a derivative. As noted in Chapter 50 at 2.4, this will involve remeasuring the derivative to its fair value each reporting period with any associated gains and losses recognised in profit or loss.

However, if the contract were a forward contract rather than an option, required physical delivery and the investor had no past practice of settling net (either in cash or by way of taking delivery and subsequently selling within a short period), the contract would not be accounted for as a derivative. *[IFRS 9.A.2]*.

4.2.4 Electricity and similar 'end-user' contracts

There have been problems in determining whether or not IAS 32, IFRS 7 and IFRS 9 apply to contracts to sell non-financial items (for example electricity or natural gas) to 'end-users' such as retail customers. The non-financial items will often be considered readily convertible to cash (see 4.1 above), at least by the supplier. Accordingly, contracts to supply such items might be considered contracts that can be settled net.

Furthermore, end-user contracts often enable the customer to purchase as much of the non-financial item as needed at a given price to satisfy its usage requirements, i.e. the supplier does not have the contractual right to control whether or not the sale will take place. This might suggest that, from the perspective of the supplier, the contract is a written option with the consequence that it could not regard it as meeting the normal sale and purchase exemption (see 4.2.3 above).

However, many argued that this was not necessarily the case, particularly in the following circumstances:

- the non-financial item is an essential item for the customer;
- the customer does not have access to a market where the non-financial item can be resold;
- the non-financial item is not easily stored in any significant amounts by the customer; and
- the supplier is the sole provider of the non-financial item for a certain period of time.

In circumstances such as these, the apparent optionality within the contract is not exercisable by the retail customer in any economic sense. The customer will purchase volumes required whether the terms in the contract are advantageous or not and would not have the practical ability to sell any excess amounts purchased. Such a contract can have both a positive value and a negative value for the supplier when compared with market conditions and therefore fails to exhibit one of the key characteristics of an option, i.e. that it has only a positive value for the holder (the customer) and only a negative value for the writer (the supplier). In many respects the positive value stems from an intangible, rather than financial, aspect of the contract, being the likelihood that the customer will exercise the option. Accordingly, it was often argued that such contracts should not be considered written options (and therefore not within the scope of IFRS 9).

Even if contracts such as these are considered to be within the scope of IFRS 9, it is common for the supplier to have the ability to increase the price charged at relatively short notice. Also, the customer may be able to cancel the contract without penalty and switch to another supplier. Features such as these are likely to reduce any fair value that the contract can have.

Only a small number of energy suppliers appeared to regard these contracts as falling within the scope of IFRS 9. The Interpretations Committee noted that the guidance already explains what constitutes a written option, essentially confirming that in this context a written option arises where a supplier does not have the contractual right to control whether or not a sale will take place.[13]

The Interpretations Committee also noted that 'in many situations these contracts are not capable of net cash settlement', and therefore would not be within the scope of IFRS 9. No detailed explanation was provided of why the ability of the supplier to readily realise the non-financial item for cash does not enable it to settle the contract net (as that term is used in IFRS 9).[14] However, we understand the reason underlying the comment to be the inability of the counterparty to realise the non-financial item (and hence the contract) for cash. This establishes a useful principle that may be applied in similar situations, i.e. a contract is not capable of net settlement if the contract is an option and the option holder cannot readily realise the non-financial item for cash.

4.2.5 Other contracts containing volume flexibility

It is not uncommon for other sales contracts, such as those with large industrial customers, to contain volume flexibility features. For example, a supplier might enter into a contract requiring it to deliver, say, 100,000 units at a given price as well as giving the counterparty the option to purchase a further 20,000 units at the same price. The customer might well have access to markets for the non-financial item and, following the guidance of the Interpretations Committee, the supplier might consider such a contract to be within the scope of IFRS 9 as it contains a written option.

However, the supplier could split the contract into two separate components for accounting purposes: a forward contract to supply 100,000 units (which may qualify as a normal sale) and a written option to supply 20,000 units (which would not). Arguments put forward include:

- the parties could easily have entered into two separate contracts, a forward contract and a written option; and
- it is appropriate to analogise to the requirements for embedded derivatives and separate a written option from the normal forward sale or purchase contract because it is not closely related (see Chapter 46 at 5).

The Interpretations Committee was asked to consider the appropriate treatment of such contracts but in spite of noting significant diversity in practice the issue has not been addressed. In our view, entities may apply either of these interpretations as an accounting policy choice.

4.2.6 Fair value option

Own use contracts are accounted for as normal sales or purchase contracts (i.e. executory contracts), with the idea that any fair value change of the contract is not relevant given that the contract is used for the entity's own use. However, participants in several industries often enter into similar contracts both for own use and for trading purposes and manage all the contracts together with derivatives on a fair value basis (so as to manage the fair value risk to close to nil). In such a situation, own use accounting leads to an accounting mismatch, as the fair value change of the derivatives and the trading positions cannot be offset against fair value changes of the own use contracts.

To eliminate the accounting mismatch, an entity could apply hedge accounting by designating own use contracts as hedged items in a fair value hedge relationship. However, hedge accounting in these circumstances is administratively burdensome and often produces less meaningful results than fair value accounting. Furthermore, entities enter into large volumes of commodity contracts and, within the large volume of contracts, some positions may naturally offset each other. An entity would therefore typically hedge on a net basis. *[IFRS 9.BCZ2.24].*

Alternatively, IFRS 9 provides a 'fair value option' for own use contracts. At inception of a contract, an entity may make an irrevocable designation to measure an own use contract at fair value through profit or loss in spite of it being entered into for the purpose of the receipt or delivery of a non-financial item in accordance with the entity's expected purchase, sale or usage requirement. However, such designation is only allowed if it eliminates or significantly reduces an accounting mismatch that would otherwise arise from not recognising that contract because it is excluded from the scope of IFRS 9. *[IFRS 9.2.5].*

On transition to IFRS 9, entities can apply the fair value option on an 'all-or-nothing' basis for similar types of (already existing) own use contracts (see Chapter 53 at 12.2). *[IFRS 9.7.2.14A].*

References

1 Information for Observers (May 2007 IFRIC meeting), *Gaming Transactions*, IASB, May 2007, paras. 25 to 27 and *IFRIC Update*, July 2007. Whilst the IFRIC discussion was held in the context of IAS 39, the discussion also holds true under IFRS 9.

2 Information for Observers (November 2007 IFRIC Meeting), *Deposits on returnable containers (Agenda Paper 7B)*, IASB, November 2007, paras. 1 and 2. Whilst the IFRIC discussion was held in the context of IAS 39, the discussion also holds true under IFRS 9.

3 *IFRIC Update*, November 2007. Whilst the IFRIC discussion was held in the context of IAS 39, the discussion also holds true under IFRS 9.
4 *IFRIC Update*, May 2008. Whilst the IFRIC discussion was held in the context of IAS 39, the discussion also holds true under IFRS 9.
5 IFRIC D23, *Distributions of Non-cash Assets to Owners*, IASB, January 2008, paras. 9-11. Whilst the IFRIC discussion was held in the context of IAS 39, the discussion also holds true under IFRS 9.
6 *IFRIC Update*, January 2013. Whilst the IFRIC discussion was held in the context of IAS 39, a similar analysis would apply under IFRS 9.
7 *IASB Update*, June 2009.
8 Information for Observers (March 2009 IASB meeting), *IAS 39 Financial Instruments: Recognition and Measurement – Scope exemption for business combination contracts (IAS 39.2(g)) (Agenda Paper 10C)*, IASB, March 2009, paras. 13 and 15. Whilst the IFRIC discussion was held in the context of IAS 39, the discussion also holds true under IFRS 9.
9 Information for Observers (March 2009 IASB meeting), *IAS 39 Financial Instruments: Recognition and Measurement – Scope exemption for business combination contracts (IAS 39.2(g)) (Agenda Paper 10C)*, IASB, March 2009, paras. 9 and 10. Whilst the IFRIC discussion was held in the context of IAS 39, the discussion also holds true under IFRS 9.
10 *IFRIC Update*, March 2016.
11 *IFRIC Update*, November 2005.
12 *IFRIC Update*, August 2005. Whilst the IFRIC discussion was held in the context of IAS 39, the discussion also holds true under IFRS 9.
13 *IFRIC Update*, March 2007 and Information for Observers (January 2007 IFRIC meeting), *IAS 39 Financial Instruments: Recognition and Measurement – Written options in retail energy contracts (Agenda Paper 14(iv))*, IASB, January 2007, paras. 9 to 11. Whilst the IFRIC discussion was held in the context of IAS 39, the discussion also holds true under IFRS 9.
14 *IFRIC Update*, March 2007 and Information for Observers (January 2007 IFRIC meeting), *IAS 39 Financial Instruments: Recognition and Measurement – Written options in retail energy contracts (Agenda Paper 14(iv))*, IASB, January 2007, para. 15. Whilst the IFRIC discussion was held in the context of IAS 39, the discussion also holds true under IFRS 9.

Chapter 46 Financial instruments: Derivatives and embedded derivatives

1 INTRODUCTION 3619
2 DEFINITION OF A DERIVATIVE 3620
   2.1 Changes in value in response to changes in underlying 3620
      2.1.1 Notional amounts 3620
      2.1.2 Underlying variables 3621
      2.1.3 Non-financial variables specific to one party to the contract 3622
   2.2 Initial net investment 3624
   2.3 Future settlement 3626
3 EXAMPLES OF DERIVATIVES 3627
   3.1 Common derivatives 3627
   3.2 In-substance derivatives 3628
   3.3 Regular way contracts 3628
4 EMBEDDED DERIVATIVES 3629
5 EMBEDDED DERIVATIVES: THE MEANING OF 'CLOSELY RELATED' 3630
   5.1 Financial instrument hosts 3630
      5.1.1 Foreign currency monetary items 3631
      5.1.2 Interest rate indices 3631
      5.1.3 Fallback provisions relating to interest rate benchmark reform 3633
      5.1.4 Term extension and similar call, put and prepayment options in debt instruments 3633
      5.1.5 Interest rate floors and caps 3637
      5.1.6 Inflation-linked debt instruments 3638

	5.1.7	Commodity- and equity-linked interest and principal payments	3639
	5.1.8	Credit-linked notes	3640
	5.1.9	Instruments with an equity kicker	3641
	5.1.10	Puttable instruments	3641
5.2	Contracts for the sale of goods or services		3642
	5.2.1	Foreign currency derivatives	3642
		5.2.1.A Functional currency of counterparty	3642
		5.2.1.B Routinely denominated in commercial transactions	3643
		5.2.1.C Commonly used currencies	3643
		5.2.1.D Examples and other practical issues	3645
	5.2.2	Inputs, ingredients, substitutes and other proxy pricing mechanisms	3646
	5.2.3	Inflation-linked features	3647
	5.2.4	Floors and caps	3647
	5.2.5	Fund performance fees	3647
5.3	Leases		3648
	5.3.1	Foreign currency derivatives	3648
	5.3.2	Inflation-linked features	3648
	5.3.3	Contingent rentals based on related sales	3648
	5.3.4	Contingent rentals based on variable interest rates	3648
5.4	Insurance contracts		3648

6 IDENTIFYING THE TERMS OF EMBEDDED DERIVATIVES AND HOST CONTRACTS ... 3649

    6.1 Embedded non-option derivatives ... 3649

    6.2 Embedded option-based derivative ... 3650

    6.3 Multiple embedded derivatives ... 3651

7 REASSESSMENT OF EMBEDDED DERIVATIVES ... 3651

    7.1 Acquisition of contracts ... 3652

    7.2 Business combinations ... 3652

    7.3 Remeasurement issues arising from reassessment ... 3653

8 LINKED AND SEPARATE TRANSACTIONS AND 'SYNTHETIC' INSTRUMENTS ... 3653

List of examples

Example 46.1: Notional amount of a derivative ... 3620

Example 46.2: Derivative containing no notional amount ... 3621

Example 46.3:	Derivative containing two underlyings	3621
Example 46.4:	Borrowing with coupons linked to revenue	3623
Example 46.5:	Currency swap – initial exchange of principal	3625
Example 46.6:	Prepaid interest rate swap (prepaid fixed leg)	3625
Example 46.7:	Prepaid interest rate swap (prepaid floating leg)	3625
Example 46.8:	Prepaid forward purchase of shares	3626
Example 46.9:	Interest rate swap – gross or net settlement	3626
Example 46.10:	In-substance derivative – offsetting loans	3628
Example 46.11:	Leveraged inverse floater – not recovering substantially all of the initial investment	3632
Example 46.12:	Leveraged inverse floater – 'double-double test'	3632
Example 46.13:	Embedded prepayment option	3634
Example 46.14:	Extension and prepayment options	3635
Example 46.15:	Bond linked to a commodity price	3639
Example 46.16:	Equity kicker	3641
Example 46.17:	Oil contract denominated in Swiss francs	3645
Example 46.18:	Oil contract, denominated in US dollars and containing a leveraged foreign exchange payment	3645
Example 46.19:	Separation of embedded derivative from a lease	3650
Example 46.20:	Investment in a synthetic fixed-rate debt	3653

Chapter 46   Financial instruments: Derivatives and embedded derivatives

1 INTRODUCTION

Under IFRS 9 – *Financial Instruments*, the question of whether an instrument is a derivative or not is an important one for accounting purposes. Derivatives are normally recorded in the statement of financial position at fair value with any changes in value reported in profit or loss (see Chapter 50 at 2), although there are some exceptions, e.g. derivatives that are designated in certain effective hedge relationships.

For many financial instruments, it will be reasonably clear whether or not they are derivatives, but there will be more marginal cases. Accordingly, the term derivative is formally defined within IFRS 9, and this definition, together with examples of derivatives, is considered further at 2 and 3 below.

IFRS 9 also contains the concept of an embedded derivative which is described as a component of a hybrid or combined instrument that also includes a non-derivative host contract. In certain circumstances embedded derivatives are required to be accounted for separately as if they were freestanding derivatives. The IASB introduced this concept because it believes that entities should not be able to circumvent the accounting requirements for derivatives merely by embedding a derivative in a non-derivative financial instrument or other non-financial contract, e.g. by placing a commodity forward in a debt instrument. In other words, it is chiefly an anti-abuse measure designed to enforce 'derivative accounting' on those derivatives that are 'hidden' in other contracts. *[IFRS 9.BCZ4.92]*.

Embedded derivatives, and the situations in which they are required to be accounted for separately, are considered in more detail at 4 to 7 below. Under IFRS 9 the concept of embedded derivatives applies to financial liabilities and non-financial items only. Embedded derivatives are not separated from financial assets within the scope of IFRS 9 and the requirements of IFRS 9 are applied to the hybrid contract as a whole.

In addition to assessing when a financial instrument or other contract should be accounted for as if it were two contracts, we consider at 8 below situations when two financial instruments should be accounted for as if they were one, together with the question of linkage (for financial reporting purposes) of transactions more generally.

This chapter does not deal with valuation of derivative financial instruments. Chapter 14 outlines the requirements of IFRS 13 – *Fair Value Measurement*, a standard that defines fair value and provides principles-based guidance on how to measure fair value under IFRS. Additional guidance affecting the valuation of derivatives can be found in Chapter 53 at 3 and 6.

This chapter refers to a number of discussions by the IASB and the Interpretations Committee on topics relevant to derivatives and embedded derivatives. A number of these discussions were held in the context of IAS 39 – *Financial Instruments: Recognition and Measurement*, prior to the effective date of IFRS 9 on 1 January 2018. Those discussions which remain relevant to IFRS 9 have been retained in this chapter.

2 DEFINITION OF A DERIVATIVE

A derivative is a financial instrument or other contract within the scope of IFRS 9 (see Chapter 45 at 2 and 3) with all the following characteristics:

(a) its value changes in response to the change in a specified interest rate, financial instrument price, commodity price, foreign exchange rate, index of prices or rates, credit rating or credit index, or other variable, provided in the case of a non-financial variable that the variable is not specific to a party to the contract (sometimes called the 'underlying');

(b) it requires no initial net investment, or an initial net investment that is smaller than would be required for other types of contracts that would be expected to have a similar response to changes in market factors; and

(c) it is settled at a future date. *[IFRS 9 Appendix A]*.

These three defining characteristics are considered further below.

2.1 Changes in value in response to changes in underlying

2.1.1 Notional amounts

A derivative usually has a notional amount, such as an amount of currency, number of shares or units of weight or volume, but does not require the holder or writer to invest or receive the notional amount at inception.

Example 46.1: Notional amount of a derivative

Company XYZ, whose functional currency is the US dollar, has placed an order with a company in France for delivery in six months' time. The price to be paid in six months' time is €2,000,000. To hedge the exposure to currency risk, Company XYZ enters into a contract with an investment bank to convert US dollars to euros at a fixed exchange rate. The contract requires the investment bank to remit €2,000,000 in exchange for US dollars at a fixed exchange rate of 1.65 (US$3,300,000). The notional amount of the contract in euro term is €2,000,000.

However, while a derivative usually has a notional amount, this is not always the case: a derivative could require a fixed payment or payment of an amount that can change (but not proportionally with a change in the underlying) as a result of some future event that is unrelated to a notional amount. For example, a contract that requires a fixed payment of €1,000 if six-month LIBOR increases by 100 basis points is a derivative, even though a notional amount is not specified (at least not in the conventional sense). [IFRS 9.BA.1]. A further example is shown below.

Example 46.2:   Derivative containing no notional amount

Company XYZ enters into a contract that requires payment of $1,000 if Company ABC's share price increases by $5 or more during a six-month period; Company XYZ will receive $1,000 if the share price decreases by $5 or more during the same six-month period; no payment will be made if the price swing is less than $5 up or down.

The settlement amount changes with an underlying, Company ABC's share price, although there is no notional amount to determine the settlement amount. Instead, there is a payment provision that is based on changes in the underlying. Provided all the other characteristics of a derivative are present, which they are in this case, such an instrument is a derivative.[1]

2.1.2   Underlying variables

It follows from the definition (see 2 above) that a derivative will always have at least one underlying variable. The following underlying variables are referred to in the standard, but this is not an exhaustive list (we have provided an example for each of the underlyings):

- specified interest rate (e.g. LIBOR);
- financial instrument price (e.g. the share price of an entity);
- commodity price (e.g. the price of a barrel of oil);
- foreign exchange rate (e.g. the £/$ spot rate);
- index of prices or rates (e.g. Consumer Price Index);
- credit rating (e.g. Fitch);
- credit index (e.g. AAA rated corporate bond index); and
- non-financial variable (e.g. index of earthquake losses or of temperatures).

A contract to receive a royalty, often in exchange for the use of certain property that is not exchange-traded, where the payment is based on the volume of related sales or service revenues and accounted for under IFRS 15 – *Revenue from Contracts with Customers* (see Chapter 31 at 2.5) is not accounted for as a derivative.

Derivatives that are based on sales volume are not necessarily excluded from the scope of IFRS 9, especially where there is another (financial) underlying, as set out in the next example.

Example 46.3:   Derivative containing two underlyings

Company XYZ, whose functional currency is the US dollar, sells products in France denominated in euros. Company XYZ enters into a contract with an investment bank to convert euros to US dollars at a fixed exchange rate. The contract requires Company XYZ to remit euros based on its sales volume in France in exchange for US dollars at a fixed exchange rate of 1.00.

The contract has two underlying variables, the foreign exchange rate and the volume of sales, no initial net investment, and a payment provision. Therefore, as the implementation guidance explains, it is a derivative. [IFRS 9.IG B.8].

However, contracts that are linked to variables that might be considered non-financial, such as an entity's revenue, can sometimes cause particular interpretative problems as discussed below.

2.1.3 Non-financial variables specific to one party to the contract

The definition of a derivative (see 2 above) refers to underlyings that are non-financial variables not specific to one party to the contract. This reference was introduced by IFRS 4 – *Insurance Contracts* – to help determine whether or not a financial instrument is an insurance contract (see Chapter 45 at 3.3). An insurance contract is likely to contain such an underlying, for example the occurrence or non-occurrence of a fire that damages or destroys an asset of a party to the contract. For periods beginning on or after 1 January 2023, IFRS 4 will be replaced by IFRS 17 – *Insurance Contracts*. Non-financial variables that are not specific to one party to the contract might include an index of earthquake losses in a particular region or an index of temperatures in a particular city. *[IFRS 9.BA.5]*. Those based on climatic variables are sometimes referred to as 'weather derivatives'. *[IFRS 9.B2.1]*.

A change in the fair value of a non-financial asset is specific to the owner if the fair value reflects not only changes in market prices for such assets (a financial variable) but also the condition of the specific non-financial asset held (a non-financial variable). For example, if a guarantee of the residual value of a specific car exposes the guarantor to the risk of changes in the car's physical condition, the change in that residual value is specific to the owner of the car, and so would not be a derivative. *[IFRS 9.BA.5]*.

Contracts with non-financial variables arise in the gaming industry where a gaming institution takes a position against a customer (rather than providing services to manage the organisation of games between two or more parties). For example, a customer will pay a stake to a bookmaker such that the bookmaker is contractually obliged to pay the customer a specified amount if the bet is a winning one, e.g. if the specified horse wins a given race. The underlying variable (the outcome of the race) is clearly non-financial in nature, but it is unlikely to be specific to either party to the contract. Accordingly, such contracts will typically be derivative financial instruments.[2]

It is not clear whether the reference to non-financial variables specific to one party to the contract means that all instruments with such an underlying would fail to meet the definition of a derivative or only those contracts that are insurance contracts, for which the reference was originally introduced. Until the standard is clarified, in our view, a legitimate case can be made for either view.

The Interpretations Committee considered this issue in the context of contracts indexed to an entity's revenue or EBITDA and initially came to a tentative conclusion that the exclusion was not restricted to insurance contracts.[3] However, that conclusion was later withdrawn and the Interpretations Committee referred the issue to the IASB, recommending that the standard be amended to limit the exclusion to insurance contracts.[4]

The IASB confirmed that it had intended the exclusion to apply only to contracts that are within the scope of IFRS 4[5] however, the IASB eventually decided not to proceed on this issue and the existing definition of a derivative (see 2 above) was incorporated into IFRS 9 without alteration, leaving the issue unaddressed.

A further issue arises in that it is not always clear whether a variable is non-financial. This is illustrated in the following example (in this case the underlying is associated with an embedded feature which might or might not meet the definition of a derivative).

Example 46.4: Borrowing with coupons linked to revenue

Company F, a manufacturing entity, issues a debt instrument for its par value of €10m. It is repayable in ten years' time at par and an annual coupon is payable that comprises two elements: a fixed amount of 2.5% of the par value and a variable amount equating to 0.01% of Company F's annual revenues. Company F does not designate the instrument at fair value through profit or loss.

It is assumed that if Company F had instead issued a more conventional fixed rate borrowing for the same amount with the same maturity it would have been required to pay an annual coupon of 4% of the par value. Therefore, on the face of it, the debt contains an embedded feature that represents a swap with an initial fair value of zero whereby Company F receives a fixed amount annually (1.5% of €10m) and pays a variable amount annually (0.01% of its revenues). The question is now whether this feature represents an embedded derivative that should be separated from the host contact by Company F and accounted for separately – see embedded derivative guidance at 4 below.

It is very hard to argue that the economic characteristics and risks of this embedded feature are closely related to the debt instrument and the variable (Company F's revenue) is clearly specific to Company F. The key issue is whether Company F's revenue is a financial or non-financial variable and therefore whether the embedded feature meets the definition of a derivative.

It is not only contracts with payments based on revenue that can cause such problems. Some contracts may require payments based on other measures taken or derived from an entity's financial statements such as EBITDA. The Interpretations Committee considered this matter in July 2006[6] and in January 2007 referred the matter to the IASB.[7] However, the IASB eventually decided not to deal with this issue.

Whilst it is tempting to regard an entity's revenue and EBITDA as financial variables, they are driven by a number of different factors many of which are clearly non-financial in nature, for example the general business risks faced by the entity. In addition, many of the drivers of EBITDA and revenue will be specific to that business, for example the location of the business, the nature of its goods or services and managements actions.

One company that has faced this issue in practice is Groupe Renault. This company has issued liabilities on which coupons are linked to revenue and net profit. As can be seen in the following extract, Groupe Renault states that its revenue-linked and net profit-linked features are not considered embedded derivatives and the liabilities are therefore carried at amortised cost. The extract below is from Groupe Renault's 2018 accounts.

> Extract 46.1: Groupe Renault (2018)
>
> **4.2.6 NOTES TO THE CONSOLIDATED FINANCIAL STATEMENT** [extract]
> **4.2.6.2 – ACCOUNTING POLICIES AND SCOPE OF CONSOLIDATION** [extract]
> Note 2 – Accounting policies [extract]
> W – Financial liabilities of the Automotive segments and sales financing debts [extract]
>
> **Redeemable shares** [extract]
>
> Redeemable shares are listed subordinated debt instruments that earn a variable return indexed on consolidated revenues.
>
> Redeemable shares are carried at amortized cost, determined by discounting forecast coupons using the effective interest rate on borrowings.
>
> It was considered that the contractual minimum return on these shares, i.e. 9%, provided the best estimate of the effective interest rate at their issue date (1983 and 1984). The variable portion is now included in estimation of the effective interest rate, with regular reassessment of the amortized cost recognized in financial income and expenses.
>
> **4.2.6.5 FINANCIAL ASSETS AND LIABILITIES, FAIR VALUE AND MANAGEMENT OF FINANCIAL RISKS** [extract]
>
> Note 23 – Financial liabilities and sales financing debts [extract]
> **Changes in redeemable shares of the Automotive (excluding AVTOVAZ) segment** [extract]
>
> The redeemable shares issued in October 1983 and April 1984 by Renault SA are subordinated perpetual shares listed on the Paris Stock Exchange. They earn a minimum annual return of 9% comprising a 6.75% fixed portion and a variable portion that depends on consolidated revenues and is calculated based on identical Group structure and methods. [...]

In 2009 the Interpretations Committee was asked to consider the accounting treatment for an instrument that contains participation rights by which the instrument holder shares in the net income and losses of the issuer. However, the Interpretations Committee considered the issue without reconsidering the assumptions described in the request, including one that the financial liability did not contain any embedded derivatives.[8] In other words, the Interpretations Committee implicitly accepted that such a feature need not be separated but did not indicate that separation was necessarily prohibited.

In practice, we believe that an entity may make an accounting policy choice as to whether the entity's revenue, EBITDA or other measures taken or derived from the entity's financial statements, are financial or non-financial variables. Once an entity elects a particular policy, it must consistently apply that approach to all similar transactions.

2.2 Initial net investment

The second key characteristic of a derivative is that it has no initial net investment, or one that is smaller than would be required for other types of contracts that would be expected to have a similar response to changes in market factors (see 2 above). *[IFRS 9 Appendix A]*.

An option contract meets the definition because the premium is less than the investment that would be required to obtain the underlying financial instrument to which the option is linked. *[IFRS 9.BA.3]*.

Financial instruments: Derivatives and embedded derivatives 3625

The implementation guidance to IAS 39 suggested that the purchase of a deeply in the money call option would fail to satisfy the original 'little net investment' test if the premium paid was equal or close to the amount required to invest in the underlying instrument. However, the implementation guidance on which Example 46.8 below is based explains that a contract is not a derivative if the initial net investment approximates the amount that an entity otherwise would be required to invest. *[IAS 39.IG B.9, IFRS 9.IG B.9]*.

Currency swaps sometimes require an exchange of different currencies of equal value at inception. This does not mean that they would not meet the definition of a derivative, i.e. no initial net investment or an initial investment that is smaller than would be required for other types of contracts that would be expected to have a similar response to changes in market factors, as the following example demonstrates.

Example 46.5: Currency swap – initial exchange of principal

Company A and Company B enter into a five year fixed-for-fixed currency swap on euros and US dollars. The current spot exchange rate is €1 = US$1. The five year interest rate in the US is 8%, while the five year interest rate in Europe is 6%. On initiation of the swap, Company A pays €2,000 to Company B, which in return pays US$2,000 to Company A. During the swap's life, Company A and Company B make periodic interest payments to each other without netting. Company B pays 6% per year on the €2,000 it has received (€120 per year), while Company A pays 8% per year on the US$2,000 it has received (US$160 per year). On termination of the swap, the two parties again exchange the original principal amounts.

The currency swap is a derivative financial instrument since the contract involves a zero initial net investment (an exchange of one currency for another of equal fair value), it has an underlying, and it will be settled at a future date. *[IFRS 9.BA.3]*.

The following examples illustrate how to assess the initial net investment characteristic in various prepaid derivatives – these can provide guidance when assessing whether what appears to be a non-derivative instrument is actually a derivative.

Example 46.6: Prepaid interest rate swap (prepaid fixed leg)

Company S enters into a €1,000 notional amount five year pay-fixed, receive-variable interest rate swap. The interest rate of the variable part of the swap resets on a quarterly basis to three month LIBOR. The interest rate of the fixed part of the swap is 10% per annum. At inception of the swap Company S prepays its fixed obligation of €500 (€1,000 × 10% × 5 years), discounted using market interest rates, while retaining the right to receive the LIBOR-based interest payments on the €1,000 over the life of the swap.

The initial net investment in the swap is significantly less than the notional amount on which the variable payments under the variable leg will be calculated and therefore requires an initial net investment that is smaller than would be required for other types of contracts that would be expected to have a similar response to changes in market conditions, such as a variable rate bond. It therefore fulfils the 'no initial net investment or an initial investment that is smaller than would be required for other types of contracts that would be expected to have similar response to change in market factors' criterion. Even though Company S has no future performance obligation, the ultimate settlement of the contract is at a future date and its value changes in response to changes in LIBOR. Accordingly, it is a derivative. *[IFRS 9.IG B.4]*.

Example 46.7: Prepaid interest rate swap (prepaid floating leg)

Instead of the transactions in Example 46.6, Company S enters into a €1,000 notional amount five year pay-variable, receive-fixed interest rate swap. The variable leg of the swap resets on a quarterly basis to three month LIBOR. The fixed interest payments under the swap are calculated as 10% of the notional amount, i.e. €100 per year. By agreement with the counterparty, Company S prepays and discharges its obligation under the variable leg of the swap at inception by paying a fixed amount determined according to current market rates, while retaining the right to receive the fixed interest payments of €100 per year.

The cash inflows under the contract are equivalent to those of a financial instrument with a fixed annuity stream since Company S knows it will receive €100 per year over the life of the swap. Therefore, all else being equal, the initial investment in the contract should equal that of other financial instruments consisting of fixed annuities. Thus, the initial net investment in the pay-variable, receive-fixed interest rate swap is equal to the investment required in a non-derivative contract that has a similar response to changes in market conditions. For this reason, the instrument does not exhibit characteristic 'no initial net investment or an initial investment that is smaller than would be required for other types of contracts that would be expected to have similar response to changes in market factors' requirement and is therefore not a derivative. *[IFRS 9.IG B.5]*.

The conclusions in Examples 46.6 and 46.7 above are fundamentally different for what, on the face of it, appear to be very similar transactions. The key difference is that in Example 46.7 all possible cash flow variances are eliminated and, consequently, the resulting cash flows exhibit the characteristics of a simple non-derivative instrument, i.e. an amortising loan.

Example 46.8: Prepaid forward purchase of shares

Company S also enters into a forward contract to purchase 100 shares in Company T in one year. The current share price is €50 per share and the one year forward price €55. Company S is required to prepay the forward contract at inception with a €5,000 payment.

The initial investment in the forward contract of €5,000 is less than the notional amount applied to the underlying, 100 shares at the forward price of €55 per share, i.e. €5,500. However, the initial net investment approximates the investment that would be required for other types of contracts that would be expected to have a similar response to changes in market factors because Company T's shares could be purchased at inception for the same price of €50. Accordingly, the prepaid forward does not exhibit characteristic 'no initial net investment or an initial investment that is smaller than would be required for other types of contracts that would be expected to have similar response to changes in market factors' criterion and is therefore not a derivative. *[IFRS 9.IG B.9]*.

Many derivative instruments, such as futures contracts and exchange traded written options, require margin payments. The implementation guidance explains that a margin payment is not part of the initial net investment in a derivative, but is a form of collateral for the counterparty or clearing-house and may take the form of cash, securities, or other specified assets, typically liquid assets. Consequently, they are separate assets that are accounted for separately. *[IFRS 9.IG B.10]*.

However, while accounted for separately, the margin call and the derivative would be presented net in the statement of financial position if the offsetting requirements of IAS 32 – *Financial Instruments: Presentation* – are met (see Chapter 54 at 7.4.1). In some jurisdictions, depending on the precise terms of the related contracts, margin payments may actually represent a partial settlement of a derivative.

2.3 Future settlement

The third characteristic is that settlement takes place at a future date. Sometimes, a contract will require gross cash settlement. However, as illustrated in the next example, it makes no difference whether the future settlements are gross or net.

Example 46.9: Interest rate swap – gross or net settlement

Company ABC is considering entering into an interest rate swap with a counterparty, Company XYZ. The proposed terms are that Company ABC pays a fixed rate of 8% and receives a variable amount based on three month LIBOR, reset on a quarterly basis; the fixed and variable amounts are determined based on a €1,000 notional amount; Company ABC and Company XYZ do not exchange the notional amount and

Company ABC pays or receives a net cash amount each quarter based on the difference between 8% and three month LIBOR. Alternatively, settlement may be on a gross basis.

The contract meets the definition of a derivative regardless of whether there is net or gross settlement because its value changes in response to changes in an underlying variable (LIBOR), there is no initial net investment and settlements occur at future dates – it makes no difference whether Company ABC and Company XYZ actually make the interest payments to each other (gross settlement) or settle on a net basis. *[IFRS 9.IG B.3]*.

The definition of a derivative also includes contracts that are settled gross by delivery of the underlying item, e.g. a forward contract to purchase a fixed rate debt instrument. An entity may have a contract to buy or sell a non-financial item that can be settled net, e.g. a contract to buy or sell a commodity at a fixed price at a future date; if that contract is within the scope of IFRS 9 (see Chapter 45 at 4), then the question of whether or not it meets the definition of a derivative will be assessed in the same way as for a financial instrument that may be settled gross. *[IFRS 9.BA.2]*.

Expiry of an option at its maturity is a form of settlement even though there is no additional exchange of consideration. Therefore, even if an option is not expected to be exercised, e.g. because it is significantly 'out of the money', it can still be a derivative. *[IFRS 9.IG B.7]*. Such an option will have some value, albeit small, because it still offers the opportunity for gain if it becomes 'in the money' before expiry even if such a possibility is remote – the more remote the possibility, the lower its value.

3 EXAMPLES OF DERIVATIVES

3.1 Common derivatives

The following table provides examples of contracts that normally qualify as derivatives. The list is not exhaustive – any contract that has an underlying may be a derivative. Moreover, as set out in Chapter 45 at 3, even if an instrument meets the definition of a derivative, it may not fall within the scope of IFRS 9.

Type of contract	*Main underlying variable*
Interest rate swap	Interest rates
Currency swap (foreign exchange swap)	Currency rates
Commodity swap	Commodity prices
Equity swap	Equity prices (equity of another entity)
Credit swap	Credit rating, credit index, or credit price
Total return swap	Total fair value of the reference asset and interest rates
Purchased or written bond option (call or put)	Interest rates
Purchased or written currency option (call or put)	Currency rates
Purchased or written commodity option (call or put)	Commodity prices
Purchased or written stock option (call or put)	Equity prices (equity of another entity)

Type of contract	Main underlying variable
Interest rate futures linked to government debt (treasury futures)	Interest rates
Currency futures	Currency rates
Commodity futures	Commodity prices
Interest rate forward linked to government debt (treasury forward)	Interest rates
Currency forward	Currency rates
Commodity forward	Commodity prices
Equity forward	Equity prices (equity of another entity) *[IFRS 9.B2]*

3.2 In-substance derivatives

The implementation guidance explains that the accounting should follow the substance of arrangements. In particular, non-derivative transactions should be aggregated and treated as a derivative when, in substance, the transactions result in a derivative. Indicators of this would include:

- they are entered into at the same time and in contemplation of one another;
- they have the same counterparty;
- they relate to the same risk; and
- there is no apparent economic need or substantive business purpose for structuring the transactions separately that could not also have been accomplished in a single transaction. *[IFRS 9.IG B.6]*.

The application of this guidance is illustrated in the following example.

Example 46.10: In-substance derivative – offsetting loans

Company A makes a five year fixed rate loan to Company B, while at the same time Company B makes a five year variable rate loan for the same amount to Company A. There are no transfers of principal at inception of the two loans, since Company A and Company B have a netting agreement.

The combined contractual effect of the loans is the equivalent of an interest rate swap arrangement, i.e. there is an underlying variable, no initial net investment, and future settlement. This meets the definition of a derivative.

This would be the case even if there was no netting agreement, because the definition of a derivative instrument does not require net settlement (see Example 46.9 at 2.3 above). *[IFRS 9.IG B.6]*.

The analysis above would be equally applicable if the loans were in different currencies – such an arrangement could synthesise a cross-currency interest rate swap and should be accounted for as a derivative if that is its substance.

3.3 Regular way contracts

A regular way purchase or sale is a purchase or sale of a financial asset under a contract whose terms require delivery of the asset within the time frame established generally by regulation or convention in the marketplace concerned. *[IFRS 9 Appendix A]*.

Such contracts give rise to a fixed price commitment between trade date and settlement date that meets the definition of a derivative. However, because of the short duration of the commitments, they are not accounted for as derivatives but in accordance with special accounting rules. These requirements are discussed in Chapter 49 at 2.2. *[IFRS 9.BA.4]*.

4 EMBEDDED DERIVATIVES

An embedded derivative is a component of a hybrid or combined instrument that also includes a non-derivative host contract; it has the effect that some of the cash flows of the combined instrument vary in a similar way to a stand-alone derivative. In other words, it causes some or all of the cash flows, that otherwise would be required by the contract, to be modified according to a specified interest rate, financial instrument price, commodity price, foreign exchange rate, index of prices or rates, credit rating or credit index, or other underlying variable (provided in the case of a non-financial variable that the variable is not specific to a party to the contract). *[IFRS 9.4.3.1]*.

Common examples of contracts that can contain embedded derivatives include non-derivative financial instruments (especially debt instruments), leases, insurance contracts as well as contracts for the supply of goods or services. In fact, they may occur in all sorts of unsuspected locations.

Under IFRS 9 the concept of embedded derivatives applies to only financial liabilities and non-financial items. Embedded derivatives are not separated from financial assets within the scope of IFRS 9 and the requirements of IFRS 9 are applied to the hybrid contract as a whole. *[IFRS 9.4.3.2]*.

Normal sale or purchase contracts (see Chapter 45 at 4) can also contain embedded derivatives. This is an important difference from US GAAP, under which a contract for the sale or purchase of a non-financial item, that can be settled net, cannot be treated as a normal sale or purchase at all if it contains an embedded pricing feature, that is not clearly and closely related to the host contract – instead the whole contract would be accounted for as a derivative.

In the basis for conclusions to IFRS 9, the IASB asserts that, in principle, all embedded derivatives that are not measured at fair value with gains and losses recognised in profit or loss ought to be accounted for separately, but explains that, as a practical expedient, they should not be where they are regarded as 'closely related' to their host contracts. In those cases, it is believed less likely that the derivative was embedded to achieve a desired accounting result. *[IFRS 9.BCZ4.92]*.

Accordingly, only where all of the following conditions are met should an embedded derivative be separated from the host contract and accounted for separately:

(a) the economic characteristics and risks of the embedded derivative are not closely related to the economic characteristics and risks of the host contract;

(b) a separate instrument with the same terms as the embedded derivative would meet the definition of a derivative; and

(c) the hybrid (combined) instrument is not measured at fair value with changes in fair value recognised in profit or loss. *[IFRS 9.4.3.3]*.

If any of these conditions are not met, the embedded derivative should not be accounted for separately, *[IFRS 9.4.3.3, IFRS 9.B4.3.8]*, i.e. an entity is prohibited from separating an embedded derivative that is closely related to its host contract. The process is similar, although not identical, to that applied when separating the equity element of a compound instrument by the issuer under IAS 32 (see Chapter 47 at 6). The assessment of the closely related criterion should be made when the entity first becomes a party to a contract or in other words, on initial recognition of the contract (see 7 below). *[IFRS 9.B4.3.11]*.

The accounting treatment for a separated embedded derivative is the same as for a standalone derivative. Such an instrument (actually, in this case, a component of an instrument) will normally be recorded in the statement of financial position at fair value with all changes in value being recognised in profit or loss (see 1 above, Chapter 50 at 2), although there are some exceptions, e.g. embedded derivatives may be designated as a hedging instrument in an effective hedge relationship in the same way as standalone derivatives (see Chapter 53 at 3.2.3).

A derivative that is attached to a financial instrument but is contractually transferable independently of that instrument, or has a different counterparty from that instrument, is not an embedded derivative, but a separate financial instrument. *[IFRS 9.4.3.1]*.

Where the embedded derivative's fair value cannot be determined reliably on the basis of its terms and conditions, it may be determined indirectly as the difference between the hybrid (combined) instrument and the host instrument, if their fair values can be determined. *[IFRS 9.4.3.7]*. If an entity is unable to measure an embedded derivative that is required to be separated from its host, either on acquisition or subsequently, the entire contract is designated at fair value through profit or loss. *[IFRS 9.4.3.6]*.

5 EMBEDDED DERIVATIVES: THE MEANING OF 'CLOSELY RELATED'

The standard does not define what is meant by 'closely related'. Instead, it illustrates what was intended by providing a series of situations where the embedded derivative is, or is not, regarded as closely related to the host. Making this determination can prove very challenging, not least because the illustrations do not always seem to be consistent with each other. This guidance is considered in the remainder of this subsection.

5.1 Financial instrument hosts

Where a host contract has no stated or predetermined maturity and represents a residual interest in the net assets of an entity, its economic characteristics and risks are those of an equity instrument. From the issuer's perspective a hybrid instrument which meets the conditions for classification as equity under IAS 32 (see Chapter 47) is excluded from the scope of IFRS 9.

More commonly, if the host is not an equity instrument and meets the definition of a financial instrument, then its economic characteristics and risks are those of a debt instrument. *[IFRS 9.B4.3.2]*. From the issuer's perspective the application of these principles to debt hosts is considered at 5.1.1 to 5.1.9 below and to instruments that may be debt or equity hosts are considered at 5.1.10 below.

The application of these principles are not relevant to the holder of debt or equity instruments as embedded derivatives are not separated from financial assets within the scope of IFRS 9 and the requirements of IFRS 9 are applied to the hybrid contract as a whole. *[IFRS 9.4.3.2].*

5.1.1 Foreign currency monetary items

A monetary item denominated in a currency other than an entity's functional currency is accounted for under IAS 21 – *The Effects of Changes in Foreign Exchange Rates* – with foreign currency gains and losses recognised in profit or loss. The embedded foreign currency derivative is considered closely related to the debt host and is not separated. In other words, it would not be considered a functional currency monetary item and a foreign currency forward contract. This also applies where the embedded derivative in a host debt instrument provides a stream of either principal or interest payments denominated in a foreign currency (e.g. a dual currency bond). *[IFRS 9.B4.3.8(c)].*

5.1.2 Interest rate indices

Many debt instruments contain embedded interest rate indices that can change the amount of interest that would otherwise be paid or received. One of the simplest examples would be a floating rate loan whereby interest is paid quarterly based on three month LIBOR. More complex examples might include the following:

- inverse floater – coupons are paid at a fixed rate minus LIBOR;
- levered inverse floater – as above but a multiplier greater than 1.0 is applied to the resulting coupon;
- delevered floater – coupons lag overall movements in a specified rate, e.g. coupons equal a proportion of the ten year constant maturity treasuries rate plus a fixed premium; or
- range floater – interest is paid at a fixed rate but only for each day in a given period that LIBOR is within a stated range.

In such cases the embedded derivative is closely related to the host debt instrument unless:

(a) the combined instrument can be settled in such a way that the holder would not recover substantially all of its recognised investment; or

(b) the embedded derivative could at least double the holder's initial rate of return on the host contract and could result in a rate of return that is at least twice what the market return would be for a contract with the same terms as the host contract (often referred to as the 'double-double test'). *[IFRS 9.B4.3.8(a)].*

If a holder is permitted, but not required, to settle the combined instrument in a manner such that it does not recover substantially all of its recognised investment, e.g. puttable debt, condition (a) is not satisfied and the embedded derivative is not separated. *[IFRS 9.IG C.10].* The standard does not define 'substantially all' and therefore judgement will need to be applied, considering all relevant facts and circumstances.

To meet condition (b), the embedded derivative must be able to double the initial return and result in a rate of return that is at least twice what would be expected for a similar contract at the time it takes effect. If it meets only one part of this condition, but not the other, the derivative is regarded as closely related to the host. Due to the requirement 'could result in a rate of return that is at least twice what the market return would be for a contract with the same terms as the host contract', the derivative embedded in a simple variable rate loan would be considered closely related to the host because the variable rate at any specific time would be a market rate.

As with all embedded derivatives, the assessment of condition (a) and (b) above is made when the entity becomes party to the contract on the basis of market conditions existing at that time (see 4 above). It is important to note that the assessment is based on the possibility of the holder not recovering its recognised investment or doubling its initial return and obtaining twice the then-market return. The likelihood of this happening is ignored in making the assessment. Therefore, even if the likelihood of this happening is low, the embedded derivative has to be separated from the host contract. The valuation of the embedded derivative would however consider the low probability of this happening, possibly resulting in a relatively low fair value at inception.

An example where the holder would not recover substantially all of its recognised investment would be a bond which becomes immediately repayable if LIBOR increases above a certain threshold, at an amount significantly lower than its issue price. A further example is set out below.

Example 46.11: Leveraged inverse floater – not recovering substantially all of the initial investment

Company A issues a leveraged inverse floater loan note for its par value of US$20m. Interest is payable annually and is calculated as 10% minus 2 times three month LIBOR. At the time Company A issues the loan note, three month LIBOR is 3%, giving an initial return of 4%. There is no floor imposed on the interest rate and the rate could therefore be negative if LIBOR increases above 5%. In such a case, the investor would need to pay interest on its investment, which would leave it unable to recover substantially all of its recognised investment. The embedded derivative is therefore not closely related to the host contract and will be accounted for separately by Company A.

An example of condition (b) above, the 'double-double test', is set out below.

Example 46.12: Leveraged inverse floater – 'double-double test'

Assume the same fact pattern as in Example 46.11, except that there is a floor imposed on the coupon rate so that rate could not be negative. In such a case, the investor would recover substantially all of its recognised investment, meaning that no embedded derivative needs to be separated based on condition (a) above. However, before Company A could conclude on whether or not an embedded derivative needs to be recognised separately, it would need to evaluate condition (b) above. The first step is to assess whether there is a possible scenario in which the initial return of the investor would at least double. If LIBOR falls to 1% or below 1%, say 0.5%, then the interest rate on the loan note would be 9%, which is more than double the investor's initial rate of return of 4%. The first part of the condition under (b) above is therefore fulfilled.

The question is now whether 9% is twice the market return for a contract with the same terms as the host contract. With LIBOR being 0.5% this will most likely be the case, leaving both parts of condition (b) above fulfilled. The embedded derivative is therefore not closely related to the host contract and will be accounted for separately. If however, it is concluded that 9% is not twice the market return for a contract with the same terms as the host contract, then only one part of the condition under (b) above would be fulfilled and the embedded feature would be considered closely related to the host with no requirement to record it separately.

5.1.3 Fallback provisions relating to interest rate benchmark reform

In October 2019, the IASB considered in the context of its project to amend IFRS in response to interest rate benchmark reform, whether any amendment to IFRS 9 was required to clarify whether fallback provisions should be separated from the host debt instrument as an embedded derivative.

Fallbacks arise where the contractual terms of financial instruments contemplate the replacement of an established interest rate benchmark with an alternative interest rate benchmark. Such a contractual term could for example state that when the entity enacts interest rate benchmark reform for the financial instrument, the interest rate will change from 3 month Sterling LIBOR plus one hundred basis points, to Sterling Overnight Interest Average (SONIA) plus one hundred and twenty basis points.

The issue is only relevant for new financial liabilities and those that have been substantially modified such that a new financial instrument is recognised. If the economic terms of the financial instrument are affected by the fallback it may not be closely related to the economic characteristics and risk of the host contract. The IASB staff suggest that where this is the case, the fallback will need to be separated and accounted for as an embedded derivative.[9]

The IASB concluded that existing IFRS provides an adequate basis to determine the accounting for fallbacks that may arise in the context of interest rate benchmark reform. Applying the guidance in IFRS 9, when a new financial liability is recognised, entities should assess whether the fallback could at least double the initial return and result in a rate of return that is at least twice what would be expected for a similar contract at the time the fallback takes effect. This assessment is described above in 5.1.2 point (b) and is often referred to as the 'double-double test'. *[IFRS 9.B4.3.8(a)]*.

It is more likely that an embedded derivative will need to be separated if the fallback includes a fixed, wide basis spread between a new interest rate benchmark and the benchmark which is being replaced. The likelihood is increased further when market interest rates are low, because the basis spread could be significant compared to the replacement benchmark interest rate. If the basis spread included in the fallback is sufficiently wide, when the new financial liability is recognised, that the rate of return for the holder of the liability would be more than double the market rate of return, the fallback would have to be separated from the host debt contract by the issuer and accounted for as an embedded derivative.

5.1.4 Term extension and similar call, put and prepayment options in debt instruments

The application guidance explains that a call, put or prepayment option embedded in a host debt instrument is closely related to the host instrument if, on each exercise date, either i) the option's exercise price is approximately equal to the debt instrument's amortised cost or ii) the exercise price reimburses the lender for an amount up to the approximate present value of lost interest for the remaining term of the host contract; otherwise it is not regarded as closely related. *[IFRS 9.B4.3.5(e)]*. For embedded derivatives with more than one exercise date, there is no requirement to apply only assessment i) or ii) above to all dates, i.e. provided that either of the assessments is met for each exercise date, the embedded option will be considered to be closely related.

There is no elaboration on what is meant by the term 'approximately equal' and so judgement will need to be applied. In assessing whether the exercise price is approximately equal to the amortised cost at each exercise date, should one consider the amortised cost of the hybrid that would reflect the entity's original expectations regarding the future exercise of the prepayment option, or potential revised estimates applying the catch up method to the amortised cost? This question is illustrated in the following simple example (which also provides further illustrations of the application of the effective interest method to instruments containing prepayment options).

Example 46.13: Embedded prepayment option

Company P borrows €1,000 on terms that require it to pay annual fixed-rate coupons of €80 and €1,000 principal at the end of ten years. The terms of the instrument also allow Company P to redeem the debt after seven years by paying the principal of €1,000 and a penalty of €100.

The debt instrument can be considered to comprise the following two components:

- a host debt instrument requiring ten annual payments of €80 followed by a €1,000 payment of principal; and
- an embedded prepayment option, exercisable only at the end of seven years with an exercise price of €1,100.

If, at inception, the prepayment option was expected *not* to be exercised, the effective interest rate of the hybrid would be 8%. This is the rate that would discount the expected cash flows of €80 per year for ten years plus €1,000 at the end of ten years to the initial carrying amount of €1,000. The table below provides information about the amortised cost, interest income and cash flows using this assumption.

Year	(a) Amortised cost at the start of the year (€)	(b = a × 8%) Interest and similar income (€)	(c) Cash flows (€)	(d = a + b − c) Amortised cost at the end of the year (€)
1	1,000	80	80	1,000
2	1,000	80	80	1,000
3	1,000	80	80	1,000
4	1,000	80	80	1,000
5	1,000	80	80	1,000
6	1,000	80	80	1,000
7	1,000	80	80	1,000
8	1,000	80	80	1,000
9	1,000	80	80	1,000
10	1,000	80	80 + 1,000	–

However if, at the outset, the option *was* expected to be exercised, the effective interest rate of the *hybrid* would be 9.08% as this is the rate that discounts the expected cash flows of €80 per year for seven years, plus €1,100 at the end of seven years, to the initial carrying amount of €1,000. The table below provides information about the amortised cost, interest income and cash flows using this alternative assumption.

Year	(a) Amortised cost at the start of the year (€)	(b = a × 9.08%) Interest and similar income (€)	(c) Cash flows (€)	(d = a + b − c) Amortised cost at the end of the year (€)
1	1,000	91	80	1,011
2	1,011	92	80	1,023
3	1,023	93	80	1,036
4	1,036	94	80	1,050
5	1,050	95	80	1,065
6	1,065	97	80	1,082
7	1,082	98	80 + 1,100	–

On the face of it, therefore, comparing the amortised cost of the hybrid with the exercise price of the option at the date it could be exercised suggests the prepayment option might be considered closely related if it was likely to be exercised (since the amortised cost will be approximately equal to the exercise price of €1,100) but not if exercise was unlikely (since the amortised cost of €1,000 is not approximately equal to the exercise price of €1,100).

Unfortunately, the standard is silent on this issue and preparers of accounts will be required to exercise judgement as to the most appropriate method to use in their individual circumstances.

The standard also says that an option or automatic provision to extend the remaining term to maturity of a debt instrument is not closely related to the host unless, at the time of the extension, there is a concurrent adjustment to the approximate current market rate of interest. *[IFRS 9.B4.3.5(b)]*. The current market rate of interest would take into consideration the credit risk of the issuer. Taken in isolation, this paragraph and the first paragraph in this section on call, put or prepayment options appear reasonably straightforward to apply. However, in some situations, they are contradictory as set out in the following example.

Example 46.14: Extension and prepayment options

Company Z borrows €1,000 from Bank A on which it is required to pay €50 per annum interest. Under the terms of the borrowing agreement, Company Z is required to repay €1,000 in three years' time unless, at repayment date, it exercises an option to extend the term of the borrowing for a further two years. If this option is exercised €50 interest per annum is payable for the additional term.

Company Z also borrows €1,000 from Bank B on which it is required to pay €50 per annum interest. Under the terms of this borrowing agreement, Company Z is required to repay €1,000 in five years' time unless, at the end of three years, it exercises an option to redeem the borrowing for €1,000.

In all practical respects these two instruments are identical – the only difference is the way in which the terms of the embedded options are expressed. In the first case the guidance indicates that the (term extension) option is not closely related to the debt as there is no concurrent adjustment to market interest rates. However, in the second case the (prepayment) option *is* considered closely related provided the amortised cost of the liability would be approximately €1,000, the exercise price of the settlement option, at the end of year three (which it should be).

As set out at 6.2 below, an embedded option-based derivative should be separated from its host contract on the basis of the stated terms of the option feature. However, in situations similar to the one described above, there is significant diversity in practice and we are aware of at least two ways in which entities have dealt with this contradiction in practice. Some entities have looked to the wording in the contract so that what is described as an extension option (or a prepayment option) is evaluated in accordance with the guidance for extension options (or prepayment options). Other entities have determined the most likely outcome of the hybrid instrument based on conditions at initial recognition and the alternative outcome is regarded as the 'option'. Under this latter approach, if Company Z in the example above considered it was likely to repay its loans from Bank A and Bank B after three years, both loans would be regarded as having a two-year extension option. The first approach is based on the contractual terms, while the second approach is substance-based.

Another complication is that, viewed as a separate instrument, a term extension option is effectively a loan commitment. As loan commitments are generally outside the scope of IFRS 9, except for derecognition and impairment provisions, (see Chapter 45 at 3), some would argue they do not meet the definition of a derivative (see 2 above). Accordingly, when embedded in a host debt instrument, a loan commitment would not be separated as an embedded derivative or, alternatively, would be separated and accounted for as a loan commitment.[10]

The Interpretations Committee discussed both above contradictions in March 2012, noting significant diversity in practice and recommended that the IASB consider this issue when it redeliberated the classification and measurement requirements of financial liabilities under IFRS 9. The Committee decided that if the Board did not address this issue as part of its redeliberations, then the Committee would revisit this issue and consider whether guidance should be provided to clarify the accounting for the issuer of a fixed-rate-debt instrument that includes a term-extending option.[11] This issue remains unaddressed in IFRS 9 with no indication from the Interpretations Committee about bringing it back onto its agenda. Preparers of financial statements are therefore left to apply their own judgement considering all the facts and circumstances.

For put, call and prepayment options, there is a further complication that the determination as to whether the option is closely related depends on the amortised cost of the instrument. It is not clear whether this reference is to the amortised cost of the host instrument, on the assumption that the option is separated, or to the amortised cost of the entire instrument on the assumption that the option is not separated. As can be seen in Chapter 50 at 3.4, the existence of such options can affect the amortised cost, especially for a portfolio of instruments. Although one trade body has published guidance explaining that where early repayment fees are included in the calculation of effective interest, the prepayment option is likely to be closely related to the loan,[12] entities are largely left to apply their own judgement to assess which appears the most appropriate in the specific circumstances.

Prepayment options are also considered closely related to the host debt instrument if the exercise price reimburses the lender for an amount up to the approximate present value of lost interest for the remaining term of the host contract. For these purposes, lost interest is the product of the principal amount prepaid multiplied by the interest rate differential, i.e. the excess of the effective interest rate of the host contract over the effective interest rate that the entity would receive at the prepayment date if it reinvested the principal amount prepaid in a similar contract for the remaining term of the host contract. *[IFRS 9.B4.3.5(e)(ii)]*. In other words, in order for the prepayment option to be considered closely related to the host, the exercise price of the prepayment option would need to compensate the lender for loss of interest by reducing the economic loss from that which would be incurred on reinvestment. *[IFRS 9.BCZ4.97]*. In making this assessment, the question may arise what interest rate should be used to discount the interest payments that would be lost if the prepayment option was exercised. If the discount rate used reflects an equivalent credit risk of the issuer, this would seem reasonable. However, the guidance does not prescribe the discount rate to be used and since the assessment is whether the lender would be reimbursed for an amount that is 'approximately equal' to the present value of lost interest, there is scope to exercise judgment in determining the appropriate discount rate.

Another question that may arise, is whether the lost interest test requires the lender to be reimbursed for lost interest over the full remaining contractual term at the date of exercise. The assessment states that the interest may be 'an amount up to' the present value of the remaining interest. This suggests that the amount may be less than the remaining contractual interest over the full remaining contractual term. Where this is the case, the prepayment option would be deemed to be closely related.

From the perspective of the issuer of a convertible debt instrument with an embedded call or put option, the assessment of whether the option is closely related to the host debt instrument is made before separating the equity element in accordance with IAS 32. *[IFRS 9.B4.3.5(e)]*. This provides a specific relaxation from the general guidance on prepayment options above because, for accounting purposes, separate accounting for the equity component results in a discount on recognition of the liability component (see Chapter 47 at 6.2), which means that the amortised cost and exercise price are unlikely to approximate to each other for much of the term of the instrument.

An embedded prepayment option in an interest-only or principal-only strip is regarded as closely related to the host contract provided the host contract (i) initially resulted from separating the right to receive contractual cash flows of a financial instrument that, in and of itself, did not contain an embedded derivative, and (ii) does not contain any terms not present in the original host debt contract. *[IFRS 9.B4.3.8(e)]*. Again, this is a specific relaxation from the general guidance on prepayment options above.

If an entity issues a debt instrument and the holder writes a call option on the debt instrument to a third party, the issuer regards the call option as extending the term to maturity of the debt instrument, provided the issuer can be required to participate in or facilitate the remarketing of the debt instrument as a result of the call option being exercised. *[IFRS 9.B4.3.5(b)]*. Such a component is presumably considered to represent part of a hybrid financial instrument contract rather than a separate instrument (see 4 above).

5.1.5 Interest rate floors and caps

An embedded floor or cap on the interest rate on a debt instrument is closely related to the host debt instrument, provided the cap is at or above the market rate of interest, and the floor is at or below the market rate of interest, when the instrument is issued (in other words it needs to be at- or out-of-the-money), and the cap or floor is not leveraged in relation to the host instrument. *[IFRS 9.B4.3.8(b)]*.

The standard does not clarify what is meant by 'market rate of interest', or whether the cap (floor) should be considered as a single derivative or a series of caplets (floorlets) to be evaluated separately. Where the cap (floor) is at a constant amount throughout the term of the debt, historically entities have often compared the cap (floor) rate with the current spot floating rate at inception of the contract to determine whether the embedded derivative is closely related. However, in the current extremely low, or negative, interest rate environment of many economies, floors are more commonly being set at higher rates than current spot rates. As a result, entities are starting to evaluate whether more sophisticated approaches to evaluate these features are more appropriate, e.g. by comparing the average forward rate over the life of the bond with the floor rate or by comparing the forward rate at each interest reset date with each floorlet rate. We do not believe it is necessary for both a cap and a floor to be present to be considered closely related. For example, a cap (or floor) on the coupon paid on a debt instrument without a corresponding floor (or cap) could be regarded as closely related to the host, provided it was above (or below) the market rate of interest on origination.

The Interpretations Committee was asked, in January 2016, to clarify the application of the embedded derivatives requirements in a negative interest rate environment. The Interpretations Committee observed that:

- paragraph B4.3.8(b) of IFRS 9 does not distinguish between positive and negative interest rate environments. As such an interest rate floor in a negative interest rate environment should be treated in the same way as in a positive interest rate environment;
- when applying paragraph B4.3.8(b) of IFRS 9 in a positive or negative interest rate environment, an entity should compare the overall interest rate floor (i.e. benchmark interest rate referenced in the contract plus contractual spreads and if applicable any premiums, discounts or other elements that would be relevant to the calculation of the effective interest rate) for the hybrid contract to the market rate of interest for a similar contract without the interest rate floor (i.e. the host contract); and
- the appropriate market rate of interest for the host contract should be determined by considering the specific forms of the host contract and the relevant spreads (including credit spreads) appropriate for the transaction. They also noted that the term market rate of interest is linked to the concept of fair value as defined in IFRS 13 and is described in IFRS 9 as the rate of interest 'for a similar instrument (similar as to currency, term, type of interest and other factors) with a similar credit rating'. [IFRS 9.B5.1.1].

The Interpretations Committee determined that neither an Interpretation nor an amendment to a Standard was necessary and did not add this issue to its agenda.[13]

In practice entities perform the assessment of whether a cap or floor is 'at or below market interest' by either considering the cap or floor as a single instrument and applying the current swap rate, or by considering the component caplets and floorlets making up the overall cap or floor using the forward rate for the payment date of each particular caplet or floorlet.

Where, in making the assessment on the cap or floor as a single instrument, an entity determines that the cap or floor is not closely related, then the whole embedded cap or floor is accounted for as a single non-closely related embedded derivative at fair value through profit or loss.

5.1.6 Inflation-linked debt instruments

It is quite common for some entities (and governments) to issue inflation-linked debt instruments, i.e. where interest and/or principal payments are linked to, say, a consumer price index. The only embedded derivative guidance in IFRS 9 relating to embedded inflation-linked features is provided in the context of leases (see 5.3.2 below). If that guidance is accepted as applying to finance leases, it should also apply to debt instruments because finance leases result in assets and liabilities that are, in substance, no different to debt instruments (see Chapter 45 at 2.2.4). Further, in much finance theory, either real (applied to current prices) or nominal (applied to inflation adjusted prices) interest rates are used, suggesting a strong link between inflation and interest rates. Finally, a government or central bank will generally raise short-term interest rates as inflation rises and reduce rates as inflation recedes, which also suggests a close relationship between the two.

Therefore, we believe it would often be appropriate to treat the embedded derivative in inflation-linked debt as similar to an interest rate index and refer to the guidance at 5.1.2 above to determine whether the index is regarded as closely related to the debt. Typically, the index will be closely related to the debt where it is based on inflation in an economic environment in which the bond is issued/denominated, it is not significantly leveraged in relation to the debt and there is a sufficiently low risk of the investor not recovering its initial investment (only sometimes do such instruments provide an absolute guarantee that the principal will not be lost, although this situation will normally only arise if, over the life of the instrument, cumulative inflation is negative). However, some may argue that even if there is a very small risk of the initial investment not being recovered, the embedded derivative should be separated.

The staff of the Interpretations Committee has expressed a view that it would be appropriate to treat the embedded derivative in inflation-linked debt as closely related in economic environments where interest rates are mainly set so as to meet inflation targets, as evidenced by strong long-run correlation between nominal interest rates and inflation. In such jurisdictions they considered the characteristics and risks of the inflation embedded derivative to be closely related to the host debt contract.[14] Further, in debating the application of the effective interest method to such instruments (see Chapter 50 at 3.6) they have implicitly acknowledged that these instruments do not necessarily contain embedded derivatives requiring separation.

5.1.7 Commodity- and equity-linked interest and principal payments

Equity-indexed or commodity-indexed interest or principal payments embedded in a host debt instrument, i.e. where the amount of interest or principal is indexed to the value of an equity instrument or commodity (e.g. gold), are not closely related to the host debt instrument because the risks inherent in the embedded derivative are dissimilar to those of the host. *[IFRS 9.B4.3.5(c)-(d)]*. This is illustrated in the following example.

Example 46.15: Bond linked to a commodity price

A mining company issues a ten year debt instrument for its par value of US$15m. Interest is payable annually and consists of guaranteed interest of 5% per annum and contingent interest of 0.5% if the price of commodity A increases above US$300 in the relevant year, 1% if the price of commodity A increases above US$400 in the relevant year or 1.5% if the price of commodity A increases above US$500 in the relevant year. The mining company could have issued the bond without the contingent interest rate feature at a rate of 6%.

The commodity price feature is a swap contract to receive 1% fixed interest and pay a variable amount of interest depending on the price of commodity A. This feature is not closely related to the debt host contract.

A common type of transaction is where refiners of commodities enter into purchase contracts for mineral ores, whereby the price is adjusted subsequent to delivery, based on the quoted market price of the refined commodity extracted from the ore. These arrangements, often called provisionally priced contracts, can provide the refiner with a hedge of the fair value of its inventories and/or related sales proceeds which vary depending on subsequent changes in quoted commodity prices. Like the debt instruments noted above, any payable (or receivable) recognised at the time of delivery will contain an embedded commodity derivative. In these circumstances, provided the payable is held at fair value through profit or loss, it is unlikely to make much difference to the amount recognised whether the embedded derivative is separated or not. Since the receivable is an asset within the scope of IFRS 9 the embedded derivative could not be separated.

However, it would not normally be regarded as necessary to account separately for such an embedded derivative prior to delivery of the non-financial item. This is because, until delivery occurs, the contract is considered executory and the pricing feature would be considered closely related to the commodity being delivered (see 5.2.2 below).

5.1.8 Credit-linked notes

Credit derivatives are sometimes embedded in a host debt instrument whereby one party (the 'beneficiary') transfers the credit risk of a particular reference asset, which it may not own, to another party (the 'guarantor'). Such credit derivatives allow the guarantor to assume the credit risk associated with the reference asset without directly owning it. *[IFRS 9.B4.3.5(f)]*.

Whilst the economic characteristics of a debt instrument will include credit risk, should the embedded derivative be a credit derivative linked to the credit standing of an entity other than the issuer, it would not normally be regarded as closely related to the host debt instrument if the issuer were not required, through the terms of the financial instrument, to own the reference asset.

For example, an entity (commonly a structured entity) may issue various tranches of debt instruments that are referenced to a group of assets, such as a portfolio of bonds, mortgages or trade receivables, and the credit exposure from those assets is allocated to the debt instruments using a so called 'waterfall' feature. The waterfall feature itself does not normally result in the separation of an embedded credit derivative; it is the location or ownership of the reference assets that is most important to the assessment.[15] If the structured entity is required to hold the reference assets, the credit risk embedded in the debt instruments is considered closely related. However, if the issuer of the debt instruments held a credit derivative over the reference assets rather than the assets themselves, the embedded credit derivative would not be regarded as closely related.

5.1.9 Instruments with an equity kicker

In some instances, venture capital entities provide subordinated loans on terms that entitle them to receive shares if and when the borrowing entity lists its shares on a stock exchange, as illustrated in the following example.

Example 46.16: Equity kicker

A venture capital investor, Company V, provides a subordinated loan to Company A and agrees that in addition to interest and repayment of principal, if Company A lists its shares on a stock exchange, Company V will be entitled to receive shares in Company A free of charge or at a very low price (an 'equity kicker'). As a result of this feature, interest on the loan is lower than it would otherwise be. The loan is not measured at fair value with changes in fair value recognised in profit or loss.

The economic characteristics and risks of an equity return are not closely related to those of the host debt instrument. The equity kicker meets the definition of a derivative because it has a value that changes in response to the change in the price of Company A's shares, requires only a relatively small initial net investment, and is settled at a future date. It does not matter that the right to receive shares is contingent upon the borrower's future listing *[IFRS 9.IG C.4]* (although the probability of this event occurring will influence the fair value of the embedded derivative).

Similarly, the derivative embedded in a bond that is convertible (or exchangeable) into equity shares of a third party will not be closely related to the host debt instrument.

5.1.10 Puttable instruments

Another example of a hybrid contract is a financial instrument that gives the holder a right to put it back to the issuer in exchange for an amount that varies on the basis of the change in an equity or commodity price or index (a 'puttable instrument'). Where the host is a debt instrument, the embedded derivative, the indexed principal payment, cannot be regarded as closely related to that debt instrument. Because the principal payment can increase and decrease, the embedded derivative is a non-option derivative whose value is indexed to the underlying variable (see 6.1 below). *[IFRS 9.B4.3.5(a), B4.3.6]*.

From the perspective of the issuer of a puttable instrument, that can be put back at any time for cash equal to a proportionate share of the net asset value of an entity (such as units of an open-ended mutual fund or some unit-linked investment products), the effect of the issuer separating an embedded derivative and accounting for each component is to measure the combined instrument at the redemption amount, that would be payable at the end of the reporting period, if the holder were to exercise its right to put the instrument back to the issuer. *[IFRS 9.B4.3.7]*.

For the holder of such an instrument, the requirements of the standard are applied to the instrument as a whole, resulting in such investments in puttable instruments being recognised at fair value through profit or loss in their entirety. *[IFRS 9.4.3.2]*.

This treatment was clarified by the Interpretations Committee in May 2017 when the Committee confirmed that the election to present subsequent changes in fair value in other comprehensive income was not available to these instruments, as they did not meet the definition of an equity instrument.[16]

Whilst it was not explicitly stated, the ineligibility of such instruments to make this election means they must be recognised at fair value through profit or loss.

5.2 Contracts for the sale of goods or services

5.2.1 Foreign currency derivatives

An embedded foreign currency derivative in a contract that is not a financial instrument is closely related to the host contract provided it is not leveraged, does not contain an option feature and requires payments denominated in one of the following currencies:

(i) the functional currency of any substantial party to the contract – see 5.2.1.A below;

(ii) the currency in which the price of the related good or service that is acquired or delivered is routinely denominated in commercial transactions around the world (such as the US dollar for crude oil transactions) – see 5.2.1.B below; or

(iii) a currency that is commonly used in contracts to purchase or sell non-financial items in the economic environment in which the transaction takes place (e.g. a relatively stable and liquid currency that is commonly used in local business transactions or external trade) – see 5.2.1.C below.

Therefore, in such cases the embedded foreign currency derivative is not accounted for separately from the host contract. *[IFRS 9.B4.3.8(d)]*. An example would be a contract for the purchase or sale of a non-financial item, where the price is denominated in a foreign currency that meets one of the three criteria outlined above.

5.2.1.A Functional currency of counterparty

In principle, the assessment of exception (i) above is straightforward. In practice, however, the functional currency of the counterparty to a contract will not always be known with certainty and, in some cases, can be a somewhat subjective assessment even for the counterparty's management (assuming the counterparty is a corporate entity) – see Chapter 15 at 4. Consequently, entities will need to demonstrate they have taken appropriate steps to make a reasonable judgement as to their counterparties' functional currencies. Where available, a counterparty's financial statements will provide evidence of its functional currency. Otherwise, it would often be appropriate to assume that an entity operating in a single country has that country's currency as its functional currency, although if there were indicators to the contrary these would have to be considered.

Another practical problem that arises in applying this exception is identifying which parties to a contract are 'substantial'. IFRS 9 does not provide any further guidance, but it is generally considered that such a party should be one that is acting as principal to the contract. Therefore if, as part of a contract, a parent provides a performance guarantee in respect of services to be provided by its operating subsidiary, the parent may be seen to be the substantial party to the contract and not the subsidiary, where the subsidiary is acting as an agent. However, if the guarantee is not expected to be called upon, the parent would not normally be considered a substantial party to the contract. Particular care is necessary when assessing a contract under which one party subcontracts an element of the work to another entity under common control, say a fellow subsidiary with a different functional currency, although in most cases it will only be the primary contractor that is considered a substantial party.

5.2.1.B Routinely denominated in commercial transactions

For the purposes of exception (ii) above, the currency must be used for similar transactions all around the world, not just in one local area. For example, if cross-border transactions in natural gas in North America are routinely denominated in US dollars and such transactions are routinely denominated in euros in Europe, neither the US dollar nor the euro is a currency in which the good or service is routinely denominated in international commerce. *[IFRS 9.IG C.9]*. Accordingly, the number of items to which this will apply will be limited – in practice it will be mainly commodities that are traded in, say, US dollars throughout much of the world. Examples include crude oil, jet fuel, certain base metals (including aluminium, copper and nickel) and some precious metals (including gold, silver and platinum). One other notable item might be wide-bodied aircraft where it appears that Boeing and Airbus, the two major manufacturers, routinely denominate sales in US dollars.

In September 2014 the Interpretations Committee received a request relating to the routinely denominated criterion. They were asked to consider whether a licensing agreement denominated in a currency, in which commercial transactions of that type were routinely denominated around the world, held an embedded foreign currency derivative that was closely related to the economic characteristics of the host contract.[17]

The Interpretations Committee noted that the issue related to a contract for a specific type of item and observed that an assessment of routinely denominated criterion is based on evidence of whether or not such commercial transactions are denominated in that currency all around the world and not merely in one local area. They further observed that the assessment of the routinely denominated criterion is a question of fact and is based on an assessment of available evidence.

5.2.1.C Commonly used currencies

The IASB noted that the requirement to separate embedded foreign currency derivatives may be burdensome for entities that operate in economies in which business contracts denominated in a foreign currency are common. For example, entities domiciled in small countries may find it convenient to denominate business contracts with entities from other small countries in an internationally liquid currency (such as the US dollar, euro or yen) rather than the local currency of any party to the transaction. Also, an entity operating in a hyperinflationary economy may use a price list in a hard currency to protect against inflation, for example an entity that has a foreign operation in a hyperinflationary economy that denominates local contracts in the functional currency of the parent. *[IFRS 9.BCZ4.94]*.

Unfortunately, however, the assessment of whether or not a particular currency meets this requirement in a particular situation has not been straightforward in practice and this question reached the attention of the Interpretations Committee in May 2007.

The Interpretations Committee debated this matter in four consecutive meetings before referring the matter to the IASB. During its debates, the Interpretations Committee noted that entities should:[18]

- Identify where the transaction takes place.

  This is not as straightforward as it might seem. For example, consider a Polish company that manufactures components in Poland and exports them to a third party in the Czech Republic. Should the sale of components be regarded as a transaction occurring in Poland or in the Czech Republic?[19] It is likely that the Polish company would regard it as occurring in Poland and the Czech entity in the Czech Republic, but this is not entirely beyond debate; and

- Identify currencies that are commonly used in the economic environment in which the transaction takes place.

  Entities need to address what the population of transactions in the economic environment is. Some might suggest that transactions to which (i) or (ii) above apply should be excluded, although this is not a view shared by the staff of the Interpretations Committee which considered that all transactions should be included.[20]

  Entities should also consider what an economic environment is. The guidance, on which Example 46.17 below is based, implies that a country could be an economic environment. The references to local business transactions and to external trade in (iii) above suggest that other examples of economic environment are the external trade or internal trade environment of the country in which the transaction takes place. The question remains as to whether there could be other economic environments, for example the luxury goods market in a country. Depending on the view taken, a different treatment could arise.[21] In considering the issue subsequently, the IASB staff noted their understanding that all of these views (and possibly more, such as the internal or external trade of a specific company) were being applied in practice.[22]

The Interpretations Committee had also been asked to provide guidance on how to interpret the term 'common', but understandably was reluctant to do so.[23] The IASB staff noted that there is no guidance as to the quantum of transactions or value that would need to be denominated in a foreign currency to conclude that the currency was commonly used and that a related matter is whether 'common' should be considered in the context of a particular entity, of an industry, or of a country.[24]

The IASB staff noted other related interpretive questions raised by constituents including the following:[25]

- What evidence does an entity require to support the notion that the use of a currency is common?
- Does the reporting entity need to investigate published statistics?
- If the reporting entity has to look for statistics, what percentage of business needs to be conducted in that currency to assert that use of the currency is common?
- Whether the consideration that a currency is commonly used should exclude from the population set those transactions falling under (i) or (ii) above.

They concluded that there are a variety of views on the appropriate interpretation of this guidance and, consequently, that there is significant diversity in practice.[26]

Ultimately, however, no additional guidance has been included within IFRS 9.

5.2.1.D   Examples and other practical issues

The application of the guidance above is illustrated in the examples below.

Example 46.17:   Oil contract denominated in Swiss francs

A Norwegian company agrees to sell oil to a company in France. The oil contract is denominated in Swiss francs, although oil contracts are routinely denominated in US dollars in international commerce and Norwegian krone are commonly used in contracts to purchase or sell non-financial items in Norway. Neither company carries out any significant activities in Swiss francs.

The Norwegian company should regard the supply contract as a host contract with an embedded foreign currency forward to purchase Swiss francs. The French company should regard it as a host contract with an embedded foreign currency forward to sell Swiss francs. [IFRS 9.IG C.7].

The implementation guidance on which this example is based does not state in which currency the host contract should be denominated (this will also be the currency of the second leg of the embedded forward contract). The currency should be chosen so that the host does not contain an embedded derivative requiring separation. In theory, therefore, it could be Norwegian krone or euro (the functional currencies of the parties to the contract) or US dollars (the currency in which oil contracts are routinely denominated in international commerce). Typically, however, an entity will use its own functional currency to define the terms of the host contract and embedded derivative.

A second issue arises where the terms of the contract require delivery and payment on different dates. For example, assume the contract was entered into on 1 January, with delivery scheduled for 30 June and payment required by 30 September. Should the embedded derivative be considered a six-month forward contract maturing on 30 June, or a nine-month forward contract maturing on 30 September? Conceptually at least, the latter approach seems more satisfactory, for example because it does not introduce into the notional terms cash flows at a point in time (i.e. on delivery) when none exist in the combined contract. In practice, however, the former approach is used far more often and is not without technical merit. For example, it avoids the recognition of an embedded foreign currency derivative between the delivery and payment dates on what would be a foreign currency denominated monetary item, something that is prohibited by IFRS 9 (see 5.1.1 above).

Example 46.18:   Oil contract, denominated in US dollars and containing a leveraged foreign exchange payment

Company A, whose functional currency is the euro, enters into a contract with Company B, whose functional currency is the Norwegian Krone, to purchase oil in six months for US$1,000. The host oil contract will be settled by making and taking delivery in the normal course of business and is not accounted for as a financial instrument because it qualifies as a normal sale or purchase contract (see Chapter 45 at 4.2). The oil contract includes a leveraged foreign exchange provision whereby the parties, in addition to the provision of, and payment for, oil will exchange an amount equal to the fluctuation in the exchange rate of the US dollar and Norwegian Krone applied to a notional amount of US$100,000.

The payment of US$1,000 under the host oil contract can be viewed as a foreign currency derivative because the dollar is neither Company A nor Company B's functional currency. However, it would not be separated as the US dollar is the currency in which crude oil transactions are routinely denominated in international commerce.

The leveraged foreign exchange provision is in addition to the required payment for the oil transaction. It is unrelated to the host oil contract and is therefore separated and accounted for as an embedded derivative. [IFRS 9.IG C.8].

In practice, all but the simplest contracts will contain other terms and features that can often make it much more difficult to isolate the precise terms of the embedded foreign currency derivative (and the host). For example, a clause may allow a purchaser to terminate the contract in return for making a specified compensation payment to the supplier – the standard offers little guidance as to whether such a feature should be included within the terms of the host, of the embedded foreign currency derivative or, possibly, of both. Other problematic terms can include options to defer the specified delivery date and options to order additional goods or services.

5.2.2 Inputs, ingredients, substitutes and other proxy pricing mechanisms

It is common for the pricing of contracts for the supply of goods, services or other non-financial items to be determined by reference to the price of inputs to, ingredients used to generate, or substitutes for the non-financial item, especially where the non-financial item is not itself quoted in an active market. For example, a provider of call centre services may determine that a large proportion of the costs of providing the service will be employee costs in a particular country. Accordingly, it may seek to link the price in a long-term contract to supply its services to the relevant wage index, effectively to provide an economic hedge of its exposure to changes in employee costs. Similarly, the producer of goods may index the price of its product to the market value of commodities that are used in the production process.

The standard contains little or no detailed guidance for determining whether or not such pricing features should be considered closely related to the host contract. However, the general requirement of the standard to assess the economic characteristics and risks would suggest that where a good link to the inputs can be established, such features will normally be considered closely related to the host, unless they were significantly leveraged.

Other proxy pricing mechanisms may arise in long-term supply agreements for commodities where there is no active market in the commodity. For example, in the 1980s, when natural gas first started to be extracted from the North Sea in significant volumes, there was no active market for that gas and thus no market price on which to base the price of long-term contracts. Because of this, suppliers and customers were willing to enter into such contracts where the price was indexed to the market price of other commodities such as crude oil that could potentially be used as a substitute for gas. For contracts entered into before the development of an active gas market, such features would normally be considered closely related, especially if similar pricing mechanisms were commonly used by other participants in the market.

Where there is an active market price for the non-financial items being supplied under the contract, different considerations apply. The use of the proxy pricing mechanism is a strong indication that the entity has entered into a speculative position and we would not normally consider such features to be closely related to the host. The separation of these types of embedded derivatives can be seen in the following extract from BP's financial statements. Although this was disclosed under IAS 39 there is no reason to believe that the outcome would be different under IFRS 9.

> *Extract 46.2: BP p.l.c. (2014)*
> Notes on financial statements [extract]
> 28.   Derivative financial instruments [extract]
> Embedded derivatives [extract]
>
> The group is a party to certain natural gas contracts containing embedded derivatives. Prior to the development of an active gas trading market, UK gas contracts were priced using a basket of available price indices, primarily relating to oil products, power and inflation. After the development of an active UK gas market, certain contracts were entered into or renegotiated using pricing formulae not directly related to gas prices, for example, oil product and power prices. In these circumstances, pricing formulae have been determined to be derivatives, embedded within the overall contractual arrangements that are not clearly and closely related to the underlying commodity. The resulting fair value relating to these contracts is recognized on the balance sheet with gains or losses recognized in the income statement.

5.2.3   Inflation-linked features

Apart from that related to leases (see 5.3.2 below), there is no reference in the guidance to contracts containing payments that are linked to inflation. Many types of contracts contain inflation-linked payments and it would appear sensible to apply the guidance in respect of leases to these contracts. Consider, for example, a long-term agreement to supply services under which payments increase by reference to a general price index and are not leveraged in any way. In cases such as this, the embedded inflation-linked derivative would normally be considered closely related to the host, provided the index related to a measure of inflation in an appropriate economic environment, such as the one in which the services were being supplied.

5.2.4   Floors and caps

Similar to debt instruments (see 5.1.5 above), provisions within a contract to purchase or sell an asset (e.g. a commodity) that establishes a cap and a floor on the price to be paid or received for the asset are closely related to the host contract if both the cap and floor were out-of-the-money at inception and are not leveraged. *[IFRS 9.B4.3.8(b)].*

5.2.5   Fund performance fees

In the investment management industry, it is common for a fund manager to receive a fee based on the performance of the assets managed in addition to a base fee. For example, if a fund's net asset value increases over its accounting year, the manager may be entitled to a percentage of that increase. The contract for providing investment management services to the fund clearly contains an embedded derivative (the underlying is the value of the fund's assets). However, whilst not addressed explicitly in the standard, we would normally consider it appropriate to regard such features as closely related to the host contract. Performance-based fees are discussed in more detail in Chapter 29 at 2.2.3 and Example 29.5.

5.3 Leases

5.3.1 Foreign currency derivatives

A lessor's finance lease receivable or a lessee's lease payable, which is recognised in accordance with IFRS 16 – *Leases*, is accounted for as a financial instrument, albeit one that is not subject to all of the measurement requirements of IFRS 9 (see Chapter 45 at 2.2.4). Therefore, a lease denominated in a foreign currency will not generally be considered to contain an embedded foreign currency derivative requiring separation, because the payable or receivable is a monetary item within the scope of IAS 21.

However, under IFRS 16, an operating lease for a lessor and a short-term lease for a lessee, is accounted for as an executory contract. Accordingly, where the lease payments are denominated in a foreign currency, the analysis at 5.2.1 above is applicable and it may be necessary to separate an embedded derivative. See Example 46.19 at 6.1 below for an example of a foreign exchange currency derivative requiring separation from a (hybrid) lease contract.

5.3.2 Inflation-linked features

An embedded derivative in a lease is considered closely related to the host if it is an inflation-related index such as an index of lease payments to a consumer price index, provided that the lease is not leveraged and the index relates to inflation in the entity's own economic environment. *[IFRS 9.B4.3.8(f)(i)]*.

5.3.3 Contingent rentals based on related sales

Where a lease requires contingent rentals based on related sales, that embedded derivative is considered to be closely related to the host lease. *[IFRS 9.B4.3.8(f)(ii)]*.

5.3.4 Contingent rentals based on variable interest rates

If a derivative embedded within a lease arises from contingent rentals based on variable interest rates, it is considered closely related. *[IFRS 9.B4.3.8(f)(iii)]*.

5.4 Insurance contracts

The guidance at 5.1.2 to 5.1.5, 5.1.7 and 5.2.1 above also applies to insurance contracts. IFRS 4 added two further illustrations to IFRS 9 that deal primarily with insurance contracts.

A unit-linking feature embedded in a host financial instrument, or host insurance contract, is closely related to the host if the unit-denominated payments are measured at current unit values that reflect the fair values of the assets of the fund. A unit-linking feature is a contractual term that requires payments denominated in units of an internal or external investment fund. *[IFRS 9.B4.3.8(g)]*.

A derivative embedded in an insurance contract is closely related to the host if the embedded derivative and host are so interdependent that the embedded derivative cannot be measured separately, i.e. without considering the host contract. *[IFRS 9.B4.3.8(h)]*.

Derivatives embedded within insurance contracts are covered in more detail in Chapter 55 at 4 for IFRS 4 and Chapter 56 at 4.1 for IFRS 17.

6 IDENTIFYING THE TERMS OF EMBEDDED DERIVATIVES AND HOST CONTRACTS

The IASB has provided only limited guidance on determining the terms of a separated embedded derivative and host contract. Accordingly, entities may find this aspect of the embedded derivative requirements particularly difficult to implement. In addition to the guidance set out below, Examples 46.17 and 46.18 above also identify the terms of an embedded derivative requiring separation.

6.1 Embedded non-option derivatives

IFRS 9 does not define the term 'non-option derivative' but suggests that it includes forwards, swaps and similar contracts. An embedded derivative of this type should be separated from its host contract on the basis of its stated or implied substantive terms, so as to result in it having a fair value of zero at initial recognition. *[IFRS 9.B4.3.3]*.

The IASB has provided implementation guidance on separating non-option derivatives in the situation where the host is a debt instrument. It is explained that, in the absence of implied or stated terms, judgement will be necessary to identify the terms of the host (e.g. whether it should be a fixed rate, variable rate or zero-coupon instrument) and the embedded derivative. However, an embedded derivative that is not already clearly present in the hybrid should not be separated, i.e. a cash flow that does not exist cannot be created. *[IFRS 9.IG C.1]*.

For example, if a five year debt instrument has fixed annual interest payments of £40 and a principal payment at maturity of £1,000 multiplied by the change in an equity price index, it would be inappropriate to identify a floating rate host and an embedded equity swap that has an offsetting floating rate leg. The host should be a fixed rate debt instrument that pays £40 annually because there are no floating interest rate cash flows in the hybrid instrument. *[IFRS 9.IG C.1]*.

Further, as noted above, the terms of the embedded derivative should be determined so that it has a fair value of zero on inception of the hybrid instrument. It is explained that if an embedded non-option derivative could be separated on other terms, a single hybrid instrument could be decomposed into an infinite variety of combinations of host debt instruments and embedded derivatives. This might be achieved, for example, by separating embedded derivatives with terms that create leverage, asymmetry or some other risk exposure not already present in the hybrid instrument. *[IFRS 9.IG C.1]*.

Finally, it is explained that the terms of the embedded derivative should be identified based on the conditions existing when the financial instrument was issued, *[IFRS 9.IG C.1]*, or when a contract is required to be reassessed (see 7 below).

The following example illustrates how a foreign currency derivative embedded in a (hybrid) lease contract, that is not closely related, could be separated.

Example 46.19: Separation of embedded derivative from a lease

Company X has Indian Rupees (INR) as its functional currency. On 1 January 2020 Company X entered into a nine month lease over an item of PP&E which required payments of US$100,000 on 31 March 2020, 30 June 2020 and 30 September 2020. The functional currency of the lessor is not US dollars; the price of such leases is not routinely denominated in US dollars and US dollars is not a currency that is commonly used in the economic environment in which the lease took place (see 5.3.1 above). Accordingly, the embedded foreign currency derivative is not closely related to the lease.

On 1 January 2020 the spot exchange rate was 40 and the forward exchange rates for settlement on 31 March 2020, 30 June 2020 and 30 September 2020 were 41, 42 and 43 respectively. The terms of the embedded derivative could be determined as follows:

31 March 2020	Pay US$100,000	Receive INR4,100,000
30 June 2020	Pay US$100,000	Receive INR4,200,000
30 September 2020	Pay US$100,000	Receive INR4,300,000

Given the terms of the embedded derivative above, the host contract will be a nine month lease over the same PP&E as the hybrid lease contract, commencing 1 January 2020 and with scheduled payments of INR 4,100,000, INR 4,200,000 and INR 4,300,000 on 31 March 2020, 30 June 2020 and 30 September 2020. It can be seen that this host, after separation of the foreign currency derivative, an INR denominated lease, does not contain an embedded derivative requiring separation and the combined terms of the two components sum to the terms of the hybrid contract.

6.2 Embedded option-based derivative

As for non-option derivatives, IFRS 9 does not define the term 'option-based derivative' but suggests that it includes puts, calls, caps, floors and swaptions. An embedded derivative of this type should be separated from its host contract on the basis of the stated terms of the option feature. *[IFRS 9.B4.3.3]*.

The implementation guidance explains that the economic nature of an option-based derivative is fundamentally different from a non-option derivative and depends critically on the strike price (or strike rate) specified for the option feature in the hybrid instrument. Therefore, the separation of such a derivative should be based on the stated terms of the option feature documented in the hybrid instrument. Consequently, in contrast to the position for non-option derivatives (see 6.1 above), an embedded option-based derivative would not normally have a fair value of zero. *[IFRS 9.IG C.2]*.

In fact, if the terms of an embedded option-based derivative were identified so as to result in it having a fair value of zero, the implied strike price would generally result in the option being infinitely out-of-the-money, i.e. it would have a zero probability of the option feature being exercised. However, since the probability of exercising the option feature is generally not zero, this would be inconsistent with the likely economic behaviour of the hybrid. *[IFRS 9.IG C.2]*.

Similarly, if the terms were identified to achieve an intrinsic value of zero, the strike price would equal the price of the underlying at initial recognition. In this case, the fair value of the option would consist only of time value. However, this may also be inconsistent with the likely economic behaviour of the hybrid, including the probability of the option feature being exercised, unless the agreed strike price was indeed equal to the price of the underlying at initial recognition. *[IFRS 9.IG C.2]*.

6.3 Multiple embedded derivatives

Generally, multiple embedded derivatives in a single instrument should be treated as a single compound embedded derivative. However, embedded derivatives that are classified as equity are accounted for separately from those classified as assets or liabilities (see Chapter 47 at 6). In addition, derivatives embedded in a single instrument that relate to different risk exposures and are readily separable and independent of each other, should be accounted for separately from each other. *[IFRS 9.B4.3.4]*.

For example, if a debt instrument has a principal amount related to an equity index and that amount doubles if the equity index exceeds a certain level, it is not appropriate to separate both a forward and an option on the equity index because those derivative features relate to the same risk exposure. Instead, the forward and option elements are treated as a single compound embedded derivative. Similarly, for an embedded call, put or prepayment option, if the risk associated with the option varies distinctly in different periods over the debt instrument's life, it would still be considered as a single embedded derivative. For the same reason, an embedded floor or cap on interest rates should not be separated into a series of 'floorlets' or 'caplets' (i.e. single interest rate options).[27]

On the other hand, if a hybrid debt instrument contains, for example, two options that give the holder a right to choose both the interest rate index on which interest payments are determined and the currency in which the principal is repaid, those two options may qualify for separation as two separate embedded derivatives since they relate to different risk exposures and are readily separable and independent of each other.[28]

7 REASSESSMENT OF EMBEDDED DERIVATIVES

On initial recognition, a contract should be reviewed to assess whether it contains one or more embedded derivatives requiring separation. However, the issue arises whether an entity is required to continue to carry out this assessment after it first becomes a party to a contract, and if so, with what frequency. *[IFRS 9.BCZ4.99]*.

The question is relevant, for example, when the terms of the embedded derivative do not change but market conditions change and the market was the principal factor in determining whether the host contract and embedded derivative are closely related. Instances when this might arise are embedded foreign currency derivatives in host contracts that are insurance contracts or contracts for the purchase or sale of a non-financial item denominated in a foreign currency. *[IFRS 9.BCZ4.100, IFRS 9.B4.3.8(d)]*.

Consider, for example, an entity that enters into a purchase contract denominated in US dollars. If, at the time the contract is entered into, US dollars are commonly used in the economic environment in which the transaction takes place, the contract will not contain an embedded foreign currency derivative requiring separation. Subsequently however, the economic environment may change such that transactions are now commonly denominated in euros, rather than US dollars. Countries joining the European Union may encounter just such a scenario.

Clearly, in this situation, an embedded foreign currency derivative would be separated from any new US dollar denominated purchase contracts, assuming they would not otherwise be considered closely related. However, should the entity separately account for derivatives embedded within its existing US dollar denominated contracts that were outstanding prior to the change in the market?

Conversely, the entity may have identified, and separately accounted for, embedded foreign currency derivatives in contracts denominated in euros that were entered into before the economic environment changed. Does the change in economic circumstances mean that the embedded derivative should now be considered closely related and not separately accounted for as a derivative? *[IFRS 9.BCZ4.100-101]*.

IFRS 9 confirms that entities should assess whether an embedded derivative is required to be separated from the host contract and accounted for as a derivative when the entity first becomes a party to the contract. Subsequent reassessment is prohibited unless there is a change in the terms of a contract that significantly modifies the cash flows that otherwise would be required under the contract, in which case an assessment is required. An entity determines whether a modification to cash flows is significant by considering the extent to which the expected future cash flows associated with the embedded derivative, the host contract or both have changed and whether the change is significant relative to the previously expected cash flows on the contract. *[IFRS 9.B4.3.11]*.

For a financial liability, a change to the terms of the contract which significantly modifies the cash flows may also require derecognition of the original instrument and recognition of a new instrument. This is discussed in more detail in Chapter 52 at 6.

7.1 Acquisition of contracts

IFRS 9 requires an entity to assess whether an embedded derivative needs to be separated from the host contract and accounted for as a derivative when it first becomes a party to that contract. Therefore, if an entity purchases a contract that contains an embedded derivative, it assesses whether the embedded derivative needs to be separated and accounted for as a derivative on the basis of conditions at the date it acquires it, not the date the original contract was established. *[IFRS 9.BCZ4.106]*.

7.2 Business combinations

From the point of view of a consolidated entity, the acquisition of a contract within a business combination accounted for using the acquisition method under IFRS 3 – *Business Combinations* – is hardly different from the acquisition of a contract in general. Consequently, an assessment of the acquiree's contracts should be made on the date of acquisition as if the contracts themselves had been acquired. *[IFRS 3.15, 16(c)]*.

Neither IFRS 9 nor IFRS 3 applies to a combination of entities or businesses under common control or the formation of a joint venture. *[IFRS 3.2, IFRS 9.B4.3.12]*.

However, in our view, if the acquisition method is applied to such arrangements, the requirements set out in IFRS 3 should be followed.

7.3 Remeasurement issues arising from reassessment

IFRS 9 does not address remeasurement issues arising from a reassessment of embedded derivatives. One of the reasons for prohibiting reassessment in general was the difficulty in determining the accounting treatment following a reassessment, which is explained in the following terms.

Assume that an entity, when it first became party to a contract, separately recognised a host asset not within the scope of IFRS 9, and an embedded derivative liability. If the entity were required to reassess whether the embedded derivative was to be accounted for separately and if the entity concluded sometime after becoming a party to the contract that the derivative was no longer required to be separated, then questions of recognition and measurement would arise. In the above circumstances, the entity could: *[IFRS 9.BCZ4.105]*

(a) remove the derivative from its statement of financial position and recognise in profit or loss a corresponding gain or loss. This would lead to recognition of a gain or loss even though there had been no transaction and no change in the value of the total contract or its components;

(b) leave the derivative as a separate item in the statement of financial position. The issue would then arise as to when the item is to be removed from the statement of financial position. Should it be amortised (and, if so, how would the amortisation affect the effective interest rate of the asset), or should it be derecognised only when the asset is derecognised?

(c) combine the derivative (which is recognised at fair value) with the asset (which may not be recognised at fair value). This would alter the carrying amount of the asset even though there had been no change in the economics of the whole contract.

IFRS 9 states that subsequent reassessment is appropriate only when there has been a change in the terms of the contract that 'significantly' modifies the cash flows, accordingly the above issues are not expected to arise. *[IFRS 9.BCZ4.105]*.

8 LINKED AND SEPARATE TRANSACTIONS AND 'SYNTHETIC' INSTRUMENTS

A derivative that is attached to a financial instrument, but is contractually transferable independently of that instrument, or has a different counterparty from that instrument, is not an embedded derivative, but a separate financial instrument. *[IFRS 9.4.3.1]*.

This is also the case where a synthetic instrument is created by using derivatives to 'alter' the nature of a non-derivative instrument, as illustrated in the following example:

Example 46.20: Investment in a synthetic fixed-rate debt

Company A issues a five year floating rate debt instrument. At the same time, it enters into a five year pay-fixed, receive-variable interest rate swap with Entity B. Company A considers the combination of the two instruments to be a synthetic fixed rate instrument.

Embedded derivatives are terms and conditions that are *included in* non-derivative host contracts and it is generally inappropriate to treat two or more separate financial instruments as a single combined, or synthetic, instrument. Each of the financial instruments has its own terms and conditions and may be transferred or settled separately. Therefore, the debt instrument and the swap must be classified separately. *[IFRS 9.IG C.6]*.

It is asserted that these transactions differ from those discussed at 3.2 above because those had no substance apart from the resulting interest rate swap. *[IFRS 9.IG C.6]*.

Although some might argue that the substance of the two transactions above is the resulting synthetic fixed rate debt instrument, this interpretation is clearly not allowed under the standard.

Interestingly, the guidance does not address a much more common situation whereby a company both borrows from, and transacts a related derivative with, the same counterparty – typically the borrowing will be floating rate and the derivative a perfectly matched pay-fixed, receive-floating interest rate swap.

In fact, the subject of linking transactions for accounting purposes is a difficult one, especially in the context of financial instruments. The IASB's *Conceptual Framework* specifies that transactions should be reported in accordance with their substance and economic reality and not merely their legal form, *[CF 2.12]*, and linking transactions can be seen as dealing with the question of how to interpret this principle.

IAS 32, and IFRS 9 deal with the subject in a piecemeal way. For example, in addition to the synthetic instrument illustration above:

- two or more non-derivative contracts that are, 'in substance', no more than a single derivative are treated as a single derivative (see 3.2 above);
- derivatives that are 'attached' to a non-derivative financial instrument may sometimes be regarded as part of a single combined instrument (see 4 above);
- in classifying an instrument in consolidated financial statements as equity or a financial liability, all terms and conditions agreed between members of the group and holders of the instrument are considered (see Chapter 47 at 4.8);
- if a loan is guaranteed by a third party, the expected credit loss determined in accordance with IFRS 9 should be calculated based on the combined credit risk of the guarantor and the guaranteed party if the guarantee is 'integral' to the contractual terms of the loan (see Chapter 51 at 5.8.1); and
- determining the appropriate accounting treatment for a transaction that involves the transfer of some or all rights associated with financial assets, without the sale of the assets themselves, inevitably involves linking separate contracts to assess whether the transaction results in derecognition of the assets. For example, there might be one contract defining the continued ownership of the asset and another obliging the owner to transfer the rights associated with the asset to a third party (see Chapter 49 at 2, Chapter 50 at 2 and Chapter 52 at 3 and 4).

The Interpretations Committee first considered the subject of linkage in 2002 and has, in the past, made certain recommendations to the IASB. In fact, the requirement to take account of linked terms when classifying instruments as debt or equity in consolidated financial statements was introduced into IAS 32 in December 2003 following the Interpretations Committee's deliberations. Despite agreeing proposed indicators for when transactions should be linked, and proposed guidance on accounting for linked transactions, these have never been published as an interpretation or standard.[29]

In August 2013 the Interpretations Committee received a request to clarify whether three different transactions should be accounted for separately or be aggregated and treated as a single derivative. The Committee decided not to add this issue to its agenda but noted that in order to determine whether to aggregate and account for the three transactions as a single derivative, reference should be made to B.6 (see 3.2 above) and C.6 (see Example 46.20 above) of the Implementation Guidance to IFRS 9 and paragraph AG39 of IAS 32. The Interpretations Committee noted that the application of the guidance in paragraph B.6 of IFRS 9 requires judgement and that the indicators in that paragraph may help an entity to determine the substance of the transaction, but that the presence or absence of any single specific indicator alone may not be conclusive.[30]

Consequently, in considering the borrowing and swap situation above, we are left principally with the guidance in IFRS 9. It is likely that the swap and the loan have their own terms and conditions and may be transferred or settled independently of each other. Therefore, the principles in Example 46.20 above would suggest separate accounting for the two instruments. Applying the guidance at 3.2 above (aggregating non-derivative transactions and treating them as a derivative) would also suggest separate accounting in most cases. Even though the instruments are transacted with the same counterparty, there will normally be a substantive business purpose for transacting the instruments separately.

It seems clear that in situations involving two separate legal contracts, in most cases, the two instruments will be regarded as separate for accounting purposes. However, in certain situations the linkage between those contracts (normally itself contractual) may be such that for accounting purposes those contracts cannot be regarded as existing independently of each other.

References

1 IGC Q&A 10-6. Whilst the Implementation Guidance Committee (IGC) discussion was held in the context of IAS 39, the discussion also holds true under IFRS 9.
2 *IFRIC Update*, July 2007. Whilst the IFRIC discussion was held in the context of IAS 39, the discussion also holds true under IFRS 9.
3 *IFRIC Update*, July 2006. Whilst the IFRIC discussion was held in the context of IAS 39, the discussion also holds true under IFRS 9.
4 *IFRIC Update*, January 2007. Whilst the IFRIC discussion was held in the context of IAS 39, the discussion also holds true under IFRS 9.
5 *IASB Update*, February 2007. Whilst the IFRIC discussion was held in the context of IAS 39, the discussion also holds true under IFRS 9.
6 *IFRIC Update*, July 2006. Whilst the IFRIC discussion was held in the context of IAS 39, the discussion also holds true under IFRS 9.
7 *IFRIC Update*, January 2007. Whilst the IFRIC discussion was held in the context of IAS 39, the discussion also holds true under IFRS 9.
8 *IFRIC Update*, May 2009. Whilst the IFRIC discussion was held in the context of IAS 39, the discussion also holds true under IFRS 9.
9 Staff paper, *Accounting implications from derecognition of a modified financial instrument*, IASB staff paper 14B, October 2019, para 69.
10 Staff paper, *Term-extending options in fixed rate debt instruments*, IFRS Interpretations Committee, March 2012. Whilst the IFRIC discussion was held in the context of IAS 39, the discussion also holds true under IFRS 9.
11 *IFRIC Update*, March 2012. Whilst the IFRIC discussion was held in the context of IAS 39, the discussion also holds true under IFRS 9.

12 *Implementation of International Accounting Standards*, British Bankers' Association, July 2004, para. 10. Whilst the guidance was provided in the context of IAS 39, it holds true under IFRS 9.
13 *IFRIC Update*, January 2016.
14 Information for Observers of March 2006 IFRIC meeting, *Hedging Inflation Risk (Agenda Paper 12)*, IASB, March 2006, para. 32. Whilst the IFRIC discussion was held in the context of IAS 39, the discussion also holds true under IFRS 9.
15 Information for Observers (December 2008 IASB meeting), *Clarification of accounting for investments in collateralised debt obligations (Agenda Paper 6E)*, IASB, December 2008 and *Q&As on accounting for some collateralised debts obligations (CDOs) – prepared by staff of the IASB*, IASB, February 2009. Whilst the IASB discussion was held in the context of IAS 39, the discussion also holds true under IFRS 9.
16 *IFRIC Update*, May 2017.
17 *IFRIC Update*, September 2014. Whilst the IFRIC discussion was held in the context of IAS 39, the discussion also holds true under IFRS 9.
18 *IFRIC Update*, May 2007. Whilst the IFRIC discussion was held in the context of IAS 39, the discussion also holds true under IFRS 9.
19 Information for Observers (May 2007 IFRIC meeting), *IAS 39: Financial Instruments: Recognition and Measurement AG33(d)(iii) of IAS 39 (Agenda Paper 11(v))*, IASB, May 2007, paras. 12-14. Whilst the IFRIC discussion was held in the context of IAS 39, the discussion also holds true under IFRS 9.
20 Information for Observers, paras. 18 to 19. Whilst the IFRIC discussion was held in the context of IAS 39, the discussion also holds true under IFRS 9.
21 Information for Observers, paras. 20-28. Whilst the IFRIC discussion was held in the context of IAS 39, the discussion also holds true under IFRS 9.
22 Information for Observers (December 2007 IASB meeting), *Application of paragraph AG33(d)(iii) – Bifurcation of embedded foreign currency derivative (Agenda Paper 3C)*, IASB, December 2007, para. 11. Whilst the IASB discussion was held in the context of IAS 39, the discussion also holds true under IFRS 9.
23 Information for Observers (May 2007 IFRIC meeting), *IAS 39: Financial Instruments: Recognition and Measurement AG33(d)(iii) of IAS 39 (Agenda Paper 11(v))*, IASB, May 2007, para. 44. Whilst the IFRIC discussion was held in the context of IAS 39, the discussion also holds true under IFRS 9.
24 Information for Observers (December 2007 IASB meeting), *Application of paragraph AG33(d)(iii) – Bifurcation of embedded foreign currency derivative (Agenda Paper 3C)*, IASB, December 2007, paras. 12-13. Whilst the IFRIC discussion was held in the context of IAS 39, the discussion also holds true under IFRS 9.
25 Information for Observers, para. 14. Whilst the IFRIC discussion was held in the context of IAS 39, the discussion also holds true under IFRS 9.
26 Information for Observers, para. 15. Whilst the IFRIC discussion was held in the context of IAS 39, the discussion also holds true under IFRS 9.
27 IGC Q&A 23-8. Whilst the IGC discussion was held in the context of IAS 39, the discussion also holds true under IFRS 9.
28 IGC Q&A 23-8. Whilst the IGC discussion was held in the context of IAS 39, the discussion also holds true under IFRS 9.
29 *IFRIC Update*, April 2002, July 2002 and February 2003 and *IASB Update*, October 2002.
30 *IFRIC Update*, March 2014. Whilst the IFRIC discussion was held in the context of IAS 39, the discussion also holds true under IFRS 9.

Chapter 47 Financial instruments: Financial liabilities and equity

1 INTRODUCTION 3663
   1.1 Background 3663
   1.2 Development of IFRS on classification of liabilities and equity 3664
2 OBJECTIVE AND SCOPE 3665
   2.1 Objective 3665
   2.2 Scope 3665
3 DEFINITIONS 3665
4 CLASSIFICATION OF INSTRUMENTS 3668
   4.1 Definition of equity instrument 3668
   4.2 Contractual obligation to deliver cash or other financial assets 3669
      4.2.1 Relationship between an entity and its members 3671
      4.2.2 Implied contractual obligation to deliver cash or other financial assets 3672
   4.3 Contingent settlement provisions 3673
      4.3.1 Contingencies that are 'not genuine' 3674
      4.3.2 Liabilities that arise only on liquidation 3675
      4.3.3 Liabilities that arise only on a change of control 3675
      4.3.4 Some typical contingent settlement provisions 3676
   4.4 Examples of equity instruments 3677
      4.4.1 Issued instruments 3677
      4.4.2 Contracts to issue equity instruments 3677
   4.5 Preference shares and similar instruments 3678
      4.5.1 Instruments redeemable mandatorily or at the holder's option 3678

	4.5.2	Instruments redeemable only at the issuer's option or not redeemable	3679
	4.5.3	Instruments with a 'dividend blocker' or a 'dividend pusher' clause	3680
		4.5.3.A Instruments with a 'dividend blocker'	3680
		4.5.3.B Instruments with a 'dividend pusher'	3682
	4.5.4	Perpetual instruments with a 'step-up' clause	3682
	4.5.5	Relative subordination	3683
	4.5.6	Economic compulsion	3683
	4.5.7	'Linked' instruments	3684
	4.5.8	'Change of control', 'taxation change' and 'regulatory change' clauses	3684
4.6	Puttable instruments and instruments repayable only on liquidation		3685
	4.6.1	The issue	3685
	4.6.2	Puttable instruments	3686
	4.6.3	Instruments entitling the holder to a pro rata share of net assets only on liquidation	3688
	4.6.4	Clarification of the exemptions in 4.6.2 and 4.6.3 above	3689
		4.6.4.A Instruments issued by a subsidiary	3689
		4.6.4.B Relative subordination of the instrument	3690
		4.6.4.C Meaning of 'identical features'	3690
		4.6.4.D No obligation to deliver cash or another financial asset	3691
		4.6.4.E Instruments that substantially fix or restrict the residual return to the holder of an instrument	3692
		4.6.4.F Transactions entered into by an instrument holder other than as owner of the entity	3692
	4.6.5	Reclassification of puttable instruments and instruments imposing an obligation only on liquidation	3693
	4.6.6	IFRIC 2	3693
4.7	Perpetual debt		3695
4.8	Differences of classification between consolidated and single entity financial statements		3695
	4.8.1	Consolidated financial statements	3695
	4.8.2	Single entity financial statements	3696
4.9	Reclassification of instruments		3697
	4.9.1	Change of terms	3697
		4.9.1.A Equity instrument to financial liability	3698
		4.9.1.B Financial liability to equity instrument	3698
	4.9.2	Change of circumstances	3698
		4.9.2.A Arguments against reclassification	3699
		4.9.2.B Arguments for reclassification	3700

5 CONTRACTS SETTLED BY DELIVERY OF THE ENTITY'S OWN EQUITY INSTRUMENTS 3701

- 5.1 Contracts accounted for as equity instruments 3703
  - 5.1.1 Comparison with IFRS 2 – Share-based Payment 3703
  - 5.1.2 Number of equity instruments issued adjusted for capital restructuring or other event 3704
  - 5.1.3 Stepped up exercise price 3706
  - 5.1.4 Exchange of fixed amounts of equity (equity for equity) 3706
- 5.2 Contracts accounted for as financial assets or financial liabilities 3707
  - 5.2.1 Variable number of equity instruments 3707
  - 5.2.2 Fixed number of equity instruments for variable consideration 3707
  - 5.2.3 Fixed amount of cash (or other financial assets) denominated in a currency other than the entity's functional currency 3707
    - 5.2.3.A Rights issues with a price fixed in a currency other than the entity's functional currency 3708
  - 5.2.4 Instrument with equity settlement alternative of significantly higher value than cash settlement alternative 3709
  - 5.2.5 Fixed number of equity instruments with variable value 3710
  - 5.2.6 Fixed amount of cash determined by reference to share price 3710
  - 5.2.7 Net-settled contracts over own equity 3710
  - 5.2.8 Derivative financial instruments with settlement options 3710
- 5.3 Liabilities arising from gross-settled contracts for the purchase of the entity's own equity instruments 3711
  - 5.3.1 Contracts to purchase own equity during 'closed' or 'prohibited' periods 3713
  - 5.3.2 Contracts to acquire non-controlling interests 3713
    - 5.3.2.A Put options over non-controlling interests – Interpretations Committee and IASB developments 3714
- 5.4 Gross-settled contracts for the sale or issue of the entity's own equity instruments 3714

6 COMPOUND FINANCIAL INSTRUMENTS 3715

- 6.1 Background 3715
  - 6.1.1 Treatment by holder and issuer contrasted 3716
- 6.2 Initial recognition – 'split accounting' 3716
  - 6.2.1 Accounting for the equity component 3719
  - 6.2.2 Temporary differences arising from split accounting 3719
- 6.3 Conversion, early repurchase and modification 3720
  - 6.3.1 Conversion at maturity 3720

	6.3.2	Conversion before maturity		3720
		6.3.2.A	'Fixed stated principal' of a bond	3720
		6.3.2.B	Accounting treatment	3720
		6.3.2.C	Treatment of embedded derivatives on conversion	3721
	6.3.3	Early redemption or repurchase		3721
		6.3.3.A	Early repurchase through negotiation with bondholders	3722
		6.3.3.B	Early repurchase through exercising an embedded call option	3724
	6.3.4	Modification		3724
6.4	The components of a compound instrument			3725
	6.4.1	Determining the components of a compound instrument		3725
	6.4.2	Compound instruments with embedded derivatives		3726
		6.4.2.A	Issuer call option – 'closely related' embedded derivatives	3727
		6.4.2.B	Issuer call option – 'not closely related' embedded derivatives	3727
6.5	Other issues			3728
6.6	Common forms of convertible bonds			3729
	6.6.1	Functional currency bond convertible into a fixed number of shares		3729
	6.6.2	Contingent convertible bond		3729
	6.6.3	Mandatorily convertible bond		3729
		6.6.3.A	Bond which is mandatorily convertible into a variable number of shares with an option for the issuer to settle early for a maximum number of shares	3730
		6.6.3.B	Bond which is mandatorily convertible into a variable number of shares upon a contingent 'non-viability' event	3732
	6.6.4	Foreign currency convertible bond		3734
		6.6.4.A	Instrument issued by foreign subsidiary convertible into equity of parent	3734
	6.6.5	Convertibles with cash settlement at the option of the issuer		3736
	6.6.6	Bond convertible into fixed percentage of equity		3736
	6.6.7	Convertible bonds with down round or ratchet features		3736
7	SETTLEMENT OF FINANCIAL LIABILITY WITH EQUITY INSTRUMENT			3737
	7.1	Scope and effective date of IFRIC 19		3737
	7.2	Requirements of IFRIC 19		3738
	7.3	Debt for equity swaps with shareholders		3739

8	INTEREST, DIVIDENDS, GAINS AND LOSSES	3739
	8.1 Transaction costs of equity transactions	3740
	8.2 Tax effects of equity transactions	3742
9	TREASURY SHARES	3742
	9.1 Transactions in own shares not at fair value	3743
	9.2 IFRS 17 treasury share election	3744
10	'HEDGING' OF INSTRUMENTS CLASSIFIED AS EQUITY	3744
11	DERIVATIVES OVER OWN EQUITY INSTRUMENTS	3745
	11.1 Forward contracts	3746
	11.1.1 Forward purchase	3746
	11.1.2 Forward sale	3748
	11.1.3 'Back-to-back' forward contracts	3751
	11.2 Call options	3752
	11.2.1 Purchased call option	3752
	11.2.2 Written call option	3754
	11.3 Put options	3756
	11.3.1 Purchased put option	3756
	11.3.2 Written put option	3758
12	POSSIBLE FUTURE DEVELOPMENTS	3762

List of examples

Example 47.1:	Share issue payable in fixed instalments	3714
Example 47.2:	Right to call for additional equity capital	3714
Example 47.3:	Convertible bond – basic 'split accounting'	3717
Example 47.4:	Early repurchase of convertible instrument	3723
Example 47.5:	Modification of the terms of a bond to induce early conversion	3725
Example 47.6:	Analysis of compound financial instrument into components	3725
Example 47.7:	Convertible bond – split accounting with multiple embedded derivative features	3727
Example 47.8:	Foreign currency denominated equity instrument with issuer's redemption right	3728
Example 47.9:	Mandatorily convertible bond classified as equity	3730
Example 47.10:	Mandatorily convertible bond classified as a compound instrument	3730
Example 47.11:	Convertible bond mandatorily convertible upon 'non-viability' event	3733

Example 47.12:	Convertible bond issued by a subsidiary with a functional currency different to that of the parent..................................	3735
Example 47.13:	Convertible bond with ratchet feature	3737
Example 47.14:	Discharge of liability for fresh issue of equity	3738
Example 47.15:	Forward purchase of shares	3746
Example 47.16:	Forward sale of shares..	3748
Example 47.17:	'Back-to-back' forward contracts...	3751
Example 47.18:	Purchased call option on own shares	3752
Example 47.19:	Written call option on own shares	3754
Example 47.20:	Purchased put option on own shares.......................................	3756
Example 47.21:	Written put option on own shares..	3759

Chapter 47   Financial instruments: Financial liabilities and equity

1 INTRODUCTION

1.1 Background

The accounting treatment of liabilities (such as loans or bonds) and equity instruments (such as shares, stock or warrants) by their issuer was not historically regarded as presenting significant problems. Essentially the accounting was dictated by the legal form of the instrument, since the traditional distinction between equity and liabilities is clear. The issue of equity creates an ownership interest in a company, remunerated by dividends, which are accounted for as a distribution of retained profit, not a charge made in arriving at the result for a particular period. Liabilities, such as loan finance, on the other hand, are remunerated by interest, which is charged to profit or loss as an expense. In general, lenders rank before shareholders in priority of claims over the assets of the company, although in practice there may also be differential rights between different categories of lenders and classes of shareholders. The two forms of finance often have different tax implications, both for the investor and the investee.

In economic terms, however, the distinction between share and loan capital can be far less clear-cut than the legal categorisation would suggest. For example, a redeemable preference share could be considered to be, in substance, much more like a liability than equity. Conversely, many would argue that a bond which can never be repaid but which will be mandatorily converted into ordinary shares deserves to be thought of as being more in the nature of equity than of debt, even before conversion has occurred.

The ambiguous economic nature of such instruments has encouraged the development of a number of complex forms of finance which exhibit characteristics of both equity and debt. The 'holy grail' is generally to devise an instrument regarded as a liability by the tax authorities (such that the costs of servicing it are tax-deductible) but treated as equity for accounting and/or regulatory purposes (so that the instrument is not considered as a component of net borrowings).

The accounting classification of an instrument as a liability or equity is much more than a matter of allocation – i.e. where particular amounts are shown in the financial statements. The requirement of IFRS for certain liabilities, in particular derivatives, to be carried at fair value means that the classification of an item as a liability can introduce significant volatility into reported results, that would not arise if the item were classified as an equity instrument. This is because changes in the fair value of an equity instrument are not recognised in the financial statements of the issuer. *[IAS 32.36]*.

Moreover, the extent to which an entity funds its operations through debt or equity is regarded as highly significant not only by investors, but also by other users of financial statements such as regulators and tax authorities. This means that the question of whether a particular instrument is a liability or equity raises issues of much greater and wider sensitivity than the mere matter of financial statement classification.

1.2 Development of IFRS on classification of liabilities and equity

Under IFRS, the classification of items as liabilities or equity is dealt with mainly in IAS 32 – *Financial Instruments: Presentation* – with some cross-reference to IFRS 9 – *Financial Instruments*.

IAS 32 was originally issued in March 1995 and subsequently amended in 1998 and 2000. However, in December 2003, the previous version of IAS 32 was withdrawn and superseded by a new version, which has itself been amended by subsequent new pronouncements, most notably IFRS 7 – *Financial Instruments: Disclosures* (see Chapter 54) and the amendment to IAS 32 – *Puttable Financial Instruments and Obligations Arising on Liquidation*.

The main text of IAS 32 is supplemented by application guidance (which is an integral part of the standard),[1] and by illustrative examples (which accompany, but are not part of, the standard).[2]

The Interpretations Committee has issued two interpretations of IAS 32 discussed in this chapter:

- IFRIC 2 – *Members' Shares in Co-operative Entities and Similar Instruments* (see 4.6.6 below); and
- IFRIC 19 – *Extinguishing Financial Liabilities with Equity Instruments* (see 7 below).

A joint attempt of the IASB and the FASB to develop a new model, in which classification of an instrument was based on whether the instrument would be settled with assets or with equity instruments of the issuer, was suspended in October 2010 due to significant challenges raised by a small group of external reviewers of a draft exposure draft.

In October 2014 the IASB resumed the *Financial Instruments with Characteristics of Equity Research Project* to explore further how to distinguish liabilities from equity claims. Following the issue of a Discussion Paper (the FICE DP) in June 2018 the IASB is now looking at addressing certain known practice issues by clarifying some of the underlying principles in IAS 32 (see 12 below).

2 OBJECTIVE AND SCOPE

2.1 Objective

The objective of IAS 32 is 'to establish principles for presenting financial instruments as liabilities or equity and for offsetting financial assets and financial liabilities.' *[IAS 32.2]*. The standard, and its associated IFRIC interpretations, address:

- the classification of financial instruments, by their issuer, into financial assets, financial liabilities and equity instruments (see 3 to 6 below);
- settling a financial liability with an equity instrument (see 7 below);
- the classification of interest, dividends, losses and gains (see 8 below);
- treasury shares – i.e. an entity's own equity instruments held by the entity (see 9 below);
- forward contracts or options for the receipt or delivery of the entity's own equity instruments (see 11 below); and
- the circumstances in which financial assets and financial liabilities should be offset (see Chapter 54 at 7.4.1).

The principles in IAS 32 complement the principles for recognising and measuring financial assets and financial liabilities in IFRS 9, and for disclosing information about them in IFRS 7. *[IAS 32.3]*.

2.2 Scope

The scope of IAS 32 is discussed in detail in Chapter 45 at 3.

3 DEFINITIONS

The following definitions in IAS 32 are relevant to the issues discussed in this chapter. Further general discussion on the meaning and implications of the definitions may be found in Chapter 45 at 2.

A *financial instrument* is any contract that gives rise to a financial asset of one entity and a financial liability or equity instrument of another entity. *[IAS 32.11]*.

A *financial asset* is any asset that is:
(a) cash;
(b) an equity instrument of another entity;
(c) a contractual right:
  (i) to receive cash or another financial asset from another entity; or
  (ii) to exchange financial assets or financial liabilities with another entity under conditions that are potentially favourable to the entity; or
(d) a contract that will or may be settled in the entity's own equity instruments and is:
  (i) a non-derivative for which the entity is or may be obliged to receive a variable number of the entity's own equity instruments; or
  (ii) a derivative that will or may be settled other than by the exchange of a fixed amount of cash or another financial asset for a fixed number of the entity's own equity instruments. For this purpose, the entity's own equity instruments do not include:
    - puttable financial instruments classified as equity instruments in accordance with paragraphs 16A and 16B of the standard (see 4.6.2 below);
    - instruments that impose on the entity an obligation to deliver to another party a *pro rata* share of the net assets of the entity only on liquidation and are classified as equity in accordance with paragraphs 16C and 16D of the standard (see 4.6.3 below); or
    - instruments that are contracts for the future receipt or delivery of the entity's own equity instruments. *[IAS 32.11]*.

A *financial liability* is any liability that is:
(a) a contractual obligation:
  (i) to deliver cash or another financial asset to another entity; or
  (ii) to exchange financial assets or financial liabilities with another entity under conditions that are potentially unfavourable to the entity; or
(b) a contract that will or may be settled in the entity's own equity instruments and is:
  (i) a non-derivative for which the entity is or may be obliged to deliver a variable number of the entity's own equity instruments; or
  (ii) a derivative that will or may be settled other than by the exchange of a fixed amount of cash or another financial asset for a fixed number of the entity's own equity instruments. For this purpose, rights, options or warrants to acquire a fixed number of the entity's own equity instruments for a fixed amount of any currency are equity instruments if the entity offers the rights, options or warrants *pro rata* to all of its existing owners of the same class of its own non-derivative equity instruments. Also, for these purposes the entity's own equity instruments do not include:

- puttable financial instruments classified as equity instruments in accordance with paragraphs 16A and 16B of the standard (see 4.6.2 below);
- instruments that impose on the entity an obligation to deliver to another party a *pro rata* share of the net assets of the entity only on liquidation and are classified as equity in accordance with paragraphs 16C and 16D of the standard (see 4.6.3 below); or
- instruments that are contracts for the future receipt or delivery of the entity's own equity instruments. *[IAS 32.11]*.

As an exception to the general definition of a financial liability, an instrument that meets the definition of a financial liability is nevertheless classified as an equity instrument if it has all the features and meets the conditions in paragraphs 16A and 16B (see 4.6.2 below) or paragraphs 16C and 16D of the standard (see 4.6.3 below). *[IAS 32.11]*.

A *puttable instrument* is a financial instrument that gives the holder the right to put the instrument back to the issuer for cash or another financial asset or is automatically put back to the issuer on the occurrence of an uncertain future event or the death or retirement of the holder. *[IAS 32.11]*.

An *equity instrument* is any contract that evidences a residual interest in the assets of an entity after deducting all of its liabilities. *[IAS 32.11]*.

A *derivative* is a financial instrument or other contract within the scope of IFRS 9 (see Chapter 46 at 2) with all three of the following characteristics:
- its value changes in response to the change in a specified interest rate, financial instrument price, commodity price, foreign exchange rate, index of prices or rates, credit rating or credit index, or other variable, provided in the case of a non-financial variable that the variable is not specific to a party of the contract (sometimes called the 'underlying');
- it requires no initial net investment or an initial net investment that is smaller than would be required for other types of contracts that would be expected to have a similar response to changes in market factors; and
- it is settled at a future date. *[IFRS 9 Appendix A]*.

Fair value is the price that would be received to sell an asset or paid to transfer a liability in an orderly transaction between market participants at the measurement date. *[IAS 32.11]*. This is the same definition as used in IFRS 13 – *Fair Value Measurement* (see Chapter 14 at 3).

In these definitions (and throughout IAS 32 and the discussion in this chapter):
- *Contract* and *contractual* refer to an agreement between two or more parties that has clear economic consequences that the parties have little, if any, discretion to avoid, usually because the agreement is enforceable by law. Contracts, and thus financial instruments, may take a variety of forms and need not be in writing; *[IAS 32.13]*
- *Entity* includes individuals, partnerships, incorporated bodies, trusts and government agencies. *[IAS 32.14]*.

4 CLASSIFICATION OF INSTRUMENTS

The most important issue dealt with by IAS 32 is the classification of financial instruments (or their components) by their issuer as financial liabilities, financial assets or equity instruments, including non-controlling interests. The rule in IAS 32 for classification of items as financial liabilities or equity is essentially simple. An issuer of a financial instrument must classify the instrument (or its component parts) on initial recognition as a financial liability, a financial asset or an equity instrument in accordance with the substance of the contractual arrangement and the definitions of a financial liability, a financial asset and an equity instrument (see 3 above). *[IAS 32.15]*. The application of this principle in practice, however, is often far from straightforward.

IAS 32 considers the question of whether a transaction is a financial liability or an equity instrument at two levels. First, it examines whether an individual instrument (or class of instruments) issued by the entity is a financial liability or equity. This is principally discussed in this section, although some of the provisions discussed at 5 and 6 below may also be relevant.

Second, where an entity settles a transaction using instruments issued by it that, when considered in isolation, would be classified as equity, IAS 32 requires the entity to consider whether the transaction considered as a whole is in fact a financial liability. This will typically be the case where a transaction is settled by issuing a variable number of equity instruments equal to an agreed value. This is principally discussed at 5 and 6 below, although some of the provisions discussed here at 4 may also be relevant.

The appropriate classification is made on initial recognition of the instrument and, in general, not changed subsequently (see 4.9 below on reclassification of instruments).

4.1 Definition of equity instrument

Application of the basic definitions in IAS 32 means that an instrument is an equity instrument only if both the following conditions are met:

- The instrument includes no contractual obligation either:
    - to deliver cash or another financial asset to another entity; or
    - to exchange financial assets or financial liabilities with another entity under conditions that are potentially unfavourable to the issuer.
- If the instrument will, or may, be settled in the issuer's own equity instruments, it is either:
    - a non-derivative that includes no contractual obligation for the issuer to deliver a variable number of its own equity instruments; or
    - a derivative that will be settled only by the issuer exchanging a fixed amount of cash or another financial asset for a fixed number of its own equity instruments. For this purpose the issuer's own equity instruments do not include instruments that have all the features and meet the conditions described in paragraphs 16A and 16B (see 4.6.2 below) or paragraphs 16C and 16D (see 4.6.3 below) of IAS 32 or instruments that are contracts for the future receipt or delivery of the issuer's own equity instruments. *[IAS 32.16]*.

As a pragmatic exception to these basic criteria, an instrument that would otherwise meet the definition of a financial liability is nevertheless classified as an equity instrument if it is either:

- a puttable instrument with all the features, and meeting the conditions described, in paragraphs 16A and 16B of IAS 32 (see 4.6.2 below); or
- an instrument entitling the holder to a *pro rata* share of assets on a liquidation with all the features, and meeting all the conditions, described in paragraphs 16C and 16D of IAS 32. *[IAS 32.16]*. This is discussed further at 4.6.3 below.

Broadly speaking, apart from this exemption, an instrument can only be classified as equity under IAS 32 if the issuer has an unconditional right to avoid delivering cash or another financial instrument (see 4.2 below) or, if it is settled through the entity's own equity instruments, it is for an exchange of a fixed amount of cash for a fixed number of the entity's own equity instruments. In all other cases it would be classified as a financial liability.

4.2 Contractual obligation to deliver cash or other financial assets

It is apparent from 4.1 above that a critical feature in differentiating a financial liability from an equity instrument is the existence of a contractual obligation of one party to the financial instrument (the issuer) either:

- to deliver cash or another financial asset to the other party (the holder); or
- to exchange financial assets or financial liabilities with the holder under conditions that are potentially unfavourable to the issuer. *[IAS 32.17]*.

IAS 32 focuses on the contractual rights and obligations arising from the terms of an instrument, rather than on the probability of those rights and obligations leading to an outflow of cash or other resources from the entity, as would be the case for a provision accounted for under IAS 37 – *Provisions, Contingent Liabilities and Contingent Assets* (see Chapter 26). Thus, IAS 32 may well:

- classify as equity: an instrument that is virtually certain to result in regular cash payments by the entity; but
- treat as a liability: an instrument which:
  - gives its holder a right to receive cash rather than equity which no rational holder would exercise; or
  - exposes the issuer to a liability to repay the instrument contingent on an external event so remote that no liability would be recognised if IAS 37 rather than IAS 32 were the applicable standard.

The holder of an equity instrument (e.g. a non-puttable share) may be entitled to receive a *pro rata* share of any dividends or other distributions of equity that are made. However, since the issuer does not have a contractual obligation to make such distributions (because it cannot be required to deliver cash or another financial asset to another party), the instrument is not a financial liability of the issuer. *[IAS 32.17]*. The price or value of such an instrument may well reflect a general expectation by market participants that distributions will be made on a regular basis, but, under IAS 32, the absence of a contractual obligation requires the instrument to be classified as equity.

IAS 32 requires the issuer of a financial instrument to classify a financial instrument by reference to its substance rather than its legal form, although it is conceded that substance and form are 'commonly', but not always, the same. Typical examples of instruments that are equity in legal form but liabilities in substance are certain types of preference share (see 4.5 below) and certain units in open-ended funds, unit trusts and similar entities (see 4.6 below). *[IAS 32.18]*. Conversely, a number of entities have issued instruments which behave in most practical respects as perpetual (or even redeemable) debt, but which IAS 32 requires to be classified as equity (see 4.5 below). IAS 32 further clarifies that a financial instrument is an equity instrument, and not a financial liability, not merely if the issuer has no legal obligation to deliver cash or other financial assets to the holder at the reporting date, but only if it has an unconditional right to avoid doing so in all future circumstances other than an unforeseen liquidation. Thus, a financial instrument (other than one classified as equity under the exceptions discussed at 4.6 below) is classified as a financial liability even if:

- the issuer's ability to discharge its obligations under the instrument is restricted (e.g. by a lack of funds, the need to obtain regulatory approval to make payments on the instrument, or a shortfall of distributable profits, or other statutory restriction); *[IAS 32.19, AG25]* or
- the holder has to perform some action (e.g. formally exercise a redemption right) in order for the issuer to become obliged to transfer cash or other financial assets. *[IAS 32.19]*.

In September 2015 the Interpretations Committee considered the classification of a prepaid card and how the unspent balance on such a card would be accounted for. The Interpretations Committee specifically considered a prepaid card with the following features:

- no expiry date;
- cannot be refunded, redeemed or exchanged for cash;
- redeemable only for goods and services;
- redeemable only at selected merchants which could include the entity;
- upon redemption by the cardholder at a merchant, the entity has a contractual obligation to pay cash to the merchant;
- no back-end fees, e.g. the balance on the prepaid card does not reduce unless spent by the cardholder; and
- is not issued as part of a customer loyalty programme.

The Interpretations Committee observed that the liability of the entity for the prepaid card meets the definition of a financial liability, because the entity has a contractual obligation to deliver cash to the merchants on behalf of the cardholder, conditional upon the cardholder using the prepaid card to buy goods or services and the entity does not have an unconditional right to avoid delivering cash to settle this contractual obligation.[3]

Following the receipt of responses to the draft agenda decision, the Interpretations Committee, in March 2016, limited the fact pattern to where the card could only be redeemed at specified third-party merchants and not at the entity itself but otherwise did not change its conclusion.

The Interpretations Committee determined that neither an interpretation nor an amendment to a standard was necessary.[4]

One of the key consequences of this decision is that if the card gives rise to a financial liability then the unspent balance on the card cannot be derecognised. Any unredeemed portion of the card will continue to be recognised as a liability in perpetuity as financial liabilities can only be derecognised when extinguished. *[IFRS 9.3.3.1]*. It is also of note that the balances on such cards are regarded as financial liabilities even though they do not meet the strict IAS 32 definition of a financial instrument, as the balance on the prepaid card will not constitute a financial asset in the hands of the cardholder.

4.2.1   Relationship between an entity and its members

The unconditional right of the entity to avoid delivering cash or another financial asset in settlement of an obligation is crucial in differentiating a financial liability from an equity instrument. In our view, the role of the entity's shareholders is critical in determining the classification of financial instruments when the shareholders can decide whether the entity delivers cash or another financial asset. It is therefore important to understand the relationship between the entity and its members. Shareholders can make decisions as part of the corporate governance decision making process of the entity (generally exercised in a general meeting) or separate from the entity's corporate governance decision making process in their capacity as holders of particular instruments.

In some entities, the right to declare dividends and/or redeem capital is reserved for the members of the entity in general meeting, as a matter either of the entity's own constitution or of general legislation in the jurisdiction concerned. The effect of such a right may be that the members can require payment of a dividend irrespective of the wishes of management. Even where management has the right to prevent a payment declared by the members, the members will generally have the right to appoint the management and can therefore appoint management that will not oppose an equity distribution declared by the members.

This raises the question whether an entity whose members have such rights should classify all its distributable retained earnings as a liability, on the grounds that the members could require earnings to be distributed as dividend, or capital to be repaid, at any time. In our view this is not appropriate, since an action reserved to the entity's shareholders in general meeting, is effectively an action of the entity itself. It is therefore at the discretion of the entity itself (as represented by the members in general meeting) that retained earnings are paid out as a dividend. Accordingly, in our view, such earnings are classified as equity, and not as a financial liability, until they become a legal liability of the entity.

If on the other hand, decisions by the shareholders are not made as part of the entity's corporate governance decision making process, but made in their capacity as holders of particular instruments, it is our view that the shareholders should be considered to be separate from the entity. The entity therefore would not have an unconditional right to avoid delivering cash or another financial asset and would have to classify the financial instrument as a financial liability.

This issue was brought to the Interpretations Committee in January 2010. The Interpretations Committee identified that diversity may exist in practice in assessing whether an entity has an unconditional right to avoid delivering cash if the contractual obligation is at the ultimate discretion of the issuer's shareholders, and consequently whether a financial instrument should be classified as a financial liability or equity. However, the Interpretations Committee concluded that the Board's then current project on financial instruments with characteristics of equity was expected to address the distinction between equity and non-equity instruments on a timely basis, and that the Interpretations Committee would therefore not add this to its agenda.[5] In October 2010 the project was suspended but was restarted in October 2014. The Board is currently considering a number of IAS 32 practice issues including those concerning contingent settlement provisions (see 12 below).

4.2.2 Implied contractual obligation to deliver cash or other financial assets

A financial instrument that does not explicitly establish a contractual obligation to deliver cash or another financial asset may nevertheless establish an obligation indirectly through its terms and conditions. [IAS 32.20].

IAS 32.20 provides two examples:

(a) A financial instrument may contain a non-financial obligation that must be settled if, and only if, the entity fails to make distributions or to redeem the instrument. If the entity can avoid a transfer of cash or another financial asset only by settling the non-financial obligation, the financial instrument is a financial liability.

(b) A financial instrument is a financial liability if it provides that on settlement the entity will deliver either:

  i. cash or another financial asset; or
  ii. its own shares whose value is determined to exceed substantially the value of the cash or other financial asset.

Although the entity does not have an explicit contractual obligation to deliver cash or another financial asset, the value of the share settlement alternative is such that the entity will settle in cash. [IAS 32.20].

The basic requirement of IAS 32.20 is for an entity to recognise a financial liability when it can only avoid using cash to settle an obligation by transferring a financial asset or a non-financial asset, in other words settlement of the obligation cannot be avoided in any other way. Then, given that the entity's own shares are not an asset, subparagraph (b)(ii) avoids a potential loophole: if the value of the shares would exceed the amount of cash that would be required to settle the liability, the entity will be economically compelled to settle the cash amount and hence, has a financial liability.

This accounting treatment was illustrated by a question put to the Interpretations Committee in 2015.[6] They considered an arrangement whereby an entity received cash from a government to fund a research and development project. The cash was repayable to the government only if the entity decided to exploit and commercialise the results of the project. If the project was not commercially exploited the entity was obliged to transfer the rights to the research to the government.

The Interpretations Committee observed in May 2016[7] that, in this case, the cash receipt gave rise to a financial liability. In reaching their conclusion the Interpretations Committee took the view that the entity could avoid transferring cash only by settling the obligation with a non-financial instrument (the rights to the research). The Interpretations Committee further noted that the cash received from the government does not meet the definition of a forgivable loan in IAS 20 – *Accounting for Government Grants and Disclosure of Government Assistance* – as the government does not undertake to waive repayment of the loan but requires settlement in cash or by transfer of the rights to research. However they also noted that the entity would be required at initial recognition to assess whether the cash received from the government is something other than a financial instrument, for example the difference between the cash received and the fair value of the financial liability may represent a government grant that should be accounted for in accordance with IAS 20.

This last sentence implies that where the fair value of the alternative settlement option is less than fair value of the cash settlement option, paragraph 20 of IAS 32 only requires a financial liability to be recorded to the extent of the fair value of the alternative settlement option. But, in this example, the Interpretations Committee did not discuss what the fair value of the research and development might be. The Interpretations Committee's discussion demonstrates that where entities receive loans with alternative repayment conditions involving settlement with a non-financial asset, judgement will be necessary in assessing the substance of the settlement requirements and determining the value at inception of the non-financial asset.

4.3 Contingent settlement provisions

Some financial instruments may require the entity to deliver cash or another financial asset, or otherwise to settle it in such a way that it would be classified as a financial liability, in the event of the occurrence or non-occurrence of uncertain future events (or on the outcome of uncertain circumstances), that are beyond the control of both the issuer and the holder of the instrument. These might include:

- a change in a stock market index or a consumer price index;
- changes in interest rates;
- changes in tax law; or
- the issuer's future revenues, net income or debt-to-equity ratio. *[IAS 32.25]*.

IAS 32 provides that, since the issuer of such an instrument does not have the unconditional right to avoid delivering cash or another financial asset (or otherwise to settle it in such a way that it would be a financial liability), the instrument is a financial liability of the issuer unless:

- the part of the contingent settlement provision that could require settlement in cash or another financial asset (or otherwise in such a way that it would be a financial liability) is not genuine (see 4.3.1 below);
- the issuer can be required to settle the obligation in cash or another financial asset (or otherwise to settle it in such a way that it would be a financial liability) only in the event of liquidation of the issuer (see 4.3.2 below); or
- the instrument is classified as equity under the exceptions discussed at 4.6 below. *[IAS 32.25]*.

Whether or not the contingency is within the control of the issuer is therefore an important consideration when classifying financial instruments with contingent settlement provisions as either financial liabilities or equity (see 4.3.4 below).

It is interesting that 'future revenues, net income or debt-to-equity ratio' are given as examples of contingencies beyond the control of both the issuer and the holder of the instrument, since, in some cases, these matters are within the control of the entity. For example, if a payment under a financial instrument is contingent upon revenue rising above a certain level, the entity could avoid the payment by ceasing to trade before revenue reaches that level. Indeed, IAS 37 argues that certain expenses (such as legally required maintenance costs) that an entity is certain to incur if it continues to trade are not liabilities until they become legally due, because the entity could avoid them by ceasing to trade by that date. As in 4.2.2 above, the analysis in IAS 32 appears to be relying on the concept of 'economic compulsion' (i.e. the entity would not rationally cease its activities merely in order to avoid making a contingent payment), even though this does not feature in the definition of 'contingent liability' in IAS 37, or indeed in the classification of many instruments under IAS 32.

4.3.1 Contingencies that are 'not genuine'

A requirement to settle an instrument in cash or another financial asset (or otherwise in such a way that it would be a financial liability) is not genuine (see 4.3 above) if the requirement would arise 'only on the occurrence of an event that is extremely rare, highly abnormal and very unlikely to occur'. *[IAS 32.AG28]*.

Similarly, if the terms of an instrument provide for its settlement in a fixed number of the entity's equity instruments, but there are circumstances, beyond the entity's control, in which such settlement may be contractually precluded, and settlement in cash or other assets required instead, those circumstances can be ignored if there is 'no genuine possibility' that they will occur. In other words, the instrument continues to be regarded as an equity instrument and not as a financial liability. *[IAS 32.AG28]*.

Guidance in IAS 32 on the meaning of 'not genuine' in this context is unfortunately restricted to the thesaurus of synonyms ('extremely rare, highly abnormal and very unlikely to occur') above. It is, however, helpful to consider the changes made when, in 2003, SIC-5 – *Classification of Financial Instruments – Contingent Settlement Provisions*[8] – was withdrawn, and its substance incorporated in these provisions of IAS 32. SIC-5 had previously required redemption terms to be ignored if they were 'remote'. Examples given by SIC-5 were where the issue of shares is contingent merely on formal approval by the authorities, or where cash settlement is triggered by an index reaching an 'extreme' level relative to its level at the time of initial recognition of the instrument.[9]

IAS 32 deliberately did not reproduce the reference to, or the examples of, 'remote' events in SIC-5. In the Basis for Conclusions to IAS 32 the IASB states that it does not believe it is appropriate to disregard events that are merely 'remote'. *[IAS 32.BC17]*. Thus it is clear that, under the revised version of IAS 32, it is not appropriate to disregard a redemption term that is triggered only when an index reaches an extreme level. This suggests that it is not open to an entity to argue (for example) that a bond that is redeemed in cash only if the entity's share price falls below, or fails to reach, a certain level can be treated as an equity instrument on the grounds that there is no genuine possibility that the share price will perform in that way.

In general, terms are included in a contract for an economic purpose and therefore are genuine. The current reference in IAS 32 to terms that are 'not genuine' is presumably intended to deal with clauses inserted into the terms of financial instruments for some legal or tax reason (e.g. so as to make conversion technically 'conditional' rather than mandatory) but having no real economic purpose or consequence.

An example of a clause that has caused some debate on this point is a 'regulatory change' clause, generally found in the terms of capital instruments issued by financial institutions such as banks and insurance companies. Such entities are generally required by local regulators to maintain certain minimum levels of equity or highly subordinated debt (generally referred to as regulatory capital) in order to be allowed to do business.

A 'regulatory change' clause will typically require an instrument which, at the date of issue, is classified as regulatory capital to be repaid in the event that it ceases to be so classified. The practice so far of the regulators in many markets has been to make changes to a regulatory classification with prospective effect only, such that any instruments already in issue continue to be regarded as regulatory capital even though they would not be under the new rules.

This has led some to question whether a 'regulatory change' clause can be regarded as a contingent settlement provision which is 'not genuine'.[10] This is ultimately a matter for the judgement of entities and their auditors in the context of the relevant regulatory environment(s). This judgement has not been made easier by the greater unpredictability of the markets (and therefore of regulators' responses to it) since the last financial crisis.

4.3.2 Liabilities that arise only on liquidation

As noted in 4.3 above, IAS 32 provides that a contingent settlement provision that comes into play only on liquidation of the issuer may be ignored in determining whether or not a financial instrument is a financial liability. IAS 32 refers specifically to 'liquidation'. In other words, if an instrument provides for redemption on the occurrence of events that are a possible precursor of liquidation (e.g. extreme insolvency, the financial statements not being prepared on a going concern basis, or the entity being placed under the protection of Chapter 11 of the United States Bankruptcy Code) but falling short of formal liquidation, the instrument must be treated as a financial liability. Also, where liquidation is in the control of the holder, the instrument will be a liability as this exception only applies to contingencies beyond the control of both the issuer and the holder.

4.3.3 Liabilities that arise only on a change of control

A number of entities have issued instruments on terms that require the issuing entity to transfer cash or other financial assets only in the event of a change in control of the issuing entity. This raises the question of whether such an event is outside the control of the issuing entity, with the effect than any instrument containing such a provision would be classified as a liability to the extent of any obligations arising on a change of control.

This issue is far from straightforward. As noted at 4.2.1 above, it is our view that, where the power to make a decision is reserved for the members of an entity in general meeting, for the purposes of such a decision, the members and the entity are one and the same. Therefore, we consider that any change of control requiring the approval of the members in general meeting should be regarded as within the control of the entity.

Conversely, in our view, a change of control is not within the control of the entity where it can be effected by one or more individual shareholders without reference to the members in general meeting, for example where a shareholder holding 40% of the ordinary equity sells its shares to another party already owning 30%.

4.3.4 Some typical contingent settlement provisions

The matrix below gives a number of contingent settlement provisions that we have encountered in practice – some common, some rather esoteric – together with our view as to whether they should be regarded as outside the control of the reporting entity. If a contingent settlement provision is regarded as outside the control of the issuing entity, the instrument will be classified as a liability by the issuer. If a contingent settlement provision is regarded as within the control of the reporting entity, the instrument will be classified as equity, provided that it has no other features requiring its classification as a liability and that the contingent settlement event is also outside the control of the holder.

Contingent settlement event	Within the issuer's control?
Issuer makes a distribution on ordinary shares.	Yes. Dividends on ordinary shares are discretionary (see also 4.2 above).
Upon the successful takeover of the issuer (i.e. a 'control event').	It depends. See 4.3.3 above.
Event of default under any of the issuer's debt facilities.	No.
Appointment of a receiver, administrator, entering a scheme of arrangement, or compromise agreement with creditors.	No. Whether this leads to the instrument being classified as equity or liability will depend on the respective requirements in each jurisdiction. In cases when these events do not necessarily result in liquidation of the issuer, this leads to classification as a liability (see 4.3.2 above).
Upon commencement of proceedings for the winding up of the issuer.	No, but this does not lead to classification as a liability due to the requirement to ignore settlement provisions arising only on liquidation (see 4.3.2 above).
Incurring a fine exceeding a given amount, or commencement of an investigation of the issuer by, a government agency or a financial regulator.	No.
A change in accounting, taxation, or regulatory regime which is expected to adversely affect the financial position of the issuer.	No.
Suspension of listing of the issuer's shares from trading on the stock exchange for more than a certain number of days.	Probably not, but it will depend on the jurisdiction and whether the reasons for suspension are always within the control of the entity.
Commencement of war or armed conflict.	No.
Issue of a subordinated security that ranks equally or in priority to the securities.	Yes.

Issue of an IPO prospectus prior to the conversion date.	Yes.
Execution of an effective IPO.	No. The execution of a successful IPO is not within the control of the issuer. However, a contractual obligation to pay cash in the event of an IPO taking place is within the control of the issuer as the issuer can determine whether an IPO occurs or not and thus can avoid the obligation to pay cash.
Disposal of all or substantially all of the issuer's business undertaking or assets.	Yes.
Change in credit rating of the issuer.	No.

4.4 Examples of equity instruments

4.4.1 Issued instruments

Under the criteria above, equity instruments under IAS 32 will include non-puttable common (ordinary) shares and some types of preference share (see 4.5 below). *[IAS 32.AG13]*.

Whilst non-puttable shares are typically equity, an issuer of non-puttable ordinary shares nevertheless assumes a liability when it formally acts to make a distribution and becomes legally obliged to the shareholders to do so. This may be the case following the declaration of a dividend, or when, on a winding up, any assets remaining after discharging the entity's liabilities become distributable to shareholders. *[IAS 32.AG13]*. For example, if an entity has issued €100 million of equity instruments on which it declares a dividend of €2 million, it recognises a liability of only €2 million. Whether or not a liability arises on declaration of a dividend will depend on local legislation or the terms of the instruments or both.

IAS 32 also treats as equity instruments some puttable instruments (see 4.6.2 below) and some instruments that impose an obligation on the issuer to deliver a *pro rata* share of net assets only on liquidation (see 4.6.3 below) that would otherwise be classified as financial liabilities. However, a contract that is required to be settled by the entity receiving or delivering either of these types of 'deemed' equity instrument is a financial asset or financial liability, even when it involves the exchange of a fixed amount of cash or other financial assets for a fixed number of such instruments. *[IAS 32.22A, AG13]*.

4.4.2 Contracts to issue equity instruments

A contract settled using equity instruments is not necessarily itself regarded as an equity instrument. The classification of contracts settled using issued equity instruments is discussed further at 5 below.

Warrants or written call options that allow the holder to subscribe for or purchase a fixed number of non-puttable common (ordinary) shares in the issuing entity in exchange for a fixed amount of cash or another financial asset, or the fixed stated principal of a bond, are classified as equity instruments. *[IAS 32.22, AG13]*. The meaning of a 'fixed' amount of cash is not as self-evident as it might appear and is discussed further at 5.2.3 below. The meaning of the 'fixed stated principal' of a bond is discussed further at 6.3.2.A below.

Conversely, an instrument is a financial liability (or financial asset) of the issuer if it gives the holder the right to obtain:

- a variable number of non-puttable common (ordinary) shares in the issuing entity in exchange for a fixed amount of cash or another financial asset; *[IAS 32.21]* or
- a fixed number of non-puttable common (ordinary) shares in the issuing entity in exchange for a variable amount of cash or another financial asset. *[IAS 32.24]*.

An obligation for the entity to issue or purchase a fixed number of its own equity instruments in exchange for a fixed amount of cash or another financial asset is classified as an equity instrument of the entity. However, if such a contract contains an obligation – or even a potential obligation – for the entity to pay cash or another financial asset, it gives rise to a liability for the present value of the redemption amount (which results in a reduction of equity, not an expense – see 5.3 below). *[IAS 32.23, AG13]*.

A purchased call option or other similar contract acquired by an entity that gives it the right to reacquire a fixed number of its own equity instruments in exchange for delivering a fixed amount of cash or another financial asset is not a financial asset of the entity. Rather, it is classified as an equity instrument, and any consideration paid for such a contract is therefore deducted from equity (see 11.2.1 below). *[IAS 32.22, AG14]*. This requirement refers only to contracts which require the entity to settle gross (i.e. the entity pays cash in exchange for its own shares). Contracts which can be net settled (i.e. the party for whom the contract is loss-making delivers cash or shares equal to the fair value of the contract to the other party) are generally treated as financial assets or financial liabilities. This is discussed in more detail at 11 below.

4.5 Preference shares and similar instruments

Whilst some of the discussion below (and the guidance in IAS 32) is, for convenience, framed in terms of 'preference shares', it should be applied equally to any financial instrument, however described, with similar characteristics. In practice, many such instruments are not described as shares (possibly to avoid weakening any argument that, for fiscal purposes, they are tax-deductible debt rather than non-deductible equity).

Preference shares may be issued with various rights. In determining whether a preference share is a financial liability or an equity instrument, IAS 32 requires an issuer to assess the particular rights attaching to the share to determine whether it exhibits the fundamental characteristic of a financial liability. *[IAS 32.AG25]*.

IAS 32 does this in part by drawing a distinction between:

- instruments mandatorily redeemable or redeemable at the holder's option (see 4.5.1 below); and
- other instruments – i.e. those redeemable only at the issuer's option or not redeemable (see 4.5.2 to 4.5.4 below).

4.5.1 Instruments redeemable mandatorily or at the holder's option

A preference share (or other instrument) that:

- provides for mandatory redemption by the issuer for a fixed or determinable amount at a fixed or determinable future date; or

- gives the holder the right to require the issuer to redeem the instrument at or after a particular date for a fixed or determinable amount,

contains a financial liability, since the issuer has an obligation, or potential obligation, to transfer cash or other financial assets to the holder. This obligation is not negated by the potential inability of an issuer to redeem a preference share when contractually required to do so, whether because of a lack of funds, a statutory restriction or insufficient profits or reserves. *[IAS 32.18(a), AG25]*.

It is more correct to say (in the words of the application guidance) that an instrument 'contains' a financial liability than to say (as the main body of the standard does) that it 'is' a financial liability. For example, if a preference share is issued on terms that it is redeemable at the holder's option, but dividends are paid entirely at the issuer's discretion, it is only the amount payable on redemption that is a liability. This would lead to a 'split accounting' treatment (see 6 below), whereby, at issue, the net present value of the amount payable on redemption would be classified as a liability and the balance of the issue proceeds as equity. *[IAS 32.AG37]*.

Non-discretionary dividends, on the other hand, establish an additional liability component. In such a case there is a contractual obligation to pay cash in respect of both the redemption of the principal and the required dividend payments up to the redemption of the instrument. The liability would be recognised at an amount equal to the present value of both the redemption amount and the non-discretionary dividends. Assuming that the dividends were set at market rate, which is generally the case, this would typically result in an overall liability classification of the whole instrument. While dividend payments might be set at a fixed percentage of the nominal value, this does not need to be the case. Any non-discretionary obligation to pay dividends creates a liability that needs to be recorded on initial recognition of the instrument. If an entity has an obligation that is non-discretionary, for example to pay out a percentage of it profits, then that gives rise to a financial liability (see Chapter 46 at 2.1.3 for discussions around embedded derivatives and non-financial variables specific to one party to the contract).

4.5.2 Instruments redeemable only at the issuer's option or not redeemable

A preference share (or other instrument) redeemable in cash only at the option of the issuer does not satisfy the definition of a financial liability in IAS 32, because the issuer does not have a present or future obligation to transfer financial assets to the shareholders. In this case, redemption of the shares is solely at the discretion of the issuer. An obligation may arise, however, when the issuer of the shares exercises its option, usually by formally notifying the shareholders of an intention to redeem the shares. *[IAS 32.AG25]*.

Likewise, where preference shares are non-redeemable, there is clearly no financial liability in respect of the 'principal' amount of the shares. In reality there may be little distinction between shares redeemable at the issuer's option and non-redeemable shares, given that in many jurisdictions an entity can 'repurchase' its 'irredeemable' shares subject to no greater restrictions than would apply to a 'redemption' of 'redeemable' shares.

Ultimately, the classification of preference shares redeemable only at the issuer's option or not redeemable according to their terms must be determined by the other rights that attach to them. IAS 32 requires the classification to be based on an assessment of the substance of the contractual arrangements and the definitions of a financial liability and an equity instrument. *[IAS 32.AG26]*.

If the share does establish a contractual right to a dividend, subject only to restrictions on payment of dividends in the relevant jurisdiction, it contains a financial liability in respect of the dividends. This would lead to a 'split accounting' treatment (see 6 below), whereby the net present value of the right to receive dividends would be shown as a liability and the balance of the issue proceeds as equity. Where the dividends are set at a market rate at the date of issue, it is likely that the issue proceeds would be equivalent to the fair value (at the date of issue) of dividends payable in perpetuity, so that the entire proceeds would be classified as a financial liability.

However, when redemption of the preference shares and distributions to holders of the preference shares, whether cumulative or non-cumulative, are at the discretion of the issuer, the shares are equity instruments. The classification of preference share distributions as an equity component or a financial liability component is not affected by, for example:

- a history of making distributions;
- an intention to make distributions in the future;
- a possible negative impact on the price of ordinary shares of the issuer if distributions are not made (because of restrictions on paying dividends on the ordinary shares if dividends are not paid on the preference shares – see 4.5.3 below);
- the amount of the issuer's reserves;
- an issuer's expectation of a profit or loss for a period; or
- an ability or inability of the issuer to influence the amount of its profit or loss for the period. *[IAS 32.AG26]*.

The treatment of non-redeemable preference shares or other instruments with preferred rights under IAS 32 is a particularly difficult issue, since such shares often inhabit the border territory between financial liabilities and equity instruments. However, the starting point is that a non-redeemable preference share whose dividend rights are simply that a dividend (whether of a fixed, capped or discretionary amount) will be paid at the issuing entity's sole discretion, is equivalent to an ordinary equity share and therefore appropriately characterised as equity.

4.5.3 Instruments with a 'dividend blocker' or a 'dividend pusher' clause

4.5.3.A Instruments with a 'dividend blocker'

A number of entities have issued non-redeemable instruments (or instruments redeemable only at the issuer's option) with the following broad terms:

- a discretionary annual coupon or dividend will be paid up to a capped maximum amount; and
- unless a full discretionary coupon or dividend is paid to holders of the instrument, no dividend can be paid to ordinary shareholders.

This restriction on dividend payments to ordinary shareholders is colloquially referred to as a 'dividend blocker' clause. Because payments of annual coupons or dividends are at the discretion of the issuer and the instrument is non-redeemable, the issuer has an unconditional right to avoid delivering cash or another financial asset. This is not negated by the fact that the issuer cannot pay dividends to ordinary shareholders if no coupon or dividend is paid to the holder of the instruments. The instrument is therefore classified as equity in its entirety.

The economic reality is that many entities that issue such instruments are able to do so at a cost not significantly higher than that of callable perpetual debt. This indicates that the financial markets regard 'dividend blocker' clauses as providing investors with reasonable security of receiving their 'discretionary' coupon or dividend, given the adverse economic consequences for the entity of not paying it (if sufficiently solvent to do so), namely:

- the disaffection of ordinary shareholders who could not receive any dividends; and
- the fact that the entity would find it very difficult to raise any similar finance again.

These factors could admit an argument that such instruments are equivalent to perpetual debt, which give rise to a financial liability of the issuer (see 4.7 below), in all respects, except that the holder has no right to sue for non-payment of the discretionary dividend. However, the analysis in IAS 32 is based on the implicit counter-argument that the position of a holder of an instrument, all payments on which are discretionary, is equivalent to that of an ordinary shareholder. Ordinary shares do not cease to be equity instruments simply because an entity that failed to pay dividends to its ordinary shareholders, when clearly able to do so, would be subject to adverse economic pressures from those shareholders, and might find it very difficult to raise additional share capital.

Aviva has issued instruments with 'dividend blocker' clauses that are accounted for as equity instruments (see, in particular, the final sentences of the Extract).

Extract 47.1: Aviva plc (2019)

IFRS financial statements [extract]
Notes to the consolidated financial statements [extract]
37   Direct capital instrument and tier 1 notes [extract]

Notional amount	2019 £m	2018 £m
5.9021% £500 million direct capital instrument – Issued November 2004	500	500
6.875% £210 million STICS – Issued November 2003	-	231
Total	500	731

The direct capital instrument (the DCI) was issued on 25 November 2004. The DCI has no fixed redemption date but the Company may, at its sole option, redeem all (but not part) of the principal amount on 27 July 2020, at which date the interest rate changes to a variable rate, or on any respective coupon payment date thereafter. The variable rate will be the six month sterling deposit rate plus margin.

[...]

No interest will accrue on any deferred coupon on the DCI. Deferred coupons on the DCI will be satisfied by the issue and sale of ordinary shares in the Company at their prevailing market value, to a sum as near as practicable to (and at least equal to) the relevant deferred coupons. In the event of any coupon deferral, the Company will not declare or pay any dividend on its ordinary or preference share capital. These instruments have been treated as equity. Please refer to accounting policy AE.

4.5.3.B Instruments with a 'dividend pusher'

A variation of the financial instrument discussed under 4.5.3.A above is one with a so called 'dividend pusher' clause which, in practice, often comes with the following broad terms:
- a discretionary annual coupon or dividend will be paid up to a capped maximum amount;
- payment of the annual coupon or dividend is required if the entity pays dividends to ordinary shareholders; and
- the instrument is non-redeemable (or redeemable only at the issuer's option).

The annual coupons or dividends are at the discretion of the issuer and the instrument is non-redeemable, indicating an unconditional right of the issuer to avoid delivering cash or another financial asset to the holder of the instrument. Whether the 'dividend pusher' clause introduces a contractual obligation to deliver cash or another financial asset depends on whether the payments of dividends to ordinary shareholders (referenced in the dividend pusher clause) are themselves discretionary. In general, payments of dividends to ordinary shareholders are at the discretion of the issuer of those shares. The 'dividend pusher' clause therefore does not introduce a contractual obligation, meaning that the issuer has an unconditional right to avoid delivering cash or another financial asset. Thus the instrument is classified as equity in its entirety.

4.5.4 Perpetual instruments with a 'step-up' clause

Some perpetual instruments are issued on terms that they are not required to be redeemed. However, if they are not redeemed on or before a given future date, any coupon or dividend paid after that date is increased, usually to a level that would give rise to a cost of finance higher than the entity would normally expect to incur. This effectively compels the issuer to redeem the instrument before the increase occurs. A provision for such an increase in the coupon or dividend is colloquially referred to as a 'step-up' clause. A 'step-up' clause is often combined with a 'dividend-blocker' or 'dividend pusher' clause (see 4.5.3.A and 4.5.3.B above).

Paragraph 22 of the version of IAS 32 in issue before its revision in December 2003 (see 1.2 above) specifically addressed 'step-up' clauses as follows:

'A preferred share that does not provide for mandatory redemption or redemption at the option of the holder may have a contractually provided accelerating dividend such that, within the foreseeable future, the dividend yield is scheduled to be so high that the issuer would be economically compelled to redeem the instrument.'[11]

The Basis for Conclusions to the current version of IAS 32 indicates that this example was removed because it was insufficiently clear, but there was no intention to alter the general principle of IAS 32 that an instrument that does not explicitly establish an obligation to deliver cash or other financial assets may establish an obligation indirectly through its terms and conditions (see 4.2.2 above). *[IAS 32.BC9]*.

This has led some to suggest that any instrument with a 'step-up' clause contains a financial liability. In our view, however, this is to misunderstand the reason for the IASB's decision to delete the old paragraph 22. The 'confusion' caused by the paragraph was that the existence of a step-up clause is in fact irrelevant to the analysis required by IAS 32. If an instrument, whether redeemable or not, contains a contractual obligation to pay a coupon or dividend, it is a liability, irrespective of the 'step-up' clause. However, if the coupon or dividend, both before and after the step-up date, is wholly discretionary, then the instrument is, absent other contractual terms that make it a liability, an equity instrument, again irrespective of the step-up clause (see 4.5.1 and 4.5.2 above).

This analysis was confirmed by the Interpretations Committee in March 2006 in its discussion of the classification of an instrument that included a 'step-up' dividend clause that would increase the dividend at a pre-determined date in the future. The Interpretations Committee agreed that this instrument included no contractual obligation ever to pay the dividends or to call the instrument and should therefore be classified as equity under IAS 32.[12]

4.5.5 Relative subordination

Some have argued that instruments with 'dividend-blocker', 'dividend-pusher' or 'step-up' clauses (see 4.5.3 and 4.5.4 above) do not meet the definition of an equity instrument. Those that take this view, point out that paragraph 11 of IAS 32 defines an equity instrument as 'any contract that evidences a residual interest in the assets of an entity after deducting all of its liabilities' (see 3 above) – whereas many instruments of the type described in 4.5.3 and 4.5.4 above are typically entitled only to a return of the amount originally subscribed on a winding up, rather than to any 'residual interest' in the assets. However, such an instrument does not meet the definition of a liability either, for all the reasons set out above.

Moreover, as noted at 4.1 above, IAS 32 paragraph 16 indicates that, in applying the definition in paragraph 11, an entity concludes that an instrument is equity if and only if the criteria in paragraph 16 are met. In other words, an instrument is equity if it satisfies the criteria of paragraph 16, whatever construction might be placed on paragraph 11.

In March 2006, the Interpretations Committee considered various issues relating to the classification of instruments under IAS 32, and agreed that IAS 32 was clear that the relative subordination on liquidation of a financial instrument was not relevant to its classification under IAS 32, even where the instrument ranks above an instrument classified as a liability.[13] This supports the view that an instrument can be classified as equity even if there are restrictions on participation by its holder in a liquidation or on winding up.

However, in February 2008, the IASB issued an amendment to IAS 32 (see 1.2 above) which, in very specific circumstances, requires the relative subordination of an instrument to be taken into account in determining its classification as debt or equity (see 4.6 below).

4.5.6 Economic compulsion

The discussion in 4.5.1 to 4.5.5 above illustrates that, while IAS 32 requires the issuer of a financial instrument to classify a financial instrument by reference to its substance rather than its legal form, in reality the substance is determined, if not by the legal form, then certainly by the precise legal rights of the holder of the financial instrument concerned. Ultimately, the key determinant of whether an instrument is a financial liability or an equity instrument of the issuer is whether the terms of the instrument give the holder a contractual right to receive cash or other financial assets which can be sued for at law, subject only to restrictions outside the terms of the instrument (e.g. statutory dividend controls).

By contrast, terms of an instrument that effectively force the issuer to transfer cash or other financial assets to the holder although not legally required to do so (often referred to as 'economic compulsion'), are not taken into account.

In response to a submission for a possible agenda item, in March 2006 the Interpretations Committee discussed the role of contractual and economic obligations in the classification of financial instruments under IAS 32.

The Interpretations Committee agreed that IAS 32 is clear that, in order for an instrument to be classified as a liability, a contractual obligation must be established (either explicitly or indirectly) through the terms and conditions of the instrument. Economic compulsion, by itself, would not result in a financial instrument being classified as a liability.

The Interpretations Committee also noted that IAS 32 restricts the role of 'substance' to consideration of the contractual terms of an instrument, and that anything outside the contractual terms is not considered for the purpose of assessing whether an instrument should be classified as a liability under IAS 32.[14]

4.5.7 'Linked' instruments

An entity may issue an instrument (the 'base' instrument) that requires a payment to be made if, and only if, a payment is made on another instrument issued by the entity (the 'linked' instrument). An example of such an instrument would be a perpetual instrument with a 'dividend blocker' clause (see 4.5.3.A above), on which the issuing entity is required to pay a coupon only if it pays a dividend to ordinary shareholders. Absent other terms requiring the perpetual instrument to be classified as a liability, it is classified as equity on the basis that the event that triggers a contractual obligation to make a payment (i.e. payment of an ordinary dividend) is itself not a contractual obligation.

If, however, where payments on the linked instrument are contractually mandatory (such that the linked instrument contains a liability), it is obvious that the base instrument must also contain a liability. This is due to the fact that, in this case, the event that triggers a contractual obligation to make a payment on the base instrument (i.e. a payment on the linked instrument) is a contractual obligation that the issuing entity cannot avoid. This analysis was confirmed by the Interpretations Committee in March 2006 following discussion of linked instruments with similar terms to these.[15]

This issue had arisen in practice in the context that the linked instrument was often very small and callable by the issuer, but on terms that required its classification as a liability under IAS 32. This would allow the issuer, with no real difficulty, to redeem the linked instrument at will and thus convert the base instrument from a liability to equity at any time. This had led some to argue that only the linked instrument should be classified as a liability.

4.5.8 'Change of control', 'taxation change' and 'regulatory change' clauses

A number of entities have issued instruments with 'dividend blocker', 'dividend pusher' and 'step-up' clauses (see 4.5.3 and 4.5.4 above), which would otherwise have been treated as equity by IAS 32, but have wished to account for them as liabilities, perhaps because they can then be hedged in a way that allows hedge accounting to be applied (see 10 below). Methods of achieving this have included the use of a *de minimis* linked liability instrument, or the inclusion of a clause requiring the repayment of the instrument in the event of a change of control. This raises the question of whether a change of control is within the control of the entity (such that the instrument is equity) or not (such that the instrument is debt), which is discussed in more detail at 4.3.3 above.

Another common method of converting an instrument that would otherwise be classified by IAS 32 as equity into debt is to add a clause requiring repayment of the instrument in the event of a fiscal or regulatory change (that in reality may be a remote possibility) – see 4.3.1 above.

4.6 Puttable instruments and instruments repayable only on liquidation

4.6.1 The issue

A 'puttable instrument' is essentially a financial instrument that gives the holder the right to put the instrument back to the issuer for cash or another financial asset (see 3 above). Prior to its amendment in February 2008 (see 1.2 above), IAS 32 classified any puttable instrument as a financial liability, including instruments the legal form of which gives the holder a right to a residual interest in the assets of the issuer.

This classification produced what some regarded as an inappropriate result in the financial statements of entities such as open-ended mutual funds, unit trusts, partnerships and some co-operative entities. Such entities often provide their unit holders or members with a right to redeem their interests in the issuer at any time for cash. Under IAS 32, prior to the February 2008 amendment, an entity whose holders had such rights might report net assets of nil, or even negative net assets, since what would, in normal usage, have been regarded as its 'equity' (i.e. assets less external borrowings) was classified as a financial liability.

For example, the owners of some co-operatives and professional partnerships are entitled to have their ownership interests repurchased at fair value. However, such entities typically do not reflect that fair value in their financial statements, because a significant part of the value may be represented by property accounted for at cost rather than fair value or by internally generated goodwill which cannot be recognised in financial statements prepared under IFRS.

Clearly, if such an entity were to recognise a liability for the right of its owners to be bought out at fair value, it would show net liabilities, which would increase (creating accounting losses) the more the fair value of the entity increases, and decrease (creating accounting profits) the more the fair value decreases. Moreover, any distributions to the owners of such entities would be shown as a charge to, rather than a distribution of, profit.

Similar concerns were raised in relation to limited-life entities. In some jurisdictions, certain types of entity are required to be wound up after a certain period of time, either automatically, or unless the members resolve otherwise. Some entities may also have a limited life under their own governing charter, or equivalent document. For example:

- a collective investment fund might be required to be liquidated on, say, the tenth anniversary of its foundation; or
- a partnership might be required to be dissolved on the death or retirement of a partner.

Such an entity arguably had no equity under IAS 32 prior to the February 2008 amendment, since its limited life imposes an obligation, outside the entity's control, to distribute all its assets. Again, some questioned whether it was very meaningful to show such an entity as having no equity.

In order to deal with these concerns, IAS 32 was amended in February 2008. In the meantime, the Interpretations Committee had published IFRIC 2 which addresses the narrower issue of the classification of certain types of puttable instrument typically issued by co-operative entities (see 4.6.6 below).

The effect of the amended standard is that certain narrowly defined categories of puttable instruments (see 4.6.2 below) and instruments repayable on a pre-determined liquidation (see 4.6.3 below) are classified as equity, notwithstanding that they have features that would otherwise require their classification as financial liabilities.

Moreover, as discussed further at 4.6.5 below, one of the criteria for classifying such an instrument as equity, is that it is the most subordinated instrument issued by the reporting entity. This represents a significant, and controversial, departure from the normal approach of IAS 32 that the classification of an instrument should be determined only by reference to the contractual terms of that instrument, rather than those of other instruments in issue. This may mean that two entities may classify an identical instrument differently, if it is the most subordinated instrument of one entity but not of the other. It may also mean that the same entity may classify the same instrument differently at different reporting dates.

It was essentially these departures from the normal requirements of IAS 32 that led two members of the IASB to dissent from the amendment. In their view, it is not based on a clear principle, but comprises 'several paragraphs of detailed rules crafted to achieve a desired accounting result ... [and] ... to minimise structuring opportunities'.[16]

Where the exceptions in 4.6.2 and 4.6.3 below do not apply, IAS 32 takes the view that the effect of the holder's option to put the instrument back to the issuer for cash or another financial asset is that the puttable instrument meets the definition of a financial liability. *[IAS 32.18(b)]*, (see 3 above).

The IASB believes that the accounting treatment required by IAS 32 for instruments not subject to the exceptions in 4.6.2 and 4.6.3 below is appropriate, but points out that the classification of members' interests in such entities as a financial liability does not preclude:

- the use of captions such as 'net asset value attributable to unitholders' and 'change in net asset value attributable to unitholders' on the face of the financial statements of an entity that has no equity capital (such as some mutual funds and unit trusts); or
- the use of additional disclosure to show that total members' interests comprise items such as reserves that meet the definition of equity and puttable instruments that do not. *[IAS 32.18(b), BC7-BC8]*.

The illustrative examples appended to IAS 32 give specimen disclosures to be used in such cases – see Chapter 54 at 7.4.6.

4.6.2 Puttable instruments

As noted above, a puttable financial instrument includes a contractual obligation for the issuer to repurchase or redeem that instrument for cash or another financial asset on exercise of the put. IAS 32 classifies a puttable instrument as an equity instrument if it has all of the following features: *[IAS 32.16A-16B]*

(a) It entitles the holder to a *pro rata* share of the entity's net assets in the event of the entity's liquidation. The entity's net assets are those assets that remain after deducting all other claims on its assets. A *pro rata* share is determined by:
   (i) dividing the entity's net assets on liquidation into units of equal amount; and
   (ii) multiplying that amount by the number of the units held by the financial instrument holder.

(b) The instrument is in the class of instruments that is subordinate to all other classes of instruments. To be in such a class the instrument:
   (i) has no priority over other claims to the assets of the entity on liquidation; and
   (ii) does not need to be converted into another instrument before it is in the class of instruments that is subordinate to all other classes of instruments.

(c) All financial instruments in the class of instruments that is subordinate to all other classes of instruments have identical features. For example, they must all be puttable, and the formula or other method used to calculate the repurchase or redemption price is the same for all instruments in that class.

(d) Apart from the contractual obligation for the issuer to repurchase or redeem the instrument for cash or another financial asset, the instrument does not include any contractual obligation to deliver cash or another financial asset to another entity, or to exchange financial assets or financial liabilities with another entity under conditions that are potentially unfavourable to the entity, and it is not a contract that will or may be settled in the entity's own equity instruments as set out in subparagraph (b) of the definition of a financial liability (see 3 above).

(e) The total expected cash flows attributable to the instrument over the life of the instrument are based substantially on the profit or loss, the change in the recognised net assets, or the change in the fair value of the recognised and unrecognised net assets of the entity over the life of the instrument (excluding any effects of the instrument). *[IAS 32.16A].* Profit or loss and the change in recognised net assets must be determined in accordance with relevant IFRSs. *[IAS 32.AG14E].*

(f) In addition to the instrument having all the features in (a) to (e) above, the issuer must have no other financial instrument or contract that has:
   (i) total cash flows based substantially on the profit or loss, the change in the recognised net assets or the change in the fair value of the recognised and unrecognised net assets of the entity (excluding any effects of such instrument or contract); and
   (ii) the effect of substantially restricting or fixing the residual return to the puttable instrument holders.

In applying this condition, the entity should not consider non-financial contracts with a holder of an instrument described in (a) to (e) above that have contractual terms and conditions that are similar to the contractual terms and conditions of an equivalent contract that might occur between a non-instrument holder and the issuing entity. If the entity cannot determine that this condition is met, it should not classify the puttable instrument as an equity instrument. *[IAS 32.16B].*

Some of these criteria raise issues of interpretation, which are addressed at 4.6.4 below.

4.6.3 Instruments entitling the holder to a pro rata share of net assets only on liquidation

Some financial instruments include a contractual obligation for the issuing entity to deliver to another entity a *pro rata* share of its net assets only on liquidation. The obligation arises because liquidation either is certain to occur and outside the control of the entity (for example, a limited life entity) or is uncertain to occur but is at the option of the instrument holder. IAS 32 classifies such an instrument as an equity instrument if it has all of the following features: *[IAS 32.16C-16D]*

(a) It entitles the holder to a *pro rata* share of the entity's net assets in the event of the entity's liquidation. The entity's net assets are those assets that remain after deducting all other claims on its assets. A *pro rata* share is determined by:

   (i) dividing the net assets of the entity on liquidation into units of equal amount; and

   (ii) multiplying that amount by the number of the units held by the financial instrument holder.

(b) The instrument is in the class of instruments that is subordinate to all other classes of instruments. To be in such a class the instrument:

   (i) has no priority over other claims to the assets of the entity on liquidation; and

   (ii) does not need to be converted into another instrument before it is in the class of instruments that is subordinate to all other classes of instruments.

(c) All financial instruments in the class of instruments that is subordinate to all other classes of instruments must have an identical contractual obligation for the issuing entity to deliver a *pro rata* share of its net assets on liquidation. *[IAS 32.16C]*.

(d) In addition to the instrument having all the features in (a) to (c) above, the issuer must have no other financial instrument or contract that has:

   (i) total cash flows based substantially on the profit or loss, the change in the recognised net assets or the change in the fair value of the recognised and unrecognised net assets of the entity (excluding any effects of such instrument or contract); and

   (ii) the effect of substantially restricting or fixing the residual return to the instrument holders.

   For the purposes of applying this condition, the entity should not consider non-financial contracts with a holder of an instrument described in (a) to (c) above that have contractual terms and conditions that are similar to the contractual terms and conditions of an equivalent contract that might occur between a non-instrument holder and the issuing entity. If the entity cannot determine that this condition is met, it should not classify the instrument as an equity instrument. *[IAS 32.16D]*.

Some of these criteria raise some issues of interpretation, which are addressed at 4.6.4 below.

Some of the criteria for classifying as equity financial instruments that entitle the holder to a *pro rata* share of assets only on liquidation are similar to those (in 4.6.2 above) for classifying certain puttable instruments as equity. The difference between these criteria and those for puttable instruments are:

- there is no requirement for there to be no contractual obligations other than those arising on liquidation;
- there is no requirement to consider the expected total cash flows throughout the life of the instrument; and
- the only feature that must be identical among the instruments in the class is the obligation for the issuing entity to deliver to the holder a *pro rata* share of its net assets on liquidation.

The reason for the more relaxed criteria in this case is that the IASB took the view that, given that the only obligation in this case arises on liquidation, there was no need to consider obligations other than those on liquidation. However, the IASB notes that, if an instrument does contain other obligations, these may need to be accounted for separately under IAS 32. [IAS 32.BC67].

4.6.4 Clarification of the exemptions in 4.6.2 and 4.6.3 above

The conditions for treating certain types of puttable instruments (see 4.6.2 above) and instruments repaying a *pro rata* share of net assets on liquidation (see 4.6.3 above) as equity are complex. IAS 32 provides some clarification in respect of the following matters:

- instruments issued by a subsidiary (see 4.6.4.A below);
- determining the level of subordination of an instrument (see condition (b) under 4.6.2 and 4.6.3 above), (see 4.6.4.B below);
- the meaning of 'no obligation to deliver cash or another financial asset' (see condition (d) under 4.6.2 above) in respect of instruments with a requirement to distribute a minimum proportion of profit to shareholders (see 4.6.4.D below);
- other instruments that substantially fix or restrict the residual return to the holder of an instrument (see condition (f)(ii) in 4.6.2 above and condition (d)(ii) in 4.6.3 above), (see 4.6.4.E below); and
- transactions entered into by an instrument holder other than as owner of the entity (see 4.6.4.F below).

One matter on which IAS 32 does not provide further clarification is the meaning of 'identical features' (see condition (c) under 4.6.2 above). This is dealt with in 4.6.4.C below.

4.6.4.A Instruments issued by a subsidiary

A subsidiary may issue an instrument that falls to be classified as equity in its separate financial statements under one of the exceptions summarised in 4.6.2 and 4.6.3 above. However, in the consolidated financial statements of the subsidiary's parent such an instrument is not recorded as a non-controlling interest, but as a financial liability. [IAS 32.AG29A]. This reflects the fact that the exceptions in 4.6.2 and 4.6.3 above are both subject to the condition that the instrument concerned is the most subordinated instrument issued by the reporting entity. The IASB took the view that a non-controlling interest, by its nature, can never be regarded as the residual ownership interest in the consolidated financial statements. [IAS 32.BC68].

4.6.4.B Relative subordination of the instrument

The exceptions in 4.6.2 and 4.6.3 above are both subject to the criterion – condition (b) – that the instrument concerned is the most subordinated instrument issued by the reporting entity. As noted at 4.6.1 above, this represents a departure from the normal principle of IAS 32 that the classification of an issued instrument as a financial liability or equity should be determined by reference only to the contractual terms of that instrument.

In order to determine whether an instrument is in the most subordinate class, the entity calculates the instrument's claim on a liquidation as at the date when it classifies the instrument. The entity reassesses the classification if there is a change in relevant circumstances (for example, if it issues or redeems another financial instrument). *[IAS 32.AG14B]*. This is discussed further at 4.6.5 below.

An instrument that has a preferential right on liquidation of the entity is not regarded as an instrument with an entitlement to a *pro rata* share of the net assets of the entity. An example might be an instrument that entitles the holder to a fixed dividend on liquidation, in addition to a share of the entity's net assets, when other instruments in the subordinate class with a right to a *pro rata* share of the net assets of the entity do not have the same right on liquidation. *[IAS 32.AG14C]*.

If an entity has only one class of financial instruments, that class is treated as if it were subordinate to all other classes. *[IAS 32.AG14D]*.

In our view, the test of whether the instrument is the most subordinated has to be applied according to the legal rights of the various classes of instrument, even where what is legally the most subordinated instrument in issue is entitled to the return of only a nominal sum on liquidation which may be dwarfed by the entitlement of other classes of shares.

It should be noted, however, that the requirement for a puttable instrument to be in the most subordinate class of instruments issued by an entity does not preclude other, non-puttable, instruments from being classified as equity at the same time. In an agenda decision issued in March 2009, the Interpretations Committee noted that a financial instrument is first classified as a liability or equity instrument in accordance with the general requirements of IAS 32. That classification is not affected by the existence of puttable instruments.[17] Thus, for example, founders' shares in an investment fund, which are entitled only to the return of their par value on liquidation, would be classified as equity even if less subordinate than a class of puttable shares which also qualify for equity classification. Conversely, if the founders' shares were the most subordinate instruments, the puttable shares would have to be classified as liabilities.

4.6.4.C Meaning of 'identical features'

Condition (c) under 4.6.2 above requires that 'all financial instruments in the class of instruments that is subordinate to all other classes of instruments have identical features. For example, they must all be puttable, and the formula or other method used to calculate the repurchase or redemption price is the same for all instruments in that class'. The word 'identical' does not normally need much further explanation in the English language. Nevertheless, some have questioned how literally the word must be interpreted in this case.

Consider, for example, an investment fund that issues several types of puttable shares, each equally subordinate, having identical redemption and dividend rights, but different minimum subscription thresholds and subscription fees. Do all these instruments have identical features for the purpose of this exemption? In our view the condition referred to above is primarily designed to ensure that the redemption rights of the shares do not differ. Accordingly, terms that take effect before the shares are issued (as in the example above), or are not financial, should not cause instruments to fail the 'identical features' test. Examples of features which are not financial might include rights to information or management powers. In our opinion, instruments with different features of this kind will not necessarily fail the 'identical features' test, provided such features do not have the potential to impact the redemption rights of the instruments.

When considering whether instruments have identical features it is important to consider whether rights and obligations arise as a result of holding the instrument or from some other cause. Consider, as an example, a closed end fund with a predetermined maturity, incorporated as a partnership limited by shares, which has two classes of shares: a management share subscribed for by the general partner; and ordinary shares subscribed for by the limited partners. Upon the dissolution of the entity, the general partner is entitled to a fixed rate management fee and a fee based on the performance of the fund, otherwise the assets are distributed to both classes of shareholder on a *pro rata* basis. As the management and ordinary shares rank *pari passu* with each other, neither is subordinate to the other and both the management share and the ordinary shares would be classified as equity. The management and performance fees payable to the general partner are returns for managing the fund rather than equity returns in their capacity as a shareholder. For transactions entered into by an instrument holder other than as an owner of equity see 4.6.4.F below. The fact that the different classes of shares have different names is irrelevant to the analysis.

4.6.4.D   No obligation to deliver cash or another financial asset

One of the conditions for classifying a financial instrument as equity under 4.6.2 above is that the instrument does not include any contractual obligation to deliver cash or another financial asset to another entity, or to exchange financial assets or financial liabilities with another entity under conditions that are potentially unfavourable to the entity.

Some entities, particularly ones with limited lives, are required by their constitution to distribute a minimum proportion of profits to shareholders or partners each year. Subject to the matters discussed at 4.2 above, such a requirement will normally result in the puttable instrument being considered a liability. It might be argued, firstly, that no obligation arises in these circumstances until profits are made, and secondly that such distributions only represent advance payments of the residual interest in the entity and so are consistent with equity classification. However, the IASB discussed this issue while developing the 2008 amendment and concluded that a contractual obligation existed, the measurement of which was uncertain. Nevertheless, the IASB declined to provide further guidance on this issue as they considered that it would have implications for other projects.

In May 2010 the Interpretations Committee considered a request to clarify whether puttable income trust units, that include contractual provisions to make distributions on a *pro rata* basis, can be classified as equity. The submission to the Interpretations

Committee argued that such *pro rata* obligations should not prevent the instrument from being classified as equity, by analogy to the *Classification of Rights Issues* amendment to IAS 32 (October 2009). The Interpretations Committee decided not to propose any amendment to IAS 32 to deal with this issue, making it fairly clear in the process that they did not believe such an instrument would qualify to be classified as equity.

4.6.4.E *Instruments that substantially fix or restrict the residual return to the holder of an instrument*

A condition for classifying a financial instrument as equity under 4.6.2 or 4.6.3 above is that the issuing entity has no other financial instrument or contract that has:

- total cash flows based substantially on the profit or loss, the change in the recognised net assets or the change in the fair value of the recognised and unrecognised net assets of the entity; and
- the effect of substantially restricting or fixing the residual return.

IAS 32 notes that the following instruments, when entered into on normal commercial terms with unrelated parties, are unlikely to prevent instruments that otherwise meet the criteria in 4.6.2 or 4.6.3 above from being classified as equity:

- instruments with total cash flows substantially based on specific assets of the entity;
- instruments with total cash flows based on a percentage of revenue;
- contracts designed to reward individual employees for services rendered to the entity; and
- contracts requiring the payment of an insignificant percentage of profit for services rendered or goods provided. *[IAS 32.AG14J]*.

4.6.4.F *Transactions entered into by an instrument holder other than as owner of the entity*

IAS 32 observes that the holder of a financial instrument subject to one of the exceptions in 4.6.2 or 4.6.3 above may enter into transactions with the entity in a role other than that of an owner. For example, an instrument holder also may be an employee of the entity. IAS 32 requires that only the cash flows and the contractual terms and conditions of the instrument that relate to the instrument holder as an owner of the entity be considered when assessing whether the instrument should be classified as equity under conditions (a) to (e) in 4.6.2 above or conditions (a) to (c) in 4.6.3 above. *[IAS 32.AG14F]*.

An example might be a limited partnership that has limited and general partners. Some general partners may provide a guarantee to the entity and be remunerated for providing that guarantee. In such situations, the guarantee and the associated cash flows relate to the instrument holders in their role as guarantors and not in their roles as owners of the entity. Therefore, such a guarantee and the associated cash flows would not result in the general partners being considered subordinate to the limited partners and would be disregarded when assessing whether the contractual terms of the limited partnership instruments and the general partnership instruments are identical. *[IAS 32.AG14G]*.

Another example might be a profit or loss sharing arrangement that allocates profit or loss to the instrument holders on the basis of services rendered or business generated during the current and previous years. Such arrangements are regarded as transactions with instrument holders in their role as non-owners and should not be considered when assessing the criteria in conditions (a) to (e) in 4.6.2 above or conditions (a) to (c) in 4.6.3 above. By contrast, profit or loss sharing arrangements, that allocate profit or loss to instrument holders based on the nominal amount of their instruments relative to others in the class, represent transactions with the instrument holders in their roles as owners and should be considered when assessing the criteria in conditions (a) to (e) in 4.6.2 above or conditions (a) to (c) in 4.6.3 above. *[IAS 32.AG14H]*.

IAS 32 notes that, in order for a transaction with an owner to be assessed as being undertaken in that person's capacity as a non-owner, the cash flows and contractual terms and conditions of the transaction must be similar to those of an equivalent transaction that might occur between a non-instrument holder and the issuing entity. *[IAS 32.AG14I]*.

4.6.5 Reclassification of puttable instruments and instruments imposing an obligation only on liquidation

As noted in 4.6.4.B above, IAS 32 requires the entity to continually reassess the classification of such an instrument. The entity classifies a financial instrument as an equity instrument from the date on which it has all the features and meets the conditions set out in 4.6.2 or 4.6.3 above, and reclassifies the instrument from the date on which it ceases to have all those features or meet all those conditions.

For example, if an entity redeems all its issued non-puttable instruments, any puttable instruments that remain outstanding and that have all of the features and meet all the conditions in 4.6.2 above, are reclassified as equity instruments from the date of redemption of the non-puttable instruments. *[IAS 32.16E]*.

Where an instrument, previously classified as an equity instrument, is reclassified as a financial liability, the financial liability is measured at fair value at the date of reclassification, with any difference between the carrying value of the equity instrument and the fair value of the financial liability at the date of reclassification being recognised in equity. *[IAS 32.16F(a)]*.

Where an instrument, previously classified as a financial liability, is reclassified as an equity instrument, the equity instrument is measured at the carrying value of the financial liability at the date of reclassification. *[IAS 32.16F(b)]*.

4.6.6 IFRIC 2

The issue that ultimately led to the publication of IFRIC 2 was the appropriate accounting treatment for the members' contributed capital of a co-operative entity, the members of which are entitled to ask for the return of their investment. However, the scope of IFRIC 2 is not confined to co-operative entities and extends to any entity whose members may ask for a return of their capital. *[IFRIC 2.1-4]*.

IFRIC 2 states that the contractual right of the holder of a financial instrument to request redemption does not, in itself, require that financial instrument to be classified as a financial liability. Rather, the entity must consider all of the terms and conditions of the financial instrument in determining its classification as a financial liability or equity. Those terms and conditions include relevant local laws, regulations and the entity's governing charter in effect at the date of classification, but not expected future amendments to those laws, regulations or charter. *[IFRIC 2.5]*.

Accordingly, IFRIC 2 provides that an instrument, that would be classified as equity if the holder did not have the right to request redemption, should be classified as an equity instrument where:

- the entity has the unconditional right to refuse redemption;
- local law, regulation or the entity's governing charter imposes an unconditional prohibition on redemption; or
- the members' shares meet the criteria in 4.6.2 or 4.6.3 above for classification as equity. *[IFRIC 2.6-8]*.

IFRIC 2 distinguishes between those prohibitions on redemption in local law, regulation or the entity's governing charter that are 'unconditional' (i.e. they apply at any time) and those which prohibit redemption only when certain conditions – such as liquidity constraints – are met or not met. Prohibitions that apply only in certain circumstances are ignored and therefore would not result in equity classification. *[IFRIC 2.8]*. This is consistent with the fact that under IAS 32 the classification of an instrument as debt or equity is not influenced by considerations of liquidity (see 4.2 above).

In some cases, there may be a partial prohibition on redemption. For example, redemption may be prohibited where its effect would be to reduce the number of members' shares or the amount of paid-in capital below a certain minimum. In such cases, only the amount subject to a prohibition on redemption is treated as equity, unless:

- the entity has the unconditional right to refuse redemption as described above; or
- the members' shares meet the criteria in 4.6.2 or 4.6.3 above for classification as equity.

If the minimum number of members' shares or amount of paid-in capital changes, an appropriate transfer is made between financial liabilities and equity. *[IFRIC 2.9]*.

Any financial liability for the redemption of instruments not classified as equity is measured at fair value. In the case of members' shares with a redemption feature, the entity measures the fair value of the financial liability for redemption at no less than the maximum amount payable under the redemption provisions of its governing charter or applicable law, discounted from the first date that the amount could be required to be paid. *[IFRIC 2.10]*.

In accordance with the general provisions of IAS 32 regarding interest and dividends (see 8 below), distributions to holders of equity instruments are recognised directly in equity, net of any income tax benefits. Interest, dividends and other returns relating to financial instruments classified as financial liabilities are expenses, regardless of whether those amounts paid are legally characterised as dividends, interest or otherwise. *[IFRIC 2.11]*.

IFRIC 2 clarifies that, where members act as customers of the entity (for example, where it is a bank and members have current or deposit accounts or similar contracts with the bank), such accounts and contracts are financial liabilities of the entity. *[IFRIC 2.6]*.

It should be noted that in the FICE DP (see 12 below), the IASB noted that the IFRS requirements to account for financial instruments have been designed around the concept of a contract. They further noted that IFRIC 2 was developed for a very specific fact pattern and that they did not believe that the analysis in IFRIC 2 should be applied more broadly.[18] The effects of laws and regulations is an area the IASB intends to clarify as part of the ongoing FICE project (see 12 below).

4.7 Perpetual debt

'Perpetual debt' instruments are those that provide the holder with the contractual right to receive payments on account of interest at fixed dates extending into the indefinite future, either with no right to receive a return of principal or a right to a return of principal under terms that make it very unlikely or very far in the future. However, this does not mean that 'perpetual debt' is to be classified as equity, since the issue proceeds will typically represent the net present value of the liability for interest payments.

For example, an entity may issue a financial instrument requiring it to make annual payments in perpetuity equal to a stated interest rate of 8% applied to a stated par or principal amount of €1 million. Assuming 8% to be the market rate of interest for the instrument when issued, the issuer assumes a contractual obligation to make a stream of future interest payments having a fair value (present value) of €1 million. Thus, perpetual debt gives rise to a financial liability of the issuer. *[IAS 32.AG6].*

4.8 Differences of classification between consolidated and single entity financial statements

4.8.1 Consolidated financial statements

In consolidated financial statements, IAS 32 requires an entity to present non-controlling interests (i.e. the interests of other parties in the equity and income of its subsidiaries) within equity, in accordance with IAS 1 – *Presentation of Financial Statements* (see Chapter 3 at 3.1.5) and IFRS 10 – *Consolidated Financial Statements* (see Chapter 7 at 4 and Chapter 9 at 8). *[IAS 32.AG29].*

When classifying a financial instrument (or a component of it) in consolidated financial statements, an entity must consider all the terms and conditions agreed between all members of the group and the holders of the instrument in determining whether the group as a whole has an obligation to deliver cash or another financial asset in respect of the instrument or to settle it in a manner that results in its classification as a financial liability. *[IAS 32.AG29].*

For example, a subsidiary in a group may issue a financial instrument and a parent or other group entity may then agree additional terms directly with the holders of the instrument so as to guarantee some or all of the payments to be made under the instrument. The effect of this is that the subsidiary may have discretion over distributions or redemption, but the group as a whole does not. *[IAS 32.AG29].*

Accordingly, the subsidiary may appropriately classify the instrument without regard to these additional terms in its individual financial statements. For the purposes of the consolidated financial statements, however, the effect of the other agreements between members of the group and the holders of the instrument is to create an obligation or settlement provision, so that the instrument (or the component of it that is subject to the obligation) is classified as a financial liability. *[IAS 32.AG29].*

Thus it is quite possible for a financial instrument to be classified as an equity instrument in the financial statements of the issuing subsidiary but as a financial liability in the financial statements of the group.

4.8.2 Single entity financial statements

The converse of the discussion in 4.8.1 above is that it is not uncommon for instruments that are classified as equity in the consolidated financial statements to give rise to liabilities and embedded derivatives in the financial statements of individual members of the group.

This is because a group wishing to raise finance for its operations will generally do so through a group entity specialising in finance-raising, which will then on-lend the proceeds of the finance raised to the relevant operating subsidiaries. The terms of the intragroup on-lending transactions will often be such that finance which constitutes equity from the perspective of group as a whole may be a liability in the individual financial statements of the finance-raising entity itself.

For example, the finance-raising entity might issue an irredeemable instrument with a 'dividend blocker' clause (see 4.5.3.A above), under the terms of which that entity is not required to make any payments to the holder unless the ultimate parent entity of the group pays a dividend to ordinary shareholders. Absent any other terms requiring its classification, in whole or in part, as a liability under IAS 32, the instrument will be treated as equity in the consolidated financial statements, since payments under the instrument are contingent on an event within the control of the group (payment of a dividend by the parent entity). In the finance-raising entity's single entity financial statements, however, the instrument should be classified as a liability, because the subsidiary cannot control the dividend policy of its parent and could therefore be forced to make payments to the holder of the instrument as a consequence of its parent entity paying a dividend.

Another common example is that a group may issue a convertible bond which is actually structured as a series of transactions along the following lines:

- a finance-raising subsidiary issues a bond, giving the holder a right to receive fixed, non-discretionary interest payments, which converts into preference shares of that subsidiary; and
- at the time that this conversion occurs, the parent entity is required to acquire the preference shares of the subsidiary from the holder (i.e. the previous bondholder) in exchange for equity of the parent.

Absent any other terms requiring classification as a liability under IAS 32, the instrument will be treated as a compound instrument, consisting of a liability and an equity component (see 6 below) in the consolidated financial statements. The instrument as a whole might be classified as a liability in the subsidiary's financial statements, if (for example) the preference shares issued on conversion by the subsidiary have terms that require them to be classified as a liability by IAS 32. In that case, the subsidiary will have issued an instrument that the holder can exchange either for cash or for a debt instrument.

From the subsidiary's perspective, therefore, there is no equity component to the instrument and the overall instrument would be classified as a liability that, under the general rules of IFRS 9, must be recorded at fair value on initial recognition, which will typically be lower than the proceeds received. This is because the pricing of the instrument as a whole considers the conversion option that the holder receives, so that the interest is typically paid at a rate below the rate that would apply to a liability without a conversion option. In other words, the holder of the instrument 'pays' for the conversion option through a reduced entitlement to interest.

The group accounts reflect the difference between the proceeds of issue and the fair value of the liability component as the equity component (see 6 below). In the financial statements of the issuing subsidiary, the most appropriate accounting treatment, in our view, would be to treat this difference as an equity contribution by the parent, reflecting the fact that the subsidiary can borrow on a reduced interest basis due to the conversion option issued by the parent. Moreover, in the period prior to conversion, the parent is required to account for its contingent forward contract to acquire the preference shares in the finance company.

4.9 Reclassification of instruments

It happens from time to time that the terms of a financial instrument are modified in such a way that an instrument that was an equity instrument at the original date of issue would be classified as a financial liability if issued at the date of modification, or *vice versa*. Alternatively, the terms of the instrument may remain unaltered, but external circumstances may change. For example:

- an instrument might have been issued subject to a contingent settlement provision (see 4.3 above) that, at the date of issue, was within the control of the issuer, but ceases to be so at a later date;
- an instrument might have been issued subject to a contingent settlement provision (see 4.3 above) that, at the date of issue, was not considered genuine, but becomes so at a later date; or
- an instrument might have been issued requiring interest payments to be made when contractually mandatory interest payments are made on another instrument issued by the entity, the 'linked' instrument (see 4.5.7 above), but this linked instrument is later repaid by the entity.

Such situations raise the question of whether such changes of terms or circumstances should lead to reclassification of the instruments affected in the financial statements and, if so, how the reclassification should be accounted for.

4.9.1 Change of terms

IAS 32 gives no guidance as to whether reclassification is required, permitted or prohibited. The requirement of IAS 32 paragraph 15 that an instrument be classified 'on initial recognition' (see 4 above) could be read as implying that classification occurs only on initial recognition and is not subsequently revisited.

However, we do not consider this an appropriate analysis. A change in the terms of an instrument is equivalent to the issue of a new instrument in settlement of the original instrument. Such an exchange transaction would be accounted for by derecognising the settled instrument and recognising (and classifying as a financial liability or equity) the new replacement instrument. This analysis has been confirmed by an agenda decision of the Interpretations Committee (see 4.9.1.A below). In our view, it would be inappropriate to apply a different accounting treatment to a change in the terms of the original instrument which has the same economic result.

4.9.1.A Equity instrument to financial liability

At its meeting in November 2006, the Interpretations Committee considered a situation in which an amendment to the contractual terms of an equity instrument resulted in the instrument being classified as a financial liability. Two issues were discussed:

- the measurement of the financial liability at the date of the amendment to the terms; and
- the treatment of any difference between the carrying amount of the previously recognised equity instrument and the amount of the financial liability recognised.

The Interpretations Committee decided not to add this issue to its agenda because, in its view, the accounting treatment is clear. The financial liability is initially recognised at fair value under the general provisions of IFRS 9 (see Chapter 49 at 3). Any difference between the carrying amount of the liability and that of the previously recognised equity instrument is recognised in equity in accordance with the general principle of IAS 32 (see 8 below) that no gain or loss is recognised in profit or loss on the purchase, sale, issue or cancellation of an entity's own equity instruments.[19]

4.9.1.B Financial liability to equity instrument

In the converse situation where the terms of a financial liability are changed such that the instrument then meets the definition of an equity instrument, we believe, as above, that the instrument should be reclassified to equity. That situation is analogous to a debt-for-equity swap as discussed at 7 below and, therefore, should be accounted for in accordance with IFRIC 19, where that interpretation applies. The most likely situation in which IFRIC 19 would not apply would be in a transaction with shareholders in their capacity as shareholders, as discussed at 7.3 below.

4.9.2 Change of circumstances

The nature and risk profile of a financial instrument may change as a result of a change in circumstances. Such a change may occur simply as the result of the passage of time. For example, in 2018 an entity might issue a bond mandatorily convertible at the end of 2021. The conversion terms are that the holder will receive a number of the issuer's equity shares, being the lower of 100 shares or a number of shares determined according to a formula based on the share price at 31 December 2018.

At the date of issue, this instrument is a financial liability since it involves an obligation to deliver a variable number of equity instruments. At 31 December 2018, however, the number of shares to be delivered on conversion can be determined and becomes fixed. Accordingly, if considered as at 31 December 2018 and later, the instrument is an equity instrument (absent any other terms requiring its continued classification as financial liability).

In our view, the liability component of the bond representing the obligation to deliver a variable number of equity instruments on 31 December 2021 expires on 31 December 2018. This liability component must therefore be derecognised (see Chapter 52 at 6), to be replaced with an equity component (see the discussion at 7 below of the appropriate accounting treatment in such circumstances).

Changes of circumstances for reasons other than the passage of time are more challenging. For example, an entity might issue a convertible bond denominated in its functional currency at that time. Such a bond would have an equity component (see 6 below). Subsequently, the entity's functional currency changes but the bond remains outstanding, now denominated in a currency other than the entity's functional currency. If a bond with these terms were issued after the change in functional currency, it would be classified in its entirety as a financial liability, since the principal of the bond would not be a 'fixed' amount by reference to the entity's functional currency (see 5.2.3 below). This raises the question of whether the equity component of the bond should be reclassified as a financial liability on the change in functional currency.

In our view, there are arguments both for and against reclassification. As the arguments for reclassification are to some extent a rebuttal of those against reclassification, we discuss the latter first.

4.9.2.A   Arguments against reclassification

The principal arguments against reclassification are:

(a) The requirement of paragraph 15 of IAS 32 to classify an instrument as a financial liability or equity 'on initial recognition' (see 4 above) could be read as implying that such classification occurs only on initial recognition and is not subsequently revisited.

(b) The implementation guidance to IFRS 1 – *First-time Adoption of International Financial Reporting Standards* – require a compound instrument to be analysed into its components, based on the substance of the contractual arrangement, as at the date on which the instrument first satisfied the recognition criteria in IAS 32. *[IFRS 1.IG35, IG36]*. Changes to the terms of the instrument after that date are taken into account on first-time adoption, but changes in circumstances are not.

This could be construed as establishing a more general principle that changes in the terms of instruments should be accounted for but changes in circumstances should not.

(c) IFRS 9 clarifies that the assessment of whether or not an embedded derivative is required to be separated from its host contract is undertaken when the entity first becomes party to the contract, and is not revisited in the light of any subsequently changing circumstances (see Chapter 48 at 7). *[IFRS 9.B4.3.1]*.

(d) IFRIC 2 and the provisions of IAS 32 requiring certain types of puttable and redeemable instrument to be classified as equity (see 4.6 above) each require accounting recognition to be given to some changes in the classification of a financial instrument as the result of changing circumstances. This implies that, absent such specific guidance, the 'default' position would be that there should be no accounting consequences, an inference reinforced by the requirement that the provisions of IAS 32 requiring certain types of puttable and redeemable instrument to be classified as equity must not be applied by analogy to other transactions.

4.9.2.B Arguments for reclassification

The principal arguments in favour of reclassification are:

(a) The definitions of financial liability and equity both use the present tense, implying that the definitions are to be applied at each reporting date, absent any more specific provision against doing so.

This is consistent with our view that some transactions falling within the scope of IFRS 2 – *Share-based Payment* – should be reclassified from equity-settled to cash-settled and *vice versa* in the light of changing circumstances (see Chapter 34 at 10.2.3). However, it could be argued that such an analogy is inappropriate given the significant differences between the definitions of equity and financial liability in IAS 32 and those of equity-settled and cash-settled share-based payment transaction in IFRS 2 (see 5.1.1 below).

(b) The provisions of IFRS 1 referred to in (b) under 4.9.2.A above are contained in implementation guidance, which is not part of the standard. Moreover, it refers only to compound financial instruments, and appears to be implicitly addressing changes in market interest rates that might alter the arithmetical split of the instrument into its financial liability and equity components (see 6 below), rather than more general changes in circumstances.

(c) The fact that IFRS 9 (see (c) under 4.9.2.A above) was issued after IFRS 1 indicates that a general prohibition on reassessment should not be inferred from IFRS 1. Had the IASB wished to clarify that this was the case, they could easily have done so in IFRS 9.

However, it is equally difficult to argue that there is an implied 'default' requirement for reclassification, given the specific requirement for reclassification of certain puttable and redeemable instruments on a change in circumstances referred to in (d) in 4.9.2.A above.

What emerges from the analysis above is a lack of definitive general guidance as to whether reclassification of an instrument is permitted, required or prohibited. Accordingly, we believe that in some circumstances, such as a change in the entity's functional currency, the entity may choose, as a matter of accounting policy, either to reclassify or not to reclassify an instrument following that change of circumstances which, had it occurred before initial recognition of the instrument, would have changed its classification. The policy adopted should, in our view, be followed consistently in respect of all changes of circumstances of a similar nature.

However, some changes in circumstances can be more fundamental to the nature of the contract. For example, the change in circumstances could lead to the instruments delivered under a contract ceasing to be equity instruments of the reporting entity. This situation could arise where a parent had entered into a derivative involving delivery of the equity instruments of a subsidiary and subsequently loses control of that subsidiary. Here the former subsidiary's equity instruments would now represent financial assets rather than non-controlling interests (equity) of the group. In these circumstances, it may be more difficult to argue that not reclassifying the derivative contract is appropriate.

5 CONTRACTS SETTLED BY DELIVERY OF THE ENTITY'S OWN EQUITY INSTRUMENTS

This Section deals with contracts, other than those within the scope of IFRS 2 (see Chapter 34), settled in equity instruments issued by the settler. Throughout the discussion here at 5, 'equity instrument(s)' excludes certain puttable and redeemable instruments classified as equity under the exceptions discussed at 4.6.2 and 4.6.3 above (any contract involving the receipt or delivery of such instruments is a financial asset or liability – see 4.1 above).

In order for an instrument to be classified as an equity instrument under IAS 32, it is not sufficient that it involves the reporting entity delivering or receiving its own equity (as opposed to cash or another financial asset). The number of equity instruments delivered, and the consideration for them, must be fixed – the so called 'fixed for fixed' requirement. Contracts that will be settled other than by delivery of a fixed number of shares for a fixed amount of cash do not generally meet the definition of equity. The IASB considered that to treat any transaction settled in the entity's own shares as an equity instrument would not deal adequately with transactions in which an entity is using its own shares as 'currency' – for example, where it has an obligation to pay a fixed or determinable amount that is settled in a variable number of its own shares. *[IAS 32.BC21(a)]*. In such transactions the counterparty bears no share price risk and is therefore not in the same position as a 'true' equity shareholder.

Where such a contract is not classified as an equity instrument by IAS 32, it will be accounted for in accordance with the general provisions of IFRS 9 as either a financial liability or a derivative.

Broadly speaking:
- a non-derivative contract involving the issue of a fixed number of own equity instruments is an equity instrument (see 5.1 below);
- a non-derivative contract involving the issue of a variable number of own equity instruments is a financial liability (see 5.2.1 below);
- a derivative contract involving the sale or purchase of a fixed number of own equity instruments for a fixed amount of cash or other financial assets is an equity instrument (see 5.1 below);
- a derivative contract for the purchase by an entity of its own equity instruments, even if for a fixed amount of cash or other financial assets (and therefore an equity instrument) may give rise to a financial liability in respect of the cash or other financial assets to be paid. However, the initial recognition of the liability results in a reduction in equity and not in an expense (see 5.3 below). In other words, whilst there is a liability to pay cash under the contract, the contract itself is an equity instrument (and is therefore not subject to periodic remeasurement to fair value);
- a derivative contract involving the delivery or receipt of:
  - a fixed number of own equity instruments for a variable amount of cash or other financial assets;
  - a variable number of own equity instruments for a variable amount of cash or other financial assets; or
  - an amount of cash or own equity instruments with a fair value equivalent to the difference between a fixed number of own equity instruments and a fixed amount of cash or other financial assets (i.e. a net-settled derivative contract),

  is a financial asset or financial liability (see 5.2 below); and
- a derivative financial instrument with settlement options is a financial asset or liability, unless all possible settlement options would result in classification as equity (see 5.2.8 below).

There are some difficulties of interpretation surrounding the treatment of certain contracts to issue equity (see 5.4 below).

In undertaking the analysis required by IAS 32, it is sometimes helpful, where the detailed guidance in the standard is not entirely clear, to consider whether the instrument or contract under discussion exposes the holder or the issuer to the risk of movements in the fair value of the issuer's equity. If the holder is at risk to the same degree as equity investors in the entity, it is likely that the instrument or contract should be classified as equity. If, however, the entity bears the risk of movements in the fair value of the entity's equity, or the holder bears some risk, but less than that borne by equity investors in the entity, it is likely that the contract should be classified, at least in part, as a liability.

It is important to remember that paragraph 16(b) of IAS 32 sets out two tests. Where an entity can control the circumstances under which a variable number of shares may be required to be delivered (e.g. as in the case of a down round clause (see 6.6.7 below)) this can lead to different accounting treatments depending on whether the instrument or compound instrument is regarded as a derivative or non-derivative. Where the instrument is a non-derivative, the requirement is that there is no contractual obligation which could result in the issuer having to deliver a variable number of shares, in other words, all contractual requirements need to be considered. Whereas, if the instrument is a derivative, the requirement is solely whether the fixed for fixed test is met, other contractual terms of the instrument are not considered. So a written option to subscribe for a variable number of shares (or a conversion option within a convertible bond) under the conditions described above would result in the derivative or component being classified as a liability.

5.1 Contracts accounted for as equity instruments

A contract that will be settled by the entity delivering or receiving a fixed number of its own equity instruments in exchange for a fixed amount of cash (see 5 above) or another financial asset is an equity instrument, although a liability may be recorded for any cash payable, by the entity on settlement of the contract. An example would be an issued share option that gives the counterparty a right to buy a fixed number of the entity's shares for a fixed price or for a fixed stated principal amount of a bond (see 6.3.2.A below). *[IAS 32.22]*.

The fair value of such a contract may change due to variations in market interest rates and the share price. However, provided that such changes in fair value do not affect the amount of cash or other financial assets to be paid or received, or the number of equity instruments to be received or delivered, on settlement of the contract, the contract is an equity instrument and accounted for as such. *[IAS 32.22]*.

Any consideration received (such as the premium received for a written option or warrant on the entity's own shares) is added directly to equity. Any consideration paid (such as the premium paid for a purchased option) is deducted directly from equity. Changes in the fair value of an equity instrument are not recognised in financial statements. *[IAS 32.22, AG27(a)]*.

IAS 32 requires some types of puttable instruments (see 4.6.2 above) and instruments that impose an obligation to deliver a *pro rata* share of net assets only on liquidation (see 4.6.3 above) to be treated as equity instruments. However, a contract that is required to be settled by the entity receiving or delivering either of these types of equity instrument is a financial asset or financial liability, even when it involves the exchange of a fixed amount of cash or other financial assets for a fixed number of such instruments. *[IAS 32.22A, AG13]*.

5.1.1 Comparison with IFRS 2 – Share-based Payment

The approach in IAS 32 differs from that in IFRS 2. IFRS 2 essentially treats any transaction that falls within its scope and can be settled only in shares (or other equity instruments) as an equity instrument, regardless of whether the number of shares to be delivered is fixed or variable (see Chapter 34 at 1.4.1). The two standards also differ as regards to:

- the classification of financial instruments that can be settled at the issuer's option in either equity instruments or cash (or other financial assets). Broadly, IFRS 2 requires the classification to be based on the likely outcome, whereas IAS 32 focuses on the strict legal obligations imposed by the contract; and
- the definition of equity instrument. IFRS 2 refers to the exchange of a 'fixed or determinable' amount of cash, whereas IAS 32 refers to the exchange of a 'fixed' amount of cash. This means that written options to issue own equity with a foreign currency strike price are typically equity instruments under IFRS 2, but financial assets or liabilities under IAS 32, subject to the limited exception for short-term rights issues (see 5.2.3.A below).

The IASB offers some (pragmatic rather than conceptual) explanation for these differences in the Basis for Conclusions to IFRS 2. First, it is argued that to apply IAS 32 to share option plans would mean that a variable share option plan (i.e. one where the number of shares varied according to performance) would give rise to more volatile (and typically greater) cost than a fixed plan (i.e. one where the number of shares to be awarded is fixed from the start), even if the same number of shares was ultimately delivered under each plan, which would have 'undesirable consequences'. [IFRS 2.BC109]. This serves only to beg the question of why it is not equally 'undesirable' for the same result to arise in accounting for share-settled contracts within the scope of IAS 32 rather than IFRS 2. Second, it is noted that this is just one of several inconsistencies between IFRS 2 and IAS 32 which will be addressed in the round as part of the IASB's review of accounting for debt and equity. [IFRS 2.BC110]. As discussed further at 12 below, this review remains somewhat more distant than was probably envisaged when IFRS 2 was issued in 2004.

5.1.2 Number of equity instruments issued adjusted for capital restructuring or other event

Entities, particularly larger listed companies, routinely restructure their equity capital. This may take many forms, including:

- structural changes in the issuer's ordinary shares (such as a share split, a share consolidation or a reclassification of the outstanding ordinary shares of the issuer);
- a repurchase of shares;
- a distribution of reserves or premiums, by way of extraordinary dividend;
- a payment of a dividend, or extraordinary dividend, in shares; or
- a bonus share or rights issue to existing shareholders.

Accordingly, contracts for the purchase or delivery of an entity's own equity often provide that the number of shares specified in the contract is modified in the event of such a restructuring. This provides protection to both the holder of the contract and to existing shareholders, by ensuring that their relative rights remain the same before and after the restructuring. For example, an entity with shares with a nominal (par) value of €1 might enter into an agreement that requires it to issue '100 shares'. If, before execution of that agreement, the entity has split each €1 share into ten €0.10 shares, it must issue 1,000, not 100, shares in order to give effect to the intention of the contract.

Such adjustment formulae are most commonly seen in the terms of convertible instruments (see 6 below for convertible instrument classification), so that the number of shares into which the bonds eventually convert will take account of any capital restructuring between issue and conversion of the bond, with the broad intention of putting the holders of the bond in the same position with respect to other equity holders before and after the restructuring. In addition, the terms of many convertible instruments provide for similar adjustment upon the occurrence of other actions or events which would affect the position of the convertible bondholders relative to other equity holders. Such actions or events may include, for example:

- the payment of ordinary dividends;
- an issue of equity at less than current market value;
- the repurchase of equity at more than current market value;
- the issue of further convertible securities at less than fair market value; or
- the acquisition of assets in exchange for equity at more than fair market value.

This raises the question of whether a contract with any such terms can be classified as equity under IAS 32, since the number of shares ultimately issued on conversion is not fixed at the outset, but may vary depending on whether a restructuring or other event occurs before conversion. In our view, an adjustment to the number of equity instruments issued in such circumstances should not be considered to result in the issue of a variable number of shares, where its purpose is to ensure that the bondholder's equity interest is not diluted or augmented. In other words, if the adjustment attempts to put the holders of the instruments into the same economic position relative to ordinary shareholders after the restructuring as they were in before the restructuring, then the fixed for fixed criterion is still met. We consider that the potential dilution or augmentation in the bondholder's equity interest which is to be adjusted for should be determined in comparison to the effect of the event on the other equity holders in aggregate. Thus, if shares are issued to new shareholders at a discount, the dilution suffered by the bondholders should be calculated by reference to the total number of shares in existence following the new issue.

The effect of such an adjustment is that the risks and rewards of the bondholder are more closely aligned to those of a holder of ordinary shares. IAS 32 generally treats contracts involving a variable number of equity instruments as a financial liability because the effect of the variability is that the counterparty is not exposed to any movement in the fair value of the equity instruments between the inception and execution of the contract. In this case, however, the variability is introduced so as to ensure that the counterparty remains exposed to any movement in the fair value of the equity instruments and maintains the same interest in the equity relative to other shareholders.

The same question arises in circumstances where a convertible bond is convertible into a fixed percentage of equity. This is discussed at 6.6.6 below.

However not all convertible securities with adjustable conversion ratios can be classified as equity. Where a convertible security has a contractual feature for the conversion ratio to be adjusted down to the lower price of any later issue in the underlying shares, the instrument will fail equity classification. The modification feature is not fixed for fixed and therefore the conversion option is a financial liability. *[IAS 32.11(b)(ii)]*. As such it is an embedded derivative of a debt host rather than an equity component. The entity's ability to control the non-fixed for fixed settlement is not relevant to the assessment. This is because a derivative instrument that gives either party the choice over settlement is a financial asset or liability unless all of the settlement alternatives would result in it being an equity instrument. *[IAS 32.26]*. The conversion option will therefore be treated as a derivative liability. This is discussed in more detail at 6.6.7 below.

The Interpretations Committee considered a number of 'fixed for fixed' issues raised by constituents at its November 2009 meeting. However, the Interpretations Committee concluded that the Board's project *Financial Instruments with Characteristics of Equity* was expected to address issues relating to the fixed for fixed condition, and that the Interpretations Committee would therefore not add this to its agenda. The IASB discussed this issue in April 2020 as part of their continuing deliberations on the FICE project (see 12 below).

5.1.3 Stepped up exercise price

Another type of adjustment which is commonly found is where an entity issues subscription shares that have a stepped exercise price, which is fixed at inception and increases with the passage of time. Such subscription shares are typically issued as bonus shares on a *pro rata* basis to existing shareholders and give the holder the right (but not the obligation) to subscribe for a certain number of ordinary shares, at a certain price and at a certain time in the future. Our view is that subscription shares that have a stepped exercise price meet the 'fixed for fixed' condition only if the exercise prices are fixed at inception and for the entire term of the instrument, such that at any point in time the exercise price is pre-determined at the issuance of the subscription shares. If the exercise price per share is linked to an index of any kind, the 'fixed for fixed' condition is not met and the contract to issue the shares would not be classified as an equity instrument.

5.1.4 Exchange of fixed amounts of equity (equity for equity)

As discussed above, IAS 32 requires a contract settled in own equity to be classified as equity if, *inter alia*, it involves the exchange of a fixed amount of cash (or other financial assets) for a fixed amount of equity. This begs the question of how to classify a contract that provides for the exchange of a fixed amount of one class of the entity's equity for a fixed amount of another class. Examples might be:

- a warrant allowing the holder of a preference share classified as equity (see 4.5 above) to exchange it for an ordinary equity share; or
- in consolidated financial statements, an option for a shareholder of a partly-owned subsidiary (classified within equity in the consolidated financial statements) to exchange a fixed number of shares in the subsidiary for a fixed number of shares in the parent.

One view might be that, as a contract to exchange equity instruments does not fall within the definition of an 'equity instrument' in accordance with IAS 32 it must therefore be accounted for as a derivative. The contrary view would be that the contract does not meet the definitions of either a financial asset or a financial liability either and given that it involves the exchange of equity instruments on a fixed for fixed basis should be accounted for as an equity instrument. Those who hold the latter view would argue that the absence of any reference to such 'fixed equity for fixed equity' contracts in IAS 32 does not reflect a conscious decision by the IASB, but rather indicates that the IASB never considered such contracts at all.

A third view might be that the analysis may depend upon the specific terms of the equity instruments. For example, if the equity instrument being exchanged has debt-like features (e.g. it pays regular, but discretionary, coupons), and is denominated in the same currency as the entity's functional currency, the contract would be classified as equity, but if it were denominated in a different currency, the contact would, for the reasons discussed at 5.2.2 below, be classified as a derivative.

It is worth noting that the IASB also discussed this issue in April 2020 as part of their continuing deliberations within the FICE project to clarify some of the principles of IAS 32 (see 12 below).

5.2 Contracts accounted for as financial assets or financial liabilities

5.2.1 Variable number of equity instruments

An entity may have a contractual right or obligation to receive or deliver a number of its own shares or other equity instruments that varies so that the fair value of the entity's own equity instruments to be received or delivered equals the amount of the contractual right or obligation.

The right or obligation may be for:
- a fixed amount – e.g. as many shares as are worth £100; or
- an amount that fluctuates in part or in full in response to changes in a variable other than the market price of the entity's own equity instruments, such as movements in interest rates, commodity prices, or the price of a financial instrument – e.g. as many shares as are worth:
  - 100 ounces of gold;
  - £100 plus interest at LIBOR plus 200 basis points;
  - 100 government bonds; or
  - 100 shares in a particular entity.

Such a contract is a financial asset or liability. Even though the contract must, or may, be settled through receipt or delivery of the entity's own equity instruments, the number of own equity instruments required to settle the contract will vary. The contract will therefore not fulfil the requirements of an equity instrument and is therefore a financial asset or financial liability. *[IAS 32.21, AG27(d)]*.

5.2.2 Fixed number of equity instruments for variable consideration

A contract that will be settled by the entity delivering or receiving a fixed number of its own equity instruments in exchange for a variable amount of cash or another financial asset is a financial asset or financial liability. An example is a contract for the entity to deliver 100 of its own equity instruments in return for an amount of cash calculated to equal the value of 100 ounces of gold, *[IAS 32.24]*, or 100 specified government bonds. As discussed at 5.2.3 below, it would also include a contract for the entity to deliver 100 of its own equity instruments in return for a fixed amount of cash denominated in a currency other than its own functional currency.

5.2.3 Fixed amount of cash (or other financial assets) denominated in a currency other than the entity's functional currency

Some contracts require an entity to issue a fixed number of equity instruments in exchange for a fixed amount of cash denominated in a currency other than the entity's functional currency. Such contracts raise a problem of interpretation illustrated by the example in paragraph 24 of IAS 32 (referred to in 5.2.1 above) of a contract being a financial asset or financial liability where the reporting entity is required 'to deliver 100 of its own equity instruments in return for an amount of cash calculated to equal the value of 100 ounces of gold'. If one substitutes '100 US dollars' for '100 ounces of gold', the latent problem becomes apparent.

Suppose a UK entity (with the pound sterling as its functional currency) issues a £100 bond convertible into a fixed number of its equity shares. As discussed in more detail at 6 below, IAS 32 requires this to be accounted for by splitting it into a liability component (the obligation to pay interest and repay principal) and an equity component (the holder's right to convert into equity). In this case the equity component is the right to convert the fixed stated £100 principal of the bond (see 6.3.2.A below) into a fixed number of shares.

Suppose instead, however, that the UK entity (with the pound sterling as its functional currency) issues a 100 US dollar bond convertible into a fixed number of its shares. The conversion feature effectively gives the bondholder the right to acquire a fixed number of shares for a fixed stated principal (see 6.3.2.A below) of $100 – is this a 'fixed amount' of cash, or is it to be regarded as being just as variable, in terms of its conversion into the functional currency of the pound sterling, as 100 ounces of gold?

If the conclusion is that $100 is a fixed amount of cash, the conversion right is accounted for as an equity component of the bond – in other words a value is assigned to it on initial recognition and it is not subsequently remeasured (see 6.2.1 below). If, on the other hand, the conclusion is that $100 is not a fixed amount of cash, then the conversion right (as an embedded derivative not regarded by IFRS 9 as closely related to the host contract – see Chapter 46 at 4) is accounted for as a separate derivative financial liability, introducing potentially significant volatility into the financial statements.

There is no obvious answer to this. A contention that the $100 is a 'fixed amount' of cash is hard to reconcile with the fact that a contract to issue shares for 'as many pounds sterling as are worth $100' would clearly involve the issue of a fixed number of shares for a variable amount of cash and would therefore not be an equity instrument.

The Interpretations Committee considered this issue at its meeting in April 2005. The Committee noted that although this matter was not directly addressed in IAS 32, it was clear that, when the question is considered in conjunction with guidance in other standards, particularly IFRS 9, any obligation denominated in a foreign currency represents a variable amount of cash. Consequently, the Interpretations Committee concluded that a contract settled by an entity delivering a fixed number of its own equity instruments in exchange for a fixed amount of foreign currency should be classified as a liability.[20]

5.2.3.A Rights issues with a price fixed in a currency other than the entity's functional currency

In July 2009, as a result of a recommendation from the Interpretations Committee, the IASB reconsidered this matter in the specific context of rights issues (options to purchase additional shares at a fixed price) where the price is denominated in a currency other than the entity's functional currency. The IASB was advised that the Interpretations Committee's conclusion was being applied to rights issues, with the result that the rights were being accounted for as derivative liabilities with changes in fair value being recognised in profit or loss. HSBC explained that such accounting would result in the recognition of a loss of $4.7 billion in the first quarter of 2009.

> Extract 47.2: HSBC Holdings plc (2009)
> Interim Management Statement Q1 2009 [extract]
> Accounting impact of HSBC's Rights Issue [extract]
>
> On 2 March 2009, HSBC announced a 5 for 12 Rights Issue of 5,060 million new ordinary shares at 254 pence per share, which was authorised by the shareholders in a general meeting on 19 March 2009. The offer period commenced on 20 March 2009, and closed for acceptance on 3 April 2009. Under IFRSs, the offer of rights is treated as a derivative because substantially all of the issue was denominated in currencies other than the Company's functional currency of US dollars, and accordingly HSBC was not able to demonstrate that it was issuing a fixed number of shares for a fixed amount of US dollars, which is the criterion under IFRSs for HSBC to account for the offer of rights in shareholders' equity. The derivative liability was measured at inception of the offer as the difference between the share price at that date and the rights price, with a corresponding debit to shareholders' equity. The revaluation of this derivative liability over the offer period, arising from an increase in the share price, has resulted in the recognition of a loss in the income statement of US$4.7 billion. The derivative liability expired on acceptance of the offer, and the closing balance was credited to shareholders' equity. Accordingly, there is no overall impact on the Group's shareholders' equity, capital position or distributable reserves.

Consequently, in October 2009, the IASB made a limited amendment to IAS 32 so as to require a rights issue granted *pro rata* to an entity's existing shareholders for a fixed amount of cash to be classified as equity, regardless of the currency in which the exercise price is denominated. [IAS 32.11].

This amendment does not apply to other instruments that grant the holder the right to purchase the entity's own equity instruments, such as the conversion feature in a convertible bond. It also does not apply to long-dated foreign currency rights issues, which are therefore classified as financial liabilities if the strike price is denominated in a foreign currency. The reason for the restricted scope of the amendment is that the IASB countenanced an exception to the 'fixed for fixed' concept in IAS 32 for short-dated rights issues only because the rights are distributed *pro rata* to existing shareholders, and can therefore be seen as a transaction with owners in their capacity as such. [IAS 32.BC4J]. The IASB does not consider long-dated transactions as primarily transactions with owners in their capacity as owners. [IAS 32.BC4K].

5.2.4 Instrument with equity settlement alternative of significantly higher value than cash settlement alternative

A financial instrument is also a financial liability if it provides that on settlement the entity will deliver either:

(a) cash or another financial asset; or

(b) a number of its own shares whose value is determined to exceed substantially the value of the cash or other financial asset.

IAS 32 explains that, although the entity does not have an explicit contractual obligation to deliver cash or another financial asset, the value of the share settlement alternative is such that the entity will settle in cash. In any event, the holder has in substance been guaranteed receipt of an amount that is at least equal to the cash settlement option. [IAS 32.20].

5.2.5 Fixed number of equity instruments with variable value

A contract is a financial asset or financial liability if it is to be settled in a fixed number of shares, the value of which will be varied (e.g. by modification of the rights attaching to them) so as to be equal to a fixed amount or an amount based on changes in an underlying variable. *[IAS 32.AG27(d)].*

5.2.6 Fixed amount of cash determined by reference to share price

An entity might enter into an option or forward contract to sell a fixed number of equity shares for a fixed price, where the price is determined by reference to the share price. For example, it might contract to sell 100 shares for £10 each if the share price is between £0 and £10, and for £15 each if the price is higher than £10. Considered as a whole, the contract provides for the exchange of a fixed number of equity instruments for a variable amount of cash and is therefore a derivative financial liability.

5.2.7 Net-settled contracts over own equity

The value of a contract over an entity's own equity instruments at the date of settlement is the difference between the value of the fixed number of equity instruments to be delivered by one party and the fixed amount of cash (or other financial assets) to be delivered by the other party. If such a contract allows for net settlement, it can then be settled by a transfer (of cash, other financial assets, or the entity's own equity) of a fair value equal to this difference. It is inherent in the general definition of an equity instrument in IAS 32 that a contract settled by a single net payment (generally referred to as net cash-settled or net equity-settled as the case may be) is a financial asset or financial liability and not an equity instrument. This is notwithstanding the fact that an economically equivalent contract settled gross (i.e. by physical delivery of the equity instruments in exchange for cash or other financial assets) would be treated as an equity instrument.

5.2.8 Derivative financial instruments with settlement options

A derivative financial instrument may have settlement options, whereby it gives one or other party a choice over how it is settled (e.g. the issuer or the holder can choose settlement net in cash, net in shares, or by exchanging shares for cash). A derivative that gives one party a choice of settlement options is required to be treated as a financial asset or a financial liability, unless all possible settlement alternatives would result in it being an equity instrument. *[IAS 32.26].* An example of a derivative financial instrument with a settlement option that is a financial liability is a share option that the issuer can decide to settle net in cash or by exchanging its own shares for cash. *[IAS 32.27].*

These provisions will apply mostly to contracts involving the sale or purchase by an entity of its own equity instruments. However, they will also be relevant to those contracts to buy or sell a non-financial item in exchange for the entity's own equity instruments that are within the scope of IAS 32 (rather than IFRS 2) because they can be settled either by delivery of the non-financial item or net in cash or another financial instrument. Such contracts are financial assets or financial liabilities and not equity instruments. *[IAS 32.27].*

Where an instrument is subject to multiple contingent events, there needs to be an assessment of whether the contingent events give rise to separate instruments embedded within the overall contract or whether there is one single instrument. If the contingent events give rise to components that are separable and independent of each other and relate to different risks, then they should be classified and accounted for separately from the host contract. If the components are not readily separable or independent of each other, then the contract will be classified based on its overall features, i.e. if the instrument does not satisfy the fixed for fixed test overall then it is classified as a liability even if individual components do meet the fixed for fixed criteria. For example, an instrument which obliges an issuer to deliver a fixed number of shares upon the consecutive occurrence of two contingent events, i.e. delivery under the second contingent event can only happen if the first contingent event has occurred, which relate to the same risks (such as interest rates, share price or performance of the entity in successive years), should be considered as one overall contract. Thus, while each individual contingency may satisfy the fixed for fixed test on their own, overall the contract will result in a variable number of shares being delivered and so would be classified as debt.

5.3 Liabilities arising from gross-settled contracts for the purchase of the entity's own equity instruments

The following discussion relates only to contracts that must be settled by the counterparty delivering equity instruments (other than those classified as such under the exceptions discussed at 4.6 above) and the entity paying cash (gross-settled contracts). Contracts which can be settled net (i.e. by payment of the difference between the fair value, at the time of settlement, of the equity instruments and that of the consideration given) are accounted for as financial assets or financial liabilities, *[IAS 32.AG27(c)]*, (see 5.2.8 above and 11 below).

IAS 32 requires some types of puttable instruments (see 4.6.2 above) and instruments that impose an obligation to deliver a *pro rata* share of net assets only on liquidation (see 4.6.3 above) to be treated as equity instruments. However, a contract that is required to be settled by the entity receiving or delivering either of these types of equity instrument is a financial asset or financial liability, even when it involves the exchange of a fixed amount of cash or other financial assets for a fixed number of such instruments. *[IAS 32.22A, AG27]*.

Entering into a gross-settled contract for the purchase of own equity instruments gives rise to a financial liability in respect of the obligation to pay the purchase or redemption price, *[IAS 32.23, AG27(a)-(b)]*, (but resulting, on initial recognition, in a reduction of equity rather than an expense). This treatment is intended to reflect the idea that a forward contract or written option to repurchase an equity share gives rise to a liability similar to that contained within a redeemable share (see 4.5 above and 11 below). *[IAS 32.BC12]*.

This is the case even if:
- the contract is an equity instrument;
- the contract is a written put option (i.e. a contract that gives the counterparty the right to require the entity to buy its own shares) rather than a forward contract (i.e. a firm commitment by the entity to purchase its own shares); or
- the number of shares subject to the contract is not fixed. *[IAS 32.23, AG27(a)-(b)]*.

The final bullet point above might refer to a put option written by the entity whereby the counterparty can require the entity to purchase between 1,000 and 5,000 of its own equity shares at €2 per share. In other words, the entity cannot avoid recognising a liability for the contract on the argument that it does not know exactly how many of its own shares it will be compelled to purchase.

When such a liability first arises it must be recognised, in accordance with IFRS 9, at its fair value, i.e. the net present value of the redemption amount. Subsequently, the financial liability is measured in accordance with IFRS 9 (see Chapter 50). *[IAS 32.23, AG27(b)]*. IAS 32 offers no guidance as to how this is to be calculated when, as might be the case with respect to a written put option such as that described in the previous paragraph, the number of shares to be purchased and/or the date of purchase is not known.

In our view, it would be consistent with the requirement of IFRS 13 that liabilities with a demand feature such as a demand bank deposit should be measured at the amount payable on demand, *[IFRS 13.47]*, (see Chapter 14 at 11.5) to adopt a 'worst case' approach. In other words, it should be assumed that the purchase will take place on the earliest possible date for the maximum number of shares. This is also consistent with IAS 32's emphasis, in the general discussion of the differences between liabilities and equity instruments, on a liability arising except to the extent that an entity has an 'unconditional' right to avoid delivering cash or other financial assets (see 4.2 above).

The treatment proposed in the previous paragraph would lead to a different accounting treatment for written 'American' put options (i.e. those that can be exercised at any time during a period ending on a future date) and written 'European' put options (i.e. those that can be exercised only at a given future date). In the case of an American option, a liability would be recorded immediately for the full potential liability. In the case of a European option, a liability would be recorded for the net present value of the full potential liability, on which interest would be accrued until the date of potential exercise. If this interpretation is correct, it has the effect that:

- a gross-settled written American put option that is an equity instrument has no effect on profit or loss (because the full amount payable on settlement would be charged to equity on inception of the contract); but
- a gross-settled European put option that is an equity instrument does affect profit or loss (because the net present value of the amount payable on settlement would be charged to equity on inception of the contract and accrued to the full settlement amount through profit or loss).

If the contract expires without delivery of the shares, the carrying amount of the financial liability is reclassified to equity. This has the rather curious effect that a share purchase contract that expires unexercised (and therefore has no impact on the entity's net assets, other than the receipt or payment of the option premium) can nevertheless give rise to a loss to the extent that interest has been recognised on the liability between initial recognition and its transfer to equity (see Example 47.21 at 11.3.2 below).

5.3.1 Contracts to purchase own equity during 'closed' or 'prohibited' periods

Financial markets often impose restrictions on an entity trading in its own listed securities for a given period (sometimes referred to as a 'closed' or 'prohibited' period) in the run-up to the announcement of its financial results for a period. However, an entity may well wish to continue to purchase its own listed equity throughout the closed period, for example as part of an ongoing share-buyback programme.

One method of achieving this may be for the entity, in advance of the closed period, to enter into a contract with a counterparty (such as a broker) whereby the counterparty purchases shares in the entity, which the entity is then obliged to acquire from the counterparty. Such a contract will give rise to a financial liability for the entity from the day on which it is entered into. As discussed above, this would initially be recorded at the net present value of the amount to be paid, with the unwinding of the discount on that liability recorded as a finance charge in profit or loss.

In addition, if the contract is for the purchase of a fixed number of shares for their market price (as opposed to the exchange of a fixed amount of cash for as many shares as are worth that amount), it will be necessary to remeasure the liability to reflect movements in the share price.

5.3.2 Contracts to acquire non-controlling interests

IFRS 10 requires non-controlling interests to be shown within equity in consolidated financial statements (see Chapter 7 at 4.3). Accordingly, the requirements of IAS 32 relating to contracts over own equity instruments also generally apply, in consolidated financial statements, to forward contracts and put and call options over non-controlling interests.

This analysis was confirmed by the Interpretations Committee in November 2006, when it considered a request to clarify the accounting treatment of contracts to acquire non-controlling interests that are put in place at the time of a business combination. It is arguable that such contracts are more appropriately accounted for under the provisions of IFRS 3 – *Business Combinations* – relating to deferred consideration. It may also be the case that such contracts have the effect that, while there is a non-controlling interest as a matter of law, the relevant subsidiary is nevertheless regarded by IFRS 10 as wholly-owned, in which case the acquirer also recognises a financial liability for the price payable to the non-controlling interest. A further discussion of these issues may be found in Chapter 7 at 5.

The Interpretations Committee agreed that there was likely to be divergence in practice in how the related equity is classified, but did not believe that it could reach a consensus on this matter on a timely basis. Accordingly, the Interpretations Committee decided not to add this item to its agenda.

However, the Interpretations Committee noted that the requirements of IAS 32 relating to the purchase of own equity apply to the purchase of a minority interest. After initial recognition any liability, to which IFRS 3 is not being applied, will be accounted for in accordance with IFRS 9. The parent will reclassify the liability to equity if a put expires unexercised.[21] Whilst this comment was made in the context of the original version of IFRS 3 (issued in 2004), it would be equally applicable where the current version (issued in 2008) is applied.

5.3.2.A Put options over non-controlling interests – Interpretations Committee and IASB developments

The accounting for put options over non-controlling interest has been the subject of much debate over the years and was one of the issues addressed in the FICE DP (see 12 below). For a summary of the Interpretations Committee and IASB developments on this issue see Chapter 7 at 5.

5.4 Gross-settled contracts for the sale or issue of the entity's own equity instruments

The following discussion in 5.4 relates only to contracts which must be settled by the entity delivering its own equity instruments (other than those classified as such under the exceptions discussed at 4.6 above) and the counterparty paying cash (gross-settled contracts). Contracts which can be settled net (i.e. by payment of the difference between the fair value, at the time of purchase, of the shares and that of the consideration given) are accounted as financial assets or financial liabilities (see 5.2.7 above). *[IAS 32.AG27(c)]*.

IAS 32 requires some types of puttable instruments (see 4.6.2 above) and instruments that impose an obligation to deliver a *pro rata* share of net assets only on liquidation (see 4.6.3 above) to be treated as equity instruments. However, a contract that is required to be settled by the entity receiving or delivering either of these types of equity instrument is a financial asset or financial liability, even when it involves the exchange of a fixed amount of cash or other financial assets for a fixed number of such instruments. *[IAS 32.22A, AG27]*.

If an entity enters into a gross-settled contract to sell its own equity instruments, the contract is economically the 'mirror image' of a contract for the purchase of own equity. However, there is no provision in IAS 32 that the contract gives rise to a financial asset in respect of the cash to be received from the counterparty, as compared to the specific provision that a contract to purchase own equity gives rise to a financial liability in respect of the cash to be paid to the counterparty (see 5.3 above). Consequently, it appears that such contracts give rise to no accounting entries until settlement. This analysis is confirmed by an illustrative example to IAS 32 (see Example 47.16 at 11.1.2 below).

Contracts for the sale or issue of an entity's own equity arise in situations such as those in Examples 47.1 and 47.2 below.

Example 47.1: Share issue payable in fixed instalments

A government intends to privatise a nationalised industry with a functional currency of euro through an initial public offering (IPO) at €5 per share. In order to encourage widespread share ownership, the terms of the issue are that shares are issued on 1 January 2018, but subscribers to the IPO are required to pay only €3 per share on 1 January 2018 followed by two further instalments of €1 per share on 1 January 2019 and 1 January 2020.

Example 47.2: Right to call for additional equity capital

A start-up technology entity with a functional currency of UK pounds sterling is unsure of its working capital requirements for the first few years of its operations. It therefore enters into an agreement with its major shareholders whereby it can require those shareholders to contribute an additional £2 per share at any time during the next seven years.

One view might be that the situation in Example 47.1 is not a contract for the future issue of equity – the share has already been issued, and so it would be quite appropriate to record a receivable for the deferred subscription payments. The accounting standard *IFRS for Small and Medium-Sized Entities* indicates that a receivable should be recognised only for shares that have been issued, but that such a receivable should be recognised as a deduction from equity, not as an asset.[22] The standard states that this proposal is derived from IAS 32[23] – an assertion difficult to reconcile with the discussion above. Interestingly, an early IASB staff draft of the exposure draft of *IFRS for Small and Medium-Sized Entities* (as made available on the IASB's website as at September 2006) admitted, with perhaps unintended candour, that this treatment is 'not in any standard'![24] In our view, current IFRS requires any receivable recognised in respect of an issued share to be shown as an asset.

On the other hand, it is clear from IAS 32 that no receivable would be recognised if the arrangement provided for the entity actually to issue further shares (*pro rata* to the shares initially issued) for €1 on 1 January 2019 and 1 January 2020.

6 COMPOUND FINANCIAL INSTRUMENTS

6.1 Background

While many financial instruments are either a liability or equity in their entirety, that is not true for all financial instruments issued by an entity. Some, referred to as compound instruments in IAS 32, contain both elements. A compound financial instrument is a non-derivative financial instrument that, from the issuer's perspective, contains both a liability and an equity component. *[IAS 32.28, AG30]*. Examples include:

- A bond, in the same currency as the functional currency of the issuing entity, convertible into a fixed number of equity instruments, which effectively comprises:
  - a financial liability (the issuer's obligation to pay interest and, potentially, to redeem the bond in cash); and
  - an equity instrument (the holder's right to call for shares of the issuer).

  IAS 32 states that the economic effect of issuing such an instrument is substantially the same as simultaneously issuing a debt instrument with an early settlement provision and warrants to purchase ordinary shares, or issuing a debt instrument with detachable share purchase warrants. *[IAS 32.29]*. However, this analysis is questionable in the sense that, if a company did issue such instruments separately, it is extremely unlikely that one would lapse as the result of the exercise of the other (as is the case on the conversion or redemption of a convertible bond);

- A mandatorily redeemable preference share with dividends paid at the issuer's discretion, which effectively comprises:
  - a financial liability (the issuer's obligation to redeem the shares in cash); and
  - an equity instrument (the holder's right to receive dividends if declared). *[IAS 32.AG37]*.

IAS 32 requires the issuer of a non-derivative financial instrument to evaluate the terms of the financial instrument to determine whether it contains both a liability and an equity component. This evaluation is based on the contractual terms of the financial instruments, the substance of the arrangement and the definition of a financial liability, financial asset and an equity instrument. If such components are identified, they must be accounted for separately as financial liabilities, financial assets or equity, *[IAS 32.28]*, and the liability and equity components shown separately in the statement of financial position. *[IAS 32.29]*.

This treatment, commonly referred to as 'split accounting', is discussed in more detail in 6.2 to 6.6 below. For simplicity, the discussion below (like that in IAS 32 itself) is framed in terms of convertible bonds, by far the most common form of compound financial instrument, but is equally applicable to other types of compound instrument, such as preference shares with different contractual terms in respect of dividends and re-payments of principal (see 4.5 above).

6.1.1 Treatment by holder and issuer contrasted

'Split accounting' is to be applied only by the issuer of a compound financial instrument. The accounting treatment by the holder is dealt with in IFRS 9 and is significantly different. *[IAS 32.AG30]*. In particular:

- In the issuer's financial statements, under IAS 32:
  - on initial recognition of the instrument, the fair value of the liability component is calculated first and the equity component is treated as a residual; and
  - the equity component is never remeasured after initial recognition.
- In the holder's financial statements, under IFRS 9:
  - the instrument fails the criteria for measurement at amortised cost (in particular the 'contractual cash flow characteristics test') and is therefore carried at fair value through profit or loss (see Chapter 48 at 6).

6.2 Initial recognition – 'split accounting'

On initial recognition of a compound instrument such as a convertible bond, IAS 32 requires the issuer to:

(a) identify the various components of the instrument;

(b) determine the fair value of the liability component (see below); and

(c) determine the equity component as a residual amount, essentially the issue proceeds of the instrument less the liability component determined in (b) above.

The liability component of a convertible bond should be measured first, at the fair value of a similar liability that does not have an associated equity conversion feature, but including any embedded non-equity derivative features, such as an issuer's or holder's right to require early redemption of the bond, if any such terms are included.

In practical terms, this will be done by determining the net present value of all potential contractually determined future cash flows under the instrument, discounted at the rate of interest applied by the market at the time of issue to instruments of comparable credit status and providing substantially the same cash flows, on the same terms, but without the conversion option. The fair value of any embedded non-equity derivative features is then determined and 'included in the liability component' – see, however, the further discussion of this point at 6.4.2 below. *[IAS 32.31]*.

Thereafter the liability component is accounted for in accordance with the requirements of IFRS 9, for the measurement of financial liabilities (see Chapter 50). *[IAS 32.31-32]*.

IAS 32 notes that:

- the equity component of a convertible bond is an embedded option to convert the liability into equity of the issuer;
- the fair value of the option comprises its time value and its intrinsic value, if any; and
- this option has value on initial recognition even when it is out of the money. *[IAS 32.AG31(b)]*.

However, not all these features are directly relevant to the accounting treatment, since the equity component is not (other than by coincidence) recorded at its fair value. Instead, in accordance with the general definition of equity as a residual, the equity component of the bond is simply the difference between the fair value of the compound instrument (total issue proceeds of the bond) and the liability component as determined above. Because of this 'residual' treatment, IAS 32 does not address the issue of how, or whether, the issue proceeds are to be allocated where more than one equity component is identified. It is important to note, that the equity component will not be remeasured subsequently.

The methodology of 'split-accounting' in IAS 32 has the effect that the sum of the carrying amounts assigned to the liability and equity components on initial recognition is always equal to the fair value that would be ascribed to the instrument as a whole. No gain or loss arises from the initial recognition of the separate components of the instrument. *[IAS 32.31]*.

This treatment is illustrated in Examples 47.3 and 47.7 below. *[IAS 32.IE34-36]*.

Example 47.3: Convertible bond – basic 'split accounting'

An entity, whose functional currency is the Euro, issues 2,000 convertible bonds. The bonds have a three-year term and are issued at par with a face value of €1,000 per bond, giving total proceeds of €2,000,000. Interest is payable annually in arrears at a nominal annual interest rate of 6% (i.e. €120,000 per annum). Each bond is convertible at any time up to maturity into 250 ordinary shares. When the bonds are issued, the prevailing market interest rate for similar debt without conversion options is 9% per annum. The entity incurs issue costs of €100,000.

The economic components of this instrument are:

- a liability component, being a discounted fixed rate debt, perhaps with an imputed holder's put option (due to the holder's right to convert at any time), and
- an equity component, representing the holder's right to convert at any time before maturity. In effect this is a written call option (from the issuer's perspective) on American terms (i.e. it can be exercised at any time until maturity of the bond).

The practical problem with this analysis is that it is not clear what is the strike price of the holder's options to put the debt and call for shares, specifically whether it is the €2,000,000 face value of the bonds or the discounted amount at which they are recorded until maturity. Perhaps for this reason, IAS 32 does not require the true fair values of these components to be calculated.

Instead the liability component is measured first at the net present value of the maximum potential cash payments that the issuer could be required to make. The difference between the proceeds of the bond issue and the calculated fair value of the liability is assigned to the equity component. The net present value (NPV) of the liability component is calculated as €1,848,122, using a discount rate of 9%, being the market interest rate for similar bonds having no conversion rights, as shown.

Year	Cash flow	€	Discount factor (at 9%)	NPV of cash flow €
1	Interest	120,000	1/1.09	110,092
2	Interest	120,000	$1/1.09^2$	101,001
3	Interest and principal	2,120,000	$1/1.09^3$	1,637,029
			Total liability component	1,848,122
			Total equity component (balance)	151,878
			Total proceeds	2,000,000

Next it is necessary to deal with the issue costs of €100,000. In accordance with the requirements of IAS 32 for such costs (see 8.1 below), these would be allocated to the liability and equity components on a *pro rata* basis. This would give the following allocation of the net issue proceeds.

	Liability component €	Equity component €	Total €
Gross proceeds (allocated as above)	1,848,122	151,878	2,000,000
Issue costs (allocated *pro rata* to gross proceeds)	(92,406)	(7,594)	(100,000)
Net proceeds	1,755,716	144,284	1,900,000

The €144,284 credited to equity is not subsequently remeasured (see 6.2.1 below). On the assumption that the liability is not classified as at fair value through profit or loss, the €1,755,716 liability component would be accounted for under the effective interest rate method. It should be borne in mind that, after taking account of the issue costs, the effective interest rate is not the 9% used to determine the gross value of the liability component, but 10.998%, as shown below.

Year	Liability b/f €	Interest at 10.998% €	Cash paid €	Liability c/f €
1	1,755,716	193,094	(120,000)	1,828,810
2	1,828,810	201,134	(120,000)	1,909,944
3	1,909,944	210,056	(2,120,000)	–
	Total finance cost	604,284		

The total finance cost can be proved as follows:

	€
Cash interest at 6%	360,000
Gross issue proceeds originally allocated to equity component	151,878
Issue costs allocated to liability component	92,406
	604,284

6.2.1 Accounting for the equity component

On initial recognition of a compound financial instrument, the equity component (i.e. the €144,284 identified in Example 47.3 above) is credited direct to equity and is not subsequently remeasured. IAS 32 does not prescribe:

- whether the credit should be to a separate component of equity (although a transitional provision relating to the February 2008 amendment of IAS 32 suggests that there is such a requirement); or
- if the entity chooses to treat it as such, how it should be described.

This ensures that there is no conflict between, on the one hand, the basic requirement of IAS 32 that there should be a credit in equity and, on the other, the legal requirements of various jurisdictions as to exactly how that credit should be allocated within equity.

After initial recognition, the classification of the liability and equity components of a convertible instrument is not revised, for example as a result of a change in the likelihood that a conversion option will be exercised, even when exercise of the option may appear to have become economically advantageous to some holders. IAS 32 points out that holders may not always act in the way that might be expected because, for example, the tax consequences resulting from conversion may differ among holders. Furthermore, the likelihood of conversion will change from time to time. The entity's contractual obligation to make future payments remains outstanding until it is extinguished through conversion, maturity of the instrument or some other transaction. *[IAS 32.30]*.

The amount originally credited to equity is subsequently neither remeasured nor reclassified to profit or loss. Thus, as illustrated by Example 47.3 above, the effective interest rate shown in profit or loss for a simple convertible bond will be equivalent to the rate that would have been paid for non-convertible debt. In effect, the dilution of shareholder value represented by the embedded conversion right is shown as an interest expense.

However, on conversion of a convertible instrument, it may be appropriate to transfer the equity component within equity (see 6.3.1 below).

6.2.2 Temporary differences arising from split accounting

In many jurisdictions it is only the cash interest paid, and sometimes also the issue costs, that are deductible for tax purposes, rather than the full amount of the finance cost charged under IAS 32. Moreover, some of these costs may be deductible in periods different from those in which they are recognised in the financial statements. These factors will give rise to temporary differences between the carrying value of the liability component of the bond and its tax base, giving rise to deferred tax required to be accounted for under IAS 12 – *Income Taxes* (see Chapter 33, particularly at 6.1.2 and 7.2.8).

6.3 Conversion, early repurchase and modification

6.3.1 Conversion at maturity

On conversion of a convertible instrument at maturity, IAS 32 requires the entity to derecognise the liability component and recognise it as equity. There is no gain or loss on conversion at maturity. [IAS 32.AG32].

Thus, for example, if the bond in Example 47.3 above were converted at maturity, the accounting entry required by IAS 32 would be:

	€	€
Liability	2,000,000	
Equity		2,000,000

The precise allocation of the credit to equity (e.g. as between share capital, additional paid-in capital, share premium, other reserves and so on) would be a matter of local legislation. In addition, IAS 32 permits the €144,284 originally allocated to the equity component in Example 47.3 above to be reallocated within equity. [IAS 32.AG32].

6.3.2 Conversion before maturity

6.3.2.A 'Fixed stated principal' of a bond

The consideration given for the issue of equity instruments on conversion of a bond is the discharge by the holder of the issuer from the liability to pay any further interest or principal payments on the bond. If conversion can take place only at maturity, the amount of the liability transferred to equity on conversion will always (as in Example 47.3 at 6.2 above) be €2,000,000. Hence, the conversion right involves the delivery of a fixed number of shares for the waiver of the right to receive a fixed amount of cash and so is clearly an equity instrument.

However, the bond in Example 47.3 allows conversion at some point before the full term. Therefore, conversion might occur at the end of year 2, when the carrying value of the bonds would have been accreted to only €1,909,944. Hence, the carrying amount of the liability that is forgiven on conversion can vary depending on when conversion occurs. This begs the question as to whether the conversion right now involves the delivery of a fixed number of shares for the waiver of the right to receive a variable amount of cash, suggesting that it is no longer an equity instrument.

It is for this reason, in our view, that IAS 32 defines an equity instrument as one that involves the exchange of a fixed number of shares for the 'fixed stated principal' rather than the 'carrying amount' of a bond. [IAS 32.22]. In other words, IAS 32 regards the 'fixed stated principal' of the bond in Example 47.3 as a constant €2,000,000. The intention is to clarify that the variation in the carrying amount of the bond during its term does not preclude the conversion right from being classified as an equity instrument.

6.3.2.B Accounting treatment

IAS 32 refers to the treatment summarised in 6.3.1 above being applied on conversion 'at maturity'. This begs the question of the treatment required if a holder converts prior to maturity (as would have been possible under the terms of the bond in Example 47.3).

As noted in 6.3.2.A above, IAS 32 concludes that the equity component of the bond is an equity instrument on the grounds that it represents the holder's right to call for a fixed number of shares for fixed consideration, in the form of the 'fixed stated principal' of the bond.

It could be argued that the logical implication of this is that, on a holder's early conversion of the bond in Example 47.3 above, the issuer should immediately recognise a finance cost for the difference between the then carrying amount of the liability component of the bond and the fixed stated principal of €2,000,000. This would create a liability of €2,000,000 immediately before conversion, so as to acknowledge that the strike price under the holder's call option is the waiver of the right to receive a fixed stated principal of €2,000,000, rather than whatever the carrying value of the bond happens to be at the time.

However, we take the view, supported by general practice, that all that is required is to transfer to equity the carrying value of the liability at the date of conversion, as calculated after accrual of finance costs on a continuous basis, rather than at the amount shown in the most recently published financial statements. In such a case, the consideration for the issue of equity instruments is the release, by the bondholder, of the issuer from its liability to make future contractual payments under the bond, measured at the net present value of those payments.

IFRIC 19 (which generally applies to debt for equity swaps) does not apply to the conversion of a convertible instrument in accordance with its original terms (see 7 below).

6.3.2.C   Treatment of embedded derivatives on conversion

IAS 32 does not specifically address the treatment of any separated non-equity embedded derivatives outstanding at the time of conversion. The issue of principle is that, when a holder exercises its right to convert, it is effectively requiring the issuer to issue equity in consideration for the bondholder ceding its rights. These may include any right to receive future payments of principal and/or interest or to require early repayment of the bond. It seems entirely appropriate that any amounts carried in respect of such rights, including those reflected in the carrying amount of separated embedded derivatives, should be transferred to equity on conversion.

Where, however, conversion has the effect of removing an issuer's right (for example, to compel early redemption or conversion), this could be seen as a loss to the issuer rather than as consideration given by the holder for an issue of equity. In our view, however, the loss of such a right by the issuer on conversion by the holder simply represents a reduction in the proceeds received for the issue of equity and should therefore by accounted for as a charge to equity (see also 8.1 below).

6.3.3   Early redemption or repurchase

It is not uncommon for the issuer of a convertible bond to redeem or repurchase it before the end of its full term, either through exercise of rights inherent in the bond, such as an embedded issuer call option, or through subsequent negotiation with bondholders.

IAS 32 contains guidance for the accounting treatment of an early redemption or repurchase of compound instruments following a tender offer to bondholders (see 6.3.3.A below).

It is not entirely clear whether this guidance applies only to redemption pursuant to a subsequent negotiation with bondholders, or whether it also applies where redemption occurs through exercise of a right inherent in the original terms of the bond. We therefore believe an entity has an accounting policy choice if redemption is based on a right inherent in original terms of the bond, such as an embedded issuer call option at par that was allocated to the liability component and considered to be clearly and closely related to the host contract (see 6.3.3.B below).

6.3.3.A Early repurchase through negotiation with bondholders

When an entity extinguishes a convertible instrument before maturity through an early redemption or repurchase in which the original conversion privileges are unchanged, IAS 32 requires the entity to allocate the consideration paid and any transaction costs for the repurchase or redemption to the liability and equity components of the instrument at the date of the transaction. *[IAS 32.AG33].*

It is not entirely clear what is meant by a 'redemption or repurchase in which the original conversion privileges are unchanged'. However, we assume that it is intended to imply that the repurchase must occur without modification of the original terms of the compound instrument, and at a price representing a fair value for the instrument on its original terms. A repurchase based on a modification of the original terms of the instrument, or at a price implying a modification of them, should presumably be dealt with according to the provisions of IAS 32 for the modification of a compound instrument (see 6.3.4 below) or those in IFRS 9 for the exchange and modification of debt (see Chapter 52 at 6.2).

The method used for allocating the consideration paid and transaction costs to the separate components should be consistent with that used in the original allocation to the separate components of the proceeds received by the entity when the convertible instrument was issued (see 6.2 above). *[IAS 32.AG33].*

The issuer is therefore required to:

- determine the fair value of the liability component and allocate this part of the purchase price to the liability component;
- allocate the remainder of the purchase price to the equity component; and
- allocate the transaction costs between the liability and equity component on a *pro rata* basis.

Once this allocation of the consideration has been made:

- the difference between the consideration allocated to the liability component and the carrying amount of the liability is recognised in profit or loss; and
- the amount of consideration relating to the equity component is recognised in equity. *[IAS 32.AG34].*

The treatment of a negotiated repurchase at fair value of a convertible instrument is illustrated by Example 47.4 below, which is based on an illustrative example in IAS 32. *[IAS 32.IE39-46].*

Example 47.4: Early repurchase of convertible instrument

For simplicity this example:
- assumes that at inception the face amount of the instrument was equal to the carrying amount of its liability and equity components in the financial statements – i.e. there was no premium or discount on issue; and
- ignores transaction costs and tax.

On 1 January 2016, an entity issued a convertible bond with a face value of €100 million maturing on 31 December 2025, at which point the holder may opt for repayment of €100 million or conversion into 4 million shares. Interest is paid half-yearly in arrears at a nominal annual interest rate of 10% (i.e. €5m per half year). At the date of issue, the entity could have issued non-convertible debt with a ten-year term bearing interest at 11%. On issue, the carrying amount of the bond was allocated as follows:

	€m
Present value of the principal – €100m payable at the end of ten years[1]	34.3
Present value of the interest – 20 6-monthly payments of €5m[2]	59.7
Total liability component	94.0
Equity component (balance)	6.0
Proceeds of the bond issue	100.0

The amounts above are discounted using a semi-annual rate of 5.5% (11%÷2) as follows:

1 €100m/1.055^{20}
2 €5m × (1/1.055 + 1/1.055^2 + 1/1.055^3 + ... 1/1.055^{20})

On 1 January 2021, the entity makes a tender offer to the holder of the bond to repurchase the bond at its then fair value of €170 million, which the holder accepts. At the date of repurchase, the entity could have issued non-convertible debt with a five-year term with interest payable half-yearly in arrears at an annual coupon interest rate of 8%.

At the time of repurchase, the carrying amount of the liability component of the bond, discounted at the original semi-annual rate of 5.5% is as follows.

	€m
Present value of the principal – €100m payable at the end of five years[1]	58.5
Present value of the interest – 10 6-monthly payments of €5m[2]	37.7
Carrying value of liability component	96.2

1 €100m/1.055^{10}
2 €5m × (1/1.055 + 1/1.055^2 + 1/1.055^3 + ... 1/1.055^{10})

The fair value of the liability component of the bond, discounted at the current semi-annual rate of 4% (8%÷2) is as follows.

	€m
Present value of the principal – €100m payable at the end of five years[1]	67.6
Present value of the interest – 10 6-monthly payments of €5m[2]	40.5
Fair value of liability component	108.1

1 €100m/1.04^{10}
2 €5m × (1/1.04 + 1/1.04^2 + 1/1.04^3 + ...1/1.04^{10})

The fair value calculation indicates that, of the repurchase price of €170 million, €108.1 million is to be treated as redeeming the liability component of the bond, and the balance of €61.9 million as redeeming the equity component. This gives rise to the accounting entry:

	€m	€m
Liability component of bond	96.2	
Equity	61.9	
Debt settlement expense (profit or loss)	11.9	
Cash		170.0

The debt settlement expense represents the difference between the carrying value of the debt component (€96.2m) and its fair value (€108.1m).

Any costs of the repurchase would have been allocated between profit or loss and equity in proportion to the fair value of the liability and equity components at the time of redemption.

6.3.3.B Early repurchase through exercising an embedded call option

It is not entirely clear whether the guidance in 6.3.3.A above applies only on early redemption or repurchase to a subsequent negotiation with bondholders, or whether it also applies where redemption occurs through exercise of rights inherent in the terms of the bond (for example an issuer call option at par allocated to the liability component and considered to be clearly and closely related to the host contract).

One way of accounting for such redemptions would be by applying the accounting treatment as discussed under 6.3.3.A above.

If, however, this early repayment option was determined, on initial recognition of the convertible bond, to be clearly and closely related to the liability host contract (see 6.4.2.A below), then it might be argued that the general measurement rules of IFRS 9 apply. In such a case the liability (including the embedded call option) would be measured at amortised cost (assuming that it was not designated at fair value through profit or loss on initial recognition). Accounting under the amortised cost method is based on an effective interest rate, calculated initially based on expected future cash flows. Any change in those expected cash flows is reflected in the carrying amount of the financial instrument, by computing the present value of the revised estimated future cash flows at the instrument's original effective interest rate, with any difference from the previous amortised cost carrying amount recorded in profit or loss. [IFRS 9.B5.4.6].

A change in the expected repayment date would therefore require the amortised cost of the financial liability component to be remeasured. This treatment has the effect that the overall repayment amount at par is allocated to the liability portion of the compound instrument.

6.3.4 Modification

An entity may amend the terms of a convertible instrument to induce early conversion, for example by offering a more favourable conversion ratio or paying other additional consideration in the event of conversion before a specified date. The difference, at the date the terms are amended, between:

- the fair value of the consideration the holder receives on conversion of the instrument under the revised terms; and
- the fair value of the consideration the holder would have received under the original terms,

is recognised as a loss in profit or loss. *[IAS 32.AG35]*. IAS 32 illustrates this treatment, as shown in Example 47.5 below. *[IAS 32.IE47-50]*.

Example 47.5: **Modification of the terms of a bond to induce early conversion**

Suppose that the entity in Example 47.4 at 6.3.3.A above wished, on 1 January 2021, to induce the bondholder to convert the bond early. The original terms of the bond allowed for conversion into 4 million shares. The entity offers the bondholder the right to convert into 5 million shares during the period 1 January to 28 February 2021. The market value of the entity's shares is €40 per share.

The enhanced conversion terms offer the bondholder the right to receive an additional 1 million shares. Accordingly, the entity recognises a cost of €40m (1m shares × share price €40/share) in profit or loss.

6.4 The components of a compound instrument

6.4.1 Determining the components of a compound instrument

The most difficult aspect of 'split accounting' is often the initial assessment of whether the instrument consists of different components and if it does, what the various components of the instrument actually are. In the examples above, it is fairly clear that the instruments consist of different components and what the various components are. However, in some instruments the analysis is far from straightforward, as illustrated by Example 47.6 below.

Example 47.6: **Analysis of compound financial instrument into components**

An entity issues a bond for €100, paying an annual cash coupon of 5% on the issue price and mandatorily convertible after five years on the following terms. If, at the date of conversion, the entity's share price is €1.25 or higher, the holder will receive 80 shares. If the entity's share price is €1.00 or lower, the holder will receive 100 shares. If the entity's share price is in the range €1.00 to €1.25, the holder will receive such number of shares (between 80 and 100) as have a fair value of €100.

Any analysis must begin by determining whether the bond as whole is a non-derivative instrument. This is the case, since the issuing entity receives full consideration for its issue. The next step is to assess whether the instrument consists of different components and, if it does, to break the instrument down into these components so as to identify any equity components in the whole.

The difficulty of this assessment is evidenced by two requests received by the Interpretations Committee to address the accounting for two instruments with substantially the same features as the one in Example 47.6 above but with an additional early settlement option for the issuer, to settle the instrument at any time by delivering a maximum (fixed) number of shares (see 6.6.3.A below).[25] While the request focused only on the additional early settlement option, and not on the classification of the 'basic' instrument (an instrument with the features described in Example 47.6 above), the accounting treatment of the 'basic instrument' was added to the Interpretations Committee's agenda. It was discussed during the January 2014 and May 2014 Interpretations Committee meetings.[26]

Four alternative views with significantly different accounting outcomes, ranging from classifying the whole financial instrument as a financial liability to various combinations of financial liabilities, equity instruments and/or derivative financial liabilities, were considered by the Interpretations Committee. In the end the Interpretations Committee noted that:

- the issuer's obligation to deliver a variable number of the entity's own equity instruments is a non-derivative that meets the definition of a financial liability in paragraph 11(b)(i) of IAS 32 in its entirety (see 3 and 4.1 above); and
- the definition of a liability in IAS 32 does not have any limits or thresholds regarding the degree of variability that is required.

Therefore, the contractual substance of the instrument is a single obligation to deliver a variable number of equity instruments at maturity, with the variation based on the value of those equity instruments. The Interpretations Committee noted further that such a single obligation to deliver a variable number of own equity instruments cannot be subdivided into components for the purposes of evaluating whether the instrument contains a component that meets the definition of equity. Even though the number of equity instruments to be delivered is limited and guaranteed by the cap and the floor, the overall number of equity instruments that the issuer is obliged to deliver is not fixed and therefore the entire obligation meets the definition of a financial liability.

The Interpretations Committee noted that the cap and the floor are embedded derivative features, whose values change in response to the price of the issuer's equity shares. Therefore, assuming that the issuer has not elected to designate the entire instrument under the fair value option, the issuer must separate those features and account for the embedded derivative features separately from the host liability contract, at fair value through profit or loss in accordance with IFRS 9 (see Chapter 46 at 4 and 5).

The fact that the issue was submitted to the Interpretations Committee in the first place together with the fact that four possible accounting views were drawn up under the guidance of IAS 32, evidences how difficult and judgemental any analysis of increasingly complex instruments can be under the provisions of IAS 32.

6.4.2 Compound instruments with embedded derivatives

As noted above, in order to qualify for split accounting, a financial instrument, when considered as a whole, must be a non-derivative instrument. However, one or more of its identified components may well be embedded derivatives. Indeed, the conversion right in any convertible bond represents a holder's call option whereby the entity can be required to issue a fixed number of shares for a fixed consideration (the 'fixed stated principal' of the bond – see 6.3.2.A above), which is accordingly identified as an equity component.

A bond may well contain other (non-equity) derivatives, such as options for either the issuer or the holder to require early repayment or conversion or to extend the period until conversion. The detailed guidance in IAS 32 requires the fair value of any embedded non-equity derivative features to be determined and included in the liability component when split accounting is applied (see 6.2 above). *[IAS 32.31]*. They are then subject to the normal requirement of IFRS 9 for embedded derivatives to be accounted for separately if they are not considered to be closely related to the host contract (see Chapter 46 at 5).

The issuer of a compound financial instrument with other embedded derivatives is therefore required to go through the following steps:

- First step: determine the fair value of the liability component that does not have an associated equity conversion feature but including any embedded non-equity derivatives features;
- Second step: determine the equity component as a residual amount by deducting the fair value of the liability component, including any embedded non-equity derivative features, from the fair value of the compound instrument (essentially its issue proceeds); and
- Third step: assess whether the embedded non-equity derivative features are closely related to the host liability component. Any not closely related embedded non-equity derivative features are accounted for separately and therefore separated from the host liability component (see Chapter 46 at 4 and 5).

Note, on initial recognition, the sum of the initial carrying amounts of the various components, determined as indicated above, must equal the overall fair value of the compound instrument.

The separation of the liability and equity components of a compound financial instrument with multiple embedded derivative features is demonstrated in Example 47.7 below which is based on an illustrative example in IAS 32. *[IAS 32.IE37-38]*.

6.4.2.A   Issuer call option – 'closely related' embedded derivatives

Example 47.7:   Convertible bond – split accounting with multiple embedded derivative features

The proceeds received on the issue of a convertible bond, callable at par, are £60 million, which equals the nominal amount of the convertible bond. The value of a similar bond without a call or equity conversion option is £57 million. Based on an option-pricing model, it is determined that the value to the entity of the embedded call feature in a similar bond without an equity conversion option is £2 million. In this case, the value is allocated to the liability component so as to reduce the liability component to £55 million (£57m – £2m) and the value allocated to the equity component is £5 million (£60m – £55m). Because IFRS 9 requires the embedded derivative assessment to be done before separating the equity component and the call option is at par, the option is considered to be clearly and closely related and therefore not separated from the liability host contract.

Where (as is often the case) a convertible bond is callable at par, the call option would not be a separable derivative. IFRS 9 states that a call option is generally closely related to the host debt contract if the exercise price is approximately equal to the amortised cost of the host on each exercise (which would not, *prima facie* be the case). However, as an exemption to the general rule, IFRS 9 requires this assessment to be made in respect of any embedded call, put or prepayment option in a convertible bond before separating the equity component. *[IFRS 9.B4.3.5(e)]*. This has the effect that an issuer's call over a convertible bond at par is effectively deemed to be equal to amortised cost for the duration of the instrument. This is discussed further in Chapter 46 at 5.

6.4.2.B   Issuer call option – 'not closely related' embedded derivatives

If a non-equity embedded derivative is considered not to be closely related to the host contract, then it should be accounted for separately. If, in Example 47.7 above, the issuer call option were at an amount that was not approximately equal to amortised cost, and not intended to reimburse the approximate present value of lost interest (see Chapter 46 at 5), say at par plus £5 million, then the call option would not be considered clearly and closely related and therefore should be accounted for separately. The issuer in Example 47.7 would therefore record a derivative financial asset at its fair value of £2 million, assuming it would have the same fair value as in Example 47.7, a liability component of £57 million and an equity component of £5 million. The call option would subsequently be remeasured at fair value through profit or loss.

There are cases where over-enthusiastic trawling for embedded derivatives may dredge up results so counter-intuitive that it is hard to believe that they were really intended by the IASB, as illustrated by Example 47.8 below.

Example 47.8: Foreign currency denominated equity instrument with issuer's redemption right

An entity with a functional currency of pounds sterling issues a euro-denominated capital instrument for €145 million (equivalent to £100 million at the date of issue). Coupons on the instrument are paid entirely at the entity's discretion. The entity has the right, but not the obligation, in certain circumstances to redeem the instrument (in Euros) for an amount equal to the original issue proceeds.

Taken as a whole, this is an equity instrument, because it gives rise to no obligation to transfer cash or other financial assets to the holder. However, the issuer's right to redeem, if considered in isolation is not an equity instrument, but a financial asset (a call option over own equity), since it is a derivative involving the purchase of a fixed number of equity instruments for €145 million which, although fixed in euros, is variable when translated into sterling. Suppose that the fair value of the call option, at the date of issue was £15 million.

This analysis would result in the following accounting entry on issue of the instrument:

	£m	£m
Cash	100	
Call option (statement of financial position)	15	
Equity		115

In our view, it would be inappropriate to show an increase in net assets of £115 million, when the only real transaction has been the raising of £100 million of equity for cash. In this particular case, this treatment is, in our view, not required since paragraph 28 of IAS 32 requires split accounting to be applied only where an instrument is determined to contain 'both a liability and an equity component'. In this case, there is no liability component, since the embedded derivative that has potentially been identified is, and can only ever be, an asset; accordingly, 'split accounting' is not required.

6.5 Other issues

The following issues discussed earlier in this chapter are of particular relevance to convertible bonds:

- the Interpretations Committee's conclusion that a fixed amount of cash denominated in a currency other than the entity's functional currency is not a 'fixed amount' of cash (see 5.2.3 above and 6.6.4 and 6.6.4.A below); and
- the treatment of instruments settled with equity instruments the number of which varies to reflect major capital restructurings before settlement (see 5.1.2 above).

These and other issues noted at various points above reinforce an increasing concern that the 'split accounting' rules in IAS 32 are implicitly based on a bond with terms much more straightforward than those of many – if not most – bonds currently in issue. See 12 below for possible future developments.

6.6 Common forms of convertible bonds

6.6.1 Functional currency bond convertible into a fixed number of shares

The most common form of convertible bond, a functional currency bond convertible into a fixed number of own equity instruments at the discretion of the holder, is discussed in Example 47.3 at 6.2 above.

6.6.2 Contingent convertible bond

A contingent convertible bond is a bond that is convertible, at the option of the holder, only on the occurrence of a contingent event outside of the control of the holder or the issuer. If the contingent event occurs then the holder has the option, but not the obligation, to convert. If the contingent event does not occur, then the bond will be settled in cash at maturity.

The fact that conversion is only contingent does not mean the instrument has no equity component. If, on occurrence of the contingent event, exercise of the conversion option would result in the exchange of a fixed number of the issuer's own equity instruments for a fixed amount of cash (in the functional currency of the issuing entity), the conversion option would meet the definition of an equity instrument under IAS 32 and the overall instrument would be treated as a compound instrument.

6.6.3 Mandatorily convertible bond

A mandatorily convertible bond is an instrument that, at a certain time in the future, converts into shares of the issuing entity, rather than the conversion being at the option of either the holder or the issuer of the bond. The classification of a mandatorily convertible bond on initial recognition as debt or equity depends on:

- how the convertible bond will be settled; and
- whether the issuer is required to pay interest up to the point of conversion.

If the fixed stated principal will be settled through delivery of a fixed number of the issuer's own shares, and the principal of the convertible bond is in the same currency as the functional currency of the issuing entity, then this feature of the bond is an equity instrument and accounted for as such (see 4.1 and 5.2.3 above). If interest on the bond is payable only at the discretion of the entity, then there is no liability component, and the entire bond is classified as an equity instrument. If, however, the entity is required to pay interest, the obligation to pay interest establishes a liability component, which is measured at the present value of the required interest payments.

If settlement can only occur through the delivery of a variable number of the issuer's own shares, calculated so that the fair value of these shares issued equals the principal amount (see 5.2.1 above), and the entity is required to pay interest then the entire bond is classified as a financial liability.

Example 47.9: Mandatorily convertible bond classified as equity

An entity, with a functional currency of Euro, issues 2,000 convertible bonds with a nominal value of €1,000 per bond, giving total proceeds of €2,000,000. The bonds have a three-year term, and interest is payable, at the discretion of the entity, annually in arrears at a nominal annual interest rate of 6% (i.e. €120,000 per annum). At maturity of the bond each bond converts into 250 ordinary shares. Because the conversion option meets the definition of an equity instrument and payment of interest is at the discretion of the entity, the entire instrument is classified as an equity instrument. The entity records the following accounting entry.

	€	€
Cash	2,000,000	
Equity		2,000,000

Example 47.10: Mandatorily convertible bond classified as a compound instrument

Assume the same fact pattern as in Example 47.9 above, except that the entity has an obligation to pay interest annually in arrears at a nominal annual interest rate of 6% (i.e. €120,000 per annum). The obligation to pay interest over three years represents a liability of the issuing entity at the net present value, using a discount rate of 9%, which is the market interest rate.

Year	Cash flow	€	Discount factor (at 9%)	NPV of cash flow €
1	Interest	120,000	$1/1.09$	110,092
2	Interest	120,000	$1/1.09^2$	101,001
3	Interest	120,000	$1/1.09^3$	92,662
		Total liability component		303,755
		Total equity component (balance)		1,696,245
		Total proceeds		2,000,000

The entity records the following accounting entry.

	€	€
Cash	2,000,000	
Equity		1,696,245
Liability		303,755

6.6.3.A Bond which is mandatorily convertible into a variable number of shares with an option for the issuer to settle early for a maximum number of shares

At its meeting in July 2013, the Interpretations Committee considered the IAS 32 classification for a financial instrument that is mandatorily convertible into a variable number of shares, subject to a cap and floor, but with an issuer option to settle by delivering the maximum (fixed) number of shares.[27] This is a financial instrument with essentially the same features as the one described in Example 47.6 above, but with an additional option for the issuer to settle the instrument at any time before maturity (see 6.4.1 above for IAS 32 classification considerations for the 'basic financial instrument', ignoring the early settlement option). If the issuer chooses to exercise its early settlement option, it must deliver the maximum number of shares specified in the contract (e.g. 100 shares in Example 47.6 and pay in cash all of the interest that would have been payable if the instrument had remained outstanding until its maturity date (a so called 'make-whole provision').

Applying the IAS 32 definitions of a financial liability and of an equity instrument to such a financial instrument would result in accounting for it as a compound instrument (i.e. a financial instrument consisting of an equity element and a financial liability element). IAS 32 states that a non-derivative financial instrument is an equity instrument if the instrument will be settled in the issuer's own equity instruments and includes no contractual obligation for the issuer to deliver a variable number of its own equity instruments. *[IAS 32.11(b)(i)]*. With the early settlement option, the issuer has the right to avoid delivering a variable number of shares. A portion of the financial instrument would therefore meet the definition of equity and would be accounted for as such. The interest payments on the instrument, on the other hand, impose a contractual obligation on the issuer to deliver cash in all cases and therefore meet the definition of a financial liability and would be accounted for as such.

However, this analysis ignores the fact that in exercising the early settlement option, the issuer must deliver at an earlier time a potentially greater number of its own shares, plus all the interest in cash which would have been payable over the instrument's life. The issuer can avoid delivering a variable number of its own shares but only by giving away a potentially larger amount of economic value. The question asked of the Interpretations Committee was whether such an early settlement option should be considered when classifying the financial instrument under IAS 32.

In its analysis, the Interpretations Committee noted that the definitions of financial asset, financial liability and equity instrument in IAS 32 are based on the financial instrument's contractual rights and contractual obligations.[28] However, IAS 32 requires the issuer of a financial instrument to classify the instrument in accordance with the substance of the contractual arrangement. *[IAS 32.15]*. An issuer cannot assume that a financial instrument (or any component) meets the definition of an equity instrument simply because the issuer has the contractual right to settle the financial instrument by delivering a fixed number of equity instruments. The issuer would need to consider whether the early settlement option is substantive and, if it was concluded that it lacks substance, then it should be ignored for the classification assessment of the instrument.

It was noted that the guidance in paragraph 20(b) of IAS 32 is relevant because it provides an example of a situation in which one of an instrument's settlement alternatives is excluded from the classification assessment. Specifically, the example in that paragraph describes an instrument that the issuer will settle by delivering either cash or its own shares, and states that one of the settlement alternatives should be excluded from the classification assessment in some circumstances (see 5.2.4 above).

To determine whether the early settlement option is substantive, the issuer would need to understand whether there are actual economic or business reasons that would lead the issuer to exercise the option. In making that assessment, the issuer could consider whether the instrument would have been priced differently if the issuer's early settlement option had not been included in the contractual terms. The Interpretations Committee also noted that factors such as the term of the instrument, the width of the range between the cap and the floor, the issuer's share price and the volatility of the share price could be relevant to the assessment of whether the issuer's early settlement option is substantive. For example, the early settlement option may be less likely to have substance – especially if the instrument is short-lived – if the range between the cap and the floor is wide and the current share price would equate to the delivery of a number of shares that is close to the floor. That is because the issuer may have to deliver significantly more shares to settle early than it may otherwise be obliged to deliver at maturity. The Interpretations Committee considered that in light of its analysis of the existing IFRS requirements, it would not add this issue to its agenda.

6.6.3.B Bond which is mandatorily convertible into a variable number of shares upon a contingent 'non-viability' event

Since the financial crisis, regulators have been looking to strengthen the capital base of financial institutions, particularly in the banking sector. Rising requirements for capital adequacy have resulted in banks looking into new forms of capital instruments. One form of such capital instruments are financial instruments that convert into a variable number of the issuer's own ordinary shares if the institution breaches a minimum regulatory requirement. This type of contingent event is called a 'non-viability' event.

While the exact terms of these instruments vary in practice, they do generally come with the following key features:

- no stated maturity but the issuer can call the instrument for the par amount of cash;
- while the instrument has a stated interest rate (e.g. 5%), payment of interest is at the discretion of the issuer; and
- if the issuer breaches a minimum regulatory requirement (e.g. 'Tier 1 Capital ratio'), the instrument mandatorily converts into a variable number of the issuer's own ordinary shares. The number of shares delivered would depend on the current share price, i.e. the issuer must deliver as many shares as are worth the par amount of the instrument at conversion.

In July 2013 the Interpretations Committee considered a request to clarify the accounting for such instruments.[29] In its tentative agenda decision, the Interpretations Committee noted that the instrument is a compound instrument that is composed of the following two components:

- a liability component, which reflects the issuer's obligation to deliver a variable number of its own equity instruments if the contingent non-viability event occurs; and
- an equity component, which reflects the issuer's discretion to pay interest.

To measure the liability component, the Interpretations Committee noted that the issuer must consider the fact that the contingent non-viability event could occur immediately because it is beyond the control of the issuer. Hence the liability component must be measured at the full amount that the issuer could be required to pay immediately. The equity component would be measured as a residual and thus would be measured at zero, because the instrument is issued at par and the value of the variable number of shares that will be delivered on conversion is equal to that fixed par amount.

The Interpretations Committee received 12 comment letters on the tentative agenda decision, many accepting that the Interpretation Committee's view is one way of analysing the financial instrument under IAS 32, but generally expressing the view that the relevant guidance in IAS 32 is unclear and that equally valid arguments could be made for other views. For instance, one view discussed at the time was that, when measuring the liability component, the issuer should consider the expected timing of the contingent non-viability event occurring and discount the liability accordingly. Therefore, if the issuer believed that the contingency would not occur in the near-term, the liability component would be recognised at an amount of less than par. The comments provided focused in particular on (a) the measurement of the liability component and (b) whether interest paid on the instrument, if any, would need to be recognised in equity or as interest in profit or loss. Based on the comments received, the Interpretations Committee decided, after further discussions in its January 2014 meeting, not to add this issue to its agenda and noted that the scope of the issues raised in the submission was too broad to be addressed in an efficient manner.[30] There is therefore the potential for diversity in practice until this issue is clarified by the IASB. This is illustrated by the following example:

Example 47.11: Convertible bond mandatorily convertible upon 'non-viability' event

A bank issues €100 million of contingent convertible bonds. The bonds notionally pay fixed interest of 7% annually however interest payments are at the sole discretion of the issuer providing that no dividend is paid on the ordinary shares of the issuer. The bonds are perpetual, but the issuer has the right to call the shares after five years and on every succeeding fifth anniversary thereafter.

The instrument is immediately converted into ordinary shares with a fair value equal to the par value of the bonds upon either:

- the bank's fully loaded Common Equity Tier 1 (CET 1) ratio falling below 7%; or
- the local regulator declaring a non-viability event.

The instrument has both debt features, such as the contingent settlement provision which requires settlement in a variable number of shares upon a non-viability event, and equity features, such as the perpetual nature of the instrument and the discretionary interest payments. As discussed above there are a number of views that could be taken on how to classify this instrument.

Based on the Interpretations Committee's discussion, the view could be taken that the bonds are a compound instrument and that because the contingent settlement provision might be activated immediately, a liability for the par amount of the bond should be recorded. The equity component of the instrument representing the discretionary interest payments would therefore have no value.

However, this could be viewed as odd given that there is usually no expectation that a trigger event will occur when the instrument is first issued. As such, it might be considered to be more reasonable to estimate when a trigger event is most likely to occur and calculate the liability component on that basis, with the residual amount being classified as equity.

There is a further argument that the whole instrument falls within the definition of a liability rather than a compound instrument as the entity may be required to deliver a variable number of shares for a non-derivative instrument. *[IAS 32.11(b)(i)]*.

The conversion trigger itself is not a separable embedded derivative as redemption at amortised cost is regarded as being closely related to the host contract. This is the case even if the debt and equity components of the instrument are separated, as the evaluation of the embedded derivative has to be performed prior to the separation of the equity component. *[IFRS 9.B4.3.5(e)]*.

Similarly, the call option exercisable to extend the term of the instrument is not a separable embedded derivative as the option is at par and so is also closely related.

Any discretionary interest payments would be classified depending on whether the host is classified as a liability, in which case the payments would be interest, or as a compound instrument, in which case payments would be dividends.

A further complication arises with the introduction of bank resolution regimes, such as the European Union's Banking Recovery and Resolution Directive (BRRD). These regimes subject certain financial instruments to bail-in, where banking regulators have the power to write down an instrument or convert it into another CET 1 instrument at their discretion.

As the right to convert the instrument is at the option of the regulator and not the issuer it is arguable that the instrument cannot be classified as equity. The exception for settlement in case of liquidation (see 4.3.2 above) does not apply here as the regulator is likely to invoke the resolution tool well before liquidation occurs. Also, IFRIC 2 specifies that local law and regulations in effect at the classification date together with the terms contained in the instrument's documentation constitute the terms and conditions of the instrument. *[IFRIC 2.BC10]*. However, in the FICE DP (see 12 below), the IASB noted that IFRIC 2 was developed for a very specific fact pattern and that they did not intend to apply the analysis in IFRIC 2 more broadly.[31]

The main conclusion to be drawn from examples such as these is that the provisions of IAS 32, which were originally drafted in the mid-1990s to deal with 'traditional' convertible instruments, are not always adequate for dealing with the increasingly complex range of instruments available in the financial markets now. However as discussed at 12 below the IASB is endeavouring to address many of these issues as part of the FICE project.

6.6.4 Foreign currency convertible bond

If an entity issues a bond in a currency other than its functional currency, the conversion option will not meet the definition of equity in IAS 32, even if the bond is convertible into a fixed number of shares. This is because a fixed amount of foreign currency (a currency different to the functional currency of the bond) is not a fixed amount of cash (see 5.2.3 above). A foreign currency convertible bond is therefore classified as a financial liability under IAS 32, and then measured under the requirements of IFRS 9. An equity conversion option embedded in a financial liability is not considered by IFRS 9 to be clearly and closely related to the host contract and should be accounted for as a separate derivative financial instrument measured at fair value through profit or loss.

6.6.4.A Instrument issued by foreign subsidiary convertible into equity of parent

The Interpretations Committee's conclusion that (other than in the context of certain rights issues – see 5.2.3.A above) a fixed amount of cash denominated in a currency other than the entity's functional currency is not a 'fixed amount' of cash (see 5.2.3 above) leads to the rather counter-intuitive result that the classification of certain instruments in consolidated financial statements depends on the functional currency of the issuing entity.

If, in the example in 5.2.3 above, the UK entity's US subsidiary (with a functional currency of US dollars) issued the same $100 bond convertible into its own equity, convertible in turn into the UK parent's equity, the conversion right would (from the perspective of the US subsidiary) involve the issue of a fixed number of shares for a fixed amount of cash and thus be an equity instrument. Moreover, this classification would not change on consolidation since IFRS has no concept of a group functional currency (see Chapter 15).

The Interpretations Committee discussed this issue at its meetings in July and November 2006. Specifically, it was asked to consider whether the fixed stated principal of the convertible instrument exchanged for equity of the parent on conversion can be considered 'fixed' if it is denominated in the functional currency of either the issuer of the exchangeable financial instruments (i.e. the US subsidiary in the example above) or the issuer of the equity instruments (i.e. the UK parent in the example).

The Interpretations Committee noted that a group does not have a functional currency. It therefore discussed whether it should add a project to its agenda to address which currency should be the reference point in determining whether the embedded conversion options are denominated in a foreign currency. The Interpretations Committee believed that the issue was sufficiently narrow that it was not expected to have widespread relevance in practice and therefore, decided not to take the issue onto its agenda.[32]

In our view, given the absence of specific guidance, an entity may, as a matter of accounting policy, determine the classification, in its consolidated financial statements, of an instrument issued by a subsidiary by reference either to that subsidiary's own functional currency or to the functional currency of the parent into whose equity the bond is convertible.

The effect of this policy choice will be that, where the debt is denominated in a currency other than the designated reference functional currency, the consolidated financial statements contain no equity component. This policy, and its consequences under IAS 32, must be applied consistently, as illustrated by Example 47.12 below.

Example 47.12: Convertible bond issued by a subsidiary with a functional currency different to that of the parent

Suppose that a UK entity with a functional currency of the pound sterling (GBP) has a US trading subsidiary with a functional currency of the US dollar (USD). The US subsidiary issues a bond convertible, at the holder's option, into equity of the UK parent.

If the parent's functional currency (GBP) is the reference currency, the accounting treatment of the holder's conversion right in the consolidated financial statements will be as follows:

- if the fixed stated principal of the bond is denominated in GBP: equity (stated principal of bond is fixed by reference to GBP); but
- if the fixed stated principal of the bond is denominated in a currency other than GBP: derivative (stated principal of bond is variable by reference to GBP).

If, however, the subsidiary's functional currency (USD) is the reference currency, a converse analysis applies, and the accounting treatment of the holder's conversion right in the consolidated financial statements will be as follows:

- if the fixed stated principal of the bond is denominated in USD: equity (stated principal of bond is fixed by reference to USD); but
- if the fixed stated principal of the bond is denominated in a currency other than USD: derivative (stated principal of bond is variable by reference to USD).

It may be that the Interpretations Committee's reluctance to issue guidance on this matter was influenced by the more subtle point that, in most cases, the issuing entity will not be, as in Example 47.12 above, a trading subsidiary, but rather a subsidiary created only for the purposes of the bond issue. IAS 21 – *The Effects of Changes in Foreign Exchange Rates* – suggests that the functional currency of such a 'single transaction' entity is the same as that of the parent for whose equity the bond will be exchanged, irrespective of the currency in which the bond is denominated (see Chapter 15 at 4). In short, the Interpretations Committee was perhaps hinting that the real problem may be the misapplication of IAS 21 in the financial statements of the issuing subsidiary rather than the interpretation of IAS 32.

6.6.5 Convertibles with cash settlement at the option of the issuer

As discussed as 5.2.8 above, IAS 32 requires a derivative with two or more settlement options to be treated as a financial asset or a financial liability unless all possible settlement alternatives would result in it being an equity instrument. Many convertible bonds currently in issue contain a provision whereby, if the holder exercises its conversion option, the issuer may instead pay cash equal to the fair value of the shares that it would otherwise have been required to deliver. This is to allow for unforeseen circumstances, such as an inability to issue the necessary number of shares to effect conversion at the appropriate time.

Where a bond has such a term, the conversion right is a derivative (in effect, a written call option over the issuer's own shares) which may potentially be settled in cash, such that there is a settlement alternative that does not result in it being an equity instrument. This means that the 'equity component' of a bond with an issuer cash settlement option is not in fact an equity instrument, but a financial liability. The financial reporting implication of this is that the conversion right must be accounted for as a derivative at fair value, with changes in value included in profit or loss – in other words the financial statements will reflect gains and losses based on the movement of the reporting entity's own share price.

6.6.6 Bond convertible into fixed percentage of equity

The terms of a convertible bond may allow conversion into a fixed percentage of outstanding shares of the issuer at the time of the conversion, so that the absolute number of shares to be issued is not fixed and is not known until conversion occurs. This raises the question of whether such a clause violates the 'fixed for fixed' criterion, or whether it can be seen as an anti-dilutive mechanism to keep the holder in the same economic position relative to other shareholders at all times (similarly to bonds whose conversion ratio is adjusted for changes in share capital, as discussed under 5.1.2 above).

Our view is that such a conversion option cannot normally be classified as equity, because the entity's capital structure could change in ways that put the convertible bond holder into a better economic position relative to other shareholders.

6.6.7 Convertible bonds with down round or ratchet features

Some instruments that are convertible at a fixed price have clauses which provide that, if additional equity is subsequently issued at a price lower than the conversion price, then the conversion price is amended down to ensure the holders of the convertible instrument are not economically disadvantaged. These clauses are often called 'down round' or 'ratchet' clauses.

When assessing instruments with down round or ratchet clauses it is necessary to know whether the instrument or component being assessed is a non-derivative or a derivative instrument. This is because, as discussed at 5 above, there are two fixed for fixed tests in paragraph 16(b) of IAS 32.

In the case of a non-derivative the test is whether there is a contractual obligation or not for the issuer to deliver a variable number of its own equity instruments. *[IAS 32.16b(i)]*. Therefore, the ability of the entity to prevent a down round or ratchet clause taking effect (by choosing not to issue shares at a lower price) is important and where that is the case the down round or ratchet feature is ignored.

In the case of a derivative instrument or derivative component of an instrument the test is simply whether it will always be settled by exchanging a fixed number of shares for a fixed amount of cash or another financial instrument. *[IAS 32.16b(ii)]*. Therefore, the entity's ability to prevent the down round or ratchet clause taking effect does not affect the classification.

Example 47.13: Convertible bond with ratchet feature

A company, issues preference shares. The preference shares carry a dividend of 2% discretionary at the option of the issuer. Preference shareholders have a right to convert the preference shares into ordinary shares if there is an IPO or earlier if agreed by 60% of the preference shareholders. If not converted, preference shares are redeemable at par at the end of eight years from the issue date. The conversion ratio is fixed at inception at one ordinary share for one preference share. However, the ratio is subject to an anti-dilution clause. If the entity in future issues any new ordinary shares or convertible shares at a price or conversion price lower than the conversion price of the existing preference shares, the conversion price of the existing preference shares is adjusted down using a prescribed formula.

The requirement to redeem the issue at par after eight years creates a liability component which would be extinguished if the conversion option is exercised. As such the presence of the redemption obligation makes the conversion option a derivative. In this case the fact that the company has control over whether the ratchet feature is triggered through the issuance of new shares is not relevant. The derivative component cannot be settled only on a fixed for fixed basis and so the redemption obligation is a liability component.

7 SETTLEMENT OF FINANCIAL LIABILITY WITH EQUITY INSTRUMENT

Neither IAS 32 nor IFRS 9 specifically addresses the accounting treatment to be adopted where an entity issues non-convertible debt, but subsequently enters into an agreement with the debt holder to discharge all or part of the liability in exchange for an issue of equity. These transactions, which are sometimes referred to as 'debt for equity swaps', most often occur when the entity is in financial difficulties.

The Interpretations Committee noted that divergent accounting treatments for such transactions were being applied and decided to address this by developing an interpretation. As a result, IFRIC 19 was published in November 2009. *[IFRIC 19.1]*.

7.1 Scope and effective date of IFRIC 19

IFRIC 19 addresses the accounting by an entity when the terms of a financial liability are renegotiated and result in the entity issuing equity instruments to a creditor to extinguish all or part of the financial liability. It does not address the accounting by the creditor. *[IFRIC 19.2]*.

Further, the interpretation does not apply to transactions in situations where: *[IFRIC 19.3]*
- the creditor is also a direct or indirect shareholder and is acting in its capacity as a direct or indirect existing shareholder (see 7.3 below);
- the creditor and the entity are controlled by the same party or parties before and after the transaction and the substance of the transaction includes an equity distribution by, or contribution to, the entity (see 7.3 below); or
- the extinguishment of the financial liability by issuing equity shares is in accordance with the original terms of the financial liability. This will most commonly arise on conversion of a convertible bond that has been subject to 'split accounting', the accounting for which is covered at 6 above.

7.2 Requirements of IFRIC 19

Equity instruments issued to a creditor to extinguish all or part of a financial liability are treated as consideration paid and should normally be measured at their fair value at the date of extinguishment. However, if that fair value cannot be reliably measured, the equity instruments should be measured to reflect the fair value of the financial liability extinguished. The difference between the carrying amount of the financial liability and the consideration paid (including the equity instruments issued) should be recognised in profit or loss and should be disclosed separately. *[IFRIC 19.5-7, 9, 11]*.

These requirements are illustrated in the following simple example.

Example 47.14: Discharge of liability for fresh issue of equity

During 2012 an entity issued £100 million bonds due to be repaid in 2022. By 2020 the entity is in some financial difficulty and reaches an agreement with the holders of the bonds whereby they will accept equity shares in the entity in full and final settlement of all amounts due under the bonds. On the date the agreement concludes, the carrying amount of the bonds is £99 million and the fair value of the equity shares issued is £60 million.

In this situation the entity would measure the equity instruments issued at their fair value of £60 million and recognise a profit on extinguishment of £39 million [£99 million – £60 million].

Debt for equity swaps often take place in situations when the terms of the financial liability such as covenants are breached and the liability has become, or will become, repayable on demand. Normally, the fair value of a financial liability with a demand feature is required by IFRS 13 to be measured at no less than the amount payable on demand, discounted from the first date that the amount could be required to be paid (see Chapter 14 at 11.5). However, in the IASB's view, the fact that a debt for equity swap has occurred indicates that the demand feature is no longer substantive. Consequently, where the fair value of the equity instruments issued is based on the fair value of the liability extinguished, this particular aspect of IFRS 13 is not applied. *[IFRIC 19.7, BC22]*.

If only part of the financial liability is extinguished, some of the consideration paid might relate to a modification of the terms of the liability that remains outstanding. If so, the consideration paid should be allocated between the part of the liability extinguished and the part of the liability that remains outstanding. All relevant facts and circumstances relating to the transaction should be considered in making this allocation. *[IFRIC 19.8]*. Any consideration so allocated forms part of the assessment of whether the terms of that remaining liability have been substantially modified. If the remaining liability has been substantially modified, the modification should be accounted for as an extinguishment of the original liability and the recognition of a new liability in accordance with IFRS 9 (see Chapter 52 at 6.2). *[IFRIC 19.10]*.

7.3 Debt for equity swaps with shareholders

As noted at 7.1 above, a debt for equity swap is outside the scope of IFRIC 19 when the creditor is a shareholder acting in its capacity as such, or where the entity and the creditor are under common control and the substance of the transaction includes a distribution by, or capital contribution to, the entity.

In our view, such transactions may be accounted for either in a manner similar to that required by IFRIC 19 or by recording the equity instruments issued at the carrying amount of the financial liability extinguished so that no profit or loss is recognised. This latter method was in fact commonly applied to debt for equity swaps before the publication of IFRIC 19.

8 INTEREST, DIVIDENDS, GAINS AND LOSSES

The basic principle of IAS 32 is that inflows and outflows of cash (and other assets) associated with equity instruments are recognised in equity and the net impact of inflows and outflows of cash (and other assets) associated with financial liabilities is ultimately recognised in profit or loss. Accordingly, IAS 32 requires:

- interest, dividends, losses and gains relating to a financial instrument or a component that is a financial liability to be recognised as income or expense in profit or loss;
- distributions to holders of an equity instrument to be debited directly to equity; and
- the transaction costs of an equity transaction to be accounted for as a deduction from equity. *[IAS 32.35]*. This applies also to the costs of issuing equity instruments that are issued in connection with the acquisition of a business. *[IFRS 3.53]*.

The treatment of the costs and gains associated with instruments is determined by their classification in the financial statements under IAS 32, and not by their legal form. Thus, dividends paid on shares classified as financial liabilities (see 4.5 above) will be recognised as an expense in profit or loss, not as an appropriation of equity.

The basic principle summarised above also applies to compound instruments and requires any payments in relation to the equity component to be recorded in equity and any payments in relation to the liability component to be recorded in profit or loss. (As discussed at 6.6.3.B above, it is not clear whether this basic principle also applies when the full amount of the issuance proceeds of a compound instrument is allocated to the liability.) A mandatorily redeemable preference share with dividends paid at the discretion of the entity results in the classification of a liability equal to the net present value of the redemption amount and an equity classification equal to the excess of the proceeds over the liability component (the net present value of the redemption amount) (see 4.5.1 above). Because the redemption obligation is classified as a liability, the unwinding of the discount on this component is recorded and classified as an interest expense. Any dividends paid, on the other hand, relate to the equity component and are therefore recorded as a distribution of profit. *[IAS 32.AG37]*.

Gains and losses associated with redemptions or refinancings of financial liabilities are recognised in profit or loss, whereas redemptions or refinancings of equity instruments are recognised as changes in equity. *[IAS 32.36]*.

Similarly, gains and losses related to changes in the carrying amount of a financial liability are recognised as income or expense in profit or loss, even when they relate to an instrument that includes a right to the residual interest in the assets of the entity in exchange for cash or another financial asset (see 4.6 above). However, IAS 32 notes that IAS 1 requires any gain or loss arising from the remeasurement of such an instrument to be shown separately in the statement of comprehensive income, where it is relevant in explaining the entity's performance. *[IAS 32.41]*.

Changes in the fair value of an instrument that meets the definition of an equity instrument are not recognised in the financial statements. *[IAS 32.36]*.

IAS 32 permits dividends classified as an expense (i.e. because they relate to an instrument, or component of an instrument, that is legally a share but classified as a financial liability under IAS 32) to be presented in the statement of comprehensive income or separate income statement (if presented), either with interest on other liabilities or as a separate item. The standard notes that, in some circumstances, separate disclosure is desirable, because of the differences between interest and dividends with respect to matters such as tax deductibility. Disclosure of interest and dividends is required by IAS 1 (see Chapter 3) and IFRS 7 (see Chapter 54). *[IAS 32.40]*.

8.1 Transaction costs of equity transactions

An entity typically incurs various costs in issuing or acquiring its own equity instruments, such as registration and other regulatory fees, amounts paid to legal, accounting and other professional advisers, printing costs and stamp duties. The transaction costs of an equity transaction are accounted for as a deduction from equity, but only to the extent they are incremental costs directly attributable to the equity transaction that otherwise would have been avoided. The costs of an equity transaction that is abandoned are recognised as an expense. *[IAS 32.37]*.

Although IAS 32 does not provide a definition of directly attributable incremental costs, IFRS 9 does define an incremental cost as 'one that would not have been incurred if the entity had not acquired, issued or disposed of the financial instrument.' *[IFRS 9 Appendix A]*. IFRS 9 also gives as examples of costs which do meet this criterion: fees and commission paid to agents, advisors, brokers and dealers, levies by regulatory agencies and security exchanges, and transfer taxes and duties. *[IFRS 9.B5.4.8]*. Such costs together with other directly related costs such as underwriting and printing costs are usually considered to be incremental and directly attributable to the issue of equity. Internal administrative or holding costs e.g. costs which would have been incurred in any case if the equity instrument had not been issued, are not considered to be incremental or directly attributable.

IAS 32 requires that only the costs of 'issuing or acquiring' equity are recognised in equity. Accordingly, it seems clear that the costs of listing shares already in issue should not be set off against equity but recognised as an expense.

The standard also requires that transaction costs that relate jointly to more than one transaction (for example, costs of a concurrent offering of some shares and a stock exchange listing of other shares) are allocated to those transactions using a basis of allocation that is rational and consistent with similar transactions. [IAS 32.38]. In its agenda decision of September 2008, the Interpretations Committee declined to provide further guidance on the extent of the transaction costs to be accounted for as a deduction from equity and how to allocate costs that relate jointly to more than one transaction, believing existing guidance to be adequate.

The Interpretations Committee noted that only incremental costs directly attributable to issuing new equity instruments or acquiring previously issued equity instruments are considered to be related to an equity transaction under IAS 32, but that the terms 'incremental' and 'directly attributable' are used with similar but not identical meanings in many Standards and Interpretations, leading to diversity in practice. It therefore recommended that the IASB develop common definitions for both terms to be added to the Glossary as part of the annual improvements process.[33] However, the IASB did not propose any such amendments in the next exposure draft published in August 2009.

It may well be that, in an initial public offering ('IPO'), for example, an entity simultaneously lists its existing equity and additional newly issued equity. In that situation the total costs of the IPO should, in our view, be allocated between the newly issued shares and the existing shares on a rational basis (e.g. by reference to the ratio of the number of new shares to the number of total shares), with only the proportion relating to the issue of new shares being deducted from equity.

Transaction costs that relate to the issue of a compound financial instrument are allocated to the liability and equity components of the instrument in proportion to the allocation of proceeds (see Example 47.3 at 6.2 above). [IAS 32.38].

IAS 32 does not specifically address the treatment of transaction costs incurred to acquire a non-controlling interest in a subsidiary, or to dispose of such an interest without loss of control in the consolidated financial statements of the parent entity. IFRS 10 indicates that 'changes in a parent's ownership interest in a subsidiary that do not result in the parent losing control of the subsidiary are equity transactions'. [IFRS 10.23]. Accordingly, we believe that the costs of such transactions should be deducted from equity in accordance with the principles described above.

IAS 32 and IFRS 10 do not specify whether such costs should be allocated to the parent's equity or to the non-controlling interest, to the extent it is still reflected in the statement of financial position. In our view, this is a matter of choice based on the facts and circumstances surrounding the transaction, and any local legal requirements. On any subsequent disposal of the subsidiary involving loss of control, the transaction costs previously recognised in equity should not be reclassified from equity to profit or loss, since they represent transactions with owners in their capacity as owners rather than components of other comprehensive income. [IAS 1.106, 109].

The amount of transaction costs accounted for as a deduction from equity in the period is required to be disclosed separately under IAS 1 (see Chapter 3 at 3.3) and IFRS 7 (see Chapter 54 at 7.3).

8.2 Tax effects of equity transactions

As originally issued, IAS 32 required distributions to shareholders and transaction costs of equity instruments to be shown net of any tax benefit. *Annual Improvements to IFRSs 2009-2011 Cycle* issued in May 2012 amended IAS 32 so as to remove the reference to income tax benefit from IAS 32. This means that all tax effects of equity transactions are allocated in accordance with the general principles of IAS 12. *[IAS 32.35A]*.

Unfortunately, it is not entirely clear how IAS 12 requires the tax effects of certain equity transactions to be dealt with and different views can be taken whether tax benefits in respect of distributions are to be recognised in equity or profit or loss (see Chapter 33 at 10.3.5).

9 TREASURY SHARES

Treasury shares are shares issued by an entity that are held by the entity. *[IAS 32.33]*. In consolidated financial statements, this will include shares issued by any group entity that are held by that entity or by any other members of the consolidated group. They will also include shares held by an employee benefit trust that is consolidated or treated as an extension of the reporting entity. Treasury shares will generally not include shares in a group entity held by any associates or the entity's pension fund. However, IAS 1 requires disclosure of own shares held by subsidiaries or associates, *[IAS 1.79(a)(vi)]*, and IAS 19 – *Employee Benefits* – requires disclosure of own shares held by defined benefit plans. *[IAS 19.143]*. Holdings of treasury shares may arise in a number of ways. For example:

- The entity holds the shares as the result of a direct transaction, such as a market purchase, or a buy-back of shares from shareholders as a whole, or a particular group of shareholders.
- The entity is in the financial services sector with a market-making operation that buys and sells its own shares along with those of other listed entities in the normal course of business, or holds them in order to 'hedge' issued derivatives.
- In consolidated financial statements:
  - the shares were purchased by another entity which subsequently became a subsidiary of the reporting entity, either through acquisition or changes in financial reporting requirements; or
  - the shares have been purchased by an entity that is a consolidated SPE of the reporting entity.

The circumstances in which an entity is permitted to hold treasury shares are a matter for legislation in the jurisdiction concerned.

Treasury shares do not include own shares held by an entity on behalf of others, such as when a financial institution holds its own equity on behalf of a client. In such cases, there is an agency relationship and as a result those holdings are not included in the entity's statement of financial position, either as assets or as a deduction from equity. *[IAS 32.AG36]*.

If an entity reacquires its own equity instruments, IAS 32 requires those instruments to be deducted from equity. They are not recognised as financial assets, regardless of the reason for which they are reacquired. No gain or loss is recognised in profit or loss on the purchase, sale, issue or cancellation of an entity's own equity instruments. Accordingly, any consideration paid or received in connection with treasury shares must be recognised directly in equity. *[IAS 32.33, AG36].*

IAS 1 requires the amount of treasury shares to be disclosed separately either on the face of the statement of financial position or in the notes (see Chapter 3 at 3.1.6). In addition, IAS 32 requires an entity to make disclosure in accordance with IAS 24 – *Related Party Disclosures* – if the entity reacquires its own equity instruments from related parties (see Chapter 39 at 2.5). *[IAS 32.34].*

As in the case of the requirements for the treatment of the equity component of a compound financial instrument (see 6 above), IAS 32 does not prescribe precisely what components of equity should be adjusted as the result of a treasury share transaction. This may have been to ensure that there was no conflict between, on the one hand, the basic requirement of IAS 32 that there should be an adjustment to equity and, on the other hand, the legal requirements of various jurisdictions as to exactly how that adjustment should be allocated within equity.

9.1 Transactions in own shares not at fair value

The requirement of IAS 32 that no profits or losses should ever be recognised on transactions in own equity instruments differs from the approach taken in IFRS 2. If an employee share award is characterised as an equity instrument under IFRS 2 (a 'share-settled' award) and settled in cash (or other assets) at more than its fair value, the excess of the consideration over the fair value is recognised as an expense (see Chapter 34).

It is not clear whether or not the IASB specifically considered transactions in own equity other than at fair value in the context of IAS 32, particularly since the relevant provisions of IAS 32 essentially reproduce requirements previously contained in SIC-16 – *Share Capital – Reacquired Own Equity Instruments (Treasury Shares)* – which was implicitly addressing market purchases and sales at fair value. In other words, the provision can be seen merely as clarifying that, if an entity buys one of its own shares in the market for £10 which it later reissues in the market at £12 or £7, it has not made, respectively, a profit of £2 or a loss of £3.

This is slightly different to the situation where an entity purchases an equity instrument for more than its fair value – i.e. if the original purchase had been for £11 when the market price was £10. Such a transaction could occur, for example where the entity wishes to rid itself of a troublesome shareholder or group of shareholders. In this case, the entity might have to offer a premium specific to the holder over and above the 'true' fair value of the equity instruments concerned. However, in general, where an entity purchases an equity instrument for more than its fair value, this can be indicative that other consideration has been received by the entity. It should be noted that IFRS 2 is explicit that any excess of the consideration over the fair value of an equity instrument is recognised as an expense. *[IFRS 2.28(b)].*

A transaction in which the entity issues shares (or reissues treasury shares) for cash or other assets with a fair value lower than the fair value of the shares would *prima facie* fall within the scope of IFRS 2, requiring the shortfall to be accounted for under IFRS 2 (see Chapter 34 at 2.2.2.C).

9.2 IFRS 17 treasury share election

An entity applying IFRS 17 – *Insurance Contracts* – may elect not to deduct a treasury share from equity, when it either:

- operates an investment fund that provides investors with benefits determined by units in the fund and recognises the amounts to be paid to those investors as financial liabilities; or
- issues groups of insurance contracts with direct participation features while holding the underlying items.

Where an entity reacquires its own equity to hold in an investment fund or as an underlying item in the above arrangements, it may elect to continue to account for the treasury share as equity with the reacquired instrument being accounted as if it were a financial asset measured through profit or loss in accordance with IFRS 9. The election is irrevocable and made on an instrument by instrument basis. *[IAS 32.33A]*. IFRS 17 is applicable for periods beginning on or after 1 January 2023 but can be early adopted by entities who have already adopted IFRS 9 and IFRS 15 – *Revenue from Contracts with Customers*.

10 'HEDGING' OF INSTRUMENTS CLASSIFIED AS EQUITY

A consequence of the requirement, discussed in 4.5.2 to 4.5.6 above, to treat discretionary instruments with certain debt-like characteristics as equity is that the issuer will not be able to adopt hedge accounting in respect of any instrument taken out as a hedge of the instrument (e.g. a receive fixed, pay floating interest rate swap taken out to hedge a fixed rate discretionary dividend on non-redeemable shares). This is because neither IFRS 9 nor IAS 39 – *Financial Instruments: Recognition and Measurement* – if applicable, recognises a hedge of own equity as a valid hedging relationship (see Chapter 53).

Accordingly, if an issuer of an equity instrument bearing a fixed-rate discretionary coupon or dividend enters into an interest rate swap to hedge its cash outflows, the swap will be accounted for under the normal rules for derivatives not forming part of a hedging relationship – i.e. at fair value with all value changes recognised in profit or loss (see Chapters 48 and 49). Although, economically speaking, any such gains and losses are offset by equal gains and losses (due to interest rate movements) on the shares, the latter, like all movements in the fair value of own equity, are ignored for financial reporting purposes under IFRS.

11 DERIVATIVES OVER OWN EQUITY INSTRUMENTS

IAS 32 provides a number of detailed examples of the accounting treatment required, under the provisions of revised IAS 32 and IFRS 9, to be adopted by an entity for derivative contracts over its own equity instruments. Examples are given of each of the main possible permutations, namely:

- a forward purchase (see 11.1.1 below);
- a forward sale (see 11.1.2 below);
- 'back-to-back' forward contracts (see 11.1.3 below);
- a purchased call option (see 11.2.1 below);
- a written call option (see 11.2.2 below);
- a purchased put option (see 11.3.1 below); and
- a written put option (see 11.3.2 below).

All such contracts can be either:

(a) net cash-settled (i.e. the contract provides that the parties will compare the fair value of the shares to be delivered by the seller to the amount of cash payable by the buyer and make a cash payment between themselves for the difference);

(b) net share-settled (i.e. the contract provides that the parties will compare the fair value of the shares to be delivered by the seller to the amount of cash payable by the buyer and make a transfer between themselves of as many of the entity's shares as have a fair value equal to the difference);

(c) gross settled (i.e. the contract provides that the seller will deliver shares to the buyer in exchange for cash); or

(d) subject to various settlement options, whereby the manner of settlement is not predetermined, and instead one or other party can choose the manner of settlement (i.e. gross, net cash or net shares).

The examples consider the above settlement options in turn for the main possible permutations of derivatives over own equity instruments.

All derivative contracts over own equity, where settlement is not exclusively by an exchange of a fixed number of shares for a fixed amount of cash, do not meet the definition of equity instruments in IAS 32 and are, in general, treated as derivative financial assets or liabilities (see 5.2.8 above). IFRS 9, requires such contracts to be accounted for at fair value through profit or loss (see Chapter 49). Exemption to this rule applies to forward purchases and written put options with an option to settle gross (see 11.1.1 and 11.3.2 below).

11.1 Forward contracts

11.1.1 Forward purchase

In a forward purchase transaction, the entity and a counterparty agree that on a given future date the counterparty will sell a given number of the entity's shares to the entity. Such a contract is illustrated in Example 47.15 below. *[IAS 32.IE2-6]*.

Example 47.15: **Forward purchase of shares**

The reporting entity (A), which has a functional currency of Euro and a year end of 31 December, and another party (B) enter into a forward contract for the purchase of A's shares by A, for which the following are the major assumptions.

Contract date	1 February 2021
Maturity date	31 January 2022
Fixed forward price to be paid on 31 January 2022	€104
Present value of forward price on 1 February 2021	€100
Number of shares under contract	1,000
Market price per share on 1 February 2021	€100
Market price per share on 31 December 2021	€110
Market price per share on 31 January 2022	€106
Fair value of forward to A on 1 February 2021	€0
Fair value of forward to A on 31 December 2021	€6,300
Fair value of forward to A on 31 January 2022	€2,000

For simplicity, it is assumed that no dividends are paid on the underlying shares (i.e. the 'carry return' is zero) so that the present value of the forward price equals the spot price when the fair value of the forward contract is zero. The fair value of the forward has been computed as the difference between the market share price and the present value of the fixed forward price. At settlement date this is €2,000 representing 1,000 shares at €2, being the difference between the market price of €106 and the contract price of €104.

A Net cash settlement

If the contract is entered into as net cash-settled on 1 February 2021, settlement on 31 January 2022 will take the form of receipt or delivery by A of a cash payment for the difference between the fair value of 1,000 of A's own shares, at 31 January 2022, and €104,000 (i.e. 1,000 shares at the forward price of €104 per share). Since IAS 32 classifies such contracts as derivative financial assets or liabilities (see 11 and 5.2.7 above), which are carried at fair value through profit or loss under IFRS 9, A records the following accounting entries:

	€	€

1 February 2021

No entry is required because the fair value of the contract is zero at inception and no cash is paid or received

31 December 2021

Forward contract (statement of financial position)	6,300	
Gain on forward (profit or loss)		6,300

To record movement in fair value of forward from zero to €6,300

31 January 2022

	€	€
Loss on forward (profit or loss)	4,300	
Forward contract (statement of financial position)		4,300

To record movement in fair value of forward from €6,300 to €2,000

Cash	2,000	
Forward contract (statement of financial position)		2,000

To record settlement of forward by payment of €2,000 by B to A

B   Net share settlement

If the contract is entered into as net share-settled on 1 February 2021, settlement on 31 January 2022 will take the form of receipt or delivery by A of as many of A's shares as have a fair value equal to the difference between the fair value, at 31 January 2022, of 1,000 of A's own shares and €104,000 (i.e. 1,000 shares at the forward price of €104 per share). Because IAS 32 classifies such contracts as derivative financial assets or liabilities (see 11 and 5.2.7 above), which are carried at fair value through profit or loss under IFRS 9, A records the following accounting entries:

	€	€

1 February 2021

No entry is required because the fair value of the contract is zero at inception and no cash is paid or received

31 December 2021

Forward contract (statement of financial position)	6,300	
Gain on forward (profit or loss)		6,300

To record movement in fair value of forward from zero to €6,300

31 January 2022

Loss on forward (profit or loss)	4,300	
Forward contract (statement of financial position)		4,300

To record movement in fair value of forward from €6,300 to €2,000

Equity	2,000	
Forward contract (statement of financial position)		2,000

To record net settlement of forward by transfer of €2,000 worth of A's shares (€2000/106=18.9 shares) by B to A. This is shown as a deduction from equity in accordance with IAS 32's requirements for treasury shares (see 9 above).

C   Gross settlement

If the contract is entered into as gross-settled on 1 February 2021, settlement on 31 January 2022 will take the form of receipt of 1,000 own shares by A in exchange for a payment of €104,000 to B. IAS 32 classifies this derivative contract as an equity instrument giving rise to a financial liability for the present value of the purchase price amount payable in one year's time (see 5.3 above). On the assumption that A accounts for this liability under the effective interest method in IFRS 9, A records the following accounting entries:

	€	€

1 February 2021

Equity	100,000	
Liability for forward contract (statement of financial position)		100,000

To record net present value of liability on forward contract

	€	€
31 December 2021		
Interest expense	3,660	
Liability for forward contract (statement of financial position)		3,660

To accrue interest, under the effective interest rate method, on the liability to settle forward contract

	€	€
31 January 2022		
Interest expense	340	
Liability for forward contract (statement of financial position)		340

To accrue further interest, under the effective interest rate method, on the liability to settle forward contract

	€	€
Liability for forward contract (statement of financial position)	104,000	
Cash		104,000

To record settlement of the liability in cash

D Settlement options

If there are settlement options (such as net in cash, net in shares or by an exchange of a fixed amount of cash for a fixed number of shares), the forward contract is a financial asset or a financial liability – see 5.2.7 above. The contract does not meet the definition of an equity instrument, because it can be settled otherwise than by delivery of a fixed amount of cash for a fixed number of equity instruments. If one of the settlement alternatives is gross settlement by an exchange of cash for shares, A recognises a liability for the obligation to deliver cash. Otherwise, A accounts for the forward contract as a derivative.

The implementation guidance to IAS 32 states that A should recognise a liability 'if one of the settlement alternatives is to exchange cash for shares'. As drafted, this applies whether the choice of settlement rests with A or B. This seems curious since, where A would always have the choice of net settlement, there would be no obligation for A to settle gross. We assume that the example is written on the presumption that the choice of settlement would normally rest with the counterparty rather than the entity or circumstances could arise in which the entity could not prevent gross settlement occurring, e.g. if the shares ceased to be listed before settlement of the contract. Paragraph 23 in the main body of the standard is clear that an equity contract gives rise to a liability for the purchase price of the shares only where there is an obligation for the entity to purchase its own equity. Accordingly, in our view, where the entity could in all circumstances chose to settle net, it is acceptable not to record a gross liability, and to account for the contract as a derivative financial asset or derivative financial liability. If the only situation in which the entity could be forced to settle gross rather than net is where the obligation is not specified in the contract but in statute or regulation, it will also be necessary to assess whether this obligation is required to be considered (see 4.2 and 4.6 above).

11.1.2 Forward sale

In a forward sale transaction, the entity and a counterparty agree that on a given future date the entity will sell (or issue) a given number of the entity's shares to the counterparty. Such a contract is illustrated in Example 47.16 below. *[IAS 32.IE7-11]*.

Example 47.16: Forward sale of shares

The reporting entity (A), which has a functional currency of Euro and a year end of 31 December, and another party (B) enter into a forward contract for the purchase of A's shares by B, for which the following are the major assumptions.

Contract date	1 February 2021
Maturity date	31 January 2022
Fixed forward price to be paid on 31 January 2022	€104
Present value of forward price on 1 February 2021	€100
Number of shares under contract	1,000
Market price per share on 1 February 2021	€100
Market price per share on 31 December 2021	€110
Market price per share on 31 January 2022	€106
Fair value of forward to A on 1 February 2021	€0
Fair value of forward to A on 31 December 2021	€(6,300)
Fair value of forward to A on 31 January 2022	€(2,000)

For simplicity, it is assumed that no dividends are paid on the underlying shares (i.e. the 'carry return' is zero) so that the present value of the forward price equals the spot price when the fair value of the forward contract is zero. The fair value of the forward has been computed as the difference between the market share price and the present value of the fixed forward price. At settlement date this is negative €2,000 representing 1,000 shares at €2, being the difference between the market price of €106 and the contract price of €104.

A   Net cash settlement

If the contract is entered into as net cash-settled on 1 February 2021, settlement on 31 January 2022 will take the form of receipt or delivery by A of a cash payment for the difference between the fair value of 1,000 of A's own shares, at 31 January 2022, and €104,000 (i.e. 1,000 shares at the forward price of €104 per share). Since IAS 32 classifies such contracts as derivative financial assets or liabilities (see 11 and 5.2.7 above), which are carried at fair value through profit or loss under IFRS 9, A records the following accounting entries:

	€	€
1 February 2021		
No entry is required because the fair value of the contract is zero at inception and no cash is paid or received.		
31 December 2021		
Loss on forward (profit or loss)	6,300	
Forward contract (statement of financial position)		6,300
To record movement in fair value of forward from zero to €(6,300)		
31 January 2022		
Forward contract (statement of financial position)	4,300	
Gain on forward (profit or loss)		4,300
To record movement in fair value of forward from €(6,300) to €(2,000)		
Forward contract (statement of financial position)	2,000	
Cash		2,000
To record net settlement of forward by payment of €2,000 cash by A to B		

B Net share settlement

If the contract is entered into as net share-settled on 1 February 2021, settlement on 31 January 2022 will take the form of receipt or delivery by A of a payment of as many of A's shares as have a fair value equal to the difference between the fair value, at 31 January 2022, of 1,000 of A's own shares and €104,000 (i.e. 1,000 shares at the forward price of €104 per share). As IAS 32 classifies such contracts as derivative financial assets or liabilities (see 11 and 5.2.7 above), which are carried at fair value through profit or loss under IFRS 9, A records the following accounting entries:

	€	€
1 February 2021		
No entry is required because the fair value of the contract is zero at inception		
31 December 2021		
Loss on forward (profit or loss)	6,300	
Forward contract (statement of financial position)		6,300
To record movement in fair value of forward from zero to €(6,300)		
31 January 2022		
Forward contract (statement of financial position)	4,300	
Gain on forward (profit or loss)		4,300
To record movement in fair value of forward from €(6,300) to €(2,000)		
Forward contract (statement of financial position)	2,000	
Equity		2,000
To record net settlement of forward by delivery of €2,000 worth of A's shares to B (€2000/106=18.9 shares)		

C Gross settlement

If the contract is entered into as gross-settled on 1 February 2021, settlement on 31 January 2022 will take the form of delivery of 1,000 own shares by A to B in exchange for a payment of €104,000. IAS 32 classifies this derivative contract as an equity instrument (see 5.4 above) and therefore no entries are recorded other than on settlement on the contract. While a forward sale is economically a 'mirror' of a forward purchase and both are classified as equity instruments, the accounting impact is different. A forward sale does not result in any accounting entries until the shares are finally issued/delivered, while a forward purchase establishes an obligation to pay the settlement amount and therefore meets the definition of a financial liability which needs to be recorded upon entering the contract (see part C of Example 47.15 above).

	€	€
31 January 2022		
Cash	104,000	
Equity		104,000
To record settlement of forward contract through delivery of 1,000 shares for the payment of €104,000		

D Settlement options

If there are settlement options (such as net in cash, net in shares or by an exchange of cash and shares), the forward contract is a financial asset or a financial liability – see 5.2.8 above. A accounts for the forward contract as a derivative (as in A and B above), with the accounting entry made on settlement determined by the manner of settlement (i.e. equity or cash).

11.1.3 'Back-to-back' forward contracts

The accounting treatment in 11.1.1 and 11.1.2 above produces rather strange results when applied to 'back-to-back' forward contracts, such as might be entered into by a financial institution with two different clients. Example 47.17 below illustrates the point.

Example 47.17: 'Back-to-back' forward contracts

Suppose that a bank entered into the forward purchase contract in Example 47.15 above with a client and laid off its risk by entering into the reciprocal forward sale contract in Example 47.16 above with a second client. If both contracts are required to be settled gross, the overall effect of the accounting entries required to be made by the bank (assuming that the bank was the reporting entity in Examples 47.15 and 47.16 can be summarised as set out below. Note that these are not the actual entries that would be made, but the arithmetical sum of all the entries:

	€	€
Profit or loss (interest expense on liability for purchase contract)	4,000	
Equity (€104,000 on sale less €100,000 on purchase)		4,000

If the purchase contract is required to be settled gross, but the sale contract net in cash, the required accounting entries (again, not the actual entries, but the arithmetical sum of all the entries) can be summarised as:

	€	€
Profit or loss (loss on sale contract €2,000 plus interest on liability for purchase contract €4,000)	6,000	
Equity (purchase contract)	100,000	
Cash (€104,000 on purchase, €2,000 on sale)		106,000

If the purchase contract is required to be settled net in cash, but the sale contract gross, the required accounting entries (again, not the actual entries, but the arithmetical sum of all the entries) can be summarised as:

	€	€
Cash (€104,000 in on sale, €2,000 in on purchase)	106,000	
Profit or loss (gain on purchase contract)		2,000
Equity (sale contract)		104,000

If both contracts are net settled, no net gain or loss arises.

Some might argue that this exposes a flaw in the requirements of IAS 32. Self-evidently, these contracts are matched and should therefore, if both run to term, give rise to no economic profit or loss, irrespective of how they are settled. However, IAS 32 requires three different results to be shown depending on whether both contracts are settled gross, or one gross and the other net. This is less understandable in the case where both contracts are settled gross. However, in cases where one contract is settled net and that contract gives rise to an initial receipt or payment of cash, then some difference is bound to occur due to interest effects.

11.2 Call options

11.2.1 Purchased call option

In a purchased call option, the entity pays a counterparty for the right, but not the obligation, to purchase a given number of its own equity instruments from the counterparty for a fixed price at a future date. The accounting for such a contract is illustrated in Example 47.18 below. *[IAS 32.IE12-16]*.

Example 47.18: Purchased call option on own shares

The reporting entity (A), which has a functional currency of Euro and a year end of 31 December, purchases a call option over its own shares from another party (B), for which the following are the major assumptions.

Contract date	1 February 2021
Exercise date (European terms – i.e. can be exercised only on maturity)	31 January 2022
Fixed exercise price to be paid on 31 January 2022	€102
Number of shares under contract	1,000
Market price per share on 1 February 2021	€100
Market price per share on 31 December 2021	€104
Market price per share on 31 January 2022	€104
Fair value of option to A on 1 February 2021	€5,000
Fair value of option to A on 31 December 2021	€3,000
Fair value of option to A on 31 January 2022	€2,000

The fair value of the option would be computed using an option pricing model and would be a function of a number of factors, principally the market value of the shares, the exercise price, and the time value of money.

A Net cash settlement

If the contract is entered into as net cash-settled on 1 February 2021, then A can, on the exercise date 31 January 2022, require B to make a cash payment to A for the excess, if any, of the fair value of 1,000 of A's own shares, as of 31 January 2022, over €102,000 (i.e. 1,000 shares at the option price of €102 per share). Since IAS 32 classifies such contracts as derivative financial assets (see 11 and 5.2.7 above), which are carried at fair value through profit or loss under IFRS 9, A records the following accounting entries:

1 February 2021	€	€
Call option asset	5,000	
Cash		5,000

Payment of option premium (equal to fair value of option) to B

31 December 2021		
Loss on option (profit or loss)	2,000	
Call option asset		2,000

To record movement in fair value of option from €5,000 to €3,000

31 January 2022	€	€
Loss on option (profit or loss)	1,000	
Call option asset		1,000

To record movement in fair value of option from €3,000 to €2,000

Cash	2,000	
Call option asset		2,000

To record net settlement of option by payment of €2,000 cash by B to A

B Net share settlement

If the contract is entered into as net share-settled on 1 February 2021, then A can, on the exercise date 31 January 2022, require B to deliver to A as many of A's own shares as have a fair value equal to any excess of 1,000 of A's own shares fair value, as of 31 January 2022 over €102,000 (i.e. 1,000 shares at the option price of €102 per share). Since IAS 32 classifies such contracts as derivative financial assets (see 11 and 5.2.7 above), which are carried at fair value through profit or loss under IFRS 9, A records the following accounting entries.

1 February 2021	€	€
Call option asset	5,000	
Cash		5,000

Payment of option premium (equal to fair value of option) to B

31 December 2021		
Loss on option (profit or loss)	2,000	
Call option asset		2,000

To record movement in fair value of option from €5,000 to €3,000

31 January 2022		
Loss on option (profit or loss)	1,000	
Call option asset		1,000

To record movement in fair value of option €3,000 to €2,000

Equity	2,000	
Call option asset		2,000

To record net settlement of option by transfer of €2,000 worth of A's shares by B to A. This is shown as a deduction from equity in accordance with IAS 32's requirements for treasury shares (see 9 above).

C Gross settlement

If the contract is entered into as gross-settled, on 1 February 2021, then A can, on the exercise date 31 January 2022, require B to deliver 1,000 of A's shares in return for a payment by A of €102,000. IAS 32 classifies such a derivative contract as an equity instrument (see 5.4 above); therefore no entries are recorded, other than to record the cash flows arising under the contract:

1 February 2021	€	€
Equity	5,000	
Cash		5,000

Payment of option premium (equal to fair value of option) to B

31 January 2022	€	€
Equity	102,000	
Cash		102,000

To record gross settlement of option by payment of €102,000 cash to B in exchange for 1,000 own shares. This is shown as a deduction from equity in accordance with IAS 32's requirements for treasury shares (see 9 above).

If the option had lapsed unexercised, because the market price of A's shares had fallen below €102 as at 31 January 2022, the €5,000 premium would remain in equity, even though it is, from an economic perspective, clearly a loss rather than an amount paid to repurchase A's own shares. This is because IFRS regards any holder of an instrument classified as equity under IAS 32 as an 'owner'.

In contrast to the treatment of a gross-settled forward purchase (see 11.1.1 above) and a gross-settled written put option (see 11.3.2 below), which also require a gross outflow of cash on settlement, there is no requirement to record a liability at the outset of the contract on which interest is accrued during the period of the contract. This is because:

- in a gross-settled forward purchase or written put option, the entity can be required to make a payment of cash; but
- in a purchased call option, there is no liability, since the entity has no obligation to exercise its right to call for the shares even if the option is 'in the money' and it is in the entity's interest to do so.

D   Settlement options

If there are different settlement options (such as net in cash, net in shares or by an exchange of cash and shares), the option is a financial asset. A accounts for the forward contract as a derivative (as in A and B above), with the accounting entry made on settlement determined by the manner of settlement (i.e. equity or cash).

11.2.2   Written call option

In a written call option, the entity receives a payment from a counterparty for granting to the counterparty the right, but not the obligation, to purchase a given number of the entity's own equity instruments from the entity for a fixed price at a future date. The accounting for such a contract is illustrated in Example 47.19 below. *[IAS 32.IE17-21].*

Example 47.19:   Written call option on own shares

The reporting entity (A), which has a functional currency of Euro and a year end of 31 December, writes a call option over its own shares with another party (B), for which the following are the major assumptions.

Contract date	1 February 20201
Exercise date (European terms – i.e. can be exercised only on maturity)	31 January 2022
Fixed exercise price to be paid on 31 January 2022	€102
Number of shares under contract	1,000
Market price per share on 1 February 2021	€100
Market price per share on 31 December 2021	€104
Market price per share on 31 January 2022	€104
Fair value of option to A on 1 February 2021	€(5,000)
Fair value of option to A on 31 December 2021	€(3,000)
Fair value of option to A on 31 January 2022	€(2,000)

The fair value of the option would be computed using an option pricing model and would be a function of a number of factors, principally the market value of the shares, the exercise price, and the time value of money.

A   Net cash settlement

If the contract is entered into as net cash-settled on 1 February 2021, then B can, on the exercise date 31 January 2022, require A to make a cash payment to B for the excess, if any, of the fair value of 1,000 of A's own shares, as of 31 January 2022, over €102,000 (i.e. 1,000 shares at the option price of €102 per share). Since IAS 32 classifies such contracts as derivative financial liabilities (see 11 and 5.2.7 above), which are carried at fair value through profit or loss under IFRS 9, A records the following accounting entries:

	€	€
1 February 2021		
Cash	5,000	
Call option liability		5,000

Receipt of option premium (equal to fair value of option) from B

	€	€
31 December 2021		
Call option liability	2,000	
Gain on option (profit or loss)		2,000

To record movement in fair value of option from €(5,000) to €(3,000)

	€	€
31 January 2022		
Call option liability	1,000	
Gain on option (profit or loss)		1,000

To record movement in fair value of option from €(3,000) to €(2,000)

	€	€
Call option liability	2,000	
Cash		2,000

To record net settlement of option by payment of €2,000 cash to B

B Net share settlement

If the contract is entered into as net share-settled on 1 February 2021, then B can, on the exercise date 31 January 2022, require A to deliver to B as many of A's own shares as have a fair value equal to any excess of 1,000 of A's own shares, as of 31 January 2022, over €102,000 (i.e. 1000 shares at the option price of €102 per share). Since IAS 32 classifies such contracts as derivative financial liabilities (see 11 and 5.2.7 above), which are carried at fair value through profit or loss under IFRS 9, A records the following accounting entries.

	€	€
1 February 2021		
Cash	5,000	
Call option liability		5,000

Receipt of option premium (equal to fair value of option) from B

	€	€
31 December 2021		
Call option liability	2,000	
Gain on option (profit or loss)		2,000

To record movement in fair value of option from €(5,000) to €(3,000)

	€	€
31 January 2022		
Call option liability	1,000	
Gain on option (profit or loss)		1,000

To record movement in fair value of option from €(3,000) to €(2,000)

	€	€
Call option liability	2,000	
Equity		2,000

To record net settlement of option by issue of €2,000 worth of A's shares to B

C Gross settlement

If the contract is entered into as gross-settled, on 1 February 2021, then B can, on the exercise date 31 January 2022, require A to deliver 1,000 of A's shares in return for a payment by B of €102,000. IAS 32 classifies this derivative contract as an equity instrument (see 5.4 above); therefore no entries are recorded, other than to record the cash flows arising under the contract:

	€	€
1 February 2021		
Cash	5,000	
Equity		5,000
Receipt of option premium (equal to fair value of option) to B		
31 January 2022		
Cash	102,000	
Equity		102,000
To record gross settlement of option by receipt of €102,000 cash from B in exchange for 1,000 of A's own shares.		

If the option had lapsed unexercised, because the market price of A's shares had fallen below €102 as at 31 January 2022, the €5,000 premium would remain in equity, even though it is, from an economic perspective, clearly a gain rather than an amount received from an owner. This is because IFRS regards any holder of an instrument classified as equity under IAS 32 as an 'owner'.

D Settlement options

If there are different settlement options (such as net in cash, net in shares or by an exchange of cash and shares), the option is a financial liability. A accounts for the forward contract as a derivative (as in A and B above), with the accounting entry made on settlement determined by the manner of settlement (i.e. equity or cash).

11.3 Put options

11.3.1 Purchased put option

In a purchased put option, the entity makes a payment to a counterparty for the right, but not the obligation, to require the counterparty to purchase a given number of the entity's own equity instruments from the entity for a fixed price at a future date. The accounting for such a contract is illustrated in Example 47.20 below. *[IAS 32.IE22-26]*.

Example 47.20: Purchased put option on own shares

The reporting entity (A), which has a functional currency of Euro and a year end of 31 December, purchases a put option over its own shares from another party (B), for which the following are the major assumptions.

Contract date	1 February 2021
Exercise date (European terms – i.e. can be exercised only on maturity)	31 January 2022
Fixed exercise price to be paid on 31 January 2022	€98
Number of shares under contract	1,000
Market price per share on 1 February 2021	€100
Market price per share on 31 December 2021	€95
Market price per share on 31 January 2022	€95
Fair value of option to A on 1 February 2021	€5,000
Fair value of option to A on 31 December 2021	€4,000
Fair value of option to A on 31 January 2022	€3,000

The fair value of the option would be computed using an option pricing model and would be a function of number of factors, principally the market value of the shares, the exercise price, and the time value of money.

A Net cash settlement

If the contract is entered into as net cash-settled on 1 February 2021, then A can, on the exercise date 31 January 2022, require B to make a cash payment to A for the excess, if any, of €98,000 (i.e. 1,000 shares at the option price of €98 per share) over the fair value of 1,000 of A's own shares, as of 31 January 2022. Because IAS 32 classifies such contracts as derivative financial assets or financial liabilities (see 11 and 5.2.7 above), which are carried at fair value through profit or loss under IFRS 9, A records the following accounting entries.

	€	€
1 February 2021		
Put option asset	5,000	
Cash		5,000
Payment of option premium (equal to fair value of option) to B		
31 December 2021		
Loss on option (profit or loss)	1,000	
Put option asset		1,000
To record movement in fair value of option from €5,000 to €4,000		
31 January 2022		
Loss on option (profit or loss)	1,000	
Put option asset		1,000
To record movement in fair value of option from €4,000 to €3,000		
Cash	3,000	
Put option asset		3,000
To record net settlement of option by receipt of €3,000 cash from B		

B Net share settlement

If the contract is entered into as net share-settled on 1 February 2021, then A can, on the exercise date 31 January 2022, require B to deliver to A as many of A's own shares as have a fair value equal to any excess of €98,000 (i.e. 1,000 shares at the option price of €98 per share) over the fair value of 1,000 of A's own shares, as of 31 January 2022. Because IAS 32 classifies such contracts as derivative financial assets (see 11 and 5.2.7 above), which are carried at fair value through profit or loss under IFRS 9, A records the following accounting entries.

	€	€
1 February 2021		
Put option asset	5,000	
Cash		5,000
Payment of option premium (equal to fair value of option) to B		
31 December 2021		
Loss on option (profit or loss)	1,000	
Put option asset		1,000
To record movement in fair value of option from €5,000 to €4,000		

	€	€
31 January 2022		
Loss on option (profit or loss)	1,000	
Put option asset		1,000

To record movement in fair value of option from €4,000 to €3,000

	€	€
Equity	3,000	
Put option asset		3,000

To record net settlement of option by receipt of €3,000 worth of A's shares from B. This is shown as a deduction from equity in accordance with IAS 32's requirements for treasury shares (see 9 above).

C Gross settlement

If the contract is entered into as gross-settled, on 1 February 2021, then A can, on the exercise date 31 January 2022, require B to take delivery 1,000 of A's shares in return for a payment by B of €98,000. IAS 32 classifies this derivative contract as an equity instrument (see 5.4 above); therefore no entries are recorded, other than to record the cash flows arising under the contract:

	€	€
1 February 2021		
Equity	5,000	
Cash		5,000

Payment of option premium (equal to fair value of option) to B

	€	€
31 January 2022		
Cash	98,000	
Equity		98,000

To record gross settlement of option by delivery of 1,000 own shares to B in exchange for €98,000.

If the option had lapsed unexercised, because the market price of A's shares had risen above €98 as at 31 January 2022, the €5,000 premium would remain in equity, even though it is, from an economic perspective, clearly a loss rather than an amount paid to repurchase A's own shares. This is because IFRS regards any holder of an instrument classified as equity under IAS 32 as an 'owner'.

D Settlement options

If there are different settlement options (such as net in cash, net in shares or by an exchange of cash and shares), the option is a financial asset. A accounts for the forward contract as a derivative (as in A and B above), with the accounting entry made on settlement determined by the manner of settlement (i.e. equity or cash).

11.3.2 Written put option

In a written put option, the entity receives a payment from a counterparty for granting to the counterparty the right, but not the obligation, to sell a given number of the entity's own equity instruments to the entity for a fixed price at a future date. The accounting for such a contract is illustrated in Example 47.21 below. *[IAS 32.IE27-31]*.

Example 47.21: Written put option on own shares

The reporting entity (A), which has a functional currency of Euros and a year end of 31 December, writes a put option over its own shares with another party (B), for which the following are the major assumptions.

Contract date	1 February 2021
Exercise date (European terms – i.e. can be exercised only on maturity)	31 January 2022
Fixed exercise price to be paid on 31 January 2022	€98
Number of shares under contract	1,000
Market price per share on 1 February 2021	€100
Market price per share on 31 December 2021	€95
Market price per share on 31 January 2022	€95
Fair value of option to A on 1 February 2021	€(5,000)
Fair value of option to A on 31 December 2021	€(4,000)
Fair value of option to A on 31 January 2022	€(3,000)

The fair value of the option would be computed using an option pricing model and would be a function of a number of factors, principally the market value of the shares, the exercise price, and the time value of money.

A Net cash settlement

If the contract is entered into as net cash-settled on 1 February 2021, then B can, on the exercise date 31 January 2022, require A to make a cash payment to B for the excess, if any, of €98,000 (i.e. 1,000 shares at the option price of €98 per share) over the fair value of 1,000 of A's own shares, as of 31 January 2022. Because IAS 32 classifies such contracts as derivative financial liabilities (see 11 and 5.2.7 above), which are carried at fair value through profit or loss under IFRS 9, A records the following accounting entries.

	€	€
1 February 2021		
Cash	5,000	
Put option liability		5,000

Receipt of option premium (equal to fair value of option) from B

	€	€
31 December 2021		
Put option liability	1,000	
Gain on option (profit or loss)		1,000

To record movement in fair value of option from €(5,000) to €(4,000)

	€	€
31 January 2022		
Put option liability	1,000	
Gain on option (profit or loss)		1,000

To record movement in fair value of option from €(4,000) to €(3,000)

	€	€
Put option liability	3,000	
Cash		3,000

To record net settlement of option by payment of €3,000 cash to B

B Net share settlement

If the contract is entered into as net share-settled on 1 February 2021, then B can, on the exercise date 31 January 2022, require A to deliver to B as many of A's own shares as have a fair value equal to any excess of €98,000 (i.e. 1,000 shares at the option price of €98 per share) over the fair value of 1,000 of A's own shares, as of 31 January 2022. Because IAS 32 classifies such contracts as derivative financial assets (see 11 and 5.2.7 above), which are carried at fair value through profit or loss under IFRS 9, A records the following accounting entries.

	€	€
1 February 2021		
Cash	5,000	
Put option liability		5,000

Receipt of option premium (equal to fair value of option) from B

	€	€
31 December 2021		
Put option liability	1,000	
Gain on option (profit or loss)		1,000

To record movement in fair value of option from €(5,000) to €(4,000)

	€	€
31 January 2022		
Put option liability	1,000	
Gain on option (profit or loss)		1,000

To record movement in fair value of option from €(4,000) to €(3,000)

	€	€
Put option liability	3,000	
Equity		3,000

To record net settlement of option by issue of €3,000 worth of own shares to B

C Gross settlement

If the contract is entered into as gross-settled on 1 February 2021, then B can, on the exercise date 31 January 2022, require A to take delivery of 1,000 of A's own shares in return for a payment by A of €98,000. IAS 32 classifies this derivative contract as an equity instrument giving rise to a financial liability for the present value of the purchase price amount payable in one year's time (see 5.3 above). On the assumption that A accounts for this liability under the effective interest method in IFRS 9, A records the following accounting entries.

	€	€
1 February 2021		
Cash	5,000	
Equity		5,000

Receipt of option premium (equal to fair value of option) from B

	€	€
Equity	95,000	
Liability (net present value of €98,000 potentially payable under option)		95,000

Recording of potential liability to settle option

31 December 2021

Interest (profit or loss)	2,750	
Liability		2,750

To accrue interest, under the effective interest rate method, on the liability

31 January 2022

Interest expense (profit or loss)	250	
Liability		250

To accrue further interest, under the effective interest rate method, on the liability

	€	€
Liability	98,000	
Cash		98,000

To record gross settlement of option by delivery of by B of 1,000 shares in A in exchange for €98,000

If the option had lapsed unexercised, because the market price of A's shares had risen above €98 as at 31 January 2022, the premium of €5,000 would remain in equity and the liability of €98,000 would be reclassified to equity. The economic consequence is clearly that A has made a profit of €5,000 – the premium that it received from B, for which it has ultimately had to give nothing in return. However the overall effect of the treatment that would be required by IAS 32 can be summarised as follows:

	€	€
Cash	5,000	
Profit or loss (interest on potential liability to pay cash)	3,000	
Equity (€98,000 carrying amount of liability transferred at date of lapse less €90,000 debited on 1 February 2020)		8,000

To record a loss on a transaction that makes a profit might seem a distortion of economic reality; but in this case is a consequence of applying the *Conceptual Framework*.

D   Settlement options

If there are different settlement options (such as net in cash, net in shares or by an exchange of cash and shares), the option is a financial liability. A accounts for the forward contract as a derivative (as in A and B above), with the accounting entry made on settlement determined by the manner of settlement (i.e. equity or cash). If one of the settlement alternatives is to exchange cash for shares, A recognises a liability for the obligation to deliver cash (as in C above). Otherwise, Entity A accounts for the put option as a derivative liability.

The implementation guidance to IAS 32 states that A should recognise a liability 'if one of the settlement alternatives is to exchange cash for shares'. *[IAS 32.IE31]*. As drafted, this applies whether the choice of settlement rests with A or B. This seems curious since, where A has the choice of settlement, there would be no obligation for A to settle gross. We assume that the example is written on the presumption that the choice of settlement of an option would normally rest with the buyer rather than the writer of the option. Paragraph 23 in the main body of the standard is clear that an equity contract gives rise to a liability for the purchase price of the shares only where there is an obligation for the entity to purchase its own equity (see 5.3 above). Accordingly, in our view, where the choice of settlement rests only with the entity, it is acceptable not to record a gross liability, and to account for the contract as a derivative financial liability.

12 POSSIBLE FUTURE DEVELOPMENTS

A number of commentators have questioned whether the current criteria used to distinguish equity from financial liabilities, both under IFRS and US GAAP, are entirely satisfactory. In an agenda paper for the IASB board meeting in January 2007, the IASB staff highlighted the following broad categories of implementation issue arising from IAS 32:

- *Issues arising from specific rules in the standard*

    The specific provisions in IAS 32 were written with particular types of capital instrument in mind. Where these rules are applied to instruments that differ from those for which they were written, the result may be the classification of an item as debt or equity that does not faithfully represent the underlying instrument.

- *Counter-intuitive results*

    The classification of an instrument under IAS 32 can produce results that conflict with the generally-held perception of how the instrument should be faithfully represented. An example is the treatment of certain puttable instruments, which was the subject of the amendment to IAS 32 in February 2008 discussed at 4.6.2 and 4.6.3 above.

- *Conflicts with the conceptual framework*

    Some provisions of IAS 32 conflict with the IASB's own conceptual framework. For example, IAS 32 requires some contracts over the entity's own equity, which are to be executed at a future date, to be accounted for as if they had been executed on inception of the contract. This contrasts with the required treatment under IFRS of nearly all other executory contracts, such as purchase orders and contracts of employment, for which no liability is recorded, except to the extent that the contract is onerous.

The IASB staff noted that the first of these issues could potentially be resolved by a more principles-based revision to the drafting of IAS 32, whilst the other two issues raised more fundamental questions about the whole approach of the standard.[34]

The Memorandum of Understanding published by the IASB and the FASB in February 2006 set as one of its goals for 2008 'to have issued one or more due process documents relating to a proposed standard' on the distinction between liabilities and equity. The IASB fulfilled that commitment by publishing a discussion paper in February 2008. Following receipt of comments on the discussion paper, the IASB and the FASB ('the Boards') began further deliberations and proposed an exposure draft. In May 2010 this was distributed to a small group of external reviewers, who raised significant challenges. The reviewers felt that the proposed approach lacked clear principles and could produce inconsistent results when applied to broadly similar instruments. In particular, many reviewers felt that the 'specified for specified' criterion was unclear and just as prone to interpretative difficulties as the 'fixed for fixed' criterion in IAS 32.

At a joint meeting in October 2010, the Boards suspended the project, acknowledging that they did not have the time necessary to deliberate the key issues. In October 2014 the IASB decided to resume the *Financial Instruments with Characteristics of Equity Research Project (FICE)*, to investigate potential improvements to:

- the classification of liabilities and equity in IAS 32, including investigating potential amendments to the definitions of liabilities and equity in the Conceptual Framework; and
- the presentation and disclosure requirements for financial instruments with characteristics of equity, irrespective of whether they are classified as liabilities or equity.

A key issue is that certain financial instruments, which have a wide range of differing characteristics, often cannot be easily classified as debt or equity as they often have features of both. The IASB looked at addressing this issue by modifying the approach in IAS 32 by:

- clarifying what set of features is most useful in distinguishing between financial liabilities and equity;
- using presentation to reflect similarities and differences not apparent from the liability and equity classification; and
- using disclosures to bring out other similarities and differences.

A Discussion Paper (the FICE DP) was published in June 2018. In it, the IASB put forward a preferred approach which would classify a financial instrument as a financial liability if it contained:

- an unavoidable contractual obligation to transfer cash or another financial asset at a specified time other than at liquidation; and/or
- an unavoidable contractual obligation for an amount independent of the entity's available economic resources.

A simple bond would satisfy both criteria. An example of an instrument that would satisfy just the first criterion would be a share that is redeemable at fair value, while an example that would satisfy just the second would be a bond with an obligation to deliver a variable number of the entity's shares, to a value equal to a fixed amount of cash. Cumulative preference shares or instruments with 'dividend blocker' arrangements would be classified as financial liabilities rather than equity as now (see 4.5.3 above).

An instrument meeting neither of these criteria would be classified as equity.

Because the FICE DP proposed to classify more instruments as liabilities, it suggested that the revaluation of such liabilities should be recorded in other comprehensive income if they did not contain an unavoidable contractual obligation for an amount independent of the entity's available economic resources. This would include, for instance, shares puttable at fair value.

The FICE DP proposed that total comprehensive income should be attributed between the different classes of equity.

In addition, the FICE DP proposed additional disclosures around:
- the priority of claims on liquidation;
- potential dilution of ordinary shares; and
- terms and conditions.

After considering comments on the DP, the IASB tentatively decided not to go ahead with the ideas proposed in the DP but to concentrate on addressing certain known practice issues by clarifying some of the underlying principles in IAS 32. In particular they identified the following areas:

- the classification of financial instruments that will or may be settled in the issuer's own equity instruments, e.g. the application of the fixed-for-fixed condition to particular derivatives on own equity and the classification of mandatorily convertible financial instruments (see 5.1, 5.2 and 6.6.3 above);
- accounting for obligations to redeem own equity instruments, e.g. accounting for put options over non-controlling interests (see 5.3.2.A above and Chapter 9 at 8.5);
- accounting for financial instruments that contain contingent settlement provisions, e.g. financial instruments with a non-viability clause (see 6.6.3.B above);
- the effect of laws and regulations on the classification of financial instruments;
- the reclassification between financial liability and equity instruments, e.g. when circumstance change, or contractual terms are modified (see 4.9 above); and
- classification of particular financial instruments that contain obligations that arise only on liquidation of the entity, e.g. perpetual financial instruments (see 4.7 above).

As at June 2020, the Board had discussed the first of the six above-mentioned issues, the classification of financial instruments that will or may be settled in the issuer's own equity instruments. The Board tentatively decided that for a derivative on own equity to meet the fixed for fixed condition in IAS 32, the number of functional currency units to be exchanged for each underlying equity instrument should be fixed or vary only due to an adjustment which:

- preserves the relative economic interest of future shareholders to an equal or lesser extent than those of existing shareholders ('preservation adjustments'); or
- is pre-determined and varies only with the passage of time and fixes the number of functional currency units per underlying equity instrument in the terms of present value ('passage of time adjustments').[35]

The Board also tentatively decided to classify as equity a contract that can be settled by exchanging a fixed number of non-derivative own equity instruments with a fixed number of another type of non-derivative equity instrument. The IASB also intends to continue with the additional disclosures proposed in the DP and discussed above.

References

1 IAS 32, Application Guidance, para. after main heading.
2 IAS 32, Illustrative Examples, para. after main heading.
3 *IFRIC Update*, September 2015.
4 *IFRIC Update*, March 2016.
5 *IFRIC Update*, January 2010.
6 *IFRIC Update*, November 2015.

7 *IFRIC Update*, May 2016.
8 SIC-5, *Classification of Financial Instruments – Contingent Settlement Provisions*, SIC, May 1998 (superseded December 2003).
9 SIC-5, para. 9.
10 *Agenda item 12B*, Information for Observers, IASB meeting, January 2007, para. 39.
11 IAS 32, (pre-2003 version – issued March 1995 and revised December 1998 and October 2000), para. 22.
12 *IFRIC Update*, March 2006.
13 *IFRIC Update*, March 2006.
14 *IFRIC Update*, March 2006.
15 *IFRIC Update*, March 2006.
16 *Amendments to IAS 32 Financial Instruments: Presentation and IAS 1 Presentation of Financial Statements – Puttable Instruments and Obligations Arising on Liquidation*, IASB, February 2008, paras. DO1-DO6.
17 *IFRIC Update*, March 2009.
18 *DP/2018/1* para. 8.33-34.
19 *IFRIC Update*, November 2006.
20 *IFRIC Update*, April 2005.
21 *IFRIC Update*, November 2006.
22 *IFRS for Small and Medium-Sized Entities*, IASB, July 2009, para. 21.2.
23 IFRS for SMEs, Derivation Table.
24 IASB staff draft of proposed exposure draft *International Financial Reporting Standard for Small and Medium-Sized Entities* (as made available on the IASB's website as at September 2006) paras. 22.2-22.4.
25 *IFRIC Update*, July 2013.
26 *IFRIC Update*, May 2014 and January 2014.
27 *IFRIC Update*, July 2013.
28 *IFRIC Update*, January 2014.
29 *IFRIC Update*, July 2013.
30 *IFRIC Update*, January 2014.
31 *DP/2018/1* para. 8.34.
32 *IFRIC Update*, July 2006.
33 *IFRIC Update*, September 2008.
34 *Overview of IAS 32 (Agenda paper 12B)*, Information for Observers, IASB meeting, January 2007, para. 48.
35 *IASB Update*, April 2020.

Chapter 48 Financial instruments: Classification

1 INTRODUCTION 3771
2 CLASSIFYING FINANCIAL ASSETS: AN OVERVIEW 3771
    2.1 Debt instruments 3774
    2.2 Equity instruments and derivatives 3775
3 CLASSIFYING FINANCIAL LIABILITIES 3775
4 FINANCIAL ASSETS AND FINANCIAL LIABILITIES HELD FOR TRADING 3777
5 FINANCIAL ASSETS: THE 'BUSINESS MODEL' ASSESSMENT 3778
    5.1 The level at which the business model assessment is applied 3779
    5.2 Hold to collect contractual cash flows 3780
        5.2.1 Impact of sales on the assessment 3780
            5.2.1.A Assessing whether sales are 'infrequent' 3781
            5.2.1.B Assessing whether sales are 'insignificant in value' 3782
        5.2.2 Transferred financial assets that are not derecognised 3783
    5.3 Hold to collect contractual cash flows and selling financial assets 3783
    5.4 Other business models 3784
    5.5 Business model for financial assets owned by a subsidiary that is held for sale 3785
    5.6 Applying the business model test in practice 3785
6 CHARACTERISTICS OF THE CONTRACTUAL CASH FLOWS OF THE INSTRUMENT 3790
    6.1 The meaning of 'principal' 3791
    6.2 The meaning of 'interest' 3792
    6.3 Contractual features that normally pass the test 3793

	6.3.1	Conventional subordination features	3793
	6.3.2	Full recourse loans secured by collateral	3794
	6.3.3	Bonds with a capped or floored interest rate	3794
	6.3.4	Lender has discretion to change the interest rate	3795
	6.3.5	Unleveraged inflation-linked bonds	3795
	6.3.6	Features which compensate the lender for changes in tax or other related costs	3796
6.4	Contractual features that may affect the classification		3796
	6.4.1	De minimis and non-genuine features	3797
		6.4.1.A De minimis features	3797
		6.4.1.B Non-genuine features	3797
	6.4.2	Contractual features that modify the consideration for the time value of money	3798
	6.4.3	Regulated interest rates	3802
	6.4.4	Other contractual features that change the timing or amount of contractual cash flows	3802
		6.4.4.A Prepayment – negative compensation	3804
		6.4.4.B Prepayment – assets originated at a premium or discount	3806
	6.4.5	Contractual features that normally do not represent payments of principal and interest	3808
	6.4.6	Loan commitments	3812
	6.4.7	Environmental, social and governance 'ESG' loans	3813
6.5	Non-recourse assets		3814
6.6	Contractually linked instruments		3816
	6.6.1	The scope of the 'contractually linked' guidance	3817
	6.6.2	Contractually linked instruments versus non-recourse instruments	3819
	6.6.3	Assessing the characteristics of the underlying pool of financial instruments	3820
		6.6.3.A Non-financial instruments in the underlying pool	3820
		6.6.3.B Liquidity facilities in the underlying pool	3820
		6.6.3.C Changes in the composition of the underlying pool	3821
		6.6.3.D Assets with prepayment options in the underlying pool	3821
		6.6.3.E Financial guarantee contracts and derivatives in the underlying pool	3822
		6.6.3.F Assets transferred to the underlying pool which have failed derecognition	3822
	6.6.4	Application of expected credit loss requirements to junior tranches	3823

	6.6.5	Assessing the exposure to credit risk in the tranche held 3823
6.7		Transferred financial assets held by a transferee and not qualifying for derecognition by the transferor..3825

7 DESIGNATION AT FAIR VALUE THROUGH PROFIT OR LOSS 3826

    7.1 Designation eliminates or significantly reduces a measurement or recognition inconsistency (accounting mismatch) that would otherwise arise 3827

    7.2 A group of financial liabilities or financial assets and financial liabilities is managed and its performance is evaluated on a fair value basis 3828

    7.3 Hybrid contracts with a host that is not a financial asset within the scope of IFRS 9 3829

8 DESIGNATION OF NON-DERIVATIVE EQUITY INVESTMENTS AT FAIR VALUE THROUGH OTHER COMPREHENSIVE INCOME......................3830

    8.1 Gains and losses on investments in equity instruments designated at fair value through other comprehensive income 3831

9 RECLASSIFICATION OF FINANCIAL ASSETS...3832

    9.1 When should reclassifications be applied? 3835

10 CONTRACTS WITH INSURANCE RISK – INTERACTION BETWEEN IFRS 17 AND IFRS 9...3835

    10.1 Loan contracts that transfer significant insurance risk only on settlement of the policyholder's obligation created by the contract.......3835

    10.2 Credit card contracts (and other similar contracts) that provide insurance coverage 3836

List of examples

Example 48.1:	Liabilities at fair value through profit or loss: accounting mismatch in profit or loss..	3776
Example 48.2:	The level at which the business model assessment should be applied	3785
Example 48.3:	Splitting portfolios...	3786
Example 48.4:	Credit risk management activities	3786
Example 48.5:	Sales to manage concentration risk..	3787
Example 48.6:	Credit-impaired financial assets in a hold to collect business model..	3787
Example 48.7:	Hedging activities in a hold to collect business model..................	3787
Example 48.8:	Securitisation	3787
Example 48.9:	Liquidity portfolio for stress case scenarios	3787
Example 48.10:	Anticipated capital expenditure...	3788

Example 48.11:	Liquidity portfolio for everyday liquidity needs	3788
Example 48.12:	Opportunistic portfolio management	3788
Example 48.13:	Replication portfolios	3789
Example 48.14:	Loans that are to be sub-participated	3789
Example 48.15:	Portfolio managed on a fair value basis	3790
Example 48.16:	Unleveraged inflation linked bond	3796
Example 48.17:	Examples of a modified time value of money component	3800
Example 48.18:	Interest rate period selected at the discretion of the borrower	3801
Example 48.19:	Five-year constant maturity bond	3801
Example 48.20:	Regulated interest rates –'Livret A'	3802
Example 48.21:	Prepayable corporate loan recognised at a premium to par	3807
Example 48.22:	Debt covenants	3808
Example 48.23:	Auction Rate Securities (ARSs)	3808
Example 48.24:	Dual currency instruments	3809
Example 48.25:	Convertible debt	3810
Example 48.26:	Inverse floater	3810
Example 48.27:	Perpetual instruments with potentially deferrable coupons	3810
Example 48.28:	Write-down or conversion imposed by regulator	3811
Example 48.29:	Multiple of a benchmark interest rate	3811
Example 48.30:	Fixed rate bond prepayable by the issuer at fair value	3812
Example 48.31:	Investment in open-ended money market or debt funds	3812
Example 48.32:	Interest payments indexed to an equity index or the debtor's performance	3812
Example 48.33:	Non-recourse loans	3814
Example 48.34:	Assessing whether instruments are contractually linked	3819
Example 48.35:	Property development company with debt and equity	3819
Example 48.36:	Assessing the exposure to credit risk in the tranche held	3823
Example 48.37:	Callable, perpetual 'Tier 1' debt instrument	3831
Example 48.38:	Change in the way a portfolio is managed	3834
Example 48.39:	Change in business model by a subsidiary	3834

Chapter 48   Financial instruments: Classification

1 INTRODUCTION

On 1 January 2018, IFRS 9 – *Financial Instruments* (IFRS 9 or the standard) came into effect. The standard includes revised classification requirements for financial assets. Classification determines how financial instruments are accounted for in the financial statements and, in particular, how they are measured on an ongoing basis.

The more principle-based approach of IFRS 9 requires the careful use of judgement in its application. Some fact patterns have no simple and distinct outcome and we highlight in this chapter the factors that need to be considered in arriving at a conclusion.

2 CLASSIFYING FINANCIAL ASSETS: AN OVERVIEW

IFRS 9 has the following measurement categories for financial assets:
- debt instruments at amortised cost;
- debt instruments at fair value through other comprehensive income with cumulative gains and losses reclassified to profit or loss upon derecognition;
- debt instruments, derivatives and equity instruments at fair value through profit or loss; and
- equity instruments designated as measured at fair value through other comprehensive income with gains and losses remaining in other comprehensive income, i.e. without recycling to profit or loss upon derecognition.

Apart from some options which are described in more detail at 7 and 8 below, the classification is based on both the entity's business model for managing the financial assets and the contractual cash flow characteristics of the financial assets. *[IFRS 9.4.1.1]*.

The diagram below illustrates the thought process on which the classification of financial assets is based:

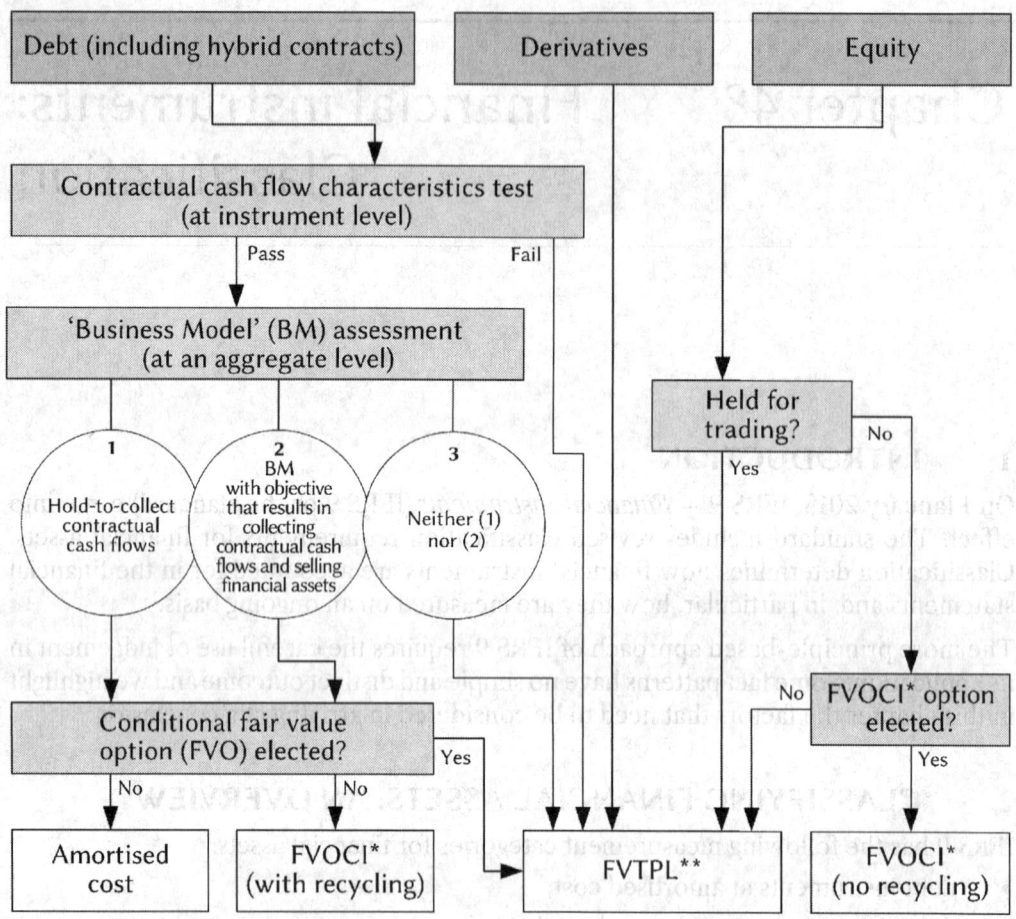

* Fair value through other comprehensive income
** Fair value through profit or loss

The following matrix summarises the outcome of the thought process depicted in the diagram above:

		Contractual cash flow characteristics test	
		Pass	Fail
Business model	Held within a business model whose objective is to hold financial assets in order to collect contractual cash flows	Amortised cost	FVTPL[1,3]
	Held within a business model whose objective is achieved by both collecting contractual cash flows and selling financial assets	FVOCI[2] (debt)	FVTPL[1,3]
	Financial assets which are neither held at amortised cost nor at fair value through other comprehensive income	FVTPL[1]	FVTPL[1,3]
Options	Equity instruments held for trading	FVTPL[1]	
	For debt instruments, the conditional fair value option is elected	FVTPL[1]	
	For equity instruments which are not held for trading, the option to elect to present changes in fair value in OCI	FVOCI[4] (equity)	

1 Fair value through profit or loss
2 Fair value through other comprehensive income
3 Financial assets which fail the contractual cash flow characteristics test are measured at fair value through profit or loss
4 Only debt instruments can pass the contractual cash flow characteristics test. The fair value through other comprehensive income option without recycling to OCI only applies to equity instruments

Measurement is covered in Chapter 50, particularly at 2.1 (debt financial assets measured at amortised cost), 2.3 (debt financial assets measured at fair value through other comprehensive income), 2.4 (financial assets measured at fair value through profit or loss) and 2.5 (investments in equity instruments designated at fair value through other comprehensive income). This includes the effective interest method and expected credit loss impairment model for financial assets measured at amortised cost and fair value through other comprehensive income. Fair value is determined in accordance with IFRS 13 – *Fair Value Measurement* – see Chapter 14.

2.1 Debt instruments

A debt instrument is normally measured at amortised cost if both of the following conditions are met: *[IFRS 9.4.1.2]*

(a) the financial asset is held within a business model whose objective is to hold financial assets in order to collect contractual cash flows; and

(b) the contractual terms of the financial asset give rise on specified dates to cash flows that are solely payments of principal and interest on the principal amount outstanding.

A debt instrument is normally measured at fair value through other comprehensive income if both of the following conditions are met: *[IFRS 9.4.1.2A]*

(a) the financial asset is held within a business model in which financial assets are managed to achieve a particular objective by both collecting contractual cash flows and selling financial assets; and

(b) the contractual terms of the financial asset give rise on specified dates to cash flows that are solely payments of principal and interest on the principal amount outstanding.

The application of these conditions (the 'business model' assessment and 'contractual cash flow characteristics' test) is covered in more detail at 5 and 6 below, respectively.

The above requirements should be applied to an entire financial asset, even if it contains an embedded derivative. *[IFRS 9.4.3.2]*.

The application of these requirements to debt instruments means that, apart from the exceptions described in 6.4 below, only relatively simple 'plain vanilla' debt instruments qualify to be measured at amortised cost or at fair value through other comprehensive income. Debt instruments that are neither measured at amortised cost nor at fair value though other comprehensive income are measured at fair value through profit or loss. *[IFRS 9.4.1.4]*. As will be shown at 5.4 below, this includes instruments that are held for trading (see 4 below).

Notwithstanding the criteria for debt instruments to be classified at amortised cost or at fair value through other comprehensive income, as described above, an entity may irrevocably designate a debt instrument as measured at fair value through profit or loss at initial recognition. This is allowed if doing so eliminates or significantly reduces a measurement or recognition inconsistency (sometimes referred to as an 'accounting mismatch'). Such mismatches would otherwise arise from measuring assets or liabilities or recognising the gains and losses on them on different bases. *[IFRS 9.4.1.5]*. This is covered further at 7 below.

In its Basis for Conclusions, the IASB noted that the fair value through other comprehensive income measurement category is intended for debt instruments for which both amortised cost information and fair value information are relevant and useful. This will be the case if their performance is affected by both the collection of contractual cash flows and the realisation of fair values through sales. *[IFRS 9.BC4.150]*.

The fair value through other comprehensive income measurement category may also help some insurers achieve consistency of measurement for assets held to back insurance liabilities under IFRS 17 – *Insurance Contracts*. Under IFRS 17, insurers may, in certain circumstances, have a policy choice between including insurance finance income or expenses for the period in profit or loss in their entirety or disaggregating insurance finance income or expenses between profit or loss and other comprehensive income. In order to minimise accounting mismatches, we expect that entities that have financial assets measured at fair value through other comprehensive income would elect to disaggregate insurance finance income and expenses. This is discussed in further detail in Chapter 56 at 15.3.1. The fair value through other comprehensive income category should also help to address concerns raised by preparers who expect to sell financial assets in greater volume than would be consistent with a business model whose objective is to hold financial assets to collect contractual cash flows and would, without this category, have to record such assets at fair value through profit or loss.

It should be noted that:

(a) the fair value through other comprehensive income classification under IFRS 9 reflects a business model evidenced by facts and circumstances and is neither a residual classification nor an election;

(b) debt instruments measured at fair value through other comprehensive income will be subject to the same impairment model as those measured at amortised cost. Accordingly, although the assets are recorded at fair value, the profit or loss treatment will be the same as for an amortised cost asset, with the difference between amortised cost, including impairment allowance, and fair value recorded in other comprehensive income; and

(c) only relatively simple debt instruments will qualify for measurement at fair value through other comprehensive income as they will also need to pass the contractual cash flow characteristics test.

2.2 Equity instruments and derivatives

Equity instruments and derivatives are normally measured at fair value through profit or loss. *[IFRS 9.5.7.1]*. However, on initial recognition, an entity may make an irrevocable election (on an instrument-by-instrument basis) to present in other comprehensive income subsequent changes in the fair value of an investment in an equity instrument within the scope of IFRS 9. This option applies to instruments that are neither held for trading (see 4 below) nor contingent consideration recognised by an acquirer in a business combination to which IFRS 3 – *Business Combinations* – applies. *[IFRS 9.5.7.1(b), 5.7.5]*. For the purpose of this election, the term equity instrument uses the definition in IAS 32 – *Financial Instruments: Presentation*. The use of this election is covered further at 8 below.

3 CLASSIFYING FINANCIAL LIABILITIES

Financial liabilities are classified and measured either at amortised cost or at fair value through profit or loss.

In addition, IFRS 9 specifies the accounting treatment for liabilities arising from certain financial guarantee contracts (see Chapter 45 at 3.4 and Chapter 50 at 2.8) and commitments to provide loans at below market rates of interest (see Chapter 45 at 3.5 and Chapter 50 at 2.8).

Financial liabilities are measured at fair value through profit or loss when they meet the definition of held for trading (see 4 below), *[IFRS 9 Appendix A]*, or when they are designated as such on initial recognition (see 7 below). Designation at fair value through profit or loss is permitted when either: *[IFRS 9.4.2.2]*

(a) it eliminates or significantly reduces a measurement or recognition inconsistency (sometimes referred to as an 'accounting mismatch'). Such mismatches would otherwise arise from measuring assets or liabilities or recognising the gains and losses on them on different bases;

(b) a group of financial liabilities or financial assets and financial liabilities is managed and its performance is evaluated on a fair value basis in accordance with a documented risk management or investment strategy, and information is provided internally on that basis to the entity's key management personnel (as defined in IAS 24 – *Related Party Disclosures* – see Chapter 39 at 2.2.1.D); or

(c) a financial liability contains one or more embedded derivatives that meet certain conditions. *[IFRS 9.4.3.5]*.

However, for financial liabilities designated as at fair value through profit or loss, the element of gains or losses attributable to changes in credit risk should normally be recognised in other comprehensive income with the remainder recognised in profit or loss. *[IFRS 9.5.7.7]*. These amounts recognised in other comprehensive income are not recycled to profit or loss if the liability is ever repurchased. However, if this treatment creates or enlarges an accounting mismatch in profit or loss the entity shall present all gains and losses on that liability (including the effects of changes in credit risk) in profit or loss. *[IFRS 9.5.7.8]*. The guidance indicates that an economic relationship is required in these cases. In other words, the liability's own credit risk must be offset by changes in the fair value of the other instrument. If there is no economic relationship between the liability's own credit risk and the fair value of the other instrument, then the gains and losses arising from the changes in credit risk cannot be recognised in profit or loss. 'Economic relationship' is not defined in the standard but the IASB noted that the relationship need not be contractual, *[IFRS 9.BC5.41]*, and that such a relationship does not arise by coincidence. *[IFRS 9.BC5.40]*. However, judging from the example given in the standard (see Example 48.1 below) it would seem that the IASB would not expect this to be very common. *[IFRS 9.B5.7.10]*.

Example 48.1: **Liabilities at fair value through profit or loss: accounting mismatch in profit or loss**

A mortgage bank provides loans to customers and funds those loans by selling bonds with matching characteristics (e.g. amount outstanding, repayment profile, term and currency) in the market. The contractual terms of the loans permit the mortgage customer to prepay its loan (i.e. satisfy its obligation to the bank) by buying the corresponding bond at fair value in the market and delivering that bond to the mortgage bank.

As a result of that contractual prepayment right, if the credit quality of the bond worsens (and, thus, the fair value of the mortgage bank's liability decreases), the fair value of the mortgage bank's loan asset also decreases. The change in the fair value of the asset reflects the mortgage customer's contractual right to prepay the mortgage loan by buying the underlying bond at fair value (which, in this example, has decreased) and delivering the bond to the mortgage bank. Therefore, the effects of changes in the credit risk of the liability (the bond) will be offset in profit or loss by a corresponding change in the fair value of a financial asset (the loan).

If the effects of changes in the liability's credit risk were presented in other comprehensive income there would be an accounting mismatch in profit or loss. Therefore, the mortgage bank is required to present all changes in fair value of the liability (including the effects of changes in the liability's credit risk) in profit or loss.

The standard also requires increased disclosure about an entity's methodology for making determinations about potential mismatches. The subsequent measurement of financial liabilities designated at fair value through profit or loss is discussed in further detail in Chapter 50 at 2.4.2.

The definition of held for trading is dealt with at 4 below and designation at fair value through profit or loss is covered further at 7 below.

All other financial liabilities, other than derivatives, are generally classified as subsequently measured at amortised cost using the effective interest method. *[IFRS 9.4.2.1]*.

In contrast to the treatment for hybrid contracts with financial asset hosts, derivatives embedded within a financial liability host within the scope of IFRS 9 will often be separately accounted for. That is, they must be separated if they are not closely related to the host contract, they meet the definition of a derivative, and the hybrid contract is not measured at fair value through profit or loss (see Chapter 46 at 4). Where an embedded derivative is separated from a financial liability host, the requirements of IFRS 9 dealing with classification of financial instruments should be applied separately to each of the host liability and the embedded derivative.

4 FINANCIAL ASSETS AND FINANCIAL LIABILITIES HELD FOR TRADING

The fact that a financial instrument is held for trading is important for its classification. For financial assets that are debt instruments, held for trading is a business model objective that results in measurement at fair value through profit or loss, as indicated at 2.1 above and covered in more detail at 5.4 below. Whether or not an asset is held for trading is also relevant for the option to designate an equity instrument as measured at fair value through other comprehensive income (see 2.2 above). Similar to financial assets, if a financial liability is held for trading it is classified as measured at fair value through profit or loss (see 3 above).

Financial assets and liabilities held for trading are defined as those that: *[IFRS 9 Appendix A]*

- are acquired or incurred principally for the purpose of sale or repurchase in the near term;
- on initial recognition are part of a portfolio of identified financial instruments that are managed together and for which there is evidence of a recent actual pattern of short-term profit-taking; or
- are derivatives (except for those that are financial guarantee contracts – see Chapter 45 at 3.4 – or are designated effective hedging instruments – see Chapter 53 at 3.2).

It follows from the definition that if an entity originates a loan with an intention of syndicating it, the amount of the loan to be syndicated should be classified as held for trading, even if the bank fails to find sufficient commitments from other participants (a so-called 'failed' loan syndication).

The term 'portfolio' in the definition of held for trading is not explicitly defined in IFRS 9, but the context in which it is used suggests that a portfolio is a group of financial assets and/or financial liabilities that are managed as part of that group. If there is evidence of a recent actual pattern of short-term profit taking on financial instruments included in such a portfolio, those financial instruments qualify as held for trading even though an individual financial instrument may, in fact, be held for a longer period of time. *[IFRS 9.IG B.11].*

A financial asset or liability held for trading will always be measured at fair value through profit or loss.

Trading generally reflects active and frequent buying and selling, and financial instruments held for trading are normally used with the objective of generating a profit from short-term fluctuations in price or a dealer's margin. *[IFRS 9.BA.6].*

In addition to derivatives that are not accounted for as hedging instruments, financial liabilities held for trading include: *[IFRS 9.BA.7]*

(a) obligations to deliver financial assets borrowed by a short seller (i.e. an entity that sells financial assets it has borrowed and does not yet own);

(b) financial liabilities that are incurred with an intention to repurchase them in the near term, such as quoted debt instruments that the issuer may buy back in the near term depending on changes in fair value; and

(c) financial liabilities that are part of a portfolio of identified financial instruments that are managed together and for which there is evidence of a recent pattern of short-term profit-taking. *[IFRS 9.BA.7(d)].* However, the fact that a liability is used merely to fund trading activities does not in itself make that liability one that is held for trading. *[IFRS 9.BA.8].*

5 FINANCIAL ASSETS: THE 'BUSINESS MODEL' ASSESSMENT

The business model assessment is one of the two steps to classify financial assets. An entity's business model reflects how it manages its financial assets in order to generate cash flows; its business model determines whether cash flows will result from collecting contractual cash flows, selling the financial assets or both. This assessment is performed on the basis of scenarios that the entity reasonably expects to occur. This means, the assessment excludes so-called 'worst case' or 'stress case' scenarios. For example, if an entity expects that it will sell a particular portfolio of financial assets only in a stress case scenario, this would not affect the entity's assessment of the business model for those assets if the entity does not reasonably expect it to occur. *[IFRS 9.B4.1.2A].*

If cash flows are realised in a way that is different from the entity's expectations at the date that the entity assessed the business model (for example, if the entity sells more or fewer financial assets than it expected when it classified the assets), this does not give rise to a prior period error in the entity's financial statements (as defined in IAS 8 – *Accounting Policies, Changes in Accounting Estimates and Errors* – see Chapter 3 at 4.6). Nor does it change the classification of the remaining financial assets held in that business model (i.e. those assets that the entity recognised in prior periods and still holds), as long as the entity considered all relevant and objective information that was available at the time that it made the business model assessment. Instead, classification of a financial asset is determined in accordance with the business model in place at the point of initial recognition and does not change thereafter except in the event of a reclassification.

Reclassifications of financial assets are only permitted, or required, in rare circumstances (see 9 below) which does not include a simple change in business model. However, when an entity assesses the business model for newly originated or newly purchased financial assets, it must consider information about how cash flows were realised in the past, along with all other relevant information. For instance, if a business model changes from being held to collect due to increasing sales out of the portfolio, any new assets recognised in the portfolio after such change would be classified in terms of the new business model (see Example 48.38 below). Existing assets within the portfolio would continue to be measured at amortised cost. This means that if there is a change in the way that cash flows are realised then this will only affect the classification of new assets when first recognised in the future. *[IFRS 9.B4.1.2A]*.

An entity's business model for managing the financial assets is a matter of fact and typically observable through particular activities that the entity undertakes to achieve its objectives. An entity will need to use judgement when it assesses its business model for managing financial assets and that assessment is not determined by a single factor or activity. Rather, the entity must consider all relevant and objective evidence that is available at the date of the assessment. Such relevant and objective evidence includes, but is not limited to: *[IFRS 9.B4.1.2B]*

(a) how the performance of the business model and the financial assets held within that business model are evaluated and reported to the entity's key management personnel;

(b) the risks that affect the performance of the business model (and the financial assets held within) and, in particular, the way those risks are managed; and

(c) how managers of the business are compensated (for example, whether the compensation is based on the fair value of the assets managed or on the contractual cash flows collected).

In addition to these three forms of evidence, in most circumstances the expected frequency, value and timing of sales are important aspects of the assessment. These are covered in more detail in 5.2.1 below. Entities will need to consider how and to what extent they document the evidence supporting the assessment of their business model.

5.1 The level at which the business model assessment is applied

The business model assessment should be performed on the basis of the entity's business model as determined by the entity's key management personnel (as defined in IAS 24 – see Chapter 39 at 2.2.1.D). *[IFRS 9.B4.1.1]*.

An entity's business model is determined at a level that reflects how groups of financial assets are managed together to achieve a particular business objective. This does not need to be the reporting entity level. The entity's business model does not depend on management's intentions for an individual instrument. Accordingly, this condition is not an instrument-by-instrument approach to classification and should be determined on a higher level of aggregation. However, a single entity may have more than one business model for managing its financial instruments (for example, one portfolio that it manages in order to collect contractual cash flows and another portfolio that it manages in order to trade to realise fair value changes). *[IFRS 9.B4.1.2]*.

Similarly, in some circumstances, it may be appropriate to split a portfolio of financial assets into sub-portfolios to reflect how an entity manages them. *[IFRS 9.B4.1.2]*. Those portfolios would be split and treated as separate portfolios, provided the assets belonging to each sub-portfolio are defined. A sub-portfolio approach would not be appropriate in cases where an entity is not able to define which assets would be held to collect contractual cash flows and which assets would potentially be sold. It is clear that judgement will need to be applied when determining the level of aggregation to which the business model assessment should be applied. Splitting a portfolio into two sub-portfolios might allow an entity to achieve amortised cost accounting for most of the assets within the portfolio, even if it is required to sell a certain volume of assets. The entity could define the assets it intends (or is required) to sell as one sub-portfolio while it defines the assets it intends to keep as another.

5.2 Hold to collect contractual cash flows

A financial asset which is held within a business model whose objective is to hold assets in order to collect contractual cash flows is measured at amortised cost (provided the asset also meets the contractual cash flow characteristics test). *[IFRS 9.4.1.2]*. An entity manages such assets to realise cash flows by collecting contractual payments over the life of the instrument instead of managing the overall return on the portfolio by both holding and selling assets. *[IFRS 9.B4.1.2C]*.

5.2.1 Impact of sales on the assessment

In determining whether cash flows are going to be realised by collecting the financial assets' contractual cash flows, it is necessary to consider the frequency, value and timing of sales in prior periods, whether the sales were of assets close to their maturity, the reasons for those sales, and expectations about future sales activity. However, the standard states that sales, in themselves, do not determine the business model and therefore cannot be considered in isolation. It goes on to say that, instead, information about past sales and expectations about future sales provide evidence related to how the entity's stated objective for managing the financial assets is achieved and, specifically, how cash flows are realised. An entity must consider information about past sales within the context of the reasons for those sales and the conditions that existed at that time as compared to current conditions. *[IFRS 9.B4.1.2C]*.

The standard is slightly cryptic concerning the role of sales. When it says that 'sales in themselves do not determine the business model', the emphasis appears to be on past sales. Given the guidance in the standard, the magnitude and frequency of sales is certainly important evidence in determining an entity's business models. However, the key point is that the standard requires the consideration of expected future sales while past sales are of relevance only as a source of evidence. Under IFRS 9 there is no concept of tainting, whereby assets are reclassified if sales activity differs from what was originally expected.

Although the objective of an entity's business model may be to hold financial assets in order to collect contractual cash flows, the entity need not hold all those instruments until maturity. Thus, an entity's business model can be to hold financial assets to collect contractual cash flows even when some sales of financial assets occur or are expected to occur in the future. *[IFRS 9.B4.1.3]*.

The following scenarios might be consistent with a hold to collect business model:

- The business model may be to hold assets to collect contractual cash flows even if the entity sells financial assets when there is an increase in the assets' credit risk. To determine whether there has been an increase in the assets' credit risk, the entity considers reasonable and supportable information, including forward looking information. Irrespective of their frequency and value, sales due to an increase in the assets' credit risk are not inconsistent with a business model whose objective is to hold financial assets to collect contractual cash flows because the credit quality of financial assets is relevant to the entity's ability to collect contractual cash flows. Credit risk management activities that are aimed at mitigating potential credit losses due to credit deterioration are integral to such a business model. Selling a financial asset because it no longer meets the credit criteria specified in the entity's documented investment policy is an example of a sale that has occurred due to an increase in credit risk. However, in the absence of such a policy, the entity may still be able to demonstrate in other ways that the sale occurred due to an increase in credit risk. *[IFRS 9.B4.1.3A]*.

- Sales that occur for other reasons, such as sales made to manage credit concentration risk (without an increase in the assets' credit risk), may also be consistent with a business model whose objective is to hold financial assets in order to collect contractual cash flows. However, such sales are likely to be consistent with a business model whose objective is to hold financial assets in order to collect contractual cash flows only if those sales are infrequent (even if significant in value) or insignificant in value both individually and in aggregate (even if frequent). *[IFRS 9.B4.1.3B]*.

- In addition, sales may be consistent with the objective of holding financial assets in order to collect contractual cash flows if the sales are made close to the maturity of the financial assets and the proceeds from the sales approximate the collection of the remaining contractual cash flows. *[IFRS 9.B4.1.3B]*. How an entity defines 'close' and 'approximate' will be a matter of judgement.

The overarching principle is whether the entity's key management personnel have made a decision that, collecting contractual cash flows rather than selling financial assets is integral to achieving the objective of the business model. Under that objective, an entity will not normally expect that sales will be more than infrequent and more than insignificant in value. IFRS 9 does not explain how 'infrequent' and 'insignificant in value' should be interpreted in practice. Those thresholds could lead to diversity in application, although it is an area where we expect that consensus and best practices will emerge over time.

5.2.1.A Assessing whether sales are 'infrequent'

If more than an infrequent number of sales are made from a portfolio and those sales are more than insignificant in value (either individually or in aggregate), the entity needs to assess whether and how such sales are consistent with an objective of collecting contractual cash flows. An increase in the frequency or value of sales in a particular period is not necessarily inconsistent with an objective to hold financial assets in order to collect contractual cash flows, if an entity can explain the reasons for those sales and demonstrate why those sales do not reflect a change in the entity's business model and, hence, sales will in future be lower in frequency or value. *[IFRS 9.B4.1.3B]*. This assessment is about expectations and not about intent. For instance, the fact that it is not the entity's objective to realise fair value gains or losses is not sufficient in itself to be able to conclude that measurement at amortised cost is appropriate.

Furthermore, whether a third party (such as a banking regulator in the case of some liquidity portfolios held by banks) imposes the requirement to sell the financial assets, or that activity is at the entity's discretion, is not relevant to the business model assessment. *[IFRS 9.B4.1.3B]*.

In contrast, if an entity manages a portfolio of financial assets with the objective of realising cash flows through the sale of the assets, the assets would not be held under a hold to collect business model. For example, an entity might actively manage a portfolio of assets in order to realise fair value changes arising from changes in credit spreads and yield curves. In this case, the entity's business model is not to hold those assets to collect the contractual cash flows. Rather, the entity's objective results in active buying and selling with the entity managing the instruments to realise fair value gains.

Many organisations hold portfolios of financial assets for liquidity purposes. Assets in those portfolios are regularly sold because sales are required by a regulator to demonstrate liquidity, because the entity needs to cover everyday liquidity needs or because the entity tries to maximise the yield of the portfolio. It follows that such portfolios (except those that may be sold only in stress case scenarios) will probably not be measured at amortised cost depending on facts and circumstances (see also 5.6 below).

5.2.1.B   Assessing whether sales are 'insignificant in value'

With reference to measuring 'insignificant in value', the standard refers to more than an infrequent number of such sales being made out of a portfolio. *[IFRS 9.B4.1.3B]*. The reference point to measuring 'insignificant in value' could therefore be considered to be the portfolio, particularly as it is the portfolio that is subject to the business model assessment. The assessment of more than insignificant in value therefore requires consideration of the sales value against the total size of the portfolio. In addition to the sales value-based assessment, an entity could also consider whether the gain or loss on sale is significant compared to the total return on the portfolio. However, the gain or loss approach, on its own, would not be an appropriate method as the standard is specific about the importance of sales in making the assessment. Loans are often sold at amounts close to their carrying value making it possible for very significant volumes of sales to generate insignificant gains or losses.

The standard is not explicit as to whether any test of insignificance should be performed period by period, or by taking into account sales over the entire life of the portfolio. However, if a period by period approach were to be used, the determination of whether sales are insignificant in value would depend on the length of the period, which means that two entities with identical portfolios but with different lengths of the reporting period would arrive at different assessments. Further, if a bank holds a portfolio of bonds with an average maturity of 20 years, sales of, say, 5% each year would mean that a considerable portion of the portfolio will have been sold before it matures, which would not seem to be consistent with a business model of holding to collect. Therefore, applying the average life of the portfolio would seem to be more relevant than applying the reporting period.

5.2.2 Transferred financial assets that are not derecognised

There are a number of circumstances where an entity may sell a financial asset, but those assets will remain on the selling entity's statement of financial position. For example, a bank may enter into a 'repo' transaction whereby it sells a debt security and at the same time agrees to repurchase it at a fixed price. Similarly, a manufacturer may sell trade receivables as part of a factoring programme and provide a guarantee to the buyer to compensate it for any defaults by the debtors. In each case, the seller retains substantially all risks and rewards of the assets and the financial assets would not be derecognised in accordance with the requirements of IFRS 9.

The inevitable question that arises in these circumstances is whether these transactions should be regarded as sales when applying the business model assessment. In this context, IFRS 9 contains in example 3 of paragraph B4.1.4 only one passing reference to derecognition, but it does suggest that it is the accounting treatment and not the legal form of a transaction that determines whether the entity has ceased to hold an asset to collect contractual cash flows (see also Example 48.8 below). Application of such an approach would give an intuitively correct answer for repo transactions, in which the seller is required to repurchase the asset at an agreed future date and price, and which are, in substance, secured financing transactions rather than sales. However, as the IASB did not provide the basis for the treatment in the example quoted above, it is not clear if accounting derecognition should always be the basis for the assessment. For instance, if a loan is sold under an agreement by which the seller will indemnify the purchaser for any credit losses (for instance if it is factored with recourse) and so the asset is not derecognised, it is not clear whether there has been a sale for the purposes of the IFRS 9 business model assessment, given that the transferor will never retake possession of the asset. In contrast, in a repo transaction the transferor will ultimately regain possession of the asset and these are generally regarded as not being a sale for the purposes of the business model test. We therefore believe that, except for instruments such as repos where the seller retains substantially all the risks and rewards of the asset, an entity has an accounting policy choice of whether it considers the legal form of the sale or the economic substance of the transaction when analysing sales within a portfolio.

5.3 Hold to collect contractual cash flows and selling financial assets

The fair value through other comprehensive income measurement category is a mandatory category for portfolios of financial assets that are held within a business model whose objective is achieved by both collecting contractual cash flows and selling financial assets (provided the asset also meets the contractual cash flow test). *[IFRS 9.4.1.2A]*.

In this type of business model, the entity's key management personnel have made a decision that both collecting contractual cash flows and selling are fundamental to achieving the objective of the business model. There are various objectives that may be consistent with this type of business model. For example, the objective of the business model may be to manage everyday liquidity needs, to maintain a particular interest yield profile or to match the duration of the financial assets to the duration of the liabilities that those assets are funding. To achieve these objectives, the entity will both collect contractual cash flows and sell the financial assets. *[IFRS 9.B4.1.4A]*.

Compared to the business model with an objective to hold financial assets to collect contractual cash flows, this business model will typically involve greater frequency and value of sales. This is because selling financial assets is integral to achieving the business model's objective rather than only incidental to it. There is no threshold for the frequency or value of sales that can or must occur in this business model. *[IFRS 9.B4.1.4B]*.

As set out in the standard, the fair value through other comprehensive income is a defined category and is neither a residual classification nor an election. However, in practice, entities may identify those debt instruments which are held to collect contractual cash flows (see 5.2 above), those which are held for trading, those managed on a fair value basis (see 5.4 below) and those for which the entity applies the fair value option to avoid a measurement mismatch, (see 7.1 below), and then measure the remaining debt instruments at fair value through other comprehensive income. As a consequence, the fair value through other comprehensive income category might, in effect, be used as a residual, just because it is far easier to articulate business models that would be classified at amortised cost or at fair value through profit or loss.

5.4 Other business models

IFRS 9 requires financial assets to be measured at fair value through profit or loss if they are not held within either a business model whose objective is to hold assets to collect contractual cash flows or within a business model whose objective is achieved by both collecting contractual cash flows and selling financial assets. A business model that results in measurement at fair value through profit or loss is where the financial assets are held for trading (see 4 above). Another is where the financial assets are managed on a fair value basis (see Example 48.15 below).

When the standard explains what it means by a portfolio of financial assets that is managed and whose performance is evaluated on a fair value basis it refers to the requirements for designating financial liabilities as measured at fair value through profit or loss. *[IFRS 9.B4.1.6]*. In order to be considered to be managed on a fair value basis, the portfolio needs to be managed in accordance with a documented risk management or investment strategy and for information, prepared on a fair value basis, about the group of instruments to be provided internally to the entity's key management personnel (this is as defined in IAS 24 see Chapter 39 at 2.2.1.D), for example the entity's board of directors and chief executive officer. *[IFRS 9.4.2.2(b)]*. Further, it is explained that if an entity manages and evaluates the performance of a group of financial assets, measuring that group at fair value through profit or loss results in more relevant information. *[IFRS 9.B4.1.33]*. Documentation of the entity's strategy need not be extensive but should be sufficient to demonstrate that the classification at fair value through profit or loss is consistent with the entity's risk management or investment strategy. *[IFRS 9.B4.1.36]*.

In each case (both where assets are held for trading and where assets are managed on a fair value basis), the entity manages the financial assets with the objective of realising cash flows through the sale of the assets. The entity makes decisions based on the assets' fair values and manages the assets to realise those fair values. As a consequence, the entity's objective will typically result in active buying and selling. Even though the entity will collect contractual cash flows while it holds financial assets in the fair value through profit or loss category, this is only incidental and not integral to achieving the business model's objective. *[IFRS 9.B4.1.5, B4.1.6]*.

5.5 Business model for financial assets owned by a subsidiary that is held for sale

A question that arises over the application of IFRS 9 concerns how to apply the business model test in the consolidated accounts to a subsidiary which is classified as held for sale in accordance with IFRS 5 – *Non-current Assets Held for Sale and Discontinued Operations*. In particular, when the financial assets of a subsidiary are held with the objective of collecting contractual cash flows but the subsidiary itself is held for sale under IFRS 5, whether the financial assets of the subsidiary should be considered to be within a hold to collect or a hold to sell business model.

The IFRS Interpretations Committee were asked precisely this question in November 2016. They noted that, in its consolidated financial statements, an entity assesses the relevant requirements of IFRS 9 from the group perspective and will advise the IASB when it comes to discuss this issue. This issue is not currently on the IASB's agenda and so until the IASB concludes on this issue, it is unclear how the business model test would be applied in these circumstances.[1]

5.6 Applying the business model test in practice

The application of the business model test is illustrated through a number of examples, in all the following examples in this section it is assumed that the instruments will meet the contractual cash flows characteristics test.

Example 48.2: The level at which the business model assessment should be applied

A global banking group operates two business lines, retail banking and investment banking. These businesses both operate in the same five locations by means of separate subsidiaries. Each subsidiary has its own Board of Directors that is responsible for carrying out the strategic objectives as set by the group's Board of Directors.

The financial assets held by the investment banking business are measured at fair value through profit or loss in line with the group's strategy, which defines the business model, to actively trade these financial assets. Within the retail banking business, four of the five subsidiaries hold debt securities in line with the group's objective to collect contractual cash flows. However, the fifth subsidiary holds a portfolio of debt securities that it expects to sell before maturity. These assets are not held for trading, but individual assets are sold if the portfolio manager believes he or she can reinvest the funds in assets with a higher yield. As a result, a more than infrequent number of sales that are significant in value are anticipated for this portfolio and it is unlikely that this portfolio would meet the amortised cost criteria if it were assessed on its own.

The bank will need to exercise judgement to determine the appropriate level at which to assess its business model(s). Hence, different conclusions are possible depending on the facts and circumstances.

This does not mean that the bank has an accounting policy choice, but it is, rather, a matter of fact that can be observed by the way the organisation is structured and managed. In many organisations, key management personnel may determine the overall strategy and then delegate their authority for executing the strategy to others. The combination of the overall strategy and the effect of the delegated authority are among the factors that can be considered in the determination of business models.

In the specified fact pattern, the determining factor is whether the fifth subsidiary is managed independently from the other four subsidiaries (and performance is assessed and management is compensated accordingly). If it is separately managed, the number of business models is three (i.e. investment banking, one business model for the first four subsidiaries and a third business model for the fifth subsidiary). If not, the number of business models is two (i.e. one for retail banking and one for investment banking). In the case of two business models, all the debt securities held by the retail banking business would be accounted for at fair value through other comprehensive income, unless the sales activity of the fifth subsidiary is not significant to the bank.

Example 48.3: Splitting portfolios

Entity A has debt instruments worth €100 million, comprising notes with maturities of three to five years. €10 million of the portfolio is sold and reinvested at least once a year, while the remaining €90 million of investments are typically held to near their maturity. First, the entity needs to use judgement to determine whether it has:

(a) Two business models: (i) €90 million of debt instruments held to near their maturity; and (ii) €10 million of debt instruments which are actively bought and sold, provided those assets can be separately identified, or

(b) One business model applied to the overall portfolio of €100 million debt investments

If scenario (a) above is considered more appropriate (e.g. the entity intends to continue to sell and reinvest a distinct part of the portfolio in the same proportions as it has in past years), the entity could achieve amortised cost classification for a majority of the debt instruments and would probably need to account for the remaining debt instruments at fair value through profit or loss. This is more likely to be the case where there is clearly a different management objective for the two groups of assets and their performance is measured, and management is compensated, accordingly.

Alternatively, if scenario (b) is considered more appropriate, the entity needs to determine whether the level of expected sales and repurchases is more than infrequent and is significant in value, requiring the whole portfolio to be measured at fair value through profit or loss or fair value through other comprehensive income (see 5.2.1 above). Whether the assets are required to be measured at fair value through profit or loss instead of fair value through other comprehensive income depends on whether the portfolio is managed on a fair value basis and fair value information is primarily used to assess asset's performance and to make decisions.

Example 48.4: Credit risk management activities

An entity holds investments to collect their contractual cash flows. The funding needs of the entity are predictable and the maturity of its financial assets is matched to its estimated funding needs.

The entity performs credit risk management activities with the objective of maintaining the credit risk of the portfolio within defined risk limits. In the past, sales have typically occurred when the financial assets' credit risk has increased such that the assets no longer meet the entity's documented investment policy.

Reports to key management personnel focus on the credit quality of the financial assets and the contractual return. The entity also monitors fair values of the financial assets, among other information.

Irrespective of their frequency and value, sales due to an increase in the assets' credit risk are not inconsistent with a business model whose objective is to hold financial assets to collect contractual cash flows, because the credit quality of financial assets is relevant to the entity's ability to collect contractual cash flows.

Credit risk management activities that are aimed at avoiding potential credit losses due to credit deterioration are integral to such a business model. Selling a financial asset because it no longer meets the credit criteria specified in the entity's documented investment policy is an example of a sale that has occurred due to an increase in credit risk. However, this conclusion cannot be extended to sales to avoid excessive credit concentration (see also Example 48.5 below).

Although the entity considers, among other information, the financial assets' fair values from a liquidity perspective (i.e. the cash amount that would be realised if the entity needs to sell assets), the entity's objective is to hold the financial assets in order to collect the contractual cash flows.

Therefore, under the fact pattern specified, the entity will still be able to measure the portfolio at amortised cost.

In the absence of a documented investment or similar policy, the entity may be able to demonstrate in other ways that a sale only occurred due to an increase in credit risk. *[IFRS 9.B4.1.4 Example 1].*

Example 48.5: Sales to manage concentration risk

An entity sells financial assets to manage the concentration of the entity's credit risk to a particular obligor, country or industrial sector, without an increase in the assets' credit risk.

Such sales may be consistent with a business model whose objective is to hold financial assets in order to collect contractual cash flows, but only to the extent that they are infrequent (even if significant in value) or insignificant in value both individually and in aggregate (even if frequent). That means such sales are treated no differently than sales for any other reason. Thus, if such sales are more than infrequent and are not insignificant in value (both individually and in aggregate), then the business model would not qualify to be held to collect, but is likely to be consistent with a business model whose objective is to hold financial assets in order to collect contractual cash flows and to sell financial assets. *[IFRS 9.B4.1.3B]*.

Example 48.6: Credit-impaired financial assets in a hold to collect business model

An entity's business model is to purchase portfolios of financial assets, such as loans. Those portfolios may or may not include financial assets that are credit-impaired, that is, there have already been one or more events occurring before purchase that have had a detrimental impact on future cash flows. If payment on the loans is not made on a timely basis, the entity attempts to realise the contractual cash flows through various means – for example, by making contact with the debtor by mail, telephone or other methods. The entity's objective is to collect contractual cash flows and the entity does not manage any of the loans in this portfolio with an objective of realising cash flows by selling them.

The objective of the entity's business model is to hold the financial assets in order to collect the contractual cash flows. *[IFRS 9.B4.1.4 Example 2]*.

Example 48.7: Hedging activities in a hold to collect business model

A bank holds a portfolio of variable rate loans and enters into interest rate swaps to change the interest rate on particular loans in the portfolio from a floating interest rate to a fixed interest rate.

The fact that the entity has entered into derivatives to modify the cash flows of the portfolio does not in itself change the entity's business model. *[IFRS 9.B4.1.4 Example 2]*.

Example 48.8: Securitisation

An entity has a business model with the objective of originating loans to customers and subsequently to sell those loans to a securitisation vehicle. The securitisation vehicle issues instruments to investors. The originating entity controls the securitisation vehicle and thus consolidates it. The securitisation vehicle collects the contractual cash flows from the loans and passes them on to its investors.

It is assumed for the purposes of this example that the loans continue to be recognised in the consolidated statement of financial position because they are recognised by the securitisation vehicle.

The consolidated group originated the loans with the objective of holding them to collect the contractual cash flows and, therefore, measures them at amortised cost. The same conclusion may be drawn if the securitisation vehicle is not consolidated but the originating entity is unable to derecognise the assets (see 5.2.2 above).

However, the originating entity has an objective of realising cash flows on the loan portfolio by selling the loans to the securitisation vehicle, so for the purposes of its separate financial statements it would not be considered to be managing this portfolio in order to collect the contractual cash flows, but to sell them. The loans would probably need to be recorded at fair value through profit or loss as long as they continue to be recognised. *[IFRS 9.B4.1.4 Example 3]*.

Example 48.9: Liquidity portfolio for stress case scenarios

A financial institution holds financial assets to meet liquidity needs in a 'stress case' scenario (e.g. a run on the bank's deposits). The entity does not anticipate selling these assets except in such a scenario. The entity monitors the credit quality of the financial assets and its objective in managing the financial assets is to collect the contractual cash flows. The entity evaluates the performance of the assets based on interest revenue earned and credit losses realised.

However, the entity also monitors the fair value of the financial assets from a liquidity perspective to ensure that the cash amount that would be realised if the entity needed to sell the assets in a stress case scenario would be sufficient to meet the entity's liquidity needs. Periodically, the entity makes sales that are insignificant in value to demonstrate liquidity.

The objective of the entity's business model is to hold the financial assets to collect contractual cash flows.

The analysis would not change even if during a previous stress case scenario, the entity made sales that were significant in value in order to meet its liquidity needs. Similarly, recurring sales activity that is insignificant in value is not inconsistent with holding financial assets to collect contractual cash flows.

However, the assessment would change if the entity periodically sells debt instruments that are significant in value to demonstrate liquidity, or if the entity sells the debt instruments to cover everyday liquidity needs. See Examples 48.10 and 48.11 below. *[IFRS 9.B4.1.4 Example 4].*

Example 48.10: Anticipated capital expenditure

A non-financial entity anticipates capital expenditure in a few years. The entity invests its excess cash in short-term and long-term financial assets so that it can fund the expenditure when the need arises. Many of the financial assets have contractual lives that exceed the entity's anticipated investment period. Therefore, the entity will need to sell some of the assets before maturity to meet those funding needs.

The objective of the business model is achieved by both collecting contractual cash flows and selling financial assets.

In contrast, consider an entity that anticipates a cash outflow in five years to fund capital expenditures and invests excess cash in short-term financial assets. When the investments mature, the entity reinvests the cash into new short-term financial assets. The entity maintains this strategy until the funds are needed, at which time the entity uses the proceeds from the maturing financial assets to fund the capital expenditures. Only insignificant sales occur before maturity (unless there is an increase in credit risk). The objective of such a business model is to hold financial assets in order to collect contractual cash flows. *[IFRS 9.B4.1.4C Example 5].*

Example 48.11: Liquidity portfolio for everyday liquidity needs

A financial institution holds financial assets to meet its everyday liquidity needs. In the past, this has resulted in frequent sales activity and such sales have been significant in value. This activity is expected to continue in the future as everyday liquidity needs can rarely be forecast with any accuracy.

The objective of the business model is meeting everyday liquidity needs. The entity achieves those objectives by both collecting contractual cash flows and selling financial assets. This means that both collecting contractual cash flows and selling financial assets are integral to achieving the business model's objective and the financial assets are measured at fair value through other comprehensive income. *[IFRS 9.B4.1.4C Example 6].* The frequent and significant sales activity does not necessarily mean that the portfolio is held for trading because under the business model objective above, assets are not sold with the intention of short-term profit taking.

Example 48.12: Opportunistic portfolio management

A financial institution holds a portfolio of financial assets. The entity actively manages the return on the portfolio on an opportunistic basis trying to increase the return, without a clear intention of holding the financial assets to collect contractual cash flows (although it might end up holding the assets if no other investment opportunities arise). That return consists of collecting contractual payments as well as gains and losses from the sale of financial assets.

As a result, the entity holds financial assets to collect contractual cash flows and sells financial assets to reinvest in higher yielding financial assets. In the past, this strategy has resulted in frequent sales activity and such sales have been significant in value. It is expected that the sales activity will continue in the future.

The entity achieves the objective stated above by both collecting contractual cash flows and selling financial assets. Both collecting contractual cash flows and selling financial assets are integral to achieving the business model's objective and, thus, the financial assets are measured at fair value through other comprehensive income. *[IFRS 9.B4.1.4C Example 6].*

Sometimes, entities may manage a portfolio to manage its yield. In such cases, the portfolio manager may be remunerated based on the overall yield of the portfolio and fair value gains or losses may not be considered in his or her remuneration. Furthermore, management's documented strategy and defined key performance indicators may emphasise optimising long-term yield rather than fair value gains or losses and accordingly, the entity's management reporting focuses on yield rather than fair value of the debt instruments within the portfolio. However, in our view, the fact that it is not the entity's objective to realise fair value gains or losses is not sufficient in itself to be able to conclude that measurement at amortised cost is appropriate as the business model objective is not only holding financial assets to collect contractual cash flows but also results in sales which are more than infrequent and significant in value. Thus, such a portfolio would be measured at fair value through other comprehensive income.

Example 48.13: Replication portfolios

Fact pattern 1: Insurance company

An insurer holds financial assets in order to fund insurance contract liabilities. The insurer uses the proceeds from the contractual cash flows on the financial assets to settle insurance contract liabilities as they come due. To ensure that the contractual cash flows from the financial assets are sufficient to settle those liabilities, the insurer undertakes significant buying and selling activity on a regular basis to rebalance its portfolio of assets and to meet cash flow needs as they arise.

The objective of the business model is to fund the insurance contract liabilities. To achieve this objective, the entity collects contractual cash flows as they come due and sells financial assets to maintain the desired profile of the asset portfolio. Thus, both collecting contractual cash flows and selling financial assets are integral to achieving the business model's objective and it follows that the financial assets are measured at fair value through other comprehensive income. *[IFRS 9.B4.1.4C Example 7].*

Fact pattern 2: Bank

A bank allocates investments into maturity bands to match the expected duration of customers' time deposits. The invested assets have a similar maturity profile and amount to the corresponding deposits. The target ratio of assets to deposits for each maturity band has pre-determined minimum and maximum levels. For example, if the ratio exceeds the maximum level because of an unexpected withdrawal of deposits, the bank will sell some assets to reduce the ratio.

Meanwhile, new assets will be acquired when necessary (i.e. when the ratio of assets to deposits falls below the pre-determined minimum level). The expected repayment profile of the deposits would be updated on a quarterly basis, based on changes in customer behaviour.

The question is whether adjusting the assets/deposits ratio by selling assets to correspond with a change in the expected repayment profile of the deposits would mean that the business model is inconsistent with the objective of holding to collect the contractual cash flows. In these circumstances, an analogy can be drawn to the insurance company above.

If the bank has a good track record of forecasting its deposit repayments, so that sales are expected to be infrequent, it is possible that the objective of the business model is to hold the investments to collect contractual cash flows. But, if significant sales take place each year, it is likely to be difficult to rationalise such practice with this objective. Due consideration will also need to be given to the magnitude of sales and the reasons for the sales.

Example 48.14: Loans that are to be sub-participated

An entity originates loans so that it holds part of the portfolio to maturity, but 'sub-participates' a portion of the loans to other banks, so that it transfers substantially all the risks and rewards and so achieves derecognition. The question arises whether, for the purposes of application of IFRS 9, the entity has one business model or two.

The entity could consider the activities of lending to hold and lending to sell or sub-participate as two separate business models, requiring different skills and processes. Whilst the financial assets resulting from the former would typically qualify for amortised cost measurement, those from the latter would probably not and would, therefore, most likely need to be measured at fair value through profit or loss. This split approach is likely to be acceptable as long as the entity is able to forecast with reasonable confidence that it will indeed hold the assets (or the proportion of a group of identical assets) that it determines to be measured at amortised cost.

If a loan is assessed, in part, to be sold or sub-participated, this raises the additional issue of whether a single financial asset can be classified into two separate business models. It was common under IAS 39 – *Financial Instruments: Recognition and Measurement* – for loans to be classified in part as held for trading and in part at amortised cost and we see this practice continuing under IFRS 9.

In some cases, an entity may fail to achieve the intended disposal, having previously classified a portion of a loan at fair value through profit or loss because of the intention to sell.

The standard requires classification to be determined in accordance with the business model applicable at the point of initial recognition of the asset. In this example, the fact that the entity fails to achieve an intended disposal does not trigger a reclassification in accordance with the standard as the threshold for reclassification is a very high hurdle. Therefore, loans or portions of loans that the entity fails to dispose of would continue to be recorded at fair value through profit or loss.

Example 48.15: Portfolio managed on a fair value basis

An entity manages a portfolio and measures its performance on a fair value basis and makes decisions based on the fair value of the financial assets. Such an objective typically results in frequent sales and purchases of financial assets.

A portfolio of financial assets that is managed and whose performance is evaluated on a fair value basis is neither held to collect contractual cash flows nor held both to collect contractual cash flows and to sell financial assets. In addition, a portfolio of financial assets that meets the definition of held for trading is not held to collect contractual cash flows or held both to collect contractual cash flows and to sell financial assets. The entity is primarily focused on fair value information and uses that information to assess the assets' performance and to make decisions.

Even though the entity will collect contractual cash flows while it holds financial assets in the fair value through profit or loss category, this is only incidental and not integral to achieving the business model's objective. Consequently, such portfolios of financial assets must be measured at fair value through profit or loss. *[IFRS 9.B4.1.5]*.

6 CHARACTERISTICS OF THE CONTRACTUAL CASH FLOWS OF THE INSTRUMENT

The assessment of the characteristics of a financial asset's contractual cash flows aims to identify whether they are 'solely payments of principal and interest on the principal amount outstanding'. Hence, the assessment is colloquially referred to as the 'SPPI test'.

The contractual cash flow characteristics test is designed to screen out financial assets on which the application of the effective interest method either is not viable from a pure mechanical standpoint or does not provide useful information about the uncertainty, timing and amount of the financial asset's contractual cash flows.

Because the effective interest method is essentially an allocation mechanism that spreads interest revenue or expense over time, amortised cost is only appropriate for simple cash flows that have low variability such as those of traditional unleveraged loans and receivables, and 'plain vanilla' debt instruments. Accordingly, the contractual cash flow characteristics test is based on the premise that it is only when the variability in the contractual cash flows maintains the holder's return in line with a 'basic lending arrangement' that the application of effective interest method provides useful information. *[IFRS 9.BC4.23, 158, 171, 172]*.

In this context, the term 'basic lending arrangement' is used broadly to capture both originated and acquired financial assets, the lender or the holder of which is looking to earn a return that compensates primarily for the time value of money and credit risk. However, such an arrangement can also include other elements that provide consideration for other basic lending risks such as liquidity risks, costs associated with holding the financial asset for a period of time (e.g. servicing or administrative costs) and a profit margin. *[IFRS 9.B4.1.7A, BC4.182(b)]*.

In contrast, contractual terms that introduce a more than *de minimis* exposure (see 6.4.1 below) to risks or volatility in the contractual cash flows that is unrelated to a basic lending arrangement, such as exposure to changes in equity prices or commodity prices, do not give rise to contractual cash flows that are solely payments of principal and interest on the principal amount outstanding. *[IFRS 9.B4.1.7A, B4.1.18]*.

The IASB noted that it believes that amortised cost would provide relevant and useful information as long as the contractual cash flows do not introduce risks or volatility that are inconsistent with a basic lending arrangement. *[IFRS 9.BC4.180]*.

The following sections cover the main aspects of the contractual cash flow characteristics test, starting with the meaning of the terms 'principal' and 'interest' in 6.1 and 6.2 below, and discusses instruments that normally pass the test at 6.3 below. So called 'modified' contractual cash flows and their effect on the contractual cash flow characteristics test are dealt with in 6.4 below. Non-recourse assets are separately covered in 6.5 below and contractually linked instruments in 6.6 below.

6.1 The meaning of 'principal'

'Principal' is not a defined term in IFRS 9. However, the standard states that, for the purposes of applying the contractual cash flow characteristics test, the principal is 'the fair value of the asset at initial recognition' and that it may change over the life of the financial asset (for example, if there are repayments of principal). *[IFRS 9.4.1.3(a), B4.1.7B]*.

The IASB believes that this usage reflects the economics of the financial asset from the perspective of the current holder; in other words, the entity would assess the contractual cash flow characteristics by comparing the contractual cash flows to the amount that it actually invested. *[IFRS 9.BC4.182(a)]*.

For example: Entity A issued a bond with a contractually stated principal of €1,000,000. The bond was originally issued at €990,000. Because interest rates have risen sharply since the bond was originally issued, Entity B, the current holder of the bond, acquired the bond in the secondary market for €975,000. From the perspective of entity B, the principal amount is €975,000. The principal will increase over time as the discount of €25,000 amortises out until it reaches the contractual amount of €1,000,000 at the bond's maturity.

The principal is, therefore, not necessarily the contractual par amount, nor (when the holder has acquired the asset subsequent to its origination) is it necessarily the amount that was advanced to the debtor when the instrument was originally issued.

The description of 'principal' as the fair value of an instrument on initial recognition avoids a concern that any financial asset acquired or issued at a substantial discount would be leveraged and hence would not have economic characteristics of interest.

A clear understanding of what the standard means by 'principal' is also necessary for the appropriate and consistent application of the contractual cash flow characteristics test to prepayable financial assets (see 6.4.4 below).

6.2 The meaning of 'interest'

IFRS 9 states that the most significant elements of interest within a basic lending arrangement are typically the consideration for the time value of money and credit risk. In addition, interest may also include consideration for other basic lending risks (for example, liquidity risk) and costs (for example, administrative costs) associated with holding the financial asset for a particular period of time. Furthermore, interest may include a profit margin that is consistent with a basic lending arrangement.

In extreme economic circumstances, interest can be negative if, for example, the holder of a financial asset effectively pays a fee for the safekeeping of its money for a particular period of time and that fee exceeds the consideration the holder receives for the time value of money, credit risk and other basic lending risks and costs.

However, contractual terms that introduce exposure to risks or volatility in the contractual cash flows that is unrelated to a basic lending arrangement, such as exposure to changes in equity prices or commodity prices, do not give rise to contractual cash flows that are solely payments of principal and interest on the principal amount outstanding. An originated or a purchased financial asset can be a basic lending arrangement irrespective of whether it is a loan in its legal form. *[IFRS 9.4.1.3(b), B4.1.7A].*

The IASB notes that the assessment of interest focuses on what the entity is being compensated for (i.e. whether the entity is receiving consideration for basic lending risks, costs and a profit margin or is being compensated for something else), instead of how much the entity receives for a particular element. For example, the Board acknowledges that different entities may price the credit risk element differently. *[IFRS 9.BC4.182(b)].* Although two entities may receive different amounts for the same element of interest, e.g. credit risk, they could both conclude that their consideration for credit risk is appropriate within a basic lending arrangement.

Time value of money is the element of interest that provides consideration for only the passage of time. That is, the time value of money element does not provide consideration for other risks or costs associated with holding the financial asset. To make this assessment, an entity applies judgement and considers relevant factors such as the currency in which the financial asset is denominated, and the period for which the interest rate is set. *[IFRS 9.B4.1.9A].*

The IASB also notes that, as a general proposition, the market in which the transaction occurs is relevant to the assessment of the time value of money element. For example, in Europe, it has been common to reference interest rates to LIBOR and in the United States it is common to reference interest rates to the prime rate. However, a particular interest rate does not necessarily reflect consideration for only the time value of money merely because that rate is considered 'normal' in a particular market. For example, if an interest rate is reset every year but the reference rate is always a 15-year rate, it would be difficult for an entity to conclude that such a rate provides consideration for only the passage of time, even if such pricing is commonly used in that particular market. Accordingly, the IASB believes that an entity must apply judgement to conclude whether the stated time value of money element meets the objective of providing consideration for only the passage of time. *[IFRS 9.BC4.178]*.

It could be argued that the standard is not entirely clear as to the status of benchmark rates such as LIBOR or EURIBOR. For such rates, the consideration for credit risk is neither fixed, nor varies over time to reflect the specific credit risk of the obligor, but instead varies to reflect the credit risks associated with a class of borrowers. However, this seems to be a purist approach and given that LIBOR has been widely used as a benchmark rate in capital markets and is cited in the standard as an example of a rate that would satisfy the criteria of the contractual cash flow characteristics test, it would seem that this is not an issue.

Moreover, this issue will to a large extent disappear with the introduction of nearly risk-free rates as part of IBOR (Interbank Offered Rates) reform. However, the precise mechanics of how such alternative rates would be calculated are presenting new accounting questions. As part of the IASB's work to address the effects of IBOR reform on financial reporting, the IASB discussed in October 2019, whether or not backward-looking interest rates would satisfy the contractual characteristics test. See 6.4.2 below for further consideration of when there are contractual features that modify the consideration for the time value of money.

Interest may include profit margin that is consistent with a basic lending arrangement. But elements that introduce exposure to risks or variability in the contractual cash flows that are unrelated to lending (such as exposure to equity or commodity price risk) are not consistent with a basic lending arrangement. The IASB also noted that the assessment of interest focusses on what the entity is being compensated for e.g. basic lending risk or something else, rather than how much the entity receives. *[IFRS 9.BC4.182(b)]*.

6.3 Contractual features that normally pass the test

The most common instruments that normally pass the test are plain vanilla debt instruments which are acquired at par, have a fixed maturity and pay interest that is fixed at inception. Instruments that pay variable interest also normally pass the test, although further consideration is required in that case (see 6.4.4 below).

There are several features that are common in many financial assets and which would not usually cause the contractual cash flow characteristics test to be failed. This section describes some of those features and instruments that are normally unproblematic but also highlights cases that might result in an asset failing the contractual cash flow characteristics test. Features that are more complex and need more consideration are described in 6.4 below.

6.3.1 Conventional subordination features

In many lending transactions the instrument is ranked relative to amounts owed by the borrower to its other creditors. An instrument that is subordinated to other instruments may be considered to have contractual cash flows that are payments of principal and interest on the principal amount outstanding if the debtor's non-payment arises only on a breach of contract and the holder has a contractual right to unpaid amounts of principal and interest on the principal amount outstanding even in the event of the debtor's bankruptcy.

For example, a trade receivable that ranks its creditor as a general creditor would qualify as having payments of principal and interest on the principal amount outstanding. This is the case even if the debtor has issued loans that are collateralised, which in the event of bankruptcy would give that loan holder priority over the claims of the general creditor in respect of the collateral but does not affect the contractual right of the general creditor to unpaid principal and other amounts due. *[IFRS 9.B4.1.19]*.

On the other hand, if the subordination feature limits the contractual cash flows in any other way or introduces any kind of leverage, the instrument would fail the contractual cash flow characteristics test.

6.3.2 Full recourse loans secured by collateral

The fact that a full recourse loan is collateralised does not in itself affect the analysis of whether the contractual cash flows are solely payments of principal and interest on the principal amount outstanding. *[IFRS 9.B4.1.13 Instrument D]*. However, a full recourse loan may, in substance, be non-recourse if the borrower has limited other assets, in which case an entity would need to assess the particular underlying assets (i.e. the collateral) to determine whether or not the contractual cash flows of the loan are payments of principal and interest on the principal amount outstanding. *[IFRS 9.B4.1.17]*. If there is insufficient collateral in the borrower to ensure that payments of the contractual cash flows are made, then the loan may fail the contractual cash flow characteristics test. However, if sufficient equity or collateral is available then the contractual cash flow characteristics test may be met (see Example 48.33 below). Judgement may be necessary in determining whether there is adequate collateral or equity to ensure that all the contractual cash payments will be made.

6.3.3 Bonds with a capped or floored interest rate

Some bonds may have a stated maturity date but pay a variable market interest rate that is subject to a cap or a floor. The contractual cash flows of such instrument could be seen as being an instrument that has a fixed interest rate and an instrument that has a variable interest rate.

These both represent payments of principal and interest on the principal amount outstanding as long as the interest reflects consideration for the time value of money, for the credit risk associated with the instrument during the term of the instrument and for other basic lending risks and costs, as well as a profit margin.

Therefore, such an instrument can have cash flows that are solely payments of principal and interest on the principal amount outstanding. A feature such as an interest rate cap or floor may reduce cash flow variability by setting a limit on a variable interest rate or increase the cash flow variability because a fixed rate becomes variable. *[IFRS 9.B4.1.13 Instrument C]*. If there is no leverage and no mismatch of term with respect to interest, then the instrument should pass the contractual cash flows characteristics test.

There is no requirement to determine whether or not the cap or floor is in the money on initial recognition.

Caps and floors will generally pass the SPPI test without further analysis, apart from some instruments, namely those with features that create leverage. These 'exotic' instruments would require detailed assessment and judgement. An instrument with a floor which is deeply in the money at origination is not seen as a problem for passing the contractual cash flows characteristics test.

We assume that a variable rate debt instrument that is subject to both a cap and a floor (known as a collar) would also satisfy the contractual cash flow characteristics test for the same reasons.

In many jurisdictions interest rates on loans are capped by law to a multiple of an absolute interest or index rate. Whereas a capped interest rate meets the contractual cash flow characteristic test when the interest reflects the time value of money as discussed above, in some cases the cap is referenced to a multiple of an index rate, so it can be argued that the cap introduces leverage into the instrument. However, it can also be argued that the feature is not intended to introduce leverage into the market but to protect consumers, as a cap it will only reduce interest rates and does not introduce volatility such as exposure to changes in equity prices or commodity prices. IFRS 9 also permits interest rates that are regulated to meet the contractual cash flow characteristic test if the interest rate represents consideration that is broadly consistent with the passage of time. *[IFRS 9.B4.1.9E]*. If the cap is introduced by the regulator to protect consumers by providing an estimate of the fair market interest rate it could be considered to represent consideration for the passage of time (see 6.4.3 below).

6.3.4 Lender has discretion to change the interest rate

In some instances, the lender may have the right to unilaterally adjust the interest rates of its loans in accordance with its own business policy. However, should the borrower disagree with the new rate, it has the right to terminate the contract and prepay the loan at par.

Such a feature does not *per se* result in the loans failing the contractual cash flow characteristic test. However, whether the loan passes the test depends on facts and circumstances which require assessment on a case-by-case basis, specifically whether interest represents considerations for the time value of money, credit risk and other basic lending risk and costs, as well as a profit margin. As such an entity might consider whether the change in interest rate applies to all similar loans, including new loans and the ones in issue, or only to one or certain individual borrowers (this excludes changes in interest rates due to changes in the credit spread of the borrower).

Note that in practice the bank is likely to be restricted as to how much it can increase the interest rate, since if it is too high the borrower will prepay, and the bank is unlikely to remain competitive. However, the lender will still need to assess whether the loan passes the contractual cash flows characteristic test.

6.3.5 Unleveraged inflation-linked bonds

For some financial instruments, payments of principal and interest on the principal amount outstanding are linked to an inflation index of the currency in which the instrument is issued. The inflation link is not leveraged. Linking payments of principal and interest on the principal amount outstanding to an unleveraged inflation index resets the time value of money to a current level. In other words, the interest rate on the instrument reflects 'real' interest. Thus, the interest amounts are consideration for the time value of money on the principal amount outstanding.

We believe measurement at amortised cost is possible even if the principal of an inflation-indexed bond is not protected, provided the inflation link is not leveraged. Payments on both the principal and interest will be inflation-adjusted and representative of 'real' interest which is consideration for the time value of money on the principal amount outstanding. *[IFRS 9.B4.1.13 Instrument A].*

Example 48.16: Unleveraged inflation linked bond

Entity A invests in euro-denominated bonds with a fixed maturity issued by Entity B. Interest on the bond is linked directly to the inflation index of Eurozone Country C, which is Entity B's principal place of business. The question arises whether Entity A can measure the euro bonds at amortised cost or fair value through other comprehensive income given that interest is not linked to the inflation index of the entire Eurozone area.

The bond is denominated in euros and Eurozone Country C is part of the Eurozone, therefore, we consider the inflation link to be acceptable. The inflation index reflects the inflation rate of the currency in which the bond is issued since it is the inflation index of Entity B's economic environment, and the euro is the currency for that economic environment.

By linking the inflation index to the inflation rate of Eurozone Country C, Entity B is reflecting 'real' interest for the economic environment in which it operates. Hence, in these circumstances, Entity A may regard the interest as consideration for the time of value of money and credit risk associated with the principal amount outstanding on the bond.

6.3.6 Features which compensate the lender for changes in tax or other related costs

Some loans include clauses which require the borrower to compensate the lender for changes in tax or regulatory costs during the life of the loan. The interest rate for such loans is usually set at a rate which takes into account the specific tax or regulatory environment, e.g. interest receivable may be exempt from tax and the lender will consequently offer the borrower a below market rate. Any change to the tax laws which affect such an arrangement could result in a loss to the lender as tax could become deductible from interest receivable. The compensation clause is therefore intended to make the lender whole in the event of such a change. As the effect of the clause is to enable the lender to maintain its profit margin it can be considered to be consistent with a normal lending arrangement.

6.4 Contractual features that may affect the classification

Sometimes, contractual provisions may affect the cash flows of an instrument such that they do not give rise to only a straightforward repayment of principal and interest. An entity is required to carefully assess those features in order to conclude whether or not the instrument passes the contractual cash flow characteristics test. It is important to note that the standard grants an exception for all features that are non-genuine or have only a *de minimis* impact and can be disregarded when making the assessment (see 6.4.1 below).

Furthermore, the standard allows the time value of money element of interest to be what is referred to as 'modified' but only when the resulting cash flows could not be significantly different from an instrument that has an unmodified time value of money element (see 6.4.2 below). It also allows regulated interest rates as long as they provide consideration that is broadly consistent with the passage of time and do not introduce risks that are inconsistent with a basic lending arrangement (see 6.4.3 below).

An instrument may have other features that change the timing or amount of contractual cash flows which need to be assessed as to whether they represent payments of principal and interest on the principal outstanding. Examples of such features are variable interest rates, interest rates that step up, prepayment and extension options (see 6.4.4 below).

Lastly, there are features that most likely result in an instrument failing the contractual cash flow characteristics test because they introduce cash flow volatility caused by risks that are inconsistent with a basic lending arrangement (see 6.4.5 below).

6.4.1 De minimis and non-genuine features

A contractual cash flow characteristic does not affect the classification of the financial asset if it could have only a *de minimis* effect on the contractual cash flows of the financial asset.

In addition, if a contractual cash flow characteristic could have an effect on the contractual cash flows that is more than *de minimis* (either in a single reporting period or cumulatively) but that cash flow characteristic is not genuine, it does not affect the classification of a financial asset. A cash flow characteristic is not genuine if it affects the instrument's contractual cash flows only on the occurrence of an event that is extremely rare, highly abnormal and very unlikely to occur. *[IFRS 9.B4.1.18]*.

Although the '*de minimis*' and 'non-genuine' thresholds are a high hurdle, allowing entities to disregard such features can result in more debt instruments qualifying for the amortised cost or fair value through other comprehensive income measurement categories. The terms will need to be interpreted by preparers in analysing the impact of the contractual cash flow characteristics test on the debt instruments they hold.

6.4.1.A De minimis features

The standard does not prescribe whether a qualitative or a quantitative analysis should be performed to determine whether a feature is *de minimis* or not. While *de minimis* is not defined in IFRS 9, one dictionary definition is 'too trivial to merit consideration'. Implicit in this definition is that if an entity has to consider whether an impact is *de minimis*, whether quantitatively or qualitatively, then it probably is not.

The *de minimis* threshold concerns the magnitude of the possible effects of the contractual cash flow characteristic. To be considered *de minimis*, the impact of the feature on the cash flows of the financial asset must be expected to be *de minimis* in each reporting period and cumulatively over the life of the financial asset.

6.4.1.B Non-genuine features

Non-genuine features, as used in this context, are contingent features. A cash flow characteristic is not genuine if it affects the instrument's contractual cash flows only on the occurrence of an event that is extremely rare, highly abnormal and very unlikely to occur. This means, although the feature can potentially lead to cash flows which are not solely payments of principal and interest, and those cash flows may even be significant, the instrument would still qualify for amortised cost or fair value through other comprehensive income measurement, depending on the business model. (See also Chapter 47 at 4.3.1).

In our view, terms are included in a contract for an economic purpose and therefore are, in general, genuine. The threshold 'not genuine' is presumably intended to deal with clauses inserted into the terms of financial instruments for some legal or tax reason but having no real economic purpose or consequence.

An example of a clause that has caused some debate in the context of paragraph AG28 of IAS 32 which uses the term non-genuine is a 'regulatory change' clause, generally found in the terms of capital instruments issued by financial institutions such as banks and insurance companies. Such entities are generally required by local regulators to maintain certain minimum levels of equity or highly subordinated debt (generally referred to as regulatory capital) in order to be allowed to do business.

A 'regulatory change' clause will typically require an instrument which, at the date of issue, is classified as regulatory capital to be repaid in the event that it ceases to be so classified. The practice so far of the regulators in many markets has been to make changes to a regulatory classification with prospective effect only, such that any instruments already in issue continue to be regarded as regulatory capital even though they would not be under the new rules.

This has led some to question whether a 'regulatory change' clause can be regarded as a contingent settlement provision which is 'not genuine'. This is ultimately a matter for the judgement of entities in the context of the relevant regulatory environment(s). This judgement has not been made easier by the greater unpredictability of the markets (and therefore of regulators' responses to it) since the financial crisis. However, as the clause was inserted to provide regulators with flexibility in their actions, even if they do not normally exercise that flexibility, it would be difficult to argue that it is 'non-genuine'.

Disregarding non-genuine features also means that the classification requirements of IFRS 9 cannot be overridden by introducing a contractual non-genuine cash flow characteristic in order to achieve a specific accounting outcome.

6.4.2 Contractual features that modify the consideration for the time value of money

In some cases, the time value of money element may be what the standard describes as 'modified' and so 'imperfect'. It cites, as an example, instances where the tenor of the interest rate does not correspond with the frequency with which it resets. In such cases, an entity must assess the modification to determine whether the contractual cash flows represent solely payments of principal and interest on the principal outstanding.

In assessing whether or not any modification to the time value of money is consistent with the SPPI test, entities need to apply their own judgement. The IASB staff paper for a Board meeting in September 2013[2] when the standard was being finalised, discussed this topic extensively. Useful points that come from this discussion which entities could consider in their assessment are the following:

- Whether rates that are determined by averaging observed rates for a particular period, or rates that are set by referencing a recent historical interest rate, as well as interest rate tenor mismatch features, could be considered to only provide consideration for the passage of time for a particular currency or whether the instrument has been structured to provide something more than just the consideration for the passage of time;[3]
- Whether the rate used is normal for the particular market (for the relevant duration and currency) in which the transaction occurs, noting however, that judgement is involved in assessing whether the stated time value component of the interest rate provides compensation for just the passage of time;[4] and
- Whether any modification to the time value of money element, has a meaningful fair value (i.e. whether the feature results in the premium or discount to the contractually stated notional amount – if it does, that would indicate consideration for other risks than just the passage of time).[5]

In some circumstances, the entity may be able to make that determination by performing a qualitative assessment whereas, in other circumstances, it may be necessary to perform a quantitative analysis. *[IFRS 9.B4.1.9B]*. The objective of a quantitative assessment is to determine whether or not the contractual (undiscounted) cash flows could be significantly different from the (undiscounted) cash flows that would arise if the time value of money element was not modified (referred to as 'the benchmark' cash flows).

For example, if the financial asset under assessment contains a variable interest rate that is reset every month to a one-year interest rate, the entity compares that financial asset to a financial instrument with identical contractual terms and credit risk, except the variable interest rate is reset monthly to a one-month interest rate. If the modified time value of money element could result in contractual (undiscounted) cash flows that are significantly different from the (undiscounted) benchmark cash flows, the financial asset fails the contractual cash flow characteristics test. To make this determination, the entity must consider the effect of the modified time value of money element in each reporting period and cumulatively over the life of the financial instrument. The reason for the interest rate being set this way is not relevant to the analysis. If it is clear, with little or no analysis, whether the contractual (undiscounted) cash flows on the financial asset under the assessment could (or could not) be significantly different from the (undiscounted) benchmark cash flows, an entity need not perform a detailed assessment. *[IFRS 9.B4.1.9C]*. 'Significantly different' is not defined in IFRS 9 and is a matter for management judgement.

The following table lists examples of modifications of the consideration for the time value of money which possibly meet the contractual cash flow characteristics test, depending on the outcome of the assessment described above.

Example 48.17: Examples of a modified time value of money component

	Modification	Fact pattern
1	Average interest rate	The stated coupon on a debt instrument is referenced to an average of long and short term benchmark interest rates for a specified period. For example, 3-month Euribor rate determined as an average of six-month and one-month rates during the previous quarter.
2	Lagging interest rate	The stated interest rate is referenced to lagging interest rates. For example, 6-month Euribor rate set for a 6 month period, but where the rate is fixed 2 months before the start of the interest period.
3	Tenor mismatch	The stated interest rate is reset to a reference interest rate, but the frequency of reset does not match the tenor of the reference rate. For example, the interest rate on a retail mortgage is reset semi-annually based on three-month Libor.
4	Combination of the above	The stated interest rate is reset monthly to an average 12-month reference rate. The interest rate is fixed based on the average 12-month rate for every working day in the month before the start of the interest period.

In October 2019[6] the IASB considered whether, as part of IBOR reform, where IBORs are replaced with backward-looking term rates (such as a rate for the next six months based on the average overnight rate for the previous six months), would this cause instruments to fail the SPPI assessment. The IASB noted that there are no specific conditions or exceptions that would automatically disqualify contractual cash flows to be SPPI. The focus on any assessment of interest should be on what the entity is being compensated for (i.e. whether the entity is receiving consideration for basic lending risks, costs and a profit margin). The IASB concluded that the current guidance in IFRS 9 provides an adequate basis to determine whether alternative benchmark rates meet SPPI and that, provided the interest rate continues to reflect the time value of money and does not reflect other risks and features, the new instrument should pass the SPPI assessment. Entities will therefore need to apply judgement in assessing whether there are any modifications to the time value of money element in replacement benchmark rates and if there are, whether these modifications will pass the SPPI test.

An example of a replacement risk free rate is SONIA ('Sterling Over Night Indexed Average') which is replacing LIBOR as the risk-free rate for sterling loans. SONIA is backward-looking, whilst LIBOR is forward-looking. Daily SONIA rates are compounded over a particular interest payment period to determine a rate for that period. The interest to be paid, is therefore only known at the end of the interest period. To facilitate timely payment of interest, it is useful for borrowers to know in advance what amount of interest is required to be paid. Therefore, the interest is determined based on a period starting and ending five working days prior to the beginning and end of the interest payment period. In this instance, an entity may be able to assess from a qualitative perspective that there is no significant modification to the time value of money.

Time value of money does not include credit risk, so it is important to exclude it from the assessment. The standard suggests this is done by comparing the instrument with a benchmark instrument with the same credit risk, but presumably the comparison could be against an instrument with a different credit risk, as long as the effect of the difference can be excluded. *[IFRS 9.B4.1.9C]*.

When assessing a modified time value of money element, an entity must consider factors that could affect future contractual cash flows. In making the assessment, it must consider every interest rate scenario that is reasonably possible instead of every scenario that could possibly arise. This requirement is illustrated in Example 48.19 below.

If an entity concludes that the contractual (undiscounted) cash flows could be significantly different from the (undiscounted) benchmark cash flows, the financial asset does not pass the contractual cash flow characteristics test and therefore cannot be measured at amortised cost or fair value through other comprehensive income. *[IFRS 9.B4.1.9D]*.

The following examples illustrate instruments with a modified time value of money element and how the benchmark test is applied to them.

Example 48.18: Interest rate period selected at the discretion of the borrower

An entity holds an instrument that is a variable interest rate instrument with a stated maturity date that permits the borrower to choose the market interest rate on an ongoing basis. For example, at each interest rate reset date, the borrower can choose to pay three-month LIBOR for a three-month term or one-month LIBOR for a one-month term.

The contractual cash flows are solely payments of principal and interest on the principal amount outstanding as long as the interest paid over the life of the instrument reflects consideration for basic lending risks and costs as well as a profit margin. Basic lending risks and costs include consideration for the time value of money, for the credit risk associated with the instrument and for other basic lending risks and costs. The fact that the LIBOR interest rate is reset during the life of the instrument does not in itself disqualify the instrument.

However, if the borrower is able to choose to pay a one-month interest rate that is reset every three months, the interest rate is reset with a frequency that does not match the tenor of the interest rate. Therefore, the time value of money element is modified. That is because the interest payable in each period is disconnected from the interest period.

In such cases, the entity must qualitatively or quantitatively assess the contractual cash flows against the cash flows of a benchmark instrument to determine whether the mismatch between the two sets of cash flows could be significantly different. The benchmark instrument is identical in all respects except that the tenor of the interest rate matches the interest period. If the analysis results in the conclusion that the two sets of cash flows could be significantly different, payments would not represent principal and interest on the principal amount outstanding.

The same analysis would apply if the borrower is able to choose between the lender's various published interest rates (e.g. the borrower can choose between the lender's published one-month variable interest rate and the lender's published three-month variable interest rate). *[IFRS 9.B4.1.13 Instrument B]*.

Example 48.19: Five-year constant maturity bond

Some bonds pay what is called a constant maturity interest rate. For example, an instrument with an original five-year maturity may pay a variable rate that is reset semi-annually but always reflects a five-year rate. In such cases, the time value of money element is modified. The entity must determine whether the instrument's cash flows could be significantly different from those on a bond with a similar maturity, credit risk and interest rate reset frequency, but that that pays a semi-annual rate of interest.

In making this assessment, the entity cannot conclude that the contractual cash flows are solely payments of principal and interest on the principal amount outstanding, simply because the interest rate curve at the time of the assessment is such that the difference between a five-year interest rate and a semi-annual interest rate is not significant. Rather, the entity must also consider whether the relationship between the five-year interest rate and the semi-annual interest rate could change over the life of the instrument such that the contractual (undiscounted) cash flows over the life of the instrument could be significantly different from the (undiscounted) benchmark cash flows. *[IFRS 9.B4.1.9D].*

In this example, if the entity considers future developments, it is unlikely that it can conclude that the contractual cash flows could not be significantly different from the benchmark cash flows, considering the magnitude of the mismatch between the interest rate tenor and reset frequency. The bond will always pay a five-year rate even though, except at the outset, this exceeds the instrument's remaining life. Therefore, the instrument is not likely to meet the SPPI test.

6.4.3 Regulated interest rates

In some jurisdictions, the government or a regulatory authority sets interest rates. For example, such government regulation of interest rates may be part of a broad macroeconomic policy or it may be introduced to encourage entities to invest in a particular sector of the economy. In some of these cases, the objective of the time value of money element is not to provide consideration for only the passage of time. However, the Board notes that the rates are set for public policy reasons and thus are not subject to structuring to achieve a particular accounting result. *[IFRS 9.BC4.180].* Consequently, as a concession, a regulated interest rate is considered by the IASB to serve as a proxy for the time value of money element for the purpose of applying the contractual cash flow characteristics test if that regulated interest rate:

- provides consideration that is broadly consistent with the passage of time; and
- does not provide exposure to risks or volatility in the contractual cash flows that are inconsistent with a basic lending arrangement. *[IFRS 9.B4.1.9E].*

As the standard does not establish criteria to determine whether a regulated rate provides consideration that is 'broadly consistent' with the passage of time, this is an area which clearly requires judgement based on the facts and circumstances. However, in the Basis for Conclusions, the board implies that the particular instrument described in the following example would satisfy the two criteria above.

Example 48.20: Regulated interest rates – 'Livret A'

In France the interest rate on 'Livret A' savings products issued by retail banks is determined by the central bank and the government according to a formula that reflects protection against inflation and an adequate remuneration to provide incentive for investment. The legislation requires a particular portion of the amounts collected by the retail banks to be lent to a governmental agency that uses the proceeds for social programmes. The IASB noted that the time value element of interest on these accounts may not provide consideration for only the passage of time; however, the IASB believes that amortised cost would provide relevant and useful information as long as the contractual cash flows do not introduce risks or volatility that are inconsistent with a basic lending arrangement. *[IFRS 9.BC4.180].*

6.4.4 Other contractual features that change the timing or amount of contractual cash flows

Some financial assets contain contractual provisions that change the timing or amount of contractual cash flows. For example, the asset may be prepaid before maturity or its term may be extended. In such cases, the entity must determine whether the contractual cash flows that could arise over the life of the instrument due to those contractual provisions are solely payments of principal and interest on the principal amount outstanding.

To make this determination, the entity must assess the contractual cash flows that could arise both before, and after, the change in contractual cash flows. The entity may also need to assess the nature of any contingent event (i.e. the trigger) that would change the timing or amount of contractual cash flows. While the nature of the contingent event in itself is not a determinative factor in assessing whether the contractual cash flows are solely payments of principal and interest, it may be an indicator.

For example, compare a financial instrument with an interest rate that is reset to a higher rate if the debtor misses a particular number of payments to a financial instrument with an interest rate that is reset to a higher rate if a specified equity index reaches a particular level. It is more likely in the former case that the contractual cash flows over the life of the instrument will be solely payments of principal and interest on the principal amount outstanding, because of the relationship between missed payments and an increase in credit risk. In contrast, in the latter case, the contingent event introduces equity price risk which is not a basic lending risk. *[IFRS 9.B4.1.10]*.

The following are examples of contractual terms that result in contractual cash flows that are solely payments of principal and interest on the principal amount outstanding: *[IFRS 9.B4.1.11]*

(a) a variable interest rate that is consideration for the time value of money and for the credit risk associated with the principal amount outstanding during a particular period of time (the consideration for credit risk may be determined at initial recognition only, and so may be fixed) and other basic lending risks and costs, as well as a profit margin (which are also likely to be fixed);

(b) a contractual term that permits the issuer (i.e. the debtor) to prepay a debt instrument or permits the holder (i.e. the creditor) to put a debt instrument back to the issuer before maturity and the prepayment amount substantially represents unpaid amounts of principal and interest on the principal amount outstanding, which may include reasonable additional compensation for the early termination of the contract; and

(c) a contractual term that permits the issuer or holder to extend the contractual term of a debt instrument (i.e. an extension option) and the terms of the extension option result in contractual cash flows during the extension period that are solely payments of principal and interest on the principal amount outstanding, which may include reasonable additional compensation for the extension of the contract.

Unfortunately, neither the standard itself nor the Basis for Conclusions specify what the IASB meant by 'reasonable additional compensation', although it seems clear that the IASB regards compensation to mean a payment by the party exercising the prepayment option to the other party. It also seems appropriate to include as reasonable additional compensation direct or indirect costs attributable to early termination or extension, ranging from costs for the additional paperwork to costs for adjusting a bank's hedging relationships. Penalties, imposed by the lender on the borrower with the aim of reducing the lender's interest rate risk and discouraging the borrower from prepaying the debt, could also, in certain circumstances, be considered to be reasonable additional compensation. This would be dependent on facts and circumstances such as whether the penalty clause was genuine and the expectation of whether the penalty would be triggered. If the borrower is not expected to exercise the prepayment option except in extremely rare or highly abnormal situations that are very unlikely to occur, then the penalty feature would not be genuine and the asset would pass the SPPI test. *[IFRS 9.B4.1.18]*.

6.4.4.A   Prepayment – negative compensation

A financial asset can still meet the SPPI condition and be eligible for classification at amortised cost even if the contractual prepayment amount is more or less than the unpaid amounts of the principal and interest. This is because IFRS 9 contemplates either the borrower or the lender terminating the contract early. If the borrower terminates the loan early, the borrower may have to compensate the lender and the prepayment amount might be more than the unpaid amount of principal and interest. If the lender terminates the loan early, then the lender may need to compensate the borrower and so, in this case, the prepayment amount might be less than the unpaid amounts of principal and interest. In other words, with these asymmetrical break clauses, depending upon which party terminates the contract early, 'reasonable additional compensation' can include a prepayment amount which is more or less than the unpaid amounts of principal and interest.

But this is not the case with a symmetrical break clause which results in the party triggering early termination of the loan receiving rather than paying compensation ('negative compensation'). This could occur if the current market interest rate is higher than the effective interest rate of the debt instrument. In that case, with a symmetrical break clause, a prepayment by the borrower will be less than the unpaid amounts of principal and interest and therefore lead to the lender effectively compensating the borrower for the increase in interest rates even if the borrower chooses to prepay the debt instrument. As set out in the version of IFRS 9 originally issued in July 2014, such a feature would fail the SPPI test and result in the instrument being measured at fair value through profit and loss.

In October 2017, the IASB issued a narrow scope amendment to IFRS 9 to address this issue. The amendment clarified that a financial asset with a symmetrical prepayment option can be measured at amortised cost or fair value through other comprehensive income. A financial asset meets the contractual cash flow requirements if a contractual term permits (or requires) the issuer to prepay, or the holder to put back to the issuer, a debt instrument before maturity and the prepayment amount substantially represents unpaid amounts of principal and interest on the principal amount outstanding including reasonable compensation for the early termination of the contract, which irrespective of the event or circumstance that causes the early termination of the contract, may be paid or received. For example, a party may pay or receive reasonable compensation when it chooses to terminate the contract early or otherwise causes the early termination to occur. *[IFRS 9.B4.1.12A]*.

This condition ensures that the amendment only captures those financial assets that would otherwise have contractual cash flows that are solely payments of principal and interest but do not meet that criterion solely because a prepayment feature may give rise to negative compensation.

The IASB noted that compensation that reflects the effect of the change in the relevant market interest rate (e.g. interest lost as a result of early terminating the contract) did not introduce any contractual cash flows that were different from cash flows which were already accomodated by the existing exemption for prepayments which contain positive compensation. *[IFRS 9.BC4.225]*.

The IASB also noted that some financial assets are prepayable at their current fair value and others are prepayable at an amount that includes the fair value cost to terminate an associated hedging instrument. The IASB acknowledged that there may be circumstances in which such features meet the contractual cash flow requirements. It provided, as an example, the case when the calculation of the prepayment amount is intended to approximate to unpaid amounts of principal and interest plus or minus an amount that reflects the effect of the change in a relevant benchmark interest rate. However the IASB also noted that this will not always be the case. *[IFRS 9.BC4.232]*. Therefore, an entity will have to assess the specific contractual cash flows for such instruments rather than automatically assuming that they will meet the contractual cash flow requirements.

The narrow scope amendment only applies to situations where the compensation is symmetrical and the signage is negative. Prepayments that include cash flows that reflect changes in an equity or commodity index will not meet this requirement.

The amendment was effective for annual periods beginning on or after 1 January 2019.

USB Group AG, in its 2018 interim consolidated financial statements, considered the classification of instruments with two-way compensation clauses.

Extract 48.1: UBS Group AG (2019)

Notes to the UBS Group AG consolidated financial statements [extract]

1   Summary of significant accounting policies [extract]

Contractual cash flow characteristics

In assessing whether the contractual cash flows are SPPI, the Group considers whether the contractual terms of the financial asset contain a term that could change the timing or amount of contractual cash flows arising over the life of the instrument, which could affect whether the instrument is considered to meet the SPPI criterion.

For example, the Group holds portfolios of private mortgage contracts and corporate loans in Personal & Corporate Banking that commonly contain clauses that provide for two-way compensation if prepayment occurs. The amount of compensation paid by or to UBS reflects the effect of changes in market interest rates. The Group has determined that the inclusion of the change in market interest rates in the compensation amount is reasonable for the early termination of the contract, and therefore results in contractual cash flows that are SPPI.

The IASB issued a webcast in June 2018, clarifying that a prepayment feature must be analysed to determine whether it gives rise to contractual cash flows that meet the contractual cashflows characteristics test, rather than relying on:

- how the feature is labelled;
- whether it is likely to be triggered; or
- whether it reflects market practice.

It also confirmed that in order to be eligible to be measured at amortised cost or fair value through other comprehensive income, a prepayable financial asset must meet the criteria outlined above or all the conditions relating to assets originated at a premium or discount described in 6.4.4.B below.

6.4.4.B Prepayment – assets originated at a premium or discount

The strict application of the definition of principal in 6.1 above would mean that debt instruments originated or acquired at a premium or discount, and which are prepayable at par, have to be measured at fair value through profit or loss. This is because, if the issuer prepays, the holder may receive a gain that is less than or in excess of a basic lending return. The IASB, however, decided to provide a narrow scope exception. Financial assets originated or acquired at a premium or discount that would otherwise have cash flows that are principal and interest, except for the effect of a prepayment option, are deemed to meet the above conditions, but only so long as:

(a) the prepayment amount substantially represents the contractual par amount and accrued (but unpaid) interest, which may include reasonable additional compensation for the early termination of the contract; and

(b) the fair value of the prepayment feature on initial recognition of the financial asset is insignificant. *[IFRS 9.B4.1.12]*.

As a result of the amendment for prepayments with negative compensation, discussed above, the IASB also amended the criteria for a) to clarify that reasonable compensation includes compensation paid or received for the early termination of a contract. *[IFRS 9.B4.1.12A]*. The amendment was effective for periods beginning on or after 1 January 2019.

The conditions described above apply regardless of whether (i) the prepayment provision is exercisable by the issuer or by the holder; (ii) the prepayment provision is voluntary or mandatory; or (iii) the prepayment feature is contingent.

This exception would allow some financial assets that otherwise do not have contractual cash flows that are solely payments of principal and interest to be measured at amortised cost or fair value through other comprehensive income (subject to the assessment of the business model in which they are held). In particular, the IASB observed that this exception will apply to many purchased credit-impaired financial assets with contractual prepayment features. If such an asset was purchased at a deep discount, the contractual cash flows would not be solely payments of principal and interest if, contractually, the asset could be repaid immediately at the par amount. However, that contractual prepayment feature would have an insignificant fair value if it is very unlikely that prepayment will occur. *[IFRS 9.BC4.193]*. Prepayment might be very unlikely because the debtor of a credit-impaired financial asset might not have the ability to prepay the financial asset.

Similarly, the IASB observed that this exception will apply to some prepayable financial assets that are originated at below-market interest rates. For example, this scenario may arise when an entity sells an item (for example, an automobile) and, as a marketing incentive, provides financing to the customer at an interest rate that is below the prevailing market rate. At initial recognition the entity would measure the financial asset at fair value and, as a result of the below-market interest rate, the fair value would be at a discount to the contractual par amount. The IASB observed that in that case a contractual prepayment feature would likely have an insignificant fair value because it is unlikely that the customer will choose to prepay; in particular, because the interest rate is below-market and thus the financing is advantageous. *[IFRS 9.BC4.194]*.

For instruments that are initially recognised at a discount, the fair value of the prepayment option will usually be insignificant, because the discount is a function of either an increased credit risk of the borrower (as in the first example above) or a below-market interest rate (as in the second example), and in each case the prepayment option is unlikely to be exercised and so will have little fair value.

For instruments that are initially recognised at a premium, because the coupon rate is above the current market rate, the application of this guidance is more difficult. While the prepayment option will likely have a more than insignificant fair value, this will usually also be reflected in the fair value at which the asset is acquired. For instance, an investor is unlikely to pay above par for a bond that pays an above market rate of interest if it can be prepaid at par at any time. It would seem that in order for the prepayment option to be relevant for the asset's classification, it would need to be constrained. The expectation would be that the borrower will exercise the option at the earliest opportunity as it will be in the economic interest of the borrower to do so. An example would be a bond that pays an above market rate of interest, with a remaining maturity of five years that can be prepaid but only after three years. Hence the bond will have an initial fair value greater than par due to the above market rate for the first three years, but will amortise to par after three years as the borrower is highly likely to exercise the prepayment option after three years. Consequently, the prepayment amount will substantially represent unpaid amounts of principal and interest on the principal amount outstanding at the point the option is exercised and will therefore pass the SPPI test. *[IFRS 9.B4.1.11(b)]*. This assessment will be performed only when the asset is first recognised. For example:

Example 48.21: Prepayable corporate loan recognised at a premium to par

Bank A buys a loan with a notional amount of £10m from another bank for £11m. The loan is to a corporate and has ten years remaining to maturity and the issuer has the right to prepay the loan at par in five years' time. The loan is acquired at a premium as interest rates have fallen significantly since the loan was first advanced.

Bank A believes that exercise of the prepayment option will be beneficial to the corporate issuer and that the borrower is highly likely to exercise the option. It therefore concludes that the premium on the loan should be amortised over the following five years and not over the full remaining contractual term of ten years. It further concludes that when the prepayment option is exercised it will substantially represent unpaid amounts of principal and interest on the principal amount outstanding and consequently classifies the loan as an amortised cost instrument.

However, it is possible that the borrower may not exercise the option even if it is beneficial to do so and this makes the assessment more complicated. If there is uncertainty over whether the prepayment option will be exercised, then the SPPI test may not be met and neither classification as amortised cost nor fair value through other comprehensive income can be applied unless the fair value of the prepayment amount is insignificant. *[IFRS 9.B4.1.12(c)]*.

This is particularly likely to be an issue with retail loans as, collectively, retail borrowers can act irrationally and not in accordance with their own best economic interests. Such behavioural factors are likely to force any entity acquiring a portfolio of retail loans at a premium to have to assess whether the fair value of the prepayment feature is insignificant or not. In practice this will probably mean that the entity will need to compare the fair value of the retail loans with the fair value of similar hypothetical instruments without the prepayment option and determine whether the difference is insignificant or not. If the difference is deemed to be significant then the portfolio would need to be classified as debt instruments at fair value through profit and loss. In contrast, an instrument which is prepayable at fair value does not fall under the exception stated above (see discussion at 6.4.4.A above).

The following examples illustrate further instruments with contractual features that modify the timing and amount of contractual cash flows such that the instruments pass the contractual cash flow characteristics test. Some examples include possible changes to the fact pattern which may change that assessment.

Example 48.22: Debt covenants

A loan agreement contains a covenant whereby the contractual spread above the benchmark rate will increase if the borrower's earnings before interest, tax, depreciation and amortisation (EBITDA) or its debt-to-equity ratio deteriorate by a specified amount by a specified date.

Whether this instrument passes the contractual cash flow characteristics test depends on the specific terms. The loan would pass the contractual cash flow characteristics test if the covenant serves to compensate the lender for taking on higher credit or liquidity risks.

However, if the covenant results in more than just credit or liquidity protection, or provides for an increase in the rate of return which is not considered appropriate under a basic lending arrangement, the instrument will fail the test. For example, an increase in interest rate to reflect an increase in EBITDA would not satisfy the criteria.

Example 48.23: Auction Rate Securities (ARSs)

ARSs have long-term maturity dates, but their interest rate resets more frequently based on the outcome of an auction. As a result of the auction process, the interest rates are short-term and the instruments are treated like short-term investments.

In the event that an auction fails (i.e. there are insufficient buyers of the bond to establish a new rate), the rate resets to a penalty rate. The penalty rate is established at inception and does not necessarily reflect the market rate when the auction fails. It is often intended to compensate the holder for the instrument's lack of liquidity as demonstrated by the auction failure. The auction process for many such securities failed during the financial crisis.

The classification at initial recognition should be based on the contractual terms over the life of the instrument. Although the presumption on acquisition may have been that the auctions were not expected to fail, the potential penalty rate should still be taken into account in the assessment of the instrument's characteristics at initial recognition. If the penalty rate could be considered to compensate the holder for the longer-term credit risk of the instrument following the auction failure as a result of a reduction in market liquidity, it may be possible that the penalty rate reflects interest. However, as such instruments usually have multiple issues with different penalty rates, each different case would need to be carefully evaluated before a conclusion could be reached.

6.4.5 Contractual features that normally do not represent payments of principal and interest

In some cases, financial assets may have contractual cash flows that are not solely payments of principal and interest. *[IFRS 9.B4.1.14]*. Unless such a feature is *de minimis* or non-genuine, the instrument would fail the contractual cash flow characteristics test. *[IFRS 9.B4.1.18]*. Examples of such instruments with contractual cash flows that may not represent solely payments of principal and interest include instruments subject to leverage and instruments that represent investments in particular assets or cash flows.

Leverage is a contractual cash flow characteristic of some financial assets. It increases the variability of the contractual cash flows with the result that they do not have the economic characteristics of just principal and interest. Stand-alone option, forward and swap contracts are examples of financial assets that include such leverage. Thus, such contracts fail the contractual cash flow characteristics test and cannot be measured at amortised cost or fair value through other comprehensive income. *[IFRS 9.B4.1.9].*

However, a variable rate asset at a deep discount will not normally fail the contractual cash flow characteristics test. When the IASB deliberated the meaning of principal in September 2013 they did not distinguish between fixed and variable rate assets and do not seem to have intended a variable rate plain vanilla instrument to fail the contractual cash flow characteristics test. Moreover, a variable rate asset which is acquired or originated at a deep discount will normally be a purchased or originated credit impaired asset. As such, the effective interest rate used will be the credit-adjusted effective interest rate. In these cases, the borrower will usually be unable to pay any increases in rates and any decrease in rates would result in the borrower repaying more principal. Either way, the loan is essentially fixed rate and, therefore not leveraged, so will not fail the contractual cash flow characteristic test.

Example 48.24: Dual currency instruments

For some financial assets the interest payments are denominated in a currency that is different from the principal of the financial asset. IFRS 9 requires the assessment of 'whether contractual cash flows are solely payments of principal and interest on the principal outstanding for the currency in which the financial asset is denominated'. *[IFRS 9.B4.1.8].*

This implies that any instrument in which interest is calculated based on a principal amount other than that payable on maturity will not pass the contractual cash flow characteristics test. For instance, if variable interest payments are computed based on a fixed principal amount in another currency, e.g. US dollars, although repayment of the principal is in sterling, the financial asset is not considered to have cash flows that are solely payments of principal and interest.

However, there may be instances where interest is denominated in a currency that is different from the principal currency, but the contractual cash flows could possibly constitute solely payments of principal and interest. For example, the principal amount of the bond is denominated (and redeemed at a fixed maturity) in Canadian dollars (CAD). Interest payments are fixed in Indian Rupees (INR) at inception based on the market interest rates and foreign exchange spot and forward rates at that time.

While not explicit in the standard, in our view, if the bond can be separated into two components that, on their own, would meet the contractual cash flow characteristics test, then the combined instrument would do so. That is, if the bond can be viewed as the combination of a zero-coupon bond denominated in CAD and a stream of fixed payments denominated in INR, and if both instruments can be analysed as a stream of cash flows that are solely payments of principal and interest, then the sum of the two would do so as well.

The defining criterion is the fact that the interest payments have been fixed at inception and there is no exposure to changes in cash flows in the currency of denomination of the cash flows.

In September 2018 the Interpretations Committee was asked whether an instrument with the features described in Example 48.24 above met the SPPI test. The Committee observed that the financial instrument described was not common and consequently decided not to add this matter to its standard-setting agenda.[7]

Example 48.25: Convertible debt

An entity holds a bond that is convertible into equity instruments of the issuer.

The holder would analyse the convertible bond in its entirety, since IFRS 9 does not separate embedded derivatives from financial assets.

The contractual cash flows are not payments of principal and interest on the principal amount outstanding because they reflect a return that is inconsistent with a basic lending arrangement (see 6 above) i.e. the return is also linked to the value of the equity of the issuer. *[IFRS 9.B4.1.14 Instrument F]*.

The assessment would change if the issuer were to use its own shares as 'currency'. That is, if the bond is convertible into a variable number of shares with a fair value equal to unpaid amounts of principal and interest on the principal amount outstanding. In this case, the bond might satisfy the contractual cash flow characteristics test and would be derecognised on conversion. However, such conversion features are often capped because, otherwise, the issuer could be required to deliver a potentially unlimited number of shares. The existence of such a cap, if genuine, would result in the failure of the test. Additionally, the use of a volume weighted average price approach to calculating the fair value of the shares at the conversion date could also result in the failure of the test.

Example 48.26: Inverse floater

An entity holds a loan that pays an inverse floating interest rate (i.e. the interest rate has an inverse relationship to market interest rates, such as 6% minus 2 times LIBOR).

The contractual cash flows are not solely payments of principal and interest on the principal amount outstanding because an inverse floating rate does not represent consideration for the time value of money. *[IFRS 9.B4.1.14 Instrument G]*.

Example 48.27: Perpetual instruments with potentially deferrable coupons

An entity holds a perpetual instrument, but the issuer may call the instrument at any time, paying the holder the par amount plus accrued interest due.

The instrument pays interest but payment of interest cannot be made unless the issuer is able to remain solvent immediately afterwards. There are two scenarios.

Scenario a) interest is accrued on the deferred amounts.

The contractual cash flows could be payments of principal and interest on the principal amount outstanding.

An example in the standard states that the fact that the instrument is perpetual does not in itself mean that the contractual cash flows are not payments of principal and interest on the principal amount outstanding. In effect, a perpetual instrument has continuous (multiple) extension options. Such options may result in contractual cash flows that are payments of principal and interest on the principal amount outstanding if interest payments are mandatory and must be paid in perpetuity.

Some may find it strange that the instrument is deemed to satisfy the contractual cash flow characteristics test even though the principal will never actually be paid. Also, the fact that the instrument is callable does not mean that the contractual cash flows are not payments of principal and interest on the principal amount outstanding, unless it is callable at an amount that does not substantially reflect payment of outstanding principal and interest on that principal amount outstanding. Even if the callable amount includes an amount that reasonably compensates the holder for the early termination of the instrument, the contractual cash flows could be payments of principal and interest on the principal amount outstanding. (See 6.4.4 above).

Scenario b) deferred interest does not accrue additional interest.

The contractual cash flows are not payments of principal and interest on the principal amount outstanding. This is because the issuer may be required to defer interest payments and additional interest does not accrue on those deferred interest amounts. As a result, interest amounts are not consideration for the time value of money on the principal amount outstanding.

Note that, in this example, the holder is not entitled to assess whether it is probable that interest may ever be deferred. As long as the feature is genuine, the deferral of interest must be taken into account in assessing whether interest amounts are consideration for the time value of money on the principal outstanding. *[IFRS 9.B4.1.14 Instrument H]*.

Example 48.28: Write-down or conversion imposed by regulator

Scenario a) the provision is not a contractual feature

A regulated bank issues an instrument with a stated maturity date. The instrument pays a fixed interest rate and all contractual cash flows are non-discretionary.

However, the issuer is subject to legislation that permits or requires a national resolution authority to impose losses on holders of particular instruments, including the above-mentioned instrument, in particular circumstances. For example, the national resolution authority has the power to write down the par amount of such an instrument or to convert it into a fixed number of the issuer's ordinary shares if the national resolution authority determines that the issuer is having severe financial difficulties, needs additional regulatory capital or is failing.

The holder would analyse the contractual terms of the financial instrument to determine whether they give rise to cash flows that are solely payments of principal and interest on the principal amount outstanding and thus are consistent with a basic lending arrangement.

According to the standard, this analysis would not consider the write-down or conversion that arise only as a result of the national resolution authority's power under statutory law to impose losses on the holders of such an instrument. That is because that power is not a contractual term of the financial instrument.

Although this example makes use of a principle that is widely applied, we note that it is not consistent with the position taken in IFRIC 2 – *Members' Shares in Co-operative Entities and Similar Instruments*, which requires an entity to include 'relevant local laws, regulations and the entity's governing charter in effect at the date of classification' when classifying a financial instrument as a liability or equity However, it should be noted that in the IASB Discussion Paper on Financial Instruments with Characteristics of Equity (see Chapter 47 at 4.6.6), the authors noted that IFRIC 2 was developed for a very specific fact pattern and that they did not believe that the analysis in IFRIC 2 should be applied more broadly.

Scenario b) the provision is a contractual feature

The contractual terms of the financial instrument permit or require the issuer or another entity to impose losses on the holder (e.g. by writing down the par amount or by converting the instrument into a fixed number of the issuer's ordinary shares), if the issuer fails to meet particular regulatory capital requirements (a non-viability event).

Provided the 'non-viability' provision is genuine, which will normally be the case, the instrument will fail the contractual cash flow characteristics test even if the probability is remote that such a loss will be imposed. *[IFRS 9.B4.1.13 Instrument E].*

Note that payments that arise as a result of a regulator's statutory power and that are either only referenced or not mentioned in the contractual terms of the instrument are not considered in the analysis of the contractual payment features of the instrument. However, where such features are specified in the contract, they clearly need to be considered in such an analysis. This typically can happen where such an instrument is entered into by entities within the same group as a way of providing a mechanism for recapitalising subsidiaries and passing losses up within the group to the ultimate shareholders. Where a regulator does not have the statutory power to enforce the terms of instruments entered into between entities within the same group, the regulator will usually require the conversion/write down features to be included in the contractual terms. This can result in such contracts failing the SPPI test.

Example 48.29: Multiple of a benchmark interest rate

An entity holds an instrument for which the interest rate is quoted as a multiple of a benchmark interest rate (e.g. 2 times 3-month EURIBOR for a 3-month term).

Such features introduce leverage and the standard is explicit that leverage increases the variability of the contractual cash flows, resulting in them not having the economic characteristics of interest. As a result, such instruments would need to be measured at fair value through profit or loss. *[IFRS 9.B4.1.9].*

Example 48.30: Fixed rate bond prepayable by the issuer at fair value

A company acquires a bond which requires the issuer to pay a fixed rate of interest and repay the principal on a fixed date. However, the issuer has the right to prepay (or call) the bond before maturity, although the amount the issuer must pay is the fair value of the bond at the time of prepayment, i.e. the fair value of the contractual interest and principal payments that remain outstanding at the point of exercise. For example, if the bond has a term of five years and the call option is exercised at the end of the second year, the fair value would be calculated by discounting the principal and interest payments due over the remaining three years at the current market interest rate for a three-year bond with similar characteristics.

The exercise price represents the fair value of unpaid amounts of principal and interest on the principal amount outstanding at the date of exercise, albeit discounted at the current market interest rate rather than the original market interest rate.

The fact that the exercise price is the fair value could be interpreted as providing reasonable additional compensation to the holder for early termination in a scenario, although this holds true only where the market rate has fallen since the issue of the bond. If interest rates rise, the holder will not receive additional compensation for early termination and will receive less than the principal amount. In these circumstances, due to the negative compensation, the bond holder would not be receiving principal and interest, however prepayments with negative compensation can meet the contractual cash flows characteristics test (see 6.4.4.A above).

Example 48.31: Investment in open-ended money market or debt funds

In an open-ended fund, new investors are accepted by the fund after inception and existing investors have the option of leaving the fund at any time. The price at which new entrants invest in the fund or leavers exit the fund is normally based on the fair value of the fund's assets. Given that investors enter and exit the fund at a price based on fair value, the cash flows of an investment in such a fund are not solely payments of principal and interest.

In addition, such investments would not normally qualify for the option for equity instruments, to present gains and losses in other comprehensive income, as they do not normally meet the definition of an equity instrument from the perspective of the fund (i.e. the issuer). See also 8 below.

Example 48.32: Interest payments indexed to an equity index or the debtor's performance

If interest payments were indexed to a variable such as an equity index, the contractual cash flows are not payments of principal and interest on the principal amount outstanding. Payments indexed to the debtor's performance (e.g. the debtor's net income) would not pass the contractual cash flows characteristics test, unless it can be demonstrated that the indexing to the debtor's performance results in an adjustment that only compensates the holder for changes in the credit risk of the instrument. That is because the contractual cash flows would otherwise reflect a return that is inconsistent with a basic lending arrangement (see 6 above). *[IFRS 9.B4.1.13 Instrument A].*

6.4.6 Loan commitments

Where a loan commitment is granted long periods may elapse before the commitment is drawn down. The question therefore arises as to whether the drawdown of loans under an irrevocable loan commitment should be assessed for classification based on when the loan commitment came into being or when the loan was actually drawn down.

IFRS 9 requires that an entity shall recognise a financial asset in its statement of financial position when the entity becomes party to the contractual provisions of the instrument. When an entity first recognises a financial asset, it shall classify it in accordance with IFRS 9. *[IFRS 9.3.1.1].* As the issuer of the irrevocable loan commitment becomes a party to the entire contractual cash flows of the loan at grant date it could be argued that any drawdowns could be treated as continuations of the original facility and that any loans drawn down should be classified on the basis of the criteria applying at the date of the origination of the loan commitment. Such an interpretation is consistent with how the time value of money on loan commitments are calculated under the expected credit loss method, 'a financial asset that is recognised following a draw down on a loan commitment shall be treated as a continuation of that commitment instead of as a new financial instrument'. [IFRS 9.B5.5.47].

However if a long period elapses between the origination of the irrevocable loan commitment and draw down it is possible that conditions affecting the assessment of classification might have changed considerably, for instance where a bank grants a loan commitment to an SPE and the SPE has sufficient equity at the date the commitment is originated but does not at the time the loan is drawn down. This is something that could be usefully clarified by the Interpretations Committee or the Board.

6.4.7 Environmental, social and governance 'ESG' loans

In order to incentivise a borrower to comply with ESG initiatives, a loan may be structured such that the interest rate varies in response to the achievement by the entity of defined ESG targets. For example, the terms may include a reduction in the interest rate if the borrower attains a certain rating on a type of green-building rating system, for an agreed number of the borrower's manufacturing buildings.

The contingent rate adjustments may introduce additional variability to the cash flows of the loan which is linked to the underlying ESG performance of the borrower, that may not be consistent with a basic lending arrangement. Careful analysis of the terms of ESG loans is required in order to assess whether the cash flows represent solely payments of principal and interest.

Instruments are more likely to meet the SPPI requirements if the attainment of the target is likely to result in the improvement of the borrower's credit risk such that the change in interest rate is commensurate with the change in credit risk of the borrower. It is often difficult to demonstrate a commensurate link between the interest rate change due to the attainment of an ESG target and the credit risk of the borrower. It may be easier to establish such a link, when the attainment of an ESG target impacts the value of the collateral of the ESG loan to such an extent that it impacts the loss given default (and hence the credit risk). For example, a loan may be advanced to a finance an asset which needs to achieve an ESG target, e.g. a loan advanced to a shipping company to finance a fleet of ships. The fleet serves as collateral for the loan and if certain carbon emissions thresholds are met then the interest rate is reduced. An entity would need to consider:

- If it can be demonstrated that the value of the collateral improves as a result of the attainment of the ESG target (i.e. there is a favourable impact on the loss given default) to such an extent that it reduces the credit risk. In the example above the consideration would be whether the value of the fleet improves if the fleet's carbon emissions are reduced to such an extent that it would change the risk of default by the borrower; and
- If there is a change in credit risk as discussed in the previous point, whether the change in interest rate in response to such change in value of the collateral can be considered appropriate compensation for the change in credit risk.

It may be difficult to establish a link between the attainment of ESG targets and an entity's credit risk, where the achievement of ESG targets does not impact the value of collateral with a resultant impact on the risk of default, but rather benefits the entity in a more broad and intangible manner (such as perceived improved social responsibility by stakeholders).

6.5 Non-recourse assets

A financial asset may have contractual cash flows that are described as principal and interest but those cash flows do not, in economic substance, represent the payment of principal and interest on the principal amount outstanding. *[IFRS 9.B4.1.15]*. For example, under some contractual arrangements, a creditor's claim is limited to specified assets of the debtor or the cash flows from specified assets (described in the standard as a 'non-recourse' financial asset). Another example given in the standard is contractual terms stipulating that the financial asset's cash flows increase as more automobiles use a particular toll road. Those contractual cash flows are inconsistent with a basic lending arrangement. *[IFRS 9.B4.1.16]*. As a result, the instrument would not pass the contractual cash flow characteristics test unless such a feature is *de minimis* or non-genuine. *[IFRS 9.B4.1.18]*.

However, the fact that a financial asset is non-recourse does not in itself necessarily preclude the financial asset from passing the contractual cash flow characteristics test (see also 6.3.2 above). Furthermore, conventional subordination features do not preclude an asset from passing the test (see 6.3.1 above).

The non-recourse provision in IFRS 9 is intended to prevent instruments that are linked to the performance of another asset from being classified as amortised cost or FVOCI. Where an asset is non-recourse the creditor is required to assess ('look through to') the particular underlying assets or cash flows to determine whether the contractual cash flows characteristics test is being met. *[IFRS 9.B4.1.17]*. When assessing a non-recourse asset, various factors could be considered, such as:

- nature of borrower and its business;
- adequacy of loss absorbing capital (particularly for SPEs);
- pricing of the loan (may indicate returns above a lending return);
- performance figures such as Loan to Value ratios (LTVs), Debt Service Coverage Ratios (DSCR) and Interest Coverage Ratios (ICR);
- expected source of repayment; or
- existence of other forms of economic recourse such as guarantees.

The following examples illustrate instruments which normally fail the contractual cash flow characteristics test because their cash flows are not solely payments of principal and interest on the principal amount outstanding.

Example 48.33: Non-recourse loans

Non-recourse loans need careful consideration and many instruments that are non-recourse will fail the test. The following examples illustrate how the guidance above might be applied to non-recourse instruments that are common in practice and under which circumstances those instruments pass the contractual cash flow characteristics test:

(a) Project finance loans

Where a loan is given for the construction and maintenance of a toll road and the payments of cash flows to the lender are reduced or cancelled if less than a certain number of vehicles travel on that road, the loan is unlikely to pass the contractual cash flow characteristics test. Similarly, a loan with cash flows specifically referenced to the performance of an underlying business will not pass the test.

In other cases, where there is no such reference and there is adequate equity in the project to absorb losses before affecting the ability to meet payments on the loan, it may well pass the contractual cash flow characteristics test. In these cases, the adequacy of equity to absorb losses will be key.

(b) Loans to a special purpose entity (SPE)

Where a loan is provided to an SPE that funds the acquisition of other assets, whether that loan passes the contractual cash flow characteristics test will depend on the specific circumstances of the arrangement.

If the assets of the SPE are all debt instruments which would themselves pass the contractual cash flow characteristics test, the loan to the SPE might well pass it too. Further, if, the SPE uses the loan from the entity to fund investments in assets which will not themselves pass the contractual cash flow characteristics test, such as equity securities or non-financial assets, but the SPE has sufficient equity to cover the losses on its investments, the loan may again pass the contractual cash flow characteristics test. However, if the loan is the only source of finance to the SPE so that it absorbs any losses from the equity securities, it would not pass the contractual cash flow characteristics test. Whether the loan is legally non-recourse does not matter in this scenario because the SPE has limited other assets to which the lender can have recourse. Therefore, the SPE must have adequate equity for the interest to represent compensation for basic lending risk.

(c) Mortgages

There are many different types of mortgage loans and some are structured so that in the event of default the lender has legal recourse only to the property provided as collateral and not to the borrower. This type of arrangement is common in some states of the USA. Other mortgages may, in substance, be non-recourse if the borrower has limited other assets.

In general, we do not believe that IFRS 9 was intended to require all normal collateralised loans such as mortgages to be accounted for at fair value through profit or loss. Consequently, if a loan is granted at a rate of interest that compensates the lender for the time value of money and for the credit risk associated with the principal amount, it would in our view usually pass the contractual cash flow characteristics test, whether or not it is legally non-recourse.

However, at inception, if the expected repayment of a loan is primarily driven by future movements in the value of the collateral so that the loan is, in substance, an investment in the real estate market, then measurement at amortised cost or fair value through other comprehensive income classification would most likely be inappropriate.

The contractual cash flow characteristics are assessed at initial recognition of the asset. If at initial recognition the asset is full recourse, there is no need to reassess whether there is any change thereafter.

Other loans could also be considered to be in substance non-recourse if the borrower has limited resources with which to repay the loan. Under certain circumstances impaired loans backed by collateral could also be considered to be non-recourse in substance, such as if the lender could only recover the loan by realising the collateral. This would in substance be similar to the lender buying the collateral directly.

Where an SPE issues non-recourse notes and uses the funding to buy an asset which is pledged as collateral for the non-recourse notes, the question arises as to how to assess whether 'a creditor's claim is limited to specified assets of the debtor or the cash flow from specified assets' and whether 'the terms of the financial asset give rise to any other cash flows or limit the cash flows in a manner inconsistent with payments representing principal and interest'. In these cases, the question revolves around whether the SPE has adequate equity such that interest represents compensation for the basic lending risks rather than asset risks.

6.6 Contractually linked instruments

In some types of transactions, an entity may prioritise payments to the holders of financial assets using multiple contractually linked instruments that create concentrations of credit risk (known as tranches). Each tranche has a subordination ranking that specifies the order in which any cash flows generated by the issuer are allocated to the tranche. In such situations, the holders of a tranche have the right to payments of principal and interest on the principal amount outstanding only if the issuer generates sufficient cash flows to satisfy higher ranking tranches. *[IFRS 9.B4.1.20]*. Examples of such types of instruments would be notes issued by securitisation structures such as collateralised debt obligations (CDOs).

Essentially such investments contain leveraged credit risk and, accordingly, the IASB believes that measuring such investments at amortised cost or fair value through other comprehensive income may be inappropriate in certain circumstances, hence the requirements for contractually linked instruments were developed.

In multi-tranche transactions that concentrate credit risk in the way described above, a tranche is considered to have cash flow characteristics that are payments of principal and interest on the principal amount outstanding only if the following three criteria are met: *[IFRS 9.B4.1.21]*

(a) the contractual terms of the tranche being assessed for classification (without looking through to the underlying pool of financial instruments) give rise to cash flows that are solely payments of principal and interest on the principal amount outstanding (e.g. the interest rate on the tranche is not linked to a commodity index);

(b) the underlying pool of financial instruments must contain one or more instruments that have contractual cash flows that are solely payments of principal and interest on the principal amount outstanding (the primary instruments) and any other instruments in the underlying pool must either: *[IFRS 9.B4.1.23-25]*

   (i) reduce the cash flow variability of the primary instruments in the pool and, when combined with the primary instruments in the pool, result in cash flows that are solely payments of principal and interest on the principal amount outstanding; or

   (ii) align the cash flows of the tranches with the cash flows of the underlying primary instruments in the pool to address differences in and only in:
   - whether the interest rate is fixed or floating;
   - the currency in which the cash flows are denominated, including inflation in that currency; or
   - the timing of the cash flows.

   For these purposes, when identifying the underlying pool of financial instruments, the holder should 'look through' the structure until it can identify an underlying pool of instruments that are creating (rather than passing through) the cash flows; *[IFRS 9.B4.1.22]*

(c) the exposure to credit risk in the underlying pool of financial instruments inherent in the tranche is equal to, or lower than, the exposure to credit risk of all of the underlying pool of instruments (for example, the credit rating of the tranche is equal to or higher than the credit rating that would apply to a single borrowing that funded the underlying pool).

If any instrument in the pool does not meet the conditions in (b) above, then the tranche fails the SPPI test. In making this assessment, a detailed instrument-by-instrument analysis of the pool may not be necessary, however an entity must use judgement and perform sufficient analysis to determine whether the instruments in the pool meet the conditions in (b) above. *[IFRS 9.B4.1.25]*.

If the holder cannot assess whether a financial asset meets criteria (a) to (c) above at initial recognition, the tranche must be measured at fair value through profit or loss. *[IFRS 9.B4.1.26]*.

An entity would apply the above criteria listed in (a) to (c) to all contractually linked tranches that it holds. Therefore, if criteria (b) is not met, it would not be met for all tranches, and this will result in all the tranches failing the SPPI test, including the most senior tranche. This result may not seem intuitive, and consequently it is important that entities carefully consider when instruments would fall within the scope of the contractually linked instruments guidance.

6.6.1 The scope of the 'contractually linked' guidance

In order to determine when the contractually linked instrument guidance as discussed in 6.6. above needs to be applied, one needs to assess what it means for instruments to be 'contractually linked'. IFRS 9 does not provide an explicit definition of contractually linked instruments but rather describes the general characteristics of such instruments. These include the following: *[IFRS 9.B4.1.20]*

- the existence of multiple contractually linked instruments that create concentrations of credit risk (so called 'tranches');
- tranche subordination ranking specifying the order in which any cash flows are allocated; and
- the holder has a right to receive payments only if the cash flows on higher-ranking tranches have been satisfied.

In addition, the Basis for Conclusions refers to such instruments being issued by 'structured investment vehicles'. *[IFRS 9.BC4.26]*. Moreover, the guidance refers to 'the pool of underlying financial instruments', which are exposed to credit risk, as opposed to other types of assets. *[IFRS 9.B4.21]*.

The reference to 'multiple' contractually linked instruments, in our view, means that there must be more than one tranche.

There are various financing structures and types of instruments that can be issued by entities and so it may be unclear when the contractually linked instrument guidance as set out in 6.6 above, should be applied. The assessment of whether there are multiple contractually linked instruments is an area of judgement which requires careful consideration of the specific facts and circumstances.

A number of questions arise when evaluating the scope of the contractually linked instruments guidance. These include:

i) whether it only applies to such instruments that are issued by structured investment vehicles, or whether it covers a broader range of entities;

ii) whether the features must be explicitly set out in the instrument's contractual terms, or whether an instrument can be 'implicitly contractually linked'. For example, a structured investment vehicle could issue two instruments, one debt and one equity or it could issue two contractually linked debt instruments where the junior debt instrument is expected to behave more like equity, due to the fact that it absorbs residual risk. Economically these two structures may be very similar; and

iii) whether the guidance only applies where the underlying assets are financial instruments (see 6.6.3 below).

The Basis for Conclusions, in discussing the development of this guidance, states that it was revised so as to focus on the economic characteristics rather than the form and legal structure, *[IFRS 9.BC4.29]*, and is not based solely on the contractual features. *[IFRS 9.BC4.33]*. Further, to make the judgement about whether an instrument has the required features to be classed as contractually linked, an entity has to understand the characteristics of the underlying issuer. *[IFRS 9.BC4.34]*. The challenge in applying this guidance is that, despite the desire of the Board not to focus on legal form, the wording, including the title, 'contractually linked', frequently refers to the contractual form.

Consequently, while we believe that the guidance might also apply to some situations other than where the instruments are issued by structured investment vehicles and that the analysis should not focus on only the instruments' legal form, it does need to be guided by the general characteristics of contractually linked instruments as set out in the standard.

Further, the Basis for Conclusions states that subordination in itself should not preclude amortised cost measurement. The ranking of an entity's instruments is a common form of subordination that affects almost all lending transactions. Commercial law (including bankruptcy law) typically sets out a basic ranking for creditors. The IASB believes that it is reasonable to assume that commercial law does not intend to create leveraged credit exposure for credit risk associated with general creditors such as trade creditors and the credit risk associated with general creditors does not preclude the contractual cash flows representing the payments of principal and interest on the principal amount outstanding. *[IFRS 9.BC4.28]*.

To make the judgement as to whether the guidance should be applied to a particular financial asset, two of the considerations that could be evaluated include the following, noting that each consideration listed below will probably not be conclusive in isolation and the evaluation will depend on the specific facts and circumstances of the structure and how the instruments that are issued are linked together:

a) Whether the subordination features are only applicable in the event of default:

If the subordination features only apply in the event of default (i.e. there is no cash flow 'waterfall' in the ordinary course of business), the subordination would not specify the order in which 'any cash flows generated by the issuer are allocated to the tranche', hence, one of the specific characteristics of contractually linked instruments referred to in paragraph B4.1.20 of IFRS 9 as discussed above, would not be met.

b) Whether non-payment of a junior tranche constitutes a breach of contract:

The nature of a contractually linked instrument is to introduce credit concentration features linked with higher yielding returns for junior instruments in exchange for providing credit protection to senior instruments. As such, if non-payment on the junior ranking instrument, because cash flows are directed to a more senior instrument, constitutes a breach of contract resulting in an event of default (so that the structure must be restructured or liquidated), it could be argued that the instrument does not provide such credit protection.

Application of some of the considerations is illustrated in the following examples:

Example 48.34: Assessing whether instruments are contractually linked

Entity X sets up a special purpose vehicle (Entity Y) in order to finance the acquisition of a pool of financial instruments. Entity Y finances the acquisition of the pool of financial instruments through the following:

- Equity of £50m from X
- Junior loan from Bank A of £30m
- Senior loan from Bank B of £20m

The terms of the loans stipulate that in the normal course of business, payments on the junior loan cannot be made unless all amounts due on the senior loan from Bank B has been settled. Non-payment of the junior loan does not trigger liquidation of Entity Y. The subordination features of the loans are not only applicable in the event of default. There is a 'waterfall' feature, that determines how profits from the pool of financial instruments should be allocated to the individual loans in the ordinary course of business.

Bank A and B would conclude, based on the terms of the junior and senior loans, that these two instruments are contractually linked. Therefore, they would need to assess both loans against the criteria as set out in paragraph B4.1.21 of IFRS 9 in order to determine whether or not they qualify to be measured at amortised cost.

Example 48.35: Property development company with debt and equity

A property development company (Entity P) sets up a separate subsidiary in order to fund each development. The subsidiary (Entity S) obtains funding in the form of ordinary shares issued to its parent and a loan from the bank. Entity S uses the funds in order to develop a property. Entity S is not permitted to declare dividends prior to the repayment of the loan and the parent funding is considered sufficient to absorb any losses that are likely to arise. In addition to this the parent is required to inject further capital if the loan-to-value ratio of the collateral, deteriorates below a certain threshold.

In this example there is only a single tranche of debt. Although the structure would result in the ordinary shares being exposed to the residual cash flows in this structure, the equity instrument is not contractually linked to the debt instrument in the ordinary course of business (i.e. there is no pre-defined 'waterfall' which would give the ordinary shareholders the right to receive payments if the cash flows on the loan have been satisfied). In addition, given that the shareholder funding is not only contractually established as equity but also imposes an obligation to inject sufficient capital to absorb any losses, the loan has the characteristics of normal bank lending. Consequently, the loan has the characteristics of a conventional bank loan and holder of the financial asset (the bank) would probably conclude that the contractually linked instrument guidance is not applicable.

6.6.2 Contractually linked instruments versus non-recourse instruments

As already mentioned, the guidance on whether a contractually linked instrument would be SPPI refers to the need to look through to 'the underlying pool of financial instruments'. *[IFRS 9.B4.1.21(b)-(c), B4.1.22]*. This has prompted the question as to whether the contractually linked instrument guidance only applies to structures where the underlying assets are financial instruments, as opposed to other assets such as property. However, the general characteristics of contractually linked instruments set out in the standard make no mention of the nature of the underlying assets. *[IFRS 9.B4.1.20]*.

Consequently, it is our view that the scope of contractually linked instruments is based on the nature of the instruments issued and not on the nature of the pool of assets underlying the instruments. As such, if a structure contains contractually linked instruments, then it would apply the contractually linked instruments guidance and not the requirements for non-recourse assets. Because of the way the standard is written the outcome of the contractual cash flow characteristics assessment will depend on the form of the arrangement. Arrangements which involve using multiple contractually linked instruments should be assessed under the contractually linked instruments requirements while arrangements with non-recourse features but without multiple tranches should be assessed under the non-recourse requirements. Therefore, the accounting outcome can vary depending on the structure employed, for instance, a non-recourse financial asset whose cash flows depend on vehicles using a toll road would be required to be assessed under the non-recourse requirement if structured as a single instrument but, if structured into tranches, would be assessed differently using the contractually linked instrument criteria. If the contractually linked instrument criteria are required to be applied, the underlying asset (the toll road in this example) would not be a financial instrument passing SPPI, and therefore criteria (b) as discussed in 6.6 above, would not be met and the tranches would therefore not pass SPPI.

6.6.3 Assessing the characteristics of the underlying pool of financial instruments

6.6.3.A Non-financial instruments in the underlying pool

The IFRS 9 contractually linked instrument guidance requires for any tranches to be SPPI that the underlying pool should consist only of financial instruments. *[IFRS 9.B4.1.21(b)]*. Contractually linked instruments referencing a pool of non-financial instruments do not meet the contractual cash flow characteristics test and cannot be classified at amortised cost. In a structure where an SPE issues contractually linked notes referenced to a note issued by another SPE referencing a pool of non-financial assets, IFRS guidance would require the entity holding the instrument to look through all contractually linked instruments.

6.6.3.B Liquidity facilities in the underlying pool

Some structures contain liquidity facilities which provide short term funding to enable interest to be paid on notes when cashflows from the underlying assets are delayed, for instance a facility which provides liquidity to cover the cashflows needed for the SPE to operate and to pay interest to the noteholders for a short period. These facilities usually have a seniority above all other notes in the structure and a failure to pay on the facility would be considered a default of the SPE. Normally these liquidity features would not be considered to be a tranche of the structure and are seen as being an instrument in the pool rather than a tranche. This is because they are short term and designed to align the cash flows in the structure in a similar way to plain vanilla derivative instruments in criterion (b) at 6.6 above, rather than to absorb risks by the holder and thereby create concentrations of credit risk.

The characteristics of the liquidity facility are sufficiently different from the notes. If the liquidity facility does not have features that would fail the contractual cash flow characteristics test, then it would be treated as a short-term loan.

6.6.3.C   Changes in the composition of the underlying pool

In practice it may be difficult for the holder to perform the look-through test because the underlying reference assets of a collateralised debt obligation (CDO) may not all have been acquired at the time of investment. In such circumstances, the holder will need to consider, amongst other things, the intended objectives of the CDO as well as the manager's investment mandate before determining whether the investment qualifies for measurement at amortised cost or fair value through other comprehensive income. If after this consideration the holder is able to conclude that all the underlying reference assets of the CDO will always have contractual cash flows that are solely payments of principal and interest on the principal amount outstanding, the interest in the CDO can qualify for measurement at amortised cost or fair value through other comprehensive income. Otherwise, the investment in the CDO must be accounted for at fair value through profit or loss because it fails the contractual cash flow characteristics test, unless the effect is *de minimis*.

If the underlying pool of instruments can change after initial recognition in a way that does not meet conditions (a) and (b) in 6.6 above, the tranche must be measured at fair value through profit or loss. However, if the underlying pool includes instruments that are collateralised by assets that do not meet the conditions above (as will often be the case), the ability to take possession of such assets is disregarded for the purposes of applying this paragraph, unless the entity acquired the tranche with the intention of controlling the collateral. *[IFRS 9.B4.1.26]*.

6.6.3.D   Assets with prepayment options in the underlying pool

The IASB noted that a key principle underlying the contractual cash flow provisions for contractually linked instruments was that an entity should not be disadvantaged simply by holding an asset indirectly if the underlying asset has cash flows that are solely principal and interest, and the holding is not subject to more-than-insignificant leverage or a concentration of credit risk relative to the underlying assets.

Accordingly, the IASB clarified that a tranche may have contractual cash flows that are solely payments of principal and interest even if the tranche is prepayable in the event that the underlying pool of financial instruments is prepaid. The Board noted that because the underlying pool of assets must have contractual cash flows that are solely payments of principal and interest, then, by extension, any prepayment features in those underlying financial assets are also required to be solely payments of principal and interest. *[IFRS 9.BC4.206(a)]*.

The Board's clarification that a prepayment feature in the underlying pool of assets does not necessarily prevent a tranche from meeting the contractual cash flow characteristics test is helpful. But, unless the underlying pool can only be acquired at origination, it may be difficult to 'look through' to the underlying pool to determine if its prepayment features would themselves be solely payments of principal and interest. This is because the information will often not be available to determine whether the assets were acquired at a premium or discount, and whether the fair value of any prepayment feature was insignificant on acquisition (see 6.4.4 above). However, there may be instances where the investment vehicle has a clearly defined investment mandate or design which will provide the investor with sufficient information as to the nature of the underlying pool of assets.

6.6.3.E Financial guarantee contracts and derivatives in the underlying pool

For the purposes of criterion (b) at 6.6 above, the underlying pool may contain financial instruments such as interest rate swaps. In order for these instruments not to preclude the use of amortised cost or fair value through other comprehensive income accounting for holders of a tranche, they must reduce the variability of cash flows, or align the cash flows of the tranches with the cash flows of the underlying pool of the primary instruments. Accordingly, an underlying pool that contains government bonds and an instrument that swaps government credit risk for (riskier) corporate credit risk would not have cash flows that represent solely principal and interest on the principal amount outstanding. *[IFRS 9.BC4.35(d)].*

If the underlying pool of financial instruments contained a purchased credit default swap, this would not prejudice the use of amortised cost or fair value through other comprehensive income accounting provided it paid out only to compensate for the loss of principal and interest, although in practice it is far more common for underlying pools to contain written rather than purchased credit default swaps. As a consequence, while it may often be possible to obtain amortised cost or fair value through other comprehensive income accounting treatment for the more senior investments in 'cash' CDOs, i.e. those where the underlying pool comprises the reference debt instruments, tranches of 'synthetic' CDOs for which the risk exposure of the tranches is generated by derivatives, would not pass the contractual characteristics test.

An underlying pool of financial instruments which contains a financial guarantee issued by the SPE to provide credit protection to the pool of financial instruments will result in the instruments supported by the pool failing the SPPI test. This is because the guarantee does not meet the SPPI test itself and does not reduce cash flow variability when combined with instruments in the pool nor align cash flows of the tranches with cash flows of the pool.

6.6.3.F Assets transferred to the underlying pool which have failed derecognition

An underlying pool containing instruments which have failed derecognition in the books of the transferee will need to be assessed carefully to understand the cash flows involved. It should be noted that just because an asset has failed derecognition does not mean that the transferee is not exposed to any of the risks and rewards of that asset. Repo balances transferred into the underlying pool will probably not impact the pool's ability to pass the SPPI test, given the nature of the cash flows in a repo. However, in other cases, the transferee could be exposed to some of the risks or rewards associated with the failed-sale asset. So, depending on the analysis of the instruments involved, it is possible that the nature of the transferred risks could result in an instrument held within the pool failing the contractual cash flows characteristic test.

6.6.4 Application of expected credit loss requirements to junior tranches

While some contractually linked instruments may pass the SPPI test and consequently may be measured at amortised cost or fair value through other comprehensive income, the contractual cash flows of the individual tranches are normally based on a pre-defined waterfall structure (i.e. principal and interest are first paid on the most senior tranche and then successively paid on more junior tranches). Accordingly, one could argue that more junior tranches could never suffer a credit loss because the contractually defined cash flows under the waterfall structure are always equal to the cash flows that an entity expects to receive, and so would never be regarded as impaired. This is, because Appendix A of IFRS 9 defines 'credit loss' as 'the difference between all contractual cash flows that are due to an entity in accordance with the contract and all the cash flows that the entity expects to receive, discounted at the original effective interest rate'.

However, consistent with treating these assets as having passed the contractual cash flow characteristics test, we believe that the impairment requirements of IFRS 9 (see Chapter 51) apply to such tranches if they are measured at amortised cost or fair value through other comprehensive income. Instead of the cash flows determined under the waterfall structure, an entity needs to consider deemed principal and interest payments as contractual cash flows when calculating expected credit losses.

6.6.5 Assessing the exposure to credit risk in the tranche held

IFRS 9 does not prescribe a method for comparing the exposure to credit risk in the tranche held to that of the underlying pool of financial instruments.

For the more senior and junior tranches, it may become obvious with relatively little analysis whether the tranche is more or less risky than the underlying assets. In some cases, it might be possible to compare the credit rating allocated to the tranche as compared with that for the underlying pool of financial instruments, provided they are all rated.

However, in some circumstances involving complex securitisation structures, a more detailed assessment may be required. For example, it might be appropriate to prepare an analysis that involves developing various credit loss scenarios for the underlying pool of financial instruments, computing the probability weighted outcomes of those scenarios, determining the probability weighted effect on the tranche held, and comparing the relative variability of the tranche held with that of the underlying assets, which is shown in the following example.

Example 48.36: Assessing the exposure to credit risk in the tranche held

Bank A is the sponsor of a securitisation vehicle (the SPE) and holds the junior notes issued by the SPE. The SPE's assets consist of a portfolio of residential mortgages that were originated and transferred to the SPE by Bank A. The SPE does not hold any derivatives. A number of other banks invest in the mezzanine, senior and super senior tranches of notes issued by the SPE. None of the banks has any further involvement with the SPE and all banks have assessed that the SPE is not required to be consolidated in their respective financial statements. The total notional amount of mortgage assets and notes issued is €1,000 million.

The following table shows a range of expected credit losses for the portfolio of mortgages as at inception and the estimated probability that those scenarios will occur.

	Loss	Estimated probability of loss	Estimated weighted average loss
	€ million	%	€ million
Scenario I	40	10%	4
Scenario II	70	25%	18
Scenario III	110	30%	33
Scenario IV	180	25%	45
Scenario V	230	10%	23
Weighted average loss expectancy			123

The probability weighted expected losses of the underlying assets therefore represent 12.3%.

The following table illustrates how an entity may compare the credit risk of the tranche with that of the underlying pool of financial instruments:

Tranche		Super senior	Senior	Mezzanine	Junior	Total
Notional amount (A) € million		630	200	90	80	1,000
	Probability	Probability weighted expected losses of the tranches (€ million) *				
Scenario I	10%	–	–	–	4	4
Scenario II	25%	–	–	–	18	18
Scenario III	30%	–	–	9	24	33
Scenario IV	25%	–	2	23	20	45
Scenario V	10%	–	6	9	8	23
Expected loss by tranche (B)		–	8	41	74	123
Expected loss % by tranche (B)/(A)		0.0%	4.0%	45.6%	92.5%	12.3%
Credit risk of tranche is less than the credit risk of the underlying assets?		Yes	Yes	No	No	
Tranche passes the contractual cash flow characteristic test		Yes	Yes	No	No	

* For each scenario, expected losses are first allocated to the junior tranches and progressively to the more senior tranches until all expected losses are absorbed. For example, in Scenario IV, the loss of €180 million would be absorbed by the Junior tranche (€80 million), mezzanine tranche (€90 million) and senior tranche (€10 million). The probability weight of 25% for Scenario IV is then applied to the expected losses allocated to each tranche.

The junior notes have an expected loss which is, in percentage terms, greater than the overall expected loss on the underlying portfolio. Therefore, these notes must be accounted for at fair value through profit or loss. Similarly, the mezzanine notes have a greater expected loss than the underlying pool and would not pass the contractual cash flow characteristics test.

The expected losses on the senior notes and the super senior notes are lower than the overall expected loss on the underlying pool of instruments and may qualify for amortised cost or fair value through other comprehensive income treatment, provided all other IFRS 9 requirements are met and the instruments are not held for trading.

In this example, it might have been possible to come to the same conclusion without a numerical calculation for the junior and super senior tranches, but the technique is helpful to determine the treatment of the intermediary notes. In practice, it may also be necessary to apply judgment through a qualitative assessment of specific facts and circumstances.

6.7 Transferred financial assets held by a transferee and not qualifying for derecognition by the transferor

IFRS 9 states that, where a financial asset is transferred from one party to another in circumstances that preclude the transferor from derecognising the asset, the transferee should not recognise the transferred asset. Instead, the transferee derecognises the cash or other consideration paid and recognises a receivable from the transferor. [IFRS 9.B3.2.15].

There may be various reasons for the transferor not achieving derecognition of transferred financial assets. Refer to Chapter 52 at 3.6 and 3.8 for further considerations on derecognition. In addition, depending on how the transfer is structured, there may be diversity in practise in terms of how the transferee accounts for the receivable and any related liabilities. Refer to Chapter 49 at 2.1.6 for initial recognition considerations.

In certain securitisations, the transferor may retain an interest in the securitisation vehicle resulting in the transferor retaining substantially all the risks and rewards of the transferred assets, and the transferred assets failing derecognition. Examples of such an interest retained by the transferor include, the provision of guarantees or put options, an obligation to substitute non-preforming loans, deferred consideration, or by the transferor investing in a junior tranche of the notes issued by the securitisation vehicle. The transferee needs to assess whether the 'failed sale' receivable it recognises as due from the transferor meets the SPPI criterion. The receivable due from the transferor, would be dependent on the cash flows of the underlying transferred asset which failed to qualify for derecognition. Therefore, it is necessary for the transferee to assess the nature of these underlying cash flows and whether it results in the transferee receiving payments on its receivable that are solely principal and interest.

In the situation where the transferor invests in a subordinated tranche of the securitisation vehicle, the transferee could consider the non-recourse guidance (as discussed in 6.5 above), as the return on the receivable due from the transferor, is limited to the cash flows from the underlying pool of transferred assets. In assessing whether the transferee's receivable meets the SPPI test, the transferee would 'look-through' to the underlying cash flows from the transferred assets that it has rights to. Alternatively, the transferee could consider whether the contractually linked instruments guidance (as discussed in 6.6 above) could be applied. In this assessment the transferee could view itself as holding the more senior tranche, with the transferor owning the junior tranche in the underlying assets (by virtue of its investment in the subordinated tranche of the securitisation), with both tranches being linked to the underlying pool of transferred assets. Applying either of these two approaches, the receivable is likely to be considered to pass the SPPI test as long as the underlying assets themselves pass the SPPI test. If the transferee is able to conclude the receivable meets the SPPI requirements and measures it at amortised cost, then it would need to apply the expected credit loss requirements to this receivable. Refer to Chapter 51 at 7.7.1 for further considerations on impairment.

7 DESIGNATION AT FAIR VALUE THROUGH PROFIT OR LOSS

Financial assets or financial liabilities may be designated as measured at fair value through profit or loss at initial recognition if doing so eliminates or significantly reduces a measurement or recognition inconsistency (sometimes referred to as an 'accounting mismatch') that would otherwise arise. *[IFRS 9.4.1.5, 4.2.2(a)]*.

Financial liabilities may also be designated at fair value through profit or loss where a group of financial liabilities or financial assets and financial liabilities is managed and its performance is evaluated on a fair value basis. *[IFRS 9.4.2.2(b)]*. Financial assets that are managed on a fair value basis will always be classified at fair value through profit or loss (see 5.4 above), hence, a designation option is not needed.

Designation at fair value through profit or loss in the two situations described above is permitted provided doing so results in the financial statements presenting more relevant information. *[IFRS 9.B4.1.27]*. Such a designation can be made only at initial recognition and cannot be revoked subsequently.

In addition, a hybrid contract with a host that is not an asset within the scope of IFRS 9 that contains one or more embedded derivatives meeting particular conditions may be designated, in its entirety, at fair value through profit or loss. *[IFRS 9.4.3.5]*. These conditions are discussed in detail at 7.3 below.

The decision to designate a financial asset or financial liability as measured at fair value through profit or loss is similar to an accounting policy choice, although, unlike an accounting policy choice, it is not required in all cases to be applied consistently to all similar transactions. However, for a group of financial assets and financial liabilities that is managed and its performance is evaluated on a fair value basis, all eligible financial liabilities that are managed together should be designated. *[IFRS 9.B4.1.35]*. When an entity has such a choice, IAS 8 requires the chosen policy to result in the financial statements providing reliable and more relevant information about the effects of transactions, other events and conditions on the entity's financial position, financial performance or cash flows. For example, in designating a financial liability at fair value through profit or loss, an entity needs to demonstrate that it falls within at least one of the circumstances set out above. *[IFRS 9.B4.1.28]*.

The fair value option cannot be applied to a portion or component of a financial instrument, e.g. changes in the fair value of a debt instrument attributable to one risk such as changes in a benchmark interest rate, but not credit risk. Further, it cannot be applied to proportions of an instrument. However, if an entity simultaneously issues two or more identical financial instruments, it is not precluded from designating only some of those instruments as being subject to the fair value option (e.g. if doing so achieves a significant reduction in an accounting mismatch). Therefore, if an entity issued a bond totalling US$100 million in the form of 100 certificates each of US$1 million, the entity could designate 10 specified certificates if to do so would meet at least one of the criteria noted above. *[IFRS 9.BCZ4.74-76]*.

The conditions under which financial instruments may be designated at fair value through profit or loss are discussed further at 7.1 to 7.3 below.

7.1 Designation eliminates or significantly reduces a measurement or recognition inconsistency (accounting mismatch) that would otherwise arise

The notion of an accounting mismatch necessarily involves two propositions. First, that an entity has particular assets and liabilities that are measured, or on which gains and losses are recognised, on different bases; and second, that there is a perceived economic relationship between those assets and liabilities. *[IFRS 9.BCZ4.61]*.

For example, absent any designation, a financial asset might be classified as subsequently measured at fair value and a liability the entity considers related would be subsequently measured at amortised cost (with changes in fair value not recognised). In such circumstances, an entity may conclude that its financial statements would provide more relevant information if both the asset and the liability were measured as at fair value through profit or loss. *[IFRS 9.B4.1.29]*.

IFRS 9 gives the following examples of situations in which designation of a financial asset or financial liability as measured at fair value through profit or loss might eliminate or significantly reduce an accounting mismatch and produce more relevant information: *[IFRS 9.B4.1.30]*

(a) an entity has liabilities under insurance contracts whose measurement incorporates current information (as permitted by IFRS 4 – *Insurance Contracts*), and financial assets it considers related that would otherwise be measured at fair value through other comprehensive income or amortised cost;

(b) an entity has financial assets, financial liabilities or both that share a risk, such as interest rate risk, that gives rise to changes in fair value that tend to offset each other. However, only some of the instruments would be measured at fair value through profit or loss (e.g. derivatives or those classified as held for trading). It may also be the case that the requirements for hedge accounting are not met, for example because the requirements for hedge effectiveness are not met;

(c) an entity has financial assets, financial liabilities or both that share a risk, such as interest rate risk, that gives rise to changes in fair value that tend to offset each other and the entity does not use hedge accounting. This could be for different reasons, for example, because items giving rise to the accounting mismatch would not qualify for hedge accounting or because the entity does not want to use hedge accounting because of operational complexity. Furthermore, in the absence of hedge accounting there is a significant inconsistency in the recognition of gains and losses. For example, the entity has financed a specified group of loans by issuing traded bonds, the changes in the fair value of which tend to offset each other. If, in addition, the entity regularly buys and sells the bonds but rarely, if ever, buys and sells the loans, reporting both the loans and the bonds at fair value through profit or loss eliminates the inconsistency in the timing of recognition of gains and losses that would otherwise result from measuring them both at amortised cost and recognising a gain or loss each time a bond is repurchased.

For practical purposes, an entity need not acquire all the assets and incur all the liabilities giving rise to the measurement or recognition inconsistency at exactly the same time. A reasonable delay is permitted provided that each transaction is designated as at fair value through profit or loss at its initial recognition and, at that time, any remaining transactions are expected to occur. *[IFRS 9.B4.1.31]*.

It would not be acceptable to designate only some of the financial assets giving rise to the inconsistency as at fair value through profit or loss if to do so would not eliminate or significantly reduce the inconsistency and would therefore not result in more relevant information. However, it would be acceptable to designate only some of a number of similar financial assets if doing so does achieve a significant reduction (and possibly a greater reduction than other allowable designations) in the inconsistency. *[IFRS 9.B4.1.32]*.

For example, assume an entity has a number of similar financial assets totalling €100 million and a number of similar financial liabilities totalling €50 million, but these are measured on a different basis. The entity may significantly reduce the measurement inconsistency by designating at initial recognition all the liabilities but only some of the assets (for example, individual assets with a combined total of €45 million) as at fair value through profit or loss. However, because designation as at fair value through profit or loss can be applied only to the whole of a financial instrument, the entity in this example must designate one or more assets in their entirety. It could not designate either a component of an asset (e.g. changes in value attributable to only one risk, such as changes in a benchmark interest rate) or a proportion (i.e. percentage) of an asset. *[IFRS 9.B4.1.32]*.

7.2 A group of financial liabilities or financial assets and financial liabilities is managed and its performance is evaluated on a fair value basis

The second situation in which the fair value option may be used (for financial liabilities) is where a group of financial liabilities or financial assets and financial liabilities is managed, and its performance evaluated, on a fair value basis. In order to meet this condition, it is necessary for the group of instruments to be managed in accordance with a documented risk management or investment strategy and for information, prepared on a fair value basis, about the group of instruments to be provided internally to the entity's key management personnel (as defined in IAS 24 – see Chapter 39 at 2.2.1.D), for example the entity's board of directors and chief executive officer. *[IFRS 9.4.2.2(b)]*.

If an entity manages and evaluates the performance of a group of financial liabilities or financial assets and financial liabilities in such a way, measuring that group at fair value through profit or loss results in more relevant information. The focus in this instance is on the way the entity manages and evaluates performance, rather than on the nature of its financial instruments. *[IFRS 9.B4.1.33]*. Accordingly, subject to the requirement of designation at initial recognition, an entity that designates financial instruments as at fair value through profit or loss on the basis of this condition should so designate all eligible financial instruments that are managed and evaluated together. *[IFRS 9.B4.1.35]*.

An entity may designate financial liabilities as at fair value through profit or loss if it has financial assets and financial liabilities that share one or more risks and those risks are managed and evaluated on a fair value basis in accordance with a documented policy of asset and liability management. For example, the entity may issue 'structured products' containing multiple embedded derivatives and manage the resulting risks on a fair value basis using a mix of derivative and non-derivative financial instruments. *[IFRS 9.B4.1.34]*.

An entity's documentation of its strategy need not be extensive (e.g. it need not be at the level of detail required for hedge accounting) but should be sufficient to demonstrate that using the fair value option is consistent with the entity's risk management or investment strategy. Such documentation is not required for each individual item, but may be on a portfolio basis. The IASB notes that in many cases, the entity's existing documentation, as approved by its key management personnel, should be sufficient for this purpose. For example, if the performance management system for a department (as approved by the entity's key management personnel) clearly demonstrates that its performance is evaluated on a total return basis, no further documentation is required. *[IFRS 9.B4.1.36]*.

The IASB made it clear in its basis for conclusions that in looking to an entity's documented risk management or investment strategy, it makes no judgement on what an entity's strategy should be. However, the IASB believes that users, in making economic decisions, would find useful a description both of the chosen strategy and of how designation at fair value through profit or loss is consistent with that strategy. Accordingly, IFRS 7 – *Financial Instruments: Disclosures* – requires these to be disclosed (see Chapter 54 at 4.1). *[IFRS 9.BCZ4.66]*.

7.3 Hybrid contracts with a host that is not a financial asset within the scope of IFRS 9

If a contract contains one or more embedded derivatives, and the host is not a financial asset within the scope of IFRS 9, an entity may designate the entire hybrid contract as at fair value through profit or loss unless:

(a) the embedded derivative does not significantly modify the cash flows that otherwise would be required by the contract; or

(b) it is clear with little or no analysis when a similar hybrid (combined) instrument is first considered that separation of the embedded derivative(s) is prohibited, such as a prepayment option embedded in a loan that permits the holder to prepay the loan for approximately its amortised cost. *[IFRS 9.4.3.5]*.

As discussed in Chapter 46 at 4 to 6, when an entity becomes a party to a hybrid financial instrument that contains one or more embedded derivatives and the host is not a financial asset within the scope of IFRS 9, the entity is required to identify any such embedded derivative, assess whether it is required to be separated from the host contract and, if so, measure it at fair value at initial recognition and subsequently. These requirements can be more complex, or result in less reliable measures, than measuring the entire instrument at fair value through profit or loss. For that reason, the entire instrument is normally permitted to be designated as at fair value through profit or loss. *[IFRS 9.B4.3.9]*.

Such designation may be used whether the entity is required to, or prohibited from, separating the embedded derivative from the host contract, except for those situations in (a) or (b) above – this is because doing so would not reduce complexity or increase reliability. *[IFRS 9.B4.3.10]*.

Little further guidance is given on what instruments might fall within (a) and (b) above. The basis for conclusions explains that, at one extreme, the terms of a prepayment option in an ordinary residential mortgage is likely to mean that the fair value option is unavailable to such a mortgage (unless it met one of the conditions in 7.1 and 7.2 above). At the other extreme, it is likely to be available for 'structured products' that contain several embedded derivatives which are typically hedged with derivatives that offset all (or nearly all) of the risks they contain irrespective of the accounting treatment applied to the embedded derivatives. *[IFRS 9.BCZ4.68-70].*

Essentially, the IASB explains, the standard seeks to strike a balance between reducing the costs of complying with the embedded derivatives provisions and the need to respond to concerns expressed regarding possible inappropriate use of the fair value option. Allowing the fair value option to be used for any instrument with an embedded derivative would make other restrictions on the use of the option ineffective, because many financial instruments include an embedded derivative. In contrast, limiting the use of the fair value option to situations in which the embedded derivative must otherwise be separated would not significantly reduce the costs of compliance and could result in less reliable measures being included in the financial statements. *[IFRS 9.BCZ4.70].*

8 DESIGNATION OF NON-DERIVATIVE EQUITY INVESTMENTS AT FAIR VALUE THROUGH OTHER COMPREHENSIVE INCOME

An entity may acquire an investment in an equity instrument that is not held for trading. At initial recognition, the entity may make an irrevocable election (on an instrument-by-instrument basis) to present in other comprehensive income subsequent changes in the fair value of such an investment. *[IFRS 9.5.7.5, B5.7.1].* For this purpose, the term equity instrument uses the definition in IAS 32, application of which for issuers is dealt with in detail in Chapter 47.

In particular circumstances a puttable instrument (or an instrument that imposes on the entity an obligation to deliver to another party a *pro rata* share of the net assets of the entity only on liquidation) is classified by the issuer as if it were an equity instrument. This is by virtue of an exception to the general definitions of financial liabilities and equity instruments. However, such instruments do not actually meet the definition of an equity instrument and therefore the related asset cannot be designated at fair value through other comprehensive income by the holder. *[IFRS 9.BC5.21].*

This was confirmed by the Interpretations Committee in May 2017 when they received a request to clarify exactly this point. The Interpretations Committee observed that 'equity instrument' is a defined term, and IAS 32 defines an equity instrument as 'any contract that evidences a residual interest in the assets of an entity after deducting all of its liabilities'. The Interpretations Committee also observed that IAS 32.11 specifies that, as an exception, an instrument that meets the definition of a financial liability is classified as an equity instrument by the issuer if it has all the features and meets the conditions in paragraphs 16A and 16B or 16C and 16D of IAS 32 (see Chapter 47 at 4.6).

Accordingly, the Interpretations Committee concluded that a financial instrument that has all the features and meets the conditions in paragraphs 16A and 16B or paragraphs 16C and 16D of IAS 32 is not eligible for the presentation election in paragraph 4.1.4 of IFRS 9 and as such does not meet the definition of an equity instrument in IAS 32.[8]

The Committee concluded that the requirements in IFRS 9 provide an adequate basis for the holder of the particular instruments described in the submission to classify such instruments. In light of the existing requirements in IFRS Standards, the Committee determined that neither an IFRIC Interpretation nor an amendment to a Standard was necessary. Consequently, the Committee decided not to add this matter to its standard-setting agenda.

Under IFRS 9 all derivatives are deemed to be held for trading. Consequently, this election cannot be applied to a derivative such as a warrant that is classified as equity by the issuer. However, it could be applied to investments in preference shares, 'dividend stoppers' and similar instruments (see Chapter 47 at 4.5) provided they are classified as equity by the issuer.

The IASB had originally intended this accounting treatment to be available only for those equity instruments that represented a 'strategic investment'. These might include investments held for non-contractual benefits rather than primarily for increases in the value of the investment, for example where there is a requirement to hold such an investment if an entity sells its products in a particular country. However, the Board concluded that it would be difficult, and perhaps impossible, to develop a clear and robust principle that would identify investments that are different enough to justify a different presentation requirement and abandoned this restriction. *[IFRS 9.BC5.25(c)]*.

The example below illustrates the requirements for the designation of a non-derivative equity investment at fair value through other comprehensive income, specifically, the requirement that the instrument meets the definition of an equity instrument in accordance with IAS 32.

Example 48.37: Callable, perpetual 'Tier 1' debt instrument

Consider the example where entity A invests in a perpetual Tier 1 debt instrument, which is redeemable at the option of the issuer (entity B). The instrument carries a fixed coupon that is deferred if entity B does not pay a dividend to its ordinary shareholders. If a coupon is not paid it will not accrue additional interest. The instrument does not have a maturity date.

Under IFRS 9, such an instrument would not be eligible for amortised cost accounting by the holder. However, given that Entity B does not have a contractual obligation to pay cash, the instrument will qualify for classification at fair value through other comprehensive income, as it meets the definition of equity from the perspective of the issuer in accordance with IAS 32.

The subsequent measurement of instruments designated in this way, including recognition of dividends, is summarised at 8.1 below and covered in detail in Chapter 50 at 2.5.

8.1 Gains and losses on investments in equity instruments designated at fair value through other comprehensive income

Although most gains and losses on investments in equity instruments designated at fair value through other comprehensive income will be recognised in other comprehensive income, dividends will normally be recognised in profit or loss. *[IFRS 9.5.7.6]*. However, the IASB noted that dividends could sometimes represent a return of investment instead of a return on investment. Consequently, the IASB decided that dividends that clearly represent a recovery of part of the cost of the investment are not recognised in profit or loss. *[IFRS 9.BC5.25(a)]*. Meanwhile, gains or losses recognised in other comprehensive income are never reclassified from equity to profit or loss on derecognition of the asset, and consequently, there is no need to review such investments for possible impairment.

Determining when a dividend does or does not clearly represent a recovery of cost could prove somewhat judgemental in practice, especially as the standard contains no further explanatory guidance. Also, because it is an exception to a principle, it could open up the possibility of structuring transactions to convert fair value gains into dividends through the use of intermediate holding vehicles. However, in the IASB's view, those structuring opportunities would be limited because an entity with the ability to control or significantly influence the dividend policy of the investee would generally not account for those investments in accordance with IFRS 9. *[IFRS 9.BC5.25(a)]*. The main exception to this would be investment entities, as defined in IFRS 10 – *Consolidated Financial Statements* – but they are required to account for investments in subsidiaries (other than those providing investment-related services or activities) at fair value through profit or loss, hence for them this issue would not arise. Furthermore, the IASB requires disclosures that would allow the user to compare the dividends recognised in profit or loss and other fair value changes easily. *[IFRS 9.BC5.25(a)]*.

9 RECLASSIFICATION OF FINANCIAL ASSETS

In certain rare circumstances, non-derivative debt assets are required to be reclassified between the amortised cost, fair value through other comprehensive income and fair value through profit or loss categories. More specifically, when (and only when) an entity changes its business model for managing financial assets, it should reclassify all affected financial assets in accordance with the requirements set out in IFRS 9. *[IFRS 9.4.4.1]*. Refer to Chapter 50 at 2.7 for further details on how the reclassification requirements should be applied. In drafting IFRS 9, the IASB debated whether reclassifications should be permissible. In the October 2009 IASB meeting, the board tentatively decided to require reclassification where there is a change in business model, however the 'Board noted that such reclassifications would be expected to occur infrequently, if ever.'[9] IFRS 9 sets out the circumstances under which changes in the business model for managing financial assets will occur and notes that these changes are expected to be very infrequent. They must be determined by an entity's senior management as a result of external or internal changes and must be significant to the entity's operations and demonstrable to external parties. Accordingly, a change in the objective of an entity's business model will occur only when an entity either begins or ceases to carry on an activity that is significant to its operations, and generally that will be the case only when the entity has acquired or disposed of a business line (see 5.5 above for the interaction between IFRS 9 and IFRS 5). Examples of a change in business model include the following: *[IFRS 9.B4.4.1]*

(a) An entity has a portfolio of commercial loans that it holds to sell in the short term. The entity acquires a company that manages commercial loans and has a business model that holds the loans in order to collect the contractual cash flows. The portfolio of commercial loans is no longer for sale, and the portfolio is now managed together with the acquired commercial loans and all are held to collect the contractual cash flows.

(b) A financial services firm decides to shut down its retail mortgage business. That business no longer accepts new business and the financial services firm is actively marketing its mortgage loan portfolio for sale.

The examples above show that there needs to be a significant activity that has commenced or ceased before assets can qualify to be reclassified. The activity that is commencing or ceasing does not refer to the act of implementing different buying or selling decisions with regards to a portfolio of financial assets, but rather the 'activity' needs to be evidenced by a fundamental change in the operation of the business.

In example (a) above, there is an acquisition of a company which ostensibly would be accompanied by the commencement of new business processes. For example, there may be new processes regarding managing the new product (such as new credit and collections process) there may also be new marketing processes to manage new clients. These changes could therefore evidence a significant change in the entity's operations. Similarly, in example (b) above, the financial services firm has ceased a significant operation by shutting down its retail mortgage business. This change in business line would be demonstrable to external parties, as there would be an entire product line of the financial services firm (with all associated business activities to support that product line) which has discontinued. In both examples above, there would be noticeably significant changes to the entity which would evidence the significant change in operations.

In the absence of these types of changes in business activity, it would not be appropriate to reclassify financial assets. In some instances, entities may be prompted to change the manner in which they manage existing assets in response to external events such as changes in regulatory requirements (e.g. criteria regarding which assets constitute high quality liquid assets), or changes that are prompted due to certain assets no longer meeting internal credit quality requirements. In these examples, even if the entity is committed to changing the way in which they manage an existing, significant portfolio of financial assets, this change in intention by management would not be accompanied by the commencement or cessation of a significant operational activity. A change in intention alone, is one of the examples provided in IFRS 9 of changes that would not result in reclassification. *[IFRS 9.B4.4.3(a)].*

The following are not considered to be changes in business model: *[IFRS 9.B4.4.3]*

(a) a change in intention related to particular financial assets (even in circumstances of significant changes in market conditions);

(b) a temporary disappearance of a particular market for financial assets; and

(c) a transfer of financial assets between parts of the entity with different business models.

Example 48.38:   Change in the way a portfolio is managed

An entity's business model objective for a portfolio meets the criteria for amortised cost measurement but, subsequently, the entity changes the way it manages the assets.

Having determined that the objective for a portfolio originally met the business model test to be classified at amortised cost, if the entity subsequently changes the way it manages the assets (which results in a more than an infrequent number of sales), so that the business model would no longer qualify for amortised cost accounting, the question of how the entity should measure the existing assets and any newly acquired assets then arises.

Although more than an infrequent number of sales have occurred, unless there has been a fundamental change in the entity's business model, the requirements of the standard regarding reclassification are unlikely to be triggered. Changes in the business model for managing financial assets that trigger reclassification of financial assets must be significant to the entity's operations and demonstrable to external parties. They are expected to be very infrequent.

Assuming that the assets are not reclassified, it is likely that the entity will have to divide the portfolio into two sub-portfolios going forward – one for the old assets and one for any new assets acquired.

Financial assets previously held will remain at amortised cost. New financial assets acquired will be measured at fair value through profit or loss or at fair value through other comprehensive income. Whether the assets are measured at fair value through profit or loss or at fair value through other comprehensive income depends on the new business model and the characteristics of the assets.

Example 48.39:   Change in business model by a subsidiary

Subsidiary S is acquired by Parent P. This is considered to be a significant acquisition of a business line. Prior to the acquisition, Subsidiary S had a significant portfolio of loans which met the criteria for amortised cost measurement. Post the acquisition of S by P, S changes the way it manages the loans in line with the strategy of the group. The group intends on managing the portfolio of loans in S together with an existing portfolio of loans held by P, that are held for sale in the short term. As a result of the alignment with the group strategy, S discontinues its debt collection function which is now no longer needed as the sales activity of the loans will be managed and performed by the existing sales division in P. The change has been assessed by the key management of S to be demonstrable to external parties as it results in a significant change in the business activities of S.

Even though Subsidiary S has not acquired a business line, but rather the subsidiary itself has been acquired, we believe that this would follow the principles established in IFRS 9.B.4.4.1 such that in the absence of any other contrary indicators, a reclassification of Subsidiary S's portfolio of loans, in the separate financial statements of S, would be permitted.

Unlike a change in business model, the contractual terms of a financial asset are known at initial recognition. However, the contractual cash flows may vary over that asset's life based on its original contractual terms. Because an entity classifies a financial asset at initial recognition based on the contractual terms over the life of the instrument, reclassification on the basis of a financial asset's contractual cash flows is not permitted, unless the asset is sufficiently modified that it is derecognised. *[IFRS 9.BC4.117].*

For instance, no reclassification is permitted or required if the conversion option of a convertible bond lapses. If, however, a convertible bond is converted into shares, the shares represent a new financial asset to be recognised by the entity. The entity would then need to determine the classification category for the new equity investment.

A related question to the above is to what extent the contractual cash flow characteristics test influences the test of whether a financial asset is sufficiently modified such that it is derecognised. It has been suggested that a modification which would result in the asset failing the contractual cash flow characteristics test is a 'substantial modification' that would result in derecognition of the asset (see also Chapter 52 at 3.4). That is because an asset that is measured at fair value through profit or loss is substantially different to an asset measured at amortised cost or fair value through other comprehensive income. Whether or not a modified asset would still meet the contractual cash flow characteristics test or not could be a helpful indicator for the derecognition assessment.

9.1 When should reclassifications be applied?

The reclassification should be applied prospectively from the 'reclassification date', *[IFRS 9.5.6.1]*, which is defined as:

'The first day of the first reporting period following the change in business model that results in an entity reclassifying financial assets.' *[IFRS 9 Appendix A]*.

Accordingly, any previously recognised gains, losses or interest should not be restated. *[IFRS 9.5.6.1]*.

In our view, the reference to reporting period includes interim periods for which the entity prepares an interim report. For example, an entity with a reporting date of 31 December might determine that there is a change in its business model in August 2020. If the entity prepares and publishes quarterly reports in accordance with IAS 34 – *Interim Financial Reporting*, the reclassification date would be 1 October 2020. However, if the entity prepares only half-yearly interim reports or no interim reports at all, the reclassification date would be 1 January 2021.

A change in the objective of an entity's business model must be effected before the reclassification date. For example, if a financial services firm decides on 15 February to shut down its retail mortgage business and hence must reclassify all affected financial assets on 1 April (i.e. the first day of the entity's next reporting period, assuming it reports quarterly), the entity must not accept new retail mortgage business or otherwise engage in activities consistent with its former business model after 15 February. *[IFRS 9.B4.4.2]*.

10 CONTRACTS WITH INSURANCE RISK – INTERACTION BETWEEN IFRS 17 AND IFRS 9

10.1 Loan contracts that transfer significant insurance risk only on settlement of the policyholder's obligation created by the contract

Some financial instruments contain features that transfer significant insurance risk which would have caused them to be within the scope of IFRS 17 as originally issued in May 2017, rather than in the scope of IFRS 9. An example of this would be a loan with a waiver in the event of the borrower's death. IFRS 17 is effective for annual reporting periods beginning on or after 1 January 2023.

In June 2020 the IASB published an amended version of IFRS 17. Based on the amendments, an entity can now elect to apply either IFRS 17 or IFRS 9 to insurance contracts that provide insurance coverage only on the settlement of a policyholder's obligation created by the contract itself, as in the above example, of a loan with a waiver upon death. The election would be made at a portfolio level and would be irrevocable. *[IFRS 17.8A]*. Refer to Chapter 56 at 2.3.3 and Chapter 45 at 3.3.5 for further detail.

If an entity elects to apply IFRS 9 to such loan contracts and the insurance element is contractual (and not imposed as a result of laws or regulations), then it would cause the contract to fail the SPPI test. Note that any terms imposed by laws or regulations would not be considered in the analysis of the contractual payment features of the loan (refer to Example 48.28 for further consideration of the impact of non-contractual features). This accounting may be different to how entities currently account for these contracts under IFRS 4 as the criteria for separating components of an insurance contract under IFRS 17 differ from those under IFRS 4. Under IFRS 4, entities may have chosen to separate the insurance element from the loan contract, with the effect that the remaining loan contract could qualify to be measured at amortised cost in terms of IFRS 9.

The insurance coverage might alternatively be issued as a separate contract to the underlying loan contract to which the coverage relates. In those situations, the loan contract could still pass the SPPI test, as it will not have the insurance cover embedded in the loan contract itself.

10.2 Credit card contracts (and other similar contracts) that provide insurance coverage

In certain jurisdictions, an entity issuing a credit card may be required to provide coverage for purchases made by the customer using the credit card. The coverage could include refunding the customer for any breach of contract by the supplier that is not rectified by the supplier. The issuer of the credit card would be entitled to be indemnified by the supplier for any loss incurred in satisfying its liability with the customer. It is common in these circumstances for the issuer of the credit card not to charge any fee for this coverage. The question then arises as to if the credit card is assessed as having transferred insurance risk that is significant, whether it would be an insurance contract within the scope of IFRS 17.

IFRS 4 had different criteria for separating components of an insurance contract when compared to IFRS 17 with the result that most entities separated the components of such contracts. For example, an entity applying IFRS 4 might account for the credit card component applying IFRS 9, the insurance component applying IFRS 4 and any other service component applying IFRS 15 – *Revenue from Contracts with Customers*. The IASB acknowledged that entities had already identified methods to separate the components of such contracts, and so concluded that changing the existing accounting for these contracts would impose costs and disruption to entities for no significant benefit. *[IFRS 17.BC94B]*.

IFRS 17 was therefore, amended to exclude from its scope, credit card contracts (and other similar contracts that provide credit or payment arrangements) that meet the definition of an insurance contract if, and only if, the entity does not reflect an assessment of the insurance risk associated with an individual customer in setting the price of the contract with that customer.

Once a credit card contract is out of scope of IFRS 17, an entity needs to determine whether it provides the insurance coverage because it is required by law or regulation, or as part of the contractual terms of the credit card contract. For insurance coverage that is provided as part of the contractual terms of the credit card contract, the June 2020 amendment (see 10.1 above) requires that the issuer: *[IFRS 17.7(h), IFRS 9.2.1(e)(iv)]*

- To separate the insurance coverage component and apply IFRS 17 to it; and
- To apply other applicable standards (such as IFRS 9, IFRS 15 or IAS 37 – *Provisions, Contingent Liabilities and Contingent Assets*) to the other components.

As a result of the amendment to IFRS 17 (as originally issued in May 2017), the issuer will (in the circumstances described above) be required to separate the insurance coverage component, and then apply IFRS 9 to the remainder of the contract. There is therefore no longer any insurance element that remains in the scope of IFRS 9 and hence the insurance element would not cause the credit card arrangement to fail the SPPI test. Refer to Chapter 56 at 2.3.1 for further detail regarding the scoping requirements of IFRS 17 and to Chapter 45 at 3.3.4 for further detail regarding the scoping of IFRS 9.

References

1 *IFRIC Update*, November 2016.
2 IASB staff paper 6D, September 2013, Project Financial Instruments: Classification and Measurement, Paper topic: Contractual cash flow characteristics: The meaning of 'interest'.
3 IASB staff paper 6D, September 2013, Project Financial Instruments: Classification and Measurement, Paper topic: Contractual cash flow characteristics: The meaning of 'interest', para. 45.
4 IASB staff paper 6D, September 2013, Project Financial Instruments: Classification and Measurement, Paper topic: Contractual cash flow characteristics: The meaning of 'interest', para. 49 and para. 51.
5 IASB staff paper 6D, September 2013, Project Financial Instruments: Classification and Measurement, Paper topic: Contractual cash flow characteristics: The meaning of 'interest', para. 51(c).
6 *IASB Update*, October 2019 IASB staff paper 14B, Project IBOR Reform and its Effects on Financial Reporting—Phase 2, Paper topic: Accounting implications from derecognition of a modified financial instrument, paras. 30-50.
7 *IFRIC Update*, September 2018.
8 *IFRIC Update*, May 2017.
9 *IASB Update*, October 2009.

Chapter 49   Financial instruments: Recognition and initial measurement

1 INTRODUCTION 3841
2 RECOGNITION 3841
  2.1 General requirements 3841
      2.1.1 Receivables and payables 3842
      2.1.2 Firm commitments to purchase or sell goods or services 3842
      2.1.3 Forward contracts 3842
      2.1.4 Option contracts 3842
      2.1.5 Planned future transactions (forecast transactions) 3842
      2.1.6 Transfers of financial assets not qualifying for derecognition by transferor – Impact on recognition 3843
      2.1.7 Cash collateral 3844
      2.1.8 Principal versus agent 3844
  2.2 'Regular way' transactions 3845
      2.2.1 Financial assets: general requirements 3845
            2.2.1.A No established market 3846
            2.2.1.B Contracts not settled according to marketplace convention: derivatives 3846
            2.2.1.C Multiple active markets: settlement provisions 3846
            2.2.1.D Exercise of a derivative 3846
      2.2.2 Financial liabilities 3847
      2.2.3 Trade date accounting 3847
      2.2.4 Settlement date accounting 3848
      2.2.5 Illustrative examples 3848
            2.2.5.A Exchanges of non-cash financial assets 3852
3 INITIAL MEASUREMENT 3853

3.1	General requirements	3853
3.2	Short-term receivables and payables and trade receivables	3854
3.3	Initial fair value, transaction price and 'day 1' profits	3854
	3.3.1 Interest-free and low-interest long-term loans	3855
	3.3.2 Measurement of financial instruments following modification of contractual terms that leads to initial recognition of a new instrument	3856
	3.3.3 Financial guarantee contracts and off-market loan commitments	3857
	3.3.4 Loans and receivables acquired in a business combination	3857
	3.3.5 Acquisition of a group of assets that does not constitute a business	3857
3.4	Transaction costs	3858
	3.4.1 Accounting treatment	3858
	3.4.2 Identifying transaction costs	3860
3.5	Embedded derivatives and financial instrument hosts	3860
3.6	Regular way transactions	3860
3.7	Assets and liabilities arising from loan commitments	3861
	3.7.1 Loan commitments outside the scope of IFRS 9	3861
	3.7.2 Loan commitments within the scope of IFRS 9	3862

List of examples

Example 49.1:	Regular way transactions – Forward contract	3846
Example 49.2:	Regular way transactions – Share purchase by call option	3846
Example 49.3:	Trade date and settlement date accounting – regular way purchase	3848
Example 49.4:	Trade date and settlement date accounting – regular way sale	3850
Example 49.5:	Trade date and settlement date accounting – exchange of non-cash financial assets	3853
Example 49.6:	Off-market loan with origination fee	3856
Example 49.7:	Changes in the contractual terms of an existing equity instrument	3856
Example 49.8:	Transaction costs – initial measurement	3859
Example 49.9:	Drawdown under a committed borrowing facility	3861

Chapter 49 Financial instruments: Recognition and initial measurement

1 INTRODUCTION

The introduction to Chapter 44 provides a general background to the development of accounting for financial instruments. Chapter 45 deals with what qualifies as financial assets and financial liabilities and other contracts that are treated as if they were financial instruments.

This chapter deals with the question of when financial instruments should be recognised in financial statements and their initial measurement under IFRS 9 – *Financial Instruments*.

Initial measurement is normally based on the fair value of an instrument and most, but not all, of the detailed requirements of IFRS governing fair values are dealt with in IFRS 13 – *Fair Value Measurement* – which is covered in Chapter 14. IFRS 9 also contains some requirements addressing fair value measurements of financial instruments and these are covered at 3.3 below.

2 RECOGNITION

2.1 General requirements

IFRS 9 provides that an entity must recognise a financial asset or a financial liability on its statement of financial position when, and only when, the entity becomes a party to the contractual provisions of the instrument. *[IFRS 9.3.1.1].* Before that, the entity does not have contractual rights or contractual obligations. Hence, there is no financial asset or a financial liability, as defined in IAS 32 – *Financial Instruments: Presentation*, to recognise. IFRS 9 provides a practical exception to the application of this general principle for 'regular way' purchases of financial assets (see 2.2 below). IFRS 9 gives the following examples of the more general application of this principle.

2.1.1 Receivables and payables

Unconditional receivables and payables are recognised as assets or liabilities when the entity becomes a party to the contract and, as a consequence, has a legal right to receive or a legal obligation to pay cash. [IFRS 9.B3.1.2(a)].

2.1.2 Firm commitments to purchase or sell goods or services

Under IFRS, assets to be acquired and liabilities to be incurred as a result of a firm commitment to purchase or sell goods or services are generally not recognised until at least one of the parties has performed under the agreement. For example, an entity that receives a firm order for goods or services does not generally recognise an asset for the consideration receivable (and the entity that places the order does not generally recognise a liability for the consideration to be paid) at the time of the commitment, but instead delays recognition until the ordered goods or services have been shipped, delivered or rendered. [IFRS 9.B3.1.2(b)].

This accounting applies on the assumption that the firm commitment to buy or sell non-financial items is not treated as if it were a derivative (see Chapter 45 at 3.5) nor designated as a hedged item in a fair value hedge (see Chapter 53 at 5.1). Where the firm commitment is treated as a derivative or designated as a hedged item in a fair value hedge, it would be recognised as an asset or liability before delivery.

2.1.3 Forward contracts

A forward contract is a contract which obliges one party to the contract to buy, and the other party to sell, the asset that is the subject of the contract for a fixed price at a future date.

A forward contract within the scope of IFRS 9 is recognised as an asset or a liability at commitment date, rather than on settlement. When an entity becomes a party to a forward contract, the fair values of the right and obligation are often equal, so that the net fair value of the forward at inception is zero. If the net fair value of the right and obligation is not zero, the contract is recognised as an asset or liability. [IFRS 9.B3.1.2(c)].

2.1.4 Option contracts

An option contract is a contract which gives one party to the contract the right, but not the obligation, to buy from, or sell to, the other party to the contract the asset that is the subject of the contract for a fixed price at a future date (or during a period of time). An option giving the right to buy an asset is referred to as a 'call' option and one giving the right to sell an asset as a 'put' option. An option is referred to as a 'bought' or 'purchased' option from the perspective of the party with the right to buy or sell (the 'holder') and as a 'written' option from the perspective of the party with the potential obligation to buy or sell.

Option contracts that are within the scope of IFRS 9 are recognised as assets or liabilities when the holder or writer becomes a party to the contract. [IFRS 9.B3.1.2(d)].

2.1.5 Planned future transactions (forecast transactions)

Planned future transactions, no matter how likely, are not assets and liabilities because the entity has not become a party to a contract. They are therefore not recognised under IFRS 9. [IFRS 9.B3.1.2(e)]. However, transactions that have been entered into as a hedge of certain 'highly probable' future transactions are recognised under IFRS 9 – this raises the issue of the accounting treatment of any gains or losses arising on such hedging transactions (see Chapter 53 at 5.2).

2.1.6 Transfers of financial assets not qualifying for derecognition by transferor – Impact on recognition

IFRS 9 states that, where a financial asset is transferred from one party to another in circumstances that preclude the transferor from derecognising the asset, the transferee should not recognise the transferred asset. Instead, the transferee derecognises the cash or other consideration paid and recognises a receivable from the transferor. [IFRS 9.B3.1.1]. If the transferor has both a right and an obligation to reacquire control of the entire transferred asset for a fixed amount (such as under a repurchase agreement – see Chapter 52 at 4.1), the transferee may account for its receivable at amortised cost if it meets the criteria for classification as measured at amortised cost. [IFRS 9.B3.2.15]. Underlying this principle appears to be a concern that more than one party cannot satisfy the criteria in IFRS 9 for recognition of the same financial asset at the same time. In fact, however, this principle may not hold in all circumstances, since it is common for the same assets to be simultaneously recognised by more than one entity – for example if the transferor adopts settlement date accounting and the transferee trade date accounting (see 2.2 below).

In addition, IFRS 9 clarifies that to the extent that a transfer does not qualify for derecognition, the transferor does not account for its contractual rights or obligations related to the transfer separately as derivatives if recognising both the derivative and either the transferred asset or the liability arising from the transfer would result in recognising the same rights or obligations twice. For example, a call option retained by the transferor may prevent a transfer of financial assets from being accounted for as a sale. In that case, the call option is not separately recognised as a derivative asset. [IFRS 9.B3.2.14].

Sometimes a transfer of financial assets can involve the transferee issuing to the transferor a non-derivative financial instrument, such as subordinated debt, the effect of which is that substantially all the risks and rewards of the assets are not transferred and therefore the transferor does not derecognise the assets. This is particularly common when the transferee is a securitisation vehicle. The subordinated debt could be issued as part of the consideration for the transferred assets, alongside the cash consideration. Alternatively, part of the cash consideration received in exchange for the transferred assets could be reinvested in the subordinated debt. In these circumstances we would expect the transferor to apply by analogy the guidance for derivatives set out above in paragraph B3.2.14, not recognise the subordinated loan as a separate asset but instead recognise a financial liability equal to the net cash received. However, IFRS 9 is less clear about the transferee's position and it will need to determine whether it should recognise the subordinated loan as a separate financial liability or to regard the subsequent cash flows on this loan as part of the cash flows arising on the receivable. The guidance in Chapter 46 at 3.2 addresses whether two financial instruments should be accounted for as one (which in those cases would lead to the recognition of a derivative) and these principles can help the transferee determine whether it recognises both a financial liability and a receivable or simply a more complex receivable.

However, this can be very judgemental and we do see a degree of diversity in the way securitisation vehicles account for these arrangements.

2.1.7 Cash collateral

The implementation guidance to IFRS 9 addresses the recognition of cash collateral. When an entity receives cash collateral that is not legally segregated (e.g. not treated as 'client money'), it must recognise the cash and a related payable to the entity providing such collateral. The reason is that the ultimate realisation of a financial asset is its conversion into cash, and hence, no further transformation is required before the economic benefits of the cash received can be realised.

On the other hand, the entity providing the cash collateral derecognises the cash and recognises a receivable from the receiving entity. *[IFRS 9.IG.D.1.1]*.

The accounting treatment of 'client money' is discussed in more detail in Chapter 52 at 3.7. The requirements related to non-cash collateral are addressed in Chapter 52 at 5.5.2.

2.1.8 Principal versus agent

When an entity acts as an intermediary in transactions involving financial instruments, the question of whether it is acting as an agent or a principal may arise. This is a particularly relevant matter for brokers and similar institutions.

The Interpretations Committee has addressed this matter in relation to clearing brokers in the context of centrally cleared client derivatives. Diversity in practice had been observed with some brokers applying the guidance on principal versus agent included in IFRS 15 – *Revenue from Contracts with Customers* – to determine whether they should account for back to back derivatives with their client and the central clearing counterparty. In June 2017, the Committee concluded that the clearing broker should first apply the requirements for financial instruments and observed that:

- if the transaction(s) results in contracts that are within the scope of IFRS 9, then the clearing member applies to those contracts the recognition requirements of IFRS 9. In the statement of financial position, the clearing member presents the assets and liabilities arising from its contracts with the clearing house separately from those arising from its contracts with its clients, unless net presentation is required pursuant to the offsetting requirements in IAS 32. This implies the clearing member is considered to act as principal in both the derivative contracts with the clearing house and its clients;

- if the transaction(s) is (are) not within the scope of IFRS 9 and another standard does not specifically apply, only then would the clearing member apply the hierarchy in paragraphs 10–12 of IAS 8 – *Accounting Policies, Changes in Accounting Estimates and Errors* – to determine an appropriate accounting policy for the transaction(s) (see Chapter 3 at 4.3), e.g. using the principal versus agent guidance in IFRS 15 (see Chapter 28 at 3.4).[1]

Therefore, the 'principal versus agent' assessment for initial recognition is largely driven by the legal form of the contract resulting in accounting treatment as a principal, even though in substance, the entity might be acting in a manner very similar to an agent.

2.2 'Regular way' transactions

2.2.1 Financial assets: general requirements

As discussed at 2.1 above, the general requirement under IFRS 9 is to recognise a financial asset or a financial liability on its statement of financial position when, and only when, the entity becomes a party to the contractual provisions of the instrument (i.e. the trade date). *[IFRS 9.3.1.1]*. However, the application of this general requirement to certain transactions known as 'regular way' purchases and sales presents some challenges. Below we discuss those challenges and the accounting policy choice that IFRS 9 has provided as a solution.

A *regular way purchase or sale* is defined as a purchase or sale of a financial asset under a contract whose terms require delivery of the asset within the time frame established generally by regulation or convention in the marketplace concerned. *[IFRS 9 Appendix A]*. By contrast, a contract that does not require delivery and can be settled by net settlement (i.e. payment or receipt of cash or other financial assets equivalent to the change in value of the contract) is not a regular way transaction, but is accounted for between the trade date and settlement date as a derivative in accordance with the requirements of IFRS 9 (see Chapter 50 at 2.4). *[IFRS 9.B3.1.4]*.

Many financial markets provide a mechanism whereby all transactions in certain financial instruments (particularly quoted equities and bonds) entered into on a particular date are settled by delivery a fixed number of days after that date. The date on which the entity commits itself to purchase or sell an asset is called the 'trade date' and the date on which it is settled by delivery of the assets that are the subject of the agreement is called the 'settlement date'. *[IFRS 9.B3.1.5, B3.1.6]*. One effect of this mechanism is that, while legal title to the assets that are the subject of the transaction passes only on or after settlement date, the buyer is effectively exposed to the risks and rewards of ownership of the assets from trade date.

Absent any special provisions, the accounting analysis for regular way transactions under IFRS 9 would therefore be that, between trade date and settlement date, an entity has a forward contract to purchase an asset (see 2.1.3 above) which, in common with all derivatives, should be recorded at fair value, with all changes in fair value recognised in profit or loss (see Chapter 48 at 4), unless the special rules for hedge accounting apply (see Chapter 53). This would not only be somewhat onerous but would also have the effect that changes in a financial asset's fair value between trade date and settlement date would be recognised in profit or loss, even though the asset itself may not be measured at fair value through profit or loss after initial recognition.

To avoid this, IFRS 9 permits assets subject to regular way transactions to be recognised, or derecognised, either as at the trade date ('trade date accounting') or as at the settlement date ('settlement date accounting'). *[IFRS 9.B3.1.3, B3.1.5, B3.1.6]*. This accounting policy choice can be made separately for each of the main categories of financial asset identified by IFRS 9, i.e. debt instruments measured at amortised cost, debt instruments at fair value through other comprehensive income (FVOCI), financial assets mandatorily measured at fair value through profit or loss, debt instruments designated as measured at fair value through profit or loss and equity investments designated as measured at FVOCI (see Chapter 48). Once chosen, the accounting policy needs to be applied consistently and symmetrically (i.e. to acquisitions and disposals) to each category. *[IFRS 9.B3.1.3]*.

IFRS 9 provides additional guidance for determining whether a transaction meets the definition of 'regular way' which is further discussed below.

2.2.1.A No established market

The definition of 'regular way' transactions refers to terms that require delivery of the asset within the time frame established generally by regulation or convention in the marketplace concerned. Marketplace in this context is not limited to a formal stock exchange or organised over-the-counter market. Rather, it means the environment in which the financial asset is customarily exchanged. An acceptable time frame would be the period reasonably and customarily required for the parties to complete the transaction and prepare and execute closing documents. For example, a market for private issue financial instruments can be a marketplace. *[IFRS 9.IG.B.28]*.

2.2.1.B Contracts not settled according to marketplace convention: derivatives

The contract must be accounted for as a derivative when it is not settled in the way established by regulation or convention in the marketplace concerned.

Example 49.1: Regular way transactions – Forward contract

Entity A enters into a forward contract to purchase 1 million of B's ordinary shares in two months for £10 per share. The contract is with an individual and is not an exchange-traded contract. The contract requires A to take physical delivery of the shares and pay the counterparty £10 million in cash. B's shares trade in an active public market at an average of 100,000 shares a day. Regular way delivery is three days. In these circumstances, the forward contract cannot be regarded as a regular way contract and must be accounted for as a derivative because it is not settled in the way established by regulation or convention in the marketplace concerned. *[IFRS 9.IG.B.29]*.

2.2.1.C Multiple active markets: settlement provisions

If an entity's financial instruments trade in more than one active market, and the settlement provisions differ in the various active markets, the provisions that apply are those in the market in which the purchase actually takes place.

For instance, an entity purchasing shares of a public company listed on a US stock exchange through a broker, where the settlement date of the contract is six business days later, could not apply the regular way trade exemption since trades for equity shares on US exchanges customarily settle in three business days. However, if the entity did the same transaction on an exchange outside the US that has a customary settlement period of six business days, the contract would meet the exemption for a regular way trade. *[IFRS 9.IG.B.30]*.

2.2.1.D Exercise of a derivative

The settlement of an option is governed by regulation or convention in the marketplace for options and, therefore, upon exercise of the option it is no longer accounted for as a derivative when the exercise is settled according to the provisions of the marketplace. In such case, the settlement of an option by delivery of the shares is a regular way transaction.

Example 49.2: Regular way transactions – Share purchase by call option

Entity A purchases a call option in a public market permitting it to purchase 100 shares of Entity X at any time over the next three months at a price of £100 per share. If Entity A exercises its option, it has 14 days to settle the transaction according to regulation or convention in the options market. X shares are traded in an active public market that requires three-day settlement.

In this case, the purchase of shares by exercising the option is a regular way purchase of shares because settlement by delivery of the shares within 14 days is a regular way transaction. *[IFRS 9.IG.B.31]*. This is the case even though if the shares had been acquired directly in the market the market convention for settlement would have been three days.

2.2.2 Financial liabilities

The above requirements apply only to transactions in financial assets. IFRS 9 does not contain any specific requirements about trade date accounting and settlement date accounting for transactions in financial instruments that are classified as financial liabilities. Therefore, the general recognition and derecognition requirements for financial liabilities in IFRS 9 normally apply. Consequently, financial liabilities are normally recognised on the date the entity 'becomes a party to the contractual provisions of the instrument' (see 2.1 above); in addition, they are not generally recognised unless one of the parties has performed or the contract is a derivative contract not exempted from the scope of IFRS 9. Financial liabilities are derecognised only when they are extinguished, i.e. when the obligation specified in the contract is discharged, cancelled or expires (see Chapter 52 at 6). *[IFRS 9.3.3.1]*.

In January 2007, the IFRS Interpretations Committee addressed the accounting for short sales of securities when the transaction terms require delivery of the securities within the time frame established generally by regulation or convention in the marketplace concerned. Constituents explained that in practice, many entities apply trade date accounting to such transactions. Specifically, industry practice recognised the short sales as financial liabilities at fair value with changes in fair value recognised in profit or loss. Profit or loss would be the same as if short sales were accounted for as derivatives, but the securities would be presented differently on the statement of financial position. Those constituents argued that a short sale is created by a transaction in a financial asset and hence the implementation guidance noted in the previous paragraph is not relevant.

The Committee acknowledged that requiring entities to account for short positions as derivatives may create considerable practical problems for their accounting systems and controls with little, if any, improvement to the quality of financial information presented. For these reasons, and because there was little diversity in practice, the Committee decided not to take the issue onto its agenda and thus industry practice remains prevalent.[2]

2.2.3 Trade date accounting

As noted above, the trade date is the date on which an entity commits itself to purchase or sell an asset. Trade date accounting requires:

(a) in respect of an asset to be bought: recognition on the trade date of the asset and the liability to pay for it, which means that during the period between trade date and settlement date, the entity accounts for the asset as if it already owned it; and

(b) in respect of an asset to be sold: derecognition on the trade date of the asset, together with recognition of any gain or loss on disposal and the recognition of a receivable from the buyer for payment.

IFRS 9 notes that, generally, interest does not start to accrue on the asset and corresponding liability until the settlement date when title passes. *[IFRS 9.B3.1.5]*.

2.2.4 Settlement date accounting

As noted above, the settlement date is the date that an asset is delivered to or by an entity. Settlement date accounting requires:

(a) in respect of an asset to be bought: the recognition of the asset on the settlement date (i.e. the date it is received by the entity). Any change in the fair value of the asset to be received during the period between the trade date and the settlement date is accounted for in the same way as the acquired asset. In other words: *[IFRS 9.5.7.4, IFRS 9.B3.1.6]*

- for assets carried at cost or amortised cost, the change in fair value is not recognised (other than impairment losses);
- for assets classified as financial assets at fair value through profit or loss, the change in fair value is recognised in profit or loss; and
- for financial assets measured at FVOCI, the change in fair value is recognised in other comprehensive income.

(b) in respect of an asset to be sold: derecognition of the asset, recognition of any gain or loss on disposal and the recognition of a receivable from the buyer for payment on the settlement date (i.e. the date it is delivered by the entity). *[IFRS 9.B3.1.6]*. A change in the fair value of the asset between trade date and settlement date is not recorded in the financial statements because the seller's right to changes in the fair value ceases on the trade date. *[IFRS 9.IG.D.2.2]*.

2.2.5 Illustrative examples

Examples 49.3 and 49.4 below (which are based on those in the implementation guidance appended to IFRS 9) illustrate the application of trade date and settlement date accounting to the various categories of financial asset identified by IFRS 9. *[IFRS 9.IG.D.2.1, IG.D.2.2]*. For simplicity purposes, these examples do not address the accounting entries related to impairment charges. The accounting treatment for these categories of assets is discussed in more detail in Chapter 50 through to Chapter 54.

Example 49.3: **Trade date and settlement date accounting – regular way purchase**

On 29 December 2021 (trade date), an entity commits itself to purchase a financial asset for €1,000, which is its fair value on trade date. On 31 December 2021 (financial year-end) and on 4 January 2022 (settlement date) the fair value of the asset is €1,002 and €1,003, respectively. The accounting entries to be recorded for the transaction will depend on how it is classified and whether trade date or settlement date accounting is used, as shown in the tables below:

A *Financial asset accounted for at amortised cost*

	Trade date accounting			Settlement date accounting		
		€	€		€	€

29 December 2021

	Financial asset	1,000				
	Liability to counterparty		1,000			
	To record purchase of asset and liability thereof			*No accounting entries*		

31 December 2021

	No accounting entries			*No accounting entries*		

4 January 2022

	Liability to counterparty	1,000		Financial asset	1,000	
	Cash		1,000	Cash		1,000
	To record settlement of liability			*To record purchase of asset*		

B *Financial asset accounted for at fair value through profit or loss*

	Trade date accounting			Settlement date accounting		
		€	€		€	€

29 December 2021

	Financial asset	1,000				
	Liability to counterparty		1,000			
	To record purchase of asset and liability thereof			*No accounting entries*		

31 December 2021

	Financial Asset	2		Receivable	2	
	Income statement		2	Income statement		2
	To record change in fair value of asset			*To record change in fair value of contract*		

4 January 2022

	Liability to counterparty	1,000				
	Cash		1,000	Financial asset	1,003	
	Financial asset	1		Cash		1,000
	Income statement		1	Receivable		2
				Income statement		1
	To record settlement of liability and change in fair value of asset			*To record purchase of asset, change in fair value and settlement of contract*		

C   *Financial asset measured at FVOCI **

	Trade date accounting		Settlement date accounting	
	€	€	€	€
29 December 2021				
Financial asset	1,000			
Liability to counterparty		1,000		
	To record purchase of asset and liability thereof		*No accounting entries*	
31 December 2021				
Financial Asset	2			
Receivable			2	
OCI		2		2
	To record change in fair value of asset		*To record change in fair value of contract*	
4 January 2022				
Liability to counterparty	1,000			
Financial asset			1,003	
Cash		1,000		
Cash				1,000
Financial asset	1			
Receivable				2
OCI		1		1
	To record settlement of liability and change in fair value of asset		*To record purchase of asset, change in fair value and settlement of contract*	

*   The same analysis applies whether the financial assets measured at FVOCI are debt instruments or equity instruments.

As illustrated above, for a regular way purchase, the key difference between trade date and settlement date accounting is the timing of recognition of a financial asset. Regardless of the method used, the impact on profit or loss, OCI and net assets is the same.

Example 49.4:   **Trade date and settlement date accounting – regular way sale**

On 29 December 2021 (trade date) an entity enters into a contract to sell a financial asset for its then current fair value of €1,010. The asset was acquired one year earlier for €1,000 and its amortised cost is €1,000. On 31 December 2021 (financial year-end), the fair value of the asset is €1,012. On 4 January 2022 (settlement date), the fair value is €1,013. The accounting entries to be recorded for this transaction will depend on how the asset is classified and whether trade date or settlement date accounting is used as shown in the tables below (any interest that might have accrued on the asset is disregarded).

A change in the fair value of a financial asset that is sold on a regular way basis is not recorded in the financial statements between trade date and settlement date, even if the entity applies settlement date accounting, because the seller's right to changes in the fair value ceases on the trade date.

A   Financial asset accounted for at amortised cost

	Trade date accounting		Settlement date accounting	
	€	€	€	€
Before 29 December 2021 (cumulative net entries)				
Financial asset	1,000		1,000	
Cash		1,000		1,000
To record acquisition of the asset a year earlier			*To record acquisition of the asset a year earlier*	
	€	€	€	€
29 December 2021				
Receivable from counterparty	1,010			
Financial asset		1,000		
Gain on disposal (income statement)		10		
To record disposal of asset			*No accounting entries*	
4 January 2022				
Cash	1,010		1,010	
Receivable from counterparty		1,010		
Financial asset				1,000
Gain on disposal (income statement)				10
To record settlement of sale contract			*To record disposal of asset*	

B   Financial asset accounted for at fair value through profit or loss

	Trade date accounting		Settlement date accounting	
	€	€	€	€
Before 29 December 2021 (cumulative net entries)				
Financial asset	1,010		1,010	
Cash		1,000		1,000
Income statement		10		10
To record acquisition and net change in fair value up to date			*To record acquisition and net change in fair value up to date*	
29 December 2021				
Receivable from counterparty	1,010			
Financial asset		1,010		
To record disposal of asset			*No accounting entries*	
4 January 2022				
Cash	1,010		1,010	
Receivable from counterparty		1,010		
Financial asset				1,010
To record settlement of sale contract			*To record disposal of asset*	

C   Debt instrument measured at FVOCI*

	Trade date accounting			Settlement date accounting		
		€	€		€	€
Before 29 December 2021 (cumulative net entries)						
	Financial asset	1,010		Financial asset	1,010	
	Cash		1,000	Cash		1,000
	OCI		10	OCI		10

	Trade date accounting			Settlement date accounting		
		€	€		€	€
29 December 2021						
	Receivable from counterparty	1,010				
	Financial asset		1,010			
**	OCI	10				
	Gain on sale (income statement)		10			
	To record disposal of asset			*No accounting entries*		
4 January 2022						
	Cash	1,010		Cash	1,010	
	Receivable from counterparty		1,010	Financial asset		1,010
**				OCI	10	
				Gain on sale (income statement)		10
	To record settlement of sale contract			*To record disposal of asset*		

*   The same analysis will apply to equity investments measured at FVOCI, except that IFRS 9 does not permit 'recycling' (i.e. transfers) of cumulative gains and losses from OCI to profit or loss. However, an entity may transfer the cumulative gains and losses within equity (e.g. from accumulated OCI to retained earnings).

**   The transfers from OCI to profit or loss (retained earnings) represent the 'recycling' of cumulative gains and losses required by IFRS 9 on disposal of a debt instrument accounted for at FVOCI (see Chapter 50 at 2.3). Disposal is regarded as occurring on trade date when trade date accounting applies and on settlement date when settlement date accounting applies.

As illustrated above, for a regular way sale, the key differences between trade date and settlement date accounting relate to the timing of derecognition of a financial asset and the timing of recognition of any gain or loss arising from the disposal of the financial asset, unless the financial asset is carried at fair value through profit or loss.

2.2.5.A   Exchanges of non-cash financial assets

The implementation guidance to IFRS 9 addresses the situation in which an entity enters into a regular way transaction whereby it commits to sell a non-cash financial asset in exchange for another non-cash financial asset.

This situation raises the question of whether, if the entity applies settlement date accounting to the asset to be delivered, it should recognise any change in the fair value of the financial asset to be received arising between trade date and settlement date. A further issue is that, due to the accounting policy choice available for each category discussed at 2.2.1 above, the asset being bought may be in a category of asset to which trade date accounting is applied.

In essence, the implementation guidance requires the buying and selling legs of the exchange transaction to be accounted for independently, as illustrated by the following example. *[IFRS 9.IG.D.2.3]*.

Example 49.5:   Trade date and settlement date accounting – exchange of non-cash financial assets

On 29 December 2021 (trade date), an entity enters into a contract to sell Note Receivable A, which is carried at amortised cost, in exchange for Bond B, which will be classified as held for trading and measured at fair value. Both assets have a fair value of €1,010 on 29 December 2021, while the amortised cost of Note Receivable A is €1,000. The entity uses settlement date accounting for financial assets at amortised cost and trade date accounting for assets held for trading.

On 31 December 2021 (financial year-end), the fair value of Note Receivable A is €1,012 and the fair value of Bond B is €1,009. On 4 January 2022 (settlement date), the fair value of Note Receivable A is €1,013 and the fair value of Bond B is €1,007.

The following entries are made:

	€	€
29 December 2021		
Bond B	1,010	
Liability to counterparty		1,010
To record purchase of Bond B (trade date accounting)		
31 December 2021		
Loss on Bond B (income statement)	1	
Bond B		1
To record change in fair value of Bond B		
4 January 2022		
Liability to counterparty	1,010	
Note Receivable A		1,000
Gain on disposal (income statement)		10
To record disposal of receivable A (settlement date accounting)		
Loss on Bond B (income statement)	2	
Bond B		2
To record change in fair value of Bond B		

The simultaneous recognition, between 29 December and 4 January, of both the asset being bought and the asset being given in consideration may seem counter-intuitive. However, it is no different from the accounting treatment of any purchase of goods for credit which results, in the period between delivery of, and payment for, the goods, in the simultaneous recognition of the goods, the liability to pay the supplier and the cash that will be used to do so.

3 INITIAL MEASUREMENT

3.1 General requirements

On initial recognition, financial assets and financial liabilities at fair value through profit or loss are normally measured at their fair value on the date they are initially recognised. The initial measurement of other financial instruments is also based on their fair value, but adjusted in respect of any transaction costs that are incremental and directly attributable to the acquisition or issue of the financial instrument. *[IFRS 9.5.1.1]*.

There are however certain exceptions and additional considerations to the general requirements that we address in the following sections.

3.2 Short-term receivables and payables and trade receivables

With the exception of trade receivables arising from transaction within the scope of IFRS 15, short-term receivables and payables with no stated interest rate may be measured at invoice amounts without discounting when the effect of not discounting is immaterial. Although a statement to this effect is no longer contained in IFRS 9, the Basis for Conclusions on IFRS 13 clarifies this approach is permitted because IAS 8 allows the application of accounting policies that are not in accordance with IFRS when the effect is immaterial. *[IFRS 13.BC138A, IAS 8.8]*.

Trade receivables that do not have a significant financing component and those for which an entity applies the practical expedient in paragraph 63 of IFRS 15 (i.e. trade receivables with a significant financing component when at contract inception the entity expects that the period between the entity transferring a promised good or service to the customer and the customer settling that trade receivable is one year or less) should be measured at initial recognition at their transaction price as defined by IFRS 15. *[IFRS 9.5.1.1, 5.1.3]*. In most cases this will be consistent with the treatment of short-term receivables discussed in the preceding paragraph.

Other trade receivables (i.e. those arising from an arrangement with a significant financing component that is accounted for as such) should be recognised at their fair value in accordance with the general requirements at 3.1 above. In principle, any differences arising from the initial recognition of these receivables at fair value and the carrying amount of the associated contract asset or transaction price determined in accordance with IFRS 15, will be recognised in profit or loss, e.g. as an impairment loss. *[IFRS 15.108]*. In practice, however, any such difference will often not be material.

3.3 Initial fair value, transaction price and 'day 1' profits

IFRS 9 and IFRS 13 acknowledge that the best evidence of the fair value of a financial instrument on initial recognition is normally the transaction price (i.e. the fair value of the consideration given or received), although this will not necessarily be the case in all circumstances (see Chapter 14 at 13.1.1). *[IFRS 9.B5.1.1, B5.1.2A, IFRS 13.58]*. Although IFRS 13 specifies how to measure fair value, IFRS 9 contains restrictions on recognising differences between the transaction price and the initial fair value as measured under IFRS 13, often called day 1 profits, which apply in addition to the requirements of IFRS 13 (see Chapter 14 at 13.2). *[IFRS 13.60, BC138]*.

If an entity determines that the fair value on initial recognition differs from the transaction price, the difference is recognised as a gain or loss only if the fair value is based on a quoted price in an active market for an identical asset or liability (i.e. a Level 1 input) or based on a valuation technique that uses only data from observable markets. Otherwise, the difference is deferred and recognised as a gain or loss only to the extent that it arises from a change in a factor (including time) that market participants would take into account when pricing the asset or liability. *[IFRS 9.5.1.1A, B5.1.2A]*. The subsequent measurement and the subsequent recognition of gains and losses should be consistent with the requirements of IFRS 9 that are covered in detail in Chapter 50. *[IFRS 9.B5.2.2A]*.

Therefore, entities that trade in financial instruments are prevented from immediately recognising a profit on the initial recognition of many financial instruments that are not quoted in active markets or whose fair value is not measured based on valuation techniques that use only observable inputs. Consequently, locked-in profits will emerge over the life of the financial instruments, although precisely how they should emerge is not at all clear. The IASB was asked to clarify that straight-line amortisation was an appropriate method of recognising the day 1 profits but decided not to do so. IFRS 9 does not discuss this at all, although IAS 39 – *Financial Instruments: Recognition and Measurement* – used to state (without further explanation) that straight-line amortisation may be an appropriate method in some cases, but will not be appropriate in others. *[IAS 39(2006).BC222(v)(ii)]*.

3.3.1 Interest-free and low-interest long-term loans

As noted in 3.3 above, the fair value of a financial instrument on initial recognition is normally the transaction price. IFRS 9 further explains that if part of the consideration given or received was for something other than the financial instrument, the entity should measure the fair value of the financial instrument in accordance with IFRS 13. For example, the fair value of a long-term loan or receivable that carries no interest could be estimated as the present value of all future cash receipts discounted using the prevailing market rate(s) of interest for instruments that are similar as to currency, term, type of interest rate, credit risk and other factors. Any additional amount advanced is an expense or a reduction of income unless it qualifies for recognition as some other type of asset. IFRS 13 requires the application of a similar approach in such circumstances. *[IFRS 9.B5.1.1, IFRS 13.60]*. For example, an entity may provide an interest free loan to a supplier in order to receive a discount on goods or services purchased in the future and the difference between the fair value and the amount advanced might well be recognised as an asset, for example under IAS 38 – *Intangible Assets* – if the entity obtains a contractual right to the discounted supplies.

Similar issues often arise from transactions between entities under common control. In fact, IFRS 13 suggests a related party transaction may indicate that the transaction price is not the same as the fair value of an asset or liability (see Chapter 14 at 13.3). For example, parents sometimes lend money to subsidiaries on an interest-free or low-interest basis where the loan is not repayable on demand. Where, in its separate financial statements, the parent (or subsidiary) is required to record a receivable (or payable) on initial recognition at a fair value that is lower than cost, the additional consideration will normally represent an additional investment in the subsidiary (or equity contribution from the parent).

Another example is a loan received from a government that has a below-market rate of interest which should be recognised and initially measured at fair value. The benefit of the below-market rate loan, i.e. the excess of the consideration received over the initial carrying amount of the loan, should be accounted for as a government grant. *[IAS 20.10A]*. The treatment of government grants is discussed further in Chapter 24.

If a financial instrument is recognised where the terms are 'off-market' (i.e. the consideration given or received does not equal the instrument's fair value) but instead a fee is paid or received in compensation, the instrument should be recognised at its fair value that includes an adjustment for the fee received or paid. *[IFRS 9.B5.1.2]*.

Example 49.6: Off-market loan with origination fee

Bank J lends $1,000 to Company K. The loan carries interest at 5% and is repayable in full in five years' time, even though the market rate for similar loans is 8%. To compensate J for the below market rate of interest, K pays J an origination fee of $120. There are no other directly related payments by either party.

The loan is recorded at its fair value of $880 (in this example, assumed to be the net present value of $50 interest payable annually for five years and $1,000 principal repaid after five years, all discounted at 8%). This equals the net amount of cash exchanged ($1,000 loan less $120 origination fee) and hence no gain or loss is recognised on initial recognition of the loan.

Applying the requirements of IFRS 9 to the simple fact pattern provided by the IASB is a relatively straightforward exercise. In practice, however, it may be more difficult to identify those fees that are required by IFRS 9 to be treated as part of the financial instrument and those that should be dealt with in another way, for example under IFRS 15. In particular it may be difficult to determine the extent to which fees associated with a financial instrument that is not quoted in an active market represent compensation for off-market terms or for the genuine provision of services.

3.3.2 Measurement of financial instruments following modification of contractual terms that leads to initial recognition of a new instrument

An entity may agree (with the holder or the issuer) to modify the terms of an instrument that it already recognises in its financial statements as a financial asset, a financial liability or an equity instrument. In such a scenario, an entity needs to consider whether the modification of the terms triggers derecognition of the existing instrument and recognition of a new instrument (see Chapter 52 at 3.4.1). If so, the new instrument would be initially measured at fair value in accordance with the general requirements discussed at 3.1 above.

For example, when the contractual terms of an issued equity instrument are modified such that it is subsequently reclassified as a financial liability, it should be measured at its fair value on the date it is initially recognised as a financial liability, with any difference between this amount and the amount recorded in equity being taken to equity. This follows IAS 32 which prohibits the recognition of gains or losses on the purchase, issue, or cancellation of an entity's own equity instrument.[3]

Example 49.7: Changes in the contractual terms of an existing equity instrument

On 1 January 2021, Company L issues a fixed rate cumulative perpetual instrument with a face value of £10 million at par. Dividends on the instrument are cumulative but discretionary and therefore it is initially classified as equity. On 1 January 2022, L adds a new clause to the instrument so that if L is subject to a change of control, L will be required to redeem the instrument at an amount equal to the face value plus any accumulated unpaid dividends. This results in a reclassification of the instrument from equity to liability. The fair value of the instrument on 1 January 2022 is £12 million.

Upon reclassification, L should recognise the financial liability at its then fair value of £12 million and the difference of £2 million is recognised in equity (e.g. retained earnings).

The accounting for a modification of a financial asset (or financial liability) that results in the recognition of a new financial asset (or financial liability) is dealt with in more detail in Chapter 52 at 3.4 and 6.2.

3.3.3 Financial guarantee contracts and off-market loan commitments

The requirement to measure financial instruments at fair value on initial recognition also applies to issued financial guarantee contracts that are within the scope of IFRS 9 as well as to commitments to provide a loan at a below-market interest rate (see Chapter 45 at 3.4 and 3.5).

When issued to an unrelated party in a stand-alone arm's length transaction, the fair value of a financial guarantee contract at inception is likely to equal the premium received, unless there is evidence to the contrary. *[IFRS 9.B2.5(a)]*. There is likely to be such evidence where, say, a parent provided to a bank a financial guarantee in respect of its subsidiary's borrowings and charged no fee.

When an off-market loan is provided to an entity's subsidiary (see 3.3.1 above), a 'spare debit' arises in the separate financial statements of the parent as a result of the recognition of the loan at fair value. The same situation can arise when a parent provides a subsidiary with an off-market loan commitment. Again, it is normally appropriate to treat this difference as an additional cost of investment in the subsidiary in the separate accounts of the parent (and as an equity contribution from the parent in the accounts of the subsidiary).

3.3.4 Loans and receivables acquired in a business combination

Consistent with IFRS 9 and IFRS 13, IFRS 3 – *Business Combinations* – requires financial assets acquired in a business combination to be measured by the acquirer on initial recognition at their fair value. *[IFRS 3.18]*.

IFRS 3 contains application guidance explaining that an acquirer should not recognise a separate valuation allowance (i.e. bad debt provision) in respect of loans and receivables for contractual cash flows that are deemed to be uncollectible at the acquisition date. This is because the effects of uncertainty about future cash flows are included in the fair value measure. However, unless the loans are deemed to be 'purchased credit-impaired', an expected credit loss allowance will also need to be recorded, with a charge to profit or loss, at the end of the first accounting period (see Chapter 9 at 5.5.5 and Chapter 51 at 7.4). *[IFRS 3.B41]*.

3.3.5 Acquisition of a group of assets that does not constitute a business

Initially, the entity should establish whether they acquired a business or an asset, this is dealt with in Chapter 9 at 3.2. Where a group of assets that does not constitute a business is acquired, IFRS 3 requires the acquiring entity to:

- identify and recognise the individual identifiable assets acquired and liabilities assumed; and
- allocate the cost of the group to the individual identifiable assets and liabilities based on their relative fair values at the date of the acquisition. *[IFRS 3.2(b)]*.

The Interpretations Committee has considered how to allocate the transaction price to the identifiable assets acquired and liabilities assumed when:

- the sum of the individual fair values of the identifiable assets and liabilities is different from the transaction price; and
- the group of assets includes identifiable assets and liabilities initially measured both at cost and at an amount other than cost, e.g. financial instruments which are measured on initial recognition at their fair value.

Such a transaction or event does not give rise to goodwill. The Committee observed that if an entity initially considers that there might be a difference between the transaction price for the group and the sum of the individual fair values of the identifiable assets and liabilities, it first reviews the procedures used to determine those individual fair values to assess whether such a difference truly exists before allocating the transaction price.

The Committee concluded that a reasonable reading of the requirements of IFRS 3 results in two possible ways of accounting for the acquisition of the group:

(a) Under the first approach, the entity accounts for the acquisition of the group as follows:
- it identifies the individual identifiable assets acquired and liabilities assumed that it recognises at the date of the acquisition;
- it determines the individual transaction price for each identifiable asset and liability by allocating the cost of the group based on the relative fair values of those assets and liabilities at the date of the acquisition; and then
- it applies the initial measurement requirements in applicable IFRS to each identifiable asset acquired and liability assumed. The entity accounts for any difference between the amount at which the asset or liability is initially measured and its individual transaction price applying the relevant requirements.

  In the case of any financial instruments within the group, the entity should treat the difference between the fair value and allocated transaction price as a 'day 1' profit, the requirements for which are discussed at 3.3 above.

(b) Under the second approach, any identifiable asset or liability that is initially measured at an amount other than cost is initially measured at the amount specified in the applicable IFRS, i.e. fair value in the case of a financial instrument. The entity first deducts from the transaction price of the group the amounts allocated to the assets and liabilities initially measured at an amount other than cost, and then determines the cost of the remaining identifiable assets and liabilities by allocating the residual transaction price based on their relative fair values at the date of the acquisition.

The Committee observed that an entity should apply its reading of the requirements consistently to all such acquisitions.[4]

3.4 Transaction costs

3.4.1 Accounting treatment

As noted at 3.1 above, the initial carrying amount of an instrument should be adjusted for transaction costs, except for financial instruments subsequently carried at fair value through profit or loss and trade receivables that do not have a significant financing component in accordance with IFRS 15. The consequences of this requirement are:

- For financial instruments subsequently measured at amortised cost and debt instruments subsequently measured at fair value through other comprehensive income, transaction costs are included in the calculation of the amortised cost using the effective interest method, in effect reducing (increasing) the amount of interest income (expense) recognised over the life of the instrument. *[IFRS 9.IG.E.1.1].*
- For investments in equity instruments that are subsequently measured at fair value through other comprehensive income, transaction costs are recognised in other comprehensive income as part of the change in fair value at the next remeasurement and they are never reclassified into profit or loss. *[IFRS 9.B5.7.1, IG.E.1.1].*
- Transaction costs relating to the acquisition or incurrence of financial instruments at fair value through profit or loss are recognised in profit or loss as they are incurred. *[IFRS 9.5.1.1].*

Transaction costs that relate to the issue of a compound financial instrument are allocated to the liability and equity components of the instrument in proportion to the allocation of proceeds. *[IAS 32.38].* This is discussed in more detail in Chapter 47 at 6.2.

IFRS 9 does not address how to allocate transaction costs that relate to a hybrid financial instrument where the embedded derivative is separated from the host. Therefore, entities should choose an accounting policy and apply it consistently. The approaches more commonly observed are to allocate the transaction costs:

- exclusively to the non-derivative host, in which case the transaction costs are included in full in its initial measurement; and
- to the non-derivative host and the embedded derivative in proportion to their fair values, i.e. in a similar fashion to compound financial instruments. Under this approach, the proportion attributable to the non-derivative host will be included in its initial measurement, while the proportion attributable to the embedded derivative will be expensed as incurred. This approach would need to be adapted if the debt host contract is a liability and the embedded derivative is an asset.

However, the choice of approach will usually only lead to a different accounting when the embedded derivative has an option feature and hence a non-zero fair value.

Transaction costs that would be incurred on transfer or disposal of a financial instrument are not included in the initial or subsequent measurement of the financial instrument. *[IFRS 9.IG.E.1.1].*

The following example illustrates the accounting treatment of transaction costs for a financial asset classified as measured at fair value through other comprehensive income.

Example 49.8: **Transaction costs – initial measurement**

Company A acquires an equity security that will be classified as measured at fair value through other comprehensive income. The security has a fair value of £100 and this is the amount A is required to pay. In addition, A also pays a purchase commission of £2. If the asset was to be sold, a sales commission of £3 would be payable.

The initial measurement of the asset is £102, i.e. the sum of its initial fair value and the purchase commission. The commission payable on sale is not considered for this purpose. If A had a reporting date immediately after the purchase of this security it would measure the security at £100 and recognise a loss of £2 in other comprehensive income. *[IFRS 9.B5.2.2].*

In the example above, if the financial asset was a debt instrument measured at fair value through other comprehensive income, the initial recognition would follow the same accounting; however, the transaction costs of £2 would subsequently be amortised to profit or loss using the effective interest method. *[IFRS 9.B5.2.2]*. This is further discussed in Chapter 50 at 2.3.

3.4.2 Identifying transaction costs

Transaction costs are defined as incremental costs that are directly attributable to the acquisition, issue or disposal of a financial asset or liability. An incremental cost is one that would not have been incurred had the financial instrument not been acquired, issued or disposed of. *[IFRS 9 Appendix A]*.

Transaction costs include fees and commissions paid to agents (including employees acting as selling agents), advisers, brokers, and dealers. They also include levies by regulatory agencies and securities exchanges, transfer taxes and duties. Debt premiums or discounts, financing costs and allocations of internal administrative or holding costs are not transaction costs. *[IFRS 9.B5.4.8]*.

Treating internal costs as transaction costs could open up a number of possibilities for abuse by allowing entities to defer expenses inappropriately. However, internal costs should be treated as transaction costs only if they are incremental and directly attributable to the acquisition, issue or disposal of a financial asset or financial liability. *[IAS 39.BC222(d)]*.[5] Therefore, it will be rare for internal costs (other than, for instance, commissions paid to sales staff in respect of a product sold that results in the origination or issuance of a financial instrument) to be treated as transaction costs.

3.5 Embedded derivatives and financial instrument hosts

In Chapter 46 at 6, it was explained that the terms of an embedded derivative that is required to be separated from a financial liability and those of the associated host should be determined. so that the derivative is initially recorded at its fair value and the host as the residual (at least for an optional derivative – a non-option embedded derivative will have a fair value and initial carrying amount of zero). *[IFRS 9.B4.3.3]*. Embedded derivatives in financial asset hosts are not accounted for separately.

3.6 Regular way transactions

When settlement date accounting is used for 'regular way' transactions (see 2.2.4 above) and those transactions result in the recognition of assets that are subsequently measured at amortised cost, there is an exception to the general requirement to measure the asset on initial recognition at its fair value (see 3.1 above).

In such circumstances, rather than being initially measured by reference to their fair value on the date they are first recognised, i.e. settlement date, these financial instruments are initially measured by reference to their fair value on the trade date. *[IFRS 9.5.1.2]*.

In practice, the difference will rarely be significant because of the short time scale involved between trade date and settlement date. It is because of this short duration that regular way transactions are not recognised as derivative financial instruments, but accounted for as set out at 2.2 above. *[IFRS 9.BA.4]*.

3.7 Assets and liabilities arising from loan commitments

Loan commitments are a form of derivative financial instrument, although for pragmatic reasons the IASB decided that certain loan commitments could be excluded from most of the recognition and measurement requirements of IFRS 9 (see Chapter 45 at 3.5). Nevertheless IFRS 9 does require issuers to apply its impairment rules to such loan commitments (see Chapter 51 at 11). *[IFRS 9.2.1(g)].*

This creates a degree of uncertainty over how assets and liabilities arising from such arrangements should be measured on initial recognition, as illustrated in the example below. For simplicity the application of the impairment requirements of IFRS 9 and any other amounts payable by the borrower to the lender (such as non-utilisation fees) have not been illustrated.

Example 49.9: Drawdown under a committed borrowing facility

Company H obtains from Bank Q a committed facility allowing it to borrow up to €10,000 at any time over the following five years, provided certain covenants specified in the facility agreement are not breached. Interest on any drawdowns is payable at LIBOR plus a fixed margin, representing Q's initial assessment of H's credit risk. Any such borrowings can be repaid at any time at the option of H, but must be repaid by the end of five years unless the facility is renegotiated and extended. They also become repayable immediately in the event that H breaches the covenants.

After one year, no drawdowns have been made and H's credit risk has increased (although it has not breached any of the covenants and there is no expectation of default). As a result of this change in credit risk, the fair value of the facility is €200 (positive value to H, negative value to Q).

Shortly afterwards H draws down the maximum €10,000 available under the facility. Because of the change in credit risk, the loan resulting from the drawdown has a fair value at that date of €9,800. The €200 difference between the fair value of €9,800 of the financial instrument created and the €10,000 cash transferred effectively represents the change in fair value of the commitment arising from the change in H's credit risk.

Should Q (H) initially measure the resulting asset (liability) at its €9,800 fair value or at €10,000, being the amount of cash actually exchanged? If it is recognised at €9,800, how is the 'spare' €200 accounted for, particularly does Q (H) recognise it as a loss (profit)?

In order to be able to answer this question, we need to consider the accounting of the loan commitment up until the date of drawdown and how its carrying amount impacts the initial measurement of the resulting loan.

3.7.1 Loan commitments outside the scope of IFRS 9

In Example 49.9, if H or Q do not designate the loan commitment at fair value through profit or loss, since the commitment cannot be settled net and it is not at a below-market interest rate, for H or Q it is outside the scope of IFRS 9.

The accounting for the loan commitment outside the scope of IFRS 9 would be as follows:

- When Q and H enter into the loan commitment, Q records a provision for expected credit losses under the impairment requirements of IFRS 9 (see Chapter 51 at 11).
- When the credit risk increases in the following year, nothing is recognised in the accounts of H in respect of the facility because the commitment is not recognised, but Q assesses and recognises any impact the increase in credit risk may have had on the provision for expected credit loss.

Therefore, until the time of drawdown, the only accounting entries for Q are in relation to the impairment requirements applicable to loan commitments.

At the time the loan is drawn down, Q classifies it within financial assets at amortised cost and H classifies it within financial liabilities at amortised cost. The general requirement under IFRS 9 as noted at 3.1 above would require the asset (liability) to initially be measured at its fair value, i.e. €9,800. This would lead to the recognition of a loss (profit) of €200 – this is because the spare €200 arising as difference between the fair value (€9,800) and the amount delivered (€10,000) does not represent any other asset or liability arising from the transaction.

However, the Basis for Conclusions on IFRS 9 explains that the effect of the loan commitment exception is to achieve consistency with the measurement basis of the resulting loan when the holder exercises its right, i.e. amortised cost. Changes in the fair value of these commitments resulting from changes in market interest rates or credit spreads will therefore not be recognised or measured, in the same manner that changes in such rates and spreads will not affect the amortised cost of the financial asset (or financial liability) recognised once the right is exercised. *[IFRS 9.BCZ2.3]*. This is exactly what the 'spare' €200 represents so, in accordance with the underlying rationale and objective of allowing loan commitments to be excluded from the scope of IFRS 9, it seems appropriate to initially measure the asset or liability arising in this case at €10,000. It is worth mentioning that the expected credit loss provision previously recognised for the loan commitment is incorporated into the allowance for the drawn down loan upon initial recognition.

The treatment under the loan commitment exception is consistent with that of similar assets arising from regular way transactions recognised using settlement date accounting (see 3.6 above). This is relevant because the IASB introduced the loan commitment exception as a result of issues identified by the IGC and the only solution the IGC could identify at the time involved treating loan commitments as regular way transactions and using settlement date accounting.[6]

3.7.2 Loan commitments within the scope of IFRS 9

If, in the above example, Q accounted for the loan commitment at fair value through profit or loss the issue of the spare €200 would not arise. At the time the loan was drawn down the commitment would have already been recognised as a €200 liability and an equivalent loss would have been recorded in profit or loss. The loan would then be recognised at its fair value of €9,800 and the €200 balance of the cash movement over this amount would be treated as the settlement of the loan commitment liability. Therefore, no further gain or loss would need to be recognised at this point. Once the loan is recognised, it will be accounted for in accordance with IFRS 9 in line with its classification.

References

1 *IFRIC Update*, June 2017.
2 *IFRIC Update*, January 2007. Whilst the IFRIC discussion was held in the context of IAS 39, the discussion also holds true under IFRS 9 as the related requirements were brought into IFRS 9 unchanged.
3 *IFRIC Update*, November 2006. Whilst the IFRIC discussion was held in the context of IAS 39, the discussion also holds true under IFRS 9 as the related requirements were brought into IFRS 9 unchanged.
4 *IFRIC Update*, November 2017.
5 This discussion was included in the Basis for Conclusions to IAS 39. However, it holds true under IFRS 9 as the related requirements were brought into IFRS 9 unchanged.
6 IAS 39 Implementation Guidance Committee (IGC), Q&A 30-1, July 2001.

Chapter 50　Financial instruments: Subsequent measurement

1	INTRODUCTION	3869
2	SUBSEQUENT MEASUREMENT AND RECOGNITION OF GAINS AND LOSSES	3869
	2.1　Debt financial assets measured at amortised cost	3870
	2.2　Financial liabilities measured at amortised cost	3871
	2.3　Debt financial assets measured at fair value through other comprehensive income	3871
	2.4　Financial assets and financial liabilities measured at fair value through profit or loss	3872
	2.4.1　Liabilities at fair value through profit or loss: calculating the gain or loss attributable to changes in credit risk	3872
	2.4.2　Liabilities at fair value through profit or loss: assessing whether an accounting mismatch is created or enlarged	3875
	2.5　Investments in equity investments designated at fair value through other comprehensive income	3877
	2.6　Unquoted equity instruments and related derivatives	3877
	2.7　Reclassifications of financial assets	3878
	2.8　Financial guarantees and commitments to provide a loan at a below-market interest rate	3879
	2.9　Exceptions to the general principles	3880
	2.9.1　Hedging relationships	3880
	2.9.2　Regular way transactions	3880
	2.9.3　Liabilities arising from failed derecognition transactions	3881
3	AMORTISED COST AND THE EFFECTIVE INTEREST METHOD	3881
	3.1　Effective interest rate (EIR)	3881

3.2	Fixed interest rate instruments		3884
3.3	Floating interest rate instruments		3885
3.4	Prepayment, call and similar options		3887
	3.4.1	Revisions to estimated cash flows	3887
3.5	Perpetual debt instruments		3889
3.6	Inflation-linked debt instruments		3890
3.7	More complex financial liabilities		3892
3.8	Modified financial assets and liabilities		3894
	3.8.1	Accounting for modifications that do not result in derecognition	3894
	3.8.2	Treatment of modification fees	3897
	3.8.3	Interbank Offered Rate (IBOR) reform	3898
4	FOREIGN CURRENCIES		3899
4.1	Foreign currency instruments		3899
4.2	Foreign entities		3902

List of examples

Example 50.1:	Estimating the change in fair value of an instrument attributable to its credit risk	3874
Example 50.2:	Liabilities at fair value through profit or loss: accounting mismatch in profit or loss	3876
Example 50.3:	Liabilities at fair value through profit or loss: no accounting mismatch in profit or loss	3877
Example 50.4:	Effective interest method – amortisation of premium or discount on acquisition	3884
Example 50.5:	Effective interest method – stepped interest rates	3884
Example 50.6:	Effective interest method – variable rate loan	3885
Example 50.7:	Fixed rate mortgage which reprices to market interest rate	3886
Example 50.8:	Bargain rate mortgage which reprices to market interest rate	3886
Example 50.9:	Effective interest method – amortisation of discount arising from credit downgrade	3886
Example 50.10:	Effective interest method – amortisation of premium arising from accrued interest	3887
Example 50.11:	Effective interest rate – embedded prepayment options	3887
Example 50.12:	Effective interest method – revision of estimates	3888
Example 50.13:	Amortised cost – perpetual debt with interest payments over a limited amount of time	3889
Example 50.14:	Application of the effective interest method to inflation-linked debt instruments	3890

Example 50.15:	Changes in credit spread	3895
Example 50.16:	Modification – troubled debt restructuring	3895
Example 50.17:	Modification – renegotiation of a fixed rate loan	3896
Example 50.18:	Accounting treatment of modification fees	3897
Example 50.19:	Foreign currency debt security measured at fair value through other comprehensive income (separation of currency component)	3901
Example 50.20:	Interaction of IAS 21 and IFRS 9: foreign currency debt investment	3902

Chapter 50   Financial instruments: Subsequent measurement

1 INTRODUCTION

This chapter discusses the subsequent measurement of financial instruments under IFRS 9 – *Financial Instruments*, including the requirements relating to amortised cost, the effective interest method and foreign currency revaluation. Subsequent measurement of contingent consideration recognised by an acquirer in a business combination to which IFRS 3 – *Business Combinations* – applies that falls within the scope of IFRS 9 is discussed in Chapter 9 at 7.1.3. The impairment of financial instruments is addressed in Chapter 51.

Most, but not all, of the detailed requirements of IFRS governing the measurement of fair values are dealt with in IFRS 13 – *Fair Value Measurement*, which is covered in Chapter 14. The measurement of a financial liability with a demand feature is also covered in Chapter 14 at 11.5. IFRS 9 contains some requirements addressing fair value measurements of financial instruments and these are covered at 2.6 below.

2 SUBSEQUENT MEASUREMENT AND RECOGNITION OF GAINS AND LOSSES

As explained in Chapter 48 at 2 and 3, following the application of IFRS 9, financial assets and financial liabilities are classified into one of the following measurement categories: [IFRS 9.4.1.1, 4.2.1]

- debt financial assets at amortised cost;
- debt financial assets at fair value through other comprehensive income (with cumulative gains and losses reclassified to profit or loss upon derecognition);
- debt financial assets, derivatives and investments in equity instruments at fair value through profit or loss;
- investments in equity instruments designated as measured at fair value through other comprehensive income (with gains and losses remaining in other comprehensive income, without recycling); or
- financial liabilities either at fair value through profit or loss or at amortised cost.

Following the initial recognition of financial assets and financial liabilities, their subsequent accounting treatment depends principally on the classification of the instrument, although there are a small number of exceptions. These requirements are summarised in Figure 50.1 below and are considered in more detail in the remainder of this section.

Figure 50.1 Classification and subsequent measurement of financial assets and financial liabilities

Classification	Instrument type	Statement of financial position	Fair value gains and losses	Interest and dividends	Impairment	Foreign exchange
Financial assets and liabilities at amortised cost	Debt	Amortised cost	–	Profit or loss: using an effective interest rate	Profit or loss (financial assets)	Profit or loss
Debt financial assets at fair value through other comprehensive income	Debt	Fair value	Other comprehensive income and recycled to profit or loss when derecognised	Profit or loss: using an effective interest rate	Profit or loss	Profit or loss
Fair value through profit or loss (including derivatives not designated in effective hedges)	Debt, equity or derivative	Fair value	Profit or loss (see Chapter 54 at 7.1.1 on presentation requirements) and other comprehensive income for changes in own credit risk (see 2.4.1 below)	Profit or loss (see Chapter 54 at 7.1.1 on presentation requirements)	–	Profit or loss
Equity investments at fair value through other comprehensive income	Equity	Fair value	Other comprehensive income (no recycling to profit or loss when derecognised)	Profit or loss: dividends receivable	–	Other comprehensive income (no recycling to profit or loss when derecognised)

In addition, IFRS 9 sets out the accounting treatment for certain financial guarantee contracts (see Chapter 45 at 3.4) and commitments to provide a loan at a below market interest rate (see Chapter 45 at 3.5).

2.1 Debt financial assets measured at amortised cost

Financial assets that are measured at amortised cost require the use of the effective interest method and are subject to the IFRS 9 impairment rules. *[IFRS 9.5.2.1, 5.2.2]*. Gains and losses are recognised in profit or loss when the instrument is derecognised or impaired, as well as through the amortisation process. *[IFRS 9.5.7.2]*. The effective interest method of accounting is dealt with at 3 below, foreign currency retranslation is discussed at 4 below, modification of financial assets is covered at 3.8 below and impairment is addressed in Chapter 51.

2.2 Financial liabilities measured at amortised cost

Liabilities that are measured at amortised cost require the use of the effective interest method with gains or losses recognised in profit or loss when the instrument is derecognised as well as through the amortisation process. *[IFRS 9.5.3.1, 5.7.2]*. The effective interest method of accounting is dealt with at 3 below, foreign currency retranslation is discussed at 4 below and modification of financial liabilities is covered at 3.8 below.

2.3 Debt financial assets measured at fair value through other comprehensive income

For financial assets that are debt instruments measured at fair value through other comprehensive income (see Chapter 48 at 2.1), the International Accounting Standards Board (IASB or Board) decided that both amortised cost and fair value information are relevant because debt instruments held by entities in this measurement category are held for both the collection of contractual cash flows and the realisation of fair values. *[IFRS 9.BC4.150]*.

After initial recognition, investments in debt instruments that are classified as measured at fair value through other comprehensive income are measured at fair value in the statement of financial position (with no deduction for sale or disposal costs). The amounts recognised in profit or loss are the same as the amounts that would have been recognised in profit or loss if the investment had been recorded at amortised cost. *[IFRS 9.5.7.11, B5.7.1A]*.

Subsequent measurement of debt instruments at fair value through other comprehensive income involves the following: *[IFRS 9.5.7.1(d), 5.7.10, B5.7.1A]*

- impairment gains and losses (see Chapter 51) are derived using the same methodology that is applied to financial assets measured at amortised cost and are recognised in profit or loss; *[IFRS 9.5.2.2, 5.5.2]*
- foreign exchange gains and losses (see 4 below) are calculated based on the amortised cost of the debt instruments and are recognised in profit or loss; *[IFRS 9.B5.7.2, B5.7.2A]*
- interest revenue is calculated using the effective interest method (see 3 below) and is recognised in profit or loss; *[IFRS 9.5.4.1]*
- other fair value gains and losses are recognised in other comprehensive income; *[IFRS 9.B5.7.1A]*
- when debt instruments are modified (see 3.8 below and Chapter 51 at 8), the modification gains or losses are recognised in profit or loss;[1] *[IFRS 9.5.4.3, 5.7.10, 5.7.11]* and
- when the debt instruments are derecognised, the cumulative gains or losses previously recognised in other comprehensive income are reclassified (i.e. recycled) from equity to profit or loss as a reclassification adjustment. *[IFRS 9.5.7.10]*.

It follows that the amount recognised in other comprehensive income is the difference between the total change in fair value and the amounts recognised in profit or loss (excluding any amounts received in cash, e.g. the coupon on a bond).

2.4 Financial assets and financial liabilities measured at fair value through profit or loss

After initial recognition, financial assets and financial liabilities that are classified as measured at fair value through profit or loss (including derivatives that are not designated in effective hedging relationships) are measured at fair value, with no deduction for sale or disposal costs (see Chapter 48 at 2, 4, 5.4 and 7). *[IFRS 9.5.2.1, 5.3.1]*.

The standard helpfully points out that if the fair value of a financial asset falls below zero it becomes a financial liability (assuming it is measured at fair value). *[IFRS 9.B5.2.1]*. The standard does not explain what happens if the fair value of a financial liability becomes positive, but it is safe to assume that it becomes a financial asset and not a negative liability.

Gains and losses arising from remeasuring a financial asset or financial liability at fair value should normally be recognised in profit or loss. *[IFRS 9.5.7.1]*. However, there is an exception for most non-derivative financial liabilities that are designated as measured at fair value through profit or loss. For these liabilities the element of the gain or loss attributable to changes in credit risk (see 2.4.1 below) should normally be recognised in other comprehensive income (with the remainder recognised in profit or loss). *[IFRS 9.5.7.7]*. These amounts presented in other comprehensive income should not be subsequently transferred to profit or loss. However, the cumulative gain or loss may be transferred within equity. *[IFRS 9.B5.7.9]*.

This exception does not apply to loan commitments or financial guarantee contracts, nor does it apply if it would create or enlarge an accounting mismatch in profit or loss (see 2.4.2 below). *[IFRS 9.5.7.8, 5.7.9]*. In these cases, all changes in the fair value of the liability (including the effects of changes in the credit risk) should be recognised in profit or loss. *[IFRS 9.B5.7.8]*.

2.4.1 Liabilities at fair value through profit or loss: calculating the gain or loss attributable to changes in credit risk

IFRS 7 – *Financial Instruments: Disclosures* – defines credit risk as 'the risk that one party to a financial instrument will cause a financial loss for the other party by failing to discharge an obligation', which is also part of non-performance risk as defined in IFRS 13 (see Chapter 14 at 11.3). *[IFRS 7 Appendix A]*. The change in fair value of a financial liability that is attributable to credit risk relates to the risk that the issuer will fail to pay that liability. It may not solely relate to the creditworthiness of the issuer but may be influenced by other factors, such as collateral.

For example, if an entity issues a collateralised liability and a non-collateralised liability that are otherwise identical, the credit risk of those two liabilities will be different, even though they are issued by the same entity. The credit risk on the collateralised liability will be less than the credit risk of the non-collateralised liability. In fact, the credit risk for a collateralised liability may be close to zero. *[IFRS 9.B5.7.13]*. It is important to distinguish between the terms 'credit risk' and 'the risk of default' as referred to in the impairment requirements of the standard (see Chapter 51 at 6.1), since the latter does not include the benefit of collateral.

For these purposes, credit risk is different from asset-specific performance risk. Asset-specific performance risk is not related to the risk that an entity will fail to discharge a particular obligation but rather it is related to the risk that a single asset or a group of assets will perform poorly (or not at all). *[IFRS 9.B5.7.14]*. For example, consider: *[IFRS 9.B5.7.15]*

(a) a liability with a unit-linking feature whereby the amount due to investors is contractually determined on the basis of the performance of specified assets. The effect of that unit-linking feature on the fair value of the liability is asset-specific performance risk, not credit risk;

(b) a liability issued by a structured entity with the following characteristics:
- the structured entity is legally isolated so the assets in the structured entity are ring-fenced solely for the benefit of its investors, even in the event of bankruptcy;
- the structured entity enters into no other transactions and the assets in the structured entity cannot be hypothecated; and
- amounts are due to the structured entity's investors only if the ring-fenced assets generate cash flows.

Thus, changes in the fair value of the liability primarily reflect changes in the fair value of the assets. The effect of the performance of the assets on the fair value of the liability is asset-specific performance risk, not credit risk.

Unless an alternative method more faithfully represents the change in fair value of a financial liability that is attributable to credit risk, the standard states that this amount should be determined as the amount of change in the fair value of the liability that is not attributable to changes in market conditions that give rise to what it defines as 'market risk'. *[IFRS 9.B5.7.16]*. Changes in market conditions that give rise to market risk include changes in a benchmark interest rate, the price of another entity's financial instrument, a commodity price, foreign exchange rate or index of prices or rates. *[IFRS 9.B5.7.17]*.

The standard says that if the only significant relevant changes in market conditions for a financial liability are changes in 'an observed (benchmark) interest rate', the amount to be recognised in other comprehensive income can be estimated as follows: *[IFRS 9.B5.7.18]*

(a) first, the liability's internal rate of return at the start of the period is computed using the fair value and contractual cash flows at that time and the observed (benchmark) interest rate at the start of the period is deducted from this, to arrive at an instrument-specific component of the internal rate of return;

(b) next, the present value of the cash flows associated with the liability is calculated using the liability's contractual cash flows at the end of the period and a discount rate equal to the sum of the observed (benchmark) interest rate at the end of the period and the instrument-specific component of the internal rate of return at the start of the period as determined in (a); and

(c) the difference between the fair value of the liability at the end of the period and the amount determined in (b) is the change in fair value that is not attributable to changes in the observed (benchmark) interest rate and this is the amount to be presented in other comprehensive income.

It should be noted that 'market risk' is defined to include movements in 'a benchmark rate'. The latter term is not itself defined but typically it would encompass both risk free rates, such as AAA rated government bond rates or overnight rates, and interbank offer rates (IBOR) such as 3-month LIBOR or EURIBOR, which include an element of credit risk. It would therefore appear that the standard is ambivalent as to whether the amount of change in fair value that is attributable to changes in credit risk of a liability is measured by reference to risk free rates, or by comparison to the credit risk already present in LIBOR. Using the former, the amount will reflect all changes in credit risk of the liability, whereas using the latter, it will only reflect a portion of the changes in credit risk to the liability. Further, the change in credit risk will differ depending on which tenor is selected such as a 3-month LIBOR, 6-month LIBOR or 12-month LIBOR. It should also be noted that regulators are encouraging benchmark rates such as LIBOR to be discontinued by December 2021, in favour of risk free benchmark rates based on actual transactions. It would follow that the change in the amount attributable to credit risk will in future reflect all changes in credit risk.

This method is illustrated in the following example, adapted from that provided in the Illustrative Examples attached to the standard. *[IFRS 9.IE1-IE5]*.

Example 50.1:   Estimating the change in fair value of an instrument attributable to its credit risk

On 1 January 2021 Company J issues a 10-year bond with a par value of €150,000 and an annual fixed coupon rate of 8%, which is consistent with market rates for bonds with similar characteristics. J uses 3-month Euro LIBOR as its observable (benchmark) interest rate. At the date of inception of the bond, 3-month Euro LIBOR is 5%. At the end of the first year:

- 3-month Euro LIBOR has decreased to 4.75%; and
- the fair value of the bond is €153,811 which is consistent with an interest rate of 7.6% (i.e. the remaining cash flows on the bond, €12,000 per year for nine years and €150,000 at the end of nine years, discounted at 7.6% equals €153,811).

For simplicity, this example assumes a flat yield curve, that all changes in interest rates result from a parallel shift in the yield curve, and that the changes in 3-month Euro LIBOR are assumed to be the only relevant changes in market conditions.

The amount of change in the fair value of the bond that is not attributable to changes in market conditions that give rise to market risk is estimated as follows:

Step (a)

The bond's internal rate of return at the start of the period is 8%. Because the observed (benchmark) interest rate (3-month Euro LIBOR) is 5%, the instrument-specific component of the internal rate of return is deemed to be 3%.

Step (b)

The contractual cash flows of the instrument at the end of the period are:

- interest: €12,000 [€150,000 × 8%] per year for each of years 2022 (year 2) to 2030 (year 10).
- principal: €150,000 in 2030 (year 10).

The discount rate to be used to calculate the present value of the bond is thus 7.75%, which is the 4.75% end of period 3-month LIBOR rate, plus the 3% instrument-specific component calculated as at the start of the period, which gives a notional present value of €152,367 (€12,000 × (1 − 1.0775^{-9}) / 0.0775 + €150,000 × 1.0775^{-9}), on the assumption that there has been no change in the instrument-specific component.

Step (c)

The market price of the liability at the end of the period (which will reflect the real instrument-specific component at the end of the period within the 7.6% yield) is €153,811, therefore J should disclose €1,444 (€153,811 – €152,367) as the increase in fair value of the bond that is not attributable to changes in market conditions that give rise to market risk.

This method assumes that changes in fair value other than those arising from changes in the instrument's credit risk or from changes in the 'observed (benchmark) interest rate' are not significant. It would not be appropriate to use this method if changes in fair value arising from other factors are significant. In such cases, an alternative method should be used that more faithfully measures the effects of changes in the liability's credit risk. For example, if the instrument in the example contained an embedded derivative, the change in fair value of the embedded derivative should be excluded in determining the amount to be presented in other comprehensive income. *[IFRS 9.B5.7.19, B5.7.16(b)]*.

The above method will also produce an amount which includes any changes in the liquidity spread charged by market participants, since such changes are not considered to be attributable to changes in market conditions that give rise to market risk. This method is applied in practice as the effect of a liquidity spread cannot normally be isolated from that of the credit spread.

As with all estimates of fair value, the measurement method used for determining the portion of the change in the liability's fair value that is attributable to changes in its credit risk should make maximum use of observable market inputs. *[IFRS 9.B5.7.20]*.

2.4.2 Liabilities at fair value through profit or loss: assessing whether an accounting mismatch is created or enlarged

If a financial liability is designated as at fair value through profit or loss, it must be determined whether presenting the effects of changes in the liability's credit risk in other comprehensive income would create or enlarge an accounting mismatch in profit or loss. An accounting mismatch would be created or enlarged if this treatment would result in a greater mismatch in profit or loss than if those amounts were presented in profit or loss. *[IFRS 9.B5.7.5]*.

In making that determination, an assessment should be made as to whether the effects of changes in the liability's credit risk are expected to be offset in profit or loss by a change in the fair value of another financial instrument measured at fair value through profit or loss. Such an expectation should be based on an economic relationship between the characteristics of the liability and the characteristics of the other financial instrument. *[IFRS 9.B5.7.6]*.

The determination should be made at initial recognition and is not reassessed. For practical purposes, all the assets and liabilities giving rise to an accounting mismatch need not be entered into at exactly the same time – a reasonable delay is permitted provided that any remaining transactions are expected to occur. An entity's methodology for making this determination should be applied consistently for similar types of transactions. IFRS 7 requires an entity to provide qualitative disclosures in the notes to the financial statements about its methodology for making that determination – see Chapter 54 at 4.4.2. *[IFRS 9.B5.7.7]*.

If an accounting mismatch would be created or enlarged, the entity is required to present all changes in fair value (including the effects of changes in the credit risk of the liability) in profit or loss. If such a mismatch would not be created or enlarged, the entity is required to present the effects of changes in the liability's credit risk in other comprehensive income. *[IFRS 9.B5.7.8]*.

The following example describes a situation in which an accounting mismatch would be created in profit or loss if the effects of changes in the credit risk of the liability were presented in other comprehensive income. *[IFRS 9.B5.7.10]*.

Example 50.2: *Liabilities at fair value through profit or loss: accounting mismatch in profit or loss*

A mortgage bank provides loans to customers and funds those loans by selling bonds with matching characteristics (e.g. amount outstanding, repayment profile, term and currency) in the market. The contractual terms of the loans permit the mortgage customer to prepay its loan (i.e. satisfy its obligation to the bank) by buying the corresponding bond at fair value in the market and delivering that bond to the mortgage bank.

As a result of that contractual prepayment right, if the credit quality of the bond worsens (and, thus, the fair value of the mortgage bank's liability decreases), the fair value of the mortgage bank's loan asset also decreases. The change in the fair value of the asset reflects the mortgage customer's contractual right to prepay the mortgage loan by buying the underlying bond at fair value (which, in this example, has decreased) and delivering the bond to the mortgage bank. Therefore, the effects of changes in the credit risk of the liability (the bond) will be offset in profit or loss by a corresponding change in the fair value of a financial asset (the loan).

If the effects of changes in the liability's credit risk were presented in other comprehensive income there would be an accounting mismatch in profit or loss. Therefore, the mortgage bank is required to present all changes in fair value of the liability (including the effects of changes in the liability's credit risk) in profit or loss.

In the example above, there is a contractual linkage between the effects of changes in the credit risk of the liability and changes in the fair value of the financial asset (i.e. as a result of the mortgage customer's contractual right to prepay the loan by buying the bond at fair value and delivering the bond to the mortgage bank). The standard states that an accounting mismatch may also occur in the absence of a contractual linkage, but does not provide any examples of when this might be the case. *[IFRS 9.B5.7.11]*.

However, the standard makes clear that a mismatch that arises solely as a result of the measurement method does not affect the determination of whether presenting the effects of changes in the liability's credit risk in other comprehensive income would create or enlarge an accounting mismatch in profit or loss. For instance, an entity may not isolate changes in a liability's credit risk from changes in liquidity risk. If the entity presents the combined effect of both factors in other comprehensive income, a mismatch may occur because changes in liquidity risk may be included in the fair value measurement of the entity's financial assets and the entire fair value change of those assets is presented in profit or loss. However, such a mismatch is caused by measurement imprecision, not an offsetting relationship, and, therefore, does not affect the determination of an accounting mismatch. *[IFRS 9.B5.7.12]*.

The following example illustrates another situation in which an accounting mismatch is not due to an economic relationship (in the sense intended by the IASB) between the movement in the fair value of the financial assets and the movement in the fair value of the financial liabilities related to the liabilities' own credit risk.

Example 50.3: **Liabilities at fair value through profit or loss: no accounting mismatch in profit or loss**

A bank issues structured products (consisting of a host debt contract and one or more embedded derivatives) in the market. These financial liabilities are designated as at fair value through profit or loss because they are managed on a fair value basis.

The bank invests the funds received in highly rated bonds, which are also designated as at fair value through profit or loss, and derivatives whose terms mirror those of the embedded derivatives in the structured products.

In periods when market credit spreads are volatile, it is expected that the effect of changes in credit spreads on the fair value of the structured products will be mainly compensated for by the effect of an offsetting credit spread movements on the bonds. This is because the credit quality of the bank is similar to the credit quality of the highly rated bonds in which the bank has invested.

Unlike Example 50.2 above, there is no direct link between the bank's own credit risk of the structured financial liabilities and the credit risk of the financial assets. The credit quality of the financial assets may be similar to that of the financial liabilities and these may move in a correlated manner as they are affected by similar movements in the general price of credit and other market risks, but the fair value of the financial assets will not move directly in response to changes in the bank's own credit risk.

Therefore, the requirements for an economic relationship are not met and all fair value changes attributable to changes in the credit risk of the financial liabilities should be taken to other comprehensive income.

2.5 Investments in equity investments designated at fair value through other comprehensive income

After initial recognition, investments in equity instruments not held for trading that are designated as measured at fair value through other comprehensive income (see Chapter 48 at 2.2) should be measured at fair value, with no deduction for sale or disposal costs. With the exception of dividends received, the associated gains and losses (including any related foreign exchange component) should be recognised in other comprehensive income. These investments are not subject to impairment testing. Amounts presented in other comprehensive income should not be subsequently transferred to profit or loss, although the cumulative gain or loss may be transferred within equity. *[IFRS 9.5.2.1, 5.7.5, B5.7.1, B5.7.3].*

Dividends from such investments should be recognised in profit or loss when the right to receive payment is probable and can be measured reliably unless the dividend clearly represents a recovery of part of the cost of the investment (see Chapter 8 at 2.4.1.C). *[IFRS 9.5.7.1A, 5.7.6, B5.7.1].* Determining when a dividend does or does not clearly represent a recovery of cost could prove somewhat judgmental in practice, especially as the standard contains no further explanatory guidance.

2.6 Unquoted equity instruments and related derivatives

IFRS 9 requires all investments in equity instruments and contracts on those instruments to be measured at fair value (see Chapter 14). However, it is recognised that in limited circumstances, cost may be an appropriate estimate of fair value. That may be the case if insufficient more recent information is available to determine fair value, or if there is a wide range of possible fair value measurements and cost represents the best estimate of fair value within that range. *[IFRS 9.B5.2.3].*

Such guidance was provided to alleviate some of the concerns expressed by constituents and also, to replace the cost exception that was not brought forward to

IFRS 9 from IAS 39 – *Financial Instruments: Recognition and Measurement*, the previous standard for accounting for financial instruments. IAS 39 contained an exception from fair value measurement for investments in equity instruments (and some derivatives linked to those investments) that did not have a quoted price in an active market and whose fair value could not be reliably measured. Those equity investments were required to be measured at cost less impairment, if any. *[IFRS 9.BC5.13, BC5.16, BC5.18].*

Indicators that cost might not be representative of fair value include: *[IFRS 9.B5.2.4]*

(a) a significant change in the performance of the investee compared with budgets, plans or milestones;

(b) changes in expectation that the investee's technical product milestones will be achieved;

(c) a significant change in the market for the investee's equity or its products or potential products;

(d) a significant change in the global economy or the economic environment in which the investee operates;

(e) a significant change in the performance of comparable entities, or in the valuations implied by the overall market;

(f) internal matters of the investee such as fraud, commercial disputes, litigation, changes in management or strategy; and

(g) evidence from external transactions in the investee's equity, either by the investee (such as a fresh issue of equity), or by transfers of equity instruments between third parties.

This list is not intended to be exhaustive. All information about the performance and operations of the investee that becomes available after the date of initial recognition should be used and to the extent that any such relevant factors exist, they may indicate that cost might not be representative of fair value. In such cases, fair value should be estimated. *[IFRS 9.B5.2.5].*

For the avoidance of doubt, IFRS 9 emphasises that cost is never the best estimate of fair value for investments in quoted equity instruments (or contracts on quoted equity instruments). *[IFRS 9.B5.2.6].* Also, the IASB noted that for financial institutions and investment funds, the cost of an equity investment cannot be considered representative of fair value. *[IFRS 9.BC5.18].*

2.7 Reclassifications of financial assets

In certain situations, financial assets classified as measured at fair value through profit or loss should be reclassified as measured at amortised cost and *vice versa*. The situations in which a reclassification might arise are considered in more detail in Chapter 48 at 9.

The reclassification should be applied prospectively from the reclassification date which is defined as 'the first day of the first reporting period following the change in business model that results in an entity reclassifying financial assets'. *[IFRS 9.5.6.1, Appendix A].*

Accordingly, any previously recognised gains, losses (including impairment gains and losses) or interest should not be restated. *[IFRS 9.5.6.1].* For example, when a financial asset is reclassified so that it is measured at fair value, its fair value is determined at the reclassification date. Any gain or loss arising from a difference between the previous carrying amount and fair value should be recognised in profit or loss of the current period without restating prior periods. *[IFRS 9.5.6.2]*. Moreover, when a financial asset is reclassified so that it is measured at amortised cost, its fair value at the reclassification date becomes its new gross carrying amount. *[IFRS 9.5.6.3]*. The effective interest rate is determined on the basis of the fair value of the asset at the date of reclassification. *[IFRS 9.B5.6.2]*.

2.8 Financial guarantees and commitments to provide a loan at a below-market interest rate

Financial guarantees issued and commitments made to provide a loan at a below-market interest rate should be measured on initial recognition at their (negative) fair value which is generally equal to the premium received where the transaction is undertaken at an arm's length. Subsequently these are measured on the balance sheet at the higher of:

- the amount of the loss allowance determined in accordance with the impairment requirements of IFRS 9 (see Chapter 51); and
- the amount initially recognised less, when appropriate, the cumulative amount of income recognised in accordance with the principles of IFRS 15 – *Revenue from Contracts with Customers* (see Chapters 27 to 32). Typically, any initial premium received will be amortised over the term of the guarantee.

This assumes that the instrument is not classified at fair value through profit or loss (in which case the requirements considered at 2.4 above apply) and, in the case of a financial guarantee contract, does not arise from a failed derecognition transaction (see 2.9.3 below). *[IFRS 9.4.2.1(a), 4.2.1(c), 4.2.1(d)]*.

Whilst the balance sheet presentation is addressed, the income statement presentation is not specified. For example, it is unclear whether the initial premium received should be recognised as 'revenue' with a separate additional remeasurement for the impairment allowance or whether a single net amount should be presented in the profit and loss account shown in the revenue or impairment line depending on the comparison of the 'higher of' test. There is a further issue of whether any amounts recorded in the impairment line should be restricted to ensure there is no reversal of impairment that would exceed the cumulative impairment losses recorded in prior periods. Due to the lack of guidance in this area, diversity may arise in practice.

Normal loan commitments issued at market interest rates are excluded from the scope of IFRS 9 except for impairment and derecognition. *[IFRS 9.2.1(g), 2.3]*. Unlike loan commitments provided at below-market interest rates, normal loan commitments are not subject to the 'higher of' test for subsequent measurement (see Chapter 51 at 11). *[IFRS 9.2.3(c), 4.2.1(d)]*.

For financial guarantees, there were discussions by the ITG on whether future premiums to be received affect the measurement of the expected credit loss (ECL) allowance and this is discussed further at Chapter 51 at 1.5 and 11. In November 2018 the IFRS Interpretations Committee (IFRIC or Committee) discussed whether the cash flows expected, in general, from a financial guarantee contract or any other credit enhancement can be included in the measurement of expected credit losses (see Chapter 51 at 5.8.1).

2.9 Exceptions to the general principles

2.9.1 Hedging relationships

Financial assets and financial liabilities that are designated as hedged items are subject to measurement under the hedge accounting requirements of IFRS 9, or IAS 39 if the entity chooses as its accounting policy to continue to apply the hedge accounting requirements of IAS 39. *[IFRS 9.5.2.3, 5.3.2, 5.7.3, 7.2.21]*.

Also, derivatives and non-derivative debt financial instruments may be designated as hedging instruments which can affect whether fair value or foreign exchange gains and losses are recognised in profit or loss or in other comprehensive income. *[IFRS 9.B5.7.2]*.

Hedge accounting is covered in Chapter 53.

2.9.2 Regular way transactions

Except for its rules on transfers of assets, IFRS 9 requires an entity to recognise a financial asset in its statement of financial position when, and only when, the entity becomes party to the contractual provisions of the instrument and to derecognise a financial asset when, and only when, the contractual rights to the cash flows from the financial asset expire (see Chapter 49 at 2.1). *[IFRS 9.3.1.1, 3.2.3]*. In other words, IFRS 9 requires a financial asset to be recognised or derecognised on a trade date basis, i.e. the date that an entity commits itself to purchase or sell an asset. *[IFRS 9.B3.1.5]*. However, the standard permits financial assets subject to so called 'regular way transactions' to be recognised, or derecognised, either as at the trade date or as at the settlement date (see Chapter 49 at 2.2). *[IFRS 9.3.1.2, B3.1.3]*. Whichever method is used, it is applied consistently and symmetrically (i.e. to acquisitions and disposals) to each of the main measurement categories of financial asset identified by IFRS 9 (see Chapter 49 at 2.2). *[IFRS 9.B3.1.3]*.

Where settlement date accounting is used for regular way transactions, any change in the fair value of the asset to be received arising between trade date and settlement date is not recognised for those assets that will be measured at amortised cost. For assets that will be recorded at fair value, such changes in value are recognised: *[IFRS 9.5.7.4, B3.1.6]*

- in profit or loss for assets classified as measured at fair value through profit or loss; and
- in other comprehensive income for debt instruments classified, and equity instruments designated, as measured at fair value through other comprehensive income.

For financial assets measured at amortised cost or at fair value through other comprehensive income, IFRS 9 requires entities to use the trade date as the date of initial recognition for the purposes of applying the impairment requirements. *[IFRS 9.5.7.4]*. This means that entities that use settlement date accounting may have to recognise a loss allowance for financial assets which they have purchased but not yet recognised and, correspondingly, no loss allowance for assets that they have sold but not yet derecognised (see Chapter 51 at 7.3.2).

On disposal, changes in value of such assets between trade date and settlement date are not recognised because the right to changes in fair value ceases on the trade date. *[IFRS 9.IG.D.2.2]*. This is discussed in Chapter 49 at 2.2.3.

2.9.3 Liabilities arising from failed derecognition transactions

There are special requirements for financial liabilities (including financial guarantee contracts) that arise when transfers of financial assets do not qualify for derecognition, or are accounted for using the continuing involvement approach. *[IFRS 9.4.2.1(b)]*. These are dealt with in Chapter 52 at 5.3.

3 AMORTISED COST AND THE EFFECTIVE INTEREST METHOD

IFRS 9 contains four key definitions relating to measurement at amortised cost, which are set out below: *[IFRS 9 Appendix A]*

- The *amortised cost* is the amount at which the financial asset or financial liability is measured at initial recognition minus any principal repayments, plus or minus the cumulative amortisation using the effective interest method of any difference between that initial amount and the maturity amount and, for financial assets, adjusted for any loss allowance.
- The *gross carrying amount* is the amortised cost of a financial asset before adjusting for any loss allowance.
- The *effective interest method* is the method that is used in the calculation of the amortised cost of a financial asset or a financial liability and in the allocation and recognition of the interest revenue or interest expense in profit or loss over the relevant period.
- The *effective interest rate (EIR)* is the rate that exactly discounts estimated future cash payments or receipts through the expected life of the financial asset or financial liability to the gross carrying amount of a financial asset or to the amortised cost of a financial liability. *[IFRS 9 Appendix A]*.

3.1 Effective interest rate (EIR)

When calculating the EIR, an entity should estimate the expected cash flows by considering all the contractual terms of the financial instrument (e.g. prepayment, extension, call and similar options). The calculation includes all fees and points paid or received between parties to the contract that are an integral part of the EIR, transaction costs, and all other premiums or discounts. *[IFRS 9 Appendix A]*. Except for purchased or originated financial assets that are credit-impaired on initial recognition, ECLs are not considered in the calculation of the EIR. This is because the recognition of ECLs is decoupled from the recognition of interest revenue (see Chapter 51 at 3.1). *[IFRS 9 Appendix A, BCZ5.67]*.

Guidance related to what fees should and should not be considered integral is also included in IFRS 9. Fees that are an integral part of the EIR of a financial instrument are treated as an adjustment to the EIR, unless the financial instrument is measured at fair value, with the change in fair value being recognised in profit or loss. In those cases, the fees are recognised as revenue or expense when the instrument is initially recognised. *[IFRS 9.B5.4.1]*. However, the recognition of day 1 profits for the difference between the transaction price and the initial fair value on initial recognition is restricted to situations where the fair value is based on a quoted price in an active market for an identical asset or liability (i.e. a Level 1 input) or based on a valuation technique that uses only data from observable markets. (See Chapter 49 at 3.3).

Fees that are an integral part of the EIR of a financial instrument include:

- origination fees received on the creation or acquisition of a financial asset. Such fees may include compensation for activities such as evaluating the borrower's financial condition, evaluating and recording guarantees, collateral and other security arrangements, negotiating the terms of the instrument, preparing and processing documents and closing the transaction. These fees are an integral part of generating an involvement with the resulting financial instrument;
- commitment fees received to originate a loan when the loan commitment is not measured at fair value through profit or loss and it is probable that the entity will enter into a specific lending arrangement. These fees are regarded as compensation for an ongoing involvement with the acquisition of a financial instrument. If the commitment expires without the entity making the loan, the fee is recognised as revenue on expiry; and
- origination fees paid on issuing financial liabilities measured at amortised cost. These fees are an integral part of generating an involvement with a financial liability. An entity distinguishes fees and costs that are an integral part of the EIR for the financial liability from origination fees and transaction costs relating to the right to provide services, such as investment management services. *[IFRS 9.B5.4.2]*.

Fees that are not an integral part of the EIR of a financial instrument and are accounted for in accordance with IFRS 15 include:

- fees charged for servicing a loan;
- commitment fees to originate a loan when the loan commitment is not measured at fair value through profit or loss and it is unlikely that a specific lending arrangement will be entered into; and
- loan syndication fees received to arrange a loan and the entity does not retain part of the loan package for itself (or retains a part at the same EIR for comparable risk as other participants). *[IFRS 9.B5.4.3]*.

For a purchased or originated credit-impaired financial asset (see Chapter 51 at 3.3), the credit-adjusted EIR is applied when calculating the interest revenue and it is the rate that exactly discounts the estimated future cash payments or receipts through the expected life of the financial asset to the amortised cost of a financial asset. An entity is required to include the initial ECLs in the estimated cash flows when calculating the credit-adjusted EIR for such assets. *[IFRS 9.5.4.1, B5.4.7, Appendix A]*.

However, this does not mean that a credit-adjusted EIR should be applied solely because the financial asset has high credit risk at initial recognition. The application guidance explains that a financial asset is only considered credit-impaired at initial recognition when the credit risk is very high or, in the case of a purchase, it is acquired at a deep discount. *[IFRS 9.B5.4.7]*.

It is important to note that the EIR is normally based on estimated, not contractual, cash flows and there is a presumption that the cash flows and the expected life of a group of similar financial instruments can be estimated reliably. However, in those rare cases when it is not possible to estimate reliably the cash flows or the expected life of a financial instrument (or group of instruments), the contractual cash flows over the full contractual term of the financial instrument (or group of instruments) should be used. [IFRS 9 Appendix A].

When applying the effective interest method, an entity generally amortises any fees, points paid or received, transaction costs and other premiums or discounts that are included in the calculation of the EIR over the expected life of the financial instrument. However, there may be situations when discounts or premiums are amortised over a shorter period (see 3.3 below).

For fair value hedges in which the hedged item is recorded at amortised cost, the adjustment to the hedged item arising from the application of hedge accounting is amortised to profit or loss. This adjustment is based on a recalculated EIR at the date amortisation begins (see Chapter 53 at 7.1.2).

For floating-rate financial assets and floating-rate financial liabilities, periodic re-estimation of cash flows to reflect the movements in the market rates of interest alters the EIR. If a floating rate financial asset or a floating rate financial liability is recognised initially at an amount equal to the principal receivable or payable on maturity, re-estimating the future interest payments normally has no significant effect on the carrying amount of the asset or the liability. [IFRS 9.B5.4.5].

In most cases, a floating rate will be specified as a benchmark rate, such as LIBOR, plus (or for a very highly rated borrower, less) a fixed credit spread. Hence it might be more accurate to say that the rate has a floating component and a fixed component. But it is also possible for the credit spread to be periodically reset to a market rate. Neither 'floating-rate' nor 'market rates of interest' are defined in the standard. However, the IFRIC noted in its January 2016 agenda decision on separation of an embedded floor from a floating rate host contract that the term 'market rate of interest' is linked to the concept of fair value as defined in IFRS 13 and is described in paragraph AG64 of IAS 39 as the rate of interest for a similar instrument (similar as to currency, term, type of interest rate and other factors) with a similar credit rating (or the equivalent in paragraph B5.1.1 of IFRS 9).[2] This implies that the market rate of interest may include the credit spread appropriate for the transaction and not just the benchmark component of the rate. [IFRS 9.B5.1.1].

The application of the effective interest method to floating-rate instruments and inflation-linked debt is considered in more detail at 3.3 and 3.6 below.

As set out in Chapter 47 at 6, an issued compound financial instrument such as a convertible bond is accounted for as a financial liability component and an equity component. In accounting for the financial liability at amortised cost, the expected cash flows should be those of the liability component only and the estimate should not take account of the bond being converted.

3.2 Fixed interest rate instruments

The effective interest method is most easily applied to instruments that have fixed payments and a fixed term. The following examples, adapted from the Implementation Guidance to the standard, illustrate this. *[IFRS 9.IG.B.26, IG.B.27]*.

Example 50.4: **Effective interest method – amortisation of premium or discount on acquisition**

At the start of 2021, a company purchases a debt instrument with five years remaining to maturity for its fair value of US$1,000 (including transaction costs). The instrument has a principal amount of US$1,250 and carries fixed interest of 4.7% payable annually (US$1,250 × 4.7% = US$59 per year). In order to allocate interest receipts and the initial discount over the term of the instrument at a constant rate on the carrying amount, it can be shown that interest needs to be accrued at the rate of 10% annually. In each period, the amortised cost at the beginning of the period is multiplied by the EIR of 10% and added to the gross carrying amount. Any cash payments in the period are deducted from the resulting balance.

The table below provides information about the gross carrying amount, interest income, and cash flows of the debt instrument in each reporting period. *[IFRS 9.IG.B.26]*.

Year	(a) Gross carrying amount at the start of the year (US$)	(b = a × 10%) Interest income (US$)	(c) Cash flows (US$)	(d = a + b − c) Gross carrying amount at the end of the year (US$)
2021	1,000	100	59	1,041
2022	1,041	104	59	1,086
2023	1,086	109	59	1,136
2024	1,136	113	59	1,190
2025	1,190	119	1,250 + 59	–

Example 50.5: **Effective interest method – stepped interest rates**

On 1 January 2021, Company A issues a debt instrument for a price of £1,250 (including transaction costs). The principal amount is £1,250 which is repayable on 31 December 2025. The rate of interest is specified in the debt agreement as a percentage of the principal amount as follows: 6% in 2021 (£75), 8% in 2022 (£100), 10% in 2023 (£125), 12% in 2024 (£150) and 16.4% in 2025 (£205). It can be shown that the interest rate that exactly discounts the stream of future cash payments to maturity is 10%. In each period, the amortised cost at the beginning of the period is multiplied by the EIR of 10% and added to the gross carrying amount. Any cash payments in the period are deducted from the resulting balance. Accordingly, the gross carrying amount, interest income and cash flows of the debt instrument in each period are as follows:

Year	(a) Gross carrying amount at the start of the year (£)	(b = a × 10%) Interest income (£)	(c) Cash flows (£)	(d = a + b − c) Gross carrying amount at the end of the year (£)
2021	1,250	125	75	1,300
2022	1,300	130	100	1,330
2023	1,330	133	125	1,338
2024	1,338	134	150	1,322
2025	1,322	133	1,250 + 205	–

It can be seen that, although the instrument is issued for £1,250 and has a maturity amount of £1,250, its gross carrying amount (i.e. the amortised cost) does not equal £1,250 at each reporting date. *[IFRS 9.IG.B.27]*.

Methods for determining the EIR for a given set of cash flows (as in the examples above) include simple trial and error techniques as well as more methodical iterative algorithms. Alternatively, many spreadsheet applications contain goal-seek or similar functions that can also be used to derive EIRs.

3.3 Floating interest rate instruments

For floating-rate instruments, the periodic re-estimation of cash flows to reflect the movements in the market interest rates alters the EIR. The standard goes on to explain that where a floating rate financial asset or a floating-rate financial liability is initially recognised at an amount equal to the principal receivable or repayable on maturity, re-estimating the future interest payments normally has no significant effect on the carrying amount of the asset or the liability. *[IFRS 9.B5.4.5]*. This is normally interpreted to mean that entities should simply account for periodic floating-rate payments on an accrual basis in the period they are earned. An alternative treatment would consist of calculating the EIR based on a market-derived yield curve applicable for the entire life of the instrument. Applying this alternative approach, the calculated EIR is applied until estimated future cash flows are revised, at which point a new EIR is calculated based on the revised cash flow expectations and the current carrying amount. This more complicated treatment is illustrated in the following example (in which it is assumed that the instrument meets the criteria for measurement at amortised cost under IFRS 9).

Example 50.6: Effective interest method – variable rate loan

At the start of July 2021, Company G originates a floating-rate debt instrument. Its fair value is equal to its principal amount of $1,000 and no transaction costs are incurred. The instrument pays, in arrears at the end of June, a variable rate coupon, determined by reference to 12-month LIBOR at the start of each previous July. It has a term of five years and is repayable at its principal amount at the end of June 2026.

On origination, 12-month LIBOR is 5% and this establishes the first payment, to be made in June 2022, at $50. Based on a market-derived yield curve, G estimates that the subsequent floating-rate payments will be $60, $70, $80 and $90 (the yield curve rises steeply). It can be demonstrated that the interest rate that exactly discounts these estimated coupon payments and the $1,000 principal at maturity to the current carrying amount of $1,000 is 6.87%. This would be the EIR for the debt instrument. The EIR is recalculated as and when the estimated future cash flows change.

Even if it is not applied widely in practice (and the effect may often not be material), such an approach seems technically correct. This was also confirmed by the IFRIC discussion on inflation-linked instruments in May 2008 (see 3.6 below).

There are financial instruments which pay a fixed or lower rate of interest in an initial period of their life and subsequently convert to a standard variable rate. An issue arises as to whether the EIR should be calculated on a 'blended' basis, so as to obtain a consistent rate of return over the instrument's expected life or whether the initial period and subsequent period of different interest rates should be treated as two discrete periods, such that blending is not necessary.

Previously, under IAS 39, entities were required to calculate the EIR by discounting estimated 'future cash payments, or receipts through the expected life of the instrument, or when appropriate, a shorter period'. Whilst IFRS 9 has removed 'when appropriate, a shorter period' in its definition in Appendix A to the standard, it has kept the phrase in IFRS 9.B5.4.4 (see below). It was, and still is, unclear as to what is meant by 'when appropriate' and this has led to some diversity in practice with some entities applying a blended rate rather than having different EIRs for discrete periods of interest.

The example below illustrates a loan whose interest is partially fixed and partially variable.

Example 50.7: Fixed rate mortgage which reprices to market interest rate

Bank E offers fixed-rate mortgages to customers with an initial fixed-rate for a term of 5 years, which is shorter than the overall term of the loan of 25 years. The fixed-rate is a market rate at the date of the mortgage offer. After the fixed 5-year term, the initial rate on the loan reverts to a market rate to be determined at that point in time.

The change in interest rate is to a current market rate and is made in accordance with the terms of the original instrument. Consequently, it may be appropriate to treat this as a change in EIR, similar to the repricing of a floating-rate instrument. Therefore, the fixed rate may be applied for the initial 5 years followed by the new market rate when applying the effective interest method.

Example 50.8: Bargain rate mortgage which reprices to market interest rate

Bank F issues the same mortgage as in Example 50.7, except that the initial fixed rate is determined to be a bargain rate. When the initial rate is a bargain rate, it may be required to calculate a blended rate, so as to obtain a consistent rate of return over the expected life of the mortgage. The blended rate would be recalculated as and when the estimated future cash flows change.

Payments, receipts, discounts and premiums included in the effective interest method calculation are normally amortised over the expected life of the instrument and it will often be acceptable to amortise transaction costs on a straight-line basis over the life of the instrument on a basis of materiality.

However, there may be situations when discounts or premiums are amortised over a shorter period if this is the period to which the fees, points paid or received, transaction costs, premiums or discounts relate. This will be the case when the related variable (e.g. interest rates) to which the fees, points paid or received, transaction costs, premiums or discounts relate is repriced to market rates before the instrument's expected maturity. In such cases, the appropriate amortisation period is to the next repricing date. [IFRS 9.B5.4.4].

For example, if a premium or discount on a floating-rate instrument reflects interest that has accrued since interest was last paid, or changes in market rates since the floating interest rate was reset to market rates, it will be amortised to the next date when the interest rate is reset to market rates. This is because the premium or discount relates to the period to the next interest reset date because, at that date, the variable to which the premium or discount relates (i.e. the interest rate) is reset to market rates. If, however, the premium or discount results from a change in the credit spread over the floating-rate specified in the financial instrument, or other variables that are not reset to market rates, it is amortised over the expected life of the instrument. [IFRS 9.B5.4.4].

The following examples illustrate the requirements of applying a discount arising on acquisition of a debt instrument resulting from: (a) a credit downgrade; and (b) accrued interest.

Example 50.9: Effective interest method – amortisation of discount arising from credit downgrade

A twenty-year bond is issued at £100, has a principal amount of £100, and requires quarterly interest payments equal to current three-month LIBOR plus 1% over the life of the instrument. The interest rate reflects the market-based required rate of return associated with the bond issue at issuance. Subsequent to issuance, the credit quality of the bond deteriorates resulting in a rating downgrade. It therefore trades at a discount, although it is assessed not to be credit-impaired (see Chapter 51 at 3.1). Company A purchases the bond for £95 and classifies it as measured at amortised cost and not determined to be purchased credit-impaired on initial recognition.

The discount of £5 is amortised to income over the period to the maturity of the bond and not to the next date interest rate payments are reset as it results from a change in credit spreads.[3] This is because it relates to an adjustment for credit quality which is not a variable that reprices to market rates before the expected maturity.

Example 50.10: Effective interest method – amortisation of premium arising from accrued interest

At the start of November 2021, Company P acquires the bond issued by Company G in Example 50.6 above – current interest rates have not changed since the end of July 2021 and G's credit risk has not changed, but $17 of coupon has accrued since the last interest reset date. Consequently, P pays $1,017 to acquire the bond.

The premium of $17 paid by P relates to interest accrued since the last reset date and so is amortised to income over the period to the next repricing date, June 2022.

Consequently, for the eight months ended June 2022, P will record additional interest income of $33 ($50 – $17), which is also the approximate equivalent of eight months interest at current rates (5%) earned on P's initial investment.

3.4 Prepayment, call and similar options

When calculating the EIR, all contractual terms of the financial instrument, for example prepayment, call and similar options, should be factored into the estimate of expected cash flows. *[IFRS 9 Appendix A]*. (This assumes that the presence of such contractual terms does not cause the contractual cash flow characteristics test to fail, i.e. the contractual terms of the debt instrument give rise on specified dates to cash flows that are solely payments of principal and interest on the principal amount outstanding (see Chapter 48 at 2 and 6)). The following simple example illustrates how this principle is applied.

Example 50.11: Effective interest rate – embedded prepayment options

Bank ABC originates 1,000 ten year loans of £10,000 with 10% stated interest, prepayable at par. Prepayments are probable and it is possible to reasonably estimate their timing and amount. ABC determines that the EIR including loan origination fees received by ABC is 10.2% based on the contractual payment terms of the loans as the fees received reduce the initial carrying amount.

However, if the *expected* prepayments were considered, the EIR would be 10.4% since the difference between the initial amount and maturity amount is amortised over a shorter period.

The EIR that should be used by ABC for the loans in this portfolio is 10.4%.[4]

3.4.1 Revisions to estimated cash flows

The standard contains an explanation of how changes to estimates of payments or receipts (e.g. because of a reassessment of the extent to which prepayments will occur) should be dealt with.

When there is a change in estimates of payments or receipts, excluding changes in estimates of ECLs, the gross carrying amount of the financial asset or amortised cost of a financial liability (or group of instruments) should be adjusted to reflect actual and revised estimated cash flows. More precisely, the gross carrying amount of the financial asset or amortised cost of the financial liability should be recalculated by computing the present value of estimated future contractual cash flows that are discounted at the financial instrument's original EIR. Any consequent adjustment should be recognised immediately in profit or loss. *[IFRS 9.B5.4.6]*.

The revision of estimates is illustrated in the following example adapted from the Implementation Guidance to the standard. [IFRS 9.IG.B.26].

Example 50.12: Effective interest method – revision of estimates

At the start of 2021, a company purchases in a quoted market a debt instrument with five years remaining to maturity for its fair value of US$1,000 (including transaction costs). The instrument has a principal amount of US$1,250 and carries fixed interest of 4.7% payable annually (US$1,250 × 4.7% = US$59 per year). In order to allocate interest receipts and the initial discount over the term of the instrument at a constant rate on the carrying amount, it can be shown that interest needs to be accrued at the rate of 10% annually. In each period, the amortised cost at the beginning of the period is multiplied by the EIR of 10% and added to the gross carrying amount. Any cash payments in the period are deducted from the resulting balance.

This instrument has the same terms as the instrument in Example 50.4 at 3.2 above, except that the contract also specifies that the borrower has an option to prepay the instrument and that no penalty will be charged for prepayment (i.e. any prepayment will be made at the principal amount of US$1,250 or a proportion thereof).

At inception, there is an expectation that the borrower will not prepay and so the information about the instrument's EIR, gross carrying amount, interest income and cash flows in each reporting period would be the same as that in Example 50.4. The table is repeated below and provides information about the gross carrying amount, interest income, and cash flows of the debt instrument in each reporting period.

Year	(a) Gross carrying amount at the start of the year (US$)	(b = a × 10%) Interest income (US$)	(c) Cash flows (US$)	(d = a + b – c) Gross carrying amount at the end of the year (US$)
2021	1,000	100	59	1,041
2022	1,041	104	59	1,086
2023	1,086	109	59	1,136
2024	1,136	113	59	1,190
2025	1,190	119	1,250 + 59	–

On the first day of 2023, the investor revises its estimate of cash flows. It now expects that 50% of the principal will be prepaid at the end of 2023 and the remaining 50% at the end of 2025. Therefore, the opening balance of the debt instrument in 2023 is adjusted to an amount calculated by discounting the amounts expected to be received in 2023 and subsequent years using the original EIR (10%). This results in a revised balance of US$1,138. The adjustment of US$52 (US$1,138 – US$1,086) is recorded in profit or loss in 2023.

The table below provides information about the gross carrying amount, interest income and cash flows as they would be adjusted taking into account this change in estimate.

Year	(a) Gross carrying amount at start of year (US$)	(b = a × 10%) Interest and similar income (US$)	(c) Cash flows (US$)	(d = a + b – c) Gross carrying amount at end of year (US$)
2021	1,000	100	59	1,041
2022	1,041	104	59	1,086
2023	1,086 + 52	114	625 + 59	568
2024	568	57	30	595
2025	595	60	625 + 30	–

This above calculation would be applicable whether the instruments were classified as measured at amortised cost or fair value through other comprehensive income under IFRS 9.

The standard and its related guidance do not state whether the catch-up adjustment in the example above (US$52 in 2023 in this case) should be classified as interest income or as some other income or expense, simply that it should be recognised in profit or loss.

This example assumes that the prepayment option does not cause the debt financial asset to fail to comply with the amortised cost classification criteria. For this to be the case, the fair value of the prepayment feature on initial recognition would have to be insignificant. [IFRS 9.4.1.2(b), B4.1.12].

If a hybrid contract contains a host that is a liability within the scope of IFRS 9, any embedded derivative (e.g. a prepayment option) that is required to be separated from the host must be accounted for as a derivative (see Chapter 46 at 4 and 5). [IFRS 9.4.3.3]. Once separated, the embedded derivative should not be taken into account in applying the effective interest method of the host. However, if the embedded derivative is closely related and not separated from the host instrument, entities that measure the whole instrument at amortised cost must apply the effective interest method inclusive of the embedded derivative to determine the amount of interest to be recognised in profit or loss for each period.

3.5 Perpetual debt instruments

Accounting for perpetual debt instruments is discussed in Chapter 47 at 4.7. The fact that an instrument is perpetual does not change how the gross carrying amount is calculated. The present value of the perpetual stream of future cash payments, discounted at the EIR, equals the gross carrying amount in each period. [IFRS 9.IG.B.24].

However, in cases where interest is only paid over a limited amount of time, some or all the interest payments are, from an economic perspective, repayments of the gross carrying amount, as illustrated in the following example. [IFRS 9.IG.B.25].

Example 50.13: **Amortised cost – perpetual debt with interest payments over a limited amount of time**

On 1 January 2021, Company A subscribes £1,000 for a debt instrument which yields 25% interest for the first five years and 0% in subsequent periods. The instrument is classified as measured at amortised cost. It can be determined that the effective yield is 7.93% and the gross carrying amount is shown in the table below.

Year	(a) Gross carrying amount at the start of the year (£)	(b = a × 7.93%) Interest income (£)	(c) Cash flows (£)	(d = a + b − c) Gross carrying amount at the end of the year (£)
2021	1,000	79	250	829
2022	829	66	250	645
2023	645	51	250	446
2024	446	36	250	232
2025	232	18	250	–
2026	–	–	–	–

3.6 Inflation-linked debt instruments

As noted in Chapter 46 at 5.1.6, the issue of debt instruments whose cash flows are linked to changes in an inflation index is quite common. IFRS 9 often allows inflation-linked financial assets to be recorded at amortised cost or at fair value through other comprehensive income, as shown in Example 48.16 at 6.3.5 in Chapter 48. Entities that record these instruments at amortised cost must apply the effective interest method to determine the amount of interest to be recognised in profit or loss each period. In May 2008, the IFRIC was asked to consider a request for guidance on this issue. The key issue is whether the changes in the cash flows on inflation-linked debt are equivalent to a repricing to the market rate and, therefore, inflation-linked debt can be treated as a floating rate instrument. Three ways of applying the effective interest method that were being used in practice were included in the request. These are summarised in the following example that has been revised to reflect the requirements in IFRS 9 instead of IAS 39.[5]

Example 50.14: Application of the effective interest method to inflation-linked debt instruments

On 1 January 2021, Company A issues a debt instrument for $100,000 that is linked to the local Consumer Prices Index (CPI). The terms of the instrument require it to be repaid in full after five years at an amount equal to $100,000 adjusted by the cumulative change in the CPI over those five years. Interest on the loan is paid at each year end at an amount equal to 5% of the principal ($100,000) adjusted by the cumulative change in the CPI from issuance of the instrument. For IFRS 9 purposes, it is assumed that the debt instrument is not held for trading or designated at fair value through profit or loss and thereby, the debt instrument is classified as subsequently measured at amortised cost.

The following table sets out the expected annual inflation rates on issuance of the instrument and one year later:

	Expected annual inflation rates	
	At start of 2021	At start of 2022
2021	0.7%	1.2%
2022	2.6%	1.4%
2023	2.8%	1.9%
2024	2.8%	3.5%
2025	2.8%	3.5%

During 2021, actual inflation is 1.2%.

Method 1 – application of IFRS 9.B5.4.6 (or the previous IAS 39 AG8 approach)

This approach follows the requirements set out at 3.4.1 above. As outlined below, it does not view the debt as a floating-rate instrument and so calculates a fixed EIR. This is established on 1 January 2021 based on expected cash flows at that time:

Date: end of	Expected cash flow ($)	Calculation
2021	5,035	=5,000 × 1.007
2022	5,166	=5,000 × 1.007 × 1.026
2023	5,311	=5,000 × 1.007 × 1.026 × 1.028
2024	5,459	=5,000 × 1.007 × 1.026 × 1.028 × 1.028
2025	117,854	=105,000 × 1.007 × 1.026 × 1.028 × 1.028 × 1.028

It can be demonstrated that these expected cash flows produce an EIR of 7.4075%, i.e. the net present value of these cash flows, discounted at 7.4075%, equals $100,000.

During 2021, A applies the EIR to the financial liability to recognise a finance charge of $7,408 ($100,000 × 7.4075%), increasing the carrying amount of the financial liability to $107,408 ($100,000 + $7,408). At the end of the year, A pays cash interest of $5,060 ($5,000 × 101.2%) reducing the liability to $102,348 ($107,408 − $5,060). In addition, A must adjust the carrying amount of the financial liability so that it equals the net present value of expected future cash flows discounted at the original expected interest rate as determined based on original expectations.

The expected future cash flows are now as follows:

Date: end of	Cash flow ($)	Calculation
2022	5,131	=5,000 × 1.012 × 1.014
2023	5,228	=5,000 × 1.012 × 1.014 × 1.019
2024	5,411	=5,000 × 1.012 × 1.014 × 1.019 × 1.035
2025	117,615	=105,000 × 1.012 × 1.014 × 1.019 × 1.035 × 1.035

The net present value of these cash flows discounted at 7.4075% is $102,050. Therefore, A recognises a gain for the revision of estimated cash flows by reducing its finance charge by $298 ($102,050 − $102,348) so that the total finance charge for 2021 is $7,110 ($7,408 − $298).

Method 2 – application of IFRS 9.B5.4.5 using forecast future cash flows (or the previous IAS 39 AG7 approach)

This approach is referred to at 3.3 above for simple floating-rate instruments. In outline, it calculates a floating-rate EIR based on current market expectations of future inflation.

The initial EIR is calculated and applied in the same way as Method 1. However, no adjustment is made to the carrying amount of the financial liability at the end of 2021 of $102,348 or to the finance charge for 2021 $7,408 ($100,000 × 7.4075%) as a result of A revising its expectations about inflation over the remaining term of the instrument at the start of 2021.

Instead, a revised EIR is calculated at the start of 2022 using the revised forecast cash flows (shown above under Method 1, i.e. $5,131 at the end of 2022, $5,228 at the end of 2023, $5,411 at the end of 2024 and $117,615 at the end of 2025) and the current carrying amount ($102,348). It can be demonstrated that this produces a revised EIR of 7.3236%, i.e. the net present value of those cash flows, discounted at 7.3236% equals $102,348.

Applying this revised rate prospectively in 2022 (and assuming estimates of future inflation are not revised again until the start of 2023) there will be a finance charge for 2022 of $7,496 ($102,348 × 7.3236%).

Method 3 – application of IFRS 9 B5.4.4-5 without forecasting future cash flows

This method is based on the traditional method of accounting for floating-rate debt instruments and is commonly used under other bodies of GAAP. Rather than taking account of expectations of future inflation it takes account of inflation only during the reporting period.

Therefore, in 2021, A would recognise a finance charge of $5,060 ($100,000 × 5% × 1.012) as a result of accruing the variable interest payment in respect of 2021. In addition, the actual inflation experienced during 2021 increases the amount of principal that will be paid from $100,000 to $101,200 ($100,000 × 1.012%). This increase, i.e. $1,200, is effectively a premium to be paid on the redemption of the financial liability. IFRS 9 explains that a premium should normally be amortised over the expected life of an instrument. However, it goes on to explain that a shorter period should be used if this is the period to which the premium relates. *[IFRS 9.B5.4.4].* In this case, the premium clearly relates to 2021 as it arises from inflation during that year and so it is appropriately amortised in that year.

Consequently, the total finance charge for 2021 using this method would be $6,260 ($5,060 + $1,200).[6]

In analysing the submission, it initially appeared as if the Committee staff completely rejected Method 3. The submission argued that Method 3 was justified by reference to IAS 29 – *Financial Reporting in Hyperinflationary Economies.* The staff concluded (quite correctly)

that it was inappropriate to apply IAS 29 because that standard applies only to the financial statements of an entity whose functional currency is the currency of a hyperinflationary economy and instead the guidance in IAS 39 should be applied.

However, in their final rejection notice the Committee noted that paragraphs AG6 to AG8 of IAS 39 provide the relevant application guidance and that judgement is required to determine whether an instrument is floating-rate and within the scope of paragraph AG7 or is within the scope of paragraph AG8.[7] Further, it was noted that IAS 39 was unclear as to whether future expectations about interest rates (and presumably, therefore, inflation) should be taken into account when applying paragraph AG7. This would appear to suggest that all three methods noted in the example would be consistent with the requirements of IAS 39 and therefore, since the requirements are unchanged, of IFRS 9.

3.7 More complex financial liabilities

Under IFRS 9, most complex financial assets are accounted for at fair value through profit or loss. The treatment of financial liabilities is, however, unchanged from that under IAS 39. The application of the effective interest method to liabilities with unusual embedded derivatives that are deemed closely related to the host, or other embedded features that are not accounted for separately, is not always straightforward or intuitive. Specifically, it is not always clear how to deal with changes in the estimated cash flows of the instrument and in any given situation one needs to assess which of the approaches set out above is more appropriate:

- the general requirements for changes in cash flows set out in paragraph B5.4.6 of IFRS 9, equivalent to the previous IAS 39 AG8 approach, assuming a fixed original EIR (see 3.4.1 above); or
- specific requirements for floating-rate instruments under paragraph B5.4.5 of IFRS 9, equivalent to the previous IAS 39 AG7 approach (see 3.3 above).

Consider an entity that issues a debt instrument for its par value of €10m which is repayable in ten years' time on which an annual coupon is payable comprising two elements: a fixed amount of 2.5% of the par value and a variable amount equating to 0.01% of the entity's annual revenues. The instrument is not designated at fair value through profit or loss and it is judged that the embedded feature is not a derivative as outlined in Example 46.4 at 2.1.3 in Chapter 46.

The requirements under paragraphs B5.4.5 and B5.4.6 of IFRS 9 could give rise to significantly different accounting treatments. In the latter case, the issuer would need to estimate the amount of payments to be made over the life of the bond (which will depend on its estimated revenues for the next ten years) in order to determine the EIR to be applied. Any changes to these estimates would result in a catch-up adjustment, based on the rate as estimated on origination, to profit or loss and the carrying amount of the bond which, potentially, could give rise to significant volatility. In the former case the annual coupon would simply be accrued each year and changes in estimated revenues of future periods would have no impact on the accounting treatment until the applicable year.

In 2009, the IFRIC was asked for guidance on how an issuer should account for a financial liability that contains participation rights by which the instrument holder shares in the net income and losses of the issuer. The holder receives a percentage of the issuer's net income and is allocated a proportional share of the issuer's losses. Losses are applied to the nominal value of the instrument to be repaid on maturity. Losses allocated to the holder in one period can be offset by profits in subsequent periods. The submission was asking how the issuer should account for such instruments in periods in which the issuer records a loss and allocates a portion of that loss to the participating financial instruments. Two possible views were submitted to IFRIC:

- In the first view the requirements in paragraph AG8 of IAS 39 (equivalent to paragraph B5.4.6 of IFRS 9) do not apply. Rather, the requirements for derecognition should be applied and a gain equal to the allocated loss should be recognised in the current period (with an offsetting reduction in the carrying amount of the instrument).

- In a second view, the requirements in paragraph AG8 (equivalent to paragraph B5.4.6 of IFRS 9) apply. Current period losses are one factor that the issuer would consider when it evaluates whether it needs to revise its estimated future cash flows and adjust the carrying amount of the participating financial instrument.

The IFRIC noted that paragraphs AG6 and AG8 of IAS 39 (equivalent to paragraphs B5.4.4. and B5.4.6 of IFRS 9) provide the relevant application guidance for measuring financial liabilities at amortised cost using the EIR method. The IFRIC also noted that it was inappropriate to analogise to the derecognition guidance in IAS 39 because the liability has not been extinguished. Therefore, a gain equal to the allocated loss should not be recognised in the current period. Rather, current period losses should be considered together with further expectations when the issuer evaluates the need to revise its estimated future cash flows and adjust the carrying amount of the participating financial instrument.

It should be noted that the IFRIC considered the issue without reconsidering the assumptions described in the request, namely that the financial liability (a) did not contain any embedded derivatives, (b) was measured at amortised cost using the effective interest method, and (c) did not meet the definition of a floating-rate instrument.[8] In other words, whilst clearly indicating that the B5.4.6 approach was acceptable, it did not explicitly preclude the use of the B5.4.5 approach. In this situation, we believe that it would often be inappropriate to apply the requirements under paragraph B5.4.5 of IFRS 9, principally because the entity's revenue does not represent a floating-rate that changes to reflect movements in market rates of interest. However, as with the examples considered in 3.6 above, judgement is required to determine which approach is appropriate.[9]

There are some financial liabilities for which re-estimation of cash flows will only reflect movements in market interest rates but for which the use of B5.4.5 would, arguably, not be appropriate. An example would be an 'inverse floater', on which coupons are paid at a fixed-rate minus LIBOR (subject to a floor of zero).

For some financial liabilities, it might be considered appropriate to apply a combination of both the B5.4.5 and B5.4.6 approaches. An example might be, for instance, a prepayable floating-rate liability on which transaction costs have been incurred and that have been included in the EIR.

3.8 Modified financial assets and liabilities

3.8.1 Accounting for modifications that do not result in derecognition

When the contractual cash flows of a financial asset are renegotiated or otherwise modified and the renegotiation or modification does not result in the derecognition of that financial asset (see Chapter 52 at 3.4.1), an entity recalculates the gross carrying amount of the financial asset and recognises a modification gain or loss in profit or loss. The gross carrying amount of the financial asset is recalculated as the present value of the renegotiated or modified contractual cash flows that are discounted at the financial asset's original effective interest rate (or credit-adjusted effective interest rate for purchased or originated credit-impaired financial assets – see 3.1 above). Any costs or fees incurred adjust the carrying amount of the modified financial asset and are amortised over the remaining term of the modified financial asset (see 3.8.2 below). *[IFRS 9.5.4.3].*

The accounting for modifications of financial assets that do not result in derecognition is similar to changes in estimates (see 3.4.1 above), i.e. the original EIR is retained and there is a catch-up adjustment to profit or loss for the change in expected cash flows discounted at the original EIR. *[IFRS 9.B5.4.6].* For example, this would be applicable where a borrower is granted a concession to delay interest payments if the entity concludes that the change in the terms is not a substantial modification and therefore does not result in the derecognition of the original loan and the recognition of a new loan.

The standard is not so clear on how to account for modifications or exchanges of financial liabilities measured at amortised cost that do not result in derecognition of the financial liability. The IFRIC received a request which asked whether, when applying IFRS 9, an entity recognises any adjustment to the amortised cost of the financial liability arising from such a modification or exchange in profit or loss at the date of the modification or exchange. The Committee decided to refer the matter to the Board.[10] In October 2017, the Board rather than making an amendment to the standard, chose to add some words to the Basis for Conclusions of IFRS 9 as part of the amendment for prepayment features with negative compensation (see Chapter 48 at 6.4.4.A). This addition states that the requirements in IFRS 9 provide an adequate basis for an entity to account for modifications and exchanges of financial liabilities that do not result in derecognition and that further standard-setting is not required. The Board highlighted that the requirements in IFRS 9 for adjusting the amortised cost of a financial liability when a modification (or exchange) does not result in derecognition are consistent with the requirements for adjusting the gross carrying amount of a financial asset when a modification does not result in the derecognition of the financial asset (see Chapter 52 at 6.2). *[IFRS 9.BC4.252-253].*

This treatment of modifications represents a change in practice for many entities compared to under IAS 39 and such entities have had to apply this change retrospectively on first time application of IFRS 9.

When the terms of a financial instrument are amended, application of the standard's guidance on modifications raises questions as to what the 'original effective interest rate' actually means, in particular when the original contractual terms introduce some form of variability in the rate. This has led to more general questions about when it may be appropriate to apply a prospective change to the effective interest rate in accordance with paragraph B5.4.5, assuming the effective interest rate has a variable component, rather than applying a fixed effective interest rate. The following examples illustrate when the changes in terms constitute a modification or when it may be appropriate to apply paragraph B5.4.5. These examples address the accounting from the lender's perspective, but are applicable to both financial assets and financial liabilities, since the same modification requirements apply to both, as discussed above.

Example 50.15: Changes in credit spread

Fact Pattern 1: A ratchet loan with a rate reset

Bank A issues a ratchet loan whereby the credit spread is increased in accordance with a scale of predetermined rates, on the occurrence of one or more predetermined events that are linked to the borrower's financial covenants (e.g. debt and equity or interest coverage ratios). These clauses are included to avoid the need to renegotiate the loan when the credit risk of the borrower changes and are considered to meet the standard's requirements for the loan to be recorded at amortised cost for the holder.

Analysis:

The credit spread is reset to reflect changes in credit risk and credit spreads are a component of a market interest rate as indicated by the January 2016 IFRIC agenda decision (see 3.1 above). For a vanilla floating rate loan (e.g. at LIBOR plus 2%), it is widely accepted that resetting only the benchmark component of the rate would be regarded as a change in EIR in accordance with paragraph B5.4.5 of IFRS 9. Similarly, resetting only the credit spread component when the reset is predetermined at inception can be regarded as a change in EIR as it is considered as a component of the market interest rate. Although the amount of the reset is specified at inception rather than being the market credit spread at the reset date, this may be accounted for as a reset of the EIR provided that the predetermined rate changes reasonably approximate the market rates for the different credit qualities as observed at inception.

Fact Pattern 2: Renegotiation of loan covenant in return for a higher credit spread

Company B has a term loan which pays interest at LIBOR plus 2% (assume the EIR is also LIBOR plus 2% as there were no transaction costs, fees, discount nor premium). Company B is close to breaching a covenant and renegotiates the loan to adjust the covenant in return for increasing the credit spread applied to the loan to 3%. The revised credit spread reflects the amended terms of the loan and Company B's current credit risk.

Analysis:

The change in rate results solely from a renegotiation of the terms and this change was not specified in the contract at inception. Unless it was specified in the original terms that the credit spread would be reset to predetermined rates based on specific events, the change should be treated as a modification in accordance with paragraph 5.4.3 of IFRS 9. This would mean retaining the original fixed EIR of LIBOR plus 2%, which requires the computation and recognition of a gain or loss based on the change of spread discounted at this rate.

Example 50.16: Modification – troubled debt restructuring

Company B enters into a fixed rate term loan. A few years later, the company is in financial difficulty and renegotiates with the lender to reduce or defer some of the payments due under the loan. The changes in the terms of the loan are not considered to result in a substantial modification and therefore it is not appropriate to derecognise the entire loan. This renegotiation is also not treated as a partial derecognition (see Chapter 52 at 3.3.4 and 3.4.1).

As the changes in payment are not a result of movements in market interest rates and this change was not specified in the contract at inception, it should be treated as a modification in accordance with paragraph 5.4.3 of IFRS 9. This would mean retaining the original fixed rate EIR, which requires the computation and recognition of a gain or loss based on the change in contractual payments discounted at this rate.

Example 50.17: Modification – renegotiation of a fixed rate loan

Fact pattern 1: Renegotiation of a non-prepayable fixed rate loan with a partial rate reset

Company C has had a fixed-rate loan for several years, during which time the market interest rate has fallen. The terms of the loan do not include any ability for the company to prepay. Company C renegotiates the loan with the bank, to reduce the future interest payments to reflect a partial reset of the benchmark rate component of the rate. There has been no change in the credit risk or credit spread applicable to the loan and there are no other changes to the terms.

Analysis:

The change in rate results solely from a renegotiation of the terms and there was no existing prepayment option that would allow Company C to prepay and re-enter into a new loan with the revised rate. Consequently, the change should be treated as a modification in accordance with paragraph 5.4.3 of IFRS 9. This would mean retaining the original fixed rate EIR, which requires the computation and recognition of a gain or loss based on the change in rate discounted at the original fixed EIR.

Fact pattern 2: Renegotiation of fixed rate loan that is prepayable at par to a current market rate

Company D has a fixed rate loan that is prepayable at par, i.e. for unpaid principal and interest, at any time with no penalty. Company D renegotiates the terms of the loan with the lender to a new fixed market rate of interest. The renegotiation is assumed not to be considered a substantial modification.

Analysis:

The standard is unclear on how to treat this fact pattern. In such circumstances, in our view, the lender may apply its judgement and select an appropriate accounting policy as follows:

- *Derecognition*: The revision of the rate is in substance a settlement of the existing loan through the exercise of the prepayment option and commencement of a new loan at the market rate of interest. The cash flows of the original loan are deemed to have expired and should be derecognised with a corresponding new loan recognised.

- *Modification – keeping the original EIR*: The revision does not represent an expiry of the contractual cash flows and there was no actual prepayment of the loan. Since the rate reset is not specifically detailed in the contract at inception, the prepayment option is not viewed as a reset option. Accordingly, the revision is treated as a modification in accordance with paragraph 5.4.3 of IFRS 9. This would mean retaining the original fixed rate EIR, which requires the computation and recognition of a gain or loss based on the change of rate discounted at the original fixed EIR.

- *Modification – prospective change in EIR*: The loan with a prepayment option at par with no penalty is considered analogous to a loan with an option to reset the interest rate to the then prevailing market rate. With such a prepayment option, Company D may prepay the fixed rate loan when interest rates decrease and refinance at a market rate of interest with the same or different lender, or force the same lender to renegotiate the existing interest rate to a market rate of interest. In both cases, the current lender is not entitled to receive the original fixed-rate over the full maturity of the loan. Accordingly, although the renegotiation is treated as a modification, the EIR is adjusted to reflect the new fixed market rate.

Fact pattern 3: Renegotiation of a fixed rate loan that is prepayable with compensation for the change in benchmark interest rate

Company E has a prepayable fixed-rate loan whereby the prepayment amount includes reasonable additional compensation to compensate for the change in benchmark interest rates. The prepayment clause is considered to meet the standard's requirements for the loan to be recorded at amortised cost. Company E renegotiates the terms of the loan with the lender to a new fixed market rate of interest. The revision is assumed not to be considered as a substantial modification.

Analysis:

In such circumstances, the lender may apply its judgement and select an appropriate accounting policy as follows:

- *Derecognition*: The revision of the rate is in substance a settlement of the existing loan through the exercise of the prepayment option to prepay at fair value and commencement of a new loan at the market rate of interest. The cash flows of the original loan are deemed to have expired and should be derecognised with a corresponding new loan recognised.

- *Modification – keeping the original EIR*: The revision does not represent an expiry of the contractual cash flows and there was no actual prepayment of the loan. In addition, the rate reset is not specifically detailed in the contract at inception and the prepayment amount requires compensation for the change in rates which differs from Fact pattern 2 above whereby it prepays at par with no penalty. Consequently, the loan cannot be analogous to a loan with an option to reset the interest rate to the then prevailing market rate. The revision should therefore be treated as a modification in accordance with paragraph 5.4.3. This would mean retaining the original fixed rate EIR, which requires the computation and recognition of a gain or loss based on the change of rate discounted at the original fixed EIR. Note that if the maturity of the renegotiated loan is at the same time extended compared to the original loan (for example from 10 years to 15 years), the penalty paid to compensate the lender for the movements in market rate over the residual maturity of the original 10-year loan should be amortised over this remaining period only and not over the extended maturity from years 11 to 15.

3.8.2 Treatment of modification fees

Assuming that the modification does not result in the derecognition of the financial asset, IFRS 9 requires that changes in the contractual cash flows of the asset are recognised in profit or loss and any costs or fees incurred adjust the carrying amount of the modified financial asset and are amortised over the remaining term of the modified financial asset together with any pre-existing unamortised fees (see Chapter 52 at 6.2.5). *[IFRS 9.5.4.3]*. Therefore, the original EIR determined at initial recognition will be revised on modification to reflect any new costs or fees incurred.

Example 50.18: Accounting treatment of modification fees

The terms of a loan are modified and the revised contractual cash flows discounted at the original EIR, determined at initial recognition, are £5,000 (£6,050 receivable in two years discounted at 10% per annum). If the bank incurs external costs related to the modification of £50, e.g. for valuation of collateral and legal services, the original EIR of 10% will be revised to approximately 9%, i.e. the discount rate that discounts £6,050 receivable in two years to a present value of £5,050.

The standard is not as clear as to the appropriate treatment by the lender when modification fees are charged to the borrower. One view could be that they should be included in the modification gain or loss as they are part of the modified contractual cash flows and do not represent 'fees incurred'. Alternatively, one might argue that the fees charged to the borrower would adjust the carrying amount of the loan. As a variation to the above example, assume £60 of fees are charged to the customer. The effect of this approach would be to revise the carrying amount of the loan to £4,940 and the EIR to 11%. This would be consistent with the principle in paragraph B5.4.2 of IFRS 9, which explains that origination and commitment fees are an integral part of the EIR and, therefore, amortised over the term of the financial asset in accordance with the effective interest method.

For modification fees paid by a borrower to a lender, IFRS 9 requires that any transaction costs or fees incurred adjust the carrying amount of the liability and are amortised over the remaining term of the modified liability. *[IFRS 9.B3.3.6]*. In contrast, paragraph BC4.253 of IFRS 9 explains that the amortised cost of a financial liability should be adjusted in the same way that the gross carrying amount of a financial asset is adjusted when a modification does not result in the derecognition of the financial asset. In its March 2017 IFRIC tentative agenda decision, the Committee confirmed that an entity recognises any adjustment to the amortised cost of a modified financial liability in profit or loss as income or expense at the date of the modification or exchange.[11] Respondents to the tentative agenda decision expressed concern that the requirements for accounting for modified cash flows and the accounting for fees and costs are different but the IFRIC did not address this concern.[12] Therefore, in certain instances judgment may need to be applied to identify whether the substance of a payment made by a borrower to the lender represents additional interest or payment of principal to be accounted for as a modification of cash flows (see 3.8.1 above) rather than a transaction cost (see also Chapter 52 at 6.2.5 to 6.2.7).

3.8.3 Interbank Offered Rate (IBOR) reform

As a result of the reforms mandated by global regulators following the financial crisis, benchmark interbank offered rates (IBORs) are being replaced by new benchmark rates known as Risk Free Rates (RFRs). In 2018, the IASB commenced a project to consider the accounting implications of the reform and divided its work into two phases:

- Phase 1 addresses issues affecting financial reporting in the period before replacement of an existing IBOR; and
- Phase 2 focused on issues that affect financial reporting when an existing interest rate benchmark is replaced with an RFR.

More detail about the project is provided in Chapter 53 at 9.

On 27 August 2020, the IASB completed phase 2 with the publication of *Interest Rate Benchmark Reform – Phase 2 Amendments to IFRS 9, IAS 39, IFRS 7, IFRS 4 and IFRS 16*. The amendments are effective for annual periods beginning on or after 1 January 2021 and earlier application is permitted.

Without the benefit of the amendments, an entity would have to first, assess whether the changes made to a financial instrument to achieve IBOR reform constitute 'a substantial modification' and so lead to its derecognition (see Chapter 52 at 3.4.3 and 6.2.2). Second, if the instrument is not derecognised and is recorded at amortised cost or at fair value through other comprehensive income, the entity would apply the requirements in paragraph 5.4.3 of IFRS 9 and recalculate the carrying amount of the financial instrument using the original EIR (i.e. the IBOR before transition to the new interest rate). This would mean that interest revenue or expense would continue to be recognised using an IBOR-based EIR over the remaining life of the instrument. The Board considered that in the context of interest rate benchmark reform this outcome would not necessarily provide useful information to users of the financial statements as the interest recognised would not reflect the economic effects on a financial instrument of a modification which has occurred as a result of the reform. *[IFRS 9.BC5.306]*.

Therefore, the phase 2 amendments require, as a practical expedient, for changes to cashflows that relate directly to the reform to be treated as changes to a floating interest rate, i.e. the EIR is updated to reflect the change in an interest rate benchmark from IBOR to an RFR without adjusting the carrying amount. In effect, the modification is akin to a movement in the market rate of interest. *[IFRS 9.BC5.308]*.

The use of the practical expedient is subject to two conditions:

- First, the modification must be as a direct consequence of the reform. This includes the addition of a fixed spread to compensate for the basis difference between an existing IBOR and an alternative benchmark rate; changes to the reset period, reset dates or the number of days between coupon payment dates that are necessary to effect the reform; and changes in cash flows arising from existing contractual terms such as a fallback provision that specifies the hierarchy of rates to be used in the event that the existing rate ceases to exist. The modification must not encompass other changes that would lead to value transfer between parties to the financial instrument. *[IFRS 9.5.4.7, BC5.309, BC5.318].*

- Second, the new basis for determining the contractual cash flows must be economically equivalent to the previous basis immediately preceding the modification. *[IFRS 9.5.4.7, BC5.311].* For example, a modification would be economically equivalent if it only involved replacing an interest rate benchmark with an alternative benchmark rate plus a fixed spread that compensated for the basis difference between the interest rate benchmark preceding replacement, and the alternative benchmark rate. *[IFRS 9.5.4.8(a), BC5.312].*

It should be noted that implicit in the amendments is the notion that, as long as the only changes made to the financial instrument are those described above as required to achieve reform, then such changes will never be regarded as sufficiently substantial that the instrument would be derecognised.

After an entity applies the practical expedient to modifications to the financial instrument required by the reform, it then separately assesses any further modifications that are not required by the reform (e.g. a change in credit spread or a maturity date) to determine if they constitute such a substantial modification that they result in derecognition of the financial instrument. If they do not result in derecognition, an entity uses the updated EIR to adjust the carrying amount of the instrument and immediately recognise a modification gain or loss in profit or loss. *[IFRS 9.5.4.9].*

4 FOREIGN CURRENCIES

4.1 Foreign currency instruments

The provisions of IAS 21 – *The Effects of Changes in Foreign Exchange Rates* – apply to transactions involving financial instruments in just the same way as they do for other transactions, although the manner in which certain hedges are accounted for can over-ride its general requirements.

Consequently, the statement of financial position measurement of a foreign currency financial instrument is determined as follows:

- First, it is recorded and measured in the foreign currency in which it is denominated, whether it is carried at fair value, cost, or amortised cost.

- Second, that amount is retranslated to the entity's functional currency using the closing rate. *[IAS 21.23].*

Profit and loss items associated with financial instruments, e.g. dividends receivable, interest payable or receivable and impairments, are recorded at the spot rate ruling when they arise (although average rates may be used when they represent an appropriate approximation to spot rates throughout the period).

The reporting of exchange differences in profit or loss or in other comprehensive income depends on whether the instrument is a monetary item (e.g. debt instruments) or a non-monetary item (e.g. an equity investment), and whether it is designated as part of a foreign currency cash flow hedge. (This excludes the translation of foreign entities which is addressed at 4.2 below).

Foreign exchange differences arising on retranslating monetary items, including debt instruments measured at fair value through other comprehensive income, are generally recognised in profit or loss. However, those exchange differences may be recognised in other comprehensive income for instruments designated as a hedging instrument in a cash flow hedge or in a hedge of a net investment in a foreign operation (except to the extent that there is hedge ineffectiveness). Exchange differences may also be recorded in other comprehensive income for a fair value hedge of an equity instrument for which an entity has elected to present changes in fair value in other comprehensive income (see 2.5 above and Chapter 53). *[IFRS 9.B5.7.2, B5.7.2A]*.

Any changes in the carrying amount of a non-monetary item are recognised in profit or loss or other comprehensive income in accordance with IFRS 9. For example, for an instrument that is measured at fair value through profit or loss, all subsequent fair value changes, including the effect of foreign exchange, are recognised in profit or loss. Similarly, for an investment in an equity instrument where an entity has made an irrevocable election to present in other comprehensive income subsequent changes in the fair value of the investment, the entire change in the carrying amount, including the effect of changes in foreign currency rates, is presented in other comprehensive income. *[IFRS 9.5.7.5, B5.7.3, IG.E.3.4]*.

In cases where some portion of the change in carrying amount is recognised in profit or loss and some in other comprehensive income, e.g. if the amortised cost of a foreign currency bond measured at fair value through other comprehensive income has increased in foreign currency (resulting in a gain in profit or loss) but its fair value has decreased in foreign currency (resulting in a loss recognised in other comprehensive income), those two components cannot be offset for the purposes of determining gains or losses that should be recognised in profit or loss or in other comprehensive income. *[IFRS 9.B5.7.2-7.2A, IG.E.3.4]*.

The Board developed the example below to illustrate the separation of the currency component for a financial asset that is measured at fair value through other comprehensive income in accordance with paragraph 4.1.2A of IFRS 9. To simplify the example, the Board did not reflect the need to record expected credit losses. *[IFRS 9.IG.E.3.2]*. A more complex illustration, including expected credit losses is included in Chapter 51 Example 51.21 at 9.2.

Example 50.19: Foreign currency debt security measured at fair value through other comprehensive income (separation of currency component)

On 31 December 2020, Company A, whose functional currency is the euro, acquires a dollar bond for its fair value of $1,000. The bond has five years to maturity and a $1,250 principal, carries fixed interest of 4.7% paid annually ($1,250 × 4.7% = $59 per year), and has an effective interest rate of 10%.

A classifies the bond as subsequently measured at fair value through other comprehensive income in accordance with paragraph 4.1.2A of IFRS 9, and thus recognises gains and losses in other comprehensive income. The exchange rate is initially $1 to €1.50 and the carrying amount of the bond is €1,500 ($1,000 × 1.50).

	€	€
Bond	1,500	
Cash		1,500

On 31 December 2021, the dollar has appreciated and the exchange rate is $1 to €2.00. The fair value of the bond is $1,060 and therefore its carrying amount is €2,120 ($1,060 × 2.00). Its amortised cost is $1,041 (or €2,082 = $1,041 × 2.00) and the cumulative gain or loss to be included in other comprehensive income is the difference between its fair value and amortised cost, i.e. a gain of €38 (€2,120 – €2,082; or, alternatively, [$1,060 – $1,041] × 2.00).

Interest received on the bond on 31 December 2021 is $59 (or €118 = $59 × 2.00). Interest revenue determined in accordance with the effective interest method is $100 ($1,000 × 10%) of which $41 ($100 – $59) is the accretion of the initial discount.

It is assumed that the average exchange rate during the year is $1 to €1.75 and that the use of an average exchange rate provides a reliable approximation of the spot rates applicable to the accrual of interest during the year. Therefore, reported interest revenue is €175 ($100 × 1.75) including accretion of the initial discount of €72 ($41 × 1.75).

The exchange difference recognised in profit or loss is €525, which comprises three elements: a €500 gain from the retranslation of the initial amortised cost ($1,000 × [2.00 – 1.50]); a €15 gain from the retranslation of interest revenue received ($59 × [2.00 – 1.75]) and a €10 gain on the retranslation of the interest revenue accreted ($41 × [2.00 – 1.75]).

	€	€
Bond	620	
Cash	118	
Interest revenue (P&L)		175
Exchange gain (P&L)		525
Fair value change in other comprehensive income (equity)		38

On 31 December 2022, the dollar has appreciated further and the exchange rate is $1 to €2.50. The fair value of the bond is $1,070 and therefore its carrying amount is €2,675 ($1,070 × 2.50). Its amortised cost is $1,086 (or €2,715 = $1,086 × 2.50) and the cumulative gain or loss to be included in other comprehensive income is the difference between its fair value and the amortised cost, i.e. a loss of €40 (€2,675 – €2,715; or, alternatively, [$1,070 – $1,086] × 2.50). Therefore, there is a debit to other comprehensive income equal to the change in the difference during 2021 of €78 (€40 + €38).

Interest received on the bond on 31 December 2022 is $59 (or €148 = $59 × 2.50). Interest revenue determined in accordance with the effective interest method is $104 ($1,041 × 10%), of which $45 ($104 – $59) is the accretion of the initial discount.

Using the same assumptions as in the previous year, interest income is €234 ($104 × 2.25) including accretion of the initial discount of €101 ($45 × 2.25).

The exchange difference recognised in profit or loss is €547, which again comprises three elements: a €521 gain from the retranslation of the opening amortised cost ($1,041 × [2.50 – 2.00]); a €15 gain from the retranslation of interest income received ($59 × [2.50 – 2.25]) and an €11 gain on the retranslation of the interest income accreted ($45 × [2.50 – 2.25]).

	€	€
Bond		555
Cash		148
Fair value change in other comprehensive income (equity)		78
Interest revenue (P&L)		234
Exchange gain (P&L)		547

The treatment would be different for equity instruments measured at fair value through other comprehensive income. Under IAS 21, these are not considered monetary items and exchange differences would form part of the change in the fair value of the instrument, which would be recognised in other comprehensive income with no recycling.

4.2 Foreign entities

IFRS 9 did not amend the application of the net investment method of accounting for foreign entities set out in IAS 21 (see Chapter 15 at 6). Therefore, for the purpose of preparing its own accounts for inclusion in consolidated accounts, a foreign entity that is part of a group applies the principles at 4.1 above by reference to its own functional currency. Consequently, the treatment of gains and losses on, say, trading assets held by a foreign entity should follow the treatment in the example below, adapted from the Implementation Guidance of IFRS 9. *[IFRS 9.IG.E.3.3]*. Another situation where foreign exchange differences on monetary items are recognised in other comprehensive income is when the long-term debt is considered to form part of the net investment in the foreign entity.

Example 50.20: Interaction of IAS 21 and IFRS 9: foreign currency debt investment

Company A is domiciled in the US and its functional currency and presentation currency is the US dollar. A has a UK domiciled subsidiary, B, whose functional currency is sterling. B is the owner of a debt instrument which is held for trading and is therefore carried at fair value through profit or loss in accordance with IFRS 9.

In B's financial statements for 2021, the fair value and carrying amount of the debt instrument is £100. In A's consolidated financial statements, the asset is translated into US dollars at the spot exchange rate applicable at the end of the reporting period, say 2.0, and the carrying amount is US$200 (£100 × 2.0).

At the end of 2022, the fair value of the debt instrument has increased to £110. B reports the trading asset at £110 in its statement of financial position and recognises a fair value gain of £10 in profit or loss. During the year, the spot exchange rate has increased from 2.0 to 3.0 resulting in an increase in the fair value of the instrument from US$200 to US$330 (£110 × 3.0). Therefore, A reports the trading asset at US$330 in its consolidated financial statements.

Since B is classified as a foreign entity, A translates B's statement of comprehensive income 'at the exchange rates at the dates of the transactions'. Since the fair value gain has accrued through the year, A uses the average rate of 2.5 (= [3.0 + 2.0] ÷ 2) as a practical approximation. Therefore, while the fair value of the trading asset has increased by US$130 (US$330 – US$200), A recognises only US$25 (£10 × 2.5) of this increase in profit or loss. The resulting exchange difference, i.e. the remaining increase in the fair value of the debt instrument of US$105 (US$130 – US$25), is recognised in other comprehensive income until the disposal of the net investment in the foreign entity.

References

1 Whilst paragraph 5.7.10 of IFRS 9 could be read as saying that the modification gains or losses should not be recognised in profit or loss, we understand that it was the IASB's intention that they should be recognised in profit or loss. This is clear from reading paragraph 5.7.11 of IFRS 9 in conjunction with paragraph 5.4.3 of IFRS 9, and therefore we view this as a drafting error in para 5.7.10 of IFRS 9.
2 *IFRIC Update*, January 2016.
3 *IGC Q&A* 76-1.
4 *IGC Q&A* 10-19.
5 *IFRIC Update*, July 2008.
6 Information for Observers (May 2008 IFRIC meeting), *Application of the Effective Interest Rate Method*, IASB, May 2008, Appendix.
7 *IFRIC Update*, July 2008.
8 *IFRIC Update*, May 2009.
9 *IFRIC Update*, July 2008.
10 *IFRIC Update*, June 2017.
11 *IFRIC Update*, March 2017.
12 IASB Staff Paper, Agenda Ref 3B, July 2017 *Prepayment Features with Negative Compensation*.

Chapter 51   Financial instruments: Impairment

1 INTRODUCTION 3911
   1.1   Brief history and background of the impairment project 3911
   1.2   Overview of the IFRS 9 impairment requirements 3915
   1.3   Key changes from the IAS 39 impairment requirements and the implications 3917
   1.4   Key differences from the FASB's standard 3919
   1.5   The IFRS Transition Resource Group for Impairment of Financial Instruments (ITG) IASB webcasts and educational materials 3920
   1.6   Other guidance on expected credit losses 3924
2 SCOPE 3924
3 APPROACHES 3925
   3.1   General approach 3925
   3.2   Simplified approach 3928
   3.3   Purchased or originated credit-impaired financial assets 3929
4 IMPAIRMENT FOR CORPORATES 3932
5 MEASUREMENT OF EXPECTED CREDIT LOSSES 3934
   5.1   Definition of default 3934
   5.2   Lifetime expected credit losses 3935
   5.3   12-month expected credit losses 3936
   5.4   Probability of default (PD) and loss rate approaches 3938
           5.4.1   Probability of default (PD) approach 3938
           5.4.2   Loss rate approach 3942
   5.5   Expected life versus contractual period 3944
   5.6   Probability-weighted outcome and multiple scenarios 3947

		5.6.1	Single versus multiple forward-looking economic scenarios	3947
		5.6.2	Approaches to incorporate multiple economic scenarios	3949
		5.6.3	Incorporating the impact of rare shock events	3951
	5.7	Time value of money		3952
	5.8	Losses expected in the event of default		3954
		5.8.1	Credit enhancements: collateral and financial guarantees	3955
			5.8.1.A Guarantees that are part of the contractual terms	3956
			5.8.1.B Guarantees that are not part of the contractual terms	3958
			5.8.1.C Government relief measures	3960
		5.8.2	Cash flows from the sale of a defaulted loan	3961
		5.8.3	Treatment of collection costs paid to an external debt collection agency	3961
	5.9	Reasonable and supportable information		3962
		5.9.1	Undue cost or effort	3962
		5.9.2	Sources of information	3963
		5.9.3	Information about past events, current conditions and forecasts of future economic conditions	3964
		5.9.4	Events and new information obtained after ECLs have been calculated	3966
		5.9.5	Other issues concerning forward-looking information	3966
6	GENERAL APPROACH: DETERMINING SIGNIFICANT INCREASES IN CREDIT RISK			3969
	6.1	Change in the risk of a default occurring		3970
		6.1.1	Impact of collateral, credit enhancements and financial guarantee contracts	3972
		6.1.2	Contractually linked instruments (CLIs) and subordinated interests	3974
		6.1.3	Determining change in the risk of a default under the loss rate approach	3975
	6.2	Factors or indicators of changes in credit risk		3975
		6.2.1	Examples of factors or indicators of changes in credit risk	3976
		6.2.2	Past due status and more than 30 days past due rebuttable presumption	3979
		6.2.3	Concessions granted to a wide range of customers	3980
		6.2.4	Illustrative examples of factors or indicators when assessing significant increases in credit risk	3982
		6.2.5	Use of behavioural factors	3986
	6.3	What is significant?		3987
	6.4	Operational simplifications		3989

		6.4.1	Low credit risk operational simplification 3989
		6.4.2	Delinquency 3994
		6.4.3	12-month risk as an approximation for change in lifetime risk 3995
		6.4.4	Assessment at the counterparty level 3996
		6.4.5	Determining maximum initial credit risk for a portfolio 3998
	6.5	Collective assessment 4000
		6.5.1	Example of individual assessment of changes in credit risk 4001
		6.5.2	Basis of aggregation for collective assessment 4002
		6.5.3	Example of collective assessment ('bottom up' and 'top down' approach) 4004
	6.6	Determining the credit risk at initial recognition of an identical group of financial assets 4007
	6.7	Multiple scenarios for the assessment of significant increases in credit risk 4008
7	OTHER MATTERS AND ISSUES IN RELATION TO THE EXPECTED CREDIT LOSS CALCULATIONS 4010
	7.1	Basel guidance on accounting for expected credit losses 4010
	7.2	Global Public Policy Committee (GPPC) guidance 4013
	7.3	Measurement dates of expected credit losses 4014
		7.3.1	Date of derecognition and date of initial recognition 4014
		7.3.2	Trade date and settlement date accounting 4016
	7.4	Interaction between the initial and subsequent measurement of debt instruments acquired in a business combination and the impairment model of IFRS 9 4016
	7.5	Interaction between expected credit losses calculations and fair value hedge accounting 4018
	7.6	Changes in ECL methodologies – errors, changes in estimates or changes in accounting policies 4019
	7.7	Securitisations and special purpose entities (SPEs) 4020
		7.7.1	ECL requirements for the SPE if the transferor is not able to derecognise the portfolio of loans 4021
		7.7.2	Accounting for a financial liability issued by an SPE 4022
	7.8	Measuring ECLs during the coronavirus (covid-19) pandemic 4023
		7.8.1	Introduction 4023
		7.8.2	Guidance 4023
		7.8.3	Calculation of ECLs 4025
		7.8.4	Determining whether there has been a significant increase in credit risk 4026
		7.8.5	Disclosures 4027
8	MODIFIED FINANCIAL ASSETS 4032

	8.1	Accounting treatment if modified financial assets are derecognised 4033
	8.2	Accounting treatment if modified financial assets are not derecognised 4034

9 FINANCIAL ASSETS MEASURED AT FAIR VALUE THROUGH OTHER COMPREHENSIVE INCOME 4036

    9.1 Accounting treatment for debt instruments measured at fair value through other comprehensive income 4036

    9.2 Interaction between foreign currency translation, fair value hedge accounting and impairment 4037

10 TRADE RECEIVABLES, CONTRACT ASSETS AND LEASE RECEIVABLES ... 4043

    10.1 Trade receivables and contract assets 4043

    10.2 Lease receivables 4044

11 LOAN COMMITMENTS AND FINANCIAL GUARANTEE CONTRACTS 4045

    11.1 Definitions and scope 4045

    11.2 The calculation of ECLs 4046

    11.3 Financial guarantee contracts that require the holder to pay further premiums in the future 4048

    11.4 Cross-company guarantees 4050

    11.5 Purchased or originated credit impaired loan commitments and financial guarantee contracts 4050

12 REVOLVING CREDIT FACILITIES 4051

    12.1 Scope of the exception 4051

    12.2 The period over which to measure ECLs 4054

        12.2.1 The requirements of the standard 4054

        12.2.2 Guidance provided by the ITG 4057

        12.2.3 Guidance provided by the IASB webcast 4058

        12.2.4 Interaction with derecognition 4060

    12.3 Exposure at default (EAD) 4062

    12.4 Time value of money 4063

    12.5 Determining significant increase in credit risk 4064

13 INTERCOMPANY LOANS 4065

    13.1 Scope of intercompany loans under IFRS 9 4065

    13.2 Intercompany loans repayable on demand 4066

    13.3 Determining the ECLs of intercompany loans 4066

14 PRESENTATION OF EXPECTED CREDIT LOSSES IN THE STATEMENT OF FINANCIAL POSITION 4067

    14.1 Allowance for financial assets measured at amortised cost, contract assets and lease receivables 4068

14.1.1 Write-off 4068
14.1.2 Presentation of the interest revenue, gross carrying amount, amortised cost, expected credit loss expense and expected credit loss allowance for credit-impaired assets 4070

14.2 Provisions for loan commitments and financial guarantee contracts 4073

14.3 Accumulated impairment amount for debt instruments measured at fair value through other comprehensive income 4073

15 DISCLOSURES 4074

List of examples

Example 51.1:	Expected credit loss allowance in stages 1, 2 and 3 under the general approach	3917
Example 51.2:	Calculation of the credit-adjusted effective interest rate and recognition of a loss allowance for a purchased credit-impaired financial asset	3931
Example 51.3:	12-month and lifetime expected credit loss measurement based on a PD approach	3938
Example 51.4:	Expected credit loss measurement using credit rating agency historical default rates	3941
Example 51.5:	12-month expected credit losses measurement based on a loss rate approach	3942
Example 51.6:	Determining the maximum contractual period when measuring expected credit losses	3945
Example 51.7:	Incorporating single versus multiple forward-looking scenarios when measuring expected credit losses	3948
Example 51.8:	Highly collateralised financial asset	3972
Example 51.9:	Significant increase in credit risk	3982
Example 51.10:	No significant increase in credit risk	3983
Example 51.11:	Assessment of a significant increase in credit risk based on a PD approach	3984
Example 51.12:	Public investment-grade bond	3992
Example 51.13:	Use of credit ratings and/or CDS spreads to determine whether there have been significant increases in credit risk and to estimate expected credit losses	3993
Example 51.14:	Counterparty assessment of credit risk	3997
Example 51.15:	Comparison to maximum initial credit risk	3998
Example 51.16:	Individual assessment in relation to responsiveness to changes in credit risk	4002
Example 51.17:	Collective assessment in relation to responsiveness to changes in credit risk ('bottom up' approach)	4004
Example 51.18:	Collective assessment in relation to responsiveness to changes in credit risk ('top down' approach)	4005

Example 51.19:	Modification of contractual cash flows	4034
Example 51.20:	Debt instrument measured at fair value through other comprehensive income	4036
Example 51.21:	Interaction between the fair value through other comprehensive income measurement category and foreign currency denomination, fair value hedge accounting and impairment	4038
Example 51.22:	Provision matrix	4044
Example 51.23:	Determining the initial and subsequent measurement of a financial guarantee contract where premiums are receivable upfront or over the life of the guarantee	4048
Example 51.24:	Revolving credit facilities	4055
Example 51.25:	Estimating the life of revolving credit facilities	4060
Example 51.26:	Partial write-offs for a loan in stage 3	4069
Example 51.27:	Disclosing the gross carrying amount and loss allowance for credit-impaired financial assets that are not purchased or originated credit-impaired	4070
Example 51.28:	Presentation of the interest revenue, gross carrying amount, amortised cost, expected credit loss expense and expected credit loss allowance for when assets move from stage 2 to stage 3 and vice versa	4072

Chapter 51 Financial instruments: Impairment

1 INTRODUCTION

This chapter discusses the forward-looking expected credit loss ('ECL') model as set out in IFRS 9 – *Financial Instruments*, accompanied by 14 illustrative examples. Since the standard was issued in 2014, a number of interpretation and application issues have been identified, many of which have been the subject of discussion by the IFRS Transition Resource Group for Impairment of Financial Instruments (ITG) established by the IASB and further guidance has been provided by the IASB in the form of webcasts and educational materials (see 1.5 below) and by banking regulators (see 1.6 and 7.1 below).

This chapter also briefly describes the credit risk disclosures in relation to the ECL model as set out in IFRS 7 – *Financial Instruments: Disclosures* – (see 15 below). A more detailed discussion of the disclosure requirements can be found in Chapter 54 at 5.3.

1.1 Brief history and background of the impairment project

During the 2007/8 global financial crisis, the delayed recognition of credit losses that are associated with loans and other financial instruments was identified as a weakness in existing accounting standards. This is primarily due to the fact that the previous impairment requirements under IAS 39 – *Financial Instruments: Recognition and Measurement* – were based on an incurred loss model, i.e. credit losses were not recognised until a credit loss event had occurred. Since losses are rarely incurred evenly over the lives of loans, there was a mismatch in the timing of the recognition of the credit spread inherent in the interest charged on the loans over their lives and any impairment losses that was only recognised at a later date. A further identified weakness was the complexity of different entities using different approaches to calculate impairment.

As part of the joint approach by the IASB and the FASB to deal with the financial reporting issues arising from the financial crisis, the boards set up the Financial Crisis Advisory Group (FCAG) in October 2008 to consider how improvements in financial reporting could help to enhance investor confidence in financial markets. Not long after, the leaders of the Group of 20 (also known as the G20) published a report *Declaration on Strengthening the Financial System* in April 2009 that called on the accounting standard setters to reduce the complexity of accounting standards for financial instruments and to strengthen accounting recognition of loan-loss provisions by incorporating a broader range of credit information.[1]

In July 2009, the FCAG presented its report to the IASB and the FASB about the standard-setting implications of the global financial crisis. Consistent with the G20's recommendations, the FCAG also recommended both the IASB and the FASB to explore alternatives to the incurred loss model for loan loss provisioning that used more forward-looking information.[2]

In June 2009, the IASB published a request for information – *Impairment of Financial Assets: Expected Cash Flow Approach* – on the feasibility of an expected loss model for the impairment of financial assets. Following this, in November 2009, the IASB issued an Exposure Draft – *Financial Instruments: Amortised Cost and Impairment* (the 2009 ED) that proposed an impairment model based on expected losses rather than on incurred losses, for all financial assets recorded at amortised cost. In this approach, the initial ECLs were to be recognised over the life of a financial asset, by including them in the computation of the effective interest rate (EIR) when the asset was first recognised. This would build an allowance for credit losses over the life of a financial asset and so match the recognition of credit losses with that of the credit spread implicit in the interest charged. Subsequent changes in credit loss expectations would be reflected in catch-up adjustments to profit or loss based on the original EIR. Because the proposals were much more closely linked to credit risk management concepts, the IASB acknowledged that this would represent a fundamental change from how entities currently operate (i.e. typically, entities operate their accounting and credit risk management systems separately). Consequently, the IASB established a panel of credit risk experts, the Expert Advisory Panel (EAP), to provide input to the project. *[IFRS 9.BC5.87]*.

Comments received on the 2009 ED and during the IASB's outreach activities indicated that constituents were generally supportive of a model that distinguished between the effect of initial estimates of ECLs and subsequent changes in those estimates. However, they were also concerned about the operational difficulties in implementing the model proposed. These included: *[IFRS 9.BC5.89]*

- estimating the full expected cash flows for all financial instruments;
- applying a credit-adjusted EIR to those cash flow estimates; and
- maintaining information about the initial estimate of ECLs.

Also, the proposals would not have been easy to apply to portfolios of loans managed on a collective basis, in particular, open portfolios to which new financial instruments are added over time, and concerns were expressed about the volatility of reported profit or loss arising from the catch-up adjustments.

To address these operational challenges and as suggested by the EAP, the IASB decided to decouple the measurement and allocation of initial ECLs from the determination of the EIR (except for purchased or originated credit-impaired financial assets). Therefore, the financial asset and the loss allowance would be measured separately, using an original EIR that is not adjusted for initial ECLs. Such an approach would help address the operational challenges raised and allow entities to leverage their existing accounting and credit risk management systems and so reduce the extent of the necessary integration between these systems. *[IFRS 9.BC5.92]*.

By decoupling ECLs from the EIR, an entity must measure the present value of ECLs using the original EIR. This presents a dilemma, because measuring ECLs using such a rate double-counts the ECLs that were priced into the financial asset at initial recognition. This is because the fair value of the loan at original recognition already reflects the ECLs, so to provide for the ECLs as an additional allowance would be to double count these losses. Hence, the IASB concluded that it was not appropriate to recognise lifetime ECLs on initial recognition. In order to address the operational challenges while trying to reduce the effect of double-counting, as well as to replicate (very approximately) the outcome of the 2009 ED, the IASB decided to pursue a dual-measurement model that would require an entity to recognise: [IFRS 9.BC5.93]

- a portion of the lifetime ECLs from initial recognition as a proxy for recognising the initial ECLs over the life of the financial asset; and
- the lifetime ECLs when credit risk had increased since initial recognition (i.e. when the recognition of only a portion of the lifetime ECLs would no longer be appropriate because the entity has suffered a significant economic loss).

It is worth noting that any approach that seeks to approximate the outcomes of the model in the 2009 ED, without the associated operational challenges, will include a recognition threshold for lifetime ECLs. This gives rise to what has been referred to as 'a cliff effect', i.e. the significant increase in allowance that represents the difference between the portion that was recognised previously and the lifetime ECLs. [IFRS 9.BC5.95].

Subsequently, the IASB and FASB spent a considerable amount of time and effort developing a converged impairment model. In January 2011, the IASB issued with the FASB a Supplementary Document – *Financial Instruments: Impairment* – reflecting a joint approach that proposed a two-tier loss allowance: [IFRS 9.BC5.96]

- for the good book, an entity would recognise the higher of a time-proportionate allowance (i.e. the lifetime ECLs over the weighted average life of the portfolio of assets) or ECLs for the 'foreseeable future'; and
- for the bad book, an entity would recognise lifetime ECLs on those financial assets when the collectability of contractual cash flows had become so uncertain that the entity's credit risk management objective had changed from receiving the regular payments to recovery of all, or a portion of, the asset.

However, this approach received only limited support, because respondents were concerned about the operational difficulties in performing the dual calculation for the good book, that it also lacked conceptual merit and, potentially, would provide confusing information to users of financial statements. Moreover, concerns were also raised as to how 'foreseeable future' should be interpreted and applied.

Many constituents emphasised the importance of achieving convergence and this encouraged the IASB and FASB to attempt to develop another joint alternative approach. In May 2011, the boards decided to develop jointly an expected credit loss model that would reflect the general pattern of increases in the credit risk of financial instruments, the so-called three-bucket model. [IFRS 9.BC5.111].

However, due to concerns raised by the FASB's constituents about the model's complexity, the FASB decided to develop an alternative expected credit loss model. [IFRS 9.BC5.112]. In December 2012, the FASB issued a proposed accounting standard update,

Financial Instruments Credit Losses (Subtopic 825-15), that would require an entity to recognise a loss allowance from initial recognition at an amount equal to lifetime ECLs (see 1.4 below).

In March 2013, the IASB published a new Exposure Draft – *Financial Instruments: Expected Credit Losses* (the 2013 ED), based on proposals that grew out of the joint project with the FASB. The 2013 ED proposed that entities should recognise a loss allowance or provision at an amount equal to 12-month credit losses for those financial instruments that had not yet seen a significant increase in credit risk since initial recognition, and lifetime ECLs once there had been a significant increase in credit risk. This new model was designed to:

- ensure a more timely recognition of ECLs than the existing incurred loss model;
- distinguish between financial instruments that have significantly deteriorated in credit quality and those that have not; and
- better approximate the economic ECLs.[3]

This two-step model was designed to approximate the build-up of the allowance as proposed in the 2009 ED, but involving less operational complexity. Figure 51.1 below illustrates the stepped profile of the new model, shown by the solid line, compared to the steady increase shown by the black dotted line proposed in the 2009 ED (based on the original ECL assumptions and assuming no subsequent revisions of this estimate). It shows that the two step model first overstates the allowance (compared to the method set out in the 2009 ED), then understates it as the credit quality deteriorates, and then overstates it once again, as soon as the deterioration is significant.

Figure 51.1 Accounting for expected credit losses – 2009 ED versus IFRS 9[4]

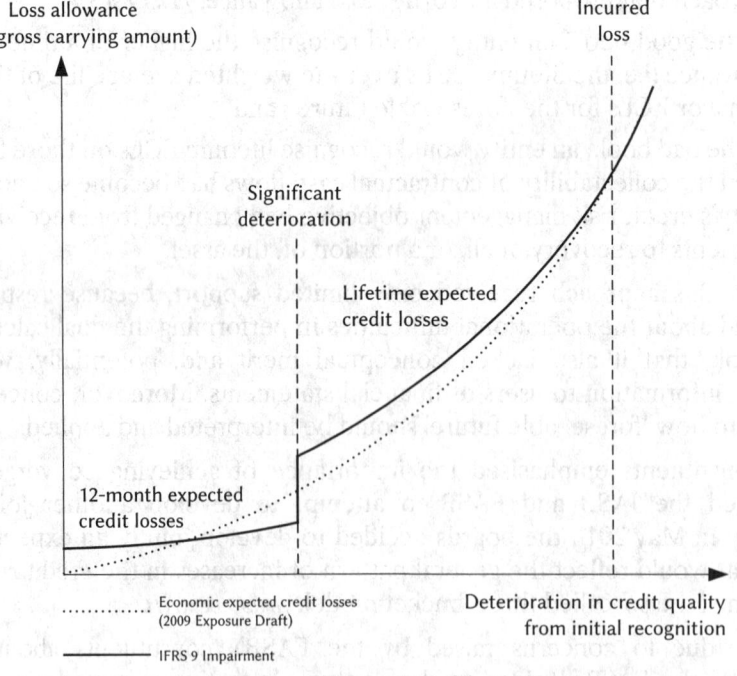

Feedback received on the IASB's 2013 ED and the FASB's 2012 Proposed Update was considered at the joint board meetings. In general, non-US constituents preferred the IASB's proposals whilst the US constituents preferred the FASB's proposals. These differences in views arose in large part because of differences in the starting point of how preparers apply US GAAP for loss allowances from that for most IFRS preparers, while the interaction between the role of prudential regulators and calculation of loss allowances is historically stronger in the US. *[IFRS 9.BC5.116]*.

Many respondents urged the IASB to finalise the proposals in the 2013 ED as soon as possible, even if convergence could not be achieved, in order to improve the accounting for the impairment of financial assets in IFRSs. *[IFRS 9.BC5.114]*. The IASB re-deliberated particular aspects of the 2013 ED proposals, with the aim of providing further clarifications and additional guidance to help entities implement the proposed requirements. The IASB finalised the impairment requirements and issued them in July 2014, as part of the final version of IFRS 9.

1.2 Overview of the IFRS 9 impairment requirements

The impairment requirements in IFRS 9 are based on an ECL model and replaced the IAS 39 incurred loss model. The ECL model applies to debt instruments (such as bank deposits, loans, debt securities and trade receivables) recorded at amortised cost or at fair value through other comprehensive income, plus lease receivables and contract assets. Loan commitments and financial guarantee contracts that are not measured at fair value through profit or loss are also included in the scope of the ECL model.

Conceptually, an impairment model is a necessary complement to an accounting model for financial assets that is based on the concept of realisation, i.e. when cash flows are received and paid. For financial assets in the scope of the impairment model, the recognition of revenue follows the effective interest method, and gains and losses relating to changes in their fair value are generally only recognised in profit or loss when the financial asset is derecognised, when that gain or loss is realised. In order to avoid delaying the recognition of impairment losses, those accounting models are complemented by an impairment model that anticipates impairment losses by recognising them before they are realised. The impairment model of IFRS 9 does this on the basis of ECLs, which means impairment losses are anticipated earlier than under the incurred loss impairment model of IAS 39. In contrast, the accounting models for financial assets in IFRS 9 that are not based on the concept of realisation, i.e. those measured at fair value through profit or loss or at fair value through other comprehensive income without recycling (under the presentation choice for fair value changes of some investments in equity instruments, see Chapter 48 at 8 and Chapter 50 at 2.5) do not involve any separate impairment accounting. Those measurement categories implicitly include impairment losses in the fair value changes that are recognised immediately (and without any later reclassification entries between other comprehensive income and profit or loss when they are realised).

The guiding principle of the ECL model is to reflect the general pattern of deterioration, or improvement, in the credit quality of financial instruments. The ECL approach has been commonly referred to as the three-bucket approach, although IFRS 9 does not use this term. Figure 51.2 below summarises the general approach in recognising either 12-month or lifetime ECLs.

Figure 51.2 General approach

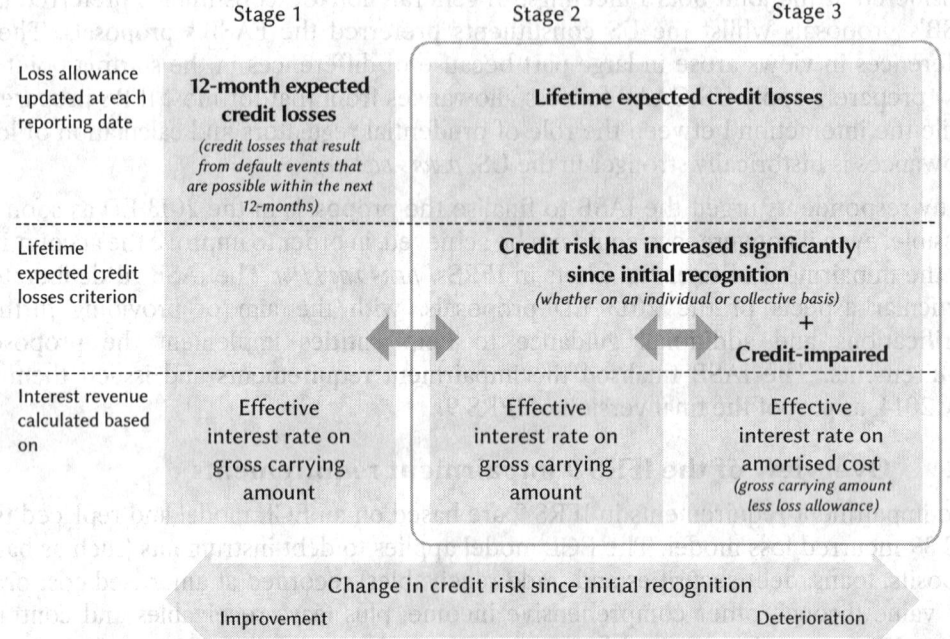

The amount of ECLs recognised as a loss allowance or provision depends on the extent of credit deterioration since initial recognition. Under the general approach (see 3.1 below), there are two measurement bases:

- 12-month ECLs (stage 1), which apply to all items as long as there is no significant deterioration in credit risk; and
- lifetime ECLs (stages 2 and 3), which apply when a significant increase in credit risk has occurred on an individual or collective basis.

When assessing significant increases in credit risk, there are a number of operational simplifications available, such as the low credit risk simplification (see 6.4.1 below).

Stages 2 and 3 differ in how interest revenue is recognised. Under stage 2 (as under stage 1), there is a full decoupling between interest recognition and impairment, and interest revenue is calculated on the gross carrying amount. A financial asset is transferred to stage 3 when it is credit-impaired, defined as when one or more events that have a detrimental impact on the estimated future cash flows of that financial asset have occurred. The criteria are set out in more detail in 3.1 below. Under stage 3, interest revenue is calculated on the amortised cost (i.e. the gross carrying amount adjusted for the impairment allowance). *[IFRS 9 Appendix A, IFRS 9.5.4.1].*

As an exception to this model, there are separate rules if a financial asset is already credit-impaired on initial recognition (see 3.3 below).

The following example illustrates how the ECL allowance changes when a loan moves from stage 1 to stage 3.

Example 51.1: *Expected credit loss allowance in stages 1, 2 and 3 under the general approach*

On 31 December 2020, Bank A originates a 10 year loan with a gross carrying amount of $1,000,000, with interest being due at the end of each year and the principal due on maturity. There are no transaction costs and the loan contracts include no options (for example, prepayment or call options), premiums or discounts, points paid, or other fees.

At origination, the loan is in stage 1 and a corresponding 12-month ECL allowance is recognised in the year ending 31 December 2020.

On 31 December 2023, the loan has shown signs of significant deterioration in credit quality and Bank A moves the loan to stage 2. A corresponding lifetime ECL allowance is recognised. In the following year, the loan defaults and is moved to stage 3.

The ECL allowance in each stage is shown below and the detailed calculation is illustrated in Example 51.3 at 5.4.1 below.

Stage 1: 12-month expected credit losses	Stage 2: lifetime expected credit losses	Stage 3: lifetime expected credit losses
On 31 December 2020, the loan is originated. An allowance of $422 is recognised.	On 31 December 2023, the loan has shown signs of a significant increase in credit risk. An allowance of $50,285 is recognised (the 12-month ECL is $3,495).	On 31 December 2024, the loan defaults. An allowance of $262,850 is recognised.

There are two alternatives to the general approach:

- the simplified approach, that is either required or available as a policy choice for trade receivables, contract assets and lease receivables (see 3.2 below); and
- the credit-adjusted effective interest rate approach, for purchased or originated credit-impaired financial assets (see 3.3 below).

ECLs are an estimate of credit losses over the next 12 months or the life of a financial instrument and, when measuring ECLs (see 5 below), an entity needs to take into account:

- the probability-weighted outcome (see 5.6 below), as ECLs should not simply be either a best or a worst-case scenario, but should, instead, reflect the possibility that a credit loss occurs and the possibility that no credit loss occurs. Following discussion at the ITG, this is understood to include a need to consider multiple economic scenarios (see 5.6.1 below);
- the time value of money (see 5.7 below); and
- reasonable and supportable information that is available without undue cost or effort at the reporting date about past events, current conditions and forecasts of future economic conditions (see 5.9 below).

1.3 Key changes from the IAS 39 impairment requirements and the implications

The IFRS 9 impairment requirements eliminated the IAS 39 threshold for the recognition of credit losses, i.e. it is no longer necessary for a credit event to have occurred before credit losses are recognised. Instead, an entity always accounts for ECLs, and updates the loss allowance for changes in these ECLs at each reporting date to reflect changes in credit risk since initial recognition. Consequently, the holder of the financial asset needs to take into account more timely and forward-looking information.

The main implications for both financial and non-financial entities are as follows:

- The scope of the impairment requirements is now much broader. Previously, under IAS 39, there were different impairment models for financial assets measured at amortised cost and available-for-sale financial assets. Under IFRS 9, there is a single impairment model for all debt instruments measured at amortised cost and at fair value through other comprehensive income. Furthermore, loan commitments and financial guarantee contracts that were previously in the scope of IAS 37 – *Provisions, Contingent Liabilities and Contingent Assets* – are now in the scope of the IFRS 9 impairment requirements (see 11 below).

- Previously, under IAS 39, loss allowances were only recorded for impaired exposures. The IFRS 9 impairment requirements result in earlier recognition of credit losses, by necessitating a 12-month ECL allowance for all credit exposures not measured at fair value through profit or loss. In addition, there is a larger allowance for all credit exposures that have significantly deteriorated (as compared to the recognition of incurred losses under IAS 39). While credit exposures in stage 3, as illustrated in Figure 51.2 above, are similar to those deemed by IAS 39 to have suffered individual incurred losses, credit exposure in stages 1 and 2 essentially replace those exposures measured under IAS 39's collective approach.

- The ECL model is more forward-looking than the IAS 39 impairment model. Holders of financial assets are not only required to consider historical information that is adjusted to reflect the effects of current conditions and information that provides objective evidence that financial assets are impaired in relation to incurred losses. They are also required to consider reasonable and supportable information that includes forecasts of future economic conditions including, where relevant, multiple scenarios, when calculating ECLs, on an individual and collective basis.

- The application of the IFRS 9 impairment requirements has led to an increase in credit loss allowances (with a corresponding reduction in equity on first-time adoption) of many entities, particularly banks and similar financial institutions. However, the increase in the loss allowance has varied by entity, depending on its portfolio and previous practices. Entities with shorter term and higher quality financial instruments are less significantly affected. Similarly, financial institutions with unsecured retail loans are generally affected to a greater extent than those with collateralised loans such as mortgages.

- Moreover, the focus on expected losses has the potential to result in higher volatility in the ECL amounts charged to profit or loss, especially for financial institutions. The level of loss allowances will increase as economic conditions are forecast to deteriorate and will decrease as economic conditions are forecast to become more favourable. This may be further compounded by the significant increase in the loss allowance when financial instruments move between 12-month and lifetime ECLs and *vice versa*.

- The need to incorporate forward-looking information, including establishing multiple macroeconomic scenarios, determining the probability of their occurrence and assessing how changes in macroeconomic factors will affect ECLs, means that the application of the standard requires considerable judgement. Also, the increased level of judgement required in making the ECL calculation and assessing when significant deterioration has occurred may mean that it will be difficult to compare the reported results of different entities. However, the more detailed disclosure requirements, that require entities to explain their inputs, assumptions and techniques used in estimating ECLs, should provide greater transparency over entities' credit risk and provisioning processes. The Enhanced Disclosures Task Force (EDTF), established in 2012 by the Financial Stability Board to recommend best practice market risk disclosures, has also published guidance to promote greater transparency and comparability about the application of the ECL model (see Chapter 54 at 9.2).

- In financial institutions, finance and credit risk management systems and processes now have to be better connected, because of the necessary alignment between risk and accounting in the IFRS 9 impairment model. Risk models and data are used more extensively to make the assessments and calculations required for accounting purposes, which are both a major change from IAS 39 and a key challenge.
- In addition, financial institutions need to fully understand the complex interactions between the IFRS 9 and regulatory capital requirements in relation to credit losses. The Basel Committee on Banking Supervision has now finalised what it calls an 'interim' approach and transitional arrangements, providing national jurisdictions with a framework for any arrangement. This is contained in the BCBS document *Standards – Regulatory treatment of accounting provisions – interim approach and transitional arrangements*. However, the long-term regulatory treatment of ECL provisions remains to be determined. In most cases, implementing the IFRS 9 ECL requirements has resulted in a reduction in the regulatory capital of financial institutions.
- The IFRS impairment requirements have had a less significant impact on corporates than on banks and similar financial institutions. To reflect this, we have set out a summary of the main implications for corporates in a separate section (see 4 below). Given that IFRS 16 – *Leases* – has retained the distinction for accounting by lessors between finance leases and operating leases, the effect of IFRS 9 is largely limited to finance leases. For these, there is a significant increase in allowances, particularly if the lessor has opted to apply the simplified approach and record lifetime allowances (see 3.2 below).

1.4 Key differences from the FASB's standard

On 16 June 2016, the FASB issued an Accounting Standard Update (ASU), *Financial Instruments – Credit Losses (Topic 326)*, that aims to address the same fundamental issue that the IASB's ECL model (in IFRS 9) addresses, namely the delayed recognition of credit losses resulting from the incurred credit loss model. It is therefore also an ECL model but it is not the same as the model in IFRS 9. The most significant differences between the FASB's and the IASB's ECL models are, as follows:

- The FASB's ECL model (known as the Current ECL or CECL model) does not apply to debt securities measured at fair value through other comprehensive income (i.e. available for sale debt securities under US GAAP). Rather, for available for sale debt securities, an allowance is recognised to reflect estimated credit losses

and is adjusted over time to reflect both positive and adverse changes in expected cash flows.
- The FASB's ECLs are calculated based on the losses expected over the remaining contractual life of an asset, considering the effect of prepayments and reasonably expected troubled debt restructurings. An allowance for lifetime ECLs is required when the loan is initially recognised instead of 12-month ECLs under IFRS 9. As a result, the FASB's model does not require an entity to assess whether there has been a significant deterioration in credit quality, in contrast to the assessment required by IFRS 9. This is similar to the IFRS 9 simplified approach (see 3.2 below).
- The FASB's standard does not require, nor does it prohibit, an entity to use probability weighted outcomes. However, entities are required to incorporate the risk of loss, even if such a risk is remote, into their estimate. It is expected that an allowance of zero will only be appropriate in very limited circumstances.
- For acquired financial assets (or acquired groups of financial assets with shared risk characteristics) that, as of the date of acquisition, have experienced a more-than-insignificant deterioration in credit quality since origination (financial assets purchased with credit deterioration (PCD)), as determined by an acquirer's assessment and that are measured at amortised cost, the FASB's model requires an entity to determine the initial amortised cost of the assets by adding the allowance for credit losses at the date of acquisition (the entity's initial estimate of ECLs) to the purchase price. The subsequent measurement of expected credit losses for PCD assets is the same as originated assets or non-PCD acquired assets. See 3.3 below for the accounting treatment of credit-impaired assets under IFRS 9.
- Unlike IFRS 9, there is no exception for revolving credit facilities (e.g. commitments connected with overdrafts and credit cards) under the FASB's model (see 12 below for the IFRS 9 treatment) and therefore, no impairment allowance is required if the commitment is unconditionally cancellable or legally revocable without any conditions.

Public companies meeting the definition of a U.S. Securities and Exchange Commission (SEC) Filer, excluding those entities which qualify as smaller reporting companies as defined by the SEC, are required to adopt the standard for fiscal years beginning after 31 December 2019. All other entities are required to adopt the standard for fiscal years beginning after 15 December 2022. Early application is permitted.

1.5 The IFRS Transition Resource Group for Impairment of Financial Instruments (ITG) IASB webcasts and educational materials

In 2014, the IASB set up an ITG that aimed to:
- provide a public discussion forum to support stakeholders on implementation issues arising from the new impairment requirements that could create diversity in practice; and
- inform the IASB about the implementation issues, to help the IASB determine what action, if any, was needed to address them.[5]

However, the ITG did not issue any guidance.

Members of the ITG included financial statement preparers and auditors from various geographical locations with expertise, skills or practical knowledge on credit risk management and accounting for impairment. Board members and observers from the Basel Committee on Banking Supervision and the International Organisation of Securities Commissions also attended the meetings.

The ITG agenda papers were prepared by the IASB staff and were made public before the meetings. The staff also provided ITG meeting summaries which are not authoritative. Both the staff papers and the meeting summaries represent educational reading on the issues submitted.

Following its inaugural meeting in December 2014 to discuss its operating procedures, the ITG met three times, on 22 April 2015, on 16 September 2015, and on 11 December 2015. IFRS 9 is now in effect and therefore the IASB has brought the work of the ITG to a conclusion. Any future support provided by the IASB for the implementation and application of IFRS 9 will be from the IFRIC, the Board and through the publication of educational materials.

On 22 April 2015, the ITG discussed eight implementation issues raised by stakeholders. These included:[6]

- when applying the impairment requirements at the reporting date, whether and how to incorporate events and forecasts that occur after economic forecasts have been made, but before the reporting date, and between the reporting period end and the date of signing the financial statements (see 5.9.4 below);
- whether the impairment requirements in IFRS 9 must also be applied to other commitments to extend credit, in particular, a commitment (on inception of a finance lease) to commence a finance lease at a date in the future and a commitment by a retailer through the issue of a store account to provide a customer with credit when the customer buys goods or services from the retailer in the future (see 11 below);
- whether there is a requirement to measure ECLs at dates other than the reporting date, namely the date of derecognition and the date of initial recognition (see 7.3.1 below);
- whether an entity should consider the ability to recover cash flows through an integral financial guarantee contract when assessing whether there has been a significant increase in the credit risk of the guaranteed debt instrument since initial recognition (see 6.1.1 below);
- the maximum period to consider when measuring ECLs on a portfolio of mortgage loans that have a stated maturity of 6 months, but contain a contractual feature whereby the term is automatically extended every 6 months subject to the lender's non-objection (see 5.5 below);
- the maximum period to consider when measuring ECLs for revolving credit facilities and the determination of the date of initial recognition of the revolving facilities for the purposes of assessing them for significant increases in credit risk (see 12.2.2 and 12.2.4 below);
- whether the measurement of ECLs for financial guarantee contracts issued should consider future premium receipts due from the holder and, if so, how (see 11 below); and
- the measurement of ECLs in respect of a modified financial asset, the calculation of the modification gain or loss and subsequent requirement to measure ECLs on the modified financial asset as well as the appropriate presentation and disclosure (see 8.2 below).

On 16 September 2015, the ITG held its third meeting to discuss six implementation issues raised by stakeholders. These included:[7]

- how to identify a significant increase in credit risk for a portfolio of retail loans when identical pricing and contractual terms are applied to customers across broad credit quality bands (see 6.2.1 below);
- the possibility of using behavioural indicators of credit risk for the purpose of the assessment of significant increases in credit risk since initial recognition (see 6.2.5 below);
- when assessing significant increases in credit risk, whether an entity would be required to perform an annual review to determine whether circumstances still support the use of the 12-month risk of a default occurring as an approximation of changes in the lifetime risk of a default occurring (see 6.4.3 below);
- when measuring ECLs for revolving credit facilities, how an entity should estimate future drawdowns on undrawn lines of credit when an entity has a history of allowing customers to exceed their contractually set credit limits on overdrafts and other revolving credit facilities (see 12.3 below);
- at what level should forward-looking information be incorporated – at the level of the entity or on a portfolio-by-portfolio basis (see 5.9.5 below); and
- how to determine what is reasonable and supportable forward-looking information and how to treat shock events with material, but uncertain, economic consequences (see 5.9.5 below).

On 11 December 2015, the ITG held its fourth meeting to discuss eleven implementation issues raised by stakeholders. These included:[8]

- what was meant by the 'current EIR' when an entity recognises interest revenue in each period based on the actual floating-rate applicable to that period (see 5.7 below);
- what was meant by 'part of the contractual terms', specifically whether a credit enhancement must be an explicit term of the related asset's contract in order for it to be taken into account in the measurement of ECLs, or whether other credit enhancements that are not recognised separately can also be taken into account (see 5.8.1.A below);
- whether cash flows that are expected to be recovered from the sale on default of a loan could be included in the measurement of ECLs (see 5.8.2 below);
- application of the revolving credit facilities exception set out in paragraph 5.5.20 of IFRS 9 to multi-purpose facilities (see 12.1 below);
- how future drawdowns should be estimated for charge cards when measuring ECLs if there is no specified credit limit in the contract (see 12.3 below);
- how an entity should determine the starting-point and the ending-point of the maximum period to consider when measuring ECLs for revolving credit facilities (see 12.2 below);
- when measuring ECLs, whether an entity can use a single forward-looking economic scenario or whether an entity needs to incorporate multiple forward-looking scenarios, and if so how (see 5.6.1 below);

- when assessing significant increases in credit risk, whether an entity can use a single forward-looking economic scenario or whether the entity needs to incorporate multiple forward-looking scenarios, and if so how (see 6.7 below);
- whether there is a requirement to assess significant increases in credit risk for financial assets with a maturity of 12 months or less (see 6 below);
- how to measure the gross carrying amount and loss allowance for credit-impaired financial assets that are not purchased or originated credit-impaired and that are measured at amortised cost (see 14.1.1 below); and
- whether an entity is required to present the loss allowance for financial assets measured at amortised cost (or trade receivables, contract assets or lease receivables) separately in the statement of financial position (see 14.1 below).

The FASB (see 1.4 above) has also set up its own Transition Resource Group (TRG) for credit losses and its discussions may prove relevant to the application of IFRS 9 in areas where the two ECL models are similar.

The IFRIC discussed two issues in relation to the IFRS 9 ECL model in November 2018:
- Whether the cash flows expected from a financial guarantee contract or any other credit enhancement can be included in the measurement of ECL if the credit enhancement is required to be recognised separately applying IFRS Standards (see 5.8.1 below).
- How an entity should present amounts recognised in the statement of profit or loss when a credit-impaired financial asset is subsequently cured, i.e. paid in full or no longer credit-impaired (see 14.1.2 below).

In addition, as part of its activities to support implementation, the IASB has published three educational webcasts since IFRS 9 was published.[9]
- The first, on forward-looking information and multiple scenarios was released on 25 July 2016. It discussed when multiple scenarios need to be considered and the concept of non-linearity, consistency of scenarios, probability-weighted assessment of significant increase in credit risk, and approaches to incorporating forward-looking scenarios (see 5.6.1 below).
- The second, on the expected life of revolving facilities was released on 16 May 2017. It focused on how credit risk management actions would affect the expected life of revolving facilities for the purpose of measuring ECLs (see 12.2 below).
- The third, on curing of a credit-impaired financial asset was released on 22 July 2019. It summarised the IFRIC's discussion and explained the conclusion it reached on how a company should present amounts in its statement of profit or loss if a credit-impaired financial asset is subsequently paid in full or no longer credit-impaired (cured) (see 14.1.2 below).

In light of the coronavirus pandemic, in March 2020, the IASB published *IFRS 9 and covid-19 – Accounting for expected credit losses applying IFRS 9 Financial Instruments in the light of current uncertainty resulting from the covid-19 pandemic*, to clarify application of the IFRS 9 ECL requirements (see 7.8.2 below).

1.6 Other guidance on expected credit losses

In November 2015, the Enhanced Disclosure Task Force (EDTF) published its report, *Impact of Expected Credit Loss Approaches on Bank Risk Disclosures*, in which it recommended disclosures for banks to provide with the implementation of the ECL requirements of IFRS 9 and US GAAP (see 15 below).

In December 2015, the Basel Committee on Banking Supervision issued its *Guidance on accounting for expected credit losses*, aimed primarily at internationally active banks, which sets out supervisory expectations regarding sound credit risk practices associated with implementing and applying an ECL accounting framework (see 7.1 below).

On 17 June 2016, the Global Public Policy Committee of representatives of the six largest accounting networks (the GPPC) published *The implementation of IFRS 9 impairment by banks – Considerations for those charged with governance of systemically important banks* (the GPPC guidance) to promote a high standard in the implementation of accounting for ECLs. It aims to help those charged with governance to evaluate management's progress during the implementation and transition phase. A year later, on 28 July 2017, the GPPC issued a paper titled *The Auditor's Response to the Risks of Material Misstatement Posed by Estimates of Expected Credit Losses under IFRS 9* to assist audit committees oversee the audit of ECLs (see 7.2 below).

2 SCOPE

IFRS 9 requires an entity to recognise a loss allowance for ECLs on: *[IFRS 9.5.5.1]*

- financial assets that are debt instruments such as loans, debt securities, bank balances and deposits and trade receivables (see 10 below) that are measured at amortised cost; *[IFRS 9.4.1.2]*
- financial assets that are debt instruments measured at fair value through other comprehensive income (see 9 below); *[IFRS 9.4.1.2A]*
- finance lease receivables (i.e. net investments in finance leases) and operating lease receivables under IFRS 16 (see 10.2 below and Chapter 23);
- contract assets under IFRS 15 – *Revenue from Contracts with Customers* – (see 10.1 below and Chapter 28). IFRS 15 defines a contract asset as an entity's right to consideration in exchange for goods or services that the entity has transferred to a customer when that right is conditional on something other than the passage of time (for example, the entity's future performance); *[IFRS 15 Appendix A, IFRS 9 Appendix A]*
- loan commitments that are not measured at fair value through profit or loss under IFRS 9 (see 11 and 12 below). The scope therefore excludes loan commitments designated as financial liabilities at fair value through profit or loss and loan commitments that can be settled net in cash or by delivering or issuing another financial instrument; *[IFRS 9.2.1(g), 2.3, 4.2.1(a), 4.2.1(d)]* and
- financial guarantee contracts that are not measured at fair value through profit or loss under IFRS 9 (see 11 below).

3 APPROACHES

In applying the IFRS 9 impairment requirements, an entity needs to follow one of the approaches below, subject to the conditions set out in each section:

- the general approach (see 3.1 below);
- the simplified approach (see 3.2 below); or
- the purchased or originated credit-impaired approach (see 3.3 below).

Figure 51.3 below, based on a diagram from the standard, summarises the process steps in recognising and measuring ECLs.

Figure 51.3 Application of the impairment requirements at a reporting date

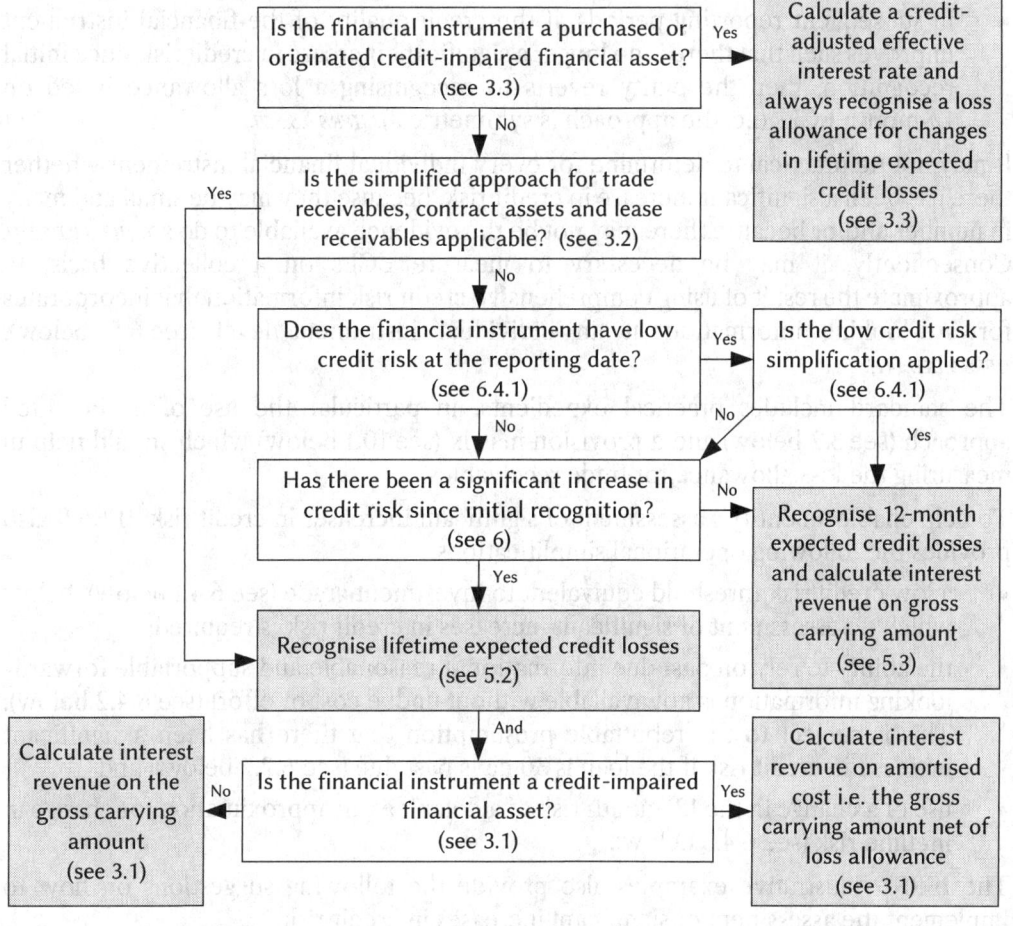

3.1 General approach

Under the general approach, at each reporting date, an entity recognises a loss allowance based on either 12-month ECLs or lifetime ECLs, depending on whether there has been a significant increase in credit risk on the financial instrument since initial recognition. *[IFRS 9.5.5.3, 5.5.5]*. The changes in the loss allowance balance are recognised in profit or loss as an impairment gain or loss. *[IFRS 9.5.5.8, Appendix A]*.

Essentially, an entity must make the following assessment at each reporting date:
- for credit exposures where there have not been significant increases in credit risk since initial recognition, an entity is required to provide for 12-month ECLs, i.e. the portion of lifetime ECLs that represent the ECLs that result from default events that are possible within the 12-months after the reporting date (stage 1 in Figure 51.2 at 1.2 above); [IFRS 9.5.5.5, Appendix A]
- for credit exposures where there have been significant increases in credit risk since initial recognition on an individual or collective basis, a loss allowance is required for lifetime ECLs, i.e. ECLs that result from all possible default events over the expected life of a financial instrument (stages 2 and 3 in Figure 51.2 at 1.2 above); [IFRS 9.5.5.4, 5.5.3, Appendix A] or
- in subsequent reporting periods, if the credit quality of the financial instrument improves such that there is no longer a significant increase in credit risk since initial recognition, then the entity reverts to recognising a loss allowance based on 12-month ECLs (i.e. the approach is symmetrical). [IFRS 9.5.5.7].

It may not be practical to determine for every individual financial instrument whether there has been a significant increase in credit risk, because they may be small and many in number and/or because there may not be the evidence available to do so. [IFRS 9.B5.5.1]. Consequently, it may be necessary to measure ECLs on a collective basis, to approximate the result of using comprehensive credit risk information that incorporates forward-looking information at an individual instrument level (see 6.5 below). [IFRS 9.BC5.141].

The standard includes practical expedients, in particular the use of a simplified approach (see 3.2 below) and a provision matrix (see 10.1 below) which should help in measuring the loss allowance for trade receivables.

To help enable an entity's assessment of significant increases in credit risk, IFRS 9 also provides the following operational simplifications:
- a low credit risk threshold equivalent to investment grade (see 6.4.1 below), below which no assessment of significant increases in credit risk is required;
- the ability to rely on past due information if reasonable and supportable forward-looking information is not available without undue cost or effort (see 6.4.2 below). This is subject to the rebuttable presumption that there has been a significant increase in credit risk if the loan is 30 days past due (see 6.2.2 below); and
- use of a change in the 12-month risk of a default as an approximation for change in lifetime risk (see 6.4.3 below).

The IFRS 9 illustrative examples also provide the following suggestions on how to implement the assessment of significant increases in credit risk:
- assessment at the counterparty level (see 6.4.4 below); and
- a set transfer threshold by determining maximum initial credit risk for a portfolio (see 6.4.5 below).

In stages 1 and 2, there is a complete decoupling between interest recognition and impairment. Therefore, interest revenue is calculated on the gross carrying amount (without deducting the loss allowance). If a financial asset subsequently becomes credit-impaired (stage 3 in Figure 51.2 at 1.2 above), an entity is required to calculate the interest revenue by applying the EIR in subsequent reporting periods to the amortised cost of the financial asset (i.e. the gross carrying amount net of loss allowance) rather than the gross carrying amount. *[IFRS 9.5.4.1, Appendix A]*. Financial assets are assessed as credit-impaired using substantially the same criteria as for the impairment assessment of an individual asset under IAS 39. *[IFRS 9 Appendix A]*.

A financial asset is credit-impaired when one or more events that have a detrimental impact on the estimated future cash flows of that financial asset have occurred. Evidence that a financial asset is impaired includes observable data about such events. IFRS 9 provides a list of events that are substantially the same as the IAS 39 loss events for an individual asset assessment: *[IFRS 9 Appendix A]*

- significant financial difficulty of the issuer or the borrower;
- a breach of contract, such as a default or past due event;
- the lender(s) of the borrower, for economic or contractual reasons relating to the borrower's financial difficulty, having granted to the borrower a concession(s) that the lender(s) would not otherwise consider;
- it is becoming probable that the borrower will enter bankruptcy or other financial reorganisation;
- the disappearance of an active market for that financial asset because of financial difficulties; or
- the purchase or origination of a financial asset at a deep discount that reflects the incurred credit losses.

It may not be possible for an entity to identify a single discrete event. Instead, the combined effect of several events may have caused the financial asset to become credit-impaired. *[IFRS 9 Appendix A]*.

There has also been some debate as to whether financial assets that are considered to be in default (e.g. because payments are more than 90 days past due) but that are fully collateralised (so that there is no ECL) would qualify as credit-impaired and therefore have to be transferred to stage 3. Although the definition of credit-impaired refers to 'a detrimental impact on the estimated future cash flows', it is not clear whether this should be read to include any recoveries from the realisation of collateral and IFRS 9 has no explicit requirements to consider collateral when assessing credit-impaired financial assets.

There are some strong arguments in favour of aligning the criteria for transferring an asset to stage 3 with those for assessing whether it is in default. First, IFRS 9 bases significant deterioration on risk of a default occurring and it would therefore seem inconsistent (and potentially confusing for users) if the value of collateral is considered for stage 3 allocation. Also, if collateral value were to influence the stage 3 allocation, this could result in some instability between stage 2 and 3, as exposures would potentially go back and forth depending on the collateral value.

Aligning stage 3 with the default status affects the scope of instruments to which the purchased or originated credit-impaired approach must be applied. However, for any exposure which is fully collateralised and where the expected loss is zero, classification as a purchased or originated credit-impaired financial asset, or classification between stage 1, 2 or 3 does not affect the accounting. If the expected loss is zero, it will not affect the EIR calculation.

Also, IFRS 7 requires a quantitative disclosure about the collateral held as security and other credit enhancements for financial assets that are credit-impaired at the reporting date (e.g. quantification of the extent to which collateral and other credit enhancements mitigate credit risk). *[IFRS 7.35K(c)]*.

In subsequent reporting periods, if the credit quality of the financial asset improves so that the financial asset is no longer credit-impaired and the improvement can be related objectively to the occurrence of an event (such as an improvement in the borrower's credit rating), then the entity should once again calculate the interest revenue by applying the EIR to the gross carrying amount of the financial asset. *[IFRS 9.5.4.2]*.

When the entity has no reasonable expectations of recovering a financial asset, in its entirety or a portion thereof, then the gross carrying amount of the financial asset should be directly reduced in its entirety. A write-off constitutes a derecognition event (see 14.1.1 below). *[IFRS 9.5.4.4]*.

3.2 Simplified approach

The simplified approach does not require an entity to track the changes in credit risk, but instead requires the entity to recognise a loss allowance based on lifetime ECLs at each reporting date. *[IFRS 9.5.5.15]*.

An entity is required to apply the simplified approach for trade receivables or contract assets that result from transactions within the scope of IFRS 15 and that do not contain a significant financing component, or when the entity applies the practical expedient for contracts that have a maturity of one year or less, in accordance with IFRS 15 (see Chapter 28). *[IFRS 9.5.5.15(a)(i)]*. Paragraphs 60-65 of IFRS 15 provide the requirements for determining the existence of a significant financing component in the contract, including the use of the practical expedient for contracts that are one year or less.

A contract asset is defined as an entity's right to consideration in exchange for goods or services that the entity has transferred to a customer when that right is conditioned on something other than the passage of time (for example, the entity's future performance). *[IFRS 15 Appendix A]*. IFRS 15 describes contracts with a significant financing component as those for which the agreed timing of payment provides the customer or the entity with a significant benefit of financing on the transfer of goods or services to the customer. Hence, in determining the transaction price, an entity is required to adjust the promised amount of consideration for the effects of the time value of money. *[IFRS 15.60]*. However, if the entity expects, at contract inception, that the period between when the entity transfers a promised good or service to a customer and when the customer pays for that good or service will be one year or less, as a practical expedient, an entity need not adjust the promised amount of consideration for the effects of a significant financing component. *[IFRS 15.63]*.

Application of the simplified approach to trade receivables and contract assets that do not contain a significant financing component intuitively makes sense. In particular, for trade receivables and contract assets that are due in 12 months or less, the 12-month ECLs are the same as the lifetime ECLs.

However, an entity has a policy choice to apply either the simplified approach or the general approach for the following: *[IFRS 9.5.5.16]*

- all trade receivables or contract assets that result from transactions within the scope of IFRS 15, and that contain a significant financing component in accordance with IFRS 15. The policy choice may be applied separately to trade receivables and contract assets (see 10.1 below and Chapter 28); *[IFRS 9.5.5.15(a)(ii)]* and
- all lease receivables that result from transactions that are within the scope of IFRS 16. The policy choice may be applied separately to finance and operating lease receivables (see 10.2 below and Chapter 23). *[IFRS 9.5.5.15(b)]*.

The IASB noted that offering this policy choice would reduce comparability. However, the IASB believes it would alleviate some of the practical concerns of tracking changes in credit risk for entities that do not have sophisticated credit risk management systems. *[IFRS 9.BC5.225]*.

In practice, trade receivables may be sold to a factoring bank, whereby all risks and rewards are transferred to the bank. Consequently, the trade receivables are derecognised by the transferring entity and recognised by the factoring bank which obtains the right to receive the payments made by the debtor for the invoiced amount. In such a case, we believe that the 'factored' trade receivables are outside the scope of the simplified approach for the purpose of the factoring bank when applying the IFRS 9 ECL model. This is because the simplified approach is limited to trade receivables that result from transactions within the scope of IFRS 15, i.e. based on a contract to obtain goods or services. This is not the case for the factoring bank since it has acquired the trade receivables through a factoring agreement. Moreover, the simplified approach was introduced to assist entities with less sophisticated credit risk management systems. *[IFRS 9.BC5.104]*. Factoring banks are likely to have more sophisticated credit risk management systems in place.

3.3 Purchased or originated credit-impaired financial assets

On initial recognition of a financial asset, an entity is required to determine whether the asset is credit-impaired. The criteria are set out at 3.1 above. *[IFRS 9.5.5.3, 5.5.5, 5.5.13]*.

A financial asset may be purchased credit-impaired because the credit risk is very high and it has already met the criteria. Such an asset is likely to be acquired at a deep discount. However, this does not mean that an entity is required to apply the credit-adjusted EIR to a financial asset solely because the financial asset has a high credit risk at initial recognition, if it has not yet met the criteria. *[IFRS 9.B5.4.7]*. Moreover, although one of the indicators that a financial asset is credit-impaired is that the asset is purchased at a deep discount, the purchased financial asset may be determined to be credit-impaired even if it is not purchased at deep discount if the other indicators (see 3.1 above) that the financial asset is credit-impaired are present. For instance, it is possible that a secured loan could be purchased credit-impaired, because one of the criteria is met, but not acquired at a deep discount due to the value of the collateral. It may be also possible that an entity originates a credit-impaired financial asset, for example following a substantial modification of a distressed financial asset that resulted in the derecognition of the original financial asset (see 8 below). *[IFRS 9.B5.5.26]*.

Again, this does not mean that the asset should be considered credit-impaired just because it is high risk. Consider an example of a bank originating a loan of €100,000 with interest of 30% per annum charged over the term of the loan, payable in monthly amortising instalments. The bank's customer has a high credit risk on origination and the bank expects a large portion of this type of customer to pay late or fail to pay some or all of their instalment payments. Although the loan is of high credit risk (which is supported by the high interest rate), none of the loss events listed above have occurred and the loan was not the result of a substantial modification and derecognition of a distressed debt, hence, the bank should assess the loan not to be credit-impaired on origination.

For financial assets that are considered to be credit-impaired on purchase or origination, the EIR (see Chapter 50 at 3) is calculated taking into account the initial lifetime ECLs in the estimated cash flows. *[IFRS 9.B5.4.7, Appendix A, BC5.214, BC5.217]*. This accounting treatment is the same as that under IAS 39 for similar assets. *[IAS 39.AG5]*. It is also consistent with the original method for measuring impairment proposed in the 2009 Exposure Draft.

Consequently, no allowance is recorded for 12-month ECLs for financial assets that are credit-impaired on initial recognition. The rationale for not recording a 12-month ECL allowance for these assets is that the losses are already reflected in the fair values at which they are initially recognised. The same logic could be applied to all the other financial assets which are not credit-impaired, arguing that they, too, are initially recognised at a fair value that reflects expectations of future losses. However, the distinction is made because the double-counting of 12-month ECLs on initial recognition would be too large for assets with such a high credit risk since default has already occurred and the 12-month ECLs are already reflected in the initial fair value. The exclusion of initial ECLs from the computation of the EIR would lead to a distortion that would be too significant to be acceptable.

For financial assets that were credit-impaired on purchase or origination, the credit-adjusted EIR is also used subsequently to discount the ECLs. In subsequent reporting periods an entity is required to recognise:

- in the statement of financial position, the cumulative changes in lifetime ECLs since initial recognition, discounted at the credit-impaired EIR (see 5.7 below), as a loss allowance; *[IFRS 9.5.5.13, B5.5.45]* and
- in profit or loss, the amount of any change in lifetime ECLs as an impairment gain or loss. An impairment gain is recognised if favourable changes result in the lifetime ECLs estimate becoming lower than the original estimate that was incorporated in the estimated cash flows on initial recognition when calculating the credit-adjusted EIR. *[IFRS 9.5.5.14]*.

For favourable changes that result in a lower lifetime ECLs than the original estimate on initial recognition, IFRS 9 does not provide guidance on where in the statement of financial position the debit entry should be booked. In our view, the impairment gain should be recognised as a direct adjustment to the gross carrying amount. This is supported by the application guidance in IFRS 9 on revision of estimates which requires adjusting the gross carrying amount of the financial asset. *[IFRS 9.B5.4.6]*. For purchased or originated credit-impaired financial assets, since the ECLs are included in the estimated cash flows when calculating the credit-adjusted EIR, it would be consistent to follow the same principle and adjust the gross carrying amount when revising the original estimates of ECLs. An alternative treatment would be to recognise a negative loss allowance which would reflect the favourable changes in lifetime ECLs.

Along with the other credit risk disclosures requirements (see 15 below and Chapter 54 at 5.3), the holder is required to explain how it has determined that assets are credit-impaired (including the inputs, assumptions and estimation techniques used). It is also required to disclose the total amount of undiscounted ECLs at initial recognition for financial assets initially recognised during the reporting period that were purchased or originated credit-impaired. *[IFRS 7.35H(c)]*.

Once a financial asset is classified as purchased or originated credit-impaired, it retains that classification until it is derecognised, i.e. when fully paid or written-off. The financial asset is never subject to a staging assessment and is required to be disclosed separately from financial assets that are subject to the general approach staging model. Therefore, a purchased or originated credit-impaired financial asset can never return to stage 1, even if the credit risk on the loan significantly improves.

The accounting treatment for a purchased credit-impaired financial asset is illustrated in the following example.

Example 51.2: **Calculation of the credit-adjusted effective interest rate and recognition of a loss allowance for a purchased credit-impaired financial asset**

On 1 January 2015, Company D issued a bond that required it to pay an annual coupon of €800 in arrears and to repay the principal of €10,000 on 31 December 2024. By 2020, Company D was in significant financial difficulties and was unable to pay the coupon due on 31 December 2020. On 1 January 2021, Company V estimates that the holder could expect to receive a single payment of €4,000 at the end of 2022. It acquires the bond at an arm's length price of €3,000. Company V determines that the debt instrument is credit-impaired on initial recognition, because of evidence of significant financial difficulty of Company D and because the debt instrument was purchased at a deep discount.

It can be shown that using the contractual cash flows (including the €800 overdue) gives rise to an EIR of 70.1% (the net present value of €800 now and annually thereafter until 2024 and €10,000 receivable at the end of 2024 equals €3,000 when discounted at 70.1%). However, because the bond is credit-impaired, V should calculate the EIR using the estimated cash flows of the instrument. In this case, the EIR is 15.5% (the net present value of €4,000 receivable in two years equals €3,000 when discounted at 15.5%).

All things being equal, interest income of €465 (€3,000 × 15.5%) would be recognised on the instrument during 2021 and its carrying amount at the end of the year would be €3,465 (€3,000 + €465). However, if at the end of the year, based on reasonable and supportable evidence, the cash flow expected to be received on the instrument had increased to, say, €4,250 (still to be received at the end of 2022), an adjustment would be made to the asset's amortised cost. Accordingly, its carrying amount would be increased to €3,681 (€4,250 discounted over one year at 15.5%) and an impairment gain of €217 would be recognised in profit or loss.

On the other hand, if at the end of the year, based on reasonable and supportable evidence, the cash flow expected to be received on the instrument had decreased to, say, €3,500 (still to be received at the end of 2022), an adjustment would be made to the asset's amortised cost. Accordingly, its carrying amount would be decreased to €3,031 (€3,500 discounted over one year at 15.5%) and an impairment loss of €433 would be recognised in profit or loss.

4 IMPAIRMENT FOR CORPORATES

For corporates, the IFRS 9 ECL model does not usually give rise to a major increase in allowances for many of the financial assets, including trade receivables, that they usually hold on their balance sheets.

There is a limit to the increase in allowances for short-term trade receivables and contract assets because of their short-term nature. Moreover, the standard includes practical expedients, in particular the use of the simplified approach and a provision matrix, which should help in measuring the loss allowance for short-term trade receivables: [IFRS 9.B5.5.35]

- The simplified approach does not require the tracking of changes in credit risk, but instead requires the recognition of lifetime ECLs at all times. [IFRS 9.5.5.15]. For trade receivables or contract assets that do not contain a significant financing component (see 10.1 below), entities are required to apply the simplified approach. [IFRS 9.5.5.15(a)(i)]. For trade receivables or contract assets that do contain a significant financing component, and lease receivables (see 10.2 below), entities have a policy choice to apply the simplified approach (see 3.2 above) or the general approach (see 3.1 above). For other debt instruments like bonds or longer-term loan receivables, the general approach is required.

- IFRS 9 allows using a provision matrix as a practical expedient for determining ECLs on trade receivables (see 10.1 below). Many corporates may already use a provision matrix to calculate their current impairment allowance, but they would need to calculate ECLs for receivables that are not yet delinquent and also consider how they can incorporate forward-looking information into their historical customer default rates (see 5.9.3 below). Entities would also need to group receivables into various customer segments that have similar loss patterns (e.g. by geography, product type, customer rating or type of collateral) (see 6.5 below).

The IFRS 9 ECL model can give rise to challenges for the measurement of other assets for which the general model applies. These include long-term trade receivables and contract assets for which the simplified approach is not applied, lease receivables and debt securities which are measured at amortised cost or at fair value through other comprehensive income (see 9 below). For example, a corporate that has a large portfolio of debt securities that were previously held as available-for-sale under IAS 39, is likely to classify its holdings as measured at fair value through other comprehensive income if the contractual cash flow characteristics and business model test are met (see Chapter 48 at 5 and 6). For these debt securities, the corporate would be required to recognise a loss allowance based on 12-month ECLs, even for debt securities that are highly rated (e.g. AAA- or AA-rated bonds).

Under the general approach, at each reporting date, an entity is required to assess whether there has been a significant increase in credit risk since initial recognition as this will determine whether a 12-month ECLs or lifetime ECLs should be recognised (see 6 below). When applying the general approach, a number of operational simplifications and presumptions are available to help entities assess significant increases in credit risk since initial recognition. These include:

- If a financial instrument has low credit risk (equivalent to investment grade quality), then an entity may assume no significant increases in credit risk have occurred (see 6.4.1 below). The low credit risk simplification may be useful for corporates as it provides relief for entities from tracking changes in the credit risk of high quality financial instruments. However, collateral does not influence whether a financial instrument has a low credit risk.
- If more forward-looking information (either on an individual or collective basis) is not available, there is a rebuttable presumption that credit risk has increased significantly when contractual payments are more than 30 DPD (see 6.2.2 below). However, contract assets, by definition, cannot be past due. Therefore, corporates cannot rely on delinquency for staging of such assets.
- The change in risk of a default occurring in the next 12 months may often be used as an approximation for the change in risk of a default occurring over the remaining life when assessing significant in credit risk (see 6.4.3 below).
- The assessment may be made on a collective basis (see 6.5 below) or at the counterparty level (see 6.4.4 below).

In measuring ECLs, financial institutions often already have sophisticated ECL models and systems for capital adequacy purposes, including data such as the probability of default (PD), loss given default (LGD) and exposure at default (EAD). Many non-financial entities do not have models and systems in place that capture such information. One possibility is to make use of credit default swap (CDS) spreads and bond spreads. For financial instruments that are rated by an external agency such as Standard & Poor's, for example, listed bonds, an entity may be able to use, as a starting point, historical default rates implied by such ratings. It should be stressed that the historical default rates implied by credit ratings assigned by agencies are historical rates for corporate debt and so they would not, without adjustment, satisfy the requirements of the standard. IFRS 9 requires the calculation of ECLs, based on current conditions and forecasts of future conditions, to be based on reasonable and supportable information. A significant challenge in applying the IFRS 9 impairment requirements to quoted bonds is that the historical experience of losses by rating grade can differ significantly from the view of the market, as reflected in, for instance, CDS spreads and bond spreads.

Even for debt instruments that are not rated, it may be possible for entities to measure ECLs by estimating how external rating agencies would rate that instrument and using external rating agency loss data as an input. See Example 51.4 below.

Bank deposits and current accounts that are classified as financial assets measured at amortised cost, are also subject to the general approach, even if treated as cash and cash equivalents. However, for most such instruments, given their maturity, the 12-month and lifetime ECLs are the same and will usually be small.

For any corporate that is a lessor, there is a significant increase in allowances on finance leases, particularly if they chose to apply the simplified approach and record lifetime allowances (see 10.2 below).

If the entity prepares separate financial statements under IFRS, then the ECL model will also apply to intercompany loans (see 13 below). Corporates will also need to determine whether guarantees and other credit-enhancements can be reflected directly in the measurement of ECLs (see 5.8.1 below).

The required impairment disclosures have been expanded significantly in comparison to the disclosures previously required under IFRS 7, including inputs, assumptions and estimation methods used, operating simplifications applied and credit risk disclosures for trade receivables, contract assets or lease receivables measured under the simplified approach. The objective of the expanded disclosures is to enable users to understand the effect of credit risk on the amount, timing and uncertainty of future cash flows (see 15 below).

5 MEASUREMENT OF EXPECTED CREDIT LOSSES

The standard defines credit loss as the difference between all contractual cash flows that are due to an entity in accordance with the contract and all the cash flows that the entity expects to receive (i.e. all cash shortfalls), discounted at the original EIR (or credit-adjusted EIR for purchased or originated credit-impaired financial assets). When estimating the cash flows, an entity is required to consider: *[IFRS 9 Appendix A]*

- all contractual terms of the financial instrument (including prepayment, extension, call and similar options) over the expected life (see 5.5 below) of the financial instrument. The maximum period to consider when measuring ECLs is the maximum contractual period (including extension options at the discretion of the borrower) over which the entity is exposed to credit risk (with an exception for revolving facilities); and
- cash flows from the sale of collateral held (see 5.8.2 below) or other credit enhancements that are integral to the contractual terms.

Also, the standard goes on to define ECLs as 'the weighted average of credit losses with the respective risks of a default occurring as the weights'. *[IFRS 9 Appendix A]*.

The standard does not prescribe specific approaches to estimate ECLs, but stresses that the approach used must reflect the following: *[IFRS 9.5.5.17]*

- an unbiased and probability-weighted amount that is determined by evaluating a range of possible outcomes (see 5.6 below);
- the time value of money (see 5.7 below); and
- reasonable and supportable information that is available without undue cost or effort at the reporting date about past events, current conditions and forecasts of future economic conditions (see 5.9 below).

5.1 Definition of default

Default is not defined for the purposes of determining the risk of a default occurring. Because it is defined differently by different institutions (for instance, 30, 90 or 180 days past due), the IASB was concerned that defining default could result in a definition that is inconsistent with that applied internally for credit risk management. In particular, since default is the anchor point used to measure probabilities of default and losses given default in Basel modelling, requiring a different definition would require building a different set of models for accounting purposes. Therefore, the standard requires an entity to apply a definition of default that is consistent with how it is defined for normal credit risk management practices, consistently from one period to another. It follows that an entity might have to use different default definitions for different types of financial instruments. However, the standard stresses that an entity needs to consider qualitative indicators of default when appropriate in addition to days past due, such as breaches of covenant. *[IFRS 9.B5.5.37]*.

The IASB did not originally expect ECL calculations to vary as a result of differences in the definition of default, because of the counterbalancing interaction between the way an entity defines default and the credit losses that arise as a result of that definition of default. *[IFRS 9.BC5.248]*. (For instance, if an entity uses a shorter delinquency period of 30 days past due instead of 60 days past due, the associated loss given default (LGD) will be correspondingly smaller as it is to be expected that more debtors that are 30 days past due will in due course recover). However, the notion of default is fundamental to the application of the model, particularly because it affects the subset of the population that is subject to the 12-month ECL measure. *[IFRS 9.BC5.249]*.

The standard restricts diversity resulting from this effect by establishing a rebuttable presumption that default does not occur later than when a financial asset is 90 days past due. This presumption may be rebutted only if an entity has reasonable and supportable information to support an alternative default criterion. *[IFRS 9.B5.5.37, BC5.252]*.

A 90-day default definition would also be consistent with that used by banks for the advanced Basel II regulatory capital calculations (with a few exceptions). We observe that most banks have aligned their regulatory and accounting definitions of default. This generally means using 90 days past due under IFRS 9, with some exceptions for certain portfolios such as mortgages for which the regulatory definition may allow longer delinquency periods. Most banks also aligned the accounting definition of credit-impaired for transfer to stage 3 with the definition of default.

5.2 Lifetime expected credit losses

IFRS 9 defines lifetime ECLs as the ECLs that result from all possible default events over the expected life of a financial instrument (i.e. an entity needs to estimate the risk of a default occurring on the financial instrument during its expected life). *[IFRS 9 Appendix A, B5.5.43]*. The expected life considered for the measurement of lifetime ECLs cannot be longer than the maximum contractual period (including extension options at the discretion of the borrower) over which the entity is exposed to credit risk. However, there is an exception for revolving facilities (see 12 below).

ECLs should be estimated based on the present value of all cash shortfalls over the remaining expected life of the financial asset, i.e. the difference between: *[IFRS 9.B5.5.29]*

- the contractual cash flows that are due to an entity under the contract; and
- the cash flows that the holder expects to receive.

As ECLs take into account both the amount and the timing of payments, a credit loss arises even if the holder expects to receive all the contractual payments due, but at a later date. *[IFRS 9.B5.5.28]*.

When estimating lifetime ECLs for undrawn loan commitments (see 11 below), the provider of the commitment needs to:

- estimate the expected portion of the loan commitment that will be drawn down over the expected life of the loan commitment. Except for revolving facilities (see 12 below), the expected life will be capped at the maximum contractual period, including extension options at the discretion of the borrower, over which the entity is exposed to credit risk (see 5.3 below for 12-month ECLs); *[IFRS 9.B5.5.31]* and
- calculate the present value of cash shortfalls between the contractual cash flows that are due to the entity if the holder of the loan commitment draws down that expected portion of the loan and the cash flows that the entity expects to receive if that expected portion of the loan is drawn down. *[IFRS 9.B5.5.30]*.

For a financial guarantee contract (see 11 below), the guarantor is required to make payments only in the event of a default by the debtor in accordance with the terms of the instrument that is guaranteed. Accordingly, the estimate of lifetime ECLs would be based on the present value of the expected payments to reimburse the holder for a credit loss that it incurs, less any amounts that the guarantor expects to receive from the holder, the debtor or any other party. If an asset is fully guaranteed, the ECL estimate for the financial guarantee contract would be consistent with the estimated cash shortfall estimate for the asset subject to the guarantee. *[IFRS 9.B5.5.32]*.

5.3 12-month expected credit losses

The 12-month ECLs is defined as a portion of the lifetime ECLs that represent the ECLs that result from default events on a financial instrument that are possible within the 12 months after the reporting date. *[IFRS 9 Appendix A]*. The standard explains further that the 12-month ECLs are a portion of the lifetime ECLs that will result if a default occurs in the 12 months after the reporting date (or a shorter period if the expected life of a financial instrument is less than 12 months), weighted by the probability of that default occurring. *[IFRS 9.B5.5.43]*.

Because the calculation is based on the probability of default (PD), the standard emphasises that the 12-month ECL is not the lifetime ECL that an entity will incur on assets that it predicts will default in the next 12 months (i.e. for which the PD over the next 12 months is greater than 50%). For instance, the PD might be only 5%, in which case this should be used to calculate 12-month ECLs, even though it is not probable that the asset will default. Also, the 12-month ECLs are not the cash shortfalls that are predicted over only the next 12 months. For an asset defaulting in the next 12 months, the lifetime ECLs that need to be included in the calculation will normally be significantly greater than just the cash flows that were contractually due in the next 12 months.

If the financial instrument has a maturity of less than 12 months, then the 12-month ECLs are the credit losses expected over the period to maturity.

For undrawn loan commitments (see 11 below), an entity's estimate of 12-month ECLs should be based on its expectations of the portion of the loan commitment that will be drawn down within 12 months of the reporting date. *[IFRS 9.B5.5.31]*.

As already mentioned at 1.2 above, the IASB believes that the 12-month ECLs serve as a proxy for the recognition of initial ECLs over time, as proposed in the 2009 Exposure Draft, and they mitigate the systematic overstatement of interest revenue that was recognised under IAS 39. *[IFRS 9.BC5.135]*. This practical approximation was necessary as a result of the decision to decouple the measurement and allocation of initial ECLs from the determination of the EIR following the re-deliberations of the 2009 Exposure Draft. *[IFRS 9.BC5.199]*.

The stage 1, 12-month allowance overstates the necessary allowance for each financial instrument after initial recognition. However, this is offset by the fact that the allowance is not further increased (except for changes in the 12-month ECLs) until the instrument's credit risk has significantly increased and it is transferred to stage 2. For a portfolio of instruments, with various origination dates, the overall provision may (very approximately) be a similar size as might be achieved using a more conceptually robust approach. Although there is no conceptual justification for an allowance based on 12-month ECLs, it was designed to be a pragmatic solution to achieve an appropriate balance between faithfully representing the underlying economics of a transaction and the cost of implementation.

How accurate a proxy the 12-month and lifetime ECL model is for a more conceptually pure approach will depend on the nature of the portfolio. Also, the effect of recording a 12-month ECL in the first reporting period that a financial instrument is recognised will not have a significant effect on reported income if the portfolio is stable in size from one period to the next. The 12-month ECL allowance may, however, significantly reduce the reported income for entities which are expanding the size of their portfolio.

Although the choice of 12 months is arbitrary, it is the same time horizon as used for the more advanced bank regulatory capital calculation under the Basel framework.[10] The definition of 12-month ECLs is similar to the Basel Committee's definition of ECL, although the modelling requirements differ significantly.[11] The 12-month requirement under IFRS 9 will always differ from that computed for regulatory capital purposes, as the IFRS 9 measure is a point-in-time estimate, reflecting currently forecast economic conditions (see 5.9.3 below), while the Basel regulatory figure is based on through-the-cycle assumptions of default and conservative estimates of losses given default. However, banks that use an advanced approach to calculate their capital requirements should be able to use their existing systems and methodologies as a starting point and make the necessary adjustments to flex the calculation to comply with IFRS 9.

As mentioned above, the 12-month ECLs is defined as a portion of the lifetime ECLs that represent the ECLs that result from default events on a financial instrument that are possible within the 12-months after the reporting date. *[IFRS 9 Appendix A]*. When measuring 12-month ECLs, one question is whether the cash shortfalls used should take into account only default events within the next 12 months or subsequent default events as well. The issue arises for instruments that are expected to default and cure (i.e. to restore to performing) and then default again after curing.

IFRS 9 does not explicitly mention the treatment of cures and subsequent defaults when calculating ECLs. However, the ITG briefly talked about this in their discussion about the life of revolving credit card portfolios in April 2015: 'As regards assets in Stage 2, it was acknowledged that the probability of assets defaulting and curing would have to be taken into account and that it would be necessary to build this into any models dealing with expected credit loss calculations. However, it was noted that materiality would need to be considered.'[12]

We conclude from the ITG discussion that cure events should only be reflected in the calculation of the LGD to the extent that they are expected to be effective. Consequently, if it is predicted that the asset will re-default in subsequent years, this need not be included in the calculation of 12-month expected losses if the defaults are expected to be unrelated to the first default. In practice, however, IFRS 9 acknowledges that a variety of techniques can be used to meet the objective of ECL and that the definition of default may vary, by product, across a bank and between banks. [IFRS 9.B5.5.37, BC5.252, BC5.265].

When measuring ECLs, the treatment of re-defaults affects both the PD and the LGD. Therefore, the same treatment should be applied consistently to determine both the PD and the LGD.

5.4 Probability of default (PD) and loss rate approaches

As mentioned above, the standard does not prescribe specific approaches to estimate ECLs. Some of the common approaches include the PD and loss rate approaches (see 5.4.1 and 5.4.2 below, respectively).

5.4.1 Probability of default (PD) approach

Following from Example 51.1 at 1.2 above, calculations of the 12-month and lifetime ECLs are illustrated below.

Example 51.3:   *12-month and lifetime expected credit loss measurement based on a PD approach*

On 31 December 2020, Bank A originates a 10 year bullet loan with a gross carrying amount of $1,000,000, with interest being due at the end of each year and the principal due at maturity. In line with IFRS 9, Bank A must recognise an impairment allowance for the ECLs, considering current and forward-looking credit risk information.

The ECLs are a probability-weighted estimate of the present value of estimated cash shortfalls – i.e. the weighted average of credit losses, with the respective risks of a default occurring used as the weights. For this purpose, the following parameters must be estimated:

- Probability of Default ('PD') – Estimate of the likelihood of default over a given time horizon (e.g. from t_{i-1} to t_i). A default may only happen at a t_i horizon if the facility has not been previously derecognized and is still in the portfolio. An early exit ('EE') may occur in case of default unless the facility reverts to performing without significant modification of the contractual terms. The marginal probability of default for the period t_{i-1} to t_i is then adjusted from the probability that an early exit occurred during the previous periods:

$$PD_{t_i} \times \prod_{J=1}^{J=j-1} (1 - EE_{t_j})$$

We note that, for simplicity, Bank A may decide to model *EE* within the PD component.

- Loss Given Default ('LGD') – Estimate of the loss arising in case a default occurs at a given time (e.g. t_i). It is based on the difference between the contractual cash flows due and those that the lender would expect to receive, including from the realisation of any collateral. It is usually expressed as a percentage of the EAD.

- Exposure at Default ('EAD') – Estimate of the exposure at a future default date, taking into account expected changes in the exposure after the reporting date, including repayments of principal and interest, whether scheduled by contract or otherwise, expected drawdowns on committed facilities, and accrued interest from missed payments.

- Discount Rate ('r') – Rate used to discount an expected loss to a present value at the reporting date, i.e. the EIR.

Based on these parameters, an ECL can be computed for any horizon – typically for each due date of an exposure. The computation formula can be expressed as follows:

$$ECL_{t_n} = \sum_{t_i=t_1}^{t_i=t_n} \frac{PD_{t_i} \times \prod_{J=1}^{J=j-1}(1 - EE_{t_j}) \times LGD_{t_i} \times EAD_{t_i}}{(1+r_i)^{t_i}}$$

Where:

- i = each future payment
- ti = maturity of the payment i
- tn = horizon considered (either 12-month or lifetime)

Note that the figures in the tables below have been rounded to one or two decimal points.

Stage 1: 12-month ECLs of $422

At origination, the loan is in stage 1. Thus, a corresponding 12-month ECL allowance is recognised, i.e. the portion of the lifetime ECLs that result from default events that are possible within 12 months after the reporting date.

Based on statistical and qualitative information, Bank A has computed the following ECL parameters at origination:

- As interest is paid on a yearly basis, ECLs are calculated using annual periods.
- Each year EAD equals the outstanding principal plus accrued interest due at the end of the year. This bullet loan does not allow any prepayment, therefore the EAD is constant.
- The effective interest rate of the loan is assumed to be the contractual rate, which is 3%.
- Bank A sets EE = PDn–1 × 0.8, on the basis that a proportion of the loans which default are expected to cure and will once again be at risk of default.
- Based on provided guarantees and collateral, LGD is estimated at 25% of EAD, whatever the date of default.

Year	EAD	Discount rate	Cumulative PD @ origination	Marginal PD	Cumulative EE t–1 @ origination	LGD	Marginal ECL	
2020	1,000,000							
2021	1,030,000	3%	0.17%	0.17%	0.00%	25%	$422	12m ECL
2022	1,030,000	3%	0.49%	0.32%	0.14%	25%	$775	
2023	1,030,000	3%	0.86%	0.37%	0.39%	25%	$877	
2024	1,030,000	3%	1.38%	0.53%	0.69%	25%	$1,196	
2025	1,030,000	3%	1.84%	0.47%	1.11%	25%	$1,027	
2026	1,030,000	3%	2.37%	0.54%	1.47%	25%	$1,141	
2027	1,030,000	3%	2.85%	0.49%	1.90%	25%	$1,014	
2028	1,030,000	3%	3.30%	0.46%	2.28%	25%	$912	
2029	1,030,000	3%	3.84%	0.56%	2.64%	25%	$1,073	
2030	1,030,000	3%	4.50%	0.69%	3.07%	25%	$1,280	
							$9,717	Lifetime ECL

$$\text{Marginal PD}_i = 1 - \frac{1 - \text{Cum PD}_i}{1 - \text{Cum PD}_{i-1}}$$

$$\text{Marginal ECL}_i = \frac{PD_i \times (1 - \text{Cum EE}_{i-1}) \times LGD_i \times EAD_i}{(1+r_i)^i}$$

Stage 2: lifetime ECLs of $50,285

On 31 December 2023 – 3 years after origination, the loan shows signs of significant deterioration in credit quality based on the creditworthiness of the obligor and forward-looking information, and Bank A moves it to stage 2. Example 51.11 below shows the calculation underlying this assessment.

Consistent with the significant increase in credit risk, the PD of the obligor has increased. In consequence, the probability of an early exist has also increased, because of the higher level of default. For the purposes of this example, we assume that there are no significant fluctuations in collateral values and the LGD remains constant.

Year	EAD	Discount rate	Cumulative PD	Marginal PD	Cumulative EE t–1	LGD	Marginal ECL	
2023	1,000,000		0.00%					
2024	1,030,000	3%	1.40%	1.40%	0.00%	25%	$3,495	12m ECL
2025	1,030,000	3%	3.87%	2.51%	1.12%	25%	$6,017	
2026	1,030,000	3%	8.82%	5.15%	3.10%	25%	$11,756	
2027	1,030,000	3%	12.84%	4.40%	7.06%	25%	$9,366	
2028	1,030,000	3%	16.04%	3.67%	10.27%	25%	$7,322	
2029	1,030,000	3%	18.98%	3.50%	12.83%	25%	$6,585	
2030	1,030,000	3%	21.60%	3.23%	15.18%	25%	$5,745	
							$50,285	Lifetime ECL

Stage 3: lifetime ECLs of $262,850

In the following year, on 31 December 2024, the obligor does not pay the amount due. Based on credit information available, it is already considered to be in default and is moved to stage 3 – credit-impaired. At this time, the exposure is $1,030,000.

Once a facility becomes credit-impaired, impairment must still represent ECLs. Therefore, it must be probability-based. At the reporting date, Bank A updates the appraisal value of the collateral and considers 3 probable scenarios:

- **Scenario 1 – Cure**: the obligor eventually pays past dues and the loan reverts to performing. In this case, ECL corresponds to lifetime losses expected from loans that have recently defaulted. Based on its historical data and using the methodology described above, Bank A expects an ECL of $130,000.

- **Scenario 2 – Restructure**: Bank A comes to a restructuring agreement with the obligor. After 6 months of negotiation, the loan is written off and a new loan is initiated with a net present value of $800,000.

- **Scenario 3 – Liquidation**: The loan is written off and the bank starts the collection of the contractual collateral. Bank A expects to sell the collateral within a year and to collect $700,000 net of recovery costs.

The ECL of each scenario can be calculated as follows:

$$ECL = EAD - \sum_{t_i=t_1}^{t_i=t_n} \frac{CF_{t_i} - RC_{t_i}}{(1+r_i)^{t_i}}$$

Where:
- CF = expected future cash flows
- RC = expected recovery costs

Probable scenarios	Probability	EAD	Discount rate	Expected net future cash flows	Expected recovery time	ECL of each scenario	Weighted ECL
Scenario 1: Cure	20%	1,030,000	3%	900,000	0.0	$130,000	$26,000
Scenario 2: Restructure	40%	1,030,000	3%	800,000	0.5	$241,737	$96,695
Scenario 3: Liquidation	40%	1,030,000	3%	700,000	1.0	$350,388	$140,155
Weighted average ECL						Lifetime ECL	$262,850
						% of EAD:	26%

$$ECL = EAD - \frac{\text{Exp. Net future CF}}{(1+r)^{\text{exp recovery time}}}$$

Most sophisticated banks have developed their IFRS 9 solutions by adjusting and extending their Basel models. This is true for all types of model component: PD, LGD and EAD. This is perhaps unsurprising given the historical investment large banks have made in their Basel models, and the fact that IFRS 9 shares fundamental similarities in expected loss modelling. But, for many banks, creating lifetime estimates and altering models to satisfy the complex and detailed IFRS 9 requirements necessitates significant work.

However, many non-financial entities do not have models and systems in place that capture such information. One possibility is to make use of historical default rates as collected by credit rating agencies such as Standard and Poor's. This is illustrated in the example below.

Example 51.4: Expected credit loss measurement using credit rating agency historical default rates

Introduction

A corporate uses a non-modelled approach to quantify the ECL of a loan issued to Borrower X.

Fact Pattern

On 1 January 2021, the corporate made a 2-year loan of $1.5m to Borrower X. It needs to estimate its ECLs on the loan for its financial statements for the year ended 31 December 2021. There is no specified collateral pledged for this loan. The lender has a general security agreement in place for the loan but it is subordinate to other bank debts of Borrower X. As a result, the loan is considered to be unsecured for the purpose of the ECL measurement.

Borrower X is an unrated private company. However, its financial condition is such that the loan would appear to fit what Standard & Poor's would rate as a B-rated instrument: the balance sheet of Borrower X indicates that while the entity currently has the capacity to meet its financial commitments on the obligation, adverse business, financial, or economic conditions will likely impair the borrower's capacity or willingness to meet its financial commitments on the obligation.

The loan is assessed to be in stage 1 as the lender assesses that there has not been a significant increase in credit risk. However, the economic environment is more uncertain than has been typical over the course of the last decade.

ECL Projection

The corporate calculates the ECLs using the normal formula ($ECL = PD \times LGD \times EAD$, discounted at the EIR):

- A PD is initially estimated based on the historical default rates for loans which have 'B' credit ratings. The S&P global ratings study indicates that 'B' rated entities have a historical aggregate cumulative 12-month PD of 3.33%.[13] Given the uncertainties in the economic environment this historical PD needs to be adjusted. The corporate adjusts the S&P historical default rate to reflect current conditions and estimates a 12-month PD range of 4-6%.

- Given the subordination of the loan to other bank debts, the majority of the amount owed would probably be lost in the event of default, therefore, LGD is estimated in the range of 80-100%.

- The EAD is known, i.e. $1.5m, and the effective interest rate of the loan for this example is assumed to be the contractual rate, which is 3%. As a simplifying assumption, it is also assumed that any default is most likely to occur at the end of the year. The discounted EAD over 1 year is $1.5m which, divided by 1.03 give a discounted amount of approximately $1.46m, that can be multiplied by the PD and the LGD.

Conclusion

With the assumptions that the discount rate is 3%, the 1-year PD is 4-6% and the LGD is 80-100%, the ECL for the loan is estimated to be in the range of $46,602 – $87,379 (see table below). However, this approach clearly acknowledges that there is a range of possible values for the ECL and significant judgement is required to reach a final determination. This judgement would need to be documented using all available information without undue cost or effort, possibly including the current spreads of similar bonds that are 'B' rated, to narrow the range of possible values for the ECL.

		LGD	
		80%	100%
PD	4%	46,602	58,252
	6%	69,903	87,379

5.4.2 Loss rate approach

Not every entity calculates a separate risk of a default occurring and an LGD, but instead uses a loss rate approach. Using this approach, the entity develops loss-rate statistics on the basis of the amount written off over the life of the financial assets. It must then adjust these historical credit loss trends for current conditions and expectations about the future. The following Illustrative Example 9 from IFRS 9 is designed to illustrate how an entity measures 12-month ECLs using a loss rate approach. *[IFRS 9 Example 9 IE53-IE57].*

Example 51.5: *12-month expected credit losses measurement based on a loss rate approach*

Bank A originates 2,000 bullet loans with a total gross carrying amount of $500,000. Bank A segments its portfolio into borrower groups (Groups X and Y) on the basis of shared credit risk characteristics at initial recognition. Group X comprises 1,000 loans with a gross carrying amount per client of $200, for a total gross carrying amount of $200,000. Group Y comprises 1,000 loans with a gross carrying amount per client of $300, for a total gross carrying amount of $300,000. There are no transaction costs and the loan contracts include no options (for example, prepayment or call options), premiums or discounts, points paid, or other fees.

Bank A measures ECLs on the basis of a loss rate approach for Groups X and Y. In order to develop its loss rates, Bank A considers samples of its own historical default and loss experience for those types of loans. In addition, Bank A considers forward-looking information, and updates its historical information for current economic conditions as well as reasonable and supportable forecasts of future economic conditions. Historically, for a population of 1,000 loans in each group, Group X's loss rates are 0.3 per cent, based on four defaults, and historical loss rates for Group Y are 0.15 per cent, based on two defaults.

Group	Number of clients in sample	Estimated per client gross carrying amount at default	Total estimated gross carrying amount at default	Historic per annum average defaults	Estimated total gross carrying amount at default	Present value of observed loss [a]	Loss rate
	A	B	C = A × B	D	E = B × D	F	G = F ÷ C
X	1,000	$200	$200,000	4	$800	$600	0.3%
Y	1,000	$300	$300,000	2	$600	$450	0.15%

(a) ECLs should be discounted using the EIR. However, for purposes of this example, the present value of the observed loss is assumed. [IFRS 9.5.5.17(b)].

At the reporting date, Bank A expects an increase in defaults over the next 12 months compared to the historical rate. As a result, Bank A estimates five defaults in the next 12 months for loans in Group X and three for loans in Group Y. It estimates that the present value of the observed credit loss per client will remain consistent with the historical loss per client.

On the basis of the expected life of the loans, Bank A determines that the expected increase in defaults does not represent a significant increase in credit risk since initial recognition for the portfolios. On the basis of its forecasts, Bank A measures the loss allowance at an amount equal to 12-month ECLs on the 1,000 loans in each group amounting to $750 and $675 respectively. This equates to a loss rate in the first year of 0.375 per cent for Group X and 0.225 per cent for Group Y.

Group	Number of clients in sample	Estimated per client gross carrying amount at default	Total estimated gross carrying amount at default	Expected defaults	Estimated total gross carrying amount at default	Present value of observed loss	Loss rate
	A	B	C = A × B	D	E = B × D	F	G = F ÷ C
X	1,000	$200	$200,000	5	$1,000	$750	0.375%
Y	1,000	$300	$300,000	3	$900	$675	0.225%

Bank A uses the loss rates of 0.375 per cent and 0.225 per cent respectively to estimate 12-month ECLs on new loans in Group X and Group Y originated during the year and for which credit risk has not increased significantly since initial recognition.

The example above illustrates that under the loss rate approach, an entity would compute its loss rates by segmenting its portfolio into appropriate groupings (or sub-portfolios) based on shared credit risk characteristics and then updating its historical loss information with more forward-looking information. The loss rate was derived simply by computing the ratio between the present value of observed losses (the numerator) and the gross carrying amount of the loans (the denominator). Although the loss rate approach does not require an explicit risk of a default occurring, there has to be an estimate of the number of defaults in order to determine whether there has been a significant increase in credit risk (see 6 below). Hence, IFRS 9 will also require any entities that intend to use this approach to track the likelihood of default.

ECLs must be discounted at the EIR. However, in this example, the present value of the observed loss is just assumed. This is an additional area of complexity that entities have to take into account when trying to build upon their existing loss rate approaches.

5.5 Expected life versus contractual period

Lifetime ECLs are defined as the ECLs that result from all possible default events over the expected life of a financial instrument. *[IFRS 9 Appendix A]*. This is consistent with the requirement that an entity should assess whether the credit risk on a financial instrument has increased significantly since initial recognition by using the change in the risk of a default occurring over the expected life of the financial instrument. *[IFRS 9.5.5.9]*.

An entity must therefore estimate cash flows and the instrument's life by considering all contractual terms of the financial instrument (for example, prepayment, extension, call and similar options). There is a presumption that the expected life of a financial instrument can be estimated reliably. In those rare cases when it is not possible to reliably estimate the expected life of a financial instrument, the entity shall use the remaining contractual term of the financial instrument. *[IFRS 9 Appendix A, B5.5.51]*.

However, the maximum period to consider when measuring ECLs should be the maximum contractual period (including extension options) over which the entity is exposed to credit risk and not a longer period, even if that longer period is consistent with business practice. *[IFRS 9.5.5.19]*. Although an exception to this principle has been added for revolving facilities (see 12 below), the IASB remains of the view that the contractual period over which an entity is committed to provide credit (or a shorter period considering prepayments) is the correct conceptual outcome. The IASB noted that most loan commitments will expire at a specified date, and if an entity decides to renew or extend its commitment to extend credit, it will be a new instrument for which the entity has the opportunity to revise the terms and conditions. *[IFRS 9.BC5.260]*.

This means that extension options should only be reflected in the measurement of ECLs as long as this does not extend the horizon beyond the maximum contractual period over which the entity is exposed to credit risk. Extension options at the discretion of the lender should therefore be excluded from the measurement of ECLs. Similarly, a lender's ability to require prepayment limits the horizon over which it is exposed to credit risk. The first prepayment date at the discretion of the lender should therefore represent the maximum period to be reflected in the expected loss calculation.

When assessing the impact of extension options at the discretion of the borrower, an entity should estimate both the probability of exercise of the extension option as well as the portion of the loan that will be extended (if the extension option can be exercised for a portion of the loan only). This is consistent with how lifetime expected losses must be assessed for loan commitments where an entity's estimate of ECLs must be consistent with its expectations of drawdowns on that loan commitment. Although the standard is not explicit on this point, the effect of extension options is best modelled not by estimating an average life of the facility but by estimating the EAD each year over the maximum lifetime. This is because use of an average life would not reflect losses expected to occur beyond the average life. *[IFRS 9.B.5.5.31]*.

Expected prepayments at the discretion of borrowers should also be reflected in the measurement of ECLs. As with extension options, an entity must estimate both the probability of exercise of the prepayment option as well as the portion of the loan that will be prepaid (if the prepayment option can be exercised for a portion of the loan only). As with extension options, the standard does not specify whether prepayment patterns should be reflected through an amortising EAD over the maximum contractual period of the financial instruments or, rather, by shortening the horizon over which to measure ECLs to the average life of the financial instruments. Similar to the treatment of extension options, described above, in our view it is more appropriate to adjust the EAD for the facility each year over the maximum lifetime. We consider this a more transparent way of incorporating product features and potential impacts of different macroeconomic scenarios that can, for example, affect pre-payment patterns and customers' ability to refinance.

Further complexity in assessing expected prepayments and extensions arises if one considers that the behaviour of borrowers is affected by their creditworthiness. This means that prepayment and extension patterns should probably be estimated separately for stage 1 and stage 2 assets. This may represent a significant challenge, as making such estimates would require distinct historical observations for each of the stage 1 and 2 populations, which are unlikely to be available given that these populations were never identified in the past. Prepayment assumptions for stage 2 assets would need to factor in the probabilities that some may subsequently default and some may cure. A further complication is that expected prepayment and extension behaviour may vary with changes in the macroeconomic outlook.

The standard is clear that, for loan commitments and financial guarantee contracts, the time horizon to measure ECLs is the maximum contractual period over which an entity has a present contractual obligation to extend credit. *[IFRS 9.B5.5.38]*. However, for revolving credit facilities (e.g. credit cards and overdrafts), as an exception to the normal rule, this period is extended beyond the maximum contractual period and includes the period over which the entity is exposed to credit risk and ECLs would not be mitigated by credit risk management actions (see 12 below). This exception is limited to facilities that include both a loan and an undrawn commitment component, that do not have a fixed term or repayment structure and usually have a short contractual cancellation period (for example, one day). *[IFRS 9.5.5.20, B5.5.39, B5.5.40]*.

At its April 2015 meeting, the ITG discussed how to determine the maximum period for measuring ECLs, by reference to the following example.[14]

Example 51.6: Determining the maximum contractual period when measuring expected credit losses

Bank A manages a portfolio of variable rate mortgages on a collective basis. The mortgage loans are issued to retail customers in Country X with the following terms:

- the stated maturity is 6 months with an automatic extension feature whereby, unless the borrower or lender take action to terminate the loan at the stated maturity date, the loan automatically extends for the following 6 months;
- the interest rate is fixed for each 6-month period at the beginning of the period. The interest rate is reset to the current market interest rate on the extension date; and
- the lender's right to refuse an extension is unrestricted.

It is assumed that the mortgage loans meet the criteria for amortised cost measurement under paragraph 4.1.2 of IFRS 9.

In practice, borrowers are generally expected not to elect to terminate their loans on the stated maturity date, because moving the mortgage to another bank, or applying for a new product, generally involves an administrative burden and has little or no economic benefit for the borrower.

Furthermore, Bank A does not complete regular credit file reviews for individual loans and as a result does not usually cancel the loans unless it receives information about an adverse credit event in respect of a particular borrower. On the basis of historical evidence, such loans extend many times and can last for up to 30 years.

The ITG noted that:
- IFRS 9 is clear that the maximum period to consider when measuring ECLs in this example would be restricted to 6 months, because this is the maximum contractual period over which the lender is exposed to credit risk, i.e. the period until the lender can next object to an extension. *[IFRS 9.5.5.19]*.
- The standard requires that extension options must be considered when determining the maximum contractual period, but does not specify whether these are lender or borrower extension options. However, if the extension option is within the control of the lender, the lender cannot be forced to continue extending credit and therefore such an option cannot be considered as lengthening the maximum period of exposure to credit risk. Conversely, if a borrower holds an extension option that could force the lender to continue extending credit, this would have the effect of lengthening that maximum contractual period of credit exposure.
- The maximum contractual period over which the entity is exposed to credit risk should be determined in accordance with the substantive contractual terms of the financial instrument. To further illustrate this point, a situation in which a lender is legally prevented from exercising a contractual right should be seen as distinct from a situation in which a lender chooses not to exercise a contractual right for practical or operational reasons.
- In the example presented, the facility is not of a revolving nature and the borrower does not have any such flexibility regarding drawdowns. Consequently, it would not be appropriate to analogise the 6-month mortgage loan to a revolving credit facility that has been fully drawn at the reporting date. Hence, the example falls outside the narrow scope exception for revolving credit facilities (e.g. credit cards and overdraft facilities) in which the maximum period to consider when measuring ECLs is over the period that the entity is exposed to credit risk and ECLs would not be mitigated by credit risk management actions, even if that period extends beyond the maximum contractual period (see 12 below). *[IFRS 9.5.5.20]*.
- Consequently, it was acknowledged that there may be a disconnect between the accounting and credit risk management view in some situations (e.g. an entity may choose to continue extending credit to a long-standing customer despite being in a position to reduce or remove the exposure). See further discussion on the application of the revolving credit facilities exception to multi-purpose facilities (see 12 below).

For demand deposits that have no fixed maturity and can be withdrawn by the holder on very short notice (e.g. one day) (assuming there is no contractual or legal constraint that could prevent the holder from withdrawing its cash at any time), the period used by the holder of such demand deposits to estimate ECLs would be limited to the contractual notice period, i.e. one day. This is the maximum contractual period over which the holder is exposed to credit risk. In accordance with paragraph 5.5.19 of IFRS 9, extension periods at the option of the holder are excluded in estimating the maximum contractual period because the holder can unilaterally choose not to extend credit and thus can limit the period over which it is exposed to credit risk. Furthermore, demand deposits do not fall under the revolving credit facility exception (see 12 below) as they do not comprise an undrawn element. *[IFRS 9.5.5.20]*.

5.6 Probability-weighted outcome and multiple scenarios

ECLs must reflect an unbiased and probability-weighted estimate of credit losses over the expected life of the financial instrument (i.e. the weighted average of credit losses with the respective risks of a default occurring as the weights). *[IFRS 9.5.5.17(a), Appendix A, B5.5.28]*.

The standard makes it clear that when measuring ECLs, in order to derive an unbiased and probability-weighted amount, an entity needs to evaluate a range of possible outcomes. *[IFRS 9.5.5.17(a)]*. This involves identifying possible scenarios that specify:

a) the amount and timing of the cash flows for particular outcomes; and

b) the estimated probability of these outcomes.

Although an entity does not need to identify every possible scenario, it will need to take into account the possibility that a credit loss occurs, no matter how low that probability is. *[IFRS 9.5.5.18]*. This is not the same as a single estimate of the worst-case or best-case scenario, or the most likely outcome (i.e. when there is a low risk or probability of a default (PD) with high loss outcomes, the most likely outcome could be no credit loss even though an allowance would be required based on probability-weighted cash flows). *[IFRS 9.B5.5.41]*. It is worthwhile noting that it is implicit that the sum of the weighted probabilities will be equal to one. A simple example of application of a probability-weighted calculation is shown in Example 51.7.

Without taking into account multiple economic scenarios (see below) calculating a probability-weighted amount may not require a complex analysis or a detailed simulation of a large number of scenarios and the standard suggests that relatively simple modelling may be sufficient. For instance, the average credit losses of a large group of financial instruments with shared risk characteristics may be a reasonable estimate of the probability-weighted amount. In other situations, the identification of scenarios that specify the amount and timing of the cash flows for particular outcomes and the estimated probability of those outcomes will probably be needed. In those situations, the ECLs shall reflect at least two outcomes in accordance with paragraph 5.5.18 of IFRS 9. *[IFRS 9.B5.5.42]*.

5.6.1 Single versus multiple forward-looking economic scenarios

At the December 2015 ITG meeting, the question was asked as to whether the use of multiple scenarios referred to in the standard relates only to what might happen to particular assets given a single forward-looking economic scenario (i.e. default or no default), or whether application of the standard requires an entity to use multiple forward-looking economic scenarios, and if so how.

The ITG members noted that the measurement of ECLs is required to reflect an unbiased and probability-weighted amount that is determined by evaluating a range of possible outcomes. Consequently, when there is a non-linear relationship between the different forward-looking scenarios and their associated credit losses, using a single forward-looking economic scenario would not meet this objective. In such cases, more than one forward-looking economic scenario would need to be used in the measurement of ECLs.[15] For each scenario the associated ECLs would need to be multiplied by the weighting allocated to that scenario.

The ITG also discussed the use of multiple economic scenarios to assess whether exposures should be measured using lifetime economic losses (see 6.7 below). It was noted by the ITG that if the same variable is relevant for determining significant increase in credit risk and for measuring ECLs, the same forward-looking scenarios should be used for both.

The ITG discussed a particular example in which there are considered to be three possible economic scenarios.[16] This is illustrated in the example below.

Example 51.7: Incorporating single versus multiple forward-looking scenarios when measuring expected credit losses

Scenario	Future unemployment	Likelihood of occurrence	ECLs
(a)	4%	20%	£30
(b)	5%	50%	£70
(c)	6%	30%	£170

Use of a single central economic scenario based on the most likely outcome of 5% unemployment, i.e. scenario (b), would give rise to an ECL of £70. However, using a probability-weighted range of scenarios, the ECL would be £92 ((£30 × 0.2) + (£70 × 0.5) + (£170 × 0.3)). Consequently, the ITG observed that in this example, using a single central forward-looking economic scenario would not result in an unbiased and probability-weighted amount in accordance with the standard.

The ITG was concerned about the distribution of possible losses often being 'non-linear', in that the increase in losses associated with those economic scenarios that are worse than the central forecast will be greater than the reduction in losses associated with those scenarios that are more benign. To use statistical terminology, the distribution is skewed. Depending on how it is calculated, a single scenario gives the mode of this distribution (i.e. the most likely outcome) or the median (the central forecast). In contrast, the standard requires the use of the mean (i.e. a probability-weighted estimation). A possible distribution of the losses in the portfolio consistent with the above example is shown in Figure 51.4 below.

Figure 51.4 Distribution of losses

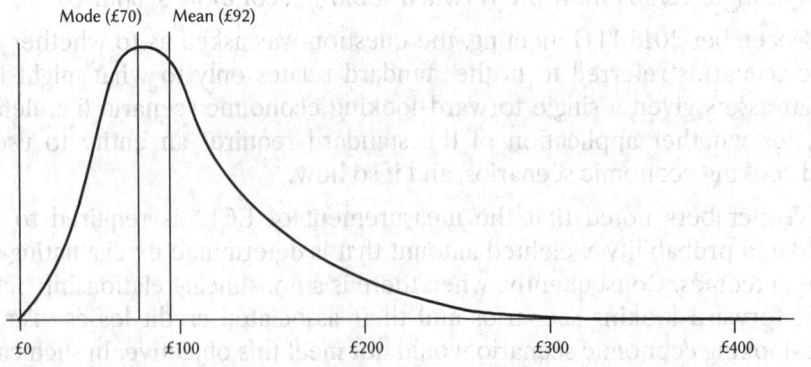

At the ITG meeting, it was noted that there are a number of possible approaches that might be used to incorporate multiple economic approaches. IFRS 9 does not prescribe any particular method of measuring ECLs and the measurement should reflect an entity's own view. What the standard does require is that the expected losses must reflect:

(a) an unbiased and probability-weighted amount that is determined using a range of possible outcomes; and

(b) reasonable and supportable information that is available without undue cost or effort at the reporting date.

With respect to reasonable and supportable information, ITG members made the following observations:

(a) although IFRS 9 does not specifically require an entity to consider external information, an entity should consider information from a variety of sources in order to ensure that the information used is reasonable and supportable;

(b) the information considered could vary depending on the facts and circumstances including the level of sophistication of the entity, geographical region and the particular features of the portfolio; and

(c) while entities are not expected to consider every possible scenario, the scenarios considered should reflect a representative sample of possible outcomes.[17]

ITG members recognised that materiality considerations would need to be taken into account.

In an IASB webcast on 25 July 2016, it was noted that, having considered:

(a) whether the effect of non-linearity is material;

(b) whether the entity has a reasonable and supportable basis for this multiple scenario analysis; and

(c) whether the application is possible without undue cost or effort;

A conclusion may sometimes be reached that it is not necessary to actually use multiple scenarios to apply the impairment requirements in IFRS 9. However, multiple scenarios must always be considered.

At the December 2015 ITG meeting, the ITG also noted that consideration should be given to the consistency of forward-looking information used for the measurement of ECLs and for other purposes within the organisation, such as budgeting and forecasting. ITG members acknowledged that there might be differences, but observed that these should be understood and explainable.

ITG members also observed that the incorporation of forward-looking scenarios will require judgement. Consequently, they emphasised the importance of the IFRS 7 disclosure requirements relating to how forward-looking information has been incorporated into the determination of ECLs (see Chapter 54 at 5.3).[18]

5.6.2 Approaches to incorporate multiple economic scenarios

Since December 2015, banks have given significant attention to how multiple economic scenarios can be incorporated into ECL calculations. We have seen three main approaches, as follows:

(a) Probability weighted scenarios – this is similar to the method discussed at the ITG meeting in December 2015 and illustrated in Example 51.7 above. It involves establishing a number of scenarios (typically three scenarios but we have seen varying numbers, generally between two and four), estimating the losses that would arise in those scenarios and allocating a weighting to each scenario. Unlike Example 51.7 above, these do not normally model economic variables such as unemployment rates in isolation – to do so, would also require complex modelling of the correlations between those variables. Instead, each scenario is normally a coherent combination of economic variables. For example, a scenario relevant to mortgage loans might include assumptions about unemployment, interest rates and house prices. This approach is transparent, but it may be difficult to assign the weightings to each scenario, requiring judgement as well as experience of the past. While selecting scenarios and respective weights, we expect banks to take into consideration the entire distribution of macroeconomic scenarios and select points (i.e. scenarios) from that distribution, with their respective weights representing the portion of the distribution represented by the scenario. We would also expect that the mean of the selected scenarios and weights is similar to that of the entire distribution.

(b) The second approach is to calculate ECLs based on a central forward-looking scenario and to adjust the outcome where necessary by a factor to reflect the non-linearity of the loss distribution. In practice it may be that a method similar to (a) above will need to be used in order to calculate this factor – so that it is not a very different approach. However, some banks view the merits of this approach as being less mechanistic and allowing more room for judgement.

(c) Monte Carlo simulation – this method seeks to calculate the expected losses associated with the entire distribution of possible scenarios around the bank's central economic forecast. It has the advantage that it does not require the bank to formulate specific scenarios or assign weightings to them, but the simulation is dependent on assumptions that may not be transparent to either users or preparers, so that this solution can seem a 'black box'. It is also very demanding as to the volume of data that has to be manipulated and it is not how most banks manage credit risk today. This method is quite rarely applied in practice.

The effect of multiple scenarios will affect not just the probability of default but also the losses given default. For instance, for property-based lending it will be necessary to forecast the value of collateral associated with each economic scenario that is modelled. A consequence of this is that there may be a need to record an ECL allowance for an asset that, based on the central forecast of future collateral values, is fully collateralised. (Also, as a result, the loss allowance for a stage 3 asset may be higher than for an impaired asset under IAS 39).

The use of multiple scenarios may also have an effect on the estimated EAD.

A number of other observations can be made about the use of multiple scenarios:

(a) Whichever approach is used to calculate the effect of non-linearity, it will be necessary for banks to communicate the result of the calculation in a manner which can be understood by readers of the financial statements. One possible approach would be for banks to report the losses associated with the central forecast and then, separately, the effect of the consideration of other scenarios. This would allow banks to communicate the amounts they expect to lose and would permit comparison between banks of the effect of the adjustment for non-linearity, even if the banks use different methods to make the calculation.

(b) It would seem that the effects of non-linearity depend on the countries in which banks operate and the economic characteristics of those countries. For instance, the effect of alternative scenarios of interest rates and unemployment may be greater in countries where there is more of a 'boom and bust' economic cycle. The size of the effect is also dependent on origination practices and the particular lending products – variable rate loans being more sensitive to interest rates than fixed-rate ones, while defaults on credit cards are more affected by unemployment rates. In some cases the issue is seen as most relevant for exposures to a particular economic variable, a topical example being lending to companies involved in the oil industry. In this example, banks might model a number of scenarios as to how oil prices could evolve. A similar approach may be relevant for non-banks with similar exposures through long term construction contracts or leasing activities. There is also more likely to be non-linearity in the calculation of ECLs when exposures are collateralised by assets whose values also change in response to the economic conditions that drive the probability of default. An example is residential mortgage loans.

(c) It should be stressed that the ITG discussion highlighted the importance of calculating the effect of non-linearity using only reasonable and supportable information, implying that if the information is not available then there is a limit to what can be done. However, banks will also need to take into account their regulators' expectations (see 1.6 above and 7.1 below for Basel Committee guidance).

The process of forecasting future economic conditions is discussed further in 5.9.3 below.

5.6.3 Incorporating the impact of rare shock events

One of the main challenges in applying the IFRS ECL model is to determine what is reasonable and supportable forward-looking information and how to treat rare shock events with material, but uncertain, economic consequences. A major example of this is the coronavirus pandemic (which is addressed in more detail at 7.8 below). On 27 March 2020, the IASB issued an education document in which it acknowledged that at the time it would likely be difficult to incorporate the specific effects of the coronavirus pandemic and government support measures on a reasonable and supportable basis. However, changes in economic conditions should be reflected in macroeconomic scenarios applied by entities and in their weightings.[19] When it is not possible to reflect such information in models, the IASB expects post-model overlays or adjustments to be considered.

Whether the impact of an event such as the coronavirus pandemic is reflected in an individual ECL assessment (estimating the probability of default on an individual basis), factored into the scenario analysis of future macroeconomic conditions on a collective basis, or adjusted through management overlays, depends on the entity's systems and processes and the facts and circumstances. In practice, entities are likely to consider a combination of these approaches. In estimating the impact of the event, entities should, however, be careful to avoid double-counting the effects of the various assumptions applied in individual assessments, macroeconomic scenarios and management overlays.

In abnormal circumstances such as those created by the coronavirus pandemic, it may take time before entities detect changes in risk indicators at a specific borrower level and are able to reassess the affected exposures. In order to accelerate the reflection of such changes in credit quality not yet detected at an individual borrower level, it may be appropriate to adjust ratings and the probabilities of default on a collective basis, considering risk characteristics such as the industry or geographical location of the borrowers (see 6.5 below). However, many methods for performing collective assessments make use of historical information, which may not be relevant in the circumstances.

One of the features of the coronavirus pandemic is that there are two sources of uncertainty: the development of the pandemic itself and also the extent and the effect of the government response. In addition to updating GDP and other macroeconomic variables in an entity's multiple economic scenarios, a challenge is to estimate how the impact of the coronavirus pandemic and any related government programmes affect specific sectors, regions and borrowers, especially as the details surrounding many government programmes continue to evolve.

The IASB educational document noted that a number of assumptions and linkages underlying the way ECLs has been implemented to date may no longer hold in the environment affected by the pandemic.[20] For example, the relationship between GDP and other macroeconomic variables, such as unemployment and interest rates, and sector-specific variables, such as oil prices, is very likely to be different from what has been experienced in the past and reflected in economic forecasting models. The probability weightings assigned to macroeconomic scenarios may also need to be revisited.

In estimating overlays, entities may need to plot several possible scenarios of what might happen over the forecasting period and assign weightings to them, to ensure that any overlay reflects the inherent uncertainty and non-linearity of potential outcomes.

5.7 Time value of money

An entity needs to consider the time value of money when measuring ECLs, by discounting the estimated losses to the reporting date using a rate that approximates the EIR of the asset. *[IFRS 9.5.5.17, B5.5.44]*. This has two components:

- discounting recoveries to the date of default, hence 'a credit loss arises even if the entity expects to be paid in full but later than when contractually due'; *[IFRS 9.B5.5.28]* and
- discounting losses from the date of default to the reporting date. This is needed as the gross amortised cost of the asset is based on the contractual cash flows discounted at the EIR, and therefore not discounting cash flows that are now not expected to be received would overstate the loss.

It is rare that customers just fail to pay amounts when due. In most cases, default also involves payments being paid late, while default can lead to the acceleration of payment of amounts that are not contractually due until a later date. Therefore, modelling losses involves modelling the timing of payments when default occurs and different patterns of timing of recoverable cash flows, such as the time it takes to foreclose on and sell collateral and complete bankruptcy proceedings, before the ECLs can be discounted back to the reporting date.

Of these two components, the first is typically included by banks in their calculation of the LGD (although not necessarily using the EIR). However, the second will also need to be calculated to comply with the standard.

The standard and its illustrative examples are silent on how the calculation should be made. In Illustrative Example 9 the present value of the observed loss is assumed and in Illustrative Example 8, a footnote states that, 'because the LGD represents a percentage of the present value of the gross carrying amount, this example does not illustrate the time value of money'.

One approach would be to model various scenarios as to how cash is collected once the loan has defaulted, and probability-weight the discounted cash flows of these various scenarios.

The discount rate is calculated as follows:

- for a fixed-rate financial asset, entities are required to determine or approximate the EIR on the initial recognition of the financial asset, while for a floating-rate financial asset, entities are required to use the current EIR; *[IFRS 9.B5.5.44]*
- for a purchased or originated credit-impaired financial asset (see 3.3 above), entities are required to discount ECLs using the credit-adjusted EIR determined on the initial recognition of the financial asset; *[IFRS 9.B5.5.45]*
- for a loan commitment (see 11 below), entities are required to use the EIR of the asset that will result once the commitment is drawn down. This would give rise to a consistent rate for a credit facility that includes both a loan (i.e. a financial asset) and an undrawn commitment (i.e. a loan commitment). If the EIR of the resulting asset is not determinable, then entities are required to use the current risk-free rate (i.e. the discount rate that reflects the current market assessment of the time value of money). This should be adjusted for risks specific to the cash flows, but only if the cash flows have not already been adjusted for these risks, in order to avoid double counting; *[IFRS 9.B5.5.47, B5.5.48]*
- for financial guarantee contracts (see 11 below) entities are required to use the current risk-free rate adjusted for risks specific to the cash flows, again to the extent that those cash flows have not already been adjusted for the risks; *[IFRS 9.B5.5.48]* and
- for lease receivables (see 10.2 below), entities are required to discount the ECLs using the same discount rate used in the measurement of the lease receivables in accordance with IFRS 16. *[IFRS 9.B5.5.46]*.

LGD data available from Basel models should include a discounting factor and sometimes this may be different from the rate required by IFRS 9. Furthermore, the discount rate used in Basel models only covers the period between default and subsequent recoveries. Therefore, entities will have to find ways to adjust their LGDs to reflect the discounting effect required by the standard (i.e. based on a rate that approximates the EIR and over the entire period from recoveries back to the reporting date). Given the requirement to use an approximation to the EIR, entities will need to work out how to determine a rate that is sufficiently accurate. One of the challenges is to interpret how much flexibility is afforded by the term 'approximation'.

At its meeting in December 2015, the ITG also discussed what was meant by the current EIR when an entity recognises interest revenue in each period based on the actual floating-rate applicable to that period. The ITG first noted that the definition of the EIR in IFRS 9 was carried forward essentially unchanged from the definition within IAS 39. Consequently, similarly to IAS 39, IFRS 9 does not specify whether an entity should use the current interest rate at the reporting date or the projected interest rates derived from the current yield curve as at the reporting date. There should be consistency between the rate used to recognise interest revenue, the rate used to project future cash flows (including cash shortfalls) and the rate used to discount those cash flows (see 5.7 above).

In relation to the guidance in paragraphs B5.5.47 and B5.5.48 on loan commitments when the EIR on the resulting asset is not determinable and for financial guarantee contracts, we make the following observations:

- Although it is not clear in the standard, any adjustment for the risks specific to the cash flows would be a *reduction* of the risk-free rate, not an increase. This would be consistent with the approach applied to provisions in IAS 37 and as was made clear in the staff paper presented to the Board when this treatment was discussed in December 2013.
- For loan commitments when the EIR on the resulting asset is not determinable, using the current risk-free rate adjusted for risks specific to the cash flows provides a prudent calculation of the ECLs, given that it is likely the entity which enters into the commitment will receive a credit spread on the loan if it is drawn down. It is in a much better position than the issuer of a financial guarantee contract, who will receive no credit spread should it be required to pay out on the guarantee.
- For financial guarantee contracts, the reduction in the risk-free discount rate will increase the present value of the obligation to pay claims to the guarantee holder. This reflects the additional compensation that would be demanded to take on this risky obligation, in particular to bear the risk that claims payments will be higher than the probability-weighted expected amount.
- The idea that the rate should be adjusted only if the cash flows have not already been adjusted for the risks may not be easy to apply in practice. This is because the cash flows should have already been estimated with regard to any non-linearities in the distribution of losses (see 5.6.1 above) and so will already have been partly adjusted for risk. It may not be easy to calculate the necessary adjustment to reflect a market assessment of the remaining risks. For this reason, the discount rate that will be applied will necessarily be an approximation of the rate required by the standard.

5.8 Losses expected in the event of default

This section discusses the measurement of ECLs taking into account credit enhancements such as collateral and financial guarantees, cash flows from the sale of a defaulted loan and collection costs paid to an external debt collection agency.

5.8.1 Credit enhancements: collateral and financial guarantees

Although credit enhancements such as collateral and guarantees play only a limited role in assessing whether there has been a significant increase in credit risk (see 6.1 below), they do affect the measurement of ECLs. For example, for a mortgage loan, even if an entity determines that there has been a significant increase in credit risk on the loan since initial recognition, if the expected proceeds from the collateral (i.e. the mortgaged property) exceeds the amount lent, then the entity may have very low or nil ECLs, and hence an allowance of close to zero.

For the purposes of measuring ECL, paragraph B5.5.55 of IFRS 9 requires the estimate of expected cash shortfalls to reflect the cash flows expected from collateral and other credit enhancements that are part of the contractual terms and are not recognised separately by the entity.

The standard specifies that the estimate of cash flows from collateral should include the effect of a foreclosure, regardless of whether foreclosure is probable, and the resulting cash flows from foreclosure on the collateral less the costs of obtaining and selling the collateral, taking into account the amount and timing of these cash flows. *[IFRS 9.B5.5.55]*. The wording does not mean that the entity is required to assume that recovery will be through foreclosure only, but rather that the entity should calculate the cash flows arising from the various ways that the asset may be recovered, only some of which may involve foreclosure, and to probability-weight these different scenarios (see Example 51.3 at 5.4 above).

Although the standard does not refer to fair value when determining the valuation of the collateral, in practice, an entity is likely to estimate the cash flows from the realisation of the collateral, based on the fair value of the collateral. In the case of illiquid collateral, such as real estate, adjustments will probably need to be made for expected changes in the fair value, depending on the economic conditions at the estimated date of selling the collateral. Also, as described at 5.6.1 and 5.6.2 above, the entity should consider multiple scenarios in ascribing value to collateral.

Also, any collateral obtained as a result of foreclosure is not recognised as an asset that is separate from the collateralised financial instrument unless it meets the relevant recognition criteria for an asset in IFRS 9 or other standards. *[IFRS 9.B5.5.55]*.

If a loan is guaranteed by a third party as part of its contractual terms, it should carry an allowance for ECLs based on the combined credit risk of the guarantor and the guaranteed party, by reflecting the effect of the guarantee in the measurement of losses expected on default.

5.8.1.A Guarantees that are part of the contractual terms

As already mentioned, paragraph B5.5.55 states that cash flows expected from a credit enhancement are included in the measurement of expected credit losses for a financial asset only if the credit enhancement is part of the asset's contractual terms. A challenge is interpreting what constitutes 'part of the contractual terms'. This was addressed by the ITG at its meeting in December 2015, specifically whether the credit enhancement must be an explicit term of the related asset's contract in order for it to be taken into account in the measurement of ECLs, or whether other credit enhancements that are not recognised separately can also be taken into account. The ITG noted that:

- The definition of credit losses states that, when estimating cash flows, an entity should include cash flows from the sale of collateral held or other credit enhancements that are 'integral to the contractual terms'. *[IFRS 9 Appendix A]*. Consequently, credit enhancements included in the measurement of ECLs should not be limited to those that are explicitly part of the contractual terms.
- An entity must apply its judgement in assessing what is meant by 'integral to the contractual terms' and in making that assessment, an entity should consider all relevant facts and circumstances.
- IFRS 7 requires disclosures to enable users of financial statements to understand the effect of collateral and other credit enhancements on the amounts arising from ECLs (see 15 below and Chapter 54 at 5.3).

Although not reflected in the official minutes of the ITG meeting, the IASB members highlighted during the course of the discussion that there was no intention to alter the treatment when drafting IFRS 9. In practice, previously under IAS 39, most banks incorporated guarantees as part of their measurement of losses given default.

The ITG also emphasised that paragraph B5.5.55 of IFRS 9 was drafted only with the intention to caution against double counting those credit enhancements that are already recognised separately, and was not intended to limit the inclusion of credit enhancements that were previously included in IAS 39 allowances for loan losses.

In November 2018, the IFRIC referred to paragraph B5.5.55 of IFRS 9 and observed that the cash flows expected from a credit enhancement are included in the measurement of expected credit losses only if the credit enhancement is both:

- part of the contractual terms; and
- not recognised separately by the entity.

Similar to the ITG, the Committee concluded that, if a credit enhancement is required to be recognised separately by IFRS Standards (an example would be a credit default swap that would need to be measured at fair value through profit or loss), an entity cannot include the cash flows expected from it in the measurement of expected credit losses. An entity applies the applicable IFRS Standard to determine whether it is required to recognise a credit enhancement separately. Paragraph B5.5.55 of IFRS 9 does not provide an exemption from applying the separate recognition requirements in IFRS 9 or other IFRS standards.

However, the ITG discussion does not fully answer the question of how to interpret when a financial guarantee is 'integral to the contractual terms' when it is not mentioned in the contractual terms of the loan.

It seems reasonably clear that a credit default swap on a loan entered into by the lender to mitigate its credit risk on the loan, would not normally be classed as integral to a loan's contractual terms. The second criteria mentioned in paragraph B5.5.55 is that the credit enhancement should not be recognised separately and separate accounting for a derivative is clearly required by IFRS 9. Also, payment under a credit default swap does not normally require the holder of the instrument to have suffered the credit loss referenced by the swap. As a result, cash flows from a credit default swap that is accounted for as a derivative would not be included in the measurement of ECLs of the associated loan.

For a financial guarantee (as defined in IFRS 9), one view is that it is integral to the contractual terms of a loan only if it is, at least implicitly, part of the contractual terms of the loan. Examples of an implicit contractual linkage might include:

- Inseparability: The financial guarantee is inseparable from the loan contract, i.e. the loan cannot be transferred without the guarantee.
- Local laws and regulations: Credit enhancements required by local laws and regulations that govern the loan contract but that are not specifically in the contract itself. For example, in some jurisdictions, legislation requires that lenders must take out financial guarantee contracts that contain little or no down payment in respect of certain loans.
- Business purpose: The guarantee and the loan have been contracted in contemplation of one another, i.e. the loan would not have been contracted without the guarantee.
- Market convention: The exposure and the financial guarantee are traded as a package in the market.

Another view might be that any contract that meets the definition of a financial guarantee under IFRS 9 can be considered 'integral to the contractual terms' of the guaranteed loan, as long as the guarantee is entered to at the same time as, or within a short time after, the loan is advanced. This is consistent with the public statement issued by the European Securities and Market Authority (ESMA) on 25 March 2020 which considered that a guarantee will be integral 'when a public guarantee is provided in conjunction with broadly applicable ex-lege moratoria or economic support and relief measures'.[21] As the definition of a financial guarantee contract requires the loan to be specified in the contractual terms of the financial guarantee and it is necessary for the lender to incur a credit loss on the loan to be reimbursed, there is a clear contractual linkage that ensures that any credit loss incurred on the loan will be compensated by the financial guarantee and no compensation will arise on the financial guarantee unless a credit loss is actually incurred by the lender on the guaranteed loan.

Whether a credit enhancement is integral depends on an assessment of the individual facts and circumstances and is likely to require judgement. If the guarantee is issued at the same time as the loan and is inseparable from it, it would generally be considered integral to the loan and therefore included in the measurement of ECL. If, instead, the guarantee is issued on existing loans, it would generally not be considered integral to that loan if it was not anticipated when the loan was originally granted.

Most guarantees require payment of a premium. To the extent that the guarantee is considered integral to the loan, it would be consistent with this notion to treat the cost of the guarantee as a transaction cost of making the loan. This means that the lender would add this cost to the initial carrying amount of the loan and so reduce the future EIR. It should not make a difference to the accounting for the loan whether the guarantee premium is paid upfront or in instalments over the life of the loan. If the premium is payable in instalments, it follows (at least, in theory, although the effect may not be material) that the full cost of the guarantee should be included in setting the loan's EIR.

5.8.1.B Guarantees that are not part of the contractual terms

Although it is not always clear as to when a financial guarantee contract would be regarded as part of the contractual terms, this may not affect the profit or loss recognition by the lender if an asset can be recognised in respect of the guarantee. Such an outcome may be achieved by following either of the two approaches described below.

A financial guarantee contract is likely to satisfy the definition of an insurance contract in both IFRS 4 – *Insurance Contracts* – and IFRS 17 – *Insurance Contracts* – as amended in June 2020 when applied but for the holder it will be excluded from the scope of IFRS 4 and IFRS 17 because it is a direct insurance contract held by a policyholder (as opposed to a policyholder of a reinsurance contract). *[IFRS 4.4(f), IFRS 17.7(g)]*. It is therefore outside the scope of IFRS 9 as well as IFRS 4. *[IFRS 9.2.1(e)]*. IAS 8 – *Accounting Policies, Changes in Accounting Estimates and Errors* – address situations where no IFRS specifically applies to a transaction, i.e. the holder of a financial guarantee contract will normally need to develop its accounting policy in accordance with the hierarchy in IAS 8. *[IAS 8.10-11]*.

Applying the IAS 8 hierarchy, one possibility would be to look to IAS 37 and treat the guarantee as a right to a reimbursement in respect of the impairment loss. IAS 37 permits a reimbursement of a liability to be recognised as an asset, not exceeding the amount of the provision, when it is virtually certain that the reimbursement will be received if the obligation for which a provision has been established is settled. *[IAS 37.53]*. In this instance, the benefit of the guarantee would be recognised as an asset to the extent it is virtually certain a recovery could be made if the lender were to suffer the impairment loss on the loan. One of the key advantages of a financial guarantee contract, compared to a normal insurance contract, is that they are typically drawn up using standard terms and conditions and there is often little doubt that an obligation would arise for the guarantor if the reference asset were to default. However, care should be taken to establish, based on the contractual terms of the arrangement, that a right to a recovery would, indeed, be virtually certain.

To record a reimbursement asset under IAS 37, it is less clear whether the credit risk of the guarantor needs to be assessed in determining whether recovery would be virtually certain, or whether the guarantor's credit risk would only be reflected in measuring the reimbursement asset. One view is that the guarantor would either have to present a very low credit risk or else the guarantee would itself need to be collateralised in order to conclude that a reimbursement right can be recognised. In this case, care should also be taken to ensure that there is no correlation between the credit risk of the loan and that of the guarantor, as would be the case if the guarantor's financial strength were to reduce at the same time that the loan is likely to default. Applying this view, if a reimbursement is considered virtually certain, there would probably be no need also to reflect the guarantor's credit risk in the measurement of the asset. In contrast, the second view imposes a less stringent criterion for recognising an asset, but would reduce the recognised asset to reflect the probability that the guarantor may be unable to meet its obligation (perhaps by applying an ECL deduction, by analogy to IFRS 9).

An alternative approach for recording an asset in respect of the guarantee would be to look to IFRS 3 – *Business Combinations* – and draw an analogy with indemnification assets. First, IFRS 3 requires all contingent liabilities to be recognised on a business combination, whether or not they are probable, which is closer to the IFRS 9 notion of an expected credit loss than the contingent liability recognition threshold under IAS 37. Second, IFRS 3 allows an indemnification asset to be recognised, measured on the same basis as the indemnified asset or liability, subject to any contractual limitations on its amount. Also, for an indemnification asset that is not subsequently measured at its fair value, the measurement is subject to management's assessment of the collectability of the indemnification asset. *[IFRS 3.57]*. Adopting this indemnification asset approach, the credit risk of the guarantor becomes a measurement, rather than a recognition issue. It would not be necessary to assess if the credit risk of the guarantor is very low, since credit risk is instead reflected in the measurement of the guarantee.

Whether an analogy is made to a reimbursement right under IAS 37 or an indemnification asset under IFRS 3, an asset may be recognised in respect of the guarantee, not exceeding the amount of the provision. *[IAS 37.53, IFRS 3.57]*. Except for the possible treatment of the guarantor's credit risk, using either of these approaches, the overall effect on profit or loss for the lender may be often the same as if the guarantee was included in the measurement of the ECL of the guaranteed asset. The right would, however, be presented as an asset rather than as a reduction of the impairment allowance.

Whereas it is relatively straightforward as to how to account for premiums paid for guarantees that are considered integral to a loan (as discussed in the previous section), it is less clear when the guarantee is not considered integral. If the entity who makes a loan and, at the same time, pays for a guarantee, records both the unamortised cost of the guarantee plus also a reimbursement or indemnification asset equivalent to the 12-month ECLs, the total amount at which the guarantee is initially recorded in the financial statements will exceed its fair value. This is because the cost of the guarantee will already include the guarantor's expectations of future losses. One view is to consider this to be 'double counting' and so, to restrict the reimbursement/ indemnification right to the excess (if any) of the ECL over the cost of the guarantee that is already reflected in the balance sheet.

There is another view that recognising both the unamortised cost of the guarantee and a reimbursement right/indemnification asset equal to the ECL is necessary to be consistent with the accounting for the loan. Another way of expressing this is to say that it is appropriate for the guarantee to be recorded at more than its initial fair value as the guaranteed loan is recorded initially at less than its fair value by a similar amount, i.e. the ECL. The subsequent amortisation of the cost of the guarantee would be balanced by the recognition of the credit spread in the interest earned on the loan.

Whatever view is taken on this issue, if the lender acquires the guarantee subsequent to making the loan and the loan has, in the meantime, increased in credit risk, it is likely that the lender will pay more for the guarantee, to reflect this increase in credit risk. If so, this additional amount will crystallise a loss for the lender and so should not be recorded as a reimbursement/ indemnification right and a reversal of a previously recognised impairment loss.

5.8.1.C Government relief measures

Entities will need to consider any form of support provided by a government and this is dependent on whether its effect is to prevent a default by the borrower, or to compensate a lender for losses it suffers due to the borrower's default. In some cases, a government may provide direct financial support to a borrower. For example, the government may offer to compensate employees who have lost their job with a portion of their previous salary for a period of time. These forms of financial support prevent or reduce the extent to which a borrower would otherwise default on a loan. These forms of financial support are considered in a lender's assessment of significant increase in credit risk and the probability of default as it reduces the credit risk associated with the underlying loan. In other cases, a guarantee may be issued to a lender to compensate it for losses it suffers due to default by a borrower. Such a guarantee does not prevent default by a borrower, but rather reduces the effect of any default.

If a guarantee is integral to the loan and is not required to be recognised separately by the lender, the guarantee is taken into account in calculating the LGD of the guaranteed loan (see 5.8.1.A above), however, it does not affect the significant increase in credit risk assessment.

If a guarantee is not considered to be integral, it may still meet the criteria to be recognised as a reimbursement asset by analogy to IAS 37. Where this applies it would have to be recognised separately in the statement of financial position and may result in an offsetting entry against ECL in profit or loss, depending on the accounting policy of the lender (see 5.8.1.B above).

Where guarantees are issued by governments for a below market rate fee, both borrowers and lenders will have to assess whether this constitutes a government grant to be accounted for and disclosed in accordance with IAS 20 – *Accounting for Government Grants and Disclosure of Government Assistance*. In performing such an assessment, entities will need to consider the level of the interest rate offered to the borrower on the guaranteed loan and whether the economics of the overall transaction provide a benefit to the lender, the borrower or to both. For example, if a benefit to a lender from a below market-rate fee on a guarantee is required to be partially offset by a reduction in the interest earned on the loan to the borrower, the value of any government grant to the lender may be reduced or eliminated. In such a case, the value of the grant accrues mainly to the borrower in the form of a below market rate loan relative to the borrower's credit risk.

5.8.2 Cash flows from the sale of a defaulted loan

At its meeting in December 2015, the ITG also discussed whether cash flows that are expected to be recovered from the sale on default of a loan could be included in the measurement of ECLs. ITG members noted that:

- such cash flows should be included in the measurement of ECLs if:
    (a) selling the loan is one of the recovery methods that the entity expects to pursue in a default scenario;
    (b) the entity is neither legally nor practically prevented from realising the loan using that recovery method; and
    (c) the entity has reasonable and supportable information upon which to base its expectations and assumptions;
- in order to support an entity's expectation that loan sales would be used as a recovery method in a default scenario, an entity's past practice would be an important consideration. However future expectations, which may differ from past practice, would also need to be considered. With respect to the amount of recovery proceeds to be included in the measurement of ECLs, an entity should consider relevant market related information relating to loan sale prices;
- in these circumstances, the inclusion of recovery sale proceeds in the measurement of ECLs would be appropriate for financial instruments in all stages; stage 1, 2 and 3 (see 3.1 above). This is because when measuring ECLs, IFRS 9 requires an entity to consider possible default scenarios for financial instruments in all three stages;
- given that it is necessary to consider multiple scenarios in measuring ECLs (see 5.6.1 above), it is possible that an entity will need to calculate the cash flows based on both a scenario in which the loan will be sold and one in which it will not. Expected sale proceeds would only be relevant when considering the possibility that a credit loss occurs (i.e. in a default scenario) and would not be relevant when considering the possibility that no credit loss occurs (i.e. in a performing scenario). For example, if, in the case of a particular loan, an entity concluded that there was a 10 per cent probability of default occurring, it would only be when considering the outcome of this default scenario that expected sale proceeds would be considered. If, in that default scenario, the entity expected to recover 30 per cent of the contractual cash flows of the loan through sale proceeds but only 25 per cent through continuing to hold, then the LGD would be 70 per cent rather than 75 per cent. In addition, the expected sale proceeds should be net of selling costs.

5.8.3 Treatment of collection costs paid to an external debt collection agency

Questions have arisen on how the collection costs paid to an external debt collection agency affect the measurement of ECLs. As an example, a bank engages the services of an external debt collection agency to recover accounts that are 90 days past due on its behalf and, in exchange, pays the agency a fee based on the amount recovered.

One view could be that in measuring the ECLs, all cash flows related to the recovery of the asset should be considered in estimating the expected cash shortfalls. Therefore, the recoveries and any incremental and directly attributable payments made to the external agency should both be considered, irrespective of whether the collections costs are deducted from the amount recovered or paid to the external debt collection agency separately. This view is based on the fact that IFRS 9 specifies that the estimate of cash flows from the realisation of collateral should include the costs of obtaining the collateral. This can be read to suggest that all cash flows relating to the various ways of recovering the asset should be considered in measuring the expected shortfall. An analogy can also be made with the ITG discussion on sales of assets where selling costs are to be included (see 5.8.2 above). This also reflects that if the cash flows expected to be received are greater than those that would be realised if the agency were not used, excluding the collection cost paid to the agency will understate the ECLs. Further, for assets that are purchased credit-impaired, these costs may already be implicit in the fair value at which they are acquired and so, unless these costs are included, the EIR would be inflated.

Another view could be that only cash flows related to the contractual terms of the financial instrument should be considered, apart from the costs of obtaining and selling collateral. This would exclude costs of an external debt collection agency. This view is based on the definition of a credit loss as 'the difference between all contractual cash flows that are due to an entity in accordance with the contracts and all the cash flows that the entity expects to receive (i.e. net of all cash shortfalls). The cash flows that are considered shall include cash flows from the sale of collateral held or other credit enhancements that are integral to the contractual terms.' Since the collection costs paid to the agency are not part of the contractual terms of the financial instrument, nor a cost for realising collateral, then they should not be considered in the calculation of ECLs. The reason for treating costs of realising collateral differently is that the proceeds from selling collateral is itself not a contractual cash flow of the instrument and the commercial value of the collateral would include provision for such costs. The analogy with sales of assets is considered irrelevant for the same reasons as they do not relate to the recovery of contractual cash flows.

Entities may take into account incremental collection costs incurred internally when measuring ECLs although this has not yet been seen widely in practice. An example of incremental internal collection costs would be incentives for employees to achieve certain collection targets. However, if the internal collection costs are not incremental, they cannot be included in the measurement of ECLs.

5.9 Reasonable and supportable information

IFRS 9 requires an entity to consider reasonable and supportable information that is available without undue cost or effort at the reporting date about past events, current conditions and forecasts of future economic conditions and that is relevant to the estimate of ECLs, including the effect of expected prepayments. *[IFRS 9.5.5.17(c), B5.5.51]*.

5.9.1 Undue cost or effort

The term undue cost or effort is not defined in the standard, although it is clear from the guidance that information available for financial reporting purposes is considered to be available without undue cost or effort. *[IFRS 9.B5.5.49]*.

Beyond that, although the standard explains that entities are not required to undertake an exhaustive search for information, it does include, as examples of relevant information, data from risk management systems, as described in 5.9.2 below.

What is available without undue cost or effort would be an area subject to management judgement in assessing the costs and associated benefits. This is consistent with the guidance in International Financial Reporting Standard for Small and Medium-sized Entities (IFRS for SMEs) in relation to the application of undue cost or effort. Paragraph 2.14B of the IFRS for SMEs states that considering whether obtaining or determining the information necessary to comply with a requirement would involve undue cost or effort depends on the entity's specific circumstances and on management's judgement of the costs and benefits from applying that requirement. This judgement requires consideration of how the economic decisions of those that are expected to use the financial statements could be affected by not having that information. Applying a requirement would involve undue cost or effort by an SME if the incremental cost (for example, valuers' fees) or additional effort (for example, endeavours by employees) substantially exceed the benefits that those that are expected to use the SME's financial statements would receive from having the information. Paragraph 232 of the Basis for Conclusions to the IFRS for SMEs further observes that:

- the undue cost or effort exemption is not intended to be a low hurdle. In particular, the IASB observed that it would expect that if an entity already had, or could easily and inexpensively acquire, the information necessary to comply with a requirement, any related undue cost or effort exemption would not be applicable. This is because, in that case, the benefits to the users of the financial statements of having the information would be expected to exceed any further cost or effort by the entity; and
- that an entity must make a new assessment of whether a requirement will involve undue cost or effort at each reporting date.

If the reporting entity is a bank, there would presumably be a higher hurdle to determine what credit risk information would require undue cost or effort, compared to a reporter that is not a bank, given that the benefit to users of its financial statements would be also expected to be higher. It is also an issue on which the Basel Committee has issued guidance (see 7.1 below).

5.9.2 Sources of information

The standard states that the information used should include factors that are specific to the borrower, general economic conditions and an assessment of both the current as well as the forecast direction of conditions at the reporting date. Entities may use various sources of data, both internal (entity-specific) data and external data that includes internal historical credit loss experience, internal ratings, credit loss experience of other entities for comparable financial instruments, and external ratings, reports and statistics. Entities that have no, or insufficient, sources of entity-specific data may use peer group experience for the comparable financial instrument (or groups of financial instruments). *[IFRS 9.B5.5.51]*.

Although the ECLs reflect an entity's own expectations of credit losses, an entity should also consider observable market information about the credit risk of particular financial instruments. *[IFRS 9.B5.5.54]*. Therefore, although entities with in-house economic teams will inevitably want to use their internal economic forecasts, while loss estimation models will be built based on historical data, they should not ignore external market data.

5.9.3 Information about past events, current conditions and forecasts of future economic conditions

One of the significant changes from the IAS 39 impairment requirements is that entities are not only required to use historical information (e.g. their credit loss experience) that is adjusted to reflect the effects of current conditions, but they are also required to consider how forecasts of future conditions would affect their historical data. A discussion of how this process needs to consider the existence of non-linearity in how expected losses will change with varying economic conditions and the need to assess multiple economic scenarios is included at 5.6.1 above. This section explores some of the other challenges in forecasting future conditions and the consequent ECLs.

The degree of judgement that is required to estimate ECLs depends on the availability of detailed information. An entity is not required to incorporate detailed forecasts of future conditions over the entire expected life of a financial instrument. The standard notes that as the forecast horizon increases, the availability of detailed information decreases and the degree of judgement required to estimate ECLs increases. Therefore, an entity is not required to perform a detailed estimate for periods that are far in the future and may extrapolate projections from available, more detailed information. *[IFRS 9.B5.5.50]*. Most banks apply a 3 to 5 year period over which macro-economic variables are considered to be capable of being forecast.

Beyond the horizon to which economic conditions can be reliably forecast, the application guidance suggests that entities may often be able to assume that economic conditions revert to their long-term average. There are at least two methods of how this might be done: either by reverting to the average immediately beyond the forecast horizon, or by adjusting the forecast data to the long-term average over a few years. The latter would, perhaps, more effectively make use of all reasonable and supportable information.

Historical information should be used as a starting point from which adjustments are made to estimate ECLs on the basis of reasonable and supportable information that incorporates both current and forward-looking information: *[IFRS 9.B5.5.52]*

- in most cases, adjustments would be needed to incorporate these effects that were not present in the past or to remove these effects that are not relevant for the future; and
- in some cases, unadjusted historical information may be the best estimate, depending on the nature of the historical information and when it was calculated, compared to circumstances at the reporting date and the characteristics of the financial instrument being considered. But it should not be assumed to be appropriate in all circumstances. *[IFRS 9.BC5.281]*.

Additionally, when considering whether historical credit losses should be adjusted, an entity needs to consider various items, including:

- whether the historical data captures ECLs that are through-the-cycle (i.e. estimates based on historical credit loss events and experience over the entire economic cycle) or point-in-time (i.e. estimates based on information, circumstances and events at the reporting date); and
- the period of time over which its historical data has been captured and the corresponding economic conditions represented in that history. The historical data period may reflect unusually benign or harsh conditions unless it is long enough. Meanwhile, products, customers and lending behaviours all change over time. When using historical credit loss experience, it is important that information about historical credit losses is applied to groups that are defined in a manner that is consistent with the groups for which the historical credit losses were observed.

The estimates of changes in ECLs should be directionally consistent with changes in related observable data from period to period (i.e. consistent with trends observed on payment status and macroeconomic data such as changes in unemployment rates, property prices, and commodity prices). Also, in order to reduce the differences between an entity's estimates and actual credit loss experience, the estimates of ECLs should be back-tested and re-calibrated, i.e. an entity should regularly review its inputs, assumptions, methodology and estimation techniques used as well as its groupings of sub-portfolios with shared credit risk characteristics (see 6.5 below).

Back-testing will be considerably more challenging for forecasts over several years than may be the case for just the 12-month risk of default, because detailed information may not be available over the forecast horizon and the degree of judgement increases as the forecast horizon increases. *[IFRS 9.B5.5.52, B5.5.53]*. Also, economic forecasts are usually wrong, as reality is much more complex than can ever be effectively modelled. Therefore, it is probably not a useful exercise to back-test macroeconomic assumptions against what actually transpires, but it is useful to back-test whether, for a given macroeconomic scenario, credit losses increased or decreased as expected.

In estimating ECLs, entities must consider how to bridge the gap between historical loss experience and current expectations. Estimating future economic conditions is only the first step of the exercise. Having decided what will happen to macroeconomic factors such as interest rates, house prices, unemployment and GDP growth, entities then need to decide how they translate into ECLs. This will need to reflect how such changes in factors affected defaults in the past. However, it is possible that the forecast combination of factors may have never been seen historically together.

We observe that banks are also trying to align IFRS 9 to their existing risk management practices. Many banks are making use of their regulatory capital calculation and stress testing frameworks for their IFRS 9 calculations. This manifests itself in many of the individual decisions that banks have made in implementing IFRS 9 (e.g. definitions of default and alignment to stress testing). It is likely that regulators and standard setters will concur with this approach. Basel PDs are used as a starting point and there is a need for a different calibration for IFRS 9, in order to transform a Basel PD into an unbiased point in time metric and include forward-looking expectations. Stress testing resources, previously working almost exclusively with capital issues, also play a role in calculating lifetime ECLs, although the scenarios modelled for IFRS 9 will not necessarily be stressed.

However, estimating losses (especially given the need to consider multiple scenarios) will still be challenging for many entities.

5.9.4 Events and new information obtained after ECLs have been calculated

In April 2015, the ITG (see 1.5 above) debated whether, and how, to incorporate events and new information about forecasts of future economic conditions that occur after the ECLs have been estimated. Due to operational practicality, entities may perform their ECL calculations before the reporting period end in order to publish their financial statements in a timely manner (e.g. forecasts of future economic conditions developed in November may be used as the basis for determining the ECLs at the reporting date as at 31 December). Further information may then become available after the period end. The ITG noted that:

- If new information becomes available before the reporting date, subject to materiality considerations in accordance with IAS 8, an entity is required to take into consideration this information in the assessment of significant increases in credit risk and the measurement of ECLs at the reporting date.

- IFRS 9 does not specifically require new information that becomes available after the reporting date to be reflected in the measurement of ECLs at the reporting date. If new information becomes available between the reporting date and the date the financial statements are authorised for issue, an entity needs to apply judgement, based on the specific facts and circumstances, to determine whether it is an adjusting or non-adjusting event in accordance with IAS 10 – *Events after the Reporting Period* (see Chapter 38). Similarly, materiality considerations apply in accordance with IAS 8.

- ECLs are similar in nature to the measurement of fair value at the reporting date, in that movements in fair value after the reporting date are generally not reflected in the measurement of fair value at the reporting date. *[IAS 10.11]*. For example, a change in interest rates or the outcome of a public vote after the reporting date would not normally be regarded as adjusting events for the ECL calculation.

- However, ECLs are a probability-weighted estimate of credit losses at the reporting date (see 5.6 above). Accordingly, the determination of ECLs should take into consideration relevant possible future scenarios based on a range of expectations at the reporting date, using the information available at that date. Hence, the probabilities attached to future expected movements in interest rates and expected outcomes of a future public vote based on information available at the reporting date would be reflected in the determination of ECLs at that date.

- Entities need robust processes and appropriate governance procedures for incorporating information, including forecasts of future economic conditions, to ensure transparent and consistent application of the impairment requirements in IFRS 9. This includes processes for updating ECLs for new information that becomes available after the initial modelling has taken place up until the reporting date.

5.9.5 Other issues concerning forward-looking information

At its meeting on 16 September 2015, the ITG examined two further questions about the use of forward-looking information:[22]

- the level at which forward-looking information should be incorporated – whether at the level of the entity or on a portfolio-by-portfolio basis; *[IFRS 9.B5.5.16, B5.5.51]* and
- how to determine what is reasonable and supportable forward-looking information and how to treat shock events with material, but uncertain, economic consequences, such as an independence referendum. The same considerations could apply to events such as natural disasters. *[IFRS 9.B5.5.49-54]*.

With respect to the first issue, the ITG members confirmed that forward-looking information should be relevant for the particular financial instrument or group of financial instruments to which the impairment requirements are being applied. Different factors may be relevant to different financial instruments and, accordingly, the relevance of particular items of information may vary between financial instruments, depending on the specific drivers of credit risk. This is highlighted in Illustrative Example 5 to IFRS 9 (see Example 51.17 below), in which expectations about future levels of unemployment in a specific industry and specific region are only relevant to a sub-portfolio of mortgage loans in which the borrowers work in that industry in that specific region. Conversely, it was also noted that if different financial instruments or portfolios being assessed share some similar risk characteristics, then relevant forward-looking information should be applied in a comparable and consistent manner to reflect those similar characteristics.

With respect to the second issue, the ITG members noted:

- There will be a spectrum of forward-looking information available, some of which will be reasonable and supportable and some of which will have little or no supportable basis. Determining the information that is relevant and reasonable and supportable and its impact on the assessment of significant increases in credit risk and measurement of ECLs can require a high level of judgement. In addition, it can be particularly challenging and difficult to determine the economic consequences (or 'second-order effects') of uncertain future outcomes. For example, while it may be possible to assess the likelihood of a particular event occurring, it may be more difficult to determine the effect of the event on the risk of a default occurring and/or on the credit loses that would be associated with that event using reasonable and supportable information.
- The objective of the IFRS 9 requirements for measuring ECLs is to reflect probability-weighted outcomes. Accordingly, information should not be excluded from the assessment of ECLs simply because:
    (a) the event has a low or remote likelihood of occurring; or
    (b) the effect of that event on the credit risk or the amount of ECLs is uncertain.
- An entity should make an effort in good faith to estimate the impact of uncertain future events, including second-order effects, on the credit risk of financial instruments and the measurement of ECLs. The estimate should be based on all reasonable and supportable information that is relevant and available without undue cost and effort. Furthermore:
    (a) estimates of ECLs should reflect an entity's own expectations of credit losses; however, entities should be able to explain how they have arrived at their estimate and how it is based on reasonable and supportable information;

(b) estimates of ECLs are, by their nature, approximations, which will be updated as more reasonable and supportable information becomes available over time; and

(c) information does not necessarily need to flow through a statistical model or credit-rating process in order to determine whether it is reasonable and supportable and relevant for a particular financial instrument or group of financial instruments.

- If an entity could determine that an uncertain event has an impact on the risk of a default occurring, then it should be possible to make an estimate of the impact on ECLs, despite the potentially large range of outcomes. However, in some exceptional cases, it was acknowledged that it may not be possible to estimate the impact on ECLs, despite an entity's best efforts.

- In this regard, the importance of disclosure of forward-looking information that is relevant, but that cannot be incorporated into the determination of significant increases in credit risk and/or the measurement of ECLs because of the lack of reasonable and supportable information was emphasised. Such disclosures should be consistent with the objective in IFRS 7, which is to enable users of the financial statements to understand the credit risk to which the entity is exposed.

- The need for good governance and processes in this area, because of the uncertainties and continually changing circumstances associated with forward-looking information. Furthermore, an entity should be able to explain what information it had considered and why that information had been included or excluded from the determination of ECLs.

This ITG discussion predated that in December 2015 on the use of probability-weighted multiple economic scenarios (see 5.6.1 above) and some of the points that were noted by the ITG probably need to be updated in the context of the later discussion. For instance, the ITG members noted that the impact of scenarios about some uncertain future events for which there is reasonable and supportable information, may need to be incorporated through the use of overlays to the 'base model' on a collective basis. In applying a multiple scenario approach, an entity will not use just one base model. Moreover, if the lender needs to estimate ECLs by considering multiple economic scenarios, it would follow that many shock events may already be included in that process (since some shock events might be assumed to occur every year), with the event and its various possible consequences occurring in some scenarios and not in others. There may still need to be cases when the effect of shock events is added through an additional 'overlay' to the modelled calculation of ECLs but, if so, as noted by the ITG members, care needs to be taken to avoid double counting the consequences of the event with what has already been assumed in the model.

Banks will also need to take account of guidance from their regulators (see 7.1 below).

The ITG members also noted that the effects of uncertain future events may need to be reflected in the assessment of whether there has been a significant increase in credit risk.

An example of an uncertain future event that arose after the ITG discussion is the coronavirus pandemic (see 7.8 below). On 27 March 2020, the IASB issued an educational document in which it acknowledged that it is likely to be difficult to incorporate the specific effects of the coronavirus pandemic and government support measures on a reasonable and supportable basis. However, changes in economic conditions should be reflected in macroeconomic scenarios applied by entities and in their weightings (see 5.6.1 and 5.6.2 above).[23] When it is not possible to reflect such information in models, the IASB expects post-model overlays or adjustments to be considered.

In addition, the IASB noted that although the circumstances of the coronavirus pandemic are difficult and create high levels of uncertainty, if ECL estimates are based on reasonable and supportable information and IFRS 9 is not applied mechanistically, useful information can be provided about ECLs. Indeed, in the stressed environment created by the pandemic, IFRS 9 and the associated disclosures can provide much needed transparency to users of financial statements (see 15 below and Chapter 54 at 5.3 and 9.1).

6 GENERAL APPROACH: DETERMINING SIGNIFICANT INCREASES IN CREDIT RISK

One of the major challenges in implementing the general approach in the IFRS 9 ECL model is to track and determine whether there have been significant increases in the credit risk of an entity's credit exposures since initial recognition.

The assessment of significant deterioration is key in establishing the point of switching between the requirement to measure an allowance based on 12-month ECLs and one that is based on lifetime ECLs. The assessment of whether there has been a significant increase in credit risk is therefore often referred to as 'the staging assessment'. The standard is prescriptive that an entity cannot align the timing of significant increases in credit risk and the recognition of lifetime ECLs with the time when a financial asset is regarded as credit-impaired or to an entity's internal definition of default. *[IFRS 9.B5.5.21]*. Financial assets should normally be assessed as having increased significantly in credit risk earlier than when they become credit-impaired (see 3.1 above) or default occurs. *[IFRS 9.B5.5.7]*.

As this area involves significant management judgement, entities are required to provide both qualitative and quantitative disclosures under IFRS 7 to explain the inputs, assumptions and estimation used to determine significant increases in credit risk of financial instruments and any changes in those assumptions and estimates (see 15 below and Chapter 54 at 5.3). *[IFRS 7.35F(a), 35G(a)(ii), 35G(c)]*.

At its meeting in December 2015, the ITG members reaffirmed that unless a more specific exception applies, IFRS 9 requires an entity to assess whether there has been a significant increase in credit risk for all financial instruments, including those with a maturity of 12 months or less. Consistently with this requirement, IFRS 7 requires corresponding disclosures that distinguish between financial instruments for which the loss allowance is equal to 12-month or lifetime ECLs. In addition, the ITG members noted that:

- the assessment of significant increases in credit risk is distinct from the measurement of ECLs as highlighted by paragraph 5.5.9 of IFRS 9. For example, a collateralised financial asset may have suffered a significant increase in credit risk, but owing to the value of the collateral there may not be an increase in the amount of ECLs even if measured on a lifetime rather than a 12-month basis;
- assessing changes in credit risk would be consistent with normal credit risk management practices; and
- the expected life of a financial instrument may change if it has suffered a significant increase in credit risk.

Finally, the ITG noted the importance of the IFRS 7 disclosure requirements and observed that disclosing information regarding the increase in credit risk since initial recognition provides users of financial statements with useful information regarding the changes in the risk of default occurring in respect of that financial instrument (see 15 below and Chapter 54 at 5.3).

6.1 Change in the risk of a default occurring

In order to make the assessment of whether there has been significant credit deterioration, an entity should consider reasonable and supportable information that is available without undue cost or effort and compare: [IFRS 9.5.5.9]

- the risk of a default occurring on the financial instrument over its life as at the reporting date; and
- the risk of a default occurring on the financial instrument over its life as at the date of initial recognition.

For loan commitments, an entity should consider changes in the risk of a default occurring on the potential loan to which a loan commitment relates.

For financial guarantee contracts, an entity should consider the changes in the risk that the specified debtor will default. [IFRS 9.B5.5.8].

An entity is required to assess significant increases in credit risk based on the change in the risk of a default occurring over the expected life of the financial instrument rather than the change in the amount of ECLs. [IFRS 9.5.5.9]. It should be noted that in a departure from the Basel regulatory wording and to avoid suggesting that statistical models are required (including the PD approach), the IASB changed the terminology from 'probability of a default occurring' to 'risk of a default occurring'. [IFRS 9.BC5.157].

In order to make the IFRS 9 impairment model operational, the IASB considered a number of alternative methods for determining significant increases in credit risk, but these were rejected for the following reasons:

- *Absolute level of credit risk*: The IASB considered whether an entity should be required to recognise lifetime ECLs on all financial instruments at, or above, a particular credit risk at the reporting date. Although this approach is operationally simpler to apply (because an entity is not required to track changes in credit risk), such an approach would provide very different information. It would not approximate the economic effect of changes in credit loss expectations subsequent to initial recognition. In addition, it may also result in overstatement or understatement of ECLs, depending on the threshold set for recognising lifetime ECLs. *[IFRS 9.BC5.160]*. However, the IASB noted that an absolute approach could be used for portfolios of financial instruments with similar credit risk at initial recognition, by determining the maximum initial credit risk accepted and then comparing the maximum initial credit risk to the credit risk at the reporting date (see 6.4.5 below). *[IFRS 9.BC5.161]*.
- *Change in the credit risk management objective*: The IASB also considered whether the assessment of significant deterioration should be based on whether an entity's credit risk management objective changes (e.g. monitoring of financial assets on an individual basis, or a change from collecting past due amounts to the recovery of these amounts). This approach is operationally relatively easy to apply. However, it is likely to have a similar effect to the IAS 39 incurred loss model and, hence, may result in a delayed recognition of ECLs. *[IFRS 9.BC5.162]*.
- *Credit underwriting policies*: The IASB further considered whether the change in the entity's credit underwriting limit for a particular class of financial instrument at the reporting date (i.e. an entity would not originate new loans on the same terms) should form the basis of assessing significant increase in credit risk. The IASB noted that this approach is similar to the absolute approach above. Moreover, the change in an entity's credit underwriting limits may be driven by other factors that are not related to a change in the credit risk of its borrowers (e.g. the entity may incorporate favourable terms to maintain a good business relationship or to increase lending), or are dependent on circumstances existing at the reporting date that are not relevant to the particular vintages of financial instruments. *[IFRS 9.BC5.163, BC5.164, BC5.165]*.

Similar to measuring ECLs, an entity may use different approaches when assessing significant increases in credit risk for different financial instruments. An approach that does not include PD as an explicit input can be consistent with the impairment requirements as long as the entity is able to separate the changes in the risk of a default occurring from changes in other drivers of ECLs (e.g. collateral) and considers the following when making the assessment: *[IFRS 9.B5.5.12]*

- the change in the risk of a default occurring since initial recognition;
- the expected life of the financial instrument; and
- reasonable and supportable information that is available, without undue cost or effort, that may affect credit risk.

In addition, because of the relationship between the expected life and the risk of default occurring, the change in credit risk cannot be assessed simply by comparing the change in the absolute risk of default over time, because the risk of default usually decreases as time passes if the credit risk is unchanged. *[IFRS 9.B5.5.11]*.

Entities that do not use probability of loss as an explicit input will have to use other criteria to identify a change in the risk of default occurring. These might include deterioration in a behavioural score, or other indicators, of a heightened risk of default. A collective approach may also be an appropriate supplement or substitute for an assessment at the individual instrument level (see 6.5 below).

A number of operational simplifications and presumptions are available to help entities make this assessment (as described further below).

6.1.1 Impact of collateral, credit enhancements and financial guarantee contracts

As already stressed, the staging assessment is based on the change in the lifetime risk of default, not the amount of ECLs. *[IFRS 9.5.5.9]*. Hence the allowance for a fully collateralised asset may need to be based on lifetime ECLs (because there has been a significant increase in the risk of default) even though no loss is expected to arise. In such instances, the fact that the asset is being measured using lifetime ECLs may have more significance for disclosure than for measurement (see 15 below).

The interaction between collateral, assessment of significant increases in credit risk and measurement of ECLs is illustrated in the following example from the standard. *[IFRS 9 Example 3 IE18-IE23]*.

Example 51.8: Highly collateralised financial asset

Company H owns real estate assets which are financed by a five-year loan from Bank Z with a loan-to-value (LTV) ratio of 50 per cent. The loan is secured by a first-ranking security over the real estate assets. At initial recognition of the loan, Bank Z does not consider the loan to be credit-impaired as defined in Appendix A of IFRS 9.

Subsequent to initial recognition, the revenues and operating profits of Company H have decreased because of an economic recession. Furthermore, expected increases in regulations have the potential to further negatively affect revenue and operating profit. These negative effects on Company H's operations could be significant and ongoing.

As a result of these recent events and expected adverse economic conditions, Company H's free cash flow is expected to be reduced to the point that the coverage of scheduled loan payments could become tight. Bank Z estimates that a further deterioration in cash flows may result in Company H missing a contractual payment on the loan and becoming past due.

Recent third party appraisals have indicated a decrease in the value of the real estate properties, resulting in a current LTV ratio of 70 per cent.

At the reporting date, the loan to Company H is not considered to have low credit risk in accordance with paragraph 5.5.10 of IFRS 9. Bank Z therefore needs to assess whether there has been a significant increase in credit risk since initial recognition in accordance with paragraph 5.5.3 of IFRS 9, irrespective of the value of the collateral it holds. It notes that the loan is subject to considerable credit risk at the reporting date because even a slight deterioration in cash flows could result in Company H missing a contractual payment on the loan. As a result, Bank Z determines that the credit risk (i.e. the risk of a default occurring) has increased significantly since initial recognition. Consequently, Bank Z recognises lifetime ECLs on the loan to Company H.

Although lifetime ECLs should be recognised, the measurement of the ECLs will reflect the recovery expected from the collateral (adjusting for the costs of obtaining and selling the collateral) on the property as required by paragraph B5.5.55 of IFRS 9 and may result in the ECLs on the loan being very small.

The ITG (see 1.5 above) discussed in April 2015 whether an entity should consider the ability to recover cash flows through a financial guarantee contract that is integral to the contract when assessing whether there has been a significant increase in the credit risk of the guaranteed debt instrument since initial recognition. IFRS 9 requires that measurement of the ECLs of the guaranteed debt instrument includes cash flows from the integral financial guarantee contract (see 5.8.1 above). *[IFRS 9.B5.5.55]*. However, some ITG members commented that IFRS 9 is clear that recoveries from integral financial guarantee contracts should be excluded from the assessment of significant increases in credit risk of the guaranteed debt instrument. *[IFRS 9.5.5.9]*. This is because the focus of the standard is about the risk of the borrower defaulting when making such an assessment, as highlighted in the examples in B5.5.17 of the standard. These examples clarify that information about a guarantee (or other credit enhancement) may be relevant to assessing changes in credit risk, but only to the extent that it affects the likelihood of the borrower defaulting on the instrument (see 6.2.1 below for the list of examples). *[IFRS 9.B5.5.17]*. Furthermore, excluding recoveries from the financial guarantee contract, when assessing significant increases in credit risk, would be consistent with the treatment of other forms of collateral.

While the value of collateral does not normally affect the assessment of significant increases in credit risk, if significant changes in the value of the collateral supporting the obligation are expected to reduce the borrower's economic incentive to make scheduled contractual payments, then this would have an effect on the risk of a default occurring. The standard provides an example where, if the value of collateral declines because house prices decline, borrowers in some jurisdictions have a greater incentive to default on their mortgages. *[IFRS 9.B5.5.17(j)]*.

The other examples provided by the standard of situations where the value of a credit enhancement could have an impact on the ability or economic incentive of the borrower to repay relate to guarantees or financial support provided by a shareholder, parent entity or other affiliate and to interests issued in securitisations:

- a significant change in the quality of the guarantee provided by a shareholder (or an individual's parent) if the shareholder (or parent) has an incentive and financial ability to prevent default by capital or cash infusion; *[IFRS 9.B5.5.17(k)]* and

- significant changes, such as reductions, in financial support from a parent entity or other affiliate or an actual or expected significant change in the quality of credit enhancement, that are expected to reduce the borrower's ability to make scheduled contractual payments. For example, such a situation could occur if a parent decides to no longer provide financial support to a subsidiary, which as a result would face bankruptcy or receivership. This could, in turn, result in that subsidiary prioritising payments for its operational needs (such as payroll and crucial suppliers) and assigning a lower priority to payments on its financial debt, resulting in an increase in the risk of default on those liabilities. Credit quality enhancements or support include the consideration of the financial condition of the guarantor and/or, for interests issued in securitisations, whether subordinated interests are expected to be capable of absorbing ECLs (for example, on the loans underlying the security). *[IFRS 9.B5.5.17(l)]*.

6.1.2 Contractually linked instruments (CLIs) and subordinated interests

The last example in the previous section, referring to the effect of subordinated interests in a securitisation deserves some comment. IFRS 9 sets out rules to determine whether an investment in a CLI such as a tranche of a securitisation, qualifies to be measured at amortised cost or at fair value through other comprehensive income (see Chapter 48 at 6.6). *[IFRS 9.4.1.2-4.1.2A, B4.1.20-B4.1.26]*. Some CLIs that are more senior tranches may pass the contractual cash flow characteristics test and consequently will be measured at amortised cost or fair value through other comprehensive income. However, the contractual cash flows of the individual tranches are normally based on a pre-defined waterfall structure (i.e. principal and interest are first paid on the most senior tranche and then successively paid on more junior tranches). To this extent, CLIs do not default. Meanwhile, Appendix A of IFRS 9 defines 'credit loss' as 'the difference between all contractual cash flows that are due to an entity in accordance with the contract and all the cash flows that the entity expects to receive (i.e. reflecting any cash shortfalls), discounted at the original effective interest rate (or credit-adjusted effective interest rate for purchased or originated credit-impaired financial assets)'. Under the contract, the issuer of a CLI only passes on cash flows that it actually receives, so the contractually defined cash flows under the waterfall structure are always equal to the cash flows that a holder expects to receive. Accordingly, one could argue that CLIs never give rise to a credit loss, and so would never be regarded as impaired.

However, consistent with recording these assets at amortised cost or FVOCI because they meet the solely payment of principal and interest (SPPI) criterion, the contractual terms of the CLI are *deemed* to give rise on specified dates to cash flows that are solely payments of principal and interest on the principal amount outstanding. Hence, we believe that for the purposes of the effective interest method and impairment requirements of IFRS 9, the lender needs to consider the deemed principal and interest payments as the contractual cash flows, instead of the contractual cash flows determined under the waterfall structure. Accordingly, any failure of the instrument to pay the investor the full amount deemed to be due must be treated as a default and an estimation of the amount of any losses that will be incurred must be reflected in the credit loss allowance.

It also follows that any changes in circumstances that may reduce the ability of the holder of a CLI to receive the principal and interest would need to be considered in assessing whether there has been a significant increase in credit risk. This would include whether more subordinated interests are expected to continue to be capable of absorbing expected credit losses on the underlying loans. Therefore, the investment should be measured based on lifetime ECLs if there are sufficient losses expected on the instruments underlying the securitisation such that they may not all be absorbed by subordinated interests in the structure, and so there is a significantly increased risk that the holder of a senior tranche will suffer a loss.

6.1.3 Determining change in the risk of a default under the loss rate approach

Under the loss rate approach, introduced at 5.4.2 above, an entity develops loss-rate statistics on the basis of the amount written off over the life of the financial assets rather than using separate PD and LGD statistics. Entities then must adjust these historical credit loss trends for current conditions and expectations about the future.

The standard is clear that although a loss rate approach may be applied, an entity needs to be able to separate the changes in the risk of a default occurring from changes in other drivers of ECLs for the purpose of assessing if there has been a significant increase in credit risk. *[IFRS 9.B5.5.12]*. Under the loss rate approach, the entity does not distinguish between a risk of a default occurring and the loss incurred following a default. This is not so much of an issue for measuring 12-month or lifetime ECLs. However, under the loss rate approach, an entity would not be able to implement the assessment of significant increases in credit risk that is based on the change in the risk of a default. Therefore, entities using the loss rate approach would need an overlay of measuring and forecasting the level of defaults, as illustrated in the extract of Example 9 from the Implementation Guidance (see Example 51.5 above). For entities that currently use only expected loss rates it may be easier to develop a PD approach than to use the method described in this example.

6.2 Factors or indicators of changes in credit risk

Similar to measuring ECLs (see 5 above), when assessing significant increases in credit risk, an entity should consider all reasonable and supportable information that is available without undue cost or effort (see 5.9.1 above) and that is relevant for an individual financial instrument, a portfolio, portions of a portfolio, and groups of portfolios. *[IFRS 9.B5.5.15, B5.5.16]*.

The IASB notes that it did not intend to prescribe a specific or mechanistic approach to assess changes in credit risk and that the appropriate approach will vary for different levels of sophistication of entities, the financial instrument and the availability of data. *[IFRS 9.BC5.157]*. It is important to stress that the assessment of significant increases in credit risk often involves a multifactor and holistic analysis. The importance and relevance of each specific factor will depend on the type of product, characteristics of the financial instruments and the borrower as well as the geographical region. *[IFRS 9.B5.5.16]*. The guidance in the standard is clear that in certain circumstances, qualitative and non-statistical quantitative information may be sufficient to determine that a financial instrument has met the criterion for the recognition of lifetime ECLs. That is, the information does not need to flow through a statistical model or credit ratings process in order to determine whether there has been a significant increase in the credit risk of the financial instrument. In other cases, the assessment may be based on quantitative information or a mixture of quantitative and qualitative information. *[IFRS 9.B5.5.18]*.

6.2.1 Examples of factors or indicators of changes in credit risk

The standard provides a non-exhaustive list of factors or indicators which an entity should consider when determining whether the recognition of lifetime ECLs is required. This list of factors or indicators is, as follows: *[IFRS 9.B5.5.17]*

- significant changes in internal price indicators of credit risk as a result of a change in credit risk since inception, including, but not limited to, the credit spread that would result if a particular financial instrument, or similar financial instrument with the same terms and the same counterparty were newly originated or issued at the reporting date;

- other changes in the rates or terms of an existing financial instrument that would be significantly different if the instrument was newly originated or issued at the reporting date (such as more stringent covenants, increased amounts of collateral or guarantees, or higher income coverage) because of changes in the credit risk of the financial instrument since initial recognition;

- significant changes in external market indicators of credit risk for a particular financial instrument or similar financial instruments with the same expected life. Changes in market indicators of credit risk include, but are not limited to: the credit spread; the credit default swap prices for the borrower; the length of time or the extent to which the fair value of a financial asset has been less than its amortised cost; and other market information related to the borrower (such as changes in the price of a borrower's debt and equity instruments). The IASB noted that market prices are an important source of information that should be considered in assessing whether credit risk has changed, although market prices themselves cannot solely determine whether significant deterioration has occurred because market prices are also affected by non-credit risk related factors such as changes in interest rates or liquidity risks; *[IFRS 9.BC5.123]*

- an actual or expected significant change in the financial instrument's external credit rating;

- an actual or expected internal credit rating downgrade for the borrower or decrease in behavioural scoring used to assess credit risk internally. Internal credit ratings and internal behavioural scoring are more reliable when they are mapped to external ratings or supported by default studies;

- existing or forecast adverse changes in business, financial or economic conditions that are expected to cause a significant change in the borrower's ability to meet its debt obligations, such as an actual or expected increase in interest rates or an actual or expected significant increase in unemployment rates;

- an actual or expected significant change in the operating results of the borrower. Examples include actual or expected declining revenues or margins, increasing operating risks, working capital deficiencies, decreasing asset quality, increased balance sheet leverage, liquidity, management problems or changes in the scope of business or organisational structure (such as the discontinuance of a segment of the business) that result in a significant change in the borrower's ability to meet its debt obligations;

- significant increases in credit risk on other financial instruments of the same borrower;

- an actual or expected significant adverse change in the regulatory, economic, or technological environment of the borrower that results in a significant change in

the borrower's ability to meet its debt obligations, such as a decline in the demand for the borrower's sales product because of a shift in technology;
- significant changes in the value of the collateral supporting the obligation or in the quality of third-party guarantees or credit enhancements, which are expected to reduce the borrower's economic incentive to make scheduled contractual payments or to otherwise have an effect on the risk of a default occurring. For example, if the value of collateral declines because house prices decline, borrowers in some jurisdictions have a greater incentive to default on their mortgages;
- a significant change in the quality of the guarantee provided by a shareholder (or an individual's parents) if the shareholder (or parents) have an incentive and financial ability to prevent default by capital or cash infusion;
- significant changes, such as reductions, in financial support from a parent entity or other affiliate or an actual or expected significant change in the quality of credit enhancement, that are expected to reduce the borrower's economic incentive to make scheduled contractual payments. For example, such a situation could occur if a parent decides to no longer provide financial support to a subsidiary, which as a result would face bankruptcy or receivership. This could in turn result in that subsidiary prioritising payments for its operational needs (such as payroll and crucial suppliers) and assigning a lower priority to payments on its financial debt, resulting in an increase in the risk of default on those liabilities. Credit quality enhancements or support include the consideration of the financial condition of the guarantor and/or, for interests issued in securitisations, whether subordinated interests are expected to be capable of absorbing ECLs (for example, on the loans underlying the security);
- expected changes in the loan documentation (i.e. changes in contract terms) including an expected breach of contract that may lead to covenant waivers or amendments, interest payment holidays, interest rate step-ups, requiring additional collateral or guarantees, or other changes to the contractual framework of the instrument;
- significant changes in the expected performance and behaviour of the borrower, including changes in the payment status of borrowers in the group (for example, an increase in the expected number or extent of delayed contractual payments or significant increases in the expected number of credit card borrowers who are expected to approach or exceed their credit limit or who are expected to be paying the minimum monthly amount);
- changes in the entity's credit management approach in relation to the financial instrument, i.e. based on emerging indicators of changes in the credit risk of the financial instrument, the entity's credit risk management practice is expected to become more active or to be focused on managing the instrument, including the instrument becoming more closely monitored or controlled, or the entity specifically intervening with the borrower; and
- past due information, including the more than 30 days past due rebuttable presumption (see 6.2.2 below).

We make the following observations:
- If entities make the staging assessment using their credit risk management systems, they will need to consider whether their systems take into account the various indicators listed above.
- Many financial institutions should have readily available information about the pricing and terms of various types of loans issued to a specific customer (e.g. overdraft, credit cards and mortgage loans) in their credit risk management systems and processes. However, in practice, it would often be difficult to use such information because changes in pricing and terms on the origination of a similar financial instrument at the reporting date may not be so obviously related to a change in credit risk as other, more commercial, factors come into play (e.g. different risk appetites, change in management approach and underwriting standards). It may be challenging to link the two sets of information (i.e. pricing processes on the one hand and credit risk management on the other).
- Some collateralised loans are subject to cash variation margining requirements, which means that the trigger for default is normally the inability to pay a margin call. Therefore, in such circumstances the PD may be driven by the value of the collateral and changes in collateral values may need to be reflected in the staging assessment.
- Some of the factors or indicators are only relevant for the assessment of significant deterioration on an individual basis and not on a portfolio basis. For example, change in external market indicators of credit risk, including the credit spread, the credit default swap prices of the borrower and the extent of decline in fair value. However, it is worth noting that external market information that is available for a quoted instrument may be useful to help assess another instrument that is not quoted but which is issued by the same debtor or one who operates in the same sector.
- It is important to stress that the approach required by the standard is more holistic and qualitative than is necessarily captured by external credit ratings, which are adjusted for discrete events and may not reflect gradual degradations in credit quality. External credit ratings should not, therefore, be used on their own but only in conjunction with other qualitative information. Furthermore, although ratings are forward-looking, it is sometimes suggested that changes in credit ratings may not be reflected in a timely matter. Therefore, entities may have to take account of expected change in ratings in assessing whether exposures are low risk. (Example 51.13 below illustrates that there could be significant differences between using agencies' credit ratings or using market data such as CDS spreads). The same point can of course be made about the use of internal credit ratings, especially if they are only reassessed on an annual basis. At the September 2015 meeting, the ITG observed that credit grading systems were not designed with the requirements of IFRS 9 in mind, and thus it should not be assumed that they will always be an appropriate means of identifying significant increases in credit risk. The appropriateness of using internal credit grading systems as a means of assessing changes in credit risk since initial recognition depends on whether the credit grades are reviewed with sufficient frequency, include all reasonable and supportable information and reflect the risk of default over the expected life of the financial instrument.

- As credit grading systems vary, care needs to be taken when referring to movements in credit grades and how this reflects an increased risk of default occurring. In addition, the assessment of whether a change in credit risk grade represents a significant increase in credit risk in accordance with IFRS 9 depends on the initial credit risk of the financial instrument being assessed. Moreover, the relationship between credit grades and changes in the risk of default occurring differs between credit grading systems. For instance, in some cases the changes in the risk of a default occurring may increase exponentially between grades whereas in others it may not.
- Also, some of the above factors or indicators are very forward-looking, such as forecasts of adverse changes in business, financial or economic conditions that are expected to result in significant future financial difficulty of the borrower in repaying its debt. In practice, the analysis may have to be performed at the level of a portfolio rather than at an individual level when forward-looking information is not available at the individual level.

With IFRS 9 not being prescriptive, we observe differences in how banks have implemented the assessment of significant increase in credit risk. These differences reflect various schools of thought along with differences in credit processes, business model, sophistication, use of advanced models for regulatory capital purposes, availability of data (e.g. historic data at origination) and consistency of definitions across businesses or multiple systems. As use of models and availability of data can vary within a bank, a number of approaches may even be adopted within a single institution.

In general, entities use a combination of quantitative and qualitative drivers to assess significant increases in credit risk. Some of these are regarded as primary, others as secondary and some as backstops. The primary driver is usually expected to be the most forward-looking indicator and is generally based on a relative measure. The most common primary drivers used by the larger banks are:

- changes in the lifetime risk of a default occurring, guided by scores and ratings;
- changes in the lifetime or 12-month probability of default; or
- changes in ratings or credit scores for retail exposures and ratings for corporate exposures.

Forbearance and watchlists are often used as secondary drivers and delinquency, usually 30 days past due, as a backstop (see 6.2.2 below).

6.2.2 Past due status and more than 30 days past due rebuttable presumption

The IASB is concerned that past due information is a lagging indicator. Typically, credit risk increases significantly before a financial instrument becomes past due or other lagging borrower-specific factors (for example, a modification or restructuring) are observed. Consequently, when reasonable and supportable information that is more forward-looking than past due information is available without undue cost or effort, it must be used to assess changes in credit risk and an entity cannot rely solely on past due information. *[IFRS 9.5.5.11, B5.5.2]*. However, the IASB acknowledged that many entities manage credit risk on the basis of information about past due status and have a limited ability to assess credit risk on an instrument-by-instrument basis in more detail on a timely basis. *[IFRS 9.BC5.192]*. Therefore, if more forward-looking information (either on an individual or collective basis) is not available without undue cost or effort, an entity may use past due information to assess changes in credit risks. *[IFRS 9.5.5.11]*. However, contract assets by definition, cannot be past due, therefore, entities cannot rely on delinquency for staging of such assets.

Whether the entity uses only past due information or also more forward-looking information (e.g. macroeconomic indicators), there is a rebuttable presumption that the credit risk on a financial asset has increased significantly since initial recognition when contractual payments are more than 30 days past due. However, the standard seems to make it clear that it is not possible to rebut the 30 days past due presumption just because of a favourable economic outlook. *[IFRS 9.5.5.11, B5.5.19]*. The IASB decided that this rebuttable presumption was required to ensure that application of the assessment of the increase in credit risk does not result in a reversion to an incurred loss notion. *[IFRS 9.BC5.190]*.

Moreover, as already stressed earlier, the standard is clear that an entity cannot align the definition and criteria used to identify significant increases in credit risk (and the resulting recognition of lifetime ECLs) to when a financial asset is regarded as credit-impaired or to an entity's internal definition of default. *[IFRS 9.B5.5.21]*. An entity should normally identify significant increases in credit risk and recognise lifetime ECLs before default occurs or the financial asset becomes credit-impaired, either on an individual or collective basis (see 6.5 below).

An entity can rebut the 30 days past due presumption if it has reasonable and supportable information that is available without undue cost or effort, that demonstrates that credit risk has not increased significantly even though contractual payments are more than 30 days past due. *[IFRS 9.5.5.11]*. Such evidence may include, for example, knowledge that a missed non-payment is because of administrative oversight rather than financial difficulty of the borrower, or historical information that suggests significant increases in credit risks only occur when payments are more than 60 days past due. *[IFRS 9.B5.5.20]*. Also, in the context of the coronavirus pandemic, the 30 days past due backstop assumption may need to be rebutted in circumstances where the borrowers are experiencing temporary liquidity issues and whose long-term credit risk is unlikely to be significant affected by the pandemic (see 7.8 below).

6.2.3 Concessions granted to a wide range of customers

In the context of the coronavirus pandemic, one of the accounting issues has been whether concessions made by lenders, such as changes in payment terms and the granting of payment holidays, should result in loans being move from stage 1 to stage 2.

The IASB noted in their educational material published on 27 March 2020 that IFRS 9 requires the application of judgement and both requires and allows entities to adjust their approach to determining ECLs in different circumstances (see 7.8.2 below).[24] A number of assumptions and linkages underlying the way ECLs have been implemented to date may no longer hold in the environment affected by the coronavirus pandemic. Entities should not continue to apply their existing ECL methodology mechanically. For example, the extension of payment holidays to all borrowers in particular classes of financial instruments should not automatically result in all those instruments being considered to have suffered a significant increase in credit risk. This would be the case even if a moratorium results in a loss for the lender (e.g. if interest payments are reduced or waived), if it is provided irrespective of the borrowers' individual circumstances and the extension of payment holidays are assessed to be modifications rather than derecognition of the financial instruments (see 8 below).

In other situations, if relief measures are available only to those who meet certain criteria, entities need to carefully assess whether such criteria themselves might indicate a significant increase in credit risk for the affected borrowers. For instance, a significant increase in credit risk is more likely to have occurred if a borrower applies for a relief measure which is available only to corporates which have suspended operations or individuals who have lost employment. Another example is if the relief, such as a deferral of loan payments, is offered to all participants in certain industries. This circumstance may indicate that borrowers in that industry are exposed to a higher risk of business failure and, thus, a higher probability of default as a class. In combination with other reasonable and supportable information, this is more likely to result in the classification of the related loans and other exposures in this portfolio, or a portion of them, into stage 2. The assessment of whether there has been a significant increase in credit risk should be made irrespective of the fact that a concession is imposed by laws or regulations. Entities are also expected to exercise judgement, in light of all facts and circumstances, including the effect of government support, to determine if the respective loans are credit impaired and should therefore be classified as stage 3.

Regulators stressed, in the context of the coronavirus pandemic, the need when assessing borrowers to differentiate a temporary liquidity need from a significant increase in credit risk. This means that lenders should distinguish between obligors whose long-term credit risk is unlikely to be significantly affected by the pandemic from those who may be more permanently impacted.

Entities whose models include payment holidays or waiver of a covenant breach as automatic significant increase in credit risk triggers may need to include overlays to unwind the effects if they determine that the significant increase in credit risk trigger is not warranted. For retail loans, data will often not be available to determine whether a significant increase in credit risk has occurred for individual borrowers. For wholesale exposures, more information is generally available on individual obligors, although the significant increase in credit risk assessment will still be difficult. A lender may consider that borrowers in certain industries (e.g. airlines, tourism and hospitality) are exposed to a higher risk of business failure and, thus, an increased PD.

When it is not practical to determine significant increase in credit risk on an individual basis, a collective approach to staging should be considered (see 6.5 below). This will also be challenging. A possible method could be to transfer to stage 2 a portion of those customers who have been given a payment holiday or a waiver of a covenant breach, whose PD was already close to the level that would trigger a significant increase in credit risk. Any approach will require considerable judgement.

Where additional rounds of relief measures are extended to existing borrowers, the same considerations which were applicable to assessing the initial relief are also applicable in determining whether the additional relief constitutes a significant increase in credit risk. If the extension of the relief measures is offered only to selected borrowers (e.g. upon individual requests), it may be harder to conclude that a significant increase in credit risk has not occurred, as the need for additional relief may be in response to further deterioration in the borrower's financial position.

6.2.4 Illustrative examples of factors or indicators when assessing significant increases in credit risk

The consideration of various factors or indicators when assessing significant increases in credit risk since initial recognition is illustrated in Examples 51.9 and 51.10, which are based on Examples 1 and 2 in the Implementation Guidance for the standard.

[IFRS 9 Example 1 IE7-11, Example 2 IE12-17].

Example 51.9: Significant increase in credit risk

Company Y has a funding structure that includes a senior secured loan facility with different tranches. The security on the loan affects the loss that would be realised if a default occurs, but does not affect the risk of a default occurring, so it is not considered when determining whether there has been a significant increase in credit risk since initial recognition as required by paragraph 5.5.3 of IFRS 9. Bank X provides a tranche of that loan facility to Company Y. At the time of origination of the loan by Bank X, although Company Y's leverage was relatively high compared with other issuers with similar credit risk, it was expected that Company Y would be able to meet the covenants for the life of the instrument. In addition, the generation of revenue and cash flow was expected to be stable in Company Y's industry over the term of the senior facility. However, there was some business risk related to the ability to grow gross margins within its existing businesses.

At initial recognition, because of the considerations outlined above, Bank X considers that despite the level of credit risk at initial recognition, the loan is not an originated credit-impaired loan because it does not meet the definition of a credit-impaired financial asset in Appendix A of IFRS 9.

Subsequent to initial recognition, macroeconomic changes have had a negative effect on total sales volume and Company Y has underperformed on its business plan for revenue generation and net cash flow generation. Although spending on inventory has increased, anticipated sales have not materialised. To increase liquidity, Company Y has drawn down more on a separate revolving credit facility, thereby increasing its leverage ratio. Consequently, Company Y is now close to breaching its covenants on the senior secured loan facility with Bank X.

Bank X makes an overall assessment of the credit risk on the loan to Company Y at the reporting date, by taking into consideration all reasonable and supportable information that is available without undue cost or effort and that is relevant for assessing the extent of the increase in credit risk since initial recognition. This may include factors such as:

(a) Bank X's expectation that the deterioration in the macroeconomic environment may continue in the near future, which is expected to have a further negative impact on Company Y's ability to generate cash flows and to de-leverage.

(b) Company Y is closer to breaching its covenants, which may result in a need to restructure the loan or reset the covenants.

(c) Bank X's assessment that the trading prices for Company Y's bonds have decreased and that the credit margin on newly originated loans have increased reflecting the increase in credit risk, and that these changes are not explained by changes in the market environment (for example, benchmark interest rates have remained unchanged). A further comparison with the pricing of Company Y's peers shows that reductions in the price of Company Y's bonds and increases in credit margin on its loans have probably been caused by company-specific factors.

(d) Bank X has reassessed its internal risk grading of the loan on the basis of the information that it has available to reflect the increase in credit risk.

Bank X determines that there has been a significant increase in credit risk since initial recognition of the loan in accordance with paragraph 5.5.3 of IFRS 9. Consequently, Bank X recognises lifetime ECLs on its senior secured loan to Company Y. Even if Bank X has not yet changed the internal risk grading of the loan it could still reach this conclusion – the absence or presence of a change in risk grading in itself is not determinative of whether credit risk has increased significantly since initial recognition.

Example 51.10: No significant increase in credit risk

Company C is the holding company of a group that operates in a cyclical production industry. Bank B provided a loan to Company C. At that time, the prospects for the industry were positive, because of expectations of further increases in global demand. However, input prices were volatile and given the point in the cycle, a potential decrease in sales was anticipated.

In addition, in the past Company C has been focused on external growth, acquiring majority stakes in companies in related sectors. As a result, the group structure is complex and has been subject to change, making it difficult for investors to analyse the expected performance of the group and to forecast the cash that will be available at the holding company level. Even though leverage is at a level that is considered acceptable by Company C's creditors at the time that Bank B originates the loan, its creditors are concerned about Company C's ability to refinance its debt because of the short remaining life until the maturity of the current financing. There is also concern about Company C's ability to continue to service interest using the dividends it receives from its operating subsidiaries.

At the time of the origination of the loan by Bank B, Company C's leverage was in line with that of other customers with similar credit risk and based on projections over the expected life of the loan, the available capacity (i.e. headroom) on its coverage ratios before triggering a default event, was high. Bank B applies its own internal rating methods to determine credit risk and allocates a specific internal rating score to its loans. Bank B's internal rating categories are based on historical, current and forward-looking information and reflect the credit risk for the tenor of the loans. On initial recognition, Bank B determines that the loan is subject to considerable credit risk, has speculative elements and that the uncertainties affecting Company C, including the group's uncertain prospects for cash generation, could lead to default. However, Bank B does not consider the loan to be originated credit-impaired.

Subsequent to initial recognition, Company C has announced that three of its five key subsidiaries had a significant reduction in sales volume because of deteriorated market conditions but sales volumes are expected to improve in line with the anticipated cycle for the industry in the following months. The sales of the other two subsidiaries were stable. Company C has also announced a corporate restructure to streamline its operating subsidiaries. This restructuring will increase the flexibility to refinance existing debt and the ability of the operating subsidiaries to pay dividends to Company C.

Despite the expected continuing deterioration in market conditions, Bank B determines, in accordance with paragraph 5.5.3 of IFRS 9, that there has not been a significant increase in the credit risk on the loan to Company C since initial recognition. This is demonstrated by factors that include:

(a) Although current sale volumes have fallen, this was as anticipated by Bank B at initial recognition. Furthermore, sales volumes are expected to improve, in the following months.

(b) Given the increased flexibility to refinance the existing debt at the operating subsidiary level and the increased availability of dividends to Company C, Bank B views the corporate restructure as being credit enhancing. This is despite some continued concern about the ability to refinance the existing debt at the holding company level.

(c) Bank B's credit risk department, which monitors Company C, has determined that the latest developments are not significant enough to justify a change in its internal credit risk rating.

As a consequence, Bank B does not recognise a loss allowance at an amount equal to lifetime ECLs on the loan. However, it updates its measurement of the 12-month ECLs for the increased risk of a default occurring in the next 12 months and for current expectations of the credit losses that would arise if a default were to occur.

A numerical illustration of how a significant increase in credit risk might be assessed is shown in Example 51.11 below.

Example 51.11: Assessment of a significant increase in credit risk based on a PD approach

This example is based on the same loan presented in Example 51.3 above.

On 31 December 2020, Bank A originates a 10-year bullet loan with a gross carrying amount of $1,000,000, interest being due at the end of each year. Based on statistical and qualitative information – including forward-looking, Bank A has estimated a **BBB rating** for the loan.

Based on this rating, Bank A has computed a PD term structure at origination. Bank A's PD term structure is estimated with the annual PD expected for each future period. The lifetime PD is the product of each marginal PD during the considered period:

$$\text{lifetime PD}_k = 1 - \prod_{k=1}^{n} (1 - \text{marginal PD}_i)$$

Finally, based on the marginal PD computed for each future period, Bank A is able to compute the forward lifetime PD as follows:

Year	Cumulative PD at origination	Marginal 12-month PD	Remaining lifetime PD	Remaining annualised lifetime PD
2020				
2021	0.17%	0.17%	4.50%	0.46%
2022	0.49%	0.32%	4.34%	0.49%
2023	0.86%	0.37%	4.03%	0.51%
2024	1.38%	0.53%	3.67%	0.53%
2025	1.84%	0.47%	3.16%	0.53%
2026	2.37%	0.54%	2.71%	0.55%
2027	2.85%	0.49%	2.18%	0.55%
2028	3.30%	0.46%	1.70%	0.57%
2029	3.84%	0.56%	1.24%	0.62%
2030	4.50%	0.69%	0.69%	0.69%

For the first year, the remaining lifetime PD is the cumulative PD at origination. Then, after a year, it starts decreasing, considering that the remaining period is shorter. After 2 years it is 4.03% and after 3 years it is only 3.67%. At the end of the loan, the remaining lifetime PD ends up at 0%.

In common with many institutions, Bank A chooses to compare an annualised lifetime PD instead of a cumulative PD. This has the advantage that business lines and risk analysts can easily map an annualised PD onto a rating scale. It also enables an absolute change in annualised lifetime PD, e.g. 20bp, to be set as a 'filter', to exclude small changes in lifetime PD from being assessed as significant that are considered to be 'noise'. For this purpose, Bank A calculates an annualised PD, using the residual cumulative curve. The annualised lifetime PD is calculated as follows:

$$\text{annualised lifetime PD}_k = 1 - (1 - \text{lifetime PD}_k)^{1/t}$$

when t = horizon of the lifetime PD expressed in years

2022: no significant increase in credit risk: Stage 1

On 31 December 2022 – 2 years after origination, Bank A updates the rating of its obligor. The rating is now BB+. A new PD term structure is estimated based on this information:

Year	Cumulative lifetime PD
2023	0.67%
2024	1.53%
2025	3.70%
2026	5.58%
2027	5.89%
2028	6.51%
2029	7.45%
2030	8.70%
Remaining annualised lifetime PD	1.13%
Forecast at origination	0.51%
Increase (multiple)	2.20

In this example, Bank A uses a significant increase in credit risk threshold of a 2.5 multiple of PD. For simplicity we ignore any qualitative or other indicators that a bank might use to make this assessment.

Comparing the remaining annualised PD estimated at origination (0.51%) with the remaining annualised PD at the reporting date (1.13%), the increase is still only ×2.2. We note that, had Bank A used a cumulative lifetime PD approach, it would compare 8.70% to 4.03%, which would also be a multiple of 2.2. The significant deterioration threshold set by Bank A is not met and therefore the loan remains in stage 1.

2023: significant increase in credit risk: stage 2

On 31 December 2023 – 3 years after origination, Bank A updates the rating of its obligor. Its rating is now BB–. Then Bank A updates its historical information for current economic conditions as well as reasonable and supportable forecasts of future economic conditions.

Year	Cumulative lifetime PD
2024	1.40%
2025	3.87%
2026	8.82%
2027	12.84%
2028	16.04%
2029	18.98%
2030	21.60%
Remaining annualised lifetime PD	3.42%
Forecast at origination	0.53%
Increase (multiple)	6.41

As before, Bank A compares the remaining annualised PD estimated at origination (0.53%) with the remaining annualised PD at the reporting date (3.42%), an increase of 6.45 times the original PD. Had Bank A used a cumulative lifetime PD approach the comparison would be of 21.6% to 3.67%, a 6.41 fold increase. This time, the threshold of significant deterioration is met and the loan is moved to stage 2.

6.2.5 Use of behavioural factors

At its meeting on 16 September 2015, the ITG (see 1.5 above) discussed whether the following behavioural indicators of credit risk could be used, on their own, as a proxy to determine if there has been a significant increase in credit risk:

- where a customer has made only the minimum monthly repayment for a specified number of months;
- where a customer has failed to make a payment on a loan with a different lender; or
- where a customer has failed to make a specified number of minimum monthly repayments.

The ITG members noted that:

- When assessing whether there has been a significant increase in credit risk, entities are required to consider a range of indicators rather than focussing on only one. Furthermore, while behavioural indicators have a role to play, the above behavioural indicators are often lagging indicators of increases in credit risk. Consequently, they should be considered in conjunction with other, more forward-looking information. In this regard, an entity must consider how to source and incorporate forward-looking information into the assessment of significant increases in credit risk and may need to do this on a collective basis if forward-looking information is not available at an individual financial instrument level.
- When considering the use of behavioural indicators, an entity should:
  (a) focus on identifying pre-delinquency behavioural indicators of increases in credit risk, e.g. increased utilisation rates or increased cash drawings on specific products;
  (b) only use indicators that are relevant to the risk of default occurring;
  (c) establish a link between the behavioural indicators of credit risk and changes in the risk of default occurring since initial recognition;
  (d) be mindful that while behavioural indicators are often predictive of defaults in the short term, they are often less predictive of defaults in the longer term, and, hence, might be lagging. Consequently, they may not, on their own, signal significant increases in credit risk in a timely manner; and
  (e) consider whether the use of behavioural indicators is appropriate for the type of product being assessed, e.g. if a loan has only back-ended payments, behavioural indicators based on timeliness of payment will not be appropriate.
- An entity is required to consider all information available without undue cost and effort and it should not be limited by the information that is available internally. For example, an entity should consider using third-party information from sources such as credit bureaus. However, information that is available to entities will vary across jurisdictions.

- When making the assessment of significant increases in credit risk, an entity should consider the possibility of segmenting the portfolio into groups of financial instruments with shared credit characteristics in such a way that similar indicators of credit risk could be used to identify increases in credit risk for specific sub-portfolios.
- It would not be appropriate to use the above behavioural indicators for the purposes of identifying low credit risk assets in accordance with paragraph 5.5.10 of IFRS 9 (see 6.4.1 below), on the basis that such measures would not constitute a globally accepted definition of low credit risk as required by IFRS 9.

Other behavioural indicators, beyond those mentioned above, including items such as the level of cash advances, changes in expected payment patterns (e.g. moving from full payment to something less than full payment), and higher-than-expected utilisation of the facility, were raised at the meeting. Individually, these kinds of behaviours may not be determinative of a significant increase in credit risk but, when observed together, they may prove to be more indicative. By combining these indicators, an entity has the potential to transfer assets between stage 1 and stage 2 more meaningfully.

We also note that that one of the challenges with using behavioural information is that it depends on the starting point. That is, if the obligor's risk of default initially is consistent with a super-prime rating, the kind of deteriorating behaviour noted above would likely signal a significant shift. However, if the obligor originally had a sub-prime rating, then such behaviour might not indicate a significant increase in risk.

As noted by the ITG, while indicators that are more lagging may show a greater correlation with subsequent default, they are also likely to be less forward-looking. Although a probability of default approach may seem more sophisticated and forward-looking, it is still generally fed by behavioural information, even if it is combined, segmented and modelled in a more sophisticated way. If the only borrower-specific information is his behaviour, a forward-looking portfolio overlay will generally be required, whether a PD or a behavioural approach is used.

6.3 What is significant?

The assessment of whether credit risk has significantly increased depends, critically, on an interpretation of the word 'significant'. Some constituents who commented on the 2013 Exposure Draft requested the IASB to quantify the term significant, however, the IASB decided not to do so, for the following reasons: *[IFRS 9.BC5.171, BC5.172]*

- specifying a fixed percentage change in the risk of default would require all entities to use the risk of default approach. As not all entities (apart from regulated financial institutions) use PDs as an explicit input, this would have increased the costs and effort for those entities that do not use such an approach; and
- defining the amount of change in the risk of a default occurring would be arbitrary and this would depend on the type of products, maturities and initial credit risk.

The standard emphasises that the determination of the significance of the change in the risk of a default occurring depends on:

- the original credit risk at initial recognition: the same absolute change in PD for a financial instrument with a lower initial credit risk will be more significant than those with a higher initial credit risk (see 6.1 above and Example 51.15 below); *[IFRS 9.B5.5.9]* and

- the expected life or term structure: the risk of a default occurring for financial instruments with similar credit risk increases the longer the expected life of the financial instruments. Due to the relationship between the expected life and the risk of a default occurring, an entity cannot simply compare the absolute risk of a default occurring over time. For example, if the risk of a default occurring for a financial instrument with an expected life of 10 years at initial recognition is the same after five years, then this indicates that the credit risk has increased. The standard also states that, for financial instruments that have significant payment obligations close to the maturity of the financial instrument (e.g. those where the principal is only repaid at maturity), the risk of a default occurring may not necessarily decrease as time passes. In such cases, an entity needs to consider other qualitative factors. We note, however, that while the risk of default may decrease less quickly for an instrument with payment obligations throughout its contractual life, normally, the risk of default will still decrease as maturity approaches. *[IFRS 9.B5.5.10, B5.5.11]*.

Some of these challenges are illustrated by examining the historical levels of default associated with the credit ratings of agencies, such as Standard & Poor's.

- It is apparent that the PDs increase at a geometrical, rather than an arithmetic, rate as the credit ratings decline. Hence, the absolute increase in the PD between two relatively low risk credit ratings is considerably less than between two relatively higher risk ratings.

- The relative increase in PD between each of these ratings might be considered significant, since most involve a doubling or trebling of the PD. In contrast, because credit rating is an art rather than a science, the smaller changes in credit risk associated with the plus or minus notches in the grading system are less likely to be viewed as significant.

- In addition, as the time horizon increases, the PDs also increase across all credit ratings (i.e. the PD increases with a longer maturity).

The majority of credit exposures that are assessed for significant credit deterioration will not have been rated by a credit rating agency. However, the same logic will apply when entities have developed their own PD models and are able to classify their exposure by PD levels.

The determination of what is significant will, for the larger banks, be influenced by the guidance issued by banking regulators (see 7.1 below).

Given the exponential shape of the PD curve relative to ratings, some banks are considering that a bigger downgrade, as measured by the number of grades, would be significant for a higher quality loan than for one with a lower quality. The extent to which this is appropriate will depend on how the different grades map to PDs. Also, the calibration of a significant deterioration has to take into account the fact that PD multiples for very good ratings only represent very small movements in absolute risk, whereas the same multiple applied to bad ratings can represent a significant change in the absolute amount of PD.

Banks have varying views on how much of an increase in PD is significant. Also, while they may view a quantitative threshold, such as a doubling of PD, to be significant, many also require a minimum absolute PD increase, such as 50 basis points so as to avoid very high quality assets moving to stage 2 as a result of a very small change and to filter out 'noise'.

Banks have also introduced various metrics to assess the effect of different approaches to assess significant increase in credit risk and for management information. Examples include the volume of stage 2 assets compared to the total portfolio and compared to 12-months of lifetime expected losses, the volume of movement (back and forth) between stages 1 and 2, the amount of assets that jump directly from stage 1 to stage 3, the proportion of assets in stage 3 which went via stage 2, and how long assets were in stage 2 before moving to stage 3.

6.4 Operational simplifications

When assessing significant increases in credit risk, there are a number of operational simplifications available. These are discussed below.

6.4.1 Low credit risk operational simplification

The standard contains an important simplification that, if a financial instrument has a low credit risk, then an entity is allowed to assume at the reporting date that no significant increases in credit risk have occurred. The low credit risk concept was intended, by the IASB, to provide relief for entities from tracking changes in the credit risk of high-quality financial instruments. This simplification is optional and the low credit risk simplification can be elected on an instrument-by-instrument basis. *[IFRS 9.BC5.184].*

This is a change from the 2013 Exposure Draft, in which a low risk exposure was deemed not to have suffered significant deterioration in credit risk. *[IFRS 9.BC5.181, BC5.182, BC5.183].* The amendment to make the simplification optional was made in response to requests from constituents, including regulators. The Basel Committee guidance (see 7.1 below) considers the use of the low credit risk simplification a low-quality implementation of the ECL model and that the use of this exemption should be limited, except for holdings in securities.

For low risk instruments for which the simplification is used, the entity would recognise an allowance based on 12-month ECLs. *[IFRS 9.5.5.10]*. However, if a financial instrument is not, or no longer, considered to have low credit risk at the reporting date, it does not follow that the entity is required to recognise lifetime ECLs. In such instances, the entity has to assess whether there has been a significant increase in credit risk since initial recognition which requires the recognition of lifetime ECLs. *[IFRS 9.B5.5.24]*.

The standard states that a financial instrument is considered to have low credit risk if: *[IFRS 9.B5.5.22]*

- the financial instrument has a low risk of default;
- the borrower has a strong capacity to meet its contractual cash flow obligations in the near term; and
- adverse changes in economic and business conditions in the longer term may, but will not necessarily, reduce the ability of the borrower to fulfil its contractual cash flow obligations.

A financial instrument is not considered to have low credit risk simply because it has a low risk of loss (e.g. for a collateralised loan, if the value of the collateral is more than the amount lent (see 5.8.1 above)) or it has lower risk of default compared to the entity's other financial instruments or relative to the credit risk of the jurisdiction within which the entity operates. *[IFRS 9.B5.5.22]*.

The description of low credit risk is equivalent to investment grade quality assets, equivalent to a Standard and Poor's rating of BBB– or better, Moody's rating of Baa3 or better and Fitch's rating of BBB– or better. When applying the low credit risk simplification, financial instruments are not required to be externally rated. However, the IASB's intention was to use a globally comparable notion of low credit risk instead of a level of risk determined, for example, by an entity or jurisdiction's view of risk based on entity-specific or jurisdictional factors. *[IFRS 9.BC5.188]*. Therefore, an entity may use its internal credit ratings to assess what is low credit risk as long as this is consistent with the globally understood definition of low credit risk (i.e. investment grade) or the market's expectations of what is deemed to be low credit risk, taking into consideration the terms and conditions of the financial instruments being assessed. *[IFRS 9.B5.5.23]*.

The Basel Committee guidance (see 7.1 below) states that the investment grade category used by ratings agencies is not considered homogeneous enough to be automatically considered low credit risk, and internationally active and sophisticated banks are expected to rely primarily on their own credit assessments.

In practice, entities with internal credit ratings will attempt to map their internal rating to the external credit ratings and definitions, such as Standard & Poor's, Moody's and Fitch. The description of the credit quality ratings by these major rating agencies are illustrated below.[25]

Figure 51.5 External credit ratings and definitions from the 3 major rating agencies

Standard & Poor's	Moody's	Fitch
Investment grade would usually refer to categories AAA to BBB (with BBB– being lowest investment grade considered by market participants).	Investment grade would usually refer to categories Aaa to Baa (with Baa3 being lowest investment grade considered by market participants).	Investment grade would usually refer to categories AAA to BBB (with BBB– being lowest investment grade considered by market participants).
BBB **Adequate capacity** to meet financial commitments, but more subject to **adverse economic conditions**.	**Baa** Obligations rated Baa are judged to be medium-grade and subject to moderate credit risk and as such may possess certain speculative characteristics.	**BBB: Good credit quality** Indicates that expectations of **default risk are currently low**. The capacity for payment of financial commitments is considered adequate but adverse business or economic conditions are more likely to impair this capacity.
The dividing line between investment grade and speculative grade		
BB Less vulnerable in the near-term but faces major on-going uncertainties to adverse business, financial and economic conditions.	**Ba** Obligations rated Ba are judged to be speculative and are subject to substantial credit risk.	**BB: Speculative** Indicates an elevated vulnerability to default risk, particularly in the event of adverse changes in business or economic conditions over time; however, business or financial flexibility exists which supports the servicing of financial commitments.

Examining the historical levels of default associated with the credit ratings of agencies such as Standard & Poor's, the PD of a BBB-rated loan is approximately treble that of one that is rated A. Hence, many entities would consider the increase in credit risk to be significant, if the low risk simplification is not used.

The low credit risk simplification will not be relevant if an entity originates or purchases a financial instrument with a credit risk which is already non-investment grade. Similarly, this simplification will also have limited use when the financial instrument is originated or purchased with a credit quality that is marginally better than a non-investment grade (i.e. at the bottom of the investment grade rating), because any credit deterioration into the non-investment grade rating would require the entity to assess whether the increase in credit risk has been significant.

Partly because of the Basel Committee guidance, most sophisticated banks are applying the low risk simplification only to securities. It is yet to be seen whether less sophisticated banks will use this operational simplification widely for their loan portfolios. Investors that hold externally rated debt instruments are more likely to rely on external rating agencies data and use the low credit risk simplification. However, some sophisticated banks are intending not to use it at all, preferring to use the same criteria as for other exposures (e.g. changes in the lifetime risk of default as the primary indicator followed by other risk metrics such as credit scores and ratings). It is also important to emphasise that although ratings are forward-looking, it is sometimes suggested that changes in credit ratings may not be reflected in a timely matter.

Therefore, entities may have to take account of expected change in ratings in assessing whether exposures are low risk.

The following example from the standard illustrates the application of the low credit risk simplification. *[IFRS 9 Example 4 IE24-IE28].*

Example 51.12: Public investment-grade bond

Company A is a large listed national logistics company. The only debt in the capital structure is a five-year public bond with a restriction on further borrowing as the only bond covenant. Company A reports quarterly to its shareholders. Entity B is one of many investors in the bond. Entity B considers the bond to have low credit risk at initial recognition in accordance with paragraph 5.5.10 of IFRS 9. This is because the bond has a low risk of default and Company A is considered to have a strong capacity to meet its obligations in the near term. Entity B's expectations for the longer term are that adverse changes in economic and business conditions may, but will not necessarily, reduce Company A's ability to fulfil its obligations on the bond. In addition, at initial recognition the bond had an internal credit rating that is correlated to a global external credit rating of investment grade.

At the reporting date, Entity B's main credit risk concern is the continuing pressure on the total volume of sales that has caused Company A's operating cash flows to decrease.

Because Entity B relies only on quarterly public information and does not have access to private credit risk information (because it is a bond investor), its assessment of changes in credit risk is tied to public announcements and information, including updates on credit perspectives in press releases from rating agencies.

Entity B applies the low credit risk simplification in paragraph 5.5.10 of IFRS 9. Accordingly, at the reporting date, Entity B evaluates whether the bond is considered to have low credit risk using all reasonable and supportable information that is available without undue cost or effort. In making that evaluation, Entity B reassesses the internal credit rating of the bond and concludes that the bond is no longer equivalent to an investment grade rating because:

(a) The latest quarterly report of Company A revealed a quarter-on-quarter decline in revenues of 20 per cent and in operating profit by 12 per cent.

(b) Rating agencies have reacted negatively to a profit warning by Company A and put the credit rating under review for possible downgrade from investment grade to non-investment grade. However, at the reporting date the external credit risk rating was unchanged.

(c) The bond price has also declined significantly, which has resulted in a higher yield to maturity. Entity B assesses that the bond prices have been declining as a result of increases in Company A's credit risk. This is because the market environment has not changed (for example, benchmark interest rates, liquidity, etc. are unchanged) and comparison with the bond prices of peers shows that the reductions are probably company specific (instead of being, for example, changes in benchmark interest rates that are not indicative of company-specific credit risk).

While Company A currently has the capacity to meet its commitments, the large uncertainties arising from its exposure to adverse business and economic conditions have increased the risk of a default occurring on the bond. As a result of the factors described above, Entity B determines that the bond does not have low credit risk at the reporting date. As a result, Entity B needs to determine whether the increase in credit risk since initial recognition has been significant. On the basis of its assessment, Company B determines that the credit risk has increased significantly since initial recognition and that a loss allowance at an amount equal to lifetime ECLs should be recognised in accordance with paragraph 5.5.3 of IFRS 9.

Some of the challenges in assessing whether there has been a significant increase in credit risk (including the use of the low credit risk simplification) and estimating the ECLs, are illustrated in the following example. It illustrates different ways of identifying a significant change in credit quality and different input parameters for calculating ECLs for a European government bond, which result in very different outcomes and volatility of the IFRS 9 ECL allowance. It should also be stressed that the default rates provided by external rating agencies are historical information. Entities need to understand the sources of these historical default rates and update the data for current and forward-looking information (see 5.9.3 above) when measuring ECLs or assessing credit deterioration.

Example 51.13: Use of credit ratings and/or CDS spreads to determine whether there have been significant increases in credit risk and to estimate expected credit losses

Introduction

A significant challenge in applying the IFRS 9 impairment requirements to quoted bonds is that the credit ratings assigned by agencies such as Standard & Poor's (S&P), and the historical experience of losses by rating grade, can differ significantly with the view of the market, as reflected in, for instance, credit default swap (CDS) spreads and bond spreads.

To illustrate the challenges of applying IFRS 9 to debt securities, we have examined how the ECL could be determined for a real bond issued by a European government on 16 September 2008 and due to mature in 2025. For three dates, we applied the IFRS 9 calculations to this bond, which is assumed to have been acquired at inception. In January 2009, the Standard & Poor's credit rating of the government was AA+, as at origination, but by January 2012, its rating was downgraded to A. The bond was further downgraded to BBB– in March 2014 before recovery to BBB in May 2014.

Three approaches

Shown below are three approaches:

- Approach 1: Use of S&P credit ratings both to determine whether the bond has significantly increased in credit risk and to estimate ECLs.

- Approach 2: Use of S&P credit ratings to determine whether the bond has significantly increased in credit risk and CDS spreads to estimate ECLs.

- Approach 3: Use of CDS spreads both to determine whether the bond has significantly increased in credit risk and to estimate ECLs.

Based on the historical corporate PDs from each assessed S&P credit rating (approach 1) and based on the CDS spreads (approaches 2 and 3), the loan loss percentages were calculated below. For the calculations, an often used LGD of 60% was applied. (Because the LGD represents a percentage of the present value of the gross carrying amount, this example does not illustrate the effect of the time value of money).

The percentage loss allowances were, as follows:

	Credit ratings	Historical 12-month PD based on ratings	12-month PD based on CDS spread	Lifetime PD based on CDS spread	Loss allowance (%)		
					Approach 1	Approach 2	Approach 3
1 January 2009	AA+	0.02%	0.44%	12.81%	–	–	–
31 January 2009	AA+	0.02%	1.84%	30.48%	0.01	1.10	18.29
31 January 2012	A	0.06%	4.96%	51,48%	0.04	2.98	30.89
31 March 2014	BBB–	0.31%	0.57%	23.01%	0.18	0.34	13.81

Approach 1

According to the credit ratings, the bond was investment grade throughout this period. Hence, using the low risk simplification, the loss allowance would have been based on 12-month ECLs. Using the corporate historical default rates implied by the credit ratings and an assumption of 60% LGD to calculate the ECLs, the 12-month allowance would have increased from 0.01% on 31 January 2009 to 0.04% three years later, increasing to 0.18% by 31 March 2014. It should be stressed that the historical default rates implied by credit ratings are historical rates for corporate debt and so they would not, without adjustment, satisfy the requirements of the standard. IFRS 9 requires the calculation of ECLs, based on current conditions and forecasts of future conditions, to be based on reasonable and supportable information. This is likely to include market indicators such as CDS and bond spreads, as illustrated by Approach 2.

Approach 2

In contrast to Approach 1, using credit default swap spreads to calculate the ECLs and the same assumption of 60% LGD to calculate the ECLs, the 12-month allowance would have increased from 1.1% on 31 January 2009 to 2.98% three years later, declining to 0.34% by 31 March 2014. The default rates implied by the CDSs are significantly higher than would have been expected given the ratings of these bonds. The loss allowances are, correspondingly, very much higher and very volatile. It might be argued that CDS spreads are too responsive to short term market sentiment to calculate long term ECLs, but it may appear difficult to find other reasonable and supportable information to adjust these rates so as to dampen the effects of market volatility.

Approach 3

Credit ratings are often viewed by the market as lagging indicators. For these bonds, the ratings are difficult to reconcile with the default probabilities as assessed by the markets. It might be argued that it is not sufficient to focus only on credit ratings when assessing whether assets are low risk since, according to CDS spreads, the bond was not low risk at any time in the period covered in this example, as it showed a significant increase in 1 year PD after inception (based on CDS spreads). The 1 year PDs increased from 0.44% on issue to 1.84% by 31 January 2009. Assessing the bond as requiring a lifetime ECL at all three dates, based on CDS spreads, would have given much higher loss allowances of 18.29%, 30.89% and 13.81%.

The counter-view might be that CDS spreads are too volatile to provide a sound basis for determining significant deterioration. Perhaps the best way to make the assessment of whether a bond has increased significantly in credit risk is to use more than one source of data and to take account of the qualitative indicators as described in the standard.

Conclusion

The calculated ECL figures differ significantly depending on the approach taken as to how to determine a significant change in credit quality and the parameters used for the calculation. Those based on CDS spreads are both large and very volatile, reflecting the investor uncertainty during the period, when the possibility of default depended more on the political will of the European Union to maintain the integrity of the Eurozone than the economic forecasts for the particular country. As a result, the disparity between the effect of the use of credit grades and CDSs is probably more marked than for most other security investments. Nevertheless, the same challenges will be found with other securities, albeit on a smaller scale.

6.4.2 Delinquency

As already described at 6.2.2 above, the standard allows use of past due information to assess whether credit risk has increased significantly, if reasonable and supportable forward-looking information (either at an individual or a collective level) is not available without undue cost or effort. This is subject to the rebuttable presumption that there has been a significant increase in credit risk if contractual payments are more than 30 days past due. *[IFRS 9.5.5.11]*. Similar to the low credit risk simplification (see 6.4.1 above), the Basel Committee guidance (see 7.1 below) considers that sophisticated banks should not use days past due information as a primary indicator, because it is a lagging indicator, but only as a backstop measure alongside other, earlier indicators.

Most sophisticated banks are following this regulatory guidance. In addition, it is a useful measure of the effectiveness of more forward-looking primary criteria to monitor the frequency that assets reach 30 days past due without having already been transferred to stage 2.

6.4.3 12-month risk as an approximation for change in lifetime risk

In determining whether there has been a significant increase in credit risk, an entity must assess the change in the risk of default occurring over the expected life of the financial instrument. Despite this, the standard states that: '...changes in the risk of a default occurring over the next 12 months may be a reasonable approximation ... unless circumstances indicate that a lifetime assessment is necessary'. [IFRS 9.B5.5.13].

The IASB observed in its Basis for Conclusions that changes in the risk of a default occurring within the next 12 months generally should be a reasonable approximation of changes in the risk of a default occurring over the remaining life of a financial instrument and thus would not be inconsistent with the requirements. Also, some entities use a 12-month PD measure for prudential regulatory requirements and these entities can continue to use their existing systems and methodologies as a starting point for determining significant increases in credit risk, thus reducing the costs of implementation. [IFRS 9.BC5.178].

However, for some financial instruments, or in some circumstances, the use of changes in the risk of default occurring over the next 12 months may not be appropriate to determine whether lifetime ECLs should be recognised. For a financial instrument with a maturity longer than 12 months, the standard gives the following examples: [IFRS 9.B5.5.14]

- the financial instrument only has significant payment obligations beyond the next 12 months;
- changes in relevant macroeconomic or other credit-related factors occur that are not adequately reflected in the risk of a default occurring in the next 12 months; or
- changes in credit-related factors only have an impact on the credit risk of the financial instrument (or have a more pronounced effect) beyond 12 months.

At its meeting on 16 September 2015, the ITG members discussed the use of changes in 12-month risk of default as a surrogate for changes in lifetime risk and commented as follows:

- An entity would be expected to complete a robust analysis up front in order to support the conclusion that changes in the 12-month risk of a default occurring was a reasonable approximation for the assessment of changes in the lifetime risk of default occurring.
- The level of initial analysis required would depend on the specific type of financial instrument being considered. Consequently, in some cases, a qualitative analysis would suffice whereas in less clear-cut cases, a quantitative analysis may be necessary. Also, it may be appropriate to segregate portfolios (e.g. by maturity) in order to facilitate the analysis for groups of similar financial instruments.
- An entity would need to be satisfied on an ongoing basis that the use of changes in the 12-month risk of a default occurring continued to be a reasonable approximation for changes in the lifetime risk of a default occurring.

At the meeting, the ITG members also discussed:
- The appropriate type of review that should be undertaken on an ongoing basis. While a quantitative review would not necessarily be required, it would depend on the specific facts and circumstances. One way of approaching an ongoing review would be as follows:
    (a) identify the key factors that would affect the appropriateness of using changes in the 12-month risk of a default occurring as an approximation of changes in the lifetime risk of default occurring;
    (b) monitor these factors on an ongoing basis as part of a qualitative review of circumstances; and
    (c) consider whether any changes in those factors indicated that changes in the 12-month risk of a default occurring was no longer an appropriate proxy for changes in a lifetime risk of default occurring.
- If it were determined that changes in the 12-month risk of a default occurring were no longer a reasonable approximation for the assessment of changes in the lifetime risk of a default occurring, an entity would be required to determine an appropriate approach to capture changes in the lifetime risk of a default occurring.
- It is important to emphasise that the guidance which permits an entity to use changes in the 12-month risk of a default as an approximation for the lifetime risk of default, is only relevant for the assessment of significant increases in credit risk and does not relate to the measurement of ECLs. When an entity is required to measure lifetime ECLs, that measurement must always reflect the lifetime risk of a default occurring.
- IFRS 9 does not prescribe how an entity should determine whether the use of changes in the 12-month risk of a default was an appropriate proxy for assessing changes in the lifetime risk of a default. However, it was noted that entities are required to disclose how they make the assessment of significant increases in credit risk, in accordance with IFRS 7.

Most sophisticated banks are using the lifetime risk of default (or an annualised equivalent) rather than the 12-month risk of default or the Basel risk of default for assessing whether there has been a significant increase in credit risk. Movements in a 12-month risk of default are, for most products and conditions, strongly correlated with movements in the lifetime risk. However, these banks appreciate that 12-month PDs may need to be adjusted or calibrated to reflect the longer-term macroeconomic outlook. Also, there are products such as interest-only mortgages and those with an introductory period in which no repayments are required, where additional procedures may need to be implemented in order to ensure that they are transferred to stage 2 appropriately.

6.4.4 Assessment at the counterparty level

As indicated by Example 7 in the Implementation Guidance of IFRS 9, assessment of significant deterioration in credit risk can be made at the level of the counterparty rather than the individual financial instrument. Such assessment at the counterparty level is only allowed if the outcome would not be different to the outcome if the financial instruments had been individually assessed. *[IFRS 9.BC5.168]*. In certain circumstances, assessment at the counterparty level would not be consistent with the impairment requirements. Both these situations are illustrated in the example below, based on Example 7 in the Implementation Guidance for the standard. *[IFRS 9 Example 7 IE43-IE47]*.

Example 51.14: Counterparty assessment of credit risk

Scenario 1

In 2014 Bank A granted a loan of $10,000 with a contractual term of 15 years to Company Q when the company had an internal credit risk rating of 4 on a scale of 1 (lowest credit risk) to 10 (highest credit risk). The risk of a default occurring increases exponentially as the credit risk rating deteriorates so, for example, the difference between credit risk rating grades 1 and 2 is smaller than the difference between credit risk rating grades 2 and 3. In 2019, when Company Q had an internal credit risk rating of 6, Bank A issued another loan to Company Q for $5,000 with a contractual term of 10 years. In 2021 Company Q fails to retain its contract with a major customer and correspondingly experiences a large decline in its revenue. Bank A considers that as a result of losing the contract, Company Q will have a significantly reduced ability to meet its loan obligations and changes its internal credit risk rating to 8.

Bank A assesses credit risk on a counterparty level for credit risk management purposes and determines that the increase in Company Q's credit risk is significant. Although Bank A did not perform an individual assessment of changes in the credit risk on each loan since its initial recognition, assessing the credit risk on a counterparty level and recognising lifetime ECLs on all loans granted to Company Q, meets the objective of the impairment requirements as stated in paragraph 5.5.4 of IFRS 9. This is because, even since the most recent loan was originated (in 2019) when Company Q had the highest credit risk at loan origination, its credit risk has increased significantly. The counterparty assessment would therefore achieve the same result as assessing the change in credit risk for each loan individually.

Scenario 2

Bank A granted a loan of $150,000 with a contractual term of 20 years to Company X in 2014 when the company had an internal credit risk rating of 4. During 2019 economic conditions deteriorate and demand for Company X's products has declined significantly. As a result of the reduced cash flows from lower sales, Company X could not make full payment of its loan instalment to Bank A. Bank A re-assesses Company X's internal credit risk rating, and determines it to be 7 at the reporting date. Bank A considered the change in credit risk on the loan, including considering the change in the internal credit risk rating, and determines that there has been a significant increase in credit risk and recognises lifetime ECLs on the loan of $150,000.

Despite the recent downgrade of the internal credit risk rating, Bank A grants another loan of $50,000 to Company X in 2020 with a contractual term of 5 years, taking into consideration the higher credit risk at that date.

The fact that Company X's credit risk (assessed on a counterparty basis) has previously been assessed to have increased significantly, does not result in lifetime ECLs being recognised on the new loan. This is because the credit risk on the new loan has not increased significantly since the loan was initially recognised. If Bank A only assessed credit risk on a counterparty level, without considering whether the conclusion about changes in credit risk applies to all individual financial instruments provided to the same customer, the objective in paragraph 5.5.4 of IFRS 9 would not be met.

Most banks manage their credit exposures on a counterparty basis and would be keen to use their existing risk management processes where they can. This is particularly the case for those banks who are seeking to use processes such as the use of watch lists to make the assessment. However, this will be challenging as the standard only allows use of a counterparty basis when it can be demonstrated that it would make no difference from making the assessment at an individual instrument level. It may be necessary for these banks to add procedures to track increase in the risk of default at the instrument level in order to comply with the standard.

6.4.5 Determining maximum initial credit risk for a portfolio

The IFRS 9 credit risk assessment that determines whether a financial instrument should attract a lifetime ECL allowance, or only a 12-month ECL allowance, is based on whether there has been a relative increase in credit risk. One of the challenges identified by some constituents in responding to the 2013 Exposure Draft is that many credit risk systems monitor absolute levels of risk, without tracking the history of individual loans (see 6.1 above). To help address this concern the standard contains an approach that turns a relative system into an absolute one, by segmenting the portfolio sufficiently by loan quality at origination.

As indicated by Illustrative Example 6 in the Implementation Guidance of IFRS 9 on which Example 51.15 below is based, an entity can determine the maximum initial credit risk accepted for portfolios with similar credit risks on initial recognition. *[IFRS 9 Example 6 IE40-IE42].* Thereby, an entity may be able to establish an absolute threshold for recognising lifetime ECLs.

Example 51.15: Comparison to maximum initial credit risk

Bank A has two portfolios of automobile loans with similar terms and conditions in Region W. Bank A's policy on financing decisions for each loan is based on an internal credit rating system that considers a customer's credit history, payment behaviour on other products with Bank A and other factors, and assigns an internal credit risk rating from 1 (lowest credit risk) to 10 (highest credit risk) to each loan on origination. The risk of a default occurring increases exponentially as the credit risk rating deteriorates so, for example, the difference between credit risk rating grades 1 and 2 is smaller than the difference between credit risk rating grades 2 and 3. Loans in Portfolio 1 were only offered to existing customers with a similar internal credit risk rating and at initial recognition all loans were rated 3 or 4 on the internal rating scale. Bank A determines that the maximum initial credit risk rating at initial recognition it would accept for Portfolio 1 is an internal rating of 4. Loans in Portfolio 2 were offered to customers that responded to an advertisement for automobile loans and the internal credit risk ratings of these customers range between 4 and 7 on the internal rating scale. Bank A never originates an automobile loan with an internal credit risk rating worse than 7 (i.e. with an internal rating of 8-10).

For the purposes of assessing whether there have been significant increases in credit risk, Bank A determines that all loans in Portfolio 1 had a similar initial credit risk. It determines that given the risk of default reflected in its internal risk rating grades, a change in internal rating from 3 to 4 would not represent a significant increase in credit risk but that there has been a significant increase in credit risk on any loan in this portfolio that has an internal rating worse than 5. This means that Bank A does not have to know the initial credit rating of each loan in the portfolio to assess the change in credit risk since initial recognition. It only has to determine whether the credit risk is worse than 5 at the reporting date to determine whether lifetime ECLs should be recognised in accordance with paragraph 5.5.3 of IFRS 9.

However, determining the maximum initial credit risk accepted at initial recognition for Portfolio 2 at an internal credit risk rating of 7, would not meet the objective of the requirements as stated in paragraph 5.5.4 of IFRS 9. This is because Bank A determines that significant increases in credit risk arise not only when credit risk increases above the level at which an entity would originate new financial assets (i.e. when the internal rating is worse than 7). Although Bank A never originates an automobile loan with an internal credit rating worse than 7, the initial credit risk on loans in Portfolio 2 is not of sufficiently similar credit risk at initial recognition to apply the approach used for Portfolio 1. This means that Bank A cannot simply compare the credit risk at the reporting date with the lowest credit quality at initial recognition (for example, by comparing the internal credit risk rating of loans in Portfolio 2 with an internal credit risk rating of 7) to determine whether credit risk has increased significantly because the initial credit quality of loans in the portfolio is too diverse. For example, if a loan initially had a credit risk rating of 4 the credit risk on the loan may have increased significantly if its internal credit risk rating changes to 6.

At its meeting on 16 September 2015, the ITG (see 1.5 above) discussed how to identify a significant increase in credit risk for a portfolio of retail loans when identical pricing and contractual terms are applied to customers across broad credit quality bands. The question was influenced by the operational simplifications described above which allows an entity to assess if there has been a significant increase in credit risk by determining the maximum initial credit risk accepted for portfolios with similar credit risks on original recognition, and by reviewing which exposures now exceed this limit. The ITG discussed an example of a retail loan portfolio (Portfolio A) comprising customers who had been assigned initial credit grades between 1 and 5 (based on a 10 grade rating scale where 1 is the highest credit quality) and had been issued loans with the same contractual terms and pricing. The question was whether it would be appropriate to make the determination of significant increases in credit risk by using a single threshold approach such as that outlined for Portfolio 1 in Illustrative Example 6 of IFRS 9, on the basis that the exposures in Portfolio A could be considered to have a similar initial credit risk, or whether there were other more appropriate approaches such as, for example, defining a significant increase in credit risk as a specific number of notch increases in credit grade.

The ITG members observed that:

- When assessing whether there has been a significant increase in credit risk, it would not be appropriate for the entity to consider only factors such as pricing and contractual terms. In this regard, while the concept of economic loss was considered in developing the IFRS 9 model, the standard requires an assessment of changes in credit risk based on a wide range of factors including internal and external indicators of credit risk, changes to contractual terms, actual and expected performance/behaviours and forecasts of future conditions.

- Credit grading systems were not necessarily designed with the requirements of IFRS 9 in mind, and thus it should not be assumed that they will always be an appropriate means of identifying significant increases in credit risk. The appropriateness of using internal credit grading systems as a means of assessing changes in credit risk since initial recognition depends on whether the credit grades are reviewed with sufficient frequency, include all reasonable and supportable information and reflect the risk of default over the expected life of the financial instrument. As credit grading systems vary, care needs to be taken when referring to movements in credit grades and how this reflects an increased risk of default occurring. In addition, the assessment of whether a change in credit risk grade represents a significant increase in credit risk in accordance with IFRS 9 depends on the initial credit risk of the financial instrument being assessed. Because the relationship between credit grades and changes in the risk of default occurring differs between credit grading systems (e.g. in some cases the changes in the risk of a default occurring may increase exponentially between grades whereas in others it may not), this requires particular consideration.

- Consequently, the impairment model is based on an assessment of changes in credit risk since initial recognition, rather than the identification of a specific level of credit risk at the reporting date and a smaller absolute change in the risk of default occurring will be more significant for an asset that is of high quality on initial recognition than for one that is of low quality.

- In Illustrative Example 6 in IFRS 9, the assessment of significant increases in credit risk of Portfolio 1 was made using a form of absolute approach. However, it was pointed out that this approach was still consistent with the objective of identifying significant increases in credit risk since initial recognition. In particular, only loans with an initial credit grade of 3 or 4 were included in Portfolio 1 and furthermore, the entity had concluded that a movement from credit grade 3 to 4 did not represent a significant increase in credit risk. Consequently, using a single threshold of credit grade 5 as a means of identifying a significant increase in credit risk since initial recognition served to capture changes in credit risk in a manner that achieved the objective of the impairment requirements.

- In contrast, in the fact pattern discussed, Portfolio A contained loans with initial credit grades ranging between 1 and 5. Questions were raised as to whether such a broad range of credit grades could be considered to represent a similar initial credit risk and the ITG members noted that in order to conclude that the assessment could be based on whether loans had a credit rating worse than 5, the entity would need to have determined that movements between credit grades 1 and 5 did not represent a significant increase in credit risk.
- Information available at an individual financial instrument level and/or built into a credit risk grading system may not incorporate forward-looking information as required by IFRS 9. Consequently, the assessment of significant increases in credit risk may need to be supplemented by a collective assessment to capture forward-looking information. However, a collective assessment should not obscure significant increases in credit risk at an individual financial instrument level. In this regard, portfolio segmentation is important and entities should ensure that sub-portfolios are not defined too widely.

6.5 Collective assessment

Banks may have hundreds of thousands, or even millions, of small exposures to retail customers and small businesses. Much of the information available to monitor them is based on whether payments are past due and behavioural information that is mostly historical rather than forward-looking. As a result such exposures tend to be managed on an aggregated basis, combining past due and behavioural data with historical statistical experience and sometimes macroeconomic indicators, such as interest rates and unemployment levels, that tend to correlate with future defaults. Also, even when exposures are managed on an individual basis, as is the case for most commercial loans, the information used to manage them may not be sufficiently forward-looking to comply with the standard.

To address these concerns, the standard introduces the idea of making a collective assessment for financial assets, to determine if there has been a significant increase in credit risk, if an entity cannot make the assessment adequately on an individual instrument level. This exercise must consider comprehensive information that incorporates not only past due data but other relevant credit information, such as forward-looking macroeconomic information. The objective is to approximate the result of using comprehensive credit information that incorporates forward-looking information at an individual instrument level. *[IFRS 9.B5.5.4]*. Hence, even if a financial asset is normally managed on an individual basis, it should also be assessed collectively (i.e. based on macroeconomic indicators), if the entity does not have sufficient forward-looking information at the individual level to make the determination. The way that this might work is not very different from the IAS 39 requirement to assess an asset collectively for impairment if it has already been assessed individually and found not to be impaired.

Some kind of collective adjustment or overlay will be needed for many retail lending portfolios, given that most customer-specific information will not be forward-looking. In contrast, for commercial loans, the lender will typically have access to much more information and a forward-looking approach may already have been built into loan grading systems. Nevertheless, we are aware of some banks who consider that they need to introduce an additional overlay for commercial loans so as to be more responsive to emerging macroeconomic and other risk developments. Other banks using their existing watch list approaches to supplement their credit grading system when assessing whether there has been a significant increase in credit risk. This is because watch list systems can be more reactive to changing circumstances than formal credit gradings. Any one bank is likely to employ a variety of methods, depending on its products, systems and data.

In abnormal circumstances, for example during the coronavirus pandemic (see 7.8 below), it may take time for an entity to detect actual changes in risk indicators for a specific counterparty. In order to accelerate the reflection of such changes in credit quality not yet detected at an individual level, it may be appropriate to adjust ratings and the PD on a collective basis, considering risk characteristics such as the industry or geographical location of the borrowers. For example, a supplier of products or services to the airline industry would likely consider, in the context of the coronavirus pandemic, that the PD (or loss rates, if a provision matrix approach is used) of its customers has increased irrespective of specific events identified at the level of individual counterparties.

It is worth noting that the language on when a collective approach is required is not entirely consistent within the standard. Paragraph B5.5.1 states that 'it *may be* necessary to perform the assessment' (emphasis added) on a collective basis, which is consistent with the requirement in paragraph 5.5.11, that 'an entity cannot rely solely on past due information if reasonable and supportable forward-looking information is available without undue cost or effort'. However, paragraph B5.5.4 states that if 'an entity does not have reasonable and supportable information that is available without undue cost or effort to measure lifetime expected credit losses on an individual instrument basis ... lifetime expected credit losses shall be recognised on a collective basis'. Banking regulators will probably ensure that this 'shall be' wording will be applied, at least for more sophisticated banks (see 1.6 above and 7.1 below). This raises a second concern: once significant deterioration has been identified for a portfolio, whether the entire portfolio would have to be measured using lifetime ECLs. This outcome would result in sudden, massive increases in provisions as soon as conditions begin to decline. Consequently, the Board, in finalising the standard, set out examples of possible methods, using which only a segment or portion of the portfolio would be changed to lifetime ECLs.

Illustrative Example 5 in the Implementation Guidance for the standard illustrates how an entity may assess whether its individual assessment should be complemented with a collective one whenever the information at individual level is not sufficiently comprehensive and up-to-date. The following examples have been adapted from that guidance.

6.5.1 Example of individual assessment of changes in credit risk

First, as a benchmark, Scenario 1 (an individual assessment) illustrates a situation where a bank has sufficient information at individual exposure level to identify a significant deterioration of credit quality.

Example 51.16: **Individual assessment in relation to responsiveness to changes in credit risk**

The bank assesses each of its mortgage loans on a monthly basis by means of an automated behavioural scoring process based on current and historical past due statuses, levels of customer indebtedness, loan-to-value (LTV) measures, customer behaviour on other financial instruments with the bank, the loan size and the time since the origination of the loan. It is said that historical data indicates a strong correlation between the value of residential property and the default rates for mortgages.

The bank updates the LTV measures on a regular basis through an automated process that re-estimates property values using recent sales in each post code area and reasonable and supportable forward-looking information that is available without undue cost or effort. Therefore, an increased risk of a default occurring due to an expected decline in residential property value adjusts the behavioural scores and the Bank is therefore able to identify significant increases in credit risk on individual customers before a mortgage becomes past due if there has been a deterioration in the behavioural score.

The example concludes that if the bank is unable to update behavioural scores to reflect the expected declines in property prices, it would use reasonable and supportable information that is available without undue cost or effort to undertake a collective assessment to determine the loans on which there has been a significant increase in credit risk since initial recognition and recognize lifetime ECLs for those loans.

It should be noted that, in this example, the main source of forward-looking information is expected future property prices. No account would appear to be taken of other economic data such as future levels of employment or interest rates. We assume that the Board took this approach to make the example simple, but it implies that future property prices are considered to provide a sufficiently good guide to future defaults that it is not necessary to take account of other data as well.

6.5.2 Basis of aggregation for collective assessment

Next, the standard sets out how financial instruments may be grouped together in order to determine whether there has been a significant increase in credit risk. Any instruments assessed collectively must possess shared credit risk characteristics. It is not permitted to aggregate exposures that have different risks and, in so doing, obscure significant increases in risk that may arise on a sub-set of the portfolio. Examples of shared credit risk characteristics given in the standard include, but are not limited to: *[IFRS 9.B5.5.5]*

- instrument type;
- credit risk ratings;
- collateral type;
- date of initial recognition;
- remaining term to maturity;
- industry;
- geographical location of the borrower; and
- the value of collateral relative to the asset (the loan-to-value or LTV ratio), if this would have an impact on the risk of a default occurring.

The standard also states that the basis of aggregation of financial instruments to assess whether there have been changes in credit risk on a collective basis may have to change over time, as new information on groups of, or individual, financial instruments becomes available. *[IFRS 9.B5.5.6]*.

We make the following observations:
- As has been stressed earlier, the assessment of significant deterioration is intended to reflect the risk of default, not the risk of loss, hence collateral should normally be ignored for the assessment. The standard nonetheless explains that the value of collateral relative to the financial asset would be relevant to the collective assessment if it has an impact on the risk of a default occurring. It cites, as an example, non-recourse loans in certain jurisdictions. The question of when such an arrangement would always meet the IFRS 9 classification and measurement characteristics of the asset test is beyond the scope of this chapter. LTV or a house price index may be a useful indicator of significant collective deterioration in a wider range of circumstances than just where the loans are non-recourse. First, house prices are themselves a useful barometer of the economy and so higher LTVs and lower indices correlate with declining economic conditions. Second, loans that were originally advanced at higher LTVs may reflect more aggressive lending practices, with the consequence that such loans may exhibit a higher PD if economic conditions decline. Third, a borrower in trouble with a lower LTV will likely sell his house to redeem the mortgage rather than defaulting on the mortgage (and, conversely, a borrower with a high LTV will have less incentive not to default).
- By date of original recognition, we assume that the Board did not intend that loans should be assessed in separate groups for each year of origination, but that vintages may be aggregated into groups that share similar credit risk characteristics. Loan products and lending practices, including the extent of due diligence, and key ratios, such as the LTV and loan to income, change over time, often reflecting the economic conditions at the time of origination. The consequence is that loans from particular years are inherently more risky than others. For some banks, this might mean isolating those loans advanced just prior to the financial crisis from those originated earlier or in the subsequent, more careful lending environment. Also, there is a phenomenon termed seasoning, which describes how loans that been serviced adequately for a number of years, over a business cycle, are statistically less likely to default in future, suggesting that older loans should be assessed separately.
- Although the examples in the standard refer to regions, as the geographical location of borrowers, the groupings could be much larger, such as by country, or much smaller, if there are particular issues associated with particular towns. Hence the choice of geographical groupings will depend very much on the environment in which a bank operates.
- Other ways that loans might be grouped according to shared credit risk characteristics could include by credit score, by payment history, whether previously restructured or subject to forbearance but subsequently restored to a 12-month ECL allowance, and manner of employment (as featured in Illustrative Example 5 in the Implementation Guidance for the standard under the bottom up assessment discussed in Example 51.17 below).
- The requirement that financial instruments that are assessed together must share similar credit risk characteristics means that a bank may have a substantial number of portfolios. Even a relatively small bank might have six different products (taking into account terms to maturity and types of collateral), three regions and three

different vintage groups which, multiplied out, would give 54 different assessment groups. A larger global bank might need to monitor many more different portfolios. However, a balance will need to be struck between ensuring that portfolios are small enough to have sufficient homogeneity and yet not so small that there is too little historical data for losses to be reliably estimated.

- Also, the requirement that groupings may have to be amended over time means that there must be processes put in place to reassess whether loans continue to share similar credit risk characteristics. Yet, in practice, there will need to be a sufficient level of stability in the construction of portfolios to allow enough historical data to be gathered for reliable estimation of losses.

Finally, paragraph B5.5.6 in IFRS 9 adds that, 'if an entity is not able to group financial instruments for which the credit risk is considered to have increased significantly since initial recognition based on shared credit risk characteristics, the entity should recognise lifetime ECLs on a portion of the financial assets for which credit risk is deemed to have increased significantly'.

As clarified by the IASB in its webcast on forward-looking information in July 2016, it is possible that a bank is aware of differences in sensitivities of credit risk to a change in a particular parameter but is unable to group the assets on the basis of such sensitivity. In such instances, the bank may determine that the expected forward-looking scenario would result in significant increases in credit risk for a certain proportion of its portfolio.

6.5.3 Example of collective assessment ('bottom up' and 'top down' approach)

The main standard does not amplify how a collective assessment would be made but Illustrative Example 5 in the Implementation Guidance of IFRS 9 provides two scenarios that explore the approach. *[IFRS 9 Example 5 IE29-IE39].*

Example 51.17: Collective assessment in relation to responsiveness to changes in credit risk ('bottom up' approach)

Region Two of Illustrative Example 5 in the Implementation Guidance for the standard introduces the so-called bottom up method. It deals with a mining community within a region that faces unemployment risk due to a decline in coal exports and, consequently, anticipated future mine closures. Although most of the loans are not yet 30 days past due and, further, the borrowers are not yet unemployed, the bank re-segments its mortgage portfolio so as to separate loans to customers employed in the mining industry (based on information in the original mortgage application form).

For these loans (plus any others that are more than 30 days past due), Bank ABC recognises lifetime ECLs, while it continues to recognise 12-month ECLs for the other mortgage loans in the region. Any new loans to borrowers who rely on the coal industry would also attract only a 12-month allowance, until they also demonstrate a significant increase in credit risk.

The bottom up method is described as an example of how to assess credit deterioration by using information that is more forward-looking than past due status. But this example also illustrates that collectively assessed groups may need to change over time, to ensure that they share similar credit risk characteristics. Once the coal mining industry begins to decline, those loans connected with it would no longer share the same risk characteristics as other loans to borrowers in the region, and so would need to be assessed separately. We also note that this example assumes that macroeconomic factors can be linked to the ECLs of a very specific portfolio. Further, in practice, most banks may not have the data to achieve this level of segmentation.

As already described above (possible criteria for grouping of financial assets with similar credit risk characteristics), the bottom up approach could be applied to sub-portfolios differentiated by type of instrument, risk rating, type of collateral, date of initial recognition, remaining term to maturity, industry, geographical location of the borrower, or the LTV ratio. A good example of this approach might be for exposures to borrowers that are expected to suffer major economic difficulties due to war or political upheaval, or borrowers with the weakest credit scores, who are expected to be more sensitive to a change in a relevant macroeconomic factor. In addition, as underwriting standards may vary or change, the portfolio might be sub-divided so as to reflect this. Note that the coal mines closures are, as yet, only anticipated, hence this example helps show how the standard is intended to look much further forward than the consequent unemployment that would probably trigger an IAS 39 impairment provision. The need to look forward is also illustrated in the next example.

Example 51.18:   Collective assessment in relation to responsiveness to changes in credit risk ('top down' approach)

For Region Three of Illustrative Example 5 in the Implementation Guidance for the standard, Bank ABC anticipates an increase in defaults following an expected rise in interest rates. Historically, an increase in interest rates has been a lead indicator of future defaults on floating-rate mortgages in the region. The bank regards the portfolio of variable rate mortgage loans in that region to be homogenous and it is incapable of identifying particular sub portfolios on the basis of shared credit risk characteristics. Hence, it uses what is described as a top down method.

Based on historical data, the bank estimates that a 200 basis points rise in interest rates will cause a significant increase in credit risk on 20 per cent of the mortgages. As a result, presumably because the bank expects a 200 basis points rise in rates, it recognises lifetime ECLs on 20 per cent of the portfolio (along with those loans that are more than 30 days past due) and 12-month ECLs on the remainder of mortgages in the region.

The challenge posed by the top down method is how to calculate the percentage of loans that have significantly deteriorated. That a rise in interest rates will likely lead to a significant deterioration in credit risk for some floating-rate borrowers, is not controversial. But working out whether they make up 5 per cent, 20 per cent or 35 per cent of the portfolio would appear to be more of an art than science, and no two banks are likely to arrive at the same figure.

The IASB brought some useful clarification on this example in its July 2016 webcast on forward-looking information:

- First, they clarified that one financial instrument cannot exist in stage 1 and in stage 2 at the same time. Therefore, the Board in the above example did not mean that each asset in the portfolio is to be regarded as 20% in stage 2 and 80% in stage 1. Instead, 20% of the assets are in stage 2, even if the bank does not yet know precisely which instruments are in stage 2.
- This allocation is intended to reflect that some assets in the portfolio will respond more adversely to a given change to the macroeconomic factor (e.g. unemployment rate) than others. Therefore, some assets in the portfolio may be considered to have significantly increased in credit risk while others have not. Judgement is required to determine how much of the portfolio should move to stage 2.

An entity may, for example, determine that given the range of possible scenarios, 20% of the portfolio moves to stage 2 considering the different level of sensitivity of the assets in the portfolio to the different relevant credit risk drivers.

- As further explained in the next section on using multiple scenarios for the staging assessment (see 6.7 below), it is important to note that the 20% is not the probability of occurrence of the more adverse scenario. Rather, it reflects the proportion of the portfolio deemed to have already significantly deteriorated based on the most recent probability-weighted average PD. This is due to the heightened sensitivity of this proportion of the portfolio to certain macroeconomic factors.

A further issue with the top down approach is the question of what the lender should do if it subsequently finds that differences in risk characteristics emerge within the portfolio, such that certain assets need to be measured using lifetime ECLs using the bottom up approach. A similar question arises if individual assets subsequently need to be measured using lifetime ECLs, for instance, because they become 30 days past due. In practice, it is likely that banks, at each reporting date, will first allocate exposures to stage 2 based on an individual assessment and then apply a collective approach to the remaining stage 1 exposures. They are unlikely to 'roll-forward' the collective allowance.

Presumably the proportion of the portfolio ECLs in stage 2 can be measured once again using 12-month ECLs if economic conditions are expected to improve. However, any assets that are 30 days past due will continue to be treated as stage 2. [IFRS 9.B5.5.19].

Because of these and similar difficulties, we are not currently aware of any banks who are using the top down approach in the manner set out in the Illustrative Example. Banks prefer to know which loans are measured using lifetime ECLs, rather than a notional percentage of the population. In practice, the methods that are being used by banks are closer to a mixture of the bottom up and top down approaches, as described in Examples 51.17 and 51.18 above. Macroeconomic indicators are assessed, as in the top down approach, but the effect is determined by assessing the effect on particular exposures. One possible method is to determine the expected migration of loans through a bank's risk classification system, by recalibrating the probabilities of default based on forward-looking data. This could be used to forecast how many additional loans will get downgraded as well as the associated ECLs. Another is to focus on more vulnerable categories of lending, such as interest-only mortgages, secured loans with high loan-to-value ratios, or property development loans, and assess how these might respond to the economic outlook. The more information about customers that a lender possesses, the more this might look like the illustrated bottom up approach. It is likely that banks will use different approaches for different portfolios, depending on how they are managed and what data is available.

All the examples in the illustrative examples simplify the fact pattern to focus on just one driver of credit losses, whereas in reality, there will be many, and it may not be possible to find a historical precedent for the combination of economic indicators that may now be present. Further, to delve into the past to predict the future requires a level of data that banks may lack. The example in the standard bases the percentage on historical experience, but it is more than 20 years since most developed countries last saw a 200 basis points rise in interest rates, and products and lending practices were then very different, as was the level of interest rates before they began to rise and the extent of the increase. Hence, the past may not be a reliable guide to the future. In practice, banks will need to determine the main macroeconomic variables that correlate with credit losses and focus on modelling these key drivers of loss. The banks can make use of work that has already been carried out for stress testing. Also, it should be stressed that banks will generally use one single model to estimate forward-looking PDs for both for the assessment of significant increases in credit risk and the measurement of ECLs (see 5.9.3 above).

The example of an anticipated increase in interest rates is very topical, given that rates in many countries are expected to rise in future from the all-time low levels that have been experienced since the financial crisis. This gives rise to an observation that is relevant to any ECL model: banks and (hopefully) borrowers have presumably known that new variable loans made since the crisis would likely increase in rate as the economy improves. If the increase was anticipated at the time of origination, expectation of a rise in interest rate should not be viewed as a significant deterioration in credit risk. Yet, there is a concern that rising rates will bring difficulty for many borrowers who have over stretched themselves, implying that the inevitable rise was not fully factored into lending decisions. With any forward-looking approach it is necessary to understand what risks were already taken into account when loans are first made, to assess whether there has been a significant increase in risk.

6.6 Determining the credit risk at initial recognition of an identical group of financial assets

In practice, entities may hold a portfolio of debt securities that are identical and cannot be distinguished individually (e.g. all securities have the same international securities identification number (ISIN)) and over the lifetime of the portfolio, entities may acquire additional securities or sell some of those previously acquired. In such instances, entities have to determine the credit risk at initial recognition of those securities that remain in the homogeneous portfolio at the reporting date.

IFRS 9 contains no specific guidance on how to calculate the cost of financial assets for derecognition purposes when they are part of a homogenous portfolio. Under IAS 39, which was also silent on this topic, entities used to choose between three cost allocation methods for available-for-sale securities: the average cost method, the first-in-first-out (FIFO) method or the specific identification method. Specific identification can be applied if the entity is able to identify the specific items sold and their costs. For example, a specific security may be identified as sold by linking the date, amount and cost of securities bought with the sale transaction, provided that there is no other evidence suggesting that the actual security sold was not the one identified under this method.

For IFRS 9, the question arises whether entities can continue to apply one of the above methods for debt instruments, not only for determining the cost of the security at derecognition but also for determining their initial credit risk. We believe that:

- the method used for recognising and measuring impairment losses should normally be the same as that used for determining the cost allocation method on derecognition;
- a FIFO approach or a specific identification method as described above constitute acceptable accounting policy choices to be applied consistently; however
- it would not normally be appropriate to use the weighted-average method to determine the credit risk at initial recognition, as averaging the different levels of

initial credit risk of debt securities purchased at different dates would result in an identical initial credit risk for each item. It therefore, would create bias when assessing whether the credit risk of debt securities has increased significantly.

6.7 Multiple scenarios for the assessment of significant increases in credit risk

At its December 2015 meeting the Impairment Transition resource Group (ITG) discussed not only the need to consider multiple scenarios for measurement of ECLs (see 5.6.1 above), but also for the purposes of assessing whether exposures should be measured on a lifetime loss basis.

Similar to the measurement of ECLs, the ITG members noted that where there is a non-linear relationship between the different forward-looking scenarios and the associated risks of default, using a single scenario would not meet the objectives of the standard. Consequently, in such cases, an entity would need to consider more than one forward-looking scenario. Further, there should be consistency, to the extent relevant, between the information used to measure ECLs and that used to assess significant increases in credit risk. An example of when the information might not be relevant is the value of collateral. It may be necessary to calculate the effect of multiple scenarios to value collateral to measure ECLs, but this information may not be relevant to assessing significant changes in credit risk unless the value has an effect on the probability of default occurring.[26]

As with the measurement of ECLs, the ITG members noted that IFRS 9 does not prescribe particular methods of assessing for significant increases in credit risk. Consequently, various methods could be applied, depending on facts and circumstances and these may include both quantitative and qualitative approaches. An entity should not restrict itself by considering only quantitative approaches when considering how to incorporate multiple forward-looking scenarios. Whichever approach is taken, it should be consistent with IFRS 9, considering reasonable and supportable information that is available without undue cost and effort. Once again, this is an area of judgement and so appropriate disclosures would need to be provided to comply with the requirements of IFRS 7 (see 15 below and Chapter 54 at 5.3).

A further issue was raised at the ITG meeting, which was not referred to in the minutes but was addressed in the 25 July 2016 IASB webcast. If a number of scenarios are applied to an individual asset, in some of which there is no significant increase in credit risk and in others there is, is it possible that it could be measured partly based on 12-month losses and partly on lifetime losses? It was not the intention of the IASB that an asset should be regarded as being in more than one stage at the same time. For staging as well as for measurement, IFRS 9 applies to the unit of account which is the individual financial instrument. The financial asset cannot be considered to have partly significantly deteriorated and partly not. Hence, for instance, if the staging assessment is based on a mechanistic approach which considers the change in the lifetime probability of default, the entity should use the multiple scenario probability-weighted lifetime probability of default to assess whether there has been a significant increase in credit risk. The asset should then be measured using the weighted 12-month probability of default if it is considered to be in stage 1, or the weighted lifetime probability of default if it is considered to be in stage 2.

However, as described in 6.5.3 above, the webcast also noted that, for a collectively assessed portfolio of assets, only a proportion of the portfolio may be deemed to have significantly deteriorated while the rest of the portfolio has not, due to differences in sensitivities of credit risk to a change in a particular parameter.

The IASB also illustrated how multiple scenarios can be reflected in a non-PD-based approach, using the example of a scorecard system. If the entity determines that there is non-linearity in the effect of the scenarios on the credit risk of the customers, one possibility is to look at the scorecard inputs and to determine which of these inputs have a non-linear relationship with the macroeconomic parameters. The entity then adjusts the scorecard, for example, using a scaling factor to reflect the impact of non-linearity, assesses whether there has been a significant increase in credit risk and measures ECL on the basis of the adjusted scorecard.

The approach set out in this discussion is broadly the same as 'the top down' approach to collective assessments illustrated by Example 51.18 in 6.5 above.

It is important to note that the ITG did not state that it is always necessary to use multiple scenarios and probability-weighted lifetime probabilities of default to assess significant increases in credit risk.

What it did state is that:

(a) it is necessary to consider more than one scenario if there is non-linearity in the possible distribution of losses;

(b) qualitative approaches may be included as well as quantitative ones, so that, for instance, it might be possible to take account of non-linearities by scaling the output from score cards; and

(c) the assessment should be based on reasonable and supportable information that is available without undue cost or effort (see 5.9.1 above).

Nevertheless, the ITG did state that there should be consistency, to the extent relevant, between the forward-looking information used for measurement and for the assessment of significant increases in credit risk. There would not always be a direct mapping of the relevant information, because in some cases information might have an impact on the measurement of ECLs but not on the assessment of significant increases in credit risk (and *vice versa*). Also, various methods of assessing for significant increases in credit risk could be applied, depending on the particular facts and circumstances, and an entity should not restrict itself by considering only quantitative approaches when considering how to incorporate multiple forward-looking scenarios.

In the July 2016 webcast, the IASB also stressed the importance of adequate disclosures. Because there is no one right approach and because this area involves a high level of judgement, disclosures are very important to enable users of financial statements to understand how entities' credit risk is affected by forward-looking scenarios and how they have affected the application of the ECL model. It would also be useful to disclose if relevant forward-looking information has not been reflected in the assessment of significant deterioration on the basis that it is not reasonable and supportable.

In practice, many banks that use multiple scenarios of lifetime probabilities of default to measure assets in stage 2, use them also for assessing if there has been a significant increase in credit risk. Moreover, as with measurement, banks will need to consider regulators' expectations (see 7.1 below).

7 OTHER MATTERS AND ISSUES IN RELATION TO THE EXPECTED CREDIT LOSS CALCULATIONS

This section discusses other matters and issues that are relevant to applying the IFRS 9 impairment requirements.

7.1 Basel guidance on accounting for expected credit losses

The Basel Committee published the final version of its *Guidance on Credit Risk and Accounting for Expected Credit Losses* (sometimes referred to as 'G-CRAECL', but in this publication, as 'the Basel guidance' or just 'the guidance') in December 2015 (see 1.6 above). The guidance deals with lending exposures, and not debt securities, and does not address the consequent capital requirements.

The guidance was originally drafted for internationally active banks and more sophisticated banks in the business of lending. The final version does not limit its scope but allows less complex banks to apply, 'a proportionate approach' that is commensurate with the size, nature and complexity of their lending exposures. It also extends this notion to individual portfolios of more complex banks. It follows that determining what is proportionate will be a key judgement to be made, which is likely to be guided in some jurisdictions by banking regulators. The guidance issued in June 2016 by the Global Public Policy Committee (GPPC) (see 7.2 below) will also be relevant in making this determination. The final version of the guidance acknowledges that due consideration may also be given to materiality.

The main section of the Basel Committee's guidance is intended to be applicable in all jurisdictions (i.e. for banks reporting under US GAAP as well as for banks reporting under IFRS) and contains 11 supervisory principles. The guidance is supplemented by an appendix that outlines additional supervisory requirements specific to jurisdictions applying the IFRS 9 ECL model.

It is important to stress that the guidance is not intended to conflict with IFRS 9 (and, indeed, this has been confirmed by the IASB), but it goes further than IFRS 9 and, in particular, removes some of the simplifications that are available in the standard. It also insists that any approximation to what would be regarded as an 'ideal' implementation of ECL accounting should be designed and implemented so as to avoid 'bias'. The term 'avoidance of bias' is used several times in the guidance and we understand it to have its normal accounting meaning of neutrality. Hence, for instance, if a bank were ever dependent on past-due information to assess whether an exposure should be measured on a lifetime ECL basis, it is guided to 'pay particular attention to their measurement of the 12-month allowance to ensure that ECLs are appropriately captured in accordance with the measurement objective of IFRS 9.'[27]

Perhaps one of the most significant pieces of guidance provided by the Basel Committee relates to the important requirement in IFRS 9 that ECLs should be measured using 'reasonable and supportable information'. The Committee accepts that in certain circumstances, information relevant to the assessment and measurement of credit risk may not be reasonable and supportable and should therefore be excluded from the ECL assessment and measurement process. But, given that credit risk management is a core competence of banks, 'these circumstances would be exceptional in nature'.[28]

This attitude pervades the guidance. It also states that management is expected 'to apply its credit judgement to consider future scenarios' and '[t]he Committee does not view the unbiased consideration of forward-looking information as speculative'.[29] The guidance, therefore, establishes a high hurdle for when it is not possible for an internationally active bank to estimate the effects of forward-looking information. It is possible that banking regulators would expect banks to make an estimate of the effects of events with an uncertain binary outcome that is highly significant, such as the result of a referendum as discussed by the ITG in September 2015 (see 5.9.5 above).

A connected piece of the guidance relates to another important principle in IFRS 9, that reasonable and supportable information should be available 'without undue cost or effort'. The guidance states that banks are not expected to read this 'restrictively'. It goes on to say that, 'Since the objective of the IFRS 9 model is to deliver fundamental improvements in the measurement of credit losses ... this will potentially require costly upfront investment in new systems and processes'. Such costs 'should therefore not be considered undue'.[30]

Much of the guidance relates to systems and controls and so is outside the scope of this publication. The requirements of the main section that relate to accounting include:

1. There should be commonality in the processes, systems, tools and data used to assess credit risk and to measure ECLs for accounting and for regulatory capital purposes.[31]

2. When a bank's individual assessment of exposures does not adequately consider forward-looking information, it is appropriate to group lending exposures with shared credit risk characteristics to estimate the impact of forward-looking information, including macroeconomic factors (see 6.5 above).[32] The grouping of lending exposures into portfolios with shared credit risk characteristics must be re-evaluated regularly (including re-segmentation in light of relevant new information or changes in the bank's expectations). Groupings must be granular enough to assess changes in credit risk and changes in a part of the portfolio must not be masked by the performance of the portfolio as a whole.[33]

3. 'Adjustments' may be used to address events, circumstances or risk factors that are not fully considered in credit rating and modelling processes. But the Committee expects that such adjustments will be temporary. If the reason for an adjustment is not expected to be temporary then the processes should be updated to incorporate that risk driver. The guidance goes on to say that adjustments require judgement and create the potential for bias. Therefore, they should be subject to appropriate governance processes.[34]

4. The 'consideration of forward-looking information and macroeconomic factors is considered essential to the proper implementation of an ECL model. It cannot be avoided on the basis that the banks consider the costs to be excessive or unnecessary or because there is uncertainty in formulating forward-looking scenarios'. However, the Committee recognises that an ECL is 'an estimate and thus may not perfectly predict actual outcomes. Accordingly, the need to incorporate such information is likely to increase the inherent degree of subjectivity in ECL estimates, compared with impairment measured using incurred loss approaches'. Also, the Basel Committee recognises that it may not always be possible to demonstrate a strong link in formal statistical terms between certain

types of information and the credit risk drivers. Consequently, a bank's experienced credit judgement will be crucial in establishing the appropriate level for the individual or collective allowance.[35]

5. Although the final version of the guidance says less about disclosures than the draft version, given the publication of the Enhanced Disclosure Task Force (EDTF) recommendations, disclosure remains one of the key principles (see 15 below or Chapter 54 at 9.2).

The guidance is supplemented by an appendix that outlines additional supervisory requirements specific to jurisdictions applying the IFRS 9 ECL model. The key requirements are outlined below:

1. A bank's definition of default adopted for accounting purposes should be guided by the definition used for regulatory purposes, which includes both a qualitative 'unlikeliness to pay' criterion and an objective 90-days-past-due criterion, described by the Committee as a 'backstop'.

2. The IFRS 9 requirement to assess whether exposures have significantly increased in credit risk 'is demanding in its requirements for data, analysis and use of experienced credit judgement'. The determination should be made 'on a timely and holistic basis', considering a wide range of current information. It is critical that banks have processes in place to ensure that financial instruments, whether assessed individually or collectively, are moved from the 12-month to the lifetime ECL measurement as soon as credit risk has increased significantly. Credit losses very often begin to deteriorate a considerable period of time before an actual delinquency occurs and delinquency data are generally backward-looking. Therefore, 'the Committee believes that they will seldom on their own be appropriate in the implementation of an ECL approach by a bank.' Instead, banks need to consider the linkages between macroeconomic factors and borrower attributes, using historical information to identify the main risk drivers, and current and forecast conditions and experienced credit judgement to determine loss expectations. This will apply not only to collective assessments of portfolios but also for assessments of individual loans. The guidance gives the example of a commercial property loan, for which the bank should assess the sensitivity of the property market to the macroeconomic environment and use information such as interest rates or vacancy rates to make the assessment.[36]

3. In assessing whether there has been a significant increase in credit risk, banks should not rely solely on quantitative analysis. The guidance draws banks' attention to the list of qualitative indicators set out in paragraph B5.5.17 of the standard. Particular consideration should be given to a list of conditions, including an increased credit spread for a particular loan, a decision to strengthen collateral and/or covenant requirements, a downgrade by a credit rating agency or within the bank's internal credit rating system, a deterioration in future cash flows, or an expectation of forbearance or restructuring. Also, the guidance stresses that the sensitivity of the risk of a default occurring to rating downgrades increases strongly as rating quality declines. Therefore, the widths of credit risk grades need to be set appropriately, so that significant increases in credit risk are not masked. Further, 'if a decision is made to intensify the monitoring of a borrower or class of

borrowers, it is unlikely that such action would have been taken ... had the increase in credit risk not been perceived as significant.'[37]

4. Exposures that are transferred to stage 2 and that are subsequently renegotiated or modified, but not derecognised, should not be moved back to stage 1 until there is sufficient evidence that the credit risk over the remaining life is no longer significantly higher than on initial recognition. 'Typically, a customer would need to demonstrate consistently good payment behaviour over a period of time before the credit risk is considered to have decreased.'[38]

5. IFRS 9 includes a number of practical expedients (see 6.4 above). However, as banks are in the business of lending and it is unlikely that obtaining relevant information will involve undue cost or effort, the Basel Committee expects their limited use by internationally active banks. For instance:

    a. The long-term benefit of a high-quality implementation of an ECL model that takes into account all reasonable and supportable information far outweighs the associated costs.

    b. The use of the low credit risk simplification is considered a low-quality implementation of the ECL model and its use should be limited (except for holdings in debt securities, which are out of scope of the guidance). Also, the reference to an investment grade rating in the standard is only given as an example of a low credit risk exposure. An investment grade rating given by a rating agenda cannot automatically be considered low credit risk because banks are expected to rely primarily on their own credit assessments.

    c. Delinquency is a lagging indicator. Therefore, the Committee expects banks not to use the more-than-30-days-past-due rebuttable presumption as a primary indicator of a significant increase in credit risk. Banks may only use the rebuttable presumption as a backstop measure, alongside other, earlier indicators, while any rebuttal of the presumption would have to be accompanied by a thorough analysis to show that 30 days past due is not correlated with a significant increase in credit risk.[39]

7.2 Global Public Policy Committee (GPPC) guidance

On 17 June 2016, the GPPC published *The implementation of IFRS 9 impairment by banks – Considerations for those charged with governance of systemically important banks* ('the GPPC guidance'). The GPPC is the Global Public Policy Committee of representatives of the six largest accounting networks. This publication was issued to promote high-quality implementation of the accounting for ECLs in accordance with IFRS and to help those charged with governance to identify the elements of a high-quality implementation. It was designed to complement other guidance such as that issued by the Basel Committee (see 7.1 above) and the EDTF (see Chapter 54 at 9.2). It does not purport to amend or interpret the requirements of IFRS 9 in any way. The first half of the GPCC guidance sets out key areas of focus for those charged with governance. This includes governance and controls, transition issues and ten questions that those charged with governance might wish to discuss. The second half of the guidance sets out a sophisticated approach to implementing each aspect of the requirements of IFRS 9, along with considerations for a simpler approach and what is not compliant. Where relevant to understanding the accounting requirements of IFRS 9, this guidance is reflected in this chapter.

The GPPC guidance regards determination of the level of sophistication of the approach to be used as one of the key areas of focus for those charged with governance. Consequently, it provides guidance on how to make this determination for particular portfolios. It sets out factors to consider at the level of the entity, such as the extent of systemic risk that the bank poses, whether it is listed or a public interest entity, the size of its balance sheet and off balance sheet credit exposures, and the level and volatility of historical credit losses. Portfolio-level factors include its size relative to that of the total balance sheet and its complexity, the sophistication of other lending-related modelling methodologies, the extent of available data, the level of historical losses and the level and volatility of losses expected in the future. The document stresses that a simpler approach is not necessarily a lower quality approach if it is applied to an appropriate portfolio.

Also, on 28 July 2017, the GPPC issued its second paper titled *The Auditor's Response to the Risks of Material Misstatement Posed by Estimates of Expected Credit Losses under IFRS 9*. This second paper was written in an effort to assist audit committees in their oversight of the bank's auditors with regard to auditing ECLs. It is addressed primarily to the audit committees of systemically-important banks (SIBs) because of the relative importance of SIBs to capital markets and global financial stability but is relevant for other banks as well. It should be read in conjunction with the initial guidance published in 2016.

7.3 Measurement dates of expected credit losses

7.3.1 Date of derecognition and date of initial recognition

Impairment must be assessed and measured at the reporting date. IFRS 9 also requires a derecognition gain or loss to be measured relative to the carrying amount at the date of derecognition (see Chapter 54 at 4.2.1 and 7.1.1). This necessitates an assessment and measurement of ECLs for that particular asset as at the date of derecognition, as was confirmed by the discussions at the April 2015 ITG meeting. Essentially, the calculation of derecognition gains or losses is a two-step process:

- Step 1: ECLs are remeasured at the date of derecognition and presented in the separate impairment line item in the statement of profit or loss as per paragraph 82(ba) of IAS 1 – *Presentation of Financial Statements*. The change in ECL estimate should still reflect the reporting entity's view rather than the market's view of credit losses based upon the remaining contractual life of the financial asset. Also, the residual life of the asset should not be deemed to be nil because of the imminent sale and impairment losses that have not materialised should not be mechanically reversed to reflect the fact that the reporting entity will no longer be holding the debt security. This is consistent with Illustrative Examples 13 and 14 of IFRS 9. In particular, a footnote to the last journal entry in Illustrative Example 14 explains that the loss on sale includes the accumulated impairment amount.
- Step 2: Gains or losses on derecognition are calculated taking into account all ECLs for financial assets measured at amortised cost and all cumulative gains or losses

previously recognised in other comprehensive income including those related to ECLs for financial assets measured at fair value through other comprehensive income. Unlike the requirement to present gains and losses arising from the derecognition of financial assets measured at amortised cost as a separate line item in the statement of profit or loss as per paragraph 82(aa) of IAS 1, there is no specific presentation requirement for financial assets measured at fair value through other comprehensive income.

Since that discussion, the ITG has discussed whether the expected sales of impaired assets should be reflected in the calculation of ECLs (see 5.8.2 above). Given their conclusion that an entity should, it is quite possible that there will be little or no additional losses to record on derecognition that have not already been reflected in the impairment cost.

A similar issue is whether impairment needs to be measured at the date that an asset is modified (see 8 below).

At the April 2015 meeting, the ITG also discussed a more difficult question, whether impairment must be measured as at the date of initial recognition for foreign currency monetary assets. The significance of this is whether subsequent gains and losses arising from foreign currency retranslation in the first accounting period should be calculated based on the initial gross amortised cost or a net amount, after deducting an impairment allowance. This would affect the allocation of subsequent gains and losses of the asset in this period to impairment or to foreign currency retranslation, so that it would be reported in different lines of the profit or loss account.

Differing views were expressed:

- A few ITG members supported the view that while IFRS 9 does not expressly require ECLs to be measured at the date of initial recognition, the requirements of other IFRSs, e.g. IAS 21 – *The Effects of Changes in Foreign Exchange Rates*, may result in an entity measuring ECLs at the date of initial recognition. Also, Illustrative Example 14 in IFRS 9 implies the need to include ECLs on initial recognition in the measurement of foreign exchange gains and losses in respect of a foreign currency-denominated asset (see Example 51.22 at 9.2 below). However, these members questioned the frequency with which an entity needed to perform that calculation and pointed out that considerations of materiality would be a key factor in making this decision.

- Some other ITG members were of the view that an entity is required to measure a financial asset at its fair value upon initial recognition and that consequently measuring ECLs at initial recognition would be inconsistent with that requirement. *[IFRS 9.5.1.1]*. IFRS 9 includes impairment as part of the subsequent measurement of a financial asset and, consequently, only requires an entity to begin measuring ECLs at the first reporting date after initial recognition (or on derecognition if that occurs earlier). *[IFRS 9.3.2.12, 5.5.3, 5.5.5, 5.5.13]*. While the requirements of other IFRSs should be applied to the loss allowance at that point, the application of those requirements should not result in an entity having to measure ECLs at a date earlier than that specifically required by IFRS 9.

The ITG also noted that the illustrative examples are non-authoritative and illustrate only one way of applying the requirements of IFRS 9. Measuring a 12-month expected loss using point in time, forward-looking information, every time that a foreign currency exposure is first recognised would not be feasible. Given that there was no consensus on this issue, we expect that there may be diversity in practice.

7.3.2 Trade date and settlement date accounting

For financial assets measured at amortised cost or at fair value through other comprehensive income, IFRS 9 requires entities to use the trade date as the date of initial recognition for the purposes of applying the impairment requirements. *[IFRS 9.5.7.4]*. This means that entities that use settlement date accounting for regular way purchases of debt securities may have to recognise a loss allowance for securities which they have purchased but not yet recognised and, correspondingly, no loss allowance for securities that they have sold but not yet derecognised. (See Chapter 49 at 2.2 for further details on trade date accounting and settlement date accounting).

Irrespective of the accounting policy choice for trade date accounting versus settlement date accounting, the recognition of the loss allowance on the trade date ensures that entities recognise the loss allowance at the same time; otherwise entities could choose settlement date accounting to delay recognising the loss allowance until the settlement date. The effect of this is similar to accounting for fair value changes on financial assets measured at fair value through other comprehensive income and those measured at fair value through profit or loss when settlement date accounting is applied (i.e. a measurement change needs to be recognised in profit or loss and the statement of financial position even if the related assets that are being measured are only recognised slightly later). It is also consistent with the treatment of ECLs in loans, where an ECL is calculated in respect of a loan commitment between the date that the commitment is made and the loan is drawn down.

For settlement date accounting, the recognition of a loss allowance for an asset that has not yet been recognised raises the question of how that loss allowance should be presented in the statement of financial position. The time between the trade date and the settlement date is somewhat similar to a loan commitment in that the accounting is off balance sheet, which suggests presentation of the loss allowance as a provision.

In practice, some entities tend to opt for settlement date accounting for regular way securities recorded at amortised cost, because they do not need the additional systems capabilities to account for the securities on trade date (i.e. they do not need to account for them until settlement date). The change from the IAS 39 incurred loss model to the IFRS 9 ECL model means that the settlement date accounting simplification for financial assets measured at amortised cost would lose much of its benefit from an operational perspective.

7.4 Interaction between the initial and subsequent measurement of debt instruments acquired in a business combination and the impairment model of IFRS 9

Consistent with IFRS 9 and IFRS 13 – *Fair Value Measurement*, IFRS 3 requires financial assets acquired in a business combination to be measured by the acquirer on initial recognition at their fair value (see Chapter 49 at 3.3.4 and Chapter 9 at 5.5.5). *[IFRS 3.18, IFRS 3.36]*.

IFRS 3 contains application guidance explaining that an acquirer should not recognise a separate valuation allowance (i.e. loss allowance for ECLs) in respect of loans and receivables acquired in a business combination for contractual cash flows that are deemed to be uncollectible at the acquisition date. This is because the effects of uncertainty about future cash flows are included in the fair value measure. *[IFRS 3.B41]*.

Consequently, the accounting for impairment of debt instruments measured at amortised cost or fair value through other comprehensive income under IFRS 9 does not affect the accounting for the business combination. At the acquisition date, the acquired debt instruments are measured at their acquisition-date fair value in accordance with IFRS 3. No loss allowance is recognised as part of the initial measurement of debt instruments that are acquired in a business combination.

In contrast, after their original recognition, the subsequent accounting for debt instruments acquired in a business combination is in the scope of IFRS 9. *[IFRS 9.5.2.1, 5.2.2, 5.5]*. At the first reporting date after the business combination, following the guidance in IFRS 9, a loss allowance is recognised. *[IFRS 9.5.5.3, 5.5.5]*. This will result in an impairment loss that is recognised in profit or loss (rather than an adjustment to goodwill), just as would be the case if the entity were to originate those assets or acquire them as a portfolio, rather than acquire them through a business combination. *[IFRS 9.5.5.8]*. The assets will all be measured on the basis of 12-month ECLs unless the assets have increased significantly in credit risk between the date of the business combination and the first reporting date.

Despite the colloquial reference to a 'day one' loss that results from the ECL impairment model in IFRS 9, it is important to understand that the recognition of a loss allowance for newly acquired (whether purchased or originated) debt instruments that are in the scope of the impairment requirements of IFRS 9 is a matter of subsequent measurement of those financial instruments. This means that the acquirer recognises the loss allowance for all debt instruments acquired in a business combination (that are subject to impairment accounting) in the reporting period that includes the business combination but not as part of that business combination, and with a corresponding impairment loss in profit or loss. As a result, these acquired assets are carried at a value below their fair value by what is often referred to as 'day two', when the 12-month ECL is booked. This may seem counter-intuitive to many preparers and users of financial statements, but is clearly what is intended by IFRS 9.

The only exception to the need to record ECLs on day two is the specific accounting for purchased or originated credit-impaired financial assets (see 3.3 above). This applies to financial assets which are already credit-impaired at the acquisition date. A financial asset is credit-impaired when one or more events that have a detrimental impact on the estimated future cash flows of that financial asset have occurred (see 3.1 above). For such assets, no allowance is initially made for ECLs, as the ECL is part of the 'credit-adjusted effective interest rate'. This differs from financial assets that are not purchased or originated credit-impaired, where an allowance must be made for expected credit losses (see 3.1 and 3.3 above).

It follows that, on a business combination, the acquirer needs to classify the acquired debt instruments that will be recorded at amortised cost or at fair value through OCI, according to whether they are purchased credit-impaired or not. If not, they will be regarded as stage 1 assets and be subject to a 12-month ECL. If they are purchased credit-impaired, then there will be no need for an additional ECL unless there is a subsequent change in estimated lifetime ECL (see 3.3 above). Furthermore, these purchased credit-impaired loans will always be treated as such and are never subsequently subject to the staging requirements. Also, none of the acquired assets, either performing or purchased credit-impaired, will be classified as stage 2 or stage 3 at the date of initial recognition.

A further issues for debt instruments acquired in a business combination is the application of the rebuttable presumption that there has been a significant increase in credit risk if the loan is 30 days past due (see 6.2.2 above) and that default does not occur later than when a financial asset is 90 days past due (see 5.1 above). For example, if loans are acquired two days before the acquirer's reporting date when they are already 29 days past due or 89 days past due, and if the acquirer were to apply the above rebuttable presumptions, such loans would be presumed to have significantly increased in credit risk (i.e. moved from stage 1 to stage 2) and have defaulted (i.e. moved from stage 1 to stage 3) respectively as at the reporting date.

- For the loans that were 29 days past due, arguably, given the heightened credit risk as at the acquisition date, the loans are unlikely to have significantly increased in credit risk over the short period of two days. Moving the loans from stage 1 to stage 2 would not be consistent with the relative measurement approach of the IFRS 9 impairment model, which is intended to track and determine whether there has been a significant increase in credit risk since initial recognition (see 6 above). However, the acquirer is permitted to rebut the presumption and apply it only to those loans that are not past due when purchased, or else 'start the clock' only at the date of acquisition (see 6.2.2 above for further discussion on the 30 day past due rebuttable presumption).

- For the loans that were 89 days past due, similar to the issue for loans that were 29 days past due, moving the loans from stage 1 directly to stage 3 may not result in useful information for the users of the accounts. Acquirers are recommended to consider all the criteria set out in the standard to determine whether such loans were actually purchased credit-impaired (see 3.3 above) and not to rely solely on the days past due.

7.5 Interaction between expected credit losses calculations and fair value hedge accounting

Previously, the implementation guidance of IAS 39 made it clear that a fair value hedge adjustment would be included in the carrying amount of a financial asset that is subject to the impairment requirements. Otherwise, a part of its carrying amount would not have a loss allowance or the loss allowance would be overstated (in case of a negative fair value hedge adjustment). This guidance stated that the effect of fair value hedge accounting is to adjust the EIR, which affects the rate used to discount expected future cash flows. *[IAS 39.E.4.4]*. The rationale given in the example is that the original interest rate before the hedge becomes irrelevant once the carrying amount of the loan is adjusted for any changes in its fair value attributable to interest rate movements.

Similarly, for a financial asset that becomes credit-impaired, IFRS 9 requires impairment to be measured by reference to the gross carrying amount of the asset, which would include the fair value hedge adjustment. Therefore, for a credit-impaired financial asset in stage 3, the EIR would be adjusted to reflect any fair value hedge adjustment. *[IFRS 9.B5.5.33]*.

However, whereas under IAS 39, most assets that are impaired would not generally be those for which fair value hedge accounting has been undertaken, under the ECL impairment model an allowance is required for all assets, i.e., including assets in stages 1 and 2, in addition to assets in stage 3. Hence, if the discount rate were to be adjusted whenever fair value hedge accounting is applied, then all fair value hedge adjustments would need to be taken into account in calculating ECLs. This would give rise to significant operational challenges.

IFRS 9 is not explicit on this matter, but two points in the standard would seem to be relevant. First, unlike IAS 39, except for credit-impaired assets, the ECL requirements are not based on an asset's 'carrying amount' but on the contractual cash flows that are expected to be lost. Second, implementation guidance E4.4 in IAS 39, which stated that a fair value hedge adjusts the EIR, was not carried forward into the new standard. We understand that removing this guidance was not intended to change the accounting treatment in this respect. However another requirement of IAS 39, carried forward into IFRS 9, is that a fair value hedge adjustment is only required to be amortised when the hedged item ceases to be adjusted for changes in fair value attributable to the risk being hedged, which can be read to imply that until then there is no need to adjust the EIR, and hence the rate used to discount ECLs. *[IFRS 9.6.5.10]*.

We believe the requirement is not clear and, so at least until it is clarified, there is an accounting policy choice for exposures that are the designated hedged items in fair value hedge relationships. One approach would be to adjust the EIR whenever a fair value hedge adjustment is made and hence change the interest rate used to discount ECLs. The other approach would be not to adjust the EIR or otherwise take into account the fair value hedge adjustment until the EIR is adjusted to amortise the fair value hedge adjustment. *[IFRS 9.6.5.8]*. Such an adjustment to the EIR is permitted to commence at any time but would, at the latest, be required when hedge accounting ceases or when the financial asset becomes credit impaired, i.e. moved to stage 3.

7.6 Changes in ECL methodologies – errors, changes in estimates or changes in accounting policies

Many entities, having now had some experience of applying IFRS 9, may be considering changing various aspects of their ECL methodologies. The potential changes could include the correction of errors found in the model, updating PD, LGD and EAD for recent experience, making changes to how significant increases in credit risk are assessed, and amending the definition of default and write-off policies. The question that these potential amendments pose is whether they should be accounted for as prior year errors or changes in accounting policies, both of which (if material) would be adjusted for retrospectively, or changes in estimates which would be accounted for as they arise.

The majority of such changes are likely to be changes in estimates. The only changes that will likely be treated as errors are those that are 'omissions from, and misstatements in, the entity's financial statements for one or more prior periods arising from a failure to use, or misuse of, reliable information that:

(a) was available when financial statements for those periods were authorised for issue; and

(b) could reasonably be expected to have been obtained and taken into account in the preparation and presentation of those financial statements'. *[IAS 8.5]*.

Examples of errors would include failure to calculate ECLs on all relevant exposures, errors in input data and incorrect spreadsheet formulae. Most amendments to ECL calculation methods, including use of more sophisticated or more up to date data, revisions to formulae or measurement on a more granular basis, are likely to be changes in estimates. It is unlikely that amendments to the calculation approach would be regarded as a change in accounting policy.

If changes are made to how credit risk is assessed for the staging assessment, care must be taken to distinguish between changes in how the risk is perceived and how it is measured, and changes in what is regarded as 'significant'. In general, it is not appropriate to reassess the credit risk of a financial asset on initial recognition. If the initial credit risk turns out to be riskier than expected, then the initial credit risk is not amended; it is possible that the asset will be transferred to stage 2 and the profit or loss impact would be accounted for as a change in estimate. On the other hand, if all that is amended is the way that the credit risk is measured, such as expressing the risk in terms of 12-month PDs as opposed to lifetime PDs, it may be necessary to recalibrate the initial credit risk using the new measurement basis, so as to measure initial and current credit risk on a consistent basis. Meanwhile, the effect on ECLs of a change in the level of risk that is deemed to be 'significant' would normally be treated as a change in estimate.

7.7 Securitisations and special purpose entities (SPEs)

Securitisation transactions are carried out to transfer risk and/or raise finance from external investors by enabling them to invest in parcels of specific financial assets such as mortgage loans, credit card receivables, other consumer loans, or lease receivables. In a relatively simple structure, a special purpose entity ('SPE') issues notes to investors and lends the money raised to an entity (the 'originator'), secured by the portfolio of assets, either with recourse to the originator should the cash flows on the portfolio be insufficient to repay the loan, or sometimes with no recourse.

A typical more complicated structure involves the originator selling the portfolio of loans to the SPE. In either case, the SPE's equity share capital, which will typically be small, will often be owned by a trustee on behalf of a charitable trust. The loans will often be issued in series of tranches, with varying levels of risk, established through a 'waterfall' of payments, and at different rates of interest to reflect the risk. The originator will often continue to administer the loans as before, for which it will receive a service fee from the SPE (see Chapter 52 at 3.6).

Some of the common issues that have arisen in practice in relation to securitisations and SPEs include contractually linked instruments and subordinated interests (see 6.1.2 above), the application by the SPE of the ECL requirements when the transferor is not able to derecognise the portfolio of loans (see 7.7.1 below), and accounting for a financial liability issued by an SPE (see 7.7.2 below).

7.7.1 ECL requirements for the SPE if the transferor is not able to derecognise the portfolio of loans

In many securitisation structures, the originator will retain some form of interest in the transferred assets which will preclude derecognition of the assets by the originator.

In the simplest types of structures, where the SPE just lends money to the originator, secured on the portfolio, the SPE will recognise this loan and measure ECLs accordingly. If the loan is without recourse to the originator, then the collateral value of the portfolio will be the most important element of the calculation.

In more complex cases, where the portfolio has been sold by the originator to the SPE, the originator may retain an interest through various different mechanisms. These can include, for example, the provision of guarantees or put options, an obligation to substitute non-preforming loans, deferred consideration, or by the originator investing in a junior tranche of the notes issued by the SPE. In each case, the SPE does not recognise the transferred assets, but recognises a 'deemed loan' receivable from the originator for the amount of the proceeds paid to buy the transferred assets (see Chapter 52 at 3.5.2 and 3.6).

The 'deemed loan' is a financial asset which, following a similar approach to the classification of contractually linked instruments (as described in Chapter 48 at 6.6), will often qualify to be recorded at amortised cost or at FVOCI. Assuming it is not measured at fair value through profit or loss, as described at 6.1.2 above, it is subject to the ECL requirements of IFRS 9. However, the standard does not set out how the ECLs on the deemed loan should be determined and whether the performance of the underlying loans should be reflected in the measurement of the deemed loan in the standalone accounts of the SPE.

The SPE is exposed to two sources of risk on the deemed loan: (1) the credit risk of the originator, in effect collateralised by the portfolio of loans, and (2) an exposure to the underlying portfolio, to the extent that the originator does not retain all the risks. For instance, if the originator indemnifies the SPE for the first 5% of impairment losses, the SPE is exposed to the originator should it be unable to pay out on the indemnity, but also to the underlying loans to the extent that losses exceed 5%. Although the second of these risks is not strictly a credit risk arising on the deemed loan, similar to the treatment of contractually linked instruments (see 6.1.2 above), both of these sources of risk would be included by the SPE in the measurement of ECLs.

It follows that, when determining whether there has been a significant increase in credit risk on the deemed loan, depending on the terms of the arrangement, the SPE is likely to need both to look through to the staging of the underlying loans but also to take into account any change in the originator's credit risk. If the originator retains all the risks associated with the underlying loans, then the determination would only consider the originator's ability to pay.

Some securitisations are structured such that the SPE is exposed to a very low risk of loss. This might be achieved, for instance, through the originator being paid deferred consideration dependent on the amounts realised from the loans or, if the SPE lends to the originator secured by the loans and ensuring that there is sufficient excess collateral to absorb any losses expected to arise. In these circumstances it is possible that the SPE's ECLs may be immaterial.

As will be apparent from this brief discussion, securitisation structures vary significantly, and each transaction will need to be assessed based on its own facts and circumstances. Disclosures will also play an important role in providing useful information to the users of the accounts with respect to the securitisation arrangements in place, the exposure to the originator, the credit quality of the underlying loans and how impairment is assessed.

7.7.2 Accounting for a financial liability issued by an SPE

In many securitisation structures, an SPE invests in a portfolio of loans and raises funds by issuing listed notes to investors. The SPE's contractual obligations on the listed notes are linked to the performance of the loans less the interest spread as, typically, the listed notes bear an interest rate slightly lower than the loans to allow the SPE to earn a spread that is sufficient to cover its operating costs and/or to provide some loss absorption capital. The retention of the interest spread and inability of the SPE to pass the cash flows received from the loan to the noteholder 'without material delay' usually result in the SPE failing the 'pass-through' test for the loans and so the SPE cannot derecognise them (see Chapter 52 at 3.5.2 and 3.6.4).

Assuming that the loans held by the SPE are recorded at amortised cost (or FVOCI), under IFRS 9 the SPE is required to record ECLs on the loans. However, any losses suffered on the loans will be borne by the noteholders, due to the contractual linkage feature. This raises the question on how the linkage feature should be accounted for.

In our view, the linkage feature should be accounted for as part of the listed notes liability. In most circumstances, the linkage feature is not a credit derivative that is embedded in a host debt instrument and required to be separated (for instance, because it would allow one party to transfer the credit risk of a particular reference asset, which it may not own, to another party). *[IFRS 9.B4.3.5(f)]*. If the linkage feature is closely related to the liability (see Chapter 46 at 5), it is not separated as an embedded derivative, and is therefore required to be accounted for as part of the amortised cost of the liability. In such instances, any revisions to the estimated contractual cash payments on the listed notes due to the linkage feature should be accounted for as an adjustment to the amortised cost of the noteholder liability that is recognised in profit or loss as per paragraph B5.4.6 of IFRS 9 (see Chapter 50 at 3.4.1).

Although the linkage feature might be thought of as a financial guarantee of the SPE's loans, as it has the effect of transferring credit losses on the loans from the SPE to the noteholders, it cannot be accounted for as a credit enhancement of the loans and thereby reduce the ECLs. Such a treatment is not consistent with the requirements of the standard and the IFRIC discussion that if a credit enhancement is required to be recognised separately by IFRS Standards, an entity cannot include the cash flows expected from it in the measurement of ECLs (see 5.8.1 above).

As a consequence of accounting for the linkage feature as part of the listed notes liability, while the SPE will recognise gains on the linkage feature if the loans deteriorate, as it records higher ECLs on the loans, the gains recognised under paragraph B5.4.6 of IFRS 9 are unlikely to match the ECL impairment expense, giving rise to some volatility of earnings. This is because the ECLs are calculated based on the probability-weighted amount of credit losses that is based on 12-month ECL if the loans are in stage 1 and lifetime ECLs if the loans are in stages 2 and 3, whilst the gains recognised under paragraph B5.4.6 of IFRS 9 are calculated based on the present value of the estimated future cash receipts. A possible approach to reduce the effect of this accounting mismatch is, on initial recognition, to irrevocably designate the loans and notes at fair value through profit or loss in order to eliminate or significantly reduces the measurement or recognition inconsistency, in accordance with paragraphs 4.1.5 and 4.2.2 of IFRS 9 (see Chapter 48 at 7).

7.8 Measuring ECLs during the coronavirus (covid-19) pandemic

7.8.1 Introduction

A major challenge in 2020 for the application of the IFRS ECL model has been the coronavirus pandemic. The virus has significantly affected the world economy and also resulted in significant volatility in the financial and commodities markets. Many countries have imposed travel bans on millions of people and many more have been subject to quarantine measures. Businesses have been dealing with lost revenue and disrupted supply chains. Whilst many countries have started to ease the lockdown, the relaxation has had to be gradual and, as at the time of writing, there is still large-scale business disruption. This has given rise to liquidity issues for many entities and also has consequential impacts on the credit quality of entities along the supply chain. This also has knock on effects on retail loan portfolios as many businesses have had to reduce staff numbers, resulting in an increase in the number of unemployed workers. In responding to these challenges, certain governments and central banks have introduced, or have directed or encouraged commercial banks to introduce, various types of relief measures. The consequence is that there are two sources of uncertainty for the calculation of ECLs: first, the potential development and consequences of the virus and, second, the extent and effect of the various relief measures.

7.8.2 Guidance

A number of prudential and securities regulators, including the European Banking Authority (EBA), the European Central Bank (ECB), the European Securities and Market Authority (ESMA), the Prudential Regulation Authority (PRA) in the United Kingdom and The Office of the Superintendent of Financial Institutions (OSFI) in Canada (the regulators) have published guidance on the regulatory and accounting implications of the pandemic. The IASB has been closely engaged with many prudential and securities regulators and others regarding the application of IFRS 9 in the context of the covid-19 pandemic and has encouraged entities whose regulators have issued guidance to consider that guidance.

In March 2020, the IASB published a document for educational purposes, *IFRS 9 and covid-19 – Accounting for expected credit losses applying IFRS 9 Financial Instruments in the light of current uncertainty resulting from the covid-19 pandemic*, to help support the consistent application of accounting standards. The document is broadly consistent with the guidance from the regulators and emphasises the following:

- IFRS 9 sets out a framework for determining the amount of ECLs that should be recognised. It requires that lifetime ECLs be recognised when there is a significant increase in credit risk on a financial instrument. However, it does not set bright lines or a mechanistic approach to determining when lifetime losses are required to be recognised. Nor does it dictate the exact basis on which entities should determine forward-looking scenarios to consider when estimating ECLs (see 5 above).
- IFRS 9 requires the application of judgement and both requires and allows entities to adjust their approach to determining ECLs in different circumstances. A number of assumptions and linkages underlying the way ECLs have been implemented to date may no longer hold in the current environment. Entities should not continue to apply their existing ECL methodology mechanically. For example, the extension of payment holidays to all borrowers in particular classes of financial instruments should not automatically result in all those instruments being considered to have suffered significant increases in credit risk (see 6.2.1 above).
- To assess significant increases in credit risks, IFRS 9 requires that entities assess changes in the risk of a default occurring over the expected life of a financial instrument. Both the assessment of significant increases in credit risk and the measurement of ECLs are required to be based on reasonable and supportable information that is available to an entity without undue cost or effort (see 5.9.5 above).
- Entities are required to develop estimates based on the best available information about past events, current conditions and forecasts of economic conditions. In assessing forecast conditions, consideration should be given both to the effects of covid-19 and the significant government support measures being undertaken (see 5.9.3, 5.9.5, and 5.8.1.C above).
- It is likely to be difficult at this time (March 2020) to incorporate the specific effects of covid-19 and government support measures on a reasonable and supportable basis. However, changes in economic conditions should be reflected in macroeconomic scenarios applied by entities and in their weightings. If the effects of covid-19 cannot be reflected in models, post-model overlays or adjustments will need to be considered. The environment is subject to rapid change and updated facts and circumstances should continue to be monitored as new information becomes available (see 5.9.5 above).
- Although current circumstances are difficult and create high levels of uncertainty, if ECL estimates are based on reasonable and supportable information and IFRS 9 is not applied mechanistically, useful information can be provided about ECLs. Indeed, in the stressed environment caused by covid-19, IFRS 9 and the associated disclosures can provide much needed transparency to users of financial statements (see 7.8.5 and 15 below and Chapter 54 at 5.3 and 9.1).

7.8.3 Calculation of ECLs

Whether the impact of an event such as the coronavirus pandemic is reflected in an individual ECL assessment (estimating the probability of default on an individual basis), factored into the scenario analysis of future macroeconomic conditions on a collective basis, or adjusted through management overlays, depends on the entity's systems and processes and the facts and circumstances. In practice, entities are likely to consider a combination of these approaches. In estimating the impact of the event, entities should, however, be careful to avoid double-counting the effects of the various assumptions applied in individual assessments, macroeconomic scenarios and management overlays.

In abnormal circumstances such as those created by the coronavirus pandemic, it may take time before entities detect changes in risk indicators at a specific borrower level and are able to reassess the affected exposures. In order to accelerate the reflection of such changes in credit quality not yet detected at an individual borrower level, it may be appropriate to adjust ratings and the probabilities of default on a collective basis, considering risk characteristics such as the industry or geographical location of the borrowers (see 6.5 above). However, many methods for performing collective assessments make use of historical information, which may not be relevant in the circumstances. Further, it may be necessary to reconsider if loans need to be segmented differently than in the past to reflect the risk characteristics.

Many financial institutions consider multiple macroeconomic scenarios in the assessment of ECLs (see 6.7 above). In addition to updating GDP expectations for the various scenarios, a challenge is to estimate how the impact of the coronavirus pandemic and any related government programmes affect specific sectors, regions and borrowers, especially as the details surrounding many government programmes has continued to evolve.

The IASB educational document noted that a number of assumptions and linkages underlying the way ECLs has been implemented to date may no longer hold in the environment affected by the pandemic. For example, the relationship between GDP and other macroeconomic variables, such as unemployment and interest rates, and sector-specific variables, such as oil prices, is very likely to be different from what has been experienced in the past and reflected in economic forecasting models. The probability weightings assigned to macroeconomic scenarios may also need to be revisited.

Lenders will also need to assess how the value of collateral, such as the homes underlying mortgages or commercial property prices, will develop over the next few years. They will also need to take into account any guarantees from governments or other parties that are considered integral to the loans (see 5.8.1.C above), having assessed the credit standing of the guarantor.

In estimating overlays, entities may consider historical experience. However, it appears clear that the widespread nature and severity of the consequences of the coronavirus pandemic is not directly comparable with any recent similar events. It may be appropriate for this purpose, to plot several possible scenarios of what might happen over the forecasting period and assign weightings to them, to ensure that any overlay reflects the inherent uncertainty and non-linearity of potential outcomes.

The IASB noted in their educational material that IFRS 9 requires the application of judgement and both requires and allows entities to adjust their approach to determining ECLs in different circumstances

7.8.4 Determining whether there has been a significant increase in credit risk

In the context of the coronavirus pandemic, one of the accounting issues has been whether concessions made by lenders, such as changes in payment terms and the granting of payment holidays, should result in loans being move from stage 1 to stage 2.

The IASB noted in their educational material that IFRS 9 requires the application of judgement and both requires and allows entities to adjust their approach to determining ECLs in different circumstances.

If payment terms are extended, the terms and conditions of the extension will have to be assessed to determine their impacts on the ECL estimate as well as any other accounting impacts. For example, if the payment terms of a receivable are extended from 90 days to 180 days, this would likely not be considered a substantial modification of the receivable (see 8 below). However, such an extension may result in an increase in PD, which would, in turn, affect the measurement of ECL. For entities which do not apply the simplified model (see 3 above), such extension may also result in moving the receivable to stage 2, depending on the extent and terms of the payment extension. However, if the same extension of payment terms is offered to an entire class of customers irrespective of individual circumstances, this should generally not result, by itself, in a stage movement.

A number of assumptions and linkages underlying the way ECLs have been implemented to date may no longer hold in the environment affected by the coronavirus pandemic. Entities should not continue to apply their existing ECL methodology mechanically. For example, the extension of payment holidays to all borrowers in particular classes of financial instruments should not automatically result in all those instruments being considered to have suffered a significant increase in credit risk. This would be the case even if a moratorium results in a loss for the lender (e.g. if interest payments are reduced or waived), if it is provided irrespective of the borrowers' individual circumstances and the extension of payment holidays are assessed to be modifications rather than derecognition of the financial instruments (see 8 below).

In other situations, if relief measures are available only to those who meet certain criteria, entities need to carefully assess whether such criteria themselves might indicate a significant increase in credit risk for the affected borrowers. For instance, a significant increase in credit risk is more likely to have occurred if a borrower applies for a relief measure which is available only to corporates which have suspended operations or individuals who have lost employment. Another example is if the relief, such as a deferral of loan payments, is offered to all participants in certain industries. This circumstance may indicate that borrowers in that industry are exposed to a higher risk of business failure and, thus, a higher probability of default as a class. In combination with other reasonable and supportable information, this is more likely to result in the classification of the related loans and other exposures in this portfolio, or a portion of them, into stage 2. The assessment of significant increase in credit risk should be made irrespective of the fact that a concession is imposed by laws or regulations. Entities are also expected to exercise judgement, in light of all facts and circumstances, including the effect of government support, to determine if the respective loans are credit impaired and should therefore be classified as stage 3.

Regulators have stressed, in the context of the coronavirus epidemic, the need when assessing borrowers to differentiate a temporary liquidity need from a significant increase in credit risk and highlighted that there may be very limited information available to make this determination at an individual borrower level. This means that lenders should distinguish between obligors whose long-term credit risk is unlikely to be significantly affected by the pandemic from those who may be more permanently impacted. In light of the above, the 30 days past due backstop assumption may need to be rebutted in these circumstances. (see 6.2.2 above).

Entities whose models include payment holidays or waiver of a covenant breach as automatic significant increase in credit risk triggers may need to include overlays to unwind the effects if they determine that the significant increase in credit risk trigger is not warranted in this situation. For retail loans, data will often not be available to determine whether a significant increase in credit risk has occurred for individual borrowers. For wholesale exposures, more information is generally available on individual obligors, although the significant increase in credit risk assessment will still be difficult. A lender may consider that borrowers in certain industries (e.g. airlines, tourism and hospitality) are exposed to a higher risk of business failure and, thus, an increased PD.

When it is not practical to determine significant increase in credit risk on an individual basis, a collective approach to staging should be considered (see 6.5 above). This will also be challenging. A possible method could be to transfer to stage 2 a portion of those customers who have been given a payment holiday or a waiver of a covenant breach, whose PD was already close to the level that would trigger a significant increase in credit risk. Any approach will require considerable judgement.

Where additional rounds of relief measures are extended to existing borrowers, the same considerations which were applicable to assessing the initial relief are also applicable in determining whether the additional relief constitutes a significant increase in credit risk. If the extension of the relief measures is offered only to selected borrowers (e.g. upon individual requests), it may be harder to conclude that a significant increase in credit risk has not occurred, as the need for additional relief may be in response to further deterioration in the borrower's financial position.

7.8.5 Disclosures

Given the level of uncertainty and the sensitivity of judgements and estimates, disclosures of the key assumptions used and judgements made in estimating ECLs, as well as the concentration of risk, liquidity risk and the impact of any relief measures, are important (see 15 below and Chapter 54 at 5.3 and 9.1). Entities should also consider any guidance and expectations on disclosures of ECLs in the current environment that may be issued by prudential and securities regulators in their jurisdictions.

An example of disclosures dealing with the impact of the coronavirus pandemic on ECLs, how economic scenarios are reflected in ECLs and post-model management adjustments of a bank is illustrated below. Note that for brevity not all the region columns, given in HSBC Holdings' interim report, have been reproduced in Extract 51.1.

Extract 51.1: HSBC Holdings plc (Interim report for the six months ended 30 June 2020)
Interim Report 2020 [extracts]
Measurement uncertainty and sensitivity analysis of ECL estimates [extract]
Methodology [extract]
[...]

The following table describes key macroeconomic variables and the probabilities assigned in the consensus Central scenario.
Central scenario (3Q20–2Q25) [extract]

	UK %	US %	Hong Kong %	Mainland China %	Canada %	France %
GDP growth						
Annual average growth rate: 2020	(7.8)	(5.2)	(4.8)	1.4	(7.1)	(8.7)
Annual average growth rate: 2021	5.9	4.1	4.2	8.1	5.5	7.2
1Q22–2Q25: average growth	1.9	2.4	2.3	5.3	2.1	1.7
3Q20–2Q22: worst quarter	(8.6) (3Q20)	(6.6) (3Q20)	(2.6) (3Q20)	3.3 (4Q21)	(8.2) (3Q20)	(8.9) (3Q20)
Unemployment rate						
Annual average: 2020	6.8	9.5	4.6	4.5	10	9.8
Annual average: 2021	6.3	7.3	4.1	4.2	8.1	10.0
1Q22–2Q25: average	4.7	5.6	3.7	3.9	6.5	8.9
3Q20–2Q22: worst quarter	8.1 (3Q20)	11.0 (3Q20)	4.8 (3Q20)	4.6 (3Q20)	11.1 (3Q20)	10.6 (3Q20)
House price index						
Annual average growth rate: 2020	(2.2)	1.7	(7.9)	1.8	0.2	(0.5)
Annual average growth rate: 2021	0.9	(2.6)	0.4	2.6	2.1	(0.3)
1Q22–2Q25: average growth	3.7	2.3	3.4	5.4	3.4	3.4
3Q20–2Q22: worst quarter	(3.4) (4Q20)	(3.6) (2Q21)	(11.5) (3Q20)	1.3 (1Q21)	(4.0) (1Q21)	(3.9) (4Q20)
10-year bond yield						
Annual average: 2020	0.5	0.9	1.2	N/A	0.8	0.0
Annual average: 2021	0.8	1.2	1.7	N/A	1.1	0.2
1Q22–2Q25: average	1.6	2.2	2.2	N/A	1.9	0.9
3Q20–2Q22: worst quarter	0.4 (3Q20)	0.8 (3Q20)	1.2 (3Q20)	N/A	0.7 (3Q20)	0.0 (3Q20)
Probability	60	70	70	70	70	70

Note: N/A – not required in credit models.

...

The range of macroeconomic projections across the various scenarios are shown in the table below:

Outer scenario ranges (3Q20–2Q25)

	UK %	US %	Hong Kong %	Mainland China %	Canada %	France %
GDP growth	(8.3) to (16.7) (3Q20) (1Q21)	(6.0) to (12.8) (3Q20) (3Q20)	(1.5) to (15.8) (3Q20) (3Q20)	3.9 to (7.2) (4Q21) (3Q20)	(8.1) to (14.3) (3Q20) (2Q21)	(8.7) to (22.0) (3Q20) (3Q20)
Unemployment rate	8.0 to 10.5 (3Q20) (2Q21)	10.5 to 18.2 (3Q20) (3Q20)	4.5 to 8.0 (3Q20) (1Q21)	4.5 to 6.1 (3Q20) (1Q22)	11 to 19.5 (3Q20) (3Q20)	10 to 11.5 (3Q20) (1Q21)
House price index	(2.8) to (24.7) (3Q20) (2Q21)	(1.7) to (15.6) (1Q21) (2Q21)	(10.3) to (26.3) (3Q20) (1Q21)	3.3 to (25.8) (3Q20) (3Q21)	(1.3) to (27.6) (3Q20) (2Q21)	(2.4) to (13.4) (4Q20) (3Q21)
10-year bond yield	0.5 to (1.7) (3Q20) (3Q21)	0.8 to (0.2) (3Q20) (2Q21)	1.2 to (0.8) (3Q20) (1Q21)	N/A	0.7 to (0.2) (3Q20) (2Q21)	0.1 to (0.5) (3Q20) (2Q22)
Consensus Upside scenario: Probability	10	5	5	10	10	10
Consensus Downside scenario: Probability	0	20	20	15	15	15
UK management Downside scenario: Probability	20					
Alternative Downside scenario: Probability	10	5	5	5	5	5

Note: The worst point refers to the quarter that is either the trough or peak in the respective variable. The figures provided represent the worst point across all four outer scenarios: the consensus Upside, the consensus Downside, the UK management Downside and the alternative Downside. These figures should not be directly compared with the annual averages presented in the previous table for the Central scenario. N/A – not required in credit models.

[…]

Critical accounting estimates and judgements

The calculation of ECL under IFRS 9 involves significant judgements, assumptions and estimates, as set out in the *Annual Report and Accounts 2019* under 'Critical accounting estimates and judgements'. The level of estimation uncertainty and judgement has increased since 31 December 2019 as a result of the economic effects of the Covid-19 outbreak, including significant judgements relating to:

- the selection and weighting of economic scenarios, given rapidly changing economic conditions in an unprecedented manner, uncertainty as to the effect of government and central bank support measures designed to alleviate adverse economic impacts, and a widening in the distribution of economic forecasts. The key judgement is whether the economic effects of the pandemic are more likely to be temporary or prolonged, and the shape of recovery;
- estimating the economic effects of those scenarios on ECL, where there is no observable historical trend that can be reflected in the models that will accurately represent the effects of the economic changes of the severity and speed brought about by the Covid-19 outbreak. Modelled assumptions and linkages between economic factors and credit losses may underestimate or overestimate ECL in these conditions, and there is significant uncertainty in the estimation of parameters such as collateral values and loss severity; and

- the identification of customers experiencing significant increases in credit risk and credit impairment, particularly where those customers have accepted payment deferrals and other reliefs designed to address short-term liquidity issues, or have extended those deferrals, given limitations in the available credit information on these customers. The use of segmentation techniques for indicators of significant increases in credit risk involves significant estimation uncertainty.

How economic scenarios are reflected in ECL

The methodologies for the application of forward economic guidance into the calculation of ECL for wholesale and retail loans and portfolios are set out on page 95 of the *Annual Report and Accounts 2019*. These models are based largely on historical observations and correlations with default rates.

The severe projections at 30 June 2020 of macroeconomic variables are outside the historical observations on which IFRS 9 models have been built and calibrated to operate. Moreover, the complexities of governmental support programmes and regulatory guidance on treatment of customer impacts (such as forbearance and payment holidays) and the unpredictable pathways of the pandemic have never been modelled. Consequently, HSBC's IFRS 9 models, in some cases, generate outputs that appear overly conservative when compared with other economic and credit metrics. Post-model adjustments are required to ensure that an appropriate amount of ECL impairment is recognised.

These data and model limitations have been addressed in the short term using in-model and post-model adjustments. This includes refining model inputs and outputs and using post-model adjustments based on management judgement and higher level quantitative analysis for impacts that are difficult to model. To ensure a consistent framework, we identified the model segments where results were overly conservative based on historical benchmarks and defined the worst economic inputs where the model output is considered reliable. For example, in the case of probability of default ('PD') models for bank and sovereign exposures, based on the historical calibration data, the model was defined as producing meaningful results when the GDP growth input is not worse than five standard deviations below the long-term average. Re-running the models with these capped economic limits established boundary conditions used by credit experts as a starting point for further adjustments based on their own structured judgement and granular analysis. For the wholesale portfolio, this analysis produced a 'credit experts best estimate' to act as a benchmark against the modelled outcomes, and inform post-model adjustments. In the short term, the focus is on refining model inputs and outputs in a consistent and explainable manner, using post-model adjustments. Wider-ranging model changes will take time to develop and need more real data on which models can be trained.

Models will be recalibrated over time once the full impacts of Covid-19 are observed, but that will not occur in 2020. Therefore, we anticipate significant in-model and post-model adjustments for the foreseeable future.

Post-model adjustments

In the context of IFRS 9, post-model adjustments are short-term increases or decreases to the ECL at either a customer or portfolio level to account for late breaking events, model deficiencies and expert credit judgement applied following management review and challenge. We have internal governance in place to regularly monitor post-model adjustments and, where possible, to reduce the reliance on these through model recalibration or redevelopment, as appropriate. Depending on the path of the Covid-19 outbreak and the shape of the economic recovery, we anticipate the composition of modelled ECL and post-model adjustments may be revised significantly over 2020, particularly when the economy resumes positive GDP growth and the uncertainty over long-term unemployment abates.

Post-model adjustments made in estimating the reported ECL at 30 June 2020 are set out in the following table. The table includes adjustments in relation to data and model limitations resulting from Covid-19 economic conditions, and as a result of the regular process of model development and implementation. It shows the adjustments applicable to the scenario-weighted ECL numbers. Adjustments in relation to Downside scenarios are more significant, as results are subject to greater uncertainty.

Net post-model reductions in ECL ($bn)	Retail	Wholesale	Total
Low-risk counterparties and economies (banks, sovereigns and government entities)	0.4	1.1	1.5
Corporate lending adjustments	–	2.8	2.8
Retail lending adjustments	0.2	–	0.2
Total	0.6	3.9	4.5

Post-model adjustments at 31 December 2019 were an increase of $75m for the wholesale portfolio and $131m for the retail portfolio.

The adjustments relating to low-credit-risk exposures are mainly to highly rated banks, sovereigns and US government-sponsored entities, where modelled credit factors do not fully reflect the underlying fundamentals of these entities or the effect of government support and economic programmes in the Covid-19 environment.

Adjustments to corporate exposures principally reflect the outcome of the 'credit experts best estimate' review on wholesale corporate exposures. Post-model adjustments, both positive and negative, have been made where modelled rating migration, and ECL outputs based on historical relationships, produced results that were overly sensitive. This can be the case when using economic inputs that are well outside the range of historical experience. For retail lending, the net impact of model adjustments was much less significant. The adjustment, under low-risk counterparties and economies, was to reduce ECL on insurance portfolios due to model over-prediction of downgrades in the bank and sovereign portfolios.

The main retail lending post-model adjustment was in relation to the UK where modelled PD outputs for the Downside scenarios were adjusted to address model limitations, so as to be consistent with longer-term relationships between unemployment and defaults.

Another example disclosure dealing with the impact of the coronavirus pandemic on ECLs and government grants of a corporate is illustrated below.

Extract 51.2: Centrica plc (Interim results for the six months ended 30 June 2020)

Notes to the condensed interim Financial Statements [extracts]

3. Accounting policies [extract]

(d) Key sources of estimation uncertainty and critical accounting judgements [extract]

With the exception of the items noted below, key areas of critical accounting judgement and estimation uncertainty that have the most significant effect on the consolidated Group Financial Statements remain as disclosed in note 3(a) and 3(b) of the Annual Report and Accounts for the year ended 31 December 2019.

Covid-19 [extract]

The Covid-19 pandemic has had a profoundly negative impact on the global economy, and there is significant uncertainty around the timing and shape of any economic recovery. This has given rise to an increase in estimation uncertainty for the Group, particularly regarding the matters noted below.

[…]

> Credit provisions for trade and other receivables
>
> The economic effects of the Covid-19 pandemic have impacted the ability of the Group's customers to pay amounts due. While the impact on customers has been mitigated by a number of government support and stimulus schemes, the level of estimation uncertainty in determining the credit provisions required for customers in different sectors and geographies has increased. Details of the approach taken to determining the level of credit provision and associated sensitivities are provided in note 14.
>
> 14. Trade and other receivables, and contract-related assets [extract]
>
> [...]
>
> The application of IFRS 9 to the Group's financial trade and other receivables and contract assets is described in the Annual Report and Accounts for the year ended 31 December 2019. The Group has continued to apply the simplified model in order to measure impairment provisions for credit losses on trade and other receivables, contract assets, and other financial assets that are not carried at fair value.
>
> The economic impacts arising from the Covid-19 pandemic and associated government responses in the geographies in which the Group operates have increased the level of uncertainty around the estimates the Group makes in measuring provisions for the impairment of financial assets. Where customers experience difficulties in settling balances, the increased aging of these amounts results in an increase in provisions held in respect of them under the provision matrix approach employed. In measuring the provision for expected losses, the Group has also considered changes in customer payment patterns, such as direct debit cancellations, and, in the case of business counterparties, the specific circumstances of the customers and the economic impacts of Covid-19 on the sectors in which they operate. Where relevant, the Group has considered macroeconomic forecasts, although government support schemes currently in place for the benefit of customers are expected to mitigate, to some degree, the near-term impacts of any forecast economic decline on financial assets recognised at 30 June 2020.
>
> During the six months to 30 June 2020, the Group incurred impairment charges of £162 million in respect of financial assets (2019: £104 million), representing 1.5% of Group revenue (2019: 0.9%).
>
> The assumptions made in estimating the impairment charge for the period and provisions held at the reporting date are felt to be appropriate, however the current high level of economic uncertainty means that impairment charges and provisions in respect of financial assets are a matter of significant judgement. The impact of any worsening of the economic outlook and any future recession could impact receivables from residential and business customers to differing extents.
>
> A provision of £426 million (31 December 2019: £387 million) has been recognised against gross current receivables from residential customers of £1,651 million (31 December 2019: £1,722 million) – a provision coverage of 25.8% (31 December 2019: 22.5%). Were this coverage to increase by one percentage point, a further impairment charge of £17 million would be recognised. A provision of £228 million (31 December 2019: £198 million) has been recognised against gross current receivables from business customers of £1,713 million (31 December 2019: £2,104 million) – a provision coverage of 13.3% (31 December 2019: 9.4%). Were this coverage to increase by one percentage point, a further impairment charge of £17 million would be recognised.

8 MODIFIED FINANCIAL ASSETS

If the contractual cash flows on a financial asset are renegotiated or modified, the holder needs to assess whether the financial asset should be derecognised (see Chapter 52 at 3.4 and 6.2 and Chapter 50 at 3.8 for further details on modification and derecognition). In summary, an entity should derecognise a financial asset if the cash flows are extinguished or if the terms of the instrument have substantially changed.

Figure 51.6 Application of the derecognition and modification requirements and their interaction with ECL assessment

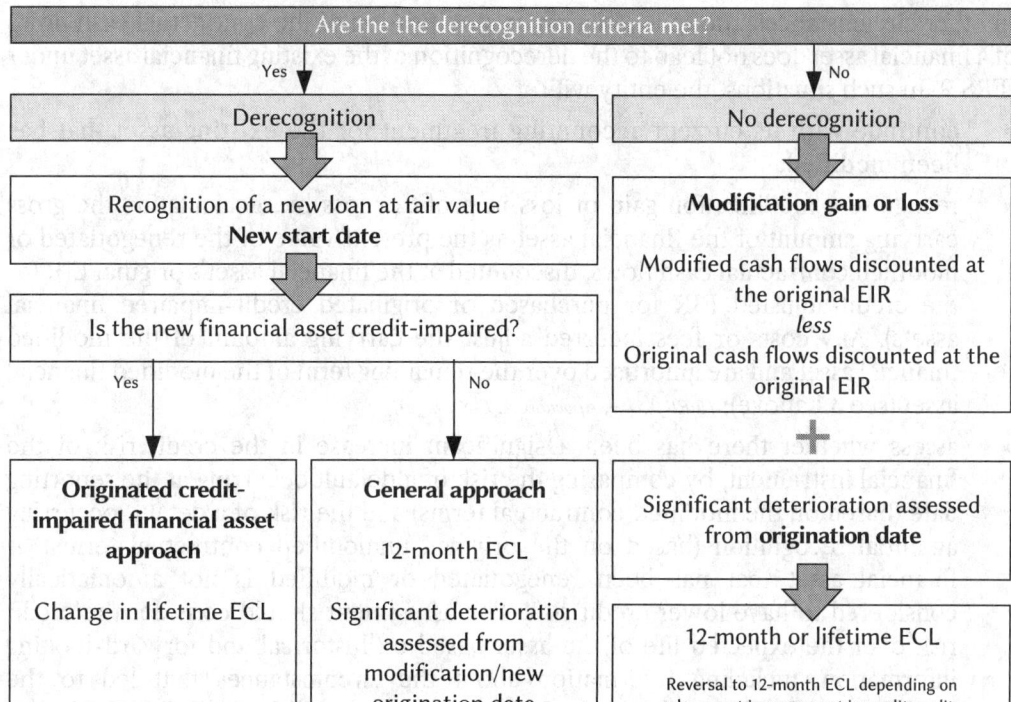

8.1 Accounting treatment if modified financial assets are derecognised

In some circumstances, the renegotiation or modification of the contractual cash flows of a financial asset can lead to the derecognition of the existing financial asset and subsequently, the recognition of a new financial asset. *[IFRS 9.B5.5.25]*. This means that the entity is starting fresh and the date of the modification will also be the date of initial recognition of the new financial asset at its fair value. Typically, the entity will recognise a loss allowance based on 12-month ECLs at each reporting date until the requirements for the recognition of lifetime ECLs are met. However, in what the standard describes as 'some unusual circumstances' following a modification that results in derecognition of the original financial asset, there may be evidence that the new financial asset is credit-impaired on initial recognition (see 3.3 above). Thus, the financial asset should be recognised as an originated credit-impaired financial asset. *[IFRS 9.B5.5.26]*.

8.2 Accounting treatment if modified financial assets are not derecognised

In other circumstances, the renegotiation or modification of the contractual cash flows of a financial asset does not lead to the derecognition of the existing financial asset under IFRS 9. In such situations, the entity will:

- continue with its current accounting treatment for the existing asset that has been modified;
- recognise a modification gain or loss in profit or loss by recalculating the gross carrying amount of the financial asset as the present value of the renegotiated or modified contractual cash flows, discounted at the financial asset's original EIR (or the credit-adjusted EIR for purchased or originated credit-impaired financial assets). Any costs or fees incurred adjust the carrying amount of the modified financial asset and are amortised over the remaining term of the modified financial asset (see 3.1 above); *[IFRS 9.5.4.3, Appendix A, IAS 1.82(a)]*
- assess whether there has been a significant increase in the credit risk of the financial instrument, by comparing the risk of a default occurring at the reporting date (based on the modified contractual terms) and the risk of a default occurring at initial recognition (based on the original, unmodified contractual terms). A financial asset that has been renegotiated or modified is not automatically considered to have lower credit risk. The assessment should consider the credit risk over the expected life of the asset based on historical and forward-looking information, including information about the circumstances that led to the modification. Evidence that the criteria for the recognition of lifetime ECLs are subsequently no longer met may include a history of up-to-date and timely payment in subsequent periods. This means a minimum period of observation will often be necessary before a financial asset may qualify to return to stage 1; *[IFRS 9.5.5.12, B5.5.27]* and
- make the appropriate quantitative and qualitative disclosures required for renegotiated or modified assets to enable users of financial statements to understand the nature and effect of such modifications (including the effect on the measurement of ECLs) and how the entity monitors its assets that have been modified (see 15 below and Chapter 54 at 5.3). *[IFRS 7.35F(f), B8B, 35J]*.

The following example has been adapted from Example 11 of the Implementation Guidance in the standard to illustrate the accounting treatment of a loan that is modified. It should be noted that it does not consider whether any of the contractual cash flows should be written off, as a partial derecognition. *[IFRS 9 Example 11 IE66-IE73]*.

Example 51.19: Modification of contractual cash flows

Bank A originates a five-year loan that requires the repayment of the outstanding contractual amount in full at maturity. Its contractual par amount is €1,000 with an interest rate of 5 per cent, payable annually. The EIR is 5 per cent. At the end of the first reporting period in Year 1, Bank A recognises a loss allowance at an amount equal to 12-month ECLs because there has not been a significant increase in credit risk since initial recognition. A loss allowance balance of €20 is recognised. In Year 2, Bank A determines that the credit risk on the loan has increased significantly since initial recognition. As a result, Bank A recognises lifetime ECLs on the loan. The loss allowance balance is €150 at the end of year 2.

At the end of Year 3, following significant financial difficulty of the borrower, Bank A modifies the contractual cash flows on the loan. It forgoes interest payments beyond year 3 until maturity and extends the contractual term of the loan by one year so that the remaining term at the date of the modification is three years. The modification does not result in the derecognition of the loan by Bank A.

As a result of that modification, Bank A recalculates the gross carrying amount of the financial asset as the present value of the modified contractual cash flows discounted at the loan's original EIR of 5 per cent. The difference between this recalculated gross carrying amount and the gross carrying amount before the modification is recognised as a modification gain or loss. Bank A recognises the modification loss (calculated as €136) against the gross carrying amount of the loan, reducing it to €864, and a modification loss of €136 in profit or loss.

Bank A also remeasures the loss allowance, taking into account the modified contractual cash flows and evaluates whether the loss allowance for the loan should continue to be measured at an amount equal to lifetime ECLs. Bank A compares the current credit risk (taking into consideration the modified cash flows) to the credit risk (on the original unmodified cash flows) at initial recognition. Bank A determines that the loan is not credit-impaired at the reporting date but that credit risk has still significantly increased compared to the credit risk at initial recognition. It continues to measure the loss allowance at an amount equal to the lifetime ECL, which is €110 at the reporting date.

At each subsequent reporting date, Bank A continues to evaluate whether there has been a significant increase in credit risk by comparing the loan's credit risk at initial recognition (based on the original, unmodified cash flows) with the credit risk at the reporting date (based on the modified cash flows).

Two reporting periods after the loan modification (Year 5), the borrower has outperformed its business plan significantly compared to the expectations at the modification date. In addition, the outlook for the business is more positive than previously envisaged. An assessment of all reasonable and supportable information that is available without undue cost or effort indicates that the overall credit risk on the loan has decreased and that the risk of a default occurring over the expected life of the loan has decreased, so Bank A adjusts the borrower's internal credit rating at the end of the reporting period.

Given the positive overall development, Bank A re-assesses the situation and concludes that the credit risk of the loan has decreased and there is no longer a significant increase in credit risk since initial recognition. As a result, Bank A once again measures the loss allowance at an amount equal to 12-month ECLs.

Year	Beginning gross carrying amount	Impairment (loss)/gain	Modification (loss)/gain	Interest revenue	Cash flows	Ending gross carrying amount	Loss allowance	Ending amortised cost amount
	A	B	C	D Gross: A × 5%	E	F = A + C + D − E	G	H = F − G
1	€1,000	(€20)		€50	€50	€1,000	€20	€980
2	€1,000	(€130)		€50	€50	€1,000	€150	€850
3	€1,000	€40	(€136)	€50	€50	€864	€110	€754
4	€864	€24		€43		€907	€86	€821
5	€907	€72		€45		€952	€14	€938
6	€952	€14		€48	€1,000	€0	€0	€0

At its meeting on 22 April 2015, the ITG (see 1.5 above) discussed the measurement of ECLs in respect of a modified financial asset where the modification does not result in derecognition, but the cash flows have been renegotiated to be consistent with those previously expected to be paid.[40]

The ITG noted that IFRS 9 is clear that an entity is required to calculate a new gross carrying amount and the gain or loss on modification taken to profit or loss should be based on the renegotiated or modified contractual cash flows and excludes ECLs unless it is a purchased or originated credit-impaired financial asset. *[IFRS 9.5.4.3, Appendix A]*. Consequently, an entity must calculate the gain or loss on modification as a first step before going on to consider the revised ECL allowance required on the modified financial asset. Thereafter, the entity is required to continue to apply the impairment requirements to the modified financial asset in the same way as it would for other unmodified financial instruments, taking into account the revised contractual terms. *[IFRS 9.5.5.12]*. The revised ECL cannot be assumed to be nil as, in accordance with paragraph 5.5.18 of IFRS 9, an entity is required to consider the possibility that a credit loss occurs, even if the likelihood of that credit loss occurring is very low. *[IFRS 9.5.5.18]*.

The ITG also discussed the appropriate presentation and disclosure requirements pertaining to modifications. These are discussed further in Chapter 54 at 7.1.1.

We note that if an entity has no reasonable expectations of recovering a portion of the financial asset, which is subsequently forgiven, then this amount should arguably be written off, as a partial derecognition. The gross carrying amount would be reduced directly before a modification gain or loss is calculated. *[IFRS 9.5.4.4, B5.4.9]*. This would mean that the loss will be recorded as an impairment loss, rather than as a loss on modification, and presented differently in the profit or loss account. In practice, it will often be difficult to disentangle the effects of modification and write off, as some forgone cash flows may be compensated for by a higher interest rate applied to the remaining contractual amounts due.

9 FINANCIAL ASSETS MEASURED AT FAIR VALUE THROUGH OTHER COMPREHENSIVE INCOME

For financial assets measured at fair value through other comprehensive income (see Chapter 48 at 5.3), the ECLs do not reduce the carrying amount of the financial assets in the statement of financial position, which remains at fair value. Instead, an amount equal to the allowance that would arise if the asset was measured at amortised cost is recognised in other comprehensive income as the 'accumulated impairment amount'. *[IFRS 9.4.1.2A, 5.5.2, Appendix A]*.

9.1 Accounting treatment for debt instruments measured at fair value through other comprehensive income

The accounting treatment and journal entries for debt instruments measured at fair value through other comprehensive income are illustrated in the following example, based on Illustrative Example 13 in the Implementation Guidance for the standard. *[IFRS 9 Example 13 IE78-IE81]*.

Example 51.20: Debt instrument measured at fair value through other comprehensive income

An entity purchases a debt instrument with a fair value of £1,000 on 15 December 2021 and measures the debt instrument at fair value through other comprehensive income (FVOCI). The instrument has an interest rate of 5 per cent over the contractual term of 10 years, and has a 5 per cent EIR. At initial recognition the entity determines that the asset is not purchased or originated credit-impaired.

	Debit	Credit
Financial asset – FVOCI	£1,000	
Cash		£1,000

(To recognise the debt instrument measured at its fair value)

On 31 December 2021 (the reporting date), the fair value of the debt instrument has decreased to £950 as a result of changes in market interest rates. The entity determines that there has not been a significant increase in credit risk since initial recognition and that ECLs should be measured at an amount equal to 12-month ECLs, which amounts to £30. For simplicity, journal entries for the receipt of interest revenue are not provided.

	Debit	Credit
Impairment loss (profit or loss)	£30	
Other comprehensive income[(a)]	£20	
Financial asset – FVOCI		£50

(To recognise 12-month ECLs and other fair value changes on the debt instrument)

(a) The cumulative loss in other comprehensive income at the reporting date was £20. That amount consists of the total fair value change of £50 (i.e. £1,000 – £950) offset by the change in the accumulated impairment amount representing 12-month ECLs that was recognised (£30).

Disclosure would be provided about the accumulated impairment amount of £30.

On 1 January 2022, the entity decides to sell the debt instrument for £950, which is its fair value at that date.

	Debit	Credit
Cash	£950	
Financial asset – FVOCI		£950
Loss (profit or loss)	£20	
Other comprehensive income		£20

(To derecognise the fair value through other comprehensive income asset and recycle amounts accumulated in other comprehensive income to profit or loss, i.e. £20).

This means that in contrast to financial assets measured at amortised cost, there is no separate allowance but, instead, impairment gains or losses are accounted for as an adjustment of the revaluation reserve accumulated in other comprehensive income, with a corresponding charge to profit or loss (which is then reflected in retained earnings). The tax implications of debt instruments measured at FVOCI is discussed further in Chapter 33 at 10.4.1 and 10.4.2.

As explained in 7.3.1 above IFRS 9 requires a derecognition gain or loss to be measured relative to the carrying amount at the date of derecognition. This necessitates an assessment and measurement of ECLs for that particular asset as at the date of derecognition.

9.2 Interaction between foreign currency translation, fair value hedge accounting and impairment

The above example is relatively straightforward. A more complicated one, based on a foreign currency denominated financial asset which is also the subject of an interest rate hedge, is provided below. It is based on Illustrative Example 14 in the Implementation Guidance for the standard but has been adjusted so as to include the effect of discounting in the measurement of ECLs (see 5.7 above). *[IFRS 9.IE82-IE102].* Note that we do not address the additional complexities that will arise from the consideration of taxation, including deferred tax. The tax accounting implications of debt instruments measured at FVOCI is discussed further in Chapter 33 at 10.4.1 and 10.4.2.

Example 51.21: Interaction between the fair value through other comprehensive income measurement category and foreign currency denomination, fair value hedge accounting and impairment

The example assumes the following fact pattern and that, on initial recognition, ECLs are included when measuring foreign exchange gains and losses (see 7.3.1 above):

- An entity purchases a bond denominated in a foreign currency (FC) for its fair value of FC100,000 on 1 January 2021.
- The bond is held within a business model whose objective is achieved by both collecting contractual cash flows and selling financial assets and has contractual cash flows which are solely payments of principal and interest on the principal amount outstanding. Therefore, the entity classifies the bond as measured at fair value through other comprehensive income.
- The bond has five years remaining to maturity and a fixed coupon of 5 per cent over its contractual life on the contractual par amount of FC100,000.
- The entity hedges the bond for its interest rate related fair value risk. The fair value of the corresponding interest rate swap at the date of initial recognition is nil.
- On initial recognition, the bond has a 5 per cent EIR which results in a gross carrying amount that equals the fair value at initial recognition.
- The entity's functional currency is its local currency (LC).
- As at 1 January 2021, the exchange rate is FC1 to LC1.
- At initial recognition, the entity determines that the bond is not purchased credit-impaired. The entity applies a 12-month PD for its impairment calculation and assumes that payment default occurs at the end of the reporting period (i.e. after 12 months). In particular, the entity estimates the PD over the next 12 months at 2 per cent and the LGD at FC60,000, resulting in an (undiscounted) expected cash shortfall of FC1,200. The discounted expected cash shortfall is FC1,143 at 5 per cent EIR (see the example below for the detailed calculation).
- For simplicity, amounts for interest revenue are not provided. It is assumed that interest accrued is received in the period. Differences of 1 in the calculations and reconciliations are due to rounding.

The entity hedges its risk exposures using the following risk management strategy:

(a) for fixed interest rate risk (in FC) the entity decides to link its interest receipts in FC to current variable interest rates in FC. Consequently, the entity uses interest rate swaps denominated in FC under which it pays fixed interest and receives variable interest in FC; and

(b) for foreign exchange (FX) risk, the entity decides not to hedge against any variability in LC arising from changes in foreign exchange rates.

The entity designates the following hedging relationship: a fair value hedge of the bond in FC as the hedged item with changes in benchmark interest rate risk in FC as the hedged risk. The entity enters into a swap that pays fixed and receives variable interest in FC on the same day and designates the swap as the hedging instrument. The tenor of the swap matches that of the hedged item (i.e. five years). This example assumes that all qualifying criteria for hedge accounting are met (see paragraph 6.4.1 of IFRS 9). The description of the designation is solely for the purpose of understanding this example (i.e. it is not an example of the complete formal documentation required in accordance with paragraph 6.4.1 of IFRS 9).

This example assumes that no hedge ineffectiveness arises in the hedging relationship. This assumption is made in order to better focus on illustrating the accounting mechanics in a situation that entails measurement at fair value through other comprehensive income of a foreign currency financial instrument that is designated in a fair value hedge relationship, and also to focus on the recognition of impairment gains or losses on such an instrument.

The entity decided not to amortise the fair value hedge adjustment to profit or loss before the hedge ceases or the asset is credit impaired. Consequently, in this example, there is no adjustment to the EIR due to fair value hedge accounting. However, such an adjustment to the EIR would at the latest be required when the entity ceases to apply hedge accounting or when the asset becomes credit-impaired, i.e. moved to stage 3. (See 7.5 above).

Situation as per 1 January 2021

The table below illustrates the amounts recognised in the financial statements as per 1 January 2021, as well as the shadow amortised cost calculation for the bond, based on the fact pattern described above (debits are shown as positive numbers and credits as negative numbers):

	Financial Statements			Shadow Calculation	
	FC	LC		FC	LC
	Statement of financial position				
Bond (FV)	100,000	100,000	Gross carrying amount	100,000	100,000
Swap (FV)	–	–	Loss allowance	(1,143)	(1,143)
			Amortised cost	98,857	98,857
	Statement of profit or loss				
Impairment	1,143	1,143	FV hedge adjustment	–	–
FV hedge (bond)	–	–	Adjusted gross carrying amt.	100,000	100,000
FX gain/loss (bond)	–	–	Adjusted amortised cost	98,857	98,857
FV hedge (swap)	–	–			
FX gain/loss (swap)	–	–			
	Statement of OCI				
FV changes	–	–			
Impairment offset	(1,143)	(1,143)			
FV hedge adjustment	–	–			

As per 1 January 2021, the entity recognises the bond and the swap at their initial fair values of LC100,000 and nil, respectively. The loss allowance of FC1,143 is recognised in profit or loss. The amount is calculated as the difference between all contractual cash flows that are due to the entity in accordance with the contract and all the cash flows that the entity expects to receive (i.e. all cash shortfalls), discounted at the original effective interest of 5 per cent, and weighted by the probability of the scenario occurring. To keep the example simple, it is assumed that default on the bond occurs one year after the date of the initial recognition, at which point the recoverable amount of the bond is received. This means that in the case of a default the entity expects cash flows of FC45,000 (which is the principal of FC100,000 plus one year of interest of FC5,000 less the LGD of FC60,000). The latter loss is discounted by the 5 per cent EIR and weighted by the 2 per cent PD to arrive at the loss allowance. The table below shows the ECL calculation:

1 January 2021 (values in FC)		Year 1	Year 2	Year 3	Year 4	Year 5
Contractual cash flows		5,000	5,000	5,000	5,000	105,000
Expected cash flows		45,000				
Expected cash shortfalls		40,000	(5,000)	(5,000)	(5,000)	(105,000)
NPV at 5%	(57,143)					
PD	2%					
Net present value (probability weighted) – this is the ECL	(1,143)					

In accordance with paragraph 16A of IFRS 7, the loss allowance for financial assets measured at fair value through other comprehensive income is not presented separately as a reduction of the carrying amount of the financial asset. As a consequence, the offsetting entry to the impairment loss of LC1,143 is recorded in other comprehensive income in the same period.

Situation as at 31 December 2021

As of 31 December 2021 (the reporting date), the entity observes the following facts:

- The fair value of the bond has decreased from FC100,000 to FC96,370, mainly because of an increase in market interest rates.
- The fair value of the swap has increased to FC1,837.
- In addition, as at 31 December 2021, the entity determines that there has been no change to the credit risk on the bond since initial recognition. The entity still estimates the PD over the next 12 months at 2 per cent and the LGD at FC60,000, resulting in an (undiscounted) expected shortfall of FC1,200.
- As at 31 December 2021, the exchange rate is FC1 to LC1.4.

The table below illustrates the amounts recognised in the financial statements between 1 January 2021 (after the entries for the impairment loss of FC1,143 at 1 January, shown above) and 31 December 2021, as well as the shadow amortised cost calculation for the bond (debits are shown as positive numbers and credits as negative numbers):

	Financial Statements			Shadow Calculation	
	FC	LC		FC	LC
Statement of financial position					
Bond (FV)	96,370	134,918	Gross carrying amount	100,000	140,000
Swap (FV)	1,837	2,572	Loss allowance	(1,143)	(1,600)
			Amortised cost	98,857	138,400
Statement of profit or loss					
Impairment	–	–	FV hedge adjustment	(1,837)	(2,572)
FV hedge (bond)	1,837	2,572	Adjusted gross carrying amount	98,163	137,428
FX gain/loss (bond)		(39,543)	Adjusted amortised cost	97,020	135,828
FV hedge (swap)	(1,837)	(2,572)			
FX gain/loss (swap)	–	–			
Statement of OCI					
FV changes	3,630	4,625			
Impairment offset	–	–			
FV hedge adjustment	(1,837)	(2,572)			

Because the entity have maintained the expected cash shortfall pattern and its probability of occurring, the change in estimate is just the effect of deferral by a year of the expected date of default, which exactly offsets the unwinding of the discount.

The bond is a monetary asset. Consequently, the entity recognises the changes arising from movements in foreign exchange rates in profit or loss in accordance with paragraphs 23(a) and 28 of IAS 21 and recognises other changes in accordance with IFRS 9. For the purposes of applying paragraph 28 of IAS 21, the asset is treated as an asset measured at amortised cost in the foreign currency.

The change in the fair value of the bond since 1 January 2021 amounts to LC34,918 and is recognised as a fair value adjustment to the carrying amount of the bond on the entity's statement of financial position.

The gain of LC39,543 due to the changes in foreign exchange rates is recognised in profit or loss. It consists of the impact of the change in the exchange rates during 2021:

- on the original gross carrying amount of the bond, amounting to LC40,000;
- offset by the loss allowance of the bond, amounting to LC457 (i.e. the difference of FC1,143 translated at the exchange rate as at 1 January 2021 of FC1 to LC1 and FC1,143 translated at the exchange rate as at 31 December 2021 of FC1 to LC1.4).

The difference between the change in fair value (LC34,918) and the gain recognised in profit or loss that is due to the changes in foreign exchange rates (LC39,543) is recognised in OCI. That difference amounts to LC4,625.

A gain of LC2,572 (FC1,837) on the swap is recognised in profit or loss and, because it is assumed that there is no hedge ineffectiveness, this amount coincides with the loss on the hedged item. Illustrative Example 14 of IFRS 9 seems to suggest that the hedging gain or loss of a debt instrument at fair value through other comprehensive income is recycled from other comprehensive income in the same period but, since paragraph 6.5.8(b) of IFRS 9 requires the hedging gain or loss on the hedged item to be recognised in profit or loss and the offsetting entry is to OCI, this is not strictly 'recycling'.

Situation as at 31 December 2022

As of 31 December 2022 (the reporting date), the entity observes the following facts:

- The fair value of the bond has further decreased from FC96,370 to FC87,114.
- The fair value of the swap has increased to FC2,092.
- Based on adverse macroeconomic developments in the industry in which the bond issuer operates, the entity assumes a significant increase in credit risk since initial recognition, and recognises the lifetime ECL for the bond.
- The entity updates its impairment estimate and now estimates the lifetime PD at 20 per cent and the LGD at FC48,500, resulting in (undiscounted) expected cash shortfalls of FC9,700. (For simplicity, this example assumes that payment default will happen on maturity when the entire face value becomes due).
- As at 31 December 2022, the exchange rate is FC1 to LC1.25.

The table below illustrates the amounts recognised in the financial statements between 31 December 2021 and 31 December 2022, as well as the shadow amortised cost calculation for the bond (debits are shown as positive numbers and credits as negative numbers):

	Financial Statements			Shadow Calculation	
	FC	LC		FC	LC
	Statement of financial position				
Bond (FV)	87,114	108,893	Gross carrying amount	100,000	125,000
Swap (FV)	2,092	2,615	Loss allowance	(8,379)	(10,474)
			Amortised cost	91,621	114,526
	Statement of profit or loss				
Impairment	7,236	9,045	FV hedge adjustment	(2,092)	(2,615)
FV hedge (bond)	255	319	Adj. gross carrying amt.	97,908	122,385
FX gain/loss (bond)		14,553	Adj. amortised cost	89,529	111,911
FV hedge (swap)	(255)	(319)			
FX gain/loss (swap)		276			
	Statement of OCI				
FV changes	9,256	11,472			
Impairment offset	(7,236)	(9,045)			
FV hedge adjustment	(255)	(319)			

The table below illustrates the ECL calculation:

31 December 2021 (values in FC)		Year 3	Year 4	Year 5
Contractual cash flows		5,000	5,000	105,000
Expected cash flows		5,000	5,000	56,500
Expected cash shortfalls		–	–	(48,500)
NPV at 5.8%	(41,896)			
PD	20%			
Net present value (probability weighted) – this is the ECL	(8,379)			

Again, the table above shows how the ECL is calculated as the net present value of the cash shortfalls, i.e. the difference between contractual and expected cash flows on each relevant date. The offsetting entry of the impairment loss FC7,236 (LC9,045) is recorded in other comprehensive income in the same period.

The change in the fair value of the bond since 31 December 2021 amounts to a decrease of LC26,026 and is recognised as a fair value adjustment to the carrying amount of the bond on the entity's statement of financial position.

The loss of LC14,553 due to the changes in foreign exchange rates is recognised in profit or loss. It consists of the impact of the change in the exchange rates during 2021:

- on the original gross carrying amount of the bond, amounting to a loss of LC15,000;
- on the loss allowance of the bond, amounting to a gain of LC171;
- on the fair value hedge adjustment, amounting to a gain of LC276.

The difference between the change in fair value (decrease of LC26,026) and the loss recognised in profit or loss that is due to the changes in foreign exchange rates (LC14,553) is recognised in OCI.

A gain of LC319 (FC255) on the swap is recognised in profit or loss and, because it is assumed that there is no hedge ineffectiveness, this amount coincides with the loss on the hedged item.

Situation as at 1 January 2023

On 1 January 2023, the entity decides to sell the bond for FC87,114, which is its fair value at that date and also closes out the swap at its fair value. For simplicity, all amounts, including the foreign exchange rate, are assumed to be the same as at 31 December 2022.

Upon derecognition, the entity reclassifies the cumulative amount recognised in OCI of LC3,018 (FC2,415) to profit or loss. This amount is equal to the difference between the fair value and the adjusted amortised cost amount of the bond, including the fair value hedge adjustment at the time of its derecognition. The table below presents a reconciliation of those amounts.

Reconciliation of loss on derecognition (values in LC) to cumulative OCI

Fair value per 1 January 2023	108,893			
Adjusted amortised cost per 1 January 2023	111,911			
Loss	**(3,018)**			
	Cum. OCI	1 January 2021	31 December 2021	31 December 2022
FV changes	16,097	–	4,625	11,472
Impairment	(10,188)	(1,143)	–	(9,045)
FV hedge adjustment	(2,891)	–	(2,572)	(319)
Total OCI to be reclassified	**3,018**			

This table presents the amount that has not yet been recycled and, therefore, must be reclassified to profit or loss on derecognition.

10 TRADE RECEIVABLES, CONTRACT ASSETS AND LEASE RECEIVABLES

The standard provides some operational simplifications for trade receivables, contract assets and lease receivables. These are the requirement or policy choice to apply the simplified approach that does not require entities to track changes in credit risk (see 3.2 above) and the practical expedient to calculate ECLs on trade receivables using a provision matrix (see 10.1 below).

10.1 Trade receivables and contract assets

It is a requirement for entities to apply the simplified approach for trade receivables or contract assets that do not contain a significant financing component. However, entities have a policy choice to apply either the general approach (see 3.1 above) or the simplified approach separately to trade receivables and contract assets that do contain a significant financing component (see 3.2 above). *[IFRS 9.5.5.15(a)].*

Also, entities are allowed to use practical expedients when measuring ECLs, as long as the approach reflects a probability-weighted outcome, the time value of money and reasonable and supportable information that is available without undue cost or effort at the reporting date about past events, current conditions and forecasts of future economic conditions. *[IFRS 9.5.5.17, B5.5.35].*

One of the approaches suggested in the standard is the use of a provision matrix as a practical expedient for measuring ECLs on trade receivables. For instance, the provision rates might be based on days past due (e.g. 1 per cent if not past due, 2 per cent if less than 30 days past due, etc.) for groupings of various customer segments that have similar loss patterns. The grouping may be based on geographical region, product type, customer rating, the type of collateral or whether covered by trade credit insurance, and the type of customer (such as wholesale or retail). To calibrate the matrix, the entity would adjust its historical credit loss experience with forward-looking information. *[IFRS 9.B5.5.35].*

In practice, many corporates use a provision matrix to calculate their current impairment allowances. However, in order to comply with the IFRS 9 requirements, corporates have needed to consider how current and forward-looking information might affect their customers' historical default rates and, consequently, how the information would affect their current expectations and estimates of ECLs. The use of the provision matrix is illustrated in the following example. *[IFRS 9 Example 12 IE74-IE77].*

Example 51.22: Provision matrix

Company M, a manufacturer, has a portfolio of trade receivables of €30 million in 2021 and operates only in one geographical region. The customer base consists of a large number of small clients and the trade receivables are categorised by common risk characteristics that are representative of the customers' abilities to pay all amounts due in accordance with the contractual terms. The trade receivables do not have a significant financing component in accordance with IFRS 15. In accordance with paragraph 5.5.15 of IFRS 9, the loss allowance for such trade receivables is always measured at an amount equal to lifetime ECLs.

To determine the ECLs for the portfolio, Company M uses a provision matrix. The provision matrix is based on its historical observed loss rates over the expected life of the trade receivables and is adjusted for forward-looking estimates. At every reporting date, the historical observed loss rates are updated and changes in the forward-looking estimates are analysed. In this case it is forecast that economic conditions will deteriorate over the next year.

On that basis, Company M estimates the following provision matrix:

	Current	1-30 days past due	31-60 days past due	61-90 days past due	More than 90 days past due
Loss rate	0.3%	1.6%	3.6%	6.6%	10.6%

The trade receivables from the large number of small customers amount to €30 million and are measured using the provision matrix.

	Gross carrying amount	Lifetime ECL allowance (Gross carrying amount × lifetime loss rate)
Current	€15,000,000	€45,000
1-30 days past due	€7,500,000	€120,000
31-60 days past due	€4,000,000	€144,000
61-90 days past due	€2,500,000	€165,000
More than 90 days past due	€1,000,000	€106,000
	€30,000,000	€580,000

It should be noted that this example, like many in the standard, ignores the need to consider explicitly the time value of money, presumably in this case because the effect is considered immaterial.

10.2 Lease receivables

For lease receivables, entities have a policy choice to apply either the general approach (see 3.1 above) or the simplified approach (see 3.2 above) separately to finance and operating lease receivables (see Chapter 23). *[IFRS 9.5.5.15(b)]*.

When measuring ECLs for lease receivables, an entity should:

- use the cash flows that are used in measuring the lease receivables in accordance with IFRS 16; *[IFRS 9.B5.5.34]* and

- discount the ECLs using the same discount rate used in the measurement of the lease receivables in accordance with IFRS 16. *[IFRS 9.B5.5.46, IAS 17.4]*.

There has been some discussion on whether the unguaranteed residual value (URV) of the asset subject to a finance lease should be included in the calculation of ECLs under IFRS 9. The URV is part of the gross investment in the finance lease, together with the minimum lease payments receivable by the lessor. Changes to URV arise from fluctuations in the price that could be received for the leased asset at the end of the lease term. Paragraph 2.1(b) of IFRS 9 scopes out rights and obligations under leases to which IFRS 16 applies, except for the impairment of finance lease receivables (i.e. net investments in finance leases) and operating lease receivables recognised by a lessor (see 2 above). IFRS 16 provides guidance on measurement of the URV, which means that such measurement is within the scope of IFRS 16 rather than the impairment requirements of IFRS 9. *[IFRS 16.77].*

The URV of the asset underlying a finance lease should be excluded from the calculation of ECLs under IFRS 9. This means that the collateral that is taken into account in measuring ECLs should exclude any amounts attributed to URV and recorded on the lessor's statement of financial position. In other words, any collateral taken into account in the calculation of ECLs should be restricted to the fair value of the right of use of the asset and not that of the underlying asset itself.

Other issues that have arisen in practice in relation to the IFRS 16 and IFRS 9 impairment requirements are covered further in Chapter 23. These include:

- Whether the finance income arising from a finance lease receivable should be calculated based on the gross lease receivable or the net amount of the lease receivable less any ECLs (see Chapter 23 at 6.2.3).
- Whether (and when) lease income should be recognised when collectability is not probable and regardless of the approach followed, IFRS 9 guidance on ECLs continues to be applicable to recognised lease receivables (see Chapter 23 at 6.3.1).
- Whether rent concessions and forgiveness of lease payments are accounted for as a modification under IFRS 16 or write-off of the impairment allowance and derecognition under IFRS 9 (see Chapter 23 at 6.4.3).

11 LOAN COMMITMENTS AND FINANCIAL GUARANTEE CONTRACTS

11.1 Definitions and scope

The description of 'loan commitment' and the definition of 'financial guarantee contract' remain unchanged from IAS 39. Loan commitments (see Chapter 45 at 3.5) are described in IFRS 9 as 'firm commitments to provide credit under pre-specified terms and conditions', while a financial guarantee contract (see Chapter 45 at 3.4) is defined as 'a contract that requires the issuer to make specified payments to reimburse the holder for a loss it incurs because a specified debtor fails to make payment when due in accordance with the original or modified terms of a debt instrument'. *[IFRS 9.BCZ2.2, Appendix A, IAS 39.9, BC15].*

The IFRS 9 impairment requirements apply to loan commitments and financial guarantee contracts that are not measured at fair value through profit or loss under IFRS 9, with some exceptions (see 2 above).

The ITG (see 1.5 above) discussed in April 2015 whether the impairment requirements in IFRS 9 must also be applied to other commitments to extend credit such as:

- a commitment (on inception of a finance lease) to commence a finance lease at a date in the future (i.e. a commitment to transfer the right to use an asset at the lease commencement date in return for a payment or series of payments in the future); and
- a commitment by a retailer through the issue of a store account to provide a customer with credit when the customer buys goods or services from the retailer in the future.

The ITG appeared to agree with the IASB's staff analysis that the impairment requirements of IFRS 9 apply to an agreement that contains a commitment to extend credit by virtue of paragraph 2.1(g) if:

- the agreement meets the description of a loan commitment; *[IFRS 9.BCZ2.2]*
- the agreement meets the definition of a financial instrument; *[IAS 32.11]* and
- none of the specific exemptions from the requirements of IFRS 9 apply. *[IFRS 9.2.1]*.

The IASB staff paper stated that some contracts, such as irrevocable finance lease agreements, might clearly contain a firm commitment at inception to provide credit under pre-specified terms and conditions. However, other cases might not be so clear cut, depending upon the specific terms of the agreement and other facts and circumstances (e.g. if the issuer of a store account has the discretion to refuse to sell products or services to a customer with a store card and hence can avoid extending credit).[41]

In the examples discussed above, the finance lease and store account do not meet the definition of a financial instrument until the contractual right to receive cash is established, that is likely to be at the commencement of the lease term or when goods or services are sold. *[IAS 32.11, AG20]*. Only lease receivables are scoped into the IFRS 9 impairment requirements (see 10.2 above). *[IFRS 9.2.1(b)]*. Consequently, there is no need to make provision for ECLs, in accordance with IFRS 9, until a financial lease receivable or a financial asset within the scope of IFRS 9 is recognised.

11.2 The calculation of ECLs

The application of the model to financial guarantees and loan commitments warrants some further specification regarding some of the key elements, such as the determination of the credit quality on initial recognition, cash shortfalls and the EIR to be used in the ECL calculations. These specifications are summarised in Figure 51.7 below, which also highlights the differences in recognising and measuring ECLs for financial assets measured at amortised cost or at fair value through other comprehensive income, loan commitments and financial guarantee contracts.

Figure 51.7   Summary of the application of the ECL model to loan commitments and financial guarantee contracts

	Financial assets measured at amortised cost or at fair value through other comprehensive income	Loan commitments	Financial guarantee contracts
Date of initial recognition in applying the impairment requirements (see 7.3.1 above)	Trade date. *[IFRS 9.5.7.4]*.	Date that an entity becomes a party to the irrevocable commitment. *[IFRS 9.5.5.6]*.	Date that an entity becomes a party to the irrevocable commitment. *[IFRS 9.5.5.6]*.
Period over which to estimate ECLs (see 5.5 above)	The expected life up to the maximum contractual period (including extension options at the discretion of the borrower) over which the entity is exposed to credit risk and not a longer period. *[IFRS 9.5.5.19]*.	The expected life up to the maximum contractual period over which an entity has a present contractual obligation to extend credit. *[IFRS 9.B5.5.38]*. However, for revolving credit facilities (see 12 below), this period extends beyond the contractual period over which the entity is exposed to credit risk and the ECLs would not be mitigated by credit risk management actions. *[IFRS 9.5.5.20, B5.5.39, B5.5.40]*.	The expected life up to the maximum contractual period over which an entity has a present contractual obligation to extend credit. *[IFRS 9.B5.5.38]*.
Cash shortfalls in measuring ECLs (see 5.2 above)	Cash shortfalls between the cash flows that are due to an entity in accordance with the contract and the cash flows that the entity expects to receive. *[IFRS 9.B5.5.28]*.	Cash shortfalls between the contractual cash flows that are due to the entity if the holder of the loan commitment draws down the loan and the cash flows that the entity expects to receive if the loan is drawn down. *[IFRS 9.B5.5.30]*.	Cash shortfalls are the expected payments to reimburse the holder for a credit loss that it incurs less any amounts that the entity (issuer) expects to receive from the holder, the debtor or any other party. *[IFRS 9.B5.5.32]*.
EIR used in discounting ECLs (see 5.7 above)	The EIR is determined or approximated at initial recognition of the financial instrument. *[IFRS 9.B5.5.44]*.	The EIR of the resulting asset will be applied and if this is not determinable, then the current rate representing the risk of the cash flows is used. *[IFRS 9.B5.5.47, B5.5.48]*.	The current rate representing the risk of the cash flows is used. *[IFRS 9.B5.5.48]*.
Assessment of significant increases in credit risk (see 6 above)	An entity considers changes in the risk of a default occurring on the financial asset. *[IFRS 9.5.5.9]*.	An entity considers changes in the risk of a default occurring on the loan to which a loan commitment relates. *[IFRS 9.B5.5.8]*.	An entity considers the changes in the risk that the specified debtor will default on the contract. *[IFRS 9.B5.5.8]*.

Further discussion on the discount rate to be used for calculating ECLs on loan commitments and financial guarantee contracts is provided at 5.7 above.

11.3 Financial guarantee contracts that require the holder to pay further premiums in the future

At its meeting in April 2015, the ITG (see 1.5 above) also discussed the measurement of ECLs for an issued financial guarantee contract that requires the holder to pay further premiums in the future. Some members of the ITG agreed with the staff's analysis that the issuer of a financial guarantee contract should exclude future premium receipts due from the holder when measuring ECLs in respect of the expected cash outflows payable under the guarantee.[42] When estimating the cash shortfalls, the amounts that the entity expects to receive from the holder should relate only to recoveries or reimbursements of claims for losses and would not include receipts of premiums. *[IFRS 9.B5.5.32]*. Moreover, the expected cash outflows under the guarantee depend upon the risk of default of the guaranteed asset, while the expected future premiums receipts are subject to the risk of default by the holder of the guarantee. Hence, these risks of default should be considered separately. In other words, the ECL measurement should be carried out gross of any premiums receivable in the future.

In addition, an ITG member noted that the terms of a financial guarantee contract may affect the period of exposure to credit risk on the guarantee, for example if the guarantee were contingent or cancellable. This should be taken into consideration when measuring the ECLs of the guarantee.

IFRS 9 requires that financial guarantees and off-market loan commitments should be measured at the 'higher of' the amount initially recognised less cumulative amortisation, and the ECL. *[IFRS 9.4.2.1(c), 4.2.1(d)]*. For a financial guarantee contract issued to an unrelated party in a stand-alone arm's length transaction, premiums that are received in full at inception will likely be the same as the fair value of the guarantee at initial recognition (see Chapter 49 at 3.3.3). In such circumstances, it is likely that no ECLs will need to be recognised immediately after initial recognition, as the initial fair value will normally exceed the lifetime ECLs. However, a financial guarantee contract for which premiums are receivable over the life of the guarantee will have a nil fair value at initial recognition. In such circumstances, the subsequent measurement of the financial guarantee contract is likely to be based on the ECL allowance. This is illustrated in the example below.

Example 51.23: Determining the initial and subsequent measurement of a financial guarantee contract where premiums are receivable upfront or over the life of the guarantee

Scenario 1: On 1 January 2021, Bank A issues a 5 year financial guarantee of a loan with a nominal value of £2,000,000 with 5% interest, with the full premium of £100,000 receivable upfront at contract inception. This premium is recognised on a straight-line basis over the life of the guarantee. As at 31 December 2023 and 2024, Bank A assesses that there has been a significant increase in credit risk of the financial guarantee contract and as at 31 December 2025, the debtor defaults and fails to make payments in accordance with the terms of the debt instrument. The lifetime ECLs estimated as at 31 December 2021 and 2022 are £75,000 and £55,000 respectively, with a significant increase in 2023 and 2024 to £200,000 and £500,000, respectively, and for the guaranteed amount of £2,100,000 (being the principal and unpaid interest) in 2025 when the debtor defaults. The 12-month ECLs are £18,000 and £25,000 as at 31 December 2021 and 2022.

Scenario 2: Same facts as in Scenario 1 except that Bank B issues a 5 year financial guarantee of a loan with a nominal value of £2,000,000, with premiums receivable over the life of the guarantee of £20,000 each year, payable on 31 December 2021, 2022, 2023, 2024 and 2025, i.e. a total of £100,000. The fair value of the guarantee is nil at origination. If a claim is paid out under the financial guarantee contract, Bank B will lose the right to receive future premiums.

	31 Dec 2021	31 Dec 2022	31 Dec 2023	31 Dec 2024	31 Dec 2025
Scenario 1: Full premium receivable at inception Initial fair value is £100,000					
(a) Fair value less cumulative income recognised*	£80,000	£60,000	£40,000	£20,000	–
(b) ECLs	£18,000	£25,000	£200,000	£500,000	£2,100,000
Recorded value: higher of (a) or (b) in accordance with IFRS 9.4.2.1(c)	£80,000	£60,000	£200,000	£500,000	£2,100,000
Scenario 2: Premium receivable over the life of contract Initial fair value is £0 in accordance with IFRS 9.5.1.1	£20,000	£20,000	£20,000	£20,000	£20,000
(a) Fair value less cumulative income recognised*	–	–	–	–	–
(b) ECLs	£18,000	£25,000	£200,000	£500,000	£2,100,000
Recorded value: higher of (a) or (b) in accordance with IFRS 9.4.2.1(c)	£18,000	£25,000	£200,000	£500,000	£2,100,000

* Based on the assumption of a straight-line amortisation of premiums received over the life of the financial guarantee.

Before there has been a significant increase in credit risk in 2021 and 2022, in Scenario 1, the measurement of the financial guarantee is based on the fair value, less cumulative income recognised in accordance with IFRS 15 whilst, in Scenario 2, the measurement is based on the ECL allowance. However, once there has been a significant increase in credit risk, the measurement of the financial guarantee is based on the ECL allowance in both scenarios. Consequently, the timing of receipt of premiums may have a significant effect on the measurement of the guarantee particularly when there has not been a significant increase in credit risk.

Although the accounting treatment in Scenario 2 in the example above may seem unintuitive, in that the guarantor must initially recognise ECLs even though it expects to receive future premium income, it is consistent with the impairment of loans on which a credit spread is also received over the life of the loan.

Normal loan commitments (i.e. those issued at market interest rates and so are excluded from the scope of IFRS 9 except for impairment and derecognition) *[IFRS 9.2.1(g), 2.3]* are not subject to the 'higher of' test for subsequent measurement. *[IFRS 9.2.3(c), 4.2.1(d)]*. The consequence is that an ECL is required for all normal loan commitments, whether or not any fees are paid upfront. This is consistent with the general requirement to provide for 12-month ECLs for any new loans that have not experienced significant increases in credit risk since initial recognition.

11.4 Cross-company guarantees

For the individual entities within a group, there may be instances where cross-company guarantee arrangements will meet the definition of financial guarantee contracts and hence will fall within the scope of the IFRS 9 ECL requirements. *[IFRS 9.4.2.1 (d)].*

Where such guarantees are provided at below market rates by holding companies or other group entities, the initial benefit provided may need to be accounted for as an equity transaction between group entities.

When estimating the ECLs on cross-company guarantees relating to loans to a group entity made by parties external to the group, each entity that is a party to the cross-company guarantee arrangement needs, for its standalone financial statements, to factor in the likelihood of it being called upon to make payments under the arrangement. A practical approach would be to determine the total ECLs and then allocate them to group entities, based on an assessment of which entities will most likely settle the guarantee if payment is required. In doing so, all reasonable and supportable information that is available, including the respective entities' relative financial strength in relation to other group entities will need to be taken into account. If one entity in the group is expected to reimburse the lender, then this will reduce the potential cash shortfall estimated by other entities within the group. For example, if the parent is in the strongest financial position and is expected to fully reimburse the lender for a loan issued to one of its subsidiaries, then the parent's estimate of cash shortfalls would be consistent with the cash shortfalls that the lender could suffer in the absence of the guarantee. However, once the expected payments from the parent are taken into account, this would significantly reduce the expected cash shortfalls estimated by other group entities. This will result in each entity recognising the appropriate probability-weighted estimate of credit losses. Requiring all entities to recognise an ECL amount which does not take into account the likelihood of being called upon would not represent a probability weighted estimate of credit losses and would not provide useful information to users of the financial statements.

Additional disclosures would be required to explain the arrangement, including the maximum amount to which the entity is exposed and how the ECL amount has been calculated. *[IFRS 7.36(a), 35G].* Also, IAS 24 – *Related Party Disclosures* – requires details of any guarantees given to, or received from, related parties to be disclosed. *[IAS 24.18, 21].*

11.5 Purchased or originated credit impaired loan commitments and financial guarantee contracts

Another question that arises in practice is whether loan commitments and financial guarantee contracts can ever be accounted for as purchased or originated credit-impaired. The definition of 'purchased or originated credit-impaired' in IFRS 9 refers only to financial assets, not financial instruments (consistent with the definition of credit-impaired) but loan commitments and financial guarantees are not financial assets. So, if such an instrument is entered into when default is highly likely or has already occurred, and the potential loss is reflected in the price, how should the ECLs be measured, so as to avoid double counting the loss?

This issue could be particularly relevant in the context of business combinations, where an entity may acquire loan commitments or financial guarantee contracts that are already credit-impaired. For financial guarantees, the 'higher of' test avoids the double-counting, as the fair value of the guarantee recognised as a liability on initial recognition will be higher than lifetime expected losses. For loan commitments, one view could be to consider they are at below-market interest rates on initial recognition (as the terms were fixed at a time where the loan commitment was not credit-impaired) and apply the higher of test; alternatively, one may consider that the guidance for financial assets may be applied by analogy to loans commitments. This would make sense as the standard treats loans that are drawn from a loan commitment as a continuation of the same financial instrument. For disclosure purposes, we believe such loan commitments and financial guarantees should also be reported as credit-impaired.

12 REVOLVING CREDIT FACILITIES

The 2013 Exposure Draft specified that the maximum period over which ECLs are to be calculated should be limited to the contractual period over which the entity is exposed to credit risk.[43] This would mean that the allowance for commitments that can be withdrawn at short notice by a lender, such as overdrafts and credit card facilities, would be limited to the ECLs that would arise over the notice period, which might be only one day. However, banks will not normally exercise their right to cancel the commitment until there is already evidence of significant deterioration, which exposes them to risk over a considerably longer period. Banks and banking regulators raised concerns on this issue and the IASB responded by introducing an exception for revolving credit facilities and setting out further guidance as well as an example addressing such arrangements.

In outline, the revolving facility exception requires the issuer of such a facility to calculate ECLs based on the period over which they expect, in practice, to be exposed to credit risk. However, the words of the exception are not very clear and it was discussed at all three ITG meetings. The IASB staff have also produced a webcast on the topic.

12.1 Scope of the exception

The guidance relates to financial instruments that 'include both a loan and an undrawn commitment component and for which the entity's contractual ability to demand repayment and cancel the commitment does not limit the entity's exposure to credit losses to the contractual notice period'. *[IFRS 9.5.5.20]*. Despite the use of the word 'both', the ITG agreed, in April 2015, that this guidance applies even if the facility has yet to be drawn down. It also applies if the facility has been completely drawn down, as it is the nature of revolving facilities that the drawn down component is periodically paid off before further amounts will be drawn down again in future.

The standard also describes three characteristics generally associated with such instruments: *[IFRS 9.B5.5.39]*

- they usually have no fixed term or repayment structure and usually have a short contractual cancellation period;
- the contractual ability to cancel the contract is not enforced in day-to-day management, but only when the lender is aware of an increase in credit risk at the facility level; and
- they are managed on a collective basis.

Products that are generally agreed to be in the scope of the exception include most credit card facilities and most retail overdrafts. However, even with these some caution needs to be applied, since we understand that there are credit card facilities which do not enable the issuer to demand repayment and cancel the facility, and which would therefore be out of scope.

What is less clear is the treatment of corporate overdrafts and similar facilities. It is relevant that all the ITG discussions as well as the webcast referred to credit cards and retail customers and not corporate exposures. The problem is partly that the guidance to the standard describes management on a collective basis as a characteristic that revolving facilities in the scope of the exception 'generally have', rather than a required feature as listed in paragraph 5.5.20 of IFRS 9. *[IFRS 9.B5.5.39]*. Some banks consider this is still a determining feature and that many of their corporate facilities are outside the scope of the exception because they are managed on an individual basis. Banks normally have a closer business relationship with their larger corporate customers than with most retail customers, and more data to manage the credit risk, such as access to regular management information. Other banks consider that facilities that are individually managed are still in the scope of the exception, notably because individual credit reviews are generally performed only on an annual basis (unless a significant event occurs). In addition, it is unclear exactly what is meant by 'managed on a collective basis' and where to draw the line between large corporates and smaller entities. It should be noted that if a corporate facility is not deemed to be a revolving facility, but can be cancelled at short notice, the ECLs will be limited to those that arise over the notice period.

At its December 2015 meeting, the ITG discussed whether:

- multi-purpose credit facilities, which have the ability to be drawn down in a number of different ways (e.g. as a revolving overdraft, a variable or fixed-rate loan (with or without a fixed term) or an amortising loan such as a mortgage) would fall within the scope exception;
- the general characteristics identified in paragraph B5.5.39 of IFRS 9 should be considered to be required characteristics, or merely examples of typical characteristics; and
- the existence of a fixed term of the loan once drawn down would prevent a facility from falling within the scope exception.

The ITG commented that:

- The supporting application guidance in paragraph B5.5.39 of IFRS 9 reinforces the features described in paragraph 5.5.20 of IFRS 9 by setting out general characteristics which, while not determinative, are consistent with those features.

- The Basis for Conclusions of IFRS 9 provides further context around the type of financial instruments that the Board envisaged would fall within the scope exception. In particular, the exception was intended to be limited in nature and that it was introduced in order to address specific concerns raised by respondents in relation to revolving credit facilities that were managed on a collective basis. Also, it was understood that these types of financial instruments included both a loan and an undrawn commitment component and that they were managed, and ECLs were estimated, on a facility level; i.e. the drawn and undrawn exposure were viewed as one single cash flow from the borrower. *[IFRS 9.BC5.254-BC5.261]*.
- Consequently, both the drawn and undrawn components of these facilities were understood to have similar short contractual maturities, i.e. the lender had both the ability to withdraw the undrawn commitment component and demand repayment of the drawn component at short notice.
- An immediately revocable facility which has a fixed maturity (e.g. 5 years) would be consistent with the type of facility within the scope exception because the fixed term feature does not negate the lender's contractual right to cancel the undrawn component at any time. In contrast, an immediately revocable facility that has no fixed maturity but when drawn, can take the form of a loan with a fixed maturity (i.e. once it has been drawn, the lender no longer has the right to demand immediate repayment at its discretion) would not be consistent with the type of facility envisaged to be within the scope exception. This is because the fixed term feature does negate the lender's contractual right to demand repayment of the undrawn component. However, regarding this characteristic, the ITG members also highlighted the following:
    (a) an entity would first need to establish the unit of account to which the requirements of IFRS 9 should be applied. In this regard, they noted that even if there was only one legal contract supporting a particular multi-purpose credit facility, there might be more than one unit of account to consider; and
    (b) if the fixed-term feature was for a shorter period, judgement would be required in order to determine whether such a fixed-term feature would prevent a particular financial instrument from falling within the scope exception (e.g. whether the borrower could consider the exposure on the drawn and undrawn components to be one single cash flow).
- IFRS 7 requires an entity to explain, among other things, the assumptions used to measure ECLs. Within the context of multi-purpose credit facilities, such disclosures are likely to be important in order to meet the disclosure objectives (see 15 below and Chapter 54 at 5.3).

While, according to the ITG, the drawn and undrawn exposures are viewed as 'one single cash flow from the borrower', the standard's Basis for Conclusions is slightly clearer. [IFRS 9.BC5.259]. It states that the loan and undrawn commitment 'are managed, and ECLs are estimated on a facility level. In other words, there is only one set of cash flows from the borrower that relates to both components'. Hence, the drawn and undrawn elements of a revolving facility within the scope of the exception would normally be viewed as only one unit of account. The ITG discussion seems to suggest that a new unit of account would be recognised if a borrower chose to draw down on a multi-purpose facility in the form of a term loan, because this is the point where this specific drawn portion ceases to share the key characteristic of a revolving facility, i.e. the entity's contractual ability to demand repayment and cancel the commitment.

At its December 2015 meeting, the ITG discussed charge cards and how ECLs on future drawdowns should be measured if there is no specified credit limit in the contract. The ITG members considered a specific fact pattern where the bank has the ability to approve each transaction at the time of sale based on the customer's perceived spending capacity using statistical models and inputs such as spending history and known income.

The ITG members noted that because the bank has the right to refuse each transaction at its discretion, and on the assumption that the bank actually exercises that right in practice, then:

- the contractual credit limit should be considered to be zero and consequently future drawdowns would not be taken into account; and furthermore,
- the facility described would not fall within the scope exception because there would be no undrawn commitment component (i.e. there is no firm commitment to extend credit).

However, the ITG members noted that their discussions focussed on the very specific fact pattern presented and observed that the conclusion could differ in other situations.

12.2 The period over which to measure ECLs

12.2.1 The requirements of the standard

According to the standard, '... some financial instruments include both a loan and an undrawn commitment component and the entity's contractual ability to demand repayment and cancel the undrawn commitment does not limit the entity's exposure to credit losses to the contractual notice period. For such financial instruments, and only those financial instruments, the entity shall measure ECLs over the period that the entity is exposed to credit risk and ECLs would not be mitigated by credit risk management actions, even if that period extends beyond the maximum contractual period'. [IFRS 9.5.5.20]. In order to calculate the period for which ECLs are assessed, 'an entity should consider factors such as historical information and experience about:

(a) the period over which the entity was exposed to credit risk on similar financial instruments;
(b) the length of time for related defaults to occur on similar financial instruments following a significant increase in credit risk; and
(c) the credit risk management actions that an entity expects to take once the credit risk on the financial instrument has increased, such as the reduction or removal of undrawn limits.' *[IFRS 9.B5.5.40]*.

The above wording in the standard is not very easy to interpret or apply.

This following example illustrates the calculation of impairment for revolving credit facilities, based on Illustrative Example 10 in the Implementation Guidance for the standard. *[IFRS 9 Example 10 IE58-IE65]*. For the sake of clarity, the assumptions and calculations have been adapted from the IASB example as it is not explicit on the source of the parameters and how they are computed. The example has also been expanded to show the calculation of the loss allowances. However, to simplify the example, we have continued to ignore the need to discount ECLs or whether the credit conversion factor would change if an exposure has significantly deteriorated in credit risk.

Example 51.24: Revolving credit facilities

Bank A provides credit cards with a one day cancellation right and manages the drawn and undrawn commitment on each card together, as a facility. Bank A sub-divides the credit card portfolio by segregating those amounts for which a significant increase in credit risk was identified at the individual facility level from the remainder of the portfolio. The remainder of this example only illustrates the calculation of ECLs for the sub-portfolio for which a significant increase in credit risk was not identified at the individual facility level. At the reporting date, the outstanding balance on the sub-portfolio is £6,000,000 and the undrawn facility is £4,000,000. The Bank determines the sub-portfolio's expected life as 30 months (using the guidance set out above) and that the credit risk on 25 per cent of the sub-portfolio has increased significantly since initial origination, making up £1,500,000 of the outstanding balance and £1,000,000 of the undrawn commitment (see the calculation of the exposure in the table below).

To calculate its EAD, Bank A uses an approach whereby it adds the amounts that are drawn at the reporting date and additional draw-downs that are expected in the case that a customer defaults. For those expected additional draw-downs, Bank A uses a credit conversion factor that represents the estimate of what percentage of that part of committed credit facilities that is unused at the reporting date would be drawn by a customer before he defaults. Using its credit models, the bank determines this credit conversion factor as 95 per cent. The EAD on the portion of facilities measured on a lifetime ECL basis is therefore £2,450,000, made up of the drawn balance of £1,500,000 and £950,000 of expected further draw-downs before the customers default. For the remainder of the facilities, the EAD that is measured on a 12-month ECL basis is £7,350,000, being the remaining drawn balance of £4,500,000 plus additional expected draw-downs for customers defaulting over the next 12 months of £2,850,000 (see the calculation for the EAD in the table below).

Bank A has estimated that the PD for the next 12 months is 5 per cent, and 30 per cent for the next 30 months. The estimate for the LGD on the credit cards in the sub-portfolio is 90 per cent. That results in lifetime ECLs of £661,500 and 12-month ECLs of £330,750 (see calculation for ECLs in the table below).

For the presentation in the statement of financial position, the ECLs against the drawn amount of £607,500 would be recognised as an allowance against the credit card receivables and the remainder of the ECLs that relates to the undrawn facilities of £384,750 would be recognised as a liability (see table below).

Determination made at facility level		Drawn	Undrawn	Total
Facility		£6,000,000	£4,000,000	£10,000,000
Exposure				
Subject to lifetime ECLs (25% of the facility has been determined to have significantly increased in credit risk)	25%	£1,500,000	£1,000,000	£2,500,000
Subject to 12-month ECLs (the remaining 75% of the facility)	75%	£4,500,000	£3,000,000	£7,500,000
Credit conversion factor (CCF)	95%			
A uniform CCF is used irrespective of deterioration, which reflects that the CCF is contingent on default which is the same reference point for a 12-month and lifetime ECL calculation				
EAD				
EAD for undrawn balances is calculated as exposure × CCF				
Subject to lifetime ECLs		£1,500,000	£950,000	£2,450,000
Subject to 12-month ECLs		£4,500,000	£2,850,000	£7,350,000
PD				
Exposures subject to lifetime ECLs	30%			
Exposures subject to 12-month ECLs	5%			
LGD	90%			
ECLs (EAD × PD × LGD)				
Exposures subject to lifetime ECLs		£405,000	£256,500	£661,500
Exposures subject to 12-month ECLs		£202,500	£128,250	£330,750
		£607,500 presented as loss allowance against assets	*£384,750 presented as provision*	£992,250

In the above calculations, we have used the same credit conversion factor, of 95%, for calculating the EAD, irrespective of whether it is an input for 12-month or lifetime ECLs. This is based on an assumption that the extent of future draw-downs in the event that the customer defaults does not differ depending on whether, at the reporting date, there has been a significant increase in credit risk. In practice, for many credit cards, the exposure in the event of default reaches close to the credit limit and may even exceed it. However, as discussed further below, the standard does not permit the use of a credit conversion factor of more than 100%. For this reason, the use of a conventional credit conversion factor model for estimating the EAD may need to be adjusted to comply with the standard.

It should be noted that:

- Example 10 of the standard (on which our Example 51.24 above is based), does not explain how the entity has concluded that 25% of the portfolio has significantly increased in credit risk. Collective assessment is discussed at 6.5 above.
- Example 10 in the standard also does not show how the 30-month period was calculated.

12.2.2 Guidance provided by the ITG

The ITG in April 2015, discussed how to determine the appropriate period when measuring ECLs for a portfolio of revolving credit card exposures in stages 1, 2 and 3 and commented that:

- An entity's ability to segment and stratify the portfolio into different sections of exposures in accordance with how those exposures are being managed will be relevant. For example, an entity may be able to identify exposures with specific attributes that are considered more likely to default and consequently would have shorter average lives than those that are expected to continue performing (see 6.5 above).
- While IFRS 9 requires a period in excess of the maximum contractual period to be used when measuring ECLs, the fundamental aim was still to determine the period over which the entity is exposed to credit risk and an entity must consider all three factors set out in paragraph B5.5.40. Consequently, expected defaults or potential credit risk management actions the entity expects to be legally and operationally able to take and that serve to terminate or limit the credit risk exposure in some way (e.g. reduction or removal of undrawn limits) could result in a shorter period of exposure than that indicated by the historical behavioural life of the facility. That is, the time horizon is not the period over which the lender expects the facility to be used, but the period over which the lender is, in practice, exposed to credit risk.

At its December 2015 meeting, the ITG continued the discussion on how an entity should determine the maximum period to consider when measuring ECLs for revolving credit facilities. This divided into two sub-questions: when does this period start and when does it end?

With respect to the starting-point, the ITG members observed that the requirements of paragraph B5.5.40 of IFRS 9 do not alter the starting-point of the maximum period to consider when measuring ECLs and consequently, the appropriate starting-point should be the reporting date.

With respect to the ending-point, ITG members focused on which credit risk management actions an entity should take into account and noted that:

- An entity should consider:
  (a) only credit risk management actions that it expects to take rather than all credit risk management actions that it is legally and operationally able to take;
  (b) only those credit risk management actions that serve to mitigate credit risk and consequently, actions that do not mitigate credit risk such as the reinstatement of previously curtailed credit limits should not be considered; and
  (c) all credit risk management actions that it expects to take and that serve to either terminate or limit the credit risk exposure in some way.

- An entity's expected actions must be based on reasonable and supportable information. In this regard, consideration should be given to an entity's normal credit risk mitigation process, past practice and future intentions.
- The ending-point could be limited by the expected timing of the entity's next review process, but only if the entity's normal business practice is to take credit risk mitigation actions as part of this review process. Consequently, it may not always be appropriate to use the timing of the entity's next review process as a basis for determining the ending-point.
- In respect of assets in stage 2, the probability of assets curing or defaulting would need to be taken into account when determining the maximum period to consider when measuring ECLs.
- It was noted that a distinction should be made between credit risk management actions such as the reinstatement of a previously curtailed credit limit (that should not be taken into account) and considering how a particular stage 2 exposure that has not yet been subject to any credit risk mitigation actions will develop. For example, an entity may have determined that there has been a significant increase in credit risk since initial recognition in respect of a particular exposure but may not yet have taken any specific credit risk mitigation actions such as the curtailment or termination of the credit limit. In this case, consideration should be given to the possibility that the exposure may cure rather than default. In contrast, if an entity had taken credit risk mitigation action in respect of that exposure such as the curtailment of the credit limit, it would not be appropriate to take into consideration the possibility that the exposure may subsequently cure, resulting in a reinstatement of the previously curtailed credit limit when determining the maximum exposure period. In this regard, appropriate portfolio segmentation is crucial, in particular in relation to financial assets in stage 2.
- There is only one maximum exposure period to consider, which applies equally to both the drawn and undrawn components of a revolving credit facility, which is consistent with the way in which the facility is managed. Nevertheless, in measuring ECLs, credit risk mitigation actions may affect the drawn and undrawn components differently. For example, when an entity cancels the undrawn component, the possibility of any future drawdowns is removed, whereas when an entity demands repayment of the drawn component the recovery period associated with that drawn exposure still needs to be considered in measuring ECLs.
- Ultimately, the estimation of the maximum period to consider would require judgement and consequently the disclosure requirements of IFRS 7 (such as those explaining inputs, assumptions and estimation techniques in relation to ECLs) would be important (see 15 below and Chapter 54 at 5.3).

12.2.3 Guidance provided by the IASB webcast

In May 2017 the IASB issued a webcast titled *IFRS 9 Impairment: The expected life of revolving facilities*. Like other IASB webcasts, this sets out the views of the speakers rather than the Board, but it will nevertheless be regarded as important educational material. The webcast indicated that the expected life will be bound by expected defaults, or when the facility is no longer used by the customer, or the next review date to the extent that credit risk mitigation actions are expected to occur.

This webcast used the example of a portfolio of 100 similar facilities, 30 of which are expected to significantly increase in credit risk by the next credit review and, at the next credit review, based on past experience, 5 of these facilities will be cut. The key messages provided were:

- The entity should assume that the expected life of the portfolio will be limited by the period to the next credit review only for those 5 facilities. This is because the expected life can only be reduced to the next review date to the extent that mitigation actions are expected to occur.
- It is not necessary to know in advance which 5 facilities will be cut.
- The expected life of the other 95 facilities will be bounded by when they are expected to default or the point at which the facility is no longer used by the customer.
- Meanwhile, the expected life for the 5 facilities may be shorter than the time to the next review if they are expected to default.
- As discussed at the ITG, it will be necessary to segment the portfolio appropriately into groups of loans with similar credit and payment expectations in order to determine its expected life. If a facility is more likely to default, then it is also more likely to be subject to risk mitigation action.
- If the entity expects, based on past experience, to cut the facility only in part, by reducing the limit, then the life of the facility will be cut only for the portion of the facility that is expected to be withdrawn.

This example only looks forward to what it expects to happen by the time of the next credit review. Presumably it would be appropriate to extend the analysis, to look beyond this to subsequent reviews and further reductions in facilities expected in the future, to help determine the expected life of the remaining 95 facilities in the portfolio. This is illustrated by Example 51.25 below.

A second example in the webcast compared two entities: entity A only cancels undrawn facilities that deteriorate to a risk classification of 20, while entity B cancels any facility as soon as it deteriorates to a classification of 15 (and so lower risk than grade 20). It was concluded that, all else being equal, the expected life for entity A's portfolio will be longer than for entity B's portfolio.

It should be stressed that estimating the expected life of a revolving facility is of relevance mostly for those facilities that are measured using lifetime credit losses. The allowance for those assets in stage 1 will be calculated based only on losses associated with default in the next twelve months, which is likely to be the period used to measure ECLs unless the entity's risk mitigation activities indicate that a shorter period should be used.

To recap, it would seem that a periodic credit review should normally be taken into account when assessing the period over which to measure losses to the extent that it is expected to result in actual limits reduction or withdrawal. Hence, for example, if normally 20% of facilities are withdrawn based on an annual review, then for 20% of the outstanding facilities the period to measure losses should be limited by the timing of this next review. For the other 80% of the facilities, three things may happen: they may someday default, the facility may someday be reduced or withdrawn, or the borrower may someday cease to use the card. For the 80% it is necessary to model each of these possibilities, which means that the period over which to measure ECLs may extend for a number of years into the future. Under this view the standard's requirement for any facilities measured using lifetime ECLs can be simply summarised as 'how much do you expect to lose'? The length of the period over which losses are measured is of secondary importance except that it is necessary to know when defaults are expected to occur, in order to determine the appropriate discounting. The application of this approach is illustrated in the following example.

Example 51.25: Estimating the life of revolving credit facilities

Of 1,000 facilities in stage 2 the entity estimates that each year:
- 10% will default every year in the first three years, but this reduces to 2% thereafter, as those facilities that do not default in the first three years are expected to have become significantly lower risk.
- 8% of holders will cease to use their card every year in the first three years but this increases to 15% thereafter once their financial position has improved.
- 15% of facilities will be withdrawn each year, as credit risk mitigation, over the first three years. After that period it is assumed that the credit risk is significantly reduced and none of the facilities are reduced thereafter.

No of facilities in Stage 2	Year 1	Year 2	Year 3	Year 4	Year 5	Year 6	Year 7
Balance brought forward	1,000	670	448	301	250	207	172
Defaults	(100)	(67)	(45)	(6)	(5)	(4)	(3)
Cease to use card	(80)	(54)	(35)	(45)	(38)	(31)	(26)
Facility withdrawn	(150)	(101)	(67)	–	–	–	–
Balance carried forward	670	448	301	250	207	172	143

In this example it is apparent that while the level of defaults quickly declines, a small portion of the portfolio has a very long life. The consequence is that the ECL could be very significant. However, the example does not take account of the time value of money. Given the high interest rate charged on credit cards, the manner in which interest is included in the estimation of cash flows and losses are discounted will have a major impact upon the ECL measurement (see 12.4 below).

One method that we have observed being applied to make this calculation is to track a portfolio of stage 2 facilities over a number of years and note how long it takes for the default rate to reduce to an immaterial level.

12.2.4 Interaction with derecognition

A further issue is the extent to which the period over which to measure ECLs is restricted by the normal derecognition principles of IFRS 9 and what could constitute a derecognition of the facility. In particular, it is unclear whether the existence of a contractual life and/or the lender's ability to revise the terms and conditions of the facility based on periodic credit reviews as thorough as that on origination, would be regarded as triggers for derecognition and so would also limit the life for ECL measurement.

In April 2015, the ITG discussed how to determine the date of initial recognition of a revolving credit facility for the purposes of the assessment of significant increases in credit risk. The challenge presented was how to determine when changes are sufficiently significant to result in a derecognition of the original facility and recognition of a new facility. The ITG members discussed some of the factors that might be taken into consideration in making that judgement, such as issuing a new card, revising credit limits or conducting credit reviews.

It was noted that judgement would be required in making this assessment and that it would depend on the specific facts and circumstances. However, the following observations were made:

(a) in some circumstances issuing a new card may be indicative that the original facility has been derecognised, but in other cases, this may be a purely operational process and thus would not indicate that a new facility has been issued; and

(b) credit reviews in themselves may not indicate that a new facility has been issued.

Although this discussion was on how to determine the reference date for assessing if there has been a significant increase in credit risk, the notion that it depends on the derecognition of one facility and the recognition of a new one would, presumably, be equally relevant for assessing the period over which to measure ECLs. This is especially relevant for corporate overdraft facilities which are considered to be in the scope of the exception (see 12.1 above). If, for instance:

i) the facility has a clearly agreed contractual life of one year (in addition to a short cancellation notice period);

ii) the bank goes through a thorough credit process each year, similar to that on original application and using detailed financial and other information specific to the customer, before deciding whether to continue with the facility, increase it, reduce it or withdraw it;

iii) the bank will at that time revise the terms and conditions of the facility to reflect the up-to-date credit quality of the borrower; and

iv) the bank derecognises the facility and recognises a new one, giving the associated required disclosures,

Intuitively, it would seem that the bank is only exposed to credit risk for the period of a year.

This is consistent with the Basis of Conclusions which confirms the general principle that, 'if an entity decides to renew or extend its commitment to extend credit, it will be a new instrument for which the entity has the opportunity to revise the terms and conditions.' *[IFRS 9.BC5.260]*. Also, while paragraph BC5.261 of IFRS 9, by starting with the word 'however', makes it clear that the revolving facilities amendment was an exception to this principle, it does not explicitly state that it is an exception to the entire principle. It only says that 'the entity's contractual ability to demand repayment and cancel the undrawn commitment does not limit the entity's exposure' remaining silent on an entity's ability to renew or extend credit. On the other hand, some believe that an ability to withdraw or cancel is in substance sufficiently similar to an ability to renew or extend, that they should be treated the same. They also consider that the IASB webcast has made it clear that only expected reductions and withdrawals of facilities can be reflected in the assessment of the risk horizon. Consequently, a decision to maintain the facility, even if based on fully revised terms and conditions, would not be considered a risk management decision that shortens the life of the facility.

There are also differences of view as to whether a revolving facility can be derecognised (and so the expected derecognition can be reflected in the ECL horizon) if the lender carries out an annual thorough periodic credit review at least equivalent to that when the facility was first granted, at which point it may revise the terms and conditions, but there is no contractual limit to the life of the facility, or if there is a contractual limit to the life of the facility but no thorough credit review at the point of renewal. In the first case, the contract allows for a periodic credit review equivalent to that on origination, performed on an individual rather than a collective basis and with an opportunity to revise the terms and conditions if the credit quality has changed, some believe that this could lead to derecognition of the facility and recognition of a new one. As a result, ECLs would only be measured over the period until the next periodic review. In the second case, the facility has a clearly agreed contractual life but its renewal is relatively automatic without a thorough review. Some believe that IFRS 9 is clear that a financial instrument is derecognised if it expires and therefore a thorough credit review is not required.

It is important for banks to disclose the basis on which they have made their calculations.

It should be stressed that this issue is of relevance mostly for those facilities that are measured using lifetime credit losses. The allowance for those assets in stage 1 will be calculated based only on losses associated with default in the next twelve months.

12.3 Exposure at default (EAD)

To measure ECLs on revolving facilities, such as credit cards, it will be necessary to estimate several components that make up the EAD:

- the credit conversion factor, to determine the portion of the facility that is drawn down in any period (limited, for facilities in stage 1 to the next twelve months);
- the speed at which drawn down facilities are paid off; and
- the level of interest expected to be charged in the future on those facilities that are drawn down.

These components will all need to be estimated based on past experience and future expectations, for sections of the portfolio that are segmented so that they have similar credit characteristics (see 6.5.2 above). The estimation of interest is addressed further in 12.4 below.

At its meeting on 16 September 2015, the ITG (see 1.5 above) discussed how an entity should estimate future drawdowns on undrawn lines of credit when an entity has a history of allowing customers to exceed their contractually set credit limits on overdrafts and other revolving credit facilities.

The ITG members noted that:

- The exception for some types of revolving credit facilities set out in paragraph 5.5.20 of IFRS 9 relates to the contractual commitment period and does not address the contractual credit limit. The standard was clear in this regard and

- consequently, it would not be appropriate to analogise this specific exception to the contractual credit limit.
- Some members of the ITG pointed out that, in practice, the tenor and amount of revolving credit facilities are inextricably linked, because banks not only extend credit for a period in excess of their maximum contractual commitment period but also allow customers to make drawdowns in excess of the maximum contractually agreed credit limit as notified to the customer. Consequently, if amounts in excess of the maximum contractually agreed credit limits are not taken into account, there would be a potential disconnect between the accounting and credit risk management view.
- However, it was concluded that IFRS 9 limits the estimation of future drawdowns to the contractually agreed credit limit.

12.4 Time value of money

The time value of money is important in measuring ECLs for revolving facilities since interest rates (when interest is charged) are high. Hence it is important that any interest that is expected to be charged on drawn balances is included in the EAD and that an appropriate rate is used to discount ECLs. An additional complexity is introduced by credit cards, because they typically have a grace period in which no interest is charged as long as the amount drawn down is repaid within a specified period of time.

According to the guidance for 'normal' loan commitments, the ECLs on a loan commitment must be discounted using the EIR, or an approximation thereof, that will be applied when recognising the financial asset resulting from the loan commitment. *[IFRS 9.B5.5.47]*. Applying this approach, the ECLs on the currently undrawn portion of a revolving facility should be discounted based on the rate that is likely to be charged if it is drawn down. If it is expected that interest will be charged at the high rate – which is likely for most facilities that are already 'revolvers', that is, those facilities where the borrower only pays off the minimum amounts permitted by the issuer (in effect, using the card to borrow money) – then the discount rate is likely to be the high rate. However, the ITG discussion on the scope of revolving credit facilities in December 2015 (see 12.1 above) noted that the drawn and undrawn balances should be viewed as one unit of account and so discounted at the same rate. If it is projected that a transactor, that is, one who repays any amount drawn down within the specified short period and so is charged no interest, will at some stage become a revolver before it defaults, then it may be appropriate to calculate a blended discount rate.

In addition, at the same meeting, the ITG discussion on the use of floating-rates of interest to measure ECLs (see 5.7 above) established a useful principle, that there should be consistency between the rate used to recognise interest revenue, the rate used to project future cash flows (including shortfalls) and the rate used to discount those cash flows.

Because the choice of interest rate used to project cash flows and to discount losses will depend on expectations of the borrower's behaviour, it will need to be made separately for segments of the portfolio with similar credit and payment characteristics.

While the high rates charged by a credit card issuer are sometimes fixed in the contract, the fact that the rate charged (nil or the high rate) depends on how quickly the customer repays the amount drawn, means that the rate can be thought of as 'floating', even if it does not vary with a benchmark rate of interest. This is important since otherwise it would be necessary to assess the EIR on initial recognition and keep this fixed unless the facility is derecognised, ignoring any changes in customer behaviour.

Applying this principle, for a credit card customer that is a 'transactor', it would not be appropriate to discount ECLs (i.e. the lender should apply an interest rate of nil). On the other hand, for a revolver, the high rate of interest should be included in the forecast cash flows and in the discount rate.

However, any transactor who goes on to default is likely to begin paying off less than the full amount for a period of time before they default. To estimate the ECLs for this scenario, it will be necessary to include any interest that will be charged in this period. A consistent discount rate will then be a blended rate, of nil for the period over which the customer is expected to pay no interest and the high rate over the period in which they will pay the higher rate.

In practice, it is likely that credit card issuers will often adopt procedures to discount their ECLs that may be less sophisticated than set out above, due to operational constraints and because the objective of the standard is to discount ECLs at an approximation of the EIR. *[IFRS 9.B5.5.44]*. However, it is necessary to understand what is theoretically required by IFRS 9 in order to be able to assess whether a pragmatic approach is a reasonable approximation when determining the discount rate.

12.5 Determining significant increase in credit risk

As already mentioned at 12.2 above, at its April 2015 meeting, the ITG discussed the starting reference date when assessing significant increases in credit risk for a portfolio of revolving credit facilities. There will typically be a diverse customer base, ranging from long-standing customers who have been with the bank for many years, to new customers who have only recently opened an account. The standard's general rule is that the starting reference date is the date of original recognition. Consequently, the date of initial recognition for this purpose is the date the facility was issued and this should only be changed if there has been a derecognition of the original facility. As discussed at 12.2 above, it is not altogether clear what would qualify as a derecognition within the context of the revolving facility exception. If the lender derecognises a facility at the end of its contractual term and recognises a new one when it decides to renew or extend credit, consistent with the Basis of Conclusions, it would be consistent to assess if there has been a significant increase in credit risk from when the current facility was first recognised. *[IFRS 9.BC5.260]*. Similarly, it may make sense to use the date that the limit was increased if a facility is now far larger than would have been granted on original recognition. There is also a view that the credit risk on the date that the facility was last increased may be a useful proxy for the credit risk on the date of original recognition. There is a particular challenge on transition to IFRS 9, since entities may have limited data on the credit risk at the date of original recognition. (See 5.9 above).

However, as discussed at 12.2 above, another view is that only a reduction or cancellation of the facility would lead to the revolving facility being derecognised. In some circumstances, issuing a new card may be indicative that the original facility has been derecognised (e.g. replacement of a student credit card with a new credit card upon graduation), but in other cases, this may be a purely operational process and thus would not indicate that a new facility has been issued.

The ITG did not conclude further on this issue and it was not discussed in the IASB's May 2017 webcast. Consequently, at the date of writing this issue had not been resolved.

13 INTERCOMPANY LOANS

For those entities that prepare separate IFRS financial statements, one of the challenges in complying with the IFRS 9 impairment requirements is the application to intercompany loans to members of the same group.

The two most common difficulties faced are the paucity of data to calculate the ECLs and the possibility that intercompany loans are either undocumented, or not documented in accordance with the substance of the arrangement. For instance, it is possible that a group entity is financed entirely by debt rather than partly through equity, so that the substance of the loan (at least in part) may be closer to an equity investment in that entity.

It should be stressed that any ECLs measured on a loan to a group entity will require a charge to profit or loss. For instance, the ECL on a loan to a subsidiary will result in an impairment expense and it cannot capitalised as part of the investment in the subsidiary.

13.1 Scope of intercompany loans under IFRS 9

All intercompany loans measured at amortised cost or FVOCI are in the scope of the ECL requirements (see Chapter 48 at 5.2 and 5.3). Paragraph 2.1(a) of IFRS 9 scopes out of the standard interests in subsidiaries accounted for in accordance with IAS 27 – *Separate Financial Statements* – and paragraph 10 of IAS 27 allows investments in subsidiaries to be accounted for at cost as an alternative to applying IFRS 9. For such investments, impairment would be calculated applying IAS 36 – *Impairment of Assets*. 'Investments' are not defined in IAS 27. Although IAS 27 is usually read to refer to investments in shares, an argument might be made that it can also cover intercompany arrangements which are, in substance, capital investments. However, in its September 2016 meeting, the IFRIC seem to have ruled against this. The Committee discussed the interaction of IFRS 9 and IAS 28 – *Investments in Associates and Joint Ventures* – where a loan is regarded as part of 'long-term interests that, in substance, forms part of the entity's net investment' as set out in paragraph 38 of IAS 28, which gives as an example, 'an item for which settlement is neither planned nor likely to occur in the foreseeable future'. The Committee concluded that although a loan is considered as 'in substance part of the investment', for the purposes of allocating losses in IAS 28, it is still in the scope of IFRS 9 as it is not 'an investment' as mentioned in scope paragraph 2.1(a) of IFRS 9 and, except for the allocation of losses, is not accounted for using the equity method. Since then, in October 2017, the IASB amended IAS 28 to clarify that IFRS 9 should be applied to long term interests in associates and joint ventures.

The IFRIC discussion was in the context of IAS 28 and not IAS 27. It is perhaps relevant that IFRS 9 in its scope paragraph refers to 'interests' in subsidiaries, rather than 'investments', although IAS 27 itself uses 'investments'. IAS 27 also allows investments to be at cost, rather than accounted for using the equity method. However, it would probably be difficult to sustain an argument that 'investments' as used in IAS 27, encompasses loans which are, in substance, part of the net investment, when the Committee has concluded that the same term in IAS 28 does not.

On balance, an undocumented interest free loan to a subsidiary, when there is no expectation of repayment, may be better characterised for accounting purposes as a capital contribution. If this is the case, then it should be documented as such and then it may be measured at cost under IAS 27 and subject to the impairment requirements of IAS 36, rather than those of IFRS 9. The amendment of a loan (if previously documented as such) to a capital contribution would be similar to a forgiveness of the debt and therefore, as already mentioned above, may have (or be constrained by) tax implications and may only be capable of being repaid in the future if there are adequate distributable profits.

In addition, there might often be cases where the contractual terms of an intercompany loan which is not 'on demand' are determined to be 'off-market' (e.g. interest-free or below market rate). In such cases, a portion is highly likely to be accounted for as a capital contribution within the scope of IAS 27, depending on the facts and circumstances. That being the case, the remaining portion would likely be within the scope of IFRS 9 (paragraphs B5.1.1 and B5.1.2 of IFRS 9), in which case measurement at amortised cost or FVOCI would require the financial instrument to pass the IFRS 9 SPPI criterion as otherwise it would need to be measured at fair value through profit and loss.

13.2 Intercompany loans repayable on demand

Assuming the intercompany loan meets the SPPI and business model criteria and is measured either at amortised cost or FVOCI, according to paragraph 5.5.19 of IFRS 9, the maximum period to consider when measuring ECLs is the maximum contractual period over which the entity is exposed to credit risk, even if a longer period is consistent with business practice. If a loan is repayable on demand, the period over which losses should be calculated would normally be no more than 24 hours. If the borrowing group entity is able to repay the loan when demanded, the PD would usually be very small and the ECL is likely to be immaterial. However, if the nature of the loan is that it provides long term finance (see Chapter 8 at 4.3) and the borrowing group entity would be unable to repay the loan if it is called at short notice, because it does not currently have access to the means to repay it or to other sources of finance, the PD would be high and close to 100%. The lender would be entitled to look to the manner of recovery of the amount due in calculating the LGD, which may mean that it would allow the subsidiary a number of years to accumulate the funds to repay the loan. In instances where the lender expects to recover the full amount of the loan, the ECL will be limited to the effect of discounting of the loan amount over the recovery period and if the loan is interest free, i.e. the EIR is 0%, then there will be no impairment loss. In addition, the lender group entity will also need to consider the staging of these loans (see 6 above).

13.3 Determining the ECLs of intercompany loans

Compared to most loans to third parties, a lender within a group is likely to have access to much more qualitative and quantitative information about the credit risk of the borrower. Consequently, the staging assessment is likely to be much better informed than for a third-party loan and will be, primarily, a qualitative exercise. In many cases, it will be reasonably clear whether there has been a significant increase in credit risk since the inception of the loan, although judgement will still be required to determine whether it is 'significant'. Circumstances that indicate a significant increase in credit risk may include a significant change in the business, financial or economic conditions, or regulatory, economic or technological environment in which the borrower operates, declining revenues and margins, or capital deficiencies. Any of these changes are likely to have a significant impact on the entity's ability to meet its debt obligations. *[IFRS 9.B5.5.17(f), B5.5.17(g), B5.5.17(i)].*

Also, the credit risk on a loan depends in part on the level of loss absorbing equity of the borrowing entity. For those intercompany loans between fellow subsidiaries that are explicitly guaranteed by a parent, the ECL may be much lower than those without a parental guarantee. Also, if the parent is listed and the guarantee is integral to the loan, the expected loss will normally be equal to the parent's PD multiplied by its LGD. That is because the parent will usually be expected to ensure, if it can do so, that its subsidiary will not default (and the subsidiary is likely to default if the parent does). It will often be much easier to calculate an ECL based on a parent PD and LGD since there may be market quoted bond spreads, credit default swap (CDS) spreads and credit ratings to draw upon. Therefore, it may be advisable to formally document guarantee arrangements between a parent and subsidiary when this is already the implicit basis on which the loan was entered into. Another scenario could be that the parent has no activities other than acting as a holding entity, in which case its PD will be closely aligned with that of its subsidiaries. There could also be situations where the subsidiary can be expected to survive even if the parent defaults.

To the extent that the lender is the parent, it cannot, for its own accounting purposes, rely on guarantees given by itself. However, any group entity that does provide a guarantee will need to measure its exposure to the guarantee, hence the existence of a guarantee does not remove the challenge of calculating the PD and LGD of the subsidiary. In general, the fact that a group intends to ensure that a subsidiary will never default does not eliminate the risk posed by that subsidiary's activities or remove the need for an ECL allowance.

If there are cross-company guarantees within the group relating to loans from external parties of the group, each entity affected by the cross-company guarantee arrangement needs, for the calculation of ECLs in its standalone financial statements to factor in the cross-company guarantees in place (see 11.4 above).

14 PRESENTATION OF EXPECTED CREDIT LOSSES IN THE STATEMENT OF FINANCIAL POSITION

IFRS 9 uses the term 'loss allowance' throughout the standard as an umbrella term for ECLs that are recognised in the statement of financial position. However, that umbrella term leaves open the question of how those ECLs should be presented in that statement. Their presentation differs by the type of the credit risk exposures that are in scope of the impairment requirements. *[IFRS 9 Appendix A].* This section explains how presentation applies in the different situations.

Any adjustment to the loss allowance balance due to an increase or decrease of the amount of ECLs recognised in accordance with IFRS 9, is reflected in profit or loss in a separate line as an impairment gain or loss. *[IAS 1.82(ba), IFRS 9.5.5.8, Appendix A].*

14.1 Allowance for financial assets measured at amortised cost, contract assets and lease receivables

ECLs on financial assets measured at amortised cost, lease receivables (see Chapter 23) and contract assets (see Chapter 28) are presented as an allowance, i.e. as an integral part of the measurement of those assets in the statement of financial position.

Unlike the requirement to show impairment losses as a separate line item in the statement of profit or loss, there is no similar consequential amendment to IAS 1 to present the loss allowance as a separate line item in the statement of financial position. *[IAS 1.82(ba)].*

It is clear from the standard that the definition of amortised cost of a financial asset is after adjusting for any loss allowance and hence, the loss allowance would reduce the gross carrying amount in the statement of financial position (which is why an allowance is sometimes referred to as a contra asset account). *[IFRS 9 Appendix A].* Accordingly, financial assets measured at amortised cost, contract assets and lease receivables should be presented net of the loss allowance at their amortised cost in the statement of financial position.

This was confirmed at the ITG meeting in December 2015, when the ITG discussed whether an entity is required to present the loss allowance for financial assets measured at amortised cost (or trade receivables, contract assets or lease receivables) separately in the statement of financial position. The ITG members first noted that irrespective of how the loss allowance is presented or how it is included in the measurement of the financial instrument, IFRS 7 contains disclosure requirements pertaining to the loss allowance for all financial instruments within the scope of the IFRS 9 impairment requirements. The ITG members also noted that, in contrast to the case of financial assets measured at fair value through other comprehensive income, neither IFRS 9 nor IFRS 7 contains any specific requirements regarding the presentation of the loss allowance for financial assets measured at amortised cost (or trade receivables, contract assets or lease receivables) on the face of the statement of financial position. In accordance with the general requirements of IAS 1, the financial statements should fairly present the financial position of an entity. However, the ITG members noted that paragraph 54 of IAS 1 does not list the loss allowance as an amount that is required to be separately presented on the face of the statement of financial position.

14.1.1 Write-off

IFRS 9 provides guidance on when the allowance should be used, i.e. when it should be applied against the gross carrying amount of a financial asset. This occurs when there is a write-off on a financial asset, which happens when the entity has no reasonable expectations of recovering the contractual cash flows on a financial asset in its entirety or a portion thereof. A write-off is considered a derecognition event. *[IFRS 9.5.4.4, B3.2.16(r)].* No similar guidance was provided previously in IAS 39 and its derecognition guidance does not refer to write-offs.

For example, a lender plans to enforce the collateral on a loan and expects to recover no more than 30 per cent of the value of the loan from selling the collateral. If the lender has no reasonable prospects of recovering any further cash flows from the loan, it should write off the remaining 70 per cent. *[IFRS 9.B5.4.9]*. The example given in the standard demonstrates that write-offs can be for only a partial amount instead of the entire gross carrying amount.

The example below illustrates how partial write-offs may be determined for a loan in stage 3.

Example 51.26: Partial write-offs for a loan in stage 3

As at 31 December 2010, the lender has an impaired loan in stage 3 and determines that it has a 75% probability of recovering nothing and a 25% probability of recovering 20% of the value of the loan. Ignoring discounting, the overall ECL would be 95% (i.e. 75% × 0% plus 25% × 20%). The probability-weighted expectation is therefore a recovery of 5% of the loan balance.

As there is still 25% probability of recovering 20% of the value of the loan, the lender writes-off a partial amount of the loan, i.e. 80% of the loan balance, leaving 20% of the loan on the balance sheet and an ECL of 15%.

Because IFRS 9 requires a loan to be written off in part when it is no longer expected that a portion of the amount due will be collected, the loan may be written off in partial amounts as stage 3 progresses. This means that there may be no single 'write off point' but instead a continuum; e.g. a loan may initially be written off 50%, then 80% and finally 100%.

Practice varies in terms of write-off and is sometimes dependent on the influence of prudential regulators. Write-off requirements in IFRS 9 should be considered at each reporting date and should not be delayed until some arbitrary past due date has been reached. On the other hand, if collection efforts continue and have some possibility of success, total write-off would also seem to be inappropriate.

If the amount of loss on write-off is greater than the accumulated loss allowance, the difference will be an additional impairment loss. In situations where a further impairment loss occurs, the question has arisen as to how it should be presented: simply as a loss in profit or loss with a credit directly to the gross carrying amount; or first, as an addition to the allowance that is then applied against the gross carrying amount. The difference between those alternatives is whether the additional impairment loss flows through the allowance, showing up in a reconciliation of the allowance as an addition and a use (i.e. a write-off), or whether such additional impairment amounts bypass the allowance. The IASB's original 2009 Exposure Draft (see 1.1 above) explicitly mandated that all write-offs could only be debited against the allowance, meaning that any direct write-offs against profit or loss without flowing through the allowance were prohibited.[44] IFRS 9 does not include any similar explicit guidance on this issue (see Chapter 50 at 3.8.1 in relation to presentation of modification losses).

Similarly, the standard does not provide guidance on accounting for subsequent recoveries of a financial asset. Arguably, there would be a higher threshold when recognising an asset that has been previously written-off and this is likely to be when cash is received rather than when the criteria for write-off are no longer met. It might also be argued that such recoveries should not often be significant, as write-off should only occur when there is no reasonable expectations of recovering the contractual cash flows. The occurrence of large recoveries subsequent to the recognition of total write-offs should give entities an indication to reconsider their approaches to future write-offs.

As the nature of recoveries are similar to reversals of impairment, it makes sense to present such recoveries in the impairment line in profit or loss as it would provide useful and relevant information to the users of the financial statements. *[IAS 1.82(ba)]*.

In addition, IFRS 7 requires an entity to disclose its policies in relation to write-offs and also, the amounts written off during the period that are still subject to enforcement activity (see 15 below and Chapter 54 at 5.3). *[IFRS 7.35F(e), 35L]*. It should be noted that there is a tension between this requirement and the criteria in IFRS 9 for write-off, since it may be difficult to argue that there is no reasonable expectation of recovering the contractual cash flows if the loan is still subject to enforcement activity.

14.1.2 Presentation of the interest revenue, gross carrying amount, amortised cost, expected credit loss expense and expected credit loss allowance for credit-impaired assets

For financial assets that are not purchased or originated credit-impaired financial assets but subsequently have become credit-impaired, i.e. moved to stage 3, in subsequent reporting periods the interest revenue is calculated by multiplying the EIR by the net amortised cost, i.e. the gross carrying amount of the financial asset net of the ECL allowance. *[IFRS 9.5.4.1(b)]*. However, the application of the EIR to the amortised cost of the financial asset applies only to the calculation and presentation of interest revenue. The Basis for Conclusions confirms that this does not affect the measurement of the loss allowance. *[IFRS 9.BC5.75]*. As long as the asset was not credit-impaired on initial recognition, the EIR is based on the contractual cash flows, excluding ECLs and this does not change when the asset becomes credit-impaired. *[IFRS 9.B5.4.4, Appendix A]*. Consequently, the calculation of the gross carrying amount and the ECL allowance, as disclosed in the notes to the financial statements, are not affected by the recognition of interest revenue moving from a gross to a net basis.

This was confirmed at a meeting of the ITG in December 2015, when a question was raised on how the disclosed figures for the gross carrying amount and loss allowance should each be calculated. The example below is based on the ITG discussion but has been amended to reflect unpaid accrued interest in the gross carrying amount.[45]

Example 51.27: **Disclosing the gross carrying amount and loss allowance for credit-impaired financial assets that are not purchased or originated credit-impaired**

The Bank originated a loan on 1 January 2021, with an amortised cost of $100 and an EIR of 10% per annum. On 31 December 2021 the loan is considered to be credit-impaired and so is moved to stage 3, and an impairment allowance is recognised of $70. Accordingly, the gross carrying amount of the loan is now $110 and the amortised cost is now $40. During 2022, no cash is received, and on 31 December 2022, there is no change in the expected cash flows. Accordingly, the amortised cost becomes $44 (being $40 + ($40 × 10%)). Three different ways could be used to reflect the changes in the net amortised cost in the gross carrying amount and the loss allowance. In Approach A, interest continues to be accrued in the measurement of the gross carrying amount at 10%, in Approach B, the interest accrued to the gross carrying amount is only the $4 recorded in profit or loss, while in Approach C, no interest is added to the gross carrying amount:

Approach	A $	B $	C $
Gross carrying amount	121 *	114	110
Loss allowance	(77)	(70)	(66)
Amortised cost	44	44	44

* The gross carrying amount of $121 is calculated by adding the EIR of 10% per annum on the 31 December 2021 gross carrying amount of $110, i.e. 10% × $110 = $11.

The ITG members appeared to agree that only Approach A is IFRS 9-compliant. Thereby, for assets in stage 3, it is necessary to 'gross up' accrued interest income, to increase both the disclosed gross carrying amount and loss allowance in the notes to the financial statements. Approach A requires the entity to calculate:

(a) the gross carrying amount by discounting the estimated contractual cash flows (without considering ECLs) using the original EIR; and

(b) the loss allowance by discounting the expected cash shortfalls using the original EIR.

Depending on the legal form of the loan, we assume that once interest is no longer contractually due, for instance when the bank moves to take possession of collateral, there would be no need to continue to make these gross up entries.

Moreover, the ITG did not consider the interaction between the recognition of interest income and the requirement to write off all or a proportion of the gross financial asset if there is no reasonable expectations of recovering the associated contractual cash flows. If there is no reasonable expectation that all of the contractual interest will be paid, then the lender should presumably not follow Approach A. Instead, a portion of the gross asset would be written off against the allowance, depending on the expectations of recovery. This could result in a lender reporting numbers closer to those in Approach B. By writing off accrued interest where there is no reasonable expectation of recovery, it may be possible to align the amounts disclosed for stage 3 loans under IFRS 9 with the figures that banking regulators require to be disclosed for non-performing loans.

The IASB is of the view that, conceptually, an entity should assess whether financial assets have become credit-impaired on an ongoing basis, thus, altering the presentation of interest revenue as the underlying economics change. However, the IASB noted that such an approach would be unduly onerous for preparers to apply. Thus, the IASB decided that an entity should be required to make the assessment of whether a financial asset is credit-impaired at the reporting date and then change the interest calculation from the beginning of the following reporting period. *[IFRS 9.BC5.78]*. Arguably, if an entity is able to change the interest calculation earlier than the reporting date, then this would be a timelier adjustment and reflection of the interest revenue. However, this is not what the standard requires.

In November 2018, the IFRIC received a request to provide guidance for how an entity presents amounts recognised in the statement of profit or loss when a credit-impaired financial asset is subsequently cured (i.e. paid in full or no longer credit-impaired), as diversity in practice had arisen.

When a financial asset becomes credit-impaired, application of the effective interest rate to the amortised cost of the financial asset results in a difference between:

(a) the interest that would be calculated by applying the effective interest rate to the gross carrying amount of the credit-impaired financial asset; and

(b) the interest revenue recognised for that asset.

If the asset cures and the full amount of interest income is subsequently received, how should this difference be recorded? The IFRIC concluded that, in the statement of profit or loss, an entity is required to present the difference as a reversal of impairment losses rather than as interest revenue. In reaching its conclusion, the IFRIC noted that paragraph 5.5.8 of IFRS 9 requires an entity to 'recognise in profit or loss, as an impairment gain or loss, the amount of expected credit losses (or reversal) that is required to adjust the loss allowance at the reporting date to the amount that is required to be recognised in accordance with this Standard.' Applying paragraph 5.5.8 of IFRS 9, an entity recognises in profit or loss as a reversal of expected credit losses the adjustment required to bring the loss allowance to the amount that is required to be recognised in accordance with IFRS 9 (zero if the asset is paid in full). The amount of this adjustment includes the effect of the unwinding of the discount on the loss allowance during the period that the financial asset was credit-impaired. This means that the reversal of impairment losses may exceed the impairment losses recognised in profit or loss over the life of the asset.

In July 2019, the IASB staff released an educational webinar which included an example explaining the accounting required to reflect the curing of a credit-impaired financial asset, consistent with the IFRIC tentative agenda decision. This is illustrated in the example below with amounts rounded to the nearest $1 and 1%.

Example 51.28: Presentation of the interest revenue, gross carrying amount, amortised cost, expected credit loss expense and expected credit loss allowance for when assets move from stage 2 to stage 3 and vice versa

On 1 January 2021, an entity originates a 5-year loan with a principal amount of $100 and annual instalments of $26 payable annually on 31 December, which results in an EIR of 10%.

The entity measures expected credit losses for the first time at the first reporting date as at 31 December 2021 after initial recognition. As at 31 December 2021, the credit risk on the loan has increased significantly since initial recognition (i.e. the loan has moved from stage 1 to stage 2) and the entity recognised lifetime expected credit losses of $66. For the reporting period to 31 December 2021, the interest revenue would be calculated by applying the 10% EIR to the gross carrying amount of the loan of $100, i.e. $10. The annual instalment of $26 was received.

As at 31 December 2022, the next annual instalment had not been paid and the loan is assessed to be credit-impaired (i.e. stage 3). For the reporting period to 31 December 2022, the interest revenue would be calculated by applying the 10% EIR to the gross carrying amount of the loan of $84, i.e. $8. To simplify the example, there is no change in the expected shortfalls in contractual cash flows between 31 December 2021 and 31 December 2023 even though the loan has deteriorated to stage 3. An impairment loss of $7 is recognised for the unwinding of the discount based on the EIR determined at initial recognition of 10%, in order to reflect the passage of time, i.e. 10% EIR on the $66 impairment loss allowance.

For the year to 31 December 2023, the interest revenue would be calculated by applying the 10% EIR to the amortised cost of the loan of $19, i.e. $2, instead of the gross carrying amount. Both the gross carrying amount and ECL loss allowance are discounted and therefore, need to reflect the effect of the unwinding of the discount. The gross carrying amount needs to increase by $9 and the ECL allowance needs to increase by $7, based on the EIR determined at initial recognition of 10%, in order to reflect the passage of time. As interest revenue of $2 has been recognised, both the gross carrying amount and ECL allowance need to increase by an additional $7 (reflected as unwinding of the discount).

To simplify the example, it is assumed that as at 1 January 2024, the entity received the contractual amount due in full of $101. $80 of impairment losses are released as a credit to the impairment expense. In this example the impairment credit exceeds the impairment losses previously recognised in profit or loss over the life of the asset ($66 + $7 = $73) due to the effect of the unwinding of the discount on the loss allowance during the period that the financial asset was credit-impaired.

	31 December 2021 Stage 2 $	31 December 2022 Stage 3 $	31 December 2023 Stage 3 $	31 December 2024 Fully repaid $
Statement of financial position				
Gross carrying amount				
As at 1 Jan	$100	$84	$92	$101
Interest accrued (EIR) on the gross carrying amount (stage 2) or amortised cost in the next reporting period (stage 3)	$10	$8	$2	–
Unwinding of discount	–	–	$7	–
Repayment	($26)	–	–	($101)
As at 31 Dec	$84	$92	$101	–
ECL allowance				
As at 1 Jan	–	$66	$73	$80
Impairment	$66	–	–	($80)
Unwinding of discount	–	$7	$7	–
As at 31 Dec	$66	$73	$80	–
Amortised cost				
As at 1 Jan	$100	$18	$19	$21
As at 31 Dec	$18	$19	$21	–
Statement of profit or loss				
Interest revenue	$10	$8	$2	–
Impairment loss / (reversal)	$66	$7	–	($80)

14.2 Provisions for loan commitments and financial guarantee contracts

In contrast to the presentation of impairment of assets, ECLs on loan commitments and financial guarantee contracts are presented as a provision in the statement of financial position, i.e. as a liability. *[IFRS 9 Appendix A]*.

For financial institutions that offer credit facilities, commitments may often be partially drawn down, i.e. an entity may have a facility that includes both a loan (a financial asset) and an undrawn commitment (a loan commitment). If the entity cannot separately identify the ECLs attributable to the drawn amount and the undrawn commitment, IFRS 7 requires an entity to present the provision for ECLs on the loan commitment together with the allowance for the financial asset. IFRS 7 states, further, that if the combined ECLs exceed the gross carrying amount of the financial asset, then the ECLs should be recognised as a provision. *[IFRS 7.B8E]*.

14.3 Accumulated impairment amount for debt instruments measured at fair value through other comprehensive income

Rather than presenting ECLs on financial assets measured at fair value through other comprehensive income as an allowance, this amount is presented as the 'accumulated impairment amount' in other comprehensive income. This is because financial assets measured at fair value through other comprehensive income are measured at fair value in the statement of financial position and the accumulated impairment amount cannot reduce the carrying amount of these assets (see 9 above for further details). *[IFRS 9.4.1.2A, 5.5.2, Appendix A]*.

15 DISCLOSURES

The credit risk disclosure requirements have expanded significantly and are supplemented by some detailed implementation guidance. The disclosure requirements in relation to the IFRS 9 ECL model are dealt with in more detail in Chapter 54 at 5.3, and this section provides only a high level summary.

The credit risk disclosure requirements will aim to enable users of financial statements to understand better an entity's credit risk management practices, its credit risk exposures, ECL estimates and changes in credit risks. *[IFRS 7.35B]*. In order to meet this objective, an entity will need to disclose both quantitative and qualitative information that includes the following:

- inputs, assumptions and estimation used (and any changes) to determine significant increases in credit risk of financial instruments, including the application of the low credit risk and more than 30 days past due operational simplifications (see 6 above); *[IFRS 7.35F(a), 35G(a)(ii), 35G(c)]*

- inputs, assumptions and techniques used (and any changes) in measuring 12-month and lifetime ECLs, including the definition of default and the incorporation of forward-looking information (see 5 above); *[IFRS 7.35F(b), 35G(a)(i), 35G(b), 35G(c), B8A]*

- how the financial instruments were grouped if the measurement of ECLs was performed on a collective basis (see 6.5 above); *[IFRS 7.35F(c)]*

- how collateral and other credit enhancements affect the estimate of ECLs, including a description of the nature and quality of collateral held and quantitative information about the collateral for financial assets that are credit-impaired (see 5.8.1 and 6.1.1 above); *[IFRS 7.35K, B8F, B8G]*

- a reconciliation of the opening and closing balance of the loss allowance and explanations of the changes. This disclosure is required to be shown separately for:
  - financial instruments that are measured using 12-month ECLs;
  - those that are measured using lifetime ECLs; financial assets that are credit-impaired on initial recognition;
  - those that are subsequently credit-impaired; and
  - trade receivables, contract assets and lease receivables measured under the simplified approach; *[IFRS 7.35H]*

- explanation of how significant changes in the gross carrying amount of financial instruments during the period contributed to changes in the loss allowance; *[IFRS 7.35I]*

- inputs, assumptions and techniques used (and any changes) to determine whether a financial asset is credit-impaired (see 3.1 and 3.3 above); *[IFRS 7.35F(d), 35G(a)(iii), 35G(c)]*

- for modified financial assets (see 8 above):

- the credit risk management practices (how an entity determines that a financial asset that is modified when its loss allowance was measured based on lifetime ECLs has improved to the extent that its allowance can now be reduced to 12-month ECLs, and how an entity monitors the extent to which such a loss allowance should subsequently be brought back to lifetime ECLs);
- the amortised cost before the modification and the net modification gain or loss recognised during the period for modified financial assets with a loss allowance measured at lifetime ECLs;
- the gross carrying amount of those modified financial assets for which the loss allowance has changed from lifetime to 12-month ECLs during the period; and
- quantitative information that will assist users to understand any subsequent increase in credit risk, including information about modified financial assets for which the loss allowance has reverted from 12-month ECLs to lifetime ECLs; *[IFRS 7.35F(f), B8B, 35J]*
- the entity's credit risk exposure and significant credit risk concentrations, including the gross carrying amount of financial assets and the exposure to credit risk on loan commitments and financial guarantee contracts, by credit risk rating grades or past due status. This disclosure is required to be shown separately for:
  - those instruments that are measured using 12-month ECLs;
  - those that are measured using lifetime ECLs;
  - financial assets that are credit-impaired on initial recognition;
  - those that are subsequently credit-impaired;
  - trade receivables, contract assets and lease receivables measured under the simplified approach; *[IFRS 7.35M, B8H, B8I]* and
- the write-off policy and amounts written off during the period that are still subject to enforcement activity (see 14.1.1 above). *[IFRS 7.35F(e), 35L]*.

It is critical for entities to align their credit risk management and financial reporting systems and processes, not only to estimate the loss allowance for ECLs, but also to produce a sufficient level of detailed information to meet the disclosure requirements in IFRS 7.

In addition, the EDTF has developed common ECL disclosure practices which are discussed in Chapter 54 at 9.2.

References

1. G20 Declaration on Strengthening the Financial System, April 2009.
2. Report of the Financial Crisis Advisory Group, July 2009.
3. IASB Snapshot: Financial Instruments: Expected Credit Losses Exposure Draft, March 2013.
4. Based on illustration provided by the IASB in its *Snapshot: Financial Instruments: Expected Credit Losses Exposure Draft*, p.9, March 2013.
5. IASB Website Announcement. IASB to establish transition resource group for impairment of financial instruments, 23 June 2014 and Transition Resource Group for Impairment of Financial Instruments – Meeting Summary, 22 April 2015.
6. IASB Transition Resource Group for Impairment of Financial Instruments, Meeting Summary, 22 April 2015.
7. IASB Transition Resource Group for Impairment of Financial Instruments, Meeting Summary, 16 September 2015.
8. IASB Transition Resource Group for Impairment of Financial Instruments, Meeting Summary, 11 December 2015.
9. IASB website, https://www.ifrs.org
10. Basel Committee on Banking Supervision, *International Convergence of Capital Measurement and Capital Standards*, June 2006 and *Basel III:A global regulatory framework for more resilient banks and banking systems*, June 2011.
11. Regulation (EU) No 575/2013 of the European Parliament and of the Council of 26 June 2013 on prudential requirements for credit institutions and investment firms and amending Regulation (EU) No 648/2012.
12. Transition Resource Group for Impairment of Financial Instruments, Meeting Summary, para. 42(b), 22 April 2015.
13. S&P Default, Transition, and Recovery: 2019 Annual Global Corporate Default and Rating Transition Study, Table 24 Global Corporate Average Cumulative Default Rates (1981-2019).
14. Transition Resource Group for Impairment of Financial Instruments, Agenda ref 1, *The maximum period to consider when measuring expected credit losses*, 22 April 2015.
15. IASB Transition Resource Group for Impairment of Financial Instruments, Meeting Summary, para. 49, 11 December 2015.
16. IASB Transition Resource Group for Impairment of Financial Instruments, Meeting Summary, paras. 50 and 51, 11 December 2015.
17. IASB Transition Resource Group for Impairment of Financial Instruments, Meeting Summary, paras. 53, 11 December 2015.
18. IASB Transition Resource Group for Impairment of Financial Instruments, Meeting Summary, paras. 56, 11 December 2015.
19. IASB, *Accounting for expected credit losses applying IFRS 9 Financial Instruments in the light of current uncertainty resulting from the covid-19 pandemic*, 27 March 2020.
20. IASB, *Accounting for expected credit losses applying IFRS 9 Financial Instruments in the light of current uncertainty resulting from the covid-19 pandemic*, 27 March 2020.
21. ESMA, *Guidance on accounting implications of COVID-19*, 25 March 2020.
22. Transition Resource Group for Impairment of Financial Instruments, Agenda ref 4, *Forward-looking information*, 16 September 2015.
23. IASB, *Accounting for expected credit losses applying IFRS 9 Financial Instruments in the light of current uncertainty resulting from the covid-19 pandemic*, 27 March 2020.
24. IASB, *Accounting for expected credit losses applying IFRS 9 Financial Instruments in the light of current uncertainty resulting from the covid-19 pandemic*, 27 March 2020.
25. IASB Agenda paper 5B, Financial Instruments: Impairment, Operational simplifications – 30dpd and low credit risk, 28 October – 1 November 2013.
26. IASB Transition Resource Group for Impairment of Financial Instruments, Meeting Summary, paras. 58 and 59, 11 December 2015.
27. Basel Committee on Banking Supervision, *Guidance on credit risk and accounting for expected credit losses*, para. A55, December 2015.
28. Basel Committee on Banking Supervision, *Guidance on credit risk and accounting for expected credit losses*, para. 22, December 2015.
29. Basel Committee on Banking Supervision, *Guidance on credit risk and accounting for expected credit losses*, para. 21, December 2015.
30. Basel Committee on Banking Supervision, *Guidance on credit risk and accounting for expected credit losses*, para. A47, December 2015.
31. Basel Committee on Banking Supervision, *Guidance on credit risk and accounting for expected credit losses*, para. 69, December 2015.
32. Basel Committee on Banking Supervision, *Guidance on credit risk and accounting for expected credit losses*, para. 57, December 2015.

33 Basel Committee on Banking Supervision, *Guidance on credit risk and accounting for expected credit losses*, paras. 46-49, December 2015.
34 Basel Committee on Banking Supervision, *Guidance on credit risk and accounting for expected credit losses*, paras. 50, 51 and 58, December 2015.
35 Basel Committee on Banking Supervision, *Guidance on credit risk and accounting for expected credit losses*, paras. 64 and 65, December 2015.
36 Basel Committee on Banking Supervision, *Guidance on credit risk and accounting for expected credit losses*, paras. A15-A21, December 2015.
37 Basel Committee on Banking Supervision, *Guidance on credit risk and accounting for expected credit losses*, paras. A23-A30, December 2015.
38 Basel Committee on Banking Supervision, *Guidance on credit risk and accounting for expected credit losses*, para. A44, December 2015.
39 Basel Committee on Banking Supervision, *Guidance on credit risk and accounting for expected credit losses*, paras. A45-A55, December 2015.
40 Transition Resource Group for Impairment of Financial Instruments, Agenda ref 8, *Measurement of expected credit losses in respect of a modified financial asset*, 22 April 2015.
41 Transition Resource Group for Impairment of Financial Instruments, Agenda ref 3, *Loan Commitments – Scope*, 22 April 2015.
42 Transition Resource Group for Impairment of Financial Instruments, Agenda ref 6, *Measurement of expected credit losses for an issued financial guarantee contract*, 22 April 2015.
43 *Exposure Draft – Financial Instruments: Expected Credit Losses*, March 2013, para. 17.
44 *Exposure Draft – Financial Instruments: Amortised Cost and Impairment*, November 2009, para. B23.
45 Transition Resource Group for Impairment of Financial Instruments, Agenda ref 9, *Measurement of the loss allowance for credit-impaired financial assets*, 11 December 2015.

Chapter 52   Financial instruments: Derecognition

1 INTRODUCTION 4085
  1.1 Off-balance sheet finance 4085
2 DEVELOPMENT OF IFRS 4087
  2.1 Definitions 4087
  2.2 Scope 4088
3 DERECOGNITION – FINANCIAL ASSETS 4089
  3.1 Background 4089
  3.2 Decision tree 4090
    3.2.1 Importance of applying tests in sequence 4092
  3.3 Derecognition principles, parts of assets and groups of assets 4092
    3.3.1 Credit enhancement through transferor's waiver of right to future cash flows 4094
    3.3.2 Derecognition of groups of financial assets 4095
      3.3.2.A The IASB's view and the Interpretations Committee's tentative conclusions 4096
      3.3.2.B What are 'similar assets'? 4097
    3.3.3 Transfer of asset (or part of asset) for only part of its life 4098
    3.3.4 'Financial asset' includes whole or part of a financial asset 4098
  3.4 Have the contractual rights to cash flows from the asset expired? 4098
    3.4.1 Renegotiation of the terms of an asset 4099
    3.4.2 Interpretations Committee discussions on asset restructuring in the context of Greek government debt 4100
    3.4.3 Interbank Offered Rate (IBOR) Reform 4101
    3.4.4 Novation of contracts to intermediary counterparties 4102
    3.4.5 Write-offs 4103
  3.5 Has the entity 'transferred' the asset? 4103

	3.5.1	Transfers of contractual rights to receive cash flows	4103
		3.5.1.A Meaning of 'transfers the contractual rights to receive the cash flows'	4104
		3.5.1.B Transfers subject to conditions	4106
	3.5.2	Retention of rights to receive cash flows subject to obligation to pay over to others (pass-through arrangement)	4107
3.6	Securitisations		4108
	3.6.1	Recourse to originator	4110
	3.6.2	Short-term loan facilities	4110
	3.6.3	Insurance protection	4110
	3.6.4	Treatment of collection proceeds	4111
	3.6.5	Transfers of non-optional derivatives along with a group of financial assets	4112
	3.6.6	'Empty' subsidiaries or SPEs	4112
3.7	Client money		4112
3.8	Has the entity transferred or retained substantially all the risks and rewards of ownership?		4114
	3.8.1	Transfers resulting in transfer of substantially all risks and rewards	4114
	3.8.2	Transfers resulting in retention of substantially all risks and rewards	4115
	3.8.3	Transfers resulting in neither transfer nor retention of substantially all risks and rewards	4116
	3.8.4	Evaluating the extent to which risks and rewards are transferred – practical example	4116
	3.8.5	Transfer of risks on a cumulative basis	4119
3.9	Has the entity retained control of the asset?		4119
	3.9.1	Transferee's 'practical ability' to sell the asset	4119
4 PRACTICAL APPLICATION OF THE DERECOGNITION CRITERIA			4120
4.1	Repurchase agreements ('repos') and securities lending		4121
	4.1.1	Agreements to return the same asset	4121
		4.1.1.A Transferee's right to pledge	4121
	4.1.2	Agreements with right to return the same or substantially the same asset	4121
	4.1.3	Agreements with right of substitution	4121
	4.1.4	Net cash-settled forward repurchase	4122
	4.1.5	Agreement to repurchase at fair value	4122
	4.1.6	Right of first refusal to repurchase at fair value	4122
	4.1.7	Wash sale	4122
4.2	Transfers subject to put and call options		4122
	4.2.1	Deeply in the money put and call options	4123

		4.2.2	Deeply out of the money put and call options	4123
		4.2.3	Options that are neither deeply out of the money nor deeply in the money	4124
			4.2.3.A Assets readily obtainable in the market	4124
			4.2.3.B Assets not readily obtainable in the market	4124
		4.2.4	Option to put or call at fair value	4125
		4.2.5	Net cash-settled options	4125
		4.2.6	Removal of accounts provision	4125
		4.2.7	Clean-up call options	4125
		4.2.8	Same (or nearly the same) price put and call options	4125
		4.2.9	Changes in probability of exercise of options after initial transfer of asset	4126
	4.3	Subordinated retained interests and credit guarantees		4127
	4.4	Transfers by way of swaps		4128
		4.4.1	Total return swaps	4128
		4.4.2	Interest rate swaps	4128
	4.5	Factoring of trade receivables		4128
5	ACCOUNTING TREATMENT			4129
	5.1	Transfers that qualify for derecognition		4129
		5.1.1	Transferred asset part of larger asset	4130
		5.1.2	Servicing assets and liabilities	4132
	5.2	Transfers that do not qualify for derecognition through retention of risks and rewards		4134
	5.3	Transfers with continuing involvement – summary		4138
		5.3.1	Guarantees	4138
		5.3.2	Options	4139
		5.3.3	Associated liability	4139
		5.3.4	Subsequent measurement of assets and liabilities	4139
		5.3.5	Continuing involvement in part only of a larger asset	4140
	5.4	Transfers with continuing involvement – accounting examples		4140
		5.4.1	Transfers with guarantees	4140
		5.4.2	Transfers of assets measured at amortised cost	4142
		5.4.3	Transfers of assets measured at fair value	4143
			5.4.3.A Transferor's call option	4144
			5.4.3.B Transferee's put option	4145
			5.4.3.C 'Collar' put and call options	4147
		5.4.4	Continuing involvement in part only of a financial asset	4149
	5.5	Miscellaneous provisions		4151
		5.5.1	Offset	4151
		5.5.2	Collateral	4152

		5.5.3	Rights or obligations over transferred assets that continue to be recognised	4152
	5.6	Reassessing derecognition		4152
		5.6.1	Reassessment of consolidation of subsidiaries and SPEs	4153

6 DERECOGNITION – FINANCIAL LIABILITIES 4153

	6.1	Extinguishment of debt		4154
		6.1.1	What constitutes 'part' of a liability?	4154
		6.1.2	Legal release by creditor	4154
		6.1.3	'In-substance defeasance' arrangements	4156
		6.1.4	Extinguishment in exchange for transfer of assets not meeting the derecognition criteria	4156
	6.2	Exchange or modification of debt by original lender		4156
		6.2.1	When is an exchange or modification of debt 'substantially' different?	4157
		6.2.2	Interbank Offered Rate (IBOR) Reform	4159
		6.2.3	Loan syndications	4160
		6.2.4	Exchange of debt through an intermediary	4161
		6.2.5	Costs and fees	4161
		6.2.6	Modification gains and losses	4163
		6.2.7	Illustrative examples	4164
		6.2.8	Settlement of financial liability with issue of new equity instrument	4166
	6.3	Gains and losses on extinguishment of debt		4166
	6.4	Derivatives that can be financial assets or financial liabilities		4167
	6.5	Supply-chain finance		4168

7 CUSIP 'NETTING' 4169

8 FUTURE DEVELOPMENTS 4170

	8.1	Conceptual Framework for Financial Reporting (the Framework)	4170
	8.2	IFRS 17 – *Insurance Contracts*	4171

List of examples

Example 52.1:	Risks and rewards analysis – variability in the amounts and timing of net cash flows	4116
Example 52.2:	Risks and rewards analysis – two separate transactions	4119
Example 52.3:	Financial asset transferred subject only to deeply out of the money call option	4126
Example 52.4:	Financial asset transferred subject only to deeply in the money call option	4126

Example 52.5:	Financial asset transferred subject to call option neither deeply in the money nor deeply out of the money	4127
Example 52.6:	Derecognition of whole of financial asset in its entirety	4130
Example 52.7:	Derecognition of part of financial asset in its entirety	4131
Example 52.8:	Servicing assets and liabilities	4133
Example 52.9:	Asset not qualifying for derecognition (risks and rewards retained)	4134
Example 52.10:	Asset not qualifying for derecognition ('repo' transaction)	4135
Example 52.11:	Continuing involvement through guarantee	4141
Example 52.12:	Asset measured at amortised cost	4142
Example 52.13:	Asset measured at fair value subject to transferor's call option	4144
Example 52.14:	Asset measured at fair value subject to transferee's put option	4146
Example 52.15:	Asset measured at fair value subject to collar put and call options	4147
Example 52.16:	Continuing involvement in part only of a financial asset	4149
Example 52.17:	Transfer of debt obligations with and without legal release	4155
Example 52.18:	Extinguishment of debt in exchange for transfer of assets not meeting derecognition criteria	4156
Example 52.19:	Fees and costs incurred on modification of debt not treated as extinguishment	4162
Example 52.20:	Modification of debt not treated as extinguishment	4164
Example 52.21:	Modification of debt treated as extinguishment	4165
Example 52.22:	Partial derecognition of debt	4167

Chapter 52 Financial instruments: Derecognition

1 INTRODUCTION

This Chapter deals with the question of when financial instruments should be removed ('derecognised') from financial statements. At what point should an item already recognised in financial statements cease to be included? If an entity sells a quoted share in the financial market, it may cease to be entitled to all the benefits, and exposed to all the risks, inherent in owning that share somewhat earlier than the date on which it ceases to be registered as the legal owner. However, the question of derecognition goes much further than this, as it encroaches on what is commonly referred to as 'off-balance sheet' finance.

1.1 Off-balance sheet finance

In order to understand the rationale for the requirements of IFRS for the derecognition of financial assets and financial liabilities, it is necessary to appreciate the fact that those requirements, and those in equivalent national standards, have their origins in the response by financial regulators to the growing use of off-balance sheet finance from the early 1980s.

'Off-balance sheet' transactions can be difficult to define, and this poses the first problem in discussing the subject. The term implies that certain things belong on the statement of financial position and that those which escape the net are deviations from this norm. The practical effect of off-balance sheet transactions is that the financial statements do not fully present the underlying activities of the reporting entity. This is generally for one of two reasons. The items in question may be included in the statement of financial position but presented 'net' rather than 'gross' – for example, by netting off loans received against the assets they finance. Alternatively, the items might be excluded from the statement of financial position altogether on the basis that they do not represent present assets and liabilities. Examples include operating lease commitments (prior to IFRS 16 – *Leases* – being effective – see Chapter 23) and certain contingent liabilities.

The result in all cases will be that the statement of financial position may suggest less exposure to assets and liabilities than really exists, with a consequential flattering effect on certain ratios, such as the debt/equity ratio and return on assets employed. There is usually an income statement dimension to be considered as well, perhaps because assets taken off-balance sheet purport to have been sold (with a possible profit effect), and also more generally because the presentation of off-balance sheet activity influences the timing or disclosure of associated revenue items. In particular, the presence or absence of items in the statement of financial position usually affects whether the finance cost implicit in a transaction is reported as such or included within another item of income or expense.

Depending on their roles, different people react differently to the term 'off-balance sheet finance'. To some accounting standard setters, or other financial regulators, the expression carries the connotation of devious accounting, intended to mislead the reader of financial statements. Off-balance sheet transactions are those which are designed to allow an entity to avoid reflecting certain aspects of its activities in its financial statements. The term is therefore pejorative and carries the slightly self-righteous inference that those who indulge in such transactions are up to no good and need to be stopped. However, there is also room for a more honourable use of the term 'off-balance sheet finance'. Entities may wish, for sound commercial reasons, to engage in transactions which share with other parties the risks and benefits associated with certain assets and liabilities.

In theory, it should be possible to determine what items belong in the statement of financial position by reference to general principles such as those in the IASB's *Conceptual Framework for Financial Reporting* and similar concepts statements. In practice, however, such principles on their own have not proved adequate to deal with off-balance sheet finance, including routine transactions such as debt factoring and mortgage securitisation.

Accordingly, standard-setters throughout the world, including the IASB, have developed increasingly detailed rules to deal with the issue. This 'anti-avoidance' aspect of the derecognition rules helps to explain why, rather unusually, IFRS considers not only the economic position of the entity at the reporting date, but also prior transactions which gave rise to that position and the reporting entity's motives in undertaking them.

For example, an entity that enters into a forward contract to purchase a specified non-derivative asset for a fixed price will normally recognise that arrangement as a derivative. However, an entity which previously owned the specified non-derivative asset and entered into an identical forward contract at the same time as selling the asset would normally recognise the entire arrangement as a financing transaction. It would leave the (sold) asset on its statement of financial position and recognise a non-derivative liability for the purchase price specified in the forward contract.

The IASB has proposed changes to its conceptual framework, including the addition of new guidance addressing derecognition which is covered in more detail at 8.1 below.

2 DEVELOPMENT OF IFRS

Under IFRS, many definitions relating to financial instruments are in IAS 32 – *Financial Instruments: Presentation* – while derecognition of financial assets and financial liabilities is currently addressed in IFRS 9 – *Financial Instruments*.

The provisions of IFRS 10 – *Consolidated Financial Statements* – are also very relevant to certain aspects of the derecognition of financial assets and financial liabilities. IFRS 10 is discussed in Chapter 6, but it is also referred to at various points below.

Whilst IFRS 9 introduced major changes to the way in which financial instruments were reflected in financial statements, its requirements relating to derecognition were substantially the same as those in IAS 39 – *Financial Instruments: Recognition and Measurement*. Accordingly, consideration by the Interpretations Committee of the application of these parts of IAS 39 continue to be relevant under IFRS 9. Therefore references to such discussions are included in this chapter as if the committee was considering IFRS 9.

Disclosure requirements in respect of transfers of financial assets are included in IFRS 7 – *Financial Instruments: Disclosures* – and these are discussed in Chapter 54 at 6.

2.1 Definitions

The following definitions abbreviated from IAS 32, IFRS 9 and IFRS 13 – *Fair Value Measurement* – are generally relevant to the discussion in this chapter.

A *financial instrument* is any contract that gives rise to a financial asset of one entity and a financial liability or equity instrument of another entity. *[IAS 32.11]*.

A *financial asset* is any asset that is:

(a) cash;

(b) an equity instrument of another entity;

(c) a contractual right:
   (i) to receive cash or another financial asset from another entity; or
   (ii) to exchange financial assets or financial liabilities with another entity under conditions that are potentially favourable to the entity; or

(d) a contract that will or may be settled in the entity's own equity instruments and is:
   (i) a non-derivative for which the entity is or may be obliged to receive a variable number of the entity's own equity instruments; or
   (ii) a derivative that will or may be settled other than by the exchange of a fixed amount of cash or another financial asset for a fixed number of the entity's own equity instruments. For this purpose the entity's own equity instruments do not include puttable financial instruments classified as equity ... instruments that impose on the entity an obligation to deliver to another party a *pro rata* share of the net assets of the entity only on liquidation and are classified as equity ... or instruments that are themselves contracts for the future receipt or delivery of the entity's own equity instruments. *[IAS 32.11]*.

A *financial liability* is any liability that is:
(a) a contractual obligation:
   (i) to deliver cash or another financial asset to another entity; or
   (ii) to exchange financial assets or financial liabilities with another entity under conditions that are potentially unfavourable to the entity; or
(b) a contract that will or may be settled in the entity's own equity instruments and is:
   (i) a non-derivative for which the entity is or may be obliged to deliver a variable number of the entity's own equity instruments; or
   (ii) a derivative that will or may be settled other than by the exchange of a fixed amount of cash or another financial asset for a fixed number of the entity's own equity instruments. For this purpose the entity's own equity instruments do not include puttable financial instruments classified as equity ... instruments that impose on the entity an obligation to deliver to another party a *pro rata* share of the net assets of the entity only on liquidation and are classified as equity ... or instruments that are themselves contracts for the future receipt or delivery of the entity's own equity instruments. *[IAS 32.11]*.

An *equity instrument* is any contract that evidences a residual interest in the assets of an entity after deducting all of its liabilities. *[IAS 32.11]*.

A *derivative* is a financial instrument or other contract within the scope of IFRS 9 (see Chapter 46 at 2) with all three of the following characteristics:

- its value changes in response to the change in a specified interest rate, financial instrument price, commodity price, foreign exchange rate, index of prices or rates, credit rating or credit index, or other variable, provided in the case of a non-financial variable that the variable is not specific to a party to the contract (sometimes called the 'underlying');
- it requires no initial net investment or an initial net investment that is smaller than would be required for other types of contracts that would be expected to have a similar response to changes in market factors; and
- it is settled at a future date. *[IFRS 9 Appendix A]*.

Fair value is the price that would be received to sell an asset or paid to transfer a liability in an orderly transaction between market participants at the measurement date. *[IFRS 13.9, Appendix A]*.

2.2 Scope

The application of IFRS 9 to financial instruments within the financial statements of all entities that are prepared in accordance with IFRS is detailed in Chapter 45 at 3. The derecognition requirements within IFRS 9 apply more widely than other requirements within IFRS 9 in that they specifically apply to the following:

- finance lease receivables (i.e. net investments in finance leases) and operating lease receivables recognised by a lessor; *[IFRS 9.2.1(b)(i)]*
- lease liabilities recognised by a lessee; *[IFRS 9.2.1(b)(ii)]* and
- loan commitments. *[IFRS 9.2.1(g)]*.

In the context of contracts with customers that fall into the scope of IFRS 15 – *Revenue from Contracts with Customers*, when an entity satisfies a performance obligation by transferring a promised good or service, the entity has earned a right to consideration from the customer. *[IFRS 15.105]*. If the right to consideration is conditional, it is a contract asset (for example, when an entity must first satisfy another performance obligation in the contract before it is entitled to payment from the customer). On the other hand, if an entity has an unconditional right to receive consideration from the customer (i.e. only the passage of time is required before payment is due), the entity has a receivable. While IFRS 9, including its derecognition requirements, applies to receivables *[IFRS 9.2.1(j), IFRS 15.108]* only the impairment requirements of IFRS 9 apply to contract assets. *[IFRS 15.107]*.

In theory, entities could also apply the derecognition guidance in IFRS 9 by analogy to contract assets. However, in practice, we believe that it is unlikely that arrangements involving contract assets would meet the requirements for derecognition in IFRS 9, particularly if they are still conditional on the entity's future performance.

3 DERECOGNITION – FINANCIAL ASSETS

3.1 Background

The requirements of IFRS 9 for derecognition of financial assets are primarily designed to deal with the accounting challenges posed by various types of off-balance sheet finance. As a result, the real focus of many of the rules for derecognition of assets is in fact the recognition of liabilities. The starting point for most of the transactions discussed below is that the reporting entity receives cash or other consideration in return for a transfer or 'sale' of all or part of a financial asset. This raises the question of whether such consideration should be treated as sales proceeds or as a liability. IFRS 9 effectively answers that question by determining whether the financial asset to which the consideration relates should be derecognised (the consideration is treated as sales proceeds and there is a gain or loss on disposal) or should continue to be recognised while the consideration is treated as a liability.

This underlying objective of the derecognition criteria helps to explain why IFRS 9 considers not only the economic position of the entity at the reporting date, but also prior transactions which gave rise to that position and the reporting entity's motives in undertaking them. For example, if, at a reporting date, an entity has two identical forward contracts for the purchase of a financial asset, the accounting treatment of the contracts may vary significantly if one contract relates to the purchase of an asset previously owned by the entity and the other does not.

This is because the derecognition rules of IFRS 9 are based on the premise that, if a transfer of an asset leaves the transferor's economic exposure to the transferred asset much as if the transfer had never taken place, the financial statements should represent that the transferor still holds the asset. Thus, if an entity sells (say) a listed bond subject to a forward contract to repurchase the bond from the buyer at a fixed price, IFRS 9 argues that the entity is exposed to the risks and rewards of that bond as if it had never sold it, but has simply borrowed an amount equivalent to the original sales proceeds secured on the bond. IFRS 9 therefore concludes that the bond should not be removed from the statement of financial position and the sale proceeds should be accounted for as a liability (in effect the obligation to repurchase the bond under the forward contract – see 4 below).

By contrast, if the entity were to enter into a second identical forward contract over another bond (i.e. one not previously owned by the entity), IFRS 9 would simply require it to be accounted for as a derivative at fair value (see Chapter 46). This might seem a rather counter-intuitive outcome of a framework that purports to report economically equivalent transactions in a consistent and objective manner. However, the IASB would argue that the two transactions are not economically equivalent; they are distinguished by the fact that, on entering into the forward contract over the originally owned asset, the entity received a separate cash inflow (i.e. the 'sale' proceeds from the counterparty), whereas, on entering into the second contract, it did not. This reinforces the point that the real focus of IFRS 9 is to determine the appropriate accounting treatment for that cash inflow and not that of the previously owned bond *per se.*

3.2 Decision tree

The provisions of IFRS 9 concerning the derecognition of financial assets are complex, but are summarised in the flowchart below. *[IFRS 9.B3.2.1].* It may be helpful to refer to this while reading the discussion that follows.

It will be seen that the process presupposes that the reporting entity has correctly consolidated all its subsidiaries in accordance with IFRS 10, including any entities identified as consolidated structured entities, often called special purpose entities (SPEs) (see Chapter 6).

Under IFRS, a vehicle (or a structured entity) that, though not meeting a traditional definition of a subsidiary based on ownership of equity, is still controlled by the entity is often referred to as a (consolidated) special purpose entity or SPE. IFRS 10 requires a reporting entity to consolidate another entity, including an SPE, when the reporting entity is exposed, or has rights, to variable returns from its involvement with the investee entity and has the ability to affect those returns through its power over the investee entity (see 3.6 below).

It is clearly highly significant from an accounting perspective that an entity to which a financial asset or liability is transferred is a subsidiary or a consolidated SPE of the transferor. A financial asset (or financial liability) transferred from an entity to its subsidiary or consolidated SPE (on whatever terms) will continue to be recognised in the entity's consolidated financial statements through the normal consolidation procedures set out in IFRS 10. Thus, the requirements discussed at 3.3 to 3.9 below are irrelevant to the treatment, in an entity's consolidated financial statements, of any transfer of a financial asset by the entity to a subsidiary or consolidated SPE. Requiring consolidation of subsidiaries and certain SPEs means that the same derecognition analysis applies whether the entity transfers the financial assets directly to a third party investor, to a subsidiary or consolidated SPE that carries out the transfer.

However, the criteria may be relevant to any onward transfer by the subsidiary or consolidated SPE, and to the transferor's separate financial statements, if prepared (see Chapter 8). Moreover, the criteria may well be relevant to determining whether the transferee is an SPE that should be consolidated. A transfer that leaves the entity, through its links with the transferee, exposed to risks and rewards similar to those arising from its former direct ownership of the transferred asset, may in itself indicate that the transferee is an SPE that should be consolidated.

Figure 52.1: Derecognition flowchart [IFRS 9.B3.2.1]

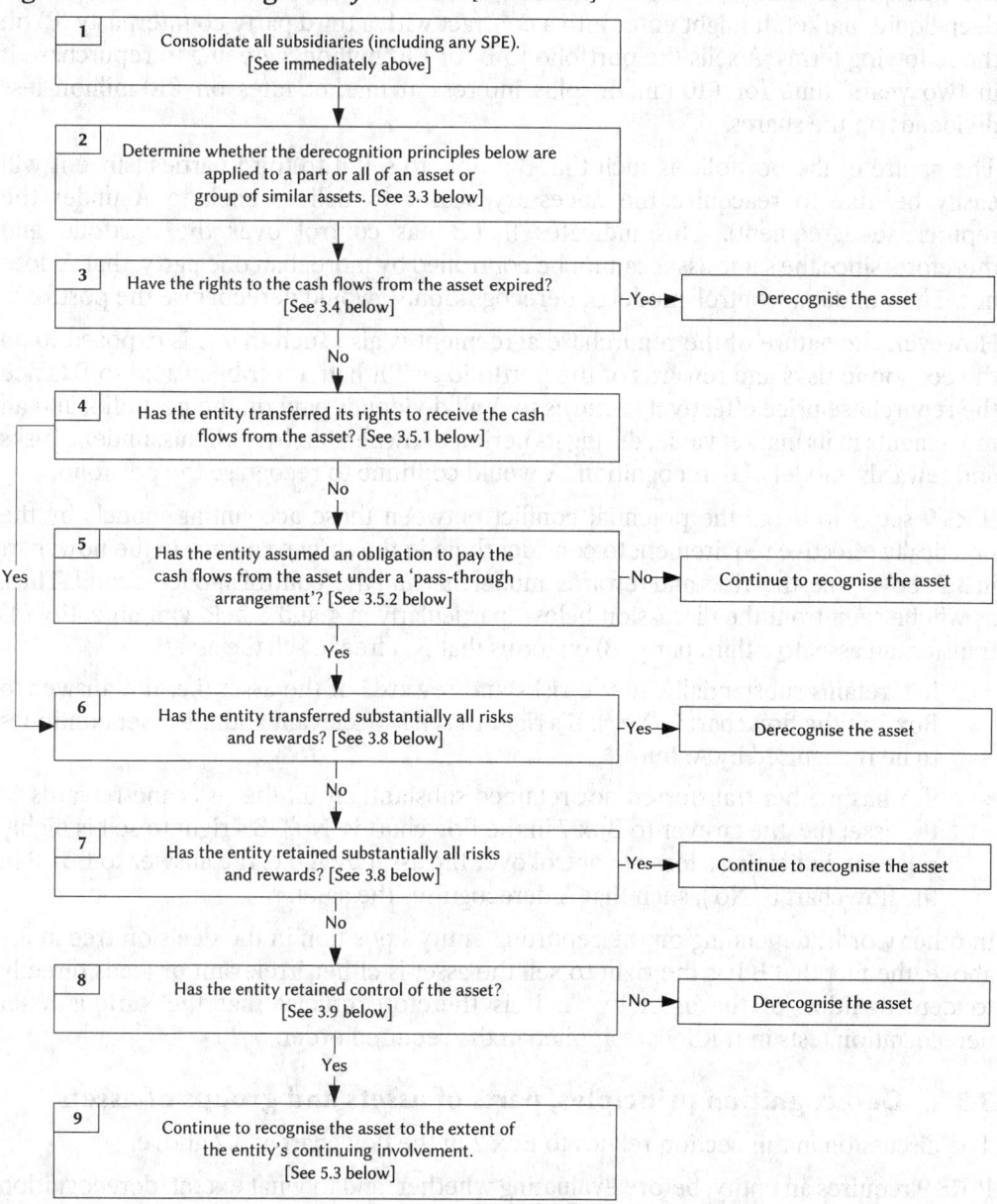

The subsequent steps towards determining whether derecognition is appropriate are discussed below. Some examples of how these criteria might be applied to some common transactions in financial assets are given in 4 below. The accounting consequences of the derecognition of a financial asset are discussed at 5 below.

3.2.1 Importance of applying tests in sequence

The derecognition rules in IFRS 9 are based on several different accounting concepts, in particular a 'risks and rewards' model and a 'control' model, which may lead to opposite conclusions.

For example, an entity (A) might have a portfolio of listed shares for which there is a deep liquid market. It might enter into a contract with a third party counterparty (B) on the following terms. A sells the portfolio to B for €10 million, agreeing to repurchase it in two years' time for €10 million plus interest at market rates on €10 million less dividends on the shares.

The nature of the portfolio is such that B is able to sell it to third parties (since it will easily be able to reacquire the necessary shares to deliver back to A under the repurchase agreement). This indicates that B has control over the portfolio and therefore, since the same asset cannot be controlled by more than one party, that A does not. Thus, under a 'control' model of derecognition, A would derecognise the portfolio.

However, the nature of the repurchase agreement is also such that A is exposed to all the economic risks and rewards of the portfolio as if it had never been sold to B (since the repurchase price effectively returns to A all dividends paid on the portfolio, and all movements in its market value, during its period of ownership by B). Thus, under a 'risks and rewards' model of derecognition, A would continue to recognise the portfolio.

IFRS 9 seeks to avoid the potential conflict between those accounting models by the practically effective requirement to consider them in the strict sequence in the flowchart in 3.2 above – i.e. the 'risks and rewards' model first and the 'control' model second. Thus, as will be seen from the discussion below (particularly at 4 and 5 below) if an entity (A) transfers an asset to a third party (B) on terms that B is free to sell the asset:

- if A retains substantially all the risks and rewards of the asset (i.e. the answer to Box 7 in the flowchart is 'Yes'), B's right to sell is irrelevant and the asset continues to be recognised by A; but
- if A has neither transferred nor retained substantially all the risks and rewards of the asset (i.e. the answer to Box 7 in the flowchart is 'No'), B's right to sell is highly relevant, indicating a loss of control over the asset by A (i.e. the answer to Box 8 in the flowchart is 'No'), such that A derecognises the asset.

In other words, depending on the reporting entity's position in the decision tree at 3.2 above, the fact that B has the right to sell the asset is either irrelevant or leads directly to derecognition of the asset by A. It is therefore crucial that the various asset derecognition tests in IFRS 9 are applied in the required order.

3.3 Derecognition principles, parts of assets and groups of assets

The discussion in this section relates to Box 2 in the flowchart at 3.2 above.

IFRS 9 requires an entity, before evaluating whether, and to what extent, derecognition is appropriate, to determine whether the provisions discussed at 3.4 below and the following sections should be applied to the whole, or a part only, of a financial asset (or the whole or, a part only, of a group of similar financial assets).

It is important to remember throughout the discussion below that these are criteria for determining at what level the derecognition rules should be applied, not for determining whether the conditions in those rules have been satisfied.

The derecognition provisions must be applied to a part of a financial asset (or a part of a group of similar financial assets) if, and only if, the part being considered for derecognition meets one of the three conditions set out in (a) to (c) below.

(a) The part comprises only specifically identified cash flows from a financial asset (or a group of similar financial assets).

For example, if an entity enters into an interest rate strip whereby the counterparty obtains the right to the interest cash flows, but not the principal cash flows, from a debt instrument, the derecognition provisions are applied to the interest cash flows.

(b) The part comprises only a fully proportionate (*pro rata*) share of the cash flows from a financial asset (or a group of similar financial assets).

For example, if an entity enters into an arrangement in which the counterparty obtains the rights to 90% of all cash flows of a debt instrument, the derecognition provisions are applied to 90% of those cash flows. The test in this case is whether the reporting entity has retained a 10% proportionate share of the total cash flows. If there is more than one counterparty, it is not necessary for each of them to have a proportionate share of the cash flows subject to such arrangements.

(c) The part comprises only a fully proportionate (*pro rata*) share of specifically identified cash flows from a financial asset (or a group of similar financial assets).

For example, if an entity enters into an arrangement whereby the counterparty obtains the rights to a 90% share of interest cash flows from a financial asset, the derecognition provisions are applied to 90% of those interest cash flows. The test is whether the reporting entity has (in this case) retained a 10% proportionate share of the interest cash flows. As in (b), if there is more than one counterparty, it is not necessary for each of them to have a proportionate share of the specifically identified cash.

If none of the criteria in (a) to (c) above is met, the derecognition provisions are applied to the financial asset in its entirety (or to the group of similar financial assets in their entirety). For example, if an entity transfers the rights to the first or the last 90% of cash collections from a financial asset (or a group of financial assets), or the rights to 90% of the cash flows from a group of receivables, but provides a guarantee to compensate the buyer for any credit losses up to 8% of the principal amount of the receivables, the derecognition provisions are applied to the financial asset (or a group of similar financial assets) in its entirety. *[IFRS 9.3.2.2]*.

The various examples above illustrate that the tests in (a) to (c) are to be applied very strictly. It is essential that the entity transfers 100%, or a lower fixed proportion, of a definable cash flow. In the arrangement in the previous paragraph, the transferor provides a guarantee the effect of which is that the transferor may have to return some part of the consideration it has already received. This has the effect that the derecognition provisions must be applied to the asset in its entirety and not just to the proportion of cash flows transferred. If the guarantee had not been given, the arrangement would have satisfied condition (b) above, and the derecognition provisions would have been applied only to the 90% of cash flows transferred.

The criteria above must be applied to the whole, or a part only, of a financial asset or the whole, or a part only, of a group of similar financial assets. This raises the question of what comprises a 'group of similar financial assets' – an issue that has been discussed by the Interpretations Committee and the IASB but without them being able to reach any satisfactory conclusions (see 3.3.2 below).

3.3.1 Credit enhancement through transferor's waiver of right to future cash flows

IFRS 9 gives an illustrative example, the substance of which is reproduced as Example 52.16 at 5.4.4 below, of the accounting treatment of a transaction in which 90% of the cash flows of a portfolio of loans are sold. All cash collections are allocated 90:10 to the transferee and transferor respectively, but subject to any losses on the loans being fully allocated to the transferor until its 10% retained interest in the portfolio is reduced to zero, and only then allocated to the transferee. IFRS 9 indicates that in this case it is appropriate to apply the derecognition criteria to the 90% sold, rather than the portfolio as whole.

At first sight, this seems inconsistent with the position in the scenario in the penultimate paragraph of 3.3 above, where application of the derecognition criteria to the 90% transferred is precluded by the transferor's having given a guarantee to the transferee. Is not the arrangement in Example 52.16 below (whereby the transferor may have to cede some of its right to receive future cash flows to the transferee) a guarantee in all but name?

Whilst IFRS 9 does not expand on this explicitly, a possible explanation could be that the two transactions can be distinguished as follows:

(a) the transaction in Example 52.16 may result in the transferor losing the right to receive a future cash inflow, whereas a guarantee arrangement may give rise to an obligation to return a past cash inflow; and

(b) the transaction in Example 52.16 gives the transferee a greater chance of recovering its full 90% share, but does not guarantee that it will do so. For example, if only 85% of the portfolio is recovered, the transferor is under no obligation to make up the shortfall.

It must be remembered that, at this stage, we are addressing the issue of whether or not the derecognition criteria should be applied to all or part of an asset, not whether derecognition is actually achieved.

In many cases an asset transferred subject to a guarantee by the transferor would not satisfy the derecognition criteria, since the guarantee would mean that the transferor had not transferred substantially all the risks of the asset. For derecognition to be possible, the scope of the guarantee would need to be restricted so that some significant risks are passed to the transferee. However, if the guarantee has been acquired from a third party, there are additional issues to consider that may affect the derecognition of the asset and/or the guarantee (see 3.3.2 below).

3.3.2 Derecognition of groups of financial assets

As described above, the derecognition provisions of IFRS 9 apply to the whole, or a part only, of a financial asset or a group, or a part of a group, of similar financial assets (our emphasis). However, transfers of financial assets, such as debt factoring or securitisations (see 3.6 below), typically involve the transfer of a group of assets (and possibly liabilities) comprising:

- the non-derivative financial assets (i.e. the trade receivables or securitised assets) that are the main focus of the transaction;
- financial instruments taken out by the transferor in order to mitigate the risk of those financial assets. These arrangements may either have already been in place for some time, or they may have been entered into to facilitate the transfer; and
- non-derivative financial guarantee contracts that are transferred with the assets. These are not always recognised separately as financial assets, e.g. mortgage indemnity guarantees which compensate the lending bank if the borrower defaults and there is a deficit when the secured property is sold. Such guarantees may be transferred together with the mortgage assets to which they relate.

Financial instruments transferred with the 'main' assets typically include derivatives such as interest rate and currency swaps. The entity may have entered into such arrangements in order to swap floating rate mortgages to fixed rate, or to change the currency of cash flows receivable from financial assets to match the currency of the borrowings, e.g. sterling into euros.

Both the Interpretations Committee and the IASB have considered whether the reference to transfers of 'similar' assets in IFRS 9 is intended to require:

- a single derecognition test for the whole 'package' of transferred non-derivative assets, and any associated financial instruments, as a whole; or
- individual derecognition tests for each type of instrument (e.g. debtor, interest rate swap, guarantee or credit insurance) transferred.

The IASB and Interpretations Committee did not succeed in clarifying the meaning of 'similar assets'. The Interpretations Committee came to a tentative decision but passed the matter to the IASB, together with some related derecognition issues, in particular, the types of transaction that are required to be treated as 'pass through' and the effect of conditions attached to the assets that have been transferred (discussed at 3.5 below). In November 2006 the Interpretations Committee issued a tentative decision not to provide formal guidance, based on the views publicly expressed by the IASB in the *IASB Update* for September 2006. The Interpretations Committee's decision not to proceed was withdrawn in January 2007 on the basis of comment letters received by the Interpretations Committee that demonstrated that the IASB's 'clarification' was, in fact, unworkable and further guidance was required after all. The Interpretations Committee announced this as follows:

> 'In November 2006, the IFRIC published a tentative agenda decision not to provide guidance on a number of issues relating to the derecognition of financial assets. After considering the comment letters received on the tentative agenda decision, the IFRIC concluded that additional guidance is required in this area. The IFRIC therefore decided to withdraw the tentative agenda decision [not to provide

further guidance] and add a project on derecognition to its agenda. The IFRIC noted that any Interpretation in this area must have a tightly defined and limited scope, and directed the staff to carry out additional research to establish the questions that such an Interpretation should address.'[1]

The next section describes the Interpretations Committee's and IASB's attempts to establish the meaning of 'similar', which demonstrated the absence of a clear principle. There is bound to be diversity in practice in the light of the failure to provide an interpretation, so it is most important that entities establish an accounting policy that they apply consistently to the derecognition of groups of financial assets.

3.3.2.A   The IASB's view and the Interpretations Committee's tentative conclusions

Although the Interpretations Committee initially tended to the view that the IASB intended a single test to be undertaken,[2] the IASB itself indicated that derivatives transferred together with non-derivative financial assets were not 'similar' to non-derivative financial assets for the purposes of what is now paragraph 3.2.2 of IFRS 9. Therefore, an entity would apply the derecognition tests in IFRS 9 to non-derivative financial assets (or groups of similar non-derivative financial assets) and derivative financial assets (or groups of similar derivative financial assets) separately, even if they were transferred at the same time.[3] The IASB also indicated that, in order to qualify for derecognition, transferred derivatives that could be assets or liabilities (such as interest rate swaps) would have to meet both the financial asset and the financial liability derecognition tests[4] – see the further discussion of this issue at 6.4 below. Whilst the IASB's published decision referred only to derivatives transferred with the main non-derivative assets, observers of the relevant meeting reported that the IASB also took the view that the derecognition tests must also be applied separately to other financial assets, such as guarantees and credit insurance, transferred with the main assets.

This could have had practical effects on many securitisations as currently structured (see 3.6 below). The interpretation could have made it easier to derecognise certain items (particularly non-derivative assets) than at present. Many derivatives themselves might not meet the appropriate derecognition criteria at all and would continue to be recognised. By contrast, a transaction might achieve a transfer of substantially all the risks and rewards (see Box 6 in Figure 52.1 at 3.2 above, and 3.8 below) of a transferred asset considered separately from any associated derivatives or guarantees, but not if the asset and the associated derivatives or guarantees are considered as a whole. However, the interpretation could well have resulted in far more arrangements falling into the category of 'continuing involvement', where the entity has neither retained nor disposed of substantially all of the risks and rewards of ownership.

Suppose that an entity transfers a fixed rate loan subject to prepayment risk and a credit guarantee, but retains prepayment risk through an amortising interest rate swap, linked to the principal amount of the transferred loan, with the transferee. On the view that the loan and guarantee should be considered for derecognition as a whole, there was no real credit risk prior to the transfer because of the guarantee. The entity was exposed to prepayment risk and the risk of failure by the counterparty to the guarantee. On the assumption that the latter risk could be considered negligible, the only real risk was prepayment risk. Thus, on the view that the loan and guarantee should be considered for derecognition as a whole, they would probably not be derecognised because the entity would retain the only substantial risk (prepayment risk) to which it was exposed before the transfer – i.e. the transaction would fail the test of transferring substantially all risks and rewards in Box 6 in Figure 52.1.

Following the IASB's decision, the implication is that the derecognition criteria would be applied separately to the loan and the guarantee. Considered individually, the loan gives rise to prepayment risk and credit risk. On this analysis, the transfer would leave the entity with only one of the two substantial risks (i.e. prepayment risk, but not credit risk) that it bore previously. This could lead to the conclusion that the entity had neither transferred nor retained substantially all the risks of the loan, and that the loan would therefore be recognised only to the extent of the entity's continuing involvement (in this example, the interest rate swap) – see Box 9 in Figure 52.1 at 3.2 above, and 5.3 below. (This assumes the transferor had retained control of the asset, which would normally be the case in a transaction such as this.)

3.3.2.B What are 'similar assets'?

There are a number of different derivative and derivative-like instruments that can be transferred together with a non-derivative, including:

- hedging instruments that are always assets, e.g. interest rate caps;
- hedging instruments that are always liabilities, e.g. written options;
- hedging instruments that may be an asset or liability at any point in time, e.g. interest rate swaps;
- purchased financial guarantee contracts and credit insurance; and
- guarantees that are not financial guarantee contracts but are commonly accounted for as derivatives, e.g. mortgage indemnity guarantee contracts.

The IASB's interpretation, repeated in its Exposure Draft – *Derecognition* – would require each of the first three to meet different derecognition treatments. Derivatives that could be financial assets or financial liabilities depending on movements in market value (e.g. interest rate and credit default swaps) would need to meet both the financial asset and financial liability derecognition requirements of IFRS 9 (even though at any one time they would be either an asset or a liability). The derecognition of liabilities requires *inter alia* legal release by the counterparty (see 6 below). In many securitisations there is no cancellation, novation or discharge of swaps 'transferred' to a structured entity, in which case the transferor would not be able to derecognise the instrument. This would raise issues regarding the treatment of the retained swap, as it does not actually expose the entity to risks and rewards. This is discussed further at 3.6.5 below.

The interpretation raises the difficulty of allocating the single cash flow received from the transferee to the various financial instruments transferred. This is discussed further at 3.5.1 below.

Given the withdrawal of the Interpretations Committee 'non-interpretation', there is no underlying principle that would prevent any of the instruments described above being considered 'similar' to the main non-derivative. Therefore, an entity must establish an accounting policy that it applies consistently to all transactions involving the derecognition of assets, not only to those associated with securitisation arrangements.

It must bear in mind that a narrow concept of 'similar', in which instruments are treated as separate assets, may make it easier to derecognise some of them but more likely to have to engage with the problems of continuing involvement and more difficult to achieve pass through (see 3.5.2 below). Regardless of the accounting policy followed, a derivative that involves two-way payments between parties (i.e. the payments are, or could be, from or to either of the parties) should be derecognised only when both the derecognition criteria for a financial asset and the derecognition criteria for a financial liability are met (see 6.4 below).

Once an entity has determined what is 'similar', it must consider the derecognition tests (pass through and transfer of risk and rewards) by reference to the same group of 'similar' assets (see 3.5 below).

3.3.3 Transfer of asset (or part of asset) for only part of its life

The examples given in IFRS 9 implicitly appear to have in mind the transfer of a tranche of cash flows from the date of transfer for the remainder of the life of an instrument. This raises the question of the appropriate accounting treatment where (for example) an entity with a loan receivable repayable in 10 years' time enters into a transaction whereby all the interest flows for the next 5 years only (or those for years 6 to 10) are transferred to a third party. There is no reason why such a transaction could not be considered for partial derecognition.

3.3.4 'Financial asset' includes whole or part of a financial asset

In the derecognition provisions in IFRS 9, as well as the discussion at 3 to 5 of this chapter, the term 'financial asset' is used to refer to either the whole, or a part, of a financial asset (or the whole or a part of a group of similar financial assets). *[IFRS 9.3.2.2]*. It is therefore important to remember throughout the following discussion that a reference to an asset being derecognised 'in its entirety' does not necessarily mean that 100% of the asset is derecognised. It may mean, for example, that there has been full derecognition of, say, 80% of the asset to which the derecognition rules have applied separately (in accordance with the criteria above).

3.4 Have the contractual rights to cash flows from the asset expired?

The discussion in this section refers to Box 3 in the flowchart at 3.2 above.

The first step in determining whether derecognition of a financial asset is appropriate is to establish whether the contractual rights to the cash flows from that asset have expired. If they have, the asset is derecognised. Examples might be:

- a loan receivable is repaid;
- the holder of a perpetual debt, whose terms provide for ten annual 'interest' payments that, in effect, provide both interest and a return of capital, receives the final payment of interest; or
- a purchased option expires unexercised.

If the cash flows from the financial asset have not expired, it is derecognised when, and only when, the entity 'transfers' the asset within the specified meaning of the term in IFRS 9 (see 3.5 below), and the transfer has the effect that the entity has either:

- transferred substantially all the risks and rewards of the asset (see 3.8 below); or
- neither transferred nor retained substantially all the risks and rewards of the asset (see 3.8 below), and has not retained control of the asset (see 3.9 below). *[IFRS 9.3.2.3].*

3.4.1 Renegotiation of the terms of an asset

It is common for an entity, particularly but not necessarily when in financial difficulties, to approach its major creditors for a restructuring of its debt commitments. The restructuring may involve a modification to the terms of a loan or an exchange of one debt instrument issued by the borrower for another. In these circumstances, IFRS 9 contains accounting requirements for the borrower to apply which address whether the restructured debt should be regarded as:

- the continuation of the original liability, albeit with recognition of a modification gain or loss in profit or loss (see 6.2 and particularly 6.2.6 below); or
- a new financial liability which replaces the original liability that is hence derecognised. In this case the borrower would recognise a gain or loss based on the difference between the fair value of the restructured debt and the carrying amount of the original liability (see 6.2 below). *[IFRS 9.3.3.1, 3.3.2, B3.3.6].*

However, IFRS 9 does not contain substantive guidance on when a modification of a financial asset should result in derecognition from a lender's perspective. Rather, the basis for conclusions simply states that some modifications of contractual cash flows result in derecognition of a financial instrument and the recognition of a new instrument, but frequently they do not. *[IFRS 9.BC5.216, BC5.227].*

The Interpretations Committee acknowledged that determining when a modification of an asset should result in its derecognition is an issue that arises in practice and considered undertaking a narrow-scope project to clarify the requirements of IFRS 9. However, in May 2016 the committee concluded that the broad nature of the issue meant it could not be resolved in an efficient manner and decided not to further consider such a project.[5]

Consequently, given the limited guidance as to which modifications of financial assets should lead to derecognition, there will be diversity in practice in this area. Entities will need to apply judgement in developing an appropriate accounting policy for determining which modifications of financial assets do, or do not, lead to derecognition of the original asset and recognition of a new asset.

Changes that may result in derecognition, individually or in tandem with others, depending on the facts and circumstances, include a change in the currency or in the basis of interest calculation (such as moving from fixed to floating) so that the original effective interest rate (EIR) would no longer provide an appropriate measure of interest income, the introduction of significant new features into the instrument, such as adding a profit participation to a loan agreement, particularly where the characteristics of the asset would no longer satisfy the criteria of IFRS 9 to be recorded at amortised cost (see Chapter 48 at 6.4.5), or a significant extension to the term of the instrument.

However, where the modification is part of a troubled debt restructuring, the objective of the changes is usually to maximise recovery of the original contractual cash flows rather than to originate a new asset on current market terms. This should also be considered when deciding if it is appropriate to derecognise the original asset and recognise a new one.

In August 2020 the IASB issued amendments to IFRS 9 to provide guidance on how to account for modifications of a financial asset due to the reform of interbank offered rates (see 3.4.3 below).

IFRS 9 contains requirements on accounting for the modification of a financial asset when its contractual cash flows are renegotiated or otherwise modified and the asset is not derecognised. In those cases the entity should recalculate the gross carrying amount of the financial asset and recognise a modification gain or loss in profit or loss. The gross carrying amount is recalculated as the present value of the renegotiated or modified contractual cash flows, discounted at the financial asset's original effective interest rate (or credit-adjusted effective interest rate for purchased or originated credit-impaired financial assets) or, when applicable, the revised effective interest rate calculated in accordance with paragraph 6.5.10 of IFRS 9. Any costs or fees incurred adjust the carrying amount of the modified financial asset and are amortised over the remaining term of the modified financial asset. *[IFRS 9.5.4.3]*. These requirements are considered in more detail in Chapter 50 at 3.8.

3.4.2 Interpretations Committee discussions on asset restructuring in the context of Greek government debt

In February 2012, the Greek government announced the terms of a restructuring of certain of its issued bonds. One aspect involved the exchange of 31.5% of the principal amount of the bonds for twenty new bonds with different maturities and interest rates. The remaining portions of the bonds were either forgiven or exchanged for other securities issued by the European Financial Stability Facility, a special purpose entity established by Eurozone states.

Soon afterwards, the Interpretations Committee was asked to address the appropriate accounting treatment for certain aspects of the restructuring, which they did initially in May 2012. One question the Committee considered was whether the exchange of 31.5% of the principal amount of the original bonds for new bonds could be regarded as a continuation of that portion of the original asset or whether that portion should also be derecognised (it being widely accepted that the remaining portions of the bonds should be derecognised).

The committee first addressed whether the exchange should be regarded as a transfer. They noted that the bonds were transferred back to the issuer rather than to a third party and, as a consequence, concluded this particular restructuring should not be regarded as a transfer (see 3.5.1 below). Instead, it should be evaluated to determine whether it amounted to an actual or in-substance expiry or extinguishment of the original cash flows.

The staff analysis was clear that a modification of terms can result in expiry of the asset's original rights to cash flows, although it would not always do so. This is because it is implicit within the requirements for measuring impairment losses that a modification would sometimes be regarded as a continuation of the original, albeit impaired, asset. Therefore an entity would assess the modifications made against the notion of 'expiry' of the rights to the cash flows.[6]

The staff analysis indicated that the 'hierarchy' in IAS 8 – *Accounting Policies, Changes in Accounting Estimates and Errors* – would be applied in developing an appropriate accounting policy. Whilst this requires the application of judgement, it is not an absolute discretion. Consequently, it would be appropriate to analogise, at least to some extent, to those requirements in IFRS 9 applying to modifications and exchanges of financial liabilities, particularly the notion of 'substantial modification' and the fact that modifications and exchanges between an existing lender and borrower are seen as equivalent (see 6.2 below). However, applying the '10% test' to determine whether a modification is substantial would not always be appropriate.

The committee did not explicitly conclude on this part of the staff analysis, particularly the question of when it would be appropriate to regard a modification or exchange as the expiry or in-substance extinguishment of the original asset. Instead they simply noted that, in their view, derecognition of the original Greek government bonds would be the appropriate accounting treatment however this particular transaction was assessed, i.e. whether it was viewed as (a) an actual expiry of the rights of the original asset or (b) as a substantial modification that should be accounted for as an extinguishment of the original asset (because of the extensive changes in the assets' terms). An agenda decision setting out the committee's conclusions was published in September 2012.[7]

Whilst that discussion resolved most of the issues associated with the restructuring of Greek government bonds, the wider topic continues to require the application of judgement and, as a result, potentially leads to inconsistent approaches being applied by different entities.

3.4.3 Interbank Offered Rate (IBOR) Reform

Following recommendations from the Financial Stability Board there are various initiatives ongoing to replace current benchmark interest rates, such as interbank offered rates like LIBOR, with nearly risk-free rates. In view of these initiatives and the resulting uncertainty around the long-term viability of IBORs, the IASB added a two-stage project to its agenda. The first stage was to consider financial reporting issues that may arise prior to the replacement of IBORs; and the second stage was to consider issues arising from changes to contractual cash flows required by the replacement of IBORs. IBOR reform and the IASB's project are discussed in more detail in Chapter 53 at 9.

One issue considered in the second stage is how the modification of a floating rate financial asset from an instrument with an IBOR benchmark rate, to an instrument with a rate of interest based on a new risk-free rate, should be accounted for under IFRS 9, particularly whether such modification would lead to the derecognition of the financial asset.

The IASB amended IFRS 9 in August 2020 to include a practical expedient whereby contractual changes to cash flows that are directly required by IBOR reform are treated as changes to a floating interest rate, equivalent to a movement in a market rate of interest. Therefore such a modification would not result in derecognition of the financial asset. Inherent in the use of this practical expedient is the requirement that the transition from an IBOR benchmark rate to a risk-free rate takes place on an economically equivalent basis. *[IFRS 9.5.4.5, 5.4.7]*.

In applying this practical expedient, an entity is required to first identify and account for modifications to the financial asset which relate directly to IBOR reform, by updating the EIR without adjusting the carrying amount of the financial asset. The amendments include examples of the type of modifications required by IBOR reform, to which the practical expedient is limited, as follows:

- The replacement of an existing interest rate with an alternative benchmark rate or effecting such a reform of an interest rate benchmark by changing the method used to calculate the interest rate benchmark;
- The addition of a fixed spread to compensate for a basis difference between an existing interest rate benchmark and an alternative benchmark rate;
- Changes to the reset period, reset dates, or the number of days between coupon payment dates that are necessary to effect the reform of an interest rate benchmark; and
- The addition of a fall-back provision to the contractual terms of a financial asset to enable any of the changes described above to be made. *[IFRS 9.5.4.8, 5.4.9]*.

Any other modifications to the financial asset that may be made at the same time, such as a change in the credit spread or maturity date, are assessed in line with the entity's existing accounting policy for determining whether modifications of financial assets result in derecognition. *[IFRS 9.5.4.9]*.

The amendments have an effective date of periods commencing 1 January 2021, although early adoption is permitted with disclosure of that fact. *[IFRS 9.7.1.9]*. The amendments should be adopted retrospectively except that there is no requirement to restate prior period figures and such figures may only be restated if this is possible without the use of hindsight. *[IFRS 9.7.2.43, 7.2.46]*.

3.4.4 Novation of contracts to intermediary counterparties

A change in the terms of a contract may take the legal form of a 'novation'. In this context novation means that the parties to a contract agree to change that contract so that an original counterparty is replaced by a new counterparty.

For example, a derivative between a reporting entity and a bank may be novated to a central counterparty (CCP) as a result of the introduction of new laws or regulations. In these circumstances, the IASB explains that through novation to a CCP the contractual rights to cash flows from the original derivative have expired and as a consequence the novation meets the derecognition criteria for a financial asset. *[IFRS 9.BC6.332-337]*.

Whilst the IASB reached the above conclusion in relation to novations of over-the-counter derivatives, it is our view that the principle is applicable to all novations of contracts underlying a financial instrument. Accordingly, when a counterparty changes as a result of a novation, the financial instrument should be derecognised and a new financial instrument should be recognised. Although such a change may not be expected to give rise to a significant gain or loss when the financial instrument derecognised and the new financial instrument recognised are both measured at fair value through profit or loss, the bid/ask spread and the effect of change in counterparty on credit risk may cause some value differences. Furthermore, a novation may result in discontinuation of hedge accounting if the original financial instrument was a derivative designated in a hedging relationship (see Chapter 53 at 8.3 for further details).

3.4.5 Write-offs

An entity is required to directly reduce the gross carrying amount of a financial asset when it has no reasonable expectations of recovery. Such a write-off is regarded as the asset being derecognised – effectively it is seen as an in-substance expiry of the associated rights. Write-offs can also relate to a portion of an asset. For example, consider an entity that plans to enforce the collateral on a financial asset and expects to recover no more than 30% of the financial asset from the collateral. If the entity has no reasonable prospects of recovering any further cash flows from the financial asset, it should write off the remaining 70%. *[IFRS 9.5.4.4, B3.2.16(r), B5.4.9]*.

3.5 Has the entity 'transferred' the asset?

An entity is regarded by IFRS 9 as 'transferring' a financial asset if, and only if, it either:

(a) transfers the contractual rights to receive the cash flows of the financial asset (see 3.5.1 below); or

(b) retains the contractual rights to receive the cash flows of the financial asset, but assumes a contractual obligation to pay the cash flows on to one or more recipients in an arrangement that meets the conditions in 3.5.2 below, *[IFRS 9.3.2.4]*, (a so-called 'pass-through arrangement').

This might be the case where the entity is a special purpose entity or trust, and issues to investors beneficial interests in financial assets that it owns and provides servicing of those assets. *[IFRS 9.B3.2.2]*.

These conditions are highly significant for securitisations and similar transactions that fall within (b) because the entity retains the contractual right to receive cash.

3.5.1 Transfers of contractual rights to receive cash flows

The discussion in this section refers to Box 4 in the flowchart at 3.2 above.

IFRS 9 does not define what is meant by the phrase 'transfers the contractual rights to receive the cash flows of the financial asset' in (a) in 3.5 above, possibly on the assumption that this is self-evident. However, this is far from the case, since the phrase raises a number of questions of interpretation.

There are two key uncertainties about the meaning of 'transferring the contractual rights' (which in turn determines whether a transaction falls within (a) or (b) in 3.5 above):

- whether it is restricted to transfers of legal title only or also encompasses transfers of equitable title or an equitable interest (see 3.5.1.A below); and
- the effect of conditions attached to the transfers (see 3.5.1.B below).

While both of these are of great significance to securitisations (see 3.6 below), they also have implications for other transactions. These issues were discussed in 2006 by both the Interpretations Committee and the IASB. However, as described at 3.3.2 above, the Interpretations Committee's tentative decision not to issue further guidance and the interpretation of the issues that had so far been published were both withdrawn in January 2007. There is no clear evidence that practice has changed as a result of the views that had been expressed by the IASB and the Interpretations

Committee but, as this has demonstrated a lack of clear underlying principles, it would be no surprise to find that entities have different interpretations of the requirements.

In the context of the restructuring of Greek government bonds (see 3.4.2 above), the Interpretations Committee considered whether an exchange of debt instruments between a borrower and a lender should be regarded as a transfer. It was noted that the bonds were transferred back to the issuer rather than to a third party and, as a consequence, it was agreed that this particular restructuring should not be regarded as a transfer.[8] However, it was noted during the committee's discussion and in the comment process that applying such a conclusion more widely might not always be appropriate, e.g. in the case of a short-term sale and repurchase agreement over a bond with the bond issuer or the simple repurchase of a bond by the issuer for cash.

3.5.1.A Meaning of 'transfers the contractual rights to receive the cash flows'

In many jurisdictions, the law recognises two types of title to property: (a) legal title; and (b) 'equitable', or beneficial title. In general, legal title defines who owns an asset at law and equitable title defines who is recognised as entitled to the benefit of the asset. Transfers of legal title give the transferee the ability to bring an action against a debtor to recover the debt in its own name. In equitable transfers, however, the transferee joins the transferor in an action to sue the debtor for recovery of debt. As noted above, the issue here is whether 'transfers of contractual rights' are limited to transfers of legal title.

In a typical securitisation transaction across many jurisdictions, the transfer of contractual rights to receive cash flows are achieved via equitable or beneficial transfer of title in that asset, as the transfer of legal title in the asset would simply not be possible without either:

- a tri-partite agreement between the corporate entity, the finance provider and the debtor; or
- a clause in the standard terms of trade allowing such a transfer at the sole discretion of the corporate entity without the express consent of the debtor, so that transfer can be effected by a subsequent bi-partite agreement between the corporate entity and the finance provider.

The consent of the debtor is not normally obtained, or indeed practically obtainable, in many securitisations and similar transactions. In these arrangements, all cash flows that are collected are contractually payable to a new eventual recipient – i.e. the debtor continues to pay the transferor, while the transferor loses the right to retain any cash collected from the debtor without actually transferring the contract itself.

In March 2006 the Interpretations Committee began to consider whether there can be a transfer of the contractual right to receive cash flows in an equitable transfer.[9] The Interpretations Committee had already concluded, in November 2005, that retaining servicing rights (i.e. continuing to administer collections and distributions of cash as agent for the transferee) does not in itself preclude derecognition.[10] However, the Interpretations Committee then considered whether retention by the transferor of the contractual right to receive the cash from debtors for distribution on to other parties (as must inevitably happen if debtors are not notified) means that such a transaction does not meet test (a) in 3.5 above, and thus must meet test (b) (pass-through) in order to achieve derecognition. The Interpretations Committee referred this issue to the IASB, which indicated in September 2006 that:

> '[a] transaction in which an entity transfers all the contractual rights to receive the cash flows (without necessarily transferring legal ownership of the financial asset), would not be treated as a pass-through. An example might be a situation in which an entity transfers all the legal rights to specifically identified cash flows of a financial asset (for example, a transfer of the interest or principal of a debt instrument). Conversely, the pass-through test would be applicable when the entity does not transfer all the contractual rights to cash flows of the financial asset, such as disproportionate transfers.'[11]

The statement that such a transaction 'would not be treated as a pass-through' means (in terms of the flowchart in Figure 52.1 at 3.2 above) that the answer to Box 4 is 'Yes', such that the pass-through test in Box 5 (see 3.5.2 below) is by-passed.

The IASB's conclusion appears to concede that the references in IFRS 9 to a transfer of the 'contractual' right to cash flows was intended to include an equitable transfer of those rights, a conclusion that the IASB repeated in its April 2009 Exposure Draft – *Derecognition*. In our view, the transfer of the contractual rights to cash flows encompass both the transfer of legal title in the asset as well as transfer of equitable or beneficial title in the asset.

The IASB commented that 'the pass-through test would be applicable when the entity does not transfer all the contractual rights to cash flows of the financial asset, such as disproportionate transfers'.

For example, if an entity transfers the rights to 90% of the cash flows from a group of receivables but provides a guarantee to compensate the buyer for any credit losses up to 8% of the principal amount of the receivables, the derecognition provisions are applied to the group of financial assets in its entirety. *[IFRS 9.3.2.2(b)]*. This means that the answer to Box 4 in the flowchart will be 'No' (since some, not all, of the cash flows of the entire group of assets have been transferred), thus requiring the pass-through test in Box 5 to be applied. In contrast, the pass-through test would not need to be applied where the entity transfers the contractual right to receive 100% of the cash flows.

It is difficult to comprehend the circumstances in which the pass-through test would ever be successfully applied to a disproportionate transfer. Accordingly, this view from the IASB would, in effect, disqualify virtually all disproportionate transfers from derecognition.

The IASB's interpretation gives no answer to an even more critical question. If the derecognition rules need to be applied separately to loans and derivatives or guarantees, how does this affect:

- the definition of a 'transfer' (if all the cash flows are transferred); or
- the application of the pass-through test (if the transfer is of a disproportionate share of the cash flow)?

Before this re-examination by the IASB of the meaning of 'transfer', it was common in some jurisdictions to apply the legal title test to transfers of financial assets to a SPE in securitisation arrangements, rather than relying on an equitable transfer. After the withdrawal of the 'non-interpretation' (see 3.3.2 above), it is likely that those entities have continued to apply their previous practice. However the discussions have, yet again, highlighted the uncertainty at the heart of the derecognition rules in IFRS 9 which means that there must be different treatments in practice. Until there is a conclusive interpretation, entities must establish an accounting policy that they apply consistently to all such transactions, whether they are transfers or pass-throughs.

The implications of the IASB's discussion on securitisation transactions are discussed further at 3.6.5 below.

3.5.1.B   Transfers subject to conditions

An entity may transfer contractual rights to cash flows but subject to conditions. The Interpretations Committee identified the following main types of condition:

- *Conditions relating to the existence and legal status of the asset at the time of the transfer*

    These include normal warranties as to the condition of the asset at the date of transfer and other guarantees affecting the existence and accuracy of the amount of the receivable that may not be known until after the date of transfer.

- *Conditions relating to the performance of the asset after the time of transfer*

    These include guarantees covering future default, late payment or changes in credit risk, guarantees relating to changes in tax, legal or regulatory requirements, where the buyer may be able to require additional payments if it is disadvantaged or – in some cases – demand reversal of the transaction, or guarantees covering future performance by the seller that might affect the recoverable amount of the debtor.

- *Offset arrangements*

    The original debtor may have the right to offset amounts against balances owed to the transferor for which the transferor will compensate the transferee. There may also be tripartite offset arrangements where a party other than the original debtor (e.g. a subcontractor) has such offset rights.[12]

All securitisations (and indeed, most derecognitions, whether of financial or non-financial assets) include express or implied warranties regarding the condition of the asset at the date of transfer. In the case of a securitisation of credit card receivables, these might include a representation that, for example, all the debtors transferred are resident in a particular jurisdiction, or have never been in arrears for more than one month in the previous two years. In our view, such warranties should not affect whether or not the transaction achieves derecognition.

It is a different matter when it comes to guarantees of post-transfer performance. In particular, one of the issues identified by the Interpretations Committee – guarantees covering future default, late payment or changes in credit risk – links to the related debate regarding the transfer of groups of financial assets where the guarantees may have been provided by a third party (see 3.3.2 above).

In July 2006 the Interpretations Committee decided to refer this issue to the IASB, which considered it at its September 2006 meeting. The IASB broadly confirmed our view as set out above. In its view neither conditions relating to the existence and value of transferred cash flows at the date of transfer nor conditions relating to the future performance of the asset would affect whether the entity has transferred the contractual rights to receive cash flows[13] (i.e. Box 4 in Figure 52.1 at 3.2 above). In other words, a transaction with such conditions that otherwise met the criteria in Box 4 would not be subject to the pass-through test in Box 5.

However, the existence of conditions relating to the future performance of the asset might affect the conclusion related to the transfer of risks and rewards (i.e. Box 6 in Figure 52.1 at 3.2 above) as well as the extent of any continuing involvement by the transferor in the transferred asset (i.e. Box 9 in Figure 52.1 at 3.2. above).[14]

These interpretations were also withdrawn by the Interpretations Committee in January 2007 together with the views that had been expressed regarding 'similar' assets and transfers of assets (see 3.3.2 above). Although the IASB repeated them in the April 2009 Exposure Draft – *Derecognition* – an entity must take a view that is consistent with its policies on these matters and, as in these other cases, hold this view consistently when considering the derecognition of any financial asset.

An example of a two-party offset arrangement is when the original debtor (e.g. a borrower or customer) has the right to offset amounts it is owed by the transferor (e.g. balances in a deposit account or arising from a credit note issued by the transferor) against the transferred asset. If such a right is exercised after the asset is transferred the transferor would be required to compensate the transferee. This would not, in our view, normally affect whether the entity has transferred the contractual rights to receive the cash flows of the original financial asset. Payments made by the transferor to the transferee as a result of the right of offset being exercised simply transfer to the transferee the value the transferor obtained when its liability to the original debtor was settled.

3.5.2 Retention of rights to receive cash flows subject to obligation to pay over to others (pass-through arrangement)

The discussion in this section refers to Box 5 in the flowchart at 3.2 above.

It is common in certain securitisation and debt sub-participation transactions (see 3.6 below) for an entity to enter into an arrangement whereby it continues to collect cash receipts from a financial asset (or more typically a pool of financial assets), but is obliged to pass on those receipts to a third party that has provided finance in connection with the financial asset. Whilst the term 'pass-through' for these arrangements does not actually appear in IFRS 9 it has become part of the language of the financial markets.

Under IFRS 9, an arrangement whereby the reporting entity retains the contractual rights to receive the cash flows of a financial asset (the 'original asset'), but assumes a contractual obligation to pay the cash flows to one or more recipients (the 'eventual recipients') is regarded as a transfer of the original asset if, and only if, all of the following three conditions are met:

(a) the entity has no obligation to pay amounts to the eventual recipients unless it collects equivalent amounts from the original asset. Short-term advances by the entity with the right of full recovery of the amount lent plus accrued interest at market rates do not violate this condition (see 3.6.1 and 3.6.2 below);

(b) the entity is prohibited by the terms of the transfer contract from selling or pledging the original asset other than as security to the eventual recipients for the obligation to pay them cash flows; and

(c) the entity has an obligation to remit any cash flows it collects on behalf of the eventual recipients without material delay. In addition, the entity is not entitled to reinvest such cash flows, except in cash or cash equivalents as defined in IAS 7 – *Statement of Cash Flows* (see Chapter 40 at 3) during the short settlement period from the collection date to the date of required remittance to the eventual recipients, with any interest earned on such investments being passed to the eventual recipients. *[IFRS 9.3.2.5]*.

These conditions are discussed further at 3.6.4 below.

IFRS 9 notes that an entity that is required to consider the impact of these conditions on a transaction is likely to be either:

- the originator of the financial asset in a securitisation transaction (see 3.6 below); or
- a group that includes a consolidated special purpose entity that has acquired the financial asset and passes on cash flows to unrelated third party investors.
[IFRS 9.B3.2.3].

IFRS 9 does not address whether it is necessary for a pass-through arrangement to be able to survive the bankruptcy of the transferor in order to be considered a transfer. Consequently, there is no explicit requirement in the standard to consider the likelihood of the transferor's bankruptcy when assessing pass-through arrangements. This issue was discussed by the IASB in its April 2009 Exposure Draft – *Derecognition* – where it was proposed that bankruptcy remoteness would not form part of the derecognition model. This was seen at the time as an intentional divergence from US GAAP, which requires transferred financial assets to be legally isolated from the transferor, its consolidated affiliates and its creditors, even in bankruptcy. In practice, if the transferred assets are held in a ring-fenced structured entity this may protect cash flows to the transferee in the event of the transferor's bankruptcy.

3.6 Securitisations

Securitisation is a process whereby finance can be raised from external investors by enabling them to invest in parcels of specific financial assets. The first main type of assets to be securitised was domestic mortgage loans, but the technique is regularly extended to other assets, such as credit card receivables, other consumer loans, or lease receivables. Securitisations are a complex area of financial reporting beyond the scope of a general text such as this to discuss in detail. However, it may assist understanding of the IASB's thinking to consider a 'generic' example of such a transaction.

A typical securitisation transaction involving a portfolio of mortgage loans would operate as follows. The entity which has initially advanced the loans in question (the 'originator') will sell them to another entity set up for the purpose (the 'issuer'). The issuer will typically be a subsidiary or consolidated SPE of the originator (and therefore consolidated – see 3.2 above) and its equity share capital, which will be small, will often be owned by a trustee on behalf of a charitable trust. The issuer will finance its purchase of these loans by issuing loan notes on interest terms which will be related to the rate of interest receivable on the mortgages and to achieve this it may need to enter into derivative instruments such as interest rate swaps. The swap counterparty may be the originator or a third party. The originator will continue to administer the loans as before, for which it will receive a service fee from the issuer.

The structure might therefore be as shown in this diagram:

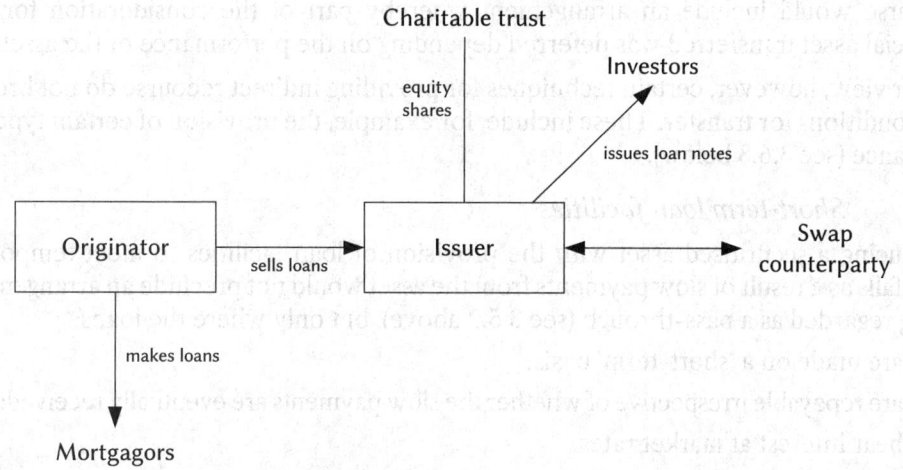

Potential investors in the mortgage-backed loan notes will want to be assured that their investment is relatively risk free and the issue will normally be supported by obtaining a high rating from a credit rating agency. This may be achieved by using a range of credit enhancement techniques which will add to the security already inherent in the quality of the mortgage portfolio. Such techniques can include the following:

- limited recourse to the originator in the event that the income from the mortgages falls short of the interest payable to the investors under the loan notes and other expenses. This may be made available in a number of ways: for example, by the provision of subordinated loan finance from the originator to the issuer; by the deferral of part of the consideration for the sale of the mortgages; or by the provision of a guarantee (see 3.6.1 below);
- the provision of loan facilities to meet temporary shortfalls as a result of slow payments of mortgage interest (see 3.6.2 below); or
- insurance against default on the mortgages (see 3.6.3 below).

The overall effect of the arrangement is that outside investors have been brought in to finance a particular portion of the originator's activities. These investors have first call on the income from the mortgages which back their investment. The originator is left with only the residual interest in the differential between the rates paid on the notes and earned on the mortgages, net of expenses. Generally, this profit element is extracted by adjustments to the service fee or through the mechanism of interest rate swaps. It has thus limited its upside interest in the mortgages, while its remaining downside risk on the whole arrangement will depend on the extent to which it has assumed obligations under the credit enhancement measures.

3.6.1 Recourse to originator

The conditions in 3.5.2 above clearly have the effect that an arrangement that does not transfer the contractual rights to receive the cash flows but provides for direct recourse to the originator does not meet the definition of a 'transfer' for the purposes of pass-through and therefore does not qualify to be considered for derecognition. Direct recourse would include an arrangement whereby part of the consideration for the financial asset transferred was deferred depending on the performance of the asset.

In our view, however, certain techniques for providing indirect recourse do not breach the conditions for transfer. These include, for example, the provision of certain types of insurance (see 3.6.3 below).

3.6.2 Short-term loan facilities

Enhancing a securitised asset with the provision of loan facilities to meet temporary shortfalls as a result of slow payments from the asset would not preclude an arrangement being regarded as a pass-through (see 3.5.2 above), but only where the loans:

- are made on a 'short-term' basis;
- are repayable irrespective of whether the slow payments are eventually received; and
- bear interest at market rates.

The purpose of these restrictions is to ensure that IFRS 9 allows derecognition of assets subject to such facilities only where the facilities are providing a short-term cash flow benefit to the investor, and not when they effectively transfer slow payment risk back to the originator (as would be the case if the originator made significant interest-free loans to the investor). Clearly, therefore, the circumstances in which such funds can be advanced must be very tightly defined if pass-through is to be achieved.

3.6.3 Insurance protection

The conditions for 'transfer' are not, in our view, breached by the originator purchasing an insurance contract for the benefit of investors in the event of a shortfall in cash collections from the securitised assets, provided that the investors' only recourse is to the insurance policy. In other words, the originator cannot give a guarantee to investors to make good any shortfalls should the insurer become insolvent, nor can the originator provide any support to the insurer through a guarantee arrangement or a reinsurance contract.

The implications of the derecognition and pass-through requirements of IFRS 9 for transfers of groups of financial assets including insurance contracts have been reconsidered by the Interpretations Committee and the IASB but their tentative conclusions were withdrawn. For a discussion of the issues and the alternative interpretations of 'similar' assets, see 3.3.2 above.

3.6.4 Treatment of collection proceeds

Securitisation contracts rarely require any amount received on the securitised assets to be immediately transferred to investors. This is for the obvious practical reason that it would be administratively inefficient, in the case of a securitisation of credit card receivables for example, to transfer the relevant portion of each individual, and relatively small, cash flow received from the hundreds, if not thousands, of cards in the portfolio. Instead, it is usual for transfers to be made in bulk on a periodic basis (e.g. weekly or monthly). This raises the question of what happens to the cash in the period between receipt by the issuer and onward transfer to the investors.

IFRS 9 requires cash flows from transferred financial assets for which derecognition is sought to be:

- passed to the eventual recipients 'without material delay'; and
- invested only in cash or cash equivalents as defined in IAS 7 entirely for the benefit of the investors (see condition (c) in 3.5.2 above).

These requirements mean that many securitisation arrangements may well fail to satisfy the pass-through test in 3.5.2 above, as explained below.

Suppose that a credit card issuer wishes to raise five year finance secured on its portfolio of credit card receivables. The assets concerned are essentially short term (being in most cases settled in full within four to eight weeks), whereas the term of the borrowings secured on them is longer. In practice, what generally happens is that, at the start of the securitisation, a 'pool' of balances is transferred to the issuer. The cash receipts from that 'pool' are used to pay interest on the borrowings, and to fund new advances on cards in the 'pool' or to purchase other balances. Such an arrangement, commonly referred to as a 'revolving' structure, appears to breach the requirement of the pass-through tests to:

- pass on cash receipts without material delay (since only the amount of cash receipts necessary to pay the interest on the borrowings is passed on, with the balance being reinvested until the principal of the borrowings falls due); and
- only invest in cash or cash equivalents as defined in IAS 7 in the period prior to passing them onto the investor. This is because the cash not required to pay interest on the borrowings is invested in further credit card receivables, which are not cash or cash equivalents as defined in IAS 7.

The Interpretations Committee confirmed in November 2005 that 'revolving' structures do not meet the requirements of the pass-through test for funds to be passed on without material delay and to be invested only in cash and cash equivalents.[15]

In practice, we have observed the pass-through tests are applied very strictly such that any arrangement that provides for even a small tranche of the interest from such short-term deposits to be retained by or for the benefit of the originator will not satisfy the criteria for transfer under IFRS 9. Moreover, IFRS 9 requires that the reporting entity 'is not entitled' to invest the cash other than in cash or cash equivalents as described above. Thus, it appears that the criteria for transfer are not satisfied merely where the entity does not in fact invest the cash in any other way – it must be contractually prohibited from doing so. In practice, this is often achieved by having the funds paid into a trustee bank account that can be used only for the benefit of the providers of finance.

The IASB does not expand further on the term 'without material delay'. It is not, in our view, intended to require settlement to noteholders on an unrealistically frequent basis such as daily, although we would normally expect payments to be made by the next quarterly coupon payment date to meet this condition.

The strict requirements of IFRS 9 in respect of cash received from assets subject to a pass-through arrangement raise the related, but broader, issue of the appropriate treatment of client money which is discussed at 3.7 below.

3.6.5 Transfers of non-optional derivatives along with a group of financial assets

As discussed at 3.3.2 above, interest rate swaps that are transferred along with a group of non-derivative financial assets may be derecognised only when any associated obligation is discharged, cancelled or expires (see 6 below). This, however, does not occur in most securitisations.

In a securitisation transaction involving the equitable transfer of an interest rate swap to an SPE, the swap would continue to be recognised by the transferor. The ongoing accounting consequences of this are less clear. The swap must clearly continue to be measured at fair value through profit or loss in accordance with the general requirement of IFRS 9 for the measurement of derivatives not in a hedging relationship (see Chapter 46). However, this would have the effect that the reporting entity reflected gains and losses in the income statement for a derivative in which it no longer has a beneficial interest. In such a case, the entity should presumably recognise the notional back-to-back swap which it has effectively entered into with the transferee, so as to offset the income statement effect of the original swap.

3.6.6 'Empty' subsidiaries or SPEs

If an entity enters into a transaction whereby:
- the entity transfers an asset to a subsidiary or SPE; and
- the subsidiary or SPE transfers the asset to noteholders on terms that satisfy the pass-through derecognition criteria in IFRS 9, as discussed at 3.5.2 and 3.6 above,

the overall effect will be that the individual financial statements of the subsidiary or SPE will include neither the transferred asset nor the finance raised from noteholders. This may well mean that the financial statements show nothing apart from the relatively small amount of equity of the entity and any related assets. This analysis is likely to be applicable only for relatively simple transfers, and not, for example, when derivatives are transferred along with the non-derivative assets.

3.7 Client money

A number of financial institutions and other entities hold money on behalf of clients. The terms on which such money is held can vary widely. In the case of normal deposits with a bank, the bank is free to use the client's money for its own purposes, with the client being protected by the capital requirements imposed by the regulatory authorities. By contrast there are cases (e.g. in the case of certain monies held by legal advisers on behalf of their clients in some jurisdictions) where funds held on behalf of clients must be kept in a bank account completely separate from that of the depositary entity itself, with all interest earned on the account being for the benefit of clients. There are also intermediate situations where, for example:

- funds are required to be segregated in separate bank accounts but the depositary entity is allowed to retain some or all of the interest on the client accounts; or
- client funds are allowed to be commingled with those of the depositary entity, but some or all income on the funds must be passed on to clients.

This raises the question of how client monies should be accounted for in the financial statements under IFRS. In particular, whether the assets should be recognised in the first place, and if so whether, in the absence of specific guidance, the rules for the treatment of funds received under a pass-through arrangement (see 3.6.4 above) should be applied.

The types of arrangement to deal with client money are so varied that it is impossible to generalise as to the appropriate treatment. Key considerations include:

- which party is at risk from the failure of assets, such as bank accounts, in which the client money is held;
- the status of the funds in the event of the insolvency of either the reporting entity or its client;
- whether the reporting entity can use the cash for its own purposes as opposed to administering the cash on behalf of the client in its capacity as an agent; and
- which party has the benefit of income from the assets.

The analysis for the two extreme cases seems relatively straightforward. In the case of a bank deposit (or any arrangement where the entity may freely use client cash for its own benefit), the general recognition criteria of IFRS 9 indicate that an asset and a liability should be recognised. Conversely, where the entity is required to hold funds held on behalf of clients in a bank account completely separate from that of the entity itself, with all interest earned on the account being for the benefit of clients, it is hard to see how such funds meet the general definition of an asset under the *Conceptual Framework for Financial Reporting*. Whilst the entity administers such funds in its capacity as an agent on behalf of the client, it can derive no economic benefits from them. The intermediate cases may be harder to deal with.

Sometimes the appropriate analysis will be that the depositary entity enjoys sufficient use of the client money that it should be recognised as an asset with a corresponding liability due to the client. This will be the case, for example, if the client money is commingled with the reporting entity's cash for a short period of time. During this period the reporting entity is exposed to the credit risk associated with the cash and is entitled to all income accruing. Hence, the reporting entity would recognise the cash as an asset and a corresponding liability. If the cash is later moved to a segregated client trust account, an analysis should be performed to determine whether or not the cash and the corresponding liability should be removed from the reporting entity's statement of financial position.

3.8 Has the entity transferred or retained substantially all the risks and rewards of ownership?

The discussion in this section refers to Boxes 6 and 7 in the flowchart at 3.2 above.

Once an entity has established that it has transferred a financial asset (see 3.5 above), IFRS 9 then requires it to evaluate the extent to which it retains the risks and rewards of ownership of the financial asset. *[IFRS 9.3.2.6]*.

If the entity transfers substantially all the risks and rewards of ownership of the financial asset, the entity must derecognise the financial asset and recognise separately as assets or liabilities any rights and obligations created or retained in the transfer. *[IFRS 9.3.2.6(a)]*. Examples of such transactions are given at 3.8.1 and 4.1 below. If an entity determines that, as a result of the transfer, it has transferred substantially all the risks and rewards of ownership of the transferred asset, it does not recognise the transferred asset again in a future period, unless it reacquires the transferred asset in a new transaction. *[IFRS 9.B3.2.6]*.

If the entity retains substantially all the risks and rewards of ownership of the financial asset, the entity continues to recognise the financial asset. *[IFRS 9.3.2.6(b)]*. Examples of such transactions are given at 3.8.2, 4.1 and 4.3 below.

If the entity neither transfers nor retains substantially all the risks and rewards of ownership of the financial asset (see 3.8.3 below), the entity determines whether it has retained control of the financial asset *[IFRS 9.3.2.6(c)]* (see 3.9 below).

IFRS 9 clarifies that the transfer of risks and rewards should be evaluated by comparing the entity's exposure, before and after the transfer, to the variability in the amounts and timing of the net cash flows of the transferred asset. *[IFRS 9.3.2.7]*. Often it will be obvious whether the entity has transferred or retained substantially all risks and rewards of ownership. In other cases, it will be necessary to determine this by computing and comparing the entity's exposure to the variability in the present value (discounted at an appropriate current market interest rate) of the future net cash flows before and after the transfer. All reasonably possible variability in net cash flows is considered, with greater weight being given to those outcomes that are more likely to occur. *[IFRS 9.3.2.8]*.

In some circumstances it may be appropriate to consider whether substantially all the risks and rewards of an asset have been transferred as a result of the cumulative effect of two separate transactions (see 3.8.5 below).

3.8.1 Transfers resulting in transfer of substantially all risks and rewards

An entity has transferred substantially all the risks and rewards of ownership of a financial asset if its exposure to the variability in the amounts and timing of the net cash flows of the transferred asset is no longer significant in relation to the total such variability. IFRS 9 gives the following examples of transactions that transfer substantially all the risks and rewards of ownership:

- an unconditional sale of a financial asset;
- a sale of a financial asset together with an option to repurchase the financial asset at its fair value at the time of repurchase (since this does not expose the entity to any risk of loss or give any opportunity for profit);
- a sale of a financial asset together with a put or call option that is deeply out of the money (i.e. an option that is so far out of the money it is highly unlikely to go into the money before expiry); or
- the sale of a fully proportionate share of the cash flows from a larger financial asset in an arrangement, such as a loan sub-participation, that satisfies the criteria for a 'transfer' in 3.5.2 above. *[IFRS 9.3.2.7, B3.2.4]*.

Such transactions are discussed in more detail at 4 below.

It is important to note that, in order for derecognition to be achieved, it is necessary that the entity's exposure to the variability in the amounts and timing of the net cash flows of the transferred asset is considered not in isolation, but 'in relation to the total such variability' (see above). Thus derecognition is not achieved simply because the entity's remaining exposure to the risks or rewards of an asset is small in absolute terms. It has also become clear, from the Interpretations Committee and IASB's discussions described at 3.3.2 above, that derecognition also depends on the interpretation of 'asset' and of groups of similar assets that is applied by the entity.

3.8.2 Transfers resulting in retention of substantially all risks and rewards

An entity has retained substantially all the risks and rewards of ownership of a financial asset if its exposure to the variability in the present value of the future net cash flows from the financial asset does not change significantly as a result of the transfer. IFRS 9 gives the following examples of transactions in which an entity has retained substantially all the risks and rewards of ownership:

- a sale and repurchase transaction where the repurchase price is a fixed price or the sale price plus a lender's return;
- a securities lending agreement;
- a sale of a financial asset together with a total return swap that transfers the market risk exposure back to the entity;
- a sale of a financial asset together with a deeply in the money put or call option (i.e. an option that is so far in the money that it is highly unlikely to go out of the money before expiry). It will be in the holder's interest to exercise such an option, so that the asset will almost certainly revert to the transferor; and
- a sale of short-term receivables in which the entity guarantees to compensate the transferee for credit losses that are likely to occur. *[IFRS 9.3.2.7, B3.2.5]*.

Such transactions are discussed in more detail at 4.1 below.

3.8.3 Transfers resulting in neither transfer nor retention of substantially all risks and rewards

IFRS 9 gives the following examples of transactions in which an entity has neither transferred nor retained substantially all the risks and rewards of ownership:

- a sale of a financial asset together with a put or call option that is neither deeply in the money nor deeply out of the money. *[IFRS 9.B3.2.16(h)-(i)].* The effect of such an option is that the transferor will have either (in the case of purchased call option) capped its exposure to a loss in value of the asset but have potentially unlimited access to increases in value or (in the case of a written put option) capped its potential access to increases in value in the asset but assumed potential exposure to a total loss in value of the asset; and

- a sale of 90% of a loan portfolio with significant transfer of prepayment risk, but retention of a 10% interest, with losses allocated first to that 10% retained interest. *[IFRS 9.B3.2.17].*

Such transactions are discussed in more detail at 4 below.

3.8.4 Evaluating the extent to which risks and rewards are transferred – practical example

The following example illustrates one approach to evaluating the extent to which risks and rewards associated with a portfolio of assets have been transferred.

Example 52.1:   Risks and rewards analysis – variability in the amounts and timing of net cash flows

Entity X sells a portfolio of trade receivables with a face value of £1 million and an average due date of 45 days from the issuance of the invoice to Entity Y, an unrelated third party. After the sale, X does not retain any residual beneficial interests in the receivables. However, X guarantees losses on the transferred portfolio up to a percentage of the total face value. Default losses, including late payments, as a percentage of face value ranged historically from 3% to 5%.

Assume the following two hypothetical situations:

- Fact pattern 1 – Entity X guarantees first losses on the portfolio up to 3.5% of the total face value.
- Fact pattern 2 – Entity X guarantees first losses on the portfolio up to 4% of the total face value.

The following calculations illustrate one possible approach for calculating the exposure to the variability in the amounts and timing of net cash flows.

Under this approach the reporting entity (Entity X) determines a number of reasonably possible scenarios that reflect the expected variability in the amounts and timing of net cash flows; these scenarios are then assigned a probability, with greater weighting being given to those outcomes that are more likely to occur. Next, Entity X calculates the expected future net cash flows for each scenario, discounted using an appropriate current market rate. The expected variability is then calculated using an appropriate statistical technique. The above steps are duplicated for net cash flows that the transferor, Entity X, remains exposed to after the transfer. Finally, the exposure to expected variability of net cash flows post transfer is compared to the corresponding expected variability before the transfer.

In this example, the expected variability is calculated by adding up the individual (negative or positive) deviations of the expected discounted future net cash flows for each scenario from the total expected value of the net cash flows for all possible scenarios. As the receivables are relatively short-term, the calculations below focus primarily on credit risk, including delinquency risk. For simplicity, the calculations below ignore the effect of discounting.

Fact pattern 1: Entity X guarantees first losses on the portfolio up to 3.5% of total face value.

Based on historical experience and supportable expectations Entity X has defined five scenarios of possible variability, each of which has been assigned a probability based on historical experience and current market information. These scenarios and probabilities are set out below.

Before Transfer

Face value = £1,000,000 = A

Possible credit loss B	Discounted expected cash flows C= A – [A×B]	Probability D	Probability weighted discounted cash flows E=C×D	Variability F=C–Σ(E)	Probability weighted negative variability G= F×D if F<0	Probability weighted positive variability H=F×D if F>0
	£		£	£	£	£
3.0%	970,000	3.5%	33,950	11,550	–	404.25
3.5%	965,000	20.0%	193,000	6,550	–	1,310.00
4.0%	960,000	30.0%	288,000	1,550	–	465.00
4.5%	955,000	35.0%	334,250	(3,450)	(1,207.50)	–
5.0%	950,000	11.5%	109,250	(8,450)	(971.75)	–
		100.0%	958,450		(2,179.25)	2,179.25
			I		K	K
			£41,550	=A – Σ(E)		

After Transfer

Face value = £1,000,000 = A

Possible credit loss B	Discounted expected cash flows C=[A×(B)], max 35,000	Probability D	Probability weighted discounted cash flows E=C×D	Variability F=C–Σ(E)	Probability weighted negative variability G=F×D if F<0	Probability weighted positive variability H=F×D if F>0
	£		£	£	£	£
3.0%	30,000	3.5%	1,050	(4,825)	(168.88)	–
3.5%	35,000	20.0%	7,000	175	–	35.00
4.0%	35,000	30.0%	10,500	175	–	52.50
4.5%	35,000	35.0%	12,250	175	–	61.25
5.0%	35,000	11.5%	4,025	175	–	20.13
		100.0%	34,825		(168.88)	168.88
			M		L	L

Percentage of variability retained by Entity X	L÷K	(7.75)%	7.75%

To avoid a mechanical determination and to leave room for judgement, IFRS 9 does not establish any bright-lines on what constitutes 'substantially all' risks and rewards of ownership. Therefore, judgement is needed to assess what is 'substantially all' in each particular situation considering, for example, the sensitivity of the calculation to certain changes in assumptions.

Assuming that Entity X determined that 'substantially all' represents 90% of total expected variability in the amounts and timing of net cash flows, it will conclude that it has transferred substantially all risks and rewards of ownership.

This conclusion may seem counterintuitive given that Entity X has retained 83.81% of the total expected losses (M ÷ I = 34,825 ÷ 41,550). However, IFRS 9 is clear that the transfer of risks and rewards should be evaluated by comparing the transferor's exposure, before and after the transfer, to the variability in the amounts and timing of net cash flows of the transferred asset. In practice, even when factoring with limited recourse, the transferor very often retains exposure to losses in excess of those reasonably expected to arise such that substantially all the variability is retained by the transferor.

Fact pattern 2: Entity X guarantees first losses on the portfolio up to 4% of the total face value.

Face value = £1,000,000 = A

Before Transfer

Possible credit loss B	Discounted expected cash flows C= A − [A×B] £	Probability D	Probability weighted discounted cash flows E=C×D £	Variability F=C−Σ(E) £	Probability weighted negative variability G= F×D if F<0 £	Probability weighted positive variability H=F×D if F>0 £
3.0%	970,000	3.5%	33,950	11,550	–	404.25
3.5%	965,000	20.0%	193,000	6,550	–	1,310.00
4.0%	960,000	30.0%	288,000	1,550	–	465.00
4.5%	955,000	35.0%	334,250	(3,450)	(1,207.50)	–
5.0%	950,000	11.5%	109,250	(8,450)	(971.75)	–
		100.0%	958,450		(2,179.25)	2,179.25
					K	K
	I		£41,550	A − Σ(E)		

After Transfer

Possible credit loss B	Discounted expected cash flows C=[A×(B), max 40,000] £	Probability D	Probability weighted discounted cash flows E=C×D £	Variability F=C−Σ(E) £	Probability weighted negative variability G=F×D if F<0 £	Probability weighted positive variability H=F×D if F>0 £
3.0%	30,000	3.5%	1,050	(8,650)	(302.75)	–
3.5%	35,000	20.0%	7,000	(3,650)	(730.00)	–
4.0%	40,000	30.0%	12,000	1,350	–	405.00
4.5%	40,000	35.0%	14,000	1,350	–	472.50
5.0%	40,000	11.5%	4,600	1,350	–	155.25
		100.0%	38,650		(1,032.75)	1,032.75
			M		L	L

Percentage of variability retained by Entity X   L÷K   (47.39)%   47.39%

Now that Entity X stands ready to cover first losses up to 4% which is in the middle of the range of expected losses (3% to 5%), it is not a surprise that its exposure to variability has increased to 47.39%. This means that Entity X has neither transferred nor retained substantially all risks and rewards of ownership in this case. Again, the fact that the seller now covers, after the sale, 93.02% (M ÷ I = 38,650 ÷ 41,550) of the total expected losses is not relevant to the analysis.

In this case, derecognition will depend on whether the transferee (Entity Y) has the practical ability to sell the trade receivables unilaterally and without imposing additional restrictions on the transfer. The conclusion needs to take into account many factors. For example: (i) whether the transferee has legal title to the transferred receivables; (ii) whether there is a market for the transferred receivables or not; (iii) whether or not the seller has a call option or has written a put option over the transferred receivables; (iv) whether or not the guarantee of Entity X is transferable with the receivables; (v) whether the receivables are 'ring-fenced' in a SPE as a pledge for securities collateralised by the transferred assets, etc. This aspect of the analysis is covered in 3.9 below.

3.8.5 Transfer of risks on a cumulative basis

The following example illustrates that derecognition may be achieved by the transfer of substantially all the risks and rewards of ownership in two separate transactions.

Example 52.2: Risks and rewards analysis – two separate transactions

Entity X owns a pool of mortgages with a fixed rate of interest of 5%. The mortgages are guaranteed by a government agency and are effectively free of credit risk, but they are subject to variability due to prepayment risk. Entity X sells part of the cash flows from the mortgages (cash flows from the principal and a proportionate share of the interest payments equivalent to a return on the principal of 3%) to Entity Y but indemnifies Entity Y such that Entity Y is not exposed to any of the prepayment variability. Entity X indemnifies Entity Y by agreeing to make a compensatory payment(s) to Entity Y for lost interest on mortgages which are prepaid.

Subsequently, Entity X enters into a second transaction with Entity Z under which Entity Z receives the remaining cash flows from the mortgages and takes on the indemnity to Entity Y such that Entity X is no longer exposed to any prepayment variability.

Entity X assesses the risks and rewards of its interests in the mortgages on a cumulative basis. At the time of the sale to Entity Y, Entity X concludes that it has retained substantially all the risks and rewards of the mortgages because it has retained the prepayment variability and therefore continues to recognise them.

At the time of the transaction with Entity Z, Entity X concludes that it has now transferred substantially all the risks and rewards of the mortgages and therefore derecognises them.

3.9 Has the entity retained control of the asset?

The discussion in this section relates to Boxes 8 and 9 of the flowchart at 3.2 above.

If the transferring entity has neither transferred nor retained substantially all the risks and rewards of a transferred financial asset, IFRS 9 requires the entity to determine whether or not it has retained control of the financial asset. If the entity has not retained control, it must derecognise the financial asset and recognise separately as assets or liabilities any rights and obligations created or retained in the transfer. If the entity has retained control, it must continue to recognise the financial asset to the extent of its continuing involvement in the financial asset (see 5.3 below). *[IFRS 9.3.2.6(c)].*

IFRS 9 requires the question of whether the entity has retained control of the transferred asset to be determined by the transferee's ability to sell the asset. If the transferee:

- has the practical ability to sell the asset in its entirety to an unrelated third party; and
- is able to exercise that ability unilaterally and without needing to impose additional restrictions on the transfer,

the entity has not retained control.

In all other cases, the entity has retained control. *[IFRS 9.3.2.9].*

3.9.1 Transferee's 'practical ability' to sell the asset

IFRS 9 provides further guidance in two scenarios. Firstly, when a transferred asset is subject to a repurchase option, second, when a transfer imposes additional restrictions on selling the transferred assets. If a transferred asset is sold subject to an option that allows the entity to repurchase it, the transferee may (subject to the further considerations discussed below) have the practical ability to sell the asset if it can readily obtain the transferred asset in the market if the option is exercised. *[IFRS 9.B3.2.7]*. For this purpose there has to be an active market for the asset.

The transferee has the practical ability to sell the transferred asset only if the transferee can sell the transferred asset in its entirety to an unrelated third party and is able to exercise that ability unilaterally and without imposing additional restrictions on the transfer. IFRS 9 requires that practical ability to sell the transferred asset be determined by considering what the transferee is able to do in practice, rather than solely by reference to any contractual rights or prohibitions. The standard notes that a contractual right to dispose of the transferred asset has little practical effect if there is no market for the transferred asset. *[IFRS 9.B3.2.8(a)]*.

An ability to dispose of the transferred asset also has little practical effect if it cannot be exercised freely. Accordingly, the transferee's ability to dispose of the transferred asset must be a unilateral ability independent of the actions of others. In other words, the transferee must be able to dispose of the transferred asset without needing to attach conditions to the transfer (e.g. conditions about how a loan asset is serviced, or an option giving the transferee the right to repurchase the asset). *[IFRS 9.B3.2.8(b)]*.

For example, the entity might sell a financial asset to a transferee but the transferee has an option to put the asset back to the entity or has a performance guarantee from the entity. IFRS 9 argues that such an option or guarantee might be so valuable to the transferee that it would not, in practice, sell the transferred asset to a third party without attaching a similar option or other restrictive conditions. Instead, the transferee would hold the transferred asset so as to obtain payments under the guarantee or put option. Under these circumstances IFRS 9 regards the transferor as having retained control of the transferred asset. *[IFRS 9.B3.2.9]*.

However, the fact that the transferee is simply unlikely to sell the transferred asset does not, of itself, mean that the transferor has retained control of the transferred asset. *[IFRS 9.B3.2.9]*.

4 PRACTICAL APPLICATION OF THE DERECOGNITION CRITERIA

IFRS 9 gives a number of practical examples of the application of the derecognition criteria, which are discussed below.

In order to provide a link with Figure 52.1 at 3.2 above we have used the following convention:

'Box 6, Yes' The transaction would result in the answer 'Yes' at Box 6 in the flowchart.

'Box 7, No' The transaction would result in the answer 'No' at Box 7 in the flowchart.

4.1 Repurchase agreements ('repos') and securities lending

4.1.1 Agreements to return the same asset

If a financial asset is:

- sold under an agreement to repurchase it at a fixed price or at the sale price plus a lender's return; or
- loaned under an agreement to return it to the transferor,

the asset is not derecognised, because the transferor retains substantially all the risks and rewards of ownership, [IFRS 9.B3.2.16(a)], (Figure 52.1, Box 7, Yes). The accounting treatment of such transactions is discussed at 5.2 below.

4.1.1.A Transferee's right to pledge

If the transferee obtains the right to sell or pledge an asset that is the subject of such a transaction, the transferor reclassifies the asset on its statement of financial position as, for example, a loaned asset or repurchase receivable. [IFRS 9.B3.2.16(a)].

It appears that this accounting treatment is required merely where the transferee has the 'right' to sell or pledge the asset. This contrasts with the requirements for determining whether an asset subject to a transaction in which the entity neither transfers nor retains substantially all the risks and rewards associated with the asset (Figure 52.1, Box 7, No) nevertheless qualifies for derecognition because the transferee has control (Figure 52.1, Box 8). In order for the transferee to be regarded as having control for the purposes of Box 8, any rights of the transferee to sell an asset must have economic substance – see 3.9 above.

The accounting treatment of such transactions is discussed at 5.2 below.

4.1.2 Agreements with right to return the same or substantially the same asset

If a financial asset is:

- sold under an agreement to repurchase the same or substantially the same asset at a fixed price or at the sale price plus a lender's return; or
- loaned under an agreement to return the same or substantially the same asset to the transferor,

the asset is not derecognised because the transferor retains substantially all the risks and rewards of ownership, [IFRS 9.B3.2.16(b)], (Figure 52.1, Box 7, Yes). The accounting treatment of such transactions is discussed at 5.2 below.

4.1.3 Agreements with right of substitution

If a financial asset is the subject of:

- a repurchase agreement at a fixed repurchase price or a price equal to the sale price plus a lender's return; or
- a similar securities lending transaction,

that provides the transferee with a right to substitute assets that are similar and of equal fair value to the transferred asset at the repurchase date, the asset sold or lent is not derecognised because the transferor retains substantially all the risks and rewards of ownership, *[IFRS 9.B3.2.16(c)]*, (Figure 52.1, Box 7, Yes). The accounting treatment of such transactions is discussed at 5.2 below.

4.1.4 Net cash-settled forward repurchase

IFRS 9 gives some guidance on the treatment of net cash-settled options over transferred assets (see 4.2.5 below), which in passing refers to net cash-settled forward contracts. This guidance indicates that the key factor for determining whether derecognition is appropriate remains whether or not the entity has transferred substantially all the risks and rewards of the transferred asset. *[IFRS 9.B3.2.16(k)]*. This suggests that an asset sold subject to a fixed price net-settled forward contract to reacquire it should not be derecognised (see 4.1.1 to 4.1.3 above) until the forward contract is settled (Figure 52.1, Box 7, Yes).

The accounting treatment of such transactions is discussed at 5.2 below.

4.1.5 Agreement to repurchase at fair value

A transfer of a financial asset subject only to a forward repurchase agreement with a repurchase price equal to the fair value of the financial asset at the time of repurchase results in derecognition because of the transfer of substantially all the risks and rewards of ownership, *[IFRS 9.B3.2.16(j)]*, (Figure 52.1, Box 6, Yes). The accounting treatment of such transactions is discussed at 5.1 below.

4.1.6 Right of first refusal to repurchase at fair value

If an entity sells a financial asset and retains only a right of first refusal to repurchase the transferred asset at fair value if the transferee subsequently sells it, the entity derecognises the asset because it has transferred substantially all the risks and rewards of ownership, *[IFRS 9.B3.2.16(d)]*, (Figure 52.1, Box 6, Yes).

IFRS 9 does not address the treatment of a financial asset sold with a right of first refusal to repurchase the transferred asset at a predetermined value that might well be lower or higher than fair value (e.g. an amount estimated, at the time at which the original transaction was entered into, as the future market value of the asset). One analysis might be that, since the transferee is under no obligation to put the asset up for sale, derecognition is still appropriate. Another analysis might be that, if the asset can ultimately only be realised by onward sale, the arrangement is nearer in substance to a transferor's call option (see 4.2 below).

4.1.7 Wash sale

A 'wash sale' is the repurchase of a financial asset shortly after it has been sold. Such a repurchase does not preclude derecognition provided that the original transaction met the derecognition requirements. However, if an agreement to sell a financial asset is entered into concurrently with an agreement to repurchase the same asset at a fixed price or the sale price plus a lender's return, then the asset is not derecognised. *[IFRS 9.B3.2.16(e)]*. Such a transaction would be equivalent to those in 4.1.1 to 4.1.4 above.

4.2 Transfers subject to put and call options

An option contract is a contract which gives one party to the contract the right, but not the obligation, to buy from, or sell to, the other party to the contract the asset that is the subject of the contract for a given price (often, but not always, a price that is fixed) at a future date (or during a longer period ending on a future date). An option giving the right to buy an asset is referred to as a 'call' option and one giving the right to sell as a 'put' option. An option is referred to as a 'bought' or 'purchased' option from the perspective of the party with the right to buy or sell (the 'holder') and as a 'written' option from the perspective of the party with the potential obligation to buy or sell. An option is referred to as 'in the money' when it would be in the holder's interest to exercise it and as 'out of the money' when it would not be in the holder's interest to exercise it.

Under IFRS 9 an option is:

- 'deeply in the money' when it is so far in the money that it is highly unlikely to go out of the money before expiry; [IFRS 9.B3.2.5(d)] and
- 'deeply out of the money' when it is so far out of the money that it is highly unlikely to become in the money before expiry. [IFRS 9.B3.2.4(c)].

IFRS 9 does not elaborate on what it means by 'highly unlikely' in this context, although the Implementation Guidance to IAS 39 clarified that 'highly probable' (in the context of a 'highly probable forecast transaction' subject to a hedge) indicates a much greater likelihood of happening than the term 'more likely than not'. [IAS 39.F.3.7].

Option contracts that are within the scope of IFRS 9 (see Chapter 46 at 2) are recognised as assets or liabilities when the holder or writer becomes a party to the contract. [IFRS 9.B3.1.2(d)].

4.2.1 Deeply in the money put and call options

If a transferred financial asset can be called back by the transferor, and the call option is deeply in the money, the transfer does not qualify for derecognition because the transferor has retained substantially all the risks and rewards of ownership (Figure 52.1, Box 7, Yes).

Similarly, if the financial asset can be put back by the transferee, and the put option is deeply in the money, the transfer does not qualify for derecognition because the transferor has retained substantially all the risks and rewards of ownership, [IFRS 9.B3.2.16(f)], (Figure 52.1, Box 7, Yes).

The accounting treatment for such transactions would be similar to that for 'repos' as set out in Example 52.10 at 5.2 below.

If a transferred asset continues to be recognised because of a transferor's call option or transferee's put option, but the option subsequently lapses unexercised, the asset and any associated liability would then be derecognised.

4.2.2 Deeply out of the money put and call options

A financial asset that is transferred subject only to a transferee's deeply out of the money put option, or a transferor's deeply out of the money call option, is derecognised. This is because the transferor has transferred substantially all the risks and rewards of ownership, [IFRS 9.B3.2.16(g)], (Figure 52.1, Box 6, Yes).

4.2.3 Options that are neither deeply out of the money nor deeply in the money

Where a financial asset is transferred subject to an option (whether a transferor's call option or a transferee's put option) that is neither deeply in the money nor deeply out of the money, the result is that the entity neither transfers nor retains substantially all the risks and rewards associated with the asset, *[IFRS 9.B3.2.16(h)-(i)]*, (Figure 52.1, Box 7, No). It is therefore necessary to determine whether or not the transferor has retained control of the asset under the criteria summarised in 3.9 above.

If a transferred asset continues to be recognised because of a transferor's call option or transferee's put option, but the option subsequently lapses unexercised, the asset and any associated liability would then be derecognised.

4.2.3.A Assets readily obtainable in the market

If the transferor has a call option over a transferred financial asset that is readily obtainable in the market, IFRS 9 considers that control of the asset has passed to the transferee (Figure 52.1, Box 8, No – see 3.9 above). *[IFRS 9.B3.2.16(h)]*. This would presumably also be the conclusion where the transferee has a put option over a transferred financial asset that is readily obtainable in the market, although IFRS 9 does not specifically address this.

4.2.3.B Assets not readily obtainable in the market

If the transferor has a call option over a transferred financial asset that is not readily obtainable in the market, IFRS 9 considers that control of the asset remains with the transferor (Figure 52.1, Box 8, Yes – see 3.9 above). Accordingly, derecognition is precluded to the extent of the amount of the asset that is subject to the call option. *[IFRS 9.B3.2.16(h)]*.

If the transferee has a put option over a transferred financial asset that is not readily obtainable in the market, IFRS 9 requires the transferee's likely economic behaviour to be assessed – in effect to determine whether the option gives the transferee the practical ability to sell the transferred asset (see 3.9.1 above).

If the put option is sufficiently valuable to prevent the transferee from selling the asset, the transferor is considered to retain control of the asset and should account for the asset to the extent of its continuing involvement, *[IFRS 9.B3.2.16(i)]*, (Figure 52.1, Box 9). The accounting treatment required is discussed at 5.3 below.

If the put option is not sufficiently valuable to prevent the transferee from selling the asset, the transferor is considered to have ceded control of the asset, and should derecognise it, *[IFRS 9.B3.2.16(i)]*, (Figure 52.1, Box 8, No).

The requirements above beg two questions. First the question of whether or not a put option is sufficiently valuable to prevent the transferee from selling the asset is not a matter of objective fact, but rather a function of the transferee's appetite for risk, its need for liquidity and so forth. It is not clear how the transferor can readily assess these factors.

Second, IFRS 9 is not explicit as to the accounting consequences (if any) of an option that was considered at the time of the original transfer to be deeply out of the money subsequently becoming neither deeply in the money nor deeply out of the money, or even deeply in the money, (or any other of the possible permutations). This is discussed further at 4.2.9 below.

4.2.4 Option to put or call at fair value

A transfer of a financial asset subject only to a put or call option with an exercise price equal to the fair value of the financial asset at the time of repurchase results in derecognition because of the transfer of substantially all the risks and rewards of ownership (Figure 52.1, Box 6, Yes). *[IFRS 9.B3.2.16(j)]*.

4.2.5 Net cash-settled options

Where a transfer of a financial asset is subject to a put or call option that will be settled net in cash, IFRS 9 requires the entity to evaluate the transfer so as to determine whether it has retained or transferred substantially all the risks and rewards of ownership. *[IFRS 9.B3.2.16(k)]*. IFRS 9 comments that 'if the entity has not retained substantially all the risks and rewards of ownership of the transferred asset, it determines whether it has retained control of the transferred asset' – a repetition of the basic principles of the standard adding no clarification specific to this type of transaction.

4.2.6 Removal of accounts provision

A 'removal of accounts provision' is an unconditional repurchase (i.e. call) option that gives an entity the right to reclaim transferred assets subject to some restrictions. Provided that such an option results in the entity neither retaining nor transferring substantially all the risks and rewards of ownership, IFRS 9 allows derecognition, except to the extent of the amount subject to repurchase (assuming that the transferee cannot sell the assets).

For example, if an entity transfers loan receivables with a carrying amount of €100,000 for proceeds of €100,000, subject only to the right to call back any individual loan(s) up to a maximum of €10,000, €90,000 of the loans would qualify for derecognition. *[IFRS 9.B3.2.16(l)]*.

4.2.7 Clean-up call options

A 'clean-up call' option is an option held by an entity that services transferred assets (and may be the transferor of those assets) to purchase remaining transferred assets when the cost of servicing the assets exceeds the entity's participation in their benefits. If such a clean-up call results in the entity neither retaining nor transferring substantially all the risks and rewards of ownership, and the transferee cannot sell the assets, IFRS 9 precludes derecognition only to the extent of the amount of assets subject to the call option. *[IFRS 9.B3.2.16(m)]*.

4.2.8 Same (or nearly the same) price put and call options

IFRS 9 does not specifically address the transfer of an asset subject to both a transferee's option to put, and a transferor's option to call, the asset at a fixed price rather than at fair value (as discussed in 4.2.4 above). Assuming that:

- both options can be exercised simultaneously; and
- both the transferor and transferee behave rationally,

it will clearly be in the interest of either the transferor or the transferee to exercise its option, so that the asset will be reacquired by the transferor. This indicates that the transferor has retained substantially all the risks and rewards of ownership.

However, if the two options were exercisable on different dates or at different prices, the effects of each option would need to be considered carefully.

4.2.9 Changes in probability of exercise of options after initial transfer of asset

As noted at 4.2.3.B above, IFRS 9 is not explicit as to the accounting consequences (if any) of an option that was considered at the time of the original transfer to be deeply out of the money subsequently becoming neither deeply in the money nor deeply out of the money, or even deeply in the money, (or any other of the possible permutations). This is explored further in Examples 52.3 to 52.5 below.

Example 52.3: Financial asset transferred subject only to deeply out of the money call option

On 1 January 2018 an entity transferred a financial asset to a counterparty, subject only to a call option to repurchase the asset at any time up to 31 December 2022. At 1 January 2018 the option was considered deeply out of the money and the asset was accordingly derecognised (see 4.2.2 above).

At 31 December 2021 market conditions have changed considerably and the option is now deeply in the money. What is the accounting consequence of this change?

There are no accounting consequences since, as noted at 3.8 above, IFRS 9 paragraph B3.2.6 specifies that an asset previously derecognised because substantially all the risks and rewards associated with the asset have been transferred (as would be the analysis for an asset transferred subject only to a deeply out of the money call – see 4.2.2 above) is not re-recognised in a future period unless it is reacquired. *[IFRS 9.B3.2.6]*. Instead the increase in the fair value of the option would be captured in the financial statements as a gain under the normal requirement of IFRS 9 to account for derivatives at fair value with changes in value reflected in profit or loss (see Chapter 48 at 2.2).

However, if the market changes were not demonstrably beyond any reasonable expectation as at 1 January 2018 there might be an argument (given the definition of a deeply out of the money option as an option that is 'highly unlikely' to become in the money before expiry – see 4.2 above) that the fact that the option is now not merely in the money, but deeply in the money, indicates that the original assessment that that option was deeply out of the money was in fact an accounting error requiring correction under IAS 8 (see Chapter 3 at 4.6).

Example 52.4: Financial asset transferred subject only to deeply in the money call option

On 1 January 2018 an entity transferred a financial asset to a counterparty, subject only to a call option to repurchase the asset at any time up to 31 December 2022. At 1 January 2018 the option was considered deeply in the money and the asset was accordingly not derecognised (see 4.2.1 above).

At 31 December 2021 market conditions have changed considerably and the option is now deeply out of the money. What is the accounting consequence of this change?

This is the mirror image of the fact pattern in Example 52.3. However, whereas IFRS 9 makes it clear that an asset previously derecognised is not re-recognised, there is no comparable provision that an asset that previously did not qualify for derecognition on the origination of a particular transaction may not later be derecognised as a result of a subsequent change in the assessed likely impact of the transaction. Because the standard does not explain the consequences, it is not clear when the asset is derecognised or whether there is any basis for derecognising the asset before the expiry of the option.

Assuming the asset in Example 52.4 above is not derecognised, the fall in the value of the option indicates an impairment of the asset which is likely to be required to be reflected in the financial statements under the normal requirements of IFRS 9 (see Chapter 51 at 5). This would in turn appear to require a corresponding adjustment to the liability recognised for the sale proceeds, so as to avoid recognising a net loss in the income statement that has not actually been suffered.

Example 52.5: Financial asset transferred subject to call option neither deeply in the money nor deeply out of the money

On 1 January 2018 an entity transferred a financial asset (an equity share) to a counterparty, subject only to a call option to repurchase the asset at any time up to 31 December 2022. At 1 January 2018 the option was considered to be neither deeply in the money nor deeply out of the money. However, the asset was readily marketable and freely transferable by the transferor and was accordingly derecognised because the entity, while neither transferring nor retaining substantially all the risks and rewards of the asset, no longer controls it (see 4.2.3 above).

At 31 December 2021 the financial asset that was the subject of the transfer ceases to be listed and is therefore not readily marketable. Had this been the case at the time of the original transfer, the entity would have been regarded as retaining control of the asset, which would not have been derecognised (see 4.2.3.B above). What is the accounting consequence of this change?

Again, matters are not entirely clear. The rule in paragraph B3.2.6 of IFRS 9 that a previously derecognised asset should not be re-recognised (other than on reacquisition of the asset) applies, as drafted, only where derecognition results from a transfer of substantially all the risks and rewards associated with the asset. In this case, derecognition has resulted from a loss of control over, not a transfer of substantially all the risks and rewards associated with, the asset. There is therefore some ambiguity as to whether B3.2.6 is to be read:

- generally as prohibiting any re-recognition of a derecognised asset; or
- specifically as referring only to circumstances where derecognition results from transfer of substantially all the risks and rewards (i.e. it applies only to 'Box 6, Yes' transactions, and not to 'Box 8, No' transactions).

Again, however, we take the view that the original decision to derecognise the asset should not be revisited, unless (in exceptional circumstances) the original assessment was an accounting error within the scope of IAS 8. The fact that the asset was transferred on terms that the transferee could freely dispose of it means that the transferor did indeed lose control.

4.3 Subordinated retained interests and credit guarantees

Where a financial asset is transferred, an entity may provide the transferee with credit enhancement by subordinating some or all of its interest retained in the transferred asset. Alternatively, an entity may provide the transferee with credit enhancement in the form of a credit guarantee that could be unlimited or limited to a specified amount. *[IFRS 9.B3.2.16(n)]*. Such techniques are commonly used in securitisation transactions (see 3.6 above).

IFRS 9 notes that, if the entity retains substantially all the risks and rewards of ownership of the transferred asset, the asset continues to be recognised in its entirety. If the entity retains some, but not substantially all, of the risks and rewards of ownership and has retained control, derecognition is precluded to the extent of the amount of cash or other assets that the entity could be required to pay. *[IFRS 9.B3.2.16(n)]*. This 'guidance' is really no more than a repetition of the basic principles of the standard, adding no real clarification specific to this type of transaction.

4.4 Transfers by way of swaps

4.4.1 Total return swaps

An entity may sell a financial asset to a transferee and enter into a total return swap with the transferee, whereby the transferor pays an amount equivalent to fixed or floating rate interest on the consideration for the transfer and receives an amount equivalent to the cash flows from, together with any increases or decreases in the fair value of, the underlying asset. In such a case, derecognition of all of the asset is prohibited, *[IFRS 9.B3.2.16(o)]*, since the transaction has the effect that substantially all the risks and rewards associated with the asset are retained by the transferor (Figure 52.1, Box 7, Yes).

4.4.2 Interest rate swaps

An entity may transfer a fixed rate financial asset and enter into an interest rate swap with the transferee to receive a fixed interest rate and pay a variable interest rate based on a notional amount equal to the principal amount of the transferred financial asset. IFRS 9 states that the interest rate swap does not preclude derecognition of the transferred asset, provided that the payments on the swap are not conditional on payments being made on the transferred asset. *[IFRS 9.B3.2.16(p)]*. It is interesting that this is included as guidance as it does not follow from the principles. There are situations in which the entity retains substantially all of the risks by retaining interest rate risk.

If, however, the transferor were to transfer an asset subject to prepayment risk (e.g. a domestic mortgage), and the transferor and transferee were to enter into an amortising interest rate swap (i.e. one whose notional amount amortises so that it equals the principal amount of the transferred financial asset outstanding at any point in time), the transferor would generally retain substantial prepayment risk through the swap. In this case, the transferor would (depending on the other facts of the transaction, such as the transfer or retention of credit risk) continue to recognise the transferred asset either in its entirety (Figure 52.1, Box 7, Yes) or to the extent of the transferor's continuing involvement (Figure 52.1, Box 9). *[IFRS 9.B3.2.16(q)]*.

Conversely, if the transferor and the transferee were to enter into an amortising interest rate swap, the amortisation of the notional amount of which is not linked to the principal amount outstanding on the transferred asset, the transferor would no longer retain prepayment risk. Therefore such a swap would not preclude derecognition of the transferred asset, provided the payments on the swap were not conditional on interest payments being made on the transferred asset and the swap did not result in the entity retaining any other significant risks and rewards of ownership on the transferred asset. *[IFRS 9.B3.2.16(q)]*.

4.5 Factoring of trade receivables

IFRS 9 does not specifically address one of the more common forms of 'off-balance sheet finance' – the factoring of trade receivables. The common aim of all factoring structures is to provide cash flow from trade receivables quicker than would arise from normal cash collections, which is generally achieved by a 'sale' of all, or certain selected, receivables to a financial institution. However, the conditions of such 'sales' are extremely varied (which may well explain the lack of any generic guidance in the standard), ranging from true outright sales and pass-through arrangements (resulting in full derecognition), to transactions with continuing involvement through guarantee or subordination arrangements. It will therefore be necessary for an entity to consider the terms of its particular debt-factoring arrangement(s) carefully in order to determine the appropriate application of the derecognition provisions of IFRS 9, particularly those discussed in sections 3.5 and 3.8 above.

Depending on circumstances, Examples 52.6 (see 5.1 below), 52.7 (see 5.1.1 below), 52.11 (see 5.4.1 below) and 52.16 (see 5.4.4 below) may also be of particular relevance.

5 ACCOUNTING TREATMENT

This part of the chapter deals with the accounting consequences of the derecognition criteria for financial assets – in other words how the principles discussed above translate into accounting entries.

In order to provide a link with Figure 52.1 at 3.2 above we have used the following convention:

'Box 6, Yes'   The transaction would result in the answer 'Yes' at Box 6 in the flowchart.

'Box 7, No'   The transaction would result in the answer 'No' at Box 7 in the flowchart.

5.1 Transfers that qualify for derecognition

It is important to remember throughout this section that references to an asset being derecognised in its entirety include situations where a part of an asset to which the derecognition criteria are applied separately is derecognised in its entirety (see 3.3 above). In this context, IFRS 9 uses the phrase 'in its entirety' in contrast to the accounting treatment applied to assets where there is continuing involvement (see 5.3 below) where some, but not all, of a financial asset, or part of an asset, is derecognised.

If, as a result of a transfer, a financial asset is derecognised in its entirety but the transfer results in the transferor obtaining a new financial asset or servicing asset or assuming a new financial liability, or a servicing liability (see 5.1.2 below), IFRS 9 requires the entity to recognise the new financial asset, servicing asset, financial liability or servicing liability at fair value. *[IFRS 9.3.2.11]*.

On derecognition of a financial asset in its entirety, IFRS 9 requires the difference between:

(a)   the carrying amount of the asset; and

(b)   the consideration received (including any new asset obtained less any new liability assumed),

to be recognised in profit or loss. *[IFRS 9.3.2.12]*. In addition, any cumulative gain or loss in respect of that asset which was previously recognised in other comprehensive income should be reclassified from equity to profit or loss if the asset is a debt instrument accounted for at fair value through other comprehensive income under IFRS 9. *[IFRS 9.5.7.10]*.

Example 52.6 illustrates these requirements.

Example 52.6: Derecognition of whole of financial asset in its entirety

At 1 October 2021 an entity has a debt instrument classified at fair value through other comprehensive income, carried at €1,400, in respect of which a cumulative gain of €200 has been recognised in equity. At that date, the asset is unconditionally sold to a third party in exchange for cash of €2,500 and a loan note issued to the third party. The loan note bears a fixed rate interest below current market rates and is repayable at €1,150 but is considered to have a fair value of €1,100. The following accounting entries are made by the entity to record the disposal:

	€	€
Cash	2,500	
Equity ('recycling' of cumulative gain on asset)	200	
Gain on disposal		200
Asset		1,400
Loan note		1,100

Thereafter the loan note will be accreted up to its repayable amount of €1,150 over its expected life using the effective interest method (see Chapter 50 at 3).

If the asset had been accounted for using the amortised cost method and had a carrying amount of (say) €1,300 at the date of the transfer, the accounting entry would have been:

	€	€
Cash	2,500	
Profit on disposal		100
Asset		1,300
Loan note		1,100

5.1.1   Transferred asset part of larger asset

If the transferred asset is part of a larger financial asset, for example when an entity transfers interest cash flows that are part of a debt instrument (see 3.3 above), and the part transferred qualifies for derecognition in its entirety, IFRS 9 requires the previous carrying amount of the larger financial asset to be allocated between the part that continues to be recognised and the part that is derecognised. The allocation is based on the relative fair values of those parts on the date of the transfer. For this purpose, a retained servicing asset (see 5.1.2 below) is to be treated as a part that continues to be recognised.

IFRS 9 requires the difference between:

(a)   the carrying amount allocated to the part derecognised; and

(b)   the sum of:

  (i)   the consideration received for the part derecognised (including any new asset obtained less any new liability assumed); and

  (ii) any cumulative gain or loss allocated to it previously recognised directly in equity,

to be recognised in profit or loss. Any cumulative gain or loss that had been recognised in equity is allocated between the part that continues to be recognised and the part that is derecognised, based on the relative fair values of those parts. *[IFRS 9.3.2.13]*.

The requirement in (b)(ii) above for 'recycling' of any cumulative gain or loss previously recognised directly in equity applies to debt instruments accounted for at fair value through other comprehensive income under IFRS 9.

Financial instruments: Derecognition

IFRS 9 notes that the accounting treatment prescribed for the derecognition of a part (or parts) of a financial asset requires an entity to determine the fair value of the part(s) that continue to be recognised. Where the entity has a history of selling parts similar to the part that continues to be recognised, or other market transactions exist for such parts, IFRS 9 requires recent prices of actual transactions to be used to provide the best estimate of its fair value. When there are no price quotations or recent market transactions to support the fair value of the part that continues to be recognised, the best estimate of the fair value is the difference between:

- the fair value of the larger financial asset as a whole; and
- the consideration received from the transferee for the part that is derecognised.

[IFRS 9.3.2.14].

The requirements of IFRS 13 that deal with the determination of fair value should also be used *[IFRS 9.B3.2.11]* – see Chapter 14.

Example 52.7 illustrates the requirements for full derecognition of a part of an asset.

Example 52.7: Derecognition of part of financial asset in its entirety

On 1 January 2017 an entity invested €1 million in a loan with a par value of €1 million. The loan pays interest of €75,000 on 31 December annually in arrears and is to be redeemed at par on 31 December 2025. The entity accounts for the loan at amortised cost.

On 1 January 2021 it unconditionally sells the right to receive the remaining five interest payments to a bank. The derecognition provisions of IFRS 9 are applied to the interest payments as an identifiable part of the asset (see 3.3.4 above), leading to the conclusion that they are required to be derecognised.

The consideration received for, and the fair value of, the future interest payments (based on the net present value, as at 1 January 2021, of the payments at the current market interest rate that would be available to the borrower of 5%, although in practice other factors might be relevant to the valuation) is €324,711 (€75,000 × [$1/1.05 + 1/1.05^2 ... + 1/1.05^5$]). By the same methodology the fair value of the principal repayment can be calculated as €783,526 (€1,000,000 × $1/1.05^5$), giving a total fair value for the loan of €1,108,237.

In order to calculate the gain or loss on disposal, the total carrying value of the loan of €1,000,000 is allocated between the part disposed of and the part retained, based on the fair values of those parts. This allocates €292,998 (€1,000,000 × 324,711 ÷ 1,108,237) to the interest payments disposed of and €707,002 (€1,000,000 × 783,526 ÷ 1,108,237) to the retained right to the repayment of principal. This generates the accounting entry:

	€	€
Cash	324,711	
Loan		
(portion of carrying amount allocated to interest payments)		292,998
Gain on disposal		31,713

If the loan had instead been a bond accounted for at fair value through other comprehensive income, it would already have been carried at €1,108,237, so that the basic disposal journal would simply be:

	€	€
Cash	324,711	
Bond		
(portion of carrying amount allocated to interest payments)		324,711

However, as the bond was accounted for at fair value through other comprehensive income, it would also be necessary to recycle that portion of the cumulative revaluation gain of €108,237 that relates to the interest 'component' of the total carrying value from equity to the income statement. IFRS 9 requires a *pro rata* allocation of the cumulative gain or loss in equity based on the total fair value of the interest and principal – this would deem €31,713 (€108,237 × €324,711 ÷ 1,108,237) of the cumulative revaluation gain to relate to interest. This would give rise to the further journal, resulting in the same gain on disposal as above:

	€	€
Equity	31,713	
Gain on disposal (income statement)		31,713

5.1.2 Servicing assets and liabilities

It is common for an entity to transfer a financial asset (or part of a financial asset) in its entirety, but to retain the right or obligation to service the asset, i.e. to collect payments as they fall due and undertake other administrative tasks, in return for a fee.

When an entity transfers a financial asset in a transfer that qualifies for derecognition in its entirety and retains the right to service the financial asset for a fee, IFRS 9 requires the entity to recognise either a servicing asset or a servicing liability for that servicing contract, as follows:

- If the fee to be received is not expected to compensate the entity adequately for performing the servicing, the entity should recognise a servicing liability for the servicing obligation at its fair value.

- If the fee to be received is expected to be more than adequate compensation for the servicing, the entity should recognise a servicing asset for the servicing right. This should be recognised at an amount determined on the basis of an allocation of the carrying amount of the larger financial asset (as described in 5.1.1 above). [IFRS 9.3.2.10].

It is not immediately clear what is meant by this requirement. The application guidance expands on the point, as follows.

An entity may retain the right to a part of the interest payments on transferred assets as compensation for servicing those assets. The part of the interest payments that the entity would give up upon termination or transfer of the servicing contract is allocated to the servicing asset or servicing liability. The part of the interest payments that the entity would not give up is an interest-only strip receivable.

For example, if the entity would not give up any interest upon termination or transfer of the servicing contract, the entire interest spread is an interest-only strip receivable. Presumably, as the entity will still have a liability to service the portfolio, it will have to account for this if it allocates none of the interest spread to a servicing asset. For the purposes of applying the requirements for disposals of part of an asset discussed in 5.1.1 above, the fair values of the servicing asset and interest-only strip receivable are used to allocate the carrying amount of the receivable between the part of the asset that is derecognised and the part that continues to be recognised. If there is no servicing fee specified, or the fee to be received is not expected to compensate the entity adequately for performing the servicing, a liability for the servicing obligation is recognised at fair value. [IFRS 9.B3.2.10].

Unfortunately, IFRS 9 does not provide examples of what exactly is meant here, but we believe that something along the lines of Example 52.8 below was intended.

Example 52.8:   Servicing assets and liabilities

An entity has a portfolio of originated domestic mortgages which are accounted for at amortised cost and have a carrying amount of £10 million. The mortgages bear interest at a fixed rate of 7.5%. The average life of the mortgages in the portfolio (taking account of prepayment risk) is 12 years and the fair value of the portfolio is £11 million, representing £4.5 million in respect of future interest payments and £6.5 million in respect of the principal amounts. The entity assesses the amount that would compensate it for servicing the assets to be £0.5 million.

The entity sells the entire portfolio to a bank (on terms such that it qualifies for derecognition under IFRS 9) but continues to service the portfolio. If the entity does not retain any part of the interest payments, the selling price would be the fair value of the assets of £11 million (or very close to it). It would then assume a servicing liability of £0.5 million, giving rise to the accounting entry:

	£m	£m
Cash	11.0	
Mortgage portfolio		10.0
Servicing liability		0.5
Profit on disposal		0.5

Alternatively, it retains interest payments of 1% and the right to service the portfolio. The entity estimates that the fair value of the right to receive interest payments of 1% is £0.6 million. In this case, the bank would be expected to pay fair value of £10.4 million (or very close to it).

The standard states – see above – that, if (as is the case here) the entity would not give up any interest on termination or transfer of the contract, then the whole of the interest spread is an interest-only strip receivable. In order to calculate the amount of the portfolio to be derecognised, the carrying value of £10 million is pro-rated (as in Example 52.7 above) as to £9.45 million disposed of (£10m × 10.4 ÷ 11) and the part retained of £0.55 million (£10m × 0.6 ÷ 11). However, as it has allocated the full amount of the interest spread to an interest-only strip receivable, it would need to recognise a servicing liability of £0.5 million in respect of its obligations under the contract. This gives rise to the following accounting entry:

	£m	£m
Cash	10.40	
Interest-only strip receivable	0.55	
Mortgage portfolio (£9.45m disposed of plus £0.55m reclassified as interest-only strip receivable)		10.00
Servicing liability		0.50
Profit on disposal		0.45

If the entity were to retain only £0.1 million of the interest spread on termination or transfer of the servicing contract, then IFRS 9 requires – see above:

- the part of the interest payments that the entity would not give up, i.e. the part which is not contingent on fulfilment of the servicing obligation (£0.1 million) to be treated as an interest-only strip receivable; and
- the part of the interest payments that the entity would give up (i.e. £0.45 million – £0.55 million as above less £0.1 million in previous bullet) upon termination or transfer of the servicing contract to be allocated to the servicing asset or servicing liability.

This suggests that the following accounting entry would be made:

	£m	£m
Cash	10.40	
Interest-only strip receivable	0.10	
Mortgage portfolio (£9.45m disposed of plus £0.1m reclassified as interest-only strip receivable and £0.45m allocated to servicing liability)		10.00
Servicing liability (£0.5m gross cost less interest payments that would be lost on termination or transfer – £0.45m)		0.05
Profit on disposal		0.45

A servicing asset is a non-financial asset representing a right to receive a higher than normal amount for performing future services. Accordingly it would normally be accounted for in accordance with IAS 38 – *Intangible Assets*. Similarly, a servicing liability represents consideration received in advance for services to be performed in the future and would normally be accounted for as deferred revenue in accordance with IFRS 15.

5.2 Transfers that do not qualify for derecognition through retention of risks and rewards

If a transfer does not result in derecognition because the entity has retained substantially all the risks and rewards of ownership of the transferred asset (see 3.8 above), IFRS 9 requires the entity to continue to recognise the transferred asset in its entirety and recognise a financial liability for any consideration received. In subsequent periods, the entity recognises any income on the transferred asset and any expense incurred on the financial liability. *[IFRS 9.3.2.15]*. This treatment is illustrated by Examples 52.9 and 52.10 below.

It should be noted that these provisions apply only where derecognition does not occur as a result of retention by the transferor of substantially all the risks and rewards of ownership of the transferred asset (Figure 52.1, Box 7, Yes). They do not apply where derecognition does not occur as a result of continuing involvement in an asset of which substantially all the risks and rewards of ownership are neither retained nor transferred (Figure 52.1, Box 8, Yes). Such transactions are dealt with by the separate provisions discussed in 5.3 and 5.4 below.

Example 52.9: Asset not qualifying for derecognition (risks and rewards retained)

An entity holds a loan of £1,000 made on 1 January 2017, paying interest of £65 annually in arrears and redeemable at par on 31 December 2021, which it accounts for at amortised cost (see Chapter 50 at 3).

On 1 January 2021 it enters into a transaction whereby the loan is sold to a bank for its then fair value of €985, but with full recourse to the entity for any default on the loan. The guarantee provided by the entity has the effect that it retains substantially all the risks and rewards of the loan, which is therefore not derecognised (Figure 52.1, Box 7, Yes – see 3.8.2 above). *[IFRS 9.B3.2.12]*.

The entity therefore continues to recognise the loan, and interest on it, as if it still held the loan. It accounts for the £985 proceeds as a liability which must be accreted up using the effective interest method (see Chapter 50 at 3) so that it will be equal to the carrying amount of the asset on the date on which it is expected that the asset will be derecognised.

In this case, the asset will be derecognised at maturity on 31 December 2021 when a payment of £1,065 (the final instalment of interest of £65 and return of principal of £1,000) is due. Accordingly, the liability must be accreted from £985 to £1,065 during the year ended 31 December 2021. The following accounting entries are made by the entity:

	£	£
1 January 2021		
Cash	985	
Liability		985
Consideration received from bank		
1 January-31 December 2021		
Loan (£1,065 at 31.12.21 – £1,000 at 1.1.21)	65	
Interest on loan (income statement)		65
Interest on liability (income statement)	80	
Liability (£1,065 at 31.12.21 – £985 at 1.1.21)		80
Accretion of interest income loan and liability		
31 December 2021		
Liability	1,065	
Loan receivable		1,065
'Redemption' of loan and 'discharge' of liability		

This accounting treatment recognises an overall loss of £15 in 2021, which would be expected, as representing the difference between the carrying value of the asset at the date of transfer (£1,000) and the consideration received (£985). However, IFRS 9 requires the various elements of the transaction to be shown separately – it would not have been acceptable for the income statement simply to show a net loss of £15.

If the transferred asset had been accounted for at fair value through profit or loss, it would already have been carried at £985 at the date of transfer – i.e. the loss of £15 would already have been reflected in the financial statements. The accounting entries at 1 January and 31 December 2021 would be the same as above. However, the following accounting entries would then have been made during the year ended 31 December:

	£	£
1 January-31 December 2021		
Interest on liability (income statement)	80	
Liability (£1,065 at 31.12.21 – £985 at 1.1.21)		80
Loan (£1,065 at 31.12.21 – £985 at 1.1.21)	80	
Interest on loan (income statement)		65
Change in fair value of loan (income statement)		15
Recognition of interest on, and change in fair value of, loan and accretion of interest on liability		

Whilst the total amounts recorded in the income statement net to nil, they are arrived at by different methodologies – the £80 increase in the carrying value of the loan receivable is recognised as it occurs whereas the £80 interest on the liability is accrued at a constant effective rate. This means that, if the entity were to prepare financial statements at an interim date, it might well show a net gain or loss on the transaction at that date, notwithstanding that ultimately no gain or loss will be reflected.

It would presumably be possible for the entity to avoid this result by designating the liability as at fair value through profit or loss (see Chapter 48 at 7), such that changes in the fair value of the liability would be matched in line with those in the fair value of the asset.

Example 52.10:   Asset not qualifying for derecognition ('repo' transaction)

An entity holds a government bond of £2,000 issued on 1 January 2017, paying interest of £50 semi-annually in arrears and redeemable at par on 31 December 2022, which it accounts for as a financial asset subsequently measured at amortised cost.

A Gross-settled transaction

On 1 January 2021 the entity enters into a transaction whereby the bond is sold to a bank for its then fair value of £1,800, and the entity agrees to repurchase it on 1 January 2022 for £1,844. As the legal owner of the loan at 30 June 2021 and 31 December 2021, the bank will receive the £100 interest payable on the bond for the calendar year 2021. This £100, together with the £44 difference between the sale and repurchase price gives the bank £144, representing a lender's return of 8% on the £1,800 sale proceeds. Accordingly, the effect of the transaction is that the entity has retained substantially all the risks and rewards of ownership of the bond (Figure 52.1, Box 7, Yes – see 4.1 above).

The entity therefore continues to recognise the bond, and interest on it, as if it still held the bond. It accounts for the £1,800 proceeds as a liability which must be accreted up to £1,844 (the repurchase price due on 31 December 2021) over the period to 31 December 2021 using the effective interest method (see Chapter 50 at 3). The following accounting entries are made by the entity:

	£	£
1 January 2021		
Cash	1,800	
Liability		1,800
Consideration received from bank		
1 January-31 December 2021		
Interest on liability (income statement)	144	
Liability (£1,944 at 31.12.21 – £1,800 at 1.1.21)		144
Bond (£2,100 at 31.12.21 – £2,000 at 1.1.21)	100	
Interest on bond (income statement)		100
Accretion of income on bond and finance cost of liability		
1 January-31 December 2021		
Liability	100	
Bond		100
Notional receipt of interest on bond at 30 June and 31 December and notional transfer thereof to bank		
1 January 2022		
Liability	1,844	
Cash		1,844
Execution of repurchase contract		

The above is arguably the strict translation into accounting entries of the accounting analysis under IFRS 9 for a situation where the entity still retains ownership of the bond throughout 2021. As a matter of practicality, however, the same overall result could have been obtained by the following 'short-cut' approach, which avoids recording the notional receipt and transfer to the bank of bond interest received on 30 June and 31 December:

	£	£
1 January 2021		
Cash	1,800	
Liability		1,800
Consideration received from bank		
1 January-31 December 2021		
Interest on liability (income statement)	144	
Interest on bond (income statement)		100
Liability (statement of financial position)		44
Accretion of income on bond and finance cost of liability		

	£	£
1 January 2022		
Liability	1,844	
Cash		1,844

Execution of repurchase contract

If (as would be likely, given the nature of the transferred asset) the bank has the right to sell or pledge the bond during the period of its legal ownership, it would be necessary to reclassify the bond as a repurchase receivable during the period of the bank's ownership (see 4.1.1.A above). In other words, the following additional accounting entries would be required.

	£	£
1 January 2021		
Repurchase receivable	2,000	
Bond		2,000
1 January 2022		
Bond	2,000	
Repurchase receivable		2,000

B   Net-settled transaction

The entity might enter into the transaction above, but on terms that the repurchase contract was to be net-settled. In other words, on 1 January 2022, a payment would be made to or by the bank for the difference between £1,844 (the notional repurchase price) and the fair value of the bond at that date. Assuming that the fair value of the bond at 1 January 2022 is £1,860, the bank would be required to pay the entity £16 (£1,860 – £1,844).

In this case, matters are further complicated by the fact that the economic effect of the net-settled forward is the same as if the entity sold the bond on 1 January 2022. The following accounting entries would be made:

	£	£
1 January 2021		
Cash	1,800	
Liability		1,800

Consideration received from bank

	£	£
1 January–31 December 2021		
Interest on liability (income statement)	144	
Interest on bond (income statement)		100
Liability (statement of financial position)		44

Accretion of income on bond and finance cost of liability

	£	£
1 January 2022		
Cash	16	
Liability	1,844	
Loss on derecognition of bond	140	
Bond		2,000

Net settlement of repurchase contract and recognition of loss on derecognition of the bond

The loss on derecognition at 1 January 2022 of £140 arises because the net-settled contract is equivalent to the entity disposing of the bond for its then fair value of £1,860, which is £140 lower than its amortised cost of £2,000.

This illustrates the point that, where the terms of net-settled forward contract over a transferred asset are such that the original asset cannot be derecognised, the result will be that the entity's statement of financial position shows a gross position – i.e. the original asset and a liability for the consideration for the transfer. This may seem a strange accounting reflection of a contract that is required to be settled net. However, the IASB was to some extent forced into this approach as an anti-avoidance measure. It is clear from the analysis in 4.1.1 to 4.1.4 above that an asset sold subject to the obligation to repurchase the same or similar asset at a fixed price should not be derecognised. If the accounting treatment were to vary merely because the contract was net-settled, it would be possible to avoid the requirements of IFRS 9 for continued recognition of assets subject to certain forward repurchase agreements simply by altering the terms of the agreement to allow net settlement.

5.3 Transfers with continuing involvement – summary

If an entity neither transfers nor retains substantially all the risks and rewards of ownership of a transferred asset, but retains control of the transferred asset (see 3.9 above), IFRS 9 requires the entity to continue to recognise the transferred asset to the extent of its 'continuing involvement' – i.e. the extent to which it is exposed to changes in the value of the transferred asset. *[IFRS 9.3.2.16]*. Such transactions fall within Box 9 of the flowchart at 3.2 above.

The concept of 'continuing involvement' was first introduced in the exposure draft of proposed amendments to IAS 32 and IAS 39 published in June 2002. The IASB's intention at that time was to move towards an accounting model for derecognition based entirely on continuing involvement. However, this approach (or at least the methodology for implementing it proposed in the exposure draft) received little support in the exposure period and the IASB decided to abandon it and revert largely to an accounting model for derecognition based on the transfer of risks and rewards. *[IFRS 9.BCZ3.4-BCZ3.12]*. Nevertheless, the continuing involvement approach remains relevant for certain transactions – mainly transfers of assets which result in the sharing, rather than the substantial transfer, of the risks and rewards.

The accounting requirements in respect of assets in which the entity has continuing involvement are particularly complex, and are summarised at 5.3.1 to 5.3.5 below, with worked examples at 5.4 below. In particular, and in contrast to the treatment for transactions that do not qualify for derecognition through retention of risks and rewards (see 5.2 above), the associated liability is often calculated as a balancing figure that will not necessarily represent the proceeds received as the result of the transfer (see 5.3.3 below).

We have a general concern regarding the required accounting treatment for a continuing involvement, namely that IFRS 9 provides examples of how to deal with certain specific transactions rather than clear underlying principles. It can be difficult to determine the appropriate treatment for a continuing involvement that does not correspond fairly exactly to one of the examples in IFRS 9.

5.3.1 Guarantees

When the entity's continuing involvement takes the form of guaranteeing the transferred asset, the extent of the entity's continuing involvement is the lower of:

- the carrying amount of the asset; and
- the maximum amount of the consideration received that the entity could be required to repay ('the guarantee amount'). *[IFRS 9.3.2.16(a)]*.

An example of this treatment is given at 5.4.1 below.

It follows that if the transferor guarantees the entire amount of the transferred asset, no derecognition would be achieved, even though it may have passed other significant risks to the transferee.

5.3.2 Options

When the entity's continuing involvement takes the form of a written and/or purchased option (including a cash-settled option or similar provision) on the transferred asset, the extent of the entity's continuing involvement is the amount of the transferred asset that the entity may repurchase. However, in case of a written put option (including a cash-settled option or similar provision) on an asset measured at fair value, the extent of the entity's continuing involvement is limited to the lower of the fair value of the transferred asset and the option exercise price. *[IFRS 9.3.2.16(b)-(c)].*

Examples of this treatment are given at 5.4.2 and 5.4.3 below.

5.3.3 Associated liability

When an entity continues to recognise an asset to the extent of its continuing involvement, IFRS 9 requires the entity to recognise an associated liability. *[IFRS 9.3.2.17].* IFRS 9 provides that 'despite the other measurement requirements in this Standard', the transferred asset and the associated liability are to be measured on a basis that reflects the rights and obligations that the entity has retained. The associated liability is measured in such a way that the net carrying amount of the transferred asset and the associated liability is equal to:

- if the transferred asset is measured at amortised cost, the amortised cost of the rights and obligations retained by the entity; or
- if the transferred asset is measured at fair value, the fair value of the rights and obligations retained by the entity when measured on a stand-alone basis. *[IFRS 9.3.2.17].*

This has the effect that the 'liability' is often calculated as a balancing figure that will not necessarily represent the proceeds received as the result of the transfer (see Examples 52.11 to 52.14 at 5.4 below). This does not fit very comfortably with the normal rules in IFRS 9 for the initial measurement of financial liabilities (see Chapter 49 at 3) – hence the comment that this treatment applies 'despite the other measurement requirements in this Standard'.

5.3.4 Subsequent measurement of assets and liabilities

IFRS 9 requires an entity to continue to recognise any income arising on the transferred asset to the extent of its continuing involvement and to recognise any expense incurred on the associated liability. *[IFRS 9.3.2.18].* This is comparable to the requirements in respect of assets not derecognised through retention of substantially all risks and rewards (see 5.2 above).

When the transferred asset and associated liability are subsequently measured, IFRS 9 requires recognised changes in the fair value of the transferred asset and the associated liability to be accounted for consistently with each other in accordance with the general provisions of IFRS 9 for measuring gains and losses (see Chapter 50 at 2) and not offset. *[IFRS 9.3.2.19].* Moreover, if the transferred asset is measured at amortised cost, the option in IFRS 9 to designate a financial liability as at fair value through profit or loss (see Chapter 48 at 7) is not applicable to the associated liability. *[IFRS 9.3.2.21]*.

5.3.5 Continuing involvement in part only of a larger asset

An entity may have continuing involvement in a part only of a financial asset, for example where the entity retains an option to repurchase part of a transferred asset, or retains a residual interest in part of an asset, such that the entity does not retain substantially all the risks and rewards of ownership, but does retain control.

In such a case, IFRS 9 requires the entity to allocate the previous carrying amount of the financial asset between the part that it continues to recognise under continuing involvement, and the part that it no longer recognises on the basis of the relative fair values of those parts on the date of the transfer. The allocation is to be made on the same basis as applies on derecognition of part only of a larger financial asset – see 5.1.1 and 5.1.2 above.

The difference between:

(a) the carrying amount allocated to the part that is no longer recognised; and
(b) the sum of:
  (i) the consideration received for the part no longer recognised; and
  (ii) any cumulative gain or loss allocated to it that had been recognised directly in equity,

is recognised in profit or loss. A cumulative gain or loss that had been recognised in equity is allocated between the part that continues to be recognised and the part that is no longer recognised on the basis of the relative fair values of those parts. *[IFRS 9.3.2.13]*.

The 'recycling' of any cumulative gain or loss previously recognised directly in equity in (b)(ii) above would apply to debt instruments accounted for at fair value through other comprehensive income under IFRS 9. This was previously an explicit requirement of IAS 39, but has not been carried over to IFRS 9, something we suspect is nothing but an oversight.

This topic is discussed further at 5.4.4 below.

5.4 Transfers with continuing involvement – accounting examples

The provisions summarised at 5.3 above, even judged by the standards of IFRS 9, are unusually impenetrable. However, the application guidance provides a number of clarifications and examples, the substance of which is reproduced below.

5.4.1 Transfers with guarantees

If a guarantee provided by an entity to pay for default losses on a transferred asset prevents the transferred asset from being derecognised to the extent of the continuing involvement, IFRS 9 requires:

(a) the transferred asset at the date of the transfer to be measured at the lower of:
  (i) the carrying amount of the asset; and
  (ii) the maximum amount of the consideration received in the transfer that the entity could be required to repay ('the guarantee amount'); and
(b) the associated liability to be initially measured at the guarantee amount plus the fair value of the guarantee (which is normally the consideration received for the guarantee).

Subsequently, the initial fair value of the guarantee is recognised in profit or loss on a time proportion basis in accordance with IFRS 15 and the carrying value of the asset is reduced by any impairment losses. *[IFRS 9.B3.2.13(a)].*

This is illustrated in Example 52.11 below (which is based on the circumstances in Example 52.16 below).

Example 52.11: Continuing involvement through guarantee

An entity has a loan portfolio carried at €10 million with a fair value of €10.5 million. It sells the rights to 100% of the cash flows to a third party for a payment of €10.55 million, which includes a payment of €50,000 in return for the entity agreeing to absorb the first €1 million of default losses on the portfolio. The loans are fixed rate loans with significant prepayment risk.

The guarantee has the effect that the entity has transferred substantially all the rewards, but not substantially all the risks, of the portfolio (Figure 52.1, Box 6, No). The prepayment risk and interest rate risk have been transferred to the transferee, so that the entity does not retain all significant risks of the loans (Figure 52.1, Box 7, No). The portfolio is not a readily marketable asset, so that the entity retains control of the asset (Figure 52.1, Box 8, Yes – see also 3.9 above), and the continuing involvement provisions of IFRS 9 apply (Figure 52.1, Box 9).

The entity turns to the requirements above. The continuing involvement in the transferred asset must be measured at the lower of:

(i) the amount of the asset transferred – i.e. €10 million; and
(ii) the maximum amount of the consideration received in the transfer that the entity could be required to repay – i.e. €1 million (the amount guaranteed).

Therefore, the entity will set up an asset that represents its continuing involvement in the transferred asset of €1 million.

The entity then considers the carrying amount of the liability. This is required to be measured at the guarantee amount (i.e. €1 million) plus the fair value of the guarantee (i.e. the €50,000 guarantee payment), a total of €1.05 million. Therefore, the entity's continuing involvement in the transaction will be reflected as follows:

	€m	€m
Cash	10.55	
Loan portfolio transferred		10.00
Continuing involvement in the transferred asset	1.00	
Liability		1.05
Profit on disposal*		0.50

* Cash received (€10.55m) less guarantee payment (€50,000) = consideration for portfolio (€10.5m) less carrying amount of portfolio (€10m).

Over the remaining life of the transaction, the €50,000 of the liability that represents the consideration received for the guarantee is amortised to the income statement on a time proportion basis. This has the effect that the income earned by the entity for entering into the guarantee arrangement is reported as revenue on a time proportion basis. This is exactly the same result as would have been obtained by simply recognising the €50,000 as a liability and amortising it (as would be required by IFRS 15).

If in a subsequent period credit losses of €0.2 million are suffered, requiring a payment under the guarantee, IFRS 9 requires the following accounting entries to be made: *[IFRS 9.B3.2.17]*

	€m	€m
Profit or loss (loss under guarantee)	0.20	
Cash (paid to transferee)		0.20
Liability	0.20	
Continuing involvement in the transferred asset		0.20

5.4.2 Transfers of assets measured at amortised cost

If a put or call option prevents derecognition (see 3.8.3 and 4.2 above) of a transferred asset measured at amortised cost, IFRS 9 requires the associated liability to be measured at cost (i.e. the consideration received) and subsequently adjusted for the amortisation of any difference between that cost and the amortised cost of the transferred asset at the expiration date of the option, as illustrated by Example 52.12 below. *[IFRS 9.B3.2.13(b)]*.

Example 52.12: Asset measured at amortised cost

An entity has a financial asset, accounted for at amortised cost, carried at £98. It transfers the asset to a third party in return for consideration of £95. The asset is subject to a call option whereby the entity can compel the transferee to sell the asset back to the entity for £102. The amortised cost of the asset on the option exercise date will be £100. The option is considered to be neither deeply in the money nor deeply out of the money. IFRS 9 therefore requires the entity to continue to recognise the asset to the extent of its continuing involvement (Figure 52.1, Box 9 – see also 4.2.3 above).

The initial carrying amount of the associated liability is £95. This is then accreted to £100 (i.e. the amortised cost of the asset on exercise date – not the £102 exercise price) through profit or loss using the effective interest method. Because the transferred asset is measured at amortised cost, the associated liability must also be accounted for at amortised cost, and not at fair value through profit or loss (see 5.3.4 above). This will give rise to the accounting entries:

	£	£
Date of transfer		
Cash	95	
Liability		95
After date of transfer		
Interest on liability	5	
Liability (£100 – £95)		5
Asset (£100 – £98)	2	
Income on asset		2

If the option is exercised, any difference between the carrying amount of the associated liability and the exercise price is recognised in profit or loss. This last requirement has the possibly counter-intuitive effect that the question of whether the entity records a profit or loss on exercise of the option is essentially a function of the difference between the liability (representing the amortised cost of the transferred asset) and the cash paid, not of whether it has in fact (i.e. in economic terms) made a gain or loss.

Thus, if the entity were to exercise its option at £102 it would apparently record the accounting entry:

	£	£
Liability	100	
Loss	2	
Cash		102

However, the entity would not have exercised the option unless the asset had been worth at least £102 (i.e. £2 more than its carrying amount), suggesting that the more appropriate treatment would be to add the £2 to the cost of the asset.

Likewise, if instead of the entity having a call option, the transferee had a put option at £98 which it exercised, the entity would apparently record the accounting entry:

	£	£
Liability	100	
Profit		2
Cash		98

However, the transferee would not have exercised its option unless the asset had been worth less than £98 (i.e. £2 less than its carrying amount). In this case, however, the IASB's thinking may have been that the exercise of the transferee's put option suggests an impairment of the asset which is required to be recognised in the financial statements (see Chapter 51 at 5). This would not necessarily be the case (e.g. where a fixed-interest asset has a fair value below cost because of movements in interest rates but is not intrinsically impaired).

If the option were to lapse unexercised, the entity would simply derecognise the transferred asset and the associated liability, i.e.:

	£	£
Liability	100	
Asset		100

5.4.3 Transfers of assets measured at fair value

IFRS 9 discusses the application of continuing involvement accounting to transferred assets measured at fair value in terms of transferred assets subject to:

- a transferor's call option (see 5.4.3.A below);
- a transferee's put option (see 5.4.3.B below); and
- a 'collar' – i.e. a transferor's call option combined with a transferee's put option (see 5.4.3.C below).

The way in which the rules are articulated in IFRS 9 is somewhat confusing, but in general the effect is that the transferred asset is recognised at:

- in the case of an asset subject to a transferor call option, its fair value (on the basis that the call option gives the transferor access to any increase in the fair value of the asset); and
- in the case of an asset subject to a transferee put option, the lower of fair value and the option exercise price (on the basis that the put option denies the transferor access to any increase in the fair value of the asset above the option price).

This methodology summarised below is applied both on the date on which the option is written and subsequently.

5.4.3.A   Transferor's call option

If a transferor's call option prevents derecognition (see 3.8.3 and 4 above) of a transferred asset measured at fair value, the asset continues to be measured at its fair value. The associated liability is measured:

- if the option is in or at the money, at the option exercise price less the time value of the option; or
- if the option is out of the money, at the fair value of the transferred asset less the time value of the option.

The adjustment to the measurement of the associated liability ensures that the net carrying amount of the asset and the associated liability is the fair value of the call option right, as illustrated by Example 52.13 below. *[IFRS 9.B3.2.13(c)]*.

Example 52.13:   Asset measured at fair value subject to transferor's call option

An entity has a financial asset, accounted for at fair value through profit or loss, carried at €80. It transfers the asset to a third party, subject to a call option whereby the entity can compel the transferee to sell the asset back to the entity for €95. At the date of transfer, the call option has a time value of €5.

The option is considered to be neither deeply in the money nor deeply out of the money. IFRS 9 therefore requires the entity to continue to recognise the asset to the extent of its continuing involvement (Figure 52.1, Box 9 – see also 4.2.3 above), and to continue recording it at fair value. At the date of transfer, the call option is out of the money. IFRS 9 therefore requires the liability to be measured at the fair value of the transferred asset less the time value of the option, i.e. €80 – €5 = €75. This has the result that the net of the carrying value of the asset (€80) and the carrying value of the liability (€75) equals the time value of the option (€5), resulting in the following accounting entry:

	€	€
Date of transfer		
Cash	75	
Liability		75

A   Transferred asset increases in value

Suppose that one year later the fair value of the asset is €100 and the time value of the option is now €3. The option is now in the money, so that the liability is measured at the option exercise price less the time value of the option, i.e. €95 – €3 = €92. This has the result that the net of the carrying value of the asset (€100) and the carrying value of the liability (€92) equals the fair value of the option (€8, representing €3 time value and €5 intrinsic value). The liability could have been more straightforwardly calculated as the fair value of the asset (€100) less the fair value of the option (€8) = €92. This gives rise to the following accounting entries:

	€	€
During year 1		
Asset (€100 – €80)	20	
Liability (€92 – €75)		17
Gain (profit or loss)		3

The €3 gain recorded in profit or loss effectively represents the increase in the fair value of the option from €5 to €8 over the period. If the entity were able to exercise the option at this point, and did so, it would record the entry:

	€	€
Liability	92	
Loss (profit or loss)	3	
Cash		95

The particular transaction results in no overall gain or loss being reflected in profit or loss (i.e. €3 gain during the year less €3 loss on exercise of option). This represents the net of the €20 gain in the fair value of the asset (€100 at the end of period less €80 at the start) and the net cash outflow of €20 (€75 in on initial transfer, €95 out on exercise of option).

B   Asset decreases in value

Suppose instead that during the first year the fair value of the asset fell to €65 and the time value of the option at the end of the year was only €1. The liability would be measured at the fair value of the transferred asset less the time value of the option, i.e. €65 – €1 = €64. This would generate the accounting entries:

	€	€
During year 1		
Liability (€64 – €75)	11	
Loss (profit or loss)	4	
Asset (€65 – €80)		15

Again the overall loss shown in profit or loss represents the movement in the fair value of the option over the period from €5 to €1. Suppose that one year later there was no change in the fair value of the asset, and the option expired unexercised. The entity would then record the accounting entry:

	€	€
At end of year 2		
Liability	64	
Loss (profit or loss)	1	
Asset (statement of financial position)		65

This results in an overall loss for the transaction as a whole of €5 (€4 in year 1 and €1 in year 2), which represents the difference between the carrying value of the asset at the date of original transfer (€80) and the proceeds received (€75).

The amount of any consideration received is in principle not relevant to the measurement of the liability. If, for example, the entity originally received consideration of €72, it would still record a liability of €75 and a 'day one' loss of €3. If it received consideration of €80, it would still record a liability of €75 and a 'day one' profit of €5. The IASB no doubt presumed that such transactions are likely to be undertaken only by sophisticated market participants such that the consideration received will always be equivalent to the fair value of the asset less the fair value of the option. However, there may well be instances where this is not the case, such as in transactions between members of the same group or other related parties.

5.4.3.B   Transferee's put option

If a transferee's put option prevents derecognition (see 3.8.3 and 4 above) of a transferred asset measured at fair value, IFRS 9 requires the asset to be measured at the lower of fair value and the option exercise price. The basis for this treatment is that the entity has no right to increases in the fair value of the transferred asset above the exercise price of the option. The associated liability is measured at the option exercise price plus the time value of the option. This ensures that the net carrying amount of the asset and the associated liability is the fair value of the put option obligation, as illustrated by Example 52.14 below. *[IFRS 9.B3.2.13(d)]*.

Example 52.14: Asset measured at fair value subject to transferee's put option

An entity has a financial asset, accounted for at fair value. On 1 January 2021 it transfers the asset, then carried at €98, to a third party, subject to a put option whereby the transferee can compel the entity to reacquire the asset for €100. The option is considered to be neither deeply in the money nor deeply out of the money. IFRS 9 therefore requires the entity to continue to recognise the asset to the extent of its continuing involvement (Figure 52.1, Box 9 – see also 4.2.3 above), and to continue recording it at the lower of (a) fair value and (b) €100 (the exercise price of the option). Assuming that the transferee pays €106 for the asset, representing €98 fair value of the asset plus €8 time value of the option, the entity would record the accounting entry:

	€	€
1 January 2021		
Cash	106	
Liability		106

A Transferred asset increases in value

Suppose that at 31 December 2021, the option has a time value of €5 and the fair value of the asset is €120. IFRS 9 requires the carrying value of the asset to be restricted to €100 (the exercise price of the option). The liability is measured at the exercise price plus the time value of the option, i.e. €100 + €5 = €105. This has the result that the net of the carrying value of the asset (€100) and the carrying value of the liability (€105) equals the fair value of the option to the transferor (–€5). The fair value of an in the money option is positive for the buyer and negative for the writer.

This gives the accounting entry:

	€	€
31 December 2021		
Asset (€100 – €98)	2	
Liability (€105 – €106)	1	
Gain (profit or loss)		3

The gain of €3 effectively represents the decrease in the time value of the option (a gain from the transferor's perspective) from €8 to €5.

If the option were then to lapse unexercised, with no further change in the fair value of the asset, the entity would record the accounting entry:

	€	€
On lapse of option		
Liability	105	
Asset		100
Gain (profit or loss)		5

The total gain on the transaction of €8 (€3 in Year 1 and €5 on lapse) represents the option premium of €8 (i.e. the difference between the total consideration of €106 and the carrying value of the asset of €98) received at the outset.

B Transferred asset decreases in value

Suppose instead that at 31 December 2021, the option has a time value of €5 but the fair value of the asset is €90. IFRS 9 requires the carrying value of the asset to be measured at its fair value of €90. The liability is measured at the exercise price plus the time value of the option (i.e. to the transferee), i.e. €100 + €5 = €105.

This gives the accounting entry:

	€	€
31 December 2021		
Liability (€105 – €106)	1	
Loss (profit or loss)	7	
Asset (€90 – €98)		8

This has the result that the net of the carrying value of the asset (€90) and the liability (€105), i.e. €(–15) represents the fair value of the option to the transferor (i.e. intrinsic value €(–10) (€100 exercise price versus €90 value of asset) + time value €(–5)). The €7 loss represents the increase in the fair value of the option (a loss to the transferor) from €8 at the outset to €15 at 31 December 2021.

If the transferee were able to, and did, exercise its option at that point, the entity would record the accounting entry:

	€	€
On exercise of option		
Liability	105	
Cash		100
Gain (profit or loss)		5

The overall €2 loss (i.e. €5 gain above and €7 loss during Year 1) represents the net cash of €8 received from the transferee (€108 in at inception less €100 out on exercise) less the €10 fall in fair value of the transferred asset (€100 at inception less €90 at exercise).

5.4.3.C 'Collar' put and call options

Assets may be transferred in a way designed to ensure that the transferee is shielded from excessive losses on the transferred asset but has to pass significant gains on the asset back to the transferor. Such an arrangement is known as a 'collar', on the basis that it allocates a range of potential value movements in the asset to the transferee, with movements outside that range accruing to the transferor. A simple example would be the transfer of an asset subject to a purchased call option (allowing the transferor to reacquire the asset if it increases in value beyond a certain level) and a written put option (allowing the transferee to compel the transferor to reacquire the asset if it falls in value beyond a certain level).

If a collar, in the form of a purchased call and written put option, prevents derecognition (see 3.8.3 and 4 above) of a transferred asset measured at fair value, IFRS 9 requires the entity to continue to measure the asset at fair value. The associated liability is measured at:

- if the call option is in or at the money, the sum of the call exercise price and the fair value of the put option less the time value of the call option; or
- if the call option is out of the money, the sum of the fair value of the asset and the fair value of the put option less the time value of the call option.

The adjustment to the associated liability ensures that the net carrying amount of the asset and the associated liability is the fair value of the options held and written by the entity, as illustrated by Example 52.15 below. *[IFRS 9.B3.2.13(e)]*.

Example 52.15: Asset measured at fair value subject to collar put and call options

An entity has a financial asset, accounted for at fair value, carried at €100. On 1 January 2021 it transfers the asset to a third party, subject to:

- a call option whereby the entity can compel the transferee to sell the asset back to the entity for €120; and
- a put option whereby the transferee can compel the entity to reacquire the asset for €80.

The options are considered to be neither deeply in the money nor deeply out of the money. IFRS 9 therefore requires the entity to continue to recognise the asset to the extent of its continuing involvement (Figure 52.1, Box 9 – see also 4.2.3 above), and to continue recording it at fair value.

At the date of transfer, the time value of the put and call are €1 and €5 respectively. At the date of transfer, the call option is out of the money, so that the associated liability is calculated as the sum of the fair value of the asset and the fair value of the put option less the time value of the call option, i.e. (€100 + €1) – €5 = €96. The net of this and the fair value of the asset (€100) is €4 which is the net fair value of the two options (call €5 less put €1). Assuming that the transaction is undertaken at arm's length, the transferee would pay €96 for the asset and the entity would record the accounting entry:

	€	€
Cash	96	
Liability		96

A Transferred asset increases in value

Suppose that, at 31 December 2021, the fair value of the asset is €140, and the time value of the put and call are €0.5 and €2 respectively. The call option is now in the money, so that IFRS 9 requires the entity to recognise a liability equal to the sum of the call exercise price and fair value of the put option less the time value of the call option, i.e. (€120 + €0.5) – €2 = €118.5. The net of this and the carrying value of the asset (€140) is €21.5 which is the net fair value of the two options (call €22 [time value €2 plus intrinsic value €20] less put €0.5 = €21.5). This gives the accounting entry:

	€	€
31 December 2021		
Asset (€140 – €100)	40.0	
Gain (profit or loss)		17.5
Liability (€118.5 – €96)		22.5

The gain represents the increase in fair value of the call option of €17 (€5 at outset and €22 at 31 December 2021) plus the €0.5 decrease (a gain from the transferor's perspective) in the fair value of the put option (€1 at outset and €0.5 at 31 December 2021).

If the entity were able to, and did, exercise its call option, it would record the entry:

	€	€
Exercise of call option		
Liability	118.5	
Loss (profit or loss)	1.5	
Cash		120.0

The overall gain of €16 on the transaction (€1.5 loss above and €17.5 profit recorded in 2021) represents the increase in fair value of the asset of €40 (€100 at outset, €140 at 31 December 2021) less the net €24 paid to the transferee (€120 paid on exercise of call less €96 received on initial transfer).

B Transferred asset decreases in value

Suppose instead that, at 31 December 2021, the fair value of the asset is €78, and the time value of the put and call are €0.5 and €2 respectively. The call option is now out of the money, so that IFRS 9 requires the entity to recognise a liability equal to the sum of the fair value of the asset and the fair value of the put option (i.e. €2.5 – time value €0.5 plus intrinsic value €2 [€80 exercise price versus €78 fair value of asset]) less the time value of the call option, i.e. (€78 + €2.5) – €2 = €78.5.

The net of this and the carrying value of the asset (€78) is €(–0.5) which is the net fair value of the two options (call €2 less put €2.5 = €(–0.5)). This gives the accounting entry:

	€	€
31 December 2021		
Liability (€78.5 – €96)	17.5	
Loss (profit or loss)	4.5	
Asset (€78 – €100)		22.0

The loss represents the decrease in the fair value of the call option of €3 (€5 at outset and €2 at 31 December 2021) plus the €1.5 increase (a decrease from the transferor's perspective) in the fair value of the put option (€1 at outset and €2.5 at 31 December 2021).

If the transferee were able to, and did, exercise its put option, the entity would record the entry:

	€	€
Exercise of put option		
Liability	78.5	
Loss (profit or loss)	1.5	
Cash		80.0

The overall loss of €6 on the transaction (€1.5 loss above and €4.5 loss recorded in 2021) represents the decrease in fair value of the asset of €22 (€100 at outset, €78 at 31 December 2021) offset by the net €16 received from the transferee (€96 received on initial transfer less €80 paid on exercise of put).

5.4.4 Continuing involvement in part only of a financial asset

IFRS 9 gives the following example of the application of the continuing involvement approach to continuing involvement in part only of a financial asset. *[IFRS 9.B3.2.17].*

Example 52.16: Continuing involvement in part only of a financial asset

An entity has a portfolio of prepayable loans whose coupon and effective interest rate is 10% and whose principal amount and amortised cost is €10 million. It enters into a transaction in which, in return for a payment of €9.115 million, the transferee obtains the right to €9 million of any collections of principal plus 9.5% interest.

The entity retains rights to €1 million of any collections of principal plus interest at 10%, plus the remaining 0.5% ('excess spread') on the remaining €9 million of principal. Collections from prepayments are allocated between the entity and the transferee proportionately in the ratio of 1:9, but any defaults are deducted from the entity's interest of €1 million until that interest is exhausted.

The fair value of the loans at the date of the transaction is €10.1 million and the estimated fair value of the excess spread of 0.5 per cent is €40,000.

The entity determines that it has transferred some significant risks and rewards of ownership (for example, significant prepayment risk) but has also retained some significant risks and rewards of ownership because of its subordinated retained interest (Figure 52.1, Box 7, No) and has retained control (Figure 52.1, Box 8, Yes). It therefore applies the continuing involvement approach (Figure 52.1, Box 9).

The entity analyses the transaction as:

- a retention of a fully proportionate retained interest of €1 million, plus
- the subordination of that retained interest to provide credit enhancement to the transferee for credit losses.

The entity calculates that €9.09 million (90% of €10.1 million) of the consideration received of €9.115 million represents the consideration for a fully proportionate 90% share. The remainder of the consideration (€25,000) received represents consideration received by the entity for subordinating its retained interest to provide credit enhancement to the transferee for credit losses. In addition, the excess spread of 0.5% represents consideration received for the credit enhancement. Accordingly, the total consideration received for the credit enhancement is €65,000 (€25,000 received from transferee plus €40,000 fair value of excess spread).

The entity first calculates the gain or loss on the sale of the 90% share of cash flows. Assuming that separate fair values of the 10% part transferred and the 90% part retained are not available at the date of the transfer, the entity allocates the carrying amount of the asset *pro rata* to the fair values of those parts (see 5.1.1, 5.1.2 and 5.3.5 above). The total fair value of the portfolio is considered to be €10.1 million (see above), and the fair value of the consideration for the part disposed of €9.09 million. The carrying amount of the whole portfolio is €10 million. This implies a carrying amount for the part disposed of €10m × 9.09 / 10.1 = €9 million, and for the part retained €1 million. The gain on the sale of the 90% is therefore €90,000 (€9.09 million – €9 million).

In addition, IFRS 9 requires the entity to recognise the continuing involvement that results from the subordination of its retained interest for credit losses. Accordingly, it recognises an asset of €1 million (the maximum amount of the cash flows it would forfeit under the subordination), and an associated liability of €1.065 million (the maximum amount of the cash flows it would forfeit under the subordination, i.e. €1 million, plus the consideration for the subordination of €65,000). It also recognises an asset for the fair value of the excess spread which forms part of the consideration for the subordination.

This gives rise to the accounting entry:

	€000	€000
Cash	9,115	
Asset for the subordination of the residual interest	1,000	
Excess spread received for subordination	40	
Loan portfolio		9,000
Liability for subordination		1,065
Gain on disposal		90

It is crucial to an understanding of this example that, as a result of the transaction, the original asset (the portfolio of prepayable loans) is being accounted for as two separate assets. Because the cash flows from the portfolio are split in fully proportionate (*pro rata*) shares (see 3.3 above), each of these assets must be considered separately.

The first of these assets, the right to cash flows of €9 million, continues to be recognised only to the extent of the entity's continuing involvement, which in this case is via the credit enhancement. The approach is very similar to continuing involvement through guarantee (see Example 52.11 at 5.4.1 above), except that the liability for subordination includes the maximum cash flow that the entity might not receive from its retained share (i.e. €1 million) rather than, as in Example 52.11, a potential cash outflow (the guarantee amount, which is the maximum amount that the entity could be required to repay). This is aggregated with the fair value of the amount received in respect of the credit enhancement, in order to calculate the full liability for subordination. This is similar to the way in which the fair value of the guarantee is added to the guarantee amount in order to calculate the associated liability. *[IFRS 9.B3.2.13(a)]*.

The second asset is the entity's proportionate retained share of €1 million. It is, seemingly, irrelevant to the accounting analysis in IFRS 9 that this has already been taken into account in calculating the entity's continuing involvement in the remaining €9 million of the portfolio.

The effect is to gross up the statement of financial position with a subordination asset and liability. As IFRS 9 notes, immediately following the transaction, the carrying amount of the asset is €2.04 million (i.e. €1 million part retained plus €1 million subordination asset plus €40,000 excess spread) – in respect of an asset whose fair value is only €1.01 million.

We have some reservations concerning the example above. First, we challenge whether, as a point of principle, it is appropriate to apply the derecognition criteria to part of an asset where the part that is retained provides credit enhancement for the transferee. As discussed more fully at 3.3.1 above, it is possible that IFRS 9 is implicitly drawing a distinction between:

- a guarantee that could result in an outflow of the total resources of the transferor, or a return of consideration for the transfer already received (which would not allow partial derecognition); and
- a guarantee that could result in the transferor losing the right to receive a specific future cash inflow, but not being obliged to make any other payment should that specific future cash inflow not materialise.

Moreover, even in the context of the analysis presented by IFRS 9, we do not understand the basis of the treatment of the excess spread. The example simply asserts that this forms part of the consideration for providing the subordination, although it is not clear that it forms any more or any less of the consideration for the subordination than the interest and principal on the 10% of the portfolio retained.

In our view, a more logical analysis would have been that:
- the entity has disposed of not 90% of the whole portfolio, but 90% of the principal balances and 9.5% interest on that 90%; and
- the consideration for the subordination is still €65,000, on the basis that if:
  - the fair value of the consideration for a fully proportionate share of 90% (i.e. including 10% interest) is €9,090,000; and
  - the fair value of the excess spread of 0.5% interest is €40,000, then

  the fair value of consideration for a fully proportionate share less the excess spread is €9,050,000 (i.e. €9,090,000 less €40,000). This in turn means that the balance of the total consideration of €9,115,000 (i.e. €65,000) relates to the subordination.

In addition, of course, Example 52.16 ignores the possibility that the excess spread is retained by the transferor because it continues to service the portfolio, although this may be an attempt to avoid overcomplicating matters even further.

A further issue is that, if the excess spread is regarded as part of the asset retained, rather than the consideration received, it would seem more appropriate to recognise it on a basis consistent with the accounting treatment of the original transferred asset (typically, amortised cost) rather than at fair value.

5.5 Miscellaneous provisions

IFRS 9 contains a number of accounting provisions generally applicable to transfers of assets, as discussed below.

5.5.1 Offset

IFRS 9 provides that, if a transferred asset continues to be recognised, the entity must not offset:
- the asset with the associated liability; or
- any income arising from the transferred asset with any expense incurred on the associated liability. *[IFRS 9.3.2.22]*.

Whilst IFRS 9 does not say so specifically, this is clearly intended to apply both to assets that continue to be recognised in full and to those that continue to be recognised to the extent of their continuing involvement.

This requirement apparently overrides the offset criteria in IAS 32, *[IAS 32.42]*, as illustrated, for example, by the various situations highlighted in the discussion at 4 and 5.1 to 5.4 above where a transaction required to be net-settled (which would normally be required to be accounted for as such under IAS 32) is accounted for as if it were to be gross-settled.

5.5.2 Collateral

If a transferor provides non-cash collateral (such as debt or equity instruments) to the transferee, the accounting treatment for the collateral by both the transferor and the transferee depends on:

- whether the transferee has the right to sell or repledge the collateral; and
- whether the transferor has defaulted.

If the transferee has the right by contract or custom to sell or repledge a collateral asset, the transferor should reclassify that asset in its statement of financial position (e.g. as a loaned asset, pledged equity instruments or repurchase receivable) separately from other assets.

If the transferee sells collateral pledged to it, it recognises the proceeds from the sale and a liability measured at fair value for its obligation to return the collateral.

If the transferor defaults under the terms of the contract and is no longer entitled to redeem the collateral, it derecognises the collateral, and the transferee either:

- recognises the collateral as its asset initially measured at fair value; or
- if it has already sold the collateral, derecognises its obligation to return the collateral.

In no other circumstances should the transferor derecognise, or the transferee recognise, the collateral as an asset. *[IFRS 9.3.2.23]*.

5.5.3 Rights or obligations over transferred assets that continue to be recognised

Where a transfer of a financial asset does not qualify for derecognition, the transferor may well have contractual rights or obligations related to the transfer, such as options or forward repurchase contracts that are derivatives of a type that would normally be required to be recognised under IFRS 9.

IFRS 9 prohibits separate recognition of such derivatives, if recognition of the derivative together with either the transferred asset or the liability arising from the transfer would result in recognising the same rights or obligations twice.

For example, IFRS 9 notes that a call option retained by the transferor may prevent a transfer of financial assets from being accounted for as a sale (see 4 above). In that case, the call option must not be separately recognised as a derivative asset. *[IFRS 9.B3.2.14]*.

We would expect a similar approach to be taken to contractual rights associated with a non-derivative financial instrument issued to the transferor by the transferee in a transfer that does not qualify for derecognition. This commonly occurs when financial assets are transferred to a securitisation vehicle which issues a subordinated loan to the transferor as a result of which substantially all risks and rewards of the financial assets are retained by the transferor.

5.6 Reassessing derecognition

IFRS 9 states that if an entity determines that, as a result of the transfer, it has transferred substantially all the risks and rewards of ownership of the transferred asset, it does not recognise the transferred asset again in a future period, unless it reacquires the transferred asset in a new transaction. *[IFRS 9.B3.2.6]*. We have noted earlier that there is some ambiguity as to whether this rule in paragraph B3.2.6 is to be read generally as prohibiting any re-recognition of a derecognised asset or specifically as referring only to circumstances where derecognition results from transfer of substantially all the risks and rewards (i.e. it applies only to 'Box 6, Yes' transactions, and not to 'Box 8, No' transactions). Our view, as expressed at 4.2 above, is that the broader interpretation should be applied and the requirement still applies if derecognition occurs for another reason, e.g. loss of control.

The risks and rewards of ownership retained by the entity may change as a result of market changes in such a way that, had the revised conditions existed at inception, they would have prevented derecognition of the asset. However, the original decision to derecognise the asset should not be revisited, unless (in exceptional circumstances) the original assessment was an accounting error within the scope of IAS 8.

5.6.1 Reassessment of consolidation of subsidiaries and SPEs

The effect of IFRS 10, combined with the derecognition provisions of IFRS 9 is that a transaction (commonly, but not exclusively, in a securitisation) may result in derecognition of the financial asset concerned in the seller's own financial statements, but the 'buyer' may be a consolidated SPE, so that the asset is immediately re-recognised in the consolidated financial statements in which the seller is included. However, an entity may derecognise assets if they are transferred to an SPE that is not consolidated because, having considered all of the facts and circumstances, the entity concludes that it does not control the SPE. The assessment as to whether a particular SPE is controlled by the reporting entity is discussed in Chapter 6.

IFRS 10 requires an investor to reassess whether it controls an investee if facts and circumstances indicate that there are changes to any elements of control, including the investor's exposure, or rights, to variable returns from its involvement with the investee (see Chapter 6). [IFRS 10.8].

6 DERECOGNITION – FINANCIAL LIABILITIES

The provisions of IFRS 9 with respect to the derecognition of financial liabilities are generally more straightforward and less subjective than those for the derecognition of financial assets. However, they are also very different from the asset derecognition rules which focus primarily on the economic substance of the transaction. By contrast, the rules for derecognition of liabilities, like the provisions of IAS 32 for the identification of instruments as financial liabilities (see Chapter 47), focus more on legal obligations than on economic substance – or, as the IASB would doubtless argue, they are based on the view that the economic substance of whether an entity has a liability to a third party is ultimately dictated by the legal rights and obligations that exist between them.

IFRS 9 contains provisions relating to:
- the extinguishment of debt (see 6.1 below);
- the substitution or modification of debt by the original lender (see 6.2 below); and
- the calculation of any profit or loss arising on the derecognition of debt (see 6.3 below).

6.1 Extinguishment of debt

IFRS 9 requires an entity to derecognise (i.e. remove from its statement of financial position) a financial liability (or a part of a financial liability – see 6.1.1 below) when, and only when, it is 'extinguished', that is, when the obligation specified in the contract is discharged, cancelled, or expires. *[IFRS 9.3.3.1]*. This will be achieved when the debtor either:

- discharges the liability (or part of it) by paying the creditor, normally with cash, other financial assets, goods or services; or
- is legally released from primary responsibility for the liability (or part of it) either by process of law or by the creditor. *[IFRS 9.B3.3.1]*. Extinguishment of liabilities by legal release is discussed further at 6.1.2 below.

If the issuer of a debt instrument repurchases the instrument, the debt is extinguished even if the issuer is a market maker in that instrument, or otherwise intends to resell or reissue it in the near term. *[IFRS 9.B3.3.2]*. IFRS 9 focuses only on whether the entity has a legal obligation to reissue the debt, not on whether there is a commercial imperative for it to do so.

6.1.1 What constitutes 'part' of a liability?

The requirements of IFRS 9 for the derecognition of liabilities apply to all or 'part' of a financial liability. It is not entirely clear what is meant by 'part' of a liability in this context. The rules, and the examples, in IFRS 9 seem to be drafted in the context of transactions that settle all remaining cash flows (i.e. interest and principal) of a proportion of a liability, such as the repayment of £25 million of a £100 million loan, together with any related interest payments.

However, these provisions are presumably also intended to apply in situations where an entity prepays the interest only (or a proportion of future interest payments) or the principal only (or a proportion of future principal payments) on a loan.

6.1.2 Legal release by creditor

A liability can be derecognised by a debtor if the creditor legally releases the debtor from the liability. It is clear that IFRS 9 regards legal release as crucial, with the effect that very similar (if not identical) situations may lead to different results purely because of the legal form.

For example, IFRS 9 provides that:

- where a debtor is legally released from a liability, derecognition is not precluded by the fact that the debtor has given a guarantee in respect of the liability; *[IFRS 9.B3.3.1(b)]* but
- if a debtor pays a third party to assume an obligation and notifies its creditor that the third party has assumed the debt obligation, the debtor derecognises the debt obligation if, and only if, the creditor legally releases the debtor from its obligations. *[IFRS 9.B3.3.4]*.

The effect of these requirements is shown by Example 52.17.

Example 52.17:   Transfer of debt obligations with and without legal release
Scenario 1
Entity A issues bonds that have a carrying amount and fair value of $1,000,000. A pays $1,000,000 to Entity B for B to assume responsibility for paying interest and principal on the bonds to the bondholders. The bondholders are informed that B has assumed responsibility for the debt. However, A is not legally released from the obligation to pay interest and principal by the bondholders. Accordingly, if B does not make payments when due, the bondholders may seek payment from A.

Scenario 2
Entity A issues bonds that have a carrying amount and fair value of $1,000,000. A pays $1,000,000 to Entity B for B to assume responsibility for paying interest and principal on the bonds to the bondholders. The bondholders are informed that B has assumed responsibility for the debt and legally release A from any further obligation under the debt. However, A enters into a guarantee arrangement whereby, if B does not make payments when due, the bondholders may seek payment from A.

It is clear, in our view, that in either scenario above the bondholders are in the same economic and legal position – they will receive payments from B and, if B defaults, they will have recourse to A.

However, IFRS 9 gives rise to the, in our view, anomalous result that:

- Scenario 1 is accounted for by the continuing recognition of the debt because no legal release has been obtained; but
- Scenario 2 is accounted for by derecognition of the debt, and recognition of the guarantee, notwithstanding that the effect of the guarantee is to put A back in the same position as if it had not been released from its obligations under the original bond.

IFRS 9 also clarifies that, if a debtor:

- transfers its obligations under a debt to a third party and obtains legal release from its obligations by the creditor; but
- undertakes to make payments to the third party so as to enable it to meet its obligations to the creditor,

it should derecognise the original debt, but recognise a new debt obligation to the third party. *[IFRS 9.B3.3.4]*.

Legal release may also be achieved through the novation of a contract to an intermediary counterparty. For example, a derivative between a reporting entity and a bank may be novated to a central counterparty (CCP). In these circumstances, the IASB explains that the novation to the CCP releases the bank from the responsibility to make payments to the reporting entity. Consequently, the original derivative meets the derecognition criteria for a financial liability and a new derivative with the CCP is recognised. *[IFRS 9.BC6.335]*. However, for hedge accounting purposes only, it is sometimes possible in these circumstances to treat the new derivative as a continuation of the original (see Chapter 53 at 8.3.5).

6.1.3 'In-substance defeasance' arrangements

Entities sometimes enter into so-called 'in-substance defeasance' arrangements in respect of financial liabilities. These typically involve a lump sum payment to a third party (other than the creditor) such as a trust, which then invests the funds in (typically) very low-risk assets to which the entity has no, or very limited, rights of access. These assets are then applied to discharge all the remaining interest and principal payments on the financial liabilities that are purported to have been defeased. It is sometimes argued that the risk-free nature of the assets, and the entity's lack of access to them, means that the entity is in substance in no different position than if it had actually repaid the original financial liability.

IFRS 9 regards such arrangements as not giving rise to derecognition of the original liability in the absence of legal release by the creditor. *[IFRS 9.B3.3.3]*.

6.1.4 Extinguishment in exchange for transfer of assets not meeting the derecognition criteria

IFRS 9 notes that in some cases legal release may be achieved by transferring assets to the creditor which do not meet the criteria for derecognition (see 3 above). In such a case, the debtor will derecognise the liability from which it has been released, but recognise a new liability relating to the transferred assets that may be equal to the derecognised liability. *[IFRS 9.B3.3.5]*. It is not entirely clear what is envisaged here, but it may be some such scenario as the following.

Example 52.18: Extinguishment of debt in exchange for transfer of assets not meeting derecognition criteria

An entity has a bank loan of €1 million. The bank agrees to accept in full payment of the loan the transfer to it by the entity of a portfolio of corporate bonds with a market value of €1 million. The entity and the bank then enter into a put and call option over the bonds, the effect of which will be that the entity will repurchase the bonds in three years' time at a price that gives the bank a lender's return on €1 million. As discussed further at 4.2.8 above, this would have the effect that the entity is unable to derecognise the bonds.

Under the provisions of IFRS 9, the entity would be able to derecognise the original bank loan, as it has been legally released from it. The provisions under discussion here have the overall result that a loan effectively continues to be recognised. Strictly, however, the analysis is that the original loan has been derecognised and a new one recognised. In effect the accounting is representing that the entity has repaid the original loan and replaced it with a new one secured on a bond portfolio.

However, as the new loan is required to be initially recognised at fair value whereas the old loan may well have been recognised at amortised cost, there may well be a gain or loss to record as the result of the different measurement bases being used – see 6.2 and 6.3 below.

6.2 Exchange or modification of debt by original lender

It is common for an entity, particularly but not necessarily when in financial difficulties, to approach its major creditors for a restructuring of its debt commitments – for example, an agreement to postpone the repayment of principal in exchange for higher interest payments in the meantime, or to roll up interest into a single 'bullet' payment of interest and principal at the end of the term. Such changes to the terms of debt can be effected in a number of ways, in particular:

- a notional repayment of the original loan followed by an immediate re-lending of all or part of the proceeds of the notional repayment as a new loan ('exchange'); or
- legal amendment of the original loan agreement ('modification').

The accounting issue raised by such transactions is essentially whether there is, in fact, anything to account for. For example, if an entity owes £100 million at floating rate interest and negotiates with its bankers to change the interest to a fixed coupon of 7%, should the accounting treatment reflect the fact that:

(a) the entity still owes £100 million to the same lender, and so is in the same position as before; or

(b) the modification of the interest profile has altered the net present value of the total obligations under the loan?

When a loan is repaid at maturity and a new loan is taken out with the same lender, this would not be a modification or exchange as the original loan was not modified or exchanged, it was settled in accordance with the original contractual terms. However, sometimes an existing loan will be replaced by a new one with the same lender shortly before its maturity date. In these circumstances judgement will be required to assess whether to regard the original loan as being modified or exchanged or whether it should be regarded as being repaid and replaced by a new loan on market terms. This judgement should involve consideration of how close to the maturity date of the original loan the transaction took place, compared to the term of the original loan. For example, if the transaction took place three months before the maturity of a 10-year loan, it is more likely to be considered a repayment and replacement than if the transaction took place six months before the maturity of a one-year loan.

IFRS 9 requires an exchange between an existing borrower and lender of debt instruments with 'substantially different' terms to be accounted for as an extinguishment of the original financial liability and the recognition of a new financial liability. Similarly, a substantial modification of the terms of an existing financial liability, or a part of it, (whether or not due to the financial difficulty of the debtor) should be accounted for as an extinguishment of the original financial liability and the recognition of a new financial liability. *[IFRS 9.3.3.2]*. The determination of whether an exchange or modification is substantially different is discussed further at 6.2.1 below.

In August 2020 the IASB issued amendments to IFRS 9 to provide guidance on how to account for modifications of a financial liability due to the reform of interbank offered rates and this is discussed further at 6.2.2 below.

Large borrowing arrangements may be transacted with multiple lenders in loan syndications and the issues arising from such arrangements are discussed further at 6.2.3 below.

Sometimes a borrower may effect an exchange of debt through an intermediary and this is discussed further at 6.2.4 below.

The accounting consequences for an exchange or a modification that results in extinguishment and one that does not lead to extinguishment are discussed in further detail at 6.2.5 to 6.2.7 below.

6.2.1 When is an exchange or modification of debt 'substantially' different?

IFRS 9 regards the terms of exchanged or modified debt as 'substantially different' if the net present value of the cash flows under the new terms (including any fees paid net of any fees received) discounted at the original effective interest rate is at least 10% different from the discounted present value of the remaining cash flows of the original debt instrument. *[IFRS 9.B3.3.6]*. This comparison is commonly referred to as 'the 10% test'.

Whilst IFRS 9 does not say so explicitly, it seems clear that the discounted present value of the remaining cash flows of the original debt instrument used in the 10% test must also be determined using the original effective interest rate, so that there is a 'like for like' comparison. This amount should also represent the amortised cost of the liability prior to modification.

Also, it was not clear originally from the standard whether the cash flows under the new terms should include only fees payable to the lender or whether they should also include other fees and costs that would be considered transaction costs, such as amounts payable to the entity's legal advisers. Read literally the standard suggests only fees should be included, but as the accounting treatment for fees and costs incurred on a modification are identical, some have argued that both should be included in the test.

However, in May 2020 the IASB issued *Annual Improvements to IFRS Standards 2018-2020*, which included amendments to IFRS 9 to clarify that only fees paid or received between the borrower and lender should be included in the 10% test. The IASB believes that the clarification aligns with the objective of the test, which is to quantitatively assess the significance of any difference between the old and new contractual terms on the basis of the changes in the contractual cash flows between the borrower and lender. The amendments should be adopted prospectively and have an effective date of periods commencing 1 January 2022, although early adoption is permitted with the appropriate disclosures. *[IFRS 9(2022).7.1.9, 7.2.35, B3.3.6]*.

Under certain circumstances extinguishment accounting for an exchange or modification of a liability may still be appropriate, even where the net present value of the cash flows under the new terms is less than 10% different from the discounted present value of the remaining cash flows of the original debt instrument. Indeed, there may be situations where the modification of the debt is so fundamental that immediate derecognition is appropriate whether or not the 10% test is satisfied. The following are examples of situations where derecognition of the original instrument could be required:

- An entity has issued a 'plain vanilla' debt instrument and restructures the debt to include an embedded equity instrument.
- An entity has issued a 5% euro-denominated debt instrument and restructures the instrument to an 18% Turkish lire-denominated debt instrument.

The present value of the cash flows of the restructured debts, discounted at the original effective interest rate, may not be significantly different from the discounted present value of the remaining cash flows of the original financial liability. However, even if the 10% test is not satisfied, the introduction of the equity-linked feature or a change in currency (unless the original and new currencies are pegged) could significantly alter the future economic risk exposure of the instrument. In these circumstances the modification of terms should, in our view, be regarded as representing a substantial change which would lead to derecognition of the original liability.

There are other modifications to the contractual terms of financial liabilities which may be considered substantial and therefore result in extinguishment accounting, for example a change in the basis of interest calculation (such as moving from fixed to floating rate) or a significant extension in the term of the debt. The assessment of such modifications will require judgement and they should be considered along with other modifications made at the same time before concluding whether the modifications should be considered substantial.

6.2.2 Interbank Offered Rate (IBOR) Reform

Following recommendations from the Financial Stability Board there are various initiatives ongoing to replace current benchmark interest rates, such as interbank offered rates like LIBOR, with nearly risk-free rates. In view of these initiatives and the resulting uncertainty around the long-term viability of IBORs, the IASB added a two-stage project to its agenda. The first stage was to consider financial reporting issues that may arise prior to the replacement of IBORs; and the second stage was to consider issues arising from changes to contractual cash flows required by the replacement of IBORs. IBOR reform and the IASB's project are discussed in more detail in Chapter 53 at 9.

One issue considered in the second stage is how the modification of a floating rate financial liability from an instrument with an IBOR benchmark rate, to an instrument with a rate of interest based on a new risk-free rate, should be accounted for under IFRS 9, particularly whether such modification would lead to the derecognition of the financial liability.

The IASB amended IFRS 9 in August 2020 to include a practical expedient whereby contractual changes to cash flows that are directly required by IBOR reform are treated as changes to a floating interest rate, equivalent to a movement in a market rate of interest. Therefore such a modification would not result in derecognition of the financial liability. Inherent in the use of this practical expedient is the requirement that the transition from an IBOR benchmark rate to a risk-free rate takes place on an economically equivalent basis. *[IFRS 9.5.4.5, 5.4.7]*.

In applying this practical expedient, an entity is required to first identify and account for modifications to the financial liability which relate directly to IBOR reform, by updating the EIR without adjusting the carrying amount of the financial liability. The amendments include examples of the type of modifications required by IBOR reform, to which the practical expedient is limited, as follows:

- The replacement of an existing interest rate with an alternative benchmark rate or effecting such a reform of an interest rate benchmark by changing the method used to calculate the interest rate benchmark;
- The addition of a fixed spread to compensate for a basis difference between an existing interest rate benchmark and an alternative benchmark rate;
- Changes to the reset period, reset dates, or the number of days between coupon payment dates that are necessary to effect the reform of an interest rate benchmark; and
- The addition of a fall-back provision to the contractual terms of a financial liability to enable any of the changes described above to be made. *[IFRS 9.5.4.8, 5.4.9]*.

Any other modifications to the financial liability that may be made at the same time, such as a change in the credit spread or maturity date, are assessed. If they are not substantial (see 6.2.1 above), the updated EIR should be used to recalculate the carrying amount of the financial liability, with any modification gain or loss recognised in profit or loss. *[IFRS 9.5.4.9]*.

The amendments have an effective date of periods commencing 1 January 2021, although early adoption is permitted with disclosure of that fact. *[IFRS 9.7.1.9]*. The amendments should be adopted retrospectively except that there is no requirement to restate prior period figures and such figures may only be restated if this is possible without the use of hindsight. *[IFRS 9.7.2.43, 7.2.46]*.

6.2.3 Loan syndications

Large borrowing arrangements for a single borrower are often funded by multiple lenders in a process referred to as 'loan syndication'. In such circumstances the borrower must determine whether this arrangement represents a single loan with a single lender (often referred to as the 'lead lender') who enters into a sub-participation arrangement with the other lenders, or whether the arrangement represents multiple loans with multiple lenders. This determination will affect how changes to the arrangement should be considered by the borrower to determine whether they represent a modification of the borrower's financial liability or an extinguishment of the original financial liability and the recognition of a new financial liability.

Where the borrower determines that it has a single loan agreement with a single lead lender, changes to this agreement must be considered by the borrower on an aggregate basis to determine whether the changes represent a modification or an extinguishment. Meanwhile, changes in the composition of the syndicate may not be relevant to the borrower, as long as the lead lender stays the same.

Where the borrower determines that it has multiple loans with multiple lenders, the borrower would consider changes to the borrowing arrangements with each lender separately. If one lender is replaced by a different lender, then the borrower must consider whether the replacement represents an extinguishment of the original loan and its replacement by another.

The assessment will require an analysis of the legal terms of the contract. Factors that need to be considered, individually or in combination, in assessing whether there is a single loan or multiple loans include the following:

- the borrower negotiates loan terms only with the lead lender or with individual lenders within the syndicate;
- the loan terms are identical or differ, depending on the lender;
- loan repayments are automatically allocated among lenders on a *pro rata* basis, or the borrower may be able to selectively repay amounts to specific lenders within the syndicate;
- the borrower can only renegotiate with the lead lender or may selectively renegotiate loans with individual lenders or subsets of lenders within the syndicate; and
- members of the syndicate may change without the permission of the borrower or such a change may require an amendment to the loan agreement.

6.2.4 Exchange of debt through an intermediary

Where a borrower repurchases a debt from an existing lender and immediately issues new debt to the same lender this is normally considered an exchange and the derecognition assessment will depend on whether the terms of the new and original debt are substantially different (see 6.2 above). However, if a borrower repurchases debt from one or more existing lenders and issues new debt to new (i.e. different) lenders, then the existing debt is derecognised.

Rather than approach the existing lenders directly a borrower may effect such an exchange through an intermediary (e.g. a bank). In such situations the intermediary might purchase existing debt held by existing lenders, and exchange it for new debt with the borrower, which is then issued to new lenders shortly afterwards. In these situations, in our view, the borrower must determine whether the intermediary is acting as a principal (i.e. as lender) or is acting as an agent of the borrower.

If the intermediary is acting as a principal, then the transaction between the issuer and the intermediary is considered a debt exchange between an existing borrower and existing lender and derecognition is assessed based on whether the terms are substantially different. If the terms are not substantially different the debt is not derecognised.

If the intermediary is acting as an agent, the derecognition is assessed assuming the intermediary does not exist. In other words the borrower will be seen as repurchasing debt from existing lenders (resulting in its derecognition) and issuing new debt to new lenders.

The determination of whether the intermediary is acting as a principal or an agent will depend on the terms of the arrangements and the extent to which the intermediary is exposed to any risks. For example, where the intermediary risks its own funds to acquire the existing debt, is responsible for placing the new debt with new investors and is required to hold any debt that it is unable to sell on, it is more likely to be acting as a principal. Alternatively, if the intermediary does not risk its own funds to any significant degree, for example by agreeing to buy only the debt that it is able to sell on, it is more likely to be acting as an agent.

6.2.5 Costs and fees

An entity will almost always be required to pay fees to the lender and incur costs (such as legal expenses) on an exchange or modification of a financial liability.

If an exchange of debt instruments or modification of terms is accounted for as an extinguishment of the original debt and the recognition of new debt, IFRS 9 requires any costs or fees incurred to be recognised as part of the gain or loss on the extinguishment (see 6.3 below). *[IFRS 9(2022).B3.3.6A]*.

However, notwithstanding a literal reading of IFRS 9, there may be very limited circumstances when fees or costs associated with the issue of new debt do not need to be included in the gain or loss on extinguishment. Where it is obvious that the fees have not been incurred as part of the modification or exchange and instead are third party costs, which are clearly incremental to the issue of new debt for example payments of taxes or listing fees on the issue of new debt, then an entity may choose to adopt a policy whereby such costs are deducted from the carrying value of the new debt and amortised over its term, as long as the new debt is not classified as held at fair value through profit or loss. Examples of such costs will be limited as they must be clearly separate from costs related to the modification or exchange, and therefore will not include costs allocated between the modification or exchange and the new debt.

Where the exchange or modification is not accounted for as an extinguishment, any costs or fees incurred adjust the carrying amount of the liability and are amortised over the remaining term of the modified liability. *[IFRS 9.B3.3.6]*. IFRS 9 does not specify a particular method for amortising such costs and fees. In our view, applying the effective interest method or another approach that approximates this such as a straight-line method would be appropriate. This is illustrated in the following example.

Example 52.19: Fees and costs incurred on modification of debt not treated as extinguishment

On 1 January 2019 an entity borrowed $100 million on, at that time, arm's length market terms, so that interest of 6% was to be paid annually in arrears and the loan repaid in full on 31 December 2023. Transaction costs of $4 million were incurred. Assuming that the loan had run to term, the entity would have recorded the following amounts using the effective interest method. The loan is originally recorded at the issue proceeds of $100 million less transaction costs of $4 million, and the effective interest rate of 6.975% is derived by a computer program or trial and error. For a more detailed discussion of the effective interest method, see Chapter 50 at 3.

Year	Liability b/f $m	Interest at 6.975% $m	Cash paid $m	Liability c/f $m
1.1.2019	96.00			96.00
2019	96.00	6.70	(6.00)	96.70
2020	96.70	6.74	(6.00)	97.44
2021	97.44	6.80	(6.00)	98.24
2022	98.24	6.85	(6.00)	99.09
2023	99.09	6.91	(106.00)	–

During the latter part of 2020 the entity considers expanding its business in a way that would crystallise the lender's right to demand immediate repayment of the loan because such an action is not permitted under the detailed terms of the loan. Therefore the entity approaches the lender with a view to amending those terms to permit the planned expansion, but without changing the cash flows on the loan. On 1 January 2021, the lender agrees to amend the terms in return for which it charges the entity a fee of $450,000. The entity also incurs directly attributable legal costs of $50,000, bringing the total fees and costs incurred to $500,000.

It can be shown that the net present value of the cash flows under the new terms, including the $0.45 million of fees paid (but excluding the $0.05 million of legal costs in line with the amendments to IFRS 9 within the *Annual Improvements to IFRS Standards 2018-2020* noted at 6.2.1 above), discounted at the original effective interest rate is $97.89 million. This compares to the carrying amount of $97.44 million and because the remaining cash flows have not changed, the difference between the two simply represents the fees paid. This difference is just 0.46% of the original carrying amount, significantly less than 10%. The entity does not consider the changes to the detailed terms of the loan to be substantial and therefore concludes the modification should not result in the extinguishment of the liability.

Accordingly the carrying amount of the liability is adjusted by the $500,000 fees and costs incurred so that the revised carrying amount is $96.94 million ($97.44 million less $0.50 million). In order to amortise this adjustment over the remaining term of the loan, the entity could reset the effective interest rate of the loan, in this case to 7.169%, so that it is amortised in accordance with the effective interest method as follows.

Year	Liability b/f $m	Interest at 7.169% $m	Cash paid $m	Liability c/f $m
1.1.2021	96.94			96.94
2021	96.94	6.95	(6.00)	97.89
2022	97.89	7.02	(6.00)	98.91
2023	98.91	7.09	(106.00)	–

Another way would be to view the liability as comprising two components: the unadjusted carrying amount of $97.44 million, to which the effective interest method would be applied using the original effective interest rate of 6.975%; and the adjustment of $500,000 which would be amortised on some other basis, such as straight line. This would give rise to substantially the same interest expense in each period, detailed calculations showing a slight change in 2021 and 2023 to $6.96 million and $7.08 million respectively.

6.2.6 Modification gains and losses

In Example 52.19 above, the remaining cash flows on the loan remained the same after the modification, but in practice they will often change. For example, in the situation set out in Example 52.19, the lender might have agreed to charge additional interest of, say, $170,000 per year for the remaining three year term of the loan instead of the $450,000 fee at the time of the modification. Detailed calculations show an almost identical outcome when applying the 10% test to these revised facts, with the net present value of the cash flows under revised terms being $97.89 million excluding the $50,000 of costs, a difference of $0.45 million or 0.46%. Again it would be concluded that the modification does not result in derecognition of the liability.

IFRS 9 requires modifications of financial liabilities that do not result in derecognition to be accounted for similarly to modifications of financial assets (see Chapter 50 at 3.8.1). The amortised cost of the financial liability should be recalculated by computing the present value of estimated future contractual cash flows that are discounted at the financial instrument's original EIR. Any consequent adjustment should be recognised immediately in profit or loss. *[IFRS 9.BC4.252, BC4.253].*

In the situation discussed above, this would result in the entity recognising a modification loss of $0.45 million, being the net present value of the additional interest payable of $170,000 per annum, discounted at the original effective interest rate of 6.975%. This might seem counter-intuitive to some when compared to the original facts in Example 52.19. The only difference between the two scenarios is that in the first the borrower makes an immediate cash payment to the lender of $0.45 million in the form of a fee, whereas in the second it makes payments to the lender over the next three years (in the form of additional interest) which have a net present value of $0.45 million.

This example highlights that the accounting treatment for costs and fees paid to the lender is different from that for changes to future cash flows paid to the lender. The former are amortised over the remaining term of the modified liability, the effects of the latter being recognised immediately in profit or loss. Therefore, in some situations, it will be necessary to consider whether the substance of a payment is different from its form, e.g. it may be more appropriate to account for a payment that is described as a fee as if it were a modification to the contractual cash flows, for example when the payment represents compensation for the lender's loss of future interest.

6.2.7 Illustrative examples

Examples 52.20 and 52.21 below illustrate some more complex modifications of debt.

Example 52.20: Modification of debt not treated as extinguishment

On 1 January 2016 an entity borrowed £100 million on, at that time, arm's length market terms, so that interest of 7% was to be paid annually in arrears and the loan repaid in full on 31 December 2025. Transaction costs of £5 million were incurred. Assuming that the loan had run to term, the entity would have recorded the following amounts using the effective interest method. The loan is originally recorded at the issue proceeds of £100 million less transaction costs of £5 million, and the effective interest rate is 7.736%.

Year	Liability b/f £m	Interest at 7.736% £m	Cash paid £m	Liability c/f £m
1.1.2016	95.00			95.00
2016	95.00	7.35	(7.00)	95.35
2017	95.35	7.38	(7.00)	95.73
2018	95.73	7.40	(7.00)	96.13
2019	96.13	7.44	(7.00)	96.57
2020	96.57	7.47	(7.00)	97.04
2021	97.04	7.51	(7.00)	97.55
2022	97.55	7.55	(7.00)	98.10
2023	98.10	7.59	(7.00)	98.69
2024	98.69	7.63	(7.00)	99.32
2025	99.32	7.68	(107.00)	–

During 2020 the entity is in financial difficulties and approaches the lender for a modification of the terms of the loan. These are agreed on 1 January 2021, as follows. No cash interest will be paid in 2021 or 2022, although a fee of £2 million must be paid to the lender immediately. From 2023 onwards interest of 9% will be paid annually in arrears and the term of the loan will be extended for two years until 31 December 2027. Legal fees and other costs incurred are not material.

The entity is required to compute the present value of the new arrangement using the original effective interest rate of 7.736%. This gives a net present value for the modified debt of £92.53 million, calculated as follows:

Year	Cash flow	£m	Discount factor	£m
1.1.2021	Fee	2.00	1	2.00
2023	Interest	9.00	$1/1.07736^3$	7.20
2024	Interest	9.00	$1/1.07736^4$	6.68
2025	Interest	9.00	$1/1.07736^5$	6.20
2026	Interest	9.00	$1/1.07736^6$	5.75
2027	Interest and principal	109.00	$1/1.07736^7$	64.70
			Total	92.53

This represents 95.4% of the current carrying value of the debt as at the end of 2020 of £97.04 million, so that the net present value of the modified loan (discounted at the effective interest rate of the original loan) is 4.6% different from that of the original loan. This is less than 10%, so that the modification is not automatically required to be treated as an extinguishment under IFRS 9.

As noted at 6.2.6 above, an entity recognises an immediate gain or loss when the cash flows on a loan are modified and the liability is not derecognised. In this situation this would result in the recognition of a gain of £6.51 million (£97.04 million current carrying value less £90.53 million recalculated net present value, excluding the fees, which as set out at 6.2.5 above adjust the carrying amount of the liability and are amortised over its remaining term). Allocating the fee based upon the effective interest method would result in an increase in the effective interest rate to 8.1213%.

The adjusted carrying amount of the liability of £88.53 million (£90.53 million net present value of cash flows on the borrowing less £2 million fee) would be accreted using the effective interest method as follows:

Year	Liability b/f £m	Interest at 8.1213% £m	Cash paid £m	Liability c/f £m
2021	88.53	7.19	–	95.72
2022	95.72	7.77	–	103.49
2023	103.49	8.41	(9.00)	102.90
2024	102.90	8.36	(9.00)	102.26
2025	102.26	8.30	(9.00)	101.56
2026	101.56	8.25	(9.00)	100.81
2027	100.81	8.19	(109.00)	–

Example 52.21: Modification of debt treated as extinguishment

Assume the same facts as in Example 52.20 above, except that on 1 January 2021 the entity comes to an arrangement with the lender to modify the terms of the loan as follows.

No cash interest will be paid in 2021 or 2022, although a fee of £2 million must be paid to the lender immediately. From 2023 onwards interest of 12.5% will be paid annually in arrears, and the term of the loan will be extended for three years until 31 December 2028. Legal fees and other costs incurred are not material.

As in Example 52.20 above, the entity is required to compute the net present value of the new arrangement using the original effective interest rate of 7.736%. This gives a net present value for the modified debt of £107.3 million calculated as follows.

Year	Cash flow	£m	Discount factor	£m
1.1.2021	Fee	2.00	1	2.00
2023	Interest	12.50	$1/1.07736^3$	10.00
2024	Interest	12.50	$1/1.07736^4$	9.28
2025	Interest	12.50	$1/1.07736^5$	8.61
2026	Interest	12.50	$1/1.07736^6$	7.99
2027	Interest	12.50	$1/1.07736^7$	7.42
2028	Interest and principal	112.50	$1/1.07736^8$	61.98
			Total	107.28

This represents 110.6% of the current carrying value of the debt as at the end of 2020 of £97.04 million, so that the net present value of the modified loan (discounted at the effective interest rate of the original loan) is 10.6% different from that of the original loan. This is greater than 10%, so the modification is required to be treated as an extinguishment.

This will involve derecognising the existing liability and recognising a new liability. The issue is then at what amount the new liability should be recognised. It is not the £107.28 million above, since this includes the fee of £2 million, which is required to be treated as integral to the cash flows of the modified loan for the purposes of comparing it with the original loan, but is then required to be expensed immediately if the test identifies an extinguishment. Moreover, as the accounting treatment is intended to represent the derecognition of an existing liability and the recognition of a new one, the modified loan must – in accordance with the initial measurement provisions of IFRS 9 (see Chapter 49) – be recognised at fair value and amortised using its own effective interest rate, not that applicable to the original loan.

The difficulty is obviously in determining the fair value of the modified loan. If the loan was in the form of a quoted bond, a market value might be available. Another possible approach might be to discount the cash flows of the modified loan at the interest rate at which the entity could have issued a new loan on similar terms to the modified loan. However, where (as may well be the case) the modification is being undertaken because the entity is in serious financial difficulty, it might be that no lender would be prepared to advance new finance, so that there is no readily available 'notional' borrowing rate. Nevertheless, IFRS 9 contains no exemption from making an estimate of the fair value of the modified loan, and it would not be appropriate to simply assume that the nominal value of the new loan is the same as its fair value.

If the view were taken that the fair value of the modified loan was £98 million, the accounting treatment for the modification would be (see also 6.3 below):

	£m	£m
Original loan	97.04	
Loss on extinguishment of debt (income statement)	2.96	
Modified loan		98.00
Cash (fee)		2.00

In this particular case, this has the result that the actual gain or loss recognised is actually somewhat smaller than the difference calculated between the net present value of the original and modified loan that led to the requirement to recognise the gain or loss in the first place. This differential will obviously be reflected in higher interest costs as the transaction matures. If the borrower was in financial difficulties, it is possible for the fair value of the modified loan to be significantly below its principal amount, which could give rise to a large profit on modification followed by very high interest charges over the remaining term.

6.2.8 Settlement of financial liability with issue of new equity instrument

A related area is the accounting treatment to be adopted where an entity issues non-convertible debt, but subsequently enters into an agreement with the debt-holder to discharge the liability under the debt in full or in part for an issue of equity instruments. This most often occurs when the entity is in financial difficulties. This topic is now dealt with in IFRIC 19 – *Extinguishing Financial Liabilities with Equity Instruments* – which is discussed in Chapter 47 at 7.

6.3 Gains and losses on extinguishment of debt

When a financial liability (or part of a liability) is extinguished or transferred to another party, IFRS 9 requires the difference between the carrying amount of the transferred financial liability (or part of a liability) and the consideration paid, including any non-cash assets transferred or liabilities assumed, to be recognised in profit or loss. *[IFRS 9.3.3.3]*.

If an entity repurchases only a part of a financial liability, it calculates the carrying value of the part disposed of (and hence the gain or loss on disposal) by allocating the previous carrying amount of the financial liability between the part that continues to be recognised and the part that is derecognised based on the relative fair values of those parts on the date of the repurchase. *[IFRS 9.3.3.4]*. In other words, the carrying amount of the liability is not simply reduced by consideration received.

This is illustrated in Example 52.22 below.

Example 52.22: Partial derecognition of debt

On 1 January 2018 an entity issues 500 million €1 10-year bonds which are traded in the capital markets. Issue costs of €15 million were incurred and the carrying value of the bonds at 31 December 2021 is €490 million. On 31 December 2021 the entity makes a market purchase of 120 million bonds at their then current market price of €0.97. The entity records the following accounting entry:

	€m	€m
Bonds (120 / 500 × €490m)	117.6	
Cash (120m × €0.97)		116.4
Gain on repurchase of debt		1.2

In some cases a creditor may release a debtor from its present obligation to make payments, but the debtor assumes an obligation to pay if the party assuming primary responsibility defaults. In such a case, IFRS 9 requires the debtor to recognise:

(a) a new liability based on the fair value for the obligation for the guarantee; and

(b) a gain or loss based on the difference between:
  (i) any proceeds; and
  (ii) the carrying amount of the original liability (including any related unamortised costs) less the fair value of the new liability. *[IFRS 9.B3.3.7]*.

6.4 Derivatives that can be financial assets or financial liabilities

A derivative which involves two-way payments between parties, i.e. the payments are or could be from and to each of the parties, should be derecognised only when it meets both the derecognition criteria for a financial asset and the derecognition criteria for a financial liability. *[IFRS 9.BC6.333]*. In practice, any transfer of such derivatives is likely to require the consent of the counterparty to the entity's legal release from its obligations under the contract, and the possible payment of a fee to compensate the counterparty for the difference between the creditworthiness of the entity and that of the transferee. Such procedures are much closer to those envisaged in the derecognition rules for financial liabilities than those implicit in the derecognition rules for financial assets.

On many occasions, the IASB has made it clear that a non-optional derivative that could be either an asset or liability can be derecognised only if the derecognition criteria for both assets and liabilities are satisfied (see 3.3.2 above).

6.5 Supply-chain finance

An increasingly common type of arrangement involves the provision of finance linked to the supply of goods or services. These arrangements, which can vary significantly in both form and substance, are often referred to as 'supply-chain finance', but other terms are also used including 'supplier finance', 'reverse factoring' and 'structured payable transactions'. Whilst the terms of such arrangements can vary widely, they typically contain a number of the following features:

- they involve a purchaser of goods and/or services, a group of its suppliers and a financial intermediary;
- the purchaser is often a large, creditworthy entity that uses a number of suppliers, many of which will have a higher credit risk than the purchaser;
- the arrangement is nearly always initiated by the purchaser rather than the supplier;
- the arrangements operate continuously for all future purchases until the arrangement is cancelled;
- they are often put in place in connection with the purchaser attempting to secure extended payment terms from its suppliers;
- the intermediary/service provider is often a financial institution who will normally make available IT systems to facilitate the arrangement;
- the intermediary makes available to suppliers an optional invoice discounting or factoring facility for invoices accepted or agreed by the purchaser, often on terms that enable the supplier to derecognise the receivable;
- the purchaser will commit to pay the invoice on the due date, sometimes by using a payment facility operated by the intermediary;
- interest terms will be included in the supply agreement to protect the intermediary in the event of the purchaser defaulting or missing the payment date;
- those interest terms will be similar to ones included in most supply agreements, although they are rarely enforced by suppliers;
- the credit risk the intermediary is taking on is that of the purchaser, but it may be able to charge a higher financing cost to the supplier (in the form of the discount) than it would if lending to the supplier directly; and
- it can be difficult to determine the overall financing costs of the arrangement, and who bears those costs, especially if the supply involves items for which the pricing is subjective/unobservable.

The primary accounting concern with these types of arrangement is whether the purchaser should present the resulting financial liability as debt or as a trade or similar payable, and how the arrangement should be presented in the statement of cash flows.

In June 2020 the Interpretations Committee issued a tentative agenda decision on reverse factoring arrangements, in which a financial institution agrees to pay amounts an entity owes to the entity's suppliers and the entity agrees to pay the financial institution at a date later than suppliers are paid. The tentative decision focused on reverse factoring arrangements because the Committee's outreach and research indicated that these are the most common supply-chain financing arrangements. While the decision only mentions reverse factoring arrangements, it may be appropriate to apply the guidance to other types of supply-chain financing. At the time of writing, the IASB was expecting feedback from constituents by September 2020.

Although the tentative agenda decision largely addresses presentation, disclosure and cash flow classification matters, it does state that an entity should assess whether and when to derecognise a liability that is (or becomes) part of a reverse factoring arrangement by applying the derecognition requirements in IFRS 9. Derecognition could occur if the purchaser is legally released from its original obligation to the supplier (see 6.1.2 above) or the terms of the original liability are amended in a way that is considered a substantial modification (see 6.2.1 above).

The tentative agenda decision goes on to state that an entity that derecognises a trade payable to a supplier and recognises a new financial liability to a financial institution still applies IAS 1 – *Presentation of Financial Statements* – in determining how to present that new liability in its statement of financial position.[16]

This indicates that even if the original liability is derecognised it may be still appropriate to present the new liability as a trade and other payable rather than as a financial liability more similar to debt, although many would consider this to be a different presentation. Conversely, even if the original liability is not derecognised, other factors may indicate that the substance and nature of the arrangements mean that the liability should no longer be presented as a trade payable. Instead the liability would be reclassified and presented as debt (in a similar way to transferred assets that are not derecognised, which IFRS 9 requires to be reclassified within the statement of financial position – see 4.1.1.A above).

Analysis of supply-chain finance is a complex exercise and requires careful examination of the individual facts and circumstances. In practice, the appropriate presentation of any such arrangement is likely to involve a high degree of judgement in the light of specific facts and circumstances.

The presentation and disclosure of supply-chain finance arrangements are discussed in more detail in Chapter 40 at 4.4.6 and Chapter 54 at 7.4.3.

7 CUSIP 'NETTING'

The CUSIP number of a security is a unique identification number assigned to all stocks and registered bonds in the United States and Canada. CUSIP 'netting' is the practice whereby the balance of a security held by an entity is reduced by the balance of that same security which the entity has sold, but not yet purchased, a so-called 'short sale'. This practice is applied to ensure that the entity properly reflects its security positions and does not reflect a financial liability to repurchase a security when in fact there is no such obligation. This practice is based on the assumption that securities with the same CUSIP number are considered to be fungible, and therefore, it would not be appropriate to present a long and a short position for the same security. This practice is equally applicable to securities with the same ISIN number, a unique identification number used in other markets.

While the practice is referred to as netting, in our view this is really a derecognition question – is it appropriate to derecognise long and short positions in the same security at the reporting date? In principle, this is different from the offsetting of separate financial assets and financial liabilities when the offsetting rules within paragraphs 42-50 of IAS 32 are met as discussed in Chapter 54 at 7.4.1.

In our view this practice is generally appropriate, i.e. the long and short positions may be derecognised, particularly where the securities are managed within the same pool of financial assets and financial liabilities, for example where internal security lending arrangements are in place to cover short positions, and both the long and short positions are classified under IFRS 9 as at fair value through profit or loss. Therefore, derecognition is appropriate when securities are managed together within the same trading book.

Where securities are not managed together, for example where the long position is held in the banking book and there is no intention of using this to settle a short position held in the trading book, we would not require derecognition. In this situation the long position may be classified as at amortised cost or at fair value through other comprehensive income (see Chapter 48 at 2) and derecognition may bring into question the business model conclusion.

8 FUTURE DEVELOPMENTS

8.1 Conceptual Framework for Financial Reporting (the Framework)

In March 2018 the IASB published the Framework. This fully revised document replaced the sections of the 2010 version previously carried-forward from the 1989 framework and also made amendments to the sections produced in 2010. The Framework contains a new chapter addressing both recognition and derecognition of assets and liabilities and highlights that accounting requirements for derecognition should aim to represent faithfully both:[17]

(a) the assets and liabilities retained after the transaction or other event that led to the derecognition (including any asset or liability acquired, incurred or created as part of the transaction or other event); and

(b) the change in the entity's assets and liabilities as a result of that transaction or other event,

and goes on to explain that those aims are normally achieved by:

- derecognising any assets or liabilities that have been transferred, consumed, collected or fulfilled, or have expired and recognising any resulting income or expense (the transferred component);

- continuing to recognise the assets or liabilities retained, if any (the retained component), which become a separate unit of account. Accordingly, no income or expenses are recognised on the retained component as a result of the derecognition of the transferred component, unless the derecognition results in a change in the measurement requirements applicable to the retained component; and

- applying one or more of the following procedures, if that is necessary to achieve one or both of those aims:
  - presenting any retained component separately in the statement of financial position;
  - presenting separately in the statement(s) of financial performance any income and expenses recognised as a result of the derecognition of the transferred component; or
  - providing explanatory information.

While this has no effect on the present requirements for derecognition of financial assets or liabilities, it may have effect in the future if and when the IASB decides to rewrite the requirements for derecognition of financial instruments.

The IASB's *Conceptual Framework for Financial Reporting* is discussed in Chapter 2 (see Chapter 2 at 8.3).

8.2 IFRS 17 – *Insurance Contracts*

There is a consequential amendment to IFRS 9 introduced by IFRS 17, although the amendment may not only affect insurance companies, which is effective for periods beginning on or after 1 January 2023. IFRS 17 is discussed in Chapter 56.

Some entities operate investment funds that provide investors with benefits determined by units in those funds, and some entities issue groups of insurance contracts with direct participation features and investment contracts with discretionary participation features. In these situations the entities may be required to include the assets within the funds, or the underlying items behind such insurance or investment contracts, on their own balance sheets, together with liabilities to investors in the funds or holders of the insurance or investment contracts.

If such an entity issues a financial liability, for example a corporate bond, that is purchased by one of the investment funds, or included within the underlying items behind the insurance contracts, that are held on the entity's balance sheet, such a purchase would normally result in derecognition of the financial liability. However, an amendment to IFRS 9 allows the entity, at the time of such a 'repurchase', to elect not to derecognise the financial liability. Instead it would continue to be recognised and the 'repurchased' instrument would be recognised as a financial asset and measured at fair value through profit or loss in accordance with IFRS 9. This election is irrevocable and made on an instrument-by-instrument basis. *[IFRS 9.3.3.5]*.

References

1 *IFRIC Update*, January 2007.
2 *IFRIC Update*, May 2006.
3 *IASB Update*, September 2006.
4 *IASB Update*, September 2006.
5 *IFRIC Update*, May 2016.
6 Staff Paper (May 2012 Interpretations Committee Meeting), *IAS 39 Financial Instruments: Recognition and Measurement – Derecognition of financial assets (Agenda reference 10-A)*, IASB, May 2012, paras. 32-36.
7 *IFRIC Update*, September 2012.
8 *IFRIC Update*, September 2012.
9 *Information for Observers*, IFRIC, March 2006.
10 *IFRIC Update*, November 2005.
11 *IASB Update*, September 2006.
12 *Information for Observers*, IFRIC, March 2006.
13 *IASB Update*, September 2006.
14 *IASB Update*, September 2006.
15 *IFRIC Update*, November 2005.
16 *IFRIC Update*, June 2020.
17 *Conceptual Framework for Financial Reporting*, IASB, paras. 5.27-5.28.

Chapter 53   Financial instruments: Hedge accounting

1 INTRODUCTION 4183
    1.1 Background 4183
    1.2 What is hedge accounting? 4183
    1.3 Development of hedge accounting standards 4185
    1.4 Objective of hedge accounting 4187
    1.5 Hedge accounting overview 4187
2 HEDGED ITEMS 4189
    2.1 General requirements 4189
    2.2 Risk components 4191
        2.2.1 General requirements 4191
        2.2.2 Contractually specified risk components 4192
        2.2.3 Non-contractually specified risk components 4193
            2.2.3.A Non-contractual risk components in financial instruments 4194
            2.2.3.B Non-contractual risk components in non-financial instruments 4195
        2.2.4 Partial term hedging 4197
        2.2.5 Foreign currency as a risk component 4198
        2.2.6 Inflation as a risk component 4200
        2.2.7 Interest rate risk component in an insurance contract 4201
    2.3 Components of a nominal amount 4201
        2.3.1 General requirement 4201
        2.3.2 Layer component for fair value hedges with prepayment risk 4203
    2.4 The 'sub-LIBOR issue' 4206

		2.4.1	Late hedges of benchmark portions of fixed rate instruments 4209
		2.4.2	Negative interest rates 4210
	2.5	Groups of items 4211
		2.5.1	General requirements 4211
		2.5.2	Hedging a component of a group 4211
		2.5.3	Cash flow hedge of a net position 4213
		2.5.4	Nil net positions 4215
	2.6	Other eligibility issues for hedged items 4216
		2.6.1	Highly probable 4216
		2.6.2	Hedged items held at fair value through profit or loss 4218
			2.6.2.A Hedged items managed on a fair value basis 4219
			2.6.2.B Hedged items held for trading 4220
			2.6.2.C Hedged items that have failed the contractual cash flows test 4220
		2.6.3	Hedges of exposures affecting other comprehensive income 4220
		2.6.4	Hedges of a firm commitment to acquire a business 4221
		2.6.5	Forecast acquisition or issuance of foreign currency monetary items 4221
		2.6.6	Own equity instruments 4222
		2.6.7	Core deposits 4222
		2.6.8	Leases and associated right of use assets 4223
	2.7	Aggregated exposures 4224
		2.7.1	Introduction 4224
		2.7.2	Background 4225
		2.7.3	Accounting for aggregated exposures 4227
3	HEDGING INSTRUMENTS 4234
	3.1	General requirements 4234
	3.2	Derivatives as hedging instruments 4234
		3.2.1	Offsetting external derivatives 4235
		3.2.2	Net written options 4235
		3.2.3	Embedded derivatives 4238
		3.2.4	Credit break clauses 4238
			3.2.4.A Principal resetting cross currency swaps 4238
		3.2.5	Basis swaps 4239
	3.3	Non-derivative financial instruments 4240
		3.3.1	Hedge of foreign currency risk by a non-derivative financial instrument 4241
	3.4	Own equity instruments 4242
	3.5	Combinations of instruments 4242

3.6	Portions and proportions of hedging instruments		4243
	3.6.1	Proportions of instruments	4243
	3.6.2	Hedging different risks with one instrument	4243
	3.6.3	Restructuring of derivatives	4246
	3.6.4	Time value of options	4246
	3.6.5	Forward element of a forward contract and foreign currency basis spread	4247
	3.6.6	Hedges of a portion of a time period	4247

4 INTERNAL HEDGES AND OTHER GROUP ACCOUNTING ISSUES 4248

4.1	Internal hedging instruments		4248
	4.1.1	Central clearing parties and ring fencing of banks	4250
4.2	Offsetting internal hedging instruments		4250
	4.2.1	Interest rate risk	4251
	4.2.2	Foreign currency risk	4252
4.3	Internal hedged items		4259
	4.3.1	Intragroup monetary items	4259
	4.3.2	Forecast intragroup transactions	4260
4.4	Hedged item and hedging instrument held by different group entities		4261

5 TYPES OF HEDGING RELATIONSHIPS 4262

5.1	Fair value hedges		4262
	5.1.1	Hedges of firm commitments	4263
	5.1.2	Hedges of foreign currency monetary items	4264
5.2	Cash flow hedges		4264
	5.2.1	All-in-one hedges	4265
	5.2.2	Hedges of firm commitments	4266
	5.2.3	Hedges of foreign currency monetary items	4266
5.3	Hedges of net investments in foreign operations		4266
	5.3.1	Nature of the hedged risk	4267
	5.3.2	Amount of the hedged item for which a hedging relationship may be designated	4268
	5.3.3	Where the hedging instrument can be held	4270

6 QUALIFYING CRITERIA 4271

6.1	General requirements		4271
6.2	Risk management strategy versus risk management objective		4272
	6.2.1	Designating 'proxy hedges'	4274
6.3	Documentation and designation		4275
	6.3.1	Business combinations	4277
	6.3.2	Dynamic hedging strategies	4277

		6.3.3	Forecast transactions	4278
	6.4	Assessing if the hedge effectiveness requirements are met		4279
		6.4.1	Economic relationship	4280
		6.4.2	Credit risk and the effectiveness assessment	4284
			6.4.2.A Credit risk on the hedging instrument	4284
			6.4.2.B Credit risk on the hedged item	4285
		6.4.3	The hedge ratio	4288
7	ACCOUNTING FOR EFFECTIVE HEDGES			4289
	7.1	Fair value hedges		4290
		7.1.1	Ongoing fair value hedge accounting	4290
		7.1.2	Dealing with adjustments to the hedged item	4292
	7.2	Cash flow hedges		4294
		7.2.1	Ongoing cash flow hedge accounting	4294
		7.2.2	Reclassification of gains and losses recognised in cash flow hedge reserve from OCI to profit or loss	4297
		7.2.3	Recycling for a hedge of foreign currency monetary items	4299
		7.2.4	Cash flow hedges within subsidiaries on acquisition or disposal	4299
	7.3	Accounting for hedges of a net investment in a foreign operation		4300
		7.3.1	Identifying the effective portion in a net investment hedge	4301
		7.3.2	Non-derivative liabilities hedging a net investment	4302
		7.3.3	Derivatives hedging a net investment	4303
			7.3.3.A Forward currency contracts hedging a net investment	4304
			7.3.3.B Cross currency interest rate swaps hedging a net investment	4304
			7.3.3.C Purchased options hedging a net investment	4306
		7.3.4	Combinations of derivative and non-derivative instruments hedging a net investment	4306
		7.3.5	Individual or separate financial statements	4306
	7.4	Measuring ineffectiveness		4307
		7.4.1	General requirements	4307
		7.4.2	The time value of money	4309
		7.4.3	Hedging using instruments with a non-zero fair value	4310
		7.4.4	Hypothetical derivatives	4310
		7.4.5	Discount rates for calculating the change in value of the hedged item	4312
		7.4.6	Detailed example of calculation of measuring ineffectiveness for a cash flow hedge of a forecast transaction in a debt instrument	4314
		7.4.7	Comparison of spot rate and forward rate methods	4320

		7.4.8	Foreign currency basis spreads 4324
		7.4.9	The impact of the hedging instrument's credit quality 4325
		7.4.10	Interest accruals and 'clean' versus 'dirty' values 4327
		7.4.11	Effectiveness of options 4327
		7.4.12	Hedged items with embedded optionality 4328
	7.5	Accounting for the costs of hedging 4329
		7.5.1	Time value of options 4330
			7.5.1.A Aligned time value 4334
		7.5.2	Forward element of forward contracts 4336
			7.5.2.A Forward element of forward contracts in a net investment hedge 4338
		7.5.3	Foreign currency basis spreads in financial instruments 4339
			7.5.3.A Measurement of the costs of hedging for foreign currency basis spread 4340
	7.6	Hedges of a firm commitment to acquire a business 4343
	7.7	Hedge accounting for a documented rollover hedging strategy 4344
	7.8	Hedge accounting for an equity instrument designated at fair value through OCI 4345
8	SUBSEQUENT ASSESSMENT OF EFFECTIVENESS, REBALANCING AND DISCONTINUATION 4346
	8.1	Assessment of effectiveness 4346
	8.2	Rebalancing 4347
		8.2.1	Definition 4347
		8.2.2	Requirement to rebalance 4349
		8.2.3	Mechanics of rebalancing 4350
	8.3	Discontinuation 4353
		8.3.1	Accounting for discontinuation of fair value hedge accounting 4355
		8.3.2	Accounting for discontinuation of cash flow hedge accounting 4355
		8.3.3	Change in risk management objective 4355
		8.3.4	Documented hedged item no longer exists 4359
		8.3.5	Impact of novation to central clearing parties on cash flow hedges 4361
		8.3.6	The impact of the introduction of settle to market derivatives on cash flow hedges 4363
		8.3.7	Change of hedging counterparty within the same consolidated group 4363
		8.3.8	Disposal of a hedged net investment 4364
9	INTEREST RATE BENCHMARK REFORM 4365
	9.1	Phase 1 reliefs 4366

		9.1.1	End of Phase 1 reliefs	4368
		9.1.2	Phase 1 reliefs for IAS 39	4369
	9.2	Phase 2 hedge accounting amendments		4369
		9.2.1	Phase 2 reliefs from discontinuing hedge relationships	4370
		9.2.2	Phase 2 temporary relief from having to meet the separately identifiable requirement	4372
			9.2.2.A Determination of whether an RFR is a separately identifiable risk component	4373
		9.2.3	Application of Phase 2 reliefs	4375
		9.2.4	Effective date and end of Phase 2 reliefs	4377
		9.2.5	Phase 2 amendments for IAS 39	4378
			9.2.5.A Determination of whether an RFR is a separately identifiable risk component under IAS 39	4378
10	PRESENTATION			4378
	10.1	Cash flow hedges		4379
	10.2	Fair value hedges		4379
	10.3	Hedges of groups of items		4380
		10.3.1	Cash flow hedges	4380
		10.3.2	Fair value hedges	4381
	10.4	Costs of hedging		4381
11	MACRO HEDGING			4382
	11.1	Accounting for dynamic risk management		4383
	11.2	Applying hedge accounting for macro hedging strategies under IFRS 9		4385
12	ALTERNATIVES TO HEDGE ACCOUNTING			4386
	12.1	Credit risk exposures		4386
	12.2	Own use contracts		4388
13	EFFECTIVE DATE AND TRANSITION			4389
	13.1	Effective date		4389
	13.2	Prospective application in general		4390
	13.3	Limited retrospective application		4391
		13.3.1	Accounting for the time value of options	4391
		13.3.2	Accounting for the forward element of forward contracts	4392
		13.3.3	Accounting for foreign currency basis spread	4392
		13.3.4	Re-designation of hedge relationships for non-financial risk components	4393
14	MAIN DIFFERENCES BETWEEN IFRS 9 AND IAS 39 HEDGE ACCOUNTING REQUIREMENTS			4394

14.1 The objective of hedge accounting 4394
14.2 Eligible hedged items 4395
14.3 Eligible hedging instruments 4396
14.4 Effectiveness criteria 4396
14.5 Discontinuation 4397
14.6 Hedge accounting mechanisms 4397

List of examples

Example 53.1:	Hedge of a contractually specified risk component – coal supply contract linked to the coal benchmark price and the Baltic Dry Index	4193
Example 53.2:	Identification of a benchmark interest rate component in fixed rate debt	4194
Example 53.3:	Identification of a benchmark interest rate component in government bonds	4195
Example 53.4:	Hedge of a non-contractually specified risk component – coffee purchases with a benchmark price risk component	4195
Example 53.5:	Partial term hedging	4197
Example 53.6:	Hedge of foreign currency denominated commodity risk	4199
Example 53.7:	Inflation risk as an eligible risk component of a debt instrument	4200
Example 53.8:	Hedging a top layer of a loan prepayable at fair value	4203
Example 53.9:	Fair value hedge accounting designation using layers with and without prepayment risk	4204
Example 53.10:	Hedging a bottom layer (no prepayment risk) of a loan portfolio	4205
Example 53.11:	Hedging a proportion of a prepayable loan portfolio	4206
Example 53.12:	Sub-LIBOR issue – selling crude oil at below benchmark price	4207
Example 53.13:	Hedge of a portion of an existing fixed rate financial asset following a rise in interest rates	4209
Example 53.14:	Negative interest rates and fair value hedges	4210
Example 53.15:	Hedging a portfolio of shares	4211
Example 53.16:	Hedging a top layer of a portfolio of financial liabilities	4212
Example 53.17:	Economic 'natural hedge' of foreign currency cash flows	4213
Example 53.18:	Cash flow hedge of a foreign currency net position	4214
Example 53.19:	Interest rate risk managed separately from a credit risk portfolio managed on a fair value basis	4219

Example 53.20:	Aggregated exposure – copper purchase in a foreign currency	4225
Example 53.21:	Fixed rate loan in a foreign currency – cash flow hedge of an aggregated exposure	4227
Example 53.22:	Floating rate loan in a foreign currency – fair value hedge of an aggregated exposure	4229
Example 53.23:	Hedge of a commodity price risk as an aggregated exposure in a cash flow hedge of foreign currency risk	4231
Example 53.24:	Aggregated exposure – interest rate pre-hedge of forecast foreign currency debt issue	4233
Example 53.25:	Cash flow hedging of an exposure that includes a net investment in a foreign operation	4234
Example 53.26:	Hedging foreign currency risk of a forecast transaction using a combined option instrument	4236
Example 53.27:	Foreign currency collar (or 'cylinder option')	4236
Example 53.28:	'Knock-out' swap	4237
Example 53.29:	Zero cost collar	4237
Example 53.30:	Hedging with a sales commitment	4238
Example 53.31:	Hedging with a principal resetting cross currency swap	4239
Example 53.32:	Hedge of a forecast commodity purchase with an investment in a commodity fund or an exchange traded commodity	4240
Example 53.33:	Hedging with a non-derivative liability	4241
Example 53.34:	Hedge of foreign currency bond	4242
Example 53.35:	Hedging with a combination of a derivative and non-derivative instrument	4242
Example 53.36:	Foreign currency forward used to hedge the position arising from two hedged items with different foreign currencies	4244
Example 53.37:	Cross-currency interest rate swap hedging two foreign currency exchange rate exposures and fair value interest rate exposure	4244
Example 53.38:	Designation of a basis swap hedging different risk positions	4245
Example 53.39:	Designation of hedging instrument with longer life than hedged item	4247
Example 53.40:	Internal derivatives	4249
Example 53.41:	Single external derivative offsets internal contracts on a net basis	4252
Example 53.42:	Using internal derivatives to hedge foreign currency risk	4253
Example 53.43:	Intragroup monetary items that will affect consolidated profit or loss	4260
Example 53.44:	Subsidiary's foreign currency exposure hedged by parent	4261
Example 53.45:	Subsidiary's foreign currency exposure hedged by parent (2)	4261

Example 53.46:	Hedge of anticipated issuance of fixed rate debt	4264
Example 53.47:	Hedge of highly probable forecast purchases	4265
Example 53.48:	Nature of the hedged risk in a net investment hedge	4268
Example 53.49:	Amount of hedged item in a net investment hedge	4268
Example 53.50:	Amount of hedged item in a net investment hedge (different hedged risks)	4269
Example 53.51:	Hedge accounting applied by intermediate parent	4270
Example 53.52:	Risk management strategies with related risk management objectives	4273
Example 53.53:	Common proxy hedging designations	4275
Example 53.54:	Hedge documentation	4276
Example 53.55:	Economic relationship between HKD and USD	4281
Example 53.56:	Designating interest rate hedges of loan assets when credit risk is expected	4287
Example 53.57:	Setting the hedge ratio	4288
Example 53.58:	Deliberate under-hedging in a cash flow hedge to avoid recognition of ineffectiveness	4288
Example 53.59:	Deliberate under-hedging in a fair value hedge to create fair value accounting	4289
Example 53.60:	Fair value hedge	4291
Example 53.61:	Hedge of a firm commitment to acquire equipment	4293
Example 53.62:	Cash flow hedge of anticipated commodity sale	4295
Example 53.63:	Cash flow hedge of a floating rate liability	4296
Example 53.64:	Hedge of a firm commitment to acquire equipment	4297
Example 53.65:	Identification of the effective portion in a net investment hedge (1)	4301
Example 53.66:	Identification of the effective portion in a net investment hedge (2)	4302
Example 53.67:	Hedge of a foreign currency net investment using a cross-currency swap	4305
Example 53.68:	Calculation of ineffectiveness	4308
Example 53.69:	Impact of time value of money when measuring ineffectiveness	4309
Example 53.70:	Determination of a hypothetical derivative in a cash flow hedge of interest rate risk	4311
Example 53.71:	Impact on ineffectiveness of changes in credit risk in the hedged item when the hedged risk is a benchmark component	4311
Example 53.72:	Measuring effectiveness for a hedge of a forecast transaction in a debt instrument	4314
Example 53.73:	Cash flow hedge of firm commitment to purchase inventory in a foreign currency	4320

Example 53.74:	Out of the money put option used to hedge forecast sales of commodity	4327
Example 53.75:	Amortisation of time value of an option hedging a time related hedged item	4331
Example 53.76:	Hedging the purchase of equipment (transaction related)	4332
Example 53.77:	Hedging interest rate risk of a bond (time period related) (1)	4332
Example 53.78:	Hedging interest rate risk of a bond (time period related) (2)	4334
Example 53.79:	Funding swaps – designating the spot risk only	4337
Example 53.80:	Calculation of the value of foreign currency basis spread	4340
Example 53.81:	Hedge of a foreign currency risk in rollover cash flow hedging strategy	4345
Example 53.82:	Rebalancing	4348
Example 53.83:	Rebalancing the hedge ratio by decreasing the volume of the hedging instrument	4351
Example 53.84:	Rebalancing the hedge ratio by decreasing the volume of hedged item	4352
Example 53.85:	Partial discontinuation as a result of a change in risk management objective	4356
Example 53.86:	Partial discontinuation of an interest margin hedge	4357
Example 53.87:	Change in risk management objective for an open portfolio of debt instruments	4358
Example 53.88:	Interruption of hedged forecast cash flows	4359
Example 53.89:	Change in forecast hedged item	4360
Example 53.90:	Change in hedged forecast debt issuance	4360
Example 53.91:	Disposal of foreign operation	4365
Example 53.92:	Application of Phase 1 relief for interest rate benchmark reform	4367
Example 53.93:	Application of Phase 2 relief to a fair value hedge	4375
Example 53.94:	Application of Phase 2 relief to a cash flow hedge relationship	4375
Example 53.95:	Processing and brokerage of soybeans and sunflowers	4389
Example 53.96:	Retrospective application of accounting for time value of option	4392

Chapter 53 Financial instruments: Hedge accounting

1 INTRODUCTION

1.1 Background

Chapter 44 provides a general background to the development of accounting for financial instruments and notes the fundamental changes that have been experienced in international financial markets. The markets for derivatives, especially, have seen remarkable and continued growth over the past two to three decades. This reflects the increasing use of such instruments by businesses, commonly to 'hedge' their financial risks. Accordingly, the accounting treatment for derivatives and hedging activities has taken on a high degree of importance.

'Hedging' itself is a much wider topic than hedge accounting and is not the primary subject of this chapter. It is an imprecise term although standard setters frequently describe hedging in terms of designating a hedging instrument that has a value that is expected, wholly or partly, to offset changes in the value or cash flows of a 'hedged position'.[1] In this context, hedged positions normally include those arising from recognised assets and liabilities, contractual commitments and expected, but uncontracted, future transactions. Whilst this may be an appropriate description for many hedges, it does not necessarily capture the essence of all risk management activities involving financial instruments. Nevertheless, it forms the basis for the hedge accounting requirements under IFRS.

1.2 What is hedge accounting?

Every entity is exposed to business risks from its daily operations. Many of those risks have an impact on the cash flows or the value of assets and liabilities, and therefore, ultimately affect profit or loss. In order to manage these risk exposures, companies often enter into derivative contracts (or, less commonly, other financial instruments) to hedge them. Hedging can therefore be seen as a risk management activity in order to change an entity's risk profile.

Applying the default IFRS accounting requirements to those risk management activities can result in accounting mismatches, when the gains or losses on a hedging instrument are not recognised in the same period(s) and/or in the same place in the financial statements as gains or losses on the hedged exposure. Many believe that the resulting accounting mismatches are not a good representation of those risk management activities. Hedge accounting is often seen as 'correcting' deficiencies in the accounting requirements that would otherwise apply to each leg of the hedge relationship. These deficiencies are an inevitable consequence of using a mixed-measurement model of accounting. Typically, hedge accounting involves recognising gains and losses on a hedging instrument in the same period(s) and in the same place in the financial statements as gains or losses on the hedged position. It may be used in a number of situations, for example to adjust (or correct) for:

- *Measurement differences*

  These might arise where the hedge is of a recognised asset or liability that is measured on a different basis to the hedging instrument. An example might be inventory that is recorded in the financial statements at cost, but whose value is hedged by a forward contract that enables inventory of the same nature to be sold at a predetermined price. In this case, both the hedging instrument and the hedged position exist and are recognised in the financial statements, but they are likely to be measured on different bases.

  Avoiding the measurement difference could in this situation theoretically be achieved in a number of ways. One alternative would be not to recognise unrealised gains or losses on the forward contract, and realised gains or losses could be deferred (e.g. separately as assets or liabilities or by including them within the carrying amount of the inventory) until the inventory is sold. On the other hand, if unrealised gains or losses on the forward contract were recognised in profit or loss, the measurement basis of the inventory could be changed to reflect changes in its fair value in profit or loss. (See 5.1 and 5.2 below for discussion of the permitted designations under IFRS 9 – *Financial Instruments*).

- *Performance reporting differences*

  Even if the measurement bases of the hedging instrument and hedged item are the same, performance reporting differences might arise if gains and losses are reported in a different place in the financial statements. An example might be where an investment in shares is classified as fair value through other comprehensive income (FVOCI) (see Chapter 48 at 8) and whose value is hedged by a put option. The investment and the put option are both measured at fair value. However, gains or losses on the investment are recognised in other comprehensive income whilst those on the put option are recognised in profit or loss, therefore resulting in a mismatch in the income statement (or statement of comprehensive income). Similarly, gains or losses on retranslating the net assets of a foreign operation are recorded in other comprehensive income whilst retranslation gains or losses on a foreign currency borrowing used to hedge that net investment are, absent any form of hedge accounting, recorded in profit or loss.

  In the case of the FVOCI investment and the put option, hedge accounting might involve reporting gains and losses on the investment in profit or loss, or gains and losses on the put option in other comprehensive income. For the foreign operation, hedge accounting normally involves reporting the retranslation gains and losses on both the borrowing and the foreign operation in other comprehensive income. (See 7.8 and 5.3 below for discussion of the permitted designations under IFRS 9).

- *Recognition differences*

    These might arise where the hedge is of contractual rights or obligations that are not recognised in the financial statements. An example is a foreign currency denominated operating lease held by the lessor, where the unrecognised future contractual lease rentals to be received in another currency are hedged by a series of forward currency contracts (i.e. each receipt is effectively 'fixed' in functional currency terms).

    In this case, one solution might be to treat the lease as a 'synthetic' functional currency denominated lease. A similar outcome would be obtained if unrealised gains and losses on each forward contract remained unrecognised or deferred until the accrual of the lease receivables it was hedging. (See 5.2 below for discussion of the permitted designation under IFRS 9).

- *Existence differences*

    These might arise where the hedge is of cash flows arising from an uncontracted future transaction, i.e. a transaction that does not yet exist. An example is a foreign currency denominated sale expected next year that is hedged by a forward currency contract.

    Again, a solution to this issue might involve treating the future sale as a 'synthetic' functional currency sale, deferring the gain or loss on the forward contract until the sale is recognised in profit or loss or it might involve not recognising the forward contract until it is settled. (See 5.2 below for discussion of the permitted designation under IFRS 9).

1.3 Development of hedge accounting standards

The first comprehensive hedge accounting requirements issued by the IASB were contained in IAS 39 – *Financial Instruments: Recognition and Measurement*. Hedge accounting under IAS 39 was often criticised as being complex and rules-based, and thus, ultimately not reflecting an entity's risk management activities. This was unhelpful for preparers and users of the financial statements alike. The IASB took this concern as the starting point of its project for a new hedge accounting model. Consequently, the objective of IFRS 9 is to reflect the effect of an entity's risk management activities in the financial statements. *[IFRS 9.6.1.1]*.

In addition, the financial crisis resulted in a significant amount of political pressure being brought to bear on standard setters in general and the IASB specifically. Responding to this pressure, in April 2009 the IASB announced a detailed six-month timetable for publishing a proposal to replace IAS 39.[2] In order to expedite the replacement of IAS 39, the IASB divided the project into three phases: classification and measurement; amortised cost and impairment of financial assets; and hedge accounting.

In December 2010, the IASB issued the Exposure Draft ('ED' or the exposure draft) *Hedge Accounting*, being the proposals for the third part of IFRS 9. After redeliberating the proposals in 2011, in September 2012 the Board published a draft of *Chapter 6 – Hedge Accounting* – of IFRS 9, together with consequential changes to other parts of

IFRS 9 and other IFRSs (the draft standard). The idea of the draft standard was to enable constituents to familiarise themselves with the new requirements.[3]

Although the IASB did not ask for comments, a number of constituents asked the IASB to clarify certain elements of the draft standard. As a result, the IASB redeliberated some elements of the IFRS 9 hedge accounting requirements in its January 2013 and April 2013 meetings.

This resulted in the third version of IFRS 9, issued in November 2013, which included the new hedge accounting requirements. Finally, in July 2014 the IASB issued the all-encompassing final version of IFRS 9 that includes the new impairment requirements (see Chapter 51) and some amendments to the classification and measurement requirements (see Chapters 48-50). This also involved some minor consequential amendments to the hedge accounting requirements in IFRS 9, mainly because of the introduction of a new category for debt instruments measured at fair value through other comprehensive income with subsequent reclassification adjustments.

IFRS 9 does not provide any particular solutions for so-called 'macro hedge' accounting, the term used to describe the more complex risk management practices used by entities such as banks to manage risk in dynamic portfolios. In May 2012 the Board decided to decouple accounting for macro hedging from IFRS 9, and a separate project was set up to develop an accounting solution for dynamic risk management – the project name adopted by the IASB for an accounting solution for macro hedging. Work is still ongoing for the Dynamic Risk Management project. A discussion paper – *Accounting for Dynamic Risk Management: a Portfolio Revaluation Approach to Macro Hedging* – was published in April 2014. No consensus was reached as a result of the discussion paper. A new model for accounting for dynamic risk management is being developed by the IASB. Having now developed the core aspects of the model, at the time of writing, the IASB has started the process of explaining and discussing the core model with stakeholders to gather their views. See 11.1 below for more details.

IFRS 9 is effective for periods beginning on or after 1 January 2018 and replaces substantially all of IAS 39, including the hedge accounting requirements. However, given the fact IFRS 9 does not include an accounting solution for dynamic risk management, entities are permitted an accounting policy choice to continue applying the hedge accounting requirements of IAS 39 instead of those in IFRS 9. *[IFRS 9.7.2.21]*. See 11.2 below.

Furthermore, for a fair value hedge of the interest rate exposure of a portfolio of financial assets or financial liabilities (and only for such a hedge), an entity may apply the related hedge accounting requirements in IAS 39 instead of those in IFRS 9. This choice relates only to a fair value portfolio hedge as described in paragraphs 81A and 89A and AG114-AG132 of IAS 39 (see 10.2 below). *[IFRS 9.6.1.3]*. A decision to continue to apply this IAS 39 guidance is not part of the accounting policy choice to defer IAS 39 mentioned above.

This chapter focuses on the hedge accounting requirements of IFRS 9. The main differences between hedge accounting under IFRS 9 and the hedge accounting requirements in IAS 39 are discussed at 14 below.

In developing IFRS 9, the IASB decided not to carry forward any of the hedge accounting related Implementation Guidance that accompanied IAS 39. However, the IASB emphasised that not carrying forward the Implementation Guidance did not mean that it had rejected the guidance. Implementation Guidance only accompanies, but is not part of, the standard. *[IFRS 9.BC6.93-95].* An entity might have relied on particular Implementation Guidance in IAS 39 as an interpretation of the IAS 39 hedge accounting guidance. Accordingly, in many instances, the entity could also interpret the same outcome based on the IFRS 9 hedge accounting guidance – in the absence of contradicting guidance within IFRS 9. Hence much of the Implementation Guidance in IAS 39 remains relevant for the application of IFRS 9.

Accordingly, whilst this chapter predominantly focuses on the guidance included with IFRS 9, on occasion IAS 39 Implementation Guidance is included where this is considered to be relevant and helpful.

1.4 Objective of hedge accounting

The objective of the IFRS 9 hedge accounting requirements is to 'represent, in the financial statements, the effect of an entity's risk management activities'. The aim of the objective is 'to convey the context of hedging instruments for which hedge accounting is applied in order to allow insight into their purpose and effect'. *[IFRS 9.6.1.1].* This is achieved by reducing the accounting mismatch by changing either the measurement or (in the case of certain firm commitments) recognition of the hedged exposure, or the accounting for the hedging instrument, but with some important improvements when compared to IAS 39.

This is a rather broad objective that focuses on an entity's risk management activities and reflects what the Board wanted to achieve with the new accounting requirements. However, this broad objective does not override any of the hedge accounting requirements, which is why the Board noted that hedge accounting is only permitted if all the new qualifying criteria are met (see 6 below). *[IFRS 9.BC6.82].*

1.5 Hedge accounting overview

Given the stated objective of IFRS 9 is for hedge accounting to represent an entity's risk management activities where possible, the first step in achieving hedge accounting under IFRS 9 is to identify the relevant risk management strategy and the objective for a particular hedge relationship. These form the foundations for hedge accounting under IFRS 9 (see 6.2 below).

The standard defines three types of hedge relationships:

- a fair value hedge: a hedge of the exposure to changes in fair value that is attributable to a particular risk and could affect profit or loss (see 5.1 below);
- a cash flow hedge: a hedge of the exposure to variability in cash flows that is attributable to a particular risk and could affect profit or loss (see 5.2 below); and
- a hedge of a net investment in a foreign operation (see 5.3 below). *[IFRS 9.6.5.2].*

An entity may choose to designate a hedging relationship between a hedging instrument and a hedged item in order to achieve hedge accounting. [IFRS 9.6.1.2]. Prior to hedge accounting being applied, all of the following steps must have been completed:
- identification of eligible hedged item(s) and hedging instrument(s) (see 2 and 3 below);
- identification of an eligible hedged risk (see 2 below);
- ensuring the hedge relationship meets the definition of one of the permitted types (a fair value, cash flow or net investment hedge) (see 5 below);
- satisfying the qualifying criteria for hedge accounting (see 6 below); and
- formal designation of the hedge relationship (see 6.3 below).

Once these requirements are met, hedge accounting can be applied prospectively, but the ongoing qualifying criteria and assessments must continue to be met, otherwise hedge accounting will cease. (See 8 below).

The table below summarises the application of hedge accounting for the three types of hedge relationships:

Figure 53.1: Accounting for hedge relationships

Hedge type	Fair value	Cash flow	Net investment
Hedged item	Carrying amount adjusted for changes in fair value with respect to the hedged risk. Adjusted through profit or loss.	N/A	N/A
Hedging instrument	N/A	No change to carrying amount, but effective portion of change in fair value is recorded in OCI.	No change to carrying amount, but effective portion of change in fair value is recorded in OCI.
Resultant profit or loss	Ineffective portion	Ineffective portion	Ineffective portion

As it can be seen from the above, for a fair value hedge, an adjustment is made to the carrying value of the hedged item to reflect the change in value due to the hedged risk, with an offset to profit or loss for the change in value of the hedging instrument. Where the offset is not complete, this will result in ineffectiveness to be recorded in profit or loss (see 7.4 below).

However, for both a cash flow and net investment hedge, the carrying amount of the hedged item, which for a cash flow hedge may not even yet be recognised, is unchanged. The effect of hedge accounting is to defer the effective portion of the change in value of the hedging instrument in other comprehensive income. Any ineffective portion will remain in profit or loss as ineffectiveness.

See 7 below for more details on accounting for eligible hedges.

2 HEDGED ITEMS

2.1 General requirements

The basic requirement for a hedged item is for it to be one of the following:
- a recognised asset or liability;
- an unrecognised firm commitment;
- a highly probable forecast transaction; or
- a net investment in a foreign operation.

The hedged item must be reliably measurable and can be a single item, or a group of items (see 2.5 below). A hedged item can also be a component of such an item(s) (see 2.2 and 2.3 below). *[IFRS 9.6.3.1, 6.3.2, 6.3.3].*

Recognised assets and liabilities can include financial items and non-financial items such as inventory. Most internally-generated intangibles (e.g. for a bank, a core deposit intangible – see 2.6.7 below) are not recognised assets and therefore cannot be hedged items. However, firm commitments that are not routinely recognised as assets or liabilities absent the effects of hedge accounting for such items can be eligible hedged items, this would include loan commitments (see Chapter 45 at 3.5). *[IFRS 9.6.3.1].*

The term 'highly probable' is not defined in IFRS 9 but is often interpreted to mean a much greater likelihood of happening than 'more likely than not'. The Implementation Guidance within IAS 39 contained some guidance as to how the term highly probable should be applied within the context of hedge accounting. This guidance can be considered relevant for IFRS 9 hedge accounting (see 2.6.1 below).

A net investment in a foreign operation is defined in paragraph 8 of IAS 21 – *The Effects of Changes in Foreign Exchange Rates* – to be the amount of the reporting entity's interest in the net assets of that operation (see Chapter 15 at 6) (see 5.3.2 below).

An aggregated exposure that is a combination of an exposure that could qualify as a hedged item and a derivative may also be designated as a hedged item (see 2.7 below). *[IFRS 9.6.3.4].*

Only assets, liabilities, firm commitments and forecast transactions with an external party qualify for hedge accounting. *[IFRS 9.6.3.5].* As an exception, a hedge of the foreign currency risk of an intragroup monetary item qualifies for hedge accounting if that foreign currency risk affects consolidated profit or loss (see 4.3.1 below). In addition, the foreign currency risk of a highly probable forecast intragroup transaction would also qualify as a hedged item if that transaction affects consolidated profit or loss. *[IFRS 9.6.3.6].* (See 4.3.2 below).

Financial assets and liabilities need not be within the scope of IFRS 9 to qualify as hedged items. For example, although rights and obligations under lease agreements are for most purposes scoped out of IFRS 9, lease payables or finance lease receivables still meet the definition of a financial instrument and could therefore be hedged items in a hedge of interest rate or foreign currency risk (see 2.6.8 below).

In the case of a financial liability containing an embedded derivative (see Chapter 46 at 4), if the embedded derivative is accounted for separately from the host instrument, the hedged item would be the host instrument or components thereof (see 2.2 and 2.3 below); basing it on the hybrid instrument (i.e. the instrument including the embedded derivative) or the cash flows from the hybrid is not permitted. This is because derivatives are only permitted as a hedged item as part of an eligible aggregated exposure. As an embedded derivative is only accounted for separately if it is not closely related to the host instrument, it is unlikely to meet the criteria for an eligible aggregated exposure (see 2.7 below).

An entity may designate an item in its entirety or a component of an item as the hedged item in a hedging relationship. An entire item comprises all changes in the cash flows or fair value of an item. A component comprises less than the entire fair value change or cash flow variability of an item. In that case an entity may designate only the following types of components (including combinations) as hedged items:

- only changes in the cash flows or fair value of an item attributable to a specific risk or risks (i.e. a risk component), including one sided risks (see 2.2 below);
- one or more selected contractual cash flows; and
- components of a nominal amount, i.e. a specified part of the amount of an item (see 2.3 below). *[IFRS 9.6.3.7]*.

The reference to one sided risks refers to an ability to designate only changes in the cash flows or fair value of a hedged item above or below a specified price or other variable. The intrinsic value of a purchased option hedging instrument (assuming that it has the same principal terms as the designated risk), but not its time value, reflects a one-sided risk in a hedged item. For example, an entity can designate the variability of future cash flow outcomes resulting from a price increase of a forecast commodity purchase, without including the risk of a price decrease within the hedge relationship. Such a situation may arise if the entity wanted to retain the opportunity to benefit from a lower commodity price, but protect itself against an increase. In such a situation, only cash flow losses that result from an increase in the price above the specified level are designated. The hedged risk does not include the time value of the purchased option. *[IFRS 9.6.3.7(a)]*. (See 3.6.4 below)

Only the portion of cash flows or fair value of a financial instrument that is designated as the hedged item are subject to the hedge accounting requirements. The accounting for other portions that are not designated as the hedged item remains unchanged.

The guidance also adds that to be eligible for hedge accounting, a risk component must be a separately identifiable component of the financial or non-financial item, and the changes in the cash flows or fair value of the item attributable to changes in that risk component must be reliably measurable. *[IFRS 9.B6.3.8]*. This is considered further at 2.2 below.

There is no requirement to designate a hedged item only on initial recognition. Designation of hedged items sometime after their initial recognition (e.g. after a previous hedge relationship is discontinued) is permitted, although some additional complexity may arise when identifying risk components (see 2.4.1 below). *[IFRS 9.B6.5.28]*.

2.2 Risk components

2.2.1 General requirements

Instead of hedging the total changes in fair values or cash flows, risk managers often enter into derivatives to hedge only specific risk components. Managing a specific risk component reflects that hedging all risks is often not economical and hence not desirable, or even not possible (because of a lack of suitable hedging instruments).

If designated, the usual hedge accounting requirement apply to a risk component in the same way as they apply to other hedged items that are not risk components. For example, the qualifying criteria apply, including that the hedging relationship must meet the hedge effectiveness requirements, and any hedge ineffectiveness must be measured and recognised, albeit only with respect to the hedged risk, and not the full item (see 6 and 7.4 below). *[IFRS 9.B6.3.11, B6.4.1]*.

IFRS 9 permits an entity to designate a risk component of a financial or non-financial item as the hedged item in a hedging relationship. Designation of a risk component means that only changes in the cash flows or fair value of the hedged item with respect to the designated risk are subject to the hedge accounting requirements. So instead of considering value changes in the hedged item with respect to all risks that are value drivers, only value changes in the hedged item with respect to the designated risk component are considered for hedge accounting purposes. This is valuable as it is common for entities to economically hedge a specific risk within a hedged item rather than its full price risk. The ability to designate risk components in a hedge relationship is an important step in enabling entities to achieve the IASB's objective for hedge accounting, which is to 'represent, in the financial statements, the effect of an entity's risk management activities'. *[IFRS 9.6.1.1]*.

It should be noted, however, that only eligible risk components can be designated in hedge relationships. IFRS 9 provides guidance on this topic which is discussed in the sections below.

The key requirements for designating a risk component are that a risk component is less than the entire item (see 2.4 below), it must be a separately identifiable component of the item and the changes in the cash flows or fair value of the item attributable to the changes in that risk component must be reliably measurable. *[IFRS 9.B6.3.7, B6.3.8]*. A risk component can be contractually specified in the contract (see 2.2.2 below) but non-contractually specified risk components may also be eligible (see 2.2.3 below). *[IFRS 9.B6.3.10]*.

When identifying what risk components qualify for designation as a hedged item, in particular whether they are separately identifiable and reliably measurable, an entity assesses such risk components within the context of the particular market structure to which the risk(s) relate and in which the hedging activity takes place. *[IFRS 9.B6.3.9]*. This assessment has increased relevance for non-contractual risk components for which is it important to undertake a careful analysis of the specific facts and circumstances of the relevant markets. *[IFRS 9.BC6.176]*.

As noted above, a risk component may be contractually specified or it may be implicit in the fair value or the cash flows of the item to which the component belongs. *[IFRS 9.B6.3.10]*. However, the mere fact that a physical component is part of the make-up of the whole item does not mean that the component necessarily qualifies as a risk component for hedge accounting purposes. A physical component is neither required nor by itself sufficient to meet the criteria for risk components that are eligible as a hedged item. However, depending on relevant market structure, a physical component can help meet those criteria. The example of an eligible risk component that is often quoted is that of the crude oil component of refined products such as jet fuel. However, just because rubber is a physical component of car tyres that does not mean that an entity can automatically designate rubber as a risk component in a hedge of forecast tyre purchases or sales, since the price of tyres may be related only indirectly to the price of rubber. Further analysis of the pricing structure of the whole car tyre would be required.

The determination of eligible non-contractually specified risk components is a judgemental area where we expect practice to continue to evolve (see 2.2.3 below).

It was reaffirmed by the IASB in developing IFRS 9 that it is not considered possible to determine that credit risk is an eligible risk component of a debt instrument. It was explained that a portion cannot be a residual; i.e. an entity is not permitted to designate as a portion the residual fair value or cash flows of a hedged item or transaction if that residual does not have a separately measurable effect on the hedged item or transaction. *[IFRS 9.BC6.470, BC6.517]*. However, IFRS 9 does introduce an alternative accounting solution for entities undertaking economic credit risk hedging activity (see 12.1 below).

2.2.2 Contractually specified risk components

Potential hedged items such as financial instruments, purchase or sales agreements may contain clauses that link the contractual cash flows via a specified formula to a benchmark rate or price. The examples below all include a contractually specified risk component:

- the interest rate on a financial instrument contractually linked to a benchmark interest rate plus a fixed incremental spread;
- the coupon on a financial instrument contractually linked to an inflation or other financial index plus a determinable incremental spread;
- the price of natural gas contractually linked in part to a gas oil benchmark price and in part to a fuel oil benchmark price;
- the price of electricity contractually linked in part to a coal benchmark price and in part to transmission charges that include an inflation indexation;
- the price of wires contractually linked in part to a copper benchmark price and in part to a variable tolling charge reflecting energy costs; and
- the price of coffee contractually linked in part to a benchmark price of Arabica coffee and in part to transportation charges that include a diesel price indexation.

In each of the above examples, for items other than financial assets, it is assumed that the contractual pricing component would not require separation as an embedded derivative (see Chapter 46 at 4 and 5). The example below provides a fuller illustration of the circumstances under which a contractually specified risk component might usefully be designated in a hedge relationship.

Example 53.1: Hedge of a contractually specified risk component – coal supply contract linked to the coal benchmark price and the Baltic Dry Index

An entity purchases coal from its coal supplier under a contract that sets out a variable price for coal linked to the coal benchmark price, represented by futures contracts for coal loaded at the Newcastle Coal Terminal in Australia, plus a logistics charge that is indexed to the Baltic Dry Index, reflecting that the delivery is at an overseas location. The contract sets out minimum purchase quantities for each month covered by its term.

The entity wishes to hedge itself against price changes related to the benchmark coal price but does not want to hedge the price variability resulting from the logistics costs represented by the indexation of the coal contract to the Baltic Dry Index. Therefore, the entity enters into Newcastle coal futures contracts whereby it purchases coal for the relevant delivery months. For each relevant delivery month the entity designates the futures contracts as a hedging instrument in a cash flow hedge of the benchmark coal price risk component of the future coal purchases under its supply contract.

In this case the risk component is contractually specified by the pricing formula in the supply contract. This means it is separately identifiable, because the entity knows exactly which part of the change in the future purchase price of coal under its particular supply contract results from changes in the benchmark price for coal and what part of the price change results from changes in the Baltic Dry Index. The risk component can also be reliably measured using the price in the futures market for the relevant delivery months as inputs for calculating the present value of the cumulative change in the hedged cash flows. An entity could also decide to hedge only its exposure to variability in the coal price that is related to transportation costs. For example, the entity could enter into forward freight agreements and designate them as hedging instruments, with the hedged item being only the variability in the coal price under its supply contract that results from the indexation to the Baltic Dry Index.

Although it is generally easier to determine that a contractually specified risk component is separately identifiable and reliably measurable, than one that is non-contractual, the requirement must still be met. When contractually specified, a risk component would usually be considered separately identifiable. *[IFRS 9.BC6.174].* Further, the risk component element of an index/price formula would usually be referenced to observable data, such as a published index/price index. Therefore, the risk component would most likely also be considered reliably measurable.

Nevertheless, difficulties can still arise where a contractual negative spread exists in the hedged item, as a risk component must be less than the entire item. *[IFRS 9.B6.3.7].* A negative spread arises when the formula for the contractual coupon/price includes a spread that is subtracted from the hedged risk component, so that the full contractual coupon/price is lower than the identified risk component. This has become termed the 'sub-LIBOR issue' (discussed at 2.4 below).

2.2.3 Non-contractually specified risk components

Not all contracts define the various pricing elements and, therefore, specify risk components. In fact, we expect most risk components of financial and non-financial items not to be contractually specified. While it is certainly easier to determine that a risk component is separately identifiable and reliably measurable if it is specified in the contract, IFRS 9 is clear that there is no need for a component to be contractually specified in order to be eligible for hedge accounting. The assessment of whether a risk component qualifies for hedge accounting (i.e. whether it is separately identifiable and reliably measurable) has to be made 'within the context of the particular market structure to which the risk or risks relate and in which the hedging activity takes place'. *[IFRS 9.B6.3.9].* We understand 'market structure' here to mean the basis upon which market prices are established or the market conventions that are in evidence. Prices are typically established through a number of 'building blocks'. So, for instance, a benchmark interest rate such as LIBOR may currently form the first building block in the valuation of a debt instrument (see 9 below), while a benchmark price, such as the LME price for copper, may form the first building block for the pricing of a non-financial item. The 'sub-LIBOR' issue, (see 2.4 below) will arise from negative spread building blocks, if as a result the identified non-contractually specified risk component is larger than the full contract itself.

2.2.3.A   Non-contractual risk components in financial instruments

It has been common practice to identify a non-contractually specified risk-free interest rate or other benchmark interest rate component of the total interest rate exposure of a fixed rate or zero coupon hedged financial instrument. This approach is supported by an example provided within the application guidance of IFRS 9, presented as Example 53.2 below, and of IAS 39 as follows 'for a fixed rate financial instrument hedged for changes in fair value attributable to changes in a risk-free or benchmark rate, the risk-free or benchmark rate is normally regarded as both a separately identifiable component of the financial instrument and reliably measurable'. *[IAS 39.AG99F(a)].*

Example 53.2:   Identification of a benchmark interest rate component in fixed rate debt

Entity A has issued five year debt with a fixed coupon of 5%. The debt is issued in an environment with a market in which a large variety of similar debt instruments are compared by their spreads to a benchmark rate (for example LIBOR) and variable rate instruments in that environment are typically indexed to that benchmark rate. Interest rate swaps are frequently used to manage interest rate risk on the basis of the benchmark rate, irrespective of the spread on the debt instruments to that benchmark rate. The price of fixed rate debt instruments vary directly in response to changes in that benchmark rate as they happen. Accordingly, Entity A concludes that the benchmark rate is a separately identifiable and reliably measurable risk component of the fixed rate debt. *[IFRS 9.B6.3.10(d)].*

When the debt was issued, the prevailing five year benchmark rate was 2%. In pricing the debt, Entity A included an additional spread of 3% above the benchmark rate to reflect credit risk and other factors. Entity A then transacted an interest rate swap at the prevailing five year benchmark rate (i.e. pay floating benchmark, receive 2%). Entity A is able to designate the benchmark interest rate component of the issued debt as the hedged item in a fair value hedge for changes in the benchmark interest rate with the interest rate swap as the hedging instrument.

Whilst in the past LIBOR has often been identified as an eligible risk component of a fixed rate or zero coupon hedged financial instrument, as part of global Interest Rate Benchmark Reform markets will move away from LIBOR as the predominant benchmark interest rate, replacing it with various Risk Free Rates (RFRs) (see 9 below). Accordingly, an assessment will be required as to whether LIBOR continues to meet the separately identifiable criteria within each market structure. The IASB have addressed this and other accounting issues arising from Interest Rate Benchmark Reform, issuing two amendments to IFRS 9, and other impacted standards (see 9.2.2.A below for further discussion).

The example below provides another example of a non-contractually specified risk component of a financial instrument. It also illustrates how the market structure might be used to support the eligibility of the benchmark rate as a risk component for the particular hedged item.

Example 53.3: *Identification of a benchmark interest rate component in government bonds*

Entity B holds Dutch government bonds and has chosen to hedge the associated interest rate risk with German government bonds futures. It is generally understood that Germany and the Netherlands are strongly linked economically. Furthermore, pricing for Dutch government bonds is generally performed in relation to German government bonds. As a result, bond yields for German government bonds and Dutch government bonds are highly correlated. In addition, German bond yields are lower than Dutch bond yields.

Based on the market structure presented above, one might conclude that for Dutch government bonds, German bond yields represent an eligible risk component as it is a separately identifiable risk component that can be reliably measured.

2.2.3.B Non-contractual risk components in non-financial instruments

An entity may be able to identify a non-contractual component in a non-financial item if within the particular market structure for that item, price negotiations ordinarily reflect a benchmark price plus other charges, similar to the contractual examples listed at 2.2.2 above, even if this formula is not explicitly stated in the contract. The existence of contractually specified risk components in similar transactions can be a relevant factor in the assessment of the market structure and so help identify risk components when they are not contractually specified.

It may also be possible to identify non-contractually specified risk components in highly probable forecast items that are the subject of a cash flow hedge. Once such forecast items become contractual commitments it is possible that the risk components will be specified in the contract. In this case, if the entity has a past practice of entering into similar contracts, it may be relatively straightforward to demonstrate that a risk component can be identified in the forecast transactions within the context of the market structure.

The following example from the application guidance of IFRS 9 illustrates the 'separately identifiable and reliably measurable' assessment.

Example 53.4: *Hedge of a non-contractually specified risk component – coffee purchases with a benchmark price risk component*

An entity purchases a particular quality of coffee of a particular origin from its supplier for the current harvest under a contract that sets out a variable price linked to the benchmark price for coffee. The price is represented by the coffee futures price plus a fixed spread, reflecting the different quality of the coffee purchased compared to the benchmark plus a variable logistics services charge reflecting that the delivery is at a specific manufacturing site of the entity. The fixed spread is set for the current harvest period only. For any deliveries that fall into the next harvest period this type of supply contract is not yet available.

The entity may wish to lock in the benchmark coffee price for future harvests, even though it does not yet have a supply contract. For such hedges of future coffee harvests, the entity analyses the market structure for its coffee supplies, taking into account how the eventual deliveries of coffee that it receives are priced. The entity has an expectation that it will enter into similar supply contracts for each future harvest period once the crop relevant for its particular purchases is known and the spread can be set. In that sense, the knowledge about the pricing under existing supply contracts also informs the entity's analysis of the market structure more widely, including forecast purchases which are not yet contractually specified. This allows the entity to conclude that its exposure to variability of cash flows resulting from changes in the benchmark coffee price is a risk component that is separately identifiable and reliably measurable for forecast coffee purchases that fall into the next harvest period (i.e. prior to the existence of a supply contract), as well as those for the current harvest period which are under a supply contract. *[IFRS 9.B6.3.10(b)]*.

In this case the entity can enter into coffee futures contracts to hedge its exposure to the variability in cash flows from the benchmark coffee price and designate that risk component as the hedged item for harvests for which the pricing is not yet subject to a supply contract. This means that changes in the contractual price due to the variable logistics services charge and future changes in the spread reflecting the quality of the coffee, would be excluded from the hedging relationship.

The assessment of whether a risk component qualifies for hedge accounting is mainly driven by an analysis of whether there are different pricing factors that have a distinguishable effect on the item as a whole (in terms of its fair value or its cash flows). This evaluation would always have to be based on relevant facts and circumstances. While it is probably not necessary that each component of the price of the non-financial item is observable in the market (for instance, transport costs may be specific to a particular transaction), it will be necessary to demonstrate that components that are designated as hedged items do have a distinguishable effect, and are not 'drowned out' by the variability of other, unobservable components.

The standard uses the refinement of crude oil to jet fuel as an example to demonstrate how the assessment of the market structure could be made to conclude that crude oil in a particular situation is an eligible risk component of jet fuel. *[IFRS 9.B6.3.10(c)]*. Crude oil is a physical input of the most common production process for jet fuel and there is a well-established price relationship between the two. The components of jet fuel will include the price of crude oil and the various 'crack spreads' relating to the refining process, plus possibly transport costs. While there may be no market to measure reliably the crack spreads beyond a certain time horizon, if it can be shown that the market does regard the crude oil price as a building block, and it has a distinguishable effect on the price of jet fuel, then the crude oil component may be designated as the hedged item for longer time periods. Similarly, it may be possible to designate the crack spread, if it can be traded or is otherwise sufficiently observable that it may be regarded as reliably measurable.

Therefore in order to conclude that benchmark components are eligible risk components of an item, there is an expectation that any residual building block component would either be relatively stable or else any fluctuations can be explained rationally within the particular market structure (e.g. quality differences or transportation costs). Accordingly, just because the full price of an item may approximate to, or is highly correlated with, a particular benchmark price, that will be insufficient on its own to demonstrate that the benchmark price can be identified as a component within the context of the particular market structure.

Extending the example of crude oil, it is also a major input in the production process for plastic. However, the manufacturing process is complex and involves a number of steps. The process starts with crude oil being distilled into its separate 'fractions', of which only one (naphtha) is used for making plastic. Naphtha then undergoes a number of further processes before the various types of plastic are finally produced. Consequently, any impact of a change in the price of crude oil on the price of plastic is likely to be significantly diluted by the costs of manufacturing and the passage of time.

Generally, the further 'downstream' in the production process an item is, the more difficult it is to find a distinguishable effect of any single pricing factor. The mere fact that a commodity is a major physical input in a production process does not automatically translate into a separately identifiable effect on the price of the item as a whole. For example, the price for pasta at food retailers in the medium to long term also responds to changes in the price for wheat, but there is no distinguishable direct effect from changes in wheat prices on the retail price for pasta, which remains unchanged for longer periods even though wheat prices are likely to change more frequently. If retail prices are only periodically adjusted in a way that directionally reflects the effect of wheat price changes, that is not sufficient to constitute a separately identifiable risk component.

Determining whether non-contractually specified risk components are eligible as hedged items requires judgement. The economic analysis ordinarily undertaken by an entity prior to undertaking risk management activity will most likely form the basis in making this judgement. However, care needs to be taken to ensure the existing economic analysis sufficiently meets the requirements of the standard, that a risk component is separately identifiable and reliably measurable within the relevant market structure. *[IFRS 9.B6.3.8, B6.3.9]*. Practice will continue to evolve in this area as to what are commonly accepted non-contractual risk components and the approach taken to determine their existence. However, judgement will need to continue to be applied to the particular facts and circumstances.

2.2.4 Partial term hedging

A common risk management technique is to hedge a risk for only a partial term for which it is outstanding, as illustrated in Example 53.5 below. The example, which is based on the Implementation Guidance of IAS 39, illustrates that a time portion of interest rate risk can be a separately identifiable and reliably measurable risk component of a financial instrument, and remains relevant under IFRS 9. Accordingly, it is possible to designate a financial instrument as a hedged item for the portion of risk that represents only part of the term that a hedged item remains outstanding.

Example 53.5: Partial term hedging

Company A acquires a 10% fixed-rate government bond with a remaining term to maturity of ten years and classifies it as at amortised cost. To hedge against the fair value exposure on the bond associated with the first five years' interest payments, it acquires a five year pay-fixed receive-floating swap.

The swap may be designated as hedging the fair value exposure of the interest rate payments on the government bond until year five and the change in value of the principal payment due at maturity to the extent affected by changes in the yield curve relating to the five years of the swap. *[IAS 39.F.2.17]*.

Whilst the above Implementation Guidance uses the example of a financial instrument, the same conclusion could be reached for hedging a partial term of a non-financial instrument. For example, an entity might wish to hedge the foreign currency risk for the next three months from a highly probable forecast purchase cash flow in six months' time. The six month forward foreign currency rate is driven by the relationship between spot rates and forward rates for any given yield curve. Furthermore, the market is built on the premise that a six-month forward rate is a combination of the three-month forward rate (i.e. the market rate for months one to three), plus the three month forward rate (i.e. the market rate for months four to six). This market structure would appear to support being able to hedge a partial risk component of a highly probable forecast purchase cash flow.

Consistent with other documented risk components, if a partial term hedge is designated, the qualifying criteria apply, including that the hedging relationship must meet the hedge effectiveness requirements, and any hedge ineffectiveness must be measured and recognised, albeit only with respect to the hedged risk (i.e. the designated partial term), and not the full item (see 2.1 above and 6 and 7.4 below). *[IFRS 9.B6.3.11, B6.4.1].*

An alternative risk management strategy would be a roll over strategy, i.e. when the maturity of the hedging instrument is intentionally shorter than the maturity of the hedged item, and there is an expectation that on expiry of the original hedging instrument it will be replaced by a new hedging instrument (see 7.7 below). Applying a roll over strategy is not the same as identifying a risk component and so it is not the same as a partial term hedge.

2.2.5 Foreign currency as a risk component

One risk component that is frequently designated as an eligible risk component is foreign currency risk. *[IFRS 9.BC6.176].* It is relatively easy to determine that foreign currency risk is a separately identifiable component of a financial instrument denominated in a foreign currency, and that the changes in the cash flows or fair value of the instrument attributable to changes in foreign currency risk are reliably measurable – at least for most frequently traded currency pairs.

Similarly, for highly probable forecast foreign currency cashflows in a cash flow hedge, it may be relatively easy to conclude that variation in foreign currency rates does have a distinguishable effect on the hedged cash flows. (See 5.2 below for more discussion on cash flow hedges.)

It is less straight forward, however, to reach a similar conclusion for non-financial items purchased or sold in a foreign currency that are designated in a fair value hedge (see 5.1 below for more discussion on fair value hedges). In June 2019, the Interpretations Committee discussed whether foreign currency risk can be a separately identifiable and reliably measurable risk component of a non-financial asset held for consumption that an entity can designate as the hedged item in a fair value hedge accounting relationship.

As part of the discussion, the Committee considered that if an entity has exposure to foreign currency risk on a non-financial asset, whether it is a separately identifiable and reliably measurable risk component. The Committee tentatively concluded that this can be the case, depending on an assessment of the particular facts and circumstances within the context of the particular market structure. A key consideration would be whether, at a global level, changes in fair value of the non-financial asset are determined only in one particular currency and that currency is not the entity's functional currency. For example, as purchases and sales of wide-bodied aircraft are routinely globally determined in US dollars, it might be possible for an entity with a functional currency other than US dollars to identify an eligible foreign currency risk component in a wide-bodied aircraft that it owns.

As noted above, the Interpretations Committee discussion as to whether foreign currency risk is a separately identifiable and reliably measurable risk component of a non-financial asset held for consumption was part of a wider debate on the eligibility of designating such a risk component in a valid hedge relationship. In order to achieve hedge accounting for such a risk component, consideration should also be given to all the qualifying criteria for hedge accounting (see 6 below) and in particular those discussed by the Interpretations Committee in June 2019.[4] These include the requirement that the changes in fair value could affect profit or loss (see 2.6.8, 5.1 and 6.2.1 below).

Prior to designation of foreign currency risk in a non-financial instrument in a fair value hedge, careful analysis and judgement will likely be required to determine that foreign currency risk is a separately identifiable component of a non-financial instrument for which the changes in the cash flows or fair value of the non-financial asset attributable to changes in that foreign currency risk are reliably measurable.

The Committee also noted, that the fact that market transactions are commonly settled in a particular currency does not necessarily mean that this is the currency in which the non-financial asset is priced – and thus the currency in which its fair value is determined. The currency may be purely a 'settlement currency'. A 'settlement currency' might arise where the price is determined in one foreign currency, but settled in another (i.e. the settlement currency) at the prevailing foreign currency rate on settlement. In that instance it is difficult to argue that changes in the foreign currency risk between an entity's functional currency and the settlement currency have a reliably measurable impact on the cash flows or fair value of the hedged item. In fact, it is the foreign currency risk between an entity's functional currency and the currency that drives the pricing of the hedged item that is more likely to be an eligible risk component.

Although the IFRIC discussion was limited to foreign currency risk in a non-financial instrument in a fair value hedge, the guidance on a settlement currency is also relevant for highly probable forecast foreign currency cash flows.

Accordingly, consideration is required to determine that any 'foreign currency risk' is an eligible risk component in a non-financial instrument or highly probable forecast foreign currency cash flow, and is not merely due to the use of a settlement currency. However, when the prices of forecast foreign currency purchases or sales are determined in the local environment in which the foreign currency is used, it is likely that the foreign currency is more than just a settlement currency and foreign currency risk is a separately identifiable component of the foreign currency purchases or sales.

Furthermore, although it is not explicit in the standard, it seems reasonable that an entity may identify a risk component of an exposure for risk(s) excluding foreign currency risk. The designation of a foreign currency risk component, and a risk component excluding foreign currency risk are both illustrated in the following example.

Example 53.6: Hedge of foreign currency denominated commodity risk

Company P has the Rand as its functional currency. It has forecast, with a high probability, the need to purchase a 1,000 barrels quantity of crude oil for US Dollars in twelve months' time.

Scenario 1: designation of a risk component excluding foreign currency risk

To hedge part of its exposure to the price risk inherent in this purchase, P enters into an exchange traded twelve-month cash-settled crude oil forward contract. The strike price of the forward is denominated in US dollars (there is no active market in Rand denominated crude oil futures) and P therefore fixes the US dollar price of the 1,000 barrels of oil to be purchased. P chooses not to hedge the risk associated with Rand to US dollar exchange rates. This might be because of illiquidity in the foreign currency markets for Rand or, perhaps, because P has forecast US dollar inflows that provide a natural hedge of the foreign currency risk.

Scenario 2: designation of foreign currency as a risk component

To hedge part of the risk associated with Rand to US dollar exchange rates, P may transact a forward contract to buy US dollar and sell Rand in twelve months' time. The forward contract can be designated as the hedging instrument in a hedge of the foreign currency risk exposure to the US dollar denominated price risk associated with its forecast purchase of crude oil.

The forward contract would hedge an amount of US dollar, e.g. USD 10,000, so Company P would also need to ensure that it was highly probable that a cash flow of at least USD 10,000 will arise from forecast purchases of oil (see 2.6.1 below).

2.2.6 Inflation as a risk component

A contractually specified inflation risk component of the cash flows of a recognised inflation-linked bond liability (assuming that there is no requirement to account for an embedded derivative separately – see Chapter 46 at 4) is separately identifiable and reliably measurable, as long as other cash flows of the instrument are not affected by the inflation risk component. *[IFRS 9.B6.3.15].*

However, IFRS 9 includes a rebuttable presumption that for financial instruments, unless contractually specified, inflation is not separately identifiable and reliably measurable. This means that there are limited cases under which it is possible to identify inflation as a non-contractually specified risk component of a financial instrument and designate that inflation component in a hedging relationship. Similar to other non-contractually specified risk components, the analysis would have to be based on the particular circumstances in the respective market, which is, in this case, the debt market. *[IFRS 9.B6.3.13].*

The example below, derived from the application guidance of IFRS 9, explains a situation in which the presumption that inflation does not qualify as a risk component of a financial instrument can be rebutted.

Example 53.7: Inflation risk as an eligible risk component of a debt instrument

An entity wishes to hedge the inflation risk component of a debt instrument. The debt instrument is issued in a currency and country in which inflation-linked bonds are actively traded in a significant volume. The volume, liquidity and term structure of these inflation-linked bonds allow the computation of a real interest yield curve. This situation supports that inflation is a factor that is separately considered in the debt market in a way that it is a separately identifiable and reliably measurable risk component. *[IFRS 9.B6.3.14].*

There are not many currencies with a liquid market for inflation-linked debt instruments, therefore limiting the availability of designating non-contractually specified inflation risk components of financial instruments. Of course, even where the presumption is successfully rebutted, the other qualifying criteria must be met in order to apply hedge accounting, as described at 6 below. In particular, demonstrating that the hedged item and the hedging instrument have values that are generally expected to move in opposite directions may prove challenging. *[IFRS 9.B6.4.4].*

While IFRS 9 defines in what circumstances inflation can be a risk component for a financial instrument, inflation can be treated as a risk component for non-financial items under IFRS 9 in the same manner as any other risk component (as described at 2.2.2 and 2.2.3 above), i.e. the rebuttable presumption described in this section applies only to financial instruments. For example, linkage to a consumer price index in a sales contract would normally qualify as a hedged item.

2.2.7 Interest rate risk component in an insurance contract

Entities that write insurance contracts often use derivatives to manage the interest rate risk they associate with those insurance liabilities. On application of IFRS 17 – *Insurance Contracts* – (see Chapter 56) insurance entities may have more inclination to apply hedge accounting to their interest rate risk management derivatives in order to avoid an accounting mismatch and better represent risk management in their financial statements.

IFRS 9 is silent on the application of hedge accounting to insurance liabilities, hence the standard IFRS 9 hedge accounting criteria must be applied. In particular, a key question will be whether there is a risk component of an insurance contract representing the risk-free interest rate risk that could be eligible as a hedged item in a fair value hedge.

In order for a risk component to be eligible, the risk component must be separately identifiable and reliably measurable. This assessment should be made within the context of a particular market structure (see 2.2.3.A above). *[IFRS 9.B6.3.8, B6.3.9]*.

Given the wide variety of insurance contracts, such an assessment will need to be undertaken for the particular facts and circumstances. Consideration as to what is the 'particular market structure' will also be important. Often there is a lack of a clear primary and, possibly, even a secondary market for insurance contracts (i.e. evidence suggests that in many markets, very few sales of insurance contracts occur post origination). Therefore, in some circumstances, it has been suggested that it may be appropriate to interpret 'market structure' as meaning the basis upon which market origination prices are established or the market conventions for fair value determination – if such common market practices exist. This is an area in which we expect practice to evolve.

2.3 Components of a nominal amount

2.3.1 General requirement

A component of a nominal amount is a specified part of the amount of an item. *[IFRS 9.6.3.7(c)]*. This could be a proportion of an entire item (such as, 60% of a fixed rate loan of EUR 100 million) or a layer component (for example, the 'bottom layer' of EUR 60 million of a EUR 100 million fixed rate loan that can be prepaid at fair value. 'Bottom layer' here refers to the portion of the loan that will be prepaid last). The type of component changes the accounting outcome. An entity must designate the component for accounting purposes consistently with its risk management objective (see 6.2 below). *[IFRS 9.B6.3.16, B6.3.17]*.

A component must be less than the entire item *[IFRS 9.B6.3.7]* and must be defined in such a way that it is possible to determine whether the usual effectiveness criteria are met and ongoing ineffectiveness can be measured. (See 6.4 and 7.4 respectively below).

Nominal layer components are frequently used in risk management activities in practice. For hedge accounting purposes it is possible to designate a layer in a defined, but open, population (see examples i) and iii) below), or from a defined nominal amount (see examples ii) and iv) below). An open population is one where the items within the population are not restricted to items that already exist. Examples of layers that could be eligible for hedge designation include:

i) part of a monetary transaction volume, for example, the first USD 1 million cash flows from sales to customers in a given period;

ii) part of a physical volume, for example, the 50 tonnes bottom layer of 200 tonnes of coal inventory in a particular location (i.e. the portion that will be used last);

iii) a part of a physical or other transaction volume, for example, the sale of the first 15,000 units of widgets during January 2022; and

iv) a layer from the nominal amount of the hedged item, for example, the top layer of a CHF 100 million fixed rate liability that can be prepaid at fair value. 'Top layer' refers to the portion of the liability that will be prepaid first. *[IFRS 9.B6.3.18]*.

The ability to designate a 'bottom layer' nominal component for a group of forecast cash flows, such as the sale of the first 15,000 units of widgets, used in example iii) above, accommodates the fact that there may be a level of uncertainty as to the quantity of the hedged item. The bottom layer designation means that any uncertainty in forecast cash flows 'above' the bottom layer does not negatively impact the assessment as to whether the bottom layer itself is eligible as a hedged item (i.e. meets the highly probable requirement) (see 2.6.1 below). However, it would not be possible to designate a 'top layer' nominal component for a group of forecast cash flows, as it is not possible to determine when that top layer occurs, as more forecast cash flows could always follow (see 6.3.3 below). *[IAS 39.F.3.10]*.

There are additional requirements if a layer is designated within a fair value hedge. An entity must specify it as a portion of a nominal amount, e.g. the top CHF 20 million layer of a CHF 100 million fixed rate liability. Accounting for a fair value hedge requires remeasurement of the hedged item for fair value changes attributable to the hedged risk (see 7.1.1 below). In addition, that fair value hedge adjustment must be recognised in profit or loss no later than when the hedged item is derecognised (see 7.1.2 below). Accordingly, it is necessary to track the designated hedged item so it can be determined when the hedged item has been derecognised. Applying this requirement to the example of a top CHF 20 million layer of a CHF 100 million fixed rate liability, the total defined nominal amount of CHF 100 million fixed rate liability must be tracked in order to identify when the specified CHF 20 million top layer is derecognised. *[IFRS 9.B6.3.19]*.

Further analysis is however required on the ability to designate layers within a fair value hedge where there is prepayment risk (see 2.3.2 below).

2.3.2 Layer component for fair value hedges with prepayment risk

Although IFRS 9 allows the designation of layer components from a defined nominal amount or a defined, but open, population as long as it is consistent with an entity's risk management objective (see 2.3.1 above), there are some additional considerations for fair value hedges where prepayment risk exists. *[IFRS 9.B6.3.18]*.

A layer component that includes a prepayment option does not qualify as a hedged item in a fair value hedge if the fair value of the prepayment option is affected by changes in the hedged risk, unless the changes in fair value of the prepayment option as a result of changes in the hedged risk are included when measuring the change in fair value of the hedged item (see Example 53.9 below). *[IFRS 9.B6.3.20]*. However, if the prepayment option with a layer component is prepayable at fair value, the fair value of the option is not affected by changes in the hedged risk, and hence it would be possible to designate a layer component in a fair value hedge with little or no ineffectiveness due to changes in the fair value of the option when measuring the hedged item (see Example 53.8 below).

Example 53.8: Hedging a top layer of a loan prepayable at fair value

An entity borrows money by issuing a $10m five-year fixed rate loan. The entity has a prepayment option to pay back $5m at fair value. The entity wants to be able to make use of the prepayment option without the amount repayable on early redemption being affected by interest rate changes. Consequently, the entity would like to hedge the fair value interest rate risk of the prepayable part of the loan. To achieve this, the entity enters into a five-year receive fixed/pay variable interest rate swap (IRS) with a notional amount of $5m. The entity designates the IRS in a fair value hedge of the interest rate risk of the $5m top layer of the loan attributable to the benchmark interest rate. As a result, the top layer is adjusted for changes in the fair value attributable to changes in the hedged risk. The bottom layer, which cannot be prepaid, remains at amortised cost.

The gain or loss on the IRS will offset the change in fair value on the top layer attributable to the hedged risk. On prepayment, the fair value hedge adjustment of the top layer is part of the gain or loss from derecognition of a part of the loan as the result of the early repayment.

The situation illustrated by Example 53.8 above, of a hedge of a top layer of a loan, would not often be found in practice as most prepayment options in loan agreements allow, in our experience, for prepayment at the nominal amount (instead of at fair value). Moreover, if a financial asset included an option that allowed prepayment at fair value, that would affect the assessment of the characteristics of the contractual cash flows. That assessment is a part of the classification of financial assets and such a prepayment option may not be consistent with payments that are solely principal and interest (see Chapter 48 at 6.4.5). However, the ability to designate a top layer in a fair value hedge could be helpful when hedging a group of fixed rate readily transferable financial instruments, see 2.5.2 below.

As already mentioned above, IFRS 9 does not preclude hedge accounting for layers including a prepayment option that are affected by changes in the hedged risk. However, in order to achieve hedge accounting for such a designation, changes in fair value of the prepayment option as a result of changes in the hedged risk have to be included in the assessment of whether the effectiveness requirements are met and when measuring the change in fair value of the hedged item. Example 53.9 illustrates what this means in practice:

Example 53.9: Fair value hedge accounting designation using layers with and without prepayment risk

A bank originates a $10m five-year fixed rate loan with a prepayment option to pay back $5m at any time at par.

For risk management purposes, the loan is considered together with variable rate borrowings of $10m. As a result, the bank is exposed to an interest margin risk resulting from the fix-to-floating rate mismatch. The bank expects the borrower to prepay $2m and, therefore, wishes to hedge $8m only. The bank enters into a five-year pay fixed/receive variable interest rate swap (IRS) with a notional amount of $8m and designates $5m of the IRS in a fair value hedge of the benchmark interest rate risk of the $5m layer of the non-prepayable loan amount. In addition, the bank enters into a five year pay variable/receive fixed interest rate swaption with a notional amount of $3m that is jointly designated with $3m of the IRS to hedge the benchmark interest rate risk of the last remaining $3m of the $5m prepayable amount of the loan (a bottom layer of the prepayable portion of the loan).

As a result, the $5m non-prepayable loan amount is adjusted for changes in the fair value attributable to changes in the hedged risk (the fixed rate benchmark interest rate risk of a fixed term instrument). This is also true for the $3m bottom layer of the prepayable amount, but in addition it must also be adjusted for the effect of changes in the fair value of the prepayment option that exists within the designated $3m layer, attributable to changes in interest rate risk. The unhedged $2m top layer remains at amortised cost.

Therefore, the first $2m of prepayments would have a gain or loss on derecognition determined as the difference between the amortised cost of the prepaid amount and par. For any further prepayments exceeding $2m, the gain or loss on derecognition would be determined as the difference between the amortised cost including the fair value hedge adjustment and par.

When deciding on which instruments to transact in order to manage the interest rate risk in a prepayable portfolio, an entity will usually consider the likelihood of prepayment in a bottom layer. In particular it will consider whether the risk of prepayment is sufficient to justify the added expense of transacting a hedging instrument that can also be cancelled (e.g. an interest rate swap cancellable at zero cost or an offsetting swaption as described in Example 53.9 above). As part of these considerations it is relatively common that from an economic perspective, an entity might view a bottom layer as having no prepayment risk attached at all and transact a non-cancellable hedging instrument accordingly.

Despite this economic view, the hedge accounting guidance requires consideration of the fair value changes of that bottom layer based on the contractual terms of the hedged item, which would include the prepayment option (see 7.4.12 below). Hence, for many economic hedges of bottom layers of prepayable hedged items, the changes in the fair values of the hedging instrument and the hedged item will not normally be the same, at least from an accounting perspective. This has the potential to distort the economic relationship between the pre-payable hedged item and the hedging instrument to the extent that hedge accounting might be precluded (see 6.4.1 below). While, it is unlikely that such a risk management objective would be undertaken unless there was an expectation that an economic relationship exists, the existence of the economic relationship would need to be demonstrated, perhaps via the use of a quantitative assessment. Additionally, as the expectation that an economic relationship exists may change over time, especially if the prepayment option looks likely to become in the money, or exercised for any other reason, this expectation would need to be periodically reassessed based on the updated facts and circumstances. Any actual ineffectiveness would be measured and recorded in profit or loss. (see 7.4 below).

'Bottom layer' hedging strategies that avoid this source of ineffectiveness can only be applied if the hedged layer is not affected by the prepayment risk. This is best demonstrated by an example (see Example 53.10 below).

Example 53.10: Hedging a bottom layer (no prepayment risk) of a loan portfolio

A bank holds a portfolio of fixed rate loans with a total nominal amount of GBP 100m. The borrowers can, at any time during the tenor, prepay 20% of their (original) loan amount at par.

For risk management purposes, the loans are considered together with variable rate borrowings of GBP 100m. As a result, the bank is exposed to an interest margin risk resulting from the fix-to-floating rate mismatch. The bank expects GBP 20m of loans to be prepaid.

As part of the risk management strategy, the bank decides to hedge a part of the interest margin by entering into a pay fixed/receive variable interest rate swap (IRS). The objective is to hedge 95% of the amount of loans that is not prepayable using an IRS with a notional amount of GBP 76m (95% of GBP 80m). The hedged layer does not include a prepayment option. Therefore, the IRS is designated in a fair value hedge of the interest rate risk of the GBP 76m bottom layer of the GBP 100m loan portfolio.

As a result, the bottom layer is adjusted for changes in the fair value attributable to changes in the hedged risk (i.e. benchmark interest rate risk). The extent to which the borrowers exercise their prepayment option (i.e. up to 20% of the original loan) does not affect the hedging relationship. Also, if the bank were to derecognise any of the loans for any other reason, the first GBP 4m of non-prepayable amount of derecognised loans would not be part of the hedged item (i.e. the GBP 76m bottom layer). However, if the nominal amount of the loan fell below GBP 76m, this would start to affect the hedging relationship.

Therefore, while IFRS 9 provides an effective solution for portfolios that feature a bottom layer that is not prepayable, as explained in Example 53.10 above, it does not provide an answer for portfolios that are fully prepayable (for example, a residential fixed rate mortgage portfolio). The IASB decided to address hedging of such portfolios in its separate macro hedging project (see 11 below). Until that project is finalised, entities are allowed to apply the portfolio fair value hedging guidance in IAS 39.

Given the current lack of an effective hedge accounting solution within IFRS 9 for portfolios that feature a bottom layer that is prepayable, it is not uncommon for entities to consider alternative 'proxy' hedge accounting designations (see 6.2.1 below). For example, an entity wishing to hedge an economic bottom layer within a group of items prepayable at par within a fair value hedge could identify specific items within the group (and designate those items only) or designate a percentage of the total as the hedged item. Both these approaches are still likely to result in ineffectiveness. If specific items within the group were designated in a fair value hedge, and those specific items prepaid, then the designated hedged item would no longer exist, even if there was sufficient 'non-designated' items within the group to cover the amount designated. The issues arising from designation of a proportion are best explained with an example (see Example 53.11 below).

Example 53.11:   Hedging a proportion of a prepayable loan portfolio

A bank holds a portfolio of fixed rate loans with a total nominal amount of $100m. The borrowers can, at any time, prepay all of their (original) loan amount at par, plus an exit fee. The bank only expects 20% of the original loan amount to be prepaid before maturity.

For risk management purposes, the loans are considered together with variable rate borrowings of $100m. As a result, the bank is exposed to an interest margin risk resulting from the fix-to-floating rate mismatch. The bank expects $20m of loans to be prepaid.

As part of the risk management strategy, the bank decides to hedge the interest margin by entering into a pay fixed/receive variable interest rate swap (IRS). The objective is to hedge the amount of loans that they do not expect to prepay using an IRS with a notional amount of $80m. The IRS is designated as a fair value hedge of 80% of the $100m loan portfolio.

After two years loans of $10m are prepaid, which is less than 20% and therefore does not affect the economic hedge in place. However, because of the proportionate designation, this is considered a reduction in the hedged amount for hedge accounting purposes. As a result, the entity now has an IRS of $80m designated as a hedge of loans of $72m ([$100m – $10m] × 80%), which will inevitably lead to some ineffectiveness.

Another source of ineffectiveness will be fair value changes attributable to the embedded prepayment option within the loan portfolio (see 7.4.12 below).

Another common approach for an entity hedging a bottom layer for risk management purposes is to identity different proxy hedged items, such as floating rate liabilities, and designate the derivatives as hedging them within a cash flow hedge (see 6.2.1 below. This avoids the inclusion of fair value changes of the embedded prepayment option in the fixed rate loans as a source of potential ineffectiveness.

2.4   The 'sub-LIBOR issue'

Some financial institutions are able to raise funding at interest rates that are below a benchmark interest rate (e.g. LIBOR minus 15 basis points (bps)). In such a scenario, the entity may wish to remove the variability in future cash flows caused by movements in the benchmark interest rates. IFRS 9 does not allow the designation of a 'full' benchmark risk component (i.e. LIBOR flat) in this situation, as a component cannot be more than the total cash flows of the entire item. This is sometimes referred to as the 'sub-LIBOR issue'. *[IFRS 9.B6.3.21-22].*

Part of the reason for this restriction is that a contractual interest rate is often 'floored' at zero, so that interest will never become negative. Hence, if debt is issued at a benchmark rate minus 15bp and the benchmark rate decreases below 15bps, any further reduction in the benchmark rate would not cause any cash flow variability for the hedged item. Consequently, any designated component has to be less than or equal to the cash flows of the entire item. *[IFRS 9.B6.3.21, BC6.226-228].*

In this scenario, the entity could instead designate, as the hedged item, the variability in cash flows of the entire liability (or a proportion of it) but only for changes attributable to the benchmark rate. *[IFRS 9.B6.3.24].* Such a designation excludes any ineffectiveness from changes in the credit risk specific to the borrower, as these are excluded from the hedge relationship, however it will not be perfectly effective. Ineffectiveness could arise as follows in the hedge designation described above:

- For financial instruments that have an interest rate floor of zero in situations in which the forward curve for a part of the remaining hedged term is below 15 basis points. This is because the hedged item will have less variability in cash flows as a result of interest rate changes than a swap without such a floor. In fact, an expectation that the benchmark rate will consistently be below 15 basis points may cause the hedge relationship to fail the effectiveness criteria as there is no economic relationship between the hedged item and hedging instrument. This would preclude hedge accounting at all (see 6.4.1 below).

However, if the benchmark rate is above 15 basis points and is not expected to go below it, this source of ineffectiveness would not be expected to arise. The hedged item will have the same cash flow variability as a liability without a floor.

- Ineffectiveness is also likely to occur from changes in the time value of the embedded floor in the hedged item, as no offset will arise from the fair value changes of a swap without a floor (see 7.4.12 below).
- Even if the variability of cash flows in the hedged item and hedging instrument may be the same, the absolute cash flows are not, due to the inclusion of the negative spread in the hedged item. Accordingly, the discounted cash flows will not perfectly offset (see 7.4 below).
- The discount curve used to discount the hedged cash flows needs to be based on a benchmark rate. However, there is a choice between discounting the hedged cash flows at the benchmark rate or at the benchmark rate minus the negative credit spread (15 basis points in the example above), as the guidance is not prescriptive. The negative credit spread would not need to be updated for changes in the borrower's credit risk as that risk is excluded from the hedge relationship. This is consistent with the general hedge accounting approach of calculating a change in the present value of the hedged item with respect to the hedged risk and not a full fair value. The second option for discounting may improve effectiveness but some ongoing ineffectiveness is likely to remain (see 7.4 below).

While the example in the standard uses LIBOR as the benchmark component, it is clear that the requirement relates not just to financial items in general, or to the LIBOR benchmark component in particular, but is a general prohibition on the cash flows of hedged risk components being larger than the cash flows of the entire hedged item. This means that the sub-LIBOR issue is also applicable to non-financial items where the contract price is linked to a benchmark price minus a differential. This is best demonstrated using an example derived from the application guidance of IFRS 9 (see Example 53.12 below).

Example 53.12: Sub-LIBOR issue – selling crude oil at below benchmark price

An entity has a long-term sales contract to sell crude oil of a specific quality to a specified location. The contract includes a clause that sets the price per barrel at West Texas Intermediate (WTI) minus USD 10 with a minimum price of USD 30. The entity wishes to hedge the WTI benchmark price risk by entering into a WTI future. As outlined above, the entity cannot designate a 'full' WTI component, i.e. a WTI component that ignores the price differential and the minimum price.

However, the entity could designate the WTI future as a hedge of the entire cash flow variability under the sales contract that is attributable to the change in the benchmark price. When doing so, the hedged item would have the same cash flow variability as a sale of crude oil at the WTI price (or above), as long as the forward price for the remaining hedged term does not fall below USD 40. *[IFRS 9.B6.3.25]*.

Where the hedged item has the same cash flow variability as the hedging instrument there may be an expectation that the hedge relationship will meet the effectiveness criteria. However, any ineffectiveness needs to be measured and recorded in profit or loss (see 7.4 below).

In some cases, the contract price may not be defined as a benchmark price minus a fixed differential but as a benchmark price plus a pricing differential (the 'basis spread') that is sometimes positive and sometimes negative. The market structure may reveal that items are priced that way and there may even be derivatives available for the basis spread (i.e. basis swaps, for example the benchmark gas oil crack spread derivative which is a derivative for the price differential between crude oil and gas oil which reflects the refining margin *[IFRS 9.B6.3.10(c)(i)]*). Similar to Example 53.12 above, an entity could not designate the benchmark price component as the hedged item given that the cash flows of the benchmark component could be more than the total cash flows of the entire item. Unfortunately, the standard does not provide any guidance as to how an entity should assess whether the basis spread could be negative or not. For example, it is not clear whether an entity is only required to look at the forward benchmark prices or whether it should consider all reasonably possible scenarios. The use of 'reasonably possible scenarios' in other places in IFRS 9 might indicate that the latter.

A related question is whether the entity could designate the entire cash flow variability that is attributable to changes in only the benchmark risk (as the entity alternatively does as shown in Example 53.12 above) if that risk is a non-contractually specified risk component. This assessment is likely to be similar to whether a non-contractually specified risk component is separately identifiable and reliably measurable (as outlined at 2.2.3 above), which would be required in order to determine the variability of the entire cash flows with respect to changes in the benchmark.

However, the presence of a spread that is sometimes negative could make this assessment more difficult. An entity needs to prove that the benchmark cash flows plus or minus the spread make up the total cash flows. This might be the case, for example, if it can be proven that there are quality differences, such that the benchmark is sometimes of better quality and sometimes worse than the hedged exposure. On the other hand, if the basis spread switches between positive and negative because of individual supply and demand drivers in the benchmark price and the price of the hedged exposure, this may indicate that the benchmark is not implicit in the fair value or cash flows of the hedged exposure. To illustrate this with an example, we could take WTI and Brent crude oil prices. While both prices might be highly correlated, WTI could not be identified as a benchmark component in Brent because both prices have their own supply and demand drivers. Furthermore, it would not be possible to determine whether either WTI is a risk component of Brent or *vice versa*, which demonstrates that there is no risk component that can be designated in a hedge relationship. In that case, hedge accounting would only be permitted if the full cash flows were designated for all changes in the contract price, and assuming the other eligibility requirements are met.

Furthermore, the prohibition on identifying a benchmark risk component in a variable instrument priced at sub-benchmark (i.e. a benchmark rate minus a spread) as outlined above has also some relevance for fixed rate instruments. Let us consider a fixed rate item that is originally priced based on a benchmark rate minus a spread, for example, a fixed-rate financial liability for which the contractual interest rate is priced at 100 basis points below the benchmark. It would not be possible to identify the hedged item as having fixed interest cash flows equal to the benchmark, however an entity can designate as the hedged item the entire liability (i.e. principal plus interest – equal to the benchmark minus 100 basis points) for changes in value attributable to changes in the benchmark. [IFRS 9.B6.3.23].

The negative interest rate environment in some countries, mainly countries in the Eurozone and Switzerland, has further implications on the designation of risk components in connection with the sub-LIBOR issue (see 2.4.2 below).

2.4.1 Late hedges of benchmark portions of fixed rate instruments

There is no requirement in IFRS 9 for hedge accounting to be designated on initial recognition of either the hedged item or the hedging instrument. [IFRS 9.B6.5.28]. In particular, it is not uncommon for risk management and/or hedge accounting to be applied sometime after initial recognition of the hedged item. This is often referred to as a 'late hedge'. There is no additional guidance in IFRS 9 on how to apply hedge accounting to 'late hedges' over and above the usual criteria. However, the identification of eligible risk components in fixed rate hedged items in late hedges can be problematic.

An example of the difficulties of such a designation is discussed in the application guidance to IFRS 9 with respect to a fixed rate financial instrument that is hedged sometime after its origination, and interest rates have changed in the meantime, such that the fixed rate on the instrument is now below LIBOR. In this case it may be possible for the entity to designate a risk component equal to the benchmark rate that is higher than the contractual rate paid on the item. This is provided that the benchmark rate is still less than the effective interest rate calculated as if the instrument had been purchased on the day it was first designated as the hedged item. [IFRS 9.B6.3.23]. This is illustrated below.

Example 53.13: Hedge of a portion of an existing fixed rate financial asset following a rise in interest rates

Company B originates a fixed rate financial asset of €100 that has an effective interest rate of 6% at a time when LIBOR is 4%. B begins to hedge that asset sometime later when LIBOR has increased to 8% and the fair value of the asset has decreased to €90.

B calculates that if it had purchased the asset on the date it first designated it as the hedged item for its then fair value of €90, the effective yield would have been 9.5%. Because LIBOR is less than this recalculated notional effective yield, the entity can designate a LIBOR component of 8% that consists partly of the contractual interest cash flows and partly of the difference between the current fair value (€90) and the amount repayable on maturity (€100). [IFRS 9.B6.3.23].

The guidance illustrated in Example 53.13 above will assist entities in designating hedges in a way that significantly reduces ineffectiveness.

2.4.2 Negative interest rates

The negative interest rate environment in some countries, mainly Switzerland and certain countries in the Eurozone, has further implications on the designation of risk components in connection with the sub-LIBOR issue (see 2.4 above). The following example illustrates this.

Example 53.14: Negative interest rates and fair value hedges

Assume the following scenarios:

a) Bank A enters into a €1 million loan to a corporate at a fixed coupon of 3.5%. The coupon has been determined considering the negative Euro Short-Term Rate (ESTR) rate (the benchmark) of –0.15% plus a credit spread of 3.65%.

b) Bank B acquires debt securities in the secondary market, issued by a highly rated corporate entity, with a €1 million notional and fixed coupon of 3.5%. In this fact pattern the debt was issued some years ago when benchmark interest rates were much higher. The purchase price of the debt is €1.185 million which results in an effective interest rate of –0.18%, consisting of the negative ESTR rate (the benchmark) when the debt is acquired of –0.15% and a credit spread of –0.03%.

Both Bank A and Bank B want to hedge the fixed rate benchmark component and enter into an interest rate swap paying fixed –0.15% and receiving ESTR. The banks wish to designate the benchmark component in a fair value hedge for changes in ESTR.

In scenario a) it seems acceptable for the bank to designate the benchmark risk component because:

- it is included in the pricing of the hedged item and is thought to meet the separately identifiable and reliably measurable criteria (see 2.2.3.A above), (or if applying the Phase 2 amendments for Interest Rate Benchmark Reform will do so within 24 months (9.2.2.A below));
- the benchmark can be positive or negative, therefore the cash flows representing that benchmark rate can also be positive or negative, even if they are part of overall positive cash flows (which is similar to a benchmark component of 4% hedging the benchmark risk in a coupon of 5%, except that the benchmark is negative in this case); and
- the benchmark cash flows are less than the cash flows in the hedged items (i.e. minus 0.15% which is less than 3.5%).

We would find it difficult to reach the same conclusion for scenario b) as the benchmark rate is higher than the effective interest rate (i.e. minus 0.15% which is greater than minus 0.18%). *[IFRS 9.B6.3.23]*. This is consistent with the fact that if a debt instrument were to be issued at par bearing a coupon of –0.18%, which included credit spread of –0.03% when the benchmark rate was –0.15% it would not be possible to identify a benchmark component for hedge accounting purposes. *[IFRS 9.B6.3.21]*.

In both scenarios, the banks would not be permitted to designate a payment of –0.15% of the principal as an eligible component of a receipt of a 3.5% coupon, as it is difficult to argue that a payment of a negative 0.15% of the principal is a portion of a receipt of 3.5% of that principal. However, this is not that relevant in scenario a) as it would be possible to designate a separately identifiable benchmark component in the total cash flows, as noted above.

Notwithstanding the above, in both cases, the banks can designate all the cash flows in the financial asset for changes in the benchmark rate, although this is likely to result in some ineffectiveness. *[IFRS 9.B6.3.21]*.

2.5 Groups of items

2.5.1 General requirements

Under IFRS 9, hedge accounting may be applied to a group of items if:

- the group consists of items or components of items that would individually qualify for hedge accounting; and
- for risk management purposes, the items in the group are managed together on a group basis. *[IFRS 9.6.6.1]*.

Example 53.15: Hedging a portfolio of shares

An entity holds a portfolio of shares of Swiss companies that replicates the Swiss Market Index (SMI). The entity elected to account for the shares at fair value through other comprehensive income without subsequent reclassification to profit or loss, as allowed by IFRS 9 (see Chapter 48 at 8). The entity decides to lock in the current value of the portfolio by entering into corresponding SMI futures contracts.

The individual shares would be eligible hedged items if hedged individually. As the objective of the portfolio is to replicate the SMI, the entity can also demonstrate that the shares are managed together on a group basis. The entity also assesses the compliance with the criteria for hedge accounting (see 6 below). Consequently, the entity designates the SMI futures contracts as the hedging instrument in a hedge of the fair value of the portfolio. As a result, the gains or losses on the SMI futures are accounted for in OCI (without subsequent reclassification to profit or loss) in the same manner as the shares, thus eliminating the accounting mismatch (see 2.6.3 below).

Whether the items in the group are managed together on a group basis is a matter of fact, i.e. it depends on an entity's behaviour and cannot be achieved by mere documentation.

The IFRS 9 eligibly criteria for groups of items for hedge accounting also permits designation of net positions, however some restrictions for cash flow hedges of net positions are retained (see 2.5.3 below). *[IFRS 9.BC6.435, BC6.436]*. Net hedged positions are permitted as eligible hedged items under IFRS 9 only if an entity hedges on a net basis for risk management purposes. Whether an entity hedges in this way is a matter of fact (not merely of assertion or documentation). Hence an entity cannot apply hedge accounting on a net basis solely to achieve a particular accounting outcome, if that would not reflect its risk management approach. *[IFRS 9.B6.6.1]*.

IFRS 9 also contains special presentation requirements when hedging net positions, which are discussed at 10.3 below.

2.5.2 Hedging a component of a group

A group designation can also consist of a component of a group of items, such as a layer component of a group. A component could also be a proportion of a group of items, such as 50% of a fixed rate bond series with a total volume of CU 100 million. Whether an entity designates a layer component or a proportionate component depends on the entity's risk management objective. *[IFRS 9.6.6.1, 6.6.2]*.

The benefits of identifying a layer component, as discussed at 2.3 above, are relevant when applied to a group of items. In fact, the bottom layer hedging strategy discussed in Example 53.10 above is, in fact, a designation of a component of a group. The following example provides a different example of designating a component of a group, this time a top layer.

Example 53.16: Hedging a top layer of a portfolio of financial liabilities

A bank completes a bond issuance of CAD 50 million that is made up of 50,000 fixed rate bonds with a face value of CAD 1,000 each. The bank expects that it will repurchase up to CAD 10 million of the issue before maturity. Therefore, it chooses to transact a receive fixed/pay variable interest rate swap with a notional amount of CAD 10 million, in order to hedge the benchmark component of the fair value interest rate risk of the volume that is expected to be repurchased. From an economic perspective, that hedge would allow repurchases of up to CAD 10 million total face value for which the gain or loss from changes in the benchmark interest rate would be compensated by the gain or loss on the swap. However, this can only be reflected in the accounting if the entity designates a CAD 10 million top layer. The entity would revalue the first CAD 10 million of face value of the bond issue for changes in the benchmark risk, and would include a fair value hedge gain or loss when determining the gain or loss on derecognition of the first CAD 10 million of bonds.

If it was not permitted to designate a layer of a group of items, entities would in such cases either have to identify individual items within the group and designate them on a standalone basis, or prorate the fair value hedge gain or loss to the entire bond issue volume, as discussed in 2.3.2 above. The IASB believes this would result in arbitrary accounting results and decided to allow a layer component designation for a group of items. *[IFRS 9.BC6.438, BC6.439]*.

A layer component of a group of items only qualifies for hedge accounting if:

- the layer is separately identifiable and reliably measurable;
- the risk management objective is to hedge a layer component;
- the items in the group from which the layer is identified are exposed to the same hedged risk (so that measurement of the hedged layer is not significantly affected by which particular items from the overall group form part of the hedged layer);
- for a hedge of existing items, the items in the group can be identified and tracked; and
- any items in the group containing prepayment options meet the requirements for components of a nominal amount (see 2.3.2 above). *[IFRS 9.6.6.3]*.

Based on the information provided, the top layer in Example 53.16 above would meet the criteria in order for a top layer to be designated.

A hedging relationship can include layers from several different groups of items. For example, in a hedge of a net position of a group of assets and a group of liabilities (see 2.5.1 above), the hedging relationship can comprise, in combination, a layer component of the group of assets and a layer component of the group of liabilities. *[IFRS 9.B6.6.12]*.

2.5.3 Cash flow hedge of a net position

Many entities are exposed to foreign currency risk arising from purchases and sales of goods or services denominated in foreign currencies. Cash inflows and outflows occurring on forecast transactions in the same foreign currency are often economically hedged on a net basis, as illustrated in the below example.

Example 53.17: Economic 'natural hedge' of foreign currency cash flows

An entity with GBP as its functional currency anticipates foreign currency denominated sales of USD 100 in 12 months and also intends to purchase fixed assets of USD 80 in 12 months. USD 80 of the cash inflows of the forecast sales are economically hedged together with the cash outflows for the forecast purchase of the fixed assets. A single foreign currency forward contract to sell USD20 in 12 months is transacted to hedge the net position arising from the sales and purchases.

In the case of a cash flow hedge of a group of items whose variabilities in cash flows are not expected to be approximately proportional to the overall variability in cash flows of the group so that offsetting or net risk positions arise, designation is only permitted for a hedge of foreign currency risk. *[IFRS 9.6.6.1(c), B6.6.7, BC6.455]*. Said differently, designation of a net position in a cash flow hedge is limited to hedges of foreign currency risk under IFRS 9.

The standard mechanics of cash flow hedge accounting cannot accommodate a hedged net position whose gross cash flows affect profit or loss in different periods (see 7.2 below). Applying standard cash flow hedge accounting to Example 53.17, the gain or loss accumulated in other comprehensive income (OCI) on the USD 20 of hedging instrument would be reclassified to profit or loss when the revenue transaction occurs. However, this will only offset the gain or loss on USD 20 of the USD 100 hedged revenue while the remaining revenue of FC 80 and the fixed asset purchase of USD 80 (i.e. the economic hedge) would still be measured at the spot rate. This would result in the bottom line profit for the period(s) not reflecting the economic hedge.

IFRS 9 amends the standard cash flow hedge accounting for such a net position in that the foreign currency gain or loss on the USD 80 revenue cash flows that affect profit or loss in the earlier period must be carried forward to offset the foreign currency gain or loss on the fixed asset purchase cash flows that will affect profit or loss in later periods. This is achieved by deferring the gain or loss on the natural hedge in OCI, with a reclassification to profit or loss once the offsetting cash flows affect profit or loss (see 9.3.1 and Example 53.18 below).

However, the gross transactions that make up the net position are recognised when they arise and will be measured at the spot foreign currency rate ruling at that time. They are not adjusted to reflect the result of the hedge. The whole impact of hedge accounting must be presented in a separate line item in profit or loss. *[IFRS 9.6.6.4]*.

This separate line item includes:
- the reclassification adjustment for gains or losses on the hedge of the net position;
- the gain or loss on the natural hedge, with the counter-entry being recognised in OCI; and
- the later reclassification adjustment of the gain or loss on the natural hedge from OCI to profit or loss.

The rather complicated accounting described above is best illustrated using an example:

Example 53.18: Cash flow hedge of a foreign currency net position

An entity having CAD as functional currency anticipates sales of GBP 100m in 12 months and also plans a major capital expenditure (fixed assets) of GBP 80m in 12 months. The anticipated sales and capital expenditure (i.e. the group of forecast transactions) are designated as the hedged item and the resulting net position is hedged with a forward contract to sell GBP 20m in 12 months. The fixed assets will be depreciated on a straight-line basis over eight years. For simplicity, assume the spot rate equals the forward rate.

GBP/CAD spot rate	
At inception of the hedge (beginning of year 1)	1.50
After 12 months (end of year 1)	1.60

The entity would record the following journal entries (amounts in millions):

Year 1

	DR CAD	CR CAD
Other comprehensive income	2	
Hedging derivative		2

To recognise the fair value loss from the hedging instrument in the statement of financial position and the cash flow hedge reserve (GBP 20 × [1.50 – 1.60]).

Cash	160	
Revenue from sales		160

To account for the sales volume of GBP 100 at the current spot rate of 1.60 (GBP 100 × 1.60).

Property, plant and equipment	128	
Cash		128

To account for the purchase of GBP 80 fixed assets at the current spot rate of 1.60 (GBP 80 × 1.60).

Hedging derivative	2	
Cash		2

To account for the settlement of the forward contract.

Net position hedging gains/losses	2	
Other comprehensive income		2

To reclassify the cash flow hedge reserve from OCI to profit or loss.

Net position hedging gains/losses	8	
Other comprehensive income		8

To defer the natural hedge gain from profit or loss to OCI (GBP 80 × [1.60 – 1.50]).

The net profit for the period is CAD 150, which represents the sale of GBP 100 at the hedged rate of 1.50 (albeit presented in two different line items).

Years 2 to 9

Depreciation	16	
Property, plant and equipment		16

To account for the straight line depreciation of the fixed assets (CAD 128 × 12.5%).

Other comprehensive income	1	
Net position hedging gains/losses		1

To reclassify part of the deferred gain from OCI to profit or loss (CAD 8 × 12.5%).

The net loss for each period is 15, which represents depreciation (at 12.5%) of a fixed asset of GBP 80 purchased at the hedged rate of 1.50.

Overview

Income statement (CAD)	Y1	Y2	Y3	Y4	Y5	Y6	Y7	Y8	Y9	Total
Revenue from sale of goods	160									160
Depreciation		(16)	(16)	(16)	(16)	(16)	(16)	(16)	(16)	(128)
Net position hedging gains/losses	(10)	1	1	1	1	1	1	1	1	(2)
Profit for the period	150	(15)	(15)	(15)	(15)	(15)	(15)	(15)	(15)	30

Statement of financial position (CAD)	Y1	Y2	Y3	Y4	Y5	Y6	Y7	Y8	Y9
Cash	30	30	30	30	30	30	30	30	30
Property, plant and equipment	128	112	96	80	64	48	32	16	0
Hedging reserve (OCI)	(8)	(7)	(6)	(5)	(4)	(3)	(2)	(1)	0

The transactions within a net position still must be measured at their spot rates, while the effect of the hedge is presented in a separate line item. *[IFRS 9.B6.6.15]*. In other words, although an entity may be economically hedged from a bottom line (or net) perspective, volatility will still arise in the amounts reported for the individual hedged transactions (on a gross basis), and it is only the bottom line of profit or loss that will reflect the benefits of the hedge.

For a net position to qualify for cash flow hedge accounting the hedge documentation has to include, for each type of item within the net position, its amount and nature as well as the reporting period in which it is expected to affect profit or loss. This is expected to be a relatively detailed record of what makes up the net position and how it will impact profit or loss, including the depreciation profile, if relevant. *[IFRS 9.6.6.1(c)(ii), B6.6.7, B6.6.8]*.

2.5.4 Nil net positions

IFRS 9 also addresses hedges of nil net positions. This refers to when entities hedge a group of items where the hedged items themselves fully offset the risk that is managed.

An example would be similar to the scenario illustrated by Example 53.17 above but where the entity anticipates sales of GBP 100m in 12 months and also plans a major capital expenditure of GBP 100m in 12 months. An entity is allowed to designate such a nil net position in a hedging relationship, provided that:

- the hedge is part of a rolling net risk hedging strategy, whereby the entity routinely hedges new positions of the same type over the course of time (for example when transactions move into the time horizon for which the entity hedges);
- hedging instruments are used to hedge the net risk when the hedged net position changes in size over the life of the rolling hedging strategy and is not a nil net position;
- the entity would normally apply hedge accounting to such net positions when the net position is not nil; and
- not applying hedge accounting to the nil net position would result in inconsistent accounting outcomes over time (because in a period in which the net position is nil, hedge accounting would not be available for what is otherwise the same type of exposure). *[IFRS 9.6.6.6]*.

2.6 Other eligibility issues for hedged items

2.6.1 Highly probable

Forecast transactions (or a component thereof) may only be eligible hedged items if they are highly probable of occurring (see 2.1 above). *[IFRS 9.6.3.3]*. The term 'highly probable' is not defined in IFRS 9 but is often interpreted to have a much greater likelihood of happening than 'more likely than not'. The Implementation Guidance within IAS 39 contained some guidance as to how the term highly probable should be applied within the context of hedge accounting and, this guidance can be considered relevant for IFRS 9 hedge accounting. The IAS 39 guidance indicates that an assessment of the likelihood that a forecast transaction will take place is not based solely on management's intention, it should be supported by observable facts and the attendant circumstances. In such an assessment, an entity should consider the following:

- the frequency of similar past transactions;
- the financial and operational ability of the entity to carry out the transaction;
- whether substantial commitments of resources have been made to a particular activity;
- the extent of loss of disruption of operations that could result if the transaction does not occur;
- the likelihood that transactions with substantially different characteristics might be used to achieve the same business purpose; and
- the entity's business plan.

In March 2019, the Interpretations Committee discussed the application of the highly probable requirement with respect to a specific derivative (a load following swap) designated as a hedging instrument.[5] In a load following swap the notional amount of the derivative designated as a hedging instrument varies depending on the outcome of the hedged item (e.g. forecast energy sales). As part of that specific discussion, the IFRIC observed more generally that the terms of the hedging instrument do not affect the highly probable assessment because the highly probable requirement is applicable to the hedged item (see 6.3.3 below). For example, an entity that wishes to hedge the foreign currency risk of a future business combination, can only achieve hedge accounting once the business combination itself is highly probable (see 2.6.4 below). This is the case even if the hedging instrument is a deal contingent foreign currency contract, such that if the business combination does not go ahead, the foreign currency contract is terminated with no cash settlement.

An entity may also need to consider the impact of wider industry and business drivers as to whether cash flows are highly probable or not. For example:

- whether forecast cash flows in a subsidiary that is due to be sold can be considered highly probable in the parent's consolidated financial statements (see 7.2.4 below); or
- if a designated benchmark interest rate is no longer expected to exist, whether forecast cash flows linked to that benchmark can be highly probable (see 9 below).

The length of time until a forecast transaction is projected to occur is also a factor. Other factors being equal, the more distant a forecast transaction is, the less likely it is that it would be considered highly probable and the stronger the evidence required to determine that it is highly probable.

For example, a transaction forecast to occur in 5 years will often be less likely to occur than a transaction forecast to occur in one year. However, forecast interest payments for the next 20 years on variable rate debt would typically be highly probable if supported by an existing contractual obligation.

An entity may also need to consider the credit risk associated with the counterparty to a forecast transaction. Even though a forecast transaction does not involve credit risk, depending on the possible counterparties for the anticipated transaction, the credit risk that affects them can indirectly affect the assessment of whether the forecast transaction is highly probable or not (see 6.4.2.B below).

In addition, other factors being equal, the greater the physical quantity or future value of the forecast transaction, in proportion to the entity's total transactions of the same nature, the less likely it is that the transaction would be considered highly probable. For example, less evidence generally would be needed to support forecast highly probable sales of 100,000 units in the next month than 950,000 units in that month, when recent sales have averaged 950,000 for the past 3 months.

A history of having designated hedges of forecast transactions and then determining that they are no longer expected to occur would call into question both an entity's ability to predict forecast transactions accurately and the propriety of using hedge accounting in the future for similar transactions. *[IAS 39 IG F.3.7]*. This is clearly common sense, however the standard contains no prescriptive 'tainting' provisions in this area. Therefore, entities are not automatically prohibited from using cash flow hedge accounting if a forecast transaction fails to occur. Instead, whenever such a situation arises the particular facts, circumstances and evidence should be assessed to determine whether doubt has, in fact, been cast on an entity's ongoing hedging strategies.

It is also explained in the IAS 39 Implementation Guidance that cash flows arising after the prepayment date on an instrument that is prepayable at the issuer's option may be highly probable for a group or pool of similar assets for which prepayments can be estimated with a high degree of accuracy, e.g. mortgage loans, or if the prepayment option is significantly out of the money. In addition, the cash flows after the prepayment date may be designated as the hedged item if a comparable option exists in the hedging instrument (see 7.4.12 below). [IAS 39.F.2.12].

Further discussion on the hedge documentation requirements for designated highly probable forecast transactions is given at 6.3.3 below.

2.6.2 Hedged items held at fair value through profit or loss

It does not immediately appear that it would be useful to designate a hedged item that is measured at fair value through profit or loss in a hedge relationship. However, because IFRS 9 may require certain variable rate assets to be measured at fair value through profit or loss (see Chapter 48 at 6), designation as the hedged item in a cash flow hedge relationship may be desirable. Although the variable hedged item would be measured at fair value through profit or loss, an entity may still seek to hedge the variability of cash flows by entering into a hedging derivative. Because of the variable nature of the hedged item, such instruments may not be significantly exposed to changes in fair value caused by movements in the hedged risk whereas the hedging derivative will be. In this instance, application of cash flow hedge accounting facilitates deferral of fair value changes in the hedging derivative to the cash flow hedge reserve, which may better reflect the risk management strategy.

IFRS 9 provides confirmation that cash flow hedge accounting is not prohibited for all hedged items measured at fair value through profit or loss. It gives as an example of an eligible cash flow hedge where an entity uses a swap to change floating rate debt to fixed-rate, even if the debt is measured at fair value. This is because there is a systematic way in which the cash flow hedge reserve can be reclassified, i.e. in the same way interest payments occur on the hedged instrument. A further example is given of a forecast purchase of an equity instrument that, once acquired, will be accounted for at fair value through profit or loss. This is mentioned as an example of an item that cannot be the hedged item in a cash flow hedge, because any gain or loss on the hedging instrument that would be deferred could not be appropriately reclassified to profit or loss during a period in which it would achieve offset. [IFRS 9.B6.5.2].

As well as providing confirmation that cash flow hedge accounting is not precluded for hedged items measured at fair value through profit or loss, the guidance in paragraph B6.5.2 of IFRS 9 also appears to introduce an additional requirement that there is a systematic way in which the cash flow hedge reserve can be reclassified for such a hedge. [IFRS 9.B6.5.2].

In addition, the reason why the instrument is measured at fair value through profit or loss will also be a factor in determining whether an instrument measured at fair value through profit or loss will be an eligible hedged item or not. Classification of an item at fair value through profit or loss could be because such an item is held for trading, managed on a fair value basis, designated as measured at fair value through profit or loss using the fair value option or because the contractual terms of the financial asset give rise on specified dates to cash flows that are not solely payments of principal and interest on the principal amount outstanding (see Chapter 48 at 2). We discuss the eligibility of such instruments measured at fair value through profit or loss in the paragraphs below.

2.6.2.A Hedged items managed on a fair value basis

For a portfolio of financial assets that is managed and whose performance is evaluated on a fair value basis, an entity is primarily focused on fair value information and uses that information to assess the assets' performance and to make decisions. *[IFRS 9.B4.1.6]*. In our view, if the hedging instrument is also part of the same portfolio (or business model), and the entity has by definition determined that fair value is the most appropriate measure for that portfolio, then this would be inconsistent with the idea of cash flow hedging, whereby part of the fair value movements would be recorded in other comprehensive income, separately from the remaining fair values movements that would be recorded in profit or loss. We therefore believe cash flow hedge accounting would not ordinarily be appropriate in this scenario.

Similarly it would not be appropriate to designate a financial asset managed on a fair value basis as a hedged item in a fair value hedge, in order to defer fair value changes in the time, forward or foreign currency basis element of the hedging instrument as a cost of hedging (see 7.5 below).

However, there may be some situations where the cash flow interest rate risk on an asset that is part of a portfolio managed on a fair value basis may be managed outside of the portfolio (or business model). In these cases the instrument hedging the interest rate risk is held separately from the managed portfolio. In such a scenario, cash flow hedge accounting is not necessarily inconsistent with the hedged asset being held at fair value through profit or loss. Such a situation is shown in the following example:

Example 53.19: Interest rate risk managed separately from a credit risk portfolio managed on a fair value basis

Entity A has excess funds to invest and spreads these across various investment portfolios for which the credit risk is managed by individual portfolio managers on a fair value basis. The individual managers are likely to manage the fair value of the portfolio using credit risk derivatives such as credit default swaps. The entity however, wishes to retain the management of interest rate risk centrally where it is aggregated with other interest rate exposures across the entity, e.g. from issued debt, and therefore instructs each portfolio manager to invest in order to achieve a 3m benchmark based rate of return. Accordingly, the majority of assets within each investment portfolio will attract a floating rate and hence most of the portfolio's fair value volatility will arise from changes in credit risk. The interest rate risk is managed centrally and so any interest rate swaps used to fix some of the variability in the future cash flows from changes in interest rate risk are transacted centrally and not part of any investment portfolio, nor are they considered when reporting or assessing the performance of the individual investment portfolios. Each investment portfolio is managed based on its fair value, has discreet fair value financial information and each portfolio manager is assessed on the fair value performance of their portfolio. The entity concludes that the business model test should be applied at the portfolio level and as such each investment portfolio is measured at fair value through profit or loss.

It is possible that in these circumstances the decision to enter into interest rate swaps and apply cash flow hedge accounting to an asset within the investment portfolios is not inconsistent with the fact the instrument is held at fair value through profit or loss, since that designation is driven by management of the fair value of credit and not the interest rate element.

2.6.2.B   Hedged items held for trading

Derivatives are deemed to be held for trading (see Chapter 48 at 4) and are therefore ineligible as hedged items on their own. *[IAS 39.F2.1]*. A portfolio that is held for trading is one where assets and liabilities are acquired or incurred principally for the purpose of selling or repurchasing or short-term profit-taking. An entity achieves those objectives by either selling or repurchasing the financial instruments or by entering into an opposite trade to lock-in a gain. We believe in this case hedge accounting will not be appropriate for the reasons set out below:

- it is consistent with the prohibition on derivatives being hedged items;
- a trading portfolio is likely to be managed on a fair value basis and so a number of the considerations in 2.6.2.A above will also apply. Furthermore, it is unlikely that any of the risks within the trading portfolio will be managed other than for trading purposes; and
- in a trading portfolio where an entity may sell an asset in the near team, the asset will usually not be eligible for cash flow hedging as the future cash flows will not be highly probable.

Although derivatives cannot on their own be designated as hedged items, they can be designated as hedged items in combination with a non-derivative item as part of an aggregated exposure if certain criteria are met. This allows hedge accounting to be applied to many common risk management strategies, such as where an entity initially only hedges the price risk of a highly probable forecast purchase of a raw material denominated in a foreign currency, then later hedges the foreign currency risk too (see 2.7 below).

2.6.2.C   Hedged items that have failed the contractual cash flows test

Where instruments are classified as fair value through profit or loss because they fail the contractual cash flow characteristics test (see Chapter 48 at 6), the above arguments do not apply and so it appears that such instruments may be designated as the hedged item.

2.6.3   Hedges of exposures affecting other comprehensive income

Only hedges of exposures that could affect profit or loss qualify for hedge accounting. *[IFRS 9.6.5.2]*. This would include hedged debt instruments measured at fair value through other comprehensive income (OCI) as although changes in fair value are initially recognised in OCI, on derecognition of such items any gains or losses held in OCI will be reclassified to profit or loss. *[IFRS 9.4.1.2A]*. Care would need to be taken to ensure the hedge designation is not inconsistent with that of the business model under which the hedged item is held. A further concern would be trying to apply hedge accounting to cash flows that are not highly probable (see 2.6.1 above and 6.1 and 6.2 below).

The sole exception to the requirement that hedges could affect profit or loss is when an entity is hedging an investment in equity instruments for which it has elected to present changes in fair value in OCI, as permitted by IFRS 9. Using that election, gains or losses on the equity investments will never be recognised in profit or loss (see Chapter 48 at 2.2). *[IFRS 9.6.5.3]*.

For such a hedge, the fair value change of the hedging instrument is recognised in OCI. *[IFRS 9.6.5.8]*. Any hedge ineffectiveness is also recognised in OCI. *[IFRS 9.6.5.3]*. On sale of the investment, gains or losses accumulated in OCI are not reclassified to profit or loss (see Chapter 48 at 2.2). Consequently, the same also applies for any accumulated fair value changes on the hedging instrument, including any ineffectiveness (see 7.8 below).

2.6.4 Hedges of a firm commitment to acquire a business

A firm commitment to acquire a business in a business combination cannot be a hedged item, except for foreign currency risk, because the other risks being hedged cannot be specifically identified and measured. *[IFRS 9.B6.3.1]*. It also follows that a forecast business combination could be a hedged item for foreign currency risk in a cash flow hedge, as long as the highly probable criterion is met (see 2.6.1 above). The other risks – i.e. other than foreign currency risk, are also said to be general business risks. IAS 39 provided additional guidance on hedging general business risks that appears relevant also to IFRS 9. A hedge of the risk of obsolescence of a physical asset or the risk of expropriation of property by a government is not eligible for hedge accounting (effectiveness cannot be measured because those risks are not reliably measurable). *[IAS 39.AG110]*. Similarly, the risk that a transaction will not occur is an overall business risk that is not eligible as a hedged item. *[IAS 39.F.2.8]*.

Nevertheless, transactions of the business to be acquired (for example floating rate interest payments on its borrowings) may potentially qualify as hedged items. For this to be the case it would need to be demonstrated that, from the perspective of the acquirer, those hedged transactions are highly probable (see 2.6.1 above) and could impact the post-acquisition profit or loss of the acquirer (see 5.1 and 5.2 below). Determining that the hedged transaction is highly probable may not be straightforward, as this requirement applies to both the business combination and the hedged transactions themselves.

2.6.5 Forecast acquisition or issuance of foreign currency monetary items

Changes in foreign currency rates prior to the acquisition or issuance of a monetary item denominated in a foreign currency do not impact profit or loss as any foreign currency risk on the issue of debt will be offset by the foreign currency risk on the cash that will be borrowed. Therefore, an entity cannot hedge the foreign currency risk associated with the forecast acquisition or issuance of a monetary item denominated in a foreign currency, such as the expected issuance of debt denominated in a currency other than the entity's functional currency. This is because there is a need for the hedged risk to have the potential to impact profit or loss in order to achieve hedge accounting. *[IFRS 9.6.5.2]*.

However, it may be possible to designate a combination of the highly probable forecast acquisition or issuance of a foreign currency monetary item and an associated highly probable forecast foreign currency derivative as an aggregated exposure within a hedge accounting relationship (see 2.7 below).

2.6.6 Own equity instruments

Transactions in an entity's own equity instruments (including distributions to holders of such instruments) are generally recognised directly in equity by the issuer (see Chapter 47) and do not affect profit or loss. Therefore, such instruments cannot be designated as a hedged item. *[IFRS 9.6.5.2]*. Similarly, a forecast transaction in an entity's own equity instruments (e.g. a forecast dividend payment) cannot qualify as a hedged item. However, a declared dividend that qualifies for recognition as a financial liability, e.g. because the entity has become legally obliged to make the payment, may qualify as a hedged item. For example, a recognised liability to pay a dividend in a foreign currency would give rise to foreign currency risk.

2.6.7 Core deposits

Financial institutions often receive a significant proportion of their funding from demand deposits, such as current account balances, savings accounts and other accounts that behave in a similar manner. Even though the total balance from all such customer deposits may vary, a financial institution typically determines a level of core deposits that it believes will be maintained for a particular time frame. These customer deposits or accounts usually pay a zero or low, stable interest rate which is generally insensitive to changes in market interest rates, and hence will behave like a fixed interest rate exposure from an interest rate risk perspective for the time frame over which they are expected to remain.

Both existing and new deposits are generally considered fungible for interest rate risk management purposes, as new deposits will usually be on the same terms as any withdrawn deposits that they replace. Financial institutions cannot determine which individual customer deposits will make up the core deposits. While these deposits can be withdrawn at little or short notice, typically they are left as a deposit for a long and generally predictable time despite the low interest paid.

Risk management of the 'deemed' fixed rate interest rate risk exposure that financial institutions attribute to core deposits will often result in the need to transact interest rate derivatives, although achieving hedge accounting for these derivatives can be difficult.[6]

In order for items to be eligible hedged items in a fair value hedge, the fair value of the hedged items must vary with the hedged risk. However, IFRS 13 – *Fair Value Measurement* – states that the fair value of a financial liability with a demand feature (e.g. a demand deposit) is not less than the amount payable on demand, discounted from the first date that the amount could be required to be paid. *[IFRS 13.47]*. Therefore, the fair value of demand deposits will not vary with the hedged risk and fair value hedge accounting is precluded.

An alternative consideration is whether it is possible to designate a core deposit intangible (representing the value of this source of funding to the financial institution) as an eligible hedged item. The term 'core deposit intangible' could be used to represent the difference between:

(a) the fair value of a portfolio of core deposits; and
(b) the aggregate of the individual fair values of the liabilities within the portfolio, normally calculated in accordance with the requirements of IFRS 13.

Generally, an internally-generated core deposit intangible cannot be a hedged item because it is not a recognised asset. However, if a core deposit intangible is acquired together with a related portfolio of deposits, it is required to be recognised separately as an intangible asset (or as part of the related acquired portfolio of deposits) if it meets the recognition criteria in IAS 38 – *Intangible Assets,* which it normally will (see Chapter 9 at 5.5.2).

Theoretically, therefore, a recognised purchased core deposit intangible asset could be designated as a hedged item. However, this will only be the case if it meets the conditions for hedge accounting, including the requirement that the effectiveness of the hedge can be measured reliably. The Implementation Guidance of IAS 39 explains that because it is often difficult to measure reliably the fair value of a core deposit intangible asset other than on initial recognition, it is unlikely that this requirement will be met. *[IAS 39.F.2.3].* In fact, this probably understates the difficulty.

For the reasons set out above, financial institutions are rarely, if ever, able to designate core deposits with the associated hedging instruments in hedge accounting relationships, despite the economic validity of these risk management activities. Accordingly, many financial institutions apply the special portfolio or macro hedge accounting guidance (see 11 below).

2.6.8 Leases and associated right of use assets

Following the introduction of IFRS 16 – *Leases* (see Chapter 23), most entities that previously hedged and designated the full foreign currency risk from future operating lease payments will no longer need to apply hedge accounting. This is because the foreign currency risk in the hedging instrument will naturally offset part of the IAS 21 retranslation of the lease liability. However, the foreign currency risk from future operating lease payments that are not economically hedged will have a previously unrecognised impact on profit or loss. As there is no hedging instrument providing offset to the IAS 21 retranslation of the lease liability, the full foreign currency risk arising from future operating lease payments will be recognised in profit or loss. Accordingly, there may be an additional incentive either to start economically hedging the foreign currency risk in the lease liability and achieve hedge accounting, or to try to achieve hedge accounting using existing foreign currency exposures. In each case, this would be subject to meeting the normal hedge accounting qualifying criteria.

Lease liabilities could be either eligible hedged items or hedging instruments (see 2.1 above and 3.3.1 below respectively). However, achieving hedge accounting for unhedged foreign currency risk in lease liabilities is likely to be problematic. For example, it may be tempting to consider designating the lease liability as the hedging instrument in a fair value hedge of foreign currency risk in the associated right of use asset. A related fact pattern was discussed in June 2019 by the Interpretations Committee when a number of difficulties were identified.[7]

The Committee considered whether foreign currency risk can be a separately identifiable and reliably measurable risk component of a non-financial asset held for consumption that an entity can designate as the hedged item in a fair value hedge accounting relationship. The Committee concluded that, although in theory such a hedge may be possible, the particular facts and circumstances would need to be considered to ensure the hedge accounting criteria were met. The Committee assessed the following key questions as part of their considerations:

Can an entity have exposure to foreign currency risk on a non-financial asset held for consumption that could affect profit or loss? IFRS 9 does not require changes in fair value to be expected to affect profit or loss but, rather, that those changes could affect profit or loss. The Committee observed that changes in fair value of a non-financial asset held for consumption could affect profit or loss if, for example, the entity were to sell the asset before the end of the asset's economic life (see 5.1 below).

If an entity has exposure to foreign currency risk on a non-financial asset, is it a separately identifiable and reliably measurable risk component? The Committee observed that foreign currency risk is separately identifiable and reliably measurable when the risk being hedged relates to changes in fair value arising from translation into an entity's functional currency of fair value that, based on an assessment within the context of the particular market structure, is determined globally only in one particular currency and that currency is not the entity's functional currency (see 2.2.5 above).

Can the designation of foreign currency risk on a non-financial asset held for consumption be consistent with an entity's risk management activities? The Committee observed that, in applying IFRS 9, an entity can apply hedge accounting only if it is consistent with the entity's risk management objective and strategy for managing its exposure (see 6.2.1 below).

In order to achieve fair value hedge accounting for a foreign currency risk component of a non-financial asset held for consumption, all three questions must be answered satisfactorily. It is unlikely that this will be the case for a fair value hedge of the foreign currency risk in a right of use asset with the associated foreign currency lease liability as the hedging instrument. In most cases, there is not an exposure to foreign currency risk in the right of use asset that will affect profit or loss, the fair value of the right of use asset is unlikely to be determined globally only in one particular currency and such a hedge is often not consistent with the entity's risk management objective.

2.7 Aggregated exposures

2.7.1 Introduction

IFRS 9 introduced a hedge accounting concept known as 'an aggregated exposure'; the purpose of which was to facilitate hedge accounting that reflects the effect of risk management undertaken for a hedged position that includes a derivative. An aggregated exposure is described as a combination of an exposure that could qualify as a hedged item, and a derivative together designated as a hedged item. *[IFRS 9.6.3.4].* The guidance does not change the unit of account for instruments making up the aggregated exposure, specifically it is not accounted for as a 'synthetic' single item. Instead, an entity should consider the combined effect of the aggregated exposure for the purpose of assessing hedge effectiveness and measuring hedge ineffectiveness.

Whilst the ability to designate an aggregated exposure as a hedged item in a hedge relationship should allow an entity to reflect better the effect of its risk management in the financial statements, the steps required to achieve this hedge accounting are quite complex. Furthermore, although some detailed examples of hedge accounting for aggregated exposures are provided in the Illustrative Examples within the Implementation Guidance of IFRS 9, there are still some areas of uncertainty. *[IFRS 9.IE115-147].* We outline below the general requirements for hedge accounting for aggregated exposures.

2.7.2 Background

Entities often purchase or sell items (in particular commodities) that expose them to more than one type of risk (e.g. commodity and foreign currency risk). When hedging those risk exposures, entities do not always hedge each risk for the same time period. This is best explained with an example:

Example 53.20: Aggregated exposure – copper purchase in a foreign currency

An entity manufacturing electrical wires is expecting to purchase copper in 12 months. The functional currency of the entity is euro (EUR). The copper price is fluctuating and is denominated in US dollars (USD), which is a foreign currency for the entity. The entity is exposed to two main risks, the copper price risk and the foreign currency risk.

The entity first decides to hedge the copper price fluctuation risk, using a copper futures contract. By doing so, the entity now has a fixed-price copper purchase denominated in a foreign currency and is therefore still exposed to foreign currency risk. (In this example we assume there is no 'basis risk' between the copper price exposures in the expected purchase and the futures contract, such as the effect of quality and the location of delivery). (See 8.2.1 below).

Three months later, the entity decides to hedge the foreign currency risk by entering into a foreign currency forward contract to buy a fixed amount of USD in nine months. By doing so, the entity is hedging the aggregated exposure, which is the combination of the original exposure to variability of the copper price and the copper futures contract. The diagram below illustrates the two economic hedging relationships.

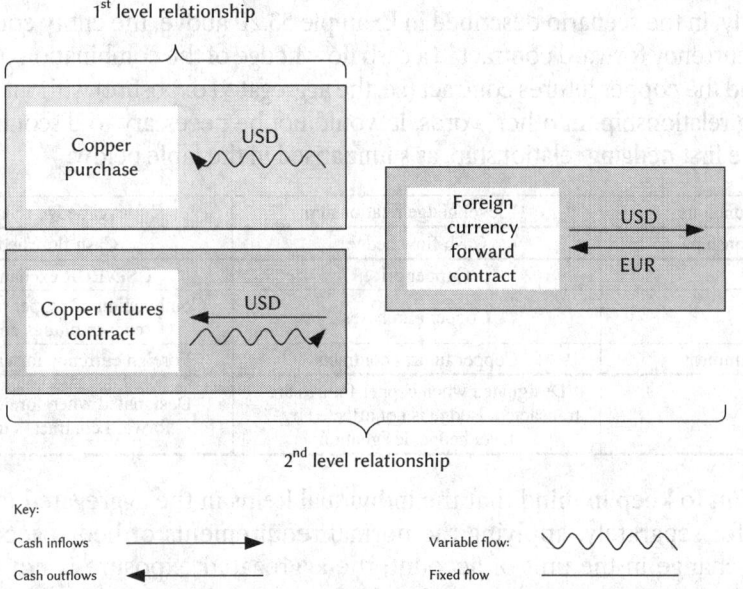

In the above example it would be possible for the entity to initially designate the copper futures contract as hedging variations in the copper purchase price in a cash flow hedge relationship. This is on the assumption that the relevant hedge accounting eligibility criteria are met. (See 6 below). However, when the entity transacts the foreign currency forward contract three months later the general hedge accounting guidance would provide the entity with two choices (see 8.3 below):

- discontinue the first hedging relationship (i.e. the copper price risk hedge) and re-designate a new relationship with joint designation of the copper futures contract and the foreign currency forward contract as the hedging instrument. This is likely to lead to some 'accounting' hedge ineffectiveness as the copper futures contract will now have a non-zero (i.e. off market) fair value on designation of the new relationship (see 7.4.3 below); or

- maintain the copper price risk hedge and designate the foreign currency forward contract in a second relationship as a hedge of the variable USD copper purchase price. Even if the other hedge accounting requirements could be met, this means that the volume of hedged item is constantly changing as it is the variable copper purchase price that is now hedged for foreign currency risk, (i.e. without consideration of the effect of the copper futures). This will likely have an impact on the effectiveness of the hedging relationship, in particular if the variable USD copper price falls, as there may not be sufficient volume of USD cash flows from the designated hedged item in order to match the foreign currency forward contract.

As mentioned above, IFRS 9 includes an additional accounting choice for such a strategy which is to permit designation as hedged items the aggregated exposures that are a combination of an exposure that could qualify as a hedged item and a derivative. *[IFRS 9.6.3.4].*

Consequently, in the scenario described in Example 53.20 above, the entity could designate the foreign currency forward contract in a cash flow hedge of the combination of the original exposure and the copper futures contract (i.e. the aggregated exposure) without affecting the first hedging relationship. In other words, it would not be necessary to discontinue and re-designate the first hedging relationship, as summarised in the table below:

IFRS 9 designations	1st level hedge relationship	2nd level hedge relationship
Hedge relationship	Cash flow hedge	Cash flow hedge
Hedged risk	Copper price	USD/EUR exchange rate
Hedged item	Copper purchases	Combination of copper purchases and copper futures contract
Hedging instrument	Copper futures contracts	Foreign currency forward contract
Designation	Designated when copper futures are transacted. Hedge is not affected by 2nd level hedge designation	Designated when foreign currency forward contract is transacted

It is important to keep in mind that the individual items in the aggregated exposure are accounted for separately, applying the normal requirements of hedge accounting (i.e. there is no change in the unit of account; the aggregated exposure is not treated as a 'synthetic' single item). For example, when hedging a combination of a variable rate loan and a pay fixed/receive variable interest rate swap (IRS), the loan would still be accounted for at amortised cost with the IRS accounted for at fair value through profit or loss, and presented separately in the statement of financial position. An entity would not be allowed to present the IRS and the loan (i.e. the aggregated exposure) together in one line item (i.e. as if it was one single fixed rate loan). *[IFRS 9.B6.3.4].*

Financial instruments: Hedge accounting

However, when assessing the effectiveness and measuring the ineffectiveness of a hedge of an aggregated exposure, the combined effect of the items in the aggregated exposure must be taken into consideration. *[IFRS 9.B6.3.4].* (See 6.4 and 7.4 below respectively). This is of particular relevance if the terms of the hedged item and the hedging instrument in the first hedging relationship do not perfectly match, e.g. if there is basis risk. Any ineffectiveness in the first level relationship would automatically also lead to some ineffectiveness in the second level relationship. However, this does not mean that the same ineffectiveness is recognised twice. The accounting for aggregated exposures is explained using a series of examples, below.

2.7.3 Accounting for aggregated exposures

The following three examples, partly derived from the Illustrative Examples in the Implementation Guidance of IFRS 9, help explain the concept of a hedge of an aggregated exposure. We have not repeated the detailed calculations provided in the Illustrative Examples, but have focused instead on explaining the required approach:

Example 53.21: *Fixed rate loan in a foreign currency – cash flow hedge of an aggregated exposure*

This fact pattern is based on Example 17 in the Illustrative Examples. *[IFRS 9.IE128-137].* An entity has a fixed rate borrowing denominated in a foreign currency (FC) and is therefore exposed to foreign currency risk and fair value risk due to changes in interest rates. The entity decides to swap the borrowing into a functional currency (LC) floating rate borrowing using a cross currency interest rate swap (CCIRS). The CCIRS is designated as the hedging instrument in a fair value hedge (first-level relationship). By doing so, the entity has eliminated both the foreign currency risk and the fair value risk due to changes in interest rates. However, it is now exposed to variable functional currency interest payments.

Later, the entity decides to fix the amount of functional currency interest payments by entering into an interest rate swap (IRS) to pay fixed and receive floating interest in its functional currency. By doing so, the entity is hedging the aggregated exposure, which is the combination of the original exposure and the CCIRS. The IRS is designated as the hedging instrument in a cash flow hedge (second-level relationship). *[IFRS 9.IE131(b)].* The diagram below illustrates the interest flows in the two hedging relationships.

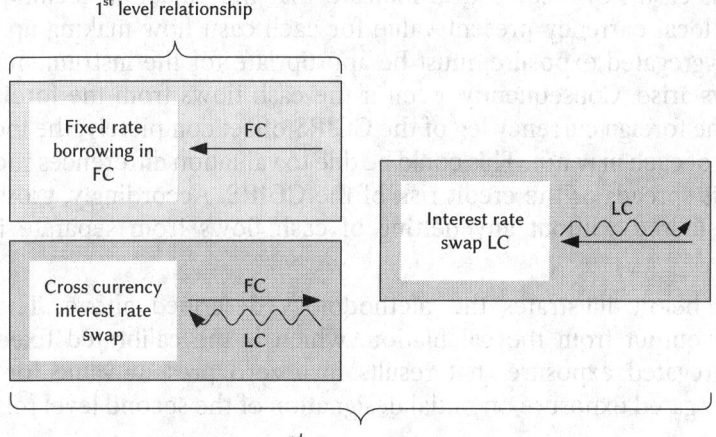

As noted above, the accounting for aggregated exposures can be complex. In this example the complexity lies in the calculation of the present value (PV) of the variability of cash flows of the aggregated exposure. This calculation is necessary in order to calculate the ineffectiveness in the second level relationship, in line with the usual hedge accounting requirements for cash flow hedges. *[IFRS 9.6.5.11(a)(ii)]*.

Example 17 in the Illustrative Examples demonstrates that the variability of the cash flows of the aggregated exposure can be calculated by creating a 'synthetic' aggregated exposure for calculation purposes only. *[IFRS 9.IE.134(a)]*. This is similar to creating what is often referred to as a 'hypothetical derivative' for hedge relationships that do not include aggregated exposures. (See 7.4.4 below).

One leg of the synthetic aggregated exposure is based on the gross cash flows from the aggregated exposure, and the other leg is 'fixed at a blended rate' such that the present value of the whole synthetic aggregated exposure is nil on initial hedge designation. Similar to the role of the fixed leg in a hypothetical derivative, the fixed leg in the synthetic aggregated exposure is designed to reflect the level at which the hedged risk in the aggregated exposure could be locked in on initial designation of the second level relationship. The purpose of this is to capture the present value of the variability of cash flows of the aggregated exposure from that point onwards.

In this particular fact pattern, the leg in the synthetic aggregated exposure that represents the cash flows of the aggregated exposure is a combination of the future foreign currency cash outflows on the liability and the local and foreign currency cash outflows and inflows on the CCIRS. The 'blended' rate for the fixed leg of the synthetic aggregated exposure is calibrated so that the present value of the synthetic aggregated exposure in total is nil on designation of the second level relationship.

In the example in the Illustrative Examples, all the cash flows contributing to the leg that represents the cash flows of the aggregated exposure, are recorded and valued on a gross basis. It follows that if the cash flows from the foreign currency fixed rate liability and those from the receive fixed foreign currency leg of the CCIRS do not exactly offset, then the resultant 'net cash flow' will contribute to the synthetic aggregated exposure leg that represents the cash flows of the aggregated exposure. However, the need to consider gross cash flows could also indicate that the valuation techniques used to calculate the local currency present value for each cash flow making up the leg that reflects the aggregated exposure, must be appropriate for the instrument from which the cash flows arise. Consequently, even if the cash flows from the foreign currency liability and the foreign currency leg of the CCIRS offset completely, the local currency present value of each may not. This could be due to valuation differences such as foreign currency basis spreads or the credit risk of the CCIRS. Accordingly, gross cash flows must be considered without any netting of cash flows from separate instruments. *[IFRS 9.IE134(a)]*.

The diagram below illustrates the methodology described above. The grey field identifies the output from the calculation, which is the calibrated fixed leg of the synthetic aggregated exposure that results in a zero present value for the overall synthetic aggregated exposure on initial designation of the second level relationship.

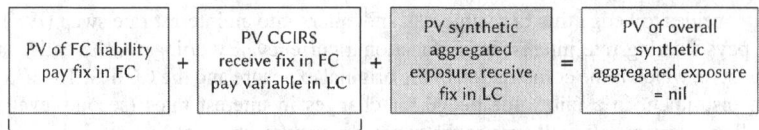

PV of cash flows representing the aggregated exposure

While, as stated above, the Illustrative Examples indicates that valuation techniques used to calculate the present value for each gross cash flow making up the leg that represents the aggregated exposure, must be appropriate for the instrument from which the cash flows arise, it is not entirely clear which valuation basis should be used when calibrating the synthetic fixed rate leg such that the overall synthetic aggregated exposure has a zero present value on designation.

In each subsequent period, the present values are updated for the changes in the cash flows representing the aggregated exposure and associated discount rates, while holding the previously calibrated blended fixed rate on the synthetic aggregated exposure constant, similar to a hypothetical derivative (see 7.4.4 below). The sum of the resulting present values of cash flows, i.e. the present value of the overall synthetic aggregated exposure (which previously was calibrated to be nil as at designation), represents the present value of the cash flow variability of the aggregated exposure which is used for measurement of ineffectiveness. *[IFRS 9.IE134]*.

This is illustrated in the diagram below. The grey field represents the output from this calculation which is the current present value of the cash flow variability of the aggregated exposure.

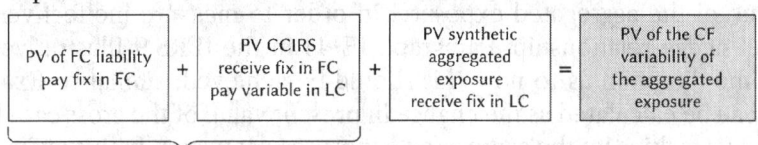

PV of cash flows representing the aggregated exposure

Ineffectiveness is then determined by comparing the change in calculated present value of the cash flow variability of the aggregated exposure and the fair value of the hedging instrument, (i.e. the local currency IRS). The normal ongoing cash flow hedge accounting treatment is applied to the change in fair value of the hedging instrument (see 7.2 below). The accounting for the first level relationship in Example 53.21 above continues unaffected by the second level relationship.

Example 53.22: Floating rate loan in a foreign currency – fair value hedge of an aggregated exposure

This fact pattern is based on Example 18 in the Illustrative Examples. *[IFRS 9.IE138-147]*. An entity has a floating rate borrowing denominated in a foreign currency (FC) and is therefore exposed to foreign currency risk and cash flow risk due to changes in interest rates. The entity decides to swap the borrowing into a functional currency (LC) fixed rate borrowing using a cross currency interest rate swap (CCIRS). The CCIRS is designated as the hedging instrument in a cash flow hedge (first-level relationship). By doing so, the entity has eliminated both the foreign currency risk and the cash flow risk due to changes in interest rates. However, it is now exposed to a fair value risk resulting from changes in the functional currency interest rate curve.

Later, the entity decides to hedge this fair value risk and enters into an interest rate swap (IRS) that receives fixed rate and pays floating rate interest in its functional currency. By doing so, the entity is hedging the aggregated exposure, which is the combination of the original exposure and the CCIRS. The IRS is designated as the hedging instrument in a fair value hedge for changes in interest rates (second-level relationship). [IFRS 9.IE139(b)]. The diagram below illustrates the two hedging relationships.

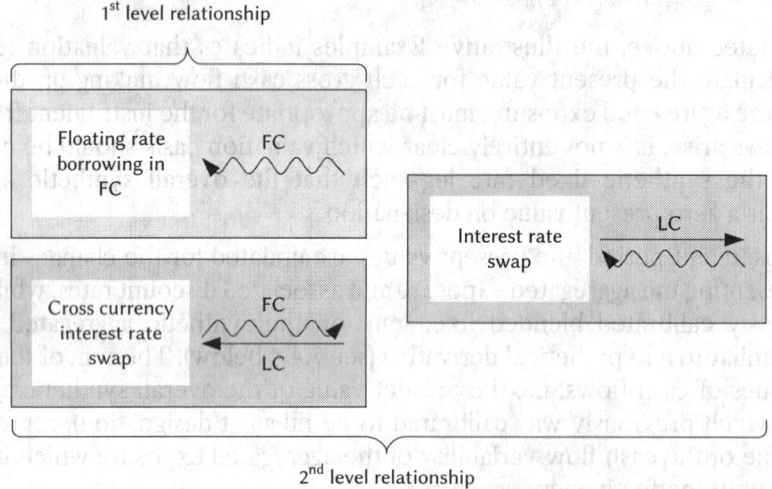

The concept of economically hedging aggregated exposures as such is straightforward. However, the accounting for such relationships includes some complexity. As for any hedge accounting relationship, there is a need to calculate the cumulative change in present value of the aggregated exposure, in order to measure ineffectiveness in the second level hedge relationship. Paragraph IE144 in the IFRS 9 Illustrative Examples provides some direction as to how this should be achieved: similar to Example 53.21 above, this can be calculated as the change in present value of the gross cash flows from the instruments making up the aggregated exposures. However, in this example there is no requirement to create a synthetic blended fixed leg, as the aggregated exposure itself is essentially fixed – it is simply the change in present value of the aggregated exposure cash flows.

An additional complexity in Example 53.22 above, is that it is a cash flow hedge in the first-level relationship that is then designated as the hedged item in a fair value hedge. This means that the cross currency interest rate swap is both a hedging instrument (first level cash flow hedge relationship) and part of a hedged item (second level fair value relationship) at the same time. Accordingly, its fair value changes are initially recognised in other comprehensive income (OCI) through the first level cash flow hedge accounting, but at the same time, should also offset the fair value changes in profit or loss of the hedging IRS in the second-level fair value relationship. This requires a reclassification of the amounts recognised in OCI to profit or loss (to the extent they relate to the second-level relationship) to achieve the offset in the second-level fair value hedge relationship. Consequently, applying fair value hedge accounting to a cross currency interest rate swap designated as the hedged item as part of an aggregated exposure affects where the hedging gains or losses from the first level cash flow hedge relationship are recognised (i.e. reclassification from the cash flow hedge reserve to profit or loss). [IFRS 9.IE143].

As explained in the Illustrative Examples, the application of hedge accounting to an aggregated exposure gets even more complicated when basis risk is involved in one of the hedging relationships, in particular if basis risk is present in the first-level relationship. This is shown in Example 53.23 below.

Example 53.23: Hedge of a commodity price risk as an aggregated exposure in a cash flow hedge of foreign currency risk

This fact pattern is based on Example 16 in the Illustrative Examples *[IFRS 9.IE116-127]*. Entity A, with functional currency (LC), enters into a coffee benchmark price forward contract to hedge its highly probable coffee purchases in foreign currency (FC) in five years. The coffee price that Entity A expects to pay for its coffee purchases is different from the benchmark price. This differential could be because of differences in one or a combination of factors such as the type of coffee, the location or delivery arrangements. Entity A designates the benchmark forward contract and the highly probably forecast transaction as a cash flow hedge (the first level relationship). The entity designates the entire price risk and not only the benchmark risk as it was not able to separately identify a benchmark component in the hedged item (see 2.2.3 above). Accordingly, basis risk exists in the first level relationship. The entity is still exposed to foreign currency risk.

One year later, the entity hedges the foreign currency risk by entering into a foreign currency forward contract. The entity designates the aggregated exposure in the first level relationship and the foreign currency forward contract as a cash flow hedge (the second level relationship). *[IFRS 9.IE119(b)]*. The diagram below illustrates the two hedging relationships.

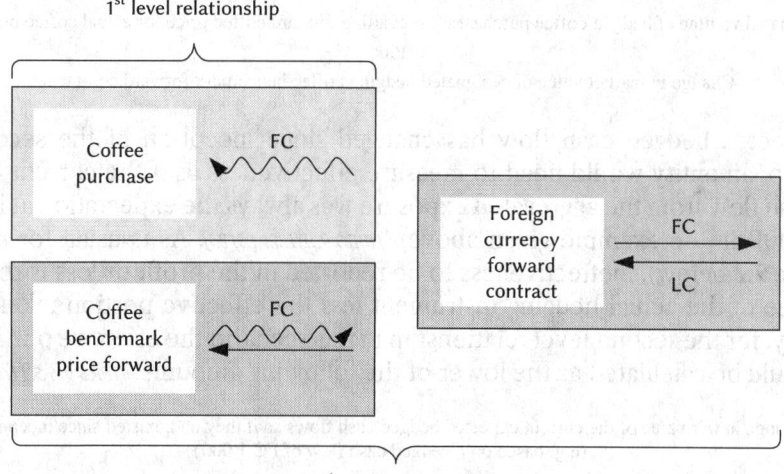

Example 16 in the Illustrative Examples of IFRS 9 demonstrates the accounting effort required in order to achieve hedge accounting for the aggregated exposure. First, the entity calculates the change in fair value of the hedged item and hedging instrument in the first level cash flow hedge relationship in foreign currency and translates them into local currency, using spot rates. Using these local currency equivalents, the entity calculates the ineffectiveness in the first level hedging relationship in the usual way. Second, the entity calculates the change in fair value of the aggregated exposure and the hedging instrument in the second-level cash flow hedge relationship in local currency. This results in the second level ineffectiveness.

The existence of basis risk within the first level relationship complicates the measurement of ineffectiveness in the second level relationship described above.

The aggregated exposure is a combination of the foreign currency cash flows expected from the highly probable coffee purchases and the gain or loss on the commodity hedging contract. If the first level relationship was a 'perfect hedge', the resultant foreign currency cash flow to be hedged in the second level relationship would be known. However, as commodity basis risk exists in the first level relationship, the hedged amount of foreign currency in the second level relationship will vary, as the basis spread between the price of the forecast coffee purchases and the underlying coffee price in the hedging contract varies. The hedging instrument in the second level relationship is just a foreign currency forward contract, and so its fair value changes are insensitive to commodity basis risk. Accordingly, additional ineffectiveness may arise in the second level relationship, due to the commodity basis risk that exists in the first level relationship. *[IFRS 9.IE119(b)]*.

For example, at inception of the second level relationship, an entity might have expected a hedged aggregated cash flow of FC 990 based on the price achieved in the commodity hedging contract and the level of basis risk that then existed. However, at the date when the entity calculates the ineffectiveness, the expected aggregated cash flow might be FC 1,000 due to changes in the commodity basis risk in the first level relationship. The expected aggregated hedged cash flow is calculated as follows:

Designated volume of hedged coffee purchases × prevailing forward coffee price for actual coffee purchases

Plus

Change in market value of designated hedging coffee benchmark forward contracts

If the expected hedged cash flow has changed since inception of the second level relationship, an entity would need to measure effectiveness as if the current expected hedged cash flow from the aggregated exposure was always the expectation at inception (i.e. FC 1,000 in the example given above). *[IFRS 9.IE122, IE123]*. As is usual for cash flow hedges (see 7.2 below), ineffectiveness to be reported in the profit or loss is the change in fair value of the actual hedging instrument less the effective portion taken to OCI. Specifically, for the second level relationship in this scenario the effective portion taken to OCI would be calculated as the lower of the following amounts: *[IFRS 9.6.5.11(a)]*

Change in fair value of the current expected hedged cash flows as if they had existed since inception.
(e.g. based on a hedged cash flow of FC 1,000)

and

Change in fair value of the actual hedging instrument
(e.g. based on original assumption of hedged flow of FC 990)

For hedge effectiveness measurement purposes, not only is the change in fair value of the hedged cash flows affected by variations in the second level relationship hedged risk, but also by ineffectiveness in the first level relationship. This second driver of fair value change can be seen in the example above as, although the hedging instrument has a notional of FC 990, the hedged cash flow is updated to FC 1,000, to reflect ineffectiveness in the first level relationship. This is likely to result in incremental ineffectiveness in the second level relationship.

Example 16 in the Illustrative Examples demonstrates that to reduce the basis risk the entity may chose a hedge ratio other than 1:1 for the first level relationship (see 6.4.3 below). In the example the entity selects the volume of foreign currency forward contract for the hedging instrument in the second level relationship based on the implied coffee forward price at the time the first level relationship was designated. This assumes the entity's original long-term expectations of the basis spread have not changed since the coffee forward was transacted, which may not always be the case. Alternatively, when identifying the optimal volume of the hedging instrument, an entity may conclude that the appropriate basis spread is the prevailing basis spread at the time of designation of the second level relationship. However, of course, the actual basis spread the entity will suffer is unknown.

Another layer of complexity would be added if the entity subsequently needed to rebalance the hedge relationship because of changes in the expected basis. The example, however, does not include this. Although the accounting for the second level relationship may be complex, the accounting for the first level hedge relationship in this example would continue to be unaffected by the existence of the second level relationship.

The definition of an aggregated exposure also includes a forecast transaction of an aggregated exposure. *[IFRS 9.6.3.4]*. An example, where this might be helpful, is when pre-hedging the interest rate risk in a forecast foreign currency debt issue:

Example 53.24: Aggregated exposure – interest rate pre-hedge of forecast foreign currency debt issue

Assume it is highly probable that an entity will issue fixed rate foreign currency debt in six months' time. It is also highly probable that on issue the entity will transact a CCIRS, converting the debt to functional currency variable rate. The combination of the forecast *foreign currency* fixed rate debt issuance and the forecast transaction of the CCIRS is economically a forecast *functional currency* variable rate debt issuance.

The entity wishes to hedge itself against increases in the variable functional currency interest rate between today and the issue of the debt in six months as well as the term of the debt. Therefore, the entity enters into a forward starting pay fixed/receive variable functional currency IRS. The entity designates the IRS as a hedging instrument in a cash flow hedge of the forecast aggregated exposure.

In this example the first level relationship does not exist yet, as both the hedged item (fixed rate foreign currency debt) and the hedging instrument (CCIRS) are forecast transactions. Hedge accounting for the 'second level hedge relationship' of the forecast aggregated exposure is still permitted though, on the condition that when the aggregated exposure occurs and is no longer forecast, it would be eligible as a hedged item. *[IFRS 9.6.3.4]*.

As an aggregated exposure is a combination of an exposure and a derivative, the aggregated exposure is often a hedging relationship itself (the first-level relationship). In order for the aggregated exposure to qualify for hedge accounting, IFRS 9 only requires that the first-level relationship could qualify for hedge accounting and not that hedge accounting is actually applied. However, applying hedge accounting to the aggregated exposure gets even more complex when hedge accounting is not applied to the first-level relationship, and the entity is also unlikely to achieve its desired accounting result. *[IFRS 9.BC6.167]*. Therefore, in many cases we expect entities to apply hedge accounting to the first-level relationship, even if not required.

However, just because an entity enters into an additional derivative transaction that relates to an existing hedging relationship it does not mean that this relationship qualifies as an aggregated exposure. This is demonstrated by the following example.

Example 53.25: *Cash flow hedging of an exposure that includes a net investment in a foreign operation*

Parent A with functional currency Australian dollars (AUD) has a US dollar (USD) net investment exposure. It transacts a pay floating USD receive floating AUD cross currency interest rate swap (CCIRS) and designates it in a hedge of a net investment in a foreign operation (see 5.3 below). By doing so, the group is exposed to cash flow variability due to the floating rate exposure in AUD and USD. Parent A also enters into a pay floating/receive fixed AUD interest rate swap (IRS) to eliminate cash flow variability from changes in AUD interest rate risk, and wishes to designate this derivative as the hedging instrument item in a cash flow hedge for the aggregated exposure including the net investment in a foreign operation.

While there is an economic relationship between the net investment exposure and the CCIRS for foreign currency risk, there is no economic relationship between the aggregated exposure and the IRS for interest rate risk. This is because the USD floating interest rate cash flows on the CCIRS are not offset by the USD net investment, as it does not have cash flow variability that is closely linked to interest rates. Furthermore, aggregated exposures can only be designated if they are managed as one exposure for a particular risk, which is unlikely to be the case in this fact pattern given the lack of interest risk associated with the net investment. *[IFRS 9.B6.3.3].*

3 HEDGING INSTRUMENTS

3.1 General requirements

The basic requirement for a hedging instrument is for it to be one of the following (or a proportion thereof (see 3.6 below)):

- a derivative measured at fair value through profit or loss, except for some written options (see 3.2 below);
- a non-derivative financial asset or liability measured at fair value through profit or loss (see 3.3 below); or
- for a hedge of foreign currency risk, the foreign currency risk component of a non-derivative financial asset or liability (see 3.3.1 below). *[IFRS 9.6.2.1, 6.2.2].*

Hedging instruments must also involve a party that is external to the reporting group. *[IFRS 9.6.2.3].* Two or more financial instruments can be jointly designated as hedging instruments (see 3.5 below). *[IFRS 9.6.2.5].*

There is no requirement to designate a hedging instrument only on initial recognition. Designation of a hedging instrument sometime after its initial recognition (e.g. after a previous hedge relationship is discontinued) is permitted, although some additional ineffectiveness may arise (see 7.4.3 below). *[IFRS 9.B6.5.28].*

3.2 Derivatives as hedging instruments

The distinction between derivative and non-derivative financial instruments is covered in Chapter 46. The standard does not restrict the circumstances in which a derivative measured at fair value through profit or loss may be designated as a hedging instrument, except for some written options. A written option does not qualify as a hedging instrument, unless the written option is designated to offset a purchased option. Purchased options include those that are embedded in another financial instrument and not required to be accounted for separately (see Chapter 46 at 5.1). *[IFRS 9.B6.2.4]*. Although not specifically mentioned, we believe that embedded purchased options in non-financial instruments that are not required to be bifurcated could also be designated as being hedged by a written option.

A single instrument combining a written option and a purchased option, such as an interest rate collar, cannot be a hedging instrument if it is a net written option at the date of the designation. Similarly, options that are transacted as legally separate contracts may be jointly designated as hedging instruments if the combined instrument is not a net written option at the date of designation. *[IFRS 9.6.2.6]*. There appears to be no requirement for the jointly designated options to be with the same counterparty. See 3.2.2 below for further discussion as to what constitutes a net written option.

A contract that is considered a normal sale or purchase, and is therefore accounted for as an executory contract (see Chapter 45 at 4), cannot be an eligible hedging instrument as it is not measured at fair value though profit or loss.

In addition, a forecast transaction or planned future transaction cannot be the hedging instrument as it is not a recognised financial instrument, *[IFRS 9.B3.1.2(e)]*, and is therefore not a derivative.

3.2.1 Offsetting external derivatives

Where two offsetting derivatives are transacted at the same time, it is generally not permitted to designate one of them as a hedging instrument in a hedge when the derivatives are viewed as one unit. *[IFRS 9.6.2.4]*. Indicators that the two derivatives should be accounted for as one unit are as follows:

- the second derivative was entered into at the same time and in contemplation of the first;
- there is a no apparent economic need or substantive business purpose for structuring the transactions separately, that could not also have been accomplished in a single transaction;
- they relate to the same risk; and
- the derivatives are with the same counterparty. *[IFRS 9.IG B.6]*.

This issue is also discussed in Chapter 46 at 3.2 and 8. It is emphasised that judgement should be applied in determining what a substantive business purpose is. For example, a centralised treasury entity may enter into third party derivative contracts on behalf of other subsidiaries to hedge their interest rate exposures and, to track those exposures within the group, enter into internal derivative transactions with those subsidiaries. It may also enter into a derivative contract with the same counterparty during the same business day with substantially the same terms as a contract entered into as a hedging instrument on behalf of another subsidiary as part of its trading operations, or because it wishes to rebalance its overall portfolio risk. In this case, there is a valid business purpose for entering into each contract. However, a desire to achieve hedge accounting for the hedged item is deemed not to be a substantive business purpose. *[IAS 39.F.1.14]*.

3.2.2 Net written options

It was explained in IAS 39 that an option an entity writes is not effective in reducing the profit or loss exposure of a hedged item. In other words, the potential loss on a written option could be significantly greater than the potential gain in value of a related hedged item. *[IAS 39.AG94, IFRS 9.BC6.151]*. This is the rationale for prohibiting a written option from qualifying as a hedging instrument unless it is designated as an offset to a purchased option, including one that is embedded in another financial instrument and not required to be accounted for separately (see Chapter 46 at 4). An example of this might be a written call option that is used to hedge a callable liability. *[IFRS 9.B6.2.4]*. In contrast, a purchased option has potential gains equal to or greater than potential losses on a related hedged item and therefore has the potential to reduce profit or loss exposure from changes in fair values or cash flows. Accordingly, a purchased option can qualify as a hedging instrument. *[IAS 39.AG94]*.

It follows that a derivative such as an interest rate collar that includes a written option cannot be designated as a hedging instrument if the interest rate collar is a net written option. However, if the interest rate collar was deemed to be a net purchased option or zero cost collar then it would be an eligible hedging instrument (see Example 53.29 below).

Example 53.26: Hedging foreign currency risk of a forecast transaction using a combined option instrument

An entity is exposed to foreign currency risk resulting from a highly probably forecast transaction in a foreign currency. In order to hedge that exposure, the entity enters into a collar by combining a long call and a short put option. The premium paid on the long call option equals the premium received on the short put option (i.e. it is what is termed a 'zero cost collar').

The entity designates the combination of the two instruments in a cash flow hedge of its highly probable forecast transaction.

Accordingly, determining whether an option contract or a combination of options (see 3.5 below) constitutes a net written option is an important step in hedge designation, and can require judgement. The following factors, taken together, indicate that an instrument or combination of instruments is not a net written option:

- no net premium is received, either at inception or over the life of the combination of options – the distinguishing feature of a written option is the receipt of a premium to compensate for the risk incurred;
- except for the strike prices, the critical terms and conditions of the written and purchased option components are the same, including underlying variable(s), currency denomination and maturity date; and
- the notional amount of the written option component is not greater than that of the purchased option component. *[IFRS 9.BC6.153, IAS 39.F.1.3(b)]*.

Applying the requirements to the scenario in Example 53.26 above, additional information would be required as consideration of premium on its own is insufficient. The application of these requirements is better illustrated in the following examples.

Example 53.27: Foreign currency collar (or 'cylinder option')

Company E, which has sterling as its functional currency, has forecast that it is highly probable it will receive €1,000 in six months' time in respect of an expected sale to a customer in France.

E is concerned that sterling might have appreciated by the time the payment is received and wishes to protect the profit margin on the sale without paying the premium that would be required with an ordinary currency option. E also wishes to benefit from some of the upside in the event that sterling depreciates, so would prefer not to use a forward contract.

Accordingly, E enters into an instrument under which it effectively:
- purchases an option that allows it to buy sterling for €1,000 from the counterparty at €1.53:£1.00; and
- sells an option that allows the counterparty to sell sterling to E for €1,000 at €1.47:£1.00.

In the foreign currency markets, such an instrument is often called a 'cylinder option' rather than a 'collar' and it operates as follows. If, in six months' time, the spot exchange rate exceeds €1.53:£1.00, E will exercise its option to sell €1,000 at €1.53:£1.00, effectively fixing its minimum proceeds on the sale (in sterling terms) at £654. Similarly, if the rate is below €1.47:£1.00, the counterparty will exercise its option to buy €1,000 at €1.47:£1.00, effectively capping E's maximum proceeds on the sale at £680. If the rate is between €1.47:£1.00 and €1.53:£1.00, both options will lapse unexercised and E will be able to sell its €1,000 for sterling at the spot rate, generating between £654 and £680.

The premium that E would pay to acquire the purchased option equals the premium it would receive to sell the written option and therefore no premium is paid or received on inception. The critical terms and conditions, including the notional amounts, of the written and purchased option components are the same except for the strike price. Therefore, E concludes that the instrument is not a net written option and, consequently, it may be used as the hedging instrument in a hedge of the foreign currency risk associated with the future sale.

It is possible that the counterparty might, instead, have offered E a variation on the instrument described above. If the notional amount on E's purchased option component had been reduced, say to €500, the counterparty could have offered a better rate on that component, say €1.51. However, in this case, the notional amount on the written option component is twice that of the purchased option component and the instrument would be seen as a net written option. Accordingly, even if E had very good business reasons for using such an instrument to manage its foreign currency risk, it could not qualify as a hedging instrument. Therefore, hedge accounting would be precluded.

Example 53.28: 'Knock-out' swap

Company Y has a significant amount of long-dated floating rate borrowings. In order to hedge the cash flow interest rate risk arising from these borrowings, Y has entered into a number of matching pay-fixed, receive-floating interest rate swaps that effectively convert the interest rates on the borrowings to fixed-rate.

Under the terms of one of these swaps, on each fifth anniversary of its inception until maturity the swap counterparty may choose to simply terminate the swap at no cost. This is often referred to as a knock-out feature. In return for agreeing to this, Y benefits by paying a lower interest rate on the fixed leg of the swap than it would on a conventional swap. In other words, Y receives a premium for taking on the risk of the counterparty cancelling the swap.

This instrument contains a net written option, i.e. the knock-out feature, and therefore cannot be used as a hedging instrument unless it is used in a hedge of an equivalent purchased option. (In practice, it is unlikely that the hedged borrowings will contain such an option feature.)

Example 53.29: Zero cost collar

Company T has 3 year floating rate debt, paying monthly coupons based on a benchmark rate. Company T wants to protect against rises in the benchmark rate but also wishes to benefit to some extent from any reduction in the that rate. In line within this risk management objective, Company T transacts a zero cost collar contract (i.e. no premium is paid or received). The terms of the collar are such that for each monthly fixing the benchmark rate is capped at 1.5% and floored at 1%. Accordingly, the contract is in fact a series of 36 purchased European collars with one collar expiring every month for the next 36 months. The critical terms such as notional, benchmark rate and fixing dates of the zero cost collar matches those of the hedged floating rate debt. The zero cost collar is designated as hedging variability in the benchmark rate with respect to the floating rate debt. The zero cost collar is not a net written option. This is despite the fact it might very well be that if the zero cost collar were to be deconstructed into 36 single collars, for one or more individual months there might be a net premium receivable. This approach is consistent with the documentation of the collar as a single financial instrument, with a single 'overall' price, and a single hedge designation.

See 3.6.4, 7.4.11 and 7.5.1 below for further discussion of the implications of using options as hedging instruments.

3.2.3 Embedded derivatives

Only derivatives that are measured at fair value through profit or loss are eligible hedging instruments. *[IFRS 9.6.2.1]*. Derivatives that are embedded in hybrid contracts, but that are not separately accounted for, cannot be designated as separate hedging instruments. *[IFRS 9.B6.2.1]*. Given that embedded derivatives in financial assets are not accounted for separately under IFRS 9 (see Chapter 48 at 6), this guidance precludes designation of embedded derivatives in financial assets as separate hedging instruments. *[IFRS 9.BC6.117-122]*.

However, an embedded derivative that is accounted for separately from its host contract (either a financial liability or non-financial host) (see Chapter 46 at 4), is measured at fair value through profit or loss, and therefore could be an eligible hedging instrument.

Example 53.30: Hedging with a sales commitment

Company J has the Japanese yen as its functional currency. J has issued a fixed-rate debt instrument with semi-annual interest payments that matures in two years with principal due at maturity of US$5 million. It has also entered into a fixed price sales commitment for US$5 million that matures in two years and is not accounted for as a derivative because it qualifies for the normal sales exemption.

Because the sales commitment is accounted for as a firm commitment (i.e. it is not recognised until at least one of the parties to the contract has performed (see Chapter 49 at 2.1.2)) rather than a derivative instrument, it cannot be a hedging instrument in a hedge of the foreign currency risk associated with the debt instrument. However, if the foreign currency component of the sales commitment was required to be separated as an embedded derivative (essentially a forward contract to buy US dollars for yen) that component could be designated as the hedging instrument in such a hedge. *[IAS 39.F.1.2]*.

3.2.4 Credit break clauses

It is not uncommon for certain derivatives (e.g. long-term interest rate swaps) to contain terms that allow the counterparties to settle the instrument at a so-called 'fair value' in certain circumstances. The 'fair value' is usually not a true fair value as it excludes changes in credit risk. Such terms, often called 'credit break clauses', enable the counterparties to manage their credit risk in markets where collateral or margin accounts and master netting agreements are not used. They are particularly common where a long-duration derivative is transacted between a financial and non-financial institution. For example, the terms of a twenty-year interest rate swap may allow either party to settle the instrument at fair value on the fifth, tenth and fifteenth anniversary of its inception.

These terms can be seen as options on counterparty credit risk. However, provided the two parties have equivalent rights to settle the instrument at 'fair value', the credit break clause will generally not prevent the derivative from qualifying as a hedging instrument. Particularly, in assessing whether a premium is received for agreeing to the incorporation of such terms into an instrument, care needs to be exercised (see 3.2.2 above). For example, marginally better underlying terms offered by one potential counterparty (as a result of market imperfections) should not be mistaken for a very small option premium.

3.2.4.A Principal resetting cross currency swaps

Another mechanism aimed at reducing ongoing credit risk in longer term derivatives, which is becoming more popular in certain geographical areas, is a principal resetting feature, typically within floating-floating cross currency swaps. The principal resetting feature allows the fair value of the swap to be settled on a quarterly basis without terminating the swap itself.

Similar to a standard cross currency swap, the fair value of a principal resetting floating-floating cross currency swap changes in response to the movements in foreign currency rates; however, the principal resetting feature means that the fair value of the swap attributable to foreign currency spot movement is cash settled at each quarterly reset date, in addition to the normal interest settlements.

Depending on changes in foreign currency spot rates, this could result in either a cash inflow (for the positive fair value) or outflow (for the negative fair value) at the end of each quarter. The notional of the principal resetting swap is then reset to the prevailing foreign currency spot rate.

The resetting feature itself does not appear to preclude the swap from being an eligible hedging instrument (see 3.2 above), however the implications of using such a swap as the hedging instrument in a hedge relationship need further consideration. This is best achieved by way of an example.

Example 53.31: Hedging with a principal resetting cross currency swap

Company A has the Australian dollar as its functional currency. Company A has issued US$ variable rate debt with principal due at maturity of US$100 million. Company A wishes to eliminate the foreign currency risk associated with the foreign currency debt and enters into a principal resetting cross currency swap; the current terms of which are to receive a specified variable benchmark rate of interest on US$100m and pay a specified variable benchmark rate of interest on AUD148m. Interest coupons are settled (and reset) on a quarterly basis.

The principal reset feature requires that the fair value of the swap attributable to the foreign currency spot movement is cash settled at each quarterly reset date, and the principal of the receive US$ leg is adjusted to reflect the prevailing spot rate.

If the foreign currency spot rate had changed such that on the first quarterly reset date it was AUD1.4:US$1, Company A would pay US$5.7m, and the US$ principal would be adjusted to US$105.7m to reflect the prevailing foreign currency spot rate (AUD148m ÷ 1.4 = US$105.7m).

Company A may wish to designate the US$ debt as the hedged item and the principal resetting swap as the hedging instrument, however, in order to achieve hedge accounting all the hedge accounting criteria must be met (see 6 below). In this case, the impact of the variation in the swap principal may be problematic, in particular where, as in this example, it is the foreign currency leg of the swap that is reset, as this will most likely require some amendment to the hedge relationship. For example, after the first quarterly reset rate the pay US$ leg of the principal reset swap is now US$105.7m, however the hedged item remains the US$100m variable rate debt.

Company A will need to consider how best to adjust the hedge relationship to reflect the ongoing risk management strategy and continue to meet the hedge accounting criteria (see 8 below).

3.2.5 Basis swaps

A derivative which does not reduce risk at the transaction level cannot be a hedging instrument. Consider a 'basis swap' that effectively converts one variable interest rate index (say a central bank base rate) on a liability to another (say SONIA). A relationship of this nature would not normally qualify for hedge accounting because the hedging instrument does not reduce or eliminate risk in any meaningful way – it simply converts one risk to another similar risk.[8] For this reason, such an economic strategy would not qualify as either a fair value or cash flow hedge relationship (see 5.1 and 5.2 below).

A basis swap or similar instrument may qualify as a hedging instrument when considered in combination with another instrument (see 3.5 below). For example, the basis swap described above and a pay-fixed, receive-SONIA interest rate swap may qualify as a hedging instrument in a cash flow hedge of a borrowing that pays interest based on a central bank rate. It may also be notionally decomposed and designated in hedges of offsetting gross asset and liability positions (see Example 53.38 at 3.6.2 below).

However, a currency basis swap that converts foreign currency variable rate interest and principal cash flows from a financial liability into variable rate interest and principal cash flows in functional currency may be eligible as a hedging instrument in a cash flow hedge, as variability in cash flows with respect to foreign currency has been reduced (or eliminated). The fact that variability in cash flows with respect to interest rate risk remains, does not preclude hedge accounting for foreign currency risk (see 2.2 above).

3.3 Non-derivative financial instruments

Under IFRS 9, entities are permitted to designate, as hedging instruments, non-derivative financial assets or non-derivative financial liabilities that are accounted for at fair value through profit or loss. This is meant in a strict sense. Consequently, a liability designated as at fair value through profit or loss (for which the amount of its change in fair value that is attributable to changes in the credit risk of that liability is presented in other comprehensive income (OCI)) does not qualify as a hedging instrument. *[IFRS 9.6.2.2]*. This is because the entire fair value change is not recognised in profit or loss, which would in effect allow the entity to ignore its own credit risk when assessing and measuring hedge ineffectiveness and thus conflict with the concepts of hedge accounting.

Example 53.32: Hedge of a forecast commodity purchase with an investment in a commodity fund or an exchange traded commodity

An entity is exposed to variability in cash flows from highly probable forecast purchases of crude oil that are indexed to Brent crude oil. The entity wants to hedge its cash flow risk from changes in the price of Brent crude oil. Instead of using derivative contracts, the entity purchases exchange traded investments that replicate the performance of Brent futures contracts such as commodity funds or exchange traded commodities (ETCs). ETCs have the legal form of bonds that are coupled to the price development of a commodity (either directly at the spot price or with a commodity futures contract). They can be traded like exchange traded funds but, because they are legally debt securities, they involve credit risk of the issuer (which is usually mitigated by collateralisation through physically deposited commodities or other suitable collateral).

These investments are financial instruments that (under IFRS 9) would be accounted for at fair value through profit or loss. Consequently, they could qualify as hedging instruments if all other qualifying criteria for hedge accounting are met. In particular, the effectiveness assessment would have to consider that the fair value change of the investments will differ from the present value of the cumulative change in the cash flows for the forecast purchases of crude oil. This is because of aspects such as 'tracking errors' (i.e. that the investments do not perfectly replicate the performance of futures contracts) and that the investments are fully funded cash-instruments whereas the cash flows on the forecast transactions will only occur in the future.

The ability to designate non-derivative hedging instruments can be helpful if an entity does not have access to derivatives markets (e.g. because of local regulations that prohibit the entity from holding such instruments), or if an entity does not want to be subject to margining requirements nor enter into uncollateralised over-the-counter derivatives. Purchasing and selling financial investments in such cases can be operationally easier for entities than transacting derivatives.

For hedges other than of foreign currency risk, when an entity designates a non-derivative financial asset or liability measured at fair value through profit or loss as a hedging instrument, it may only designate the non-derivative financial instrument in its entirety or a proportion of it (see 3.6 below). *[IFRS 9.B6.2.5]*.

3.3.1 Hedge of foreign currency risk by a non-derivative financial instrument

For a hedge of foreign currency risk, the foreign currency component of a non-derivative financial asset or liability may be designated, as a hedging instrument. *[IFRS 9.6.2.2]*. Non-derivative financial assets and liabilities need not be within the scope of IFRS 9 to qualify as hedging instruments. For example, although rights and obligations under lease agreements are for most purposes scoped out of IFRS 9, lease payables or finance lease receivables denominated in a foreign currency still meet the definition of a non-derivative financial instrument and are therefore eligible as hedging instruments in a hedge of foreign currency risk. Consideration should be given to all the qualifying criteria before hedge accounting is applied (see 6 below), in particular as to whether the designation is consistent with the risk management objective and strategy for managing the hedged exposure (see 2.6.8 above).

An equity instrument for which an entity has elected to present changes in fair value in OCI does not qualify as a hedging instrument in a hedge of foreign currency risk. *[IFRS 9.6.2.2]*. This reflects that fair value changes (including from foreign currency risk) are not recognised in profit or loss, which is incompatible with the mechanics of fair value hedges and cash flow hedges.

For hedges of foreign currency risk, the foreign currency risk component of a non-derivative financial instrument is determined in accordance with IAS 21. *[IFRS 9.B6.2.3]*. This means that an entity could, for example, hedge the spot risk of highly probable forecast sales in 12 months' time that are denominated in a foreign currency with a 7-year financial liability in the same foreign currency. However, when measuring ineffectiveness, IFRS 9 is explicit that the revaluation of the forecast sales for foreign currency risk would have to be on a discounted basis (i.e. a present value calculation of the spot revaluation, reflecting the time between the reporting date and the future cash flow date), whereas the hedging instrument (i.e. the IAS 21-based foreign currency component of the financial liability) would not. This would result in some ineffectiveness (see 7.4.7 below). *[IFRS 9.B6.5.4]*.

The following two examples illustrate the types of permitted hedge relationships for foreign currency risk where the hedging instrument is a non-derivative financial instrument.

Example 53.33: Hedging with a non-derivative liability

Company J, which has GBP as its functional currency, has issued a fixed rate debt instrument with a principal due at maturity in two years of US$5 million. The debt is accounted for at amortised cost. J had also entered into a fixed price sales commitment, accounted for as an executory contract, for US$5 million that matures in two years as well.

J could not designate the debt instrument as a hedge of the exposure to *all* fair value changes of the fixed price sales commitment because the hedging instrument is a non-derivative liability that is not measured at fair value through profit or loss (and it would not be a good economic hedge anyway). However, J could designate the fixed rate debt instrument as a hedge of the foreign currency exposure associated with the future receipt of US dollars on the fixed price sales commitment.

Example 53.34: Hedge of foreign currency bond

Company J has also issued US$10 million five-year fixed rate debt and owns a US$10 million five year fixed rate bond, both measured at amortised cost.

J's bond has exposure to changes in both foreign currency and interest rates, as does the liability. However, the liability can only be designated as a hedge of the bond's foreign currency, not interest rate, risk because it is a non-derivative instrument.

In Example 53.34 above, hedge accounting is unnecessary because the amortised cost of the hedging instrument and the hedged item are both remeasured using closing rates with differences recognised in profit or loss as required by IAS 21.

In principle, there is no reason why a non-derivative financial instrument cannot be a hedging instrument in one hedge (of foreign currency risk) and a hedged item in another hedge (for example in a hedge of interest rate risk).

3.4 Own equity instruments

An entity's own equity instruments are not financial assets or liabilities of the entity and therefore cannot be designated as hedging instruments. *[IFRS 9.B6.2.2]*.

This prohibition would also apply to instruments that give rise to non-controlling interests in consolidated financial statements – under IFRS it is clear that non-controlling interests are part of a reporting entity's equity.

3.5 Combinations of instruments

An entity may view in combination, and jointly designate as the hedging instrument, any combination of the following (including those circumstances in which the risk or risks arising from some hedging instruments offset those arising from others):

- derivatives (or a proportion of them); and
- non-derivatives (or a proportion of them). *[IFRS 9.6.2.5]*.

Further discussion on designation of proportions is provided in 3.6 below. There is a requirement that any combination can only be designated as a hedging instrument if the combination is not a net written option (see 3.2.2 above).

Example 53.35: Hedging with a combination of a derivative and non-derivative instrument

Entity J with the euro as its functional currency has issued a yen denominated floating rate borrowing and entered into a matching receive-yen floating (plus principal at maturity), pay-US dollar floating (plus principal at maturity) cross currency interest rate swap. These instruments, which effectively synthesise a US dollar floating rate borrowing, contain offsetting terms, i.e. the whole of the borrowing and the yen leg of the swap.

Entity J could designate the combination of these two instruments in a hedge of the entity's foreign currency risk arising from, say, an asset with an identifiable exposure to US dollar exchange rates.

Designation of a combination of instruments as the hedging instrument does not change the unit of account for each individual instrument within the designated combination. Classification and measurement (see Chapter 48) and the usual eligibility criteria for hedge accounting (see 3.1 above) are applied to the individual instruments designated in combination as the hedging instrument. The incremental hedge accounting entries however, are applied in consideration of the combination of instruments (see 7 below).

3.6 Portions and proportions of hedging instruments

In contrast to the position for hedged items (see 2 above), there are significant restrictions on what components of an individual financial instrument can be carved out and designated as a hedging instrument. A qualifying instrument must be designated in its entirety as a hedging instrument, with only the following exceptions:

- a proportion of a hedging instrument (see 3.6.1 below);
- the time value of options may be separated (see 3.6.4 below);
- forward elements of forwards may be separated (see 3.6.5 below);
- foreign currency basis spread may be separated (see 3.6.5 below); *[IFRS 9.6.2.4]*
- the spot rate retranslation risk of a foreign currency non-derivative financial instrument may be separated (see 3.3.1 above); and
- a derivative may be separated into notional component parts when each part is designated as a hedge and qualifies for hedge accounting (see 3.6.2 below).

The hedge accounting guidance is applied only to the designated portion or proportion of the hedging instrument. However, should an entity choose to separate the time value of an option, the forward element of a forward contract or the foreign currency basis spread from a hedge relationship, the costs of hedging guidance should also be applied (see 7.5 below).

3.6.1 Proportions of instruments

It is possible to designate a proportion of the entire hedging instrument, such as 50% of the notional amount, in a hedging relationship. *[IFRS 9.6.2.4(c)]*. The proportion that is not designated is available for designation within other hedge relationships, such that a maximum of 100% of the notional is designated as a hedging instrument. Any proportions of an instrument not designated within hedge relationships are accounted under the usual IFRS 9 classification and measurement guidance.

3.6.2 Hedging different risks with one instrument

A single instrument may be designated as a hedging instrument of more than one type of risk, provided that there is specific designation of:

- the hedging instrument; and
- the different risk positions.

Those hedged items can be in different hedging relationships. *[IFRS 9.B6.2.6]*. A single hedging instrument can also be used to hedge different risks within the same hedge relationship; one such frequent designation is of a single cross currency swap used to hedge both foreign currency and interest rate risk in foreign currency debt.

An example where a single hedging derivative is used to hedge more than one risk in different hedging relationships is the use of a foreign currency forward to eliminate the resulting foreign currency risk from payables and receivables in two different foreign currencies, see Example 53.36 below, which is based on an example given in IAS 39. *[IAS 39.F1.13]*.

Example 53.36: *Foreign currency forward used to hedge the position arising from two hedged items with different foreign currencies*

Company J, which has Japanese yen as its functional currency, issues five year floating rate US dollar debt and acquires a ten year fixed rate sterling bond. The principal amounts of the asset and liability, when converted into Japanese yen, are the same. J enters into a single foreign currency forward contract to hedge its foreign currency exposure on both instruments under which it receives US dollars and pays sterling at the end of five years.

Company J designates the foreign currency forward as the hedging instrument in a cash flow hedge of foreign currency risk on both the sterling bond and the US dollar debt.

Designating a single hedging instrument as a hedge of multiple types of risk is permitted if there is specific designation of the hedging instrument and the different risk positions.

Company J has Japanese yen as its functional currency, hence it is exposed to JPY/GBP and USD/JPY foreign currency risk from the sterling bond and the US dollar debt respectively. Separation of these different risk positions can be achieved by documentation of the principal repayment of the bond and debt in their respective currency of denomination as the hedged items in separate cash flow hedge relationships.

In order to achieve specific designation of the hedging instrument, it is effectively decomposed and viewed as two forward contracts, each with an offsetting position in yen, i.e. J's functional currency. Each of the decomposed forward contracts is then designated in an eligible hedge accounting relationship.

Even though the bond has a ten year life and the foreign currency forward only protects it for the first five years, hedge accounting is permitted for only a portion of the exposure (see 2.2.4 above).

Accordingly hedge accounting may be achieved, but only if all the hedge accounting qualification criteria continue to be met (see 6 below).

In the above example a single hedging instrument is designated in a hedge of foreign currency risk arising from two separate hedged items. The hedges in the example could both be designated as either cash flow or fair value hedges (see 5.1.2 and 5.2.3 below). There is no reason why a single hedging instrument may not be designated in both a cash flow hedge and a fair value hedge for different risks, provided the usual conditions for achieving hedge accounting are met.

Example 53.37: *Cross-currency interest rate swap hedging two foreign currency exchange rate exposures and fair value interest rate exposure*

Applying the same fact pattern as in Example 53.36 above, but in this case Company J wishes to hedge not only the foreign currency exposure on both the bond and the debt, but the fair value interest rate exposure on the bond as well. To do this Company J enters into a matching cross currency interest rate swap to receive floating rate US dollars, pay fixed rate sterling and exchange the US dollars for sterling at the end of five years.

Similar to Example 53.36 above, the cross currency interest rate swap is effectively decomposed and viewed as two cross currency swaps, each with an offsetting leg in yen, i.e. J's functional currency, as follows:

- Decomposed swap 1: receive floating rate yen, pay fixed rate sterling and exchange the sterling for yen at the end of five years; and
- Decomposed swap 2: receive floating rate US dollars, pay floating rate yen and exchange the US dollars for yen at the end of five years.

Therefore, the swap may be designated as a hedging instrument in separate hedges of the sterling bond and the US dollar liability as follows:

- Decomposed swap 1 designated in a fair value hedge (see 5.1 above) as the hedging instrument against exposure to changes in present value of the sterling bond associated with the interest rate payments on the bond until year five and the change in present value of the principal payment due at maturity to the extent affected by changes in the yield curve relating to the five years of the swap (see Example 53.5 at 2.2.4 above) as well as the exchange rate between sterling and yen.

- Decomposed swap 2 designated in a cash flow hedge (see 5.2 above) as the hedging instrument against changes in all cash flows on the US dollar liability associated with forward USD/JPY foreign currency risk.

Accordingly hedge accounting may be achieved, but only if all the hedge accounting qualification criteria continue to be met (see 6 below).

As can be seen in Examples 53.36 and 53.37 above, decomposition of a derivative hedging instrument by imputing notional legs is an acceptable means of splitting the fair value of a derivative hedging instrument into multiple components in order to achieve hedge accounting, as long as:

- the split does not result in the recognition of cash flows that are not evident from contractual terms of the derivative instrument;
- the notional legs introduced must be offsetting;
- all decomposed elements of the derivative instrument are included within an eligible hedge relationship; and
- the designation is consistent with risk management (see 6.2 below).

The IFRS Interpretations Committee confirmed such an approach to be acceptable under IAS 39 and there is no reason to believe that this would not also be the case under IFRS 9.[9] Consideration of the hedge accounting qualifying criteria for all relationships that include decomposed elements of a derivative instrument should be captured in the hedge documentation on designation, as normal.

The qualifying criteria assessment may be carried out for the total hedged position, i.e. incorporating all risks identified if these risks are inextricably linked, or for the decomposed parts separately, i.e. individually for each hedge relationship that includes a decomposed part of the derivative. However, if the assessment is undertaken separately, each hedge relationship that includes a decomposed part would need to meet the qualifying criteria. Otherwise the derivative would not qualify for hedge accounting as part of it would not be included within an eligible hedge relationship. This restriction is necessary as a financial instrument can only be designated as a hedging instrument in its entirety or an eligible portion or proportion thereof (see 3.6 above). For example, the 'knock-out swap' in Example 53.28 above could not be split into, on the one hand, a conventional interest rate swap, to be used as a hedging instrument and, on the other hand, the knock-out feature (a written swaption, i.e. an option for the counterparty to enter into an offsetting interest rate swap with the same terms as the conventional swap). This is because the knock-out feature is unlikely to be designated and qualify for hedge accounting at all.

If the IFRIC analysis of the decomposition of derivatives is applied to a basis swap, hedge accounting for that swap may be possible (see 3.2.5 above). The swap would be designated as a hedge of appropriate asset and liability positions.

Example 53.38: Designation of a basis swap hedging different risk positions

Entity X has made a $1m loan that earns LIBOR based interest and incurred a $1m liability that pays interest based on the central bank rate. Entity X transacts a basis swap under which it pays LIBOR based interest and receives interest based on the central bank rate on a notional amount of $1m in order to eliminate the interest rate mismatch between the loan and the liability. In this case, the basis swap could be decomposed into two interest rate swaps, both with an offsetting $1m fixed rate leg, to facilitate hedge designations for each of the LIBOR loan and central bank deposit within separate cash flow hedges.

The guidance above discussed various combinations of cash flow and fair value hedge relationships. However, there appears to be no reason why a single instrument could not, in theory, be designated in other combinations of hedges, for example a cash flow hedge and a hedge of a net investment.

3.6.3 Restructuring of derivatives

An entity may exchange a derivative that does not qualify as a hedging instrument (say, the knock-out swap in Example 53.28 above) for two separate derivatives that, together, have the same fair value as the original instrument (say, a conventional interest rate swap and a written swaption). Such an exchange is likely to be motivated by a desire to obtain hedge accounting for one of these new instruments.

In order to determine whether the new arrangement can be treated as two separate derivatives, rather than a continuation of the original derivative, we believe it is necessary to determine whether the exchange transaction has any substance, which is clearly a matter of judgement. If the exchange has no substance, then hedge accounting would still be precluded as the two 'separate' derivatives would in substance be a continuation of the original derivative (see 3.2.1 above and Chapter 46 at 3.2 and 8).

In the case of the knock-out swap, if the two new contracts had the same counterparty and, in aggregate, the same terms as the original contract this would not necessarily lead to the conclusion that the exchange lacked substance. However if, in addition, the swaption would be settled by delivery of the conventional interest rate swap in the event that it was exercised, this is a strong indicator that the exchange does lack substance.

3.6.4 Time value of options

An entity may choose to hedge for risk management purposes the variability of future cash flow outcomes resulting from a price increase (but not a decrease) of a forecast commodity purchase. This hedge of a 'one-sided risk' could be achieved by transacting a purchased option as the hedging instrument (see 3.2.2 above). In such a situation, it is permitted that only cash flow losses in the hedged item that result from an increase in the price above the specified level are designated within a hedge relationship. However, only the intrinsic value of a purchased option hedging instrument, not its time value, reflects this one-sided risk in the hedged item (assuming that it has the same principal terms as the designated risk). The hedged risk for a one-sided risk does not include the time value of a purchased option, because the time value is not a component of the forecast transactions that affects profit or loss (see 7.4.12 below). [IFRS 9.B6.3.12]. As a result, changes in the time value of the option would give rise to hedge ineffectiveness.

To address this problem, an entity is permitted to designate as the hedging instrument only the change in the intrinsic value of an option and not the change in its time value. [IFRS 9.6.2.4(a)].

If it does so, the entity accounts for the time value of the option as a cost of hedging (see 7.5 below). [IFRS 9.6.5.15]. No prescriptive guidance is provided as to how the intrinsic value of an option should be calculated. We believe it is acceptable to calculate the intrinsic value with respect to either the prevailing relevant spot or forward price, consistent with the risk management objective. The chosen approach should also be documented and consistently applied for that hedge relationship.

Excluding the time value may make it administratively easier to process the hedges and it can certainly improve a hedge's effectiveness from an accounting perspective. However, accounting for the option time value as a cost of hedging does involve some complexity, in particular where the terms of the hedged item and hedging option are what is described in the standard as not 'closely aligned' (see 7.5.1.A below).

The use of this exception is not mandatory. For example, a dynamic hedging strategy that assesses both the intrinsic value and time value of an option contract can qualify for hedge accounting (see 6.3.2 below), although the time value is still likely to result in some ineffectiveness. In addition, an entity may use an option to hedge an exposure that itself contains optionality – see 7.4.12 below for the challenges that arise with such a designation.

3.6.5 Forward element of a forward contract and foreign currency basis spread

IFRS 9 also permits (but does not require) an entity to separate the forward element and the spot element of a forward contract and designate only the change in the value of the spot element of a forward contract and not the forward element as the hedging instrument. In addition, the foreign currency basis spread may be separated and excluded from the designation of a financial instrument as the hedging instrument. *[IFRS 9.6.2.4(b)]*.

Where the forward element or foreign currency basis are excluded from the designation as a hedging instrument, IFRS 9 permits a choice as to whether to account for the excluded portion as a cost of hedging (see 7.5 below) or to continue measurement at fair value through profit or loss. This is, however, not an accounting policy choice, but an election for each designation. *[IFRS 9.6.5.16]*.

3.6.6 Hedges of a portion of a time period

A hedging instrument may not be designated for a part of its change in fair value that results from only a portion of the time period during which the hedging instrument remains outstanding. This clarifies that an entity cannot designate a 'partial-term' component of a financial instrument as the hedging instrument, but only the entire instrument for its remaining life (notwithstanding that an entity may exclude from designation the time value of an option, the forward element of a forward contract or the foreign currency basis spread, see 3.6.4 and 3.6.5 above). *[IFRS 9.6.2.4]*. This does not mean that the hedge relationship must necessarily continue for the entire remaining life of the hedging instrument – the usual hedge discontinuation requirements apply (see 8.3 below).

Example 53.39: Designation of hedging instrument with longer life than hedged item

Entity T has an interest rate swap with a remaining maturity of five years and 6 months. Entity T wishes to designate the swap as the hedging instrument with respect to interest rate risk in issued debt that matures in five years.

It would not be possible for Entity T to designate only payments and receipts from the swap that occur over the next five years (i.e. ignoring those after year five) as the hedging instrument. Instead, the whole derivative (i.e. including payments and receipts after year five) could be designated as the hedging instrument, although the hedging relationship may itself last for only five years.

However, hedge accounting can only be applied if the hedge effectiveness criteria are met (see 6.4 below), which may not necessarily be immediately obvious from a qualitative assessment if there are significant mismatches in maturity between the hedged item and the hedging instrument (see 6.4.1 below).

4 INTERNAL HEDGES AND OTHER GROUP ACCOUNTING ISSUES

One of the most pervasive impacts that hedge accounting can have on groups, especially those operating centralised treasury functions, is the need to reassess hedging strategies that involve intra-group transactions. To a layman this might come as something of a surprise because the standard does little more than reinforce the general principle that transactions between different entities within a group should be eliminated in the consolidated financial statements of that group. Nevertheless, where risk is centrally managed the requirement to identify eligible hedged items and hedging instruments with counterparties that are external to the reporting group, and to ensure the qualifying criteria are met, can be a challenge.

IAS 39 included a significant volume of Implementation Guidance devoted to the subject of internal hedges. The requirements in IFRS 9 for hedged items and hedging instruments to be with a party external to the reporting group (and the associated exemptions to this rule) are unchanged from the requirements in IAS 39. Therefore, much of the IAS 39 guidance is still relevant under IFRS 9, and is frequently referred to within this section.

4.1 Internal hedging instruments

The starting point for this guidance is the principle of preparing consolidated financial statements in IFRS 10 – *Consolidated Financial Statements* – that requires 'intragroup assets and liabilities, equity, income, expenses and cash flows to be eliminated in full'. *[IFRS 10.B86]*.

Although individual entities within a consolidated group (or divisions within a single legal entity) may enter into hedging transactions with other entities within the group (or divisions within the entity), such as internal derivative contracts to transfer risk exposures between different companies (or divisions), any such intragroup (or intra-entity) transactions are eliminated on consolidation. Therefore, such hedging transactions do not qualify for hedge accounting in the consolidated financial statements of the group, *[IFRS 9.6.3.5, IAS 39.F.1.4]*, (or in the individual or separate financial statements of an entity for hedging transactions between divisions of the entity). Effectively, this is because they do not exist in an accounting sense.

Accordingly, IFRS 9 is very clear that for hedge accounting purposes only instruments that involve a party external to the reporting entity (i.e. external to the group or individual entity that is being reported on) can be designated as hedging instruments (see 3.1 above). *[IFRS 9.6.2.3]*.

The Implementation Guidance of IAS 39 explains that the standard does not specify how an entity should manage its risk. Accordingly, where an internal contract is offset with an external contract, the external contract may be regarded as the hedging instrument. In such cases, the hedging relationship (which is between the external transaction and the item that is the subject of the internal hedge) may qualify for hedge accounting, as long as such a representation is directionally consistent with the actual risk management activities. Where the hedge designation does not exactly mirror an entity's risk management activities it is commonly referred to as 'proxy hedging'. The eligibly of proxy hedging designations was discussed by the IASB in their deliberations in developing IFRS 9 (see 6.2.1 below).

The following example illustrates the proposed approach.

Example 53.40: Internal derivatives

The banking division of Bank A enters into an internal interest rate swap with A's trading division. The purpose is to hedge the interest rate risk exposure of a loan (or group of similar loans) in the banking division's loan portfolio. Under the swap, the banking division pays fixed interest payments to the trading division and receives variable interest rate payments in return.

Assuming a hedging instrument is not acquired from an external party, hedge accounting treatment for the hedging transaction undertaken by the banking and trading divisions is not allowed, because only derivatives that involve a party external to the entity can be designated as hedging instruments. Further, any gains or losses on intragroup or intra-entity transactions should be eliminated on consolidation. Therefore, transactions between different divisions within A cannot qualify for hedge accounting treatment in Bank A's financial statements. Similarly, transactions between different entities within a group cannot qualify for hedge accounting treatment in A's consolidated financial statements.

However, if, in addition to the internal swap in the above example, the trading division entered into an interest rate swap or other contract with an external party that offset the exposure hedged in the internal swap, hedge accounting would be permitted. For the purposes of hedge accounting, the hedged item is the loan (or group of similar loans) in the banking division and the hedging instrument is the external interest rate swap or other contract.

The trading division may aggregate several internal swaps or portions of them that are not offsetting each other (see 4.2 below) and enter into a single third-party derivative contract that offsets the aggregate exposure. Such external hedging transactions may qualify for hedge accounting treatment provided that the hedged items in the banking division are identified and the other conditions for hedge accounting are met. *[IAS 39.F.1.4]*.

It follows that internal hedges may qualify for hedge accounting in the individual or separate financial statements of individual entities within the group, provided they are external to the individual entity that is being reported on. *[IFRS 9.6.2.3]*.

The IAS 39 Implementation Guidance contains the following summary of the application of IAS 39 to internal hedging transactions:

- IAS 39 does not preclude an entity from using internal derivative contracts for risk management purposes and it does not preclude internal derivatives from being accumulated at the treasury level or some other central location so that risk can be managed on an entity-wide basis or at some higher level than the separate legal entity or division.
- Internal derivative contracts between two separate entities within a consolidated group can qualify for hedge accounting by those entities in their individual or separate financial statements, even though the internal contracts are not offset by derivative contracts with a party external to the consolidated group.
- Internal derivative contracts between two separate divisions within the same legal entity can qualify for hedge accounting in the individual or separate financial statements of that legal entity only if those contracts are offset by derivative contracts with a party external to the legal entity.
- Internal derivative contracts between separate divisions within the same legal entity and between separate legal entities within the consolidated group can qualify for hedge accounting in the legal entity or consolidated financial statements only if the internal contracts are offset by derivative contracts with a party external to the legal entity or consolidated group.
- If the internal derivative contracts are not offset by derivative contracts with external parties, the use of hedge accounting by group entities and divisions using internal contracts must be reversed on consolidation. *[IAS 39.F.1.4]*.

The premise on which the restriction on internal hedging instruments is based does not always hold. Foreign currency intragroup balances may well give rise to gains and losses in profit or loss under IAS 21 that are not fully eliminated on consolidation. To address this, such intra-group monetary items, as well as forecast intragroup transactions, may qualify as a hedged item in the consolidated financial statements if the other conditions for hedge accounting are met (see 4.3 below).

However, although internal transactions are sometimes permitted to be hedged items, even those internal transactions that affect consolidated profit or loss cannot be used in consolidated financial statements as hedging instruments. This is somewhat surprising as one might consider the same arguments that led to the exception permitting intragroup monetary items and forecast intragroup transactions to be hedged items to support allowing intragroup monetary items to be hedging instruments. However, during its deliberations of the hedge accounting model under IFRS 9 the IASB decided to retain this restriction, and so the guidance is equally relevant in applying IFRS 9. [IFRS 9.BC6.142-150].

IFRS 8 – *Operating Segments* – requires disclosure of segment information that is reported to the chief operating decision maker even if this is on a non-GAAP basis (see Chapter 36 at 3.1). Consequently, for a hedge to qualify for hedge accounting in segment reporting, it is not always necessary for the hedging instrument to involve a party external to the segment.

4.1.1 Central clearing parties and ring fencing of banks

Following the introduction of legal or regulatory requirements requiring over-the-counter (OTC) derivatives to be novated to a central clearing party (CCP) or incentivising financial institutions to do so (see 8.3.5 below) coupled with additional legislation in various jurisdictions for banks to separate core retail banking activities from investment banking activities, additional focus has arisen on 'internal derivatives' within a banking group.

When derivatives transacted between the retail banking and investment banking legal entities within a banking group are novated to a CCP, the CCP becomes the counterparty to the derivatives. This does not automatically mean that the external derivatives with the CCP are eligible for hedge accounting, judgement will be required as to whether the offsetting external derivatives should be considered in substance as a single contract in the consolidated financial statements. As part of this judgement, consideration should be given to the substantive business purpose for the practice of transacting derivatives between the retail banking and investment banking legal entities and, in particular, novating derivatives to a CCP – other than to achieve hedge accounting (see 3.2.1 above). The assessment as to whether such a substantive business purpose exists or not must be made based on the particular facts and circumstances, including consideration of the regulatory environment, and the judgement documented accordingly.

4.2 Offsetting internal hedging instruments

As noted at 4.1 above, if an internal contract used in a hedging relationship is offset with an external party, the external contract may be regarded as a hedging instrument and the hedge may qualify for hedge accounting. The IAS 39 Implementation Guidance elaborates on this further in the context of both interest rate and foreign currency risk management, particularly in the situation where the exposure from internal derivatives are offset before being laid off with a third party.

4.2.1 Interest rate risk

Sometimes, central treasury functions enter into internal derivative contracts with subsidiaries and, perhaps, divisions within the consolidated group to manage interest rate risk on a centralised basis. If, before laying off the risk, the internal contracts are first netted against each other and only the net exposure is offset in the marketplace with external derivative contracts, the internal contracts cannot qualify for hedge accounting in the consolidated financial statements.

Where two or more internal derivatives used to manage interest rate risk on assets or liabilities at the subsidiary or division level are offset at the treasury level, the effect of designating the internal derivatives as hedging instruments is that the hedged non-derivative exposures at the subsidiary or division levels would be used to offset each other on consolidation. Accordingly, since IAS 39 did not permit designating non-derivatives as hedging instruments (except for foreign currency exposures), the results of hedge accounting from the use of internal derivatives at the subsidiary or division level that are not laid off with external parties must be reversed on consolidation. *[IAS 39.F.1.5]*. Although IFRS 9 does permit designation of non-derivative instruments as hedging instruments, this is only for financial instruments measured at fair value through profit or loss, which is unlikely to be the case in this scenario (see 3.3 above).

It should be noted, however, that if internal derivatives offset each other on consolidation; are used in the same type of hedging relationship at the subsidiary or division level; if the hedged items affect profit or loss in the same period (in the case of cash flow hedges); and if the hedges are perfectly effective at the subsidiary level; then there will be no effect on profit or loss and equity of reversing the effect of hedge accounting on consolidation. Just as the internal derivatives offset at the treasury level, their use as fair value hedges by two separate entities or divisions within the consolidated group will also result in the offset of the fair value amounts recognised in profit or loss. Similarly, their use as cash flow hedges by two separate entities or divisions within the consolidated group will also result in the fair value amounts being offset against each other in other comprehensive income. *[IAS 39.F.1.5]*.

However, reversal of subsidiary hedge accounting on consolidation may affect individual line items in both the consolidated income statement (or statement of comprehensive income) and the consolidated statement of financial position. This will be the case, for example, when internal derivatives that hedge assets (or liabilities) in a fair value hedge are offset by internal derivatives that are used as a fair value hedge of other assets (or liabilities) that are recognised in a different line item in the statement of financial position or income statement (or statement of comprehensive income). In addition, to the extent that one of the internal contracts is used as a cash flow hedge and the other is used in a fair value hedge, the effect on profit or loss and equity would not offset since the gain (or loss) on the internal derivative used as a fair value hedge would be recognised in profit or loss and the corresponding loss (or gain) on the internal derivative used as a cash flow hedge would be recognised in other comprehensive income. *[IAS 39.F.1.5]*.

Notwithstanding this, under the principles set out at 4.1 above, it may be possible to designate the external derivative as a hedge of some of the underlying exposures as illustrated in the following example.

Example 53.41: Single external derivative offsets internal contracts on a net basis

Company A uses internal derivative contracts to transfer interest rate risk exposures from individual divisions to a central treasury function. The central treasury function aggregates the internal derivative contracts and enters into a single external derivative contract that offsets the internal derivative contracts on a net basis.

On one particular day the central treasury function enters into three internal receive-fixed, pay-variable interest rate swaps that lay off the exposure to variable interest cash flows on variable rate liabilities in other divisions and one internal receive-variable, pay-fixed interest rate swap that lays off the exposure to variable interest cash flows on variable rate assets in another division. It enters into an interest rate swap with an external counterparty that exactly offsets the four internal swaps.

A cash flow hedge of an overall net position for interest rate risk does not qualify for hedge accounting under IFRS 9 (see 2.5.3 above). However, designating a part of the variable rate assets or liabilities as the hedged position on a gross basis is permitted if the designation is directionally consistent with the actual risk management activities (see 6.2.1 below). Therefore, even though the purpose of entering into the external derivative was to offset internal derivative contracts on a net basis, hedge accounting is permitted if the hedging relationship is defined and documented as a hedge of a part of the underlying cash inflows or cash outflows on a gross basis and assuming that the hedge accounting criteria are met. *[IAS 39.F.2.15]*.

4.2.2 Foreign currency risk

Although much of the discussion at 4.2.1 above applies equally to hedges of foreign currency risk, there is one important distinction between the two situations. Non-derivative financial instruments are permitted to be used as the hedging instrument in the hedge of foreign currency risk. Therefore, in this case, internal derivatives may be used as a basis for identifying non-derivative external transactions that could qualify as hedging instruments or hedged items, provided that the internal derivatives represent the transfer of foreign currency risk on underlying non-derivative financial assets or liabilities (see Case 3 in Example 53.41 above). However, for consolidated financial statements, it is necessary to designate the hedging relationship so that it involves only external transactions.

Forecast transactions and unrecognised firm commitments cannot qualify as hedging instruments (see 3.1 above). Accordingly, to the extent that two or more offsetting internal derivatives represent the transfer of foreign currency risk on such items, hedge accounting cannot be applied. As a result, if any cumulative net gain or loss on an internal derivative has been included in the initial carrying amount of an asset or liability (a 'basis adjustment') (see 7.2.2 below), it would have to be reversed on consolidation if it cannot be demonstrated that the offsetting internal derivative represented the transfer of a foreign currency risk on a financial asset or liability to an external hedging instrument. *[IAS 39.F.1.6]*.

The following example illustrates this principle – it also illustrates the mechanics of accounting for fair value hedges and cash flow hedges, which are discussed in more detail at 7.1 and 7.2 below. *[IAS 39.F.1.7]*.

Financial instruments: Hedge accounting

Example 53.42: Using internal derivatives to hedge foreign currency risk

In each of the following cases, 'FC' represents a foreign currency, 'LC' represents the local currency (which is the entity's functional currency) and 'TC' the group's treasury centre.

Case 1: Offset of fair value hedges

Subsidiary A has trade receivables of FC100, due in 60 days, which it hedges using a forward contract with TC. Subsidiary B has payables of FC50, also due in 60 days, which it hedges using a forward contact with TC.

TC nets the two internal derivatives and enters into a net external forward contract to pay FC50 and receive LC in 60 days.

At the end of month 1, FC weakens against LC. A incurs a foreign currency loss of LC10 on its receivables, offset by a gain of LC10 on its forward contract with TC. B makes a foreign currency gain of LC5 on its payables, offset by a loss of LC5 on its forward contract with TC. TC makes a loss of LC10 on its internal forward contract with A, a gain of LC5 on its internal forward contract with B and a gain of LC5 on its external forward contract.

Accordingly, the following entries are made in the individual or separate financial statements of A, B and TC at the end of month 1 (assuming that forward foreign currency and spot exchange rates are exactly the same, which is unlikely in reality). Entries reflecting intra-group transactions or events are shown in italics.

A's entries

	LC	LC
Foreign currency loss	10	
Receivables		10
Internal contract (TC)	*10*	
Internal gain (TC)		*10*

B's entries

	LC	LC
Payables	5	
Foreign currency gain		5
Internal loss (TC)	*5*	
Internal contract (TC)		*5*

TC's entries

	LC	LC
Internal loss (A)	*10*	
Internal contract (A)		*10*
Internal contract (B)	*5*	
Internal gain (B)		*5*
External forward contract	5	
Foreign currency gain		5

Both A and B could apply hedge accounting in their individual financial statements provided all the necessary conditions were met. However, because gains and losses on the internal derivatives and the offsetting losses and gains on the hedged receivables and payables are recognised immediately in profit or loss without hedge accounting (as required by IAS 21), hedge accounting is unnecessary (see 7.1.1 below for further information on hedges of foreign currency denominated monetary items).

In the consolidated financial statements, the internal derivative transactions are eliminated. In economic terms, B's payable hedges FC50 of A's receivables. The external forward in TC hedges the remaining FC50 of A's receivable. In the consolidated financial statements, hedge accounting is again unnecessary because monetary items are measured at spot foreign currency rates under IAS 21 irrespective of whether hedge accounting is applied.

The net balances, before and after elimination of the accounting entries relating to the internal derivatives, are the same, as set out below. Accordingly, there is no need to make any further accounting entries to meet the requirements of IAS 39.

	LC	LC
Receivables	–	10
Payables	5	–
External forward contract	5	–
Gains and losses	–	–
Internal contracts	–	–

Case 2: Offset of cash flow hedges

To extend the example, A also has highly probable future revenues of FC200 on which it expects to receive cash in 90 days. B has highly probable future expenses of FC500 (advertising cost), also to be paid for in 90 days. A and B enter into separate forward contracts with TC to hedge these exposures and TC enters into an external forward contract to receive FC300 in 90 days.

As before, FC weakens at the end of month 1. A incurs a 'loss' of LC20 on its anticipated revenues because the LC value of these revenues decreases and this is offset by a gain of LC20 on its forward contract with TC. Similarly, B incurs a 'gain' of LC50 on its anticipated advertising cost because the LC value of the expense decreases and this is offset by a loss of LC50 on its transaction with TC.

TC incurs a gain of LC50 on its internal transaction with B, a loss of LC20 on its internal transaction with A and a loss of LC30 on its external forward contract.

Both A and B satisfy the hedge accounting criteria and qualify for hedge accounting in their individual financial statements. A recognises the gain of LC20 on its internal derivative transaction in other comprehensive income and B does the same with its loss of LC50. TC does not claim hedge accounting, but measures both its internal and external derivative positions at fair value, which net to zero.

Accordingly, the following entries are made in the individual or separate financial statements of A, B and TC at the end of month 1. Entries reflecting intra-group transactions or events are shown in italics.

A's entries

	LC	LC
Internal contract (TC)	*20*	
Other comprehensive income		20

B's entries

	LC	LC
Other comprehensive income	50	
Internal contract (TC)		*50*

TC's entries

	LC	LC
Internal loss (A)	*20*	
Internal contract (A)		*20*
Internal contract (B)	*50*	
Internal gain (B)		*50*
Foreign currency loss	30	
External forward contract		30

IAS 39 (and IFRS 9) requires that, in the consolidated financial statements, the accounting effects of the internal derivative transactions must be eliminated.

If there were no hedge designation for the consolidated financial statements, the gains and losses recognised in other comprehensive income and profit or loss on the internal derivatives would be reversed. Consequently, a loss of LC30 would be recognised in profit or loss in respect of the external forward contract held by TC.

However, for the consolidated financial statements, TC's external forward contract on FC300 can be designated, at the beginning of month 1, as a hedging instrument of the first FC300 of B's highly probable future expenses. Therefore, LC30 of the gain recognised in other comprehensive income by B may remain in other comprehensive income on consolidation, because it involves an external derivative. Accordingly, the net balances, before and after elimination of the accounting entries relating to the internal derivatives, are as set out below and there is no need to make any further accounting entries.

	LC	LC
External forward contract	–	30
Other comprehensive income	30	–
Gains and losses	–	–
Internal contracts	–	–

Case 3: Offset of fair value and cash flow hedges

The example is extended further and it is assumed that the exposures and the internal derivative transactions are the same as in Cases 1 and 2. In other words, Subsidiary A has trade receivables of FC100, due in 60 days, and highly probable future revenues of FC200 on which it expects to receive cash in 90 days. Subsidiary B has payables of FC50, due in 60 days, and highly probable future expenses of FC500 to be paid for in 90 days. Each of these exposures is hedged using forward contacts with TC. However, in this case, instead of entering into two external derivatives to hedge separately the fair value and cash flow exposures, TC enters into a single net external derivative to receive FC250 in exchange for LC in 90 days.

Consequently, TC has four internal derivatives, two maturing in 60 days and two maturing in 90 days. These are offset by a net external derivative maturing in 90 days. The interest rate differential (and hence forward points) between FC and LC is minimal, and therefore the ineffectiveness resulting from the mismatch in maturities is expected to have a minimal effect on profit or loss in TC, and so has been ignored for the purposes of this example.

As in Cases 1 and 2, A and B apply hedge accounting for their cash flow hedges and TC measures its derivatives at fair value. A recognises a gain of LC20 on its internal derivative transaction in other comprehensive income and B does the same with its loss of LC50.

Accordingly, the following entries are made in the individual or separate financial statements of A, B and TC at the end of month 1. Entries reflecting intra-group transactions or events are shown in italics.

A's entries

	LC	LC
Foreign currency loss	10	
Receivables		10
Internal contract (TC)	*10*	
Internal gain (TC)		*10*
Internal contract (TC)	*20*	
Other comprehensive income		*20*

B's entries

	LC	LC
Payables	5	
Foreign currency gain		5
Internal loss (TC)	*5*	
Internal contract (TC)		*5*
Other comprehensive income	*50*	
Internal contract (TC)		*50*

TC's entries

	LC	LC
Internal loss (A)	10	
Internal contract (A)		10
Internal loss (A)	20	
Internal contract (A)		20
Internal contract (B)	5	
Internal gain (B)		5
Internal contract (B)	50	
Internal gain (B)		50
Foreign currency loss	25	
External forward contract		25

The gains and losses recognised on the internal contracts in A and B can be summarised as follows:

	A LC	B LC	Total LC
Profit or loss (fair value hedges)	10	(5)	5
Other comprehensive income (cash flow hedges)	20	(50)	(30)
Total	30	(55)	(25)

In the consolidated financial statements, IAS 39 (and IFRS 9) requires the accounting effects of the internal derivative transactions to be eliminated.

If there were no hedge designation for the consolidated financial statements, the gains and losses recognised in other comprehensive income and profit or loss on the internal derivatives would be reversed. Consequently, a loss of LC30 would be recognised in profit or loss in respect of the external receivable and payable held by A (loss LC10) and B (gain LC5) respectively and the external forward contract held by TC (loss LC25).

However, for the consolidated financial statements, the following designations can be made at the beginning of month 1:

- the payable of FC50 in B is designated as a hedge of the first FC50 of the highly probable future revenues in A.

  Therefore, at the end of month 1, the following entries are made in the consolidated financial statements: Dr Payable LC5; Cr Other comprehensive income LC5;

- the receivable of FC100 in A is designated as a hedge of the first FC100 of the highly probable future expenses in B.

  Therefore, at the end of month 1, the following entries are made in the consolidated financial statements: Dr Other comprehensive income LC10, Cr Receivable LC10; and

- the external forward contract on FC250 in TC is designated as a hedge of the next FC250 of highly probable future expenses in B.

  Therefore, at the end of month 1, the following entries are made in the consolidated financial statements: Dr Other comprehensive income LC25; Cr External forward contract LC25.

Combining these entries produces the total net balances as follows:

	LC	LC
Receivables	–	10
Payables	5	–
External forward contract	–	25
Other comprehensive income	30	–
Gains and losses	–	–
Internal contracts	–	–

Based on this designation, the total net balances achieved in the consolidated financial statements at the end of month 1 are the same as those that would be recognised if the hedge accounting effect of the internal derivatives were not eliminated. However, it should be noted this is a simplified example and any difference in timing between the hedged item and hedging instrument is assumed to have a minimal effect on profit or loss, and so no effect has been reflected here. This will not necessarily be the case in reality, therefore some additional ineffectiveness is likely to occur in the consolidated financial statements. This would arise, for example, if the FC50 payable in B due in 60 days is designated as a hedge of the first FC50 of the highly probable future revenues in A expected to occur in 90 days.

Case 4: Offset of fair value and cash flow hedges with adjustment to carrying amount of inventory

Similar transactions to those in Case 3 are assumed except that the anticipated cash outflow of FC500 in B relates to the purchase of inventory that is delivered after 60 days. The entity applies a basis adjustment to the hedged forecast non-financial items (see 7.2.1 below).

To recap, Subsidiary A has trade receivables of FC100, due in 60 days, and highly probable future revenues of FC200 on which it expects to receive cash in 90 days. Subsidiary B has payables of FC50, due in 60 days, and a highly probable future purchase of inventory for FC500, to be delivered in 60 days and paid for in 90 days. Each of these exposures is hedged using forward contracts with TC, and TC enters into a single net external derivative to receive FC250 in exchange for LC in 90 days.

At the end of month 2, there are no further changes in exchange rates or fair values. At that date, the inventory is delivered and the loss of LC50 on B's internal derivative, recognised in other comprehensive income in month 1, is removed from equity and adjusts the carrying amount of inventory in B. The gain of LC20 on A's internal derivative is recognised in other comprehensive income as before.

In the consolidated financial statements, there is now a mismatch compared with the result that would have been achieved by unwinding and redesignating the hedges. The external derivative (FC250) and the proportion of receivable (FC50) in A offset FC300 of the anticipated inventory purchase in B. Offset will occur between the FC50 payable in B and a FC50 proportion of the receivable in A. There is a natural hedge between the remaining FC200 of anticipated cash outflow in B (inventory) and the anticipated cash inflow of FC200 in A (revenue). This last relationship does not qualify for hedge accounting under IAS 39 (or IFRS 9) as no valid hedging instrument exists, hence this time there is only a partial offset between gains and losses on the internal derivatives that hedge these amounts.

Accordingly, the following entries are made in the individual or separate financial statements of A, B and TC at the end of month 1. Entries reflecting intra-group transactions or events are shown in italics.

A's entries (all at the end of month 1)

	LC	LC
Foreign currency loss	10	
Receivables		10
Internal contract (TC)	*10*	
Internal gain (TC)		*10*
Internal contract (TC)	*20*	
Other comprehensive income		*20*

B's entries (at the end of month 1)

	LC	LC
Payables	5	
Foreign currency gain		5
Internal loss (TC)	*5*	
Internal contract (TC)		*5*
Other comprehensive income	*50*	
Internal contract (TC)		*50*

B's entries (at the end of month 2)

	LC	LC
Inventory	50	
Other comprehensive income		50

TC's entries (all at the end of month 1)

	LC	LC
Internal loss (A)	10	
Internal contract (A)		10
Internal loss (A)	20	
Internal contract (A)		20
Internal contract (B)	5	
Internal gain (B)		5
Internal contract (B)	50	
Internal gain (B)		50
Foreign currency loss	25	
External forward contract		25

The gains and losses recognised on the internal contracts in A and B can be summarised as follows:

	A LC	B LC	Total LC
Profit or loss (fair value hedges)	10	(5)	5
Other comprehensive income (cash flow hedges)	20	–	20
Basis adjustment (inventory)	–	(50)	(50)
Total	30	(55)	(25)

Combining these amounts with the external transactions (i.e. those not marked in italics above) produces the total net balances before elimination of the internal derivatives as follows:

	LC	LC
Receivables	–	10
Payables	5	–
External forward contract	–	25
Other comprehensive income	–	20
Basis adjustment (inventory)	50	–
Gains and losses	–	–
Internal contracts	–	–

For the consolidated financial statements, the following designations can be made at the beginning of month 1:

- The payable of FC50 in B is designated as a hedge of the first FC50 of the highly probable future revenues in A.

    Therefore, at the end of month 1, the following entry is made in the consolidated financial statements: Dr Payables LC5; Cr Other comprehensive income LC5.

- The receivable of FC100 in A is designated as a hedge of the first FC100 of the highly probable future inventory purchase in B.

    Therefore, at the end of month 1, the following entries are made in the consolidated financial statements: Dr Other comprehensive income LC10; Cr Receivable LC10; and at the end of month 2, Dr Inventory LC10; Cr Other comprehensive income LC10.

- The external forward contract on FC250 in TC is designated as a hedge of the next FC250 of highly probable future inventory purchase in B.

    Therefore, at the end of month 1, the following entry is made in the consolidated financial statements: Dr Other comprehensive income LC25; Cr External forward contract LC25; and at the end of month 2, Dr Inventory LC25; Cr Other comprehensive income LC25.

This leaves FC150 of the future revenue in A and FC150 of future inventory purchase in B not designated in a hedge accounting relationship in the consolidated financial statements.

The total net balances after elimination of the accounting entries relating to the internal derivatives are as follows:

	LC	LC
Receivables	–	10
Payables	5	–
External forward contract	–	25
Other comprehensive income	–	5
Basis adjustment (inventory)	35	–
Gains and losses	–	–
Internal contracts	–	–

These total net balances are different from those that would be recognised if the internal derivatives were not eliminated, and it is these net balances that IAS 39 (and IFRS 9) requires to be included in the consolidated financial statements. The accounting entries required to adjust the total net balances before elimination of the internal derivatives are as follows:

- to reclassify LC15 of the loss on B's internal derivative that is included in inventory to reflect that FC150 of the forecast purchase of inventory is not hedged by an external instrument (neither the external forward contract of FC250 in TC nor the external payable of FC100 in A); and
- to reclassify the gain of LC15 on A's internal derivative to reflect that the forecast revenues of FC150 to which it relates is not hedged by an external instrument.

The net effect of these two adjustments is as follows:

	LC	LC
Other comprehensive income	15	
Inventory		15

It is apparent that extending the principles set out in this relatively simple example to the more complex and higher volume situations that are likely to be encountered in practice is not going to be straightforward.

4.3 Internal hedged items

Only assets, liabilities, firm commitments or highly probable forecast transactions that involve a party external to the entity can be designated as hedged items. It follows that hedge accounting can be applied to transactions between entities in the same group only in the individual or separate financial statements of those entities and not in the consolidated financial statements of the group. *[IFRS 9.6.3.5]*. However, there are two exceptions – intragroup monetary items and forecast intragroup transactions, discussed at 4.3.1 and 4.3.2 below.

4.3.1 Intragroup monetary items

IFRS 9 allows the foreign currency risk of an intra-group monetary item (e.g. a payable or receivable between two subsidiaries) to qualify as a hedged item in the consolidated financial statements if it results in an exposure to foreign exchange rate gains or losses under IAS 21 that are not fully eliminated on consolidation. Foreign exchange gains and losses on such items are not fully eliminated on consolidation when they are transacted between two group entities that have different functional currencies (see Chapter 15 at 6.3), *[IFRS 9.6.3.6]*, as illustrated in the following example.

Example 53.43: Intragroup monetary items that will affect consolidated profit or loss

Company A has two subsidiaries, Company B and Company C. A and B have the euro as their functional currencies, while C has the US dollar as its functional currency. On 31 March, C purchases goods from B for US$110, payable on 30 June.

In this case, the intragroup monetary item of US$110 may be designated as a hedged item in a hedge of foreign currency risk both by B in its separate financial statements and by A in its consolidated financial statements.

While B's foreign currency receivable is eliminated against C's foreign currency payable on consolidation, the exchange differences that arise for B cannot be eliminated since C has no corresponding exchange differences.

Thus, the intragroup monetary item results in an exposure to variability in the foreign currency amount of the intra-group monetary item that will affect profit or loss in the consolidated financial statements. Therefore, the intragroup monetary item may be designated as a hedged item in a foreign currency hedge.[10]

4.3.2 Forecast intragroup transactions

IFRS 9 also contains a second exception allowing the foreign currency risk of a highly probable forecast intragroup transaction to qualify as a hedged item in a cash flow hedge in consolidated financial statements in certain circumstances. The transaction must be denominated in a currency other than the functional currency of the entity entering into that transaction (e.g. parent, subsidiary, associate, joint venture or branch) and the foreign currency risk must affect consolidated profit or loss (otherwise it cannot qualify as a hedged item). *[IFRS 9.6.3.6]*.

Normally, royalty payments, interest payments and management charges between members of the same group will not affect consolidated profit or loss unless there is a related external transaction. However, by way of example, a forecast sale or purchase of inventory between members of the same group will affect profit or loss if there is an onward sale of the inventory to a party external to the group. Similarly, a forecast intragroup sale of plant and equipment from the group entity that manufactured it to a group entity that will use it in its operations may affect consolidated profit or loss. This could occur, for example, because the plant and equipment will be depreciated by the purchasing entity and the amount initially recognised for the plant and equipment may change if the forecast intragroup transaction is denominated in a currency other than the functional currency of the purchasing entity. *[IFRS 9.B6.3.5]*.

Therefore, in order that a forecast intragroup transaction to be eligible as a hedged item, a related external transaction must also exist. It is clear that the designated hedged item is the forecast intragroup transaction, which is therefore subjected to the usual eligibility criteria for hedge accounting (see 2 above). However, the highly probable criterion (see 2.6.1 above) is also relevant for the external transaction in order to meet the requirement that the forecast foreign currency risk will affect consolidated profit or loss. The related external transaction also drives the timing of recycling of the effective portion of the hedge relationship (see 7.2.2 below).

Although the standard refers exclusively to forecast intragroup transactions, we believe there is no reason why these provisions should not also apply to intragroup firm commitments.

4.4 Hedged item and hedging instrument held by different group entities

The IAS 39 Implementation Guidance explained that, in a group, it is not necessary for the hedging instrument to be held by the same entity as the one that has the exposure being hedged in order to qualify for hedge accounting in the consolidated financial statements. *[IAS 39.F.2.14]*. This is illustrated in the following example.

Example 53.44: Subsidiary's foreign currency exposure hedged by parent

Company S is based in Switzerland and prepares consolidated financial statements in Swiss francs. It has an Australian subsidiary, Company A, whose functional currency is the Australian dollar and is included in the consolidated financial statements of S. A has forecast purchases in Japanese yen that are highly probable and S enters into a forward contract to hedge the change in yen relative to the Australian dollar.

Because A did not hedge the foreign currency exchange risk associated with the forecast purchases in yen, the effects of exchange rate changes between the Australian dollar and the yen will affect A's profit or loss and, therefore, would also affect consolidated profit or loss. Therefore that hedge may qualify for hedge accounting in S's consolidated financial statements provided the other hedge accounting criteria are met. *[IAS 39.F.2.14]*.

By contrast, if Company A also has forecast purchases in Australian dollar, and S enters into a forward contract to hedge the change in Australian dollar relative to the Swiss francs, hedge accounting would not be permitted as changes between the Australian dollar and Swiss francs will not affect A's profit or loss nor consequently S's consolidated profit or loss. Whilst the above is based on Implementation Guidance from IAS 39, we believe that it is still relevant under IFRS 9. This position was explicitly confirmed for hedges of net investments within IFRIC 16 – *Hedges of a Net Investment in a Foreign Operation*. (See 5.3.3 below.)

One of the key qualifying criteria that must be met when a hedging instrument is held by a different group entity in a fair value or cash flow hedge, is that the hedged risk could affect profit or loss (see 5.1. and 5.2 below). This is illustrated using the fact pattern in Example 53.45.

Example 53.45: Subsidiary's foreign currency exposure hedged by parent (2)

Using the same fact pattern as in Example 53.44 above, but in this case S has instead entered into a forward contract to hedge the change in Swiss francs relative to the Australian dollar.

S cannot achieve cash flow hedge accounting for the forward contract to sell Swiss francs and buy yen in S's consolidated financial statements as there is no cash flow variability with respect to the Swiss francs/yen exchange rates that will affect consolidated profit or loss.

Consolidated profit or loss will be impacted by movements in the yen/Australian dollar exchange rates, as subsidiary A will recognise the purchase at the prevailing yen/Australian dollar exchange rate, consistent with the designated risk in the hedging strategy in Example 53.44 above. *[IAS 21.21]*.

S is only exposed to Australian dollar/Swiss franc exchange rates on translation of the purchase on consolidation, which is not a cash flow exposure. *[IAS 21.39(b)]*. Hence cash flow hedge accounting cannot be achieved.

5 TYPES OF HEDGING RELATIONSHIPS

There are three types of hedging relationship defined in IFRS 9: *[IFRS 9.6.5.2]*

- *fair value hedge:* a hedge of the exposure to changes in the fair value of a recognised asset or liability or an unrecognised firm commitment, or a component of any such item, that is attributable to a particular risk and could affect profit or loss (see 5.1 below);
- *cash flow hedge:* a hedge of the exposure to variability in cash flows that is attributable to a particular risk associated with all or a component of recognised asset or liability (such as all or some future interest payments on variable rate debt) or a highly probable forecast transaction and could affect profit or loss (see 5.2 below); and
- *hedge of a net investment in a foreign operation:* as defined in IAS 21 (see Chapter 15 at 2.3 and 5.3 below).

These definitions are considered further in the remainder of this section.

5.1 Fair value hedges

An example of a fair value hedge is a hedge of the exposure to changes in the fair value of a fixed rate debt instrument (not measured at fair value through profit or loss) as a result of changes in interest rates – if interest rates increase, the fair value of the debt decreases and *vice versa*. Such a hedge could be entered into either by the issuer or by the holder. *[IFRS 9.B6.5.1]*.

On the face of it, if a fixed rate loan that is measured at amortised cost or fair value through OCI and is held until it matures (as is the case for many such loans), changes in the fair value of the loan would not affect profit or loss. However, the fact that the loan could be sold, in which case fair value changes would affect profit or loss means that such a hedge relationship meets the definition set out in 5 above, that variability in the hedged risk and could affect profit or loss. The same would be true of a fixed rate borrowing for which settlement before maturity is very unlikely.

A variable rate debt may be the hedged item in a fair value hedge in certain circumstances. For example, the fair value of such an instrument will change if the issuer's credit risk changes. Accordingly, variable rate debt could be designated in a hedge of all changes in its fair value. There may also be changes in its fair value relating to movements in the market rate in the periods between which the variable rate is reset. For example, if a debt instrument provides for annual interest payments reset to the market rate each year, a portion of the debt instrument has an exposure to changes in fair value during the year. *[IAS 39.F.3.5]*.

In June 2019, within the context of a fair value hedge of foreign currency risk of a non-financial asset held for consumption, the IFRS Interpretations Committee discussed the requirement that to designate a hedged risk, an entity must conclude that the hedged risk 'could affect profit or loss'.[11]

IFRS 9 does not require changes in fair value to be expected to affect profit or loss but, rather, that those changes could affect profit or loss. The Committee observed that changes in fair value of a non-financial asset held for consumption could affect in consolidated subsidiaries cannot be hedged items in a fair value hedge because changes in the investments' fair value are not recognised in profit or loss, they may be designated in a net investment hedge relationship. A hedge of a net investment in a foreign operation is said to be different because it is a hedge of the foreign currency exposure, not a fair value hedge of the change in the value of the investment. *[IFRS 9.B6.3.2].*

Conceptually, net investment hedging is somewhat unsatisfactory, as it mixes foreign currency translation risk (largely an accounting exposure) with transactional risk (much more an economic exposure). IFRIC 16 – *Hedges of a Net Investment in a Foreign Operation* – addresses the question of what does and does not constitute a valid hedging relationship, a topic on which IFRS 9 provides very little guidance.

IFRIC 16 applies to any entity that hedges the foreign currency risk arising from its net investments in foreign operations and wishes to qualify for hedge accounting in accordance with IFRS 9. *[IFRIC 16.7].* It only applies to those hedges and should not be applied by analogy to other types of hedge accounting. *[IFRIC 16.8].* For the avoidance of doubt, IFRIC 16 explains that such a hedge can be applied only when the net assets of that foreign operation are included in the financial statements. This will be the case for consolidated financial statements, financial statements in which investments such as associates or joint ventures are accounted for using the equity method or those that include a branch or a joint operation (as defined in IFRS 11 – *Joint Arrangements*). *[IFRIC 16.2].* For convenience, IFRIC 16 refers to such an entity as a parent entity and to the financial statements in which the net assets of foreign operations are included as consolidated financial statements and this section follows this convention. *[IFRIC 16.7].*

Investments in foreign operations may be held directly by a parent entity or indirectly by its subsidiary or subsidiaries (see 5.3.1 below). *[IFRIC 16.12].*

The requirements of IFRIC 16 are discussed in more detail at 5.3.1 to 5.3.3 below and, in the case of accounting for such a hedge, at 7.3 below.

5.3.1 Nature of the hedged risk

Perhaps the most important decision made by the Interpretations Committee was that hedge accounting may be applied only to the foreign exchange differences arising between the functional currency of the foreign operation and the parent entity's functional currency. *[IFRIC 16.10].* Furthermore, the hedged risk may be designated as the foreign currency exposure arising between the functional currency of the foreign operation and the functional currency of any parent entity (the immediate, intermediate or ultimate parent entity) of that foreign operation. The fact that the net investment may be held through an intermediate parent does not affect the nature of the economic risk arising from the foreign currency exposure to the ultimate parent entity. *[IFRIC 16.12].* This principle is illustrated in the following example.

Example 53.48: Nature of the hedged risk in a net investment hedge

Company P is the ultimate parent entity of a group and presents its consolidated financial statements in its functional currency of euro. It has two direct wholly owned subsidiaries, Company A whose functional currency is Japanese yen and Company B whose functional currency is sterling. B has a wholly owned subsidiary, Company C, whose functional currency is US dollars. P's net investment in A is ¥400,000 million which includes A's external borrowings of US$300 million. P's net investment in B is £500 million including the equivalent of £159 million representing B's net investment in C of US$300 million. This corporate structure is illustrated as follows:

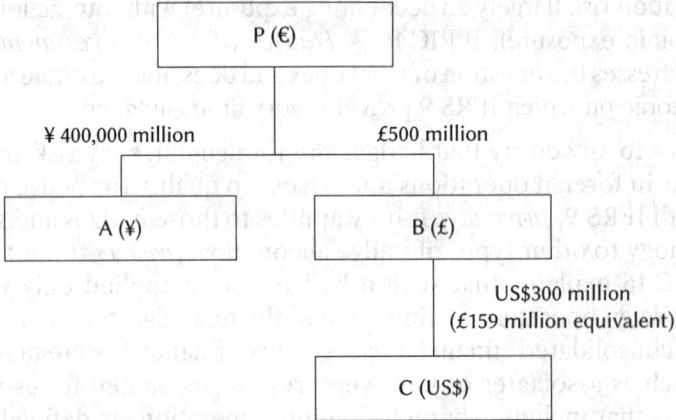

P, in its consolidated financial statements, could hedge its net investment in each of A, B and C for the foreign exchange risk between their functional currencies (Japanese yen, sterling and US dollars respectively) and euro. P could, as an alternative to hedging P's investment in C, hedge the foreign exchange risk between the functional currencies of B (sterling) and C (US dollars).

In its consolidated financial statements, B could hedge its net investment in C for the foreign exchange risk between C's functional currency (US dollars) and its own (sterling). *[IFRIC 16.AG1-AG3].*

Where a non-derivative instrument is used as the hedging instrument, the designated risk should be the spot foreign exchange risk; if the hedging instruments were forward contracts, the forward or the spot foreign exchange risk could be designated as the hedged risk (see 7.3.3 below). *[IFRIC 16.AG2].*

5.3.2 Amount of the hedged item for which a hedging relationship may be designated

In a hedge of the foreign currency risks arising from a net investment in a foreign operation, the hedged item can be an amount of net assets equal to or less than the carrying amount of the net assets of the foreign operation in the consolidated financial statements of the parent entity. *[IFRIC 16.11].* Also, although the hedged item is described here with reference to the net assets, there is nothing within the guidance to suggest that a hedge of negative net assets would be precluded.

Example 53.49: Amount of hedged item in a net investment hedge

The facts are as in Example 53.48 above. If P wished to hedge the foreign exchange risk from its net investment in C, it could use A's external borrowing of US$300 million as a hedging instrument and the hedged item could be an amount of net assets equal to or less than the US$300 million carrying amount of C in P's consolidated financial statements. *[IFRIC 16.AG4].*

The carrying amount of the net investment takes account of monetary items receivable from or payable to a foreign operation for which settlement is neither planned nor likely to occur in the future. These balances are considered to be, in substance, part of the reporting entity's net investment in the foreign operation. *[IAS 21.15]*. A loan made to the foreign operation, for which settlement is neither planned nor likely to occur in the future, will increase the amount that can be hedged; if a loan is made by the foreign operation, the amount that can be hedged will be reduced. *[IFRIC 16.AG14]*.

In many cases the full economic value of a net investment will not be recognised in the financial statements. The most common reason will be the existence of, say, goodwill or intangible assets that are either not recognised or measured at an amount below their current value (see Chapters 9 and 17). In these situations, if an investor hedges the entire economic value of its net investment it will not be able to obtain hedge accounting for the proportion of the hedging instrument that exceeds the recognised net assets.

A single hedging instrument can hedge the same designated risk only once. Consequently, in Examples 53.48 and 53.49 above, P could not in its consolidated financial statements designate A's external borrowing in a hedge of both the €/US$ spot foreign exchange risk and the £/US$ spot foreign exchange risk in respect of its net investment in C. *[IFRIC 16.AG6]*.

The carrying amount of the net assets of a foreign operation that may be designated as the hedged item in the consolidated financial statements of a parent depends on whether any lower level parent of the foreign operation has applied hedge accounting for all or part of the net assets of that foreign operation and whether that accounting has been maintained in the parent's consolidated financial statements. *[IFRIC 16.11]*. An exposure to foreign currency risk arising from a net investment in a foreign operation may qualify for hedge accounting only once in the consolidated financial statements. Therefore, if the same net assets of a foreign operation are hedged by more than one parent entity within the group (for example, both a direct and an indirect parent entity) for the same risk, only one hedging relationship will qualify for hedge accounting in the consolidated financial statements of the ultimate parent. *[IFRIC 16.13]*. This is illustrated in the following example.

Example 53.50:   Amount of hedged item in a net investment hedge (different hedged risks)

The facts are the same as in Examples 53.48 and 53.49 above except that P's net assets include £500 million and US$300 million of external borrowings. If P wished to hedge the foreign exchange risk in relation to its net investments in B and C, the designations it could make in its consolidated financial statements include the following: *[IFRIC 16.AG10]*

- US$300 million of the US dollar borrowings designated as a hedge of the net investment in C with the risk being the spot foreign exchange exposure (€/US$) between P and C and up to £341 million of the sterling borrowings designated as a hedge of the net investment in B with the risk being the spot foreign exchange exposure (€/£) between P and B; or

- US$300 million of the US dollar borrowings as a hedge of the net investment in C with the risk being the spot foreign exchange exposure (£/US$) between B and C and up to £500 million of the sterling borrowings designated as a hedge of the net investment in B with the risk being the spot foreign exchange exposure (€/£) between P and B.

The €/US$ risk from P's net investment in C is a different risk from the €/£ risk from P's net investment in B. However, in the first case described above, P would have already fully hedged the €/US$ risk from its net investment in C and if P also designated its £500 million of borrowings as a hedge of its net investment in B, £159 million of that net investment, representing the sterling equivalent of its US dollar net investment in C, would be hedged twice for £/€ risk in P's consolidated financial statements. *[IFRIC 16.AG11]*. The £341 million that may be designated is just £500 million less £159 million.

In the second case described above, because the designation of the US$/£ risk between B and C does not include the £/€ risk, P is also able to designate up to £500 million of its net investment in B with the risk being the spot foreign currency exposure (£/€) between P and B. *[IFRIC 16.AG12]*.

A hedging relationship designated by one parent entity in its consolidated financial statements need not be maintained by another higher level parent entity. However, if it is not maintained by the higher level parent entity, the hedge accounting applied by the lower level parent must be reversed before the higher level parent's hedge accounting is recognised. *[IFRIC 16.13]*. This is illustrated in the following example.

Example 53.51: Hedge accounting applied by intermediate parent

The facts are the same as in Examples 53.48 and 53.49 above, except that P's net assets include £500 million of external borrowings and B's net assets of £341 million include US$300 million of external borrowings which it designates as a hedge of the £/US$ risk of its net investment in C in its own consolidated financial statements.

P could maintain B's designation of that hedging instrument as a hedge of its net investment in C for the £/US$ risk and P could designate its £500 million external borrowings as a hedge of its entire net investment in B. The first hedge, designated by B, would be assessed by reference to B's functional currency (sterling) and the second hedge, designated by P, would be assessed by reference to P's functional currency (euro). In this case, only the £/US$ risk from P's net investment in C has been hedged in its consolidated financial statements by B's US dollar borrowings, not the entire €/US$ risk. Therefore, the entire €/£ risk from P's net investment in B may be hedged in P's consolidated financial statements. *[IFRIC 16.AG13]*.

Alternatively, P could reverse the hedging relationship designated by B. In this case, it could designate B's US$300 million external borrowing as a hedge of its net investment in C for the €/US$ risk and designate £341 million of its borrowings as a hedge of part of the net investment in B. In this case the effectiveness of both hedges would be computed by reference to P's functional currency (euro). Consequently, both the US$/£ and £/€ changes in value of B's US$300 million borrowing would be included in P's foreign currency translation reserve. Because P has already fully hedged the €/US$ risk from its net investment in C, it could hedge only up to £341 million for the €/GBP risk of its net investment in B. *[IFRIC 16.AG15]*.

5.3.3 Where the hedging instrument can be held

The hedging instrument(s) may be held by any entity or entities within the group, including the foreign operation being hedged, provided the designation, documentation and qualification criteria of IFRS 9 are satisfied. The hedging strategy of the group should be clearly documented because of the possibility of different designations at different levels of the group (see 5.3.2 above). *[IFRIC 16.14, BC24A, BC24B]*.

Where the entity holding the hedging instrument has a functional currency that is not the same as the parent by which the hedged risk is defined, this could result in some of the foreign exchange difference on the hedging instrument remaining in profit or loss – this is discussed further at 7.3.1 below.

Clearly the reporting entity (which, in the case of consolidated financial statements, includes any subsidiary consolidated by the parent) must be a party to the hedging instrument. In Examples 53.48 and 53.49 above, therefore, B could not apply hedge accounting in its consolidated financial statements in respect of a hedge involving the US$300 million borrowing issued by A because the hedging instrument is held outside of the group headed by B. *[IFRIC 16.AG6]*.

6 QUALIFYING CRITERIA

6.1 General requirements

In order to qualify for hedge accounting as set out at 7 below, all of the following criteria must be met:

- the hedging relationship consists only of eligible hedging instruments and eligible hedged items (see 2 and 3 above);
- at inception of the hedging relationship, there is formal designation and documentation of the hedging relationship and entity's risk management objective and strategy for undertaking the hedge (see 6.2 below). That documentation shall include an identification of the hedging instrument, the hedged item, the nature of the risk being hedged and how the entity will assess the effectiveness requirements (including its analysis of the sources of hedge ineffectiveness and how it determines the hedge ratio (see 6.3 below)); and
- the hedging relationship meets all the following hedge effectiveness requirements (see 6.4 below):
  - there is an economic relationship between the hedged item and the hedging instrument (see 6.4.1 below);
  - the effect of credit risk does not dominate the value changes that result from that economic relationship (see 6.4.2 below); and
  - the hedge ratio of the hedging relationship is the same as that resulting from the quantity of the hedged item that the entity actually hedges and the quantity of the hedging instrument that the entity actually uses to hedge that quantity of the hedged item. However, that designation shall not reflect an imbalance between the weightings of the hedged item and the hedging instrument that would create hedge ineffectiveness (irrespective of whether recognised or not) that could result in an accounting outcome that would be inconsistent with the purpose of hedge accounting. The second part of this requirement is an anti-abuse clause that is explained in more detail in at 6.4.3 below. *[IFRS 9.6.4.1]*.

The required steps for designating a hedging relationship can be summarised in a flow chart as follows:

Figure 53.2: How to achieve hedge accounting

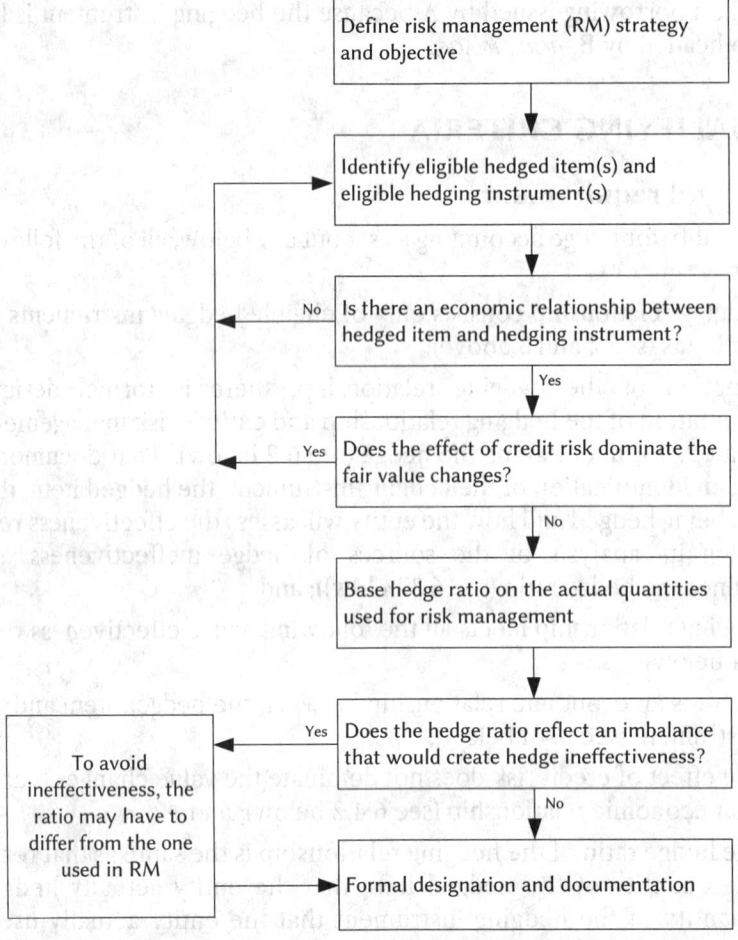

The initial effectiveness requirements also form the basis for the subsequent effectiveness assessment in order to continue to achieve hedge accounting, which is discussed at 8 below.

6.2 Risk management strategy versus risk management objective

Linking hedge accounting with an entity's risk management activities requires an understanding of what those risk management activities are. IFRS 9 distinguishes between the risk management strategy and the risk management objective. One of the qualifying criteria for hedge accounting is that the risk management objective and strategy are documented. [IFRS 9.6.4.1(b)].

The risk management strategy is established at the highest level of an entity and identifies the risks to which the entity is exposed, and whether and how the risk management activities should address those risks. For example, a risk management strategy could identify changes in interest rates of loans as a risk and define a specific target range for the fixed to floating rate ratio for those loans. The strategy is typically maintained for a relatively long period of time. However, it may include some flexibility to react to changes in circumstances. *[IFRS 9.B6.5.24]*.

IFRS 9 refers to the risk management strategy as normally being set out in 'a general document that is cascaded down through an entity through policies containing more specific guidelines.' *[IFRS 9.B6.5.24]*. However, in our view, this does not need to be a formal written risk management strategy document in all circumstances. Small and medium-sized entities with limited risk management activities that use financial instruments may not have a formal written document outlining their overall risk management strategy that they have in place. In some instances, there might be an informal risk management strategy empowering an individual within the entity to decide on what is done for risk management purposes. In such situations entities do not have the benefit of being able to incorporate the risk management strategy in their hedge documentation by reference to a formal policy document, but instead have to include a description of their risk management strategy directly in their hedge documentation. Also, there are disclosure requirements for the risk management strategy that apply irrespective of whether an entity uses a formal written policy document as part of its risk management activities. Consequently, a more informal risk management strategy should be both reflected in the disclosures and 'compensated' by a more detailed documentation of the hedging relationships.

The risk management strategy is an important cornerstone of the hedge accounting requirements in IFRS 9. Consequently, the Board added specific disclosure requirements that should allow users of the financial statements to understand the risk management activities of an entity and how they affect the financial statements (see Chapter 54 at 4.3.1). *[IFRS 7.21A(a)]*.

The risk management objective, on the contrary, is set at the level of an individual hedging relationship. It defines how a particular hedging instrument is designated to hedge a particular hedged item, and how that hedging instrument is used to achieve the risk management strategy. For example, this would define how a specific interest rate swap is used to 'convert' a specific fixed rate liability into a floating rate liability. Hence, a risk management strategy can involve many different hedging relationships whose risk management objective relates to executing that overall risk management strategy. *[IFRS 9.B6.5.24]*.

Example 53.52: Risk management strategies with related risk management objectives

The table below shows two examples of a risk management strategy with a related risk management objective.

Risk management strategy	Risk management objective
Maintain 40% of financial debt at floating interest rate	Designate an interest rate swap as a fair value hedge of a GBP 100m fixed rate liability
Hedge foreign currency risk of up to 70% of forecast sales in USD up to 12 months in advance	Designate a foreign currency forward contract to hedge the foreign currency risk of the first USD 100 sales in June 2021

It is essential to understand the difference between the risk management strategy and the risk management objective. In particular, a change in a risk management objective, is likely to affect the entity's ability to continue applying hedge accounting (see 8.3.3 below).

Furthermore, voluntary discontinuation of a hedging relationship without a respective change in the risk management objective is not allowed. This is described at 8.3 below.

The Implementation Guidance within IAS 39 contained some guidance that risk reduction on an entity-wide basis was not a condition for hedge accounting, within the context of the risk management objective, that guidance remains relevant under IFRS 9. *[IAS 39.F.2.6]*. However, as the risk management strategy is established at the highest level of an entity, it would seem contrary to the objective of the hedge accounting if the strategy was to increase entity-wide risk. *[IFRS 9.6.1.1]*.

6.2.1 Designating 'proxy hedges'

The objective of the standard is 'to represent, in the financial statements, the effect of an entity's risk management activities'. *[IFRS 9.6.1.1]*. However, this does not mean that an entity can only designate hedging relationships that exactly mirror its risk management activities. The Basis for Conclusions notes that, in some circumstances, the designation for hedge accounting purposes is inevitably not the same as an entity's risk management view of its hedging, but that the designation reflects risk management in that it relates to the same type of risk that is being managed and the instruments used for this purpose. The IASB refer to this situation as 'proxy hedging' (i.e. designations that do not exactly represent the actual risk management). In redeliberating the September 2012 draft standard, the Board decided that proxy hedging is permitted, provided the designation is directionally consistent with the actual risk management activities.[12] Furthermore, where there is a choice of accounting hedge designation, there is no apparent requirement for an entity to select the designation that most closely matches the risk management view of hedging as long as the chosen approach is still directionally consistent with actual risk management. *[IFRS 9.BC6.97-101]*.

In June 2019, within the context of a fair value hedge of foreign currency risk of a non-financial asset held for consumption, the IFRS Interpretations Committee discussed the extent to which a designated hedge relationship should be consistent with an entity's risk management activities.[13]

Paragraph 6.4.1(b) of IFRS 9 requires that, at the inception of a hedging relationship, 'there is formal designation and documentation of the hedging relationship and the entity's risk management objective and strategy for undertaking the hedge'. Accordingly, the Committee observed that, in applying IFRS 9, an entity can apply hedge accounting only if it is consistent with the entity's risk management objective and strategy for managing its exposure. An entity therefore cannot apply hedge accounting solely on the basis that it identifies items in its statement of financial position that are measured differently but are subject to the same type of risk.

The Committee observed that to the extent that an entity intends to consume a non-financial asset (rather than to sell it), changes in the fair value of the non-financial asset may be of limited significance to the entity. In such cases, an entity may not be economically managing or hedging risk exposures on the non-financial asset and, in that case, it cannot apply hedge accounting.

However, although the Interpretations Committee has reiterated the importance of consistency between designation of a hedge relationship and the entity's risk management objective, proxy hedging is still permitted, as long as the hedge designation is still directionally consistent with actual risk management. The examples below are common proxy hedging designations:

Example 53.53: Common proxy hedging designations

Net position cash flow hedging

IFRS 9 limits the designation of net positions in cash flow hedges to hedges of foreign currency risk (see 2.5.3 above). However, in practice, entities often hedge other types of risk on a net cash flow basis. Such entities could still designate the net position as a gross designation. *[IFRS 9.BC6.100(a)]*.

For example, an entity holds Australian Dollar (AUD) 2m of variable rate loan assets and AUD 10m of variable rate borrowings. The treasurer is hedging the cash flow risk exposure on the net position of AUD 8m, by entering into a pay fixed/receive variable interest rate swap (IRS) with a nominal amount of AUD 8m. Rather than designate the net AUD 8m as the hedged item, the entity could designate the IRS in a hedge of variable rate interest payments on a portion of AUD 8m of its AUD 10m borrowing.

The same approach could be applied when hedging the net foreign currency risk from forecast purchases and sales.

Risk components

An entity that hedges on a risk component basis in accordance with its risk management view might not meet the criteria for designating the hedged item as a risk component (see 2.2 above). This does not mean that the entity is prohibited from applying hedge accounting altogether. The entity could designate the item in its entirety as the hedged item and apply hedge accounting, if all the qualifying criteria are met. *[IFRS 9.BC6.100(b)]*.

Macro hedging strategies

Permitting proxy hedging is of particular relevance for banks wishing to apply macro cash flow hedging strategies (see 10 below). Typically, banks manage the interest margin risk resulting from fixed-floating mismatches of financial assets and financial liabilities held at amortised cost on their banking books. Assume the assets are floating rate and the liabilities are fixed rate. The fixed-floating mismatches are offset by entering into receive fixed/pay variable interest rate swaps. Currently there is no hedge accounting model that perfectly accommodates such hedges of the interest margin. Consequently, banks are forced to use either fair value hedge accounting for the liabilities or cash flow hedge accounting for the assets, although the actual risk management activity is neither to hedge fair values nor cash flows, but to hedge the interest margin. Both cash flow hedge accounting and fair value hedge accounting would be directionally consistent with the risk management activity and so acceptable as proxy hedging designations. *[IFRS 9.BC6.98]*.

6.3   Documentation and designation

An entity may choose to designate a hedging relationship between a hedging instrument and a hedged item in order to achieve hedge accounting. *[IFRS 9.6.1.2]*. At inception of the hedging relationship the documentation supporting the hedge should include the identification of:

- the hedging relationship and entity's risk management objective and strategy for undertaking the hedge (see 6.2 above);
- the hedging instrument (see 3 above);
- the hedged item (see 2 above);
- the nature of the risk being hedge (see 2.2 above); and
- how the entity will assess the effectiveness requirements (including its analysis of the sources of hedge ineffectiveness and how it determines the hedge ratio (see 6.4 below). *[IFRS 9.6.4.1(b)]*.

All the criteria at 6.1 above, including the documentation requirements, must be met in order to achieve hedge accounting. *[IFRS 9.6.4.1]*. Accordingly hedge accounting can be applied only from the date all the necessary documentation is completed and designation of a hedge relationship takes effect prospectively from that date. In particular, hedge relationships cannot be designated retrospectively.

Example 53.54:   Hedge documentation

In order to meet the above documentation requirements, the hedge documentation should include definitive information on the following, where relevant:

IFRS 9.6.4.1 requirement	Detailed documentation required
Risk management objective and strategy (see 6.2 above)	• Risk management strategy (could reference a formal policy document) • Risk management objective (specific to the hedge relationship)
Hedging instrument	• Specific identification of hedging instrument(s), including whether hedging instrument(s) might be replaced (see 8.3 below) • Specified proportion • Exclusion of time value, forward element or foreign currency basis (see 3.6.4 and 3.6.5 above) • Whether part of a rollover strategy (see 7.7 below) • Whether part of a dynamic strategy (see 6.3.2 below)
Hedged item	• Identification of hedged item(s) with sufficient specificity to determine whether/when the hedged item has occurred (see 6.3.3 and 8.3.4 below) • Specified proportion or layer (see 2.3 above) • Specified risk component (see 2.2 above) • Which contractual cash flows (if not all) • Timing of and rationale for forecast transactions being highly probable (see 2.6.1 above)
Risk being hedged	• Hedge type (e.g. fair value, cash flow or net investment hedge) (see 5 above) • Specific identification of hedged risk • Designation of a one side risk (see 2.1 above)
Approach to effectiveness assessment (see 6.4 below)	• Rationale for existence of an economic relationship • Hedge ratio and how determined • The effects of credit risk and how determined • Method for assessing the effectiveness qualification criteria • Sources of hedge ineffectiveness • Frequency of assessment
Date of designation	• Date of designation • Approval signature

Hedge effectiveness is the extent to which changes in the fair value or the cash flows of the hedging instrument offset changes in the fair value or the cash flows of the hedged item. When the hedged item is a risk component, the relevant change in fair value or cash flow of an item is the one that is attributable to the hedged risk (see 2.2.1 above). *[IFRS 9.B6.4.1].*

If there are changes in circumstances that affect the hedge effectiveness, an entity may have to change the method for assessing whether a hedge relationship meets the hedge effectiveness requirements, in order to ensure that the relevant characteristics of the hedging relationship, including the sources of ineffectiveness are still captured. The hedge documentation must be updated to reflect any such changes. *[IFRS 9.B6.4.2, B6.4.17, B6.4.19].*

An entity can designate a new hedging relationship that involves the hedging instrument or hedged item of a previous hedging relationship, for which hedge accounting was (in part or in its entirety) discontinued. This does not constitute a continuation, but is a restart and requires redesignation. *[IFRS 9.B6.5.28].* Hedge accounting will apply prospectively from redesignation, provided all other qualifying criteria are met. Even where the qualifying criteria are met, a hedge relationship in which an existing hedging instrument is designated, may result in higher levels of ineffectiveness (see 7.4.3 below).

The need to meet the documentation requirements should not just be seen as a compliance exercise in order to achieve hedge accounting. The way in which the hedge relationship is documented can have significant implications on the way in which hedge accounting is applied, in particular in consideration of whether the hedge relationship should be discontinued (see 8.3 below).

6.3.1 Business combinations

In a business combination accounted for using the purchase method of accounting, where the acquiree has designated hedging relationships, the question arises of whether the acquirer should:

- be permitted to continue to apply the hedge accounting model to hedge relationships designated previously by the acquiree, assuming it is consistent with the acquirer's strategies and policies; or
- be required to re-designate hedge relationships at the acquisition date.[14]

IFRS 3 – *Business Combinations* – provides guidance that in order to obtain hedge accounting in their consolidated financial statements, acquirers are required to redesignate the acquiree's hedges. *[IFRS 3.15, 16(b)]*. Further, the acquirer should not recognise in its consolidated financial statements any amounts in equity in respect of any cash flow hedges of the acquiree relating to the period prior to acquisition (see 7.2.4 below).

Redesignating the hedge relationships at the acquisition date means that if the hedging instrument has a fair value other than zero (see 7.4.3 below), it is likely that ineffectiveness will be introduced in a hedge that may have been nearly 100% effective prior to the acquisition, particularly for cash flow hedges. To mitigate this, the acquirer may, subsequent to the combination, choose to settle the existing hedging instruments and replace them with similar 'on market' contracts with a zero fair value. Furthermore, the existence of this source of ineffectiveness may influence the chosen methodology used to demonstrate the existence of an economic relationship in order to qualify for hedge accounting in the acquirer's consolidated financial statements (see 6.4.1 below). *[IFRS 9.B6.4.15]*.

For business combinations under common control, for which IFRS 3 is not applicable, see further discussion in Chapter 10 at 3.

6.3.2 Dynamic hedging strategies

A dynamic risk management strategy is one where the entity uses a dynamic process in which the exposure and the hedging instruments used to manage the exposure do not remain the same for long. *[IFRS 9.B6.5.24(b), IFRS 7.23C]*.

One such dynamic hedging strategy is where an entity assesses both the intrinsic value and time value of option contracts when hedging a risk exposure. Consider, as an example, a delta-neutral option hedging strategy (i.e. a strategy that is designed to create a net risk position (including the full option value) that is unlikely to be affected by small movements in the price of the underlying). In this situation it is helpful that there is no requirement to exclude the time value of hedging option contracts from the hedge relationship. IFRS 9 permits, but does not require, separation of the intrinsic and time value of an option contract and designation only of the intrinsic value as the hedging instrument (see 3.6.4 above). *[IFRS 9.6.2.4(a)]*. Accordingly, for a delta-neutral option hedging strategy, it is possible to achieve hedge accounting without excluding the option time value, as long as the other qualifying criteria are met (see 6.1 above).

Similarly, other dynamic hedging strategies under which the quantity of the hedging instrument is constantly adjusted in line with the risk management strategy in order to maintain a desired hedge ratio (e.g. to achieve a delta-neutral position, insensitive to changes in the fair value of the hedged item), may qualify for hedge accounting.

For a dynamic hedging strategy to qualify for hedge accounting, the documentation must specify how the hedge will be monitored and updated and how the effectiveness criteria will be assessed (see 6.4. below).

Consideration must also be made as to whether the periodic changes made as part of dynamic hedging strategy should be treated as a rebalancing of the hedge relationship (see 8.2 below) or a discontinuation and redesignation of the hedge relationship (see 8.3 below). Such a determination is not a choice but based on facts and circumstances; for example, treatment as rebalancing is only permitted where changes to the hedge ratio are made (i.e. the quantity of hedged item compared to the quantity of hedging instrument). In contrast, the introduction of new types of hedging instruments would most likely be treated as a discontinuation and redesignation.

The guidance on rebalancing is applicable when the quantity of the hedging instrument is constantly adjusted in order to maintain a desired hedge ratio for the existing hedged item(s), often referred to as a closed portfolio (see 8.2 below). Accounting for dynamic risk management of the associated risk in an open portfolio, to which new exposures are frequently added, existing exposures mature, where frequent changes also occur to the hedged item(s) is the subject of a live project for the IASB (see 11.1 below).

For any designated dynamic hedging strategies that do meet the IFRS 9 hedge accounting requirements, additional disclosures are required (see Chapter 54 at 4.3.2). *[IFRS 7.23C]*.

6.3.3 Forecast transactions

In the case of a hedge of a forecast transaction, the documentation should identify the date on, or time period in which, the forecast transaction is expected to occur. This is because, in order to qualify for hedge accounting:

- the hedge must relate to a specific identified and designated risk;
- it must be possible to measure its effectiveness reliably; and
- the hedged forecast transaction must be highly probable (see 2.6.1 above).

To meet these criteria, entities are not required to predict and document the exact date a forecast transaction is expected to occur. However, the time period in which the forecast transaction is expected to occur should be identified and documented within a reasonably specific and generally narrow range of time from a most probable date, as a basis for measuring hedge ineffectiveness. Consideration of the effectiveness criteria would need to reflect differences in timing of the hedged and hedging cash flows in a manner consistent with the designated hedged risk (see 6.4.1 and 7.4.2 below).

If a forecast transaction such as a commodity sale is properly designated in a cash flow hedge relationship and, subsequently, its expected timing changes to an earlier (or later) period, this does not affect the validity of the original designation. If the entity can conclude that this transaction is the same as the one designated as being hedged, then hedge accounting may be able to continue (see 8.3.4 below). However, ineffectiveness may arise due to the change in timing, as the calculation of the change in fair value of the hedged item would be based on the up to date expectation of the timing of the hedged forecast transaction. For example, if a forecast transaction was originally thought to occur in five months but is now expected one month earlier, the hedging instrument (still with five months remaining) will be designated for the remaining period of its existence, which will exceed the period to the forecast sale. Ineffectiveness will arise from the comparison of the change in value of the hedged item (with four months remaining) to the hedging instrument with a residual maturity of five months.

Further, hedged forecast transactions must be identified and documented with sufficient specificity so that when the transaction occurs, it is clear whether the transaction is, or is not, the hedged transaction. Therefore, a forecast transaction may be identified as the sale of the first 15,000 units of a specific product during a specified three-month period (see 2.3.1 above), but it could not be identified as the last 15,000 units of that product sold because they cannot be identified when they occur. For the same reason, a forecast transaction cannot be specified solely as a percentage of sales or purchases during a period, without also specifying the forecast value of forecast sales or purchases. The need for documented specificity of the hedged item was reiterated by the Interpretations Committee in March 2019 in a discussion within the context of the Application of the Highly Probable Requirement when a Specific Derivative is Designated as a Hedging Instrument (IFRS 9 Financial Instruments and IAS 39 Financial instruments: Recognition and Measurement)[15] (see 2.6.1 above).

6.4 Assessing if the hedge effectiveness requirements are met

A hedging relationship can only qualify for hedge accounting if all the hedge effectiveness requirements are met, assuming the other qualifying criteria are also met (see 6.1 above).

The hedge effectiveness requirements are as follows:

- there is an economic relationship between the hedged item and the hedging instrument (see 6.4.1 below);
- the effect of credit risk does not dominate the value changes that result from that economic relationship (see 6.4.2 below); and
- the hedge ratio of the hedging relationship is the same as that resulting from the quantity of the hedged item that the entity actually hedges and the quantity of the hedging instrument that the entity actually uses to hedge that quantity of the hedged item. However, that designation shall not reflect an imbalance between the weightings of the hedged item and the hedging instrument that would create hedge ineffectiveness (irrespective of whether recognised or not) that could result in an accounting outcome that would be inconsistent with the purpose of hedge accounting. The second part of this requirement is an anti-abuse clause that is explained in more detail in at 6.4.3 below. *[IFRS 9.6.4.1(c)]*.

An entity shall assess at the inception of the hedging relationship, and on an ongoing basis whether the hedge effectiveness requirements are met (see 8.1 below). The assessment relates to expectations about hedge effectiveness and is therefore only forward looking. The standard does not specify a particular method for assessing whether the effectiveness requirements are met, however the methods selected must be documented within the hedge documentation (see 6.3 above). *[IFRS 9.B6.4.12, B6.4.13, B6.4.19]*.

6.4.1 Economic relationship

The first effectiveness requirement means that the hedging instrument and the hedged item must generally be expected to move in opposite directions as a result of a change in the hedged risk. This is within the context of how the hedged item and hedging instrument have been designated as described at 2 and 3 above. *[IFRS 9.B6.4.1]*. The guidance does not require a belief that the value changes of the hedging instrument and the hedged item move in the opposite direction for the hedged risk in all circumstances, but that generally there is an expectation that they will systematically move in opposite directions. It is clear therefore, that there can be instances where the value changes in the hedged item and hedging instrument move in the same direction, although they should typically be expected to move in opposite directions.

IFRS 9 does not specify a method for assessing whether there is an economic relationship. An entity should use a method capturing all the relevant characteristics of the hedging relationship including the sources of ineffectiveness. *[IFRS 9.B6.4.13]*. Which methods, including statistical methods such as regression or sensitivity analysis, as well as the thresholds attached to them, will require judgement. No 'bright lines' are mandated by the guidance, nor is there a requirement for an entity to determine their own bright lines. Instead, judgement is required in determining whether an economic relationship exists or not. However, it follows from the objective of the hedge accounting requirements, to represent the effect of an entity's risk management activities, that the main source of information to perform the assessment would be an entity's risk management activities. *[IFRS 9.6.1.1, B6.4.18]*. In practice, an entity will normally have assessed the economic relationship for risk management purposes and, in most cases, assuming sound risk management, we would expect that this assessment to be appropriate for accounting purposes as well. However, in some cases, existing risk management techniques might not adequately consider all sources of ineffectiveness, such that additional quantitative analysis may be required, although this is likely to be rare. The chosen quantitative technique should depend on the complexity of the relationship, availability of data, the time value of money and the level of uncertainty of offset in the hedge relationship. If there are changes in circumstances that affect hedge effectiveness, an entity may have to change the method for assessing whether an economic relationship exists. *[IFRS 9.B6.4.17]*. However, if the economic relationship has in fact broken down, a change in assessment methodology would be insufficient to fix it, and the hedge relationship must be discontinued (see 8.3 below).

The standard also mentions that a quantitative method, (e.g. regression analysis), might help demonstrate a suitable hedge ratio (see 6.4.3 below). *[IFRS 9.B6.4.16]*.

The following example illustrates an approach that uses a qualitative assessment.

Example 53.55: Economic relationship between HKD and USD

An entity has foreign currency exposures in both Hong Kong dollars (HKD) and US dollars (USD). The entity aggregates its exposures in the two currencies and only uses USD linked hedges to hedge those currency exposures.

Because the HKD is pegged to the USD in a way that allows fluctuations only within a very narrow band (between HKD 7.75 – HKD 7.85 per USD) the entity concludes that an economic relationship exists between its USD linked hedges (with the USD as the underlying) and its HKD denominated foreign currency exposures.

The entity monitors the currency peg for changes and treats the movements of the HKD within the narrow band as a source of some ineffectiveness for all hedges in which the hedged item relates to amounts denominated in HKD.

The standard discusses an example where the price of the hedged instrument is based on the West Texas Intermediate (WTI) price of oil whereas the price of the hedged item is based on the Brent crude oil price. The values of the hedging instrument and the hedged item can both move in the same direction if, for example, there is only a minor change in the relative underlyings of each of the hedged item and hedging instrument (i.e. the WTI and Brent oil prices) but there is a change in the price differential between the two. However, no guidance is provided as to how frequently this would have to happen so as to lead us to reject the expectation that they would 'generally' move in opposite directions. One possibility might be to use correlation analysis to demonstrate that there is, over time, a reliable and systematic price relationship. *[IFRS 9.B6.4.4, B6.4.5, BC6.238]*.

The assessment of whether there is an economic relationship should be based on an economic rationale rather than it just arising by chance, as could be the case if the relationship is based only on a statistical correlation. That is, causality cannot be assumed purely from correlation or, to quote the IASB, 'the mere existence of a statistical correlation between two variables does not, by itself, support a valid conclusion that an economic relationship exists'. *[IFRS 9.B6.4.6]*.

Conversely, a statistical correlation may provide corroboration of an economic rationale. For example, if it can be seen that value drivers exist such that there is an expectation that the value of the hedged item and hedging instrument would generally move in opposite directions, but that significant sources of ineffectiveness exist within a relationship that may counteract the offset, then quantitative analysis may assist in determining whether an economic relationship exists or not. For example, in the case of a fair value hedge of an inflation risk component in a fixed rate bond (assuming it is determined that an eligible risk component exists (see 2.2.6 above)), quantitative analysis may provide additional evidence as to whether an economic relationship exists or not. In summary, a quantitative assessment alone is not enough to establish an economic relationship, but it may be useful in a small number of cases to support a qualitative analysis that an economic relationship exists.

The requirement of an economic relationship will automatically be fulfilled for many hedging relationships, as the underlying of the hedging instrument often matches, or is closely aligned with, the hedged risk. *[IFRS 9.B6.4.14]*. Even though it is not sufficient to focus solely on changes in value due to the hedged risk, the economic relationship will often still be capable of being demonstrated using a qualitative assessment. However, value drivers of fair value movements that are excluded from the hedge relationship (e.g. a change in credit risk on a hedged bond, if the designated risk is the benchmark rate), can be ignored for the purposes of the assessment of whether there is an economic relationship.

A qualitative assessment may also be used to determine that an economic relationship does not exist. For example, a hedge of one-sided risk in forecast purchases is designated as being hedged by an out-of-the-money call option. If the main driver of value change in the option is expected to be the time value of the option, (perhaps because the option is expected to remain out of the money) then it can easily be seen the hedged item and hedging instrument are generally not expected to move in opposite directions with respect to the hedged risk. Of course, in this example, if the time value of the option were to be excluded from the hedge relationship (see 3.6.4 above), then it would be easier to demonstrate that there is an economic relationship.

When the critical terms of the hedging instrument and hedged item are not closely aligned, and there is increased uncertainty about the extent of offset, such that hedge effectiveness is more difficult to predict, as noted above, IFRS 9 suggests that 'it might only be possible for an entity to conclude [that there is an economic relationship] on the basis of a quantitative assessment.' *[IFRS 9.B6.4.16, BC6.269]*. The standard does not provide any further guidance on when a quantitative assessment might be required or how it would be made. However, it would seem to be most relevant when the hedged item and the hedging instrument are each based on prices derived from different markets, as in the example of WTI and Brent crude oil, cited earlier, where there is a reasonable chance that the value changes of the hedging instrument and the hedged item will frequently move in the same direction. Although judgement will be required, we expect the need for a quantitative assessment over and above what is already undertaken for risk management purposes, to be relatively infrequent. *[IFRS 9.B6.4.18]*.

The standard also mentions hedging relationships where a derivative with a non-zero fair value is designated as the hedging instrument, as an example of a situation where a quantitative assessment might be required to establish an economic relationship. It depends on the particular circumstances as to whether hedge effectiveness arising from the non-zero fair value could potentially have a magnitude that a qualitative assessment would not adequately capture. *[IFRS 9.B6.4.15]*. However, as noted above, the standard does not provide guidance on how large the non-zero fair value would have to be for a quantitative assessment to be required, or for an economic relationship to be considered not to exist.

The assessment of the economic relationship, whether qualitative or quantitative, would need to consider, amongst other possible sources of mismatch between the designated hedged item and the hedging instrument, the following:

- maturity;
- volume or nominal amount;
- cash flow dates;
- interest rate basis, or quality and location basis differences;
- day count methods;
- features that arise only in either the designated hedged item or hedging instrument;
- differences in valuation methods and inputs such as discount rates or credit risk; and
- the extent that the hedging instrument is already 'in the money', or 'out of the money' when designated.

The assessment must be forward looking at all times. This does not mean that retrospective offset is never relevant, but it should only be relied upon if there is a reasonable expectation that it is representative of the future. *[IFRS 9.B6.4.12]*.

The assessment should include an analysis of the possible behaviour of the hedging relationship during its term to ascertain whether it can be expected to meet the risk management objective. *[IFRS 9.B6.4.6]*.

In some cases, it may be difficult to demonstrate that an economic relationship exists for the entire life of the hedged item and hedging instrument, for example in the case of a hedging instrument with a longer life than the hedged item (see 3.6.6 above), where there is a prepayment option within the hedged item, which is not matched by the hedging instrument (see 2.3.2 above) or in a documented rollover strategy (see 7.7 below). The assessment as to whether an economic relationship exists must consider possible behaviours over the 'term' of the hedging relationship. *[IFRS 9.B6.4.6]*.

The meaning of the 'term' of the hedging relationship is not explicitly defined. In some cases it would be appropriate to assume that it refers to the remaining life of the hedging instrument or hedged item, however, the importance of the risk management objective in the assessment should not be ignored. *[IFRS 9.B6.4.18]*.

For a documented dynamic hedging strategy using a process, in which the hedged item(s) and the hedging instruments do not remain the same for long (see 6.3.2 above), there is an expectation that changes will be required in future to the hedge designation in order to continue to meet the risk management objective. IAS 39 contained some explicit guidance on effectiveness testing for dynamic hedging strategies, that an entity 'must be able to demonstrate an expectation that the hedge will be highly effective for a specified short period of time during which the hedge is not expected to be adjusted'. *[IAS 39.AG107, F1.9]*. Whilst this guidance has not explicitly been carried forward into IFRS 9, it appears consistent with the requirement to consider the risk management objective when assessing whether an economic relationship exists.

Accordingly, we believe that the term of the hedging relationship and the assessment of whether there is an economic relationship should be consistent with the risk management objective. Hence if it is the case, and is documented as such, that a source of ineffectiveness, for example, prepayment risk or duration mismatches, are expected to result in changes to the risk management objective for that hedge relationship, then the relevant term of the hedging relationship for assessment purposes is until the hedge is expected to be reset or reassessed, rather than the life of the hedging instrument or hedged item. However, all ineffectiveness must be measured and recorded in the usual way, irrespective of whether the hedge term for assessment purpose is considered to be shorter than the life of either the hedged item of instrument (see 7.4 below).

When using a statistical method such as regression analysis, either to corroborate an economic relationship or to determine a suitable hedging ratio, an entity is required to consider its expectations of future developments. A prominent recent example is negative interest rates in some European countries. Many variable debt instruments such as mortgages include an explicit or implicit floor while the interest rates swaps used to hedge the variability of cash flows of those exposures usually do not. Although the interest cash flows of the hedged item and the variable leg of the hedging instrument may well have been highly correlated in the past, in an environment where interest rates are expected to be negative in the foreseeable future, this may no longer be expected because of the floor in the hedged item. This means that an entity needs to incorporate changes in expectations and re-calibrate its regression analysis accordingly.

It might also be necessary to ensure any expectations or rationale applied when undertaking a qualitative assessment to determine whether an economic relationship exists continue to be relevant for the current economic environment.

6.4.2 Credit risk and the effectiveness assessment

IFRS 9 requires that, to achieve hedge accounting, the impact of credit risk should not be of a magnitude such that it dominates the value changes, even if there is an economic relationship between the hedged item and hedging instrument. Credit risk can arise on both the hedging instrument and the hedged item in the form of counterparty credit risk or the entity's own credit risk.

Judgement must be used in determining when the impact of credit risk is 'dominating' the value changes. But clearly, to 'dominate' would mean that there would have to be a very significant effect on the fair value of the hedged item or the hedging instrument (i.e. 'the loss (or gain) from credit risk frustrating the effect of changes in the underlyings on the value of the hedging instrument or hedged item, even if those changes were significant'). [IFRS 9.B6.4.7]. The standard provides guidance that small effects should be ignored even when, in a particular period, they affect the fair values more than changes in the hedged risk. An example of credit risk dominating a hedging relationship would be when an entity hedges an exposure to commodity price risk with an uncollateralised derivative and the credit standing of the counterparty to that derivative deteriorates severely, such that the effect of the changes in the counterparty's credit standing might outweigh the effect of changes in the commodity price on the fair value of the hedging instrument. [IFRS 9.B6.4.8].

The assessment of the effect of credit risk on value changes for hedge effectiveness purposes, which often may be made on a qualitative basis, should not be confused with the requirement to measure and recognise the impact of credit risk on the hedging instrument and, where appropriate, the designated hedged item, which will normally give rise to hedge ineffectiveness recognised in profit or loss (see 7.4.9 below).

The sections below provide more discussion on the assessment of whether credit risk arising in either the hedging instrument or hedged item dominates the value changes in the hedge relationship.

6.4.2.A Credit risk on the hedging instrument

IFRS 13 is clear that the effect of credit risk, both the counterparty's credit risk and the entity's own credit risk, must be reflected in the measurement of fair value (see Chapter 14 at 11.3.2). The effect of counterparty and own credit risk on the measurement of the hedging instrument will obviously result in some hedge ineffectiveness, as the same credit risk does not usually arise in the hedged item. The expected effect of that ineffectiveness should not be of a magnitude that it frustrates the offsetting impact of a change in the values of the hedging instrument and the hedged item that results from the economic relationship (as explained at 6.4.2 above).

We expect the assessment of the effect of credit risk to be a qualitative assessment in most cases. For example, entities typically have counterparty risk limits defined as part of their risk management policy. The credit standing of the counterparties is monitored on a regular basis. However, a quantitative assessment of the impact of credit risk on the value changes of the hedging relationship might be required in some instances, if the counterparty's credit standing deteriorates.

Nowadays, most over-the-counter derivative contracts between financial institutions are cash collateralised. Furthermore, current initiatives in several jurisdictions, such as, the European Market Infrastructure Regulation (EMIR) in the European Union or the Dodd-Frank Act in the United States, have resulted in more derivative contracts being collateralised by cash (see 8.3.5 below). Similarly, since December 2015, when the London Clearing House (LCH) changed its rule book to introduce a new type of settled-to-market (STM) interest rate swap, in which the daily variation margin is used to settle the interest rate swap's outstanding fair value, more transactions are settled in this way (see 8.3.6 below).

Both cash collateralisation and STM significantly reduce the credit risk for both parties involved, meaning that credit risk is unlikely to dominate the change in fair value of such hedging instruments.

6.4.2.B Credit risk on the hedged item

The analysis of the hedged item is somewhat different, as credit risk does not apply to all types of hedged items. For example, while loan assets typically have counterparty credit risk and financial liabilities bear the issuing entity's own credit risk, inventory and forecast transactions do not pose credit risk.

Credit risk is defined as 'risk that one party to a financial instrument will cause a financial loss for the other party by failing to discharge an obligation'. *[IFRS 7 Appendix A]*. Credit risk cannot dominate the value change in a hedge of a forecast transaction as the transaction is, by definition, only anticipated but not committed. *[IFRS 9 Appendix A]*. Similarly, inventory does not involve credit risk.

This should be contrasted with the assessment of whether a forecast transaction is highly probable (see 2.6.1 above). Even though such a transaction does not involve credit risk, depending on the possible counterparties for the anticipated transaction, the credit risk that affects them can indirectly affect the assessment of whether the forecast transaction is highly probable. For example, assume an entity sells a product to only one particular customer abroad for which the sales are denominated in a foreign currency and the entity does not have alternative customers to sell the product to in that currency (or other sales in that currency). In that case, the credit risk of that particular customer would indirectly affect the likelihood of the entity's forecast sales in that currency occurring. Conversely, if the entity has a wider customer base for sales of its product that are denominated in the foreign currency then the potential loss of a particular customer would not significantly (or even not at all) affect the likelihood of the entity's forecast sales in that currency occurring.

It is noted in IFRS 9 that a magnitude that gives rise to dominance is one that would result in the loss (or gain) from credit risk frustrating the effect of changes in the underlying on the value of the hedging instrument or the hedged item, even if those changes were significant. *[IFRS 9.B6.4.7]*. The guidance refers to both a loss and a gain due to changes in credit risk for the hedged item and the hedging instrument. However, it will only be relevant to consider a decrease in credit risk for the hedged item, if such a change in credit risk would frustrate the hedge relationship. For example, a decrease in credit risk in a hedged financial asset is unlikely to cause the level of offset within the hedge relationship to become erratic, if credit risk is excluded from the hedge relationship. In contrast, this would not be the case for an increase in the credit risk of hedged financial assets, as higher levels of credit risk could affect the hedged cash flows themselves.

For regulatory and accounting purposes, banks usually have systems in place to determine the credit risk on their loan portfolios. Therefore, banks should be able to identify loans for which credit risk is so high that it would require an assessment of whether credit risk is dominating the value changes in the hedging relationship.

The introduction of the impairment model of IFRS 9 (see Chapter 51) raised the question of whether there is a linkage between:

- the impairment model concept of a significant increase in credit risk (i.e. the move from 'stage one' to 'stage two') and the subsequent transfer of a credit-impaired financial assets to 'stage three'; and

- the concept of when the effect of credit risk dominates the value changes of the hedged item that represent the hedged risk.

There is no direct link between the stages of the impairment model and credit risk eligibility criterion of the hedge accounting model. However, in practice, an entity may consider the indicators cited in the definition of a credit-impaired financial asset (see Chapter 51 at 3.1). This is because those indicators characterise situations with a magnitude of credit risk that normally suggests that its effect would dominate the value changes of the hedged item that represent the hedged risk. This suggests that normally the hedge effectiveness criteria would cease to be met no later than when a financial asset is classified as credit-impaired (i.e. in stage three). How much earlier the hedge effectiveness criteria might be failed is a matter of judgement, which may need to be supported by quantitative assessment in some situations. But also, in the context of stage three of the impairment model, it should be remembered that the effect of credit risk on the fair value of an item involves not only the probability of default but also the loss given default, whereas the indicators cited in the definition of a credit-impaired financial asset relate only to the probability of default. That difference is relevant when assessing whether credit risk is dominant in the case of items that are highly collateralised.

In practice, we expect that entities with a sound risk management would be unlikely to struggle with the assessment of when the effect of credit risk dominates the value changes of the hedged item that represent the hedged risk. This is because such entities would have developed suitable criteria for when risk exposures can no longer be economically hedged because credit risk creates too much uncertainty as to whether that exposure will eventually crystallise as per the terms in the contract from which it arises. Entities normally evaluate this for risk management purposes because they want to avoid being 'over-hedged' as a result of the offset from the hedged item for the gains or losses on the hedging instrument being eroded by credit risk. In other words, this is predominantly an economic question rather than an accounting consideration (similar to the discussion at 6.4.2.A above regarding the credit risk of hedging instruments and entities' criteria for selecting counterparties for those instruments).

It has been suggested that there is also interaction between the hedge accounting model and the impairment model regarding the effect that a fair value hedge might have on the measurement of the expected credit loss (ECLs). Specifically, as IFRS 9 requires that expected cash flows are discounted at the effective interest rate (EIR) for the purposes of calculation of the ECL, the question is whether fair value hedge accounting changes the EIR of hedged financial assets for this purpose.

If an accounting policy choice was made that fair value hedges do change the EIR, then the EIR used for discounting the ECL should be adjusted for the effect of fair value hedging. Under IFRS 9 every debt instrument recorded at amortised cost or at fair value through other comprehensive income has an associated ECL. This would mean, for every fair value hedge in relation to such financial assets, the measurement of the ECL would require taking into account the effect of the fair value hedge accounting.

However, as a fair value hedge adjustment is only required to be amortised when the hedged item ceases to be adjusted for changes in fair value attributable to the risk being hedged, arguably there is no need to adjust the EIR until then, and hence the rate used to discount ECLs. We believe the requirement is not clear and that there is an accounting policy choice on the matter (see Chapter 51 at 7.5.).

The systems used to assess the credit risk of loans would also usually permit banks to determine the appropriate economic hedge when hedging the interest rate risk of such loans, as illustrated by Example 53.56 below:

Example 53.56: Designating interest rate hedges of loan assets when credit risk is expected

Assume a bank wishes to hedge the interest rate risk of a portfolio of non-pre-payable loans that have similar credit risk characteristics. Economically, the bank should hedge only the cash flows it expects to collect. When expecting to collect 95% of all cash flows in a loan portfolio, the bank should designate the first 95% of cash flows only. A designation of more than 95% would result in an economic over-hedge and would also increase the risk of credit risk dominating the value changes of the hedging relationship.

The designation of such a nominal component (often referred to as a bottom layer) is possible under IFRS 9 (as discussed at 2.3 above). This type of designation would require that all items included in the layer are exposed to the same hedged risk so that the measurement of the hedged layer is not significantly affected by items that make up the 95% layer from the overall 100% of the portfolio. *[IFRS 9.6.6.3(c)]*. Therefore, the entity has to designate the same kind of benchmark interest rate risk component of each loan to make up the bottom layer. If there is a deterioration in the credit risk of a particular loan that results in credit risk dominating the economic relationship with the benchmark interest rate, such that its benchmark interest rate risk component will no longer qualify to be designated as a hedged item, it would not be considered to be part of the bottom layer unless and until those loans for which credit risk dominates the economic relationship would exceed 5% of the portfolio.

The example should not be taken to imply that for an individual loan with an expected loss of, say, 5% an entity may not hedge the interest rate risk using an interest rate swap that has a notional amount equal to the loan's face value. However, if the loan deteriorated in its credit quality to an extent where the credit risk-related changes in fair value start to dominate the interest rate risk-related changes, the hedging relationship would have to be discontinued.

6.4.3 The hedge ratio

The hedge ratio is the ratio between the amount of hedged item and the amount of hedging instrument. For many hedging relationships, the hedge ratio would be 1:1 as the underlying of the hedging instrument perfectly matches the designated hedged risk.

Some hedging relationships may include basis risk such that the fair value changes of the hedged item and the hedging instrument do not have a simple 1:1 relationship. In such cases, risk managers will generally set the hedge ratio so as to be other than 1:1, in order to improve the effectiveness of the hedge. Consequently, the third effectiveness requirement is that the hedge ratio used for accounting should ordinarily be the same as that used for risk management purposes. *[IFRS 9.6.4.1(c)(iii)]*.

Example 53.57: Setting the hedge ratio

An entity purchases a raw material whose price is at a discount to the commodity benchmark price, reflecting that the raw material is not yet processed to the same extent as the benchmark commodity, as well as quality differences. The entity runs a rolling 12-month regression analysis at each month end to ascertain that the price of the commodity in the futures market and the price of the raw material remain highly correlated. The slopes of the regression analyses (commodity benchmark price to raw material price) over recent months varied between 1.237 and 1.276.

The entity considers that the pattern of its regression analyses is consistent with its longer term view that the raw material trades at an approximately 20% discount to the commodity benchmark price and does not indicate a change in trend but fluctuations around that discount. Therefore, the entity uses a notional amount of 1 tonne of a forward contract for the benchmark commodity to hedge highly probable forecast purchases of 1.25 tonnes of the raw material. Note that this is not exactly the same as the particular slope of the most recent monthly regression, which is not required because the standard requires only that the entity uses the hedge ratio that it actually uses for risk management purposes, and not that it is required to minimise ineffectiveness. The example also illustrates what the standard acknowledges: there is no 'right' answer, as different entities would run different regression analyses (e.g. in terms of frequency and data inputs used, which means there is no one hedge ratio that could be required). The fluctuation of the actual discount around the particular hedge ratio chosen for designating the hedging relationship will give rise to some ineffectiveness that will need to be recorded.

However, the standard requires the hedge ratio for accounting purposes to be different from the hedge ratio used for risk management if the latter hedge ratio reflects an imbalance that would create hedge ineffectiveness 'that could result in an accounting outcome that would be inconsistent with the purpose of hedge accounting.' *[IFRS 9.6.4.1(c)(iii), B6.4.10]*. This complex language was introduced because the Board is specifically concerned with deliberate 'under-hedging', either to minimise recognition of ineffectiveness in cash flow hedges or the creation of additional fair value adjustments to the hedged item in fair value hedges. *[IFRS 9.B6.4.11(a)]*.

Example 53.58: Deliberate under-hedging in a cash flow hedge to avoid recognition of ineffectiveness

IFRS 9 requires the cash flow hedge reserve to be adjusted for the lower of (a) the cumulative gain or loss on the hedging instrument or (b) the cumulative change in fair value of the hedged item (see 7.2 below). *[IFRS 9.6.5.11(a)]*. If (a) exceeds (b), the difference is recognised in profit or loss as ineffectiveness. On the other hand, no ineffectiveness is recognised if (b) exceeds (a).

An entity has highly probable forecast purchases of a raw material used in its manufacturing process. The average volume of raw material purchases is expected to be Russian Rouble (RUB) 200 million per month. The entity wishes to hedge the commodity price risk on those forecast purchases. The only derivative available does not have an underlying risk exactly matching the one from the actual raw material hedged. The slope of a linear regression analysis is 0.93, indicating the ideal hedge ratio.

To seek to avoid recognition of accounting ineffectiveness, the entity ensures (b) will exceed (a), applying the accounting requirement discussed above. It enters into derivatives with a notional amount of only RUB 150m per month and designates the RUB 150 million of derivatives as hedging instruments in cash flow hedges of highly probable forecast purchases of RUB 200 million (thereby setting the hedge ratio at 0.75:1).

In this scenario, the hedge ratio would be considered unbalanced and only entered into to avoid recognition of accounting ineffectiveness. For hedge accounting purposes, the hedge ratio would have to be based on the expected sensitivity between the hedged item and the hedging instrument (in this example possibly around the 0.93:1 based on the linear regression analysis, which would give a hedged volume of RUB 161m). As a result, if the relative change in the fair value of the hedging instrument is greater than that on the hedged item because the relationship between the underlyings changes, some ineffectiveness will have to be recognised.

Example 53.59: Deliberate under-hedging in a fair value hedge to create fair value accounting

An entity acquires a CU 50 million portfolio of debt instruments. The debt instruments fail the 'cash flow characteristics test' of IFRS 9 (i.e. the contractual cash flows do not solely represent payments of principal and interest on the principal amount outstanding) and are therefore accounted for at fair value through profit or loss (see Chapter 48 at 6). *[IFRS 9.4.1.2(b), 4.1.2A(b), 4.1.4].*

The treasurer dislikes the profit or loss volatility resulting from the fair value accounting. He realises that one of the entity's fixed rate bank borrowings has a similar term structure and that fair value changes on the liability would more or less offset the fair value changes on the asset portfolio. However, at the time of entering into the bank borrowing, the entity did not apply the fair value option to this liability (see Chapter 48 at 7).

The treasurer enters into a CU 1 million receive fixed/pay variable interest rate swap (IRS) and designates the IRS in a fair value hedge of CU 50 million of fixed rate liability (thereby setting the hedge ratio at 0.02:1). As a result, the entire CU 50 million of liability would be adjusted for changes in the hedged interest rate risk.

In this scenario, the hedge ratio is unbalanced as the real purpose of the hedging relationship is to achieve fair value accounting (related to changes in interest rate risk) for CU 49 million of the liability. The hedge ratio used for hedge accounting purposes would have to be different (likely close to 1:1).

Alternatively, the entity could consider designating the CU 50 million portfolio of debt instruments as the hedging instrument in a fair value hedge of the fixed rate bank borrowings for interest rate risk (see 3.3 above), in that case a 1:1 hedge ratio may also be required.

The above examples are of course extreme scenarios and instances of unbalanced hedge designations are likely to be rare; IFRS 9 does not however require an entity to designate a 'perfect hedge'. For instance, if the hedging instrument is only available in multiples of 25 metric tonnes as the standard contract size, an imbalance due to using, say, 400 metric tonnes nominal value of hedging instrument to hedge 409 metric tonnes of forecast purchases, would not be regarded as resulting in an outcome 'that would be inconsistent with the purpose of hedge accounting' and so would meet the qualifying criteria. *[IFRS 9.B6.4.11(b)].*

The subsequent prospective effectiveness assessment requires consideration as to whether the accounting hedge ratio is still appropriate, or indeed whether a change is required. This 'rebalancing' of a live hedge relationship is further discussed at 8.2 below.

7 ACCOUNTING FOR EFFECTIVE HEDGES

If any entity chooses to designate a hedging relationship of a type described at 5 above, between a hedging instrument and a hedged item as described at 2 and 3 above and it meets the qualifying criteria set out at 6 above, the accounting for the gain or loss on the hedging instrument and the hedged item will be as set out in the remainder of this section. *[IFRS 9.6.1.2, 6.5.1].*

7.1 Fair value hedges

7.1.1 Ongoing fair value hedge accounting

If a fair value hedge (see 5.1 above) meets the qualifying conditions set out at 6 above during the period, it should be accounted for as follows:

- the gain or loss on the hedging instrument shall be recognised in profit or loss (or OCI if the hedging instrument hedges an equity instrument for which an entity has elected to present changes in fair value in OCI in accordance with paragraph 5.7.5 of IFRS 9 (see Chapter 48 at 2.2)); and

- the hedging gain or loss on the hedged item shall adjust the carrying amount of the hedged item (if applicable) and be recognised in profit or loss.

If the hedged item is a debt instrument (or a component thereof) that is measured at fair value through OCI in accordance with paragraph 4.1.2.A of IFRS 9 (see Chapter 48 at 2.1) the hedging gain or loss on the hedged item shall be recognised in profit or loss.

If the hedged item is an equity instrument for which an entity has elected to present changes in fair value in OCI, those amounts shall remain in OCI.

Where a hedged item is an unrecognised firm commitment (or a component thereof), the cumulative change in the fair value of the hedged item subsequent to its designation is recognised as an asset or liability with a corresponding gain or loss recognised in profit or loss. *[IFRS 9.6.5.8]*.

The hedging gain or loss on the hedged item is not necessarily the full fair value change in the hedged item, but reflects the change in value since designation of the designated portion or component of the hedged item (see 2.2 and 2.3 above) attributable to the hedged risk. Any changes in the fair value of the hedged item that are unrelated to the hedged risk (or occurred prior to the hedge designation) should only be recognised in compliance with normal IFRS requirements. *[IFRS 9.B6.3.11]*.

The gain or loss on the hedging instrument for the purposes of accounting for a fair value hedge, refers to all changes in fair value of the hedging instrument since designation in the hedge relationship. Only fair value changes with respect to the time value of an option, forward element of a forward contract or foreign currency basis spreads if excluded from the hedge designation (see 3.6.4 and 3.6.5 above), or a documented excluded proportion of the instrument (see 3.6.1 above) are not included within the gain or loss on the hedging instrument.

Hedge ineffectiveness is the extent to which the changes in the fair value or the cash flow of the hedging instrument are greater or less that those on the hedged item. *[IFRS 9.B6.4.1, B6.3.11]*. Where hedge ineffectiveness arises in a fair value hedge, a net amount will be recognised in profit or loss, (unless the hedged item is an equity instrument for which an entity has elected to present changes in fair value in OCI in accordance with paragraph 5.7.5 of IFRS 9, in which case it will be recognised in OCI). Hedge ineffectiveness is an important concept with IFRS 9, and measurement of it is considered more fully at 7.4 below.

Although not clearly evident from the standard, we believe the gain or loss on the hedging instrument and the hedging gain or loss on the hedged item should be recognised in the same line item in profit or loss to reflect the offsetting effect of hedge accounting (see Chapter 54 at 7.1.3).

The following simple example illustrates how the treatment above might apply to a hedge of fair value interest rate risk on an investment in fixed rate debt.

Example 53.60: Fair value hedge

At the beginning of Year 1 an investor purchases a fixed rate debt security for £100 and classifies it as measured at fair value thorough OCI in accordance with paragraph 4.1.2A of IFRS 9. At the end of Year 1, the fair value of the asset is £110. To protect this value, the investor enters into a hedge by acquiring an interest rate derivative with a nil fair value and designates it in a fair value hedge of interest rate risk. By the end of Year 2, the derivative has a fair value of £5 and the debt security has a corresponding decline in fair value. Fair value changes in both the fixed rate security and the derivative have only occurred due to interest rates.

The investor would record the following accounting entries:

Year 1

	DR £	CR £
Beginning of year		
Debt security	100	
Cash		100

To reflect the acquisition of the security.

	DR £	CR £
End of year		
Debt security	10	
Other comprehensive income		10

To record the increase in the security's fair value in other comprehensive income.

Year 2

	DR £	CR £
Beginning of year		
Derivative	–	
Cash		–

To record the acquisition of the derivative at its fair value of nil.

	DR £	CR £
End of year		
Derivative	5	
Profit or loss		5

To recognise the increase in the derivative's fair value in profit or loss.

	DR £	CR £
Profit or loss	5	
Debt security		5

To recognise the decrease in the security's fair value in profit or loss.

The £5 credit to the carrying amount of the debt security in Example 53.60 above, reflects application of the usual accounting for instruments measured at fair value thorough OCI in accordance with paragraph 4.1.2A of IFRS 9 (see Chapter 50 at 2.3). The effect of fair value hedge accounting in this example, is just that the reduction in fair value is recognised in profit or loss, rather than OCI. For hedged items not held at fair value, the adjustment to both the carrying amount of the hedged item and profit or loss would only occur as a result of the application of fair value hedge accounting.

Conversely, when hedging the foreign currency risk on a foreign currency monetary item, IAS 21 retranslation gains or losses would be recognised in profit or loss in any event, accordingly any incremental adjustment to the carrying amount as part of fair value hedge accounting should not include the retranslation effect again.

Example 53.60 above also includes an assumption that fair value changes only occurred as a result of changes in interest rates. No ineffectiveness was recorded as the effect of changes in interest rates on both the hedged item and hedging instrument offset perfectly, however this is a simplified example and is unlikely to be the case.

The basic hedge accounting treatment above applies equally to fair value hedges of unrecognised firm commitments. Therefore, where an unrecognised firm commitment is designated as a hedged item in a fair value hedge, the subsequent cumulative change in its fair value attributable to the hedged risk should be recognised as an asset or liability with a corresponding gain or loss recognised in profit or loss. Thereafter, the firm commitment would be a recognised asset or liability (albeit that its carrying amount will not represent either its cost or, necessarily, its fair value). The changes in the fair value of the hedging instrument would also be recognised in profit or loss. *[IFRS 9.6.5.8(b)]*.

It can be seen that applying fair value hedge accounting adjustments does not change the accounting for the hedging instrument (unless it hedges an equity instrument for which an entity has elected to present changes in fair value in OCI, or if the time value of an option, forward element of a forward contract or foreign currency basis spreads are excluded from the hedge and accounting for the costs of hedging is applied (see 7.5 below)). This is true whether the hedging instrument is a derivative or non-derivative instrument. For example, if a foreign currency cash instrument was designated as the hedging instrument in a fair value hedge (see 3.3.1 above), the foreign currency component of its carrying amount would continue to be measured in accordance with IAS 21.

7.1.2 Dealing with adjustments to the hedged item

In general, adjustments to the hedged asset or liability arising from the application of hedge accounting as described at 7.1.1 above are dealt with in accordance with the normal accounting treatment for that item. For example, copper inventory might be the hedged item in a fair value hedge of the exposure to changes in the copper price. In this case, the adjusted carrying amount of the copper inventory becomes the cost basis for the purpose of applying the lower of cost and net realisable value test under IAS 2 – *Inventories* (see Chapter 22 at 3). *[IAS 39.F.3.6]*. See also 8.3.1 below for further discussion on the accounting for discontinuation of fair value hedges.

Where the hedged item is a financial instrument (or component thereof) for which the effective interest method of accounting is used, the adjustment should be amortised to profit or loss. Amortisation may begin as soon as the adjustment exists and should begin no later than when the hedged item ceases to be adjusted for hedging gains and losses. The adjustment should be based on a recalculated effective interest rate at the date amortisation begins and should be fully amortised by maturity. If the hedged item is measured at fair value through OCI in accordance with paragraph 4.1.2A of IFRS 9, it is the cumulative gain or loss previously recognised in OCI that is adjusted, not the carrying amount. *[IFRS 9.6.5.10]*. See Chapter 51 at 7.5 for details on how the recalculated effective interest rate interacts with the IFRS 9 expected credit loss calculation.

When a hedged item in a fair value hedge is a firm commitment (or component thereof) to acquire an asset or assume a liability, the initial carrying amount of the asset or liability that results from the entity meeting the firm commitment is adjusted to include the cumulative change in the fair value of the hedged item that was recognised in the statement of financial position. *[IFRS 9.6.5.9].*

Example 53.61: Hedge of a firm commitment to acquire equipment

Company X has the euro as its functional currency. It has chosen to treat all hedges of foreign currency risk associated with firm commitments as fair value hedges. In January 2021 it contracts with a US supplier (with the US dollar as its functional currency) to purchase an item of machinery it intends to use in its business. The machine will be delivered at the start of July 2021 and the contracted price, payable on delivery, is US$1,000.

X has no appetite to take on foreign currency exchange risk in relation to euro/US dollar exchange rates and so contracts with a bank to purchase US$1,000 at the start of July in exchange for €900 (six month forward exchange rate is US$1:€0.90). In other words, X has effectively fixed the price it will pay for the machine (in euro terms) at €900.

If the fair value of the forward contract at the end of March 2021 (X's year end) is €30 positive to X, on delivery is €50 positive to X (spot exchange rate is US$1:€0.95) and assuming the hedge is perfectly effective (this might be the case if the hedged risk is identified as the forward exchange rate – see 7.4.7 below, and it is assumed that no sources of ineffectiveness such as foreign currency basis spreads exist – see 7.4.8 below) and meets all the requirements for hedge accounting, the journal entries to record this hedging relationship would be as follows:

January 2021

No entries are required as the firm commitment is unrecognised, the forward contract is recognised but has a zero fair value and no cash is paid or received.

March 2021

	DR €	CR €
Forward contract	30	
Profit or loss		30

To recognise the change in fair value of the forward contract in profit or loss.

	€	€
Profit or loss	30	
Firm commitment		30

To recognise the change in fair value of the (previously) unrecognised firm commitment in respect of changes in forward exchange rates in profit or loss.

July 2021

	€	€
Forward contract	20	
Profit or loss		20

To recognise the change in fair value of the forward contract in profit or loss.

	€	€
Profit or loss	20	
Firm commitment		20

To recognise the change in fair value of the (now recognised) firm commitment in respect of changes in forward exchange rates in profit or loss.

	DR €	CR €
Cash	50	
Forward contract		50

To record the settlement of the forward contract at its fair value.

	€	€
Machine	950	
Cash		950

To record the settlement of the firm commitment at the contracted price of US$1,000 at the spot rate of US$1:€0.95.

	€	€
Firm commitment	50	
Machine		50

To remove the carrying amount of the firm commitment from the statement of financial position and adjust the initial carrying amount of the machine that results from the firm commitment.

In summary, the result of these accounting entries is as follows:

	€	€
Machine	900	
Cash		900

which is somewhat reassuring given the starting presumption, i.e. that X had effectively fixed the purchase price of its machine at €900.

7.2 Cash flow hedges

7.2.1 Ongoing cash flow hedge accounting

If a cash flow hedge (see 5.2 above) meets the qualifying conditions set out at 6 above during the period, it should be accounted for as follows:

(a) the separate component of equity associated with the hedged item (cash flow hedge reserve) is adjusted to the lesser of the following (in absolute amounts):

   (i) the cumulative gain or loss on the hedging instrument from inception of the hedge; and

   (ii) the cumulative change in fair value (present value) of the hedged item (i.e. the present value of the cumulative change in the hedged expected future cash flows) from inception of the hedge;

(b) the portion of the gain or loss on the hedging instrument that is determined to be an effective hedge (i.e. the portion that is offset by the change in the cash flow hedge reserve calculated in accordance with (a) shall be recognised in other comprehensive income;

(c) any remaining gain or loss on the hedging instrument (or any gain or loss required to balance the change in cash flow hedge reserve in accordance with (a)) is hedge ineffectiveness and shall be recognised in profit or loss; and

(d) if the amount accumulated in the cash flow hedge reserve is a loss and an entity expects that all or a portion of that loss will not be recovered in one or more future periods, it shall immediately reclassify the amount that is not expected to be received into profit or loss as a reclassification adjustment, the 'recoverability test'. *[IFRS 9.6.5.11, IAS 1.92].*

No specific guidance is provided on how to perform the recoverability test, hence a hierarchy of guidance should be considered in the selection of an appropriate accounting policy, in line with IAS 8 – *Accounting Policies, Changes in Accounting Estimates and Errors* (see Chapter 3 at 4.3). *[IAS 8.10].* Accordingly, consideration is likely to be given to the guidance on the recoverability of assets which is contained in other IFRS such as IAS 2 on determining net realisable value of inventory, IAS 36 – *Impairment of Assets* – on impairment testing of non–financial assets or IAS 37 – *Provisions, Contingent Liabilities and Contingent Assets* – on onerous contracts. The outcome of applying these different methodologies may differ. Therefore, judgement is required in determining the most appropriate methodology based on the specific facts and circumstances of the hedge relationship.

Unlike fair value hedge accounting (see 7.1.1 above), the application of cash flow hedge accounting does not amend the accounting for the hedged items, it is the accounting for the hedging instrument that is changed. However, cash flow hedge accounting only changes the accounting for the designated portion of the hedging instrument. For example, if the time value of an option, forward element of a forward contract or foreign currency basis spreads are excluded from the hedge (see 7.5 below) or a proportion of the instrument is not designated (see 3.6.1 above), the accounting for those excluded elements remains unchanged by cash flow hedge accounting.

The requirements set out in (a) above are often referred to as the 'lower of' requirements. This accounting treatment is illustrated in the following examples.

Example 53.62: Cash flow hedge of anticipated commodity sale

On 30 September 2021, Company A hedges the anticipated sale of 24 tonnes of pulp on 1 March 2022 by entering into a short forward contract. The contract requires net settlement in cash, determined as the difference between the future spot price of 24 tonnes of pulp on a specified commodity exchange and £1m. A expects to sell the pulp in a different, local market.

A designates the forward contract as the hedging instrument in a cash flow hedge of changes in the pulp price on the cash flows from the anticipated sales. A determines that the hedge effectiveness requirements and the other hedge accounting criteria are met.

On 31 December 2021, the spot price of pulp has increased both in the local market and on the exchange, although the increase in the local market exceeds the increase on the exchange. As a result, the present value of the expected cash inflow from the sale on the local market is £1.1 million and the fair value of the forward is £85,000 negative. The hedge is still determined to meet the hedge effectiveness criteria. In particular Company A considers the difference in relative value changes in the local and exchange market price of pulp to be fluctuations around an appropriate hedge ratio, rather than an indication that the existing 1:1 hedge ratio is no longer appropriate (see 6.4.3 above). *[IFRS 9.B6.5.11].*

The cumulative change in the fair value of the forward contract is £85,000, while the fair value of the cumulative change in expected future cash flows on the hedged item is £100,000. Ineffectiveness is not recognised in the financial statements because the cumulative change in the fair value of the hedged cash flows exceeds the cumulative change in the value of the hedging instrument. The whole of the fair value change in the forward contract would be recognised in other comprehensive income.

December 2021

	DR £'000	CR £'000
Other comprehensive income	85	
Forward contract		85

Example 53.63: Cash flow hedge of a floating rate liability

Company A has a floating rate liability of £1 million with five years remaining to maturity. It enters into a five year pay-fixed, receive-floating interest rate swap with the same principal terms to hedge the exposure to variable cash flow payments on the floating rate liability attributable to interest rate risk.

At inception, the swap's fair value is £nil. Subsequently, there is an increase of £49,000 which consists of a change of £50,000 resulting from an increase in market interest rates and a change of minus £1,000 resulting from an increase in the credit risk of the swap counterparty. There is no change in the fair value of the floating rate liability, but the fair value (present value) of the future cash flows needed to offset the exposure to variable interest cash flows on the liability increases by £50,000.

Even if A determines that the hedge of interest rate risk meets the hedge effectiveness requirements (which is quite likely based on the fact pattern), it is not fully effective if part of the change in the fair value of the derivative is due to the counterparty's credit risk (see 7.4.9 below). The accounting will be to credit the effective portion of the swap's fair value change, £49,000, to other comprehensive income. There is no debit to profit or loss for the change in fair value of the swap attributable to the deterioration in the credit quality of the swap counterparty because the cumulative change in the present value of the future cash flows needed to offset the exposure to variable interest cash flows on the hedged item, £50,000, exceeds the cumulative change in value of the hedging instrument, £49,000.

Alternatively, if the fair value of the swap increased to £51,000 of which £50,000 results from the increase in market interest rates and £1,000 from a decrease in the swap counterparty's credit risk, there would be a credit to profit or loss of £1,000 for the change in the swap's fair value attributable to the improvement in the counterparty's credit quality. This is because the cumulative change in the value of the hedging instrument, £51,000, exceeds the cumulative change in the present value of the future cash flows needed to offset the exposure to variable interest cash flows on the hedged item, £50,000. The difference of £1,000 represents the ineffectiveness attributable to the swap, and is recognised in profit or loss. *[IAS 39 IG F.5.2]*.

The above example illustrates that measurement of hedge ineffectiveness differs for a cash flow hedge when compared to a fair value hedge. In a cash flow hedge, if the fair value of the derivative increases by €10 and the present value of the hedged expected cash flows change by only €8, the €2 difference is recognised in profit or loss (as would be the case for a fair value hedge). However, in a cash flow hedge, if the present value of the hedged expected cash flows changes by €10, but the fair value of the derivative changes by only €8, this €2 of hedge ineffectiveness is not recognised in profit or loss (which would not be the case for a fair value hedge).

Because of this, an entity might consider deliberately under-hedging an exposure in a cash flow hedge. It might do this by targeting an offset of, say, 85% to 90%, however, whilst it still might be possible to demonstrate the existence of an economic relationship for such a designation (see 6.4.1 above), it is unlikely to meet the hedge ratio requirements (as it seems the hedge ratio was established to avoid recognising ineffectiveness in a cash flow hedge) and so would most likely be precluded (see 6.4.3 above). *[IFRS 9.B6.4.11(a)]*.

7.2.2 Reclassification of gains and losses recognised in cash flow hedge reserve from OCI to profit or loss

The amount that has been accumulated in the cash flow hedge reserve in accordance with 7.2.1 above shall be accounted for as follows:

(a) if a hedged forecast transaction subsequently results in the recognition of a non-financial asset or liability, or a hedged forecast transaction for a non-financial asset or liability becomes a firm commitment for which fair value hedge accounting is applied, the entity shall remove that amount from the cash flow hedge reserve and include it directly in the initial cost or other carrying amount of the asset or liability, this is often referred to as a 'basis adjustment'. This is not a reclassification adjustment and hence it does not affect OCI for the period; and

(b) for a hedged transaction in a cash flow hedge other than those covered in (a) above, that amount shall be reclassified from the cash flow hedge reserve to profit or loss as a reclassification adjustment in the same period(s) during which the hedged expected future cash flows affect profit or loss, e.g. in the periods that interest income or interest expense is recognised or when a forecast sale occurs. [IFRS 9.6.5.11(d), IAS 1.92].

The treatments for (a) above is illustrated in the following example.

Example 53.64: Hedge of a firm commitment to acquire equipment

Consider a variation of the situation in Example 53.61 at 7.1.2 above whereby Company X has chosen to treat all hedges of foreign currency risk associated with firm commitments as cash flow hedges, rather than as fair value hedges, as permitted by the standard (see 5.2.2 above). Otherwise, the underlying facts and assumptions are the same. The accounting entries made at the end of March 2021 have not been shown separately (as they were in Example 53.61) because they are not relevant to the issue being illustrated.

The journal entries to record this hedging relationship would be as follows:

January 2021

No entries are required as the firm commitment is unrecognised, the forward contract is recognised but has a zero fair value and no cash is paid or received.

July 2021

	DR €	CR €
Forward contract	50	
Other comprehensive income		50

To recognise the change in fair value of the forward contract and, because no ineffectiveness arises, the whole of this change is recognised in other comprehensive income.

	€	€
Cash	50	
Forward contract		50

To record the settlement of the forward contract at its fair value.

	€	€
Machine	950	
Cash		950

To record the settlement of the firm commitment at the contracted price of US$1,000 at the spot rate of US$1:€0.95.

	€	€
Other comprehensive income	50	
Machine		50

To remove the gain recognised in other comprehensive income and adjust the carrying amount of the machine that results from the hedged transaction by this amount. This is not a reclassification adjustment as per IAS 1 – *Presentation of Financial Statements*. *[IFRS 9.6.5.11(d)(i)]*.

In summary, the result of these accounting entries is as follows:

	€	€
Machine	900	
Cash		900

which again reflects the starting presumption, i.e. that X had effectively fixed the purchase price of its machine at €900.

In applying treatment (b) above to hedged items that are not forecast transactions that subsequently result in the recognition of a non-financial asset or liability, or a hedged forecast transaction for a non-financial asset or liability becomes a firm commitment for which fair value hedge accounting is applied, an appropriate reclassification method must be applied. When instruments such as conventional interest rate swaps are used as a hedging instrument in a cash flow hedge, it is common for entities to recognise net interest income or expense on the hedging instrument directly in profit or loss on an accruals basis. Other changes in fair value of the hedging instrument (i.e. the 'clean value' – excluding accrued interest) are recognised in other comprehensive income, subject to the 'lower of' requirements (see 7.2.1 above). Such an approach avoids the need to reclassify from cash flow hedge reserve to profit or loss the net interest as the hedged item impacts profit or loss. However, care must be taken to ensure the portion of the gain or loss on the hedging instrument that is recognised in the cash flow hedge reserve appropriately excludes ineffectiveness, which should be recognised in profit or loss. The hedging derivative would still be recognised in the statement of financial position at the full fair value.

Although not clearly evident from the standard, we believe the reclassification from cash flow hedge reserve to profit or loss should be recognised in the same line item in profit or loss as the hedged transaction to reflect the offsetting effect of hedge accounting (see Chapter 54 at 7.1.3).

If a hedge of a foreign currency forecast intragroup transaction qualifies for hedge accounting (see 4.3.2 above), any gain or loss that is recognised in other comprehensive income should be reclassified from cash flow hedge reserve to profit or loss in the same period(s) during which the foreign currency risk of the hedged transaction affects consolidated profit or loss. *[IFRS 9.B6.3.6]*. In order for the consolidated profit or loss to be affected by a foreign currency forecast intragroup transaction, an associated external forecast transaction must also exist. Accordingly, that external transaction also drives the timing of recycling of the effective portion of the hedge relationship.

Guidance is provided on the accounting for the amount that has been accumulated in the cash flow hedge reserve on discontinuation of hedge accounting (see 8.3.2 below). *[IFRS 9.6.5.12]*.

7.2.3 Recycling for a hedge of foreign currency monetary items

It was stated at 5.2.3 above that using a forward exchange contract to hedge a foreign currency payable or receivable could be treated either as a fair value hedge, or a cash flow hedge. In a fair value hedge, the gain or loss on remeasurement of both the forward contract and the hedged item are recognised immediately in profit or loss. Even if the forward foreign currency risk was the designated hedged risk, then ineffectiveness would arise from changes in the forward points, as the retranslation of the foreign currency payable or receivable is restricted to the IAS 21 spot revaluation (see 7.1.1 above and 7.4.7 below).

However, in a cash flow hedge of the forward foreign currency risk, the cumulative gain or loss on remeasuring the forward contract is recognised in the cash flow hedge reserve (assuming no sources of ineffectiveness) and reclassified from the cash flow hedge reserve to profit or loss when the payable or receivable affects profit or loss (see 7.2.2 above). Because the payable or receivable is remeasured continuously in respect of changes in foreign currency rates per IAS 21, there is a requirement for the gain or loss on the forward contract to be reclassified from the cash flow hedge reserve to profit or loss as the payable or receivable is remeasured, not when the payment occurs. There is variation in practice as to the method used to facilitate the reclassification over the period the payable or receivable affects profit or loss.

The forward element of a forward contract may be excluded from a designated fair value or cash flow hedge relationship (designation of the spot exchange risk only – see 3.6.5 above). In that case any fair value changes attributable to the forward element may be recognised in other comprehensive income if accounted for as costs of hedging (see 7.5.2 below). *[IFRS 9.6.5.16]*.

Designating the forward exchange rate or the spot exchange rate as the hedged risk could result in different results as illustrated in Example 53.72 at 7.4.6 below.

7.2.4 Cash flow hedges within subsidiaries on acquisition or disposal

Where a reporting entity acquires a subsidiary that is applying cash flow hedge accounting, additional considerations arise. In applying the purchase method of accounting in its consolidated financial statements, the reporting entity does not inherit the subsidiary's existing cash flow hedge reserve, since this clearly represents cumulative pre-acquisition gains and losses (see Chapter 9 at 5.4).[16] This has implications for the assessment of hedge effectiveness and the measurement of ineffectiveness because, so far as the group is concerned, it has effectively started a new hedge relationship with a hedging instrument that is likely to have a non-zero fair value (see 6.3.1 above and 7.4.3 below).

The standard does not address the situation when a subsidiary is disposed of. In November 2016, the Interpretations Committee discussed the issue of whether a group should discontinue hedge accounting in the consolidated financial statements where the group applies cash flow hedge accounting to forecast transactions that are anticipated in a subsidiary after the expected date of disposal of that subsidiary. The Interpretations Committee were of the tentative view that the assessment of a qualifying hedging relationship should be performed from the group's perspective based on whether the transaction is highly probable and could affect the group's profit or loss. Given that the forecast transactions are expected to occur only after the expected date of disposal of the subsidiary, these transactions are no longer expected to occur from the group's perspective as soon as the subsidiary is classified as held for sale. According to the Interpretation Committee's tentative view the forecast transactions would no longer be eligible hedged items and the group would discontinue hedge accounting from the date the subsidiary is classified as held for sale.[17] The Interpretations Committee suggested that outreach would be helpful to understand if diverse accounting is currently applied in practice. If the Interpretation Committee's view is confirmed, existing accounting policies may need to be changed retrospectively, although this has still not happened at the time of writing.

7.3 Accounting for hedges of a net investment in a foreign operation

Hedges of a net investment in a foreign operation (see 5.3 above), including a hedge of a monetary item that is accounted for as part of the net investment (see Chapter 15 at 6.3.1), shall be accounted for similarly to cash flow hedges:

- the portion of the gain or loss on the hedging instrument that is determined to be an effective hedge should be recognised in other comprehensive income and (as clarified by IFRIC 16) included with the foreign exchange differences arising on translation of the results and financial position of the foreign operation; *[IFRIC 16.3]* and
- the ineffective portion should be recognised in profit or loss. *[IFRS 9.6.5.13]*.

The cumulative gain or loss on the hedging instrument relating to the effective portion of the hedge that has been accumulated in the foreign currency translation reserve shall be reclassified from equity to profit or loss as a reclassification adjustment on disposal or, in certain circumstances, partial disposal of the foreign operation in accordance with IAS 21 (see Chapter 15 at 6.6). *[IFRS 9.6.5.14]*.

The meaning of 'similarly to cash flow hedges' is not immediately clear, and has been the subject of some debate. It is readily understood that the portion of the gain or loss on the hedging derivative that is determined to be an effective hedge should be recognised in other comprehensive income (as it would for a cash flow hedge). However, the wording in the standard also seems to indicate that ineffectiveness should be measured in the same way as for cash flow hedges, i.e. no ineffectiveness is recognised in profit or loss if the gain or loss on the hedging instrument is less, in absolute terms, than the gain or loss on the hedged item, (see 7.2.1 above). This is despite the fact that there appears to be no good reason why ineffectiveness should not also be recognised in profit or loss if the gain or loss on the hedging instrument is less, in absolute terms, than the gain or loss on the hedged item. This is different to the accounting for net investment hedges under US GAAP,[18] for which it is clear that ineffectiveness should be recognised in profit or loss for under-hedges as well as over-hedges.

In its March 2016 meeting, the Interpretations Committee discussed this issue. The Interpretations Committee concluded that the guidance in IFRS 9 is sufficiently clear and would require an entity to apply the lower of test for net investment hedges. One of the arguments put forward was that the application of the lower of test in determining the effective portion of the gains or losses arising from the hedging instrument when accounting for net investment hedges, avoids the recycling of exchange differences arising from the hedged item that have been recognised in other comprehensive income before the disposal of the foreign operation. Such an outcome would be consistent with the requirements of IAS 21.[19]

Whilst the above accounting may appear relatively straight forward at first consideration, a number of additional complexities arise in the accounting for net investment hedges. The complexity is largely driven by the requirement to apply guidance written for a cash flow hedge to a situation where no cash flow arises, and the accounting for net investments in foreign operations within complex groups. These are further considered in the following sections.

7.3.1 Identifying the effective portion in a net investment hedge

In accounting for a hedge of a net investment, IFRS 9 requires that the portion of the gain or loss on the hedging instrument that is determined to be an effective hedge should be recognised in other comprehensive income. *[IFRS 9.6.5.13]*. IFRIC 16 provides some helpful guidance in calculating the effective portion of the gain or loss on the hedging instrument.

As set out at 5.3.1 above, IFRIC 16 explains that the hedged risk in a net investment hedge is defined by reference to the functional currency of a parent of the foreign operation that is the subject of the hedge. The cumulative gain or loss on the hedging instrument that is determined to be effective is the change in value of the hedging instrument in respect of foreign exchange risk, this should be computed by reference to the functional currency of this parent entity. *[IFRIC 16.15]*.

Depending on where the hedging instrument is held, in the absence of hedge accounting the total change in its value might be recognised in profit or loss, in other comprehensive income, or both. The interpretation states that the calculation of the effective portion should not be affected by where the change in value of the hedging instrument would be recognised. In applying hedge accounting, the total effective portion of the change should be included in other comprehensive income. *[IFRIC 16.15]*.

Example 53.65: Identification of the effective portion in a net investment hedge (1)

Consider the situation outlined in Example 53.48 above (see 5.3.1 above). In addition, A's borrowings were designated in a hedge of the €/US$ spot risk associated with P's net investment in C. In the absence of hedge accounting, the total US$/€ foreign exchange difference on A's US$300 million external borrowing would be recognised in P's consolidated financial statements as follows: *[IFRIC 16.AG5]*

- US$/¥ spot foreign exchange rate change, translated to euro, in profit or loss; and
- ¥/€ spot foreign exchange rate change in other comprehensive income.

The fact that gain or loss on the hedging instrument is split between profit or loss and OCI does not affect the calculation of the effective portion in applying paragraph 6.5.13 of IFRS 9.

The cumulative gain or loss on the hedging instrument that is determined to be effective is computed by reference to the functional currency of P, the hedging parent, which is euro. *[IFRIC 16.15]*. Hence all of the €/US$ foreign exchange difference on A's US$300 million external borrowing would, after the application of hedge accounting, be recognised in other comprehensive income and be included in the foreign currency translation reserve relating to C.

The guidance says this is because the change in value of both the hedging instrument and the hedged item are computed by reference to the functional currency of P (euro) against the functional currency of C (US dollars). *[IFRIC 16.AG4, AG7]*.

Example 53.66: Identification of the effective portion in a net investment hedge (2)

Using the same fact pattern as in Example 53.65 above, but if A's US$300 million external borrowing was designated as a hedge of the £/US$ spot foreign exchange risk between C and B, the guidance states that the total US$/€ foreign exchange difference on A's borrowing would instead be recognised in P's consolidated financial statements as follows:

- the £/US$ spot foreign exchange rate change (the effective portion of the hedging instrument) in the foreign currency translation reserve relating to C;
- £/¥ spot foreign exchange rate change, translated to euro, in profit or loss; and
- ¥/€ spot foreign exchange rate change in other comprehensive income. *[IFRIC 16.AG5]*.

Finally, the interpretation states that if P held the US$ denominated borrowings and designated them in a hedge of the spot foreign exchange exposure (£/US$) between B and C, only the £/US$ part of the change in the value of the borrowings (the effective portion of the hedging instrument) would be included in P's foreign currency translation reserve relating to C. The remainder of the change (equivalent to the £/€ change on £159 million) would be included in P's consolidated profit or loss. *[IFRIC 16.AG12]*.

The calculation of the effective portion is not affected by whether the hedging instrument is a derivative or a non-derivative instrument or by the method of consolidation. *[IFRIC 16.15]*.

7.3.2 Non-derivative liabilities hedging a net investment

A foreign currency denominated non-derivative financial liability, such as a borrowing, can be used as the hedging instrument in a hedge of a net investment in a foreign operation (see 3.3.1 above). *[IFRIC 16.14]*. This can be seen as purely an 'accounting' hedge, i.e. the retranslation gain or loss on the borrowing (an accounting entry representing a part of its change in fair value that is accounted for on a continuous basis) can offset the retranslation gain or loss on the net investment (another accounting entry). In fact, if the liability is:

- denominated in the same currency as the functional currency of the hedged net investment;
- held by an entity with the same functional currency as the parent by which the hedged risk is defined;
- has an amortised cost that is lower than the net investment in the foreign operation; and
- is designated appropriately,

the hedge is likely to be perfectly effective in terms of the offsetting retranslation gains and losses on the liability and the hedged proportion of the net investment.

If a borrowing or similar liability is denominated in a different currency to the functional currency of the net investment, it may still be possible to designate it as the hedging instrument. However, it will need to be demonstrated that the two currencies are sufficiently correlated so that the hedging instrument is expected to result in offsetting gains and losses over the period that the hedge is designated, i.e. an economic relationship exists (see 6.4.1 above). This might be the case if the two currencies are formally pegged or otherwise linked to one another or if the relevant exchange rates move in tandem because of, say, similarities in the underlying economies.

Even if such a hedge meets the hedge effectiveness requirements (see 6.4 above), it is likely to result in some ineffectiveness. Under US GAAP it is suggested that the retranslation gains and losses on the actual instrument should be compared to those on a hypothetical non-derivative (e.g. a borrowing in the correct currency) with any difference recognised in profit or loss.[20] This approach should normally be acceptable under IFRS 9, if applied in conjunction with the accounting requirements for net investment hedges (see 7.3 above).

For hedges of foreign currency risk, the foreign currency risk component of a non-derivative financial instrument is determined in accordance with IAS 21. *[IFRS 9.B6.2.3]*. Therefore, when designating a foreign currency denominated non-derivative financial liability as the hedging instrument in a hedge of a net investment, it is only possible to designate the spot foreign exchange risk, and not a forward foreign exchange risk. *[IFRIC 16.AG2]*.

7.3.3 Derivatives hedging a net investment

It is clear that a derivative instrument may be designated as the hedging instrument in a hedge of a net investment. *[IFRIC 16.14]*. What is harder to determine is how various types of derivative may be designated in a hedge of a net investment in order that the hedge relationship meets the usual hedge accounting criteria, and how the relationship should be accounted for. For example:

- Is it possible to designate the forward foreign currency risk as the hedged risk in a net investment hedge?
- How should the hedged risk in the net investment be represented for ineffectiveness measurement purposes when the hedging instrument is a derivative?
- What is the accounting treatment for any excluded portions of a derivative hedging instrument in a net investment hedge?

These questions will be considered in the remainder of this section.

In the application guidance to IFRIC 16, it is noted that if the hedging instrument is a forward contract, then it is possible to designate a forward foreign currency risk as the hedged risk in a hedge of a net investment (see 3.6.5 above). *[IFRIC 16.AG2]*. Forward foreign currency risk must therefore be deemed to exist within the net investment. If the forward foreign currency risk is designated for a net investment hedge, then the entire change in fair value of the hedging instrument, (including changes in the forward element) should be included in the calculation of the portion of the gain or loss on the hedging instrument that is determined to be an effective hedge. *[IFRS 9.6.5.13]*. This could be achieved by using a hypothetical derivative that is also a forward foreign contract (see 7.4.4 below).

Like forward contracts, cross currency interest rate swaps are sometimes used as hedging instruments in net investment hedges. It is often said that cross currency swaps are essentially a series of forward contracts and so arguably the treatment for forwards should be equally applicable to cross currency swaps. However, it is difficult to rationalise why a cross currency swap, for which there are periodic gross settlements is a good representation of the forward foreign currency risk within the retranslation of a net investment, and therefore an appropriate hypothetical derivative (see 7.3.3.B and 7.4.4 below).

There is no reason why an option contract, that is not a written option, cannot be designated as the hedging instrument in a hedge of a net investment (see 3.2.2 above). In fact such a hedge is included as an example in the IFRS 9 application guidance. *[IFRS 9.B6.5.29(b)]*.

A qualifying instrument may be designated with the following portions excluded: time value of options, forward elements of forwards, and/or foreign currency basis spread (see 3.6 above). Where such portions are excluded they may be treated as costs of hedging (see 7.5 below), or, alternatively, the excluded forward elements of forwards and/or foreign currency basis spread may remain at fair value through profit or loss. *[IFRS 9.6.5.16]*. This treatment for hedges of a net investment is discussed in more detail in 7.5.2.A below. It is worth noting that unless the foreign currency basis spread is excluded from the derivative hedging instrument in a net investment hedge, ineffectiveness will occur as foreign currency basis spread cannot be assumed to exist in a non-derivative hedged item (see 7.4.8 below).

7.3.3.A Forward currency contracts hedging a net investment

It is very common for forward currency contracts to be used as the hedging instrument in a hedge of a net investment, and it is acknowledged in the IFRIC 16 application guidance that it is possible to designate a forward foreign currency risk for such a hedge (see 7.3.3 above). Therefore, permitting the hedged foreign currency risk in the net investment hedge to be represented by a hypothetical forward foreign currency contract seems relatively uncontroversial and has effectively been endorsed in IFRIC 16. *[IFRIC 16. AG2]*.

If on the other hand the spot risk is designated (i.e. the hedged foreign currency risk in the net investment hedge is represented by a hypothetical spot foreign currency exposure), the costs of hedging guidance may be applied to the excluded portion rather than fair value changes in the excluded portion being recognised immediately profit or loss (see 7.5 below).

It is clear under IFRS 9 that foreign currency basis spread cannot be assumed to exist in a non-derivative hedged item (including a foreign currency net investment), hence this will be an additional source of ineffectiveness, unless foreign currency basis spread is excluded from the hedging instrument. *[IFRS 9.B6.5.5]*.

7.3.3.B Cross currency interest rate swaps hedging a net investment

Like forward contracts, cross currency interest rate swap instruments are commonly used as hedging instruments in net investment hedges. As noted above, it is often said that cross currency swaps are essentially a series of forward contracts. However, what the appropriate hypothetical derivative would be for measuring ineffectiveness when hedging with a cross currency interest rate swap depends very much on the type of cross currency interest rate swaps.

At a conceptual level, it is easy to see that the changes in value of a cross currency swap with two floating-rate legs are likely to offset the spot retranslation gains and losses of a net investment, provided the floating rate resets sufficiently frequently. Hence such a designation will most probably meet the requirement to demonstrate that an economic relationship exists, although some residual ineffectiveness is likely to occur from the floating rate legs of the cross currency swap and foreign currency basis spread (if not excluded from the hedge relationship (see 7.4.8 below)).

It is also reasonably easy to see that a swap with one floating-rate leg and one fixed-rate leg could result in levels of ineffectiveness that contradict the existence of an economic relationship between the hedged item and hedging instrument, which would preclude hedge accounting (see 6.4.1 above). This is because the fair value of a swap with one floating-rate leg and one fixed-rate leg will change due to factors unrelated to changes in forward exchange rates.

It is less easy to see how hedge accounting will be applied using a swap with two fixed-rate legs as a hedge of the retranslation gains and losses in a net investment (since again the fixed-rate legs will give rise to changes in the swap's value that are unrelated to changes in forward exchange rates). As noted above, such an instrument is often viewed as a combination of a series of forward contracts, (i.e. each interest and principal fixed foreign currency cash flow and associated fixed functional currency cash flow is a forward contract, albeit based on a blended forward rate across the life of the instrument). Applying this perspective, combined with the guidance that net investment hedges should be accounted for similarly as cash flow hedges, *[IFRS 9.6.5.13]*, we believe it is possible to designate a fixed-for-fixed currency swap in a net investment hedge, whereby the amount of the hedged item would be equal to the sum of the undiscounted foreign currency interest and principal payments, (i.e. an amount higher than just the notional amount of the swap).

Example 53.67: Hedge of a foreign currency net investment using a cross-currency swap

Entity P, functional currency euro, has a £120m foreign currency net investment in Subsidiary S. S's functional is GBP. In order to hedge a proportion of the foreign currency EUR/GBP translation risk associated with P's net investment in S, P has transacted a 2 year fixed-for-fixed cross-currency swap as follows: a foreign currency leg with a notional amount of £100 million, paying 3% annually, and a functional currency leg with €110m notional receiving 2.5% annually.

P chooses to designate the forward foreign currency risk in £106 million of the net investment (i.e. a proportion of the net investment is hedged by each foreign currency cash flow arising from the cross currency swap, in this case the £100 million plus the two payments of interest of £3 million). The foreign currency risk for such a designated hedged item could be represented by a fixed-for-fixed cross-currency swap (this would be for both the hypothetical derivative used to measure the effective portion and the aligned hedging derivative if the costs of hedging guidance is applied) (see 7.4.4. and 7.5.2 below).

If a fixed-for-fixed cross-currency swap with a foreign currency notional amount of £100m is designated as a hedge of the forward foreign currency risk in a net investment of only £100m, it is harder to argue that the hedged risk could be represented by fixed-for-fixed cross-currency swap also with a foreign currency notional amount of £100m. Given that there are no periodic settlements in the hedged item, it might be argued that the forward foreign currency risk in the hedged item would be better represented by a simple forward contract with notional amount of £100m, for both measurement of ineffectiveness and application of the costs of hedging guidance.

It would of course be possible to designate only the spot element of a cross-currency swap as a hedging instrument in a hedge of a net investment (see 3.6.5 above). In Example 53:67 above, the cross-currency swap with a foreign currency notional amount of £100m could be designated as hedging the spot foreign currency risk in £100m of a net investment. Changes in the undesignated component of the cross-currency swap would remain in profit or loss, to the extent that costs of hedging guidance was not applied (see 7.5 below).

When hedging forward foreign currency risk in a foreign currency net investment using cross currency swaps, some ineffectiveness is likely to arise unless the foreign currency basis spread is excluded from the relationship and the costs of hedging guidance is applied (see 7.4.8 below). *[IFRS 9.B6.5.5]*.

7.3.3.C Purchased options hedging a net investment

It is possible to designate the intrinsic value of a purchased option as the hedging instrument (i.e. its time value is excluded from the hedge relationship) (see 3.6.4 above). Such a designation would require the costs of hedging treatment to be applied. The costs of hedging accounting would require changes in fair value of the excluded time value to be initially recorded in other comprehensive income (see 7.5.1 below).

As discussed at 3.6.4 above, designating the entire purchased option as the hedging instrument is likely to result in high levels of ineffectiveness and could challenge the existence of an economic relationship (see 6.4.1 above). This is because no offset will arise for changes in the time value of the purchased option, as the time value is not a component of the hedged net investment. *[IFRS 9.B6.3.12]*.

7.3.4 Combinations of derivative and non-derivative instruments hedging a net investment

It is not uncommon for entities to hedge their net investments using synthetic foreign currency debt instruments. For example, consider a parent with the euro as its functional currency that has a net investment in a Japanese subsidiary with yen as its functional currency. The parent might borrow in US dollars and enter into a pay-Japanese yen, receive-US dollar cross currency interest rate swap. In this way the two instruments might be considered a synthetic Japanese yen borrowing, although they are required to be accounted for separately (see Chapter 46 at 8).

As noted at 3.5 above, a combination of derivatives and non-derivatives may be viewed in combination and jointly designated as a hedging instrument. *[IFRS 9.6.2.5]*. However, all the hedging instruments must be clearly identified in the hedge documentation (see 6.3 above). *[IFRS 9.6.4.1(b)]*.

The European parent in the above fact pattern may wish to designate the spot rate only when hedging a net investment with a combination of derivatives and non-derivatives. Designation of the combination as hedging a forward rate is more problematic as the foreign currency risk component of a non-derivative financial instrument is restricted to the spot rate, in accordance with IAS 21 (see 3.3.1 above). *[IFRS 9.B6.2.3]*.

Another alternative may be to notionally decompose the cross currency swap by introducing an interest bearing functional currency denominated leg and designating one part as a hedge of the borrowing and the other as a hedge of the net investment (see 3.6.2 above).

7.3.5 Individual or separate financial statements

The discussion so far has concentrated on the accounting for a hedge of the foreign currency risk in a foreign operation in the parent's consolidated financial statements. However, all references to consolidated financial statements in the guidance on accounting for net investment hedges apply equally to standalone financial statements in which the net assets of a foreign operation are included. This will include financial statements in which investments in a foreign operation that is a joint venture, an associate or a branch are accounted for using the equity method. *[IFRIC 16.2, 7]*. Although not explicitly stated in IFRIC 16, it would also include standalone financial statements in which investments in subsidiaries are accounted for the using the equity method. *[IFRS 9.6.5.2(c), IAS 21.44].*

Where net investment hedges have been designated in a parent's consolidated financial statements there is also the question of whether hedge accounting can be applied in that parent's individual or separate financial statements if the equity method is not applied. This question is only likely to arise where an eligible hedging instrument exists within the parent entity (e.g. the parent entity has foreign currency external borrowings which are designated as the hedging instrument in a net investment hedge in the consolidated financial statements).

In a parent's individual or separate financial statements there is an accounting policy choice as to how the investment in the foreign operation is accounted for:

- as an asset measured at cost;
- as a financial asset in accordance with IFRS 9; or
- using the equity method as described in IAS 28 – *Investments in Associates and Joint Ventures* (see Chapter 11 at 7). *[IAS 27.10].*

In the reporting entity's individual or separate financial statements, if the accounting policy choice is to measure the investment either at cost or in accordance with IFRS 9, it is not accounted for as a net investment in a foreign operation and hence net investment hedge accounting is precluded. *[IFRS 9.6.5.2(c), IAS 21.8].* This means a borrowing designated as the hedging instrument in a net investment hedge in the consolidated financial statements, could not be similarly designated in a net investment hedge for the purposes of the separate financial statements.

However, if hedge accounting is desirable, it may be possible to designate the borrowing as the hedging instrument in another type of hedge. Typically, this would be a fair value hedge of the foreign currency risk arising from the investment (see 5.1 above). This will be an independent hedge relationship, separate from the net investment hedge in the consolidated financial statements. Therefore, all of the other hedge accounting criteria (including the documentation requirements) will need to be met for this hedge too. Of course, the effects of this hedge accounting will need to be reversed when preparing the group's consolidated financial statements (otherwise those financial statements will reflect as an asset or liability certain changes in the fair value of a parent's investment in its subsidiary which would be contrary to the general principles of IFRS 10 – see Chapter 7).

7.4 Measuring ineffectiveness

7.4.1 General requirements

Hedge ineffectiveness is the extent to which the changes in the fair value or cash flows of the hedging instrument are greater or less than those on the hedged item. *[IFRS 9.B6.4.1].*

All hedge ineffectiveness is recognised in the profit or loss for fair value hedges (except where the hedged item is an equity instrument measured at fair value through OCI) (see 7.1.1 above). For cash flow and net investment hedges ineffectiveness is recognised in the profit or loss to the extent that the cumulative change in the fair value or cash flows of the hedging instrument are greater than those on the hedged item (see 7.2.1 and 7.3 above). Accordingly, the measurement of ineffectiveness is an important aspect of IFRS 9.

Although, for many hedge relationships, it will be acceptable to undertake a qualitative assessment as to whether the hedge effectiveness requirements are met (see 6.4 above) there is still a requirement to measure and record ineffectiveness appropriately within the financial statements.

In determining the ineffectiveness of a hedge relationship, it is important to closely follow the hedge designation. In particular it is necessary to determine the hedged risk, and whether any portions or proportions have been excluded from hedged item (see 2.2 and 2.3 above) and/or the hedging instrument (see 3.6 above). Hedge ineffectiveness only relates to those elements not excluded from the hedge relationship, and for the hedged item only, with respect to changes in the hedged risk, not the full price risk. *[IFRS 9.B6.3.11, B6.4.1]*. The initial designation of a hedge relationship is therefore very important and can in some cases significantly reduce the expected ineffectiveness levels from hedge relationships. However, it should be noted that not all sources of ineffectiveness can be eliminated via clever hedge designation. All sources of ineffectiveness must be documented as part of the hedged documentation. *[IFRS 9.6.4.1(b)]*.

The calculation of ineffectiveness compares the monetary amount of the change in fair value of the hedging instrument with the monetary amount of the change in fair value or cash flows of the hedged item or transactions attributable to the hedged risk, over the assessment period. This is illustrated by the following simplified example:

Example 53.68: Calculation of ineffectiveness

An entity issues fixed rate debt at par of £100, with annual fixed interest of 3%. On the same day, the entity designates an existing interest rate swap in a hedge relationship with the issued debt, for changes in SONIA. The existing swap has a notional of £100, a receive leg of 2.5% annually and a floating leg paying a compounded SONIA rate every 6 months. At the first reporting period after designation, (but prior to settlement of any coupons on the debt or interest rate swap) the effectiveness would be calculated as follows:

	Hedged item (issued debt)	Hedging instrument (existing swap)
Fair value on initial designation	£100 CR	£4.5 CR
Fair value on first reporting date	£107 CR	£2.4 DR
Change in fair value of the hedging instrument over the assessment period		£6.9 gain
Change in fair value of the hedged item attributable to the hedged risk over the assessment period	£7 loss	

Hedge ineffectiveness is calculated by comparing the £6.9 gain on the hedging instrument with £7 loss on the hedged item over the assessment period.

Whilst it may be relatively obvious how to calculate the change in fair value or cash flows of a hedged item with fixed flows for changes in the hedged risk since designation (typically a fair value hedge) (see 5.1 above), it is less obvious how this might be achieved where the hedged flows are not fixed, in particular, as hedged items with variable flows do not tend to attract fair value risk. This is discussed in more detail at 7.4.4 and 7.4.6 below.

7.4.2 The time value of money

Entities must consider the time value of money when measuring hedge ineffectiveness. This means that an entity must determine the value of the hedged item on a present value basis (thereby including the effect of the time value of money). *[IFRS 9.B6.5.4]*. The inclusion of the words 'the changes in the fair value or cash flows' in the definition of ineffectiveness is unhelpful (see 7.4.1 above), but the need for consideration of the time value of money is clear based on the noted application guidance of IFRS 9. In valuation practice, the effect of the time value of money is also included when measuring the fair value of financial instruments. Consequently, it is logical to apply the same principle to the hedged item as well.

It is possible to designate a spot element of a hedged item if it can be determined to be an eligible risk component (see 2.2 above). Whilst a spot designation is relatively common place for both foreign currency and commodity risk, the need to consider the time value of money for effectiveness purposes for spot designations has been a matter of some debate. The IAS 39 Implementation Guidance contains an example in which an entity designates changes in the spot element only (see 7.4.7 below). The example indicates that the time value of money is still relevant for the measurement of ineffectiveness even when the spot element is designated in a hedge relationship. See Example 53.73 below for the detailed example in the IAS 39 Implementation Guidance, but Example 53.69 immediately below more simply demonstrates how ineffectiveness can arise when there are differences in the timing of hedged and hedging cash flows.

Example 53.69: Impact of time value of money when measuring ineffectiveness

A manufacturing company in India, having the Indian Rupee as its functional currency, is expecting forecast sales in USD. The company assesses sales of USD 1m per month for the next twelve months to be highly probable and wishes to hedge the related foreign currency exposure. The company also holds a borrowing of USD 20m with a bullet repayment in fourteen months' time. Instead of entering into foreign currency forward contracts, the company designates the US dollar borrowing as a hedging instrument in hedges of the spot risk of the monthly highly probable US dollar sales.

When measuring hedge ineffectiveness, the revaluation of the forecast sales for foreign currency spot risk would have to be made on a discounted basis (i.e. a present value calculation reflecting the time between the reporting date and the individual future cash flow dates), whereas the revaluation of the hedging instrument would not (as this follows the requirements of IAS 21) (see 3.3.1 above).

Similarly, if instead of using a US dollar borrowing as the hedging instrument, the entity transacted a forward foreign currency contract to sell USD 12m for Indian Rupee in 12 months' time, ineffectiveness will arise due to the differences in the timing of hedged and hedging cash flows. For the hedged cash flows, the revaluation for foreign currency spot risk would have to be a present value calculation reflecting the time between the reporting date and the individual future cash flow dates. In the same way, to measure hedge effectiveness, the present value of the spot foreign currency revaluation of the hedging instrument would reflect the time value to the ultimate maturity of the forward contract, which is not the same as the timing of the hedged individual monthly forecast cash flows. The treatment of the excluded forward element of the forward contract is discussed further at 7.5.2 below.

The requirement to calculate ineffectiveness on a present value basis intuitively makes sense in cases where the cash flows of the hedged item and hedging instrument are not aligned. It would seem inappropriate to have no ineffectiveness under a spot designation, for example in the situation described at 3.3.1 above, where a 7-year financial liability denominated in a foreign currency is used as the hedging instrument for a 12 month forecast sale in that foreign currency.

7.4.3 Hedging using instruments with a non-zero fair value

There is no requirement for hedge accounting to be designated on initial recognition of either the hedged item or the hedging instrument. *[IFRS 9.B6.5.28]*. However, there is often a hidden danger when designating a derivative as a hedging instrument subsequent to its inception. For non-option derivatives, such as forwards or interest rate swaps, any fair value is likely to create 'noise' in measuring hedge ineffectiveness that may not be fully offset by changes in the hedged item, especially in the case of a cash flow hedge. This is because the derivative contains a 'financing' element (the initial fair value), gains and losses on which will not be replicated in the hedged item and therefore the hedge contains an inherent source of ineffectiveness. For example, if applying the hypothetical derivative method for measurement of ineffectiveness (see 7.4.4 below) this financing element will be evident as the hypothetical derivative will be based on the prevailing market rates on designation, which will result in cash flows that differ from those of the actual now 'off market' derivative.

Consequently, there is likely to be more ineffectiveness recognised and, in extremis, a quantitative assessment may be needed to demonstrate the existence of an economic relationship (see 6.4.1 above). It depends on the circumstances whether hedge ineffectiveness arising from the financing element on designation could have a magnitude that a qualitative assessment would not adequately capture. *[IFRS 9.B6.4.15]*. Only by coincidence will a derivative that was entered into previously still have a fair value that is zero, or close to zero, on the date of designation which would minimise this problem.

This situation can not only arise when a derivative is designated or redesignated in a hedging relationship subsequent to its initial recognition, but also in a business combination (see 6.3.1 above).

This same issue does not arise for hedged items that are designated after initial recognition, however difficulties can occur identifying eligible risk components (see 2.4.1 above).

7.4.4 Hypothetical derivatives

A method commonly used in practice to calculate ineffectiveness of cash flow hedges (and net investment hedges) is the use of a so-called 'hypothetical derivative'. The method involves establishing a notional derivative that has terms that match the critical terms of the hedged exposure (normally an interest rate swap or forward contract with no unusual terms) and a zero fair value at inception of the hedging relationship. The fair value of the hypothetical derivative is then used as a proxy to measure the change in the value of the hedged item against which changes in value of the actual hedging instrument are compared to calculate ineffectiveness. The use of a hypothetical derivative is one possible way of determining the change in the value of the hedged item when measuring ineffectiveness. *[IFRS 9.B6.5.5]*.

IFRS 9 is clear that a hypothetical derivative has to be a replication of the hedged item and not the 'perfect hedge'. Also the standard makes clear that any different method for determining the change in the value of the hedged item would have to give the same outcome. Consequently, an entity cannot include features in the hypothetical derivative that only exist in the hedging instrument, but not in the hedged item. *[IFRS 9.B6.5.5]*. Whilst this appears to be a logical requirement, it may have wider implications for cash flow hedges than many would have expected. An entity cannot simply assume no ineffectiveness for a cash flow hedge because the principal terms of the hedging instrument exactly match the principal terms of a hedged item, if there are differences in other features of the hedging instrument and the hedged item. For example, IFRS 13 requires an entity to reflect both the counterparty's credit risk and the entity's own credit risk when determining the fair value of a derivative. The same credit risk cannot be assumed in the hypothetical derivative. This difference in credit risk would result in some ineffectiveness (see 7.4.5 and 7.4.9 below).

It is possible to exclude the credit risk in the hedged item from the hedge relationship, for example by designating interest rate risk as the hedged risk (see 2.2 above). This does not eliminate ineffectiveness from changes in the credit risk of the hedging derivative, but prevents additional ineffectiveness from changes in the credit risk of the hedged item. (This assumes that credit risk is not of a magnitude such that it dominates the value changes of the hedged item (see 6.4.2 above)).

Examples 53.69 and 53.70 below provide simple illustrations of how an entity might establish and apply a hypothetical derivative for the calculation of ineffectiveness in a hedge relationship.

Example 53.70: Determination of a hypothetical derivative in a cash flow hedge of interest rate risk

Company X has purchased £200m of variable rate 5-year debt securities. The debt securities yield 1-month LIBOR plus 100 basis points. Company X wishes to mitigate cash flow variability from the debt securities by transacting a 5-year interest rate swap with £200m notional, receiving a fixed coupon of 2% quarterly and paying a 3-month LIBOR rate. The swap and the debt securities were acquired on the same day at prevailing market rates and designated in a cash flow hedge relationship for changes in LIBOR, i.e. excluding credit risk from the debt securities.

The hypothetical derivative representing the hedged risk in the issued debt might be determined as follows:

A 5-year interest rate swap with £200m notional, receiving 1-month LIBOR, and paying a 2.25% fixed coupon monthly. The fixed coupon of 2.25% is calculated such that the hypothetical derivative has a zero fair value on the date of designation. (See 7.4.5 below for a discussion on the selection of an appropriate discounting curve for calculation of fair value changes in the hypothetical derivative.)

The fact that the actual hedging derivative is referenced to LIBOR and cash flows occurs quarterly has no impact on the determination of the hypothetical derivative. The hypothetical derivative can only be based on features that arise in the hedged item, which attracts a monthly coupon. The difference between the hypothetical derivative and the hedging derivative is likely to lead to ineffectiveness (see 7.4.1 above).

Example 53.71: Impact on ineffectiveness of changes in credit risk in the hedged item when the hedged risk is a benchmark component

Entity A has issued floating rate debt, paying a benchmark floating rate plus a credit spread of 1%. Entity A also transacts a pay fixed, receive benchmark interest rate swap in order to eliminate variability in cash flows from changes in the benchmark rate. The entity designates this swap as a hedge of the benchmark component of the issued debt and excludes credit risk on the debt from the hedge relationship. Accordingly, if subsequently Entity A's credit rating changes such that the current credit spread is now 0.95%, this will have no impact on the change in value of the hedged item for the purposes of measuring ineffectiveness, as credit risk in the hedged item has been excluded from the hedge relationship. Conversely, if there is a change in the credit risk with respect to the interest rate swap (either that of the counterparty or the entity itself), resulting in a change in the fair value of the interest rate swap, this would affect the measurement of hedge ineffectiveness. The credit risk associated with the interest rate swap includes both counterparty and own credit risk (see 7.4.9 below).

When considering the credit risk of the hedged item, any changes must not be of a magnitude that it dominates the value changes in the hedged item (see 6.4.2.B above). That is unlikely to be the case for a change in credit spread from 1% to 0.95%.

One other example of when the features of the hedging instrument and the hedging item are likely to differ is when an entity hedges a debt instrument denominated in a foreign currency in a cash flow hedge (irrespective of whether it is fixed-rate or variable-rate debt). IFRS 9 is explicit that when using a hypothetical derivative to calculate ineffectiveness, the hypothetical derivative cannot simply impute a charge for exchanging different currencies (i.e. the foreign currency basis spread) even though actual derivatives (for example, cross currency interest rate swaps) under which different currencies are exchanged might include such a charge. *[IFRS 9.B6.5.5]*. Although cross currency interest rate swaps are used to highlight the fact that foreign currency basis spreads should not be replicated in hypothetical derivatives, this issue is also likely to arise in other foreign currency contacts settled in the future. To address this, IFRS 9 includes the ability to account for the foreign currency basis spread as a cost of hedging (see 7.5 below).

In many cases where the critical terms of the hedged item are closely matched by a hedging instrument which had a zero fair value on designation, the hypothetical derivative is likely to have similar terms to the actual hedging derivative – subject to the known differences mentioned above (e.g. foreign currency basis spreads and credit risk).

Example 53.72 (see 7.4.6 below) contains a very comprehensive illustration of the calculation of infectiveness based on Implementation Guidance in IAS 39, which remains relevant under IFRS 9.

7.4.5 Discount rates for calculating the change in value of the hedged item

The standard is clear that entities must consider the time value of money when measuring hedge ineffectiveness. This means that an entity must determine the value of the hedged item on a present value basis (thereby including the effect of the time value of money) (see 7.4.2 above). *[IFRS 9.B6.5.4]*. Although capturing the effect of the time value of money is a key aspect of the application of hedge accounting, little guidance is provided on how to calculate the time value in the hedged item. By contrast, guidance is given on how to calculate the fair value changes for hedging instruments in various places: in IFRS 13 for those held at fair value through profit or loss (see Chapter 14), and in IAS 21 for non-derivative hedging instruments of foreign currency risk (see 3.3.1 above).

For example, a key consideration for market participants in calculating the fair value of derivatives is the selection of an appropriate discount rate. Historically, the fair values of interest rate swaps (IRS) have been calculated using LIBOR-based discount rates. As per its definition, LIBOR is the average rate at which the reference banks can fund unsecured cash in the interbank market for a given currency and maturity.[21] However, the use of LIBOR as the standard discount rate ignores the fact that many derivative transactions are now collateralised and have therefore a lower credit risk than LIBOR would suggest. For cash-collateralised trades, a more relevant discount rate is an overnight rate rather than LIBOR. Overnight index swaps (OIS) are interest rate swaps where the floating leg is linked to a benchmark interest rate for overnight unsecured lending. OIS rates much better reflect the credit risk of cash collateralised IRS. So although an IRS might be referenced to one benchmark rate (e.g. LIBOR) the appropriate discount rates for calculating fair value in line with IFRS 13 guidance, may be derived from a different benchmark rate (e.g. OIS) if that is how market participants would calculate the fair value.

The way in which the time value of a hedged item is captured can have a significant impact on the measurement of ineffectiveness. This is illustrated in the following two examples.

Consider firstly the example of a fair value hedge of a fixed rate bond for changes in an eligible benchmark interest rate risk component (see 2.2.3.A above). It is clear that in order to capture the change in value of the hedged fixed cash flows attributable to changes in the benchmark interest rate, the discounting curve would have to be based on the designated benchmark interest rate. For a fair value hedge of a specified interest rate, to choose any other discounting curve would reflect a risk other than the designated hedged risk. For such hedges, in order to reflect the hedged risk, that choice of hedged risk predetermines the discounting rate to be applied to the hedged item. Hence for a fair value hedge, unless the benchmark rate designated as the hedged risk is the same as the discounting curve applied to the hedging instrument, ineffectiveness will arise. This is the case even if the hedged fixed cash flows match exactly the fixed cash flows of the hedging instrument.

Now contrast this with the example of a benchmark interest rate (e.g. LIBOR) floating rate debt, swapped into a fixed rate of interest using a receive-benchmark, pay-fixed interest rate swap, designated in a cash flow hedge for changes in the benchmark interest rate. For the purposes of calculating the change in the value of the hedged item due to the hedged risk, the entity may use a hypothetical derivative (see 7.4.4 above). When measuring the fair value of the actual and hypothetical interest rate swaps, the entity would start by using the specified benchmark forward curve to forecast the future floating cash flows. However potentially the discount rate applied to those future cash flows may not be the same as that used for forecasting. In the case of a collateralised swap (for which the relevant discount rate is likely to be an overnight rate (e.g. OIS), unless the value of the hypothetical derivative is also calculated using an OIS discounting curve, even though the future cash flows might be the same, changes in value of the hypothetical derivative and the fair value of the actual swap will not be same – resulting in ineffectiveness.

For those hedge relationships where the discounting curve is not predetermined by the hedged risk (e.g. a cash flow hedge of a benchmark interest rate) the standard is not prescriptive, and practice has evolved such that there appears to be an element of choice as to which benchmark interest rate is used as the basis for discounting in the calculation of changes in value of the hedged item. We believe this choice is limited to a benchmark interest rate. For example, it is not permissible to use a discount rate that exactly mirrors the ongoing specific credit risk inherent in the hedging instrument, as this would reflect a feature in the hedging instrument that is unlikely to exist in the hedged item (see 7.4.4 above). *[IFRS 9.B6.5.5].* Put differently, although it may be possible to choose the discounting benchmark rate for the hedged item to be that which is used for discounting purposes for the actual derivative, no such choice exists to reflect elements of the valuation of the actual derivative such as the credit valuation adjustment (CVA) in determining value changes in the hedged item (see Chapter 14 at 11.3.2). Hence changes in the specific credit risk inherent in the hedging instrument will still result in ineffectiveness. However, if the hedging derivative is collateralised, the use of an OIS curve for discounting the hedged item may result in very little ineffectiveness.

Similarly, the ability to choose a benchmark rate curve for discounting purposes when calculating a change in value of the hedged item, does not permit the inclusion of cross currency spreads within such a curve – unless for a hedge of foreign currency risk and the cross currency basis occurs in the hedged item (see 7.4.4 above).

Any choice of discounting benchmark rate should be documented at the inception of the hedge relationship (see 6.3 above).

As a result of the reforms mandated by the Financial Stability Board following the financial crisis, regulators are pushing for IBOR (including LIBOR) to be replaced by new 'official' benchmark rates, known as Risk Free Rates (RFRs). Such a change will necessarily affect both forecasting and discounting curves for financial instruments, and may reduce the instances of where there is a difference between discounting curves for the valuation of hedging derivatives and hedged items. However, this change in benchmark rates raises a number of accounting issues, including some related to hedge accounting. The IASB has published two amendments to IFRS 9 and other standards to address these issues: in September 2019, *Interest Rate Benchmark Reform, Amendments to IFRS 9, IAS 39 and IFRS 7*, and in August 2020 *Interest Rate Benchmark Reform Phase 2, Amendments to IFRS 9, IAS 39, IFRS 7, IFRS 4 and IFRS 16* (see 9 below).

7.4.6 Detailed example of calculation of measuring ineffectiveness for a cash flow hedge of a forecast transaction in a debt instrument

Example 53.72 below contains a very comprehensive illustration of the calculation of ineffectiveness for a cash flow hedge that is based on the Implementation Guidance to IAS 39. Method B describes, without explicitly naming it, as the hypothetical derivative method. Method A in the example is also an acceptable of calculating ineffectiveness for a cash flow hedge, but is not widely applied.

Although the example is somewhat esoteric, and many accountants will find the calculations difficult to follow, it is an important example that remains relevant under IFRS 9.

Example 53.72: Measuring effectiveness for a hedge of a forecast transaction in a debt instrument

A forecast investment in an interest-earning asset or forecast issue of an interest-bearing liability creates a cash flow exposure to interest rate changes because the related interest payments will be based on the market rate that exists when the forecast transaction occurs. The objective of a cash flow hedge of the exposure to interest rate changes is to offset the effects of future changes in interest rates so as to obtain a single fixed rate, usually the rate that existed at the inception of the hedge that corresponds with the term and timing of the forecast transaction. However, during the period of the hedge, it is not possible to determine what the market interest rate for the forecast transaction will be at the time the hedge is terminated or when the forecast transaction occurs.

During this period, effectiveness can be measured on the basis of changes in interest rates between the designation date and the interim effectiveness measurement date. The interest rates used to make this measurement are the interest rates that correspond with the term and occurrence of the forecast transaction that existed at the inception of the hedge and that exist at the measurement date as evidenced by the term structure of interest rates.

Generally it will not be sufficient simply to compare cash flows of the hedged item with cash flows generated by the derivative hedging instrument as they are paid or received, since such an approach ignores the entity's expectations of whether the cash flows will offset in subsequent periods and whether there will be any resulting ineffectiveness.

It is assumed that Company X expects to issue a €100,000 one-year debt instrument in three months. The instrument will pay interest quarterly with principal due at maturity. X is exposed to interest rate increases and establishes a hedge of the interest cash flows of the debt by entering into a forward starting interest rate swap. The swap has a term of one year and will start in three months to correspond with the terms of the forecast debt issue. X will pay a fixed rate and receive a variable rate, and it designates the risk being hedged as the LIBOR-based interest component in the forecast issue of the debt.

Yield curve

The yield curve provides the foundation for computing future cash flows and the fair value of such cash flows both at the inception of, and during, the hedging relationship. It is based on current market yields on applicable reference bonds that are traded in the marketplace. Market yields are converted to spot interest rates ('spot rates' or 'zero coupon rates') by eliminating the effect of coupon payments on the market yield. Spot rates are used to discount future cash flows, such as principal and interest rate payments, to arrive at their fair value. Spot rates also are used to compute forward interest rates that are used to compute the estimated variable future cash flows. The relationship between spot rates and one-period forward rates is shown by the following formula:

Spot-forward relationship

$$F = \frac{(1 + SR_t)^t}{(1 + ST_{t-1})^{t-1}} - 1$$

where   F = forward rate (%)

SR = spot rate (%)

t = period in time (e.g. 1, 2, 3, 4, 5)

It is assumed that the following quarterly-period term structure of interest rates using quarterly compounding exists at the inception of the hedge.

Yield curve at inception (beginning of period 1)

Forward periods	1	2	3	4	5
Spot rates	3.75%	4.50%	5.50%	6.00%	6.25%
Forward rates	3.75%	5.25%	7.51%	7.50%	7.25%

The one-period forward rates are computed on the basis of spot rates for the applicable maturities. For example, the current forward rate for Period 2 calculated using the formula above is equal to [1.0450² ÷ 1.0375] – 1 = 5.25%. The current one-period forward rate for Period 2 is different from the current spot rate for Period 2, since the spot rate is an interest rate from the beginning of Period 1 (spot) to the end of Period 2, while the forward rate is an interest rate from the beginning of Period 2 to the end of Period 2.

Hedged item

In this example, X expects to issue a €100,000 one-year debt instrument in three months with quarterly interest payments. X is exposed to interest rate increases and would like to eliminate the effect on cash flows of interest rate changes that may happen before the forecast transaction takes place. If that risk is eliminated, X would obtain an interest rate on its debt issue that is equal to the one-year forward coupon rate currently available in the marketplace in three months. That forward coupon rate, which is different from the forward (spot) rate, is 6.86%, computed from the term structure of interest rates shown above. It is the market rate of interest that exists at the inception of the hedge, given the terms of the forecast debt instrument. It results in the fair value of the debt being equal to par at its issue.

At the inception of the hedging relationship, the expected cash flows of the debt instrument can be calculated on the basis of the existing term structure of interest rates. For this purpose, it is assumed that interest rates do not change and that the debt would be issued at 6.86% at the beginning of Period 2. In this case, the cash flows and fair value of the debt instrument would be as follows at the beginning of Period 2.

Issue of fixed rate debt (beginning of period 2) – no rate changes (spot based on forward rates)

	Total	1	2	3	4	5
Original forward periods						
Remaining periods			1	2	3	4
Spot rates			5.25%	6.38%	6.75%	6.88%
Forward rates			5.25%	7.51%	7.50%	7.25%
	€		€	€	€	€
Cash flows:						
Fixed interest at 6.86%			1,716	1,716	1,716	1,716
Principal						100,000
Fair value:						
Interest*	6,592		1,694	1,663	1,632	1,603
Principal*	93,408					93,408
	100,000					

* cash flow discounted at the spot rate for the relevant period, e.g. fair value of principal is calculated as €100,000 ÷ (1 + [0.0688 ÷ 4])^4 = €93,408

Since it is assumed that interest rates do not change, the fair value of the interest and principal amounts equals the par amount of the forecast transaction. The fair value amounts are computed on the basis of the spot rates that exist at the inception of the hedge for the applicable periods in which the cash flows would occur had the debt been issued at the date of the forecast transaction. They reflect the effect of discounting those cash flows on the basis of the periods that will remain after the debt instrument is issued. For example, the spot rate of 6.38% is used to discount the interest cash flow that is expected to be paid in Period 3, but it is discounted for only two periods because it will occur two periods after the forecast transaction.

The forward interest rates are the same as shown previously, since it is assumed that interest rates do not change. The spot rates are different but they have not actually changed. They represent the spot rates one period forward and are based on the applicable forward rates.

Hedging instrument

The objective of the hedge is to obtain an overall interest rate on the forecast transaction and the hedging instrument that is equal to 6.86%, which is the market rate at the inception of the hedge for the period from Period 2 to Period 5. This objective is accomplished by entering into a forward starting interest rate swap that has a fixed rate of 6.86%. Based on the term structure of interest rates that exist at the inception of the hedge, the interest rate swap will have such a rate. At the inception of the hedge, the fair value of the fixed rate payments on the interest rate swap will equal the fair value of the variable rate payments, resulting in the interest rate swap having a fair value of zero. The expected cash flows of the interest rate swap and the related fair value amounts are shown as follows:

Interest rate swap

	Total	1	2	3	4	5
Original forward periods						
Remaining periods			1	2	3	4
	€		€	€	€	€
Cash flows:						
Fixed interest at 6.86%			1,716	1,716	1,716	1,716
Forecast variable interest*			1,313	1,877	1,876	1,813
Forecast based on forward rate			5.25%	7.51%	7.50%	7.25%
Net interest			(403)	161	160	97

Fair value

Discount rate (spot)		5.25%	6.38%	6.75%	6.88%
Fixed interest	6,592	1,694	1,663	1,632	1,603
Forecast variable interest	6,592	1,296	1,819	1,784	1,693
Fair value of interest rate swap	0	(398)	156	152	90

* forecast variable rate cash flow based on forward rate, e.g. €1,313 = €100,000 × (0.0525 ÷ 4)

At the inception of the hedge, the fixed rate on the forward swap is equal to the fixed rate X would receive if it could issue the debt in three months under terms that exist today.

Measuring hedge effectiveness

If interest rates change during the period the hedge is outstanding, the effectiveness of the hedge can be measured in various ways.

Assume that interest rates change as follows immediately before the debt is issued at the beginning of Period 2 (this effectively uses the yield curve existing at Period 1 with a 200 basis point (2%) shift).

Yield curve assumption

Forward periods	1	2	3	4	5
Remaining periods		1	2	3	4
Spot rates		5.75%	6.50%	7.50%	8.00%
Forward rates		5.75%	7.25%	9.51%	9.50%

Under the new interest rate environment, the fair value of the pay-fixed at 6.86%, receive-variable interest rate swap that was designated as the hedging instrument would be as follows.

Fair value of interest rate swap

	Total					
Original forward periods		1	2	3	4	5
Remaining periods			1	2	3	4
	€		€	€	€	€
Cash flows:						
Fixed interest at 6.86%			1,716	1,716	1,716	1,716
Forecast variable interest			1,438	1,813	2,377	2,376
Forecast based on new forward rate			5.75%	7.25%	9.51%	9.50%
Net interest			(279)	97	661	660

	Total					
Original forward periods		1	2	3	4	5
Remaining periods			1	2	3	4
	€		€	€	€	€
Fair value						
New discount rate (spot)			5.75%	6.50%	7.50%	8.00%
Fixed interest	6,562		1,692	1,662	1,623	1,585
Forecast variable interest	7,615		1,417	1,755	2,248	2,195
Fair value of interest rate swap	1,053		(275)	93	625	610

In order to compute the effectiveness of the hedge, it is necessary to measure the change in the present value of the cash flows or the value of the hedged forecast transaction. There are at least two methods of accomplishing this measurement.

Method A – Compute change in fair value of debt

	Total	1	2	3	4	5
Original forward periods		1	2	3	4	5
Remaining periods			1	2	3	4
	€		€	€	€	€
Cash flows:						
Fixed interest at 6.86%			1,716	1,716	1,716	1,716
Principal						100,000
Fair value:						
New discount rate (spot)			5.75%	6.50%	7.50%	8.00%
Interest	6,562		1,692	1,662	1,623	1,585
Principal	92,385					*92,385
Total	98,947					
Fair value at inception	100,000					
Difference	(1,053)					

* €100,000 ÷ (1 + [0.08 ÷ 4])^4

Under Method A, a computation is made of the fair value in the new interest rate environment of debt that carries interest that is equal to the coupon interest rate that existed at the inception of the hedging relationship (6.86%). This fair value is compared with the expected fair value as of the beginning of Period 2 that was calculated on the basis of the term structure of interest rates that existed at the inception of the hedging relationship, as illustrated above, to determine the change in the fair value. Note that the difference between the change in the fair value of the swap and the change in the expected fair value of the debt (€1,053) exactly offset in this example, since the terms of the swap and the forecast transaction match each other.

Method B – Compute change in fair value of cash flows

	Total	1	2	3	4	5
Original forward periods		1	2	3	4	5
Remaining periods			1	2	3	4
Market rate at inception			6.86%	6.86%	6.86%	6.86%
Current forward rate			5.75%	7.25%	9.51%	9.50%
Rate difference			1.11%	(0.39%)	(2.64%)	(2.64%)
Cash flow difference (principal × rate)			€279	(€97)	(€661)	(€660)
Discount rate (spot)			5.75%	6.50%	7.50%	8.00%
Fair value of difference	(€1,053)		€275	(€93)	(€625)	(€610)

Under Method B, the present value of the change in cash flows is computed on the basis of the difference between the forward interest rates for the applicable periods at the effectiveness measurement date and the interest rate that would have been obtained if the debt had been issued at the market rate that existed at the inception of the hedge. The market rate that existed at the inception of the hedge is the one-year forward coupon rate in three months. The present value of the change in cash flows is computed on the basis of the current spot rates that exist at the effectiveness measurement date for the applicable periods in which the cash flows are expected to occur. This method also could be referred to as the 'theoretical swap' method (or 'hypothetical derivative' method) because the comparison is between the hedged fixed rate on the debt and the current variable rate, which is the same as comparing cash flows on the fixed and variable rate legs of an interest rate swap.

As before, the difference between the change in the fair value of the swap and the change in the present value of the cash flows exactly offset in this example.

Other considerations

There is an additional computation that should be performed to compute ineffectiveness before the expected date of the forecast transaction that has not been considered for the purpose of this illustration. The fair value difference has been determined in each of the illustrations as of the expected date of the forecast transaction immediately before the forecast transaction, i.e. at the beginning of Period 2. If the assessment of hedge effectiveness is performed before the forecast transaction occurs, the difference should be discounted to the current date to arrive at the actual amount of ineffectiveness. For example, if the measurement date were one month after the hedging relationship was established and the forecast transaction is now expected to occur in two months, the amount would have to be discounted for the remaining two months before the forecast transaction is expected to occur to arrive at the actual fair value. This step would not be necessary in the examples provided above because there was no ineffectiveness. Therefore, additional discounting of the amounts, which net to zero, would not have changed the result.

Under Method B, ineffectiveness is computed on the basis of the difference between the forward coupon interest rates for the applicable periods at the effectiveness measurement date and the interest rate that would have been obtained if the debt had been issued at the market rate that existed at the inception of the hedge. Computing the change in cash flows based on the difference between the forward interest rates that existed at the inception of the hedge and the forward rates that exist at the effectiveness measurement date is inappropriate if the objective of the hedge is to establish a single fixed rate for a series of forecast interest payments. This objective is met by hedging the exposures with an interest rate swap as illustrated in the above example. The fixed interest rate on the swap is a blended interest rate composed of the forward rates over the life of the swap. Unless the yield curve is flat, the comparison between the forward interest rate exposures over the life of the swap and the fixed rate on the swap will produce different cash flows whose fair values are equal only at the inception of the hedging relationship. This difference is shown in the table below.

	Total	1	2	3	4	5
Original forward periods		1	2	3	4	5
Remaining periods			1	2	3	4
Forward rate at inception			5.25%	7.51%	7.50%	7.25%
Current forward rate			5.75%	7.25%	9.51%	9.50%
Rate difference			(0.50%)	0.26%	(2.00%)	(2.25%)
Cash flow difference (principal × rate)			(€125)	€64	(€501)	(€563)
Discount rate (spot)			*5.75%*	*6.50%*	*7.50%*	*8.00%*
Fair value of difference	€1,055		(€123)	€62	(€474)	(€520)
Fair value of interest rate swap	€1,053					
Ineffectiveness	(€2)					

If the objective of the hedge is to obtain the forward rates that existed at the inception of the hedge, the interest rate swap is ineffective because the swap has a single blended fixed coupon rate that does not offset a series of different forward interest rates. However, if the objective of the hedge is to obtain the forward coupon rate that existed at the inception of the hedge, the swap is effective, and the comparison based on differences in forward interest rates suggests ineffectiveness when none may exist. Computing ineffectiveness based on the difference between the forward interest rates that existed at the inception of the hedge and the forward rates that exist at the effectiveness measurement date would be an appropriate measurement of ineffectiveness if the hedging objective is to lock in those forward interest rates. In that case, the appropriate hedging instrument would be a series of forward contracts each of which matures on a repricing date that corresponds with the date of the forecast transactions.

It also should be noted that it would be inappropriate to compare only the variable cash flows on the interest rate swap with the interest cash flows in the debt that would be generated by the forward interest rates. That methodology has the effect of measuring ineffectiveness only on a portion of the derivative, and IAS 39 does not permit the bifurcation of a derivative for the purposes of assessing effectiveness in this situation[22] – see 3.6 above. It is recognised, however, that if the fixed interest rate on the interest rate swap is equal to the fixed rate that would have been obtained on the debt at inception, there will be no ineffectiveness assuming that there are no differences in terms and no change in credit risk or it is not designated in the hedging relationship. *[IAS 39.F.5.5]*.

7.4.7 Comparison of spot rate and forward rate methods

It was explained at 3.6.5 above that the spot and forward elements of a forward contract may be treated separately for the purposes of hedge designation. The next example, based on the Implementation Guidance of IAS 39, contrasts calculation of ineffectiveness for two hedge relationships using the same hedging instrument, but designated in different ways (see 7.4.1 above). Case 1 can be used when the whole of a forward contract is treated as the hedging instrument and the hedged risk is identified by reference to changes attributable to the forward rate (the forward rate method). Case 2 can be used when the forward element is excluded and the hedged risk is identified by reference to changes attributable to the spot rate (the spot rate method).

To demonstrate these methods, the IAS 39 Implementation Guidance uses a type of hedge that is very common in practice, the hedging of foreign currency risk associated with future purchases using a forward exchange contract. The example also illustrates the difference in the accounting for such hedges depending on whether the spot and forward elements of a forward contract are treated separately for the purposes of hedge designation.

Although the example is based on IAS 39 Implementation Guidance it is still relevant under IFRS 9 if we assume that the entity has chosen not to apply the costs of hedging guidance in Case 2. There is also an assumption that there is no impact from changes in foreign currency basis spreads.

Example 53.73: Cash flow hedge of firm commitment to purchase inventory in a foreign currency

Company A has the Local Currency (LC) as its functional and presentation currency. A chooses to treat hedges of the foreign currency risk of a firm commitment as cash flow hedges.

On 30 June 2021, A enters into a forward exchange contract to receive Foreign Currency (FC) 100,000 and deliver LC109,600 on 30 June 2022 at an initial cost and fair value of zero. On inception, it designates the forward exchange contract as a hedging instrument in a cash flow hedge of a firm commitment to purchase a certain quantity of paper for FC100,000 on 31 March 2022 and, thereafter, as a fair value hedge of the resulting payable of FC100,000, which is to be paid on 30 June 2022. It is assumed that all hedge accounting conditions in IFRS 9 are met.

The relevant foreign currency rates and associated fair values for the forward exchange contract are provided in the following table:

Date	Spot rate	Forward rate to 30 June 2022	Fair value of forward contract
30 June 2021	1.072	1.096	–
31 December 2021	1.080	1.092	(388)
31 March 2022	1.074	1.076	(1,971)
30 June 2022	1.072	–	(2,400)

The applicable yield curve in the local currency is flat at 6% per annum throughout the period. The fair value of the forward exchange contract is negative LC388 on 31 December 2021 ($\{[1.092 \times 100,000] - 109,600\} \div 1.06^{(6/12)}$), negative LC1,971 on 31 March 2022 ($\{[1.076 \times 100,000] - 109,600\} \div 1.06^{(3/12)}$), and negative LC2,400 on 30 June 2022 ($1.072 \times 100,000 - 109,600$).

Case 1: Changes in the fair value of the forward contract are designated in the hedge

Ignoring ineffectiveness that may arise from other elements that have an impact on the fair value of the hedging instrument, the hedge is expected to be fully effective because the critical terms of the forward exchange contract and the purchase contract are otherwise the same. The assessments of hedge effectiveness are based on the forward price.

The accounting entries are as follows.

30 June 2021

	LC	LC
Forward	–	
Cash		–

To record the forward exchange contract at its initial fair value, i.e. zero.

31 December 2021

	LC	LC
Other comprehensive income	388	
Forward – liability		388

To recognise the change in the fair value of the forward contract between 30 June 2021 and 31 December 2021, i.e. $388 - 0 = LC388$, in other comprehensive income. The hedge is fully effective because the loss on the forward exchange contract, LC388, exactly offsets the change in cash flows associated with the purchase contract based on the forward price $\{([1.092 \times 100,000] - 109,600) \div 1.06^{(6/12)}\} - \{([1.096 \times 100,000] - 109,600) \div 1.06\} = -LC388$. The negative figure denotes a reduction in the net present value of cash outflows and, therefore, effectively represents a 'gain' to offset the loss on the forward in other comprehensive income.

31 March 2022

	LC	LC
Other comprehensive income	1,583	
Forward – liability		1,583

To recognise the change in the fair value of the forward contract between 1 January 2022 and 31 March 2022, i.e. $1,971 - 388 = LC1,583$, in other comprehensive income. The hedge is fully effective because the loss on the forward exchange contract, LC1,583, exactly offsets the change in cash flows associated with the purchase contract based on the forward price $\{([1.076 \times 100,000] - 109,600) \div 1.06^{(3/12)}\} - \{([1.092 \times 100,000] - 109,600) \div 1.06^{(6/12)}\} = -LC1,583$. The negative figure denotes a reduction in the net present value of cash outflows and, therefore, effectively represents a 'gain' to offset the loss on the forward in other comprehensive income.

	LC	LC
Paper (purchase price)	107,400	
Paper (hedging loss)	1,971	
Other comprehensive income		1,971
Payable		107,400

To record the purchase of the paper at the spot rate ($1.074 \times 100,000$ = LC 107,400) and remove the cumulative loss on the forward recognised in other comprehensive income from equity, LC1,971, and include it in the initial measurement of the purchased paper. Accordingly, the initial measurement of the purchased paper is LC 109,371 consisting of a purchase consideration of LC 107,400 and a hedging loss of LC 1,971. The payable is recorded as a foreign currency monetary item of FC100,000, equivalent to LC107,400 ($100,000 \times 1.074$) on initial recognition.

30 June 2022

	LC	LC
Payable	107,400	
Cash		107,200
Profit or loss		200

To record the settlement of the payable at the spot rate (100,000 × 1.072 = LC107,200) and recognise the associated exchange gain of LC200 = 107,400 – 107,200 in profit or loss.

	LC	LC
Profit or loss	429	
Forward – liability		429

To recognise the loss on the forward exchange contract between 1 April 2022 and 30 June 2022, i.e. 2,400 – 1,971 = LC429) in profit or loss. The hedge is considered to be fully effective because the loss on the forward exchange contract, LC429, exactly offsets the change in the fair value of the payable based on the forward price $[1.072 \times 100{,}000] - 109{,}600 - \{([1.076 \times 100{,}000] - 109{,}600) \div 1.06^{(3/12)}\} = -LC429$. The negative figure denotes a reduction in the net present value of the payable and, therefore represents a gain to offset the loss on the forward contract.

	LC	LC
Forward – liability	2,400	
Cash		2,400

To record the net settlement of the forward exchange contract.

Although this arrangement has been set up to be a 'perfect hedge', the loss on the forward in the last three months is significantly different from the exchange gain recognised on retranslating the hedged payable. The principal reason for this is that the change in the fair value of the forward contract includes changes in its interest element, as well as its currency element, whereas the payable is translated at the spot foreign currency rate. *[IAS 21.23(a)]*.

Case 2: Changes in the spot element of the forward contract only are designated in the hedge

Ignoring ineffectiveness that may arise from other elements that have an impact on the fair value of the hedging instrument, the hedge is expected to be fully effective because the critical terms of the forward exchange contract and the purchase contract are the same and the change in the premium or discount on the forward contract is excluded from the assessment of effectiveness.

30 June 2021

	LC	LC
Forward	–	
Cash		–

To record the forward exchange contract at its initial fair value, i.e. zero.

31 December 2021

	LC	LC
Profit or loss (interest element of forward)	1,165	
Other comprehensive income (spot element)		777
Forward – liability		388

To recognise the change in the fair value of the forward contract between 30 June 2021 and 31 December 2021, i.e. 388 – 0 = LC388. The change in the present value of spot settlement of the forward exchange contract is a gain of LC777 = $\{([1.080 \times 100{,}000] - 107{,}200) \div 1.06^{(6/12)}\} - \{([1.072 \times 100{,}000] - 107{,}200) \div 1.06\}$), which is recognised in other comprehensive income. The present value of the spot settlement of the forward exchange contract is calculated as there is a need to consider the time value of money for effectiveness purposes (see 7.4.2 above).

The change in the interest element of the forward exchange contract (the residual change in fair value) is a loss of LC1,165 = 388 + 777, which is recognised in profit or loss. The hedge is fully effective because the gain in the spot element of the forward contract, LC777, exactly offsets the change in the purchase price at spot rates $\{([1.080 \times 100,000] - 107,200) \div 1.06^{(6/12)}\} - \{([1.072 \times 100,000] - 107,200) \div 1.06\} = $ LC777. The positive figure denotes an increase in the net present value of cash outflows and, therefore, effectively represents a 'loss' to offset the gain on the forward in other comprehensive income.

31 March 2022

	LC	LC
Other comprehensive income (spot element)	580	
Profit or loss (interest element)	1,003	
Forward – liability		1,583

To recognise the change in the fair value of the forward contract between 1 January 2022 and 31 March 2022, i.e. 1,971 – 388 = LC1,583. The change in the present value of spot settlement of the forward exchange contract is a loss of LC580 = $\{([1.074 \times 100,000] - 107,200) \div 1.06^{(3/12)}\} - \{([1.080 \times 100,000] - 107,200) \div 1.06^{(6/12)}\}$, which is recognised in other comprehensive income. The change in the interest element of the forward contract (the residual change in fair value) is a loss of LC1,003 = 1,583 – 580), which is recognised in profit or loss. The hedge is fully effective because the loss in the spot element of the forward contract, LC580, exactly offsets the change in the purchase price at spot rates $\{([1.074 \times 100,000] - 107,200) \div 1.06^{(3/12)}\} - \{([1.080 \times 100,000] - 107,200) \div 1.06^{(6/12)}\} = -$LC580. The negative figure denotes a reduction in the net present value of cash outflows and, therefore, effectively represents a 'gain' to offset the loss on the forward in other comprehensive income.

	LC	LC
Paper (purchase price)	107,400	
Other comprehensive income	197	
Paper (hedging gain)		197
Payable		107,400

To recognise the purchase of the paper at the spot rate (1.074 × 100,000 = LC 107,400) and remove the cumulative gain on the spot element of the forward contract that has been recognised in other comprehensive income (777 – 580 = LC197) and include it in the initial measurement of the purchased paper. Accordingly, the initial measurement of the purchased paper is LC107,203 consisting of a purchase consideration of LC107,400 and a hedging gain of LC197.

30 June 2022

	LC	LC
Payable	107,400	
Cash		107,200
Profit or loss		200

To record the settlement of the payable at the spot rate (100,000 × 1.072 = LC107,200) and recognise the associated exchange gain of LC200 (= – [1.072 – 1.074] × 100,000) in profit or loss.

	LC	LC
Profit or loss (spot element)	197	
Profit or loss (interest element)	232	
Forward – liability		429

To recognise the change in the fair value of the forward between 1 April 2022 and 30 June 2022, i.e. 2,400 – 1,971 = LC429). The change in the present value of spot settlement of the forward exchange contract is a loss of LC197 = $\{[1.072 \times 100,000] - 107,200 - \{([1.074 \times 100,000] - 107,200) \div 1.06^{(3/12)}\}$, which is recognised in profit or loss. The change in the interest element of the forward contract (the residual change in fair value) is a loss of LC232 = 429 – 197, which is recognised in profit or loss. The hedge is fully effective because the loss in the spot element of the forward contract, LC197, exactly offsets the gain on the payable reported using spot rates = $\{[1.072 \times 100{,}000] - 107{,}200 - \{([1.074 \times 100{,}000] - 107{,}200) \div 1.06^{(3/12)}\}\} = -LC197$. The negative figure denotes a reduction in the net present value of the payable and, therefore represents a gain to offset the loss on the forward contract.

	LC	LC
Forward – liability	2,400	
Cash		2,400

To record the net settlement of the forward exchange contract.

The following table provides an overview of the components of the change in fair value of the hedging instrument over the term of the hedging relationship. It illustrates that the way in which a hedging relationship is designated affects the subsequent accounting for that hedging relationship, including the assessment of hedge effectiveness and the recognition of gains and losses. *[IAS 39.F.5.6]*.

Period ending	Change in spot settlement LC	Fair value of change in spot settlement LC	Change in forward settlement LC	Fair value of change in forward settlement LC	Fair value of change in interest element LC
30 June 2021	–	–	–	–	–
31 December 2021	800	777	(400)	(388)	(1,165)
31 March 2022	(600)	(580)	(1,600)	(1,583)	(1,003)
30 June 2022	(200)	(197)	(400)	(429)	(232)
Total	–	–	(2,400)	(2,400)	(2,400)

Ignoring ineffectiveness that may arise from elements that affect the fair value of the hedging instrument only or that may be different from the hedged item to the hedging instrument (e.g. foreign currency basis spreads), both designations result in effective hedges as a result of the way effectiveness is measured. The example also sets out how a single hedge can initially be a cash flow hedge of the future purchase and then become a fair value hedge of the associated payable, provided it is documented as such.

The example also indicates that the time value of money is relevant for the assessment of effectiveness even when the spot element is designated in a hedge relationship (see 7.4.2 above). Although in many circumstances the effect of discounting the revaluation of the spot element may not be material.

7.4.8 Foreign currency basis spreads

One phenomenon of the financial crisis was the increase in foreign currency basis spreads. The foreign currency basis is the charge above the risk-free rate in a foreign country to compensate for country and liquidity risk. Historically, basis spreads had been low, but increased significantly after the financial crisis and the following sovereign debt crisis. Volatility in foreign currency basis can create hedge ineffectiveness when using a cross currency interest rate swap (CCIRS) to hedge the foreign currency and interest rate risk of a debt instrument issued in a foreign currency.

When designating the CCIRS in a fair value hedge, the gain or loss on the hedged item attributable to changes in the hedged interest rate risk is determined based on the foreign currency interest rate curve, therefore excluding currency basis. IAS 21 then requires such a monetary item in a foreign currency to be translated to the functional currency using the spot exchange rate. *[IAS 21.23]*. Conversely, the fair value of the CCIRS incorporates the foreign currency basis spread which results in ineffectiveness.

For a cash flow hedge, IFRS 9 is explicit that when using a hypothetical derivative to calculate ineffectiveness, the hypothetical derivative cannot simply impute a charge for exchanging different currencies (i.e. the foreign currency basis spread) even though actual derivatives (for example, cross currency interest rate swaps) under which different currencies are exchanged might include such a charge (see 7.4.4 above). *[IFRS 9.B6.5.5]*.

Although cross currency interest rate swaps are used to highlight the fact that foreign currency basis spreads should not be replicated in hypothetical derivatives, this issue is also likely to arise in other foreign currency contacts settled in the future. This is also an issue for net investment hedges for which the hedging instrument is a derivative (see 7.5.2.A below).

To address this, IFRS 9 identifies foreign currency basis spread as a 'cost of hedging'. Application of the costs of hedging accounting permits an appropriate portion of the change in the fair value of foreign currency basis spread to be taken to OCI rather than immediately recognised in profit or loss, see 7.5.3 below.

7.4.9 The impact of the hedging instrument's credit quality

One of the key hedge effectiveness requirements in IFRS 9 is that the impact of credit risk should not be of a magnitude such that it dominates the value changes (see 6.4.2 above). *[IFRS 9.6.4.1(c)(ii)]*. It is therefore clear that the credit quality of the hedging instrument, and hedged item are both relevant in determining the ongoing eligibility of a hedge relationship. However, the assessment of the effect of credit risk on value changes for hedge effectiveness purposes, which often may be made on a qualitative basis, should not be confused with the requirement to measure and recognise the impact of credit risk on the hedging instrument and, where appropriate, the designated hedged item, which will normally give rise to hedge ineffectiveness recognised in profit or loss (see 7.4.1 and 7.4.5 above).

Hedge ineffectiveness is the extent to which the changes in the fair value or cash flows of the hedging instrument are greater or less than those on the hedged item. *[IFRS 9.B6.4.1]*. Although it is permissible to exclude some components from a designated hedging instrument, and associated fair value changes, counterparty credit risk is not one of the permitted exclusions (see 3.6 above). Accordingly, unless the hedged item attracts the same credit risk as the hedging instrument, it will be a source of ineffectiveness (see 7.4.1 above). It is very unlikely to be the case that the hedged item and hedging instrument both attract the same credit risk. In particular, they will often not share the same counterparty, credit enhancement arrangements, term, exposure to credit risk and even contractual status. In addition to changes in the hedging instrument's counterparty credit risk, changes in the reporting entity's own credit risk may also affect the fair value of the hedging instrument in ways that are not replicated in the hedged item (see Chapter 14 at 11.3.2).

For a fair value hedge, the implications of this requirement are clear. If there is a change in the hedging instrument's credit risk, the hedging instrument's fair value will change, but there is unlikely to be an offsetting change in fair value for the hedged item. This will affect its effectiveness as measured. In most cases, credit risk in the hedged item does not form part of the designated hedged risk (see 2.2 above) and so changes in fair value of the hedged item due to credit risk will not provide any offset to changes in the fair value of the hedging instrument due to its credit risk. However, as noted above, even if credit risk is not part of the designated risk, if changes in the fair value of the hedged item due to credit risk dominate the value changes in the hedge relationship, then the hedge must be discontinued (see 6.4.2.B above and 8.3 below).

For a cash flow hedge, the implications might not immediately be so obvious. It is relatively common for the measurement of ineffectiveness in a cash flow hedge to be calculated using a hypothetical derivative (see 7.4.4 above). Hence, the effect of changes in the hedging instrument's credit risk on the measurement of ineffectiveness might be best explained in the context of a hypothetical derivative. The application guidance of IFRS 9 states that when applying the hypothetical derivative method, one cannot include features in the value of the hedged item that only exist in the hedging instrument, but not in the hedged item. *[IFRS 9.B6.5.5]*. Arguably, both the hedged item and the hedging instrument include credit risk. However, the credit risk in the hedged item is likely to be different from the credit risk in the hedging instrument. This is true even when the specific credit risk that exists in the hedged item is not included in the hedge relationship as a benchmark interest rate has been designated as the hedged risk (see 2.2 above).

Given the prohibition on reflecting terms in the hypothetical derivative that do not exist in the hedged item, it is clear that, when using a hypothetical derivative for measuring ineffectiveness in a cash flow hedge, the counterparty credit risk on the hedging instrument should not, as a matter of course be deemed to be equally present in the hedged item (see 7.4.5 above). *[IFRS 9.B6.5.5]*. For example, if the hedged item is a highly probable forecast transaction it may not involve any credit risk at all (see 6.4.2.B above), so that there is no offset for the specific credit risk affecting the fair value of the hedging instrument. This would give rise to some ineffectiveness recorded in profit or loss.

The impact will be more pronounced where the hedging instrument is longer term, has a significant fair value and there exist no other credit enhancements such as collateral agreements or credit break clauses.

Nowadays, most over-the-counter derivative contracts between financial institutions are cash collateralised. Furthermore, current initiatives in several jurisdictions, such as, the European Market Infrastructure Regulation (EMIR) in the European Union or the Dodd-Frank Act in the United States, have resulted in more derivative contracts being collateralised by cash. Cash collateralisation significantly reduces the credit risk for both parties involved (see 8.3.5 below). Similarly, since December 2015, when the London Clearing House (LCH) changed its rule book to introduce a new type of settled-to-market (STM) interest rate swap, in which the daily variation margin is used to settle the interest rate swap's outstanding fair value derivative position, more transactions are settled in this way (see 8.3.6 below).

Accordingly the residual credit risk to these cash collateralised and STM derivatives are much less likely to be a significant source of ineffectiveness.

7.4.10 Interest accruals and 'clean' versus 'dirty' values

When measuring ineffectiveness in hedge relationships for which the designated hedging instruments is an interest rate swap or similar, fair value 'noise' is often generated between the dates on which the variable leg is reset to market, in particular for a fair value hedge. Currently the payments on an interest rate swap are typically established at the beginning of a reset period and paid at the end of that period. Between these two dates the swap is no longer a pure pay-fixed receive-variable (or *vice versa*) instrument because both the next payment and the next receipt are fixed. Accordingly, the corresponding changes in the fair value of the hedged item (e.g. fixed rate debt) will not strictly mirror that of the swap. This problem becomes more acute the less frequently variable interest rates are re-fixed to market rates.

This 'noise' is unlikely to be significant enough to influence whether there is an economic relationship or not, especially where the interval between re-pricings is frequent enough, e.g. quarterly rather than yearly, in order to minimise the changes in fair value from the fixed net settlement or next interest payment (see 6.4.1 above). However, ineffectiveness should always be measured and recognised in profit or loss (see 7.4 above). This ineffectiveness is likely to be more significant when interest rates are more volatile, as experienced by a number of entities during the 'credit crunch' starting in the second half of 2007.

However, as a result of the reforms mandated by the Financial Stability Board following the Financial Crisis, regulators are pushing for IBORs to be replaced by new 'official' benchmark rates, known as Risk Free Rates (RFRs) (see 9 below). In many jurisdictions, the nature of term structures for RFRs remains an area of development at the time of writing. In particular it is unclear whether a 'term RFR' will exist at all (e.g. a 3 month RFR rate set in advance, similar to existing 3 month LIBOR) or if there will only be a compounded RFR rate with regular settlements (e.g. a rate equal to daily cumulative accrual at the overnight RFR rate, settled every 3 months). It also seems likely that term RFRs will develop in some currencies and not others. Where a cumulative accrual RFR is applied this will reduce or fully eliminate the 'noise' from the revaluation of the floating leg, as the floating rate never becomes 'fixed' given the ongoing cumulative accrual at the prevailing overnight rate.

7.4.11 Effectiveness of options

It was explained at 3.6.4 above that the time value of an option may be excluded from the hedge relationship and, in many cases, this may make it easier to demonstrate an expectation of offset from changes in the hedged item and the hedging instrument (see 6.4.1 above). In such cases, if the documented hedged risk is appropriately customised there will, in many cases, be very little ineffectiveness to recognise (other than that arising from changes in credit risk), as set out in the following example.

Example 53.74: Out of the money put option used to hedge forecast sales of commodity

Company A expects highly probable forecast sales of 100 tonnes of commodity X in 6 months' time. The current unit price of commodity X is £100 per tonne. To partially protect itself against a decrease in the price of the commodity, A acquires a put option, which gives it the right to sell 100 tonnes of commodity X at £90 per tonne. Company A's objective is only to provide protection for price changes below £90 per tonne, and such a strategy is often referred to as a hedge of a one-sided risk. *[IFRS 9.B6.3.12]*.

A is permitted to designate changes in the option's intrinsic value as the hedging instrument to reflect the one-sided risk in the hedged item. The changes in the intrinsic value of the option provide protection against the risk of variability in the price of commodity X below or equal to the strike price of the put of £90 per tonne. For prices above £90 per tonne, the option is out of the money and has no intrinsic value. Accordingly, gains and losses on the forecast sales of commodity X for prices above £90 are not attributable to the hedged risk for the purposes of assessing whether an economic relationship exists or not, nor are they relevant when measuring ineffectiveness.

Therefore, when calculating the cumulative change in fair value (present value) of the hedged forecast sales for the purposes of measuring ineffectiveness, no present value change would arise for variation in the price of commodity X above £90 per tonne. Changes in the fair value (present value) of the hedged forecast sales associated with price declines below £90 per tonne form part of the designated cash flow hedge and hence are included within the calculation of ineffectiveness.

Assuming there are no sources of ineffectiveness (i.e. including no change in credit risk), those changes are offset by changes in the intrinsic value of the put, resulting in zero ineffectiveness to be recognised in profit or loss (see 7.2 above).

Changes in the time value of the put option are excluded from the designated hedging relationship and the costs of hedging guidance is applied (see 7.5.1 below).

When hedging a one-sided risk, the hedged risk cannot include the time value of a purchased option, because the time value is not a component of the forecast transaction. *[IFRS 9.B6.3.12]*. Hence if, a purchased option is designated in its entirety as the hedging instrument of a one-sided risk arising from a forecast transaction, additional ineffectiveness will arise, as changes in the fair value of the hedged item will not provide any offset to changes in time value of the hedging instrument. This is consistent with the Implementation Guidance on hypothetical derivatives in IFRS 9 that prohibits the inclusion of features in the value of the hedged item that only exist in the hedging instrument (see 7.4.4 above). *[IFRS 9.B6.5.5]*.

7.4.12 Hedged items with embedded optionality

As described at 3.6.4 above, an entity can exclude the time value of the hedging instrument from the hedging relationship when hedging with options. Changes in value of the excluded time value must then be treated as a cost of hedging (see 7.5 below). Such a strategy is sometimes applied when hedging highly probable forecast cash flows, in which case excluding the time value of the hedging option would most likely achieve a lower level of ineffectiveness from an accounting perspective (see 7.4.11 above).

However, if the hedged item contains embedded optionality, which is matched by optionality within the hedging instrument, including the time value from both the hedged item and hedging instrument in the hedge relationship may result in a highly effective hedge. This is because there will be a level of offset from changes in time value of the hedging option and changes in the embedded time value in the hedged item. The following fact patterns provide examples of where there may be offsetting changes in time value:

- Entity A has purchased 10-year fixed rate debt. At the end of years five and seven, the issuer has the option to prepay the debt at par. Entity A may choose to eliminate variability in the fair value of the fixed rate debt by transacting a pay fixed receive floating interest rate swap, with matching prepayment options at five and seven years.
- Entity B has issued floating rate debt which includes an embedded floor (e.g. interest is floored at 0%). Entity B could choose to eliminate the variability in the cash flows above the floor (and lock in current low rates), by transacting a pay fixed swap with an embedded floor.

In the case of Entity A above, it is relatively easy to conclude that the change in value of the embedded prepayment option should form part of the effectiveness assessment and measurement of ineffectiveness, as a fair value hedge. However, it is less clear in the case of Entity B since the arrangement would be a cash flow hedge.

IFRS 9 provides guidance on hedge accounting for purchased options hedging a one-sided risk in a forecast transaction. The guidance explains that the hedged risk cannot include option time value because time value is not a component of the forecast transaction that affects profit or loss. Therefore, if an entity designates a purchased option in its entirety, as the hedging instrument of a one-sided risk arising from a forecast transaction, the hedging relationship will not be perfectly effective. In this situation, there will be no offset between the cash flows relating to the time value of the option premium paid and the designated hedged risk. *[IFRS 9.B6.3.12]*.

This might indicate that including the change in the time value of the embedded option in the hedged item as part of the change in value of the hedged item when measuring ineffectiveness is also not permitted. However, the above guidance was written specifically for forecast transactions that do not include time value, whereas hedged items with embedded optionality do include time value. Therefore, we believe that the guidance referred to above is not relevant for hedged items that do include optionality.

IFRS 9 defines a cash flow hedge as a hedge of an exposure to variability in cash flows that could affect profit or loss. *[IFRS 9.6.5.2(b)]*. Arguably, a change in the time value of an embedded option within the hedged item does not affect profit or loss, nor does it result in cash flow variability. However, we believe that cash flow variability and the potential to affect profit or loss must be demonstrated for the designated hedged risk, which in this case is the underlying of the host hedged item and the embedded option. The measurement of ineffectiveness should incorporate the cumulative change in fair value (present value) of the expected future cash flows of the entire hedged item, with respect to the designated hedged risk. *[IFRS 9.6.5.11(a)(ii)]*. The fair value of the hedged cash flows, which include the embedded optionality, includes the time value and not just the intrinsic value.

Furthermore, when calculating ineffectiveness, it is not acceptable only to compare cash flows, since it is also necessary to consider the time value of money by discounting the cash flows. *[IFRS 9.B6.5.4]*. This is despite the fact that the time value of money does not affect profit or loss or cause variability in the cash flows in a cash flow hedge, but is considered a factor in the cumulative fair value (present value) of the future cash flows (consistent with paragraph 6.5.11(a)(ii) of IFRS 9). This is also consistent with the requirement that the time value of any embedded optionality within the hedged item with respect to the hedged risk should be considered when measuring ineffectiveness, irrespective of whether the associated hedging instrument also has optionality.

7.5 Accounting for the costs of hedging

From a risk management perspective, entities typically consider the premium paid on an option (which, on inception, is often only time value), forward element in a forward, and foreign currency basis spread as a cost of hedging rather than a trading position. Economically, these 'costs' could be considered as a premium for protection against risk (i.e. an 'insurance premium'). *[IFRS 9.BC6.387]*. The IASB acknowledged these concerns when developing IFRS 9 and included a specific accounting treatment for changes in the fair value of the time value, forward element in a forward, and foreign currency basis spread if not designated in a hedging relationship.

The IFRS 9 hedging model permits the time value of options, forward elements of forwards, and foreign currency basis spread to be excluded from the hedging instrument (see 3.6 above). *[IFRS 9.6.2.4]*. The excluded portions can either remain at fair value through profit or loss, or be treated as 'costs of hedging'. The 'costs of hedging' guidance in IFRS 9 is included in paragraphs 6.5.15 and 6.5.16 and the associated application guidance in B6.5.29-39, it should not be used by analogy more widely for other portions not explicitly identified in the guidance. *[IFRS 9.BC6.297]*.

On application of the costs of hedging accounting, fluctuations in the fair value of the time value of options, the forward element of forwards or foreign currency basis spreads over time is recorded in other comprehensive income instead of affecting profit or loss immediately. Although the costs of hedging will ultimately be recognised in profit or loss, this will be in a manner consistent with the risk management activity.

It is important to note that because this accounting for 'costs of hedging' only applies if the time value of the option, the forward element of forwards or foreign currency basis spreads are excluded from the designation of the hedging relationship, the amounts deferred in accumulated other comprehensive income are not part of the cash flow hedge (or foreign currency reserve) but instead a different component of equity. The cash flow hedge reserve (or foreign currency reserve) only includes amounts that are gains or losses on hedging instruments that are determined to be an effective hedge (i.e. amounts that are included in the designation of a hedging relationship).

7.5.1 Time value of options

The fair value of an option consists of its intrinsic value and its time value. An entity can either designate an option as a hedging instrument in its entirety, or it can separate the intrinsic value and the time value and designate only the intrinsic value (see 3.6.4 above). *[IFRS 9.6.2.4(a)]*.

If the option is designated in its entirety as a hedge of a non-option item, changes in the portion of the fair value attributable to the option time value result in ineffectiveness (see 7.4.11 above). This is because only changes in the intrinsic value of the option will provide offset to the fair value changes attributable to the hedged risk (the situation is different if the hedged item also includes optionality, see 7.4.12 above, or if a delta-neutral hedging strategy is applied, see 6.3.2 above). Depending on the level of ineffectiveness from changes in the time value, an entity may have difficulty determining that an economic relationship existed between the hedged item and the hedging option (see 6.4.1 above).

If an entity chooses to exclude the time value from the designated hedging instrument it must apply the costs of hedging guidance, such that changes in the fair value of the time value of options to the extent that they relate to the hedged item, are first recognised in other comprehensive income (OCI). *[IFRS 9.6.5.15]*. It is worth noting that this treatment is not an accounting policy choice, as the treatment must be applied for all hedge relationships for which only the intrinsic value of the hedging instrument is designated within the hedge relationship. The subsequent treatment depends on the nature of the hedged transaction.

The standard differentiates between transaction related hedged items and time-period related hedged items: *[IFRS 9.6.5.15, B6.5.29]*

- Transaction related hedged items: the time value of an option used to hedge such an item has the character of part of the cost of the transaction. Examples would be a hedge of forecast purchases of inventory or property, plant and equipment, and forecast sales or purchases, as well as purchases or sales resulting from firm commitments.

  The amount that is accumulated in OCI is removed similarly to amounts accumulated in the cash flow hedge reserve (see 7.2.2 above). I.e. if the hedged transaction subsequently results in the recognition of a non-financial item (e.g. purchase of inventory or property, plant and equipment) the amount becomes a 'basis adjustment', otherwise the amount is reclassified to profit or loss in the same period or periods during which the hedged cash flows affect profit or loss (e.g. forecast sales);

- Time-period related hedged items: the time value of an option used to hedge such an item has the character of the cost of protection against a risk over a particular period of time (rather than a hedge of a transaction for which the transactions costs are accounted for as part of a one-off event).

  The amount that will be accumulated in OCI is amortised on a systematic and rational basis to profit or loss as a reclassification adjustment. The amortisation period is the period during which the hedge adjustment for the option's intrinsic value could affect profit or loss (or other comprehensive income if the option is designated as a hedge of an equity instrument accounted for at fair value through other comprehensive income). The appropriate amortisation period is illustrated in Example 53.75 below.

  Examples are hedges of interest expense or income in particular periods, already existing inventory hedged for fair value changes or a hedge of a net investment in a foreign operation. In the case of a forward starting interest rate option, the time value would be amortised over the interest periods that the option covers (i.e. the amortisation period would exclude the initial part of the option's life). *[IFRS 9.B6.5.30]*.

Example 53.75: Amortisation of time value of an option hedging a time related hedged item

If an interest rate option (a cap) is used to provide protection against increases in the interest expense on a floating rate bond, and for which the critical terms of the option and hedged item match, the time value of the cap is amortised to profit or loss as follows:

a) If the cap hedges increases in interest rates for the first three years out of a total life of the floating rate bond of five years, the time value of that cap is amortised over the first three years; or

b) If the cap is a forward starting option that hedges increases in interest rates for years two and three out of a total life of the floating rate bond of five years, the time value of that cap is amortised during years two and three. *[IFRS 9.B6.5.30]*.

By default, the time value will be zero at expiry of an option contract. For a transaction related hedged item, recognising the fair value changes of the time value in OCI means that on expiry, the aligned time value that existed at designation will have accumulated in OCI (see 7.5.1.A below). As mentioned above, once the hedged transaction happens, the accounting for the accumulated time value follows the accounting for any changes in fair value of the intrinsic value of the option recorded in the cash flow hedge reserve. *[IFRS 9.6.5.15].* Example 53.76 below illustrates how the costs of hedging accounting might be applied for a transaction related hedged item.

Example 53.76: Hedging the purchase of equipment (transaction related)

In the first quarter of a year, a manufacturing entity plans to purchase a new machine for its manufacturing process. Delivery of the machine is expected in the third quarter and the purchase price will be Swedish Krona (SEK) 5m. The entity has the Norwegian Krone (NOK) as its functional currency and, therefore, is exposed to foreign currency risk on this forecast transaction. The entity buys a call option to purchase SEK 5m in the third quarter, as it wishes to hedge the downside risk only. The terms of the option match the terms of the forecast transaction. The entity designates only the intrinsic value of the call option in a cash flow hedge of the highly probable forecast purchase of the machine.

At inception, the time value of the option amounts to NOK 30,000. The time value of the option amounts to NOK 16,000 at the end of the first quarter, NOK 7,000 at the end of the second quarter and zero at maturity.

Applying the IFRS 9 accounting requirements to the time value of the option results in the following movement within other comprehensive income (OCI), specifically the reserve within equity for accumulating amounts in relation to the time value of options associated with transaction related hedged items:

(All amounts in NOK thousands)	Q1	Q2	Q3
Reserve at beginning of quarter	–	(14)	(23)
Change in time value of option	(14)	(9)	(7)
Basis adjustment to machine			30
Reserve at end of quarter	(14)	(23)	–
Effect on OCI for the period	(14)	(9)	23

As noted above, by default, the time value will be zero at expiry of an option contract. For a time-period related hedged item, recognising the fair value changes of the time value in OCI means that on expiry, the time value that existed at designation will have accumulated in OCI. For time-period related hedged items, the amount accumulated in OCI is amortised on a 'systematic and rational basis' to profit or loss, however the standard does not prescribe what 'on a systematic and rational basis' means in this context. We believe a straight-line amortisation to be appropriate in most cases.

Example 53.77: Hedging interest rate risk of a bond (time period related) (1)

An entity issues a seven-year floating rate bond and wishes to protect itself against increases in the interest expense for the first two years. Therefore, the entity purchases an interest rate cap with a maturity of two years. The terms of the option match all other terms of the floating rate bond. Only the intrinsic value of the cap is designated as a hedging instrument in a cash flow hedge.

The time value on designation is CU 20, which is amortised to profit or loss on a straight-line basis over the protection period (i.e. the first two years). The time value of the option amounts to CU 13 at the end of the first year and zero at maturity.

Applying the IFRS 9 accounting requirements to the time value of the option results in the following movement within other comprehensive income (OCI), specifically the reserve within equity for accumulating amounts in relation to the time value of options associated with time-period related hedged items:

	Year 1	Year 2
Reserve at beginning of year	–	3
Change in time value of option	(7)	(13)
Amortisation of time value at inception	10	10
Reserve at end of year	3	–
Effect on OCI for the year	3	(3)
Effect on profit or loss for the year	(10)	(10)

The standard is, however, not wholly prescriptive as to where in profit or loss the costs of hedging accumulated in OCI should be recycled. The distinction between transaction related hedged items and time-period related hedged items reflects that the accounting for the time value of the option should follow general IFRS principles for how to account for payments that are akin to insurance premiums (the 'insurance premium view' mentioned above). So, in making the distinction, an entity needs to consider how the accounting for the hedged item will eventually affect profit or loss. This would be an accounting policy choice since the standard is not clear. However, when hedging forecast sales or purchases, one acceptable treatment would be presentation within the financial expense/income line item.

If hedge accounting is discontinued for a time-period related hedge relationship for which the costs of hedging treatment has been applied to the time value of the hedging option, the net amount (i.e. including cumulative amortisation) that has been accumulated in OCI must be immediately reclassified to profit or loss as a reclassification adjustment. This appears to be the case whether or not the hedged item is still expected to occur. *[IFRS 9.6.5.15(c), BC6.399].* In contrast there is no equivalent guidance for discontinuation of transaction related hedges when the transaction is still expected to take place, and so there does not seem to be a need to reclassify the net amount accumulated in OCI immediately to profit or loss in that scenario, although this is an area of uncertainty given the standard as drafted.

The accounting for the time value of options would also apply to combinations of options, for example, when hedging a highly probable forecast transaction with a zero-cost collar. When designating the intrinsic value only, the volatility resulting from changes in the time values of the two options would be recognised in other comprehensive income. However, the amortisation (in the case of time-period related hedged items) or the transaction costs deferred at the end of the life of the hedging relationship (for transaction related hedged items) would be nil when using a zero-cost collar, as the cumulative change in time value over the period would be nil. *[IFRS 9.B6.5.31]*.

7.5.1.A Aligned time value

Examples 53.76 and 53.77 above both assume that the critical terms of the option match the hedged item. However, in practice, this is not always the case. The accounting treatment described above applies only to the extent the time value relates to the hedged item. An additional assessment has to be made if the critical terms of the option do not match the hedged item. For that purpose, the actual time value has to be compared with that of a hypothetical option that perfectly matches the critical terms of the hedged item (in IFRS 9 referred to as the 'aligned time value'). *[IFRS 9.B6.5.32]*.

When the terms of the option are not aligned with the hedged item, the accounting for the time value in situations in which the aligned time value exceeds the actual time value is different to situations in which the actual time value exceeds the aligned time value. *[IFRS 9.B6.5.33]*.

If, at inception, the actual time value exceeds the aligned time value:

- the aligned time value at inception is treated in line with the general requirements outlined in 7.5.1 above, depending on whether it is a time period or transaction related hedged item;
- the change in the fair value of the aligned time value is recognised in OCI; and
- the remaining difference in change in fair value between the actual time value and the aligned time value is recognised in profit or loss.

If, at inception, the aligned time value exceeds the actual time value:

- the actual time value at inception is treated in line with the general requirements outlined in 7.5.1 above, depending on whether it is a time period or transaction related hedged item except as follows:
  - the lower of the cumulative change in the fair value of the actual time value and the aligned time value is recognised in OCI; and
  - the remaining difference in change in fair value between the actual time value and the aligned time value, if any, is recognised in profit or loss. *[IFRS 9.B6.5.33]*.

For the hedging strategy introduced in Example 53.77 above, this would change the accounting as follows:

Example 53.78: Hedging interest rate risk of a bond (time period related) (2)

Scenario 1: Actual time value exceeds aligned time value

The actual time value at inception is CU 20, and over time follows the same pattern as in Example 53.77 above. The aligned time value at inception is CU 15. The aligned time value of the option amounts to CU 9 at the end of the first year and zero at maturity.

	Year 1	Year 2
Change in actual time value of option	(7)	(13)
Change in aligned time value of option	(6)	(9)
Reserve in equity at beginning of year	–	1.5
Change in time value of option (based on aligned time value)	(6)	(9)
Amortisation of time value at inception (based on aligned time value)	7.5	7.5
Reserve in equity at end of year	1.5	–
Effect on OCI for the year	1.5	(1.5)
Remaining change in (actual) time value recognised in profit or loss (difference between the change in aligned time value and the actual time value of the option)	(1)	(4)
Effect on profit or loss for the year	(8.5)	(11.5)

The above accounting treats the difference between the actual and the aligned time value, consistent with its default classification, as a derivative at fair value through profit or loss.

Scenario 2: Actual time value is lower than aligned time value

The actual time value at inception is CU 20, and over time follows the same pattern as in Example 53.77 above. The aligned time value at inception is CU 24. The aligned time value of the option amounts to CU 10 at the end of the first year and zero at maturity.

	Year 1	Year 2
Change in actual time value of option	(7)	(13)
Change in aligned time value of option	(14)	(10)
Reserve in equity at beginning of year	–	3
Change in time value of option (based on the lower of the cumulative change in aligned time value and actual time value)	(7)	(13)
Amortisation of time value at inception (based on actual time value)	10	10
Reserve in equity at end of year	3	–
Effect on OCI for the year	3	(3)
Remaining change in (actual) time value recognised in profit or loss (zero, because the aligned time value of the option exceeds the actual time value of the option at inception)	–	–
Effect on profit or loss for the year	(10)	(10)

The above 'lower of test' for the accounting of the time value ensures that the entity does not recognise more expense in profit or loss than the entity actually incurs (based on the time value at inception). *[IFRS 9.BC6.398].* In this scenario, over the life of the option the cumulative change in fair value of the actual time value will always be lower than the cumulative change in fair value of the aligned time value, because the actual time value was lower at inception of the hedge relationship.

IFRS 9 does not define the 'aligned time value' in much detail but it is clear that it is part of the concept of 'costs of hedging'. Therefore, regular pricing features, such as dealer margins, are part of the aligned time value of an option, reflecting that they are part of the fair value of the financial instrument whose intrinsic value is designated as the hedging instrument. This is different from using a hypothetical derivative, which has the purpose of measuring the hedged item. For that purpose, features that are only in the hedging instrument but not the hedged item cannot be taken into account, whereas the same rationale does not apply for the purpose of accounting for the costs of hedging. This becomes clearer from the example of the foreign currency basis spread (see 7.5.3 below); it cannot be included as part of a hypothetical derivative to measure the hedged item but it is a cost of hedging.

However, similar to the need to update a hypothetical derivative to reflect changes in the timing of a forecast hedged item (see 7.4.4 above), if expectations of the forecast transaction are revised, the terms of the 'aligned' instrument will need to be updated to reflect the change in timing. The updated aligned instrument should match all of the critical terms of the forecast transaction, as if the amended terms were known at inception of the hedge. A true up to the costs of hedging reserve and associated profit or loss for the cumulative effect of the revised aligned time value will be required.

7.5.2 Forward element of forward contracts

Entities using foreign currency forward contracts in hedging relationships can designate the instrument in their entirety or exclude the forward element by designating the spot element only. When only the spot element is designated, an entity has a choice to apply costs of hedging accounting to the excluded forward element. This is, however, not an accounting policy choice, but an election for each designation. *[IFRS 9.6.5.16]*. If the costs of hedging guidance is not applied, designating the spot element of a forward contract results in the forward points (often also called the 'forward element') being accounted for at fair value through profit or loss (see 3.6.5 above).

When designating the entire hedging instrument, it is usually desirable for the hedged item also to be measured at the forward rate instead of the spot rate in order to enhance effectiveness. For example, when hedging a highly probable forecast transaction, the hedged item, once transacted, could be measured with respect to the forward rate if the 'forward rate method' is designated (see 7.4.7 above). However, IAS 21 requires monetary financial assets and liabilities denominated in a foreign currency to be measured at the spot rate. As a result, the forward rate method does not provide a similar solution for hedges of such monetary items because of the IAS 21 requirement for such assets and liabilities to be measured at the spot rate. *[IFRS 9.BC6.422]*. Some assistance is provided in the Implementation Guidance of IAS 39 as to how the spot and forward elements of a simple forward contract can be identified (see also Example 53.73 at 7.4.7 above). *[IAS 39.F.5.6]*. This guidance remains relevant under IFRS 9.

When designating the spot element and applying the costs of hedging to the forward element, the change in fair value of the forward element is recognised in other comprehensive income (OCI) and accumulated in a separate component of equity. The accounting for the forward element that exists at inception also follows the distinction between transaction related hedged items and time-period related hedged items that is made when accounting for the time value of an option (see at 7.5.1 above). This means, in the case of a transaction related hedged item, that the change in the fair value of the forward element is deferred in OCI and included, like transaction costs, in the measurement of the hedged item (or it is reclassified to profit or loss when a hedged sale occurs). In case of a time-period related hedged item, the forward element that exists at inception is amortised from the separate component of equity to profit or loss on a systematic and rational basis. For example, if commodity inventory is hedged against changes in fair value for six months using a commodity forward contract with a corresponding life, the forward element of the forward contract will be amortised over that six month period. *[IFRS 9.6.5.16, B6.5.34-36]*.

As a result of the above accounting, fluctuations in the fair value of the forward element over time will affect other comprehensive income, and the amount accumulated in OCI will be recognised in profit or loss when the hedged item affects profit or loss (in case of a transaction related hedged item), or be amortised to profit or loss (in case of a time-period related hedged item). The following example is designed to demonstrate the accounting for the forward element of a hedging derivative, as a cost of hedging. The fact pattern is intentionally simplified in order to isolate the costs of hedging accounting.

Example 53.79: Funding swaps – designating the spot risk only

A bank, having the Singapore Dollar (SGD) as its functional currency, borrows money by entering into a two-year zero coupon loan denominated in Japanese Yen (JPY). The loan is accounted for at amortised cost. The bank transfers the JPY funds into its functional currency and lends the money as a SGD denominated two-year zero coupon loan. To hedge the SGD/JPY exchange risk, the bank enters into a foreign currency forward contract to buy JPY against SGD in two years' time and designates it as a hedge of the spot JPY foreign currency risk. The fair value of the forward element at inception is SGD 20,000 and it is SGD 13,000 at the end of the first year and zero at maturity.

From an economic standpoint, the bank has now hedged the foreign currency risk and locked in the interest margin for the entire two-year period.

In economic theory, the forward points represent the difference in interest rates between the two currencies involved. Hence, the forward element that exists at inception is seen as one element of the interest margin, although other elements also exist (see 7.5.3 below).

Applying the accounting for costs of hedging to the forward element of the forward contract results in the following movement within other comprehensive income (OCI):

(All amounts in SGD thousands)	Year 1	Year 2
Reserve in equity at beginning of year	–	3
Change in fair value of forward element	(7)	(13)
Amortisation of forward element at inception	10	10
Reserve in equity at end of year	3	–
Effect on OCI for the year	3	(3)
Effect on profit or loss for the year	(10)	(10)

The bank could present the amortisation of the forward element in the income statement within the interest margin, together with the interest income from the loan and the interest expense from the borrowing, showing the interest margin from the combined transaction, economically fixed in SGD (see Chapter 54 at 7.1.3).

The forward element costs of hedging treatment is not solely applicable for simple foreign currency forward contracts, but applies equally to forward contracts with respect to other risks, such as commodity or interest rate. *[IFRS 9.BC6.416]*. We would also expect the treatment to apply to a fixed-for-fixed currency swap as arguably that is no more than a series of forward contracts applying a blended rate.

Just like the accounting for the time value of an option, the accounting for the forward element as a cost of hedging applies only to the extent of the so-called 'aligned' forward element (i.e. only to the extent that the forward element relates to the hedged item – see 7.5.1.A above). *[IFRS 9.B6.5.37]*. Although not explicitly mentioned in the guidance, we believe that the aligned forward element must be based on prevailing forward rates on designation, as otherwise the aligned forward element would include a period that does not relate to the hedged item. This means that if an existing forward contact with a non-zero fair value is designated as hedging a hedged item for which the notional, residual life, and underlying all match the forward contract, it cannot be assumed that the forward element of the off-market hedging forward contract will be the same as the aligned forward contract. Further we believe it is acceptable for the type of aligned instrument to match that of the actual instrument where that makes sense, for example if a fixed-for-fixed cross currency swap is the hedging instrument it is likely to be acceptable for the aligned instrument to also be a fixed-for-fixed cross currency swap, rather than a series of individual aligned forward contracts.

The above discussion focuses on the costs of hedging accounting where the forward element is excluded from the hedging instrument. It should be noted that most foreign currency instruments also include foreign currency basis spreads which can also be excluded from hedging instruments (see 7.5.3 below).

7.5.2.A Forward element of forward contracts in a net investment hedge

It is possible to designate the forward rate as the hedged risk in a net investment hedge (see 7.3.3 above), but for some entities it may be preferable to designate only the spot rate, so a question arises as to the accounting treatment of the excluded forward element in a net investment hedge. The costs of hedging guidance (see 7.5 above) is not specific to a particular type of hedge relationship, accordingly it can be applied to fair value, cash flow and net investment hedges (see 5 above). In fact, the application guidance to IFRS 9, includes a net investment hedge as an example of a fact pattern for which the costs of hedging accounting could be applied. The example given is of a time-related hedge: a net investment that is hedged for 18 months using a foreign-exchange option, which would result in allocating the time value of the option over that 18-month period. *[IFRS 9.B6.5.29(b)]*. This guidance also confirms that for the purposes of accounting for the costs of hedging, a hedge of a net investment would ordinarily be treated as time-period related hedge, in particular as in most cases there is no expectation of a hedged transaction (see 7.5.1 above).

The application of the costs of hedging guidance to the excluded forward element of a forward contract is not an accounting policy choice, but an election for each designation. *[IFRS 9.6.5.16]*. If the costs of hedging guidance is not applied, designating the spot element of a forward contract in a net investment hedge results in the forward element being accounted for at fair value through profit or loss (see 3.6.5 above).

The costs of hedging accounting can only be applied to the extent that it relates to the hedged item, this is achieved by comparison with an 'aligned hedging instrument' (see 7.5.1.A above). *[IFRS 9.6.5.15]*. The aligned hedging instrument should match the critical terms of the hedged item. *[IFRS 9.B6.5.37]*. Where the hedged item is a financial instrument or a forecast transaction for which specific terms exist, determining the aligned hedging instrument is relatively straight forward. However, given that a net investment hedge is largely an accounting concept, identifying appropriate terms for an aligned hedging instrument is more judgemental.

Given that it is possible to designate the forward rate as the hedged risk in a net investment hedge and assess effectiveness using a hypothetical forward contract (see 7.3.3.A above), it is relatively easy to conclude that an aligned hedging instrument for a net investment hedge could similarly be a simple forward. It is harder to conclude that where a cross currency swap is designated as hedging an amount of net investment equal to the swap notional, the aligned instrument could similarly be a cross currency swap. This is due to the existence of periodic settlements in the swap that are not evident in the net investment (see 7.3.3.B above).

Although the above analysis focuses on accounting for any excluded forward element in a net investment hedge, it is also relevant to foreign currency basis spreads (see 7.5.3 below).

7.5.3 Foreign currency basis spreads in financial instruments

The foreign currency basis spread, a phenomenon that became very significant during the financial crisis, is a charge embedded in financial instruments that compensates for aspects such as country and liquidity risk as well as demand and supply factors. This charge only applies to transactions involving the exchange of foreign currencies at a future point in time (as, for example, in currency forward contracts or cross currency interest rate swaps (CCIRS)).

Historically, the difference between the spot and forward prices of currency forward contracts and CCIRS represented the differential between the interest rates of the two currencies involved. However, basis spreads increased significantly during the financial crisis and during the subsequent sovereign debt crisis, and have become a significant and volatile component of the pricing of longer term forward contracts and CCIRS.

The standard cites currency basis spread as an example of an element that is only present in the hedging instrument, but not in a hedged item that is a single currency instrument. Consequently, this would result in some ineffectiveness even when using a hypothetical derivative for measuring ineffectiveness (see 7.4.8 above). *[IFRS 9.B6.5.5]*.

When using a foreign currency forward contract or a CCIRS in a hedge, the foreign currency basis spread is an unavoidable 'cost' of the hedging instrument. Hence IFRS 9 permits the accounting for foreign currency basis spreads as a 'cost of hedging', similar to the time value of options and the forward element of forward contracts.[23] This means that, when designating a hedging instrument, an entity may exclude the foreign currency basis spread and account for it separately in the same way as the accounting for time value of options or the forward element of the forward rate, as described in 7.5.1 and 7.5.2 above. *[IFRS 9.6.5.16]*.

Consistent with the approach to designation of the forward element as a cost of hedging, designation of foreign currency basis as a cost of hedging is not an accounting policy choice, but an election for each designation. However, if an entity designates the entire hedging instrument, fair value changes due to changes in the foreign currency basis spread would result in some ineffectiveness.

It may be the case for some hedging instruments that contain both a forward element and foreign currency basis that it is more operationally efficient to designate only the spot risk and calculate the combined cost of hedging, rather than the forward element and foreign currency basis individually or designating the forward rate and excluding only the foreign currency basis spread. The standard does not explicitly permit a combined treatment, but for many scenarios the aggregate of the individual costs of hedging accounting will equate to the costs of hedging accounting calculated on a combined basis.

7.5.3.A Measurement of the costs of hedging for foreign currency basis spread

Although the standard is clear that the 'costs of hedging' accounting method can be applied to the foreign currency basis spread within hedging instruments, it is less clear as to how to identify the foreign currency basis spread for this purpose. We outline below two possible approaches for the identification of the foreign currency basis spread; other acceptable approaches may exist:

Approach 1: Based on the difference between the fair value of the actual foreign currency hedging instrument and the value of a hypothetical instrument derived and valued using market data excluding foreign currency basis spread.

Approach 2: Based on the difference between the fair value of the actual foreign currency hedging instrument and its value calculated using market data excluding foreign currency basis spread.

Example 53.80: Calculation of the value of foreign currency basis spread

Entity A has functional currency of GBP and issued three year USD100m fixed rate debt on 31/12/20, paying a semi-annual coupon of 3.75%. In order to eliminate variability in the fair value of the debt with respect to interest rate and foreign currency risk, Entity A transacted a foreign currency swap (Swap A) on the same day as follows:

Pay leg – GBP 64.2m paying 6m benchmark interest rate +2.757% (semi-annual) maturing on 31/12/23

Receive leg – USD100m paying 3.75% (semi-annual) maturing on 31/12/23

The spread of 2.757% on the GBP floating leg includes an amount of –0.103% that represents the foreign currency basis spread priced into the swap contract. (Quoted prices for foreign currency basis spreads for many currency pairs are widely available.)

Entity A designates the debt and Swap A in a fair value hedge of foreign currency and interest rate risk, and wishes to apply the costs of hedging approach to the foreign currency basis spread. The hedge appears to be a time-period related hedge (see 7.5.1 above).

The receive leg of Swap A matches the cash flows from the debt exactly. As the critical terms of the foreign currency basis swap are aligned with the hedged debt, there is no need to create an aligned foreign currency basis swap (see 7.5.1.A above). For the purposes of this example no other valuation sources of ineffectiveness arise, although this is unlikely to be the case in practice.

Below are two possible approaches to calculating the value of the foreign currency basis spread to be recognised in other comprehensive income as part of the costs of hedging:

Approach 1 – Swap B

Entity A creates hypothetical Swap B. The receive leg of Swap B should exactly match the receive leg of Swap A (which also matches the debt). The pay leg of Swap B should be derived to achieve an overall zero fair value for Swap B on designation, based on market curves, excluding foreign currency basis spread. Accordingly, Swap B might look like the following:

Pay leg – GBP 64.2m paying 6m benchmark interest rate +2.86% (semi-annual) maturing on 31/12/23

Receive leg – USD100m paying 3.75% (semi-annual) maturing on 31/12/23

(The spread of 2.86% on the GBP floating leg does not include an amount representing foreign currency basis spread.)

The accounting for the hedge relationship would be as follows:

Instrument	Fair value on designation	Accounting
Debt	nil	Value changes due to foreign currency and interest rate risk (using discount curves that do not reflect foreign currency basis spread) are recognised in profit or loss, and adjust the carrying value of the debt.
		(The recognised changes in value of the debt will be offset by changes in the fair value of Swap B's receive leg.)
Swap B (hypothetical swap)	nil	Changes in fair value due to foreign currency and interest rate risk (using discount curves that do not reflect foreign currency basis spread) are recognised in profit or loss.
Swap A (actual swap)	nil	Changes in fair value of Swap A (i.e. using discount curves that reflect foreign currency basis spreads) LESS the calculated changes in the fair value of Swap B, are recognised in other comprehensive income as the costs of hedging.
		In the statement of financial position, Swap A is recognised at its fair value at all times.
Other comprehensive income		As the fair value of the foreign currency basis spread is zero at inception, there is no requirement for a systematic and rational amortisation of the costs of hedging from other comprehensive income into profit or loss. *[IFRS 9.6.5.15(c)]*.
		The value of the foreign currency basis spreads at inception (nil) equals the initial fair value of Swap A (nil) less the initial fair value of Swap B (nil).

Approach 2 – Swap C

Entity A creates hypothetical Swap C. The terms of Swap C exactly match the terms of Swap A, but Swap C would be fair valued based on market curves excluding foreign currency basis spread. (It should be noted that the receive leg of Swap C in this example also matches the debt). Swap C will have a fair value on designation which is equal to the net present value of the foreign currency basis spread included within the GBP pay leg (e.g. a negative spread of 0.103% in this example). Accordingly Swap C will look like the following:

Pay leg – GBP 64.2m paying 6m benchmark interest rate +2.757% (semi-annual) maturing on 31/12/22.

Receive leg – USD100m paying 3.75% (semi-annual) maturing on 31/12/22

The fair value of Swap C on designation is an asset of £132k, this is calculated using market curves excluding foreign currency basis spread.

The accounting for the hedge relationship would be as follows:

Instrument	Fair value on designation	Accounting
Debt	nil	Value changes due to foreign currency and interest rate risk (using discount curves that do not reflect foreign currency basis spread) are recognised in profit or loss, and adjust the carrying value of the debt. (The recognised changes in value of the debt will be offset by changes in the fair value of Swap C's receive leg.)
Swap C (hypothetical swap)	£132k DR	Changes in fair value due to foreign currency and interest rate risk (using discount curves that do not reflect foreign currency basis spread) are recognised in profit or loss.
Swap A (actual swap)	nil	Changes in fair value of Swap A (i.e. using discount curves that reflect foreign currency basis spreads) LESS the calculated changes in the fair value of Swap C, are recognised in other comprehensive income as the costs of hedging. In the statement of financial position, Swap A is recognised at its fair value at all times.
Other comprehensive income		The value of the foreign currency basis spread at inception must be amortised from other comprehensive income into profit or loss on a systematic and rational basis. *[IFRS 9.6.5.15(c)]*. The value of the foreign currency basis spread at inception (GBP 132k CR) is the initial fair value of Swap A (nil) less the initial fair value of Swap C (GBP 132k DR). Over the life of the hedge relationship the cumulative amortisation will result in the following: DR other comprehensive income GBP 132k CR profit or loss GBP 132k

The above fact pattern assumes that there are no sources of ineffectiveness and that the hedging derivative exactly matches the critical terms of the hedged item. In reality this is unlikely to always be the case, therefore additional complexity may need to be incorporated into the chosen approach for identifying the foreign currency basis spread. In particular, where the critical terms of the hedging derivative do not match those of the hedged item, it is the aligned foreign currency basis spread which is eligible for the costs of hedging treatment. In that case swap A, B and C (above) should be based on an aligned foreign currency derivative, i.e. one that would perfectly match the hedged item. Differences in fair value changes between the actual foreign currency derivative and the aligned foreign currency derivative will be an additional source of ineffectiveness (see 7.5.2 above). *[IFRS 9.B6.5.37,B6.5.38]*.

Although quoted prices for foreign currency basis spreads for many currency pairs are widely available, entities should not underestimate the complexities involved in eliminating the effect of foreign currency basis spreads from market forward foreign currency rates which generally do reflect foreign currency basis spreads.

7.6 Hedges of a firm commitment to acquire a business

A firm commitment to acquire a business in a business combination cannot be a hedged item, except for foreign currency risk (see 2.6.4 above).

Consider the situation where an entity with euro as its functional currency enters into a binding agreement to purchase a subsidiary in six months. The subsidiary's functional currency is the US dollar. The consideration is denominated in US dollars and is payable in cash. The entity decides to enter into a forward contract to buy US dollars for euros to hedge its foreign currency risk on the firm commitment. The following options exist and the entity may choose the most appropriate accounting treatment:

- because the hedge is a purchase of US dollars, it is, arguably, not a fair value hedge of the acquisition, since the acquisition is itself naturally hedged for changes in the fair value in the US dollar – that is, the entity is committed to buy a group of US dollar denominated assets and liabilities for a price denominated in US dollars. Nevertheless, the entity may still designate the transaction as the hedged item in a fair value hedge relationship, although this may not make intuitive sense; *[IFRS 9.B6.5.3]*

- the entity could instead designate the forward contract as a hedge of the cash flows associated with the committed purchase, which is a cash flow hedge (see 5.2.2 above); *[IFRS 9.B6.3.1]* or

- if the anticipated business combination in this example is only a highly probable forecast transaction and not a firm commitment, then the entity can only apply cash flow hedging (see 2.6.1 above).

If the transaction is a fair value hedge, then the carrying amount of the hedged item is adjusted for the gain or loss attributable to the hedged risk (see 7.1 above). Since separately identifiable assets acquired and liabilities assumed must be recognised on initial consolidation at fair value in the consolidated financial statements of the acquirer, it follows that the gain or loss attributable to the hedged risk must be included in the consideration paid. In other words, the impact of the hedge affects the calculation of goodwill that is otherwise determined by the application of IFRS 3 (see Chapter 9 at 6).[24]

During the hedging period, the effective portion of the gain or loss on a hedging instrument in a cash flow hedge is recognised in other comprehensive income (see 7.2 above). Upon initial recognition of the acquisition, gains or losses recognised in other comprehensive income are included in the consideration paid for the business combination that is designated as the hedged item. *[IFRS 9.6.5.11(d)(i)]*.

The adjusted carrying amount of goodwill, including the gain or loss from hedge accounting, will then be subject to the normal requirements to test for annual impairment (see Chapter 20 at 8).

Once the purchase price is paid and the transaction is completed, the entity is 'long' US dollars as a result of recognising the US dollar net assets of the acquired entity. Those net assets would then be eligible for net investment hedging which would require selling US dollars to create an eligible hedging instrument, for example by entering into a foreign currency forward (see 5.3 and 7.3 above).

7.7 Hedge accounting for a documented rollover hedging strategy

The standard is clear that the replacement or rollover of a hedging instrument into another hedging instrument is not an expiration or termination of a hedge relationship if such replacement or rollover is part of the entity's documented risk management objective (see 8.3 below). *[IFRS 9.6.5.6]*. However, there is minimal additional specific guidance provided on what is meant by, or the accounting for, a documented rollover hedging strategy. We believe that a rollover hedging strategy refers to a strategy whereby the maturity of the hedging instrument is intentionally shorter than the maturity of the hedged item, and there is an expectation that on expiry of the original hedging instrument it will be replaced by a new hedging instrument. The replacement hedging instrument is likely to have similar characteristics to the instrument being replaced. Whether the risk management strategy is to be achieved through a rollover strategy is a matter of fact, and must have been documented as such at inception of the initial hedge and the usual qualifying conditions for hedge accounting should be met (see 6 above). An alternative risk management strategy would be a partial term hedge, i.e. for a specified portion of the life of the hedged item (see 2.2.4 above), which is not the same as a rollover strategy.

An entity's risk management strategy is the main source of information to perform an assessment of whether a hedging relationship meets the effectiveness requirements, for example whether an economic relationship exists between the hedged item and the hedging instrument. *[IFRS 9.B6.4.18]*. Therefore, when making this assessment for a rollover hedging strategy, it will be necessary to consider whether the risk management strategy does envisage rolling over the hedging instrument (see 6.4.1 above). *[IFRS 9.B6.4.6]*.

The measurement of hedge ineffectiveness is undertaken on a cumulative basis (see 7.1.1 and 7.2.1 above). *[IFRS 9.6.5.8, 6.5.11]*. 'Cumulative' is generally understood to mean over the life of the hedge relationship. This will include historic gains and losses from previous periods in which the hedging instruments were rolled over, for as long as the hedge continues to remain live. The cumulative period is not reset just because a new rollover hedging instrument is transacted if it is part of a documented rollover strategy, as it is not an event that requires discontinuation of the hedge relationship. This is particularly relevant for a cash flow hedge in the identification of the hypothetical derivative, as demonstrated in Example 53.81 below (see also 7.4.4 above).

Example 53.81: Hedge of a foreign currency risk in rollover cash flow hedging strategy

Company A has sterling as its functional currency. Company A expects highly probable foreign currency sales resulting in a forecast cash inflow of €2m in 9 months' time. Company A chooses to hedge the foreign currency risk and transacts an FX forward to sell €2m and receive GBP in 3 months' time. This is with an expectation that as the initial contract matures another 3-month contract will be transacted and then again a third contract on maturity of the second contract. As part of the usual hedge documentation Company A has identified this as being a rollover strategy for foreign currency risk. Company A has determined that the effectiveness criteria are met on initial designation.

The hedge relationship is not discontinued when the second and third FX contracts are transacted. The effectiveness requirements are assessed throughout the life of the hedge relationship, including consideration of the expected roll-over of the hedging instruments (see 6.4.1 above). The amount of ineffectiveness recorded is determined by a comparison of the change in fair value of the hedging instruments (the aggregate of the changes in fair value of the 3-month FX contracts) and the change in value of the hedged item (the highly probable cash flow in 9 months' time) for changes in foreign currency risk. This cumulative approach means the calculation would include fair value changes since designation of the hedge relationship, which would include the realised changes in fair value of the matured 3-month FX forwards.

If the hypothetical derivative method (see 7.4.4 above) is adopted to calculate the change in value of the hedged item, a single hypothetical derivative would be used based on the expected timing of the forecast transaction (i.e. a 9-month FX contract).

An alternative risk management objective would be a partial term hedge, i.e. when the entity chooses to manage the hedged risk for only a partial term, perhaps because there is an expectation that a natural hedge will occur at some point in the future (see 2.2.4 above). In that case there is no expectation that on expiry of the original hedging instrument it will be replaced by a new hedging instrument with similar characteristics to the instrument being replaced, hence it is not the same as a roll-over strategy.

Accordingly, the documented risk management objective for a hedge relationship (see 6.2 above) should highlight if it is either a roll-over strategy or a partial term hedge, and the assessment of the effectiveness requirements (see 6.4 above) and measurement of ineffectiveness (see 7.4 above) will be assessed on that basis.

Amortisation of any fair value adjustment made to the hedged item under a fair value hedge of a documented roll-over strategy need not commence until the rollover hedge strategy is discontinued (see 7.1.2 above).

7.8 Hedge accounting for an equity instrument designated at fair value through OCI

It is clear from the standard that it is possible to designate as the hedged item in a fair value hedge, an investment in an equity instrument for which the entity has elected on initial recognition to present changes in fair value in OCI (see 2.6.3 above). *[IFRS 9.6.5.3]*. Applying that initial recognition election, with the exception of dividends received, subsequent gains or losses on the equity investments will never be recognised in profit or loss, (see Chapter 50 at 2.5). However, for such a hedge, all fair value changes of the hedging instrument are recognised in OCI. *[IFRS 9.6.5.8]*.

This treatment can lead to an accounting mismatch as value changes for the hedged item when a dividend is recognised will be reflected in profit or loss but remain in OCI for the hedging instrument.

8 SUBSEQUENT ASSESSMENT OF EFFECTIVENESS, REBALANCING AND DISCONTINUATION

8.1 Assessment of effectiveness

A prospective effectiveness assessment is required on an ongoing basis, in a similar manner as at the inception of the hedging relationship (see 6 above) and, as a minimum, at each reporting date or upon a significant change in circumstances, whichever comes first, in order to continue to apply hedge accounting. *[IFRS 9.B6.4.12]*. The flow chart below illustrates the assessment life cycle.

Figure 53.3: Effectiveness assessment and rebalancing

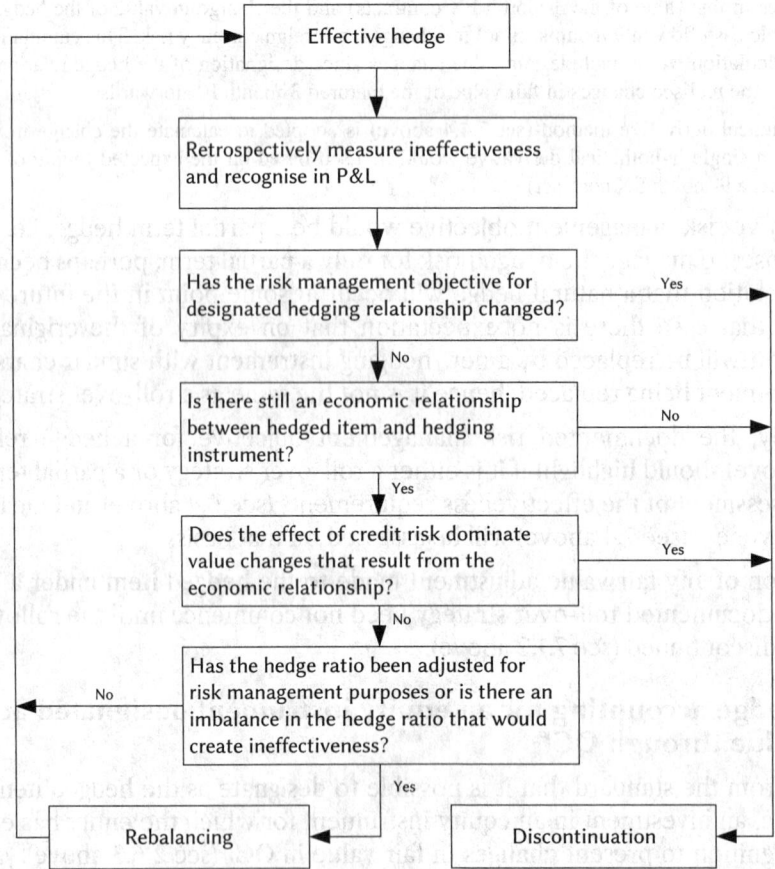

Each accounting period an entity first must assess whether the risk management objective for the hedging relationship has changed. A change in risk management objective is a matter of fact that triggers discontinuation prospectively. Discontinuation of hedging relationships is discussed at 8.3 below.

An entity would also have to discontinue hedge accounting prospectively if it turns out that there is no longer an economic relationship (see 6.4.1 above). This makes sense as whether there is an economic relationship is a matter of fact that cannot be altered by adjusting the hedge ratio (see 6.4.3 above). The same is true for the impact of credit risk;

if credit risk is now dominating the hedging relationship, then the entity must discontinue hedge accounting prospectively (see 6.4.2 above). *[IFRS 9.6.5.6]*.

The hedge ratio may need to be adjusted if it turns out that the hedged item and hedging instrument do not move in relation to each other as expected, or if the ratio has changed for risk management purposes. This is referred to as 'rebalancing' and is discussed at 8.2 below.

It can be seen from the above flow chart that hedge accounting can only continue prospectively if the risk management objective has not changed, and the effectiveness requirements continue to be met. Otherwise the hedge relationship must be discontinued (see 8.3 below).

8.2   Rebalancing

8.2.1   Definition

An entity is required to 'rebalance' the hedge ratio to reflect a change in the relationship between the hedged item and hedging instrument if it expects the new relationship to continue going forward. Rebalancing refers to the adjustments made to the designated quantities of the hedged item or hedging instrument of an already existing hedging relationship for the purpose of maintaining a hedge ratio that complies with the hedge effectiveness requirements. Changes to the designated quantities of either the hedged item or hedging instrument for other purpose is not rebalancing within the context of IFRS 9. *[IFRS 9.B6.5.7]*.

Rebalancing allows entities to refine their hedge ratio without discontinuation and redesignation, so reducing the need for designation of 'late hedges' and the associated accounting issues that can arise with such a hedge (see 2.4.1 and 7.4.3 above).

The concept of rebalancing only comprises prospective changes to the hedge ratio (i.e. the quantity of hedged item compared to the quantity of hedging instrument) in response to changes in the economic relationship between the hedged item and hedging instrument, when the risk management otherwise continues as originally designated. *[IFRS 9.BC6.303]*. For instance, an entity may have designated a hedging relationship in which the hedging instrument and the hedged item have different but related underlying reference indices, rates or prices. If the relationship or correlation between those two underlyings change, the hedge ratio may need to change to better reflect the revised correlation. *[IFRS 9.B6.5.9]*.

By way of an example; an entity hedges an exposure to Foreign Currency A using a currency derivative that references Foreign Currency B. Foreign Currency A and B are pegged (i.e. their exchange rate is maintained within a band or at an exchange rate set by a central bank or other authority). If the exchange rate between Foreign Currency A and Foreign Currency B were changed (i.e. a new band or rate was set), rebalancing the hedging ratio to reflect the new exchange rate would ensure that the hedging relationship would continue to meet the hedge effectiveness requirements. *[IFRS 9.B6.5.10]*.

Any other changes made to the quantities of the hedged item or hedging instrument, for instance, a reduction in the quantity of the hedged item because some cash flows are no longer highly probable, would not be rebalancing. Such other changes to the designated quantities would need to be treated as a partial discontinuation if the entity reduces the extent to which it hedges, and a new designation of a hedging relationship if the entity increases it. *[IFRS 9.B6.5.7]*.

Changes that risk managers may make to improve hedge effectiveness but that do not alter the quantities of the hedged item or the hedging instrument are not rebalancing either. An example of such a change is the transaction of derivatives related to a risk that was not considered in the original hedge relationship.

Therefore, rebalancing is only relevant if there is basis risk between the hedged item and the hedging instrument. Basis risk, in the context of hedge accounting, refers to any difference in price sensitivity of the underlyings of the hedging instrument and the hedged item. The existence of basis risk in a hedge relationship usually results in a degree of hedge ineffectiveness (see 7.4 above). For example, hedging a cotton purchase in India with NYMEX cotton futures contracts is likely to result in some ineffectiveness, as the hedged item and the hedging instrument do not share exactly the same underlying price. Rebalancing only affects the expected relative sensitivity between the hedged item and the hedging instrument going forward, as ineffectiveness from past changes in the sensitivity will have already been recognised in profit or loss.

The following example provides some indications as to how to distinguish rebalancing from other changes to a hedge relationship:

Example 53.82: Rebalancing

Fact pattern 1

An entity is exposed to price changes in commodity A which is not widely traded as a derivative. The entity has proven that there is an economic relationship between commodity A and commodity B. Commodity B is widely traded as a derivative. In that case, the entity may use commodity B derivatives to hedge the price risk in commodity A. An initial hedge ratio of 1:1.1 is based on the expected relationship between the prices of commodity A and commodity B. The relationship subsequently changes such that a ratio of 1:1.15 is expected to be more effective.

The entity can account for the changes in the hedging relationship as rebalancing because the difference between the prices is caused by basis risk.

Fact pattern 2

An entity swaps a base rate floating rate loan into a fixed interest rate using a pay LIBOR receive fixed swap. At inception, the entity is able to prove that there is an economic relationship between the base rate and LIBOR and designates the swap and the loan in a cash flow hedge, although it expects some level of ineffectiveness (see 6.4.1 above). Similar to fact pattern 1, the entity may use rebalancing to account for changes in the basis spread between the base rate and LIBOR.

However, the entity subsequently transacts a LIBOR versus base rate swap in order to eliminate the basis risk. The accounting consequences would depend on the reason for doing so and here we consider two scenarios:

a) The entity can no longer prove that there is an economic relationship between the base rate and LIBOR (although this is unlikely in practice).

b) The entity can still prove that there is an economic relationship between the base rate and LIBOR, but no longer wishes to suffer the resultant ineffectiveness arising from the basis risk.

In scenario a), the hedging relationship no longer meets the eligibility criteria and needs to be discontinued, as there is no longer an economic relationship between the hedged item and the hedging instrument. The entity cannot use rebalancing to avoid discontinuation because the hedge no longer meets the qualifying criteria (see 8.3 below).

In scenario b), the entity tries to avoid ineffectiveness by contracting another hedging instrument. Arguably, the entity could continue with the original designation and account for the LIBOR versus base rate swap as a derivative measured at fair value through profit or loss. However, given that the entity seeks to avoid ineffectiveness, it might want to apply hedge accounting to the base rate swap as well. If the entity wants to include the LIBOR versus base rate swap in the original hedging relationship, it would represent a change in the documented risk management objective which requires discontinuation of the existing and re-designation of a new hedging relationship. Alternatively, the entity may be able to designate the base rate swap as hedging the aggregated exposure of the base rate floating rate loan and pay LIBOR interest rate swap (see 2.7 above).

Fact pattern 3

An entity with US dollars as its functional currency designated a fix rate loan denominated in EUR and a US dollars /euro forward exchange contract in a cash flow hedge. Subsequently, the borrower suffers significant financial difficulties and the entity only expects to receive 90% of the contractual cash flows on the loan.

The entity cannot apply rebalancing because the changes in the cash flows of the hedged item are not caused by basis risk but by credit risk. Instead, the entity is required to assess whether credit risk dominates the fair value changes of the hedged item in which case the hedging relationship needs to be discontinued (see 8.1 above). The entity might, however, simply adjust the amount of the hedging instrument to reflect the reduced volume of the hedged risk and treat this as a partial dedesignation (see 8.3 below).

Fact pattern 4

An airline with a functional currency of Swiss francs enters into a firm commitment to purchase ten new wide-bodied airplanes in two years' time. The contract to purchase those airplanes is denominated in US dollars and the airline enters into a forward exchange contract to hedge the foreign currency exposure. There is no embedded foreign currency derivative to bifurcate, as sales of wide-bodied aircrafts appear to be routinely denominated in US dollars around the world (see Chapter 46 at 5.2.1.B). The airline designates the firm commitment and the derivative in a fair value hedge. Six months into the contract, the aircraft manufacturer informs the airline that it has suffered significant delays in production and that the aircrafts will not be delivered in two years as originally planned but in three years. Payment is due when the airplanes are delivered.

The delay in payment may result in some ineffectiveness as the forward exchange and discounting rates for two years and three years are likely to be different. However, the airline could not avoid this ineffectiveness by rebalancing, because the ineffectiveness is caused by the timing difference and not basis risk that was present in the original designation.

8.2.2 Requirement to rebalance

Whether an entity is required to rebalance a hedging relationship is first and foremost a matter of fact, which is, whether the hedge ratio has changed for risk management purposes. An entity must rebalance a hedging relationship if that relationship has an unchanged risk management objective but no longer meets the hedge effectiveness requirements regarding the hedge ratio. This will, in effect, be the case if the hedge ratio is no longer the one that is actually used for risk management (see 6.4.3 above). *[IFRS 9.6.5.5]*.

However, consistent with initial designation, the hedge ratio used for hedge accounting purposes may have to differ from the hedge ratio used for risk management if the latter would result in ineffectiveness that could result in an accounting outcome that would be inconsistent with the purpose of hedge accounting (see 6.4.3 above). *[IFRS 9.B6.5.14]*. The guidance in IFRS 9 clarifies that an accounting outcome that would be inconsistent with the purpose of hedge accounting as the result of failing to adjust the hedge ratio for risk management purposes, would not meet the qualifying criteria for hedge accounting. This simply means that the qualifying criteria treat inappropriate hedge ratios in the same way, irrespective of whether they were achieved by acting (inappropriate designation) or failure to act (by not adjusting a designation that has become inappropriate). *[IFRS 9.B6.5.13]*.

IFRS 9 also clarifies that not every change in the extent of offset between the hedging instrument and the hedged item constitutes a change in the relationship that requires rebalancing. For example, hedge ineffectiveness arising from a fluctuation around an otherwise valid hedge ratio cannot be reduced by adjusting the hedge ratio. *[IFRS 9.B6.5.11, B6.5.12]*. A trend in the amount of ineffectiveness on the other hand might suggest that retaining the hedge ratio would result in increased ineffectiveness going forward.

Accordingly, in order to continue to apply hedge accounting, an entity must rebalance the hedge ratio for accounting purposes if required as part of the prospective effectiveness assessment. IFRS 9 acknowledges that such an assessment is usually inherent in effective risk management monitoring, and so in many cases existing risk management process may be sufficient to determine whether accounting rebalancing is required or not. *[IFRS 9.BC6.301]*.

IFRS 9 does not specify the nature of the assessment to determine if rebalancing is required. Therefore, the nature of the assessment requires judgement based on the facts and circumstances of the hedge relationship. For example, a hedge involving two underlyings with correlation that has been historically volatile would likely require more robust analysis than two underlyings that have shown consistent correlation over many years. As another example, a relationship that has been under-hedging for four consecutive quarters would likely require more robust analysis than a relationship constantly moving to and from an over- and under-hedge position.

Regardless of the chosen assessment methodology, it is clear that rebalancing is not a mathematical optimization exercise. *[IFRS 9.BC6.310]*. Accordingly, hedges are not required to be perfectly effective, but judgement will be required to determine if rebalancing is necessary or not. Therefore, at each reporting date, entities should document the work performed to determine whether rebalancing is necessary or not, and any judgements made.

8.2.3   Mechanics of rebalancing

Rebalancing is accounted for as a continuation of the hedging relationship. On rebalancing, any hedge ineffectiveness arising from the hedging relationship is determined and recognised immediately before adjusting the hedging relationship. *[IFRS 9.B6.5.8]*.

Once any hedge ineffectiveness has been recognised, rebalancing can be achieved by:

- increasing the volume of the hedged item;
- increasing the volume of the hedging instrument;
- decreasing the volume of the hedged item; or
- decreasing the volume of the hedging instrument. *[IFRS 9.B6.5.16]*.

Decreasing the volume of the hedging instrument or hedged item does not mean that the respective transactions or items no longer exist or are no longer expected to occur. As demonstrated in Examples 53.83 and 53.84 below, rebalancing only changes what is designated in the particular hedging relationship.

Example 53.83: **Rebalancing the hedge ratio by decreasing the volume of the hedging instrument**

1 January

An entity expects to purchase 1m barrels of West Texas Intermediate (WTI) crude oil in 12 months. The entity designates a futures contract of 1.05m barrels of Brent crude oil in a cash flow hedge to hedge the highly probable forecast purchase of 1m barrels of WTI crude oil (hedge ratio of 1.05:1) in a cash flow hedge. This hedge ratio is consistent with risk management and is not designed to result in an accounting outcome that would be inconsistent with the purpose of hedge accounting.

30 June

At 30 June, the cumulative change in the value of the hedged item is CU 200, while the cumulative change in the fair value of the hedging instrument is CU 229.

The entity would account for the hedging relationship as follows (see 7.2 above):

	CU	CU
Cash flow hedge reserve – OCI	200	
Hedge ineffectiveness – profit or loss	29	
Derivatives – hedging instruments		229

The treasurer of the entity is very sensitive to ineffectiveness and therefore considers rebalancing the hedging relationship.

The analysis of the treasurer shows that the sensitivity of Brent crude oil to WTI crude oil prices was not as expected. Going forward, the treasurer expects a different relationship between the two benchmark prices and decides to reset the hedge ratio to 0.98:1.

Rebalancing on 30 June

The treasurer can either designate more WTI exposure or de-designate part of the Brent crude oil hedging instrument. The entity decides to do the latter, that is, discontinue hedge accounting for 0.07m barrels of Brent crude oil derivatives.

Of the total of 1.05m barrels of Brent derivative, 0.07m are no longer part of the hedging relationship. Therefore, the entity needs to reclassify 7/105 (or 6.7%) of the hedging instrument in the statement of financial position to a held for trading derivative, measured at fair value through profit or loss. The hedge documentation is updated accordingly.

The entity accounts for the rebalancing as follows:

	CU	CU
Derivatives – hedging instruments	15	
Derivatives – trading		15

To reflect that a part of the derivative is no longer part of a hedging relationship.

In Example 53.83 above, the entity no longer needs to hold this portion of the derivative any longer for hedging purposes and could, therefore, close it out. If the entity chooses to keep that portion of the derivative it will of course continue to result in volatility in the profit or loss, although it would no longer be presented as hedge ineffectiveness. As mentioned, the entity could have also rebalanced by designating more WTI exposure (assuming that the higher level of exposure is highly probable of occurring). In that case, there would not be any immediate accounting entries; the entity would simply designate more WTI exposure. However, the ongoing accounting can be more complex, which is discussed in more detail below. The same would be true when rebalancing by increasing the volume of hedging instrument, in which case the entity would simply designate more of the same hedging instruments within the hedge relationship. This could be achieved either by entering into additional hedging instruments via a market transaction, or by designating existing derivatives that are not currently designated within a hedge relationship. *[IFRS 9.B6.5.16-20].*

Example 53.84: Rebalancing the hedge ratio by decreasing the volume of hedged item

1 April

An entity has highly probable forecast purchases of diesel over the next 12 months. The entity expects to get monthly deliveries of 10,000 metric tonnes at the local market price. The entity designates a futures contract referenced to the Platts Diesel D2 price with a nominal amount of 9,500 metric tonnes in a cash flow hedge, to hedge 10,000 metric tonnes of highly probable diesel purchases in September (giving a hedge ratio of 1:0.95).

30 June

At 30 June, the cumulative change in the value of hedged item is CU 820, while the cumulative change in the fair value of hedging instrument is CU 650.

The entity would account for the hedging relationship as follows:

	CU	CU
Cash flow hedge reserve – OCI	650	
Derivatives – hedging instruments		650

To account for the fair value change of the hedging instrument.

Despite the hedge only being 79% effective, no hedging ineffectiveness is recorded as a result of the 'lower of test' in the standard. *[IFRS 9.6.5.11(a)].* As per that paragraph, the amount accumulated in other comprehensive income has to be the lower of:

i) the cumulative gain or loss on the hedging instrument; and

ii) the cumulative change in fair value of the hedged item, with any remaining gain or loss on the hedging instrument being recorded in profit or loss (see 7.2 above).

Based on an analysis, the entity now believes that the appropriate hedge ratio going forward is 1:1.05. Consequently, the entity can either increase the volume of hedging instrument or decrease the volume of hedged item. Based on a cost-benefit analysis the entity decides to reduce the volume of hedged item by 952 metric tonnes.

Rebalancing on 30 June

Rebalancing a hedge ratio by decreasing the volume of hedged item is considered a partial discontinuation of the hedging relationship. *[IFRS 9.B6.5.27(a)].* The entity is discontinuing 952 (10,000 – (9,500/1.05) = 952) metric tonnes of diesel purchases while 9,048 metric tonnes of forecast purchases remain in the hedging relationship. The hedge documentation is updated accordingly. No accounting entry is required (however, the entity would have to retain the information that 952 metric tonnes of diesel were the hedged item for some part of the total life of the hedging relationship and which amount in the cash flow hedge reserve relates to this quantity of diesel).

Even though the standard allows adjusting either the quantity of hedging instrument or the quantity of the hedged item, when rebalancing, entities should consider that adjusting the hedged item will be operationally more complex than adjusting the hedging instrument because of the need to track the history of different quantities that were designated during the term of the hedging relationship. For example, if a quantity of 10 tonnes of a hedged item were added to increase the quantity of hedged item and later deducted to decrease it, those 10 tonnes would have been part of the hedged item for only a part of the life of the hedging relationship. However, the amount accumulated in the cash flow hedge reserve, would still, in part, relate to that quantity, even though it is not currently part of a cash flow hedge. Therefore, ongoing tracking of the 10 tonnes is required to ensure appropriate recycling of the amounts previously taken to the cash flow hedge reserve (see 7.2.2 above). This can get more complex in situations in which the hedging relationship needs frequent rebalancing, if not all hedged transactions occur at the same time, or in conjunction with the cost formulas used for the measurement of the cost of inventory (for example a first in first out formula) (see Chapter 22 at 3.2). In addition, risk management would normally adjust the quantity of the designated hedging instruments when rebalancing, since the hedged exposure is normally the 'given' and drives what hedges are needed.

When rebalancing a hedging relationship, an entity must update its analysis of the sources of ineffectiveness in the hedge documentation. *[IFRS 9.B6.5.21]*.

8.3 Discontinuation

An entity must discontinue hedge accounting prospectively if either of the following occurs:
- the hedging relationship ceases to meet the qualifying criteria (after taking into account any rebalancing of the hedging relationship, if applicable) (see 8.1 and 8.2 above). An example would include where an eligible hedged item no longer exists (see 8.3.4 below); or
- the hedging instrument expires or is sold, terminated, or exercised.

For the purpose of the second of these two occurrences, the replacement or a rollover of a hedging instrument into another hedging instrument is not an expiration or termination if that is part of and consistent with a documented risk management objective, such as a rollover hedging strategy (see 7.7 above).

There is a further exception, introduced when regulators began to mandate the clearing of over the counter derivatives through a central clearing house (see 8.3.3 below).

These two occurrences are the only circumstances when a hedge is discontinued, as voluntary discontinuation is not permitted under IFRS 9.

Discontinuing hedge accounting can either affect a hedging relationship in its entirety or only a part of it (in which case hedge accounting continues for the remainder of the hedging relationship). *[IFRS 9.6.5.6]*.

The table below summarises the main scenarios resulting in either full or partial discontinuation:

Scenario	Discontinuation
The risk management objective has changed (see 8.3.3. below)	Full or partial
There is no longer an economic relationship between the hedged item and the hedging instrument (see 6.4.1 above)	Full
The effect of credit risk dominates the value changes of the hedging relationship (see 6.4.2 above)	Full
As part of rebalancing, the volume of the hedged item or the hedging instrument is reduced (see 8.2 above)	Partial
The hedging instrument expires	Full
The hedging instrument is (in full or in part) sold, terminated or exercised	Full or partial
The hedged item (or part of it) no longer exists or is no longer highly probable (see 8.3.4 below)	Full or partial

A logical consequence of linking the discontinuation to the risk management objective is that, as already mentioned, voluntary discontinuations are not permitted just for accounting purposes. In developing the standard, the IASB noted that hedge accounting is an exception to the general accounting principles in IFRS, in order to (better) present in the financial statements a particular risk management objective of a risk management activity. If that risk management objective is unchanged and the qualifying criteria for hedge accounting are still met, a voluntary discontinuation would be inconsistent with the original (valid) reason for applying hedge accounting. The Board believes that hedge accounting, including its discontinuation, should have a meaning and should not be a mere accounting exercise. *[IFRS 9.BC6.327]*. Based on this, the IASB decided not to allow voluntary discontinuation for hedges with unchanged risk management objectives. *[IFRS 9.BC6.331]*.

This change gave rise to concern among some constituents who argued that, given hedge accounting is optional, voluntary discontinuation should be permitted (as it was previously under IAS 39). *[IFRS 9.BC6.324]*.

However, many of the circumstances in which an entity applying IAS 39 might have voluntarily discontinued hedge accounting do not arise in the same way under IFRS 9. For example, it is not necessary to discontinue hedge accounting in order:

- to adjust the hedge ratio for a change in the expected relationship between the hedged item and the hedging instrument (see 8.2 above);
- to hedge a secondary risk (e.g. where an entity first hedges the commodity price risk in a commodity purchase contract in foreign currency but later decides to hedge the foreign currency risk as well (see 2.7 above));
- to amend the chosen effectiveness method if it becomes no longer appropriate (see 6.3 above); or
- because some of the hedged cash flows are no longer expected to occur (see 8.3.4 below).

These circumstances are all addressed in IFRS 9 by inclusion of: rebalancing, the ability to achieve hedge accounting for aggregated exposures, no longer requiring hedges to be 'highly effective' and partial discontinuation. Hence, voluntary discontinuation is not needed in such situations.

It is important to note that the risk management objective of an individual hedging relationship can change although the risk management strategy of the entity remains unchanged (see 6.2 above and 8.3.3 below)). *[IFRS 9.BC6.330]*. In fact, in most cases where an entity might wish to 'voluntarily dedesignate' a hedging relationship, this is usually driven by a change in the risk management objective, in which case the entity would actually be required to amend its hedge accounting under IFRS 9. The standard prohibits voluntary dedesignations when they are only made for accounting purposes.

As a result of the reforms mandated by the Financial Stability Board following the financial crisis, regulators are pushing for benchmark interbank offered rates (IBORs) such as LIBOR to be replaced by new 'official' benchmark rates, known as Risk Free Rates (RFRs). Such a change will necessarily affect future cash flows in both contractual floating rate financial instruments currently referenced to IBOR, and highly probably forecast transactions for which IBOR is designated as the hedged risk. This raises a number of accounting questions, not least whether changes to the hedged or hedging instrument required by the reform might lead to the discontinuation of hedge relationships. In September 2019 and August 2020 the IASB issued amendments to IFRS 9 (and IAS 39) to address the accounting issues that arise as result of the reform (see 9 below).

8.3.1 Accounting for discontinuation of fair value hedge accounting

On discontinuation of a hedge relationship for which the hedged item is a financial instrument (or component thereof) measured at amortised cost, any adjustment arising from a hedging gain or loss on the hedged item must be amortised to profit or loss. The amortisation is based on a recalculated effective interest rate at the date the amortisation begins. The treatment of any fair value hedge adjustments on discontinuation should also be applied to partial discontinuations. *[IFRS 9.6.5.10]*.

In the case of a debt instrument (or component thereof) that is a hedged item measured at fair value through other comprehensive income (see 7.1.1 above), the amortisation is applied in the same manner as for financial instruments measured at amortised cost, but to other comprehensive income instead of by adjusting the carrying amount. *[IFRS 9.6.5.10]*.

On discontinuation of a fair value hedge for which the hedged item is not a financial instrument, the entity ceases to make any further adjustment arising from a hedging gain or loss on the hedged item, and any previous adjustment from fair value hedge accounting becomes part of the carrying amount of the hedged item, as per the general requirements when accounting for fair value hedges (see 7.1.1 above). *[IFRS 9.6.5.8(b)]*.

If the hedged item no longer exists, which may be the reason the hedge relationship has been discontinued (see 8.3.4 below), any hedging gain or loss on the hedged item will be accounted for on application of the usual derecognition guidance for the hedged item, as the gain or loss forms part of its carrying amount.

8.3.2 Accounting for discontinuation of cash flow hedge accounting

When an entity discontinues hedge accounting for a cash flow hedge, it must account for the amount that has been accumulated in the cash flow hedge reserve as follows:

- the amount remains in accumulated OCI if the hedged future cash flows are still expected to occur; or
- the amount is immediately reclassified to profit or loss as a reclassification adjustment if the hedged future cash flows are no longer expected to occur. *[IFRS 9.6.5.12]*.

After discontinuation, once the previously expected hedged cash flow occurs, any amount remaining in accumulated OCI must be accounted for depending on the nature of the underlying transaction consistent with the accounting for cash flow hedge relationships that are not discontinued (see 7.2.2 above). *[IFRS 9.6.5.12]*. The treatment of the cash flow hedge reserve on discontinuation should also be applied to partial discontinuations.

8.3.3 Change in risk management objective

An entity must discontinue hedge accounting prospectively for a hedge relationship if there is a change in the risk management objective for that hedge relationship (see 8.3 above). A change in risk management objective must be a matter of fact that can be observed in the entity's actual risk management (see 6.2 above). The examples below, the first of which is derived from the application guidance to IFRS 9, demonstrate how this could be assessed in practice. *[IFRS 9.B6.5.24]*.

Example 53.85: Partial discontinuation as a result of a change in risk management objective

ABC Ltd is currently fully financed with variable rate borrowings (the tables in this example show nominal amounts in millions of euro (EUR)):

Non-current financial liabilities as of 1 January 2021	Variable rate	Fixed rate
Variable rate borrowings	100	
Fixed rate borrowings		0
Total	100	0
	100%	0%

Risk management strategy

To maintain between 20% and 40% of long term debt at a fixed rate.

Risk management activity

To implement the strategy, the treasurer of ABC enters into a pay fixed/receive variable interest rate swap (IRS) with a notional amount of EUR 30m and designates the IRS in a hedging relationship.

Risk management objective

Use a pay fixed/receive floating interest rate swap with a notional amount of EUR 30m in a cash flow hedge of the interest payments on EUR 30m of the variable rate borrowings in order to maintain 30% of the long-term borrowings at a fixed rate.

Non-current financial liabilities as of 1 January 2021	Variable rate	Fixed rate
Variable rate borrowings	100	
Fixed rate borrowings		0
Pay fixed/receive variable interest rate swap	(30)	30
Total	70	30
	70%	30%

On 31 March 2022, the entity needs further funding and takes advantage of lower interest rates by issuing a EUR 50m fixed rate bond. At the same time, the entity decides to set its fixed rate exposure at 40% of total borrowings, still being within the existing risk management strategy.

Non-current financial liabilities as of 31 March 2022	Variable rate	Fixed rate
Variable rate borrowings	100	
Fixed rate borrowings		50
Pay fixed/receive variable interest rate swap	(30)	30
Total	70	80
	47%	53%

It is evident that ABC is no longer within the target range of its risk management strategy. In order to execute the risk management strategy, ABC no longer needs part of its interest rate swap. In other words, the risk management objective for the hedging relationship has changed. Consequently, ABC discontinues EUR 20m of the hedging relationship (a partial discontinuation). ABC may close out the risk from EUR 20m of the IRS or ABC may choose to use the EUR 20m of the IRS to hedge a different exposure or to transfer it to a trading book.

Going forward, ABC's debt financing and risk profile will be as follows: *[IFRS 9.B6.5.24(a)]*

Non-current financial liabilities as of 31 March 2022	Variable rate	Fixed rate
Variable rate borrowings	100	
Fixed rate borrowings		50
Pay fixed/receive floating interest rate swap	(10)	10
Total	90	60
	60%	40%

The above example only illustrates the outcome of one particular course of action. The entity could also have adjusted its interest rate exposure in a different way in order to remain in the target range for its fixed rate funding, for instance by swapping EUR 20m of the new fixed rate bond into variable rate funding. In that case, instead of discontinuing a part of the already existing cash flow hedge, the entity could have designated a new fair value hedge. The example in the application guidance of the standard is obviously a simplified one. In practice, entities tend to have staggered maturities for different parts of their financing. In such situations it would often be obvious from the maturity of the new interest rate swaps if they are a fair value hedge of the debt or a reduction of the already existing cash flow hedge volume. For example, if the new EUR 50m fixed rate bond is for a longer period than the existing debt and the new interest rate swap is for the same longer period, it would suggest that it is a fair value hedge of the new fixed rate bond instead of a reduction of the cash flow hedge for the already existing debt. Conversely, a reduction of the cash flow hedge volume would be consistent with entering into a new interest rate swap that has the same remaining maturity as the existing interest rate swap and offsets its fair value changes on a part of the notional amount. Whichever way an entity chooses to incorporate a change in risk management activity into its hedge accounting solution, it must be directionally consistent with its risk management strategy (see 6.2.1 above).

Example 53.86: Partial discontinuation of an interest margin hedge

XYZ Bank is holding a combination of fixed and variable rate assets and liabilities on its banking book. For risk management purposes, the bank allocates all the assets and liabilities to time bands based on their contractual maturity. As of 1 January 2021 the bank holds the following instruments in the 5-year time band (the tables in this example show nominal amounts in millions of euro (EUR)). For simplicity the example only reflects a single time band. In reality this is highly unlikely to be the case. Further, the risk management activity is also simpler than might be the case when considering numerous time bands:

Summary of instruments with a 5-year maturity	Assets: fixed rate	Liabilities: fixed rate	Assets: variable rate	Liabilities: variable rate
Bonds held			20	
Mortgages	30		10	
Retail loans	30		10	
Client term deposits				(60)
Bonds issued		(30)		(10)
Total	60	(30)	40	(70)
Fixed-variable interest mismatch		30		(30)

The fixed-variable mismatch results in interest margin risk due to changes in interest rates.

Risk management strategy

To eliminate the interest margin risk resulting from fixed-variable interest mismatches.

Risk management activity

In order to achieve the risk management strategy, XYZ Bank enters into a pay fixed/receive variable interest rate swap (IRS) with a notional amount of EUR 30m. For accounting purposes, the bank could either designate the IRS in a cash flow hedge of EUR 30m of specific variable rate liabilities or in a fair value hedge of EUR 30m of specific fixed rate assets (see 6.2.1 above). Under the local regulatory requirements, fair value hedges are more favourable for the bank's regulatory capital.

Risk management objective

Using a EUR 30m pay fixed/receive variable IRS in a fair value hedge of EUR 30m of fixed rate retail loans to hedge a fixed-variable interest mismatch on fixed and variable rate assets and liabilities in the 5-year time band of XYZ Bank's banking book.

At the beginning of year 2023, XYZ Bank attracts EUR 10m of client term deposits as a result of a successful marketing campaign. The new term deposits all have a fixed interest rate for a maturity of three years, therefore, matching the (remaining) maturity of the instruments in the above time bucket. The XYZ Bank uses the proceeds from the new term deposits to buy back EUR 10m of variable rate bonds that it has issued. The new situation in the (now) 3-year time band is:

Summary of instruments with a 3-year maturity	Assets: fixed rate	Liabilities: fixed rate	Assets: variable rate	Liabilities: variable rate
Bonds held			20	
Mortgages	30		10	
Retail loans	30		10	
Client term deposits		(10)		(60)
Bonds issued		(30)		(0)
Total	60	(40)	40	(60)
Fixed-variable interest mismatch		20		(20)
Pay fixed/receive variable interest rate swap		(30)		30

As a result of the change in funding, the risk management objective of the hedging relationship has changed. XYZ Bank is over-hedged and needs to discontinue EUR10m of its hedging relationship.

As stated above, whether the risk management objective has changed for a particular hedge relationship should be a matter of fact, and for many scenarios this will be obvious, as demonstrated in Examples 53.85 and 53.86 above. However, for more complex risk management approaches, judgement will be required to determine whether the risk management objective has changed or not. An example would be when managing the risk from a portfolio on a dynamic basis but for which 'proxy' hedge accounting relationships have been designated (see 6.2.1 above). The application guidance in IFRS 9 provides an example of how a change in the risk management objective should be considered for a dynamic risk management approach.

Example 53.87: Change in risk management objective for an open portfolio of debt instruments

An entity manages the interest rate risk of an open portfolio of debt instruments. The resultant exposure from the open portfolio frequently changes due to the addition of new debt instruments and the derecognition of debt instruments (i.e. it is different from simply running off a position as it matures). Entity A applies a dynamic process in which both the exposure and the hedging instruments used to manage it do not remain the same for long. Consequently, Entity A frequently adjusts the hedging instruments used to manage the interest rate risk as the exposure changes. For example, debt instruments with 24 months' remaining maturity are designated as the hedged item for interest rate risk for 24 months. The same procedure is applied to other time buckets or maturity periods. After a short period of time, Entity A discontinues all, some or a part of the previously designated hedging relationships and designates new hedging relationships for maturity periods on the basis of their size and the hedging instruments that exist at that time. The discontinuation of hedge accounting in this situation reflects that those hedging relationships are established in such a way that Entity A looks at a new hedging instrument and a new hedged item instead of the hedging instrument and the hedged item that were designated previously. The risk management strategy remains the same, but there is no risk management objective that continues for those previously designated hedging relationships, which as such no longer exist.

In such a situation, the discontinuation of hedge accounting applies to the extent to which the risk management objective has changed. This depends on the situation of an entity and could, for example, affect all or only some hedging relationships of a maturity period, or only part of a hedging relationship. *[IFRS 9.B6.5.24(b)].*

The above example would, in particular, appear to be relevant if an entity with a dynamic risk management approach to interest rate risk within an open portfolio designates its risk management activity as a macro cash flow hedge (see 10.2 below).

8.3.4 Documented hedged item no longer exists

Hedge accounting is only permitted for eligible hedged items, hence hedge accounting must be discontinued if the hedged item no longer exists (see 8.3 above). Partial discontinuation is required if only a part of the hedged item no longer exists. *[IFRS 9.6.5.6].* For partial discontinuations, it is important that the hedge relationship containing the remaining hedged item continues to meet the qualifying criteria in order to continue hedge accounting (see 6 above).

Specific guidance is provided on the accounting for the adjustment arising from a hedging gain or loss on the hedged item in a fair value hedge or the amount accumulated in OCI in a cash flow hedge on discontinuation of a hedge relationship (see 8.3.1 and 8.3.2 above).

In many cases it will be straight forward to determine whether the hedged item exists or not, but in all cases that determination will need to be made with respect to the documented description of the hedged item made on initial designation (see 6.3 above). The importance of the initial documentation of hedged items and the impact it can have over the life the hedge relationship is illustrated below in Examples 53.88-53.90. In all the examples below, it is assumed that the qualifying criteria for application of hedge accounting are met on initial designation (see 6 above).

Example 53.88: Interruption of hedged forecast cash flows

An entity with sterling as its functional currency documents the designation of its forecast euro highly probable sales of €100,000 each month throughout 2021 as hedged items in a cash flow hedge of the risk of changes in foreign currency rates (see 2.6.1 and 6.3.3 above). It hedges these sales by entering into a series of forward foreign currency contracts, one for each month. Business is severely interrupted for a number of months (e.g. from a fire in the warehouse or a global pandemic) such that sales in May, June and July are now expected to be zero. The hedged cash flows for May, June and July therefore no longer exist. Hedge accounting for those cash flows should be discontinued and the associated amounts in OCI recycled to profit or loss immediately. This is despite the fact that the entity may have unhedged euro sales in subsequent months, as they do not meet the description of the hedged item as documented. This is the case even if there is a belief that greater than originally expected euro sales in subsequent months would arise as a catch up of sales that did not take place in earlier months.

Example 53.89: Change in forecast hedged item

Entity X, a specialist supplier and fitter of luxury vehicles, with euro functional currency has negotiated a sale of a bespoke luxury yacht. It is highly probable the sale will be made to a particular US customer in September 2021. Given the customized nature of the yacht specifications and the currency of the customer, the sales price was negotiated in US dollars (see 2.2.5 above). Entity X designates the highly probable forecast sale of the bespoke luxury yacht for USD 10m as the hedged item in a cash flow hedge of the risk of changes in foreign currency rates.

Subsequently the sale is delayed due to delivery issues, and it is now expected to occur in December 2021. Although the expected timing has changed, the sale of the bespoke luxury yacht to the particular US customer is still highly probable and so the documented hedged item still exists. The change in timing may however result in some additional ineffectiveness (see 7.4.2 above).

Whilst Examples 53.88 and 53.89 above both include a scenario in which the expectations of the entity undertaking the risk management activity have changed with respect to timing of foreign currency cash flows, it can be seen from the above that the outcome for the hedge relationship is quite different. In Example 53.88 in which the hedged item is defined by its timing, i.e. sales in May, June and July 2021, a change in timing would redefine the hedged item such that it is different to the original documented hedged item. By contrast, in Example 53.89 the definition of the hedged item is the highly probable sale of a bespoke luxury yacht itself. The time period in which a forecast transaction is expected to occur must be identified and documented within a reasonably specific and generally narrow range of time from a most probable date in order to determine that the forecast transaction is highly probable (see 6.3.3 above). *[IAS 39.F.3.11]*. However, a change in the estimate of the timing of the sale of a bespoke luxury yacht does not of itself redefine the hedged item, hence it is still highly probable the original hedged item will occur.

Example 53.90: Change in hedged forecast debt issuance

As at 1 January 2021 Entity A expects to issue highly probable 10 year floating rate debt in June 2021. In order to hedge cash flow variability from changes in SONIA, Entity A transacts a forward starting 10 year pay fixed, receive SONIA interest rate swap (IRS) from June 2021. The IRS is designated in a cash flow hedge for changes in SONIA interest rates.

There are a number of ways in which the hedged item (i.e. the forecast debt) might be documented for that hedge relationship. For the purposes of illustration, set out below are two possible ways key aspects of the hedged items might be described in the documentation. Additional information, not provided here, is likely to be required in order to meet all of the requirements of the standard (see 6.3 above):

a) the variability of cash flows on 10 year £100m debt expected to be issued in June 2021 attributable to the risk of changes in SONIA; or

b) the variability of cash flows arising on forecast GBP interest flows (based on £100m principal) between June 2021 and June 2031, attributable to the risk of changes in SONIA

Let us now consider various scenarios that might arise sometime after designation of the hedge relationship, and how the documentation of the hedged item would affect the outcome for hedge accounting:

(i) £100m debt was issued in June 2021, but at a fixed interest rate based on SONIA plus a spread.

For both a) and b) it appears the documented hedged item still exists.

However, it is likely that the IRS would be closed out once the debt was issued. This would have no bearing on the hedge relationship, which would already have ended as there is no further variability in cash flows from the issued fixed rate debt. As the hedged items are still expected to occur, the amount accumulated in OCI must be reclassified from the cash flow hedge reserve to profit or loss as a reclassification adjustment in the periods that interest expense is recognised in profit or loss (see 7.2.2 above).

(ii)   £100m floating rate debt (monthly coupons) was issued in September 2021

If the issued debt met the description under a) in all areas other than timing, it is likely that the hedged item in a) still exists. However, some ineffectiveness will arise due to the change in timing of the hedged item. This case is similar to that of the specialist supplier and fitter of luxury vehicles in Example 53.89 above, for which the forecast sale of the bespoke luxury yacht was delayed. In both cases, the identification of the documented hedged item was defined by the transaction itself, rather than its timing.

For hedged item b) the hedged interest flows from June to August 2021 do not exist (similar to the conclusion in Example 53.88 above), but the remaining interest flows until June 2031 are still highly probable of occurring. Assessment of the effectiveness requirements and measurement of ineffectiveness must reflect the fact that the June to August 2021 flows no longer exist. If a hypothetical derivative is used for assessment and measurement purposes it will need to be updated to reflect the fact that no interest flows will occur from June to August 2021. This will lead to an additional source of ineffectiveness which must be considered within the economic relationship assessment and is likely to lead to the recognition of ineffectiveness (see 6.4.1 and 7.2.1 above). Any amounts remaining in OCI relating to the June to August 2021 cash flows that are no longer expected to occur should be recycled immediately to profit or loss (see 8.3.2 above).

It can be seen that documentation of the hedged item on initial designation requires careful consideration, as it is a key determinant through the life of the hedge relationship as to whether the hedged item continues to exist.

Although it may seem potentially beneficial to be intentionally vague when documenting a hedged item in order to reduce the possibility that some unforeseen circumstance might require discontinuation of a hedge relationship, the documentation must be sufficiently specific in order to ascertain whether the hedged item has occurred or not. Having said that, this does not mean the hedge documentation needs to specify the hedged item in every single detail. As mentioned above, the key aim of the documentation is to provide clarity as to whether the hedged item has occurred or not, hence a balance needs to be struck to achieve an appropriate level of specificity. The Implementation Guidance within IAS 39 contained some guidance on the need for sufficient specificity of the documented hedged item, this guidance can be considered relevant for IFRS 9 hedge accounting (see 6.3 above). *[IAS 39.F.3.10, IFRS 9.BC6.200].*

8.3.5   Impact of novation to central clearing parties on cash flow hedges

The collapse of some financial institutions during the financial crisis highlighted the potential impact of credit risk on the global derivatives markets. In response to this, several jurisdictions have introduced, legal or regulatory requirements that require or incentivise over-the-counter (OTC) derivatives to be novated to a central clearing party (CCP). The CCP would usually require the derivatives to be collateralised, thereby reducing (potentially significantly) the counterparty credit risk.

Following an urgent request, the IFRS Interpretation Committee concluded in January 2013 that an entity is required to discontinue hedge accounting where an OTC derivative that is designated as hedging instrument in a hedging relationship is novated to a CCP (unless, very unusually, the novation represented a replacement or rollover of the hedging instrument as part of a documented hedging strategy (see 7.7 above)). This is because the novated derivative is derecognised and the new derivative contract, with the CCP as a counterparty, is recognised at the time of the novation. However, if the new derivative was designated in a cash flow hedge relationship accounting ineffectiveness would likely arise if the derivative is off market (see 7.4.3 above). Consequently, the Interpretations Committee decided to recommend that the IASB make a narrow-scope amendment to IAS 39 to permit continuation of hedge accounting in such narrow circumstances.[25] In July 2013 the IASB amended IAS 39 after the publication of an exposure draft in February 2013 and the changes were also incorporated in IFRS 9 when the hedge accounting chapter was added in November 2013.

The relevant guidance in IFRS 9 states that an expiration or termination of the hedging instrument does not require discontinuation of the hedge relationship if:

- as a consequence of changes in laws or regulations, the original counterparty to the hedging instrument is replaced by a clearing counterparty (sometimes called a 'clearing organisation' or 'clearing agency') or a clearing member of a clearing organisation or a client of a clearing member of a clearing organisation, that are acting as counterparty in order to effect clearing by a central counterparty;
- each of the original counterparties to the hedging instrument effects clearing with the same central counterparty; and
- other changes, if any, to the hedging instrument are limited to those that are necessary to effect such a replacement of the counterparty. Such changes are limited to those that are consistent with the terms that would be expected if the hedging instrument were originally cleared with the clearing counterparty. These changes include changes in the collateral requirements, rights to offset receivables and payables balances, and charges levied. *[IFRS 9.6.5.6]*.

It can be seen from the guidance that the exception applies to some, but not all, voluntary novations to a CCP. In order for hedge accounting to continue, a voluntary novation should at least be associated with laws or regulations that are relevant to central clearing of derivatives. For example, a voluntary novation could be in anticipation of regulatory changes. However, the mere possibility of laws or regulations being introduced is not, in the view of the IASB, a sufficient basis for continuation of hedge accounting. *[IAS 39.BC220O-BC220Q]*.

Further, the exception also applies to so-called 'indirect clearing' arrangements whereby a clearing member of a CCP provides an indirect clearing service to its client or where a group entity is clearing on behalf of another entity within the same group since they are consistent with the objective of the amendments. *[IAS 39.BC220R, BC220S]*.

A further impact of novating derivatives to a CCP is that the derivatives are likely to become collateralised by cash. The July 2013 amendments to IFRS 9 acknowledged this and provided clarity that such a change on novation to a CCP would not result in derecognition if such changes are limited to those that are consistent with the terms that would be expected if the hedging instrument were originally cleared with the clearing counterparty. *[IFRS 9.6.5.6]*.

Cash collateralisation significantly reduces the credit risk for both parties involved, which will influence the fair value of derivatives novated. The application guidance clarifies that the change in the fair value of the hedging instrument that results from the changes to the contract in connection with the novation (e.g. a change in the collateral arrangements) must be included in the measurement of hedge ineffectiveness. *[IFRS 9.B6.4.3]*.

The other criteria for achieving hedge accounting will still need to be met in order to continue hedge accounting (see at 6 above).

8.3.6 The impact of the introduction of settle to market derivatives on cash flow hedges

In December 2015, the London Clearing House (LCH) changed its rule book to introduce a new type of settled-to-market (STM) interest rate swap in addition to the previously existing collateralized-to-market (CTM) swaps.

In the existing CTM model, transactions cleared through LCH are subject to daily cash variation margining. This means that the replacement value of the trade is in effect paid or received as cash each day and there is no ability to recover any of the variation margin unless the fair value of the interest rate swap changes. In addition, the variation margin is also used to settle the periodic swaps payments, and, in case of early settlement, the variation margin is used to settle the outstanding derivative position. Interest is paid on the variation margin based on a risk free overnight rate.

In the STM model, transactions have the same economic exposure and overall cash flows as in the CTM model, except that the previous daily variation margin is now treated as a settlement of the interest rate swap's outstanding fair value. While the swap is gradually settled, it remains the same swap with the same original terms (e.g. the fixed rate, maturity date etc.). In order to maintain the same economics, a new feature of the STM swap pricing is the Price Alignment Interest (PAI) that essentially replicates what would have been the interest on the collateral for a CTM swap into the STM swap pricing.

The introduction of the STM swaps was primarily driven by the potentially different regulatory treatment they attract and at first sight it may appear that the accounting impact is limited since the existing CTM swap replacement values and related cash collateral are already normally offset in the statement of financial position. There are however some important accounting considerations if swaps designated in on-going hedging relationships are migrated from the CTM model to the STM model. The first question that arises is whether the change results in the de-designation of the existing hedge relationship and hence the need to re-designate a new hedging relationship with a derivative that is now likely to have a non-zero fair value (and so give rise to ineffectiveness if designated in a cash flow hedge). We consider that the amendment of each swap from being CTM to STM is not a substantial modification and so does not result in derecognition of one swap and the recognition of another. Accordingly, we believe that there is no requirement to de-designate the existing hedging relationship. The second question that arises is how the PAI should be considered in the hedge effectiveness measurement and whether any hypothetical derivative can be assumed to reflect these new terms (see 7.4.4 above). No consistent interpretation of the accounting requirements has yet emerged with respect to the measurement of ineffectiveness from the PAI. This is an area where we expect practice to continue to evolve.

8.3.7 Change of hedging counterparty within the same consolidated group

An entity may be required to, or choose to, novate a hedging instrument from one entity within a consolidated group, to another entity within the same group. For example, following the vote by the United Kingdom to leave the European Union in June 2016, commonly known as 'Brexit', Corporate A (the hedging entity) might plan to novate existing hedging derivatives with Bank UK (the hedging counterparty entity), to Bank EU, both Bank UK and Bank EU are subsidiaries of the same global banking group. Alternatively, a banking group may undertake an internal reorganisation such that a portfolio of derivatives (or a whole business) is transferred into a different entity within the same banking group. In both instances a question arises as to whether such a change in hedging derivative counterparty will result in the discontinuation of a hedge relationship.

We set out below the accounting requirement from the perspective of the various parties in the fact pattern – on the assumption that all parties designate the novated derivative in an eligible hedge relationship, consistent with their risk management objective.

- In the standalone financial statements of the original hedging counterparty, (i.e. Bank UK in the Brexit example above), it is clear that a hedge relationship would be discontinued, as an eligible hedging instrument no longer exists within that hedging counterparty legal entity.

- In the standalone financial statements of the new hedging counterparty (i.e. Bank EU in the Brexit example above), it is clear that a new hedge relationship would need to be designated (including identification of an eligible hedged item), as this entity is not party to the instruments designated in the previous hedge relationship (unless the derivative and designated hedged item were both included in a business transferred as part of the common control transaction (see Chapter 8 at 4.4.2)).

- In the consolidated financial statements of a parent that consolidates both the original hedging counterparty (i.e. Bank UK) and the new hedging counterparty (i.e. Bank EU), (i.e. the global banking group in the Brexit example above) the hedge relationship will continue. This is because an entity first consolidates all subsidiaries and then applies the derecognition guidance to financial instruments. *[IFRS 9.3.2.1]*. Accordingly, the hedging derivative still exists within the consolidated financial statement, hence there is no requirement to discontinue the hedge relationship.

- From the perspective of the hedging entity (i.e. Corporate A), the transfer of a derivative from one counterparty to another would ordinarily result in derecognition and hence a de-designation and re-designation of a hedge relationship. However, the appropriate treatment will depend on the specific facts and circumstances.

8.3.8 Disposal of a hedged net investment

The amount relating to a net investment hedge that has been accumulated in the foreign currency translation reserve must be reclassified from equity to profit or loss as a reclassification adjustment on disposal or, in certain circumstances, partial disposal of the foreign operation in accordance with IAS 21 (see Chapter 15 at 6.6 and 7.3 above). *[IFRS 9.6.5.14]*.

When a foreign operation that was hedged is disposed of, the amount reclassified from the foreign currency translation reserve to profit or loss is as follows:

- in respect of the hedging instrument in the consolidated financial statements, the cumulative gain or loss on the hedging instrument that was determined to be an effective hedge (see 7.3.1 above); and *[IFRIC 16.16]*

- in respect of the net investment, the cumulative amount of exchange differences relating to that foreign operation. *[IAS 21.48, IFRIC 16.17]*.

If an intermediate parent exists within the ultimate consolidation group, there is a choice of applying either the direct or step-by-step method of consolidation (see Chapter 15 at 6.1.5 and at 6.6). If the step by step method of consolidation is used, the cumulative amount of exchange differences relating to that foreign operation accumulated in the foreign currency transaction reserve could be different to the equivalent amount had the direct method of consolidation been applied. This potential difference in the accounting outcome on disposal of a foreign operation is illustrated in Example 53.91 below.

This difference in accounting treatment could be eliminated, but there is no requirement to do so. An accounting policy choice must be taken as to whether the difference is eliminated or not, and such a choice must be applied consistently on disposal of all net investments. *[IFRIC 16.17].*

Example 53.91: Disposal of foreign operation

Based on the same facts as in Examples 53.48 and 53.49 at 5.3.1 and 5.3.2 above, the group has designated US$300 million of the US dollar borrowings of A as a hedge of the net investment in C with the risk being the spot foreign currency exposure (€/US$) between P and C. If C were disposed of, the amounts reclassified to profit or loss in P's consolidated financial statements from its foreign currency translation reserve would be: *[IFRIC 16.17, AG8]*

- in respect of A's borrowing (the hedging instrument), the total change in value in respect of foreign currency risk that was recognised in other comprehensive income as the effective portion of the hedge (i.e. the retranslation effect on the US$300 million borrowing with respect to the EUR/USD foreign currency rate since initial designation); and
- in respect of the net investment in C, the amount determined by the entity's consolidation method:
  - If P uses the direct method, its foreign currency translation reserve ('FCTR') in respect of C will be determined directly by the EUR/USD foreign currency rate.
  - If P uses the step-by-step method, its FCTR in respect of C will be determined by the FCTR recognised by B reflecting the GBP/USD foreign currency rate, translated to P's functional currency using the EUR/GBP foreign currency rate.

P's use of the step-by-step method for consolidation in prior periods does not require it to or preclude it from determining the amount of FCTR to be reclassified when it disposes of C to be the amount that it would have recognised if it had always used the direct method. However, it is an accounting policy choice which should be followed consistently on disposal of all net investments.

9 INTEREST RATE BENCHMARK REFORM

As a result of the reforms mandated by the Financial Stability Board following the financial crisis, regulators are pushing for benchmark interbank offered rates (IBORs) such as LIBOR to be replaced by new 'official' benchmark rates, known as Risk Free Rates (RFRs). For instance, in the UK, the new official benchmark is the reformed Sterling Overnight Interest Average (SONIA) and panel banks will no longer be required to submit the quotes used to build LIBOR beyond the end of 2021. Such a change will affect future cash flows in both contractual floating rate financial instruments currently referenced to IBOR, and highly probably forecast transactions for which IBOR is designated as the hedged risk. This raises a number of accounting questions, many of which relate to hedge accounting.

In 2018, the IASB noted the increasing level of uncertainty about the long-term viability of some interest rate benchmarks and decided to add a project to its agenda to consider the financial reporting implications of the reform. The IASB identified two groups of accounting issues that could have financial reporting implications. These are:

- *Phase 1:* pre-replacement issues – issues affecting financial reporting in the period before the replacement of an existing interest rate benchmark with an alternative RFR; and
- *Phase 2:* replacement issues – issues that might affect financial reporting when an existing interest rate benchmark is replaced with an alternative RFR.

The IASB prioritised the Phase 1 issues because they were more urgent, and in September 2019 the IASB issued *Interest Rate Benchmark Reform, Amendments to IFRS 9, IAS 39 and IFRS 7* (the Phase 1 amendments) to address them. The Phase 1 amendments provided a number of temporary exceptions from applying specific hedge accounting requirements of both IFRS 9 (see 9.1 below) and IAS 39 (see 9.1.2 below), but added some additional disclosure requirements to IFRS 7 – *Financial Instruments: Disclosures*. The disclosure requirements are covered in Chapter 54 at 4.3.5.

In August 2020 the IASB issued *Interest Rate Benchmark Reform Phase 2, Amendments to IFRS 9, IAS 39, IFRS 7, IFRS 4 and IFRS 16* (the Phase 2 amendments). The Phase 2 amendments provide the following with respect to changes in financial instruments that are directly required by the reform:

- a practical expedient when accounting for the modification of financial assets and liabilities (see Chapter 50 at 3.8.3 and Chapter 52 at 3.4.3);
- reliefs from discontinuing hedge relationships (see 9.2.1 below);
- temporary relief from having to meet the separately identifiable requirement when an RFR instrument is designated as a hedge of a risk component (see 9.2.2 below); and
- additional disclosures (see Chapter 54 at 5.7).

9.1 Phase 1 reliefs

The reliefs apply to all hedging relationships that are directly affected by uncertainties due to IBOR reform about the timing or amount of interest rate benchmark-based cash flows of the hedged item or hedging instrument (i.e. uncertainty about what the new benchmark will be and when it will take effect). *[IFRS 9.6.8.1]*. However, if the hedged item or hedging instrument is designated for risks other than just interest rate risk, the exceptions only apply to the interest rate benchmark-based cash flows. The relief does not therefore apply to net investment hedges, as the hedged item must have interest-based cashflows to be eligible.

Application of the reliefs is mandatory. *[IFRS 9.7.1.8]*. The first three reliefs for IFRS 9 provide for:

1. The assessment of whether a forecast transaction (or component thereof) is highly probable (see 2.6.1 above); *[IFRS 9.6.8.4]*
2. Assessing when to reclassify the amount in the cash flow hedge reserve to profit and loss (see 8.2.2 above); *[IFRS 9.6.8.5]* and
3. The assessment of the economic relationship between the hedged item and the hedging instrument (see 6.4.1 above). *[IFRS 9.6.8.6]*.

On application of each of these reliefs, it must be assumed that the benchmark on which the hedged cash flows are based (whether or not contractually specified) and/or, for relief three, the benchmark on which the cash flows of the hedging instrument are based, are not altered as a result of IBOR reform.

Example 53.92: Application of Phase 1 relief for interest rate benchmark reform

Entity A is hedging an eight year floating rate borrowing referenced to 3m IBOR, and it is known that any interest coupons payable after the loan has been renegotiated will not be determined with reference to IBOR, but according to the new RFR. The borrowing was previously designated in a cash flow hedge of 3m IBOR interest rate risk. There is still uncertainty due to IBOR reform about the timing or amount of interest rate benchmark-based cash flows of the loan and the associated hedging instrument. While that uncertainty exists, the Phase 1 amendment requires Entity A to ignore that fact and assume the hedged interest coupons on the borrowing and associated hedging instrument will remain IBOR flows for the purpose of assessing and measuring effectiveness.

The fourth relief provides that, for a benchmark component of interest rate risk that is affected by IBOR reform, the requirement that the risk component is separately identifiable (see 2.2.3 above) need be met only at the inception of the hedging relationship. For 'macro' hedging strategies (i.e. where hedging instruments and hedged items may be added to or removed from an open portfolio in a continuous hedging strategy resulting in frequent de-designations and re-designations) the entity need only satisfy the separately identifiable requirement when hedged items are initially designated within the hedging relationship. The entity does not subsequently need to reassess this requirement for any hedged items that have been re-designated. *[IFRS 9.6.8.7, 6.8.8].* However, the Phase 1 amendments do not provide any relief from the requirement that changes in the fair value or cash flows of the risk component must be reliably measurable. *[IFRS 9.BC6.575].*

The reliefs are intended to be narrow in their effect, such that other than the specific reliefs provided, the usual requirements within the IFRS 9 hedge accounting guidance must be applied. The Basis for Conclusions contains an example of where relief will not be available: benchmark-based cash flows cannot be assumed to still be highly probable if an entity decides not to issue forecast debt due to the uncertainties arising from IBOR reform. *[IFRS 9.BC6.560].* Also, to the extent that a hedging instrument is altered so that its cash flows are based on an RFR, but the hedged item is still based on IBOR (or *vice versa*), there is no relief from measuring and recording any ineffectiveness that arises due to differences in their changes in fair value. *[IFRS 9.BC6.567, BC6.568].*

The effective date of the amendments is for annual periods beginning on or after 1 January 2020, although earlier application was permitted. The requirements must be applied retrospectively, however, the reliefs only apply to hedging relationships that existed at the beginning of the reporting period in which an entity first applies those requirements or were designated thereafter, and to the amount accumulated in the cash flow hedge reserve that existed at the beginning of the reporting period in which an entity first applies those requirements. It follows that it is not possible to apply the requirements retroactively to hedge relationships that were not previously designated as such. *[IFRS 9.7.2.26(d)].*

9.1.1 End of Phase 1 reliefs

Reliefs one and two above will cease to apply prospectively at the earlier of when the uncertainty arising from IBOR reform is no longer present with respect to the timing and amount of the benchmark-based cash flows of the hedged item, and:

- for relief one, when the hedging relationship that the hedged item is part of is discontinued; and
- for relief two, when the entire amount accumulated in the cash flow hedge reserve has been reclassified to profit and loss. *[IFRS 9.6.8.9, 6.8.10]*.

Relief three will cease prospectively:

- for a hedged item when the uncertainty arising from IBOR reform is no longer present with respect to the timing and amount of benchmark-based cash flows of the hedged item;
- for a hedging instrument, when the uncertainty arising from IBOR reform is no longer present with respect to the timing and amount of benchmark-based cash flows of the hedging instrument; and
- if the hedging relationship is discontinued before either of the two above events occur, at the date of discontinuation. *[IFRS 9.6.8.11]*.

When an entity designates a group of items as the hedged item, the end of relief requirements would be applied prospectively to each individual item within the designated group of items. *[IFRS 9.6.8.12]*.

Relief four ceases either when the formal designation of the hedge relationship is amended applying the Phase 2 relief (see 9.2.1 below) or when the hedging relationship is discontinued, applying the normal IFRS 9 discontinuation guidance (see 8.3 above). This means that until either of these occur, the risk component may continue to be designated, even if it is no longer separately identifiable. This is particularly relevant for fair value hedges as the hedged items will generally not need to be amended for the reform. *[IFRS 9.6.8.13]*.

The reliefs will continue indefinitely in the absence of any of the events described above. The Basis for Conclusions sets out a number of different fact patterns, which could arise as contracts are amended in anticipation of IBOR reform, to illustrate when uncertainties due to IBOR reform will end. *[IFRS 9.BC6.587-593]*. The key message is that, in most cases, relief will only end when a contract is amended to specify both what the new benchmark will be and when it will take effect.

It is noted that there could be situations in which the uncertainty for particular elements of a single hedging relationship could end at different times. For example, assume an entity is required to apply the relevant exceptions to both the hedged item and the hedging instrument, as will typically be the case for a cash flow hedge. If the hedging instrument in that hedging relationship is amended through market protocols covering all derivatives in that market, and will be based on an RFR such that the uncertainty about the timing and the amount of interest rate RFR-based cash flows of the hedging instrument is eliminated, the relevant exceptions would continue to apply to the hedged item, but would no longer apply to the hedging instrument. *[IFRS 9.BC6.594]*. The consequence of this is that any delay between the modification of the hedging instrument and the hedged item will introduce a new source of hedge ineffectiveness, specifically any changes in the basis risk between the RFR interest on the hedging instrument and the IBOR interest on the hedged item. This must be considered as part of the assessment of whether the hedge effectiveness criteria are met (see 6.4 above) and, while perhaps unlikely to result in the entity concluding that there is no longer an 'economic relationship', may lead to the recognition of additional ineffectiveness.

9.1.2 Phase 1 reliefs for IAS 39

As many entities remain under the hedge accounting requirements of IAS 39 (see 1.3 above), amendments are also proposed to IAS 39 (see 13 below). *[IAS 39.102A-102N, 108G]*. The amendments to IAS 39 are consistent with those for IFRS 9, but with the following differences:

- For the retrospective assessment of effectiveness, an entity may continue to apply hedge accounting to a hedging relationship for which effectiveness is outside of the 80–125% range during the period of uncertainty arising from the reform. This may be particularly important if there is a delay between when a hedging instrument is amended for IBOR reform and the amendment of the hedged item (or *vice versa*). All other hedge accounting requirements, including the amended prospective assessment requirements, would need to be met and any actual ineffectiveness would need to be measured and recognised in the financial statements. This should be calculated based on how market participants would value the hedged items and hedging instruments. This includes the effect of any increase in discount rates that the market requires due to the uncertainties arising from IBOR reform. *[IAS 39.102G]*.

- For the prospective assessment of hedge effectiveness, it is assumed that the benchmark on which the hedged cash flows are based (whether or not it is contractually specified) and/or the benchmark on which the cash flows of the hedging instrument are based, are not altered as a result of IBOR reform. *[IAS 39.102F]*.

- For a hedge of a benchmark portion (rather than a risk component under IFRS 9) of interest rate risk that is affected by IBOR reform, the requirement that the portion is separately identifiable need be met only at the inception of the hedge. *[IAS 39.102H]*.

9.2 Phase 2 hedge accounting amendments

As noted above, the Phase 1 amendments only cover pre-replacement issues. The issues that affect financial reporting when an existing interest rate benchmark is replaced with a RFR, are covered in a separate set of amendments, the Phase 2 amendments issued by the IASB in August 2020.

For those amendments affecting the accounting for the modification of financial instruments due to interest rate benchmark reform see Chapter 50 at 3.8.3 and Chapter 52 at 3.4.3. We discuss below only the hedge accounting issues that arise when an existing interest rate benchmark is replaced with an RFR.

The Phase 2 amendments for IFRS 9 provide the following reliefs (the 'Phase 2 reliefs'):

1. relief from discontinuing hedge relationships for changes to hedge documentation required by the RFR reform (see 9.2.1 below); and
2. temporary relief from having to meet the separately identifiable requirement (see 9.2.2 below).

The Phase 2 reliefs can only be applied to hedge relationships including a financial asset, financial liability or derivative for which contractual changes, or changes to cash flows are directly required by the reform. Changes to contractual cashflows could change either in a way not originally specified on initial recognition, or as a result of activation of an existing contractual term such as a fallback clause. Changes are only directly required by the reform if, and only if, both of the following conditions are met:

i. the change is necessary as a direct consequence of interest rate benchmark reform; and
ii. the new basis for determining the contractual cash flows is 'economically equivalent' to the previous basis (i.e. the basis immediately preceding the change). [IFRS 9.5.4.5-5.4.7].

The amendments include examples of the type of changes required by interest rate reform that are considered to be economically equivalent to the previous basis, as follows:

- the replacement of an existing interest rate with a RFR or effecting such a reform of an interest rate benchmark by changing the method used to calculate the interest rate benchmark, with the addition of a fixed spread to compensate for a basis difference between the existing interest rate benchmark and the RFR.

  For example, the floating rate on a debt instrument for which the coupon was previously based on IBOR plus 100bp may be replaced with a coupon that is based on RFR plus 120bp, when the basis spread between IBOR and the RFR is 20bp;

- changes to the reset period, reset dates, or the number of days between coupon payment dates that are necessary to effect the reform of an interest rate benchmark.

  For example, an interest rate previously based on a 3m term IBOR rate paid quarterly may be replaced with one based on a 3m compounded RFR paid quarterly, or a 1m compounded RFR paid monthly; and

- the addition of a fallback provision to the contractual terms of a financial asset or liability to enable any of the changes described above to be made (see also Chapter 46 at 5.1.3). [IFRS 9.5.4.8].

9.2.1 Phase 2 reliefs from discontinuing hedge relationships

The Phase 2 amendments require that as and when an entity ceases to apply the Phase 1 reliefs (see 9.1.1 above) to a hedging relationship, the entity must amend the formal designation of that hedging relationship to reflect the changes that are required by interest rate benchmark reform (see 9.2 above). The hedge designation must be amended by the end of the reporting period during which the applicable requirements cease to apply. The principal phase 2 relief is that such changes to the hedge documentation do not result in the discontinuation of hedge accounting nor the designation of a new hedge relationship, as long as the only changes are those permitted by the Phase 2 amendments. Permitted changes include redefining the hedged risk to reference an RFR and redefining the description of the hedging instruments and/or the hedged items to reflect the RFR. This would include amendments such as the addition of a fixed spread to compensate for the basis difference between the previous benchmark and the RFR, as described above. [IFRS 9.6.9.1, 6.9.3, 6.9.4].

If changes are made in addition to those changes required by interest rate benchmark reform to the financial asset or financial liability designated in a hedging relationship (see 9.2 above) or to the designation of the hedging relationship, an entity must first apply the normal requirements in IFRS 9 to determine if those additional changes result in the discontinuation of hedge accounting (see 8.3 above). If the additional changes do not result in the discontinuation of hedge accounting, an entity must amend the formal designation of the hedging relationship. *[IFRS 9.6.9.5]*.

A hedging instrument may alternatively be changed as required by IBOR reform, not by amending the basis on which its contractual cash flows are calculated but by, for instance, terminating an existing IBOR-related derivative and replacing it, with a new derivative with the same counterparty, referencing an RFR. Clarification was provided in the phase 2 amendments that in such situations the phase 2 reliefs apply if and only if:

- the original hedging instrument is not derecognised, applying the usual accounting derecognition criteria (see Chapter 52 at 6.4); and
- the chosen approach is economically equivalent to changing the basis for determining the contractual cash flows of the original hedging instrument (see 9.2 above). *[IFRS 9.6.9.2,]*.

This means that, in order for the original hedge relationship to be regarded as continued, the fair value of the new RFR derivative at initial recognition must be equivalent to the fair value of the original derivative. It would not be possible to replace the older derivative with a new one at a market rate of interest.

Although this clarification will primarily apply to derivatives cleared by a central clearing counterparty, according to the Basis for Conclusions, it will also apply to where the addition of a new basis swap, specific to a particular instrument, swaps the existing interest rate benchmark for that instrument to the RFR. It should be noted that although the IASB introduced the condition that the replacement of the derivative does not result in its derecognition, it provided no additional guidance on when such a replacement would satisfy this condition. *[IFRS 9.BC6.616-BC6.619]*.

Changes required by IBOR reform to be made to hedge designations and hedge documentation may be required at different times for different hedge relationships, and more than once for individual hedge relationships. For instance, for a cash flow hedge, it is possible that the hedge designation and documentation will need to be amended twice: once when the derivative is modified to refer to an RFR and again when the hedged item is renegotiated to refer to an RFR. An entity must apply the relief from discontinuing hedge relationships on each occasion the criteria are met. *[IFRS 9.6.9.3]*.

At the end of the reporting period in which the hedge designation is amended to reference an RFR, the usual IFRS 9 requirements for accounting for changes in the fair value of the hedged item or hedging instrument apply:

- For fair value hedges, the hedging instrument and hedged item are remeasured based on the RFR, and a gain or loss recognised in profit or loss (see 7.1 above).
- For cash flow hedges, the cash flow hedge reserve is remeasured based on the RFR to the lower of the cumulative gain or loss on the hedging instrument and the cumulative change in fair value of the hedged item (see 7.2 above). *[IFRS 9.6.9.3]*.

Any hedge ineffectiveness is recognised in profit and loss as normal.

When the hedge designation is amended (or if the hedge has previously been discontinued, when the contractual cash flows of the previously designated item are modified), amounts accumulated in the cash flow hedge reserve are deemed to be based on the RFR. This results in the release of the cash flow hedge reserve to profit or loss in the same period or periods in which the hedged cash flows that are now based on the RFR affect profit or loss. To achieve this, a hypothetical derivative in a cash flow hedge may be updated, although any valuation adjustment on transition may need to be recognised in profit or loss in the period when the hedge documentation is amended. This will be recorded as part of the normal recognition in OCI of the lower of the cumulative gain or loss on the hedging instrument and the cumulative change in fair value of the hedged item. *[IFRS 9.6.9.7, 6.9.8]*.

The Phase 2 amendments also provide reliefs for items within a designated group of items (such as those forming part of a macro cash flow hedging strategy) that are amended for modifications directly required by IBOR reform. The reliefs allow the hedging strategy to remain and not be discontinued. As items within the hedged group transition at different times from IBORs to RFRs, they will be transferred to sub-groups of instruments that reference RFRs as the hedged risk. The existing IBOR would remain designated as the hedged risk for the other sub-group of hedged items, until they too are updated to reference to the new RFR. At each transition, the hypothetical derivative for the subgroup will require updating. Each sub-group must meet the eligibility requirements for a group of items to be designated as a hedged item, however application of the usual hedge accounting requirements (see 7.1 and 7.2 above) must be applied to the hedge relationship in its entirety. *[IFRS 9.6.9.9, 6.9.10]*.

The phase 2 reliefs for accounting for cash flow hedges and groups of items provides exceptions only to the circumstances described and all the other qualifying criteria for hedge accounting must be applied (see 6 above). *[IFRS 9.6.9.6]*.

9.2.2 Phase 2 temporary relief from having to meet the separately identifiable requirement

IFRS 9 requires that a risk component is not only reliably measurable but also 'separately identifiable' to be eligible for hedge accounting (see 2.2.3 above). The Phase 2 amendments provide temporary relief to entities from having to meet the separately identifiable requirement, when an RFR instrument is designated as a hedge of a risk component, both upon designation of a new hedge relationship, and for existing hedge relationships when changes required by IBOR reform are made to hedge designations and hedge documentation (see 9.2.1 above). The relief allows entities to assume that the separately identifiable requirement is met, provided the entity reasonably expects the RFR risk component to become separately identifiable within the next 24 months. The 24-month period applies to each RFR separately (i.e. it applies on a rate-by-rate basis) and starts from the date an entity designates the RFR as a risk component for the first time.

If an entity reasonably expects that a RFR will not be separately identifiable within 24 months after initial designation, the relief will end for that RFR. Hedge accounting should be discontinued prospectively from the date of that reassessment for all hedging relationships in which the RFR was designated as a risk component. *[IFRS 9.6.9.11, 6.9.12]*.

In either of these cases, the hedge would have to be prospectively discontinued. No relief is provided from the requirement for the risk component to be reliably measurable throughout the life of the hedging relationship.

The relief only applies for uncertainty arising directly from IBOR reform, as to whether an RFR risk component is separately identifiable. The relief is not available for hedging relationships where there is uncertainty whether the risk component is separately identifiable, but the uncertainty is not as a direct result of IBOR reform.

The relief from having to satisfy the separately identifiable requirement should significantly ease the transition to RFRs by allowing hedging relationships to continue. However, entities must ensure they are comfortable making the appropriate judgements at the time of transition, over the subsequent 24 months and have suitable processes and governance to update their assessment.

9.2.2.A   Determination of whether an RFR is a separately identifiable risk component

Although the Phase 1 and 2 amendments provide reliefs for the assessment of whether a non-contractually specified risk component is separately identifiable, and so can be designated as a hedged risk, they do not provide guidance on what is meant by 'separately identifiable' (see 2.2.3 above). Therefore, there should generally be no change in how this criterion is interpreted. There are, however, a couple of points made in the Phase 2 amendments that may be relevant.

The first point is that, as the relief is provided only for 'separately identifiable' and not for 'reliably measurable', the two criteria are clearly different. It is to be expected that an RFR might become sufficiently liquid that it is reliably measurable, but without yet being separately identifiable. *[IFRS 9.B6.3.9]*.

Whilst much of the guidance in IFRS 9 on how to determine whether a risk component is separately identifiable or not was written primarily to permit hedging of components of non-financial items (see 2.2.3.B above), one example appears particularly relevant for interest rate hedges, as follows:

'Entity D holds a fixed-rate debt instrument. This instrument is issued in an environment with a market in which a large variety of similar debt instruments are compared by their spreads to a benchmark rate (for example, LIBOR) and variable rate instruments in that environment are typically indexed to that benchmark rate. Interest rate swaps are frequently used to manage interest rate risk on the basis of that benchmark rate. The price of fixed-rate debt instruments varies directly in response to changes in the benchmark as they happen. Consequently, Entity D may designate hedge relationships for the fixed rate debt instrument on a risk component basis for the benchmark interest rate risk.' *[IFRS 9.B6.3.10(d)]*.

This paragraph is cited only as 'an example', so this should not be read as a list of criteria for a rate to qualify as separately identifiable. Nevertheless, this example could be read to imply that for a benchmark interest rate to qualify as a risk component it has to be the basis on which fixed rate debt instruments are frequently priced and floating ones frequently vary in rate, and that it would be insufficient for the rate to be used only in the swap market. At the time of writing there have already been a number of SONIA-based bond issues and SONIA swaps already make up half the sterling swaps market by volume. It is possible that an entity might conclude that SONIA is already separately identifiable and, if not yet, will be within 24 months. In contrast, swaps referenced to Secured Overnight Financing Rate (SOFR) (the chosen US dollar RFR) are far fewer in volume. Although it is not clear when or if it will form the basis on which fixed rate debt instruments are priced, there is an expectation that SOFR will become the reference index for many variable rate instruments. Further, the US dollar swap market is expected to move to be SOFR-based and, to that extent, SOFR will become a major interest rate benchmark and the main one used for hedging purposes. On this basis, given that the guidance in IFRS 9 is only 'an example', we expect that most entities applying IFRS 9 for hedge accounting purposes will conclude that SOFR will be separately identifiable within 24 months.

Although the guidance in IFRS 9 as to the criterion for a risk component to be separately identifiable is very similar to that in IAS 39 for a risk portion, the wording is not exactly the same (see 9.2.5.A below). The IASB never said that it had intended the application of 'separately identifiable' to interest rates to change on the application of IFRS 9, which could imply that if a benchmark risk portion was separately identifiable under IAS 39 then it would also be a separately identifiable risk component under IFRS 9. However, the guidance in IFRS 9.B6.3.10(d) arguably provides more restrictive guidance on what constitutes a 'benchmark'. Further, if SOFR is already separately identifiable by virtue of being a benchmark, that would make the 24-month exception largely unnecessary.

An assessment will need to be made for each RFR as to when that RFR is expected to meet the separately identifiable criteria for fixed rate debt (see 9.2.2 above). This assessment is likely to include consideration of the prevalence of transactions referenced to that RFR and how the associated debt market adjusts to accommodate RFR transactions.

The second point is that it is clear that the exception for identifying risk components in the Phase 1 and 2 amendments apply to cash flow hedges as well as fair value hedges. *[IFRS 9.BC6.647]*. This leads to the question of whether it is possible to designate an RFR as a risk component of a LIBOR floating rate debt instrument? The relevance of this question arises mainly where there is a mismatch in the timing of the amendment of a hedging derivative and the floating rate instrument which is the hedged item, so that the derivative is amended to refer to an RFR before the hedged item. The issue here is not whether, for instance, SONIA or SOFR will be separately identifiable as a component within 24 months, but whether it will ever be regarded as a separately identifiable component of a LIBOR-based floating rate.

In the deliberations about the Phase 2 amendments, on the subject of timing mismatches, it was suggested in a Staff Paper that hedge ineffectiveness could be minimised in the period before the hedged item is amended, by adjusting the hedged risk to the RFR rather than the contractual interest rate. This might be read to endorse the possibility of designating an RFR a component of LIBOR.[26]

However, there is no guidance specifically on this issue within the IBOR reform amendments. Unlike fair value hedges, in the past there has been much less practice of designation of risk components in floating rate instruments, unless the risk was already contractually specified (e.g. LIBOR risk in a loan that was indexed to LIBOR). Also, the examples in both IFRS 9 and IAS 39 only address fair value hedges. Therefore, it is more difficult to draw on past precedent or practice to support designating an RFR as a component of LIBOR.

The case for SONIA as a component of sterling LIBOR is perhaps easier to make, since it can be thought of as 'overnight sterling LIBOR' and so 'a building block' of term LIBOR. SOFR, on the other hand, based on the repo rate, is somewhat different in nature from US dollar LIBOR. Practice will emerge on this issue and it is possible that the IASB or regulators may provide guidance on the topic, but, for the purpose of Example 53.93 below, it has been assumed that SOFR cannot be designated as a component of US dollar LIBOR.

As illustrated by Example 53.94, unless an RFR can be designated as a component of LIBOR, entities are recommended to seek to ensure that there are no mismatches in the timing of the amendment of hedging instruments and hedged items, to minimise the level of recorded hedge ineffectiveness.

9.2.3 Application of Phase 2 reliefs

The following two examples illustrate the key features of the Phase 2 amendments.

Example 53.93: Application of Phase 2 relief to a fair value hedge

Company A has previously entered into an interest rate swap paying fixed 3% and receiving 3-month US dollar LIBOR. It had been designated in a hedge of the exposure to changes in fair value attributable to US dollar LIBOR, of cash flows equivalent to a 3% coupon plus principal of a 4% fixed US dollar asset.

On 1 November 2020 3-month US dollar LIBOR is 0.5% and SOFR is 0.2%, i.e. the basis difference between the two rates is 30 basis points. The swap is accordingly amended to pay fixed 2.7%, receive SOFR. The amendment of the derivative is not considered to be a substantial modification and so it is not derecognised. *[IFRS 9.BC6.619]*. The new swap is considered 'economically equivalent' to the old swap, since the only change has been to refer to SOFR instead of LIBOR and to adjust the spread based on the current market rates (see 9.2 above). As a result, the formal designation of the hedge is amended, and although the LIBOR hedged risk designation ends, the hedge continues, but with SOFR as the designated risk component (see 9.2.1 above).

SOFR is expected to be a separately identifiable component of US dollar interest rates within 24 months, and therefore may now be designated as the hedged risk component (see 9.2.2 above). Consequently, the description of the hedge designation is amended, to refer to the new hedging instrument and, the hedged item is amended to a hedge of changes in fair value attributable to SOFR, of the component of the 4% asset equivalent to a 2.7% coupon plus principal, (see 9.2. above). (An entity applying IAS 39 for hedge accounting must also update how hedge effectiveness will be assessed in future (see 9.2.5 below).)

At the next period end the swap is remeasured to its new fair value, based on SOFR, consistent with the normal hedge accounting requirements. This remeasurement will include any difference in fair value of the swap immediately before and after its modification, but as the derivative has been modified on an 'economically equivalent basis' the effect should be small. The asset is also adjusted for the difference in its fair value with respect to the designated hedged risk. This will include the difference in fair value between the 3% coupon plus principal discounted at 3-month US dollar LIBOR and the 2.7% coupon plus principal discounted at SOFR. This difference should also be small. Any net change of fair value on the amendment of the swap and of the designated hedged component, is recorded in profit or loss as part of the recorded hedge ineffectiveness for the period (see 9.2.1 above).

Example 53.94: Application of Phase 2 relief to a cash flow hedge relationship

The initial fact pattern is the same as that in the Example 53.93 above, except that it is a cash flow hedge of the US dollar LIBOR risk of a US dollar LIBOR plus 20bp liability. Ineffectiveness has been assessed and measured using a hypothetical derivative on which Company A receive 3% fixed and pays 3-month US dollar LIBOR.

As in Example 53.93, on 1 November 2020 the derivative is amended to pay fixed 2.7%, receive SOFR. Again, the amendment of the derivative is not considered to be a substantial modification and so it is not derecognised. The main difference in this example is that the US dollar LIBOR liability will also need to be amended as part of IBOR reform, through bilateral negotiation, but it is assumed that this does not happen for several months.

The hedge documentation may need to be amended to describe the amended swap as the hedging instrument in a cash flow hedge of the US dollar LIBOR liability (see 9.2.1 above). Whether this will be necessary will depend on the specificity of the original hedge documentation. SOFR is expected to be a separately identifiable component of US dollar interest rates within 24 months. However, Company A does not consider SOFR will ever be a separately identifiable component of US dollar LIBOR (see 9.2.2.A above). As a result, the hypothetical derivative is not amended at this time and continues to be based on LIBOR (see 9.1 above).

The original hedge relationship continues (see 9.2.1 above), and the amount recorded in the cash flow hedge reserve continues to be considered to be based on LIBOR as required by the Phase 1 amendments (see 9.1 above).

At the end of each accounting period from when the swap is amended until the liability is also renegotiated, the cash flow hedge reserve is remeasured to the lower of:

- the cumulative gain or loss in fair value of the SOFR swap; and
- the cumulative gain or loss in fair value of the US dollar LIBOR hypothetical derivative.

Because the swap is valued based on SOFR and the liability based on LIBOR, this remeasurement will give rise to a degree of ineffectiveness which may need to be recorded in profit or loss. However, the entity considers that there is still an 'economic relationship' between SOFR and US dollar LIBOR, such that hedge accounting continues to be permitted (see 6.4.1 above). (An entity applying IAS 39 would need to meet the prospective effectiveness assessment (see 9.1.2 below).)

The liability is renegotiated on 15 January 2021, on which date the basis difference between 3-month US dollar LIBOR and SOFR is 25 basis points. However, as part of the bilateral negotiation to amend the liability, the credit spread is also reduced by 6bp. The liability is accordingly amended to pay SOFR plus 39bp (where 39bp is the previous 20bp plus the current 3-month US dollar LIBOR-SOFR basis of 25bp, less the change in credit spread of 6bp).

Apart from the 6bp change in credit spread, the amendment is considered to be required as a direct consequence of IBOR reform and the new basis for determining the contractual flows is considered to be economically equivalent to the old basis (see 9.2 above). Applying the Phase 2 relief on modification of a financial instrument, the effective interest rate (EIR) on the liability is amended to SOFR plus 45bp (where 45bp is the previous 20bp plus the current 3-month LIBOR-SOFR basis of 25bp) (see Chapter 50 at 3.8.3).

The 6bp change in credit spread is not considered to be a substantial modification of the liability, since quantitatively, the change in net present value discounted at the new EIR is less than 10% and the change is also judged to be not substantial from a qualitative perspective. Hence, the liability is not derecognised (see Chapter 52 at 6). The 6bp change in credit spread is however not covered by the Phase 2 relief and the net present value of the 6bp reduction, discounted at the revised EIR of SOFR plus 45bp, is recorded as an immediate credit to profit or loss.

The hedge documentation is amended for a second time (see 9.2.1 above). The Phase 1 relief requiring the hedged risk to continue to be based on LIBOR comes to an end (see 9.1.1 above), and the hedge is now documented as a cash flow hedge of the SOFR component of the SOFR plus 39bp liability. (An entity applying IAS 39 for hedge accounting will also need to update the hedge documentation for any change in how hedge effectiveness will be assessed (see 9.2.5 below)). Again, the amendment of the hedge documentation, to refer to the modified hedged item and the new designated risk component, does not constitute a discontinuation of the original hedging relationship (see 9.2.1 above). Hence the amended hypothetical derivative does not need to be based on the current rate of SOFR. Instead it is amended to be a receive 2.75%, pay SOFR swap (where 2.75% is the previous 3% less the 25bp basis difference between 3-month US dollar LIBOR and SOFR when the hedge is amended).

The amount accumulated in the cash flow hedge reserve is now deemed to be based on SOFR (see 9.2.1 above). The cash flow hedge reserve is remeasured at the next period end, to the lower of:

- the cumulative gain or loss in fair value of the amended swap; and
- the cumulative gain or loss in fair value of the revised hypothetical derivative.

Note that because of the timing mismatch, the derivative (pay 2.70%, receive SOFR) and the hypothetical derivative (receive 2.75%, pay SOFR) have a different fixed rate, a degree of hedge ineffectiveness will arise:

- in this period, due mostly to a 'catch up' due to the difference in the fixed rates of the derivative and the hypothetical derivative and hence their fair values on redesignation; and
- in the future, as changes in the fair values of the derivative and the hypothetical derivative will not be the same. Going forward, although the entity considers that there is an 'economic relationship' between the derivative and the hypothetical derivative, for entities applying IAS 39, the level of ineffectiveness will need to be monitored to ensure that the hedge continues to qualify for accounting purposes as there is no relief from the 80/125% effectiveness requirements (see 9.2.5 below).

Because this is a cash flow hedge, the amount of ineffectiveness actually recorded will depend on whether the change in the fair value of the derivative is greater than that on the hypothetical derivative (see 7.2.1 above).

9.2.4 Effective date and end of Phase 2 reliefs

The Phase 2 amendments are effective for annual periods beginning on or after 1 January 2021, with earlier application permitted. *[IFRS 9.7.1.9]*. Application of the Phase 2 amendments are mandatory, to ensure comparability.

Application is retrospective and discontinued hedging relationships must be reinstated if, and only if, the following conditions are met:

- the hedging relationship was discontinued solely due to changes required by IBOR reform, and therefore the entity would not have been required to discontinue that hedging relationship if the Phase 2 amendments had been applied at that time; and
- at the date of initial application of the Phase 2 amendments, that discontinued hedge relationship continues to meet all the qualifying criteria for hedge accounting, after taking account of the Phase 2 amendments. *[IFRS 9.7.2.36, 7.2.37]*.

Continuing to meet all the qualifying criteria will include the need for the risk management objective of the discontinued hedge relationship to remain unchanged (see 6.2 above), this is unlikely to be the case if either the hedging item or hedging instrument has subsequently been designated in a new hedge relationship.

The requirement to reinstate discontinued hedge relationships that meet the above criteria may be operationally onerous as each discontinued hedge relationship will need to be identified and assessed in order to determine whether the criteria are met or not. Further, for any relationships that do meet the criteria for reinstatement, calculation of retrospective hedge accounting entries may also be challenging for accounting systems.

If discontinued hedges for which RFR instruments are designated as a hedge of a risk components are reinstated, the 24-month period to which the relief for being separately identifiable shall begin from the date of initial application of the Phase 2 amendments (see 9.2.2 above). *[IFRS 9.7.2.37(b)]*.

As instruments transition to RFRs, for a single benchmark interest rate there could be more than one change arising directly as a result of IBOR reform. The reliefs would not be restricted to one application, but could be applied each time a hedging relationship is modified as a direct result of IBOR reform. The phase two reliefs will cease to apply once all changes have been made to financial instruments and hedging relationships, as required by IBOR reform. *[IFRS 9.BC7.88]*.

9.2.5 Phase 2 amendments for IAS 39

As is the case for the Phase 1 amendments (see 9.1.2 above), the Phase 2 amendments also include changes to IAS 39. The corresponding amendments to IAS 39 are consistent with those for IFRS 9, but with the following differences:

- The Phase 1 relief from the retrospective 80-125% assessment (see 9.1.2 above) will end at the earlier of when there is no longer uncertainty with respect to the cash flows of both the hedged item and the hedging instrument, and when the hedging relationships is discontinued. *[IAS 39.102M]*.

- IAS 39 is also amended so that for the assessment of retrospective hedge effectiveness, cumulative fair value changes may be reset to zero when the exception to the retrospective assessment ends. This election is made separately for each hedging relationship (i.e. on a hedge-by-hedge basis). However, actual hedge ineffectiveness will continue to be measured and recognised in full in profit or loss. *[IAS 39.102V]*.

- The Phase 2 amendments also clarify that changes to the method for assessing hedge effectiveness due to modifications required by IBOR reform, will not result in the discontinuation of hedge accounting. *[IAS 39.102P(d)]*.

9.2.5.A Determination of whether an RFR is a separately identifiable risk component under IAS 39

Similar to the Phase 1 and 2 amendments for IFRS 9 (see 9.1 and 9.2.2.A above), although the amendments to IAS 39 provide reliefs for the assessment of whether a non-contractually specified risk component is separately identifiable, and so can be designated as a hedged risk, they do not provide guidance on what is meant by 'separately identifiable'. Whilst the guidance in IFRS 9 as to the criterion for a risk component to be separately identifiable is very similar to that in IAS 39 for a risk portion, the wording is not exactly the same. In particular, IAS 39 contains an additional example that was not carried forward into IFRS 9:

'for a fixed rate financial instrument hedged for changes in fair value attributable to changes in a risk-free or benchmark rate, the risk-free or benchmark rate is normally regarded as both a separately identifiable component of the financial instrument and reliably measurable'. *[IAS 39.AG99F(a)]*.

Given the reference to 'risk-free or benchmark', it has been established practice to designate other benchmarks, such as the overnight interest rate swap rate ('OIS'). It is possible that those entities still applying IAS 39 will consider RFRs such as SONIA and SOFR as separately identifiable, on the basis that they are already benchmarks and SOFR is also (nearly) risk-free.

10 PRESENTATION

For a comprehensive overview of the financial instruments related presentation requirements of IFRS 7 see Chapter 54. We present below only some of the key requirements for hedge accounting.

IFRS 9 includes plenty of guidance as to when gains and losses from hedge accounting should be recognised in the profit or loss. The standard is much more imprecise as to where in the profit or loss such gains and losses should be presented. However, it can be inferred that gains and losses from hedging instruments in hedging relationships would be presented in the same line item that is affected by the hedged item (at least to the extent the hedge is effective) rather than being shown separately, although this is not explicitly stated in IFRS 9 (see Chapter 54 at 7.1.3).

The IFRS Interpretations Committee clarified in March 2018 that only interest on financial assets measured at amortised cost or on debt instruments measured at fair value through other comprehensive income should be included in the amount of interest revenue presented separately for items calculated using the effective interest method (see Chapter 54 at 7.1.1). *[IAS 1.82(a)]*. At this meeting it was also concluded that the separate interest revenue line would encompass any effect of a qualifying hedging relationship applying the hedge accounting requirements.[27]

10.1 Cash flow hedges

IFRS 9 requires that those amounts accumulated in the cash flow hedging reserve shall be reclassified from the cash flow hedge reserve as a reclassification adjustment in the same period or periods during which the hedged future cash flows affect profit or loss. The guidance provides as an example of the period over which such a reclassification should occur as the 'periods that interest income or interest expense is recognised' (see 7.2.2 above). *[IFRS 9.6.5.11(d)(ii)]*. This clarifies that entities cannot simply account for the net interest payment on an interest rate swap straight into profit or loss but would have to present this as a reclassification adjustment between OCI and profit or loss. There is a requirement to disclose reclassification adjustments in the statement of comprehensive income (see Chapter 54 at 7.2). *[IAS 1.92]*.

If the hedged transaction subsequently results in the recognition of a non-financial item, the amount accumulated in equity is removed from the separate component of equity and included in the initial cost or other carrying amount of the hedged asset or liability. This accounting entry, sometimes referred to as 'basis adjustment', does not affect OCI of the period (see 7.2.2 above). *[IFRS 9.6.5.11(d)(i)]*.

A similar approach would equally apply to situations where the hedged forecast transaction of a non-financial asset or non-financial liability subsequently becomes a firm commitment for which fair value hedge accounting is applied.

For any other cash flow hedges, the amount accumulated in equity is reclassified to profit or loss as a reclassification adjustment in the same period or periods during which the hedged cash flows affect profit or loss. This accounting entry does affect OCI of the period and should be disclosed as a reclassification adjustment in OCI. *[IFRS 9.6.5.11(d), IAS 1.92]*.

10.2 Fair value hedges

Entities recognise the gain or loss on the hedging instrument in profit or loss and adjust the carrying amount of the hedged item for the hedging gain or loss with the adjustment being recognised in profit or loss (see 7.1.1 above).

For hedged items that are debt instruments measured at fair value through OCI in accordance with paragraph 4.1.2A of IFRS 9 (see Chapter 50 at 2.3), the gain or loss on the hedged item results in recognition of that amount in profit or loss rather than accumulating in OCI. This means fair value hedge accounting changes the presentation of gains or loss on the hedged item, but the measurement of the debt instrument at fair value remains unaffected. *[IFRS 9.6.5.8(b)]*.

For hedged items that are equity instruments for which an entity has elected to present fair value changes in OCI without subsequent reclassification to profit or loss, the accounting for a fair value hedge is different because it does not affect profit or loss but, instead, OCI. There is no change to the accounting for the hedged item and the gain or loss on the hedging instrument is recognised in OCI (see 2.6.3, 7.1.1 and 7.8 above). *[IFRS 9.6.5.8]*.

10.3 Hedges of groups of items

10.3.1 Cash flow hedges

The designation of a group of items within a cash flow hedge, has no effect on the presentation in profit or loss of those designated hedged items. However, the presentation of the related hedging gains or losses in the statement of profit or loss depends on the nature of the group position. *[IFRS 9.B6.6.13-15]*. The required presentation for hedges of groups of items is discussed in more detail in Chapter 54 at 7.1.3, and is summarised in the table below.

Figure 53.4: Presentation for a hedge of groups of items

Nature of position	Line items affected in profit or loss	Presentation in the income statement
	One line item	The amount reclassified from equity to profit or loss has to be presented in the same line item as the underlying hedged transaction.
Gross position	Multiple line items	The amount reclassified from equity to profit or loss has to be allocated to the line items affected by the hedged items on a systematic and rational basis and shall not result in a gross up of the net gains or losses on the hedging instrument.
Net position	Multiple line items	The amount reclassified from equity to profit or loss has to be presented in a separate line item.

Note that the designation of a net position cash flow hedge is only permitted when hedging foreign currency risk (see 2.5.3 above).

For net position cash flow hedges, as the hedging gains and losses will be presented in a different line to that which the hedged items are presented in profit or loss, such a hedge designation might not seem very attractive, as the presentation of the hedged transactions will not reflect the effect of the hedge. However, the Board was concerned that grossing-up the hedging gain or loss would result in non-existing gains or losses being recognised in the statement of profit or loss, which would be in conflict with general accounting principles. *[IFRS 9.BC6.457]*. The Board also considered that such a presentation makes it transparent that an entity is hedging on a net basis and would clearly present the effect of those hedges of net positions on the face of the statement of profit or loss. *[IFRS 9.BC6.461]*. However, because of this presentation, in practice some entities may choose to continue to designate a proportion of a gross position rather than a net designation. Such a 'proxy designation' would be permitted provided the designation is directionally consistent with the actual risk management activities (see 6.2.1 above). *[IFRS 9.BC6.98, BC6.100(a)].*

10.3.2 Fair value hedges

A special presentation in the income statement is prescribed for fair value hedges of groups of items with offsetting risk positions (i.e. hedges of a net position), whose hedged risk affects different profit or loss line items. Entities must present the hedging gains or losses of such a hedge in a separate line item in the income statement in order to avoid grossing up the hedging gain or loss on a single instrument into multiple line items. Hence in that situation the amount in the line item that relates to the hedged item itself remains unaffected. *[IFRS 9.6.6.4, B6.6.16].*

However, the treatment in the statement of financial position is different, in that the individual items in the group are separately adjusted for the change in fair value due to changes in the hedged risk. *[IFRS 9.6.6.5].*

10.4 Costs of hedging

When applying the costs of hedging accounting to the time value of an option contract, the forward element of a forward contract or the foreign currency basis spread the treatment for the amount accumulated in a separate component of equity is dependent on the nature of the underlying hedged item (see 7.5 above).

For transaction related hedges:

- If the hedged item subsequently results in the recognition of a non-financial asset or liability, or a firm commitment for a non-financial asset or liability for which fair value hedging will be applied, the amount accumulated in a separate component of equity is removed from equity and included directly in the carrying amount of the asset or liability. This is not a reclassification adjustment, and so does not affect OCI of the period.

- For other transaction related hedging relationships (such as the hedge of highly probable forecast sales), the amount accumulated in a separate component of equity is be reclassified to profit or loss as a reclassification adjustment in the same period or periods during which the hedged expected future cash flows affect profit or loss. This is a reclassification adjustment, and so does affect OCI of the period.

- If all or a portion of the amount accumulated in a separate component of equity is not expected to be recovered, the amount that is not expected to be recovered is immediately reclassified into profit or loss (see 7.2.1 above). This is a reclassification adjustment, and so does affect OCI of the period. *[IFRS 9.6.5.15(b)].*

For time-period related hedges, the costs of hedging at the date of designation as a hedging instrument is to be amortised on a systematic and rational basis over the period during which the hedged item impacts profit or loss (see 7.5.1 above). The 'costs of hedging' in this context is the time value of an option contract, the forward element of a forward contract or the foreign currency basis spread, to the extent that it relates to the hedged item, (see 7.5.1.A above). However, if the hedge relationship is discontinued, the net amount remaining in OCI (i.e. including cumulative amortisation) is immediately reclassified into profit or loss. Both are reclassification adjustments, and so do affect OCI of the period. *[IFRS 9.6.5.15(c)]*. The standard is however silent on where in profit or loss the costs of hedging accumulated in OCI should be recycled.

11 MACRO HEDGING

At a detailed level, the topic of portfolio (or macro) hedging for banks and similar financial institutions is beyond the scope of a general financial reporting publication such as this. However, no discussion of hedge accounting would be complete without an overview of the high level issues involved and an explanation of how the standard setters have tried to accommodate these entities.

Financial institutions, especially retail banks, usually have as a core business the collection of funds by depositors that are subsequently invested as loans to customers. This typically includes instruments such as current and savings accounts, deposits and borrowings, loans and mortgages that are usually accounted for at amortised cost. The difference between interest received and interest paid on these instruments (i.e. the net interest margin) is a main source of profitability.

A bank's net interest margin is exposed to changes in interest rates, a risk most banks (economically) hedge by entering into derivatives (mainly interest rate swaps). Applying the hedge accounting requirements as set out in IFRS 9 (or IAS 39) to such hedging strategies on an individual item-by-item basis can be difficult as a result of the characteristics of the underlying financial assets and liabilities:

- Prepayment options are common features of many fixed rate loans to customers (see 2.3.2 above). Customers exercise these options for many reasons, such as when they move house, and so not necessarily in response to interest rate movements. Their behaviour can be predicted better on a portfolio basis rather than an item-by-item basis.

- As a result of the sheer number of financial instruments involved, banks typically apply their hedging strategies on a macro (or portfolio), dynamic basis, with the number of individual instruments in the hedged portfolio constantly churning.

In addition, not all exposures that form part of a bank's risk management of net interest margin are eligible as hedged items. For example, it is common for banks to attribute a 'deemed' fixed rate interest rate risk from their demand deposits, such as current account balances, savings accounts and other accounts, consistent with the bank's expectations as to how they will behave. These deemed fixed rate liabilities are often referred to as 'core demand deposits'. However, banks are prohibited by IFRS 9 (or IAS 39) from including core demand deposits in a manner that is consistent with their risk management strategy (see 2.6.7 above). *[IAS 39.F.2.3]*.

IAS 39 includes some specific guidance originally designed with macro hedging in mind. Currently some of this guidance can still be applied even when IFRS 9 is applied (see 11.2 below). *[IFRS 9.6.1.3]*. The IAS 39 macro hedging guidance exists for portfolio fair value, *[IAS 39.81A, 89A, AG114-132]*, and cash flow hedge accounting, *[IAS 39 IG F.6.1-F.6.3]*, for interest rate risk. However, banks did not always use the IAS 39 macro hedge accounting solutions. This is because: not all sources of interest rate risk qualify for hedge accounting, the use of IAS 39 can be operationally complex and cash flow hedge solutions result in volatility of other comprehensive income. Some European banks, instead, made use of the European Union's carve out of certain sections of the IAS 39 hedge accounting rules (see Chapter 1 at 4.2.1.A).

The accounting for macro hedging was originally part of the IASB's project to replace IAS 39 with IFRS 9. However, the IASB realised that developing the new accounting model would take time and probably be a different concept from hedge accounting. In May 2012, the Board therefore decided to decouple the part of the project that is related to accounting for macro hedging from IFRS 9, allowing more time to develop an accounting model without affecting the timeline for the completion of the other elements of IFRS 9.[28] This separate project is referred to as Accounting for Dynamic Risk Management. The status of the project is discussed at 11.1 below.

11.1 Accounting for dynamic risk management

In April 2014, the IASB issued the Discussion Paper – *Accounting for Dynamic Risk Management: a Portfolio Revaluation Approach to Macro Hedging*. Most respondents supported the need for the project, but there was no consensus on a solution. Given the diversity in views, in July 2015 the IASB concluded that the insights that it had received from the comment letters and feedback so far did not enable it to develop proposals for an exposure draft. Accordingly, the IASB decided that the project should remain in the research programme, with the aim of publishing a second discussion paper, most likely with a new accounting model, without further developing the Portfolio Revaluation Approach to Macro Hedging.

Since November 2017 the IASB has been developing a new accounting model for the recognition and measurement for dynamic risk management (the model). The Board is exploring whether it can develop an accounting model that will enable investors to understand a company's dynamic risk management activities and to evaluate the effectiveness of those activities.

The aim of the model is to faithfully represent, in the financial statements, the impact of risk management activities of a financial institution in the area of dynamic risk management rather than perfectly capture every aspect of the risk management activity. It has been tentatively agreed that because accounting for the interest rate risk management activities of financial institutions is where the greatest need arises, any accounting model developed will be based on that scenario. The IASB also tentatively decided that the application of the model should be optional.

Through the various IASB meetings since November 2017, the model has been developed recognising that interest rate risk management activities of financial institutions focus on achieving a particular net interest margin profile; transforming the existing profile to one that meets the financial institution's risk management strategy. At a high level, the model being developed requires the identification of the financial assets that are managed as part of the dynamic risk management. Then in consideration of the financial liabilities also included within dynamic risk management, and the financial institution's risk management strategy, a target asset profile is determined.

The target asset profile is a hypothetical asset portfolio that would deliver the desired net interest margin profile, consistent with the financial institution's risk management strategy, in combination with the actual financial liabilities included within dynamic risk management. The target asset profile would be an amount equal to the actual asset portfolio, although the tenor of the assets within the target portfolio would differ in most cases. The derivatives actually transacted for the purposes of dynamic risk management must also be identified and designated as such.

When an entity perfectly achieves its risk management strategy, the model should reflect in the statement of profit or loss (i.e. net interest margin) the entity's target asset profile, because that is the quantification of the entity's risk management strategy. This is achieved through the recognition of interest income and expense from the designated financial assets and liabilities in scope of the model, and the deferral to OCI and reclassification of the changes in fair values of the designated derivatives. The intended process for the accounting for changes in fair value of the designated derivatives is similar, but not identical, to the cash flow hedge mechanics (see 7.2 above).

However, if the entity does not perfectly achieve its risk management strategy (i.e. there is imperfect alignment), that should be evident to users of the financial statements. The magnitude of imperfect alignment provides information about the extent to which an entity has not achieved its risk management strategy and therefore quantifies the potential impact on the entity's future economic resources.

In order to measure imperfect alignment, the model uses 'benchmark derivatives' for comparison with the designated derivatives. 'Benchmark derivatives' are those that achieve a perfect transformation of the asset profile to the target asset profile. The difference between the change in clean fair value of the benchmark and designated derivatives captures the imperfect alignment, and is recognised in the statement of profit or loss to the extent the change in clean fair value of the designated derivative is greater than that of the benchmark, (i.e. an 'over-hedge'). This accounting is similar, but not identical, to the 'lower of' accounting for cash flow hedges (see 7.2 above).

The IASB have discussed various eligibility criteria for application of the model, including criteria for eligible financial assets, liabilities and designated derivatives. These criteria are too detailed for this discussion, however it is worth noting that core demand deposits are eligible financial liabilities for the purposes of determining the target asset profile, subject to some conditions.

Given the dynamic nature of the financial assets and liabilities under dynamic risk management, designation and documentation of these within the model should be undertaken in a manner that accommodates that dynamic behaviour, while providing clarity as to which items are in scope and which are not. Accordingly, the proposal is that designation of financial assets and liabilities within the model will be based on portfolios rather than individual instruments.

The risk management strategy ultimately drives the target asset profile and hence is a key component of the model. Furthermore, one of the aims of the model is to faithfully represent in the financial statements the impact of risk management activities of a financial institution. Accordingly, when management change that risk management strategy (other than to accommodate changes in assumptions (e.g. of prepayment) or inputs (e.g. new and/or expired financial assets), the IASB has tentatively decided that the accumulated balance recognised in OCI should be reclassified to profit or loss over the life of the target asset profile as defined prior to the change in risk management strategy. The IASB expect a change in risk management strategy to be rare.

The IASB's objective of enabling investors to understand a company's dynamic risk management activities and to evaluate the effectiveness of those activities, cannot be met by accounting mechanisms alone. Accordingly, the IASB has developed areas of focus for disclosure requirements for dynamic risk management, that require further development. They are as follows:

- understand and evaluate an entity's risk management strategy;
- evaluate management's ability to achieve that strategy;
- understand the impact on current and future economic resources; and
- understand the impact on an entity's financial statements from the application of the model.

Having developed the core aspects of the model, the IASB planned to undertake outreach on the core model to gather stakeholders' views prior to developing a consultation document. Given the effects of the coronavirus pandemic, to allow sufficient time for banks to consider the outreach materials and provide high-quality responses during those meetings, the outreach was postponed. At the time of writing, the outreach process has begun, with a target of providing feedback to the IASB by December 2020.

11.2 Applying hedge accounting for macro hedging strategies under IFRS 9

Because of its pending project on an accounting model specifically tailored to macro hedging situations (see 11.1 above), the IASB created a scope exception from the IFRS 9 hedging accounting requirements that allows entities to use the fair value hedge accounting for portfolio hedges of interest rate risk, and only for such hedges, as defined and set out in IAS 39, until the project is finalised and becomes effective. *[IFRS 9.6.1.3]*. The specific guidance that defines what is meant by the fair value hedge accounting for portfolios of interest rate risk is set out in paragraphs 81A, 89A and AG114 to AG132 of IAS 39. The application of this guidance for banks and similar financial institutions is beyond the scope of a general financial reporting publication such as this and so is not covered further within this publication.

However, IFRS 9 does not include a similar scope exception for the 'macro' cash flow hedge accounting set out in the Implementation Guidance to IAS 39, often applied by financial institutions to interest rate positions for which interest rate risk is managed on a net basis. *[IAS 39 IG F.6.1-F.6.3]*. The IASB is of the view that as the macro cash flow hedge accounting model is an application of the general hedge accounting model under IAS 39, the macro cash flow hedge accounting model should remain an application of the IFRS 9 hedge accounting guidance. Accordingly, the IASB did not want to make an exception for the macro cash flow hedge accounting approach and so decided to retain an earlier decision not to carry forward any IAS 39 Implementation Guidance on hedge accounting to IFRS 9. *[IFRS 9.BC6.91-95]*.

However, many financial institutions were concerned that their understanding of the IAS 39 macro cash flow hedge accounting model was not totally consistent with IFRS 9 and that they would not be able to continue with their existing macro cash flow hedging strategies under IFRS 9.

In its January 2013 meeting, the IASB confirmed its earlier decision and clarified that not carrying forward the Implementation Guidance was without prejudice (i.e. it did not mean that the IASB had rejected that guidance and so had not intended to imply that entities cannot apply macro cash flow hedge accounting under IFRS 9).[29]

This was, however, not the end of the story. Several constituents continued to lobby EFRAG and the IASB to allow entities to either apply the hedge accounting requirements in IAS 39 or IFRS 9 until the project on accounting for macro hedging is finalised.[30]

Eventually, the IASB gave entities the following choices until the project on accounting for macro hedging is completed:

- to apply the hedge accounting requirements as set out in IFRS 9, in full;
- to apply the hedge accounting requirements as set out in IFRS 9 to all hedges except fair value hedges of the interest rate exposure of a portfolio of financial assets or financial liabilities; in that case an entity must also apply the paragraphs that were added to IAS 39 when that particular type of hedge was introduced (paragraphs 81A, 89A and AG114-AG132 of IAS 39) – i.e. an entity must apply all the hedge accounting requirements of IAS 39 (including the 80%-125% bright line effectiveness test as well) including the paragraphs that specifically address fair value hedges of the interest rate exposure of a portfolio of financial assets or financial liabilities); the choice to apply IAS 39 in these situations is the result of the scope of the hedge accounting requirements of IFRS 9 and available on a case-by-case basis (i.e. it is not an accounting policy choice); *[IFRS 9.6.1.3]* or
- to continue applying hedge accounting as set out in IAS 39 until the project on accounting for macro hedging is completed, to all hedges; this is an accounting policy choice. *[IFRS 9.7.2.21]*. Because it is an accounting policy choice, an entity may later change its policy and start applying the hedge accounting requirements of IFRS 9 (subject to the transition requirements of IFRS 9 for hedge accounting). However, even if an entity chooses to continue to apply the hedge accounting requirements of IAS 39, the entity still must provide the hedge accounting disclosures that were developed during the IFRS 9 project because those disclosure requirements have become a part of IFRS 7 for which no similar accounting policy choice to continue to apply the previous requirements was provided. *[IFRS 9.BC6.104]*. Once an entity changes its accounting policy and starts to apply the hedge accounting requirements of IFRS 9, it cannot go back to applying IAS 39 (see 13.1 below).

12 ALTERNATIVES TO HEDGE ACCOUNTING

12.1 Credit risk exposures

Many financial institutions hedge the credit risk arising from loans or loan commitments using credit default swaps (CDS). This would often result in an accounting mismatch, as loans and loan commitments are typically not accounted for at fair value through profit or loss. The most natural approach to hedge accounting would be to designate the credit risk as a risk component in a hedging relationship. However, the IASB noted that due to the difficulty in isolating the credit risk as a separate risk it does not meet the eligibility criteria for risk components (see 2.2.1 above). As a result, the accounting mismatch creates profit or loss volatility. [IFRS 9.BC6.470]. The Exposure Draft leading up to IFRS 9 did not propose any changes in this area, however, the IASB asked its constituents to comment on three alternative approaches, none of which were that credit risk could be deemed an eligible risk component for hedge accounting. The feedback from constituents showed that accounting for credit risk hedging strategies is a major concern for many financial institutions. [IFRS 9.BC6.491].

In its redeliberations the Board reconfirmed its view that credit risk does not qualify as a separate risk component for hedge accounting purposes. [IFRS 9.BC6.504]. However, the IASB decided that an entity undertaking economic credit risk hedging may, at any time, elect to account for all or a proportion of a debt instrument (such as a loan or a bond), a loan commitment or a financial guarantee contract, to the extent that any of these instruments is managed for changes in its credit risk, at fair value through profit or loss. This was one of the alternative approaches set out in the Exposure Draft. This election can only be made if the asset referenced by the credit derivative has the same issuer and subordination as the hedged exposure (i.e. both the issuer's name and seniority of the exposure match). The accounting for the credit derivative would not change, i.e. it would continue to be accounted at fair value through profit or loss. [IFRS 9.6.7.1].

If the election is made, the difference at that time between the carrying value (if any) and the fair value of the financial instrument designated as at fair value through profit or loss is immediately recognised in profit or loss; in case of a debt instrument accounted for as at fair value through other comprehensive income the carrying amount (i.e. fair value) does not change but instead the gain or loss that has been accumulated in the revaluation reserve has to be reclassified to profit or loss. [IFRS 9.6.7.2]. This gain or loss would not only reflect any change in credit risk, but also any change in other risks such as interest rate risk. Also different to a fair value hedge, once elected, the financial instruments hedged for credit risk are measured at their full fair value instead of just being adjusted for changes in the risk actually hedged. As a result, by economically hedging the credit risk exposure and applying the fair value option consistent with the guidance in paragraph 6.7.1 of IFRS 9, the entity also has to revalue the financial instrument for the general effect of interest rate risk, which may result in profit or loss volatility.

An entity must discontinue the specific accounting for credit risk hedges in line with its actual risk management. This would be the case when the credit risk either no longer exists or if the credit risk is no longer managed using credit derivatives (irrespective of whether the credit derivative still exists or is sold, terminated or settled). [IFRS 9.6.7.3].

On discontinuation, the accounting for the financial instrument reverts to the same measurement category that had applied before the designation as at fair value through profit or loss. However, the fair value of the financial instrument on the date of discontinuing the accounting at fair value through profit or loss becomes the new carrying amount on that date. [IFRS 9.6.7.4]. For example, the fair value of a loan at the time of discontinuation becomes its new deemed amortised cost which is the basis to determine its new effective interest rate. This applies also to a debt instrument that reverts to accounting at fair value through other comprehensive income because it is required to affect profit or loss in the same way as a financial instrument at amortised cost. *[IFRS 9.5.7.11]*. This means the revaluation reserve only includes the gains and losses that arise after the date on which the accounting at fair value through profit or loss ceased.

For a loan commitment or a financial guarantee contract the fair value at the date on which the accounting at fair value through profit or loss ceased is amortised over the remaining life of the instrument in accordance with the principles of IFRS 15 – *Revenue from Contracts with Customers* – unless the impairment requirements of IFRS 9 would require a higher amount than the remaining unamortised balance (see Chapter 50 at 2.8). *[IFRS 9.4.2.1(c)-(d)]*.

In contrast to the fair value option under IFRS 9 (see Chapter 48 at 7), the possibility to elect to measure at fair value through profit or loss those financial instruments whose credit risk is managed using credit derivatives, has the following advantages:

- the election can be made after initial recognition of the financial instrument;
- the election is available for a proportion of the instrument (instead of only the whole instrument); and
- the fair value through profit or loss accounting can be discontinued if credit risk hedging no longer occurs.

Consequently, even though it is not an equivalent to fair value hedge accounting, this accounting does address several, but not all, concerns of entities that use CDSs for hedging credit exposures.

If credit exposures are designated as measured at fair value through profit or loss additional disclosure requirements apply (see Chapter 54 at 4.3.4). *[IFRS 7.24G]*.

12.2 Own use contracts

Contracts accounted for in accordance with IFRS 9 include those contracts to buy or sell non-financial items that can be settled net in cash, as if they were financial instruments (i.e. they are in substance similar to financial derivatives). Many commodity purchase and sale contracts meet the criteria for net settlement in cash because the commodities are readily convertible to cash. However, such contracts are excluded from the scope of IFRS 9 if they were entered into and continue to be held for the purpose of the receipt or delivery of a non-financial item in accordance with the entity's expected purchase, sale or usage requirements. *[IFRS 9.2.4]*. This is commonly referred to as the 'own use' scope exception. Own use contracts are further discussed in Chapter 45 at 4.2.

Own use contracts are accounted for as normal sales or purchase contracts (i.e. executory contracts), with the idea that any fair value change of the contract is not relevant given the contract is used for the entity's own use. However, some entities in certain industries enter into contracts for own use and similar financial derivatives for risk management purposes and manage all these contracts together. In such a situation, own use accounting leads to an accounting mismatch as the fair value change of the derivative positions used for risk management purposes cannot be offset against fair value changes of the own use contracts.

To eliminate the accounting mismatch, an entity could apply hedge accounting by designating an own use contract as the hedged item in a fair value hedging relationship. However, hedge accounting in these circumstances is administratively burdensome. Furthermore, entities often enter into large volumes of commodity contracts and, within the large volume of contracts, some positions may offset each other. An entity would therefore typically hedge on a net basis.

To address this issue, IFRS 9 includes a fair value option for own use contracts. At inception of a contract, an entity may make an irrevocable designation to measure an own use contract at fair value through profit or loss (the 'fair value option'). However, such designation is only allowed if it eliminates or significantly reduces an accounting mismatch. [IFRS 9.2.5].

Example 53.95: Processing and brokerage of soybeans and sunflowers

An entity is in the business of procuring, transporting, storing, processing and merchandising soybeans and sunflower seeds. The inputs and the outputs are agricultural commodities which are traded in liquid markets. The entity has both a broker business and a processing business, which are operationally distinct. However, the entity analyses and monitors its net commodity risk position, comprising inventories, physically settled forward purchase and sales contracts and exchange traded futures and options. The target is to keep the net fair value risk position close to nil.

Applying the guidance in IFRS 9 paragraph 2.4, the physically settled forward contracts from the processing business have to be accounted for as own use contracts, whereas all other contracts are accounted for at fair value through profit or loss. The resulting accounting mismatch does not reflect how the entity is managing the overall fair value risk of those contracts.

If the entity applied the fair value option to the physically settled contracts, this would eliminate the accounting mismatch.

Some entities, especially in the power and utilities sector, enter into long-term own use contracts, sometimes for as long as 15 years. The business model of those entities would often be to manage those contracts together with other contracts on a fair value basis. However, there are often no derivatives available with such long maturities, while fair values for longer dated contracts may be difficult to determine. Hence, for risk management purposes a fair value based approach might only be used for the time horizon in which derivatives are available, i.e. sometime after inception of the contract. The fair value option is, however, only available on inception of the own use contract. As risk management of longer term own use contracts on a fair value basis usually occurs sometime after inception of the contract, the fair value option will mainly be useful for shorter-term own use contracts.

13 EFFECTIVE DATE AND TRANSITION

13.1 Effective date

IFRS 9 is effective for periods beginning on or after 1 January 2018 and replaces substantially all of IAS 39, including the hedge accounting requirements. However, as stated at 1.3 above, an entity has the accounting policy choice to continue applying hedge accounting as set out in IAS 39 to all hedges until the project on accounting for macro hedging is completed, instead of the requirements of Chapter 6 of IFRS 9. [IFRS 9.7.2.21]. We believe that an entity can chose to adopt the IFRS 9 hedge accounting requirements subsequent to the initial adoption of IFRS 9, as there is nothing in the transition guidance that indicates that an entity must continue to apply the accounting policy choice until the macro hedging project is finished. *[IFRS 9.BC6.104]*. Adoption of IFRS 9 hedge accounting can only start from the beginning of a reporting period, and although not explicit in the standard, we believe that the reporting period can be an annual reporting period or an interim reporting period. *[IFRS 9.7.2.2]*. However, it is not possible to switch back to the hedge accounting provisions of IAS 39 once Chapter 6 of IFRS 9 has been applied.

The IFRS 9 transition guidance is applicable when an entity first applies the requirements of the standard, and it is noted that more than one date of initial application may arise for the different requirements of IFRS 9. *[IFRS 9.7.2.2]*. Hence, we believe the transition guidance for IFRS 9 hedge accounting (Chapter 6) is applicable when an entity changes its accounting policy to apply IFRS 9 hedge accounting subsequent to the initial adoption of IFRS 9. *[IFRS 9.7.2.21-26]*. However, for first time adopters of IFRS, the transition guidance in IFRS 9 is not relevant, and hence the accounting policy choice to apply the hedge accounting requirements of IAS 39 is not available.

It should also be noted that on subsequent adoption of IFRS 9 hedge accounting, comparatives will need to be restated for any retrospective application (albeit retrospective application is limited (see 13.2 and 13.3 below)). The transition guidance that permitted entities not to restate comparatives was only relevant on adoption of the classification and measurement requirements of IFRS 9. *[IFRS 9.7.2.15]*.

The accounting policy choice to continue to apply the hedge accounting requirements of IAS 39, effectively defers all of Chapter 6 of IFRS 9, (although not the IFRS 7 disclosure requirements on hedge accounting introduced by IFRS 9 (see Chapter 54)). As the guidance on designating credit exposures at fair value through profit or loss is included within Chapter 6 of IFRS 9, we believe it cannot be applied if an entity chooses to remain on IAS 39 for hedge accounting. See 12.1 above for more details on designating credit exposures at fair value through profit or loss.

Furthermore, if an entity has an equity instrument classified at fair value through other comprehensive income as permitted by paragraph 5.7.5 of IFRS 9, and has chosen to continue to apply the IAS 39 hedge accounting requirements; we believe that such an equity instrument is not an eligible hedged item as it will not impact profit or loss (see 14.2 below). *[IAS 39.86]*. This is because the specific guidance in paragraph 6.5.8 of IFRS 9 which permits designation of an equity instrument for which an entity has elected to present changes in fair value in other comprehensive income in a fair value hedges is not applicable if the entity remains on IAS 39 hedge accounting (see 2.6.3 above and 14.2 below).

13.2 Prospective application in general

A hedging relationship can only be designated on a prospective basis, in order to avoid the use of hindsight. The same concern about using hindsight would also apply if the IFRS 9 hedge accounting requirements were to be applied retrospectively. Consequently, the IASB decided that hedge accounting in accordance with IFRS 9 has to be applied prospectively, with some limited exceptions. *[IFRS 9.7.2.22]*. Because the date of initial application can only be the beginning of a reporting period, an entity can only start applying the hedge accounting requirements of IFRS 9 prospectively from the beginning of a reporting period, and only if all qualifying criteria – including the hedge accounting documentation that conforms to IFRS 9 are met on that date. *[IFRS 9.7.2.2, 7.2.23].*

When transitioning from applying hedge accounting under IAS 39 to IFRS 9, the standard clarifies that hedging relationships under IAS 39 which also qualify for hedge accounting under IFRS 9, are treated as continuing hedging relationships. *[IFRS 9.7.2.24].* Hedge accounting under IAS 39 ceases in the very same second as hedge accounting under IFRS 9 starts, therefore resulting in no accounting entries on transition. However, entities might have to rebalance their hedges on transition to fulfil the effectiveness requirements under IFRS 9 (see 7.4 above) in which case any resulting gain or loss must be recognised in profit or loss. *[IFRS 9.7.2.25].*

Entities will need to ensure the existing IAS 39 hedge documentation is updated to meet the requirements of IFRS 9 on the date of initial application (see 6.3 above). As a minimum this would include the following:

- reconsideration of the documented risk management strategy and objective;
- the approach and rationale for concluding the eligibility criteria are met, specifically an explanation of the economic relationship, the effect of credit risk, and the hedge ratio;
- identification of all major sources of ineffectiveness;
- justification for designation of any risk components;
- deletion of retrospective effectiveness assessment; and
- the approach to costs of hedging (if applicable).

13.3 Limited retrospective application

The exceptions from prospective application of IFRS 9 are for the accounting treatment for the time value of options, when only the intrinsic value is designated; and, at the option of the entity, for the forward element of forward contracts, when only the spot element is designated, and the foreign currency basis spread of financial instruments (see 7.5 above). However, retrospective application shall not be applied to items that have already been derecognised at the date of application. *[IFRS 9.7.2.1].*

13.3.1 Accounting for the time value of options

Entities must apply the new accounting treatment for the time value of options retrospectively, if in accordance with IAS 39, only the hedging option's intrinsic value was designated as part of the hedge relationship (see 14 below). However, retrospective treatment is only applied to hedging relationships that existed at the beginning of the earliest comparative period and hedging relationships designated thereafter. *[IFRS 9.7.2.26(a)].* There is also the restriction that IFRS 9 shall only be applied to items that have not been derecognised by the date of application, which would preclude any retrospective application to hedge relationships for which either of the hedging instrument or hedged item have been derecognised prior to that date. *[IFRS 9.7.2.1].*

For those foreign entities registered with and reporting to the United States Securities and Exchange Commission and required to present two comparative years of income statements, this means they would have a longer period to adjust for the retrospective application of the new requirements.

Applying the new accounting requirement retrospectively may have a much wider impact on comparative periods than is at first apparent. Depending on the type of hedging relationship, many line items in the primary statements and many disclosures in the notes may be affected.

Example 53.96: Retrospective application of accounting for time value of option

An entity applies the IFRS 9 hedge accounting requirements for the first time in its accounting period beginning 1 September 2021 and 1 September 2020 is the beginning of its earliest comparative period presented.

As of 1 September 2020, the entity had a hedging relationship in place in which the intrinsic value of an option was designated as the hedging instrument of a highly probable forecast purchase of a machine on 30 November 2021. For the purposes of this example, there is an assumption that no sources of ineffectiveness exist. When preparing the August 2022 financial statements, the entity would have to:

- determine the change in the time value of that option as of 1 September 2020 and restate accumulated other comprehensive income (OCI) against retained earnings as of that date;
- determine the change in time value of that option from 1 September 2020 to 31 August 2021 and restate accumulated OCI against retained earnings as of that date;
- reflect the restatement in the statement of profit or loss and other comprehensive income and the statement of changes in equity for the comparative period; and
- reflect the restatement in the notes disclosures.

13.3.2 Accounting for the forward element of forward contracts

Different to the accounting for the time value of options, entities have a choice of whether to apply retrospectively the new costs of hedging accounting for the forward element of forward contracts or not (see at 7.5.2 above). This is exclusively relevant for hedge relationships where, in accordance with IAS 39, only changes in the spot element of a hedging forward contract were designated within the hedge relationship. The choice applies on an all or nothing basis (i.e. if an entity elects to apply the accounting retrospectively, it must be applied to all hedging relationships that qualify for the election). The retrospective application would also only apply to those hedging relationships that 'existed' at the beginning of the earliest comparative period or that were designated thereafter. *[IFRS 9.7.2.26(b), BC7.49]*. We believe that in order for a hedge relationship to 'exist' as at the beginning of the earliest comparative period, it must have met all the hedge accounting conditions in paragraph 88 of IAS 39 on that date, including demonstration of effectiveness (see 14 below). Assets and liabilities cannot be adjusted to reflect hedges that had already finished at the start of the comparative period. Furthermore, if under IAS 39 a forward designation was made, yet on application of IFRS 9 a spot designation is deemed preferable, we believe that such a change to the designation should be treated as discontinuation of the original relationship and the re-designation of a new relationship, hence this retrospective application will not apply in that case, see 13.3.4 below.

13.3.3 Accounting for foreign currency basis spread

Similar to the retrospective transition guidance for the accounting for the forward element of forward contracts, it is also possible to apply retrospectively the accounting for foreign currency basis spreads (see at 7.5.3 above) on transition to IFRS 9 hedge accounting. However, in contrast to the transition requirements for the forward element of forward contracts, the decision to apply retrospectively the costs of hedging guidance on foreign currency basis spreads can be made on a hedge by hedge basis, without a requirement that foreign currency basis had been excluded from the designation under IAS 39. This is owing to the differences in circumstances: IAS 39 did not have an exception for excluding a foreign currency basis spread from the designation of a financial instrument as a hedging instrument. The hedge by hedge choice can be made for those hedging relationships that 'existed' at the beginning of the earliest comparative period or that were designated thereafter. *[IFRS 9.7.2.26(b), BC7.49]*.

13.3.4 Re-designation of hedge relationships for non-financial risk components

IFRS 9 permits the designation of eligible risk components in non-financial hedged items (see 2.2 above). Such a designation was not possible under IAS 39. This means, even if entities were economically hedging a risk component, they were obliged to designate the change in the entire hedged item as the hedged risk in order to achieve hedge accounting. Such a designation was likely to result in the recognition of ineffectiveness in profit or loss and in some cases failure of the effectiveness requirements.

On transition to IFRS 9 hedge accounting, entities may wish to amend hedge accounting relationships such that the hedged risk is an eligible risk component for non-financial hedged items. The question is whether that change in the documented hedged risk must result in the discontinuation of the original hedge relationship and the start of a new hedge relationship, or whether it can be treated as an amendment to the original designation such that the original hedge relationship continues. This question is particularly relevant for cash flow hedges, as on re-designation the non-zero fair value of the hedging instrument can result in subsequent ineffectiveness recorded in profit or loss (see 7.4.3 above).

We believe that such a change in the documented hedged risk should be treated as a discontinuation of the original hedge relationship and the re-designation of a new hedge relationship because it can be seen as either a change in the hedged item or a change in the documented risk management objective which both require discontinuation of a hedging relationship (see 8.3 above). *[IFRS 9.B6.5.26(a)]*.

The IASB was nervous of permitting any retrospective application of the IFRS 9 hedge accounting requirements, as such an application could involve the use of hindsight, for example as to whether it is beneficial or not to change the hedged risk to be an eligible risk component. The specific scenarios where retrospective application is permitted are those that either do not involve the use of hindsight as IFRS 9 application relied on particular choices that had already been made under IAS 39 (e.g. the designation of the intrinsic value of an option or the spot element of a forward) or where retrospective application was already permitted in IAS 39 (novation of a derivative through a central counterparty). *[IFRS 9.BC7.44-51]*. Due to the absence of a specific respective transition relief, it follows that a hedge relationship cannot continue if an eligible risk component under IFRS 9 is introduced into an existing IAS 39 hedge relationship.

The question has been asked as to whether this transition issue could be resolved by 'dual-designating' the hedge relationship, at the inception of the hedge, under both IAS 39 and IFRS 9. The IAS 39 designation would be for the full price risk, while the IFRS 9 designation would be of just the eligible risk component. Unfortunately this does not work, because the switch from the IAS 39 hedge designation to the IFRS 9 hedge designation would reflect a change in risk management objective, which would result in discontinuation of the first hedge relationship (see 8.3 above).

The logical follow-on question is whether an entity can continue with the original IAS 39 designation although it does not exactly represent the entity's risk management objective. We note that although the objective of hedge accounting under IFRS 9 is to represent an entity's risk management activities, *[IFRS 9.6.1.1]*, it does not require that it is an exact match. The Basis for Conclusions notes that, in some circumstances, the designation for hedge accounting purposes is inevitably not the same as an entity's risk management view of its hedging, but that the designation reflects risk management in that it relates to the same type of risk that is being managed and the instruments used for this purpose. The IASB refer to this situation as 'proxy hedging', which is an eligible way of designating the hedged item under IFRS 9 provided that it still reflects risk management (see 6.2.1 above). One example of proxy hedging mentioned is those instances where the risk management objective is to hedge a risk component but the accounting hedge designation is for the full price risk. Where there is a choice of accounting hedge designation, there is no requirement for an entity to select the designation that most closely matches the risk management view of hedging as long as the chosen approach still reflects risk management. *[IFRS 9.BC6.97, BC6.98, BC6.100(b)]*. Consequently, we believe that it is permitted, on transition, to continue with an accounting designation of the full price risk even if the management objective was always to hedge a component of risk, provided all the other qualifying criteria are met (see 6.1 above).

Both questions above were debated by the IFRS Interpretations Committee in September 2015 and January 2016. The final agenda decision reached by the Interpretations Committee is consistent with the analysis presented above.[31]

14 MAIN DIFFERENCES BETWEEN IFRS 9 AND IAS 39 HEDGE ACCOUNTING REQUIREMENTS

Most of the basics of hedge accounting are the same under both IFRS 9 and IAS 39, however there are some significant differences. We discuss the main differences between IFRS 9 and IAS 39 hedge accounting below.

IAS 39 includes some specific guidance originally designed with portfolio fair value hedges of interest rate risk. Equivalent guidance does not appear in IFRS 9 – see 11 above for further details.

IAS 39 includes extensive Implementation Guidance on the application of hedge accounting. In developing IFRS 9, the IASB decided not to carry forward any of the hedge accounting related Implementation Guidance that accompanied IAS 39. However the IASB emphasised that not carrying forward the Implementation Guidance did not mean that it had rejected the guidance for the application of IFRS 9. *[IFRS 9.BC6.93-95]*. Much, but not all, of the Implementation Guidance in IAS 39 therefore remains relevant on application of IFRS 9 (see 1.3 above).

14.1 The objective of hedge accounting

The objective of IFRS 9 hedge accounting is to represent in the financial statements, the effect of an entity's risk management activities that use instruments to manage exposures arising from particular risks that could affect profit or loss (or OCI in the case of equity investment designated at FVOCI). This approach aims to convey the context of hedging instruments for which hedge accounting is applied in order to provide insight into their purpose and effect. *[IFRS 9.6.1.1]*. There is no such objective within IAS 39.

The perceived purpose of hedge accounting under IAS 39 is to reduce the accounting mismatches caused by risk management activity, but it has no conceptual objective. Consequently it is a more rules-based standard, which is particularly evident in the 80-125% quantitative threshold for the hedge effectiveness assessment (see 14.4 below).

Similar to IFRS 9, IAS 39 includes a requirement to document the risk management strategy and risk management objective for undertaking the hedge (see 6.2 above). *[IAS 39.88(a)]*. However, whereas, under IFRS 9, the risk management objective is rooted in risk management practice and determines whether the hedge relationship can be or should be discontinued, under IAS 39 it is just part of the accounting designation.

14.2 Eligible hedged items

The hedge accounting guidance under IAS 39 has a number of additional restrictions on the eligibility of hedged items that do not appear within the IFRS 9 guidance. Most important is the preclusion of designating any risk components in non-financial hedged items, other than foreign currency risk. The rationale at the time was the difficulty of isolating and measuring the appropriate portion of cash flows or fair value changes attributable to specific risks (other than foreign currency risks) in a non-financial asset or liability. *[IAS 39.82, AG100]*. This preclusion has been removed in IFRS 9 (see 2.2 above).

The ability to designate an aggregated exposure, which includes a derivative as the hedged item in a second hedging relationship is not possible under IAS 39 (see 2.7 above). In order to achieve hedge accounting for the hedging instrument in the 'second hedge relationship', under IAS 39 the first hedge relationship would need to be de-designated and a new hedge relationship with a combined hedge instrument (i.e. the hedging instrument from the first and second hedge relationship) would need to be designated. The combined hedging derivative is likely to have a non-zero fair value which could result in additional ineffectiveness for a cash flow hedge (see 7.4.3 above).

In addition, IAS 39 includes a complete prohibition on designating inflation as a risk component unless there is a contractually specified inflation portion, which is a harsher position than in IFRS 9 (see 2.2.6 above). *[IAS 39.AG99F]*.

IAS 39 also permits designation of groups of hedged items, however the designation of a net position is prohibited under IAS 39, only gross designations are allowed. *[IAS 39.84]*. In addition, groups of hedged items are only eligible for designation if the change in fair value attributable to the hedged risk for each individual item in the group was expected to be approximately proportional to the overall change in fair value attributable to the hedged risk of the group of items. *[IAS 39.83]*. This requirement does not form part of IFRS 9 hedge accounting (see 2.5 above).

Although a hedge of a component is permitted under IAS 39, the type of eligible component is more restrictive than under IFRS 9 (see 2.3 above). For example, it is not possible to designate a layer of a hedged item in a fair value hedge. In order to achieve hedge accounting, designation of a proportion or specific cash flows within the hedged item would be required.

IFRS 9 includes an exception to the requirement that hedges could affect profit or loss, that is when an entity is hedging an investment in equity instruments for which it has elected to present changes in fair value in OCI (see 2.6.3 above and Chapter 48 at 2.2). *[IFRS 9.6.5.3]*. No such exception exists under IAS 39, hence hedge accounting is precluded for equity investments for which the entity has elected to present changes in fair value in OCI. *[IAS 39.86]*.

14.3 Eligible hedging instruments

Under IFRS 9 it is possible to designate, as hedging instruments, non-derivative financial assets or non-derivative financial liabilities that are accounted for at fair value through profit or loss (except for financial liabilities designated at fair value through profit or loss) (see 3.3 above). *[IFRS 9.6.2.2]*. However, this is not possible under IAS 39. It was previously possible only to designate a non-derivative financial instrument as the hedging instrument for a hedge of foreign currency risk, which is of course still permitted under IFRS 9 (see 3.3.1 above). *[IAS 39.72]*.

Similar to IFRS 9, a standalone written option is prohibited from qualifying as a hedging instrument under IAS 39, unless it is as an offset to a purchased option, including one that is embedded in another financial instrument (see 3.2 above). However, IAS 39 does not allow standalone written options to be designated within a combination of other hedging derivatives, even if the combination of all the derivatives is not a net written option. *[IAS 39.AG94]*.

14.4 Effectiveness criteria

Perhaps the most significant difference between IAS 39 and IFRS 9 is the criteria as to whether a hedge relationship is eligible for hedge accounting or not. Whilst IFRS 9 takes a principle-based approach (see 6.4 and 14.1 above), the eligibility criteria under IAS 39 are more rules based. In particular, IAS 39 requires that:

- the entity should expect the hedge to be highly effective in achieving offsetting changes in fair value or cash flows attributable to the hedged risk, consistent with the originally documented risk management strategy for that particular hedging relationship;
- the hedge should be assessed on an ongoing basis and determined actually to have been highly effective throughout the financial reporting periods for which the hedge was designated; *[IAS 39.88]*
- a hedge is regarded as highly effective only if both of the following conditions are met:
    i) at the inception of the hedge, and in subsequent periods, the hedge is expected to be highly effective in achieving offsetting changes in fair value or cash flows attributable to the hedged risk during the period for which the hedge is designated; and
    ii) the actual results of the hedge are within a range of 80% to 125%.

    For example, if actual results are such that the loss on the hedging instrument is €120 and the gain on the cash instrument is €100, offset can be measured by 120 ÷ 100, which is 120%, or by 100 ÷ 120, which is 83%. In this example, assuming the hedge meets the condition in (i), it would be concluded that the hedge has been highly effective. *[IAS 39.AG105(b)]*.

It can be seen that IAS 39 requires that hedge relationships pass both a retrospective and prospective effectiveness test in order to achieve hedge accounting. The test itself is more restrictive, as it includes the requirement to achieve an arbitrary 80%-125% level of offset. The IFRS 9 effectiveness requirements are only forward looking, will normally be qualitative and permit judgement as to whether the requirements are met (see 8 above). Hence many more hedge relationships are precluded from hedge accounting under the stricter IAS 39 effectiveness tests. However, the requirement to measure and record any ineffectiveness is consistent under both IFRS 9 and IAS 39 (see 7.4 above). *[IAS 39.89, 96]*.

14.5 Discontinuation

There is significant overlap in the guidance on discontinuation of hedge accounting under IAS 39 and IFRS 9, however there are some important differences. Whilst discontinuation of a hedge relationship is only permitted under IFRS 9 if one of the mandatory discontinuation criteria occur (see 8.3 above), there is no prohibition on voluntary discontinuation of designated hedge relationships under IAS 39. An entity can just choose to prospectively stop hedge accounting. *[IAS 39.91(c), 101(d)]*.

If the IAS 39 effectiveness test is failed (see 14.4. above), then the hedge relationship must be discontinued and hedge accounting ceases from the last time the hedge relationship was effective. Under IAS 39 there is no opportunity to rebalance the hedge relationship, amend the method of assessing effectiveness or undertake a partial discontinuation (see 8.2, 6.3 and 8.3 above). *[IAS 39.91(b), 101(b)]*. In addition, under IFRS 9, if discontinuation is required, this is only applied prospectively (see 8.3 above).

The risk management objective plays a much more important role within IFRS 9 hedge accounting than under IAS 39 (see 14.1 above). For example, there is no requirement to monitor whether the risk management objective has changed under IAS 39, as such a change is not one of the mandatory discontinuation criteria as it is under IFRS 9 (see 8.3 above).

14.6 Hedge accounting mechanisms

The basic IAS 39 hedge accounting mechanics are the same as those under IFRS 9 (see 7 above). However IFRS 9 contains some accounting mechanisms that do not appear within IAS 39.

Although it is possible under IAS 39 to exclude the time value of a hedging option and the forward element of a forward contract from the hedging derivative, similar to IFRS 9 (see 3.6.4 and 3.6.5 above), the accounting treatment of the excluded components differ. Under IAS 39, it is not possible to apply the costs of hedging accounting to the excluded time value of an option or the forward element of a forward contract (see 7.5 above). Accordingly the excluded portions will remain at fair value through profit or loss. So, although the excluded time value or forward element do not affect the hedge effectiveness assessment (see 14.4 above), they are likely to result in profit or loss volatility under IAS 39. *[IAS 39.74]*. It is also worth noting that under IAS 39 there is no opportunity to exclude the foreign currency basis from a hedging derivative (see 7.4.8 and 7.5.3 above).

IFRS 9 includes two alternatives to hedge accounting: the fair value option for credit risk exposures (see 12.1 above) and a fair value option for own use contracts (see 12.2 above). Neither of these alternatives are available under IAS 39.

References

1. For example, see IAS 39 (2000), *Financial Instruments: Recognition and Measurement*, IASC, December 1998 to October 2000, para. 10.
2. Press Release, *IASB sets out timetable for IAS 39 replacement and its conclusions on FASB FSPs*, IASB, April 2009.
3. Press Release, *Draft of forthcoming IFRS on general hedge accounting*, September 2012.
4. *IFRIC Update*, June 2019.
5. *IFRIC Update*, March 2019.
6. *DP/2014/1* paras. 1.14-1.15 and 3.9.1-3.9.16.
7. *IFRIC Update*, June 2019.
8. Dynamic Risk Management: Derivatives used for DRM purposes, *IASB staff paper 4B*, June 2018, para. 11.
9. *IFRIC Update*, July 2007.
10. IGC Q&A 137-13.
11. *IFRIC Update*, June 2019.
12. *IASB Update*, January 2013.
13. *IFRIC Update*, June 2019.
14. Information for Observers (February 2007 IASB meeting), *Business Combinations II: Reassessments (Agenda Paper 2B)*, IASB, February 2007, para. 25.
15. *IFRIC Update*, March 2019.
16. Information for Observers (February 2007 IASB meeting), *Business Combinations II: Reassessments (Agenda Paper 2B)*, IASB, February 2007, para. 28 and Information for Observers (April 2007 IASB meeting), *Classification and Designation of Assets, Liabilities and Equity Instruments Acquired or Assumed in a Business Combination (Agenda Paper 2B)*, IASB, April 2007, item #5, table following para. 14.
17. *IFRIC Update*, November 2016.
18. ASC 815-35-35-1 through 35-26 (formerly, Statement 133 Implementation Issue H8, *Foreign Currency Hedges: Measuring the Amount of Ineffectiveness in a Net Investment Hedge*).
19. *IFRIC Update*, March 2016.
20. ASC 815-35-35-1 to 35-26 (formerly, Statement 133 Implementation Issue H8, *Foreign Currency Hedges: Measuring the Amount of Ineffectiveness in a Net Investment Hedge*).
21. www.bbalibor.com/explained/definitions (24 July 2013).
22. *IFRIC Update*, March 2007.
23. *IASB Update*, January 2013.
24. *IFRIC Update*, January 2011.
25. *IFRIC Update*, January 2013.
26. Staff paper 14A prepared for the January 2020 Board meeting.
27. *IFRIC Update*, March 2018.
28. *IASB Update*, May 2012.
29. *IASB Update*, January 2013.
30. For example: *Request to allow hedge accounting to comply with either IAS 39 or IFRS 9 while the macro hedging project is developed*, letter from EFRAG to the IASB, 22 March 2013.
31. *IFRIC Update*, January 2016.

Chapter 54 Financial instruments: Presentation and disclosure

1 INTRODUCTION 4405
   1.1   IAS 32 4405
   1.2   IFRS 7 4405
2 SCOPE OF IFRS 7 4406
   2.1   Entities required to comply with IFRS 7 4406
   2.2   Financial instruments within the scope of IFRS 7 4406
   2.3   Interim reports 4406
3 STRUCTURING THE DISCLOSURES 4407
   3.1   Level of detail 4408
   3.2   Materiality 4408
   3.3   Classes of financial instrument 4408
4 SIGNIFICANCE OF FINANCIAL INSTRUMENTS FOR AN ENTITY'S FINANCIAL POSITION AND PERFORMANCE 4409
   4.1   Accounting policies 4409
   4.2   Income, expenses, gains and losses 4410
       4.2.1   Gains and losses by measurement category 4410
       4.2.2   Interest income and expense 4411
       4.2.3   Fee income and expense 4411
   4.3   Hedge accounting 4412
       4.3.1   The risk management strategy 4413
       4.3.2   The amount, timing and uncertainty of future cash flows 4415
       4.3.3   The effects of hedge accounting on financial position and performance 4416

		4.3.4	Option to designate a credit exposure as measured at fair value through profit or loss	4423
		4.3.5	Uncertainty arising from interest rate benchmark (IBOR) reform	4423
	4.4	Statement of financial position		4424
		4.4.1	Categories of financial assets and financial liabilities	4424
		4.4.2	Financial liabilities designated at fair value through profit or loss	4425
		4.4.3	Financial assets designated as measured at fair value through profit or loss	4426
		4.4.4	Investments in equity instruments designated at fair value through other comprehensive income	4426
		4.4.5	Reclassification	4427
		4.4.6	Collateral	4427
		4.4.7	Compound financial instruments with multiple embedded derivatives	4428
		4.4.8	Defaults and breaches of loans payable	4428
		4.4.9	Interests in associates and joint ventures accounted for in accordance with IFRS 9	4429
	4.5	Fair values		4429
		4.5.1	General disclosure requirements	4429
		4.5.2	Day 1 profits	4430
	4.6	Business combinations		4432
		4.6.1	Acquired receivables	4432
		4.6.2	Contingent consideration and indemnification assets	4433
5	NATURE AND EXTENT OF RISKS ARISING FROM FINANCIAL INSTRUMENTS			4433
	5.1	Qualitative disclosures		4435
	5.2	Quantitative disclosures		4438
	5.3	Credit risk		4439
		5.3.1	Scope and objectives	4439
		5.3.2	Credit risk management practices	4440
		5.3.3	Quantitative and qualitative information about amounts arising from expected credit losses	4441
		5.3.4	Credit risk exposure	4446
		5.3.5	Collateral and other credit enhancements obtained	4449
		5.3.6	Credit risk: illustrative disclosures	4450
	5.4	Liquidity risk		4454
		5.4.1	Information provided to key management	4454
		5.4.2	Maturity analyses	4454
			5.4.2.A Time bands	4454

	5.4.2.B	Cash flows: general requirements 4456
	5.4.2.C	Cash flows: borrowings 4457
	5.4.2.D	Cash flows: derivatives 4457
	5.4.2.E	Cash flows: embedded derivatives 4458
	5.4.2.F	Cash flows: financial guarantee contracts and written options 4458
	5.4.2.G	Examples of disclosures in practice 4459
5.4.3	Management of associated liquidity risk 4462
5.4.4	Puttable financial instruments classified as equity 4463

5.5 Market risk 4463
    5.5.1 'Basic' sensitivity analysis 4463
    5.5.2 Value-at-risk and similar analyses 4469
    5.5.3 Other market risk disclosures 4470

5.6 Quantitative disclosures: other matters 4471
    5.6.1 Concentrations of risk 4471
    5.6.2 Operational risk 4472
    5.6.3 Capital disclosures 4472

5.7 Interest rate benchmark (or IBOR) reform 4473

6 TRANSFERS OF FINANCIAL ASSETS 4474

6.1 The meaning of 'transfer' 4474

6.2 Transferred financial assets that are not derecognised in their entirety 4475

6.3 Transferred financial assets that are derecognised in their entirety 4477
    6.3.1 Meaning of continuing involvement 4477
    6.3.2 Disclosure requirements 4478

7 PRESENTATION ON THE FACE OF THE FINANCIAL STATEMENTS AND RELATED DISCLOSURES 4481

7.1 Gains and losses recognised in profit or loss 4481
    7.1.1 Presentation on the face of the statement of comprehensive income (or income statement) 4481
    7.1.2 Further analysis of gains and losses recognised in profit or loss 4485
    7.1.3 Offsetting and hedges 4486
    7.1.4 Embedded derivatives 4488
    7.1.5 Entities whose share capital is not equity 4488

7.2 Gains and losses recognised in other comprehensive income 4489

7.3 Statement of changes in equity 4490

7.4 Statement of financial position 4491
    7.4.1 Offsetting financial assets and financial liabilities 4491
        7.4.1.A Criterion (a): Enforceable legal right of set-off 4492

	7.4.1.B	Master netting agreements	4495
	7.4.1.C	Criterion (b): Intention to settle net or realise the gross amount simultaneously ('the net settlement criterion')	4495
	7.4.1.D	Situations where offset is not normally appropriate	4497
	7.4.1.E	Cash pooling arrangements	4498
	7.4.1.F	Offsetting collateral amounts	4499
	7.4.1.G	Unit of account	4500
7.4.2	Offsetting financial assets and financial liabilities: disclosure		4500
	7.4.2.A	Objective	4500
	7.4.2.B	Scope	4500
	7.4.2.C	Disclosure requirements	4501
	7.4.2.D	Offsetting disclosures – illustrative examples	4503
7.4.3	Assets and liabilities		4508
	7.4.3.A	Supply chain financing and reverse factoring arrangements – introduction	4509
	7.4.3.B	Supply chain financing and reverse factoring arrangements – presentation in the statement of financial position	4511
	7.4.3.C	Supply chain financing and reverse factoring arrangements – derecognition of a financial liability	4512
	7.4.3.D	Supply chain financing and reverse factoring arrangements – presentation in the statement of cash flows	4512
	7.4.3.E	Supply chain financing and reverse factoring arrangements – notes to the financial statements	4513
	7.4.3.F	Supply chain financing and reverse factoring arrangements – summary and example disclosure	4514
7.4.4	The distinction between current and non-current assets and liabilities		4515
	7.4.4.A	Derivatives	4515
	7.4.4.B	Convertible loans	4515
	7.4.4.C	Long-term loans with repayment on demand terms	4516
	7.4.4.D	Debt with refinancing or roll over agreements	4516
	7.4.4.E	Loan covenants	4517
7.4.5	Equity		4517
7.4.6	Entities whose share capital is not equity		4518
7.5 Statement of cash flows			4520

8   EFFECTIVE DATES AND TRANSITIONAL PROVISIONS 4520
9   FUTURE DEVELOPMENTS 4521
    9.1   General developments 4521
    9.2   Enhanced Disclosure Task Force.. 4522

List of examples

Example 54.1:	Illustrative disclosure of risk management strategy for commodity price risk...	4414
Example 54.2:	Illustrative disclosure of timing, nominal amount and average price of coffee futures contracts	4415
Example 54.3:	Amounts related to hedged instruments	4416
Example 54.4:	Amounts related to hedged items..	4417
Example 54.5:	Amounts affecting the statement of comprehensive income...	4419
Example 54.6:	Illustrative disclosure of the effects of hedge accounting on the financial position and performance	4419
Example 54.7:	Disclosure of deferred day 1 profits	4431
Example 54.8:	Information about changes in the loss allowance.......................	4443
Example 54.9:	Information about credit risk exposures and significant credit risk concentrations	4447
Example 54.10:	Information about credit risk exposures using a provision matrix	4448
Example 54.11:	Certain disclosures of impairment allowances by a bank for one class of lending..	4450
Example 54.12:	Maturity analysis: floating rate borrowing	4457
Example 54.13:	Illustration of how sensitivity disclosures can be determined..	4465
Example 54.14:	Illustrative disclosure of sensitivity analyses...............................	4467
Example 54.15:	Quantitative disclosures for transferred assets not fully derecognised	4476
Example 54.16:	Quantitative disclosures for transferred assets fully derecognised	4480
Example 54.17:	Physical settlement of sales contract that is accounted for as a derivative financial instrument...	4484
Example 54.18:	Statement of comprehensive income (or income statement) format for a mutual fund	4488
Example 54.19:	Statement of comprehensive income (income statement) format for a co-operative...	4489
Example 54.20:	Illustration of offsetting disclosures	4504
Example 54.21:	Statement of financial position format for a mutual fund..........	4518
Example 54.22:	Statement of financial position format for a co-operative	4519

Chapter 54   Financial instruments: Presentation and disclosure

1 INTRODUCTION

Disclosure of financial instruments is largely dealt with in IFRS 7 – *Financial Instruments: Disclosures* – and presentation in IAS 32 – *Financial Instruments: Presentation*. The development of these standards is outlined below.

1.1 IAS 32

The original version of IAS 32 – *Financial Instruments: Disclosure and Presentation* – was published in March 1995 and, as its title suggested, contained requirements about the disclosures entities should make about financial instruments. These requirements were superseded by IFRS 7 (see 1.2 below) which also changed the name of the standard.

One of the topics IAS 32 continues to address is when entities should offset financial assets and financial liabilities, the associated requirements for which are discussed at 7.4.1 below. It also addresses the classification of financial instruments as equity, financial liabilities or financial assets, a topic covered in Chapter 47. IAS 32 has been amended a number of times since publication, including in December 2011 when the IASB addressed certain practical problems it had identified in its offsetting requirements.

1.2 IFRS 7

IFRS 7 emerged from a project principally focused on revising IAS 30 – *Disclosures in the Financial Statements of Banks and Similar Financial Institutions* – a standard which, at the time, set out additional disclosure requirements for banks and similar entities. It was published in August 2005 and superseded IAS 30.

The standard has been subject to significant amendment since its original publication, in particular to address concerns raised during the financial crisis. These amendments aimed to improve the disclosures entities provide in a number of areas including liquidity risk, transfers of financial assets, offsetting and fair values (most of the disclosures for which are now included in IFRS 13 – *Fair Value Measurement* – see Chapter 14).

In July 2014, the IASB published a substantially final version of IFRS 9 – *Financial Instruments* – its replacement for IAS 39 – *Financial Instruments: Recognition and Measurement*. The new standard changed the framework for classifying and measuring financial assets and financial liabilities; introduced an expected loss approach for determining impairment losses on financial assets and amended the requirements for applying hedge accounting. It also made a number of consequential amendments to IFRS 7, introducing extensive new disclosures in respect of impairment (see 5.3 below) and hedge accounting (see 4.3 below) as well as making other changes.

The objective of IFRS 7 is to require entities to provide disclosures in their financial statements that enable users to evaluate: *[IFRS 7.1]*

- the significance of financial instruments for the entity's financial position and performance; and
- the nature and extent of risks arising from financial instruments to which the entity is exposed during the period and at the reporting date, and how the entity manages those risks.

These objectives manifest themselves in two disclosure principles (see 4 and 5 below) which are designed to complement those for recognising, measuring and presenting financial assets and financial liabilities in IAS 32 and IFRS 9. *[IFRS 7.2]*.

2 SCOPE OF IFRS 7

2.1 Entities required to comply with IFRS 7

Although IFRS 7 evolved from a project to update IAS 30 (which applied only to banks and similar financial institutions) it applies to all entities preparing their financial statements in accordance with IFRS that have financial instruments. *[IFRS 7.BC6]*. The IASB considered exempting certain entities, including insurers, subsidiaries and those that are small or medium-sized (SMEs), but decided that IFRS 7 should apply to all entities applying IFRS. *[IFRS 7.BC9, BC10, BC11]*. Entities applying the IFRS for SMEs are required to provide only reduced disclosures about financial instruments.

2.2 Financial instruments within the scope of IFRS 7

Chapter 45 at 3 and 4 contains a detailed explanation of the scope of IFRS 7. It is important to recognise that the scope of IFRS 7 is generally somewhat wider than that of IFRS 9. Therefore IFRS 7 can apply to instruments that are not subject to the recognition and measurement provisions of IFRS 9. *[IFRS 7.4]*. For example, lease liabilities and certain loan commitments are within the scope of IFRS 7 even though they are not, or not wholly, within the scope of IFRS 9. Conversely, some financial instruments within the scope of IFRS 9, particularly those held in disposal groups or as part of discontinued operations, are not subject to all of the requirements in IFRS 7.

2.3 Interim reports

IAS 34 – *Interim Financial Reporting* – sets out the minimum content of an interim financial report. When an event or transaction is significant to an understanding of the changes in an entity's financial position or performance since the last annual financial period, IAS 34 requires the report to provide an explanation of, and update to, the information included in the last annual financial statements. *[IAS 34.15]*. The standard emphasises that relatively insignificant updates need not be provided. *[IAS 34.15A]*. The following disclosures which relate to financial instruments are required if significant: *[IAS 34.15B]*

- losses recognised from the impairment of financial assets;
- changes in the business or economic circumstances that affect the fair value of the entity's financial assets and financial liabilities, whether recognised at fair value or amortised cost;
- any loan default or breach of a loan agreement that has not been remedied on or before the end of the reporting period;
- transfers between levels of the fair value hierarchy used in the measurement of the fair value of financial instruments; and
- changes in the classification of financial assets as a result of a change in the purpose or use of those assets.

In considering the extent of disclosures necessary to meet the requirements above, IAS 34 refers to the guidance included in other IFRSs, *[IAS 34.15C]*, which would include IFRS 7, but does not ordinarily require compliance with all the requirements in those standards.

IAS 34 also specifies additional disclosures to be given (normally on a financial year-to-date basis) about the fair value of financial instruments, including those discussed at 4.5 below and a number required by IFRS 13. *[IAS 34.16A(j)]*. This requirement is not subject to the qualifications noted above and so, as discussed in further detail in Chapter 41 at 4.5, these disclosures should always be given unless the information is not material.

The disclosures about offsetting of financial assets and financial liabilities (see 7.4.2 below) need not be provided in condensed interim financial statements unless required by the more general requirements of IAS 34. *[IFRS 7.BC72B, BC72C]*.

3 STRUCTURING THE DISCLOSURES

The main text of IFRS 7 is supplemented by application guidance, which is an integral part of the standard,[1] and by implementation guidance, which accompanies, but is not part of, the standard.[2] The implementation guidance suggests possible ways of applying some of the requirements of the standard but, it is emphasised, does not create additional requirements. *[IFRS 7.IG1]*.

Although the implementation guidance discusses each disclosure requirement in IFRS 7 separately, disclosures would normally be presented as an integrated package and individual disclosures might satisfy more than one requirement. For example, information about concentrations of risk might also convey information about exposure to credit or other risk. *[IFRS 7.IG2]*. This chapter follows a similar approach whereby each topic is considered individually in the context of the requirements of the standard as well as related application and implementation guidance.

3.1 Level of detail

Entities need to decide, in the light of their circumstances, how much detail to provide to satisfy the requirements of IFRS 7, how much emphasis to place on different aspects of the requirements and how information is aggregated to display the overall picture without combining information with different characteristics. It is necessary to strike a balance between overburdening financial statements with excessive detail that may not assist users of financial statements and obscuring important information as a result of too much aggregation. For example, important information should not be obscured by including it among a large amount of insignificant detail. Similarly, information should not be aggregated so that it obscures important differences between individual transactions or associated risks. *[IFRS 7.B3]*.

This means that not all of the information suggested, say, in the implementation guidance is necessarily required. *[IFRS 7.IG5]*. On the other hand, there is a reminder that IAS 1 – *Presentation of Financial Statements* – requires additional disclosures when compliance with the specific requirements in IFRSs is insufficient to enable users to understand the impact of particular transactions, other events and conditions on the entity's financial position and financial performance (see Chapter 3 at 4.1.1.A). *[IFRS 7.IG6]*.

3.2 Materiality

The implementation guidance to the original version of IFRS 7 drew attention to the definition of materiality in IAS 1 (see Chapter 3 at 4.1.5.A), noting that a specific disclosure requirement need not be satisfied if the information is not material. *[IFRS 7(2010).IG3]*. The inclusion of such guidance was intended to provide a degree of reassurance that entities with few financial instruments and few risks (for example a manufacturer whose only financial instruments are accounts receivable and accounts payable) will give few disclosures, something that was borne out in other references within the standard and accompanying material. *[IFRS 7.BC10]*. Nevertheless, in May 2010, the IASB removed all references to materiality from IFRS 7 because they thought that they could imply that other disclosures in IFRS 7 are required even if those disclosures are not material, which was not the intention. *[IFRS 7.BC47A]*.

3.3 Classes of financial instrument

Certain disclosures required by IFRS 7 should be provided by class of financial instrument (see 4.5.1, 4.5.2, 5.3 and 6 below). For these, entities should group financial instruments into classes that are appropriate to the nature of the information disclosed and take into account the characteristics of those instruments. *[IFRS 7.6]*. It is clear from this requirement that the classes used need not be the same for each disclosure provided, e.g. one set of classes may be used to present information about credit risk (see 5.3 below) and another for information about day 1 profits (see 4.5.2 below).

It is emphasised that these classes should be determined by the entity and are, thus, distinct from the categories of financial instruments specified in IFRS 9 which determine how financial instruments are measured and where changes in fair value are recognised. *[IFRS 7.B1]*. However, in determining classes of financial instrument an entity should, as a minimum, distinguish instruments measured at amortised cost from those measured at fair value and treat as a separate class or classes those financial instruments outside the scope of IFRS 7. *[IFRS 7.B2]*.

For disclosures given by class of instrument, sufficient information should be provided to permit the information to be reconciled to the line items presented in the statement of financial position. *[IFRS 7.6]*.

4 SIGNIFICANCE OF FINANCIAL INSTRUMENTS FOR AN ENTITY'S FINANCIAL POSITION AND PERFORMANCE

The IASB decided that the disclosure requirements in this area should result from the following disclosure principle:

> 'An entity shall disclose information that enables users of its financial statements to evaluate the significance of financial instruments for its financial position and performance.'

Further, they concluded that this principle could not be satisfied unless other specified disclosures (which are dealt with at 4.1 to 4.5 below) are also provided. *[IFRS 7.7, BC13]*.

4.1 Accounting policies

The main body of IFRS 7 contains a reminder of IAS 1's requirement for an entity to disclose its significant accounting policies, comprising the measurement basis (or bases) used in preparing the financial statements and the other accounting policies used that are relevant to an understanding of the financial statements. *[IFRS 7.21]*.

For financial assets and financial liabilities designated as measured at fair value through profit or loss (see Chapter 48 at 7), such disclosure may include: *[IFRS 7.B5(a), B5(aa)]*

- the nature of the financial assets or financial liabilities designated as measured at fair value through profit or loss;
- the criteria for so designating financial liabilities on initial recognition; and
- how the conditions or criteria in IFRS 9 for such designation have been satisfied.

Other policies that might be appropriate include: *[IFRS 7.B5(c), B5(e), B5(f), B5(g)]*

- whether regular way purchases and sales of financial assets are accounted for at trade date or at settlement date (see Chapter 49 at 2.2); and
- how net gains or net losses on each category of financial instrument are determined (see 4.2.1 below), for example whether the net gains or net losses on items measured at fair value through profit or loss include interest or dividend income.

  In our view, interest income and interest expense (including, for example, that arising on short positions) should be treated consistently, i.e. both included or both excluded from the net gains and losses disclosed.

  Although related, different considerations will apply to the requirement to present separately on the face of the statement of comprehensive income (or income statement) interest revenue calculated using the effective interest method – see 7.1.1 below.

The application guidance also contains a reminder that IAS 1 requires entities to disclose the judgements, apart from those involving estimations, that management has made in the process of applying the entity's accounting policies and that have the most significant effect on the amounts recognised in the financial statements (see Chapter 3 at 5.1.1.B). *[IFRS 7.B5]*. These might include those an entity has used in applying hedge accounting requirements of IFRS 9, for example those made in determining whether an economic relationship exists between the hedged item and the hedging instrument, how the hedge ratio was set and how risk components were identified.

4.2 Income, expenses, gains and losses

Under IFRS 7, entities are required to disclose various items of income, expense, gains and losses. The disclosures below may be provided either on the face of the financial statements or in the notes. *[IFRS 7.20]*.

4.2.1 Gains and losses by measurement category

The IASB concluded that information about the gains and losses arising on the various measurement categories of instrument is necessary to understand the financial performance of an entity's financial instruments given the different measurement bases used. Consequently, disclosure should be given of net gains or net losses arising on the following categories of instrument: *[IFRS 7.20]*

- financial assets or financial liabilities measured at fair value through profit or loss, showing separately those on financial assets or liabilities:
  - designated as such upon initial recognition (or subsequently when the credit risk of a financial asset is managed using a credit derivative); and
  - mandatorily measured at fair value in accordance with IFRS 9, e.g. liabilities held for trading.

  In our view, these amounts should not be shown net of funding costs if the associated financial liabilities are not classified at fair value through profit or loss.

  For financial liabilities designated at fair value through profit or loss, the amount of gain or loss recognised in other comprehensive income, i.e. relating to changes in fair value attributable to changes in credit risk (see Chapter 50 at 2.4.1), should be shown separately;

- financial assets measured at amortised cost.

  IFRS 7 requires disclosure of an analysis of the gain or loss arising from derecognition of such assets showing separately gains and losses. The reasons for derecognition should also be given. *[IFRS 7.20A]*. These gains and losses should also be shown separately on the face of the income statement or statement of comprehensive income (see 7.1.1 below); *[IAS 1.82(aa)]*

- financial liabilities measured at amortised cost;
- investments in equity instruments designated at fair value through other comprehensive income; and
- debt instruments measured at fair value through other comprehensive income, showing separately:
  - the amount of gain or loss recognised in other comprehensive income during the period; and

- the amount reclassified upon derecognition from accumulated other comprehensive income to profit or loss for the period.

These disclosures are designed to complement the statement of financial position disclosure requirement described at 4.4.1 below. *[IFRS 7.BC33]*.

Some entities include interest and dividend income in gains and losses on financial assets and financial liabilities held for trading and others do not. To assist users in comparing income arising from financial instruments across different entities, entities are required to disclose how the income statement amounts are determined. For example, an entity should disclose whether net gains and losses on financial assets or financial liabilities held for trading include interest and dividend income (see 4.1 above). *[IFRS 7.BC34]*.

4.2.2 Interest income and expense

For financial assets or financial liabilities that are not measured at fair value through profit or loss, total interest income and total interest expense (calculated using the effective interest method) should be disclosed. Interest revenue for financial assets measured at amortised cost should be shown separately from interest revenue on debt instruments measured at fair value through other comprehensive income. *[IFRS 7.20(b)]*. This disclosure requirement is similar, but different, to the requirement to present separately on the face of the statement of comprehensive income (or income statement) interest revenue calculated using the effective interest method – see 7.1.1 below.

Financial instruments containing discretionary participation features fall within the scope of IFRS 4 – *Insurance Contracts* – rather than IFRS 9 (see Chapter 45 at 3.3.2 and Chapter 55 at 6) or IAS 39 for those insurers continuing to apply that standard (see Chapter 55 at 10.1). However, IFRS 7 does apply to such instruments and IFRS 4 acknowledges that the interest expense disclosed need not be calculated using the effective interest method. *[IFRS 4.35(d)]*. When IFRS 17 – *Insurance Contracts* – is applied, such contracts would only rarely be within the scope of IFRS 7 (see Chapter 45 at 3.3.2).

Similarly, lease liabilities and finance lease receivables are within the scope of IFRS 7 (see Chapter 45 at 3.2) but are not accounted for using the effective interest method. There is no equivalent acknowledgement in IFRS 16 – *Leases* – or IFRS 9 that the disclosure of interest income and interest expense should be made on the basis of the finance cost and finance revenue recognised under the relevant standard for leases. However, this seems little more than an oversight and we consider it appropriate to include in the disclosure the amounts actually recognised rather than amounts calculated in accordance with the effective interest method.

4.2.3 Fee income and expense

Entities should disclose fee income and expense (excluding amounts included in the effective interest rate calculation) arising from: *[IFRS 7.20(c)]*

- financial assets or financial liabilities that are not measured at fair value through profit or loss; and
- trust and other fiduciary activities that result in the holding or investing of assets on behalf of individuals, trusts, retirement benefit plans, and other institutions.

This information is said to indicate the level of such activities and help users to estimate possible future income of the entity. *[IFRS 7.BC35]*.

4.3 Hedge accounting

When developing IFRS 9 many constituents, users in particular, asked for improved disclosures that link more clearly an entity's risk management activities and how it applies hedge accounting. *[IFRS 7.BC35C]*. Consequently, IFRS 9 has expanded significantly the disclosure requirements in respect of hedge accounting when compared to the requirements under IAS 39. Those requirements are also supplemented by some detailed implementation guidance. The hedge accounting requirements of IFRS 9 are dealt with in Chapter 53.

Under IFRS 9 an entity may choose to continue applying certain, or all, of the hedge accounting requirements of IAS 39 rather than those in IFRS 9 (see Chapter 53 at 11.2). In these circumstances the disclosure requirements introduced by IFRS 9 should be followed, rather than those that previously applied under IAS 39. *[IFRS 9.BC6.104]*.

The requirements set out at 4.3.1 to 4.3.4 below apply for those risk exposures that an entity hedges and for which it elects to apply hedge accounting. The objective of these disclosures is to provide information about: *[IFRS 7.21A]*

- the entity's risk management strategy and how it is applied to manage risk.

    Linking the application of hedge accounting to the entity's risk management strategy requires an understanding of the entity's risk management strategy and to facilitate this the IASB has introduced more guidance about the information to be included in a description of the risk management strategy of the entity (see 4.3.1 below); *[IFRS 7.BC35P]*

- how the entity's hedging activities may affect the amount, timing and uncertainty of its future cash flows (see 4.3.2 below); and

- the effect that hedge accounting has had on the entity's statement of financial position, statement of comprehensive income and statement of changes in equity (see 4.3.3 and 4.3.4 below).

In order to meet these objectives, an entity will need to determine how much detail to disclose, how much emphasis to place on different aspects of the disclosure requirements, the appropriate level of aggregation or disaggregation and whether additional explanations are needed to evaluate the quantitative information disclosed. The level of aggregation or disaggregation should be consistent with that used for meeting the disclosure requirements of related information elsewhere in IFRS 7 and in IFRS 13 (see Chapter 14 at 20.1.2). *[IFRS 7.21D]*.

Some of the disclosure requirements at 4.3.1 to 4.3.3 below are required to be given by 'risk category'. This is not a defined term, but appears to refer to the type of risk being hedged rather than, say, the type of hedge relationship such as cash flow hedges and fair value hedges. Each risk category should be determined on the basis of the risk exposures an entity decides to hedge and for which hedge accounting is applied. These categories should be determined consistently for all hedge accounting disclosures. *[IFRS 7.21C]*. This should enable users to follow the various disclosures by type of risk, resulting in a much better understanding of the hedging activities and their impact on the financial statements.

These disclosures should be presented in a single note or separate section of the financial statements. To avoid duplication, IFRS 7 allows this information to be incorporated by cross-reference from the financial statements to some other statement that is available to users of the financial statements on the same terms and at the same time, such as a management commentary or risk report. Without the information incorporated by cross-reference, the financial statements are incomplete. *[IFRS 7.21B]*.

4.3.1 The risk management strategy

An entity should explain its risk management strategy for each risk category of risk exposures that it decides to hedge and for which hedge accounting is applied. This explanation should enable users of financial statements to evaluate, for example: *[IFRS 7.22A]*

- how each risk arises;
- how each risk is managed.
    This includes whether the entity hedges an item in its entirety for all risks or hedges a risk component (or components) of an item and why; and
- the extent of risk exposures that are managed.

To meet these requirements, the information should include, but is not limited to, a description of: *[IFRS 7.22B]*

- the hedging instruments that are used (and how they are used) to hedge risk exposures;
- how the economic relationship between the hedged item and the hedging instrument is determined for the purpose of assessing hedge effectiveness;
- how the hedge ratio is established; and
- the sources of hedge ineffectiveness.

When a specific risk component is designated as a hedged item, qualitative or quantitative information should be provided about: *[IFRS 7.22C]*

- how the risk component that is designated as the hedged item was determined, including a description of the nature of the relationship between the risk component and the item as a whole; and
- how the risk component relates to the item in its entirety. For example, the designated risk component may historically have covered on average 80% of the changes in fair value of the item as a whole.

This information could include a description of whether the risk component is contractually specified, and if not, how the entity determined that the non-contractually specified risk component is separately identifiable and reliably measurable.

The following example shows how an entity might present some of this information.

Example 54.1: Illustrative disclosure of risk management strategy for commodity price risk

Coffee price risk

Fluctuations in the coffee price are the main source of market risk for the Alpha Beta Coffee Group (the Group). The Group purchases Arabica coffee from various suppliers in South America. For this purpose, the Group enters into long-term contracts (for between one and three years) with its suppliers, in which the future coffee price is indexed to the USD Arabica benchmark coffee price, adjusted for transport cost that are indexed to diesel prices plus a quality coefficient that is reset annually for a crop period. In order to secure the volume of coffee needed, supply contracts are always entered into (or renewed) at least one year prior to harvest.

The Group forecasts the monthly volume of expected coffee purchases for a period of 18 months and manages the coffee price risk exposure on a 12-month rolling basis. For this purpose, the Group enters into futures contracts on the Arabica benchmark price and designates the futures contracts in cash flow hedges of the USD Arabica benchmark price risk component of its future coffee purchases. Some of those purchases are committed minimum volumes under the contracts and some purchases are highly probable forecast transactions (i.e. quantities in excess of the minimum purchases volumes and sometimes for periods for which no contract has yet been entered into). The underlying risk of the coffee futures contracts is identical to the hedged risk component (i.e. the USD Arabica benchmark price). Therefore, the Group has established a hedge ratio of 1:1 for all its hedging relationships. The USD Arabica benchmark price risk component is contractually specified in its purchase contracts, therefore, the Group considers the risk component to be separately identifiable and reliably measurable based on the price of coffee futures.

The Group does not hedge its exposure to the variability in the purchase price of coffee that results from the annual reset of the quality coefficient, because hedging that risk would require highly bespoke financial instruments that in the Group's view are not economical.

The Group's exposure to the variability in the purchase price of coffee that results from the diesel price indexation of the transport costs is integrated into its general risk management of logistics costs that aggregates exposures resulting from various logistics processes of the Group.

The Group determined the USD Arabica benchmark coffee price risk component that it designates as the hedged item on the basis of the pricing formula in the Group's coffee supply contracts (see the above description). That benchmark component is the largest pricing element. The quality coefficient depends on the particular crop in the region from which the Group sources its coffee, depending mainly on weather conditions that affect size and quality of the crop. Sometimes pest and plant diseases can have similar effects. Over the last 10 crop periods the quality coefficient ranged between US cents 2-27 per pound (lb). For the effect of the diesel price indexation, refer to the section 'Logistics costs management' in the Risk Management Report that is included in this Annual Report.

More information about how the Group manages its risk, including the extent to which the Group hedges, the hedging instruments used and sources of ineffectiveness, is provided in the Risk Management Report (see section 'Commodity Price Risk Management').

Disclosures about an entity's risk management strategy are an important cornerstone of the new hedge accounting model, as they provide the link between an entity's risk management activities and how they affect the financial statements.

4.3.2 The amount, timing and uncertainty of future cash flows

For most hedge relationships, quantitative information should be disclosed by risk category that allows the evaluation of the terms and conditions of the hedging instruments and how they affect the amount, timing and uncertainty of future cash flows. *[IFRS 7.23A]*. This should include a breakdown disclosing: *[IFRS 7.23B]*

- the profile of the timing of the hedging instrument's nominal amount; and
- if applicable, its average price or rate (e.g. strike or forward prices).

This requirement applies to cash flow hedges, fair value hedges, and hedges of a net investment, and meeting this requirement with concise information could prove challenging where an entity's use of hedge accounting is extensive. The following example shows how an entity might present some of this information.

Example 54.2: Illustrative disclosure of timing, nominal amount and average price of coffee futures contracts

As of 31 December 2020, Alpha Beta Coffee Group is holding the following coffee futures contracts to hedge the exposure on its coffee purchases over the next twelve months:

	Jan	Feb	Mar	Apr	May	...	Dec	Total
Notional amount of coffee futures contracts (in lb thousands) by month of their maturity	1,275	1,425	1,350	1,312	1,350	...	1,200	16,275
Average hedged rate (in US cents per lb)	122	125	128	133	135	...	139	133

Different information should be given where a dynamic hedging process is used. A dynamic process may be used in which both the exposure and the hedging instruments used to manage that exposure remain the same for only short periods of time because both the hedging instrument and the hedged item frequently change and the hedging relationship is frequently reset (or discontinued and restarted). This might occur, for example, when hedging the interest rate risk of an open portfolio of debt instruments. In these situations, the following should be disclosed: *[IFRS 7.23C]*

- information about what the ultimate risk management strategy is in relation to those hedging relationships;
- a description of how the risk management strategy is reflected by using hedge accounting and designating those particular hedging relationships; and
- an indication of how frequently the hedging relationships are discontinued and restarted as part of the process in relation to those hedging relationships.

When the volume of hedging relationships in a dynamic process is unrepresentative of normal volumes during the period (i.e. the volume at the reporting date does not reflect the volumes during the period) that fact should be disclosed along with the reason volumes are believed to be unrepresentative. *[IFRS 7.24D]*.

For all hedges, a description of the sources of hedge ineffectiveness that are expected to affect the hedging relationship during its term should be disclosed by risk category. *[IFRS 7.23D]*. If other sources of hedge ineffectiveness emerge in a hedging relationship, those sources should be disclosed by risk category along with an explanation of the resulting hedge ineffectiveness. *[IFRS 7.23E]*.

For cash flow hedges, a description of any forecast transaction for which hedge accounting had been used in the previous period, but which is no longer expected to occur, should be disclosed. *[IFRS 7.23F]*.

Originally the IASB had proposed that entities should disclose the total volume of risk the entity managed, irrespective of whether the entity actually hedges the full exposure. However, they were persuaded by many constituents saying this could result in disclosure of commercially sensitive information and did not to carry this requirement forward to the final standard. *[IFRS 7.BC35U, BC35W, BC35X]*.

4.3.3 The effects of hedge accounting on financial position and performance

The following amounts related to designated hedging instruments should be disclosed:

- the carrying amount of the hedging instruments, presenting financial assets separately from financial liabilities;
- the line item in the statement of financial position that includes the hedging instrument;
- the change in fair value of the hedging instrument used as the basis for recognising hedge ineffectiveness for the period; and
- the nominal amounts (including quantities such as tonnes or cubic metres) of the hedging instruments.

This information should be given in a tabular format, separately by risk category and for fair value hedges, cash flow hedges and hedges of a net investment in a foreign operation, *[IFRS 7.24A]*, and the implementation guidance suggests it might be given in the following format. *[IFRS 7.IG13C]*.

Example 54.3: Amounts related to hedged instruments

	Nominal amount of the hedging instrument	Carrying amount of the hedging instrument		Line item in the statement of financial position where the hedging instrument is located	Changes in fair value used for calculating hedge ineffectiveness for 20X1
		Assets	Liabilities		
Cash flow hedges					
Commodity price risk					
– Forward sales contracts	xx	xx	xx	Line item XX	xx
Fair value hedges					
Interest rate risk					
– Interest rate swaps	xx	xx	xx	Line item XX	xx
Foreign exchange risk					
– Foreign currency loan	xx	xx	xx	Line item XX	xx

Financial instruments: Presentation and disclosure 4417

The following amounts related to hedged items should be disclosed:
- for fair value hedges:
    - the carrying amount of the hedged item recognised in the statement of financial position, presenting assets separately from liabilities;
    - the accumulated amount of adjustments to the hedged item included in its carrying amount, again presenting assets separately from liabilities;
    - the line item in the statement of financial position that includes the hedged item;
    - the change in value of the hedged item used as the basis for recognising hedge ineffectiveness for the period; and
    - the accumulated amount of adjustments to hedged financial instruments measured at amortised cost that have ceased to be adjusted for hedging gains and losses and which remain in the statement of financial position;
- for cash flow hedges and hedges of a net investment in a foreign operation:
    - the change in value of the hedged item used as the basis for recognising hedge ineffectiveness for the period;
    - the balances in the cash flow hedge reserve and the foreign currency translation reserve for continuing hedges; and
    - the balances remaining in the cash flow hedge reserve and the foreign currency translation reserve from any hedging relationships for which hedge accounting is no longer applied.

This information should be given in a tabular format, separately by risk category, *[IFRS 7.24B]*, and the implementation guidance suggests it might be given in the following format. *[IFRS 7.IG13D].*

Example 54.4: Amounts related to hedged items

	Carrying amount of the hedged item		Accumulated amount of fair value hedge adjustments on the hedged item included in the carrying amount of the hedged item		Line item in the statement of financial position in which the hedged item is included	Change in value used for calculating hedge ineffectiveness for 20X1	Cash flow hedge reserve
	Assets	Liabilities	Assets	Liabilities			
Cash flow hedges							
Commodity price risk							
– Forecast sales	n/a	n/a	n/a	n/a	n/a	xx	xx
– Discontinued hedges (forecast sales)	n/a	n/a	n/a	n/a	n/a	n/a	xx
Fair value hedges							
Interest rate risk							
– Loan payable	–	xx	–	xx	Line item XX	xx	n/a
– Discontinued hedges (Loan payable)	–	xx	–	xx	Line item XX	n/a	n/a
Foreign exchange risk							
– Firm commitment	xx	xx	xx	xx	Line item XX	xx	n/a

The following amounts affecting the statement of comprehensive income should be disclosed:
- for fair value hedges:
  - hedge ineffectiveness, i.e. the difference between the hedging gains or losses of the hedging instrument and the hedged item, recognised in profit or loss (or other comprehensive income for hedges of an equity instrument for which changes in fair value are presented in other comprehensive income); and
  - the line item in the statement of comprehensive income that includes the recognised hedge ineffectiveness;
- for cash flow hedges and hedges of a net investment in a foreign operation:
  - hedging gains or losses that were recognised in other comprehensive income in the reporting period;
  - hedge ineffectiveness recognised in profit or loss;
  - the line item in the statement of comprehensive income that includes the recognised hedge ineffectiveness;
  - the amount reclassified from the cash flow hedge reserve or the foreign currency translation reserve into profit or loss as a reclassification adjustment, differentiating in the case of cash flow hedges between:
    - amounts for which hedge accounting had previously been used, but for which the hedged future cash flows are no longer expected to occur; and
    - amounts that have been transferred because the hedged item has affected profit or loss;
  - the line item in the statement of comprehensive income that includes the reclassification adjustment; and
  - for hedges of net positions, the hedging gains or losses recognised in a separate line item in the statement of comprehensive income.

This information should be given in a tabular format, separately by risk category, *[IFRS 7.24C]*, and the implementation guidance suggests it might be given in the following format. *[IFRS 7.IG13E]*.

Financial instruments: Presentation and disclosure 4419

Example 54.5: Amounts affecting the statement of comprehensive income.

Cash flow hedges (a)	Separate line item recognised in profit or loss as a result of a hedge of a net position (b)	Change in the value of the hedging instrument recognised in other comprehensive income	Hedge ineffectiveness recognised in profit or loss	Line item in profit or loss (that includes hedge ineffectiveness)	Amount reclassified from the cash flow hedge reserve to profit or loss	Line item affected in profit or loss because of the reclassification
Commodity price risk						
Commodity X	n/a	xx	xx	Line item XX	xx	Line item XX
– Discontinued hedge	n/a	n/a	n/a	n/a	xx	Line item XX

(a) The information disclosed in the statement of changes in equity (cash flow hedge reserve) should have the same level of detail as these disclosures.
(b) This disclosure only applies to cash flow hedges of foreign currency risk.

Fair value Hedges	Ineffectiveness recognised in profit or loss	Line item(s) in profit or loss (that include(s) hedge ineffectiveness)
Interest rate risk	xx	Line item XX
Foreign exchange risk	xx	Line item XX

The following example shows another way an entity might present this information.

Example 54.6: Illustrative disclosure of the effects of hedge accounting on the financial position and performance

The impact of hedging instruments designated in hedging relationships as of 31 December 2021 on the statement of financial position of Alpha Beta Coffee Group (the Group) is as follows:

Cash flow hedges	Notional amount	Carrying amount	Line item in the statement of financial position	Change in fair value used for measuring ineffectiveness for the period
Coffee price risk Arabica coffee futures	16,275lbs (thousands)	(4.5)	Short-term derivative financial liabilities	(1.0)
Interest rate risk Pay fixed/receive variable interest rate swap	EUR 50m	4.0	Long-term derivative financial assets	1.0

Fair value hedges	Notional amount	Carrying amount	Line item in the statement of financial position	Change in fair value used for measuring ineffectiveness for the period
Interest rate risk Receive fixed/pay variable interest rate swap	EUR 200m	(10.0)	Long-term derivative financial liabilities	(2.0)

The impact of hedged items designated in hedging relationships as of 31 December 2021 on the statement of financial position of the Group is as follows:

Cash flow hedges	Change in value used for measuring ineffectiveness	Cash flow hedge reserve
Coffee price risk		
Coffee purchases	1.0	4.5
Interest rate risk		
Forecast interest payments	(0.9)	(3.9)

Fair value hedges	Carrying amount	Thereof accumulated fair value adjustments	Line item in the statement of financial position	Change in fair value used for measuring ineffectiveness for the period
Interest rate risk				
Fixed rate borrowings	211.0	11.0	Long-term borrowings	2.1

The above hedging relationships affected profit or loss and other comprehensive income as follows:

Cash flow hedges	Hedging gain or loss recognised in OCI	Ineffectiveness recognised in profit or loss	Line item in the statement of profit or loss for ineffectiveness	Amount reclassified from OCI to profit or loss	Line item in the statement of profit or loss for reclassification
Coffee price risk					
Hedges of forecast coffee purchases	(1.0)				
Interest rate risk					
Forecast interest payments	0.9	0.1	Other financial income	0.5	Interest expense

Fair value hedges	Ineffectiveness recognised in profit or loss	Line item in the statement of profit or loss for ineffectiveness
Interest rate risk		
Hedge of fixed rate borrowings	(0.1)	Other financial expenses

IAS 1 requires the presentation of a reconciliation of each component of equity and an analysis of other comprehensive income (see 7.2 and 7.3 below). The level of information given in the reconciliation and analysis should: *[IFRS 7.24E]*

- differentiate between hedging gains or losses recognised in other comprehensive income and amounts reclassified to profit or loss, separately for:
    - cash flow hedges for which the hedged future cash flows are no longer expected to occur;
    - those hedges for which the hedged item has affected profit or loss; and
    - amounts related to hedged forecast transactions that subsequently result in the recognition of a non-financial asset or liability, or a hedged forecast transaction for a non-financial asset or liability becomes a firm commitment for which fair value hedge accounting is applied, that are included directly in the initial cost or other carrying amount of the asset or the liability.

As noted at 7.2 and at 7.3 below, this adjustment should not be included within other comprehensive income. *[IFRS 9.BC6.380]*. Instead it should be presented within the statement of changes of equity, albeit separately from other comprehensive income;

- differentiate between amounts associated with the time value of options that hedge transaction related hedged items and those that hedge time-period related hedged items where the time value of the option is recognised initially in other comprehensive income; and
- differentiate between amounts associated with forward elements of forward contracts and the foreign currency basis spreads of financial instruments that hedge transaction related hedged items and those that hedge time-period related hedged items where those amounts are recognised initially in other comprehensive income.

The information in the bullets above should be disclosed separately by risk category, although this disaggregation may be provided in the notes to the financial statements. *[IFRS 7.24F]*.

The following extract from the financial statements of Vodafone shows the type of disclosure about hedge accounting and hedge relationships that can be seen in practice. In addition to the information shown below, the table in the financial statements also includes, where relevant, the average maturity year, average foreign currency rate and average euro interest rate for each of the relevant line items.

Extract 54.1: Vodafone Group Plc (2019)

Notes to the consolidated financial statements [extract]

21. Capital and financial risk management [extract]

Risk management strategy of hedge relationships [extract]

The risk strategies of the denominated cash flow, fair value, and net investment hedges reflect the above market risk strategies.

The objective of the cash flow hedges is principally to convert foreign currency denominated fixed rate borrowings in US dollar, Pound Sterling, Australian dollar, Swiss Franc, Hong Kong dollar, Japanese yen, Norwegian krona and euro and US dollar borrowings into euro fixed rate borrowings and hedge the foreign exchange spot rate and interest rate risk. Derivative financial instruments designated in cash flow hedges are cross-currency interest rate swaps and foreign exchange swaps. The swap maturity dates and liquidity profiles of the nominal cash flows match those of the underlying borrowings.

The objective of the net investment hedges is to hedge foreign exchange risk in foreign operations. Derivative financial instruments designated in net investment hedges are cross-currency interest rate swaps and foreign exchange swaps. The hedging instruments are rolled on an ongoing basis as determined by the nature of the business.

The objective of the fair value hedges is to hedge a proportion of the Group's fixed rate euro denominated borrowing to a euro floating rate borrowing. The swap maturity dates match those of the underlying borrowing and the nominal cash flows are converted to quarterly payments.

Hedge effectiveness is determined at the inception of the hedge relationship and through periodic prospective effectiveness assessments to ensure that an economic relationship exists between the hedged item and hedging instrument.

For hedges of foreign currency denominated borrowings and investments, the Group uses a combination of cross-currency and foreign exchange swaps to hedge its exposure to foreign exchange risk and interest rate risk and enters into hedge relationships where the critical terms of the hedging instrument match exactly with the terms of the hedged item. Therefore the Group expects a highly effective hedging relationship with the swap contracts and the value of the corresponding hedged items to change systematically in the opposite direction in response to movements in the underlying exchange rates and interest rates. The Group therefore performs a qualitative assessment of effectiveness. If changes in circumstances affect the terms of the hedged item such that the critical terms no longer match exactly with the critical terms of the hedging instrument, the Group uses the hypothetical derivative method to assess effectiveness.

Hedge ineffectiveness may occur due to:

a) The fair value of the hedging instrument on the hedge relationship designation date if the fair value is not nil;

b) Changes in the contractual terms or timing of the payments on the hedged item; and

c) A change in the credit risk of the Group or the counterparty with the hedged instrument.

The hedge ratio for each designation will be established by comparing the quantity of the hedging instrument and the quantity of the hedged item to determine their relative weighting; for all of the Group's existing hedge relationships the hedge ratio has been determined as 1:1.

The fair values of the derivative financial instruments are calculated by discounting the future cash flows to net present values using appropriate market rates and foreign currency rates prevailing at 31 March. The valuation basis is level 2. This classification comprises items where fair value is determined from inputs other than quoted prices that are observable for the asset and liability, either directly or indirectly. Derivative financial assets and liabilities are included within trade and other receivables and trade and other payables in the statement of financial position.

The following table represents the corresponding carrying values and nominal amounts of derivatives in a continued hedge relationship as at 31 March 2019.

At 31 March 2019	Nominal amounts €m	Carrying value Assets €m	Carrying value Liabilities €m	Opening balance 1 April 2018 €m	(Gain)/ Loss deferred to OCI €m	Gain/ (Loss) recycled to financing costs €m	Closing balance 31 March 2019[1] €m
Cash flow hedges – foreign currency risk[2]							
Cross-currency and foreign exchange swaps							
US dollar bonds	18,444	1,273	83	132	(1,410)	1,099	(179)
Australian dollar bonds	736	14	2	(4)	(21)	8	(17)
Swiss franc bonds	624	–	43	16	(25)	31	22
Pound sterling bonds	2,720	76	112	8	(39)	69	38
Hong Kong dollar bonds	233	3	7	15	(23)	21	13
Japanese yen bonds	78	1	–	–	(3)	5	2
Norwegian krona bonds	241	2	14	(4)	5	–	1
Cash flow hedges – foreign currency and interest rate risk[2]							
Cross currency swaps – US dollar bonds	905	33	–	1	(40)	51	12
Cash flow hedges – interest rate risk[2]							
Interest rate swaps – Euro loans	668	–	17	15	1	(5)	11
Fair value hedges – interest rate risk[3]							
Interest rate swaps – Eurobonds	186	117	–	–	–	–	–
Net investment hedge – foreign exchange risk[4]							
Cross-currency and foreign exchange swaps – South African rand investment	1,952	120	3	918	(108)	–	810
	26,787	1,639	281	1,097	(1,663)	1,279	713

> Notes:
> 1 Fair value movement deferred into other comprehensive income includes €754 million loss (2018: €572 million loss) and €1 million gain (2018: €19 million gain) of foreign currency basis outside the cash flow and net investment hedge relationships respectively.
> 2 For cash flow hedges, the movement in the hypothetical derivative (hedged item) mirrors that of the hedging instrument. Hedge ineffectiveness of swaps designated in a cash flow hedge during the period was €nil (2018: €nil).
> 3 The carrying value of the bond includes €86 million loss (2018: €92 million loss) of cumulative fair value adjustment for the hedged interest rate risk. Net ineffectiveness on the fair value hedges, €2 million loss (2018: €12 million loss) is recognised in the income statement. The carrying value of bonds includes an additional €749 million loss (2018: €727 million loss) in relation to fair value of bonds previously designated in fair value hedge relationships.
> 4 Hedge ineffectiveness of swaps designated in a net investment hedge during the period was €nil (2018: €nil).

4.3.4 Option to designate a credit exposure as measured at fair value through profit or loss

If a financial instrument, or a proportion of it, has been designated as measured at fair value through profit or loss because a credit derivative is used to manage the credit risk of that financial instrument, the following should be disclosed: *[IFRS 7.24G]*

- a reconciliation of each of the nominal amount and the fair value of the credit derivative at the beginning and end of the period;
- the gain or loss recognised in profit or loss on initial designation; and
- on discontinuation of measuring a financial instrument, or a proportion of it, at fair value through profit or loss, the fair value of that financial instrument that becomes the new carrying amount and the related nominal or principal amount.

Except for providing comparative information in accordance with IAS 1, this information need not be given in subsequent periods.

4.3.5 Uncertainty arising from interest rate benchmark (IBOR) reform

Replacing interbank offered rates (IBOR) with alternative rates was one of the recommendations following the financial crisis and some jurisdictions have been making clear progress towards this. IBOR reform gives rise to a number of financial reporting issues which the IASB approached in two phases. In September 2019, the IASB issued its first amendments to IFRS 9 that were designed to mitigate the effects of these reforms on hedge accounting in the period before financial instruments are issued or modified to reference alternative rates and these mitigants are addressed in Chapter 53 at 9. Consequential amendments were also made to IFRS 7 requiring the following information to be disclosed in respect of hedging relationships to which the mitigants in IFRS 9 are applied: *[IFRS 7.24H]*

- the significant interest rate benchmarks to which the entity's hedging relationships are exposed;
- the extent of the risk exposure the entity manages that is directly affected by the interest rate benchmark reform;
- how the entity is managing the process to transition to alternative benchmark rates;
- a description of significant assumptions or judgements the entity made in applying these paragraphs (for example, assumptions or judgements about when the uncertainty

arising from interest rate benchmark reform is no longer present with respect to the timing and the amount of the interest rate benchmark-based cash flows); and
- the nominal amount of the hedging instruments in those hedging relationships.

Disclosures introduced by the second phase of the IASB's project to address IBOR reform are considered at 5.7 below.

4.4 Statement of financial position

4.4.1 Categories of financial assets and financial liabilities

The carrying amounts of each of the following categories of financial instrument should be disclosed, either on the face of the statement of financial position or in the notes: *[IFRS 7.8]*

- financial assets measured at fair value through profit or loss, showing separately:
  - those designated as such upon initial recognition; and
  - those mandatorily measured at fair value in accordance with IFRS 9;
- financial liabilities at fair value through profit or loss, showing separately:
  - those designated as such upon initial recognition; and
  - those that meet the definition of held for trading in IFRS 9;
- financial assets measured at amortised cost;
- financial liabilities measured at amortised cost; and
- financial assets measured at fair value through other comprehensive income, showing separately:
  - debt instruments held within a business model to both collect contractual cash flows from, and to sell, the assets.

    The carrying amount of debt instruments measured at fair value through other comprehensive income should not be reduced by a loss allowance and the loss allowance should not be presented separately in the statement of financial position as a reduction of the carrying amount of the financial asset. However, the loss allowance should be disclosed in the notes to the financial statements; and *[IFRS 7.16A]*
  - investments in equity instruments designated to be measured as such upon initial recognition.

The IASB concluded that such disclosure would assist users in understanding the extent to which accounting policies affect the amounts at which financial assets and financial liabilities are recognised. *[IFRS 7.BC14]*.

Although accounted for identically, the carrying amounts of financial instruments that are classified as held for trading and those designated at fair value through profit or loss are shown separately because designation is at the discretion of the entity. *[IFRS 7.BC15]*.

A derivative that is designated as a hedging instrument in an effective hedge relationship does not fall within any of the above categories and, strictly, is not required to be included in these disclosures. Disclosure requirements for hedges are set out at 4.3 above.

4.4.2 Financial liabilities designated at fair value through profit or loss

Where a (non-derivative) financial liability has been designated at fair value through profit or loss, i.e. it is not classified as held for trading, the amount of change during the period and cumulatively (i.e. since initial recognition) in its fair value that is attributable to changes in credit risk should be disclosed. This disclosure should be provided for financial liabilities where the change is recognised in other comprehensive income (see Chapter 50 at 2.4.1) and it should also be provided for financial liabilities where the change is recognised in profit or loss because recognising it in other comprehensive income would create or enlarge an accounting mismatch within profit or loss (see Chapter 50 at 2.4.2). *[IFRS 7.10(a), 10A(a)].*

Further, if the disclosure is not considered to represent faithfully the change in the fair value of the financial liability attributable to changes in credit risk, the reasons for reaching this conclusion and the factors believed to be relevant should also be disclosed. *[IFRS 7.11(b)].*

The IASB concluded that the difference between the carrying amount of such a liability and the amount the entity would be contractually required to pay at maturity to the holder of the obligation should also be disclosed. This disclosure is also required for liabilities where the change in fair value attributable to credit risk is recognised in other comprehensive income and for those where the change is recognised in profit or loss. *[IFRS 7.10(b), 10A(b)].* The fair value may differ significantly from the settlement amount, particularly for liabilities with a long duration when the entity has experienced a significant deterioration in creditworthiness subsequent to issuance and the IASB concluded that knowledge of this difference would be useful. Also, the settlement amount is important to some financial statement users, particularly creditors. *[IFRS 7.BC22].*

Where changes in the fair value of a financial liability attributable to credit risk are recognised in other comprehensive income, any transfers of the cumulative gain or loss within equity should be disclosed, including the reason for such transfers. *[IFRS 7.10(c)].* Also, if such a financial liability is derecognised during the period, the amount (if any) presented in other comprehensive income that was realised at derecognition should be disclosed. *[IFRS 7.10(d)].*

A detailed description of the methods used to calculate the changes in fair value attributable to changes in credit risk should be given, including an explanation of why the method is appropriate. This disclosure is required irrespective of whether those changes are recognised in other comprehensive income or in profit or loss. *[IFRS 7.11(a)].*

Entities should also provide a detailed description of the methodology or methodologies used to determine whether presenting changes in the fair value of a liability attributable to credit risk in other comprehensive income would create or enlarge an accounting mismatch in profit or loss (see Chapter 50 at 2.4.2). Where an entity is required to present such changes in profit or loss, this disclosure should include a detailed description of the economic relationship between the financial liability and other financial instrument(s) measured at fair value through profit or loss that are expected to offset those changes. *[IFRS 7.11(c)].*

4.4.3 Financial assets designated as measured at fair value through profit or loss

Additional disclosure requirements apply to financial assets (or groups of such assets) that are designated at fair value through profit or loss if they would otherwise be measured at fair value through other comprehensive income or at amortised cost, namely: *[IFRS 7.9]*

- the maximum exposure to credit risk (see 5.3.3 below) at the reporting date of the financial asset (or group of financial assets);
- the amount by which any related credit derivatives or similar instruments mitigate that maximum exposure to credit risk;
- the amount of change during the period and cumulatively (i.e. since initial recognition) in the fair value of the financial assets (or group of financial assets) that is attributable to changes in credit risk (see below); and
- the amount of change in the fair value of any related credit derivative or similar instrument that has occurred during the period and cumulatively since the financial asset was designated.

Calculating the change in fair value attributable to changes in credit risk is approached in much the same way as for financial liabilities (see 4.4.2 above). It may be determined either as the amount of change in fair value that is not attributable to changes in market conditions that give rise to market risk or by using an alternative method that more faithfully represents the amount of change in its fair value that is attributable to changes in credit risk. *[IFRS 7.9]*.

A detailed description of the chosen method(s), including an explanation of why the method is appropriate should be disclosed. If the disclosure is not considered to represent faithfully the change in the fair value of the financial asset attributable to changes in credit risk, the reasons for reaching this conclusion and the factors believed to be relevant should be disclosed. *[IFRS 7.11]*.

4.4.4 Investments in equity instruments designated at fair value through other comprehensive income

Where investments in equity instruments have been designated to be measured at fair value through other comprehensive income (see Chapter 48 at 2.2 and 8), the following should be disclosed: *[IFRS 7.11A]*

- which investments in equity instruments have been designated to be measured at fair value through other comprehensive income;
- the reasons for using this presentation alternative;
- the fair value of each such investment at the end of the reporting period;

    This requirement, applying as it does to each such investment, may be onerous if an entity makes significant use of the fair value through other comprehensive income option. However, as noted at 3.2 above, the concept of materiality does apply to disclosures, therefore this information could be provided separately only for those investments that are themselves material whilst aggregated disclosures may suffice for immaterial items;

- dividends recognised during the period, showing separately those related to investments derecognised during the reporting period and those related to investments held at the end of the reporting period; and
- any transfers of the cumulative gain or loss within equity during the period, including the reason for such transfers.

Where such investments are derecognised during the reporting period, the following should also be disclosed: *[IFRS 7.11B]*

- the reasons for disposing of the investments;
- the fair value of the investments at the date of derecognition; and
- the cumulative gain or loss on disposal.

4.4.5 Reclassification

The circumstances in which financial assets should or may be reclassified from one category to another in response to a change in an entity's business model are discussed in Chapter 48 at 9. If, in the current or previous reporting periods, any such reclassifications have occurred, the following should be disclosed: *[IFRS 7.12B]*

- the date of reclassification;
- a detailed explanation of the change in business model and a qualitative description of its effect on the entity's financial statements; and
- the amount reclassified into and out of each category.

For assets previously measured at fair value through profit or loss that are reclassified so that they are measured at amortised cost or at fair value through other comprehensive income, the following information should be disclosed in each reporting period following reclassification until derecognition: *[IFRS 7.12C]*

- the effective interest rate determined on the date of reclassification; and
- the interest income or expense recognised.

Where financial assets previously measured at fair value through other comprehensive income have been reclassified since the last annual reporting date so that they are measured at amortised cost, the following should be disclosed:

- the fair value of the financial assets at the end of the reporting period; and
- the fair value gain or loss that would have been recognised in profit or loss during the reporting period if the financial assets had not been reclassified.

The same information should be given where financial assets previously measured at fair value through profit or loss have been reclassified since the last annual reporting date so that they are measured at amortised cost or at fair value through other comprehensive income. *[IFRS 7.12D]*.

4.4.6 Collateral

Where an entity has pledged financial assets as collateral for liabilities or contingent liabilities it should disclose the carrying amount of those assets and the terms and conditions relating to its pledge. This also applies to transfers of non-cash collateral where the transferee has the right, by contract or custom, to sell or repledge the collateral (see Chapter 52 at 5.5.2). *[IFRS 7.14]*.

When an entity holds collateral (of financial or non-financial assets) and is permitted to sell or repledge the collateral in the absence of default by the owner of the collateral, it should disclose: *[IFRS 7.15]*

- the fair value of the collateral held;
- the fair value of any such collateral sold or repledged, and whether the entity has an obligation to return it; and
- the terms and conditions associated with its use of the collateral.

Although some respondents to the exposure draft that preceded IFRS 7 (ED 7) argued for an exemption from this disclosure in cases where it is impracticable to obtain the fair value of the collateral held, the IASB concluded that it is reasonable to expect an entity to know the fair value of collateral that it holds and can sell even where there is no default. *[IFRS 7.BC25]*.

4.4.7 Compound financial instruments with multiple embedded derivatives

Where an instrument has been issued that contains both a liability and an equity component and the instrument has multiple embedded derivatives whose values are interdependent, such as a callable convertible debt instrument (see Chapter 47 at 6.4.2), the existence of these features should be disclosed. *[IFRS 7.17]*. Accordingly, the impact on the amounts reported as liabilities and equity will be highlighted, something the IASB sees as important given the acknowledged arbitrary nature of the allocation under IAS 32 of the joint value attributable to this interdependence. *[IFRS 7.BC31]*.

4.4.8 Defaults and breaches of loans payable

Loans payable are defined as 'financial liabilities other than short-term trade payables on normal credit terms.' *[IFRS 7 Appendix A]*. It is considered that disclosures about defaults and breaches of loans payable and other loan agreements provide relevant information about the entity's creditworthiness and its prospects of obtaining future loans. *[IFRS 7.BC32]*.

Accordingly, for any loans payable recognised at the reporting date, an entity is required to disclose: *[IFRS 7.18]*

- details of any defaults during the period of principal, interest, sinking fund, or redemption terms;
- the carrying amount of the loans payable in default at the reporting date; and
- whether the default was remedied, or the terms of the loans payable were renegotiated, before the financial statements were authorised for issue.

If, during the period, there were breaches of loan agreement terms other than those described above, the same information should be disclosed if those breaches permitted the lender to demand accelerated repayment (unless the breaches were remedied, or the terms of the loan were renegotiated, on or before the reporting date). *[IFRS 7.19].*

It is noted that any defaults or breaches may affect the classification of the liability as current or non-current in accordance with IAS 1 (see Chapter 3 at 3.1.4). *[IFRS 7.IG12].*

4.4.9 Interests in associates and joint ventures accounted for in accordance with IFRS 9

IAS 28 – *Investments in Associates and Joint Ventures* – allows an interest in an associate or a joint venture held by a venture capital or similar organisation to be measured at fair value through profit or loss in accordance with IFRS 9 (see Chapter 11 at 5.3). In these circumstances, IFRS 12 – *Disclosure of Interests in Other Entities* – contains additional disclosure requirements, over and above those in IFRS 7, which are dealt with in Chapter 13 at 2.2.3.D and 5.

4.5 Fair values

4.5.1 General disclosure requirements

The IASB sees the disclosure of information about the fair value of financial assets and liabilities as being an important requirement. It is explained in the following terms:

> 'Many entities use fair value information internally in determining their overall financial position and in making decisions about individual financial instruments. It is also relevant to many decisions made by users of financial statements because, in many circumstances, it reflects the judgement of the financial markets about the present value of expected future cash flows relating to an instrument. Fair value information permits comparisons of financial instruments having substantially the same economic characteristics, regardless of why they are held and when and by whom they were issued or acquired. Fair values provide a neutral basis for assessing management's stewardship by indicating the effects of its decisions to buy, sell or hold financial assets and to incur, maintain or discharge financial liabilities.'

Therefore, when financial assets or liabilities are not measured on a fair value basis, information on fair values should be given by way of supplementary disclosures to assist users in comparing entities on a consistent basis. *[IFRS 7.BC36].*

More specifically, except as set out below, the fair value of each class of financial assets and liabilities should be disclosed in a way that permits comparison with the corresponding carrying amounts. *[IFRS 7.25].* In providing this disclosure, instruments should be offset only to the extent that their related carrying amounts are also offset in the statement of financial position. *[IFRS 7.26].* IFRS 13 contains guidance on determining fair values and includes more extensive disclosure requirements about the fair values disclosed. These are discussed in Chapter 14 at 20.

Pragmatically, disclosure of fair values is not required for instruments whose carrying amount reasonably approximates their fair value, for example short-term trade receivables and payables. [IFRS 7.29(a)]. Where an entity has material amounts of longer term receivables or payables the carrying amount will often not represent a reasonable approximation of fair value and in such cases the use of this concession will not be appropriate.

Similarly, disclosure need not be given of the fair value of lease liabilities. [IFRS 7.29(d)].

As set out in Chapter 45 at 3.3.2 some instruments within the scope of IFRS 4 (normally life insurance policies) contain a discretionary participation feature. If the fair value of that feature cannot be reliably measured, disclosures of fair value are not required. [IFRS 7.29(c)]. However, additional disclosures should be given to assist users of the financial statements in making their own judgements about the extent of possible differences between the carrying amount of such contracts and their fair value. In particular, the following should be disclosed: [IFRS 7.30]

- the fact that fair value has not been disclosed because it cannot be reliably measured;
- a description of the instruments, their carrying amount, and an explanation of why fair value cannot be measured reliably;
- information about the market for the instruments;
- information about whether and how the entity intends to dispose of the instruments; and
- for instruments whose fair value previously could not be reliably measured that are derecognised:
  - that fact;
  - their carrying amount at the time of derecognition; and
  - the amount of gain or loss recognised.

When IFRS 17 is applied such contracts would only rarely be within the scope of IFRS 7 (see Chapter 45 at 3.3.2) and consequently these requirements are deleted from the standard.

4.5.2 Day 1 profits

In certain situations there will be a difference between the transaction price for a financial asset or financial liability and the fair value that would be determined at that date in accordance with IFRS 13 (commonly known as a day 1 profit). [IFRS 7.28]. As set out in Chapter 49 at 3.3, an entity should not recognise a day 1 profit on initial recognition of the financial instrument if the fair value is neither evidenced by a quoted price in an active market for an identical asset or liability (known as a Level 1 input) nor based on a valuation technique that uses only data from observable markets. Instead, the difference will be recognised in profit or loss in subsequent periods in accordance with IFRS 9 and the entity's accounting policy. [IFRS 7.IG14].

Where such a difference exists, IFRS 7 requires disclosure, by class of financial instrument, of: [IFRS 7.28]

- the accounting policy for recognising that difference in profit or loss to reflect a change in factors (including time) that market participants would take into account when setting a price for the financial instrument;
- the aggregate difference yet to be recognised in profit or loss at the beginning and end of the period and a reconciliation of changes in the amount of this difference; and
- why it was concluded that the transaction price was not the best evidence of fair value, including a description of the evidence that supports the fair value.

In other words, disclosure is required of the profits an entity might think it has made but which it is prohibited from recognising, at least for the time being. This disclosure is illustrated in the following example based on the implementation guidance. It is rather curious in that it illustrates a day 1 loss, not profit.

Example 54.7: Disclosure of deferred day 1 profits

On 1 January 2020 Company R purchases financial assets that are not traded in an active market for €15 million which represents their fair value at initial recognition. After initial recognition, R applies a valuation technique to measure the fair value of the financial assets. This valuation technique uses inputs other than data from observable markets. At initial recognition, the same valuation technique would have resulted in an amount of €14 million, which differs from fair value by €1 million. R has only one class of such financial assets with existing differences of €5 million at 1 January 2020. The disclosure in R's 2021 financial statements would include the following: *[IFRS 7.IG14]*

Accounting policies

R uses the following valuation technique to measure the fair value of financial instruments that are not traded in an active market: [insert description of technique, not included in this example] Differences may arise between the fair value at initial recognition (which, in accordance with IFRS 13 and IFRS 9, is normally the transaction price) and the amount determined at initial recognition using the valuation technique. Any such differences are [description of R's accounting policy].

In the notes to the financial statements

As discussed in note X, [insert name of valuation technique] is used to measure the fair value of the following financial instruments that are not traded in an active market. However, in accordance with IFRS 13 and IFRS 9, the fair value of an instrument at inception is normally the transaction price. If the transaction price differs from the amount determined at inception using the valuation technique, that difference is [description of R's accounting policy].

The differences yet to be recognised in profit or loss are as follows:

	2021 €m	2020 €m
Balance at beginning of year	5.3	5.0
New transactions	–	1.0
Recognised in profit or loss during the year	(0.7)	(0.8)
Other increases	–	0.2
Other decreases	(0.1)	(0.1)
Balance at end of year	4.5	5.3

UBS discloses the following information about recognition of day 1 profits.

> **Extract 54.2: UBS Group AG (2018)**
>
> **Notes to the UBS AG consolidated financial statements** [extract]
>
> 24   Fair value measurement [extract]
> d)   Valuation adjustments [extract]
> Deferred day-1 profit or loss reserves [extract]
>
> For new transactions where the valuation technique used to measure fair value requires significant inputs that are not based on observable market data, the financial instrument is initially recognized at the transaction price. The transaction price may differ from the fair value obtained using a valuation technique, where any such difference is deferred and not initially recognized in the income statement. These day-1 profit or loss reserves are reflected, where appropriate, as valuation adjustments.
>
> Deferred day-1 profit or loss related to financial instruments other than financial assets measured at fair value through other comprehensive income is released into *Other net income from fair value changes on financial instruments* when pricing of equivalent products or the underlying parameters become observable or when the transaction is closed out.
>
> Deferred day-1 profit or loss related to financial assets measured at fair value through other comprehensive income is released into *Other comprehensive income* when pricing of equivalent products or the underlying parameters become observable and is released into *Other income* when the assets are sold.
>
> The table on the next page summarizes the changes in deferred day-1 profit or loss reserves during the respective period.
>
> **Deferred day-1 profit or loss reserves**
>
> | USD million | 2018 | 2017 | 2016 |
> | --- | --- | --- | --- |
> | Reserve balance at the beginning of the year | 338 | 365 | 420 |
> | Profit/(loss) deferred on new transactions | 341 | 247 | 257 |
> | (Profit)/loss recognized in the income statement | (417) | (279) | (293) |
> | (Profit)/loss recognized in other comprehensive income | | | (23) |
> | Foreign currency translation | (6) | 6 | 4 |
> | Reserve balance at the end of the year | 255 | 338 | 365 |

4.6 Business combinations

IFRS 3 – *Business Combinations* – requires an acquirer to disclose additional information about financial instruments arising from business combinations that occur during the reporting period. These requirements are discussed below.

4.6.1 Acquired receivables

Some constituents were concerned that prohibiting the use of an allowance account when accounting for acquired receivables at fair value (see Chapter 49 at 3.3.4) could make it impossible to determine the contractual cash flows due on those assets and the amount of those cash flows not expected to be collected. They asked for additional disclosure to help in assessing considerations of credit quality used in estimating those fair values, including expectations about receivables that will be uncollectible. *[IFRS 3.BC258]*. Consequently, the IASB decided to require the following disclosures to be made about such assets acquired in a business combination:

- fair value of the receivables;
- gross contractual amounts receivable; and

- the best estimate at the acquisition date of the contractual cash flows not expected to be collected.

This information should be provided by major class of receivable, such as loans, direct finance leases and any other class of receivables. *[IFRS 3.B64(h)]*.

Although these requirements will produce some of the information users need to evaluate the credit quality of receivables acquired, the IASB acknowledged that it may not provide all such information. This was seen as an interim measure and the IASB said it would monitor a related FASB project with a view to improving the disclosure requirements in the future. *[IFRS 3.BC260]*. The FASB project was completed in July 2010, but IFRS 3 was not subsequently changed, although the disclosure requirements in IFRS 7 about credit risk were expanded significantly by IFRS 9 (see 5.3 below).

4.6.2 Contingent consideration and indemnification assets

The following information about contingent consideration arrangements and indemnification assets (see Chapter 45 at 3.7.1 and 3.12 respectively) should be given: *[IFRS 3.B64(g)]*

- the amount recognised as at the acquisition date;
- a description of the arrangement and the basis for determining the amount of the payment; and
- an estimate of the range of outcomes (undiscounted) or, if a range cannot be estimated, that fact and the reasons why a range cannot be estimated.

If the maximum amount of the payment is unlimited, that fact should be disclosed.

These are requirements of IFRS 3 and apply irrespective of whether such items meet the definition of a financial instrument (which they normally will).

5 NATURE AND EXTENT OF RISKS ARISING FROM FINANCIAL INSTRUMENTS

IFRS 7 establishes a second key principle, namely:

> 'An entity shall disclose information that enables users of its financial statements to evaluate the nature and extent of risks arising from financial instruments to which the entity is exposed at the reporting date.' *[IFRS 7.31]*.

Again this is supported by related disclosure requirements which focus on qualitative and quantitative aspects of the risks arising from financial instruments and how those risks have been managed. *[IFRS 7.32]*.

Providing qualitative disclosures in the context of quantitative disclosures enables users to link related disclosures and hence form an overall picture of the nature and extent of risks arising from financial instruments. The interaction between qualitative and quantitative disclosures contributes to disclosure of information in a way that better enables users to evaluate an entity's exposure to risks. *[IFRS 7.32A]*.

These risks typically include, but are not limited to, credit risk, liquidity risk and market risk, which are defined as follows: *[IFRS 7 Appendix A]*

(a) *Credit risk*, the risk that one party to a financial instrument will cause a financial loss for the other party by failing to discharge an obligation.

(b) *Liquidity risk*, the risk that an entity will encounter difficulty in meeting obligations associated with financial liabilities that are settled by delivering cash or another financial asset.

(c) *Market risk*, the risk that the fair value or future cash flows of a financial instrument will fluctuate because of changes in market prices. It comprises three separate types of risk:

   (i) *Currency risk*, the risk that the fair value or future cash flows of a financial instrument will fluctuate because of changes in foreign exchange rates.

   Currency risk (or foreign exchange risk) arises on financial instruments that are denominated in a foreign currency, i.e. in a currency other than the functional currency in which they are measured. For the purpose of IFRS 7, currency risk does not arise from financial instruments that are non-monetary items or from financial instruments denominated in an entity's functional currency. *[IFRS 7.B23]*. Therefore if a parent with the euro as its functional and presentation currency owns a subsidiary with the pound sterling as its functional currency, monetary items held by the subsidiary that are denominated in sterling do not give rise to any currency risk in the consolidated financial statements of the parent.

   (ii) *Interest rate risk*, the risk that the fair value or future cash flows of a financial instrument will fluctuate because of changes in market interest rates.

   It is explained that interest rate risk arises on interest-bearing financial instruments recognised in the statement of financial position (e.g. debt instruments acquired or issued) and on some financial instruments not recognised in the statement of financial position (e.g. some loan commitments). *[IFRS 7.B22]*.

   (iii) *Other price risk*, the risk that the fair value or future cash flows of a financial instrument will fluctuate because of changes in market prices (other than those arising from interest rate risk or currency risk), whether those changes are caused by factors specific to the individual financial instrument or its issuer, or factors affecting all similar financial instruments traded in the market.

   Other price risk arises on financial instruments because of changes in, for example, commodity prices, equity prices, prepayment risk (i.e. the risk that one party to a financial asset will incur a financial loss because the other party repays earlier or later than expected), and residual value risk (e.g. a lessor of motor cars that writes residual value guarantees is exposed to residual value risk). *[IFRS 7.B25, IG32]*.

   Two examples of financial instruments that give rise to equity price risk are a holding of equities in another entity, and an investment in a trust, which in turn holds investments in equity instruments. Other examples include forward contracts and options to buy or sell specified quantities of an equity instrument and swaps that are indexed to equity prices. The fair values of such financial instruments are affected by changes in the market price of the underlying equity instruments. *[IFRS 7.B26]*.

The specified disclosures can be provided either in the financial statements or may be incorporated by cross-reference from the financial statements to some other statement that is available to users of the financial statements on the same terms and at the same time, such as a management commentary or risk report (preparation of which might be required by a regulatory authority). Without the information incorporated by cross-reference, the financial statements are incomplete. *[IFRS 7.B6, BC46]*.

Consistent with the approach outlined at 3 above, it is emphasised that the extent of these disclosures will depend on the extent of an entity's exposure to risks arising from financial instruments. *[IFRS 7.BC41]*. Therefore, entities with many financial instruments and related risks should provide more disclosure and those with few financial instruments and related risks may provide less extensive disclosure. *[IFRS 7.BC40(b)]*.

The IASB recognised that entities view and manage risk in different ways and that some entities undertake limited management of risks. Therefore, disclosures based on how risk is managed are unlikely to be comparable between entities and, for some entities, would convey little or no information about the risks assumed. Accordingly, whilst at a high level the disclosures are approached from the perspective of information provided to management (see 5.2 below), certain minimum disclosures about risk exposures are specified to provide a common and relatively easy to implement benchmark across different entities. Obviously, those entities with more developed risk management systems would provide more detailed information. *[IFRS 7.BC42]*.

It is explained in the basis for conclusions that the implementation guidance, which illustrates how an entity might apply IFRS 7, is consistent with the disclosure requirements for banks developed by the Basel Committee (known as Pillar 3), so that banks can prepare, and users receive, a single co-ordinated set of disclosures about financial risk. *[IFRS 7.BC41]*. The standard was originally written before the financial crisis and there have been a number of subsequent initiatives to improve the reporting of risk by financial institutions, both from a regulatory and a financial reporting perspective, for example as set out at 9 below.

In developing the standard, the IASB considered various arguments that risk disclosures should not be included within the financial statements (even by cross-reference). For example, concerns were expressed that the information would be difficult and costly to audit and that it did not meet the criteria of comparability, faithful representation and completeness because it is subjective, forward-looking and based on management's judgement. It was also suggested that the subjectivity involved in the sensitivity analyses could undermine the credibility of the fair values recognised in the financial statements. However, the IASB was not persuaded and these arguments were rejected. *[IFRS 7.BC43, BC44, BC45, BC46]*.

5.1 Qualitative disclosures

For each type of risk arising from financial instruments, an entity is required to disclose: *[IFRS 7.33(a), (b)]*

(a) the exposures to risk and how they arise; and
(b) its objectives, policies and processes for managing the risk and the methods used to measure the risk.

Any changes in either (a) or (b) above compared to the previous period, together with the reasons for the change, should be disclosed. These changes may result from changes in exposure to risk or the way those exposures are managed. [IFRS 7.33(c), IG17].

The type of information that might be disclosed to meet these requirements includes, but is not limited to, a narrative description of: [IFRS 7.IG15]

- the entity's exposures to risk and how they arose, which might include details of exposures, both gross and net of risk transfer and other risk-mitigating transactions;
- the entity's policies and processes for accepting, measuring, monitoring and controlling risk, which might include:
  - the structure and organisation of the entity's risk management function(s), including a discussion of independence and accountability;
  - the scope and nature of the entity's risk reporting or measurement systems;
  - the entity's policies for hedging or mitigating risk, including its policies and procedures for taking collateral; and
  - the entity's processes for monitoring the continuing effectiveness of such hedges or mitigating devices; and
- the entity's policies and procedures for avoiding excessive concentrations of risk.

It is noted that information about the nature and extent of risks arising from financial instruments is more useful if it highlights any relationship between financial instruments that can affect the amount, timing or uncertainty of an entity's future cash flows. The extent to which a risk exposure is altered by such relationships might be apparent from other required disclosures, but in some cases further disclosures might be useful. [IFRS 7.IG16].

The following extract from the financial statements of Hunting PLC shows the type of disclosure that can be seen in practice.

Extract 54.3: Hunting PLC (2018)

Notes to the consolidated financial statements [extract]

27   Financial Risk Management [extract]

The Group's activities expose it to certain financial risks, namely market risk (including currency risk, fair value interest rate risk and cash flow interest rate risk), credit risk and liquidity risk. The Group's risk management strategy seeks to mitigate potential adverse effects on its financial performance. As part of its strategy, both primary and derivative financial instruments are used to hedge certain risk exposures.

There are clearly defined objectives and principles for managing financial risk established by the Board of Directors, with policies, parameters and procedures covering the specific areas of funding, banking relationships, foreign currency and interest rate exposures and cash management.

The Group's treasury function is responsible for implementing the policies and providing a centralised service to the Group for funding, foreign exchange and interest rate management and counterparty risk management. It is also responsible for identifying, evaluating and hedging financial risks in close co-operation with the Group's operating companies.

(a)   Market Risk: Foreign Exchange Risk

The Group's international base is exposed to foreign exchange risk from its investing, financing and operating activities, particularly in respect of Sterling, Canadian dollars and Chinese Yuan Renminbi. Foreign exchange risks arise from future transactions and cash flows, and from recognised monetary assets and liabilities that are not denominated in the functional currency of the Group's local operations.

(i) Transactional Risk

The exposure to exchange rate movements in significant future transactions and cash flows is hedged by using forward foreign exchange contracts. Certain forward foreign exchange contracts have been designated as hedging instruments of highly probable forecast transactions. Operating companies prepare quarterly rolling 12-month cash flow forecasts to enable working capital currency exposures to be identified. Exposures are also identified and hedged, if necessary, on an ad-hoc basis, such as when a purchase order in a foreign currency is placed. Currency exposures arise where the cash flows are not in the functional currency of the entity. Exposures arising from committed long-term projects beyond a 12-month period are also identified. The currency flows to be hedged are committed foreign currency transactions greater than $50,000 equivalent. Exposures of less than $50,000 equivalent will also be hedged but only where the underlying foreign currency cash flow is expected to occur 60 days or more from the point of entering into the transaction.

(ii) Translational Risk

Foreign exchange risk also arises from financial assets and liabilities not denominated in the functional currency of an entity's operations and forward foreign exchange contracts are used to manage the exposure to changes in foreign exchange rates. Where appropriate, hedge accounting is applied to the forward foreign exchange contracts and the hedged item to remove any accounting mismatch.

Foreign exchange risk also arises from the Group's investments in foreign operations. During the year, foreign currency swaps have been designated in a fair value hedge to hedge the foreign exchange rate changes in a pseudo-equity Canadian dollar inter-company loan.

The foreign exchange exposure arising from the translation of its net investments in foreign operations into the Group's presentation currency of US dollars has also previously been managed by designating any borrowings that are not US dollar denominated as a hedge of the net investment in foreign operations. The foreign exchange exposure primarily arises from Sterling and Canadian dollar denominated net investments.

(b)   **Market Risk: Interest Rate Risk**

Variable interest rates on cash at bank, short-term deposits, overdrafts and borrowings expose the Group to cash flow interest rate risk and fixed interest rates on loans and short-term deposits expose the Group to fair value interest rate risk. The treasury function manages the Group's exposure to interest rate risk and uses interest rate swaps and caps, when considered appropriate.

(c)   **Credit Risk**

The Group's credit risk arises from its cash at bank and in hand, Money Market Funds, short-term deposits, investments, derivative financial instruments, the loan note, accrued revenue, outstanding trade receivables and contract assets.

At the year-end, the Group had credit risk exposures to a wide range of counterparties. Credit risk exposure is continually monitored and no individual exposure is considered to be significant in the context of the ordinary course of the Group's activities. Exposure limits are set for each approved counterparty, as well as the types of transactions that may be entered into. Approved institutions that the treasury function can invest surplus cash with must all have a minimum A2, P2 or F2 short-term rating from Standard and Poor's, Moody's or Fitch rating agencies respectively and AAAm S&P rating for Money Market Funds. The Net Asset Value of the Money Market Funds aims be a minimum of 1 (this means that for every $1 that is in the fund there will be an asset to cover it) and the funds have overnight liquidity. At the year-end, deposits in Money Market Funds totalled $26.1m (2017 – $nil).

The credit risk of foreign exchange contracts is calculated before the contract is acquired and compared to the credit risk limit set for each counterparty. Credit risk is calculated as a fixed percentage of the nominal value of the instrument.

Trade and other receivables are continuously monitored. Credit account limits are primarily based on the credit quality of the customer and past experience through trading relationships. To reduce credit risk exposure from outstanding receivables, the Group has taken out credit insurance with an external insurer, subject to certain conditions.

(d)   **Liquidity Risk**

The Group needs to ensure that it has sufficient liquid funds available to support its working capital and capital expenditure requirements. All subsidiaries submit weekly and bi-monthly cash forecasts to the treasury function to enable them to monitor the Group's requirements.

5.2 Quantitative disclosures

For each type of risk arising from financial instruments (see 5 above), entities are required to disclose summary quantitative data about their exposure to that risk at the reporting date. It should be based on the information provided internally to key management personnel of the entity as defined in IAS 24 – *Related Party Disclosures* (see Chapter 39 at 2.2.1.D), for example the board of directors or chief executive officer and should include the matters set out at 5.3 to 5.5 below. *[IFRS 7.34(a), (b)]*.

This 'management view' approach was adopted by the IASB because it was considered to: *[IFRS 7.BC47]*

- provide a useful insight into how the entity views and manages risk;
- result in information that has more predictive value than information based on assumptions and methods that management does not use, for instance, in considering the entity's ability to react to adverse situations;
- be more effective in adapting to changes in risk measurement and management techniques and developments in the external environment;
- have practical advantages for preparers of financial statements, because it allows them to use the data they use in managing risk; and
- be consistent with the approach used in segment reporting (see Chapter 36).

When several methods are used to manage a risk exposure, the information disclosed should use the method(s) that provide the most relevant and reliable information. It is noted, in this context, that IAS 8 – *Accounting Policies, Changes in Accounting Estimates and Errors* – discusses relevance and reliability (see Chapter 3 at 4.3). *[IFRS 7.B7]*.

Where the quantitative data disclosed as at the reporting date are unrepresentative of an entity's exposure to risk during the period, further information that is representative should be provided. *[IFRS 7.35]*. For example, if an entity typically has a large exposure to a particular currency, but at year-end unwinds the position, the entity might disclose a graph that shows the exposure at various times during the period, or it might disclose the highest, lowest and average exposures. *[IFRS 7.IG20]*.

In developing IFRS 7, the IASB considered whether quantitative information about average risk exposures during the period should be given in all cases. However, they considered that such information is more informative only if the risk exposure at the reporting date is not representative of the exposure during the period. They also considered it would be onerous to prepare. Consequently, they decided that IFRS 7 would only require disclosure by exception, i.e. when the position at the reporting date was unrepresentative of the exposure during the reporting period. *[IFRS 7.BC48]*.

5.3 Credit risk

The disclosure requirements in respect of impairment are expanded significantly when compared to those under IAS 39. Those requirements are also supplemented by some detailed implementation guidance. The requirements of IFRS 9 relating to the measurement of impairments are dealt with in Chapter 51.

5.3.1 Scope and objectives

The objective of these disclosures is to enable users to understand the effect of credit risk on the amount, timing and uncertainty of future cash flows. To achieve this objective, the disclosures should provide: *[IFRS 7.35B]*

- information about the entity's credit risk management practices and how they relate to the recognition and measurement of expected credit losses, including the methods, assumptions and information used to measure those losses (see 5.3.2 below);
- quantitative and qualitative information that allows users of financial statements to evaluate the amounts in the financial statements arising from expected credit losses, including changes in the amount of those losses and the reasons for those changes (see 5.3.3 below); and
- information about the entity's credit risk exposure, i.e. the credit risk inherent in its financial assets and commitments to extend credit, including significant credit risk concentrations (see 5.3.4 below).

An entity will need to determine how much detail to disclose, how much emphasis to place on different aspects of the disclosure requirements, the appropriate level of aggregation or disaggregation and whether additional explanations are necessary to evaluate the quantitative information disclosed. *[IFRS 7.35D]*. If the disclosures provided are insufficient to meet the objectives above, additional information that is necessary to meet those objectives should be disclosed. *[IFRS 7.35E]*.

To avoid duplication, IFRS 7 allows this information to be incorporated by cross-reference from the financial statements to some other statement that is available to users of the financial statements on the same terms and at the same time, such as a management commentary or risk report. Without the information incorporated by cross-reference, the financial statements are incomplete. *[IFRS 7.35C]*.

A number of the disclosures about credit risk are required to be given by class (see 3.3 above). In determining these classes, financial instruments in the same class should reflect shared economic characteristics with respect to credit risk. A lender, for example, might determine that residential mortgages, unsecured consumer loans and commercial loans each have different economic characteristics. *[IFRS 7.IG21]*.

Unless otherwise stated, the disclosure requirements set out at 5.3.2 to 5.3.4 below are applicable only to financial instruments to which the impairment requirements in IFRS 9 are applied. *[IFRS 7.35A]*.

5.3.2 Credit risk management practices

An entity should explain its credit risk management practices and how they relate to the recognition and measurement of expected credit losses. To meet this objective it should disclose information that enables users to understand and evaluate: *[IFRS 7.35F]*

- how it has determined whether the credit risk of financial instruments has increased significantly since initial recognition, including if and how:
  - financial instruments are considered to have low credit risk, including the classes of financial instruments to which it applies; and
  - the presumption that there have been significant increases in credit risk since initial recognition when financial assets are more than 30 days past due has been rebutted;
- its definitions of default, including the reasons for selecting those definitions. This may include: *[IFRS 7.B8A]*
  - the qualitative and quantitative factors considered in defining default;
  - whether different definitions have been applied to different types of financial instruments; and
  - assumptions about the cure rate, i.e. the number of financial assets that return to a performing status, after a default has occurred on the financial asset;
- how the instruments were grouped if expected credit losses were measured on a collective basis;
- how it has determined that financial assets are credit-impaired; and
- its write-off policy, including the indicators that there is no reasonable expectation of recovery and information about the policy for financial assets that are written-off but are still subject to enforcement activity.

  An asset (or portion thereof) should be written off only if there is no reasonable expectation of recovery; *[IFRS 9.5.4.4]* and
- how the requirements for the modification of contractual cash flows of financial instruments have been applied, including how the entity:
  - determines whether the credit risk on a financial asset that has been modified while the loss allowance was measured at an amount equal to lifetime expected credit losses has improved to the extent that the loss allowance reverts to being measured at an amount equal to 12-month expected credit losses; and
  - monitors the extent to which the loss allowance on financial assets meeting the criteria in the previous bullet is subsequently remeasured at an amount equal to lifetime expected credit losses.

    Quantitative information that will assist users in understanding the subsequent increase in credit risk of modified financial assets may include information about modified financial assets meeting the criteria above for which the loss allowance has reverted to being measured at an amount equal to lifetime expected credit losses, i.e. a deterioration rate. *[IFRS 7.B8B]*. Including qualitative information can also be a useful way of meeting this disclosure requirement.

An entity should also explain the inputs, assumptions and estimation techniques used to apply the impairment requirements of IFRS 9. For this purpose it should disclose: *[IFRS 7.35G]*

- the basis of inputs and assumptions and the estimation techniques used to:
  - measure 12-month and lifetime expected credit losses;
  - determine whether the credit risk of financial instruments has increased significantly since initial recognition; and
  - determine whether a financial asset is credit-impaired.

  This may include information obtained from internal historical information or rating reports and assumptions about the expected life of financial instruments and the timing of the sale of collateral *[IFRS 7.B8C]* or information about the estimated maximum period considered when determining estimated credit losses in respect of revolving credit facilities;[3]
- how forward-looking information has been incorporated into the determination of expected credit losses, including the use of macroeconomic information. Where relevant this will include information about the use of multiple economic scenarios in determining those expected credit losses (see Chapter 51, particularly at 5.6).

  In rare circumstances, there may be relevant forward-looking information that cannot be incorporated into the determination of significant increases in credit risk or the measurement of expected credit losses because of a lack of reasonable and supportable information. In such cases disclosures should be made that are consistent with the objective in IFRS 7, i.e. to enable users of the financial statements to understand the credit risk to which the entity is exposed;[4] and
- changes in estimation techniques or significant assumptions made during the reporting period and the reasons for those changes.

5.3.3 Quantitative and qualitative information about amounts arising from expected credit losses

An entity should explain the changes in the loss allowance and reasons for those changes by presenting a reconciliation of the opening balance to the closing balance. This should be given in a table for each relevant class of financial instruments, showing separately the changes during the period for: *[IFRS 7.35H]*

- the loss allowance measured at an amount equal to 12-month expected credit losses;
- the loss allowance measured at an amount equal to lifetime expected credit losses for:
  - financial instruments for which credit risk has increased significantly since initial recognition but that are not credit-impaired financial assets;
  - financial assets that are credit-impaired at the reporting date (but were not credit-impaired when purchased or originated); and
  - trade receivables, contract assets or lease receivables for which the loss allowance is measured using a simplified approach based on lifetime expected credit losses; and
- financial assets (or, potentially, loan commitments or financial guarantee contracts – see Chapter 51 at 11) that were credit-impaired when purchased or originated.

The total amount of undiscounted expected credit losses on initial recognition of any such assets during the reporting period should also be disclosed.

In addition, it may be necessary to provide a narrative explanation of the changes in the loss allowance during the period. This narrative explanation may include an analysis of the reasons for changes in the loss allowance during the period, including: [IFRS 7.B8D]

- the portfolio composition;
- the volume of financial instruments purchased or originated; and
- the severity of the expected credit losses.

For loan commitments and financial guarantee contracts the loss allowance is recognised as a provision. Information about changes in the loss allowance for financial assets should be shown separately from those for loan commitments and financial guarantee contracts. However, if a financial instrument includes both a loan (i.e. financial asset) and an undrawn loan commitment (i.e. loan commitment) component and the expected credit losses on the loan commitment component cannot be separately identified from those on the financial asset component, the expected credit losses on the loan commitment should be recognised together with the loss allowance for the financial asset. To the extent that the combined expected credit losses exceed the gross carrying amount of the financial asset, the expected credit losses should be recognised as a provision. [IFRS 7.B8E].

An explanation should also be provided of how significant changes in the gross carrying amount of financial instruments during the period contributed to changes in the loss allowance. This information should be provided separately for each class of financial instruments for which loss allowances are analysed (see above). It should also include relevant qualitative and quantitative information. Examples of changes in the gross carrying amount of financial instruments that contribute to changes in the loss allowance may include: [IFRS 7.35I]

- changes because of financial instruments originated or acquired during the reporting period;
- the modification of contractual cash flows on financial assets that do not result in a derecognition of those financial assets;
- changes because of financial instruments that were derecognised, including those that were written-off during the reporting period; and
- changes arising from the measurement of the loss allowance moving from 12-month expected credit losses to lifetime losses (or *vice versa*).

The information disclosed should provide an understanding of the nature and effect of modifications of contractual cash flows on financial assets that have not resulted in derecognition as well as the effect of such modifications on the measurement of expected credit losses. The following information should therefore be given: [IFRS 7.35J]

- the amortised cost before the modification and the net modification gain or loss recognised for financial assets for which the contractual cash flows have been modified during the reporting period while they had a loss allowance based on lifetime expected credit losses; and

- the gross carrying amount at the end of the reporting period of financial assets that have been modified since initial recognition at a time when the loss allowance was based on lifetime expected credit losses and for which the loss allowance has changed during the reporting period to an amount equal to 12-month expected credit losses.

These requirements apply to all modifications whether they are as a result of credit related or other commercial reasons. However, if an entity has the ability to separately identify different types of modifications and considers that the separate disclosure of these items is relevant to achieving the overall objective of the disclosures in this section, the entity could provide this additional detail as part of the disclosure.[5]

The following example illustrates how this information might be presented. *[IFRS 7.IG20B]*.

Example 54.8:   Information about changes in the loss allowance

Mortgage loans – loss allowance	12-month expected credit losses	Lifetime expected credit losses (collectively assessed)	Lifetime expected credit losses (individually assessed)	Credit-impaired financial assets (lifetime expected credit losses)
CU'000				
Loss allowance as at 1 January	X	X	X	X
Changes due to financial instruments recognised as at 1 January:				
– Transfer to lifetime expected credit losses	(X)	X	X	–
– Transfer to credit-impaired financial assets	(X)	–	(X)	X
– Transfer to 12-month expected credit losses	X	(X)	(X)	–
– Financial assets that have been derecognised during the period	(X)	(X)	(X)	(X)
New financial assets originated or purchased	X	–	–	–
Write-offs	–	–	(X)	(X)
Changes in models/risk parameters	X	X	X	X
Foreign exchange and other movements	X	X	X	X
Loss allowance as at 31 December	X	X	X	X

Significant changes in the gross carrying amount of mortgage loans that contributed to changes in the loss allowance were:

- The acquisition of the ABC prime mortgage portfolio increased the residential mortgage book by x per cent, with a corresponding increase in the loss allowance measured on a 12-month basis.
- The write off of the CUXX DEF portfolio following the collapse of the local market reduced the loss allowance for financial assets with objective evidence of impairment by CUX.
- The expected increase in unemployment in Region X caused a net increase in financial assets whose loss allowance is equal to lifetime expected credit losses and caused a net increase of CUX in the lifetime expected credit losses allowance.

The significant changes in the gross carrying amount of mortgage loans are further explained below:

Mortgage loans – gross carrying amount	12-month expected credit losses	Lifetime expected credit losses (collectively assessed)	Lifetime expected credit losses (individually assessed)	Credit impaired financial assets (lifetime expected credit losses)
CU'000				
Gross carrying amount as at 1 January	X	X	X	X
Individual financial assets transferred to lifetime expected credit losses	(X)	–	X	–
Individual financial assets transferred to credit-impaired financial assets	(X)	–	(X)	X
Individual financial assets transferred from credit-impaired financial assets	X	–	X	(X)
Financial assets assessed on collective basis	(X)	X	–	–
New financial assets originated or purchased	X	–	–	–
Write-offs	–	–	(X)	(X)
Financial assets that have been derecognised	(X)	(X)	(X)	(X)
Changes due to modifications that did not result in derecognition	(X)	–	(X)	(X)
Other changes	X	X	X	X
Gross carrying amount as at 31 December	X	X	X	X

Where the loss allowance for trade receivables or lease receivables is measured using a simplified approach based on lifetime expected credit losses, the information about modifications need be given only if those financial assets are modified while more than 30 days past due. *[IFRS 7.35A(a)]*.

To provide an understanding of the effect of collateral and other credit enhancements on the amounts arising from expected credit losses, the following should be disclosed by class of financial instrument: *[IFRS 7.35K]*

- the amount that best represents the maximum exposure to credit risk at the end of the reporting period without taking account of any collateral held or other credit enhancements (e.g. netting agreements that do not qualify for offset in accordance with IAS 32);
- a narrative description of collateral held as security and other credit enhancements, including:
    - a description of the nature and quality of the collateral held;
    - an explanation of any significant changes in the quality of that collateral or credit enhancements as a result of deterioration or changes in the entity's collateral policies during the reporting period; and

- information about financial instruments for which a loss allowance has not been recognised because of the collateral.

This might include information about: *[IFRS 7.B8G]*
- the main types of collateral held as security and other credit enhancements, examples of the latter being guarantees, credit derivatives and netting agreements that do not qualify for offset in accordance with IAS 32;
- the volume of collateral held and other credit enhancements and its significance in terms of the loss allowance;
- the policies and processes for valuing and managing collateral and other credit enhancements;
- the main types of counterparties to collateral and other credit enhancements and their creditworthiness; and
- information about risk concentrations within the collateral and other credit enhancements; and
- quantitative information about the collateral held as security and other credit enhancements, e.g. quantification of the extent to which collateral and other credit enhancements mitigate credit risk, on financial assets that are credit-impaired at the reporting date.

Disclosure of information about the fair value of collateral and other credit enhancements is not required, nor is a quantification of the exact value of the collateral included in the calculation of expected credit losses (i.e. the loss given default). *[IFRS 7.B8F]*. Further, these requirements do not apply to lease receivables. *[IFRS 7.35A(b)]*.

For a financial asset, the maximum exposure to credit risk is typically the gross carrying amount, net of any amounts offset in accordance with IAS 32 and any impairment losses recognised in accordance with IFRS 9. *[IFRS 7.B9]*. Activities that give rise to credit risk and the associated maximum exposure to credit risk include, but are not limited to: *[IFRS 7.B10]*
- granting loans to customers and placing deposits with other entities. In these cases, the maximum exposure to credit risk is the carrying amount of the related financial assets;
- entering into derivative contracts, e.g. foreign exchange contracts, interest rate swaps and purchased credit derivatives. When the resulting asset is measured at fair value, the maximum exposure to credit risk at the reporting date will equal the carrying amount;
- granting financial guarantees. In this case, the maximum exposure to credit risk is the maximum amount the entity could have to pay if the guarantee is called on, which may be significantly greater than the amount recognised as a liability; and
- making a loan commitment that is irrevocable over the life of the facility or is revocable only in response to a material adverse change. If the issuer cannot settle the loan commitment net in cash or another financial instrument, the maximum credit exposure is the full amount of the commitment. This is because it is uncertain whether the amount of any undrawn portion may be drawn upon in the future. This may be significantly greater than the amount recognised as a liability.

The contractual amount outstanding on financial assets that were written off during the reporting period and which are still subject to enforcement activity should be disclosed. [IFRS 7.35L].

5.3.4 Credit risk exposure

Users should be able to assess an entity's credit risk exposure and understand its significant credit risk concentrations. Therefore, an entity should disclose, by 'credit risk rating grades' (see below), the gross carrying amount of financial assets and the exposure to credit risk on loan commitments and financial guarantee contracts. This information should be provided separately for financial instruments: [IFRS 7.35M]

- for which the loss allowance is measured at an amount equal to 12-month expected credit losses;
- for which the loss allowance is measured at an amount equal to lifetime expected credit losses and that are:
  - financial instruments for which credit risk has increased significantly since initial recognition but are not credit-impaired financial assets;
  - financial assets that are credit-impaired at the reporting date (but were not credit-impaired when purchased or originated); and
  - trade receivables, contract assets or lease receivables for which the loss allowances are measured using a simplified approach based on lifetime expected credit losses. Information for these assets may be based on a provision matrix; [IFRS 7.35N] and
- that are financial assets (or, potentially, loan commitments or financial guarantee contracts – see Chapter 51 at 11) that were credit-impaired when purchased or originated.

These disclosures should distinguish between financial instruments for which the loss allowance is equal to 12-month or lifetime expected credit losses even where the maturity of a financial instrument is twelve months or less in spite of the fact that the loss allowance should be the same under either approach.[6]

The following examples illustrate how this information might be presented. [IFRS 7.IG20C, IG20D].

Example 54.9: Information about credit risk exposures and significant credit risk concentrations

Consumer loan credit risk exposure by internal rating grades

20XX CU'000	Consumer–credit card Gross carrying amount		Consumer–automotive Gross carrying amount	
	Lifetime	12-month	Lifetime	12-month
Internal Grade 1-2	X	X	X	X
Internal Grade 3-4	X	X	X	X
Internal Grade 5-6	X	X	X	X
Internal Grade 7	X	X	X	X
Total	X	X	X	X

Corporate loan credit risk profile by external rating grades

20XX CU'000	Corporate–equipment Gross carrying amount		Corporate–construction Gross carrying amount	
	Lifetime	12-month	Lifetime	12-month
AAA-AA	X	X	X	X
A	X	X	X	X
BBB-BB	X	X	X	X
B	X	X	X	X
CCC-CC	X	X	X	X
C	X	X	X	X
D	X	X	X	X
Total	X	X	X	X

Corporate loan risk profile by probability of default

20XX CU'000	Corporate–unsecured Gross carrying amount		Corporate–secured Gross carrying amount	
	Lifetime	12-month	Lifetime	12-month
0.00-0.10	X	X	X	X
0.11-0.40	X	X	X	X
0.41-1.00	X	X	X	X
1.01-3.00	X	X	X	X
3.01-6.00	X	X	X	X
6.01-11.00	X	X	X	X
11.01-17.00	X	X	X	X
17.01-25.00	X	X	X	X
25.01-50.00	X	X	X	X
50.00+	X	X	X	X
Total	X	X	X	X

Example 54.10: Information about credit risk exposures using a provision matrix

The reporting entity manufactures cars and provides financing to both dealers and end customers. It discloses its dealer financing and customer financing as separate classes of financial instruments and applies the simplified approach to its trade receivables so that the loss allowance is always measured at an amount equal to lifetime expected credit losses. The following table illustrates the use of a provision matrix as a risk profile disclosure under the simplified approach:

20XX CU'000		Trade receivables days past due			
	Current	More than 30 days	More than 60 days	More than 90 days	Total
Dealer financing					
Expected credit loss rate	0.10%	2%	5%	13%	
Estimated total gross carrying amount at default	CU20,777	CU1,416	CU673	CU235	CU23,101
Lifetime expected credit losses – dealer financing	CU21	CU28	CU34	CU31	CU114
Customer financing					
Expected credit loss rate	0.20%	3%	8%	15%	
Estimated total gross carrying amount at default	CU19,222	CU2,010	CU301	CU154	CU21,687
Lifetime expected credit losses – customer financing	CU38	CU60	CU24	CU23	CU145

Credit risk rating grades are defined as ratings of credit risk based on the risk of a default occurring on the financial instrument. *[IFRS 7 Appendix A]*. The number of credit risk rating grades used to disclose the information above should be consistent with the number that the entity reports to key management personnel for credit risk management purposes. If past due information is the only borrower-specific information available and past due information is used to assess whether credit risk has increased significantly since initial recognition, an analysis by past due status should be provided for that class of financial assets. *[IFRS 7.B8I]*.

When expected credit losses are measured on a collective basis, it may not be possible to allocate the gross carrying amount of individual financial assets or the exposure to credit risk on loan commitments and financial guarantee contracts to the credit risk rating grades for which lifetime expected credit losses are recognised. In that case, the disclosure requirement above should be applied to those financial instruments that can be directly allocated to a credit risk rating grade and separate disclosure should be given of the gross carrying amount of financial instruments for which lifetime expected credit losses have been measured on a collective basis. *[IFRS 7.B8J]*.

A concentration of credit risk exists when a number of counterparties are located in a geographical region or are engaged in similar activities and have similar economic characteristics that would cause their ability to meet contractual obligations to be similarly affected by changes in economic or other conditions. Information should be provided to enable users to understand whether there are groups or portfolios of financial instruments with particular features that could affect a large portion of that group of financial instruments, such as concentration to particular risks. This could include, for example, loan-to-value groupings, geographical, industry or issuer-type concentrations. *[IFRS 7.B8H]*.

For financial instruments within the scope of IFRS 7 to which the impairment requirements in IFRS 9 are *not* applied, disclosure should be given by class of instrument of the amount that best represents the entity's maximum exposure to credit risk at the reporting date (see 5.3.3 above). The amount disclosed should not take account of any collateral held or other credit enhancements (e.g. netting agreements that do not qualify for offset in accordance with IAS 32). This disclosure is not required for financial instruments whose carrying amount best represents this amount, *[IFRS 7.36(a)]*, but will be required, for example, for written credit default swaps measured at fair value through profit or loss.

Entities should also provide, by class of financial instrument to which the impairment requirements in IFRS 9 are not applied, a description of collateral held as security and of other credit enhancements, and their financial effect (e.g. a quantification of the extent to which collateral and other credit enhancements mitigate credit risk) in respect of the amount that best represents the maximum exposure to credit risk. This applies irrespective of whether the maximum exposure to credit risk is disclosed separately or is represented by the carrying amount of a financial instrument. *[IFRS 7.36(b)]*. The requirement may be met by disclosing: *[IFRS 7.IG22]*

- the policies and processes for valuing and managing collateral and other credit enhancements obtained;
- a description of the main types of collateral and other credit enhancements (examples of the latter being guarantees and credit derivatives, as well as netting agreements that do not qualify for offset in accordance with IAS 32);
- the main types of counterparties to collateral and other credit enhancements and their creditworthiness; and
- information about risk concentrations within the collateral or other credit enhancements.

Whilst the standard suggests this information should, or at least could, involve disclosure of quantitative information, the implementation guidance implies more discursive disclosures might suffice in some cases. Therefore entities will need to make a judgement based on their own specific circumstances.

5.3.5 Collateral and other credit enhancements obtained

When an entity obtains financial or non-financial assets during the period by taking possession of collateral it holds as security, or calling on other credit enhancements such as guarantees, and these assets meet the recognition criteria in other standards, it should disclose for such assets held at the reporting date: *[IFRS 7.38]*

- the nature and carrying amount of the assets; and
- when the assets are not readily convertible into cash, its policies for disposing of such assets or for using them in its operations.

This disclosure is intended to provide information about the frequency of such activities and the entity's ability to obtain and realise the value of the collateral. *[IFRS 7.BC56]*.

5.3.6 Credit risk: illustrative disclosures

The following example illustrates what some of the disclosures about credit risk and loss allowances for one class of a bank's lending might look like. In preparing this example the following approach has been taken:

- although not explicitly required by IFRS 7, in order to provide relevant qualitative and quantitative information (see 5.3.3 above) and in line with the examples to the standard:
  - a reconciliation of movements in the gross carrying amounts in a tabular format has been provided; and
  - loans that are assessed on a specific basis and those assessed collectively have been shown separately;
- IFRS 7 does not require disclosure of the proportion of stage 2 loans that are 30 days past due, but this is regarded as useful information by users and has therefore been included;
- in order to avoid excessive detail only the net effect of using multiple scenarios has been provided rather than providing details of the scenarios and their weightings; and
- in practice the various parameters used are unlikely to be independent and, in line with the EDTF's recommendations (see 9.2 below), sensitivity to only one parameter has been disclosed.

Example 54.11: Certain disclosures of impairment allowances by a bank for one class of lending

Small business lending

The table below shows the credit quality and the maximum exposure to credit risk based on the Bank's internal credit rating system and year-end stage classification. Except for POCI loans, the amounts presented are gross of impairment allowances. The table analyses separately those loans which are assessed and measured individually and those which are assessed and measured on a collective basis:

In $ million							2021	2020
Internal rating grade	Stage 1 Individual	Stage 1 Collective	Stage 2 Individual	Stage 2 Collective	Stage 3	POCI	Total	Total
Performing								
High grade	1,168	832	–	–	–	–	2,000	2,358
Standard grade	728	340	299	358	–	–	1,725	1,886
Sub-standard grade	–	–	213	321	–	23	557	180
Low grade	–	–	75	194	–	–	269	120
Non-performing								
Individually impaired	–	–	–	–	205	31	236	208
Total	1,896	1,172	587	873	205	54	4,787	4,752

Financial instruments: Presentation and disclosure 4451

The following is a reconciliation of the gross carrying amounts at the beginning and end of year:

In $ million	Stage 1 Individual	Stage 1 Collective	Stage 2 Individual	Stage 2 Collective	Stage 3	POCI	Total
Gross carrying amount as at 1/1/2021	1,871	1,129	626	938	188	–	4,752
Assets originated/purchased	167	163	–	–	–	56	386
Assets de-recognised or repaid	(137)	(125)	(59)	(81)	(35)	(4)	(441)
Transfers to Stage 1	16	8	(16)	(8)	–	–	–
Transfers to Stage 2	(48)	(19)	62	19	(14)	–	–
Transfers to Stage 3	(5)	(4)	(36)	(12)	57	–	–
Modifications to contractual cash flows	–	–	–	–	(9)	–	(9)
Change in interest charged but not received	21	12	4	13	27	–	77
Amounts written-off	–	–	–	–	(12)	–	(12)
Foreign exchange revaluation	11	8	6	4	3	2	34
At 31/12/2021	1,896	1,172	587	873	205	54	4,787

The following is a reconciliation of the ECL allowances as at the beginning and end of the year. The effect on ECLs of transfers between stages has been calculated based on the allowances recorded at the date of transfer:

In $ million	Stage 1 Individual	Stage 1 Collective	Stage 2 Individual	Stage 2 Collective	Stage 3	POCI	Total
ECL allowances as at 1/1/2021	48	41	36	47	79	–	251
Assets originated/purchased	5	15	–	–	–	–	20
Assets de-recognised or repaid	(4)	(12)	(5)	(3)	(4)	–	(28)
Transfers to Stage 1	1	–	(2)	(1)	–	–	(2)
Transfers to Stage 2	(4)	(1)	21	5	–	–	21
Transfers to Stage 3	(1)	(1)	(10)	(4)	20	–	4
Unwind of discount	9	10	5	6	13	–	43
Modifications to contractual cash flows	–	–	–	–	(6)	–	(6)
Changes to models and inputs used for ECL calculations	7	10	6	5	18	3	49
Amounts written off	–	–	–	–	(12)	–	(12)
Foreign exchange	2	2	1	1	1	–	7
At 31/12/2021	63	64	52	56	109	3	347

Of the $587m of loans classified as stage 2 on an individual basis, $37m (1 January: $33m) of loans and $17m (1 January: $16m) of ECLs are more than 30 days past due.

The credit risk for the bank's small business customers is mostly affected by factors specific to individual borrowers, but, given the available information, the ECLs for the majority of the loans are measured on a collective basis. The key inputs in the ECL model, apart from the bank's own credit risk appraisal process, are assumptions about changes in Gross Domestic Product (GDP) and future interest rates. As at 1 January 2021, the base scenario assumed that GDP will increase by 2.6% in 2021 and 2.0% in 2022, with the rate of increase declining over the next four years to 1.5%. GDP grew during 2021 by only 2.0% and is now forecast to grow by only 1.3% in 2022, increasing to 1.5% over the next four years. The base rate of interest assumed in the base scenario as at 1 January 2021 was 1.2% for 2021 and 1.4% for 2022, increasing to 2.2% over the next four years. The average rate for 2021 was 1.4% and the forecast for 2022 is now 1.5%, increasing to 2.3% over the next four years.

The allowance was calculated using, in addition to the base scenario, an upside scenario and two downside scenarios, all weighted to reflect their likelihood of occurrence. The allowance as at 31 December 2021, based upon the bank's base case scenario, is $312.5m. The effect of applying multiple economic scenarios is to increase the allowance by $34.5m (11%). (As at 1 January the equivalents were: $230m, $40m and 14.8%).

Based upon past experience, reducing the growth in GDP over the next three years by 1% (keeping interest rates constant) would increase the ECLs by approximately $14m (1 January: $18m).

The largest contribution to the increase in ECLs of the portfolio during the year was the update to inputs to models to reflect the deterioration in economic conditions. However, the result of changes in the base scenario has been partly offset by a small reduction in the effect of using multiple economic scenarios.

The following extract from the financial statements of Volkswagen shows the type of disclosure addressing credit risk that can be seen in practice.

> *Extract 54.4: Volkswagen Aktiengesellschaft (2018)*
> **Notes to the Consolidated Financial Statements** [extract]
> **Other disclosures** [extract]
> **34. Financial risk management and financial instruments** [extract]
> **2. CREDIT AND DEFAULT RISK** [extract]
> **LOSS ALLOWANCE**
>
> The Volkswagen Group consistently uses the expected credit loss model of IFRS 9 for all financial assets and other risk exposures.
>
> Regarding this, IFRS 9 differentiates between the general approach and the simplified approach. The expected credit loss model under IFRS 9 takes in both loss allowances for financial assets for which there are no objective indications of impairment and loss allowances for financial assets that are already impaired. For the calculation of impairment losses, IFRS 9 distinguishes between the general approach and the simplified approach.
>
> Under the general approach, financial assets are allocated to one of three stages, plus an additional stage for financial assets that are already impaired when acquired (stage 4). Stage 1 comprises financial assets that are recognized for the first time or for which the probability of default has not increased significantly. The expected credit losses for the next twelve months are calculated at this stage. Stage 2 comprises financial assets with a significantly increased probability of default, while financial assets with objective indications of default are allocated to stage 3. The lifetime expected credit losses are calculated at these stages. Stage 4 financial assets, which are already impaired when acquired, are subsequently measured by recognizing a loss allowance on the basis of the accumulated lifetime expected losses. Financial assets classified as impaired on acquisition remain in this category until they are derecognized.
>
> The Volkswagen Group applies the simplified approach to trade receivables and contract assets with a significant financing component in accordance with IFRS 15. The same applies to receivables under operating or finance leases accounted for under IAS 17. Under the simplified approach, the expected losses are consistently determined for the entire life of the asset.
>
> The tables below show the reconciliation of the loss allowance for various financial assets and financial guarantees and credit commitments:

CHANGES IN LOSS ALLOWANCE FOR FINANCIAL ASSETS MEASURED AT AMORTIZED COST FROM JANUARY 1 TO DECEMBER 31, 2018

€ million	Stage 1	Stage 2	Stage 3	Simplified approach	Stage 4	Total
Carrying amount at Jan. 1, 2018	800	802	1,002	622	138	3,364
Foreign exchange differences	–2	–7	–35	–15	–4	–63
Changes in consolidated group	4	6	15	8	0	33
Newly extended/purchased financial assets (additions)	253	–	–	176	30	459
Other changes within a stage	–69	132	195	1	16	275
Transfers to						
Stage 1	22	–67	–13	–	–	–58
Stage 2	–102	275	–39	–	–	134
Stage 3	–33	–51	445	–	–	361
Financial instruments derecognized during the period (disposals)	–120	–148	–226	–127	–33	–653
Utilization	–	–	–459	–34	–1	–493
Changes to models or risk parameters	–1	4	10	3	–2	13
Carrying amount at Dec. 31, 2018	750	946	896	634	146	3,372

CHANGES IN LOSS ALLOWANCE FOR FINANCIAL GUARANTEES AND CREDIT COMMITMENTS FROM JANUARY 1 TO DECEMBER 31, 2018

€ million	Stage 1	Stage 2	Stage 3	Stage 4	Total
Carrying amount at Jan. 1, 2018	11	4	1	0	16
Foreign exchange differences	0	0	0	–	0
Changes in consolidated group	–	–	–	–	–
Newly extended/purchased financial assets (additions)	11	–	–	1	12
Other changes within a stage	0	0	0	0	0
Transfers to					
Stage 1	0	0	0	–	0
Stage 2	–1	0	0	–	0
Stage 3	0	0	1	–	1
Financial instruments derecognized during the period (disposals)	–4	–4	0	–1	–9
Utilization	–	–	0	–	0
Changes to models or risk parameters	0	0	0	0	0
Carrying amount at Dec. 31, 2018	18	1	1	0	19

CHANGES IN LOSS ALLOWANCE FOR LEASE RECEIVABLES FROM JANUARY 1 TO DECEMBER 31, 2018

€ million	Simplified approach
Carrying amount at Jan. 1, 2018	1,250
Foreign exchange differences	–6
Changes in consolidated group	–
Newly extended/purchased financial assets (additions)	450
Other changes	0
Financial instruments derecognized during the period (disposals)	–465
Utilization	–54
Changes to models or risk parameters	18
Carrying amount at Dec. 31, 2018	1,193

The loss allowance on "assets measured at fair value" amounted to €2 million in January 2018 (Stage 1) and did not change in the course of the fiscal year.

The amount contractually outstanding for financial assets that have been derecognized in the current year and are still subject to enforcement proceedings is €293 million.

5.4 Liquidity risk

5.4.1 Information provided to key management

As set out at 5.2 above, an entity should disclose summary quantitative data about its exposure to risk on the basis of the information provided internally to key management personnel and IFRS 7 emphasises that this requirement applies to liquidity risk too. *[IFRS 7.B10A, BC58A(b)]*.

Entities should provide an explanation of how the data disclosed are determined. If the outflows of cash (or other financial assets) included in the data could occur significantly earlier than indicated, that fact should be stated and quantitative information should be provided to enable users of the financial statements to evaluate the extent of this risk, unless that information is included in the contractual maturity analyses (see 5.4.2 below). Similar information should be given if the outflows of cash (or other financial assets) could be for significantly different amounts than those indicated in the data. This might be required, for example, if a derivative is included in the data on a net settlement basis, but the counterparty has the option of requiring gross settlement. *[IFRS 7.B10A]*.

5.4.2 Maturity analyses

To illustrate liquidity risk, the principal minimum numerical disclosures required are: *[IFRS 7.39(a), (b)]*

- a maturity analysis for non-derivative financial liabilities (including issued financial guarantee contracts) that shows their remaining contractual maturities; and
- a maturity analysis for derivative financial liabilities which includes the remaining contractual maturities for those derivative financial liabilities for which contractual maturities are essential for an understanding of the timing of the cash flows.

  The contractual maturities of the following would be essential for an understanding of the timing of the cash flows: *[IFRS 7.B11B]*
  - an interest rate swap with a remaining maturity of five years in a cash flow hedge of a variable rate financial asset or liability; and
  - all loan commitments.

  Derivatives entered into for trading purposes that are typically settled before their contractual maturity (e.g. in response to fair value movements) are an example of the type of instrument that might not need to be included in the maturity analysis.[7]

These requirements are discussed further in the remainder of this sub-section.

Although these minimum disclosures address only financial liabilities, other aspects of IFRS 7 mean that most financial institutions will be required to disclose a maturity analysis of financial assets too (see 5.4.3 below).

5.4.2.A Time bands

The time bands to be used in the maturity analyses are not specified. Rather, entities should use their judgement to determine what is appropriate. For example, an entity might determine that the following are appropriate: *[IFRS 7.B11]*

- not later than one month;
- later than one month and not later than three months;
- later than three months and not later than one year; and
- later than one year and not later than five years.

In practice it is rare for entities outside of the financial services sector to present more than one time band covering amounts payable within one year. However, it is quite common for more than one time band to be given covering amounts payable later than one year and within five years as Unilever and Nestlé have done (see Extracts 54.6 and 54.7 respectively at 5.4.2.G below). For banks and similar institutions an 'on demand' category could also be relevant.

IFRS 16 requires lessees to disclose a maturity analysis of lease liabilities applying paragraphs 39(a) and B11 of IFRS 7 separately from the maturity analyses of other financial liabilities. *[IFRS 16.58]*. Guidance in IFRS 7 illustrates a number of different approaches, each of which takes into account the maturity of the financial liabilities being presented. Two of these examples simply show lease liabilities as a separate line within a table. A third example illustrates an entity with all financial liabilities due within three years except lease liabilities which extend for 25 years. For this entity, two tables are presented, one including all financial liabilities using the following time bands:

- less than 1 month;
- 1-6 months;
- 6 months – 1 year;
- 1-2 years;
- 2-3 years; and
- more than 3 years;

and a second analysing only the lease liabilities but using the following time bands:

- less than 1 year;
- 1-5 years;
- 5-10 years;
- 10-15 years;
- 15-20 years; and
- 20-25 years. *[IFRS 7.IG31A]*.

When a counterparty has a choice of when an amount is paid, the liability should be included on the basis of the earliest date on which the entity can be required to pay. For example, financial liabilities such as demand deposits that an entity can be required to repay on demand should be included in the earliest time band. *[IFRS 7.B11C(a)]*. This means that the disclosure shows a worst case scenario, even if there is only a remote possibility that the entity could be required to pay its liabilities earlier than expected, *[IFRS 7.BC57]*, (although the disclosures at 5.4.3 below may be relevant in these circumstances, i.e. those which are based on the information used by management to manage liquidity risk).

No guidance is given on how to deal with instruments where the issuer has a choice of when an amount is paid. For example, borrowings containing embedded issuer call or issuer prepayment options might be included in the analysis for non-derivative financial liabilities based on the earliest, latest or expected contractual payment dates. Where an entity has a material amount of such instruments it would be appropriate to explain the basis of the analyses presented.

When an entity is committed to make amounts available in instalments, each instalment should be allocated to the earliest period in which the entity can be required to pay. For example, an undrawn loan commitment would be included in the time band containing the earliest date it could be drawn down. *[IFRS 7.B11C(b)]*.

For issued financial guarantee contracts, amounts included in the maturity analysis should be allocated to the earliest period in which the guarantee could be called. *[IFRS 7.B11C(c)]*.

5.4.2.B Cash flows: general requirements

The amounts that should be disclosed in the maturity analyses are the contractual undiscounted cash flows, for example:

- gross finance lease obligations (before deducting finance charges);
- prices specified in forward agreements to purchase financial assets for cash;
- net amounts for pay-floating/receive-fixed interest rate swaps for which net cash flows are exchanged;
- contractual amounts to be exchanged in a derivative financial instrument (e.g. a currency swap) for which gross cash flows are exchanged; and
- gross loan commitments.

These undiscounted cash flows will differ from the amount included in the statement of financial position because the latter amount is based on discounted cash flows. *[IFRS 7.B11D]*.

When the amount payable is not fixed, the amount disclosed should be determined by reference to the conditions existing at the reporting date. For example, if the amount payable varies with changes in an index, the amount disclosed may be based on the level of the index at the reporting date. *[IFRS 7.B11D]*. The standard does not explain whether the amount should be based on the spot or forward price of the index and, in practice, both approaches are used. Where a material difference between the two approaches could arise it would be appropriate to explain the basis on which the information is prepared as Berendsen plc does.

> *Extract 54.5: Berendsen plc (2016)*
> Notes to the consolidated financial statements [extract]
> 17.   Financial risk management [extract]
> 17.1   Financial risk factors [extract]
> c)   Liquidity risk [extract]
>
> The table below analyses the group's financial liabilities, excluding break clauses, which will be settled on a net basis into relative maturity groupings based on the remaining period at the balance sheet to the contract maturity date. The amounts disclosed in the table are contractual undiscounted cash flows using spot interest and foreign exchange rates at 31 December 2016. Balances due within 12 months equal their carrying balances as the impact of the discount is not significant.

Berendsen applied IAS 39 in these financial statements but the disclosure requirements in respect of liquidity risk are unchanged under IFRS 9.

The definition of liquidity risk includes only financial liabilities that will result in the outflow of cash or another financial asset (see 5 above) which means that financial liabilities that will be settled in the entity's own equity instruments and liabilities within the scope of IFRS 7 that are settled with non-financial assets will not be included in the maturity analysis. *[IFRS 7.BC58A(a)]*.

5.4.2.C Cash flows: borrowings

It follows from the requirements at 5.4.2.B above that the cash flows included in the analysis of non-derivative financial liabilities in respect of interest-bearing borrowings should reflect coupon as well as principal payments (although the standard does not say this explicitly). Quite how perpetual debt obligations should be dealt with in this analysis is not clear because the amount the standard requires to be included in the latest maturity category is infinity.

A number of companies show coupon payments separately from payments of principal, for example Unilever (see Extract 54.6 at 5.4.2.G below). However, separate disclosure is not required and coupon payments are commonly aggregated with principal payments as Nestlé and Volkswagen have (see Extracts 54.7 and 54.8 respectively).

The following example illustrates the cash flows that should be included in the maturity analysis for non-derivative financial liabilities for a simple floating rate borrowing.

Example 54.12: Maturity analysis: floating rate borrowing

On 1 January 2021, Company P borrowed €100 million from a bank on the following terms: coupons are payable on the entire principal on 30 June and 31 December each year at the annual rate of LIBOR plus 1% as determined on the previous 1 January and 1 July; the principal is repayable on 31 December 2024.

At the end of 2021, P's reporting period, LIBOR is 5% and there is no difference between spot and forward interest rates (i.e. the yield curve is flat). Accordingly, P would include the following cash flows in its maturity analysis:

	€ million
30 June 2022	3
31 December 2022	3
30 June 2023	3
31 December 2023	3
30 June 2024	3
31 December 2024	103
Total	118

5.4.2.D Cash flows: derivatives

In the case of derivatives that are settled by a gross exchange of cash flows, it is not entirely clear whether entities should disclose the related cash inflow as well as the cash outflow, although such information might be considered useful. Further, because the analysis is of financial liabilities, it seems clear that, strictly, cash outflows from a derivative asset that is settled by a gross exchange of cash should not be included. However, the contractual cash flows on these instruments would appear to be no less relevant than on those that have a negative fair value and should be disclosed where relevant.

A number of approaches to these issues were seen in practice as illustrated in Extracts 54.6 to 54.9 at 5.4.2.G below. Unilever and Nestlé both included cash inflows as well as outflows whereas Volkswagen showed only the cash outflows; Unilever included only derivative liabilities whereas Nestlé and Volkswagen included gross-settled derivative assets too. The size of the figures disclosed by entities with gross-settled derivatives can be staggering – Volkswagen, for example, disclosed gross cash outflows of nearly €110 billion from its derivatives.

The IASB staff has been clear that disclosure of only the outflow on derivatives that were in a liability position was explicitly required. However, IFRS 7 emphasises the need to provide a maturity analysis of assets where such information is necessary to enable users of financial statements to evaluate the nature and extent of the entity's liquidity risk (see 5.4.3 below). This change is likely to bring derivative assets within the scope of the maturity analyses[8] and, by analogy, related gross cash inflows. Similar issues can arise on commodity contracts that are accounted for under IFRS 9 which will often be settled by exchanging the commodity for cash. An additional complication with these is that one leg of the contract may not involve a cash flow.

Further issues can arise in the case of a derivative liability settled by exchanging net cash flows in a number of future periods. For example, the relevant index for a long-term interest rate swap might predict that in some periods the entity could have cash inflows. Although this issue was identified by the IASB staff,[9] it has not been addressed and it remains unclear whether and how these inflows should be included within the analyses.

5.4.2.E Cash flows: embedded derivatives

The application guidance to IFRS 7 explains that where an embedded derivative is separated from a hybrid (combined) financial instrument (see Chapter 46 at 4), the entire instrument should be dealt with in the maturity analysis for non-derivative instruments. *[IFRS 7.B11A]*.

No guidance is given for dealing with embedded derivatives separated from non-financial contracts. However, applying a similar approach to those separated from financial instruments would result in them being excluded from the maturity analyses altogether. This is because the hypothecated cash flows of the embedded derivative would be treated as cash flows of the non-financial contract and such contracts are not within the scope of IFRS 7. This is consistent with the IASB staff analysis when developing the above requirement: they planned to exclude from the maturity analysis all separated embedded derivatives except those for which the hybrid contract was a financial liability because including them was unhelpful in understanding the liquidity information provided.[10]

5.4.2.F Cash flows: financial guarantee contracts and written options

For issued financial guarantee contracts, IFRS 7 requires the maximum amount of the guarantee to be included in the maturity analysis, *[IFRS 7.B11C(c)]*, but credit default swaps and written options are not directly addressed. However, the IASB staff have noted that the question of what to include in the maturity analysis is the same for such instruments and, in our view, the maximum amount that could be payable should be included in the analysis.[11]

5.4.2.G Examples of disclosures in practice

The following extracts from the financial statements of Unilever, Nestlé, Volkswagen and Royal Bank of Scotland show a variety of ways that companies applied the requirements of IFRS 7 in practice.

Extract 54.6: Unilever PLC and Unilever N.V. (2018)

NOTES TO THE CONSOLIDATED FINANCIAL STATEMENTS [extract]

16A.   MANAGEMENT OF LIQUIDITY RISK [extract]

The following table shows Unilever's contractually agreed undiscounted cash flows, including expected interest payments, which are payable under financial liabilities at the balance sheet date:

Undiscounted cash flows	€ million Due within 1 year	€ million Due between 1 and 2 years	€ million Due between 2 and 3 years	€ million Due between 3 and 4 years	€ million Due between 4 and 5 years	€ million Due after 5 years	€ million Total	€ million Net carrying amount as shown in balance sheet
2018								
Non-derivative financial liabilities:								
Bank loans and overdrafts	(529)	(12)	(1)	(278)	–	–	(820)	(814)
Bonds and other loans	(2,888)	(2,748)	(2,572)	(2,646)	(2,387)	(14,090)	(27,331)	(23,391)
Finance lease creditors	(20)	(19)	(18)	(17)	(17)	(96)	(187)	(128)
Other financial liabilities	(149)	(1)	–	–	–	–	(150)	(150)
Trade payables, accruals and other liabilities	(13,945)	(140)	(10)	(5)	(4)	(14)	(14,118)	(14,118)
Deferred consideration	(14)	(79)	(70)	(6)	–	(45)	(214)	(187)
	(17,545)	(2,999)	(2,671)	(2,952)	(2,408)	(14,245)	(42,820)	(38,788)
Derivative financial liabilities:								
Interest rate derivatives:								
Derivatives contracts – receipts	67	760	163	788	37	1,406	3,221	
Derivative contracts – payments	(23)	(756)	(138)	(797)	(17)	(1,423)	(3,154)	
Foreign exchange derivatives:								
Derivatives contracts – receipts	17,108	–	–	–	–	–	17,108	
Derivative contracts – payments	(17,317)	–	–	–	–	–	(17,317)	
Commodity derivatives:								
Derivatives contracts – receipts	–	–	–	–	–	–	–	
Derivative contracts – payments	(74)	–	–	–	–	–	(74)	
	(239)	4	25	(9)	20	(17)	(216)	(542)
Total	(17,784)	(2,995)	(2,646)	(2,961)	(2,388)	(14,262)	(43,036)	(39,330)

Extract 54.7: Nestlé S.A. (2018)

Notes [extract]
12. Financial instruments [extract]
12.2b Liquidity risk [extract]
Contractual maturities of financial liabilities and derivatives (including interest) [extract]

In millions of CHF

	In the first year	In the second year	In the third to the fifth year	After the fifth year	Contractual amount	Carrying amount
Trade and other payables	(17,800)	(58)	(303)	(29)	(18,190)	(18,190)
Commercial paper [a]	(9,193)	–	–	–	(9,193)	(9,165)
Bonds [a]	(2,510)	(2,771)	(11,099)	(14,293)	(30,673)	(24,869)
Lease liabilities	(788)	(637)	(1,146)	(1,105)	(3,676)	(3,253)
Other financial debt	(3,013)	(109)	(80)	(12)	(3,214)	(3,107)
Total financial debt	(15,504)	(3,517)	(12,325)	(15,410)	(46,756)	(40,394)
Financial liabilities (excluding derivatives)	(33,304)	(3,575)	(12,628)	(15,439)	(64,946)	(58,584)
Non-currency derivative assets	45	6	12	–	63	62
Non-currency derivative liabilities	(83)	(6)	(2)	–	(91)	(90)
Gross amount receivable from currency derivatives	14,448	1,080	667	1,689	17,884	17,765
Gross amount payable from currency derivatives	(14,501)	(1,370)	(812)	(1,835)	(18,518)	(18,002)
Net derivatives	(91)	(290)	(135)	(146)	(662)	(265)
Of which derivatives under cash flow hedges [b]	(39)	(6)	(2)	–	(47)	(46)

(a) Commercial paper of CHF 7698 million and bonds of CHF 720 million have maturities of less than three months.
(b) The periods when the cash flow hedges affect the income statement do not differ significantly from the maturities disclosed above.

Extract 54.8: Volkswagen Aktiengesellschaft (2018)

Notes to the Consolidated Financial Statements [extract]
34. Financial risk management and financial instruments [extract]
3. LIQUIDITY RISK [extract]

The solvency and liquidity of the Volkswagen Group are ensured at all times by rolling liquidity planning, a liquidity reserve in the form of cash, confirmed credit lines and the issuance of securities on the international money and capital markets. The volume of confirmed bilateral and syndicated credit lines stood at €16.8 billion as of December 31, 2018, of which €3.4 billion was drawn down.

Local cash funds in certain countries (e.g. China, Brazil, Argentina, South Africa and India) are only available to the Group for cross-border transactions subject to exchange controls. There are no significant restrictions over and above these.

The following overview shows the contractual undiscounted cash flows from financial instruments.

MATURITY ANALYSIS OF UNDISCOUNTED CASH FLOWS FROM FINANCIAL INSTRUMENTS

€ million	Remaining contractual maturities			
	up to one year	within one to five years	more than five years	2018
Put options and compensation rights granted to noncontrolling interest shareholders	1,853	–	–	1,853
Financial liabilities	91,891	84,965	23,380	200,235
Trade payables	23,607	0	–	23,607
Other financial liabilities	8,010	1,916	154	10,080
Derivatives	63,059	42,984	3,036	109,078
	188,419	129,865	26,570	344,854

When calculating cash outflows related to put options and compensation rights, it was assumed that shares would be tendered at the earliest possible date. The cash outflows on other financial liabilities include outflows on liabilities for tax allocations amounting to €33 million.

Derivatives comprise both cash flows from derivative financial instruments with negative fair values and cash flows from derivatives with positive fair values for which gross settlement has been agreed. Derivatives entered into through offsetting transactions are also accounted for as cash outflows. The cash outflows from derivatives for which gross settlement has been agreed are matched in part by cash inflows. These cash inflows are not reported in the maturity analysis. If these cash inflows were also recognized, the cash outflows presented would be substantially lower. This applies in particular also if hedges have been closed with offsetting transactions.

The cash outflows from irrevocable credit commitments are presented in section entitled "Other financial obligations", classified by contractual maturities.

As of December 31, 2018, the maximum potential liability under financial guarantees amounted to €315 million. Financial guarantees are assumed to be due immediately in all cases.

Extract 54.9: The Royal Bank of Scotland Group plc (2018)

Notes on the consolidated accounts [extract]

13. Financial instruments – maturity analysis [extracts]

Assets and liabilities by contractual cash flow maturity [extract]

The tables below show the contractual undiscounted cash flows receivable and payable, up to a period of 20 years, including future receipts and payments of interest of financial assets and liabilities by contractual maturity. The balances in the following tables do not agree directly with the consolidated balance sheet, as the tables include all cash flows relating to principal and future coupon payments, presented on an undiscounted basis. The tables have been prepared on the following basis:

Financial assets have been reflected in the time band of the latest date on which they could be repaid, unless earlier repayment can be demanded by RBS. Financial liabilities are included at the earliest date on which the counterparty can require repayment, regardless of whether or not such early repayment results in a penalty. If the repayment of a financial instrument is triggered by, or is subject to, specific criteria such as market price hurdles being reached, the asset is included in the time band that contains the latest date on which it can be repaid, regardless of early repayment.

The liability is included in the time band that contains the earliest possible date on which the conditions could be fulfilled, without considering the probability of the conditions being met.

For example, if a structured note is automatically prepaid when an equity index exceeds a certain level, the cash outflow will be included in the less than three months period, whatever the level of the index at the year end. The settlement date of debt securities in issue, issued by certain securitisation vehicles consolidated by RBS, depends on when cash flows are received from the securitised assets. Where these assets are prepayable, the timing of the cash outflow relating to securities assumes that each asset will be prepaid at the earliest possible date. As the repayments of assets and liabilities are linked, the repayment of assets in securitisations is shown on the earliest date that the asset can be prepaid, as this is the basis used for liabilities.

The principal amounts of financial assets and liabilities that are repayable after 20 years or where the counterparty has no right to repayment of the principal are excluded from the table, as are interest payments after 20 years.

MFVTPL assets of £207.9 billion and HFT liabilities of £198.3 billion have been excluded from the following tables.

2018	0-3 months £m	3-12 months £m	1-3 years £m	3-5 years £m	5-10 years £m	10-20 years £m
Liabilities by contractual maturity						
Bank deposits	7,417	21	13,785	2,003	–	59
Settlement balance	3,066	–	–	–	–	–
Other financial liabilities	1,736	7,226	10,724	11,658	9,316	2,029
Subordinated liabilities	131	637	1,476	7,532	1,737	1,422
Other liabilities	2,152	–	–	–	–	–
Total maturing liabilities	14,502	7,884	25,985	21,193	11,053	3,510
Customer deposits	351,054	8,114	1,727	14	6	26
Derivatives held for hedging	181	306	1,062	416	637	531
	365,737	16,304	28,774	21,623	11,696	4,067
Guarantees and commitments – notional amounts						
Guarantees	3,952	–	–	–	–	–
Commitments	116,843	–	–	–	–	–
	120,795	–	–	–	–	–

5.4.3 Management of associated liquidity risk

In addition to the maturity analyses for financial liabilities, the entity should provide a description of how it manages the liquidity risk inherent in those analyses. *[IFRS 7.39(c)]*. These disclosures are, in effect, intended to 'reconcile' the maturity analyses which are prepared on a worst case scenario notion (see 5.4.2 above) with how an entity actually manages liquidity risk (see 5.4.1 above).[12]

It is emphasised that a maturity analysis of financial assets held for managing liquidity risk (e.g. financial assets that are readily saleable or expected to generate cash inflows to meet cash outflows on financial liabilities) is required if that information is necessary to enable users of financial statements to evaluate the nature and extent of the entity's liquidity risk. *[IFRS 7.B11E, BC58D]*. IFRS 7 does not specify the basis on which such an analysis should be provided and in practice they are often prepared on the basis of expected rather than contractual maturities as this is considered more relevant information.

Other factors that might be considered when making this disclosure include, but are not limited to, whether the entity: *[IFRS 7.B11F]*

- has committed borrowing facilities (e.g. commercial paper facilities) or other lines of credit (e.g. stand-by credit facilities) that it can access to meet liquidity needs;
- holds deposits at central banks to meet liquidity needs;
- has very diverse funding sources;
- has significant concentrations of liquidity risk in either its assets or its funding sources;
- has internal control processes and contingency plans for managing liquidity risk;

- has instruments that include accelerated repayment terms (e.g. on the downgrade of the entity's credit rating);
- has instruments that could require the posting of collateral (e.g. margin calls for derivatives);
- has instruments that allow the entity to choose whether it settles its financial liabilities by delivering cash (or another financial asset) or by delivering its own shares; or
- has instruments that are subject to master netting agreements.

5.4.4 Puttable financial instruments classified as equity

Certain puttable financial instruments that meet the definition of financial liabilities are classified as equity instruments (see Chapter 47 at 4.6). In spite of this classification, the IASB recognises that these instruments give rise to liquidity risk and consequently requires the following disclosures about them: *[IAS 1.136A]*

- summary quantitative data about the amount classified as equity;
- the entity's objectives, policies and processes for managing its obligation to repurchase or redeem the instruments when required to do so by the instrument holders, including any changes from the previous period;
- the expected cash outflow on redemption or repurchase of that class of financial instruments; and
- information about how the expected cash outflow on redemption or repurchase was determined.

5.5 Market risk

IFRS 7 requires entities to provide disclosure of their sensitivity to market risk in one of two ways which are set out at 5.5.1 and 5.5.2 below. The sensitivity analyses should cover the whole of an entity's business, but different types of sensitivity analysis may be provided for different classes of financial instruments. *[IFRS 7.B21]*. This is considered by the IASB to be simpler and more suitable than the disclosure of terms and conditions of financial instruments previously required by IAS 32 and for which there is no direct equivalent within IFRS 7. *[IFRS 7.BC59]*.

No sensitivity analysis is required for financial instruments that an entity classifies as equity instruments. Such instruments are not remeasured so that neither profit or loss nor equity will be affected by the equity price risk of those instruments. *[IFRS 7.B28]*.

5.5.1 'Basic' sensitivity analysis

Except where the disclosures set out at 5.5.2 below are provided, entities should disclose: *[IFRS 7.40]*

- a sensitivity analysis for each type of market risk to which the entity is exposed at the reporting date, showing how profit or loss and equity would have been affected by changes in the relevant risk variable that were reasonably possible at that date.

    The sensitivity of profit or loss (which arises, for example, from instruments measured at fair value through profit or loss) should be disclosed separately from the sensitivity of equity (which arises, for example, from investments in equity instruments whose changes in fair value are presented in other comprehensive income). *[IFRS 7.B27].*

The term 'profit or loss' is used in IAS 1 to mean profit after tax. Therefore, it might well be argued that the amounts disclosed should take account of any related tax effects, a view corroborated by the illustrative disclosures in the implementation guidance to IFRS 7 (see Example 54.13 below). However, as noted below, the application guidance suggests this requirement should (and the implementation guidance might suggest it could) be met by disclosing the impact on interest expense, a pre-tax measure of profit. Given this conflicting guidance, it is difficult to say that a pre-tax approach fails to comply with the standard and, in practice, both approaches are seen.

Where a post-tax figure is disclosed, it will not always be straightforward to determine the related tax effects, especially for a multinational group, and it may be appropriate to use the guidance in Chapter 33 at 10 which deals with the allocation of income tax between profit or loss, other comprehensive income and equity.

This requirement focuses exclusively on accounting sensitivity, and does not include market risk sensitivities that do not directly impact profit and loss or equity, e.g. interest rate risk arising on fixed rate financial assets held at amortised cost. In December 2008, the IASB considered encouraging entities to discuss the effect of changes in the relevant risk variable on economic value not manifest in profit and loss or equity, but decided not to;[13]

- the methods and assumptions used in preparing the sensitivity analysis; and
- changes from the previous period in the methods and assumptions used, and the reasons for such changes.

The standard contains a reminder of the general guidance at 3.1 above and explains that an entity should decide how it aggregates information to display the overall picture without combining information with different characteristics about exposures to risks from significantly different economic environments. For example, an entity that trades financial instruments might disclose this information separately for financial instruments held for trading and those not held for trading. Similarly, an entity would not aggregate its exposure to market risks from areas of hyperinflation with its exposure to the same market risks from areas of very low inflation. However, an entity that has exposure to only one type of market risk in only one economic environment, would not show disaggregated information. *[IFRS 7.B17].*

Risk variables that are relevant to disclosing market risk include, but are not limited to: *[IFRS 7.IG32]*

- the yield curve of market interest rates.

    It may be necessary to consider both parallel and non-parallel shifts in the yield curve;
- foreign exchange rates.

    The standard requires a sensitivity analysis to be disclosed for each currency to which an entity has significant exposure; *[IFRS 7.B24]*
- prices of equity instruments; and
- market prices of commodities.

When disclosing how profit or loss and equity would have been affected by changes in the relevant risk variable, there is no requirement to determine what the profit or loss for the period would have been if the relevant risk variables had been different during the reporting period. The requirement is subtly different because the effect that is disclosed assumes that a reasonably possible change in the relevant risk variable had occurred at the reporting date and had been applied to the risk exposures in existence at that date. For example, if an entity has a floating rate liability at the reporting date, the entity would disclose the effect on profit or loss (i.e. interest expense) for the current year if interest rates had varied by reasonably possible amounts. Further, this disclosure is not required for each change within a range of reasonably possible changes, only at the limits of the reasonably possible range. *[IFRS 7.B18]*.

The following example illustrates how the amounts to be included in these disclosures in respect of a number of different instruments might be determined – for simplicity, tax effects are ignored.

Example 54.13: Illustration of how sensitivity disclosures can be determined

Company X, which has the euro as its functional currency, is party to the following instruments at 31 December 2021, X's reporting date:

- a €100m floating rate borrowing;
- a forward contract to sell US$10m in July 2022 that is designated in an effective hedge of a highly probable forecast sale that is denominated in US dollars;
- a short-term loan of £10m made to a related party;
- an interest rate swap that is not designated as a hedge;
- investments in fixed rate debt securities that are classified as financial assets measured at amortised cost;
- investments in similar securities that are classified as debt instruments measured at fair value through other comprehensive income; and
- investments in a portfolio of US equities with a fair value of US$50m.

Floating rate borrowing

Changes in interest rates will result in this instrument impacting on X's profit or loss. If X concludes that a reasonably possible change in interest rates is 50 basis points (0.5%), €0.5m [€100m × 0.5%] would be included in the amount disclosed as the impact on profit or loss of this reasonably possible change.

Forward contract

Changes in exchange rates will have an impact on the fair value (and carrying value) of this instrument, but this would be recognised in other comprehensive income, not profit or loss (assuming ineffectiveness is insignificant). If a reasonably possibly change in exchange rates would change the value of the contract by €0.3m, this would be included in the amount disclosed as the impact on equity of this reasonably possible change.

Foreign currency loan

Changes in spot exchange rates will have an impact on the carrying amount of this asset with changes recognised in profit or loss as a result of the application of IAS 21 – *The Effects of Changes in Foreign Exchange Rates*. If a reasonably possible change in the exchange rate would alter the carrying value of the contract by €1.0m, this would be included in the amount disclosed as the impact on profit or loss of this reasonably possible change.

If the loan were made to a subsidiary of X that had sterling as its functional currency, the loan itself would eliminate on consolidation but the impact of retranslating it into euros in X's own financial statements would remain in consolidated profit or loss. Therefore, in these circumstances, the loan would still be included in the sensitivity analysis for X's consolidated financial statements.

Interest rate swap

Changes in interest rates will have an impact on the fair value (and carrying value) of this instrument and such changes would be recognised in profit or loss. If a reasonably possible change of 50 basis points in interest rates would change the value of the contract by €0.4m, this would be included in the amount disclosed as the impact on profit or loss of this reasonably possible change.

Fixed rate debt securities

Changes in interest rates will have an impact on the fair value of all these instruments. However, because those classified as measured at amortised cost are not measured at fair value, the carrying amount only of those that are classified as debt instruments measured at fair value through other comprehensive income will change as interest rates move and such change will normally be recognised in other comprehensive income. Therefore, if a reasonably possible 50 basis point change in interest rates would change the fair value of each group of instruments by €0.5m, only the amount in respect of the debt instruments measured at fair value through other comprehensive income would be included in the sensitivity disclosure as an impact on equity. Of course there would be nothing to preclude disclosure, as additional information (if considered relevant), of the sensitivity of the fair value of those classified as measured at amortised cost to changes in interest rates.

US equity securities

The impact of a reasonably possible change in the market prices of these securities should be included in the amount disclosed as X's sensitivity to equity price risk. Changes in exchange rates might be considered to impact the fair value of these investments. However, as noted at (c)(i) at 5 above, financial instruments that are non-monetary items do not give rise to foreign currency risk for the purposes of IFRS 7 – essentially the foreign currency risk is seen as part of the market price risk associated with such instruments. Therefore, X should take no account of these investments when disclosing its sensitivity to changes in the euro/US dollar exchange rate. Nevertheless, this information may be provided as additional disclosure where it is considered relevant.

Relevant risk variables for the purpose of this disclosure might include: *[IFRS 7.IG33]*

- prevailing market interest rates, for interest-sensitive financial instruments such as a variable-rate loan; or
- currency rates and interest rates, for foreign currency financial instruments such as foreign currency bonds.

For interest rate risk, the sensitivity analysis might show separately the effect of a change in market interest rates on:

- interest income and expense;
- other line items of profit or loss (such as trading gains and losses); and
- when applicable, equity.

An entity might disclose a sensitivity analysis for interest rate risk for each currency in which the entity has material exposures to interest rate risk. *[IFRS 7.IG34]*.

In determining what a reasonably possible change in the relevant risk variable is, the economic environment(s) in which the entity operates and the time frame over which it is making the assessment should be considered. A reasonably possible change should not include remote or 'worst case' scenarios or 'stress tests'. Moreover, if the rate of change in the underlying risk variable is stable, the chosen reasonably possible change in the risk variable need not be altered.

For example, assume that interest rates are 5 percent and an entity determines that a fluctuation in interest rates of ±50 basis points is reasonably possible. It would disclose the effect on profit or loss and equity if interest rates were to change to 4.5 percent or 5.5 percent. In the next period, interest rates have increased to 5.5 percent. The entity continues to believe that interest rates may fluctuate by ±50 basis points (i.e. that the rate of change in interest rates is stable). The entity would disclose the effect on profit or loss and equity if interest rates were to change to 5 percent or 6 percent. The entity would not be required to revise its assessment that interest rates might reasonably fluctuate by ±50 basis points, unless there is evidence that interest rates have become significantly more volatile. *[IFRS 7.B19].*

However, when market conditions change significantly, for example as occurred in many markets in the second half of 2008, an entity's assessment of what constitutes a reasonably possible change should be reassessed.[14]

The time frame over which a reasonably possible change should be assessed is defined by the period until these disclosures will next be presented. This will normally coincide with the next annual reporting period, *[IFRS 7.B19],* although in some jurisdictions such information may be included in interim reports.

Because the factors affecting market risk will vary according to the specific circumstances of each entity, the appropriate range to be considered in providing a sensitivity analysis of market risk will also vary for each entity and for each type of market risk. *[IFRS 7.IG35].*

Where an entity has exposure to other price risk, it might disclose the effect of a decrease in a specified stock market index, commodity price, or other risk variable. For example, if residual value guarantees that are financial instruments are given, the disclosure could include an increase or decrease in the value of the assets to which the guarantee applies. *[IFRS 7.B25].*

The following example from the implementation guidance illustrates the type of disclosure that might be provided.

Example 54.14:   Illustrative disclosure of sensitivity analyses

Interest rate risk

At 31 December 2021, if interest rates at that date had been 10 basis points lower with all other variables held constant, post-tax profit for the year would have been €1.7 million (2020: €2.4 million) higher, arising mainly as a result of lower interest expense on variable borrowings.

If interest rates had been 10 basis points higher, with all other variables held constant, post-tax profit would have been €1.5 million (2020: €2.1 million) lower, arising mainly as a result of higher interest expense on variable borrowings.

Profit is more sensitive to interest rate decreases than increases because of borrowings with capped interest rates. The sensitivity is lower in 2021 than in 2020 because of a reduction in outstanding borrowings that has occurred as the entity's debt has matured (see note X).

Foreign currency exchange rate risk

At 31 December 2021, if the euro had weakened 10 percent against the US dollar with all other variables held constant, post-tax profit for the year would have been €2.8 million (2020: €6.4 million) lower, and other comprehensive income would have been €1.2 million (2020: €1.1 million) higher.

Conversely, if the euro had strengthened 10 percent against the US dollar with all other variables held constant, post-tax profit would have been €2.8 million (2020: €6.4 million) higher, and other comprehensive income would have been €1.2 million (2020: €1.1 million) lower.

The lower foreign currency exchange rate sensitivity in profit in 2021 compared with 2020 is attributable to a reduction in foreign currency denominated debt. Equity is more sensitive in 2021 than in 2020 because of the increased use of hedges of foreign currency purchases, offset by the reduction in foreign currency debt. *[IFRS 7.IG36].*

The following extracts from the financial statements of Hunting illustrates how one company has addressed this disclosure requirement in respect of certain of its interest rate and foreign currency exposures.

> Extract 54.10: Hunting PLC (2018)
> **Notes to the consolidated financial statements** [extract]
> 28.   **Financial Instruments: Sensitivity Analysis** [extract]
>
> The following sensitivity analysis is intended to illustrate the sensitivity to changes in market variables on the Group's financial instruments and show the impact on profit or loss and shareholders' equity. Financial instruments affected by market risk include cash at bank and in hand, Money Market Funds, short-term deposits, trade and other receivables, trade and other payables, borrowings and derivative financial instruments. The sensitivity analysis relates to the position as at 31 December 2018. The analysis excludes the impact of movements in market variables on the carrying value of pension and other post-retirement obligations, provisions and non-financial assets and liabilities of foreign operations.
>
> The following assumptions have been made in calculating the sensitivity analysis:
> - Foreign exchange rate and interest rate sensitivities have an asymmetric impact on the Group's results, that is, an increase in rates does not result in the same amount of movement as a decrease in rates.
> - For floating rate assets and liabilities, the amount of asset or liability outstanding at the balance sheet date is assumed to be outstanding for the whole year.
> - Fixed-rate financial instruments that are carried at amortised cost are not subject to interest rate risk for the purpose of this analysis.
> - The carrying values of financial assets and liabilities carried at amortised cost do not change as interest rates change.
>
> Positive figures represent an increase in profit or equity.
>
> **(a) Interest Rate Sensitivity**
>
> The sensitivity rate of 0.5% (2017 – 0.75%) for US interest rates represents management's assessment of a reasonably possible change, based on historical volatility and a review of analysts' research and banks' expectations of future interest rates.
>
> The post-tax impact on the income statement, with all other variables held constant, at 31 December, for an increase or decrease of 0.5% (2017 – 0.75%) in US interest rates, is not material (2017 – not material). There is no impact on other comprehensive income ("OCI") for a change in interest rates.
>
> **(b) Foreign Exchange Rate Sensitivity**
>
> The sensitivity rate of 10% (2017 – 10%) for Sterling and 10% (2017 – 5%) for Canadian dollar exchange rates represents management's assessment of a reasonably possible change, based on historical volatility and a review of analysts' research and banks' expectations of future foreign exchange rates.
>
> The table below shows the post-tax impact for the year of a reasonably possible change in foreign exchange rates, with all other variables held constant, at 31 December.
>
> | | 2018 | | 2017 | |
> | --- | --- | --- | --- | --- |
> | | Income statement | OCI | Income statement | OCI |
> | | $m | $m | $m | $m |
> | Sterling exchange rates +10% (2017: +10%) | (0.4) | – | (0.3) | – |
> | Sterling exchange rates –10% (2017: –10%) | 0.4 | – | 0.3 | – |
> | Canadian dollar exchange rates +10% (2017: +5%) | – | 0.2 | 0.7 | 0.2 |
> | Canadian dollar exchange rates –10% (2017: –5%) | – | – | (0.7) | (0.2) |

> The movements in the income statement arise from cash, intra-Group balances, trade and other receivables, payables, accrued expenses and provisions, where the functional currency of the entity is different from the currency that the monetary items are denominated in. The movements in OCI mainly arise from foreign exchange contracts designated in a cash flow hedge.
>
> The post-tax impact on the income statement of reasonably possible changes in the Singapore dollar and UAE Dirham exchange rates were considered and were immaterial.

5.5.2 Value-at-risk and similar analyses

Where an entity prepares a sensitivity analysis, such as value-at-risk, that reflects interdependencies between risk variables (e.g. interest rates and exchange rates) and uses it to manage financial risks, it may disclose that analysis in place of the information specified at 5.5.1 above. *[IFRS 7.41]*. If this disclosure is given, the effects on profit or loss and equity at 5.5.1 above need not be given. *[IFRS 7.BC61]*.

In these cases the following should also be disclosed: *[IFRS 7.41]*

- an explanation of the method used in preparing such a sensitivity analysis, and of the main parameters and assumptions underlying the data provided; and
- an explanation of the objective of the method used and of limitations that may result in the information not fully reflecting the fair value of the assets and liabilities involved.

This applies even if such a methodology measures only the potential for loss and does not measure the potential for gain. Such an entity might comply with the disclosure requirements above by detailing the type of value-at-risk model used (e.g. whether the model relies on Monte Carlo simulations), an explanation about how the model works and the main assumptions (e.g. the holding period and confidence level). Entities might also disclose the historical observation period and weightings applied to observations within that period, an explanation of how options are dealt with in the calculations, and which volatilities and correlations (or, alternatively, Monte Carlo probability distribution simulations) are used. *[IFRS 7.B20]*.

The basic sensitivity analysis considered at 5.5.1 above incorporates only the effects of financial instruments and other contracts within the scope of IFRS 7. In contrast, value-at-risk and similar analyses can incorporate the effects of items outside the scope of IFRS 7, for example trading inventories, own use contracts and insurance contracts. This is because the standard requires entities to disclose the analysis actually used in the management of the business which will often include such items.

It has been suggested that disclosure of potential losses due to stress conditions would be of greater use than the disclosure requirements for value-at-risk and similar methodologies that do not contemplate extraordinary market movements. However, in December 2008, the IASB noted this would be inconsistent with the 'basic' sensitivity analysis (see 5.5.1 above) and decided not to add such a requirement to IFRS 7.[15]

BP provides the following market risk disclosures which includes the value-at-risk limit it uses to manage that risk.

> **Extract 54.11: BP p.l.c. (2018)**
>
> Notes on financial statements [extract]
>
> 29   Financial instruments and financial risk factors [extract]
> (a)   Market risk [extract]
>
> Market risk is the risk or uncertainty arising from possible market price movements and their impact on the future performance of a business. The primary commodity price risks that the group is exposed to include oil, natural gas and power prices that could adversely affect the value of the group's financial assets, liabilities or expected future cash flows. The group enters into derivatives in a well-established entrepreneurial trading operation. In addition, the group has developed a control framework aimed at managing the volatility inherent in certain of its natural business exposures. In accordance with the control framework the group enters into various transactions using derivatives for risk management purposes.
>
> The major components of market risk are commodity price risk, foreign currency exchange risk and interest rate risk, each of which is discussed below.
> (i)   Commodity price risk
>
> The group's integrated supply and trading function uses conventional financial and commodity instruments and physical cargoes and pipeline positions available in the related commodity markets. Oil and natural gas swaps, options and futures are used to mitigate price risk. Power trading is undertaken using a combination of over-the-counter forward contracts and other derivative contracts, including options and futures. This activity is on both a standalone basis and in conjunction with gas derivatives in relation to gas-generated power margin. In addition, NGLs are traded around certain US inventory locations using over-the-counter forward contracts in conjunction with over-the-counter swaps, options and physical inventories.
>
> The group measures market risk exposure arising from its trading positions in liquid periods using value-at-risk techniques. These techniques make a statistical assessment of the market risk arising from possible future changes in market prices over a one-day holding period. The value-at-risk measure is supplemented by stress testing. Trading activity occurring in liquid periods is subject to value-at-risk limits for each trading activity and for this trading activity in total. The board has delegated a limit of $100 million value at risk in support of this trading activity. Alternative measures are used to monitor exposures which are outside liquid periods and which cannot be actively risk-managed.

5.5.3   Other market risk disclosures

When the sensitivity analyses discussed at 5.5.1 and 5.5.2 above are unrepresentative of a risk inherent in a financial instrument, that fact should be disclosed together with the reason for believing the sensitivity analyses are unrepresentative. *[IFRS 7.42]*.

This can occur when the year-end exposure does not reflect the exposure during the year *[IFRS 7.42]* or a financial instrument contains terms and conditions whose effects are not apparent from the sensitivity analysis, e.g. options that remain out of (or in) the money for the chosen change in the risk variable. *[IFRS 7.IG37(a)]*. Additional disclosures in this second case might include:

- the terms and conditions of the financial instrument (e.g. the options);

- the effect on profit or loss if the term or condition were met (i.e. if the options were exercised); and
- a description of how the risk is hedged.

For example, an entity may acquire a zero-cost interest rate collar that includes an out-of-the-money leveraged written option (e.g. the entity pays ten times the amount of the difference between a specified interest rate floor and the current market interest rate if that current rate is below the floor). The entity may regard the collar as an inexpensive economic hedge against a reasonably possible increase in interest rates. However, an unexpectedly large decrease in interest rates might trigger payments under the written option that, because of the leverage, might be significantly larger than the benefit of lower interest rates. Neither the fair value of the collar nor a sensitivity analysis based on reasonably possible changes in market variables would indicate this exposure. In this case, the entity might provide the additional information described above. *[IFRS 7.IG38]*.

Where financial assets are illiquid, e.g. when there is a low volume of transactions in similar assets and it is difficult to find a counterparty, additional disclosures might be required, *[IFRS 7.IG37(b)]*, for example the reasons for the lack of liquidity and how the risk is hedged. *[IFRS 7.IG39]*.

A large holding of a financial asset that, if sold in its entirety, would be sold at a discount or premium to the quoted market price for a smaller holding could also require additional disclosure. *[IFRS 7.IG37(c)]*. This might include: *[IFRS 7.IG40]*

- the nature of the security (e.g. entity name);
- the extent of holding (e.g. 15 percent of the issued shares);
- the effect on profit or loss; and
- how the entity hedges the risk.

5.6 Quantitative disclosures: other matters

5.6.1 Concentrations of risk

Concentrations of risk should be disclosed if not otherwise apparent from the disclosures made to comply with the requirements set out at 5.2 to 5.5 above. *[IFRS 7.34(c)]*. This should include:

- a description of how management determines concentrations;
- a description of the shared characteristic that identifies each concentration (for example, counterparty, geographical area, currency or market).

  For example, the shared characteristic may refer to geographical distribution of counterparties by groups of countries, individual countries or regions within countries; *[IFRS 7.IG19]* and
- the amount of the risk exposure associated with all financial instruments sharing that characteristic.

Concentrations of risk arise from financial instruments that have similar characteristics and are affected similarly by changes in economic or other conditions. It is emphasised that the identification of concentrations of risk requires judgement taking into account the circumstances of the entity. *[IFRS 7.B8]*. For example, they may arise from:

- Industry sectors.

    If an entity's counterparties are concentrated in one or more industry sectors (such as retail or wholesale), it would disclose separately exposure to risks arising from each concentration of counterparties;

- Credit rating or other measure of credit quality.

    If an entity's counterparties are concentrated in one or more credit qualities (such as secured loans or unsecured loans) or in one or more credit ratings (such as investment grade or speculative grade), it would disclose separately exposure to risks arising from each concentration of counterparties;

- Geographical distribution.

    If an entity's counterparties are concentrated in one or more geographical markets (such as Asia or Europe), it would disclose separately exposure to risks arising from each concentration of counterparties; and

- A limited number of individual counterparties or groups of closely related counterparties.

Similar principles apply to identifying concentrations of other risks, including liquidity risk and market risk. For example, concentrations of liquidity risk may arise from the repayment terms of financial liabilities, sources of borrowing facilities or reliance on a particular market in which to realise liquid assets. Concentrations of foreign exchange risk may arise if an entity has a significant net open position in a single foreign currency, or aggregate net open positions in several currencies that tend to move together. *[IFRS 7.IG18]*.

5.6.2 Operational risk

In developing IFRS 7, the IASB considered whether disclosure of information about operational risk should be required by the standard. However, the definition and measurement of operational risk were considered to be in their infancy and were not necessarily related to financial instruments. Also, such disclosures were believed to be more appropriately located outside the financial statements. Consequently, this issue was deferred for consideration in the management commentary project. *[IFRS 7.BC65]*.

5.6.3 Capital disclosures

The IASB considers that the level of an entity's capital and how it is managed are important factors for users of financial statements to consider in assessing the risk profile of an entity and its ability to withstand unexpected adverse events. It might also affect an entity's ability to pay dividends. Consequently, ED 7 contained proposed disclosures about capital. *[IAS 1.BC86]*.

However, some commentators questioned the relevance of the capital disclosures in a standard dealing with disclosures relating to financial instruments and the IASB noted that an entity's capital does not relate solely to financial instruments and, thus, they have more general relevance. Accordingly, whilst these disclosures were retained, they were included in IAS 1, rather than IFRS 7. *[IAS 1.BC88]*. Those disclosures required by IAS 1 are dealt with in Chapter 3 at 5.4.

5.7 Interest rate benchmark (or IBOR) reform

Replacing interbank offered rates (IBOR) with alternative rates was one of the recommendations following the financial crisis and some jurisdictions have been making clear progress towards this. IBOR reform gives rise to a number of financial reporting issues which the IASB approached in two phases. In August 2020, the IASB issued a second set of amendments to IFRS 9 addressing changes made to contractual cash flows, including modifications of financial assets and financial liabilities, and to hedging relationships that occur when interest rate benchmarks are replaced with alternative benchmarks. These amendments, which are effective for periods commencing on or after 1 January 2021 but are available for earlier adoption, are discussed in Chapter 50 at 3.8.3, in Chapter 52 at 3.4.3 and at 6.2.2 and in Chapter 53 at 9. Consequential amendments were made to IFRS 7 to enable users of financial statements to understand the effect of interest rate benchmark reform on an entity's financial instruments and risk management strategy. As a result, entities should disclose information about: *[IFRS 7.24I]*

- the nature and extent of risks to which the entity is exposed arising from financial instruments subject to interest rate benchmark reform, and how the entity manages those risks; and
- the entity's progress in completing the transition to alternative benchmark rates, and how the entity is managing that transition.

To meet these two objectives the following should be disclosed: *[IFRS 7.24J]*

- how the entity is managing the transition to alternative benchmark rates, its progress at the reporting date and the risks to which it is exposed arising from financial instruments because of the transition;
- disaggregated by significant interest rate benchmark subject to interest rate benchmark reform, quantitative information about financial instruments that have yet to transition to an alternative benchmark rate as at the end of the reporting period, showing separately:
  - non-derivative financial assets;
  - non-derivative financial liabilities; and
  - derivatives; and
- if the risks described in the first objective above have resulted in changes to an entity's risk management strategy, a description of those changes.

Disclosures introduced by the first phase of the IASB's project to address IBOR reform are considered at 4.3.5 above.

6 TRANSFERS OF FINANCIAL ASSETS

The objective of these requirements, which were introduced into IFRS 7 in October 2010, is that entities should disclose information that enables users of its financial statements: *[IFRS 7.42B]*

(a) to understand the relationship between transferred financial assets that are not derecognised in their entirety and the associated liabilities; and

(b) to evaluate the nature of, and risks associated with, the entity's continuing involvement in derecognised financial assets.

The standard specifies detailed disclosure requirements to support objectives (a) and (b) which are discussed below at 6.2 and 6.3 respectively. However, these may not be sufficient to meet these objectives, in which case an entity should disclose any additional information, over and above that specified by IFRS 7, that it considers necessary. The entity should decide, in the light of its circumstances, how much additional information it needs to provide to satisfy the information needs of users and how much emphasis it places on different aspects of the additional information. It is necessary to strike a balance between burdening financial statements with excessive detail that may not assist users of financial statements and obscuring information as a result of too much aggregation. *[IFRS 7.42H, B39]*.

Rather unusually, the standard specifies that these disclosures should be presented in a single note to the financial statements. *[IFRS 7.42A]*. Presumably this is to prevent entities 'hiding' these disclosures by having the detailed information scattered across a number of notes.

These requirements supplement the other requirements of IFRS 7 and apply when an entity transfers financial assets. They apply for all transferred financial assets that are not derecognised, and for any continuing involvement in a transferred asset, that exist at the reporting date, irrespective of when the related transfer occurred. *[IFRS 7.42A]*.

6.1 The meaning of 'transfer'

For the purposes of applying the disclosure requirements in this section, an entity transfers all or a part of a financial asset (the transferred financial asset) if, and only if, it either: *[IFRS 7.42A]*

(a) transfers the contractual rights to receive the cash flows of that financial asset; or

(b) retains the contractual rights to receive the cash flows of that financial asset, but assumes a contractual obligation to pay the cash flows to one or more recipients in an arrangement.

The transactions encompassed by (a) should be the same ones that would be regarded as transfers under the derecognition requirements of IFRS 9 (see Chapter 52 at 3.5.1).

However, the transactions falling within (b) represent a larger group than those which would be regarded as 'pass-through arrangements' for the purposes of those requirements (see Chapter 52 at 3.5.2).

6.2 Transferred financial assets that are not derecognised in their entirety

Financial assets may have been transferred in such a way that part or all of the financial assets do not qualify for derecognition. This might occur if:

- the contractual rights to the cash flows have been transferred but substantially all risks and rewards are retained, e.g. a sale and repurchase agreement, so that the assets are not derecognised;
- the rights to the cash flows have been transferred, the risks and rewards partially transferred and control of the assets has been retained so that the assets continue to be recognised to the extent of the entity's continuing involvement; or
- an obligation has been assumed to pay the cash flows from the asset to other parties but in a way that does not meet the 'pass-through' requirements (see Chapter 52 at 3.5.2).

Where securitisations and similar arrangements do not meet the pass-through requirements, careful analysis will be required to determine whether they are within the scope of these disclosures. If such a transaction is not considered to be within the scope of these requirements, the disclosures about collateral discussed at 4.4.6 above are likely to be applicable.

The following disclosures should be given for each class of transferred financial assets that are not derecognised in their entirety: *[IFRS 7.42D]*

(a) the nature of the transferred assets;

(b) the nature of the risks and rewards of ownership to which the reporting entity is exposed;

(c) a description of the nature of the relationship between the transferred assets and the associated liabilities, including restrictions arising from the transfer on the reporting entity's use of the transferred assets;

(d) when the counterparty (counterparties) to the associated liabilities has (have) recourse only to the transferred assets, a schedule that sets out the fair value of the transferred assets, the fair value of the associated liabilities and the net position, i.e. the difference between the fair value of the transferred assets and the associated liabilities;

(e) when the reporting entity continues to recognise all of the transferred assets, the carrying amounts of the transferred assets and the associated liabilities; and

(f) when the reporting entity continues to recognise the assets to the extent of its continuing involvement, the total carrying amount of the original assets before the transfer, the carrying amount of the assets that the entity continues to recognise, and the carrying amount of the associated liabilities.

These disclosures should be given at each reporting date at which the entity continues to recognise the transferred financial assets, regardless of when the transfers occurred. *[IFRS 7.B32]*.

The above requirements clearly apply to transfers of entire financial assets where the transferred assets continue to be recognised in their entirety. They also apply to transfers of entire assets where the transferred assets are recognised to the extent of the transferor's continuing involvement.

However, the derecognition criteria in IFRS 9 are sometimes applied to specified parts of a financial asset (or group of similar financial assets). For example, an entity might transfer a proportion of an entire financial asset, such as 50% of all cash flows on a bond. Similarly, it may transfer specified cash flows from a financial asset, such as all the coupon payments or only the principal payment on a bond, commonly known as an interest strip and principal strip respectively. Further, if the derecognition criteria are met, it is possible for the specified parts of the financial asset to be derecognised whilst the remainder of the asset remains on the statement of financial position (see Chapter 52, particularly at 3.3). This begs the question of whether the disclosure requirements in this section should be applied to such transfers.

Whilst the financial asset has not been derecognised in its entirety, it will normally be the case that the asset has not been transferred in its entirety either. Therefore, it might seem more appropriate for the disclosure requirements to follow the way in which the derecognition requirements of IFRS 9 have been applied, i.e. they should focus on the specified part of the asset that has been transferred. Nevertheless, in the absence of specific guidance, we believe the alternative view could be supported too so that the disclosures would address the entire asset.

In our view these disclosure requirements do not apply where an entity provides non-cash financial assets as collateral to a third party and the transferee's right to control the asset (normally evidenced by its ability to resell or repledge those assets) is conditional on default of the transferor. Instead the disclosures about collateral set out at 4.4.6 above would apply.

The following example illustrates how an entity might meet the quantitative disclosure requirements in (d) and (e) above. *[IFRS 7.IG40C]*.

Example 54.15: Quantitative disclosures for transferred assets not fully derecognised

	Financial assets at fair value through profit or loss		Financial assets at amortised cost		Equity investments designated at fair value through OCI
	CU million		CU million		CU million
	Trading securities	Derivatives	Mortgages	Consumer loans	Equity investments
Carrying amount of assets	X	X	X	X	X
Carrying amount of associated liabilities	(X)	(X)	(X)	(X)	(X)
For those liabilities that have recourse only to the transferred assets:					
Fair value of assets	X	X	X	X	X
Fair value of associated liabilities	(X)	(X)	(X)	(X)	(X)
Net position	X	X	X	X	X

6.3 Transferred financial assets that are derecognised in their entirety

An entity may have transferred financial assets in such a way that they are derecognised in their entirety but the entity has 'continuing involvement' in those assets. Where this is the case, the additional disclosures set out at 6.3.2 below should be given. In this context, the term continuing involvement has a different meaning to that used in the derecognition requirements of IFRS 9 (see Chapter 52 at 3.2 and 5.3) which is discussed at 6.3.1 below.

In practice the application of these requirements might be limited given that few transfers with any form of continuing involvement (as that term is used here) will qualify for full derecognition. One example is a transfer of a readily obtainable financial asset subject to a call option that is neither deeply in the money nor deeply out of the money (see Chapter 52 at 4.2.3.A), but others could certainly be encountered in practice.

6.3.1 Meaning of continuing involvement

In this context, continuing involvement arises if, as part of the transfer, the entity retains any of the contractual rights or obligations inherent in the transferred financial asset or obtains any new contractual rights or obligations relating to it. *[IFRS 7.42C]*.

For example, a financial asset transferred subject only to either (a) a deeply out of the money put option granted to the transferee or (b) a deeply out of the money call option retained by the transferor would be derecognised. This is because substantially all the risks and rewards of ownership have been transferred. *[IFRS 9.B3.2.16(g)]*. However, the put or call option would constitute continuing involvement in the asset.

Similarly, a readily obtainable asset transferred subject to a call option that is neither deeply in the money nor deeply out of the money would also be derecognised. This is because the entity has neither transferred nor retained substantially all of the risks and rewards of ownership and has not retained control. *[IFRS 9.B3.2.16(h)]*. However, the call option would constitute continuing involvement in the asset.

The following do not constitute continuing involvement for these purposes: *[IFRS 7.42C]*

(a) normal representations and warranties relating to fraudulent transfer and concepts of reasonableness, good faith and fair dealings that could invalidate a transfer as a result of legal action;

(b) forward, option and other contracts to reacquire the transferred financial asset for which the contract price (or exercise price) is the fair value of the transferred financial asset; or

(c) an arrangement whereby an entity retains the contractual rights to receive the cash flows of a financial asset but assumes a contractual obligation to pay the cash flows to one or more entities in a 'pass-through arrangement' (see Chapter 52 at 3.5.2).

An entity does not have a continuing involvement in a transferred financial asset if, as part of the transfer, it neither retains any of the contractual rights or obligations inherent in the transferred financial asset nor acquires any new contractual rights or obligations relating to the transferred financial asset. Also, an entity does not have continuing involvement in a transferred financial asset if it has neither an interest in the future performance of the transferred financial asset nor a responsibility under any circumstances to make payments in respect of the transferred financial asset in the future. The term 'payment' in this context does not include cash flows of the transferred financial asset that an entity collects and is required to remit to the transferee. [IFRS 7.B30].

When an entity transfers a financial asset, it may retain the right to service that financial asset for a fee, e.g. by entering into a servicing contract. Such a contract should be assessed in accordance with the guidance above to determine whether it gives rise to continuing involvement for the purposes of these disclosures. For example, a servicer will have continuing involvement in the transferred financial asset if the servicing fee is dependent on the amount or timing of the cash flows collected from the transferred financial asset. Similarly, the right to a fixed fee that would not be paid in full as a result of non-performance of the transferred financial asset would also represent continuing involvement. This is because the servicer has an interest in the future performance of the transferred financial asset. Any such assessment is independent of whether the fee to be received is expected to compensate the entity adequately for performing the servicing. [IFRS 7.B30A].

An entity might transfer a fixed rate financial asset and at the same time enter into an interest rate swap with the transferee that has the same notional amount as the transferred asset. If payments on the swap are not conditional on payments being made on the transferred financial asset and the notional of the swap is not linked to the notional amount of the loan this would not, in our view, represent continuing involvement.

The assessment of continuing involvement in a transferred financial asset should be made at the level of the reporting entity. For example, a subsidiary may transfer to an unrelated third party a financial asset in which the parent of the subsidiary has continuing involvement. In the subsidiary's stand-alone financial statements the parent's involvement should not be included in the assessment of whether the reporting entity (the subsidiary) has continuing involvement in the transferred asset. However, in the parent's consolidated financial statements, its continuing involvement (or that of another member of the group) in a financial asset transferred by its subsidiary would be included in determining whether the group has continuing involvement in the transferred asset. [IFRS 7.B29].

Continuing involvement in a transferred financial asset may result from contractual provisions in the transfer agreement or in a separate agreement with the transferee or a third party entered into in connection with the transfer. [IFRS 7.B31]. In our view it would not encompass arrangements entered into some time after the financial asset was transferred that were not contemplated at the time of the transfer.

6.3.2 Disclosure requirements

When an entity derecognises transferred financial assets in their entirety but has continuing involvement in those assets, it should disclose, as a minimum, the following for each type of continuing involvement at each reporting date: [IFRS 7.42E]

(a) the carrying amount of the assets and liabilities that are recognised in the entity's statement of financial position and represent the entity's continuing involvement in the derecognised financial assets, and the line items in which the carrying amount of those assets and liabilities are recognised;

(b) the fair value of the assets and liabilities that represent the entity's continuing involvement in the derecognised financial assets;

(c) the amount that best represents the entity's maximum exposure to loss from its continuing involvement in the derecognised financial assets, and information showing how the maximum exposure to loss is determined;

(d) the undiscounted cash outflows that would or may be required to repurchase derecognised financial assets (e.g. the strike price in an option agreement) or other amounts payable to the transferee in respect of the transferred assets.

If the cash outflow is variable then the amount disclosed should be based on the conditions that exist at each reporting date;

(e) a maturity analysis of the undiscounted cash outflows that would or may be required to repurchase the derecognised financial assets or other amounts payable to the transferee in respect of the transferred assets, showing the remaining contractual maturities of the entity's continuing involvement.

This analysis should distinguish between cash flows that are required to be paid (e.g. forward contracts), cash flows the entity may be required to pay (e.g. written put options) and cash flows the entity might choose to pay (e.g. purchased call options). *[IFRS 7.B34].*

Entities should use judgement to determine an appropriate number of time bands in preparing the maturity analysis. For example, it might be determined that the following maturity time bands are appropriate: *[IFRS 7.B35]*

(i) not later than one month;
(ii) later than one month and not later than three months;
(iii) later than three months and not later than six months;
(iv) later than six months and not later than one year;
(v) later than one year and not later than three years;
(vi) later than three years and not later than five years; and
(vii) more than five years.

If there is a range of possible maturities, the cash flows should be included on the basis of the earliest date on which the entity can be required or is permitted to pay; *[IFRS 7.B36]* and

(f) qualitative information that explains and supports the quantitative disclosures set out in (a) to (e) above.

This should include a description of the derecognised financial assets and the nature and purpose of the continuing involvement retained after transferring those assets. It should also include a description of the risks to which an entity is exposed, including: *[IFRS 7.B37]*

(i) a description of how the entity manages the risk inherent in its continuing involvement in the derecognised financial assets;

(ii) whether the entity is required to bear losses before other parties, and the ranking and amounts of losses borne by parties whose interests rank lower than the entity's interest in the asset (i.e. its continuing involvement in the asset); and

(iii) a description of any triggers associated with obligations to provide financial support or to repurchase a transferred financial asset.

The types of continuing involvement into which these disclosures and those referred to below are analysed should be representative of the entity's exposure to risks. For example, the analysis may be given by type of financial instrument (e.g. guarantees or call options) or by type of transfer (e.g. factoring of receivables, securitisations and securities lending). *[IFRS 7.B33]*.

If an entity has more than one type of continuing involvement in respect of a particular derecognised financial asset the information above may be aggregated and reported under one type of continuing involvement. *[IFRS 7.42F]*.

The following example illustrates how an entity might meet the quantitative disclosure requirements in (a) to (e) above. *[IFRS 7.IG40C]*.

Example 54.16: Quantitative disclosures for transferred assets fully derecognised

Type of continuing involvement	Cash outflows to repurchase transferred (derecognised) assets CU million	Carrying amount of continuing involvement in statement of financial position CU million			Fair value of continuing involvement CU million		Maximum exposure to loss CU million
		Held for trading	Debt instruments at fair value through OCI	Financial liabilities at fair value through profit or loss	Assets	Liabilities	
Written put options	(X)			(X)		(X)	X
Purchased call options	(X)	X			X		X
Securities lending	(X)		X	(X)	X	(X)	X
	X	X	(X)	X	(X)		X

Undiscounted cash flows to repurchase transferred assets
Maturity of continuing involvement
CU million

Type of continuing involvement	Total	less than 1 month	1-3 months	3-6 months	6 months- 1 year	1-3 years	3-5 years	more than 5 years
Written put options	X		X	X	X	X		
Purchased call options	X			X	X	X		X
Securities lending	X	X	X					

In addition to the information above, the following should be disclosed for each type of continuing involvement: *[IFRS 7.42G]*

(a) the gain or loss recognised at the date of transfer of the assets.

Disclosure should also be given if a gain or loss on derecognition arose because the fair values of the components of the previously recognised asset (i.e. the interest in the asset derecognised and the interest retained by the entity) were different from the fair value of the previously recognised asset as a whole. In that situation, disclosure should be made of whether the fair value measurements included significant inputs that were not based on observable market data; [IFRS 7.B38]

(b) income and expenses recognised, both in the reporting period and cumulatively, from the entity's continuing involvement in the derecognised financial assets (e.g. fair value changes in derivative instruments); and

(c) if the total amount of proceeds from transfer activity (that qualifies for derecognition) in a reporting period is not evenly distributed throughout the reporting period (e.g. if a substantial proportion of the total amount of transfer activity takes place in the closing days of a reporting period):

   (i) when the greatest transfer activity took place within that reporting period (e.g. the last five days before the end of the reporting period);

   (ii) the amount (e.g. related gains or losses) recognised from transfer activity in that part of the reporting period; and

   (iii) the total amount of proceeds from transfer activity in that part of the reporting period.

This information should be provided for each period for which a statement of comprehensive income is presented. [IFRS 7.42G].

7 PRESENTATION ON THE FACE OF THE FINANCIAL STATEMENTS AND RELATED DISCLOSURES

Although it requires certain minimum disclosures, IFRS 7 provides little guidance as to where financial instruments and related gains and losses should be presented on the face of the financial statements nor how such items should be disaggregated. Further, the disclosures required need not always reflect how items are presented on the face of the statements. Therefore, for the time being at least, management must use its judgement in deciding how best to present much of the information relating to financial instruments, taking account of the minimum requirements of IFRS 7 and other related standards such as IAS 1.

7.1 Gains and losses recognised in profit or loss

7.1.1 Presentation on the face of the statement of comprehensive income (or income statement)

The effects of an entity's various activities, transactions and other events (including those relating to financial instruments) differ in frequency, potential for gain or loss and predictability. Accordingly, IAS 1 explains, disclosing the components of financial performance assists in providing an understanding of the financial performance achieved and in making projections of future results. [IAS 1.86].

IAS 1 prescribes requirements for line items to be included on the face of the statement of comprehensive income (or income statement) which include:

- revenue, presenting separately interest revenue calculated using the effective interest method; *[IAS 1.82(a)]*

  The IFRS Interpretations Committee clarified in March 2018 that only interest on financial assets measured at amortised cost or on debt instruments measured at fair value through other comprehensive income should be included in the amount of interest revenue presented separately (subject to the effects of qualifying hedging relationships under IFRS 9). In particular, it should not include, for example, interest revenue from financial assets measured at fair value through profit or loss.[16]

  In March 2019 the Interpretations Committee issued an agenda decision addressing the measurement of revenue arising from the physical settlement of a contract to sell a non-financial asset when that contract is in the scope of IFRS 9 and accounted for at fair value through profit or loss. The committee concluded that any such revenue should be measured at an amount reflecting the cash price received adjusted by the fair value of the contract at the settlement date – this should equal, or at least approximate, the fair value of the non-financial item delivered at the date of delivery.[17] This is illustrated in Example 54.17 below;

- gains and losses arising from the derecognition of financial assets measured at amortised cost. *[IAS 1.82(aa)]*. In order to determine the amount of this gain or loss, the carrying amount of the financial asset should, in principle, be updated to the date of derecognition. It should, therefore, include a revised estimate of expected credit losses determined as at the date of derecognition. However, as noted at 3.2 above, considerations of materiality would also need to be taken into account;[18]

  There is no equivalent requirement to present separately gains and losses arising from derecognition of debt instruments measured at fair value through other comprehensive income. However, the amount of such gains and losses should be determined in the same way as for financial assets measured at amortised cost, i.e. by updating expected credit losses to the date of derecognition; *[IFRS 9.5.7.11]*

- impairment losses (including reversals of impairment losses or impairment gains) determined in accordance with IFRS 9. *[IAS 1.82(ba)]*. This will include losses in respect of loan commitments and financial guarantee contracts as well as financial assets.

  Some might argue this line item should also include modification gains or losses, particularly if the reason for the modification was credit-related. However, a summary of the April 2015 meeting of the Transition Resource Group for Impairment of Financial Instruments, published on the IASB's website, suggests this would not be appropriate. Instead, it says that if disclosing gains and losses from impairments and modifications on a net basis would provide relevant information (for example, if the reason for the modification was credit-related), this could be dealt with through additional disclosure in the notes.

The summary also says that modification gains and losses should be presented separately if considered appropriate.[19] Consequently, another way in which a net figure could be presented on the face of the income statement involves presenting modification gains and losses (or at least those arising from credit-related events) in a separate line item that is adjacent to the one showing impairment losses and gains, together with a subtotal that includes these two amounts.

Another view is that because modification gains and losses are determined consistently with the effective interest method, they could be presented as a component of interest revenue. However, if the amounts included were material, we would expect separate disclosure of the amounts involved;

- where a financial asset previously measured at amortised cost is reclassified so that it is measured at fair value through profit or loss, any gain or loss arising from a difference between the previous carrying amount and its fair value at the reclassification date; *[IAS 1.82(ca)]*
- where a financial asset previously classified at fair value through other comprehensive income is reclassified as measured at fair value through profit or loss, any cumulative gain or loss previously recognised in other comprehensive income that is reclassified to profit or loss; *[IAS 1.82(cb)]* and
- finance costs. *[IAS 1.82(b)]*.

The implementation guidance to IFRS 7 explains that this caption includes total interest expense (see 4.2.2 above) but may also include amounts associated with non-financial liabilities, for example the unwinding of the discount on long-term provisions (see Chapter 26 at 4.3.5). *[IFRS 7.IG13]*.

The IFRS Interpretations Committee concluded that it is not permissible to present a line item 'net finance costs' (or a similar term) on the face of the statement without showing the finance costs and finance revenue composing it. However, the presentation of finance revenue followed immediately by finance costs and a subtotal, e.g. 'net finance costs', is allowed.[20]

The demand for safe investments can sometimes result in a negative yield on very high quality financial assets (e.g. certain government bonds or reserve bank deposits). The Interpretations Committee has considered this phenomenon and in January 2015 noted that interest resulting from a negative effective interest rate on a financial asset does not meet the definition of interest revenue because it reflects a gross outflow, not a gross inflow, of economic benefits. Consequently, such expenses should not be presented as interest revenue, but in an appropriate expense classification.[21] This might be a separate line item titled, for example, 'financial expenses on liquid short term assets' or 'other financial expenses' or using another appropriate description. Alternatively, it could be appropriate to include within another expense line, for example, 'other expenses'. Similarly, we believe negative interest on financial liabilities, which will represent a form of income, should not be offset against positive interest expense.

Example 54.17: **Physical settlement of sales contract that is accounted for as a derivative financial instrument**

On 1 December 20X1, Entity A enters into a contract to sell a commodity for a fixed price of $100 on 5 January 20X2. The contract is not considered to be for the entity's normal sale requirements and is therefore accounted for as a derivative in accordance with IFRS 9. At inception, the contract is at the money and its fair value is nil.

Entity A's reporting period ends on 31 December 20X1. On that date, the forward price of the commodity has decreased and, as a result, the fair value of the contract has increased by $10. Entity A presents gains and losses on commodity contracts accounted for as derivatives within other operating income/expense. Therefore, the following journal is recorded for the year ended 31 December 20X1:

	$	$
Derivative asset	10	
Other operating income/expense		10

On 5 January 20X2, Entity A settles the contract by delivering the commodity and receiving $100 in cash. The fair value of the contract has not changed between 31 December 20X1 and 5 January 20X2 and Entity A presents revenue on delivery of the commodity. The carrying value of the commodity delivered, measured at the lower of cost and net realisable value, is $85. Therefore, Entity A records the following to reflect the settlement:

	$	$
Cash	100	
Derivative asset		10
Revenue		90
Cost of sales	85	
Inventory		85

Prior to the Interpretations Committee finalising the agenda decision referred to above, many entities measured revenue recognised in these circumstances at the cash price receivable ($100 in this example). They would also have reversed the previously recognised gains or losses on the commodity contract, typically in the line item in which those gains or losses were originally recognised (resulting in other operating expenses of $10 in this example).

The Interpretations Committee did not address whether this revenue is within the scope of IFRS 15 – *Revenue from Contracts with Customers* – and hence whether it should be included in the disclosures required by that standard. In practice many entities do consider this revenue to be within the scope of IFRS 15 and consequently their financial statements do not necessarily distinguish it from other revenue from contracts with customers that is clearly within scope of IFRS 15.

Another matter the agenda decision does not address is when, or in what circumstances, revenue should be recognised when an entity settles such a sales contract by physical delivery. Some entities do not (or do not in all circumstances) recognise revenue but instead present the settlement of the contract on a net basis. If, in this example, Entity A followed such an approach it would not present revenue of $90 and cost of sales of $85, but instead show a net gain on settlement of $5. In practice many entities (or components of an entity) that do not present revenue on physical settlement of such contracts are broker-traders that measure their inventory at fair value less costs to sell in accordance with IAS 2 – *Inventories* – in which case there should be no net gain or loss on settlement.

Additional line items, headings and subtotals should be presented on the face of the statement of comprehensive income (or income statement) when such presentation is relevant to an understanding of the elements of an entity's financial performance. Factors that should be considered include materiality and the nature and function of the components of income and expenses. For example, a financial institution may amend the descriptions to provide information that is relevant to the operations of a financial institution. *[IAS 1.85, 86]*. This may also be relevant where an entity recognises negative interest on financial assets or financial liabilities.[22]

Any additional subtotals presented should: *[IAS 1.85A]*

- comprise line items made up of amounts recognised and measured in accordance with IFRS;
- be presented and labelled in a manner that makes the line items that constitute the subtotal clear and understandable;
- be consistent from period to period, as required by IAS 1 (see Chapter 3 at 4.1.4); and
- not be displayed with more prominence than the subtotals and totals required in IFRS for the statement(s) presenting profit or loss and other comprehensive income.

The following items should also be disclosed on the face of the statement of comprehensive income (or income statement) as allocations of profit or loss for the period: *[IAS 1.81B(a)]*

- profit or loss attributable to non-controlling interests; and
- profit or loss attributable to owners of the parent.

7.1.2 Further analysis of gains and losses recognised in profit or loss

As noted at 4.2.2 above, entities are required to disclose total interest income and total interest expense, calculated using the effective interest method, for financial assets and financial liabilities that are not at fair value through profit or loss. Whilst leases are included within the scope of IFRS 7, strictly they are not accounted for using the effective interest method (although for many leases the method prescribed in IFRS 16 results in a very similar treatment). Accordingly, where material, it appears that finance income (charges) arising on leases should be disclosed separately from the interest income (expense) disclosed above. In fact, it will sometimes be appropriate to include such items within the same caption on the face of the statement of comprehensive income (or income statement) and include a sub-analysis in the notes, albeit having regard to the restrictions on what may be presented within the separate line item containing interest revenue calculated using the effective interest method – see 7.1.1 above.

Dividends classified as an expense (for example those payable to holders of redeemable preference shares) may be presented either with interest on other liabilities or as a separate item. Such items are subject to the requirements of IAS 1. In some circumstances, because of the differences between interest and dividends with respect to matters such as tax deductibility, it is desirable to disclose them separately in the statement of comprehensive income (or income statement). *[IAS 32.40]*.

The following gains and losses reported in profit or loss should also be disclosed:

- the amount of dividends recognised from equity investments designated at fair value through other comprehensive income, showing separately the amounts arising on investments derecognised during the reporting period and those related to investments held at the end of the reporting period; *[IFRS 7.11A(d)]*

- changes in fair value that relate to instruments at fair value through profit or loss (see 4.2.1 above).

    Little guidance is given on disaggregating gains and losses from instruments classified as at fair value through profit or loss. For example, the components of the change in fair value of a debt instrument can include:

    - interest accruals;
    - foreign currency retranslation;
    - movements arising from changes in the issuer's credit risk; and
    - changes in market interest rates.

    An entity is neither required to disaggregate, nor prohibited from disaggregating, these components on the face of the statement of comprehensive income (or income statement) provided the minimum disclosure requirements are met (e.g. see 4.2 above) and the restrictions on what may be presented within the separate line item containing interest revenue calculated using the effective interest method are followed (see 7.1.1 above). Accordingly, in our view the interest accrual component, say, of a financial liability may be included separately within an interest expense caption or it may be included within the same caption as other components of the gain or loss such as dealing profit. As noted at 4.1 above, whatever the entity's approach, it should be explained in its accounting policies; and

- the amount of exchange differences recognised in profit or loss under IAS 21 except for those arising on financial instruments measured at fair value through profit or loss. *[IAS 21.52(a)]*.

In IAS 1 it is explained that when items of income and expense are material, their nature and amount are required to be disclosed separately. *[IAS 1.97]*. Circumstances that can give rise to separate disclosure include the disposal of investments *[IAS 1.98]* and the early settlement of liabilities. However, gains and losses should not be reported as extraordinary items, either on the face of the statement of comprehensive income (or income statement) or in the notes. *[IAS 1.87]*.

7.1.3 Offsetting and hedges

IAS 1 explains that income and expenses should not be offset unless required or permitted by another standard. This is because offsetting detracts from the ability of users to understand fully the transactions, other events and conditions that have occurred and to assess the entity's future cash flows (except where it reflects the substance of the transaction or other event). *[IAS 1.32, 33]*. It goes on to explain that gains and losses on the disposal of non-current investments (such as many debt instruments measured at fair value through other comprehensive income) are reported by deducting the carrying amount of the asset and related selling expenses from the proceeds on disposal rather than showing gross proceeds as revenue *[IAS 1.34]* – in the case of debt instruments measured at fair value through other comprehensive income the profit or loss on disposal will also include any gains and losses that are reclassified from equity. It also explains that gains and losses arising from groups of similar transactions should be reported on a net basis, for example gains and losses arising on financial instruments held for trading or foreign exchange differences. The individual transactions should, however, be reported separately if they are material. *[IAS 1.35]*.

Whilst IAS 32 prescribes when financial assets and liabilities should be offset in the statement of financial position (see 7.4.1 below) it contains no guidance on when related income and expenses should be offset. However, IFRS 9 is more prescriptive, specifying the following:

- if a group of hedged items in a cash flow hedge contains no offsetting risk positions and will affect different line items in profit or loss, the gains or losses on the hedging instrument should be apportioned to the line items affected by the hedged items when reclassified to profit or loss.

    This might be the case, for example, if a group of foreign currency expense transactions are hedged for foreign currency risk and those expenses will affect, say, both distribution costs and administrative expenses.

    The basis of apportionment between line items should be systematic and rational and not result in the grossing up of net gains or losses arising from a single hedging instrument; *[IFRS 9.B6.6.13, B6.6.14]*

- if a group of hedged items contains offsetting risk positions, i.e. a net position is hedged and the hedged risk affects different line items in profit or loss, the gains or losses on the hedging instrument should be presented in a line separate from those affected by the hedged items. Consequently, the line item relating to the hedged item will remain unaffected by the hedge accounting. *[IFRS 9.6.6.4, B6.6.13]*.

    This would apply, for example, to a cash flow hedge of a group of foreign currency denominated sales and expenses. The hedging gains or losses would be presented in a line item that is separate from both revenue and the relevant expense line item(s). *[IFRS 9.B6.6.15]*.

    Another example would be a fair value hedge of a net position involving a fixed-rate asset and a fixed-rate liability. Hedge accounting would normally involve recognising the net interest accrual on the interest rate swap in profit or loss. In this case the net interest accrual should be presented in a line item separate from gross interest revenue and gross interest expense.

    This is to avoid the grossing up of net gains or losses on a single instrument into offsetting gross amounts and recognising them in different line items. *[IFRS 9.B6.6.16]*.

These requirements imply that gains and losses from hedging instruments in other hedging relationships would be presented in the same line item that is affected by the hedged item (at least to the extent the hedge is effective) rather than being shown separately, although this is not explicitly stated in IFRS 9.

7.1.4 Embedded derivatives

IFRS 9 explicitly states that it does not address whether embedded derivatives should be presented separately in the statement of financial position. However, the standard is silent about the presentation in profit or loss. *[IFRS 9.4.3.4]*. In practice, it will depend on the nature both of the hybrid and the host whether related gains and losses are included in the same or separate captions within profit or loss.

For example, a borrowing with commodity-linked coupons that is accounted for as a simple debt host and an embedded commodity derivative might give rise to interest expense and other finance income (or expense) respectively that would often be reported in separate captions within profit or loss. Alternatively, changes in the fair value of an embedded prepayment option in a host borrowing that is accounted for separately may be included in the same caption within profit or loss as interest expense on the host debt instrument if the value of the option varies largely as a result of change in interest rates.

7.1.5 Entities whose share capital is not equity

Gains and losses related to changes in the carrying amount of a financial liability are recognised as income or expense in profit or loss even when they relate to an instrument that includes a right to the residual interest in the assets of the entity in exchange for cash or another financial asset, such as shares in mutual funds and co-operatives (see Chapter 47 at 4.6). Any gain or loss arising from the remeasurement of such an instrument (including the impact of dividends paid, where appropriate) should be presented separately on the face of the statement of comprehensive income (or income statement) when it is relevant in explaining the entity's performance. *[IAS 32.41]*.

The following example illustrates a format for a statement of comprehensive income (or income statement) that may be used by entities such as mutual funds that do not have equity as defined in IAS 32, although other formats may be acceptable.

Example 54.18: Statement of comprehensive income (or income statement) format for a mutual fund

Statement of comprehensive income (income statement) for the year ended 31 December 2021 *[IAS 32.IE32]*

	2021 €	2020 €
Revenue	2,956	1,718
Expenses (classified by nature or function)	(644)	(614)
Profit from operating activities	2,312	1,104
Finance costs		
– other finance costs	(47)	(47)
– distributions to members	(50)	(50)
Change in net assets attributable to unit holders	2,215	1,007

Although it may not be immediately clear, the final line item in this format is an expense. Therefore the entity's 'profit or loss' (as that term is used in IAS 1) for 2021 is €2,312 – €47 – €50 – €2,215 = €nil.

The next example illustrates a format for a statement of comprehensive income (or income statement) that may be used by entities whose share capital is not equity as defined in IAS 32 because the entity has an obligation to repay the share capital on demand, for example co-operatives, but which do have some equity (such as other reserves). Again, other formats may be acceptable.

Example 54.19: Statement of comprehensive income (income statement) format for a co-operative

Statement of comprehensive income (income statement) for the year ended 31 December 2021 [IAS 32.IE33]

	2021 €	2020 €
Revenue	472	498
Expenses (classified by nature or function)	(367)	(396)
Profit from operating activities	105	102
Finance costs		
– other finance costs	(4)	(4)
– distributions to members	(50)	(50)
Change in net assets attributable to members	51	48

In this example, the line item 'Finance costs – distributions to members' is an expense and the final line item is equivalent to 'profit or loss'.

Corresponding statement of financial position formats for both of these examples are shown at 7.4.6 below.

7.2 Gains and losses recognised in other comprehensive income

IAS 1 requires income and expense not recognised within profit or loss to be included in a statement of comprehensive income. [IAS 1.82A]. Material items of income and expense and gains and losses that result from financial assets and financial liabilities which are included in other comprehensive income are required to be disclosed separately and should include at least the following:

- the amount of gain or loss attributable to changes in a liability's credit risk for those financial liabilities designated as at fair value through profit or loss; [IFRS 7.20(a)(i)]
- the revaluation gain or loss arising on equity investments designated at fair value through other comprehensive income; [IFRS 7.20(a)(vii)] and
- revaluation gains or losses arising on debt instruments measured at fair value through other comprehensive income, showing separately: [IFRS 7.20(a)(viii)]
  - the amount of gain or loss recognised in other comprehensive income during the period; and
  - the amount reclassified upon derecognition from accumulated other comprehensive income to profit or loss for the period.

The application of hedge accounting can also result in the recognition in other comprehensive income of gains and losses arising on hedging instruments and the reclassification thereof. However, when an entity removes such a gain or loss that was recognised in other comprehensive income and includes it in the initial cost or other carrying amount of a non-financial asset or liability, that should not be regarded as a reclassification adjustment and hence should not affect, or be included within, other comprehensive income. *[IAS 1.96, IFRS 9.BC6.380]*.

The following items should also be disclosed on the face of the statement of comprehensive income as allocations of total comprehensive income for the period: *[IAS 1.81B(b)]*

- total comprehensive income attributable to non-controlling interests; and
- total comprehensive income attributable to owners of the parent.

7.3 Statement of changes in equity

The following information should be included in the statement of changes in equity: *[IAS 1.106]*

- total comprehensive income for the period, showing separately the total amounts attributable to owners of the parent and to non-controlling interests; and
- for each component of equity, a reconciliation between the carrying amount at the beginning and the end of the period, separately disclosing changes resulting from:
    - profit or loss;
    - other comprehensive income; and
    - transactions with owners acting in their capacity as owners, showing separately:
        - contributions by and distributions to owners; and
        - changes in ownership interests in subsidiaries that do not result in a loss of control.

An analysis of other comprehensive income by item should be presented for each component of equity, either in the statement or in the notes. *[IAS 1.106A]*.

Where hedge accounting is applied, IFRS 7 specifies additional information that should be presented within the reconciliation and analysis noted above or the notes thereto. This is covered in more detail at 4.3.3 above.

As noted at 7.2 above, when an entity applying IFRS 9 removes a gain or loss on a cash flow hedge that was recognised in other comprehensive income in order to include it in the initial cost or other carrying amount of a non-financial asset or liability, that adjustment should not be included within other comprehensive income. *[IFRS 9.BC6.380]*. Such an entry should instead be presented within the statement of changes of equity (because it affects an entity's net assets and hence its equity), albeit separately from other comprehensive income.

The amount of dividends recognised as distributions to owners during the period should be disclosed on the face of the statement of changes in equity or in the notes. *[IAS 1.107]*.

In addition, IAS 32 notes that IAS 1 requires the amount of transaction costs accounted for as a deduction from equity in the period to be disclosed separately. *[IAS 32.39].*

If an entity reacquires its own equity instruments from related parties disclosure should be provided in accordance with IAS 24 (see Chapter 39). *[IAS 32.34].*

If an entity such as a mutual fund or a co-operative has no issued equity instruments, it may still need to present a statement of changes in equity. For example, such an entity may have gains or losses arising on debt instruments measured at fair value through other comprehensive income that are recognised in equity; also co-operatives, for example, may have a balance on equity.

7.4 Statement of financial position

7.4.1 Offsetting financial assets and financial liabilities

It is common for reporting entities to enter into offsetting arrangements with their counterparties. Offsetting arrangements allow market participants to manage counterparty credit risks, and manage liquidity risk. In particular, netting arrangements generally reduce the credit risk exposures of market participants to counterparties relative to their gross exposures. Such mechanisms also permit the management of existing market risk exposures by taking on offsetting contracts with the same counterparty rather than assuming additional counterparty risk by entering into an offsetting position with a new counterparty. Furthermore, for a regulated financial institution, position netting may also have regulatory capital implications.

IAS 1 sets out a general principle that assets and liabilities should not be offset except where such offset is permitted or required by an accounting standard or interpretation (see Chapter 3 at 4.1.5.B). *[IAS 1.32].* This general prohibition on offset is due to the fact that net presentation of assets and liabilities generally does not provide a complete depiction of the assets and liabilities of an entity. In particular, offsetting obscures the existence of some assets and liabilities in the statement of financial position and it impacts key financial ratios such as gearing, and measures such as total assets or liabilities.

IAS 32 provides some exceptions to this general rule in the case of financial assets and liabilities. IAS 32 requires a financial asset and a financial liability to be offset and the net amount reported in the statement of financial position when, and only when, an entity:

(a) currently has a legally enforceable right to set off the recognised amounts; and

(b) intends either to settle on a net basis, or to realise the asset and settle the liability simultaneously.

These two conditions are often called the IAS 32 Offsetting Criteria. There is, however, one exception to the offsetting requirement. This exception arises when a transferred financial asset does not qualify for derecognition. In such a circumstance, the transferred asset and the associated liability must not be offset, *[IAS 32.42],* even if they otherwise satisfy the offsetting criteria (see Chapter 52 at 5.5.1).

IAS 32 argues that offset is appropriate in the circumstances set out in (a) and (b) above, because the entity has, in effect, a right to, or an obligation for, only a single net future cash flow and, hence, a single net financial asset or financial liability. In other circumstances, financial assets and financial liabilities are presented separately from each other, consistently with their characteristics as resources or obligations of the entity. *[IAS 32.43]*. Furthermore, the amount resulting from offsetting must also reflect the reporting entity's expected future cash flows from settling two or more separate financial instruments. *[IAS 32.BC94]*.

Offset is not equivalent to derecognition, since offsetting does not result in the financial asset or the financial liability being removed from the statement of financial position, but in net presentation of a net financial asset or a net financial liability. Moreover, no gain or loss can ever arise on offset, but may arise on derecognition. *[IAS 32.44]*.

IAS 32 acknowledges that an enforceable right to set off a financial asset and a financial liability affects the rights and obligations associated with that asset and liability and may affect an entity's exposure to credit and liquidity risk. However, such a right is not, in itself, a sufficient basis for offsetting. The entity may still realise the asset and liability separately and, in the absence of an intention to exercise the right or to settle simultaneously, the amount and timing of an entity's future cash flows are not affected. Similarly, an intention by one or both parties to settle on a net basis without the legal right to do so is not sufficient to justify offsetting because the rights and obligations associated with the individual financial asset and financial liability remain unaltered. *[IAS 32.46, AG38E]*.

IAS 32 elaborates further on the detail of the offsetting criteria as set out in the following subsections.

7.4.1.A   Criterion (a): Enforceable legal right of set-off

IAS 32 describes a right of set-off as a debtor's legal right, by contract or otherwise (for example, it may arise as a result of a provision in law or a regulation), to settle or otherwise eliminate all or a portion of an amount due to a creditor by applying against that amount an amount due from the creditor. The enforceability of the right of set-off is thus essentially a legal matter, so that the specific conditions supporting the right may vary from one legal jurisdiction to another. *[IAS 32.45]*. Care must therefore be taken to establish which laws apply to the relationships between the parties.

In unusual circumstances, a debtor (A) may have a legal right to apply an amount due from a third party (B) against an amount due to a creditor (C), provided that there is an agreement among A, B and C that clearly establishes A's right to set off amounts due from B against those due to C. *[IAS 32.45]*. For example, a foreign branch of a US bank makes a loan to a foreign subsidiary of a US parent with the parent required to deposit an amount equal to the loan in the US bank for the same term. The terms of the transactions may give the bank a legal right to set off the amount due to the parent against the amount owed by the foreign subsidiary. Another example is bank accounts maintained for a group of companies where each member of the group agrees that its credit balance may be the subject of set-off in respect of debit balances of other members of the group. In our experience, not all jurisdictions recognise this type of contractual multilateral set-off arrangement, particularly in bankruptcy scenarios.

A right of set-off may currently be available or it may be contingent on a future event (e.g. the right may be triggered or exercisable only on the occurrence of some future event, such as the default, insolvency or bankruptcy of one of the counterparties). Even if the right of set-off is not contingent on a future event, it may only be legally enforceable in the normal course of business, or in the event of default, or in the event of insolvency or bankruptcy, of one or all of the counterparties. *[IAS 32.AG38A]*.

The revised application guidance makes it clear that, in order for an entity to currently have a legally enforceable right of set-off, the right: *[IAS 32.AG38B]*

- must not be contingent on a future event; and
- must be legally enforceable in all of the following circumstances:
  - the normal course of business;
  - the event of default; and
  - the event of insolvency or bankruptcy of the entity and all of the counterparties.

The nature and extent of the right of set-off, including any conditions attached to its exercise and whether it would remain in the event of default or insolvency or bankruptcy, may vary from one legal jurisdiction to another. Consequently, it cannot be assumed that the right of set-off is automatically available outside of the normal course of business. For example, the bankruptcy or insolvency laws of a jurisdiction may prohibit, or restrict, the right of set-off in the event of bankruptcy or insolvency in some circumstances. *[IAS 32.AG38C]*. Therefore, contractual provisions, the laws governing the contract, or the default, insolvency or bankruptcy laws applicable to the parties need to be considered to ascertain whether the right of set-off is enforceable in the circumstances set out above. *[IAS 32.AG38D]*. In assessing whether an agreement meets these conditions, entities will need to make a legal determination, which may involve obtaining legal advice.

The basis for conclusions suggests that to meet the criteria for offsetting, these rights must exist for all counterparties. Thus, if one party, including the reporting entity, will not or cannot perform under the contract, the other counterparties will be able to enforce that right to set-off against the party that has defaulted or become insolvent or bankrupt. *[IAS 32.BC80]*. However, the revised application guidance above appears to focus only on whether the rights of the reporting entity are legally enforceable. It is also clear that the above reference to 'all of the counterparties' pertains to the legal enforceability in the circumstances listed (i.e. the normal course of business, the events of default, insolvency or bankruptcy), and not who holds the set-off right.

In our view, normally the standard and its application guidance would prevail over the basis for conclusions and we consider that the IASB's most likely intention, consistent with the wording in the body and application guidance of the standard, was to require only the reporting entity to have a legal right to set off in the circumstances noted above – including, in the event of the reporting entity's own default, insolvency or bankruptcy.

The requirement that a reporting entity must be able to legally enforce a right of set-off in the event of its own bankruptcy means that the counterparty (or counterparties) to a netting agreement must not have the ability to force gross settlement in the event of the reporting entity's default, insolvency or bankruptcy. It also means that the reporting entity may need to obtain legal advice as to whether its legal right to net settle will survive the bankruptcy laws of the jurisdiction in which it is located.

Many contracts give only the non-defaulting party the right to enforce the netting provisions in case of default, insolvency or bankruptcy of any of the parties to the agreement. Unless the insolvency laws in the relevant jurisdiction would force net settlement, such contracts would fail the IAS 32 criteria because the reporting entity cannot enforce such rights of set-off in the event of its own bankruptcy, regardless of the fact that in practice it is highly unlikely that the non-defaulting party would insist on gross settlement. In practice, most of these contracts would not achieve offsetting under IAS 32 anyway, because the legal right of set-off available under such contracts is usually not enforceable in the normal course of business. Generally speaking, these contracts are structured this way because entities do not intend to settle net other than in situations of default. In other circumstances, entities need to determine if the right to enforce net settlement would survive their own bankruptcy.

A right of set-off that can be exercised only upon the occurrence of a future event is often referred to as a 'conditional' right of set-off. For example, an entity may have a right of set-off that is exercisable on changes to particular legislation or change in control of the counterparties. Conditional rights of set-off such as these do not meet the offsetting criteria and, hence, the financial asset and financial liability subject to such rights of set-off would not qualify to be offset.

As the description of a right of set-off itself envisages an amount being due to each party either now or in the future, the passage of time and uncertainties relating to amounts to be paid do not preclude an entity from currently having a legally enforceable right of set-off. The fact that payments subject to a right of set-off will only arise at a future date is not in itself a condition or form of contingency that prevents offsetting. *[IAS 32.BC83]*.

However, if the right of set-off is not exercisable during a period when amounts are due and payable, then the entity does not meet the offsetting criterion as it has no right to set off those payments. Similarly, a right of set-off that could disappear or that would no longer be enforceable after a future event that could take place in the normal course of business or in the event of default, or in the event of insolvency or bankruptcy, such as a ratings downgrade, would not meet the currently (legally enforceable) criterion. *[IAS 32.BC84]*.

Some contracts include representation clauses under which the right to set-off is automatically invalidated if any undertakings or representations in the contract turns out to be incorrect in a material respect. In our view, such clauses would generally not render the right of set-off a conditional right of set-off.

In certain circumstances, an entity may, in order to exercise its right of set-off, need to unilaterally take a procedural action within its control. For example, an entity may be required to notify the counterparty, in the form of a letter in advance, in order to effect net settlement under the terms of the contract. In some cases, an entity may need to apply to a court to effect set-off when a counterparty becomes bankrupt (as a matter of process), although that right is assured and is upheld in the event of default of a counterparty in that jurisdiction. In our view, the mere fact that such actions are needed before an entity can exercise the right of set-off would not make the exercisability of that right contingent on a future event. However, in the latter example, the probability of favourable or unfavourable judgement from the court would have to be assessed separately as part of the 'legal enforceability' requirement to conclude whether the right of set-off meets the offsetting criteria in IAS 32.

Unlike US GAAP, IAS 32 does not specify a particular level of assurance required to meet the 'legally enforceable' criterion. Instead, it leaves such determination to judgement and consideration of the relevant facts and circumstances. In practice, entities are expected, in their day to day business, to obtain reasonable assurance on enforceability of contractual rights as part of prudent risk management regardless of the accounting requirements.

7.4.1.B Master netting agreements

It is common practice for an entity that undertakes a number of financial instrument transactions with a single counterparty to enter into a 'master netting arrangement' with that counterparty. These arrangements are typically used by financial institutions to restrict their exposure to loss in the event of bankruptcy or other events that result in a counterparty being unable to meet its obligations. Such an agreement commonly creates a conditional right of set-off that becomes enforceable, and affects the realisation or settlement of individual financial assets and financial liabilities, only following a specified event of default or in other circumstances not expected to arise in the normal course of business. Entities who enter into such master netting agreements other than not meeting the legal right of set-off requirement also typically do not intend to settle net in the normal course of business.

Where an entity has entered into such an agreement, the agreement does not provide the basis for the offset of assets and liabilities unless both of the offsetting criteria are satisfied. *[IAS 32.50]*. For enforceable master netting arrangements that create a conditional right of set off, this will typically be the case only if the default (or other event specified in the contract) has actually occurred. When financial assets and financial liabilities subject to a master netting arrangement are not offset, the effect of the arrangement falls within the scope of the disclosure requirements of IFRS 7 (see 7.4.2 below).

7.4.1.C Criterion (b): Intention to settle net or realise the gross amount simultaneously ('the net settlement criterion')

An entity's intention to settle net or settle simultaneously may be demonstrated through its past experience of executing set-off or simultaneous settlement in similar situations, its usual operating practices or by reference to its documented risk policies. Thus, incidental net or simultaneous settlement of a financial asset or financial liability does not meet the criterion above.

The requirement for an intention to settle net or to settle simultaneously is, however, considered only from the reporting entity's perspective.

IAS 32 notes that an entity's intentions with respect to settlement of particular assets and liabilities may be influenced by its normal business practices, the requirements of the financial markets and other circumstances that may limit the ability to settle net or simultaneously. *[IAS 32.47]*. In practice, even though a reporting entity has the right to settle net, it may settle gross either because of lack of appropriate arrangements or systems to effect net settlement or to facilitate operations which would likely preclude offsetting.

Simultaneous settlement of two financial instruments may occur through, for example, the operation of a clearing house in an organised financial market or a face-to-face exchange. *[IAS 32.48]*. The procedures of the clearing house or exchange may provide that the amount to be paid or received for different products be settled gross. However, such payments may be made simultaneously. Hence, even though the parties may make payment or receive payment separately for different product types, settlement occurs at the same moment and there is exposure only to the net amount.

The standard states that the reference to 'simultaneous' settlement in the conditions for offset above is to be interpreted literally, as applying only to the realisation of a financial asset and settlement of a financial liability at the same moment. *[IAS 32.48]*. For example, the settlement of a financial asset and a financial liability at the same nominal time but in different time zones is not considered to be simultaneous.

Nevertheless, it became apparent to the IASB that there was diversity in practice related to the interpretation of 'simultaneous' settlement in IAS 32. In practice, due to processing constraints, settlement of gross amounts rarely occurs at exactly the same moment, even when using a clearing house or settlement system. Rather, actual settlement takes place over a period of time (e.g. clearing repos and reverse repos in batches during the day). Arguably, therefore, 'simultaneous' is not operational and ignores settlement systems that are established to achieve what is economically equivalent to net settlement. Consequently, IAS 32 has often been interpreted to mean that settlement through a clearing house does meet the simultaneous settlement criterion, even if not occurring at the same moment. The IASB agreed that some, but not all, settlement systems should be seen as equivalent to net settlement and, in order to reduce diversity of accounting treatment, introduced guidance into IAS 32 in December 2011 to clarify how criterion (b) should be assessed in these circumstances. *[IAS 32.BC94-BC100]*.

The amendments explain that if an entity can settle amounts in a manner such that the outcome is, in effect, equivalent to net settlement, the entity will meet the net settlement criterion. This will occur if, and only if, the gross settlement mechanism has features that: (i) eliminate or result in insignificant credit and liquidity risk, and (ii) will process receivables and payables in a single settlement process or cycle. For example, a gross settlement system that has all of the following characteristics would meet the net settlement criterion: *[IAS 32.AG38F]*

- financial assets and financial liabilities eligible for set-off are submitted at the same point in time for processing;
- once the financial assets and financial liabilities are submitted for processing, the parties are committed to fulfil the settlement obligation;
- there is no potential for the cash flows arising from the assets and liabilities to change once they have been submitted for processing (unless the processing fails – see next item below);
- assets and liabilities that are collateralised with securities will be settled on a securities transfer or similar system (e.g. delivery versus payment), so that if the transfer of securities fails, the processing of the related receivable or payable for which the securities are collateral will also fail (and *vice versa*);
- any transactions that fail, as outlined in the previous item above, will be re-entered for processing until they are settled;

- settlement is carried out through the same settlement institution (e.g. a settlement bank, a central bank or a central securities depository); and
- an intraday credit facility is in place that will provide sufficient overdraft amounts to enable the processing of payments at the settlement date for each of the parties, and it is virtually certain that the intraday credit facility will be honoured if called upon.

The IASB deliberately chose the language above so that it was clear that settlement systems established by clearing houses or other central counterparties should not automatically be assumed to meet the net settlement criterion. Conversely, irrespective of the names used in a particular jurisdiction, other settlement systems may meet the net settlement criterion if that system eliminates or results in insignificant credit and liquidity risk and processes receivables and payables in the same settlement process or cycle. [IAS 32.BC101].

7.4.1.D   Situations where offset is not normally appropriate

An entity may enter into a number of different financial instruments designed to replicate, as a group, the features of a single financial instrument (such a replication is sometimes referred to as creating a 'synthetic instrument'). For example, if an entity issues floating rate debt and then enters into a 'pay fixed/receive floating' interest rate swap, the combined economic effect is that the entity has issued fixed rate debt.

IAS 32 argues that each of the individual financial instruments that together constitute a 'synthetic instrument':

- represents a contractual right or obligation with its own terms and conditions;
- may be transferred or settled separately; and
- is exposed to risks that may differ from those to which the other financial instruments in the 'synthetic instrument' are exposed.

Accordingly, when one financial instrument in a 'synthetic instrument' is an asset and another is a liability, they are not offset and presented on an entity's statement of financial position on a net basis unless they meet the offsetting criteria. [IAS 32.49(a), AG39].

Other circumstances where the offsetting criteria are generally not met, and therefore offsetting is usually inappropriate, include: [IAS 32.49(b), 49(c), 49(d), 49(e)]

(a) financial assets and financial liabilities which arise from financial instruments having the same primary risk exposure (e.g. assets and liabilities within a portfolio of forward contracts or other derivative instruments) but involving different counterparties;

(b) financial or other assets that are pledged as collateral for non-recourse financial liabilities (see 7.4.1.F below);

(c) financial assets which are set aside in trust by a debtor for the purpose of discharging an obligation without those assets having been accepted by the creditor in settlement of the obligation (e.g. a sinking fund arrangement); or

(d) obligations incurred as a result of events giving rise to losses that are expected to be recovered from a third party by virtue of a claim made under an insurance policy.

Derivative assets and liabilities that are not transacted through central clearing systems are very unlikely to qualify for offsetting. For example, it is rare that they will be settled net in the normal course of business and even where associated offsetting agreements exist they are usually conditional on the default of one of the counterparties.

7.4.1.E Cash pooling arrangements

Groups often use what are commonly known as cash pooling arrangements. Typically these will involve a number of subsidiaries within a group each having a legally separate bank account with the same bank that may have positive or negative (overdrawn) balances. In many respects these accounts will be managed on an aggregated basis, for example interest will normally be determined on a notional basis using the net balance of all accounts; similarly any overdraft limit will normally apply to the net balance.

These arrangements may or may not give the group a legally enforceable right to set off the balances in these accounts. Clearly if there is no such right the balances should not be offset in the group financial statements. However, where such a right exists and meets criterion (a), the entity should assess whether there is an intention to settle the balances net or simultaneously, i.e. to what extent criterion (b) is met.

The Interpretations Committee considered criterion (b) for a particular cash pooling arrangement where:

- the group instigated regular physical transfers of balances into a single netting account;
- such transfers were not required under the terms of the cash-pooling arrangement and were not performed at the reporting date; and
- at the reporting date, the group expected that its subsidiaries would use their bank accounts before the next net settlement date by placing further cash on deposit or by withdrawing cash to settle other obligations.

The committee observed that the group expects cash movements to take place on individual bank accounts before the next net settlement date because the group expects its subsidiaries to use those bank accounts in their normal course of business. Consequently, to the extent the group did not expect to settle its subsidiaries' period-end account balances on a net basis, it would not be appropriate for the group to assert it had the intention to settle the entire period-end balances on a net basis at the reporting date. Therefore, presenting these balances net would not appropriately reflect the amounts and timings of the expected future cash flows, taking into account the entity's normal business practices.

In other cash-pooling arrangements, a group's expectations regarding how subsidiaries will use their bank accounts before the next net settlement date may be different. Consequently, in those circumstances, the group would be required to apply judgement in determining whether there was an intention to settle on a net basis at the reporting date. The committee also noted that many different cash pooling arrangements exist in practice and the determination of what constitutes an intention to settle on a net basis would depend on the individual facts and circumstances of each case. The related disclosure requirements (see 7.4.2 below) should also be considered.[23]

7.4.1.F   Offsetting collateral amounts

Many central counterparty clearing houses require cash collateral in the form of variation margin to cover the fluctuations in the market value of 'over-the-counter' and exchange-traded derivatives. Historically IAS 32 has not addressed the offsetting of collateral although entities sometimes did offset the market values of the derivatives against the cash collateral, on the basis that all payments on the derivatives will be made net using the cash collateral already provided. In effect, the collateral is represented as an advance payment for settlement of the cash flows arising on the derivatives.

In the basis for conclusions to the 2011 amendment, the IASB clarified that the offsetting criteria do not give special consideration to items referred to as 'collateral'. Accordingly, a recognised financial instrument designated as collateral should be set off against the related financial asset or financial liability if, and only if, it meets the offsetting criteria in IAS 32. This might be the case, for instance, if variation margin is used to settle cash flows on derivative contracts. However, the IASB also noted that if an entity can be required to return or receive back collateral, the entity would not currently have a legally enforceable right of set-off in all relevant circumstances and therefore offsetting would not be appropriate. *[IAS 32.BC103].*

In practice, to set off collateral against related financial assets and liabilities, a reporting entity would also need to assess, among other factors: (i) whether the amounts paid or received (however they might be described) actually represent a partial settlement of the amounts due under the derivative contracts (see below); (ii) whether the right of offset is legally enforceable in the event of default, insolvency or bankruptcy of either party as well as in the normal course of business; (iii) whether the right to offset the collateral and the open position is conditional on a future event; (iv) whether the collateral will form part of the actual net settlement of the underlying contracts; and (v) whether there is a single process for both the settlement of the underlying contracts and the transfer of the collateral.

The analysis of whether payments or receipts, whether described as margin payments or otherwise, are in fact partial settlements of an open position and hence result in partial derecognition of the derivative, can require the application of significant judgement, including particularly an assessment of the legal relationship between the clearing member and the clearing house. When the strike price of a derivative contract is effectively reset each day following a margin payment based on the contract's change in fair value, this might indicate it is appropriate to regard the margin payment as a partial settlement of the derivative. This situation sometimes occurs with exchange traded futures for which gains and losses on the open position are realised over time as opposed to being accumulated until the final settlement date.

The accounting outcome for a payment mechanism considered to represent a partial settlement is unlikely to be significantly different from one that is considered to give rise to collateral if the collateral qualifies for offset. However, the regulatory capital consequences can be very different (and the disclosure requirements are different too – see 7.4.2 below). Consequently, many clearing houses provide their members with a choice of payment mechanisms, one of which is designed to achieve partial settlement and the other the provision of collateral.

7.4.1.G Unit of account

IAS 32 does not specify the 'unit of account' to which the offsetting requirements should be applied. For example, they could be applied to individual financial instruments, such as entire derivative assets or liabilities, or they could be applied to identifiable cash flows arising on those financial instruments. In practice, both approaches are seen with the former being more commonly applied by financial institutions and the latter by energy producers and traders. This diversity became apparent to the IASB during its project that amended IAS 32 in December 2011. Nevertheless, whilst the IASB considered imposing an approach based on individual cash flows (which, on a conceptual level, it favoured), it concluded that the different interpretations applied today do not result in inappropriate application of the offsetting criteria. The Board also concluded that the benefits of amending IAS 32 would not outweigh the costs for preparers. *[IAS 32.BC105-BC111].* Accordingly, IAS 32 was not amended, thereby allowing this diversity to continue. Reporting entities should establish an accounting policy and apply that policy consistently.

7.4.2 Offsetting financial assets and financial liabilities: disclosure

This section discusses the requirements of IFRS 7 introduced by the IASB in December 2011. These requirements are similar to requirements introduced into US GAAP by the FASB at around the same time and are intended to assist users in identifying major differences between the effects of the IFRS and US GAAP offsetting requirements (without requiring a full reconciliation). *[IAS 32.BC77].*

7.4.2.A Objective

The objective of these requirements is to disclose information to enable users of financial statements to evaluate the effect or potential effect of netting arrangements, including rights of set-off associated with recognised financial assets and liabilities, on the reporting entity's financial position. *[IFRS 7.13B].*

To meet this objective, the minimum quantitative disclosure requirements considered at 7.4.2.C below may need to be supplemented with additional (qualitative) disclosures. Whether such disclosures are necessary will depend on the terms of an entity's enforceable master netting arrangements and related agreements, including the nature of the rights of set-off, and their effect or potential effect on the entity's financial position. *[IFRS 7.B53].*

7.4.2.B Scope

The disclosure requirements considered at 7.4.2.C below are applicable not only to all recognised financial instruments that are set off in accordance with IAS 32 (see 7.4.1 above), but also to recognised financial instruments that are subject to an enforceable master netting arrangement or 'similar agreement' that covers similar financial instruments and transactions, irrespective of whether they are set off in accordance with IAS 32. *[IFRS 7.13A, B40].*

In this context, enforceability has two elements: first, enforceability as a matter of law under the governing laws of the contract; and second, consistency with the bankruptcy laws of the jurisdictions where the reporting entity and counterparty are located. The latter is critical since, regardless of the jurisdiction selected to govern the contract, local insolvency laws in an insolvent counterparty's jurisdiction can override contractual terms in the event of insolvency. Determining whether an agreement is enforceable for the purposes of these disclosures may require judgement based on a legal analysis that is sometimes, but not necessarily, based on legal advice.

These 'similar agreements' include, but are not limited to, derivative clearing agreements, global master repurchase agreements, global master securities lending agreements, and any related rights to financial collateral. The 'similar financial instruments and transactions' include, but are not restricted to, derivatives, sale and repurchase agreements, reverse repurchase agreements, securities borrowing and securities lending agreements. However, loans and customer deposits with the same financial institution would not be within the scope of these disclosure requirements, unless they are set off in the statement of financial position; nor would financial instruments that are subject only to a collateral agreement. [IFRS 7.B41].

The scope of equivalent disclosures in US GAAP is restricted to derivatives, repurchase and reverse repurchase agreements and securities lending and borrowing arrangements. In November 2012, the IASB considered this and effectively confirmed that the scope of IFRS 7 is broader than US GAAP. As a result, trade or other receivables and payables, such as balances with brokers, that are subject to an umbrella netting arrangement (normally where an entity's customer is also a supplier, and *vice versa*), are likely to fall within the scope of these disclosure requirements. Extract 54.12 (BP) at 7.4.2.D below illustrates one company's disclosures about receivables and payables in addition to derivatives.

7.4.2.C   Disclosure requirements

To meet the objective at 7.4.2.A above, the standard requires entities to disclose, at the end of the reporting period, in a tabular format unless another format is more appropriate, the following information separately for recognised financial assets and for recognised financial liabilities: *[IFRS 7.13C]*

- the gross amounts of those recognised financial assets and recognised financial liabilities within the scope of the disclosures (see 7.4.2.B above) [Amount (a)].

  This excludes any amounts recognised as a result of collateral agreements that do not meet the offsetting criteria in IAS 32. Instead these will be disclosed in Amount (d) (see below); *[IFRS 7.B43]*

- the amounts that are set off in accordance with the criteria in IAS 32 when determining the net amounts presented in the statement of financial position [Amount (b)].

  These amounts will be disclosed in both the financial asset and financial liability disclosures. However, the amounts disclosed (in, for example, a table) should be limited to the amounts subject to set-off. For example, an entity may have a recognised derivative asset and a recognised derivative liability that meet the offsetting criteria. If the gross amount of the asset is larger than the gross amount of the liability, the financial asset disclosure table will include the entire amount of the derivative asset in Amount (a) and the entire amount of the derivative liability in Amount (b). However, while the financial liability disclosure table will include the entire amount of the derivative liability in Amount (a), it will only include the amount of the derivative asset that is equal to the amount of the derivative liability in Amount (b); *[IFRS 7.B44]*

- the net amounts presented in the statement of financial position [Amount (c) = Amount (a) – Amount (b)].

For instruments that are within the scope of these disclosure requirements but which do not meet the offsetting criteria in IAS 32, the amounts included in Amount (c) would equal the amounts included in Amount (a). *[IFRS 7.B45]*.

Amount (c) should be reconciled to the individual line item amounts presented in the statement of financial position. For example, if an entity determines that the aggregation or disaggregation of individual line item amounts provides more relevant information, it should reconcile the aggregated or disaggregated amounts included in Amount (c) back to the individual line item amounts presented in the statement of financial position; *[IFRS 7.B46]*

- the amounts subject to an enforceable master netting arrangement or similar agreement that are not included in the amounts subject to set-off above [Amount (d)], including:
    - amounts related to recognised financial instruments that do not meet some or all of the offsetting criteria in IAS 32 [Amount (d)(i)].

    This might include, for example, current rights of set-off where there is no intention to settle the open positions subject to these rights net or simultaneously, or conditional rights of set-off that are enforceable and exercisable only in the event of the default, insolvency or bankruptcy of any of the counterparties; *[IFRS 7.B47]* and
    - amounts related to financial collateral (including cash collateral) [Amount (d)(ii)].

    The fair value of those financial instruments that have been pledged or received as collateral should be disclosed. To ensure that the disclosures reflect the maximum net exposure to credit risk, the amendments require the amounts disclosed for financial collateral not offset to include actual collateral received, whether recognised or not as well as actual collateral pledged. The amounts disclosed should not relate to any payables or receivables recognised to return or receive back such collateral. *[IFRS 7.B48]*. The amounts disclosed for collateral would exclude non-financial collateral, for instance, land and buildings.

References to Amounts (a), (b), *et seq.* can be traced through to Example 54.20 at 7.4.2.D below.

The total amount included in Amount (d) for any instrument is limited to the amount included in Amount (c) for that instrument. *[IFRS 7.13D]*. In other words, an entity takes into account the effects of over-collateralisation by financial instrument, so that, for example, an over-collateralisation on one asset does not make an under-collateralisation on another. To do so, it first deducts the amounts included in Amount (d)(i) from the amount included in Amount (c).

It then limits the amounts included in Amount (d)(ii) to the remaining amount in Amount (c) for the related financial instrument. However, if rights to collateral are available to cover multiple contracts with the same counterparty, for example through a cross collateralisation agreement, such rights can be taken into account in arriving at Amount (d)(ii). *[IFRS 7.B49]*.

Entities should provide a description of the rights of set-off associated with the entity's financial instruments included in Amount (d), including the nature and type of those rights. For example, conditional rights would need to be described. For instruments subject to rights of set-off that are not contingent on a future event but that do not meet the remaining criteria in IAS 32, the description should include the reasons why the criteria are not met. For any financial collateral received or pledged, it would be appropriate to disclose the terms of the collateral (such as why the collateral is restricted); *[IFRS 7.13E, B50]* and

- the net amount after deducting Amount (d) from Amount (c) [Amount (e)].

The financial instruments disclosed in accordance with the requirements above may be subject to different measurement requirements, for example a payable related to a repurchase agreement may be measured at amortised cost, while a derivative will be measured at fair value. Instruments should be included at their recognised amounts and any resulting measurement differences should be described in the related disclosures. *[IFRS 7.B42]*.

The disclosures may be grouped by type of financial instrument or transaction (e.g. derivatives, repurchase and reverse repurchase agreements or securities borrowing and securities lending agreements). *[IFRS 7.B51]*.

Alternatively, disclosure of Amounts (a) to (c) may be grouped by type of financial instrument with disclosure of Amounts (c) to (e) by counterparty. Amounts that are individually significant in terms of total counterparty amounts should be separately disclosed with the remaining individually insignificant counterparty amounts aggregated into one line item. Names of the counterparties need not be given, although designation of counterparties (Counterparty P, Counterparty Q, Counterparty R, etc.) should remain consistent from year to year for the periods presented to maintain comparability. Qualitative disclosures should be considered so that further information can be given about the types of counterparties. *[IFRS 7.B52]*.

If the above quantitative and qualitative disclosures are included in more than one note to the financial statements, the amendments require the information in the individual notes to be cross-referenced to each other. This is intended to increase the transparency of the disclosures and enhance the value of information. *[IFRS 7.13F]*.

7.4.2.D Offsetting disclosures – illustrative examples

The amendment that introduced the disclosures related to offsetting financial instruments provides the following example illustrating ways in which an entity might provide the required quantitative disclosures described above. However, these illustrations do not address all possible ways of applying the disclosure requirements. *[IFRS 7.IG40D]*.

Example 54.20: Illustration of offsetting disclosures

Background

An entity has entered into transactions subject to an enforceable master netting arrangement or similar agreement with the following counterparties. The entity has the following recognised financial assets and financial liabilities resulting from those transactions that meet the scope of the disclosure requirements.

Counterparty A:

The entity has a derivative asset (fair value of CU100 million) and a derivative liability (fair value of CU80 million) with Counterparty A that meet the IAS 32 offsetting criteria. Consequently, the gross derivative liability is set off against the gross derivative asset, resulting in the presentation of a net derivative asset of CU20 million in the entity's statement of financial position. Cash collateral has also been received from Counterparty A for a portion of the net derivative asset (CU10 million). The cash collateral of CU10 million does not meet the IAS 32 offsetting criteria, but it can be set off against the net amount of the derivative asset and derivative liability in the case of default and insolvency or bankruptcy, in accordance with an associated collateral arrangement.

Counterparty B:

The entity has a derivative asset (fair value of CU100 million) and a derivative liability (fair value of CU80 million) with Counterparty B that do not meet the IAS 32 offsetting criteria, but which the entity has the right to set off in the case of default and insolvency or bankruptcy. Consequently, the gross amount of the derivative asset (CU100 million) and the gross amount of the derivative liability (CU80 million) are presented separately in the entity's statement of financial position.

Cash collateral has also been received from Counterparty B for the net amount of the derivative asset and derivative liability (CU20 million). The cash collateral of CU20 million does not meet the IAS 32 offsetting criteria, but it can be set off against the net amount of the derivative asset and derivative liability in the case of default and insolvency or bankruptcy, in accordance with an associated collateral arrangement.

Counterparty C:

The entity has entered into a sale and repurchase agreement with Counterparty C that is accounted for as a collateralised borrowing. The carrying amount of the financial assets (bonds) used as collateral and posted by the entity for the transaction is CU79 million and their fair value is CU85 million. The carrying amount of the collateralised borrowing (repo payable) is CU80 million.

The entity has also entered into a reverse sale and repurchase agreement with Counterparty C that is accounted for as a collateralised lending. The fair value of the financial assets (bonds) received as collateral (and not recognised in the entity's statement of financial position) is CU105 million. The carrying amount of the collateralised lending (reverse repo receivable) is CU90 million.

The transactions are subject to a global master repurchase agreement with a right of set-off only in default and insolvency or bankruptcy and therefore do not meet the IAS 32 offsetting criteria. Consequently, the related repo payable and repo receivable are presented separately in the entity's statement of financial position.

Illustration of the disclosures by type of financial instrument

Financial assets subject to offsetting, enforceable master netting arrangements and similar agreements

CU million

As at 31 December 20XX	(a) Gross amounts of recognised financial assets	(b) Gross amounts of recognised financial liabilities set off in the statement of financial position	(c)=(a)–(b) Net amounts of financial assets presented in the statement of financial position	(d) Related amounts not set off in the statement of financial position		(e)=(c)–(d) Net amount
				(d)(i), (d)(ii) Financial instruments	(d)(ii) Cash collateral received	
Description						
Derivatives	200	(80)	120	(80)	(30)	10
Reverse repurchase, securities borrowing and similar agreements	90	–	90	(90)	–	–
Other financial instruments	–	–	–	–	–	–
Total	290	(80)	210	(170)	(30)	10

Financial liabilities subject to offsetting, enforceable master netting arrangements and similar agreements

CU million

As at 31 December 20XX	(a) Gross amounts of recognised financial liabilities	(b) Gross amounts of recognised financial assets set off in the statement of financial position	(c)=(a)–(b) Net amounts of financial liabilities presented in the statement of financial position	(d) Related amounts not set off in the statement of financial position		(e)=(c)–(d) Net amount
				(d)(i), (d)(ii) Financial instruments	(d)(ii) Cash collateral pledged	
Description						
Derivatives	160	(80)	80	(80)	–	–
Repurchase, securities lending and similar agreements	80	–	80	(80)	–	–
Other financial instruments	–	–	–	–	–	–
Total	240	(80)	160	(160)	–	–

Illustration of amounts offset disclosed by type of financial instrument and amounts not offset by counterparty

Financial assets subject to offsetting, enforceable master netting arrangements and similar agreements

CU million

As at 31 December 20XX	(a) Gross amounts of recognised financial assets	(b) Gross amounts of recognised financial liabilities set off in the statement of financial position	(c)=(a)–(b) Net amounts of financial assets presented in the statement of financial position
Description			
Derivatives	200	(80)	120
Reverse repurchase, securities borrowing and similar agreements	90	–	90
Other financial instruments	–	–	–
Total	290	(80)	210

Net financial assets subject to enforceable master netting arrangements and similar agreements, by counterparty

CU million

As at 31 December 20XX	(c) Net amounts of financial assets presented in the statement of financial position	(d) Related amounts not set off in the statement of financial position		(e)=(c)–(d) Net amount
		(d)(i), (d)(ii) Financial instruments	(d)(ii) Cash collateral received	
Counterparty A	20	–	(10)	10
Counterparty B	100	(80)	(20)	–
Counterparty C	90	(90)	–	–
Other	–	–	–	–
Total	210	(170)	(30)	10

Financial liabilities subject to offsetting, enforceable master netting arrangements and similar agreements

CU million

As at 31 December 20XX	(a) Gross amounts of recognised financial liabilities	(b) Gross amounts of recognised financial assets set off in the statement of financial position	(c)=(a)–(b) Net amounts of financial liabilities presented in the statement of financial position
Description			
Derivatives	160	(80)	80
Repurchase, securities lending and similar agreements	80	–	80
Other financial instruments	–	–	–
Total	240	(80)	160

Net financial liabilities subject to enforceable master netting arrangements and similar agreements, by counterparty

CU million

As at 31 December 20XX	(c) Net amounts of financial liabilities presented in the statement of financial position	Related amounts not set off in the statement of financial position		(e)=(c)–(d) Net amount
		(d)(i), (d)(ii) Financial instruments	(d)(ii) Cash collateral pledged	
Counterparty A	–	–	–	–
Counterparty B	80	(80)	–	–
Counterparty C	80	(80)	–	–
Other	–	–	–	–
Total	160	(160)	–	–

BP provides the following disclosures about the extent of its offsetting.

Extract 54.12: BP p.l.c. (2018)

Notes on financial statements [extract]

29. Financial instruments and financial risk factors [extract]

(b) Credit risk [extract]

Financial instruments subject to offsetting, enforceable master netting arrangements and similar agreements

The following table shows the amounts recognized for financial assets and liabilities which are subject to offsetting arrangements on a gross basis and the amounts offset in the balance sheet.

Amounts which cannot be offset under IFRS, but which could be settled net under the terms of master netting agreements if certain conditions arise, and collateral received or pledged, are also presented in the table to show the total net exposure of the group.

$ million

At 31 December 2018	Gross amounts of recognized financial assets (liabilities)	Amounts set off	Net amounts presented on the balance sheet	Related amounts not set off in the balance sheet		Net amount
				Master netting arrangements	Cash collateral (received) pledged	
Derivative assets	11,502	(2,511)	8,991	(2,079)	(299)	6,613
Derivative liabilities	(11,337)	2,511	(8,826)	2,079	–	(6,747)
Trade and other receivables	11,296	(5,390)	5,906	(1,020)	(169)	4,717
Trade and other payables	(10,797)	5,390	(5,407)	1,020	–	(4,387)

7.4.3 Assets and liabilities

IAS 1 does not prescribe the order or format in which items are to be presented on the face of the statement of financial position, but states that the following items relating to financial instruments, are sufficiently different in nature or function to warrant separate presentation: [IAS 1.54, 57]

- trade and other receivables;
- cash and cash equivalents;
- other financial assets;
- trade and other payables;
- provisions; and
- other financial liabilities.

IAS 1 does not list the loss allowance in respect of financial assets measured at amortised cost as an amount to be separately presented on the face of the statement.[24] Rather, it is an integral part of the amortised cost measurement. [IAS 1.33]. However, additional line items, headings and subtotals should be presented on the face of the statement of financial position when the size, nature or function of an item or aggregation of similar items is such that separate presentation is relevant to an understanding of the entity's financial position. Additional line items may also be presented by disaggregating the line items noted above. [IAS 1.55, 57(a)].

Any additional subtotals presented should: *[IAS 1.55A]*
- comprise line items made up of amounts recognised and measured in accordance with IFRS;
- be presented and labelled in a manner that makes the line items that constitute the subtotal clear and understandable;
- be consistent from period to period, as required by IAS 1 (see Chapter 3 at 4.1.4); and
- not be displayed with more prominence than the subtotals and totals required in IFRS for the statement of financial position.

The judgement on whether additional items are presented separately should be based on an assessment of: *[IAS 1.58]*
- the nature and liquidity of assets;
- the function of assets within the entity; and
- the amounts, nature and timing of liabilities.

The descriptions used and the ordering of items or aggregation of similar items may be amended according to the nature of the entity and its transactions, to provide information that is relevant to an understanding of the entity's financial position. For example, a financial institution may amend the descriptions to provide information that is relevant to the operations of a financial institution. *[IAS 1.57(b)]*. Consequently entities need not necessarily use categorisations that are the same as the measurement categories in IFRS 9, something that was stated explicitly in IAS 39.[25]

However, the use of different measurement bases for different classes of assets suggests that their nature or function differs and, therefore, that they should be presented as separate line items. *[IAS 1.59]*. For example, financial assets measured at amortised cost would normally be presented separately from debt instruments measured at fair value through other comprehensive income, particularly by a financial institution.

As noted at 7.1.4 above, IFRS 9 explicitly states that it does not address whether embedded derivatives should be presented separately in the statement of financial position. *[IFRS 9.4.3.4]*. Although the guidance in the previous paragraph suggests that embedded derivatives will often be presented separately on the face of the statement of financial position, this will not always be the case, e.g. for the 'puttable instruments' shown in Example 54.21 at 7.4.6 below, which is based on IAS 32.

Further sub-classifications of the line items presented should be disclosed, either on the face of the statement of financial position or in the notes, classified in a manner appropriate to the entity's operations. *[IAS 1.77]*. The detail provided in sub-classifications will depend on the size, nature and function of the amounts involved and will vary for each item. For example, receivables should be disaggregated into amounts receivable from trade customers, receivables from related parties and other amounts. Assets included within receivables that are not financial instruments, such as many prepayments, should also be shown separately. *[IAS 1.78(b)]*.

7.4.3.A   Supply chain financing and reverse factoring arrangements – introduction

An increasingly common type of arrangement involves the provision of finance linked to the supply of goods or services which can be referred to be a variety of names including 'supply-chain finance', 'supplier finance', and 'structured payable transactions' which to some extent reflects the wide variety of such arrangements. One of more common types of arrangement, often referred to as 'reverse factoring', will typically contain a number of the following features:

- the involvement of a purchaser of goods and/or services, a group of its suppliers and a financial intermediary which enter into tri-partite or a series of bilateral agreements;
- the purchaser is often a large, creditworthy entity that uses a number of suppliers, many of which will have a higher credit risk than the purchaser;
- the arrangement is nearly always initiated by the purchaser rather than the supplier;
- the arrangements operate continuously for all future purchases until the arrangement is cancelled;
- they are often put in place in connection with the purchaser attempting to secure extended payment terms from its suppliers;
- the intermediary/service provider is often a financial institution who will normally make available IT systems to facilitate the arrangement (or secure another party to do this);
- the intermediary makes available to suppliers an optional invoice discounting or factoring facility for invoices accepted or agreed by the purchaser, often on terms that enable the supplier to derecognise the receivable;
- the purchaser will commit to pay the invoice on the due date, sometimes by using a payment facility operated by the intermediary which may be called an irrevocable payment undertaking;
- interest and cross-default terms are included in the supply agreement to protect the intermediary in the event of the purchaser defaulting or missing the payment date;
- those interest terms will be similar to ones included in most supply agreements, although they are rarely enforced by suppliers;
- the credit risk the intermediary is taking on is that of the purchaser, but it may be able to charge a higher financing cost to the supplier (in the form of the discount) than it would if lending to the supplier directly; and
- it can be difficult to determine the overall financing costs of the arrangement, and who bears those costs, especially if the supply involves items for which the pricing is subjective/unobservable.

The primary accounting concern with these types of arrangement is whether the purchaser should present the resulting financial liability as a trade or similar payable or as a debt-like liability. This determination could have a significant impact on the purchaser's financial position, particularly its leverage or gearing ratios. However, as can be seen from the guidance at 7.4.3 above, and as acknowledged by the IASB, debt is neither defined in, nor required to be disclosed by, IFRS. *[IAS 7.BC11]*. In fact, the need for clear disclosure of complex supplier arrangements under IFRS is something that has been emphasised by a number of European and US regulators.[26]

More recently, in early 2020, Moody's Investors Service wrote to the Interpretations Committee highlighting their concerns about the classification and disclosure of liabilities and liquidity risks arising from supply chain financing arrangements such as reverse factoring and asked the committee to consider providing guidance.[27] The committee soon started to discuss this topic and in June 2020 issued a tentative agenda decision setting out its analysis of:

- how an entity presents liabilities to which reverse factoring arrangements relate (i.e. how it presents liabilities to pay for goods or services received when the related invoices are part of a reverse factoring arrangement); and
- what information about reverse factoring arrangements an entity should disclose in its financial statements.

The committee described reverse factoring arrangements simply as ones in which a financial institution agrees to pay amounts an entity owes to the entity's suppliers and the entity agrees to pay the financial institution at a date later than suppliers are paid. It addressed four separate matters: presentation in the statement of financial position; derecognition of a financial liability; presentation in the statement of cash flows; and notes to the financial statements which are covered in turn below.[28]

7.4.3.B Supply chain financing and reverse factoring arrangements – presentation in the statement of financial position

The committee noted that an entity should present trade and other payables separately from other financial liabilities. *[IAS 1.54]*. This is because they are sufficiently different in nature or function from each other to warrant separate presentation. *[IAS 1.57]*. Trade payables are liabilities to pay for goods or services that have been received or supplied and have been invoiced or formally agreed with the supplier. Some current liabilities, such as trade payables, are part of the working capital used in the entity's normal operating cycle. *[IAS 37.11(a), IAS 1.70]*. Therefore an entity should present a financial liability as a trade payable only when it:

- represents a liability to pay for goods or services;
- is invoiced or formally agreed with the supplier; and
- is part of the working capital used in the entity's normal operating cycle.

An entity should present separately items of a dissimilar nature or function unless they are immaterial. *[IAS 1.29]*. Also, line items should be included in the statement of financial position when the size, nature or function of an item (or aggregation of similar items) is such that separate presentation is relevant to an understanding of the entity's financial position. *[IAS 1.57]*. Accordingly, an entity should present:

- other payables together with trade payables only when those other payables have a similar nature and function to trade payables, for example when other payables are part of the working capital used in the entity's normal operating cycle; and
- liabilities that are part of a reverse factoring arrangement separately when the size, nature or function of those liabilities makes separate presentation relevant to an understanding of the entity's financial position.

    In assessing whether to present such liabilities separately (including whether to disaggregate trade and other payables) an entity should consider the amounts, nature and timing of those liabilities. *[IAS 1.55, 58]*.

When assessing whether to present liabilities that are part of a reverse factoring arrangement separately an entity might consider factors including, for example:

- whether additional security is provided as part of the arrangement that would not be provided without the arrangement; and
- whether the terms of liabilities that are part of the arrangement are substantially different from the terms of the entity's trade payables that are not part of the arrangement.[29]

7.4.3.C Supply chain financing and reverse factoring arrangements – derecognition of a financial liability

The tentative agenda decision explains that an entity should assess whether and when to derecognise a liability that is (or becomes) part of a reverse factoring arrangement by applying the derecognition requirements in IFRS 9 (see Chapter 52 at 6.2 and at 6.5). If a trade payable to a supplier is derecognised and a new financial liability to a financial institution recognised, the entity should determine how to present that new liability in its statement of financial position by applying IAS 1 as set out at 7.4.3.B above.[30]

7.4.3.D Supply chain financing and reverse factoring arrangements – presentation in the statement of cash flows

The tentative agenda decision explains that cash flows from a reverse factoring arrangement should be classified as operating or financing. However, this omits the possibility of the cost of goods or services forming part of the cost of an item of property, plant or equipment, or maybe an intangible asset, in which case the cash flow would be classified as either investing or financing.

The committee observed that the nature of the liabilities that are part of the arrangement may help in determining the nature of the related cash flows as arising from operating or financing activities. For example, if the related liability is considered to be a trade or other payable that is part of the working capital used in the entity's principal revenue-producing activities, payments to settle the liability would be classified as operating (or possibly investing). In contrast, if the related liability is not a trade or other payable because the liability represents borrowings, payments to settle the liability would be classified as financing.

Investing and financing transactions that do not require the use of cash or cash equivalents should be excluded from the statement of cash flows. Consequently, if a cash inflow and cash outflow occur when an invoice is factored as part of a reverse factoring arrangement, those cash flows are presented in the statement of cash flows. If no cash flows are involved the transaction should be disclosed elsewhere in the financial statements in a way that provides all the relevant information about the financing activity (see 7.4.3.E below). *[IAS 7.43]*.[31]

The treatment of reverse factoring arrangements in the statement of cash flows is discussed further in Chapter 40 at 4.4.6.

7.4.3.E Supply chain financing and reverse factoring arrangements – notes to the financial statements

The committee highlighted a number of disclosure requirements that could be relevant for reverse factoring arrangements. Firstly, IAS 7 – *Statement of Cash Flows* – requires disclosures that enable users of financial statements to evaluate changes in liabilities arising from financing activities, including both changes arising from cash flows and non-cash changes. *[IAS 7.44A]*. This will be relevant if the cash flows for liabilities that are part of a reverse factoring arrangement were, or future cash flows will be, classified as financing.

Next, reverse factoring arrangements will often give rise to liquidity risk because:

- the entity will have concentrated a portion of its liabilities with one financial institution rather than a diverse group of suppliers.

    The entity may also obtain other sources of funding from the financial institution which could increase the risk of the entity having to pay a significant amount, at one time, to one counterparty, especially if it were to encounter any difficulty in meeting its obligations; or

- some suppliers may have become accustomed to, or reliant on, earlier payment of their trade receivables under the reverse factoring arrangement.

    If the financial institution were to withdraw the reverse factoring arrangement, those suppliers could demand shorter credit terms which could affect the entity's ability to settle liabilities, particularly if the entity were already in financial distress.

In this context the committee drew attention to the requirements in IFRS 7, addressed in more detail at 5.4 above, for an entity to disclose how exposures to risk arising from financial instruments (including liquidity risk) arise, what the entity's objectives, policies and processes are for managing the risk, summary quantitative data about the entity's exposure to liquidity risk at the end of the reporting period (including further information if this data is unrepresentative of the entity's exposure to liquidity risk during the period) and concentrations of risk.

The committee also observed that an entity should:

- disclose the judgements that management has made in assessing how to present liabilities and cash flows related to reverse factoring arrangements if those judgements are among the ones that have the most significant effect on the amounts recognised in the financial statements; and *[IAS 1.122]*
- provide information about reverse factoring arrangements to the extent they have a material effect on an entity's financial statements and such information is relevant to an understanding of those financial statements. *[IAS 1.112]*.

Finally in this context, the committee noted that making materiality judgements involves both quantitative and qualitative considerations.[32]

7.4.3.F Supply chain financing and reverse factoring arrangements – summary and example disclosure

Determining the appropriate presentation of liabilities that are part of reverse factoring arrangements, the presentation of related cash flows, and the information to be disclosed in the notes about, for example, liquidity risks that arise in such arrangements will require the application of judgement. However, the committee tentatively concluded that IFRS provides an adequate basis for an entity to make these judgements and therefore the matter should not be added to its standard-setting agenda. The committee provided an extended comment period with responses due to be submitted by the end of September 2020.

The committee was also asked for views on whether a narrow-scope standard setting project should be carried out to develop disclosure requirements for arrangements entered into to fund payables to suppliers. However, no formal decisions were made during the meeting nor, at the time of writing, had any such decisions been made.[33]

AstraZeneca includes in its annual report and financial statements the following information about its supply chain financing arrangements which has been identified as an example of good disclosure by the company's local regulatory body.[34]

Extract 54.13: AstraZeneca PLC (2019)

Business Review [extract]

Supply chain management [extract]

Supply chain financing

AstraZeneca has a supply chain finance programme to support the cash flow of its supply base. This programme, supported by Taulia Inc. and Greensill Capital, provides suppliers with visibility of invoices and payment dates. Suppliers can access this platform free of charge and have full optionality and flexibility on an invoice-by-invoice basis to request early payment of invoices. On election of an early payment, a charge is incurred by the supplier based on the period of acceleration, central bank interest rate, and the rate agreed between Taulia Inc. and each supplier. All early payments are paid by Greensill Capital, and AstraZeneca settles the original invoice amount with Greensill Capital at maturity of the original invoice due date.

We believe this programme offers a benefit to our suppliers, as it provides visibility and flexibility to manage their cash flow, and the rates offered can be preferential to their cost of funding. The programme is live in the US, UK, Sweden and Germany. As of December 2019, the programme had 3,032 suppliers enrolled and a potential early payment balance of $492 million.

For more information on supply chain financing, see Note 20 on page 199

Notes to the Group Financial Statements [extract]

20 Trade and other payables [extracts]

	2019 $m	2018 $m	2017 $m
Current liabilities			
Trade payables	1,774	1,720	2,285
Value-added and payroll taxes and social security	323	204	243
Rebates, chargebacks, returns and other revenue accruals	4,410	4,043	3,264
Clinical trial accruals	736	993	922
Other accruals	4,026	3,951	3,324
Collaboration revenue contract liabilities	28	92	–
Contingent consideration	897	867	555
Other payables	1,793	971	1,048
Total	13,987	12,841	11,641

> Trade payables includes $492m (2018: $166m; 2017: $64m) due to suppliers that have signed up to a supply chain financing programme, under which the suppliers can elect on an invoice-by-invoice basis to receive a discounted early payment from the partner bank rather than being paid in line with the agreed payment terms. If the option is taken the Group's liability is assigned by the supplier to be due to the partner bank rather than the supplier. The value of the liability payable by the Group remains unchanged. The Group assesses the arrangement against indicators to assess if debts which vendors have sold to the funder under the supplier financing scheme continue to meet the definition of trade payables or should be classified as borrowings. At 31 December 2019 the payables met the criteria of Trade payables.

7.4.4 The distinction between current and non-current assets and liabilities

For entities presenting a statement of financial position that distinguishes between current and non-current assets and liabilities, the requirements of IAS 1 for determining whether items are classified as current or non-current are dealt with in Chapter 3 at 3.1.1 to 3.1.4. This section deals with five interpretive issues that have arisen in applying those requirements to financial instruments, some of which have resulted in amendments being made to IAS 1.

7.4.4.A Derivatives

IAS 1 requires assets and liabilities held 'primarily for the purpose of trading' to be classified as current. *[IAS 1.66, 69]*. Where a derivative is not designated as a hedging instrument in an effective hedge, it is classified by IFRS 9 as held for trading irrespective of the purpose for which it is held (see Chapter 48 at 4). *[IFRS 9 Appendix A]*. This does not mean that any derivative not designated as a hedging instrument in an effective hedge must always be classified as current because the IFRS 9 classification is for measurement purposes only. Whilst a derivative held primarily for trading purposes should be presented as current regardless of its maturity date, other derivatives should be classified as current or non-current on the basis of their settlement date. Accordingly, derivatives that have maturities of less than 12 months from the end of the reporting period, or derivatives that have maturities of more than 12 months from the end of the reporting period but are expected to be settled within 12 months should be presented as a current asset or liability. Conversely, derivatives that have a maturity of more than twelve months and are expected to be held for more than twelve months after the reporting period should be presented as non-current assets or liabilities. *[IAS 1.BC38I, BC38J]*.

Although the Interpretations Committee and the IASB have considered how to split into current and non-current components the carrying amount of derivatives with staggered payment dates, both have decided not to address this issue. Consequently, entities will need to apply judgement in determining an appropriate split. For example, the current component of a five-year interest rate swap with interest payments exchanged quarterly could be determined as the present value of the net interest cash flows of the swap for the forthcoming twelve months after the reporting date.[35]

7.4.4.B Convertible loans

Where an entity issues convertible bonds that are accounted for as an equity component (i.e. the holders' rights to convert the bonds into a fixed number of the issuer's equity instruments) and a liability component (i.e. the entity's obligation to deliver cash to holders at the maturity date), the issue arises whether the liability component should be classified as current or non-current if the conversion option may be exercised at any time before maturity. The extant version of IAS 1 explains that any terms of a liability which could, at the option of the counterparty, result in its settlement by the issue of equity instruments do not affect its classification. *[IAS 1.69(d)]*. In other words, provided the entity could not be required to settle the liability component in cash within one year, it would be classified as non-current even if the holder could exercise the conversion option (thereby requiring the liability component to be derecognised) within one year.

It has not been clear whether a similar approach could be applied to convertible bonds and similar instruments for which the conversion option is classified as a liability. However, in January 2020, the IASB amended IAS 1 to clarify that the potential settlement of a liability by the issue of equity instruments does affect its classification unless it arises from a counterparty conversion option recognised separately from the liability as an equity component of a compound financial instrument. *[IAS 1(2023).76A, 76B]*. This amendment, adoption of which is required for periods beginning on or after 1 January 2023, is likely to change some entities' presentation of, for example, convertible bonds that are denominated in a currency other than their functional currency and for which the conversion option is accounted for as an embedded derivative.

7.4.4.C   Long-term loans with repayment on demand terms

IAS 1 requires liabilities for which the entity does not have an unconditional right to defer settlement for at least twelve months after the reporting date to be classified as current. *[IAS 1.69(d)]*. Some long-term loan agreements, particularly in Hong Kong, contain clauses allowing the lender an absolute right to demand repayment at any time before maturity. Historically, borrowers often approached these clauses in the same way as more conventional covenants because the risk of exercise was considered very low (except in situations that might adversely affect the borrower's ability to repay). Consequently, the clause would result in classification of a loan as current only if such adverse matters relating to the borrower existed at the end of the reporting period.[36]

However, in 2010, the Interpretations Committee addressed this situation, noting that the requirements of IAS 1 are clear, i.e. such terms should always result in the loan being classified as current.[37]

7.4.4.D   Debt with refinancing or roll over agreements

The extant version of IAS 1 states that if an entity expects, and has the discretion, to refinance or roll over an obligation for at least twelve months after the reporting period under an existing loan facility, the obligation should be classified as non-current even if it would otherwise be due within a shorter period *[IAS 1.73]* and the Interpretations Committee and IASB have been considering the circumstances in which this guidance should apply for some time.

One particular area of concern has been the classification of liabilities arising from a short-term commercial paper programme that is backed by a long-term loan facility. In these arrangements the commercial paper is typically issued for a term of 90 or 180 days; the issuer will normally attempt to issue new instruments to replace those maturing; and a bank (often the sponsor or manager of the scheme) will have provided the entity with a longer-term loan facility that may be drawn down if any issue of commercial paper is under-subscribed. In this situation, *prima facie* the entity has in place an agreement (the loan facility) that can be used to refinance the short-term liability (from the commercial paper) on a long-term basis and might consider classifying the liability arising from commercial paper as non-current.

However, in January 2011 after analysing outreach requests, the Interpretations Committee noted that there was no charted diversity in practice where an agreement is reached to refinance an existing borrowing with a different lender – here paragraph 73 is not considered applicable, whatever the terms of the new facility, and the existing borrowing would be classified as current. Therefore the commercial paper liabilities should be classified as current.[38] In January 2020 the IASB amended IAS 1 to remove the reference in paragraph 73 to 'refinance' and bring the wording of the standard into line with the committee's view on how it should be (and is being) applied.

7.4.4.E   Loan covenants

If an entity does not have an unconditional right to defer settlement of the liability for at least twelve months after the reporting period the liability should be reported as current. *[IAS 1.69(d)]*. Further, when an entity breaches a provision of a long-term loan arrangement (commonly called a covenant) on or before the end of the reporting period with the effect that the liability becomes payable on demand, the liability should be classified as current because, at the end of the reporting period, it does not have an unconditional right to defer settlement for at least twelve months after that date. *[IAS 1.73]*.

The application of these requirements, including in some commonly occurring situations, has sometimes proved challenging and the IASB in January 2020 issued clarifying amendments to IAS 1, adoption of which is required for periods beginning on or after 1 January 2023. These requirements are discussed in more detail in Chapter 3 at 3.1.4.

7.4.5   Equity

IAS 1 explains that the face of the statement of financial position should include line items that present the following amounts within equity: *[IAS 1.54(q), (r)]*

- non-controlling interests, presented within equity; and
- issued capital and reserves attributable to owners of the parent.

As for assets and liabilities, additional line items, headings and subtotals should be presented on the face of the statement of financial position when such presentation is relevant to an understanding of the entity's financial position and additional line items may also be presented by disaggregating the line items noted above. *[IAS 1.55]*. Further sub-classifications of the line items presented should be disclosed, either on the face of the statement of financial position or in the notes, classified in a manner appropriate to the entity's operations. *[IAS 1.77]*. The detail provided in the sub-classifications will depend on the size, nature and function of the amounts involved and will vary for each item. For example, equity capital and reserves should be disaggregated into various classes, such as paid-in capital, share premium and reserves. *[IAS 1.78(e)]*. A description of the nature and purpose of each reserve within equity should also be provided. *[IAS 1.79(b)]*.

For each class of share capital, the following information should be disclosed, either on the face of the statement of financial position or in the notes: [IAS 1.79(a)]

- the number of shares authorised;
- the number of shares issued and fully paid, and issued but not fully paid;
- par value per share, or that the shares have no par value;
- a reconciliation of the number of shares outstanding at the beginning and at the end of the period;
- the rights, preferences and restrictions attaching to that class including restrictions on the distribution of dividends and the repayment of capital;
- shares in the entity held by the entity or by its subsidiaries (treasury shares [IAS 32.34]) or associates; and
- shares reserved for issue under options and contracts for the sale of shares, including the terms and amounts.

An entity without share capital, such as a partnership or trust, should disclose equivalent information, showing changes during the period in each category of equity interest, and the rights, preferences and restrictions attaching to each category of equity interest, [IAS 1.80], (assuming of course it has actually issued instruments that meet the definition of equity).

Where puttable financial instruments and obligations arising on liquidation (see Chapter 47 at 4.6) are reclassified between financial liabilities and equity, entities are required to disclose the amount reclassified into and out of each category and the timing and reason for that reclassification. [IAS 1.80A]. This requirement was introduced by the amendments to IAS 32 and IAS 1 dealing with the classification of puttable financial instruments and obligations arising on liquidation.

7.4.6 Entities whose share capital is not equity

Continuing Example 54.18 and Example 54.19 at 7.1.5 above, the following examples illustrate corresponding statement of financial position formats that may be used by entities such as mutual funds that do not have equity as defined in IAS 32, or entities such as co-operatives whose share capital is not equity as defined in IAS 32 because the entity has an obligation to repay the share capital on demand.

Example 54.21: Statement of financial position format for a mutual fund

Statement of financial position at 31 December 2021 [IAS 32.IE32]

	2021 €	2021 €	2020 €	2020 €
ASSETS				
Non-current assets (classified in accordance with IAS 1)	91,374		78,484	
Total non-current assets		91,374		78,484
Current assets (classified in accordance with IAS 1)	1,422		1,769	
Total current assets		1,422		1,769
Total assets		92,796		80,253

LIABILITIES				
Current liabilities (classified in accordance with IAS 1)	647		66	
Total current liabilities		(647)		(66)
Non-current liabilities excluding net assets attributable to unit holders (classified in accordance with IAS 1)	280		136	
		(280)		(136)
Net assets attributable to unit holders		91,869		80,051

As for the equivalent income statement format, it may not be immediately clear what the final line item in this format represents. It is, in fact, a liability and therefore the entity's 'equity' (as that term is used in IAS 1) at the end of 2021 is €92,796 – €647 – €280 – €91,869 = €nil.

Example 54.22: *Statement of financial position format for a co-operative*

Statement of financial position at 31 December 2021 *[IAS 32.IE33]*	2021		2020	
	€	€	€	€
ASSETS				
Non-current assets (classified in accordance with IAS 1)	908		830	
Total non-current assets		908		830
Current assets (classified in accordance with IAS 1)	383		350	
Total current assets		383		350
Total assets		1,291		1,180
LIABILITIES				
Current liabilities (classified in accordance with IAS 1)	372		338	
Share capital repayable on demand	202		161	
Total current liabilities		(574)		(499)
Total assets less current liabilities		717		681
Non-current liabilities (classified in accordance with IAS 1)	187		196	
		187		196
RESERVES*				
Reserves, e.g. revaluation reserve, retained earnings	530		485	
		530		485
		717		681
MEMORANDUM NOTE				
TOTAL MEMBERS' INTERESTS				
Share capital repayable on demand		202		161
Reserves		530		485
		732		646

* In this example, the entity has no obligation to deliver a share of its reserves to its members.

The line item 'Share capital repayable on demand' is part of the entity's liabilities and the items within 'Reserves' represent its equity.

Although not required by IAS 1, an entity adopting this type of format for its statement of financial position may choose to present an analysis of movements in (or reconciliation of) total members' interests (often defined as equity plus share capital repayable on demand, perhaps adjusted for other balances with members) if this is considered to provide useful information; this would not remove the need to present a statement of changes in equity.

7.5 Statement of cash flows

The implementation guidance to IFRS 9 acknowledges that the terminology in IAS 7 was not updated to reflect publication of the standard, but does explain that the classification of cash flows arising from hedging instruments within the statement of cash flows should be consistent with the classification of these instruments as hedging instruments. In other words, such cash flows should be classified as operating, investing or financing activities, on the basis of the classification of the cash flows arising from the hedged item. [IFRS 9.IG G.2].

The classification of cash flows arising from supply chain financing and reverse factoring arrangements has been considered by the IFRS Interpretations Committee. This is discussed at 7.4.3.D above, alongside other presentation and disclosure aspects of such arrangements.

8 EFFECTIVE DATES AND TRANSITIONAL PROVISIONS

In September 2019 and August 2020, the IASB issued amendments to IFRS 9 (and IAS 39) designed to mitigate the accounting effects of IBOR reform and at the same time made consequential amendments to IFRS 7 (see 4.3.5 and 5.7 respectively above). The amendments are effective for periods commencing on or after 1 January 2020 and 1 January 2021 respectively with earlier application permitted, albeit an entity would be required to disclose it had done so. [IFRS 7.44DE, 44GG]. In the reporting period in which these amendments are first applied an entity is not required to present the quantitative information required by paragraph 28(f) of IAS 8, i.e. information about the amount of any adjustment to financial statement line items and earning per share figures in the current and comparative periods from applying the amendments. [IFRS 7.44DF, 44HH]. The amendments to IFRS 9 are to be applied largely retrospectively, although entities need not restate comparatives when first applying the second set of amendments. If comparatives are not restated, the disclosures addressed at 5.7 above need not be given for the comparative period. [IFRS 7.BC350].

IAS 1 was amended in January 2020 to clarify when financial liabilities should be classified as current or non-current (see 7.4.4.B, 7.4.4.D and 7.4.4.E above). The amendments are effective for periods commencing on or after 1 January 2023 and should be applied retrospectively in accordance with IAS 8. Earlier application is permitted, although an entity would be required to disclose it had done so. [IAS 1(2023).136U].

9 FUTURE DEVELOPMENTS

9.1 General developments

Disclosure requirements are considered important by the IASB and those in respect of financial instruments have been expanded significantly as a result of changes made following the financial crisis. However, it seems unlikely that further major changes to IFRS 7 will be forthcoming in the near term.

At the time of writing the world was coming to terms with the effects of the coronavirus pandemic and companies were addressing the associated financial reporting effects. The IASB has emphasised that disclosures about expected credit losses, along with the requirements of IFRS 9, can help provide much needed transparency to users of financial statements[39] and this will be a continuing area of focus for companies and regulators. A number of regulators published guidance in the first half of 2020 emphasising the importance of clear and transparent disclosures in interim reports, particularly in respect of entities' exposure to credit risk and the determination of expected credit loss provisions. It therefore seems extremely likely that more regulatory pronouncements will be forthcoming as the main 2020 reporting season approaches. These may well include guidance on:

- identifying and providing appropriate disclosures about concentrations of credit risk, potentially including additional information by geography or sector especially for exposures to those industries such as airlines, hospitality and tourism that are more exposed to the coronavirus pandemic;
- highlighting changes in liquidity risk exposures such as any increase in the risk of breaching loan covenants or being unable to refinance maturing loans;
- significant estimates and judgements, particularly when estimating expected credit loss provisions which for lenders might include the values of the key macroeconomic inputs used in the multiple economic scenario analysis and the probability weights of these scenarios, as well as the assumptions used to determine how the different challenges for specific sectors and regions have been taken into account and the effect of any management overlays; and
- for lenders, the impact of material reliefs such as payment holidays provided to borrowers, including how that has manifested itself in the accounting treatment.

The IASB's disclosure initiative (see Chapter 3 at 6.2.3) may influence the way entities present their disclosures about financial instruments. Initiatives by other bodies, such as reports and surveys of the Enhanced Disclosure Task Force of the Financial Stability Board (see 9.2 below) and the Basel Committee on Banking Supervision, may also influence the disclosures provided, particularly by financial institutions, as could other regulatory actions and initiatives. In addition, we may see a gradual evolution of disclosure requirements in the light of practical experience. For example, as discussed at 7.4.3.F above, the IFRS Interpretations Committee was asked for views in June 2020 on whether a narrow-scope standard setting project should be carried out to develop disclosure requirements for arrangements entered into to fund payables to suppliers. However, at the time of writing, no decisions had been made.

In the longer term, any new accounting requirements arising from the IASB's projects addressing financial instruments with the characteristics of equity (see Chapter 47 at 12) and macro hedge accounting (see Chapter 53 at 11) will likely result in extensive new disclosure requirements.

9.2 Enhanced Disclosure Task Force

The Enhanced Disclosure Task Force ('EDTF') was a private sector group comprising representatives from financial institutions, investors and analysts, credit rating agencies and external auditors. It was formed by the Financial Stability Forum in May 2012 and its objectives included the development of principles for enhanced disclosures about market conditions and risks, including ways to enhance the comparability of those disclosures and identifying those disclosures seen as leading practice.

In October 2012 the EDTF issued its first report – *Enhancing the Risk Disclosures of Banks* – in which seven fundamental principles for achieving enhanced risk disclosures were identified, namely that disclosures should:

- be clear, balanced and understandable;
- be comprehensive and include all of the bank's key activities and risks;
- present relevant information;
- reflect how the bank manages its risks;
- be consistent over time;
- be comparable among banks; and
- be provided on a timely basis.

The report also identified 32 detailed recommendations for enhancing risk disclosures, grouped under the following subjects (as well as addressing more general matters):

- risk governance and risk management strategies/business model;
- capital adequacy and risk-weighted assets;
- liquidity;
- funding;
- market risk;
- credit risk; and
- other risks.

These were accompanied by illustrative examples as well as observations on and extracts from recent reports issued by banks and were followed by three further reports charting the progress of a number of banks in applying the principles and recommendations set out in the first report. The latest of these reports noted that banks should continue to improve their credit risk disclosures. In November 2015, a few months before the EDTF was disbanded having completed its work, it published another report – *Impact of Expected Credit Loss Approaches on Bank Risk Disclosures* – containing guidance for banks in this area.

The aims of the November 2015 guidance were to enhance banks' disclosures, help the market understand the then upcoming change in provisioning based on expected credit losses (whether under IFRS or US GAAP) and promote consistency and comparability of disclosures across internationally-active banks. It built on the existing fundamental principles and recommendations noted above and addressed the following key areas of user focus:

- concepts, interpretations and policies developed to implement the new expected credit loss approaches, including the significant credit deterioration assessment required by IFRS 9;
- the specific methodologies and estimation techniques developed;
- the impact of moving from an incurred to an expected credit loss approach;
- understanding the dynamics of changes in impairment allowances and their sensitivity to significant assumptions, including those as a result of the application of macro-economic assumptions;
- any changes made to the governance over financial reporting, and how they link with existing governance over other areas including credit risk management and regulatory reporting; and
- understanding the differences between the expected credit losses applied in the financial statements and those used in determining regulatory capital.

In particular, it contained additional considerations regarding the application of certain of the existing 32 recommendations. Some of these were temporary, addressing the transition to an expected credit loss framework, and some are more permanent which will continue to apply following the adoption of the new accounting standards.

Whilst the EDTF is not a standard setter and its recommendations are not mandatory, regulators in a number of countries have strongly encouraged their implementation, and analysts, investors and other stakeholders continue to show an interest in them. Whilst some of the recommended disclosures overlap with those required by IFRS 7, many of them are not included in any other framework or authoritative guidance. Also, although the recommendations are designed for large international banks, they should be equally relevant for other banks that actively access the major public equity or debt markets. Therefore all major banks should assess the availability and quality of data that are necessary to provide these disclosures and, more generally, the full range of the EDTF disclosures.

References

1 IFRS 7, Appendix B, Application guidance, para. after main heading.
2 IFRS 7, Guidance on implementing, para. after main heading.
3 Transition Resource Group for Impairment of Financial Instruments, *Meeting Summary – 16 September 2015*, IASB, September 2015, para. 48.
4 Transition Resource Group for Impairment of Financial Instruments, *Meeting Summary – 11 December 2015*, IASB, December 2015, para. 46.
5 Transition Resource Group for Impairment of Financial Instruments, *Meeting Summary – 22 April 2015*, IASB, April 2015, para. 57(b).
6 Transition Resource Group for Impairment of Financial Instruments, *Meeting Summary – 11 December 2015*, IASB, December 2015, para. 64.
7 Information for Observers (January 2009 IASB Meeting), *Proposed amendments on liquidity risk disclosures (Agenda paper 14B)*, IASB, January 2009, para. 32.

8 Information for Observers (September 2008 IASB Meeting), *IFRS 7 Financial Instruments: Disclosures, Liquidity risk (Agenda paper 2A)*, IASB, September 2008, para. 34(b) and Information for Observers (January 2009 IASB Meeting), *Proposed amendments on liquidity risk disclosures (Agenda paper 14B)*, IASB, January 2009, para. 35(a).
9 Information for Observers (September 2008 IASB Meeting), *IFRS 7 Financial Instruments: Disclosures, Liquidity risk (Agenda paper 2A)*, IASB, September 2008, para. 34(c).
10 Information for Observers (September 2008 IASB Meeting), *IFRS 7 Financial Instruments: Disclosures, Liquidity risk (Agenda paper 2A)*, IASB, September 2008, paras. 40 and 41.
11 Information for Observers (September 2008 IASB Meeting), *IFRS 7 Financial Instruments: Disclosures, Liquidity risk (Agenda paper 2A)*, IASB, September 2008, para. 34(d).
12 Information for Observers (September 2008 IASB Meeting), *IFRS 7 Financial Instruments: Disclosures, Liquidity risk (Agenda paper 2A)*, IASB, September 2008, para. 25.
13 Information for Observers (December 2008 IASB Meeting), *IFRS 7 Financial Instruments: Disclosures – Minor Amendments (Agenda paper 14)*, IASB, December 2008, paras. 71 to 79 and *IASB Update*, December 2008.
14 Information for Observers (December 2008 IASB Meeting), *IFRS 7 Financial Instruments: Disclosures – Minor Amendments (Agenda paper 14)*, IASB, December 2008, para. 86.
15 Information for Observers (December 2008 IASB Meeting), *IFRS 7 Financial Instruments: Disclosures – Minor Amendments (Agenda paper 14)*, IASB, December 2008, paras. 80 to 88 and *IASB Update*, December 2008.
16 *IFRIC Update*, March 2018.
17 *IFRIC Update*, March 2019.
18 Transition Resource Group for Impairment of Financial Instruments, *Meeting Summary – 22 April 2015*, IASB, April 2015, paras. 24 and 25.
19 Transition Resource Group for Impairment of Financial Instruments, *Meeting Summary – 22 April 2015*, IASB, April 2015, para. 57(a).
20 *IFRIC Update*, October 2004 and November 2006.
21 *IFRIC Update*, January 2015.
22 *IFRIC Update*, January 2015.
23 *IFRIC Update*, March 2016.
24 Transition Resource Group for Impairment of Financial Instruments, *Meeting Summary – 11 December 2015*, IASB, December 2015, para. 77.
25 IAS 39, para. 45.
26 For example, Press Release 74/14, *FRC urges clarity in the reporting of complex supplier arrangements by retailers and other businesses*, FRC, December 2014.
27 *Classification and Disclosure of Liabilities and Liquidity Risks Arising from Supply Chain Financing Arrangements*, Moody's Investors Service, January 2020.
28 *IFRIC Update*, June 2020.
29 *IFRIC Update*, June 2020.
30 *IFRIC Update*, June 2020.
31 *IFRIC Update*, June 2020.
32 *IFRIC Update*, June 2020.
33 *IFRIC Update*, June 2020.
34 *Disclosures on the sources and uses of cash (A Lab project report)*, FRC, September 2019.
35 Information for Observers (March 2007 IFRIC meeting), *Current or non-current presentation of derivatives that are not designated as hedging instruments in effective hedges*, IASB, March 2007, paras. 14 and 17 and Information for Observers (11 March 2008 IASB meeting), *ED Annual improvements process – Comment analysis: IAS 1 Current/non-current classification of derivatives (Q6)*, IASB, March 2008, para. 12.
36 Staff Paper (September 2010 IFRS Interpretations Committee Meeting), *Current/non-current classification of callable term loan*, IASB, September 2010.
37 *IFRIC Update*, September 2010.
38 *IFRIC Update*, January 2011 and Staff Paper (January 2011 IFRS Interpretations Committee Meeting), *IAS 1 Presentation of Financial Statements – current/non-current classification of debt (rollover agreements) – outreach results*, IASB, January 2011.
39 *IFRS 9 and covid-19*, Accounting for expected credit losses applying IFRS 9 *Financial Instruments* in the light of current uncertainty resulting from the covid-19 pandemic, IASB, March 2020.

Chapter 55   Insurance contracts (IFRS 4)

1 INTRODUCTION 4533
   1.1   The history of the IASB's insurance project 4533
   1.2   The development of IFRS 4 4535
   1.3   Mitigating the impact on insurers of applying IFRS 9 before applying IFRS 17 4535
   1.4   Existing accounting practices for insurance contracts 4535
        1.4.1   Non-life insurance 4536
        1.4.2   Life insurance 4536
        1.4.3   Embedded value 4536

2 THE OBJECTIVES AND SCOPE OF IFRS 4 4537
   2.1   The objectives of IFRS 4 4537
   2.2   The scope of IFRS 4 4537
        2.2.1   Definitions 4537
        2.2.2   Transactions within the scope of IFRS 4 4538
        2.2.3   Transactions not within the scope of IFRS 4 4540
                2.2.3.A   Product warranties 4540
                2.2.3.B   Assets and liabilities arising from employment benefit plans 4541
                2.2.3.C   Contingent rights and obligations related to non-financial items 4541
                2.2.3.D   Financial guarantee contracts 4541
                2.2.3.E   Contingent consideration payable or receivable in a business combination 4542
                2.2.3.F   Direct insurance contracts in which the entity is the policyholder 4542
        2.2.4   The product classification process 4542

3 THE DEFINITION OF AN INSURANCE CONTRACT 4543

    3.1   The definition 4543
    3.2   Significant insurance risk 4544
            3.2.1   The meaning of 'significant' 4545
            3.2.2   The level at which significant insurance risk is assessed 4546
                    3.2.2.A   Self insurance 4547
                    3.2.2.B   Insurance mutuals 4547
                    3.2.2.C   Intragroup insurance contracts 4547
            3.2.3   Significant additional benefits 4548
    3.3   Changes in the level of insurance risk 4549
    3.4   Uncertain future events 4550
    3.5   Payments in kind 4550
            3.5.1   Service contracts 4550
    3.6   The distinction between insurance risk and financial risk 4551
    3.7   Adverse effect on the policyholder 4552
            3.7.1   Lapse, persistency and expense risk 4553
            3.7.2   Insurance of non-insurance risks 4553
    3.8   Accounting differences between insurance and non-insurance contracts 4554
    3.9   Examples of insurance and non-insurance contracts 4554
            3.9.1   Examples of insurance contracts 4554
            3.9.2   Examples of transactions that are not insurance contracts 4556
    3.10   Ex-gratia payments 4559
4   EMBEDDED DERIVATIVES 4559
    4.1   Unit-linked features 4563
5   UNBUNDLING OF DEPOSIT COMPONENTS 4563
    5.1   The unbundling requirements 4564
    5.2   Unbundling illustration 4564
    5.3   Practical difficulties 4567
6   DISCRETIONARY PARTICIPATION FEATURES 4568
    6.1   Discretionary participation features in insurance contracts 4571
    6.2   Discretionary participation features in financial instruments .. 4573
    6.3   Practical issues 4574
            6.3.1   Unallocated DPF liabilities which are negative 4574
            6.3.2   Contracts with switching features 4574
7   SELECTION OF ACCOUNTING POLICIES 4575
    7.1   The hierarchy exemption 4576
    7.2   Limits on the hierarchy exemption 4577
            7.2.1   Catastrophe and equalisation provisions 4577

	7.2.2	Liability adequacy testing		4578
		7.2.2.A	Using a liability adequacy test under existing accounting policies	4579
		7.2.2.B	Using the liability adequacy test specified in IFRS 4	4580
		7.2.2.C	Investment contracts with a discretionary participation feature	4581
		7.2.2.D	Interaction between the liability adequacy test and shadow accounting	4581
	7.2.3	Insurance liability derecognition		4582
	7.2.4	Offsetting of insurance and related reinsurance contracts		4583
	7.2.5	Impairment of reinsurance assets		4583
	7.2.6	Accounting policy matters not addressed by IFRS 4		4584
		7.2.6.A	Derecognition of insurance and reinsurance assets	4584
		7.2.6.B	Impairment of insurance assets	4585
		7.2.6.C	Gains and losses on buying reinsurance	4585
		7.2.6.D	Acquisition costs	4586
		7.2.6.E	Salvage and subrogation	4586
		7.2.6.F	Policy loans	4586
		7.2.6.G	Investments held in a fiduciary capacity	4587

8 CHANGES IN ACCOUNTING POLICIES 4587

8.1	Criteria for accounting policy changes			4587
8.2	Specific issues			4588
	8.2.1	Continuation of existing practices		4588
		8.2.1.A	Measuring insurance liabilities on an undiscounted basis	4588
		8.2.1.B	Measuring contractual rights to future investment management fees in excess of their fair value	4588
		8.2.1.C	Introducing non-uniform accounting policies for the insurance contracts of subsidiaries	4589
	8.2.2	Current market interest rates		4590
	8.2.3	Prudence		4590
	8.2.4	Future investment margins		4591
8.3	Shadow accounting			4592
8.4	Redesignation of financial assets			4595
8.5	Practical issues			4595
	8.5.1	Changes to local GAAP		4595

9 INSURANCE CONTRACTS ACQUIRED IN BUSINESS COMBINATIONS AND PORTFOLIO TRANSFERS 4596

9.1	Expanded presentation of insurance contracts		4596
	9.1.1	Practical issues	4598
		9.1.1.A The difference between a business combination and a portfolio transfer	4598
		9.1.1.B Fair value of an insurer's liabilities	4599
		9.1.1.C Deferred taxation	4599
		9.1.1.D Negative intangible assets	4599
9.2	Customer lists and relationships not connected to contractual insurance rights and obligations		4599

10 APPLYING IFRS 9 WITH IFRS 4 4600

10.1	The temporary exemption from IFRS 9		4601
	10.1.1	Activities that are predominantly connected with insurance	4603
	10.1.2	Initial assessment and reassessment of the temporary exemption	4606
	10.1.3	First-time adopters	4608
	10.1.4	Relief for investors in associates and joint ventures	4608
	10.1.5	Disclosures required for entities using the temporary exemption	4609
		10.1.5.A Disclosures required to understand how an insurer qualified for the temporary exemption	4610
		10.1.5.B Disclosures required in order to compare insurers applying the temporary exemption with entities applying IFRS 9	4613
	10.1.6	Interest rate benchmark reform	4616
10.2	The overlay approach		4617
	10.2.1	Designation and de-designation of eligible financial assets	4619
	10.2.2	First-time adopters	4620
	10.2.3	Disclosures required for entities applying the overlay approach	4620

11 DISCLOSURE 4621

11.1	Explanation of recognised amounts		4623
	11.1.1	Disclosure of accounting policies	4623
	11.1.2	Recognised assets, liabilities, income and expense	4626
		11.1.2.A Assets and liabilities	4626
		11.1.2.B Income and expense	4630
		11.1.2.C Cash flows	4633
	11.1.3	Gains or losses on buying reinsurance	4633
	11.1.4	Process used to determine significant assumptions	4633
	11.1.5	The effects of changes in assumptions	4637
	11.1.6	Reconciliations of changes in insurance assets and liabilities	4639

11.2	Nature and extent of risks arising from insurance contracts		4643
	11.2.1	Objectives, policies and processes for managing insurance contract risks	4645
	11.2.2	Insurance risk – general matters	4648
	11.2.3	Insurance risk – sensitivity information	4650
	11.2.4	Insurance risk – concentrations of risk	4652
	11.2.5	Insurance risk – claims development information	4654
	11.2.6	Credit risk, liquidity risk and market risk disclosures	4658
		11.2.6.A Credit risk disclosures	4658
		11.2.6.B Liquidity risk disclosures	4661
		11.2.6.C Market risk disclosures	4662
	11.2.7	Exposures to market risk from embedded derivatives	4664
	11.2.8	Other disclosure matters	4665
		11.2.8.A IAS 1 capital disclosures	4665
		11.2.8.B Financial guarantee contracts	4666
		11.2.8.C Fair value disclosures	4667
		11.2.8.D Key performance indicators	4667
12. FUTURE DEVELOPMENTS			4668

List of examples

Example 55.1:	Significant insurance risk	4545
Example 55.2:	Loan contract with prepayment fee	4548
Example 55.3:	Deferred annuity with policyholder election	4549
Example 55.4:	Residual value insurance	4551
Example 55.5:	Contract with insurance and financial risk	4552
Example 55.6:	Reinsurance contract with 'original loss warranty' clause	4553
Example 55.7:	Insurance of non-insurance risks	4553
Example 55.8:	Deferred annuity with guaranteed rates	4556
Example 55.9:	Guarantee fund established by contract	4556
Example 55.10:	Insurance contract issued to employees related to a defined contribution pension plan	4556
Example 55.11:	No market value adjustment for maturity benefits	4556
Example 55.12:	No market value adjustment for death benefits	4556
Example 55.13:	Investment contract linked to asset pool	4557
Example 55.14:	Credit-related guarantee	4557
Example 55.15:	Guarantee fund established by law	4558
Example 55.16:	Right to recover future premiums	4558
Example 55.17:	Catastrophe bond linked to index	4558
Example 55.18:	Insurance policy issued to defined benefit pension plan	4558

Example 55.19:	Market value adjustment without death or maturity benefits	4559
Example 55.20:	Death or annuitisation benefit linked to equity prices or index	4561
Example 55.21:	Life contingent annuity option	4562
Example 55.22:	Policyholder option to surrender contract for cash surrender value	4562
Example 55.23:	Policyholder option to surrender contract for value based on a market index	4562
Example 55.24:	Persistency bonus	4562
Example 55.25:	Unbundling	4564
Example 55.26:	Unbundling a deposit component of a reinsurance contract	4565
Example 55.27:	Unitised with-profits policy	4568
Example 55.28:	DPF with minimum interest rates	4568
Example 55.29:	DPF recognition	4571
Example 55.30:	Shadow loss recognition	4581
Example 55.31:	Shadow accounting	4594
Example 55.32:	Business combination under IFRS 4	4597
Example 55.33:	Purchase of portfolio of one-year motor insurance contracts	4600
Example 55.34:	Determination of eligibility for the temporary exemption at reporting entity level when the group is eligible for the temporary exemption	4602
Example 55.35:	Determination of eligibility for the temporary exemption at reporting entity level when the group is not eligible for the temporary exemption	4602
Example 55.36:	Calculation of the predominance ratio	4606
Example 55.37:	Discontinuation of the temporary exemption	4607
Example 55.38:	Illustrative disclosure explaining how an insurer qualified for the temporary exemption – where the gross liabilities within the scope of IFRS 4 exceed 90% of total liabilities	4611
Example 55.39:	Illustrative disclosure explaining how an insurer qualified for the temporary exemption – where the gross liabilities within the scope of IFRS 4 are less than 90% of total liabilities but liabilities connected with insurance are in excess of 90% of total liabilities	4611
Example 55.40:	Illustrative disclosure explaining how an insurer qualified for the temporary exemption – where the total carrying amount of liabilities connected with insurance are greater than 80% but less than 90% of total liabilities	4612
Example 55.41:	Illustrative disclosures required in order to compare insurers applying the temporary exemption with entities applying IFRS 9	4614

Example 55.42:	Disclosure of claims development	4654
Example 55.43:	Contract containing a guaranteed annuity option	4664
Example 55.44:	Contract containing minimum guaranteed death benefits	4664

Chapter 55   Insurance contracts (IFRS 4)

1 INTRODUCTION

IFRS 4 – *Insurance Contracts* – issued in March 2004, is an interim accounting standard for insurance contracts. Subsequent to the issue of IFRS 4, the IASB spent many years developing a new accounting standard for insurance contracts to address the various deficiencies within IFRS 4, including the absence of a measurement model.

The new insurance accounting standard, IFRS 17 – *Insurance Contracts* – was issued in May 2017. In June 2020, the IASB amended IFRS 17 with targeted changes to respond to concerns and challenges raised in the implementation process, including delaying the mandatory effective date to accounting periods beginning on or after 1 January 2023. When IFRS 17 is applied, IFRS 4 is withdrawn. IFRS 17 is discussed in Chapter 56. This chapter discusses only IFRS 4.

1.1 The history of the IASB's insurance project

The IASB and its predecessor, the IASC, have been developing a comprehensive standard on insurance contracts since 1997 when a Steering Committee was established to carry out the initial project work. *[IFRS 4.BC3]*. It was decided to develop a standard on insurance contracts because:

(a) there was no standard on insurance contracts, and insurance contracts were excluded from the scope of existing standards that would otherwise have been relevant; and

(b) accounting practices for insurance contracts are diverse, and also often differ from practices in other sectors. *[IFRS 4.BC2]*.

Historically, the IASB and its predecessor avoided dealing with specific accounting issues relating to insurance contracts by excluding them from the scope of their accounting standards. Currently, insurance contracts are excluded from the scope of the following standards:

- IFRS 7 – *Financial Instruments: Disclosures*;
- IFRS 9 – *Financial Instruments*;
- IFRS 15 – *Revenue from Contracts with Customers*;

- IAS 32 – *Financial Instruments: Presentation*;
- IAS 36 – *Impairment of Assets*;
- IAS 37 – *Provisions, Contingent Liabilities and Contingent Assets*;
- IAS 38 – *Intangible Assets*; and
- IAS 39 – *Financial Instruments: Recognition and Measurement*.

In addition, contractual rights from insurance contracts are excluded from the measurement requirements of IFRS 5 – *Non-current Assets Held for Sale and Discontinued Operations*.

Contracts within the scope of IFRS 4 are not excluded from the scope of IFRS 13 – *Fair Value Measurement* – which means that any reference to fair value in IFRS 4 should be fair value as defined and measured by IFRS 13. However, IFRS 4 does not require that insurance liabilities are measured at fair value.

An alternative to developing a standard on insurance contracts would have been for the IASB to remove the insurance contract scope exemptions from these standards. Revenue would then have to be measured in accordance with IFRS 15 and most insurance contract liabilities would have to be recognised in accordance with either IAS 39 or IFRS 9 or IAS 37 depending on their nature. However, the IASB and its predecessor were persuaded that an insurance contract is sufficiently unique to warrant its own accounting standard and spent many years deciding what accounting that standard should require.

The Steering Committee established in 1997 published an Issues Paper – *Insurance* – in December 1999 which attracted 138 comment letters. Following a review of the comment letters, the committee developed a report to the IASB that was published in 2001 as a *Draft Statement of Principles – Insurance Contracts* (DSOP). The DSOP was never approved. *[IFRS 4.BC3]*.

The IASB began discussing the DSOP in November 2001. However, at its May 2002 meeting the IASB concluded that it would not be realistic to expect the implementation of a full recognition and measurement standard for insurance contracts by 2005 (in time for the adoption of IFRS in the EU).[1]

Consequently, the insurance project was split into two phases: Phase I, which became IFRS 4 and Phase II, which resulted in the publication of IFRS 17 in May 2017. IFRS 17 (see Chapter 56) has an effective date applicable to accounting periods beginning on or after 1 January 2023, as discussed at 1 above.

Amendments made to IFRS 4, designed to mitigate the impact on insurers of applying IFRS 9 before applying IFRS 17, are discussed at 1.3 and 10 below.

1.2 The development of IFRS 4

IFRS 4 was finalised in a relatively short period by the IASB once it became clear that a standard was required in time for the EU adoption of IFRS in 2005. An exposure draft, ED 5 – *Insurance Contracts* – was issued in July 2003 with a comment period expiring on 31 October 2003. The IASB was extremely responsive to comment letters with most of the major concerns of the insurance industry being addressed in the final standard when it was issued in March 2004. IFRS 4 was first applicable for accounting periods beginning on or after 1 January 2005 with earlier adoption encouraged. *[IFRS 4.41]*.

1.3 Mitigating the impact on insurers of applying IFRS 9 before applying IFRS 17

The time it has taken to issue IFRS 17 means that the effective date of this standard is five years after the effective date of IFRS 9. Consequently, the IASB was asked to address concerns that additional accounting mismatches and profit or loss volatility could result if IFRS 9 was applied before the new insurance accounting standard. The IASB agreed that these concerns should be addressed and, in September 2016, issued *Applying IFRS 9 Financial Instruments with IFRS 4 Insurance Contracts* that amends IFRS 4 in order to address these concerns. An entity applies these amendments for annual periods beginning on or after 1 January 2018. These amendments are discussed at 10 below.

In June 2020, the IASB issued *Amendments to IFRS 17* which defers the effective date of IFRS 17 to accounting periods beginning on or after 1 January 2023 (see 1 above). The IASB also issued *Extension of the Temporary Exemption from Applying IFRS 9 – Amendments to IFRS 4 –* which extends the temporary exemption from applying IFRS 9 and permits these amendments to IFRS 4 to be used until an insurer's first accounting period beginning on or after 1 January 2023 see 10 below). As a result of these amendments, many insurers will continue to apply IAS 39 until 2022. Therefore, this chapter refers to both IAS 39 and IFRS 9, but all extracts illustrate the application of IAS 39 and not IFRS 9.

1.4 Existing accounting practices for insurance contracts

Existing local accounting practices for insurance contracts are diverse. Typically, such practices, including the definition of what constitutes an insurance contract, are driven by regulatory requirements. There may also be separate GAAP and regulatory rules for insurers.

Many jurisdictions have also evolved different accounting rules for non-life (property/casualty) or short-term insurance and life or long-term insurance. However, the boundaries between what is considered non-life and life insurance can vary between jurisdictions and even within jurisdictions.

1.4.1 Non-life insurance

Non-life or short-term insurance transactions under local GAAP are typically accounted for on a deferral and matching basis. This means that premiums are normally recognised as revenue over the contract period, usually on a time apportionment basis. Claims are usually recognised on an incurred basis with no provision for claims that have not occurred at the reporting date. Within this basic model, differences exist across local GAAPs on various points of detail which include:

- whether or not claims liabilities are discounted;
- the basis for measuring claims liabilities (e.g. best estimate or a required confidence level);
- whether and what acquisition costs are deferred;
- whether a liability adequacy test (see 7.2.2 below) is performed on the unearned revenue or premium balance and the methodology and level of aggregation applied in such a test; and
- whether reinsurance follows the same model as direct insurance and whether immediate gains on retroactive reinsurance contracts are permitted or not (see 7.2.6.C below).

1.4.2 Life insurance

Most local GAAP life insurance accounting models recognise premiums when receivable and insurance contract liabilities are typically measured under some form of discounted cash flow approach that calculates the cash flows expected over the lifetime of the contract. In many jurisdictions the key inputs to the calculation (e.g. discount rates, mortality rates) are set by regulators. Key assumptions may be current or 'locked-in' at the contract inception. Differences across jurisdictions also include:

- whether or not certain investment-type products are subject to 'deposit accounting' (i.e. only fees are recognised as revenue rather than all cash inflows from policyholders);
- if, and how (contracts with) discretionary participation features are accounted for (discussed at 6 below);
- whether and what acquisition costs are deferred;
- how to account for options and guarantees embedded within contracts; and
- the use of contingency reserves or provisions for adverse deviation.

1.4.3 Embedded value

The embedded value (EV) of a life insurance business is an estimate of its economic worth excluding any value which may be attributed to future new business. The EV is the sum of the value placed on the entity's equity and the value of the in-force business. Typically, an embedded value calculation would involve discounting the value of the stream of after tax profits. For insurance liabilities the income stream would normally be calculated by using the income stream from the backing invested assets as a proxy.

EV is used as an alternative (non-GAAP) performance measure by some life insurers to illustrate the performance and value of their business because local accounting is rarely seen as providing this information. This is because local accounting is often driven by what management consider are 'unrealistic' regulatory rules and assumptions. *[IFRS 4.BC140]*.

There is no standardised global measure of embedded value and embedded value practices are diverse. For example, in Europe, the European Insurance CFO Forum, an organisation comprising the Chief Financial Officers of Europe's leading life and property and casualty insurers, has published both *European Embedded Values (EEV)* and *Market Consistent Embedded Value Principles (MCEV)*. Either of these embedded value models can be applied by Forum members.[2]

The potential use of embedded value under IFRS 4 is discussed at 8.2.4 below.

2 THE OBJECTIVES AND SCOPE OF IFRS 4

2.1 The objectives of IFRS 4

The stated objectives of IFRS 4 are:

(a) to make limited improvements to accounting by insurers for insurance contracts; and

(b) to require disclosures that identify and explain the amounts in an insurer's financial statements arising from insurance contracts and help users of those financial statements understand the amount, timing and uncertainty of future cash flows from insurance contracts. *[IFRS 4.1]*.

It is not IFRS 4's stated objective to determine, in a comprehensive way, how insurance contracts are recognised, measured and presented. This is addressed by IFRS 17. Instead, issuers of insurance contracts are permitted, with certain limitations, to continue to apply their existing, normally local, GAAP. This is discussed further at 7 and 8 below.

2.2 The scope of IFRS 4

2.2.1 Definitions

The following definitions are relevant to the application of IFRS 4. *[IFRS 4 Appendix A]*.

An *insurer* is the party that has an obligation under an insurance contract to compensate a policyholder if an insured event occurs.

An *insurance contract* is a contract under which one party (the insurer) accepts significant insurance risk from another party (the policyholder) by agreeing to compensate the policyholder if a specified uncertain future event (the insured event) adversely affects the policyholder.

A *reinsurer* is the party that has an obligation under a reinsurance contract to compensate a cedant if an insured event occurs.

A *reinsurance contract* is an insurance contract issued by one insurer (the reinsurer) to compensate another insurer (the cedant) for losses on one or more contracts issued by the cedant.

An *insured event* is an uncertain future event that is covered by an insurance contract and creates insurance risk.

An *insurance asset* is an insurer's net contractual rights under an insurance contract.

A *reinsurance asset* is a cedant's net contractual rights under a reinsurance contract.

An *insurance liability* is an insurer's net contractual obligations under an insurance contract.

A *cedant* is the policyholder under a reinsurance contract.

A *policyholder* is a party that has a right to compensation under an insurance contract if an insured event occurs.

Fair value is the price that would be received to sell an asset or paid to transfer a liability in an orderly transaction between market participants at the measurement date. This definition of fair value is the same as in IFRS 13.

Guaranteed benefits are payments or other benefits to which a particular policyholder or investor has an unconditional right that is not subject to the contractual discretion of the issuer.

A *discretionary participation feature* (DPF) is a contractual right to receive, as a supplement to guaranteed benefits, additional benefits:

(a) that are likely to be a significant portion of the total contractual benefits;
(b) whose amount or timing is contractually at the discretion of the issuer; and
(c) that are contractually based on:
   (i) the performance of a specified pool of contracts or a specified type of contract;
   (ii) realised and/or unrealised investment returns on a specified pool of assets held by the issuer; or
   (iii) the profit or loss of the company, fund or other entity that issues the contract.

A *financial guarantee contract* is a contract that requires the issuer to make specified payments to reimburse the holder for a loss it incurs because a specified debtor fails to make payment when due in accordance with the original or modified terms of a debt instrument.

2.2.2 Transactions within the scope of IFRS 4

Unless specifically excluded from its scope (see 2.2.3 below) IFRS 4 must be applied to:

(a) insurance contracts (including reinsurance contracts) issued by an entity and reinsurance contracts that it holds; and
(b) financial instruments that an entity issues with a discretionary participation feature (see 6.2 below). *[IFRS 4.2]*.

It can be seen from this that IFRS 4 applies to insurance contracts and not just to entities that specialise in issuing insurance contracts. Consistent with other IFRSs it is a transaction-based standard. Consequently, non-insurance entities will be within its scope if they issue contracts that meet the definition of an insurance contract.

IFRS 4 describes any entity that issues an insurance contract as an insurer whether or not the entity is regarded as an insurer for legal or supervisory purposes. *[IFRS 4.5]*.

Often an insurance contract will meet the definition of a financial instrument but IAS 39 and IFRS 9 contain a scope exemption for both insurance contracts and for contracts that would otherwise be within its scope but are within the scope of IFRS 4 because they contain a discretionary participation feature (see 6 below). *[IAS 39.2(e), IFRS 9.2.1(e)]*.

Although the recognition and measurement of financial instruments (or investment contracts) with a discretionary participation feature is governed by IFRS 4, for disclosure purposes they are within the scope of IFRS 7. *[IFRS 4.2(b)]*.

Contracts that fail to meet the definition of an insurance contract are within the scope of IAS 39 or IFRS 9 if they meet the definition of a financial instrument (unless they contain a DPF). This will be the case even if such contracts are regulated as insurance contracts under local legislation. These contracts are commonly referred to as 'investment contracts'.

Consequently, under IFRS, many insurers have different measurement and disclosure requirements applying to contracts that, under local GAAP or local regulatory rules, might, or might not, have been subject to the same measurement or disclosure requirements. The following table illustrates the standards applying to such contracts.

Type of contract	Recognition and Measurement	Disclosure
Insurance contract issued (both with and without a DPF)	IFRS 4	IFRS 4
Reinsurance contract held and issued	IFRS 4	IFRS 4
Investment contract with a DPF	IFRS 4	IFRS 7/IFRS 13
Investment contract without a DPF	IAS 39/IFRS 9	IFRS 7/IFRS 13

Many local GAAPs and local regulatory regimes prescribe different accounting requirements for life (long-term) and non-life (short-term) insurance contracts (see 1.4 above). However, IFRS 4 does not distinguish between different types of insurance contracts.

IFRS 4 confirms that a reinsurance contract is a type of insurance contract and that all references to insurance contracts apply equally to reinsurance contracts. *[IFRS 4.6]*.

Because all rights and obligations arising from insurance contracts and investment contracts with a DPF are also scoped out of IAS 39 and IFRS 9, IFRS 4 applies to all the assets and liabilities arising from insurance contracts. *[IAS 39.2(e), IFRS 9.2.1(e)]*. These include:

- insurance and reinsurance receivables owed by the policyholder direct to the insurer;
- insurance claims agreed with the policyholder and payable;
- insurance contract policy liabilities;
- claims handling cost provisions;
- the present value of acquired in-force business (discussed at 9.1 below);
- deferred or unearned premium reserves;
- reinsurance assets (i.e. expected reinsurance recoveries in respect of claims incurred);
- deferred acquisition costs; and
- discretionary participation features (DPF).

Receivables not arising from insurance contracts (such as those arising from a contractual relationship with an agent) would be within the scope of IAS 39 or IFRS 9. When an insurer uses an agent, judgement may be required to determine whether insurance receivables, payable by an agent on behalf of a policyholder are within the scope of IFRS 4 or IAS 39/IFRS 9. Such receivables might include:

- balances with intermediaries for premiums received from policyholders but not yet remitted to the insurer by the intermediary;
- funds withheld amounts with intermediaries (e.g. claims funds); and
- loans to intermediaries.

Payables and receivables arising out of investment contracts fall within the scope of IAS 39 or IFRS 9 and the capitalisation and deferral of costs arising from such contracts currently fall within the scope of IFRS 15, IAS 38 and IAS 39 or IFRS 9.

2.2.3 Transactions not within the scope of IFRS 4

IFRS 4 does not address other aspects of accounting by insurers, such as accounting for financial assets held by insurers and financial liabilities issued by insurers (which are within the scope of IAS 32, IAS 39, IFRS 7 and IFRS 9), except: *[IFRS 4.3]*

- insurers that meet specified criteria are permitted to apply a temporary exemption from IFRS 9 for annual periods beginning on or after 1 January 2018 (see 10.1 below);
- insurers are permitted to apply what the IASB describes as the 'overlay approach' to designated financial assets for annual periods beginning on or after 1 January 2018 (see 10.2 below); and
- insurers are permitted to reclassify in specified circumstances some or all of their financial assets so that the assets are measured at fair value through profit or loss (see 8.4 below).

In addition, although not mentioned in IFRS 4, IAS 40 – *Investment Property* – permits an entity to separately choose between the fair value model or the cost model for all investment property backing liabilities that pay a return linked directly to the fair value of, or returns from, specified assets including that investment property (e.g. contracts with discretionary participation features as discussed at 6 below). The choice to use either the fair value model or the cost model for all other investment property is a separate election. *[IAS 40.32A]*. See Chapter 19 at 5.1.

IFRS 4 also describes transactions to which IFRS 4 is not applied. These primarily relate to transactions covered by other standards that could potentially meet the definition of an insurance contract. It was not the intention of the IASB in issuing IFRS 4 to reopen issues addressed by other standards unless the specific features of insurance contracts justified a different treatment. *[IFRS 4.BC10(c)]*. These transactions are discussed below.

2.2.3.A Product warranties

Product warranties issued directly by a manufacturer, dealer or retailer are outside the scope of IFRS 4. These are accounted for under IFRS 15 and IAS 37. *[IFRS 4.4(a)]*.

Without this exception many product warranties would have been covered by IFRS 4 as they would normally meet the definition of an insurance contract. The IASB has excluded them from the scope of IFRS 4 because they are closely related to the underlying sale of goods and because IAS 37 addresses product warranties while IFRS 15 deals with the revenue received for such warranties. *[IFRS 4.BC71]*.

However, a product warranty is within the scope of IFRS 4 if an entity issues it on behalf of another party i.e. the contract is issued indirectly. *[IFRS 4.BC69]*.

Other types of warranty are not specifically excluded from the scope of IFRS 4. However, since IFRS 4 does not prescribe a specific accounting treatment, issuers of such warranties are likely to be able to apply their existing accounting policies.

2.2.3.B   Assets and liabilities arising from employment benefit plans

Employers' assets and liabilities under employee benefit plans and retirement benefit obligations reported by defined benefit retirement plans are excluded from the scope of IFRS 4. These are accounted for under IAS 19 – *Employee Benefits*, IFRS 2 – *Share-based Payment* – and IAS 26 – *Accounting and Reporting by Retirement Benefit Plans*. *[IFRS 4.4(b)]*.

Many defined benefit pension plans and similar post-employment benefits meet the definition of an insurance contract because the payments to pensioners are contingent on uncertain future events such as the continuing survival of current or retired employees. Without this exception they would have been within the scope of IFRS 4.

2.2.3.C   Contingent rights and obligations related to non-financial items

Contractual rights or contractual obligations that are contingent on the future use of, or right to use, a non-financial item (for example, some licence fees, royalties, contingent or variable lease payments and similar items) are excluded from the scope of IFRS 4, as well as a lessee's residual value guarantee embedded in a lease (see IFRS 15, IFRS 16 – *Leases,* and IAS 38). *[IFRS 4.4(c)]*.

2.2.3.D   Financial guarantee contracts

Financial guarantee contracts are excluded from the scope of IFRS 4 unless the issuer has previously asserted explicitly that it regards such contracts as insurance contracts and has used accounting applicable to insurance contracts, in which case the issuer may elect to apply either IAS 32, IAS 39 or IFRS 9 and IFRS 7 or IFRS 4 to them. The issuer may make that election contract by contract, but the election for each contract is irrevocable. *[IFRS 4.4(d)]*.

Where an insurer elects to use IFRS 4 to account for its financial guarantee contracts, its accounting policy defaults to its previous GAAP for such contracts (subject to any limitations discussed at 7.2 below) unless subsequently modified as permitted by IFRS 4 (see 8 below).

IFRS 4 does not elaborate on the phrase 'previously asserted explicitly'. However, the application guidance to IAS 39 and IFRS 9 states that assertions that an issuer regards contracts as insurance contracts are typically found throughout the issuer's communications with customers and regulators, contracts, business documentation and financial statements. Furthermore, insurance contracts are often subject to accounting requirements that are distinct from the requirements for other types of transaction, such as contracts issued by banks or commercial companies. In such cases, an issuer's financial statements typically include a statement that the issuer has used those accounting requirements. *[IAS 39.AG4A, IFRS 9.B2.6]*. Therefore, it is likely that insurers that have previously issued financial guarantee contracts and accounted for them under an insurance accounting and regulatory framework will meet these criteria. It is unlikely that an entity not subject to an insurance accounting and regulatory framework, or new insurers (start-up companies) and existing insurers that had not previously issued financial guarantee contracts would meet these criteria because they would not have previously made the necessary assertions.

Accounting for financial guarantee contracts by issuers that have not elected to use IFRS 4 is discussed in Chapter 45 at 3.4.2.

2.2.3.E Contingent consideration payable or receivable in a business combination

Contingent consideration payable or receivable in a business combination is outside the scope of IFRS 4. *[IFRS 4.4(e)]*. Contingent consideration in a business combination is required to be recognised at fair value at the acquisition date with subsequent remeasurements of non equity consideration included in profit or loss. *[IFRS 3.58]*.

2.2.3.F Direct insurance contracts in which the entity is the policyholder

Accounting by policyholders of direct insurance contracts (i.e. those that are not reinsurance contracts) is excluded from the scope of IFRS 4 because the IASB did not regard this as a high priority for Phase I. *[IFRS 4.4(f), BC73]*. However, holders of reinsurance contracts (cedants) are required to apply IFRS 4. *[IFRS 4.4(f)]*.

A policyholder's rights and obligations under an insurance contract are also excluded from the scope of IAS 32, IAS 39 or IFRS 9 and IFRS 7. However, the IAS 8 – *Accounting Policies, Changes in Accounting Estimates and Errors* – hierarchy does apply to policyholders when determining an accounting policy for direct insurance contracts. IAS 37 addresses accounting for reimbursements from insurers for expenditure required to settle a provision and IAS 16 – *Property, Plant and Equipment* – addresses some aspects of compensation from third parties for property, plant and equipment that is impaired, lost or given up. *[IFRS 4.BC73]*.

The principal outlined in IAS 37 is that reimbursements and contingent assets can only be recognised if an inflow of economic benefits is virtually certain. *[IAS 37.33, 56]*. IAS 16 requires that compensation from third parties for property, plant and equipment impaired, lost or given up is included in profit or loss when it 'becomes receivable'. *[IAS 16.66(c)]*. These are likely to be more onerous recognition tests than any applied under IFRS 4 for cedants with reinsurance assets which will be based on local insurance GAAP.

2.2.4 The product classification process

Because of the need to determine which transactions should be within the scope of IFRS 4, and which transactions are not within its scope, one of the main procedures required of insurers as part of their first-time adoption of IFRS 4 is to conduct a product classification review.

Many large groups developed a product classification process to determine the appropriate classification on a consistent basis. In order to ensure consistency, the product classification process is typically set out in the group accounting manual.

The assessment of the appropriate classification for a contract will include an assessment of whether the contract contains significant insurance risk (discussed at 3 below), and whether the contract contains embedded derivatives (discussed at 4 below), deposit components (discussed at 5 below) or discretionary participation features (discussed at 6 below).

The diagram below illustrates a product classification decision tree, assuming that the entity continues to apply IAS 39.

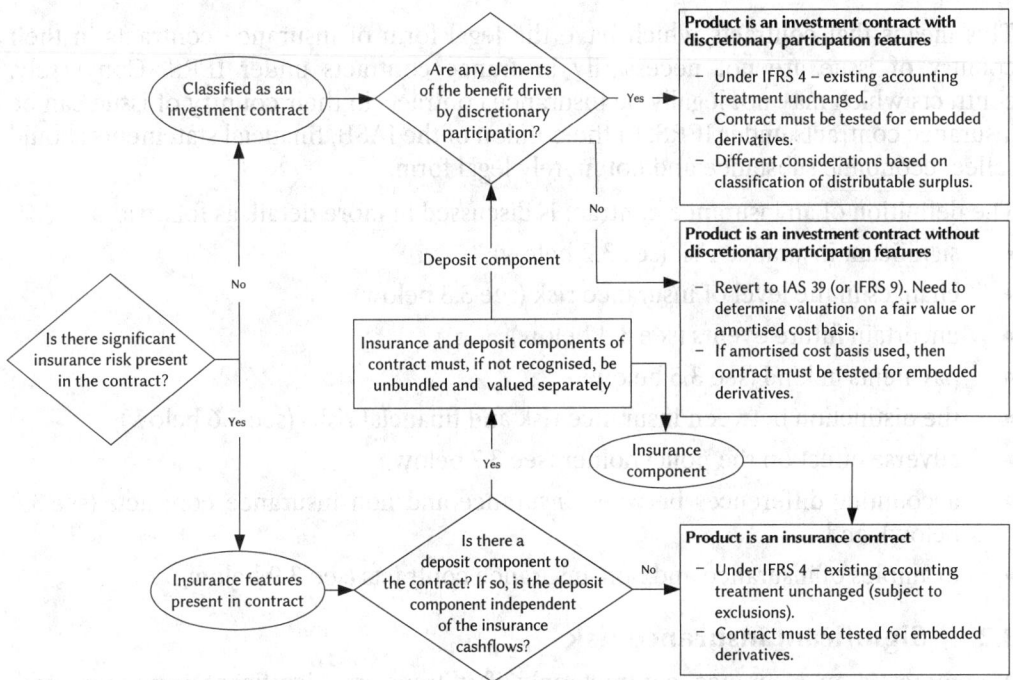

3 THE DEFINITION OF AN INSURANCE CONTRACT

3.1 The definition

The definition of an insurance contract in IFRS 4 is:

'A contract under which one party (the insurer) accepts significant insurance risk from another party (the policyholder) by agreeing to compensate the policyholder if a specified uncertain future event (the insured event) adversely affects the policyholder'.
[IFRS 4 Appendix A].

This definition determines which contracts are within the scope of IFRS 4 rather than other standards.

The IASB rejected using existing national definitions because they believed it unsatisfactory to base the definition used in IFRS on definitions that may vary from country to country and may not be the most relevant for deciding which IFRS ought to apply to a particular type of contract. *[IFRS 4.BC12]*.

In response to concerns that the definition in IFRS 4 could ultimately lead to changes in definitions used for other purposes, such as insurance law, insurance supervision or tax, the IASB made it clear that any definition within IFRS is solely for financial reporting and is not intended to change or pre-empt definitions used for other purposes. *[IFRS 4.BC13]*.

This means that contracts which have the legal form of insurance contracts in their country of issue are not necessarily insurance contracts under IFRS. Conversely, contracts which may not legally be insurance contracts in their country of issue can be insurance contracts under IFRS. In the opinion of the IASB, financial statements should reflect economic substance and not merely legal form.

The definition of an insurance contract is discussed in more detail, as follows:

- significant insurance risk (see 3.2 below);
- changes in the level of insurance risk (see 3.3 below);
- uncertain future events (see 3.4 below);
- payments in kind (see 3.5 below);
- the distinction between insurance risk and financial risks (see 3.6 below);
- adverse effect on the policyholder (see 3.7 below);
- accounting differences between insurance and non-insurance contracts (see 3.8 below); and
- examples of insurance and non-insurance contracts (see 3.9 below).

3.2 Significant insurance risk

A contract is an insurance contract only if it transfers 'significant insurance risk'. *[IFRS 4.B22]*.

Insurance risk is 'significant' if, and only if, an insured event could cause an insurer to pay significant additional benefits in any scenario, excluding scenarios that lack commercial substance (i.e. have no discernible effect on the economics of the transaction). *[IFRS 4.B23]*.

If significant additional benefits would be payable in scenarios that have commercial substance, this condition may be met even if the insured event is extremely unlikely or even if the expected (i.e. probability-weighted) present value of contingent cash flows is a small proportion of the expected present value of all the remaining contractual cash flows. *[IFRS 4.B23]*.

From this, we consider the IASB's intention was to make it easier, not harder, for contracts regarded as insurance contracts under most local GAAPs to be insurance contracts under IFRS 4.

Local GAAP in many jurisdictions prohibit insurance contract accounting if there are restrictions on the timing of payments or receipts. IFRS 4 has no such restrictions, provided there is significant insurance risk, although clearly the existence of restrictions on the timing of payments may mean that the policy does not transfer significant insurance risk.

3.2.1 The meaning of 'significant'

No quantitative guidance supports the determination of 'significant' in IFRS 4. This was a deliberate decision because the IASB considered that if quantitative guidance was provided it would create an arbitrary dividing line that would result in different accounting treatments for similar transactions that fall marginally on different sides of that line and would therefore create opportunities for accounting arbitrage. *[IFRS 4.BC33]*.

The IASB also rejected defining the significance of insurance risk by reference to the definition of materiality within IFRS because, in their opinion, a single contract, or even a single book of similar contracts, could rarely generate a loss that would be material to the financial statements as a whole. *[IFRS 4.BC34]*. The IASB also rejected the notion of defining significance of insurance risk by expressing the expected (probability weighted) average of the present values of the adverse outcomes as a proportion of the expected present value of all outcomes, or as a proportion of the premium. This idea would have required the constant monitoring of contracts over their life to see whether they continued to transfer insurance risk. As discussed at 3.3 below, an assessment of whether significant insurance risk has been transferred is normally only required at the inception of a contract. *[IFRS 4.BC35]*.

The IASB believes that 'significant' means that the insured benefits certainly must be greater than 101% of the benefits payable if the insured event did not occur and it expressed this in the implementation guidance as illustrated below. It is, however, unclear how much greater than 101% the insured benefits must be to meet the definition of 'significant'.

Example 55.1: Significant insurance risk

Entity A issues a unit-linked contract that pays benefits linked to the fair value of a pool of assets. The benefit is 100% of the unit value on surrender or maturity and 101% of the unit value on death.

In this situation the implementation guidance states that if the insurance component (the additional death benefit of 1%) is not unbundled then the whole contract is an investment contract. The insurance component in this arrangement is insignificant in relation to the whole contract and so would not meet the definition of an insurance contract in IFRS 4. *[IFRS 4.IG2 E1.3]*.

Some jurisdictions have their own guidance as to what constitutes significant insurance risk. However, as with IFRS 4, other jurisdictions offer no quantitative guidance. Some US GAAP practitioners apply a guideline that a reasonable possibility of a significant loss is a 10% probability of a 10% loss although this guideline does not appear in US GAAP itself. *[IFRS 4.BC32]*. It is not disputed in the basis for conclusions that a 10% chance of a 10% loss results in a transfer of significant insurance risk and, indeed, the words 'extremely unlikely' and 'a small proportion' (see 3.2 above) suggests to us that the IASB envisages that significant insurance risk can exist at a different threshold than a 10% probability of a 10% loss.

This lack of a quantitative definition means that insurers must apply their own judgement as to what constitutes significant insurance risk. Although the IASB did not want to create an 'arbitrary dividing line', the practical impact of this lack of guidance is that insurers have to apply their own criteria to what constitutes significant insurance risk and there probably is inconsistency in practice as to what these dividing lines are, at least at the margins.

There is no requirement under IFRS 4 for insurers to disclose any thresholds used in determining whether a contract has transferred significant insurance risk. However, IAS 1 – *Presentation of Financial Statements* – requires an entity to disclose the judgements that management has made in the process of applying the entity's accounting policies that have the most significant effect on the amounts recognised in the financial statements (see Chapter 3 at 5.1.1.B). Liverpool Victoria made the following disclosures about significant insurance risk in its 2016 financial statements.

> *Extract 55.1: Liverpool Victoria Friendly Society Limited (2016)*
> Notes to the Financial Statements [extract]
> 1.   Significant accounting policies [extract]
> b)   Contract classification [extract]
>
> Insurance contracts are those contracts that transfer significant insurance risk. Such contracts may also transfer financial risk. As a general guideline, the Group defines as significant insurance risk the possibility of having to pay benefits on the occurrence of an insured event that are at least 10% more than the benefits payable if the insured event did not occur.

3.2.2 The level at which significant insurance risk is assessed

Significant insurance risk must be assessed by individual contract, rather than by blocks of contracts or by reference to materiality to the financial statements. Thus, insurance risk may be significant even if there is a minimal probability of material losses for a whole book of contracts. *[IFRS 4.B25]*.

The IASB's reasons for defining significant insurance risk in relation to a single contract were that:

(a)   although contracts are often managed and measured on a portfolio basis, the contractual rights and obligations arise from individual contracts; and

(b)   an assessment contract by contract is likely to increase the proportion of contracts that qualify as insurance contracts. The IASB intended to make it easier, not harder, for a contract previously regarded as an insurance contract under local GAAP to meet the IFRS 4 definition. *[IFRS 4.BC34]*.

However, where a relatively homogeneous book of small contracts is known to consist of contracts that all transfer insurance risk, the standard does not require that an insurer examine each contract within that book to identify a few non-derivative contracts that transfer insignificant insurance risk. *[IFRS 4.B25]*.

Multiple, mutually linked contracts entered into with a single counterparty (or contracts that are otherwise interdependent) should be considered a single contract for the purposes of assessing whether significant insurance risk is transferred. *[IFRS 4.B25 fn7]*. This requirement is intended to prevent entities entering into contracts that individually transfer significant insurance risk but collectively do not and accounting for part(s) of what is effectively a single arrangement as (an) insurance contract(s).

If an insurance contract is unbundled (see 5 below) into a deposit component and an insurance component, the significance of insurance risk transferred is assessed by reference only to the insurance component. The significance of insurance risk transferred by an embedded derivative is assessed by reference only to the embedded derivative (see 4 below). *[IFRS 4.B28]*.

3.2.2.A   Self insurance

An insurer can accept significant insurance risk from a policyholder only if it issues an insurance contract to an entity separate from itself. Therefore, 'self insurance', such as a self-insured deductible where the insured cannot claim for losses below the excess limit of an insurance policy, is not insurance because there is no insurance contract. Accounting for self insurance and related provisions is covered by IAS 37 which requires that a provision is recognised only if there is a present obligation as a result of a past event, if it is probable that an outflow of resources will occur and a reliable estimate can be determined. *[IAS 37.14]*.

3.2.2.B   Insurance mutuals

A mutual insurer accepts risk from each policyholder and pools that risk. Although policyholders bear the pooled risk collectively in their capacity as owners, the mutual has still accepted the risk that is the essence of an insurance contract and therefore IFRS 4 applies to those contracts. *[IFRS 4.B17]*.

3.2.2.C   Intragroup insurance contracts

Where there are insurance contracts between entities in the same group these would be eliminated in the consolidated financial statements as required by IFRS 10 – *Consolidated Financial Statements*. If any intragroup insurance contract is reinsured with a third party that is not part of the group, this third party reinsurance contract should be accounted for as a direct insurance contract in the consolidated financial statements of a non-insurer because the intragroup contract will be eliminated on consolidation. This residual direct insurance contract (i.e. the policy with the third party) is outside the scope of IFRS 4 from the viewpoint of the consolidated financial statements of a non-insurer because policyholder accounting is excluded from IFRS 4 as discussed at 2.2.3.F above.

3.2.3 Significant additional benefits

The 'significant additional benefits' described at 3.2 above refer to amounts that exceed those that would be payable if no insured event occurred. These additional amounts include claims handling and claims assessment costs, but exclude:

(a) the loss of the ability to charge the policyholder for future services, for example where the ability to collect fees from a policyholder for performing future investment management services ceases if the policyholder of an investment-linked life insurance contract dies. This economic loss does not reflect insurance risk and the future investment management fees are not relevant in assessing how much insurance risk is transferred by a contract;

(b) the waiver on death of charges that would be made on cancellation or surrender of the contract. Because the contract brought these charges into existence, the waiver of them does not compensate the policyholder for a pre-existing risk. Hence, they are not relevant in determining how much insurance risk is transferred by a contract;

(c) a payment conditional on an event that does not cause a significant loss to the holder of the contract, for example where the issuer must pay one million currency units if an asset suffers physical damage causing an insignificant economic loss of one currency unit to the holder. The holder in this case has transferred to the insurer the insignificant insurance risk of losing one currency unit. However, at the same time the contract creates non-insurance risk that the issuer will need to pay 999,999 additional currency units if the specified event occurs;

(d) possible reinsurance recoveries. The insurer will account for these separately; *[IFRS 4.B24]* and

(e) the original policy premium (but not additional premiums payable in the event of claims experience – see Example 55.26 below).

The definition of insurance risk refers to risk that the insurer accepts from the policyholder. Consequently, insurance risk must be a pre-existing risk transferred from the policyholder to the insurer. A new risk, such as the inability to charge the policyholder for future services, is not insurance risk. *[IFRS 4.B12]*. The following example illustrates this.

Example 55.2: Loan contract with prepayment fee

A loan contract contains a prepayment fee that is waived if the prepayment results from the borrower's death.

This is not an insurance contract since before entering into the contract the borrower faced no risk corresponding to the prepayment fee. Hence, although the loan contract exposes the lender to mortality risk, it does not transfer a pre-existing risk from the borrower. Thus, the risk associated with the possible waiver on death of the prepayment fee is not insurance risk. *[IFRS 4.IG2 E1.23]*.

It follows from this that if a contract pays a death benefit exceeding the amount payable on survival (excluding waivers under (b) above), the contract is an insurance contract unless the additional death benefit is insignificant (judged by reference to the contract rather than to an entire book of contracts). Similarly, an annuity contract that pays out regular sums for the rest of a policyholder's life is an insurance contract, unless the aggregate life-contingent payments are insignificant. In this case, the insurer could suffer a significant loss on an individual contract if the annuitant survives longer than expected. *[IFRS 4.B26]*.

Additional benefits could include a requirement to pay benefits earlier than expected if the insured event occurs earlier provided the payment is not adjusted for the time value of money. An example could be whole life insurance cover that provides a fixed death benefit whenever a policyholder dies. Whilst it is certain that the policyholder will die, the timing of death is uncertain and the insurer will suffer a loss on individual contracts when policyholders die early, even if there is no overall expected loss on the whole book of contracts. *[IFRS 4.B27]*.

3.3 Changes in the level of insurance risk

It is implicit within IFRS 4 that an assessment of whether a contract transfers significant insurance risk should be made at the inception of a contract. *[IFRS 4.B29]*. Further, a contract that qualifies as an insurance contract at inception remains an insurance contract until all rights and obligations are extinguished or expire. *[IFRS 4.B30]*. This applies even if circumstances have changed such that insurance contingent rights and obligations have expired. The IASB considered that requiring insurers to set up systems to continually assess whether contracts continue to transfer significant insurance risk imposed a cost that far outweighed the benefit that would be gained from going through the exercise. *[IFRS 4.BC38]*.

Conversely, contracts that do not transfer insurance risk at inception may become insurance contracts if they transfer insurance risk at a later time, as explained in the following example. This is because IFRS 4 imposes no limitations on when contracts can be assessed for significant insurance risk. The reclassification of contracts as insurance contracts occurs based on changing facts and circumstances, although there is no guidance on accounting for the reclassification.

Example 55.3: Deferred annuity with policyholder election

Entity A issues a deferred annuity contract whereby the policyholder will receive, or can elect to receive, a life-contingent annuity at rates prevailing when the annuity begins.

This is not an insurance contract at inception if the insurer can reprice the mortality risk without constraints. However, it will become an insurance contract when the annuity rate is fixed (unless the contingent amount is insignificant in all scenarios that have commercial substance). *[IFRS 4.IG2 E1.7]*.

In practice, in the accumulation phase of an annuity, there are other guaranteed benefits such as premium refunds that might still make this an insurance contract prior to the date when the annuity rate is fixed.

Some respondents to ED 5 suggested that a contract should not be regarded as an insurance contract if the insurance-contingent rights and obligations expire after a very short time. The IASB considered that the requirement to ignore scenarios that lack commercial substance in assessing significant insurance risk and the fact that there is no significant transfer of pre-existing risk in some contracts that waive surrender penalties on death is sufficient to cover this issue. *[IFRS 4.BC39]*.

IFRS 3 – *Business Combinations* – confirms that there should be no reassessment of the classification of contracts previously classified as insurance contracts under IFRS 4 which are acquired as a part of a business combination. *[IFRS 3.17(b)]*.

3.4 Uncertain future events

Uncertainty (or risk) is the essence of an insurance contract. Accordingly, IFRS 4 requires at least one of the following to be uncertain at the inception of an insurance contract:

(a) whether an insured event will occur;
(b) when it will occur; or
(c) how much the insurer will need to pay if it occurs. *[IFRS 4.B2]*.

An insured event will be one of the following:

- the discovery of a loss during the term of the contract, even if the loss arises from an event that occurred before the inception of the contract;
- a loss that occurs during the term of the contract, even if the resulting loss is discovered after the end of the contract term; *[IFRS 4.B3]* or
- the discovery of the ultimate cost of a claim which has already occurred but whose financial effect is uncertain. *[IFRS 4.B4]*.

This last type of insured event arises from 'retroactive' contracts, i.e. those providing insurance against events which have occurred prior to the policy inception date. An example is a reinsurance contract that covers a direct policyholder against adverse development of claims already reported by policyholders. In this case the insured event is the discovery of the ultimate cost of those claims.

Local GAAP in some jurisdictions, including the US, prohibits the recognition of gains on inception of retroactive reinsurance contracts. IFRS 4 contains no such prohibition. Therefore, such gains would be recognised if that was required by an insurer's existing accounting policies. However, as discussed at 11.1.3 below, the amount of any such gains recognised should be disclosed.

3.5 Payments in kind

Insurance contracts that require or permit payments to be made in kind are treated the same way as contracts where payment is made directly to the policyholder. For example, some insurers replace an article directly rather than compensating the policyholder. Others use their own employees, such as medical staff, to provide services covered by the contract. *[IFRS 4.B5]*.

3.5.1 Service contracts

Some fixed-fee service contracts in which the level of service depends on an uncertain event may meet the definition of an insurance contract. However, in some jurisdictions these are not regulated as insurance contracts. For example, a service provider could enter into a maintenance contract in which it agrees to repair specified equipment after a malfunction. The fixed service fee is based on the expected number of malfunctions but it is uncertain whether a particular machine will break down. Similarly, a contract for car breakdown services in which the provider agrees, for a fixed annual fee, to provide roadside assistance or tow the car to a nearby garage could meet the definition of an insurance contract even if the provider does not agree to carry out repairs or replace parts. *[IFRS 4.B6]*.

In respect of the type of service contracts described above, their inclusion within IFRS 4 seems an unintended consequence of the definition of an insurance contract.

However, the IASB stresses that applying IFRS 4 to these contracts should be no more burdensome than applying other IFRSs since:

(a) there are unlikely to be material liabilities for malfunctions and breakdowns that have already occurred;

(b) if the service provider applied accounting policies consistent with IFRS 15, this would be acceptable either as an existing accounting policy or, possibly, an improvement of existing policies (see 8 below);

(c) whilst the service provider would be required to apply the liability adequacy test discussed at 7.2.2 below if the cost of meeting its contractual obligation to provide services exceeded the revenue received in advance, it would have been required to apply IAS 37 to determine whether its contracts were onerous if IFRS 4 did not apply; and

(d) the disclosure requirements in IFRS 4 are unlikely to add significantly to the disclosures required by other IFRSs. *[IFRS 4.B7]*.

3.6 The distinction between insurance risk and financial risk

The definition of an insurance contract refers to 'insurance risk' which is defined as 'risk, other than financial risk, transferred from the holder of a contract to the issuer'. *[IFRS 4 Appendix A]*.

A contract that exposes the reporting entity to financial risk without significant insurance risk is not an insurance contract. *[IFRS 4.B8]*. 'Financial risk' is defined as 'the risk of a possible future change in one or more of a specified interest rate, financial instrument price, foreign exchange rate, index of prices or rates, credit rating or credit index or other variable, provided in the case of a non-financial variable that the variable is not specific to a party to the contract'. *[IFRS 4 Appendix A]*.

An example of a non-financial variable that is not specific to a party to the contract is an index of earthquake losses in a particular region or an index of temperature in a particular city. An example of a non-financial variable that is specific to a party to the contract is the occurrence or non-occurrence of a fire that damages or destroys an asset of that party.

The risk of changes in the fair value of a non-financial asset is not a financial risk if the fair value reflects not only changes in the market prices for such assets (a financial variable) but also the condition of a specific non-financial asset held by a party to the contract (a non-financial variable). For example if a guarantee of the residual value of a specific car exposes the guarantor to the risk of changes in that car's condition, that risk is insurance risk. *[IFRS 4.B9]*.

Example 55.4: Residual value insurance

Entity A issues a contract to Entity B that provides a guarantee of the fair value at the future date of an aircraft (a non-financial asset) held by B. A is not the lessee of the aircraft (residual value guarantees given by a lessee under a lease within the scope of IFRS 16).

This is an insurance contract (unless changes in the condition of the asset have an insignificant effect on its value). The risk of changes in the fair value of the aircraft is not a financial risk because the fair value reflects not only changes in market prices for similar aircraft but also the condition of the specific asset held.

However, if the contract compensated B only for changes in market prices and not for changes in the condition of B's asset, the contract would be a derivative and within the scope of IAS 39 or IFRS 9. *[IFRS 4.IG2 E1.15]*.

Contracts that expose the issuer to both financial risk and significant insurance risk can be insurance contracts. *[IFRS 4.B10]*.

Example 55.5: Contract with insurance and financial risk

Entity A issues a catastrophe bond to Entity B under which principal, interest payments or both are reduced significantly if a specified triggering event occurs and the triggering event includes a condition that B has suffered a loss.

The contract is an insurance contract because the triggering event includes a condition that B has suffered a loss, and contains an insurance component (with the issuer as policyholder and the holder as the insurer) and a deposit component. A discussion of the separation of these two components is set out at 5 below. *[IFRS 4.IG2 E1.20]*.

Contracts where an insured event triggers the payment of an amount linked to a price index are insurance contracts provided the payment that is contingent on the insured event is significant.

An example would be a life contingent annuity linked to a cost of living index. Such a contract transfers insurance risk because payment is triggered by an uncertain future event, the survival of the annuitant. The link to the price index is an embedded derivative but it also transfers insurance risk. If the insurance risk transferred is significant, the embedded derivative meets the definition of an insurance contract (see 4 below for a discussion of derivatives embedded within insurance contracts). *[IFRS 4.B11]*.

3.7 Adverse effect on the policyholder

For a contract to be an insurance contract the insured event must have an adverse effect on the policyholder. In other words, there must be an insurable interest.

Without the notion of insurable interest the definition of an insurance contract would have encompassed gambling. The IASB believed that without this notion the definition of an insurance contract might have captured any prepaid contract to provide services whose cost is uncertain and that would have extended the scope of the term 'insurance contract' too far beyond its traditional meaning. *[IFRS 4.BC26-28]*. In the IASB's opinion the retention of insurable interest gives a principle-based distinction, particularly between insurance contracts and other contracts that happen to be used for hedging and they preferred to base the distinction on a type of contract rather than the way an entity manages a contract or group of contracts. *[IFRS 4.BC29]*.

The adverse effect on the policyholder is not limited to an amount equal to the financial impact of the adverse event. So, the definition includes 'new for old' coverage that replaces a damaged or lost asset with a new asset. Similarly, the definition does not limit payment under a term life insurance contract to the financial loss suffered by a deceased's dependents, nor does it preclude the payment of predetermined amounts to quantify the loss caused by a death or accident. *[IFRS 4.B13]*.

A contract that requires a payment if a specified uncertain event occurs which does not require an adverse effect on the policyholder as a precondition for payment is not an insurance contract. Such contracts are not insurance contracts even if the holder uses the contract to mitigate an underlying risk exposure. Conversely, the definition of an insurance contract refers to an uncertain event for which an adverse effect on the policyholder is a contractual precondition for payment. This contractual precondition does not require the insurer to investigate whether the uncertain event actually caused an adverse effect, but permits the insurer to deny payment if it is not satisfied that the event caused an adverse effect. *[IFRS 4.B14]*.

The following example illustrates the concept of insurable interest.

Example 55.6:   Reinsurance contract with 'original loss warranty' clause

Entity A agrees to provide reinsurance cover to airline insurer B for $5m against losses suffered. The claims are subject to an original loss warranty of $50m meaning that only losses suffered by B up to $5m from events exceeding a cost of $50m in total can be recovered under the contract. This is an insurance contract as B can only recover its own losses arising from those events.

If the contract allowed B to claim up to $5m every time there was an event with a cost exceeding $50m regardless of whether B had suffered a loss from that event then this would not be an insurance contract because there would be no insurable interest in this arrangement.

3.7.1   Lapse, persistency and expense risk

Lapse or persistency risk (the risk that the policyholder will cancel the contract earlier or later than the issuer had expected in pricing the contract) is not insurance risk because, although this can have an adverse effect on the issuer, the cancellation is not contingent on an uncertain future event that adversely affects the policyholder. *[IFRS 4.B15]*.

Similarly, expense risk (the risk of unexpected increases in the administrative costs incurred by the issuer associated with the serving of a contract, rather than the costs associated with insured events) is not insurance risk because an unexpected increase in expenses does not adversely affect the policyholder. *[IFRS 4.B15]*.

Therefore, a contract that exposes the issuer to lapse risk, persistency risk or expense risk is not an insurance contract unless it also exposes the issuer to significant insurance risk. *[IFRS 4.B16]*.

3.7.2   Insurance of non-insurance risks

If the issuer of a contract which does not contain significant insurance risk mitigates the risk of that contract by using a second contract to transfer part of that first contract's risk to another party, this second contract exposes that other party to insurance risk because the policyholder of the second contract (the issuer of the first contract) is subject to an uncertain event that adversely affects it and thus it meets the definition of an insurance contract. *[IFRS 4.B16]*. This is illustrated by the following example.

Example 55.7:   Insurance of non-insurance risks

Entity A agrees to compensate Entity B for losses on a series of contracts issued by B that do not transfer significant insurance risk. These could be investment contracts or, for example, a contract to provide services.

The contract is an insurance contract if it transfers significant insurance risk from B to A, even if some or all of the underlying individual contracts do not transfer significant insurance risk to B. The contract is a reinsurance contract if any of the contracts issued by B are insurance contracts. Otherwise, the contract is a direct insurance contract. *[IFRS 4.IG2 E1.29]*.

3.8 Accounting differences between insurance and non-insurance contracts

Making a distinction between insurance and non-insurance contracts is important because the accounting treatment will usually differ.

Insurance contracts under IFRS 4 will normally be accounted for under local GAAP (see 7 below). Typically, local GAAP (see 1.4 above) will recognise funds received or due from a policyholder as premiums (revenue) and amounts due to a policyholder as claims (an expense). However, if a contract does not transfer significant insurance risk and is therefore not an insurance contract under IFRS 4, it will probably be accounted for as an investment contract under IAS 39 or IFRS 9. Under IAS 39 or IFRS 9 the receipt of funds relating to financial assets or financial liabilities will result in the creation of a liability for the value of the remittance rather than a credit to profit or loss. This accounting treatment is sometimes called 'deposit accounting'. *[IFRS 4.B20]*.

A financial liability within the scope of IAS 39 or IFRS 9 is measured at either amortised cost or fair value or possibly a mixture (e.g. if the instrument contains an embedded derivative). However, under IFRS 4, an insurance liability is measured under the entity's previous local GAAP accounting policies, unless these have been subsequently changed as discussed at 8 below. These may well result in the measurement of a liability that is different from that obtained by applying IAS 39 or IFRS 9.

Additionally, the capitalisation of any acquisition costs related to the issuance of a contract is also likely to be different for insurance and investment contracts. IFRS 15 permits only incremental costs associated with obtaining an investment management contract to be capitalised. IAS 39 or IFRS 9 requires transaction costs directly attributable to a financial asset or financial liability not at fair value through profit or loss to be included in its initial measurement. Transaction costs relating to financial assets and financial liabilities held at fair value through profit or loss are required to be expensed immediately. IFRS 4 does not provide any guidance as to what acquisition costs can be capitalised so reference to existing local accounting policies should apply (see 7.2.6.D below). In most cases, these will differ from the requirements outlined in IFRS 15 and IAS 39 or IFRS 9.

If non-insurance contracts (see 3.9.2 below) do not create financial assets or financial liabilities, then IFRS 15 applies to the recognition of associated revenue. The principle outlined in IFRS 15 is to recognise revenue associated with a transaction involving the rendering of services when (or as) an entity satisfies a performance obligation by transferring the promised service to a customer in an amount that reflects the consideration to which the entity expects to be entitled. *[IFRS 4.B21]*. This could differ from revenue recognition for insurance contracts measured under local GAAP.

3.9 Examples of insurance and non-insurance contracts

The section contains examples given in IFRS 4 of insurance and non-insurance contracts.

3.9.1 Examples of insurance contracts

The following are examples of contracts that are insurance contracts, if the transfer of insurance risk is significant:

(a) insurance against theft or damage to property;
(b) insurance against product liability, professional liability, civil liability or legal expenses;
(c) life insurance and prepaid funeral plans (although death is certain, it is uncertain when death will occur or, for some types of life insurance, whether death will occur within the period covered by the insurance);
(d) life-contingent annuities and pensions (contracts that provide compensation for the uncertain future event – the survival of the annuitant or pensioner – to assist the annuitant or pensioner in maintaining a given standard of living, which would otherwise be adversely affected by his or her survival);
(e) disability and medical cover;
(f) surety bonds, fidelity bonds, performance bonds and bid bonds (i.e. contracts that provide compensation if another party fails to perform a contractual obligation, for example an obligation to construct a building);
(g) credit insurance that provides for specified payments to be made to reimburse the holder for a loss it incurs because a specified debtor fails to make payment when due under the original or modified terms of a debt instrument. These contracts could have various legal forms, such as that of a guarantee, some types of letter of credit, a credit derivative default contract or an insurance contract. Although these contracts meet the definition of an insurance contract they also meet the definition of a financial guarantee contract and are within the scope of IAS 39 or IFRS 9 and IFRS 7 and not IFRS 4 unless the issuer has previously asserted explicitly that it regards such contracts as insurance contracts and has used accounting applicable to such contracts (see 2.2.3.D above);
(h) product warranties issued by another party for goods sold by a manufacturer, dealer or retailer are within the scope of IFRS 4. However, as discussed at 2.2.3.A above, product warranties issued directly by a manufacturer, dealer or retailer are outside the scope of IFRS 4;
(i) title insurance (insurance against the discovery of defects in title to land that were not apparent when the contract was written). In this case, the insured event is the discovery of a defect in the title, not the title itself;
(j) travel assistance (compensation in cash or in kind to policyholders for losses suffered while they are travelling);
(k) catastrophe bonds that provide for reduced payments of principal, interest or both if a specified event adversely affects the issuer of the bond (unless the specified event does not create significant insurance risk, for example if the event is a change in an interest rate or a foreign exchange rate);
(l) insurance swaps and other contracts that require a payment based on changes in climatic, geological and other physical variables that are specific to a party to the contract; and
(m) reinsurance contracts. *[IFRS 4.B18]*.

These examples are not intended to be an exhaustive list.

The following illustrative examples provide further guidance on situations where there is significant insurance risk:

Example 55.8: Deferred annuity with guaranteed rates

Entity A issues a contract to a policyholder who will receive, or can elect to receive, a life-contingent annuity at rates guaranteed at inception.

This is an insurance contract unless the transfer of insurance risk is not significant. The contract transfers mortality risk to the insurer at inception, because the insurer might have to pay significant additional benefits for an individual contract if the annuitant elects to take the life-contingent annuity and survives longer than expected. *[IFRS 4.IG2 E1.6].*

This example contrasts with Example 55.3 above where the rates were not set at the inception of the policy and therefore that was not an insurance contract at inception.

Example 55.9: Guarantee fund established by contract

A guarantee fund is established by contract. The contract requires all participants to pay contributions to the fund so that it can meet obligations incurred by participants (and, perhaps, others). Participants would typically be from a single industry, e.g. insurance, banking or travel.

The contract that establishes the guarantee fund is an insurance contract. *[IFRS 4.IG2 E1.13].*

This example contrasts with Example 55.15 below where a guarantee fund has been established by law and not by contract.

Example 55.10: Insurance contract issued to employees related to a defined contribution pension plan

An insurance contract is issued by an insurer to its employees as a result of a defined contribution pension plan. The contractual benefits for employee service in the current and prior periods are not contingent on future service. The insurer also issues similar contracts on the same terms to third parties.

This is an insurance contract. However, if the insurer pays part or all of its employee's premiums, the payment by an insurer is an employee benefit within the scope of IAS 19 and is not accounted for under IFRS 4 because the insurer is the employer and would be paying its own insurance premiums. *[IFRS 4.IG2 E1.22].*

Defined benefit pension liabilities are outside the scope of IFRS 4 as discussed at 2.2.3.B above.

Example 55.11: No market value adjustment for maturity benefits

A contract permits the issuer to deduct a market value adjustment (MVA), a charge which varies depending on a market index, from surrender values or death benefits to reflect current market prices for the underlying assets. It does not permit an MVA for maturity benefits.

The policyholder obtains an additional survival benefit because no MVA is applied at maturity. That benefit is a pure endowment because the insured person receives a payment on survival to a specified date but beneficiaries receive nothing if the insured person dies before then. If the risk transferred by that benefit is significant, the contract is an insurance contract. *[IFRS 4.IG2 E1.25].*

Example 55.12: No market value adjustment for death benefits

A contract permits the issuer to deduct a market value adjustment (MVA) from surrender values or maturity payments to reflect current market prices for the underlying assets. It does not permit an MVA for death benefits.

The policyholder obtains an additional death benefit because no MVA is applied on death. If the risk transferred by that benefit is significant, the contract is an insurance contract. *[IFRS 4.IG2 E1.26].*

3.9.2 Examples of transactions that are not insurance contracts

The following are examples of transactions that are not insurance contracts:

(a) investment contracts that have the legal form of an insurance contract but do not expose the insurer to significant insurance risk, for example life insurance contracts in which the insurer bears no significant mortality risk;

(b) contracts that have the legal form of insurance, but pass all significant risk back to the policyholder through non-cancellable and enforceable mechanisms that adjust future payments by the policyholder as a direct result of insured losses, for example some financial reinsurance contracts or some group contracts;

(c) self insurance, in other words retaining a risk that could have been covered by insurance. There is no insurance contract because there is no agreement with another party (see 3.2.2.A above);

(d) contracts (such as gambling contracts) that require a payment if an unspecified uncertain future event occurs, but do not require, as a contractual precondition for payment, that the event adversely affects the policyholder. However, this does not preclude the specification of a predetermined payout to quantify the loss caused by a specified event such as a death or an accident (see 3.7 above);

(e) derivatives that expose one party to financial risk but not insurance risk, because they require that party to make payment based solely on changes in one or more of a specified interest rate, financial instrument price, commodity price, foreign exchange rate, index of prices or rates, credit rating or credit index or other variable, provided in the case of a non-financial variable that the variable is not specific to a party to the contract;

(f) a credit-related guarantee (or letter of credit, credit derivative default contract or credit insurance contract) that requires payments even if the holder has not incurred a loss on the failure of a debtor to make payments when due;

(g) contracts that require a payment based on a climatic, geological or other physical variable that is not specific to a party to the contract. These are commonly described as weather derivatives and are accounted for under IAS 39 or IFRS 9 (see Chapter 45 at 3.3.1); and

(h) catastrophe bonds that provide for reduced payments of principal, interest or both, based on a climatic, geological or other physical variable that is not specific to a party to the contract. *[IFRS 4.B19]*.

The following examples illustrate further situations where IFRS 4 is not applicable.

Example 55.13: Investment contract linked to asset pool

Entity A issues an investment contract in which payments are contractually linked (with no discretion) to returns on a pool of assets held by the issuer.

This contract is within the scope of IAS 39 or IFRS 9 because the payments are based on asset returns and there is no significant insurance risk. *[IFRS 4.IG2 E1.10]*.

Example 55.14: Credit-related guarantee

Entity A issues a credit-related guarantee that does not, as a precondition for payment, require that the holder is exposed to, and has incurred a loss on, the failure of the debtor to make payments on the guaranteed asset when due.

This is a derivative within the scope of IAS 39 or IFRS 9 because there is no insurable interest. *[IFRS 4.IG2 E1.12]*.

Example 55.15: Guarantee fund established by law

Guarantee funds established by law exist in many jurisdictions. Typically they require insurers to contribute funds into a pool in order to pay policyholder claims in the event of insurer insolvencies. They may be funded by periodic (usually annual) levies or by levies only when an insolvency arises. The basis of the funding requirement varies although typically most are based on an insurer's premium income.

The commitment of participants to contribute to the fund is not established by contract so there is no insurance contract. Obligations to guarantee funds are within the scope of IAS 37. *[IFRS 4.IG2 E1.14].*

Example 55.16: Right to recover future premiums

Entity A issues an insurance contract which gives it an enforceable and non-cancellable contractual right to recover all claims paid out of future premiums, with appropriate compensation for the time value of money.

Insurance risk is insignificant because all claims can be recovered from future premiums and consequently the insurer cannot suffer a significant loss. Therefore, the contract is a financial instrument within the scope of IAS 39 or IFRS 9. *[IFRS 4.IG2 E1.18].*

Example 55.17: Catastrophe bond linked to index

Entity A issues a catastrophe bond in which principal, interest payments or both are reduced if a specified triggering event occurs and that triggering event does not include a condition that the issuer of the bond suffered a loss.

This is a financial instrument with an embedded derivative. Both the holder and the issuer, measure the embedded derivative at fair value through profit or loss under IAS 39 or IFRS 9. *[IFRS 4.IG2 E1.19].*

Example 55.18: Insurance policy issued to defined benefit pension plan

Entity A issues an insurance contract to either (a) a defined benefit pension plan, covering the employees of A, and/or (b) the employees of another entity consolidated within the same group financial statements as A.

This contract will generally be eliminated on consolidation from the group financial statements which will include:

(a) the full amount of the pension obligation under IAS 19 with no deduction for the plan's right under the contract;

(b) no liability to policyholders under the contract; and

(c) the assets backing the contract. *[IFRS 4.IG2 E1.21].*

In January 2008, the Interpretations Committee considered a request for guidance on the accounting for investment or insurance policies that are issued by an entity to a pension plan covering its own employees (or the employees of an entity that is consolidated into the same group as the entity issuing the policy). The Interpretations Committee noted the definitions of plan assets, assets held by a long-term employee benefit plan and a qualifying insurance policy as defined by IAS 19 and considered that, if a policy was issued by a group company to the employee benefit fund then the treatment would depend on whether the policy was a 'non-transferable financial instrument issued by the reporting entity'. Since the policy was issued by a related party, the Interpretations Committee concluded that it could not meet the definition of a qualifying insurance policy as defined by IAS 19. Because of the narrow scope of this issue the Interpretations Committee declined to either issue an Interpretation or to add the issue to its agenda.[3]

Example 55.19: Market value adjustment without death or maturity benefits

A contract permits the issuer to deduct an MVA from surrender payments to reflect current market prices for the underlying assets. The contract does not permit an MVA for death and maturity benefits. The amount payable on death or maturity is the amount originally invested plus interest.

The policyholder obtains an additional benefit because no MVA is applied on death or maturity. However, that benefit does not transfer insurance risk from the policyholder because it is certain that the policyholder will live or die and the amount payable on death or maturity is adjusted for the time value of money. Therefore, the contract is an investment contract because there is no significant insurance risk. This contract combines the two features discussed in Examples 55.11 and 55.12 at 3.9.1 above. When considered separately, these two features transfer insurance risk. However, when combined, they do not transfer insurance risk. Therefore, it is not appropriate to separate this contract into two insurance components.

If the amount payable on death were not adjusted in full for the time value of money, or were adjusted in some other way, the contract might transfer insurance risk. *[IFRS 4.IG2 E1.27].*

3.10 Ex-gratia payments

An ex-gratia payment is a payment to the policyholder where, based on the terms and conditions of the policy, an insurer would not be obliged to make a payment to the policyholder. This would be a voluntary payment made by the insurer in response to a loss for which the insurer is not technically liable under the terms and conditions of its policy.

Ex-gratia payments should be accounted for in accordance with the insurer's local GAAP applied under IFRS 4, where this is available; otherwise, the insurer should select an accounting policy for such payments under IFRS 4.

4 EMBEDDED DERIVATIVES

Insurance contracts may contain policyholder options or other clauses that meet the definition of an embedded derivative under IAS 39 or IFRS 9. A derivative is a financial instrument within the scope of IAS 39 or IFRS 9 with all three of the following characteristics:

- its value changes in response to a change in a specified interest rate, financial instrument price, commodity price, foreign exchange rate, index of prices or rates, credit rating or credit index, or other variable, provided in the case of a non-financial variable that the variable is not specific to the underlying of the contract;
- it requires no initial net investment or an initial net investment that would be smaller than would be required for other types of contracts that would be expected to have a similar response to changes in market factors; and
- it is settled at a future date. *[IAS 39.9, IFRS 9 Appendix A].*

An embedded derivative is a component of a hybrid (combined) instrument that also includes a non-derivative host contract. An embedded derivative causes some or all of the cash flows that would otherwise be required by the contract to be modified according to a specified interest rate, financial instrument price, commodity price, foreign exchange rate, index of prices or rates, credit rating or credit index, or other variable provided in the case of a non-financial variable that the variable is not specific to a party to the contract. *[IAS 39.10, IFRS 9.4.3.1].*

The following are examples of embedded derivatives that may be found in insurance contracts:
- benefits, such as death benefits, linked to equity prices or an equity index;
- options to take life-contingent annuities at guaranteed rates;
- guarantees of minimum interest rates in determining surrender or maturity values;
- guarantees of minimum annuity payments where the annuity payments are linked to investment returns or asset prices;
- a put option for the policyholder to surrender a contract. These can be specified in a schedule, based on the fair value of a pool of interest-bearing securities or based on an equity or commodity price index;
- an option to receive a persistency bonus (an enhancement to policyholder benefits for policies that remain in-force for a certain period);
- an industry loss warranty where the loss trigger is an industry loss as opposed to an entity specific loss;
- a catastrophe trigger where a trigger is defined as a financial variable such as a drop in a designated stock market;
- an inflation index affecting policy deductibles;
- contracts where the currency of claims settlement differs from the currency of loss; and
- contracts with fixed foreign currency rates.

IAS 39 requires that an embedded derivative is separated from its host contract and measured at fair value with changes in fair value included in profit or loss if:
- its economic characteristics and risks are not closely related to the economic characteristics and risks of the host contract;
- it meets the definition of a derivative; and
- the combined instrument is not measured at fair value through profit or loss. [IAS 39.11].

IFRS 9 has identical requirements, although they do not apply to contracts that are financial assets. [IFRS 9.4.3.3].

The IASB considered and rejected arguments that insurers should be exempt from the requirement to separate embedded derivatives contained in a host insurance contract under IAS 39 or IFRS 9 because, in the IASB's opinion, fair value is the only relevant measure for derivatives. [IFRS 4.BC190].

However, the IASB decided to exclude derivatives embedded in an insurance contract from the IAS 39 or IFRS 9 measurement requirements, if the embedded derivative is itself an insurance contract. [IFRS 4.7].

The IASB determined that it would be contradictory to require the measurement at fair value of an embedded derivative that met the definition of an insurance contract when such accounting is not required for a stand-alone insurance contract. Similarly, the IASB concluded that an embedded derivative is closely related to the host insurance contract if the embedded derivative and the host insurance contract are so interdependent that an entity cannot measure the embedded derivative separately. Without this conclusion

IAS 39 or IFRS 9 would have required an insurer to measure the entire insurance contract at fair value. *[IFRS 4.BC193].*

This means that derivatives embedded within insurance contracts do not have to be separated and accounted for under IAS 39 or IFRS 9 if the policyholder benefits from the embedded derivative only when the insured event occurs.

IFRS 4 also states that an insurer need not (but may) separate, and measure at fair value, a policyholder's option to surrender an insurance contract for a fixed amount (or for an amount based on a fixed amount and an interest rate) even if the exercise price differs from the carrying amount of the host insurance liability. This appears to overrule the requirement in IAS 39 or IFRS 9 that a call, put or prepayment option embedded in a host insurance contract must be separated from the host insurance contract unless the option's exercise price is approximately equal on each exercise date to the carrying amount of the host insurance contract. *[IAS 39.AG30(g), IFRS 9.B4.3.5(e)].* Because surrender values of insurance contracts often do not equal their amortised cost, without this concession in IFRS 4 fair value measurement of the surrender option would be required. *[IFRS 4.8].* This relief also applies to investment contracts with a discretionary participation feature. *[IFRS 4.9].*

The diagram below illustrates an embedded derivative decision tree.

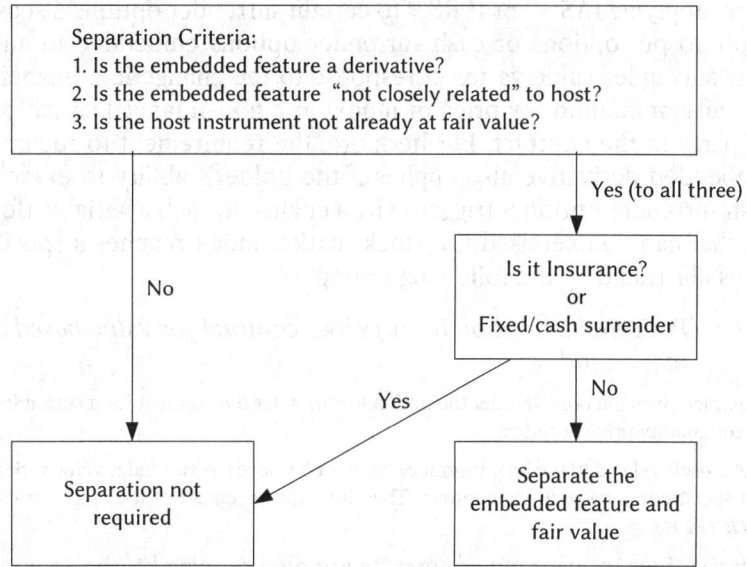

The example below illustrates an embedded derivative in an insurance contract that is not required to be separated and accounted for under IAS 39 or IFRS 9.

Example 55.20: Death or annuitisation benefit linked to equity prices or index

A contract has a death benefit linked to equity prices or an equity index and is payable only on death or when annuity payments begin and not on surrender or maturity.

The equity-index feature meets the definition of an insurance contract (unless the life-contingent payments are insignificant) because the policyholder benefits from it only when the insured event occurs. The embedded derivative is not required to be separated for accounting purposes. *[IFRS 4.IG4 E2.1].*

The following two examples illustrate the application of the concession that IFRS 4 gives from the requirements in IAS 39 or IFRS 9 to separate and measure at fair value, surrender options for which the exercise price is not amortised cost as discussed above.

Example 55.21: Life contingent annuity option

An insurance contract gives the policyholder the option to take a life-contingent annuity at a guaranteed rate i.e. a combined guarantee of interest rates and mortality changes.

The embedded option is an insurance contract (unless the life-contingent payments are insignificant) because the option is derived from mortality changes. Fair value measurement is not required (but not prohibited) even though the guaranteed rate may differ from the carrying amount of the insurance liability. [IFRS 4.IG4 E2.3].

Example 55.22: Policyholder option to surrender contract for cash surrender value

An insurance contract gives the policyholder the option to surrender the contract for a cash surrender value specified in a schedule i.e. not indexed and does not accumulate interest.

Fair value measurement is not required (but not prohibited) because the surrender option is for a fixed amount even though that fixed amount may differ from the carrying amount of the insurance liability. The surrender value may be viewed as a deposit component, but IFRS 4 does not require an insurer to unbundle a contract if it recognises all its obligations arising under the deposit component (see 5 below).

If this was an investment contract measured at amortised cost then fair value measurement of the option would be required if the surrender value was not approximately equal to the amortised cost at each exercise date. [IFRS 4.IG4 E2.12].

The relief from applying IAS 39 or IFRS 9 to certain surrender options discussed above does not apply to put options or cash surrender options embedded in an insurance contract if the surrender value varies in response to the change in a financial variable (such as an equity or commodity price or index) or a non-financial variable that is not specific to a party to the contract. Furthermore, the requirement to separate and fair value the embedded derivative also applies if the holder's ability to exercise the put option or cash surrender option is triggered by a change in such a variable (for example, a put option that can be exercised if a stock market index reaches a specified level). [IFRS 4.8]. This is illustrated by the following example.

Example 55.23: Policyholder option to surrender contract for value based on a market index

An insurance contract gives the policyholder the option to surrender the contract for a surrender value based on an equity or commodity price or index.

The option is not closely related to the host insurance contract because the surrender value is derived from an index and is not specific to a party to the contract. Therefore, measurement of the option at its fair value is required. [IFRS 4.IG4 E2.14].

Embedded derivatives in insurance contracts are also required to be separated where they do not relate to insurance risk and are not otherwise closely related to the host contract. An example of this is illustrated below.

Example 55.24: Persistency bonus

An insurance contract gives policyholders a persistency bonus paid at maturity in cash (or as a period-certain annuity).

The embedded derivative (the option to receive the persistency bonus) is not an insurance contract because, as discussed at 3.7 above, insurance risk does not include lapse or persistency risk. Therefore, measurement of the option at its fair value is required. [IFRS 4.IG4 E2.17].

If the persistency bonus was paid at maturity as an enhanced life-contingent annuity, then the embedded derivative would be an insurance contract and separate accounting would not be required. [IFRS 4.IG4 E2.18].

Non-guaranteed participating dividends contained in an insurance contract are discretionary participation features rather than embedded derivatives and are discussed at 6 below.

Although IFRS 4 provides relief from the requirements of IAS 39 or IFRS 9 to separately account for embedded derivatives, some derivatives embedded in insurance contracts may still be required to be separated from the host instrument and accounted for at fair value under IAS 39 or IFRS 9 as illustrated in Examples 55.23 and 55.24 above. In some circumstances this can be a challenging and time-consuming task.

4.1 Unit-linked features

A unit-linked feature (i.e. a contractual term that requires payments denominated in units of an internal or external investment fund) embedded in a host insurance contract (or financial instrument) is considered to be closely related to the host contract if the unit-denominated payments are measured at current unit values that reflect the fair values of the assets of the fund. *[IAS 39.AG33(g), IFRS 9.B4.3.8(g)].*

IAS 39 or IFRS 9 also considers that unit-linked investment liabilities should be normally regarded as puttable instruments that can be put back to the issuer at any time for cash equal to a proportionate share of the net asset value of an entity, i.e. they are not closely related. Nevertheless, the effect of separating an embedded derivative and accounting for each component is to measure the combined instrument at the redemption amount that is payable at the reporting date if the unit holders had exercised their right to put the instrument back to the issuer. *[IAS 39.AG32, IFRS 9.B4.3.7].* This seems to somewhat contradict the fact that the unit-linked feature is regarded as closely related (which means no separation of the feature is required) but the accounting treatment is substantially the same.

5 UNBUNDLING OF DEPOSIT COMPONENTS

The definition of an insurance contract distinguishes insurance contracts within the scope of IFRS 4 from investments and deposits within the scope of IAS 39 or IFRS 9. However, most insurance contracts contain both an insurance component and a 'deposit component'. *[IFRS 4.10].* Indeed, virtually all insurance contracts have an implicit or explicit deposit component, because the policyholder is generally required to pay premiums before the period of the risk and therefore the time value of money is likely to be one factor that insurers consider in pricing contracts. *[IFRS 4.BC40].*

A deposit component is 'a contractual component that is not accounted for as a derivative under IAS 39 or IFRS 9 and would be within the scope of IAS 39 or IFRS 9 if it were a separate instrument'. *[IFRS 4 Appendix A].*

IFRS 4 requires an insurer to 'unbundle' those insurance and deposit components in certain circumstances, *[IFRS 4.10],* i.e. to account for the components of a contract as if they were separate contracts. *[IFRS 4 Appendix A].* In other circumstances unbundling is either allowed (but not required) or is prohibited.

Unbundling has the following accounting consequences:

(a) the insurance component is measured as an insurance contract under IFRS 4;

(b) the deposit component is measured under IAS 39 or IFRS 9 at either amortised cost or fair value, which may not be consistent with the measurement basis used for the insurance component;

(c) premiums for the deposit component are not recognised as revenue, but rather as changes in the deposit liability. Premiums for the insurance component are typically recognised as revenue (see 3.8 above); and

(d) a portion of the transaction costs incurred at inception is allocated to the deposit component if this allocation has a material effect. *[IFRS 4.12, BC41]*.

The IASB's main reason for making unbundling mandatory only in limited circumstances was to give relief to insurers from having to make costly systems changes. These changes have been needed to identify and separate the various deposit components in certain contracts (e.g. surrender values in traditional life insurance contracts) which may then have needed to be reversed when an entity applied what became IFRS 17. However, the IASB generally regards unbundling as appropriate for all large customised contracts, such as some financial reinsurance contracts, because a failure to unbundle them might lead to the complete omission of material contractual rights and obligations from the statement of financial position. *[IFRS 4.BC44-46]*.

5.1 The unbundling requirements

Unbundling is required only if both the following conditions are met:

(a) the insurer can measure the deposit component (including any embedded surrender options) separately (i.e. without considering the insurance component); and

(b) the insurer's accounting policies do not otherwise require it to recognise all obligations and rights arising from the deposit component. *[IFRS 4.10(a)]*.

Unbundling is permitted, but not required, if the insurer can measure the deposit component separately as in (a) but its accounting policies require it to recognise all obligations and rights arising from the deposit component. This is regardless of the basis used to measure those rights and obligations. *[IFRS 4.10(b)]*.

Unbundling is prohibited when an insurer cannot measure the deposit component separately. *[IFRS 4.10(c)]*.

Example 55.25: Unbundling

A cedant receives compensation for losses from a reinsurer but the contract obliges the cedant to repay the compensation in future years. That obligation arises from a deposit component.

If the cedant's accounting policies would otherwise permit it to recognise the compensation as income without recognising the resulting obligation, unbundling is required. *[IFRS 4.11]*.

5.2 Unbundling illustration

The implementation guidance accompanying IFRS 4 provides an illustration of the unbundling of the deposit component of a reinsurance contract which is reproduced in full below.

Insurance contracts (IFRS 4) 4565

Example 55.26: Unbundling a deposit component of a reinsurance contract

Background

A reinsurance contract has the following features:

(a) the cedant pays premiums of CU10 every year for five years;

(b) an 'experience account' is established equal to 90% of the cumulative premiums (including the additional premiums discussed in (c) below) less 90% of the cumulative claims;

(c) if the balance in the experience account is negative (i.e. cumulative claims exceed cumulative premiums), the cedant pays an additional premium equal to the experience account balance divided by the number of years left to run on the contract;

(d) at the end of the contract, if the experience account balance is positive (i.e. cumulative premiums exceed cumulative claims), it is refunded to the cedant; if the balance is negative, the cedant pays the balance to the reinsurer as an additional premium;

(e) neither party can cancel the contract before maturity; and

(f) the maximum loss that the reinsurer is required to pay in any period is CU200.

The contract is an insurance contract because it transfers significant risk to the reinsurer. For example, in case 2 discussed below, the reinsurer is required to pay additional benefits with a present value, in year 1, of CU35, which is clearly significant in relation to the contract.

The following discussion addresses the accounting by the reinsurer. Similar principles apply to the accounting by the cedant.

Application of requirements: case 1 – no claims

If there are no claims, the cedant will receive CU45 in year 5 (90% of the cumulative premiums of CU50). In substance, the cedant has made a loan, which the reinsurer will repay in one instalment of CU45 in year 5.

If the reinsurer's accounting policies require it to recognise its contractual liability to repay the loan to the cedant, unbundling is permitted but not required. However, if the reinsurer's accounting policies would not require it to recognise the liability to repay the loan, the reinsurer is required to unbundle the contract.

If the reinsurer is required, or elects, to unbundle the contract, it does so as follows. Each payment by the cedant has two components: a loan advance (deposit component) and a payment for insurance cover (insurance component). Applying IAS 39 or IFRS 9 to the deposit component, the reinsurer is required to measure it initially at fair value. Fair value could be determined by discounting the future cash flows from the deposit component. Assume that an appropriate discount rate is 10% and that the insurance cover is equal in each year, so that the payment for insurance cover is the same in each year. Each payment of CU10 by the cedant is then made up of a loan advance of CU6.7 and an insurance premium of CU3.3.

The reinsurer accounts for the insurance component in the same way it accounts for a separate insurance contract with an annual premium of CU3.3.

The movements in the loan are shown below.

Year	Opening balance	Interest at 10%	Advance (repayment)	Closing balance
	CU	CU	CU	CU
0	0.00	0.00	6.70	6.70
1	6.70	0.67	6.70	14.07
2	14.07	1.41	6.70	22.18
3	22.18	2.21	6.70	31.09
4	31.09	3.11	6.70	40.90
5	40.90	4.10	(45.00)	0.00
Total		11.50	(11.50)	

Application of requirements: case 2 – claim of CU150 in year 1

Consider now what happens if the reinsurer pays a claim of CU150 in year 1. The changes in the experience account, and the resulting additional premiums, are as follows:

Year	Premium	Additional premium	Total premium	Cumulative premium	Claims	Cumulative claims	Cumulative premiums less claims	Experience account
	CU	CU	CU	CU	CU	CU	CU	CU
0	10	0	10	10	0	0	10	9
1	10	0	10	20	(150)	(150)	(130)	(117)
2	10	39	49	69	0	(150)	(81)	(73)
3	10	36	46	115	0	(150)	(35)	(31)
4	10	31	41	156	0	(150)	6	6
Total		106	156		(150)			

Incremental cash flows because of the claim in year 1

The claim in year 1 leads to the following incremental cash flows, compared with case 1:

Year	Additional premium	Claims	Refund in case 2	Refund in case 1	Net incremental cash flow	Present value at 10%
	CU	CU	CU	CU	CU	CU
0	0	0			0	0
1	0	(150)			(150)	(150)
2	39	0			39	35
3	36	0			36	30
4	31	0			31	23
5	0	0	(6)	(45)	39	27
Total	106	(150)	(6)	(45)	(5)	(35)

The incremental cash flows have a present value, in year 1, of CU35 (assuming a discount rate of 10% is appropriate). Applying paragraphs 10-12 of IFRS 4, the cedant unbundles the contract and applies IAS 39 or IFRS 9 to this deposit component (unless the cedant already recognises its contractual obligation to repay the deposit component to the reinsurer). If this were not done, the cedant might recognise the CU150 received in year 1 as income and the incremental payments in years 2-5 as expenses. However, in substance, the reinsurer has paid a claim of CU35 and made a loan of CU115 (CU150 less CU35) that will be repaid in instalments.

The following table shows the changes in the loan balance. The table assumes that the original loan shown in case 1 and the new loan shown in case 2 meet the criteria for offsetting in IAS 32. Amounts shown in the table are rounded.

Year	Opening balance	Interest at 10%	Payments per original schedule	Additional payments in case 2	Closing balance
	CU	CU	CU	CU	CU
0	–	–	6	–	6
1	6	1	7	(115)	(101)
2	(101)	(10)	7	39	(65)
3	(65)	(7)	7	36	(29)
4	(29)	(3)	6	31	5
5	5	1	(45)	39	0
Total		(18)	(12)	30	

Although the example refers to 'in year' the calculations indicate that most of the cash flows occur at the end of each year. The present value table showing the incremental cash flows resulting from the claim 'in year 1' appear to show the present values at the end of year 1. *[IFRS 4.IG5 E3]*.

5.3 Practical difficulties

In unbundling a contract the principal difficulty is identifying the initial fair value of any deposit component. In the IASB's illustration at 5.2 above, a discount rate is provided but in practice contracts will not have a stated discount rate. The issuer and the cedant will therefore have to determine an appropriate discount rate in order to calculate the fair value of the deposit component. The IASB illustration is also unclear as to whether the discount rate is a risk adjusted rate. Fair value measurement would require an adjustment for credit risk.

However, the potential burden on insurers is reduced by the fact that the IASB has limited the requirement to unbundle to only those contracts where the rights and obligations arising from the deposit component are not recognised under insurance accounting. As noted above, the IASB is principally concerned with ensuring that large reinsurance contracts with a significant financing element have all of their obligations properly recorded, although the requirements apply equally to direct insurance contracts. *[IFRS 4.IG5]*.

Some examples of clauses within insurance contracts that might indicate the need for unbundling are:

- 'funds withheld' clauses where part or all of the premium is never paid to the reinsurer or claims are never received;
- 'no claims bonus', 'profit commission' or 'claims experience' clauses which guarantee that the cedant will receive a refund of some of the premium;
- 'experience accounts' used to measure the profitability of the contract. These are often segregated from other funds and contain interest adjustments that may accrue to the benefit of the policyholder;
- 'finite' clauses that limit maximum losses or create a 'corridor' of losses not reinsured under a contract;
- contracts that link the eventual premium to the level of claims;
- commutation clauses whose terms guarantee that either party will receive a refund of amounts paid under the contract; and
- contracts of unusual size where the economic benefits to either party are not obviously apparent.

The unbundling requirements in IFRS 4 do not specifically address the issue of contracts artificially separated through the use of side letters, the separate components of which should be considered together. The IASB believes that it is a wider issue for a future project on linkage (accounting for separate transactions that are connected in some way). However, IFRS 4 does state that linked contracts entered into with a single counterparty (or contracts that are otherwise interdependent) form a single contract, for the purposes of assessing whether significant insurance risk is transferred, although the standard is silent on linked transactions with different counterparties (see 3.2.2 above). *[IFRS 4.BC54]*.

6 DISCRETIONARY PARTICIPATION FEATURES

A discretionary participation feature (DPF) is a contractual right to receive, as a supplement to guaranteed benefits, additional benefits:

(a) that are likely to be a significant portion of the total contractual benefits;
(b) whose amount or timing is contractually at the discretion of the issuer; and
(c) that are contractually based on:
 (i) the performance of a specified pool of contracts or a specified type of contract;
 (ii) realised and/or unrealised investment returns on a specified pool of assets held by the issuer; or
 (iii) the profit or loss of the company, fund or other entity that issues the contract.
 [IFRS 4 Appendix A].

Guaranteed benefits are payments or other benefits to which the policyholder or investor has an unconditional right that is not subject to the contractual discretion of the issuer. Guaranteed benefits are always accounted for as liabilities.

Insurance companies in many countries have issued contracts with discretionary participation features. For example, in Germany, insurance companies must return to the policyholders at least 90% of the investment profits on certain contracts, but may give more. In France, Italy, the Netherlands and Spain, realised investment gains are distributed to the policyholder, but the insurance company has discretion over the timing of realising the gains. In the United Kingdom, bonuses are added to the policyholder account at the discretion of the insurer. These are normally based on the investment return generated by the underlying assets but sometimes include allowance for profits made on other contracts. The following are two examples of contracts with a DPF.

Example 55.27: Unitised with-profits policy

Premiums paid by the policyholder are used to purchase units in a 'with-profits' fund at the current unit price. The insurer guarantees that each unit added to the fund will have a minimum value which is the bid price of the unit. This is the guaranteed amount. In addition, the insurer may add two types of bonus to the with-profits units. These are a regular bonus, which may be added daily as a permanent increase to the guaranteed amount, and a final bonus that may be added on top of those guaranteed amounts when the with-profits units are cashed in. Levels of regular and final bonuses are adjusted twice per year. Both regular and final bonuses are discretionary amounts and are generally set based on expected future returns generated by the funds.

Example 55.28: DPF with minimum interest rates

An insurance contract provides that the insurer must annually credit each policyholder's 'account' with a minimum interest rate (3%). This is the guaranteed amount. The insurer then has discretion with regard to whether and what amount of the remaining undistributed realised investment returns from the assets backing the participating policies are distributed to policyholders in addition to the minimum. The contract states that the insurer's shareholders are only entitled to share up to 10% in the underlying investment results associated with the participating policies. As that entitlement is up to 10%, the insurer can decide to credit the policyholders with more than the minimum sharing rate of 90%. Once any additional interest above the minimum interest rate of 3% is credited to the policyholder it becomes a guaranteed liability.

DPF can appear in both insurance contracts and investment contracts. However, to qualify as a DPF, the discretionary benefits must be likely to be a 'significant' portion of the total contractual benefits. The standard does not quantify what is meant by 'significant' but it could be interpreted in the same sense as in the definition of an insurance contract (see 3.2.1 above).

The definition of a DPF does not capture an unconstrained contractual discretion to set a 'crediting rate' that is used to credit interest or other returns to policyholders (as found in contracts described in some countries as 'universal life' contracts). For example, some contracts may not meet the criterion of (c) above if the discretion to set crediting rates is not contractually bound to the performance of a specified pool of assets or the profit or loss of the entity or fund that issues the contract. The IASB, however, acknowledges that some view these features as similar to a DPF because crediting rates are constrained by market forces and it proposed to revisit the treatment of these features in what became IFRS 17. *[IFRS 4.BC162]*.

With contracts that have discretionary features, the issuer has discretion over the amount and/or timing of distributions to policyholders although that discretion may be subject to some contractual constraints (including related legal and regulatory constraints) and competitive constraints. Distributions are typically made to policyholders whose contracts are still in force when the distribution is made. Thus, in many cases, a change in the timing of a distribution, apart from the change in the value over time, means that a different generation of policyholders might benefit. *[IFRS 4.BC154]*.

Although the issuer has contractual discretion over distributions it is usually likely that current or future policyholders will ultimately receive some, if not most, of the accumulated surplus available at the reporting date. In Example 55.28 above, policyholders are contractually entitled to a minimum of 90% of any discretionary distribution. Management can decide on any (total) amount. The main accounting question is whether that part of the discretionary surplus is a liability or a component of equity. *[IFRS 4.BC155]*.

The problem caused by discretionary features is that it is difficult to argue they meet the definition of a liability under IFRS. However, they can be integral to the economics of a contract and would clearly have to be considered in determining its fair value.

The IASB's *Conceptual Framework for Financial Reporting ('Framework')* published in 2018 defines a liability as a present obligation of the entity to transfer an economic resource as a result of past events. *[CF 4.2, 4.26]*. An obligation is a duty or responsibility that an entity has no practical ability to avoid. *[CF 4.28, 29]*. This can be contractual or constructive (see Chapter 2 at 7.3.1). However, a financial liability under IAS 32 must be a 'contractual obligation' *[IAS 32.11]* and discretionary obligations normally would not meet this requirement because of their discretionary nature.

IAS 37 requires provisions to be established once an 'obligating event' has occurred. Obligating events can be constructive but constructive obligations do require an entity to have indicated its responsibilities to other parties by an established pattern of past practice, published policies, or a sufficiently specific current statement, such that the entity has created a valid expectation on the part of those other parties that it will discharge those responsibilities. *[IAS 37.10]*. Say, for example, that an entity has previously paid discretionary bonuses to policyholders in the past five years of 5%, 15%, 0%, 10% and 5%. What 'valid expectation' has it created at the reporting date to policyholders in the absence of any public statement of management intent or, say, a published policy that discretionary bonuses will be linked to a particular profit figure?

If a DPF does not meet the definition of a liability then, under IAS 32, it would default to being equity, which is the residual interest in an entity's assets after deduction of its liabilities. This appears counter-intuitive and would result in discretionary distributions to policyholders being recorded as equity transactions outside of profit or loss or other comprehensive income. Taking this approach, a contract with a DPF would be bifurcated between liability and equity components like a bond convertible into equity shares.

The IASB's response to this difficult conceptual issue was to ignore it altogether in IFRS 4 and permit entities a choice as to whether to present contracts with a DPF within liabilities or equity. The IASB considered that the factor making it difficult to determine the appropriate accounting for these features is 'constrained discretion', being the combination of discretion and constraints on that discretion. If participation features lack discretion, they are embedded derivatives and are within the scope of IAS 39 or IFRS 9. *[IFRS 4.BC161]*.

There may be timing differences between accumulated profits under IFRS and distributable surplus (i.e. the accumulated amount that is contractually eligible for distribution to holders of a DPF), for example, because distributable surplus excludes unrealised investment gains that are recognised under IAS 39 or IFRS 9. IFRS 4 does not address the classification of such timing differences. *[IFRS 4.BC160]*.

In November 2005, the Interpretations Committee rejected a request for further interpretative guidance on the definition of a DPF. The Interpretations Committee had been informed of concerns that a narrow interpretation of a DPF would fail to ensure clear and comprehensive disclosure about contracts that included these features. In response, the Interpretations Committee noted that disclosure was particularly important in this area, drawing attention to the related implementation guidance, discussed at 11 below, but declined to add the topic to its agenda because it involved some of the most difficult questions that the IASB would need to resolve in what became IFRS 17.[4]

In January 2010, the Interpretations Committee also rejected a request to provide guidance on whether features contained in ownership units issued by certain Real Estate Investment Trusts (REITs) met the definition of a DPF. In some of the trusts, the contractual terms of the ownership units require the REIT to distribute 90% of the Total Distributable Income (TDI) to investors. The remaining 10% may be distributed at the discretion of management. The request was to provide guidance on whether the discretion to distribute the remaining 10% of TDI met the definition of a DPF. If so, IFRS 4 would permit the ownership units to be classified as a liability in its entirety rather than a compound instrument with financial liability and equity components under IAS 32. The Interpretations Committee noted that the definition of a DPF in IFRS 4 requires, among other things, that the instrument provides the holder with guaranteed benefits and that the DPF benefits are in addition to these guaranteed benefits. Furthermore, it noted that such guaranteed benefits were typically found in insurance contracts. In other words, the Interpretations Committee was very sceptical about this presentation. However, it considered that providing guidance on this issue would be in the nature of application guidance, rather than interpretive guidance, and therefore declined to add the issue to its agenda.[5]

The lack of interpretative guidance as to what constitutes a DPF has led to diversity in practice as to what is recognised as a DPF liability. For example, IFRS 4 is silent as to whether that part of an undistributed surplus on a participating contract which does not belong to policyholders should be treated as a liability or equity. This is illustrated by the following example.

Example 55.29: DPF recognition

A minimum of 90% of an investment surplus on a participating contract may be distributed to policyholders although any distribution is entirely at the discretion of the insurer. However, IFRS 4 is silent as to whether the 10% of the surplus which does not belong to policyholders is part of the DPF if it has not been distributed and consequentially there is diversity in practice among insurers as to whether the undistributed DPF liability includes the amount attributable to shareholders. Some insurers recognise the 90% as a liability and the 10% as a component of equity whereas others recognise the entire 100% as a liability until it is distributed.

6.1 Discretionary participation features in insurance contracts

Whilst IFRS 4 permits previous accounting practices for insurance contracts (see 7 below), the IASB considered there was a need to specify special accounting requirements for DPF features within these contracts. This might seem odd but the IASB's main concerns were:

- to prevent insurers classifying contracts with a DPF as an intermediate category that is neither liability nor equity as may have been permitted under some existing local accounting practices, such an intermediate category being incompatible with the *Framework*; *[IFRS 4.BC157]* and

- to ensure consistency with the treatment of DPF in investment contracts. *[IFRS 4.BC158]*.

IFRS 4 requires any guaranteed element (i.e. the obligation to pay guaranteed benefits included in a contract that contains a DPF) within an insurance contract to be recognised as a liability. However, insurers have an option as to whether to present a DPF either as a liability or as a component of equity. The following requirements apply:

(a) where the guaranteed element is not recognised separately from the DPF the whole contract must be classified as a liability;

(b) where the DPF is recognised separately from the guaranteed element, the DPF can be classified as either a liability or as equity. IFRS 4 does not specify how an insurer determines whether the DPF is a liability or equity. The insurer may split the DPF into liability and equity components but must use a consistent accounting policy for such a split; and

(c) a DPF cannot be classified as an intermediate category that is neither liability nor equity. *[IFRS 4.34(a)-(b)]*.

An insurer may recognise all premiums received as revenue without separating any portion that relates to the equity component. *[IFRS 4.34(c)]*. The use of the word 'may' means that an insurer can classify some of the DPF as equity but continue to record all of the contract premiums as income. Conceptually, the IASB has admitted that if part or all of the DPF is classified as a component of equity, then the related portion of the premium should not be included in profit or loss. However, it concluded that requiring each incoming premium on a contract with a DPF to be split between liability and equity would require systems changes beyond the scope of Phase I. Therefore, it decided that an issuer could recognise the entire premium as revenue without separating the portion that relates to the equity component. *[IFRS 4.BC164]*. This conclusion is inconsistent with those discussed at 4 and 5 above where IFRS 4 requires the separation of embedded derivatives and deposit elements of contracts in certain circumstances regardless of the 'systems changes' that may be required as a result.

Subsequent changes in the measurement of the guaranteed element and in the portion of the DPF classified as a liability must be recognised in profit or loss. If part or all of the

DPF is classified in equity, that portion of profit or loss may be attributable to that feature (in the same way that a portion may be attributable to a non-controlling interest). The insurer must recognise the portion of profit or loss attributable to any equity component of a DPF as an allocation of profit or loss, not as expense or income. *[IFRS 4.34(c)]*.

IFRS 4 also requires an insurer to:

(a) apply IAS 39 or IFRS 9 to a derivative embedded within an insurance contract containing a DPF if it is within the scope of IAS 39 or IFRS 9 (see 4 above); and

(b) continue its existing accounting policies for such contracts, unless it changes those accounting policies in a way that complies with IFRS 4 (subject to the constraints noted above and those discussed at 8 below). *[IFRS 4.34(d)-(e)]*.

AMP provide the following detail as to how DPF contracts have been allocated in their income statement and statement of financial position.

Extract 55.2: AMP Limited (2016)

Notes to the financial statements
for the year ended 31 December 2016 [extract]
Section 4: Life insurance and investment contracts
4.1   Accounting for life insurance contracts and investment contracts [extract]

Allocation of operating profit and unvested policyholder benefits

The operating profit arising from discretionary participating contracts is allocated between shareholders and participating policyholders by applying the MoS principles in accordance with the *Life Insurance Act 1995* (Cth) (Life Act) and the Participating Business Management Framework applying to NMLA.

Once profit is allocated to participating policyholders it can only be distributed to these policyholders.

Profit allocated to participating policyholders is recognised in the Income statement as an increase in policy liabilities. The policy liabilities include profit that has not yet been allocated to specific policyholders (i.e. unvested) and that which has been allocated to specific policyholders by way of bonus distributions (i.e. vested).

Bonus distributions to participating policyholders do not alter the amount of profit attributable to shareholders. These are merely changes to the nature of the liability from unvested to vested.

The principles of allocation of the profit arising from discretionary participating business are as follows:

(i) investment income (net of tax and investment expenses) on retained earnings in respect of discretionary participating business is allocated between policyholders and shareholders in proportion to the balances of policyholders' and shareholders' retained earnings. This proportion is, mostly, 80% to policyholders and 20% to shareholders;

(ii) other MoS profits arising from discretionary participating business are allocated 80% to policyholders and 20% to shareholders, with the following exceptions:

- the profit arising from New Zealand corporate superannuation business is apportioned such that shareholders are allocated 15% of the profit allocated to policyholders;

- the profit arising in respect of preservation superannuation account business is allocated 92.5% to policyholders and 7.5% to shareholders;

- the profits arising from NMLA's discretionary participating investment account business where 100% of investment profit is allocated to policyholders and 100% of any other profit or loss is allocated to shareholders, with the over-riding provision being that at least 80% of any profit and not more than 80% of any loss be allocated to policyholders' retained profits of the relevant statutory fund;

- the underwriting profit arising in respect of NMLA's participating super risk business is allocated 90% to policyholders and 10% to shareholders.

6.2 Discretionary participation features in financial instruments

As discussed at 2.2.2 above, a financial instrument containing a DPF is also within the scope of IFRS 4, not IAS 39 or IFRS 9, and issuers of these contracts are permitted to continue applying their existing accounting policies to them rather than apply the rules in IAS 39 or IFRS 9.

The requirements discussed at 6.1 above apply equally to financial instruments that contain a DPF. However, in addition:

(a) if the issuer classifies the entire DPF as a liability, it must apply the liability adequacy test discussed at 7.2.2 below to the whole contract, i.e. to both the guaranteed element and the DPF. The issuer need not determine separately the amount that would result from applying IAS 39 or IFRS 9 to the guaranteed element;

(b) if the issuer classifies part or all of the DPF of that instrument as a separate component of equity, the liability recognised for the whole contract should not be less than the amount that would result from applying IAS 39 or IFRS 9 to the guaranteed element. That amount should include the intrinsic value of an option to surrender the contract but need not include its time value if IFRS 4 exempts that option from fair value measurement (see 4 above). The issuer need not disclose the amount that would result from applying IAS 39 or IFRS 9 to the guaranteed element, nor need it present the guaranteed amount separately. Furthermore, it need not determine the guaranteed amount if the total liability recognised for the whole contract is clearly higher; and

(c) the issuer may continue to recognise all premiums (including the premiums from the guaranteed element) as revenue and recognise as an expense the resulting increase in the carrying amount of the liability even though these contracts are financial instruments.

The IASB has admitted that, conceptually, the premium for the guaranteed element of these investment contracts is not revenue but believes that the treatment of the discretionary element could depend on matters that will not be resolved until Phase II. It has also decided to avoid requiring entities to make systems changes in order to split the premium between the guaranteed and discretionary elements, which might later become redundant. Therefore, entities can continue to present premiums or deposits received from investment contracts with a DPF as revenue, with an expense representing the corresponding change in the liability. *[IFRS 4.BC163].*

AXA's accounting policy for revenue recognition gives an example of an accounting policy that includes premiums from investment contracts with a DPF as revenue.

> *Extract 55.3: AXA SA (2016)*
> **NOTES TO THE CONSOLIDATED FINANCIAL STATEMENTS** [extract]
> 1.19.   REVENUE RECOGNITION [extract]
> **1.19.1. Gross written premiums**
>
> Gross written premiums correspond to the amount of premiums written by insurance and reinsurance companies on business incepted in the year with respect to both insurance contracts and investment contracts with discretionary participating features, net of cancellations and gross of reinsurance ceded. For reinsurance, premiums are recorded on the basis of declarations made by the ceding company, and may include estimates of gross written premiums.

The disclosure requirements of IFRS 7 and IFRS 13 apply to financial instruments containing a DPF even though they are accounted for under IFRS 4. *[IFRS 4.2(b)]*. However, disclosure of the fair value of a contract containing a DPF (as described in IFRS 4) is not required if the fair value of that DPF cannot be measured reliably. *[IFRS 7.29(c)]*. Further, IFRS 4 allows the disclosed amount of interest expense for such contracts to be calculated on a basis other than the effective interest method. *[IFRS 4.35(d)]*. All of the other disclosure requirements of IFRS 7 and IFRS 13 apply to investment contracts with a DPF without modification, for example the contractual maturity analysis showing undiscounted cash flows and the fair value hierarchy categorisation if the contracts are measured at fair value.

6.3 Practical issues

6.3.1 Unallocated DPF liabilities which are negative

Cumulative unallocated realised and unrealised returns on investments backing insurance and investment contracts with a DPF may become negative and result in an unallocated amount that is negative (a cumulative unallocated loss).

Negative DPF is not addressed in IFRS 4 and does not appear to have been contemplated by the IASB at the time the standard was issued.

Assuming an insurer normally classifies contracts with a DPF as a liability, where such amounts become negative we believe that the insurer is prohibited from recognising an asset or debiting the contract liability related to the cumulative unallocated losses (realised or unrealised) on the investments backing contracts that include DPF features except to the extent that:

- the insurer is contractually entitled to pass those losses to the contract holders; or
- the insurer's previous local GAAP accounting for insurance or investment contracts with a DPF permitted the recognition of such an asset or the debiting of the contract liability when the unallocated investment results of the investments backing a DPF contract were negative.

An insurer is permitted to continue existing GAAP accounting for insurance contracts and investment contracts with a DPF as discussed at 7 below. If an existing GAAP accounting policy specifically allows the recognition of an asset or the reduction of contract liabilities related to cumulative unallocated DPF losses, then in our view continuation of that policy is permitted because IFRS 4 specifically excludes accounting policies for insurance contracts from paragraphs 10-12 of IAS 8. If the existing GAAP accounting policy does not permit the recognition of an asset or the reduction of contract liabilities in such circumstances, then the introduction of such a policy would need to satisfy the relevance and reliability criteria discussed at 8.1 below to be permissible.

Examples of situations in which an insurer is contractually entitled to (partially) recover losses can include contracts with a fixed surrender charge or a market value adjustment feature.

6.3.2 Contracts with switching features

Some contracts may contain options for the counterparty to switch between terms that would, *prima facie*, result in classification as an investment contract without DPF features (accounted for under IAS 39 or IFRS 9) and terms that would result in a classification as an investment contract with DPF features (accounted for under IFRS 4).

We believe that the fact that this switch option makes these contracts investment contracts with a DPF means that the issuer should continuously be able to demonstrate that the DPF feature still exists and also be able to demonstrate actual switching to a DPF in order to classify these contracts as investment contracts with a DPF under IFRS 4.

7 SELECTION OF ACCOUNTING POLICIES

IFRS 4 provides very little guidance on accounting policies that should be used by an entity that issues insurance contracts or investment contracts with a DPF (hereafter for convenience, at 7 and 8 below, referred to as 'insurance contracts').

Instead of providing detailed guidance, the standard:

(a) creates an exemption from applying the hierarchy in IAS 8 (the 'hierarchy exemption') that specifies the criteria an entity should use in developing an accounting policy if no IFRS applies specifically to an item (see 7.1 below);

(b) limits the impact of the hierarchy exemption by imposing five specific requirements relating to catastrophe provisions, liability adequacy, derecognition, offsetting and impairment of reinsurance assets (see 7.2 below); and

(c) permits some existing practices to continue but prohibits their introduction (see 8.2.1 below).

The importance of the hierarchy exemption is that without it certain existing accounting practices would be unlikely to be acceptable under IFRS as they would conflict with the *Framework* or other standards such as IAS 37, IAS 39 or IFRS 9 or IFRS 15. For example, the deferral of acquisition costs that are not incremental or directly attributable to the issue of an insurance contract are unlikely to meet the *Framework's* definition of an asset. Similarly, a basis of liability measurement, such as the gross premium valuation, which includes explicit estimates of future periods' cash inflows in respect of policies which are cancellable at the policyholder's discretion would be unlikely to be acceptable.

The IASB considered that, without the hierarchy exemption, establishing acceptable accounting policies for insurance contracts could have been costly and that some insurers might have made major changes to their policies on adoption of IFRS followed by further significant changes in what became IFRS 17. *[IFRS 4.BC77].*

The practical result of the hierarchy exemption is that an insurer is permitted to continue applying the accounting policies that it was using when it first applied IFRS 4, subject to the exceptions noted at 7.2 below. *[IFRS 4.BC83].*

Usually, but not exclusively, these existing accounting policies will be the insurer's previous GAAP, but IFRS 4 does not specifically require an insurer to follow its local accounting pronouncements. This is mainly because of the problems in defining local GAAP. Additionally, some insurers, such as non-US insurers with a US listing, apply US GAAP to their insurance contracts rather than the GAAP of their own country which would have given rise to further definitional problems. *[IFRS 4.BC81].* The IASB also wanted to give insurers the opportunity to improve their accounting policies even if there was no change to their local GAAP. *[IFRS 4.BC82].*

The practical result of this is a continuation of the diversity in accounting practices whose elimination was one of the primary objectives of the IASC's project on insurance contracts originally initiated in 1997.

To illustrate this point, below are extracts from the financial statements of Prudential and Münchener Rück (Munich Re), both of which apply IFRS. Prudential is a UK insurance group which applies previously extant UK GAAP to its UK insurance contracts whereas Munich Re is a German insurance group that applies US GAAP (as at 1 January 2005) to its insurance contracts.

> Extract 55.4: Prudential plc (2016)
>
> Notes to Primary statements [extract]
> Section A: Background and critical accounting policies [extract]
> A3.1 Critical accounting policies, estimates and judgements [extract]
> Measurement of policyholder liabilities and unallocated surplus of with-profits [extract]
>
> IFRS 4 permits the continued usage of previously applied Generally Accepted Accounting Practices (GAAP) for insurance contracts and investment contracts with discretionary participating features.
>
> A modified statutory basis of reporting was adopted by the Group on first-time adoption of IFRS in 2005. This was set out in the Statement of Recommended Practice issued by the Association of British Insurers (ABI SORP). An exception was for UK regulated with-profits funds which were measured under FRS 27 as discussed below.
>
> FRS 27 and the ABI SORP were withdrawn in the UK for the accounting periods beginning in or after 2015. As used in these consolidated financial statements, the terms 'FRS 27' and the 'ABI SORP' refer to the requirements of these pronouncements prior to their withdrawal.

> Extract 55.5: Allianz SE (2016)
>
> Notes to the consolidated financial statements [extract]
> GENERAL INFORMATION [extract]
> 1 – Nature of operations and basis of presentation [extract]
>
> In accordance with the provisions of IFRS 4 insurance contracts are recognized and measured on the basis of accounting principles generally accepted in the United States of America (US GAAP) as at first-time adoption of IFRS 4 on 1 January 2005.

7.1 The hierarchy exemption

Paragraphs 10-12 of IAS 8 provide guidance on the development and application of accounting policies in the absence of a standard or interpretation that specifically applies to a transaction. In particular, it explains the applicability and relative weighting to be given to other IFRS sources, the use of guidance issued by other standard-setting bodies and other accounting literature and accepted industry practices.

An insurer is not required to apply paragraphs 10-12 of IAS 8 for:

(a) insurance contracts that it issues (including related acquisition costs and related intangible assets); and

(b) reinsurance contracts that it holds. *[IFRS 4.13]*.

What this means is that an insurer need not consider:

- whether its existing accounting policies are consistent with the *Framework*;

- whether those accounting policies regarding insurance contracts are consistent with other standards and interpretations dealing with similar and related issues; or
- whether they result in information that is 'relevant' or 'reliable'.

This exemption was controversial within the IASB and resulted in five members of the IASB dissenting from the issue of the standard. It was also opposed by some respondents to ED 5 on the grounds that it would permit too much diversity in practice and allow fundamental departures from the *Framework* that could prevent an insurer's financial statements from presenting information that is understandable, relevant, reliable and comparable. The IASB admitted that the exemption is 'unusual' but believed that it was necessary to minimise disruption in 2005 for both users and preparers. *[IFRS 4.BC79].*

7.2 Limits on the hierarchy exemption

In order to prevent insurers continuing with accounting policies that the IASB considered would either not be permitted by what became IFRS 17 or which conflict too greatly with other standards, such as IAS 39 or IFRS 9 or IAS 37, IFRS 4 imposes several limits on the hierarchy exception. These are in respect of:

- catastrophe and equalisation provisions;
- liability adequacy testing;
- derecognition of insurance liabilities;
- offsetting of reinsurance contracts against relating direct insurance contracts; and
- impairment of reinsurance assets. *[IFRS 4.14].*

These are discussed below.

7.2.1 Catastrophe and equalisation provisions

Catastrophe provisions are provisions that are generally built up over the years out of premiums received, perhaps following a prescribed regulatory formula, until an amount, possibly specified by the regulations, is reached. These provisions are usually intended to be released on the occurrence of a future catastrophic loss that is covered by current and future contracts. Equalisation provisions are usually intended to cover random fluctuations of claim expenses around the expected value of claims for some types of insurance contract (such as hail, credit guarantee and fidelity insurance) perhaps using a formula based on experience over a number of years. *[IFRS 4.BC87].* Consequently, these provisions tend to act as income smoothing mechanisms that reduce profits in reporting periods in which insurance claims are low and reduce losses in reporting periods in which insurance claims are high. As catastrophe and/or equalisation provisions are normally not available for distribution to shareholders, the solvency position of an insurer can be improved.

The recognition of a liability (such as catastrophe and equalisation provisions) for possible future claims, if these claims arise from insurance contracts that are not in existence at the end of the reporting period, is prohibited. *[IFRS 4.14(a)].*

The IASB considers there is no credible basis for arguing that equalisation or catastrophe provisions are recognisable liabilities under IFRS. Such provisions are not liabilities as defined in the *Framework* because the insurer has no present obligation for losses that will occur after the end of the contract period. Therefore, without the hierarchy exemption discussed at 7.1 above, the recognition of these provisions as liabilities would have been prohibited and the requirement described in the paragraph above preserves that prohibition. *[IFRS 4.BC90]*.

The IASB views the objective of financial statements as not to enhance solvency but to provide information that is useful to a wide range of users for economic decisions. *[IFRS 4.BC89(d)]*. Present imperfections in the measurement of insurance liabilities do not, in the IASB's opinion, justify the recognition of items that do not meet the definition of a liability. *[IFRS 4.BC92(a)]*.

Although the recognition of catastrophe and equalisation provisions in respect of claims arising from insurance contracts that are not in force at the end of the reporting period are prohibited, such provisions are permitted to the extent that they were permitted under previous accounting policies and they are attributable to policies in force at the end of the reporting period.

Although IFRS 4 prohibits the recognition of these provisions as a liability, it does not prohibit their segregation as a component of equity. Consequently, insurers are free to designate a proportion of their equity as an equalisation or catastrophe provision. *[IFRS 4.BC93]*.

When a catastrophe or equalisation provision has a tax base but is not recognised in the IFRS financial statements, then a taxable temporary difference will arise that should be accounted for under IAS 12 – *Income Taxes*.

7.2.2 Liability adequacy testing

Many existing insurance accounting models have mechanisms to ensure that insurance liabilities are not understated, and that related amounts recognised as assets, such as deferred acquisition costs, are not overstated. However, because there is no guarantee that such tests are in place in every jurisdiction and are effective, the IASB was concerned that the credibility of IFRS could suffer if an insurer claims to comply with IFRS but fails to recognise material and reasonably foreseeable losses arising from existing contractual obligations.

Therefore, a requirement for the application of a 'liability adequacy test' (an assessment of whether the carrying amount of an insurance liability needs to be increased, or the carrying amount of related deferred acquisition costs or related intangible assets decreased, based on a review of future cash flows) was introduced into IFRS 4. This assessment of liability adequacy is required at each reporting date. *[IFRS 4.BC94]*.

If the assessment shows that the carrying amount of the recognised insurance liabilities (less related deferred acquisition costs and related intangible assets such as those acquired in a business combination or portfolio transfer discussed at 9 below) is inadequate in the light of the estimated future cash flows, the entire deficiency must be recognised immediately in profit or loss. *[IFRS 4.15]*.

The purpose of this requirement is to prevent material liabilities being unrecorded.

7.2.2.A Using a liability adequacy test under existing accounting policies

As many existing insurance accounting models have some form of liability adequacy test, the IASB was keen to ensure that insurers using such models, as far as possible, did not have to make systems changes. Therefore, if an insurer applies a liability adequacy test that meets specified minimum requirements, IFRS 4 imposes no further requirements. The minimum requirements are the following:

(a) the test considers current estimates of all contractual cash flows, and of related cash flows such as claims handling costs, as well as cash flows resulting from embedded options and guarantees; and

(b) if the test shows that the liability is inadequate, the entire deficiency is recognised in profit or loss. *[IFRS 4.16]*.

If the insurer's liability adequacy test meets these requirements then the test should be applied at the level of aggregation specified in that test. *[IFRS 4.18]*.

The standard does not specify:

- what criteria in the liability adequacy test determine when existing contracts end and future contracts start;
- at what level of aggregation the test should be performed;
- whether or how the cash flows are discounted to reflect the time value of money or adjusted for risk and uncertainty;
- whether the test considers both the time value and intrinsic value of embedded options and guarantees; or
- whether additional losses recognised because of the test are recognised by reducing the carrying amount of deferred acquisition costs or by increasing the carrying amount of the related insurance liabilities. *[IFRS 4.BC101]*.

Additionally, IFRS 4 does not state whether this existing liability adequacy test can be performed net of expected related reinsurance recoveries. However, the liability adequacy test discussed at 7.2.2.B below explicitly excludes reinsurance.

IFRS 4 provides only minimum guidelines on what a liability adequacy test comprises. This was to avoid insurers having to make systems changes that may have had to be reversed when what became IFRS 17 was applied but allows the continuation of a diversity of practice among insurers, for example in the use (or not) of discounting. However, some existing practices may not meet these minimum requirements, for example if they use cash flows locked-in at inception rather than current estimates.

An example of the details of a liability adequacy test can be found in the financial statements of Allianz.

> **Extract 55.6: Allianz SE (2016)**
> Notes to the consolidated financial statements [extract]
> 2 – Accounting policies and new accounting pronouncements [extract]
> Summary of significant accounting policies [extract]
> Insurance, investment and reinsurance contracts [extract]
> Liability adequacy tests
>
> Liability adequacy tests are performed for each insurance portfolio on the basis of estimates of future claims, costs, premiums earned, and proportionate investment income. For short-duration contracts, a premium deficiency is recognized if the sum of expected claim costs and claim adjustment expenses, expected dividends to policyholders, DAC, and maintenance expenses exceeds related unearned premiums while considering anticipated investment income.
>
> For long-duration contracts a premium deficiency is recognized, if actual experience regarding investment yields, mortality, morbidity, terminations or expense indicates that existing contract liabilities, along with the present value of future gross premiums, will not be sufficient to cover the present value of future benefits and to recover DAC.

7.2.2.B Using the liability adequacy test specified in IFRS 4

If an insurer's accounting policies do not require a liability adequacy test that meets the minimum criteria discussed, it should:

(a) determine the carrying amount of the relevant insurance liabilities less the carrying amount of:

  (i) any related deferred acquisition costs; and

  (ii) any related intangible assets. However, related reinsurance assets are not considered because an insurer assesses impairment for them separately (see 7.2.5 below);

(b) determine whether the amount described in (a) is less than the carrying amount that would be required if the relevant insurance liabilities were within the scope of IAS 37. If it is less, the entire difference should be recognised in profit or loss and the carrying amount of the related deferred acquisition costs or related intangible assets should be reduced or the carrying amount of the relevant insurance liabilities should be increased. *[IFRS 4.17]*.

This test should be performed at the level of a portfolio of contracts that are subject to broadly similar risks and managed together as a single portfolio. *[IFRS 4.18]*.

Investment margins should be reflected in the calculation if, and only if, the carrying amounts of the liabilities and any related deferred acquisition costs and intangible assets also reflect those margins. *[IFRS 4.19]*.

IAS 37 was used as a basis for this liability adequacy test as it was an existing measurement basis that minimised the need for exceptions to existing IFRS principles. *[IFRS 4.BC95, 104]*.

IAS 37 requires an amount to be recognised as a provision that is the best estimate of the expenditure required to settle the present obligation. This is the amount that an entity would rationally pay to settle the obligation at the reporting date or transfer it to a third party at that time. *[IAS 37.36-47]*. Although IAS 37 refers to 'expenditure' there appears to be no specific prohibition from considering future premiums. This might be appropriate if it can be argued that the expenditures are a function of the future premiums.

The end result is that the IAS 37 requirements are potentially more prescriptive and onerous than those where an insurer has an existing liability adequacy test which meets the minimum IFRS 4 criteria discussed above.

7.2.2.C Investment contracts with a discretionary participation feature

As discussed at 6.2 above the accounting requirements for investment contracts with a DPF depend on whether the entity has classified the DPF as a liability or as equity. Where the DPF is classified entirely as a liability then the liability adequacy test is applied to the whole contract, i.e. both the guaranteed element and the DPF. Where the DPF is classified in part or in total as a separate component of equity then IFRS 4 states that the amount recognised as a liability for the whole contract should be not less than the amount that would result from applying IAS 39 or IFRS 9 to the guaranteed element. IFRS 4 does not specify whether the IAS 39 or IFRS 9 measurement basis should be amortised cost or fair value. It is also not clear if this requirement relates to the gross liability or to the net carrying amount, i.e. less any related deferred acquisition costs or related intangible assets. *[IFRS 4.35(b)]*.

7.2.2.D Interaction between the liability adequacy test and shadow accounting

IFRS 4 does not address the interaction between the liability adequacy test ('LAT') and shadow accounting (discussed at 8.3 below). The liability adequacy test requires all deficiencies to be recognised in profit or loss, whereas shadow accounting permits certain unrealised losses to be recognised in other comprehensive income.

We believe that a company can apply shadow accounting to offset an increase in insurance liabilities to the extent that the increase is caused directly by market interest rate movements that lead to changes in the value of investments that are recognised directly in other comprehensive income. Although IFRS 4 does not specify the priority of shadow accounting over the LAT, because the LAT is to be applied as a final test to the amount recognised under the insurer's accounting policies, it follows that shadow accounting has to be applied first. This is illustrated in the example below.

Example 55.30: Shadow loss recognition

An insurer has classified certain investments backing insurance liabilities as available-for-sale financial assets. It has issued a guaranteed single premium product backed by an investment in a government bond with the same effective interest rate, duration and currency.

The opening position in the statement of financial position, perfectly matched in currency, interest rates and duration is as follows:

	CU		CU
Bond @ 6% effective rate, initial value	100	Equity	10
Other assets	10	Contract @ 6% guarantee	100
Total assets	110	Total liabilities and equity	110

The position in the statement of financial position, one year after issuance, after a significant decline in market interest rates is as follows:

	CU		CU
Bond @ market value	116	Equity	20
Other assets	10	Contract @ 6% guarantee	106
Total assets	126	Total liabilities and equity	126

Given the market interest rate movement, the 'matched' situation no longer shows in the statement of financial position as the investment is valued at CU 116 and the liability at CU 106. The current market return on the assets funding the insurance contract at the time of performing the liability adequacy test (LAT) is no longer 6%. It is now 5.2% (CU 6 ÷ CU 116).

The increase in shareholders' equity could be used for, or considered available for, dividend payments. Part of the cash value of the investment is no longer allocated to the insurance liability, but to shareholders' equity. This is not correct because the entire investment, regardless of its carrying amount, is needed to provide the annual investment return (CU 6) to fund the growth of the liability (CU 6).

The bond's unrealised gain results in a decline in its market interest yield to below 6%. Therefore the liability needs to increase (in other words, a higher amount of the investment needs to be allocated to it) to the level where the nominal CU 6 is earned.

IFRS 4 states that any increase in the liability needs to be charged to profit or loss. However, in this case the increase is caused by a market interest movement that has produced an unrealised gain on an investment. This unrealised gain has been credited to other comprehensive income rather than profit or loss. If the liability increase is charged to profit or loss there will be a mismatch between this and the related unrealised gain in other comprehensive income.

To the extent that the increase in the liability is related to other causes, the insurer should recognise a loss in the income statement.

This example assumes that the effect of the change in market interest rates on the fair value of investments is recorded in other comprehensive income and was exactly the same as the opposite change in the fair value of the liability. In reality these two effects may not match exactly, so there could be a difference between the change in the fair value of the available-for-sale (AFS) assets and the change required in the carrying amount of the liability before the LAT is performed. The impact of shadow accounting needs to be limited to the change in value that was directly recorded in other comprehensive income arising from changes in the fair value carrying amount of the AFS assets.

7.2.3 Insurance liability derecognition

An insurance liability, or a part of such a liability, can be removed from the statement of financial position (derecognised) when, and only when, it is extinguished i.e. when the obligation specified in the contract is discharged, cancelled or expires. *[IFRS 4.14(c)]*.

This requirement is identical to that contained in IAS 39 or IFRS 9 for the derecognition of financial liabilities. *[IAS 39.39, IFRS 9.3.3.1]*. The IASB said it could identify no reasons for the derecognition requirements for insurance liabilities to differ from those for financial liabilities. *[IFRS 4.BC105]*.

Accordingly, insurance liabilities should not normally be derecognised as a result of entering into a reinsurance contract because this does not usually discharge the insurer's liability to the policyholder. This applies even if the insurer has delegated all claims settlement authority to the reinsurer or if a claim has been fully reinsured.

Derecognition should be distinguished from remeasurement. The carrying amounts of many insurance liabilities are estimates and an insurer should re-estimate its claims liabilities, and hence change their carrying amounts, if that is required by its accounting policies. However, in certain situations the distinction between the two concepts can be blurred, for example where there is a dispute or other uncertainty over the contractual terms of an insurance policy.

IFRS 4 contains no guidance on when or whether a modification of an insurance contract might cause derecognition of the assets and liabilities in respect of that contract.

7.2.4 Offsetting of insurance and related reinsurance contracts

IFRS 4 prohibits offsetting of:

(a) reinsurance assets against the related insurance liabilities; and

(b) income or expense from reinsurance contracts against the expense or income from the related insurance contracts. *[IFRS 4.14(d)]*.

This prohibition broadly aligns the offsetting criteria for insurance assets and liabilities with those required for financial assets and financial liabilities under IAS 32, which requires that financial assets and financial liabilities can only be offset where an entity:

(a) has a legally enforceable right to set-off the recognised amounts; and

(b) intends to settle on a net basis, or to realise both the asset and settle the liability simultaneously. *[IAS 32.42]*.

Because a cedant normally has no legal right to offset amounts due from a reinsurer against amounts due to the related underlying policyholder, the IASB considers a gross presentation gives a clearer picture of the cedant's rights and obligations. *[IFRS 4.BC106]*.

As a result, balances due from reinsurers should be shown as assets in the statement of financial position, whereas the related insurance liabilities should be shown as liabilities. Because of the relationship between the two, some insurers provide linked disclosures in the notes to their IFRS financial statements as discussed at 11.1.2.A below.

The IFRS 4 requirements, however, appear to be less flexible than those in IAS 32 in that they provide no circumstances in which offsetting can be acceptable. So, for example, 'pass through' contracts that provide for reinsurers to pay claims direct to the underlying policyholder would still have to be shown gross in the statement of financial position. IAS 32 also does not address offsetting in the income statement.

7.2.5 Impairment of reinsurance assets

If the IASB had required that the impairment model in IAS 36 be applied to reinsurance assets (as proposed in ED 5) many cedants would have been compelled to change their accounting model for reinsurance contracts in a way that was inconsistent with the accounting for the underlying direct insurance liability. This would have required the cedant to address matters such as discounting and risk, together with the attendant systems implications. Consequently, the IASB concluded that the impairment test should focus on credit risk (arising from the risk of default by the reinsurer and also from disputes over coverage) and not address matters arising from the measurement of the underlying direct insurance liability. It decided the most appropriate way to achieve this was to introduce an incurred loss model based on that contained in IAS 39. *[IFRS 4.BC107-108]*.

Consequently, a reinsurance asset should be impaired if, and only if:

(a) there is objective evidence, as a result of an event that occurred after initial recognition of the asset, that the cedant may not receive all amounts due to it under the terms of the contract; and

(b) that event has a reliably measurable impact on the amounts that the cedant will receive from the reinsurer. *[IFRS 4.20]*.

Where a reinsurance asset is impaired, its carrying amount should be reduced accordingly and the impairment loss recognised in profit or loss.

IAS 39 provides various indicators of impairment for financial assets, such as the significant financial difficulty of the obligor and a breach of contract, such as a default in interest or principal payments. IFRS 4 does not provide any specific indicators of impairment relating to reinsurance assets. In the absence of such indicators, it would seem appropriate for insurers to refer to those in IAS 39 as a guide to determining whether reinsurance assets are impaired.

The use of this impairment model means that provisions cannot be recognised in respect of credit losses expected to arise from future events.

IAS 39 permits a portfolio approach to determining impairment provisions for financial assets carried at amortised cost. More specifically, IAS 39 permits a collective evaluation of impairment for assets that are grouped on the basis of similar credit risk characteristics that are indicative of the debtors' ability to pay all amounts due according to the contractual terms (for example on the basis of a credit risk evaluation or grading process that considers asset type, industry, geographical location, collateral type, past-due status and other relevant factors). *[IAS 39.AG87]*.

It is questionable whether an insurer's reinsurance assets would normally exhibit sufficiently similar credit risk characteristics to permit such an approach to determining impairment. That said, IAS 39 is clear that impairment losses recognised on a group basis represent an interim step pending the identification of impairment losses on individual assets in the group of financial assets that are collectively assessed for impairment. As soon as information is available that specifically identifies losses on individually impaired assets in a group, those assets are removed from the group. *[IAS 39.AG88]*.

IFRS 9 does not contain any consequential amendments to IFRS 4 in respect of impairment of reinsurance assets. Therefore, if an insurer applying IFRS 4 adopts IFRS 9 it must continue to use an incurred loss impairment model for reinsurance assets notwithstanding the fact that an expected loss model will be used for financial assets within the scope of IFRS 9.

7.2.6 Accounting policy matters not addressed by IFRS 4

7.2.6.A Derecognition of insurance and reinsurance assets

IFRS 4 does not address the derecognition of insurance or reinsurance assets. The IASB could identify no reason why the derecognition criteria for insurance assets should differ from those for financial assets accounted for under IAS 39 or IFRS 9 but declined to address the issue 'because derecognition of financial assets is a controversial topic'. *[IFRS 4.BC105]*. Consequently, derecognition of insurance assets should be dealt with under existing accounting practices which may differ from the requirements of IAS 39 or IFRS 9.

7.2.6.B   Impairment of insurance assets

IFRS 4 is silent on the impairment model to be used for receivables arising under insurance contracts that are not reinsurance assets (discussed at 7.2.5 above). An example of these would be premium receivables due from policyholders. Receivables arising from insurance contracts are not within the scope of either IAS 39 or IFRS 9 (see 2.2.2 above). Insurers should therefore apply their existing accounting policies to determine impairment provisions for these assets. Any changes in accounting policy (e.g. to move from an incurred loss model to an expected loss model on adoption of IFRS 9) must satisfy the criteria for changes in accounting policy discussed at 8.1 below and should be applied retrospectively as required by IAS 8 since IFRS 4 has no specific transitional rules. Impairment of financial receivables not within the scope of IFRS 4 are subject to either IAS 39 or IFRS 9 requirements (depending on which standard is being applied).

7.2.6.C   Gains and losses on buying reinsurance

Some local accounting requirements often define reinsurance contracts more strictly than direct insurance contracts to avoid income statement distortion caused by contracts that have the legal form of reinsurance but do not transfer significant insurance risk. Such contracts are sometimes described as financial reinsurance. One such source of distortion is caused because many local GAAPs do not require the discounting of non-life insurance claims liabilities. If the insurer buys reinsurance, the premium paid to the reinsurer reflects the present value of the underlying liability and is, therefore, potentially less than the existing carrying amount of the liability. This could result in a gain on the initial recognition of the reinsurance contract (a 'day 1' gain) where a reinsurance asset is recognised at an amount equivalent to the undiscounted liability and this is less than the premium payable for the reinsurance contract. This day 1 gain arises largely because of the inability to discount the underlying liability. Initial recognition of gains could also arise if the underlying insurance liability is measured with excessive prudence. *[IFRS 4.BC110]*.

IFRS 4 defines a reinsurance contract using the same terms as an insurance contract. The IASB decided not to use the definition of a reinsurance contract to address the problems described above because it found no conceptual reason to define a reinsurance contract any differently to a direct insurance contract. It considered making a distinction for situations where significant distortions in reported profit were most likely to occur, such as retroactive contracts, but eventually considered that developing such a distinction would be time-consuming and difficult, and there would have been no guarantee of success. *[IFRS 4.BC111, 113]*.

Consequently, IFRS 4 does not restrict the recognition of gains on entering into reinsurance contracts but instead requires specific disclosure of the gains and losses that arise (see 11.1.3 below).

Insurers are therefore permitted to continue applying their existing accounting policies to gains and losses on the purchase of reinsurance contracts (which may or may not prohibit gains on initial recognition) and are also permitted to change those accounting policies according to the criteria discussed at 8 below.

7.2.6.D Acquisition costs

IFRS 4 is silent on how to account for the costs of acquiring insurance contracts. 'Acquisition costs' are not defined within the standard, although the Basis for Conclusions states that they are 'the costs that an insurer incurs to sell, underwrite and initiate a new insurance contract', [IFRS 4.BC116], a description that would appear to exclude costs associated with amending an existing contract.

IFRS 4 neither prohibits nor requires the deferral of acquisition costs, nor does it prescribe what acquisition costs should be deferred, the period and method of their amortisation, or whether an insurer should present deferred acquisition costs as an asset or as a reduction in insurance liabilities. [IFRS 4.BC116].

The IASB decided that the treatment of acquisition costs was an integral part of existing insurance models that could not easily be amended without a more fundamental review of these models in IFRS 17. [IFRS 4.BC116].

Insurers are therefore permitted to continue applying their existing accounting policies for deferring the costs of acquiring insurance contracts.

Under IFRS 15 only incremental costs that are associated with obtaining an investment management contract are recognised as an asset. An incremental cost is one that would not have been incurred if the entity had not secured the investment management contract. [IFRS 15.91-93].

7.2.6.E Salvage and subrogation

Some insurance contracts permit the insurer to sell (usually damaged) property acquired in settling the claim (salvage). The insurer may also have the right to pursue third parties for payment of some or all costs (subrogation). IFRS 4 contains no guidance on whether potential salvage and subrogation recoveries should be presented as separate assets or netted against the related insurance liability. [IFRS 4.BC120].

Royal & SunAlliance is an example of an entity which discloses that its insurance liabilities are stated net of anticipated salvage and subrogation.

> Extract 55.7: RSA Insurance Group plc (2016)
> Basis of preparation and significant accounting policies [extract]
> 4) Significant accounting policies [extract]
> Gross claims incurred and insurance contract liabilities [extract]
>
> Gross claims incurred represent the cost of agreeing and settling insurance claims on insurance contracts underwritten by the Group. Provisions for losses and loss adjustment expenses are recognised at the estimate ultimate cost, net of expected salvage and subrogation recoveries when a claim is incurred.

7.2.6.F Policy loans

Some insurance contracts permit the policyholder to obtain a loan from the insurer with the insurance contract acting as collateral for the loan. IFRS 4 is silent on whether an insurer should treat such loans as a prepayment of the insurance liability or as a separate financial asset. This is because the IASB does not regard the issue as a priority. [IFRS 4.BC122].

Consequently, insurers can present these loans either as separate assets or as a reduction of the related insurance liability depending on their local GAAP requirements.

7.2.6.G   Investments held in a fiduciary capacity

Insurers often make investments on behalf of policyholders as well as on behalf of shareholders. In some cases, this can result in the insurer holding an interest in an entity which, either on its own, or when combined with the interest of the policyholder, gives the insurer control of that entity (as defined by IFRS 10).

8   CHANGES IN ACCOUNTING POLICIES

IFRS 4 imposes a number of constraints that apply whenever an insurer wishes to change its accounting policies for insurance contracts. These requirements apply both to changes made by an insurer that already applies IFRS and to changes made by an insurer adopting IFRS for the first time. *[IFRS 4.21]*.

They reflect the IASB's concern that insurers might change their existing policies to ones that are less relevant or reliable, contrary to the requirements of IAS 8. One option would have been for the IASB to prohibit any changes in accounting policies to prevent lack of comparability (especially within a country) and management discretion to make arbitrary changes. However, it decided to permit changes in accounting policies for insurance contracts provided they can be justified, as is required for any change in accounting policy under IFRS. *[IFRS 4.BC123, 125]*.

The general and specific requirements relating to changes in accounting policies are discussed below.

8.1   Criteria for accounting policy changes

An insurer may change its accounting policies for insurance contracts if, and only if, the change makes the financial statements more relevant to the economic decision-making needs of users and no less reliable, or more reliable and no less relevant to those needs. Relevance and reliability should be judged by the criteria in IAS 8. *[IFRS 4.22]*.

Relevance relates to the economic decision-making needs of users and reliability, in reference to the financial statements, relates to faithful representation, the economic substance of transactions and not merely their legal form, freedom from bias, prudence and completion in all material respects. *[IAS 8.10]*. In making judgements regarding relevance and reliability management should refer to the requirements in IFRSs dealing with similar and related issues and the definitions, recognition criteria and measurement concepts in the IASB *Framework*. Management may also consider the most recent pronouncements of other standard-setting bodies that use a similar conceptual framework to develop accounting standards, other accounting literature and accepted industry practices to the extent that they do not conflict with IFRS. *[IAS 8.11-12]*.

The Board also considered that, as what became IFRS 17 developed, the expected requirements of the new standard would give insurers further context for judgements about whether a change in accounting policy would make the financial statements more relevant and reliable (i.e. in determining whether a new accounting policy was more relevant an entity could look to what became IFRS 17). *[IFRS 4.BC123]*. Any such change in an insurer's accounting policies should have brought the insurer's financial statements closer to meeting the relevance and reliability criteria in IAS 8, but did not need to achieve full compliance with those criteria. *[IFRS 4.23]*. Now that IFRS 17 has been issued it is possible that some insurers, whilst still applying IFRS 4, will consider changing their accounting policies to better align them with the requirements of IFRS 17.

IAS 8 requires changes in accounting policies for which there are no specific transitional provisions to be applied retrospectively. As IFRS 4 does not contain any transitional provisions for changes in accounting policies for insurance contracts, any such changes will have to be retrospective, unless impracticable. *[IAS 8.19]*.

8.2 Specific issues

In addition to the more general criteria considered at 8.1 above, certain changes of accounting policy are specifically addressed in IFRS 4. The need for the IASB to establish requirements in respect of these issues perhaps indicates that the criteria above are not as clear-cut on certain matters as the IASB would like.

The following are discussed below:
- continuation of existing practices;
- current market interest rates;
- prudence; and
- future investment margins. *[IFRS 4.23]*.

Shadow accounting is discussed separately at 8.3 below.

8.2.1 Continuation of existing practices

An insurer may continue the following practices but the introduction of any of them after IFRS has been adopted is not permitted because the IASB believes that they do not satisfy the criteria discussed at 8.1 above. *[IFRS 4.25]*.

8.2.1.A Measuring insurance liabilities on an undiscounted basis

Under many bodies of local GAAP, non-life insurance liabilities are not discounted to reflect the time value of money. In the IASB's view, discounting of insurance liabilities results in financial statements that are more relevant and reliable. Hence, a change from a policy of discounting to not discounting liabilities is not permitted. *[IFRS 4.25(a)]*. The IASB decided against requiring insurance liabilities to be discounted in IFRS 4 because it had not addressed the issue of the discount rate(s) to be used and the basis for any risk adjustments. *[IFRS 4.BC126]*.

8.2.1.B Measuring contractual rights to future investment management fees in excess of their fair value

It is not uncommon to find insurance contracts that give the insurer an entitlement to receive a periodic investment management fee. Some local GAAP accounting policies permit the insurer, in determining the value of its contractual rights and obligations under the insurance contract, to discount the estimated cash flows related to those fees at a discount rate that reflects the risks associated with the cash flows. This approach is found in some embedded value methodologies. *[IFRS 4.BC128]*.

In the IASB's opinion, however, this approach can lead to results that are not consistent with fair value measurement. The IASB considers that if the insurer's contractual asset management fee is in line with the fee charged by other insurers and asset managers for comparable asset management services, the fair value of the contractual right to that fee would be approximately equal to what it would cost insurers and asset managers to acquire similar contractual rights. This approach is considered by the IASB to be consistent with how to account for servicing rights and obligations in IAS 39 or IFRS 9. Therefore, IFRS 4 does not permit an insurer to introduce an accounting policy that measures those contractual rights at more than their fair value as implied by fees charged by others for comparable services. *[IFRS 4.BC129].*

The reasoning behind this requirement is that the fair value at inception of such contractual rights will equal the origination costs paid, unless future investment management fees and related costs are out of line with market comparables. *[IFRS 4.25(b)].*

8.2.1.C   Introducing non-uniform accounting policies for the insurance contracts of subsidiaries

IFRS 10 requires consolidated financial statements to be prepared using uniform accounting policies for like transactions. *[IFRS 10.19].* However, under current local requirements, some insurers consolidate subsidiaries without using the parent company's accounting policies for the measurement of the subsidiaries' insurance liabilities (and related deferred acquisition costs and intangible assets) which continue to be measured under the relevant local GAAP applying in each jurisdiction. *[IFRS 4.BC131].*

The use of non-uniform accounting policies in consolidated financial statements reduces the relevance and reliability of financial statements and is not permitted by IFRS 10. However, prohibiting this practice in IFRS 4 would have forced some insurers to change their accounting policies for the insurance liabilities for some of their subsidiaries, requiring systems changes now that might not be subsequently required following what became IFRS 17. Therefore, the IASB decided that an insurer could continue to use non-uniform accounting policies to account for insurance contracts. If those accounting policies are not uniform, an insurer may change them if the change does not make the accounting policies more diverse and also satisfies the criteria set out at 8.1 above. *[IFRS 4.25(c), BC132].*

There is one exception to this requirement which is discussed at 8.2.2 below.

Old Mutual is an example of a company that applies non-uniform accounting policies to the measurement of its insurance contract liabilities.

> **Extract 55.8: Old Mutual plc (2016)**
> Notes to the consolidated financial statements [extract]
> G: Analysis of financial assets and liabilities [extract]
> G6: Insurance and investment contracts [extract]
> Insurance contract liabilities [extract]
>
> Insurance contract liabilities for African businesses have been computed using a gross premium valuation method. Provisions in respect of African business have been made in accordance with the Financial Soundness Valuation basis as set out in the guidelines issued by the Actuarial Society of South Africa in Standard of Actuarial Practice (SAP) 104 (2012). Under this guideline, provisions are valued using realistic expectations of future experience, with margins for prudence and deferral of profit emergence.
>
> [...]
>
> For other territories, the valuation bases adopted are in accordance with local actuarial practices and methodologies.

8.2.2 Current market interest rates

An insurer is permitted, but not required, to change its accounting policies so that it remeasures designated insurance liabilities (including related deferred acquisition costs and related intangible assets) to reflect current market interest rates. Any changes in these rates would need to be recognised in profit or loss. At that time, it may also introduce accounting policies that require other current estimates and assumptions for the designated liabilities. An insurer may change its accounting policies for designated liabilities without applying those policies consistently to all similar liabilities as IAS 8 would otherwise require. If an insurer designates liabilities for this election, it should apply current market interest rates (and, if applicable, the other current estimates and assumptions) consistently in all periods to all those liabilities until they are extinguished. [IFRS 4.24].

The purpose of this concession is to allow insurers to move, in whole or in part, towards the use of fair value-based measures for insurance contracts.

AXA is an example of an insurance group which has used this option for some of its insurance contracts.

Extract 55.9: AXA SA (2016)

5.6 Notes to the consolidated financial statements [extract]

1.14.2. Insurance contracts and investment contracts with discretionary participating features [extract]

Some guaranteed benefits such as Guaranteed Minimum Death or Income Benefits (GMDB or GMIB), or certain guarantees on return proposed by reinsurance treaties, are covered by a Risk Management program using derivative instruments. In order to minimize the accounting mismatch between liabilities and hedging derivatives, AXA has chosen to use the option allowed under IFRS 4.24 to re-measure its provisions: this revaluation is carried out at each accounts closing based on guarantee level projections and considers interest rates and other market assumptions. The liabilities revaluation impact in the current period is recognized through income, symmetrically with the impact of the change in value of hedging derivatives. This change in accounting principles was adopted on the first time application of IFRS on January 1, 2004 for contracts portfolios covered by the Risk Management program at that date. Any additional contract portfolios covered by the Risk Management program after this date are valued on the same terms as those that applied on the date the program was first applied.

Our view is that, where an entity has elected to account for some, but not all, of its insurance products using current market interest rates, or other current estimates and assumptions, it cannot selectively disregard an input variable, such as a change in interest rates, to determine the value of those liabilities. The input variable must be used every time those insurance contracts are valued.

8.2.3 Prudence

In the IASB's opinion, insurers sometimes measure insurance liabilities on what is intended to be a highly prudent basis that lacks the neutrality required by the IASB's *Framework*. This may be particularly true for insurers who are required under local GAAP to measure their liabilities on a regulatory basis. However, IFRS 4 does not define how much prudence is 'sufficient' and therefore does not require the elimination of 'excessive prudence'. [IFRS 4.BC133]. As a result, insurers are not required under IFRS 4 to change their accounting policies to eliminate excessive prudence. However, if an insurer already measures its insurance contracts with sufficient prudence, it should not introduce additional prudence. [IFRS 4.26].

The liability adequacy test requirements discussed at 7.2.2 above address the converse issue of understated insurance liabilities.

8.2.4 Future investment margins

An insurer need not change its accounting policies for insurance contracts to eliminate the recognition of future investment margins (which may occur under some forms of embedded value accounting). However, IFRS 4 imposes a rebuttable presumption that an insurer's financial statements will become less relevant and reliable if it introduces an accounting policy that reflects future investment margins in the measurement of insurance contracts, unless those margins directly affect the contractual payments.

Two examples of accounting policies that reflect those margins are:

(a) using a discount rate that reflects the estimated return on the insurer's assets; and

(b) projecting the returns on those assets at an estimated rate of return, discounting those projected returns at a different rate and including the result in the measurement of the liability. *[IFRS 4.27]*.

Such accounting policies are used in some embedded value methodologies. For example, the European Insurance CFO Forum European Embedded Value (EEV) Principles state that the value of future cash flows from in-force covered business should be the present value of future shareholder cash flows projected to emerge from the assets backing the liabilities of the in-force covered business reduced by the value of financial options and guarantees.[6] The EEV methodology is considered to be an indirect method of measuring the insurance liability because the measurement of the liability is derived from the related asset. In contrast, direct methods measure the liability by discounting future cash flows arising from the book of insurance contracts only. If the same assumptions are made in both direct and indirect methods, they can produce the same results. *[IFRS 4.BC138]*.

The IASB appears to have been concerned that insurers might take advantage of the lack of specific accounting guidance for insurance contracts in IFRS 4 as an opportunity to change their accounting policies to an embedded value basis on the grounds that this was more relevant and no less reliable, or more reliable and no less relevant than their existing accounting policies (possibly prepared on an 'excessively prudent' regulatory basis). The use of embedded value measures by insurers is discussed at 1.4.3 above.

The IASB's view is that the cash flows arising from an asset are irrelevant for the measurement of a liability unless those cash flows affect (a) the cash flows arising from the liability or (b) the credit characteristics of the liability. Therefore, the IASB considers that the following two embedded value approaches involve practices that are incompatible with IFRS, namely:

- applying an asset discount rate to insurance liabilities; and
- measuring contractual rights to investment management fees at an amount that exceeds their fair value (see 8.2.1.B above).

However, the IASB concluded that it could not eliminate these practices, where they were existing accounting policies, until IFRS 17 gives guidance on the appropriate discount rates and the basis for risk adjustments and therefore the use of asset-based discount rates for the measurement of insurance liabilities is not prohibited. *[IFRS 4.BC142]*.

In addition, where embedded values are generally determined on a single best estimate basis, the IASB considers that they do not reflect a full range of possible outcomes and do not generally adequately address liabilities arising from embedded guarantees and options. Further, the IASB believes that existing embedded value approaches are largely unregulated and there is diversity in their application. *[IFRS 4.BC141]*.

It is possible for insurers to introduce accounting policies that use an embedded value approach even if that involves the use of asset-based discount rates for liabilities if they can overcome the rebuttable presumption described above. This will be if, and only if, the other components of a change in accounting policies increase the relevance and reliability of its financial statements sufficiently to outweigh the decrease in relevance and reliability caused by the inclusion of future investment margins. For example, suppose an insurer's existing accounting policies for insurance contracts involves excessively prudent assumptions set at inception and a discount rate prescribed by a regulator without direct reference to market conditions, and the assumptions ignore some embedded options and guarantees. The insurer might make its financial statements more relevant and no less reliable by switching to a basis of accounting that is widely used and involves:

(a) current estimates and assumptions;

(b) a reasonable (but not excessively prudent) adjustment to reflect risk and uncertainty;

(c) measurements that reflect both the intrinsic value and time value of embedded options and guarantees; and

(d) a current market discount rate, even if that discount rate reflects the estimated return on the insurer's assets. *[IFRS 4.28]*.

In some measurement approaches, the discount rate is used to determine the present value of a future profit margin. That profit margin is then attributed to different periods using a formula. In those approaches, the discount rate affects the measurement of the liability only indirectly. In these circumstances, the IASB has concluded that the use of a less appropriate discount rate has a limited or no effect on the measurement of the liability at inception. However, in other approaches, the IASB considers that the discount rate determines the measurement of the liability directly. In the latter case, because the introduction of an asset-based discount rate has a more significant effect, the IASB believes that it is highly unlikely that an insurer could overcome the rebuttable presumption described above. *[IFRS 4.29]*.

The IASB believes that in most applications of embedded value, the discount rate determines the measurement of the liability directly; and therefore, it is highly unlikely that an insurer could overcome the rebuttable presumption described above if it wanted to change its accounting policies for insurance contracts to an embedded value basis. *[IFRS 4.BC144]*.

8.3 Shadow accounting

IFRS 4 grants relief to insurers allowing them to mitigate an accounting mismatch occurring when unrealised gains or losses on assets backing insurance contracts affect the measurement of the insurance contracts. This relief, known as 'shadow accounting', ensures that all gains and losses on investments affect the measurement of the insurance assets and liabilities in the same way, regardless of whether they are realised or unrealised and regardless of whether the unrealised investment gains and losses are recognised in profit or loss or in other comprehensive income using a revaluation reserve. In particular, the relief permits certain gains or losses arising from remeasuring insurance contracts to be recognised in other comprehensive income whereas IFRS 4 otherwise requires all gains and losses arising from insurance contracts to be recognised in profit or loss. Normally, this change in accounting policy would be adopted upon transition to IFRS. Application of shadow accounting is always voluntary and in practice it is also applied selectively.

In many local GAAP accounting models, gains or losses on an insurer's assets have a direct effect on the measurement of some or all of its insurance liabilities, related deferred acquisition costs and related intangible assets. *[IFRS 4.30]*. In some of these models, prior to the introduction of IFRS, the insurer's assets were measured at cost or amortised cost and unrealised fair value movements were not recognised. Under IFRS, most of an insurer's assets are likely to be held at either fair value through profit or loss or available-for-sale with unrealised fair value gains recognised in profit or loss or other comprehensive income respectively. If the unrealised gains on the insurance liabilities (or deferred acquisition costs and intangible assets) which the assets back were not also recognised there would be an accounting mismatch.

The IASB believe that, in principle, gains or losses on an asset should not influence the measurement of an insurance liability unless the gains or losses on the asset alter the amounts payable to policyholders. Nevertheless, this was a feature of some existing measurement models for insurance liabilities and the IASB decided that it was not feasible to eliminate this practice. The IASB also acknowledged that shadow accounting might mitigate volatility caused by differences between the measurement basis for assets and the measurement basis for insurance liabilities. However, that is a by-product of shadow accounting and not its primary purpose. *[IFRS 4.BC183]*.

IFRS 4 permits, but does not require, a change in accounting policies so that a recognised but unrealised gain or loss on an asset affects the related insurance liabilities in the same way that a realised gain or loss does. In other words, a measurement adjustment to an insurance liability (or deferred acquisition cost or intangible asset) arising from the remeasurement of an asset would be recognised in other comprehensive income if, and only if, the unrealised gains or losses on the asset are also recognised in other comprehensive income. *[IFRS 4.30]*.

Recognition of movements in insurance liabilities (or deferred acquisition costs or intangible assets) in other comprehensive income only applies when unrealised gains on assets are recognised in other comprehensive income such as for available-for-sale investments accounted for under IAS 39, debt or equity securities classified at fair value through other comprehensive income under IFRS 9 or property, plant and equipment accounted for using the revaluation model under IAS 16. *[IFRS 4.IG10]*.

Shadow accounting is not applicable for liabilities arising from investment contracts accounted for under IAS 39 or IFRS 9. However, shadow accounting may be applicable for a DPF within an investment contract if the measurement of that feature depends on asset values or asset returns. *[IFRS 4.IG8]*.

Further, shadow accounting may not be used if the measurement of an insurance liability is not driven by realised gains and losses on assets held, for example if the insurance liabilities are measured using a discount rate that reflects a current market rate but that measurement does not depend directly on the carrying amount of any assets held. *[IFRS 4.IG9]*.

The implementation guidance to IFRS 4 includes an illustrative example to show how shadow accounting through other comprehensive income might be applied. This example is reproduced in full below.

Example 55.31: Shadow accounting

Background

Under some national requirements for some insurance contracts, deferred acquisition costs (DAC) are amortised over the life of the contract as a constant proportion of estimated gross profits (EGP). EGP includes investment returns, including realised (but not unrealised) gains and losses. Interest is applied to both DAC and EGP, to preserve present value relationships. For simplicity, this example ignores interest and ignores re-estimation of EGP.

At the inception of a contract, insurer A has DAC of CU20 relating to that contract and the present value, at inception, of EGP is CU100. In other words, DAC is 20 per cent of EGP at inception. Thus, for each CU1 of realised gross profits, insurer A amortises DAC by CU0.20. For example, if insurer A sells assets and recognises a gain of CU10, insurer A amortises DAC by CU2 (20 per cent of CU10).

Before adopting IFRSs for the first time in 2013, insurer A measured financial assets on a cost basis. (Therefore, EGP under those national requirements considers only realised gains and losses.) However, under IFRSs, it does not apply IFRS 9 and classifies its financial assets as available for sale. Thus, insurer A measures the assets at fair value and recognises changes in their fair value directly in other comprehensive income. In 2013, insurer A recognises unrealised gains of CU10 on the assets backing the contract.

In 2014, insurer A sells the assets for an amount equal to their fair value at the end of 2013 and, to comply with IAS 39, transfers the now-realised gain of CU10 from other comprehensive income to profit or loss.

Application of paragraph 30 of IFRS 4

Paragraph 30 of IFRS 4 permits, but does not require, insurer A to adopt shadow accounting. If insurer A adopts shadow accounting, it amortises DAC in 2013 by an additional CU2 (20 per cent of CU10) as a result of the change in the fair value of the assets. Because insurer A recognised the change in the assets' fair value in other comprehensive income, it recognises the additional amortisation of CU2 directly in other comprehensive income.

When insurer A sells the assets in 2014, it makes no further adjustment to DAC, but transfers DAC amortisation of CU2 relating to the now-realised gain from other comprehensive income to profit or loss.

In summary, shadow accounting treats an unrealised gain in the same way as a realised gain, except that the unrealised gain and resulting DAC amortisation are (a) recognised in other comprehensive income rather than in profit or loss and (b) transferred to profit or loss when the gain on the asset becomes realised.

If insurer A does not adopt shadow accounting, unrealised gains on assets do not affect the amortisation of DAC (i.e. the CU2 of DAC amortisation would have been recognised in profit or loss in 2013). *[IFRS 4.IG10, IE4]*.

Old Mutual is an example of an entity that applies shadow accounting.

Extract 55.10: Old Mutual plc (2016)

Notes to the consolidated financial statements [extract]

G: Analysis of financial assets and liabilities [extract]

G6: Insurance and investment contracts [extract]

Insurance contract liabilities [extract]

In respect of the South Africa life assurance, shadow accounting is applied to insurance contract liabilities where the underlying measurement of the policyholder liability depends directly on the value of owner-occupied property and the unrealised gains and losses on such property, which are recognised in other comprehensive income. The shadow accounting adjustment to insurance contract liabilities is recognised in other comprehensive income to the extent that the unrealised gains or losses on owner-occupied property backing insurance contract liabilities are also recognised directly in other comprehensive income.

IFRS 4 does not specifically address the interaction between shadow accounting and the liability adequacy test. We believe that shadow accounting is applied before the liability adequacy test and the implications of this are discussed at 7.2.2.D above.

8.4 Redesignation of financial assets

IAS 39 generally prohibits the reclassification of a financial asset into the 'fair value through profit or loss' category while it is held or issued. *[IAS 39.50]*. IFRS 9 allows such reclassifications only when an entity changes its business model for financial assets. *[IFRS 9.4.4.1]*. However, when an insurer changes its accounting policies for insurance liabilities, it is permitted, but not required, to reclassify some or all of its financial assets at fair value through profit or loss. This reclassification is permitted if an insurer changes its accounting policies when it first applies IFRS 4 and also if it makes a subsequent policy change permitted by IFRS 4. This reclassification is a change in accounting policy and the requirements of IAS 8 apply, i.e. it must be performed retrospectively unless impracticable. *[IFRS 4.45, IAS 39.50A(c)]*.

The IASB decided to grant this exemption from IAS 39 or IFRS 9 in order to allow an insurer to avoid an accounting mismatch when it improves its accounting policies for insurance contracts and to remove unnecessary barriers for insurers wishing to move to a measurement basis that reflects fair values. *[IFRS 4.BC145]*.

This concession cannot be used to reclassify financial assets out of the fair value through profit or loss category. These remain subject to the normal IAS 39 or IFRS 9 requirements.

8.5 Practical issues

8.5.1 Changes to local GAAP

As most entities are applying some form of local GAAP for their insurance contracts under IFRS 4, a common issue is whether an entity is obliged to change its accounting policy when local GAAP changes or whether the decision to change an accounting policy for IFRS purposes is one that remains solely with the insurer.

In our view, the decision to change an accounting policy established on the initial adoption of IFRS is at the discretion of the entity. Accordingly, any change in local GAAP for insurance contracts that was used as the basis for the initial adoption of IFRS does not oblige the insurer to change its accounting policies.

Although an entity is not required to change its policies when local GAAP changes, it can make voluntary changes provided the revised accounting policy makes the financial statements more relevant and no less reliable or more reliable and no less relevant, as discussed at 8.1 above.

When a local accounting standard is changed, it is likely that the change is made for a reason. Therefore, there would normally be a rebuttable presumption that any change in local GAAP is an improvement to the existing standard and so is more relevant and no less reliable or more reliable and no less relevant to users than the previous standard would have been.

The fact that an entity can decide whether or not to apply changes in local GAAP has, over time, led to further diversity in practice.

An entity should not state that it fully applies a particular local GAAP for insurance contracts if it no longer complies with that GAAP due to it not implementing a local GAAP accounting policy change.

9 INSURANCE CONTRACTS ACQUIRED IN BUSINESS COMBINATIONS AND PORTFOLIO TRANSFERS

9.1 Expanded presentation of insurance contracts

IFRS 3 requires most assets and liabilities, including insurance liabilities assumed and insurance assets acquired, in a business combination to be measured at fair value. *[IFRS 4.31]*. The IASB saw no compelling reason to exempt insurers from these requirements. *[IFRS 4.BC153]*.

However, an insurer is permitted, but not required, to use an expanded presentation that splits the fair value of acquired insurance contracts into two components:

(a) a liability measured in accordance with the acquirer's accounting policies for insurance contracts that it issues; and

(b) an intangible asset, representing the difference between (i) the fair value of the contractual insurance rights acquired and insurance obligations assumed and (ii) the amount described in (a). The subsequent measurement of this asset should be consistent with the measurement of the related insurance liabilities. *[IFRS 4.31(a), (b)]*.

We note that technically this IFRS 4 intangible has no intrinsic value that can be actuarially calculated. It is no more than the balancing number between the purchase price allocated to the insurance liability and the amount recorded for the insurance liability by the purchaser under the purchaser's existing GAAP. The more prudent (higher) the basis of liability measurement, the higher the value of the intangible.

This alternative presentation had often been used in practice under many local GAAPs. Life insurers have variously described this intangible asset as the 'present value of in-force business' (PVIF), 'present value of future profits' (PVFP or PVP) or 'value of business acquired' (VOBA). Similar principles apply in non-life insurance, for example, if claims liabilities are not discounted. *[IFRS 4.BC147]*.

The IASB decided to allow these existing practices to continue because:

- they wished to avoid insurers making systems changes for IFRS 4 that might need to be reversed by what became IFRS 17. In the IASB's opinion the disclosures about the intangible asset provide transparency for users;

- IFRS 4 gives no guidance on how to determine fair values (although IFRS 13 does not exclude insurance contracts from its scope – see 9.1.1.B below); and
- it might be difficult for insurers to integrate a fair value measurement at the date of a business combination into subsequent insurance contract accounting without requiring systems changes that could become obsolete as a result of IFRS 17. *[IFRS 4.BC148].*

An insurer acquiring a portfolio of insurance contracts (separate from a business combination) may also use the expanded presentation described above. *[IFRS 4.32].*

An illustration of how a business combination might be accounted for using the expanded presentation is given below.

Example 55.32: Business combination under IFRS 4

Insurance entity A purchases an insurance business owned by Entity B for €10 million. Under A's existing accounting policies for insurance contracts, the carrying value of the insurance contract liabilities held by B is €8 million. Entity A estimates the fair value of the insurance contract liabilities to be €6 million. The fair value of other net assets acquired, including intangible assets, after recognising any additional deferred tax, is €13 million. The tax rate is 25%.

This gives rise to the following journal entry to record the acquisition of B in A's consolidated financial statements:

	€m	€m
Cash		10.0
Present value of in-force (PVIF) business intangible (£8m less £6m)	2.0	
Carrying value of insurance liabilities (A's existing accounting policies)		8.0
Goodwill	3.5	
Other net assets acquired	13.0	
Deferred taxation on PVIF		0.5

The intangible asset described at (b) above is excluded from the scope of both IAS 36 and IAS 38; instead, IFRS 4 requires its subsequent measurement to be consistent with the measurement of the related insurance liabilities. *[IFRS 4.33].* As a result, it is generally amortised over the estimated life of the contracts. Some insurers use an interest method of amortisation, which the IASB considers is appropriate for an asset that essentially comprises the present value of a set of contractual cash flows. However, the IASB considers it doubtful whether IAS 38 would have permitted such a method, hence the scope exclusion from IAS 38. This intangible asset is included within the scope of the liability adequacy test discussed at 7.2.2 above which acts as a quasi-impairment test on its carrying amount and hence is also excluded from the scope of IAS 36. *[IFRS 4.BC149].*

Generali is one entity that uses the expanded presentation discussed above and its accounting policy for acquired insurance contracts is reproduced below.

> **Extract 55.11: Assicurazioni Generali S.p.A. (2016)**
>
> Notes to the consolidated financial statements [extract]
> Balance sheet – Assets [extract]
> Contractual relations with customers – insurance contracts acquired in a business combination or portfolio transfer [extract]
>
> In case of acquisition of life and non-life insurance contract portfolios in a business combination or portfolio transfer, the Group recognises an intangible asset, i.e. the value of the acquired contractual relationships (Value Of Business Acquired).
>
> The VOBA is the present value of the pre-tax future profit arising from the contracts in force at the purchase date, taking into account the probability of renewals of the one year contracts in the non-life segment. The related deferred taxes are accounted for as liabilities in the consolidated balance sheet.
>
> The VOBA is amortised over the effective life of the contracts acquired, by using an amortization pattern reflecting the expected future profit recognition. Assumptions used in the development of the VOBA amortization pattern are consistent with the ones applied in its initial measurement. The amortization pattern is reviewed on a yearly basis to assess its reliability and, if applicable, to verify the consistency with the assumptions used in the valuation of the corresponding insurance provisions.
>
> [...]
>
> The Generali Group applies this accounting treatment to the insurance liabilities assumed in the acquisition of life and non-life insurance portfolios.
>
> The future VOBA recoverable amount is nonetheless tested on yearly basis.

Investment contracts within the scope of IAS 39 or IFRS 9 are required to be measured at fair value when acquired in a business combination.

As discussed at 3.3 above, there should be no reassessment of the classification of contracts previously classified as insurance contracts under IFRS 4 which are acquired as a part of a business combination.

9.1.1 Practical issues

9.1.1.A The difference between a business combination and a portfolio transfer

When an entity acquires a portfolio of insurance contracts, the main accounting consideration is to determine whether that acquisition meets the definition of a business. IFRS 3 defines a business as 'an integrated set of activities and assets that is capable of being conducted and managed for the purpose of providing a return in the form of dividends, lower costs or other economic benefits directly to investors, or other owners, members or participants'. *[IFRS 3 Appendix A]*. The application guidance to IFRS 3 notes that a business consists of inputs and processes applied to those inputs that have the ability to create outputs. Although businesses usually have outputs they do not need to be present for an integrated set of assets and activities to be a business. *[IFRS 3.B7]*. Where it is considered that a business is acquired, goodwill may need to be recognised as may deferred tax liabilities in respect of any acquired intangibles. For an isolated portfolio transfer, neither goodwill nor deferred tax should be recognised.

The determination of whether a portfolio of contracts or a business has been acquired will be a matter of judgement based on the facts and circumstances. Acquisitions of contracts that also include the acquisition of underwriting systems and/or the related organised workforce are more likely to meet the definition of a business than merely the acquisition of individual or multiple contracts.

Rights to issue or renew contracts in the future (as opposed to existing insurance contracts) are separate intangible assets and the accounting for the acquisition of such rights is discussed at 9.2 below.

9.1.1.B Fair value of an insurer's liabilities

IFRS 4 does not prescribe a method for determining the fair value of insurance liabilities. However, the definition of fair value in IFRS 4 is the same as that in IFRS 13 and insurance contracts are not excluded from the scope of IFRS 13. Therefore, any calculation of fair value must be consistent with IFRS 13's valuation principles.

Deferred acquisition costs (DAC) are generally considered to have no value in a business combination and are usually subsumed into the PVIF intangible. The fair value of any unearned premium reserve will include any unearned profit element as well as the present value of the claims obligation in respect of the unexpired policy period at the acquisition date which is likely to be different from the value under existing accounting policies.

9.1.1.C Deferred taxation

IAS 12 requires deferred tax to be recognised in respect of temporary differences arising in business combinations, for example if the tax base of the asset or liability remains at cost when the carrying amount is fair value. IFRS 4 contains no exemption from these requirements. Therefore, deferred tax will often arise on temporary differences created by the recognition of insurance liabilities at their fair value or on the related intangible asset. The deferred tax adjusts the amount of goodwill recognised as illustrated in Example 55.32 at 9.1 above. *[IAS 12.19]*.

9.1.1.D Negative intangible assets

There are situations where the presentation described at 9.1 above will result in the creation of a negative intangible asset. This could arise, for example, where the acquirer's existing accounting policies are such that the contractual liabilities acquired are measured at an amount less than their fair value, although this is likely to raise questions about whether the carrying value of the liabilities are adequate (see 7.2.2 above). IFRS 4 is silent on the subject of negative intangible assets but there is no prohibition on their recognition.

9.2 Customer lists and relationships not connected to contractual insurance rights and obligations

The requirements discussed at 9.1 above apply only to contractual insurance rights and obligations that existed at the date of a business combination or portfolio transfer.

Therefore, they do not apply to customer lists and customer relationships reflecting the expectation of future contracts that are not part of the contractual insurance rights and contractual insurance obligations existing at the date of the transaction. *[IFRS 4.33]*. IAS 36 and IAS 38 apply to such transactions as they apply to other intangible assets.

The following example deals with customer relationships acquired together with a portfolio of one-year motor insurance contracts.

Example 55.33: Purchase of portfolio of one-year motor insurance contracts

Background

Parent A obtained control of insurer B in a business combination on 31 December 2018. B has a portfolio of one-year motor insurance contracts that are cancellable by policyholders.

Analysis

Because B establishes its relationships with policyholders through insurance contracts, the customer relationship with the policyholders meets the contractual-legal criterion for recognition as an intangible asset. IAS 36 and IAS 38 apply to the customer relationship intangible asset. *[IFRS 3.IE30(d)].*

10 APPLYING IFRS 9 WITH IFRS 4

Even before IFRS 17 was published, it had become clear that its effective date would be three years after the effective date of IFRS 9. Consequently, the IASB was asked to address concerns expressed by various parties that additional accounting mismatches and profit or loss volatility could result if IFRS 9 was applied before IFRS 17. The IASB agreed that these concerns should be addressed. *[IFRS 4.BC229].*

Consequently, in September 2016, the IASB issued *Applying IFRS 9 Financial Instruments with IFRS 4 Insurance Contracts* to address these concerns by amending IFRS 4 to introduce the temporary exemption and the overlay approach as explained in the bullet points below. In June 2020, the IASB further amended IFRS 4 by issuing an *Extension of the Temporary Exemption from Applying IFRS 9* in order to permit insurers with the option to align the implementation of IFRS 9 with IFRS 17, for annual reporting periods beginning on or after 1 January 2023.

- The optional temporary exemption from IFRS 9 for insurers whose activities are predominantly connected with insurance. The temporary exemption is available until an insurer's first accounting period beginning on or after 1 January 2023 which is the effective date of IFRS 17 (see 10.1 below), and
- the optional overlay approach that permits insurers to reclassify between profit or loss and other comprehensive income an amount equal to the difference between the amount reported in profit or loss for designated financial assets applying IFRS 9 and the amount that would have been reported in profit or loss for those assets if the insurer had applied IAS 39 (see 10.2 below).

As both the temporary exemption and the overlay approach are optional, an insurer can still apply IFRS 9 as issued by the IASB and not use either of the permitted alternatives.

In this context, an insurer includes an entity that issues financial instruments that contain a discretionary participation feature. *[IFRS 4.5].* Therefore, if the qualifying criteria are met, both the temporary exemption and the overlay approach are also available to an issuer of a financial instrument that contains a discretionary participation feature. *[IFRS 4.35A].*

An entity should apply these amendments for annual periods beginning on or after 1 January 2018 (i.e. the effective date of IFRS 9). *[IFRS 4.46].* The overlay approach may be applied only when an entity first applies IFRS 9 and therefore an insurer that early applies IFRS 9 may also adopt the overlay approach at the same time. *[IFRS 4.35C, 48].* An entity that has previously applied any version of IFRS 9, other than only the requirements for the presentation in OCI of gains and losses arising from changes in own credit risk on financial liabilities designated at fair value through profit or loss (see Chapter 50 at 2.4), is not permitted to use either the temporary exemption or the overlay approach. *[IFRS 4.20B, 35C(b)]*.

IAS 8 requires an entity to disclose information when it has not applied a new IFRS that has been issued but is not yet effective. *[IAS 8.30]*. Accordingly, the IASB believes that insurers are required to provide information about the expected date of these amendments before they are effective, including whether the insurer expects to apply the temporary exemption from IFRS 9. *[IFRS 4.BC273]*.

As discussed at 1 above, in June 2020, the IASB amended IFRS 17 with targeted changes, including amending IFRS 4 to extend the temporary exemption from applying IFRS 9 so that an entity applying the exemption would only be required to apply IFRS 9 for annual reporting periods beginning on or after 1 January 2023.

The diagram below summarises the various options available until 2022, when IFRS 17, as amended in 2020, is effective and IFRS 9 must be applied. Note that an insurer may transition from option 3 to option 2 or option 1 (see 10.1.2 below); and from option 2 to option 1 (as explained above) during the period. However, an insurer that has previously applied any version of IFRS 9 (option 1), is not permitted to use either the temporary exemption (option 3) or the overlay approach (option 2) (as explained above).

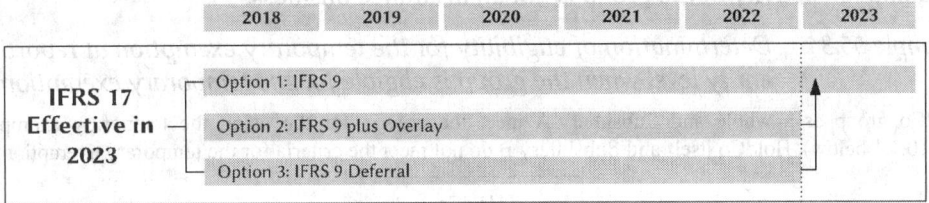

10.1 The temporary exemption from IFRS 9

For an insurer that meets the eligibility criteria, the temporary exemption permits, but does not require, the insurer to apply IAS 39 rather than IFRS 9 for annual reporting periods beginning before 1 January 2023. Therefore, an insurer that applies the temporary exemption does not adopt IFRS 9. *[IFRS 4.20A]*. As a result, an insurer applies one standard to all its financial assets and financial liabilities: IAS 39 if it applies the temporary exemption; or IFRS 9 if it does not. However, one exception has resulted from the interest rate benchmark reform phase 2 amendments to IFRS 4, which requires an insurer applying the temporary exemption from IFRS 9 to apply the requirements in paragraphs 5.4.6 to 5.4.9 of IFRS 9 to a financial asset or financial liability if the basis for determining the contractual cash flows of that financial asset or financial liability changes as a result of interest rate benchmark reform, and this is discussed at 10.1.6 below.

An insurer that applies the temporary exemption from IFRS 9 should: *[IFRS 4.20A]*

- use the requirements in IFRS 9 that are necessary to provide the disclosures discussed at 10.1.5 below; and
- apply all other applicable IFRSs to its financial instruments except as described below.

Eligibility for the temporary exemption is assessed at the reporting entity level. That is, an entity as a whole is assessed by considering all of its activities. *[IFRS 4.BC252].* So, for example, a conglomerate financial institution assesses its eligibility to apply the temporary exemption in its consolidated financial statements by reference to the entire group. This indicates that a separate eligibility assessment is required for the separate financial statements of the parent company of the group. Subsidiaries within the conglomerate that issue their own separate, individual or consolidated financial statements must also assess the eligibility criteria at the relevant reporting entity level. Consequently, it is unlikely that all reporting entities consolidated within group financial statements will meet the criteria for the temporary exemption even if the criteria are met in the group financial statements. This means that conglomerates that elect to use the temporary exemption, where permitted, are likely to have some subsidiaries required to apply IFRS 9 in the subsidiaries' own financial statements.

The impact of the temporary exemption on financial conglomerates has proved controversial in some jurisdictions. Consequently, the EU-adopted version of IFRS permits a 'financial conglomerate' to use a mixed accounting model for financial instruments in its consolidated financial statements – see Chapter 1 at 4.2.1.A.

The following examples illustrate how eligibility would be determined at the reporting entity level. Example 55.34 illustrates the situation when the predominant activity of the group is an insurance business and Example 55.35 illustrates the situation when the predominant activity of the group is not an insurance business.

Example 55.34:   Determination of eligibility for the temporary exemption at reporting entity level when the group is eligible for the temporary exemption

HoldCo group as a whole and Subsidiary A meet the criteria for the using the temporary exemption (see 10.1.1 below). HoldCo itself and Subsidiary B do not meet the criteria for the temporary exemption.

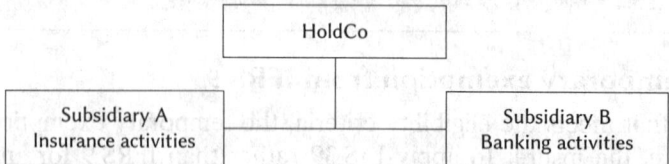

The temporary exemption is available for HoldCo's consolidated financial statements and Subsidiary A's individual financial statements. However, the temporary exemption is not available for HoldCo's separate financial statements and Subsidiary B's individual financial statements. In those financial statements IFRS 9 must be applied, although the overlay approach may be available for designated financial assets (see 10.2 below).

Example 55.35:   Determination of eligibility for the temporary exemption at reporting entity level when the group is not eligible for the temporary exemption

HoldCo group as a whole, HoldCo itself and Subsidiary B do not meet the criteria for the use of the temporary exemption. Subsidiary A does meet the criteria for the use of the temporary exemption (see 10.1.1 below).

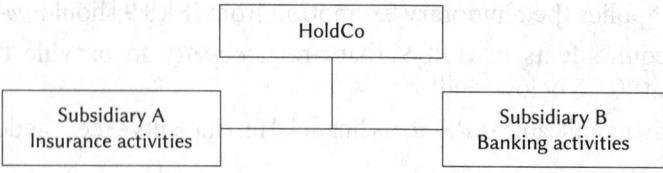

HoldCo and Subsidiary B are not eligible to apply the temporary exemption and must apply IFRS 9, in HoldCo's case, in both its consolidated and separate financial statements. However, they may be eligible to apply the overlay approach to designated financial assets (see 10.2 below). Subsidiary A is eligible to apply the temporary exemption.

An insurer may apply the temporary exemption from IFRS 9 if, and only if: *[IFRS 4.20B]*

- it has not previously applied any version of IFRS 9, other than only the requirements for the presentation in OCI of gains and losses attributable to changes in the entity's own credit risk on financial liabilities designated at fair value through profit or loss; and
- its activities are predominantly connected with insurance (see 10.1.1 below) at its annual reporting date that immediately precedes 1 April 2016, or at a subsequent reporting date when reassessed (see 10.1.2 below).

An insurer applying the temporary exemption from IFRS 9 is permitted to elect to apply only the requirements of IFRS 9 for the presentation in OCI of gains and losses attributable to changes in an entity's own credit risk on financial liabilities designated as at fair value through profit or loss. If an insurer elects to apply those requirements, it should apply the relevant transition provisions in IFRS 9, disclose the fact that it has applied those requirements and provide on an ongoing basis the related disclosures set out in IFRS 7 and discussed in Chapter 54 at 4.4.2. *[IFRS 4.20C]*.

The ability to use the temporary exemption from IFRS 9 ceases automatically when an entity first applies IFRS 17 (i.e. for periods beginning on or after 1 January 2023 based on the amendments issued in June 2020). At that time a reporting entity must apply IFRS 9 to its financial instruments (using the associated transitional rules in the standard).

10.1.1 Activities that are predominantly connected with insurance

An insurer's activities must be predominantly connected with insurance for the temporary exemption from IFRS 9 to be used. An insurer's activities are predominantly connected with insurance if, and only if: *[IFRS 4.20D]*

- the carrying amount of its liabilities arising from contracts within the scope of IFRS 4, which includes any deposit components or embedded derivatives unbundled from insurance contracts (see 4 and 5 above), is significant compared to the total carrying amount of all its liabilities; and
- the percentage of the total carrying amount of its liabilities connected with insurance relative to the total carrying amount of all its liabilities is:
  - greater than 90%; or
  - less than or equal to 90% but greater than 80%, and the insurer does not engage in a significant activity unconnected with insurance.

It is observed in the Basis for Conclusions that the IASB decided to require that liabilities within the scope of IFRS 4 be significant compared to total liabilities as a condition for use of the temporary exemption in order to prevent entities with very few such contracts qualifying for the exemption. 'Significant' in this context is not quantified. The Board acknowledges that determining significance will require judgement but decided not to provide additional guidance on its meaning because this term is used in other IFRSs and is already applied in practice. *[IFRS 4.BC258]*.

For example, IAS 28 – *Investments in Associates and Joint Ventures* – defines 'significant influence' and provides a rebuttable presumption that a holding of 20 per cent or more of the voting power of an investee gives the investor significant influence. *[IAS 28.5]*.

In assessing whether an insurer engages in a significant activity unconnected with insurance, it should consider: *[IFRS 4.20F]*

- only those activities from which it may earn income and incur expenses; and
- quantitative or qualitative factors (or both), including publicly available information such as industry classification that users of financial statements apply to the insurer.

For this purpose, liabilities connected with insurance comprise: *[IFRS 4.20E]*

- liabilities arising from contracts within the scope of IFRS 4, which includes any deposit components or embedded derivatives that are unbundled from insurance contracts (see 4 and 5 above);
- non-derivative investment contract liabilities measured at fair value through profit or loss (FVPL) applying IAS 39, including those liabilities designated at fair value through profit or loss to which the insurer has elected to apply the requirements in IFRS 9 for the presentation of gains and losses (see 10.1 above); and
- liabilities that arise because the insurer issues, or fulfils obligations arising from, the contracts noted in the preceding two bullet points. Examples of such liabilities include derivatives used to mitigate risks arising from those contracts and from the assets backing those contracts, relevant tax liabilities such as the deferred tax liabilities for taxable temporary differences on liabilities arising from those contracts, and debt instruments that are included in the insurer's regulatory capital.

Although not specifically mentioned in the standard, the Basis for Conclusions states that other connected liabilities include liabilities for salaries and other employment benefits for the employees of the insurance activities. *[IFRS 4.BC255(b)]*. Employee benefit liabilities would include, for example, defined benefit pension liabilities.

The Basis for Conclusions observes that, although non-derivative investment contract liabilities measured at FVPL applying IAS 39 (including those designated at fair value through profit or loss to which the insurer has applied the requirements in IFRS 9 for the presentation in OCI of gains and losses arising from changes in the entity's own credit risk) do not meet the definition of an insurance contract, those investment contracts are sold alongside similar products with significant insurance risk and are regulated as insurance contracts in many jurisdictions. Accordingly, the IASB concluded that insurers with significant investment contracts measured at FVPL should not be precluded from applying the temporary exemption.

However, the IASB noted that insurers generally measure at amortised cost most non-derivative financial liabilities that are associated with non-insurance activities and therefore decided that such financial liabilities (i.e. non-derivative financial liabilities associated with non-insurance liabilities measured at amortised cost) cannot be treated as connected with insurance. *[IFRS 4.BC255(a)]*.

In our view, this would not preclude non-derivative financial liabilities measured at amortised cost being included within the numerator provided such liabilities are connected with insurance. Determining whether such liabilities measured at amortised cost are connected with insurance is a matter of judgement based on facts and circumstances.

The 90% threshold for predominance was set to avoid ambiguity and undue effort in determining eligibility for the temporary exemption from IFRS 9. Nevertheless, the IASB acknowledged that an assessment based solely on this 90% threshold has shortcomings. Accordingly, the IASB decided that when an insurer narrowly fails to meet the threshold, the insurer is still able to qualify for the temporary exemption as long as more than 80% of its liabilities are connected with insurance and it does not engage in a significant activity unconnected with insurance. *[IFRS 4.BC256].*

When a reporting entity's liabilities connected with insurance are greater than 80% but less than 90% of all of its liabilities and the insurer wishes to apply the temporary exemption, additional disclosures are required (see 10.1.5 below). A reporting entity is not permitted to apply the temporary exemption if its liabilities connected with insurance are less than 80% of all of its liabilities at initial assessment (see 10.1.2 below).

The diagram below illustrates the assessment of the temporary exemption.

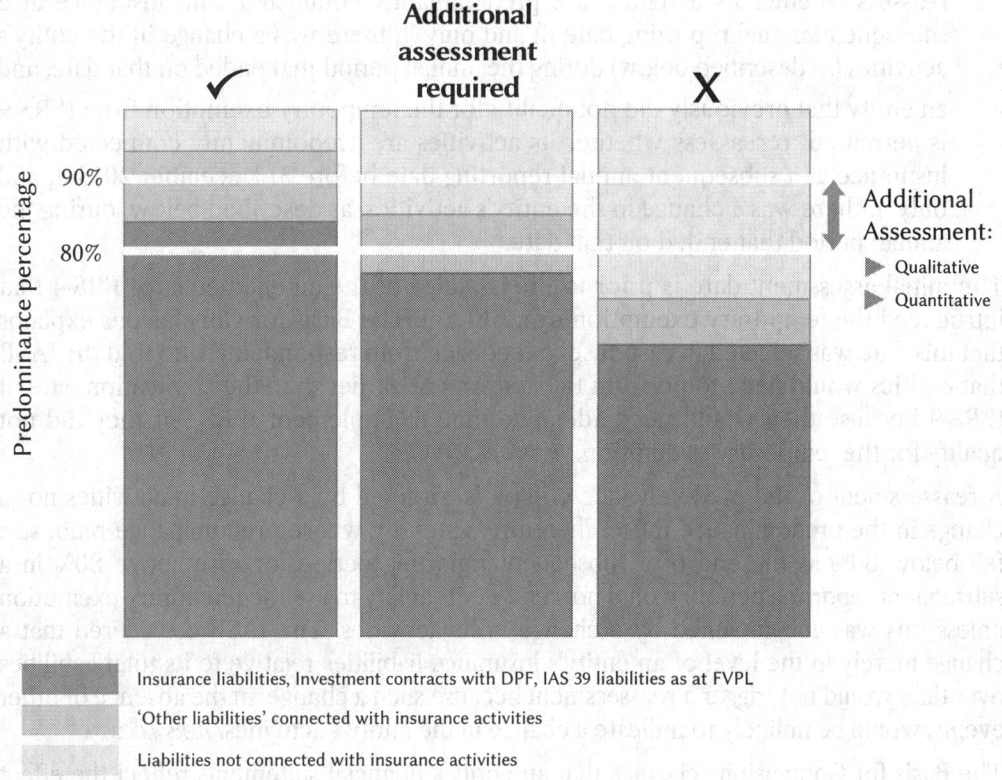

An example of how the predominance calculation works is illustrated below.

Example 55.36: Calculation of the predominance ratio

A reporting entity has the following liabilities at its annual reporting date that immediately precedes 1 April 2016.

	CU
Insurance contract liabilities	500
Investment contract liabilities at FVPL	200
Debt issued for regulatory capital	100
Derivatives used for hedges of insurance liabilities	60
Employee benefit liabilities of insurance employees	50
Banking liabilities at amortised cost	90
Total liabilities	**1,000**

Predominance ratio = 91% (i.e. 500 + 200 + 100 + 60 + 50 ÷ 1,000).
Therefore, the reporting entity's liabilities are predominantly connected with insurance activities.

10.1.2 Initial assessment and reassessment of the temporary exemption

An insurer is required to assess whether it qualifies for the temporary exemption from IFRS 9 at its annual reporting date that immediately precedes 1 April 2016. After that date: *[IFRS 4.20G]*

- an entity that previously qualified for the temporary exemption from IFRS 9 should reassess whether its activities are predominantly connected with insurance at a subsequent annual reporting date if, and only if, there was a change in the entity's activities (as described below) during the annual period that ended on that date; and

- an entity that previously did not qualify for the temporary exemption from IFRS 9 is permitted to reassess whether its activities are predominantly connected with insurance at a subsequent annual reporting date before 31 December 2018 if, and only if, there was a change in the entity's activities, as described below, during the annual period that ended on that date.

The initial assessment date is prior to the issuance of the amendments to IFRS 4 that introduced the temporary exemption from IFRS 9. The Basis for Conclusions explains that this date was selected in response to feedback from respondents who told the IASB that entities would need to perform the assessment earlier than the application date of IFRS 9 because they would need adequate time to implement IFRS 9 if they did not qualify for the temporary exemption. *[IFRS 4.BC264].*

A reassessment of the predominance criteria is triggered by a change in activities not a change in the predominance ratio. Therefore, an entity whose predominance ratio, say, fell below 80% at the end of a subsequent reporting period (or rose above 80% in a subsequent reporting period) would not reassess its ability to use the temporary exemption unless this was accompanied by a change in its activities. The IASB considered that a change merely in the level of an entity's insurance liabilities relative to its total liabilities over time would not trigger a reassessment because such a change, in the absence of other events, would be unlikely to indicate a change in the entity's activities. *[IFRS 4.BC265].*

The Basis for Conclusions clarifies that an entity's financial statements reflect the effect of a change in its activities only after the change has been completed. Therefore, an entity performs the reassessment using the carrying amounts of its liabilities at the annual reporting date immediately following the completion of the change in its activities. For example, an entity would reassess whether its activities are predominantly connected with insurance at the annual reporting date immediately following the completion of an acquisition. *[IFRS 4.BC266]*.

A change in an entity's activities that would result in a reassessment is a change that: *[IFRS 4.20H]*
- is determined by the entity's senior management as a result of internal or external changes;
- is significant to the entity's operations; and
- is demonstrable to external parties.

Accordingly, such a change occurs only when the entity begins or ceases to perform an activity that is significant to its operations or significantly changes the magnitude of one of its activities; for example, when the entity has acquired, disposed of or terminated a business line.

The IASB expects a change in an entity's activities that would result in reassessment to occur very infrequently. The following are examples of changes that would not result in a reassessment: *[IFRS 4.20I]*
- a change in the entity's funding structure that in itself does not affect the activities from which the entity earns income and incurs expenses; and
- the entity's plan to sell a business line, even if the assets and liabilities are classified as held for sale applying IFRS 5. A plan to sell a business activity could change the entity's activities and give rise to a reassessment in the future but has yet to affect the liabilities recognised on its balance sheet. This means that a disposal must have completed for it to trigger a reassessment.

If an entity no longer qualifies for the temporary exemption from IFRS 9 as a result of reassessment, then the entity is permitted to continue to apply IAS 39 only until the end of the annual period that began immediately after that reassessment. Nevertheless, the entity must apply IFRS 9 for annual periods beginning on or after 1 January 2023, based on the amendments issued in June 2020. This is illustrated in the following example. *[IFRS 4.20J]*.

Example 55.37: Discontinuation of the temporary exemption

A reporting entity has a 31 December reporting date and qualifies for the temporary exemption in its annual reporting period ending 31 December 2015 (i.e. its reporting period immediately preceding 1 April 2016). Following a reassessment, after a change in its activities, the reporting entity determines that it no longer qualifies for the temporary exemption from IFRS 9 at the end of its annual reporting period ending 31 December 2019. As a result, it is permitted to continue using the temporary exemption from IFRS 9 only until 31 December 2020. For the 31 December 2021 financial statements, the entity can either apply IFRS 9 or apply IFRS 9 with the overlay approach.

When an entity, having previously qualified for the temporary exemption, concludes that its activities are no longer predominantly connected with insurance, additional disclosures are required – see 10.1.5.A below.

An insurer that previously elected to apply the temporary exemption from IFRS 9 may always, at the beginning of any subsequent annual period, irrevocably elect to apply

IFRS 9 rather than IAS 39. *[IFRS 4.20K]*. The transitional requirements of IFRS 9 would apply in those circumstances. An insurer ceasing to use the temporary exemption may also elect to use the overlay approach in the first reporting period in which it applies IFRS 9.

10.1.3 First-time adopters

A first-time adopter, as defined in IFRS 1 – *First-time Adoption of International Financial Reporting Standards*, may apply the temporary exemption if, and only if, it meets the criteria described at 10.1 above. A first-time adopter is required to assess and reassess predominance on the same reporting dates as an existing user of IFRS. This means that a first-time adopter initially performs the predominance calculation (see 10.1.1 above) using the carrying amounts determined applying IFRSs as at its annual reporting date that immediately precedes 1 April 2016. This reporting period is used even if the entity first applies IFRS 1 with a later date of transition to IFRSs (e.g. the period ended 31 December with a 1 January 2017 date of transition). A first-time adopter that qualifies for the temporary exemption at its annual reporting date that immediately precedes 1 April 2016 must reassess eligibility if there is a change in its activities (see 10.1.2 above). A first-time adopter that does not qualify for the temporary exemption on initial assessment is permitted to reassess whether its activities are predominantly connected with insurance at a subsequent annual reporting date before 31 December 2018 if, and only if, there is a change in its activities. *[IFRS 4.20L]*. The Basis for Conclusions states that the IASB was prepared to allow first-time adopters to use the temporary exemption if, and only if, those first-time adopters met the same criteria as existing users of IFRS (i.e. the initial assessment of eligibility for the temporary exemption was performed for the same reporting period). *[IFRS 4.BC282]*.

A first-time adopter may apply the temporary exemption if the entity qualified for the temporary exemption in a financial year ending before 31 December 2018 in accordance with the eligibility criteria (see 10.1 above). For example, a new company which begins trading in 2019 or later will not have qualified for the temporary exemption in a financial year ending before 31 December 2018 and therefore should apply IFRS 9.

Other requirements in IFRS 1, for example the elections available to a subsidiary that becomes a first-time adopter later than its parent or to an entity that becomes a first-time adopter later than its subsidiary (discussed in Chapter 5 at 5.9), do not override the conditions for using the temporary exemption. Therefore, nothing overrides the requirement that a first-time adopter must meet the predominance criteria at an annual reporting date that immediately precedes 1 April 2016, or, in certain circumstances, at a later date, to apply the temporary exemption from IFRS 9. *[IFRS 4.20M]*.

When making the disclosure required by entities using the temporary exemption (see 10.1.5 below), a first-time adopter should use the requirements and exemptions in IFRS 1 that are relevant to making the assessments required for those disclosures. *[IFRS 4.20N]*.

10.1.4 Relief for investors in associates and joint ventures

IAS 28 requires an entity to use uniform accounting policies when applying the equity method to account for interests in associates and joint ventures. Nevertheless, for accounting periods beginning before 1 January 2023, based on the amendments issued

in June 2020, an entity is permitted, but not required, to retain the relevant accounting policies applied by the associate or joint venture as follows: *[IFRS 4.20O]*
- the entity applies IFRS 9 but the associate or joint venture uses the temporary exemption from IFRS 9; or
- the entity applies the temporary exemption from IFRS 9 but the associate or joint venture applies IFRS 9.

These reliefs are intended to reduce the costs of applying the equity method when an entity does not qualify for the temporary exemption from IFRS 9, and thus applies IFRS 9, but one or more of its associates and joint ventures is eligible and chooses to continue to apply IAS 39 (or *vice versa*). *[IFRS 4.BC279]*. The effect is that the underlying financial assets and liabilities held by individual associates and joint ventures, which contribute to the equity accounted result, can be valued on a different basis to those of the reporting entity. This election may be applied separately to each associate or joint venture. *[IFRS 4.20Q]*.

The following accounting applies when an entity uses the equity method to account for its investment in an associate or joint venture: *[IFRS 4.20P]*
- if IFRS 9 was previously applied in the financial statements used to apply the equity method to that associate or joint venture (after reflecting any adjustments made by the entity), then IFRS 9 should continue to be applied; and
- if the temporary exemption from IFRS 9 was previously applied in the financial statements used to apply the equity method to that associate or joint venture (after reflecting any adjustments made by the entity), then IFRS 9 may be subsequently applied.

The elections described above may be applied separately for each associate or joint venture. *[IFRS 4.20Q]*.

This relief is not limited to consolidated financial statements and could also be applied under the temporary exemption in separate or individual financial statements when associates and joint ventures are accounted for using the equity method.

When an entity uses fair value through profit or loss to measure an investment in associate or joint venture, as permitted by paragraph 18 of IAS 28, this election does not apply (as the election applies only to associates and joint ventures accounted for using the equity method).

10.1.5 Disclosures required for entities using the temporary exemption

Insurers that apply the temporary exemption should disclose information to enable users of their financial statements to: *[IFRS 4.39B]*
- understand how the insurer qualified for the temporary exemption; and
- compare insurers applying the temporary exemption with entities applying IFRS 9.

The standard contains detailed disclosure requirements for each of these principles which are described at 10.1.5.A and 10.1.5.B below. An insurer that uses the temporary exemption from IFRS 9 should use the transitional provisions in IFRS 9 that are relevant to making the assessments required for these disclosures. The date of initial application for that purpose should be deemed to be the beginning of the first annual period beginning on or after 1 January 2018. *[IFRS 4.47]*. In our view, comparative period disclosures in the first year of application (i.e. a financial year beginning on or after 1 January 2018) are not required since IFRS 9 does not require restatement of prior periods in the year of application. However, comparative disclosures are required for subsequent accounting periods.

There have been no consequential amendments to IAS 34 – *Interim Financial Reporting* – and therefore the disclosures detailed at 10.1.5.A and 10.1.5.B below are not required specifically in interim financial statements.

10.1.5.A Disclosures required to understand how an insurer qualified for the temporary exemption

In order to comply with the overall disclosure objective an insurer should disclose: *[IFRS 4.39C]*

- the fact that it is applying the temporary exemption from IFRS 9; and
- how it concluded on the relevant date (see 10.1.2 above) that it qualifies for the temporary exemption from IFRS 9, including:
  - if the carrying amount of its liabilities arising from contracts within the scope of IFRS 4 was less than or equal to 90% of the total carrying amount of all its liabilities, the nature and carrying amount of the liabilities connected with insurance that are not liabilities arising from contracts within the scope of IFRS 4 (e.g. non-derivative investment contract liabilities measured at fair value through profit or loss applying IAS 39, liabilities that arise because the insurer issues or fulfils obligations arising from contracts within the scope of IFRS 4 and non-derivative investment contract liabilities measured at fair value through profit or loss) – see 10.1.1 above;
  - if the percentage of the total carrying amount of its liabilities connected with insurance relative to the total carrying amount of all its liabilities was less than or equal to 90% but greater than 80%, how the insurer determined that it did not engage in a significant activity unconnected with insurance, including what information it considered; and
  - if the insurer qualified for the temporary exemption from IFRS 9 on the basis of a reassessment (see 10.1.2 above):
    - the reason for the reassessment;
    - the date on which the relevant change in its activities occurred; and
    - a detailed explanation of the change in its activities and a qualitative description of the effect of that change on the insurer's financial statements.

The following examples illustrates the application of the disclosure requirements above and in particular:

- Example 55.38 provides illustrative disclosures for an entity whose carrying amount of liabilities within the scope of IFRS 4 exceeds 90% of total liabilities;
- Example 55.39 provides illustrative disclosures for an entity whose carrying amount of its liabilities connected with insurance relative to the total carrying amount of all its liabilities was greater than 90% but whose liabilities arising from contracts within the scope of IFRS 4 was less than or equal to 90% of the total carrying amount of all its liabilities; and

- Example 55.40 provides illustrative disclosures for an entity whose total carrying amount of its liabilities connected with insurance relative to the total carrying amount of all its liabilities was less than or equal to 90% but greater than 80% of the total carrying amount of all its liabilities.

Example 55.38: Illustrative disclosure explaining how an insurer qualified for the temporary exemption – where the gross liabilities within the scope of IFRS 4 exceed 90% of total liabilities

The Group applies the temporary exemption from IFRS 9 as permitted by the amendments to IFRS 4 *Applying IFRS 9 Financial Instruments with IFRS 4 Insurance Contracts* issued in September 2016 and amended in June 2020. The temporary exemption permits the Group to continue applying IAS 39 rather than IFRS 9 for annual periods beginning before 1 January 2023.

The Group concluded that it qualified for the temporary exemption from IFRS 9 because its activities are predominantly connected with insurance. As at 31 December 2015, the Group's gross liabilities arising from contracts within the scope of IFRS 4 represented 96% of the total carrying amount of all its liabilities. Since 31 December 2015, there has been no change in the activities of the Group that requires reassessment of the use of the temporary exemption.

Example 55.39: Illustrative disclosure explaining how an insurer qualified for the temporary exemption – where the gross liabilities within the scope of IFRS 4 are less than 90% of total liabilities but liabilities connected with insurance are in excess of 90% of total liabilities

The Group applies the temporary exemption from IFRS 9 as permitted by the amendments to IFRS 4 *Applying IFRS 9 Financial Instruments with IFRS 4 Insurance Contracts* issued in September 2016 and amended in June 2020. The temporary exemption permits the Group to continue applying IAS 39 rather than IFRS 9 for annual periods beginning before 1 January 2023.

The Group concluded that it qualified for the temporary exemption from IFRS 9 because its activities are predominantly connected with insurance. As at 31 December 2015, the Group's percentage of its gross liabilities connected with insurance represented 96% of its total liabilities. Since 31 December 2015, there has been no change in the activities of the Group that requires reassessment of the use of the temporary exemption.

As at 31 December 2015, the gross liabilities connected with insurance relative to total liabilities were as follows:

Liability type	*CU'm*	*% of total liabilities*
Liabilities arising from contracts within the scope of IFRS 4	750	75
Liabilities from non-derivative investment contracts measured at fair value through profit or loss	100	10
Debt instruments issued included in regulatory capital	50	5
Liabilities for derivatives used to mitigate risks arising from contracts within the scope of IFRS 4, investment contracts measured at fair value through profit or loss and from the assets backing those contracts	25	2.5
Relevant tax liabilities	25	2.5
Relevant other liabilities including employee benefits	10	1

Example 55.40: *Illustrative disclosure explaining how an insurer qualified for the temporary exemption – where the total carrying amount of liabilities connected with insurance are greater than 80% but less than 90% of total liabilities*

The Group applies the temporary exemption from IFRS 9 as permitted by the amendments to IFRS 4 *Applying IFRS 9 Financial Instruments with IFRS 4 Insurance Contracts* issued in September 2016 and amended in June 2020. The temporary exemption permits the Group to continue applying IAS 39 rather than IFRS 9 for annual periods beginning before 1 January 2023.

The Group concluded that it qualified for the temporary exemption from IFRS 9 because its activities are predominantly connected with insurance. As at 31 December 2015, the Group's percentage of its gross liabilities connected with insurance represented 86% of its total liabilities. Since 31 December 2015, there has been no change in the activities of the Group that requires reassessment of the use of the temporary exemption.

As at 31 December 2015, the gross liabilities connected with insurance relative to total liabilities were as follows:

Liability type	CU'm	% of total liabilities
Liabilities arising from contracts within the scope of IFRS 4	650	65
Liabilities from non-derivative investment contracts measured at fair value through profit or loss	100	10
Debt instruments issued included in regulatory capital	50	5
Liabilities for derivatives used to mitigate risks arising from contracts within the scope of IFRS 4, investment contracts measured at fair value through profit or loss and from the assets backing those contracts	25	2.5
Relevant tax liabilities	25	2.5
Relevant other liabilities including employee benefits	10	1

The Group has determined that it does not engage in significant activities unconnected with insurance, primarily based on a consideration of the following factors:

- its principal subsidiaries are all regulated insurance entities;
- liabilities not connected with insurance relate primarily to debt instruments not included in regulatory capital. These liabilities do not relate to a significant activity unconnected with insurance; and
- the Group is classified as a regulated insurance company by the insurance regulator of Euroland and is therefore considered as an insurer for the purposes of prudential supervision.

If an entity, having previously qualified for the temporary exemption, concludes that its activities are no longer predominantly connected with insurance, it should disclose the following information in each reporting period before it begins to apply IFRS 9: *[IFRS 4.39D]*

- the fact that it no longer qualifies for the temporary exemption from IFRS 9;
- the date on which the relevant change in its activities occurred; and
- a detailed explanation of the change in its activities and a qualitative description of the effect of that change on the entity's financial statements.

10.1.5.B Disclosures required in order to compare insurers applying the temporary exemption with entities applying IFRS 9

To comply with this disclosure principle, an insurer should disclose the fair value at the end of the reporting period and the amount of change in fair value during that period for the following two groups of financial assets separately: *[IFRS 4.39E]*

- financial assets with contractual terms that give rise on specified dates to cash flows that are solely payments of principal and interest on the principal amount outstanding, i.e. any financial asset which should be measured at either amortised cost or fair value through comprehensive income (excluding any financial asset that meets the IFRS 9 definition of held for trading or that is managed and whose performance is evaluated on a fair value basis); and
- all financial assets other than those specified above; that is, any financial asset:
  - with contractual terms that do not give rise on specified dates to cash flows that are solely payments of principal and interest on the principal amount outstanding (which includes equity instruments measured at fair value through OCI under IFRS 9);
  - that would meet the definition of held for trading under IFRS 9; or
  - that is managed or whose performance is evaluated on a fair value basis.

When disclosing the fair value at the end of the reporting period and the change in fair value of the two groups, the insurer: *[IFRS 4.39F]*

- may use the carrying amount of a financial asset measured at amortised cost as its fair value if that is a reasonable approximation (e.g. for short-term receivables); and
- should consider the level of detail necessary to enable users of the financial statements to understand the characteristics of the financial assets.

This disclosure requirement means that insurers applying the temporary exemption need to allocate their financial assets into the two groups above, an exercise that will be of similar complexity to that required on adoption of IFRS 9.

There is no explicit requirement to distinguish between the different measurement models used under IFRS 9 for financial assets in each group (e.g. to distinguish between those assets measured at amortised cost and those at fair value through OCI or fair value through profit or loss) although there is a requirement to consider the detail necessary to enable users of the financial statements to understand the characteristics of the financial assets. In addition, there is no requirement to sub-analyse the change in fair value of the financial assets within each group (e.g. between realised and unrealised gains or losses). As IFRS 7 and IFRS 13 already require disclosure of the fair value of financial assets measured at amortised cost (see Chapter 14 at 20.4) information about fair values at each reporting date should generally be available although not analysed by the two groupings required.

As well as disclosing fair values and changes in fair values, an insurer should also disclose information about credit risk exposure, including significant credit risk concentration, inherent in the first group of financial assets. At a minimum, an insurer should disclose the following information for those financial assets at the end of the reporting period: *[IFRS 4.39G]*

- the carrying amounts applying IAS 39 (before adjusting for any impairment allowances in the case of financial assets measured at amortised cost) by credit risk rating grades as defined in IFRS 7; and
- the fair value and carrying amount applying IAS 39 (before adjusting for any impairment allowances in the case of financial assets measured at amortised cost) for those financial assets that do not have low credit risk at the end of the reporting period. IFRS 9 sets out guidance assessing whether the credit risk on a financial instrument is considered low (see Chapter 51 at 6.4.1).

As with the requirement to disclose fair values and changes in fair values, there is no explicit requirement to distinguish between the different measurement models used under IFRS 9 for financial assets in each group (e.g. to distinguish between those assets measured at amortised cost, those at fair value through OCI or those at fair value through profit or loss). Details of impairment losses for those financial assets under IFRS 9 are also not required. In addition, there is no requirement for credit risk information for the second group of financial assets in addition to the disclosures required already by IFRS 7.

The following example illustrates the disclosure requirements above (for simplicity no comparative disclosures are made):

Example 55.41: *Illustrative disclosures required in order to compare insurers applying the temporary exemption with entities applying IFRS 9*

The table below presents an analysis of the fair value of classes of financial assets as at the end of the reporting period, as well as the corresponding change in fair value during the reporting period. The financial assets are divided into two categories:

- Assets for which their contractual cash flows represent solely payments of principal and interest (SPPI), excluding any financial assets that are held for trading or that are managed and whose performance is evaluated on a fair value basis; and
- All financial assets other than those specified in SPPI above (i.e. those for which contractual cash flows do not represent SPPI, assets that are held for trading and assets that are managed and whose performance is evaluated on a fair value basis).

In the table the amortised cost of cash and cash equivalents and short-term receivables has been used as a reasonable approximation to fair value.

Asset type (CU'm)	SPPI financial assets		Other financial assets	
	Fair value	Fair Value change	Fair value	Fair value change
Cash and cash equivalents	50	1	–	–
Debt securities	200	10	100	10
Equity securities	–	–	200	20
Short-term receivables	20	–	–	–
Derivatives	–	–	40	(6)
Total	270	11	340	24

The following table shows the carrying amount of the SPPI assets included in the table above by credit risk rating grades reported to key management personnel. The carrying amount is measured in accordance with IAS 39 although this is prior to any impairment allowance for those measured at amortised cost.

Asset type (CU'm)			Credit rating			
	Total	AAA	AA/A	BBB	BB/B	Unrated
Cash and cash equivalents	50	5	43	1	1	–
Debt securities	210	20	120	30	10	30
Short-term receivables	20	–	–	–	–	20
Total	280	25	163	31	11	50

The following table provides information on the fair value and carrying amount under IAS 39 for those SPPI assets which the Group has determined do not have a low credit risk. The carrying amount is measured in accordance with IAS 39 although this is prior to any impairment allowance for those measured at amortised cost.

Asset type (CU'm)	Fair value	Carrying amount
Cash and cash equivalents	1	1
Debt securities	45	40
Short-term receivables	5	5
Total	51	46

An insurer should also disclose information about where a user of financial statements can obtain any publicly available IFRS 9 information that relates to an entity within the group that is not already provided in the group's consolidated financial statements for the relevant reporting period. Such information could be obtained from publicly available individual or separate financial statement of an entity within the group that has applied IFRS 9. *[IFRS 4.39H]*.

When an entity elects to apply the exemption from using uniform accounting policies for associates and joint ventures, discussed at 10.1.4 above, it should disclose that fact. *[IFRS 4.39I]*.

In addition, if an entity applied the temporary exemption from IFRS 9 when accounting for its investment in an associate or joint venture using the equity method it should disclose the following in addition to the information required by IFRS 12 – *Disclosure of Interests in Other Entities*: *[IFRS 4.39J]*

- the information required above (e.g. fair value analysis and credit risk disclosures) for each associate or joint venture that is material to the entity. The amounts disclosed should be those included in the IFRS financial statements of the associate or joint venture after reflecting any adjustments made by the entity when using the equity method rather than the entity's share of those amounts (see Chapter 13 at 5.1.1); and
- the quantitative information required above (e.g. fair value analysis and credit risk disclosures) in aggregate for individually immaterial associates or joint ventures. The aggregate amounts:
    - disclosed should be the entity's share of those amounts; and
    - for associates should be disclosed separately from the aggregate amounts disclosed for joint ventures.

If applicable, this requires disclosure of financial assets which are not shown separately on the reporting entity's balance sheet (as only the net equity investment in an associate or joint venture is disclosed). Therefore, this will require the reporting entity to have access to the underlying records of the associate(s) and joint venture(s). As worded, these disclosure requirements apply only for an associate or joint venture where the reporting entity applies IFRS 9 but elects to apply the temporary exemption in equity accounting for its associate or joint venture. They do not apply for any associate and joint venture when the reporting entity applies the temporary exemption but elects to apply IFRS 9 when equity accounting for an associate or joint venture. As discussed at 10.1.4 above, this election can be made separately for each associate or joint venture.

10.1.6 Interest rate benchmark reform

Interest Rate Benchmark Reform – Phase 2, Amendments to IFRS 9, IAS 39, IFRS 7, IFRS 4 and IFRS 16 – (the Phase 2 amendments), issued in August 2020, added paragraphs 20R to 20S and paragraphs 50 to 51 to IFRS 4. *[IFRS 4.50]*. The Phase 2 amendments to specific requirements in IFRS 9, IAS 39, IFRS 7, IFRS 4 and IFRS 16 address issues that might affect financial reporting during the reform of an interest rate benchmark, including the replacement of an interest rate benchmark with an alternative benchmark rate. The term 'interest rate benchmark reform' refers to the market-wide reform of an interest rate benchmark as described in Chapter 53 at 9.1.2. *[IAS 39.102B]*. The background to these amendments is discussed in Chapter 53 at 9. *[IFRS 4.BC277D]*.

As discussed at 10.1 above, the temporary exemption from applying IFRS 9 permits an insurer that meets specific criteria to apply IAS 39 rather than IFRS 9 for annual periods beginning before the effective date of IFRS 17. *[IFRS 4.20A]*. However, the IASB maintained that due to the temporary nature of the exemption and its relatively narrow application, a version of IAS 39 (except for its hedge accounting requirements) would not be maintained and updated for any subsequent amendments to other IFRS Standards. This means that an insurer applying the temporary exemption would be required to apply the requirements in IAS 39 to account for changes in the basis for determining contractual cash flows as a result of the reform; i.e. such an insurer would not be able to apply the amendments set out in paragraphs 5.4.5 to 5.4.9 of IFRS 9 – see Chapter 50 at 3.8.3. *[IFRS 4.BC277E-F]*.

The financial assets and financial liabilities of such an insurer could be affected by the interest rate benchmark reform in the same way as those for other entities. The Board therefore decided the amendments in paragraphs 5.4.5 to 5.4.9 of IFRS 9 should apply to insurers that apply the IAS 39 requirements. The Board noted that amending the superseded paragraphs in IAS 39 would be inconsistent with its previous decisions that IAS 39 (except for its hedge accounting requirements) would not be maintained. However, the Board decided to amend IFRS 4 to require insurers applying the temporary exemption from IFRS 9 to apply requirements that are comparable to paragraphs 5.4.5 to 5.4.9 of the Phase 2 amendments to financial assets and financial liabilities for which the basis for determining the contractual cash flows of those financial assets or financial liabilities change as a result of the reform. The Board noted that this decision was due to the significance of the potential effect of the reform on insurers and reaffirmed its overall position that it will not update the classification and measurement requirements of IAS 39. *[IFRS 4.BC277F]*.

Consequently, an insurer applying the temporary exemption from IFRS 9 should apply the requirements in paragraphs 5.4.6 to 5.4.9 of IFRS 9 to a financial asset or financial liability if, and only if, the basis for determining the contractual cash flows of that financial asset or financial liability changes as a result of interest rate benchmark reform. *[IFRS 4.20R]*. For the purpose of applying paragraphs 5.4.6 to 5.4.9 of the amendments to IFRS 9, the references to paragraph B5.4.5 of IFRS 9 should be read as referring to paragraph AG7 of IAS 39; and the references to paragraphs 5.4.3 and B5.4.6 of IFRS 9 should be read as referring to paragraph AG8 of IAS 39. *[IFRS 4.20S]*.

An entity should apply the Phase 2 amendments for annual periods beginning on or after 1 January 2021. Earlier application is permitted. If an entity applies these amendments for an earlier period, it should disclose that fact. An entity should apply these amendments retrospectively in accordance with IAS 8, except as specified below. *[IFRS 4.50]*.

An entity is not required to restate prior periods to reflect the application of these amendments. The entity may restate prior periods if, and only if, it is possible without the use of hindsight. If an entity does not restate prior periods, the entity should recognise any difference between the previous carrying amount and the carrying amount at the beginning of the annual reporting period that includes the date of initial application of these amendments in the opening retained earnings (or other component of equity, as appropriate) of the annual reporting period that includes the date of initial application of these amendments. *[IFRS 4.51]*.

10.2 The overlay approach

An insurer is permitted, but not required, to apply the overlay approach to designated financial assets. *[IFRS 4.35B]*. The overlay approach is intended to address the additional accounting mismatches and volatility in profit or loss that may arise if an insurer applies IFRS 9 before IFRS 17. *[IFRS 4.BC240]*.

The overlay approach is elective on an instrument-by-instrument basis. Insurers may therefore choose whether to apply the overlay approach and to what extent. There is no 'predominance test' (see 10.1.1 above) and therefore the overlay approach can be applied to designated financial instruments by any reporting entity, such as a financial conglomerate, that has activities which are not predominantly connected with insurance. The IASB acknowledged that the availability of choice reduces comparability among insurers but decided not to require insurers to apply the overlay approach to all eligible financial assets because there is no loss of information when an insurer applies the overlay approach to only some financial assets. *[IFRS 4.BC241]*.

An insurer may elect to apply the overlay approach only when it first applies IFRS 9, including when it first applies IFRS 9 after previously applying: *[IFRS 4.35C]*

- the temporary exemption discussed at 10.1 above; or
- only the requirements in IFRS 9 for the presentation in OCI of gains and losses attributable to changes in the entity's own credit risk on financial liabilities designated at fair value through profit or loss.

An insurer that applies the overlay approach when applying IFRS 9 should: *[IFRS 4.35B]*

- reclassify between profit or loss and other comprehensive income an amount that results in the profit or loss at the end of the reporting period for the designated financial assets being the same as if the entity had applied IAS 39 to the designated financial assets. Accordingly, the amount reclassified is equal to the difference between:
  - the amount reported in profit or loss for the designated financial assets applying IFRS 9; and
  - the amount that would have been reported in profit or loss for the designated financial assets if the insurer had applied IAS 39.
- apply all other applicable IFRSs to its financial instruments, except for the application of the overlay approach.

An insurer should present the amount reclassified between profit and loss and other comprehensive income applying the overlay approach: *[IFRS 4.35D]*

- in profit or loss as a separate line item; and
- in other comprehensive income as a separate component of other comprehensive income.

The use of the overlay approach will result in financial instruments in the statement of financial position being recognised and measured in accordance with IFRS 9 but profit or loss and other comprehensive income will reflect a mixed measurement model (i.e. gains and losses from some financial assets will reflect the requirements of IAS 39 whilst gains and losses on other financial assets and all financial liabilities will reflect the requirements of IFRS 9). The IASB has acknowledged that different entities could use different approaches to designating financial assets (see 10.2.1 below) but notes that all financial assets will be accounted for in the statement of financial position under IFRS 9 and considers that the proposed presentation and disclosure requirements (see 10.2.3 below) will make the effect of the overlay approach transparent.

Unlike the temporary exemption from IFRS 9 (see 10.1 above), there is no expiry date for the overlay approach so an insurer is able to continue to use this approach until IFRS 17 supersedes IFRS 4. The overlay approach is available only for designated financial assets. Financial liabilities cannot be designated for the overlay approach.

When an entity elects to apply the overlay approach it should: *[IFRS 4.49]*

- apply that approach retrospectively to designated financial assets on transition to IFRS 9. Accordingly, for example, an entity should recognise as an adjustment to the opening balance of accumulated other comprehensive income an amount equal to the difference between the fair value of designated financial assets determined applying IFRS 9 and their carrying amount determined applying IAS 39; and
- restate comparative amounts to reflect the overlay approach if, and only if, the entity restated comparative information applying IFRS 9.

If an insurer applies the overlay approach, shadow accounting (see 8.3 above) may be applicable. *[IFRS 4.35L]*.

The reclassification between profit or loss and other comprehensive income may have consequential effects for including other amounts in other comprehensive income, such as income taxes. The relevant IFRS (e.g. IAS 12) should be applied to determine any such consequential effects. *[IFRS 4.35M]*.

10.2.1 Designation and de-designation of eligible financial assets

Eligible financial assets can be designated for the overlay approach on an instrument-by-instrument basis. *[IFRS 4.35G]*.

A financial asset is eligible for the overlay approach if, and only if, the following criteria are met: *[IFRS 4.35E]*

- it is measured at fair value through profit or loss applying IFRS 9 but would not have been measured at fair value through profit or loss in its entirety applying IAS 39; and
- it is not held in respect of an activity that is unconnected with contracts within the scope of IFRS 4. Examples of financial assets that would not be eligible for the overlay approach are those assets held in respect of banking activities or financial assets held in funds relating to investment contracts that are outside the scope of IFRS 4.

The first criterion above limits the application of the overlay approach to those financial assets for which application of IFRS 9 may result in additional volatility in profit or loss. The Basis for Conclusions states that an example of such a financial asset is one that is measured at fair value through profit or loss applying IFRS 9 but that would have been bifurcated into a derivative and a host applying IAS 39. *[IFRS 4.BC240(b)(i)]*.

The second criterion above is expressed in the negative (i.e. an asset is eligible if it is not held in respect of an activity that is unconnected with contracts within the scope of IFRS 4). Logically, this means that a financial asset is eligible for the overlay approach if it is held in respect of a business activity that is connected with contracts within the scope of IFRS 4. In the majority of situations this is likely to be obvious (e.g. the assets are held to back insurance liabilities). In other situations, application depends on the specific facts and circumstances. Although not mentioned in the text of the standard, the Basis for Conclusions clarifies that financial assets held for insurance regulatory requirements (or for internal capital requirements for the insurance business) are eligible for the overlay approach on the grounds that what became IFRS 17 may affect them. *[IFRS 4.BC240(b)(ii)]*.

An insurer may designate an eligible financial asset for the overlay approach when it elects to apply the overlay approach (see 10.2 above). Subsequently, it may designate an eligible financial asset for the overlay approach when, and only when: *[IFRS 4.35F]*

- that asset is initially recognised; or
- that asset newly meets the criteria above having previously not met that criteria.

For the purpose of applying the overlay approach to a newly designated financial asset: *[IFRS 4.35H]*

- its fair value at the date of designation should be its new amortised cost carrying amount; and
- the effective interest rate should be determined based on its fair value at the date of designation (i.e. the new amortised cost carrying amount).

An entity should continue to apply the overlay approach to a designated financial asset until that financial asset is derecognised. However, an entity: *[IFRS 4.35I]*

- should de-designate a financial asset if the financial asset no longer meets the second criterion specified above. For example a financial asset will no longer meet that criterion when an entity transfers that asset so that it is held in respect of its banking activities or when an entity ceases to be an insurer. When an entity de-designates a financial asset in this way it should reclassify from other comprehensive income to profit or loss as a reclassification adjustment any balance relating to that financial asset; *[IFRS 4.35J]* and
- may, at the beginning of any annual period, stop applying the overlay approach to all designated financial assets. An entity that elects to stop applying the overlay approach should apply IAS 8 to account for the change in accounting policy (i.e. account for the change retrospectively unless impracticable).

An entity that stops using the overlay approach because it elects to do so or because it is no longer an insurer should not subsequently apply the overlay approach. However, an insurer that has elected to apply the overlay approach but has no eligible financial assets may subsequently apply the overlay approach when it has eligible financial assets. *[IFRS 4.35K]*.

10.2.2 First-time adopters

First-time adopters are permitted to apply the overlay approach. A first-time adopter that elects to apply the overlay approach should restate comparative information to reflect the overlay approach if, and only if, it restates comparative information to comply with IFRS 9. IFRS 1 allows a first-time adopter not to apply IFRS 9 to its comparative period if its first IFRS reporting period begins before 1 January 2019. *[IFRS 4.35N]*.

10.2.3 Disclosures required for entities applying the overlay approach

Insurers that apply the overlay approach should disclose information to enable users of the financial statements to understand: *[IFRS 4.39K]*

- how the amount reclassified from profit or loss to other comprehensive income in the reporting period is calculated; and
- the effect of that reclassification on the financial statements.

To comply with these principles an insurer should disclose: *[IFRS 4.39L]*

- the fact that it is applying the overlay approach;
- the carrying amount at the end of the reporting period of financial assets to which the entity applies the overlay approach by class of financial assets ('class' is explained in Chapter 54 at 3.3);
- the basis for designating financial assets for the overlay approach, including an explanation of any designated financial assets held outside the legal entity that issues contracts within the scope of IFRS 4;
- an explanation of the total amount reclassified between profit or loss and other comprehensive income in the reporting period in a way that enables users of the financial statements to understand how that amount is derived, including:

- the amount reported in profit or loss for the designated financial assets applying IFRS 9; and
- the amount that would have been reported in profit or loss for the designated financial assets if the insurer had applied IAS 39;
- the effect of the reclassification and consequential effects (e.g. income taxes) on each affected line item in profit or loss; and
- if during the reporting period the insurer has changed the designation of financial assets:
  - the amount reclassified between profit or loss and other comprehensive in the reporting period relating to newly designated financial assets applying the overlay approach;
  - the amount that would have been reclassified between profit or loss and other comprehensive income in the reporting period if the financial assets had not been de-designated; and
  - the amount reclassified in the reporting period to profit or loss from accumulated other comprehensive income for financial assets that have been de-designated.

If an entity applies the overlay approach when accounting for its investment in an associate or joint venture using the equity method it should disclose the following, in addition to information required by IFRS 12: *[IFRS 4.39M]*

- the information set out above for each associate or joint venture that is material to the entity. The amounts disclosed should be those included in the IFRS financial statements of the associate or joint venture after reflecting any adjustments made by the entity when using the equity method rather than the reporting entity's share of those amounts (see Chapter 13 at 5.1.1); and
- the quantitative information set out above and the effect of the reclassification on profit and loss and other comprehensive income in aggregate for all individually immaterial associates or joint ventures. The aggregate amounts:
  - disclosed should be the entity's share of those amounts; and
  - for associates should be disclosed separately from the aggregate amounts disclosed for joint ventures.

Designation of financial assets is always voluntary on an instrument-by-instrument basis under the overlay approach. Therefore, an entity could always avoid the need for these disclosures for associates and joint ventures by not designating an investee's financial assets for the overlay approach.

11 DISCLOSURE

One of the two main objectives of IFRS 4 is to require entities issuing insurance contracts to disclose information about those contracts that identifies and explains the amounts in an insurer's financial statements arising from these contracts and helps users of those financial statements understand the amount, timing and uncertainty of future cash flows from those insurance contracts. *[IFRS 4.1]*.

For many insurers, the disclosure requirements of the standard had a significant impact when IFRS 4 was applied for the first time because they significantly exceeded what was required under most local GAAP financial reporting frameworks.

In drafting the disclosure requirements, the main objective of the IASB appears to have been to impose similar requirements for insurance contracts as for financial assets and financial liabilities under IFRS 7.

The requirements in the standard itself are relatively high-level and contain little specific detail. For example, reconciliations of changes in insurance liabilities, reinsurance assets and, if any, related deferred acquisition costs are required but no details about the line items those reconciliations should contain are specified. In comparison, IFRS 17 requires details of items required to be included in its equivalent reconciliations for amounts included in the statement of financial position.

The lack of specific disclosure requirements is probably attributable to the diversity of accounting practices permitted under IFRS 4. We suspect the IASB probably felt unable to give anything other than generic guidance within the standard to avoid the risk that local GAAP requirements may not fit in with more specific guidance.

However, the disclosure requirements outlined in the standard are supplemented by sixty-nine paragraphs of related implementation guidance which explains how insurers may or might apply the standard. According to this guidance, an insurer should decide in the light of its circumstances how much emphasis to place on different aspects of the requirements and how information should be aggregated to display the overall picture without combining information that has materially different characteristics. Insurers should strike a balance so that important information is not obscured either by the inclusion of a large amount of insignificant detail or by the aggregation of items that have materially different characteristics. To satisfy the requirements of the standard an insurer would not typically need to disclose all the information suggested in the guidance. *[IFRS 4.IG12]*.

The implementation guidance does not, however, create additional disclosure requirements. *[IFRS 4.IG12]*. On the other hand, there is a reminder that IAS 1 requires additional disclosures when compliance with the specific requirements in IFRSs is insufficient to enable users to understand the impact of particular transactions, other events and conditions on the entity's financial position and financial performance. *[IFRS 4.IG13]*. The guidance also draws attention to the definition and explanation of materiality in IAS 1. *[IFRS 4.IG15-16]*.

The disclosure requirements are sub-divided into two main sections:

(a) information that identifies and explains the amounts in the financial statements arising from insurance contracts; and

(b) information that enables users of its financial statements to evaluate the nature and extent of risks arising from insurance contracts.

Each of these is discussed in detail below. They are accompanied by examples illustrating how some of disclosure requirements have been applied in practice.

As discussed at 2.2.2 above, disclosures for investment contracts with a DPF are within the scope of IFRS 7 and IFRS 13, not IFRS 4.

11.1 Explanation of recognised amounts

The first disclosure principle established by the standard is that an insurer should identify and explain the amounts in its financial statements arising from insurance contracts. *[IFRS 4.36]*.

To comply with this principle an insurer should disclose:

(a) its accounting policies for insurance contracts and related assets, liabilities, income and expense;

(b) the recognised assets, liabilities, income and expense (and cash flows if its statement of cash flows is presented using the direct method) arising from insurance contracts. Furthermore, if the insurer is a cedant it should disclose:
   (i) gains or losses recognised in profit or loss on buying reinsurance; and
   (ii) if gains and losses on buying reinsurance are deferred and amortised, the amortisation for the period and the amounts remaining unamortised at the beginning and the end of the period;

(c) the process used to determine the assumptions that have the greatest effect on the measurement of the recognised amounts described in (b). When practicable, quantified disclosure of these assumptions should be given;

(d) the effect of changes in assumptions used to measure insurance assets and insurance liabilities, showing separately the effect of each change that has a material effect on the financial statements; and

(e) reconciliations of changes in insurance liabilities, reinsurance assets and, if any, related deferred acquisitions costs. *[IFRS 4.37]*.

Each of these is discussed below.

11.1.1 Disclosure of accounting policies

As noted at 11.1 above, IFRS 4 requires an insurer's accounting policies for insurance contracts and related liabilities, income and expense to be disclosed. *[IFRS 4.37(a)]*. The implementation guidance suggests that an insurer might need to address the treatment of some or all of the following:

(a) premiums (including the treatment of unearned premiums, renewals and lapses, premiums collected by agents and brokers but not passed on and premium taxes or other levies on premiums);

(b) fees or other charges made to policyholders;

(c) acquisition costs (including a description of their nature);

(d) claims incurred (both reported and unreported), claims handling costs (including a description of their nature) and liability adequacy tests (including a description of the cash flows included in the test, whether and how the cash flows are discounted and the treatment of embedded options and guarantees in those tests – see 7.2.2 above). Disclosure of whether insurance liabilities are discounted might be given together with an explanation of the methodology used;

(e) the objective of methods used to adjust insurance liabilities for risk and uncertainty (for example, in terms of a level of assurance or level of sufficiency), the nature of those models, and the source of information used in those models;

(f) embedded options and guarantees including a description of whether:
  (i) the measurement of insurance liabilities reflects the intrinsic value and time value of these items; and
  (ii) their measurement is consistent with observed current market prices;

(g) discretionary participation features (including an explanation of how the insurer classifies those features between liabilities and components of equity) and other features that permit policyholders to share in investment performance;

(h) salvage, subrogation or other recoveries from third parties;

(i) reinsurance held;

(j) underwriting pools, coinsurance and guarantee fund arrangements;

(k) insurance contracts acquired in business combinations and portfolio transfers, and the treatment of related intangible assets; and

(l) the judgements, apart from those involving estimations, management has made in the process of applying the accounting policies that have the most significant effect on the amounts recognised in the financial statements as required by IAS 1. The classification of a DPF is an example of an accounting policy that might have a significant effect. *[IFRS 4.IG17]*.

Because an insurer's accounting policies will normally be based on its previous local GAAP, the policies for such items will vary from entity to entity.

Set out below are the accounting policies for premiums and claims for Aviva. These are based on UK GAAP which has different requirements for recognition of premiums from life and general (non-life) insurance business.

Extract 55.12: Aviva plc (2016)
Accounting policies [extract]
(H) Premiums earned

Premiums on long-term insurance contracts and participating investment contracts are recognised as income when receivable, except for investment-linked premiums which are accounted for when the corresponding liabilities are recognised. For single premium business, this is the date from which the policy is effective. For regular premium contracts, receivables are recognised at the date when payments are due. Premiums are shown before deduction of commission and before any sales-based taxes or duties. Where policies lapse due to non-receipt of premiums, then all related premium income accrued but not received from the date they are deemed to have lapsed is offset against premiums.

General insurance and health premiums written reflect business incepted during the year, and exclude any sales-based taxes or duties. Unearned premiums are those proportions of the premiums written in a year that relate to periods of risk after the statement of financial position date. Unearned premiums are calculated on either a daily or monthly pro rata basis. Premiums collected by intermediaries, but not yet received, are assessed based on estimates from underwriting or past experience, and are included in premiums written.

Deposits collected under investment contracts without a discretionary participation feature (non-participating contracts) are not accounted for through the income statement, except for fee income (covered in accounting policy I) and the investment income attributable to those contracts, but are accounted for directly through the statement of financial position as an adjustment to the investment contract liability.

(L) Insurance and participating investment contract liabilities [extract]

Claims

Long-term business claims reflect the cost of all claims arising during the year, including claims handling costs, as well as policyholder bonuses accrued in anticipation of bonus declarations.

General insurance and health claims incurred include all losses occurring during the year, whether reported or not, related handling costs, a reduction for the value of salvage and other recoveries, and any adjustments to claims outstanding from previous years.

Claims handling costs include internal and external costs incurred in connection with the negotiation and settlement of claims. Internal costs include all direct expenses of the claims department and any part of the general administrative costs directly attributable to the claims function.

Long-term business provisions

Under current IFRS requirements, insurance and participating investment contract liabilities are measured using accounting policies consistent with those adopted previously under existing accounting practices, with the exception of liabilities remeasured to reflect current market interest rates to be consistent with the value of the backing assets, and those relating to UK with-profit and non-profit contracts.

The long-term business provisions are calculated separately for each life operation, based either on local regulatory requirements or existing local GAAP (at the later of the date of transition to IFRS or the date of acquisition of the entity); and actuarial principles consistent with those applied in each local market. Each calculation represents a determination within a range of possible outcomes, where the assumptions used in the calculations depend on the circumstances prevailing in each life operation. The principal assumptions are disclosed in note 40(b). For the UK with-profit funds, FRS 27 required liabilities to be calculated on the realistic basis adjusted to remove the shareholders' share of future bonuses. FRS 27 was grandfathered from UK regulatory requirements prior to the adoption of Solvency II. For UK non-profit insurance contracts, the liabilities are calculated using the gross premium valuation method. This method uses the amount of contractual premiums payable and includes explicit assumptions for interest and discount rates, mortality and morbidity, persistency and future expenses. These assumptions are set on a prudent basis and can vary by contract type and reflect current and expected future experience. The liabilities are based on the UK regulatory requirements prior to the adoption of Solvency II, adjusted to remove certain regulatory reserves and margins in assumptions, notably for annuity business.

General insurance and health provisions [extract]

Outstanding claims provisions [extract]

General insurance and health outstanding claims provisions are based on the estimated ultimate cost of all claims incurred but not settled at the statement of financial position date, whether reported or not, together with related claims handling costs. Significant delays are experienced in the notification and settlement of certain types of general insurance claims, particularly in respect of liability business, including environmental and pollution exposures, the ultimate cost of which cannot be known with certainty at the statement of financial position date. As such, booked claim provisions for general insurance and health insurance are based on the best estimate of the cost of future claim payments plus an explicit allowance for risk and uncertainty. Any estimate represents a determination within a range of possible outcomes. Further details of estimation techniques are given in note 40(c).

Provisions for latent claims and claims that are settled on an annuity type basis such as structured settlements are discounted, in the relevant currency at the reporting date, having regard to the expected settlement dates of the claims and the nature of the liabilities. The discount rate is set at the start of the accounting period with any change in rates between the start and end of the accounting period being reflected below operating profit as an economic assumption change. The range of discount rates used is described in note 40(c)(ii).

Provision for unearned premiums

The proportion of written premiums, gross of commission payable to intermediaries, attributable to subsequent periods is deferred as a provision for unearned premiums. The change in this provision is taken to the income statement as recognition of revenue over the period of risk.

The following example from Allianz illustrates an accounting policy for reinsurance contracts based on US GAAP.

> **Extract 55.13: Allianz SE (2016)**
> Notes to the consolidated financial statements [extract]
> 2 – Accounting policies and new accounting pronouncements [extract]
> Summary of significant accounting policies [extract]
> **Reinsurance contracts**
> The Allianz Group's consolidated financial statements reflect the effects of ceded and assumed reinsurance contracts. Assumed reinsurance premiums, commissions and claim settlements, as well as the reinsurance element of technical provisions are accounted for in accordance with the conditions of the reinsurance contracts, and in consideration of the original contracts for which the reinsurance was concluded. When the reinsurance contracts do not transfer significant insurance risk, deposit accounting is applied as required under the related reinsurance accounting provisions of US GAAP or under IAS 39.

An example of an accounting policy showing a split of contracts with a DPF between liability and equity (AMP) is shown at 6.1 above.

An example of an accounting policy for a liability adequacy test (Allianz) is shown at 7.2.2.A above.

An example of an accounting policy for salvage and subrogation (Royal & SunAlliance) is shown at 7.2.6.E above.

If the financial statements disclose supplementary information, for example embedded value information, that is not prepared on the basis used for other measurements in the financial statements, it would be appropriate to explain the basis of preparation. Disclosures about embedded value methodology might include information similar to that described above, as well as disclosure of whether, and how, embedded values are affected by estimated returns from assets and by locked-in capital and how those effects are estimated. *[IFRS 4.IG18]*.

11.1.2 Recognised assets, liabilities, income and expense

As noted at 11.1 above, IFRS 4 requires disclosure of the recognised assets, liabilities, income and expense (and cash flows if using the direct method) arising from insurance contracts. *[IFRS 4.37(b)]*.

11.1.2.A Assets and liabilities

IAS 1 requires minimum disclosures on the face of the statement of financial position. *[IAS 1.54]*. In order to satisfy these requirements, an insurer may need to present separately on the face of its statement of financial position the following amounts arising from insurance contracts:

(a) liabilities under insurance contracts and reinsurance contracts issued;
(b) assets under insurance contracts and reinsurance contracts issued; and
(c) assets under reinsurance contracts ceded which, as discussed at 7.2.4 above, should not be offset against the related insurance liabilities. [IFRS 4.IG20].

Neither IAS 1 nor IFRS 4 prescribe the descriptions and ordering of the line items presented on the face of the statement of financial position. An insurer could amend the descriptions and ordering to suit the nature of its transactions. [IFRS 4.IG21].

IAS 1 requires the presentation of current and non-current assets and liabilities as separate classifications on the face of the statement of financial position except where a presentation based on liquidity provides information that is reliable and more relevant. [IAS 1.60]. In practice, a current/non-current classification is not normally considered relevant for insurers, and they usually present their IFRS statements of financial position in broad order of liquidity.

IAS 1 permits disclosure, either on the face of the statement of financial position or in the notes, of sub-classifications of the line items presented, classified in a manner appropriate to the entity's operations. The appropriate sub-classifications of insurance liabilities will depend on the circumstances, but might include items such as:

(a) unearned premiums;
(b) claims reported by policyholders;
(c) claims incurred but not reported (IBNR);
(d) provisions arising from liability adequacy tests;
(e) provisions for future non-participating benefits;
(f) liabilities or components of equity relating to discretionary participating features. If these are classified as a component of equity, IAS 1 requires disclosure of the nature and purpose of each reserve within equity;
(g) receivables and payables related to insurance contracts (amounts currently due to and from agents, brokers and policyholders); and
(h) non-insurance assets acquired by exercising rights to recoveries. [IFRS 4.IG22].

Similar sub-classifications may also be appropriate for reinsurance assets, depending on their materiality and other relevant circumstances. For assets under insurance contracts and reinsurance contracts issued, an insurer might need to distinguish:

(a) deferred acquisition costs; and
(b) intangible assets relating to insurance contracts acquired in business combinations or portfolio transfers. [IFRS 4.IG23].

If non-uniform accounting policies for the insurance liabilities of subsidiaries are adopted, it might be necessary to disaggregate the disclosures about the amounts reported to give meaningful information about amounts determined using different accounting policies. *[IFRS 4.IG30]*.

Munich Re's gross technical provisions on the face of the statement of financial position are illustrated below, together with some further detail shown in selected notes.

Extract 55.14: Münchener Rückversicherungs – Gesellschaft Aktiengesellschaft (2016)

Consolidated balance sheet [extract]
Equity and liabilities [extract]

	Notes	31.12.2016		Prev. year		Change	
		€m	€m	€m	€m		%
C. Gross technical provisions							
I. Unearned premiums	(20)	8,984		8,841	143		1.6
II. Provision for future policy benefits	(21)	108,108		108,572	–463		–0.4
III. Provision for outstanding claims	(22)	61,362		59,756	1,606		2.7
IV. Other technical provisions	(23)	19,026		17,413	1,612		9.3
			197,480	194,582		2,898	1.5
D. Gross technical provisions for unit-linked life insurance	(24)		8,429	8,201		228	2.8

21 Provision for future policy benefits [extract]

Gross provision for future policy benefits according to type of insurance cover

€m	31.12.2016	Prev. year
Life	74,878	77,142
Reinsurance	11,206	12,924
ERGO	63,672	64,218
Term life insurance	3,363	3,293
Other life insurance	26,718	28,343
Annuity insurance	32,268	31,277
Disability insurance	1,292	1,281
Contracts with combination of more than one risk	31	25
Health	32,558	30,962
Munich Health	1,196	1,118
ERGO	31,362	29,844
Property-casualty	672	468
Reinsurance	26	26
ERGO	646	442
Total	108,108	108,572

The provision for future policy benefits in life reinsurance largely involves contracts where the mortality or morbidity risk predominates. In reinsurance, annuity contracts have a significantly lower weight than in primary insurance.

Essentially the same actuarial assumptions have been used as in the previous year for measuring the provisions for future policy benefits for business in force.

In the ERGO Life and Health Germany segment, there was an adjustment in 2016 to the assumptions regarding future lapses, future administration expenses, and to long-term interest-rate levels that are geared to the long-term regular return on investments. This resulted in an increase to the provision for future policy benefits.

Further information on the underwriting risks can be found in the risk report in the section "Significant Risks".

CNP Assurances provided the following analysis of its insurance and financial liabilities.

Extract 55.15: CNP Assurances (2016)

ASSETS, EQUITY AND LIABILITIES [extract]

Note 10   Analysis of insurance and financial liabilities [extract]

The following tables show the sub-classifications of insurance liabilities that require separate disclosure under IFRS.

10.1.1   Analysis of insurance and financial liabilities at 31 December 2016 [extract]

(in € millions)	Before reinsurance	Net of reinsurance	Reinsurance
Non-life technical reserves	8,372.9	6,917.1	1,455.8
Unearned premium reserves	892.0	802.8	89.2
Outstanding claims reserves	5,480.8	4,400.1	1,080.7
Bonuses and rebates (including claims equalisation reserve on group business maintained in liabilities)	43.9	42.3	1.6
Other technical reserves	1,956.2	1,672.0	284.2
Liability adequacy test reserves	0.0	0.0	0.0
Life technical reserves	183,734.5	166,998.6	16,735.9
Unearned premium reserves	1,495.9	1,367.0	128.9
Life premium reserves	175,339.1	158,949.2	16,390.0
Outstanding claims reserves	2,263.7	2,086.9	176.8
Policyholder surplus reserves	3,978.5	3,948.6	29.9
Other technical reserves	657.3	647.0	10.3
Liability adequacy test reserves	0.0	0.0	0.0
Financial instruments with DPF	134,126.5	129,617.8	4,508.6
Life premium reserves	126,670.6	122,442.6	4,228.0
Outstanding claims reserves	2,566.7	2,450.2	116.5
Policyholder surplus reserves	4,889.1	4,725.0	164.2
Other technical reserves	0.0	0.0	0.0
Liability adequacy test reserves	0.0	0.0	0.0
Financial instruments without DPF	4,800.7	4,468.5	332.3
Derivative instruments separated from the host contract	0.0	0.0	0.0
Deferred participation reserve	30,713.6	30,713.6	0.0
Total insurance and financial liabilities	361,748.3	338,715.7	23,032.6

IFRS 7 requires an entity to disclose the carrying amount of financial assets pledged as collateral for liabilities, the carrying amount of financial assets pledged as collateral for contingent liabilities, and any terms and conditions relating to assets pledged as collateral. *[IFRS 7.14-15]*. In complying with this requirement, it might be necessary to disclose segregation requirements that are intended to protect policyholders by restricting the use of some of the insurer's assets. *[IFRS 4.IG23A]*.

Prudential makes the following disclosures in respect of the segregation requirements applying to its assets and liabilities.

> **Extract 55.16: Prudential plc (2016)**
> **Notes to Primary statements** [extract]
> **C12 Capital** [extract]
> **(c) Transferability of available capital**
>
> In the UK, the Solvency II regime became effective on 1 January 2016. PAC is required to meet the Solvency II capital requirements as a company as a whole, i.e. covering both its ring-fenced with-profit funds and non-profit funds. Further, the surplus of the with-profits funds is ring-fenced from the shareholder balance sheet with restrictions as to its distribution. Distributions from the with-profits funds to shareholders continue to reflect the shareholders' one-ninth share of the cost of declared policyholders' bonuses.
>
> For Jackson, capital retention is maintained at a level consistent with an appropriate rating by Standard & Poor's. Currently, Jackson is rated AA. Jackson can pay dividends on its capital stock only out of earned surplus unless prior regulatory approval is obtained. Furthermore, dividends which exceed the greater of statutory net gain from operations less net realised investment losses for the prior year or 10 per cent of Jackson's prior year end statutory surplus, excluding any increase arising from the application of permitted practices, require prior regulatory approval.
>
> For Asia subsidiaries, the amounts retained within the companies are at levels that provide an appropriate level of capital strength in excess of the local regulatory minimum. For ring-fenced with-profits funds, the excess of assets over liabilities is retained with distribution tied to the shareholders' share of bonuses through declaration of actuarially determined surplus. The businesses in Asia may, in general, remit dividends to the UK, provided the statutory insurance fund meets the local regulatory solvency targets.
>
> Available capital of the non-insurance business units is transferable to the life assurance businesses after taking account of an appropriate level of operating capital, based on local regulatory solvency targets, over and above basis liabilities.

11.1.2.B   Income and expense

IAS 1 lists minimum line items that an entity should present on the face of its income statement. It also requires the presentation of additional line items when this is necessary to present fairly the entity's financial performance. To satisfy these requirements, disclosure of the following amounts on the face of the income statement might be required:

(a) revenue from insurance contracts issued (without any deduction for reinsurance held);

(b) income from contracts with reinsurers;

(c) expense for policyholder claims and benefits (without any reduction for reinsurance held); and

(d) expenses arising from reinsurance held. *[IFRS 4.IG24]*.

The extracts below show two alternative methods of presenting revenue and expense on the face of the income statement. Royal & Sun Alliance presents sub-totals of net earned premiums (premiums net of reinsurance premiums) and net claims (claims net of reinsurance claims) on the face of its income statement. AEGON presents reinsurance premiums within expenses and reinsurance claims within income on the face of its income statement.

Extract 55.17: RSA Insurance Group plc (2016)

Consolidated Income Statement for the year ended 31 December 2016 [extract]

	Notes	2016 £m	2015 £m
Income			
Gross written premiums		7,220	6,858
Less: reinsurance premiums		(981)	(906)
Net written premiums	8	6,239	5,952
Change in the gross provision for unearned premiums		109	(97)
Less: change in provision for unearned reinsurance premiums		(8)	305
Change in provision for unearned premiums		101	208
Net earned premiums		6,340	6,160
Net investment return	9	347	381
Other operating income	11	170	142
Total income		**6,857**	**6,683**
Expenses			
Gross claims incurred		(4,826)	(4,496)
Less: claims recoveries from reinsurers		707	367
Net claims	10	(4,119)	(4,129)
Underwriting and policy acquisition costs		(1,977)	(1,986)
Unwind of discount		(59)	(52)
Other operating expenses	12	(229)	(308)
		(6,384)	**(6,475)**

Extract 55.18: AEGON N.V. (2016)

Consolidated Income Statement of AEGON N.V [extract]
For The Year Ended December 31

Amount in EUR million (except per share data)	Note	2016	2015	2014
Premium income	6	23,453	22,925	19,864
Investment income	7	7,788	8,525	8,148
Fee and commission income	8	2,408	2,438	2,137
Other revenues		7	14	7
Total revenues		*33,655*	*33,902*	*30,157*
Income from reinsurance ceded	9	3,687	3,321	2,906
Results from financial transactions	10	15,949	401	13,772
Other income	11	66	83	61
Total Income		**53,357**	**37,707**	**46,896**
Premiums paid to reinsurers	6	3,176	2,979	3,011
Policyholder claims and benefits	12	41,974	26,443	36,214
Profit sharing and rebates	13	49	31	17
Commissions and expenses	14	6,351	6,598	5,629
Impairment charges/(reversals)	15	95	1,251	87
Interest charges and related fees	16	347	412	371
Other charges	17	700	774	172
Total Charges		**52,693**	**38,489**	**45,502**

IFRS 4 does not prescribe a particular method for recognising revenue and recording expenses so a variety of models are used, the most common ones being:

- recognising premiums earned during the period as revenue and recognising claims arising during the period (including estimates of claims incurred but not reported) as an expense;
- recognising premiums received as revenue and at the same time recognising an expense representing the resulting increase in the insurance liability; and
- initially recognising premiums received as deposit receipts. Revenue will include charges for items such as mortality, and expenses will include the policyholder claims and benefits related to those charges. *[IFRS 4.IG25].*

IAS 1 requires additional disclosures of various items of income and expense. To meet this requirement the following additional items might need to be disclosed, either on the face of the income statement or in the notes:

(a) acquisition costs (distinguishing those recognised as an expense immediately from the amortisation of deferred acquisition costs);

(b) the effects of changes in estimates and assumptions (see 11.1.5 below);

(c) losses recognised as a result of applying liability adequacy tests;

(d) for insurance liabilities measured on a discounted basis:

  (i) accretion of interest to reflect the passage of time; and

  (ii) the effect of changes in discount rates; and

(e) distributions or allocations to holders of contracts that contain a DPF. The portion of profit or loss that relates to any equity component of those contracts is an allocation of profit or loss, not expense or income (see 6.1 above). *[IFRS 4.IG26].*

These items should not be offset against income or expense arising from reinsurance held. *[IFRS 4.IG28].*

Some insurers present a detailed analysis of the sources of their earnings from insurance activities, either in the income statement, or in the notes. Such an analysis may provide useful information about both the income and expense of the current period and risk exposures faced during the period. *[IFRS 4.IG27].*

To the extent that gains or losses from insurance contracts are recognised in other comprehensive income, e.g. as a result of applying shadow accounting (see 8.3 above), similar considerations to those discussed above will apply.

If non-uniform accounting policies for the insurance liabilities of subsidiaries are adopted, it might be necessary to disaggregate the disclosures about the amounts reported to give meaningful information about amounts determined using different accounting policies. *[IFRS 4.IG30].*

11.1.2.C   Cash flows

If an insurer presents its cash flow statement using the direct method, IFRS 4 also requires it to disclose the cash flows that arise from insurance contracts although it does not require disclosure of the component cash flows associated with its insurance activity. *[IFRS 4.IG19]*.

11.1.3   Gains or losses on buying reinsurance

Gains or losses on buying reinsurance may, using some measurement models, arise from imperfect measurements of the underlying direct insurance liability. Furthermore, some measurement models require a cedant to defer some of those gains and losses and amortise them over the period of the related risk exposures, or some other period. *[IFRS 4.IG29]*.

Therefore, a cedant is required to provide specific disclosure about gains or losses on buying reinsurance as discussed at 7.2.6.C and 11.1 above. In addition, if gains and losses on buying reinsurance are deferred and amortised, disclosure is required of the amortisation for the period and the amounts remaining unamortised at the beginning and end of the period. *[IFRS 4.37(b)(i)-(ii)]*.

11.1.4   Process used to determine significant assumptions

As noted at 11.1 above, IFRS 4 requires disclosure of the process used to determine the assumptions that have the greatest effect on the measurement of the recognised amounts. Where practicable, quantified disclosure of these assumptions should also be given. *[IFRS 4.37(c)]*.

Some respondents to ED 5 expressed concern that information about assumptions and changes in assumptions (see 11.1.5 below) might be costly to prepare and of limited usefulness. They argued that there are many possible assumptions that could be disclosed and excessive aggregation would result in meaningless information, whereas excessive disaggregation could be costly, lead to information overload, and reveal commercially sensitive information. In response to these concerns, the IASB determined that disclosure about assumptions should focus on the process used to derive them. *[IFRS 4.BC212]*. Further, the standard refers only to those assumptions 'that have the greatest effect on the measurement of' the recognised amounts.

IFRS 4 does not prescribe specific assumptions that should be disclosed, because different assumptions will be more significant for different types of contracts. *[IFRS 4.IG33]*.

For some disclosures, such as discount rates or assumptions about future trends or general inflation, it may be relatively easy to disclose the assumptions used (aggregated at a reasonable but not excessive level, when necessary). For other assumptions, such as mortality rates derived from tables, it may not be practicable to disclose quantified assumptions because there are too many, in which case it is more important to describe the process used to generate the assumptions. *[IFRS 4.IG31]*.

The description of the process used to describe assumptions might include a summary of the most significant of the following:

(a) the objective of the assumptions, for example, whether the assumptions are intended to be neutral estimates of the most likely or expected outcome ('best estimates') or to provide a given level of assurance or level of sufficiency. If they are intended to provide a quantitative or qualitative level of assurance, that level could be disclosed;

(b) the source of data used as inputs for the assumptions that have the greatest effect, for example, whether the inputs are internal, external or a mixture of the two. For data derived from detailed studies that are not carried out annually, the criteria used to determine when the studies are updated and the date of the latest update could be disclosed;

(c) the extent to which the assumptions are consistent with observable market prices or other published information;

(d) a description of how past experience, current conditions and other relevant benchmarks are taken into account in developing estimates and assumptions. If a relationship would normally be expected between past experience and future results, the reasons for using assumptions that differ from past experience and an indication of the extent of the difference could be explained;

(e) a description of how assumptions about future trends, such as changes in mortality, healthcare costs or litigation awards were developed;

(f) an explanation of how correlations between different assumptions are identified;

(g) the policy in making allocations or distributions for contracts with discretionary participation features. In addition, the related assumptions that are reflected in the financial statements, the nature and extent of any significant uncertainty about the relative interests of policyholders and shareholders in the unallocated surplus associated with those contracts, and the effect on the financial statements of any changes during the period in that policy or those assumptions could be disclosed; and

(h) the nature and extent of uncertainties affecting specific assumptions. In addition, to comply with IAS 1, an insurer may need to disclose the assumptions it makes about the future, and other major sources of estimation uncertainty, that have a significant risk of resulting in a material adjustment to the carrying amounts of insurance assets and liabilities within the next financial year. *[IFRS 4.IG32]*.

Ping An disclose the following assumptions in relation to their insurance liabilities together with further detail about those assumptions.

> *Extract 55.19: Ping An Insurance (Group) Company of China Ltd (2016)*
>
> Notes to Consolidated Financial Statements [extract]
>
> 4. Critical accounting estimates and judgements in applying accounting policies [extract]
>
> (4) **Measurement unit and valuation of insurance contract liabilities** [extract]
>
> The Group makes significant judgments on whether a group of insurance contracts' insurance risks are of the same nature. Different measurement units would affect the measurement of insurance contract liabilities.
>
> At the end of the reporting period, when measuring the insurance contract liabilities, the Group needs to make a reasonable estimate of amounts of the payments which the Group is required to make in fulfilling the obligations under the insurance contracts, based on information currently available at the end of the reporting period.

At the end of the reporting period, the Group shall make an estimate of the assumptions used in the measurement of insurance contract liabilities. Such assumptions shall be determined based on information currently available at the end of the reporting period. To determine these assumptions, the Group selects proper risk margins according to both uncertainties and degree of impact of expected future cash outflows. Refer to note 3. (2) for the changes in accounting policies and estimates.

The main assumptions used in the measurement of policyholders' reserves and unearned premium reserves are as follows:

> For long term life insurance contracts where the future insurance benefits are not affected by investment return of the underlying asset portfolio, the discount rate assumption is based on the benchmarking yield curve for the measurement of insurance contract liabilities published by China Central Depository and Clearing Co., Ltd., with consideration of the impact of the tax and liquidity premium. The current discount rate assumption for the measurement as at 31 December 2016 ranged from 3.12%-5.00% (31 December 2015: 3.55%-5.29%).

For long-term non-life insurance contracts where the future policy benefits are not affected by investment return of the underlying asset portfolio, as the risk margin has no material impact on the reserve measurement, the discount rate assumption is the benchmarking yield curve for the measurement of insurance contract liabilities published by China Central Depository and Clearing Co., Ltd.

For long term life insurance contracts where the future insurance benefits are affected by investment return of the underlying asset portfolio, the discount rates are determined based on expected future investment returns of the asset portfolio backing those liabilities. The future investment returns assumption for the measurement as at 31 December 2016 ranged from 4.75%-5.00% (31 December 2015: 4.75%-5.50%).

For short term insurance contracts liabilities whose duration is within one year, the future cash flows are not discounted.

The discount rate and investment return assumptions are affected by the future macro-economy, capital market, investment channels of insurance funds, investment strategy, etc., and therefore subject to uncertainty.

> The Group uses reasonable estimates, based on market and actual experience and expected future development trends, in deriving assumptions of mortality rates, morbidity rates, disability rates, etc.

The assumption of mortality rates is based on the industrial benchmark or Group's prior experience data on mortality rates, estimates of current and future expectations, the understanding of the China insurance market as well as a risk margin. The assumption of mortality rates is presented as a percentage of 'China Life Insurance Mortality Table (2000-2003)', which is the industry standard for life insurance in China.

The assumption of morbidity rates is determined based on the Group's assumptions used in product pricing, experience data of morbidity rates, and estimates of current and future expectation as well as a risk margin.

The assumptions of mortality and morbidity rates are affected by factors such as changes in lifestyles of national citizens, social development, and improvement of medical treatment, and hence subject to uncertainty.

> The Group uses reasonable estimates, based on actual experience and future development trends, in deriving lapse rate assumptions.

The assumptions of lapse rates are determined by reference to different pricing interest rates, product categories and sale channels separately. They are affected by factors such as future macro-economy and market competition, and hence subject to uncertainty.

> The Group uses reasonable estimates, based on an expense study and future development trends, in deriving expense assumptions. If the future expense level becomes sensitive to inflation, the Group will consider the inflation factor as well in determining expense assumptions.

The expense assumptions include assumptions of acquisition costs and maintenance costs. The assumption of maintenance costs also has a risk margin.

> The Group uses reasonable estimates, based on expected investment returns of participating insurance accounts, participating dividend policy, policyholders' reasonable expectations, etc. in deriving policy dividend assumptions.

The assumption of participating insurance accounts is affected by the above factors, and hence bears uncertainty. The future assumption of life and bancassurance participating insurance with a risk margin based on a dividend rate of 85%.

> In the measurement of unearned premium reserves for the property and casualty insurance and short term life insurance business, the Group applies the cost of capital approach and the insurance industry guideline ranged from 3% to 6% to determine risk margins.

> The major assumptions needed in measuring claim reserves include the claim development factor and expected claim ratio, which can be used to forecast trends of future claims so as to estimate the ultimate claim expenses. The loss claim development factors and expected loss ratio of each measurement unit are based on the Group's historical claim development experiences and claims paid, with consideration of adjustments to company policies like underwriting policies, level of premium rates, claim management and the changing trends of external environments such as macroeconomic regulations, and legislation. In the measurement of claim reserves, the Group applies the cost of capital approach and insurance industry guideline ranged from 2.5% to 5.5% to determine risk margins.

Some life insurers give details of the mortality tables used for measuring their insurance contract liabilities and changes in those tables during the reporting period. AMP provide an example of the type of disclosures made.

> **Extract 55.20: AMP Limited (2016)**
>
> **Notes to the financial statements** [extract]
> For the year ended 31 December 2016
> **4.3. Life insurance contracts – assumptions and valuation methodology** [extract]
> **(g) Mortality and morbidity** [extract]
>
> Standard mortality tables, based on national or industry-wide data, are used.
>
> Rates of mortality assumed at 31 December 2016 for AMP Life and NMLA are as follows:
>
> – Retail risk mortality rates for AMP Life Australia and NMLA Australia have been reviewed and strengthened for some business lines from those assumed at 31 December 2015, as indicated in the tables below. Retail risk mortality rates for AMP Life and NMLA New Zealand are unchanged from those assumed at 31 December 2015. The rates are based on the Industry standard IA04-08 Death Without Riders;
>
> – Conventional business mortality rates are unchanged from those assumed at 31 December 2015;
>
> – Annuitant mortality rates are unchanged from those assumed at 31 December 2015.
>
> For Australian income protection business, the assumptions have been updated and based on the recently released AD107-11 standard table modified for AMP Life and NMLA with overall specific adjustment factors. For New Zealand income protection business, the assumptions are unchanged from those assumed at 31 December 2015. These assumptions are based on the IAS89-93 standard table.
>
> For Australian TPD and Trauma business, the AMP Life and NMLA retail risk products assumptions have been strengthened for some business lines from those assumed at 31 December 2015. For New Zealand TPD and Trauma business, the retail risk products assumptions are unchanged from those assumed at 31 December 2015. These assumptions are based on the latest industry table IA04-08.
>
> The assumptions are summarised in the following table:
>
> | Conventional | Conventional – % of IA95-97 (AMP Life) | | Conventional – % of IA95-97 (NMLA) | |
> |---|---|---|---|---|
> | | Male | Female | Male | Female |
> | **31 December 2016** | | | | |
> | Australia | 67.5 | 67.5 | 67.5 | 67.5 |
> | New Zealand | 73.0 | 73.0 | 73.0 | 73.0 |
>
> | Risk products | Retail Lump Sum – % of table (AMP Life) | | Retail Lump Sum – % of table (NMLA) | |
> |---|---|---|---|---|
> | | Male | Female | Male | Female |
> | **31 December 2016** | | | | |
> | Australia | 94-148 | 94-148 | 100-106 | 100-106 |
> | New Zealand | 100 | 82 | 120 | 98 |

The impact of interest rates on long-term business relates primarily to annuities in the UK (including any change in credit default and reinvestment risk provisions), where a decrease in the valuation interest rate, in response to decreasing risk-free rates and narrowing credit spreads, has increased liabilities. The overall impact on profit also depends on movements in the value of assets backing the liabilities, which is not included in this disclosure.

In the UK, expense reserves have reduced and persistency reserves have increased following a review of recent experience. There has been a release of annuitant mortality reserves in the UK following a review of recent experience (including the exposure to anti-selection risk) and the adoption of CML_2015 mortality improvement assumptions, partially offset by a change in base mortality assumptions in response to revisions in the calculation of mortality exposure.

Tax and other assumptions include the profit arising from a change in estimate related to the recoverability testing of the deferred acquisition cost assets (DAC) in the UK. The allowance for risk for non-participating investment contracts and the level of prudence for insurance contracts has been re-assessed, resulting in amortisation or impairment of DAC in prior reporting periods being reversed (subject to the original amortisation profile).

The adverse change in discount rate assumptions on general insurance and health business of £242 million arises as a result of a decrease in the real interest rates used to discount claim reserves for periodic payment orders and latent claims. Market interest rates used to discount periodic payment orders and latent claims have reduced and the estimated future inflation rate used to value periodic payment orders has been increased to be consistent with market expectations. This has, in part, been offset by a change in estimate for the interest rate used to discount periodic payment orders to allow for the illiquid nature of these liabilities.

11.1.6 Reconciliations of changes in insurance assets and liabilities

As noted at 11.1 above, IFRS 4 requires reconciliations of changes in insurance liabilities, reinsurance assets and, if any, related deferred acquisition costs, although it does not prescribe the line items that should appear in the reconciliations. *[IFRS 4.37(e)]*.

The changes need not be disaggregated into broad classes, but they might be if different forms of analysis are more relevant for different types of liability. For insurance liabilities the changes might include:

(a) the carrying amount at the beginning and end of the period;
(b) additional insurance liabilities arising during the period;
(c) cash paid;
(d) income and expense included in profit or loss;
(e) liabilities acquired from, or transferred to, other insurers; and
(f) net exchange differences arising on the translation of the financial statements into a different presentation currency, and on the translation of a foreign operation into the presentation currency of the reporting entity. *[IFRS 4.IG37]*.

This reconciliation is also required for each period for which comparative information is presented. *[IFRS 4.IG38]*.

The reconciliations given by CNP Assurances for life insurance, non-life insurance and financial instruments with a DPF are shown below.

In the tables the amounts are shown before and after the impact of reinsurance.

> **Extract 55.23: CNP Assurances (2016)**
> ASSETS, EQUITY AND LIABILITIES [extract]
> Note 10. Analyses of insurance and financial liabilities [extract]
> 10.2 Change in technical reserves [extract]
>
> This note presents changes in technical reserves by category, such as those arising from changes in the assumptions applied to measure insurance liabilities. Each change with a material impact on the consolidated financial statements is shown separately. Movements are presented before and after reinsurance.
>
> 10.2.1.1 Changes in mathematical reserves – life insurance – at 31 December 2016 [extract]
>
> | (in € millions) | Before reinsurance | Net of reinsurance | Reinsurance |
> |---|---|---|---|
> | Mathematical reserves at the beginning of the period | 293,987.3 | 284,559.5 | 9,427.7 |
> | Premiums | 27,029.7 | 13,657.2 | 13,372.5 |
> | Extinguished liabilities (benefit payments) | (26,483.8) | (24,387.0) | (2,096.8) |
> | Locked-in gains | 6,903.8 | 6,412.8 | 491.0 |
> | Change in value of linked portfolios | 409.1 | 409.1 | 0.0 |
> | Changes in scope (acquisitions/divestments) | 685.9 | 687.1 | (1.2) |
> | Outstanding fees | (1,763.6) | (1,686.1) | (77.5) |
> | Surpluses/deficits | (2.4) | (2.4) | 0.0 |
> | Currency effect | 2,014.7 | 2,014.7 | 0.0 |
> | Changes in assumptions | 0.0 | 0.0 | 0.0 |
> | Newly-consolidated companies | 0.0 | 0.0 | 0.0 |
> | Deconsolidated companies | 0.0 | 0.0 | 0.0 |
> | Non-current liabilities related to assets held for sale and discontinued operations | 0.0 | 0.0 | 0.0 |
> | Other | (770.9) | (273.1) | (497.8) |
> | Mathematical reserves at the end of the period | 302,009.7 | 281,391.8 | 20,618.0 |

10.2.2.1 Changes in technical reserves – non-life insurance – at 31 December 2016 [extract]

(in € millions)	Before reinsurance	Net of reinsurance	Reinsurance
Outstanding claims reserves at the beginning of the period	5,911.7	4,948.1	963.6
Claims expenses for the period	2,210.3	1,959.8	250.5
Prior period surpluses/deficits	(0.0)	(0.0)	(0.0)
Total claims expenses	**2,210.2**	**1,959.8**	**250.4**
Current period claims settled during the period	(2,645.5)	(2,508.8)	(136.6)
Prior period claims settled during the period	(40.0)	(37.4)	(2.6)
Total paid claims	**(2,685.5)**	**(2,546.2)**	**(139.3)**
Changes in scope (acquisitions/divestments)	0.0	0.0	0.0
Currency effect	38.4	32.4	6.0
Newly-consolidated companies	0.0	0.0	0.0
Non-current liabilities related to assets held for sale and discontinued operations	0.0	0.0	0.0
Other	0.0	0.0	0.0
Outstanding claims reserves at the end of the period	**5,474.9**	**4,394.1**	**1,080.7**

10.2.3 Changes in mathematical reserves – financial instruments with DPF [extract]

	31.12.2016		
(in € millions)	Before reinsurance	Net of reinsurance	Reinsurance
Mathematical reserves at the beginning of the period	4,793.4	4,646.3	147.1
Premiums	451.8	447.2	4.6
Extinguished liabilities (benefit payments)	(885.2)	(852.6)	(32.6)
Locked-in gains	45.8	45.8	0.0
Change in value of linked liabilities	386.1	395.7	(9.6)
Changes in scope (acquisitions/divestments)	(67.8)	(67.8)	0.0
Currency effect	151.4	151.4	0.0
Newly-consolidated companies	0.0	0.0	0.0
Deconsolidated companies	0.0	0.0	0.0
Non-current liabilities related to assets held for sale and discontinued operations	0.0	0.0	0.0
Other	(74.8)	(297.5)	222.8
Mathematical reserves at the end of the period	**4,800.7**	**4,468.5**	**332.3**

A reconciliation of deferred acquisition costs might include:
(a) the carrying amount at the beginning and end of the period;
(b) the amounts incurred during the period;
(c) the amortisation for the period;
(d) impairment losses recognised during the period; and
(e) other changes categorised by cause and type. [IFRS 4.IG39].

Aviva's reconciliation of deferred acquisition costs is illustrated below.

> Extract 55.24: Aviva plc (2016)
> **Notes to the consolidated financial statements** [extract]
> **28 – Deferred acquisition costs, other assets, prepayments and accrued income** [extract]
> (b) Deferred acquisition costs – movements in the year [extract]
> The movements in deferred acquisition costs (DAC) during the year were:
>
> | | 2016 | | | | Restated 2015 | | | |
> |---|---|---|---|---|---|---|---|---|
> | | Long-term business | General insurance and health business | Retail fund management business | Total | Long-term business | General insurance and health business | Retail fund management business | Total |
> | | £m | £m | £m | £m | £m | £m | £m | £m |
> | Carrying amount at 1 January | 1,604 | 812 | 5 | 2,421 | 1,453 | 852 | 7 | 2,312 |
> | Acquisition costs deferred during the year | 283 | 2,264 | – | 2,547 | 263 | 1,952 | – | 2,215 |
> | Amortisation | (377) | (2,118) | (2) | (2,497) | (167) | (1,950) | (2) | (2,119) |
> | Impact of assumption changes | 40 | – | – | 40 | 73 | – | – | 73 |
> | Effect of portfolio transfers, acquisitions and disposals | (29) | (8) | – | (37) | – | – | – | – |
> | Foreign exchange rate movements | 53 | 87 | – | 140 | (18) | (42) | – | (60) |
> | Carrying amount at 31 December | 1,574 | 1,037 | 3 | 2,614 | 1,604 | 812 | 5 | 2,421 |
>
> The balance of deferred acquisition costs for long-term business decreased over 2016 mainly due to increased amortisation as a result of projected future profits being reduced in response to an adjustment to the allocation of fixed costs between product lines in our UK Life business. The balance of deferred acquisition costs for general insurance and health business increased over 2016 mainly due to a new partnership distribution deal and increased new business sales.

An insurer may have intangible assets related to insurance contracts acquired in a business combination or portfolio transfer. IFRS 4 does not require any disclosures for intangible assets in addition to those required by IAS 38 (see 9.2 above). *[IFRS 4.IG40]*.

11.2 Nature and extent of risks arising from insurance contracts

The second key disclosure principle established by IFRS 4 is that information should be disclosed to enable the users of the financial statements to evaluate the nature and extent of risks arising from insurance contracts. *[IFRS 4.38]*.

To comply with this principle, an insurer needs to disclose:

(a) its objectives, policies and processes for managing risks arising from insurance contracts and the methods used to manage those risks;

(b) information about insurance risk (both before and after risk mitigation by reinsurance), including information about:

　(i) sensitivity to insurance risk;

　(ii) concentrations of insurance risk, including a description of how management determines concentrations and a description of the shared characteristic that identifies each concentration (e.g. type of insured event, geographical area or currency); and

　(iii) actual claims compared with previous estimates (i.e. claims development). This disclosure has to go back to the period when the earliest material claim arose for which there is still uncertainty about the amount and timing of the claims payments, but need not go back more than ten years. Information about claims for which uncertainty about the amount and timing of claims payments is typically resolved within one year need not be disclosed;

(c) information about credit risk, liquidity risk and market risk that would be required by IFRS 7 if insurance contracts were within the scope of that standard. However:

　(i) an insurer need not provide the maturity analyses required by IFRS 7 if it discloses information about the estimated timing of the net cash outflows resulting from recognised insurance liabilities instead. This may take the form of an analysis, by estimated timing, of the amounts recognised in the statement of financial position rather than gross undiscounted cash flows; and

　(ii) if an alternative method to manage sensitivity to market conditions, such as an embedded value analysis is used, an insurer may use that sensitivity analysis to meet the requirements of IFRS 7. However, disclosures are still required explaining the methods used in preparing that alternative analysis, its main parameters and assumptions, and an explanation of the objectives of the method and of its limitations; and

(d) information about exposures to market risk arising from embedded derivatives contained in a host insurance contract if the insurer is not required to, and does not, measure the embedded derivatives at fair value. *[IFRS 4.39]*.

These disclosures are based on two foundations:

(a) there should be a balance between quantitative and qualitative disclosures, enabling users to understand the nature of risk exposures and their potential impact; and

(b) disclosures should be consistent with how management perceives its activities and risks, and the objectives, policies and processes that management uses to manage those risks so that they:

   (i) generate information that has more predictive value than information based on assumptions and methods that management does not use, for example, in considering the insurer's ability to react to adverse situations; and

   (ii) are more effective in adapting to the continuing change in risk measurement and management techniques and developments in the external environment over time. [IFRS 4.IG41].

In developing disclosures to satisfy the requirements, it might be useful to group insurance contracts into broad classes appropriate for the nature of the information to be disclosed, taking into account matters such as the risks covered, the characteristics of the contracts and the measurement basis applied. These broad classes may correspond to classes established for legal or regulatory purposes, but IFRS 4 does not require this. [IFRS 4.IG42].

Under IFRS 8 – *Operating Segments* – the identification of operating segments reflects the way in which management allocates resources and assesses performance. It might be useful to adopt a similar approach to identify broad classes of insurance contracts for disclosure purposes, although it might be appropriate to disaggregate disclosures down to the next level. For example, if life insurance is identified as an operating segment for IFRS 8, it might be appropriate to report separate information about, say, life insurance, annuities in the accumulation phase and annuities in the payout phase. [IFRS 4.IG43].

In identifying broad classes for separate disclosure, it is useful to consider how best to indicate the level of uncertainty associated with the risks underwritten, so as to inform users whether outcomes are likely to be within a wider or a narrower range. For example, an insurer might disclose information about exposures where there are significant amounts of provisions for claims incurred but not reported (IBNR) or where outcomes and risks are unusually difficult to assess, e.g. for asbestos-related claims. [IFRS 4.IG45].

It may also be useful to disclose sufficient information about the broad classes identified to permit a reconciliation to relevant line items on the statement of financial position. [IFRS 4.IG46].

Information about the nature and extent of risks arising from insurance contracts will be more useful if it highlights any relationship between classes of insurance contracts (and between insurance contracts and other items, such as financial instruments) that can affect those risks. If the effect of any relationship would not be apparent from disclosures required by IFRS 4, additional disclosure might be useful. *[IFRS 4.IG47].*

A more detailed analysis of risk disclosures made by insurers is discussed below.

11.2.1 Objectives, policies and processes for managing insurance contract risks

As noted at 11.2 above, IFRS 4 requires an insurer to disclose its objectives, policies and processes for managing risks arising from insurance contracts and the methods used to manage those risks. *[IFRS 4.39(a)].*

Such disclosure provides an additional perspective that complements information about contracts outstanding at a particular time and might include information about:

(a) the structure and organisation of the entity's risk management function(s), including a discussion of independence and accountability;

(b) the scope and nature of its risk reporting or measurement systems, such as internal risk measurement models, sensitivity analyses, scenario analysis, and stress testing, and how these are integrated into the entity's operating activities. Useful disclosure might include a summary description of the approach used, associated assumptions and parameters (including confidence intervals, computation frequencies and historical observation periods) and strengths and limitations of the approach;

(c) the processes for accepting, measuring, monitoring and controlling insurance risks and the entity's underwriting strategy to ensure that there are appropriate risk classification and premium levels;

(d) the extent to which insurance risks are assessed and managed on an entity-wide basis;

(e) the methods employed to limit or transfer insurance risk exposures and avoid undue concentrations of risk, such as retention limits, inclusion of options in contracts, and reinsurance;

(f) asset and liability management (ALM) techniques; and

(g) the processes for managing, monitoring and controlling commitments received (or given) to accept (or contribute) additional debt or equity capital when specified events occur.

It might be useful to provide disclosures both for individual types of risks insured and overall. They might include a combination of narrative descriptions and specific quantified data, as appropriate to the nature of the contracts and their relative significance to the insurer. *[IFRS 4.IG48].*

The following extract from AMP provides an example of disclosures concerning the management of life insurance risks.

Extract 55.25: AMP Limited (2016)

Notes to the financial statements [extract]
for the year ended 31 December 2016
4.4. Life insurance contracts – risk [extract]
(a) Life insurance risk

AMP Life and NMLA life insurance entities issue contracts that transfer significant insurance risk from the policyholder, covering death, disability or longevity of the insured, often in conjunction with the provision of wealth management products.

The products carrying insurance risk are designed to ensure that policy wording and promotional materials are clear, unambiguous and do not leave AMP Life and NMLA open to claims from causes that were not anticipated. The variability inherent in insurance risk, including concentration risk, is managed by having a large geographically diverse portfolio of individual risks, underwriting and the use of reinsurance.

Underwriting is managed through a dedicated underwriting department, with formal underwriting limits and appropriate training and development of underwriting staff. Individual policies carrying insurance risk are generally underwritten individually on their merits. Individual policies which are transferred from a group scheme are generally issued without underwriting. Group risk insurance policies meeting certain criteria are underwritten on the merits of the employee group as a whole.

Claims are managed through a dedicated claims management team, with formal claims acceptance limits and appropriate training and development of staff with an objective to ensure payment of all genuine claims. Claims experience is assessed regularly and appropriate actuarial reserves are established to reflect up-to-date experience and any anticipated future events. This includes reserves for claims incurred but not yet reported.

AMP Life and NMLA reinsure (cede) to reinsurance companies a proportion of their portfolio or certain types of insurance risk, including catastrophe. This serves primarily to:

– reduce the net liability on large individual risks;
– obtain greater diversification of insurance risks;
– provide protection against large losses;
– reduce overall exposure to risk;
– reduce the amount of capital required to support the business;

The reinsurance companies are regulated by the Australian Prudential Regulation Authority (APRA), or industry regulators in other jurisdictions and have strong credit ratings from A+ to AA+.

This extract from Beazley plc illustrates the disclosure of non-life insurance and reinsurance risk policies and processes.

Extract 55.26: Beazley plc (2016)

Notes to the financial statements [extract]
2 Risk management [extract]
2.1 Insurance risk [extract]

The group's insurance business assumes the risk of loss from persons or organisations that are directly exposed to an underlying loss. Insurance risk arises from this risk transfer due to inherent uncertainties about the occurrence, amount and timing of insurance liabilities. The four key components of insurance risk are underwriting, reinsurance, claims management and reserving.

Each element is considered below.

a) Underwriting risk [extract]

Underwriting risk comprises four elements that apply to all insurance products offered by the group:
- cycle risk – the risk that business is written without full knowledge as to the (in)adequacy of rates, terms and conditions;
- event risk – the risk that individual risk losses or catastrophes lead to claims that are higher than anticipated in plans and pricing;
- pricing risk – the risk that the level of expected loss is understated in the pricing process; and
- expense risk – the risk that the allowance for expenses and inflation in pricing is inadequate.

We manage and model these four elements in the following three categories; attritional claims, large claims and catastrophe events.

The group's underwriting strategy is to seek a diverse and balanced portfolio of risks in order to limit the variability of outcomes. This is achieved by accepting a spread of business over time, segmented between different products, geographies and sizes.

The annual business plans for each underwriting team reflect the group's underwriting strategy, and set out the classes of business, the territories and the industry sectors in which business is to be written. These plans are approved by the board and monitored by the underwriting committee.

Our underwriters calculate premiums for risks written based on a range of criteria tailored specifically to each individual risk. These factors include but are not limited to the financial exposure, loss history, risk characteristics, limits, deductibles, terms and conditions and acquisition expenses.

The group also recognises that insurance events are, by their nature, random, and the actual number and size of events during any one year may vary from those estimated using established statistical techniques.

To address this, the group sets out the exposure that it is prepared to accept in certain territories to a range of events such as natural catastrophes and specific scenarios which may result in large industry losses. This is monitored through regular calculation of realistic disaster scenarios (RDS). The aggregate position is monitored at the time of underwriting a risk, and reports are regularly produced to highlight the key aggregations to which the group is exposed.

The group uses a number of modelling tools to monitor its exposures against the agreed risk appetite set and to simulate catastrophe losses in order to measure the effectiveness of its reinsurance programmes. Stress and scenario tests are also run using these models. The range of scenarios considered includes natural catastrophe, cyber, marine, liability, political, terrorism and war events.

One of the largest types of event exposure relates to natural catastrophe events such as windstorm or earthquake. Where possible the group measures geographic accumulations and uses its knowledge of the business, historical loss behaviour and commercial catastrophe modelling software to assess the expected range of losses at different return periods. Upon application of the reinsurance coverage purchased, the key gross and net exposures are calculated on the basis of extreme events at a range of return periods.

The group's high level catastrophe risk appetite is set by the board and the business plans of each team are determined within these parameters. The board may adjust these limits over time as conditions change. In 2016 the group operated to a catastrophe risk appetite for a probabilistic 1-in-250 years US event of $412.0m (2015: $462.0m) net of reinsurance. This represented a reduction in our catastrophe risk appetite of 11% compared to 2015.

[...]

To manage underwriting exposures, the group has developed limits of authority and business plans which are binding upon all staff authorised to underwrite and are specific to underwriters, classes of business and industry. In 2016, the maximum line that any one underwriter could commit the managed syndicates to was $100m. In most cases, maximum lines for classes of business were much lower than this.

These authority limits are enforced through a comprehensive sign-off process for underwriting transactions including dual sign-off for all line underwriters and peer review for all risks exceeding individual underwriters' authority limits. Exception reports are also run regularly to monitor compliance.

All underwriters also have a right to refuse renewal or change the terms and conditions of insurance contracts upon renewal. Rate monitoring details, including limits, deductibles, exposures, terms and conditions and risk characteristics are also captured and the results are combined to monitor the rating environment for each class of business.

> *b) Reinsurance risk* [extract]
>
> Reinsurance risk to the group arises where reinsurance contracts put in place to reduce gross insurance risk do not perform as anticipated, result in coverage disputes or prove inadequate in terms of the vertical or horizontal limits purchased. Failure of a reinsurer to pay a valid claim is considered a credit risk which is detailed in the credit risk section on page 153.
>
> The group's reinsurance programmes complement the underwriting team business plans and seek to protect group capital from an adverse volume or volatility of claims on both a per risk and per event basis. In some cases the group deems it more economic to hold capital than purchase reinsurance. These decisions are regularly reviewed as an integral part of the business planning and performance monitoring process.
>
> The reinsurance security committee (RSC) examines and approves all reinsurers to ensure that they possess suitable security. The group's ceded reinsurance team ensures that these guidelines are followed, undertakes the administration of reinsurance contracts and monitors and instigates our responses to any erosion of the reinsurance programmes.

11.2.2 Insurance risk – general matters

As noted at 11.2 above, IFRS 4 requires disclosure about insurance risk (both before and after risk mitigation by reinsurance). *[IFRS 4.39(c)]*.

These disclosures are intended to be consistent with the spirit of the disclosures required by financial instruments. The usefulness of particular disclosures about insurance risk depends on individual circumstances. Therefore, the requirements have been written in general terms to allow practice in this area to evolve. *[IFRS 4.BC217]*.

Disclosures made to satisfy this requirement might build on the following foundations:

(a) information about insurance risk might be consistent with (though less detailed than) the information provided internally to the entity's key management personnel as defined in IAS 24 – *Related Party Disclosures* – so that users can assess the entity's financial position, performance and cash flows 'through the eyes of management';

(b) information about risk exposures might report exposures both gross and net of reinsurance (or other risk mitigating elements, such as catastrophe bonds issued or policyholder participation features). This is especially relevant if a significant change in the nature or extent of an entity's reinsurance programme is expected or if an analysis before reinsurance is relevant for an analysis of the credit risk arising from reinsurance held;

(c) in reporting quantitative information about insurance risk, disclosure of the strengths and limitations of those methods, the assumptions made, and the effect of reinsurance, policyholder participation and other mitigating elements might be useful;

(d) risk might be classified according to more than one dimension. For example, life insurers might classify contracts by both the level of mortality risk and the level of investment risk. It may sometimes be useful to display this information in a matrix format;

(e) if risk exposures at the reporting date are unrepresentative of exposures during the period, it might be useful to disclose that fact; and

(f) the following disclosures required by IFRS 4 might also be relevant:
  (i) the sensitivity of profit or loss and equity to changes in variables that have a material effect on them (see 11.2.3 below);
  (ii) concentrations of insurance risk (see 11.2.4 below); and
  (iii) the development of prior year insurance liabilities (see 11.2.5 below). *[IFRS 4.IG51]*.

Disclosures about insurance risk might also include:

(a) information about the nature of the risk covered, with a brief summary description of the class (such as annuities, pensions, other life insurance, motor, property and liability);

(b) information about the general nature of participation features whereby policyholders share in the performance (and related risks) of individual contracts or pools of contracts or entities. This might include the general nature of any formula for the participation and the extent of any discretion held by the insurer; and

(c) information about the terms of any obligation or contingent obligation for the insurer to contribute to government or other guarantee funds established by law which are within the scope of IAS 37 as illustrated by Example 55.15 at 3.9.2 above.

[IFRS 4.IG51A].

An extract of the narrative disclosures provided by Legal & General about the types of life insurance contracts that it issues is shown below.

Extract 55.27: Legal & General Group plc (2017)

Group consolidated financial statements [extract]

Balance sheet management [extract]

7 Principal products [extract]

Legal & General Insurance (LGI) [extract]

UK protection business (retail and group)

The group offers protection products which provide mortality or morbidity benefits. They may include health, disability, critical illness and accident benefits; these additional benefits are commonly provided as supplements to main life policies but can also be sold separately. The benefit amounts would usually be specified in the policy terms. Some sickness benefits cover the policyholder's mortgage repayments and are linked to the prevailing mortgage interest rates. In addition to these benefits, some contracts may guarantee premium rates, provide guaranteed insurability benefits and offer policyholders conversion options.

US protection business

Protection consists of individual term assurance, which provides death benefits over the medium to long term. The contracts have level premiums for an initial period with premiums set annually thereafter. During the initial period, there is generally an option to convert the contract to a universal life contract. After the initial period, the premium rates are not guaranteed, but cannot exceed the age-related guaranteed premium.

Reinsurance is used within the protection businesses to manage exposure to large claims. These practices lead to the establishment of reinsurance assets on the group's balance sheet. Within LGIA, reinsurance and securitisation is also used to provide regulatory solvency relief (including relief from regulation governing term insurance and universal life reserves).

US universal life

Universal life contracts written by LGIA provide savings and death benefits over the medium to long term. The savings element has a guaranteed minimum growth rate. LGIA has exposure to loss in the event that interest rates decrease and it is unable to earn enough on the underlying assets to cover the guaranteed rate. LGIA is also exposed to loss should interest rates increase, as the underlying market value of assets will generally fall without a change in the surrender value. The reserves for universal life totalled $557m (£412m) at 31 December 2017 ($596m (£482m) at 31 December 2016). The guaranteed interest rates associated with these reserves ranged from 1.5% to 6%, with the majority of the policies having guaranteed rates ranging from 3% to 4% (2016: 3% to 4%).

The following extract from the financial statements of Amlin illustrates a tabular presentation of insurance risk showing information about premiums and line sizes by class of business.

> **Extract 55.28: MS Amlin plc (2016)**
>
> Notes to the financial statements [extract]
> for the year ended 31 December 2016
> **13. Insurance liabilities and reinsurance assets** [extract]
> **g) Underwriting risk** [extract]
> **Marine & Aviation portfolios (unaudited)** [extract]
>
> | | | UK Gross written premium | Europe Gross written premium | UK Max line size | Europe Max line size | UK Average line size | Europe Average line size |
> |---|---|---|---|---|---|---|---|
> | 2016 | | £m | £m | £m | £m | £m | £m |
> | (i) | Hull | 45 | 52 | 50 | 50 | 3 | 2 |
> | (ii) | Cargo | 46 | 30 | 50 | 33 | 9 | 2 |
> | (iii) | Energy | 34 | – | 73 | – | 6 | – |
> | (iv) | War and Terrorism | 51 | – | 50 | – | 15 | – |
> | (v) | Yacht | 52 | 3 | 67 | 33 | 7 | 8 |
> | (vi) | Marine Liability | 81 | 19 | 67 | 67 | 12 | 6 |
> | (vii) | Specie | 15 | – | 43 | – | 7 | – |
> | (viii) | Aviation | 47 | – | 87 | – | 17 | – |
> | Total Marine & Aviation | | 371 | 104 | | | | |

11.2.3 Insurance risk – sensitivity information

As noted at 11.2 above, IFRS 4 requires disclosures about sensitivity to insurance risk. *[IFRS 4.39(c)(i)]*.

To comply with this requirement, disclosure is required of either:

(a) a sensitivity analysis that shows how profit or loss and equity would have been affected had changes in the relevant risk variable that were reasonably possible at the end of the reporting period occurred; the methods and assumptions used in preparing that sensitivity analysis; and any changes from the previous period in the methods and assumptions used. However, if an insurer uses an alternative method to manage sensitivity to market conditions, such as an embedded value analysis, it may meet this requirement by disclosing that alternative sensitivity analysis. Where this is done, the methods used in preparing that alternative analysis, its main parameters and assumptions, and its objectives and limitations should be explained; or

(b) qualitative information about sensitivity, and information about those terms and conditions of insurance contracts that have a material effect on the amount, timing and uncertainty of future cash flows. *[IFRS 4.39A]*.

Quantitative disclosures may be provided for some insurance risks and qualitative information about sensitivity and information about terms and conditions for other insurance risks. *[IFRS 4.IG52A]*.

Although sensitivity tests can provide useful information, such tests have limitations. Disclosure of the strengths and limitations of the sensitivity analyses performed might be useful. *[IFRS 4.IG52]*.

Insurers should avoid giving a misleading sensitivity analysis if there are significant non-linearities in sensitivities to variables that have a material effect. For example, if a change of 1% in a variable has a negligible effect, but a change of 1.1% has a material effect, it might be misleading to disclose the effect of a 1% change without further explanation. *[IFRS 4.IG53]*.

Further, if a quantitative sensitivity analysis is disclosed and that sensitivity analysis does not reflect significant correlations between key variables, the effect of those correlations may need to be explained. *[IFRS 4.IG53A]*.

If qualitative information about sensitivity is provided, disclosure of information about those terms and conditions of insurance contracts that have a material effect on the amount, timing and uncertainty of cash flows should be made. This might be achieved by disclosing the information discussed at 11.2.2 above and 11.2.6 below. An entity should decide in the light of its circumstances how best to aggregate information to display an overall picture without combining information with different characteristics. Qualitative information might need to be more disaggregated if it is not supplemented with quantitative information. *[IFRS 4.IG54A]*.

QBE provide the following quantitative information about non-life insurance sensitivities in their financial statements:

> **Extract 55.29: QBE Insurance Group (2016)**
> **Notes to the financial statements** [extract]
> for the year ended 31 December 2016
> **2.3.7. Impact of changes in key variables on the net outstanding claims liability** [extract]
> **Overview**
> The impact of changes in key variables used in the calculation of the outstanding claims liability is summarised in the table below. Each change has been calculated in isolation from the other changes and shows the after tax impact on profit assuming that there is no change to any of the other variables. In practice, this is considered unlikely to occur as, for example, an increase in interest rates is normally associated with an increase in the rate of inflation. Over the medium to longer term, the impact of a change in discount rates is expected to be largely offset by the impact of a change in the rate of inflation.
>
> The sensitivities below assume that all changes directly impact profit after tax. In practice, however, if the central estimate was to increase, at least part of the increase may result in an offsetting change in the level of risk margin rather than in a change to profit after tax, depending on the nature of the change in the central estimate. Likewise, if the coefficient of variation were to increase, it is possible that the probability of adequacy would reduce from its current level rather than result in a change to net profit after income tax.

	SENSITIVITY %	PROFIT (LOSS) [1] 2016 US$M	2015 US$M
Net discounted central estimate	+5	(444)	(494)
	−5	444	494
Risk margin	+5	(38)	(44)
	−5	38	44
Inflation rate	+0.5	(130)	(145)
	−0.5	124	139
Discount rate	+0.5	124	139
	−0.5	(130)	(145)
Coefficient of variation	+1	(114)	(124)
	−1	114	124
Probability of adequacy	+1	(37)	(43)
	−1	35	40
Weighted average term to settlement	+10	43	58
	−10	(43)	(59)

1 Net of tax at the Group's prima facie income tax rate of 30%.

11.2.4 Insurance risk – concentrations of risk

As noted at 11.2 above, IFRS 4 requires disclosure of concentrations of insurance risk, including a description of how management determines concentrations and a description of the shared characteristic that identifies each type of concentration (e.g. type of insured event, geographical area, or currency). *[IFRS 4.39(c)(ii)]*.

Such concentrations could arise from, for example:

(a) a single insurance contract, or a small number of related contracts, for example when an insurance contract covers low-frequency, high-severity risks such as earthquakes;

(b) single incidents that expose an insurer to risk under several different types of insurance contract. For example, a major terrorist incident could create exposure under life insurance contracts, property insurance contracts, business interruption and civil liability;

(c) exposure to unexpected changes in trends, for example unexpected changes in human mortality or in policyholder behaviour;

(d) exposure to possible major changes in financial market conditions that could cause options held by policyholders to come into the money. For example, when interest rates decline significantly, interest rate and annuity guarantees may result in significant losses;

(e) significant litigation or legislative risks that could cause a large single loss, or have a pervasive effect on many contracts;

(f) correlations and interdependencies between different risks;

(g) significant non-linearities, such as stop-loss or excess of loss features, especially if a key variable is close to a level that triggers a material change in future cash flows; and

(h) geographical and sectoral concentrations. *[IFRS 4.IG55]*.

Disclosure of concentrations of insurance risk might include a description of the shared characteristic that identifies each concentration and an indication of the possible exposure, both before and after reinsurance held, associated with all insurance liabilities sharing that characteristic. *[IFRS 4.IG56]*.

Disclosure about the historical performance of low-frequency, high-severity risks might be one way to help users assess cash flow uncertainty associated with those risks. For example, an insurance contract may cover an earthquake that is expected to happen, on average, once every 50 years. If the earthquake occurs during the current reporting period the insurer will report a large loss. If the earthquake does not occur during the current reporting period the insurer will report a profit. Without adequate disclosure of long-term historical performance, it could be misleading to report 49 years of large profits, followed by one large loss, because users may misinterpret the insurer's long-term ability to generate cash flows over the complete cycle of 50 years. Therefore, describing the extent of the exposure to risks of this kind and the estimated frequency of losses might be useful. If circumstances have not changed significantly, disclosure of the insurer's experience with this exposure may be one way to convey information about estimated frequencies. *[IFRS 4.IG57]*. However, there is no specific requirement to disclose a probable maximum loss (PML) in the event of a catastrophe because there is no widely agreed definition of PML. *[IFRS 4.BC222]*.

Brit Limited discloses the potential impact of modelled realistic disaster scenarios (estimated losses incurred from a hypothetical catastrophe).

Extract 55.30: Brit Limited (2016)

NOTES TO THE CONSOLIDATED FINANCIAL STATEMENTS [extract]

4 RISK MANAGEMENT POLICIES [extract]

(v) Aggregate exposure management [extract]

The Group is exposed to the potential of large claims from natural catastrophe events. The Group's catastrophe risk tolerance is reviewed and set by the Board on an annual basis. The Board has last reviewed its natural and non-natural catastrophe risk tolerances in April 2016.

Overall, the Group has a maximum catastrophe risk tolerance for major catastrophe events (as measured through world wide all perils 1-in-30 AEP) of 25% of Brit Limited Group level net tangible assets. This equates to a maximum acceptable loss (after all reinsurance) of US$268.7m at 31 December 2016.

The Group closely monitors aggregation of exposure to natural catastrophe events against agreed risk appetites using stochastic catastrophe modelling tools, along with knowledge of the business, historical loss information, and geographical accumulations. Analysis and monitoring also measures the effectiveness of the Group's reinsurance programmes. Stress and scenario tests are also run, such as Lloyd's and internally developed Realistic Disaster Scenarios (RDS). The selection of the RDS is adjusted with development of the business. Below are the key RDS losses to the Group for all classes combined (unaudited).

	Estimated industry loss US$m	Gross US$m	Modelled Group loss at 1 October 2016 Net US$m	Gross US$m	Modelled Group loss at 1 October 2015 Net US$m
Gulf of Mexico windstorm	113,500	829	191	813	174
Florida Miami windstorm	128.250	654	168	601	149
US North East windstorm	80,500	748	156	737	155
San Francisco earthquake	87,750	716	282	716	222
Japan earthquake	44,716	237	156	207	150
Japan windstorm	13,329	92	58	79	52
European windstorm	25,595	228	163	190	127

11.2.5 Insurance risk – claims development information

As noted at 11.2 above, IFRS 4 requires disclosure of actual claims compared with previous estimates (i.e. claims development). The disclosure about claims development should go back to the period when the earliest material claim arose for which there is still uncertainty about the amount and the timing of the claims payments, but need not go back more than ten years. Disclosure need not be provided for claims for which uncertainty about claims payments is typically resolved within one year. *[IFRS 4.39(c)(iii)]*.

These requirements apply to all insurers, not only to property and casualty insurers. However, the IASB consider that because insurers need not disclose the information for claims for which uncertainty about the amount and timing of payments is typically resolved within a year, it is unlikely that many life insurers will need to give the disclosure. *[IFRS 4.IG60, BC220]*. Additionally, the implementation guidance to IFRS 4 states that claims development disclosure should not normally be needed for annuity contracts because each periodic payment is regarded as a separate claim about which there is no uncertainty. *[IFRS 4.IG60]*.

It might also be informative to reconcile the claims development information to amounts reported in the statement of financial position and disclose unusual claims expenses or developments separately, allowing users to identify the underlying trends in performance. *[IFRS 4.IG59]*.

The implementation guidance to IFRS 4 provides an illustrative example of one possible format for presenting claims development which is reproduced in full below. From this it is clear that the IASB is expecting entities to present some form of claims development table. This example presents discounted claims development information by underwriting year. *[IFRS 4.IG61 IE5]*. Other formats are permitted, including for example, presenting information by accident year or reporting period rather than underwriting year. *[IFRS 4.IG61]*.

Example 55.42: Disclosure of claims development

This example illustrates a possible format for a claims development table for a general insurer. The top half of the table shows how the insurer's estimates of total claims for each underwriting year develop over time. For example, at the end of 2016, the insurer estimated that it would pay claims of CU680 for insured events relating to insurance contracts underwritten in 2016. By the end of 2017, the insurer had revised the estimate of cumulative claims (both those paid and those still to be paid) to CU673.

The lower half of the table reconciles the cumulative claims to the amount appearing in the statement of financial position. First, the cumulative payments are deducted to give the cumulative unpaid claims for each year on an undiscounted basis. Second, if the claims liabilities are discounted, the effect of discounting is deducted to give the carrying amount in the statement of financial position.

Underwriting year	2016 CU	2017 CU	2018 CU	2019 CU	2020 CU	Total CU
Estimate of cumulative claims:						
At end of underwriting year	680	790	823	920	968	
One year later	673	785	840	903		
Two years later	692	776	845			
Three years later	697	771				
Four years later	702					
Estimate of cumulative claims	702	771	845	903	968	
Cumulative payments	(702)	(689)	(570)	(350)	(217)	
	–	82	275	553	751	1,661
Effect of discounting	–	(14)	(68)	(175)	(285)	(542)
Present value recognised in the statement of financial position	–	68	207	378	466	1,119

The example appears to be gross of reinsurance but IFRS 4 is silent on whether development information should be given on both a gross basis and a net basis. If the effect of reinsurance is significant it would seem appropriate to provide such information both gross and net of reinsurance.

The illustrative example also provides only five years of data although the standard itself requires ten (subject to the transitional relief upon first-time adoption). Given the long tail nature of many non-life insurance claims liabilities, it is likely that many non-life insurers will still have claims outstanding at the reporting date that are more than ten years old and which will need to be included in a reconciliation of the development table to the statement of financial position.

IFRS 4 is also silent on the presentation of:

- exchange differences associated with insurance liabilities arising on retranslation;
- claims liabilities acquired in a business combination or portfolio transfer; and
- claims liabilities disposed of in a business combination or portfolio transfer.

As IFRS 4 is silent on these matters, a variety of treatments would appear to be permissible provided they are adequately explained to the users of the financial statements and consistently applied in each reporting period. For example, exchange rates could be fixed at the date the claims are incurred, the original reporting period dates or amounts could be retranslated at each reporting date. Claims liabilities acquired in a business combination or portfolio transfer could be reallocated to the prior reporting periods in which they were originally incurred by the acquiree or all liabilities could be allocated to the reporting period in which the acquisition/portfolio transfer occurred.

Aviva's loss (claims) development tables are shown below (although, for brevity, the extract illustrates only six years of data). These are presented on an accident year basis. Aviva discloses both gross and net insurance liabilities in this format.

> **Extract 55.31: Aviva plc (2016)**
>
> **Notes to the consolidated financial statements** [extract]
>
> **40 – Insurance liabilities** [extract]
>
> **(d) Loss development tables** [extract]
>
> (i) Description of tables
>
> The tables that follow present the development of claim payments and the estimated ultimate cost of claims for the accident years 2007 to 2016. The upper half of the tables shows the cumulative amounts paid during successive years related to each accident year. For example, with respect to the accident year 2007, by the end of 2016 £8,278 million had actually been paid in settlement of claims. In addition, as reflected in the lower section of the table, the original estimated ultimate cost of claims of £8,530 million was re-estimated to be £8,380 million at 31 December 2016.
>
> The original estimates will be increased or decreased, as more information becomes known about the individual claims and overall claim frequency and severity.
>
> The Group aims to maintain reserves in respect of its general insurance and health business that protect against adverse future claims experience and development. The Group establishes reserves in respect of the current accident year (2016), where the development of claims is less mature, that allow for the greater uncertainty attaching to the ultimate cost of current accident year claims. As claims develop and the ultimate cost of claims become more certain, the absence of adverse claims experience will result in a release of reserves from earlier accident years, as shown in the loss development tables and movements table (c)(iv) above. Releases from prior accident year reserves are also due to an improvement in the estimated cost of claims.
>
> Key elements of the release from prior accident year general insurance and health net provisions during 2016 were:
> - £208 million strengthening from UK & Ireland due to the impact of the change in the Ogden discount rate in the UK partly offset by other favourable developments on personal motor and commercial liability claims.
> - £154 million release from Canada mainly due to continued favourable experience on motor, following the legislative changes in Ontario.
> - £90 million release from Europe mainly due to favourable development in France and Italy.
>
> There was also a £78 million reduction in net claim reserves relating to an outwards reinsurance contract completed by the UK General Insurance business.
>
> (ii) Gross figures
>
> Before the effect of reinsurance, the loss development table is:
>
> | Accident year | All prior years £m | [...] | 2011 £m | 2012 £m | 2013 £m | 2014 £m | 2015 £m | 2016 £m | Total £m |
> |---|---|---|---|---|---|---|---|---|---|
> | Gross cumulative claim payments | | | | | | | | | |
> | At end of accident year | | | (3,420) | (3,055) | (3,068) | (3,102) | (2,991) | (3,534) | |
> | One year later | | | (4,765) | (4,373) | (4,476) | (4,295) | (4,285) | | |
> | Two years later | | | (5,150) | (4,812) | (4,916) | (4,681) | | | |
> | Three years later | | | (5,457) | (5,118) | (5,221) | | | | |
> | Four years later | | | (5,712) | (5,376) | | | | | |
> | Five years later | | | (5,864) | | | | | | |
> | [...] | | | | | | | | | |
> | Estimate of gross ultimate claims | | | | | | | | | |
> | At end of accident year | | | 6,428 | 6,201 | 6,122 | 5,896 | 5,851 | 6,947 | |
> | One year later | | | 6,330 | 6,028 | 6,039 | 5,833 | 5,930 | | |
> | Two years later | | | 6,315 | 6,002 | 6,029 | 5,865 | | | |
> | Three years later | | | 6,292 | 5,952 | 6,067 | | | | |
> | Four years later | | | 6,262 | 6,002 | | | | | |
> | Five years later | | | 6,265 | | | | | | |
> | [...] | | | | | | | | | |

Accident year	All prior years £m	[...]	2011 £m	2012 £m	2013 £m	2014 £m	2015 £m	2016 £m	Total £m
Estimate of gross ultimate claims			6,265	6,002	6,067	5,865	5,930	6,947	
Cumulative payments			(5,864)	(5,376)	(5,221)	(4,681)	(4,285)	(3,534)	
	2,568		401	626	846	1,184	1,645	3,413	11,465
Effect of discounting	(400)		(2)	1	(3)	–	–	–	(487)
Present value	2,168		399	627	843	1,184	1,645	3,413	10,978
Cumulative effect of foreign exchange movements	–		(3)	5	22	64	176	–	263
Effect of acquisitions	73		39	33	46	61	68	41	468
Present value recognised in the statement of financial position	2,241		435	665	911	1,309	1,889	3,454	11,709

(iii)   Net of reinsurance

After the effect of reinsurance, the loss development table is:

Accident year	All prior years £m	[...]	2011 £m	2012 £m	2013 £m	2014 £m	2015 £m	2016 £m	Total £m
Net cumulative claim payments									
At end of accident year			(3,300)	(2,925)	(2,905)	(2,972)	(2,867)	(3,309)	
One year later			(4,578)	(4,166)	(4,240)	(4,079)	(4,061)		
Two years later			(4,963)	(4,575)	(4,649)	(4,432)			
Three years later			(5,263)	(4,870)	(4,918)				
Four years later			(5,485)	(5,110)					
Five years later			(5,626)						
[...]									
Estimate of net ultimate claims									
At end of accident year			6,202	5,941	5,838	5,613	5,548	6,489	
One year later			6,103	5,765	5,745	5,575	5,635		
Two years later			6,095	5,728	5,752	5,591			
Three years later			6,077	5,683	5,733				
Four years later			6,034	5,717					
Five years later			6,005						
[...]									
Estimate of net ultimate claims			6,005	5,717	5,733	5,591	5,635	6,489	
Cumulative payments			(5,626)	(5,110)	(4,918)	(4,432)	(4,061)	(3,309)	
	928		379	607	815	1,159	1,574	3,180	9,377
Effect of discounting	(191)		3	1	3	–	–	–	(249)
Present value	737		382	608	818	1,159	1,574	3,180	9,128
Cumulative effect of foreign exchange movements	–		(3)	5	22	62	170	–	254
Effect of acquisitions	61		39	33	46	61	68	26	442
Present value recognised in the statement of financial position	798		418	646	886	1,282	1,812	3,206	9,824

In the loss development tables shown above, the cumulative claim payments and estimates of cumulative claims for each accident year are translated into sterling at the exchange rates that applied at the end of that accident year. The impact of using varying exchange rates is shown at the bottom of each table. Disposals are dealt with by treating all outstanding and IBNR claims of the disposed entity as "paid" at the date of disposal.

> The loss development tables above include information on asbestos and environmental pollution claims provisions from business written before 2007. The undiscounted claim provisions, net of reinsurance, in respect of this business at 31 December 2016 were £134 million (*2015: £237 million*). The movement in the year reflects a reduction of £78 million due to the reinsurance contract completed by the UK General Insurance business covering a proportion of these liabilities, favourable claims development of £34 million, claim payments net of reinsurance recoveries and foreign exchange rate movements.

11.2.6 Credit risk, liquidity risk and market risk disclosures

As noted at 11.2 above, IFRS 4 also requires disclosure of information about credit risk, liquidity risk and market risk that would be required by IFRS 7 if insurance contracts were within the scope of that standard. *[IFRS 4.39(d)]*.

Such disclosure should include:

- summary quantitative data about exposure to those risks based on information provided internally to key management personnel; and
- to the extent not already covered by the disclosures discussed above, the information required by IFRS 7.

IFRS 7 allows disclosures about credit risk, liquidity risk and market risk to be either provided in the financial statements or incorporated by cross-reference to some other statement, such as a management commentary or risk report, that is available to users of the financial statements on the same terms as the financial statements and at the same time. This approach is also permitted for the equivalent disclosures about insurance contracts. *[IFRS 4.IG62]*.

To be informative, the disclosure about credit risk, liquidity risk and market risk might include:

(a) information about the extent to which features such as policyholder participation features might mitigate or compound those risks;

(b) a summary of significant guarantees, and of the levels at which guarantees of market prices or interest rates are likely to alter cash flows; and

(c) the basis for determining investment returns credited to policyholders, such as whether the returns are fixed, based contractually on the return of specified assets or partly or wholly subject to the insurer's discretion. *[IFRS 4.IG64]*.

11.2.6.A Credit risk disclosures

Credit risk is defined in IFRS 7 as 'the risk that one party to a financial instrument will fail to discharge an obligation and cause the other party to incur a financial loss'.

For a reinsurance contract, credit risk includes the risk that the insurer incurs a financial loss because a reinsurer defaults on its obligations under a reinsurance contract. Furthermore, disputes with reinsurers could lead to impairments of the cedant's reinsurance assets. The risk of such disputes may have an effect similar to credit risk. Thus, similar disclosure might be relevant. Balances due from agents or brokers may also be subject to credit risk. *[IFRS 4.IG64A]*.

The specific disclosure requirements about credit risk in IFRS 7 are:

(a) an amount representing the maximum exposure to credit risk at the reporting date without taking account of any collateral held or other credit enhancements;

(b) in respect of the amount above, a description of the collateral held as security and other credit enhancements;

(c) information about the credit quality of financial assets that are neither past due nor impaired;

(d) the carrying amount of financial assets that would otherwise be past due or impaired whose terms have been renegotiated;

(e) for financial assets:
   (i) an analysis of the age of those that are past due at the reporting date but not impaired;
   (ii) an analysis of those that are individually determined to be impaired as at the reporting date, including the factors considered in determining that they are impaired; and
   (iii) for the amounts disclosed above a description of collateral held as security and other credit enhancements and, unless impracticable, an estimate of the fair value of this collateral or credit enhancement.

(f) when possession is taken of financial or non-financial assets during the reporting period either by taking possession of collateral held as security or calling on other credit enhancements and such assets meet the recognition criteria in other IFRSs, for such assets held at the reporting date disclosure is required of:
   (i) the nature and carrying amount of the assets obtained; and
   (ii) when the assets are not readily convertible into cash, the entity's policies for disposing of such assets or for using them in its operations.

The disclosures in (a) to (e) above are to be given by class of financial instrument. [IFRS 7.36-38].

IFRS 7 also contains a requirement to disclose a reconciliation of an entity's allowance account for credit losses. However, this requirement does not apply to insurance contracts as the relevant paragraph in IFRS 7 is not specified in IFRS 4 as one of those that should be applied to insurance contracts. Nevertheless, this requirement does apply to financial assets held by insurers that are within the scope of IAS 39 or IFRS 9, such as mortgages and other loans and receivables due from intermediaries which have a financing character or are due from those not acting in a fiduciary capacity.

Zurich provides the following disclosures about the credit risk for reinsurance assets and insurance receivables.

> **Extract 55.32: Zurich Insurance Group, Zurich (2016)**
>
> **Risk review** [extract]
>
> **Credit risk related to reinsurance assets** [extract]
>
> The Group's Corporate Reinsurance Security Committee manages the credit quality of our cessions and reinsurance assets. The Group typically cedes new business to authorized reinsurers with a minimum rating of 'A–'. As of December 31, 2016 and 2015 respectively, 66 percent and 73 per cent of the business ceded to reinsurers that fall below 'A–' or are not rated is collateralized. Of the business ceded to reinsurers that fall below 'A–' or are not rated, 32 percent was ceded to captive insurance companies, in 2016 and in 2015.
>
> Reinsurance assets included reinsurance recoverables (the reinsurers' share of reserves for insurance contracts) of USD 18.4 billion and USD 17.9 billion, and receivables arising from ceded reinsurance of USD 1.4 billion and USD 0.9 billion as of December 31, 2016 and 2015, respectively, gross of allowance for impairment. Reserves for potentially uncollectable reinsurance assets amounted to USD 94 million as of December 31, 2016 and USD 149 million as of December 31, 2015. The Group's policy on impairment charges takes into account both specific charges for known situations (e.g. financial distress or litigation) and a general, prudent provision for unanticipated impairments.
>
> Reinsurance assets in table 11 are shown before taking into account collateral such as cash or bank letters of credit and deposits received under ceded reinsurance contracts. Except for an immaterial amount, letters of credit are from banks rated 'A–' and better. Compared with December 31, 2015, collateral decreased by USD 0.6 billion to USD 8.4 billion. In 2015, reinsurance assets and collateral increased due to the sale of a run-off portfolio.
>
> Table 11 shows reinsurance premiums ceded and reinsurance assets split by rating.
>
> **Table 11 – Reinsurance premiums ceded and reinsurance assets by rating of reinsurer and captive**
>
> | as of December 31 | 2016 | | | | 2015 | | | |
> |---|---|---|---|---|---|---|---|---|
> | | Premiums ceded | | Reinsurance assets | | Premiums ceded | | Reinsurance assets | |
> | | USD millions | % of total | USD millions | % of total | USD millions | % of total | USD millions | % of total |
> | **Rating** | | | | | | | | |
> | AAA | 68 | 0.9% | 29 | 0.1% | 72 | 0.9% | 36 | 0.2% |
> | AA | 2,178 | 27.9% | 5,402 | 27.3% | 1,188 | 14.7% | 4,770 | 25.6% |
> | A | 2,883 | 36.9% | 8,625 | 43.6% | 2,284 | 28.3% | 8,271 | 44.3% |
> | BBB | 933 | 11.9% | 1,366 | 6.9% | 861 | 10.7% | 1,244 | 6.7% |
> | BB | 267 | 3.4% | 566 | 2.9% | 325 | 4.0% | 530 | 2.8% |
> | B | 310 | 4.0% | 379 | 1.9% | 258 | 3.2% | 194 | 1.0% |
> | Unrated | 1,205 | 15.0% | 3,383 | 17.3% | 3,090 | 38.3% | 3,617 | 19.4% |
> | **Total** | **7,843** | **100.0%** | **19,749** | **100.0%** | **8,078** | **100.0%** | **18,662** | **100.0%** |
>
> **Credit risk related to receivables**
>
> The Group's largest credit-risk exposure to receivables is related to third-party agents, brokers and other intermediaries. It arises where premiums are collected from customers to be paid to the Group, or to pay claims to customers on behalf of the Group. The Group has policies and standards to manage and monitor credit risk related to intermediaries. The Group requires intermediaries to maintain segregated cash accounts for policyholder money. The Group also requires that intermediaries satisfy minimum requirements in terms of capitalization, reputation and experience and provide short-dated business credit terms.
>
> Receivables that are past due but not impaired should be regarded as unsecured, but some of these receivable positions may be offset by collateral. The Group reports internally on Group past-due receivable balances and strives to keep the balance of past-due positions as low as possible, while taking into account customer satisfaction.

11.2.6.B Liquidity risk disclosures

Liquidity risk is defined in IFRS 7 as 'the risk that an entity will encounter difficulty in meeting obligations associated with financial liabilities that are settled by delivering cash or another financial asset'.

The specific disclosure requirements in IFRS 7 relating to liquidity risk are:

(a) a maturity analysis for non-derivative financial liabilities (including issued financial guarantee contracts) that shows the remaining contractual maturities;

(b) a maturity analysis for derivative financial liabilities. The maturity analysis should include the remaining contractual maturities for those derivative financial liabilities for which contractual maturities are essential for an understanding of the timing of cash flows; and

(c) a description of how the liquidity risk inherent in (a) and (b) is managed. *[IFRS 7.39]*.

IFRS 7 also requires disclosure of a maturity analysis of financial assets an entity holds for managing liquidity risk (e.g. financial assets that are readily saleable or expected to generate cash inflows to meet cash outflows on financial liabilities) if that information is necessary to enable users of its financial statements to evaluate the nature and extent of liquidity risk. *[IFRS 7.B11E]*. As most insurers hold financial assets in order to manage liquidity risk (i.e. to pay claims) they are likely to have to provide such an analysis and, indeed, some insurers have historically provided such an analysis.

For financial liabilities within the scope of IFRS 7 the maturity analysis should present undiscounted contractual amounts. *[IFRS 7.B11D]*. However, an insurer need not present the maturity analyses of insurance liabilities using undiscounted contractual cash flows if it discloses information about the estimated timing of the net cash outflows resulting from recognised insurance liabilities instead. This may take the form of an analysis, by estimated timing, of the amounts recognised in the statement of financial position. *[IFRS 4.39(d)(i)]*. The guidance in respect of the maturity analysis for financial assets is silent as to whether such analysis should be on a contractual undiscounted basis or on the basis of the amounts recognised in the statement of financial position.

The reason for this concession is to avoid insurers having to disclose detailed cash flow estimates for insurance liabilities that are not required for measurement purposes. Because various accounting practices for insurance contracts are permitted, an insurer may not need to make detailed estimates of cash flows to determine the amounts recognised in the statement of financial position. *[IFRS 4.IG65B]*.

However, this concession is not available for investment contracts whether or not they contain a DPF. These contracts are within the scope of IFRS 7 not IFRS 4. Consequently, a maturity analysis of contractual undiscounted amounts is required for these liabilities.

An insurer might need to disclose a summary narrative description of how the flows in the maturity analysis (or analysis by estimated timing) could change if policyholders exercised lapse or surrender options in different ways. If lapse behaviour is likely to be sensitive to interest rates, that fact might be disclosed as well as whether the disclosures about market risk (see 11.2.6.C below) reflect that interdependence. *[IFRS 4.IG65C]*.

Prudential's liability maturity analysis for its UK insurance operations is shown below. The disclosure is on a discounted basis and includes investment contracts although an undiscounted maturity profile of those investment contracts is disclosed elsewhere in the financial statements.

Extract 55.33: Prudential plc (2016)

Notes to Primary statements [extract]
C4. Policyholder liabilities and unallocated surplus [extract]
C4.1(d). UK insurance operations [extract]
(ii) Duration of liabilities [extract]

With the exception of most unitised with-profit bonds and other whole of life contracts the majority of the contracts of the UK insurance operations have a contract term. In effect, the maturity term of the other contracts reflects the earlier of death, maturity, or the policy lapsing. In addition, as described in note A3.1, with-profits contract liabilities include projected future bonuses based on current investment values. The actual amounts payable will vary with future investment performance of SAIF and the WPSF.

The following tables show the carrying value of the policyholder liabilities and the maturity profile of the cash flows, on a discounted basis for 2016 and 2015:

2016 £m

	With-profits business			Annuity business (insurance contracts)			Other		
	Insurance contracts	Investment contracts	Total	Non-profit annuities within WPSF	Shareholder-backed annuity	Total	Insurance contracts	Investment contracts	Total
Policyholder liabilities	37,848	52,495	90,343	11,153	33,881	45,034	6,111	16,166	22,277

2016%

Expected maturity:									
0 to 5 years	37	37	37	29	25	26	40	34	37
5 to 10 years	23	29	26	24	22	23	23	23	23
10 to 15 years	15	16	16	18	18	18	12	17	15
15 to 20 years	9	10	10	12	14	13	7	12	10
20 to 25 years	7	4	5	7	9	9	4	7	6
Over 25 years	9	4	6	10	12	11	14	7	9

[...]

- The cash flow projections of expected benefit payments used in the maturity profile table above are from value of in-force business and exclude the value of future new business, including vesting of internal pension contracts.
- Benefit payments do not reflect the pattern of bonuses and shareholder transfers in respect of the with-profits business.
- Shareholder-backed annuity business includes the ex-PRIL and the legacy PAC shareholder annuity business.
- Investment contracts under 'Other' comprise certain unit-linked and similar contracts accounted for under IAS 39 and IAS 18.
- For business with no maturity term included within the contracts; for example with-profits investment bonds such as Prudence Bonds, an assumption is made as to likely duration based on prior experience.

11.2.6.C   Market risk disclosures

Market risk is defined in IFRS 7 as 'the risk that the fair value or future cash flows of a financial instrument will fluctuate because of changes in market prices'. Market risk comprises three types of risk: currency risk, interest rate risk and other price risk.

The specific disclosure requirements in respect of market risk are:

(a) a sensitivity analysis for each type of market risk to which there is exposure at the reporting date, showing how profit or loss and equity would have been affected by changes in the relevant risk variable that were reasonably possible at that date;

(b) the methods and assumptions used in preparing that sensitivity analysis; and

(c) changes from the previous reporting period in the methods and assumptions used, and the reasons for such changes. *[IFRS 7.40]*.

These disclosures are required for insurance contracts. However, if an insurer uses an alternative method to manage sensitivity to market conditions, such as an embedded value analysis, it may use that sensitivity analysis to meet the requirements of IFRS 4. *[IFRS 4.39(d)(ii)]*. In addition, it should also disclose:

(a) an explanation of the method used in preparing such a sensitivity analysis, and of the main parameters and assumptions underlying the data provided; and

(b) an explanation of the objective of the method used and of limitations that may result in the information not fully reflecting the fair value of the assets and liabilities involved. *[IFRS 7.41]*.

Because two approaches are permitted, an insurer might use different approaches for different classes of business. *[IFRS 4.IG65G]*.

Where the sensitivity analysis disclosed is not representative of the risk inherent in the instrument (for example because the year-end exposure does not reflect the exposure during the year), that fact should be disclosed together with the reasons the sensitivity analyses are unrepresentative. *[IFRS 7.42]*.

If no reasonably possible change in a relevant risk variable would affect either profit or loss or equity, that fact should be disclosed. A reasonably possible change in the relevant risk variable might not affect profit or loss in the following examples:

- if a non-life insurance liability is not discounted, changes in market interest rates would not affect profit or loss; and

- some entities may use valuation factors that blend together the effect of various market and non-market assumptions that do not change unless there is an assessment that the recognised insurance liability is not adequate. In some cases a reasonably possible change in the relevant risk variable would not affect the adequacy of the recognised insurance liability. *[IFRS 4.IG65D]*.

In some accounting models, a regulator may specify discount rates or other assumptions about market risk variables that are used in measuring insurance liabilities and the regulator may not amend those assumptions to reflect current market conditions at all times. In such cases, compliance with the requirements might be achieved by disclosing:

(a) the effect on profit or loss or equity of a reasonably possible change in the assumption set by the regulator; and

(b) the fact that the assumption set by the regulator would not necessarily change at the same time, by the same amount, or in the same direction, as changes in market prices, or market rates, would imply. *[IFRS 4.IG65E]*.

An insurer might be able to take action to reduce the effect of changes in market conditions. For example, it may have discretion to change surrender values or maturity benefits, or to vary the amount or timing of policyholder benefits arising from discretionary participation features. There is no requirement for entities to consider the potential effect of future management actions that may offset the effect of the disclosed changes in any relevant risk variable. However, disclosure is required of the methods and assumptions used to prepare any sensitivity analysis. To comply with this requirement, disclosure of the extent of available management actions and their effect on the sensitivity analysis might be required. *[IFRS 4.IG65F]*.

Because some insurers manage sensitivity to market conditions using alternative methods as discussed above, different sensitivity approaches may be used for different classes of insurance contracts. *[IFRS 4.IG65G]*.

Many life insurance contract liabilities are backed by matching assets. In these circumstances giving isolated disclosures about the variability of, say, interest rates on the valuation of the liabilities without linking this to the impact on the assets could be misleading to users of the financial statements. In these circumstances it may be useful to provide information as to the linkage of market risk sensitivities.

11.2.7 Exposures to market risk from embedded derivatives

As noted at 11.2 above, disclosure is required if there are exposures to market risk arising from embedded derivatives contained in a host insurance contract if the insurer is not required to, and does not, measure the embedded derivatives at fair value. *[IFRS 4.39(e)]*.

Fair value measurement is not required for derivatives embedded in an insurance contract if the embedded derivative is itself an insurance contract (see 4 above). Examples of these include guaranteed annuity options and guaranteed minimum death benefits as illustrated below. *[IFRS 4.IG66]*.

Example 55.43: Contract containing a guaranteed annuity option

An insurer issues a contract under which the policyholder pays a fixed monthly premium for thirty years. At maturity, the policyholder can elect to take either (a) a lump sum equal to the accumulated investment value or (b) a lifetime annuity at a rate guaranteed at inception (i.e. when the contract started). This is an example of a contract containing a guaranteed annuity option.

For policyholders electing to receive the annuity, the insurer could suffer a significant loss if interest rates decline substantially or if the policyholder lives much longer than the average. The insurer is exposed to both market risk and significant insurance risk (mortality risk) and the transfer of insurance risk occurs at inception of the contract because the insurer fixed the price for mortality risk at that date. Therefore, the contract is an insurance contract from inception. Moreover, the embedded guaranteed annuity option itself meets the definition of an insurance contract, and so separation is not required. *[IFRS 4.IG67]*.

Example 55.44: Contract containing minimum guaranteed death benefits

An insurer issues a contract under which the policyholder pays a monthly premium for 30 years. Most of the premiums are invested in a mutual fund. The rest is used to buy life cover and to cover expenses. On maturity or surrender, the insurer pays the value of the mutual fund units at that date. On death before final maturity, the insurer pays the greater of (a) the current unit value and (b) a fixed amount. This is an example of a contract containing minimum guaranteed death benefits. It is an insurance contract because the insurer is exposed to significant insurance risk as the fixed amount payable on death before maturity could be greater than the unit value.

It could be viewed as a hybrid contract comprising (a) a mutual fund investment and (b) an embedded life insurance contract that pays a death benefit equal to the fixed amount less the current unit value (but zero if the current unit value is more than the fixed amount). *[IFRS 4.IG68]*.

Both of the examples of embedded derivatives above meet the definition of an insurance contract where the insurance risk is deemed significant. However, in each case, market risk or interest rate risk may be much more significant than the mortality risk. So, if interest rates or equity markets fall substantially, these guarantees would have significant value. Given the long-term nature of the guarantees and the size of the exposures, an insurer might face extremely large losses in certain scenarios. Therefore, particular emphasis on disclosures about such exposures might be required. *[IFRS 4.IG69]*.

To be informative, disclosures about such exposures may include:
- the sensitivity analysis discussed at 11.2.6.C above;
- information about the levels where these exposures start to have a material effect on the insurer's cash flows; and
- the fair value of the embedded derivative, although this is not a required disclosure. *[IFRS 4.IG70]*.

An extract of Aviva's disclosures in respect of financial guarantees and options is shown below.

> Extract 55.34: Aviva plc (2016)
> Notes to the consolidated financial statements [extract]
> 42 –   Financial guarantees and options [extract]
> (c) Overseas life business [extract]
> (ii) Spain and Italy
> *Guaranteed investment returns and guaranteed surrender values*
> The Group has also written contracts containing guaranteed investment returns and guaranteed surrender values in both Spain and Italy. Traditional profit-sharing products receive an appropriate share of the investment return, assessed on a book value basis, subject to a guaranteed minimum annual return of up to 6% in Spain and up to 4% in Italy on existing business, while on new business the maximum guaranteed rate is lower. Liabilities are generally taken as the face value of the contract plus, if required, an explicit provision for guarantees calculated in accordance with local regulations. At 31 December 2016, total liabilities for the Spanish business were £1 billion *(2015: £1 billion)* with a further reserve of £15 million *(2015: £14 million)* for guarantees. Total liabilities for the Italian business were £18 billion *(2015: £14 billion)*, with a further provision of £47 million *(2015: £41 million)* for guarantees. Liabilities are most sensitive to changes in the level of interest rates. It is estimated that provisions for guarantees would need to increase by £14 million *(2015: £12 million)* in Spain and decrease by £5 million *(2015: £1 million decrease)* in Italy if interest rates fell by 1% from end 2016 values. Under this sensitivity test, the guarantee provision in Spain is calculated conservatively, assuming a long-term market interest rate of 0.39% and no lapses or premium discontinuances. In the local valuation there is no allowance for stochastic modelling of guarantees and options.

11.2.8   Other disclosure matters

11.2.8.A   IAS 1 capital disclosures

Most insurance entities are exposed to externally imposed capital requirements and therefore the IAS 1 disclosures in respect of these requirements are likely to be applicable.

Where an entity is subject to externally imposed capital requirements, disclosures are required of the nature of these requirements and how these requirements are incorporated into the management of capital. Disclosure of whether these requirements have been complied with in the reporting period is also required and, where they have not been complied with, the consequences of such non-compliance. *[IAS 1.135]*.

Many insurance entities operate in several jurisdictions. When an aggregate disclosure of capital requirements, and how capital is managed, would not provide useful information or distorts a financial statement user's understanding of an entity's capital resources, separate information should be disclosed for each capital requirement to which an entity is subject. *[IAS 1.136]*.

Although there is no explicit requirement to disclose the amounts of the regulatory capital requirements, some insurers do so to assist users of the financial statements. Ping An is an example of an entity that discloses its externally imposed regulatory capital requirements.

Extract 55.35: Ping An Insurance (Group) Company of China, Ltd (2016)

Notes to consolidated financial statements [extract]
for the year ended 31 December 2016
45. RISK AND CAPITAL MANAGEMENT [extract]
(7) CAPITAL MANAGEMENT [extract]

The Group's capital requirements are primarily dependent on the scale and the type of business that it undertakes, as well as the industry and geographic location in which it operates. The primary objectives of the Group's capital management are to ensure that the Group complies with externally imposed capital requirements and to maintain healthy capital ratios in order to support its business and to maximize shareholders' value.

The Group manages its capital requirements by assessing shortfalls, if any, between the reported and the required capital levels on a regular basis. Adjustments to current capital levels are made in light of changes in economic conditions and risk characteristics of the Group's activities. In order to maintain or adjust the capital structure, the Group may adjust the amount of dividends paid, return capital to ordinary shareholders or issue capital securities.

The Group has formally implemented China Risk Oriented Solvency System since 1 January 2016 by reference to the 'Notice on the Formal Implementation of China Risk Oriented Solvency System by CIRC'. The Group adjusted the objective, policy and process of capital management. As at 31 December 2016, the Group was compliant with the relevant regulatory capital requirements.

The table below summarizes the minimum regulatory capital for the Group and its major insurance subsidiaries and the regulatory capital held against each of them.

	31 December 2016		
	The Group	Ping An Life	Ping An Property & Casualty
Core capital	889,883	501,710	63,439
Regulatory capital held	929,883	533,710	71,439
Minimum regulatory capital	442,729	236,304	26,725
Core solvency margin ratio	201.0%	212.3%	237.4%
Comprehensive solvency margin ratio	210.0%	225.9%	267.3%

As discussed at 7.2.1 above, equalisation and catastrophe provisions are not liabilities but are a component of equity. Therefore, they are subject to the disclosure requirements in IAS 1 for equity. IAS 1 requires disclosure of a description of the nature and purpose of each reserve within equity. *[IFRS 4.IG58]*.

11.2.8.B Financial guarantee contracts

A financial guarantee contract reimburses a loss incurred by the holder because a specified debtor fails to make payment when due. The holder of such a contract is exposed to credit risk and is required by IFRS 7 to make disclosures about that credit risk. However, from the perspective of the issuer, the risk assumed by the issuer is insurance risk rather than credit risk. *[IFRS 4.IG64B]*.

As discussed at 2.2.3.D above, the issuer of a financial guarantee contract should provide disclosures complying with IFRS 7 if it applies IAS 39 or IFRS 9 in recognising and measuring the contract. However, if the issuer elects, when permitted, to apply IFRS 4 in recognising and measuring the contract, it provides disclosures complying with IFRS 4. The main implications are as follows:

(a) IFRS 4 requires disclosure about actual claims compared with previous estimates (claims development), but does not require disclosure of the fair value of the contract; and

(b) IFRS 7 requires disclosure of the fair value of the contract, but does not require disclosure of claims development. *[IFRS 4.IG65A]*.

11.2.8.C Fair value disclosures

Insurance contracts are not excluded from the scope of IFRS 13 and therefore any insurance contracts measured at fair value are also subject to the disclosures required by IFRS 13. However, insurance contracts are excluded from the scope of IFRS 7.

Disclosure of the fair value of investment contracts with a DPF is not required by IFRS 7 if the fair value of that feature cannot be measured reliably. *[IFRS 7.29(c)]*. However, IFRS 7 does require additional information about fair value in these circumstances including disclosure that fair value information has not been provided because fair value cannot be reliably measured, an explanation of why fair value cannot be reliably measured, information about the market for the instruments, information about whether and how the entity intends to dispose of the financial instruments and any gain or loss recognised on derecognition. *[IFRS 7.30]*.

For insurance contracts and investment contract liabilities with and without a DPF which are measured at fair value, disclosures required by IFRS 13 include the level in the fair value hierarchy in which the liabilities are categorised. *[IFRS 13.93]*. Very few insurance or investment contract liabilities are likely to have quoted prices (unadjusted) in active markets and are therefore likely to be Level 2 or Level 3 measurements under IFRS 13.

For investment contract liabilities without a DPF measured at amortised cost, disclosure of the fair value of those contracts is required as well as the assumptions applied in determining those fair values and the level of the fair value hierarchy in which those fair value measurements are categorised. *[IFRS 13.97]*.

When unit-linked investment liabilities are matched by associated financial assets some have argued that there is no fair value adjustment for credit risk as the liability is simply the value of the asset. However, there will be at least some risk, however small, of non-payment with regard to the liability. Therefore, it would be appropriate to provide some form of qualitative disclosure that credit risk was taken into account in assessing the fair value of the liability or why it was thought to be immaterial and/or relevant only in extreme situations.

11.2.8.D Key performance indicators

IFRS 4 does not require disclosure of key performance indicators. However, such disclosures might be a useful way for an insurer to explain its financial performance during the period and to give an insight into the risks arising from insurance contracts. *[IFRS 4.IG71]*.

12. FUTURE DEVELOPMENTS

As discussed at 1 and 10 above, in June 2020, the IASB amended IFRS 17 with targeted changes including a deferral of the effective date to accounting periods beginning on or after 1 January 2023 and consequential amendments to IFRS 4 which extends the use of the temporary exemption from IFRS 9 and the use of the overlay approach (see 10 above) by two years to annual periods beginning before 1 January 2023.

References

1 *IASB Update*, May 2002.
2 www.cfoforum.eu (accessed on 6 August 2020).
3 *IFRIC Update*, January 2008, p.3.
4 *IFRIC Update*, November 2005, p.6.
5 *IFRIC Update*, January 2010, p.2.
6 *European Embedded Value Principles*, European Insurance CFO Forum, May 2004, p.3.

Chapter 56 Insurance contracts (IFRS 17)

1 INTRODUCTION 4681
2 THE OBJECTIVE, DEFINITIONS AND SCOPE OF IFRS 17 4683
   2.1 The objective of IFRS 17 4683
   2.2 Definitions 4684
   2.3 Scope 4686
       2.3.1 Transactions not within the scope of IFRS 17 4688
           2.3.1.A Product warranties 4689
           2.3.1.B Assets and liabilities arising from employment benefit plans 4689
           2.3.1.C Contingent contractual rights and obligations related to non-financial items 4689
           2.3.1.D Residual value guarantees 4689
           2.3.1.E Financial guarantee contracts 4690
           2.3.1.F Contingent consideration payable or receivable in a business combination 4691
           2.3.1.G Direct insurance contracts in which the entity is the policyholder 4691
           2.3.1.H Credit card contracts (or similar contracts) that provide insurance coverage 4691
       2.3.2 Fixed fee service contracts 4693
       2.3.3 Loan contracts that transfer significant insurance risk only on settlement of the policyholder's obligation created by the contract 4694
       2.3.4 Other accounting standards which affect insurers 4694
3 THE DEFINITION OF AN INSURANCE CONTRACT 4695
   3.1 The definition 4695
   3.2 Uncertain future events 4697

	3.3	Payments in kind	4697
	3.4	The distinction between insurance risk and financial risk	4698
		3.4.1 Insurable interest	4699
		3.4.2 Lapse, persistency and expense risk	4700
		3.4.3 Insurance of non-insurance risks	4700
	3.5	Significant insurance risk	4701
		3.5.1 Quantity of insurance risk	4701
		3.5.2 The level at which significant insurance risk is assessed	4703
		3.5.2.A Self insurance	4703
		3.5.2.B Insurance mutuals	4703
		3.5.2.C Intragroup insurance contracts	4704
		3.5.3 Significant additional amounts	4704
	3.6	Changes in the level of insurance risk	4705
	3.7	Examples of insurance and non-insurance contracts	4706
		3.7.1 Examples of insurance contracts	4706
		3.7.2 Examples of transactions that are not insurance contracts	4708
4	SEPARATING COMPONENTS FROM AN INSURANCE CONTRACT		4710
	4.1	Separating embedded derivatives from an insurance contract	4712
	4.2	Separating investment components from an insurance contract	4715
		4.2.1 The definition of an investment component	4715
		4.2.2 Separable investment components	4716
		4.2.3 Measurement of the non-distinct investment component	4719
	4.3	Separating a promise to provide distinct goods or services other than insurance contract services	4720
5	LEVEL OF AGGREGATION		4722
	5.1	Identifying portfolios	4723
		5.1.1 Separation of insurance components within an insurance contract	4723
		5.1.2 Combining insurance contracts	4724
	5.2	Groups of insurance contracts	4725
		5.2.1 Identifying groups based on profitability	4726
		5.2.2 'Annual cohorts'	4728
		5.2.2.A Contracts with intergenerational sharing of risks	4730
	5.3	Identifying groups for contracts applying the premium allocation approach	4732
6	INITIAL RECOGNITION		4732
	6.1	Initial recognition of insurance and reinsurance contracts issued	4732
	6.2	Initial recognition of reinsurance contracts held	4733

	6.3	Initial recognition of insurance acquisition cash flows............................. 4735		
	6.4	Initial recognition of investment contracts with discretionary participation features 4737		
7	MEASUREMENT – OVERVIEW 4737			
	7.1	Overview of the general model... 4737		
	7.2	Modifications to the general model.. 4738		
	7.3	Insurance contracts in a foreign currency 4739		
8	MEASUREMENT – GENERAL MODEL 4740			
	8.1	The contract boundary 4740		
		8.1.1	Options to add insurance coverage... 4745	
		8.1.2	Constraints or limitations relevant in assessing repricing 4746	
		8.1.3	Contracts between an entity and customers of an association or bank 4747	
		8.1.4	Contract boundary matters related to insurance acquisition cash flows... 4748	
		8.1.5	Contract boundary matters related to reinsurance contracts issued and held.. 4749	
	8.2	Estimates of expected future cash flows.. 4749		
		8.2.1	Market and non-market variables.. 4752	
			8.2.1.A	Market variables... 4752
			8.2.1.B	Non-market variables... 4753
		8.2.2	Using current estimates 4754	
		8.2.3	Cash flows within the contract boundary 4756	
			8.2.3.A	Premium cash flows... 4758
			8.2.3.B	Payments to (or on behalf of) a policyholder 4758
			8.2.3.C	Payments to (or on behalf of) a policyholder that vary depending on returns on underlying items 4758
			8.2.3.D	Payments to (or on behalf of) a policyholder resulting from derivatives.. 4758
			8.2.3.E	Insurance acquisition cash flows....................... 4759
			8.2.3.F	Claims handling costs 4759
			8.2.3.G	Costs incurred in providing contractual benefits in kind 4759
			8.2.3.H	Policy administration and maintenance costs 4759
			8.2.3.I	Transaction-based taxes..................................... 4759
			8.2.3.J	Payments by the insurer in a fiduciary capacity 4760
			8.2.3.K	Potential inflows from recoveries 4760
			8.2.3.L	An allocation of fixed and variable overheads........ 4760

| | | 8.2.3.M | Costs incurred in providing investment activity, investment-return and investment-related services .... 4761 |
| | | 8.2.3.N | Any other costs .... 4761 |

- 8.2.4 Cash flows excluded from the contract boundary 4761
- 8.3 Discount rates 4762
- 8.4 The risk adjustment for non-financial risk 4770
  - 8.4.1 Techniques used to estimate the risk adjustment for non-financial risk 4772
  - 8.4.2 The level at which the risk adjustment should be determined 4773
  - 8.4.3 Consideration of reinsurance held in the risk adjustment 4774
  - 8.4.4 Presentation of the risk adjustment for non-financial risk in the statement of comprehensive income 4775
- 8.5 The contractual service margin 4775
- 8.6 Subsequent measurement 4777
  - 8.6.1 The liability for remaining coverage 4778
  - 8.6.2 The liability for incurred claims 4779
  - 8.6.3 Subsequent measurement of the contractual service margin (for insurance contracts without direct participation features) 4780
- 8.7 Allocation of the contractual service margin to profit or loss 4785
  - 8.7.1 Determining the quantity of benefits for identifying coverage units 4787
  - 8.7.2 Allocating the contractual service margin on the basis of coverage units determined by considering both insurance coverage and any investment-return service 4791
- 8.8 Measurement of onerous contracts 4793
- 8.9 Reinsurance contracts issued 4796
  - 8.9.1 The boundary of a reinsurance contract issued 4796
  - 8.9.2 Issued adverse loss development covers 4797
  - 8.9.3 Accounting for ceding commissions and reinstatement premiums 4798
  - 8.9.4 Determining the quantity of benefits for identifying coverage units 4800
- 8.10 Impairment of assets recognised for insurance acquisition cash flows 4801
- 8.11 Insurance contracts issued by mutual entities 4804
- 8.12 Other matters 4805
  - 8.12.1 Impairment of insurance receivables 4805
  - 8.12.2 Policyholder loans 4806

9	MEASUREMENT – PREMIUM ALLOCATION APPROACH		4806
	9.1	Criteria for use of the premium allocation approach	4808
		9.1.1 Main sources of difference between the premium allocation approach and the general approach	4811
		9.1.1.A Changing expectations of profitability for the period of remaining coverage	4811
		9.1.1.B Changing interest rates	4811
		9.1.1.C Uneven revenue recognition patterns	4812
		9.1.2 Applying materiality for the premium allocation approach eligibility assessment	4812
	9.2	Initial measurement	4812
	9.3	Subsequent measurement – liability for remaining coverage	4814
	9.4	Subsequent measurement – liability for incurred claims	4816
10	MEASUREMENT – REINSURANCE CONTRACTS HELD		4817
	10.1	Level of aggregation	4819
	10.2	The boundary of a reinsurance contract held	4819
		10.2.1 Reinsurance contracts held with repricing clauses	4821
	10.3	Measurement – initial recognition	4822
		10.3.1 Initial measurement – fulfilment cash flows	4822
		10.3.2 Measurement at initial recognition – contractual service margin	4822
		10.3.3 Initial measurement of reinsurance held of underlying onerous insurance contracts that are onerous at initial recognition	4824
		10.3.4 Initial measurement of the effect of the risk of non-performance	4828
	10.4	Subsequent measurement	4829
		10.4.1 Subsequent measurement of non-performance risk	4832
		10.4.2 Subsequent measurement of a loss-recovery component	4832
	10.5	Allocation of the contractual service margin to profit or loss	4835
	10.6	Premium allocation approach for reinsurance contracts held	4836
	10.7	Reinsurance contracts held and the variable fee approach	4837
11	MEASUREMENT – CONTRACTS WITH PARTICIPATION FEATURES		4837
	11.1	Contracts with cash flows that affect or are affected by cash flows to policyholders of other contracts (mutualisation)	4840
	11.2	Insurance contracts with direct participation features	4842
		11.2.1 Definition of an insurance contract with direct participation features	4843
		11.2.1.A A share of a clearly defined pool of underlying items	4844

| | | 11.2.1.B | A substantial share of the fair value returns on the underlying items .... 4845 |
| | | 11.2.1.C | A substantial proportion of any change in the amounts to be paid to the policyholder to vary with the change in fair value of the underlying items .... 4848 |

	11.2.2	Measurement of the risk adjustment for non-financial risk using the variable fee approach 4848
	11.2.3	Measurement of the contractual service margin using the variable fee approach 4849
	11.2.4	Allocation of the contractual service margin to profit or loss 4851
	11.2.5	Risk mitigation 4852
	11.2.6	Disaggregation of insurance finance income or expenses between profit or loss and other comprehensive income 4854

| 11.3 | Investment contracts with discretionary participation features .... 4855 |
| | 11.3.1 | Contracts with switching features .... 4857 |

12 MODIFICATION AND DERECOGNITION 4857
- 12.1 Modification of an insurance contract 4858
- 12.2 Derecognition of an insurance contract 4859
- 12.3 Accounting for derecognition 4860
  - 12.3.1 Derecognition resulting from extinguishment 4860
  - 12.3.2 Derecognition resulting from transfer 4860
  - 12.3.3 Derecognition resulting from modification 4861
  - 12.3.4 Reclassification adjustments arising from derecognition 4862
  - 12.3.5 Contracts applying the premium allocation approach that are derecognised 4862
- 12.4 Derecognition of assets for insurance acquisition cash flows paid before the related group of insurance contracts is recognised as an asset 4862

13 ACQUISITIONS OF INSURANCE CONTRACTS 4863
- 13.1 Assets for insurance acquisition cash flows acquired in a business combination within the scope of IFRS 3 or a transfer 4867
- 13.2 Subsequent treatment of contracts acquired in their settlement period 4868
- 13.3 Business combinations under common control 4870
- 13.4 Practical issues 4870
  - 13.4.1 The difference between a business combination and a transfer 4870
  - 13.4.2 Deferred taxation 4871
  - 13.4.3 Customer lists and relationships not connected to contractual insurance contracts 4871

14	PRESENTATION IN THE STATEMENT OF FINANCIAL POSITION	4872
15	PRESENTATION IN THE STATEMENT OF FINANCIAL PERFORMANCE	4874
	15.1 Insurance revenue	4876
	15.1.1 Insurance revenue related to the provision of services in a period under the general model	4877
	15.1.2 Insurance revenue under the premium allocation approach	4879
	15.1.3 Income or expenses from reinsurance contracts held	4880
	15.2 Insurance service expenses	4880
	15.3 Insurance finance income or expenses	4881
	15.3.1 Presentation of insurance finance income or expenses in the statement of comprehensive income	4883
	15.3.2 Allocating insurance finance income or expenses for contracts except those with direct participation features for which the entity holds the underlying items	4886
	15.3.2.A Allocating insurance finance income or expenses for contracts for which changes that relate to financial risk do not have a substantial effect on the amounts paid to the policyholder	4887
	15.3.2.B Allocating insurance finance income or expenses for contracts for which changes in assumptions that relate to financial risk have a substantial effect on amounts paid to policyholders	4888
	15.3.3 Allocating insurance finance income or expenses for incurred claims when applying the premium allocation approach	4892
	15.3.4 Allocating finance income or expenses for insurance contracts with direct participation features for which the entity holds the underlying items	4892
	15.4 Reporting the contractual service margin in interim financial statements	4896
16	DISCLOSURE	4898
	16.1 Explanation of recognised amounts	4900
	16.1.1 Reconciliations required for contracts applying the general model	4900
	16.1.2 Disclosures and reconciliations required for contracts applying the premium allocation approach	4906
	16.1.2.A Accounting policies adopted for contracts applying the premium allocation approach	4906
	16.1.2.B Reconciliations required for contracts applying the premium allocation approach	4906
	16.1.3 Insurance finance income or expenses	4907

	16.2	Transition amounts		4908
	16.3	Significant judgements made in applying IFRS 17		4909
	16.4	Disclosure of accounting policies		4910
	16.5	Nature and extent of risks arising from contracts within the scope of IFRS 17		4912
		16.5.1	Concentrations of risk	4913
		16.5.2	Insurance and market risks – sensitivity analysis	4914
		16.5.3	Insurance risk – claims development	4915
		16.5.4	Credit risk – other information	4917
		16.5.5	Liquidity risk – other information	4917
		16.5.6	Regulatory disclosures	4918
		16.5.7	Disclosures required by IFRS 7 and IFRS 13	4918
		16.5.8	Key performance indicators	4919
17	EFFECTIVE DATE AND TRANSITION			4919
	17.1	Effective date		4919
	17.2	Transition – general requirements		4919
		17.2.1	Transitional relief and prohibition – all entities	4921
			17.2.1.A Disclosure relief	4921
			17.2.1.B Prohibition from applying risk mitigation prior to the transition date	4922
			17.2.1.C Business combinations within the scope of IFRS 3	4922
		17.2.2	Disclosures about the effect of transition	4922
	17.3	Retrospective application of transition		4923
	17.4	The modified retrospective approach		4925
		17.4.1	Assessments at inception or initial recognition	4927
		17.4.2	Determining the contractual service margin or loss component for groups of insurance contracts without direct participation features	4927
		17.4.3	The contractual service margin or loss component for groups of insurance contracts with direct participation features	4931
		17.4.4	Insurance finance income or expenses	4933
			17.4.4.A Groups of insurance contracts that include contracts issued more than one year apart	4933
			17.4.4.B Groups of insurance contracts that do not include contracts issued more than one year apart	4934
	17.5	The fair value approach		4935
		17.5.1	Disaggregated insurance finance income or expenses using the fair value approach	4937

17.5.2 Asset for insurance acquisition cash flows using the fair value approach 4937

17.6 Redesignation of financial assets and financial liabilities– when IFRS 9 has been applied previously 4938

    17.6.1 Redesignation of financial assets 4938

    17.6.2 Redesignation of financial liabilities 4940

17.7 Entities that have not previously applied IFRS 9 4941

18 FUTURE DEVELOPMENTS 4941

List of examples

Example 56.1:	Residual value insurance	4698
Example 56.2:	Contract with life contingent annuity linked to price index	4699
Example 56.3:	Reinsurance contract with 'original loss warranty' clause	4700
Example 56.4:	Insurance of non-insurance risks	4700
Example 56.5:	Deferred annuity with policyholder election	4706
Example 56.6:	Guarantee fund established by contract	4707
Example 56.7:	No market value adjustment for maturity benefits	4707
Example 56.8:	No market value adjustment for death benefits	4708
Example 56.9:	Investment contract linked to asset pool	4709
Example 56.10:	Guarantee fund established by law	4709
Example 56.11:	Right to recover future premiums	4709
Example 56.12:	Market value adjustment without death or maturity benefits	4710
Example 56.13:	Death or annuitisation benefit linked to equity prices or index	4714
Example 56.14:	Policyholder option to surrender contract for value based on a market index	4714
Example 56.15:	Investment component in a life cover contract	4715
Example 56.16:	Investment component in deferred annuity contract	4716
Example 56.17:	Pure protection contract	4716
Example 56.18:	Investment component in a life cover contract	4717
Example 56.19:	Investment component in deferred annuity contract	4717
Example 56.20:	Separating components from a life insurance contract with an account balance	4718
Example 56.21:	Separating components from a stop-loss contract with claims processing services	4721
Example 56.22:	Identifying groups when profitability constrained by law	4727
Example 56.23:	Determining the date of recognition of a group of insurance contracts (1)	4733

Example 56.24:	Determining the date of recognition of a group of insurance contracts (2)	4733
Example 56.25:	Determining the date of recognition of a group of insurance contracts (3)	4733
Example 56.26:	Recognition of reinsurance contract held providing proportionate coverage	4734
Example 56.27:	Recognition of reinsurance contract held which does not provide proportionate coverage	4734
Example 56.28:	Recognition of reinsurance contract held when the underlying insurance contracts are onerous	4735
Example 56.29:	Contract boundary of a stepped premium life insurance contract	4743
Example 56.30:	Contract boundary of a level premium life insurance contract	4743
Example 56.31:	Credit life loan insurance	4788
Example 56.32:	Credit life product with variable amount of cover	4788
Example 56.33:	Mortgage loss cover	4789
Example 56.34:	Product warranty	4789
Example 56.35:	Extended product warranty	4789
Example 56.36:	Health cover	4789
Example 56.37:	Transaction liability	4789
Example 56.38:	Combination of different types of cover	4790
Example 56.39:	Life contingent annuity	4790
Example 56.40:	Forward purchase of fixed rate annuity	4791
Example 56.41:	Insurance services and investment-return services with different durations	4792
Example 56.42:	Deferred annuity contract without an investment component which provides an investment-return service	4793
Example 56.43:	Application of the loss component for a group of onerous contracts	4796
Example 56.44:	Proportional reinsurance issued	4800
Example 56.45:	Reinsurance adverse development of claims with claim limit	4801
Example 56.46:	Reinsurance adverse development of claims without claim limit	4801
Example 56.47:	Applying the two impairment tests for an insurance acquisition cash flow asset	4803
Example 56.48:	Measurement at initial recognition of a group of insurance contracts using the premium allocation approach	4814
Example 56.49:	Subsequent measurement of a group of insurance contracts using the premium allocation approach	4816
Example 56.50:	Subsequent measurement of the liability for incurred claims using the premium allocation approach	4817
Example 56.51:	Measurement on initial recognition of groups of reinsurance contracts held	4824

Example 56.52:	Initial measurement of a group of reinsurance contracts held that provides coverage for groups of underlying insurance contracts, including an onerous group	4826
Example 56.53:	Measurement subsequent to initial recognition of groups of reinsurance contracts held	4830
Example 56.54:	Subsequent measurement of a loss recovery component	4833
Example 56.55:	Treatment of changes in reinsurance recoveries arising from past events	4836
Example 56.56:	Unitised with-profits policy	4839
Example 56.57:	Participation policy with minimum interest rates	4839
Example 56.58:	Calculation of the expected fair value returns without and with mortality charge	4847
Example 56.59:	Insurance services and investment component with different durations	4852
Example 56.60:	Contract derecognition resulting from modification	4861
Example 56.61:	Measurement on initial recognition of insurance contracts acquired in a transfer (that is not a business combination) from another entity	4866
Example 56.62:	Measurement on initial recognition of insurance contracts acquired in a business combination [IFRS 17.IE146-151]	4867
Example 56.63:	Purchase of portfolio of one-year motor insurance contracts	4871
Example 56.64:	Allocating a portion of premiums to insurance acquisition cash flows	4878
Example 56.65:	Allocating insurance finance income or expenses for contracts where the impact of financial risk on the amounts paid to policyholders is not substantial	4887
Example 56.66:	Allocating insurance finance income or expenses for contracts where the impact of financial risk on the amounts paid to policyholders is substantial – effective yield approach	4890
Example 56.67:	Allocating insurance finance income or expenses for contracts where the impact of financial risk on the amounts paid to policyholders is substantial – projected crediting rate approach	4890
Example 56.68:	Allocating insurance finance income and expense for contracts using the current book yield approach	4893
Example 56.69:	The contractual service margin and interim reporting	4896
Example 56.70:	Disclosure of claims development	4916
Example 56.71:	Measurement of groups of insurance contracts without direct participation features applying the modified retrospective approach	4930
Example 56.72:	Measurement of groups of insurance contracts with direct participation features applying the modified retrospective approach	4932

Chapter 56   Insurance contracts (IFRS 17)

1 INTRODUCTION

The IASB issued IFRS 17 – *Insurance Contracts* – in May 2017. IFRS 17 establishes principles for the recognition, measurement, presentation and disclosure of insurance contracts issued, reinsurance contracts held and investment contracts with discretionary participation features issued. In June 2020, IFRS 17 was amended by *Amendments to IFRS 17* (the June 2020 amendments). The amendments made targeted changes to the requirements in IFRS 17 to respond to concerns and challenges raised by stakeholders as IFRS 17 was being implemented. This chapter incorporates the June 2020 amendments, which also change the mandatory effective date of IFRS 17 to accounting periods beginning on or after 1 January 2023.

The previous IFRS standard on insurance contracts, IFRS 4 – *Insurance Contracts*, issued in March 2004, was an interim standard that allowed entities to use a wide variety of accounting practices for insurance contracts, reflecting national accounting requirements and variations of those requirements. The IASB had always intended to replace IFRS 4. The differences in accounting treatment across jurisdictions and practices have made it difficult for investors and analysts to understand and compare insurers' results. Most stakeholders agreed on the need for a common global insurance accounting standard even though opinions varied as to what it should be. Long-term and complex insurance risks are difficult to reflect in the measurement of insurance contracts. In addition, insurance contracts are subject to several measurement challenges. Some previous accounting practices under IFRS 4 did not adequately reflect the true underlying financial position or the financial performances of these insurance contracts. *[IFRS 17.IN4]*. IFRS 4 is discussed in Chapter 55.

IFRS 17 reflects the Board's view that an insurance contract combines features of both a financial instrument and a service contract. In addition, many insurance contracts generate cash flows with substantial variability over a long period. To provide useful information about these features the Board developed an approach that: *[IFRS 17.IN5]*

- combines current measurement of the future cash flows with the recognition of profit over the period services are provided under the contract;
- presents insurance service results (including presentation of insurance revenue) separately from insurance finance income or expenses; and

- requires an entity to make an accounting policy choice portfolio-by-portfolio of whether to recognise all insurance finance income or expense for the reporting period in profit or loss or to recognise some of that income or expense in other comprehensive income.

The measurement required by IFRS 17 results in: *[IFRS 17.IN7]*

- the liability for a group of insurance contracts relating to performance obligations for remaining service being measured broadly consistent with IFRS 15 – *Revenue from Contracts with Customers* – except that:
    - the measurement is updated for changes in financial assumptions (to differing degrees depending on the type of insurance contract); and
    - the liability often includes an investment component typically not in contracts within the scope of IFRS 15; and
- the liability for a group of insurance contracts relating to incurred claims being measured is broadly consistent with IAS 37 – *Provisions, Contingent Liabilities and Contingent Assets*, except that the liability often includes an investment component that is typically not in contracts within the scope of IAS 37.

An entity may apply a simplified measurement approach (the premium allocation approach) to some insurance contracts. This simplified measurement approach allows an entity to measure the amount relating to remaining service by allocating the premium over the coverage period. *[IFRS 17.IN8]*.

IFRS 17 will have a significant effect on many insurers as their existing accounting policies for recognition and measurement under IFRS 4, usually derived from their local GAAP, are likely to differ from those required by IFRS 17. The costs involved in implementing IFRS 17 are likely to be substantial because of the need for significant systems development in order to capture the required information.

IFRS 17 was effective originally for annual accounting periods beginning on or after 1 January 2021. As a result of the June 2020 amendments, IFRS 17 is effective for accounting periods beginning on or after 1 January 2023. Early application is permitted for entities that apply IFRS 9 – *Financial Instruments* – on or before the date of initial application.

IFRS 17's transition provisions require a full retrospective application of the standard unless it is impracticable, in which case entities should apply either a modified retrospective approach or a fair value approach (see 17 below).

Following issuance of IFRS 17, the IASB created a Transition Resource Group (TRG). The members of the TRG include financial-statement preparers and auditors with both practical and direct knowledge of implementing IFRS 17. The TRG members work in different countries and regions. The TRG's purpose is to:

- provide a public forum for stakeholders to follow the discussion of questions raised on implementation; and
- inform the IASB in order to help the IASB determine what, if any, action will be needed to address those questions. Possible actions include providing supporting materials such as webinars, case studies and/or referral to the Board or Interpretations Committee.

The TRG met three times in 2018 and once in 2019. As of the date of the last TRG meeting, in April 2019, a total of 127 issues had been submitted by constituents of which the TRG discussed 22 in detail. The rest are questions that:

- have been answered by IASB staff applying only the words in IFRS 17; or
- do not meet the submission criteria; or
- were considered through a process other than a TRG discussion (e.g. annual improvement or outreach).

At the time of writing, there are no further TRG meetings scheduled although the TRG submission process remains open for stakeholders to submit questions that they believe meet the TRG submission criteria. The TRG members' views are non-authoritative, but entities should consider them as they implement the new standard.

During the period to May 2019, as a result of the TRG discussions and issues identified by constituents, the IASB discussed and agreed a number of amendments to IFRS 17. In June 2019, the IASB issued an Exposure Draft – *ED/2019/4 Amendments to IFRS 17* (the ED) containing the proposed amendments. The IASB discussed comments on the ED in the period to May 2020 and then issued the June 2020 amendments to IFRS 17. The June 2020 amendments have been reflected throughout the applicable sections of this chapter.

The views expressed in this chapter may evolve as implementation continues and additional issues are identified. Conclusions in seemingly similar situations may differ from those reached in the illustrations due to differences in the underlying facts and circumstances.

2 THE OBJECTIVE, DEFINITIONS AND SCOPE OF IFRS 17

2.1 The objective of IFRS 17

The objective of IFRS 17 is to ensure that an entity provides relevant information that faithfully represents the recognition, measurement, presentation and disclosure principles for insurance contracts within its scope. This information gives a basis for users of financial statements to assess the effect that insurance contracts have on the entity's financial position, financial performance and cash flows. *[IFRS 17.1]*.

2.2 Definitions

The following definitions are relevant to the application of IFRS 17. *[IFRS 17 Appendix A]*. These are the definitions as amended in June 2020.

Figure 56.1: IFRS 17 Definitions

Term	Definition
Contractual service margin	A component of the carrying amount of the asset or liability for a group of insurance contracts representing the unearned profit the entity will recognise as it provides insurance contract services under the insurance contracts in the group.
Coverage period	The period during which the entity provides insurance contract services. This period includes the insurance contract services that relate to all premiums within the boundary of the insurance contract.
Experience adjustment	A difference between: (a) for premium receipts (and any related cash flows such as insurance acquisition cash flows and insurance premium taxes) – the estimate at the beginning of the period of the amounts expected in the period and the actual cash flows in the period; or (b) for insurance service expenses (excluding insurance acquisition expenses) – the estimate at the beginning of the period of the amounts expected to be incurred in the period and the actual amounts incurred in the period.
Financial risk	The risk of a possible future change in one or more of a specified interest rate, financial instrument price, commodity price, currency exchange rate, index of prices or rates, credit rating or credit index or other variable, provided in the case of a non-financial variable that the variable is not specific to a party to the contract.
Fulfilment cash flows	An explicit, unbiased and probability-weighted estimate (i.e. expected value) of the present value of the future cash outflows minus the present value of the future cash inflows that will arise as the entity fulfils insurance contracts, including a risk adjustment for non-financial risk.
Group of insurance contracts	A set of insurance contracts resulting from the division of a portfolio of insurance contracts into, at a minimum, contracts issued within a period of no longer than one year and that, at initial recognition: (a) are onerous, if any; (b) have no significant possibility of becoming onerous subsequently, if any; or (c) do not fall into either (a) or (b), if any.
Insurance acquisition cash flows	Cash flows arising from the costs of selling, underwriting and starting a group of insurance contracts (issued or expected to be issued) that are directly attributable to the portfolio of insurance contracts to which the group belongs. Such cash flows include cash flows that are not directly attributable to individual contracts or groups of insurance contracts within the portfolio.

Insurance contract	A contract under which one party (the issuer) accepts significant insurance risk from another party (the policyholder) by agreeing to compensate the policyholder if a specified uncertain future event (the insured event) adversely affects the policyholder.
Insurance contract services	The following services that an entity provides to a policyholder of an insurance contract: (a) coverage for an insured event (insurance coverage); (b) for insurance contracts without direct participation features, the generation of an investment return for the policyholder, if applicable (investment-return service); and (c) for insurance contracts with direct participation features, the management of underlying items on behalf of the policyholder (investment-related service).
Insurance contract with direct participation features	An insurance contract for which, at inception: (a) the contractual terms specify that the policyholder participates in a share of a clearly identified pool of underlying items; (b) the entity expects to pay to the policyholder an amount equal to a substantial share of the fair value returns on the underlying items; and (c) the entity expects a substantial proportion of any change in the amounts paid to the policyholder to vary with the change in the fair value of the underlying items.
Insurance contract without direct participation features	An insurance contract that is not an insurance contract with direct participation features.
Insurance risk	Risk, other than financial risk, transferred from the holder of a contract to the issuer.
Insured event	An uncertain future event covered by an insurance contract that creates insurance risk.
Investment component	The amounts that an insurance contract requires the entity to repay to a policyholder in all circumstances, regardless of whether an insured event occurs.

Investment contract with discretionary participation features	A financial instrument that provides a particular investor with the contractual right to receive, as a supplement to an amount not subject to the discretion of the issuer, additional amounts:
	(a) that are expected to be a significant portion of the total contractual benefits;
	(b) the timing or amount of which are contractually at the discretion of the issuer; and
	(c) that are contractually based on:
	    (i) the returns on a specified pool of contracts or a specified type of contract;
	    (ii) realised and/or unrealised investment returns on a specified pool of assets held by the issuer; or
	    (iii) the profit or loss of the entity or fund that issues the contract.

Term	Definition
Liability for incurred claims	An entity's obligation to: (a) investigate and pay valid claims for insured events that have already occurred, including events that have occurred but for which claims have not been reported, and other incurred insurance expenses; and (b) pay amounts that are not included in (a) and that relate to: 　(i) insurance contract services that have already been provided; or 　(ii) any investment components or other amounts that are not related to the provision of insurance contract services and that are not in the liability for remaining coverage.
Liability for remaining coverage	An entity's obligation to: (a) investigate and pay valid claims under existing insurance contracts for insured events that have not yet occurred (i.e. the obligation that relates to the unexpired portion of the insurance coverage); and (b) pay amounts under existing insurance contracts that are not included in (a) and that relate to: 　(i) insurance contract services not yet provided (i.e. the obligations that relate to future provision of insurance contract services); or 　(ii) any investment components or other amounts that are not related to the provision of insurance contract services and that have not been transferred to the liability for incurred claims.
Policyholder	A party that has a right to compensation under an insurance contract if an insured event occurs.
Portfolio of insurance contracts	Insurance contracts subject to similar risks and managed together.
Reinsurance contract	An insurance contract issued by one entity (the reinsurer) to compensate another entity for claims arising from one or more insurance contracts issued by that other entity (underlying contracts).
Risk adjustment for non-financial risk	The compensation an entity requires for bearing the uncertainty about the amount and timing of the cash flows that arises from non-financial risk as the entity fulfils insurance contracts.
Underlying items	Items that determine some of the amounts payable to a policyholder. Underlying items can comprise any items; for example, a reference portfolio of assets, the net assets of the entity, or a specified subset of the net assets of the entity.

2.3 Scope

An entity should apply IFRS 17 to: *[IFRS 17.3]*

- insurance contracts, including reinsurance contracts, it issues;
- reinsurance contracts it holds; and
- investment contracts with discretionary participation features it issues, provided the entity also issues insurance contracts.

IFRS 17 specifies that all references to insurance contracts throughout the standard also apply to: *[IFRS 17.4]*
- reinsurance contracts held, except:
  - for references to insurance contracts issued; and
  - the specific requirements for reinsurance contracts held discussed at 10 below;
- investment contracts with a discretionary participation feature (DPF) as set out above except for the reference to insurance contracts as described at 11.3 below.

In addition, all references to insurance contracts also apply to insurance contracts acquired by an entity in a transfer of insurance contracts or a business combination other than reinsurance contracts held. *[IFRS 17.5]*.

It can be seen from this that IFRS 17 applies to all insurance contracts (as defined in IFRS 17) throughout the duration of those contracts, regardless of the type of entity issuing the contracts. *[IFRS 17.BC64]*. Consistent with other IFRSs it is a transaction-based standard. Consequently, non-insurance entities will be within its scope if they issue contracts that meet the definition of an insurance contract.

The Board decided to base its approach on the type of activity rather than on the type of the entity because: *[IFRS 17.BC63]*

- a robust definition of an insurer that could be applied consistently from country to country would be difficult to create;
- entities that might meet the definition frequently have major activities in other areas as well as in insurance, and would need to determine how and to what extent these non-insurance activities would be accounted for in a manner similar to insurance activities or in a manner similar to how other entities account for their non-insurance activities; and
- if an entity that issues insurance contracts accounted for a transaction in one way and an entity that does not issue insurance contracts accounted for the same transaction in a different way, comparability across entities would be reduced.

Conversely, contracts that fail to meet the definition of an insurance contract are within the scope of IFRS 9 if they meet the definition of a financial instrument (unless they contain discretionary participation features and the entity also issues insurance contracts). This will be the case even if such contracts are regulated as insurance contracts under local legislation. Such contracts are commonly referred to as 'investment contracts'. If an investment contract contains an insignificant amount of insurance risk, that insignificant insurance risk is not within the scope of IFRS 17 since the contract is an investment contract and not an insurance contract.

The assessment of whether a contract is an insurance contract will include an assessment of whether the contract contains significant insurance risk (discussed at 3.5 below). In addition, even if the contract contains significant insurance risk, an entity needs to assess whether the contract also contains embedded derivatives (discussed at 4.1 below), distinct investment components (discussed at 4.2 below) or a promise to provide distinct goods or services other than insurance contract services (discussed at 4.3 below) that need to be separated and accounted for under other standards.

Contracts within the scope of IFRS 17 are excluded from the scope of the following IFRSs (except for specific exceptions which are discussed separately elsewhere in this chapter):
- IFRS 7 – *Financial Instruments: Disclosures*;
- IFRS 9 – *Financial Instruments*;
- IFRS 15 – *Revenue from Contracts with Customers*;
- IAS 32 – *Financial Instruments: Presentation*;
- IAS 36 – *Impairment of Assets*;
- IAS 37 – *Provisions, Contingent Liabilities and Contingent Assets*; and
- IAS 38 – *Intangible Assets*.

Any assets for insurance acquisition cash flows (see 6.3 below) are also excluded from the scope of IAS 38.

Contracts within the scope of IFRS 17 are excluded from the measurement provisions of IFRS 5 – *Non-current Assets Held for Sale and Discontinued Operations*.

Contracts within the scope of IFRS 17 are not excluded from the scope of IFRS 13 – *Fair Value Measurement* – which means that any reference to fair value in IFRS 17 should be fair value as defined and measured by IFRS 13. However, IFRS 17 does not generally require that insurance liabilities are measured at fair value except on transition in certain circumstances and, in those circumstances, IFRS 13's measurement requirements are modified to exclude the demand deposit floor (see 17.5 below).

2.3.1 Transactions not within the scope of IFRS 17

IFRS 17 also describes transactions to which IFRS 17 is not applied. These are primarily transactions covered by other standards that could potentially meet the definition of an insurance contract. These transactions are as follows: *[IFRS 17.7]*

- warranties provided by a manufacturer, dealer or retailer in connection with the sale of its goods or services to a customer (see 2.3.1.A below);
- employers' assets and liabilities from employee benefit plans and retirement benefit obligations reported by defined benefit retirement plans (see 2.3.1.B below);
- contractual rights or contractual obligations contingent on the future use of, or right to use, a non-financial item (for example, some licence fees, royalties, variable and other contingent lease payments and similar items) (see 2.3.1.C below);
- residual value guarantees provided by a manufacturer, dealer or retailer and a lessee's residual value guarantees when they are embedded in a lease (see 2.3.1.D below);
- financial guarantee contracts, unless the issuer has previously asserted explicitly that it regards such contracts as insurance contracts and has used accounting applicable to insurance contracts (see 2.3.1.E below);
- contingent consideration payable or receivable in a business combination (see 2.3.1.F below);
- insurance contracts in which the entity is the policyholder, unless those contracts are reinsurance contracts (see 2.3.1.G below); and
- credit card contracts (or similar contracts) that provide insurance coverage (see 2.3.1.H below).

2.3.1.A   Product warranties

Warranties provided by a manufacturer, dealer or retailer in connection with the sale of its goods or services to a customer are outside the scope of IFRS 17. *[IFRS 17.7(a)]*. Such warranties might provide a customer with assurance that the related product will function as the parties intended because it complies with agreed-upon specifications, or they might provide the customer with a service in addition to the assurance that the product complies with agreed-upon specifications. *[IFRS 17.BC89]*. See Chapter 31 at 3.

Without this exception, many product warranties would have been covered by IFRS 17 as they would normally meet the definition of an insurance contract. The Basis for Conclusions observes that the IASB has excluded them from the scope of IFRS 17 because if the standard were to apply, entities would generally apply the premium allocation approach to such contracts, which would result in accounting similar to that resulting from applying IFRS 15. Further, in the Board's view, accounting for such contracts in the same way as other contracts with customers would provide comparable information for the users of financial statements for the entities that issue such contracts. Hence, the Board concluded that changing the existing accounting for these contracts would impose costs and disruption for no significant benefit. *[IFRS 17.BC90]*.

Conversely, a product warranty is within the scope of IFRS 17 if it is not issued by a manufacturer, dealer or retailer in connection with the sale of its goods or services to a customer. See 3.7.1 below.

Other types of warranty are not specifically excluded from the scope of IFRS 17.

2.3.1.B   Assets and liabilities arising from employment benefit plans

Employers' assets and liabilities under employee benefit plans and retirement benefit obligations reported by defined benefit retirement plans are excluded from the scope of IFRS 17. These are accounted for under IAS 19 – *Employee Benefits*, IFRS 2 – *Share-based Payment* – and IAS 26 – *Accounting and Reporting by Retirement Benefit Plans*. *[IFRS 17.7(b)]*.

Many defined benefit pension plans and similar post-employment benefits meet the definition of an insurance contract because the payments to pensioners are contingent on uncertain future events such as the continuing survival of current or retired employees. Without this exception they would have been within the scope of IFRS 17.

2.3.1.C   Contingent contractual rights and obligations related to non-financial items

Contractual rights or contractual obligations that are contingent on the future use of, or right to use, a non-financial item (for example, some licence fees, royalties, variable and other contingent lease payments and similar items) are excluded from the scope of IFRS 17. These are accounted for under IFRS 15, IFRS 16 – *Leases* – and IAS 38. *[IFRS 17.7(c)]*.

2.3.1.D   Residual value guarantees

Residual value guarantees provided by a manufacturer, dealer or retailer and a lessee's residual value guarantees when they are embedded in a lease are excluded from the scope of IFRS 17. They are accounted for under IFRS 15 and IFRS 16. *[IFRS 17.7(d)]*.

However, stand-alone residual value guarantees that transfer insurance risk are not addressed by other IFRSs and are within the scope of IFRS 17. *[IFRS 17.BC87(d)]*.

2.3.1.E   Financial guarantee contracts

A financial guarantee contract is defined as a contract that requires the issuer to make specified payments to reimburse the holder for a loss it incurs because a specified debtor fails to make payment when due in accordance with the original or modified terms of a debt instrument. *[IFRS 9 Appendix A]*. These contracts transfer credit risk and may have various legal forms, such as a guarantee, some types of letter of credit, a credit default contract or an insurance contract. *[IFRS 17.BC91]*.

Financial guarantee contracts are excluded from the scope of IFRS 17 unless the issuer has previously asserted explicitly that it regards such contracts as insurance contracts and has used accounting applicable to insurance contracts. If so, the issuer may elect to apply either IFRS 17 or IAS 32, IFRS 7 and IFRS 9 to the financial guarantee contracts. The issuer may make that choice contract by contract, but the choice for each contract is irrevocable. *[IFRS 17.7(e)]*.

This accounting policy election is the same as that previously in IFRS 4. The Board decided to carry forward to IFRS 17 the option to account for a financial guarantee contract as if it were an insurance contract, without any substantive changes, because the option has worked in practice and results in consistent accounting for economically similar contracts issued by the same entity. The Board did not view it as a high priority to address the inconsistency that results from accounting for financial guarantee contracts differently depending on the issuer. *[IFRS 17.BC93]*.

IFRS 17 does not elaborate on the phrase 'previously asserted explicitly'. However, the application guidance to IFRS 9 states that assertions that an issuer regards contracts as insurance contracts are typically found throughout the issuer's communications with customers and regulators, contracts, business documentation and financial statements. Furthermore, insurance contracts are often subject to accounting requirements that are distinct from the requirements for other types of transaction, such as contracts issued by banks or commercial companies. In such cases, an issuer's financial statements typically include a statement that the issuer has used those accounting requirements. *[IFRS 9.B2.6]*. Therefore, it is likely that insurers that have previously issued financial guarantee contracts and accounted for them under an insurance accounting and regulatory framework will meet this requirement. It is unlikely that an entity not subject to an insurance accounting and regulatory framework and existing insurers that had not previously issued financial guarantee contracts would meet this requirement because they would not have previously made the necessary assertions.

In our view, on transition to IFRS 17, an entity that has previously asserted explicitly that it regards such contracts as insurance contracts and has used accounting applicable to insurance contracts may reconsider its previous election regarding accounting for financial guarantee contracts made under IFRS 4 and decide whether it would prefer to account for those contracts under IFRS 17 or IFRS 9. This is because there are no specific transition provisions either within IFRS 17 or IFRS 9 as to whether previous elections made under a different standard, i.e. IFRS 4, should be continued. Hence, IFRS 17 would not prevent an entity from making new elections on application of IFRS 17. An entity which had not previously asserted explicitly that it regards such contracts as insurance contracts or which it had not previously used accounting applicable to insurance contracts (i.e. IAS 39 – *Financial Instruments: Recognition and Measurement* – or IFRS 9 accounting was applied under IFRS 4) may not reconsider its previous election (either implicitly or explicitly made).

It is observed in the Basis for Conclusions that some credit-related contracts lack the precondition for payment that the holder has suffered a loss. One example of such a contract is one that requires payments in response to changes in a specified credit rating or credit index. The Board concluded that those contracts are derivatives and do not meet the definition of an insurance contract. Therefore, such contracts will continue to be accounted for as derivatives under IFRS 9. The Board noted that these contracts were outside the scope of the policy choice in IFRS 4 carried forward into IFRS 17, so continuing to account for them as derivatives would not create further diversity. *[IFRS 17.BC94]*.

Accounting for financial guarantee contracts by issuers that have not elected to use IFRS 17 is discussed in Chapter 45 at 3.4.2.

2.3.1.F Contingent consideration payable or receivable in a business combination

Contingent consideration payable or receivable in a business combination is outside the scope of IFRS 17. *[IFRS 17.7(f)]*. Contingent consideration in a business combination is required to be recognised at fair value at the acquisition date with subsequent remeasurements of non-equity consideration included in profit or loss (see Chapter 9 at 7.1.3). *[IFRS 3.58]*.

2.3.1.G Direct insurance contracts in which the entity is the policyholder

Accounting by policyholders of direct insurance contracts (i.e. those that are not reinsurance contracts) is excluded from the scope of IFRS 17. However, holders of reinsurance contracts (cedants) are required to apply IFRS 17. *[IFRS 17.7(g)]*.

The IASB originally intended to address accounting by policyholders of direct insurance contracts in IFRS 17 but changed its mind. The Basis for Conclusions observes that other IFRSs include requirements that may apply to some aspects of contracts in which the entity is the policyholder. For example, IAS 37 sets requirements for reimbursements from insurance contracts held that provide cover for expenditure required to settle a provision and IAS 16 – *Property, Plant and Equipment* – sets requirements for some aspects of reimbursement under an insurance contract held that provides coverage for the impairment or loss of property, plant and equipment. Furthermore, IAS 8 – *Accounting Policies, Changes in Accounting Estimates and Errors* – specifies a hierarchy that an entity should use when developing an accounting policy if no IFRS standard applies specifically to an item. Accordingly, the Board did not view work on policyholder accounting as a high priority. *[IFRS 17.BC66]*.

2.3.1.H Credit card contracts (or similar contracts) that provide insurance coverage

Credit card contracts (or similar contracts that provide credit or payment arrangements) that meet the definition of an insurance contract are excluded from the scope of IFRS 17 if, and only if, the entity does not reflect an assessment of the insurance risk associated with an individual customer in setting the price of the contract with that customer. If excluded from IFRS 17, these contracts would be within the scope of IFRS 9 and other applicable standards. However, if, and only if, the insurance component is a contractual term of such a financial instrument (rather than, say, required by local legislation), IFRS 9 requires an entity to separate and apply IFRS 17 to that insurance component. *[IFRS 17.7(h), IFRS 9.2.1(e)(iv)].*

An example of a credit card contract (or similar contract) that provides insurance coverage is one in which the entity:

- must refund the customer for some claims against a supplier in respect of a misrepresentation or breach of the purchase agreement (for example, if the goods are defective or if the supplier fails to deliver the goods) if the supplier does not rectify; and
- is entitled to be indemnified by the supplier for any loss suffered in satisfying its liability with its customer.

As a result, the entity and the supplier are jointly and severally liable to the customer, i.e. the customer can choose whether to claim from the entity or from the supplier. In addition, subject to a maximum amount, the customer can claim from the entity or from the supplier an amount in excess of the amount paid using the specific credit card (for example, the entire purchase price, even if only part of the purchase price was paid using the credit card, and any additional costs reasonably incurred as a result of the supplier failure). Normally, the entity does not charge any fee to the customer or charges an annual fee to the customer that does not reflect an assessment of the insurance risk associated with that individual customer.[1]

This scope exclusion was added to IFRS 17 by the June 2020 amendments. The Board noted that IFRS 9 and IFRS 17 both have requirements that can address credit risk and insurance risk, which are the prominent features of such contracts. Further, the Board was aware that applying IFRS 4 – which had different criteria for separating components of an insurance contract when compared to IFRS 17 – most entities separated the components of such contracts. For example, an entity applying IFRS 4 might account for the credit card component applying IFRS 9, the insurance component applying IFRS 4 and any other service components applying IFRS 15. Acknowledging that entities had already identified methods to separate the components of such contracts, the Board concluded that changing the existing accounting for these contracts would impose costs and disruption to entities that typically do not issue contracts in the scope of IFRS 17, other than some credit card contracts and similar contracts that meet the definition of an insurance contract, for no significant benefit. *[IFRS 17.BC94B].*

In the Board's view, applying IFRS 17 to the insurance coverage components in these contracts will result in the most useful information for users of financial statements. In addition, it will increase comparability between insurance coverage provided as part of the contractual terms of a credit card contract and insurance coverage provided as a separate stand-alone contract. Other IFRS Standards, such as IFRS 15 or IAS 37 might apply to other components of the contract, such as service components or insurance components required by law or regulation. *[IFRS 17.BC94C].*

2.3.2 Fixed fee service contracts

A fixed-fee service contract is a contract in which the level of service depends on an uncertain event but the fee does not. Examples include some types of roadside assistance programmes and maintenance contracts in which the service provider agrees to repair specified equipment after a malfunction. It is stated in the Basis for Conclusions that such contracts meet the definition of an insurance contract because: *[IFRS 17.BC95]*

- it is uncertain whether, or when, assistance or a repair will be needed;
- the owner is adversely affected by the occurrence; and
- the service provider compensates the owner if assistance or repair is needed.

Although these are insurance contracts their primary purpose is the provision of services for a fixed fee. Consequently, IFRS 17 permits entities a choice of applying IFRS 15 instead of IFRS 17 to such contracts that it issues if, and only if, specified conditions are met. The entity may make that choice contract by contract, but the choice for each contract is irrevocable. The conditions are: *[IFRS 17.8]*

- the entity does not reflect an assessment of the risk associated with an individual customer in setting the price of the contract with that customer;
- the contract compensates the customer by providing services, rather than by making cash payments to the customer; and
- the insurance risk transferred by the contract arises primarily from the customer's use of services rather than from uncertainty over the cost of those services.

The Board had proposed originally to exclude fixed fee service contracts whose primary purpose is the provision of services from the scope of IFRS 17. However, some stakeholders noted that some entities issue both fixed-fee service contracts and other insurance contracts. For example, some entities issue both roadside assistance contracts and insurance contracts for damage arising from accidents. Therefore, the Board decided to allow entities a choice of whether to apply IFRS 15 or IFRS 17 to fixed-fee service contracts to enable such entities to account for both types of contract in the same way. In the view of the Board, if IFRS 17 is applied to fixed-fee service contracts, entities would generally apply the premium allocation approach (see 9 below) to such contracts which would result in accounting similar to that resulting from applying IFRS 15. *[IFRS 17.BC96-97]*.

In many cases service agreements are priced using some form of risk assessment and therefore the conditions above which require that IFRS 17 must be applied (and the entity would not have a choice between IFRS 17 and IFRS 15) to fixed fee service contracts may require the exercise of judgement. Despite the comment in the Basis for Conclusions that the choice of whether to apply IFRS 15 or IFRS 17 was introduced to assist entities that issue both roadside assistance contracts and insurance contracts, it is possible that other types of service contracts are within the scope of IFRS 17.

The election described above is in respect of fixed fee service contracts (i.e. contracts where the fee is fixed regardless of the level of service required during the contract period). IFRS 17 does not refer to service contracts in which the level of fee varies according to the level of service. These contracts are normally within the scope of IFRS 15 as they should not contain significant insurance risk.

2.3.3 Loan contracts that transfer significant insurance risk only on settlement of the policyholder's obligation created by the contract

Some contracts meet the definition of an insurance contract but limit the compensation for insured events to the amount otherwise required to settle the policyholder's obligation created by the contract (for example, loans with death waivers). An entity shall choose to apply either IFRS 17 or IFRS 9 to such contracts that it issues unless such contracts are excluded from the scope of IFRS 17 (see 2.3.1.A-2.3.1.H above). The entity shall make that choice for each portfolio (see 5 below) of insurance contracts, and the choice for each portfolio is irrevocable. *[IFRS 17.8A]*.

Examples of such contracts are:

- mortgages when the outstanding balance of the mortgage is waived if the borrower dies;
- lifetime mortgages (sometimes called equity release mortgages) where the entity's recourse is limited to the mortgaged property and if the property is sold for less than the mortgage balance (when the customer dies or moves into long-term care) then the loss is borne by the entity;
- student loan contracts where repayments are income and/or life contingent and may not be made at all if the borrower's income never exceeds the repayment threshold or the borrower dies;[2] and
- a loan provided to a customer to buy a non-financial asset which is repaid via low instalments over the period of the loan with a final, higher 'balloon' payment at maturity but where the customer can choose to return the non-financial asset to the entity instead of making the 'balloon' payment. If the contract compensates the entity only for changes in market prices and not for changes in the condition of the beneficiary's asset, then it would not provide insurance coverage and meet the definition of a derivative within the scope of IFRS 9.[3]

This accounting policy choice was added to IFRS 17 by the June 2020 amendments. This was as a result of stakeholder concerns that such contracts are typically issued by non-insurers who might be expected to be in a less advanced stage of IFRS 17 implementation and might not have fully assessed the implications of IFRS 17 on their business, and because these contracts do not usually have the legal form of insurance contracts. It is observed in the Basis for Conclusions that applying either IFRS 17 or IFRS 9 would provide useful information about such contracts. Hence, the Board concluded requiring an entity to apply IFRS 17 to those contracts, when the entity had previously been applying an accounting policy consistent with IFRS 9 or IAS 39 to those contracts (or *vice versa*), could impose costs and disruption with no significant benefit. *[IFRS 17.BC94E]*.

It is further observed in the Basis for Conclusions that the accounting policy choice for each portfolio was made irrevocable in order to mitigate the lack of comparability that might otherwise arise between similar contracts issued by the same entity, and between similar contracts issued by different entities. *[IFRS 17.BC94F]*.

2.3.4 Other accounting standards which affect insurers

IFRS 17 does not address other aspects of accounting by insurers, such as accounting for financial assets held by insurers and financial liabilities issued by insurers which are within the scope of IFRS 7, IFRS 9 and IAS 32. However:

- IFRS 9 permits an entity that operates an investment fund that provides investors with benefits determined by units in that fund and recognises liabilities for the amounts to be paid to those investors (e.g. some insurance contracts with direct participation features and some investment contracts with discretionary participation features) to elect not to derecognise any underlying items held by the funds that include the entity's own financial liabilities. Normally, if an entity issues a financial liability, for example a corporate bond, that is purchased by one of its investment funds, or included within the underlying items behind the insurance contracts that are held on the entity's balance sheet, such a purchase should result in derecognition of the financial liability. This election is irrevocable and made on an instrument-by-instrument basis. *[IFRS 9.3.3.5]*. See Chapter 52 at 8.2.
- IAS 40 – *Investment Property* – permits an entity to separately choose between the fair value model or the cost model for all investment property backing liabilities that pay a return linked directly to the fair value of, or returns from, specified assets including that investment property (e.g. insurance contracts with direct participation features as discussed at 11.2 below). *[IAS 40.32A]*. The choice to use either the fair value model or the cost model for all other investment property is a separate election. See Chapter 19 at 5.1.

3 THE DEFINITION OF AN INSURANCE CONTRACT

3.1 The definition

The definition of an insurance contract in IFRS 17 is:

'A contract under which one party (the insurer) accepts significant insurance risk from another party (the policyholder) by agreeing to compensate the policyholder if a specified uncertain future event (the insured event) adversely affects the policyholder'. *[IFRS 17 Appendix A]*.

This definition determines which contracts are within the scope of IFRS 17 as opposed to other standards.

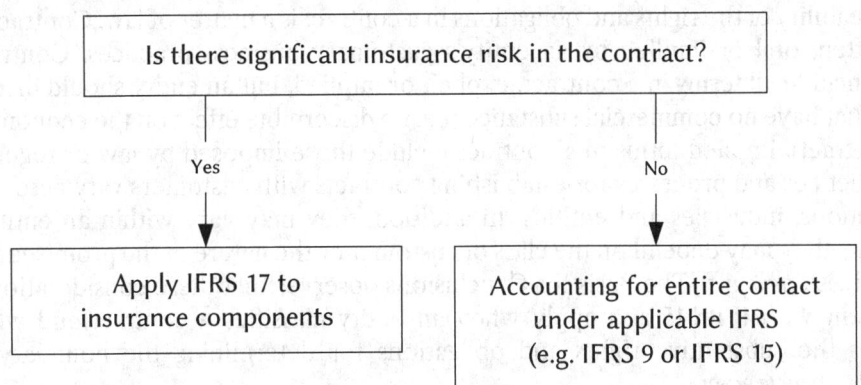

The definition of an insurance contract is, in essence, the same as in IFRS 4. Therefore, in many cases, contracts that were insurance contracts under IFRS 4 are expected to be insurance contracts under IFRS 17 although IFRS 17 contains no transitional provisions which 'grandfather' conclusions made under IFRS 4 (except for the consequential amendments to IFRS 3 – *Business Combinations* – see 13 below).

However, there have been clarifications to the related application guidance explaining the definition to require that: *[IFRS 17.BC67]*

- an insurer should consider the time value of money in assessing whether the additional benefits payable in any scenario are significant (see 3.5 below); and
- a contract does not transfer significant insurance risk if there is no scenario with commercial substance in which the insurer can suffer a loss on a present value basis (see 3.5 below).

Both of these clarifications are intended to ensure that the determination of insurance risk is made on a present value basis as it was considered that IFRS 4 was unclear on the matter. Additionally, the definition of significant insurance risk (see 3.5 below) uses the word 'amounts' instead of 'benefits' in order to capture payments that may not necessarily be payable to policyholders (for example claim handling expenses).

While the definition of an insurance contract has not changed much from IFRS 4, the consequences of qualifying as an insurance contract have changed. This is because IFRS 4 allowed entities to use their previous accounting policies for contracts that qualified as insurance contracts. Hence, under IFRS 4, many non-insurance entities, such as banks and service companies, applied guidance from other standards, such as IFRS 9 and IFRS 15, to recognise and measure insurance contracts. This will no longer be possible since IFRS 17 has specific recognition, measurement and presentation requirements for financial statements. As discussed at 2.3.1.H and 2.3.3 above, IFRS 17 has a scope exemption for certain credit card contracts (or similar contracts) that provide insurance coverage and an accounting policy choice to apply either IFRS 9 or IFRS 17 to loan contracts that transfer significant insurance risk only on settlement of the policyholder's obligation created by the contract.

An entity should consider its substantive rights and obligations, whether they arise from a contract, law or regulation, when applying IFRS 17. A contract is an agreement between two or more parties that creates enforceable rights and obligations. Enforceability of the rights and obligations in a contract is a matter of law. Contracts can be written, oral or implied by an entity's customary business practices. Contractual terms include all terms in a contract, explicit or implied, but an entity should disregard terms that have no commercial substance (i.e. no discernible effect on the economics of the contract). Implied terms in a contract include those imposed by law or regulation. The practices and processes for establishing contracts with customers vary across legal jurisdictions, industries and entities. In addition, they may vary within an entity (for example, they may depend on the class of customer or the nature of the promised goods or services). *[IFRS 17.2]*. The Basis for Conclusions observes that these considerations are consistent with IFRS 15 and apply when an entity classifies a contract and when it assesses the substantive rights and obligations for determining the boundary of a contract. *[IFRS 17.BC69]*.

In a paper submitted to the TRG in September 2018, the IASB staff discussed whether a service fee contract for hotel management services which also guarantees the hotel owner a specified level of EBITDA was an insurance contract because the amount payable under the guarantee may exceed the service fee receivable. The IASB staff noted that IFRS 17 includes a scope exclusion for warranties provided by a manufacturer, dealer or retailer in connection with the sale of its services to a customer and also excludes contractual obligations contingent on the future use of a non-financial item (for example contingent payments)[4] – see 2.3.1.C above. The implication from the IASB staff's response is that the EBITDA guarantee is excluded from the scope of IFRS 17 as it is a guarantee given by a retailer in connection with the sale of its services to a customer.

The definition of an insurance contract is discussed in more detail as follows: *[IFRS 17.B2]*

- uncertain future events (see 3.2 below);
- payments in kind (see 3.3 below);
- the distinction between insurance risk and other risks (see 3.4 below);
- significant insurance risk (see 3.5 below);
- changes in the level of insurance risk (see 3.6 below); and
- examples of insurance and non-insurance contracts (see 3.7 below).

3.2 Uncertain future events

Uncertainty (or risk) is the essence of an insurance contract. Accordingly, IFRS 17 requires at least one of the following to be uncertain at the inception of an insurance contract: *[IFRS 17.B3]*

(a) the probability of an insured event occurring;
(b) when the insured event will occur; or
(c) how much the entity will need to pay if the insured event occurs.

An insured event will be one of the following:

- the discovery of a loss during the term of the contract, even if the loss arises from an event that occurred before the inception of the contract;
- a loss that occurs during the term of the contract, even if the resulting loss is discovered after the end of the contract term; *[IFRS 17.B4]* or
- the determination of the ultimate cost of a claim which has already occurred but whose financial effect is uncertain. *[IFRS 17.B5]*.

This last type of insured event above arises from 'retroactive' contracts, i.e. those providing insurance coverage against an adverse development of an event which has occurred prior to the policy inception date. An example is a reinsurance contract that covers a direct policyholder against adverse development of claims already reported by policyholders. In those contracts, the insured event is the determination of the ultimate cost of those claims. The implications of this on measurement is discussed at 8.9.2 below.

3.3 Payments in kind

Some insurance contracts require or permit payments to be made in kind. In such cases, the entity provides goods or services to the policyholder to settle the entity's obligation to compensate the policyholder for insured events. Such contracts are insurance contracts, even though the claims are settled in kind, and are treated the same way as insurance contracts when payment is made directly to the policyholder. For example, some insurers replace a stolen article directly rather than compensating the policyholder for the amount of its loss. Another example is when an entity uses its own hospitals and medical staff to provide medical services covered by the insurance contract. *[IFRS 17.B6]*.

Although these are insurance contracts, if they meet the conditions for fixed-fee service contracts (see 2.3.2 above) entities can elect to apply either IFRS 15 or IFRS 17.

3.4 The distinction between insurance risk and financial risk

The definition of an insurance contract refers to 'insurance risk' which is defined as 'risk, other than financial risk, transferred from the holder of a contract to the issuer'. *[IFRS 17 Appendix A]*.

A contract that exposes the reporting entity to financial risk without significant insurance risk is not an insurance contract. *[IFRS 17.B7]*. 'Financial risk' is defined as 'the risk of a possible future change in one or more of a specified interest rate, financial instrument price, foreign exchange rate, index of prices or rates, credit rating or credit index or other variable, provided in the case of a non-financial variable that variable is not specific to a party to the contract'. *[IFRS 17 Appendix A]*.

An example of a non-financial variable that is not specific to a party to the contract is an index of earthquake losses in a particular region or an index of temperatures in a particular city. An example of a non-financial variable that is specific to a party to the contract is the occurrence or non-occurrence of a fire that damages or destroys an asset of that party. Furthermore, the risk of changes in the fair value of a non-financial asset is not a financial risk if the fair value reflects changes in the market prices for such assets (i.e. a financial variable) and the condition of a specific non-financial asset held by a party to the contract (i.e. a non-financial variable). For example, if a guarantee of the residual value of a specific car exposes the guarantor to the risk of changes in that car's condition, that risk is insurance risk, not financial risk. *[IFRS 17.B8]*. This is illustrated by the following example:

Example 56.1:   Residual value insurance

Entity A issues a contract to Entity B that provides a guarantee of the fair value at a future date of an aircraft (a non-financial asset) held by Entity B. Entity A is not the manufacturer, dealer or retailer of the aircraft and also is not the lessee of the aircraft (residual value guarantees given by a lessee under a lease are within the scope of IFRS 16).

This is an insurance contract (unless changes in the condition of the asset have an insignificant effect on its value). The risk of changes in the fair value of the aircraft is not a financial risk because the fair value reflects not only changes in market prices for similar aircraft but also the condition of the specific asset held.

However, if the contract compensated Entity B only for changes in market prices and not for changes in the condition of Entity B's asset, the contract would be a derivative and within the scope of IFRS 9.

Contracts that expose the issuer to both financial risk and significant insurance risk can be insurance contracts. For example, many life insurance contracts guarantee a minimum rate of return to policyholders, creating financial risk, and at the same time promise death benefits that may significantly exceed the policyholder's account balance, creating insurance risk in the form of mortality risk. Such contracts are insurance contracts. *[IFRS 17.B9]*.

Under some contracts, an insured event triggers the payment of an amount linked to a price index. Such contracts are insurance contracts provided that the payment contingent on the insured event could be significant. This is illustrated by the following example: *[IFRS 17.B10]*

Example 56.2: Contract with life contingent annuity linked to price index

Entity A issues a life-contingent annuity the value of which is linked to a cost of living index.

The contract is an insurance contract because the payment is triggered by an uncertain future event – the survival of the person who receives the annuity. The link to the price index is a derivative, but it also transfers insurance risk because the number of payments to which the index applies depends on the survival of the annuitant. If the resulting transfer of insurance risk is significant, the derivative meets the definition of an insurance contract in which case it should not be separated from the host contract (see 4.1 below).

The definition of an insurance contract requires risk to be transferred from the policyholder to the insurer. This means that the insurer must accept, from the policyholder, a risk to which the policyholder was already exposed. Any new risk created by the contract for the entity or the policyholder is not insurance risk. *[IFRS 17.B11]*.

3.4.1 Insurable interest

For a contract to be an insurance contract the insured event must have an adverse effect on the policyholder. *[IFRS 17.B12]*. In other words, there must be an 'insurable interest'. *[IFRS 17.BC73]*.

The IASB considered whether it should eliminate the notion of insurable interest and replace it with the notion that insurance involves assembling risks into a pool in which they can be managed together. *[IFRS 17.BC74]*. However, the IASB decided to retain the notion of insurable interest contained in IFRS 4 because without the reference to 'adverse effect' the definition might have captured any prepaid contract to provide services with uncertain costs. In addition, the notion of insurable interest is needed to avoid including gambling in the definition of insurance. Furthermore, the definition of an insurance contract is a principle-based distinction, particularly between insurance contracts and those used for hedging. *[IFRS 17.BC75]*.

The adverse effect on the policyholder is not limited to an amount equal to the financial impact of the adverse event. So, for example, the definition includes 'new for old' insurance coverage that pays the policyholder an amount that permits the replacement of a used or damaged asset with a new asset. Similarly, the definition does not limit payment under a life insurance contract to the financial loss suffered by a deceased's dependents, nor does it preclude the payment of predetermined amounts to quantify the loss caused by a death or accident. *[IFRS 17.B12]*.

A contract that requires a payment if a specified uncertain event occurs which does not require an adverse effect on the policyholder as a precondition for payment is not an insurance contract. Such contracts are not insurance contracts even if the holder of the contract uses the contract to mitigate an underlying risk exposure. For example, if the holder of the contract uses a derivative to hedge an underlying financial or non-financial variable correlated with the cash flows from an asset of the entity, the derivative is not conditional on whether the holder is adversely affected by a reduction in the cash flows from the asset. Conversely, the definition of an insurance contract refers to an uncertain future event for which an adverse effect on the policyholder is a contractual precondition for payment. This contractual precondition does not require the insurer to investigate whether the uncertain event actually caused an adverse effect, but it does permit the insurer to deny payment if it is not satisfied that the event caused an adverse effect. *[IFRS 17.B13]*.

The following example illustrates the concept of an adverse effect on the policyholder:

Example 56.3:   Reinsurance contract with 'original loss warranty' clause

Entity A agrees to issue a contract to Entity B to provide reinsurance cover for £5m against losses suffered. The insurance losses suffered by Entity B which are recoverable under the contract are limited to those arising from events where the industry-wide insured loss exceeds a threshold of £100m (sometimes described as an 'original loss warranty'). This means that only losses suffered by Entity B up to £5m from events exceeding an industry-wide insured loss of £100m can be recovered under the contract.

Assuming insurance risk is significant, this is an insurance contract as Entity B can only recover its own insurance claims arising from those events.

If the contract allowed Entity B to claim up to £5m every time there was an event with an industry-wide loss exceeding a threshold of £100m regardless of whether Entity B had suffered insurance claims from that event then this would not be an insurance contract because there would be no insurable interest in the arrangement.

3.4.2   Lapse, persistency and expense risk

Lapse or persistency risk (the risk that the policyholder will cancel the contract earlier or later than the issuer had expected in pricing the contract) is not insurance risk. This is because the resulting variability in the payment to the policyholder is not contingent on an uncertain future event that adversely affects the policyholder. *[IFRS 17.B14]*.

Similarly, expense risk (the risk of unexpected increases in the administrative costs incurred by the issuer associated with the servicing of a contract, rather than in the costs associated with insured events) is not insurance risk because an unexpected increase in expenses does not adversely affect the policyholder. *[IFRS 17.B14]*.

Therefore, a contract that exposes an entity to lapse risk, persistency risk or expense risk is not an insurance contract unless it also exposes the entity to significant insurance risk. *[IFRS 17.B15]*.

3.4.3   Insurance of non-insurance risks

If the issuer of a contract which does not contain significant insurance risk mitigates the risk of that contract by using a second contract to transfer part of that first contract's risk to another party, this second contract exposes that other party to insurance risk. This is because the policyholder of the second contract (the issuer of the first contract) is subject to an uncertain event that adversely affects it and thus it meets the definition of an insurance contract. *[IFRS 17.B15]*. This is illustrated by the following example:

Example 56.4:   Insurance of non-insurance risks

Entity A agrees to compensate Entity B for losses on a series of contracts issued by Entity B that do not transfer significant insurance risk. These could be investment contracts or, for example, a contract to provide services.

The contract issued by Entity A is an insurance contract if it transfers significant insurance risk from Entity B to Entity A, even if some or all of the underlying individual contracts do not transfer significant insurance risk to Entity B. The contract is a reinsurance contract if any of the underlying contracts issued by Entity B are insurance contracts. Otherwise, the contract is a direct insurance contract.

3.5 Significant insurance risk

A contract is an insurance contract only if it transfers 'significant insurance risk'. *[IFRS 17.B17]*.

Insurance risk is 'significant' if, and only if, an insured event could cause an insurer to pay significant additional amounts in any scenario, excluding scenarios that lack commercial substance (i.e. have no discernible effect on the economics of the transaction). If an insured event could mean significant additional amounts would be payable in scenarios that have commercial substance, this condition may be met even if the insured event is extremely unlikely or even if the expected (i.e. probability-weighted) present value of contingent cash flows is a small proportion of the expected present value of all the remaining contractual cash flows. *[IFRS 17.B18]*.

In addition, a contract transfers significant insurance risk only if there is a scenario that has commercial substance in which the issuer has a possibility of a loss on a present value basis. However, even if a reinsurance contract does not expose the issuer to the possibility of a significant loss, that contract is deemed to transfer significant insurance risk if it transfers to the reinsurer substantially all the insurance risk relating to the reinsured portions of the underlying insurance contracts. *[IFRS 17.B19]*.

The additional amounts described above are determined on a present value basis. If an insurance contract requires payment when an event with uncertain timing occurs and if the payment is not adjusted for the time value of money, there may be scenarios in which the present value of the payment increases, even if its nominal value is fixed. An example is insurance that provides a fixed death benefit when the policyholder dies, with no expiry date for the cover (often referred to as whole-life insurance for a fixed amount). It is certain that the policyholder will die, but the date of death is uncertain. Payments may be made when an individual policyholder dies earlier than expected. Because those payments are not adjusted for the time value of money, significant insurance risk could exist even if there is no overall loss on the portfolio of contracts. Similarly, contractual terms that delay timely reimbursement to the policyholder can eliminate significant insurance risk. An entity should use the discount rates required as discussed at 8.3 below to determine the present value of the additional amounts. *[IFRS 17.B20]*.

IFRS 17 does not prohibit a contract from being an insurance contract if there are restrictions on the timing of payments or receipts. However, the existence of restrictions on the timing of payments may mean that the policy does not transfer significant insurance risk if it results in the lack of a scenario that has commercial substance in which the issuer has a possibility of a loss on a present value basis.

3.5.1 Quantity of insurance risk

No quantitative guidance supports the determination of 'significant' in IFRS 17. This was a deliberate decision because the IASB considered that if quantitative guidance was provided it would create an arbitrary dividing line that would result in different accounting treatments for similar transactions that fall marginally on different sides of that line and would therefore create opportunities for accounting arbitrage. *[IFRS 17.BC78]*.

The IASB also rejected defining the significance of insurance risk by reference to the definition of materiality within the *Conceptual Framework for Financial Reporting* because, in its opinion, a single contract, or even a single book of similar contracts, would rarely generate a loss that would be material to the financial statements as a whole. Consequently, IFRS 17 defines the significance of insurance risk in relation to individual contracts (see 3.5.2 below). *[IFRS 17.BC79]*.

The IASB also rejected the notion of defining the significance of insurance risk by expressing the expected (probability weighted) average of the present values of the adverse outcomes as a proportion of the expected present value of all outcomes, or as a proportion of the premium. This definition would mean that a contract could start as a financial liability and become an insurance contract as time passes or probabilities are reassessed. This idea would have required the constant monitoring of contracts over their life to see whether they continued to transfer insurance risk. The IASB considered that it would be too burdensome to require an entity to continuously monitor whether a contract meets the definition of an insurance contract over its duration. Consequently, as discussed at 3.6 below, an assessment of whether significant insurance risk has been transferred is normally required only at the inception of a contract. *[IFRS 17.BC80]*.

IFRS 4 contained an illustrative example which implied that insured benefits must be greater than 101% of the benefits payable if the insured event did not occur for there to be insurance risk in an insurance contract. *[IFRS 4.IG2 E 1.3]*. However, no equivalent example has been included in IFRS 17.

Some jurisdictions have their own guidance as to what constitutes significant insurance risk. However, other jurisdictions offer no quantitative guidance. Some US GAAP practitioners apply a guideline that a reasonable possibility of a significant loss is a 10% probability of a 10% loss, although this guideline does not appear in US GAAP itself. *[IFRS 17.BC77]*. It is not disputed in the Basis for Conclusions that a 10% chance of a 10% loss results in a transfer of significant insurance risk and, indeed, the words 'extremely unlikely' and 'a small proportion' (see 3.5 above) suggests that the IASB envisages that significant insurance risk could exist at a lower threshold than a 10% probability of a 10% loss.

This lack of a quantitative definition means that insurers must apply their own judgement as to what constitutes significant insurance risk. Although the IASB did not want to create an 'arbitrary dividing line', the practical impact of this lack of guidance is that insurers have to apply their own criteria to determine what constitutes significant insurance risk and there will probably be inconsistency in practice as to what these dividing lines are, at least at the margins.

There is no specific requirement under IFRS 17 for insurers to disclose any thresholds used in determining whether a contract contains significant insurance risk. However, IFRS 17 requires an entity to disclose the significant judgements made in applying IFRS 17 (see 16.3 below) whilst IAS 1 – *Presentation of Financial Statements* – requires an entity to disclose the judgements that management has made in the process of applying the entity's accounting policies that have the most significant effect on the amounts recognised in the financial statements (see Chapter 3 at 5.1.1.B).

3.5.2 The level at which significant insurance risk is assessed

Significant insurance risk must be assessed by individual contract, rather than by portfolios or groups of contracts or by reference to materiality to the financial statements. Thus, insurance risk may be significant even if there is a minimal probability of significant losses for a portfolio or group of contracts. *[IFRS 17.B22]*. There is no exception to the requirement for assessment at an individual contract level, unlike IFRS 4 which permitted an insurer to make an assessment based on a small book of contracts if those contracts were relatively homogeneous.

The IASB decided to define significant insurance risk in relation to a single contract rather than at a higher level of aggregation because, although contracts are usually managed on a portfolio basis, the contractual rights and obligations arise from individual contracts. Materiality by reference to the financial statements was considered an inappropriate basis to define significant insurance risk because a single contract, or even a single book of similar contracts, would rarely generate a material loss in relation to the financial statements as a whole. *[IFRS 17.BC79]*.

A set or series of insurance contracts with the same or a related counterparty may achieve, or be designed to achieve, an overall commercial effect. In those circumstances, it may be necessary to treat the set or series of contracts as a whole in order to report the substance of such contracts. For example, if the rights or obligations in one contract do nothing other than entirely negate the rights or obligations of another contract entered into at the same time with the same counterparty, the combined effect is that no rights or obligations exist. *[IFRS 17.9]*. This requirement is intended to prevent entities entering into contracts that individually transfer significant insurance risk, but collectively do not, and accounting for part(s) of what is effectively a single arrangement as (an) insurance contract(s).

If an insurance contract is separated into non-insurance components and insurance components (see 4 below) the significance of insurance risk transferred is assessed by reference only to the remaining components of the host insurance contract. *[IFRS 17.13]*.

3.5.2.A Self insurance

An insurer can accept significant insurance risk from a policyholder only if it issues an insurance contract to an entity separate from itself. Therefore, 'self insurance', such as a self-insured deductible where the insured cannot claim for losses below the excess limit of an insurance policy, is not insurance because there is no insurance contract with a third party. *[IFRS 17.B27(c)]*. Accounting for self insurance and related provisions is covered by IAS 37 which requires that a provision is recognised only if there is a present obligation as a result of a past event, if it is probable that an outflow of resources will occur and a reliable estimate can be determined. *[IAS 37.14]*.

3.5.2.B Insurance mutuals

A mutual insurer accepts risk from each policyholder and pools that risk. Although policyholders bear the pooled risk collectively in their capacity as owners, the mutual has still accepted the risk that is the essence of an insurance contract and therefore IFRS 17 applies to those contracts. *[IFRS 17.B16]*. Accounting for insurance contracts issued by mutual entities is discussed at 8.11 below.

3.5.2.C Intragroup insurance contracts

Where there are insurance contracts between entities in the same group, these would be eliminated in the consolidated financial statements as required by IFRS 10 – *Consolidated Financial Statements*. If any intragroup insurance contract is reinsured with a third party that is not part of the group, this third party reinsurance contract should be accounted for as a direct insurance contract in the consolidated financial statements of a non-insurer because the intragroup contract will be eliminated on consolidation. This residual direct insurance contract (i.e. the policy with the third party) is outside the scope of IFRS 17 from the viewpoint of the consolidated financial statements of a non-insurer because policyholder accounting is excluded from IFRS 17 as discussed at 2.3.1.G above.

3.5.3 Significant additional amounts

The 'significant additional amounts' described at 3.5 above refer to the present value of amounts that exceed those that would be payable if no insured event occurred (excluding scenarios that lack commercial substance). These additional amounts include claims handling and claims assessment costs, but exclude: *[IFRS 17.B21]*

(a) the loss of the ability to charge the policyholder for future service. For example, in an investment-linked life contract, the death of the policyholder means that the entity can no longer perform investment management services and collect a fee for doing so. However, the economic loss for the entity does not result from insurance risk. Consequently, the potential loss or future investment management fees is not relevant when assessing how much insurance risk is transferred by a contract;

(b) the waiver, on death, of charges that would be made on cancellation or surrender of the contract. Because the contract brought these charges into existence, their waiver does not compensate the policyholder for a pre-existing risk. Hence, they are not relevant in determining how much insurance risk is transferred by a contract;

(c) a payment conditional on an event that does not cause a significant loss to the holder of the contract. For example where the issuer must pay £1m if an asset suffers physical damage causing an insignificant economic loss of £1 to the holder. The holder in this case has transferred to the insurer the insignificant insurance risk of losing £1. At the same time the contract creates non-insurance risk that the issuer will need to pay an additional £999,999 if the specified event occurs. Because there is no scenario in which an insured event causes a significant loss to the holder of the contract, the issuer does not accept significant insurance risk from the holder and this contract is not an insurance contract; and

(d) possible reinsurance recoveries. The insurer will account for these separately.

It follows from this that if a contract pays a death benefit exceeding the amount payable on survival (excluding any waiver or surrender charges as per (b) above), the contract is an insurance contract unless the additional death benefit is insignificant (judged by reference to the contract rather than to an entire portfolio of contracts). Similarly, an annuity contract that pays out regular sums for the rest of a policyholder's life is an insurance contract, unless the aggregate life-contingent payments are insignificant. In this case, the insurer could suffer a significant loss on an individual contract if the annuitant survives longer than expected. *[IFRS 17.B23]*.

In September 2018, the TRG members considered an IASB staff paper which discussed whether a contract that contains a provision that waives the payment of a premium under certain circumstances is an insurance contract. In these cases, the main insured event in the contract differs from the event triggering a premium waiver (for example, the primary coverage may be a term life contract covering mortality risk and premiums are waived if the policyholder has been disabled for six consecutive months, although the policyholder continues to receive the benefits originally promised under the insurance contract despite the waiver of premiums). The TRG members agreed with the IASB staff analysis and observed that:

- there is an insurance risk when an entity provides a waiver of premiums if a specified event occurs; and
- the waiver of premiums differs from the situations discussed above (i.e. the loss of the ability to charge the policyholder for future service and the waiver, on death, of contract surrender or cancellation charges).

This is because the risk of the events giving rise to the waiver exists before the contract is issued. It is not a risk created by the contract and the contract does not increase the potential adverse effects. In addition, the events that trigger a waiver are contractual pre-conditions without which the entity can deny the waiver.

The TRG members observed that the consequences of such a waiver of premiums are:

- the inclusion of a clause in an investment contract in which premiums are waived by contractual pre-conditions makes the investment contract an insurance contract; and
- the inclusion of such a waiver in a contract that would also be an insurance contract without the waiver would impact the quantity of benefits provided by the contract and the coverage period, affecting the recognition of the contractual service margin in profit or loss.[5]

In April 2019, in response to a submission to the TRG, the IASB staff clarified that, to the extent that a premium waiver results from an insured event, it is a claim and therefore recognised as an insurance service expense.[6]

3.6 Changes in the level of insurance risk

IFRS 17 requires the assessment of whether a contract transfers significant insurance risk to be made only once. The Basis for Conclusions states that this assessment is made 'at inception'. *[IFRS 17.BC80]*. We interpret this phrase to mean that the assessment is made when the contract is issued rather than the start of the coverage period since a contract can be recognised at an earlier date than the start of the coverage period (see 6 below).

As the assessment of significant insurance risk is made only once, a contract that qualifies as an insurance contract remains an insurance contract until all rights and obligations are extinguished, i.e. discharged, cancelled or expired, unless the contract is derecognised because of a modification (see 12.1 below). *[IFRS 17.B25]*. This applies even if circumstances have changed such that insurance contingent rights and obligations have expired. The IASB considered that requiring insurers to set up systems to continually assess whether contracts continue to transfer significant insurance risk imposed a cost that far outweighed the benefit that would be gained from going through the exercise. *[IFRS 17.BC80]*. For a contract acquired in a business combination or transfer, the assessment of whether the contract transfers significant insurance risk is made at the date of acquisition or transfer (see 13 below).

For some contracts, the transfer of insurance risk to the issuer occurs after a period of time, as explained in the following example: *[IFRS 17.B24]*

Example 56.5: Deferred annuity with policyholder election

Entity A issues a deferred annuity contract which provides a specified investment return to the policyholder and includes an option for the policyholder to use the proceeds of the investment on maturity to buy a life-contingent annuity at the same rates Entity A charges other new annuitants at the time the policyholder exercises that option.

This is not an insurance contract at inception because it does not contain significant insurance risk. Entity A remains free to price the annuity on a basis that reflects the insurance risk that will be transferred to it at that time. Such a contract transfers insurance risk to the issuer only after the option is exercised. Consequently, the cash flows that would occur on the exercise of the option fall outside the boundary of the contract, and before exercise there are no insurance cash flows within the boundary of the contract. Consequently, on inception, the contract is a financial instrument within the scope of IFRS 9.

However, if the contract specifies the annuity rates (or a basis other than market rates for setting the annuity rates), the contract transfers insurance risk to Entity A (the issuer) because Entity A is exposed to the risk that the annuity rates will be unfavourable when the policyholder exercises the option. In that case, the cash flows that would occur when the option is exercised are within the boundary of the contract.

In April 2019, an IASB staff paper presented to the TRG, confirmed that contracts that transfer insurance risk only after an option is exercised do not meet the definition of an insurance contract at inception and an entity should consider the requirements of other IFRSs in order to account for such contracts until they become insurance contracts. A contract which only transfers insurance risk after a period of time is different to an insurance contract that provides an option to add further insurance coverage.[7]

Some stakeholders suggested to the IASB that a contract should not be accounted for as an insurance contract if the insurance-contingent rights and obligations expire after a very short time. IFRS 17 addresses aspects of this by requiring scenarios that lack commercial substance are ignored in the assessment of significant insurance risk and stating that there is no significant transfer of insurance risk in some contracts that waive surrender penalties on death (see 3.5.3 above and 11.3.1 below). *[IFRS 17.BC81]*.

3.7 Examples of insurance and non-insurance contracts

This section contains examples given in IFRS 17 of insurance and non-insurance contracts.

3.7.1 Examples of insurance contracts

The following are examples of contracts that are insurance contracts, if the transfer of insurance risk is significant: *[IFRS 17.B26]*

- insurance against theft or damage;
- insurance against product liability, professional liability, civil liability or legal expenses;
- life insurance and prepaid funeral plans (although death is certain, it is uncertain when death will occur or, for some types of life insurance, whether death will occur within the period covered by the insurance);

- life-contingent annuities and pensions (contracts that provide compensation for the uncertain future event – the survival of the annuitant or pensioner – to assist the annuitant or pensioner in maintaining a given standard of living, which would otherwise be adversely affected by his or her survival);
- insurance against disability and medical costs;
- surety bonds, fidelity bonds, performance bonds and bid bonds (i.e. contracts that provide compensation if another party fails to perform a contractual obligation, for example an obligation to construct a building);
- product warranties issued by another party for goods sold by a manufacturer, dealer or retailer are within the scope of IFRS 17. However, as discussed at 2.3.1.A above, product warranties issued directly by a manufacturer, dealer or retailer are outside the scope of IFRS 17 and are instead within the scope of IFRS 15 or IAS 37;
- title insurance (insurance against the discovery of defects in title to land that were not apparent when the insurance contract was issued). In this case, the insured event is the discovery of a defect in the title, not the defect itself;
- travel assistance (compensation in cash or in kind to policyholders for losses suffered in advance of, or during travel);
- catastrophe bonds that provide for reduced payments of principal, interest or both if a specified event adversely affects the issuer of the bond (unless the specified event does not create significant insurance risk, for example if the event is a change in an interest rate or a foreign exchange rate); and
- insurance swaps and other contracts that require a payment based on changes in climatic, geological and other physical variables that are specific to a party to the contract;

These examples are not intended to be an exhaustive list.

The following illustrative examples, based on examples contained previously in IFRS 4, provide further guidance on situations where there is significant insurance risk:

Example 56.6: Guarantee fund established by contract

A guarantee fund is established by contract. The contract requires all participants to pay contributions to the fund so that it can meet obligations incurred by participants (and, perhaps, others). Participants would typically be from a single industry, e.g. insurance, banking or travel.

The contract that establishes the guarantee fund is an insurance contract.

This example contrasts with Example 56.10 below where a guarantee fund has been established by law and not by contract.

Example 56.7: No market value adjustment for maturity benefits

A contract permits the issuer to deduct a market value adjustment (MVA), a charge which varies depending on a market index, from surrender values or death benefits. The contract does not permit the issuer to deduct a MVA for maturity benefits.

The policyholder obtains an additional survival benefit because no MVA is applied at maturity. That benefit is a pure endowment because the insured person receives a payment on survival to a specified date but beneficiaries receive nothing if the insured person dies before then. If the risk transferred by that benefit is significant, the contract is an insurance contract.

Example 56.8: No market value adjustment for death benefits

A contract permits the issuer to deduct a MVA from surrender values or maturity payments. The contract does not permit the issuer to deduct a MVA for death benefits.

The policyholder obtains an additional death benefit because no MVA is applied on death. If the risk transferred by that benefit is significant, the contract is an insurance contract.

3.7.2 Examples of transactions that are not insurance contracts

The following are examples of transactions that are not insurance contracts: *[IFRS 17.B27]*

- investment contracts that have the legal form of an insurance contract but do not transfer significant insurance risk to the issuer. For example, life insurance contracts in which the insurer bears no significant mortality or morbidity risk are not insurance contracts. Investment contracts with discretionary participation features do not meet the definition of an insurance contract; however, they are within the scope of IFRS 17 provided they are issued by an entity that also issues insurance contracts (see 11 below);

- contracts that have the legal form of insurance, but return all significant risk back to the policyholder through non-cancellable and enforceable mechanisms that adjust future payments by the policyholder as a direct result of insured losses, for example, some financial reinsurance contracts or some group contracts. Such contracts are normally financial instruments or service contracts;

- self-insurance, in other words retaining a risk that could have been covered by insurance. See 3.5.2.A above;

- contracts (such as gambling contracts) that require a payment if an unspecified uncertain future event occurs, but do not require, as a contractual precondition for payment, that the event adversely affects the policyholder. However, this does not preclude the specification of a predetermined payout to quantify the loss caused by a specified event such as a death or an accident. See 3.4.1 above;

- derivatives that expose one party to financial risk but not insurance risk, because the derivatives require that party to make payment based solely on the changes in one or more of a specified interest rate, a financial instrument price, a commodity price, a foreign exchange rate, an index of prices or rates, a credit rating or a credit index or other variable, provided that, in the case of a non-financial variable, the variable is not specific to a party to the contract;

- credit-related guarantees that require payments even if the holder has not incurred a loss on the failure of a debtor to make payments when due;

- contracts that require a payment that depends on a climatic, geological or any other physical variable not specific to a party to the contract (commonly described as weather derivatives); and

- contracts that provide for reduced payments of principal, interest or both, that depend on a climatic, geological or any other physical variable that is not specific to a party to the contract (commonly referred to as catastrophe bonds).

An entity should apply other IFRSs, such as IFRS 9 and IFRS 15, to the contracts described above. *[IFRS 17.B28]*.

The credit-related guarantees and credit insurance contracts referred to above can have various legal forms, such as that of a guarantee, some types of letters of credit, a credit default contract or an insurance contract. As discussed at 2.3.1.E above, those contracts are insurance contracts if they require the issuer to make specified payments to reimburse the holder for a loss that the holder incurs because a specified debtor fails to make payment when due to the policyholder applying the original or modified terms of a debt instrument. However, such insurance contracts are excluded from the scope of IFRS 17 unless the issuer has previously asserted explicitly that it regards the contracts as insurance contracts and has used accounting applicable to insurance contracts. *[IFRS 17.B29]*.

Credit-related guarantees and credit insurance contracts that require payment, even if the policyholder has not incurred a loss on the failure of the debtor to make payments when due, are outside the scope of IFRS 17 because they do not transfer significant insurance risk. Such contracts include those that require payment: *[IFRS 17.B30]*

- regardless of whether the counterparty holds the underlying debt instrument; or
- on a change in the credit rating or the credit index, rather than on the failure of a specified debtor to make payments when due.

The following examples, based on examples contained previously in IFRS 4, illustrate further situations where IFRS 17 is not applicable.

Example 56.9:   Investment contract linked to asset pool

Entity A issues an investment contract in which payments are contractually linked (with no discretion) to returns on a pool of assets held by the issuer (Entity A).

This contract is within the scope of IFRS 9 because the payments are based on asset returns and there is no transfer of significant insurance risk.

Example 56.10:   Guarantee fund established by law

Guarantee funds established by law exist in many jurisdictions. Typically they require insurers to contribute funds into a pool in order to pay policyholder claims in the event of insurer insolvencies. They may be funded by periodic (usually annual) levies or by levies only when an insolvency arises. The basis of the funding requirement varies although typically most are based on an insurer's premium income.

The commitment of participants to contribute to the fund is not established by contract so there is no insurance contract. Obligations to guarantee funds are within the scope of IAS 37.

Example 56.11:   Right to recover future premiums

Entity A issues an insurance contract which gives it an enforceable and non-cancellable contractual right to recover all claims paid out of future premiums, with appropriate compensation for the time value of money.

Insurance risk is insignificant because all claims can be recovered from future premiums and consequently the insurer cannot suffer a significant loss. Therefore, the contract is a financial instrument within the scope of IFRS 9.

Example 56.12: Market value adjustment without death or maturity benefits

A contract permits the issuer to deduct an MVA from surrender payments. The contract does not permit a MVA for death and maturity benefits. The amount payable on death or maturity is the amount originally invested plus interest.

The policyholder obtains an additional benefit because no MVA is applied on death or maturity. However, that benefit does not transfer insurance risk from the policyholder because it is certain that the policyholder will live or die and the amount payable on death or maturity is adjusted for the time value of money. Therefore, the contract is an investment contract because there is no significant insurance risk. This contract combines the two features discussed in Examples 56.7 and 56.8 at 3.7.1 above. When considered separately, these two features transfer insurance risk. However, when combined, they do not transfer insurance risk. Therefore, it is not appropriate to separate this contract into two insurance components. *[IFRS 17.9].*

If the amount payable on death were not adjusted in full for the time value of money, or were adjusted in some other way, the contract might transfer significant insurance risk.

4 SEPARATING COMPONENTS FROM AN INSURANCE CONTRACT

Insurance contracts may contain one or more components that would be within the scope of another IFRS if they were separate contracts. Such components may be embedded derivatives, an investment component or a component for services other than insurance contract services.

IFRS 17 requires an insurer to identify and separate components in certain circumstances. When separated, those components must be accounted for under the relevant IFRS instead of under IFRS 17. *[IFRS 17.10].* The IASB considers that accounting for such components separately using other applicable IFRSs makes them more comparable to similar contracts that are issued as separate contracts and allows users of financial statements to better compare the risks undertaken by entities in different businesses or industries. *[IFRS 17.BC99].*

Therefore, an insurer should:

- apply IFRS 9 to determine whether there is an embedded derivative to be bifurcated (i.e. be separated) and, if there is, account for that separate derivative (see 4.1 below);
- separate from a host insurance contract an investment component if, and only if, that investment component is distinct and apply IFRS 9 to account for the separated component unless it is an investment contract with discretionary participation features (see 4.2 below); *[IFRS 17.11]* and then
- separate from the host insurance contract any promise to transfer to a policyholder distinct goods or services other than insurance contract services applying paragraph 7 of IFRS 15 (see 4.3 below). *[IFRS 17.12].*

After separating the components described above (i.e. distinct non-insurance components), an entity should apply IFRS 17 to all remaining components of the host insurance contract. *[IFRS 17.13].* The recognition and measurement criteria of IFRS 17 are discussed at 6 and 7 below.

Insurance contracts (IFRS 17) 4711

This is illustrated by the following decision tree:

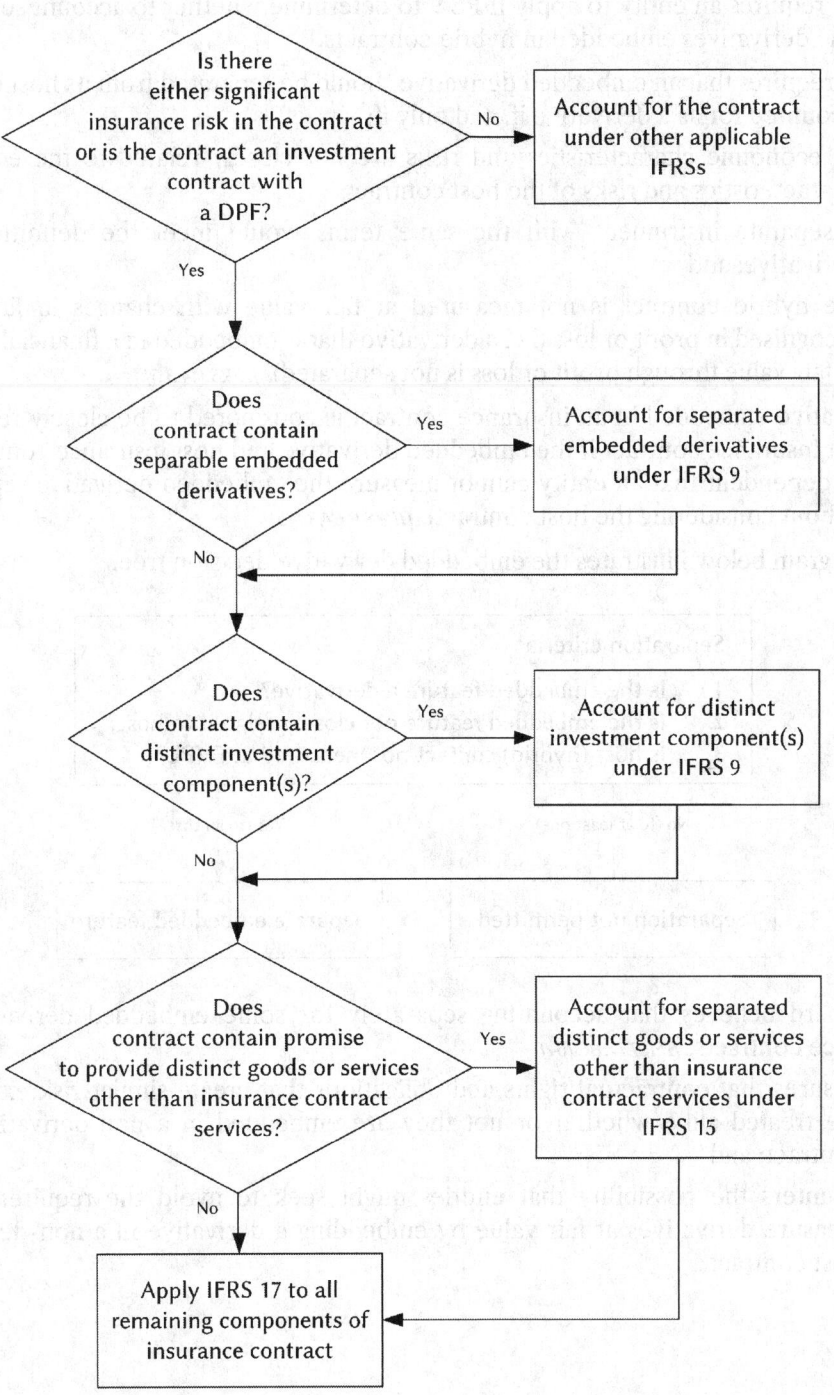

4.1 Separating embedded derivatives from an insurance contract

IFRS 17 requires an entity to apply IFRS 9 to determine whether to account separately for some derivatives embedded in hybrid contracts.

IFRS 9 requires that an embedded derivative should be separated from its host contract and accounted for as a derivative if, and only if:

- its economic characteristics and risks are not closely related to the economic characteristics and risks of the host contract;
- a separate instrument with the same terms would meet the definition of a derivative; and
- the hybrid contract is not measured at fair value with changes in fair value recognised in profit or loss (i.e. a derivative that is embedded in a financial liability at fair value through profit or loss is not separated). *[IFRS 9.4.3.3].*

A derivative embedded in an insurance contract is considered to be closely related to the host insurance contract if the embedded derivative and host insurance contract are so interdependent that an entity cannot measure the embedded derivative separately (i.e. without considering the host contract). *[IFRS 9.B4.3.8(h)].*

The diagram below illustrates the embedded derivative decision tree.

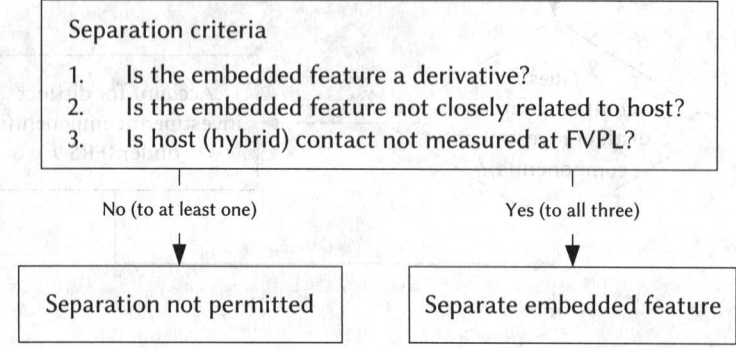

The Board believes that accounting separately for some embedded derivatives in insurance contracts: *[IFRS 17.BC104]*

- ensures that contractual rights and obligations that create similar risk exposures are treated alike whether or not they are embedded in a non-derivative host contract; and
- counters the possibility that entities might seek to avoid the requirement to measure derivatives at fair value by embedding a derivative in a non-derivative host contract.

IFRS 4 had previously required IFRS 9 or IAS 39 to be applied to derivatives embedded in a host insurance contract unless the embedded derivative was itself an insurance contract. *[IFRS 4.7]*. By applying IFRS 9 to determine whether an embedded derivative should be separated, the Board replaced this option of separating an embedded derivative that was an insurance contract with a prohibition from separating such closely related embedded derivatives from the host contract. This is because the Board concluded that when embedded derivatives are closely related to the host insurance contract, the benefits of separating those embedded derivatives fail to outweigh the costs (and, under IFRS 17 such embedded derivatives are measured using current market-consistent information). *[IFRS 17.BC105(a)]*. In practice, this change is unlikely to have a measurement impact because any separated insurance component would also be measured under IFRS 17.

IFRS 17 has also removed the exception in IFRS 4 which allowed an insurer not to separate and measure at fair value, a policyholder's option to surrender an insurance contract for a fixed amount (or for an amount based on a fixed amount and an interest rate), even if the exercise price differed from the carrying amount of the host insurance liability. *[IFRS 4.8]*. Instead, the requirements of IFRS 9 are used to determine whether an entity needs to separate a surrender option. *[IFRS 17.BC105(b)]*. However, the value of a typical surrender option and the host insurance contract are likely to be interdependent because one component cannot usually be measured without the other. Therefore, these requirements will very often result in not separating the surrender option from the host insurance contract.

A derivative is a financial instrument within the scope of IFRS 9 with all three of the following characteristics:

- its value changes in response to a change in a specified interest rate, financial instrument price, commodity price, foreign exchange rate, index of prices or rates, credit rating or credit index, or other variable, provided in the case of a non-financial variable that the variable is not specific to the underlying of the contract; and
- it requires no initial net investment or an initial net investment that would be smaller than would be required for other types of contracts that would be expected to have a similar response to changes in market factors; and
- it is settled at a future date. *[IFRS 9 Appendix A]*.

An embedded derivative is a component of a hybrid contract that also includes a non-derivative host with the effect that some of the cash flows of the combined instrument vary in a way similar to a stand-alone derivative. An embedded derivative causes some or all of the cash flows that otherwise would be required by the contract to be modified according to a specified interest rate, financial instrument price, commodity price, foreign exchange rate, index of prices or rates, credit rating or credit index, or other variable, provided in the case of a non-financial variable that the variable is not specific to a party to the contract. A derivative that is attached to a financial instrument but is contractually transferable independently of that instrument, or has a different counterparty, is not an embedded derivative, but a separate financial instrument. *[IFRS 9.4.3.1]*.

The following are examples of embedded derivatives that may be found in insurance contracts:
- benefits, such as death benefits, linked to equity prices or an equity index;
- options to take life-contingent annuities at guaranteed rates;
- guarantees of minimum interest rates in determining surrender or maturity values;
- guarantees of minimum annuity payments where the annuity payments are linked to investment returns or asset prices;
- a put option for the policyholder to surrender a contract. These can be specified in a schedule, based on the fair value of a pool of interest-bearing securities or based on an equity or commodity price index;
- an option to receive a persistency bonus (an enhancement to policyholder benefits for policies that remain in-force for a certain period);
- an industry loss warranty where the loss trigger is an industry loss as opposed to an entity specific loss;
- a catastrophe trigger where a trigger is defined as a financial variable such as a drop in a designated stock market;
- an inflation index affecting policy deductibles;
- contracts where the currency of claims settlement differs from the currency of loss; and
- contracts with fixed foreign currency rates.

The following example illustrates an embedded derivative in an insurance contract that is not required to be separated and accounted for under IFRS 9.

Example 56.13: Death or annuitisation benefit linked to equity prices or index

A contract has a death benefit linked to equity prices or an equity index and is payable only on death or when annuity payments begin and not on surrender or maturity.

The equity-index feature meets the definition of an insurance contract (unless the life-contingent payments are insignificant) because the policyholder benefits from it only when the insured event occurs and therefore the derivative and the host insurance contract are interdependent. The embedded derivative is not required to be separated and will be accounted for under IFRS 17. *[IFRS 9.B4.3.8(h)]*.

The following example illustrates an embedded derivative in an insurance contract that is required to be separated and accounted for under IFRS 9.

Example 56.14: Policyholder option to surrender contract for value based on a market index

An insurance contract gives the policyholder the option to surrender the contract for a surrender value based on an equity or commodity price or index.

The option is not closely related to the host insurance contract because the surrender value is derived from an index and is therefore not interdependent with the insurance contract. Therefore, the surrender option is required to be accounted for under IFRS 9. *[IFRS 9.B4.3.5(c)-(d)]*.

The meaning of 'closely related' is discussed more generally in Chapter 46 at 5.

A unit-linking feature (i.e. a contractual term that requires payments denominated in units of an internal or external investment fund) embedded in a host financial instrument or host insurance contract is closely related to the host instrument or host contract if the unit-denominated payments are measured at current unit values that reflect the fair values of the assets of the fund. *[IFRS 9.B4.3.8(g)]*.

IFRS 9 also considers that unit-linked investment liabilities should normally be regarded as puttable instruments that can be put back to the issuer at any time for cash equal to a proportionate share of the net asset value of an entity, i.e. they are not closely related. Nevertheless, the effect of separating an embedded derivative and accounting for each component is to measure the hybrid contract at the redemption amount that is payable at the reporting date if the unit holder had exercised its right to put the instrument back to the issuer. *[IFRS 9.B4.3.7]*. This seems somewhat to contradict the fact that the unit-linked feature is regarded as closely related (which means no separation of the feature is required) but the accounting treatment is substantially the same.

4.2 Separating investment components from an insurance contract

IFRS 4 referred to the notion of a deposit component, *[IFRS 4.10-12]*. IFRS 17 does not refer to a deposit component but, instead, introduces the new concept of an investment component.

IFRS 17 requires distinct investment components to be separated from the host insurance contract and accounted for under IFRS 9. Investment components that are not distinct are accounted for under IFRS 17. However, investment components accounted for under IFRS 17 are excluded from the insurance service result (i.e. they are not accounted for as either insurance revenue or insurance service expenses). *[IFRS 17.85]*.

4.2.1 The definition of an investment component

The definition of an investment component, as a result of the June 2020 amendments, is now 'The amounts that an insurance contract requires the entity to repay to a policyholder in all circumstances, regardless of whether an insured event occurs.' *[IFRS 17 Appendix A]*.

The definition was amended because the explanation of an insurance component in the Basis for Conclusions was not entirely captured by the original wording of the definition.

At the April 2019 meeting of the TRG, the TRG members considered that, in assessing whether a contract requires the entity to repay amounts in all circumstances, an entity considers the following factors:

- whether scenarios in which no payments are made have commercial substance; and
- if there are circumstances in which a payment could be determined to be zero, what the terms of the contract indicate about that payment of zero.[8]

The following examples illustrate how the definition applies in practice:[9]

Example 56.15: Investment component in a life cover contract

In exchange for a single premium of $1,000 paid by a 60 year-old policyholder, the life cover contract promises to pay an amount of $2,000 when the policyholder reaches 80 years old or when the policyholder dies before reaching 80 years old. The policyholder cannot terminate the contract.

The life cover contract includes an investment component because the contract requires the insurer to make a payment to the policyholder in all circumstances, i.e. whether the policyholder reaches 80 years old or dies before reaching 80 years old.

Example 56.16: Investment component in deferred annuity contract

The deferred annuity contract promises to pay a surrender amount to the policyholder if the policyholder dies or terminates the contract before reaching 60 years old or, if the policyholder reaches 60 years old, to make regular payments to the policyholder for the remainder of the policyholder's life. In addition, if the policyholder dies before reaching 80 years old, the contract requires the entity to pay an amount at least equal to the amount accumulated to the policyholder through deposits less payments already made. It is assumed that if the policyholder reaches 80 years old, the regular payments received between the ages of 60 years old and 80 years old at least equal the amount accumulated through deposits and the amount accumulated through deposits does not accrue interest after the policyholder reaches 60 years old. The policyholder cannot terminate the contract after reaching 60 years old.

The deferred annuity contract includes an investment component because the contract requires the entity to pay a fixed amount in all circumstances, either a surrender amount if the policyholder dies or terminates the contract before reaching 60 years old or an amount that is equal to the amount accumulated by the policyholder through deposits, if the policyholder dies between the ages of 60 and 80 or reaches 80 years old.

Example 56.17: Pure protection contract

In exchange for premiums, the pure protection contract promises to pay a fixed amount of $1,000 to the policyholder on the death of the policyholder, if the policyholder dies within a 5-year coverage period or a variable surrender amount to the policyholder if the policyholder opts to surrender the contract before the end of Year 4. No amount is paid to the policyholder if the policyholder keeps the contract to Year 5 and survives.

The pure protection contract does not contain an investment component because there are circumstances with commercial substance in which no amount is paid.

A contract which does not require a payment to a policyholder if it continues to the end of the coverage period without a claim being made does not contain an investment component. There may be a payment upon surrender but this payment is regardless of whether the insured event occurs. However, because there is no payment on maturity there is a scenario where no payment to the policyholder is made (provided this scenario has commercial substance). Therefore, a pure protection contract does not contain an investment component because there are circumstances with commercial substance in which no amount is paid. The same would apply to a contract where there is no payment upon death before maturity (i.e. a pure endowment contract).[10]

4.2.2 Separable investment components

Many insurance contracts have an implicit or explicit investment component that would, if it were a separable financial instrument, be within the scope of IFRS 9. However, the Board decided that it would be difficult to routinely separate such investment components from insurance contracts. *[IFRS 17.BC108]*.

Accordingly, IFRS 17 requires an entity to separate from a host insurance contract an investment component if, and only if, that investment component is distinct from the host insurance contract. *[IFRS 17.11(b)]*. The Board concluded that, in all cases, entities would be able to measure the stand-alone value for a separated investment component by applying IFRS 9. *[IFRS 17.BC109]*.

The words 'if, and only if' mean that voluntary separation of investment components which are not distinct is prohibited. This is a change from IFRS 4, which permitted voluntary unbundling of deposit components if the deposit component could be measured separately. The Board considered whether to permit an entity to separate a non-insurance component when not required to do so by IFRS 17; for example, some investment components with interrelated cash flows, such as policy loans. Such components may have been separated when applying previous accounting practices. However, the Board concluded that it would not be possible to separate in a non-arbitrary way a component that is not distinct from the insurance contract nor would such a result be desirable. The Board also noted that when separation ignores interdependencies between insurance and non-insurance components, the sum of the values of the components may not always equal the value of the contract as a whole, even on initial recognition. That would reduce the comparability of the financial statements across entities. *[IFRS 17.BC114].*

An investment component is distinct if, and only if, both the following conditions are met: *[IFRS 17.B31]*

- the investment component and the insurance component are not highly interrelated; and
- a contract with equivalent terms is sold, or could be sold, separately in the same market or the same jurisdiction, either by entities that issue insurance contracts or by other parties. The entity should take into account all information reasonably available in making this determination. The entity is not required to undertake an exhaustive search to identify whether an investment component is sold separately.

An investment component and an insurance component are highly interrelated if, and only if: *[IFRS 17.B32]*

- the entity is unable to measure one component without considering the other. Thus, if the value of one component varies according to the value of the other, an entity should apply IFRS 17 to account for the combined investment and insurance component; or
- the policyholder is unable to benefit from one component unless the other is also present. Thus, if the lapse or maturity of one component in a contract causes the lapse or maturity of the other, the entity should apply IFRS 17 to account for the combined investment component and insurance component.

The requirements above are illustrated by the following examples.

Example 56.18: Investment component in a life cover contract

Assume the same fact pattern as Example 56.15 above.

The value of the insurance component varies according to the value of the investment component because the insured event in this example is the timing of death. Although the payment of $2,000 is certain, it is uncertain when the policyholder will die and, therefore whether the entity will pay the amount of $2,000 before the policyholder reaches 80 years old and how soon that may be after the inception of the contract. Therefore, the entity cannot measure the insurance component without considering the investment component and, as a result, the investment component is not distinct and the entity cannot separate it from the insurance contract.

The IASB staff further observed that the policyholder cannot benefit from one component when the other component is not present because both components lapse together.

Example 56.19: Investment component in deferred annuity contract

Assume the same fact pattern as in Example 56.16 above.

In this contract the investment component is (i) a surrender amount if the policyholder dies or terminates the contract before reaching 60 years old; or (ii) an amount that is equal to the amount accumulated by the policyholder through deposits, if the policyholder reaches 60 years old. The insurance component is possible payments exceeding the amount accumulated by the policyholder through deposits.

If the policyholder dies after reaching 60 years old and before reaching 80 years old, the entity makes a payment reflecting the amount accumulated by the policyholder through deposits. The timing of that payment depends on the death of the policyholder. Therefore, the entity cannot measure the investment contract without considering the insurance component. As a result, the investment component is not distinct and the entity cannot separate it from the insurance contract.

The IASB staff also observed that the death of the policyholder causes the maturity of both the insurance component in the contract and the investment component in the contract.

The following example is taken from Example 4 accompanying IFRS 17: *[IFRS 17.IE43-51]*

Example 56.20: Separating components from a life insurance contract with an account balance

An entity issues a whole life insurance contract with an account balance. The contract does not have a fixed term. The entity receives a premium of $1,000 when the contract is issued. The account balance is increased annually by voluntary amounts paid by the policyholder, increased or decreased by amounts calculated using the returns from specified assets and decreased by fees charged by the entity (e.g. asset management fees).

The contract promises to pay the following:

- a death benefit of $5,000 plus the amount of the account balance if the insured person dies during the coverage period; and
- the account balance, if the contract is cancelled (i.e. there are no surrender charges).

The entity has a claims processing department to process the claims received and an asset management department to manage investments. An investment product that has equivalent terms to the account balance, but without the insurance coverage, is sold by another financial institution.

Analysis

The contract contains an investment component because an amount is paid to the policyholder in all circumstances (i.e. either the account balance if the contract is cancelled or the death benefit plus the account balance if the insured person dies during the coverage period).

The existence of an investment product with equivalent terms indicates that the components may be distinct. However, if the right to provide death benefits provided by the insurance coverage either lapses or matures at the same time as the account balance, the insurance and investment components are highly interrelated and are therefore not distinct. Consequently, the account balance would not be separated from the insurance contract and would be accounted for by applying IFRS 17.

Claims processing activities are part of the activities the entity must undertake to fulfil the contract and the entity does not transfer a good or service to the policyholder because the entity performs those activities. Thus, the entity would not separate the claims processing component from the insurance contract.

Asset management activities, similar to claims processing activities, are part of the activities the entity must undertake to fulfil the contract and the entity does not transfer a good or service other than insurance contract services to the policyholder because the entity performs those activities. Thus, the entity would not separate the asset management component from the insurance contract.

At the April 2019 meeting of the TRG, the TRG members observed that, in their view, the hurdle for separation of investment components from an (host) insurance contract is high.[11]

The requirements in IFRS 17 for separating investment components do not specifically address the issue of contracts artificially separated through the use of side letters, the separate components of which should be considered together. However, IFRS 17 does state that it may be necessary to treat a set or series of contracts as a whole in order to report the substance of such contracts. For example, if the rights or obligations in one contract do nothing other than entirely negate the rights or obligations of another contract entered into at the same time with the same counterparty, the combined effect is that no rights or obligations exist (see 3.5.2 above). *[IFRS 17.9]*.

4.2.3 Measurement of the non-distinct investment component

Although an entity applies IFRS 17 to account for both the combined investment and insurance components of an insurance contract if those components are highly interrelated, insurance revenue and insurance service expenses presented in profit or loss must exclude any non-separated investment component. *[IFRS 17.85, BC108(b)].*

IFRS 17 does not explain how to determine the amount of non-distinct investment components that an entity is required to exclude from insurance revenue and insurance service expense.

This issue was discussed at the April 2019 meeting of the TRG. The IASB staff observed that there could be circumstances in which the investment component is not explicitly identified by the contractual terms or where the amount of the investment component varies over time. The staff observed that, in these circumstances an approach for determining the investment component that is based on a present value basis as at the time of making this determination would be consistent with the requirements of paragraph B21 of IFRS 17, which refers to the present value of significant additional amounts that result in a contract being defined as an insurance contract (see 3.5.3 above). The staff consider that if the amounts that would be payable if no insurance event had occurred are determined on a present value basis, it would be consistent to determine the investment component on a present value basis too.

The TRG members observed that:

- In some cases, it may be reasonable to determine the amount of the investment component that an entity is required to exclude from insurance revenue and insurance service expenses using the explicit amount identified by contractual terms. For example, the amounts of a non-distinct investment component can be identified as an explicit surrender amount or explicit guaranteed payments.

- In other cases, it may be appropriate to determine the amount of the investment component that an entity is required to exclude from insurance revenue and insurance service expenses on a present value basis at the time of making the determination. For example, in an uncancellable contract that requires an entity to pay the policyholder an amount when the policyholder dies or reaches the age of 80 (see Examples 56.15 and 56.18 above), using the present value of the payments the contract requires the entity to make at the age of 80 would result in a reasonable outcome because death in the early periods of coverage would reflect a higher insurance claim than in later periods.

The TRG members also observed that if an entity uses an explicit surrender amount for determining the amounts to be excluded from insurance revenue and insurance service expense, it should not be required to determine whether a part of that amount reflects a premium refund. The TRG members noted that both an investment component and a premium refund will be excluded from revenue and expenses recognised from a contract in these circumstances.[12] However, there is no requirement to separately disclose any premium refund from the non-distinct investment component (see 16.1.1 below).

It is observed in the Basis for Conclusions that non-distinct investment components need be identified only at the time revenue and incurred claims are recognised, so as to exclude the investment components so identified. *[IFRS 17.BC34].* However, since the contractual service margin in the general model is determined by considering both insurance coverage and investment return service, if any (see 8.7.2 below), an entity might also need to determine whether an insurance contract includes a non-distinct investment component before an incurred claim is recognised.

Despite the fact that insurance revenue and insurance service expenses excludes any non-distinct investment component, the contractual service margin for a group of insurance contracts without direct participation features is adjusted for differences between any investment component expected to become payable in the period (adjusted for the effect of the time value of money and financial risk) and the actual investment component that becomes payable in the period (see 8.6.3 below). *[IFRS 17.B96]*.

4.3 Separating a promise to provide distinct goods or services other than insurance contract services

After applying IFRS 9 to embedded derivatives and separating a distinct investment component from a host insurance contract, an entity is required to separate from the host insurance contract any promise to transfer to a policyholder distinct goods or services other than insurance contract services (i.e. non-insurance services) by applying the requirements of IFRS 15 for a contract that is partially within the scope of IFRS 15 and partially within the scope of other standards. *[IFRS 17.12]*. See Chapter 27 at 3.5.

This means that, on initial recognition, an entity should: *[IFRS 17.12]*

- apply IFRS 15 to attribute the cash inflows between the insurance component and any promises to provide distinct goods or services other than insurance contract services; and

- attribute the cash outflows between the insurance component and any promised goods or services other than insurance contract services accounted for applying IFRS 15 so that:

  - cash outflows that relate directly to each component are attributed to that component; and

  - any remaining cash outflows are attributed on a systematic and rational basis, reflecting the cash outflows the entity would expect to arise if that component were a separate contract.

The allocation of the cash inflows between the host insurance contract and the distinct good or service other than an insurance contract service should be based on the stand-alone selling price of the components. The Board believes that in most cases entities would be able to determine an observable stand-alone selling price for the bundled goods or services if those components meet the separation criteria. *[IFRS 17.BC111]*. If the stand-alone selling price is not directly observable, an entity would need to estimate the stand-alone selling price of each component to allocate the transaction price. This stand-alone selling price might not be directly observable if the entity does not sell the insurance and the goods or components separately, or if the consideration charged for the two components together differs from the stand-alone selling prices for each component. In this case, applying IFRS 15 results in any discounts and cross-subsidies being allocated to components proportionately or on the basis of observable evidence. *[IFRS 17.BC112]*. IFRS 17 requires that cash outflows should be allocated to their related component, and that cash outflows not clearly related to one of the components should be systematically and rationally allocated between components. Insurance acquisition cash flows and some fulfilment cash flows relating to overhead costs do not clearly relate to one of the components. A systematic and rational allocation of such cash flows is consistent with the requirements in IFRS 17 for allocating acquisition and fulfilment cash flows that cover more than one group of insurance contracts to the individual groups of contracts, and is also consistent with the requirements in other IFRSs for allocating the costs of production – the requirements in IFRS 15 and IAS 2 – *Inventories*, for example. *[IFRS 17.BC113].*

For the purpose of separation an entity should not consider activities that an entity must undertake to fulfil a contract unless the entity transfers a good or service other than insurance contract services to the policyholder as those activities occur. For example, an entity may need to perform various administrative tasks to set up a contract. The performance of those tasks does not transfer a service to the policyholder as the tasks are performed. *[IFRS 17.B33].*

A good or service other than an insurance contract service promised to a policyholder is distinct if the policyholder can benefit from the good or service either on its own or together with other resources readily available to the policyholder. Readily available resources are goods or services that are sold separately (by the entity or by another entity), or resources that the policyholder has already got (from the entity or from other transactions or events). *[IFRS 17.B34].*

A good or service other than an insurance contract service that is promised to the policyholder is not distinct if: *[IFRS 17.B35]*

- the cash flows and the risks associated with the good or service are highly interrelated with the cash flows and risks associated with the insurance components in the contract; and
- the entity provides a significant service in integrating the good or service with the insurance components.

The Board considered, but rejected, the possibility to separate non-insurance components that are not distinct because it would not be possible to separate in a non-arbitrary way a component that is not distinct from the insurance contract nor would such a result be desirable. *[IFRS 17.BC114].*

The following example, based on Example 5 accompanying IFRS 17, illustrates the requirements for separating non-insurance components from insurance contracts. *[IFRS 17.IE51-55].*

Example 56.21: Separating components from a stop-loss contract with claims processing services

An entity issues a stop-loss contract to a policyholder (which is an employer). The contract provides health coverage for the policyholder's employees and has the following features:

- insurance coverage of 100% for the aggregate claims from employees exceeding €25 million (the 'stop loss' threshold). The employer will self-insure claims from employees up to €25 million; and
- claims processing services for employees' claims during the next year, regardless of whether the claims have passed the stop-loss threshold of €25 million. The entity is responsible for processing the health insurance claims of employees on behalf of the employer.

Analysis

The entity considers whether to separate the claims processing services from the insurance contract. The entity notes that similar services to process claims on behalf of customers are sold on the market.

The criteria for identifying distinct non-insurance services are met in this example because:

- claims processing services, similar to the services to process the employers' claims on behalf of the employer, are sold as a standalone service without any insurance coverage;
- the claims processing services benefit the policyholder independently of the insurance coverage. Had the entity not agreed to provide those services, the policyholder would have to process its employees' medical claims itself or engage other service providers to do this; and
- the cash flows associated with the claims processing services are not highly interrelated with the cash flows associated with the insurance coverage, and the entity does not provide a significant service of integrating the claims processing services with the insurance components.

Accordingly, the entity separates the claims processing services from the insurance contract and accounts for them applying IFRS 15.

5 LEVEL OF AGGREGATION

IFRS 17 defines the level of aggregation to be used for measuring insurance contracts and their related profitability. This is a key issue in identifying onerous contracts and in determining the recognition of profit or loss and presentation in the financial statements.

The starting point for aggregation is a portfolio of insurance contracts. A portfolio comprises contracts that are subject to similar risks and are managed together. *[IFRS 17.14]*.

Once an entity has identified its portfolios of insurance contracts it should divide, on initial recognition, each portfolio, at a minimum, into the following three 'buckets' referred to as groups: *[IFRS 17.16]*

- those contracts that are onerous at initial recognition (except for those contracts to which an entity applies the premium allocation approach – see 5.3 below);
- those contracts that have no significant possibility of becoming onerous subsequently; and
- all remaining contracts in the portfolio.

This can be illustrated as follows:

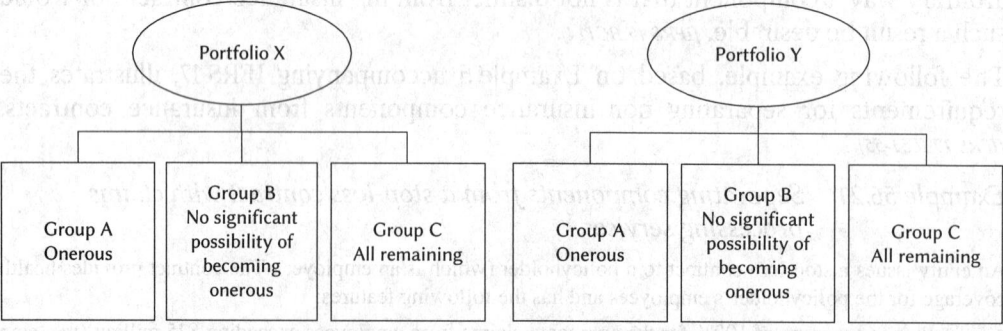

An entity is permitted, but not required, to divide the portfolio into more groups based on profitability if the entity's internal reporting provides information of profitability at a more detailed level. See 5.2.1 below. *[IFRS 17.21]*.

Groups of contracts are established at initial recognition and are not reassessed. *[IFRS 17.24].*

An entity is prohibited from grouping contracts issued more than one year apart (except in certain circumstances when applying IFRS 17 for the first time – see 17.4 and 17.5 below). See 5.2.2 below. This means that separate groups for each portfolio are created at least annually in the 'buckets' identified above.

Current practices applied under IFRS 4 for recognising losses from onerous contracts are likely to be based on wider groupings of contracts than those required by IFRS 17. For example, liability adequacy tests are often applied at product or legal entity level. We believe the level of aggregation requirements under IFRS 17 will lead to a more granular grouping and, as such, the requirements under IFRS 17 are likely to result in earlier identification of losses on onerous contracts compared to current reporting under IFRS 4.

5.1 Identifying portfolios

A portfolio comprises contracts that are subject to similar risks and managed together. Contracts have similar risks if the entity expects their cash flows will respond similarly in amount and timing to changes in key assumptions. Contracts within a product line would be expected to have similar risks and, thus, would be in the same portfolio if they are managed together. Contracts in different product lines (for example, single premium fixed annuities as opposed to regular-term life assurance) would not be expected to have similar risks and would be in different portfolios. *[IFRS 17.14].*

Deciding which contracts have 'similar risks' will be a matter of judgement. Many insurance products provide a basic level of insurance cover with optional 'add-ons' (or 'riders') at the discretion of the policyholder. For example, a home contents insurance policy may provide legal costs protection or additional accidental damage cover at the policyholder's discretion in return for additional premiums. The question therefore arises as to the point at which policies of a similar basic type have been tailored to the level at which the risks have become dissimilar. Riders that are issued and priced separately from the host insurance contract may need to be accounted for as separate contracts (see 5.1.1 below).

For presentation purposes only, insurance contracts are aggregated in the statement of financial position at portfolio level (see 14 below).

5.1.1 Separation of insurance components within an insurance contract

Insurers may combine different types of products or coverages that have different risks into one insurance contract. Examples include a contract that includes both life insurance and motor insurance and a contract that includes both pet insurance and home insurance. In some situations, separation of a single insurance contract into separate risk components may be required for regulatory reporting purposes. Although IFRS 17 provides guidance on separating non-insurance components within an insurance contract (see 4 above) the standard is silent as to whether an insurance contract can be separated into different insurance components (i.e. allocated to different portfolios for aggregation purposes) and, if so, the basis for such a separation.[13]

This issue was discussed at the February 2018 meeting of the TRG. The TRG members discussed the analysis of an IASB staff paper and observed that:

- the lowest unit of account that is used in IFRS 17 is the contract that includes all insurance components;
- entities would usually design contracts in a way that reflects their substance. Therefore, a contract with the legal form of a single contract would generally be considered a single contract in substance. However:
  - there might be circumstances where the legal form of a single contract would not reflect the substance of its contractual rights and obligations; and
  - overriding the contract unit of account presumption by separating insurance components of a single insurance contract involves significant judgement and careful consideration of all relevant facts and circumstances. It is not an accounting policy choice;
- combining different types of products or coverages that have different risks into one legal insurance contract is not, in itself, sufficient to conclude that the legal form of the contract does not reflect the substance of its contractual rights and obligations. Similarly, the availability of information to separate cash flows for different risks is not, in itself, sufficient to conclude that the contract does not reflect the substance of its contractual rights and obligations;
- the fact that a reinsurance contract held provides cover for underlying contracts that are included in different groups is not, in itself, sufficient to conclude that accounting for the reinsurance contract held as a single contract does not reflect the substance of its contractual rights and obligations.

The TRG members also observed that considerations that might be relevant in the assessment of whether the legal form of a single contract reflects the substance of its contractual rights and contractual obligations include:

- interdependency between the different risks covered;
- whether components lapse together; and
- whether components can be priced and sold separately.

The TRG members considered that an example of when it may be appropriate to override the presumption that a single legal contract is the lowest unit of account is when more than one type of insurance cover is included in one legal contract solely for the administrative convenience of the policyholder and the price is simply the aggregate of the standalone prices for the different insurance covers provided.[14]

5.1.2 Combining insurance contracts

The inverse situation of separating components of insurance contracts (see 5.1.1 above) is consideration as to when insurance contracts might need to be combined.

This issue was discussed at the May 2018 meeting of the TRG. The TRG members discussed the analysis of an IASB staff paper and observed that:

- a contract with the legal form of a single contract would generally be considered on its own to be a single contract in substance. However, there may be circumstances where a set or series of insurance contracts with the same or a related counterparty reflect a single contract in substance;

- the fact that a set or series of insurance contracts with the same counterparty are entered into at the same time is not, in itself, sufficient to conclude that they achieve, or are designed to achieve, an overall commercial effect. Determining whether it is necessary to treat a set or series of insurance contracts as a single contract involves significant judgement and careful consideration of all relevant facts and circumstances. No single factor is determinative in applying this assessment;
- the following considerations might be relevant in assessing whether a set or series of insurance contracts achieve, or are designed to achieve, an overall commercial effect:
  - the rights and obligations are different when looked at together compared to when looked at individually. For example, if the rights and obligations of one contract negate the rights and obligations of another contract;
  - the entity is unable to measure one contract without considering the other. This may be the case where there is interdependency between the different risks covered in each contract and the contracts lapse together. When cash flows are interdependent, separating them can be arbitrary;
  - the existence of a discount, in itself, does not mean that a set or series of contracts achieve an overall commercial effect.[15]

The TRG members also observed that the principles for combining insurance contracts in paragraph 9 of IFRS 17 are consistent with the principles for separating insurance components from a single contract, as discussed at the February 2018 meeting of the TRG (see 5.1.1 above).

5.2 Groups of insurance contracts

A group of insurance contracts is the main unit of account for determining measurement. Measurement of insurance contracts occurs at the group level within each portfolio (see 7 below) and each portfolio, to the extent relevant, will consist usually of a minimum of three separate types of groups.

An entity will typically enter into transactions for individual contracts, not groups, and therefore IFRS 17 includes requirements that specify how to recognise groups that include contracts issued in more than one reporting period (see 6 below) and how to derecognise contracts from within a group (see 12.3 below). *[IFRS 17.BC139]*.

The Board concluded that groups should be established on the basis of profitability in order to avoid offsetting of profitable and unprofitable contracts because information about onerous contracts provided useful information about an entity's pricing decisions. *[IFRS 17.BC119]*.

Once groups are established at initial recognition an entity should not reassess the composition of the groups subsequently. Additional contracts should be added to the group after initial recognition of the group following the criteria discussed at 6 below. *[IFRS 17.24]*. A group of contracts should comprise a single contract if that is the result of applying the requirements. *[IFRS 17.23]*.

An entity need not determine the grouping of each contract individually. If an entity has reasonable and supportable information to conclude that all contracts in a set of contracts will be in the same group, it may perform the classification based on a measurement of this set of contracts ('top-down'). If the entity does not have such reasonable and supportable information, it must determine the group to which contracts belong by evaluating individual contracts ('bottom-up'). *[IFRS 17.17]*.

5.2.1 Identifying groups based on profitability

Dividing a portfolio into the three minimum groups on inception based on an assessment of profitability will require judgement, using quantitative factors, qualitative factors or a combination of such factors. For example, identifying (sets of) contracts that can be grouped together could require some form of expected probability-weighted basis of assessment as insurance contracts are measured on this basis (see 8 below). Alternatively, it may be possible to do this assessment based on the characteristics of the types of policyholders that are more or less prone to make claims than other types of policyholders (e.g. based on age, gender, geographical location or occupation). This assessment is therefore likely to represent a significant effort for insurers and is likely to be different to any form of aggregation used previously under IFRS 4 when many entities will not have performed aggregation at a level lower than portfolio.

For contracts issued to which an entity does not apply the premium allocation approach, an entity should assess whether contracts that are not onerous at initial recognition or have no significant possibility of becoming onerous: *[IFRS 17.19]*

- based on the likelihood of changes in assumptions which, if they occurred, would result in the contract becoming onerous; and

- using information about estimates prepared by the entity's internal reporting. Hence, in assessing whether contracts that are not onerous at initial recognition have no significant possibility of becoming onerous:

  - an entity should not disregard information provided by its internal reporting about the effect of changes in assumptions on different contracts on the possibility of their becoming onerous; but

  - an entity is not required to gather additional information beyond that provided by the entity's internal reporting about the effect of changes in assumptions on different contracts.

The objective of the requirement to identify contracts that are onerous at initial recognition is to identify contracts that are onerous measured as individual contracts. An entity typically issues individual contracts and it is the characteristics of the individual contracts that determine how they should be grouped. However, the Board concluded this does not mean that the contracts must be measured individually. If an entity can determine, using reasonable and supportable information, that a set of contracts will all be in the same group, the entity can measure that set to determine whether the contracts are onerous or not, because there will be no offsetting effects in the measurement of the set. The same principle applies to the identification of contracts that are not onerous at initial recognition and that have no significant possibility of becoming onerous subsequently – the objective is to identify such contracts at an individual contract level, but this objective can be achieved by assessing a set of contracts if the entity can conclude using reasonable and supportable information that the contracts in the set will all be in the same group. *[IFRS 17.BC129]*.

Insurance contracts (IFRS 17)

In a paper submitted to the TRG in May 2018, the IASB staff observed that the term 'no significant possibility' (of becoming onerous) should be interpreted in the context of the objective of the requirement. The objective is to identify contracts with no significant possibility of becoming onerous at initial recognition in order to group such contracts separately from contracts that are onerous at initial recognition and any remaining contracts in the portfolio that are not onerous at initial recognition. 'No significant possibility of becoming onerous' is different from 'significant insurance risk' and the concept of significant insurance risk should not be used by analogy.[16]

An entity is permitted, but not required, to subdivide the groups into further groups. For example, an entity may choose to divide portfolios into: [IFRS 17.21]

- more groups that are not onerous at initial recognition if the entity's internal reporting provides information that distinguishes:
  - different levels of profitability; or
  - or different possibilities of contracts becoming onerous after initial recognition; and
- more than one group of contracts that are onerous at initial recognition if the entity's internal reporting information at a more detailed level about the extent to which the contracts are onerous.

This can be illustrated as follows:

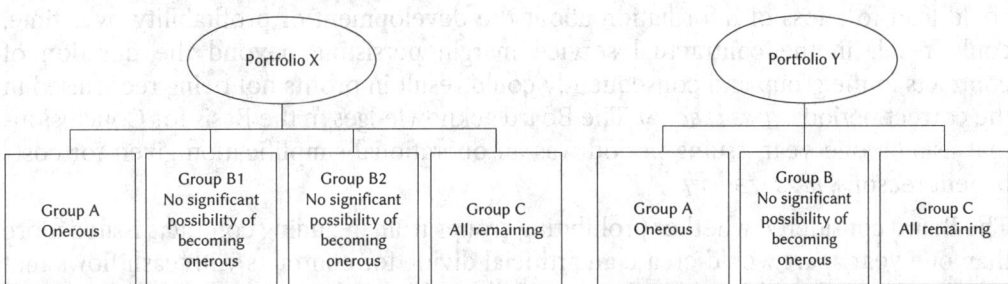

If contracts within a portfolio would fall into different groups *only* because law or regulation specifically constrains the entity's practical ability to set a different price or level of benefits for policyholders with different characteristics, the entity may include these contracts in the same group. [IFRS 17.20]. This expedient has been provided because the Board concluded that it would not provide useful information to group separately contracts that an entity is required by law or regulation to group together for determining the pricing or level of benefits. In the Board's opinion, all market participants will be constrained in the same way, particularly if such entities are unable to provide insurance coverage solely on the basis of differences in that characteristic. [IFRS 17.BC132]. This can be illustrated by the following example.

Example 56.22: Identifying groups when profitability constrained by law

An insurer is not permitted by law from pricing car insurance based on gender. Assume that the premium/risk relationship for motor contracts differs materially depending on gender. Without the relief provided by paragraph 20 of IFRS 17, the insurer would be required to split the motor contracts into separate groups based on gender as profitability varies by gender. However, paragraph 20 of IFRS 17 allows the insurer to combine them in one group as the law constrains the entity's ability from setting a different price based on gender and hence equalising profitability

This expedient should not be applied by analogy to other items. *[IFRS 17.20]*. For example, an entity might set the price for contracts without considering differences in a specific characteristic because it believes using that characteristic in pricing may result in a law or regulation prohibiting its use in the future or because doing so is likely to fulfil a public policy objective. These practices, sometimes referred to as 'self-regulatory practices', do not qualify for grouping exception caused by regulatory constraints. *[IFRS 17.BC133]*.

Each group (or sub-group) of insurance contracts is measured separately (whether under the general model discussed at 8 below, the premium allocation approach discussed at 9 below, reinsurance contracts held discussed at 10 below or the variable fee approach discussed at 11.2 below).

5.2.2 'Annual cohorts'

An entity is prohibited from grouping contracts *issued* (emphasis added) more than one year apart (except in certain circumstances when grouping insurance contracts on transition using either the modified retrospective approach or the fair value approach – see 17.4 and 17.5 below, respectively). To achieve this, the entity should, if necessary, further divide the groups described at 5.2.1 above. *[IFRS 17.22]*.

The prohibition on grouping together contracts issued more than one year apart is one of the more contentious requirements of IFRS 17. It was included because the Board was concerned that, without it, entities could have perpetually open portfolios and this could lead to a loss of information about the development of profitability over time, could result in the contractual service margin persisting beyond the duration of contracts in the group and consequently could result in profits not being recognised in the correct periods. *[IFRS 17.BC136]*. The Board acknowledges in the Basis for Conclusions that using a one-year issuing period was an operational simplification given for cost-benefit reasons. *[IFRS 17.BC137]*.

The Board considered whether prohibiting groups from including contracts issued more than one year apart would create an artificial divide for contracts with cash flows that affect or are affected by cash flows to policyholders of contracts in another group (sometimes referred to as 'mutualisation'). Some stakeholders asserted that such a division would distort the reported result of those contracts and would be operationally burdensome. However, the Board concluded that applying the requirements of IFRS 17 to determine the fulfilment cash flows for groups of such contracts provides an appropriate depiction of the results of such contracts. The Board acknowledged that, for contracts that fully share risks, the groups together will give the same results as a single combined risk-sharing portfolio, and therefore considered whether IFRS 17 should give an exception to the requirement to restrict groups to include only contracts issued within one year. However, the Board concluded that setting the boundary for such an exception would add complexity to IFRS 17 and create the risk that the boundary would not be robust or appropriate in all circumstances. Hence, IFRS 17 does not include such an exception. Nonetheless, the Board noted that the requirements specify the amounts to be reported, not the methodology to be used to arrive at those amounts. Therefore, it may not be necessary for an entity to restrict groups in this way to achieve the same accounting outcome in some circumstances. *[IFRS 17.BC138]*.

One way to divide the groups is to use an annual period that coincides with an entity's financial reporting period (e.g. contracts issued between 1 January and 31 December comprise a group for an entity with an annual reporting period ending 31 December). This is illustrated below. However, IFRS 17 does not require any particular approach and entities are also not required to use a twelve-month period when grouping insurance contracts. In addition, an entity that produces interim financial statements is not required to restrict the grouping of contracts issued to those contracts issued in that interim period.

	Portfolio A	Portfolio B	...
2021 / 2022 / 2023	No significant possibility of becoming onerous	No significant possibility of becoming onerous	No significant possibility of becoming onerous
	Other profitable	Other profitable	Other profitable
	Onerous at inception	Onerous at inception	Onerous at inception

There is no requirement in IFRS 17 that an entity must use the same issue period for each group.

In its deliberations on the June 2020 amendments to IFRS 17, the IASB considered but rejected a suggestion to amend the annual cohort requirement to base it on the date contracts are 'recognised', instead of the date they are 'issued'. In doing so, the Board confirmed that it intended annual cohorts to be determined based on the date of issue of the contract and not the date of initial recognition. This is because the objective of the annual cohort requirement is to facilitate timely recognition of profits, losses and trends in profitability. The profitability of a contract is initially set when the contract is issued, based on facts and circumstances at that date, for example interest rates, underwriting expectations and pricing. Hence, the Board concluded that determining annual cohorts based on the date that contracts are issued is necessary to provide useful information about trends in profitability. *[IFRS 17.BC139T]*.

This means, for example, that a profitable contract issued on 1 January 2022 which has a coverage period beginning 1 January 2022 will be in the same annual cohort (i.e. group) as a profitable contract issued on 1 January 2022 which has a coverage period beginning on 1 January 2025 (assuming both contracts are part of the same portfolio). However, a profitable contract issued on 1 January 2023 (within the same portfolio) with a coverage period beginning 1 January 2023 will be in a different group to the other contracts as it was issued more than one year apart from the issue date of the other two contracts. As a result, if an entity issues profitable contracts for coverage that does not start for several years and premiums are not due until the coverage starts, the date of initial recognition will be several years after the date of issue.

The IASB staff acknowledge that the use of the term 'issued' has consequences for the practical relief available for determining the discount rate at the date of initial recognition of the group, since the weighted average discount rates used only cover the period that the contracts were issued which cannot exceed one year (see 8.3 below). The IASB staff observed that these effects are a consequence of the unit of account being the group of insurance contracts rather than the individual contract, and an entity could choose to further divide the annual cohort and thereby avoid these effects.[17]

To measure a group of contracts, an entity may estimate the fulfilment cash flows (see 8.2 below) at a higher level of aggregation than the group or portfolio provided the entity is able to include the appropriate fulfilment cash flows in the measurement of the group by allocating such estimates to groups of contracts. *[IFRS 17.24]*.

5.2.2.A   Contracts with intergenerational sharing of risks

Some stakeholders have expressed the view that the level of aggregation requirements artificially segregate portfolios and will not properly depict business performance, particularly when applying the annual cohort requirement to insurance contracts with risk sharing between different generations of policyholders. As a result, the IASB reconsidered the IFRS 17 aggregation requirements during its deliberations on the June 2020 amendments to IFRS 17 but decided that the requirements should be unchanged.

In the view of the Board, intergenerational sharing of risks between policyholders is reflected in the fulfilment cash flows and therefore, also reflected in the contractual service margin of each generation of mutualised contracts as discussed at 11 below. However, each generation of contracts may be more or less profitable for an entity than other generations. Even if the policyholders across all annual cohorts share equally in the returns, the amount of the entity's share in those returns created by each generation may differ, reflecting the contractual terms of each annual cohort and the economic conditions during the coverage period of each annual cohort. For example, an entity's share of 20 per cent of the returns of underlying items is a higher amount for annual cohorts for which the coverage period includes periods in which the returns are 5 per cent than it is for annual cohorts for which the coverage period includes only periods in which the fair value returns are 1 per cent. Accordingly, removing the requirement for annual cohorts for those groups of contracts with intergenerational sharing of risks between policyholders would average higher or lower profits across generations, resulting in a loss of information about changes in profitability over time. *[IFRS 17.BC139J]*.

It is observed in the Basis for Conclusions that two aspects of applying the annual cohort requirement to some contracts with intergenerational sharing of risks between policyholders that could increase the costs of applying the requirement and reduce the benefits of the resulting information were identified. These were: *[IFRS 17.BC139K]*

- distinguishing between the effect of sharing of risks and the effect of discretion; and
- allocating changes in the amount of the entity's share of the fair value of underlying items across annual cohorts that share in the same pool of underlying items.

The aspect of the annual cohort requirement in respect of the first bullet point above relates to circumstances in which an entity has discretion over the portion of the fair value returns on underlying items that is paid to policyholders and the portion that is retained by the entity. For example, an entity may be required under the terms of the insurance contracts to pay policyholders a minimum of 90 per cent of the total fair value returns on a specified pool of underlying items with discretion to pay more to policyholders. The Board acknowledged that an entity that has such discretion is required to apply additional judgement to allocate changes in fulfilment cash flows between groups in a way that appropriately reflects the effect of sharing of risks and the effect of the discretion. However, an entity would be required to make that judgement to measure new contracts recognised in the period even if the entity was not required to apply the annual cohort requirement. *[IFRS 17.BC139L].*

The concern set out in the second bullet point above relates to insurance contracts with direct participation features. For those contracts an entity adjusts the contractual service margin for changes in the amount of the entity's share of the fair value of underlying items. IFRS 17 does not include requirements on how to allocate those changes across annual cohorts that share in the same pool of underlying items. The Board observed that an entity needs to exercise judgement to identify an allocation approach that provides useful information about the participation of each annual cohort in the underlying items and to avoid allocation approaches that do not provide useful information. *[IFRS 17.BC139M].*

In the Board's view, the information that results from the judgements an entity makes in determining the allocation approaches discussed above will provide useful insights about how management expects businesses to develop and could assist users of financial statements to hold management to account based on those expectations. *[IFRS 17.BC139N].*

The Board also considered that the benefits of the information provided by the annual cohort requirement are particularly high for some specific insurance contracts with intergenerational sharing of risks. Those specific contracts: *[IFRS 17.BC139O]*

- include features such as financial guarantees on the returns from underlying items and/or other cash flows that do not vary with returns on underlying items (for example, insurance claims); and
- do not share the effect of changes in those features between the entity and policyholders or share the effect between the entity and policyholders in a way that does not result in the entity's share being small.

The Board observed that information about the effect of financial guarantees is particularly important in low interest rate environments. The Board acknowledged that for some insurance contracts with substantial intergenerational sharing of risks, it is likely to be rare for the effect of financial guarantees and other cash flows that do not vary with returns on underlying items to cause an annual cohort to become onerous. However, it is exactly that rarity that makes the information particularly useful to users of financial statements when such an event occurs and information about the effect of financial guarantees is particularly important when interest rates are low. *[IFRS 17.BC139P].*

5.3 Identifying groups for contracts applying the premium allocation approach

For a group of insurance contracts to which the premium allocation approach applies (see 9 below), an entity assesses aggregation of insurance contracts as discussed at 5.2 above except that the entity should assume that no contracts in the portfolio are onerous at initial recognition unless facts and circumstances indicate otherwise. *[IFRS 17.18]*.

An entity should assess whether contracts that are not onerous at initial recognition have no significant possibility of becoming onerous subsequently by assessing the likelihood of changes in applicable facts and circumstances.

6 INITIAL RECOGNITION

6.1 Initial recognition of insurance and reinsurance contracts issued

An entity should recognise a group of insurance contracts (and reinsurance contracts) it issues from the earliest of the following: *[IFRS 17.25]*

- the beginning of the coverage period of the group of contracts;
- the date when the first payment from a policyholder in the group is due; and
- for a group of onerous contracts, when the group becomes onerous.

If there is no contractual due date, the first payment from the policyholder is deemed to be due when it is received. An entity is required to determine whether any contracts form a group of onerous contracts before the earlier of the first two dates above (i.e. before the earlier of the beginning of the coverage period and the date when the first payment from a policyholder in the group is due) if facts and circumstances indicate there is such a group. *[IFRS 17.26]*.

IFRS 17, as amended in June 2020, states that that in recognising a group of insurance contracts in a reporting period an entity shall include only contracts that individually meet one of the three recognition criteria (see above). *[IFRS 17.28]*. This clarifies that an individual contract has to be recognised initially and measured at a time which is specific to the contract. This means that the date of initial recognition of an individual contract added to a group of insurance contracts has to be determined for that individual insurance contract using the measurement assumptions at that date rather than determined by the date of initial recognition of the group to which individual contracts will be added.

In addition, an entity shall make estimates for the discount rates at the date of initial recognition (see 8.3 below) and for the coverage units provided in the reporting period (see 8.7 below). *[IFRS 17.28]*.

An entity may include more contracts in the group after the end of a reporting period (subject to the constraint that contracts within a group cannot be issued more than a year apart – see 5.2.2 above). An entity shall add contracts to the group in the reporting period in which the contracts meet the recognition criteria set out above, applied to each contract individually. *IFRS 17.28]*.

When new contracts are added to a group, this may result in a change to the determination of the weighted-average discount rates at the date of initial recognition (see 8.3 below). An entity shall apply any revised discount rates from the start of the reporting period in which the new contracts are added to the group. *[IFRS 17.28]*. There is no retrospective 'catch-up' adjustment for previous reporting periods, the effect of any change in average discount rates is therefore recognised prospectively.

For reinsurance contracts held, the group consists of the reinsurance contracts, not the underlying direct contracts which are subject to the reinsurance.

The requirements for initial recognition can be illustrated by the following examples.

Example 56.23: Determining the date of recognition of a group of insurance contracts (1)

An entity issues a group of insurance contracts to policyholders beginning on 25 December 2022. The coverage period of the group begins on 1 January 2023 and the first premium from a policyholder in the group is due on 5 January 2023. The group of insurance contracts is not onerous.

The group of insurance contracts is recognised on 1 January 2023 (i.e. the start of the coverage period of the group) which is earlier than the date that the first premium is due.

Example 56.24: Determining the date of recognition of a group of insurance contracts (2)

An entity issues a group of insurance contracts to policyholders beginning on 25 December 2022. The coverage period of the group begins on 1 January 2023 and the first premium from a policyholder in the group is due on 30 December 2022. The group of insurance contracts is not onerous.

The group of insurance contracts is recognised on 30 December 2022 (i.e. the date that the first premium is due) which is earlier than the date of the beginning of the coverage period. However, if the entity has a reporting date of 31 December 2022, only those contracts within the group issued as at the reporting date will be recognised in the financial statements for the period ending 31 December 2022.

Example 56.25: Determining the date of recognition of a group of insurance contracts (3)

An entity issues a group of insurance contracts to policyholders beginning on 25 December 2022. On 25 December 2022 the entity determines that the group of insurance contracts is onerous. The coverage period of the group begins on 1 January 2023 and the first premium from a policyholder in the group is due on 5 January 2023.

The group of insurance contracts is recognised on 25 December 2022, which is when the group of insurance contracts is determined to be onerous. However, if the entity has a reporting date of 31 December 2022, only those contracts within the group that are issued as at the reporting date will be recognised in the financial statements for the period ending 31 December 2022.

Examples 56.23 to 56.25 above demonstrate how the period of a group of insurance contracts may differ from year to year depending on whether the group is onerous and when the first contract premium is due. This is important because contracts issued more than one year apart cannot be in the same group (see 5.2.2 above).

6.2 Initial recognition of reinsurance contracts held

IFRS 17, as amended in June 2020, states that for a group of reinsurance contracts held the requirements discussed at 6.1 above do not apply. Instead, a group of reinsurance contracts held is recognised from the earliest of the following: *[IFRS 17.62]*

- the beginning of the coverage period of the group of reinsurance contracts held; and
- the date the entity recognises an onerous group of underlying insurance contracts (see 6.1 above) if the entity entered into the related reinsurance contract held in the group of reinsurance contracts held at or before that date.

However, notwithstanding the above requirements, an entity should delay the recognition of a group of reinsurance contracts held that provide proportionate coverage until the date that any underlying insurance contract is initially recognised, if that date is later than the beginning of the coverage period of the group of reinsurance contracts held. [IFRS 17.62A].

IFRS 17 does not include guidance on when a contract provides proportionate coverage. In the Basis for Conclusions, it is observed that many reinsurance arrangements are designed to cover the claims incurred under underlying insurance contracts written during a specified period. In some cases, the reinsurance contract held covers the losses of separate contracts on a proportionate basis. In other cases, the reinsurance contract held covers aggregate losses from a group of underlying contracts that exceed a specified amount. [IFRS 17.BC304].

When a reinsurance contract held provides proportionate coverage, the initial recognition of the (group of) reinsurance contract(s) will, as a simplification, be later than the beginning of the coverage period if no underlying contracts have been recognised as at that date. [IFRS 17.BC305(a)].

However, when the group of reinsurance contracts held covers aggregate losses arising from a group of insurance contracts over a specified amount, the group of reinsurance contracts held is recognised when the coverage period of the group of reinsurance contracts begins. In these contracts the entity benefits from coverage – in case the underlying losses exceed the threshold – from the beginning of the group of reinsurance contracts held because such losses accumulate throughout the coverage period. In the Board's view, the coverage benefits the entity from the beginning of the coverage period of the group of reinsurance contracts held because such losses accumulate throughout the coverage period. [IFRS 17.BC305(b)].

The following examples illustrate application of the recognition criteria for reinsurance contracts held when the general model is used.

Example 56.26: Recognition of reinsurance contract held providing proportionate coverage

An entity holds a reinsurance contract in respect of a term life insurance portfolio on a quota share basis whereby 20% of all premiums and all claims from the underlying insurance contracts are ceded to the reinsurer. The reinsurance contract is considered to be a group for the purpose of aggregation and incepts on 1 January 2023. The first underlying insurance contract is recognised on 1 February 2023.

As the reinsurance contract held provides proportionate coverage initial recognition of the contract is delayed until the later of the beginning of the coverage period of the contract and the initial recognition of any underlying contract, i.e. 1 February 2023.

Contracts that do not provide proportionate coverage (often referred to as non-proportional or excess of loss) usually provide insurance for claim events exceeding a certain underlying limit. A non-proportional contract is illustrated in the following example.

Example 56.27: Recognition of reinsurance contract held which does not provide proportionate coverage

An entity holds a reinsurance contract which provides excess of loss protection for a motor insurance portfolio. In exchange for a fixed premium of €100 the reinsurance contract provides cover for claims arising from individual events in the portfolio in excess of €500 up to a limit of €200. The reinsurance contract is considered to be a group for the purpose of aggregation and incepts on 1 January 2023. The first underlying motor insurance contract is recognised on 1 February 2023.

As the reinsurance contract held does not provide proportionate coverage (because neither the premiums nor the claims are a proportion of the premiums and claims from the underlying insurance contracts) the contract is recognised at the beginning of the coverage period of the contract, i.e. 1 January 2023.

Example 56.28: Recognition of reinsurance contract held when the underlying insurance contracts are onerous

An entity holds a reinsurance contract in respect of a term life insurance portfolio on a quota share basis whereby 20% of all premiums and all claims from the underlying insurance contracts are ceded to the reinsurer. The reinsurance contract is considered to be a group for the purpose of aggregation. The reinsurance contract was entered into on 1 December 2022 and incepts on 1 January 2023. The first underlying insurance contract were entered into on 1 December 2022 and incept on 1 January 2023. On 15 December 2022, the group of underlying insurance contracts are determined to be onerous.

As the group of underlying insurance contracts are onerous and the reinsurance held was entered into at the same time as the underlying insurance contracts, the date of initial recognition of the reinsurance contract held is 15 December 2022.

6.3 Initial recognition of insurance acquisition cash flows

Insurance acquisition cash flows are cash flows arising from the costs of selling, underwriting and starting a group of insurance contracts that are directly attributable to the portfolio of insurance contracts to which the group belongs. Such cash flows include cash flows that are not directly attributable to individual contracts or groups of insurance contracts within the portfolio. *[IFRS 17 Appendix A]*.

An entity which does not elect to expense acquisition cash flows as incurred for premium allocation approach contracts (see 9 below) shall recognise an asset for insurance acquisition cash flows paid (or insurance acquisition cash flows for which a liability has been recognised under another IFRS standard) before the related group of insurance contracts is recognised. An entity should recognise such an asset for each related group of insurance contracts. *[IFRS 17.28B]*. An entity shall allocate insurance acquisition cash flows to a group of insurance contracts using a systematic and rational method. *[IFRS 17.28A]*.

If an entity recognises in a reporting period only some of the insurance contracts expected to be included in the group (see 6.1 above), the entity should determine the related portion of an asset for insurance acquisition cash flows for the group on a systematic and rational basis considering the expected timing of recognition of contracts in the group. *[IFRS 17.28D]*.

Any insurance acquisition cash flows paid at the date of initial recognition of the group of insurance contracts are recognised as part of the contractual service margin of the group of insurance contracts (see 8.5 below).

Any insurance acquisition cash flows an entity expects to pay after the related group of insurance contracts is recognised are part of the fulfilment cash flows of the group of insurance contracts (see 8.2 below).

The systematic and rational method of allocating insurance acquisition cash flows to groups referred to above shall be used to allocate: [IFRS 17.B35A]

- insurance acquisition cash flows that are directly attributable to a group of insurance contracts:
    - to that group; and
    - to groups that will include insurance contracts that are expected to arise from renewals of the insurance contracts in that group.
- insurance acquisition cash flows directly attributable to a portfolio of insurance contracts that are not directly attributable to individual contracts or groups of contracts to groups in the portfolio.

The last bullet point above means that insurance acquisition cash flows directly attributable to a portfolio of insurance contracts but not directly attributable to a group of insurance contracts are systematically and rationally allocated to groups of insurance contracts in the portfolio. [IFRS 17.BC184B].

It is observed in the Basis for Conclusions that, prior to the June 2020 amendments, IFRS 17 did not allow insurance acquisition cash flows to be allocated to expected contract renewals. However, in some situations, an entity issues an insurance contract with a short coverage period, such as one year, but might incur high up-front costs, such as commissions to sales agents, relative to the premium the entity will charge for that contract. The entity agrees to those costs because it anticipates that some policyholders will renew their contracts. Often, those costs are fully directly attributable to the initial insurance contract issued because these costs are non-refundable and are not contingent on the policyholder renewing the contracts. In some circumstances, such commissions are higher than the premium charged and applying IFRS 17, as issued in May 2017, would have resulted in the contract being identified as onerous. The Board considered that recognising a loss in those circumstances would provide useful information to policyholders as it reflects that the entity does not have the right to charge policyholders to renew the contracts or to reclaim the commission from the sales agents if policyholders choose not to renew their contracts. [IFRS 17.BC184C-D].

However, the Board was persuaded that an amendment to IFRS 17 requiring an entity to allocate insurance acquisition cash flows to expected renewals of contracts would also provide useful information to users of financial statements about insurance acquisition cash flows. This approach depicts the payment of up-front costs such as commission as an asset that an entity expects to recover through expected renewals of contracts. The asset reflects the right of an entity to not pay again costs it has already paid to obtain renewals. The Board noted that the information resulting from the amendment is comparable to the information provided by IFRS 15 for the incremental costs of obtaining a contract. [IFRS 17.BC184E].

The Board considered whether it should develop requirements to specify how to allocate insurance acquisition cash flows to expected renewals of contracts. However, it concluded that requiring allocation applying a systematic and rational method, consistent with the requirements for allocating fixed and variable overheads (see 8.2.3.L below), was sufficient. [IFRS 17.BC184F].

An entity might add insurance contracts to a group of insurance contracts across more than one reporting period. In those circumstances, an entity shall derecognise the portion of an asset for insurance acquisition cash flows that relates to insurance contracts added to the group in that period and continue to recognise an asset for insurance acquisition cash flows to the extent that the asset relates to insurance contracts expected to be added to the group in a future reporting period. *[IFRS 17.B35C]*.

Impairment and derecognition of insurance acquisition cash flow assets is discussed at 8.10 and 12.4 below respectively.

6.4 Initial recognition of investment contracts with discretionary participation features

The date of initial recognition of an investment contract with discretionary participation features (see 11.3 below) is the date the entity becomes party to the contract. This is consistent with the requirements for recognition of a financial instrument in IFRS 9 and is likely to be earlier than the date of initial recognition for an insurance contract. *[IFRS 17.71]*.

7 MEASUREMENT – OVERVIEW

IFRS 17 has a default approach to measuring groups of insurance contracts (which is the unit of account for measurement as discussed at 5.2 above) described in this publication as the 'general model'. The general model does not distinguish between so-called short duration and long duration (or life and non-life) insurance contracts. It also does not distinguish between insurance products.

IFRS 17 also includes modifications and a simplification to the general model that are applicable in specific circumstances.

The basic revenue recognition principle under IFRS 17 is that no profit is recognised on initial recognition of a group of insurance contracts, but that a loss must be recognised if the group of contracts is onerous (see 6 above for the timing of initial recognition). Subsequently, profit and revenue are recognised as services are performed under the contract.

7.1 Overview of the general model

The general model measures a group of insurance contracts as the sum of the following components, or 'building blocks', for each group of insurance contracts: *[IFRS 17.32]*

- fulfilment cash flows, which comprise:
    - estimates of expected future cash flows over the life of the contract;
    - an adjustment to reflect the time value of money and the financial risks related to the future cash flows to the extent that the financial risks are not included in the estimates of the future cash flows; and
    - a risk adjustment for non-financial risk;
- a contractual service margin (CSM), representing the unearned profit on the group of contracts.

This can be illustrated in the diagram below.

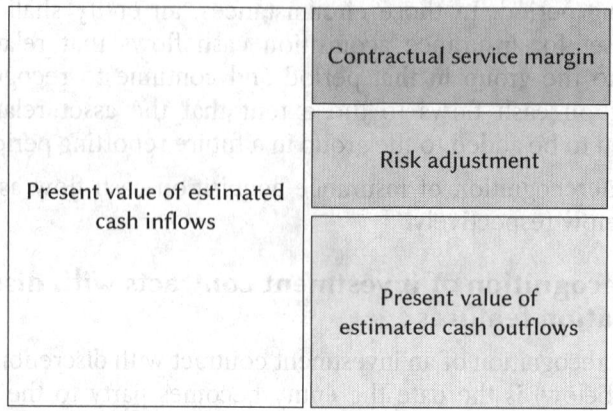

After initial recognition of a group of insurance contracts, the carrying amount of the group at each reporting date is the sum of:
- the liability for remaining coverage, comprising:
  - the fulfilment cash flows related to future service allocated to the group at that date; and
  - the CSM of the group at that date; and
- the liability for incurred claims comprising the fulfilment cash flows related to past service allocated to the group at that date.

The components of the liability for remaining coverage and the liability for incurred claims are as follows:

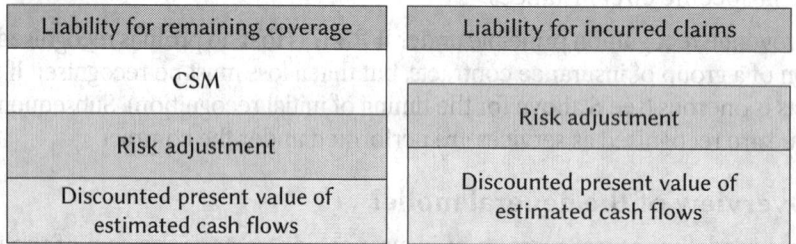

The general model is discussed further at 8 below.

7.2 Modifications to the general model

An entity should apply the general model to all groups of insurance contracts except as follows: *[IFRS 17.29]*
- a simplified or premium allocation approach may be applied for groups of insurance contracts meeting either of the specified criteria for that approach (see 9 below);
- for groups of reinsurance contracts held, an entity should apply either the general model or the premium allocation approach as modified by separate measurement requirements (see 10 below);

- an adaptation of the general model, the 'variable fee approach' is applied to insurance contracts with direct participation features (see 11.2 below); and
- for groups of investment contracts with discretionary participation features, an entity applies the general model (as modified) because of the lack of insurance risk in the contracts (see 11.3 below).

7.3 Insurance contracts in a foreign currency

IFRS 17 states that when applying IAS 21 – *The Effects of Changes in Foreign Exchange Rates* – to a group of insurance contracts that generate cash flows in a foreign currency, an entity should treat the group of contracts, including the contractual service margin, as a monetary item. *[IFRS 17.30]*.

The Basis for Conclusions observes that the contractual service margin (see 8.5 below) might otherwise be classified as non-monetary, because it is similar to a prepayment for goods and services. However, in the Board's view, it was simpler to treat all components of the measurement of an insurance contract in the same way and, since the measurement in IFRS 17 is largely based on cash flow estimates, the Board concluded that it was more appropriate to view the insurance contract as a whole as a monetary item. *[IFRS 17.BC277]*. The Board's conclusion that the insurance contract is a monetary item does not change if an entity measures a group of insurance contracts using the simplified approach (i.e. the premium allocation approach) for the measurement of the liability for the remaining coverage. *[IFRS 17.BC278]*.

Treating insurance contracts as monetary items means that groups of insurance contracts in a foreign currency are retranslated to the entity's functional currency using the exchange rate applying at each reporting date. Exchange differences arising on retranslation are accounted for in profit or loss. IFRS 4 contained no similar assertion and therefore many insurers, following the guidance on monetary and non-monetary items in IAS 21, treated unearned premium provisions (i.e. deferred revenue) and deferred acquisition costs in a foreign currency as non-monetary items and did not retranslate these balances subsequent to initial recognition.

IFRS 17 does not provide any further guidance on accounting for the contractual service margin (CSM) if a group of contracts generates cash flows in multiple currencies. There are several concepts that could be applied in this situation some of which involve the concept of a 'CSM currency' (for example making the CSM currency the predominant currency of the group of insurance contracts) although the concept is not mentioned by IFRS 17.

Neither IAS 21 nor IFRS 17 specify where exchange differences on insurance contract liabilities should be presented in the statement of financial performance and, as discussed in Chapter 15 at 10.1, entities should apply judgement to determine the appropriate line item(s) in which exchange differences are recorded where IFRS 17 specifies that changes of financial risk should be included in insurance finance income or expenses. Foreign currency risk is considered to be financial risk by IFRS 17 and so presenting exchange differences in insurance service expenses would not be appropriate.

8 MEASUREMENT – GENERAL MODEL

As explained at 7.1 above, the general model is based on the following building blocks for each group of insurance contracts: *[IFRS 17.32]*

- fulfilment cash flows, which comprise:
  - estimates of expected future cash flows over the life of the contract (see 8.2 below);
  - an adjustment to reflect the time value of money and the financial risks related to the future cash flows to the extent that the financial risks are not included in the estimates of the future cash flows (see 8.3 below); and
  - a risk adjustment for non-financial risk (see 8.4 below).
- a contractual service margin (CSM), representing the unearned profit on the group of contracts (see 8.5 below).

The contractual service margin is released to profit or loss over the period that services are provided to the policyholder. Therefore, at initial recognition, no profit should normally be recognised. However, a loss is recognised if the group of contracts is onerous at the date that the group is determined to be onerous (see 6 above). Measurement of onerous contracts is discussed at 8.8 below. The contractual service margin for insurance contracts with direct participation features is adjusted over the service period in a different way from the contractual service margin for insurance contracts without direct participation features. Contracts with direct participation features are discussed at 11.2 below. Once the contractual service margin is utilised, the group of insurance contracts will be measured using only the fulfilment cash flows.

8.1 The contract boundary

Establishing the boundary of a contract is crucial as it determines the cash flows that will be included in its measurement.

Estimates of cash flows in a scenario should include all cash flows within the boundary of an existing contract and no other cash flows. In determining the boundary of a contract an entity should consider its substantive rights and obligations and whether they arise from a contract, law or regulation (see 3.1 above). *[IFRS 17.B61]*.

Cash flows are within the boundary of an insurance contract if they arise from substantive rights and obligations that exist during the reporting period in which the entity can compel the policyholder to pay the premiums or in which the entity has a substantive obligation to provide the policyholder with insurance contract services. A substantive obligation to provide insurance contract services ends when: *[IFRS 17.34]*

(a) the entity has the practical ability to reassess the risks of the particular policyholder and, as a result, can set a price or level of benefits that fully reflects those risks; or

(b) both of the following criteria are satisfied:

    (i) the entity has the practical ability to reassess the risks of the portfolio of insurance contracts that contains the contract and, as a result, can set a price or level of benefits that fully reflects the risk of that portfolio; and

(ii) the pricing of the premiums up to the date when the risks are reassessed does not take into account the risks that relate to periods after the reassessment date.

A liability or asset relating to expected premiums or expected claims outside the boundary of the existing insurance contract should not be recognised. Such amounts relate to future insurance contracts. *[IFRS 17.35]*. However, an asset should be recognised for acquisition cash flows paid before the related group of insurance contracts is recognised (see 6.3 above and 8.1.4 below).

IFRS 17 does not explicitly state whether the boundary condition relating to repricing for risk refers to insurance risk only or whether it also reflects other types of risk under the contract. At the February 2018 meeting of the TRG, the TRG members noted that paragraph (b) above should be read as an extension of the risk assessment in paragraph (a) above from the individual to portfolio level, without extending policyholder risks to all types of risks and considerations applied by an entity when pricing a contract. The TRG members observed that the IASB staff noted that policyholder risk includes both the insurance risk and the financial risk transferred from the policyholder to the entity and therefore excludes lapse risk and expense risk as these are not risks which are transferred by the policyholder.[18]

In April 2019, the IASB staff responded to a TRG submission by confirming that the reference to a 'portfolio of insurance contracts' in the substantive obligation criteria above means the same as a 'portfolio of insurance contracts' as defined in IFRS 17 (i.e. it should not be interpreted at a more granular level).[19]

When an issuer of an insurance contract is required by the contract to renew or otherwise continue the contract, it should assess whether premiums and related cash flows that arise from the renewed contract are within the boundary of the original contract. *[IFRS 17.B63]*.

An entity has the practical ability to set a price at a future date (a renewal date) that fully reflects the risk in the contract from that date in the absence of constraints that prevent the entity from setting the same price it would for a new contract with the same characteristics as the existing contract issued on that date, or if it can amend the benefits to be consistent with the price it will charge. Similarly, an entity has the practical ability to set a price when it can reprice an existing contract so that the price reflects overall changes in the risks in a portfolio of insurance contracts, even if the price set for each individual policyholder does not reflect the change in risk for that specific policyholder. When assessing whether the entity has the practical ability to set a price that fully reflects the risks in the contract or portfolio, it should consider all the risks that it would consider when underwriting equivalent contracts on the renewal date for the remaining service. In determining the estimates of future cash flows at the end of a reporting period, an entity should reassess the boundary of an insurance contract to include the effect of changes in circumstances on the entity's substantive rights and obligations. *[IFRS 17.B64]*.

It is acknowledged in the Basis for Conclusions that it may be more difficult to decide the contract boundary if the contract binds one party more tightly than the other. Examples of circumstances in which it is more difficult are: *[IFRS 17.BC162]*

- An entity may price a contract so that the premiums charged in early periods subsidise the premiums charged in later periods, even if the contract states that each premium relates to an equivalent period of coverage. This would be the case if the contract charges level premiums and the risks covered by the contract increase with time. The Board concluded that the premiums charged in later periods would be within the boundary of the contract because, after the first period of coverage, the policyholder has obtained something of value, namely the ability to continue coverage at a level price despite increasing risk.

- An insurance contract might bind the entity, but not the policyholder, by requiring the entity to continue to accept premiums and provide coverage (without the ability to reprice the contract) but permitting the policyholder to stop paying premiums, although possibly incurring a penalty. In the Board's view, the premiums the entity is required to accept and the resulting coverage it is required to provide fall within the boundary of the contract.

- An insurance contract may permit an entity to reprice the contract on the basis of general market experience (for example, mortality experience), without permitting the entity to reassess the individual policyholder's risk profile (for example, the policyholder's health). In this case, the insurance contract binds the entity by requiring it to provide the policyholder with something of value: continuing insurance coverage without the need to undergo underwriting again. Although the terms of the contract are such that the policyholder has a benefit in renewing the contract, and thus the entity expects that renewals will occur, the contract does not require the policyholder to renew the contract. As a result, the repriced cash flows are outside the contract boundary provided both the criteria in (b) above are met.

Even when an entity is prevented from repricing an existing contract using an individual policyholder's risk assessment, the entity may nonetheless be able to reprice a portfolio to which the contract belongs with the result that the price charged for the portfolio as a whole fully reflects the risk of the portfolio. As a result, some stakeholders argued that in such cases the entity is no longer bound by the existing portfolio of contracts and that any cash flows that arise beyond that repricing point should be considered to be beyond the boundary of the existing contract. To the extent that an entity would not be able to charge a price that fully reflects the risks of the portfolio as a whole, it would be bound by the existing contract. The Board was persuaded by this view and therefore such cash flows are considered to be outside the contract boundary, provided the pricing of the premiums for coverage up to the date when the risks are reassessed does not take into account the risks that relate to periods subsequent to the reassessment date. *[IFRS 17.BC163]*.

The assessment of the contract boundary is made in each reporting period. This is because an entity updates the measurement of the group of insurance contracts to which the individual contract belongs and, hence, the portfolio of contracts in each reporting period. For example, in one reporting period an entity may decide that a renewal premium for a portfolio of contracts is outside the contract boundary because the restriction on the entity's ability to reprice the contract has no commercial substance. However, if circumstances change so that the same restrictions on the entity's ability to reprice the portfolio take on commercial substance, the entity may conclude that future renewal premiums for that portfolio of contracts are within the boundary of the contract. *[IFRS 17.BC164].*

The following examples illustrate the application of the contract boundary.

Example 56.29: Contract boundary of a stepped premium life insurance contract

An entity issues a group of annual insurance contracts which provide cover for death, and total and permanent disablement. The cover is guaranteed renewable every year (i.e. the entity must accept renewal) for twenty years regardless as to changes in health of the insured. However, the premiums increase annually with the age of the policyholder and the insurer may increase premium rates annually provided that the increase is applied to the entire portfolio of contracts (premium rates for an individual policyholder cannot be increased after the policy is underwritten).

Analysis

The contract boundary is one year.

The guaranteed renewable basis means that the entity has a substantive obligation to provide the policyholder with services. However, the substantive obligation ends at the end of each year. This is because the entity has the practical ability to reassess the risks of the portfolio that contains the contract and, therefore, can set a price that reflects the risk of that portfolio and the pricing of the premiums for coverage up to the date when the risks are reassessed do not take into account the risks that relate to premiums after the reassessment date (as premiums are adjusted annually for age). Therefore, both criteria in paragraph (b)(i) and (b)(ii) above are satisfied.

Example 56.30: Contract boundary of a level premium life insurance contract

An entity issues a group of insurance contracts which provide cover for death, and total and permanent disablement. The cover is guaranteed renewable (i.e. the entity must accept renewal) for twenty years regardless as to changes in health of the insured. The premium rates are level for the life of the policy irrespective of policyholder age. Therefore, the insurer will generally 'overcharge' younger policyholders and 'undercharge' older policyholders. In addition, the insurer may increase premium rates annually provided that the increase is applied to the entire portfolio of contracts (premium rates for an individual policyholder cannot be increased after the policy is underwritten).

Analysis

The contract boundary is twenty years.

The guaranteed renewable basis means that the entity has a substantive obligation to provide the policyholder with services. The substantive obligation does not end until the period of the guaranteed renewable basis expires. Although the entity has the practical ability to reassess the risks of the portfolio that contains the contract and, therefore, can set a price that reflects the risk of that portfolio, the pricing of the premiums does take into account the risks that relate to premiums after the reassessment date. The entity charges premiums in the early years to recover the expected cost of death claims in later years. Therefore, the second criterion in (b)(ii) above for drawing a shortened contract boundary when an entity can reassess the premiums or benefits for a portfolio of insurance contracts is not satisfied.

In February 2018, the TRG discussed an IASB staff paper which analysed specific fact patterns of two insurance contracts where the insurance entity assesses the risk at the level of a portfolio of insurance contracts and not at an individual contract level. The TRG members noted that, in the specific fact patterns, the entity can reset the premiums of the portfolios to which both of the example contracts belong annually to reflect the reassessed risk of those portfolios. The entity has the practical ability to reassess the risks of the specific portfolio of insurance contracts that contains the contract and, as a result, can set a price that fully reflects the risk of that portfolio and therefore meets the requirements of (b)(i) above. Additionally, premiums increase in line with age each year based on the step-rated table – i.e. the contract does not charge level premiums, consequently the staff analysis assumes that the requirements in (b)(ii) above are also met. Accordingly, for those two situations discussed at the TRG meeting, the cash flows resulting from the renewal terms should not be included within the boundary of the existing insurance contract (i.e. a 'short' contract boundary applies. However, the TRG members observed that if, conversely, the fact patterns of the two contracts described in the submission was changed such that the entity instead has a practical ability to reassess risks only at a general level (for example, at a portfolio level) and, as a result, can set a price for the portfolio of insurance contracts that contains the contract (for example, using a step-rate table for the portfolio) then this would provide the individual policyholders within the portfolios with a substantive right and consequently, the cash flows resulting from these renewal terms should be included within the boundary of the existing contract (i.e. a 'long' contract boundary applies). The TRG members also observed that the two situations described in the IASB staff paper are for specific fact patterns. In practice, the features of contracts and their repricing might be different from those examples. The facts and circumstance of each contract should be assessed to reach an appropriate conclusion applying the requirements of IFRS 17.[20]

In September 2018, the TRG members discussed an IASB staff paper which considered how to account for cash flows of an insurance contract issued that, at initial recognition, are outside the boundary of the contract when facts or circumstances change over time. In particular, the staff paper considered the interaction between the statement in paragraph 35 of IFRS 17 that cash flows outside the boundary of a contract at initial recognition are cash flows of a new contract and the final sentence of paragraph B64 which permits an entity to re-assess the boundary of an insurance contract to include the effect of changes in circumstances. The IASB staff observed that:

- the requirements in the two paragraphs are different because they address two different circumstances;
- when paragraph 35 of IFRS 17 applies, additional cash flows will be recognised as a new contract when the recognition criteria of a new group of contracts are met;
- paragraph B64 of IFRS 17 discusses the assessment of the practical ability of an entity to reprice a contract considering constraints that might limit that ability and, therefore, applies to the reassessment of the contract boundary in this context. For example, a contract boundary reassessment may occur when, in one reporting period, repricing restrictions that have no commercial substance but in the next reporting period facts and circumstances come to light that would have led to a different conclusion at inception (if known then). When paragraph B64 applies, the fulfilment cash flows are updated to reflect changes in cash flows that are within the (revised) contract boundary. When such changes relate to future service they are recognised by adjusting the carrying amount of the contractual service margin of the group of contracts to which the contract belongs.

The TRG members agreed with the IASB staff observations, but noted the apparent conflict between the two paragraphs which stems from a lack of clarity of the meaning of paragraph B64. IASB staff observed that the meaning of the last sentence in paragraph B64 should be considered in the context of the preceding sentences in paragraph B64, paragraphs B61-B63 and the Basis for Conclusions. The TRG members also expressed different views as to the applicability of the distinction between paragraphs 35 and B64 of IFRS 17 in circumstances where cash flows that are outside the contract boundary at initial recognition relate to an additional type of coverage that may be provided over the coverage period of the contract.[21]

In September 2018, the IASB staff discussed a question submitted to the TRG regarding a type of entity in which parties become members by purchasing an insurance contract. Members of the entity are also provided with free additional insurance coverage. The entity can cancel the free additional insurance coverage at any time and the question arises as to whether cash flows related to the free additional coverage are within the boundary of the insurance contracts purchased by policyholders. The IASB staff concluded that the right of an entity to cancel coverage at any time means that the entity does not have a substantive obligation to provide future service related to the free additional insurance coverage. The expected cash flows related to future free additional insurance coverage are therefore not included in the boundary of the insurance contract and are not included in the liability for remaining coverage. If the entity has a substantive obligation for the free additional insurance coverage that has already been provided, such as unpaid claims, the cash flows related to that coverage are within the boundary of the contract and are included in the liability for incurred claims.[22]

8.1.1 Options to add insurance coverage

In May 2018, the TRG discussed an IASB staff paper that analysed how to determine the contract boundary of insurance contracts that include an option to add insurance coverage at a later date. The TRG members observed that:

- an option to add insurance coverage at a future date is a feature of the insurance contract;
- an entity should focus on substantive rights and obligations arising from that option to determine whether the cash flows related to the option are within or outside the contract boundary;
- unless the entity considers that an option to add coverage at a future date is a separate contract, the option is an insurance component that is not measured separately from the remainder of the insurance contract;
- if an option to add insurance coverage is not a separate contract and the terms are guaranteed by the entity, the cash flows arising from the option would be within the boundary of the contract because the entity cannot reprice the contract to reflect the reassessed risks when it has guaranteed the price for one of the risks included in the contract;
- if an option to add insurance coverage is not a separate contract and the terms are not guaranteed by the entity, the cash flows arising from the option might be either within or outside of the contract boundary, depending on whether the entity has the practical

ability to set a price that fully reflects the reassessed risks of the entire contract. The analysis in the IASB staff paper: (i) assumed that the option to add insurance coverage at a future date created substantive rights and obligations; and (ii) noted that, if an entity does not have the practical ability to reprice the whole contract when the policyholder exercises the option to add coverage, the cash flows arising from the premiums after the option exercise date would be within the contract boundary. The TRG members expressed different views about whether an option with terms that are not guaranteed by the entity would create substantive rights and obligations; and

- if the cash flows arising from an option to add coverage at a future date are within the contract boundary, the measurement of a group of insurance contracts is required to reflect, on an expected value basis, the entity's current estimates of how the policyholders in the group will exercise the option.[23]

In April 2019, the IASB staff considered a TRG submission which described a feature that provides a policyholder of a contract that lapsed (due to failure to pay premiums) an option to reinstate the contract within a contractually specified period, as long as the contract had not been surrendered. In the fact pattern, the entity may agree to reinstate the contract only after new underwriting, but once agreed the contractual premium is not repriced, the premiums for previous periods are paid and the coverage is reinstated. The IASB staff declined to provide further analysis of the specific transaction but observed that an entity should assess whether its substantive obligation to provide services ends when a contract with such features lapses applying the criteria set out at 8.1 above (and discussed further above) and that cash flows related to the unexpired portion of the coverage period, such as the expected reinstatement of contracts, are part of the liability for remaining coverage.[24]

8.1.2 Constraints or limitations relevant in assessing repricing

In May 2018, the TRG discussed an IASB staff paper which addresses what constraint or limitations, other than those arising from the terms of an insurance contract, would be relevant in assessing the practical ability of an entity to reassess the risks of the particular policyholder (or of the portfolio of insurance contracts that contains the contract) and set a price or level of benefits that fully reflects those risks. The TRG members observed that:

- a constraint that equally applies to new contracts and existing contracts would not limit an entity's practical ability to reprice existing contracts to reflect their reassessed risks;
- when determining whether it has the practical ability to set a price at a future date that fully reflects the reassessed risks of a contract or portfolio, an entity shall (i) consider contractual, legal and regulatory restrictions; and (ii) disregard restrictions that have no commercial substance;

- IFRS 17 does not limit pricing constraints to contractual, legal and regulatory constraints. Market competitiveness and commercial considerations are factors that an entity typically considers when pricing new contracts and repricing existing contracts. As such, sources of constraints may also include market competitiveness and commercial considerations, but constraints are irrelevant to the contract boundary if they apply equally to new and existing policyholders in the same market; and
- a constraint that limits an entity's practical ability to price or reprice contracts differs from choices that an entity makes (pricing decisions), which may not limit the entity's practical ability to reprice existing contracts in the way envisaged by paragraph B64 of IFRS 17.

The TRG members also observed that an entity should apply judgement to decide whether commercial considerations are relevant when considering the contract boundary requirements of IFRS 17.[25]

8.1.3 Contracts between an entity and customers of an association or bank

In September 2018, the TRG members considered an IASB staff paper which discussed a submission about the boundary of a contract for an agreement between an entity and an association or bank (referred to as a group insurance policy) under which the entity provides insurance coverage to members of an association or to customers of a bank (referred to as 'certificate holders').

In the case of group association policies, the insurance entity has a policy with an association or bank to sell insurance coverage to individual members or customers. Although the legal contract is between the entity and the association or bank, the insurance coverage for each certificate holder is priced as if it were an individual contract. In the case of group creditor policies with a bank, the entity can sell insurance coverage to individual customers of the bank. These policies have the same facts and circumstances as the group association policy, other than insurance cover being linked to the remaining outstanding balance of the loan or mortgage issued by the bank to the certificate holder. The entity pays the remaining outstanding loan balance to the bank when an insured event occurs (rather than the certificate holder or their beneficiaries who are liable for paying the outstanding balances). In the fact pattern submitted, the entity can terminate the policy with a 90-day notice period. In such arrangements, the question arises as to whether the cash flows related to periods after the notice period of 90 days are within the boundary of an insurance contract and is the policyholder the bank or association or is it the individual certificate holders?

The TRG members agreed with the analysis and conclusion of the staff paper including the steps that an entity should perform in its analysis and observed that:
- for group insurance policies an entity should consider whether the policyholder is the association or bank, or the certificate holders. This is the case regardless as to whether that compensation is received directly or indirectly by paying amounts on the policyholder's behalf;
- for group insurance policies an entity should consider whether the arrangement reflects a single insurance contract or multiple insurance contracts (i.e. with each certificate holder). Rebutting the presumption that the contract is a single contract by separating components requires judgement and careful consideration of all facts and circumstances (see 5.1.1 above);
- for the group insurance policies described in the submission, the following facts and circumstances are indicative that the arrangement reflects multiple insurance contracts (i.e. an insurance contract with each certificate holder) for the purpose of applying IFRS 17:
  - the insurance coverage is priced and sold separately;
  - other than being members of the association or customers of the bank the individuals are not related to one another; and
  - purchase of the insurance coverage is an option for each individual;
- an entity should assess the boundary of each insurance contract. For the group insurance policies described in the submission, the entity's substantive obligation to provide services under the contract ends at the point the entity can terminate the contract. This means that, in these examples, the substantive obligation ends after 90 days and cash flows within the boundary are those related to the obligation to provide services over the 90-day period. The certificate holder's expectation that the group insurance policy will not be terminated earlier than the contract term is not relevant to the assessment of the contract boundary.

The TRG members also observed that in practice there are many group insurance contracts with different terms and the assessment of whether a group insurance policy arrangement reflects a single insurance contract or multiple insurance contracts should be applied to group insurance policies considering all relevant facts and circumstances.[26]

8.1.4 Contract boundary matters related to insurance acquisition cash flows

As discussed at 6.3 above, in some circumstances, an insurer may pay insurance acquisition cash flows on insurance contracts which are expected to last for many years but where the contract boundary is much shorter. For example, an insurer may pay significant up-front insurance acquisition cash flows in the first year of a contract on the basis that the contract will last for a number of years but the contract boundary may be only one year (for example, because of the reasons explained in Example 56.29 above). In some cases, part of the commission is refundable from the agent if the future renewals do not occur as expected. In other circumstances the commission is not refundable.

As a result of the June 2020 amendments, IFRS 17 requires an entity to allocate insurance acquisition cash flows to groups of insurance contracts using a systematic and rational method unless, as permitted under the premium allocation approach (see 9.1 below), it chooses to recognise them as an expense. *[IFRS 17.28A]*. The systematic and rational method should be used to allocate: *[IFRS 17.B35A]*

- insurance acquisition cash flows directly attributable to a group of insurance contracts:
  - to that group; and
  - to groups that will include insurance contracts that are expected to arise from renewals of the insurance contracts in that group; and
- insurance acquisition cash flows directly attributable to a portfolio of insurance contracts, other than those in the bullet points above, to groups of contracts in that portfolio.

As discussed at 6.3 above, IFRS 17 does not contain specific requirements on how to allocate parts of the acquisition cash flows to anticipated contract renewals of different groups of insurance contracts on a systematic and rational basis. Therefore, determining such an allocation will be a matter of judgement based on facts and circumstances.

At the end of each reporting period, an entity shall revise amounts allocated to each group using the systematic and rational method specified above to reflect any changes in assumptions that determine the inputs to the method of allocation used. An entity shall not change amounts allocated to a group of insurance contracts after all contracts have been added to the group. *[IFRS 17.B35B]*.

A distinction can be made when an insurer has paid an intermediary separately for exclusivity or future services as these costs are not attributable to an insurance contract and these payments would be outside the scope of IFRS 17 and may be within the scope of another IFRS.

8.1.5 Contract boundary matters related to reinsurance contracts issued and held

Contract boundary issues related to reinsurance contracts issued are discussed at 8.9.1 below.

Contracts boundary issues related to reinsurance contracts held are discussed at 10.2 below.

8.2 Estimates of expected future cash flows

The first element of the building blocks in the general model discussed at 8 above is an estimate of the future cash flows over the life of each contract.

This assessment should include all the future cash flows within the boundary of each contract (see 8.1 above). *[IFRS 17.33]*. However, the fulfilment cash flows should not reflect the non-performance risk (i.e. own credit) of the entity. *[IFRS 17.31]*. As discussed at 5 above, an entity is permitted to estimate the future cash flows at a higher level of aggregation than a group and then allocate the resulting fulfilment cash flows to individual groups of contracts.

The estimates of future cash flows should: *[IFRS 17.33]*
- incorporate, in an unbiased way, all reasonable and supportable information available without undue cost or effort about the amount, timing and uncertainty of those future cash flows. To do this, an entity should estimate the expected value (i.e. the probability-weighted mean) of the full range of possible outcomes;
- reflect the perspective of the entity, provided that the estimates of any relevant market variables are consistent with observable market prices for those variables (see 8.2.1 below);
- be current – the estimates should reflect conditions existing at the measurement date, including assumptions at that date about the future (see 8.2.2 below); and
- be explicit – the entity should estimate the adjustment for non-financial risk separately from the other estimates. The entity also should estimate the cash flows separately from the adjustment for the time value of money and financial risk, unless the most appropriate measurement technique combines these estimates (see 8.4 below).

The objective of estimating future cash flows is to determine the expected value, or probability-weighted mean, of the full range of possible outcomes, considering all reasonable and supportable information available at the reporting date without undue cost or effort. Reasonable and supportable information available at the reporting date without undue cost or effort includes information about past events and current conditions, and forecasts of future conditions. Information available from an entity's own information systems is considered to be available without undue cost or effort. *[IFRS 17.B37]*.

The estimates of future cash flows must be on an expected value basis and therefore should be unbiased. This means that they should not include any additional estimates above the probability-weighted mean for 'uncertainty', 'prudence' or what is sometimes described as a 'management loading'. Separately, a risk adjustment for non-financial risk (see 8.4 below) is determined to reflect the compensation for bearing the non-financial risk resulting from the uncertain amount and the timing of the cash flows.

The starting point for an estimate of future cash flows is a range of scenarios that reflects the full range of possible outcomes. Each scenario specifies the amount and timing of the cash flows for a particular outcome, and the estimated probability of that outcome. The cash flows from each scenario are discounted and weighted by the estimated probability of that outcome to derive an expected present value. Consequently, the objective is not to develop a most likely outcome, or a more-likely-than-not outcome, for future cash flows. *[IFRS 17.B38]*.

When considering the full range of possible outcomes, the objective is to incorporate all reasonable and supportable information available without undue cost or effort in an unbiased way, rather than to identify every possible scenario. In practice, developing explicit scenarios is unnecessary if the resulting estimate is consistent with the measurement objective of considering all reasonable and supportable information available without undue cost or effort when determining the mean. For example, if an entity estimates that the probability distribution of outcomes is broadly consistent with a probability distribution that can be described completely with a small number of parameters, it will be sufficient to estimate the smaller number of parameters. Similarly, in some cases, relatively simple modelling may give an answer within an acceptable range of precision, without the need for many detailed simulations. However, in some cases, the cash flows may be driven by complex underlying factors and may respond in a non-linear fashion to changes in economic conditions. This may happen if, for example, the cash flows reflect a series of interrelated options that are implicit or explicit. In such cases, more sophisticated stochastic modelling is likely to be necessary to satisfy the measurement objective. *[IFRS 17.B39]*.

The scenarios developed should include unbiased estimates of the probability of catastrophic losses under existing contracts. Those scenarios exclude possible claims under possible future contracts. *[IFRS 17.B40]*. Therefore, consistent with IFRS 4 (see Chapter 55 at 7.2.1), catastrophe provisions and equalisation provisions (provisions generally build up over years following a prescribed regulatory formula which are permitted to be released in years when claims experience is high or abnormal) are not permitted to the extent that they relate to contracts that are not in force at the reporting date. Although IFRS 17 prohibits the recognition of these provisions as a liability, it does not prohibit their segregation as a component of equity. Consequently, insurers are free to designate a proportion of their equity as an equalisation or catastrophe reserve. When a catastrophe or equalisation provision has a tax base but is not recognised in the IFRS financial statements, then a taxable temporary difference will arise that should be accounted for under IAS 12 – *Income Taxes*.

An entity should estimate the probabilities and amounts of future payments under existing contracts on the basis of information obtained including: *[IFRS 17.B41]*

- information about claims already reported by policyholders;
- other information about the known or estimated characteristics of the insurance contracts;
- historical data about the entity's own experience, supplemented when necessary with historical data from other sources. Historical data is adjusted to reflect current conditions, for example, if:
    - the characteristics of the insured population differ (or will differ, for example, because of adverse selection) from those of the population that has been used as a basis for the historical data;
    - there are indications that historical trends will not continue, that new trends will emerge or that economic, demographic and other changes may affect the cash flows that arise from the existing insurance contracts; or
    - there have been changes in items such as underwriting procedures and claims management procedures that may affect the relevance of historical data to the insurance contracts;
- current price information, if available, for reinsurance contracts and other financial instruments (if any) covering similar risks, such as catastrophe bonds and weather derivatives, and recent market prices for transfers of insurance contracts. This information should be adjusted to reflect the differences between the cash flows that arise from those reinsurance contracts or other financial instruments, and the cash flows that would arise as the entity fulfils the underlying contracts with the policyholder.

8.2.1 Market and non-market variables

IFRS 17 identifies two types of variables that can affect estimates of cash flows: *[IFRS 17.B42]*

- market variables (i.e. variables that can be observed in, or derived directly from markets (for example, prices of publicly traded securities and interest rates)); and
- non-market variables (i.e. all other variables, such as the frequency and severity of insurance claims and mortality).

Market variables will generally give rise to financial risk (for example, observable interest rates) and non-market variables will generally give rise to non-financial risk (for example, mortality rates). However, this will not always be the case, there may be assumptions that relate to financial risks for which variables cannot be observed in, or derived directly from, markets (for example, interest rates that cannot be observed in, or derived directly from, markets). *[IFRS 17.B43]*.

8.2.1.A Market variables

Market variables are variables that can be observed in, or derived directly from markets (for example, prices of publicly traded securities and interest rates).

Estimates of market variables should be consistent with observable market prices at the measurement date. An entity should maximise the use of observable inputs and should not substitute its own estimates for observable market data except in the limited circumstances as permitted by IFRS 13 (see Chapter 14 at 17.1). Consistent with IFRS 13, if variables need to be derived (for example, because no observable market variables exist) they should be as consistent as possible with observable market variables. *[IFRS 17.B44]*.

Market prices blend a range of views about possible future outcomes and also reflect the risk preferences of market participants. Consequently, they are not a single-point forecast of the future outcome. If the actual outcome differs from the previous market price, IFRS 17 argues that this does not mean that the market price was 'wrong'. *[IFRS 17.B45]*.

An important application of market variables is the notion of a replicating asset or a replicating portfolio of assets. A replicating asset is one whose cash flows exactly match, in all scenarios, the contractual cash flows of a group of insurance contracts in amount, timing and uncertainty. In some cases, a replicating asset may exist for some of the cash flows that arise from a group of insurance contracts. The fair value of that asset reflects both the expected present value of the cash flows from the asset and the risk associated with those cash flows. If a replicating portfolio of assets exists for some of the cash flows that arise from a group of insurance contracts, the entity can use the fair value of those assets to measure the relevant fulfilment cash flows instead of explicitly estimating the cash flows and discount rate. *[IFRS 17.B46]*. IFRS 17 does not require an entity to use a replicating portfolio technique. However, if a replicating asset or portfolio does exist for some of the cash flows that arise from insurance contracts and an entity chooses to use a different technique, the entity should satisfy itself that a replicating portfolio technique would be unlikely to lead to a materially different measurement of those cash flows. *[IFRS 17.B47]*. In practice, we believe that the use of a replicating portfolio is likely to be rare as IFRS 17 refers to an asset whose cash flows exactly match those of the liability.

Techniques other than a replicating portfolio technique, such as stochastic modelling techniques, may be more robust or easier to implement if there are significant interdependencies between cash flows that vary based on returns on assets and other cash flows. Judgement is required to determine the technique that best meets the objective of consistency with observable market variables in specific circumstances. In particular, the technique used must result in the measurement of any options and guarantees included in the insurance contracts being consistent with observable market prices (if any) for such options and guarantees. *[IFRS 17.B48]*.

In May 2018, the IASB staff responded to a submission to the TRG which asked whether 'risk neutral' (i.e. based on an assumed distribution of scenarios that is intended to reflect realistic assumptions about actual future asset returns) or 'real world' (i.e. based on an underlying assumption that, on average, all assets earn the same risk-free return, with a range of scenarios analysed reflecting the assumed volatility of returns for an asset price consistent with volatility implied by option prices) scenarios should be used for stochastic modelling techniques to project future returns on assets. The IASB staff clarified that IFRS 17 does not require an entity to divide estimated cash flows into those that vary based on the returns on underlying items and those that do not (see 8.3 below) and, if not divided, the discount rate should be appropriate for the cash flows as a whole. The IASB staff observed that any consideration beyond this is actuarial (i.e. operational measurement implementation) in nature and therefore does not fall within the remit of the TRG. The TRG members did not disagree with the IASB staff's observations.[27]

8.2.1.B   Non-market variables

Non-market variables are all other variables (other than market variables) such as the frequency and severity of insurance claims and mortality.

Estimates of non-market variables should reflect all reasonable and supportable evidence available without undue cost or effort, both external and internal. *[IFRS 17.B49]*.

Non-market external data (for example, national mortality statistics) may have more or less relevance than internal data (for example, internally developed mortality statistics), depending on the circumstances. For example, an entity that issues life insurance contracts should not rely solely on national mortality statistics, but should consider all other reasonable and supportable internal and external sources of information available without undue cost or effort when developing unbiased estimates of probabilities for mortality scenarios for its insurance contracts. In developing those probabilities, an entity should give more weight to the more persuasive information. For example: *[IFRS 17.B50]*

- Internal mortality statistics may be more persuasive than national mortality data if national data is derived from a large population that is not representative of the insured population. This might be because, for example, the demographic characteristics of the insured population could significantly differ from those of the national population, meaning that an entity would need to place more weight on the internal data and less weight on the national statistics.

- Conversely, if the internal statistics are derived from a small population with characteristics that are believed to be close to those of the national population, and the national statistics are current, an entity should place more weight on the national statistics.

Estimated probabilities for non-market variables should not contradict observable market variables. For example, estimated probabilities for future inflation rate scenarios should be as consistent as possible with probabilities implied by market interest rates. *[IFRS 17.B51].*

In some cases, an entity may conclude that market variables vary independently of non-market variables. If so, the entity should consider scenarios that reflect the range of outcomes for the non-market variables, with each scenario using the same observed value of the market variable. *[IFRS 17.B52].*

In other cases, market variables and non-market variables may be correlated. For example, there may be evidence that lapse rates (a non-market variable) are correlated with interest rates (a market variable). Similarly, there may be evidence that claim levels for house or car insurance are correlated with economic cycles and therefore with interest rates and expense amounts. The entity should ensure that the probabilities for the scenarios and the risk adjustments for the non-financial risk that relates to the market variables are consistent with the observed market prices that depend on those market variables. *[IFRS 17.B53].*

8.2.2 Using current estimates

In estimating each cash flow scenario and its probability, an entity should use all reasonable and supportable information available without undue cost or effort. *[IFRS 17.B54].* Undue cost and effort is discussed at 17.4 below.

An entity should review the estimates that it made at the end of the previous reporting period and update them. In doing so, an entity should consider whether: *[IFRS 17.B54]*

- the updated estimates faithfully represent the conditions at the end of the reporting period; and
- the changes in estimates faithfully represent the changes in conditions during the period. For example, suppose that estimates were at one end of a reasonable range at the beginning of the period. If the conditions have not changed, shifting the estimates to the other end of the range at the end of the period would not faithfully represent what has happened during the period. If an entity's most recent estimates are different from its previous estimates, but conditions have not changed, it should assess whether the new probabilities assigned to each scenario are justified. In updating its estimates of those probabilities, the entity should consider both the evidence that supported its previous estimates and all newly available evidence, giving more weight to the more persuasive evidence.

The probability assigned to each scenario should reflect the conditions at the end of the reporting period. Consequently, applying IAS 10 – *Events after the Reporting Period*, an event occurring after the end of the reporting period that resolves an uncertainty that existed at the end of the reporting period does not provide evidence of the conditions that existed at that date. For example, there may be a 20 per cent probability at the end of the reporting period that a major storm will strike during the remaining six months of an insurance contract. After the end of the reporting period but before the financial statements are authorised for issue, a major storm occurs. The fulfilment cash flows under that contract should not reflect the storm that, with hindsight, is known to have occurred. Instead, the cash flows included in the measurement include the 20 per cent probability apparent at the end of the reporting period (with disclosure applying IAS 10 that a non-adjusting event occurred after the end of the reporting period). *[IFRS 17.B55]*.

Current estimates of expected cash flows are not necessarily identical to the most recent actual experience. For example, suppose that mortality experience in the reporting period was 20 per cent worse than the previous mortality experience and previous expectations of mortality experience. Several factors could have caused the sudden change in experience, including: *[IFRS 17.B56]*

- lasting changes in mortality;
- changes in the characteristics of the insured population (for example, changes in underwriting or distribution, or selective lapses by policyholders in unusually good health);
- random fluctuations; or
- identifiable non-recurring causes.

An entity should investigate the reasons for the change in experience and develop new estimates of cash flows and probabilities in the light of the most recent experience, the earlier experience and other information. The result for the example above when mortality experience worsened by 20 per cent in the reporting period would typically be that the expected present value of death benefits changes, but not by as much as 20 per cent. However, if mortality rates continue to be significantly higher than the previous estimates for reasons that are expected to continue, the estimated probability assigned to the high-mortality scenarios will increase. *[IFRS 17.B57]*.

Estimates of non-market variables should include information about the current level of insured events and information about trends. For example, mortality rates have consistently declined over long periods in many countries. The determination of the fulfilment cash flows reflects the probabilities that would be assigned to each possible trend scenario, taking account of all reasonable and supportable information available without undue cost or effort. *[IFRS 17.B58]*.

In a similar manner, if cash flows allocated to a group of insurance contracts are sensitive to inflation, the determination of the fulfilment cash flows should reflect current estimates of possible future inflation rates. Because inflation rates are likely to be correlated with interest rates, the measurement of fulfilment cash flows should reflect the probabilities for each inflation scenario in a way that is consistent with the probabilities implied by the market interest rates used in estimating the discount rate (see 8.2.1.A above). *[IFRS 17.B59]*.

When estimating the cash flows, an entity should take into account current expectations of future events that might affect those cash flows. The entity should develop cash flow scenarios that reflect those future events, as well as unbiased estimates of the probability of each scenario. However, an entity should not take into account current expectations of future changes in legislation that would change or discharge the present obligation or create new obligations under the existing insurance contract until the change in legislation is substantively enacted. *[IFRS 17.B60]*.

8.2.3 Cash flows within the contract boundary

As discussed at 8.1 above, estimates of cash flows should include all cash flows within the boundary of an insurance contract and in determining the contract boundary, an entity should consider its substantive rights and obligations and whether those rights and obligations arise from contract, law or regulation.

Many insurance contracts have features that enable policyholders to take actions that change the amount, timing, nature or uncertainty of the amounts they will receive. Such features include renewal options, surrender options, conversion options and options to stop paying premiums while still receiving benefits under the contracts. The measurement of a group of insurance contracts should reflect, on an expected value basis, the entity's current estimates of how the policyholders in the group will exercise the options available, and the risk adjustment for non-financial risk (see 8.4 below) should reflect the entity's current estimates of how the actual behaviour of the policyholders may differ from the expected behaviour. This requirement to determine the expected value applies regardless of the number of contracts in a group; for example it applies even if the group comprises a single contract. Thus, the measurement of a group of insurance contracts should not assume a 100 per cent probability that policyholders will: [IFRS 17.B62]

- surrender their contracts, if there is some probability that some of the policyholders will not; or
- continue their contracts, if there is some probability that some of the policyholders will not.

It is observed in the Basis for Conclusions that IFRS 17 does not require or allow the application of a deposit floor when measuring insurance contracts. If a deposit floor were to be applied the resulting measurement would ignore all scenarios other than those involving the exercise of policyholder options in the way that is least favourable to the entity. This would contradict the principle that an entity should incorporate in the measurement of an insurance contract future cash flows on a probability-weighted basis. [IFRS 17.BC166]. The expected cash outflows include outflows over which the entity has discretion. [IFRS 17.BC168]. The Board considered whether payments that are subject to the entity's discretion meet the definition of a liability in the *Conceptual Framework for Financial Reporting* (the Conceptual Framework). The contract, when considered as a whole, clearly meets the Conceptual Framework's definition of a liability. Some components, if viewed in isolation, may not meet the definition of a liability. However, in the Board's view, including such components in the measurement of insurance contracts would generate more useful information for users of financial statements. [IFRS 17.BC169].

Cash flows within the boundary of an insurance contract are those that relate directly to the fulfilment of the contract, including cash flows for which the entity has discretion over the amount or timing.

IFRS 17 provides the following examples of such cash flows: *[IFRS 17.B65]*
- premiums – see 8.2.3.A below;
- payments, including claims, to a policyholder – see 8.2.3.B below;
- payments to a policyholder that vary based on underlying items – see 8.2.3.C below;
- payments to a policyholder resulting from derivatives – see 8.2.3.D below;
- insurance acquisition cash flows – see 8.2.3.E below;
- claims handling costs – see 8.2.3.F below;
- costs incurred in providing contractual benefits in kind – see 8.2.3.G below;
- policy administration and maintenance costs – see 8.2.3.H below;
- transaction-based taxes and levies – see 8.2.3.I below;
- payments by the insurer of tax in a fiduciary capacity – see 8.2.3.J below;
- potential cash inflows from recoveries – see 8.2.3.K below;
- an allocation of fixed and variable overheads – see 8.2.3.L below;
- costs the entity will incur in providing an investment activity, an investment-return service or an investment-related service – see 8.2.3.M below; and
- any other costs specifically chargeable to the policyholder – see 8.2.3.N below.

The list of examples of cash flows within the boundary of an insurance contract is more extensive than permitted under many local GAAPs (and hence applied previously under IFRS 4). For example, some local GAAP's permit only incremental costs to be included. Some local GAAPs also permit entities an accounting policy choice in whether or not to treat certain costs as insurance acquisition cash flows (and hence deferred over the policy period). IFRS 17 does not allow a choice as to whether or not to include these cash flows that are within the boundary of the insurance contract.

The Board decided not to include only insurance cash flows that are incremental at a contract level as that would mean that entities would recognise different contractual service margins and expenses depending on the way they structure their acquisition activities. *[IFRS 17.BC182(a)]*. For example, there would be different liabilities reported if the entity had an internal sales department rather than outsourcing sales to external agents as the costs of an internal sales department, such as fixed salaries, are less likely to be incremental than amounts paid to an agent.

At initial recognition of an insurance contract, the fulfilment cash flows will include estimates for these cash flows. Subsequently, as services are provided under the contract, the liability for remaining coverage is reduced and insurance revenue is recognised except for those changes that do not relate to services provided in the period (premiums received, investment component changes, changes related to transaction-based taxes, insurance finance income or expenses, and insurance acquisition cash flows) – see 15.1 below.

In September 2018, the IASB staff considered a submission to the TRG which asked whether cash flows from insurance contracts with direct participation features that relate to periods when insurance coverage is no longer provided and the policyholder bears all of the risks related to the investment related services are within the boundary of the contract. In particular, if the cash flows within the boundary of the contract extends to include the period in which the investment component exists but no insurance coverage is provided. The IASB staff observed that cash flows within the boundary of a contract may relate to periods in which coverage is no longer provided, such as when claims are expected to be settled in the future that relate to premium within the boundary of the contract and that periods of coverage may be outside the boundary of a contract if, for example, an entity can fully reprice premiums.[28]

8.2.3.A   Premium cash flows

Premium cash flows include premium adjustments, instalment premiums from a policyholder and any additional cash flows that result from those premiums.

Some insurance contracts charge a higher premium to policyholders who pay by (say) monthly instalments compared to those who pay a single amount on policy inception. The increased amount billed to those paying by instalments may include an implicit interest charge. Under IFRS 4, accounting practices for the higher premium charged to those who pay by instalments have been diverse. Under IFRS 17, the fulfilment cash flows arising from any incremental premium chargeable to policyholders is insurance revenue as it does not meet the definition of insurance finance income or expenses (see 15.3 below) nor is it a distinct non-insurance service as the insurance and financing is not usually sold separately (see 4.3 above).

8.2.3.B   Payments to (or on behalf of) a policyholder

These payments include claims that have already been reported but have not yet been paid (i.e. reported claims), incurred claims for future events that have occurred but for which claims have not been reported (i.e. incurred but not reported or IBNR claims) and all future claims for which an entity has a substantive obligation.

8.2.3.C   Payments to (or on behalf of) a policyholder that vary depending on returns on underlying items

Some insurance contracts give policyholders the right to share in the returns on specified underlying items. Underlying items are items that determine some of the amounts payable to a policyholder. Underlying items can comprise any items; for example, a reference portfolio of assets, the net assets of the entity, or a specified subset of the net assets of the entity. *[IFRS 17 Appendix A]*.

Payments to policyholders that vary depending on returns from underlying items are found most frequently in contracts with participation features. These are discussed at 11 below.

8.2.3.D   Payments to (or on behalf of) a policyholder resulting from derivatives

Examples of such derivatives include options and guarantees embedded into the contract, to the extent that those options and guarantees are not separated from the contract (see 4.1 above).

8.2.3.E   Insurance acquisition cash flows

These cash flows comprise an allocation of insurance acquisition cash flows attributable to the portfolio to which the contract belongs.

There is no restriction of insurance acquisition cash flows to those resulting from successful efforts. So, for example the directly attributable costs of an underwriter of a portfolio of motor insurance contracts do not need to be apportioned between those costs relating to efforts that result in the issuance of a contract and those relating to unsuccessful efforts. The Basis for Conclusions observes that the Board considered whether to restrict insurance acquisition cash flows included in the measurement of a group of insurance contracts to those cash flows directly related to the successful acquisition of new or renewed insurance contracts. However, it was concluded that this was not consistent with an approach that measured profitability of a group of contracts over the duration of the group and, in addition, the Board wanted to avoid measuring liabilities and expenses at different amounts depending on how an entity structures its insurance activities. *[IFRS 17.BC183]*.

Changes in estimates of insurance acquisition cash flows are adjusted against the liability for remaining coverage but do not adjust insurance revenue as they do not relate to services provided by the entity. *[IFRS 17.B123]*. Separately, insurance revenue related to insurance acquisition cash flows is determined by allocating (or amortising) the portion of the premiums that relates to recovering these cash flows to each reporting period in a systematic way on the basis of passage of time, with a corresponding entry to insurance service expenses (i.e. DR insurance service expense, CR insurance revenue). *[IFRS 17.B125]*. See 15.1.1 below.

8.2.3.F   Claims handling costs

These are costs that an entity will incur in investigating, processing and resolving claims under existing insurance contracts (as opposed to claim payments to policyholders – see 8.2.3.B above). Claims handling costs include legal and loss adjusters' fees and the internal costs of investigating claims and processing claims payments.

8.2.3.G   Costs incurred in providing contractual benefits in kind

These costs are those related to the type of payments in kind discussed at 3.3 above.

8.2.3.H   Policy administration and maintenance costs

These costs include the costs of billing premiums and handling policy changes (for example, conversions and reinstatements). Such costs also include recurring commissions that are expected to be paid to intermediaries if a particular policyholder continues to pay the premiums within the boundary of the insurance contract.

8.2.3.I   Transaction-based taxes

These include such taxes as premium tax, value added taxes and goods and service taxes and levies (such as fire service levies and guarantee fund assessments) that arise directly from existing insurance contracts, or that can be attributed to them on a reasonable and consistent basis. See also 8.2.3.J below.

Premium or sales taxes are typically billed to the policyholder and then passed onto the tax authorities with the insurer usually acting as an agent for the tax authorities. The cash flows within the contract boundary would therefore include both the tax in-flow and the tax out-flow. Guarantee fund or similar assessments are usually billed to the insurer directly based on a calculation made by the tax authority often derived from the insurer's market share of particular types of insurance business. There is usually only a cash out-flow for these assessments.

Changes in cash flows that relate to transaction-based taxes collected on behalf of third parties (such as premium taxes, value added taxes and goods and services taxes) adjust the liability for remaining coverage (i.e. are included within the balance of portfolios of insurance contracts included in the statement of financial position) but do not adjust insurance revenue as these do not relate to services expected to be covered by the consideration received by the entity. *[IFRS 17.B123]*.

8.2.3.J Payments by the insurer in a fiduciary capacity

These are payments (and related receipts) made by the insurer to meet tax obligations of the policyholder. In some jurisdictions, the insurer is required to make these payments (e.g. to pay the policyholder's tax on gains made on underlying items). Income tax obligations which are not paid in a fiduciary capacity (e.g. the insurer's own income tax obligations) are not cash flows within the boundary of an insurance contracts. See 8.2.4 below.

8.2.3.K Potential inflows from recoveries

Some insurance contracts permit the insurer to sell, usually damaged, property acquired in settling the claim (salvage). The insurer may also have the right to pursue third parties for payment of some or all costs (subrogation). Potential cash inflows from both salvage and subrogation are included with the cash flows of the boundary of an insurance contract and, to the extent that they do not qualify for recognition as separate assets, potential cash inflows from recoveries on past claims.

8.2.3.L An allocation of fixed and variable overheads

Fixed and variable overheads included with the cash flows of the boundary of an insurance contract include the directly attributable costs of:

- accounting;
- human resources;
- information technology and support;
- building depreciation;
- rent; and
- maintenance and utilities.

These overheads should be allocated to groups of contracts using methods that are systematic and rational and are consistently applied to all costs that have similar characteristics.

8.2.3.M Costs incurred in providing investment activity, investment-return and investment-related services

These are costs the entity will incur:

- performing investment activity, to the extent the entity performs that activity to enhance benefits from insurance coverage for policyholders. Investment activities enhance benefits from insurance coverage if the entity performs those activities expecting to generate an investment return from which policyholders will benefit if an insured event occurs;
- providing investment-return service to policyholders of insurance contracts without direct participation features (see 8.7.2 below); and
- providing investment-related service to policyholders of insurance contracts with direct participation features (see 11.2.4 below).

Investment activity costs that an entity incurs are included in the fulfilment cash flows to the extent that the entity incurs those costs to provide investment-return service or investment-related service. It is acknowledged in the Basis for Conclusions that an entity may also incur investment activity costs to enhance benefits from insurance coverage from customers. Therefore, IFRS 17, as amended in June 2020 specifies that an entity is required to include investment activity costs in the fulfilment cash flows to the extent that the entity performs those activities to enhance benefits from insurance coverage for policyholders. IFRS 17 also specifies when investment activities enhance benefits from insurance coverage. In determining whether investment activity costs enhance benefits from insurance coverage for policyholders, an entity needs to apply judgement in a similar manner to when an entity determines whether an investment-return service exists. *[IFRS 17.BC283I]*.

Costs resulting from investment activity performed for the benefit of shareholders, rather than policyholders, are excluded from the list above. Therefore, it can be inferred by omission that the IASB does not consider shareholder-related investment costs to be fulfilment cash flows directly related to insurance contracts.

8.2.3.N Any other costs

These are any other costs specifically chargeable to the policyholder under the insurance contract.

The IASB has clarified that the other costs include income tax payments and receipts that are specifically chargeable to the policyholder under the terms of an insurance contract (see 8.2.4 below). The consequence of this is that an entity will recognise insurance revenue for the consideration paid by the policyholder for these tax payments and receipts consistent with the recognition of insurance revenue for other incurred expenses. The IASB staff's view is that for income tax payments specifically chargeable to the policyholder under the contract terms, when the tax expense is incurred applying IAS 12, the entity will treat it as an incurred expense applying IFRS 17 (see also 15.1 below).[29]

8.2.4 Cash flows excluded from the contract boundary

Having provided a list of cash flows that are within the boundary of an insurance contract, IFRS 17 then provides a list of cash flows that should not be included when estimating the cash flows that will arise as an entity fulfils an existing insurance contract. These are as follows: *[IFRS 17.B66]*

- investment returns. Investments are recognised, measured and presented separately;
- cash flows (payments or receipts) that arise under reinsurance contracts held. Reinsurance contracts held are recognised, measured and presented separately;
- cash flows that may arise from future insurance contracts, i.e. cash flows outside the boundary of existing contracts (see 8.2.3 above);
- cash flows relating to costs that cannot be directly attributed to the portfolio of insurance contracts that contain the contract, such as some product development and training costs. Such costs are recognised in profit or loss when incurred;
- cash flows that arise from abnormal amounts of wasted labour or other resources that are used to fulfil the contract. Such costs are recognised in profit or loss when incurred;
- income tax payments and receipts the insurer does not pay or receive in a fiduciary capacity or that are not specifically chargeable to the policyholder under the terms of the contract;
- cash flows between different components of the reporting entity, such as policyholder funds and shareholder funds, if those cash flows do not change the amount that will be paid to the policyholders; and
- cash flows arising from components separated from the insurance contract and accounted for using other applicable IFRSs (see 4 to 4.3 above).

IFRS 17, as amended in June 2020, resolves an inconsistency between the description of cash flows within the boundary of an insurance contract (see 8.2.3.N above) and the description of cash flows outside the boundary of an insurance contract. IFRS 17, as issued in May 2017, required an entity exclude income tax payments and receipts not paid or received in a fiduciary capacity from the estimate of the cash flows that will arise as the entity fulfils an insurance contract. The Board received feedback that some income tax payments and receipts, although not paid or received in a fiduciary capacity, are costs specifically chargeable to the policyholder under the terms of the contract. Accordingly, those costs should be included in the boundary of an insurance contract. The Board agreed that any costs specifically chargeable to the policyholder are cash flows that will arise as the entity fulfils an insurance contract. Therefore, the Board amended IFRS 17 to clarify that income tax payments or receipts not specifically chargeable to the policyholder under the terms of the contract should be excluded from the estimate of the cash flows that will arise as the entity fulfils an insurance contract. *[IFRS 17.BC170A]*.

8.3 Discount rates

The second element of the building blocks in the general model (discussed at 8 above) is an adjustment (i.e. discount) to the estimates of future cash flows to reflect the time value of money and the financial risks related to those cash flows, to the extent that the financial risks are not included in the estimates of cash flows.

The discount rates applied to the estimates of the future cash flows should: *[IFRS 17.36]*

- reflect the time value of money, the characteristics of the cash flows and the liquidity characteristics of the insurance contracts;

- be consistent with observable current market prices (if any) for financial instruments with cash flows whose characteristics are consistent with those of the insurance contracts, in terms of, for example, timing, currency and liquidity; and
- exclude the effect of factors that influence such observable market prices but do not affect the future cash flows of the insurance contracts.

The discount rates calculated according to the requirements above should be determined as follows: *[IFRS 17.B72-B73]*

Insurance liability measurement component	Discount rate for liability
Fulfilment cash flows.	Current rate at reporting date.
Contractual service margin interest accretion for contracts without direct participation features (including insurance and reinsurance contracts issued and reinsurance contracts held).	Rate at date of initial recognition of group.
Changes in the fulfilment cash flows for contracts without direct participation features which relate to future service that affect the contractual service margin (including insurance and reinsurance contracts issued and reinsurance contracts held).	Rate at date of initial recognition of group.
Liability for remaining coverage under the premium allocation approach for groups of insurance contracts that have a significant financing component.	Rate at date of initial recognition of group.

Insurance finance income or expenses	Discount rate used for disaggregation between profit or loss and other comprehensive income
Insurance finance income or expenses for which disaggregation between profit or loss and other comprehensive income is optional and for which changes in financial risk do not have a substantial effect on amounts paid to policyholders (see 15.3.1 below).	Rate at date of initial recognition of group.
Insurance finance income or expenses for which disaggregation between profit or loss and other comprehensive income is optional and for which changes in financial risk assumptions have a significant effect on amounts paid to policyholders (see 15.3.1 below).	Rate that allocates the remaining revised finance income or expense over the duration of the group at a constant rate ('effective yield approach') or, for contracts that use a crediting rate, uses an allocation based on the amounts credited in the period and expected to be credited in future periods ('projected crediting approach').
Insurance finance income or expenses for which disaggregation between profit or loss and other comprehensive income is optional for incurred claims of groups of contracts applying the premium allocation approach (see 15.3.3 below).	Rate at date of incurred claim.
Insurance finance income or expenses for which disaggregation between profit or loss and other comprehensive income is optional for groups of insurance contracts with direct participation features for which the entity holds the underlying items (see 15.3.4 below).	An amount that eliminates accounting mismatches with income or expenses on the underlying items, i.e. the net of the two should be nil ('current period book yield approach').

IFRS 17 does not specify requirements for accretion of interest on assets for insurance acquisition cash flows. The Board decided against specifying such requirements because doing so would be inconsistent with IFRS 15. *[IFRS 17.BC184H]*. Consequently, entities have an accounting policy choice as to whether to accrete interest on such assets and the rate to use for such accretion.

For insurance contracts without direct participation features, the Board concluded that changes in the effects of the time value of money and financial risk do not affect the amount of unearned profit. This is the case even if the payments to policyholders vary with returns on underlying items through a participation mechanism. Accordingly, the entity does not adjust the contractual service margin to reflect the effects of changes in these assumptions and hence a locked-in discount rate is used. *[IFRS 17.BC228]*.

Discount rates should reflect the rate at initial recognition of the group, considering that contracts may be added to the group after its initial recognition. This can be achieved by applying locked in rates that correspond to the initial recognition date over the period that the contracts in the group are issued, or a weighted-average locked-in rate that reflects these rates which apply over the period that contracts in the group are issued, which cannot exceed one year. *[IFRS 17.B73]*. As explained at 6 above, this can result in a change in the discount rates during the period of the contracts as newly recognised contracts are added to the group. When contracts are added to a group in a subsequent reporting period (because the period of the group spans across two reporting periods) and weighted-average discount rates are revised, an entity should apply the revised discount rates from the start of the reporting period in which the new contracts are added to the group. *[IFRS 17.28]*. This means that there is no retrospective catch-up adjustment for previous reporting periods (see 15.4 below).

In April 2019, the IASB staff responded to a submission to the TRG which asked how to account for a discrepancy between:

- the current discount rate used to measure the fulfilment cash flows of each contract when it joins a group of insurance contracts; and
- the weighted average discount rates used at initial recognition of a group of insurance contracts.

The IASB staff observed that entities which apply the other comprehensive income disaggregation option use the discount rates determined at the date of initial recognition to determine the amounts recognised in profit or loss using a systematic allocation. An entity is permitted to use weighted-average discount rates over the period that contracts in a group are issued to determine the discount rate at the date of initial recognition of a group of contracts. The weighted average discount rate used should achieve the outcome that the amounts recognised in other comprehensive income over the duration of the group of contracts total zero.[30]

IFRS 17 does not state whether the discount rate should be a yield curve or a single discount rate. In May 2018, the IASB staff responded to a submission to the TRG which asked whether, for a group of insurance contracts for which changes in financial risk do not have a substantial effect on the amounts paid to policyholders (and the entity chooses to disaggregate insurance finance income or expenses between profit or loss and other comprehensive income) an entity should use an effective yield rate or a yield curve. The IASB staff confirmed that, in using the discount rate determined at the date of initial recognition to nominal cash flows that do not vary based on returns from underlying items, IFRS 17 does not mandate the use of an effective yield rate or a yield curve. In response to the IASB staff, a few TRG members commented that using an effective yield rate compared to using a yield curve could result in a significant difference to insurance finance income or expense to be included in profit or loss over the reporting periods subsequent to initial recognition.[31]

Estimates of discount rates should be consistent with other estimates used to measure insurance contracts to avoid double counting or omissions; for example: *[IFRS 17.B74]*

- cash flows that do not vary based on the returns on any underlying items should be discounted at rates that do not reflect any such variability;
- cash flows that vary based on the returns on any financial underlying items should be:
  - discounted using rates that reflect that variability; or
  - adjusted for the effect of that variability and discounted at a rate that reflects the adjustment made;
- nominal cash flows (i.e. those that include the effect of inflation) should be discounted at rates that include the effect of inflation; and
- real cash flows (i.e. those that exclude the effect of inflation) should be discounted at rates that exclude the effect of inflation.

However, discount rates should not reflect the non-performance (i.e. own credit) risk of the entity. *[IFRS 17.31]*.

As explained in the second bullet point above, cash flows that vary based on the returns on underlying items should be discounted using rates that reflect that variability, or to be adjusted for the effect of that variability and discounted at a rate that reflects the adjustment made. The variability is a relevant factor regardless of whether it arises because of contractual terms or because the entity exercises discretion, and regardless of whether the entity holds the underlying items. *[IFRS 17.B75]*.

Cash flows that vary with returns on underlying items with variable returns, but that are subject to a guarantee of a minimum return, do not vary solely based on the returns on the underlying items, even when the guaranteed amount is lower than the expected return on the underlying items. Hence, an entity should adjust the rate that reflects the variability of the returns on the underlying items for the effect of the guarantee, even when the guaranteed amount is lower than the expected return on the underlying items. *[IFRS 17.B76]*. In May 2018, in response to a submission to the TRG which had asked whether minimum guarantees are reflected through adjusting the discount rate (rather than through adjustments to the cash flows) the IASB staff stated that although IFRS 17 requires the time value of a guarantee to be reflected in the measurement of fulfilment cash flows, it does not require the use of a specific approach to achieve this objective. Financial risk is included in the estimates of future cash flows or the discount rate used to adjust the cash flows. Judgement is required to determine the technique for measuring market variables and that the technique must result in the measurement of any options and guarantees being consistent with observable market prices for such options and guarantees. Any consideration beyond this is actuarial (i.e. operational measurement implementation) in nature. The TRG members did not disagree with the IASB staff's observations.[32]

IFRS 17 does not require an entity to divide estimated cash flows into those that vary based on the returns on underlying items and those that do not. If an entity does not divide the estimated cash flows in this way, the entity should apply discount rates appropriate for the estimated cash flows as a whole; for example, using stochastic modelling techniques or risk-neutral measurement techniques. *[IFRS 17.B77]*

Discount rates should include only relevant factors, i.e. factors that arise from the time value of money, the characteristics of the cash flows and the liquidity characteristics of the insurance contracts. Such discount rates may not be directly observable in the market. Hence, when observable market rates for an instrument with the same characteristics are not available, or observable market rates for similar instruments are available but do not separately identify the factors that distinguish the instrument from the insurance contracts, an entity should estimate the appropriate rates. IFRS 17 does not require a particular estimation technique for determining discount rates. In applying an estimation technique, an entity should: *[IFRS 17.B78]*

- maximise the use of observable inputs and reflect all reasonable and supportable information on non-market variables available without undue cost or effort, both external and internal. In particular, the discount rates used should not contradict any available and relevant market data, and any non-market variables used should not contradict observable market variables;
- reflect current market conditions from the perspective of a market participant; and
- exercise judgement to assess the degree of similarity between the features of the insurance contracts being measured and the features of the instrument for which observable market prices are available and adjust those prices to reflect the differences between them.

For cash flows of insurance contracts that do not vary based on the returns on underlying items, the discount rate reflects the yield curve in the appropriate currency for instruments that expose the holder to no or negligible credit risk, adjusted to reflect the liquidity characteristics of the group of insurance contracts. That adjustment should reflect the difference between the liquidity characteristics of the group of insurance contracts and the liquidity characteristics of the assets used to determine the yield curve. Yield curves reflect assets traded in active markets that the holder can typically sell readily at any time without incurring significant costs. In contrast, under some insurance contracts the entity cannot be forced to make payments earlier than the occurrence of insured events, or dates specified in the contracts. *[IFRS 17.B79]*

IFRS 17 proposes two methods for determining discount rates for cash flows of insurance contracts that do not vary based on the returns on underlying items as follows:

- a 'bottom-up' approach; and
- a 'top-down' approach.

The 'bottom-up' approach determines discount rates by adjusting a liquid risk-free yield curve to reflect the differences between the liquidity characteristics of the financial instruments that underlie the rates observed in the market and the liquidity characteristics of the insurance contracts. *[IFRS 17.B80]*.

The 'top-down' approach determines the appropriate discount rates for insurance contracts based on a yield curve that reflects the current market rates of return implicit in a fair value measurement of a reference portfolio of assets. An entity should adjust that yield curve to eliminate any factors that are not relevant to the insurance contracts, but is not required to adjust the yield curve for differences in liquidity characteristics of the insurance contracts and the reference portfolio. *[IFRS 17.B81]*.

In theory, when considering all required adjustments, both the 'top-down' and 'bottom-up' approaches should give the same result although in practice this is not necessarily the case.

An example of the approaches giving the same result is illustrated below where the overall liability discount rate is 2.5% in each case. The example assumes that there are no differences between the liquidity characteristics of the liability and the reference portfolio of assets. The 'top down' approach starts with a current asset yielding 4% and this rate is reduced by 1.5% for expected and unexpected losses while the 'bottom up' approach starts with a risk-free rate of 2% which is increased by a liquidity premium of 0.5%.

Assume a current asset yield of a reference instrument of 4% composed of:

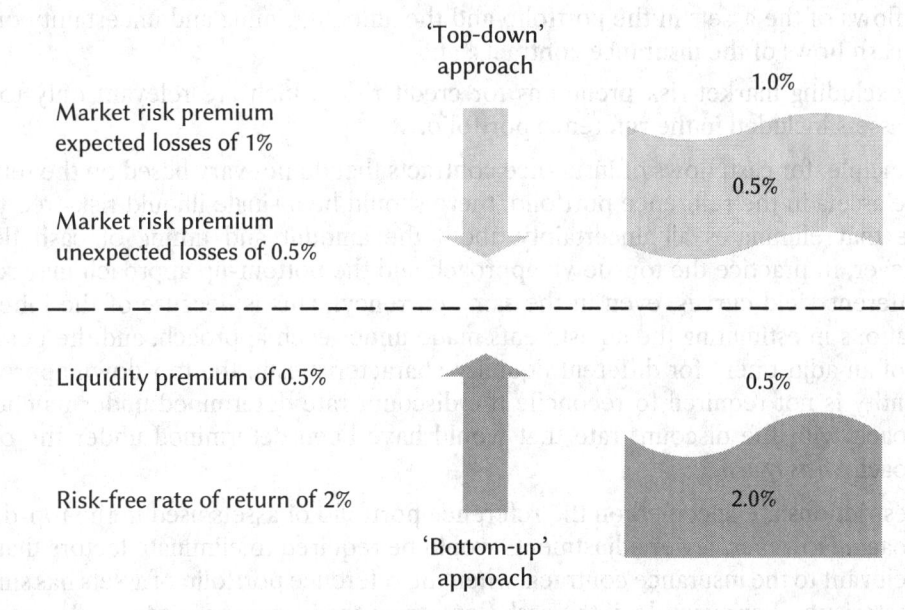

In estimating the yield curve on a 'top down' basis an entity should use measurement bases consistent with IFRS 13 as follows: *[IFRS 17.B82]*

- if there are observable market prices in active markets for assets in the reference portfolio, an entity should use those prices;
- if a market is not active, an entity should adjust observable market prices for similar assets to make them comparable to market prices for the assets being measured;
- if there is no market for assets in the reference portfolio, an entity should apply an estimation technique. For such assets an entity should:
  - develop unobservable inputs using the best information available in the circumstances. Such inputs might include the entity's own data and, in the context of IFRS 17, the entity might place more weight on long-term estimates than on short-term fluctuations; and
  - adjust the data to reflect all information about market participant assumptions that is reasonably available.

In adjusting the yield curve, an entity should adjust market rates observed in recent transactions in instruments with similar characteristics for movements in market factors since the transaction date, and should adjust observed market rates to reflect the degree of dissimilarity between the instrument being measured and the instrument for which transaction prices are observable. For cash flows of insurance contracts that do not vary based on the returns on the assets in the reference portfolio, such adjustments include: *[IFRS 17.B83]*

- adjusting for differences between the amount, timing and uncertainty of the cash flows of the assets in the portfolio and the amount, timing and uncertainty of the cash flows of the insurance contracts; and
- excluding market risk premiums for credit risk, which are relevant only to the assets included in the reference portfolio.

In principle, for cash flows of insurance contracts that do not vary based on the returns of the assets in the reference portfolio, there should be a single illiquid risk-free yield curve that eliminates all uncertainty about the amount and timing of cash flows. However, in practice the top-down approach and the bottom-up approach may result in different yield curves, even in the same currency. This is because of the inherent limitations in estimating the adjustments made under each approach, and the possible lack of an adjustment for different liquidity characteristics in the top-down approach. An entity is not required to reconcile the discount rate determined under its chosen approach with the discount rate that would have been determined under the other approach. *[IFRS 17.B84]*.

No restrictions are specified on the reference portfolio of assets used in the top-down approach. However, fewer adjustments would be required to eliminate factors that are not relevant to the insurance contracts when the reference portfolio of assets has similar characteristics. For example, if the cash flows from the insurance contracts do not vary based on the returns on underlying items, fewer adjustments would be required if an entity used debt instruments as a starting point rather than equity instruments. For debt instruments, the objective would be to eliminate from the total bond yield the effect of credit risk and other factors that are not relevant to the insurance contracts. One way to estimate the effect of credit risk is to use the market price of a credit derivative as a reference point. *[IFRS 17.B85]*.

In September 2018, the TRG members discussed an IASB staff paper which responded to a submission that asked whether, in applying a top-down approach to determine the discount rates for insurance contracts with cash flows that do not vary based on the returns of underlying items:

- an entity could use the assets it holds as a reference portfolio of assets;
- an entity could ignore the liquidity characteristics of insurance contracts; and
- changes in the assets the entity holds result in changes in the discount rates used to measure insurance contracts under specific circumstances.

The TRG members agreed with the IASB staff analysis and conclusion in this paper that an entity can use the assets it holds as a reference portfolio when determining a top-down discount rate to measure its insurance liabilities. The TRG members observed that:

- IFRS 17 does not specify restrictions on the reference portfolio of assets used in applying a top-down approach to determine discount rates and also does not define 'a reference portfolio of assets'. Consequently, a portfolio of assets an entity holds can be used as a reference portfolio to determine the discount rates provided that the discount rates achieve the objectives of reflecting the characteristics of the insurance contracts and are consistent with observable current market prices.
- IFRS 17 requires that discount rates reflect, among other factors, the liquidity characteristics of the insurance contracts. However, when using the top-down approach, as a simplification, IFRS 17 permits an entity not to adjust the yield curve derived from a reference portfolio of assets for differences in liquidity characteristics of the insurance contracts and the reference portfolio. The IASB expected a reference portfolio of assets typically to have liquidity characteristics closer to the liquidity characteristics for a group of insurance contracts than would be the case for highly-liquid, high-quality bonds.
- In determining the appropriate discount rates for cash flows that do not vary based on underlying items, an entity ensures that at each reporting date those discount rates reflect the characteristics of the insurance contracts, even when the entity chooses to use a portfolio of assets that it holds to determine the discount rates.
- An entity needs to make adjustments to the yield curve of the reference portfolio of assets at each reporting date to eliminate any effect on discount rates of credit risk and differences in liquidity characteristics of the insurance contracts and the reference portfolio. However, if the entity uses the simplification related to liquidity, fluctuations in the liquidity of the reference portfolio are mirrored in the changes in discount rates used to measure the group of insurance contracts.
- The TRG members also observed that, when an entity uses the simplification related to liquidity (i.e. the top-down approach discussed above), small changes in discount rates that result from changes in the composition of the reference portfolio could result in significant changes to the insurance contract liabilities measured using those rates, particularly with respect to long-term insurance contracts.

Both the IASB staff and the TRG members note that IFRS 17 contains disclosure requirements for qualitative and quantitative information about the significant judgements and changes in those judgements (see 16.3 below) and consider that, if the effect of illiquidity were to be significant, entities would be expected to disclose such information in their financial statements.[33]

In April 2019, in response to a submission to the TRG, the IASB staff further observed that identifying a reference portfolio that will enable an entity to meet the objectives required for setting a discount rate is dependent on specific facts and circumstances and providing specific application guidance is not within the remit of the TRG.[34]

Some insurance contracts will have a contract boundary which extends beyond the period for which observable market data is available. In these situations, the entity will have to determine an extrapolation of the discount rate yield curve beyond that period. IFRS 17 provides no specific guidance on the estimation techniques for interest rates in these circumstances. The general guidance above for unobservable inputs is that an entity should use the best information available in the circumstances and adjust that data to reflect all information about market participant assumptions that is reasonably available.

In some jurisdictions, a liquid risk-free yield curve (or interest rate) might be negative. An entity should use the current market rates even if those are negative and this results in the present value of future payments exceeding, rather than reducing, the value of the undiscounted fulfilment cash flows.

8.4 The risk adjustment for non-financial risk

The third element of the building blocks in the general model discussed at 8 above is the risk adjustment for non-financial risk.

The risk adjustment for non-financial risk is the compensation that the entity requires for bearing the uncertainty about the amount and timing of cash flows that arises from non-financial risk. *[IFRS 17.37]*. Non-financial risk is risk arising from insurance contracts other than financial risk, which is included in the estimates of future cash flows or the discount rate used to adjust the cash flows. The risks covered by the risk adjustment for non-financial risk are insurance risk and other non-financial risks such as lapse risk and expense risk. *[IFRS 17.B86]*.

In theory, the risk adjustment for non-financial risk for insurance contracts measures the compensation that the entity would require to make the entity indifferent between: *[IFRS 17.B87]*

- fulfilling a liability that has a range of possible outcomes arising from non-financial risk; and
- fulfilling a liability that will generate fixed cash flows with the same expected present value as the insurance contracts.

In developing the objective of the risk adjustment for non-financial risk, the Board concluded that a risk adjustment for non-financial risk should not represent: *[IFRS 17.BC209]*

- the compensation that a market participant would require for bearing the non-financial risk that is associated with the contract. This is because the measurement model is not intended to measure the current exit value or fair value, which reflects the transfer of the liability to a market participant. Consequently, the risk

- adjustment for non-financial risk should be determined as the amount of compensation that the entity, not a market participant, would require; and
- an amount that would provide a high degree of certainty that the entity would be able to fulfil the contract. Although such an amount might be appropriate for some regulatory purposes, it is not compatible with the Board's objective of providing information that will help users of financial statements make decisions about providing resources to the entity.

To illustrate the objective, the Application Guidance explains that a risk adjustment for non-financial risk would measure the compensation the entity would require to make it indifferent between fulfilling a liability that, because of non-financial risk, has a 50% probability of being CU90 and a 50% probability of being CU110, and fulfilling a liability that is fixed at CU100. As a result, the risk adjustment for non-financial risk conveys information to users of financial statements about the amount charged by the entity for the uncertainty arising from non-financial risk about the amount and timing of cash flows. *[IFRS 17.B87]*.

In addition, because the risk adjustment for non-financial risk reflects the compensation the entity would require for bearing the non-financial risk arising from the uncertain amount and timing of the cash flows, the risk adjustment for non-financial risk also reflects: *[IFRS 17.B88]*
- the degree of diversification benefit the entity includes when determining the compensation it requires for bearing that risk; and
- both favourable and unfavourable outcomes, in a way that reflects the entity's degree of risk aversion.

The purpose of the risk adjustment for non-financial risk is to measure the effect of uncertainty in the cash flows that arise from insurance contracts, other than uncertainty arising from financial risk. Consequently, the risk adjustment for non-financial risk should reflect all non-financial risks associated with the insurance contracts. It should not reflect the risks that do not arise from the insurance contracts, such as general operational risk. *[IFRS 17.B89]*.

The risk adjustment for non-financial risk should be included in the measurement in an explicit way. The risk adjustment for non-financial risk is conceptually separate from the estimates of future cash flows and the discount rates that adjust those cash flows. The entity should not double-count the risk adjustment for non-financial risk by, for example, also including the risk adjustment for non-financial risk implicitly when determining the estimates of future cash flows or the discount rates. The yield curve (or range of yield curves) used to discount cash flows that do not vary based on the returns on underlying items which are required to be disclosed (see 16.1.5 below) should not include any implicit adjustments for non-financial risk. *[IFRS 17.B90]*.

In April 2019, the IASB staff responded to a submission to the TRG which asked whether the risk adjustment for non-financial risk takes into account uncertainty related to how management will apply discretion. The IASB staff observed that the risk adjustment for non-financial risk does not reflect risks that do not arise from insurance contracts such as general operational risk. Uncertainty related to how management applies discretion for a group of insurance contracts, if not considered a general operational risk, should be captured in the risk adjustment for non-financial risk (e.g. to the extent management discretion reduces the amount it would charge for uncertainty, the discretion would reduce the risk adjustment for non-financial risk). The risk adjustment for non-financial risk should reflect favourable and unfavourable outcomes in a way that reflects the entity's degree of risk aversion.[35]

8.4.1 Techniques used to estimate the risk adjustment for non-financial risk

IFRS 17 does not specify the estimation technique(s) used to determine the risk adjustment for non-financial risk. This is because the Board decided that a principle-based approach, rather than identifying specific techniques, would be consistent with the Board's approach on how to determine a similar risk adjustment for non-financial risk in IFRS 13. Furthermore, the Board concluded that limiting the number of risk-adjustment techniques would conflict with the Board's desire to set principle-based IFRSs and, given that the objective of the risk adjustment is to reflect an entity-specific perception of non-financial risk, specifying a level of aggregation that was inconsistent with the entity's view would also conflict with that requirement. *[IFRS 17.BC213]*.

Therefore, the risk adjustment under IFRS 17 should be determined based on the principle of the compensation that an entity requires for bearing the uncertainty arising from non-financial risk inherent in the cash flows arising from the fulfilment of the group of insurance contracts. According to this principle, the risk adjustment for non-financial risk reflects any diversification benefit the entity considers when determining the amount of compensation it requires for bearing that uncertainty. *[IFRS 17.BC214]*.

Different entities may determine different risk adjustments for similar groups of insurance contracts because the risk adjustment for non-financial risk is an entity specific perception, rather than a market participant's perception, based on the compensation that a particular entity requires for bearing the uncertainty about the amount and timing of the cash flows that arise from the non-financial risks. Accordingly, to allow users of financial statements to understand how entity-specific assessments of risk aversion might differ from entity to entity, disclosure is required of the confidence level used to determine the risk adjustment for non-financial risk or, if a technique other than confidence level is used, the technique used and the confidence level corresponding to the technique (see 16.3 below).

IFRS 17 states that risk adjustment for non-financial risk should have the following characteristics: *[IFRS 17.B91]*

- risks with low frequency and high severity will result in higher risk adjustments for non-financial risk than risks with high frequency and low severity;
- for similar risks, contracts with a longer duration will result in higher risk adjustments for non-financial risk than contracts with a shorter duration;
- risks with a wider probability distribution will result in higher risk adjustments for non-financial risk than risks with a narrower distribution;
- the less that is known about the current estimate and its trend, the higher the risk adjustment will be for non-financial risk; and
- to the extent that emerging experience reduces uncertainty about the amount and timing of cash flows, risk adjustments for non-financial risk will decrease and *vice versa*.

An entity should apply judgement when determining an appropriate estimation technique for the risk adjustment for non-financial risk. When applying that judgement, an entity should also consider whether the technique provides concise and informative disclosure so that users of financial statements can benchmark the entity's performance against the performance of other entities. *[IFRS 17.B92]*.

It is likely that some entities will want to apply a cost of capital approach technique to estimate the risk adjustment for non-financial risk because this will be the basis of local regulatory capital requirements. It is observed in the Basis for Conclusions that although the usefulness of a confidence level technique diminishes when the probability distribution is not statistically normal, as is often the case for insurance contracts, the cost of capital approach would be more complicated to calculate than a confidence level disclosure. However, the Board expects that many entities will have the information necessary to apply the cost of capital technique. *[IFRS 17.BC217]*. This implies that the Board is anticipating some, or perhaps many, entities will use a cost of capital technique to measure the risk adjustment for non-financial risk.

8.4.2 The level at which the risk adjustment should be determined

IFRS 17 does not specify the level within an insurance group at which to determine the risk adjustment for non-financial risk. Therefore, the question arises as to whether, in the individual financial statements of a subsidiary, the risk adjustment for non-financial risk should reflect the degree of risk diversification available to the entity or to the consolidated group as a whole and whether, in the consolidated financial statements of a group of entities, the risk adjustment for non-financial risk issued by entities in the group should reflect the degree of risk diversification available only to the consolidated group as a whole. This issue was discussed by the TRG in May 2018 and the results of the discussion were as follows:

- In respect of individual financial statements, the degree of risk diversification that occurs at a level higher than the issuing entity level is required to be considered if, and only if, it is considered when determining the compensation the issuing entity would require for bearing non-financial risk related to the insurance contracts it issues. Equally, risk diversification that occurs at a level higher than the issuing entity level must not be considered when determining the risk adjustment for non-financial risk if it is not considered when determining the compensation the issuing entity would require for bearing non-financial risk related to the insurance contracts it issues.

- In respect of consolidated financial statements, the IASB staff opinion is that the risk adjustment for non-financial risk is the same as the risk adjustment for non-financial risk at the individual entity level because determining the compensation that the entity would require for bearing non-financial risk related to insurance contracts issued by the entity is a single decision that is made by the entity that is party to the contract (i.e. the issuer of the insurance contract). However, differing views were expressed by TRG members. Some TRG members agreed with the IASB staff but other TRG members read the requirements as requiring different measurement of the risk adjustment for non-financial risk for a group of insurance contracts at different reporting levels if the issuing entity would require different compensation for bearing non-financial risk than the consolidated group would require. The TRG members also observed that in some cases the compensation an entity requires for bearing non-financial risk could be evidenced by capital allocation in a group of entities.[36]

Subsequently, the IASB decided not to amend IFRS 17 on the grounds that it was considered that the risk adjustment was likely to be the same at both consolidated and individual financial statements in the vast majority of situations.

In September 2018, the TRG members also discussed an IASB staff paper which addressed a submission about the level at which the risk adjustment for non-financial risk should be determined for insurance contracts that are within industry pools managed by an association (i.e. at the association level or the individual member level). In the fact pattern an association manages two industry pools:

- Pool 1 – in which some members are appointed to issue contracts on behalf of all members; and
- Pool 2 – to which members can choose to transfer some insurance contracts they have issued.

The IASB staff considered that there should be only one risk adjustment for each insurance contract and that the risk adjustment is at either at an individual member or an association level depending on who has issued the contract. Consistent with the discussion at the May 2018 TRG meeting above, some TRG members disagreed with the IASB staff's view that there is one single risk adjustment for a group of insurance contracts that reflects the degree of diversification that the issuer of the contract considers in determining the compensation required for bearing non-financial risk. Those TRG members expressed the view that each entity would consider the compensation it would require for non-financial risk, rather than the compensation required by the association. This would mean that the risk adjustment would not necessarily be determined by the entity that issued the contract (e.g. the pool or individual member of the association that priced the risk). As noted above, the IASB does not propose to amend or clarify IFRS 17 on this matter.[37]

In addition, since IFRS 17 does not specify the level of aggregation at which to determine the risk adjustment for non-financial risk, the question arises as to whether the risk adjustment for non-financial risk could be negative for a group of insurance contracts. This situation could, in theory, arise where a diversification benefit is allocated between two or more groups of insurance contracts and the additional diversification risk for one group may be negative as the insurer would accept a lower price for taking on these liabilities given that it reduces the risk for the entity in total. IFRS 17 is silent as to whether a risk adjustment could be negative. However, a negative risk adjustment would normally be inappropriate as it would not reflect the purpose of the risk adjustment for non-financial risk which is to measure the effect of uncertainty in the cash flows (see 8.4 above). So, for example, a risk adjustment should not reduce fulfilment cash flows below the best estimate of the expected future cash flows.

8.4.3 Consideration of reinsurance held in the risk adjustment

In April 2019, the IASB staff responded to a TRG submission which questions whether the effect of reinsurance should be considered in calculating the risk adjustment for non-financial risk for contracts that have been reinsured. The IASB staff observed that the risk adjustment for non-financial risk reflects the degree of diversification benefit the entity includes when determining the compensation it requires for bearing that risk.

Therefore, if an entity considers reinsurance when determining the compensation it requires for bearing non-financial risk related to underlying insurance contracts, the effect of reinsurance (both cost and benefit) would be reflected in the risk adjustment for non-financial risk of the underlying insurance contracts. The IASB staff further observed that IFRS 17 requires that the risk adjustment for non-financial risk for reinsurance contracts held represents the amount of risk being transferred by the holder of the group of reinsurance contracts to the issuer of those contracts. Therefore, the risk adjustment for non-financial risk of the reinsurance contract held could not be nil, unless:

- the entity considers reinsurance when determining the compensation it requires for bearing non-financial risk related to underlying insurance contracts; and
- the cost of acquiring the reinsurance is equal or less than the expected recoveries.[38]

The TRG members agreed with the IASB staff observations that if an entity considers reinsurance when determining the compensation it requires for non-financial risk, the effect of the reinsurance would be included in the risk adjustment and that the measurement of the risk adjustment for non-financial risk of a reinsurance contract held is the amount of risk transferred to the reinsurer.[39]

8.4.4 Presentation of the risk adjustment for non-financial risk in the statement of comprehensive income

The change in risk adjustment for non-financial risk is not required to be disaggregated between the insurance service result and the insurance finance income or expense. When an entity decides not to disaggregate the change in risk adjustment for non-financial risk, the entire change should be included as part of the insurance service result. *[IFRS 17.81]*.

When the risk adjustment for non-financial risk is disaggregated between profit or loss and other comprehensive income the method of disaggregation is determined by the disaggregation policy applied to that portfolio (see 15.3.1 below).

8.5 The contractual service margin

The fourth element of the building blocks in the general model discussed at 8 above is the contractual service margin. The contractual service margin is a new concept to IFRS, introduced in IFRS 17 to identify the expected profitability of a group of contracts and recognise this profitability over time in an explicit manner, based on the pattern of services provided under the contract.

The contractual service margin is a component of the asset or liability for the group of insurance contracts that represents the unearned profit the entity will recognise as it provides insurance contract services in the future. Hence, the contractual service margin would usually be calculated at the level of a group of insurance contracts rather than at an individual insurance contract level.

An entity should measure the contractual service margin on initial recognition of a group of insurance contracts at an amount that, unless the group of contracts is onerous (see 8.8 below) or where there is insurance revenue and expenses recognised from the

derecognition of an asset for other cash flows (see 15.3.1 below), results in no income or expenses arising from: *[IFRS 17.38]*
- the initial recognition of an amount for the fulfilment cash flows (see 8.2 above);
- any cash flows arising from the contracts in the group at that date;
- the derecognition at the date of initial recognition of:
    - any asset recognised for insurance acquisition cash flows (see 6.3 above); and
    - any other asset or liability previously recognised for cash flows related to the group of contracts.

For insurance contracts acquired in a transfer of insurance contracts or in a business combination with the scope of IFRS 3 an entity shall apply the above in accordance with the requirements for acquisitions of insurance contracts (see 13 below). *[IFRS 17.39]*.

Before the recognition of a group of insurance contracts, an entity might be required to recognise an asset or liability for cash flows related to the group of insurance contracts other than insurance acquisition cash flows either because of the occurrence of the cash flows or because of the requirements of another IFRS Standard. Cash flows are related to the group of insurance contracts if those cash flows would have been included in the fulfilment cash flows at the date of initial recognition of the group had they been paid or received after that date. To apply the requirement in the last bullet point above, an entity should derecognise such an asset or liability to the extent that the asset or liability would not be recognised separately from the group of insurance contracts if the cash flow or the application of the IFRS Standard occurred at the date of initial recognition of the group of insurance contracts. *[IFRS 17.B66A]*. For example, an entity that recognised a liability for premiums received in advance of the recognition of a group of insurance contracts would derecognise that liability when the entity recognises a group of insurance contracts to the extent the premiums relate to the contracts in the group. The performance obligation that was depicted by the liability would not be recognised separately from the group of insurance contracts had the premium been received on the date of initial recognition of the group. No insurance revenue arises on the derecognition of the liability. *[IFRS 17.BC184N]*.

As a result of the measurement requirements, the contractual service margin on initial recognition, assuming a contract is not onerous and there is no insurance revenue or expense due to derecognition of another asset, is no more than the balancing number needed to eliminate any day 1 differences and thereby avoiding a day 1 profit being recognised. The contractual service margin cannot depict unearned losses. Instead, IFRS 17 requires an entity to recognise a loss in profit or loss for any excess of the expected present value of the future cash flows above the expected future value of the premium inflows adjusted for risk – see 8.8 below.

The approach above on initial recognition applies to contracts with and without participation features including investment contracts with discretionary participation features.

A contractual service margin is not specifically identified for contracts subject to the premium allocation approach, although the same principle of profit recognition applies (i.e. no day 1 profits and recognition over the coverage period as insurance contract services are provided) – see 9 below.

For groups of reinsurance contracts held, the calculation of the contractual service margin at initial recognition is modified to take into account the fact that such groups are usually assets rather than liabilities and that a margin payable to the reinsurer rather than making profits is an implicit part of the premium – see 10 below.

For insurance contracts acquired in a business combination or transfer the contractual service margin at initial recognition is calculated in the same way except that initial recognition is the date of the business combination or transfer – see 13 below.

8.6 Subsequent measurement

The carrying amount of a group of insurance contracts at the end of each reporting period should be the sum of: *[IFRS 17.40]*

- the liability for remaining coverage comprising:
  - the fulfilment cash flows related to future service allocated to the group at that date, measured applying the requirements discussed at 8.2 above – see 8.6.1 below;
  - the contractual service margin of the group at that date, measured applying the requirements discussed at 8.6.3 below; and
- the liability for incurred claims, comprising the fulfilment cash flows related to past service allocated to the group at that date, measured applying the requirements discussed at 8.2 above – see 8.6.2 below.

Hence, after initial recognition, the fulfilment cash flows comprise two components:

- those relating to future service (the liability for remaining coverage); and
- those relating to past service (the liability for incurred claims).

In some circumstances an incurred claim can create insurance risk for an entity that would not exist if no claim was made. Two examples cited of this situation are:

- insurance coverage for disability that provides an annuity for the period when a policyholder is disabled; and
- insurance coverage for fire that provides compensation for the cost of rebuilding a house after a fire.

The question therefore arises whether the entity's obligation to pay these amounts, that are subject to insurance risk, should be treated as a liability for incurred claims or a liability for remaining coverage. One view is that the liability for incurred claims is the entity's obligation to pay for a policyholder's claim (on becoming disabled or upon a fire occurring). The alternative view is that the liability for incurred claims is the policyholder's obligation to settle a claim that has already been made by a policyholder (for a period of disability or to pay for the cost of the house damaged by fire) and the liability for remaining coverage is the obligation to pay claims relating to future events that have not yet occurred (such as future periods of disability or claims relating to fire events that have not occurred). In September 2018, the TRG members discussed an IASB staff paper which argued that both approaches represent valid interpretations of IFRS 17 and are a matter of judgement for the entity as to which interpretation provides the most useful information about the service provided to the policyholder. The TRG members observed that:

- the classification of an obligation as a liability for incurred claims or a liability for remaining coverage does not affect the determination of fulfilment cash flows. However, the classification does affect the determination of the coverage period. Consequently, the classification affects whether some changes in fulfilment cash flows adjust the contractual service margin and allocation of the contractual service margin;

- the definitions in IFRS 17 allow an entity to use judgement when determining whether the obligation to pay an annuity after a disability event and the obligation to pay the costs of rebuilding a house after a fire event are part of the liability for remaining coverage or liability for incurred claims;

- it is a matter of judgement for an entity to develop an accounting policy that reflects the insurance service provided by the entity to the policyholder under the contract in accordance with IFRS 17. The requirements of IAS 8 apply and hence the entity should apply an approach consistently for similar transactions and over time;

- whatever approach an entity applies, IFRS 17 requires disclosure of significant judgements made in applying the standard and requires disclosures relating to the contractual service margin, which will enable users to understand the effects of the approach required; and

- these observations are also relevant when law or regulation impose a requirement for an entity to settle a claim by life-contingent annuity.[40]

Although leaving the decision open to the entity allows preparers to determine which approach provides more useful information given the facts and circumstances around their products, the accounting policy choice may result in identical contracts being accounted for differently in the financial statements of different insurers.

8.6.1 The liability for remaining coverage

IFRS 17, as amended in June 2020, states that the liability for remaining coverage is an entity's obligation to: *[IFRS 17 Appendix A]*

- investigate and pay valid claims for insured events that have not yet occurred (i.e. the obligation that relates to the unexpired portion of the insurance coverage); and

- pay amounts under existing contracts that are not included above and that relate to:
  - insurance contract services not yet provided (i.e. the obligations that relate to future provision of insurance contract services); or
  - any investment components or other amounts that are not related to the provision of insurance contract services and that have not been transferred to the liability for incurred claims.

At initial recognition, the liability for remaining coverage includes all remaining cash inflows and outflows under an insurance contract. Subsequently, at each reporting date, the liability for remaining coverage, excluding the contractual service margin, is re-measured using the fulfilment cash flow requirements discussed at 8.2 above. That is, it comprises the present value of the best estimate of the cash flows required to settle the obligation together with an adjustment for non-financial risk. The fulfilment cash flows for the liability for remaining coverage for contracts without direct participation features are discounted at the date of initial recognition of the group (under both the general model and the premium allocation approach where applicable) – see 8.3 above.

Usually, the fulfilment cash flows should reduce over the contract period as the number of future insured events that have not occurred decline. When future insured events can no longer occur then the fulfilment cash flows of the liability for remaining coverage should be nil.

An entity should recognise income and expenses for the following changes in the carrying amount of the liability for remaining coverage: *[IFRS 17.41]*

- insurance revenue – for the reduction in the liability for remaining coverage because of services provided in the period (see 15.1.1 below for measurement);
- insurance service expenses – for losses on groups of onerous contracts, and reversals of such losses (see 8.8 below); and
- insurance finance income or expenses – for the effect of the time value of money and the effect of financial risk (see 15.3 below).

8.6.2 The liability for incurred claims

IFRS 17, as amended in 2020, states that the liability for incurred claims is an entity's obligation to: *[IFRS 17 Appendix A]*

- investigate and pay valid claims for insured events that have already occurred, including events that have occurred but for which claims have not been reported, and other incurred insurance expenses; and
- pay amounts that are not included above and that relate to:
  - insurance contract services that have already been provided: or
  - any investment components or other amounts that are not related to the provision of insurance contract services and that are not in the liability for remaining coverage.

At initial recognition of a group of contracts, the liability for incurred claims is usually nil as no insured events covered under the contracts have occurred. Subsequently, at each reporting date, the liability for incurred claims is measured using the fulfilment cash flow requirements discussed at 8.2 and 8.4 above. That is, it comprises the present value of the expected cash flows required to settle the obligation together with an adjustment for non-financial risk. This includes unpaid incurred cashflows allocated to the group of contracts (including expenses) as discussed at 8.2.4 above.

The liability for incurred claims under the general model, including claims arising from contracts with direct participation features, is discounted at a current rate (i.e. the rate applying as at the reporting date). The liability for incurred claims under the premium allocation approach need not be discounted if certain conditions are met (see 9.4 below). Otherwise, the liability for incurred claims under the premium allocation approach is also discounted at a current rate.

There is no direct relationship between the liability for incurred claims and the liability for remaining coverage. That is, the creation of a liability for incurred claims (or a reduction in the value of incurred claims) does not necessarily result in an equal and opposite reduction to the liability for remaining coverage. There is no contractual service margin attributable to the liability for incurred claims as the contractual service margin relates to remaining (i.e. future) service provided over the coverage period and incurred claims relate to past service.

Consequently, the establishment of a liability for incurred claims should give rise to the following accounting entry:

	CU	CU
Dr. Insurance service expense – profit or loss	X	
Cr. Liability for incurred claims		X

Subsequent to initial recognition, an entity should recognise income and expenses for the following changes in the carrying amount of the liability for incurred claims: *[IFRS 17.42]*

- insurance service expenses – for the increase in the liability because of claims and expenses incurred in the period, excluding any investment components (see 15.2 below);
- insurance service expenses – for any subsequent changes in fulfilment cash flows relating to incurred claims and incurred expenses (see 15.2 below); and
- insurance finance income or expenses – for the effect of the time value of money and the effect of financial risk (see 15.3 below).

IFRS 17 does not distinguish between or require separate disclosure of the components of the liability for incurred claims which represent claims notified to the insurer (sometimes described as 'outstanding claims') and claims incurred but not reported (sometimes described as 'IBNR claims'). IFRS 17 also does not distinguish between, or require, separate disclosure of those components of the liability for incurred claims that represent the entity's liability for expected payments to the policyholder and those that represent an allocation of expenses.

Disclosure of the liability for incurred claims is required showing the development of actual claims compared with previous estimates of the liability for incurred claims, except for those claims for which uncertainty about the amount and timing of payments is typically resolved within one year (see 16.5.3 below).

8.6.3 Subsequent measurement of the contractual service margin (for insurance contracts without direct participation features)

The contractual service margin at the end of the reporting period represents the profit in the group of insurance contracts that has not yet been recognised in profit or loss because it relates to the future service to be provided under the contracts in the group. *[IFRS 17.43]*.

At the end of each reporting period, the carrying amount of the contractual service margin of a group of insurance contracts without direct participation features comprises the carrying amount at the start of the reporting period adjusted for: *[IFRS 17.44]*

- the effect of any new contracts added to the group (see 6 above);
- interest accreted on the carrying amount of the contractual service margin during the reporting period, measured at the discount rates at initial recognition (see 8.3 above);
- the changes in fulfilment cash flows relating to future service (see below), except to the extent that:
    - such increases in the fulfilment cash flows exceed the carrying amount of the contractual service margin, giving rise to a loss (see 8.8 below); or
    - such decreases in the fulfilment cash flows are allocated to the loss component of the liability for remaining coverage (see 8.8 below);
- the effect of any currency exchange differences (see 7.3 above) on the contractual service margin; and
- the amount recognised as insurance revenue because of the transfer of insurance contract services in the period, determined by the allocation of the contractual service margin remaining at the end of the reporting period (before any allocation) over the current and remaining coverage period (see 8.7 below)

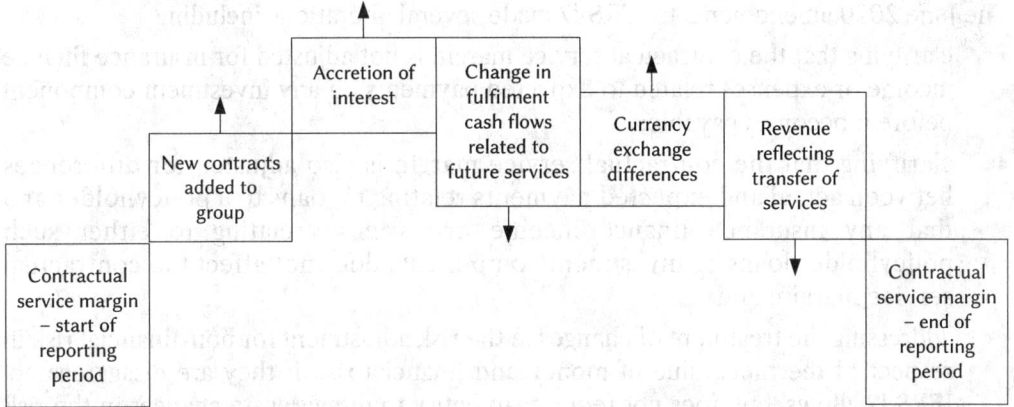

The changes in fulfilment cash flows that relate to future events which adjust the contractual service margin for a group of insurance contracts without direct participation features are as follows: [IFRS 17.B96]

- Experience adjustments arising from premiums received in the period that relate to future service, and related cash flows such as insurance acquisition cash flows and premium-based taxes, measured at the discount rates applying at the date of initial recognition.
- Changes in estimates of the present value of the future cash flows in the liability for remaining coverage (except those changes described in paragraph B97 and discussed below) measured at the discount rates applying at the date of initial recognition.
- Differences between any investment component expected to become payable or repayable in the period and the actual investment component or loan to a policyholder that becomes payable or repayable in the period. Those differences are determined by comparing (i) the actual investment component that becomes

payable in the period with (ii) the payment in the period that was expected at the start of the period plus an insurance finance income or expense related to that expected payment before it becomes payable.

- Differences between any loan to a policyholder expected to become repayable in the period and the actual loan to a policyholder that becomes repayable in the period. Those differences are determined by comparing (i) the actual loan to a policyholder that becomes repayable in a period with (ii) the repayment in the period that was expected at the start of the period plus an insurance finance income or expense related to that expected repayment before it becomes repayable.

- Changes in the risk adjustment for non-financial risk that relate to future service. An entity is not required to disaggregate the change in the risk adjustment for non-financial risk between (i) a change related to non-financial risk and (ii) the effect of the time value of money and changes in the time value of money. If an entity makes such a disaggregation, it should adjust the contractual service margin for the change related to non-financial risk, measured at the discount rates applying at the date of initial recognition.

The June 2020 amendments to IFRS 17 made several alterations including:

- clarifying that the contractual service margin is not adjusted for insurance finance income or expenses related to expected payments on any investment component before it becomes payable;

- clarifying that the contractual service margin is also adjusted for differences between actual and expected payments relating to loans to a policyholder and that any insurance finance income or expense relating to either such policyholder loans or investment components does not affect the contractual service margin; and

- addressing the treatment of changes in the risk adjustment for non-financial risk in respect of the time value of money and financial risk if they are disaggregated. IFRS 17 allows, but does not require, an entity to disaggregate changes in the risk adjustment for non-financial risk into those caused by the time value of money and those caused by changes in non-financial risk (see 8.4.4 above).

In February 2018, the IASB staff responded to a submission made to the TRG asking whether the adjustment of the contractual service margin for a difference in the investment component as a result of the acceleration or delay of repayment was appropriate since the contractual service margin is adjusted for changes solely in timing of payments which appears to conflict with the principle underlying insurance revenue recognition by referring to the Board's reasons for this treatment in the Basis for Conclusions.[41] It is stated in the Basis for Conclusions that the Board did not regard as useful information, for example, the recognition of a gain for a delay in repaying an investment component accompanied by a loss that adjusts the contractual service margin for the expected later repayment. Acceleration or delay in repayments of investment components only gives rise to a gain or loss for the entity to the extent that the amount of the repayment is affected by its timing. As IFRS 17 does not require an entity to determine the amount of an investment component until a claim is incurred, accordingly, when a claim is incurred, IFRS 17 requires an entity to determine how much of that claim is an investment component, and whether it was expected to become payable in that period. IFRS 17 requires any unexpected repayment of an investment component to adjust the contractual service margin. The contractual service margin will also be adjusted for changes in future estimates of cash flows which will include (but not separately identify) the reduction in future repayments of investment components. This achieves the desired result of the net effect on the contractual service margin being the effect of the change in timing of the repayment of the investment component. *[IFRS 17.BC235]*. However, the Board did amend IFRS 17 to specify that the adjustment of the contractual service margin for a difference in the investment component does not apply to insurance finance income or expenses that depict the effect on the investment component of the time value of money and financial risk between the beginning of the period and the unexpected payment or non-payment of the investment component. *[IFRS 17.BC235fn]*.

In September 2018, the IASB staff responded to a submission to the TRG as to whether a difference between the expected and actual crediting rate applied to a policyholder's account balance is included in insurance finance income or expenses or adjusts the contractual service margin as above. The question related to an insurance contract without direct participation features for which the account balance is expected to become payable in the future and ignores the effect of any discretion. The IASB staff observed that paragraph 96 of IFRS 17 is applicable for differences between any investment component expected to become payable in the period and the actual investment component that becomes payable in the period. However, in the fact pattern provided, the account balance is not expected to become payable in the period and does not become payable in the period and therefore the requirement to adjust the contractual service margin does not apply in that period.[42]

The contractual service margin for contracts without direct participation features should not be adjusted for the following changes in fulfilment cash flows because they do not relate to future service: *[IFRS 17.B97]*

- the effect of the time value of money and changes in the time value of money, and the effect of financial risk and changes in financial risk. These effects comprise:
  - the effect, if any, on estimated future cash flows;
  - the effect, if disaggregated, on the risk adjustment for non-financial risk; and
  - the effect of a change in discount rate.
- changes in estimates of fulfilment cash flows in the liability for incurred claims; and
- experience adjustments, except those described above that relate to future service.

In September 2018, the TRG members discussed an IASB staff paper in respect of a submission which asked how differences between expected premiums and actual premiums (i.e. premium experience adjustments) which relate to current or past service should be accounted for (i.e. should these adjust the contractual service margin or be recognised in the statement of profit or loss immediately as part of either insurance revenue or insurance service expenses). The TRG members agreed with the analysis in the IASB staff paper and observed that:

- applying the general model, experience adjustments arising from premiums received in the period that relate to future services adjust the contractual service margin. Premium adjustments related to current or past service should be recognised immediately in the statement of profit or loss as part of insurance revenue;
- although premium experience adjustments are not specifically referenced in paragraph B124 of IFRS 17 the purpose of that paragraph is to demonstrate an alternative analysis of insurance revenue as determined by paragraph B123 of IFRS 17 (see 15.1.1 below). Hence, applying the requirements in IFRS 17 should result in premium experience adjustments relating to current and past service being included in insurance revenue despite the lack of a specific reference in paragraph B124 of IFRS 17; and
- for the premium allocation approach, the requirements for allocating premium adjustments above, apply to expected premium receipts, including premium experience adjustments (see 15.1.2 below).

The TRG members also observed that:

- Given an entity is required to disclose an analysis of insurance revenue recognised in the period, an additional line item may be necessary in the reconciliation to reflect the effect of premium experience adjustments on the revenue recognised in the period (see 16.1.1 below).
- In some circumstances, judgement may be required to determine whether premium experience adjustments relate to future service and therefore adjust the contractual service margin rather than are recognised in the statement of profit or loss.[43]

The June 2020 amendments to IFRS 17 added a specific reference to experience adjustments for premium receipts consistent with the TRG comments. See 15.1.1 below.

IFRS 17 notes that some changes in the contractual service margin offset changes in the fulfilment cash flows for the liability for remaining coverage, resulting in no change in the total carrying amount of the liability for remaining coverage. To the extent that changes in the contractual service margin do not offset changes in the fulfilment cash flows for the liability for remaining coverage, an entity should recognise income and expenses for the changes, applying the requirements at 8.6.1 above. *[IFRS 17.46]*.

The terms of some insurance contracts without direct participation features give an entity discretion over the cash flows to be paid to policyholders. A change in the discretionary cash flows is regarded as relating to future service, and accordingly adjusts the contractual service margin. To determine how to identify a change in discretionary cash flows, an entity should specify at inception of the contract the basis on which it expects to determine its commitment under the contract; for example, based on a fixed interest rate, or on returns that vary based on specified asset returns. *[IFRS 17.B98]*.

An entity should use that specification to distinguish between the effect of changes in assumptions that relate to financial risk on that commitment (which do not adjust the contractual service margin) and the effect of discretionary changes to that commitment (which adjust the contractual service margin). *[IFRS 17.B99]*.

If an entity cannot specify at inception of the contract what it regards as its commitment under the contract and what it regards as discretionary, it should regard its commitment to be the return implicit in the estimate of the fulfilment cash flows at inception of the contract, updated to reflect current assumptions that relate to financial risk. *[IFRS 17.B100]*.

8.7 Allocation of the contractual service margin to profit or loss

Determining how to release the contractual service margin to profit or loss is a key aspect of IFRS 17 and one of the key challenges implementing the standard.

The basic principle is that an amount of the contractual service margin for a group of insurance contracts is recognised in profit or loss in each period to reflect the insurance contract services provided under the group of insurance contracts in that period.

The amount recognised in profit or loss is determined by: *[IFRS 17.B119]*

- identifying the coverage units in the group. The number of coverage units in a group is the quantity of insurance contract services provided by the contracts in the group, determined by considering for each contract the quantity of the benefits provided under a contract and its expected coverage period;
- allocating the contractual service margin at the end of the period (before recognising any amounts in profit or loss to reflect the insurance contract services provided in the period) equally to each coverage unit provided in the current period and expected to be provided in the future; and
- recognising in profit or loss the amount allocated to coverage units provided in the period.

In February 2018, responding to a submission to the TRG as to how to allocate contractual service margin to coverage units, the IASB staff observed that the contractual service margin is allocated equally to each coverage unit provided in the current period and expected to be provided in the future. Therefore, the allocation is performed at the end of the period, identifying coverage units that were actually provided in the current period and coverage units that are expected at this date to be provided in the future.[44]

It is observed in the Basis for Conclusions that the Board views the contractual service margin as depicting the unearned profit for coverage and other services provided over the coverage period. Insurance coverage is the defining service provided by insurance contracts and an entity provides this service over the whole of the coverage period, and not just when it incurs a claim. Consequently, the contractual service margin should be recognised over the coverage period in a pattern that reflects the provision of coverage as required by the contract. To achieve this, the contractual service margin for a group of insurance contracts remaining (before any allocation) at the end of the reporting period is allocated over the coverage provided in the current period and expected remaining future coverage, on the basis of coverage units, reflecting the expected duration and quantity of benefits provided by contracts in the group. The Board considered whether: [IFRS 17.BC279]

- the contractual service margin should be allocated based on the pattern of expected cash flows or on the change in the risk adjustment for non-financial risk caused by the release of risk. However, the Board decided the pattern of expected cash flows and the release of the risk adjustment for non-financial risk are not relevant factors in determining the satisfaction of the performance obligation of the entity. They are already included in the measurement of the fulfilment cash flows and do not need to be considered in the allocation of the contractual service margin. Hence, the Board concluded that coverage units better reflect the provision of insurance coverage; and

- the contractual service margin should be allocated before any adjustments made because of changes in fulfilment cash flows that relate to future service. However, the Board concluded that allocating the amount of the contractual service margin adjusted for the most up-to-date assumptions provides the most relevant information about the profit earned from service provided in the period and the profit to be earned in the future from future service.

The Board also considered whether the allocation of the contractual service margin based on coverage units would result in profit being recognised too early for insurance contracts with fees determined based on the returns on underlying items. For such contracts, IFRS 17 requires the contractual service margin to be determined based on the total expected fee over the duration of the contracts, including expectations of an increase in the fee because of an increase in underlying items arising from investment returns and additional policyholder contributions over time. The Board rejected the view that the allocation based on coverage units results in premature profit recognition. The Board noted that the investment component of such contracts is accounted for as part of the insurance contract only when the cash flows from the investment component and from insurance and other services are highly interrelated and hence cannot be accounted for as distinct components. In such circumstances, the entity provides multiple services in return for an expected fee based on the expected duration of contracts, and the Board concluded the entity should recognise that fee over the coverage period as the insurance services are provided, not when the returns on the underlying items occur. [IFRS 17.BC280].

IFRS 17 requires the contractual service margin remaining at the end of the reporting period to be allocated equally to the coverage units provided in the period and the expected remaining coverage units. IFRS 17 does not specify whether an entity should consider the time value of money in determining that equal allocation and consequently does not specify whether that equal allocation should reflect the timing of the expected provision of the coverage units. The Board concluded that should be a matter of judgement by an entity. [IFRS 17.BC282].

Consistent with the requirements in IFRS 15, the settlement of a liability is not considered to be a service provided by the entity. Thus, the recognition period for the contractual service margin is the coverage period over which the entity provides the coverage promised in the insurance contract, rather than the period over which the liability is expected to be settled. The risk margin the entity recognises for bearing risk is recognised in profit or loss as the entity is released from risk in both the coverage period and the settlement period. For contracts with a coverage period of one year, this means that the contractual service margin will be released over that one-year period (possibly, a single reporting period). *[IFRS 17.BC283]*. For longer-term contracts, with a coverage period lasting many years, an entity will have to use judgement in order to determine an appropriate allocation of the contractual service margin to each reporting period.

8.7.1 Determining the quantity of benefits for identifying coverage units

The question of how to determine the quantity of benefits for coverage units was discussed by the TRG in both February 2018 and May 2018. In May 2018, the TRG analysed an IASB staff paper that contained the IASB staff's views on sixteen examples of different types of insurance contracts. The TRG members observed that:

- IFRS 17 established a principle (to reflect the services provided in a period under a group of insurance contracts), not detailed requirements, and that it would not be possible to develop detailed requirements that would apply appropriately to the wide variety of insurance products existing globally.
- The determination of coverage units is not an accounting policy choice but involves judgement and estimates to best achieve the principle of reflecting the services provided in each period. Those judgements and estimates should be applied systematically and rationally.
- The analysis of the examples in the IASB Staff paper depends on the fact patterns in that paper, and would not necessarily apply to other fact patterns. In addition, which method would best reflect the services provided in each period would be a matter of judgement based on facts and circumstances.
- In considering how to achieve the principle, the TRG members observed:
  - the period in which an entity bears insurance risk is not necessarily the same as the insurance coverage period;
  - expectations of lapses of contracts are included in the determination of coverage units because they affect the expected duration of the coverage. Consistently, coverage units reflect the likelihood of insured events occurring to the extent that they affect the expected duration of coverage for contracts in the group;
  - because the objective is to reflect the insurance services provided in each period, different levels of service across periods should be reflected in the determination of coverage units;
  - determining the quantity of benefits provided under a contract requires an entity to consider the benefits expected to be received by the policyholder, not the costs of providing those benefits expected to be incurred by the entity;
  - a policyholder benefits from the entity standing ready to meet valid claims, not just from making a claim if an insured event occurs. The quantity of benefits provided therefore relates to the amounts that can be claimed by the policyholder;
  - different probabilities of an insured event occurring in different periods do not affect the benefit provided in those periods of the entity standing ready to meet valid claims for that insured event. Different probabilities of different

types of insured events occurring might affect the benefit provided by the entity standing ready to meet valid claims for the different types of insured events; and

- IFRS 17 does not specify a particular method or methods to determine the quantity of benefits. Different methods may achieve the objective of reflecting the services provided in each period, depending on facts and circumstances.

The TRG members considered that the following methods might achieve the objective if they are reasonable proxies for the services provided under the groups of insurance contracts in each period:

- a straight-line allocation over the passage of time, but reflecting the number of contracts in a group;
- a method based on the maximum contractual cover in each period;
- a method based on the amount the entity expects the policyholder to be able to validly claim in each period if an insured event occurs;
- methods based on premiums. However, premiums will not be reasonable proxies when comparing services across periods if they are receivable in different periods to those in which insurance services are provided, or reflect different probabilities of claims for the same type of insured event in different periods rather than different levels of service of standing ready to meet claims. Additionally, premiums will not be reasonable proxies when comparing contracts in a group if the premiums reflect different levels of profitability in contracts. The level of profitability in a contract does not affect the services provided by the contract; and
- methods based on expected cash flows. However, methods that result in no allocation of the contractual service margin to periods in which the entity is standing ready to meet valid claims do not meet the objective.[45]

The following examples apply the principles above to specific fact patterns for insurance contracts issued without direct participation features. Examples for reinsurance contracts issued and insurance contracts with direct participation features are discussed at 8.9.4 and 11.2.4 below respectively.[46]

Example 56.31: Credit life loan insurance

A life insurance policy pays a death benefit equal to the principal and interest outstanding on a loan at the time of death. The balance of the loan will decline because of contractually scheduled payments and cannot be increased.

Applying the principles above the method suggested for determining the quantity of benefits is the cover for the contractual balance outstanding because it is both the maximum contractual cover and the amount the entity expects the policyholder to be able to make a valid claim for if the insured event occurs.

Example 56.32: Credit life product with variable amount of cover

A credit life insurance policy where the amount payable on an insured event varies (for example, claims might relate to an outstanding credit card balance). In these cases the sum assured will vary over time, rather than simply reducing. In addition, the sum assured may be limited based on the lender's credit limits.

Applying the principles above, the methods suggested for determining the quantity of benefits are either the constant cover of the contractual maximum amount of the credit limit or cover based on the expected credit card balances (i.e. the amount the entity expects the policyholder to be able to make a valid claim for if the insured event occurs).

Example 56.33: Mortgage loss cover

An insurance contract provides cover for five years for default losses on a mortgage, after recovering the value of the property on which the mortgage is secured. The balance of the mortgage will decline because of contractually scheduled payments and cannot be increased.

Applying the principles above, the methods suggested for determining the quantity of benefits are either the maximum contractual cover (the contractual balance of mortgage) or the amount the entity expects the policyholder to be able to make a valid claim for if the insured event occurs (the contractual balance of the mortgage less the expected value of the property).

Example 56.34: Product warranty

A five-year warranty coverage insurance contract provides for replacement of a purchased item if it fails to work properly within five years of the date of purchase. Claims are typically skewed toward the end of the coverage period as the purchased item ages.

Applying the principles above, the quantity of benefits are constant over the five year coverage period if the price of replacement product is expected to remain constant. However, if the cost of the replacement product rises over the coverage period (e.g. inflation costs) then the coverage units should include expectations about the cost of replacing the item.

Example 56.35: Extended product warranty

Extended warranty policies cover the policyholders after the manufacturer's original warranty has expired. The policies provide new for old cover in the event of a major defect to the covered asset.

Applying the principles above, the expected coverage duration does not start until the manufacturer's original warranty has expired. The policyholder cannot make a valid claim to the entity until then.

Example 56.36: Health cover

An insurance contract provides health cover for 10 years for specified types of medical costs up to €1m over the life of the contract, with the expected amount and expected number of claims increasing with age.

Applying the principles above, the expected coverage duration is the 10 years during which cover is provided, adjusted for any expectations of the limit being reached during the ten years and lapses. For determining the quantity of benefits the following two methods are suggested:

- comparing the contractual maximum amount that could have been claimed in the period with the remaining contractual maximum amount that can be claimed as a constant amount for each future coverage period. So, if a claim of €100,000 were made in the first year, at the end of the year the entity would compare €1m coverage provided in the year with coverage of €900,000 for the following nine years, resulting in an allocation of 1/9.1 of the contractual service margin for the first year; or

- comparing the maximum amount that could be claimed in the period with the expected maximum amounts that could be claimed in each of the future coverage periods, reflecting the expected reduction in cover because of claims made. This approach involves looking at the probabilities of claims in different periods to determine the expected maximum amounts in future periods. However, in this fact pattern, the probability of claims in one period affects the amount of cover for future periods, thereby affecting the level of service provided in those periods.

Example 56.37: Transaction liability

A transaction liability policy will pay claims for financial losses arising as a result of breaches of representations and warranties made in a specified and executed acquisition transaction. The policy period (contract term) is for 10 years from the policy start date. The insurer will pay claims for financial losses reported during the 10-year policy period up to the maximum sum insured.

Applying the principles above the insured event is the discovery of breaches of representations and warranties (consistent with the definition of title insurance – see 3.7 above). Coverage starts at the moment the contract is signed and lasts for 10 years. The IASB staff rejected the view that the coverage period is just one day (i.e. the transaction closing date, which is the date on which the representations and warranties were made).

Example 56.38: Combination of different types of cover

This example assumes there are five different contracts (A-E) in a single group of insurance contracts. Each contract has a different combination of four coverages (accidental death, cancer diagnosis, surgery and inpatient treatment). Each contract has a different coverage period. Coverages have a high level of interdependency in the same insurance contract; if a coverage of an insurance contract in the group of insurance contracts lapses, other coverages of the same insurance contract lapse simultaneously. Presented in the table below is the summary of the contracts.

Contract	Coverage				Coverage period
	Accidental death	Cancer diagnosis	Surgery	Inpatient treatment	
A	Cover of 2000	Cover of 1000	Cover of 500	Cover of 50	2 years
B	N/A	Cover of 1000	Cover of 500	N/A	5 years
C	N/A	N/A	Cover of 500	Cover of 50	2 years
D	N/A	N/A	Cover of 500	Cover of 50	5 years
E	Cover of 2000	N/A	N/A	N/A	10 years

The entity charges the same annual premium amount for each type of cover, and the total annual premium amount for a contract is the sum of the premiums for each type of cover included in the contract.

Applying the principles above the expected coverage duration is the period in which cover is provided, adjusted for expectations of lapses. The quantity of benefits for each contract is the sum of all the levels of cover provided. So, based on the cover set out in the table, the total coverage units for contract A for each year would be $3,550 (i.e. 2,000 + 1,000 + 500 + 50) and for contract B 1,500 (i.e. 1,000 + 500). Methods which do not reflect the different amounts of cover provided by each contract would not appear to be valid. A method based on annual premiums may be valid depending on the factors mentioned in the TRG analysis above.

In this example, in all scenarios the coverage period is the same for all coverage components so the probability of the insured event does not affect the coverage period and can be ignored. If the coverage period for the various covers is different, then the probability of the insured event becomes relevant as some coverage components will expire before other coverage components.

Example 56.39: Life contingent annuity

A life contingent pay out annuity pays a fixed monthly amount of €10 each period until the annuitant dies.

Applying the principles above the expected coverage duration is the probability weighted average expected duration of the contract. The expected coverage duration is reassessed in each period. The quantity of benefits is the fixed monthly amount of €10. An approach that does not reassess the expected coverage period would appear to be inconsistent with the current measurement principle of IFRS 17.

The IASB staff rejected the view that there is a constant level of benefits provided over the life of the annuitant and that the contractual service margin should be amortised straight line over the remaining expected life of the annuitant (i.e. the quantity of benefits is €10 per year and the coverage period is the length of time until there will no longer be any payments made to the policyholder which is estimated at 40 years) because it does not reflect the expected duration of the contract. The IASB staff also rejected the view that the contract is a series of individual promises to pay a fixed amount at a future point in time if the annuitant is still alive at that point in time because it requires an entity to split a contract into multiple individual contracts and also does not appear to require reassessment of the expected coverage duration.

Example 56.40: Forward purchase of fixed rate annuity

A forward contract to buy an annuity in the future at a fixed rate. The premium is payable when the annuity is bought. If the policyholder dies, or cancels the contract, before the date the annuity can be purchased, the policyholder receives no benefit.

Applying the principles above the entity bears insurance risk from the date the forward contract is issued, but the coverage period does not start until the date the annuity starts (as a claim cannot be made before that date). The insured event is that the policyholder lives long enough (i.e. survives) to receive payments under the annuity.

8.7.2 Allocating the contractual service margin on the basis of coverage units determined by considering both insurance coverage and any investment-return service

IFRS 17, as amended in June 2020, defines insurance contract services as the following services that an entity provides to the policyholder of an insurance contract: *[IFRS 17 Appendix A]*

- coverage for an insured event (insurance coverage);
- for insurance contracts without direct participation features, the generation of an investment return for the policyholder, if applicable (investment-return service); and
- for insurance contracts with direct participation features, the management of underlying items on behalf of the policyholder (investment-related service).

As the contractual service margin is recognised in profit or loss to reflect the provision of insurance contract services, this means that the period over which the contractual service margin is amortised includes both the period in which the entity provides insurance contract services and the period over which it provides an investment-return service (for insurance contracts without direct participation features) or an investment-related service (for insurance contracts with direct participation features). The coverage period of insurance contracts with direct participation features is discussed at 11.2.4 below.

In IFRS 17, as issued in 2017, the coverage period of an insurance contract without direct participation features included only the period in which an entity provided insurance contract services and did not include the period in which an entity provided investment return-services. In May 2018, most TRG members disagreed that insurance contracts under the general model should be treated as providing only insurance services.[47] Stakeholders also expressed concerns that contracts which provide insurance coverage that ends significantly before the investment-return service ended would result in 'front-end' revenue recognition and deferred annuity contracts with an account balance accumulating in the period before the annuity payments start could result in 'back-end' revenue recognition if insurance coverage is provided only during the annuity periods. As a result, the Board was persuaded that some insurance contracts outside the scope of the variable fee approach (i.e. those that do not contain direct participation features) provide an investment-return service and that recognising the contractual service margin considering both insurance coverage and an investment-return service will provide useful information to users of the financial statements. *[IFRS 17.BC283B]*.

Insurance contracts without direct participation features may provide an investment-return service if, and only if: *[IFRS 17.B119B]*

- an investment component exists or the policyholder has a right to withdraw an amount;
- the entity expects the investment component, or amount the policyholder has a right to withdraw, to include an investment return (an investment return could be below zero, for example in a negative interest rate environment); and
- the entity expects to perform investment activity to generate that investment return.

In this context, a 'right to withdraw an amount from the entity' includes a policyholder's right to: *[IFRS 17.BC283C]*

- receive a surrender value or refund of premiums on cancellation of a policy; or
- transfer an amount to another insurance provider.

The Board admits that specifying conditions for an investment-return service creates the risk that an appropriate outcome may not be achieved in all scenarios (for example, entities might also conclude that an investment-return service exists in circumstances in which the Board would conclude otherwise such as when an entity provides only custodial services relating to an investment component). Balancing those potential risks, the Board decided to specify conditions that are necessary to identify, but not determinative of, the existence of an investment-return service. An entity is required to apply judgement, considering the facts and circumstances, to determine whether an insurance contract meets the conditions to provide an investment-return service. *[IFRS 17.BC283D-E]*

For the purpose of amortising the contractual service margin, the period of investment-return service ends at or before the date that all amounts due to current policyholders relating to those services have been paid, without considering payments to future policyholders included in the fulfilment cash flows as a result of mutualisation (see 11.1 below). *[IFRS 17.B119A]*

The following example illustrates the impact of the change on the contractual service margin.

Example 56.41: Insurance services and investment-return services with different durations

An insurance contract matures in year 10 and pays the customer the account value at maturity. The contract also includes a death benefit that varies depending on which year in the 10 year period the death occurs. Specifically, if the customer dies in years 1-5, the customer's beneficiary would receive a death benefit that is the higher of 110% of the premium paid or the accumulated account value (assume that the death benefit for years 1-5 results in significant insurance risk). However, if the customer dies in years 6-10 the customer's beneficiary receives only the account value. There is no surrender penalty.

Does the insurer only have to consider years 1-5 for determining the coverage units to determine the amortisation of the contractual service margin? Or does the insurer need to consider all 10 years for determining coverage units and amortisation of the contractual service margin?

Based on IFRS 17, as amended in June 2020, the coverage units should be determined reflecting the benefits to the policyholder during the period of both the insurance coverage and the investment return services (i.e. 10 years). Under IFRS 17 as issued in 2017, the insurer would only consider years 1-5 for determining the coverage units since that is the period of the insurance benefits.

The impact on profit in Example 56.41 can be illustrated graphically below.

Recognition of profit considering both insurance coverage and investment-return service

Year	1	2	3	4	5	6	7	8	9	10
IFRS 17 (as amended in June 2020)	Insurance coverage									
	Investment-return service									
	Recognition of profit									

Recognition of profit considering insurance coverage only

Year	1	2	3	4	5	6	7	8	9	10
IFRS 17 (as originally issued)	Insurance coverage									
	Investment component									
	Recognition of profit									

As discussed above, an investment-return service only exists if the contract includes an investment component or if the policyholder has a right to withdraw an amount from the entity. This is illustrated by the following example based on an example in an IASB staff paper:[48]

Example 56.42: Deferred annuity contract without an investment component which provides an investment-return service

A deferred annuity contract under which premiums are paid up-front. The premiums earn a return during the accumulation phase and the accumulated amount can be converted into an annuity at a fixed conversion rate at a future date. The accumulation phase could be a substantial number of years. During the accumulation phase the policyholder has the right to transfer the accumulated amount to another annuity provider or to receive the accumulated amount if (s)he dies. After conversion into an annuity, there is no period of guaranteed payments, i.e. if the policyholder dies after conversion but before the first annuity payment the policyholder receives nothing. Hence, the contract does not have an investment component. However, although there is no investment component, the policyholder has the right during the accumulation phase to withdraw an amount from the entity that includes an investment return.

8.8 Measurement of onerous contracts

As discussed at 8 above, a loss must be recognised on initial recognition of a group of insurance contracts if that group is onerous.

An insurance contract is onerous at the date of initial recognition if the fulfilment cash flows allocated to the contract, any previously recognised insurance acquisition cash flows and any cash flows arising from the contract at the date of initial recognition in total are a net outflow. As discussed at 5 above, an entity should group such contracts in a portfolio separately from contracts that are not onerous. To the extent that an entity has reasonable and supportable information to conclude that all contracts in a set of contracts will be in the same group, an entity may identify the group of onerous contracts by measuring a set of contracts rather than individual contracts.

When a group of insurance contracts are onerous, an entity should recognise a loss component and book the corresponding loss in profit or loss for the net outflow for the group of onerous contracts, resulting in the carrying amount of the liability for remaining coverage of the group being equal to the fulfilment cash flows and the contractual service margin of the group being zero. *[IFRS 17.47]*.

Subsequent to initial recognition, a group of insurance contracts becomes onerous (or more onerous) if the following amounts exceed the carrying amount of the contractual service margin: *[IFRS 17.48]*

- unfavourable changes relating to future service in the fulfilment cash flows allocated to the group arising from changes in estimates of future cash flows and the risk adjustment for non-financial risk; and
- for a group of insurance contracts with direct participation features, the decrease in the amount of the entity's share of the fair value of the underlying items.

An entity should recognise a loss in profit or loss to the extent of that excess.

For losses under onerous groups of insurance contracts recognised either on initial recognition or subsequently, an entity should establish (or increase) a loss component of the liability for remaining coverage for an onerous group depicting the losses recognised. A 'loss component' means a notional record of the losses attributable to each group of onerous insurance contracts. The liability for the expected loss is contained within the liability for remaining coverage for the onerous group (as it is within the fulfilment cash flows). Keeping a record of the loss component of the liability for remaining coverage is necessary in order to account for subsequent reversals, if any, of the onerous group and any loss component is required to be separately disclosed (see 16.1.1 below). The loss component determines the amounts that are presented in profit or loss as reversals of losses on onerous groups and are consequently excluded from the determination of insurance revenue and, instead, credited to insurance service expenses. *[IFRS 17.49]*.

After an entity has recognised a loss on an onerous group of insurance contracts, it should allocate: *[IFRS 17.50]*

- the subsequent changes in fulfilment cash flows of the liability for remaining coverage on a systematic basis between:
    - the loss component of the liability for remaining coverage; and
    - the liability for remaining coverage, excluding the loss component.
- solely to the loss component until that component is reduced to zero:
    - any subsequent decrease relating to future service in fulfilment cash flows allocated to the group arising from changes in estimates of future cash flows and the risk adjustment for non-financial risk; and
    - any subsequent increases in the amount of the entity's share of the fair value of the underlying items.

IFRS 17 does not specify the order in which an entity allocates the fulfilment cash flows in the bullet points above (i.e. whether paragraph 50(a) or 50(b) is applied first). [IFRS 17.IE95(c)].

An entity should adjust the contractual service margin only for the excess of the decrease over the amount allocated to the loss component.

The subsequent changes in the fulfilment cash flows of the liability for remaining coverage to be allocated are: [IFRS 17.51]

- estimates of the present value of future cash flows for claims and expenses released from the liability for remaining coverage because of incurred insurance service expenses;
- changes in the risk adjustment for non-financial risk recognised in profit or loss because of the release from risk; and
- insurance finance income or expenses.

The systematic allocation required above should result in the total amounts allocated to the loss component being equal to zero by the end of the coverage period of a group of contracts (since the loss component will have been realised in the form of incurred claims). [IFRS 17.52].

IFRS 17 does not prescribe specific methods to track the loss component. The IASB considered whether to require specific methods but concluded that any such methods would be inherently arbitrary. The IASB therefore decided to require an entity to make a systematic allocation of changes in the fulfilment cash flows for the liability for remaining coverage that could be regarded as affecting either the loss component or the rest of the liability. [IFRS 17.BC287].

Tracking the loss component of the liability for remaining coverage for each group of onerous contracts will be a new and complex task, particularly for many life insurers. Most non-life insurers will be familiar with the concept of running off provisions for unearned premiums and unexpired risks, and we expect that tracking a loss component should be easier for short duration contracts. Maintaining the loss component is not equivalent to maintaining a negative contractual service margin because the purpose of the loss component is to separately account for and present the shortfall in the insurance liability and, in contrast to the contractual service margin, is not directly driven by the performance of services under the group of contracts.

Changes in the liability for remaining coverage due to insurance finance income or expenses, release from risk, and incurred claims and other insurance service expenses, need to be allocated between the loss component and the remainder of the liability for remaining coverage on a systematic basis. An entity could allocate the effect of these changes to the loss component in proportion to the total liability, although other bases could be appropriate. Whichever approach is adopted, it should be applied consistently. This also implies that insurance finance income or expenses must be allocated to the loss component to reflect the accretion of interest.

Changes in the liability for incurred claims are not allocated to the liability for remaining coverage.

The treatment of onerous contracts can be illustrated in the following example.

Example 56.43: Application of the loss component for a group of onerous contracts

An entity determines that a group of insurance contracts without direct participation features is onerous at initial recognition. On initial recognition, the fulfilment cash flows (ignoring discounting and other adjustments) are a net cash outflow of €50 and therefore this is recognised as a loss in profit or loss. There is no contractual service margin. The loss component of the liability for remaining coverage is €50.

At the entity's next reporting date, the entity calculates that the fulfilment cash flows for the liability for remaining coverage have decreased by €60. Applying paragraph 50 of IFRS 17, the entity decides that it will first allocate the subsequent changes in fulfilment cash flows of the liability for remaining coverage in a systematic way between the loss component and the liability for remaining coverage excluding the loss component. The entity then decides to allocate any subsequent decrease relating to future service in the fulfilment cash flows solely to the loss component. As a result, €40 adjusts the loss component of the liability for remaining coverage by a release (i.e. a credit) to profit or loss. The remaining €20 reduction does not adjust the loss component of the liability for remaining coverage. Consequently, at the reporting date, the loss component of the liability for remaining coverage is €10 (i.e. €50 less €40).

8.9 Reinsurance contracts issued

A reinsurance contract is a contract issued by one entity (the reinsurer) to compensate another entity for claims arising from one or more insurance contracts issued by that other entity (underlying contracts). *[IFRS 17 Appendix A]*.

The requirements for recognition and measurement of reinsurance contracts issued are the same as for insurance contracts. This means that the issuer should make an estimate of the fulfilment cash flows including estimates of expected future cash flows. At initial recognition (and at each reporting date) this will include estimates of future cash flows arising from underlying insurance contracts expected to be issued by the reinsured entity (and covered by the issued reinsurance contract) that are within the contract boundary of the reinsurance contract. This is because the issuer of the reinsurance contract has a substantive obligation to provide insurance cover (i.e. services) for those unissued policies. However, the unit of account for measurement is the reinsurance contract rather than the underlying individual direct contracts.

8.9.1 The boundary of a reinsurance contract issued

Some reinsurance contracts issued may contain break clauses which allow either party to cancel the contract at any time following a specified notice period. In February 2018, TRG members observed that, in an example of a reinsurance contract where the reinsurer can terminate coverage at any time with a three month notice period, the initial contract boundary for the issuer of the reinsurance contract would exclude cash flows related to underlying insurance premiums outside of that three month notice period.[49]

In September 2018, the IASB staff clarified to TRG members that if, after three months, neither the entity nor the reinsurer had given notice to terminate the reinsurance contract with respect to new business ceded, this would not cause a reassessment of the contract boundary. The cash flows related to underlying contracts that are expected to be issued and ceded in the next three-month period are cash flows outside the existing contract boundary. In response to a concern that this may result in daily reinsurance contracts being issued, the IASB staff observed that reinsurance contracts held are recognised only when the recognition criteria for reinsurance contracts are met. The contract boundary is determined at initial recognition and in this example that will result in a new reinsurance contract held being recognised after the end of the first three-month period with a contract boundary of cash flows arising from contracts expected to be issued in the following three months. See also 10.2 below.

The submission to the IASB staff in September 2018 included an additional fact pattern in which there is (or there is not) a unilateral right for the reinsurer to amend the rate of the ceding commission it pays, in addition to unilateral termination rights. The IASB staff observed that in this fact pattern, the existence of the right to terminate the contract with a three month notice period determines the cash flows within the contract boundary regardless of the existence of a right to amend the rate of the ceding commission if the contract is not terminated. Therefore, the same accounting would apply to the additional fact pattern provided.[50]

8.9.2 Issued adverse loss development covers

For reinsurance contracts which cover events that have already occurred, but for which the financial effect is uncertain, IFRS 17 states that the insured event is the determination of the ultimate costs of the claim. *[IFRS 17.B5]*. As the claim has occurred already, the question arises as to how insurance revenue and insurance service expenses should be presented for these insurance contracts when they are acquired in a business combination or similar acquisition in their settlement period. More specifically, whether insurance revenue should reflect the entire expected claims or not. This issue is not specific to reinsurance contracts issued; it is also relevant to direct adverse development covers issued. In February 2018, this question was submitted to the TRG and the IASB staff stated that for insurance contracts that cover events that have already occurred but the financial effect of which is uncertain the claims are incurred when the financial effect is certain. This is not when an entity has a reliable estimate if there is still uncertainty involved. Conversely this is not necessarily when the claims are paid if certainty has been achieved prior to settlement. Accordingly, insurance revenue would reflect the entire expected claims as the liability for remaining coverage reduces because of services provided. If some cash flows meet the definition of an investment component, those cash flows will not be reflected in insurance revenue or insurance service expenses.[51]

This results in entities accounting differently for similar contracts, depending on whether those contracts are issued originally by the entity or whether the entity acquired those contracts in their settlement period. The potential consequences of this distinction include:

- an entity applies the general model for contracts acquired in their settlement period because the period over which claims would develop is much longer than one year, whilst entities expect to apply the premium allocation approach for similar contracts that they issue; and
- an entity recognises revenue for the contracts acquired in their settlement period over the period the claims are expected to develop, while revenue is no longer recognised over this period for similar contracts issued.

The TRG members observed that, although the requirements in IFRS 17 are clear, applying the requirements reflects a significant change from existing practice and this change results in implementation complexities and costs. In May 2018, the IASB staff prepared an outreach report which included implementation concerns regarding the subsequent treatment of insurance contracts issued and acquired in their settlement period.[52] Subsequently, the IASB decided not to change IFRS 17 for this issue but has amended IFRS 17 to provide transitional relief for these contracts when the modified retrospective approach (see 17.4.2 below) or the fair value approach (see 17.5 below) is applied.

Some reinsurance contracts issued (as well as direct insurance contracts issued) may contain a mixture of both retrospective and prospective coverage. In these circumstances an entity would need to apply judgement as to (i) the portfolio of contracts to which a contract with such a mixture should be allocated and (ii) whether the 'mixed' contract could be split into separate retrospective and prospective components, with each component allocated to different portfolios, applying the guidance discussed at 5.1.1. above.

8.9.3 Accounting for ceding commissions and reinstatement premiums

In September 2018, a question as to how to account for ceding commissions and reinstatement premiums was discussed by the TRG. The question asked how the following should be accounted for in the financial statements of the reinsurer:

- common types of commission due to the cedant; and
- reinstatement premiums charged to the cedant in order to continue coverage following the occurrence of an insured event.

The TRG members discussed the analysis in an IASB staff paper and observed that:

- The requirements set out in paragraph 86 of IFRS 17 for the presentation of income and expenses from reinsurance contracts held are based on the economic effects of exchanges between the reinsurer and the cedant and it would be appropriate to apply an assessment of the economic effect of such exchanges to reinsurance contracts issued as well.
- The economic effect of amounts exchanged between a reinsurer and a cedant that are not contingent on claims is equivalent to the effect of charging a different premium. Therefore, these amounts would be recognised as part of insurance revenue.

- The economic effect of amounts exchanged between a reinsurer and a cedant that are contingent on claims is equivalent to reimbursing a different amount of claims than expected. Therefore, these amounts would be recognised as part of insurance service expenses.
- Unless a cedant provides a distinct service to the reinsurer that results in a cost to the reinsurer for selling, underwriting and starting a group of reinsurance contracts that it issues, a ceding commission is not an insurance acquisition cash flow of the insurer. The IASB staff observed that, unlike insurance acquisition costs that are paid to a third-party intermediary, ceding commissions are paid by the reinsurer to the cedant who is the policyholder of the contract.
- Amounts exchanged between the reinsurer and the cedant that are not contingent on claims may meet the definition of an investment component if they are repaid to the cedant in all circumstances. However, an amount deducted from the initial premium up-front is not an investment component (although the impact on insurance revenue is the same).

The TRG members observed that applying the requirements in IFRS 17 for amounts exchanged between a reinsurer and a cedant has practical implications because the requirements are different from existing practice. The TRG members also observed that applying the requirements of IFRS 17 may affect key performance measures currently used to assess the performance of reinsurers.[53]

Applying the guidance above in practice to the reinsurer:

- A ceding commission charged as a fixed amount or as a percentage of premiums on the underlying insurance contracts is a reduction in insurance revenue. If paid after the premium is received, the ceding commission may meet the definition of an investment component, provided the amounts are repaid to the policyholder in all circumstances.
- A ceding commission contingent on claims (i.e. excluding any minimum amounts that are, in effect, non-contingent) is part of claims and recognised as part of insurance service expenses.
- A mandatory reinstatement premium contingent on a claim amount and settled net with the claims paid to the cedant is equivalent to reimbursing a different amount of claims to the cedant and should be recognised as part of insurance service expenses when incurred.
- A voluntary reinstatement premium which is not contingent on claims (i.e. the cedant can decide not to pay the additional premium and the contract terminates) is equivalent to the effect of charging a higher premium to extend the contract coverage to an additional period, or higher level of exposure, and is recognised as insurance revenue. The IASB staff observed that when the reinsurer has no right to exit or reprice the contract (the reinstatement premium is at predetermined rates), the expected cash flows related to the reinstatement premium are within the boundary of the initial reinsurance contract and voluntary reinstatement premiums cannot be considered cash flows related to a future contract.[54]

The following flowchart may assist in the assessment of how to account for exchanges between a reinsurer and a cedant.

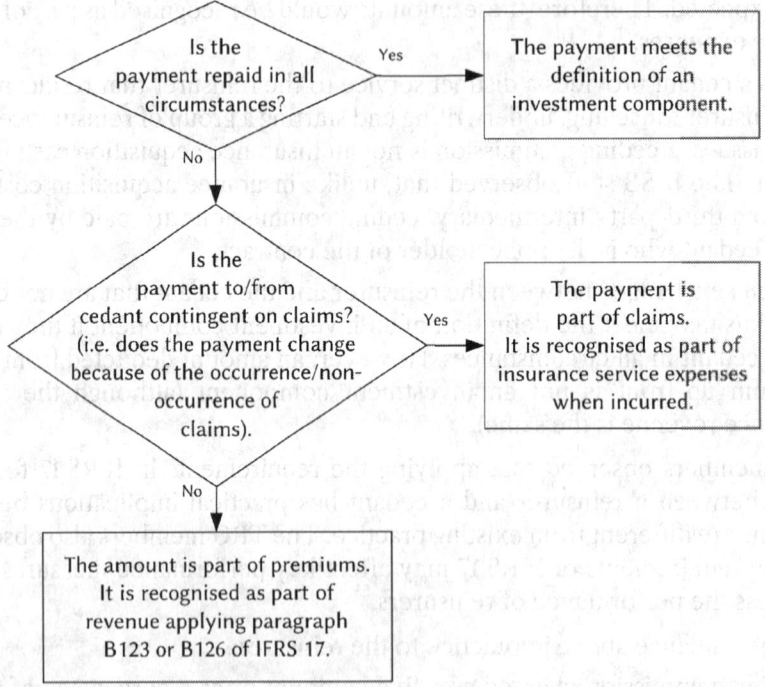

8.9.4 Determining the quantity of benefits for identifying coverage units

As discussed at 8.7.1 above, the question of how to determine the quantity of benefits for coverage units was discussed by the TRG in both February 2018 and May 2018. In May 2018, the TRG analysed an IASB staff paper that contained the IASB staff's views on sixteen examples of different types of insurance contracts.

The following examples apply the principles discussed at 8.7.1 above to specific fact patterns for reinsurance contracts issued.[55]

Example 56.44: Proportional reinsurance issued

A reinsurance contract issued provides proportional cover for underlying contracts issued during the contract period. The reinsurance contract issued is for a period of one year. Underlying contracts are written uniformly throughout the year and are annual policies that are reasonably homogenous and provide relatively even cover over their one-year coverage periods.

Applying the principles at 8.7.1 above the expected coverage duration of the reinsurance contract issued is two years. This is because the reinsurer has a substantive obligation to provide services under the contract for a period of two years as the risks attaching over a single policy year will cover two years of exposure to risk. A valid method for determining the quantity of benefits is the amount for which the policyholder has the ability to make a valid claim. This is because the pattern of coverage should reflect the expected pattern of underwriting of the underlying contracts because the level of service provided depends on the number of underlying contracts in-force. Therefore, the more contracts in force, the higher the level of service.

Example 56.45: Reinsurance adverse development of claims with claim limit

A reinsurance adverse development cover contract will pay claims in excess of a stated aggregate amount on a group of underlying property and casualty contracts where the claim event has already been incurred. There is a total aggregate limit to the amount payable under the contract. Because there is uncertainty in the ultimate amount and timing of the final settlements of the underlying claims, the insured event is the determination of the ultimate cost of settling those claims.

Applying the principles at 8.7.1 above the expected coverage duration would be the period from inception of the contract to the time at which the limit of cover is expected to be reached, adjusted for expected lapses, if any. Valid methods for determining the quantity of benefits are:

- comparing the contractual maximum amount that could have been claimed in the period with the remaining contractual maximum amount that can be claimed as a constant amount for each future coverage period; or
- comparing the expected amount of underlying claims covered in the period with the expected amount of underlying claims remaining to be covered in future periods.

A straight-line method over the expected coverage duration might not be valid because it would not reflect the different levels of cover provided across periods.

Example 56.46: Reinsurance adverse development of claims without claim limit

A reinsurance adverse development cover contract will pay claims in excess of a stated aggregate amount on a group of underlying property and casualty contracts where the claim event has already been incurred. There is no total aggregate limit to the amount payable under the contract. Because there is uncertainty in the ultimate amount and timing of the final settlements of the underlying claims, the insured event is the determination of the ultimate cost of settling those claims.

Applying the principles at 8.7.1 above the expected coverage duration would be the period to when the financial effect of the claims becomes certain. This may be before the claims are paid if certainty has been achieved prior to the actual payment. An entity will need to estimate the expected duration of the period in which claims will be made and payments will be made to estimate the fulfilment cash flows. Valid methods for determining the quantity of benefits are:

- equal benefits in each coverage period, which would end at the date of the last expected settlement payment; or
- compare the expected amount of underlying claims covered in the period with the expected amount of underlying claims remaining to be covered in future periods; or
- if the underlying claims were of equal size, comparing the number of underlying claims covered in the period with the number of underlying claims remaining to be covered in future periods.

8.10 Impairment of assets recognised for insurance acquisition cash flows

As discussed at 6.3 above, an entity should recognise as an asset insurance acquisition cash flows paid (or insurance acquisition cash flows for which a liability has been recognised under another IFRS standard) before the related group of insurance contracts is recognised.

As a result, IFRS 17 requires, an entity to assess the recoverability of any insurance acquisition cash flow asset recognised before the related group of insurance contracts is recognised at the end of each reporting period, if facts and circumstances indicate the asset may be impaired. If an entity identifies an impairment loss, the entity should adjust the carrying amount of the asset and recognise any impairment loss identified in profit and loss. If an impairment loss is reversed, an entity shall adjust the carrying amount of the asset and recognise the reversal of any such loss in profit and loss. *[IFRS 17.28E-F]*.

In assessing the recoverability: *[IFRS 17.B35D]*

(a) an entity shall recognise that impairment loss in profit or loss and reduce the carrying amount of an asset for insurance acquisition cash flows so that the carrying amount of each asset does not exceed the expected net fulfilment cash inflows (see 8.2 above) for the related group of insurance contracts;

(b) when an entity allocates insurance acquisition cash flows to groups of insurance contracts that will include insurance contracts that are expected to arise from renewals of the insurance contracts in that group, the entity shall recognise an impairment loss in profit or loss and reduce the carrying amount of the related assets for insurance acquisition cash flows to the extent that:

- the entity expects those insurance acquisition cash flows to exceed the net fulfilment cash inflows for the expected renewals; and
- the excess determined in the preceding bullet point has not already been recognised as an impairment loss applying the requirements above for assets directly attributable to a group.

An entity shall recognise in profit or loss a reversal of some or all of an impairment loss previously recognised applying the requirements above and increase the carrying amount of the asset, to the extent that the impairment conditions no longer exist or have improved. *[IFRS 17.28F]*.

It is observed in the Basis for Conclusions that the impairment test is intended to be consistent with the impairment test for capitalised contract costs in IFRS 15 (see Chapter 32 at 5.4) and therefore an entity recognises an impairment loss in profit or loss and reduces the carrying amount of an asset for insurance acquisition cash flows so that it does not exceed the expected net cash inflow for the related group. *[IFRS 17.BC184J]*.

The Basis for Conclusions also observes that an asset for insurance acquisition cash flows is measured at a group level. An impairment test at a group level compares the carrying amount of an asset for insurance acquisition cash flows allocated to a group with the expected net cash inflow of the group. That net cash inflow includes cash flows for contracts unrelated to any expected renewals but expected to be in that group. The Board therefore decided to require an additional impairment test specific to cash flows for expected renewals. The additional impairment test results in the recognition of any impairment losses when the entity no longer expects the renewals supporting the asset to occur or expects the net cash inflows to be lower than the amount of the asset. Without the additional impairment test, cash flows unrelated to any expected renewals might prevent the recognition of such an impairment loss. *[IFRS 17.BC184K]*.

The following example, based on an example in an IASB staff paper, illustrates how the two impairment tests would identify any impairment losses on an asset for insurance acquisition cash flows.[56]

Example 56.47: Applying the two impairment tests for an insurance acquisition cash flow asset

At the beginning of Year 1 an entity pays commissions of $38 relating to a group of contracts yet to be issued. Those commissions meet the definition of insurance acquisition cash flow assets.

The commissions are directly attributable to insurance contracts the entity expected to issue later in Year 1 (Group 1). The entity expects that some policyholders of those insurance contracts that will be issued in Year 1 will renew those contracts in Year 2 (Group 2), Year 3 (Group 3) and Year 4 (Group 4). Accordingly, at the beginning of Year 1, the entity allocates the commissions of $38 on a systematic and rational basis to the expected future groups of insurance contracts as follows:

- Group 1 – $25
- Group 2 – $5
- Group 3 – $5
- Group 4 – $3

The entity recognises assets for insurance acquisition cash flows of $38 at the beginning of Year 1.

At the end of Year 1, the entity derecognises the asset of $25 allocated to Group 1 and includes the insurance acquisition cash flows in the measurement of Group 1. At the end of Year 1, there are no facts and circumstances indicating that the assets for insurance acquisition cash flows allocated to each of Groups 2 to 4 may be impaired. Therefore, at the end of Year 1, the carrying amount of the assets for insurance acquisition cash flows is $13 (i.e. $5 + $5 + $3 as per above).

At the end of Year 2, the entity derecognises the asset of $5 allocated to Group 2 and includes the insurance acquisition cash flows in the measurement of Group 2. At the end of Year 2, facts and circumstances indicate that the assets for insurance acquisition cash flows for Groups 3 and 4 may be impaired. The carrying amount of the assets for insurance acquisition cash flows subject to impairment testing is $8 (i.e. $5 + $3 as per above).

To perform the impairment tests the entity estimates the following amounts:

	Year 3 (Group 3) $	Year 4 (Group 4) $
Expected net fulfilment cash inflows		
Expected renewals	3	1
Other than renewals	6	1
Total expected net cash inflows	9	2
Asset for insurance acquisition cash flows	5	3
Impairment	–	(1)

Applying the additional impairment test specific to insurance acquisition cash flows allocated to expected contracts renewals, the entity compares the amount of insurance acquisition cash flows allocated to expected renewals to the total expected net cash inflows for those expected renewals, as follows:

	Year 3 (Group 3)	Year 4 (Group 4)	Total
	$	$	$
Expected net fulfilment cash inflows			
Amount of insurance acquisition cash flows allocated to expected renewals	5	3	8
Expected net cash inflows for expected renewals	3	1	4
Impairment			(4)

Accordingly, the entity recognises an expense in profit or loss an impairment of $4 comprising of:
- $1 identified applied paragraph B35D(a) of IFRS 17; and
- $4 identified applying paragraph B35D(b)(i) of IFRS 17 less $1 already identified above applying paragraph B35D(ii) of IFRS 17.

After recognising the total impairment loss of $4, the entity will allocate the total amount of insurance acquisition cash flows remaining in assets of $4 to groups of contracts still to be recognised (Group 3 and Group 4) on a systematic and rational basis.

8.11 Insurance contracts issued by mutual entities

A mutual entity accepts risks from each policyholder and pools that risk. However, a defining feature of a mutual entity is that the most residual interest of the entity is due to a policyholder and not to a shareholder. Thus, the fulfilment cash flows of an insurer that is a mutual entity generally include the rights of policyholders to the whole of any surplus of assets over liabilities. This means that, for an insurer that is a mutual entity, there should, in principle, normally be no equity remaining and no net comprehensive income reported in any accounting period. *[IFRS 17.BC265]*. In addition, the Basis for Conclusions clarifies that not all entities that may be described as mutual entities have the feature that the most residual interest of the entity is due to a policyholder. *[IFRS 17.BC265FN27]*.

Payments to policyholders with a residual interest in a mutual entity vary depending on the returns on underlying items – the net asset of the mutual entity. These cash flows (i.e. the payments that vary with the underlying items) are within the boundary of an insurance contract. *[IFRS 17.B65(c)]*. Although policyholders with a residual interest in the entity bear the pooled risk collectively, the mutual, as a separate entity has accepted risk from each individual policyholder and therefore the risk adjustment for non-financial risk for these contracts reflects the compensation the mutual entity requires for bearing the uncertainty from non-financial risk in those contracts. However, because the net cash flows of the mutual entity are returned to policyholders, applying IFRS 17 to contracts with policyholders with a residual interest in the mutual entity will result in no contractual service margin for those contracts.[57]

Mutual entities may also issue insurance contracts that do not provide the policyholder with a residual interest in the mutual entity. Consequently, groups of such contracts are expected to have a contractual service margin. Determining whether a contract provides the policyholder with a residual interest in the mutual entity requires consideration of all substantive rights and obligations.

The IASB also suggested that to provide useful information about its financial position a mutual can distinguish between:

- liabilities attributable to policyholders in their capacity as policyholders; and
- liabilities attributable to policyholders with the most residual interest in the entity.

The statement of financial performance could include a line item 'income or expenses attributable to policyholders in their capacity as policyholders before determination of the amounts attributable to policyholders with the most residual interest in the entity'.[58]

The IASB decided not to develop specific guidance for, or defining mutual entities because: [IFRS 17.BC269B]

- a core principle of IFRS 17 is the requirement to include in the fulfilment cash flows all the expected future cash flows that arise within the boundary of insurance contracts, including discretionary cash flows and those due to future policyholders;
- if entities were required to account for the same insurance contract differently depending on the type of entity issuing the contract, comparability among entities would be reduced; and
- a robust definition of a mutual entity to which different requirements would apply would be difficult to create.

8.12 Other matters

8.12.1 Impairment of insurance receivables

IFRS 17 does not refer to impairment of insurance receivables (e.g. amounts due from policyholders or agents in respect of insurance premiums).

A premium receivable (including premium adjustments and instalment premiums) is a right arising from an insurance (or reinsurance) contract. Rights and obligations under contracts within the scope of IFRS 17 are excluded from the scope of IFRS 9 (see 2.3 above). As a premium receivable is a cash flow it is measured on an expected present value basis (see 8.2 above) which should include an assessment of credit risk. This cash flow is remeasured at each reporting date. Receivables from insurance contracts are not required to be disclosed separately on the statement of financial position but are subsumed within the overall insurance contract balances (see 14 below).

Receivables not arising from insurance contracts (such as those arising from a contractual relationship with an intermediary) are within the scope of IFRS 9. When an insurer uses an intermediary, judgement may be required to determine whether insurance receivables from an intermediary on behalf of a policyholder are within the scope of IFRS 17 or IFRS 9. A similar judgement is necessary for other amounts held by intermediaries such as funds withheld to pay future claims as well as loans to intermediaries. For example, if the policyholder has remitted premiums due to the insurer, under the terms of an insurance contract, to an intermediary and the intermediary defaults on remitting those premiums to the insurer, can the insurer enforce payment of the premiums by the policyholder? In other words, is the intermediary acting on behalf of the policyholder (in which case any balances held by the intermediary are expected to be within the scope of IFRS 17) or on behalf of the insurer (in which cases any balances held by the intermediary are expected to be within the scope of IFRS 9)?

8.12.2 Policyholder loans

Some insurance contracts permit the policyholder to obtain a loan from the insurer with the insurance contract acting as collateral for the loan. Under IFRS 4 policyholder loans may have been separated from insurance contract balances and shown as separate assets. IFRS 17 regards a policyholder loan as an example of an investment component with interrelated cash flows which is not separated from the host insurance contract. *[IFRS 17.BC114]*. Consequently, a policyholder loan is included within the overall insurance contract balance and is part of the fulfilment cash flows (and is not within the scope of IFRS 9).

The repayment or receipt of amounts lent to and repaid by policyholders does not give rise to insurance revenue (see 15.1.1 below). However, the contractual service margin is adjusted for any difference between a loan to a policyholder expected to become payable or repayable in a period and the actual loan that becomes payable or repayable in a period, after adjusting for insurance finance income or expense related to that expected payment or repayment before it becomes payable or repayable (see 8.6.3 above).

A waiver of a loan to a policyholder would be treated the same way as any other claim.[59]

There may be situations when an insurance policy is collateral for a stand-alone loan, not stemming from the contractual terms of an insurance contract and not highly interrelated with an insurance contract. Such a loan would be within the scope of IFRS 9.

9 MEASUREMENT – PREMIUM ALLOCATION APPROACH

The premium allocation approach is a simplified form of measurement of insurance contracts. The premium allocation approach is intended to produce an accounting outcome similar to that which resulted from the unearned premium approach used by many non-life or short-duration insurers under previous local GAAP and, hence, continued under IFRS 4. The Board considers that it is similar to the customer consideration approach in IFRS 15. However, as shown at 9.1 below, the criteria required for use of the premium allocation approach means that not all contracts regulated as 'non-life' or 'short-duration' by local regulators will qualify.

Use of the premium allocation approach is optional for each group of insurance contracts that meets the eligibility criteria (see 9.1 below). The criteria are assessed for each group and the election is made for each group meeting the criteria at inception. In April 2019, the IASB staff responded to a submission to the TRG which questioned whether an entity is required, or permitted, to reassess a group's eligibility for the premium allocation approach and, as a result, to revoke its election to apply the approach. The IASB staff observed that given the eligibility criteria are assessed at inception, IFRS 17 does not require or permit reassessment of the eligibility criteria or the election to apply the approach.[60]

The main advantage of the simplified method, in accounting terms, is that the premium allocation approach does not require separate identification of the components (i.e. the building blocks) of the general model until a claim is incurred. Only a total amount for a liability for remaining coverage on initial recognition is determined, rather than a separate calculation of the components of the fulfilment cash flows performed with the contractual service margin as a balancing item which eliminates any expected profit. Therefore, compared to the general model, using the premium allocation approach results in a simpler accounting method. Further, as discussed at 9.2 below, an entity also has the option not to adjust liabilities for incurred claims for the effect of time value of money and financial risk in certain circumstances. Consequently, the premium allocation approach produces results which are generally more similar to current accounting practices applied under IFRS 4 than the general model, and therefore likely to be more readily understood.

The premium allocation approach can be applied to any insurance or reinsurance contract issued that meets the criteria, including contracts that would otherwise be required to apply the variable fee approach discussed at 11.2 below. The premium allocation approach can also be used for reinsurance contracts held. However, the ability to use the premium allocation approach for reinsurance contracts held must be assessed separately from the use of the premium allocation approach for the related underlying insurance contracts covered by reinsurance. See 10.6 below for discussion of the application of the premium allocation approach to reinsurance contracts held.

Although the accounting model for the premium allocation approach is broadly similar to the accounting model used by most non-life or short-duration insurers under IFRS 4 there are some important differences as follows:

- the liability for remaining coverage is measured using premiums received minus any insurance acquisition cash flows at the measurement date. The word 'received' is interpreted literally, rather than interpreted to mean amounts due (see below). Under local GAAP (and hence IFRS 4) the unearned premium provision would have often been set up based on premiums receivable, with a separate asset recorded for the premiums receivable;

- no separate asset is recognised for deferred acquisition costs (except for those assets in respect of insurance acquisition cash flows paid before the related group of insurance contracts is recognised – see 6.3 above). Instead, any acquisition cash flows are subsumed within the liability for remaining coverage (unless the entity elects to expense insurance acquisition cash flows – see 9.1 below);

- most non-life or short-duration insurers would not usually have discounted their insurance liabilities under local GAAP (a practice permitted to continue under IFRS 4); and

- the fulfilment cash flows model required for incurred claims, which is the same as the general model except for one simplification, is likely to be different than the incurred claim model used under local GAAP (and therefore IFRS 4).

A comparison of the general model with the premium allocation approach on initial recognition is shown below.

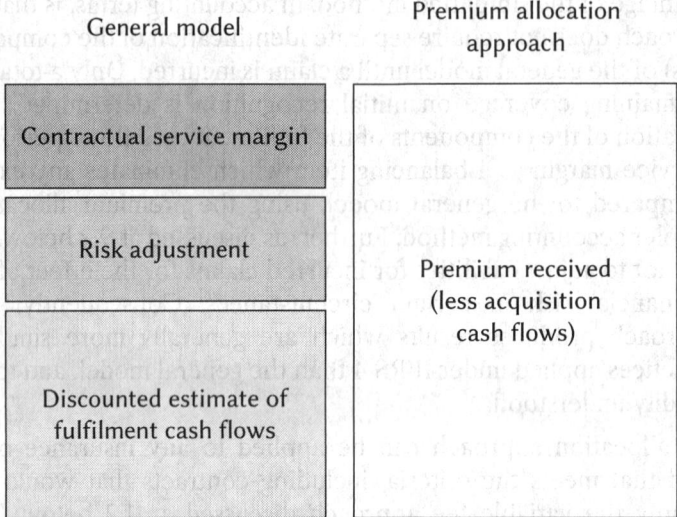

In February 2018, the TRG members agreed with the IASB staff view that the words 'premiums, if any, received' in paragraphs 55(a) and 55(b)(i) of IFRS 17 means premiums actually received at the reporting date. It does not include premiums due or premiums expected. However, the TRG members noted that applying these requirements reflects a significant change from existing practice and this change will result in implementation complexities and costs.[61] Subsequently, the IASB staff included this matter in an implementation challenges outreach report (issued in May 2018) which was provided to the IASB within the papers for the May 2018 IASB Board meeting. However, the IASB concluded not to amend the standard.

9.1 Criteria for use of the premium allocation approach

The premium allocation approach is permitted if, and only if, at the inception of the group of contracts: *[IFRS 17.53]*

- the entity reasonably expects that such simplification would produce a measurement of the liability for remaining coverage for the group that would not differ materially from the one that would be produced applying the requirements for the general model discussed at 8 above (i.e. the fulfilment cash flows related to future service plus the contractual service margin); *or*
- the coverage period of each contract in the group (including insurance contract services arising from all premiums within the contract boundary determined at that date applying the requirements discussed at 8.1. above) is one year or less.

The second criterion means that all contracts with a one-year coverage period or less should qualify for the premium allocation approach regardless as to whether the first criterion is met. However, for insurance contracts with a coverage period greater than one year (e.g. long term construction insurance contracts or extended warranty-type contracts) entities will need to meet the first criterion in order to be eligible for the premium allocation approach.

IFRS 17 states that the first criterion is not met if, at the inception of the group of contracts, an entity expects significant variability in the fulfilment cash flows that would affect the measurement of the liability for the remaining coverage during the period before a claim is incurred. Variability in the fulfilment cash flows increases with, for example: *[IFRS 17.54]*

- the extent of future cash flows related to any derivatives embedded in the contracts; and
- the length of the coverage period of the group of contracts.

A discussion identifying the main sources of variability between the premium allocation approach and the general model is included at 9.1.1 below. A discussion of the meaning of 'differ materially in these circumstances' is included at 9.1.2 below.

Once an entity decides to use the premium allocation approach for a group of insurance contracts, the following accounting policy choices are available separately in certain circumstances:

- whether to recognise insurance acquisition cash flows as an expense when it incurs those costs or to include those cash flows within the liability for remaining coverage (and hence amortise those cash flows over the coverage period). The ability of an entity to recognise insurance acquisition cash flows as an expense when it incurs those costs is available provided that the coverage period of each contract in the group on initial recognition is no more than one year. Otherwise acquisition cash flows must be included within the liability for remaining coverage; *[IFRS 17.59(a)]* and
- whether or not to adjust the liability for remaining coverage to reflect the time value of money and the effect of financial risk. An entity is not required to adjust the liability for remaining coverage to reflect the time value of money and the effect of financial risk if, at initial recognition, the entity expects that the time between providing each part of the services and the related premium due date is no more than one year. Otherwise, the liability for remaining coverage must be adjusted to reflect the time value of money and the effect of financial risk using the discount rates as determined on initial recognition if the insurance contracts in the group have a significant financing component. *[IFRS 17.56]*.

These choices can be shown graphically as follows:

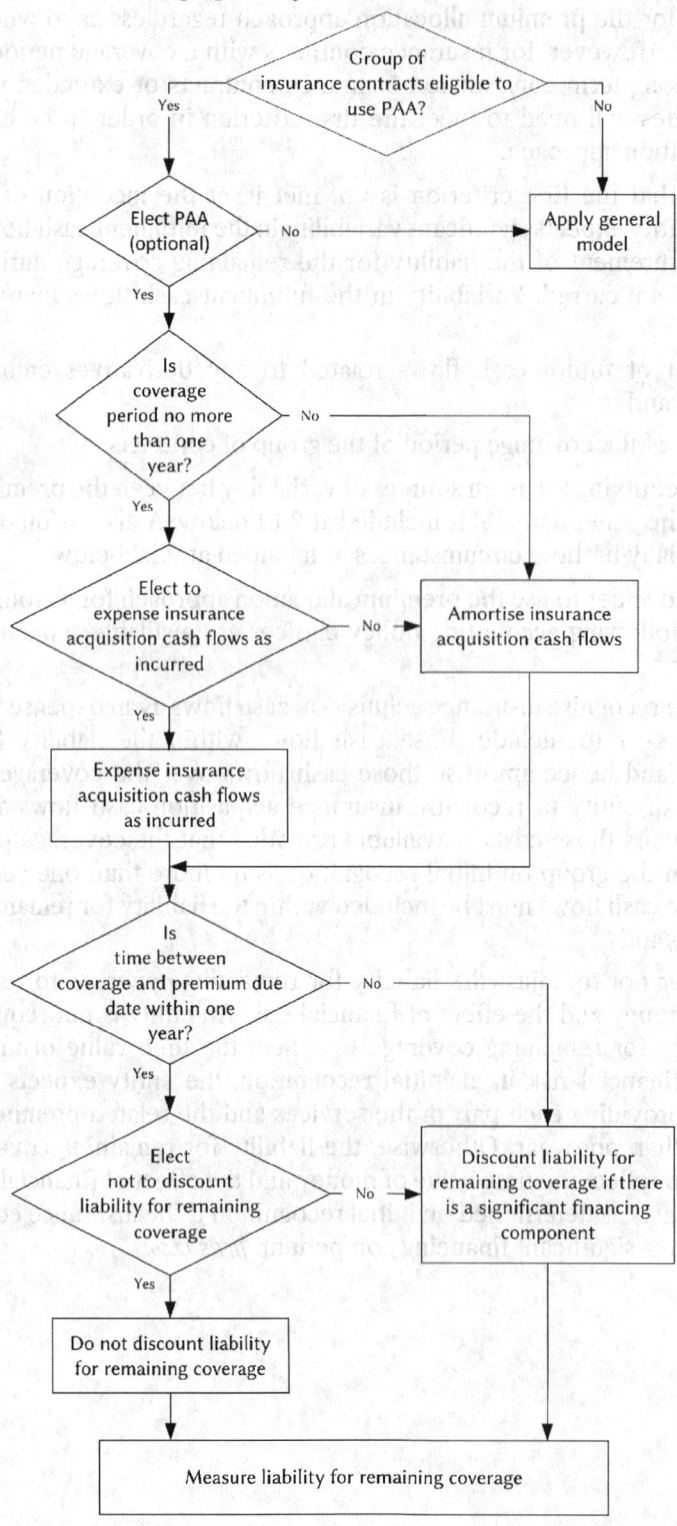

A further accounting policy choice is available when applying the PAA to elect not to adjust the liability for incurred claims for the time value of money and the effect of financial risk if those cash flows are expected to be paid or received within one year or less from the date that the claims are incurred (see 9.4 below).

9.1.1 Main sources of difference between the premium allocation approach and the general approach

The first criterion for use of the premium allocation approach discussed at 9.1 above involves a comparison of the liability for remaining coverage under the general model and the premium allocation approach over the expected period of the liability for remaining coverage. This assessment is made at inception and is not reassessed subsequently.

Under all situations the liability for incurred claims is the same between the premium allocation approach and general model. This means that after the coverage period has expired there will be no difference between the two approaches unless the election not to discount incurred claims, discussed at 9.4 below, is used. However, a number of situations exist under which the premium allocation approach and the general model could produce different measurements for the liability for remaining coverage during the coverage period, and therefore could impact the eligibility of the premium allocation approach. These should be considered when designing the approach used for assessing the applicability of the premium allocation approach. Three examples of potential sources of differences are as follows:

- changing expectations of profitability for the period of remaining coverage – see 9.1.1.A below;
- changing interest rates – see 9.1.1.B below; and
- uneven revenue recognition – see 9.1.1.C below.

9.1.1.A Changing expectations of profitability for the period of remaining coverage

When the expectation of the remaining profitability changes during the coverage period of a group of insurance contacts, so that it is still profitable, the results can differ under the premium allocation approach and general model. In this situation, the premium allocation approach will not recognise this improvement or deterioration in profitability in an explicit way until the exposure is earned, whereas the general model will recognise a portion of this change in expectations now through the unwinding of the contractual service margin even though the exposure has not yet been earned.

The significance of this difference will vary depending on how likely it is that the expected profitability of the remaining coverage might change and how much it may vary by. However, if the change in expectation of future profitability is to such an extent that the contract becomes onerous under the general model, then both approaches will give the same results.

9.1.1.B Changing interest rates

Under the premium allocation approach, if there is a significant financing component, an amount should be included for accretion of interest although this is based on the interest rate at the date of initial recognition of the group (see 8.3 above). As a result, the premium allocation approach never considers the current interest rates for the liability for remaining coverage, unlike the general model. So, if the discount rate changes significantly from the initial recognition of the contract this will result in a difference in the liability for remaining coverage between the premium allocation approach and the general model. The impact of this difference and its significance will depend on various factors including how large the discounting impact was originally, how large a change might reasonably be expected in the currency of the liabilities during the coverage period and the length of term of the liabilities, as longer-tailed contracts are more likely to be affected by discounting than shorter-tailed contracts.

9.1.1.C Uneven revenue recognition patterns

Under the premium allocation approach revenue is based on the passage of time or expected pattern of release of risk (see 9.3 below). However, under the general model, the contractual service margin is allocated based on coverage units reflecting the expected quantity of benefits and duration of each group of insurance contracts (see 8.7 above).

One example of where differences in revenue recognition between the two approaches could occur is contracts where the timing of when claims occur is not evenly spread over the passage of time due to the seasonality of claims. This could arise if the release of risk is 'significantly different from the passage of time'. For example, property insurance contracts exposed to catastrophes tend to have uneven earnings patterns.

9.1.2 Applying materiality for the premium allocation approach eligibility assessment

In order to qualify for the premium allocation approach under the first criteria at 9.1 above, the measurement for the liability for remaining coverage should not 'differ materially' from that produced applying the general model. Materiality in this context should be as defined by IAS 1 and IAS 8 (see Chapter 3 at 4.1.5.A). In addition to the general requirements of IAS 1 and IAS 8, there are specific materiality requirements in IFRS 17. Eligibility for the application of premium allocation approach must be assessed for each group of insurance contracts [IFRS 17.53] and therefore materiality should be considered at the group level. If the measurement of the liability for remaining coverage is not materially different for a group of insurance contracts measured using the premium allocation approach compared to that calculated using the general model in a range of scenarios that have a reasonable possibility of occurring, then the premium allocation approach can be adopted for that particular group.

9.2 Initial measurement

An entity should measure the liability for remaining coverage on initial recognition as follows: [IFRS 17.55]

- the premium, if any, received at initial recognition;
- minus any insurance acquisition cash flows at that date, unless the entity chooses to recognise the payments as an expense (see 9.1 above); and
- plus or minus any amount arising from the derecognition at that date of:
  - any asset for insurance acquisition cash flows that the entity paid before the related group of insurance contracts is recognised (see 6.3 above); and
  - any other asset or liability previously recognised for cash flows related to the group of contracts (see 8.5 above).

As discussed at 9 above, premiums received means 'received' rather than receivable or due.

If the entity is not able to does not use the policy choice not to adjust the liability for remaining coverage to reflect the time value of money and the effect of financial risk (see 9.1 above), the carrying amount of the liability for remaining coverage must be adjusted to reflect the time value of money and the effect of financial risk using the discount rate as determined at initial recognition of the group when the insurance contracts in the group have a significant financing component. The discount rate is the rate at the date of initial recognition of the group determined using the requirements discussed at 8.3 above.

If the entity is not able to, or chooses not to, recognise insurance acquisition cash flows as an expense when incurred, then the insurance acquisition cash flows are included in the measurement of the liability for remaining coverage. The effect of recognising insurance acquisition cash flows as an expense when incurred is to increase the liability for remaining coverage and hence reduce the likelihood of any subsequent onerous contract loss. There would be an increased profit or loss expense at the date the expense is incurred (which may be before the initial recognition of the contract) followed by an increase in profit released from the liability for remaining coverage over the coverage period.

An entity applying the premium allocation approach should assume that no contracts in the portfolio are onerous at initial recognition unless facts and circumstances indicate otherwise. An entity should assess whether contracts that are not onerous at initial recognition have no significant possibility of becoming onerous subsequently by assessing the likelihood of changes in applicable facts and circumstances. *[IFRS 17.18]*.

If at any time during the coverage period, including at initial recognition, facts and circumstances indicate that a group of insurance contracts is onerous, an entity should calculate the difference between: *[IFRS 17.57]*

- the carrying amount of the liability for the remaining coverage as determined above; and
- the fulfilment cash flows (see 8.2 to 8.4 above) that relate to the remaining coverage of the group of contracts.

Any difference arising is recognised as a loss in profit or loss and increases the liability for remaining coverage. *[IFRS 17.58]*. In performing the fulfilment cash flows calculation, above, if an entity does not adjust the liability for incurred claims to reflect the time value of money and the effect of financial risk, it should also not include any such adjustment in the fulfilment cash flows. *[IFRS 17.57]*.

The following diagram provides an overview of the premium allocation approach on initial recognition assuming the entity does not expense insurance acquisition cash flows as incurred.

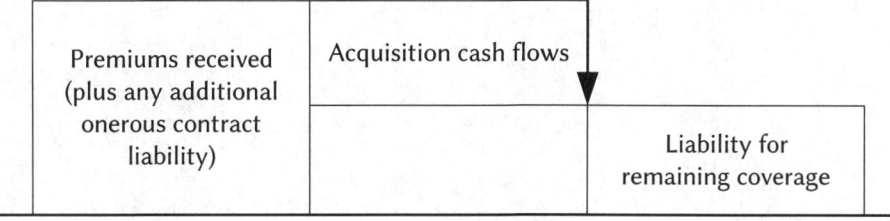

The following example, based on an example accompanying IFRS 17, illustrates the measurement at initial recognition of a group of insurance contracts measured using the premium allocation approach.

Example 56.48: Measurement at initial recognition of a group of insurance contracts using the premium allocation approach

An entity issues a group of insurance contracts on 1 July 2023. The insurance contracts have a coverage period of 10 months that ends on 30 April 2024. The entity's annual reporting period ends on 31 December each year and the entity prepares interim financial statements as of 30 June each year.

The entity expects to receive premiums of £1,220 and to pay directly attributable acquisition cash flows of £20. It is anticipated that no contracts will lapse during the coverage period and that facts and circumstances do not indicate that the group of contracts is onerous.

The group of insurance contracts qualifies for the premium allocation approach. As the time between providing each part of the coverage and the related premium due is no more than a year, the entity chooses not to adjust the carrying amount of the liability for remaining coverage to reflect the time value of money and the effect of financial risk (therefore no discounting or interest accretion is applied). Further, the entity chooses to recognise the insurance acquisition cash flows as an expense when it incurs the relevant costs. All other amounts, including the investment component, are ignored for simplicity.

On initial recognition, assuming the premiums were received and the acquisition cash flows paid, the liability for remaining coverage is £1,220 (i.e. the premium received). The acquisition cash flows of £20 are expensed as incurred. If the premiums were not received on initial recognition (i.e. they are receivable at a later date) then the liability for remaining coverage is £0.

9.3 Subsequent measurement – liability for remaining coverage

At the end of each reporting period subsequent to initial recognition, assuming the group of insurance contracts is not onerous, the carrying amount of the liability for remaining coverage is the carrying amount at the start of the reporting period: *[IFRS 17.55(b)]*

- plus the premiums received in the period;
- minus insurance acquisition cash flows unless the entity chooses to recognise the payments as an expense (see 9.2 above);
- plus any amounts relating to the amortisation of the insurance acquisition cash flows recognised as an expense in the reporting period unless the entity chooses to recognise insurance acquisition cash flows as an expense (see 9.2 above);
- plus any adjustment to the financing component;
- minus the amount recognised as insurance revenue for services provided in that period; and
- minus any investment component paid or transferred to the liability for incurred claims.

This can be illustrated by the following diagram:

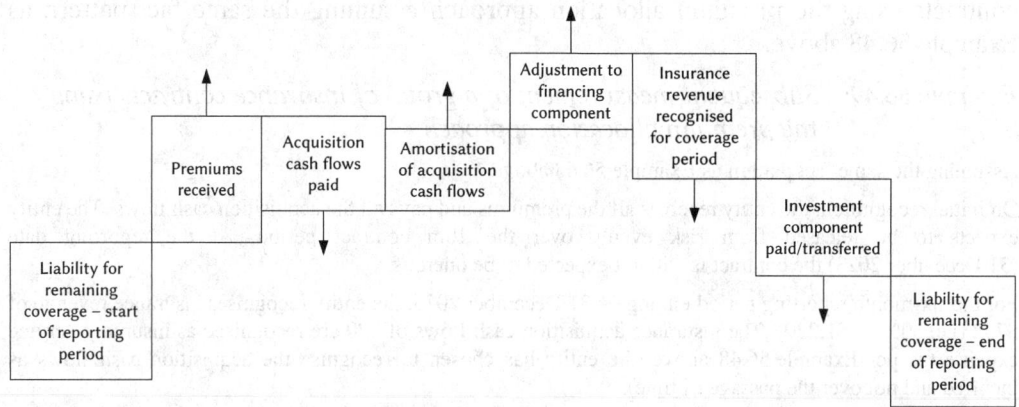

If a group of insurance contracts was onerous at initial recognition, then an entity would continue to compare the carrying amount of the liability for remaining coverage as calculated above with the fulfilment cash flows and recognise any further deficits or surpluses (to the extent that the fulfilment cash flows still exceed the liability for remaining coverage on a cumulative basis) in profit or loss.

Under the premium allocation approach, insurance revenue for the period is the amount of expected premium receipts (excluding any investment component and after adjustment to reflect the time value of money and the effect of financial risk, if applicable) allocated to the period for services provided. An entity should allocate the expected premium receipts to each period of insurance contract services: *[IFRS 17.B126]*

- on the basis of the passage of time; but
- if the expected pattern of release of risk during the coverage period differs significantly from the passage of time (which might be the case for example if claims were skewed towards a particular time of year such as the 'hurricane season'), on the basis of the expected timing of incurred insurance service expenses.

The liability for remaining coverage may be an asset if premiums are received after the recognition of revenue. This is because revenue is recognised independent of the receipt of cash but is determined by the provision of services.

An entity should change the basis of allocation between the two methods (passage of time and incurred insurance service expenses) as necessary if facts and circumstances change. *[IFRS 17.B127]*. This change results from new information and accordingly is not a correction of an error and will be accounted for prospectively as a change in accounting estimate. Judgement will be required in interpreting 'differs significantly from the passage of time'.

The following example illustrates the subsequent measurement of a group of insurance contracts using the premium allocation approach assuming the same fact pattern as Example 56.48 above.

Example 56.49: Subsequent measurement of a group of insurance contracts using the premium allocation approach

Assuming the same fact pattern as Example 56.48 above.

On initial recognition, the entity receives all the premiums and pays all the acquisition cash flows. The entity expects to be released from risk evenly over the 10m contract period. At the reporting date (31 December 2023) the contract is still not expected to be onerous.

For the six-month reporting period ending on 31 December 2023, the entity recognises insurance revenue of $732 (i.e. 60% of $1,220). The insurance acquisition cash flows of $20 are recognised as insurance service expense (as per Example 56.48 above, the entity has chosen to recognise the acquisition cash flows as incurred and not over the passage of time).

As at 31 December 2023, the liability for remaining coverage is $488 (i.e. $1,220 – $732 or 40% of $1,220). Note that, alternatively, if premiums were not received until 1 January 2024, the liability for remaining coverage would be an asset of $732 at 31 December 2023.

For the six-month reporting period ending on 30 June 2024, the entity recognises the remaining $488 as insurance revenue and there is no liability for remaining coverage as at 30 June 2024.

In September 2018, the TRG agreed with an IASB staff paper which stated that premium experience adjustments under the premium allocation approach are part of expected premium receipts and are therefore allocated to insurance revenue on the basis of either the passage of time or the expected release from risk (see above). If the expected pattern of release of risk differs significantly from the passage of time, the expected premium receipts are allocated over the coverage period on the basis of the expected timing of the incurred insurance service expense.[62] This approach does not appear to preclude an entity from allocating any premium experience adjustment to both past and future services and hence recognise the resulting revenue relating to past services in the current period. The result of splitting the premium experience adjustment between past and future periods adds complexity.

9.4 Subsequent measurement – liability for incurred claims

The liability for incurred claims for a group of insurance contracts subject to the premium allocation approach (which should usually be nil on initial recognition) is measured in the same way as the liability for incurred claims using the general model (i.e. a discounted estimate of future cash flows with a risk adjustment for non-financial risk). See 8.6.2 above.

However, when applying the premium allocation method to the liability for incurred claims, an entity is not required to adjust future cash flows for the time value of money and the effect of financial risk if those cash flows (for that group of insurance contracts) are expected to be paid or received in one year or less from the date the claims are incurred. *[IFRS 17.59(b)]*. This is a separate policy choice from the choice not to adjust the carrying amount of the liability for remaining coverage to reflect the time value of money and the effect of financial risk at initial recognition (see 9.2 above). It is possible that a group of insurance contracts would be eligible to not adjusting the liability for remaining coverage for time value of money (because the coverage period and the premium due date are within one year) but have to discount the liability for incurred claims (because the claims are not expected to settle within one year or less from the date in which they are incurred). This would likely be the case for products with short coverage periods and long-tail claim settlement periods.

IFRS 17 does not state whether the discounting election above is irrevocable. There may be circumstances in which groups of claims that were expected originally to be settled within one year (and hence not discounted) subsequently turn out to take much longer to settle. In those circumstances, we believe that an entity should start discounting the claims in the period in which it identifies such change and account for it prospectively (as this is a change in estimate).

When the entire insurance finance income or expenses is included in profit or loss, incurred claims are discounted at current rates (i.e. the rate at the reporting date). When insurance finance income or expenses is disaggregated between profit or loss and other comprehensive income (see 15.3.3 below) the amount of insurance finance income or expenses included in profit or loss is determined using the discount rate at the date of the incurred claim. See 8.3 above.

Example 56.50: Subsequent measurement of the liability for incurred claims using the premium allocation approach

Assuming the same fact pattern as Example 56.48 above.

For the six-month reporting period ending on 31 December 2023, there were claims incurred of £636 including a risk adjustment for non-financial risk related to those claims of £36. None of the claims have been paid at the reporting date. The claims will be paid within one year after the claims are incurred and therefore the entity chooses not to adjust the liability for incurred claims for the time value of money and the effect of financial risk.

At 31 December 2023 the liability for incurred claims is £636 which is also the amount for incurred claims recorded in profit or loss as insurance service expenses.

For the six month reporting period ending on 30 June 2024, there were claims incurred of £424 including a risk adjustment for non-financial risk related to those claims of £24. During the period claims of £800 were paid.

At 30 June 2024 the total liability for incurred claims and the risk adjustment for future risk is £260 (i.e. £636 + £400 + £24 – £800). The total incurred claims recognised in profit or loss as insurance service expenses for the six-month reporting period ending on 30 June 2024 is £424 (i.e. £400 + £24).

10 MEASUREMENT – REINSURANCE CONTRACTS HELD

A reinsurance contract is an insurance contract issued by one entity (the reinsurer) to compensate another entity for claims arising from one or more insurance contracts issued by that other entity (underlying contracts). *[IFRS 17 Appendix A]*.

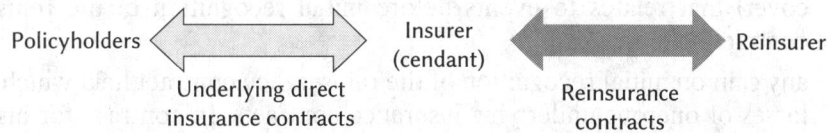

IFRS 17 requires a reinsurance contract held to be accounted for separately from the underlying insurance contracts to which it relates. This is because an entity that holds a reinsurance contract does not normally have a right to reduce the amounts it owes to the underlying policyholder by amounts it expects to receive from the reinsurer. It is acknowledged in the Basis for Conclusions that separate accounting for the reinsurance contracts and their underlying insurance contracts might create mismatches that some regard as purely accounting, for example; on the timing of recognition, the measurement of the reinsurance contracts and the recognition of profit. However, the Board concluded that accounting for a reinsurance contract held separately from the underlying insurance contracts gives a faithful representation of the entity's rights and obligations and the related income and expenses from both contracts. *[IFRS 17.BC298]*. Examples of potential accounting mismatches are:

- Contract boundaries for reinsurance held may differ from those of the underlying direct insurance contracts as the accounting for reinsurance held requires the cedant (insurer) to estimate cash flows for underlying direct contracts that have not been issued yet but are within the boundary of the reinsurance contract (see 10.2 below).

- Underlying insurance contracts may meet one of the criteria to apply the premium allocation approach but the related reinsurance contracts do not, possibly because the contract boundary of the reinsurance contract differs from that of the underlying insurance contracts (see 10.6 below).

- Reinsurance held cannot be accounted for under the variable fee approach, even if the underlying direct insurance contracts are accounted for under the variable fee approach (see 10.7 below).

A modified version of the general model is applied by cedants for reinsurance contracts held. This is to reflect that: *[IFRS 17.BC302]*

- groups of reinsurance contracts held are usually assets rather than liabilities; and
- entities holding reinsurance contracts generally pay a margin to the reinsurer as an implicit part of the premium rather than making profits from the reinsurance contracts.

A further consideration is that most reinsurance contracts held will be 'loss making' if the underlying insurance contracts to which they relate are profitable. Given that IFRS 17 does not permit gains on initial recognition of insurance contracts issued, it would seem inappropriate to require anticipated losses on related reinsurance contracts held to be expensed on initial recognition. This would create an accounting mismatch.

Consequently, the overall result of the modifications of the general model for reinsurance contracts held are that:

- both day 1 gains and day 1 differences are initially recognised in the statement of financial position as a contractual service margin and recognised in profit or loss as the reinsurer renders services except for:
  - any portion of a day 1 difference (i.e. the net cost of purchasing reinsurance cover) that relates to events before initial recognition of the reinsurance contract held or;
  - any gain on initial recognition of the reinsurance contract held which covers losses of onerous underlying insurance contracts. In contrast, for insurance and reinsurance contracts issued all day 1 losses are recognised in profit or loss immediately;
- assumptions used for measurement should be consistent with the assumptions used for measurement of the underlying insurance contracts issued;

- non-performance risk of the reinsurer should be included in the measurement of the fulfilment cash flows of the reinsurance asset (as this would not have been included within the measurement of the underlying insurance contracts issued);
- the risk adjustment for non-financial risk reflects the amount of the risk transferred from the insurer to the reinsurer; and
- changes in the fulfilment cash flows adjust the contractual service margin if they relate to future coverage and other future services. However, changes in fulfilment cash flows are recognised in profit or loss if the related changes in the underlying contracts are also recognised in profit or loss when the underlying contracts are onerous.

As noted above, a key consideration arising for insurers will be the extent of any accounting mismatches arising from the different treatment of reinsurance contracts held with underlying insurance contracts and whether the model used by the underlying insurance contracts can be used by the related reinsurance contracts held (see 10.6 and 10.7 below).

10.1 Level of aggregation

An entity should divide portfolios of reinsurance contracts held by applying the same criteria as the general model (see 6 above) except that references to onerous contracts (see 8.8 above) should be replaced with a reference to contracts on which there is a net gain on initial recognition. *[IFRS 17.61]*. This appears to mean that a portfolio of reinsurance contracts held should be divided into a minimum of:

- a group of contracts on which there is a net gain on initial recognition, if any;
- a group of contracts that have no significant possibility of a net gain arising subsequent to initial recognition, if any; and
- a group of the remaining contracts in the portfolio.

An entity is not allowed to group contracts purchased more than a year apart. A group of contracts is not reassessed after initial recognition. It is acknowledged by IFRS 17 that for some reinsurance contracts held, applying the general model, as modified, will result in a group that comprises a single contract. *[IFRS 17.61]*.

A reinsurance contract held cannot be onerous. Therefore, the requirements for onerous contracts in the general model (see 8.8 above) do not apply. *[IFRS 17.68]*.

10.2 The boundary of a reinsurance contract held

The contract boundary requirements of IFRS 17 (see 8.1 above) apply also to reinsurance contracts held.

In some cases, reinsurance contracts held will offer protection for underlying contracts that an entity has not yet issued. The question therefore arises as to whether the boundary of a reinsurance contract held should include those anticipated cash flows from unissued underlying contracts (which will not have been recognised as underlying insurance contracts by the entity). In February 2018, this issue was discussed by the TRG who agreed with the IASB staff's conclusion that the application of the contract boundary requirements to reinsurance contracts held means that cash flows within the boundary of a reinsurance contract held arise from substantive rights and obligations of the entity, i.e. the holder of the contract. Therefore:

- A substantive right to receive services from the reinsurer ends when the reinsurer has the practical ability to reassess the risks transferred to the reinsurer and can set a price or level of benefits for the contract to fully reflect the reassessed risk or the reinsurer has a substantive right to terminate the contract.
- Accordingly, the boundary of a reinsurance contract held could include cash flows from underlying contracts covered by the reinsurance contract that are expected to be issued by the cedant in the future.[63]

This means that an entity will need to estimate the fulfilment cash flows of contracts it expects to issue that will give rise to cash flows within the boundary of the reinsurance contracts that it holds. Some stakeholders argued that this will result in an accounting mismatch between the direct insurance contracts issued and the reinsurance contracts held. However, the Basis for Conclusions states that the IASB disagreed that differences between the carrying amount of the reinsurance contract held and the underlying insurance contracts are accounting mismatches. The carrying amount of a reinsurance contract held is nil before any cash flows occur or any service is received. Thereafter any difference that arise between the carrying amount of the reinsurance contract held and the underlying insurance contracts are not accounting mismatches but differences caused by: *[IFRS 17.BC309E]*

- the provision of coverage, for example because the reinsurer provides coverage for less than 100% of the risks the entity covers;
- the timing of cash flows; and
- interest accreted on the contractual service margin of the reinsurance contract held from an earlier period than, and at a different discount rate from, the interest accreted on the contractual service margin of the underlying insurance contracts, reflecting the different effects of the time value of money on the contractual service margin and fulfilment cash flows.

The TRG members observed that applying this requirement is likely to result in operational complexity because it is a change from existing practice under IFRS 4. This increase in cost and complexity resulting from a change in existing practice is acknowledged in the Basis for Conclusions but the IASB concluded that the benefits of appropriately reflecting an entity's rights and obligations as the holder of a reinsurance contract outweigh those costs. *[IFRS 17.BC309F]*.

Additionally, some reinsurance contracts held may contain break clauses which allow either party to cancel the contract at any time following a specified notice period. In February 2018, the TRG members observed that, in an example of a reinsurance contract which:

- is issued and recognised on 1 January;
- covers a proportion of all risks arising from underlying insurance contracts issued in a 24-month period; and

- provides the unilateral right to both the cedant and the reinsurer to terminate the contract with a three-month notice period to the other party with respect to only new business ceded,

the initial contract boundary would exclude cash flows related to premiums outside of that three month notice period.[64]

In September 2018, the IASB staff clarified to TRG members that, if as at 31 March (i.e. after three months) neither the entity nor the reinsurer had given notice to terminate the reinsurance contract with respect to new business ceded, this would not cause a reassessment of the contract boundary. This is because the contract boundary determination at initial recognition (i.e. three months) was not based on an assessment of the practical ability to set a price that fully reflected the risk in the contract. The cash flows related to underlying contracts that are expected to be issued and ceded in the next three-month period are cash flows outside the existing contract boundary. In response to a concern that this may result in daily reinsurance contracts being issued, the IASB staff observed that reinsurance contracts held are recognised only when the recognition criteria are met. In the fact pattern provided, this is likely to be 1 April or later. The contract boundary is determined at initial recognition and, in this example, that will result in a new reinsurance contract held being recognised after the end of the first three-month period with a contract boundary of cash flows arising from contracts expected to be issued in the following three months. Both of these contracts held could belong to an annual group of contracts applying the level of aggregation criteria.

The submission to the IASB staff in September 2018 included an additional fact pattern in which there is a unilateral right for the reinsurer to amend the rate of the ceding commission it pays, in addition to unilateral termination rights. The IASB staff observe that in this fact pattern, the existence of the right to terminate the contract with a three-month notice period determines the cash flows within the contract boundary regardless of the existence of a right to amend the rate of the ceding commission if the contract is not terminated. Therefore, the same accounting would apply to the additional fact pattern provided.[65]

10.2.1 Reinsurance contracts held with repricing clauses

In May 2018, the TRG discussed an IASB staff paper concerning the determination of the boundary of a reinsurance contract held when the reinsurer has the right to reprice remaining coverage prospectively. In the fact pattern provided, the reinsurer can adjust premium rates at any time, subject to a minimum three month notice period and could choose either (i) not to exercise the right to reprice, in which case the holder of the reinsurance contract is committed to continue paying premiums to the reinsurer, or (ii) to exercise the right to reprice in which case the holder has the right to terminate coverage. The TRG members observed that:

- For reinsurance contracts held, cash flows are within the contract boundary if they arise from substantive rights and obligations that exist during the reporting period in which the entity (i.e. the holder) is compelled to pay amounts to the reinsurer or in which the entity has a substantive right to receive services from the reinsurer.
- A right to terminate coverage that is triggered by the reinsurer's decision to reprice the reinsurance contract is not relevant when considering whether a substantive

obligation to pay premiums exists. Such a right is not within the entity's control and therefore the entity would continue to be compelled to pay premiums for the entire contractual term.

- The entity's expectations about the amount and timing of future cash flows, including with respect to the probability of the reinsurer repricing the contract, would be reflected in the fulfilment cash flows.

The TRG members also observed that although the fact pattern in this example was limited in scope, it demonstrates the principle that both rights and obligations need to be considered when assessing the boundary of a contract.[66]

10.3 Measurement – initial recognition

10.3.1 Initial measurement – fulfilment cash flows

A reinsurance contract held should be measured using the same criteria for fulfilment cash flows and contractual service margin as an insurance contract issued to the extent that the underlying contracts are also measured using this approach. However, the entity should use consistent assumptions to measure the estimates of the present value of future cash flows for the group of reinsurance contracts held and the estimates of the present value of the underlying insurance contracts. *[IFRS 17.63].*

In February 2018, in answer to a TRG submission, the IASB staff stated that 'consistent' in this context does not necessarily mean 'identical' (i.e. the use of an identical discount rate for measurement of the group of underlying insurance contracts and the related group of reinsurance contracts held was not mandated). The extent of dependency between the cash flows of the reinsurance contract held and the underlying cash flows should be evaluated in applying the requirements of paragraph 63 of IFRS 17.[67] In May 2018, in answer to a TRG submission, the IASB staff further noted that consistency is required to the extent that the same assumptions apply to both the underlying contracts and the reinsurance contracts held. In the IASB staff's view, this requirement does not require or permit the entity to use the same assumptions used (e.g. the same discount rates) for measuring the underlying contracts when measuring the reinsurance contracts held if those assumptions are not valid for the term of the reinsurance contracts held. If different assumptions apply for reinsurance contracts held, the entity uses those different assumptions when measuring the contract. The TRG members did not disagree with either of the IASB staff statements.[68]

10.3.2 Measurement at initial recognition – contractual service margin

In determining the contractual service margin on initial recognition, the requirements of the general model are modified to reflect the fact that there is no unearned profit but instead a net gain or net cost on purchasing the reinsurance.

Hence, on initial recognition, unless the net cost of purchasing reinsurance coverage relates to events that occurred before the purchase of the group of reinsurance contracts, the entity should recognise any net cost or net gain on purchasing the group of reinsurance contracts held as a contractual service margin measured at an amount equal to the sum of: *[IFRS 17.65]*

- the fulfilment cash flows;
- the amount derecognised at that date of any asset or liability previously recognised for cash flows related to the group of reinsurance contracts held;
- any cash flows arising at that date; and
- any income recognised in profit or loss when an entity recognises a loss on initial recognition of an onerous group of underlying contracts (see 10.3.3 below).

If the net cost of purchasing reinsurance coverage relates to events that occurred before the purchase of the group of reinsurance contracts held, an entity should recognise such a cost immediately in profit or loss as an expense. *[IFRS 17.65A]*.

It is stated in the Basis for Conclusions that the IASB decided that the net expense of purchasing reinsurance should be recognised over the coverage period as services are received unless the reinsurance covers events that have already occurred. For such reinsurance contracts held, the Board concluded that entities should recognise the whole of the net expense at initial recognition, to be consistent with the treatment of the net expense of purchasing reinsurance before an insured event has occurred. The Board acknowledged that this approach does not treat the coverage period of the reinsurance contract consistently with the view that for some insurance contracts the insured event is the discovery of a loss during the term of the contract, if that loss arises from an event that had occurred before the inception of the contract. However, the Board concluded that consistency of the treatment of the net expense across all reinsurance contracts held would result in more relevant information. *[IFRS 17.BC312]*.

IFRS 17 provides no guidance as to how a cedant should account for the net cost of a reinsurance contract held which provides both prospective and retrospective coverage. In these circumstances an entity would need to apply judgement as to the portfolio to which a contract providing both prospective and retrospective coverage should be allocated and whether the legal contract could be split into separate retrospective and prospective insurance components, with each component allocated to different portfolios as an in-substance separate contract for accounting purposes, applying the guidance discussed at 5.1.1. above.

Measurement of a reinsurance contract held on initial recognition is illustrated by the following example, based on Example 11 in IFRS 17. *[IFRS 17.IE124-129]*. The initial recognition of reinsurance contracts in situations where a group of underlying insurance contracts is onerous at initial recognition is discussed at 10.3.3 below.

Example 56.51: **Measurement on initial recognition of groups of reinsurance contracts held**

An entity enters into a reinsurance contract that in return for a premium of £300m covers 30% of each claim from the underlying insurance contracts. Applying the relevant criteria, the entity considers that the group comprises a single contract held. For simplicity, this example ignores the risk of non-performance of the reinsurer and all other amounts.

The entity measures the estimates of the present value of future cash flows for the group of reinsurance contracts held using assumptions consistent with those used to measure the estimates of the present value of the future cash flows for the group of the underlying insurance contracts as shown in the table below.

	Underlying contracts £m	Reinsurance contract £m
Estimates of the present value of future cash inflows	1,000	270
Estimates of the present value of future cash outflows/premium paid	(900)	(300)
Risk adjustment for non-financial risk	(60)	18
Contractual service margin	(40)	12
Insurance contract asset/liability on initial recognition	–	–

The entity measures the present value of the future cash inflows consistent with the assumptions of the cash outflows of the underlying insurance contracts. Consequently, the estimate of cash inflows is £270m (i.e. 30% of £900m). The risk adjustment is determined to represent the amount of risk being transferred by the holder of the reinsurance contract to the issuer of the contract and consequently the risk adjustment, which is treated as an inflow rather than an outflow, is £18m (i.e. 30% of 60).

The contractual service margin (CSM) is an amount equal to the sum of the fulfilment cash flows and any cash flows arising at that date. In this example, cash outflows exceed cash inflows and therefore there is a net loss on purchasing the reinsurance and so the CSM is an asset.

If the premium was, say, only £260m then there would be a net gain of £28m on purchasing the reinsurance (i.e. inflows of £270m plus the risk adjustment of £18m less outflows of £260m) and the CSM would represent a liability of £28m in order to eliminate the net gain on inception.

10.3.3 Initial measurement of reinsurance held of underlying onerous insurance contracts that are onerous at initial recognition

IFRS 17, as amended in June 2020 states that an entity should adjust the contractual service margin of a group of reinsurance contracts held and as a result recognise income when the entity recognises a loss on initial recognition of an onerous group of underlying contracts or on addition of onerous underlying insurance contracts to that group. *[IFRS 17.66A]*. This requirement applies to all reinsurance contracts held and is irrespective of the measurement model used by the underlying contracts.

It is clarified in the Basis of Conclusions that, for this accounting to apply, an entity must enter into the reinsurance contract held before or at the same time as the entity recognises the onerous underlying insurance contracts. The Board concluded that it would not be appropriate for an entity to recognise a recovery of loss when the entity does not hold a reinsurance contract. *[IFRS 17.BC315C]*. This does not preclude the entity from recognising the gain for underlying contracts that are added to the group subsequently as these contracts are initially recognised after the entity entered into the reinsurance held contract.

The amount of the adjustment to the contractual service margin of a group of reinsurance contracts held and resulting income is determined by multiplying: *[IFRS 17.B119D]*

- the loss recognised on the underlying contracts; and
- the percentage of claims on underlying insurance contracts the entity expects to recover from the group of reinsurance contracts held.

An entity should also establish (or adjust) a loss-recovery component of the asset for remaining coverage for a group of reinsurance contracts held depicting the recovery of losses recognised applying the requirements above. The loss-recovery component determines the amounts that are presented in profit or loss as reversals of recoveries of losses from reinsurance contracts held and are consequently excluded from the allocation of premiums paid to the reinsurer. *[IFRS 17.66B]*.

An entity might include in an onerous group of insurance contracts both onerous insurance contracts covered by a group of reinsurance contracts held and onerous insurance contracts not covered by the group of reinsurance contracts held. In such cases, the entity shall apply a systematic and rational method of allocation to determine the portion of losses recognised on the group of insurance contracts that relates to insurance contracts covered by the group of reinsurance contracts held. *[IFRS 17.B119E]*.

It is observed in the Basis for Conclusions that IFRS 17 does not require an entity to track insurance contracts at a lower level than the level of the group of insurance contracts. Accordingly, the Board specified that, in these circumstances, an entity applies a systematic and rational method of allocation to determine the portion of losses on a group of insurance contracts that relates to underlying insurance contracts covered by a reinsurance contract held. Requiring a systematic and rational method of allocation is consistent with other requirements in IFRS 17. *[IFRS 17.BC315H]*.

Applying the requirements for reinsurance contracts held based on IFRS 17, as issued in May 2017, an entity would not have recognised corresponding income representing the expected recovery of losses at initial recognition of the underlying insurance contracts despite the entity's right to recover from a reinsurer some or all the claims that contribute to those losses. Some stakeholders perceived the previous IFRS 17 treatment to result in an accounting mismatch between the recognition of losses on underlying insurance contracts and the recognition of the contractual service margin of the reinsurance contract held. *[IFRS 17.BC315E]*.

The Board was persuaded that amending IFRS 17 was justified because: *[IFRS 17.BC315F]*

- IFRS 17 provides a similar exception for changes in the measurement of underlying insurance contracts on subsequent measurement of a group of reinsurance contracts held.

- The amendment provides users of financial statements with useful information about expected loss recoveries on reinsurance contracts held in addition to the information provided to users of financial statements about expected losses on underlying insurance contracts. The information provided about onerous underlying contracts is unchanged. Losses and loss recoveries are presented in separate line items in the statement(s) of financial performance and are disclosed separately in the notes to the financial statements.

It is acknowledged in the Basis for Conclusions that this requirement adds complexity to IFRS 17 because it requires an entity to track a loss-recovery component. However, the Board concluded that the added complexity was justified given the strong stakeholder support for the information that entities will provide to users of financial statements as a result of the amendment. In addition, the Board noted that the loss-recovery component of a reinsurance contract held is treated similarly to the loss component on insurance contracts issued. *[IFRS 17.BC315G]*.

The following example, based on Example12C in the Illustrative Examples on IFRS 17, shows the application of these requirements at initial measurement. *[IFRS 17.IE138A-138K]*.

Example 56.52: Initial measurement of a group of reinsurance contracts held that provides coverage for groups of underlying insurance contracts, including an onerous group

At the beginning of Year 1, an entity enters into a reinsurance contract that in return for a fixed premium covers 30 per cent of each claim from the groups of underlying insurance contracts. The reinsurance held is the only contract in the group. The underlying insurance contracts are issued at the same time as the entity enters into the reinsurance contract held. For simplicity it is assumed that no contracts will lapse before the end of the coverage period, there are no changes in estimates and all other amounts, including the effect of discounting, the risk adjustment for non-performance risk and the risk of non-performance of the reinsurer are ignored.

Some of the underlying insurance contracts are onerous at initial recognition. Thus, the entity establishes a group comprising the onerous contracts. The remainder of the underlying insurance contracts are expected to be profitable and, in this example, the entity establishes a single group comprising the profitable contracts. The coverage period of the underlying insurance contracts and the reinsurance contract held is three years from the beginning of Year 1. Service is provided evenly over the coverage periods.

The entity expects to receive $1,110 on the underlying insurance contracts immediately after initial recognition. Claims on the underlying insurance contracts are expected to be incurred evenly across the coverage period and are paid immediately after claims are incurred.

The entity measures the group of underlying insurance contracts on initial recognition as follows:

	Profitable group of insurance contracts	Onerous group of insurance contracts	Total
	$	$	$
Estimates of present value of future cash inflows	(900)	(210)	(1,110)
Estimates of present value of future cash outflows	600	300	900
Fulfilment cash flows	(300)	90	(210)
Contractual service margin	300	–	300
Loss on initial recognition	–	90	90

The entity establishes a group comprising a single reinsurance contract held that provides proportionate coverage. The entity pays a premium of $315 to the reinsurer immediately after initial recognition. The entity expects to receive recoveries of claims from the reinsurer on the same day that the entity pays claims on the underlying insurance contracts.

Applying IFRS 17, the entity measures the estimates of the present value of the future cash flows for the group of reinsurance contracts held using assumptions consistent with those used to measure the estimates of the present value of the future cash flows for the groups of underlying insurance contracts. Consequently, the estimate of the present value of the future cash inflows is $270 (recovery of 30 per cent of the estimates of the present value of the future cash outflows for the groups of underlying insurance contracts of $900).

The entity measures the group of reinsurance contracts held on initial recognition as follows:

	Initial recognition
	$
Estimates of present value of future cash inflows (recoveries) being 900 × 30%	(270)
Estimates of present value of future cash outflows (premiums)	315
Fulfilment cash flows	45
Contractual service margin of the reinsurance contract held (before the loss recovery adjustment)	(45)
Loss-recovery component (being 90 × 30%)	27
Contractual service margin of the reinsurance contract held (after the loss-recovery adjustment)	(72)
Reinsurance contract asset on initial recognition	(27)
Income on initial recognition	27

Applying IFRS 17, the entity adjusts the contractual service margin of the reinsurance contract held and recognises income to reflect the loss recovery. The entity determines the adjustment to the contractual service margin and the income recognised as $27 (the loss of $90 recognised for the onerous group of underlying insurance contracts multiplied by 30 per cent, the fixed percentage of claims the entity expects has the right to recover). The contractual service margin of $45 is adjusted by $27, resulting in a contractual service margin of $72, reflecting a net cost on the reinsurance contract held. The reinsurance contract asset of $27 comprises the fulfilment cash flows of $45 (net outflows) and a contractual service margin reflecting a net cost of $72. The entity establishes a loss-recovery component of the asset for remaining coverage of $27 depicting the recovery of losses recognised.

10.3.4 Initial measurement of the effect of the risk of non-performance

In addition to using consistent assumptions, an entity should make the following modifications in calculating the fulfilment cash flows:

- the estimates of the present value of the future cash flows for the group of reinsurance contracts held should reflect the effect of any risk of non-performance by the issuer of the reinsurance contract, including the effects of collateral and losses from disputes. *[IFRS 17.63]*. This is because an entity holding a reinsurance contract faces the risk that the reinsurer may default or may dispute whether a valid claim exists for an insured event. *[IFRS 17.BC308]*. The estimates of expected credit losses are based on expected values; and

- the estimate of the risk adjustment for non-financial risk should be determined so that it represents the amount of risk being transferred by the holder of the group of insurance contracts to the issuer of those contracts. *[IFRS 17.64]*. The risk adjustment does not include an adjustment for the risk of non-performance (which is already contained within the estimates of the present value of future cash flows), a fact confirmed by the IASB staff to TRG members in May 2018 (the TRG members did not disagree with the IASB staff's statement).[69]

In April 2019, the IASB staff discussed a TRG submission which explained that the non-performance risk of a reinsurer may incorporate different risks such as insolvency risk and the risk related to disputes and further negotiations. The submission questioned whether these risks are identified as financial or non-financial risks and the impact this determination has on the measurement of reinsurance contracts held when determining the risk being transferred from the holder of the reinsurance contract to the issuer of the reinsurance contract. The IASB staff observed that paragraph 63 of IFRS 17 specifically requires that estimates of the present value of future cash flows should include the effect of the risk of any non-performance by the issuer including the effects of collateral and losses from disputes. Thus, the risk adjustment for non-financial risk of a reinsurance contract held reflects only the risks that the cedant transfers to the reinsurer. The risk of non-performance by the reinsurer is not a risk transferred to the reinsurer nor does it reduce the risk transferred to the reinsurer. Hence, the risk of non-performance is only reflected in the present value of the future cash flows of the reinsurance contracts held, similar to the treatment of financial risks. The IASB staff further observed that IFRS 17 does not provide specific requirements on how to determine the risk of any non-performance.[70] Nevertheless, changes in fulfilment cash flows that relate to the risk of non-performance will affect the risk adjustment for non-financial risk to the extent that the underlying expected cash flows have reduced (for example, because of insolvency of the reinsurer). This is because the risk inherent in those revised cash flows has changed. As a result, we would expect the risk adjustment for non-financial risk to be calculated on the expected fulfilment cash flows after the fulfilment cash flows have been adjusted for the effect of non-performance.

10.4 Subsequent measurement

Instead of applying the subsequent measurement requirements for the general model, an entity should measure the contractual service margin at the end of the reporting period for a group of reinsurance contracts held as the carrying amount determined at the start of the reporting period, adjusted for: *[IFRS 17.66]*

- the effect of any new contracts added to the group;
- interest accreted on the carrying amount of the contractual service margin, measured at the discount rates determined at the date of initial recognition of a group of contracts using the discount rates as determined by the general model (see 8.3 above);
- income recognised in profit or loss when an entity offsets a loss on an onerous group of underlying contracts (see 10.3.3 above);
- reversals of a loss-recovery component recognised (see 10.3.3 above) to the extent those reversals are not changes in the fulfilment cash flows of the group of reinsurance contracts held;
- changes in the fulfilment cash flows measured at the discount rates applying on initial recognition (see 8.3 above) to the extent that the change relates to future service, unless:
    - the change results from a change in fulfilment cash flows allocated to a group of underlying insurance contracts that does not adjust the contractual service margin for the group of underlying insurance contracts ; or
    - the change results from applying the onerous contract requirements to the measurement of a group of underlying insurance contracts using the premium allocation approach.
- the effect of any currency exchange differences arising on the contractual service margin; and
- the amount recognised in profit or loss because of services received in the period, determined by the allocation of the contractual service margin remaining at the end of the reporting period (before any allocation) over the current and remaining coverage period of the group of reinsurance contracts held.

The contractual service margin of a group of insurance contracts issued can never be negative. In contrast, IFRS 17 does not include a limit on the amount by which the contractual service margin of a group of reinsurance contracts held could be adjusted as a result of changes in estimates of cash flows. In the Board's view, the contractual service margin for a group of reinsurance contracts held is different from that for a group of insurance contracts issued – the contractual service margin for the group of reinsurance contracts held depicts the expense the entity incurs when purchasing reinsurance coverage rather than the profit it will make by providing services under the insurance contract. Accordingly, the Board placed no limit on the amount of the adjustment to the contractual service margin for the group of reinsurance contracts held, subject to the amount of premium paid to the reinsurer. *[IFRS 17.BC314]*.

It is stated in the Basis for Conclusions in IFRS 17, as issued in 2017, that the Board considered the situation that arises when the underlying group of insurance contracts becomes onerous after initial recognition because of adverse changes in estimates of fulfilment cash flows relating to future service. In such a situation, the entity recognises a loss on the group of underlying insurance contracts (this situation would also apply to the subsequent accounting of underlying direct contracts that were already onerous at their initial recognition). The Board concluded that corresponding changes in cash inflows from a group of reinsurance contracts held should not adjust the contractual service margin of the group of reinsurance contracts held, with the result that the entity recognises no net effect of the loss and gain in the profit or loss for the period. This means that, to the extent that the change in the fulfilment cash flows of the group of underlying contracts is matched with a change in fulfilment cash flows on the group of reinsurance contracts held, there is no net effect on profit or loss. *[IFRS 17.BC315]*.

These requirements are illustrated by the following example, based on Examples 12A and 12B in IFRS 17. *[IFRS 17.IE130-138]*.

Example 56.53: Measurement subsequent to initial recognition of groups of reinsurance contracts held

An entity enters into a reinsurance contract that in return for a fixed premium covers 30% of each claim from the underlying insurance contracts (the entity assumes that it could transfer 30% of non-financial risk from the underlying contracts to the reinsurer). In this example the effect of discounting, the risk of non-performance of the reinsurer and other amounts are ignored, for simplicity. Applying the relevant criteria, the entity considers that the group comprises a single contract held.

Immediately before the end of Year 1, the entity measures the group of insurance contracts and the reinsurance contract held as follows:

	Insurance contract liability	Reinsurance contract asset
	$m	$m
Fulfilment cash flows (before the effect of any change in estimates)	300	(90)
Contractual service margin (CSM)	100	(25)
Insurance contract liability/(reinsurance contract asset) immediately before the end of Year 1	400	(115)

In this example, the difference between the CSM for the reinsurance contract held of $25m and 30% of the underlying group of insurance contracts of $30m (30% × $100m) arises because of a different pricing policy between the underlying group of insurance contracts and the reinsurance contract held.

At the end of year 1, the entity revises its estimates of the fulfilment cash flows of the underlying group of contracts as follows:

- In Example A, the entity estimates there is an increase in the fulfilment cash flows of the underlying contracts of $50m and a decrease in the contractual service margin by the same amount (the group of underlying insurance contracts is not onerous).

- In Example B, the entity estimates that there is an increase in the fulfilment cash flows of the underlying group of insurance contracts of $160m. This change makes the underlying group of insurance contracts onerous and the entity decreases the contractual service margin by $100m to zero and recognises the remaining $60m as a loss in profit or loss.

Example A

The entity increases the fulfilment cash flows of the reinsurance contract held by 30 per cent of the change in fulfilment cash flows of the underlying group of insurance contracts ($15m = 30% × $50m).

Applying paragraph 66, the entity adjusts the contractual service margin of the reinsurance contract held by the whole amount of the change in the fulfilment cash flows of this reinsurance contract held of CU15m from $(25)m to $(10)m. This is because the whole change in the fulfilment cash flows allocated to the group of underlying insurance contracts adjusts the contractual service margin of those underlying insurance contracts.

At the end of Year 1, the entity measures the insurance contracts liability and the reinsurance contract asset as follows:

	Insurance contract liability	Reinsurance contract asset
	$m	$m
Fulfilment cash flows (including the effect of any change in estimates)	350	(105)
Contractual service margin (CSM)	50	(10)
Insurance contract liability/(reinsurance contract asset) immediately before the end of Year 1	400	(115)

There is no effect of these change in estimates on profit and loss as all changes in the fulfilment cash flows go to the CSM.

Example B

The entity increases the fulfilment cash flows of the reinsurance contract held by $48m which equals 30 per cent of the fulfilment cash flows of the underlying group of insurance contracts ($48m=30% of $160m).

Applying paragraph 66, the entity adjusts the contractual service margin of the reinsurance contract held for the change in fulfilment cash flows that relate to future services to the extent this change results from a change in the fulfilment cash flows of the group of underlying insurance contracts that adjusts the contractual service margin for that group.

Consequently, the change in the fulfilment cash flows of the reinsurance contract held of $48m are recognised as follows by:

- Adjusting the contractual service margin of the reinsurance contract held for $30m of the change in the fulfilment cash flows. The $30m is equivalent to the change in the fulfilment cash flows that adjusts the CSM of the underlying contracts of $100m ($30m = 30% × $100m). Consequently, the contractual service margin of the reinsurance contract held of $5m equals the contractual service margin on initial recognition of $25m adjusted for the part of the change in the fulfilment cash flows of $30m ($5m = $(25)m + $30m). This represents a CSM 'asset'.
- Recognising the remaining change in the fulfilment cash flows of the reinsurance contract held, $18m (i.e. $48m − $30m) immediately in profit or loss.

Therefore, at the end of Year 1, using these alternative estimates, the entity measures the insurance contracts liability and the reinsurance contract asset as follows:

	Insurance contract liability $m	Reinsurance contract asset $m
Fulfilment cash flows (including the effect of any change in estimates)	460	(138)
Contractual service margin (CSM)	–	5
Insurance contract liability/(reinsurance contract asset) at the end of Year 1	460	(133)
The effect on profit or loss will be:		
Profit/(loss) at the end of Year 1	(60)	18

10.4.1 Subsequent measurement of non-performance risk

Any changes in expected credit losses are economic events that should be reflected as gains and losses in profit or loss when they occur.

To this end, IFRS 17 prohibits changes in fulfilment cash flows that relate to the risk of non-performance adjusting the contractual service margin. In the Board's view, differences in expected credit losses do not relate to future service. *[IFRS 17.67]*. Accordingly, this results in consistent accounting for expected credit losses between reinsurance contracts held and purchased, and originated credit-impaired financial assets accounted for in accordance with IFRS 9 (which does not apply to rights and obligations arising under a contract within the scope of IFRS 17 such as a receivable due under a reinsurance contract held – see 2.3 above). *[IFRS 17.BC309]*.

As noted at 10.3.4 above, the risk adjustment for non-financial risk does not include an adjustment for the risk of non-performance (which is already contained within the estimates of the present value of future cash flows). However, changes in fulfilment cash flows that relate to the risk of non-performance will affect the risk adjustment for non-financial risk to the extent that the underlying expected cash flows have reduced because the risk inherent in those revised cash flows has changed.

10.4.2 Subsequent measurement of a loss-recovery component

As discussed at 10.3.3 above, at initial recognition, an entity shall establish (or adjust) a loss-recovery component of the asset for remaining coverage for a group of reinsurance contracts held depicting the recovery of losses recognised. This loss-recovery component should be accounted for in a manner consistent with the loss component of the group of underlying insurance contracts issued. As such, after the entity has established a loss component, it should adjust the loss-recovery component to reflect changes in the loss component of an onerous group of underlying insurance contracts.

The carrying amount of the loss-recovery component shall not exceed the portion of the carrying amount of the loss component of the onerous group of underlying insurance contracts that the entity expects to recover from the group of reinsurance contracts held. [IFRS 17.B119F].

A loss-recovery component reverses, consistent with reversal of the loss component of underlying groups of contracts issued, even when those reversals are not changes in the fulfilment cash flows of the group of reinsurance contracts held. Such reversals adjust the contractual service margin. [IFRS 17.66(bb)]. For example, a loss-recovery component might be reversed by a change in fulfilment cash flows in the underlying group of insurance contracts that has no corresponding change in fulfilment cash flows in the reinsurance contract held (e.g. because of a favourable change in expense assumptions not covered under the reinsurance agreement). The following example, based on Example 12C in the Illustrative Examples on IFRS 17 show how this operates in practice. [IFRS 17.IE138L-138M].

Example 56.54: Subsequent measurement of a loss recovery component

Assuming the same fact pattern as Example 56.52 above.

At the end of Year 1, the entity measures the insurance contract liability and the reinsurance contract asset as follows:

	Insurance contract liability		Reinsurance contract asset
	Profitable group of insurance contracts	Onerous group of insurance contracts	
	$'m	$'m	$'m
Estimates of future cash inflows (recoveries)	–	–	(180)
Estimates of present value of future cash outflows (claims)	400	200	–
Contractual service margin	200	–	(48)
Insurance contract liability/(reinsurance contract asset)	600	200	(228)

Applying paragraphs 66(e) and B119 of IFRS 17, the entity determines the amount of the contractual service margin recognized in profit or loss for the service received in Year 1 as $24m, which is calculated by dividing the contractual service margin on initial recognition of $72m by the coverage period of three years. Consequently, the contractual service margin of the reinsurance contract held at the end of Year 1 of $48m equals the contractual service margin on initial recognition of $72m minus $24m.

At the end of Year 2, the entity revises its estimates of the remaining fulfilment cash outflows of the groups of underlying insurance contracts. The entity estimates that the fulfilment cash flows of the groups of underlying insurance contracts increase by 10 per cent, from future cash outflows of $300m (see Example 56.52) to future cash outflows of $330m (see below). Consequently, the entity estimates the fulfilment cash flows of the reinsurance contract held also increase, from future cash inflows of $90m to future cash inflows of $99m.

At the end of Year 2, the entity measures the insurance contract liability and the reinsurance contract asset as follows:

	Insurance contract liability		Reinsurance contract asset
	Profitable group of insurance contracts	Onerous group of insurance contracts 1	
	$	$	$
Estimates of future cash inflows (recoveries)	–	–	(99)
Estimates of present value of future cash outflows (claims)	220	110	–
Contractual service margin	90	–	(21)
Insurance contract liability/(reinsurance contract asset)	310	110	(120)
Recognition of loss and recovery of loss	–	(10)	3

As a result of the changes in the estimates of the remaining fulfilment cash flows:

- The entity increases the expected remaining cash outflows of the groups of underlying insurance contracts by 10 per cent for each group ($30m in total) and increases the expected remaining cash inflows of the reinsurance contract held by 10 per cent of the expected recoveries of $90m ($9m).

- Applying paragraph 44(c) of IFRS 17, the entity adjusts the carrying amount of the contractual service margin of $200m by $20m for the changes in fulfilment cash flows relating to future service. Applying paragraph 44(e), the entity also adjusts the carrying amount of the contractual service margin by $90m for the amount recognised as insurance revenue (($200m – $20m = $180m) ÷ 2). The resulting contractual service margin at the end of year 2 is $90m ($200m – $20m – $90m).

- Applying paragraph 48 of IFRS 17, the entity recognises in profit or loss an amount of $10 for the changes in the fulfilment cash flows relating to future services of the onerous group of underlying insurance contracts.

- Applying paragraph 66(c)(i) of IFRS 17, the entity adjusts the contractual service margin of the reinsurance contract held for the change in fulfilment cash flows that relate to future service unless the change results from a change in fulfilment cash flows allocated to a group of underlying insurance contracts that does not adjust the contractual service margin for that group. Consequently, the entity recognises the change in the fulfilment cash flows of the reinsurance contract held of $9m by:

    - recognising immediately in profit or loss $3 of the change in the fulfilment cash flows of the reinsurance contract held (30 per cent of the $10m change in the fulfilment cash flows of the onerous group of underlying insurance contracts that does not adjust the contractual service margin of those contracts); and

    - adjusting the contractual service margin of the reinsurance contract held by CU6m of the change in the fulfilment cash flows ($9m – $3m).

- Consequently, the contractual service margin of the reinsurance contract held of $(21)m equals the contractual service margin at the end of Year 1 of $(48m) adjusted for $6m and for $21m of the contractual service margin recognised for the service received in Year 2 ($(21)m = ($(48)m + $6m) ÷ 2).

As discussed at 10.3.3 above, an entity might include in an onerous group of insurance contracts both onerous insurance contracts covered by a group of reinsurance contracts held and onerous insurance contracts not covered by the group of reinsurance contracts held. To adjust the contractual service margin for changes in fulfilment cash flows allocated to a group of underlying insurance contracts that do not adjust the contractual service margin for that group of underlying insurance contracts, an entity should apply a systematic and rational method of allocation to determine the portion of losses recognised on the group of insurance contracts that relate to insurance contracts covered by the group of reinsurance contracts held. [IFRS 17.B119E].

10.5 Allocation of the contractual service margin to profit or loss

The principles for release of the contractual service margin for reinsurance contracts held follows the same principles as for insurance and reinsurance contracts issued, i.e. the contractual service margin is released to revenue as the reinsurer renders service For a reinsurance contract held, the period that the reinsurer renders services is the coverage period of the reinsurance contract which includes both the period of insurance coverage as well as the period of any investment return service.

The coverage period of a reinsurance contract held ends when the coverage periods of all underlying contracts are expected to end. This could be up to two years for reinsurance contracts written on a twelve-months 'risks attaching' basis where underlying insurance contracts incepting in a twelve month period are covered by a single reinsurance contract.

In May 2018, the IASB staff confirmed that, applying the requirements of the general model (see 8.7 above), the coverage units in a group of reinsurance contracts held is the coverage received by the insurer from those reinsurance contracts held and not the coverage provided by the insurer to its policyholders through the underlying insurance contracts. When determining the quantity of benefits received from a reinsurance contract, an entity may consider relevant facts and circumstances related to the underlying insurance contracts.[71]

For retroactive reinsurance contracts held, the coverage period of the underlying insurance contracts may have expired prior to the inception of the reinsurance contract held. In respect of these contracts, the coverage is provided against an adverse development of an event that has already occurred. [IFRS 17.B5]. This means that the contractual service margin should be released over the expected settlement period of the claims of the underlying insurance contracts (since that is, in effect, the coverage period for the reinsurance contract).

Since incurred claims are treated as a liability for incurred claims on the underlying direct/assumed side but as part of the liability for remaining coverage on the reinsurance held side, the question arises as to whether this creates an asymmetry in the recognition of changes in claims between the direct contract issued (relating to past service) and the reinsurance contract held. There should be no asymmetry because paragraph 66 of IFRS 17 (see 10.5 above) indicates that the contractual service margin of reinsurance contracts held is not adjusted by the change that results from a change in fulfilment cash flows allocated to a group of underlying insurance contracts that does not adjust the contractual service margin for the group of underlying insurance contracts. These fulfilment cash flows include the liability for incurred claims, as changes in the liability for incurred claims do not adjust the contractual service margin for the underlying contracts as there is no contractual service margin on the liability for incurred claims. Accordingly, any change in the fulfilment cashflows of the reinsurance contract held due to the changes of the liability for incurred claims of the underlying contracts will impact profit and loss and not the contractual service margin of the reinsurance contract held. This is illustrated by the following example:

Example 56.55:   Treatment of changes in reinsurance recoveries arising from past events

Company A (the cedant) has a liability for incurred claims of $100. It decides to enter into a reinsurance contract under which it cedes 50% of the liability for incurred claims.

The cedant pays a reinsurance premium of $55 to the reinsurer at inception and cedes an amount of $50 (i.e. 50%) of its liability for incurred claims. This results in a net cost of reinsurance of $5 at initial recognition. The net cost of $5 goes immediately through profit and loss following paragraph 65A of IFRS 17 (net cost of purchasing reinsurance coverage recognised as an expense).

In Year 1, the liability for incurred claims of the underlying direct contracts increases from $100 to $115. As a consequence, the share of liability for incurred claims ceded to the reinsurer increases by $7.5 (50% of $15) and implies a favourable change (increase) in the asset for remaining coverage of the reinsurance contract held of $7.5.

The favourable change in the asset for remaining coverage of $7.5 should be credited direct to profit or loss to match the treatment for the change of the underlying liability for incurred claims and not to the contractual service margin. This accounting (i.e. direct to profit or loss) should be the same if the deviation was unfavourable.

10.6 Premium allocation approach for reinsurance contracts held

An entity may use the premium allocation approach discussed at 9 above (adapted to reflect the features of reinsurance contracts held that differ from insurance contracts issued, for example the generation of expenses or reduction in expenses rather than revenue) to simplify the measurement of a group of reinsurance contracts held, if at the inception of the group: *[IFRS 17.69]*

- the entity reasonably expects the resulting measurement would not differ materially from the result of applying the requirements in the general model for reinsurance contracts held discussed above; or
- the coverage period of each contract in the group of reinsurance contracts held (including insurance coverage from all premiums within the contract boundary determined at that date applying the definition in the general model) is one year or less.

Assessment of eligibility for groups of reinsurance contracts held to be able to use the premium allocation approach is independent of whether the entity applies the premium allocation approach to the underlying groups of insurance contracts issued by an entity. Therefore, for example, reinsurance contracts which are written on a twelve months risks attaching basis (i.e. the underlying insurance contracts subject to the reinsurance contract incept over a twelve month period) will have a contract boundary of up to two years if each of the underlying insurance contracts have a coverage period of one year. The two year contract boundary means that those reinsurance contracts held will not meet the twelve month criterion for use of the premium allocation approach and would have to qualify for the premium allocation approach on the basis that the resulting measurement would not differ materially from the result of applying the requirements in the general model. As a consequence, a mismatch in measurement models may arise if the underlying contracts are accounted for under the premium allocation approach.

IFRS 17 confirms that an entity cannot meet the first condition above if, at the inception of the group, an entity expects significant variability in the fulfilment cash flows that would affect the measurement of the asset for remaining coverage during the period before a claim is incurred. Variability in the fulfilment cash flows increases with, for example: *[IFRS 17.70]*

- the extent of future cash flows relating to any derivatives embedded in the contracts; and
- the length of the coverage period of the group of reinsurance contracts held.

When a group of reinsurance contracts held is accounted for applying the premium allocation approach and an entity has a group of underlying insurance contracts that are onerous on initial recognition (see 10.3.3 above), the carrying amount of the asset for remaining coverage is adjusted instead of the contractual service margin. *[IFRS 17.70A]*.

10.7 Reinsurance contracts held and the variable fee approach

An entity is not permitted to use the variable fee approach for reinsurance contracts held. The variable fee approach also cannot be applied to reinsurance contracts issued. *[IFRS 17.B109]*. This will therefore cause an accounting mismatch when an entity has reinsured contracts subject to the variable fee approach discussed at 11 below. It is stated in the Basis for Conclusions that the IASB considers that the entity and the reinsurer do not share in the returns on underlying items and therefore the criteria for the variable fee approach are not met, even if the underlying insurance contracts issued are insurance contracts with direct participation features. The IASB therefore decided not to modify the scope of the variable fee approach to include reinsurance contracts held as it was considered that such an approach would be inconsistent with the Board's view that a reinsurance contract held should be accounted for separately from the underlying contracts issued. *[IFRS 17.BC248]*.

11 MEASUREMENT – CONTRACTS WITH PARTICIPATION FEATURES

Many entities issue participating contracts (referred to in IFRS 17 as contracts with participation features) that is, to say, contracts in which both the policyholder and the entity benefit from the financial return on the premiums paid by sharing the performance of the underlying items over the contract period. Participating contracts can include cash flows with different characteristics, for example:

- cash flows that do not vary with returns from underlying items, e.g. death benefits and financial guarantees;
- cash flows that vary with returns on underlying items, either through a contractual link to the returns on underlying items or through an entity's right to exercise discretion in determining payments made to policyholders.

Insurance companies in many countries have issued contracts with participation features. An example of an insurance contract with a participation feature is a contract with a death cover in which the policyholder pays annual premiums into an account held by the insurer and receives the higher of a specified death benefit or the account balance (less fees), the return on which is based on the return generated by specified investments. Participating contracts may also contain discretionary participation features. For example, in some countries, insurance companies must return to the policyholders at least a specified proportion of the investment profits on certain contracts, but may give more. In other countries, bonuses are added to the policyholder account at the discretion of the insurer. In a third example, insurance companies distribute realised investment gains to the policyholder, but the companies have discretion over the timing of realising the gains. These gains are normally based on the investment return generated by the underlying assets but sometimes include allowance for profits made on other contracts.

For measurement and presentation purposes, IFRS 17 does not distinguish between those participating insurance contracts that have discretionary features and those insurance contracts which do not have discretionary features. This is a change from IFRS 4 which had separate requirements for insurance contracts with discretionary participating features.

IFRS 17 includes:

- a mandatory adaptation to the general model (the variable fee approach) for insurance contracts that include direct participation features (see 11.2 below). In addition, within the variable fee approach, contracts with certain features are permitted to use a different method to calculate the insurance finance income or expenses through profit or loss when insurance finance income or expenses is disaggregated between profit or loss and other comprehensive income (see 11.2.6 below); and

- specific requirements within the general model for investment contracts with discretionary participation features (see 11.3 below).

Insurance contracts without direct participation features are not permitted to apply the variable fee approach, even if such contracts contain participation features (sometimes referred to as indirect participating contracts). For example, an insurance contract where the profit sharing is not based on a share of a clearly identified pool of underlying items. Consequently, there will be a difference between the recognition of insurance revenue for insurance contracts without direct participation features but that have some asset dependent cash flows and for insurance contracts with direct participation features accounted for using the variable fee approach, not least because different discount rates should be used for re-measuring the contractual service margin (see 8.3 above).

Contracts with participation features, including those contracts that meet the criteria for the variable fee approach, are not excluded from applying the premium allocation approach (see 9 above) but IFRS 17 appears to assume that they will typically not meet the eligibility criteria (as, usually, the contract boundary will be significantly in excess of one year).

The following diagram compares accounting for direct participating contracts to other insurance contracts (assuming the premium allocation approach is not applied).

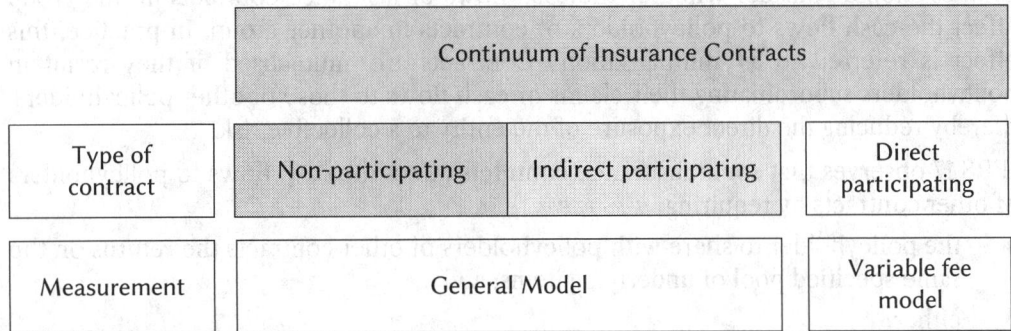

Reinsurance contracts issued and held cannot be insurance contracts with direct participation features for the purposes of IFRS 17 (see 10.7 above). *[IFRS 17.B109]*.

Many participation contracts also contain an element of discretion which means that the entity can choose whether or not to pay additional benefits to policyholders. However, contracts without participation features may also contain discretion. As discussed at 8 above, the expected cash outflows of an insurance contract should include outflows over which the entity has discretion. IFRS 4 permitted the discretionary component of an insurance contract with participation features to be classified in its entirety as either a liability or as equity. *[IFRS 4.34(b)]*. As a result, under IFRS 4, many insurers classified the entire contract (including amounts potentially due to shareholders) as a liability. This treatment is not available under IFRS 17. Under IFRS 17, entities must make a best estimate of the liability due to policyholders (both current and future) under the contracts and amounts attributable to shareholders are part of shareholders' equity.

The following are two examples of contracts with participation features.

Example 56.56: Unitised with-profits policy

Premiums paid by the policyholder are used to purchase units in a 'with-profits' fund at the current unit price. The insurer guarantees that each unit added to the fund will have a minimum value which is the bid price of the unit. This is the guaranteed amount. In addition, the insurer may add two types of bonuses to the with-profits units. These are a regular bonus, which may be added daily as a permanent increase to the guaranteed amount, and a final bonus that may be added on top of those guaranteed amounts when the with-profits units are cashed in. Levels of regular and final bonuses are adjusted twice per year. Both regular and final bonuses are discretionary amounts and are generally set based on expected future returns generated by the funds.

Example 56.57: Participation policy with minimum interest rates

An insurance contract provides that the insurer must annually credit each policyholder's 'account' with a minimum interest rate (3%). This is the guaranteed amount. The insurer then has discretion with regard to whether and what amount of the remaining undistributed realised investment returns from the assets backing the participating policies are distributed to policyholders in addition to the minimum. The contract states that the insurer's shareholders are only entitled to share up to 10% in the underlying investment results associated with the participating policies. As that entitlement is up to 10%, the insurer can decide to credit the policyholders with more than the minimum sharing rate of 90%. Once any additional interest above the minimum interest rate of 3% is credited to the policyholder it becomes a guaranteed liability.

11.1 Contracts with cash flows that affect or are affected by cash flows to policyholders of other contracts (mutualisation)

Entities should consider whether the cash flows of insurance contracts in one group affect the cash flows to policyholders of contracts in another group. In practice, this effect is referred to as 'mutualisation'. Contracts are 'mutualised' if they result in policyholders subordinating their claims or cash flows to those of other policyholders, thereby reducing the direct exposure of the entity to a collective risk.

IFRS 17 observes that some insurance contracts affect the cash flows to policyholders of other contracts by requiring: *[IFRS 17.B67]*

- the policyholder to share with policyholders of other contracts the returns on the same specified pool of underlying items; and
- either:
    - the policyholder to bear a reduction in their share of the returns on the underlying items because of payments to policyholders of other contracts that share in that pool, including payments arising under guarantees made to policyholders of those other contracts; or
    - policyholders of other contracts to bear a reduction in their share of returns on the underlying items because of payments to the policyholder, including payments arising from guarantees made to the policyholder.

Sometimes, such contracts will affect the cash flows to policyholders of contracts in other groups. The fulfilment cash flows of each group reflect the extent to which the contracts in the group cause the entity to be affected by expected cash flows, whether to policyholders in that group or to policyholders in another group. Hence the fulfilment cash flows for a group: *[IFRS 17.B68]*

- include payments arising from the terms of existing contracts to policyholders of contracts in other groups, regardless of whether those payments are expected to be made to current or future policyholders; and
- exclude payments to policyholders in the group that, applying the above, have been included in the fulfilment cash flows of another group.

It is stated in the Basis for Conclusions that the reference to future policyholders is necessary because sometimes the terms of an existing contract are such that the entity is obliged to pay to policyholders amounts based on underlying items, but with discretion over the timing of the payments. That means that some of the amounts based on underlying items may be paid to policyholders of contracts that will be issued in the future that share in the returns on the same underlying items, rather than to existing policyholders. From the entity's perspective, the terms of the existing contract require it to pay the amounts, even though it does not yet know when or to whom it will make the payments. *[IFRS 17.BC172]*.

For example, to the extent that payments to policyholders in one group are reduced from a share in the returns on underlying items of €350 to €250 because of payments of a guaranteed amount to policyholders in another group, the fulfilment cash flows of the first group would include the payments of €100 (i.e. would be €350) and the fulfilment cash flows of the second group would exclude €100 of the guaranteed amount. [IFRS 17.B69].

Different practical approaches can be used to determine the fulfilment cash flows of groups of contracts that affect or are affected by cash flows to policyholders of contracts in other groups. In some cases, an entity might be able to identify the change in the underlying items and resulting change in the cash flows only at a higher level of aggregation than the groups. In such cases, the entity should allocate the effect of the change in the underlying items to each group on a systematic and rational basis. [IFRS 17.B70].

After all insurance contract services have been provided to the contracts in a group, the fulfilment cash flows may still include payments expected to be made to current policyholders in other groups or future policyholders. An entity is not required to continue to allocate such fulfilment cash flows to specific groups but can instead recognise and measure a liability for such fulfilment cash flows arising from all groups. [IFRS 17.B71].

It is observed in the Basis for Conclusions that the Board considered whether to provide specific guidance on amounts that have accumulated over many decades in participating funds and whose 'ownership' may not be attributable definitively between shareholders and policyholders. It concluded that it would not. In principle, IFRS 17 requires an entity to estimate the cash flows in each scenario. If that requires difficult judgements or involves unusual levels of uncertainty, an entity would consider those matters in deciding what disclosures it must provide to satisfy the disclosure objective in IFRS 17 (see 16.3 below). [IFRS 17.BC170].

The Board considered whether prohibiting groups from including contracts issued more than one year apart would create an artificial divide for contracts with cash flows that affect or are affected by cash flows to policyholders in another group. The Board acknowledged that, for contracts that fully share risks, the groups together will give the same results as a single combined risk-sharing portfolio and therefore considered whether IFRS 17 should give an exception to the requirement to restrict groups to include only contracts issued within one year. However, the Board concluded that setting the boundary for such an exception would add complexity to IFRS 17 and create the risk that the boundary would not be robust or appropriate in all circumstances. Nonetheless, the Board noted that the requirements specify the amounts to be reported, not the methodology to be used to arrive at those amounts. Therefore, it may not be necessary for an entity to restrict groups in this way to achieve the same accounting outcome in some circumstances. [IFRS 17.BC138]. Further detail about IFRS 17's requirements for annual cohorts and inter-generational sharing of risk is contained at 5.2.2.A above.

In September 2018, the TRG members discussed an IASB staff paper which considered a submission about annual groups of contracts which all share a return on a specified pool of underlying items with some of the return contractually passing from one group of policyholders to another. The question asked in what circumstances would measuring the contractual service margin at a higher level than an annual cohort level, such as a portfolio level, achieve the same accounting outcome as measuring the contractual service margin at an annual cohort level. The TRG members observed that:

- when a specified pool of underlying items consists of insurance contracts issued to the policyholders that share in the returns of that pool, the criteria for mutualisation is met regardless of whether the policyholders' share is 100% of the return of the pool of underlying items or only part of the pool of underlying items;

- for contracts that share in 100% of the return of a pool of underlying items consisting of insurance contracts, the contractual service margin will be nil. Therefore, measuring the contractual service margin at a higher level than the annual cohort level, such as a portfolio level, would achieve the same accounting outcome as measuring the contractual service margin at an annual cohort level; and

- when contracts share to a lesser extent in the return on a pool of underlying items consisting of insurance contracts, an entity could be affected by the expected cash flows of each contract issued. Therefore, the contractual service margin of the groups of contracts may differ from the contractual service margin measured at a higher level, such as a portfolio level. To assess whether measuring the contractual service margin at a higher level would achieve the same accounting outcome as measuring the contractual service margin at an annual cohort level, an entity would need to determine what the effect would be (i.e. the accounting outcome would need to be the same in all circumstances, regardless of how assumptions and experience develop over the life of the contract).

However, TRG members expressed concern that in practice cash flows would be determined at a higher-level of measurement than in the examples provided in the IASB staff paper and then the entity would have to allocate the effect of the change in the underlying items to each group on a systematic and rational basis (see above).[72]

11.2 Insurance contracts with direct participation features

IFRS 17 identifies a separate set of insurance contracts with participation features described as insurance contracts with direct participation features. These contracts apply an adapted version of the general model commonly referred to as the 'variable fee' approach. For contracts using the variable fee approach, the changes in the contractual service margin are mostly driven by the movements in the assets 'backing' the contracts or other profit-sharing items (referred to as 'underlying items') rather than by the fulfilment cash flows of the insurance contract liability. Use of the variable fee approach instead of the general model is mandatory for those insurance contracts that meet the criteria of the variable fee approach (see 11.2.1 below). The assessment of eligibility for the variable fee approach should be performed at individual contract level although practice this could be applied to 'clusters' of contracts as long as the outcome would not be different. This was clarified by the June 2020 amendments to IFRS 17. *[IFRS 17.B107(b)(i)].*

The variable fee approach applies to insurance contracts that meet its criteria; the fact that participation features are discretionary does not necessarily preclude contracts from meeting the criteria. However, contracts with participation features are significantly different across jurisdictions. Not all contracts with participation features will meet the criteria to be accounted for as direct participation contracts.

Conceptually, insurance contracts with direct participation features are contracts under which an entity's obligation to the policyholder is net of: *[IFRS 17.B104]*

- the obligation to pay the policyholder an amount equal to the fair value of the underlying items; and
- a variable fee that the entity will deduct from the obligation in exchange for the future service provided by the insurance contract comprising:
  - the amount of the entity's share of the fair value of the underlying items; less
  - fulfilment cash flows that do not vary based on the returns on underlying items.

The Board concluded that returns to the entity from underlying items should be viewed as part of the compensation the entity charges the policyholder for service provided under the insurance contract, rather than as a share of returns from an unrelated investment, in a narrow set of circumstances in which the policyholders directly participate in a share of the returns on the underlying items. In such cases, the fact that the fee for the contract is determined by reference to a share of the returns on the underlying items is incidental to its nature as a fee. The Board concluded, therefore, that depicting the gains and losses on the entity's share of the underlying items as part of a variable fee for service faithfully represents the nature of the contractual arrangement. *[IFRS 17.BC244]*.

IFRS 17 requires the contractual service margin for insurance contracts with direct participation features to be updated for more changes than those affecting the contractual service margin for other insurance contracts. In addition to the adjustments made for other insurance contracts, the contractual service margin for insurance contracts with direct participation features is also adjusted for the effect of changes in: *[IFRS 17.BC240]*

- the entity's share of the underlying items; and
- financial risks other than those arising from the underlying items, for example the effect of financial guarantees.

It is observed in the Basis for Conclusions that the Board decided that these differences are necessary to give a faithful representation of the different nature of the fee in these contracts. The Board concluded that for many insurance contracts it is appropriate to depict the gains and losses on any investment portfolio related to the contracts in the same way as gains and losses on an investment portfolio unrelated to insurance contracts. *[IFRS 17.BC241]*.

11.2.1 Definition of an insurance contract with direct participation features

An entity should assess whether the conditions for meeting the definition of an insurance contract with direct participation features are met using its expectations at inception of the contract. This assessment should not be reassessed afterwards unless the contract is modified (see 12 below for modifications). *[IFRS 17.B102]*. As noted at 11.2 above, the assessment is made at individual contract level.

Insurance contracts with direct participation features are insurance contracts that are substantially investment-related service contracts under which an entity promises an investment return based on underlying items (i.e. items that determine some of the amounts payable to a policyholder). Hence, they are defined as insurance contracts for which: *[IFRS 17.B101]*

- the contractual terms specify that the policyholder participates in a share of a clearly identified pool of underlying items (see 11.2.1.A below);
- the entity expects to pay to the policyholder an amount equal to a substantial share of the fair value returns on the underlying items (see 11.2.1.B below); and
- the entity expects a substantial proportion of any change in the amounts to be paid to the policyholder to vary with the change in fair value of the underlying items (see 11.2.1.C below).

When an insurance contract is acquired in a business combination or transfer, the criteria as to whether the contract applies the variable fee approach should be assessed at the business combination or transfer date (see 13 below).

Situations where cash flows of insurance contracts in a group affect the cash flows of contracts in other groups are discussed at 11.1 above.

11.2.1.A   A share of a clearly defined pool of underlying items

The pool of underlying items can comprise any items, for example a reference portfolio of assets, the net assets of the entity, or a specified subset of the net assets of the entity, as long as they are clearly identified by the contract. An entity need not hold the identified pool of underlying items (although there are accounting consequences of this – see 15.3.1 below). However, a clearly identified pool of underlying items does not exist when: *[IFRS 17.B106]*

- an entity can change the underlying items that determine the amount of the entity's obligation with retrospective effect; or
- there are no underlying items identified, even if the policyholder could be provided with a return that generally reflects the entity's overall performance and expectations, or the performance and expectations of a subset of assets the entity holds. An example of such a return is a crediting rate or dividend payment set by the entity at the end of the period to which it relates. In this case, the obligation to the policyholder reflects the crediting rate or dividend amounts the entity has set and does not reflect identified underlying items.

The word 'share' referred to in the section heading above does not preclude the existence of the entity's discretion to vary amounts paid to the policyholder. However, the link to the underlying items must be enforceable. *[IFRS 17.B105]*.

It is explained in the Basis for Conclusions that the Board believes that, for the variable fee approach to be applied, the contract must specify a determinable fee and because of this a clearly identified pool of underlying items must exist. Without a determinable fee, which can be expressed as a percentage of portfolio returns or portfolio asset values rather than only as a monetary amount, the share of the return on the underlying items the entity retains would be entirely at the discretion of the entity and, in the Board's view, this would not be consistent with being equivalent to a fee. *[IFRS 17.BC245(a)]*. However, IFRS 17 does not mention a stated minimum determinable fee.

There is no requirement that underlying items have to be measured at fair value. There is also no restriction on the type of asset which can be an underlying item. This means that underlying items can be, for example, a subsidiary of the group, assets such as financial assets measured at amortised cost or non-participating insurance contracts measured in accordance with the general model in IFRS 17. In February 2020, the IASB confirmed that non-participating insurance contracts held as underlying items should be measured in accordance with IFRS 17 rather than at fair value on the grounds that creating an exception for these assets would add significant complexity to IFRS 17.[73] However, as discussed at 11.2.1.B below, a substantial portion of the fair value returns of underlying items, regardless as to how they are measured for accounting purposes, must be payable to the policyholder.

11.2.1.B   A substantial share of the fair value returns on the underlying items

The Basis for Conclusions observes that the entity should expect to pay to the policyholder an amount equal to a substantial share of the fair value returns on the underlying items. It further observes that it would not be a faithful representation to depict an obligation to pay an amount equal to the fair value of the underlying items if the policyholder does not expect to receive a substantial part of the fair value returns on the underlying items. *[IFRS 17.BC245(b)]*.

IFRS 17 provides no specific quantitative threshold for 'substantial'. However, an entity should interpret the word 'substantial' as in both 'substantial share' and 'substantial proportion' (see 11.2.1.C below): *[IFRS 17.B107]*

- in the context of the objective of insurance contracts with direct participation features being contracts under which the entity provides investment-related services and is compensated for the services by a fee that is determined by reference to the underlying items; and
- assess the variability in the amounts:
  - over the duration of the insurance contract; and
  - on a present value probability-weighted average basis, not a best or worst outcome basis.

As discussed at 11.2.1.A above, there is no requirement that underlying items have to be measured at fair value. This raises the question as to whether the variable fee approach can be applied to contracts where the return to policyholders is determined on a basis other than fair value (e.g. at amortised cost). In February 2018, in response to a submission to the TRG, the IASB staff observed that contracts which provide a return that is based on an amortised cost measurement of the underlying items would not automatically fail the definition of an insurance contract with direct participation features. Entities expectations of returns would be assessed over the duration of the contract and therefore returns based on an amortised cost measurement might equal returns based on the fair value of the underlying items over the contract duration. The TRG members agreed with the IASB's staff conclusion that the variable fee approach could be met when the return is based on amortised cost measurement of the underlying items.[74]

IFRS 17 further explains that if, for example, the entity expects to pay a substantial share of the fair value returns on underlying items, subject to a guarantee of a minimum return, there will be scenarios in which: *[IFRS 17.B108]*

- the cash flows that the entity expects to pay to the policyholder vary with the changes in the fair value of the underlying items because the guaranteed return and other cash flows that do not vary based on the returns on underlying items do not exceed the fair value return on the underlying items; and
- the cash flows that the entity expects to pay to the policyholder do not vary with the changes in the fair value of the underlying items because the guaranteed return and other cash flows that do not vary based on the returns on underlying items exceed the fair value return on the underlying items.

The entity's assessment of the variability will reflect a present value probability-weighted average of all these scenarios.

In reality, as many participation contracts contain guarantees, the question as to whether a contract is one with direct participation features or not depends on the effect of the guarantee on the expected value of the cash flows at inception. It does not mean that there can be no scenarios in which the guarantee 'kicks in'. Instead, it does mean that the effect of those scenarios on a probability-weighted basis should be such that a substantial share of the expected returns payable to the policyholder are still based on the fair value of the underlying items. Considering the impact of options and guarantees on the eligibility criteria will have to be based on the specific facts and circumstances and requires the use of judgement.

When the cash flows of insurance contracts in a group affect the cash flows to policyholders of contracts in other groups (see 11.1 above), an entity should assess whether the conditions for meeting the classification of the contracts as insurance contracts with direct participation features are met by considering the cash flows that the entity expects to pay to the policyholders. *[IFRS 17.B103]*.

In April 2019, the IASB staff considered a submission to the TRG which provided an example of a contract for which an entity charges an asset management fee determined as a percentage of the fair value of the underlying items plus a fixed premium charge for mortality cover which reduces the underlying items at the beginning of each period. The submission asked, firstly, how to determine the share of the fair value returns on the underlying items ignoring the fixed premium charge for mortality cover and, secondly, whether and how the premium for mortality cover deducted from the underlying items impacts the calculation of the fair value returns. The IASB staff stated that, in this example, the fixed annual charge for mortality cover is, in effect, an amount paid out of the policyholder's share and therefore the policyholder's share includes that charge. However, an entity needs to also consider whether the entity expects a substantial proportion of any change in the amounts paid to the policyholder to vary with the change in the fair value of the underlying items (see 11.2.1.C below) in determining whether the definition of an insurance contract with direct participation features is met. For the purposes of this condition, an entity considers changes in any amounts to be paid to the policyholder regardless of whether they have been paid from the underlying items or not.[75] The TRG members observed that a distinguishing feature in this example is that the premium for mortality is fixed rather than varying with the fair value of the underlying items. The IASB staff confirmed that the analysis might differ had the charge varied with the fair value of the underlying items. The TRG members also observed that when determining whether an insurance contract is in the scope of the variable fee approach, in some circumstances it may be necessary to consider the way a charge is determined, rather than the way it is labelled in the contract, to identify what the charge represents. The IASB staff also noted that one of the other conditions of assessing eligibility for the variable fee approach is that a substantial proportion of the changes in amounts paid to policyholders should vary with the changes in the fair value of the underlying items, regardless of whether they have been paid from the underlying items or not.[76]

The table below illustrates the calculations in the IASB staff's example.

Example 56.58: *Calculation of the expected fair value returns without and with mortality charge*

(a) Without mortality charge

An insurance contract gives the policyholder the returns on underlying items, after paying an annual management fee of 0.75% of the assets. The expected duration of the contract is 10 years and the expected returns on underlying items are 5%. The expected account balance is calculated in the following table:

Year	1	2	3	4	5	6	7	8	9	10	Total
	£	£	£	£	£	£	£	£	£	£	£
Opening balance	15,000	15,632	16,290	16,977	17,692	18,437	19,214	20,023	20,867	21,746	
Returns on underlying items	750	782	815	849	885	922	961	1,001	1,043	1,087	9,094
Annual management fee	(118)	(123)	(128)	(134)	(139)	(145)	(151)	(158)	(164)	(171)	(1,432)
Closing balance	15,632	16,290	16,977	17,692	18,437	19,214	20,023	20,867	21,746	22,662	

To apply paragraph B101(b) of IFRS 17, the fair value returns are £9,094, of which the entity expects to pay to the policyholder £7,662 (£22,662 – £15,000).

(b) With mortality charge

An insurance contract gives the policyholder the returns on underlying items, after paying an annual management fee of 0.75% of the fair value of the underlying items. The expected duration of the contract is 10 years and the expected returns on underlying items are 5%. An annual charge for mortality cover of 100 reduces the underlying items at the start of each year. The expected account balance is calculated in the following table:

Year	1 £	2 £	3 £	4 £	5 £	6 £	7 £	8 £	9 £	10 £	Total £
Opening balance	15,000	15,527	16,076	16,648	17,245	17,866	18,514	19,189	19,892	20,625	
Mortality charge	(100)	(100)	(100)	(100)	(100)	(100)	(100)	(100)	(100)	(100)	(1,000)
Returns on underlying items	745	771	799	827	857	888	921	954	990	1,026	8,779
Annual management fee	(118)	(122)	(127)	(131)	(136)	(141)	(146)	(151)	(157)	(162)	(1,390)
Closing balance	15,527	16,067	16,648	17,245	17,866	18,514	19,189	19,892	20,625	21,389	

To apply paragraph B101(b) of IFRS 17, the fair value returns are £8,779. The entity expects to pay to the policyholders £6,389 (21,389 – 15,000) having deducted the mortality charge. Hence, in total, the share of the fair value of fair value returns the entity expects to pay to the policyholder is £7,789 (£6,389 + £1,000).

11.2.1.C A substantial proportion of any change in the amounts to be paid to the policyholder to vary with the change in fair value of the underlying items

The Basis for Conclusions observes that the entity should expect a substantial proportion of any change in the amounts to be paid to the policyholder to vary with the change in fair value of the underlying items. It would not be a faithful representation to depict an obligation to pay an amount equal to the fair value of the underlying items if the entity were not to expect changes in the amount to be paid to vary with the change in fair value of the underlying items. *[IFRS 17.BC245(b)(ii)]*.

The discussion at 11.2.1.B above applies here also, including how to apply the words 'substantial proportion'.

11.2.2 Measurement of the risk adjustment for non-financial risk using the variable fee approach

IFRS 17's guidance for the measurement of the risk adjustment for non-financial risk (see 8.4 above) does not prescribe how the risk adjustment should be calculated for contracts where the entity shares in the results from underlying items with policyholders. However, the risk adjustment for non-financial risk is the compensation that the entity requires for bearing the uncertainty about the amount and timing of cash flows that arise from non-financial risk as the entity fulfils the insurance contract. Consequently, the risk adjustment for non-financial risk should reflect only the risk of the entity and not also the additional risk of the policyholder. However, the entity's risk is not limited to the shareholder's share in the underlying items but would also include the risk of any returns which do not vary with underlying items (e.g. the effect of guarantees).

11.2.3 Measurement of the contractual service margin using the variable fee approach

At initial recognition, the contractual service margin for a group of insurance contracts with direct participation features is measured in the same way as a group of insurance contracts without direct participation features (i.e. as a balancing figure intended to eliminate any day 1 profits unless the contract is onerous – see 8.5 above). However, the contractual service margin is adjusted based on changes in the fair value of underlying items, which includes the impact of discount rate changes rather than discount rates at the measurement date of the group (see 8.3 above). *[IFRS 17.B113(a)].*

At the end of a reporting period, for insurance contracts with direct participation features, the carrying amount of a group of contracts equals the carrying amount at the beginning of the reporting period adjusted for the following amounts: *[IFRS 17.45]*

- the effect of any new contracts added to the group (see 6 above);
- the change in the amount of the entity's share of fair value of the underlying items (see 11.2.1 above), except to the extent that:
    - the entity opts to and applies risk mitigation (see 11.2.5 below);
    - the decrease in the amount of the entity's share of the fair value of the underlying items exceeds the carrying amount of the contractual service margin, giving rise to an onerous contract loss (see 8.8 above); or
    - the increase in the amount of the entity's share of the fair value of the underlying items reverses any onerous contract loss above;
- the changes in fulfilment cash flows relating to future service, except to the extent that:
    - risk mitigation is applied (see 11.2.5 below);
    - such increases in the fulfilment cash flows exceed the carrying amount of the contractual service margin, giving rise to an onerous contract loss (see 8.8 above); or
    - such decreases in the fulfilment cash flows are allocated to the loss component of the liability for remaining coverage;
- the effect of any currency exchange differences (see 7.3 above) arising on the contractual service margin; and
- the amount recognised as insurance revenue because of the transfer of insurance contract services in the period, determined by the allocation of the contractual service margin remaining at the end of the reporting period (before any allocation) over the current and remaining coverage period.

IFRS 17 further states that:

- changes in the obligation to pay the policyholder an amount equal to the fair value of the underlying items do not relate to future service and do not adjust the contractual service margin; *[IFRS 17.B111]* and
- changes in the amount of the entity's share of the fair value of the underlying items relate to future service and adjust the contractual service margin. *[IFRS 17.B112].*

Changes in fulfilment cash flows that do not vary based on returns on underlying items comprise: *[IFRS 17.B113]*

- the change in the effect of the time value of money and financial risks not arising from the underlying items. An example of this would be the effect of financial guarantees. These relate to future service and adjust the contractual service margin except to the extent that the entity applies risk mitigation; and
- other changes in estimates of fulfilment cash flows. An entity applies the same requirements consistent with insurance contracts without direct participation features to determine what extent they relate to future service and therefore adjust the contractual service margin (see 8.6.3 above).

An entity is not required to identify the separate components of the adjustments to the contractual service margin resulting from changes in the entity's share of the fair value of underlying items that relate to future service and changes in the fulfilment cash flows relating to future service. Instead, a combined amount may be determined for some or all of the adjustments. *[IFRS 17.B114]*.

Except in situations when a group of contracts is onerous, or to the extent the entity applies the risk mitigation exception (see 11.2.5 below), the effect of the general model and the variable fee approach may be compared, as follows:

Comparison of	General model	Variable fee approach
Insurance finance income or expenses (total) recognised in statement of financial performance	Change in the carrying amount of fulfilment cash flows arising from the time value of money and financial risk Accretion of interest on the contractual service margin at rate locked in at initial recognition Any difference between the present value of a change in fulfilment cash flows measured at current rates and locked in rates that adjust the contractual service margin	Change in the fair value of underlying items
Changes in the carrying amount of fulfilment cash flows arising from the time value of money and financial risk	Recognised immediately in the statement of financial performance	Adjusts the contractual service margin unless risk mitigation applied (in which case it adjusts profit or loss or other comprehensive income)
Discount rates for accretion of, and adjustment to, the contractual service margin	Rates determined at initial recognition	Rate included in the balance sheet measurement (i.e. current rates)

In April 2019, the IASB staff responded to a TRG submission which described a specific fact pattern for a contract applying the variable fee approach where the entity shares returns with policyholders by paying dividends. The dividends scale varies based on the market value returns with respect to economic experience of the investments and a statutory basis for the non-economic experience (such as expenses and reinsurance contracts held). The questions asked were whether the measurement of the change in non-economic experience for the purpose of the variable fee approach is determined on an IFRS, statutory or fair value basis and whether the option to disaggregate insurance finance income or expenses between profit or loss and other comprehensive income is limited to financial income or expense on underlying items held or any income or expense arising from underlying items.

The IASB staff observed that under the variable fee approach an entity adjusts the contractual service margin of a group of contracts based on changes in the fair value of underlying items. Therefore, a statutory basis or an IFRS measure which are not fair value measurements cannot be used to determine the adjustment to the contractual service margin. The IASB staff also observed that, when disaggregation is applied, the amount of income or expense included in profit or loss should exactly match the income or expense included in profit or loss for the underlying items, resulting in the net of the two separately presented items being nil. Therefore, income or expense on underlying items is not limited to financial income or expense.[77]

11.2.4 Allocation of the contractual service margin to profit or loss

The contractual service margin for an insurance contract with direct participation features is allocated to profit or loss using the same methodology discussed at 8.7 above for the general model. That is, by identifying the coverage units in the group and releasing the contractual service margin in profit and loss to reflect the insurance contract services in the period.

IFRS 17, as amended in June 2020, defines insurance contract services in respect of contracts with direct participation features as: *[IFRS 17 Appendix A]*

- coverage for an insured event (insurance coverage); and
- the management of underlying items on behalf of the policyholder (investment-related service).

This means that the period over which the contractual service margin is amortised for contracts with direct participation features includes both the period in which the entity provides insurance coverage and the period over which it provides an investment-related service.

For the purpose of amortising the contractual service margin, the period of investment-related service ends at or before the date that all amounts due to current policyholders relating to those services have been paid, without considering payments to future policyholders included in the fulfilment cash flows as a result of mutualisation (see 11.1 above). *[IFRS 17.B119A]*.

IFRS 17, as issued in May 2017, was less clear as to whether the contractual service margin was amortised over only the coverage period or whether the investment-related service period was also included. In May 2018, the TRG members expressed different views on whether it was necessary to clarify that the definition of coverage period for variable fee approach contracts includes the period in which investment services are provided.[78] However, the IASB decided to amend IFRS 17 in order to resolve this matter.

The effect of the amendment can be illustrated by the following example.

Example 56.59:   Insurance services and investment component with different durations

An insurance contract with direct participation features matures in year 10 and pays the customer the account value at maturity. The contract also includes a death benefit that varies depending on which year in the 10 year period the death occurs. Specifically, if the customer dies in years 1-5, the customer's beneficiary would receive a death benefit that is the higher of 110% of the premium paid or the accumulated account value (assume that the death benefit for years 1-5 results in significant insurance risk). However, if the customer dies in years 6-10 the customer's beneficiary receives only the account value. There is no surrender policy.

In IFRS 17, as amended in June 2020, the insurer needs to consider all 10 years for determining coverage units and amortisation of the contractual service margin rather than only years 1-5.

See also 8.7.2 above for discussion of the similar amendment for insurance contracts without direct participation features.

11.2.5   Risk mitigation

For contracts with direct participation features, IFRS 17 requires changes in the shareholder's share of underlying items to adjust the contractual service margin (see 11.2.3 above). However, amounts payable to policyholders create risks for an entity, particularly if the amounts payable are independent of the amounts that the entity receives from investments; for example, if the insurance contract includes guarantees. An entity is also at risk from possible changes in its share of the fair value returns on underlying items. An entity may purchase derivatives to mitigate such risks. When applying IFRS 9, such derivatives are measured at fair value through profit or loss. Consequently, because the change in the carrying amount of the insurance liability (i.e. the hedged item) does not go through profit or loss an accounting mismatch arises. A similar accounting mismatch arises if the entity uses instruments other than derivatives to mitigate risk such as reinsurance contracts held because the variable fee approach cannot be used for reinsurance contracts held. *IFRS 17.BC250-253].*

To address these mismatches, IFRS 17, as amended in June 2020, permits entities relief from these accounting mismatches. This relief allows an entity to choose not to recognise a change in the contractual service margin to reflect some or all of the changes in the time value of money or the effect of financial risk on: *[IFRS 17.B115]*

- the amount of the entity's share of the underlying items if the entity mitigates the effect of financial risk on that amount using derivatives or reinsurance contracts held; and
- the fulfilment cash flows arising from a change in the effect of the time value of money and financial risk arising from the underlying items, for example the effect of financial guarantees, if the entity mitigates the effect of financial risk on those fulfilment cash flows using derivatives, non-derivative financial instruments measured at fair value through profit or loss or reinsurance contracts held.

An entity that elects to use this approach should determine the eligible fulfilment cash flows in a group of contracts in a consistent manner in each reporting period. *[IFRS 17.B117].*

When risk mitigation is applied using derivatives or non-derivative financial instruments, any insurance finance income or expenses arising should be included in profit or loss. If an entity mitigates the effect of financial risk using reinsurance contracts held, it should apply the same accounting policy for the presentation of insurance finance income or expenses as the entity applies to the reinsurance contracts held (i.e. profit and loss if disaggregation is not applied or split between profit and loss and other comprehensive income if disaggregation is applied – see 15.3 below). *[IFRS 17.B117A]*.

Use of this relief is conditional on the entity having a previously documented risk management objective and strategy for the mitigating financial risk described above and, in applying that objective and strategy: *[IFRS 17.B116]*

- An economic offset exists between the insurance contracts and the derivative, non-derivative financial instrument measured at fair value or reinsurance contract held (i.e. the values of the insurance contracts and the risk mitigating items generally move in opposite directions because they respond in a similar way to the changes in the risk being mitigated). An entity should not consider accounting measurement differences in assessing the economic offset.
- Credit risk does not dominate the economic offset.

If, and only if, any of the conditions above cease to be met, an entity should cease to apply the risk mitigation accounting prospectively from that date. An entity should not make any adjustment for changes previously recognised in profit or loss. *[IFRS 17.B118]*. This means that an entity can discontinue the use of risk mitigation option only if any of the eligibility criteria cease to apply and not on a voluntary basis. The application of risk mitigation is intended to be aligned with the hedge accounting requirements in IFRS 9 and IFRS 9 does not allow an entity to discontinue hedge accounting unless the hedging relationship ceases to meet the qualifying criteria.[79]

IFRS 17, as issued in May 2017, permitted the risk mitigation exception to apply only to derivatives. It is explained in the Basis for Conclusions that the Board received feedback that applying the requirements in IFRS 17 when an entity holds a reinsurance contract that covers insurance contracts with direct participation features results in an accounting mismatch. The underlying insurance contracts issued are accounted for applying the variable fee approach and the reinsurance contract held is not. Reinsurance contracts that cover insurance contracts with direct participation features transfer both non-financial risk and financial risk to the reinsurer. However, the Board rejected a suggestion to permit an entity to apply the variable fee approach to those reinsurance contracts held. Despite this, the Board acknowledged that an accounting mismatch could arise when an entity mitigates the effect of financial risk using a reinsurance contract held that is similar to the mismatch that could arise when an entity uses derivatives. Accordingly, the Board amended IFRS 17 so that the risk mitigation option applies when an entity uses reinsurance. *[IFRS 17.BC256B]*.

The Basis for Conclusions also explains that the Board received feedback that some entities mitigate the effect of some financial risk on fulfilment cash flows that do not vary with returns on underlying items using non-derivative financial instruments. The Board was persuaded that if those non-derivative financial instruments are measured at fair value through profit or loss, an accounting mismatch could arise, which is similar to the accounting mismatch for derivatives. Accordingly, the Board extended the risk mitigation option to apply in that circumstance. The Board decided to limit the extension to only those non-derivative financial instruments measured at fair value through profit or loss. For those non-derivative financial instruments, the extension resolves the accounting mismatch in the same way it resolves the accounting mismatch for derivatives (measured at fair value through profit or loss). *[IFRS 17.BC256C].*

In contrast, the Board considered but rejected a suggestion that an entity should be permitted to apply the risk mitigation option when it uses non-derivative financial instruments measured at fair value through other comprehensive income. The Board noted that in most circumstances the risk mitigation option would not resolve perceived mismatches between amounts recognised in profit or loss for insurance contracts with direct participation features using the other comprehensive income option in IFRS 17 and assets measured at fair value through other comprehensive income. Further, the suggestion would have resulted in the ineffectiveness of the risk mitigation strategy being recognised in other comprehensive income. That would be inconsistent with the hedge accounting requirements in IFRS 9. The Board observed than an entity could avoid mismatches by applying together the fair value option in IFRS 9 (to designate financial assets at fair value through profit or loss) and the risk mitigation option in IFRS 17. The Board was also not persuaded by the view that an entity should be permitted to apply the risk mitigation option when it uses non-derivative financial instruments to mitigate the effect of financial risk on the entity's share of the fair value of the underlying items, for example, when the entity mitigates such financial risk by investing premiums in assets other than the underlying items, for example, through an investment in fixed rate bonds. In the Board's view, permitting an entity to apply the risk mitigation option in that circumstance would contradict the principle that an entity need not hold the underlying items for the variable fee approach to apply. *[IFRS 17.BC256D-F].*

11.2.6 Disaggregation of insurance finance income or expenses between profit or loss and other comprehensive income

As discussed at 15.3 below, entities have an accounting policy choice, per portfolio of insurance contracts, between:

- including insurance finance income or expenses in profit or loss; or
- disaggregating insurance finance income or expenses between profit or loss and other comprehensive income.

For insurance contracts with direct participation features, when disaggregation is selected, allocation of the insurance finance income or expenses between profit or loss and other comprehensive income is different depending on whether or not the underlying items are held as follows:

- If the underlying items are not held, then the insurance finance income or expenses included in profit or loss is calculated using a systematic allocation arising from the estimates of future cash flows that that can be determined in one of two ways (known as the 'effective yield approach' and the 'projected crediting approach'). See 15.3.1 below.

- If the underlying items are held, then the insurance finance income or expenses included in profit or loss is an amount that eliminates accounting mismatches with income and expenses on the underlying items held. This means that the expenses or income from the movement of the insurance liability should exactly match the income or expenses included in profit or loss for the underlying items, resulting in the net of the two separately presented items being nil. This approach is sometimes referred to as the 'current period book yield approach' (see 15.3.4 below).

11.3 Investment contracts with discretionary participation features

An investment contract with discretionary participation features does not include a transfer of insurance risk and therefore is a financial instrument. Nevertheless, these contracts are within the scope of IFRS 17 provided the entity also issues insurance contracts. *[IFRS 17.3(c)].*

There is no *de minimis* limit on the number of insurance contracts that an entity must issue in order to ensure that its investment contracts with discretionary participation features are within the scope of IFRS 17. In theory, an entity need only issue one insurance contract.

An investment contract with discretionary participation features is a financial instrument that provides a particular investor with the contractual right to receive, as a supplement to an amount not subject to the discretion of the issuer, additional amounts: *[IFRS 17 Appendix A]*

- that are expected to be a significant portion of the total contractual benefits;
- the timing or amount of which are contractually at the discretion of the issuer; and
- that are contractually based on:
  - the returns on a specified pool of contracts or a specified type of contract;
  - realised and/or unrealised investment returns on a specified pool of assets held by the issuer; or
  - the profit or loss of the entity or fund that issues the contract.

The Basis for Conclusions observes that although investment contracts with discretionary participation features do not meet the definition of insurance contracts, the advantages of treating them the same as insurance contracts rather than as financial instruments when they are issued by entities that issue insurance contracts are that: *[IFRS 17.BC83]*

- Investment contracts with discretionary participation features and insurance contracts that specify a link to returns on underlying items are sometimes linked to the same underlying pool of assets. Sometimes investment contracts with discretionary participation features share in the performance of insurance contracts. Using the same accounting for both types of contracts will produce more useful information for users of financial statements because it enhances comparability within an entity. It also simplifies the accounting for those contracts. For example, some cash flow distributions to participating policyholders are made in aggregate both for insurance contracts that specify

- a link to returns on underlying items and for investment contracts with discretionary participation features. This makes it challenging to apply different accounting models to different parts of that aggregate participation.
- Both of these types of contract often have characteristics, such as long maturities, recurring premiums and high acquisition cash flows that are more commonly found in insurance contracts than in most other financial instruments. The Board developed the model for insurance contracts specifically to generate useful information about contracts containing such features.
- If investment contracts with discretionary participation features were not accounted for by applying IFRS 17, some of the discretionary participation features might be separated into an equity component in accordance with the Board's existing requirements for financial instruments. Splitting these contracts into components with different accounting treatments would cause the same problems that would arise if insurance contracts were separated. Also, in the Board's view, the accounting model it has developed for insurance contracts, including the treatment of discretionary cash flows is more appropriate than using any other model for these types of contracts.

Investment contracts with discretionary participation features are accounted for in the same way as other insurance contracts. That is to say, the general model is applied (as discussed at 8 above) and, at initial recognition, an entity should assess whether the contracts contain direct participation features and hence should apply the variable fee approach (discussed at 11.2 above).

However, as investment contracts with discretionary participation features do not transfer insurance risk, IFRS 17 requires certain modifications as follows: *[IFRS 17.71]*

- the date of initial recognition is the date the entity becomes party to the contract (see 6.4 above);
- the contract boundary (see 8.1 above) is modified so that cash flows are within the contract boundary if they result from a substantive obligation of the entity to deliver cash at a present or future date. The entity has no substantive obligation to deliver cash if it has the practical ability to set a price for the promise to deliver the cash that fully reflects the amount of cash promised and related risks; and
- the allocation of the contractual service margin is modified so that the entity should recognise the contractual service margin over the duration of a group of contracts in a systematic way that reflects the transfer of investment services under the contract. This requirement is similar to the revenue recognition guidance contained in IFRS 15 which seems logical as IFRS 15 would apply to the asset management component of an investment contract without discretionary participation features.

In April 2019, the IASB staff considered a submission to the TRG which described an investment contract in a specific jurisdiction that is linked to a crediting rate and asked whether the product meets the third criteria of the definition of an investment contract with discretionary participation features (see above). The crediting rate in the example was based on returns of assets held and weighted average rates on local treasury bonds and can be adjusted by the entity to some extent, based on future expected revenue and returns (the discretionary feature). The IASB staff observed that the definition of an investment contract with discretionary participation features requires that the additional discretionary amounts are contractually based on specified pools of contracts, specified pools of assets or the profit or loss of the entity or fund that issues the contract and that the discretionary features in each investment contract need to be assessed against these criteria considering all relevant facts and circumstances[80] (i.e. the IASB staff were sceptical that the investment contract in the example met the criteria of an investment contract with discretionary participation features).

11.3.1 Contracts with switching features

Some contracts may contain options for the policyholder to switch between funds over the lifetime of the contract and therefore change from holding an investment contract measured under IFRS 9 to holding an investment contract with discretionary participation features measured under IFRS 17 (or *vice versa*) provided the entity also issues insurance contracts. Where the assessment at contract inception has concluded that the contract is not an investment contract with discretionary participation features the question arises as to whether the existence of the option means that the contract is accounted for under IFRS 17 (as an investment contract with discretionary participation features) or under IFRS 9. If the option contains features (for example in terms of pricing) that require it to be considered within the boundary of the contract (see 8.1 above) the option may already scope the contract within IFRS 17 from inception as an investment contract with discretionary participation features.

IFRS 17 states that once a contract is within its scope then it is not subsequently reassessed even if, at a later date, it is no longer a contract within its scope if the contract would have been reassessed at that date. Therefore, investment contracts with discretionary participation features, issued by an entity that also issues insurance contracts, that subsequently lose their 'discretionary feature' as the result of the exercise of a policyholder option will remain within the scope of IFRS 17.

12 MODIFICATION AND DERECOGNITION

IFRS 17 states that a contract which qualifies as an insurance contract remains an insurance contract until all rights and obligations are extinguished (i.e. discharged, cancelled or expired) unless the contract is derecognised because of a contract modification. *[IFRS 17.B25]*.

IFRS 4 contained no guidance on when or whether a modification of an insurance contract might cause derecognition of that contract. Therefore, prior to IFRS 17, most insurers would have applied the requirements, if any, contained in local GAAP.

12.1 Modification of an insurance contract

An insurance contract can be modified either by agreement between the parties or as result of regulation. If the terms of an insurance contract are modified, an entity should derecognise the original insurance contract and recognise the modified contract as a new contract, if and only if, any of the conditions listed below are satisfied. The conditions are that: *[IFRS 17.72]*

- if the modified terms had been included at contract inception:
  - the modified contract would have been excluded from the scope of IFRS 17;
  - an entity would have separated different components from the host insurance contract (see 4 above) resulting in a different insurance contract to which IFRS 17 would have applied;
  - the modified contract would have had a substantially different contract boundary; or
  - the modified contract would have been included in a different group of contracts at initial recognition (e.g. the contracts would have been onerous at initial recognition rather than had no significant possibility of being onerous subsequently – see 5 above);
- the original contract met the definition of an insurance contract with direct participation features but the modified contract no longer meets that definition or *vice versa;* or
- the entity applied the premium allocation approach (see 9 above) to the original contract but the modifications mean that the contract no longer meets the eligibility criteria for that approach.

In summary, any contract modification which changes the accounting model or the accounting standards measuring the components of the insurance contract is likely to result in derecognition. This is probably a different treatment compared to current practices applied under IFRS 4.

If a contract modification meets none of the conditions above for derecognition, the entity should treat any changes in cash flows caused by the modification as changes in the estimates of the fulfilment cash flows. *[IFRS 17.73]*. In practical terms, this means that an entity will need to determine whether the change in the estimate of the fulfilment cash flows arising from the modification is a past service event (which affects profit or loss in the current period) or a future service event (which affects the contractual service margin). For contracts applying the premium allocation approach any adjustments to premium receipts or insurance acquisition cash flows arising from a modification adjust the liability for remaining coverage and insurance revenue is allocated to the period for services provided (which would also require judgement in determining the period to which the modification applies) See 8.6, 9.3 and 11.2.3 above for the accounting for changes in the fulfilment cash flows.

The exercise of a right included in the terms of a contract is not a modification. *[IFRS 17.72]*. This includes the exercise of a right that could change the nature of the insurance contract. In February 2020, the IASB discussed a staff paper prepared on this issue as a result of feedback from respondents who stated that an accounting mismatch could arise from a contract that changes in nature over time. In particular, such a contract could change its nature due to the policyholder exercising an option. An example of such a contract noted in the staff paper is a contract with a savings phase with profit sharing that provides the policyholder with an option to subsequently convert the account balance into an annuity at a guaranteed rate. At inception, that contract might meet the scope of the variable fee approach. Subsequently, when the policyholder exercises the annuity option, the entity will still be required to continue applying the variable fee approach. In contrast, at inception of an annuity contract without a savings phase the entity would normally apply the general model.

The IASB staff observed that different respondents favoured different suggested ways of amending IFRS 17 to address this matter such as excluding cash flows generated from exercising some options from the contract boundary, providing an accounting election to separate some components of an insurance contract or other changes. In conclusion, the IASB agreed with the IASB staff recommendation not to amend IFRS 17 as the suggested changes touched on key aspects of IFRS 17 and the IASB staff believed these were likely to result in unintended consequences and some of the options suggested would significantly reduce comparability across entities and would increase the complexity of IFRS 17. In addition, the IASB agreed with the IASB staff decision to decline to provide further application guidance or educational material on the matter, as suggested by some respondents, on the grounds that such guidance could be disruptive at this stage of IFRS 17 implementation.[81]

Accounting for derecognition of a modified contract is discussed at 12.3 below.

12.2 Derecognition of an insurance contract

An insurance contract is derecognised when, and only when *[IFRS 17.74]*

- it is extinguished, i.e. when the obligation specified in the insurance contract expires or is discharged or cancelled; or
- any of the conditions for modifications which result in derecognition (see 12.1 above) are met.

The treatment of contract derecognition differs depending on which of the scenarios above applies. See 12.3 below.

When an insurance contract is extinguished, the entity is no longer at risk and is therefore no longer required to transfer any economic resources to satisfy the insurance contract. Therefore, the settlement of the last claim outstanding on a contract does not necessarily result in derecognition of the contract *per se* although it may result in the remaining fulfilment cash flows under a contract being immaterial. For derecognition to occur all obligations must be discharged or cancelled. When an entity purchases reinsurance, it should derecognise the underlying insurance contracts only when those underlying insurance contracts are extinguished. *[IFRS 17.75]*.

12.3 Accounting for derecognition

There are three different ways to treat the derecognition of a contract, depending on the circumstances discussed at 12.3.1 to 12.3.3 below.

The reclassification of balances previously recognised in other comprehensive income as a result of derecognition is discussed at 12.3.4 below.

12.3.1 Derecognition resulting from extinguishment

An entity derecognises an insurance contract from within a group of insurance contracts by applying the following requirements: *[IFRS 17.76]*

- the fulfilment cash flows allocated to the group for both the liability for remaining coverage and the liability for incurred claims are adjusted to eliminate the present value of the future cash flows and risk adjustment for non-financial risk relating to the rights and obligations that have been derecognised from the group;
- the contractual service margin of the group is adjusted for the change in fulfilment cash flows described above, to the extent required by the general model as discussed at 8.6.2 above (for contracts without direct participation features) and 11.2.3 above (for contracts with direct participation features); and
- the number of coverage units for expected remaining insurance contract services is adjusted to reflect the coverage units derecognised from the group, and the amount of the contractual service margin recognised in profit or loss in the period is based on that adjusted number to reflect services provided in the period (see 8.7 above).

In practice, contracts derecognised as a result of extinguishment should no longer have a contractual service margin (or liability for remaining coverage). In these circumstances, extinguishment will result in the elimination of any fulfilment cash flows for the liability for incurred claims with a corresponding adjustment to profit or loss. It is observed in the Basis for Conclusions that an entity might not know whether a liability has been extinguished because claims are sometimes reported years after the end of the coverage period. As a result, an entity might be unable to derecognise those liabilities. In the Board's view, ignoring contractual obligations that remain in existence and can generate valid claims would not give a faithful representation of an entity's financial position. However, it is expected that when the entity has no information to suggest there are unasserted claims on a contract with an expired coverage period, the entity would measure the insurance contract liability at a very low amount. Accordingly, there may be little practical difference between recognising an insurance liability measured at a very low amount and derecognising the liability. *[IFRS 17.BC322]*.

12.3.2 Derecognition resulting from transfer

When an entity derecognises an insurance contract because it transfers the contract to a third party the entity should: *[IFRS 17.77]*

- adjust the fulfilment cash flows allocated to the group relating to the rights and obligations that have been derecognised as discussed at 12.3.1 above; and
- adjust the contractual service margin of the group from which the contract has been derecognised for the difference between the change in the contractual cash

flows resulting from derecognition and the premium charged by the third party (unless the decrease in fulfilment cash flows are allocated to the loss component of the liability for remaining coverage).

If there is no contractual service margin to be adjusted then the difference between the fulfilment cash flows derecognised and the premium charged by the third party are recognised in profit or loss.

12.3.3 Derecognition resulting from modification

When an entity derecognises an insurance contract and recognises a new insurance contract as a result of a modification described at 12.1 above the entity should: [IFRS 17.77]

- adjust the fulfilment cash flows allocated to the group relating to the rights and obligations that have been derecognised as discussed at 12.3.1 above;
- adjust the contractual service margin of the group from which the contract has been derecognised for the difference between the change in the contractual cash flows resulting from derecognition and the hypothetical premium the entity would have charged had it entered into a contract with equivalent terms as the new contract at the date of the contract modification, less any additional premium charged for the modification (unless the decrease in fulfilment cash flows are allocated to the loss component of the liability for remaining coverage); and
- measure the new contract recognised assuming that the entity received the hypothetical premium that the entity would have charged had it entered into the modified contract at the date of the contract modification.

This can be illustrated by the following example.

Example 56.60: Contract derecognition resulting from modification

An entity modifies an insurance contract issued such that there is a substantial change in the contract boundary and, applying the guidance in IFRS 17, determines that the contract should be derecognised and replaced by a new contract. The modified contract was part of a group of insurance contracts that were not onerous.

At the date of modification the fulfilment cash flows in respect of the contract were £100 and the present value of the additional premium received for the contract modification is £10. The entity estimates that a hypothetical premium that it would have charged had it entered into the modified contract at the date of the contract modification was £105.

This gives rise to the following accounting entries:

	£	£
Dr. Cash	10	
Dr. Derecognition of original contract fulfilment cash flows	100	
Cr. Initial recognition of new contract at hypothetical premium		105
Cr. Contractual service margin		5

Determining any hypothetical premium will require the exercise of judgement by the reporting entity.

In April 2019, responding to a submission to the TRG, the IASB staff clarified that when, as a result of a modification that results in a derecognition of an existing contract, an entity recognises new contracts that are in their settlement period, and therefore cover events that have already occurred but the financial effect of which is uncertain, the insured event is the determination of the ultimate cost of the claims.[82] This means that an entity recognises a liability for remaining coverage rather than a liability for incurred claims. See 8.9.2 above.

12.3.4 Reclassification adjustments arising from derecognition

When an entity transfers a group of insurance contracts or derecognises an insurance contract because it either transfers that contract to a third party (see 12.3.2 above) or derecognises the insurance contract and recognises a new insurance contract (see 12.3.3 above) it should: *[IFRS 17.91]*

- for insurance contracts without direct participation features, reclassify to profit or loss as a reclassification adjustment any remaining amounts for the group (or contract) that were previously recognised in other comprehensive income as a result of its accounting policy choice, if any, to disaggregate the finance income or expenses of a group of insurance contracts (see 15.3.1 below); or

- for insurance contracts with direct participation features, not reclassify to profit or loss as a reclassification adjustment any remaining amounts for the group (or contract) that were previously recognised in other comprehensive income as a result of its accounting policy choice, if any, to disaggregate the finance income or expenses of a group of insurance contracts (see 15.3.1 below).

12.3.5 Contracts applying the premium allocation approach that are derecognised

IFRS 17 does not contain guidance on how contracts accounted for under the premium allocation approach (see 9 above) should apply the requirements at 12.3.1 to 12.3.4 above in circumstances in which the derecognised contracts are part of a group which has a liability for remaining coverage but no separate contractual service margin (as a contractual service margin is not recognised separately under the premium allocation approach).

12.4 Derecognition of assets for insurance acquisition cash flows paid before the related group of insurance contracts is recognised as an asset

An entity should derecognise an asset recognised for insurance acquisition cash flows paid before the related group of insurance contracts is recognised as an asset when the insurance acquisition cash flows allocated to the group of insurance contracts are included in the measurement of the group. The derecognition should be allocated against the contractual margin and not taken to profit or loss unless the contract is onerous (see 8.5 above). *[IFRS 17.28C]*.

If an entity recognises in a reporting period only some of the insurance contracts expected to be included in the group, the entity should determine the related portion of an asset for insurance acquisition cash flows for the group on a systematic and rational basis considering the expected timing of recognition of contracts in the group. The entity should derecognise that portion of the asset and include it in the measurement of a group of insurance contracts as above. *[IFRS 17.28C]*. In this situation it would also be necessary to perform an impairment test on any remaining asset for acquisition cash flows that relates to the group (see 8.10 above).

13 ACQUISITIONS OF INSURANCE CONTRACTS

Insurance contracts may be acquired in a transfer (often referred to as a portfolio transfer) or in a business combination as defined in IFRS 3.

In summary, insurance contracts acquired in a transfer or a business combination are measured in the same way as insurance contracts issued by the entity except that the fulfilment cash flows are recognised at date of the combination or transfer. IFRS 3 requires a group of insurance contracts acquired in a business combination to be measured at the acquisition date under IFRS 17 rather than at fair value. *[IFRS 3.31A].*

This results in the following key differences for insurance contracts acquired in a business combination within the scope of IFRS 3 compared with the accounting used previously under IFRS 4:

- contracts acquired in a business combination within the scope of IFRS 3 after the date of initial application of IFRS 17 (i.e. accounting periods beginning on or after 1 January 2023) are classified as insurance contracts based on the contractual terms, economic conditions, operating or accounting policies and other pertinent factors and conditions as they exist at the acquisition date. *[IFRS 3.15, 64N].* Previously, when IFRS 4 applied, IFRS 3 had an exception for insurance contracts from this requirement and stated that insurance contracts acquired in a business combination within its scope should be classified on the basis of the contractual terms and other factors at the inception of the contract rather than at the date of acquisition. Other assessments like the eligibility for the premium allocation approach or variable fee approach for direct participation contracts should be based on the contractual terms and conditions at the date of acquisition;

- contracts acquired in a transfer that is not a business combination are classified as insurance contracts based on the contractual terms, economic conditions, operating or accounting policies and other pertinent factors and conditions as they exist at the acquisition date (i.e. there is no transitional relief – see 17.2.1.C below); and

- contracts are measured under the requirements of IFRS 17 rather than at fair value. Consequently, no option is available to split the value of the acquired insurance contracts into two components (i.e. between a liability in according with the insurer's accounting policies and an intangible asset representing the difference between fair value and the value of that liability under the IFRS 17 measurement model) as was permitted under IFRS 4.

IFRS 17 does not explicitly state that contracts acquired in a business combination within the scope of IFRS 3 should be classified based on the contractual terms and conditions as they exist at the acquisition date. However, neither do other standards in similar circumstances. The amendments to IFRS 3 which apply on application of IFRS 17 are clear that, in a business combination, an entity is required to classify contracts (i.e. assess whether a contract transfers significant insurance risk or is an investment contract with discretionary participation features) based on the contractual terms and other factors at the date of acquisition rather than the original inception date of the contract.[83]

When considering feedback from entities implementing IFRS 17, the Board considered but rejected a suggestion to reinstate the previous IFRS 4 exception in IFRS 3. In the Board's opinion, removing that exception, IFRS 17 makes the accounting for the acquisition of insurance contracts consistent with the accounting for acquisitions of other contracts acquired in a business combination. The Board was not persuaded by the argument that applying the requirement will result in differences in accounting between an acquirer's consolidated financial statements and an acquiree's financial statements. In the Board's view, differences in accounting between an acquirer's financial statements and an acquiree's financial statements depict differences arising from the economics of the acquisition, are not unique to insurance contracts and are not unusual when applying IFRS Standards. Those differences reflect changes in facts and circumstances at the acquisition date compared to facts and circumstances at the date the acquiree recognised the contracts. In addition, differences between an acquirer's financial statements and an acquiree's financial statements can arise for other reasons, for example, because of the elimination of intragroup transactions. *[IFRS 17.BC327B-C].*

As IFRS 3 also refers to 'groupings' and 'operating and accounting policies', this implies that other assessments like the eligibility for the premium allocation approach or variable fee approach for direct participation contracts (see 9.1 and 11.2 above) should be based on the contractual terms and conditions at the date of acquisition rather than at the date of the original inception of the contract. This approach may result in, for example, contracts that are insurance contracts of the acquiree being investment contracts of the acquirer and consequently there will be a different accounting treatment between the consolidated financial statements that include the acquiree and the separate financial statements of the acquiree. However, this would reflect the substance that the acquirer has purchased investment contracts rather than insurance contracts. This also applies to business combinations within the scope of IFRS 3 that occurred before the date of initial application.

When insurance contracts issued or reinsurance contracts held are acquired in a transfer of insurance contracts that do not form a business or in a business combination within the scope of IFRS 3, an entity should also apply the aggregation requirements for the identification of portfolios of insurance contracts and divide those into groupings as explained at 5 above as if it had entered into the contracts on the date of transaction. *[IFRS 17.B93].* In our view, this also implies that these contracts should be classified (i.e. assessed for significant insurance risk and eligibility for the variable fee approach and the premium allocation approach) based on the terms and conditions at the transaction date. This is consistent with the requirements in IFRS 3 for allocating of the cost of a group of assets acquired that does not constitute a business to individual identifiable assets and liabilities based on their relative fair values at the date of purchase. *[IFRS 3.2(b)].*

IFRS 17 requires an entity to treat the consideration received or paid for insurance contracts acquired in a transfer of business or a business combination within the scope of IFRS 3, including contracts in their settlement period, as a proxy for the premiums received. This means that the entity determines the contractual service margin in accordance with all other requirements of IFRS 17 in a way that reflects the premium paid for the contracts. In a business combination within the scope of IFRS 3 the consideration received or paid is the fair value of the contracts at that date. However, IFRS 17 states that the entity does not apply the requirement in IFRS 13 and that the fair value of a financial liability with a demand feature cannot be less than the amount payable on demand, discounted from the first date that the amount could be required to be paid. [IFRS 17.B94].

The consideration received or paid for the contracts excludes the consideration received or paid for any other assets or liabilities acquired in the same transaction. Therefore, an acquirer will have to allocate the consideration received or paid between contracts within the scope of IFRS 17, other assets and liabilities outside the scope of IFRS 17 and goodwill, if any. [IFRS 17.B94].

For insurance contracts measured using the general model, including the variable fee approach, on initial recognition (i.e. acquisition) the contractual service margin is calculated: [IFRS 17.B95]

- for acquired insurance contracts issued based on the requirements of the general model (see 8.5 above); and
- for acquired reinsurance contracts held based on the requirements of the general model as modified (see 10.3 above) using the consideration received or paid for the contracts as a proxy for the premiums received or paid at the date of initial recognition.

If the premium allocation approach applies to insurance contracts acquired in a transfer or business combination then the premium received is the initial carrying amount of the liability for remaining coverage and the liability for incurred claims. [IFRS 17.B94]. If facts and circumstances indicate that the contract is onerous, the difference between the carrying amount of the liability for remaining coverage and the fulfilment cash flows that relate to the remaining coverage should be treated the same way as a contract under the general model (i.e. recognised within goodwill or the gain on bargain purchase in a business combination or recognised as a loss in profit or loss on a transfer).

If the acquired insurance contracts issued are onerous: [IFRS 17.B95A]

- for contracts acquired in a business combination within the scope of IFRS 3 the excess of the fulfilment cash flows over the consideration paid or received should be recognised as part of goodwill or the gain on a bargain purchase; or
- for contracts acquired in a transfer the excess of the fulfilment cash flows over the consideration paid or received is recognised as a loss in profit or loss. The entity should establish a loss component of the liability for remaining coverage for that excess (i.e. the onerous group) and apply the guidance discussed at 8.8 above to allocate subsequent changes in fulfilment cash flows to that loss component.

For a group of reinsurance contracts held when the underlying insurance contracts issued are onerous and a loss-recovery component has been recognised, an entity shall determine the loss-recovery component of the asset for remaining coverage at the date of transaction by multiplying: [IFRS 17.B95B]

- the loss component of the liability for remaining coverage of the group of underlying insurance contracts at the date of transaction; and
- the percentage of claims on the underlying insurance contracts the entity expects at the date of transaction to recover from the group of reinsurance contracts held.

Any loss-recovery component determined above is part of goodwill or the gain on a bargain purchase for reinsurance contracts held acquired in a business combination within the scope of IFRS 3, or as income in profit or loss for contracts acquired in a transfer. *[IFRS 17.B95C]*.

At the date of the transaction, onerous underlying insurance contracts might be included in a group of insurance contracts with other onerous contracts not covered by the group of reinsurance contracts held. In that situation, for the purposes of applying the requirements above, the entity shall use a systematic and rational basis of allocation to determine the portion of the loss component of the group of insurance contracts that relates to insurance contracts covered by the group of reinsurance contracts held. *[IFRS 17.B95D]*.

Investment contracts within the scope of IFRS 9 are required to be measured at fair value when acquired in a business combination.

The following two examples, based on Illustrative Examples 13 and 14 of IFRS 17 demonstrate the measurement on initial recognition for insurance contracts acquired. *[IFRS 17.IE139-151]*.

Example 56.61: Measurement on initial recognition of insurance contracts acquired in a transfer (that is not a business combination) from another entity

An entity acquires insurance contracts in a transfer from another entity. The seller pays €30 to the entity to take on those insurance contracts. The entity determines that the acquired contracts form a group, as if it had entered into the contracts on the date of the transaction. The entity applies the general model to the measurement of the insurance contracts.

On initial recognition the entity estimates the fulfilment cash flows to be:

- in Example A – net outflow (or liability) of €20; and
- in Example B – net outflow (or liability) of €45.

For simplicity, this example ignores all other amounts.

The consideration of €30 received from the seller is a proxy for the premium received. Consequently, on initial recognition, the entity measures the insurance contract liability as follows:

	Example A €	Example B €
Fulfilment cash flows	20	45
Contractual service margin (CSM)	10	–
Insurance contract liability on initial recognition	30	45
The effect on profit or loss will be:		
Profit/(loss) on initial recognition	–	(15)

For contracts that are not onerous, the contractual service margin is the difference between the premium and the fulfilment cash flows (i.e. 30 less 20 resulting in a contractual service margin of 10 in Example A). Consequently, in Example A the total insurance contract liability is equal to the premium received.

In Example B, the premium received (30) is less than the fulfilment cash flows (45) and therefore the entity concludes that the contract is onerous. Consequently, the difference between 30 and 45 (15) is an expense in profit or loss and the insurance contract liability is equal to the fulfilment cash flows.

Example 56.62: **Measurement on initial recognition of insurance contracts acquired in a business combination**

An entity acquires insurance contracts as part of a business combination within the scope of IFRS 3 and estimates that the transaction results in goodwill applying IFRS 3. The entity determines that the acquired contracts form a group, as if it had entered into the contracts on the date of the transaction. The entity applies the general model to the measurement of the insurance contracts.

On initial recognition the entity estimates that the fair value (i.e. deemed premium) of the group of insurance contracts is €30 and the fulfilment cash flows are as follows:

- in Example A – outflow (or liability) of €20; and
- in Example B – outflow (or liability) of €45.

For simplicity, this example ignores all other amounts.

The consideration of €30 received from the seller is a proxy for the fair value of the group of contracts. Consequently, on initial recognition, the entity measures the liability for the group of contracts as follows:

	Example A €	Example B €
Fulfilment cash flows	20	45
Contractual service margin (CSM)	10	–
Insurance contract liability on initial recognition	30	45
The effect on profit or loss will be:		
Profit/(loss) on initial recognition	–	–

In Example A, the entity measures the contractual service margin as the difference between the deemed premium (30) and the fulfilment cash flows (20). Consequently, in Example A the contractual service margin is 10 and the total insurance contract liability is equal to the deemed premium.

In Example B, the fulfilment cash flows exceed the deemed premium. Consequently, the contractual service margin is zero and the excess of the fulfilment cash flows (45) over the deemed premium (30) is an adjustment against goodwill since there cannot be a 'loss' on initial recognition of a business combination.

13.1 Assets for insurance acquisition cash flows acquired in a business combination within the scope of IFRS 3 or a transfer

The asset for insurance acquisition cash flows should be excluded from the measurement of insurance contracts acquired in a business combination within the scope of IFRS 3 or in a transfer of insurance contracts that do not form a business. *[IFRS 17.B95F].*

However, when an entity acquires insurance contracts in a transfer of insurance contracts that do not form a business or in a business combination within the scope of IFRS 3, the entity should recognise an asset for insurance acquisition cash flows at fair value at the date of transaction for the rights to obtain: *[IFRS 17.B95E]*

- future insurance contracts that are renewals of insurance contracts recognised at the date of transaction; and
- future insurance contracts, other than those above, after the date of the transaction without paying again insurance acquisition cash flows the acquiree has already paid that are directly attributable to the related portfolio of insurance contracts.

These insurance acquisition cash flow assets recognised for the rights to obtain future insurance contracts are excluded from the scope of IAS 38. *[IAS 38.3(g)]*.

IFRS 17, as issued in May 2017, did not specify any requirements in respect of assets for insurance acquisition cash flows acquired in a transfer or business or business combination. It is observed in the Basis for Conclusions that the IASB concluded that requiring an entity to recognise assets for insurance acquisition cash flows for rights to obtain future insurance contracts and future renewals at the acquisition date ensures that the contractual service margin of groups of insurance contracts the entity recognises subsequent to the acquisition appropriately reflect the rights the entity paid for relating to those future groups as part of the consideration for the acquisition. Requiring an entity to recognise any such assets at the acquisition date is consistent with the other requirements in IFRS 17 for recognising an asset for insurance acquisition cash flows (see 6.3 above). The Board decided that to achieve that consistency it is necessary to determine the rights described in the first bullet point above by reference to insurance acquisition cash flows the acquiree has already paid. Otherwise broader rights to obtain future contracts from intangible assets such as customer relationships, unconnected to any previously paid insurance acquisition cash flows, could be included in the insurance acquisition cash flow assets. In contrast, the Board decided that such reference is not needed to determine the rights described in the subsequent bullet point above. The fact that these rights relate only to renewals means they are sufficiently constrained. *[IFRS 17.BC327I]*.

13.2 Subsequent treatment of contracts acquired in their settlement period

For retroactive insurance contracts which cover events that have already occurred, but for which the financial effect is uncertain, IFRS 17 states that the insured event is the determination of the ultimate costs of the claim. *[IFRS 17.B5]*. As the claim has occurred already, the question arises as to how insurance revenue and insurance service expense should be presented for these insurance contracts when they are acquired in a business combination or similar acquisition in their settlement period. More specifically, whether insurance revenue should reflect the entire expected claims or not. In February 2018, this question was submitted to the TRG and the IASB staff stated that acquiring contracts in their settlement period is essentially providing coverage for the adverse development of claims. Therefore, the settlement period for the entity that issued the original contract becomes the coverage period for the entity that acquires the contracts. Therefore, contracts acquired in their settlement period will be considered part of the liability for remaining coverage for the entity that acquired the contract and not part of the liability for incurred claims. Accordingly, insurance revenue would reflect the entire expected claims as the liability for remaining coverage reduces because of services provided. If some cash flows meet the definition of an investment component, those cash flows will not be reflected in insurance revenue or insurance service expenses.[84]

This results in entities accounting differently for similar contracts, depending on whether those contracts are issued by the entity or whether the entity acquired those contracts in their settlement period. The most notable outcomes of this distinction include:

- an entity applies the general model for contracts acquired in their settlement period because the period over which claims could develop is longer than one year whilst entities expect to apply the premium allocation approach for similar contracts that they issue; and
- an entity recognises revenue for the contracts acquired in their settlement period over the period the claims can develop, while revenue is no longer recognised over this period for similar contracts issued.

In May 2018, in response to a TRG submission, the IASB staff further clarified that, for contracts acquired in their settlement period, claims are incurred (and, hence, the liability for remaining coverage is reduced) when the financial effect becomes certain. This is not when the entity has a reliable estimate if there is still uncertainty involved. Conversely, this is not necessarily when the claims are paid if certainty has been achieved prior to the actual payment. Additionally, for contracts acquired in their settlement period where the liability for remaining coverage is determined to have nil contractual service margin at initial recognition (i.e. insurance contracts are measured at zero with nil contractual service margin) and estimates of future cash flows decrease subsequently (i.e. positive fulfilment cash flows), the IASB staff stated that a contractual service margin larger than zero may be recognised post acquisition.[85]

The TRG members had no specific comments on the IASB staff observations although the TRG members had previously observed that the requirements reflect a significant change from existing practice and this change results in implementation complexities and costs. In May 2018, the IASB staff prepared an outreach report which included implementation concerns regarding the subsequent treatment of insurance contracts acquired in their settlement period.[86] However, the IASB declined to create an exception to the general classification and measurement requirements in IFRS 17 for contracts acquired in their settlement period. The Board concluded that an entity that acquires a contract should, at the acquisition date, apply the requirements for identifying whether a contract has an insured event and meets the definition of an insurance contract, just as an entity that issues a contract applies the requirement at the issue date. *[IFRS 17.BC327E]*.

It is observed in the Basis for Conclusions that some contracts acquired in their settlement period will not meet the definition of an insurance contract at the acquisition date. This is because, in some circumstances, all claim amounts are known at the acquisition date but remain unpaid. In such circumstances, the acquirer is not providing insurance coverage, the contract does not meet the definition of an insurance contract and the acquirer would account for the contract as a financial liability applying IFRS 3 and subsequently IFRS 9. The Board also observed that for contracts that meet the definition of an insurance contract at the acquisition date, an entity would need to consider whether any amounts payable to the policyholder meet the definition of an investment component (and are therefore excluded from insurance revenue). *[IFRS 17.BC327G]*.

However, the IASB amended IFRS 17 to provide transitional relief for the settlement of claims incurred before an insurance contract is acquired when the modified retrospective approach or fair value approach is used (see 17.4.1 and 17.5 below).

13.3 Business combinations under common control

IFRS 3 does not apply to a combination of entities or businesses under common control (i.e. a common control business combination). *[IFRS 3.2(c)]*.

Similarly, IFRS 17, as amended in June 2020, limits the accounting requirements in respect of business combinations (discussed at 13 above) to a 'business combination in the scope of IFRS 3'. This amendment is intended to exclude business combinations outside the scope of IFRS 3, such as business combinations under common control, from the specific requirements of IFRS 17 for determining the contractual service margin for insurance contracts acquired in a transfer of insurance contracts or a business combination. IFRS 17, as issued in 2017, did not mention common control business combinations as such and the requirements for accounting for business combinations were stated to apply to a 'business combination' without any qualification. *[IFRS 17.BC327A]*.

The result of the amendment is that business combinations under common control are outside the scope of IFRS 17. Consequently, an entity will need to develop an appropriate accounting policy for business combinations under common control. Accounting for business combinations under common control is discussed in Chapter 10 at 3 and the application and use of the pooling of interests method is discussed in Chapter 10 at 3.3.1.

13.4 Practical issues

13.4.1 The difference between a business combination and a transfer

When an entity acquires a portfolio of insurance contracts the main accounting consideration is to determine whether that acquisition meets the definition of a business. IFRS 3 defines a business as 'an integrated set of activities and assets that is capable of being conducted and managed for the purpose of providing goods or services to customers, generating investment income (such as dividends or interest) or generating other income from ordinary activities'. *[IFRS 3 Appendix A]*. The application guidance to IFRS 3 notes that a business consists of inputs and processes applied to those inputs that have the ability to contribute to the creation of outputs. Although businesses usually have outputs they are not required for an integrated set of assets and activities to be a business. *[IFRS 3.B7-8]*. Where it is considered that a business is acquired, goodwill may need to be recognised, as may deferred tax liabilities, in respect of any acquired intangibles. For an isolated transfer, neither goodwill nor deferred tax should be recognised.

The determination of whether a portfolio of contracts or a business has been acquired will be a matter of judgement based on the facts and circumstances. Acquisitions of contracts that also include the acquisition of underwriting systems and/or the related organised workforce are more likely to meet the definition of a business than merely the acquisition of individual or multiple contracts.

Rights to issue or renew contracts in the future (as opposed to existing insurance contracts) are separate intangible assets and the accounting for the acquisition of such rights is discussed at 13.4.3 below.

An entity should recognise an asset at fair value for insurance acquisition cash flows that relate to future insurance contracts and future renewals acquired in a transfer that is not a business as discussed at 13.1 above.

13.4.2 Deferred taxation

For transactions that meet the definition of a business combination, IAS 12 requires deferred tax to be recognised in respect of temporary differences arising in business combinations, for example if the tax base of the asset or liability remains at cost when the carrying amount is fair value. IFRS 17 contains no exemption from these requirements. Therefore, deferred tax will often arise on temporary differences created by the recognition of insurance contracts at a value different from that applied previously by the acquiree (e.g. because the fulfilment cash flows at the date of acquisition for the insurance contracts acquired, calculated on the basis of the contractual terms at the date of the acquisition, is different from the carrying value of the fulfilment cash flows calculated by the acquiree on the basis of contractual terms on initial recognition of the insurance contract). The deferred tax adjusts the amount of goodwill recognised as discussed in Chapter 33 at 12. For transactions that do not meet the definition of a business combination the initial recognition exemption applies and no deferred tax is recognised on initial recognition (as discussed at 13.4.1 above).

13.4.3 Customer lists and relationships not connected to contractual insurance contracts

The requirements discussed at 13 above apply only to recognised insurance contracts that exist at the date of a business combination or transfer and the requirements discussed at 13.1 above apply to insurance acquisition cash flows related for the rights to obtain future insurance contracts.

Therefore, they do not apply to customer lists and customer relationships reflecting the expectation of future insurance contracts and related insurance acquisition cash flows that do not meet the IFRS 17 recognition criteria. IAS 36 and IAS 38 apply to such transactions just as they apply to other intangible assets.

The following example deals with customer relationships acquired together with a portfolio of one-year motor insurance contracts.

Example 56.63: Purchase of portfolio of one-year motor insurance contracts

Background

Parent A obtained control of insurer B in a business combination on 31 December 2021. B has a portfolio of one-year motor insurance contracts that are cancellable by policyholders.

Analysis

Because Insurer B establishes its relationships with policyholders through insurance contracts, the customer relationship with the policyholders meets the contractual-legal criterion for recognition as an intangible asset. IAS 36 and IAS 38 apply to the customer relationship intangible asset. *[IFRS 3.IE30(d)]*.

14 PRESENTATION IN THE STATEMENT OF FINANCIAL POSITION

IFRS 17 specifies minimum amounts of information that need to be presented on the face of the statement of financial position. This minimum information is supplemented by disclosures to explain the amounts recognised on the face of the primary financial statements (see 16 below).

For presentation in the statement of financial position, IFRS 17 as amended in June 2020, requires insurance contracts to be aggregated by portfolios and presented separately as follows: *[IFRS 17.78]*

- insurance contracts issued that are assets;
- insurance contracts issued that are liabilities;
- reinsurance contracts held that are assets; and
- reinsurance contracts held that are liabilities.

This presentation is also required by IAS 1. *[IAS 1.54(da), (ma)]*.

A portfolio is a group of insurance contracts that are subject to similar risks and managed together (see 5 above). *[IFRS 17.14]*.

Any assets for insurance acquisition cash flows (see 6.3 above) and any other assets or liabilities for cash flows related to a group of contracts that occur before the group is recognised are subsumed in the carrying amount of the related portfolios of insurance contracts issued, and any other assets or liabilities for cash flows related to portfolios of reinsurance contracts held are subsumed in the carrying amount of the portfolios of reinsurance contracts held. *[IFRS 17.79]*.

There is no requirement for disclosure of balances in respect of the general model, the premium allocation model or the variable fee approach to be shown separately on the face of the statement of financial position. Nor is there a requirement for the components of the balances (such as the contractual service margin or the risk adjustment for non-financial risk) to be presented separately on the face of the statement of financial position. However, an entity should disclose reconciliations in the notes to the financial statements that show how the amounts disclosed on the face of the statement of financial position (i.e. the net carrying amount of contracts within the scope of IFRS 17) changed during the reporting period because of cash flows and income and expenses recognised in the statement of financial performance. Separate reconciliations are required for insurance contracts issued and reinsurance contracts held. *[IFRS 17.98]*. The detailed requirements of these reconciliations are discussed at 16.1 below. In summary, separate reconciliations are required for contracts subject to the general model and the premium allocation approach together with reconciliations for the individual components of the contract balances. An entity is required to consider the level of aggregation of these reconciliations necessary to meet the overall disclosure objectives of the disclosure requirements of IFRS 17. *[IFRS 17.95]*.

The presentation requirements are significantly different to those required by IFRS 9 in respect of financial instruments. They are also likely to differ significantly from any presentation applied previously by an insurer under IFRS 4. For example:

- individual positive and negative contract balances with different counterparties within one portfolio are aggregated (netted) on the statement of financial position; and
- all rights and obligations arising from an insurance contract are included in the presentation of the portfolio on a single net contract basis unless the components of the contract are separated and accounted for under a different IFRS (see 4 above). The rights and obligations presented net would include, for example, policyholder loans, insurance premiums receivable, liabilities for incurred claims and deferred acquisition cash flows.

Applying IFRS 4, some entities presented separately in the statement of financial position different amounts arising from an insurance contract, as if those different amounts were separate assets or liabilities. For example, some entities presented line items labelled as premiums receivable, claims payable and deferred acquisition costs separately from the insurance contract liability. Different entities presented different line items and had different definitions of what those line items were (for example, some entities presented as premiums receivable amounts that were not yet billed while other entities presented only billed amounts that remain outstanding). Some stakeholders expressed the view that they would like to continue that practice of further disaggregation because they view such disaggregated line items as providing meaningful information to users of financial statements. The Board disagreed with this approach to presentation because it could result in the presentation of amounts that are not separable assets or liabilities. For example, premiums receivable for future coverage is not a gross asset separable from the related liability for the future coverage. *[IFRS 17.BC330D]*. IAS 1 permits the presentation of additional line items including by disaggregation of required line items, headings and subtotals in the statement of financial position only when such presentation is relevant to an understanding of the entity's financial position. *[IAS 1.55]*.

The Board also considered some stakeholders' suggestions that entities should be permitted to present one insurance contract asset or liability for all insurance contracts issued by the entity (that is, present insurance contracts at an entity level). The Board rejected that suggestion because that would risk an unacceptable loss of useful information for users of financial statements. *[IFRS 17.BC330C]*.

IFRS 17, as issued in May 2017, required insurance contracts to be aggregated by groups, rather than portfolios in the statement of financial position. This presentation requirement prior to the June 2020 amendments was consistent with the requirements for recognising and measuring groups of insurance contracts. However, the Board noted that an entity would need to allocate some fulfilment cash flows to groups only for the purpose of presentation (for example, fulfilment cash flows for incurred claims). In addition, feedback while IFRS 17 was being implemented indicated that an amendment to require an entity to present insurance contracts at a portfolio level would provide significant operational relief and suggested that the amendment would not significantly diminish the usefulness of information compared to that which would have been provided by IFRS 17 without the amendment. *[IFRS 17.BC330B]*.

15 PRESENTATION IN THE STATEMENT OF FINANCIAL PERFORMANCE

An entity is required to disaggregate the amounts recognised in the statement of profit and loss and the statement of other comprehensive income (collectively, the statement of financial performance) into: *[IFRS 17.80]*

- insurance service result comprised of:
  - insurance revenue; and
  - insurance service expenses.
- insurance finance income or expenses.

In addition, income or expenses from reinsurance contracts held should be presented separately from the expenses or income from insurance contracts issued. *[IFRS 17.82]*.

This presentation is also required by IAS 1. *[IAS 1.82(a)(ii), (ab)-(ac)]*.

An entity may present the income or expense from a group of reinsurance contracts held, other than insurance finance income or expenses, as either: *[IFRS 17.86]*

- a single amount (netted); or
- separately:
  - the amounts recovered from the reinsurer; and
  - an allocation of the premium paid.

When the gross presentation for reinsurance held is used, an entity is not allowed to present the allocation of the reinsurance premiums paid as a reduction in revenue. *[IFRS 17.86(c)]*.

Insurance finance income or expenses must be presented separately for insurance contracts issued and reinsurance contracts held on the face of the statement of profit or loss. *[IAS 1.82(bb)-(bc)]*. When insurance finance income or expenses is disaggregated it must also be shown separately for insurance contracts issued and reinsurance contracts held in other comprehensive income, within items of other comprehensive income that will be classified subsequently to profit or loss when specific conditions are met. *[IAS 1.7(i)-(j)]*.

The following table illustrates a summary statement of financial performance under IFRS 17.

Statement of profit or loss and other comprehensive income	2023 €'m	2022 €'m
Insurance revenue	10,304	8,894
Insurance service expenses	(9,069)	(8,489)
Insurance service result before reinsurance contracts held	1,235	405
Income (expenses) from reinsurance contracts held	(448)	(327)
Insurance service result	787	78
Insurance finance income or expenses from contracts issued within the scope of IFRS 17	394	353
Finance income or expenses from reinsurance contracts held	200	300
Net financial result	594	653
Profit before tax	1,381	731
Other comprehensive income		
Items that may be reclassified subsequently to profit or loss		
Insurance finance income or expenses from contracts issued within the scope of IFRS 17	50	(25)
Finance income or expenses from reinsurance contracts held	(25)	50
Other comprehensive income for the year net of tax	25	25
Total comprehensive income for the year	1,406	756

The following example illustrates the presentation of the insurance service result if the result from reinsurance contracts held is shown on a gross basis.

Statement of profit or loss and other comprehensive income	2023 €'m	2022 €'m
Insurance revenue	10,304	8,894
Insurance service expenses	(9,069)	(8,489)
Insurance service result before reinsurance contracts held	1,235	405
Income (expenses) from reinsurance contracts held		
Amounts recovered from the reinsurer	300	200
Allocation of reinsurance premiums paid	(748)	(527)
Reinsurance held subtotal	(448)	(327)
Insurance service result	787	78

There is nothing to prevent an entity from providing further sub-analysis of the components of the insurance service result (which may make the relationship of the reconciliations discussed at 16 below to the face of the statement of financial performance more understandable). Indeed, IAS 1 states that an entity should present additional line items (including by disaggregating the line items specified by the standard), headings and subtotals in the statement(s) presenting profit or loss and other comprehensive income when such presentation is relevant to an understanding of the entity's financial performance. *[IAS 1.85]*.

The following diagram illustrates the high-level relationship of the movements in the building clocks of the general model (discussed at 8 above) and their relationship with the presentation in the statement of financial performance.

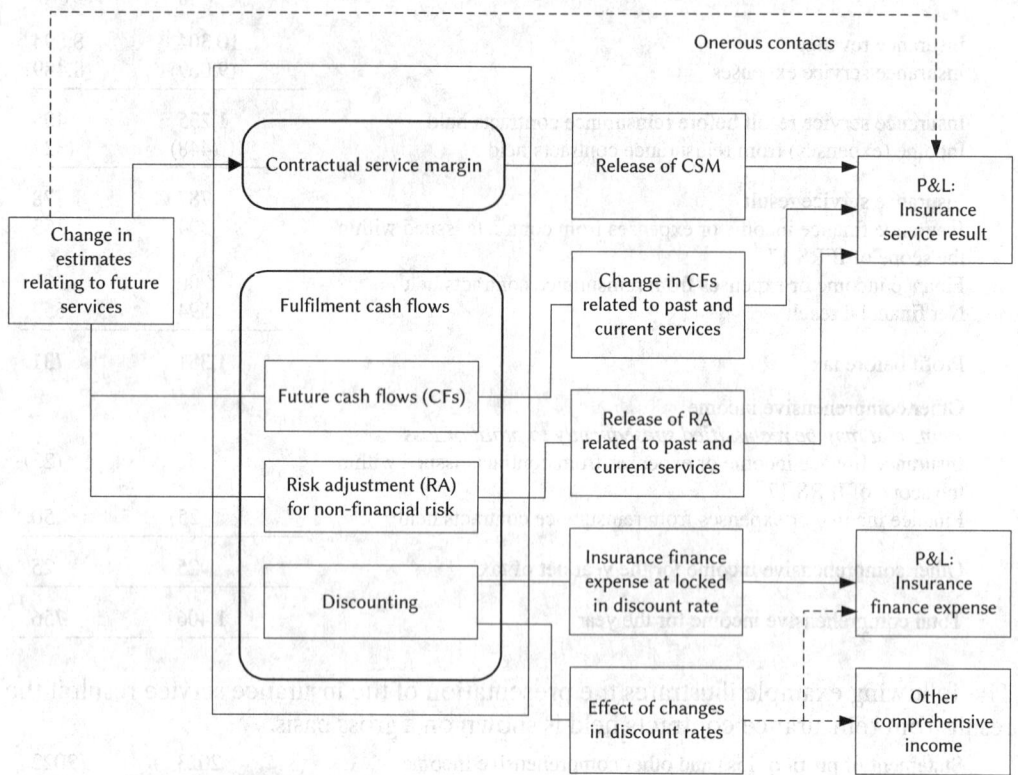

Each of the amounts required to be reported in the statement of financial performance are discussed at 15.1 to 15.3 below.

15.1 Insurance revenue

Insurance revenue should depict the provision of services arising from the group of insurance contracts at an amount that reflects the consideration to which the entity expects to be entitled in exchange for those services. *[IFRS 17.83]*.

Insurance revenue from a group of insurance contracts is therefore the consideration for the contracts, i.e. the amount of premiums paid to the entity: *[IFRS 17.B120]*

- adjusted for financing effect (i.e. adjusted for the time value of money); and
- excluding any investment components.

Investment components are accounted for separately and are not part of the insurance service result.

The amount of insurance revenue recognised in a period depicts the transfer of promised services at an amount that reflects the consideration to which the entity expects to be entitled in exchange for those services. The total consideration for a group of contracts covers the following amounts: *[IFRS 17.B121]*

- amounts related to the provision of services, comprising:
  - insurance service expenses, excluding any amounts related to the risk adjustment for non-financial risk included below and any amounts allocated to the loss component of the liability for remaining coverage;
  - amounts related to income tax that are specifically chargeable to the policyholder;
  - the risk adjustment for non-financial risk, excluding any amounts allocated to the loss component of the liability for remaining coverage; and
  - the contractual service margin; and
- amounts related to insurance acquisition cash flows.

Expected costs for insurance service expenses will be included in the fulfilment cash flows. For example, an entity might include building costs in the fulfilment cash flows (see 8.2.3.L above). The entity will determine depreciation costs over the period of the useful life of the building applying the requirements of IAS 16. When these costs are incurred applying IAS 16, the entity will treat them as an incurred expense under IFRS 17. i.e. the entity will reduce the liability for remaining coverage and recognise revenue. An entity accounts for income tax applying IAS 12. When income tax expenses that are specifically chargeable to the policyholder under the terms of an insurance contract are recognised applying IAS 12, an entity recognises insurance revenue for the consideration paid by the policyholder for such income tax amounts when the entity recognises in profit or loss the income tax amounts. This means that when an entity incurs income tax expenses that are specifically chargeable to the policyholder under the terms of an insurance contract, the entity will need to reduce the liability for remaining coverage and recognise insurance revenue accordingly.[87]

15.1.1 Insurance revenue related to the provision of services in a period under the general model

When an entity provides services in a period, it reduces the liability for remaining coverage for the services provided and recognises insurance revenue. This is consistent with IFRS 15 in which revenue is recognised when an entity derecognises the performance obligation for services that it provides. *[IFRS 17.B123]*.

The reduction in the liability for remaining coverage that gives rise to insurance revenue excludes changes in the liability that do not relate to services expected to be covered by the consideration received by the entity. Those changes are: *[IFRS 17.B123]*

- Changes that do not relate to services provided in the period, for example:
  - changes resulting from cash inflows from premiums received;
  - changes that relate to investment components in that period;
  - changes resulting from cash flows from loans to policyholders;
  - changes that relate to transaction-based taxes collected on behalf of third parties (such as premium taxes, value added taxes and goods and services taxes);
  - insurance finance income or expenses;
  - insurance acquisition cash flows; and
  - derecognition of liabilities transferred to a third party.
- Changes that relate to services, but for which the entity does not expect consideration, i.e. increases and decreases in the loss component of the liability for remaining coverage.

Additionally, any insurance revenue presented in profit or loss should exclude any investment components as well as amounts not arising from the provision of insurance services. [IFRS 17.85].

To the extent that an entity derecognises an asset for cash flows other than insurance acquisition cash flows at the date of initial recognition of a group of insurance contracts, it should recognise insurance revenue and expenses for the amount derecognised at that date. [IFRS 17.B123A].

After having explained what insurance revenue is not, IFRS 17 then explains which changes in the liability for remaining coverage in the period relates to services for which the entity expects to receive compensation. Those changes are: [IFRS 17.B124]

- insurance service expenses incurred in the period (measured at the amounts expected at the beginning of the period), excluding:
    - amounts allocated to the loss component of the liability for remaining coverage;
    - repayments of investment components;
    - amounts that relate to transaction-based taxes collected on behalf of third parties (such as premium taxes, value added taxes and goods and services taxes);
    - insurance acquisition expenses; and
    - the amount related to the risk adjustment for non-financial risk;
- the change in the risk adjustment for non-financial risk, excluding:
    - changes included in insurance finance income or expenses;
    - changes that adjust the contractual service margin because they relate to future service; and
    - amounts allocated to the loss component of the liability for remaining coverage; and
- the amount of the contractual service margin recognised in profit or loss in the period; and
- other amounts, if any, for example, experience adjustments for premium receipts other than those that relate to future service.

Insurance revenue related to insurance acquisition cash flows should be determined by allocating the portion of the premiums that relate to recovering those cash flows to each reporting period in a systematic way on the basis of passage of time. An entity should recognise the same amount as insurance service expenses. [IFRS 17.B125]. The purpose of this is to separately identify and recognise the recovery of the insurance acquisition cash flows through insurance revenue over the coverage period. The following example illustrates how insurance acquisition cash flows are allocated to revenue.

Example 56.64: Allocating a portion of premiums to insurance acquisition cash flows

An entity issues a group of insurance contracts with a coverage period of four years. The entity pays initial acquisition cash flows of ¥200 and expects to pay trail commission of ¥50 at the end of year 4. The group of contracts is not determined to be onerous. The entity estimates, at the time of initial recognition of the group of contracts, that the discount rate that applies to nominal cash flows that do not vary based on the returns on any underlying items is 3% per year.

The present value of expected insurance acquisition cash flows at initial recognition is ¥244 [¥200 + (¥50 ÷ 1.03^4)] which is part of the initial liability for remaining coverage. This is reduced when the insurance acquisition cash flows occur. The entity elects to accrete interest on the insurance acquisition cash flows (see 8.3 above) and estimates the portion of premiums that relates to the recovery of insurance acquisition cash flows in each of the four years of coverage after accreting interest on the opening balance to be ¥63, ¥65, ¥67 and ¥68. The entity recognises the same amounts as insurance service expenses in each year (i.e. insurance revenue and insurance service expenses are grossed-up for the same amount of ¥263).

In September 2018, the TRG members discussed an IASB staff paper which considered a submission about accounting for changes in insurance acquisition cash flows. The IASB staff paper noted that insurance acquisition cash flows are included in the determination of the contractual service margin or loss component for a group of insurance contracts on initial recognition. They are treated the same way as other cash flows incurred in fulfilling insurance contracts and an entity is therefore not required to identify whether it will recover the acquisition cash flows at each reporting date since the measurement model captures any lack of recoverability automatically. It does this by limiting the contractual service margin from becoming negative. When expected cash inflows are less than the total of expected cash outflows (including acquisition cash flows) and the risk adjustment for non-financial risk, a loss component is recognised along with a charge to profit or loss. The TRG members observed that:

- An entity is not required separately to identify whether it will recover insurance acquisition cash flows at each reporting date.
- IFRS 17 assumes that the portion of premiums relating to the recovery of insurance acquisition cash flows is equal to the current estimate of total expected insurance acquisition cash flows at each reporting period.

The TRG members also noted that experience adjustments arising from premiums received in the period that relate to future service, and the related cash flows such as insurance acquisition cash flows, adjust the contractual service margin.[88]

This means that, for example, if initial estimates of acquisition cash flows, payable at the end of a one-year coverage period, were $100 and at six months into the coverage period the entity now expects to pay $120 for acquisition cash flows at the end of the coverage period compared to the initial expectation of $100 then the amount of insurance service expenses related to the amortisation of acquisition cash flows (and insurance revenue recognised) at six months is $60.

In April 2019, the IASB staff discussed a TRG submission which asked whether IFRS 17 requires or permits an entity to accrete interest on the amount of acquisition cash flows paid for determining insurance revenue and insurance services expenses. The IASB staff observed that an entity is required to determine insurance revenue related to insurance acquisition cash flows by allocating the portion of premiums that relate to recovering those cash flows to each reporting period on a systematic way on the basis of passage of time and such a systematic way does not preclude a way that considers interest accretion.[89]

15.1.2 Insurance revenue under the premium allocation approach

When an entity applies the premium allocation approach, insurance revenue for the period is the amount of expected premium receipts (excluding any investment component and adjusted to reflect the time value of money and the effect of financial risk, if applicable) allocated to the period. The entity should allocate the expected premium receipts to each period of insurance contract service: [IFRS 17.B126]

- on the basis of the passage of time; but
- if the expected pattern of release of risk during the coverage period differs significantly from the passage of time, then on the basis of the expected timing of incurred insurance service expenses.

An entity should change the basis of allocation between the two methods above as necessary if facts and circumstances change. [IFRS 17.B127]. As discussed at 9.3 above, any change in the basis of allocation is a change in accounting estimate and applied prospectively.

If an entity using the premium allocation approach does not expense insurance acquisition cash flows as incurred (see 9.1 above) the same guidance applies for allocating these to revenue as discussed at 15.1.1 above for the general approach.

15.1.3 Income or expenses from reinsurance contracts held

IFRS 17 permits an entity to present income or expenses from a group of reinsurance contracts held, other than insurance finance income or expenses, either:

- as a single amount; or
- separately, the amounts recovered from the reinsurer and an allocation of the premiums paid that together give a net amount equal to that single amount. [IFRS 17.86].

If an entity presents separately the amounts recovered from the reinsurer and an allocation of the premiums paid, it should: [IFRS 17.86]

- treat reinsurance cash flows that are contingent on claims on the underlying contracts (which would include profit commission payable or receivable) as part of the claims that are expected to be reimbursed under the reinsurance contract held;
- treat amounts from the reinsurer that it expects to receive that are not contingent on the claims of the underlying contracts (for example, some types of ceding commissions) as a reduction in the premiums to be paid to the reinsurer;
- treat amounts recognised relating to recovery of losses when an entity has a group of reinsurance contracts held providing coverage for an onerous group of underlying insurance contracts as amounts recovered from the reinsurer (see 10.4.2 above); and
- not present the allocation of premiums paid as a reduction in revenue.

15.2 Insurance service expenses

Insurance service expenses comprise the following: [IFRS 17.84]

- incurred claims (excluding repayments of investment components);
- other incurred service expenses;
- amortisation of insurance acquisition cash flows;

- changes that relate to past services, i.e. changes in fulfilment cash flows relating to the liability for incurred claims; and
- changes that relate to future service, i.e. losses on onerous groups of contracts and reversals of such losses.

As discussed at 15 above, an entity should disaggregate this information (for example to show insurance acquisition cash flows separately from other insurance service expenses) when such presentation is relevant to an understanding of the entity's financial performance.

With respect to the change in risk adjustment for non-financial risk, the entire charge is included as part of insurance service result unless the entity has decided to disaggregate this change between the insurance service result and the insurance finance income or expense. *[IFRS 17.81]*.

15.3 Insurance finance income or expenses

Insurance finance income or expenses comprises the change in the carrying amount of the group of insurance contracts arising from: *[IFRS 17.87]*
- the effect of the time value of money and changes in the time value of money; and
- the effect of financial risk and changes in financial risk; but
- excluding any such changes for groups of insurance contracts with direct participation features that would adjust the contractual service margin but do not do so in certain circumstances. These circumstances are when the entity's share of a decrease in the fair value of the underlying items exceeds the carrying amount of the contractual service margin and gives rise to a loss (or a reversal of that loss), increases in the fulfilment cash flows which exceed the carrying amount of the contractual service margin and give rise to a loss and decreases in fulfilment cash flows which are allocated to the loss component of the liability for remaining coverage. These are included in insurance service expenses.

Insurance finance income or expenses do not include income or expenses related to financial assets or liabilities within the scope of IFRS 9 such as investment finance income on underlying items. This is disclosed separately under IAS 1 (see Chapter 3 at 3.2.2).

An entity is required to include in insurance finance income or expenses the effect of the time value of money and financial risk and changes therein For this purpose: *[IFRS 17.B128]*
- assumptions about inflation based on an index of prices or rates or on prices of assets with inflation-linked returns are assumptions that relate to financial risk;
- assumptions about inflation based on an entity's expectation of specific price changes are not assumptions that relate to financial risk; and
- changes in the measurement of a group of insurance contracts caused by changes in the value of underlying items (excluding additions and withdrawals) are changes arising from the effect of the time value of money and financial risk and changes therein.

The words in the last bullet point above mean that changes in the measurement of insurance contracts arising from changes in underlying items, including changes in the value of underlying items not caused by the time value of money or the effect of financial risks, for example where the underlying items include non-financial assets should be treated as insurance finance income or expenses. This is because the underlying items are regarded as investments that determine the amount of some payments to policyholders. The underlying items referred to are those that affect measurement of all insurance contracts and not only underlying items in respect of contracts with direct participation features. The Basis for Conclusions observes that without this requirement changes in underlying items could adjust the contractual service margin of insurance contracts without direct participation features. The Board considered a view that, although it would be complex, the effects of changes in cash flows from participating in underlying items that are not financial in nature (for example, insurance contracts) should be presented within the insurance service result, rather than within insurance finance income or expenses. The Board disagreed with this view because the requirement to reflect changes from participation in underlying items in insurance finance income or expenses appropriately depicts the nature of the participation, as an investment. In the Board's view, policyholder participation in underlying items that are not solely financial in nature, such as insurance contracts, should not change the underlying insurance service result. Further, splitting the effect of changes in cash flows resulting from the participation in underlying items that are not solely financial in nature into an amount that should be included in the insurance service result and an amount that should be included in insurance finance income or expense would be complex and could disrupt implementation for some entities. [IFRS 17.BC342A.].

In April 2019, the IASB staff considered a submission to the TRG which questioned whether changes in fulfilment cash flows as a result of changes in inflation assumptions are treated as changes in non-financial risk (and adjust the contractual service margin) or changes in financial risk for contracts measured under the general approach. The submission provided examples of cash flows such as claims contractually linked to a specified consumer price inflation index and cash flows that are not contractually linked to an index but which are expected to increase with inflation. The IASB staff observed that cash flows that an entity expects to increase with an index are considered to be an assumption that relates to financial risks, even if the cash flows are not contractually linked to a specific index. The TRG members did not disagree with the IASB staff's observation.[90]

Exchange differences on changes in the carrying amount of groups of insurance contracts, including the contractual service margin, are included in the statement of profit or loss, unless they relate to changes in the carrying amount of groups of insurance contracts in other comprehensive income, in which case they should be included in other comprehensive income. [IFRS 17.92]. Neither IAS 21 nor IFRS 17 specify where, in profit or loss, exchange differences should be presented – see 7.3 above.

15.3.1 Presentation of insurance finance income or expenses in the statement of comprehensive income

Except for insurance finance income or expenses arising from insurance contracts under the variable fee approach when risk mitigation is applied, entities have an accounting policy choice between presenting insurance finance income or expenses in profit or loss or disaggregated between profit or loss and other comprehensive income. [IFRS 17.88].

If an entity mitigates the effect of financial risk under the variable fee approach (see 11.2.5 above) using derivatives and non-derivative financial assets measured at fair value through profit or loss, it should include insurance finance income or expenses for the period in profit or loss. If an entity mitigates the effect of financial risk using reinsurance contracts held insurance finance income or expenses should be allocated between profit and loss and other comprehensive income on the basis of the allocation used by the reinsurance contract. [IFRS 17.B117A].

An entity should apply its choice of accounting policy to portfolios of insurance contracts. The choice is then applied to all groups of contracts within that portfolio. In assessing the appropriate accounting policy for a portfolio of insurance contracts, applying the requirements of IAS 8 (see Chapter 3 at 4.3) the entity should consider for each portfolio the assets that the entity holds and how it accounts for those assets. [IFRS 17.B129].

A summary of the policy choices that apply when allocating insurance finance income or expenses in the statement of comprehensive income are as follows:

Type of contract	Accounting	Unit of account
General model		
Present value of future cash flows	All in profit or loss unless disaggregated between profit and loss and other comprehensive income	Disaggregation choice per portfolio
Risk adjustment for non-financial risk	Follows the present value or future cash flows as per above for insurance finance income or expenses (i.e. all in profit and loss or disaggregated) if the entity has elected to disaggregate the risk adjustment between insurance service result and insurance finance income or expenses (see 15.2 above).	Disaggregation choice per portfolio
Contractual service margin	All in profit and loss as not revalued at current interest rates.	N/A

Type of contract	Accounting	Unit of account
Premium allocation approach		
Liability for remaining coverage	All in profit and loss as not revalued at current interest rates.	N/A
Liability for incurred claims	All in profit or loss unless disaggregated between profit and loss and other comprehensive income	Disaggregation choice per portfolio
Variable fee approach		
Present value of future cash flows	All in profit or loss unless disaggregated between profit and loss and other comprehensive income	Disaggregation choice per portfolio
Risk adjustment for non-financial risk	Follows the present value of future cash flows for insurance finance income or expenses as per above (i.e. all in profit and loss or disaggregated) if the entity has elected to disaggregate the risk adjustment between insurance service result and insurance finance income or expenses (see 15.2 above).	Disaggregation choice per portfolio
Contractual service margin	The contractual service margin is at current interest rates so this leads to an offset between fulfilment cash flows and contractual service margin rather than being presented in insurance finance income or expenses.	N/A

In April 2019, the IASB staff responded to a question submitted to the TRG about a situation in which portfolios of insurance contracts change due to the manner in which an entity manages its contracts and questioned the impact of such a change on the application of the option to disaggregate insurance finance income or expenses. The IASB staff observed that applying the requirements of IAS 8, an entity should select and apply an accounting policy consistently for similar portfolios of insurance contracts. This implies that when an entity decides to choose a policy of disaggregation (or decides to cease a policy of disaggregation) that policy change or choice should be applied to all similar portfolios.[91]

As explained above, an entity should consider, for each portfolio, the assets that it holds and how it accounts for them. Entities would typically try to minimise accounting mismatches between assets and liabilities. For example, entities that have financial assets held within a business model whose objective is achieved by both collecting contractual cash flows and selling financial assets and therefore record the effect of fair value fluctuations on those securities in other comprehensive income under IFRS 9 would be expected to disaggregate insurance finance income or expenses between profit or loss and other comprehensive income on related insurance contract liabilities in order to minimise accounting mismatches. Conversely, an entity would be less inclined to disaggregate insurance finance income or expenses for portfolios of insurance contracts where the assets backing those liabilities include a substantial proportion of equity instruments which are held at fair value with changes in fair value through profit or loss under IFRS 9.

When disaggregation is selected, the methodology required for allocating insurance finance income or expenses between profit and loss and other comprehensive income is different depending on the entity's accounting policy choices based on the nature of the insurance contract liabilities in the portfolio.

The disaggregation approaches for each type of insurance contract are discussed at 15.3.2 to 15.3.4 below.

In summary, the approaches determining what portion of insurance finance income or expenses are attributed to profit and loss for portfolios of contracts, except those to which risk mitigation is applied under the variable fee approach, are as follows:

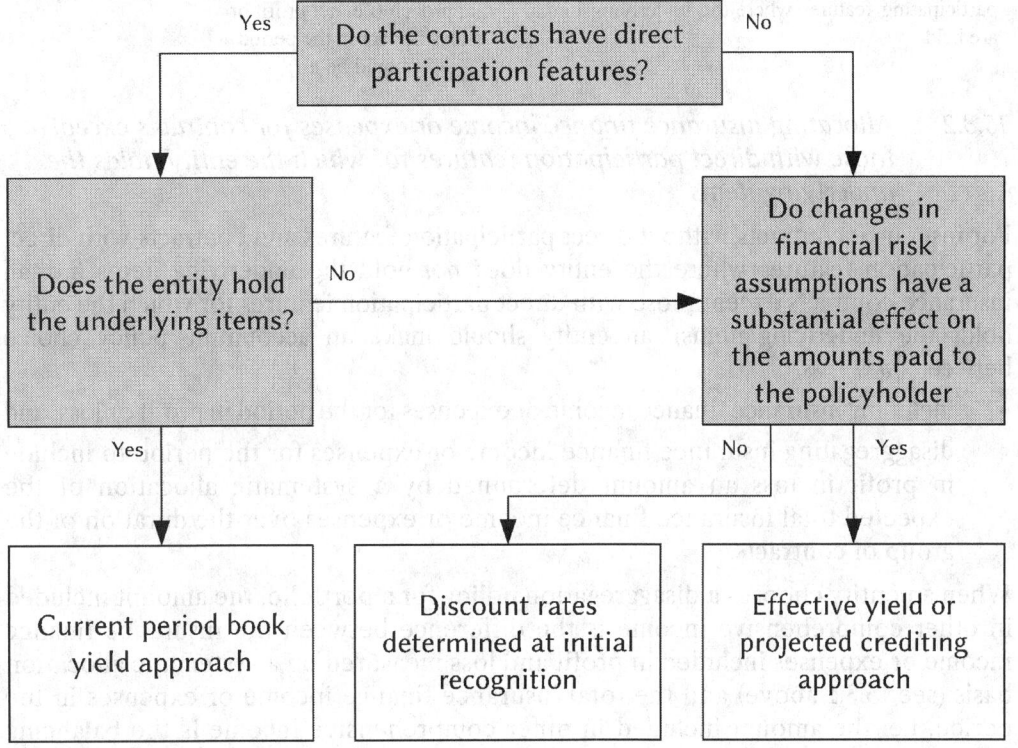

This can be further illustrated as follows:

Contract type	Amount recognised in profit or loss	OCI element recycled
Groups of insurance contracts without direct participating features where the effect of financial risk assumptions does not have a substantial effect on the policyholder	Using discount rates determined on initial recognition	Yes
Groups of insurance contracts without direct participating features where the effect of financial risk assumptions has a substantial effect on the policyholder	Choice of (a) effective yield or (b) projected crediting approach	Yes
Contracts accounted for under the premium allocation approach (incurred claims)	Using discount rates determined at date of incurred claim	Yes
Groups of insurance contracts with direct participating features where the underlying items are not held but the effect of financial risk assumptions has a substantial effect on the policyholder	Choice of (a) effective yield or (b) projected crediting approach	Yes
Groups of insurance contracts with direct participating features where the underlying items are held	Current period book yield approach (i.e. net profit or loss impact in the period should be nil)	No

15.3.2 Allocating insurance finance income or expenses for contracts except those with direct participation features for which the entity holds the underlying items

For insurance contracts without direct participation features and contracts with direct participation features where the entity does *not* hold the underlying items (i.e. all insurance contracts except those with direct participation features for which the entity holds the underlying items), an entity should make an accounting policy choice between: *[IFRS 17.88]*

- including insurance finance income or expenses for the period in profit or loss; and
- disaggregating insurance finance income or expenses for the period to include in profit in loss an amount determined by a systematic allocation of the expected total insurance finance income or expenses over the duration of the group of contracts.

When an entity chooses a disaggregation policy for a portfolio, the amount included in other comprehensive income is the difference between the insurance finance income or expenses included in profit and loss measured on a systematic allocation basis (see 15.3.1 above) and the total insurance finance income or expenses in the period, i.e. the amount included in other comprehensive income is the balancing figure. *[IFRS 17.90]*.

This approach applies to both the liability for remaining coverage and the liability for incurred claims under the general model. Under the premium allocation model, it applies only to the liability for incurred claims. It does not apply to the liability for remaining coverage under the premium allocation approach unless the group of contracts becomes onerous as the liability for remaining coverage is discounted using the rates at initial recognition of the group and not at current rates. Disaggregating discount rates for the liability for incurred claims under the premium allocation approach is discussed at 15.3.3 below.

A systematic allocation means an allocation of the total expected insurance finance income or expenses of a group of insurance contracts over the duration of the group that: *[IFRS 17.B130]*

- is based on characteristics of the contracts, without reference to factors that do not affect the cash flows expected to arise under the contracts. For example, the allocation of the insurance finance income or expenses should not be based on expected recognised returns on assets if those expected recognised returns do not affect the cash flows of the contracts in the group; and

- results in the amounts recognised in other comprehensive income over the duration of the group of contracts totalling zero. The cumulative amount recognised in other comprehensive income at any date is the difference between the carrying amount of the group of contracts and the amount that the group would be measured at when applying the systematic allocation.

When an entity that has disaggregated insurance finance income or expenses of a group of insurance contracts transfers that group of insurance contracts or derecognises an insurance contract (see 12.3.1 to 12.3.3 above), it should reclassify to profit or loss as a reclassification adjustment any remaining amounts for the group (or contract) that were previously recognised in other comprehensive income as a result of its accounting policy choice. *[IFRS 17.91(a)]*.

15.3.2.A Allocating insurance finance income or expenses for contracts for which changes that relate to financial risk do not have a substantial effect on the amounts paid to the policyholder

For groups of insurance contracts for which changes in assumptions that relate to financial risk do not have a substantial effect on the amounts paid to the policyholder, the systematic allocation (i.e. the amount presented in profit or loss) is determined using the discount rates determined at the date of initial recognition of the group of contracts. *[IFRS 17.B131]*. This can be illustrated by the following example.

Example 56.65: **Allocating insurance finance income or expenses for contracts where the impact of financial risk on the amounts paid to policyholders is not substantial**

On initial recognition of a group of insurance contracts an entity expects to pay policyholders €1,890 at the end of Year 3. The impact of financial risk on the amounts paid to the policyholders is not substantial and is not affected by changes in discount rates. The interest rate at initial recognition of the group of contracts is 10% and there are no changes to this applying a weighted average discount rate. For simplicity it is assumed that all premiums (cash inflows) are received at the date of initial recognition and all other amounts, including the risk adjustment for non-financial risk, are ignored. Applying paragraph B131 of IFRS 17, the entity disaggregates insurance finance income or expenses using the discount rates determined on initial recognition of the group.

At initial recognition the present value of expected future cash flows is €1,420 (i.e. €1,890 discounted for 3 years at 10%, being €1,562 after one year, €1,718 after 2 years and €1,890 after 3 years).

At the end of year 1, the present value of expected future cash flows is €1,562 (i.e. €1,890 discounted for 2 years at 10%). The insurance finance income or expenses of €142 (i.e. €1,562 less €1,420) is debited to profit or loss as there is no difference between current discount rates and the discount rate at initial recognition.

At the end of year 2, market interest rates have reduced to 5%. As a result, the present value of expected future cash flows at the end of year 2 is €1,800. The insurance finance income or expenses of €238 (i.e. €1,800 less €1,562) is allocated as follows:

- €156 is debited to profit or loss being the difference between €1,800 and €1,562 at the discount rate at initial recognition of 10%.
- €82 is debited to other comprehensive income being the difference being total insurance finance income or expenses of €238 and the amount allocated to profit or loss of €156.

At the end of year 3, market interest rates are still 5%. As a result, the insurance finance income or expenses of €90 (i.e. €1,890 less €1,800) is allocated as follows:

- €172 is debited to profit or loss being the difference between €1,718 and €1,890 using the discount rate and cash flows at initial recognition of 10%.
- €82 is credited to other comprehensive income being the difference being total insurance finance income or expenses of €90 and the amount allocated to profit or loss of €172.

The net cumulative amount in other comprehensive income at the end of year 3 is €nil.

For contracts applying the general approach, as the contractual margin is not retranslated using current rates, all insurance finance income or expenses arising from the accretion of interest of the contractual service margin is recorded in profit or loss.

In April 2019, the IASB staff responded to a submission to the TRG which asked whether accumulated other comprehensive income on insurance contracts measured applying the general model should be reclassified to profit or loss when experience does not unfold as expected, and if so, how. The IASB staff observed that the cumulative amount recognised in other comprehensive income at any date is the difference between the carrying amount of the group of contracts and the amount that the group would be measured at when applying the systematic allocation of the expected total insurance finance income or expenses over the duration of the group.[92] In other words, when the insurance liability is increased or decreased as a result of experience adjustments, the discount rate used for the systematic allocation of the expected total insurance finance income or expenses continues to be calculated as before (e.g. based on the discount rates determined at initial recognition for a group of insurance contracts for which changes in assumptions that relate to financial risk do not have a substantial effect on the amounts paid to the policyholder) and a reclassification adjustment occurs only on derecognition.

15.3.2.B Allocating insurance finance income or expenses for contracts for which changes in assumptions that relate to financial risk have a substantial effect on amounts paid to policyholders

For groups of insurance contracts for which changes in assumptions that relate to financial risk have a substantial effect on the amounts paid to the policyholders, which will include contracts with direct participation features for which the underlying items are not held, a systematic allocation for the finance income or expenses arising from the estimates of future cash flows can be determined in one of the following ways: *[IFRS 17.B132(a)]*

- using a rate that allocates the remaining revised expected finance income or expenses over the remaining duration of the group of contracts at a constant rate ('effective yield approach'); or
- for contracts that use a crediting rate to determine amounts due to the policyholders, using an allocation that is based on the amounts credited in the period and expected to be credited in future periods to the policyholder ('projected crediting approach').

IFRS 17 does not provide guidance how to determine 'substantial effect' although it is presumably intended to be interpreted similarly to the words 'substantial share' and 'substantial proportion' discussed in the context of insurance contracts with direct participation features at 11.2.1 above. That is to say, a group of insurance contracts with direct participation features will usually be a group for which changes in assumptions that relate to financial risk have a substantial effect on the amounts paid to the policyholders. In addition, a group of insurance contracts that have failed to meet the criteria for applying the variable fee approach because of, for example, a lack of a clearly identified pool of underlying items (see 11.2.1 above) might also be groups of contracts for which changes in assumptions that relate to financial risk (e.g. a change in the crediting rate or dividend amount) have a substantial effect on the amounts paid to policyholders.

The decision to elect either an effective yield approach or a projected crediting approach is an accounting policy choice and is applied to eligible groups according to the criteria in IAS 8.

A systematic allocation for the finance income or expenses arising from the risk adjustment for non-financial risk, if separately disaggregated from other changes in the risk adjustment for non-financial risk, is determined using an allocation consistent with that used for the allocation for the finance income or expenses arising from the future cash flows. *[IFRS 17.B132(b)].*

A systematic allocation for the finance income or expenses arising from the contractual service margin is determined: *[IFRS 17.B132(c)]*

- for insurance contracts that do not have direct participation features, using the discount rates determined at the date of initial recognition of the group of contracts (which results in the entire insurance finance income or expenses allocated to profit or loss since the contractual service margin is not remeasured at current rates); and
- for insurance contracts with direct participation features, using an allocation consistent with that used for the allocation for the interest income or expenses arising from future cash flows.

Examples 56.66 and 67 below, based on Examples 15A and B in the Illustrative Examples on IFRS 17, illustrate the application of the effective yield approach and the projected crediting rate approach respectively. *[IFRS 17.IE155-IE172].*

Example 56.66: *Allocating insurance finance income or expenses for contracts where the impact of financial risk on the amounts paid to policyholders is substantial – effective yield approach*

On initial recognition of a group of insurance contracts an entity expects to pay policyholders €1,890 at the end of Year 3. The interest rate at initial recognition of the group of contracts is 10% and there are no changes to this applying a weighted average discount rate. For simplicity it is assumed that all premiums (cash inflows) are received at the date of initial recognition and all other amounts, including the risk adjustment for non-financial risk, are ignored. The entity choses to disaggregate insurance finance income or expenses using a systematic allocation of the total expected insurance finance income or expenses over the remaining duration of the group.

At initial recognition the present value of expected future cash flows is €1,420 (i.e. €1,890 discounted for 3 years at 10%, being €1,562 after one year, €1,718 after 2 years and €1,890 after 3 years)).

At the end of year 1, market interest rates have reduced to 5%. Consequently, the entity revises its expectations as to the future cash flows it will pay its policyholders and now expects to pay only €1,802 at the end of year 3. The revised constant interest rate is calculated at 7.42% a year (i.e. the rate required to accrete €1,562 up to €1,802). As a result, the revised present value of future cash flows at the end of year 1 is €1,635.

Applying paragraph B132(a)(i) the entity recognizes in profit or loss the insurance finance income or expenses calculated as the change in estimates of the present value of the future cash flows at the constant rate of return. In year 1, the finance expenses of €142 in profit or loss is the difference between the estimates of the present value of future cash flows at the original constant rate of 10% at the end of the year 1 of €1,562 and the corresponding amount at the beginning of the period of €1,420. Applying paragraph B130(b), the entity recognises in other comprehensive income the difference between the total insurance finance expense of €215 (i.e. the difference between opening fulfilment cash flows of €1,420 and the current fulfilment cash flows of €1,635) and the amount included in profit or loss of €142, i.e. €73.

At the end of year 2, market interest rates are still 5%. The present value of expected future cash flows discounted at current rates is €1,716. The insurance finance income or expenses of €81 (i.e. the difference between €1,716 and the opening revised cashflows of €1,635) is allocated as follows:

- €116 is debited to profit or loss being the difference between the estimates of future cash flows of €1,562 and €1,678 using the constant rate of return of 7.34%; and
- €35 is credited to other comprehensive income being the difference being total insurance finance income or expenses of €81 and the amount allocated to profit or loss of €116.

At the end of year 3, market interest rates are still 5%. As a result, the insurance finance income or expenses of €86 (i.e. €1,802 less €1,716) is allocated as follows:

- €124 is debited to profit or loss being the difference between the final cash flows of €1,802 and the previous discounted figure of €1,678 using the constant rate of return of 7.34%; and
- €38 is credited to other comprehensive income being the difference being total insurance finance income or expenses of €86 and the amount allocated to profit or loss of €124.

The net cumulative amount in other comprehensive income at the end of year 3 is €nil.

Example 56.67: *Allocating insurance finance income or expenses for contracts where the impact of financial risk on the amounts paid to policyholders is substantial – projected crediting rate approach*

On initial recognition of a group of insurance contracts an entity receives a single premium of €15 for 100 insurance contracts with a coverage period of three years. The total premium for the group of contracts is €1,500. On initial recognition, the entity expects to achieve rate of return on underlying items of 10% each year and to credit the policyholder account balances by 8% each year (the expected crediting rate). Consequently, the entity expects to pay policyholders €1,890 at the end of Year 3 (€1,500 × 1.08 × 1.08 × 1.08).

In Year 1, the entity credits the policyholder account balances with a return of 8% a year, as expected at the date of initial recognition.

At the end of Year 1, the market interest rate falls from 10% per year to 5% per year. Consequently, the entity revises its expectations about cash flows as follows:

- it will achieve a return of 5% in Year 3 after reinvesting the maturity proceeds of the bonds that mature at the end of Year 2.
- it will credit the policyholder account balances 8% in Year 2 and 3% in Year 3; and
- it will pay policyholders €1,802 at the end of Year 3 (€1,500 × 1.08 × 1.08 × 1.03).

The entity elects to disaggregate insurance finance income or expenses using an allocation to profit or loss based on amounts credited in the period and expected to be credited in future periods (a 'projected crediting rate approach').

Therefore, the entity allocates the remaining expected insurance finance income and expenses over the remaining life of the contracts using the series of discount rates calculated as the projected crediting rates multiplied by the constant factor. The constant factor and the series of discount rates based on crediting rates at the end of Year 1 are as follows:

- the product of the actual crediting rate in Year 1 and the expected crediting rates in Years 2 and 3 equals 1.20 (1.08 × 1.08 × 1,03);
- the carrying amount of the liability increases by a factor of 1.269 over three years because of the interest accretion (€1,802 ÷ €1,420);
- consequently, each crediting rate needs to be adjusted by a constant factor (K), as follows 1.08.K × 1.08.K × 1.03K = 1.269;
- the constant K equals 1.0184 calculated as $(1.269 \div 1.20)^{1/3}$; and
- the resulting interest accretion rate for Year 1 is 10% (calculated as 1.08 × 1.0184).

The carrying amount of the liability at the end of Year 1 for the purposes of allocating insurance finance income or expenses to profit or loss is €1,562 (€1,420 × 1.08 × 1.0184).

The actual crediting rate for Years 2 and 3 are as expected at the end of Year 1. The resulting accretion rate for Year 2 is 10% (calculated as (1.08 × 1.0184) – 1) and for Year 3 is 4.9% (calculated as (1.03 × 1.0184) – 1).

	Initial recognition €	Year 1 €	Year 2 €	Year 3 €
Estimates of future cash flows at the end of Year 3	1,890	1,802	1,802	1,802
Estimates of the present value of future cash flows at current discount rates (A)	1,420	1,635	1,716	1,802
Estimates of future cash flows at discount rates based on projected crediting (B)	1,420	1,562	1,718	1,802
Amount accumulated in other comprehensive income (A-B)	–	73	(2)	–

In the table above, €1,716 equals the estimate of the future cash flows at the end of Year 3 of €1,802 discounted at the current market rate of 5% a year, i.e. €1,802 ÷ 1.05 = €1,716.

€1,718 equals the estimates of future cash flows at the end of Year 3 of €1,802 discounted at the projected crediting rate of 4.9% a year, i.e. €1,802 ÷ 1,049 = €1,718.

There is an amount of €2 accumulated in other comprehensive income at the end of Year 2 because the discount rate based on projected crediting of 4.9% a year (1.03 × K) is different from the current discount rate of 5% per year.

The insurance finance income or expenses included in profit or loss and other comprehensive income are as follows:

Insurance income and expensed arising from fulfilment cash flows	Year 1 €	Year 2 €	Year 3 €
In profit or loss	(142)	(156)	(84)
In other comprehensive income	(73)	75	(2)
In total comprehensive income	(215)	(81)	(86)

The entity recognises in profit or loss the insurance finance expenses calculated as the change in the estimates of the present value of the future cash flows at the projected crediting rate. In Year 1, the insurance finance expenses of €142 is the difference between the estimates of the present value of the future cash flows at the original crediting rate of 10 per cent at the end of Year 1 of €1,562 and the corresponding amount at the beginning of the period of €1,420.

The entity includes in other comprehensive income the difference between the amount recognised in total comprehensive income and the amount recognised in profit or loss. For example, in Year 1 the amount included in other comprehensive income of €(73) is €(215) minus €(142). In Years 1-3, the total other comprehensive income equals zero (€0 = €(73) + €75 + €(2)).

The entity recognises in total comprehensive income the change in estimates of the present value of the future cash flows at the current discount rate. In Year 1, for example, the total insurance finance expenses of €(215) is the difference between the estimates of the present value of the future cash flows at the current discount rate at the beginning of Year 1 of €1,420 and the corresponding amount at the end of Year 1 of €1,635.

15.3.3 Allocating insurance finance income or expenses for incurred claims when applying the premium allocation approach

When the premium allocation approach is applied (see 9 above), an entity may be required, or may choose to discount the liability for incurred claims (see 9.4 above). In such cases, it may also choose to disaggregate the insurance finance income or expenses as discussed at 15.3.1 above. If the entity makes this choice, it should determine the insurance finance income or expenses in profit or loss using the discount rate determined at the date of the incurred claim. *[IFRS 17.B133]*.

15.3.4 Allocating finance income or expenses for insurance contracts with direct participation features for which the entity holds the underlying items

For insurance contracts with direct participation features, for which the entity holds the underlying items, an entity should make an accounting policy choice between: *[IFRS 17.89]*

- including insurance finance income or expenses for the period in profit or loss; or
- disaggregating insurance finance income or expenses for the period to include in profit or loss an amount that eliminates accounting mismatches with income or expenses included in profit or loss on the underlying items held.

This means that, when disaggregation is applied, the amount included in profit or loss insurance finance income or expenses in respect of the insurance contracts with direct participation features exactly matches the insurance finance income or expenses included in profit or loss for the underlying items, resulting in the net of the separately presented items being nil. *[IFRS 17.B134]*. This is sometimes described as the current period book yield approach.

This is illustrated by the following example based on Example 16 in the Illustrative Examples on IFRS 17. *[IFRS 17.IE173-IE185]*.

Example 56.68: Allocating insurance finance income and expense for contracts using the current book yield approach

An entity issues 100 insurance contracts with a coverage period of three years. The coverage period starts when the insurance contracts are issued. The contracts meet the criteria for insurance contracts with direct participation features.

The entity receives a single premium of $15 for each contract at the beginning of the coverage period (total future cash inflows of $1,500). The entity promises to pay policyholders on maturity of the contract an accumulated amount of returns on a specified pool of bonds minus a charge equal to 5% of the premium and accumulated returns calculated at that date. Thus, policyholders that survive to maturity of the contract receive 95% of the premium and accumulated returns. In this example all other amounts, including the risk adjustment for non-financial risk are ignored for simplicity.

The entity invests premiums received of $1,500 in zero coupon fixed income bonds with a duration of three years (the same as the returns promised to policyholders). The bonds return a market interest rate of 10% a year. At the end of Year 1, market interest rates fall from 10% to 5%. The entity measures the bonds at fair value through other comprehensive income applying IFRS 9. The effective interest rate of the bonds acquired is 10% a year, and that rate is used to calculate investment income in profit or loss. For simplicity, this example excludes the effect of accounting for expected credit losses on financial assets. The value of the bonds held by the entity is illustrated in the table below:

Bonds held	Initial recognition $	Year 1 $	Year 2 $	Year 3 $
Fair value	1,500	1,811	1,902	1,997
Amortised cost	1,500	1,650	1,815	1,997
Cumulative amounts recognised in other comprehensive income	–	161	87	–
Change in other comprehensive income		161	(74)	(87)
Investment income recognised in profit or loss (effective interest rate)		150	165	182

The entity elects to disaggregate insurance finance income or expenses for each period to include in profit or loss an amount that eliminates accounting mismatches with income or expense included in profit or loss on underlying items held. Therefore, the entity needs to analyse the changes in fulfilment cash flows to decide whether each change adjusts the contractual service margin. The source of the fulfilment cash flows is as follows:

Fulfilment cash flows	Year 1 $	Year 2 $	Year 3 $
Opening balance	–	1,720	1,806
Change related to future service: new contracts	(75)	–	–
Change in the policyholders' share in the fair value of the underlying items	295	86	90
Cash flows	1,500	–	(1,896)
Closing balance	1,720	1,806	–

Fulfilment cash flows are the estimate of the present value of the future cash inflows and the estimate of the present value of the future cash outflows (in this example all cash outflows vary based on the returns on underlying items). For example, at initial recognition the fulfilment cash flows of $(75) are the sum of the estimates of the present value of the future cash inflows of $(1,500) and the estimates of the present value of the future cash outflows of $1,425 (the policyholders' share of 95% of the fair value of the underlying items at initial recognition of $1,500).

The change in the policyholders' share in the fair value of the underlying items is 95% of the change in fair value of the underlying items. For example, in Year 1 the change in the policyholders' share in the underlying items of $295 is 95% of the change in fair value in Year 1 of $311 ($1,811 – $1,500). The entity does not adjust the contractual service margin for the change in the obligation to pay policyholders an amount equal to the fair value of the underlying items because it does not relate to future service.

The entity determines the carrying amount of the contractual service margin at the end of each reporting period as follows:

Contractual service margin	Year 1 $	Year 2 $	Year 3 $
Opening balance	–	61	33
Change related to future service: new contracts	75	–	–
Change in the entity's share in the fair value of the underlying items	16	5	6
Change relating to current service: recognition in profit or loss for the service provided	(30)	(33)	(38)
Closing balance	61	33	–

The entity adjusts the contractual service margin for the change in the amount of the entity's share of the fair value of the underlying items because those changes relate to future service. For example, in Year 1 the change in the amount of the entity's share of the fair value of the underlying items of $16 is 5% of the change in fair value of the underlying items of $311 ($1,811 – $1,500). (This example does not include cash flows that do not vary based on the returns on underlying items).

The entity determines the amount of contractual service margin recognised in profit or loss by allocating the contractual service margin at the end of the period (before recognising any amounts in profit or loss) equally to each coverage unit provided in the current period and expected to be provided in the future. In this example, the coverage provided in each period is assumed to be the same; hence, the contractual service margin recognised in profit or loss for Year 1 of $U30 is the contractual service margin before allocation of $U91 ($75 + $16), divided by three years of coverage.

The amounts recognised in the statement(s) of financial performance for the periods are as follows:

Statement(s) of financial performance	Year 1 $	Year 2 $	Year 3 $
Profit or loss			
Contractual service margin recognised in profit or loss for the service provided	30	33	38
Insurance service result	30	33	38
Investment income	150	165	182
Insurance finance expense	(150)	(165)	(182)
Profit	30	33	38
Other comprehensive income			
Gain/(loss) on financial assets measured at fair value through other comprehensive income	161	(74)	(87)
Gain/(loss) on insurance contracts	(161)	74	87
Total other comprehensive income	–	–	–

The entity does not adjust the contractual service margin for the changes in the obligation to pay the policyholders an amount equal to the fair value of the underlying items because those changes do not relate to future service. Consequently, the entity recognises those changes as insurance finance income or expenses in the statement(s) of financial performance. For example, in Year 1 the change in fair value of the underlying items is $311 ($1,811 – $1,500).

Furthermore, the entity disaggregates the insurance finance income or expenses for the period between profit or loss and other comprehensive income to include in profit or loss an amount that eliminates accounting mismatches with the income or expenses included in profit or loss on the underlying items held. This amount exactly matches the income or expenses included in profit or loss for the underlying items, resulting in the net of the two separately presented items being zero. For example, in Year 1 the total amount of the insurance finance income or expenses of $311 is disaggregated and the entity presents in profit or loss the amount of $150 that equals the amount of finance income for the underlying items. The remaining amount of insurance finance income or expenses of $161 is recognised in other comprehensive income.

An entity may qualify for the accounting policy choice above in some periods but not in others because of a change in whether it holds the underlying items. If such a change occurs, the accounting policy choice available to the entity changes from that set out above to that set out at 15.3.1 above or *vice versa*. Hence, an entity might change its accounting policy between that set out above and that set out at 15.3.1 above. In making such a change an entity should: *[IFRS 17.B135]*

- include the accumulated amount previously included in other comprehensive income by the date of the change as a reclassification adjustment in profit or loss in the period of change and in future periods, as follows:
  - if the entity had previously applied the requirements described at 15.3.1 above the entity should include in profit or loss the accumulated amount included in other comprehensive income before the change as if the entity were continuing the approach described at 15.3.1 above based on the assumptions that applied immediately before the change; and
  - if the entity had previously applied the requirements above, the entity should include in profit or loss the accumulated amount included in other comprehensive income before the change as if the entity were continuing the approach above based on the assumptions that applied immediately before the change; and
- not restate prior period comparative information.

An entity should not recalculate the accumulated amount previously included in other comprehensive income as if the new disaggregation had always applied; and the assumptions used for the reclassification in future periods should not be updated after the date of the change. *[IFRS 17.B136]*.

When an entity which has disaggregated the finance income or expenses of a group of insurance contracts with direct participation features using the current book yield approach, transfers that group of insurance contracts or derecognises an insurance contract (see 12.3.2 and 12.3.3 above) it should not reclassify to profit or loss as a reclassification adjustment any remaining amounts for the group (or contract) that were previously recognised in other comprehensive income as a result of its accounting policy choice. *[IFRS 17.91(b)]*. This is a different accounting treatment than for contracts which do not apply the current book yield approach (see 15.3.2 above).

15.4 Reporting the contractual service margin in interim financial statements

IFRS 17, as amended in June 2020, states that if an entity prepares interim financial statements applying IAS 34 – *Interim Financial Reporting*, the entity shall make an accounting policy choice as to whether to change the treatment of accounting estimates made in previous interim financial statements when applying IFRS 17 in subsequent interim financial statements and in the annual reporting period. The entity shall apply its choice of accounting policy to all groups of insurance contracts it issues and groups of reinsurance contracts it holds. *[IFRS 17.B137]*.

An entity which elects not to change the treatment of estimates made in previous interim financial statements is likely to have a different accounting result than an entity which does change estimates made in previous interim reporting periods. This is because adjusting the contractual service margin for changes in estimates of the fulfilment cash flows but not for experience adjustments has the consequence that the accounting depends on the timing of a reporting date. *[IFRS 17.BC236]*.

When an entity elects not to change estimates made in previous interim financial statements, the amounts presented in any annual report should equal the values as of the end of the last interim period and the cumulative profit or loss for the year should be the sum of the profit or loss amounts for each interim period. Each interim period is determined separately as if it were a discrete period and the annual period is simply the total of the profit or loss of the discrete interim periods.

When an entity does restate estimates made in previous interim periods, each interim report includes information which in aggregate results in the year-to-date figures since the end value of the last interim report equals the value which would have been the result if IFRS 17 had been applied to the full year to date without any interim periods. The cumulative profit and loss to date of the interim period would equal the cumulative amount on an annual basis to date.

The effect of this accounting policy choice on profit or loss is illustrated in the following example:

Example 56.69: The contractual service margin and interim reporting

This example focuses on the impact of the release of the contractual service margin on insurance revenue and not on the impact on profit or loss of other components of an insurance contract liability. The example also assumes there are no other changes in expectations and ignores accretion of interest for simplicity

An entity with an annual reporting period ending on 31 December publishes half-yearly interim financial statements.

At 31 December 2022, the entity has issued a group of insurance contracts with a CSM of $1,200 and an expected coverage period of two years. The entity expects to provide coverage evenly over the coverage period and expects to incur claims in H2 2023 of $300.

At the end of H1 2023, the entity increases its estimate of claims to be incurred in H2 of 2023 by $200 to $500. The entity adjusts (reduces) the related contractual service margin by $200 and reduces the contractual service margin by $250 for services provided in H1 ($1,200 – CU200) ÷ 4. At the end of H1 2023, the entity carries forward a contractual service margin of $750.

The entity incurs claims in H2 2023 of $300 (as originally expected).

Option A – the entity elects not to change the treatment of its previous estimates in subsequent interim financial statements and in the annual financial report

As a result of incurring claims in H2 2023 of $300, the entity recognises a favourable experience adjustment in profit or loss (i.e. a credit to insurance service expenses) of $200 in H2.

The entity releases $250 from the contractual service margin to profit or loss (insurance revenue) in H2 and carries forward a contractual service margin of $500 ($750 – $250) at 31 December 2023 in the H2 2023 interim as well as annual 2023 financial statements.

In summary, in 2023 the entity recognises $500 as part of insurance revenue, a positive experience adjustment in profit or loss of $200 and carries forward a contractual service margin of $500 in both its interim financial statements for H2 2023, as well as its annual financial statements for that year.

Option B – the entity elects to change the treatment of its previous estimates in subsequent interim financial statements and in the annual financial report

If the entity does change its previous estimates then the position at the end of the H2 2023 interims and the 2023 financial report is the cumulative result for the calendar year. Therefore, the impact on the annual financial statements is as follows:

- There is no experience adjustment in the year – claims in 2023 are as expected at 31 December 2022.
- The entity would release $600 from the contractual service margin to profit or loss in the calendar year 2023 and would carry forward a contractual service margin of $600 ($1,200 brought forward – $600 release to P&L = $600).

In summary, in 2023 the entity recognises $600 as part of insurance revenue in 2023 and carries forward a contractual service margin of $600 at 31 December 2023 instead of recognising insurance revenue of $500 and a positive experience adjustment in insurance service expenses of $200 and carrying forward a contractual service margin of $500 under option A above.

In September 2018, an IASB staff paper submitted to the TRG in response to a submission confirmed that the requirements of paragraph B137 of IFRS 17 described above applies only to interim reports prepared applying IAS 34. This can cause a particular issue for groups where the parent does, but the subsidiary does not, prepare IAS 34 interim financial statements. If the parent prepares IAS 34 interim financial statements but the subsidiary does not, (e.g. the subsidiary prepares interim internal management reports that do not comply with IAS 34) then the choice of changing the treatment of previous estimates in subsequent interim financial statements is available only to the parent and not applicable to the subsidiary.[93] The TRG members agreed with the IASB staff's interpretation but highlighted the significant operational challenges of applying it in practice.[94]

IFRS 17, as issued in May 2017, stated that an entity could not change the treatment of accounting estimates made in previous interim financial statements when applying IFRS 17 in subsequent interim financial statements and in the annual reporting period. However, the IASB received feedback from entities who expressed the view that the requirement resulted in a practical burden that was more significant than the burden the Board had intended to alleviate with the requirement. They expressed the view this is particularly the case for entities in a consolidated group with different frequency of reporting because of a need to maintain two sets of accounting estimates. Considering that feedback, the Board concluded that permitting an accounting policy choice would ease IFRS 17 implementation by enabling an entity to assess which accounting policy is less burdensome. To avoid a significant loss of useful information for users of financial statements, the Board concluded that the entity is required to apply consistently its choice of accounting policy to all groups of insurance contracts it issues and groups of reinsurance contracts it holds (i.e. accounting policy choice at reporting entity level). *[IFRS 17.BC236B-C]*.

There is also related transitional relief available upon applying IFRS 17 for entities applying the modified retrospective approach that elect an accounting policy not to change the treatment of estimates made in previous interim reporting periods. See 17.4 below.

16 DISCLOSURE

One of the main objectives of IFRS 17 is to establish principles for the disclosure of insurance contracts which gives a basis for users of the financial statements to assess the effect that insurance contracts have on an entity's financial position, financial performance and cash flows. *[IFRS 17.1]*.

Hence, the objective of the disclosure requirements is for an entity to disclose information in the notes that, together with the information provided in the statement of financial position, statement(s) of financial performance and statement of cash flows, gives a basis for users of financial statements to assess the effect of contracts within the scope of IFRS 17. To achieve that objective, an entity should disclose qualitative and quantitative information about: *[IFRS 17.93]*

- the amounts recognised in its financial statements for contracts within the scope of IFRS 17 (see 16.1 below);
- disclosures showing the effect of transition (see 16.2 below);
- the significant judgements, and changes in those judgements, made when applying IFRS 17 (see 16.3 below); and
- the nature and extent of the risks from contracts within the scope of IFRS 17 (see 16.5 below).

The disclosure objective is supplemented with some specific disclosure requirements designed to help the entity satisfy this objective. By specifying the objective of the disclosures, the Board aims to ensure that entities provide the information that is most relevant for their circumstances and to emphasise the importance of communication to users of financial statements rather than compliance with detailed and prescriptive disclosure requirements. In situations in which the information provided to meet the specific disclosure requirements is not sufficient to meet the disclosure objective, the entity is required to disclose additional information necessary to achieve that objective. *[IFRS 17.BC347]*.

The Board used the disclosure requirements in IFRS 4, including the disclosure requirements in IFRS 7 that are incorporated in IFRS 4 by cross-reference, as a basis for the requirements in IFRS 17. This is because stakeholders have indicated that such disclosures provide useful information to users of financial statements for understanding the amount, timing and uncertainty of future cash flows from insurance contracts. The disclosure requirements brought forward from IFRS 4 include information about significant judgements in applying the standard as well as most of the disclosures about the nature and extent of risks that arise from insurance contracts. *[IFRS 17.BC348]*. In addition, when developing IFRS 17, the Board identified key items it views as critical to understanding the financial statements of entities issuing insurance contracts, in the light of the requirement to update the measurement of insurance contracts at each reporting date. Consequently, additional disclosures have been added requiring: *[IFRS 17.BC349]*

- reconciliations of opening to closing balances of the various components of the liability for remaining coverage and the liability for incurred claims;
- an analysis of insurance revenue;
- information about initial recognition of insurance contracts in the statement of financial position;
- an explanation of when an entity expects to recognise the contractual service margin remaining at the end of the reporting period in profit or loss;
- an explanation of the total amount of insurance finance income or expenses in profit or loss and the composition and fair value of underlying items for contracts with direct participation features;
- information about the entity's approach to determining various inputs into the fulfilment cash flows;
- the confidence level used to determine the risk adjustment for non-financial risk;
- information about yield curves used to discount cash flows that do not vary based on returns from underlying items; and
- information about the effect of the regulatory framework in which the entity operates.

The result of this is that the disclosure requirements of IFRS 17 are likely to be more extensive compared to the requirements of IFRS 4. They comprise forty paragraphs of the standard and many of these disclosures will not have previously been applied by insurance entities. In summary, complying with the disclosure requirements will be challenging.

IFRS 17 requires a reporting entity to consider the level of detail necessary to satisfy the disclosure objective and how much emphasis to place on each of the various requirements. Preparers are informed that if the mandatory disclosures required are not enough to meet the disclosure objective, additional information should be disclosed as necessary to meet that objective. *[IFRS 17.94]*.

An entity should aggregate or disaggregate information so that useful information is not obscured either by the inclusion of a large amount of insignificant detail or by the aggregation of items that have different characteristics. *[IFRS 17.95]*.

Preparers are also reminded of the requirements in IAS 1 relating to materiality and aggregation of information (see Chapter 3 at 4.1.5.A). IFRS 17 states that examples of aggregation bases that might be appropriate for information disclosed about insurance contracts are: *[IFRS 17.96]*

- type of contract (for example, major product lines);
- geographical area (for example, country or region); or
- reportable segment, as defined in IFRS 8 – *Operating Segments*.

16.1 Explanation of recognised amounts

The first part of the disclosure objective established by the standard is that an entity should disclose qualitative and quantitative information about the amounts recognised in its financial statements for contracts within its scope. *[IFRS 17.93]*.

The principal method by which the disclosure objective is achieved is by the disclosure of reconciliations that show how the net carrying amounts of contracts within the scope of IFRS 17 changed during the period because of cash flows and income and expenses recognised in the statement(s) of financial performance. Separate reconciliations should be disclosed for insurance contracts issued and reinsurance contracts held. An entity should adapt the requirements of the reconciliations described below to reflect the features of reinsurance contracts held that differ from insurance contracts issued; for example, the generation of expenses or reduction in expenses rather than revenue. *[IFRS 17.98]*.

Enough information should be provided in the reconciliations to enable users of financial statements to identify changes from cash flows and amounts that are recognised in the statement(s) of financial performance. To comply with this requirement, an entity should: *[IFRS 17.99]*

- disclose, in a table, the reconciliations set out at 16.1.1 to 16.1.2 below; and
- for each reconciliation, present the net carrying amounts at the beginning and at the end of the period, disaggregated into a total for portfolios of contracts that are assets and a total for portfolios of contracts that are liabilities, that equal the amounts presented in the statement of financial position as set out at 14 above.

The objective of the reconciliations detailed in 16.1.1 to 16.1.2 below is to provide different types of information about the insurance service result. *[IFRS 17.102]*.

16.1.1 Reconciliations required for contracts applying the general model

These reconciliations are required for all contracts other than those to which the premium allocation approach is applied including contracts with direct participation features.

Firstly, an entity must provide overall reconciliations from the opening to the closing balances separately for each of: *[IFRS 17.100]*

- the net liabilities (or assets) for the remaining coverage component, excluding any loss component;
- any loss component (see 8.8 above); and
- the liabilities for incurred claims.

Within the overall reconciliations above, an entity should separately disclose each of the following amounts related to services, if applicable: *[IFRS 17.103]*

- insurance revenue;
- insurance service expenses, showing separately:
  - incurred claims (excluding investment components) and other incurred insurance service expenses;

- amortisation of insurance acquisition cash flows;
- changes that relate to past service, i.e. changes in fulfilment cash flows relating to the liability for incurred claims; and
- changes that relate to future service, i.e. losses on onerous groups of contracts and reversals of such losses; and

• investment components excluded from insurance revenue and insurance service expenses (combined with refunds of premiums unless refunds of premiums are presented as part of the cash flows in the period).

Below is an example of this overall reconciliation, based on an illustrative disclosure in the IASB's *IFRS 17 Effects Analysis*.

Figure 56.2   Movements in insurance contract liabilities analysed between the liability for remaining coverage and the liabilities for incurred claims.

	Liability for remaining coverage		Liabilities for incurred claims	Total
	Excluding onerous contracts component	Onerous contracts component		
Insurance contract liabilities 2023	161,938	15,859	1,021	178,818
Insurance revenue	(9,856)	–	–	(9,856)
Insurance services expenses	1,259	(623)	7,985	8,621
Incurred claims and other expenses	–	(840)	7,945	7,105
Acquisition expenses	1,259	–	–	1,259
Changes that relate to future service: loss on onerous contracts and reversals of those losses	–	217	–	217
Changes that relate to past service: changes to liability for incurred claims	–	–	40	40
Investment components	(6,465)	–	6,465	–
Insurance service result	(15,062)	(623)	14,450	(1,235)
Insurance finance expenses	8,393	860	55	9,308
Total changes in the statement of comprehensive income	(6,669)	237	14,505	8,073
Cash flows				
Premiums received	33,570	–	–	33,570
Claims, benefits and other expenses paid	–	–	(14,336)	(14,336)
Acquisition cash flows paid	(401)	–	–	(401)
Total cash flows	33,169	–	(14,336)	18,833
Insurance contract liabilities 2024	188,438	16,096	1,190	205,724

Secondly, an entity should also disclose reconciliations from the opening to the closing balances separately for each of: *[IFRS 17.101]*
- the estimates of the present value of the future cash flows;
- the risk adjustment for non-financial risk; and
- the contractual service margin.

Within these reconciliations, an entity should disclose the following amounts related to services, if applicable: *[IFRS 17.104]*
- changes that relate to future service, showing separately:
  - changes in estimates that adjust the contractual service margin;
  - changes in estimates that do not adjust the contractual service margin, i.e. losses on groups of onerous contracts and reversals of such losses; and
  - the effects of contracts initially recognised in the period.
- changes that relate to current service, i.e.:
  - the amount of the contractual service margin recognised in profit or loss to reflect the transfer of services;
  - the change in the risk adjustment for non-financial risk that does not relate to future service or past service; and
  - experience adjustments, excluding amounts relating to the risk adjustment for non-financial risk included above; and
- changes that relate to past service, i.e. changes in fulfilment cash flows relating to incurred claims.

In April 2019, the IASB staff considered a submission to the TRG which asked whether a gross disclosure should be made of the component parts which make up the changes that relate to future service. In the example submitted there was a premium experience adjustment related to future service that would increase a loss component and a change in fulfilment cash flows related to future service that would decrease a loss component. The IASB staff observed that IFRS 17 requires an entity to provide disclosure of changes that relate to future service separately from those related to current or past service and in the example submitted all changes relate to future service. In other words, no sub-analysis of the changes that relate to future service was required for the example included in the submission.[95]

Figure 56.3 contains an example of these reconciliations, based on an illustrative disclosure in the IASB's *IFRS 17 Effects Analysis*.

Figure 56.3 Movements in insurance contract liabilities analysed by components.

	Estimates of the present value of future cash flows	Risk adjustment	Contractual service margin	Total
Insurance contract liabilities 2023	163,962	5,998	8,858	178,818
Changes that relate to current service	35	(604)	(923)	(1,492)
Contractual service margin recognised for service period	–	–	(923)	(923)
Risk adjustment recognised for the risk expired	–	(604)	–	(604)
Experience adjustments	35	–	–	35
Changes that relate to future service	(784)	1,117	(116)	217
Contracts initially recognised in the period	(2,329)	1,077	1,375	123
Changes in estimates reflected in the contractual service margin	1,452	39	(1,491)	–
Changes in estimates that result in onerous contract losses	93	1	–	94
Changes that relate to past service	47	(7)	–	40
Adjustments to liabilities for incurred claims	47	(7)	–	40
Insurance service result	(702)	506	(1,039)	(1,235)
Insurance finance expenses	9,087	–	221	9,308
Total changes in the statement of comprehensive income	8,385	506	(818)	8,073
Cash flows	18,833	–	–	18,833
Insurance contract liabilities 2024	191,180	6,504	8,040	205,724

In April 2019, the IASB staff responded to a TRG submission which asked whether changes disclosed as relating to past service in an interim reporting period, when an entity did not change its treatment of accounting estimates made in previous interim financial statements when applying IFRS 17 in subsequent interim reporting periods or in the annual reporting period (see 15.4 above), should be disclosed in the reconciliations above as changes relating to current service in the annual reporting. The IASB staff stated the amounts disclosed in the reconciliations above reflected the amounts included in the measurement of insurance contracts and that the description of the amount as relating to past or current service does not affect the measurement.[96]

In addition, to complete the reconciliations above, an entity should also disclose separately each of the following amounts not related to services provided in the period, if applicable: [IFRS 17.105]

- cash flows in the period, including:
  - premiums received for insurance contracts issued (or paid for reinsurance contracts held);
  - insurance acquisition cash flows; and
  - incurred claims paid and other insurance service expenses paid for insurance contracts issued (or recovered under reinsurance contracts held), excluding insurance acquisition cash flows;
- the effect of changes in the risk of non-performance by the issuer of reinsurance contracts held;
- insurance finance income or expenses; and
- any additional line items that may be necessary to understand the change in the net carrying amount of the insurance contracts.

When an entity recognises an asset for insurance acquisition cash flows paid for existing or future groups of insurance contracts before those insurance contracts are recognised (see 6.3 above), an entity should disclose a reconciliation from the opening to the closing balance of assets recognised for those insurance acquisition cash flows. The information should be aggregated at a level which is consistent with that for the other reconciliations of insurance contracts discussed above. [IFRS 17.105A].

The reconciliation of the insurance acquisition cash flows above should disclose separately any recognition of impairment losses and reversals of impairment losses of the insurance acquisition cash flow assets. [IFRS 17.105B].

In respect of insurance revenue recognised in the period, entities need to provide the following analysis: [IFRS 17.106]

- the amounts relating to the changes in the liability for remaining coverage as discussed at 15.1.1 above, separately disclosing:
  - the insurance service expenses incurred during the period;
  - the change in the risk adjustment for non-financial risk;
  - the amount of the contractual service margin recognised in profit or loss because of the transfer of insurance contract services in the period; and
  - other amounts, if any, for example experience adjustments for premium receipts other than those that relate to future service.
- the allocation of the portion of the premiums that relate to the recovery of insurance acquisition cash flows.

Figure 56.4 contains an example of this insurance revenue analysis, based on an illustrative disclosure in the IASB's *IFRS 17 Effects Analysis*.

Figure 56.4   Analysis of insurance revenue.

	2023
Amounts related to liabilities for remaining coverage	8,597
Expected incurred claims and other expenses	7,070
Contractual service margin for the service provided	923
Risk adjustment for the risk expired	604
Recovery of acquisition cash flows	1,259
Insurance revenue	9,856

The effect on the statement of financial position for insurance contracts issued and reinsurance contracts held that are initially recognised in the period should be shown separately, disclosing the effect at initial recognition on: [IFRS 17.107]

- the estimates of the present value of future cash outflows, showing separately the amount of the insurance acquisition cash flows;
- the estimates of the present value of future cash inflows;
- the risk adjustment for non-financial risk; and
- the contractual service margin.

In the reconciliation showing the effect of insurance contracts issued and reinsurance contracts held, there should be separate disclosure of: [IFRS 17.108]

- contracts acquired from other entities in transfers of insurance contracts or business combinations; and
- groups of contracts that are onerous.

Below is an example of this analysis, based on an illustrative disclosure in the IASB's *IFRS 17 Effects Analysis*. The example shows insurance contracts issued only for an entity which has not acquired contracts in the period via transfers or business combinations.

Figure 56.5   Analysis of contracts initially recognised in the period.

Contracts initially recognised in 2023		Of which contracts acquired	Of which onerous contracts
Estimates of the present value of futures cash inflows	(33,570)	(19,155)	(1,716)
Estimates of the present value of future cash outflows			
Insurance acquisition cash flows	401	122	27
Claims payable and other expenses	30,840	17,501	1,704
Risk adjustment	1,077	658	108
Contractual service margin	1,375	896	–
Total	123	22	123

Additionally, an entity should disclose when it expects to recognise the contractual service margin remaining at the end of the reporting period in profit or loss *quantitatively* (emphasis added) in appropriate time bands. Such information should be provided separately for insurance contracts issued and reinsurance contracts held. [IFRS 17.109].

An entity is also required to disclose quantitatively, in appropriate time bands, when it expects to derecognise an asset for insurance acquisition cash flows. [IFRS 17.109A].

16.1.2 Disclosures and reconciliations required for contracts applying the premium allocation approach

16.1.2.A Accounting policies adopted for contracts applying the premium allocation approach

When an entity uses the premium allocation approach it must disclose the following: [IFRS 17.97]

- which of the criteria for the use of the premium allocation approach for insurance contracts issued and reinsurance contracts held it has satisfied;
- whether it makes an adjustment for the time value of money and the effect of financial risk for the liability for remaining coverage and the liability for incurred claims; and
- whether it recognises insurance acquisition cash flows as expenses when it incurs those costs or whether it amortises insurance acquisition cash flows over the coverage period.

These choices are discussed at 9.1 and 9.4 above.

16.1.2.B Reconciliations required for contracts applying the premium allocation approach

The reconciliations described below apply to contracts using the premium allocation approach. Most also apply for contracts using the general model – see 16.1.1 above. As with the general model, for each reconciliation, an entity should present the net carrying amounts at the beginning and at the end of the period, disaggregated into a total for portfolios of contracts that are assets and a total for portfolios of contracts that are liabilities, that equal the amounts presented in the statement of financial position as set out at 14 above. [IFRS 17.99].

Overall reconciliations from the opening to the closing balances are required separately for each of: [IFRS 17.100]

- the net liabilities (or assets) for the remaining coverage component, excluding any loss component;
- any loss component (see 8.8 above); and
- the liabilities for incurred claims with separate reconciliations for:
  - the estimates of the present value of the future cash flows; and
  - the risk adjustment for non-financial risk.

Within the overall reconciliations above, separate disclosure of each of the following amounts related to services, if applicable: *[IFRS 17.103]*

- insurance revenue;
- insurance service expenses, showing separately:
  - incurred claims (excluding investment components) and other incurred insurance service expenses;
  - amortisation of insurance acquisition cash flows;
  - changes that relate to past service, i.e. changes in fulfilment cash flows relating to the liability for incurred claims; and
  - changes that relate to future service, i.e. losses on onerous groups of contracts and reversals of such losses; and
- investment components excluded from insurance revenue and insurance service expenses (combined with refunds of premiums unless refunds of premiums are presented as part of the cash flows in the period).

Disclosure is also required of each of the following amounts that are not related to services provided in the period, if applicable: *[IFRS 17.105]*

- cash flows in the period, including:
  - premiums received for insurance contracts issued (or paid for reinsurance contracts held);
  - insurance acquisition cash flows; and
  - incurred claims paid and other insurance service expenses paid for insurance contracts issued (or recovered under reinsurance contracts held), excluding insurance acquisition cash flows;
- the effect of changes in the risk of non-performance by the issuer of reinsurance contracts held;
- insurance finance income or expenses; and
- any additional line items that may be necessary to understand the change in the net carrying amount of the insurance contracts.

The disclosures required when an entity recognises an asset for acquisition cash flows paid for existing or future groups of insurance contracts before those insurance contracts are recognised insurance acquisition cash flow assets also apply to contracts accounted for under the premium allocation approach (see 16.1.1 above).

16.1.3 Insurance finance income or expenses

The total amount of insurance finance income or expenses in the reporting period should be disclosed and explained. In particular, an entity should explain the relationship between insurance finance income or expenses and the investment return on its assets, to enable users of its financial statements to evaluate the sources of finance income or expenses recognised in profit or loss and other comprehensive income. *[IFRS 17.110]*.

Specifically, for contracts with direct participation features, an entity should:
- Describe the composition of the underlying items and disclose their fair value. *[IFRS 17.111]*.
- Disclose the effect of any adjustment to the contractual service margin in the current period as a result of the application of risk mitigation whereby a choice has been made not to adjust the contractual service margin to reflect some or all of the changes in the effect of financial risk on the entity's share of underlying items for the effect of the time value of money and financial risks not arising from the underlying items, (see 11.2.6 above). *[IFRS 17.112]*.
- Disclose, in the period when an entity changes the basis of disaggregation of insurance finance income or expense between profit or loss and other comprehensive income because of a change in whether it holds the underlying items (see 15.3.4 above): *[IFRS 17.113]*
    - the reason why the entity was required to change the basis of aggregation;
    - the amount of any adjustment for each financial statement line item affected; and
    - the carrying amount of the group of insurance contracts to which the change applied at the date of the change.

16.2 Transition amounts

An entity should provide disclosures that enable users of financial statements to identify the effect of groups of insurance contracts measured at the transition date applying the modified retrospective approach (see 17.4 below) or the fair value approach (see 17.5 below) on the contractual service margin and insurance revenue in subsequent periods. As a result, IFRS 17 requires various disclosures that must continue to be made each reporting period until the contracts which exist at transition have expired or been extinguished.

Hence an entity should disclose the reconciliation of the contractual service margin and the amount of insurance revenue required at 16.1.1 above separately for: *[IFRS 17.114]*
- insurance contracts that existed at the transition date to which the entity has applied the modified retrospective approach;
- insurance contracts that existed at the transition date to which the entity has applied the fair value approach; and
- all other insurance contracts (i.e. including those to which the entity has accounted for fully retrospectively).

In addition, for all periods in which disclosures are made for contracts which, on transition, were accounted for using either the modified retrospective approach or the fair value approach, an entity should explain how it determined the measurement of insurance contracts at the transition date. The purpose of this is to enable users of financial statements to understand the nature and significance of the methods used and judgements applied in determining the transition amounts. *[IFRS 17.115]*.

An entity that chooses to disaggregate insurance finance income or expenses between profit or loss and other comprehensive income applies the requirements discussed at 17.4 below (for the modified retrospective approach) or 17.5 below (for the fair value approach) to determine the cumulative difference between the insurance finance income or expenses that would have been recognised in profit or loss and the total insurance finance income or expenses at the transition date for the groups of insurance contracts to which the disaggregation applies. For all periods in which amounts determined by applying these transitional approaches exist, the entity should disclose a reconciliation of the opening to the closing balance of the cumulative amounts included in other comprehensive income for financial assets measured at fair value through other comprehensive income related to the groups of insurance contracts. The reconciliation should include, for example, gains or losses recognised in other comprehensive income in the period and gains or losses previously recognised in other comprehensive income in previous periods reclassified in the period to profit or loss. *[IFRS 17.116]*.

16.3 Significant judgements made in applying IFRS 17

IAS 1 requires that an entity should disclose the judgements that management has made in the process of applying the entity's accounting policies and that have the most significant effect on the amounts recognised in the financial statements. *[IAS 1.122]*.

Consistent with IAS 1, the second part of the disclosure objective established by IFRS 17 is that an entity should disclose the significant judgements and changes in judgements made by an entity in applying the standard. *[IFRS 17.93(b)]*.

Specifically, an entity should disclose the inputs, assumptions and estimation techniques used, including: *[IFRS 17.117]*

- the methods used to measure insurance contracts within the scope of IFRS 17 and the processes for estimating the inputs to those methods. Unless impracticable, an entity should also provide quantitative information about those inputs;
- any changes in the methods and processes for estimating inputs used to measure contracts, the reason for each change, and the type of contracts affected;
- to the extent not covered above, the approach used:
  - to distinguish changes in estimates of future cash flows arising from the exercise of discretion from other changes in estimates of future cash flows for contracts without direct participation features;
  - to determine the risk adjustment for non-financial risk, including whether changes in the risk adjustment for non-financial risk are disaggregated into an insurance service component and an insurance finance component or are presented in full in the insurance service result;
  - to determine discount rates;
  - to determine investment components; and
  - to determine the relative weighting of the benefits provided by insurance coverage and investment-return service (for insurance contracts without direct participation features) or insurance coverage and investment-related service (for insurance contracts with direct participation features).

If, an entity chooses to disaggregate insurance finance income or expenses into amounts presented in profit or loss and amounts presented in other comprehensive income (see 15.3.1 to 15.3.4 above), the entity should disclose an explanation of the methods used to determine the insurance finance income or expenses recognised in profit or loss. *[IFRS 17.118]*.

An entity should also disclose the confidence level used to determine the risk adjustment for non-financial risk. If the entity uses a technique other than the confidence level technique for determining the risk adjustment for non-financial risk, it should disclose: *[IFRS 17.119]*

- the technique used; and
- the confidence level corresponding to the results of that technique.

An entity should disclose the yield curve (or range of yield curves) used to discount cash flows that do not vary based on the returns on underlying items. When an entity provides this disclosure in aggregate for a number of groups of insurance contracts, it should provide such disclosures in the form of weighted averages, or relatively narrow ranges. *[IFRS 17.120]*.

16.4 Disclosure of accounting policies

Unlike IFRS 4, IFRS 17 does not contain an explicit requirement for an insurer's accounting policies for insurance contracts and related liabilities, income and expense to be disclosed. However, IAS 1 requires an entity to disclose its significant accounting policies comprising: *[IAS 1.117]*

- the measurement basis (or bases) used in preparing the financial statements; and
- the other accounting policies used that are relevant to an understanding of the financial statements.

In addition, certain specific disclosures concerning accounting policy choices in respect of discounting and insurance acquisition cash flows are required when the premium allocation approach is used (see 16.1.2.A above).

IFRS 17 contains a number of specific accounting policy elections, the exercise of which (or not) may be relevant to an understanding of the financial statements. Some of these are contained in the table below. Accounting policy elections applicable only on transition are discussed at 17 below.

Accounting policy choice	*Unit of Account*	*Revocable?*
Election to apply IFRS 17 or IAS 32/IFRS 9 to financial guarantee contracts if previously asserted to be insurance contracts (see 2.3.1.E above)	Individual contract	No
Election to apply either IFRS 15 or IFRS 17 to certain fixed-fee service contracts (see 2.3.2 above)	Individual contract	No
Election to apply either IFRS 17 or IFRS 9 to certain loan contracts that only transfer insurance risk on settlement (see 2.3.3 above)	Accounting policy choice at level of portfolio of contracts	No
Period of cohort – group of contracts can be grouped into any period of one year or less (see 5.2.1 above)	IAS 8 accounting policy choice	IAS 8 applies

Accretion of interest on insurance acquisition cash flows – voluntary election (see 8.3 above)	IAS 8 applies	IAS 8 applies
Use of the premium allocation approach (see 9 above)	Group of contracts	No – unless contract modified (see 12.1 above).
Premium allocation approach – election to expense insurance acquisition cash flows as incurred for contracts where coverage period of each contract in group is no more than one year as opposed to including within the liability for remaining coverage (see 9.1 above)	Group of contracts	IAS 8 applies
Premium allocation approach – election to not adjust the liability for remaining coverage to reflect the time value of money and effect of financial risk if, on initial recognition the time between providing services and premium due date is no more than one year (see 9.1 above).	IAS 8 applies	IAS 8 applies
Premium allocation approach – election to not adjust the liability for incurred claims to reflect the time value of money and effect of financial risk if the cash flows are expected to be paid or received in one year or less from the date the claims are incurred (see 9.4 above).	IAS 8 applies	Yes – if eligibility criteria failed in subsequent periods
Use of risk mitigation for eligible contracts applying the variable fee approach (see. 11.2.5 above)	Group of contracts	If, and only if, conditions cease to apply (see 11.2.5).
Present changes in the risk adjustment for non-financial risk in insurance service expenses or disaggregate between insurance service expenses and insurance finance income or expenses (see 15.2 above)	Apply IAS 8 as no specific guidance	Yes – provided change satisfies IAS 8 criteria.
Present insurance finance income or expenses in profit or loss or disaggregate between profit or loss and other comprehensive income (see 15.3.1 above)	Portfolio of contracts	Yes – provided change satisfies IAS 8 criteria. If underlying items now held or no longer held by variable fee approach change is compulsory (see 15.3.4 above).
Election as to whether to change the treatment of accounting estimates made in previous interim financial statements when applying IFRS 17 in subsequent interim financial statements and in the annual reporting period (see 15.4 above)	Reporting entity	Yes – provided change satisfies IAS 8 criteria.
Net or gross presentation of reinsurance held in profit or loss (see 15 above)	Reporting entity	Yes – provided change satisfies IAS 8 criteria.

16.5 Nature and extent of risks arising from contracts within the scope of IFRS 17

The third part of the disclosure objective established by the standard is that an entity should disclose the nature and extent of the risks from contracts within the scope of IFRS 17. *[IFRS 17.93]*.

To comply with this objective, an entity should disclose information that enables users of its financial statements to evaluate the nature, amount, timing and uncertainty of future cash flows that arise from contracts within the scope of IFRS 17. *[IFRS 17.121]*.

The disclosures detailed below are considered to be those that would normally be necessary to meet this requirement. These disclosures focus on the insurance and financial risks that arise from insurance contracts and how they have been managed. Financial risks typically include, but are not limited to, credit risk, liquidity risk and market risk. *[IFRS 17.122]*. Many similar disclosures were contained in IFRS 4, often phrased to the effect that an insurer should make disclosures about insurance contracts assuming that insurance contracts were within the scope of IFRS 7. The equivalent disclosures required by IFRS 17 are tailored to the recognition and measurement of the standard and do not cross-refer to IFRS 7.

For each type of risk arising from contracts within the scope of IFRS 17, an entity should disclose: *[IFRS 17.124]*

- the exposures to risks and how they arise;
- the entity's objectives, policies and processes for managing the risks and the methods used to measure the risks; and
- any changes in the above from the previous period.

An entity should also disclose, for each type of risk: *[IFRS 17.125]*

- summary quantitative information about its exposure to that risk at the end of the reporting period. This disclosure should be based on the information provided internally to the entity's key management personnel; and
- the disclosures detailed at 16.5.1 to 16.5.5 below, to the extent not provided by the summary quantitative information required above.

If the information disclosed about an entity's exposure to risk at the end of the reporting period is not representative of its exposure to risk during the period, the entity should disclose that fact, the reason why the period-end exposure is not representative, and further information that is representative of its risk exposure during the period. *[IFRS 17.123]*.

Disclosure of an entity's objectives, policies and processes for managing risks and the methods used to manage the risk provides an additional perspective that complements information about contracts outstanding at a particular time and might include information about:

- the structure and organisation of the entity's risk management function(s), including a discussion of independence and accountability;
- the scope and nature of its risk reporting or measurement systems, such as internal risk measurement models, sensitivity analyses, scenario analysis, and stress testing, and how these are integrated into the entity's operating activities. Useful disclosures might include a summary description of the approach used, associated assumptions and parameters (including confidence intervals, computation frequencies and historical observation periods) and strengths and limitations of the approach;

- the processes for accepting, measuring, monitoring and controlling insurance risks and the entity's underwriting strategy to ensure that there are appropriate risk classification and premium levels;
- the extent to which insurance risks are assessed and managed on an entity-wide basis;
- the methods employed to limit or transfer insurance risk exposures and avoid undue concentrations of risk, such as retention limits, inclusion of options in contracts, and reinsurance;
- asset and liability management (ALM) techniques; and
- the processes for managing, monitoring and controlling commitments received (or given) to accept (or contribute) additional debt or equity capital when specified events occur.

Additionally, it might be useful to provide disclosures both for individual types of risks insured and overall. These disclosures might include a combination of narrative descriptions and specific quantified data, as appropriate to the nature of the contracts and their relative significance to the insurer.

Quantitative information about exposure to insurance risk might include:

- information about the nature of the risk covered, with a brief summary description of the class (such as annuities, pensions, other life insurance, motor, property and liability);
- information about the general nature of participation features whereby policyholders share in the performance (and related risks) of individual contracts or pools of contracts or entities. This might include the general nature of any formula for the participation and the extent of any discretion held by the insurer; and
- information about the terms of any obligation or contingent obligation for the insurer to contribute to government or other guarantee funds established by law which are within the scope of IAS 37.

16.5.1 Concentrations of risk

An entity should disclose information about concentrations of risk arising from contracts within the scope of IFRS 17, including a description of how the entity determines the concentrations, and a description of the shared characteristic that identifies each concentration (for example, the type of insured event, industry, geographical area, or currency).

It is further explained that concentrations of financial risk might arise, for example, from interest-rate guarantees that come into effect at the same level for a large number of contracts. Concentrations of financial risk might also arise from concentrations of non-financial risk; for example, if an entity provides product liability protection to pharmaceutical companies and also holds investments in those companies (i.e. a sectoral concentration). *[IFRS 17.127]*.

Other concentrations could arise from, for example:

- a single insurance contract, or a small number of related contracts, for example when an insurance contract covers low-frequency, high-severity risks such as earthquakes;
- single incidents that expose an insurer to risk under several different types of insurance contract. For example, a major terrorist incident could create exposure

under life insurance contracts, property insurance contracts, business interruption and civil liability;
- exposure to unexpected changes in trends, for example unexpected changes in human mortality or in policyholder behaviour;
- exposure to possible major changes in financial market conditions that could cause options held by policyholders to come into the money. For example, when interest rates decline significantly, interest rate and annuity guarantees may result in significant losses;
- significant litigation or legislative risks that could cause a large single loss, or have a pervasive effect on many contracts;
- correlations and interdependencies between different risks;
- significant non-linearities, such as stop-loss or excess of loss features, especially if a key variable is close to a level that triggers a material change in future cash flows; and
- geographical concentrations.

Disclosure of concentrations of insurance risk might include a description of the shared characteristic that identifies each concentration and an indication of the possible exposure, both before and after reinsurance held, associated with all insurance liabilities sharing that characteristic.

Disclosure about the historical performance of low-frequency, high-severity risks might be one way to help users assess cash flow uncertainty associated with those risks. For example, an insurance contract may cover an earthquake that is expected to happen, on average, once every 50 years. If the earthquake occurs during the current reporting period the insurer will report a large loss. If the earthquake does not occur during the current reporting period the insurer will report a profit. Without adequate disclosure of long-term historical performance, it could be misleading to report 49 years of large profits, followed by one large loss, because users may misinterpret the insurer's long-term ability to generate cash flows over the complete cycle of 50 years. Therefore, describing the extent of the exposure to risks of this kind and the estimated frequency of losses might be useful. If circumstances have not changed significantly, disclosure of the insurer's experience with this exposure may be one way to convey information about estimated frequencies. However, there is no specific requirement to disclose a probable maximum loss (PML) in the event of a catastrophe.

16.5.2 Insurance and market risks – sensitivity analysis

An entity should disclose information about sensitivities to changes in risk variables arising from contracts within the scope of IFRS 17. To comply with this requirement, an entity should disclose: *[IFRS 17.128]*
- a sensitivity analysis that shows how profit or loss and equity would have been affected by changes in risk variables that were reasonably possible at the end of the reporting period:
    - for insurance risk – showing the effect for insurance contracts issued, before and after risk mitigation by reinsurance contracts held; and

- for each type of market risk – in a way that explains the relationship between the sensitivities to changes in risk variables arising from insurance contracts and those arising from financial assets held by the entity.
- the methods and assumptions used in preparing the sensitivity analysis; and
- changes from the previous period in the methods and assumptions used in preparing the sensitivity analysis, and the reasons for such changes.

Market risk comprises three types of risk: currency risk, interest rate risk and other price risk. *[IFRS 7 Appendix A]*.

If an entity prepares a sensitivity analysis (e.g. an embedded value analysis) that shows how amounts different from those above are affected by changes in risk variables and uses that sensitivity analysis to manage risks arising from contracts within the scope of IFRS 17, it may use that sensitivity analysis in place of the analysis specified above. The entity should also disclose: *[IFRS 17.129]*

- an explanation of the method used in preparing such a sensitivity analysis and of the main parameters and assumptions underlying the information provided; and
- an explanation of the objective of the method used and of any limitations that may result in the information provided.

16.5.3 Insurance risk – claims development

An entity should disclose actual claims compared with previous estimates of the undiscounted amount of the claims (i.e. claims development). The disclosure about claims development should start with the period when the earliest material claim(s) arose and for which there is still uncertainty about the amount and timing of the claims payments at the end of the reporting period; but the disclosure is not required to start more than 10 years before the end of the reporting period (although there is transitional relief for first-time adopters – see 17.2.1.A below). An entity is not required to disclose information about the development of claims for which uncertainty about the amount and timing of the claims payments is typically resolved within one year. *[IFRS 17.130]*.

An entity should reconcile the disclosure about claims development with the aggregate carrying amount of the groups of insurance contracts which comprise the liabilities for incurred claims (see 16.1.1 and 16.1.2 above). *[IFRS 17.130]*. Hence, only incurred claims are required to be compared with previous estimates and not any amounts within the liability for remaining coverage. In this context incurred claims appears to include those arising from reinsurance contracts held as well as those arising from insurance and reinsurance contracts issued. *[IFRS 17.100]*.

These requirements apply to incurred claims arising from all models (i.e. general model, premium allocation approach and variable fee approach). However, because insurers need not disclose the information about claims for which uncertainty about the amount and timing of payments is typically resolved within a year, it is unlikely that many life insurers will need to give the disclosure.

The claims development table is required to be shown undiscounted. Hence, any discounting adjustment will be a reconciling item between the claims development table and the carrying amount of the liability for incurred claims. In addition, given the long tail nature of many non-life insurance claims liabilities, it is likely that many non-life insurers will still have claims outstanding at the reporting date that are more than ten years old and which will also need to be included in a reconciliation of the claims development table to the carrying amount of the liability for incurred claims.

IFRS 17 does not contain an illustrative example of a claims development table (or, indeed, specifically require disclosure in a tabular format). The example below is based on an illustrative example contained in the Implementation Guidance to IFRS 4. This example, as a simplification for illustration purposes, presents five years of claims development information by underwriting year although the standard itself requires ten (subject to the transitional relief upon first-time adoption) and assumes no reinsurance held. Other formats are permitted, including for example, presenting information by accident year or reporting period rather than underwriting year.

Example 56.70: Disclosure of claims development

The top half of the table shows how the insurer's estimates of incurred claims for each underwriting year develop over time. For example, at the end of 2019, the insurer's estimate of the undiscounted liability for incurred claims that it would pay for insured events relating to insurance contracts underwritten in 2019 was €680. By the end of 2020, the insurer had revised the estimate of incurred claims (both those paid and those still to be paid) to €673.

The lower half of the table reconciles the cumulative incurred claims to the amount appearing in the statement of financial position. First, the cumulative payments are deducted to give the cumulative unpaid claims for each year on an undiscounted basis. Second, the effect of discounting is deducted to give the carrying amount in the statement of financial position.

Incurred claim year	2019 €	2020 €	2021 €	2022 €	2023 €	Total €
Estimate of incurred claims:						
At end of underwriting year	680	790	823	920	968	
One year later	673	785	840	903		
Two years later	692	776	845			
Three years later	697	771				
Four years later	702					
Estimate of incurred claims	702	771	845	903	968	
Cumulative payments	(702)	(689)	(570)	(350)	(217)	
	–	82	275	553	751	1,661
Effect of discounting	–	(14)	(68)	(175)	(265)	(562)
Liabilities for which uncertainty is expected to be settled within one year						20
Liabilities for incurred claims recognised in the statement of financial position	–	68	207	378	486	1,119

In addition, IFRS 17 does not address the presentation in the claims development table of:

- exchange differences associated with insurance liabilities arising on retranslation (e.g. whether previous years' incurred claims should be retranslated at the current reporting period date);
- claims liabilities acquired in a business combination or transfer (as discussed at 13.1 above, for contracts acquired in their settlement period, claims are incurred only when the financial effect becomes certain); and
- claims liabilities disposed of in a business disposal or transfer.

As IFRS 17 is silent on these matters, a variety of treatments would appear to be permissible provided they are adequately explained to the users of the financial statements and consistently applied in each reporting period.

16.5.4 Credit risk – other information

For credit risk that arises from contracts within the scope of IFRS 17, an entity should disclose: *[IFRS 17.131]*

- the amount that best represents its maximum exposure to credit risk at the end of the reporting period, separately for insurance contracts issued and reinsurance contracts held; and
- information about the credit quality of reinsurance contracts held that are assets.

Credit risk is defined in IFRS 7 as 'the risk that one party to a financial instrument will fail to discharge an obligation and cause the other party to incur a financial loss'. IFRS 17 provides no further detail about what is considered to be the maximum exposure to credit risk for an insurance contract or reinsurance contract held at the end of the reporting period (such as whether it is the maximum possible loss, the maximum expected loss or the fulfilment cash flows). The equivalent IFRS 7 requirement for financial instruments requires disclosure of credit risk gross of collateral or other credit enhancements. *[IFRS 7.35K(a)]*. However, IFRS 17 does not specify that the maximum credit risk should be disclosed gross of collateral or other credit enhancements.

Information about the credit quality of reinsurance could be provided by an analysis based on credit risk rating grades.

16.5.5 Liquidity risk – other information

For liquidity risk arising from contracts within the scope of IFRS 17, an entity should disclose: *[IFRS 17.132]*

- a description of how it manages the liquidity risk;
- separate maturity analyses for portfolios of insurance contracts issued that are liabilities and portfolios of reinsurance contracts held that are liabilities that show, as a minimum, net cash flows of the portfolios for each of the first five years after the reporting date and in aggregate beyond the first five years. An entity is not required to include in these analyses liabilities for remaining coverage measured applying the premium allocation approach. The analyses may take the form of:
    - an analysis, by estimated timing, of the remaining contractual undiscounted net cash flows; or
    - an analysis, by estimated timing, of the estimates of the present value of the future cash flows;
- the amounts that are payable on demand, explaining the relationship between such amounts and the carrying amount of the related portfolios of contracts, if not disclosed in the maturity analysis above.

There is no equivalent disclosure required for portfolios of insurance contracts and reinsurance contracts held that are in an asset position.

IFRS 7 does not contain an equivalent requirement to disclose 'amounts that are payable on demand' so the nature of this requirement in IFRS 17 is not entirely clear (i.e. whether it is intended to include gross liabilities payable at the reporting date in respect of portfolios of insurance contracts and reinsurance assets held that are assets or whether the requirement is intended to show only those net cash outflows payable at the reporting date included within the maturity analysis).

16.5.6 Regulatory disclosures

Most insurance entities are exposed to externally imposed capital requirements and therefore the IAS 1 disclosures in respect of these requirements are likely to be applicable.

Where an entity is subject to externally imposed capital requirements, disclosures are required of the nature of these requirements and how these requirements are incorporated into the management of capital. Disclosure of whether these requirements have been complied with in the reporting period is also required and, where they have not been complied with, the consequences of such non-compliance. [IAS 1.135].

Many insurance entities operate in several jurisdictions. Where an aggregate disclosure of capital requirements and how capital is managed would not provide useful information or distorts a financial statement user's understanding of an entity's capital resources, separate information should be disclosed for each capital requirement to which an entity is subject. [IAS 1.136].

In addition to the requirements of IAS 1, an entity should disclose information about the effect of the regulatory frameworks in which it operates; for example, minimum capital requirements or required interest-rate guarantees. [IFRS 17.126]. These extra disclosures do not contain an explicit requirement for an insurer to quantify its regulatory capital requirements. The IASB considered whether to add a requirement for insurers to quantify regulatory capital on the grounds that such disclosures might be useful for all entities operating in a regulated environment. However, the Board was concerned about developing such disclosures in isolation in a project on accounting for insurance contracts that would go beyond the existing requirements in IAS 1. Accordingly, the Board decided to limit the disclosures about regulation to those set out above. [IFRS 17.BC369-371].

Additionally, if an entity includes contracts within the same group which would have been in different groups only because law or regulation specifically constrains the entity's practical ability to set a different price or level of benefits for policyholders with different characteristics (see 6 above), it should disclose that fact. [IFRS 17.126].

16.5.7 Disclosures required by IFRS 7 and IFRS 13

Contracts within the scope of IFRS 17 are not excluded from the scope of IFRS 13 and therefore any of those contracts measured at fair value are also subject to the disclosures required by IFRS 13. In practice, this is unlikely as IFRS 17 does not require contracts within its scope to be measured at fair value. In addition, all contracts within the scope of IFRS 17 are excluded from the scope of IFRS 7. [IFRS 7.3(d)]. Under IFRS 4, investment contracts with a DPF were within the scope of IFRS 7.

However, IFRS 7 applies to: [IFRS 7.3(d)]

- derivatives that are embedded in contracts within the scope of IFRS 17, if IFRS 9 requires the entity to account for them separately; and
- investment components that are separated from contracts within the scope of IFRS 17, if IFRS 17 requires such separation.

16.5.8 Key performance indicators

IFRS 17 does not require disclosure of key performance indicators. However, such disclosures might be a useful way for an insurer to explain its financial performance during the period and to give an insight into the risks arising from insurance contracts.

17 EFFECTIVE DATE AND TRANSITION

17.1 Effective date

An entity should apply IFRS 17 for annual reporting periods beginning on or after 1 January 2023. *[IFRS 17.C1]*. When IFRS 17 is applied, IFRS 4 is withdrawn. *[IFRS 17.C34]*.

If an entity applies IFRS 17 earlier than reporting periods beginning on or after 1 January 2023 it should disclose that fact. However, early application is permitted only for entities that also apply IFRS 9 on or before the date of initial application of IFRS 17. *[IFRS 17.C1]*.

For the purposes of the transition requirements discussed at 17.2 below: *[IFRS 17.C2]*

- the date of initial application is the beginning of the annual reporting period in which an entity first applies IFRS 17 (i.e. 1 January 2023 for an entity first applying the standard with an annual reporting period ending 31 December 2023); and
- the transition date is the beginning of the annual reporting period immediately preceding the date of initial application (i.e. 1 January 2022 for an entity first applying the standard with an annual reporting period ending 31 December 2023 which reports only one comparative period).

17.2 Transition – general requirements

An entity should apply IFRS 17 retrospectively from the transition date unless: *[IFRS 17.C3]*
- impracticable; or
- the entity chooses to apply the fair value approach for a group of insurance contracts with direct participation features (to which it could apply IFRS 17 retrospectively) when risk mitigation has been applied prospectively to the group from the transition date and the entity has used derivatives, non-derivative financial instruments measured at fair value through profit or loss, or reinsurance contracts held to mitigate financial risk arising from that group of contracts before transition date. *[IFRS 17.C5A]*.

Notwithstanding the requirement for retrospective application, if it is impracticable (as defined in IAS 8), to apply IFRS 17 retrospectively for a group of insurance contracts, an entity should apply one of the two following approaches instead: *[IFRS 17.C5]*
- a modified retrospective approach (see 17.4 below); or
- a fair value approach (see 17.5 below).

An entity should also apply either the modified retrospective approach or the fair value approach to measure an asset for insurance acquisition cash flows if, and only if, it is impracticable to identify, recognise and measure any assets for insurance acquisition cash flows retrospectively. *[IFRS 17.C5B]*.

IAS 8 states that applying a requirement is 'impracticable' when an entity cannot apply it after making every reasonable effort to do so. *[IAS 8.5]*. Guidance on what impracticable means in the context of restatement of prior periods following a change in accounting policy is discussed in Chapter 3 at 4.7.

The Board permitted these alternative options to the full retrospective approach on the grounds that measuring the remaining amount of the contractual service margin for contracts acquired in prior periods, as well as the information needed in the statement of financial performance in subsequent periods, was likely to be challenging for preparers. This is because these amounts reflect a revision of estimates for all periods after the initial recognition of a group of contracts. *[IFRS 17.BC377]*. In the Board's opinion, measuring the following amounts needed for retrospective application would often be impracticable: *[IFRS 17.BC378]*

- the estimates of cash flows at the date of initial recognition;
- the risk adjustment for non-financial risk at the date of initial recognition;
- the changes in estimates that would have been recognised in profit or loss for each accounting period because they did not relate to future service, and the extent to which changes in the fulfilment cash flows would have been allocated to the loss component;
- the discount rates at the date of initial recognition; and
- the effect of changes in discount rates on estimates of future cash flows for contracts for which changes in financial assumptions have a substantial effect on the amounts paid to policyholders.

The choice of applying either a modified retrospective approach or a fair value approach exists separately for each group of insurance contracts when it is impracticable to apply IFRS 17 retrospectively to that group. An entity is permitted to use either of these two methods although use of the modified retrospective approach is conditional on the availability of reasonable and supportable information. *[IFRS 17.C6(a)]*.

Within the two permitted methods there are also measurement choices available depending on the level of prior year information. Consequently, there is likely to be considerable diversity of practice across entities in calculating the contractual service margin at transition date. In turn, this will result in potentially different releases of the contractual service margin (i.e. different profit) for similar types of contract in subsequent accounting periods. The Board has acknowledged that the choice of transition methods results in a lack of comparability of transition amounts. *[IFRS 17.BC373]*. This explains why the Board included a requirement for disclosures that track the effects of the modified retrospective approach and the fair value approach on the contractual service margin and insurance revenue in future periods (see 16.2 above).

It is observed in the Basis for Conclusions that no simplification has been provided for contracts that have been derecognised before transition. This is because the Board considers that reflecting the effect of contracts derecognised before the transition date on the remaining contractual service margin was necessary to provide a faithful representation of the remaining profit of the group of insurance contracts. *[IFRS 17.BC390]*.

An overview of the transition methods is illustrated below:

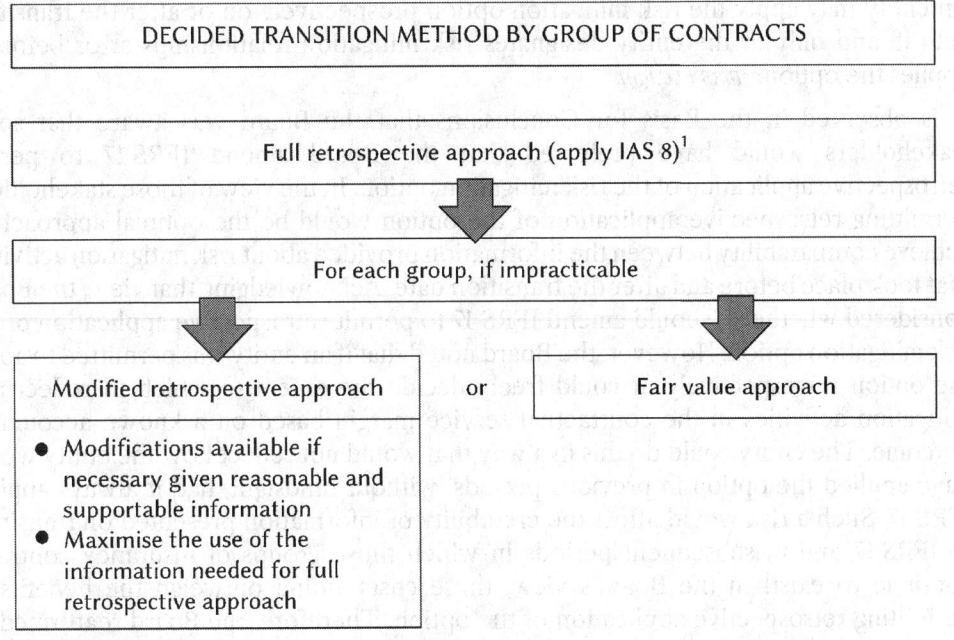

1 An entity eligible to apply the full retrospective approach can also elect to use the fair value approach for a group of insurance contracts with direct participation features when risk mitigation has been applied prospectively to the group from the transition date.

17.2.1 Transitional relief and prohibition – all entities

IFRS 17 provides disclosure exemptions for all entities, a prohibition from applying risk mitigation retrospectively prior to the transition date and measurement exemptions or modifications on transition. Consequential amendments to IFRS 3 provide transitional relief for business combinations within the scope of IFRS 3 prior to the date of initial application of IFRS 17.

17.2.1.A Disclosure relief

IFRS 17 contains the following disclosure relief on transition:

- An entity is exempt from the IAS 8 requirement to present the amount of the adjustment resulting from applying IFRS 17 affecting each financial line item to either the current period or each prior period presented and the impact of applying IFRS 17 in those periods on earnings per share. *[IFRS 17.C3(a)]*.

- An entity need not disclose previously unpublished information about claims development that occurred earlier than five years before the end of the annual reporting period in which it first applies IFRS 17 (i.e. information about claims that occurred prior to 1 January 2019 for an entity first applying the standard with an annual reporting period ending 31 December 2023). An entity that elects to take advantage of this disclosure relief should disclose that fact. *[IFRS 17.C28]*.

17.2.1.B Prohibition from applying risk mitigation prior to the transition date

An entity must not apply the risk mitigation option available for insurance contracts with direct participation features (see 11.2.5 above) before the transition date of IFRS 17. An entity may apply the risk mitigation option prospectively on or after the transition date if, and only if, the entity designates risk mitigation relationships at or before it applies the option. *[IFRS 17.C3(b)]*.

It is observed in the Basis for Conclusions that the Board was aware that some stakeholders would have preferred that the Board amend IFRS 17 to permit retrospective application of the risk mitigation option. In the view of those stakeholders, permitting retrospective application of the option would be the optimal approach to achieve comparability between the information provided about risk mitigation activities that took place before and after the transition date. Acknowledging that view, the Board considered whether it should amend IFRS 17 to permit retrospective application of the risk mitigation option. However, the Board noted that if an entity was permitted to apply the option retrospectively, it could freely decide the extent to which to reflect risk mitigation activities in the contractual service margin based on a known accounting outcome. The entity could do this in a way that would not reflect how the entity would have applied the option in previous periods, without hindsight, had it always applied IFRS 17. Such a risk would affect the credibility of information presented on transition to IFRS 17 and in subsequent periods in which those groups of insurance contracts continue to exist. In the Board's view, these costs would outweigh the benefits of permitting retrospective application of the option. Therefore, the Board reaffirmed its decision to prohibit retrospective application of the option because of the risk of the use of hindsight. *[IFRS 17.BC393C]*. Some stakeholders suggested alternative approaches that would avoid the risk of the use of hindsight. However, the Board also rejected these approaches as unworkable. *[IFRS 17.BC393D-E]*.

17.2.1.C Business combinations within the scope of IFRS 3

For contracts acquired in business combinations within the scope of IFRS 3 before the date of initial application of IFRS 17 an entity classifies and groups those contracts based on the contractual terms, economic conditions, operating or accounting policies or other factors as they existed at the date of initial recognition of those contracts rather than at the acquisition date of the business combination. *[IFRS 3.64N]*. This relief allows entities to continue to apply their previous IFRS 4 classification of contracts acquired in a business combination before the date of initial application of IFRS 17.

This relief applies only to business combinations. It does not apply to other transfers of contracts (e.g. portfolio transfers) that are not business combinations.

17.2.2 Disclosures about the effect of transition

At transition to IFRS 17, entities should provide the disclosures required by IAS 8 applicable to changes in accounting policies apart from the exemption discussed above (i.e. there is no requirement to present the amount of the adjustment resulting from applying IFRS 17 affecting each financial line item to either the current period or each prior period presented and the impact of applying IFRS 17 in those periods on earnings per share).

IAS 8 requires the following disclosures upon initial application of an IFRS: *[IAS 8.28]*

- the title of the IFRS (i.e. IFRS 17);
- a statement that the change in accounting policy is made in accordance with the transitional provisions;
- the nature of the change in accounting policy;
- where applicable, a description of the transitional provisions (which means that an entity would need to explain whether and how it had applied the retrospective, modified retrospective and fair value approaches);
- when applicable, the transitional provisions that might have an effect on future periods;
- the amount of any adjustment relating to periods prior to the accounting periods presented in the financial statements, to the extent practicable; and
- if retrospective application is impracticable, the circumstances that led to the existence of that condition and a description of how and from when the change in accounting policy is consistently applied.

In addition, as discussed at 16.2 above, entities are required to provide disclosures to enable users of the financial statements to identify the effects of groups of insurance contracts measured at transition date applying the modified retrospective approach or the fair value approach on the contractual service margin in subsequent periods. This information is provided in the form of reconciliations. In all periods for which disclosures are made for those contracts which used the modified retrospective or fair value approach on transition, an entity should continue to explain how it determined the measurement requirements at transition date.

17.3 Retrospective application of transition

When applying IFRS 17 retrospectively, an entity should: *[IFRS 17.C4]*

- identify, recognise and measure each group of insurance contracts as if IFRS 17 had always applied;
- identify, recognise and measure any assets for insurance acquisition cash flows as if IFRS 17 had always applied (except that an entity is not required to apply the recoverability assessment test discussed at 8.10 above before the transition date);
- derecognise any existing balances that would not exist had IFRS 17 always applied; and
- recognise any resulting net difference in equity.

The balances derecognised upon application of IFRS 17 would include balances recognised previously under IFRS 4 as well as items such as deferred acquisition costs, deferred origination costs (for investment contracts with discretionary participation features) and some intangible assets that relate solely to existing contracts. The requirement to recognise any net difference in equity means that no adjustment is made to the carrying amounts of goodwill from any previous business combination. *[IFRS 17.BC374]*. However, the value of contracts within the scope of IFRS 17 acquired in prior period business combinations or transfers would have to be adjusted by the acquiring entity from the date of acquisition (i.e. initial recognition) together with any intangible related to those in-force contracts. Any intangible asset derecognised would include an intangible asset that represented the difference between the fair value of insurance contracts acquired in a business combination or transfer and a liability measured in accordance with an insurer's previous accounting practices for insurance contracts where an insurer previously chose the option in IFRS 4 to use an expanded presentation that split the fair value of acquired insurance contracts into two components. *[IFRS 4.31]*.

Applying the standard retrospectively means that comparative period (i.e. the annual reporting period immediately preceding the date of initial application) must be restated and comparative disclosures made in full in the first year of application subject to the exemptions noted below. An entity may also present adjusted comparative information applying IFRS 17 for any earlier periods presented (i.e. any periods earlier than the annual reporting period immediately preceding the date of initial application) but is not required to do so. If an entity does present adjusted comparative information for any prior periods, the reference to 'the beginning of the annual reporting period immediately preceding the date of initial application' (see 17.1 above) should be read as 'the beginning of the earliest adjusted comparative period presented'. *[IFRS 17.C25]*. However, an entity is not required to provide the disclosures specified at 16 above for any period presented before the beginning of the annual accounting period immediately preceding the date of initial application. *[IFRS 17.C26]*. This relief is intended for entities which are required to present more than one comparative period in their annual financial statements.

If an entity presents unadjusted comparative information and disclosures for any earlier periods, it should clearly identify the information that has not been adjusted, disclose that it has been prepared on a different basis, and explain that basis. *[IFRS 17.C27]*.

The requirement to apply IFRS 17 retrospectively as if it has always applied means that an entity which elects not to change estimates made in previous interim financial statements (see 15.4 above) should estimate the contractual service margin for all individual interim periods previously presented, in order to get to a number for the contractual service margin that reflects that as if IFRS 17 had always been applied. *[IFRS 17.B137]*. This is based on the fact that only a fully retrospective interim contractual service margin roll-forward would provide the outcome that corresponds to a situation as if IFRS 17 had always been applied. Applying the standard retrospectively by an entity that issues interim financial statements may present significant additional operational challenges for insurers upon transition. This is because the contractual service margin for each interim reporting period subsequent to initial recognition of a group of contracts would need to be tracked and estimated in accordance with the requirements in IFRS 17 to determine the contractual service margin on transition date. Therefore, for entities applying the modified retrospective approach, transitional relief is available from this requirement (see 17.4 below).

The Basis for Conclusions observes that the IASB considered that some stakeholders implementing IFRS 17 thought that the inclusion of specified modifications in IFRS 17 implies that an entity cannot make estimates in applying IFRS 17 retrospectively. The Board noted that paragraph 51 of IAS 8, which states that '...the objective of estimates related to prior periods remains the same as estimates related to the current period, namely, for the estimates to reflect the circumstances that existed when the transaction, other event or condition occurred' specifically acknowledges the need for estimates in retrospective application and that this paragraph applies to entities applying IFRS 17 for the first time just as it does to entities applying other IFRS Standards for the first time. *[IFRS 17.BC380C]*.

In addition, some stakeholders suggested that the Board could reduce the burden of applying the transition requirements by specifying methods that can be used, for example, methods using information from embedded value reporting or information prepared for regulatory reporting purposes. However, the Board rejected this suggestion. The Board concluded that specifying methods would conflict with the approach in IFRS 17 of establishing measurement objectives that can be satisfied using different approaches. In particular situations, some methods may be more applicable, or may be easier to implement, and it would not be practicable for an IFRS Standard to specify in detail every situation in which particular methods would be appropriate. The appropriateness of any method depends on the particular facts and circumstances. Furthermore, specifying methods could risk incorrectly implying other methods that would satisfy the requirements of IFRS 17 cannot be used. *[IFRS 17.BC380D]*.

17.4 The modified retrospective approach

This approach contains a series of permitted modifications to retrospective application as follows: *[IFRS 17.C7]*

- assessment of insurance contracts or groups of insurance contracts that would have been made at the date of inception or initial recognition – see 17.4.1 below;
- amounts related to the contractual service margin or loss component for insurance contracts without direct participation features – see 17.4.2 below;
- amounts related to the contractual service margin or loss component for insurance contracts with direct participation features – see 17.4.3 below; and
- insurance finance income or expenses – see 17.4.4 below.

An entity is permitted to use each modification listed above only to the extent that it does not have reasonable and supportable information to apply a retrospective approach. *[IFRS 17.C8]*.

The objective of the modified retrospective approach is to achieve the closest outcome to retrospective application possible using reasonable and supportable information available without undue cost or effort. Accordingly, in applying this approach, an entity should: *[IFRS 17.C6]*

- use reasonable and supportable information. If the entity cannot obtain reasonable and supportable information necessary to apply the modified retrospective approach, it should apply the fair value approach; and
- maximise the use of information that would have been used to apply a fully retrospective approach but need only use information available without undue cost or effort.

'Undue cost and effort' is not defined in IFRS. However, the *IFRS for Small and Medium-sized Entities* states that considering whether obtaining or determining the information necessary to comply with a requirement would involve undue cost or effort depends on the entity's specific circumstances and on management's judgement of the costs and benefits from applying that requirement. This judgement requires consideration of how the economic decisions of those that are expected to use the financial statements could be affected by not having that information. Applying a requirement would involve undue cost or effort by a Small and Medium sized entity (SME) if the incremental cost (for example, valuers' fees) or additional effort (for example, endeavours by employees) substantially exceed the benefits those that are expected to use the SME's financial statements would receive from having the information. The Basis for Conclusions to the IFRS for SMEs further observes that:

- the undue cost or effort exemption is not intended to be a low hurdle. This is because an entity is required to carefully weigh the expected effects of applying the exemption on the users of the financial statements against the cost or effort of complying with the related requirement. In particular, the IASB observed that it would expect that if an entity already had, or could easily and inexpensively acquire, the information necessary to comply with a requirement, any related undue cost or effort exemption would not be applicable. This is because, in that case, the benefits to the users of the financial statements of having the information would be expected to exceed any further cost or effort by the entity; and
- that an entity must make a new assessment of whether a requirement will involve undue cost or effort at each reporting date.[97]

The IASB's Conceptual Framework also notes that although cost is a pervasive constraint on the information provided by financial reporting and that the cost of producing information must be justified by the benefits that it provides, the cost is ultimately borne by the users (not the preparers) and implies that any cost constraint should be seen from a user's viewpoint. See Chapter 2 at 5.3.

To use each modification, an entity must have the reasonable and supportable information necessary to apply that modification. If not, the entity is required to apply the fair value approach to the group of insurance contracts. The Basis for Conclusions observes that the Board expects that estimates will often be needed when applying a specified modification in the modified retrospective approach. [IFRS 17.BC380A, BC380C].

The Board considered feedback from entities implementing IFRS 17 that said the requirement to use reasonable and supportable information significantly increases the costs of applying the modified retrospective approach. The Board acknowledged that removing the requirements relating to the use of reasonable and supportable information might provide significant cost relief for those entities. However, the Board disagreed with suggestions to amend IFRS 17 in that regard because, in its view, entities should use information that is reasonable and supportable. Permitting an entity to use information that is not reasonable and supportable would undermine the credibility of the information that results from applying IFRS 17. In addition, permitting an entity to ignore reasonable and supportable information available without undue cost or effort that the entity would have used to apply a retrospective approach would be contrary to the objective of the modified retrospective approach and would reduce comparability between contracts issued before and after the transition date. [IFRS 17.BC380B].

17.4.1 Assessments at inception or initial recognition

When it is impracticable for an entity to apply the retrospective approach, an entity should determine the following matters using information available at the transition date: *[IFRS 17.C9]*

- how to identify groups of contracts (see 5 above);
- whether an insurance contract meets the definition of an insurance contract with direct participation features (see 11 above);
- how to identify discretionary cash flows for insurance contracts without direct participation features (see 8 above); and
- whether an investment contract meets the definition of an investment contract with discretionary participation features (see 11.3 above)

To apply IFRS 17 retrospectively, an entity needs to determine the group of insurance contracts to which individual contracts would have belonged on initial recognition. IFRS 17 requires entities to group only contracts written within one year. *[IFRS 17.BC391]*. The IASB considered that it may not always be practicable for entities to group contracts written in the same one-year period retrospectively. *[IFRS 17.BC392]*. Consequently, in aggregating contracts when it is impracticable to apply a retrospective approach, an entity is permitted (to the extent that reasonable and supportable information does not exist) to aggregate contracts in a portfolio issued more than one year apart into a single group. *[IFRS 17.C10]*. This may mean that a single group of, say, term life contracts, could span many years to the extent reasonable and supportable information would not be available to aggregate the contracts into groups that only contain contracts issued within one year.

To the extent there is no reasonable and supportable information as discussed above, an entity should classify as a liability for incurred claims, a liability for settlement of claims incurred before an insurance contract was acquired in a transfer of business contracts that do not form a business or in a business combination within the scope of IFRS 3 (see 13.2 above). *[IFRS 17.C9A]*. This relief was added in June 2020 in response to feedback that suggested that it would often be impracticable for an entity to apply IFRS 17 retrospectively to contracts acquired before the transition date (that is, to classify and measure those contracts as a liability for remaining coverage). *[IFRS 17.BC382A]*.

17.4.2 Determining the contractual service margin or loss component for groups of insurance contracts without direct participation features

When it is impracticable for an entity to apply the retrospective approach at initial recognition to determine the contractual service margin or the loss component of the liability for remaining coverage, an entity is permitted to determine these at transition date using a modified approach to determine the components of the liability for remaining coverage. *[IFRS 17.C11]*.

The modified retrospective approach requires that reasonable and supportable information exists for the cash flows prior to transition up until the date of initial recognition (i.e. the date past which reasonable and supportable information is no longer available). This means all of the cash flows within the boundary of the insurance contract, as discussed at 8.2 above, including, for example, internally allocated directly attributable insurance acquisition cash flows, claims handling costs, policy maintenance and administration costs and an allocation of fixed and variable overheads.

The modified retrospective approach allows considerable judgement as it permits an entity to go back as far as it is able in order to determine reliable accounting estimates for the fulfilment cash flows. Inevitably, this will result in diversity of practice being applied by first time adopters and some lack of comparability in the release of the contractual margin in future periods between entities with longer-term contracts.

The process applied is as follows:

- The future cash flows at the date of initial recognition of a group of insurance contracts should be estimated as the amount of the future cash flows at the transition date (or earlier date, if the future cash flows at that earlier date can be determined retrospectively), adjusted by the cash flows that are known to have occurred between the date of initial recognition of a group of insurance contracts and the transition date (or earlier date). The cash flows that are known to have occurred include cash flows resulting from contracts that were derecognised before the transition date. *[IFRS 17.C12]*.

- The discount rates that applied at the date of initial recognition of a group of insurance contracts (or subsequently) should be determined: *[IFRS 17.C13]*

    - using an observable yield curve that, for at least three years immediately before the transition date, approximates the yield curve estimated applying a basis comparable with the general model to calculating discount rates (see 8.2 above), if such an observable yield curve exists; or

    - if the observable yield curve described above does not exist, the discount rates that applied at the date of initial recognition (or subsequently) should be estimated by determining an average spread between an observable yield curve and the yield curve estimated applying the general model, and applying that spread to that observable yield curve. That spread should be an average over at least three years immediately before the transition date.

- The risk adjustment for non-financial risk at the date of initial recognition of a group of insurance contracts (or subsequently) should be determined by adjusting the risk adjustment for non-financial risk at the transition date by the expected release of risk before the transition date. The expected release of risk should be determined by reference to the release of risk for similar insurance contracts that the entity issues at the transition date. *[IFRS 17.C14]*.

An entity should use the same systematic and rational method that it expects to use after transition date to allocate any insurance acquisition cash flows paid (or for which a liability has been recognised applying another IFRS standard) before the transition date (excluding any amount relating to insurance contracts that ceased to exist before the transition date) to: *[IFRS 17.C14B]*

- groups of insurance contracts recognised at the transition date; and
- groups of insurance contracts that are expected to be recognised after the transition date.

Insurance acquisition cash flows paid before the transition date that are allocated to a group of insurance contracts that is recognised at the transition date adjust the contractual service margin of that group, to the extent insurance contracts expected to be in the group have been recognised at that date. Other insurance acquisition cash flows paid before the transition date, including those that are allocated to a group of insurance contracts that is expected to be recognised after the transition date, are also recognised as an asset (see 6.3 above). [IFRS 17.C14C].

This systematic and rational method mentioned above should be the same systematic and rational method as the entity expects to apply after the transition date (see 6.3 above). To the extent that the entity does not have reasonable and supportable information to use a systematic and rational method, the following amounts should be determined to be nil at the transition date: [IFRS 17.C14D]

- the adjustment to the contractual service margin of groups of insurance contracts that are recognised at the transition date and any asset for insurance acquisition costs relating to that group; and
- the asset for insurance acquisition cash flows for groups of insurance contracts that are expected to be recognised after the transition date.

An entity that makes an accounting policy choice not to change the treatment of accounting estimates made in previous interim financial statements (see 15.4 above) should determine the contractual service margin or loss component at the transition date as if the entity has not prepared interim financial statements before the transition date if there is not reasonable and supportable information to apply a retrospective approach. [IFRS 17.C14A]. This means that entities without reasonable and supportable retrospective information do not have to recalculate insurance contract liabilities prior to transition date on a more frequent basis than annual.

If applying the modified requirements above (including those relating to insurance acquisition cash flows) results in a contractual service margin at initial recognition (i.e. there is a profit on initial recognition) then the entity should determine the contractual service margin at transition date as follows: [IFRS 17.C15]

- use the modified discount rates calculated above to accrete interest on the contractual service margin; and
- determine the amount of the contractual service margin recognised in profit or loss because of the transfer of services before the transition date, by comparing the remaining coverage units at that date with the coverage units provided under the group of contracts before the transition date (see 8.7 above).

If applying the modified requirements above results in a loss component of that liability for remaining coverage at the date of initial recognition, an entity should determine any amounts allocated to that loss component before the transition date applying the modified requirements above and using a systematic basis of allocation. [IFRS 17.C16].

For a group of reinsurance contracts held that provides coverage for an onerous group of insurance contracts and was acquired before or at the same time that the insurance contracts were issued, an entity should establish a loss-recovery component of the asset for remaining coverage at the transition date (see 10 above).

To the extent that there is not reasonable and supportable information to apply a retrospective approach, an entity shall determine the loss-recovery component by multiplying: *[IFRS 17.C16A]*

- the loss component of the liability for remaining coverage for the underlying insurance contracts at the transition date; and
- the percentage of claims for the group of underlying insurance contracts the entity expects to recover from the group of reinsurance contracts held.

However, if an entity does not have reasonable and supportable information to determine the loss recovery, an entity is not permitted to identify a loss-recovery component for the group of reinsurance contracts held. *[IFRS 17.C16C]*.

At the transition date onerous underlying insurance contracts might include in an onerous group of insurance contracts both onerous insurance contracts covered by the group of reinsurance contracts held and onerous insurance contracts not covered by a group of reinsurance contracts held. In that case, for the purpose of determining the loss-recovery component, the entity should use a systematic and rational basis of allocation to determine the portion of the loss component of the group of insurance contracts that relates to insurance contracts covered by the group of reinsurance contracts held. *[IFRS 17.C16B]*.

In addition, an entity should also apply the same methodology described at 17.4.2 above to recognise an asset for insurance acquisition cash flows, and any adjustment to the contractual service margin of a group of insurance contracts with direct participation features for insurance acquisition cash flows. *[IFRS 17.C17A]*.

The following example, based on Example 17 in the Illustrative Examples to IFRS 17, shows the transition requirements for a group of insurance contracts without direct participation features applying the modified retrospective approach. *[IFRS 17.IE186-IE191]*.

Example 56.71:   Measurement of groups of insurance contracts without direct participation features applying the modified retrospective approach

An entity issues insurance contracts without direct participation features and aggregates those contracts into groups. The entity estimates the fulfilment cash flows at the transition date applying the general model as the sum of:

- an estimate of the present value of future cash flows of €620 (including the effect of discounting of €(150)); and
- a risk adjustment for non-financial risk of €100.

The entity concludes that it is impracticable to apply IFRS 17 retrospectively. As a result, the entity chooses to apply the modified retrospective approach to measure the contractual service margin at the transition date. The entity uses reasonable and supportable information to achieve the closest outcome to retrospective application.

Analysis

The entity determines the contractual service margin at the transition date by estimating the fulfilment cash flows on initial recognition as follows:

- the future cash flows at the date of initial recognition of the group of insurance contracts are estimated to be the sum of the estimates of future cash flows of €770 at the transition date and cash flows of €800 that are known to have occurred between the date of initial recognition of the group of insurance contracts and transition date (including premiums paid on initial recognition of €1,000 and cash outflows of €200 paid during the period). This amount includes cash flows resulting from contracts that ceased to exist before the transition date.

- the entity determines the effect of discounting at the date of initial recognition of the group of insurance contracts to equal €(200) calculated as the discounting effect on estimates of future cash flows at the date of initial recognition determined above. The entity determines the effect of discounting by using a yield curve that, for at least 3 years immediately before the transition date, approximates the yield curve estimated applying the methodology described at 8.3 above. The entity estimates this amount to equal €50 reflecting the fact that the premium was received on initial recognition, hence, the discounting effect relates only to future cash outflows.
- the entity determines the risk adjustment for non-financial risk on initial recognition of €120 as the risk adjustment for the non-financial risk at the transition date of €100 adjusted by €20 to reflect the expected release of risk before the transition date. The entity determines the expected release of risk by reference to the release of risk for similar insurance contracts that the entity issues at the transition date.
- the contractual service margin on initial recognition is €110, the amount that would result in no profit or loss on initial recognition of the fulfilment cash flows of €110. The subsequent movement in the contractual margin, using the discount rates derived above to accrete interest and recognising the amount in profit or loss because of the transfer of services, by comparing the remaining coverage units at the transition date with the coverage units provided by the group before the transition date, is €90. Consequently, the contractual service margin on transition date is €20.

This is illustrated as follows:

	Transition date €	Adjustment to initial recognition €	Initial recognition €
Estimates of future cash flows	770	(800)	(30)
Effect of discounting	(150)	(50)	(200)
Risk adjustment for non-financial risk	100	20	120
Fulfilment cash flows	720	(830)	(110)
Contractual service margin:	20	90	110
Liability for remaining coverage	740		–

17.4.3 The contractual service margin or loss component for groups of insurance contracts with direct participation features

When it is impracticable for an entity to apply the retrospective approach at initial recognition to determine the contractual service margin or the loss component of the liability for remaining coverage for groups of contracts with direct participation features, these should be determined as: *[IFRS 17.C17]*

- the total fair value of the underlying items at the transition date (a); minus
- the fulfilment cash flows at the transition date (b); plus or minus
- an adjustment for (c):
    - amounts charged by the entity to the policyholders (including amounts deducted from the underlying items) before that date;
    - amounts paid before that date that would not have varied based on the underlying items;
    - the change in the risk adjustment for non-financial risk caused by the release from risk before that date. An entity should estimate this amount by reference

to the release of risk for similar insurance contracts that the entity issues at the transition date; and

- insurance acquisition cash flows paid (for which a liability has been recognised under another IFRS standard) before the transition date that are allocated to the group.

- if the sum of (a) – (c) above result in a contractual service margin – minus the amount of the contractual service margin that relates to services provided before that date. The sum of (a)–(c) above is a proxy for the total contractual service margin for all services to be provided under the group of contracts, i.e. before any amounts that would have been recognised in profit or loss for services provided. An entity should estimate the amounts that would have been recognised in profit or loss for services provided by comparing the remaining coverage units at the transition date with the coverage units provided under the group of contracts before the transition date; or

- if the sum of (a) – (c) results in a loss component, adjust the loss component to nil and increase the liability for remaining coverage excluding the loss component by the same amount.

The following example, based on Example 18 in the Illustrative Examples to IFRS 17, shows the transition requirements for a group of insurance contracts with direct participation features when applying the modified retrospective approach. *[IFRS 17.IE192-IE199].*

Example 56.72: Measurement of groups of insurance contracts with direct participation features applying the modified retrospective approach

An entity issues 100 insurance contracts with direct participation features five years before the transition date and aggregates these contracts into a group.

Under the terms of the contracts:

- a single premium is paid at the beginning of the coverage period of 10 years;
- the entity maintains account balances for policyholders and deducts charges from those account balances at the end of each year;
- a policyholder will receive an amount equal to the higher of the account balance and the minimum death benefit if an insured person dies during the coverage period; and
- if an insured person survives the coverage period, the policyholder receives the value of the account balance.

The following events occurred in the five-year period prior to the transition date:

- the entity paid death benefits and other expenses of £239 comprising:
  - £216 of cash flows that vary based on the returns from underlying items; and
  - £23 of cash flows that do not vary based on the returns from underlying items; and
- The entity deducted charges from the underlying items of £55.

The entity estimates the fulfilment cash flows at the transition date to be £922, comprising the estimates of the present value of the future cash flows of £910 and a risk adjustment for non-financial risk of £12. The fair value of the underlying items at that date is £948.

The entity makes the following estimates:

- Based on an analysis of similar contracts that the entity issues at transition date, the estimated change in the risk adjustment for non-financial risk caused by the release from risk in the five-year period before transition date is £14; and

- The units of coverage provided before the transition date is approximately 60% of the total coverage units of the group of contracts.

Analysis

The entity applies a modified retrospective approach to determine the contractual service margin at transition date and determines that the contractual service margin that relates to services provided before transition date of £26 as the percentage of the coverage units provided before the transition date and the total coverage units of 60% multiplied by the contractual service margin before recognition in profit or loss of £44. This is illustrated as follows:

	£
Fair value of the underlying items at transition date	948
Fulfilment cash flows at the transition date	(922)
Adjustments:	
– Charges deducted from underlying items before the transition date	55
– Amounts paid before transition date that would not have varied based on the returns on underlying items	(23)
– Estimated change in the risk adjustment for non-financial risk caused by the release from risk before transition date	(14)
Contractual service margin of the group of contracts before recognition in profit or loss	44
Estimated amount of the contractual service margin that relates to services provided before the transition date	(26)
Estimated contractual service margin at the transition date	18

The total insurance contract liability at the transition date is £940, which is the sum of the fulfilment cash flows of £922 and the contractual service margin of £18.

17.4.4 Insurance finance income or expenses

The modified requirements for insurance finance income or expenses are different depending on whether, as a result of applying the modified retrospective approach, groups of insurance contracts include contracts issued more than one year apart (see 17.4.1 above).

17.4.4.A Groups of insurance contracts that include contracts issued more than one year apart

When an entity has aggregated a group of insurance contracts on a basis that includes contracts issued more than one year apart in the same group: *[IFRS 17.C18]*

- the entity is permitted to determine the discount rates at the date of initial recognition for the contractual service margin, the liability for remaining coverage and for incurred claims for contracts applying the premium allocation approach, as at the transition date instead of at the date of initial recognition or incurred claim date;
- if an entity chooses to disaggregate insurance finance income or expenses between amounts included in profit or loss and amounts included in other comprehensive income (see 15.3.1 to 15.3.4 above), the entity needs to determine the cumulative amount of insurance finance income or expenses recognised in other comprehensive income at the transition date in order to be able to reclassify any remaining amounts from other comprehensive income to profit or loss upon subsequent transfer

or derecognition. The entity is permitted to determine that cumulative difference on transition either by applying the requirements for groups of contracts that do not include contracts issued more than one year apart – see 17.4.4.B below; or

- as nil; except for
- insurance contracts with direct participation features where the entity holds the underlying items when the cumulative difference is equal to the cumulative amount recognised in other comprehensive income on the underlying items.

17.4.4.B   *Groups of insurance contracts that do not include contracts issued more than one year apart*

When an entity has aggregated a group of insurance contracts on a basis that does not include contracts issued more than one year apart in the same group: *[IFRS 17.C19]*

- if an entity applies the requirements at 17.4.2 above for groups of insurance contracts without direct participation features to estimate the discount rates that applied at initial recognition (or subsequently), it should also determine the discount rates specified for accreting the interest on the contractual service margin, measuring the changes in the contractual service margin, discounting the liability for remaining coverage under the premium allocation approach and for disaggregated insurance finance or expenses in the same way; and

- if an entity chooses to disaggregate insurance finance income or expenses between amounts included in profit or loss and amounts included in other comprehensive income (see 15.3.1 to 15.3.4 above), the entity needs to determine the cumulative amount of insurance finance income or expenses recognised in other comprehensive income at the transition date in order to be able to reclassify any remaining amounts from other comprehensive income to profit or loss upon subsequent transfer or derecognition in future periods. The entity should determine that cumulative difference:

    - for insurance contracts for which changes in assumptions that relate to financial risk do not have a substantial effect on the amounts paid to policyholders – if it applies the requirements at 17.4.2 above to estimate the discount rates at initial recognition – using the discount rates that applied at the date of initial recognition, also applying the requirements at 17.4.2 above;

    - for groups of insurance contracts for which changes in assumptions that relate to financial risk have a substantial effect on the amounts paid to policyholders, on the basis that the assumptions that relate to financial risk that applied at the date of initial recognition are those that apply on the transition date, i.e. as nil;

    - for insurance contracts for which an entity will apply the premium allocation approach to discount the liability for incurred claims – if the entity applies the requirements at 17.4.2 above to estimate the discount rates at initial recognition (or subsequently) – using the discount rates that applied at the date of the incurred claim, also applying the requirements at 17.4.2 above; and

    - for insurance contracts with direct participation features where the entity holds the underlying items – as equal to the cumulative amount recognised in other comprehensive income on the underlying items.

Although entities are permitted to set the cumulative balance in other comprehensive income for disaggregated insurance finance income or expenses at nil on transition in certain circumstances, the same option is not permitted under IFRS 9 for any related financial assets. Therefore, an accounting mismatch will arise. It is observed in the Basis for Conclusions that the Board considered feedback from some stakeholders that preferred alternative modifications to those modifications set out above for determining the amount of insurance finance income or expenses accumulated in other comprehensive income at the transition date in order to resolve the accounting mismatch. The Board disagreed with these suggestions on various grounds and declined to amend either IFRS 9 or IFRS 17. *[IFRS 17.BC384A-B]*.

In addition, to the extent that an entity has made an accounting policy choice not to change the treatment of accounting estimates made in previous interim financial statements and is unable to apply this treatment retrospectively (see 17.4.1 above) it should determine amounts related to insurance finance income or expenses at the transition date as if it had not prepared interim financial statements before the transition date.

17.5 The fair value approach

The fair value approach is:

- permitted as an alternative to the modified retrospective approach for a group of contracts when full retrospective application of that group of contracts is impracticable (see 17.2 above); or

- required when full retrospective application of a group of contracts is impracticable and an entity cannot obtain reasonable and supportable information for that group of contracts necessary to use the modified retrospective approach (see 17.4 above); or

- permitted for a group of insurance contracts with direct participation features when risk mitigation has been applied prospectively to the group from the transition date and the entity has used derivatives, reinsurance contracts held or non-derivative financial instruments at fair value through profit or loss to mitigate financial risk arising from that group of contracts before transition date (see 17.2 above).

To apply the fair value approach, an entity should determine the contractual service margin or loss component of the liability for remaining coverage at the transition date as the difference between the fair value of a group of insurance contracts at that date and the fulfilment cash flows measured at that date. In determining fair value, an entity must apply the requirements of IFRS 13 except for the requirement that the fair value of a financial liability with a demand feature (e.g. a demand deposit) cannot be less than the amount payable on demand, discounted from the first date that the amount could be required to be paid. *[IFRS 17.C20]*. This means that insurance contract liabilities can be measured at an amount lower than the discounted amount repayable on demand.

In April 2019, the IASB staff considered a TRG submission on the fair value approach and confirmed that when, in applying the fair value approach, an entity determines the contractual service margin by comparing the fulfilment cash flows and the fair value of a group of insurance contracts, the fair value measurement in this situation reflects the effect of non-performance risk as required by IFRS 17 (but not the requirements relating to demand features). However, the fulfilment cash flows of an entity do not reflect the non-performance risk of the entity and this applies also to the fulfilment cash flows of an entity using the fair value approach on transition (i.e. the fulfilment cash flows of an entity that applies the fair value approach on transition exclude non-performance risk but non-performance risk is considered when determining the fair value of a group of contracts at transition date for the purpose of the calculation of the contractual service margin as the difference between the fulfilment cash flows and fair value).[98]

For a group of reinsurance contracts held to which the underlying insurance contracts are onerous at the transition date, an entity should determine the loss-recovery component of the asset for remaining coverage by multiplying: *[IFRS 17.C20A]*

- the loss component for the liability for remaining coverage for the underlying insurance contracts at the transition date; and
- the percentage of claims for the group of underlying insurance contracts the entity expects to recover from the group of reinsurance contracts held.

At the transition date onerous underlying insurance contracts might be included in a group of insurance contracts with other onerous insurance contracts that are not covered by the group of reinsurance contracts held. In that case, for the purpose of applying the calculation above, an entity should use a systematic and rational basis of allocation to determine the portion of the loss component of the group of insurance contracts that relates to insurance contracts covered by the group of reinsurance contracts held. *[IFRS 17.C20B]*.

In applying the fair value approach an entity may use reasonable and supportable information for what the entity would have determined given the terms of the contract and the market conditions at the date of inception or initial recognition, as appropriate or, alternatively, reasonable and supportable information at the transition date in determining: *[IFRS 17.C21-22]*

- how to identify groups of insurance contracts;
- whether an insurance contract meets the definition of an insurance contract with direct participation features;
- how to identify discretionary cash flows for insurance contracts without direct participation features; and
- whether an investment contract meets the definition of an investment contract with discretionary participation features (see 11.3 above).

In addition, the general requirements of IFRS 17 are modified as follows when the fair value approach is used:

- An entity may choose to classify as a liability for incurred claims, a liability for settlement of claims incurred before an insurance contract was acquired in a transfer of insurance contracts that do not form a business or in a business combination within the scope of IFRS 3. *[IFRS 17.C22A]*.
- When determining groups of insurance contracts, an entity may include as a group contracts issued more than one year apart. An entity is only allowed to divide groups into those only including contracts issued within a year or less if it has reasonable and supportable information to make the decision. This reflects the Board's expectation that grouping of contracts issued within a year (or less) will be challenging in situations where the fair value approach is applied. *[IFRS 17.C23]*.

- An entity determines the discount rate at the date of initial recognition of a group of contracts and the discount rates of the date of the incurred claims under the premium allocation approach (when discounting has been elected – see 9.4 above) at the transition date instead of the date of the initial recognition or incurred claim. *[IFRS 17.C23]*.

17.5.1 Disaggregated insurance finance income or expenses using the fair value approach

If an entity chooses to disaggregate insurance finance income or expenses between profit or loss and other comprehensive income, it is permitted to determine the cumulative amount of insurance finance income or expenses recognised in other comprehensive income at the transition date: *[IFRS 17.C24]*

- retrospectively, but only if it has reasonable and supportable information to do so; or
- as nil, unless the below applies; and
- for insurance contracts with direct participation features where the entity holds the underlying items, as equal to the cumulative amount recognised in other comprehensive income from the underlying items.

Although there is the option above to set other comprehensive income at nil on transition no equivalent option exists under transition in IFRS 9 for financial assets held at fair value through other comprehensive income.

17.5.2 Asset for insurance acquisition cash flows using the fair value approach

The amount of any asset for insurance acquisition cash flows should not be included in the measurement of any groups of insurance contracts recognised at the transition date. *[IFRS 17.C24B]*.

In applying the fair value approach for an asset for insurance acquisition cash flows, an entity should determine an asset for insurance acquisition cash flows at the transition date at an amount equal to the amount of insurance acquisition cash flows the entity would incur at the transition date for the rights to obtain: *[IFRS 17.C24A]*

- recoveries of insurance acquisition cash flows from premiums of insurance contracts issued before the transition date but not yet recognised at the transition date, (a);
- future insurance contracts that are renewals of insurance contracts recognised at the date of transition and insurance contracts described in (a) above, (b); and
- future insurance contracts, other than those in (b) above, after the date of transition without paying again insurance acquisition cash flows the entity has already paid that are directly attributable to the related portfolio of insurance contracts:

In May 2018, the TRG discussed the analysis in an IASB staff paper that considered whether, when applying the fair value approach to transition, insurance acquisition cash flows that occurred prior to the transition date are recognised as revenue and expenses for reporting periods subsequent to the transition date. The TRG members noted that:

- applying the fair value transition approach meant that the amount of insurance acquisition cash flows included in the measurement of the contractual service margin will only be the amount occurring after the transition date that is also included in the fulfilment cash flows. When this approach to transition is applied the entity is not required nor permitted to include in the measurement of the

contractual service margin any insurance acquisition cash flows occurring prior to the date of transition;
- the fair value approach is intended to provide an entity with a 'fresh start' approach to transition; and
- since insurance acquisition cash flows that occurred prior to the transition date are not included in the measurement of the contractual service margin at the transition date, they are not included in the presentation of insurance revenue and expenses for reporting periods subsequent to the transition date.

The IASB staff noted that this analysis applies in all situations that the fair value transition approach is taken, irrespective of whether the entity can identify and measure the insurance acquisition cash flows that applied prior to the transition date.[99]

17.6 Redesignation of financial assets and financial liabilities– when IFRS 9 has been applied previously

IFRS 17 allows a generous amount of dispensation for entities to redesignate their financial assets within the scope of IFRS 9 when IFRS 17 is applied. In addition, a consequential change to IFRS 9 allows redesignation of financial liabilities in certain circumstances.

17.6.1 Redesignation of financial assets

At the date of initial application of IFRS 17, an entity that had applied IFRS 9 to annual reporting periods before the initial application of IFRS 17: *[IFRS 17.C29]*

- may reassess whether an eligible financial asset meets the condition to be held within a business model whose objective is to hold financial assets in order to collect contractual cash flows or held within a business model whose objective is achieved by both collecting contractual cash flows and selling financial assets. A financial asset is eligible only if the financial asset is held in respect of an activity that is connected with contracts within the scope of IFRS 17. Examples of financial assets that would not be eligible for reassessment are financial assets held in respect of banking activities or financial assets held in respect of investment contracts that are outside the scope of IFRS 17;
- should revoke its designation of a financial asset measured at fair value through profit or loss if the original designation was made to avoid or reduce an accounting mismatch and that accounting mismatch no longer exists because of the application of IFRS 17;
- may designate a financial asset as measured at fair value through profit or loss if in doing so eliminates or significantly reduces an accounting mismatch that would otherwise arise from measuring assets or liabilities or recognising the gains and losses on them on different bases;
- may make an irrevocable election to designate an investment in an equity instrument as at fair value through other comprehensive income provided that equity instrument is neither held for trading nor contingent consideration recognised by an acquirer in a business combination to which IFRS 3 applies; and
- may revoke its previous designation of an investment in an equity instrument as at fair value through other comprehensive income.

An entity should apply the above on the basis of the facts and circumstances that exist at the date of initial application of IFRS 17. An entity should apply those designations and classifications retrospectively. In doing so, the entity should apply the relevant transition requirements in IFRS 9. The date of initial application for that purpose should be deemed to be the date of initial application of IFRS 17. *[IFRS 17.C30]*.

Any changes resulting from applying the above do not require the restatement of prior periods. The entity may restate prior periods only if it is possible without the use of hindsight. This may result in a situation whereby the comparative period is restated for the effect of IFRS 17 (which may include changes that affect financial instruments within the scope of IFRS 9, for example accounting for investment components that are separated) but not for consequential changes resulting to the classification of financial assets (this situation will also potentially arise when an entity has not previously applied IFRS 9 – see 17.7 below). If an entity does restate prior periods, the restated financial statements must reflect all the requirements of IFRS 9 for those affected financial assets. If an entity does not restate prior periods, the entity should recognise, in the opening restated earnings (or other component of equity, as appropriate) at the date of initial application, any difference between:

- the previous carrying amount of those financial assets; and
- the carrying amount of those financial assets at the date of initial application. *[IFRS 17.C31]*.

Other disclosure requirements when redesignation of financial assets is applied are as follows:

- the basis for determining financial assets eligible for redesignation;
- the measurement category and carrying amount of the affected financial assets determined immediately before the date of initial application of IFRS 17;
- the new measurement category and carrying amount of the affected financial assets determined after redesignation;
- the carrying amount of financial assets in the statement of financial position that were previously designated as measured at fair value through profit or loss in order to significantly reduce or avoid an accounting mismatch that are no longer so designated; *[IFRS 17.C32]* and
- qualitative information that would enable users of the financial statements to understand: *[IFRS 17.C33]*
    - how the entity applied the various options available for reassessment, revocation and designation described above;
    - the reasons for any designation or de-designation of financial assets measured at fair value through profit or loss in order to significantly reduce or avoid an accounting mismatch; and
    - why the entity came to any different conclusion in the new assessments applying the requirements of the business model test.

A simplified summary of the IFRS 9 redesignations above when initially applying IFRS 17 is as follows:

IFRS 9 asset class	Re-designate?	New category
Amortised cost	Yes – mandatory reclassification if business model has changed and assets held in respect of an activity that is connected with contracts within the scope of IFRS 17	Fair value through other comprehensive income or fair value through profit or loss depending on business model
	Yes – instrument-by-instrument election if eliminates or reduces an accounting mismatch that would otherwise arise from amortised cost measurement	Fair value through profit or loss
Fair value through other comprehensive income (debt securities)	Yes – mandatory if business model has changed and assets held in respect of an activity that is connected with contracts within the scope of IFRS 17	Amortised cost or fair value through profit or loss depending on business model
	Yes – instrument-by-instrument election if eliminates or reduces an accounting mismatch that would otherwise arise from fair value through other comprehensive income measurement	Fair value through profit or loss
Fair value through profit or loss (debt securities)	Yes – if designated due to accounting mismatch and accounting mismatch has ceased	Amortised cost or fair value through other comprehensive income depending on business model
Fair value through profit or loss (equity securities)	Yes – free election instrument by instrument	Fair value through other comprehensive income
Fair value through other comprehensive income (equity securities)	Yes – free election instrument by instrument	Fair value through profit or loss

17.6.2 Redesignation of financial liabilities

When IFRS 17 is applied, IFRS 9 states that:

- a previous designation of a financial liability measured at fair value through profit or loss should be revoked if that designation was previously made in order to eliminate or reduce an accounting mismatch, but the condition which caused the mismatch is no longer satisfied as a result of the application of IFRS 17; and

- a financial liability may be designated as measured at fair value through profit or loss if that designation would not have previously been permitted because it did not satisfy the condition (i.e. because there was no accounting mismatch) and that condition is now satisfied as a result of the application of these amendments.

Such a designation and revocation should be made on the basis of the facts and circumstances that exist at the date of initial application of these amendments. That classification shall be applied retrospectively. *[IFRS 9.7.2.39]*. However, prior periods may only be restated if it is possible to do so without the use of hindsight. *[IFRS 9.7.2.40]*.

17.7 Entities that have not previously applied IFRS 9

Most entities meeting the eligibility criteria for the temporary exemption from IFRS 9 in IFRS 4 (see Chapter 55 at 10) are expected to elect to defer IFRS 9 until IFRS 17 becomes effective.

An entity that adopts IFRS 9 at the same time that it adopts IFRS 17 will be able to assess financial asset classifications, elections and designations while, at the same time, assessing the implications of the requirements of IFRS 17. An entity adopting IFRS 9 at the same time that it adopts IFRS 17 will also be able to apply the various transitional provisions of IFRS 9.

IFRS 17 requires any net differences resulting from its application to be recorded in net equity at the date of transition (i.e. 1 January 2022 for an entity applying IFRS 17 for the first time in its annual reporting period ending 31 December 2023). In contrast, IFRS 9's starting point is that the net differences resulting from its application are recorded in net equity at the date of initial application (i.e. 1 January 2023 for an entity applying IFRS 9 for the first time in its annual reporting period ending 31 December 2023). Comparative periods may only be restated if it is possible to do so without the use of hindsight. *[IFRS 9.7.2.15]*.

However, even if comparative periods are restated IFRS 9 cannot be applied to items already derecognised at the date of initial application (i.e. 1 January 2023 if IFRS 9 is first applied in a calendar year ending 31 December 2023). *[IFRS 9.7.2.1]*. This means that IAS 39 accounting, for example available-for-sale accounting, will remain in the comparative statement of comprehensive income for financial assets derecognised in that comparative period. The Board considered feedback from entities implementing IFRS 17 suggesting that an entity that, on initial application of IFRS 17, first applied IFRS 9 at the same time it first applied IFRS 17, be permitted to apply IFRS 9 to financial assets that were derecognised during the IFRS 17 comparative period. However, the Board disagreed with the suggestion on the grounds that the requirements in IFRS 9 relating to transition were subject to extensive deliberation and consultation by the Board. *[IFRS 17.BC398A-B]*.

As a result, some care may therefore be needed by preparers to explain the presentation of financial instruments in the comparative period to users of the financial statements in the year of initial application of IFRS 17.

18 FUTURE DEVELOPMENTS

As discussed at 1 above, in June 2020, the IASB issued *Amendments to IFRS 17* which is reflected in this chapter.

At the time of writing this chapter, no further TRG meetings have been scheduled.

References

1. *Amendments to IFRS 17 Insurance Contracts – Credit cards that provide insurance coverage,* IASB staff paper 2D, March 2019, pp.5-7.
2. *Amendments to IFRS 17 Insurance Contracts – Loans that transfer significant insurance risk,* IASB staff paper 2A, February 2019, pp.6-9.
3. *IASB staff Paper AP11, Transition Resource Group for IFRS 17 Insurance contracts; reporting on other questions submitted,* IASB, September 2018, Log S33.
4. *IASB staff Paper AP11, Transition Resource Group for IFRS 17 Insurance contracts; reporting on other questions submitted,* IASB, September 2018, Log S33.
5. *Summary of the Transition Resource Group for IFRS 17 Insurance Contracts meeting held on 26-27 September 2018,* IASB, September 2018, pp.9-10.
6. *IASB staff Paper AP02, Transition Resource Group for IFRS 17 Insurance contracts: Reporting on other questions submitted,* IASB, April 2019, Log S117.
7. *IASB staff Paper AP02, Transition Resource Group for IFRS 17 Insurance contracts: Reporting on other questions submitted,* IASB, April 2019, Log S96, S107.
8. *Summary of the Transition Resource Group for IFRS 17 Insurance Contracts meeting held on 4 April 2019,* IASB, April 2019, p.2.
9. *IASB staff Paper AP01, Transition Resource Group for IFRS 17 Insurance contracts: Investment components within an insurance contract,* IASB, April 2019.
10. *Amendments to IFRS 17 Insurance Contracts – Annual improvements,* IASB staff paper 2D, April 2019, p.3.
11. *Summary of the Transition Resource Group for IFRS 17 Insurance Contracts meeting held on 4 April 2019,* IASB, April 2019, p.3.
12. *Summary of the Transition Resource Group for IFRS 17 Insurance Contracts meeting held on 4 April 2019,* IASB, April 2019, pp.3-4.
13. *Insurance contracts: Responding to the external editorial review,* IASB staff paper 2C, February 2017, Issue A8.
14. *Summary of the Transition Resource Group for IFRS 17 Insurance Contracts meeting held on 6 February 2018,* IASB, February 2018, pp.1-4.
15. *Summary of the Transition Resource Group for IFRS 17 Insurance Contracts meeting held on 2 May 2018,* IASB, May 2018, pp.2-3.
16. *IASB staff Paper AP07, Transition Resource Group for IFRS 17 Insurance contracts; reporting on other questions submitted,* IASB, May 2018, Log S35.
17. *Amendments to IFRS 17 Insurance Contracts – Annual improvements,* IASB staff paper 2D, April 2019, p 5-6.
18. *Summary of the Transition Resource Group for IFRS 17 Insurance Contracts meeting held on 6 February 2018,* IASB, February 2018, p.4.
19. *IASB staff Paper AP02, Transition Resource Group for IFRS 17 Insurance contracts: Reporting on other questions submitted,* IASB, April 2019, Log S86.
20. *Summary of the Transition Resource Group for IFRS 17 Insurance Contracts meeting held on 6 February 2018,* IASB, February 2018, pp.4-5.
21. *Summary of the Transition Resource Group for IFRS 17 Insurance Contracts meeting held on 26-27 September 2018,* IASB, September 2018, p.8.
22. *IASB staff Paper AP11, Transition Resource Group for IFRS 17 Insurance contracts; reporting on other questions submitted,* IASB, September 2018, Log S62.
23. *Summary of the Transition Resource Group for IFRS 17 Insurance Contracts meeting held on 2 May 2018,* IASB, May 2018, pp.6-7.
24. *IASB staff Paper AP02, Transition Resource Group for IFRS 17 Insurance contracts: Reporting on other questions submitted,* IASB, April 2019, Log S111.
25. *Summary of the Transition Resource Group for IFRS 17 Insurance Contracts meeting held on 2 May 2018,* IASB, May 2018, p.5.
26. *Summary of the Transition Resource Group for IFRS 17 Insurance Contracts meeting held on 26-27 September 2018,* IASB, September 2018, pp.10-11.
27. *IASB staff Paper AP07, Transition Resource Group for IFRS 17 Insurance contracts; reporting on other questions submitted,* IASB, May 2018, Log S14, S37.
28. *IASB staff Paper AP11, Transition Resource Group for IFRS 17 Insurance contracts; reporting on other questions submitted,* IASB, September 2018, Log S79.
29. *IASB staff Paper 2F, Amendments to IFRS 17: Other topics raised by respondents to the Exposure Draft Amendments to IFRS 17,* IASB, February 2020, p. 5.

30 *IASB staff Paper AP02, Transition Resource Group for IFRS 17 Insurance contracts; reporting on other questions submitted*, IASB, April 2019, Log S93.
31 *IASB staff Paper AP07, Transition Resource Group for IFRS 17 Insurance contracts; reporting on other questions submitted*, IASB, May 2018, Log S29.
32 *IASB staff Paper AP07, Transition Resource Group for IFRS 17 Insurance contracts; reporting on other questions submitted*, IASB, May 2018, Log S38.
33 *Summary of the Transition Resource Group for IFRS 17 Insurance Contracts meeting held on 26-27 September 2018*, IASB, September 2018, pp.3-5.
34 *IASB staff Paper AP02, Transition Resource Group for IFRS 17 Insurance contracts; reporting on other questions submitted*, IASB, April 2019, Log S91.
35 *IASB staff Paper AP02, Transition Resource Group for IFRS 17 Insurance contracts: Reporting on other questions submitted*, IASB, April 2019, Log S110.
36 *Summary of the Transition Resource Group for IFRS 17 Insurance Contracts meeting held on 2 May 2018*, IASB, May 2018, pp.3-4.
37 *Summary of the Transition Resource Group for IFRS 17 Insurance Contracts meeting held on 26-27 September 2018*, IASB, September 2018, pp.12-13.
53 *IASB staff Paper AP02, Amendments to IFRS 17: Sweep Issues*, IASB, May 2020, pp.6-7.
38 *IASB staff Paper AP02, Transition Resource Group for IFRS 17 Insurance contracts; reporting on other questions submitted*, IASB, April 2019, Log S118.
39 *Summary of the Transition Resource Group for IFRS 17 Insurance Contracts meeting held on 4 April 2019*, IASB, April 2018, p.7.
40 *Summary of the Transition Resource Group for IFRS 17 Insurance Contracts meeting held on 26-27 September 2018*, IASB, September 2018, pp.2-3.
41 *IASB staff Paper AP07, Transition Resource Group for IFRS 17 Insurance contracts; reporting on other questions submitted*, IASB, February 2018, Log S25.
42 *IASB staff Paper AP11, Transition Resource Group for IFRS 17 Insurance contracts – reporting on other questions submitted*, IASB, September 2018, Log S57.
43 *Summary of the Transition Resource Group for IFRS 17 Insurance Contracts meeting held on 26-27 September 2018*, IASB, September 2018, pp.6-7.
44 *IASB staff Paper AP07, Transition Resource Group for IFRS 17 Insurance contracts; reporting on other questions submitted*, IASB, February 2018, Log S09.
45 *Summary of the Transition Resource Group for IFRS 17 Insurance Contracts meeting held on 2 May 2018*, IASB, May 2018, pp.8-11.
46 *IASB staff Paper AP05, Determining the quantity of benefits for applying coverage units; Transition Resource Group for IFRS 17 Insurance contracts*, IASB, May 2018, pp.20-41.
47 *Summary of the Transition Resource Group for IFRS 17 Insurance Contracts meeting held on 2 May 2018*, IASB, May 2018, pp.12-13.
48 *Amendments to IFRS 17 Insurance Contracts – Sweep issue*, IASB staff paper 2C, May 2019, pp.2-4.
49 *Summary of the Transition Resource Group for IFRS 17 Insurance Contracts meeting held on 6 February 2018*, IASB, February 2018, p.6.
50 *IASB staff Paper AP05, Transition Resource Group for IFRS 17 Insurance contracts; Cash flows that are outside the contract boundary at initial recognition*, IASB, September 2018, pp.16-18.
51 *IASB staff Paper AP07, Transition Resource Group for IFRS 17 Insurance contracts; reporting on other questions submitted*, IASB, February 2018, Log S04.
52 *IASB staff Paper AP06, Transition Resource Group for IFRS 17 Implementation challenges outreach report*, IASB, May 2018.
53 *Summary of the Transition Resource Group for IFRS 17 Insurance Contracts meeting held on 26-27 September 2018*, IASB, September 2018, pp.5-6.
54 *IASB staff Paper AP03, Commissions and reinstatement premiums in reinsurance contracts issued; Transition Resource Group for IFRS 17 Insurance contracts*, IASB, September 2018.
55 *IASB staff Paper AP05, Determining the quantity of benefits for applying coverage units; Transition Resource Group for IFRS 17 Insurance contracts*, IASB, May 2018, pp.20-41.
56 *Amendments to IFRS 17 – Insurance Contracts Expected recovery of insurance acquisition cash flows*, IASB staff paper 2B, IASB, December 2019, pp.17-19.
57 *Insurance contracts issued by mutual entities*, IASB, July 2018.
58 *Insurance contracts issued by mutual entities*, IASB, July 2018.
59 *Amendments to IFRS 17 Insurance Contracts – Sweep issues*, IASB staff paper 2C, May 2019, pp.6-7.

60 *IASB staff Paper AP02, Transition Resource Group for IFRS 17 Insurance contracts; reporting on other questions submitted*, IASB, April 2019, Log S123.
61 *Summary of the Transition Resource Group for IFRS 17 Insurance Contracts meeting held on 6 February 2018*, IASB, February 2018, p.11.
62 *IASB staff Paper AP04, Transition Resource Group for IFRS 17 Insurance contracts; Premium experience adjustments related to current and past service*, IASB, September 2018, p.10.
63 *Summary of the Transition Resource Group for IFRS 17 Insurance Contracts meeting held on 6 February 2018*, IASB, February 2018, pp.5-6.
64 *Summary of the Transition Resource Group for IFRS 17 Insurance Contracts meeting held on 6 February 2018*, IASB, February 2018, p.6.
65 *IASB staff Paper AP05, Transition Resource Group for IFRS 17 Insurance contracts; Cash flows that are outside the contract boundary at initial recognition*, IASB, September 2018, pp.16-18.
66 *Summary of the Transition Resource Group for IFRS 17 Insurance Contracts meeting held on 2 May 2018*, IASB, May 2018, pp.7-8.
67 *IASB staff Paper AP07, Transition Resource Group for IFRS 17 Insurance contracts; reporting on other questions submitted*, IASB, February 2018, Log S17.
68 *IASB staff Paper AP07, Transition Resource Group for IFRS 17 Insurance contracts; reporting on other questions submitted*, IASB, May 2018, Log S40.
69 *IASB staff Paper AP07, Transition Resource Group for IFRS 17 Insurance contracts; reporting on other questions submitted*, IASB, May 2018, Log S42.
70 *IASB staff Paper AP02, Transition Resource Group for IFRS 17 Insurance contracts; reporting on other questions submitted*, IASB, April 2019, Log S119.
71 *IASB staff Paper AP07, Transition Resource Group for IFRS 17 Insurance contracts; reporting on other questions submitted*, IASB, May 2018, Log S41.
72 *Summary of the Transition Resource Group for IFRS 17 Insurance Contracts meeting held on 26-27 September 2018*, IASB, September 2018, pp.14-15.
73 *IASB staff Paper 2F, Amendments to IFRS 17: Other topics raised by respondents to the Exposure Draft*, IASB, February 2020, Appendix A, p.11.
74 *IASB staff Paper AP07, Transition Resource Group for IFRS 17 Insurance contracts; reporting on other questions submitted*, IASB, February 2018, Log S26.
75 *IASB staff Paper AP02, Transition Resource Group for IFRS 17 Insurance contracts; reporting on other questions submitted*, IASB, April 2019, Log S115.
76 *Summary of the Transition Resource Group for IFRS 17 Insurance Contracts meeting held on 4 April 2019*, IASB, April 2019, pp.6-7.
77 *IASB staff Paper AP02, Transition Resource Group for IFRS 17 Insurance contracts; reporting on other questions submitted*, IASB, April 2019, Log S114.
78 *Summary of the Transition Resource Group for IFRS 17 Insurance Contracts meeting held on 2 May 2018*, IASB, May 2018, p.11.
79 *Amendments to IFRS 17 Insurance Contracts – Annual improvement*, IASB staff paper 2D, April 2019. p.3.
80 *IASB staff Paper AP02, Transition Resource Group for IFRS 17 Insurance contracts; reporting on other questions submitted*, IASB, April 2019, Log S94-95.
81 *IASB staff Paper 2F, Amendments to IFRS 17: Other topics raised by respondents to the Exposure Draft*, IASB, February 2020, pp.7-8.
82 *IASB staff Paper AP02, Transition Resource Group for IFRS 17 Insurance contracts; reporting on other questions submitted*, IASB, April 2019, Log S82.
83 *Insurance contracts: Responding to the external editorial review*, IASB staff paper 2C, February 2017, Issue A12.
84 *IASB staff Paper AP07, Transition Resource Group for IFRS 17 Insurance contracts; reporting on other questions submitted*, IASB, February 2018, Log S04.
85 *IASB staff Paper AP07, Transition Resource Group for IFRS 17 Insurance contracts; reporting on other questions submitted*, IASB, May 2018, Log S32.
86 *IASB staff Paper AP06, Transition Resource Group for IFRS 17 Implementation challenges outreach report*, IASB, May 2018.
87 *Amendments to IFRS 17 – Sweep issues*, IASB staff paper 2, May 2020, p.6.
88 *Summary of the Transition Resource Group for IFRS 17 Insurance Contracts meeting held on 26-27 September 2018*, IASB, September 2018, pp.8-9.
89 *IASB staff Paper AP02, Transition Resource Group for IFRS 17 Insurance contracts; reporting on other questions submitted*, IASB, April 2019, Log S121.
90 *IASB staff Paper AP02, Transition Resource Group for IFRS 17 Insurance contracts; reporting on other questions submitted*, IASB, April 2019, Log S122.

91 *IASB staff Paper AP02, Transition Resource Group for IFRS 17 Insurance contracts; reporting on other questions submitted*, IASB, April 2019, Log S106.
92 *IASB staff Paper AP02, Transition Resource Group for IFRS 17 Insurance contracts; reporting on other questions submitted*, IASB, April 2019, Log S102.
93 *IASB staff Paper AP11, Transition Resource Group for IFRS 17 Insurance contracts; reporting on other questions submitted*, IASB, September 2018, Log S56, 67.
94 *Summary of the Transition Resource Group for IFRS 17 Insurance Contracts meeting held on 26-27 September 2018*, IASB, September 2018, p.16.
95 *IASB staff Paper AP02, Transition Resource Group for IFRS 17 Insurance contracts; reporting on other questions submitted*, IASB, April 2019, Log S125.
96 *IASB staff Paper AP02, Transition Resource Group for IFRS 17 Insurance contracts; reporting on other questions submitted*, IASB, April 2019, Log S83.
97 *International Financial Reporting Standard for Small and Medium-sized Entities*, IASB, May 2015, paras. 2.14B, BC231.
98 *IASB staff Paper AP02, Transition Resource Group for IFRS 17 Insurance contracts; reporting on other questions submitted*, IASB, April 2019, Log S127.
99 *Summary of the Transition Resource Group for IFRS 17 Insurance Contracts meeting held on 2 May 2018*, IASB, May 2018, pp.9-10.

Index of extracts from financial statements

3i Group plc	956
A.P. Møller – Mærsk A/S	1530, 3174
Accelerate Property Fund Ltd	1487
adidas AG	683
AEGON N.V.	4631
African Rainbow Minerals Limited	3149
AGF Mutual Funds	233
Airbus SE	2419
Akzo Nobel N.V.	1395, 1840, 1992
Alkane Resources Limited	3475
Allianz SE	3184, 4576, 4580, 4626
Allied Electronics Corporation	684
AMP Limited	4572, 4636, 4646
Angel Mining plc	3425
Anglo American Platinum Limited	3482
Anglo American plc	3459, 3465, 3484, 3485, 3522
AngloGold Ashanti Limited	1683, 1980, 3416, 3489, 3491
Anheuser-Busch InBev NV/SA	1314, 1841, 3150, 3217, 3257
ArcelorMittal	1413
Ardagh Group S.A.	3216
ARINSO International SA	383
ASML Holding N.V.	2421, 2426
ASOS Plc	1328
Assicurazioni Generali S.p.A.	4598
AstraZeneca PLC	3146, 4514
Aveng Limited	816
Aviva plc	986, 2849, 3681, 4624, 4638, 4642, 4656, 4665

Index of extracts from financial statements

AXA SA 4573, 4590
BAE Systems plc 3014, 3015
Barclays PLC 981
Barrick Gold Corporation 3456, 3554
Bayer Aktiengesellschaft 976, 1326, 3076
BBA Aviation plc 1241
Beazley plc 4646
Belarusian National Reinsurance Organisation 1276
Berendsen plc 4456
BHP Billiton plc 3477
BHP Group Plc 3366, 3389, 3430, 3515, 3560
BMW Group 3225
Bombardier Inc. 344, 348, 364, 2393, 2429
BP p.l.c. 955, 977, 1154, 2619, 2620, 3120, 3127, 3208, 3359,
.... 3370, 3438, 3478, 3488, 3493, 3647, 4470, 4508
Brit Limited 4653
British Airways Plc 1396
British Sky Broadcasting Group plc 3126
BT Group plc 2960, 2963
Canadian Imperial Bank of Commerce 362
Capita plc 2413, 2438
Capital & Counties Properties PLC 1506
Centrais Elétricas Brasileiras S.A. – Eletrobras 320
Centrica plc 1940, 4031
China Mobile Limited 3167
CNP Assurances 4629, 4640
Coca-Cola FEMSA S.A.B. de C.V. 305
Coca-Cola HBC AG 3260
Cranswick plc 3084
CRH plc 1693
Daimler AG 3001, 3006, 3215, 3222
Dairy Crest Group plc 2846
Deutsche Bank Aktiengesellschaft 962, 3212
Deutsche Lufthansa AG 3139, 3210
Deutsche Post AG 1777, 1816

Downer EDI Limited 3214
E.ON SE 1398
Enersource Corporation 300
ENGIE SA 428, 1883, 3487, 3555
Eni S.p.A. 1431
Equinor ASA 3004, 3013, 3209, 3390, 3452, 3463, 3468
Eskom Holdings SOC Ltd 1844
Fédération Internationale de Football Association 2398, 2416
Ferrovial, S.A. 2406
Forthnet S.A. 3210
Fortum Oyj 1989
Glencore plc 3369, 3413
Greencore Group plc 1840
Groupe Renault 3624
Harmony Gold Mining Company Limited 3400, 3481
Heineken N.V. 1389
Hochschild Mining PLC 2620
HOCHTIEF Aktiengesellschaft 2990, 3007
Hongkong Land Holdings Limited 3173
HSBC Holdings plc 964, 983, 1942, 3214, 3709, 4028
Hunting PLC 4436, 4468
Husky Energy Inc. 269
IAMGOLD Corporation 3490
Icade 1488
Infosys Technologies Limited 235
ING Groep N.V. 1082, 1137, 1196
Inspired Energy PLC 3172
InterContinental Hotels Group PLC 2944, 3145
International Consolidated Airlines Group, S.A. 1354, 3211, 3248
Intrepid Mines Limited 3398
ITV plc 1300
J Sainsbury plc 3126
KAZ Minerals PLC 1666, 1671
Kendrion N.V. 1401
Kinross Gold Corporation 3491

Klépierre 1484, 1485
Koninklijke Philips N.V. 2004, 2424
LafargeHolcim Ltd 3075
Land Securities Group PLC 1481, 1489, 1492
Legal & General Group plc 4649
Liverpool Victoria Friendly Society Limited 4546
Lloyds Banking Group plc 1208, 3144
Lonmin Plc 3516
Lucas Bols N.V. 1432
Manulife Financial Corporation 289
MERCK Kommanditgesellschaft auf Aktien 1310, 1325
MOL Hungarian Oil and Gas Plc. 1363
Mondi plc 3314
Mowi ASA 3320
MS Amlin plc 4650
Münchener Rückversicherungs – Gesellschaft Aktiengesellschaft 4628
Naspers Limited 3176
National Australia Bank Limited 3008
Nestlé S.A. 884, 1357, 1779, 3010, 3218, 3224, 4460
Netcare Limited 3186
Newcrest Mining Limited 3439
Nexen Inc. 293
Nine Entertainment Co. Holdings Limited 3219
Nokia Corporation 883
Norsk Hydro ASA 3557
Old Mutual plc 4589, 4594
Pearson plc 1228
PGS ASA 3085
Ping An Insurance 4634, 4666
Poste Italiane SpA 1812, 1817
Premier Oil plc 3364, 3389
Priorbank JSC 1282
ProSiebenSat.1 Media SE 2420
Proton Power Systems plc 3197
Prudential plc 4576, 4630, 4637, 4662

Index of extracts from financial statements

PSA Peugeot Citroën	1833
QBE Insurance Group	4651
Quilter plc	980
RAI – Radiotelevisione italiana SpA	1344
RELX PLC	1298
Repsol, S.A.	1364
Rio Tinto plc	1155, 3423, 3459, 3464, 3468, 3470, 3484, 3512, 3523
Robert Bosch Gesellschaft mit beschränkter Haftung	961
Roche Holding Ltd	2010, 2985, 3015, 3220
Rolls-Royce Holdings plc	3220, 3599
Royal Dutch Shell plc	2618, 3520
Royal Schiphol Group N.V.	3143
RSA Insurance Group plc	4586, 4631
RWE Aktiengesellschaft	883
Sanofi	1324
SAP SE	2430, 2434
Sappi Limited	3318
Sberbank of Russia	1211
Schroders plc	3125
Siemens Aktiengesellschaft	3003
Sirius Minerals Plc	3233
Skanska AB	1388, 1409
Slater and Gordon Limited	2405, 2436
Société nationale SNCF	2415
Spotify Technology S.A.	2423
Stagecoach Group plc	1845
Stora Enso Oyj	1699
Suncor Energy Inc	293
T&G Global Limited	3310
Telefónica, S.A.	1283
Telenor ASA	1901
The British Land Company PLC	1464, 1477
The Crown Estate	1479
The Go-Ahead Group plc	2984
The Rank Group Plc	678

Index of extracts from financial statements

The Royal Bank of Scotland Group plc 3129, 4461
The Toronto-Dominion Bank 270
The Village Building Co. Limited 2405
thyssenkrupp, AG 3218
TOTAL S.A. 975, 3380
Tullow Oil plc 3375, 3521
UBS Group AG 958, 985, 988, 1151, 1240, 2962, 3805, 4432
Unibail-Rodamco-Westfield SE 1470, 1499, 1507
Unilever PLC and Unilever N.V. 1698, 4459
Vivendi SE 1304, 1345
Vodafone Group Plc 1636, 3002, 3011, 4421
Volkswagen Aktiengesellschaft 4452, 4460
VTech Holdings Limited 3139
Woodside Petroleum Ltd. 3424, 3560
Yorkshire Building Society 3211
Zargon Oil & Gas Ltd. 299
Zurich Insurance Group, Zurich 4660

Index of standards

SP 1

SP 1.1 .... Ch.2, p.48
SP 1.2 .... Ch.2, p.48
SP 1.3 .... Ch.2, p.48
SP 1.4 .... Ch.2, p.48
SP 1.5 .... Ch.2, p.48

Conceptual Framework (2001)

CF(2001) 4.4 .... Ch.9, p.667

Conceptual Framework (2010)

CF(2010) 4.29 .... Ch.27, p.2018
CF(2010) 4.29 .... Ch.27, p.2027
CF(2010) 4.29 .... Ch.32, p.2406
CF(2010) 4.31 .... Ch.27, p.2018
CF(2010) 4.55(b) Ch.16, p.1260
CF(2010) 4.59(a) Ch.16, p.1251
CF(2010) BC3.28 .... Ch.26, p.1949
CF(2018) BC4.96 .... Ch.32, p.2406
CF(2010) QC12 .... Ch.26, p.1949
CF(2010) QC14 .... Ch.26, p.1949

Conceptual Framework

CF 1.1 .... Ch.2, p.49
CF 1.1-1.2 .... Ch.2, p.59
CF 1.2 .... Ch.2, p.49
CF 1.2 .... Ch.5, p.231
CF 1.3 .... Ch.2, p.50
CF 1.4 .... Ch.2, p.50
CF 1.5 .... Ch.2, p.49
CF 1.6 .... Ch.2, p.50
CF 1.7 .... Ch.2, p.50
CF 1.8 .... Ch.2, p.50
CF 1.9 .... Ch.2, p.50
CF 1.9 .... Ch.5, p.231
CF 1.10 .... Ch.2, p.49
CF 1.11 .... Ch.2, p.50
CF 1.12 .... Ch.2, p.50
CF 1.13 .... Ch.2, p.51
CF 1.14 .... Ch.2, p.51
CF 1.15 .... Ch.2, p.51
CF 1.16 .... Ch.2, p.51
CF 1.17 .... Ch.2, p.52
CF 1.17 .... Ch.3, p.156
CF 1.18 .... Ch.2, p.51
CF 1.19 .... Ch.2, p.52
CF 1.20 .... Ch.2, p.52
CF 1.20 .... Ch.40, p.3136
CF 1.21 .... Ch.2, p.51
CF 1.22 .... Ch.2, p.52
CF 1.23 .... Ch.2, p.52
CF 2.1 .... Ch.2, p.52
CF 2.2 .... Ch.2, p.53
CF 2.3 .... Ch.2, p.53
CF 2.4 .... Ch.2, p.53
CF 2.4 .... Ch.2, p.56
CF 2.4 .... Ch.2, p.92
CF 2.5 .... Ch.2, p.52
CF 2.6 .... Ch.2, p.54
CF 2.7 .... Ch.2, p.54
CF 2.8 .... Ch.2, p.54
CF 2.9 .... Ch.2, p.54
CF 2.10 .... Ch.2, p.54
CF 2.11 .... Ch.2, p.54
CF 2.12 .... Ch.2, p.54
CF 2.12 .... Ch.46, p.3654
CF 2.13 .... Ch.2, p.54
CF 2.13 .... Ch.26, p.1949
CF 2.14 .... Ch.2, p.55
CF 2.15 .... Ch.2, p.55
CF 2.15 .... Ch.3, p.165
CF 2.15 .... Ch.26, p.1949
CF 2.16 .... Ch.2, p.55
CF 2.16 .... Ch.3, p.165
CF 2.17 .... Ch.2, p.55
CF 2.18 .... Ch.2, p.55
CF 2.19 .... Ch.2, p.53
CF 2.20 .... Ch.2, p.56
CF 2.21 .... Ch.2, p.56
CF 2.22 .... Ch.2, p.56
CF 2.23 .... Ch.2, p.52
CF 2.23 .... Ch.2, p.56
CF 2.24 .... Ch.2, p.57
CF 2.25-2.27 .... Ch.2, p.57
CF 2.26-2.28 .... Ch.2, p.57
CF 2.29 .... Ch.2, p.57
CF 2.30 .... Ch.2, p.57
CF 2.31 .... Ch.2, p.57
CF 2.32 .... Ch.2, p.57
CF 2.33 .... Ch.2, p.57
CF 2.34 .... Ch.2, p.58

Index of standards

CF 2.35	Ch.2, p.58
CF 2.36	Ch.2, p.49
CF 2.36	Ch.2, p.58
CF 2.37	Ch.2, p.58
CF 2.38	Ch.2, p.58
CF 2.39	Ch.2, p.52
CF 2.39	Ch.2, p.58
CF 2.40	Ch.2, p.58
CF 2.41	Ch.2, p.58
CF 2.42	Ch.2, p.58
CF 2.42	Ch.2, p.59
CF 2.43	Ch.2, p.59
CF 3.1	Ch.2, p.59
CF 3.2	Ch.2, p.59
CF 3.3	Ch.2, p.59
CF 3.4	Ch.2, p.60
CF 3.5	Ch.2, p.60
CF 3.6	Ch.2, p.60
CF 3.7	Ch.2, p.60
CF 3.8	Ch.2, p.60
CF 3.9	Ch.2, p.60
CF 3.9	Ch.38, p.3083
CF 3.10	Ch.2, p.59
CF 3.10	Ch.2, p.60
CF 3.10	Ch.6, p.391
CF 3.10	Ch.6, p.402
CF 3.10	Ch.9, p.752
CF 3.10	Ch.10, p.774
CF 3.11	Ch.2, p.61
CF 3.12	Ch.2, p.61
CF 3.12	Ch.6, p.401
CF 3.13	Ch.2, p.61
CF 3.13-14	Ch.6, p.403
CF 3.14	Ch.2, p.61
CF 3.15	Ch.2, p.62
CF 3.16	Ch.2, p.62
CF 3.17	Ch.2, p.62
CF 3.18	Ch.2, p.62
CF 4.1-4.4	Ch.2, p.62
CF 4.2	Ch.2, p.70
CF 4.2	Ch.55, p.4569
CF 4.3	Ch.25, p.1862
CF 4.5	Ch.2, p.66
CF 4.6	Ch.2, p.66
CF 4.7	Ch.2, p.67
CF 4.8	Ch.2, p.67
CF 4.9	Ch.2, p.67
CF 4.10	Ch.2, p.67
CF 4.11	Ch.2, p.67
CF 4.12	Ch.2, p.67
CF 4.13	Ch.2, p.68
CF 4.14	Ch.2, p.68
CF 4.15	Ch.2, p.68
CF 4.16	Ch.2, p.68
CF 4.17	Ch.2, p.68
CF 4.18	Ch.2, p.68
CF 4.19	Ch.2, p.69
CF 4.20	Ch.2, p.69
CF 4.21	Ch.2, p.69
CF 4.22	Ch.2, p.69
CF 4.23	Ch.2, p.69
CF 4.24	Ch.2, p.69
CF 4.25	Ch.2, p.69
CF 4.26	Ch.2, p.62
CF 4.26	Ch.2, p.70
CF 4.26	Ch.26, p.1932
CF 4.26	Ch.55, p.4569
CF 4.27	Ch.2, p.70
CF 4.27	Ch.26, p.1932
CF 4.28	Ch.2, p.70
CF 4.28	Ch.55, p.4569
CF 4.29	Ch.2, p.70
CF 4.29	Ch.55, p.4569
CF 4.30	Ch.2, p.70
CF 4.31	Ch.2, p.70
CF 4.32	Ch.2, p.70
CF 4.33	Ch.2, p.70
CF 4.34	Ch.2, p.71
CF 4.35	Ch.2, p.71
CF 4.36	Ch.2, p.71
CF 4.37	Ch.2, p.71
CF 4.38	Ch.2, p.71
CF 4.39	Ch.2, p.71
CF 4.40	Ch.2, p.71
CF 4.41	Ch.2, p.71
CF 4.42	Ch.2, p.72
CF 4.43	Ch.2, p.72
CF 4.44	Ch.2, p.72
CF 4.45	Ch.2, p.72
CF 4.46	Ch.2, p.72
CF 4.46	Ch.43, p.3473
CF 4.47	Ch.2, p.72
CF 4.48	Ch.2, p.63
CF 4.49	Ch.2, p.63
CF 4.49	Ch.3, p.160
CF 4.50	Ch.2, p.63
CF 4.51	Ch.2, p.64
CF 4.52	Ch.2, p.64
CF 4.53	Ch.2, p.64
CF 4.54	Ch.2, p.64
CF 4.55	Ch.2, p.65
CF 4.56	Ch.2, p.65
CF 4.56	Ch.17, p.1302
CF 4.57	Ch.2, p.65
CF 4.57	Ch.17, p.1302
CF 4.58	Ch.2, p.65
CF 4.58	Ch.17, p.1302
CF 4.59	Ch.2, p.65
CF 4.60	Ch.2, p.66
CF 4.61	Ch.2, p.66
CF 4.62	Ch.2, p.66
CF 4.63	Ch.2, p.62
CF 4.63	Ch.2, p.72
CF 4.63-4.64	Ch.7, p.540
CF 4.64	Ch.2, p.72
CF 4.65	Ch.2, p.73

Index of standards

CF 4.66	Ch.2, p.73
CF 4.67	Ch.2, p.73
CF 4.68	Ch.2, p.62
CF 4.68	Ch.3, p.160
CF 4.68	Ch.27, p.2018
CF 4.68-70	Ch.2, p.73
CF 4.69	Ch.2, p.62
CF 4.71	Ch.2, p.73
CF 4.72	Ch.2, p.73
CF 5.1	Ch.2, p.74
CF 5.2	Ch.2, p.74
CF 5.2	Ch.2, p.101
CF 5.3	Ch.2, p.74
CF 5.3	Ch.2, p.103
CF 5.4	Ch.2, p.75
CF 5.5	Ch.2, p.75
CF 5.6	Ch.2, p.75
CF 5.7	Ch.2, p.75
CF 5.8	Ch.2, p.76
CF 5.9	Ch.2, p.76
CF 5.10	Ch.2, p.76
CF 5.11	Ch.2, p.76
CF 5.12	Ch.2, p.76
CF 5.13	Ch.2, p.76
CF 5.14	Ch.2, p.77
CF 5.15	Ch.2, p.77
CF 5.16	Ch.2, p.77
CF 5.17	Ch.2, p.77
CF 5.18	Ch.2, p.77
CF 5.19	Ch.2, p.77
CF 5.20	Ch.2, p.78
CF 5.21	Ch.2, p.78
CF 5.22	Ch.2, p.78
CF 5.23	Ch.2, p.78
CF 5.24	Ch.2, p.79
CF 5.25	Ch.2, p.79
CF 5.26	Ch.2, p.79
CF 5.27	Ch.2, p.79
CF 5.27	Ch.2, p.80
CF 5.28	Ch.2, p.80
CF 5.29	Ch.2, p.80
CF 5.30	Ch.2, p.80
CF 5.31	Ch.2, p.81
CF 5.32	Ch.2, p.81
CF 5.33	Ch.2, p.81
CF 6.1	Ch.2, p.81
CF 6.2	Ch.2, p.82
CF 6.3	Ch.2, p.82
CF 6.4	Ch.2, p.82
CF 6.5	Ch.2, p.82
CF 6.6	Ch.2, p.83
CF 6.7	Ch.2, p.83
CF 6.8	Ch.2, p.83
CF 6.9	Ch.2, p.83
CF 6.10	Ch.2, p.83
CF 6.11	Ch.2, p.83
CF 6.12	Ch.2, p.84
CF 6.13	Ch.2, p.84
CF 6.14	Ch.2, p.84
CF 6.15	Ch.2, p.84
CF 6.16	Ch.2, p.84
CF 6.17	Ch.2, p.85
CF 6.18	Ch.2, p.85
CF 6.19	Ch.2, p.85
CF 6.20	Ch.2, p.85
CF 6.21	Ch.2, p.85
CF 6.22	Ch.2, p.85
CF 6.23	Ch.2, p.86
CF 6.24	Ch.2, p.90
CF 6.25	Ch.2, p.90
CF 6.26	Ch.2, p.90
CF 6.27	Ch.2, p.90
CF 6.28	Ch.2, p.90
CF 6.29	Ch.2, p.90
CF 6.30	Ch.2, p.91
CF 6.31	Ch.2, p.91
CF 6.32	Ch.2, p.91
CF 6.33	Ch.2, p.91
CF 6.34	Ch.2, p.91
CF 6.35	Ch.2, p.91
CF 6.36	Ch.2, p.91
CF 6.37	Ch.2, p.91
CF 6.38	Ch.2, p.91
CF 6.39	Ch.2, p.92
CF 6.40	Ch.2, p.92
CF 6.41	Ch.2, p.92
CF 6.42	Ch.2, p.92
CF 6.43	Ch.2, p.92
CF 6.44	Ch.2, p.92
CF 6.45	Ch.2, p.92
CF 6.46	Ch.2, p.93
CF 6.47	Ch.2, p.92
CF 6.48	Ch.2, p.93
CF 6.49	Ch.2, p.93
CF 6.50	Ch.2, p.93
CF 6.51	Ch.2, p.93
CF 6.52	Ch.2, p.93
CF 6.53	Ch.2, p.94
CF 6.54	Ch.2, p.94
CF 6.55	Ch.2, p.94
CF 6.56	Ch.2, p.94
CF 6.57	Ch.2, p.94
CF 6.58	Ch.2, p.95
CF 6.59	Ch.2, p.95
CF 6.60	Ch.2, p.95
CF 6.61	Ch.2, p.95
CF 6.62	Ch.2, p.95
CF 6.63	Ch.2, p.95
CF 6.64	Ch.2, p.95
CF 6.65	Ch.2, p.95
CF 6.66	Ch.2, p.96
CF 6.67	Ch.2, p.96
CF 6.68	Ch.2, p.96
CF 6.69	Ch.2, p.96
CF 6.70	Ch.2, p.96
CF 6.71	Ch.2, p.96

CF 6.72	Ch.2, p.96
CF 6.73	Ch.2, p.96
CF 6.74	Ch.2, p.97
CF 6.75	Ch.2, p.97
CF 6.76	Ch.2, p.97
CF 6.77	Ch.2, p.93
CF 6.78	Ch.2, p.98
CF 6.79	Ch.2, p.98
CF 6.80	Ch.2, p.98
CF 6.81	Ch.2, p.98
CF 6.82	Ch.2, p.98
CF 6.83	Ch.2, p.98
CF 6.84	Ch.2, p.98
CF 6.85	Ch.2, p.99
CF 6.86	Ch.2, p.99
CF 6.87	Ch.2, p.99
CF 6.88	Ch.2, p.99
CF 6.89	Ch.2, p.99
CF 6.90	Ch.2, p.100
CF 6.91	Ch.2, p.100
CF 6.92	Ch.2, p.100
CF 6.93	Ch.2, p.100
CF 6.94	Ch.2, p.100
CF 6.95	Ch.2, p.100
CF 7.1	Ch.2, p.101
CF 7.2	Ch.2, p.101
CF 7.3	Ch.2, p.101
CF 7.4	Ch.2, p.101
CF 7.5	Ch.2, p.102
CF 7.6	Ch.2, p.102
CF 7.7	Ch.2, p.102
CF 7.8	Ch.2, p.102
CF 7.9	Ch.2, p.102
CF 7.10	Ch.2, p.102
CF 7.10	Ch.43, p.3550
CF 7.11	Ch.2, p.102
CF 7.12	Ch.2, p.102
CF 7.13	Ch.2, p.103
CF 7.14	Ch.2, p.103
CF 7.15	Ch.2, p.103
CF 7.16	Ch.2, p.103
CF 7.17	Ch.2, p.103
CF 7.18	Ch.2, p.104
CF 7.19	Ch.2, p.104
CF 7.20	Ch.2, p.104
CF 7.21	Ch.2, p.104
CF 7.22	Ch.2, p.101
CF 7.22	Ch.2, p.104
CF 8.1	Ch.2, p.105
CF 8.2	Ch.2, p.105
CF 8.3(a)	Ch.2, p.105
CF 8.3(b)	Ch.2, p.106
CF 8.4	Ch.2, p.104
CF 8.5	Ch.2, p.105
CF 8.5	Ch.2, p.106
CF 8.6	Ch.2, p.104
CF 8.6	Ch.2, p.105
CF 8.7	Ch.2, p.105
CF 8.7	Ch.2, p.106
CF 8.8	Ch.2, p.106
CF 8.9	Ch.2, p.105
CF 8.10	Ch.2, p.105
CF Appendix	Ch.6, p.391
CF Appendix	Ch.6, p.400
CF Appendix	Ch.6, p.402
CF BC0.27	Ch.2, p.46
CF BC0.28	Ch.2, p.47
CF BC3.21	Ch.2, p.61
CF BC3.21	Ch.6, p.401
CF BC4.96	Ch.27, p.2018
CF BC6.1	Ch.2, p.82
CF BC6.10	Ch.2, p.82
CF BC7.29	Ch.2, p.104
CF BC7.24	Ch.2, p.103

IFRS 1

IFRS 1.1	Ch.5, p.227
IFRS 1.2-3	Ch.5, p.233
IFRS 1.2(a)	Ch.5, p.232
IFRS 1.2(b)	Ch.5, p.232
IFRS 1.3	Ch.5, p.229
IFRS 1.3(a)	Ch.5, p.229
IFRS 1.3(b)	Ch.5, p.232
IFRS 1.3(b)-(c)	Ch.5, p.231
IFRS 1.3(d)	Ch.5, p.232
IFRS 1.4	Ch.5, p.230
IFRS 1.5	Ch.5, p.232
IFRS 1.6	Ch.5, p.236
IFRS 1.7	Ch.5, p.238
IFRS 1.7	Ch.5, p.266
IFRS 1.7	Ch.5, p.268
IFRS 1.7	Ch.5, p.291
IFRS 1.7	Ch.5, p.302
IFRS 1.7	Ch.5, p.364
IFRS 1.7	Ch.33, p.2599
IFRS 1.8	Ch.5, p.238
IFRS 1.9	Ch.5, p.240
IFRS 1.9	Ch.5, p.249
IFRS 1.10	Ch.5, p.239
IFRS 1.10	Ch.5, p.281
IFRS 1.10	Ch.5, p.296
IFRS 1.11	Ch.5, p.239
IFRS 1.11	Ch.5, p.367
IFRS 1.11	Ch.5, p.368
IFRS 1.11	Ch.33, p.2572
IFRS 1.12	Ch.5, p.241
IFRS 1.12(b)	Ch.5, p.266
IFRS 1.13	Ch.5, p.238
IFRS 1.13	Ch.5, p.240
IFRS 1.13-17	Ch.5, p.241
IFRS 1.14	Ch.5, p.244
IFRS 1.14	Ch.5, p.377
IFRS 1.14	Ch.5, p.379
IFRS 1.14-15	Ch.5, p.369

IFRS 1.14-17	Ch.5, p.365	IFRS 1.32(b)	Ch.5, p.358
IFRS 1.14-17	Ch.5, p.377	IFRS 1.32(c)	Ch.5, p.365
IFRS 1.4(a)	Ch.5, p.235	IFRS 1.32-33	Ch.5, p.356
IFRS 1.4A	Ch.5, p.233	IFRS 1 Appendix A	Ch.5, p.228
IFRS 1.4B	Ch.5, p.233	IFRS 1 Appendix A	Ch.5, p.229
IFRS 1.15	Ch.5, p.244	IFRS 1 Appendix A	Ch.5, p.232
IFRS 1.16	Ch.5, p.244	IFRS 1 Appendix A	Ch.5, p.234
IFRS 1.17	Ch.5, p.245	IFRS 1 Appendix A	Ch.5, p.236
IFRS 1.18	Ch.5, p.238	IFRS 1 Appendix A	Ch.5, p.240
IFRS 1.18	Ch.5, p.240	IFRS 1 Appendix B	Ch.5, p.241
IFRS 1.18	Ch.5, p.243	IFRS 1 Appendix C	Ch.5, p.242
IFRS 1.20	Ch.5, p.342	IFRS 1 Appendix C	Ch.5, p.266
IFRS 1.21	Ch.5, p.237	IFRS 1 Appendix C	Ch.5, p.267
IFRS 1.21	Ch.5, p.342	IFRS 1 Appendix C	Ch.5, p.307
IFRS 1.21-30	Ch.5, p.290	IFRS 1 Appendix D	Ch.5, p.242
IFRS 1.22	Ch.5, p.343	IFRS 1.B2	Ch.5, p.247
IFRS 1.23	Ch.5, p.343	IFRS 1.B2	Ch.5, p.271
IFRS 1.23	Ch.5, p.347	IFRS 1.B3	Ch.5, p.247
IFRS 1.23	Ch.5, p.360	IFRS 1.B4(a)	Ch.5, p.250
IFRS 1.23	Ch.5, p.365	IFRS 1.B4(b)	Ch.5, p.250
IFRS 1.23-28	Ch.5, p.322	IFRS 1.B5	Ch.5, p.248
IFRS 1.23A	Ch.5, p.233	IFRS 1.B5	Ch.5, p.252
IFRS 1.23B	Ch.5, p.233	IFRS 1.B6	Ch.5, p.248
IFRS 1.24(a)	Ch.5, p.345	IFRS 1.B6	Ch.5, p.252
IFRS 1.24(a)	Ch.5, p.358	IFRS 1.B6	Ch.5, p.253
IFRS 1.24(a)-(b)	Ch.5, p.365	IFRS 1.B6	Ch.5, p.256
IFRS 1.24(b)	Ch.5, p.345	IFRS 1.B7	Ch.5, p.262
IFRS 1.24(b)	Ch.5, p.358	IFRS 1.B7	Ch.5, p.268
IFRS 1.24(c)	Ch.5, p.356	IFRS 1.B8	Ch.5, p.262
IFRS 1.24(c)	Ch.5, p.376	IFRS 1.B8A	Ch.5, p.262
IFRS 1.25	Ch.5, p.345	IFRS 1.B8A	Ch.5, p.356
IFRS 1.25	Ch.5, p.358	IFRS 1.B8B	Ch.5, p.263
IFRS 1.25	Ch.5, p.364	IFRS 1.B8B	Ch.5, p.357
IFRS 1.26	Ch.5, p.245	IFRS 1.B8C	Ch.5, p.263
IFRS 1.26	Ch.5, p.345	IFRS 1.B8D	Ch.5, p.264
IFRS 1.26	Ch.5, p.358	IFRS 1.B8E	Ch.5, p.264
IFRS 1.26	Ch.5, p.365	IFRS 1.B8F	Ch.5, p.264
IFRS 1.27	Ch.5, p.346	IFRS 1.B8F(a)	Ch.5, p.264
IFRS 1.27	Ch.5, p.365	IFRS 1.B8G	Ch.5, p.264
IFRS 1.27A	Ch.5, p.347	IFRS 1.B9	Ch.5, p.265
IFRS 1.27A	Ch.5, p.365	IFRS 1.B10	Ch.5, p.265
IFRS 1.28	Ch.5, p.345	IFRS 1.B11	Ch.5, p.265
IFRS 1.29	Ch.5, p.314	IFRS 1.B12	Ch.5, p.265
IFRS 1.29-29A	Ch.5, p.356	IFRS 1.B13	Ch.5, p.266
IFRS 1.29A	Ch.5, p.315	IFRS 1.C1	Ch.5, p.262
IFRS 1.30	Ch.5, p.295	IFRS 1.C1	Ch.5, p.268
IFRS 1.30	Ch.5, p.296	IFRS 1.C1	Ch.5, p.271
IFRS 1.31	Ch.5, p.357	IFRS 1.C1	Ch.5, p.283
IFRS 1.32	Ch.5, p.360	IFRS 1.C2	Ch.5, p.282
IFRS 1.32	Ch.43, p.3550	IFRS 1.C2	Ch.5, p.283
IFRS 1.33	Ch.5, p.361	IFRS 1.C3	Ch.5, p.283
IFRS 1.30. D5	Ch.5, p.357	IFRS 1.C4(a)	Ch.5, p.271
IFRS 1.31A	Ch.5, p.298	IFRS 1.C4(a)	Ch.5, p.276
IFRS 1.31A	Ch.5, p.357	IFRS 1.C4(b)	Ch.5, p.271
IFRS 1.31B	Ch.5, p.300	IFRS 1.C4(b)	Ch.5, p.273
IFRS 1.31B	Ch.5, p.357	IFRS 1.C4(b)	Ch.5, p.277
IFRS 1.31C	Ch.5, p.358	IFRS 1.C4(b)	Ch.5, p.281
IFRS 1.32(a)	Ch.5, p.358	IFRS 1.C4(b)	Ch.5, p.286

IFRS 1.C4(b)(ii)	Ch.5, p.278	IFRS 1.D5	Ch.5, p.292
IFRS 1.C4(b)(ii)	Ch.5, p.280	IFRS 1.D5	Ch.5, p.293
IFRS 1.C4(b)(ii)	Ch.5, p.281	IFRS 1.D5	Ch.5, p.375
IFRS 1.C4(b)(ii)	Ch.5, p.378	IFRS 1.D5-D7	Ch.5, p.295
IFRS 1.C4(c)	Ch.5, p.272	IFRS 1.D5-D8	Ch.5, p.294
IFRS 1.C4(c)	Ch.5, p.281	IFRS 1.D5-D8	Ch.5, p.296
IFRS 1.C4(c)(i)	Ch.5, p.277	IFRS 1.D6	Ch.5, p.292
IFRS 1.C4(c)(i)	Ch.5, p.278	IFRS 1.D6	Ch.5, p.293
IFRS 1.C4(c)(ii)	Ch.5, p.281	IFRS 1.D7	Ch.5, p.292
IFRS 1.C4(d)	Ch.5, p.276	IFRS 1.D7	Ch.5, p.294
IFRS 1.C4(d)	Ch.5, p.277	IFRS 1.D7	Ch.5, p.296
IFRS 1.C4(e)	Ch.5, p.263	IFRS 1.D7	Ch.5, p.357
IFRS 1.C4(e)	Ch.5, p.274	IFRS 1.D7	Ch.5, p.375
IFRS 1.C4(e)	Ch.5, p.277	IFRS 1.D8	Ch.5, p.295
IFRS 1.C4(f)	Ch.5, p.272	IFRS 1.D8	Ch.5, p.296
IFRS 1.C4(f)	Ch.5, p.273	IFRS 1.D8	Ch.5, p.297
IFRS 1.C4(f)	Ch.5, p.277	IFRS 1.D9	Ch.5, p.273
IFRS 1.C4(f)	Ch.5, p.278	IFRS 1.D9	Ch.5, p.302
IFRS 1.C4(f)	Ch.5, p.280	IFRS 1.D12	Ch.5, p.304
IFRS 1.C4(f)	Ch.5, p.281	IFRS 1.D12	Ch.5, p.305
IFRS 1.C4(f)	Ch.5, p.286	IFRS 1.D12	Ch.5, p.310
IFRS 1.C4(f)	Ch.5, p.378	IFRS 1.D13	Ch.5, p.304
IFRS 1.C4(g)	Ch.5, p.272	IFRS 1.D13	Ch.5, p.305
IFRS 1.C4(g)	Ch.5, p.276	IFRS 1.D13	Ch.5, p.310
IFRS 1.C4(g)	Ch.5, p.277	IFRS 1.D13	Ch.5, p.311
IFRS 1.C4(g)	Ch.5, p.279	IFRS 1.D13	Ch.5, p.312
IFRS 1.C4(g)(i)	Ch.5, p.273	IFRS 1.D13A	Ch.5, p.304
IFRS 1.C4(g)(i)	Ch.5, p.278	IFRS 1.D13A	Ch.5, p.310
IFRS 1.C4(g)(i)	Ch.5, p.281	IFRS 1.D13A	Ch.5, p.312
IFRS 1.C4(g)(i)	Ch.5, p.286	IFRS 1.D14	Ch.5, p.306
IFRS 1.C4(g)(ii)	Ch.5, p.375	IFRS 1.D15	Ch.5, p.284
IFRS 1.C4(g)(ii)	Ch.5, p.376	IFRS 1.D15	Ch.5, p.306
IFRS 1.C4(h)	Ch.5, p.279	IFRS 1.D15	Ch.5, p.307
IFRS 1.C4(h)	Ch.5, p.280	IFRS 1.D15	Ch.5, p.357
IFRS 1.C4(h)	Ch.5, p.281	IFRS 1.D15	Ch.8, p.597
IFRS 1.C4(h)(i)	Ch.5, p.275	IFRS 1.D15A	Ch.5, p.307
IFRS 1.C4(i)	Ch.5, p.281	IFRS 1.D15A	Ch.8, p.598
IFRS 1.C4(i)(i)	Ch.5, p.281	IFRS 1.D16	Ch.5, p.307
IFRS 1.C4(i)(i)	Ch.5, p.282	IFRS 1.D16	Ch.5, p.308
IFRS 1.C4(i)(ii)	Ch.5, p.282	IFRS 1.D16-D17	Ch.5, p.307
IFRS 1.C4(j)	Ch.5, p.283	IFRS 1.D16(a)	Ch.5, p.304
IFRS 1.C4(j)	Ch.5, p.284	IFRS 1.D16(a)	Ch.5, p.313
IFRS 1.C4(j)	Ch.5, p.306	IFRS 1.D17	Ch.5, p.277
IFRS 1.C4(k)	Ch.5, p.273	IFRS 1.D17	Ch.5, p.283
IFRS 1.C4(k)	Ch.5, p.277	IFRS 1.D17	Ch.5, p.306
IFRS 1.C4(k)	Ch.5, p.278	IFRS 1.D17	Ch.5, p.307
IFRS 1.C4(k)	Ch.5, p.281	IFRS 1.D17	Ch.5, p.311
IFRS 1.C4(k)	Ch.5, p.285	IFRS 1.D17	Ch.5, p.313
IFRS 1.C4(k)	Ch.5, p.286	IFRS 1.D17	Ch.5, p.314
IFRS 1.C5	Ch.5, p.271	IFRS 1.D18	Ch.5, p.314
IFRS 1.C5	Ch.5, p.279	IFRS 1.D19	Ch.5, p.315
IFRS 1.C5	Ch.5, p.285	IFRS 1.D19	Ch.5, p.356
IFRS 1.C5	Ch.5, p.375	IFRS 1.D19-D19C	Ch.5, p.265
IFRS 1.D2	Ch.5, p.287	IFRS 1.D19A	Ch.5, p.314
IFRS 1.D2	Ch.5, p.289	IFRS 1.D19A	Ch.5, p.356
IFRS 1.D2	Ch.34, p.2884	IFRS 1.D19B	Ch.5, p.315
IFRS 1.D3	Ch.5, p.287	IFRS 1.D19C	Ch.5, p.315
IFRS 1.D4	Ch.5, p.290	IFRS 1.D20	Ch.5, p.316

IFRS 1.D21	Ch.5, p.316
IFRS 1.D21A	Ch.5, p.298
IFRS 1.D21A	Ch.5, p.319
IFRS 1.D22	Ch.5, p.319
IFRS 1.D23	Ch.5, p.320
IFRS 1.D25	Ch.5, p.321
IFRS 1.D26	Ch.5, p.321
IFRS 1.D26-D30	Ch.5, p.358
IFRS 1.D27	Ch.5, p.321
IFRS 1.D27	Ch.16, p.1276
IFRS 1.D28	Ch.5, p.321
IFRS 1.D29	Ch.5, p.321
IFRS 1.D30	Ch.5, p.322
IFRS 1.D31	Ch.5, p.285
IFRS 1.D31	Ch.5, p.322
IFRS 1.D32	Ch.5, p.322
IFRS 1.D33	Ch.5, p.342
IFRS 1.D34	Ch.5, p.335
IFRS 1.D34	Ch.5, p.336
IFRS 1.D34	Ch.5, p.371
IFRS 1.D35	Ch.5, p.335
IFRS 1.D35	Ch.5, p.336
IFRS 1.D35	Ch.5, p.337
IFRS 1.D35	Ch.5, p.371
IFRS 1.D36	Ch.5, p.342
IFRS 1.D8(b)	Ch.5, p.297
IFRS 1.D8A	Ch.5, p.298
IFRS 1.D8A(b)	Ch.5, p.357
IFRS 1.D8B	Ch.5, p.299
IFRS 1.D8B	Ch.5, p.300
IFRS 1.D8B	Ch.5, p.357
IFRS 1.D9B	Ch.5, p.302
IFRS 1.D9B	Ch.5, p.303
IFRS 1.D9B-D9E	Ch.5, p.273
IFRS 1.D9C	Ch.5, p.303
IFRS 1.D9D	Ch.5, p.303
IFRS 1.D9E	Ch.5, p.303
IFRS 1.IG3	Ch.5, p.244
IFRS 1.IG4	Ch.5, p.245
IFRS 1.IG7	Ch.5, p.277
IFRS 1.IG7	Ch.5, p.369
IFRS 1.IG9	Ch.5, p.295
IFRS 1.IG10	Ch.5, p.370
IFRS 1.IG11	Ch.5, p.294
IFRS 1.IG11	Ch.5, p.296
IFRS 1.IG12	Ch.5, p.292
IFRS 1.IG12	Ch.5, p.371
IFRS 1.IG13	Ch.5, p.316
IFRS 1.IG14	Ch.5, p.371
IFRS 1.IG17	Ch.5, p.372
IFRS 1.IG19	Ch.5, p.372
IFRS 1.IG20	Ch.5, p.373
IFRS 1.IG21	Ch.5, p.372
IFRS 1.IG21A	Ch.5, p.282
IFRS 1.IG23	Ch.5, p.320
IFRS 1.IG24	Ch.5, p.320
IFRS 1.IG26	Ch.5, p.305
IFRS 1.IG27(a)	Ch.5, p.283
IFRS 1.IG27(a)	Ch.5, p.306
IFRS 1.IG27(b)	Ch.5, p.306
IFRS 1.IG27(c)	Ch.5, p.284
IFRS 1.IG27(c)	Ch.5, p.306
IFRS 1.IG28	Ch.5, p.306
IFRS 1.IG30	Ch.5, p.312
IFRS 1.IG31	Ch.5, p.309
IFRS 1.IG32	Ch.5, p.375
IFRS 1.IG33	Ch.5, p.375
IFRS 1.IG34	Ch.5, p.375
IFRS 1.IG35	Ch.47, p.3699
IFRS 1.IG35-IG36	Ch.5, p.314
IFRS 1.IG36	Ch.47, p.3699
IFRS 1.IG37	Ch.5, p.358
IFRS 1.IG39	Ch.5, p.376
IFRS 1.IG40	Ch.5, p.376
IFRS 1.IG40	Ch.5, p.377
IFRS 1.IG41	Ch.5, p.376
IFRS 1.IG41	Ch.5, p.377
IFRS 1.IG43	Ch.5, p.376
IFRS 1.IG44	Ch.5, p.378
IFRS 1.IG46	Ch.5, p.378
IFRS 1.IG47	Ch.5, p.378
IFRS 1.IG48	Ch.5, p.378
IFRS 1.IG49	Ch.5, p.378
IFRS 1.IG51	Ch.5, p.379
IFRS 1.IG53	Ch.5, p.247
IFRS 1.IG53	Ch.5, p.248
IFRS 1.IG54	Ch.5, p.247
IFRS 1.IG55	Ch.5, p.264
IFRS 1.IG56	Ch.5, p.262
IFRS 1.IG57	Ch.5, p.263
IFRS 1.IG58A	Ch.5, p.250
IFRS 1.IG58A	Ch.5, p.263
IFRS 1.IG58B	Ch.5, p.245
IFRS 1.IG58B	Ch.5, p.250
IFRS 1.IG59	Ch.5, p.263
IFRS 1.IG60	Ch.5, p.248
IFRS 1.IG60	Ch.5, p.256
IFRS 1.IG60	Ch.5, p.257
IFRS 1.IG60	Ch.5, p.258
IFRS 1.IG60A	Ch.5, p.254
IFRS 1.IG60B	Ch.5, p.253
IFRS 1.IG60B	Ch.5, p.254
IFRS 1.IG60B	Ch.5, p.255
IFRS 1.IG60B	Ch.5, p.256
IFRS 1.IG62	Ch.5, p.369
IFRS 1.IG201	Ch.5, p.316
IFRS 1.IG201-IG203	Ch.5, p.316
IFRS 1.IG Example 1	Ch.5, p.246
IFRS 1.IG Example 10	Ch.5, p.359
IFRS 1.IG Example 11	Ch.5, p.345
IFRS 1.IG Example 12	Ch.5, p.265
IFRS 1.IG Example 2	Ch.5, p.276
IFRS 1.IG Example 3	Ch.5, p.272
IFRS 1.IG Example 4	Ch.5, p.285
IFRS 1.IG Example 4	Ch.5, p.286
IFRS 1.IG Example 5	Ch.5, p.281

Index of standards

IFRS 1.IG Example 6	Ch.5, p.284
IFRS 1.IG Example 7	Ch.5, p.273
IFRS 1.IG Example 8	Ch.5, p.308
IFRS 1.IG Example 9	Ch.5, p.277
IFRS 1.IG Example 9	Ch.5, p.311
IFRS 1.IG5-IG6	Ch.5, p.365
IFRS 1.BC3	Ch.5, p.227
IFRS 1.BC5	Ch.5, p.230
IFRS 1.BC6	Ch.5, p.230
IFRS 1.BC9	Ch.5, p.228
IFRS 1.BC10	Ch.5, p.228
IFRS 1.BC11	Ch.5, p.238
IFRS 1.BC14	Ch.5, p.240
IFRS 1.BC36	Ch.5, p.274
IFRS 1.BC39	Ch.5, p.279
IFRS 1.BC43	Ch.5, p.302
IFRS 1.BC45	Ch.5, p.292
IFRS 1.BC45	Ch.5, p.376
IFRS 1.BC47	Ch.5, p.294
IFRS 1.BC62	Ch.5, p.309
IFRS 1.BC63	Ch.5, p.311
IFRS 1.BC67	Ch.5, p.375
IFRS 1.BC75	Ch.5, p.252
IFRS 1.BC84	Ch.5, p.244
IFRS 1.BC91	Ch.5, p.343
IFRS 1.BC94	Ch.5, p.356
IFRS 1.BC97	Ch.5, p.347
IFRS 1.BC11A	Ch.5, p.238
IFRS 1.BC12(a)	Ch.5, p.242
IFRS 1.BC12(b)	Ch.5, p.241
IFRS 1.BC3B	Ch.5, p.228
IFRS 1.BC46B	Ch.5, p.297
IFRS 1.BC47A	Ch.5, p.298
IFRS 1.BC47B	Ch.5, p.298
IFRS 1.BC47D	Ch.5, p.298
IFRS 1.BC47F	Ch.5, p.299
IFRS 1.BC47G	Ch.5, p.300
IFRS 1.BC47H	Ch.5, p.300
IFRS 1.BC47I	Ch.5, p.299
IFRS 1.BC55C	Ch.5, p.310
IFRS 1.BC63CA	Ch.5, p.319
IFRS 1.BC63J	Ch.5, p.322
IFRS 1.BC6C	Ch.5, p.233
IFRS 1.BC83A	Ch.5, p.316
IFRS 1.BC89B	Ch.5, p.342

IFRS 2

IFRS 2.1	Ch.34, p.2642
IFRS 2.2	Ch.34, p.2643
IFRS 2.2	Ch.34, p.2651
IFRS 2.2	Ch.34, p.2662
IFRS 2.2	Ch.34, p.2855
IFRS 2.2(c)	Ch.34, p.2794
IFRS 2.3A	Ch.34, p.2644
IFRS 2.4	Ch.34, p.2654
IFRS 2.5	Ch.8, p.619
IFRS 2.5	Ch.34, p.2644
IFRS 2.5	Ch.34, p.2654
IFRS 2.5	Ch.34, p.2655
IFRS 2.6	Ch.34, p.2655
IFRS 2.6A	Ch.34, p.2674
IFRS 2.6A	Ch.34, p.2693
IFRS 2.6A	Ch.34, p.2740
IFRS 2.6A	Ch.34, p.2775
IFRS 2.7	Ch.34, p.2663
IFRS 2.7	Ch.34, p.2709
IFRS 2.8	Ch.34, p.2663
IFRS 2.9	Ch.34, p.2663
IFRS 2.10	Ch.8, p.615
IFRS 2.10	Ch.9, p.750
IFRS 2.10	Ch.34, p.2674
IFRS 2.11	Ch.34, p.2676
IFRS 2.11	Ch.34, p.2677
IFRS 2.12	Ch.34, p.2677
IFRS 2.13	Ch.9, p.750
IFRS 2.13	Ch.34, p.2691
IFRS 2.13A	Ch.9, p.750
IFRS 2.13A	Ch.34, p.2651
IFRS 2.13A	Ch.34, p.2662
IFRS 2.13A	Ch.34, p.2794
IFRS 2.14	Ch.34, p.2693
IFRS 2.15	Ch.34, p.2694
IFRS 2.15(b)	Ch.34, p.2699
IFRS 2.15(b)	Ch.34, p.2708
IFRS 2.16	Ch.34, p.2692
IFRS 2.17	Ch.34, p.2692
IFRS 2.18	Ch.34, p.2692
IFRS 2.19	Ch.34, p.2695
IFRS 2.19-20	Ch.34, p.2695
IFRS 2.19-21	Ch.34, p.2707
IFRS 2.19-21A	Ch.34, p.2693
IFRS 2.21	Ch.34, p.2704
IFRS 2.21A	Ch.34, p.2712
IFRS 2.22	Ch.34, p.2693
IFRS 2.23	Ch.34, p.2696
IFRS 2.24(a)	Ch.34, p.2766
IFRS 2.24(b)	Ch.34, p.2767
IFRS 2.25	Ch.34, p.2768
IFRS 2.25(a)	Ch.34, p.2768
IFRS 2.25(b)	Ch.34, p.2768
IFRS 2.26	Ch.34, p.2714
IFRS 2.26-28	Ch.34, p.2734
IFRS 2.26-29	Ch.5, p.287
IFRS 2.26-29	Ch.5, p.289
IFRS 2.27	Ch.34, p.2715
IFRS 2.27	Ch.34, p.2716
IFRS 2.27	Ch.34, p.2725
IFRS 2.28	Ch.34, p.2726
IFRS 2.28	Ch.34, p.2727
IFRS 2.28	Ch.34, p.2732
IFRS 2.28	Ch.34, p.2734
IFRS 2.28(a)	Ch.34, p.2729
IFRS 2.28(b)	Ch.47, p.3743
IFRS 2.28(c)	Ch.34, p.2731

IFRS 2.28A	Ch.34, p.2713
IFRS 2.28A	Ch.34, p.2714
IFRS 2.29	Ch.34, p.2726
IFRS 2.30	Ch.34, p.2777
IFRS 2.30-33D	Ch.34, p.2775
IFRS 2.31	Ch.34, p.2770
IFRS 2.31	Ch.34, p.2775
IFRS 2.32	Ch.34, p.2777
IFRS 2.32-33	Ch.34, p.2777
IFRS 2.33	Ch.34, p.2775
IFRS 2.33A-33B	Ch.34, p.2777
IFRS 2.33C	Ch.34, p.2779
IFRS 2.33D	Ch.34, p.2777
IFRS 2.33D	Ch.34, p.2779
IFRS 2.33E	Ch.34, p.2860
IFRS 2.33F	Ch.34, p.2860
IFRS 2.33G	Ch.34, p.2860
IFRS 2.33H(a)	Ch.34, p.2861
IFRS 2.33H(b)	Ch.34, p.2860
IFRS 2.34	Ch.34, p.2788
IFRS 2.35	Ch.34, p.2788
IFRS 2.35	Ch.34, p.2789
IFRS 2.35	Ch.34, p.2794
IFRS 2.36	Ch.34, p.2789
IFRS 2.37	Ch.34, p.2790
IFRS 2.38	Ch.34, p.2790
IFRS 2.39-40	Ch.34, p.2792
IFRS 2.40	Ch.34, p.2792
IFRS 2.41	Ch.34, p.2795
IFRS 2.41-42	Ch.34, p.2795
IFRS 2.43	Ch.34, p.2796
IFRS 2.43A	Ch.34, p.2644
IFRS 2.43A	Ch.34, p.2815
IFRS 2.43B	Ch.34, p.2647
IFRS 2.43B	Ch.34, p.2648
IFRS 2.43B	Ch.34, p.2811
IFRS 2.43B	Ch.34, p.2815
IFRS 2.43B-43C	Ch.34, p.2645
IFRS 2.43B-43C	Ch.34, p.2648
IFRS 2.43C	Ch.34, p.2649
IFRS 2.43C	Ch.34, p.2816
IFRS 2.43D	Ch.34, p.2815
IFRS 2.44	Ch.5, p.287
IFRS 2.44	Ch.34, p.2845
IFRS 2.45	Ch.5, p.287
IFRS 2.45	Ch.34, p.2845
IFRS 2.46	Ch.34, p.2846
IFRS 2.47	Ch.34, p.2847
IFRS 2.48	Ch.34, p.2848
IFRS 2.49	Ch.34, p.2848
IFRS 2.50	Ch.34, p.2848
IFRS 2.51	Ch.34, p.2848
IFRS 2.52	Ch.34, p.2848
IFRS 2.52	Ch.34, p.2861
IFRS 2.62	Ch.34, p.2638
IFRS 2.63	Ch.34, p.2638
IFRS 2.64	Ch.34, p.2638
IFRS 2.63A	Ch.34, p.2643
IFRS 2.63D	Ch.34, p.2638
IFRS 2 Appendix A	Ch.34, p.2642
IFRS 2 Appendix A	Ch.34, p.2664
IFRS 2 Appendix A	Ch.34, p.2671
IFRS 2 Appendix A	Ch.34, p.2674
IFRS 2 Appendix A	Ch.34, p.2676
IFRS 2 Appendix A	Ch.34, p.2677
IFRS 2 Appendix A	Ch.34, p.2678
IFRS 2 Appendix A	Ch.34, p.2692
IFRS 2 Appendix A	Ch.34, p.2693
IFRS 2 Appendix A	Ch.34, p.2704
IFRS 2 Appendix A	Ch.34, p.2727
IFRS 2 Appendix A	Ch.34, p.2771
IFRS 2 Appendix A	Ch.34, p.2789
IFRS 2.B1	Ch.34, p.2739
IFRS 2.B2	Ch.34, p.2765
IFRS 2.B3	Ch.34, p.2765
IFRS 2.B4-5	Ch.34, p.2744
IFRS 2.B5	Ch.34, p.2746
IFRS 2.B6	Ch.34, p.2754
IFRS 2.B7-9	Ch.34, p.2754
IFRS 2.B10	Ch.34, p.2754
IFRS 2.B11-12	Ch.34, p.2755
IFRS 2.B13-15	Ch.34, p.2755
IFRS 2.B16-17	Ch.34, p.2755
IFRS 2.B18	Ch.34, p.2757
IFRS 2.B19-21	Ch.34, p.2758
IFRS 2.B22-24	Ch.34, p.2759
IFRS 2.B25	Ch.34, p.2760
IFRS 2.B26	Ch.34, p.2761
IFRS 2.B27-29	Ch.34, p.2761
IFRS 2.B30	Ch.34, p.2659
IFRS 2.B30	Ch.34, p.2761
IFRS 2.B31	Ch.34, p.2765
IFRS 2.B31-32	Ch.34, p.2762
IFRS 2.B33-34	Ch.34, p.2765
IFRS 2.B34	Ch.34, p.2762
IFRS 2.B35	Ch.34, p.2762
IFRS 2.B36	Ch.34, p.2763
IFRS 2.B37	Ch.34, p.2763
IFRS 2.B38-39	Ch.34, p.2764
IFRS 2.B40-41	Ch.34, p.2764
IFRS 2.B42	Ch.34, p.2715
IFRS 2.B42	Ch.34, p.2716
IFRS 2.B42	Ch.34, p.2725
IFRS 2.B42-43	Ch.34, p.2716
IFRS 2.B42-44	Ch.34, p.2716
IFRS 2.B43	Ch.34, p.2715
IFRS 2.B43(a)	Ch.34, p.2717
IFRS 2.B43(a)	Ch.34, p.2718
IFRS 2.B43(b)	Ch.34, p.2718
IFRS 2.B43(c)	Ch.34, p.2718
IFRS 2.B43-44	Ch.34, p.2725
IFRS 2.B44	Ch.34, p.2715
IFRS 2.B44	Ch.34, p.2725
IFRS 2.B44(a)	Ch.34, p.2720
IFRS 2.B44(b)	Ch.34, p.2721
IFRS 2.B44(b)	Ch.34, p.2724

Index of standards

IFRS 2.B44(c)	Ch.34, p.2720
IFRS 2.B44(c)	Ch.34, p.2721
IFRS 2.B44A	Ch.34, p.2786
IFRS 2.B44B	Ch.34, p.2787
IFRS 2.B44C	Ch.34, p.2787
IFRS 2.B45	Ch.34, p.2815
IFRS 2.B45	Ch.34, p.2816
IFRS 2.B45-46	Ch.34, p.2815
IFRS 2.B48-49	Ch.34, p.2772
IFRS 2.B48(b)	Ch.34, p.2646
IFRS 2.B49	Ch.34, p.2648
IFRS 2.B50	Ch.34, p.2648
IFRS 2.B50	Ch.34, p.2817
IFRS 2.B52	Ch.34, p.2817
IFRS 2.B52(a)	Ch.34, p.2645
IFRS 2.B52(b)	Ch.34, p.2647
IFRS 2.B52(b)	Ch.34, p.2811
IFRS 2.B53	Ch.34, p.2817
IFRS 2.B53-B54	Ch.34, p.2645
IFRS 2.B54	Ch.34, p.2817
IFRS 2.B55	Ch.34, p.2647
IFRS 2.B55	Ch.34, p.2811
IFRS 2.B55	Ch.34, p.2817
IFRS 2.B56-B57	Ch.34, p.2818
IFRS 2.B56-B58	Ch.34, p.2649
IFRS 2.B58	Ch.34, p.2818
IFRS 2.B59	Ch.34, p.2840
IFRS 2.B60	Ch.34, p.2840
IFRS 2.B61	Ch.34, p.2841
IFRS 2.IG1-3	Ch.34, p.2678
IFRS 2.IG2	Ch.34, p.2678
IFRS 2.IG4	Ch.34, p.2679
IFRS 2.IG5	Ch.34, p.2691
IFRS 2.IG5D	Ch.34, p.2651
IFRS 2.IG6-7	Ch.34, p.2691
IFRS 2.IG11	Ch.34, p.2696
IFRS 2.IG11	Ch.34, p.2698
IFRS 2.IG12	Ch.34, p.2699
IFRS 2.IG12	Ch.34, p.2702
IFRS 2.IG13	Ch.34, p.2704
IFRS 2.IG13	Ch.34, p.2707
IFRS 2.IG14	Ch.34, p.2708
IFRS 2.IG15	Ch.34, p.2717
IFRS 2.IG15	Ch.34, p.2721
IFRS 2.IG19	Ch.34, p.2775
IFRS 2.IG24	Ch.34, p.2669
IFRS 2.IG24	Ch.34, p.2713
IFRS 2.IG24	Ch.34, p.2714
IFRS 2.IG Example 1	Ch.34, p.2651
IFRS 2.IG Example 1	Ch.34, p.2652
IFRS 2.IG Example 2	Ch.34, p.2700
IFRS 2.IG Example 3	Ch.34, p.2701
IFRS 2.IG Example 4	Ch.34, p.2700
IFRS 2.IG Example 4	Ch.34, p.2702
IFRS 2.IG Example 5	Ch.34, p.2707
IFRS 2.IG Example 6	Ch.34, p.2708
IFRS 2.IG Example 7	Ch.34, p.2717
IFRS 2.IG Example 8	Ch.34, p.2721
IFRS 2.IG Example 9	Ch.34, p.2792
IFRS 2.IG Example 9A	Ch.34, p.2713
IFRS 2.IG Example 10	Ch.34, p.2767
IFRS 2.IG Example 12	Ch.34, p.2775
IFRS 2.IG Example 12A	Ch.34, p.2775
IFRS 2.IG Example 12B	Ch.34, p.2778
IFRS 2.IG Example 12B	Ch.34, p.2860
IFRS 2.IG Example 12C	Ch.34, p.2787
IFRS 2.IG Example 13	Ch.34, p.2791
IFRS 2.BC8-17	Ch.34, p.2653
IFRS 2.BC18C	Ch.34, p.2652
IFRS 2.BC18D	Ch.34, p.2652
IFRS 2.BC22E	Ch.34, p.2643
IFRS 2.BC22G	Ch.34, p.2647
IFRS 2.BC24	Ch.34, p.2739
IFRS 2.BC54-BC57	Ch.37, p.3049
IFRS 2.BC70-74	Ch.34, p.2822
IFRS 2.BC88-96	Ch.34, p.2675
IFRS 2.BC109	Ch.34, p.2641
IFRS 2.BC109	Ch.47, p.3704
IFRS 2.BC110	Ch.34, p.2641
IFRS 2.BC110	Ch.47, p.3704
IFRS 2.BC126	Ch.34, p.2675
IFRS 2.BC126-127	Ch.34, p.2676
IFRS 2.BC130	Ch.34, p.2740
IFRS 2.BC131	Ch.34, p.2744
IFRS 2.BC152	Ch.34, p.2744
IFRS 2.BC153-169	Ch.34, p.2753
IFRS 2.BC171A	Ch.34, p.2668
IFRS 2.BC171B	Ch.34, p.2669
IFRS 2.BC171B	Ch.34, p.2670
IFRS 2.BC183-184	Ch.34, p.2705
IFRS 2.BC188-192	Ch.34, p.2769
IFRS 2.BC218-221	Ch.34, p.2696
IFRS 2.BC222-237	Ch.34, p.2715
IFRS 2.BC233	Ch.34, p.2732
IFRS 2.BC237A	Ch.34, p.2713
IFRS 2.BC237H	Ch.34, p.2787
IFRS 2.BC237K	Ch.34, p.2782
IFRS 2.BC246-251	Ch.34, p.2775
IFRS 2.BC255G	Ch.34, p.2858
IFRS 2.BC255G-I	Ch.34, p.2860
IFRS 2.BC255J	Ch.34, p.2861
IFRS 2.BC256	Ch.34, p.2803
IFRS 2.BC268H-268K	Ch.34, p.2818
IFRS 2.BC311-BC329	Ch.33, p.2589
IFRS 2.BC311-BC329	Ch.33, p.2593
IFRS 2.BC330-333	Ch.34, p.2673
IFRS 2.BC341	Ch.34, p.2670
IFRS 2.BC353-BC358	Ch.34, p.2669
IFRS 2.BC364	Ch.34, p.2668

IFRS 3 (2000)

IFRS 3(2000).21B	Ch.9, p.669

IFRS 3 (2007)

IFRS 3(2007).B8	Ch.8, p.595
IFRS 3(2007).B8	Ch.9, p.744
IFRS 3(2007).BC28	Ch.10, p.771

IFRS 3 (2022)

IFRS 3(2022).11	Ch.9, p.668
IFRS 3(2022).11	Ch.9, p.686
IFRS 3(2022).23A	Ch.9, p.686
IFRS 3(2022).BC114D	Ch.9, p.686

IFRS 3

IFRS 3.1	Ch.10, p.768
IFRS 3.2	Ch.9, p.647
IFRS 3.2	Ch.9, p.648
IFRS 3.2	Ch.10, p.766
IFRS 3.2	Ch.12, p.932
IFRS 3.2	Ch.46, p.3652
IFRS 3.2(a)	Ch.11, p.856
IFRS 3.2(a)	Ch.12, p.893
IFRS 3.2(b)	Ch.6, p.393
IFRS 3.2(b)	Ch.7, p.504
IFRS 3.2(b)	Ch.8, p.620
IFRS 3.2(b)	Ch.18, p.1397
IFRS 3.2(b)	Ch.19, p.1457
IFRS 3.2(b)	Ch.33, p.2516
IFRS 3.2(b)	Ch.33, p.2609
IFRS 3.2(b)	Ch.43, p.3418
IFRS 3.2(b)	Ch.49, p.3857
IFRS 3.2(b)	Ch.56, p.4864
IFRS 3.2(c)	Ch.6, p.393
IFRS 3.2(c)	Ch.10, p.768
IFRS 3.2(c)	Ch.56, p.4870
IFRS 3.2A	Ch.5, p.267
IFRS 3.2A	Ch.9, p.647
IFRS 3.3	Ch.5, p.267
IFRS 3.3	Ch.7, p.504
IFRS 3.3	Ch.7, p.514
IFRS 3.3	Ch.9, p.650
IFRS 3.3	Ch.10, p.768
IFRS 3.4	Ch.5, p.271
IFRS 3.4	Ch.9, p.659
IFRS 3.5	Ch.5, p.271
IFRS 3.5	Ch.9, p.659
IFRS 3.5	Ch.10, p.777
IFRS 3.6	Ch.9, p.659
IFRS 3.7	Ch.9, p.659
IFRS 3.7	Ch.9, p.752
IFRS 3.8	Ch.6, p.393
IFRS 3.8	Ch.7, p.503
IFRS 3.8	Ch.9, p.665
IFRS 3.9	Ch.9, p.665
IFRS 3.10	Ch.7, p.541
IFRS 3.10	Ch.9, p.666
IFRS 3.10	Ch.9, p.710
IFRS 3.10	Ch.33, p.2605
IFRS 3.11	Ch.2, p.47
IFRS 3.11	Ch.9, p.667
IFRS 3.11	Ch.43, p.3414
IFRS 3.12	Ch.9, p.667
IFRS 3.12	Ch.9, p.726
IFRS 3.13	Ch.9, p.667
IFRS 3.14	Ch.9, p.666
IFRS 3.15	Ch.9, p.670
IFRS 3.15	Ch.46, p.3652
IFRS 3.15	Ch.53, p.4277
IFRS 3.15	Ch.56, p.4863
IFRS 3.16	Ch.9, p.670
IFRS 3.16(b)	Ch.53, p.4277
IFRS 3.16(c)	Ch.46, p.3652
IFRS 3.17	Ch.9, p.670
IFRS 3.17(b)	Ch.55, p.4549
IFRS 3.18	Ch.9, p.666
IFRS 3.18	Ch.17, p.1365
IFRS 3.18	Ch.33, p.2605
IFRS 3.18	Ch.49, p.3857
IFRS 3.18	Ch.51, p.4016
IFRS 3.19	Ch.7, p.504
IFRS 3.19	Ch.7, p.541
IFRS 3.19	Ch.7, p.554
IFRS 3.19	Ch.9, p.666
IFRS 3.19	Ch.9, p.710
IFRS 3.19	Ch.9, p.714
IFRS 3.19	Ch.20, p.1602
IFRS 3.20	Ch.9, p.666
IFRS 3.20	Ch.9, p.669
IFRS 3.21	Ch.9, p.690
IFRS 3.22	Ch.9, p.690
IFRS 3.23	Ch.9, p.691
IFRS 3.23	Ch.26, p.1935
IFRS 3.23	Ch.26, p.1942
IFRS 3.23	Ch.26, p.1961
IFRS 3.24	Ch.9, p.692
IFRS 3.24	Ch.33, p.2562
IFRS 3.24	Ch.33, p.2605
IFRS 3.25	Ch.9, p.692
IFRS 3.25	Ch.33, p.2605
IFRS 3.26	Ch.9, p.692
IFRS 3.26	Ch.20, p.1584
IFRS 3.27	Ch.9, p.693
IFRS 3.27	Ch.45, p.3606
IFRS 3.27-28	Ch.9, p.693
IFRS 3.28	Ch.9, p.693
IFRS 3.29	Ch.9, p.695
IFRS 3.30	Ch.7, p.541
IFRS 3.30	Ch.9, p.695
IFRS 3.30	Ch.20, p.1584
IFRS 3.30	Ch.34, p.2804
IFRS 3.31	Ch.9, p.695
IFRS 3.31A	Ch.56, p.4863
IFRS 3.32	Ch.9, p.697

IFRS 3.32	Ch.9, p.708
IFRS 3.32	Ch.10, p.777
IFRS 3.33	Ch.9, p.699
IFRS 3.33	Ch.9, p.709
IFRS 3.33	Ch.9, p.741
IFRS 3.33	Ch.10, p.779
IFRS 3.34	Ch.9, p.697
IFRS 3.34	Ch.9, p.724
IFRS 3.34	Ch.10, p.777
IFRS 3.35	Ch.9, p.724
IFRS 3.36	Ch.9, p.724
IFRS 3.36	Ch.51, p.4016
IFRS 3.37	Ch.8, p.584
IFRS 3.37	Ch.9, p.698
IFRS 3.37	Ch.10, p.779
IFRS 3.37	Ch.11, p.828
IFRS 3.38	Ch.9, p.698
IFRS 3.39	Ch.7, p.539
IFRS 3.39	Ch.9, p.700
IFRS 3.39	Ch.40, p.3178
IFRS 3.39-40	Ch.9, p.703
IFRS 3.40	Ch.5, p.287
IFRS 3.40	Ch.7, p.539
IFRS 3.40	Ch.9, p.704
IFRS 3.40	Ch.9, p.706
IFRS 3.40	Ch.40, p.3178
IFRS 3.41	Ch.9, p.717
IFRS 3.41-42	Ch.11, p.836
IFRS 3.41-42	Ch.11, p.870
IFRS 3.42	Ch.9, p.717
IFRS 3.42A	Ch.9, p.723
IFRS 3.42A	Ch.12, p.937
IFRS 3.43	Ch.9, p.708
IFRS 3.44	Ch.9, p.709
IFRS 3.45	Ch.9, p.736
IFRS 3.45	Ch.9, p.737
IFRS 3.45	Ch.20, p.1589
IFRS 3.45	Ch.43, p.3562
IFRS 3.46	Ch.9, p.736
IFRS 3.46	Ch.20, p.1589
IFRS 3.47	Ch.9, p.737
IFRS 3.48	Ch.9, p.738
IFRS 3.49	Ch.9, p.737
IFRS 3.50	Ch.9, p.738
IFRS 3.51	Ch.9, p.726
IFRS 3.51-53	Ch.9, p.708
IFRS 3.52	Ch.9, p.727
IFRS 3.52	Ch.9, p.731
IFRS 3.52	Ch.34, p.2804
IFRS 3.53	Ch.9, p.707
IFRS 3.53	Ch.14, p.1051
IFRS 3.53	Ch.40, p.3148
IFRS 3.53	Ch.40, p.3177
IFRS 3.53	Ch.41, p.3238
IFRS 3.53	Ch.47, p.3739
IFRS 3.54	Ch.9, p.690
IFRS 3.54	Ch.9, p.739
IFRS 3.55	Ch.9, p.695
IFRS 3.56	Ch.9, p.691
IFRS 3.56	Ch.26, p.1942
IFRS 3.56	Ch.26, p.1962
IFRS 3.57	Ch.9, p.693
IFRS 3.57	Ch.51, p.3959
IFRS 3.58	Ch.5, p.287
IFRS 3.58	Ch.7, p.539
IFRS 3.58	Ch.9, p.707
IFRS 3.58	Ch.40, p.3178
IFRS 3.58	Ch.55, p.4542
IFRS 3.58	Ch.56, p.4691
IFRS 3.58(b)(i)	Ch.45, p.3602
IFRS 3.59	Ch.9, p.753
IFRS 3.59(b)	Ch.41, p.3207
IFRS 3.60	Ch.9, p.753
IFRS 3.61	Ch.9, p.756
IFRS 3.62	Ch.9, p.756
IFRS 3.63	Ch.9, p.757
IFRS 3.64	Ch.20, p.1602
IFRS 3.64N	Ch.56, p.4863
IFRS 3.64N	Ch.56, p.4922
IFRS 3.67	Ch.20, p.1597
IFRS 3 Appendix A	Ch.5, p.267
IFRS 3 Appendix A	Ch.6, p.393
IFRS 3 Appendix A	Ch.7, p.503
IFRS 3 Appendix A	Ch.7, p.504
IFRS 3 Appendix A	Ch.7, p.514
IFRS 3 Appendix A	Ch.8, p.619
IFRS 3 Appendix A	Ch.9, p.639
IFRS 3 Appendix A	Ch.9, p.650
IFRS 3 Appendix A	Ch.9, p.665
IFRS 3 Appendix A	Ch.9, p.672
IFRS 3 Appendix A	Ch.9, p.694
IFRS 3 Appendix A	Ch.9, p.697
IFRS 3 Appendix A	Ch.9, p.699
IFRS 3 Appendix A	Ch.9, p.703
IFRS 3 Appendix A	Ch.9, p.709
IFRS 3 Appendix A	Ch.9, p.710
IFRS 3 Appendix A	Ch.9, p.752
IFRS 3 Appendix A	Ch.10, p.768
IFRS 3 Appendix A	Ch.10, p.789
IFRS 3 Appendix A	Ch.17, p.1296
IFRS 3 Appendix A	Ch.43, p.3412
IFRS 3 Appendix A	Ch.55, p.4598
IFRS 3 Appendix A	Ch.56, p.4870
IFRS 3.B1	Ch.10, p.768
IFRS 3.B1	Ch.20, p.1623
IFRS 3.B1-B4	Ch.9, p.649
IFRS 3.B1-B4	Ch.10, p.768
IFRS 3.B2	Ch.10, p.769
IFRS 3.B2	Ch.39, p.3114
IFRS 3.B3	Ch.10, p.769
IFRS 3.B4	Ch.10, p.769
IFRS 3.B4	Ch.10, p.787
IFRS 3.B5	Ch.9, p.650
IFRS 3.B6	Ch.9, p.650
IFRS 3.B7	Ch.9, p.651
IFRS 3.B7	Ch.55, p.4598

IFRS 3.B7-B12D	Ch.7, p.514	IFRS 3.B37	Ch.9, p.685
IFRS 3.B7A	Ch.9, p.651	IFRS 3.B37	Ch.20, p.1584
IFRS 3.B7A	Ch.19, p.1454	IFRS 3.B38	Ch.9, p.686
IFRS 3.B7A	Ch.19, p.1456	IFRS 3.B38	Ch.20, p.1584
IFRS 3.B7B	Ch.9, p.652	IFRS 3.B39	Ch.9, p.739
IFRS 3.B7B	Ch.19, p.1455	IFRS 3.B40	Ch.9, p.686
IFRS 3.B7C	Ch.9, p.653	IFRS 3.B41	Ch.9, p.687
IFRS 3.B7-B8	Ch.56, p.4870	IFRS 3.B41	Ch.49, p.3857
IFRS 3.B7-B12D	Ch.7, p.504	IFRS 3.B41	Ch.51, p.4017
IFRS 3.B8	Ch.9, p.651	IFRS 3.B42	Ch.9, p.671
IFRS 3.B8	Ch.9, p.654	IFRS 3.B43	Ch.9, p.687
IFRS 3.B8	Ch.9, p.655	IFRS 3.B44	Ch.9, p.711
IFRS 3.B8A	Ch.9, p.654	IFRS 3.B45	Ch.9, p.711
IFRS 3.B9	Ch.9, p.651	IFRS 3.B46	Ch.9, p.709
IFRS 3.B11	Ch.9, p.655	IFRS 3.B47	Ch.9, p.709
IFRS 3.B11	Ch.19, p.1454	IFRS 3.B47	Ch.9, p.710
IFRS 3.B12B	Ch.9, p.654	IFRS 3.B48	Ch.9, p.710
IFRS 3.B12B	Ch.9, p.658	IFRS 3.B49	Ch.9, p.710
IFRS 3.B12C	Ch.9, p.655	IFRS 3.B50	Ch.9, p.727
IFRS 3.B12D(a)	Ch.9, p.654	IFRS 3.B50	Ch.34, p.2805
IFRS 3.B12D(b)	Ch.9, p.655	IFRS 3.B51	Ch.9, p.728
IFRS 3.B12D(c)	Ch.9, p.655	IFRS 3.B52	Ch.9, p.728
IFRS 3.B13	Ch.9, p.659	IFRS 3.B53	Ch.9, p.730
IFRS 3.B14	Ch.9, p.660	IFRS 3.B54	Ch.9, p.731
IFRS 3.B14	Ch.9, p.748	IFRS 3.B55	Ch.9, p.732
IFRS 3.B15	Ch.9, p.660	IFRS 3.B55(a)	Ch.9, p.732
IFRS 3.B16	Ch.9, p.660	IFRS 3.B55(a)	Ch.9, p.733
IFRS 3.B17	Ch.9, p.660	IFRS 3.B55(e)	Ch.9, p.733
IFRS 3.B18	Ch.9, p.661	IFRS 3.B56	Ch.9, p.707
IFRS 3.B18	Ch.10, p.789	IFRS 3.B56	Ch.34, p.2805
IFRS 3.B19	Ch.5, p.271	IFRS 3.B56	Ch.34, p.2808
IFRS 3.B19	Ch.9, p.740	IFRS 3.B56-B62	Ch.9, p.707
IFRS 3.B19	Ch.9, p.750	IFRS 3.B56-B62	Ch.9, p.734
IFRS 3.B19	Ch.9, p.752	IFRS 3.B56-B62	Ch.9, p.749
IFRS 3.B19	Ch.10, p.789	IFRS 3.B57-59	Ch.34, p.2805
IFRS 3.B20	Ch.9, p.740	IFRS 3.B59	Ch.34, p.2805
IFRS 3.B21	Ch.9, p.742	IFRS 3.B59	Ch.34, p.2809
IFRS 3.B22	Ch.9, p.743	IFRS 3.B60	Ch.34, p.2806
IFRS 3.B23	Ch.9, p.745	IFRS 3.B60	Ch.34, p.2809
IFRS 3.B24	Ch.9, p.745	IFRS 3.B61-62	Ch.34, p.2806
IFRS 3.B25	Ch.9, p.746	IFRS 3.B62A	Ch.7, p.541
IFRS 3.B25	Ch.37, p.3033	IFRS 3.B62A	Ch.9, p.707
IFRS 3.B26	Ch.9, p.747	IFRS 3.B62A	Ch.9, p.714
IFRS 3.B26	Ch.37, p.3033	IFRS 3.B62A-B62B	Ch.34, p.2811
IFRS 3.B27	Ch.9, p.747	IFRS 3.B62B	Ch.7, p.541
IFRS 3.B27	Ch.37, p.3033	IFRS 3.B62B	Ch.9, p.707
IFRS 3.B31	Ch.9, p.672	IFRS 3.B62B	Ch.9, p.714
IFRS 3.B31	Ch.9, p.673	IFRS 3.B63	Ch.9, p.698
IFRS 3.B32	Ch.9, p.673	IFRS 3.B63	Ch.9, p.739
IFRS 3.B32	Ch.17, p.1315	IFRS 3.B63(a)	Ch.7, p.498
IFRS 3.B32(b)	Ch.17, p.1299	IFRS 3.B63(a)	Ch.20, p.1582
IFRS 3.B33	Ch.9, p.672	IFRS 3.B63(d)	Ch.34, p.2809
IFRS 3.B33	Ch.17, p.1315	IFRS 3.B64	Ch.9, p.753
IFRS 3.B34	Ch.9, p.672	IFRS 3.B64(g)	Ch.54, p.4433
IFRS 3.B34	Ch.17, p.1315	IFRS 3.B64(h)	Ch.54, p.4433
IFRS 3.B35	Ch.9, p.684	IFRS 3.B64(o)(i)	Ch.9, p.753
IFRS 3.B36	Ch.9, p.685	IFRS 3.B65	Ch.9, p.755
IFRS 3.B36	Ch.9, p.695	IFRS 3.B65	Ch.41, p.3207

IFRS 3.B66	Ch.9, p.756	IFRS 3.BC149-BC156	Ch.9, p.679
IFRS 3.B66	Ch.41, p.3207	IFRS 3.BC178	Ch.9, p.685
IFRS 3.B67	Ch.9, p.756	IFRS 3.BC180	Ch.9, p.685
IFRS 3.B69(e)	Ch.5, p.281	IFRS 3.BC182-BC184	Ch.9, p.685
IFRS 3.IE1-IE5	Ch.9, p.740	IFRS 3.BC217	Ch.9, p.712
IFRS 3.IE9	Ch.9, p.747	IFRS 3.BC218	Ch.9, p.713
IFRS 3.10	Ch.9, p.747	IFRS 3.BC245	Ch.9, p.691
IFRS 3.IE11-IE15	Ch.9, p.745	IFRS 3.BC258	Ch.54, p.4432
IFRS 3.IE16	Ch.17, p.1315	IFRS 3.BC260	Ch.54, p.4433
IFRS 3.IE16-IE44	Ch.9, p.673	IFRS 3.BC275	Ch.9, p.691
IFRS 3.IE16-44	Ch.17, p.1315	IFRS 3.BC276	Ch.9, p.686
IFRS 3.IE23-31	Ch.17, p.1297	IFRS 3.BC276	Ch.20, p.1584
IFRS 3.IE28	Ch.9, p.676	IFRS 3.BC296-BC300	Ch.9, p.692
IFRS 3.IE30	Ch.9, p.675	IFRS 3.BC298	Ch.9, p.696
IFRS 3.IE30	Ch.17, p.1317	IFRS 3.BC302-BC303	Ch.9, p.693
IFRS 3.IE30(d)	Ch.55, p.4600	IFRS 3.BC 303	Ch.9, p.694
IFRS 3.IE30(d)	Ch.56, p.4871	IFRS 3.BC308	Ch.9, p.695
IFRS 3.IE34	Ch.9, p.675	IFRS 3.BC310	Ch.9, p.695
IFRS 3.IE45-IE49	Ch.9, p.725	IFRS 3.BC311	Ch.9, p.696
IFRS 3.IE50-IE53	Ch.9, p.737	IFRS 3.BC311B	Ch.34, p.2808
IFRS 3.IE54-IE57	Ch.9, p.729	IFRS 3.BC313	Ch.9, p.697
IFRS 3.IE57	Ch.9, p.729	IFRS 3.BC313	Ch.20, p.1584
IFRS 3.IE58-IE60	Ch.9, p.733	IFRS 3.BC316	Ch.9, p.697
IFRS 3.IE61-IE71	Ch.9, p.734	IFRS 3.BC317	Ch.20, p.1584
IFRS 3.IE61-71	Ch.34, p.2806	IFRS 3.BC323	Ch.20, p.1583
IFRS 3.IE72	Ch.9, p.758	IFRS 3.BC328	Ch.9, p.697
IFRS 3.IE73-123	Ch.9, p.653	IFRS 3.BC337-342	Ch.9, p.699
IFRS 3.IE74	Ch.19, p.1456	IFRS 3.BC338-BC342	Ch.9, p.699
IFRS 3.IE75-76	Ch.19, p.1456	IFRS 3.BC342	Ch.9, p.699
IFRS 3.IE77	Ch.19, p.1456	IFRS 3.BC347	Ch.9, p.701
IFRS 3.IE78	Ch.19, p.1457	IFRS 3.BC348	Ch.9, p.701
IFRS 3.BC21F	Ch.9, p.655	IFRS 3.BC349	Ch.9, p.701
IFRS 3.BC21G	Ch.19, p.1454	IFRS 3.BC357	Ch.9, p.706
IFRS 3.BC21H-21I	Ch.9, p.655	IFRS 3.BC360I	Ch.9, p.707
IFRS 3.BC21M	Ch.9, p.654	IFRS 3.BC370	Ch.9, p.708
IFRS 3.BC21Q	Ch.9, p.658	IFRS 3.BC370	Ch.9, p.734
IFRS 3.BC21V	Ch.19, p.1455	IFRS 3.BC371	Ch.9, p.724
IFRS 3.BC21W	Ch.19, p.1455	IFRS 3.BC372-BC375	Ch.9, p.724
IFRS 3.BC21Y	Ch.19, p.1456	IFRS 3.BC376-BC377	Ch.9, p.724
IFRS 3.BC23	Ch.10, p.773	IFRS 3.BC379	Ch.9, p.724
IFRS 3.BC58	Ch.9, p.647	IFRS 3.BC384	Ch.8, p.589
IFRS 3.BC60	Ch.9, p.647	IFRS 3.BC384	Ch.9, p.717
IFRS 3.BC61B-BC61D	Ch.9, p.647	IFRS 3.BC384	Ch.11, p.836
IFRS 3.BC71-BC72	Ch.9, p.647	IFRS 3.BC392	Ch.9, p.736
IFRS 3.BC79	Ch.9, p.647	IFRS 3.BC393	Ch.9, p.736
IFRS 3.BC110	Ch.9, p.665		
IFRS 3.BC112	Ch.9, p.667		
IFRS 3.BC120	Ch.9, p.734		
IFRS 3.BC122	Ch.9, p.728		

IFRS 4

IFRS 4.1	Ch.55, p.4537
IFRS 4.1	Ch.55, p.4621
IFRS 4.2	Ch.55, p.4538
IFRS 4.2(b)	Ch.45, p.3594
IFRS 4.2(b)	Ch.55, p.4539
IFRS 4.2(b)	Ch.55, p.4574
IFRS 4.3	Ch.55, p.4540
IFRS 4.4(a)	Ch.55, p.4540
IFRS 4.4(b)	Ch.55, p.4541

IFRS 3.BC125-BC130	Ch.9, p.667
IFRS 3.BC132	Ch.9, p.667
IFRS 3.BC132	Ch.9, p.734
IFRS 3.BC137	Ch.9, p.667
IFRS 3.BC137	Ch.9, p.734
IFRS 3.BC146	Ch.9, p.671
IFRS 3.BC148	Ch.9, p.671
IFRS 3.BC148	Ch.19, p.1461
IFRS 3.BC149-BC156	Ch.9, p.673

IFRS 4.4(c)	Ch.55, p.4541
IFRS 4.4(d)	Ch.45, p.3598
IFRS 4.4(d)	Ch.55, p.4541
IFRS 4.4(e)	Ch.55, p.4542
IFRS 4.4(f)	Ch.45, p.3599
IFRS 4.4(f)	Ch.51, p.3958
IFRS 4.4(f)	Ch.55, p.4542
IFRS 4.5	Ch.55, p.4538
IFRS 4.5	Ch.55, p.4600
IFRS 4.6	Ch.55, p.4539
IFRS 4.7	Ch.55, p.4560
IFRS 4.7	Ch.56, p.4713
IFRS 4.8	Ch.55, p.4561
IFRS 4.8	Ch.55, p.4562
IFRS 4.8	Ch.56, p.4713
IFRS 4.9	Ch.55, p.4561
IFRS 4.10	Ch.55, p.4563
IFRS 4.10-12	Ch.56, p.4715
IFRS 4.10(a)	Ch.55, p.4564
IFRS 4.10(b)	Ch.55, p.4564
IFRS 4.10(c)	Ch.55, p.4564
IFRS 4.11	Ch.55, p.4564
IFRS 4.12	Ch.55, p.4564
IFRS 4.13	Ch.55, p.4576
IFRS 4.14	Ch.55, p.4577
IFRS 4.14(a)	Ch.55, p.4577
IFRS 4.14(c)	Ch.55, p.4582
IFRS 4.14(d)	Ch.55, p.4583
IFRS 4.15	Ch.55, p.4578
IFRS 4.16	Ch.55, p.4579
IFRS 4.17	Ch.55, p.4580
IFRS 4.18	Ch.55, p.4579
IFRS 4.18	Ch.55, p.4580
IFRS 4.19	Ch.55, p.4580
IFRS 4.20	Ch.55, p.4584
IFRS 4.20A	Ch.26, p.1935
IFRS 4.20A	Ch.55, p.4601
IFRS 4.20A	Ch.55, p.4616
IFRS 4.20B	Ch.26, p.1935
IFRS 4.20B	Ch.55, p.4601
IFRS 4.20B	Ch.55, p.4603
IFRS 4.20C	Ch.55, p.4603
IFRS 4.20D	Ch.55, p.4603
IFRS 4.20E	Ch.55, p.4604
IFRS 4.20F	Ch.55, p.4604
IFRS 4.20G	Ch.55, p.4606
IFRS 4.20H	Ch.55, p.4607
IFRS 4.20I	Ch.55, p.4607
IFRS 4.20J	Ch.55, p.4607
IFRS 4.20K	Ch.55, p.4608
IFRS 4.20L	Ch.55, p.4608
IFRS 4.20L-20N	Ch.5, p.291
IFRS 4.20M	Ch.55, p.4608
IFRS 4.20N	Ch.55, p.4608
IFRS 4.20O	Ch.11, p.861
IFRS 4.20O	Ch.55, p.4609
IFRS 4.20P	Ch.11, p.861
IFRS 4.20P	Ch.55, p.4609
IFRS 4.20Q	Ch.11, p.861
IFRS 4.20Q	Ch.55, p.4609
IFRS 4.20R	Ch.55, p.4617
IFRS 4.20S	Ch.55, p.4617
IFRS 4.21	Ch.55, p.4587
IFRS 4.22	Ch.55, p.4587
IFRS 4.23	Ch.55, p.4588
IFRS 4.24	Ch.55, p.4590
IFRS 4.25	Ch.55, p.4588
IFRS 4.25(a)	Ch.55, p.4588
IFRS 4.25(b)	Ch.55, p.4589
IFRS 4.25(c)	Ch.7, p.503
IFRS 4.25(c)	Ch.55, p.4589
IFRS 4.26	Ch.55, p.4590
IFRS 4.27	Ch.55, p.4591
IFRS 4.28	Ch.55, p.4592
IFRS 4.29	Ch.55, p.4592
IFRS 4.30	Ch.55, p.4593
IFRS 4.31	Ch.55, p.4596
IFRS 4.31	Ch.56, p.4924
IFRS 4.31(a)	Ch.55, p.4596
IFRS 4.31(b)	Ch.55, p.4596
IFRS 4.32	Ch.55, p.4597
IFRS 4.33	Ch.55, p.4597
IFRS 4.33	Ch.55, p.4599
IFRS 4.34(a)-(b)	Ch.55, p.4571
IFRS 4.34(b)	Ch.56, p.4839
IFRS 4.34(c)	Ch.55, p.4571
IFRS 4.34(c)	Ch.55, p.4572
IFRS 4.34(d)-(e)	Ch.55, p.4572
IFRS 4.35(b)	Ch.55, p.4581
IFRS 4.35(d)	Ch.54, p.4411
IFRS 4.35(d)	Ch.55, p.4574
IFRS 4.35A	Ch.55, p.4600
IFRS 4.35B	Ch.55, p.4617
IFRS 4.35B	Ch.55, p.4618
IFRS 4.35C	Ch.55, p.4600
IFRS 4.35C	Ch.55, p.4617
IFRS 4.35C(b)	Ch.55, p.4601
IFRS 4.35D	Ch.55, p.4618
IFRS 4.35E	Ch.55, p.4619
IFRS 4.35F	Ch.55, p.4619
IFRS 4.35G	Ch.55, p.4619
IFRS 4.35H	Ch.55, p.4619
IFRS 4.35I	Ch.55, p.4620
IFRS 4.35J	Ch.55, p.4620
IFRS 4.35K	Ch.55, p.4620
IFRS 4.35L	Ch.55, p.4618
IFRS 4.35M	Ch.55, p.4619
IFRS 4.35N	Ch.5, p.291
IFRS 4.35N	Ch.55, p.4620
IFRS 4.36	Ch.55, p.4623
IFRS 4.37	Ch.55, p.4623
IFRS 4.37(a)	Ch.55, p.4623
IFRS 4.37(b)	Ch.40, p.3185
IFRS 4.37(b)	Ch.40, p.3186
IFRS 4.37(b)	Ch.55, p.4626
IFRS 4.37(b)(i)-(ii)	Ch.55, p.4633

IFRS 4.37(c)	Ch.55, p.4633	IFRS 4.B10	Ch.55, p.4552
IFRS 4.37(d)	Ch.55, p.4637	IFRS 4.B11	Ch.55, p.4552
IFRS 4.37(e)	Ch.55, p.4639	IFRS 4.B12	Ch.55, p.4548
IFRS 4.38	Ch.55, p.4643	IFRS 4.B13	Ch.55, p.4552
IFRS 4.39	Ch.55, p.4643	IFRS 4.B14	Ch.55, p.4553
IFRS 4.39(a)	Ch.55, p.4645	IFRS 4.B15	Ch.55, p.4553
IFRS 4.39(c)	Ch.55, p.4648	IFRS 4.B16	Ch.55, p.4553
IFRS 4.39(c)(i)	Ch.55, p.4650	IFRS 4.B17	Ch.55, p.4547
IFRS 4.39(c)(ii)	Ch.55, p.4652	IFRS 4.B18	Ch.55, p.4555
IFRS 4.39(c)(iii)	Ch.55, p.4654	IFRS 4.B18(l)	Ch.45, p.3594
IFRS 4.39(d)	Ch.55, p.4658	IFRS 4.B19	Ch.55, p.4557
IFRS 4.39(d)(i)	Ch.55, p.4661	IFRS 4.B19(a)	Ch.45, p.3594
IFRS 4.39(d)(ii)	Ch.55, p.4663	IFRS 4.B19(f)	Ch.45, p.3596
IFRS 4.39(e)	Ch.55, p.4664	IFRS 4.B19(g)	Ch.45, p.3594
IFRS 4.39D	Ch.55, p.4612	IFRS 4.B20	Ch.55, p.4554
IFRS 4.39A	Ch.55, p.4651	IFRS 4.B21	Ch.55, p.4554
IFRS 4.39B	Ch.55, p.4609	IFRS 4.B22	Ch.55, p.4544
IFRS 4.39C	Ch.55, p.4610	IFRS 4.B23	Ch.55, p.4544
IFRS 4.39E	Ch.55, p.4613	IFRS 4.B24	Ch.55, p.4548
IFRS 4.39F	Ch.55, p.4613	IFRS 4.B25	Ch.55, p.4546
IFRS 4.39G	Ch.55, p.4613	IFRS 4.B25 fn7	Ch.55, p.4547
IFRS 4.39H	Ch.55, p.4615	IFRS 4.B26	Ch.55, p.4548
IFRS 4.39I	Ch.55, p.4615	IFRS 4.B27	Ch.55, p.4549
IFRS 4.39J	Ch.55, p.4615	IFRS 4.B28	Ch.55, p.4547
IFRS 4.39K	Ch.55, p.4620	IFRS 4.B29	Ch.55, p.4549
IFRS 4.39L	Ch.55, p.4620	IFRS 4.B30	Ch.55, p.4549
IFRS 4.39M	Ch.55, p.4621	IFRS 4.IG2 E 1.3	Ch.55, p.4545
IFRS 4.40-45	Ch.5, p.290	IFRS 4.IG2 E 1.3	Ch.56, p.4702
IFRS 4.41	Ch.55, p.4535	IFRS 4.IG2 E 1.6	Ch.55, p.4556
IFRS 4.42	Ch.40, p.3185	IFRS 4.IG2 E 1.7	Ch.55, p.4549
IFRS 4.42	Ch.40, p.3186	IFRS 4.IG2 E 1.10	Ch.55, p.4557
IFRS 4.44	Ch.5, p.290	IFRS 4.IG2 E 1.11	Ch.45, p.3599
IFRS 4.45	Ch.55, p.4595	IFRS 4.IG2 E 1.12	Ch.55, p.4557
IFRS 4.46	Ch.55, p.4600	IFRS 4.IG2 E 1.13	Ch.55, p.4556
IFRS 4.46-49	Ch.5, p.291	IFRS 4.IG2 E 1.14	Ch.55, p.4558
IFRS 4.47	Ch.55, p.4610	IFRS 4.IG2 E 1.15	Ch.55, p.4551
IFRS 4.48	Ch.55, p.4600	IFRS 4.IG2 E 1.18	Ch.55, p.4558
IFRS 4.49	Ch.55, p.4618	IFRS 4.IG2 E 1.19	Ch.55, p.4558
IFRS 4.50	Ch.55, p.4616	IFRS 4.IG2 E 1.20	Ch.55, p.4552
IFRS 4.50	Ch.55, p.4617	IFRS 4.IG2 E 1.21	Ch.35, p.2909
IFRS 4.51	Ch.55, p.4617	IFRS 4.IG2 E 1.21	Ch.55, p.4558
IFRS 4 Appendix A	Ch.45, p.3593	IFRS 4.IG2 E 1.22	Ch.55, p.4556
IFRS 4 Appendix A	Ch.45, p.3594	IFRS 4.IG2 E 1.23	Ch.55, p.4548
IFRS 4 Appendix A	Ch.45, p.3596	IFRS 4.IG2 E 1.25	Ch.55, p.4556
IFRS 4 Appendix A	Ch.55, p.4537	IFRS 4.IG2 E 1.26	Ch.55, p.4556
IFRS 4 Appendix A	Ch.55, p.4543	IFRS 4.IG2 E 1.29	Ch.55, p.4553
IFRS 4 Appendix A	Ch.55, p.4551	IFRS 4.IG2 E 1.27	Ch.55, p.4559
IFRS 4 Appendix A	Ch.55, p.4563	IFRS 4.IG4 E 2.1	Ch.55, p.4561
IFRS 4 Appendix A	Ch.55, p.4568	IFRS 4.IG4 E 2.3	Ch.55, p.4562
IFRS 4 Appendix B	Ch.45, p.3593	IFRS 4.IG4 E 2.12	Ch.55, p.4562
IFRS 4.B2	Ch.55, p.4550	IFRS 4.IG4 E 2.14	Ch.55, p.4562
IFRS 4.B3	Ch.55, p.4550	IFRS 4.IG4 E 2.17	Ch.55, p.4562
IFRS 4.B4	Ch.55, p.4550	IFRS 4.IG4 E 2.18	Ch.55, p.4562
IFRS 4.B5	Ch.55, p.4550	IFRS 4.IG5	Ch.55, p.4567
IFRS 4.B6	Ch.55, p.4550	IFRS 4.IG5 E 3	Ch.55, p.4567
IFRS 4.B7	Ch.55, p.4551	IFRS 4.IG8	Ch.55, p.4593
IFRS 4.B8	Ch.55, p.4551	IFRS 4.IG9	Ch.55, p.4594
IFRS 4.B9	Ch.55, p.4551	IFRS 4.IG10	Ch.55, p.4593

IFRS 4.IG10	Ch.55, p.4594	IFRS 4.IG65B	Ch.55, p.4661
IFRS 4.IG10 E 4	Ch.55, p.4594	IFRS 4.IG65C	Ch.55, p.4661
IFRS 4.IG12	Ch.55, p.4622	IFRS 4.IG65D	Ch.55, p.4663
IFRS 4.IG13	Ch.55, p.4622	IFRS 4.IG65E	Ch.55, p.4663
IFRS 4.IG15-16	Ch.55, p.4622	IFRS 4.IG65F	Ch.55, p.4664
IFRS 4.IG17	Ch.55, p.4624	IFRS 4.IG65G	Ch.55, p.4663
IFRS 4.IG18	Ch.55, p.4626	IFRS 4.IG65G	Ch.55, p.4664
IFRS 4.IG19	Ch.55, p.4633	IFRS 4.IG66	Ch.55, p.4664
IFRS 4.IG20	Ch.55, p.4627	IFRS 4.IG67	Ch.55, p.4664
IFRS 4.IG21	Ch.55, p.4627	IFRS 4.IG68	Ch.55, p.4664
IFRS 4.IG22	Ch.55, p.4627	IFRS 4.IG69	Ch.55, p.4665
IFRS 4.IG23	Ch.55, p.4627	IFRS 4.IG70	Ch.55, p.4665
IFRS 4.IG23A	Ch.55, p.4629	IFRS 4.IG71	Ch.55, p.4667
IFRS 4.IG24	Ch.55, p.4630	IFRS 4.BC2	Ch.55, p.4533
IFRS 4.IG25	Ch.55, p.4632	IFRS 4.BC3	Ch.55, p.4533
IFRS 4.IG26	Ch.55, p.4632	IFRS 4.BC3	Ch.55, p.4534
IFRS 4.IG27	Ch.55, p.4632	IFRS 4.BC10(c)	Ch.55, p.4540
IFRS 4.IG28	Ch.55, p.4632	IFRS 4.BC12	Ch.55, p.4544
IFRS 4.IG29	Ch.55, p.4633	IFRS 4.BC13	Ch.55, p.4544
IFRS 4.IG30	Ch.55, p.4628	IFRS 4.BC26-28	Ch.55, p.4552
IFRS 4.IG30	Ch.55, p.4632	IFRS 4.BC29	Ch.55, p.4552
IFRS 4.IG31	Ch.55, p.4633	IFRS 4.BC32	Ch.55, p.4545
IFRS 4.IG32	Ch.55, p.4634	IFRS 4.BC33	Ch.55, p.4545
IFRS 4.IG33	Ch.55, p.4633	IFRS 4.BC34	Ch.55, p.4545
IFRS 4.IG34	Ch.55, p.4637	IFRS 4.BC34	Ch.55, p.4546
IFRS 4.IG35	Ch.55, p.4637	IFRS 4.BC35	Ch.55, p.4545
IFRS 4.IG36	Ch.55, p.4638	IFRS 4.BC38	Ch.55, p.4549
IFRS 4.IG37	Ch.55, p.4639	IFRS 4.BC39	Ch.55, p.4549
IFRS 4.IG38	Ch.55, p.4639	IFRS 4.BC40	Ch.55, p.4563
IFRS 4.IG39	Ch.55, p.4642	IFRS 4.BC41	Ch.55, p.4564
IFRS 4.IG40	Ch.55, p.4643	IFRS 4.BC44-46	Ch.55, p.4564
IFRS 4.IG41	Ch.55, p.4644	IFRS 4.BC54	Ch.55, p.4567
IFRS 4.IG42	Ch.55, p.4644	IFRS 4.BC69	Ch.55, p.4541
IFRS 4.IG43	Ch.55, p.4644	IFRS 4.BC71	Ch.55, p.4541
IFRS 4.IG45	Ch.55, p.4644	IFRS 4.BC73	Ch.55, p.4542
IFRS 4.IG46	Ch.55, p.4644	IFRS 4.BC77	Ch.55, p.4575
IFRS 4.IG47	Ch.55, p.4645	IFRS 4.BC79	Ch.55, p.4577
IFRS 4.IG48	Ch.55, p.4645	IFRS 4.BC81	Ch.55, p.4575
IFRS 4.IG51	Ch.55, p.4648	IFRS 4.BC82	Ch.55, p.4575
IFRS 4.IG51A	Ch.55, p.4649	IFRS 4.BC83	Ch.55, p.4575
IFRS 4.IG52	Ch.55, p.4651	IFRS 4.BC87	Ch.55, p.4577
IFRS 4.IG52A	Ch.55, p.4651	IFRS 4.BC89(d)	Ch.55, p.4578
IFRS 4.IG53	Ch.55, p.4651	IFRS 4.BC90	Ch.55, p.4578
IFRS 4.IG53A	Ch.55, p.4651	IFRS 4.BC92(a)	Ch.55, p.4578
IFRS 4.IG54A	Ch.55, p.4651	IFRS 4.BC93	Ch.55, p.4578
IFRS 4.IG55	Ch.55, p.4652	IFRS 4.BC94	Ch.55, p.4578
IFRS 4.IG56	Ch.55, p.4653	IFRS 4.BC95	Ch.55, p.4580
IFRS 4.IG57	Ch.55, p.4653	IFRS 4.BC101	Ch.55, p.4579
IFRS 4.IG58	Ch.55, p.4666	IFRS 4.BC104	Ch.55, p.4580
IFRS 4.IG59	Ch.55, p.4654	IFRS 4.BC105	Ch.55, p.4582
IFRS 4.IG60	Ch.55, p.4654	IFRS 4.BC105	Ch.55, p.4584
IFRS 4.IG61	Ch.55, p.4654	IFRS 4.BC106	Ch.55, p.4583
IFRS 4.IG61 IE 5	Ch.55, p.4654	IFRS 4.BC107-108	Ch.55, p.4583
IFRS 4.IG62	Ch.55, p.4658	IFRS 4.BC110	Ch.55, p.4585
IFRS 4.IG64	Ch.55, p.4658	IFRS 4.BC111	Ch.55, p.4585
IFRS 4.IG64A	Ch.55, p.4658	IFRS 4.BC113	Ch.55, p.4585
IFRS 4.IG64B	Ch.55, p.4666	IFRS 4.BC116	Ch.55, p.4586
IFRS 4.IG65A	Ch.55, p.4667	IFRS 4.BC120	Ch.55, p.4586

IFRS 4.BC122	Ch.55, p.4586
IFRS 4.BC123	Ch.55, p.4587
IFRS 4.BC125	Ch.55, p.4587
IFRS 4.BC126	Ch.55, p.4588
IFRS 4.BC128	Ch.55, p.4588
IFRS 4.BC129	Ch.55, p.4589
IFRS 4.BC131	Ch.55, p.4589
IFRS 4.BC132	Ch.7, p.503
IFRS 4.BC132	Ch.55, p.4589
IFRS 4.BC133	Ch.55, p.4590
IFRS 4.BC138	Ch.55, p.4591
IFRS 4.BC140	Ch.55, p.4537
IFRS 4.BC141	Ch.55, p.4592
IFRS 4.BC142	Ch.55, p.4591
IFRS 4.BC144	Ch.55, p.4592
IFRS 4.BC145	Ch.55, p.4595
IFRS 4.BC147	Ch.55, p.4596
IFRS 4.BC148	Ch.55, p.4597
IFRS 4.BC149	Ch.55, p.4597
IFRS 4.BC153	Ch.55, p.4596
IFRS 4.BC154	Ch.55, p.4569
IFRS 4.BC155	Ch.55, p.4569
IFRS 4.BC157	Ch.55, p.4571
IFRS 4.BC158	Ch.55, p.4571
IFRS 4.BC160	Ch.55, p.4570
IFRS 4.BC161	Ch.55, p.4570
IFRS 4.BC162	Ch.55, p.4569
IFRS 4.BC163	Ch.55, p.4573
IFRS 4.BC164	Ch.55, p.4571
IFRS 4.BC183	Ch.55, p.4593
IFRS 4.BC190	Ch.55, p.4560
IFRS 4.BC193	Ch.55, p.4561
IFRS 4.BC212	Ch.55, p.4633
IFRS 4.BC217	Ch.55, p.4648
IFRS 4.BC220	Ch.55, p.4654
IFRS 4.BC222	Ch.55, p.4653
IFRS 4.BC229	Ch.55, p.4600
IFRS 4.BC240	Ch.55, p.4617
IFRS 4.BC240(b)(i)	Ch.55, p.4619
IFRS 4.BC240(b)(ii)	Ch.55, p.4619
IFRS 4.BC241	Ch.55, p.4617
IFRS 4.BC252	Ch.55, p.4602
IFRS 4.BC255(a)	Ch.55, p.4604
IFRS 4.BC255(b)	Ch.55, p.4604
IFRS 4.BC256	Ch.55, p.4605
IFRS 4.BC258	Ch.55, p.4603
IFRS 4.BC264	Ch.55, p.4606
IFRS 4.BC265	Ch.55, p.4606
IFRS 4.BC266	Ch.55, p.4607
IFRS 4.BC273	Ch.55, p.4601
IFRS 4.BC277D	Ch.55, p.4616
IFRS 4.BC277E-F	Ch.55, p.4616
IFRS 4.BC277F	Ch.55, p.4616
IFRS 4.BC279	Ch.55, p.4609
IFRS 4.BC282	Ch.55, p.4608

IFRS 5

IFRS 5.1	Ch.4, p.189
IFRS 5.2	Ch.4, p.189
IFRS 5.2	Ch.4, p.191
IFRS 5.2	Ch.4, p.198
IFRS 5.3	Ch.3, p.122
IFRS 5.3	Ch.4, p.205
IFRS 5.4	Ch.4, p.190
IFRS 5.4	Ch.4, p.198
IFRS 5.5	Ch.4, p.189
IFRS 5.5	Ch.4, p.198
IFRS 5.5	Ch.7, p.532
IFRS 5.5	Ch.8, p.602
IFRS 5.5A	Ch.4, p.189
IFRS 5.5A	Ch.4, p.191
IFRS 5.5A	Ch.4, p.193
IFRS 5.5A	Ch.7, p.532
IFRS 5.5A	Ch.7, p.533
IFRS 5.5A	Ch.8, p.602
IFRS 5.5B	Ch.4, p.214
IFRS 5.5B	Ch.33, p.2621
IFRS 5.5B	Ch.36, p.3010
IFRS 5.5B	Ch.45, p.3606
IFRS 5.6	Ch.4, p.190
IFRS 5.6	Ch.4, p.191
IFRS 5.6	Ch.18, p.1427
IFRS 5.7	Ch.4, p.191
IFRS 5.7	Ch.18, p.1427
IFRS 5.8	Ch.4, p.193
IFRS 5.8	Ch.18, p.1427
IFRS 5.8A	Ch.4, p.196
IFRS 5.8A	Ch.5, p.262
IFRS 5.9	Ch.4, p.194
IFRS 5.10	Ch.4, p.191
IFRS 5.11	Ch.4, p.191
IFRS 5.12	Ch.4, p.191
IFRS 5.12	Ch.4, p.213
IFRS 5.12	Ch.38, p.3080
IFRS 5.12A	Ch.4, p.193
IFRS 5.12A	Ch.7, p.532
IFRS 5.12A	Ch.8, p.602
IFRS 5.13	Ch.4, p.191
IFRS 5.13	Ch.4, p.196
IFRS 5.13	Ch.4, p.207
IFRS 5.14	Ch.4, p.196
IFRS 5.14	Ch.4, p.207
IFRS 5.15	Ch.4, p.198
IFRS 5.15	Ch.11, p.824
IFRS 5.15	Ch.19, p.1486
IFRS 5.15A	Ch.4, p.199
IFRS 5.15A	Ch.7, p.532
IFRS 5.15A	Ch.8, p.602
IFRS 5.16	Ch.4, p.199
IFRS 5.17	Ch.4, p.198
IFRS 5.18	Ch.4, p.198
IFRS 5.18	Ch.20, p.1545
IFRS 5.19	Ch.4, p.200

IFRS 5.20	Ch.4, p.200
IFRS 5.21	Ch.4, p.200
IFRS 5.22	Ch.4, p.200
IFRS 5.23	Ch.4, p.200
IFRS 5.24	Ch.4, p.202
IFRS 5.25	Ch.4, p.199
IFRS 5.25	Ch.19, p.1486
IFRS 5.26	Ch.4, p.191
IFRS 5.26	Ch.4, p.205
IFRS 5.26A	Ch.4, p.206
IFRS 5.27	Ch.4, p.205
IFRS 5.28	Ch.4, p.206
IFRS 5.28	Ch.4, p.212
IFRS 5.28	Ch.12, p.938
IFRS 5.29	Ch.4, p.205
IFRS 5.30	Ch.3, p.123
IFRS 5.30	Ch.4, p.202
IFRS 5.31	Ch.4, p.207
IFRS 5.32	Ch.4, p.207
IFRS 5.33	Ch.5, p.327
IFRS 5.33	Ch.33, p.2611
IFRS 5.33	Ch.37, p.3062
IFRS 5.33(a)	Ch.4, p.208
IFRS 5.33(a)(ii)	Ch.3, p.136
IFRS 5.33(b)	Ch.4, p.208
IFRS 5.33(b)(ii)	Ch.33, p.2584
IFRS 5.33(c)	Ch.4, p.210
IFRS 5.33(c)	Ch.40, p.3185
IFRS 5.33(d)	Ch.4, p.208
IFRS 5.33A	Ch.4, p.208
IFRS 5.34	Ch.4, p.208
IFRS 5.34	Ch.4, p.211
IFRS 5.35	Ch.4, p.210
IFRS 5.36	Ch.4, p.213
IFRS 5.36A	Ch.4, p.196
IFRS 5.37	Ch.4, p.206
IFRS 5.37	Ch.4, p.208
IFRS 5.37	Ch.4, p.212
IFRS 5.38	Ch.4, p.203
IFRS 5.38-39	Ch.3, p.124
IFRS 5.39	Ch.4, p.203
IFRS 5.40	Ch.4, p.211
IFRS 5.41	Ch.4, p.213
IFRS 5.42	Ch.4, p.214
IFRS 5 Appendix A	Ch.4, p.190
IFRS 5 Appendix A	Ch.4, p.193
IFRS 5 Appendix A	Ch.4, p.195
IFRS 5 Appendix A	Ch.4, p.198
IFRS 5 Appendix A	Ch.4, p.205
IFRS 5 Appendix A	Ch.4, p.207
IFRS 5 Appendix A	Ch.17, p.1301
IFRS 5 Appendix A	Ch.26, p.1944
IFRS 5 Appendix A	Ch.29, p.2180
IFRS 5 Appendix A	Ch.33, p.2491
IFRS 5 Appendix B	Ch.4, p.194
IFRS 5.IG1-3	Ch.4, p.192
IFRS 5.IG4	Ch.4, p.194
IFRS 5.IG5-7	Ch.4, p.195
IFRS 5.IG8	Ch.4, p.196
IFRS 5.IG9	Ch.4, p.207
IFRS 5.IG10	Ch.4, p.200
IFRS 5.IG11	Ch.4, p.209
IFRS 5.IG12	Ch.4, p.203
IFRS 5.IG13	Ch.4, p.199
IFRS 5.BC24B-24C	Ch.4, p.197
IFRS 5.BC58	Ch.4, p.203

IFRS 6 (2010)

IFRS 6(2010).IN1	Ch.43, p.3338

IFRS 6

IFRS 6.2(b)	Ch.20, p.1521
IFRS 6.3	Ch.43, p.3401
IFRS 6.4	Ch.43, p.3393
IFRS 6.4	Ch.43, p.3397
IFRS 6.5	Ch.43, p.3360
IFRS 6.6	Ch.43, p.3361
IFRS 6.7	Ch.43, p.3361
IFRS 6.7	Ch.43, p.3401
IFRS 6.8	Ch.43, p.3367
IFRS 6.8	Ch.43, p.3418
IFRS 6.9	Ch.43, p.3362
IFRS 6.9	Ch.43, p.3368
IFRS 6.10	Ch.43, p.3362
IFRS 6.10	Ch.43, p.3368
IFRS 6.11	Ch.43, p.3369
IFRS 6.12	Ch.43, p.3367
IFRS 6.13	Ch.43, p.3367
IFRS 6.14	Ch.43, p.3367
IFRS 6.15	Ch.43, p.3365
IFRS 6.15	Ch.43, p.3370
IFRS 6.15	Ch.43, p.3373
IFRS 6.16	Ch.43, p.3371
IFRS 6.17	Ch.43, p.3363
IFRS 6.17	Ch.43, p.3365
IFRS 6.17	Ch.43, p.3371
IFRS 6.17	Ch.43, p.3373
IFRS 6.18	Ch.43, p.3372
IFRS 6.18-20	Ch.43, p.3372
IFRS 6.20	Ch.43, p.3372
IFRS 6.20	Ch.43, p.3373
IFRS 6.20	Ch.43, p.3563
IFRS 6.21	Ch.43, p.3372
IFRS 6.22	Ch.43, p.3372
IFRS 6.23	Ch.43, p.3374
IFRS 6.24	Ch.43, p.3374
IFRS 6.24(b)	Ch.40, p.3187
IFRS 6.25	Ch.43, p.3376
IFRS 6 Appendix A	Ch.43, p.3338
IFRS 6 Appendix A	Ch.43, p.3360
IFRS 6.BC6	Ch.43, p.3361
IFRS 6.BC17	Ch.43, p.3361

IFRS 6.BC17	Ch.43, p.3362	IFRS 7.11A	Ch.54, p.4426
IFRS 6.BC19	Ch.43, p.3361	IFRS 7.11A(d)	Ch.54, p.4486
IFRS 6.BC22	Ch.43, p.3362	IFRS 7.11B	Ch.54, p.4427
IFRS 6.BC23	Ch.43, p.3362	IFRS 7.12B	Ch.54, p.4427
IFRS 6.BC23B	Ch.43, p.3376	IFRS 7.12C	Ch.54, p.4427
IFRS 6.BC27	Ch.43, p.3368	IFRS 7.12D	Ch.54, p.4427
IFRS 6.BC28	Ch.43, p.3368	IFRS 7.13A	Ch.54, p.4500
IFRS 6.BC29-BC30	Ch.43, p.3368	IFRS 7.13B	Ch.54, p.4500
IFRS 6.BC33	Ch.43, p.3371	IFRS 7.13C	Ch.54, p.4501
IFRS 6.BC37	Ch.43, p.3371	IFRS 7.13D	Ch.54, p.4502
IFRS 6.BC40-BC47	Ch.43, p.3372	IFRS 7.13E	Ch.54, p.4503
IFRS 6.BC48	Ch.43, p.3374	IFRS 7.13F	Ch.54, p.4503
IFRS 6.BC49	Ch.43, p.3367	IFRS 7.14	Ch.54, p.4428
IFRS 6.BC53	Ch.43, p.3376	IFRS 7.14-15	Ch.55, p.4629
		IFRS 7.15	Ch.54, p.4428
		IFRS 7.16A	Ch.54, p.4424

IFRS 7 (2010)

IFRS 7(2010).IG3	Ch.54, p.4408	IFRS 7.17	Ch.54, p.4428
		IFRS 7.18	Ch.54, p.4428
		IFRS 7.19	Ch.54, p.4429
		IFRS 7.20	Ch.54, p.4410

IFRS 7

		IFRS 7.20(a)(i)	Ch.54, p.4489
		IFRS 7.20(a)(vii)	Ch.54, p.4489
		IFRS 7.20(a)(viii)	Ch.54, p.4489
IFRS 7.1	Ch.44, p.3577	IFRS 7.20(b)	Ch.54, p.4411
IFRS 7.1	Ch.54, p.4406	IFRS 7.20(c)	Ch.54, p.4411
IFRS 7.2	Ch.54, p.4406	IFRS 7.20A	Ch.54, p.4410
IFRS 7.3	Ch.14, p.1010	IFRS 7.21	Ch.54, p.4409
IFRS 7.3	Ch.45, p.3591	IFRS 7.21A	Ch.54, p.4412
IFRS 7.3	Ch.45, p.3594	IFRS 7.21A(a)	Ch.53, p.4273
IFRS 7.3(a)	Ch.45, p.3592	IFRS 7.21B	Ch.54, p.4413
IFRS 7.3(a)	Ch.45, p.3593	IFRS 7.21C	Ch.54, p.4413
IFRS 7.3(a)	Ch.45, p.3602	IFRS 7.21D	Ch.54, p.4412
IFRS 7.3(b)	Ch.45, p.3605	IFRS 7.22A	Ch.54, p.4413
IFRS 7.3(d)	Ch.45, p.3593	IFRS 7.22B	Ch.54, p.4413
IFRS 7.3(d)	Ch.45, p.3595	IFRS 7.22C	Ch.54, p.4414
IFRS 7.3(d)	Ch.45, p.3598	IFRS 7.23A	Ch.54, p.4415
IFRS 7.3(d)	Ch.56, p.4918	IFRS 7.23B	Ch.54, p.4415
IFRS 7.3(e)	Ch.45, p.3605	IFRS 7.23C	Ch.53, p.4277
IFRS 7.4	Ch.45, p.3600	IFRS 7.23C	Ch.53, p.4278
IFRS 7.4	Ch.54, p.4406	IFRS 7.23C	Ch.54, p.4415
IFRS 7.5	Ch.45, p.3607	IFRS 7.23D	Ch.54, p.4416
IFRS 7.5	Ch.45, p.3608	IFRS 7.23E	Ch.54, p.4416
IFRS 7.5A	Ch.45, p.3607	IFRS 7.23F	Ch.54, p.4416
IFRS 7.6	Ch.54, p.4408	IFRS 7.24A	Ch.54, p.4416
IFRS 7.6	Ch.54, p.4409	IFRS 7.24B	Ch.54, p.4417
IFRS 7.7	Ch.54, p.4409	IFRS 7.24C	Ch.54, p.4418
IFRS 7.8	Ch.54, p.4424	IFRS 7.24D	Ch.54, p.4415
IFRS 7.9	Ch.54, p.4426	IFRS 7.24E	Ch.54, p.4420
IFRS 7.10(a)	Ch.54, p.4425	IFRS 7.24F	Ch.54, p.4421
IFRS 7.10(b)	Ch.54, p.4425	IFRS 7.24G	Ch.53, p.4388
IFRS 7.10(c)	Ch.54, p.4425	IFRS 7.24G	Ch.54, p.4423
IFRS 7.10(d)	Ch.54, p.4425	IFRS 7.24H	Ch.54, p.4423
IFRS 7.10A(a)	Ch.54, p.4425	IFRS 7.24I	Ch.54, p.4473
IFRS 7.10A(b)	Ch.54, p.4425	IFRS 7.24J	Ch.54, p.4473
IFRS 7.11	Ch.54, p.4426	IFRS 7.25	Ch.14, p.1009
IFRS 7.11(a)	Ch.54, p.4425	IFRS 7.25	Ch.14, p.1010
IFRS 7.11(b)	Ch.54, p.4425	IFRS 7.25	Ch.41, p.3223
IFRS 7.11(c)	Ch.54, p.4425	IFRS 7.25	Ch.54, p.4429

IFRS 7.26	Ch.41, p.3223
IFRS 7.26	Ch.54, p.4429
IFRS 7.28	Ch.41, p.3223
IFRS 7.28	Ch.54, p.4430
IFRS 7.29	Ch.14, p.1009
IFRS 7.29(a)	Ch.14, p.1010
IFRS 7.29(a)	Ch.41, p.3223
IFRS 7.29(a)	Ch.54, p.4430
IFRS 7.29(c)	Ch.41, p.3223
IFRS 7.29(c)	Ch.54, p.4430
IFRS 7.29(c)	Ch.55, p.4574
IFRS 7.29(c)	Ch.55, p.4667
IFRS 7.29(d)	Ch.14, p.1010
IFRS 7.29(d)	Ch.54, p.4430
IFRS 7.30	Ch.54, p.4430
IFRS 7.30	Ch.55, p.4667
IFRS 7.31	Ch.54, p.4433
IFRS 7.31-42	Ch.15, p.1244
IFRS 7.32	Ch.54, p.4433
IFRS 7.32A	Ch.54, p.4433
IFRS 7.33(a)	Ch.54, p.4435
IFRS 7.33(b)	Ch.54, p.4435
IFRS 7.33(c)	Ch.54, p.4436
IFRS 7.33-35	Ch.40, p.3158
IFRS 7.34(a)	Ch.54, p.4438
IFRS 7.34(b)	Ch.54, p.4438
IFRS 7.34(c)	Ch.54, p.4471
IFRS 7.35	Ch.54, p.4438
IFRS 7.35A	Ch.54, p.4439
IFRS 7.35A(a)	Ch.32, p.2399
IFRS 7.35A(a)	Ch.54, p.4444
IFRS 7.35A(b)	Ch.54, p.4445
IFRS 7.35B	Ch.51, p.4074
IFRS 7.35B	Ch.54, p.4439
IFRS 7.35C	Ch.54, p.4439
IFRS 7.35D	Ch.54, p.4439
IFRS 7.35E	Ch.54, p.4439
IFRS 7.35F	Ch.54, p.4440
IFRS 7.35F(a)	Ch.51, p.3969
IFRS 7.35F(a)	Ch.51, p.4074
IFRS 7.35F(b)	Ch.51, p.4074
IFRS 7.35F(c)	Ch.51, p.4074
IFRS 7.35F(d)	Ch.51, p.4074
IFRS 7.35F(e)	Ch.51, p.4070
IFRS 7.35F(e)	Ch.51, p.4075
IFRS 7.35F(f)	Ch.51, p.4034
IFRS 7.35F(f)	Ch.51, p.4075
IFRS 7.35G	Ch.51, p.4050
IFRS 7.35G	Ch.54, p.4440
IFRS 7.35G(a)(i)	Ch.51, p.4074
IFRS 7.35G(a)(ii)	Ch.51, p.3969
IFRS 7.35G(a)(ii)	Ch.51, p.4074
IFRS 7.35G(a)(iii)	Ch.51, p.4074
IFRS 7.35G(b)	Ch.51, p.4074
IFRS 7.35G(c)	Ch.51, p.3969
IFRS 7.35G(c)	Ch.51, p.4074
IFRS 7.35H	Ch.51, p.4074
IFRS 7.35H	Ch.54, p.4441
IFRS 7.35H(c)	Ch.51, p.3931
IFRS 7.35I	Ch.51, p.4074
IFRS 7.35I	Ch.54, p.4442
IFRS 7.35J	Ch.54, p.4442
IFRS 7.35K	Ch.51, p.4074
IFRS 7.35K	Ch.54, p.4444
IFRS 7.35K(a)	Ch.56, p.4917
IFRS 7.35K(c)	Ch.51, p.3928
IFRS 7.35L	Ch.51, p.4070
IFRS 7.35L	Ch.51, p.4075
IFRS 7.35L	Ch.54, p.4446
IFRS 7.35M	Ch.51, p.4075
IFRS 7.35M	Ch.54, p.4446
IFRS 7.35N	Ch.54, p.4446
IFRS 7.36	Ch.13, p.987
IFRS 7.36-38	Ch.55, p.4659
IFRS 7.36(a)	Ch.51, p.4050
IFRS 7.36(a)	Ch.54, p.4449
IFRS 7.36(b)	Ch.54, p.4449
IFRS 7.38	Ch.54, p.4449
IFRS 7.39	Ch.40, p.3152
IFRS 7.39	Ch.40, p.3158
IFRS 7.39	Ch.55, p.4661
IFRS 7.39(a)	Ch.54, p.4454
IFRS 7.39(b)	Ch.54, p.4454
IFRS 7.39(c)	Ch.54, p.4462
IFRS 7.40	Ch.54, p.4463
IFRS 7.40	Ch.55, p.4663
IFRS 7.41	Ch.54, p.4469
IFRS 7.41	Ch.55, p.4663
IFRS 7.42	Ch.54, p.4470
IFRS 7.42	Ch.55, p.4663
IFRS 7.42A	Ch.54, p.4474
IFRS 7.42B	Ch.54, p.4474
IFRS 7.42C	Ch.54, p.4477
IFRS 7.42D	Ch.54, p.4475
IFRS 7.42E	Ch.54, p.4478
IFRS 7.42F	Ch.54, p.4480
IFRS 7.42G	Ch.54, p.4480
IFRS 7.42G	Ch.54, p.4481
IFRS 7.42H	Ch.54, p.4474
IFRS 7.42R	Ch.5, p.262
IFRS 7.42R	Ch.5, p.356
IFRS 7.42S	Ch.5, p.263
IFRS 7.42S	Ch.5, p.357
IFRS 7.44DE	Ch.54, p.4520
IFRS 7.44DF	Ch.54, p.4520
IFRS 7.44GG	Ch.54, p.4520
IFRS 7.44HH	Ch.54, p.4520
IFRS 7 Appendix A	Ch.50, p.3872
IFRS 7 Appendix A	Ch.53, p.4285
IFRS 7 Appendix A	Ch.54, p.4428
IFRS 7 Appendix A	Ch.54, p.4434
IFRS 7 Appendix A	Ch.54, p.4448
IFRS 7 Appendix A	Ch.56, p.4915
IFRS 7.B1	Ch.54, p.4408
IFRS 7.B2	Ch.54, p.4409
IFRS 7.B3	Ch.54, p.4408

IFRS 7.B5	Ch.54, p.4410	IFRS 7.B29	Ch.54, p.4478
IFRS 7.B5(a)	Ch.54, p.4409	IFRS 7.B30	Ch.54, p.4478
IFRS 7.B5(c)	Ch.54, p.4409	IFRS 7.B30A	Ch.54, p.4478
IFRS 7.B5(e)	Ch.54, p.4409	IFRS 7.B31	Ch.54, p.4478
IFRS 7.B5(f)	Ch.54, p.4409	IFRS 7.B32	Ch.54, p.4475
IFRS 7.B5(g)	Ch.54, p.4409	IFRS 7.B33	Ch.54, p.4480
IFRS 7.B5(aa)	Ch.54, p.4409	IFRS 7.B34	Ch.54, p.4479
IFRS 7.B6	Ch.54, p.4435	IFRS 7.B35	Ch.54, p.4479
IFRS 7.B6-B24	Ch.15, p.1244	IFRS 7.35J	Ch.51, p.4034
IFRS 7.B7	Ch.54, p.4438	IFRS 7.35J	Ch.51, p.4075
IFRS 7.B8	Ch.54, p.4472	IFRS 7.B36	Ch.54, p.4479
IFRS 7.B8A	Ch.51, p.4074	IFRS 7.B37	Ch.54, p.4479
IFRS 7.B8A	Ch.54, p.4440	IFRS 7.B38	Ch.54, p.4481
IFRS 7.B8B	Ch.51, p.4034	IFRS 7.B39	Ch.54, p.4474
IFRS 7.B8B	Ch.51, p.4075	IFRS 7.B40	Ch.54, p.4500
IFRS 7.B8B	Ch.54, p.4440	IFRS 7.B41	Ch.54, p.4501
IFRS 7.B8C	Ch.54, p.4441	IFRS 7.B42	Ch.54, p.4503
IFRS 7.B8D	Ch.54, p.4442	IFRS 7.B43	Ch.54, p.4501
IFRS 7.B8E	Ch.51, p.4073	IFRS 7.B44	Ch.54, p.4502
IFRS 7.B8E	Ch.54, p.4442	IFRS 7.B45	Ch.54, p.4502
IFRS 7.B8F	Ch.51, p.4074	IFRS 7.B46	Ch.54, p.4502
IFRS 7.B8F	Ch.54, p.4445	IFRS 7.B47	Ch.54, p.4502
IFRS 7.B8G	Ch.51, p.4074	IFRS 7.B48	Ch.54, p.4502
IFRS 7.B8G	Ch.54, p.4445	IFRS 7.B49	Ch.54, p.4503
IFRS 7.B8H	Ch.51, p.4075	IFRS 7.B50	Ch.54, p.4503
IFRS 7.B8H	Ch.54, p.4448	IFRS 7.B51	Ch.54, p.4503
IFRS 7.B8I	Ch.51, p.4075	IFRS 7.B52	Ch.54, p.4503
IFRS 7.B8I	Ch.54, p.4448	IFRS 7.B53	Ch.54, p.4500
IFRS 7.B8J	Ch.54, p.4448	IFRS 7.IG1	Ch.54, p.4407
IFRS 7.B9	Ch.54, p.4445	IFRS 7.IG2	Ch.54, p.4407
IFRS 7.B10	Ch.54, p.4445	IFRS 7.IG5	Ch.54, p.4408
IFRS 7.B10A	Ch.54, p.4454	IFRS 7.IG6	Ch.54, p.4408
IFRS 7.B11	Ch.54, p.4454	IFRS 7.IG12	Ch.54, p.4429
IFRS 7.B11A	Ch.54, p.4458	IFRS 7.IG13	Ch.54, p.4483
IFRS 7.B11B	Ch.54, p.4454	IFRS 7.IG13C	Ch.54, p.4416
IFRS 7.B11C(a)	Ch.54, p.4455	IFRS 7.IG13D	Ch.54, p.4417
IFRS 7.B11C(b)	Ch.54, p.4456	IFRS 7.IG13E	Ch.54, p.4418
IFRS 7.B11C(c)	Ch.54, p.4456	IFRS 7.IG14	Ch.54, p.4430
IFRS 7.B11C(c)	Ch.54, p.4458	IFRS 7.IG14	Ch.54, p.4431
IFRS 7.B11D	Ch.54, p.4456	IFRS 7.IG15	Ch.54, p.4436
IFRS 7.B11D	Ch.55, p.4661	IFRS 7.IG16	Ch.54, p.4436
IFRS 7.B11E	Ch.54, p.4462	IFRS 7.IG17	Ch.54, p.4436
IFRS 7.B11E	Ch.55, p.4661	IFRS 7.IG18	Ch.54, p.4472
IFRS 7.B11F	Ch.40, p.3158	IFRS 7.IG19	Ch.54, p.4471
IFRS 7.B11F	Ch.54, p.4462	IFRS 7.IG20	Ch.54, p.4438
IFRS 7.B17	Ch.54, p.4464	IFRS 7.IG20B	Ch.54, p.4443
IFRS 7.B18	Ch.54, p.4465	IFRS 7.IG20C	Ch.54, p.4446
IFRS 7.B19	Ch.54, p.4467	IFRS 7.IG20D	Ch.54, p.4446
IFRS 7.B20	Ch.54, p.4469	IFRS 7.IG21	Ch.54, p.4439
IFRS 7.B21	Ch.54, p.4463	IFRS 7.IG22	Ch.54, p.4449
IFRS 7.B22	Ch.54, p.4434	IFRS 7.IG31A	Ch.54, p.4455
IFRS 7.B23	Ch.54, p.4434	IFRS 7.IG32	Ch.54, p.4434
IFRS 7.B24	Ch.54, p.4464	IFRS 7.IG32	Ch.54, p.4464
IFRS 7.B25	Ch.54, p.4434	IFRS 7.IG33	Ch.54, p.4466
IFRS 7.B25	Ch.54, p.4467	IFRS 7.IG34	Ch.54, p.4466
IFRS 7.B26	Ch.54, p.4434	IFRS 7.IG35	Ch.54, p.4467
IFRS 7.B27	Ch.54, p.4464	IFRS 7.IG36	Ch.54, p.4467
IFRS 7.B28	Ch.54, p.4463	IFRS 7.IG37(a)	Ch.54, p.4470

IFRS 7.IG37(b)	Ch.54, p.4471	IFRS 8.2	Ch.36, p.2982
IFRS 7.IG37(c)	Ch.54, p.4471	IFRS 8.2(b)	Ch.36, p.2982
IFRS 7.IG38	Ch.54, p.4471	IFRS 8.3	Ch.36, p.2983
IFRS 7.IG39	Ch.54, p.4471	IFRS 8.4	Ch.36, p.2983
IFRS 7.IG40	Ch.54, p.4471	IFRS 8.5	Ch.20, p.1587
IFRS 7.IG40C	Ch.54, p.4476	IFRS 8.5	Ch.20, p.1588
IFRS 7.IG40C	Ch.54, p.4480	IFRS 8.5	Ch.36, p.2978
IFRS 7.IG40D	Ch.54, p.4503	IFRS 8.5	Ch.36, p.2980
IFRS 7.BC6	Ch.54, p.4406	IFRS 8.5	Ch.36, p.2984
IFRS 7.BC8	Ch.45, p.3602	IFRS 8.5	Ch.36, p.2996
IFRS 7.BC9	Ch.54, p.4406	IFRS 8.5(a)	Ch.36, p.2979
IFRS 7.BC10	Ch.54, p.4406	IFRS 8.5(b)	Ch.32, p.2411
IFRS 7.BC10	Ch.54, p.4408	IFRS 8.5(b)	Ch.36, p.2987
IFRS 7.BC11	Ch.54, p.4406	IFRS 8.5(b)	Ch.36, p.2989
IFRS 7.BC13	Ch.54, p.4409	IFRS 8.5(c)	Ch.36, p.2987
IFRS 7.BC14	Ch.54, p.4424	IFRS 8.6	Ch.36, p.2984
IFRS 7.BC15	Ch.54, p.4424	IFRS 8.7	Ch.36, p.2980
IFRS 7.BC22	Ch.54, p.4425	IFRS 8.7	Ch.36, p.2984
IFRS 7.BC25	Ch.54, p.4428	IFRS 8.7	Ch.36, p.2985
IFRS 7.BC31	Ch.54, p.4428	IFRS 8.8	Ch.36, p.2983
IFRS 7.BC32	Ch.54, p.4428	IFRS 8.8	Ch.36, p.2986
IFRS 7.BC33	Ch.54, p.4411	IFRS 8.8	Ch.36, p.2988
IFRS 7.BC34	Ch.54, p.4411	IFRS 8.9	Ch.36, p.2980
IFRS 7.BC35	Ch.54, p.4412	IFRS 8.9	Ch.36, p.2985
IFRS 7.BC35C	Ch.54, p.4412	IFRS 8.9	Ch.36, p.2988
IFRS 7.BC35O	Ch.54, p.4520	IFRS 8.10	Ch.20, p.1587
IFRS 7.BC35P	Ch.54, p.4412	IFRS 8.10	Ch.36, p.2979
IFRS 7.BC35U	Ch.54, p.4416	IFRS 8.10	Ch.36, p.2988
IFRS 7.BC35W	Ch.54, p.4416	IFRS 8.11	Ch.36, p.2981
IFRS 7.BC35X	Ch.54, p.4416	IFRS 8.11	Ch.36, p.3000
IFRS 7.BC36	Ch.54, p.4429	IFRS 8.11-12	Ch.20, p.1587
IFRS 7.BC40(b)	Ch.54, p.4435	IFRS 8.12	Ch.20, p.1588
IFRS 7.BC41	Ch.54, p.4435	IFRS 8.12	Ch.36, p.2981
IFRS 7.BC42	Ch.54, p.4435	IFRS 8.12	Ch.36, p.2986
IFRS 7.BC43	Ch.54, p.4435	IFRS 8.12	Ch.36, p.2992
IFRS 7.BC44	Ch.54, p.4435	IFRS 8.12	Ch.36, p.2995
IFRS 7.BC45	Ch.54, p.4435	IFRS 8.13	Ch.36, p.2981
IFRS 7.BC46	Ch.54, p.4435	IFRS 8.13	Ch.36, p.2996
IFRS 7.BC47	Ch.54, p.4438	IFRS 8.13	Ch.36, p.2997
IFRS 7.BC47A	Ch.54, p.4408	IFRS 8.14	Ch.36, p.2997
IFRS 7.BC48	Ch.54, p.4438	IFRS 8.15	Ch.36, p.2998
IFRS 7.BC56	Ch.54, p.4449	IFRS 8.16	Ch.36, p.2997
IFRS 7.BC57	Ch.54, p.4455	IFRS 8.16	Ch.36, p.2998
IFRS 7.BC58A(a)	Ch.54, p.4457	IFRS 8.16	Ch.36, p.3001
IFRS 7.BC58A(b)	Ch.54, p.4454	IFRS 8.16	Ch.36, p.3007
IFRS 7.BC58D	Ch.54, p.4462	IFRS 8.17	Ch.36, p.2990
IFRS 7.BC59	Ch.54, p.4463	IFRS 8.18	Ch.36, p.2998
IFRS 7.BC61	Ch.54, p.4469	IFRS 8.19	Ch.36, p.2998
IFRS 7.BC65	Ch.54, p.4472	IFRS 8.20	Ch.32, p.2411
IFRS 7.BC72B	Ch.54, p.4407	IFRS 8.20	Ch.36, p.3000
IFRS 7.BC72C	Ch.54, p.4407	IFRS 8.21	Ch.36, p.3000
		IFRS 8.22	Ch.36, p.2979

IFRS 8

		IFRS 8.22	Ch.36, p.3001
		IFRS 8.22(aa)	Ch.36, p.3001
IFRS 8.1	Ch.36, p.2981	IFRS 8.23	Ch.36, p.2979
IFRS 8.1	Ch.36, p.2989	IFRS 8.23	Ch.36, p.2997
IFRS 8.1	Ch.36, p.3012	IFRS 8.23	Ch.36, p.3002

IFRS 8.23	Ch.36, p.3003	IFRS 9.2.1	Ch.45, p.3591
IFRS 8.23-24	Ch.36, p.3004	IFRS 9.2.1	Ch.51, p.4046
IFRS 8.23(g)	Ch.36, p.2989	IFRS 9.2.1(a)	Ch.7, p.499
IFRS 8.24	Ch.36, p.3005	IFRS 9.2.1(a)	Ch.7, p.550
IFRS 8.24(a)	Ch.36, p.2989	IFRS 9.2.1(a)	Ch.11, p.876
IFRS 8.25	Ch.36, p.2999	IFRS 9.2.1(a)	Ch.11, p.877
IFRS 8.25	Ch.36, p.3010	IFRS 9.2.1(a)	Ch.45, p.3592
IFRS 8.26	Ch.36, p.2999	IFRS 9.2.1(a)	Ch.45, p.3593
IFRS 8.27	Ch.36, p.3005	IFRS 9.2.1(b)	Ch.45, p.3593
IFRS 8.27	Ch.36, p.3006	IFRS 9.2.1(b)	Ch.51, p.4046
IFRS 8.27-28	Ch.36, p.3000	IFRS 9.2.1(b)(i)	Ch.52, p.4088
IFRS 8.27(f)	Ch.36, p.2999	IFRS 9.2.1(b)(ii)	Ch.52, p.4088
IFRS 8.28	Ch.36, p.3007	IFRS 9.2.1(c)	Ch.45, p.3605
IFRS 8.29	Ch.36, p.3009	IFRS 9.2.1(d)	Ch.45, p.3602
IFRS 8.30	Ch.36, p.3009	IFRS 9.2.1(e)	Ch.26, p.1935
IFRS 8.31	Ch.36, p.2979	IFRS 9.2.1(e)	Ch.45, p.3593
IFRS 8.31	Ch.36, p.3012	IFRS 9.2.1(e)	Ch.45, p.3594
IFRS 8.32	Ch.36, p.3013	IFRS 9.2.1(e)	Ch.45, p.3595
IFRS 8.32-34	Ch.36, p.2979	IFRS 9.2.1(e)(iv)	Ch.45, p.3595
IFRS 8.32-33	Ch.36, p.3012	IFRS 9.2.1(e)	Ch.45, p.3598
IFRS 8.33	Ch.36, p.3013	IFRS 9.2.1(e)	Ch.45, p.3599
IFRS 8.33	Ch.36, p.3014	IFRS 9.2.1(e)(iv)	Ch.48, p.3837
IFRS 8.34	Ch.36, p.3014	IFRS 9.2.1(e)	Ch.51, p.3958
IFRS 8.34	Ch.36, p.3015	IFRS 9.2.1(e)	Ch.55, p.4539
IFRS 8.35	Ch.36, p.2977	IFRS 9.2.1(e)(iv)	Ch.56, p.4692
IFRS 8.36	Ch.36, p.2981	IFRS 9.2.1(f)	Ch.45, p.3603
IFRS 8 Appendix A	Ch.36, p.2980	IFRS 9.2.1(g)	Ch.45, p.3600
IFRS 8.D01-D04	Ch.36, p.2977	IFRS 9.2.1(g)	Ch.49, p.3861
IFRS 8.IG7	Ch.36, p.2991	IFRS 9.2.1(g)	Ch.50, p.3879
IFRS 8.BC22	Ch.36, p.2983	IFRS 9.2.1(g)	Ch.51, p.3924
IFRS 8.BC23	Ch.36, p.2982	IFRS 9.2.1(g)	Ch.51, p.4049
IFRS 8.BC27	Ch.36, p.2988	IFRS 9.2.1(g)	Ch.52, p.4088
IFRS 8.BC30	Ch.36, p.2992	IFRS 9.2.1(h)	Ch.45, p.3605
IFRS 8.BC32	Ch.36, p.2992	IFRS 9.2.1(i)	Ch.45, p.3606
IFRS 8.BC43-45	Ch.36, p.2979	IFRS 9.2.1(j)	Ch.45, p.3606
IFRS 8.BC43-45	Ch.36, p.2992	IFRS 9.2.1(j)	Ch.52, p.4089
IFRS 8.BC44	Ch.36, p.3012	IFRS 9.2.3	Ch.50, p.3879
IFRS 8.BC46-47	Ch.36, p.3012	IFRS 9.2.3	Ch.51, p.3924
IFRS 8.BC Appendix A 72	Ch.36, p.2979	IFRS 9.2.3	Ch.51, p.4049
IFRS 8.BC Appendix A 73	Ch.36, p.2992	IFRS 9.2.3(a)	Ch.45, p.3600
		IFRS 9.2.3(b)	Ch.45, p.3600
		IFRS 9.2.3(b)	Ch.45, p.3601
		IFRS 9.2.3(c)	Ch.45, p.3600

IFRS 9 (2012)

IFRS 9(2012).B5.4.12	Ch.14, p.1009

IFRS 9 (2022)

IFRS 9(2022).7.1.9	Ch.52, p.4158
IFRS 9(2022).7.2.35	Ch.52, p.4158
IFRS 9(2022).B3.3.6	Ch.52, p.4158
IFRS 9(2022).B3.3.6A	Ch.52, p.4161

IFRS 9

IFRS 9.1.1	Ch.44, p.3577

IFRS 9.2.3(c)	Ch.50, p.3879
IFRS 9.2.3(c)	Ch.51, p.4049
IFRS 9.2.4	Ch.17, p.1366
IFRS 9.2.4	Ch.42, p.3297
IFRS 9.2.4	Ch.43, p.3456
IFRS 9.2.4	Ch.43, p.3473
IFRS 9.2.4	Ch.45, p.3607
IFRS 9.2.4	Ch.45, p.3608
IFRS 9.2.4	Ch.45, p.3609
IFRS 9.2.4	Ch.53, p.4388
IFRS 9.2.5	Ch.5, p.342
IFRS 9.2.5	Ch.43, p.3474
IFRS 9.2.5	Ch.45, p.3613
IFRS 9.2.5	Ch.53, p.4389
IFRS 9.2.6	Ch.43, p.3473

IFRS 9.2.6	Ch.43, p.3474
IFRS 9.2.6	Ch.45, p.3608
IFRS 9.2.6	Ch.45, p.3609
IFRS 9.2.6(b)	Ch.43, p.3457
IFRS 9.2.6(c)	Ch.43, p.3457
IFRS 9.2.7	Ch.43, p.3474
IFRS 9.2.7	Ch.45, p.3610
IFRS 9.3.1.1	Ch.15, p.1188
IFRS 9.3.1.1	Ch.48, p.3812
IFRS 9.3.1.1	Ch.49, p.3841
IFRS 9.3.1.1	Ch.49, p.3845
IFRS 9.3.1.1	Ch.50, p.3880
IFRS 9.3.1.2	Ch.50, p.3880
IFRS 9.3.2.1	Ch.53, p.4364
IFRS 9.3.2.2	Ch.52, p.4093
IFRS 9.3.2.2	Ch.52, p.4098
IFRS 9.3.2.2(b)	Ch.52, p.4105
IFRS 9.3.2.3	Ch.50, p.3880
IFRS 9.3.2.3	Ch.52, p.4099
IFRS 9.3.2.4	Ch.52, p.4103
IFRS 9.3.2.5	Ch.52, p.4108
IFRS 9.3.2.6	Ch.52, p.4114
IFRS 9.3.2.6(a)	Ch.52, p.4114
IFRS 9.3.2.6(b)	Ch.52, p.4114
IFRS 9.3.2.6(c)	Ch.52, p.4114
IFRS 9.3.2.6(c)	Ch.52, p.4119
IFRS 9.3.2.7	Ch.52, p.4114
IFRS 9.3.2.7	Ch.52, p.4115
IFRS 9.3.2.8	Ch.52, p.4114
IFRS 9.3.2.9	Ch.52, p.4119
IFRS 9.3.2.10	Ch.52, p.4132
IFRS 9.3.2.11	Ch.52, p.4129
IFRS 9.3.2.12	Ch.51, p.4015
IFRS 9.3.2.12	Ch.52, p.4129
IFRS 9.3.2.13	Ch.52, p.4130
IFRS 9.3.2.13	Ch.52, p.4140
IFRS 9.3.2.14	Ch.52, p.4131
IFRS 9.3.2.15	Ch.52, p.4134
IFRS 9.3.2.16	Ch.52, p.4138
IFRS 9.3.2.16(a)	Ch.52, p.4138
IFRS 9.3.2.16(b)-(c)	Ch.52, p.4139
IFRS 9.3.2.17	Ch.52, p.4139
IFRS 9.3.2.18	Ch.52, p.4139
IFRS 9.3.2.19	Ch.52, p.4139
IFRS 9.3.2.21	Ch.52, p.4140
IFRS 9.3.2.22	Ch.40, p.3155
IFRS 9.3.2.22	Ch.52, p.4151
IFRS 9.3.2.23	Ch.52, p.4152
IFRS 9.3.3.1	Ch.47, p.3671
IFRS 9.3.3.1	Ch.49, p.3847
IFRS 9.3.3.1	Ch.52, p.4099
IFRS 9.3.3.1	Ch.52, p.4154
IFRS 9.3.3.1	Ch.55, p.4582
IFRS 9.3.3.2	Ch.52, p.4099
IFRS 9.3.3.2	Ch.52, p.4157
IFRS 9.3.3.3	Ch.52, p.4166
IFRS 9.3.3.4	Ch.52, p.4166
IFRS 9.3.3.5	Ch.52, p.4171
IFRS 9.3.3.5	Ch.56, p.4695
IFRS 9.4.1.1	Ch.48, p.3771
IFRS 9.4.1.1	Ch.50, p.3869
IFRS 9.4.1.2	Ch.5, p.262
IFRS 9.4.1.2	Ch.48, p.3774
IFRS 9.4.1.2	Ch.48, p.3780
IFRS 9.4.1.2	Ch.51, p.3924
IFRS 9.4.1.2-2A	Ch.51, p.3974
IFRS 9.4.1.2(b)	Ch.50, p.3889
IFRS 9.4.1.2(b)	Ch.53, p.4289
IFRS 9.4.1.2A	Ch.5, p.262
IFRS 9.4.1.2A	Ch.5, p.263
IFRS 9.4.1.2A	Ch.33, p.2579
IFRS 9.4.1.2A	Ch.48, p.3774
IFRS 9.4.1.2A	Ch.48, p.3783
IFRS 9.4.1.2A	Ch.51, p.3924
IFRS 9.4.1.2A	Ch.51, p.4036
IFRS 9.4.1.2A	Ch.51, p.4074
IFRS 9.4.1.2A	Ch.53, p.4220
IFRS 9.4.1.2A(b)	Ch.53, p.4289
IFRS 9.4.1.3(a)	Ch.48, p.3791
IFRS 9.4.1.3(b)	Ch.48, p.3792
IFRS 9.4.1.4	Ch.43, p.3410
IFRS 9.4.1.4	Ch.48, p.3774
IFRS 9.4.1.4	Ch.53, p.4289
IFRS 9.4.1.5	Ch.5, p.314
IFRS 9.4.1.5	Ch.48, p.3774
IFRS 9.4.1.5	Ch.48, p.3826
IFRS 9.4.2.1	Ch.7, p.555
IFRS 9.4.2.1	Ch.48, p.3777
IFRS 9.4.2.1	Ch.50, p.3869
IFRS 9.4.2.1-2	Ch.7, p.539
IFRS 9.4.2.1(a)	Ch.51, p.3924
IFRS 9.4.2.1(a)	Ch.50, p.3879
IFRS 9.4.2.1(b)	Ch.50, p.3881
IFRS 9.4.2.1(c)	Ch.50, p.3879
IFRS 9.4.2.1(c)	Ch.51, p.4048
IFRS 9.4.2.1(c)-(d)	Ch.53, p.4388
IFRS 9.4.2.1(d)	Ch.51, p.3924
IFRS 9.4.2.1(d)	Ch.50, p.3879
IFRS 9.4.2.1(d)	Ch.51, p.4049
IFRS 9.4.2.1(d)	Ch.45, p.3600
IFRS 9.4.2.1(d)	Ch.51, p.4048
IFRS 9.4.2.1(d)	Ch.51, p.4050
IFRS 9.4.2.1(e)	Ch.7, p.539
IFRS 9.4.2.2	Ch.5, p.315
IFRS 9.4.2.2	Ch.7, p.555
IFRS 9.4.2.2	Ch.48, p.3776
IFRS 9.4.2.2(a)	Ch.48, p.3826
IFRS 9.4.2.2(b)	Ch.48, p.3784
IFRS 9.4.2.2(b)	Ch.48, p.3826
IFRS 9.4.2.2(b)	Ch.48, p.3828
IFRS 9.4.3.1	Ch.43, p.3475
IFRS 9.4.3.1	Ch.46, p.3629
IFRS 9.4.3.1	Ch.46, p.3630
IFRS 9.4.3.1	Ch.46, p.3653
IFRS 9.4.3.1	Ch.55, p.4559
IFRS 9.4.3.1	Ch.56, p.4713

IFRS 9.4.3.2	Ch.46, p.3629	IFRS 9.5.4.1	Ch.51, p.3927
IFRS 9.4.3.2	Ch.46, p.3631	IFRS 9.5.4.1(b)	Ch.51, p.4070
IFRS 9.4.3.2	Ch.46, p.3641	IFRS 9.5.4.2	Ch.51, p.3928
IFRS 9.4.3.2	Ch.48, p.3774	IFRS 9.5.4.3	Ch.50, p.3871
IFRS 9.4.3.3	Ch.5, p.264	IFRS 9.5.4.3	Ch.50, p.3894
IFRS 9.4.3.3	Ch.46, p.3629	IFRS 9.5.4.3	Ch.50, p.3897
IFRS 9.4.3.3	Ch.46, p.3630	IFRS 9.5.4.3	Ch.51, p.4034
IFRS 9.4.3.3	Ch.50, p.3889	IFRS 9.5.4.3	Ch.51, p.4035
IFRS 9.4.3.3	Ch.55, p.4560	IFRS 9.5.4.3	Ch.52, p.4100
IFRS 9.4.3.3	Ch.56, p.4712	IFRS 9.5.4.4	Ch.51, p.3928
IFRS 9.4.3.4	Ch.54, p.4488	IFRS 9.5.4.4	Ch.51, p.4036
IFRS 9.4.3.4	Ch.54, p.4509	IFRS 9.5.4.4	Ch.51, p.4068
IFRS 9.4.3.5	Ch.48, p.3776	IFRS 9.5.4.4	Ch.52, p.4103
IFRS 9.4.3.5	Ch.48, p.3826	IFRS 9.5.4.4	Ch.54, p.4440
IFRS 9.4.3.5	Ch.48, p.3829	IFRS 9.5.4.5	Ch.52, p.4101
IFRS 9.4.3.6	Ch.5, p.264	IFRS 9.5.4.5	Ch.52, p.4159
IFRS 9.4.3.6	Ch.46, p.3630	IFRS 9.5.4.5-7	Ch.53, p.4370
IFRS 9.4.3.7	Ch.46, p.3630	IFRS 9.5.4.7	Ch.50, p.3899
IFRS 9.4.4.1	Ch.48, p.3832	IFRS 9.5.4.7	Ch.52, p.4101
IFRS 9.4.4.1	Ch.55, p.4595	IFRS 9.5.4.7	Ch.52, p.4159
IFRS 9.5.1.1	Ch.7, p.509	IFRS 9.5.4.8(a)	Ch.50, p.3899
IFRS 9.5.1.1	Ch.8, p.627	IFRS 9.5.4.8	Ch.52, p.4102
IFRS 9.5.1.1	Ch.8, p.629	IFRS 9.5.4.8	Ch.52, p.4159
IFRS 9.5.1.1	Ch.14, p.1052	IFRS 9.5.4.8	Ch.53, p.4370
IFRS 9.5.1.1	Ch.24, p.1832	IFRS 9.5.4.9	Ch.52, p.4102
IFRS 9.5.1.1	Ch.25, p.1875	IFRS 9.5.4.9	Ch.52, p.4159
IFRS 9.5.1.1	Ch.25, p.1909	IFRS 9.5.4.9	Ch.52, p.4160
IFRS 9.5.1.1	Ch.25, p.1910	IFRS 9.5.5	Ch.51, p.4017
IFRS 9.5.1.1	Ch.25, p.1913	IFRS 9.5.5.1	Ch.33, p.2579
IFRS 9.5.1.1	Ch.26, p.2007	IFRS 9.5.5.1	Ch.51, p.3924
IFRS 9.5.1.1	Ch.32, p.2399	IFRS 9.5.5.2(a)	Ch.33, p.2579
IFRS 9.5.1.1	Ch.49, p.3854	IFRS 9.5.5.2	Ch.50, p.3871
IFRS 9.5.1.1	Ch.49, p.3859	IFRS 9.5.5.2	Ch.51, p.4036
IFRS 9.5.1.1	Ch.51, p.4015	IFRS 9.5.5.2	Ch.51, p.4074
IFRS 9.5.1.1A	Ch.7, p.509	IFRS 9.5.5.3	Ch.33, p.2579
IFRS 9.5.1.1A	Ch.49, p.3855	IFRS 9.5.5.3	Ch.51, p.3925
IFRS 9.5.1.2	Ch.7, p.509	IFRS 9.5.5.3	Ch.51, p.3926
IFRS 9.5.1.2	Ch.49, p.3860	IFRS 9.5.5.3	Ch.51, p.3929
IFRS 9.5.1.3	Ch.7, p.509	IFRS 9.5.5.3	Ch.51, p.4015
IFRS 9.5.1.3	Ch.32, p.2399	IFRS 9.5.5.3	Ch.51, p.4017
IFRS 9.5.1.3	Ch.49, p.3854	IFRS 9.5.5.4	Ch.51, p.3926
IFRS 9.5.2.1	Ch.11, p.835	IFRS 9.5.5.5	Ch.33, p.2579
IFRS 9.5.2.1	Ch.50, p.3870	IFRS 9.5.5.5	Ch.51, p.3925
IFRS 9.5.2.1	Ch.50, p.3872	IFRS 9.5.5.5	Ch.51, p.3926
IFRS 9.5.2.1	Ch.50, p.3877	IFRS 9.5.5.5	Ch.51, p.3929
IFRS 9.5.2.1	Ch.51, p.4017	IFRS 9.5.5.5	Ch.51, p.4015
IFRS 9.5.2.2	Ch.50, p.3870	IFRS 9.5.5.5	Ch.51, p.4017
IFRS 9.5.2.2	Ch.50, p.3871	IFRS 9.5.5.6	Ch.5, p.264
IFRS 9.5.2.2	Ch.51, p.4017	IFRS 9.5.5.6	Ch.51, p.4047
IFRS 9.5.2.3	Ch.50, p.3880	IFRS 9.5.5.7	Ch.51, p.3926
IFRS 9.5.3.1	Ch.50, p.3871	IFRS 9.5.5.8	Ch.51, p.3925
IFRS 9.5.3.1	Ch.50, p.3872	IFRS 9.5.5.8	Ch.51, p.4017
IFRS 9.5.3.2	Ch.50, p.3880	IFRS 9.5.5.8	Ch.51, p.4068
IFRS 9.5.4.1	Ch.5, p.338	IFRS 9.5.5.9	Ch.51, p.3944
IFRS 9.5.4.1	Ch.27, p.2039	IFRS 9.5.5.9	Ch.51, p.3970
IFRS 9.5.4.1	Ch.50, p.3871	IFRS 9.5.5.9	Ch.51, p.3972
IFRS 9.5.4.1	Ch.50, p.3882	IFRS 9.5.5.9	Ch.51, p.3973
IFRS 9.5.4.1	Ch.51, p.3916	IFRS 9.5.5.9	Ch.51, p.4047

Index of standards

IFRS 9.5.5.10	Ch.5, p.264
IFRS 9.5.5.10	Ch.51, p.3990
IFRS 9.5.5.11	Ch.5, p.264
IFRS 9.5.5.11	Ch.51, p.3979
IFRS 9.5.5.11	Ch.51, p.3980
IFRS 9.5.5.11	Ch.51, p.3994
IFRS 9.5.5.12	Ch.51, p.4034
IFRS 9.5.5.12	Ch.51, p.4036
IFRS 9.5.5.13	Ch.51, p.3929
IFRS 9.5.5.13	Ch.51, p.3930
IFRS 9.5.5.13	Ch.51, p.4015
IFRS 9.5.5.14	Ch.51, p.3930
IFRS 9.5.5.15	Ch.51, p.3928
IFRS 9.5.5.15	Ch.51, p.3932
IFRS 9.5.5.15(a)	Ch.51, p.4043
IFRS 9.5.5.15(a)(i)	Ch.51, p.3928
IFRS 9.5.5.15(a)(i)	Ch.51, p.3932
IFRS 9.5.5.15(a)(ii)	Ch.51, p.3929
IFRS 9.5.5.15(b)	Ch.51, p.3929
IFRS 9.5.5.15(b)	Ch.51, p.4044
IFRS 9.5.5.16	Ch.51, p.3929
IFRS 9.5.5.17	Ch.51, p.3934
IFRS 9.5.5.17	Ch.51, p.3952
IFRS 9.5.5.17	Ch.51, p.4043
IFRS 9.5.5.17(a)	Ch.51, p.3947
IFRS 9.5.5.17(b)	Ch.51, p.3943
IFRS 9.5.5.17(c)	Ch.51, p.3962
IFRS 9.5.5.18	Ch.51, p.3947
IFRS 9.5.5.18	Ch.51, p.4036
IFRS 9.5.5.19	Ch.51, p.3944
IFRS 9.5.5.19	Ch.51, p.3946
IFRS 9.5.5.19	Ch.51, p.4047
IFRS 9.5.5.20	Ch.51, p.3945
IFRS 9.5.5.20	Ch.51, p.3946
IFRS 9.5.5.20	Ch.51, p.4047
IFRS 9.5.5.20	Ch.51, p.4051
IFRS 9.5.5.20	Ch.51, p.4054
IFRS 9.5.6.1	Ch.48, p.3835
IFRS 9.5.6.1	Ch.50, p.3878
IFRS 9.5.6.2	Ch.50, p.3879
IFRS 9.5.6.3	Ch.50, p.3879
IFRS 9.5.7.1	Ch.48, p.3775
IFRS 9.5.7.1	Ch.50, p.3872
IFRS 9.5.7.1(b)	Ch.48, p.3775
IFRS 9.5.7.1(d)	Ch.50, p.3871
IFRS 9.5.7.1A	Ch.5, p.338
IFRS 9.5.7.1A	Ch.27, p.2039
IFRS 9.5.7.1A	Ch.38, p.3081
IFRS 9.5.7.1A	Ch.50, p.3877
IFRS 9.5.7.2	Ch.50, p.3870
IFRS 9.5.7.2	Ch.50, p.3871
IFRS 9.5.7.3	Ch.50, p.3880
IFRS 9.5.7.4	Ch.49, p.3848
IFRS 9.5.7.4	Ch.50, p.3880
IFRS 9.5.7.4	Ch.51, p.4016
IFRS 9.5.7.4	Ch.51, p.4047
IFRS 9.5.7.5	Ch.5, p.263
IFRS 9.5.7.5	Ch.5, p.315
IFRS 9.5.7.5	Ch.11, p.835
IFRS 9.5.7.5	Ch.48, p.3775
IFRS 9.5.7.5	Ch.48, p.3830
IFRS 9.5.7.5	Ch.50, p.3877
IFRS 9.5.7.5	Ch.50, p.3900
IFRS 9.5.7.6	Ch.5, p.338
IFRS 9.5.7.6	Ch.48, p.3831
IFRS 9.5.7.6	Ch.50, p.3877
IFRS 9.5.7.7	Ch.14, p.1076
IFRS 9.5.7.7	Ch.48, p.3776
IFRS 9.5.7.7	Ch.50, p.3872
IFRS 9.5.7.7-8	Ch.5, p.315
IFRS 9.5.7.8	Ch.48, p.3776
IFRS 9.5.7.8	Ch.50, p.3872
IFRS 9.5.7.9	Ch.50, p.3872
IFRS 9.5.7.10	Ch.50, p.3871
IFRS 9.5.7.10	Ch.52, p.4129
IFRS 9.5.7.11	Ch.50, p.3871
IFRS 9.5.7.11	Ch.53, p.4388
IFRS 9.5.7.11	Ch.54, p.4482
IFRS 9.6.1.1	Ch.53, p.4185
IFRS 9.6.1.1	Ch.53, p.4187
IFRS 9.6.1.1	Ch.53, p.4191
IFRS 9.6.1.1	Ch.53, p.4274
IFRS 9.6.1.1	Ch.53, p.4280
IFRS 9.6.1.1	Ch.53, p.4394
IFRS 9.6.1.1	Ch.53, p.4395
IFRS 9.6.1.2	Ch.53, p.4188
IFRS 9.6.1.2	Ch.53, p.4275
IFRS 9.6.1.2	Ch.53, p.4289
IFRS 9.6.1.3	Ch.53, p.4186
IFRS 9.6.1.3	Ch.53, p.4382
IFRS 9.6.1.3	Ch.53, p.4385
IFRS 9.6.1.3	Ch.53, p.4386
IFRS 9.6.2.1	Ch.53, p.4234
IFRS 9.6.2.1	Ch.53, p.4238
IFRS 9.6.2.2	Ch.53, p.4234
IFRS 9.6.2.2	Ch.53, p.4240
IFRS 9.6.2.2	Ch.53, p.4241
IFRS 9.6.2.2	Ch.53, p.4396
IFRS 9.6.2.3	Ch.53, p.4234
IFRS 9.6.2.3	Ch.53, p.4248
IFRS 9.6.2.3	Ch.53, p.4249
IFRS 9.6.2.4	Ch.53, p.4235
IFRS 9.6.2.4	Ch.53, p.4243
IFRS 9.6.2.4	Ch.53, p.4247
IFRS 9.6.2.4	Ch.53, p.4330
IFRS 9.6.2.4(a)	Ch.53, p.4246
IFRS 9.6.2.4(a)	Ch.53, p.4278
IFRS 9.6.2.4(a)	Ch.53, p.4330
IFRS 9.6.2.4(b)	Ch.53, p.4247
IFRS 9.6.2.4(c)	Ch.53, p.4243
IFRS 9.6.2.5	Ch.53, p.4234
IFRS 9.6.2.5	Ch.53, p.4242
IFRS 9.6.2.5	Ch.53, p.4306
IFRS 9.6.2.6	Ch.53, p.4235
IFRS 9.6.3.1	Ch.53, p.4189
IFRS 9.6.3.2	Ch.53, p.4189

IFRS 9.6.3.3	Ch.53, p.4189	IFRS 9.6.5.8	Ch.53, p.4221
IFRS 9.6.3.3	Ch.53, p.4216	IFRS 9.6.5.8	Ch.53, p.4290
IFRS 9.6.3.4	Ch.53, p.4189	IFRS 9.6.5.8	Ch.53, p.4344
IFRS 9.6.3.4	Ch.53, p.4224	IFRS 9.6.5.8	Ch.53, p.4345
IFRS 9.6.3.4	Ch.53, p.4226	IFRS 9.6.5.8	Ch.53, p.4380
IFRS 9.6.3.4	Ch.53, p.4233	IFRS 9.6.5.8(b)	Ch.53, p.4292
IFRS 9.6.3.5	Ch.53, p.4189	IFRS 9.6.5.8(b)	Ch.53, p.4355
IFRS 9.6.3.5	Ch.53, p.4248	IFRS 9.6.5.8(b)	Ch.53, p.4380
IFRS 9.6.3.5	Ch.53, p.4259	IFRS 9.6.5.9	Ch.53, p.4293
IFRS 9.6.3.6	Ch.53, p.4189	IFRS 9.6.5.10	Ch.5, p.258
IFRS 9.6.3.6	Ch.53, p.4259	IFRS 9.6.5.10	Ch.51, p.4019
IFRS 9.6.3.6	Ch.53, p.4260	IFRS 9.6.5.10	Ch.53, p.4292
IFRS 9.6.3.7	Ch.53, p.4190	IFRS 9.6.5.10	Ch.53, p.4355
IFRS 9.6.3.7(a)	Ch.53, p.4190	IFRS 9.6.5.11	Ch.53, p.4295
IFRS 9.6.3.7(c)	Ch.53, p.4201	IFRS 9.6.5.11	Ch.53, p.4344
IFRS 9.6.4.1	Ch.5, p.248	IFRS 9.6.5.11(a)	Ch.53, p.4232
IFRS 9.6.4.1	Ch.5, p.252	IFRS 9.6.5.11(a)	Ch.53, p.4288
IFRS 9.6.4.1	Ch.5, p.256	IFRS 9.6.5.11(a)	Ch.53, p.4352
IFRS 9.6.4.1	Ch.53, p.4271	IFRS 9.6.5.11(a)(ii)	Ch.53, p.4228
IFRS 9.6.4.1	Ch.53, p.4275	IFRS 9.6.5.11(a)(ii)	Ch.53, p.4329
IFRS 9.6.4.1(a)	Ch.5, p.248	IFRS 9.6.5.11(d)	Ch.53, p.4297
IFRS 9.6.4.1(a)	Ch.5, p.252	IFRS 9.6.5.11(d)	Ch.53, p.4379
IFRS 9.6.4.1(b)	Ch.5, p.248	IFRS 9.6.5.11(d)(i)	Ch.53, p.4298
IFRS 9.6.4.1(b)	Ch.5, p.252	IFRS 9.6.5.11(d)(i)	Ch.53, p.4343
IFRS 9.6.4.1(b)	Ch.53, p.4272	IFRS 9.6.5.11(d)(i)	Ch.53, p.4379
IFRS 9.6.4.1(b)	Ch.53, p.4275	IFRS 9.6.5.11(d)(ii)	Ch.53, p.4379
IFRS 9.6.4.1(b)	Ch.53, p.4306	IFRS 9.6.5.12	Ch.5, p.253
IFRS 9.6.4.1(b)	Ch.53, p.4308	IFRS 9.6.5.12	Ch.53, p.4298
IFRS 9.6.4.1(c)	Ch.5, p.248	IFRS 9.6.5.12	Ch.53, p.4355
IFRS 9.6.4.1(c)	Ch.5, p.252	IFRS 9.6.5.12(b)	Ch.5, p.253
IFRS 9.6.4.1(c)	Ch.53, p.4279	IFRS 9.6.5.13	Ch.5, p.255
IFRS 9.6.4.1(c)(ii)	Ch.53, p.4325	IFRS 9.6.5.13	Ch.53, p.4300
IFRS 9.6.4.1(c)(iii)	Ch.53, p.4288	IFRS 9.6.5.13	Ch.53, p.4301
IFRS 9.6.5.1	Ch.5, p.256	IFRS 9.6.5.13	Ch.53, p.4303
IFRS 9.6.5.1	Ch.53, p.4289	IFRS 9.6.5.13	Ch.53, p.4305
IFRS 9.6.5.2	Ch.53, p.4187	IFRS 9.6.5.14	Ch.53, p.4300
IFRS 9.6.5.2	Ch.53, p.4220	IFRS 9.6.5.14	Ch.53, p.4364
IFRS 9.6.5.2	Ch.53, p.4221	IFRS 9.6.5.15	Ch.5, p.259
IFRS 9.6.5.2	Ch.53, p.4222	IFRS 9.6.5.15	Ch.53, p.4246
IFRS 9.6.5.2	Ch.53, p.4262	IFRS 9.6.5.15	Ch.53, p.4330
IFRS 9.6.5.2(b)	Ch.53, p.4329	IFRS 9.6.5.15	Ch.53, p.4331
IFRS 9.6.5.2(c)	Ch.53, p.4307	IFRS 9.6.5.15	Ch.53, p.4332
IFRS 9.6.5.3	Ch.53, p.4220	IFRS 9.6.5.15	Ch.53, p.4338
IFRS 9.6.5.3	Ch.53, p.4221	IFRS 9.6.5.15(b)	Ch.53, p.4381
IFRS 9.6.5.3	Ch.53, p.4345	IFRS 9.6.5.15(c)	Ch.53, p.4333
IFRS 9.6.5.3	Ch.53, p.4396	IFRS 9.6.5.15(c)	Ch.53, p.4341
IFRS 9.6.5.5	Ch.53, p.4349	IFRS 9.6.5.15(c)	Ch.53, p.4342
IFRS 9.6.5.6	Ch.5, p.248	IFRS 9.6.5.15(c)	Ch.53, p.4382
IFRS 9.6.5.6-7	Ch.5, p.253	IFRS 9.6.5.16	Ch.5, p.259
IFRS 9.6.5.6-7	Ch.5, p.256	IFRS 9.6.5.16	Ch.53, p.4247
IFRS 9.6.5.6	Ch.53, p.4344	IFRS 9.6.5.16	Ch.53, p.4299
IFRS 9.6.5.6	Ch.53, p.4347	IFRS 9.6.5.16	Ch.53, p.4304
IFRS 9.6.5.6	Ch.53, p.4353	IFRS 9.6.5.16	Ch.53, p.4336
IFRS 9.6.5.6	Ch.53, p.4359	IFRS 9.6.5.16	Ch.53, p.4338
IFRS 9.6.5.6	Ch.53, p.4362	IFRS 9.6.5.16	Ch.53, p.4339
IFRS 9.6.5.7	Ch.5, p.248	IFRS 9.6.6.1	Ch.5, p.252
IFRS 9.6.5.8	Ch.5, p.258	IFRS 9.6.6.1	Ch.53, p.4211
IFRS 9.6.5.8	Ch.51, p.4019	IFRS 9.6.6.1(c)	Ch.53, p.4213

IFRS 9.6.6.1(c)(ii)	Ch.53, p.4215	IFRS 9.7.2.25	Ch.53, p.4391
IFRS 9.6.6.2	Ch.53, p.4211	IFRS 9.7.2.26(a)	Ch.53, p.4391
IFRS 9.6.6.3	Ch.53, p.4212	IFRS 9.7.2.26(b)	Ch.53, p.4392
IFRS 9.6.6.3(c)	Ch.53, p.4287	IFRS 9.7.2.26(b)	Ch.53, p.4393
IFRS 9.6.6.4	Ch.53, p.4213	IFRS 9.7.2.26(d)	Ch.53, p.4367
IFRS 9.6.6.4	Ch.53, p.4381	IFRS 9.7.2.36	Ch.53, p.4377
IFRS 9.6.6.4	Ch.54, p.4487	IFRS 9.7.2.37(b)	Ch.53, p.4377
IFRS 9.6.6.5	Ch.53, p.4381	IFRS 9.7.2.37	Ch.53, p.4377
IFRS 9.6.6.6	Ch.53, p.4216	IFRS 9.7.2.39	Ch.56, p.4941
IFRS 9.6.7.1	Ch.53, p.4387	IFRS 9.7.2.40	Ch.56, p.4941
IFRS 9.6.7.2	Ch.53, p.4387	IFRS 9.7.2.43	Ch.52, p.4102
IFRS 9.6.7.3	Ch.53, p.4387	IFRS 9.7.2.43(a)	Ch.52, p.4160
IFRS 9.6.7.4	Ch.53, p.4387	IFRS 9.7.2.46	Ch.52, p.4102
IFRS 9.6.8.1	Ch.53, p.4366	IFRS 9.7.2.46	Ch.52, p.4160
IFRS 9.6.8.4	Ch.53, p.4366	IFRS 9 Appendix A	Ch.5, p.338
IFRS 9.6.8.5	Ch.53, p.4366	IFRS 9 Appendix A	Ch.27, p.2039
IFRS 9.6.8.6	Ch.53, p.4366	IFRS 9 Appendix A	Ch.33, p.2579
IFRS 9.6.8.7	Ch.53, p.4367	IFRS 9 Appendix A	Ch.39, p.3122
IFRS 9.6.8.8	Ch.53, p.4367	IFRS 9 Appendix A	Ch.40, p.3142
IFRS 9.6.8.9	Ch.53, p.4368	IFRS 9 Appendix A	Ch.45, p.3596
IFRS 9.6.8.10	Ch.53, p.4368	IFRS 9 Appendix A	Ch.46, p.3620
IFRS 9.6.8.11	Ch.53, p.4368	IFRS 9 Appendix A	Ch.46, p.3624
IFRS 9.6.8.12	Ch.53, p.4368	IFRS 9 Appendix A	Ch.46, p.3628
IFRS 9.6.8.13	Ch.53, p.4368	IFRS 9 Appendix A	Ch.47, p.3667
IFRS 9.6.9.1	Ch.53, p.4370	IFRS 9 Appendix A	Ch.47, p.3740
IFRS 9.6.9.2	Ch.53, p.4371	IFRS 9 Appendix A	Ch.48, p.3776
IFRS 9.6.9.3	Ch.53, p.4371	IFRS 9 Appendix A	Ch.48, p.3777
IFRS 9.6.9.3-4	Ch.53, p.4370	IFRS 9 Appendix A	Ch.48, p.3835
IFRS 9.6.9.5	Ch.53, p.4371	IFRS 9 Appendix A	Ch.49, p.3845
IFRS 9.6.9.6	Ch.53, p.4372	IFRS 9 Appendix A	Ch.49, p.3860
IFRS 9.6.9.7	Ch.53, p.4372	IFRS 9 Appendix A	Ch.50, p.3878
IFRS 9.6.9.8	Ch.53, p.4372	IFRS 9 Appendix A	Ch.50, p.3881
IFRS 9.6.9.9	Ch.53, p.4372	IFRS 9 Appendix A	Ch.50, p.3882
IFRS 9.6.9.10	Ch.53, p.4372	IFRS 9 Appendix A	Ch.50, p.3883
IFRS 9.6.9.11	Ch.53, p.4372	IFRS 9 Appendix A	Ch.50, p.3887
IFRS 9.6.9.12	Ch.53, p.4372	IFRS 9 Appendix A	Ch.51, p.3916
IFRS 9.7.1.8	Ch.53, p.4366	IFRS 9 Appendix A	Ch.51, p.3924
IFRS 9.7.1.9	Ch.52, p.4102	IFRS 9 Appendix A	Ch.51, p.3925
IFRS 9.7.1.9	Ch.52, p.4160	IFRS 9 Appendix A	Ch.51, p.3926
IFRS 9.7.1.9	Ch.53, p.4377	IFRS 9 Appendix A	Ch.51, p.3927
IFRS 9.7.2.1	Ch.53, p.4391	IFRS 9 Appendix A	Ch.51, p.3930
IFRS 9.7.2.1	Ch.56, p.4941	IFRS 9 Appendix A	Ch.51, p.3934
IFRS 9.7.2.2	Ch.53, p.4390	IFRS 9 Appendix A	Ch.51, p.3935
IFRS 9.7.2.2	Ch.53, p.4391	IFRS 9 Appendix A	Ch.51, p.3936
IFRS 9.7.2.14A	Ch.45, p.3613	IFRS 9 Appendix A	Ch.51, p.3937
IFRS 9.7.2.15	Ch.53, p.4390	IFRS 9 Appendix A	Ch.51, p.3944
IFRS 9.7.2.15	Ch.56, p.4941	IFRS 9 Appendix A	Ch.51, p.3947
IFRS 9.7.2.19(a)	Ch.5, p.264	IFRS 9 Appendix A	Ch.51, p.3956
IFRS 9.7.2.20	Ch.5, p.264	IFRS 9 Appendix A	Ch.51, p.4034
IFRS 9.7.2.21	Ch.5, p.249	IFRS 9 Appendix A	Ch.51, p.4035
IFRS 9.7.2.21	Ch.50, p.3880	IFRS 9 Appendix A	Ch.51, p.4036
IFRS 9.7.2.21	Ch.53, p.4186	IFRS 9 Appendix A	Ch.51, p.4045
IFRS 9.7.2.21	Ch.53, p.4386	IFRS 9 Appendix A	Ch.51, p.4067
IFRS 9.7.2.21	Ch.53, p.4389	IFRS 9 Appendix A	Ch.51, p.4068
IFRS 9.7.2.21-26	Ch.53, p.4390	IFRS 9 Appendix A	Ch.51, p.4070
IFRS 9.7.2.22	Ch.53, p.4390	IFRS 9 Appendix A	Ch.51, p.4073
IFRS 9.7.2.23	Ch.53, p.4391	IFRS 9 Appendix A	Ch.51, p.4074
IFRS 9.7.2.24	Ch.53, p.4391	IFRS 9 Appendix A	Ch.52, p.4088

IFRS 9 Appendix A	Ch.53, p.4285	IFRS 9.B3.2.13(c)	Ch.52, p.4144
IFRS 9 Appendix A	Ch.54, p.4515	IFRS 9.B3.2.13(d)	Ch.52, p.4145
IFRS 9 Appendix A	Ch.55, p.4559	IFRS 9.B3.2.13(e)	Ch.52, p.4147
IFRS 9 Appendix A	Ch.56, p.4690	IFRS 9.B3.2.13(a)	Ch.52, p.4150
IFRS 9 Appendix A	Ch.56, p.4713	IFRS 9.B3.2.14	Ch.49, p.3843
IFRS 9.B1	Ch.45, p.3587	IFRS 9.B3.2.14	Ch.52, p.4152
IFRS 9.B2	Ch.46, p.3628	IFRS 9.B3.2.15	Ch.48, p.3825
IFRS 9.B2.1	Ch.45, p.3594	IFRS 9.B3.2.15	Ch.49, p.3843
IFRS 9.B2.1	Ch.46, p.3622	IFRS 9.B3.2.16(r)	Ch.51, p.4068
IFRS 9.B2.3	Ch.45, p.3593	IFRS 9.B3.2.16(r)	Ch.52, p.4103
IFRS 9.B2.4	Ch.45, p.3594	IFRS 9.B3.2.16(h)-(i)	Ch.52, p.4116
IFRS 9.B2.5	Ch.45, p.3598	IFRS 9.B3.2.16(a)	Ch.52, p.4121
IFRS 9.B2.5(a)	Ch.45, p.3594	IFRS 9.B3.2.16(b)	Ch.52, p.4121
IFRS 9.B2.5(a)	Ch.45, p.3598	IFRS 9.B3.2.16(c)	Ch.52, p.4122
IFRS 9.B2.5(a)	Ch.49, p.3857	IFRS 9.B3.2.16(d)	Ch.52, p.4122
IFRS 9.B2.5(b)	Ch.45, p.3596	IFRS 9.B3.2.16(e)	Ch.52, p.4122
IFRS 9.B2.5(c)	Ch.45, p.3599	IFRS 9.B3.2.16(j)	Ch.52, p.4122
IFRS 9.B2.6	Ch.45, p.3599	IFRS 9.B3.2.16(k)	Ch.52, p.4122
IFRS 9.B2.6	Ch.55, p.4542	IFRS 9.B3.2.16(f)	Ch.52, p.4123
IFRS 9.B2.6	Ch.56, p.4690	IFRS 9.B3.2.16(g)	Ch.52, p.4123
IFRS 9.B3.1.1	Ch.49, p.3843	IFRS 9.B3.2.16(h)	Ch.52, p.4124
IFRS 9.B3.1.2(b)	Ch.15, p.1188	IFRS 9.B3.2.16(h)-(i)	Ch.52, p.4124
IFRS 9.B3.1.2(a)	Ch.49, p.3842	IFRS 9.B3.2.16(i)	Ch.52, p.4124
IFRS 9.B3.1.2(b)	Ch.49, p.3842	IFRS 9.B3.2.16(j)	Ch.52, p.4125
IFRS 9.B3.1.2(c)	Ch.49, p.3842	IFRS 9.B3.2.16(k)	Ch.52, p.4125
IFRS 9.B3.1.2(d)	Ch.49, p.3842	IFRS 9.B3.2.16(l)	Ch.52, p.4125
IFRS 9.B3.1.2(e)	Ch.49, p.3842	IFRS 9.B3.2.16(m)	Ch.52, p.4125
IFRS 9.B3.1.2(d)	Ch.52, p.4123	IFRS 9.B3.2.16(n)	Ch.52, p.4127
IFRS 9.B3.1.2(e)	Ch.53, p.4235	IFRS 9.B3.2.16(o)	Ch.52, p.4128
IFRS 9.B3.1.3	Ch.49, p.3845	IFRS 9.B3.2.16(p)	Ch.52, p.4128
IFRS 9.B3.1.3	Ch.50, p.3880	IFRS 9.B3.2.16(q)	Ch.52, p.4128
IFRS 9.B3.1.4	Ch.49, p.3845	IFRS 9.B3.2.16(g)	Ch.54, p.4477
IFRS 9.B3.1.5	Ch.49, p.3845	IFRS 9.B3.2.16(h)	Ch.54, p.4477
IFRS 9.B3.1.5	Ch.49, p.3848	IFRS 9.B3.2.17	Ch.52, p.4116
IFRS 9.B3.1.5	Ch.50, p.3880	IFRS 9.B3.2.17	Ch.52, p.4142
IFRS 9.B3.1.6	Ch.49, p.3845	IFRS 9.B3.2.17	Ch.52, p.4149
IFRS 9.B3.1.6	Ch.49, p.3848	IFRS 9.B3.3.1	Ch.52, p.4154
IFRS 9.B3.1.6	Ch.50, p.3880	IFRS 9.B3.3.1(b)	Ch.52, p.4154
IFRS 9.B3.2.1	Ch.52, p.4090	IFRS 9.B3.3.2	Ch.52, p.4154
IFRS 9.B3.2.1	Ch.52, p.4091	IFRS 9.B3.3.3	Ch.52, p.4156
IFRS 9.B3.2.2	Ch.52, p.4103	IFRS 9.B3.3.4	Ch.52, p.4154
IFRS 9.B3.2.3	Ch.52, p.4108	IFRS 9.B3.3.4	Ch.52, p.4155
IFRS 9.B3.2.4	Ch.52, p.4115	IFRS 9.B3.3.5	Ch.52, p.4156
IFRS 9.B3.2.4(c)	Ch.52, p.4123	IFRS 9.B3.3.6	Ch.50, p.3897
IFRS 9.B3.2.5	Ch.52, p.4115	IFRS 9.B3.3.6	Ch.52, p.4099
IFRS 9.B3.2.5(d)	Ch.52, p.4123	IFRS 9.B3.3.6	Ch.52, p.4157
IFRS 9.B3.2.6	Ch.52, p.4114	IFRS 9.B3.3.6	Ch.52, p.4162
IFRS 9.B3.2.6	Ch.52, p.4126	IFRS 9.B3.3.7	Ch.52, p.4167
IFRS 9.B3.2.6	Ch.52, p.4152	IFRS 9.B4.1.1	Ch.48, p.3779
IFRS 9.B3.2.7	Ch.52, p.4120	IFRS 9.B4.1.2	Ch.48, p.3779
IFRS 9.B3.2.8(a)	Ch.52, p.4120	IFRS 9.B4.1.2	Ch.48, p.3780
IFRS 9.B3.2.8(b)	Ch.52, p.4120	IFRS 9.B4.1.2A	Ch.48, p.3778
IFRS 9.B3.2.9	Ch.52, p.4120	IFRS 9.B4.1.2A	Ch.48, p.3779
IFRS 9.B3.2.10	Ch.52, p.4132	IFRS 9.B4.1.2B	Ch.48, p.3779
IFRS 9.B3.2.11	Ch.52, p.4131	IFRS 9.B4.1.2C	Ch.48, p.3780
IFRS 9.B3.2.12	Ch.52, p.4134	IFRS 9.B4.1.3	Ch.48, p.3781
IFRS 9.B3.2.13(a)	Ch.52, p.4141	IFRS 9.B4.1.3A	Ch.48, p.3781
IFRS 9.B3.2.13(b)	Ch.52, p.4142	IFRS 9.B4.1.3B	Ch.48, p.3781

IFRS 9.B4.1.3B	Ch.48, p.3782
IFRS 9.B4.1.3B	Ch.48, p.3787
IFRS 9.B4.1.4A	Ch.48, p.3784
IFRS 9.B4.1.4B	Ch.48, p.3784
IFRS 9.B4.1.4 Example 1	Ch.48, p.3786
IFRS 9.B4.1.4 Example 2	Ch.48, p.3787
IFRS 9.B4.1.4 Example 3	Ch.48, p.3787
IFRS 9.B4.1.4 Example 4	Ch.48, p.3788
IFRS 9.B4.1.4C Example 5	Ch.48, p.3788
IFRS 9.B4.1.4C Example 6	Ch.48, p.3788
IFRS 9.B4.1.4C Example 7	Ch.48, p.3789
IFRS 9.B4.1.5	Ch.48, p.3785
IFRS 9.B4.1.5	Ch.48, p.3790
IFRS 9.B4.1.6	Ch.48, p.3784
IFRS 9.B4.1.6	Ch.48, p.3785
IFRS 9.B4.1.6	Ch.53, p.4219
IFRS 9.B4.1.7A	Ch.25, p.1876
IFRS 9.B4.1.7A	Ch.48, p.3791
IFRS 9.B4.1.7A	Ch.48, p.3792
IFRS 9.B4.1.7B	Ch.48, p.3791
IFRS 9.B4.1.8	Ch.48, p.3809
IFRS 9.B4.1.9	Ch.48, p.3809
IFRS 9.B4.1.9	Ch.48, p.3811
IFRS 9.B4.1.9A	Ch.48, p.3792
IFRS 9.B4.1.9B	Ch.48, p.3799
IFRS 9.B4.1.9B-9D	Ch.5, p.262
IFRS 9.B4.1.9B-9D	Ch.5, p.356
IFRS 9.B4.1.9C	Ch.48, p.3799
IFRS 9.B4.1.9C	Ch.48, p.3801
IFRS 9.B4.1.9D	Ch.48, p.3801
IFRS 9.B4.1.9D	Ch.48, p.3802
IFRS 9.B4.1.9E	Ch.48, p.3795
IFRS 9.B4.1.9E	Ch.48, p.3802
IFRS 9.B4.1.10	Ch.48, p.3803
IFRS 9.B4.1.11	Ch.48, p.3803
IFRS 9.B4.1.11(b)	Ch.48, p.3807
IFRS 9.B4.1.12	Ch.5, p.263
IFRS 9.B4.1.12	Ch.5, p.357
IFRS 9.B4.1.12	Ch.48, p.3806
IFRS 9.B4.1.12	Ch.50, p.3889
IFRS 9.B4.1.12(c)	Ch.48, p.3807
IFRS 9.B4.1.12A	Ch.48, p.3804
IFRS 9.B4.1.12A	Ch.48, p.3806
IFRS 9.B4.1.13 Instrument C	Ch.48, p.3794
IFRS 9.B4.1.13 Instrument D	Ch.48, p.3794
IFRS 9.B4.1.13 Instrument A	Ch.48, p.3796
IFRS 9.B4.1.13 Instrument B	Ch.48, p.3801
IFRS 9.B4.1.13 Instrument E	Ch.48, p.3811
IFRS 9.B4.1.13 Instrument A	Ch.48, p.3812
IFRS 9.B4.1.14	Ch.48, p.3808
IFRS 9.B4.1.14 Instrument F	Ch.48, p.3810
IFRS 9.B4.1.14 Instrument G	Ch.48, p.3810
IFRS 9.B4.1.14 Instrument H	Ch.48, p.3810
IFRS 9.B4.1.15	Ch.48, p.3814
IFRS 9.B4.1.16	Ch.48, p.3814
IFRS 9.B4.1.17	Ch.48, p.3794
IFRS 9.B4.1.17	Ch.48, p.3814
IFRS 9.B4.1.18	Ch.25, p.1876
IFRS 9.B4.1.18	Ch.48, p.3791
IFRS 9.B4.1.18	Ch.48, p.3797
IFRS 9.B4.1.18	Ch.48, p.3804
IFRS 9.B4.1.18	Ch.48, p.3808
IFRS 9.B4.1.18	Ch.48, p.3814
IFRS 9.B4.1.19	Ch.48, p.3794
IFRS 9.B4.1.20	Ch.48, p.3816
IFRS 9.B4.1.20	Ch.48, p.3817
IFRS 9.B4.1.20	Ch.48, p.3820
IFRS 9.B4.1.20-26	Ch.51, p.3974
IFRS 9.B4.1.21	Ch.48, p.3816
IFRS 9.B4.1.21	Ch.48, p.3817
IFRS 9.B4.1.21(b)	Ch.48, p.3820
IFRS 9.B4.1.21(b)-(c)	Ch.48, p.3819
IFRS 9.B4.1.22	Ch.48, p.3816
IFRS 9.B4.1.22	Ch.48, p.3819
IFRS 9.B4.1.23-25	Ch.48, p.3816
IFRS 9.B4.1.25	Ch.48, p.3817
IFRS 9.B4.1.26	Ch.48, p.3817
IFRS 9.B4.1.26	Ch.48, p.3821
IFRS 9.B4.1.27	Ch.48, p.3826
IFRS 9.B4.1.28	Ch.48, p.3826
IFRS 9.B4.1.29	Ch.48, p.3827
IFRS 9.B4.1.30	Ch.48, p.3827
IFRS 9.B4.1.31	Ch.48, p.3828
IFRS 9.B4.1.32	Ch.48, p.3828
IFRS 9.B4.1.33	Ch.48, p.3784
IFRS 9.B4.1.33	Ch.48, p.3828
IFRS 9.B4.1.34	Ch.48, p.3828
IFRS 9.B4.1.35	Ch.48, p.3826
IFRS 9.B4.1.35	Ch.48, p.3828
IFRS 9.B4.1.36	Ch.48, p.3784
IFRS 9.B4.1.36	Ch.48, p.3829
IFRS 9.B4.3.1	Ch.47, p.3699
IFRS 9.B4.3.2	Ch.46, p.3630
IFRS 9.B4.3.3	Ch.46, p.3649
IFRS 9.B4.3.3	Ch.46, p.3650
IFRS 9.B4.3.3	Ch.49, p.3860
IFRS 9.B4.3.4	Ch.46, p.3651
IFRS 9.B4.3.5(a)	Ch.46, p.3641
IFRS 9.B4.3.5(b)	Ch.46, p.3635
IFRS 9.B4.3.5(b)	Ch.46, p.3637
IFRS 9.B4.3.5(c)-(d)	Ch.46, p.3639
IFRS 9.B4.3.5(c)-(d)	Ch.56, p.4714
IFRS 9.B4.3.5(e)	Ch.46, p.3633
IFRS 9.B4.3.5(e)	Ch.46, p.3637
IFRS 9.B4.3.5(e)	Ch.47, p.3727
IFRS 9.B4.3.5(e)	Ch.47, p.3734
IFRS 9.B4.3.5(e)	Ch.55, p.4561
IFRS 9.B4.3.5(e)(ii)	Ch.46, p.3636
IFRS 9.B4.3.5(f)	Ch.46, p.3640
IFRS 9.B4.3.5(f)	Ch.51, p.4022
IFRS 9.B4.3.6	Ch.46, p.3641
IFRS 9.B4.3.7	Ch.46, p.3641
IFRS 9.B4.3.7	Ch.55, p.4563
IFRS 9.B4.3.7	Ch.56, p.4715
IFRS 9.B4.3.8	Ch.46, p.3630
IFRS 9.B4.3.8(a)	Ch.46, p.3631

IFRS 9.B4.3.8(a)	Ch.46, p.3633	IFRS 9.B5.4.6	Ch.47, p.3724
IFRS 9.B4.3.8(b)	Ch.46, p.3637	IFRS 9.B5.4.6	Ch.50, p.3887
IFRS 9.B4.3.8(b)	Ch.46, p.3647	IFRS 9.B5.4.6	Ch.50, p.3894
IFRS 9.B4.3.8(c)	Ch.46, p.3631	IFRS 9.B5.4.6	Ch.51, p.3931
IFRS 9.B4.3.8(d)	Ch.43, p.3476	IFRS 9.B5.4.7	Ch.50, p.3882
IFRS 9.B4.3.8(d)	Ch.46, p.3642	IFRS 9.B5.4.7	Ch.51, p.3929
IFRS 9.B4.3.8(d)	Ch.46, p.3651	IFRS 9.B5.4.7	Ch.51, p.3930
IFRS 9.B4.3.8(e)	Ch.46, p.3637	IFRS 9.B5.4.8	Ch.47, p.3740
IFRS 9.B4.3.8(f)(i)	Ch.46, p.3648	IFRS 9.B5.4.8	Ch.49, p.3860
IFRS 9.B4.3.8(f)(ii)	Ch.46, p.3648	IFRS 9.B5.4.9	Ch.51, p.4036
IFRS 9.B4.3.8(f)(iii)	Ch.46, p.3648	IFRS 9.B5.4.9	Ch.51, p.4069
IFRS 9.B4.3.8(g)	Ch.46, p.3648	IFRS 9.B5.4.9	Ch.52, p.4103
IFRS 9.B4.3.8(g)	Ch.55, p.4563	IFRS 9.B5.5.1	Ch.51, p.3926
IFRS 9.B4.3.8(g)	Ch.56, p.4715	IFRS 9.B5.5.1-6	Ch.5, p.264
IFRS 9.B4.3.8(h)	Ch.46, p.3648	IFRS 9.B5.5.2	Ch.51, p.3979
IFRS 9.B4.3.8(h)	Ch.56, p.4712	IFRS 9.B5.5.4	Ch.51, p.4000
IFRS 9.B4.3.8(h)	Ch.56, p.4714	IFRS 9.B5.5.5	Ch.51, p.4002
IFRS 9.B4.3.9	Ch.48, p.3829	IFRS 9.B5.5.6	Ch.51, p.4002
IFRS 9.B4.3.10	Ch.48, p.3829	IFRS 9.B5.5.7	Ch.51, p.3969
IFRS 9.B4.3.11	Ch.5, p.265	IFRS 9.B5.5.8	Ch.51, p.3970
IFRS 9.B4.3.11	Ch.43, p.3477	IFRS 9.B5.5.8	Ch.51, p.4047
IFRS 9.B4.3.11	Ch.46, p.3630	IFRS 9.B5.5.9	Ch.51, p.3988
IFRS 9.B4.3.11	Ch.46, p.3652	IFRS 9.B5.5.10	Ch.51, p.3988
IFRS 9.B4.3.12	Ch.46, p.3652	IFRS 9.B5.5.11	Ch.51, p.3972
IFRS 9.B4.4.1	Ch.48, p.3832	IFRS 9.B5.5.11	Ch.51, p.3988
IFRS 9.B4.4.2	Ch.48, p.3835	IFRS 9.B5.5.12	Ch.51, p.3971
IFRS 9.B4.4.3	Ch.48, p.3833	IFRS 9.B5.5.12	Ch.51, p.3975
IFRS 9.B4.4.3(a)	Ch.48, p.3833	IFRS 9.B5.5.13	Ch.51, p.3995
IFRS 9.B5.1.1	Ch.8, p.627	IFRS 9.B5.5.14	Ch.51, p.3995
IFRS 9.B5.1.1	Ch.24, p.1832	IFRS 9.B5.5.15	Ch.51, p.3975
IFRS 9.B5.1.1	Ch.46, p.3638	IFRS 9.B5.5.16	Ch.51, p.3967
IFRS 9.B5.1.1	Ch.49, p.3854	IFRS 9.B5.5.16	Ch.51, p.3975
IFRS 9.B5.1.1	Ch.49, p.3855	IFRS 9.B5.5.17	Ch.51, p.3973
IFRS 9.B5.1.1	Ch.50, p.3883	IFRS 9.B5.5.17	Ch.51, p.3976
IFRS 9.B5.1.2	Ch.49, p.3856	IFRS 9.B5.5.17(f)	Ch.51, p.4067
IFRS 9.B5.1.2A	Ch.49, p.3854	IFRS 9.B5.5.17(g)	Ch.51, p.4067
IFRS 9.B5.1.2A	Ch.49, p.3855	IFRS 9.B5.5.17(i)	Ch.51, p.4067
IFRS 9.B5.1.2A(b)	Ch.5, p.316	IFRS 9.B5.5.17(j)	Ch.51, p.3973
IFRS 9.B5.2.1	Ch.50, p.3872	IFRS 9.B5.5.17(k)	Ch.51, p.3973
IFRS 9.B5.2.2	Ch.49, p.3859	IFRS 9.B5.5.17(l)	Ch.51, p.3973
IFRS 9.B5.2.2	Ch.49, p.3860	IFRS 9.B5.5.18	Ch.51, p.3975
IFRS 9.B5.2.2A	Ch.49, p.3855	IFRS 9.B5.5.19	Ch.51, p.3980
IFRS 9.B5.2.3	Ch.50, p.3877	IFRS 9.B5.5.19	Ch.51, p.4006
IFRS 9.B5.2.4	Ch.50, p.3878	IFRS 9.B5.5.20	Ch.51, p.3980
IFRS 9.B5.2.5	Ch.50, p.3878	IFRS 9.B5.5.21	Ch.51, p.3969
IFRS 9.B5.2.6	Ch.50, p.3878	IFRS 9.B5.5.21	Ch.51, p.3980
IFRS 9.B5.4.1	Ch.50, p.3882	IFRS 9.B5.5.22	Ch.51, p.3990
IFRS 9.B5.4.1-3	Ch.5, p.338	IFRS 9.B5.5.22-24	Ch.5, p.264
IFRS 9.B5.4.1-7	Ch.5, p.338	IFRS 9.B5.5.23	Ch.51, p.3990
IFRS 9.B5.4.1-7	Ch.27, p.2039	IFRS 9.B5.5.24	Ch.51, p.3990
IFRS 9.B5.4.2	Ch.50, p.3882	IFRS 9.B5.5.25	Ch.51, p.4033
IFRS 9.B5.4.3	Ch.50, p.3882	IFRS 9.B5.5.26	Ch.51, p.3930
IFRS 9.B5.4.4	Ch.50, p.3886	IFRS 9.B5.5.26	Ch.51, p.4033
IFRS 9.B5.4.4	Ch.50, p.3891	IFRS 9.B5.5.27	Ch.51, p.4034
IFRS 9.B5.4.4	Ch.51, p.4070	IFRS 9.B5.5.28	Ch.51, p.3935
IFRS 9.B5.4.5	Ch.50, p.3883	IFRS 9.B5.5.28	Ch.51, p.3952
IFRS 9.B5.4.5	Ch.50, p.3885	IFRS 9.B5.5.28	Ch.51, p.4047
IFRS 9.B5.4.6	Ch.43, p.3394	IFRS 9.B5.5.28	Ch.51, p.3947

IFRS 9.B5.5.29	Ch.32, p.2399	IFRS 9.B5.7.1	Ch.48, p.3830
IFRS 9.B5.5.29	Ch.51, p.3935	IFRS 9.B5.7.1	Ch.49, p.3859
IFRS 9.B5.5.30	Ch.51, p.3936	IFRS 9.B5.7.1	Ch.50, p.3877
IFRS 9.B5.5.30	Ch.51, p.4047	IFRS 9.B5.7.1A	Ch.50, p.3871
IFRS 9.B5.5.31	Ch.51, p.3936	IFRS 9.B5.7.2	Ch.50, p.3871
IFRS 9.B5.5.31	Ch.51, p.3944	IFRS 9.B5.7.2	Ch.50, p.3880
IFRS 9.B5.5.32	Ch.51, p.3936	IFRS 9.B5.7.2	Ch.50, p.3900
IFRS 9.B5.5.32	Ch.51, p.4047	IFRS 9.B5.7.2-2A	Ch.50, p.3900
IFRS 9.B5.5.32	Ch.51, p.4048	IFRS 9.B5.7.2A	Ch.50, p.3871
IFRS 9.B5.5.33	Ch.51, p.4019	IFRS 9.B5.7.2A	Ch.50, p.3900
IFRS 9.B5.5.34	Ch.51, p.4044	IFRS 9.B5.7.3	Ch.11, p.835
IFRS 9.B5.5.35	Ch.51, p.3932	IFRS 9.B5.7.3	Ch.15, p.1197
IFRS 9.B5.5.35	Ch.51, p.4043	IFRS 9.B5.7.3	Ch.15, p.1198
IFRS 9.B5.5.37	Ch.51, p.3935	IFRS 9.B5.7.3	Ch.16, p.1258
IFRS 9.B5.5.37	Ch.51, p.3938	IFRS 9.B5.7.3	Ch.50, p.3877
IFRS 9.B5.5.38	Ch.51, p.3945	IFRS 9.B5.7.3	Ch.50, p.3900
IFRS 9.B5.5.38	Ch.51, p.4047	IFRS 9.B5.7.5	Ch.50, p.3875
IFRS 9.B5.5.39	Ch.51, p.3945	IFRS 9.B5.7.6	Ch.50, p.3875
IFRS 9.B5.5.39	Ch.51, p.4047	IFRS 9.B5.7.7	Ch.50, p.3875
IFRS 9.B5.5.39	Ch.51, p.4051	IFRS 9.B5.7.8	Ch.50, p.3872
IFRS 9.B5.5.39	Ch.51, p.4052	IFRS 9.B5.7.8	Ch.50, p.3876
IFRS 9.B5.5.40	Ch.51, p.3945	IFRS 9.B5.7.9	Ch.50, p.3872
IFRS 9.B5.5.40	Ch.51, p.4047	IFRS 9.B5.7.10	Ch.48, p.3776
IFRS 9.B5.5.40	Ch.51, p.4055	IFRS 9.B5.7.10	Ch.50, p.3876
IFRS 9.B5.5.41	Ch.51, p.3947	IFRS 9.B5.7.11	Ch.50, p.3876
IFRS 9.B5.5.42	Ch.51, p.3947	IFRS 9.B5.7.12	Ch.50, p.3876
IFRS 9.B5.5.43	Ch.51, p.3936	IFRS 9.B5.7.13	Ch.50, p.3872
IFRS 9.B5.5.43	Ch.51, p.3935	IFRS 9.B5.7.14	Ch.50, p.3873
IFRS 9.B5.5.44	Ch.51, p.3952	IFRS 9.B5.7.15	Ch.50, p.3873
IFRS 9.B5.5.44	Ch.51, p.3953	IFRS 9.B5.7.16	Ch.50, p.3873
IFRS 9.B5.5.44	Ch.51, p.4047	IFRS 9.B5.7.16(b)	Ch.50, p.3875
IFRS 9.B5.5.44	Ch.51, p.4064	IFRS 9.B5.7.17	Ch.50, p.3873
IFRS 9.B5.5.45	Ch.51, p.3930	IFRS 9.B5.7.18	Ch.50, p.3873
IFRS 9.B5.5.45	Ch.51, p.3953	IFRS 9.B5.7.19	Ch.50, p.3875
IFRS 9.B5.5.46	Ch.51, p.3953	IFRS 9.B5.7.20	Ch.50, p.3875
IFRS 9.B5.5.46	Ch.51, p.4044	IFRS 9.B6.2.1	Ch.53, p.4238
IFRS 9.B5.5.47	Ch.48, p.3813	IFRS 9.B6.2.2	Ch.53, p.4242
IFRS 9.B5.5.47	Ch.51, p.3953	IFRS 9.B6.2.3	Ch.53, p.4241
IFRS 9.B5.5.47	Ch.51, p.4047	IFRS 9.B6.2.3	Ch.53, p.4303
IFRS 9.B5.5.47	Ch.51, p.4063	IFRS 9.B6.2.3	Ch.53, p.4306
IFRS 9.B5.5.48	Ch.51, p.3953	IFRS 9.B6.2.4	Ch.53, p.4235
IFRS 9.B5.5.48	Ch.51, p.4047	IFRS 9.B6.2.4	Ch.53, p.4236
IFRS 9.B5.5.49	Ch.51, p.3962	IFRS 9.B6.2.5	Ch.53, p.4241
IFRS 9.B5.5.49-54	Ch.51, p.3967	IFRS 9.B6.2.6	Ch.53, p.4243
IFRS 9.B5.5.50	Ch.51, p.3964	IFRS 9.B6.3.1	Ch.9, p.698
IFRS 9.B5.5.51	Ch.51, p.3962	IFRS 9.B6.3.1	Ch.53, p.4221
IFRS 9.B5.5.51	Ch.51, p.3963	IFRS 9.B6.3.1	Ch.53, p.4343
IFRS 9.B5.5.51	Ch.51, p.3967	IFRS 9.B6.3.2	Ch.53, p.4263
IFRS 9.B5.5.51	Ch.51, p.3944	IFRS 9.B6.3.2	Ch.53, p.4267
IFRS 9.B5.5.52	Ch.51, p.3964	IFRS 9.B6.3.3	Ch.53, p.4234
IFRS 9.B5.5.52	Ch.51, p.3965	IFRS 9.B6.3.4	Ch.53, p.4226
IFRS 9.B5.5.53	Ch.51, p.3965	IFRS 9.B6.3.4	Ch.53, p.4227
IFRS 9.B5.5.54	Ch.51, p.3964	IFRS 9.B6.3.5	Ch.53, p.4260
IFRS 9.B5.5.55	Ch.45, p.3599	IFRS 9.B6.3.6	Ch.53, p.4298
IFRS 9.B5.5.55	Ch.51, p.3955	IFRS 9.B6.3.7	Ch.53, p.4191
IFRS 9.B5.5.55	Ch.51, p.3973	IFRS 9.B6.3.7	Ch.53, p.4193
IFRS 9.B5.6.2	Ch.50, p.3879	IFRS 9.B6.3.7	Ch.53, p.4202
IFRS 9.B5.7.1	Ch.11, p.835	IFRS 9.B6.3.8	Ch.53, p.4190

IFRS 9.B6.3.8	Ch.53, p.4191
IFRS 9.B6.3.8	Ch.53, p.4197
IFRS 9.B6.3.8	Ch.53, p.4201
IFRS 9.B6.3.9	Ch.53, p.4191
IFRS 9.B6.3.9	Ch.53, p.4194
IFRS 9.B6.3.9	Ch.53, p.4197
IFRS 9.B6.3.9	Ch.53, p.4201
IFRS 9.B6.3.9	Ch.53, p.4373
IFRS 9.B6.3.10	Ch.53, p.4191
IFRS 9.B6.3.10	Ch.53, p.4192
IFRS 9.B6.3.10(b)	Ch.53, p.4195
IFRS 9.B6.3.10(c)	Ch.53, p.4196
IFRS 9.B6.3.10(c)(i)	Ch.53, p.4208
IFRS 9.B6.3.10(d)	Ch.53, p.4194
IFRS 9.B6.3.10(d)	Ch.53, p.4373
IFRS 9.B6.3.11	Ch.53, p.4191
IFRS 9.B6.3.11	Ch.53, p.4198
IFRS 9.B6.3.11	Ch.53, p.4290
IFRS 9.B6.3.11	Ch.53, p.4308
IFRS 9.B6.3.12	Ch.53, p.4246
IFRS 9.B6.3.12	Ch.53, p.4306
IFRS 9.B6.3.12	Ch.53, p.4327
IFRS 9.B6.3.12	Ch.53, p.4328
IFRS 9.B6.3.12	Ch.53, p.4329
IFRS 9.B6.3.13	Ch.53, p.4200
IFRS 9.B6.3.14	Ch.53, p.4200
IFRS 9.B6.3.15	Ch.53, p.4200
IFRS 9.B6.3.16	Ch.53, p.4201
IFRS 9.B6.3.17	Ch.53, p.4201
IFRS 9.B6.3.18	Ch.53, p.4202
IFRS 9.B6.3.18	Ch.53, p.4203
IFRS 9.B6.3.19	Ch.53, p.4202
IFRS 9.B6.3.20	Ch.53, p.4203
IFRS 9.B6.3.21	Ch.53, p.4206
IFRS 9.B6.3.21	Ch.53, p.4210
IFRS 9.B6.3.21-22	Ch.53, p.4206
IFRS 9.B6.3.23	Ch.53, p.4209
IFRS 9.B6.3.23	Ch.53, p.4210
IFRS 9.B6.3.24	Ch.53, p.4206
IFRS 9.B6.3.25	Ch.53, p.4207
IFRS 9.B6.4.1	Ch.53, p.4191
IFRS 9.B6.4.1	Ch.53, p.4198
IFRS 9.B6.4.1	Ch.53, p.4276
IFRS 9.B6.4.1	Ch.53, p.4280
IFRS 9.B6.4.1	Ch.53, p.4290
IFRS 9.B6.4.1	Ch.53, p.4307
IFRS 9.B6.4.1	Ch.53, p.4308
IFRS 9.B6.4.1	Ch.53, p.4325
IFRS 9.B6.4.2	Ch.53, p.4276
IFRS 9.B6.4.3	Ch.53, p.4362
IFRS 9.B6.4.4	Ch.53, p.4200
IFRS 9.B6.4.4	Ch.53, p.4281
IFRS 9.B6.4.5	Ch.53, p.4281
IFRS 9.B6.4.6	Ch.53, p.4281
IFRS 9.B6.4.6	Ch.53, p.4283
IFRS 9.B6.4.6	Ch.53, p.4344
IFRS 9.B6.4.7	Ch.53, p.4284
IFRS 9.B6.4.7	Ch.53, p.4286
IFRS 9.B6.4.8	Ch.53, p.4284
IFRS 9.B6.4.10	Ch.53, p.4288
IFRS 9.B6.4.11(a)	Ch.53, p.4288
IFRS 9.B6.4.11(a)	Ch.53, p.4296
IFRS 9.B6.4.11(b)	Ch.53, p.4289
IFRS 9.B6.4.12	Ch.53, p.4280
IFRS 9.B6.4.12	Ch.53, p.4283
IFRS 9.B6.4.12	Ch.53, p.4346
IFRS 9.B6.4.13	Ch.53, p.4280
IFRS 9.B6.4.14	Ch.53, p.4281
IFRS 9.B6.4.15	Ch.53, p.4277
IFRS 9.B6.4.15	Ch.53, p.4282
IFRS 9.B6.4.15	Ch.53, p.4310
IFRS 9.B6.4.16	Ch.53, p.4280
IFRS 9.B6.4.16	Ch.53, p.4282
IFRS 9.B6.4.17	Ch.53, p.4276
IFRS 9.B6.4.17	Ch.53, p.4280
IFRS 9.B6.4.18	Ch.53, p.4280
IFRS 9.B6.4.18	Ch.53, p.4282
IFRS 9.B6.4.18	Ch.53, p.4283
IFRS 9.B6.4.18	Ch.53, p.4344
IFRS 9.B6.4.19	Ch.53, p.4276
IFRS 9.B6.4.19	Ch.53, p.4280
IFRS 9.B6.5.1	Ch.53, p.4262
IFRS 9.B6.5.2	Ch.53, p.4218
IFRS 9.B6.5.2	Ch.53, p.4264
IFRS 9.B6.5.3	Ch.53, p.4263
IFRS 9.B6.5.3	Ch.53, p.4266
IFRS 9.B6.5.3	Ch.53, p.4343
IFRS 9.B6.5.4	Ch.53, p.4241
IFRS 9.B6.5.4	Ch.53, p.4309
IFRS 9.B6.5.4	Ch.53, p.4312
IFRS 9.B6.5.4	Ch.53, p.4329
IFRS 9.B6.5.5	Ch.53, p.4304
IFRS 9.B6.5.5	Ch.53, p.4305
IFRS 9.B6.5.5	Ch.53, p.4310
IFRS 9.B6.5.5	Ch.53, p.4312
IFRS 9.B6.5.5	Ch.53, p.4313
IFRS 9.B6.5.5	Ch.53, p.4325
IFRS 9.B6.5.5	Ch.53, p.4326
IFRS 9.B6.5.5	Ch.53, p.4328
IFRS 9.B6.5.5	Ch.53, p.4339
IFRS 9.B6.5.7	Ch.53, p.4347
IFRS 9.B6.5.7	Ch.53, p.4348
IFRS 9.B6.5.8	Ch.53, p.4350
IFRS 9.B6.5.9	Ch.53, p.4347
IFRS 9.B6.5.10	Ch.53, p.4347
IFRS 9.B6.5.11	Ch.53, p.4295
IFRS 9.B6.5.11	Ch.53, p.4350
IFRS 9.B6.5.12	Ch.53, p.4350
IFRS 9.B6.5.13	Ch.53, p.4349
IFRS 9.B6.5.14	Ch.53, p.4349
IFRS 9.B6.5.16	Ch.53, p.4350
IFRS 9.B6.5.16-20	Ch.53, p.4352
IFRS 9.B6.5.21	Ch.53, p.4353
IFRS 9.B6.5.24	Ch.53, p.4273
IFRS 9.B6.5.24	Ch.53, p.4356
IFRS 9.B6.5.24(a)	Ch.53, p.4357

IFRS 9.B6.5.26(a)	Ch.53, p.4393
IFRS 9.B6.5.27(a)	Ch.53, p.4352
IFRS 9.B6.5.24(b)	Ch.53, p.4277
IFRS 9.B6.5.24(b)	Ch.53, p.4359
IFRS 9.B6.5.28	Ch.53, p.4190
IFRS 9.B6.5.28	Ch.53, p.4209
IFRS 9.B6.5.28	Ch.53, p.4234
IFRS 9.B6.5.28	Ch.53, p.4276
IFRS 9.B6.5.28	Ch.53, p.4310
IFRS 9.B6.5.29	Ch.53, p.4331
IFRS 9.B6.5.29-39	Ch.5, p.259
IFRS 9.B6.5.29(b)	Ch.53, p.4303
IFRS 9.B6.5.29(b)	Ch.53, p.4338
IFRS 9.B6.5.30	Ch.53, p.4331
IFRS 9.B6.5.31	Ch.53, p.4334
IFRS 9.B6.5.32	Ch.53, p.4334
IFRS 9.B6.5.33	Ch.53, p.4334
IFRS 9.B6.5.34-36	Ch.53, p.4336
IFRS 9.B6.5.37	Ch.53, p.4337
IFRS 9.B6.5.37	Ch.53, p.4338
IFRS 9.B6.5.37	Ch.53, p.4343
IFRS 9.B6.5.38	Ch.53, p.4343
IFRS 9.B6.6.1	Ch.53, p.4211
IFRS 9.B6.6.7	Ch.53, p.4213
IFRS 9.B6.6.7	Ch.53, p.4215
IFRS 9.B6.6.8	Ch.53, p.4215
IFRS 9.B6.6.12	Ch.53, p.4212
IFRS 9.B6.6.13	Ch.54, p.4487
IFRS 9.B6.6.13-15	Ch.53, p.4380
IFRS 9.B6.6.14	Ch.54, p.4487
IFRS 9.B6.6.15	Ch.53, p.4215
IFRS 9.B6.6.15	Ch.54, p.4487
IFRS 9.B6.6.16	Ch.53, p.4381
IFRS 9.B6.6.16	Ch.54, p.4487
IFRS 9.B7.2.2	Ch.5, p.264
IFRS 9.B7.2.2-3	Ch.5, p.264
IFRS 9.B7.2.3	Ch.5, p.264
IFRS 9.BA.1	Ch.46, p.3621
IFRS 9.BA.2	Ch.46, p.3627
IFRS 9.BA.3	Ch.46, p.3624
IFRS 9.BA.3	Ch.46, p.3625
IFRS 9.BA.4	Ch.46, p.3629
IFRS 9.BA.4	Ch.49, p.3860
IFRS 9.BA.5	Ch.46, p.3622
IFRS 9.BA.6	Ch.48, p.3778
IFRS 9.BA.7	Ch.48, p.3778
IFRS 9.BA.7(d)	Ch.48, p.3778
IFRS 9.BA.8	Ch.48, p.3778
IFRS 9.IE1-IE5	Ch.50, p.3874
IFRS 9.IE7-11 Example 1	Ch.51, p.3982
IFRS 9.IE12-17 Example 2	Ch.51, p.3982
IFRS 9.IE18-IE23 Example 3	Ch.51, p.3972
IFRS 9.IE24-IE28 Example 4	Ch.51, p.3992
IFRS 9.IE29-IE39 Example 5	Ch.51, p.4004
IFRS 9.IE40-IE42 Example 6	Ch.51, p.3998
IFRS 9.IE43-IE47 Example 7	Ch.51, p.3997
IFRS 9.IE53-IE57 Example 9	Ch.51, p.3942
IFRS 9.IE58-IE65 Example 10	Ch.51, p.4055
IFRS 9.IE66-IE73 Example 11	Ch.51, p.4034
IFRS 9.IE74-IE77 Example 12	Ch.51, p.4043
IFRS 9.IE78-IE81 Example 13	Ch.33, p.2580
IFRS 9.IE78-IE81 Example 13	Ch.51, p.4036
IFRS 9.IE82-IE102	Ch.51, p.4037
IFRS 9.IE115-147	Ch.53, p.4225
IFRS 9.IE116-127	Ch.53, p.4231
IFRS 9.IE119(b)	Ch.53, p.4231
IFRS 9.IE119(b)	Ch.53, p.4232
IFRS 9.IE122	Ch.53, p.4232
IFRS 9.IE123	Ch.53, p.4232
IFRS 9.IE128-137	Ch.53, p.4227
IFRS 9.IE131(b)	Ch.53, p.4227
IFRS 9.IE134	Ch.53, p.4229
IFRS 9.IE134(a)	Ch.53, p.4228
IFRS 9.IE138-147	Ch.53, p.4229
IFRS 9.IE139(b)	Ch.53, p.4230
IFRS 9.IE143	Ch.53, p.4230
IFRS 9.IG A.1	Ch.45, p.3609
IFRS 9.IG A.2	Ch.45, p.3611
IFRS 9.IG B.3	Ch.46, p.3627
IFRS 9.IG B.4	Ch.46, p.3625
IFRS 9.IG B.5	Ch.46, p.3626
IFRS 9.IG B.6	Ch.46, p.3628
IFRS 9.IG B.6	Ch.53, p.4235
IFRS 9.IG B.7	Ch.46, p.3627
IFRS 9.IG B.8	Ch.46, p.3621
IFRS 9.IG B.9	Ch.46, p.3625
IFRS 9.IG B.9	Ch.46, p.3626
IFRS 9.IG B.10	Ch.46, p.3626
IFRS 9.IG B.11	Ch.48, p.3778
IFRS 9.IG B.24	Ch.50, p.3889
IFRS 9.IG B.25	Ch.50, p.3889
IFRS 9.IG B.26	Ch.50, p.3884
IFRS 9.IG B.26	Ch.50, p.3888
IFRS 9.IG B.27	Ch.50, p.3884
IFRS 9.IG B.28	Ch.49, p.3846
IFRS 9.IG B.29	Ch.49, p.3846
IFRS 9.IG B.30	Ch.49, p.3846
IFRS 9.IG B.31	Ch.49, p.3847
IFRS 9.IG C.1	Ch.46, p.3649
IFRS 9.IG C.2	Ch.46, p.3650
IFRS 9.IG C.2	Ch.46, p.3651
IFRS 9.IG C.4	Ch.46, p.3641
IFRS 9.IG C.6	Ch.46, p.3653
IFRS 9.IG C.6	Ch.46, p.3654
IFRS 9.IG C.7	Ch.46, p.3645
IFRS 9.IG C.8	Ch.46, p.3645
IFRS 9.IG C.9	Ch.46, p.3643
IFRS 9.IG C.10	Ch.46, p.3631
IFRS 9.IG D.1.1	Ch.49, p.3844
IFRS 9.IG D.2.1	Ch.49, p.3848
IFRS 9.IG D.2.2	Ch.49, p.3848
IFRS 9.IG D.2.2	Ch.50, p.3881
IFRS 9.IG D.2.3	Ch.49, p.3853
IFRS 9.IG E.1.1	Ch.49, p.3859
IFRS 9.IG E.3.2	Ch.50, p.3900
IFRS 9.IG E.3.3	Ch.50, p.3902

IFRS 9.IG E.3.4	Ch.50, p.3900	IFRS 9.BC4.193	Ch.48, p.3806
IFRS 9.IG G.2	Ch.40, p.3161	IFRS 9.BC4.194	Ch.48, p.3807
IFRS 9.IG G.2	Ch.54, p.4520	IFRS 9.BC4.206(a)	Ch.48, p.3821
IFRS 9.BCZ2.2	Ch.45, p.3600	IFRS 9.BC4.225	Ch.48, p.3805
IFRS 9.BCZ2.2	Ch.45, p.3601	IFRS 9.BC4.232	Ch.48, p.3805
IFRS 9.BCZ2.2	Ch.51, p.4045	IFRS 9.BC4.252	Ch.52, p.4163
IFRS 9.BCZ2.2	Ch.51, p.4046	IFRS 9.BC4.252-253	Ch.50, p.3894
IFRS 9.BCZ2.3	Ch.45, p.3600	IFRS 9.BC4.253	Ch.52, p.4163
IFRS 9.BCZ2.3	Ch.49, p.3862	IFRS 9.BC5.13	Ch.50, p.3878
IFRS 9.BCZ2.6	Ch.45, p.3601	IFRS 9.BC5.16	Ch.50, p.3878
IFRS 9.BCZ2.7	Ch.45, p.3601	IFRS 9.BC5.18	Ch.50, p.3878
IFRS 9.BCZ2.12	Ch.45, p.3598	IFRS 9.BC5.21	Ch.48, p.3830
IFRS 9.BCZ2.14	Ch.45, p.3600	IFRS 9.BC5.25(a)	Ch.48, p.3832
IFRS 9.BCZ2.18	Ch.43, p.3474	IFRS 9.BC5.25(c)	Ch.48, p.3831
IFRS 9.BCZ2.18	Ch.45, p.3608	IFRS 9.BC5.40	Ch.48, p.3776
IFRS 9.BCZ2.18	Ch.45, p.3609	IFRS 9.BC5.41	Ch.48, p.3776
IFRS 9.BCZ2.18	Ch.45, p.3610	IFRS 9.BCZ5.67	Ch.50, p.3881
IFRS 9.BCZ2.24	Ch.45, p.3613	IFRS 9.BC5.75	Ch.51, p.4070
IFRS 9.BCZ2.39	Ch.45, p.3603	IFRS 9.BC5.78	Ch.51, p.4071
IFRS 9.BCZ2.40	Ch.45, p.3603	IFRS 9.BC5.87	Ch.51, p.3912
IFRS 9.BCZ2.41	Ch.45, p.3603	IFRS 9.BC5.89	Ch.51, p.3912
IFRS 9.BCZ2.42	Ch.11, p.827	IFRS 9.BC5.92	Ch.51, p.3912
IFRS 9.BCZ2.42	Ch.45, p.3604	IFRS 9.BC5.93	Ch.51, p.3913
IFRS 9.BCZ3.4-12	Ch.52, p.4138	IFRS 9.BC5.95	Ch.51, p.3913
IFRS 9.BC4.23	Ch.48, p.3790	IFRS 9.BC5.96	Ch.51, p.3913
IFRS 9.BC4.26	Ch.48, p.3817	IFRS 9.BC5.104	Ch.51, p.3929
IFRS 9.BC4.28	Ch.48, p.3818	IFRS 9.BC5.111	Ch.51, p.3913
IFRS 9.BC4.29	Ch.48, p.3818	IFRS 9.BC5.112	Ch.51, p.3913
IFRS 9.BC4.33	Ch.48, p.3818	IFRS 9.BC5.114	Ch.51, p.3915
IFRS 9.BC4.34	Ch.48, p.3818	IFRS 9.BC5.116	Ch.51, p.3915
IFRS 9.BC4.35(d)	Ch.48, p.3822	IFRS 9.BC5.123	Ch.51, p.3976
IFRS 9.BCZ4.61	Ch.48, p.3827	IFRS 9.BC5.135	Ch.51, p.3937
IFRS 9.BCZ4.66	Ch.48, p.3829	IFRS 9.BC5.141	Ch.51, p.3926
IFRS 9.BCZ4.68-70	Ch.48, p.3830	IFRS 9.BC5.154	Ch.32, p.2398
IFRS 9.BCZ4.70	Ch.48, p.3830	IFRS 9.BC5.157	Ch.51, p.3970
IFRS 9.BCZ4.74-76	Ch.48, p.3826	IFRS 9.BC5.157	Ch.51, p.3975
IFRS 9.BCZ4.92	Ch.46, p.3629	IFRS 9.BC5.160	Ch.51, p.3971
IFRS 9.BCZ4.92	Ch.46, p.3619	IFRS 9.BC5.161	Ch.51, p.3971
IFRS 9.BCZ4.94	Ch.46, p.3643	IFRS 9.BC5.162	Ch.51, p.3971
IFRS 9.BCZ4.97	Ch.46, p.3636	IFRS 9.BC5.163	Ch.51, p.3971
IFRS 9.BCZ4.99	Ch.46, p.3651	IFRS 9.BC5.164	Ch.51, p.3971
IFRS 9.BCZ4.100	Ch.46, p.3651	IFRS 9.BC5.165	Ch.51, p.3971
IFRS 9.BCZ4.100-101	Ch.46, p.3652	IFRS 9.BC5.168	Ch.51, p.3997
IFRS 9.BCZ4.105	Ch.46, p.3653	IFRS 9.BC5.171	Ch.51, p.3987
IFRS 9.BCZ4.106	Ch.46, p.3652	IFRS 9.BC5.172	Ch.51, p.3987
IFRS 9.BC4.117	Ch.48, p.3834	IFRS 9.BC5.178	Ch.51, p.3995
IFRS 9.BC4.150	Ch.48, p.3774	IFRS 9.BC5.181	Ch.51, p.3989
IFRS 9.BC4.150	Ch.50, p.3871	IFRS 9.BC5.182	Ch.51, p.3989
IFRS 9.BC4.158	Ch.48, p.3790	IFRS 9.BC5.183	Ch.51, p.3989
IFRS 9.BC4.171	Ch.48, p.3790	IFRS 9.BC5.184	Ch.51, p.3989
IFRS 9.BC4.172	Ch.48, p.3790	IFRS 9.BC5.188	Ch.51, p.3990
IFRS 9.BC4.178	Ch.48, p.3793	IFRS 9.BC5.190	Ch.51, p.3980
IFRS 9.BC4.180	Ch.48, p.3791	IFRS 9.BC5.192	Ch.51, p.3980
IFRS 9.BC4.180	Ch.48, p.3802	IFRS 9.BC5.199	Ch.51, p.3937
IFRS 9.BC4.182(a)	Ch.48, p.3791	IFRS 9.BC5.214	Ch.51, p.3930
IFRS 9.BC4.182(b)	Ch.48, p.3791	IFRS 9.BC5.216	Ch.52, p.4099
IFRS 9.BC4.182(b)	Ch.48, p.3792	IFRS 9.BC5.217	Ch.51, p.3930
IFRS 9.BC4.182(b)	Ch.48, p.3793	IFRS 9.BC5.225	Ch.51, p.3929

IFRS 9.BC5.227	Ch.52, p.4099	IFRS 9.BC6.380	Ch.54, p.4490
IFRS 9.BC5.248	Ch.51, p.3935	IFRS 9.BC6.387	Ch.53, p.4329
IFRS 9.BC5.249	Ch.51, p.3935	IFRS 9.BC6.398	Ch.53, p.4335
IFRS 9.BC5.252	Ch.51, p.3935	IFRS 9.BC6.399	Ch.53, p.4333
IFRS 9.BC5.252	Ch.51, p.3938	IFRS 9.BC6.416	Ch.53, p.4337
IFRS 9.BC5.254-261	Ch.51, p.4053	IFRS 9.BC6.422	Ch.53, p.4336
IFRS 9.BC5.259	Ch.51, p.4054	IFRS 9.BC6.435	Ch.53, p.4211
IFRS 9.BC5.260	Ch.51, p.4064	IFRS 9.BC6.436	Ch.53, p.4211
IFRS 9.BC5.260	Ch.51, p.4061	IFRS 9.BC6.438	Ch.53, p.4212
IFRS 9.BC5.260	Ch.51, p.3944	IFRS 9.BC6.439	Ch.53, p.4212
IFRS 9.BC5.265	Ch.51, p.3938	IFRS 9.BC6.455	Ch.53, p.4213
IFRS 9.BC5.281	Ch.51, p.3964	IFRS 9.BC6.457	Ch.53, p.4380
IFRS 9.BC5.306	Ch.50, p.3898	IFRS 9.BC6.461	Ch.53, p.4380
IFRS 9.BC5.309	Ch.50, p.3899	IFRS 9.BC6.470	Ch.53, p.4387
IFRS 9.BC5.311	Ch.50, p.3899	IFRS 9.BC6.470	Ch.53, p.4192
IFRS 9.BC5.312	Ch.50, p.3899	IFRS 9.BC6.491	Ch.53, p.4387
IFRS 9.BC5.318	Ch.50, p.3899	IFRS 9.BC6.504	Ch.53, p.4387
IFRS 9.BC6.327	Ch.53, p.4354	IFRS 9.BC6.517	Ch.53, p.4192
IFRS 9.BC6.330	Ch.53, p.4354	IFRS 9.BC6.560	Ch.53, p.4367
IFRS 9.BC6.82	Ch.53, p.4187	IFRS 9.BC6.567	Ch.53, p.4367
IFRS 9.BC6.91-95	Ch.53, p.4385	IFRS 9.BC6.568	Ch.53, p.4367
IFRS 9.BC6.93-95	Ch.53, p.4394	IFRS 9.BC6.575	Ch.53, p.4367
IFRS 9.BC6.93-95	Ch.53, p.4187	IFRS 9.BC6.594	Ch.53, p.4368
IFRS 9.BC6.94-95	Ch.53, p.4265	IFRS 9.BC6.619	Ch.53, p.4375
IFRS 9.BC6.97	Ch.53, p.4394	IFRS 9.BC6.647	Ch.53, p.4374
IFRS 9.BC6.97-101	Ch.53, p.4274	IFRS 9.BC6.587-593	Ch.53, p.4368
IFRS 9.BC6.98	Ch.53, p.4275	IFRS 9.BC6.616-619	Ch.53, p.4371
IFRS 9.BC6.98	Ch.53, p.4381	IFRS 9.BC7.44-51	Ch.53, p.4393
IFRS 9.BC6.98	Ch.53, p.4394	IFRS 9.BC7.49	Ch.53, p.4393
IFRS 9.BC6.100(a)	Ch.53, p.4381	IFRS 9.BC7.49	Ch.53, p.4392
IFRS 9.BC6.100(a)	Ch.53, p.4275	IFRS 9.BC7.52	Ch.5, p.249
IFRS 9.BC6.100(b)	Ch.53, p.4394	IFRS 9.BC7.52	Ch.5, p.252
IFRS 9.BC6.100(b)	Ch.53, p.4275	IFRS 9.BC7.88	Ch.53, p.4377
IFRS 9.BC6.104	Ch.54, p.4412		
IFRS 9.BC6.104	Ch.53, p.4386		
IFRS 9.BC6.104	Ch.53, p.4390	**IFRS 10**	
IFRS 9.BC6.117-122	Ch.53, p.4238		
IFRS 9.BC6.142-150	Ch.53, p.4250	IFRS 10.1	Ch.6, p.394
IFRS 9.BC6.151	Ch.53, p.4236	IFRS 10.2	Ch.6, p.394
IFRS 9.BC6.153	Ch.53, p.4236	IFRS 10.2	Ch.27, p.2035
IFRS 9.BC6.167	Ch.53, p.4233	IFRS 10.3	Ch.6, p.394
IFRS 9.BC6.174	Ch.53, p.4193	IFRS 10.4	Ch.5, p.313
IFRS 9.BC6.331	Ch.53, p.4354	IFRS 10.4	Ch.6, p.394
IFRS 9.BC6.176	Ch.53, p.4198	IFRS 10.4	Ch.8, p.577
IFRS 9.BC6.176	Ch.53, p.4191	IFRS 10.4-4B	Ch.27, p.2035
IFRS 9.BC6.200	Ch.53, p.4361	IFRS 10.4(a)	Ch.6, p.395
IFRS 9.BC6.226-228	Ch.53, p.4206	IFRS 10.4(a)	Ch.8, p.577
IFRS 9.BC6.238	Ch.53, p.4281	IFRS 10.4A	Ch.6, p.398
IFRS 9.BC6.269	Ch.53, p.4282	IFRS 10.4B	Ch.6, p.399
IFRS 9.BC6.297	Ch.53, p.4330	IFRS 10.5	Ch.6, p.405
IFRS 9.BC6.301	Ch.53, p.4350	IFRS 10.6	Ch.6, p.405
IFRS 9.BC6.303	Ch.53, p.4347	IFRS 10.6	Ch.9, p.659
IFRS 9.BC6.310	Ch.53, p.4350	IFRS 10.7	Ch.6, p.405
IFRS 9.BC6.324	Ch.53, p.4354	IFRS 10.7	Ch.6, p.410
IFRS 9.BC6.332-337	Ch.52, p.4102	IFRS 10.7	Ch.6, p.436
IFRS 9.BC6.333	Ch.52, p.4167	IFRS 10.7	Ch.6, p.439
IFRS 9.BC6.335	Ch.52, p.4155	IFRS 10.7	Ch.6, p.445
IFRS 9.BC6.380	Ch.54, p.4421	IFRS 10.7	Ch.7, p.508

IFRS 10.8	Ch.6, p.406
IFRS 10.8	Ch.6, p.410
IFRS 10.8	Ch.6, p.467
IFRS 10.8	Ch.7, p.508
IFRS 10.8	Ch.52, p.4153
IFRS 10.9	Ch.6, p.406
IFRS 10.10	Ch.6, p.408
IFRS 10.10	Ch.6, p.409
IFRS 10.10	Ch.6, p.432
IFRS 10.11	Ch.6, p.413
IFRS 10.11	Ch.6, p.434
IFRS 10.12	Ch.6, p.415
IFRS 10.13	Ch.6, p.409
IFRS 10.14	Ch.6, p.409
IFRS 10.14	Ch.6, p.414
IFRS 10.14	Ch.6, p.416
IFRS 10.15	Ch.6, p.439
IFRS 10.16	Ch.6, p.439
IFRS 10.17	Ch.6, p.445
IFRS 10.18	Ch.6, p.445
IFRS 10.18	Ch.6, p.446
IFRS 10.19	Ch.5, p.335
IFRS 10.19	Ch.7, p.497
IFRS 10.19	Ch.55, p.4589
IFRS 10.20	Ch.6, p.399
IFRS 10.20	Ch.6, p.405
IFRS 10.20	Ch.7, p.497
IFRS 10.20	Ch.7, p.503
IFRS 10.20	Ch.8, p.578
IFRS 10.20	Ch.27, p.2035
IFRS 10.21	Ch.7, p.497
IFRS 10.21	Ch.7, p.498
IFRS 10.21	Ch.7, p.499
IFRS 10.21	Ch.7, p.501
IFRS 10.21	Ch.7, p.502
IFRS 10.21	Ch.7, p.503
IFRS 10.21	Ch.7, p.523
IFRS 10.21	Ch.7, p.547
IFRS 10.21	Ch.7, p.549
IFRS 10.21	Ch.7, p.550
IFRS 10.22	Ch.7, p.498
IFRS 10.22	Ch.7, p.545
IFRS 10.22	Ch.11, p.840
IFRS 10.22	Ch.11, p.867
IFRS 10.23	Ch.5, p.262
IFRS 10.23	Ch.7, p.498
IFRS 10.23	Ch.7, p.533
IFRS 10.23	Ch.7, p.538
IFRS 10.23	Ch.8, p.623
IFRS 10.23	Ch.10, p.788
IFRS 10.23	Ch.11, p.868
IFRS 10.23	Ch.20, p.1606
IFRS 10.23	Ch.33, p.2600
IFRS 10.23	Ch.47, p.3741
IFRS 10.24	Ch.7, p.498
IFRS 10.24	Ch.7, p.499
IFRS 10.24	Ch.7, p.533
IFRS 10.24	Ch.7, p.538
IFRS 10.24	Ch.7, p.546
IFRS 10.24	Ch.7, p.547
IFRS 10.24	Ch.7, p.548
IFRS 10.24	Ch.7, p.549
IFRS 10.25	Ch.6, p.405
IFRS 10.25	Ch.6, p.488
IFRS 10.25	Ch.7, p.509
IFRS 10.25	Ch.7, p.514
IFRS 10.25	Ch.7, p.518
IFRS 10.25	Ch.7, p.519
IFRS 10.25	Ch.7, p.520
IFRS 10.25	Ch.7, p.565
IFRS 10.25	Ch.11, p.857
IFRS 10.25	Ch.12, p.933
IFRS 10.26	Ch.7, p.509
IFRS 10.26	Ch.7, p.514
IFRS 10.26	Ch.7, p.518
IFRS 10.26	Ch.7, p.519
IFRS 10.26	Ch.7, p.520
IFRS 10.26	Ch.7, p.524
IFRS 10.26	Ch.7, p.525
IFRS 10.26	Ch.7, p.526
IFRS 10.26	Ch.7, p.527
IFRS 10.26	Ch.7, p.531
IFRS 10.26	Ch.7, p.565
IFRS 10.27	Ch.6, p.473
IFRS 10.28	Ch.6, p.473
IFRS 10.29	Ch.6, p.473
IFRS 10.30	Ch.6, p.474
IFRS 10.30	Ch.6, p.488
IFRS 10.31	Ch.5, p.313
IFRS 10.31	Ch.6, p.485
IFRS 10.31	Ch.8, p.583
IFRS 10.31	Ch.45, p.3592
IFRS 10.31-33	Ch.7, p.497
IFRS 10.31-33	Ch.7, p.540
IFRS 10.32	Ch.5, p.313
IFRS 10.32	Ch.6, p.475
IFRS 10.32	Ch.6, p.485
IFRS 10.33	Ch.5, p.313
IFRS 10.33	Ch.6, p.489
IFRS 10 Appendix A	Ch.5, p.285
IFRS 10 Appendix A	Ch.5, p.313
IFRS 10 Appendix A	Ch.6, p.394
IFRS 10 Appendix A	Ch.6, p.405
IFRS 10 Appendix A	Ch.6, p.416
IFRS 10 Appendix A	Ch.7, p.497
IFRS 10 Appendix A	Ch.7, p.498
IFRS 10 Appendix A	Ch.7, p.540
IFRS 10 Appendix A	Ch.7, p.544
IFRS 10 Appendix A	Ch.8, p.577
IFRS 10 Appendix A	Ch.12, p.898
IFRS 10 Appendix A	Ch.13, p.951
IFRS 10 Appendix A	Ch.13, p.959
IFRS 10 Appendix A	Ch.27, p.2035
IFRS 10 Appendix A	Ch.39, p.3102
IFRS 10 Appendix A	Ch.39, p.3104
IFRS 10 Appendix A	Ch.40, p.3174

IFRS 10.B1	Ch.6, p.457	IFRS 10.B35	Ch.6, p.421
IFRS 10.B2	Ch.6, p.406	IFRS 10.B36	Ch.6, p.421
IFRS 10.B2	Ch.6, p.410	IFRS 10.B37	Ch.6, p.421
IFRS 10.B2	Ch.6, p.436	IFRS 10.B38	Ch.6, p.421
IFRS 10.B3	Ch.6, p.406	IFRS 10.B39	Ch.6, p.433
IFRS 10.B3	Ch.12, p.897	IFRS 10.B40	Ch.6, p.433
IFRS 10.B4	Ch.6, p.406	IFRS 10.B41	Ch.6, p.423
IFRS 10.B5	Ch.6, p.407	IFRS 10.B42	Ch.6, p.423
IFRS 10.B6	Ch.6, p.406	IFRS 10.B42	Ch.6, p.429
IFRS 10.B6	Ch.6, p.408	IFRS 10.B43	Ch.6, p.424
IFRS 10.B6	Ch.6, p.409	IFRS 10.B43 Example 4	Ch.6, p.424
IFRS 10.B6	Ch.6, p.420	IFRS 10.B43 Example 5	Ch.6, p.433
IFRS 10.B7	Ch.6, p.408	IFRS 10.B44	Ch.6, p.424
IFRS 10.B8	Ch.6, p.408	IFRS 10.B44 Example 6	Ch.6, p.424
IFRS 10.B8	Ch.6, p.441	IFRS 10.B45	Ch.6, p.425
IFRS 10.B9	Ch.6, p.408	IFRS 10.B45 Example 7	Ch.6, p.425
IFRS 10.B10	Ch.6, p.409	IFRS 10.B45 Example 8	Ch.6, p.426
IFRS 10.B11-B12	Ch.6, p.409	IFRS 10.B46	Ch.6, p.423
IFRS 10.B13	Ch.6, p.409	IFRS 10.B47	Ch.6, p.428
IFRS 10.B13 Example 1	Ch.6, p.409	IFRS 10.B47	Ch.6, p.430
IFRS 10.B13 Example 1	Ch.12, p.898	IFRS 10.B48	Ch.6, p.428
IFRS 10.B13 Example 2	Ch.6, p.410	IFRS 10.B49	Ch.6, p.429
IFRS 10.B14	Ch.6, p.413	IFRS 10.B50	Ch.6, p.429
IFRS 10.B14	Ch.6, p.430	IFRS 10.B50 Example 9	Ch.6, p.431
IFRS 10.B15	Ch.6, p.414	IFRS 10.B50 Example 10	Ch.6, p.429
IFRS 10.B16	Ch.6, p.414	IFRS 10.B51	Ch.6, p.438
IFRS 10.B17	Ch.6, p.434	IFRS 10.B52	Ch.6, p.434
IFRS 10.B18	Ch.6, p.437	IFRS 10.B53	Ch.6, p.435
IFRS 10.B19	Ch.6, p.437	IFRS 10.B53 Example 11	Ch.6, p.436
IFRS 10.B19	Ch.6, p.440	IFRS 10.B53 Example 12	Ch.6, p.436
IFRS 10.B20	Ch.6, p.420	IFRS 10.B54	Ch.6, p.420
IFRS 10.B20	Ch.6, p.438	IFRS 10.B54	Ch.6, p.436
IFRS 10.B20	Ch.6, p.440	IFRS 10.B55	Ch.6, p.439
IFRS 10.B21	Ch.6, p.437	IFRS 10.B56	Ch.6, p.439
IFRS 10.B22	Ch.6, p.414	IFRS 10.B56	Ch.6, p.440
IFRS 10.B22	Ch.6, p.430	IFRS 10.B56	Ch.13, p.947
IFRS 10.B23	Ch.6, p.414	IFRS 10.B56	Ch.13, p.948
IFRS 10.B23	Ch.6, p.451	IFRS 10.B57	Ch.6, p.439
IFRS 10.B23(a)	Ch.6, p.431	IFRS 10.B57	Ch.6, p.444
IFRS 10.B23(a)(ii)	Ch.6, p.430	IFRS 10.B57(c)	Ch.6, p.444
IFRS 10.B23(a)(vi)	Ch.6, p.451	IFRS 10.B58	Ch.6, p.446
IFRS 10.B23(b)	Ch.6, p.450	IFRS 10.B58	Ch.6, p.447
IFRS 10.B24	Ch.6, p.415	IFRS 10.B59	Ch.6, p.447
IFRS 10.B24	Ch.6, p.430	IFRS 10.B59	Ch.6, p.454
IFRS 10.B24	Ch.6, p.432	IFRS 10.B60	Ch.6, p.447
IFRS 10.B24 Example 3-3D	Ch.6, p.415	IFRS 10.B60	Ch.6, p.457
IFRS 10.B25	Ch.6, p.416	IFRS 10.B61	Ch.6, p.447
IFRS 10.B26	Ch.6, p.416	IFRS 10.B62	Ch.6, p.448
IFRS 10.B26-27	Ch.12, p.898	IFRS 10.B63	Ch.6, p.448
IFRS 10.B27	Ch.6, p.416	IFRS 10.B64	Ch.6, p.449
IFRS 10.B28	Ch.6, p.416	IFRS 10.B64	Ch.6, p.451
IFRS 10.B29	Ch.6, p.417	IFRS 10.B65	Ch.6, p.450
IFRS 10.B30	Ch.6, p.418	IFRS 10.B66	Ch.6, p.449
IFRS 10.B31	Ch.6, p.418	IFRS 10.B67	Ch.6, p.450
IFRS 10.B32	Ch.6, p.418	IFRS 10.B68	Ch.6, p.452
IFRS 10.B33	Ch.6, p.418	IFRS 10.B69	Ch.6, p.453
IFRS 10.B34	Ch.6, p.420	IFRS 10.B70	Ch.6, p.453
IFRS 10.B34	Ch.6, p.421	IFRS 10.B71	Ch.6, p.454

IFRS 10.B72	Ch.6, p.455	IFRS 10.B85U	Ch.6, p.481
IFRS 10.B72 Example 13	Ch.6, p.449	IFRS 10.B85V	Ch.6, p.481
IFRS 10.B72 Example 13	Ch.6, p.453	IFRS 10.B85W	Ch.6, p.482
IFRS 10.B72 Example 13	Ch.6, p.457	IFRS 10.B86	Ch.7, p.498
IFRS 10.B72 Example 14	Ch.6, p.453	IFRS 10.B86	Ch.11, p.846
IFRS 10.B72 Example 14	Ch.6, p.457	IFRS 10.B86	Ch.11, p.847
IFRS 10.B72 Example 14-14A	Ch.6, p.449	IFRS 10.B86	Ch.40, p.3174
IFRS 10.B72 Example 14A	Ch.6, p.458	IFRS 10.B86	Ch.53, p.4248
IFRS 10.B72 Example 14B	Ch.6, p.458	IFRS 10.B86(c)	Ch.7, p.501
IFRS 10.B72 Example 14C	Ch.6, p.458	IFRS 10.B86(c)	Ch.7, p.502
IFRS 10.B72 Example 15	Ch.6, p.450	IFRS 10.B87	Ch.7, p.497
IFRS 10.B72 Example 15	Ch.6, p.453	IFRS 10.B87	Ch.7, p.503
IFRS 10.B72 Example 15	Ch.6, p.459	IFRS 10.B87	Ch.10, p.780
IFRS 10.B72 Example 16	Ch.6, p.460	IFRS 10.B88	Ch.7, p.497
IFRS 10.B72 Example 16	Ch.13, p.982	IFRS 10.B88	Ch.7, p.498
IFRS 10.B73	Ch.6, p.462	IFRS 10.B88	Ch.7, p.503
IFRS 10.B73	Ch.6, p.463	IFRS 10.B88	Ch.7, p.523
IFRS 10.B74	Ch.6, p.462	IFRS 10.B88	Ch.10, p.783
IFRS 10.B74	Ch.6, p.463	IFRS 10.B88	Ch.40, p.3174
IFRS 10.B75	Ch.6, p.462	IFRS 10.B89	Ch.7, p.499
IFRS 10.B75(f)	Ch.6, p.463	IFRS 10.B89	Ch.7, p.547
IFRS 10.B76	Ch.6, p.464	IFRS 10.B89	Ch.7, p.549
IFRS 10.B77	Ch.6, p.464	IFRS 10.B90	Ch.7, p.499
IFRS 10.B78	Ch.6, p.467	IFRS 10.B90	Ch.7, p.547
IFRS 10.B79	Ch.6, p.467	IFRS 10.B90	Ch.7, p.549
IFRS 10.B80	Ch.6, p.467	IFRS 10.B91	Ch.7, p.499
IFRS 10.B80	Ch.7, p.508	IFRS 10.B91	Ch.7, p.550
IFRS 10.B81	Ch.6, p.467	IFRS 10.B91	Ch.45, p.3592
IFRS 10.B82	Ch.6, p.467	IFRS 10.B92	Ch.7, p.502
IFRS 10.B82	Ch.6, p.471	IFRS 10.B93	Ch.7, p.503
IFRS 10.B83	Ch.6, p.467	IFRS 10.B94	Ch.5, p.262
IFRS 10.B84	Ch.6, p.467	IFRS 10.B94	Ch.7, p.498
IFRS 10.B85	Ch.6, p.468	IFRS 10.B94	Ch.7, p.499
IFRS 10.B85A	Ch.6, p.473	IFRS 10.B94	Ch.7, p.546
IFRS 10.B85A	Ch.6, p.485	IFRS 10.B94	Ch.7, p.547
IFRS 10.B85B	Ch.6, p.474	IFRS 10.B94	Ch.7, p.548
IFRS 10.B85C	Ch.6, p.475	IFRS 10.B94	Ch.7, p.549
IFRS 10.B85D	Ch.6, p.475	IFRS 10.B94	Ch.11, p.840
IFRS 10.B85E	Ch.6, p.475	IFRS 10.B94	Ch.11, p.867
IFRS 10.B85F	Ch.6, p.477	IFRS 10.B95	Ch.7, p.547
IFRS 10.B85G	Ch.6, p.477	IFRS 10.B96	Ch.5, p.262
IFRS 10.B85H	Ch.6, p.477	IFRS 10.B96	Ch.7, p.533
IFRS 10.B85H	Ch.6, p.485	IFRS 10.B96	Ch.7, p.538
IFRS 10.B85I	Ch.6, p.478	IFRS 10.B96	Ch.7, p.548
IFRS 10.B85J	Ch.6, p.479	IFRS 10.B96	Ch.10, p.788
IFRS 10.B85K	Ch.6, p.479	IFRS 10.B96	Ch.11, p.868
IFRS 10.B85L	Ch.6, p.479	IFRS 10.B96	Ch.33, p.2600
IFRS 10.B85L	Ch.12, p.892	IFRS 10.B97	Ch.7, p.524
IFRS 10.B85L	Ch.12, p.929	IFRS 10.B97	Ch.7, p.525
IFRS 10.B85L(b)	Ch.11, p.820	IFRS 10.B97	Ch.9, p.715
IFRS 10.B85M	Ch.6, p.479	IFRS 10.B97-B99	Ch.5, p.262
IFRS 10.B85N	Ch.6, p.473	IFRS 10.B98	Ch.7, p.509
IFRS 10.B85O	Ch.6, p.480	IFRS 10.B98	Ch.7, p.514
IFRS 10.B85P	Ch.6, p.480	IFRS 10.B98	Ch.7, p.518
IFRS 10.B85Q	Ch.6, p.480	IFRS 10.B98	Ch.7, p.565
IFRS 10.B85R	Ch.6, p.480	IFRS 10.B98(a)	Ch.7, p.527
IFRS 10.B85S	Ch.6, p.480	IFRS 10.B98(b)	Ch.7, p.531
IFRS 10.B85T	Ch.6, p.481	IFRS 10.B98(b)(i)	Ch.45, p.3605

IFRS 10.B98(d)	Ch.7, p.527	IFRS 10.BC240F	Ch.6, p.475
IFRS 10.B99	Ch.7, p.509	IFRS 10.BC240H	Ch.6, p.476
IFRS 10.B99	Ch.7, p.518	IFRS 10.BC242	Ch.6, p.478
IFRS 10.B99	Ch.7, p.526	IFRS 10.BC243	Ch.6, p.479
IFRS 10.B99	Ch.7, p.527	IFRS 10.BC248	Ch.6, p.477
IFRS 10.B99	Ch.7, p.565	IFRS 10.BC250	Ch.6, p.479
IFRS 10.B99A	Ch.7, p.514	IFRS 10.BC251	Ch.6, p.479
IFRS 10.B99A	Ch.7, p.519	IFRS 10.BC252	Ch.6, p.478
IFRS 10.B99A	Ch.7, p.520	IFRS 10.BC260	Ch.6, p.480
IFRS 10.B99A	Ch.7, p.565	IFRS 10.BC261	Ch.6, p.481
IFRS 10.B100	Ch.6, p.489	IFRS 10.BC263	Ch.6, p.481
IFRS 10.B101	Ch.6, p.488	IFRS 10.BC264	Ch.6, p.481
IFRS 10.C1A	Ch.6, p.393	IFRS 10.BC266	Ch.6, p.481
IFRS 10.C1B	Ch.6, p.393	IFRS 10.BC271	Ch.8, p.589
IFRS 10.C1B	Ch.6, p.472	IFRS 10.BC272	Ch.6, p.476
IFRS 10.C1C	Ch.7, p.514	IFRS 10.BC276-278	Ch.6, p.489
IFRS 10.C1C	Ch.7, p.565	IFRS 10.BC280	Ch.6, p.489
IFRS 10.C1D	Ch.6, p.393	IFRS 10.BC281	Ch.6, p.489
IFRS 10.C1D	Ch.6, p.397	IFRS 10.BC282	Ch.6, p.489
IFRS 10.C1D	Ch.6, p.473	IFRS 10.BC283	Ch.6, p.489
IFRS 10.IE1-IE6	Ch.6, p.483	IFRS 10.BC298-BC300	Ch.6, p.472
IFRS 10.IE7-IE8	Ch.6, p.483		
IFRS 10.IE12-IE15	Ch.6, p.485		

IFRS 11

IFRS 10.BCZ18	Ch.6, p.396	IFRS 11.1	Ch.12, p.892
IFRS 10.BCZ21	Ch.6, p.471	IFRS 11.2	Ch.12, p.892
IFRS 10.BC28A-B	Ch.6, p.397	IFRS 11.3	Ch.12, p.892
IFRS 10.BC28A-28B	Ch.8, p.578	IFRS 11.4	Ch.12, p.891
IFRS 10.BC28D	Ch.6, p.398	IFRS 11.4	Ch.43, p.3403
IFRS 10.BC37-BC39	Ch.6, p.445	IFRS 11.5	Ch.12, p.891
IFRS 10.BC63	Ch.6, p.456	IFRS 11.5	Ch.43, p.3543
IFRS 10.BC66	Ch.6, p.442	IFRS 11.5(a)	Ch.43, p.3404
IFRS 10.BC69	Ch.6, p.406	IFRS 11.6	Ch.12, p.891
IFRS 10.BC124	Ch.6, p.431	IFRS 11.6	Ch.12, p.904
IFRS 10.BC124	Ch.6, p.469	IFRS 11.7	Ch.12, p.895
IFRS 10.BC130	Ch.6, p.455	IFRS 11.7	Ch.43, p.3404
IFRS 10.BC132	Ch.6, p.454	IFRS 11.7	Ch.43, p.3543
IFRS 10.BC152	Ch.6, p.468	IFRS 11.8	Ch.12, p.898
IFRS 10.BCZ162-164	Ch.7, p.548	IFRS 11.8	Ch.43, p.3404
IFRS 10.BCZ165	Ch.7, p.548	IFRS 11.9	Ch.12, p.901
IFRS 10.BCZ168	Ch.40, p.3175	IFRS 11.10	Ch.12, p.897
IFRS 10.BCZ173	Ch.7, p.533	IFRS 11.10	Ch.12, p.901
IFRS 10.BCZ173	Ch.33, p.2600	IFRS 11.11	Ch.12, p.895
IFRS 10.BCZ175	Ch.7, p.500	IFRS 11.11	Ch.13, p.953
IFRS 10.BCZ180	Ch.7, p.509	IFRS 11.12	Ch.12, p.896
IFRS 10.BCZ182	Ch.7, p.512	IFRS 11.13	Ch.12, p.897
IFRS 10.BCZ185	Ch.7, p.524	IFRS 11.13	Ch.12, p.931
IFRS 10.BCZ186	Ch.7, p.525	IFRS 11.14	Ch.12, p.904
IFRS 10.BC190I	Ch.7, p.518	IFRS 11.15	Ch.12, p.904
IFRS 10.BC190I	Ch.7, p.565	IFRS 11.16	Ch.12, p.904
IFRS 10.BC190J	Ch.7, p.520	IFRS 11.17	Ch.12, p.906
IFRS 10.BC190L-190O	Ch.7, p.565	IFRS 11.18	Ch.12, p.894
IFRS 10.BC190M-190N	Ch.7, p.565	IFRS 11.19	Ch.12, p.931
IFRS 10.BC190N	Ch.18, p.1429	IFRS 11.20	Ch.8, p.580
IFRS 10.BC190O	Ch.7, p.514	IFRS 11.20	Ch.12, p.923
IFRS 10.BC190O	Ch.18, p.1429	IFRS 11.20	Ch.27, p.2037
IFRS 10.BC239	Ch.6, p.475	IFRS 11.20	Ch.40, p.3180
IFRS 10.BC240B	Ch.6, p.476		
IFRS 10.BC240E	Ch.6, p.475		

IFRS 11.20-23	Ch.5, p.375
IFRS 11.20-23	Ch.12, p.929
IFRS 11.21	Ch.12, p.923
IFRS 11.21	Ch.27, p.2037
IFRS 11.21	Ch.43, p.3450
IFRS 11.21A	Ch.12, p.936
IFRS 11.21A	Ch.40, p.3181
IFRS 11.22	Ch.7, p.523
IFRS 11.22	Ch.12, p.928
IFRS 11.23	Ch.8, p.580
IFRS 11.23	Ch.12, p.927
IFRS 11.23	Ch.18, p.1430
IFRS 11.23	Ch.43, p.3399
IFRS 11.23	Ch.43, p.3407
IFRS 11.23	Ch.43, p.3408
IFRS 11.24	Ch.12, p.929
IFRS 11.25	Ch.12, p.929
IFRS 11.25	Ch.43, p.3408
IFRS 11.26	Ch.8, p.580
IFRS 11.26(a)	Ch.12, p.929
IFRS 11.26(b)	Ch.12, p.930
IFRS 11.27(a)	Ch.12, p.929
IFRS 11.27(b)	Ch.12, p.930
IFRS 11 Appendix A	Ch.6, p.410
IFRS 11 Appendix A	Ch.6, p.433
IFRS 11 Appendix A	Ch.12, p.891
IFRS 11 Appendix A	Ch.12, p.892
IFRS 11 Appendix A	Ch.12, p.893
IFRS 11 Appendix A	Ch.12, p.895
IFRS 11 Appendix A	Ch.12, p.906
IFRS 11 Appendix A	Ch.13, p.951
IFRS 11 Appendix A	Ch.39, p.3102
IFRS 11 Appendix A	Ch.39, p.3105
IFRS 11 Appendix A	Ch.43, p.3403
IFRS 11 Appendix A	Ch.43, p.3404
IFRS 11 Appendix A	Ch.43, p.3406
IFRS 11 Appendix C	Ch.5, p.322
IFRS 11.B2	Ch.10, p.769
IFRS 11.B2	Ch.12, p.893
IFRS 11.B2	Ch.43, p.3404
IFRS 11.B3	Ch.12, p.893
IFRS 11.B4	Ch.12, p.893
IFRS 11.B5	Ch.12, p.897
IFRS 11.B5	Ch.12, p.898
IFRS 11.B5	Ch.43, p.3404
IFRS 11.B6	Ch.12, p.901
IFRS 11.B7	Ch.12, p.901
IFRS 11.B8	Ch.12, p.902
IFRS 11.B8 Example 1	Ch.12, p.902
IFRS 11.B8 Example 2	Ch.12, p.902
IFRS 11.B8 Example 3	Ch.12, p.902
IFRS 11.B9	Ch.12, p.901
IFRS 11.B9	Ch.43, p.3404
IFRS 11.B10	Ch.12, p.896
IFRS 11.B10	Ch.12, p.903
IFRS 11.B11	Ch.12, p.897
IFRS 11.B14	Ch.12, p.906
IFRS 11.B14	Ch.12, p.914
IFRS 11.B15	Ch.12, p.906
IFRS 11.B16	Ch.12, p.923
IFRS 11.B17	Ch.12, p.923
IFRS 11.B18	Ch.12, p.923
IFRS 11.B19	Ch.12, p.906
IFRS 11.B20	Ch.12, p.906
IFRS 11.B21	Ch.12, p.907
IFRS 11.B22	Ch.12, p.908
IFRS 11.B23	Ch.12, p.908
IFRS 11.B24	Ch.12, p.907
IFRS 11.B25	Ch.12, p.909
IFRS 11.B26	Ch.12, p.909
IFRS 11.B27	Ch.12, p.908
IFRS 11.B27	Ch.12, p.910
IFRS 11.B27	Ch.12, p.913
IFRS 11.B28	Ch.12, p.910
IFRS 11.B29	Ch.12, p.911
IFRS 11.B30	Ch.12, p.911
IFRS 11.B31	Ch.12, p.911
IFRS 11.B31-B32	Ch.12, p.914
IFRS 11.B31-B32	Ch.12, p.916
IFRS 11.B32	Ch.12, p.912
IFRS 11.B32	Ch.12, p.916
IFRS 11.B32-B33	Ch.12, p.914
IFRS 11.B32 Example 5	Ch.12, p.911
IFRS 11.B33A	Ch.12, p.936
IFRS 11.B33B	Ch.12, p.936
IFRS 11.B33C	Ch.12, p.936
IFRS 11.B33CA	Ch.12, p.937
IFRS 11.B33D	Ch.12, p.936
IFRS 11.B34	Ch.7, p.523
IFRS 11.B34	Ch.12, p.928
IFRS 11.B34	Ch.18, p.1429
IFRS 11.B35	Ch.7, p.523
IFRS 11.B35	Ch.12, p.928
IFRS 11.B36	Ch.12, p.928
IFRS 11.B37	Ch.12, p.928
IFRS 11.C14	Ch.12, p.897
IFRS 11.C14	Ch.12, p.929
IFRS 11.C14	Ch.43, p.3408
IFRS 11.IE1	Ch.12, p.917
IFRS 11.IE2-IE52	Ch.12, p.917
IFRS 11 Examples 1-6	Ch.12, p.917
IFRS 11 Example 4	Ch.12, p.909
IFRS 11 Example 5	Ch.12, p.916
IFRS 11.BC14	Ch.12, p.897
IFRS 11.BC15-18	Ch.12, p.892
IFRS 11.BC20	Ch.12, p.894
IFRS 11.BC24	Ch.12, p.891
IFRS 11.BC25	Ch.12, p.891
IFRS 11.BC27	Ch.12, p.907
IFRS 11.BC28	Ch.12, p.891
IFRS 11.BC29	Ch.12, p.906
IFRS 11.BC31	Ch.12, p.907
IFRS 11.BC32	Ch.12, p.907
IFRS 11.BC35	Ch.12, p.894
IFRS 11.BC36	Ch.12, p.894
IFRS 11.BC38	Ch.12, p.923

IFRS 11.BC43	Ch.12, p.908	IFRS 12.21	Ch.13, p.971
IFRS 11.BC43	Ch.12, p.915	IFRS 12.21A	Ch.13, p.971
IFRS 11.BC45A	Ch.43, p.3417	IFRS 12.22	Ch.13, p.971
IFRS 11.BC45E	Ch.12, p.936	IFRS 12.22	Ch.15, p.1244
IFRS 11.BC45F	Ch.12, p.936	IFRS 12.22(a)	Ch.40, p.3187
IFRS 11.BC45H	Ch.43, p.3417	IFRS 12.24	Ch.13, p.978
IFRS 11.BC45I	Ch.43, p.3417	IFRS 12.25	Ch.13, p.979
		IFRS 12.25A	Ch.13, p.978
		IFRS 12.26	Ch.13, p.979

IFRS 12

IFRS 12.27	Ch.13, p.982		
IFRS 12.28	Ch.13, p.982		
IFRS 12.1	Ch.13, p.945	IFRS 12.29	Ch.13, p.987
IFRS 12.2	Ch.13, p.945	IFRS 12.30	Ch.13, p.989
IFRS 12.3	Ch.13, p.946	IFRS 12.31	Ch.13, p.989
IFRS 12.4	Ch.13, p.951	IFRS 12 Appendix A	Ch.6, p.407
IFRS 12.5	Ch.13, p.946	IFRS 12 Appendix A	Ch.6, p.435
IFRS 12.5A	Ch.4, p.214	IFRS 12 Appendix A	Ch.13, p.983
IFRS 12.5A	Ch.13, p.950	IFRS 12 Appendix A	Ch.13, p.992
IFRS 12.6(a)	Ch.13, p.953	IFRS 12.B3	Ch.13, p.951
IFRS 12.6(b)	Ch.8, p.604	IFRS 12.B4	Ch.13, p.950
IFRS 12.6(b)	Ch.13, p.953	IFRS 12.B5	Ch.13, p.951
IFRS 12.6(c)	Ch.13, p.953	IFRS 12.B6	Ch.13, p.951
IFRS 12.6(d)	Ch.13, p.954	IFRS 12.B7	Ch.13, p.947
IFRS 12.7	Ch.12, p.896	IFRS 12.B8	Ch.13, p.947
IFRS 12.7	Ch.12, p.906	IFRS 12.B8	Ch.13, p.948
IFRS 12.7	Ch.13, p.954	IFRS 12.B9	Ch.6, p.442
IFRS 12.8	Ch.13, p.954	IFRS 12.B9	Ch.13, p.948
IFRS 12.9	Ch.13, p.954	IFRS 12.B10	Ch.5, p.333
IFRS 12.9A	Ch.6, p.473	IFRS 12.B10	Ch.13, p.959
IFRS 12.9A	Ch.13, p.956	IFRS 12.B10(b)	Ch.40, p.3187
IFRS 12.9B	Ch.13, p.968	IFRS 12.B11	Ch.13, p.959
IFRS 12.9(d)	Ch.11, p.816	IFRS 12.B11	Ch.40, p.3187
IFRS 12.9(e)	Ch.11, p.816	IFRS 12.B12	Ch.13, p.972
IFRS 12.10	Ch.13, p.957	IFRS 12.B12(a)	Ch.40, p.3187
IFRS 12.10	Ch.15, p.1244	IFRS 12.B12-13	Ch.5, p.333
IFRS 12.11	Ch.13, p.957	IFRS 12.B13	Ch.13, p.973
IFRS 12.12	Ch.5, p.333	IFRS 12.B13(a)	Ch.40, p.3187
IFRS 12.12	Ch.13, p.959	IFRS 12.B14	Ch.13, p.973
IFRS 12.12(e)	Ch.5, p.332	IFRS 12.B15	Ch.13, p.974
IFRS 12.13	Ch.13, p.962	IFRS 12.B16	Ch.5, p.333
IFRS 12.13	Ch.15, p.1244	IFRS 12.B16	Ch.13, p.976
IFRS 12.14	Ch.13, p.964	IFRS 12.B17	Ch.4, p.214
IFRS 12.15	Ch.13, p.965	IFRS 12.B17	Ch.13, p.950
IFRS 12.16	Ch.13, p.966	IFRS 12.B17	Ch.13, p.976
IFRS 12.17	Ch.13, p.966	IFRS 12.B18	Ch.13, p.977
IFRS 12.18	Ch.13, p.966	IFRS 12.B18	Ch.39, p.3122
IFRS 12.19	Ch.5, p.333	IFRS 12.B19	Ch.13, p.977
IFRS 12.19	Ch.13, p.967	IFRS 12.B19-20	Ch.39, p.3123
IFRS 12.19A	Ch.13, p.968	IFRS 12.B22	Ch.6, p.435
IFRS 12.19B	Ch.13, p.968	IFRS 12.B22	Ch.13, p.949
IFRS 12.19C	Ch.13, p.968	IFRS 12.B23	Ch.6, p.435
IFRS 12.19D	Ch.13, p.969	IFRS 12.B23	Ch.13, p.949
IFRS 12.19E	Ch.13, p.969	IFRS 12.B24	Ch.6, p.435
IFRS 12.19F	Ch.13, p.969	IFRS 12.B24	Ch.13, p.950
IFRS 12.19G	Ch.13, p.969	IFRS 12.B25-26	Ch.13, p.990
IFRS 12.20	Ch.13, p.970	IFRS 12.BC16	Ch.13, p.956
IFRS 12.20	Ch.15, p.1244	IFRS 12.BC19	Ch.13, p.956
IFRS 12.21	Ch.5, p.333	IFRS 12.BC27	Ch.13, p.959

IFRS 12.BC28	Ch.13, p.959	IFRS 13.7(c)	Ch.20, p.1546
IFRS 12.BC29	Ch.13, p.959	IFRS 13.8	Ch.14, p.1008
IFRS 12.BC31	Ch.13, p.962	IFRS 13.9	Ch.4, p.198
IFRS 12.BC32	Ch.13, p.962	IFRS 13.9	Ch.10, p.779
IFRS 12.BC33	Ch.13, p.962	IFRS 13.9	Ch.14, p.1016
IFRS 12.BC34	Ch.13, p.963	IFRS 13.9	Ch.19, p.1468
IFRS 12.BC35	Ch.13, p.963	IFRS 13.9	Ch.24, p.1830
IFRS 12.BC38-39	Ch.13, p.967	IFRS 13.9	Ch.42, p.3277
IFRS 12.BC49	Ch.13, p.974	IFRS 13.9	Ch.52, p.4088
IFRS 12.BC50-51	Ch.13, p.974	IFRS 13.11	Ch.14, p.1025
IFRS 12.BC52	Ch.13, p.974	IFRS 13.11	Ch.14, p.1110
IFRS 12.BC52	Ch.39, p.3106	IFRS 13.11	Ch.20, p.1546
IFRS 12.BC60	Ch.13, p.974	IFRS 13.11	Ch.42, p.3304
IFRS 12.BC61C	Ch.13, p.969	IFRS 13.12	Ch.14, p.1025
IFRS 12.BC61I	Ch.13, p.968	IFRS 13.13	Ch.14, p.1019
IFRS 12.BC69	Ch.13, p.952	IFRS 13.14	Ch.14, p.1019
IFRS 12.BC72	Ch.13, p.979	IFRS 13.15	Ch.14, p.1017
IFRS 12.BC77	Ch.13, p.952	IFRS 13.15	Ch.14, p.1038
IFRS 12.BC82	Ch.13, p.949	IFRS 13.16	Ch.14, p.1029
IFRS 12.BC83	Ch.13, p.950	IFRS 13.16	Ch.14, p.1033
IFRS 12.BC83-85	Ch.13, p.950	IFRS 13.17	Ch.14, p.1030
IFRS 12.BC87	Ch.13, p.982	IFRS 13.17	Ch.42, p.3304
IFRS 12.BC90	Ch.13, p.983	IFRS 13.18	Ch.14, p.1029
IFRS 12.BC94	Ch.13, p.986	IFRS 13.18	Ch.42, p.3300
IFRS 12.BC96	Ch.13, p.979	IFRS 13.18	Ch.42, p.3306
IFRS 12.BC96	Ch.13, p.980	IFRS 13.19	Ch.14, p.1031
IFRS 12.BC97	Ch.13, p.987	IFRS 13.20	Ch.14, p.1031
IFRS 12.BC98-99	Ch.13, p.987	IFRS 13.20	Ch.14, p.1038
IFRS 12.BC100	Ch.13, p.987	IFRS 13.21	Ch.14, p.1030
IFRS 12.BC104	Ch.13, p.966	IFRS 13.22	Ch.14, p.1034
IFRS 12.BC105-106	Ch.13, p.965	IFRS 13.22	Ch.14, p.1035
IFRS 12.BC113-114	Ch.13, p.990	IFRS 13.22	Ch.19, p.1469
		IFRS 13.23	Ch.14, p.1034
		IFRS 13.23	Ch.42, p.3304
		IFRS 13.24	Ch.14, p.1050

IFRS 13

IFRS 13.1	Ch.14, p.1003	IFRS 13.25	Ch.14, p.1017
IFRS 13.1	Ch.24, p.1838	IFRS 13.25	Ch.14, p.1050
IFRS 13.2	Ch.9, p.669	IFRS 13.25	Ch.19, p.1469
IFRS 13.2	Ch.9, p.682	IFRS 13.25	Ch.19, p.1476
IFRS 13.2	Ch.14, p.1006	IFRS 13.25	Ch.42, p.3292
IFRS 13.2	Ch.14, p.1007	IFRS 13.25	Ch.42, p.3305
IFRS 13.2	Ch.14, p.1017	IFRS 13.26	Ch.14, p.1050
IFRS 13.2	Ch.18, p.1419	IFRS 13.27	Ch.14, p.1053
IFRS 13.2	Ch.19, p.1469	IFRS 13.27	Ch.18, p.1419
IFRS 13.2	Ch.20, p.1546	IFRS 13.27	Ch.19, p.1460
IFRS 13.3	Ch.14, p.1007	IFRS 13.27	Ch.20, p.1546
IFRS 13.3	Ch.14, p.1045	IFRS 13.27	Ch.42, p.3299
IFRS 13.4	Ch.14, p.1008	IFRS 13.27-28	Ch.19, p.1482
IFRS 13.5	Ch.10, p.779	IFRS 13.28	Ch.14, p.1053
IFRS 13.5	Ch.14, p.1007	IFRS 13.28	Ch.18, p.1419
IFRS 13.5	Ch.24, p.1830	IFRS 13.28	Ch.42, p.3299
IFRS 13.6	Ch.9, p.695	IFRS 13.29	Ch.14, p.1056
IFRS 13.6	Ch.14, p.1007	IFRS 13.29	Ch.14, p.1057
IFRS 13.6	Ch.20, p.1546	IFRS 13.29	Ch.18, p.1419
IFRS 13.6(c)	Ch.19, p.1473	IFRS 13.29	Ch.19, p.1481
IFRS 13.6(c)	Ch.20, p.1581	IFRS 13.29	Ch.20, p.1546
IFRS 13.7	Ch.14, p.1008	IFRS 13.29	Ch.42, p.3299
		IFRS 13.30	Ch.14, p.1057

IFRS 13.31	Ch.42, p.3299	IFRS 13.62	Ch.20, p.1546
IFRS 13.31(a)-(b)	Ch.18, p.1420	IFRS 13.62	Ch.42, p.3305
IFRS 13.31(a)(i)	Ch.14, p.1059	IFRS 13.63	Ch.14, p.1101
IFRS 13.31(a)(ii)	Ch.14, p.1062	IFRS 13.63	Ch.42, p.3305
IFRS 13.31(a)(iii)	Ch.14, p.1060	IFRS 13.64	Ch.14, p.1105
IFRS 13.31(b)	Ch.14, p.1059	IFRS 13.65	Ch.14, p.1105
IFRS 13.32	Ch.14, p.1062	IFRS 13.65	Ch.14, p.1106
IFRS 13.32	Ch.42, p.3300	IFRS 13.65	Ch.14, p.1114
IFRS 13.34	Ch.9, p.699	IFRS 13.66	Ch.14, p.1106
IFRS 13.34	Ch.14, p.1064	IFRS 13.66	Ch.18, p.1421
IFRS 13.34(a)	Ch.9, p.700	IFRS 13.66	Ch.20, p.1547
IFRS 13.36	Ch.10, p.779	IFRS 13.67	Ch.14, p.1109
IFRS 13.36	Ch.14, p.1066	IFRS 13.67	Ch.19, p.1472
IFRS 13.37	Ch.9, p.701	IFRS 13.67	Ch.42, p.3300
IFRS 13.37	Ch.14, p.1066	IFRS 13.68	Ch.14, p.1109
IFRS 13.38	Ch.14, p.1066	IFRS 13.69	Ch.14, p.1109
IFRS 13.39	Ch.14, p.1067	IFRS 13.69	Ch.14, p.1111
IFRS 13.40	Ch.14, p.1066	IFRS 13.69	Ch.14, p.1112
IFRS 13.40	Ch.14, p.1069	IFRS 13.69	Ch.14, p.1113
IFRS 13.41	Ch.14, p.1070	IFRS 13.70	Ch.14, p.1114
IFRS 13.42	Ch.9, p.704	IFRS 13.71	Ch.14, p.1114
IFRS 13.42-44	Ch.14, p.1073	IFRS 13.72	Ch.14, p.1117
IFRS 13.44	Ch.14, p.1078	IFRS 13.72	Ch.18, p.1421
IFRS 13.45	Ch.14, p.1087	IFRS 13.72	Ch.20, p.1547
IFRS 13.46	Ch.14, p.1087	IFRS 13.73	Ch.14, p.1119
IFRS 13.47	Ch.7, p.552	IFRS 13.73	Ch.14, p.1120
IFRS 13.47	Ch.14, p.1088	IFRS 13.74	Ch.14, p.1100
IFRS 13.47	Ch.47, p.3712	IFRS 13.74	Ch.14, p.1118
IFRS 13.47	Ch.53, p.4222	IFRS 13.74	Ch.42, p.3305
IFRS 13.48	Ch.14, p.1085	IFRS 13.75	Ch.14, p.1119
IFRS 13.48	Ch.14, p.1088	IFRS 13.75	Ch.14, p.1121
IFRS 13.48	Ch.14, p.1092	IFRS 13.75	Ch.14, p.1126
IFRS 13.48	Ch.14, p.1094	IFRS 13.75	Ch.42, p.3307
IFRS 13.49	Ch.14, p.1089	IFRS 13.76	Ch.14, p.1125
IFRS 13.50	Ch.14, p.1090	IFRS 13.76	Ch.18, p.1421
IFRS 13.51	Ch.14, p.1090	IFRS 13.77	Ch.14, p.1125
IFRS 13.52	Ch.14, p.1089	IFRS 13.78	Ch.14, p.1126
IFRS 13.53	Ch.14, p.1096	IFRS 13.79	Ch.14, p.1125
IFRS 13.54	Ch.14, p.1091	IFRS 13.79(a)	Ch.14, p.1126
IFRS 13.54	Ch.14, p.1095	IFRS 13.79(b)	Ch.14, p.1127
IFRS 13.55	Ch.14, p.1095	IFRS 13.79(c)	Ch.14, p.1126
IFRS 13.56	Ch.14, p.1096	IFRS 13.80	Ch.14, p.1112
IFRS 13.57	Ch.14, p.1096	IFRS 13.80	Ch.14, p.1127
IFRS 13.57-59	Ch.42, p.3305	IFRS 13.81	Ch.14, p.1127
IFRS 13.58	Ch.14, p.1096	IFRS 13.82	Ch.14, p.1127
IFRS 13.58	Ch.49, p.3854	IFRS 13.83	Ch.14, p.1130
IFRS 13.59	Ch.14, p.1096	IFRS 13.84	Ch.14, p.1130
IFRS 13.60	Ch.14, p.1097	IFRS 13.86	Ch.14, p.1131
IFRS 13.60	Ch.49, p.3854	IFRS 13.87	Ch.14, p.1131
IFRS 13.60	Ch.49, p.3855	IFRS 13.87	Ch.14, p.1132
IFRS 13.61	Ch.9, p.682	IFRS 13.87-89	Ch.20, p.1547
IFRS 13.61	Ch.14, p.1100	IFRS 13.88	Ch.14, p.1132
IFRS 13.61	Ch.18, p.1420	IFRS 13.89	Ch.14, p.1049
IFRS 13.61	Ch.20, p.1546	IFRS 13.89	Ch.14, p.1131
IFRS 13.62	Ch.9, p.681	IFRS 13.89	Ch.14, p.1132
IFRS 13.62	Ch.14, p.1100	IFRS 13.89	Ch.20, p.1548
IFRS 13.62	Ch.18, p.1420	IFRS 13.91	Ch.9, p.669
IFRS 13.62	Ch.19, p.1471	IFRS 13.91	Ch.14, p.1134

IFRS 13.91	Ch.41, p.3223	IFRS 13 Appendix A	Ch.14, p.1043
IFRS 13.91	Ch.42, p.3292	IFRS 13 Appendix A	Ch.14, p.1050
IFRS 13.91(a)	Ch.9, p.753	IFRS 13 Appendix A	Ch.14, p.1053
IFRS 13.92	Ch.14, p.1134	IFRS 13 Appendix A	Ch.14, p.1115
IFRS 13.92	Ch.19, p.1505	IFRS 13 Appendix A	Ch.14, p.1118
IFRS 13.92	Ch.41, p.3224	IFRS 13 Appendix A	Ch.17, p.1293
IFRS 13.93	Ch.7, p.533	IFRS 13 Appendix A	Ch.17, p.1335
IFRS 13.93	Ch.14, p.1138	IFRS 13 Appendix A	Ch.18, p.1419
IFRS 13.93	Ch.14, p.1139	IFRS 13 Appendix A	Ch.19, p.1497
IFRS 13.93	Ch.14, p.1140	IFRS 13 Appendix A	Ch.20, p.1534
IFRS 13.93	Ch.14, p.1146	IFRS 13 Appendix A	Ch.20, p.1547
IFRS 13.93	Ch.18, p.1434	IFRS 13 Appendix A	Ch.24, p.1825
IFRS 13.93	Ch.18, p.1435	IFRS 13 Appendix A	Ch.42, p.3301
IFRS 13.93	Ch.41, p.3223	IFRS 13 Appendix A	Ch.42, p.3304
IFRS 13.93	Ch.42, p.3320	IFRS 13 Appendix A	Ch.52, p.4088
IFRS 13.93	Ch.55, p.4667	IFRS 13.B2	Ch.14, p.1017
IFRS 13.93(a)	Ch.14, p.1136	IFRS 13.B2	Ch.42, p.3298
IFRS 13.93(b)	Ch.19, p.1498	IFRS 13.B3	Ch.14, p.1061
IFRS 13.93(b)	Ch.38, p.3085	IFRS 13.B4(a)-(b)	Ch.14, p.1097
IFRS 13.93(c)	Ch.14, p.1122	IFRS 13.B4(c)	Ch.14, p.1096
IFRS 13.93(c)	Ch.14, p.1144	IFRS 13.B4(c)	Ch.14, p.1099
IFRS 13.93(c)	Ch.19, p.1498	IFRS 13.B4(d)	Ch.14, p.1097
IFRS 13.93(d)	Ch.14, p.1137	IFRS 13.B5	Ch.14, p.1106
IFRS 13.93(d)	Ch.14, p.1146	IFRS 13.B5	Ch.18, p.1420
IFRS 13.93(d)	Ch.19, p.1498	IFRS 13.B5	Ch.20, p.1547
IFRS 13.93(d)	Ch.38, p.3085	IFRS 13.B6	Ch.14, p.1106
IFRS 13.93(e)	Ch.19, p.1498	IFRS 13.B6	Ch.18, p.1420
IFRS 13.93(e)(iv)	Ch.14, p.1122	IFRS 13.B6	Ch.20, p.1547
IFRS 13.93(e)(iv)	Ch.14, p.1144	IFRS 13.B7	Ch.14, p.1106
IFRS 13.93(f)	Ch.19, p.1499	IFRS 13.B8	Ch.9, p.682
IFRS 13.93(g)	Ch.19, p.1499	IFRS 13.B8	Ch.14, p.1107
IFRS 13.93(g)	Ch.38, p.3086	IFRS 13.B8	Ch.18, p.1421
IFRS 13.93(h)	Ch.19, p.1499	IFRS 13.B8	Ch.20, p.1547
IFRS 13.93(i)	Ch.14, p.1056	IFRS 13.B9	Ch.9, p.682
IFRS 13.93(i)	Ch.14, p.1156	IFRS 13.B9	Ch.14, p.1107
IFRS 13.93(i)	Ch.19, p.1498	IFRS 13.B9	Ch.18, p.1421
IFRS 13.93(i)	Ch.38, p.3086	IFRS 13.B9	Ch.20, p.1547
IFRS 13.94	Ch.14, p.1135	IFRS 13.B10	Ch.14, p.1108
IFRS 13.94	Ch.19, p.1504	IFRS 13.B10	Ch.18, p.1421
IFRS 13.94	Ch.19, p.1505	IFRS 13.B10	Ch.20, p.1547
IFRS 13.94-96	Ch.41, p.3223	IFRS 13.B11	Ch.14, p.1108
IFRS 13.95	Ch.14, p.1122	IFRS 13.B11	Ch.18, p.1421
IFRS 13.95	Ch.14, p.1137	IFRS 13.B11	Ch.20, p.1547
IFRS 13.95	Ch.14, p.1144	IFRS 13.B12	Ch.14, p.1160
IFRS 13.96	Ch.14, p.1137	IFRS 13.B13	Ch.14, p.1161
IFRS 13.97	Ch.14, p.1156	IFRS 13.B13(c)	Ch.14, p.1162
IFRS 13.97	Ch.55, p.4667	IFRS 13.B14	Ch.14, p.1162
IFRS 13.98	Ch.14, p.1156	IFRS 13.B15	Ch.14, p.1162
IFRS 13.98	Ch.41, p.3223	IFRS 13.B16	Ch.9, p.703
IFRS 13.99	Ch.7, p.533	IFRS 13.B16	Ch.14, p.1115
IFRS 13.99	Ch.14, p.1135	IFRS 13.B16	Ch.14, p.1162
IFRS 13.99	Ch.38, p.3086	IFRS 13.B17	Ch.14, p.1163
IFRS 13.99	Ch.41, p.3224	IFRS 13.B18	Ch.14, p.1163
IFRS 13 Appendix A	Ch.5, p.292	IFRS 13.B19	Ch.14, p.1163
IFRS 13 Appendix A	Ch.14, p.1014	IFRS 13.B19	Ch.14, p.1164
IFRS 13 Appendix A	Ch.14, p.1030	IFRS 13.B20-21	Ch.14, p.1165
IFRS 13 Appendix A	Ch.14, p.1033	IFRS 13.B22	Ch.14, p.1164
IFRS 13 Appendix A	Ch.14, p.1034	IFRS 13.B23	Ch.14, p.1166

IFRS 13.B24	Ch.14, p.1166	IFRS 13.IE66	Ch.14, p.1153
IFRS 13.B25	Ch.14, p.1167	IFRS 13.BC6	Ch.14, p.1170
IFRS 13.B25-B29	Ch.14, p.1115	IFRS 13.BC8	Ch.14, p.1011
IFRS 13.B26	Ch.14, p.1167	IFRS 13.BC21	Ch.14, p.1010
IFRS 13.B27-B29	Ch.14, p.1168	IFRS 13.BC22	Ch.14, p.1010
IFRS 13.B30	Ch.14, p.1168	IFRS 13.BC24	Ch.19, p.1473
IFRS 13.B31	Ch.14, p.1070	IFRS 13.BC29	Ch.14, p.1016
IFRS 13.B32	Ch.14, p.1070	IFRS 13.BC31	Ch.14, p.1017
IFRS 13.B33	Ch.14, p.1070	IFRS 13.BC36	Ch.14, p.1016
IFRS 13.B34	Ch.14, p.1109	IFRS 13.BC39	Ch.14, p.1017
IFRS 13.B34	Ch.36, p.2983	IFRS 13.BC40	Ch.14, p.1017
IFRS 13.B35	Ch.14, p.1128	IFRS 13.BC46	Ch.14, p.1025
IFRS 13.B35(g)	Ch.19, p.1497	IFRS 13.BC52	Ch.14, p.1030
IFRS 13.B36	Ch.14, p.1132	IFRS 13.BC52	Ch.14, p.1033
IFRS 13.B37	Ch.14, p.1040	IFRS 13.BC55-BC59	Ch.14, p.1034
IFRS 13.B38	Ch.14, p.1046	IFRS 13.BC57	Ch.14, p.1035
IFRS 13.B39	Ch.14, p.1115	IFRS 13.BC63	Ch.14, p.1053
IFRS 13.B40	Ch.14, p.1045	IFRS 13.BC69	Ch.14, p.1055
IFRS 13.B40	Ch.14, p.1102	IFRS 13.BC81	Ch.14, p.1065
IFRS 13.B41	Ch.14, p.1017	IFRS 13.BC82	Ch.14, p.1065
IFRS 13.B42	Ch.14, p.1045	IFRS 13.BC88	Ch.14, p.1067
IFRS 13.B43	Ch.14, p.1039	IFRS 13.BC89	Ch.9, p.702
IFRS 13.B43	Ch.14, p.1043	IFRS 13.BC89	Ch.14, p.1067
IFRS 13.B43	Ch.14, p.1044	IFRS 13.BC91	Ch.14, p.1116
IFRS 13.B43	Ch.19, p.1472	IFRS 13.BC92	Ch.14, p.1075
IFRS 13.B43	Ch.20, p.1548	IFRS 13.BC93	Ch.14, p.1075
IFRS 13.B44	Ch.14, p.1043	IFRS 13.BC94	Ch.14, p.1075
IFRS 13.B44	Ch.14, p.1044	IFRS 13.BC95	Ch.14, p.1076
IFRS 13.B44	Ch.14, p.1046	IFRS 13.BC96-BC98	Ch.14, p.1076
IFRS 13.B44(c)	Ch.14, p.1044	IFRS 13.BC99	Ch.14, p.1028
IFRS 13.B45	Ch.14, p.1122	IFRS 13.BC99	Ch.14, p.1087
IFRS 13.B46	Ch.14, p.1116	IFRS 13.BC100	Ch.14, p.1028
IFRS 13.B47	Ch.14, p.1123	IFRS 13.BC100	Ch.14, p.1087
IFRS 13.C1	Ch.14, p.1003	IFRS 13.BCZ102-BCZ103	Ch.14, p.1088
IFRS 13.IE3-IE6	Ch.14, p.1036	IFRS 13.BC106	Ch.14, p.1063
IFRS 13.IE7-IE8	Ch.14, p.1056	IFRS 13.BC119A	Ch.14, p.1089
IFRS 13.IE7-IE8	Ch.18, p.1420	IFRS 13.BC119B	Ch.14, p.1089
IFRS 13.IE9	Ch.14, p.1057	IFRS 13.BC121	Ch.14, p.1090
IFRS 13.IE11-IE14	Ch.14, p.1103	IFRS 13.BC138	Ch.14, p.1097
IFRS 13.IE11-IE14	Ch.14, p.1108	IFRS 13.BC138	Ch.49, p.3854
IFRS 13.IE15-IE17	Ch.14, p.1102	IFRS 13.BC138A	Ch.14, p.1010
IFRS 13.IE19-IE20	Ch.14, p.1029	IFRS 13.BC138A	Ch.49, p.3854
IFRS 13.IE19.21-IE22	Ch.14, p.1033	IFRS 13.BC145	Ch.14, p.1105
IFRS 13.IE24-IE26	Ch.14, p.1098	IFRS 13.BC157	Ch.14, p.1113
IFRS 13.IE28-IE29	Ch.14, p.1026	IFRS 13.BC164	Ch.14, p.1114
IFRS 13.IE31	Ch.14, p.1073	IFRS 13.BC165	Ch.14, p.1099
IFRS 13.IE32	Ch.14, p.1074	IFRS 13.BC184	Ch.14, p.1133
IFRS 13.IE34	Ch.14, p.1074	IFRS 13.BC208	Ch.14, p.1170
IFRS 13.IE35-IE39	Ch.14, p.1070	IFRS 13.BC238(a)	Ch.14, p.1172
IFRS 13.IE40-IE42	Ch.14, p.1067	IFRS 13.BC238(b)	Ch.14, p.1172
IFRS 13.IE43-IE47	Ch.14, p.1068	IFRS 13.BC238(c)	Ch.14, p.1172
IFRS 13.IE49-IE58	Ch.14, p.1047		
IFRS 13.IE60	Ch.14, p.1142		
IFRS 13.IE61	Ch.14, p.1150		
IFRS 13.IE62	Ch.14, p.1151		
IFRS 13.IE63	Ch.14, p.1147		
IFRS 13.IE64(a)	Ch.14, p.1134		
IFRS 13.IE65	Ch.14, p.1152		

IFRS 14

IFRS 14.5	Ch.5, p.323
IFRS 14.5	Ch.26, p.1966
IFRS 14.6	Ch.5, p.323

IFRS 14.6	Ch.26, p.1966
IFRS 14.7	Ch.5, p.325
IFRS 14.8	Ch.5, p.323
IFRS 14.8	Ch.5, p.335
IFRS 14.9	Ch.5, p.324
IFRS 14.9	Ch.5, p.325
IFRS 14.9-10	Ch.5, p.324
IFRS 14.11	Ch.5, p.324
IFRS 14.11	Ch.5, p.326
IFRS 14.11	Ch.5, p.334
IFRS 14.12	Ch.5, p.334
IFRS 14.12-15	Ch.5, p.324
IFRS 14.13	Ch.2, p.47
IFRS 14.13	Ch.5, p.325
IFRS 14.13	Ch.5, p.326
IFRS 14.13	Ch.26, p.1966
IFRS 14.13-15	Ch.5, p.324
IFRS 14.14	Ch.5, p.325
IFRS 14.15	Ch.5, p.325
IFRS 14.16	Ch.5, p.333
IFRS 14.17	Ch.5, p.333
IFRS 14.18-19	Ch.5, p.324
IFRS 14.20	Ch.5, p.326
IFRS 14.20-24	Ch.5, p.328
IFRS 14.21	Ch.5, p.326
IFRS 14.22	Ch.5, p.326
IFRS 14.23	Ch.5, p.326
IFRS 14.24	Ch.5, p.326
IFRS 14.24	Ch.5, p.327
IFRS 14.24	Ch.5, p.331
IFRS 14.25	Ch.5, p.327
IFRS 14.26	Ch.5, p.327
IFRS 14.26	Ch.5, p.328
IFRS 14.27	Ch.5, p.331
IFRS 14.28	Ch.5, p.331
IFRS 14.29	Ch.5, p.331
IFRS 14.29(a)	Ch.5, p.332
IFRS 14.30	Ch.5, p.331
IFRS 14.31	Ch.5, p.332
IFRS 14.32	Ch.5, p.332
IFRS 14.33	Ch.5, p.327
IFRS 14.33	Ch.5, p.332
IFRS 14.34	Ch.5, p.332
IFRS 14.35	Ch.5, p.332
IFRS 14.35	Ch.5, p.333
IFRS 14.36	Ch.5, p.333
IFRS 14 Appendix A	Ch.5, p.299
IFRS 14 Appendix A	Ch.5, p.322
IFRS 14.B1	Ch.5, p.323
IFRS 14.B2	Ch.5, p.323
IFRS 14.B3	Ch.5, p.325
IFRS 14.B4	Ch.5, p.324
IFRS 14.B5	Ch.5, p.325
IFRS 14.B6	Ch.5, p.326
IFRS 14.B7-B28	Ch.5, p.333
IFRS 14.B8	Ch.5, p.333
IFRS 14.B9	Ch.5, p.334
IFRS 14.B10	Ch.5, p.334
IFRS 14.B11	Ch.5, p.326
IFRS 14.B12	Ch.5, p.327
IFRS 14.B12	Ch.5, p.331
IFRS 14.B14	Ch.5, p.327
IFRS 14.B15	Ch.5, p.334
IFRS 14.B15-B16	Ch.5, p.334
IFRS 14.B16	Ch.5, p.334
IFRS 14.B17-B18	Ch.5, p.334
IFRS 14.B19	Ch.5, p.334
IFRS 14.B20	Ch.5, p.327
IFRS 14.B21	Ch.5, p.327
IFRS 14.B22	Ch.5, p.327
IFRS 14.B23	Ch.5, p.335
IFRS 14.B24	Ch.5, p.335
IFRS 14.B25	Ch.5, p.332
IFRS 14.B26-B27	Ch.5, p.333
IFRS 14.B28	Ch.5, p.333
IFRS 14.C1	Ch.26, p.1966
IFRS 14.IE1	Ch.5, p.326
IFRS 14.IE1	Ch.5, p.328
IFRS 14.IE1	Ch.5, p.329
IFRS 14.IE1	Ch.5, p.333
IFRS 14.IE2	Ch.5, p.328
IFRS 14.BC10	Ch.2, p.47
IFRS 14.BC10	Ch.26, p.1966
IFRS 14.BC22	Ch.5, p.323
IFRS 14.BC23	Ch.5, p.323
IFRS 14.BC32	Ch.5, p.324
IFRS 14.BC33	Ch.5, p.325

IFRS 15 (2016)

IFRS 15(2016).IN5	Ch.27, p.2020

IFRS 15

IFRS 15.1	Ch.27, p.2021
IFRS 15.2	Ch.27, p.2021
IFRS 15.2	Ch.31, p.2345
IFRS 15.3	Ch.27, p.2022
IFRS 15.4	Ch.28, p.2068
IFRS 15.5	Ch.27, p.2024
IFRS 15.5(c)	Ch.27, p.2035
IFRS 15.5(d)	Ch.18, p.1406
IFRS 15.5(d)	Ch.43, p.3449
IFRS 15.5(d)	Ch.43, p.3450
IFRS 15.6	Ch.27, p.2028
IFRS 15.6	Ch.43, p.3450
IFRS 15.6	Ch.43, p.3453
IFRS 15.6	Ch.43, p.3460
IFRS 15.7	Ch.27, p.2029
IFRS 15.7	Ch.29, p.2249
IFRS 15.7	Ch.31, p.2327
IFRS 15.7	Ch.43, p.3457
IFRS 15.8	Ch.25, p.1896
IFRS 15.8	Ch.27, p.2026

IFRS 15.8	Ch.31, p.2358
IFRS 15.9	Ch.28, p.2053
IFRS 15.9	Ch.28, p.2054
IFRS 15.9(e)	Ch.28, p.2058
IFRS 15.10	Ch.25, p.1869
IFRS 15.10	Ch.25, p.1914
IFRS 15.10	Ch.28, p.2052
IFRS 15.10	Ch.28, p.2055
IFRS 15.11	Ch.28, p.2052
IFRS 15.11	Ch.28, p.2061
IFRS 15.12	Ch.28, p.2061
IFRS 15.13	Ch.28, p.2053
IFRS 15.14	Ch.28, p.2083
IFRS 15.15	Ch.28, p.2066
IFRS 15.15	Ch.28, p.2082
IFRS 15.16	Ch.28, p.2082
IFRS 15.18	Ch.28, p.2065
IFRS 15.18	Ch.28, p.2069
IFRS 15.18	Ch.28, p.2077
IFRS 15.18	Ch.29, p.2172
IFRS 15.19	Ch.28, p.2069
IFRS 15.20	Ch.28, p.2071
IFRS 15.20(a)	Ch.28, p.2072
IFRS 15.20(b)	Ch.28, p.2072
IFRS 15.20-21	Ch.5, p.335
IFRS 15.21	Ch.28, p.2073
IFRS 15.21(a)	Ch.29, p.2248
IFRS 15.22	Ch.25, p.1870
IFRS 15.22	Ch.25, p.1906
IFRS 15.22	Ch.28, p.2084
IFRS 15.22(b)	Ch.28, p.2109
IFRS 15.22(b)	Ch.28, p.2116
IFRS 15.23	Ch.28, p.2084
IFRS 15.23	Ch.28, p.2109
IFRS 15.23	Ch.28, p.2116
IFRS 15.24	Ch.28, p.2085
IFRS 15.24	Ch.28, p.2089
IFRS 15.25	Ch.28, p.2085
IFRS 15.25	Ch.28, p.2086
IFRS 15.25	Ch.28, p.2089
IFRS 15.26	Ch.25, p.1870
IFRS 15.26	Ch.25, p.1906
IFRS 15.26	Ch.28, p.2085
IFRS 15.26(e)	Ch.28, p.2087
IFRS 15.26(g)	Ch.28, p.2087
IFRS 15.27	Ch.25, p.1870
IFRS 15.27	Ch.25, p.1906
IFRS 15.28	Ch.28, p.2097
IFRS 15.29	Ch.28, p.2098
IFRS 15.29	Ch.28, p.2099
IFRS 15.29	Ch.28, p.2104
IFRS 15.29(a)	Ch.28, p.2100
IFRS 15.29(b)	Ch.28, p.2102
IFRS 15.29(c)	Ch.28, p.2102
IFRS 15.30	Ch.25, p.1870
IFRS 15.30	Ch.25, p.1906
IFRS 15.30	Ch.28, p.2095
IFRS 15.30	Ch.28, p.2120
IFRS 15.31	Ch.19, p.1492
IFRS 15.31	Ch.25, p.1908
IFRS 15.31	Ch.30, p.2257
IFRS 15.31	Ch.43, p.3450
IFRS 15.32	Ch.19, p.1492
IFRS 15.32	Ch.25, p.1908
IFRS 15.32	Ch.30, p.2258
IFRS 15.32	Ch.30, p.2259
IFRS 15.33	Ch.28, p.2125
IFRS 15.33	Ch.30, p.2257
IFRS 15.33	Ch.30, p.2258
IFRS 15.34	Ch.30, p.2298
IFRS 15.35	Ch.30, p.2259
IFRS 15.35(a)	Ch.25, p.1908
IFRS 15.35(a)	Ch.25, p.1916
IFRS 15.35(a)	Ch.28, p.2092
IFRS 15.35(b)	Ch.25, p.1908
IFRS 15.35(b)	Ch.25, p.1915
IFRS 15.35(c)	Ch.5, p.337
IFRS 15.35(c)	Ch.30, p.2264
IFRS 15.36	Ch.30, p.2264
IFRS 15.36	Ch.30, p.2266
IFRS 15.36	Ch.30, p.2276
IFRS 15.37	Ch.30, p.2267
IFRS 15.37	Ch.30, p.2276
IFRS 15.38	Ch.23, p.1802
IFRS 15.38	Ch.28, p.2126
IFRS 15.38	Ch.30, p.2291
IFRS 15.39	Ch.25, p.1898
IFRS 15.39	Ch.30, p.2278
IFRS 15.40	Ch.30, p.2278
IFRS 15.40	Ch.38, p.3088
IFRS 15.41	Ch.30, p.2279
IFRS 15.41	Ch.30, p.2280
IFRS 15.42	Ch.30, p.2278
IFRS 15.43	Ch.30, p.2278
IFRS 15.44	Ch.30, p.2279
IFRS 15.45	Ch.25, p.1908
IFRS 15.45	Ch.30, p.2279
IFRS 15.46	Ch.29, p.2164
IFRS 15.47	Ch.19, p.1493
IFRS 15.47	Ch.25, p.1871
IFRS 15.47	Ch.25, p.1907
IFRS 15.47	Ch.29, p.2164
IFRS 15.47	Ch.29, p.2166
IFRS 15.47	Ch.33, p.2459
IFRS 15.47	Ch.43, p.3458
IFRS 15.47	Ch.43, p.3558
IFRS 15.48	Ch.29, p.2164
IFRS 15.49	Ch.29, p.2164
IFRS 15.49	Ch.31, p.2384
IFRS 15.50	Ch.25, p.1871
IFRS 15.50	Ch.25, p.1907
IFRS 15.50	Ch.29, p.2175
IFRS 15.50-51	Ch.29, p.2167
IFRS 15.51	Ch.25, p.1871
IFRS 15.51	Ch.25, p.1907
IFRS 15.51	Ch.29, p.2167

IFRS 15.51	Ch.29, p.2172	IFRS 15.74	Ch.25, p.1908
IFRS 15.51	Ch.29, p.2174	IFRS 15.74	Ch.25, p.1915
IFRS 15.52	Ch.29, p.2167	IFRS 15.74	Ch.29, p.2222
IFRS 15.53	Ch.25, p.1871	IFRS 15.75	Ch.29, p.2222
IFRS 15.53	Ch.25, p.1907	IFRS 15.76	Ch.29, p.2222
IFRS 15.53	Ch.29, p.2176	IFRS 15.76	Ch.29, p.2235
IFRS 15.54	Ch.29, p.2176	IFRS 15.77	Ch.29, p.2222
IFRS 15.55	Ch.9, p.689	IFRS 15.77	Ch.29, p.2223
IFRS 15.55	Ch.26, p.2006	IFRS 15.77	Ch.29, p.2224
IFRS 15.55	Ch.29, p.2188	IFRS 15.77	Ch.29, p.2225
IFRS 15.56	Ch.25, p.1871	IFRS 15.78	Ch.29, p.2223
IFRS 15.56	Ch.25, p.1907	IFRS 15.78	Ch.29, p.2224
IFRS 15.56	Ch.29, p.2179	IFRS 15.78	Ch.29, p.2225
IFRS 15.57	Ch.29, p.2179	IFRS 15.78	Ch.29, p.2228
IFRS 15.58	Ch.29, p.2180	IFRS 15.79	Ch.25, p.1872
IFRS 15.59	Ch.29, p.2187	IFRS 15.79	Ch.25, p.1908
IFRS 15.60	Ch.29, p.2192	IFRS 15.79	Ch.25, p.1915
IFRS 15.60	Ch.51, p.3928	IFRS 15.79	Ch.29, p.2224
IFRS 15.60-65	Ch.40, p.3167	IFRS 15.79	Ch.29, p.2225
IFRS 15.61	Ch.29, p.2192	IFRS 15.79(c)	Ch.29, p.2226
IFRS 15.61(a)	Ch.29, p.2201	IFRS 15.80	Ch.29, p.2225
IFRS 15.62	Ch.25, p.1871	IFRS 15.80	Ch.29, p.2227
IFRS 15.62	Ch.25, p.1915	IFRS 15.81	Ch.29, p.2244
IFRS 15.62	Ch.29, p.2193	IFRS 15.82	Ch.29, p.2244
IFRS 15.62(a)	Ch.28, p.2154	IFRS 15.82(b)	Ch.29, p.2215
IFRS 15.62(c)	Ch.29, p.2201	IFRS 15.83	Ch.29, p.2244
IFRS 15.63	Ch.25, p.1909	IFRS 15.84	Ch.29, p.2237
IFRS 15.63	Ch.29, p.2193	IFRS 15.85	Ch.28, p.2153
IFRS 15.63	Ch.29, p.2202	IFRS 15.85	Ch.29, p.2237
IFRS 15.63	Ch.51, p.3928	IFRS 15.85	Ch.29, p.2238
IFRS 15.64	Ch.25, p.1872	IFRS 15.85	Ch.31, p.2347
IFRS 15.64	Ch.25, p.1876	IFRS 15.86	Ch.29, p.2237
IFRS 15.64	Ch.25, p.1907	IFRS 15.86	Ch.29, p.2246
IFRS 15.64	Ch.25, p.1909	IFRS 15.87	Ch.29, p.2222
IFRS 15.64	Ch.25, p.1911	IFRS 15.88	Ch.29, p.2223
IFRS 15.64	Ch.25, p.1913	IFRS 15.88-89	Ch.28, p.2079
IFRS 15.64	Ch.29, p.2193	IFRS 15.88-89	Ch.29, p.2247
IFRS 15.64	Ch.29, p.2196	IFRS 15.89	Ch.28, p.2152
IFRS 15.65	Ch.29, p.2205	IFRS 15.90	Ch.29, p.2248
IFRS 15.66	Ch.18, p.1402	IFRS 15.90(a)	Ch.29, p.2248
IFRS 15.66	Ch.25, p.1880	IFRS 15.90(b)	Ch.29, p.2249
IFRS 15.66	Ch.29, p.2206	IFRS 15.91	Ch.25, p.1896
IFRS 15.67	Ch.25, p.1880	IFRS 15.91-93	Ch.31, p.2359
IFRS 15.67	Ch.25, p.1915	IFRS 15.91-93	Ch.55, p.4586
IFRS 15.67	Ch.29, p.2206	IFRS 15.92	Ch.25, p.1896
IFRS 15.68	Ch.29, p.2207	IFRS 15.92	Ch.31, p.2359
IFRS 15.69	Ch.29, p.2207	IFRS 15.93	Ch.25, p.1896
IFRS 15.70	Ch.29, p.2210	IFRS 15.94	Ch.31, p.2363
IFRS 15.70	Ch.29, p.2214	IFRS 15.95	Ch.25, p.1897
IFRS 15.70	Ch.29, p.2215	IFRS 15.95	Ch.31, p.2365
IFRS 15.70-72	Ch.25, p.1864	IFRS 15.95	Ch.41, p.3243
IFRS 15.71	Ch.29, p.2210	IFRS 15.95-96	Ch.22, p.1687
IFRS 15.71	Ch.29, p.2214	IFRS 15.95-96	Ch.31, p.2365
IFRS 15.72	Ch.29, p.2211	IFRS 15.97	Ch.26, p.1974
IFRS 15.72	Ch.29, p.2212	IFRS 15.97	Ch.31, p.2367
IFRS 15.72	Ch.29, p.2215	IFRS 15.98	Ch.26, p.1974
IFRS 15.73	Ch.29, p.2222	IFRS 15.98	Ch.31, p.2368
IFRS 15.74	Ch.25, p.1872	IFRS 15.99	Ch.31, p.2375

IFRS 15.99	Ch.31, p.2376	IFRS 15.117	Ch.32, p.2417
IFRS 15.99	Ch.31, p.2380	IFRS 15.118	Ch.32, p.2417
IFRS 15.99	Ch.31, p.2384	IFRS 15.119	Ch.29, p.2168
IFRS 15.100	Ch.31, p.2376	IFRS 15.119-120	Ch.32, p.2422
IFRS 15.101	Ch.31, p.2384	IFRS 15.119(a)	Ch.30, p.2260
IFRS 15.101(a)	Ch.31, p.2384	IFRS 15.120	Ch.5, p.335
IFRS 15.102	Ch.31, p.2384	IFRS 15.120	Ch.32, p.2432
IFRS 15.102	Ch.31, p.2385	IFRS 15.121	Ch.32, p.2430
IFRS 15.103	Ch.31, p.2385	IFRS 15.121	Ch.32, p.2432
IFRS 15.104	Ch.31, p.2385	IFRS 15.122	Ch.32, p.2430
IFRS 15.105	Ch.9, p.689	IFRS 15.123	Ch.3, p.175
IFRS 15.105	Ch.32, p.2393	IFRS 15.123	Ch.29, p.2168
IFRS 15.105	Ch.32, p.2395	IFRS 15.123	Ch.32, p.2433
IFRS 15.105	Ch.52, p.4089	IFRS 15.123(a)	Ch.30, p.2260
IFRS 15.106	Ch.9, p.688	IFRS 15.124	Ch.30, p.2260
IFRS 15.106-107	Ch.32, p.2394	IFRS 15.124	Ch.32, p.2433
IFRS 15.107	Ch.9, p.689	IFRS 15.125	Ch.32, p.2433
IFRS 15.107	Ch.25, p.1876	IFRS 15.126	Ch.29, p.2168
IFRS 15.107	Ch.25, p.1883	IFRS 15.126	Ch.32, p.2435
IFRS 15.107	Ch.25, p.1910	IFRS 15.127-128	Ch.32, p.2437
IFRS 15.107	Ch.25, p.1912	IFRS 15.129	Ch.32, p.2439
IFRS 15.107	Ch.25, p.1913	IFRS 15 Appendix A	Ch.8, p.627
IFRS 15.107	Ch.25, p.1916	IFRS 15 Appendix A	Ch.9, p.689
IFRS 15.107	Ch.32, p.2395	IFRS 15 Appendix A	Ch.25, p.1869
IFRS 15.107	Ch.32, p.2398	IFRS 15 Appendix A	Ch.25, p.1905
IFRS 15.107	Ch.45, p.3607	IFRS 15 Appendix A	Ch.25, p.1906
IFRS 15.107	Ch.52, p.4089	IFRS 15 Appendix A	Ch.25, p.1914
IFRS 15.108	Ch.25, p.1875	IFRS 15 Appendix A	Ch.27, p.2018
IFRS 15.108	Ch.25, p.1876	IFRS 15 Appendix A	Ch.27, p.2023
IFRS 15.108	Ch.25, p.1877	IFRS 15 Appendix A	Ch.27, p.2027
IFRS 15.108	Ch.25, p.1885	IFRS 15 Appendix A	Ch.27, p.2033
IFRS 15.108	Ch.25, p.1909	IFRS 15 Appendix A	Ch.28, p.2057
IFRS 15.108	Ch.25, p.1910	IFRS 15 Appendix A	Ch.42, p.3315
IFRS 15.108	Ch.25, p.1911	IFRS 15 Appendix A	Ch.43, p.3452
IFRS 15.108	Ch.25, p.1912	IFRS 15 Appendix A	Ch.43, p.3467
IFRS 15.108	Ch.32, p.2395	IFRS 15 Appendix A	Ch.43, p.3469
IFRS 15.108	Ch.32, p.2399	IFRS 15 Appendix A	Ch.51, p.3924
IFRS 15.108	Ch.32, p.2404	IFRS 15 Appendix A	Ch.51, p.3928
IFRS 15.108	Ch.45, p.3606	IFRS 15.B3	Ch.30, p.2261
IFRS 15.108	Ch.49, p.3854	IFRS 15.B4	Ch.25, p.1908
IFRS 15.108	Ch.52, p.4089	IFRS 15.B4	Ch.30, p.2261
IFRS 15.109	Ch.32, p.2396	IFRS 15.B5	Ch.30, p.2263
IFRS 15.110	Ch.32, p.2408	IFRS 15.B6	Ch.30, p.2264
IFRS 15.111	Ch.32, p.2408	IFRS 15.B7	Ch.30, p.2264
IFRS 15.112	Ch.32, p.2408	IFRS 15.B7	Ch.30, p.2265
IFRS 15.112	Ch.32, p.2410	IFRS 15.B8	Ch.30, p.2265
IFRS 15.112	Ch.36, p.2980	IFRS 15.B9	Ch.30, p.2267
IFRS 15.113	Ch.32, p.2404	IFRS 15.B10	Ch.30, p.2268
IFRS 15.113	Ch.43, p.3458	IFRS 15.B11	Ch.30, p.2268
IFRS 15.113(a)	Ch.43, p.3450	IFRS 15.B12	Ch.30, p.2267
IFRS 15.113(b)	Ch.29, p.2206	IFRS 15.B12	Ch.30, p.2269
IFRS 15.113(b)	Ch.32, p.2399	IFRS 15.B13	Ch.30, p.2269
IFRS 15.113(b)	Ch.32, p.2400	IFRS 15.B14	Ch.30, p.2279
IFRS 15.114	Ch.32, p.2409	IFRS 15.B15	Ch.30, p.2279
IFRS 15.114	Ch.36, p.2980	IFRS 15.B16	Ch.30, p.2280
IFRS 15.115	Ch.32, p.2411	IFRS 15.B16	Ch.30, p.2281
IFRS 15.115	Ch.36, p.2980	IFRS 15.B17	Ch.30, p.2280
IFRS 15.116	Ch.32, p.2417	IFRS 15.B18	Ch.25, p.1908

IFRS 15.B18	Ch.25, p.1915	IFRS 15.B41	Ch.28, p.2150
IFRS 15.B18	Ch.30, p.2280	IFRS 15.B42	Ch.29, p.2231
IFRS 15.B19	Ch.25, p.1898	IFRS 15.B43	Ch.29, p.2231
IFRS 15.B19	Ch.30, p.2283	IFRS 15.B43	Ch.29, p.2232
IFRS 15.B19	Ch.30, p.2284	IFRS 15.B44-B47	Ch.28, p.2154
IFRS 15.B19(a)	Ch.30, p.2284	IFRS 15.B44-B47	Ch.43, p.3472
IFRS 15.B20	Ch.28, p.2154	IFRS 15.B45	Ch.30, p.2309
IFRS 15.B20	Ch.29, p.2188	IFRS 15.B46	Ch.28, p.2066
IFRS 15.B21	Ch.29, p.2188	IFRS 15.B46	Ch.30, p.2309
IFRS 15.B21	Ch.29, p.2189	IFRS 15.B46	Ch.30, p.2311
IFRS 15.B22	Ch.28, p.2154	IFRS 15.B46	Ch.31, p.2348
IFRS 15.B22	Ch.29, p.2188	IFRS 15.B48	Ch.29, p.2218
IFRS 15.B23	Ch.29, p.2189	IFRS 15.B49	Ch.28, p.2089
IFRS 15.B24	Ch.29, p.2189	IFRS 15.B49	Ch.29, p.2218
IFRS 15.B25	Ch.29, p.2189	IFRS 15.B50	Ch.29, p.2218
IFRS 15.B25	Ch.32, p.2402	IFRS 15.B51	Ch.29, p.2218
IFRS 15.B26	Ch.28, p.2154	IFRS 15.B52	Ch.31, p.2320
IFRS 15.B26	Ch.29, p.2188	IFRS 15.B53	Ch.31, p.2321
IFRS 15.B27	Ch.28, p.2154	IFRS 15.B54	Ch.28, p.2096
IFRS 15.B27	Ch.29, p.2188	IFRS 15.B54	Ch.31, p.2324
IFRS 15.B28	Ch.31, p.2350	IFRS 15.B56	Ch.31, p.2320
IFRS 15.B28-B33	Ch.28, p.2096	IFRS 15.B58	Ch.31, p.2328
IFRS 15.B29	Ch.31, p.2350	IFRS 15.B59	Ch.31, p.2328
IFRS 15.B29	Ch.31, p.2353	IFRS 15.B59A	Ch.31, p.2329
IFRS 15.B30	Ch.25, p.1906	IFRS 15.B60	Ch.31, p.2333
IFRS 15.B30	Ch.25, p.1914	IFRS 15.B61	Ch.31, p.2333
IFRS 15.B30	Ch.26, p.1936	IFRS 15.B61	Ch.31, p.2335
IFRS 15.B30	Ch.26, p.2003	IFRS 15.B61	Ch.31, p.2336
IFRS 15.B30	Ch.31, p.2350	IFRS 15.B62(a)	Ch.31, p.2324
IFRS 15.B30	Ch.31, p.2354	IFRS 15.B62(b)	Ch.31, p.2326
IFRS 15.B31	Ch.31, p.2350	IFRS 15.B63	Ch.31, p.2337
IFRS 15.B32	Ch.31, p.2353	IFRS 15.B63	Ch.31, p.2348
IFRS 15.B32	Ch.31, p.2355	IFRS 15.B63A	Ch.31, p.2338
IFRS 15.B33	Ch.26, p.1936	IFRS 15.B63B	Ch.31, p.2340
IFRS 15.B33	Ch.31, p.2350	IFRS 15.B64	Ch.30, p.2298
IFRS 15.B33	Ch.31, p.2351	IFRS 15.B64	Ch.43, p.3466
IFRS 15.B34	Ch.28, p.2121	IFRS 15.B65	Ch.30, p.2298
IFRS 15.B34	Ch.28, p.2123	IFRS 15.B65	Ch.43, p.3466
IFRS 15.B34	Ch.28, p.2124	IFRS 15.B66-B67	Ch.30, p.2299
IFRS 15.B34A(a)	Ch.28, p.2123	IFRS 15.B68-B69	Ch.30, p.2300
IFRS 15.B34A(b)	Ch.28, p.2125	IFRS 15.B70	Ch.30, p.2301
IFRS 15.B34A	Ch.28, p.2121	IFRS 15.B70	Ch.30, p.2302
IFRS 15.B35	Ch.28, p.2121	IFRS 15.B70-B71	Ch.30, p.2301
IFRS 15.B35	Ch.28, p.2122	IFRS 15.B72	Ch.30, p.2302
IFRS 15.B35A	Ch.28, p.2126	IFRS 15.B73	Ch.30, p.2302
IFRS 15.B35B	Ch.28, p.2131	IFRS 15.B74	Ch.30, p.2302
IFRS 15.B36	Ch.28, p.2121	IFRS 15.B75	Ch.30, p.2301
IFRS 15.B36	Ch.28, p.2131	IFRS 15.B76	Ch.30, p.2302
IFRS 15.B37	Ch.28, p.2129	IFRS 15.B77	Ch.30, p.2304
IFRS 15.B37A	Ch.28, p.2129	IFRS 15.B77	Ch.30, p.2305
IFRS 15.B38	Ch.28, p.2132	IFRS 15.B78	Ch.30, p.2304
IFRS 15.B39	Ch.28, p.2140	IFRS 15.B79	Ch.30, p.2305
IFRS 15.B39-B43	Ch.28, p.2096	IFRS 15.B79-B82	Ch.43, p.3448
IFRS 15.B40	Ch.28, p.2140	IFRS 15.B80	Ch.30, p.2305
IFRS 15.B40	Ch.28, p.2148	IFRS 15.B81	Ch.30, p.2306
IFRS 15.B40	Ch.28, p.2154	IFRS 15.B82	Ch.30, p.2306
IFRS 15.B41	Ch.28, p.2141	IFRS 15.B82	Ch.43, p.3448
IFRS 15.B41	Ch.28, p.2148	IFRS 15.B83	Ch.30, p.2295

Index of standards

IFRS 15.B84	Ch.30, p.2296	IFRS 15.IE238A-IE238G	Ch.28, p.2133
IFRS 15.B85	Ch.30, p.2296	IFRS 15.IE239-IE243	Ch.28, p.2134
IFRS 15.B86	Ch.30, p.2296	IFRS 15.IE244-IE248	Ch.28, p.2134
IFRS 15.B87	Ch.32, p.2410	IFRS 15.IE248A-IE248F	Ch.28, p.2135
IFRS 15.B87-B89	Ch.32, p.2410	IFRS 15.IE250-IE253	Ch.28, p.2141
IFRS 15.C1	Ch.27, p.2020	IFRS 15.IE257-IE266	Ch.28, p.2151
IFRS 15.C5	Ch.5, p.335	IFRS 15.IE267-IE270	Ch.30, p.2310
IFRS 15.C5(a)(ii)	Ch.5, p.339	IFRS 15.IE281	Ch.31, p.2322
IFRS 15.C5(a)(ii)	Ch.5, p.341	IFRS 15.IE281-IE284	Ch.31, p.2331
IFRS 15.C5(c)	Ch.5, p.336	IFRS 15.IE285-IE288	Ch.31, p.2322
IFRS 15.C6	Ch.5, p.336	IFRS 15.IE297-IE302	Ch.31, p.2334
IFRS 15.C10	Ch.27, p.2020	IFRS 15.IE303-IE306	Ch.31, p.2335
IFRS 15.IE3-IE6	Ch.28, p.2059	IFRS 15.IE307-IE308	Ch.31, p.2340
IFRS 15.IE7-IE9	Ch.29, p.2169	IFRS 15.IE309-IE313	Ch.31, p.2342
IFRS 15.IE14-IE17	Ch.28, p.2061	IFRS 15.IE315	Ch.30, p.2303
IFRS 15.IE17	Ch.28, p.2061	IFRS 15.IE315-IE318	Ch.30, p.2300
IFRS 15.IE19	Ch.28, p.2074	IFRS 15.IE319-IE321	Ch.30, p.2303
IFRS 15.IE19-IE21	Ch.28, p.2073	IFRS 15.IE323-IE327	Ch.30, p.2307
IFRS 15.IE22-IE24	Ch.28, p.2074	IFRS 15.BC32	Ch.28, p.2052
IFRS 15.IE33-IE36	Ch.28, p.2074	IFRS 15.BC32	Ch.28, p.2086
IFRS 15.IE37-IE41	Ch.28, p.2076	IFRS 15.BC33	Ch.28, p.2053
IFRS 15.IE42-IE43	Ch.28, p.2069	IFRS 15.BC34	Ch.28, p.2053
IFRS 15.IE45-IE48C	Ch.28, p.2116	IFRS 15.BC35	Ch.28, p.2055
IFRS 15.IE49-IE58	Ch.28, p.2117	IFRS 15.BC36	Ch.28, p.2056
IFRS 15.IE58A-IE58K	Ch.28, p.2118	IFRS 15.BC37	Ch.28, p.2056
IFRS 15.IE59-IE65A	Ch.28, p.2087	IFRS 15.BC40	Ch.28, p.2056
IFRS 15.IE67-IE68	Ch.28, p.2114	IFRS 15.BC43	Ch.28, p.2057
IFRS 15.IE67-IE68	Ch.30, p.2262	IFRS 15.BC45	Ch.28, p.2057
IFRS 15.IE69-IE72	Ch.30, p.2269	IFRS 15.BC46	Ch.28, p.2058
IFRS 15.IE73-IE76	Ch.30, p.2265	IFRS 15.BC46C	Ch.28, p.2058
IFRS 15.IE77-IE80	Ch.30, p.2270	IFRS 15.BC46E	Ch.28, p.2057
IFRS 15.IE81-IE90	Ch.30, p.2270	IFRS 15.BC46E	Ch.28, p.2058
IFRS 15.IE92-IE94	Ch.30, p.2286	IFRS 15.BC46H	Ch.28, p.2083
IFRS 15.IE95-IE100	Ch.30, p.2284	IFRS 15.BC46H	Ch.28, p.2084
IFRS 15.IE98	Ch.30, p.2286	IFRS 15.BC47	Ch.28, p.2083
IFRS 15.IE102-IE104	Ch.29, p.2173	IFRS 15.BC48	Ch.28, p.2066
IFRS 15.IE110-IE115	Ch.29, p.2190	IFRS 15.BC48	Ch.28, p.2083
IFRS 15.IE116-IE123	Ch.29, p.2182	IFRS 15.BC52-BC56	Ch.43, p.3450
IFRS 15.IE124-IE128	Ch.29, p.2167	IFRS 15.BC54	Ch.27, p.2028
IFRS 15.IE129-IE133	Ch.29, p.2184	IFRS 15.BC54	Ch.43, p.3453
IFRS 15.IE135-IE140	Ch.29, p.2197	IFRS 15.BC56	Ch.27, p.2028
IFRS 15.IE141-IE142	Ch.29, p.2198	IFRS 15.BC58	Ch.27, p.2026
IFRS 15.IE143-IE147	Ch.29, p.2199	IFRS 15.BC69	Ch.28, p.2068
IFRS 15.IE148-IE151	Ch.29, p.2199	IFRS 15.BC71	Ch.28, p.2067
IFRS 15.IE152-IE154	Ch.29, p.2200	IFRS 15.BC73	Ch.28, p.2068
IFRS 15.IE156-IE158	Ch.29, p.2207	IFRS 15.BC74	Ch.28, p.2067
IFRS 15.IE160-IE162	Ch.29, p.2216	IFRS 15.BC75	Ch.28, p.2067
IFRS 15.IE164-IE166	Ch.29, p.2227	IFRS 15.BC76	Ch.28, p.2070
IFRS 15.IE167-IE177	Ch.29, p.2244	IFRS 15.BC79	Ch.27, p.2024
IFRS 15.IE178-IE187	Ch.29, p.2242	IFRS 15.BC79	Ch.28, p.2071
IFRS 15.IE178-IE187	Ch.31, p.2340	IFRS 15.BC83	Ch.29, p.2248
IFRS 15.IE189-IE191	Ch.31, p.2362	IFRS 15.BC85	Ch.28, p.2084
IFRS 15.IE192-IE196	Ch.31, p.2368	IFRS 15.BC87	Ch.28, p.2086
IFRS 15.IE198-IE200	Ch.32, p.2396	IFRS 15.BC87	Ch.28, p.2088
IFRS 15.IE201-IE204	Ch.32, p.2397	IFRS 15.BC88	Ch.28, p.2086
IFRS 15.IE210-IE211	Ch.32, p.2412	IFRS 15.BC89	Ch.28, p.2086
IFRS 15.IE212-IE219	Ch.32, p.2430	IFRS 15.BC90	Ch.28, p.2090
IFRS 15.IE220-IE221	Ch.32, p.2432	IFRS 15.BC92	Ch.28, p.2087

IFRS 15.BC100	Ch.28, p.2097	IFRS 15.BC171	Ch.30, p.2286
IFRS 15.BC100	Ch.28, p.2104	IFRS 15.BC172	Ch.30, p.2284
IFRS 15.BC101	Ch.28, p.2097	IFRS 15.BC172	Ch.30, p.2285
IFRS 15.BC102	Ch.28, p.2096	IFRS 15.BC172	Ch.30, p.2286
IFRS 15.BC102	Ch.28, p.2099	IFRS 15.BC174	Ch.30, p.2284
IFRS 15.BC105	Ch.28, p.2104	IFRS 15.BC174	Ch.30, p.2285
IFRS 15.BC107	Ch.28, p.2101	IFRS 15.BC179	Ch.30, p.2279
IFRS 15.BC108	Ch.28, p.2101	IFRS 15.BC180	Ch.30, p.2279
IFRS 15.BC109	Ch.28, p.2102	IFRS 15.BC185	Ch.29, p.2164
IFRS 15.BC110	Ch.28, p.2102	IFRS 15.BC187	Ch.29, p.2164
IFRS 15.BC112	Ch.28, p.2103	IFRS 15.BC188D	Ch.28, p.2136
IFRS 15.BC113	Ch.28, p.2109	IFRS 15.BC188D	Ch.29, p.2166
IFRS 15.BC113	Ch.28, p.2112	IFRS 15.BC191	Ch.29, p.2167
IFRS 15.BC114	Ch.28, p.2109	IFRS 15.BC194	Ch.28, p.2059
IFRS 15.BC115	Ch.28, p.2111	IFRS 15.BC194	Ch.29, p.2170
IFRS 15.BC116	Ch.28, p.2112	IFRS 15.BC200	Ch.29, p.2176
IFRS 15.BC116D	Ch.28, p.2090	IFRS 15.BC200	Ch.29, p.2177
IFRS 15.BC116J	Ch.28, p.2099	IFRS 15.BC201	Ch.29, p.2177
IFRS 15.BC116J	Ch.28, p.2104	IFRS 15.BC202	Ch.29, p.2176
IFRS 15.BC116J-BC116L	Ch.28, p.2100	IFRS 15.BC203	Ch.29, p.2179
IFRS 15.BC116K	Ch.28, p.2099	IFRS 15.BC204	Ch.29, p.2179
IFRS 15.BC116K	Ch.28, p.2104	IFRS 15.BC211	Ch.29, p.2180
IFRS 15.BC116L	Ch.28, p.2099	IFRS 15.BC212	Ch.29, p.2180
IFRS 15.BC116N	Ch.28, p.2100	IFRS 15.BC215	Ch.29, p.2185
IFRS 15.BC116N	Ch.28, p.2104	IFRS 15.BC219	Ch.31, p.2337
IFRS 15.BC116U	Ch.28, p.2090	IFRS 15.BC228	Ch.29, p.2187
IFRS 15.BC118	Ch.30, p.2257	IFRS 15.BC228	Ch.29, p.2249
IFRS 15.BC120	Ch.30, p.2257	IFRS 15.BC229	Ch.29, p.2193
IFRS 15.BC121	Ch.30, p.2258	IFRS 15.BC230	Ch.29, p.2193
IFRS 15.BC125	Ch.30, p.2260	IFRS 15.BC232	Ch.29, p.2194
IFRS 15.BC126	Ch.30, p.2261	IFRS 15.BC233	Ch.29, p.2194
IFRS 15.BC127	Ch.30, p.2262	IFRS 15.BC233	Ch.29, p.2195
IFRS 15.BC129	Ch.30, p.2263	IFRS 15.BC234	Ch.29, p.2196
IFRS 15.BC130	Ch.30, p.2263	IFRS 15.BC235	Ch.29, p.2194
IFRS 15.BC135	Ch.30, p.2265	IFRS 15.BC236	Ch.29, p.2194
IFRS 15.BC136	Ch.30, p.2266	IFRS 15.BC238	Ch.29, p.2195
IFRS 15.BC137	Ch.30, p.2265	IFRS 15.BC239	Ch.29, p.2196
IFRS 15.BC138	Ch.30, p.2265	IFRS 15.BC244	Ch.29, p.2205
IFRS 15.BC138-BC139	Ch.27, p.2025	IFRS 15.BC247	Ch.29, p.2206
IFRS 15.BC139	Ch.30, p.2266	IFRS 15.BC252	Ch.29, p.2209
IFRS 15.BC141	Ch.30, p.2266	IFRS 15.BC254C	Ch.29, p.2208
IFRS 15.BC142	Ch.30, p.2267	IFRS 15.BC254E	Ch.29, p.2208
IFRS 15.BC142	Ch.30, p.2268	IFRS 15.BC254H	Ch.29, p.2209
IFRS 15.BC144	Ch.30, p.2268	IFRS 15.BC257	Ch.29, p.2213
IFRS 15.BC145	Ch.30, p.2269	IFRS 15.BC266	Ch.29, p.2222
IFRS 15.BC145	Ch.30, p.2273	IFRS 15.BC272	Ch.29, p.2226
IFRS 15.BC146	Ch.30, p.2273	IFRS 15.BC273	Ch.29, p.2226
IFRS 15.BC148	Ch.30, p.2293	IFRS 15.BC278	Ch.29, p.2237
IFRS 15.BC154	Ch.30, p.2293	IFRS 15.BC279-BC280	Ch.29, p.2243
IFRS 15.BC155	Ch.30, p.2292	IFRS 15.BC280	Ch.29, p.2237
IFRS 15.BC160	Ch.30, p.2280	IFRS 15.BC283	Ch.29, p.2244
IFRS 15.BC161	Ch.30, p.2278	IFRS 15.BC296	Ch.31, p.2356
IFRS 15.BC161	Ch.30, p.2288	IFRS 15.BC307	Ch.31, p.2365
IFRS 15.BC163	Ch.30, p.2281	IFRS 15.BC307	Ch.31, p.2367
IFRS 15.BC165	Ch.30, p.2280	IFRS 15.BC308	Ch.25, p.1897
IFRS 15.BC166	Ch.30, p.2281	IFRS 15.BC308	Ch.31, p.2367
IFRS 15.BC171	Ch.30, p.2284	IFRS 15.BC309	Ch.31, p.2377
IFRS 15.BC171	Ch.30, p.2285	IFRS 15.BC312	Ch.31, p.2370

IFRS 15.BC313	Ch.31, p.2371
IFRS 15.BC315	Ch.31, p.2371
IFRS 15.BC317	Ch.32, p.2400
IFRS 15.BC323	Ch.32, p.2396
IFRS 15.BC323-BC324	Ch.32, p.2395
IFRS 15.BC325	Ch.32, p.2395
IFRS 15.BC327	Ch.32, p.2408
IFRS 15.BC331	Ch.32, p.2408
IFRS 15.BC332	Ch.32, p.2404
IFRS 15.BC334	Ch.32, p.2404
IFRS 15.BC336	Ch.32, p.2410
IFRS 15.BC340	Ch.32, p.2411
IFRS 15.BC340	Ch.36, p.2980
IFRS 15.BC341	Ch.32, p.2417
IFRS 15.BC346	Ch.32, p.2417
IFRS 15.BC347	Ch.32, p.2418
IFRS 15.BC348	Ch.32, p.2428
IFRS 15.BC350	Ch.32, p.2428
IFRS 15.BC354	Ch.32, p.2421
IFRS 15.BC355	Ch.32, p.2433
IFRS 15.BC355	Ch.32, p.2435
IFRS 15.BC364	Ch.28, p.2154
IFRS 15.BC371	Ch.31, p.2353
IFRS 15.BC376	Ch.31, p.2353
IFRS 15.BC376	Ch.31, p.2354
IFRS 15.BC383-BC385	Ch.28, p.2132
IFRS 15.BC385B	Ch.28, p.2123
IFRS 15.BC385D	Ch.28, p.2121
IFRS 15.BC385E	Ch.28, p.2121
IFRS 15.BC385H	Ch.28, p.2129
IFRS 15.BC385O	Ch.28, p.2123
IFRS 15.BC385O	Ch.28, p.2127
IFRS 15.BC385Q	Ch.28, p.2123
IFRS 15.BC385R	Ch.28, p.2128
IFRS 15.BC385S	Ch.28, p.2125
IFRS 15.BC385U	Ch.28, p.2126
IFRS 15.BC385V	Ch.28, p.2127
IFRS 15.BC385Z	Ch.28, p.2136
IFRS 15.BC386	Ch.28, p.2140
IFRS 15.BC390	Ch.29, p.2231
IFRS 15.BC391	Ch.28, p.2064
IFRS 15.BC394	Ch.29, p.2231
IFRS 15.BC 394	Ch.29, p.2232
IFRS 15.BC395	Ch.29, p.2232
IFRS 15.BC398	Ch.30, p.2309
IFRS 15.BC400	Ch.30, p.2309
IFRS 15.BC405-BC406	Ch.31, p.2325
IFRS 15.BC407	Ch.31, p.2320
IFRS 15.BC407	Ch.31, p.2330
IFRS 15.BC412(b)	Ch.28, p.2094
IFRS 15.BC413	Ch.31, p.2329
IFRS 15.BC414	Ch.31, p.2333
IFRS 15.BC414	Ch.31, p.2336
IFRS 15.BC414I	Ch.31, p.2329
IFRS 15.BC414K	Ch.31, p.2330
IFRS 15.BC414N	Ch.31, p.2330
IFRS 15.BC414O	Ch.31, p.2325
IFRS 15.BC414P	Ch.31, p.2325
IFRS 15.BC414P	Ch.31, p.2326
IFRS 15.BC414Q	Ch.31, p.2325
IFRS 15.BC414S	Ch.31, p.2336
IFRS 15.BC414T	Ch.31, p.2337
IFRS 15.BC414U	Ch.31, p.2337
IFRS 15.BC414X	Ch.31, p.2321
IFRS 15.BC414X	Ch.31, p.2331
IFRS 15.BC414Y	Ch.31, p.2332
IFRS 15.BC415	Ch.31, p.2338
IFRS 15.BC416	Ch.31, p.2338
IFRS 15.BC421	Ch.31, p.2343
IFRS 15.BC421E	Ch.31, p.2338
IFRS 15.BC421F	Ch.31, p.2343
IFRS 15.BC421G	Ch.31, p.2338
IFRS 15.BC421I	Ch.31, p.2337
IFRS 15.BC421I	Ch.31, p.2341
IFRS 15.BC421J	Ch.31, p.2340
IFRS 15.BC423	Ch.30, p.2299
IFRS 15.BC425	Ch.30, p.2300
IFRS 15.BC427	Ch.30, p.2299
IFRS 15.BC427	Ch.30, p.2303
IFRS 15.BC431	Ch.30, p.2304
IFRS 15.BC441	Ch.5, p.338
IFRS 15.BC445D	Ch.5, p.338

IFRS 16

IFRS 16.1	Ch.23, p.1710
IFRS 16.2	Ch.23, p.1710
IFRS 16.2	Ch.43, p.3540
IFRS 16.3	Ch.17, p.1294
IFRS 16.3	Ch.23, p.1710
IFRS 16.3	Ch.43, p.3528
IFRS 16.3(a)	Ch.43, p.3336
IFRS 16.3(a)	Ch.43, p.3361
IFRS 16.3(b)	Ch.42, p.3280
IFRS 16.3(c)	Ch.25, p.1857
IFRS 16.4	Ch.23, p.1710
IFRS 16.5	Ch.23, p.1710
IFRS 16.6	Ch.5, p.303
IFRS 16.6	Ch.23, p.1752
IFRS 16.6	Ch.23, p.1753
IFRS 16.6	Ch.43, p.3547
IFRS 16.7	Ch.23, p.1752
IFRS 16.8	Ch.23, p.1752
IFRS 16.8	Ch.23, p.1753
IFRS 16.9	Ch.17, p.1373
IFRS 16.9	Ch.23, p.1713
IFRS 16.9	Ch.23, p.1714
IFRS 16.9	Ch.25, p.1857
IFRS 16.9	Ch.43, p.3539
IFRS 16.9	Ch.43, p.3553
IFRS 16.9-11	Ch.5, p.302
IFRS 16.10	Ch.23, p.1714
IFRS 16.11	Ch.5, p.302
IFRS 16.11	Ch.23, p.1728
IFRS 16.12	Ch.23, p.1728

IFRS 16.12	Ch.27, p.2030	IFRS 16.47	Ch.18, p.1388
IFRS 16.12	Ch.43, p.3531	IFRS 16.47	Ch.23, p.1774
IFRS 16.12	Ch.43, p.3554	IFRS 16.48	Ch.18, p.1388
IFRS 16.13	Ch.23, p.1731	IFRS 16.48	Ch.19, p.1445
IFRS 16.14	Ch.23, p.1731	IFRS 16.48	Ch.23, p.1774
IFRS 16.15	Ch.23, p.1730	IFRS 16.49	Ch.23, p.1774
IFRS 16.15-16	Ch.26, p.1977	IFRS 16.50	Ch.23, p.1775
IFRS 16.16	Ch.23, p.1729	IFRS 16.50	Ch.40, p.3168
IFRS 16.17	Ch.23, p.1734	IFRS 16.50	Ch.40, p.3169
IFRS 16.17	Ch.27, p.2030	IFRS 16.51	Ch.23, p.1776
IFRS 16.18	Ch.23, p.1736	IFRS 16.52	Ch.23, p.1776
IFRS 16.19	Ch.23, p.1736	IFRS 16.53	Ch.23, p.1776
IFRS 16.20	Ch.23, p.1741	IFRS 16.53(i)	Ch.23, p.1807
IFRS 16.21	Ch.23, p.1742	IFRS 16.53(g)	Ch.23, p.1778
IFRS 16.22	Ch.23, p.1751	IFRS 16.53(g)	Ch.40, p.3168
IFRS 16.22	Ch.45, p.3587	IFRS 16.54	Ch.23, p.1776
IFRS 16.23	Ch.23, p.1754	IFRS 16.55	Ch.23, p.1778
IFRS 16.24	Ch.19, p.1463	IFRS 16.55	Ch.38, p.3080
IFRS 16.24	Ch.23, p.1754	IFRS 16.56	Ch.19, p.1445
IFRS 16.24(b)	Ch.19, p.1462	IFRS 16.56	Ch.23, p.1778
IFRS 16.24(b)	Ch.23, p.1743	IFRS 16.57	Ch.23, p.1778
IFRS 16.24(d)	Ch.26, p.1986	IFRS 16.58	Ch.23, p.1778
IFRS 16.25	Ch.23, p.1754	IFRS 16.58	Ch.54, p.4455
IFRS 16.25	Ch.26, p.1986	IFRS 16.59	Ch.23, p.1779
IFRS 16.26	Ch.23, p.1749	IFRS 16.60	Ch.23, p.1751
IFRS 16.26	Ch.23, p.1754	IFRS 16.61	Ch.23, p.1781
IFRS 16.26	Ch.45, p.3587	IFRS 16.62	Ch.23, p.1781
IFRS 16.27	Ch.23, p.1755	IFRS 16.63	Ch.23, p.1782
IFRS 16.27(a)	Ch.19, p.1462	IFRS 16.64	Ch.23, p.1782
IFRS 16.27(a)	Ch.23, p.1743	IFRS 16.65	Ch.23, p.1782
IFRS 16.28	Ch.23, p.1744	IFRS 16.66	Ch.5, p.371
IFRS 16.29	Ch.23, p.1755	IFRS 16.66	Ch.23, p.1783
IFRS 16.29-35	Ch.18, p.1426	IFRS 16.67	Ch.23, p.1784
IFRS 16.30	Ch.23, p.1755	IFRS 16.67	Ch.23, p.1796
IFRS 16.31	Ch.23, p.1755	IFRS 16.67	Ch.25, p.1856
IFRS 16.31	Ch.26, p.2003	IFRS 16.67-97	Ch.42, p.3280
IFRS 16.32	Ch.23, p.1755	IFRS 16.68	Ch.23, p.1785
IFRS 16.33	Ch.20, p.1521	IFRS 16.68	Ch.23, p.1799
IFRS 16.33	Ch.23, p.1756	IFRS 16.69	Ch.23, p.1751
IFRS 16.33	Ch.23, p.1773	IFRS 16.69	Ch.23, p.1785
IFRS 16.34	Ch.19, p.1444	IFRS 16.70	Ch.23, p.1785
IFRS 16.34	Ch.23, p.1756	IFRS 16.70(a)	Ch.23, p.1743
IFRS 16.35	Ch.23, p.1756	IFRS 16.70(c)	Ch.23, p.1745
IFRS 16.36	Ch.23, p.1756	IFRS 16.71	Ch.23, p.1785
IFRS 16.37	Ch.23, p.1756	IFRS 16.72	Ch.23, p.1786
IFRS 16.38	Ch.23, p.1756	IFRS 16.73	Ch.23, p.1786
IFRS 16.38(b)	Ch.23, p.1746	IFRS 16.74	Ch.23, p.1786
IFRS 16.39	Ch.23, p.1748	IFRS 16.75	Ch.23, p.1787
IFRS 16.39	Ch.23, p.1758	IFRS 16.76	Ch.23, p.1787
IFRS 16.40	Ch.23, p.1758	IFRS 16.77	Ch.23, p.1787
IFRS 16.41	Ch.23, p.1758	IFRS 16.77	Ch.23, p.1789
IFRS 16.42	Ch.23, p.1758	IFRS 16.77	Ch.51, p.4045
IFRS 16.42(a)	Ch.23, p.1745	IFRS 16.78	Ch.23, p.1788
IFRS 16.42(b)	Ch.23, p.1744	IFRS 16.79	Ch.23, p.1793
IFRS 16.43	Ch.23, p.1758	IFRS 16.80	Ch.23, p.1793
IFRS 16.44	Ch.23, p.1759	IFRS 16.81	Ch.19, p.1462
IFRS 16.45	Ch.23, p.1760	IFRS 16.81	Ch.23, p.1791
IFRS 16.46	Ch.23, p.1760	IFRS 16.81-88	Ch.42, p.3280

IFRS 16.82	Ch.23, p.1791	IFRS 16.B7	Ch.23, p.1753
IFRS 16.83	Ch.19, p.1463	IFRS 16.B7	Ch.23, p.1799
IFRS 16.83	Ch.23, p.1791	IFRS 16.B8	Ch.23, p.1753
IFRS 16.84	Ch.23, p.1791	IFRS 16.B9	Ch.17, p.1373
IFRS 16.85	Ch.23, p.1791	IFRS 16.B9	Ch.23, p.1714
IFRS 16.86	Ch.23, p.1791	IFRS 16.B9	Ch.25, p.1857
IFRS 16.87	Ch.23, p.1793	IFRS 16.B10	Ch.23, p.1714
IFRS 16.88	Ch.23, p.1796	IFRS 16.B11	Ch.23, p.1714
IFRS 16.89	Ch.23, p.1797	IFRS 16.B12	Ch.23, p.1714
IFRS 16.90	Ch.23, p.1797	IFRS 16.B13	Ch.23, p.1716
IFRS 16.91	Ch.23, p.1797	IFRS 16.B14	Ch.23, p.1720
IFRS 16.92	Ch.23, p.1797	IFRS 16.B14	Ch.43, p.3531
IFRS 16.93	Ch.23, p.1797	IFRS 16.B14	Ch.43, p.3541
IFRS 16.94	Ch.23, p.1797	IFRS 16.B14(a)-(b)	Ch.43, p.3531
IFRS 16.95	Ch.23, p.1798	IFRS 16.B15	Ch.23, p.1720
IFRS 16.96	Ch.23, p.1798	IFRS 16.B16	Ch.23, p.1720
IFRS 16.97	Ch.23, p.1798	IFRS 16.B17	Ch.23, p.1720
IFRS 16.98	Ch.23, p.1801	IFRS 16.B18	Ch.23, p.1721
IFRS 16.99	Ch.23, p.1801	IFRS 16.B19	Ch.23, p.1721
IFRS 16.99	Ch.40, p.3170	IFRS 16.B19	Ch.43, p.3531
IFRS 16.100	Ch.23, p.1803	IFRS 16.B19	Ch.43, p.3541
IFRS 16.100	Ch.40, p.3170	IFRS 16.B20	Ch.23, p.1717
IFRS 16.101	Ch.23, p.1805	IFRS 16.B21	Ch.23, p.1722
IFRS 16.101	Ch.40, p.3170	IFRS 16.B22	Ch.23, p.1722
IFRS 16.102	Ch.23, p.1805	IFRS 16.B23	Ch.23, p.1722
IFRS 16.103	Ch.23, p.1807	IFRS 16.B24	Ch.23, p.1722
IFRS 16.103	Ch.40, p.3170	IFRS 16.B24	Ch.23, p.1724
IFRS 16 Appendix A	Ch.5, p.303	IFRS 16.B24	Ch.43, p.3545
IFRS 16 Appendix A	Ch.17, p.1373	IFRS 16.B25	Ch.23, p.1723
IFRS 16 Appendix A	Ch.19, p.1462	IFRS 16.B26	Ch.23, p.1723
IFRS 16 Appendix A	Ch.19, p.1463	IFRS 16.B27	Ch.23, p.1724
IFRS 16 Appendix A	Ch.23, p.1711	IFRS 16.B28	Ch.23, p.1725
IFRS 16 Appendix A	Ch.23, p.1713	IFRS 16.B29	Ch.23, p.1726
IFRS 16 Appendix A	Ch.23, p.1720	IFRS 16.B30	Ch.23, p.1726
IFRS 16 Appendix A	Ch.23, p.1735	IFRS 16.B31	Ch.23, p.1726
IFRS 16 Appendix A	Ch.23, p.1742	IFRS 16.B32	Ch.23, p.1728
IFRS 16 Appendix A	Ch.23, p.1743	IFRS 16.B32	Ch.27, p.2030
IFRS 16 Appendix A	Ch.23, p.1749	IFRS 16.B33	Ch.23, p.1728
IFRS 16 Appendix A	Ch.23, p.1750	IFRS 16.B33	Ch.23, p.1729
IFRS 16 Appendix A	Ch.23, p.1751	IFRS 16.B33	Ch.27, p.2030
IFRS 16 Appendix A	Ch.23, p.1752	IFRS 16.B34	Ch.23, p.1739
IFRS 16 Appendix A	Ch.23, p.1759	IFRS 16.B35	Ch.23, p.1739
IFRS 16 Appendix A	Ch.23, p.1780	IFRS 16.B36	Ch.23, p.1736
IFRS 16 Appendix A	Ch.23, p.1784	IFRS 16.B37	Ch.23, p.1736
IFRS 16 Appendix A	Ch.23, p.1792	IFRS 16.B37	Ch.23, p.1737
IFRS 16 Appendix A	Ch.23, p.1798	IFRS 16.B38	Ch.23, p.1737
IFRS 16 Appendix A	Ch.23, p.1806	IFRS 16.B39	Ch.23, p.1738
IFRS 16 Appendix A	Ch.40, p.3169	IFRS 16.B40	Ch.23, p.1738
IFRS 16 Appendix A	Ch.43, p.3530	IFRS 16.B41	Ch.23, p.1741
IFRS 16 Appendix A	Ch.43, p.3553	IFRS 16.B42	Ch.23, p.1743
IFRS 16.B1	Ch.23, p.1773	IFRS 16.B43	Ch.23, p.1735
IFRS 16.B1	Ch.23, p.1796	IFRS 16.B44	Ch.23, p.1735
IFRS 16.B2	Ch.23, p.1734	IFRS 16.B45	Ch.23, p.1735
IFRS 16.B3	Ch.23, p.1753	IFRS 16.B46	Ch.23, p.1735
IFRS 16.B3-B8	Ch.5, p.303	IFRS 16.B47	Ch.23, p.1736
IFRS 16.B4	Ch.23, p.1753	IFRS 16.B48	Ch.23, p.1779
IFRS 16.B5	Ch.23, p.1753	IFRS 16.B49	Ch.23, p.1780
IFRS 16.B6	Ch.23, p.1753	IFRS 16.B50	Ch.23, p.1780

IFRS 16.B51	Ch.23, p.1780	IFRS 16.BC182	Ch.19, p.1445
IFRS 16.B52	Ch.23, p.1807	IFRS 16.BC199	Ch.23, p.1773
IFRS 16.B53	Ch.23, p.1781	IFRS 16.BC222	Ch.23, p.1778
IFRS 16.B54	Ch.23, p.1783	IFRS 16.BC235	Ch.23, p.1800
IFRS 16.B55	Ch.23, p.1783	IFRS 16.BC236	Ch.23, p.1800
IFRS 16.B56	Ch.23, p.1729	IFRS 16.BC262	Ch.23, p.1802
IFRS 16.B56	Ch.23, p.1783	IFRS 16.BC266	Ch.40, p.3170
IFRS 16.B57	Ch.23, p.1729	IFRS 16.BC287	Ch.23, p.1811
IFRS 16.B57	Ch.23, p.1783	IFRS 16.BC298	Ch.23, p.1808
IFRS 16.B58	Ch.23, p.1799		
IFRS 16.C1	Ch.23, p.1808		
IFRS 16.C1	Ch.41, p.3240		

IFRS 17

IFRS 16.C2	Ch.23, p.1809	IFRS 17.IN4	Ch.56, p.4681
IFRS 16.C3	Ch.23, p.1809	IFRS 17.IN5	Ch.56, p.4681
IFRS 16.C4	Ch.23, p.1809	IFRS 17.IN7	Ch.56, p.4682
IFRS 16.C4	Ch.25, p.1857	IFRS 17.IN8	Ch.56, p.4682
IFRS 16.C5	Ch.23, p.1809	IFRS 17.1	Ch.56, p.4683
IFRS 16.C6	Ch.23, p.1809	IFRS 17.1	Ch.56, p.4898
IFRS 16.C7	Ch.23, p.1810	IFRS 17.2	Ch.56, p.4696
IFRS 16.C8	Ch.23, p.1810	IFRS 17.3	Ch.56, p.4686
IFRS 16.C9	Ch.23, p.1811	IFRS 17.3(c)	Ch.45, p.3594
IFRS 16.C10	Ch.23, p.1811	IFRS 17.3(c)	Ch.56, p.4855
IFRS 16.C11	Ch.23, p.1816	IFRS 17.4	Ch.56, p.4687
IFRS 16.C12	Ch.23, p.1819	IFRS 17.5	Ch.56, p.4687
IFRS 16.C13	Ch.23, p.1819	IFRS 17.7	Ch.56, p.4688
IFRS 16.C14	Ch.23, p.1818	IFRS 17.7(a)	Ch.56, p.4689
IFRS 16.C15	Ch.23, p.1818	IFRS 17.7(b)	Ch.56, p.4689
IFRS 16.C16	Ch.23, p.1818	IFRS 17.7(c)	Ch.56, p.4689
IFRS 16.C17	Ch.23, p.1818	IFRS 17.7(d)	Ch.56, p.4689
IFRS 16.C18	Ch.23, p.1818	IFRS 17.7(e)	Ch.26, p.1935
IFRS 16.C19	Ch.23, p.1819	IFRS 17.7(e)	Ch.45, p.3598
IFRS 16.C20	Ch.23, p.1819	IFRS 17.7(e)	Ch.56, p.4690
IFRS 16.IE4	Ch.23, p.1732	IFRS 17.7(f)	Ch.56, p.4691
IFRS 16.IE7	Ch.23, p.1760	IFRS 17.7(g)	Ch.45, p.3599
IFRS 16.IE8	Ch.23, p.1800	IFRS 17.7(g)	Ch.51, p.3958
IFRS 16.IE11	Ch.23, p.1807	IFRS 17.7(g)	Ch.56, p.4691
IFRS 16.BC58-BC66	Ch.42, p.3280	IFRS 17.7(h)	Ch.45, p.3595
IFRS 16.BC68(a)	Ch.43, p.3528	IFRS 17.7(h)	Ch.48, p.3837
IFRS 16.BC68(b)	Ch.42, p.3280	IFRS 17.7(h)	Ch.56, p.4692
IFRS 16.BC69	Ch.25, p.1857	IFRS 17.8	Ch.27, p.2025
IFRS 16.BC100	Ch.23, p.1753	IFRS 17.8	Ch.56, p.4693
IFRS 16.BC113	Ch.23, p.1720	IFRS 17.8A	Ch.45, p.3596
IFRS 16.BC113	Ch.43, p.3531	IFRS 17.8A	Ch.48, p.3835
IFRS 16.BC120	Ch.23, p.1723	IFRS 17.8A	Ch.56, p.4694
IFRS 16.BC121	Ch.23, p.1724	IFRS 17.9	Ch.56, p.4703
IFRS 16.BC126	Ch.43, p.3542	IFRS 17.9	Ch.56, p.4710
IFRS 16.BC130-BC132	Ch.23, p.1734	IFRS 17.9	Ch.56, p.4718
IFRS 16.BC135 (b)	Ch.23, p.1730	IFRS 17.10	Ch.56, p.4710
IFRS 16.BC139-BC140	Ch.40, p.3168	IFRS 17.11	Ch.56, p.4710
IFRS 16.BC165	Ch.23, p.1744	IFRS 17.11(a)	Ch.45, p.3595
IFRS 16.BC170	Ch.23, p.1745	IFRS 17.11(b)	Ch.45, p.3595
IFRS 16.BC173	Ch.23, p.1736	IFRS 17.11(b)	Ch.56, p.4716
IFRS 16.BC178	Ch.19, p.1444	IFRS 17.12	Ch.56, p.4710
IFRS 16.BC178	Ch.19, p.1467	IFRS 17.12	Ch.56, p.4720
IFRS 16.BC179	Ch.19, p.1471	IFRS 17.13	Ch.56, p.4703
IFRS 16.BC179(b)	Ch.19, p.1443	IFRS 17.13	Ch.56, p.4710
IFRS 16.BC180	Ch.19, p.1471	IFRS 17.14	Ch.56, p.4722
IFRS 16.BC181	Ch.19, p.1471		

IFRS 17.14	Ch.56, p.4723	IFRS 17.54	Ch.56, p.4809
IFRS 17.14	Ch.56, p.4872	IFRS 17.55	Ch.56, p.4812
IFRS 17.16	Ch.56, p.4722	IFRS 17.55(b)	Ch.56, p.4814
IFRS 17.17	Ch.56, p.4726	IFRS 17.56	Ch.56, p.4809
IFRS 17.18	Ch.56, p.4732	IFRS 17.57	Ch.56, p.4813
IFRS 17.18	Ch.56, p.4813	IFRS 17.58	Ch.56, p.4813
IFRS 17.19	Ch.56, p.4726	IFRS 17.59(a)	Ch.56, p.4809
IFRS 17.20	Ch.56, p.4727	IFRS 17.59(b)	Ch.56, p.4816
IFRS 17.20	Ch.56, p.4728	IFRS 17.61	Ch.56, p.4819
IFRS 17.21	Ch.56, p.4722	IFRS 17.62	Ch.56, p.4733
IFRS 17.21	Ch.56, p.4727	IFRS 17.62A	Ch.56, p.4734
IFRS 17.22	Ch.56, p.4728	IFRS 17.63	Ch.56, p.4822
IFRS 17.23	Ch.56, p.4725	IFRS 17.63	Ch.56, p.4828
IFRS 17.24	Ch.56, p.4723	IFRS 17.64	Ch.56, p.4828
IFRS 17.24	Ch.56, p.4725	IFRS 17.65	Ch.56, p.4823
IFRS 17.24	Ch.56, p.4730	IFRS 17.65A	Ch.56, p.4823
IFRS 17.25	Ch.56, p.4732	IFRS 17.66	Ch.56, p.4829
IFRS 17.26	Ch.56, p.4732	IFRS 17.66A	Ch.56, p.4824
IFRS 17.28	Ch.56, p.4732	IFRS 17.66B	Ch.56, p.4825
IFRS 17.28	Ch.56, p.4733	IFRS 17.66(bb)	Ch.56, p.4833
IFRS 17.28	Ch.56, p.4764	IFRS 17.67	Ch.56, p.4832
IFRS 17.28A	Ch.56, p.4735	IFRS 17.68	Ch.56, p.4819
IFRS 17.28A	Ch.56, p.4749	IFRS 17.69	Ch.56, p.4836
IFRS 17.28B	Ch.56, p.4735	IFRS 17.70	Ch.56, p.4837
IFRS 17.28C	Ch.56, p.4862	IFRS 17.70A	Ch.56, p.4837
IFRS 17.28D	Ch.56, p.4735	IFRS 17.71	Ch.56, p.4737
IFRS 17.28E-F	Ch.56, p.4801	IFRS 17.71	Ch.56, p.4856
IFRS 17.28F	Ch.56, p.4802	IFRS 17.72	Ch.56, p.4858
IFRS 17.29	Ch.56, p.4738	IFRS 17.72	Ch.56, p.4859
IFRS 17.30	Ch.15, p.1190	IFRS 17.73	Ch.56, p.4858
IFRS 17.30	Ch.56, p.4739	IFRS 17.74	Ch.56, p.4859
IFRS 17.31	Ch.56, p.4749	IFRS 17.75	Ch.56, p.4859
IFRS 17.31	Ch.56, p.4765	IFRS 17.76	Ch.56, p.4860
IFRS 17.32	Ch.56, p.4737	IFRS 17.77	Ch.56, p.4860
IFRS 17.32	Ch.56, p.4740	IFRS 17.77	Ch.56, p.4861
IFRS 17.33	Ch.56, p.4749	IFRS 17.78	Ch.56, p.4872
IFRS 17.33	Ch.56, p.4750	IFRS 17.79	Ch.56, p.4872
IFRS 17.34	Ch.56, p.4740	IFRS 17.80	Ch.56, p.4874
IFRS 17.35	Ch.56, p.4741	IFRS 17.81	Ch.56, p.4775
IFRS 17.36	Ch.56, p.4762	IFRS 17.81	Ch.56, p.4881
IFRS 17.37	Ch.56, p.4770	IFRS 17.82	Ch.56, p.4874
IFRS 17.38	Ch.56, p.4776	IFRS 17.83	Ch.56, p.4876
IFRS 17.39	Ch.56, p.4776	IFRS 17.84	Ch.56, p.4880
IFRS 17.40	Ch.56, p.4777	IFRS 17.85	Ch.56, p.4715
IFRS 17.41	Ch.56, p.4779	IFRS 17.85	Ch.56, p.4719
IFRS 17.42	Ch.56, p.4780	IFRS 17.85	Ch.56, p.4878
IFRS 17.43	Ch.56, p.4780	IFRS 17.86	Ch.56, p.4874
IFRS 17.44	Ch.56, p.4780	IFRS 17.86	Ch.56, p.4880
IFRS 17.45	Ch.56, p.4849	IFRS 17.86(c)	Ch.56, p.4874
IFRS 17.46	Ch.56, p.4784	IFRS 17.87	Ch.56, p.4881
IFRS 17.47	Ch.56, p.4794	IFRS 17.88	Ch.56, p.4883
IFRS 17.48	Ch.56, p.4794	IFRS 17.88	Ch.56, p.4886
IFRS 17.49	Ch.56, p.4794	IFRS 17.89	Ch.56, p.4892
IFRS 17.50	Ch.56, p.4794	IFRS 17.90	Ch.56, p.4886
IFRS 17.51	Ch.56, p.4795	IFRS 17.91	Ch.56, p.4862
IFRS 17.52	Ch.56, p.4795	IFRS 17.91(a)	Ch.56, p.4887
IFRS 17.53	Ch.56, p.4808	IFRS 17.91(b)	Ch.56, p.4895
IFRS 17.53	Ch.56, p.4812	IFRS 17.92	Ch.56, p.4882

IFRS 17.93	Ch.56, p.4898
IFRS 17.93	Ch.56, p.4900
IFRS 17.93	Ch.56, p.4912
IFRS 17.93(b)	Ch.56, p.4909
IFRS 17.94	Ch.56, p.4899
IFRS 17.95	Ch.56, p.4872
IFRS 17.95	Ch.56, p.4899
IFRS 17.96	Ch.56, p.4899
IFRS 17.97	Ch.56, p.4906
IFRS 17.98	Ch.56, p.4872
IFRS 17.98	Ch.56, p.4900
IFRS 17.99	Ch.56, p.4900
IFRS 17.99	Ch.56, p.4906
IFRS 17.100	Ch.56, p.4900
IFRS 17.100	Ch.56, p.4906
IFRS 17.100	Ch.56, p.4915
IFRS 17.101	Ch.56, p.4902
IFRS 17.102	Ch.56, p.4900
IFRS 17.103	Ch.56, p.4900
IFRS 17.103	Ch.56, p.4907
IFRS 17.104	Ch.56, p.4902
IFRS 17.105	Ch.56, p.4904
IFRS 17.105	Ch.56, p.4907
IFRS 17.105A	Ch.56, p.4904
IFRS 17.105B	Ch.56, p.4904
IFRS 17.106	Ch.56, p.4904
IFRS 17.107	Ch.56, p.4905
IFRS 17.108	Ch.56, p.4905
IFRS 17.109	Ch.56, p.4906
IFRS 17.109A	Ch.56, p.4906
IFRS 17.110	Ch.56, p.4907
IFRS 17.111	Ch.56, p.4908
IFRS 17.112	Ch.56, p.4908
IFRS 17.113	Ch.56, p.4908
IFRS 17.114	Ch.56, p.4908
IFRS 17.115	Ch.56, p.4908
IFRS 17.116	Ch.56, p.4909
IFRS 17.117	Ch.56, p.4909
IFRS 17.118	Ch.56, p.4909
IFRS 17.119	Ch.56, p.4910
IFRS 17.120	Ch.56, p.4910
IFRS 17.121	Ch.56, p.4912
IFRS 17.122	Ch.56, p.4912
IFRS 17.123	Ch.56, p.4912
IFRS 17.124	Ch.56, p.4912
IFRS 17.125	Ch.56, p.4912
IFRS 17.126	Ch.56, p.4918
IFRS 17.127	Ch.56, p.4913
IFRS 17.128	Ch.56, p.4914
IFRS 17.129	Ch.56, p.4915
IFRS 17.130	Ch.56, p.4915
IFRS 17.131	Ch.56, p.4917
IFRS 17.132	Ch.56, p.4917
IFRS 17 Appendix A	Ch.45, p.3593
IFRS 17 Appendix A	Ch.56, p.4684
IFRS 17 Appendix A	Ch.56, p.4695
IFRS 17 Appendix A	Ch.56, p.4698
IFRS 17 Appendix A	Ch.56, p.4715
IFRS 17 Appendix A	Ch.56, p.4735
IFRS 17 Appendix A	Ch.56, p.4758
IFRS 17 Appendix A	Ch.56, p.4778
IFRS 17 Appendix A	Ch.56, p.4779
IFRS 17 Appendix A	Ch.56, p.4791
IFRS 17 Appendix A	Ch.56, p.4796
IFRS 17 Appendix A	Ch.56, p.4817
IFRS 17 Appendix A	Ch.56, p.4851
IFRS 17 Appendix A	Ch.56, p.4855
IFRS 17.B2	Ch.56, p.4697
IFRS 17.B2-B30	Ch.45, p.3593
IFRS 17.B3	Ch.56, p.4697
IFRS 17.B4	Ch.56, p.4697
IFRS 17.B5	Ch.56, p.4697
IFRS 17.B5	Ch.56, p.4797
IFRS 17.B5	Ch.56, p.4835
IFRS 17.B5	Ch.56, p.4868
IFRS 17.B6	Ch.56, p.4698
IFRS 17.B7	Ch.56, p.4698
IFRS 17.B8	Ch.56, p.4698
IFRS 17.B9	Ch.56, p.4698
IFRS 17.B10	Ch.56, p.4699
IFRS 17.B11	Ch.56, p.4699
IFRS 17.B12	Ch.56, p.4699
IFRS 17.B13	Ch.56, p.4700
IFRS 17.B14	Ch.56, p.4700
IFRS 17.B15	Ch.56, p.4700
IFRS 17.B16	Ch.56, p.4703
IFRS 17.B17	Ch.56, p.4701
IFRS 17.B18	Ch.56, p.4701
IFRS 17.B19	Ch.56, p.4701
IFRS 17.B20	Ch.56, p.4701
IFRS 17.B21	Ch.56, p.4704
IFRS 17.B22	Ch.56, p.4703
IFRS 17.B23	Ch.56, p.4704
IFRS 17.B24	Ch.56, p.4706
IFRS 17.B25	Ch.56, p.4705
IFRS 17.B25	Ch.56, p.4857
IFRS 17.B26	Ch.56, p.4706
IFRS 17.B26(k)	Ch.45, p.3594
IFRS 17.B27	Ch.56, p.4708
IFRS 17.B27(a)	Ch.45, p.3594
IFRS 17.B27(c)	Ch.56, p.4703
IFRS 17.B27(f)	Ch.45, p.3596
IFRS 17.B27(g)	Ch.45, p.3594
IFRS 17.B28	Ch.56, p.4709
IFRS 17.B29	Ch.56, p.4709
IFRS 17.B30	Ch.45, p.3596
IFRS 17.B30	Ch.56, p.4709
IFRS 17.B31	Ch.56, p.4717
IFRS 17.B32	Ch.56, p.4717
IFRS 17.B33	Ch.56, p.4721
IFRS 17.B34	Ch.56, p.4721
IFRS 17.B35	Ch.56, p.4721
IFRS 17.B35A	Ch.56, p.4736
IFRS 17.B35A	Ch.56, p.4749
IFRS 17.B35B	Ch.56, p.4749
IFRS 17.B35C	Ch.56, p.4737

IFRS 17.B35D	Ch.56, p.4802	IFRS 17.B91	Ch.56, p.4772
IFRS 17.B37	Ch.56, p.4750	IFRS 17.B92	Ch.56, p.4773
IFRS 17.B38	Ch.56, p.4750	IFRS 17.B93	Ch.56, p.4864
IFRS 17.B39	Ch.56, p.4751	IFRS 17.B94	Ch.56, p.4865
IFRS 17.B40	Ch.56, p.4751	IFRS 17.B95	Ch.56, p.4865
IFRS 17.B41	Ch.56, p.4751	IFRS 17.B95A	Ch.56, p.4865
IFRS 17.B42	Ch.56, p.4752	IFRS 17.B95B	Ch.56, p.4865
IFRS 17.B43	Ch.56, p.4752	IFRS 17.B95C	Ch.56, p.4866
IFRS 17.B44	Ch.56, p.4752	IFRS 17.B95D	Ch.56, p.4866
IFRS 17.B45	Ch.56, p.4752	IFRS 17.B95E	Ch.56, p.4867
IFRS 17.B46	Ch.56, p.4752	IFRS 17.B95F	Ch.56, p.4867
IFRS 17.B47	Ch.56, p.4752	IFRS 17.B96	Ch.56, p.4720
IFRS 17.B48	Ch.56, p.4753	IFRS 17.B96	Ch.56, p.4781
IFRS 17.B49	Ch.56, p.4753	IFRS 17.B97	Ch.56, p.4783
IFRS 17.B50	Ch.56, p.4753	IFRS 17.B98	Ch.56, p.4784
IFRS 17.B51	Ch.56, p.4754	IFRS 17.B99	Ch.56, p.4785
IFRS 17.B52	Ch.56, p.4754	IFRS 17.B100	Ch.56, p.4785
IFRS 17.B53	Ch.56, p.4754	IFRS 17.B101	Ch.56, p.4844
IFRS 17.B54	Ch.56, p.4754	IFRS 17.B102	Ch.56, p.4844
IFRS 17.B55	Ch.56, p.4755	IFRS 17.B103	Ch.56, p.4846
IFRS 17.B56	Ch.56, p.4755	IFRS 17.B104	Ch.56, p.4843
IFRS 17.B57	Ch.56, p.4755	IFRS 17.B105	Ch.56, p.4844
IFRS 17.B58	Ch.56, p.4755	IFRS 17.B106	Ch.56, p.4844
IFRS 17.B59	Ch.56, p.4755	IFRS 17.B107	Ch.56, p.4845
IFRS 17.B60	Ch.56, p.4755	IFRS 17.B107(b)(i)	Ch.56, p.4842
IFRS 17.B61	Ch.56, p.4740	IFRS 17.B108	Ch.56, p.4846
IFRS 17.B62	Ch.56, p.4756	IFRS 17.B109	Ch.56, p.4837
IFRS 17.B63	Ch.56, p.4741	IFRS 17.B109	Ch.56, p.4839
IFRS 17.B64	Ch.56, p.4741	IFRS 17.B111	Ch.56, p.4849
IFRS 17.B65	Ch.56, p.4757	IFRS 17.B112	Ch.56, p.4849
IFRS 17.B65(c)	Ch.56, p.4804	IFRS 17.B113	Ch.56, p.4850
IFRS 17.B66	Ch.56, p.4762	IFRS 17.B113(a)	Ch.56, p.4849
IFRS 17.B66A	Ch.56, p.4776	IFRS 17.B114	Ch.56, p.4850
IFRS 17.B67	Ch.56, p.4840	IFRS 17.B115	Ch.56, p.4852
IFRS 17.B68	Ch.56, p.4840	IFRS 17.B116	Ch.56, p.4853
IFRS 17.B69	Ch.56, p.4841	IFRS 17.B117	Ch.56, p.4852
IFRS 17.B70	Ch.56, p.4841	IFRS 17.B117A	Ch.56, p.4853
IFRS 17.B71	Ch.56, p.4841	IFRS 17.B117A	Ch.56, p.4883
IFRS 17.B72-B73	Ch.56, p.4763	IFRS 17.B118	Ch.56, p.4853
IFRS 17.B73	Ch.56, p.4764	IFRS 17.B119	Ch.56, p.4785
IFRS 17.B74	Ch.56, p.4765	IFRS 17.B119A	Ch.56, p.4792
IFRS 17.B75	Ch.56, p.4765	IFRS 17.B119A	Ch.56, p.4851
IFRS 17.B76	Ch.56, p.4765	IFRS 17.B119B	Ch.56, p.4792
IFRS 17.B77	Ch.56, p.4766	IFRS 17.B119D	Ch.56, p.4825
IFRS 17.B78	Ch.56, p.4766	IFRS 17.B119E	Ch.56, p.4825
IFRS 17.B79	Ch.56, p.4766	IFRS 17.B119E	Ch.56, p.4835
IFRS 17.B80	Ch.56, p.4767	IFRS 17.B119F	Ch.56, p.4833
IFRS 17.B81	Ch.56, p.4767	IFRS 17.B120	Ch.56, p.4876
IFRS 17.B82	Ch.56, p.4768	IFRS 17.B121	Ch.56, p.4877
IFRS 17.B83	Ch.56, p.4768	IFRS 17.B123	Ch.56, p.4759
IFRS 17.B84	Ch.56, p.4768	IFRS 17.B123	Ch.56, p.4760
IFRS 17.B85	Ch.56, p.4769	IFRS 17.B123	Ch.56, p.4877
IFRS 17.B86	Ch.56, p.4770	IFRS 17.B123A	Ch.56, p.4878
IFRS 17.B87	Ch.56, p.4770	IFRS 17.B124	Ch.56, p.4878
IFRS 17.B87	Ch.56, p.4771	IFRS 17.B125	Ch.56, p.4759
IFRS 17.B88	Ch.56, p.4771	IFRS 17.B125	Ch.56, p.4878
IFRS 17.B89	Ch.56, p.4771	IFRS 17.B126	Ch.56, p.4815
IFRS 17.B90	Ch.56, p.4771	IFRS 17.B126	Ch.56, p.4880

IFRS 17.B127	Ch.56, p.4815	IFRS 17.C25	Ch.56, p.4924
IFRS 17.B127	Ch.56, p.4880	IFRS 17.C26	Ch.56, p.4924
IFRS 17.B128	Ch.56, p.4881	IFRS 17.C27	Ch.56, p.4924
IFRS 17.B129	Ch.56, p.4883	IFRS 17.C28	Ch.56, p.4921
IFRS 17.B130	Ch.56, p.4887	IFRS 17.C29	Ch.56, p.4938
IFRS 17.B131	Ch.56, p.4887	IFRS 17.C30	Ch.56, p.4939
IFRS 17.B132(a)	Ch.56, p.4888	IFRS 17.C31	Ch.56, p.4939
IFRS 17.B132(b)	Ch.56, p.4889	IFRS 17.C32	Ch.56, p.4939
IFRS 17.B132(c)	Ch.56, p.4889	IFRS 17.C33	Ch.56, p.4939
IFRS 17.B133	Ch.56, p.4892	IFRS 17.C34	Ch.56, p.4919
IFRS 17.B134	Ch.56, p.4893	IFRS 17.IE43-51	Ch.56, p.4718
IFRS 17.B135	Ch.56, p.4895	IFRS 17.IE51-55	Ch.56, p.4721
IFRS 17.B136	Ch.56, p.4895	IFRS 17.IE95(c)	Ch.56, p.4795
IFRS 17.B137	Ch.56, p.4896	IFRS 17.IE124-129	Ch.56, p.4823
IFRS 17.B137	Ch.56, p.4924	IFRS 17.IE130-138	Ch.56, p.4830
IFRS 17.C1	Ch.56, p.4919	IFRS 17.IE138A-138K	Ch.56, p.4826
IFRS 17.C2	Ch.56, p.4919	IFRS 17.IE138L-138M	Ch.56, p.4833
IFRS 17.C3	Ch.56, p.4919	IFRS 17.IE139-151	Ch.56, p.4866
IFRS 17.C3(a)	Ch.56, p.4921	IFRS 17.IE155-IE172	Ch.56, p.4889
IFRS 17.C3(b)	Ch.56, p.4922	IFRS 17.IE173-IE185	Ch.56, p.4893
IFRS 17.C4	Ch.56, p.4923	IFRS 17.IE186-IE191	Ch.56, p.4930
IFRS 17.C5	Ch.56, p.4919	IFRS 17.IE192-IE199	Ch.56, p.4932
IFRS 17.C5A	Ch.56, p.4919	IFRS 17.BC34	Ch.56, p.4719
IFRS 17.C5B	Ch.56, p.4920	IFRS 17.BC63	Ch.56, p.4687
IFRS 17.C6	Ch.56, p.4925	IFRS 17.BC64	Ch.56, p.4687
IFRS 17.C6(a)	Ch.56, p.4920	IFRS 17.BC65(a)	Ch.45, p.3594
IFRS 17.C7	Ch.56, p.4925	IFRS 17.BC65(c)	Ch.18, p.1408
IFRS 17.C8	Ch.56, p.4925	IFRS 17.BC66	Ch.45, p.3599
IFRS 17.C9	Ch.56, p.4927	IFRS 17.BC66	Ch.56, p.4691
IFRS 17.C9A	Ch.56, p.4927	IFRS 17.BC67	Ch.56, p.4696
IFRS 17.C10	Ch.56, p.4927	IFRS 17.BC69	Ch.56, p.4696
IFRS 17.C11	Ch.56, p.4927	IFRS 17.BC73	Ch.56, p.4699
IFRS 17.C12	Ch.56, p.4928	IFRS 17.BC74	Ch.56, p.4699
IFRS 17.C13	Ch.56, p.4928	IFRS 17.BC75	Ch.56, p.4699
IFRS 17.C14	Ch.56, p.4928	IFRS 17.BC77	Ch.56, p.4702
IFRS 17.C14A	Ch.56, p.4929	IFRS 17.BC78	Ch.56, p.4701
IFRS 17.C14B	Ch.56, p.4928	IFRS 17.BC79	Ch.56, p.4702
IFRS 17.C14C	Ch.56, p.4929	IFRS 17.BC79	Ch.56, p.4703
IFRS 17.C14D	Ch.56, p.4929	IFRS 17.BC80	Ch.56, p.4702
IFRS 17.C15	Ch.56, p.4929	IFRS 17.BC80	Ch.56, p.4705
IFRS 17.C16	Ch.56, p.4929	IFRS 17.BC80	Ch.56, p.4706
IFRS 17.C16A	Ch.56, p.4930	IFRS 17.BC81	Ch.56, p.4706
IFRS 17.C16B	Ch.56, p.4930	IFRS 17.BC83	Ch.56, p.4855
IFRS 17.C16C	Ch.56, p.4930	IFRS 17.BC87(d)	Ch.56, p.4690
IFRS 17.C17	Ch.56, p.4931	IFRS 17.BC89	Ch.56, p.4689
IFRS 17.C17A	Ch.56, p.4930	IFRS 17.BC90	Ch.56, p.4689
IFRS 17.C18	Ch.56, p.4933	IFRS 17.BC91	Ch.56, p.4690
IFRS 17.C19	Ch.56, p.4934	IFRS 17.BC93	Ch.56, p.4690
IFRS 17.C20	Ch.56, p.4935	IFRS 17.BC94	Ch.56, p.4691
IFRS 17.C20A	Ch.56, p.4936	IFRS 17.BC94B	Ch.45, p.3595
IFRS 17.C20B	Ch.56, p.4936	IFRS 17.BC94B	Ch.48, p.3836
IFRS 17.C21-C22	Ch.56, p.4936	IFRS 17.BC94B	Ch.56, p.4692
IFRS 17.C22A	Ch.56, p.4936	IFRS 17.BC94C	Ch.45, p.3595
IFRS 17.C23	Ch.56, p.4936	IFRS 17.BC94C	Ch.56, p.4692
IFRS 17.C23	Ch.56, p.4937	IFRS 17.BC94E	Ch.56, p.4694
IFRS 17.C24	Ch.56, p.4937	IFRS 17.BC94F	Ch.56, p.4694
IFRS 17.C24A	Ch.56, p.4937	IFRS 17.BC95	Ch.56, p.4693
IFRS 17.C24B	Ch.56, p.4937	IFRS 17.BC96-97	Ch.56, p.4693

IFRS 17.BC99	Ch.56, p.4710	IFRS 17.BC236B-C	Ch.56, p.4898
IFRS 17.BC104	Ch.56, p.4712	IFRS 17.BC240	Ch.56, p.4843
IFRS 17.BC105(a)	Ch.56, p.4713	IFRS 17.BC241	Ch.56, p.4843
IFRS 17.BC105(b)	Ch.56, p.4713	IFRS 17.BC244	Ch.56, p.4843
IFRS 17.BC108	Ch.45, p.3595	IFRS 17.BC245(a)	Ch.56, p.4845
IFRS 17.BC108	Ch.56, p.4716	IFRS 17.BC245(b)	Ch.56, p.4845
IFRS 17.BC108(b)	Ch.56, p.4719	IFRS 17.BC245(b)(ii)	Ch.56, p.4848
IFRS 17.BC109	Ch.56, p.4716	IFRS 17.BC248	Ch.56, p.4837
IFRS 17.BC111	Ch.56, p.4720	IFRS 17.BC256B	Ch.56, p.4853
IFRS 17.BC112	Ch.56, p.4720	IFRS 17.BC256C	Ch.56, p.4854
IFRS 17.BC113	Ch.56, p.4721	IFRS 17.BC256D-F	Ch.56, p.4854
IFRS 17.BC114	Ch.56, p.4717	IFRS 17.BC265	Ch.56, p.4804
IFRS 17.BC114	Ch.56, p.4721	IFRS 17.BC265fn27	Ch.56, p.4804
IFRS 17.BC114	Ch.56, p.4806	IFRS 17.BC269B	Ch.56, p.4805
IFRS 17.BC119	Ch.56, p.4725	IFRS 17.BC277	Ch.56, p.4739
IFRS 17.BC129	Ch.56, p.4726	IFRS 17.BC278	Ch.56, p.4739
IFRS 17.BC132	Ch.56, p.4727	IFRS 17.BC279	Ch.56, p.4786
IFRS 17.BC133	Ch.56, p.4728	IFRS 17.BC280	Ch.56, p.4786
IFRS 17.BC136	Ch.56, p.4728	IFRS 17.BC282	Ch.56, p.4786
IFRS 17.BC137	Ch.56, p.4728	IFRS 17.BC283	Ch.56, p.4787
IFRS 17.BC138	Ch.56, p.4728	IFRS 17.BC283B	Ch.56, p.4791
IFRS 17.BC138	Ch.56, p.4841	IFRS 17.BC283C	Ch.56, p.4792
IFRS 17.BC139	Ch.56, p.4725	IFRS 17.BC283D-E	Ch.56, p.4792
IFRS 17.BC139J	Ch.56, p.4730	IFRS 17.BC283I	Ch.56, p.4761
IFRS 17.BC139K	Ch.56, p.4730	IFRS 17.BC287	Ch.56, p.4795
IFRS 17.BC139L	Ch.56, p.4731	IFRS 17.BC298	Ch.56, p.4818
IFRS 17.BC139M	Ch.56, p.4731	IFRS 17.BC302	Ch.56, p.4818
IFRS 17.BC139N	Ch.56, p.4731	IFRS 17.BC304	Ch.56, p.4734
IFRS 17.BC139O	Ch.56, p.4731	IFRS 17.BC305(a)	Ch.56, p.4734
IFRS 17.BC139P	Ch.56, p.4731	IFRS 17.BC305(b)	Ch.56, p.4734
IFRS 17.BC139T	Ch.56, p.4729	IFRS 17.BC308	Ch.56, p.4828
IFRS 17.BC162	Ch.56, p.4742	IFRS 17.BC309	Ch.56, p.4832
IFRS 17.BC163	Ch.56, p.4742	IFRS 17.BC309E	Ch.56, p.4820
IFRS 17.BC164	Ch.56, p.4743	IFRS 17.BC309F	Ch.56, p.4820
IFRS 17.BC166	Ch.56, p.4756	IFRS 17.BC312	Ch.56, p.4823
IFRS 17.BC168	Ch.56, p.4756	IFRS 17.BC314	Ch.56, p.4829
IFRS 17.BC169	Ch.56, p.4756	IFRS 17.BC315	Ch.56, p.4830
IFRS 17.BC170	Ch.56, p.4841	IFRS 17.BC315C	Ch.56, p.4825
IFRS 17.BC170A	Ch.56, p.4762	IFRS 17.BC315E	Ch.56, p.4825
IFRS 17.BC172	Ch.56, p.4840	IFRS 17.BC315F	Ch.56, p.4826
IFRS 17.BC182(a)	Ch.56, p.4757	IFRS 17.BC315G	Ch.56, p.4826
IFRS 17.BC183	Ch.56, p.4759	IFRS 17.BC315H	Ch.56, p.4825
IFRS 17.BC184B	Ch.56, p.4736	IFRS 17.BC322	Ch.56, p.4860
IFRS 17.BC184C-D	Ch.56, p.4736	IFRS 17.BC327A	Ch.56, p.4870
IFRS 17.BC184E	Ch.56, p.4736	IFRS 17.BC327B-C	Ch.56, p.4864
IFRS 17.BC184F	Ch.56, p.4736	IFRS 17.BC327E	Ch.56, p.4869
IFRS 17.BC184H	Ch.56, p.4764	IFRS 17.BC327G	Ch.56, p.4869
IFRS 17.BC184J	Ch.56, p.4802	IFRS 17.BC327I	Ch.56, p.4868
IFRS 17.BC184K	Ch.56, p.4802	IFRS 17.BC330B	Ch.56, p.4874
IFRS 17.BC184N	Ch.56, p.4776	IFRS 17.BC330C	Ch.56, p.4873
IFRS 17.BC209	Ch.56, p.4770	IFRS 17.BC330D	Ch.56, p.4873
IFRS 17.BC213	Ch.56, p.4772	IFRS 17.BC342A	Ch.56, p.4882
IFRS 17.BC214	Ch.56, p.4772	IFRS 17.BC347	Ch.56, p.4898
IFRS 17.BC217	Ch.56, p.4773	IFRS 17.BC348	Ch.56, p.4899
IFRS 17.BC228	Ch.56, p.4764	IFRS 17.BC349	Ch.56, p.4899
IFRS 17.BC235	Ch.56, p.4783	IFRS 17.BC369-371	Ch.56, p.4918
IFRS 17.BC235fn	Ch.56, p.4783	IFRS 17.BC373	Ch.56, p.4920
IFRS 17.BC236	Ch.56, p.4896	IFRS 17.BC374	Ch.56, p.4923

IFRS 17.BC377	Ch.56, p.4920	IAS 1.7(i)-(j)	Ch.56, p.4874
IFRS 17.BC378	Ch.56, p.4920	IAS 1.8	Ch.3, p.133
IFRS 17.BC380A	Ch.56, p.4926	IAS 1.9	Ch.3, p.116
IFRS 17.BC380B	Ch.56, p.4926	IAS 1.10	Ch.3, p.134
IFRS 17.BC380C	Ch.56, p.4925	IAS 1.10	Ch.40, p.3138
IFRS 17.BC380C	Ch.56, p.4926	IAS 1.10(f)	Ch.41, p.3232
IFRS 17.BC380D	Ch.56, p.4925	IAS 1.10-10A	Ch.3, p.121
IFRS 17.BC382A	Ch.56, p.4927	IAS 1.10-11	Ch.3, p.116
IFRS 17.BC384A-B	Ch.56, p.4935	IAS 1.10-11	Ch.3, p.121
IFRS 17.BC390	Ch.56, p.4921	IAS 1.10A	Ch.3, p.134
IFRS 17.BC391	Ch.56, p.4927	IAS 1.10A	Ch.37, p.3061
IFRS 17.BC392	Ch.56, p.4927	IAS 1.10A	Ch.41, p.3228
IFRS 17.BC393C	Ch.56, p.4922	IAS 1.11	Ch.40, p.3135
IFRS 17.BC393D-E	Ch.56, p.4922	IAS 1.13	Ch.3, p.117
IFRS 17.BC398A-B	Ch.56, p.4941	IAS 1.14	Ch.3, p.117
IFRS 17.BC407	Ch.5, p.266	IAS 1.15	Ch.3, p.152
		IAS 1.15	Ch.45, p.3606
		IAS 1.15-35	Ch.41, p.3203
		IAS 1.16	Ch.1, p.22

IAS 1 (2023)

IAS 1(2023).74	Ch.38, p.3086	IAS 1.16	Ch.3, p.120
IAS 1(2023).76	Ch.38, p.3086	IAS 1.16	Ch.41, p.3224
IAS 1(2023).76A	Ch.15, p.1219	IAS 1.17	Ch.3, p.153
IAS 1(2023).76A	Ch.54, p.4516	IAS 1.17	Ch.36, p.3012
IAS 1(2023).76B	Ch.54, p.4516	IAS 1.17(c)	Ch.43, p.3357
IAS 1(2023).136U	Ch.54, p.4520	IAS 1.18	Ch.3, p.153
IAS 1(2023).139U	Ch.3, p.126	IAS 1.19	Ch.3, p.154
		IAS 1.19	Ch.36, p.3012
		IAS 1.20-21	Ch.3, p.154
		IAS 1.22	Ch.3, p.154

IAS 1

IAS 1.1	Ch.3, p.114	IAS 1.23	Ch.3, p.155
IAS 1.2	Ch.3, p.114	IAS 1.24	Ch.3, p.153
IAS 1.2	Ch.5, p.231	IAS 1.25	Ch.3, p.155
IAS 1.3	Ch.3, p.114	IAS 1.25	Ch.38, p.3083
IAS 1.4	Ch.3, p.114	IAS 1.25	Ch.41, p.3226
IAS 1.4	Ch.41, p.3203	IAS 1.26	Ch.3, p.155
IAS 1.4	Ch.41, p.3226	IAS 1.26	Ch.41, p.3226
IAS 1.5	Ch.3, p.114	IAS 1.27	Ch.3, p.156
IAS 1.6	Ch.3, p.114	IAS 1.28	Ch.3, p.156
IAS 1.7	Ch.3, p.114	IAS 1.29	Ch.3, p.157
IAS 1.7	Ch.3, p.115	IAS 1.29	Ch.33, p.2568
IAS 1.7	Ch.3, p.117	IAS 1.29	Ch.54, p.4511
IAS 1.7	Ch.3, p.119	IAS 1.30	Ch.3, p.157
IAS 1.7	Ch.3, p.133	IAS 1.30	Ch.3, p.158
IAS 1.7	Ch.3, p.134	IAS 1.30A	Ch.2, p.50
IAS 1.7	Ch.3, p.140	IAS 1.30A	Ch.3, p.157
IAS 1.7	Ch.3, p.144	IAS 1.30A	Ch.3, p.161
IAS 1.7	Ch.3, p.157	IAS 1.31	Ch.3, p.158
IAS 1.7	Ch.3, p.158	IAS 1.31	Ch.39, p.3115
IAS 1.7	Ch.5, p.231	IAS 1.32	Ch.3, p.159
IAS 1.7	Ch.7, p.502	IAS 1.32	Ch.23, p.1800
IAS 1.7	Ch.8, p.600	IAS 1.32	Ch.24, p.1841
IAS 1.7	Ch.16, p.1278	IAS 1.32	Ch.32, p.2406
IAS 1.7	Ch.36, p.3012	IAS 1.32	Ch.42, p.3315
IAS 1.7	Ch.39, p.3115	IAS 1.32	Ch.43, p.3409
IAS 1.7	Ch.41, p.3235	IAS 1.32	Ch.54, p.4487
IAS 1.7	Ch.41, p.3239	IAS 1.32	Ch.54, p.4491
		IAS 1.32-33	Ch.24, p.1841
		IAS 1.33	Ch.3, p.159

IAS 1.33	Ch.54, p.4487	IAS 1.54(ma)	Ch.56, p.4872
IAS 1.33	Ch.54, p.4508	IAS 1.54(n)	Ch.33, p.2568
IAS 1.34	Ch.3, p.159	IAS 1.54(n)	Ch.33, p.2611
IAS 1.34	Ch.27, p.2018	IAS 1.54(o)	Ch.33, p.2568
IAS 1.34	Ch.32, p.2406	IAS 1.54(o)	Ch.33, p.2611
IAS 1.34	Ch.42, p.3315	IAS 1.54(q)	Ch.54, p.4517
IAS 1.34	Ch.54, p.4487	IAS 1.54(r)	Ch.54, p.4517
IAS 1.34(a)	Ch.32, p.2406	IAS 1.55	Ch.3, p.128
IAS 1.35	Ch.3, p.159	IAS 1.55	Ch.17, p.1356
IAS 1.35	Ch.54, p.4487	IAS 1.55	Ch.40, p.3163
IAS 1.36	Ch.3, p.116	IAS 1.55	Ch.54, p.4508
IAS 1.36	Ch.5, p.237	IAS 1.55	Ch.54, p.4511
IAS 1.37	Ch.3, p.116	IAS 1.55	Ch.54, p.4517
IAS 1.37	Ch.5, p.238	IAS 1.55	Ch.56, p.4873
IAS 1.38	Ch.3, p.117	IAS 1.55A	Ch.3, p.130
IAS 1.38	Ch.3, p.118	IAS 1.55A	Ch.54, p.4509
IAS 1.38	Ch.5, p.237	IAS 1.56	Ch.3, p.124
IAS 1.38	Ch.5, p.343	IAS 1.56	Ch.3, p.125
IAS 1.38	Ch.39, p.3115	IAS 1.57	Ch.3, p.128
IAS 1.38	Ch.40, p.3145	IAS 1.57	Ch.3, p.129
IAS 1.38	Ch.41, p.3198	IAS 1.57	Ch.33, p.2568
IAS 1.38	Ch.41, p.3231	IAS 1.57	Ch.54, p.4508
IAS 1.38A	Ch.3, p.118	IAS 1.57	Ch.54, p.4511
IAS 1.38A	Ch.41, p.3198	IAS 1.57(a)	Ch.54, p.4508
IAS 1.38B	Ch.3, p.119	IAS 1.57(b)	Ch.54, p.4509
IAS 1.38C	Ch.3, p.118	IAS 1.58	Ch.3, p.128
IAS 1.38D	Ch.3, p.118	IAS 1.58	Ch.3, p.130
IAS 1.40A	Ch.3, p.118	IAS 1.58	Ch.54, p.4509
IAS 1.40A-40D	Ch.41, p.3198	IAS 1.58	Ch.54, p.4511
IAS 1.40C	Ch.3, p.118	IAS 1.59	Ch.3, p.128
IAS 1.41	Ch.3, p.119	IAS 1.59	Ch.54, p.4509
IAS 1.41	Ch.36, p.3010	IAS 1.60	Ch.3, p.122
IAS 1.41	Ch.41, p.3242	IAS 1.60	Ch.3, p.123
IAS 1.42	Ch.3, p.119	IAS 1.60	Ch.17, p.1356
IAS 1.43	Ch.3, p.119	IAS 1.60	Ch.55, p.4627
IAS 1.45	Ch.3, p.156	IAS 1.61	Ch.3, p.123
IAS 1.45	Ch.41, p.3242	IAS 1.62	Ch.3, p.122
IAS 1.46	Ch.3, p.156	IAS 1.63	Ch.3, p.123
IAS 1.48	Ch.3, p.121	IAS 1.64	Ch.3, p.123
IAS 1.49-50	Ch.3, p.120	IAS 1.65	Ch.3, p.123
IAS 1.51	Ch.3, p.120	IAS 1.66	Ch.3, p.122
IAS 1.52	Ch.3, p.120	IAS 1.66	Ch.3, p.124
IAS 1.53	Ch.3, p.120	IAS 1.66	Ch.42, p.3309
IAS 1.54	Ch.3, p.128	IAS 1.66	Ch.54, p.4515
IAS 1.54	Ch.3, p.129	IAS 1.67	Ch.3, p.122
IAS 1.54	Ch.7, p.546	IAS 1.67	Ch.17, p.1356
IAS 1.54	Ch.13, p.961	IAS 1.68	Ch.3, p.122
IAS 1.54	Ch.13, p.970	IAS 1.68	Ch.3, p.124
IAS 1.54	Ch.17, p.1356	IAS 1.68	Ch.22, p.1678
IAS 1.54	Ch.33, p.2568	IAS 1.69	Ch.3, p.122
IAS 1.54	Ch.41, p.3199	IAS 1.69	Ch.3, p.125
IAS 1.54	Ch.42, p.3308	IAS 1.69	Ch.32, p.2398
IAS 1.54	Ch.54, p.4508	IAS 1.69	Ch.54, p.4515
IAS 1.54	Ch.54, p.4511	IAS 1.69(d)	Ch.54, p.4516
IAS 1.54	Ch.55, p.4626	IAS 1.69(d)	Ch.54, p.4517
IAS 1.54-56	Ch.33, p.2609	IAS 1.70	Ch.3, p.122
IAS 1.54(da)	Ch.56, p.4872	IAS 1.70	Ch.3, p.125
IAS 1.54(e)	Ch.11, p.882	IAS 1.70	Ch.54, p.4511

IAS 1.71	Ch.3, p.125	IAS 1.85	Ch.40, p.3163
IAS 1.72	Ch.3, p.126	IAS 1.85	Ch.42, p.3283
IAS 1.73	Ch.3, p.126	IAS 1.85	Ch.54, p.4485
IAS 1.73	Ch.54, p.4516	IAS 1.85	Ch.56, p.4875
IAS 1.73	Ch.54, p.4517	IAS 1.85-86	Ch.3, p.134
IAS 1.74	Ch.3, p.126	IAS 1.85A	Ch.3, p.135
IAS 1.74	Ch.38, p.3086	IAS 1.85A	Ch.54, p.4485
IAS 1.75	Ch.3, p.126	IAS 1.85B	Ch.3, p.135
IAS 1.76	Ch.3, p.126	IAS 1.86	Ch.3, p.134
IAS 1.76	Ch.3, p.183	IAS 1.86	Ch.3, p.135
IAS 1.76	Ch.38, p.3079	IAS 1.86	Ch.54, p.4481
IAS 1.76	Ch.38, p.3080	IAS 1.86	Ch.54, p.4485
IAS 1.76	Ch.38, p.3086	IAS 1.87	Ch.3, p.148
IAS 1.77	Ch.3, p.130	IAS 1.87	Ch.54, p.4486
IAS 1.77	Ch.39, p.3124	IAS 1.88	Ch.3, p.133
IAS 1.77	Ch.54, p.4509	IAS 1.88	Ch.3, p.160
IAS 1.77	Ch.54, p.4517	IAS 1.88	Ch.35, p.2947
IAS 1.78	Ch.3, p.130	IAS 1.88	Ch.40, p.3150
IAS 1.78(b)	Ch.54, p.4509	IAS 1.89	Ch.3, p.160
IAS 1.78(e)	Ch.54, p.4517	IAS 1.90	Ch.3, p.145
IAS 1.79	Ch.3, p.131	IAS 1.90	Ch.33, p.2611
IAS 1.79(a)	Ch.54, p.4518	IAS 1.90	Ch.33, p.2613
IAS 1.79(a)(vi)	Ch.47, p.3742	IAS 1.91	Ch.3, p.140
IAS 1.79(b)	Ch.54, p.4517	IAS 1.91	Ch.3, p.145
IAS 1.80	Ch.3, p.131	IAS 1.91	Ch.33, p.2611
IAS 1.80	Ch.54, p.4518	IAS 1.92-93	Ch.3, p.144
IAS 1.80A	Ch.3, p.131	IAS 1.92	Ch.53, p.4295
IAS 1.80A	Ch.54, p.4518	IAS 1.92	Ch.53, p.4297
IAS 1.81A	Ch.3, p.136	IAS 1.92	Ch.53, p.4379
IAS 1.81A	Ch.3, p.140	IAS 1.94	Ch.3, p.141
IAS 1.81B	Ch.3, p.136	IAS 1.94	Ch.3, p.144
IAS 1.81B	Ch.3, p.141	IAS 1.95	Ch.3, p.144
IAS 1.81B	Ch.7, p.546	IAS 1.96	Ch.3, p.145
IAS 1.81B	Ch.13, p.961	IAS 1.96	Ch.54, p.4490
IAS 1.81B(a)	Ch.54, p.4485	IAS 1.97	Ch.3, p.119
IAS 1.81B(b)	Ch.54, p.4490	IAS 1.97	Ch.3, p.148
IAS 1.82	Ch.3, p.135	IAS 1.97	Ch.19, p.1509
IAS 1.82	Ch.13, p.970	IAS 1.97	Ch.21, p.1671
IAS 1.82	Ch.41, p.3199	IAS 1.97	Ch.40, p.3163
IAS 1.82(a)	Ch.51, p.4034	IAS 1.97	Ch.54, p.4486
IAS 1.82(a)	Ch.53, p.4379	IAS 1.98	Ch.3, p.148
IAS 1.82(a)	Ch.54, p.4482	IAS 1.98	Ch.54, p.4486
IAS 1.82(a)(ii)	Ch.56, p.4874	IAS 1.99	Ch.3, p.137
IAS 1.82(aa)	Ch.54, p.4410	IAS 1.99	Ch.42, p.3283
IAS 1.82(aa)	Ch.54, p.4482	IAS 1.99-100	Ch.3, p.136
IAS 1.82(ab)-(ac)	Ch.56, p.4874	IAS 1.100	Ch.3, p.137
IAS 1.82(b)	Ch.54, p.4483	IAS 1.101	Ch.3, p.137
IAS 1.82(ba)	Ch.51, p.4068	IAS 1.102	Ch.3, p.138
IAS 1.82(ba)	Ch.51, p.4069	IAS 1.103	Ch.3, p.140
IAS 1.82(ba)	Ch.54, p.4482	IAS 1.104	Ch.3, p.140
IAS 1.82(bb)-(bc)	Ch.56, p.4874	IAS 1.105	Ch.3, p.137
IAS 1.82(c)	Ch.11, p.883	IAS 1.105	Ch.3, p.138
IAS 1.82(ca)	Ch.54, p.4483	IAS 1.106	Ch.3, p.148
IAS 1.82(cb)	Ch.54, p.4483	IAS 1.106	Ch.7, p.546
IAS 1.82A	Ch.3, p.140	IAS 1.106	Ch.13, p.961
IAS 1.82A	Ch.11, p.884	IAS 1.106	Ch.47, p.3741
IAS 1.82A	Ch.54, p.4489	IAS 1.106	Ch.54, p.4490
IAS 1.85	Ch.20, p.1612	IAS 1.106(d)	Ch.13, p.967

IAS 1.106A	Ch.3, p.149	IAS 1.125-129	Ch.33, p.2473
IAS 1.106A	Ch.54, p.4490	IAS 1.125-129	Ch.33, p.2540
IAS 1.107	Ch.3, p.149	IAS 1.125-133	Ch.15, p.1244
IAS 1.107	Ch.54, p.4490	IAS 1.126	Ch.3, p.177
IAS 1.108	Ch.3, p.149	IAS 1.127	Ch.3, p.178
IAS 1.109	Ch.3, p.149	IAS 1.128	Ch.3, p.178
IAS 1.109	Ch.7, p.538	IAS 1.129	Ch.3, p.178
IAS 1.109	Ch.47, p.3741	IAS 1.130	Ch.3, p.178
IAS 1.110	Ch.3, p.149	IAS 1.131	Ch.3, p.179
IAS 1.111	Ch.3, p.121	IAS 1.132	Ch.3, p.178
IAS 1.112	Ch.3, p.151	IAS 1.133	Ch.3, p.178
IAS 1.112	Ch.40, p.3158	IAS 1.134	Ch.3, p.180
IAS 1.112	Ch.54, p.4513	IAS 1.135	Ch.3, p.180
IAS 1.113	Ch.3, p.151	IAS 1.135	Ch.55, p.4665
IAS 1.114	Ch.3, p.151	IAS 1.135	Ch.56, p.4918
IAS 1.116	Ch.3, p.151	IAS 1.136	Ch.3, p.180
IAS 1.117	Ch.3, p.174	IAS 1.136	Ch.55, p.4666
IAS 1.117	Ch.17, p.1361	IAS 1.136	Ch.56, p.4918
IAS 1.117	Ch.21, p.1671	IAS 1.136A	Ch.3, p.182
IAS 1.117	Ch.23, p.1780	IAS 1.136A	Ch.54, p.4463
IAS 1.117	Ch.32, p.2391	IAS 1.137	Ch.3, p.182
IAS 1.117	Ch.43, p.3511	IAS 1.137	Ch.38, p.3081
IAS 1.117	Ch.56, p.4910	IAS 1.137	Ch.39, p.3121
IAS 1.117-121	Ch.15, p.1244	IAS 1.138	Ch.3, p.183
IAS 1.117-124	Ch.42, p.3283	IAS 1.138(b)	Ch.13, p.957
IAS 1.118	Ch.3, p.163	IAS 1.138(c)	Ch.39, p.3113
IAS 1.118	Ch.3, p.174	IAS 1.IG3	Ch.3, p.131
IAS 1.119	Ch.3, p.174	IAS 1.IG6	Ch.33, p.2611
IAS 1.121	Ch.3, p.174	IAS 1.IG10-11	Ch.3, p.180
IAS 1.121	Ch.17, p.1361	IAS 1.IG Part I	Ch.3, p.131
IAS 1.122	Ch.3, p.175	IAS 1.IG Part I	Ch.3, p.138
IAS 1.122	Ch.13, p.956	IAS 1.IG Part I	Ch.3, p.141
IAS 1.122	Ch.15, p.1244	IAS 1.IG Part I	Ch.3, p.144
IAS 1.122	Ch.16, p.1267	IAS 1.IG Part I	Ch.3, p.146
IAS 1.122	Ch.19, p.1453	IAS 1.IG Part I	Ch.3, p.150
IAS 1.122	Ch.21, p.1672	IAS 1.BC13L	Ch.3, p.161
IAS 1.122	Ch.23, p.1781	IAS 1.BC13Q	Ch.3, p.157
IAS 1.122	Ch.26, p.1936	IAS 1.BC30F	Ch.3, p.161
IAS 1.122	Ch.33, p.2475	IAS 1.BC32C	Ch.3, p.118
IAS 1.122	Ch.35, p.2895	IAS 1.BC33	Ch.41, p.3232
IAS 1.122	Ch.40, p.3158	IAS 1.BC38G	Ch.3, p.130
IAS 1.122	Ch.43, p.3379	IAS 1.BC38I	Ch.54, p.4515
IAS 1.122	Ch.43, p.3438	IAS 1.BC38J	Ch.54, p.4515
IAS 1.122	Ch.43, p.3441	IAS 1.BC38L-P	Ch.3, p.125
IAS 1.122	Ch.54, p.4513	IAS 1.BC55	Ch.3, p.137
IAS 1.122	Ch.56, p.4909	IAS 1.BC56	Ch.3, p.137
IAS 1.122-133	Ch.32, p.2433	IAS 1.BC64	Ch.3, p.148
IAS 1.123	Ch.3, p.175	IAS 1.BC76D	Ch.3, p.151
IAS 1.124	Ch.3, p.175	IAS 1.BC84	Ch.3, p.179
IAS 1.125	Ch.3, p.177	IAS 1.BC86	Ch.3, p.180
IAS 1.125	Ch.23, p.1781	IAS 1.BC86	Ch.54, p.4472
IAS 1.125	Ch.26, p.2009	IAS 1.BC88	Ch.54, p.4473
IAS 1.125	Ch.33, p.2475	IAS 1.BC100B	Ch.3, p.182
IAS 1.125	Ch.42, p.3292	IAS 1.BC103	Ch.37, p.3039
IAS 1.125	Ch.43, p.3438		
IAS 1.125	Ch.43, p.3441		
IAS 1.125	Ch.43, p.3511		
IAS 1.125	Ch.45, p.3606		

IAS 2

IAS 2.1	Ch.22, p.1675
IAS 2.2	Ch.22, p.1676
IAS 2.3	Ch.17, p.1366
IAS 2.3	Ch.22, p.1676
IAS 2.3(a)	Ch.43, p.3336
IAS 2.3(a)	Ch.43, p.3361
IAS 2.3(a)	Ch.43, p.3451
IAS 2.3(a)	Ch.43, p.3480
IAS 2.3(a)	Ch.43, p.3487
IAS 2.3(b)	Ch.22, p.1688
IAS 2.3(b)	Ch.22, p.1694
IAS 2.3(b)	Ch.43, p.3480
IAS 2.3(b)	Ch.43, p.3487
IAS 2.4	Ch.22, p.1676
IAS 2.4	Ch.43, p.3336
IAS 2.4	Ch.43, p.3361
IAS 2.5	Ch.22, p.1676
IAS 2.6	Ch.17, p.1299
IAS 2.6	Ch.17, p.1366
IAS 2.6	Ch.22, p.1676
IAS 2.6	Ch.22, p.1678
IAS 2.6	Ch.22, p.1682
IAS 2.6	Ch.32, p.2407
IAS 2.7	Ch.22, p.1683
IAS 2.8	Ch.22, p.1677
IAS 2.8	Ch.43, p.3481
IAS 2.9	Ch.17, p.1344
IAS 2.9	Ch.22, p.1682
IAS 2.9	Ch.29, p.2215
IAS 2.9	Ch.43, p.3451
IAS 2.9	Ch.43, p.3488
IAS 2.10	Ch.22, p.1683
IAS 2.10	Ch.43, p.3428
IAS 2.11	Ch.22, p.1683
IAS 2.12	Ch.22, p.1684
IAS 2.12	Ch.22, p.1696
IAS 2.12	Ch.22, p.1697
IAS 2.12	Ch.26, p.1974
IAS 2.13	Ch.22, p.1684
IAS 2.13	Ch.41, p.3243
IAS 2.14	Ch.22, p.1685
IAS 2.14	Ch.22, p.1696
IAS 2.14	Ch.43, p.3483
IAS 2.15	Ch.22, p.1685
IAS 2.15	Ch.22, p.1686
IAS 2.16	Ch.22, p.1685
IAS 2.16	Ch.22, p.1694
IAS 2.16	Ch.43, p.3428
IAS 2.16(b)	Ch.22, p.1685
IAS 2.16(c)	Ch.22, p.1686
IAS 2.16(c)	Ch.26, p.1974
IAS 2.17	Ch.22, p.1686
IAS 2.18	Ch.22, p.1687
IAS 2.20	Ch.22, p.1676
IAS 2.21	Ch.22, p.1689
IAS 2.22	Ch.22, p.1689
IAS 2.23	Ch.22, p.1690
IAS 2.24	Ch.22, p.1690
IAS 2.25	Ch.22, p.1690
IAS 2.25	Ch.43, p.3486
IAS 2.26	Ch.22, p.1690
IAS 2.27	Ch.22, p.1691
IAS 2.28	Ch.22, p.1692
IAS 2.28	Ch.29, p.2215
IAS 2.29	Ch.22, p.1692
IAS 2.30	Ch.22, p.1692
IAS 2.30	Ch.43, p.3488
IAS 2.31	Ch.22, p.1692
IAS 2.32	Ch.22, p.1692
IAS 2.32	Ch.22, p.1693
IAS 2.33	Ch.22, p.1693
IAS 2.34	Ch.22, p.1697
IAS 2.34	Ch.43, p.3447
IAS 2.35	Ch.22, p.1697
IAS 2.36	Ch.22, p.1697
IAS 2.37	Ch.22, p.1698
IAS 2.37	Ch.43, p.3481
IAS 2.38	Ch.22, p.1685
IAS 2.38	Ch.22, p.1698
IAS 2.39	Ch.22, p.1699
IAS 2.BC9	Ch.22, p.1691

IAS 7

IAS 7 Objective	Ch.40, p.3137
IAS 7.1	Ch.40, p.3182
IAS 7.3	Ch.40, p.3138
IAS 7.4	Ch.40, p.3137
IAS 7.5	Ch.40, p.3138
IAS 7.6	Ch.16, p.1272
IAS 7.6	Ch.40, p.3137
IAS 7.6	Ch.40, p.3138
IAS 7.6	Ch.40, p.3141
IAS 7.6	Ch.40, p.3147
IAS 7.6	Ch.40, p.3151
IAS 7.6	Ch.40, p.3152
IAS 7.6-8	Ch.5, p.363
IAS 7.7	Ch.40, p.3138
IAS 7.7	Ch.40, p.3140
IAS 7.7	Ch.40, p.3141
IAS 7.8	Ch.5, p.363
IAS 7.8	Ch.40, p.3142
IAS 7.9	Ch.40, p.3138
IAS 7.10	Ch.16, p.1272
IAS 7.10	Ch.40, p.3135
IAS 7.10	Ch.40, p.3145
IAS 7.11	Ch.40, p.3145
IAS 7.11	Ch.40, p.3152
IAS 7.12	Ch.40, p.3146
IAS 7.13	Ch.40, p.3147
IAS 7.13	Ch.40, p.3154
IAS 7.14	Ch.18, p.1427
IAS 7.14	Ch.27, p.2041

IAS 7.14	Ch.40, p.3147
IAS 7.14	Ch.40, p.3148
IAS 7.14	Ch.40, p.3153
IAS 7.14	Ch.40, p.3159
IAS 7.14	Ch.40, p.3160
IAS 7.14	Ch.40, p.3161
IAS 7.14(a)	Ch.40, p.3155
IAS 7.14(d)	Ch.40, p.3155
IAS 7.15	Ch.40, p.3148
IAS 7.15	Ch.40, p.3184
IAS 7.16	Ch.40, p.3148
IAS 7.16	Ch.40, p.3151
IAS 7.16	Ch.40, p.3161
IAS 7.16	Ch.40, p.3168
IAS 7.16	Ch.40, p.3177
IAS 7.16	Ch.40, p.3178
IAS 7.16	Ch.40, p.3179
IAS 7.16	Ch.40, p.3180
IAS 7.16	Ch.43, p.3376
IAS 7.16(b)	Ch.40, p.3159
IAS 7.16(e)	Ch.40, p.3184
IAS 7.16(f)	Ch.40, p.3184
IAS 7.17	Ch.40, p.3152
IAS 7.17	Ch.40, p.3160
IAS 7.17	Ch.40, p.3162
IAS 7.17	Ch.40, p.3179
IAS 7.17	Ch.40, p.3180
IAS 7.17(a)	Ch.40, p.3161
IAS 7.17(c)	Ch.40, p.3155
IAS 7.17(e)	Ch.40, p.3169
IAS 7.18	Ch.40, p.3148
IAS 7.18	Ch.40, p.3165
IAS 7.19	Ch.40, p.3148
IAS 7.19	Ch.40, p.3175
IAS 7.19	Ch.40, p.3185
IAS 7.20	Ch.40, p.3149
IAS 7.20	Ch.40, p.3150
IAS 7.20	Ch.40, p.3175
IAS 7.21	Ch.40, p.3152
IAS 7.21	Ch.40, p.3153
IAS 7.21	Ch.40, p.3164
IAS 7.22	Ch.40, p.3164
IAS 7.23	Ch.40, p.3164
IAS 7.23A	Ch.40, p.3164
IAS 7.23A(c)	Ch.40, p.3155
IAS 7.24	Ch.40, p.3185
IAS 7.25	Ch.40, p.3165
IAS 7.26	Ch.40, p.3165
IAS 7.27	Ch.40, p.3165
IAS 7.28	Ch.40, p.3140
IAS 7.28	Ch.40, p.3165
IAS 7.31	Ch.40, p.3153
IAS 7.32	Ch.40, p.3154
IAS 7.33	Ch.40, p.3153
IAS 7.33	Ch.40, p.3184
IAS 7.34	Ch.40, p.3153
IAS 7.34	Ch.40, p.3154
IAS 7.35	Ch.33, p.2612
IAS 7.35	Ch.40, p.3154
IAS 7.36	Ch.33, p.2612
IAS 7.36	Ch.40, p.3154
IAS 7.37	Ch.40, p.3180
IAS 7.37	Ch.40, p.3181
IAS 7.38	Ch.40, p.3180
IAS 7.39	Ch.40, p.3176
IAS 7.39-42	Ch.9, p.757
IAS 7.40	Ch.40, p.3176
IAS 7.40-40A	Ch.40, p.3181
IAS 7.41	Ch.40, p.3176
IAS 7.42	Ch.40, p.3176
IAS 7.42A	Ch.40, p.3153
IAS 7.42A	Ch.40, p.3175
IAS 7.42A	Ch.40, p.3176
IAS 7.42B	Ch.40, p.3175
IAS 7.43	Ch.40, p.3157
IAS 7.43	Ch.40, p.3166
IAS 7.43	Ch.40, p.3178
IAS 7.43	Ch.54, p.4512
IAS 7.44	Ch.40, p.3167
IAS 7.44A	Ch.40, p.3171
IAS 7.44A	Ch.54, p.4513
IAS 7.44B	Ch.40, p.3171
IAS 7.44C	Ch.40, p.3171
IAS 7.44D	Ch.40, p.3171
IAS 7.44E	Ch.40, p.3172
IAS 7.45	Ch.40, p.3139
IAS 7.45	Ch.40, p.3143
IAS 7.46	Ch.40, p.3139
IAS 7.48	Ch.15, p.1244
IAS 7.48	Ch.40, p.3143
IAS 7.49	Ch.15, p.1244
IAS 7.49	Ch.40, p.3143
IAS 7.50	Ch.40, p.3173
IAS 7.51	Ch.40, p.3173
IAS 7.52	Ch.40, p.3173
IAS 7 Appendix A part D	Ch.40, p.3174
IAS 7.IE Example A	Ch.3, p.138
IAS 7.BC3	Ch.40, p.3152
IAS 7.BC5-7	Ch.40, p.3179
IAS 7.BC7	Ch.40, p.3152
IAS 7.BC9	Ch.40, p.3171
IAS 7.BC11	Ch.54, p.4510

IAS 8

IAS 8.1	Ch.3, p.115
IAS 8.2	Ch.3, p.115
IAS 8.3	Ch.3, p.114
IAS 8.4	Ch.3, p.115
IAS 8.5	Ch.3, p.114
IAS 8.5	Ch.3, p.157
IAS 8.5	Ch.3, p.163
IAS 8.5	Ch.3, p.166
IAS 8.5	Ch.3, p.168
IAS 8.5	Ch.3, p.169

IAS 8.5	Ch.3, p.171	IAS 8.16	Ch.3, p.167
IAS 8.5	Ch.3, p.172	IAS 8.17	Ch.18, p.1425
IAS 8.5	Ch.5, p.244	IAS 8.17	Ch.41, p.3241
IAS 8.5	Ch.5, p.365	IAS 8.17-18	Ch.3, p.167
IAS 8.5	Ch.5, p.368	IAS 8.19	Ch.55, p.4588
IAS 8.5	Ch.30, p.2279	IAS 8.19-20	Ch.3, p.166
IAS 8.5	Ch.33, p.2473	IAS 8.21	Ch.3, p.167
IAS 8.5	Ch.33, p.2540	IAS 8.22	Ch.3, p.166
IAS 8.5	Ch.33, p.2573	IAS 8.23	Ch.3, p.166
IAS 8.5	Ch.43, p.3498	IAS 8.23	Ch.3, p.172
IAS 8.5	Ch.43, p.3518	IAS 8.23	Ch.33, p.2572
IAS 8.5	Ch.43, p.3563	IAS 8.24	Ch.3, p.172
IAS 8.5	Ch.51, p.4020	IAS 8.25	Ch.3, p.172
IAS 8.5	Ch.56, p.4920	IAS 8.26	Ch.3, p.166
IAS 8.7	Ch.3, p.164	IAS 8.26	Ch.3, p.172
IAS 8.7	Ch.10, p.765	IAS 8.27	Ch.3, p.172
IAS 8.7	Ch.43, p.3344	IAS 8.28	Ch.3, p.176
IAS 8.8	Ch.3, p.153	IAS 8.28	Ch.56, p.4923
IAS 8.8	Ch.3, p.164	IAS 8.29	Ch.3, p.176
IAS 8.8	Ch.5, p.239	IAS 8.29	Ch.40, p.3148
IAS 8.8	Ch.14, p.1010	IAS 8.29	Ch.41, p.3242
IAS 8.8	Ch.49, p.3854	IAS 8.30	Ch.3, p.177
IAS 8.9	Ch.3, p.114	IAS 8.30	Ch.38, p.3087
IAS 8.10	Ch.3, p.164	IAS 8.30	Ch.55, p.4601
IAS 8.10	Ch.5, p.324	IAS 8.31	Ch.3, p.177
IAS 8.10	Ch.5, p.325	IAS 8.32-33	Ch.3, p.167
IAS 8.10	Ch.8, p.586	IAS 8.32-38	Ch.43, p.3518
IAS 8.10	Ch.17, p.1309	IAS 8.32-40	Ch.5, p.245
IAS 8.10	Ch.18, p.1403	IAS 8.32-40	Ch.5, p.250
IAS 8.10	Ch.19, p.1465	IAS 8.32(d)	Ch.18, p.1415
IAS 8.10	Ch.43, p.3344	IAS 8.34	Ch.3, p.167
IAS 8.10	Ch.43, p.3361	IAS 8.34	Ch.20, p.1588
IAS 8.10	Ch.43, p.3421	IAS 8.34	Ch.30, p.2279
IAS 8.10	Ch.53, p.4295	IAS 8.35	Ch.3, p.163
IAS 8.10	Ch.55, p.4587	IAS 8.35	Ch.3, p.164
IAS 8.10-11	Ch.51, p.3958	IAS 8.35	Ch.3, p.167
IAS 8.10-12	Ch.5, p.239	IAS 8.36	Ch.3, p.168
IAS 8.10-12	Ch.7, p.517	IAS 8.36	Ch.17, p.1347
IAS 8.10-12	Ch.31, p.2383	IAS 8.36	Ch.17, p.1349
IAS 8.11	Ch.3, p.165	IAS 8.36	Ch.18, p.1415
IAS 8.11	Ch.5, p.324	IAS 8.36	Ch.26, p.1957
IAS 8.11	Ch.17, p.1308	IAS 8.36	Ch.33, p.2476
IAS 8.11	Ch.43, p.3344	IAS 8.36	Ch.33, p.2567
IAS 8.11	Ch.43, p.3514	IAS 8.36-37	Ch.30, p.2279
IAS 8.11-12	Ch.55, p.4587	IAS 8.36-38	Ch.3, p.168
IAS 8.11(a)	Ch.7, p.504	IAS 8.38	Ch.3, p.163
IAS 8.12	Ch.3, p.165	IAS 8.38	Ch.17, p.1347
IAS 8.13	Ch.42, p.3283	IAS 8.39	Ch.3, p.179
IAS 8.12	Ch.5, p.324	IAS 8.40	Ch.3, p.179
IAS 8.12	Ch.5, p.325	IAS 8.41	Ch.3, p.168
IAS 8.12	Ch.43, p.3344	IAS 8.42	Ch.3, p.169
IAS 8.13	Ch.3, p.157	IAS 8.42	Ch.33, p.2476
IAS 8.13	Ch.24, p.1831	IAS 8.43	Ch.3, p.170
IAS 8.14	Ch.3, p.166	IAS 8.43	Ch.3, p.173
IAS 8.14	Ch.22, p.1690	IAS 8.44	Ch.3, p.173
IAS 8.14-15	Ch.5, p.325	IAS 8.45	Ch.3, p.173
IAS 8.14(b)	Ch.41, p.3240	IAS 8.46	Ch.3, p.169
IAS 8.15	Ch.3, p.157	IAS 8.47	Ch.3, p.174

IAS 8.48	Ch.3, p.164	IAS 10.17	Ch.38, p.3086
IAS 8.48	Ch.3, p.168	IAS 10.17	Ch.41, p.3219
IAS 8.49	Ch.3, p.179	IAS 10.18	Ch.38, p.3086
IAS 8.50	Ch.3, p.171	IAS 10.19	Ch.38, p.3082
IAS 8.51	Ch.3, p.171	IAS 10.20	Ch.38, p.3082
IAS 8.52	Ch.3, p.172	IAS 10.21	Ch.33, p.2474
IAS 8.53	Ch.3, p.171	IAS 10.21	Ch.33, p.2476
IAS 8.IG1	Ch.3, p.169	IAS 10.21	Ch.33, p.2542
IAS 8.IG3	Ch.3, p.172	IAS 10.21	Ch.38, p.3074
		IAS 10.21	Ch.38, p.3083
		IAS 10.21	Ch.39, p.3115
		IAS 10.22	Ch.38, p.3079
		IAS 10.22(e)	Ch.26, p.1968
		IAS 10.22(f)	Ch.38, p.3079
		IAS 10.22(h)	Ch.33, p.2474
		IAS 10.22(h)	Ch.33, p.2475
		IAS 10.22(h)	Ch.33, p.2541
		IAS 10.22(h)	Ch.38, p.3090
		IAS 10.22(h)	Ch.41, p.3252
		IAS 10.BC4	Ch.38, p.3081

IAS 10

IAS 10.1	Ch.38, p.3074
IAS 10.2	Ch.38, p.3073
IAS 10.3	Ch.33, p.2473
IAS 10.3	Ch.33, p.2541
IAS 10.3	Ch.33, p.2567
IAS 10.3	Ch.38, p.3073
IAS 10.3	Ch.38, p.3074
IAS 10.3	Ch.43, p.3518
IAS 10.3	Ch.43, p.3561
IAS 10.3(a)	Ch.38, p.3073
IAS 10.3(a)	Ch.38, p.3078
IAS 10.3(a)	Ch.43, p.3419
IAS 10.3(b)	Ch.38, p.3074
IAS 10.3(b)	Ch.38, p.3079
IAS 10.4	Ch.38, p.3074
IAS 10.5	Ch.38, p.3074
IAS 10.5-6	Ch.38, p.3075
IAS 10.6	Ch.38, p.3074
IAS 10.7	Ch.38, p.3077
IAS 10.8	Ch.38, p.3073
IAS 10.8	Ch.38, p.3082
IAS 10.9	Ch.26, p.1939
IAS 10.9	Ch.26, p.1945
IAS 10.9	Ch.38, p.3078
IAS 10.9(b)(i)	Ch.38, p.3088
IAS 10.9(b)(ii)	Ch.22, p.1692
IAS 10.9(b)(ii)	Ch.38, p.3087
IAS 10.9(e)	Ch.38, p.3089
IAS 10.10	Ch.5, p.244
IAS 10.10	Ch.38, p.3074
IAS 10.10	Ch.38, p.3083
IAS 10.11	Ch.38, p.3079
IAS 10.11	Ch.38, p.3080
IAS 10.11	Ch.38, p.3089
IAS 10.11	Ch.51, p.3966
IAS 10.12	Ch.33, p.2535
IAS 10.12	Ch.38, p.3079
IAS 10.13	Ch.8, p.599
IAS 10.13	Ch.38, p.3081
IAS 10.14	Ch.38, p.3074
IAS 10.14	Ch.38, p.3082
IAS 10.14	Ch.38, p.3083
IAS 10.15	Ch.38, p.3082
IAS 10.16(a)	Ch.38, p.3083
IAS 10.16(b)	Ch.38, p.3083

IAS 12 (2018)

IAS 12(2018).52A	Ch.33, p.2577

IAS 12

IAS 12 Objective	Ch.33, p.2455
IAS 12 Objective	Ch.33, p.2456
IAS 12.1-2	Ch.33, p.2458
IAS 12.1-2	Ch.43, p.3557
IAS 12.2	Ch.33, p.2457
IAS 12.2	Ch.33, p.2461
IAS 12.4	Ch.24, p.1828
IAS 12.4	Ch.33, p.2458
IAS 12.4	Ch.33, p.2462
IAS 12.5	Ch.33, p.2457
IAS 12.5	Ch.33, p.2471
IAS 12.5	Ch.33, p.2478
IAS 12.5	Ch.33, p.2482
IAS 12.5	Ch.33, p.2494
IAS 12.5	Ch.33, p.2519
IAS 12.5	Ch.33, p.2522
IAS 12.5	Ch.33, p.2523
IAS 12.5	Ch.33, p.2568
IAS 12.7	Ch.33, p.2479
IAS 12.7	Ch.33, p.2530
IAS 12.8	Ch.33, p.2480
IAS 12.9	Ch.33, p.2481
IAS 12.10	Ch.33, p.2456
IAS 12.10	Ch.33, p.2481
IAS 12.10	Ch.33, p.2546
IAS 12.11	Ch.33, p.2478
IAS 12.11	Ch.33, p.2560
IAS 12.12	Ch.33, p.2471
IAS 12.12	Ch.33, p.2569

IAS 12.13	Ch.41, p.3255	IAS 12.29(b)	Ch.33, p.2604
IAS 12.13-14	Ch.33, p.2471	IAS 12.29A	Ch.33, p.2522
IAS 12.15	Ch.5, p.365	IAS 12.30	Ch.33, p.2520
IAS 12.15	Ch.33, p.2491	IAS 12.31	Ch.33, p.2518
IAS 12.15	Ch.33, p.2516	IAS 12.32A	Ch.9, p.692
IAS 12.15	Ch.33, p.2531	IAS 12.32A	Ch.33, p.2495
IAS 12.15(a)	Ch.5, p.277	IAS 12.33	Ch.33, p.2488
IAS 12.15(b)	Ch.33, p.2515	IAS 12.33	Ch.33, p.2498
IAS 12.15(b)	Ch.33, p.2516	IAS 12.34	Ch.33, p.2464
IAS 12.16	Ch.33, p.2453	IAS 12.34	Ch.33, p.2526
IAS 12.16	Ch.33, p.2456	IAS 12.35	Ch.33, p.2526
IAS 12.17-20	Ch.33, p.2482	IAS 12.35	Ch.33, p.2527
IAS 12.19	Ch.55, p.4599	IAS 12.36	Ch.33, p.2527
IAS 12.20	Ch.33, p.2516	IAS 12.37	Ch.33, p.2528
IAS 12.20	Ch.33, p.2517	IAS 12.38	Ch.33, p.2531
IAS 12.20	Ch.33, p.2522	IAS 12.39	Ch.33, p.2534
IAS 12.20	Ch.33, p.2528	IAS 12.39	Ch.33, p.2535
IAS 12.21	Ch.33, p.2495	IAS 12.39	Ch.33, p.2537
IAS 12.21A	Ch.33, p.2495	IAS 12.39	Ch.33, p.2601
IAS 12.21A	Ch.33, p.2499	IAS 12.39(b)	Ch.33, p.2536
IAS 12.21A	Ch.33, p.2503	IAS 12.40	Ch.33, p.2534
IAS 12.21B	Ch.33, p.2496	IAS 12.41	Ch.15, p.1242
IAS 12.22	Ch.33, p.2497	IAS 12.41	Ch.33, p.2572
IAS 12.22(a)	Ch.20, p.1593	IAS 12.41	Ch.43, p.3421
IAS 12.22(c)	Ch.33, p.2493	IAS 12.42	Ch.33, p.2534
IAS 12.22(c)	Ch.33, p.2499	IAS 12.43	Ch.33, p.2534
IAS 12.22(c)	Ch.33, p.2508	IAS 12.44	Ch.33, p.2535
IAS 12.22(c)	Ch.33, p.2609	IAS 12.45	Ch.33, p.2535
IAS 12.23	Ch.33, p.2515	IAS 12.46	Ch.33, p.2471
IAS 12.24	Ch.5, p.365	IAS 12.46	Ch.33, p.2473
IAS 12.24	Ch.33, p.2488	IAS 12.46	Ch.33, p.2475
IAS 12.24	Ch.33, p.2491	IAS 12.46	Ch.33, p.2561
IAS 12.24	Ch.33, p.2492	IAS 12.46	Ch.33, p.2564
IAS 12.24	Ch.33, p.2516	IAS 12.46	Ch.33, p.2569
IAS 12.24	Ch.33, p.2531	IAS 12.47	Ch.33, p.2475
IAS 12.24	Ch.41, p.3256	IAS 12.47	Ch.33, p.2539
IAS 12.24-31	Ch.5, p.367	IAS 12.47	Ch.33, p.2540
IAS 12.25	Ch.33, p.2456	IAS 12.47	Ch.33, p.2561
IAS 12.26	Ch.33, p.2482	IAS 12.47	Ch.33, p.2564
IAS 12.26(d)	Ch.33, p.2522	IAS 12.47	Ch.41, p.3253
IAS 12.27	Ch.33, p.2492	IAS 12.48	Ch.33, p.2471
IAS 12.27	Ch.33, p.2517	IAS 12.48	Ch.33, p.2539
IAS 12.27	Ch.33, p.2523	IAS 12.48	Ch.41, p.3251
IAS 12.27A	Ch.33, p.2518	IAS 12.49	Ch.33, p.2539
IAS 12.27A	Ch.33, p.2524	IAS 12.51	Ch.33, p.2542
IAS 12.28	Ch.33, p.2518	IAS 12.51A	Ch.33, p.2544
IAS 12.28	Ch.33, p.2525	IAS 12.51A	Ch.33, p.2551
IAS 12.28	Ch.33, p.2526	IAS 12.51B	Ch.33, p.2547
IAS 12.28	Ch.33, p.2528	IAS 12.51C	Ch.33, p.2549
IAS 12.29	Ch.33, p.2512	IAS 12.51C	Ch.33, p.2550
IAS 12.29	Ch.33, p.2518	IAS 12.51D	Ch.33, p.2550
IAS 12.29	Ch.33, p.2525	IAS 12.51E	Ch.33, p.2547
IAS 12.29	Ch.33, p.2604	IAS 12.51E	Ch.33, p.2550
IAS 12.29(a)(i)	Ch.33, p.2519	IAS 12.52A	Ch.33, p.2536
IAS 12.29(a)(i)	Ch.33, p.2523	IAS 12.52A	Ch.33, p.2554
IAS 12.29(a)(ii)	Ch.33, p.2519	IAS 12.53	Ch.33, p.2477
IAS 12.29(b)	Ch.33, p.2542	IAS 12.53	Ch.33, p.2556
IAS 12.29(b)	Ch.33, p.2543	IAS 12.54	Ch.33, p.2556

IAS 12.55	Ch.33, p.2556	IAS 12.80(d)	Ch.33, p.2541
IAS 12.56	Ch.33, p.2528	IAS 12.81	Ch.33, p.2613
IAS 12.57	Ch.33, p.2570	IAS 12.81(c)	Ch.33, p.2460
IAS 12.57A	Ch.33, p.2536	IAS 12.81(c)	Ch.33, p.2617
IAS 12.57A	Ch.33, p.2554	IAS 12.81(d)	Ch.33, p.2474
IAS 12.57A	Ch.33, p.2574	IAS 12.81(d)	Ch.33, p.2541
IAS 12.58	Ch.15, p.1242	IAS 12.81(e)	Ch.33, p.2620
IAS 12.58	Ch.33, p.2570	IAS 12.81(f)	Ch.33, p.2620
IAS 12.58	Ch.33, p.2573	IAS 12.81(g)	Ch.33, p.2619
IAS 12.58	Ch.33, p.2582	IAS 12.82	Ch.33, p.2616
IAS 12.58	Ch.33, p.2601	IAS 12.82A	Ch.33, p.2617
IAS 12.58(a)	Ch.33, p.2600	IAS 12.84	Ch.33, p.2614
IAS 12.58(a)	Ch.33, p.2601	IAS 12.85	Ch.33, p.2615
IAS 12.60	Ch.33, p.2570	IAS 12.86	Ch.33, p.2613
IAS 12.60	Ch.33, p.2573	IAS 12.87	Ch.33, p.2616
IAS 12.61A	Ch.5, p.365	IAS 12.87A	Ch.33, p.2617
IAS 12.61A	Ch.5, p.366	IAS 12.87A-87C	Ch.33, p.2617
IAS 12.61A	Ch.5, p.368	IAS 12.88	Ch.26, p.1935
IAS 12.61A	Ch.33, p.2528	IAS 12.88	Ch.33, p.2541
IAS 12.61A	Ch.33, p.2541	IAS 12.88	Ch.33, p.2614
IAS 12.61A	Ch.33, p.2570	IAS 12.88	Ch.33, p.2619
IAS 12.61A	Ch.33, p.2571	IAS 12.98I	Ch.33, p.2455
IAS 12.61A	Ch.33, p.2580	IAS 12.98I	Ch.33, p.2577
IAS 12.61A	Ch.33, p.2581	IAS 12.IE.A-C	Ch.33, p.2482
IAS 12.61A	Ch.33, p.2582	IAS 12.IE.A.18	Ch.16, p.1266
IAS 12.61A(b)	Ch.33, p.2601	IAS 12 IE Example 4	Ch.33, p.2515
IAS 12.62	Ch.33, p.2570	IAS 12 IE Example 6	Ch.33, p.2597
IAS 12.62A	Ch.33, p.2570	IAS 12 IE Example 7	Ch.33, p.2524
IAS 12.62A(a)	Ch.33, p.2573	IAS 12.BC1A	Ch.33, p.2520
IAS 12.63	Ch.33, p.2571	IAS 12.BC6	Ch.33, p.2545
IAS 12.64	Ch.33, p.2571	IAS 12.BC6	Ch.33, p.2547
IAS 12.65	Ch.33, p.2571	IAS 12.BC37	Ch.33, p.2520
IAS 12.65A	Ch.33, p.2574	IAS 12.BC38	Ch.33, p.2521
IAS 12.65A	Ch.33, p.2575	IAS 12.BC39	Ch.33, p.2521
IAS 12.65A	Ch.33, p.2576	IAS 12.BC40	Ch.33, p.2522
IAS 12.66	Ch.33, p.2604	IAS 12.BC42-44	Ch.33, p.2522
IAS 12.67	Ch.33, p.2607	IAS 12.BC47	Ch.33, p.2521
IAS 12.68	Ch.9, p.692	IAS 12.BC49	Ch.33, p.2523
IAS 12.68	Ch.20, p.1597	IAS 12.BC50	Ch.33, p.2523
IAS 12.68	Ch.33, p.2607	IAS 12.BC52	Ch.33, p.2521
IAS 12.68A	Ch.33, p.2587	IAS 12.BC53	Ch.33, p.2521
IAS 12.68A-68C	Ch.5, p.367	IAS 12.BC53	Ch.33, p.2523
IAS 12.68A-68C	Ch.33, p.2570	IAS 12.BC55	Ch.33, p.2521
IAS 12.68B	Ch.33, p.2587	IAS 12.BC55	Ch.33, p.2523
IAS 12.68C	Ch.5, p.367	IAS 12.BC56	Ch.33, p.2519
IAS 12.68C	Ch.33, p.2587	IAS 12.BC56	Ch.33, p.2523
IAS 12.68C	Ch.33, p.2589	IAS 12.BC57	Ch.33, p.2521
IAS 12.68C	Ch.33, p.2593	IAS 12.BC58	Ch.33, p.2523
IAS 12.71	Ch.33, p.2610	IAS 12.BC59	Ch.33, p.2524
IAS 12.72	Ch.33, p.2610	IAS 12.BC67	Ch.33, p.2577
IAS 12.73	Ch.33, p.2610	IAS 12.BC69	Ch.33, p.2578
IAS 12.74	Ch.33, p.2610	IAS 12.BC70	Ch.33, p.2577
IAS 12.75	Ch.33, p.2611		
IAS 12.76	Ch.33, p.2611		
IAS 12.77	Ch.33, p.2611		
IAS 12.78	Ch.33, p.2612		
IAS 12.79-80	Ch.33, p.2613		
IAS 12.79-80	Ch.33, p.2617		

IAS 16 (2022)

IAS 16(2022).17(e)	Ch.18, p.1405
IAS 16(2022).BC16F-G	Ch.43, p.3448

IAS 16(2022).BC16J Ch.43, p.3448

IAS 16

IAS 16.1	Ch.18, p.1385
IAS 16.2	Ch.43, p.3513
IAS 16.2-3	Ch.18, p.1386
IAS 16.3	Ch.18, p.1386
IAS 16.3	Ch.43, p.3513
IAS 16.3(b)	Ch.18, p.1393
IAS 16.3(c)	Ch.43, p.3361
IAS 16.3(d)	Ch.43, p.3336
IAS 16.3(d)	Ch.43, p.3361
IAS 16.3(d)	Ch.43, p.3502
IAS 16.5	Ch.18, p.1386
IAS 16.5	Ch.18, p.1418
IAS 16.6	Ch.8, p.585
IAS 16.6	Ch.18, p.1387
IAS 16.6	Ch.18, p.1393
IAS 16.6	Ch.18, p.1410
IAS 16.6	Ch.18, p.1419
IAS 16.6	Ch.32, p.2407
IAS 16.6	Ch.33, p.2545
IAS 16.6	Ch.43, p.3395
IAS 16.6	Ch.43, p.3418
IAS 16.7	Ch.18, p.1388
IAS 16.7	Ch.18, p.1428
IAS 16.8	Ch.18, p.1389
IAS 16.9	Ch.5, p.292
IAS 16.9	Ch.5, p.371
IAS 16.9	Ch.18, p.1389
IAS 16.9	Ch.18, p.1428
IAS 16.10	Ch.18, p.1394
IAS 16.11	Ch.18, p.1390
IAS 16.12	Ch.5, p.371
IAS 16.12	Ch.18, p.1395
IAS 16.12	Ch.43, p.3492
IAS 16.13	Ch.5, p.371
IAS 16.13	Ch.18, p.1395
IAS 16.13	Ch.43, p.3492
IAS 16.14	Ch.18, p.1396
IAS 16.14	Ch.18, p.1397
IAS 16.14	Ch.43, p.3492
IAS 16.15	Ch.18, p.1397
IAS 16.15	Ch.21, p.1647
IAS 16.15	Ch.43, p.3367
IAS 16.15	Ch.43, p.3395
IAS 16.15	Ch.43, p.3398
IAS 16.16	Ch.18, p.1397
IAS 16.16	Ch.18, p.1399
IAS 16.16	Ch.18, p.1405
IAS 16.16	Ch.18, p.1414
IAS 16.16	Ch.26, p.1941
IAS 16.16	Ch.26, p.1979
IAS 16.16(a)	Ch.26, p.2001
IAS 16.16(b)	Ch.18, p.1403
IAS 16.16(b)	Ch.19, p.1457
IAS 16.16(b)	Ch.21, p.1647
IAS 16.16(b)	Ch.42, p.3285
IAS 16.16(b)	Ch.43, p.3443
IAS 16.16(b)	Ch.43, p.3486
IAS 16.16(c)	Ch.5, p.316
IAS 16.16(c)	Ch.26, p.1947
IAS 16.16(c)	Ch.26, p.1985
IAS 16.16(c)	Ch.33, p.2509
IAS 16.16(c)	Ch.43, p.3428
IAS 16.17	Ch.18, p.1399
IAS 16.17	Ch.18, p.1404
IAS 16.17(e)	Ch.43, p.3444
IAS 16.18	Ch.18, p.1398
IAS 16.18	Ch.26, p.1947
IAS 16.18	Ch.26, p.1986
IAS 16.18	Ch.43, p.3428
IAS 16.19	Ch.18, p.1400
IAS 16.20	Ch.18, p.1400
IAS 16.20	Ch.18, p.1404
IAS 16.20	Ch.43, p.3444
IAS 16.20A	Ch.17, p.1308
IAS 16.20A	Ch.18, p.1404
IAS 16.21	Ch.18, p.1403
IAS 16.21	Ch.18, p.1404
IAS 16.21	Ch.19, p.1466
IAS 16.21	Ch.43, p.3444
IAS 16.21(b)	Ch.43, p.3445
IAS 16.22	Ch.18, p.1399
IAS 16.22	Ch.18, p.1400
IAS 16.22	Ch.42, p.3286
IAS 16.22A	Ch.18, p.1393
IAS 16.22A	Ch.42, p.3284
IAS 16.22A	Ch.42, p.3286
IAS 16.23	Ch.16, p.1261
IAS 16.23	Ch.18, p.1401
IAS 16.24	Ch.8, p.613
IAS 16.24	Ch.8, p.616
IAS 16.24	Ch.18, p.1406
IAS 16.24	Ch.18, p.1408
IAS 16.24	Ch.43, p.3402
IAS 16.25	Ch.11, p.852
IAS 16.25	Ch.18, p.1407
IAS 16.26	Ch.8, p.613
IAS 16.26	Ch.8, p.615
IAS 16.26	Ch.18, p.1408
IAS 16.28	Ch.18, p.1408
IAS 16.29	Ch.18, p.1408
IAS 16.29	Ch.18, p.1417
IAS 16.29	Ch.18, p.1418
IAS 16.29	Ch.42, p.3284
IAS 16.29A-29B	Ch.18, p.1409
IAS 16.30	Ch.18, p.1408
IAS 16.30	Ch.19, p.1483
IAS 16.31	Ch.14, p.1136
IAS 16.31	Ch.18, p.1417
IAS 16.31	Ch.21, p.1647
IAS 16.34	Ch.14, p.1136
IAS 16.34	Ch.18, p.1418

IAS 16.35	Ch.18, p.1423
IAS 16.36	Ch.18, p.1418
IAS 16.37	Ch.18, p.1418
IAS 16.37	Ch.42, p.3310
IAS 16.38	Ch.18, p.1418
IAS 16.39	Ch.18, p.1422
IAS 16.39	Ch.18, p.1424
IAS 16.40	Ch.18, p.1422
IAS 16.41	Ch.18, p.1422
IAS 16.41	Ch.18, p.1426
IAS 16.41	Ch.27, p.2040
IAS 16.42	Ch.18, p.1423
IAS 16.43	Ch.5, p.371
IAS 16.43	Ch.18, p.1394
IAS 16.43	Ch.18, p.1409
IAS 16.43	Ch.26, p.1963
IAS 16.43	Ch.43, p.3514
IAS 16.44	Ch.17, p.1299
IAS 16.44	Ch.18, p.1394
IAS 16.44	Ch.18, p.1409
IAS 16.44	Ch.19, p.1485
IAS 16.44	Ch.26, p.1964
IAS 16.44	Ch.26, p.2003
IAS 16.45	Ch.18, p.1392
IAS 16.45	Ch.18, p.1410
IAS 16.45	Ch.43, p.3514
IAS 16.46	Ch.18, p.1410
IAS 16.47	Ch.18, p.1410
IAS 16.48	Ch.18, p.1410
IAS 16.49	Ch.18, p.1410
IAS 16.50	Ch.18, p.1411
IAS 16.51	Ch.5, p.369
IAS 16.51	Ch.5, p.370
IAS 16.51	Ch.18, p.1410
IAS 16.51	Ch.18, p.1411
IAS 16.51	Ch.19, p.1483
IAS 16.51	Ch.42, p.3284
IAS 16.52	Ch.18, p.1411
IAS 16.53	Ch.18, p.1411
IAS 16.53	Ch.42, p.3293
IAS 16.54	Ch.18, p.1411
IAS 16.55	Ch.18, p.1414
IAS 16.55	Ch.18, p.1415
IAS 16.56	Ch.18, p.1412
IAS 16.56	Ch.18, p.1414
IAS 16.56(c)	Ch.18, p.1414
IAS 16.57	Ch.18, p.1411
IAS 16.57	Ch.18, p.1412
IAS 16.57	Ch.18, p.1414
IAS 16.58	Ch.18, p.1413
IAS 16.59	Ch.18, p.1413
IAS 16.59	Ch.18, p.1414
IAS 16.60-62	Ch.18, p.1415
IAS 16.61	Ch.5, p.369
IAS 16.61	Ch.18, p.1414
IAS 16.61	Ch.18, p.1415
IAS 16.62	Ch.18, p.1416
IAS 16.62	Ch.41, p.3244
IAS 16.62A	Ch.18, p.1415
IAS 16.63	Ch.18, p.1417
IAS 16.63	Ch.42, p.3284
IAS 16.65	Ch.18, p.1417
IAS 16.65	Ch.18, p.1431
IAS 16.66	Ch.18, p.1417
IAS 16.66	Ch.18, p.1431
IAS 16.66(c)	Ch.55, p.4542
IAS 16.67	Ch.18, p.1426
IAS 16.67	Ch.18, p.1428
IAS 16.67	Ch.43, p.3395
IAS 16.67	Ch.43, p.3399
IAS 16.68	Ch.18, p.1406
IAS 16.68	Ch.18, p.1426
IAS 16.68	Ch.27, p.2018
IAS 16.68	Ch.27, p.2040
IAS 16.68	Ch.36, p.2999
IAS 16.68A	Ch.3, p.122
IAS 16.68A	Ch.18, p.1406
IAS 16.68A	Ch.18, p.1427
IAS 16.68A	Ch.19, p.1509
IAS 16.68A	Ch.22, p.1677
IAS 16.68A	Ch.22, p.1681
IAS 16.68A	Ch.27, p.2040
IAS 16.68A	Ch.27, p.2041
IAS 16.68A	Ch.40, p.3159
IAS 16.69	Ch.18, p.1426
IAS 16.69	Ch.27, p.2040
IAS 16.70	Ch.18, p.1394
IAS 16.70	Ch.18, p.1426
IAS 16.71	Ch.18, p.1426
IAS 16.71	Ch.25, p.1865
IAS 16.71	Ch.27, p.2040
IAS 16.71	Ch.43, p.3399
IAS 16.72	Ch.18, p.1427
IAS 16.72	Ch.25, p.1865
IAS 16.72	Ch.27, p.2040
IAS 16.72	Ch.43, p.3400
IAS 16.72	Ch.45, p.3605
IAS 16.73	Ch.41, p.3232
IAS 16.73	Ch.42, p.3310
IAS 16.73(a)	Ch.18, p.1431
IAS 16.73(b)	Ch.18, p.1431
IAS 16.73(c)	Ch.18, p.1432
IAS 16.73(d)	Ch.18, p.1432
IAS 16.73(d)	Ch.20, p.1612
IAS 16.73(e)	Ch.18, p.1432
IAS 16.73(e)	Ch.41, p.3205
IAS 16.73(e)(iv)	Ch.20, p.1612
IAS 16.74	Ch.18, p.1433
IAS 16.74(c)	Ch.38, p.3080
IAS 16.74(c)	Ch.39, p.3123
IAS 16.74A	Ch.18, p.1434
IAS 16.75	Ch.18, p.1431
IAS 16.75	Ch.18, p.1432
IAS 16.76	Ch.18, p.1434
IAS 16.77	Ch.18, p.1434
IAS 16.78	Ch.18, p.1436

IAS 16.79	Ch.18, p.1436	IAS 19.11	Ch.35, p.2948
IAS 16.80D	Ch.18, p.1405	IAS 19.13	Ch.41, p.3248
IAS 16.81N	Ch.18, p.1405	IAS 19.13(b)	Ch.35, p.2949
IAS 16.BC19	Ch.18, p.1406	IAS 19.14	Ch.35, p.2948
IAS 16.BC21	Ch.17, p.1311	IAS 19.15	Ch.35, p.2948
IAS 16.BC21	Ch.18, p.1407	IAS 19.16	Ch.35, p.2949
IAS 16.BC22	Ch.11, p.852	IAS 19.17	Ch.35, p.2949
IAS 16.BC23	Ch.18, p.1408	IAS 19.18	Ch.35, p.2949
IAS 16.BC29	Ch.18, p.1410	IAS 19.19	Ch.35, p.2949
IAS 16.BC35C	Ch.27, p.2041	IAS 19.19	Ch.41, p.3246
IAS 16.BC67	Ch.42, p.3293	IAS 19.20	Ch.35, p.2950
IAS 16.BC81	Ch.42, p.3285	IAS 19.21	Ch.34, p.2864
IAS 16.BC82	Ch.42, p.3286	IAS 19.21	Ch.35, p.2950
IAS 16.BC83	Ch.42, p.3277	IAS 19.22	Ch.35, p.2950
		IAS 19.23	Ch.35, p.2950
		IAS 19.24	Ch.35, p.2950
		IAS 19.25	Ch.35, p.2967
IAS 17		IAS 19.26	Ch.35, p.2894
IAS 17.4	Ch.51, p.4044	IAS 19.27	Ch.35, p.2894
		IAS 19.28	Ch.35, p.2895
		IAS 19.29	Ch.35, p.2894
IAS 18		IAS 19.29(b)	Ch.35, p.2902
IAS 18.12	Ch.43, p.3449	IAS 19.30	Ch.35, p.2894
IAS 18.16	Ch.5, p.341	IAS 19.30	Ch.35, p.2895
		IAS 19.30	Ch.35, p.2897
		IAS 19.32	Ch.35, p.2898
IAS 19		IAS 19.33	Ch.35, p.2898
IAS 19.1	Ch.35, p.2891	IAS 19.34	Ch.35, p.2899
IAS 19.2	Ch.35, p.2892	IAS 19.35	Ch.35, p.2898
IAS 19.3	Ch.35, p.2892	IAS 19.36	Ch.35, p.2898
IAS 19.4	Ch.35, p.2892	IAS 19.36	Ch.35, p.2899
IAS 19.5	Ch.35, p.2892	IAS 19.37	Ch.35, p.2899
IAS 19.6	Ch.35, p.2892	IAS 19.37	Ch.35, p.2907
IAS 19.7	Ch.35, p.2892	IAS 19.38	Ch.35, p.2898
IAS 19.8	Ch.34, p.2855	IAS 19.39	Ch.35, p.2900
IAS 19.8	Ch.35, p.2892	IAS 19.40	Ch.35, p.2900
IAS 19.8	Ch.35, p.2894	IAS 19.41	Ch.35, p.2900
IAS 19.8	Ch.35, p.2895	IAS 19.42	Ch.35, p.2901
IAS 19.8	Ch.35, p.2898	IAS 19.43	Ch.35, p.2901
IAS 19.8	Ch.35, p.2908	IAS 19.44	Ch.35, p.2901
IAS 19.8	Ch.35, p.2909	IAS 19.44	Ch.35, p.2902
IAS 19.8	Ch.35, p.2910	IAS 19.45	Ch.35, p.2902
IAS 19.8	Ch.35, p.2912	IAS 19.46	Ch.35, p.2896
IAS 19.8	Ch.35, p.2929	IAS 19.47	Ch.35, p.2896
IAS 19.8	Ch.35, p.2930	IAS 19.48	Ch.35, p.2896
IAS 19.8	Ch.35, p.2941	IAS 19.48	Ch.35, p.2897
IAS 19.8	Ch.35, p.2942	IAS 19.49	Ch.35, p.2896
IAS 19.8	Ch.35, p.2943	IAS 19.50	Ch.35, p.2906
IAS 19.8	Ch.35, p.2945	IAS 19.51	Ch.35, p.2906
IAS 19.8	Ch.35, p.2946	IAS 19.52	Ch.35, p.2906
IAS 19.8	Ch.35, p.2947	IAS 19.53	Ch.35, p.2957
IAS 19.8	Ch.35, p.2951	IAS 19.54	Ch.35, p.2957
IAS 19.8	Ch.35, p.2953	IAS 19.55	Ch.35, p.2907
IAS 19.9	Ch.35, p.2948	IAS 19.56	Ch.35, p.2895
IAS 19.9(a)	Ch.34, p.2855	IAS 19.56	Ch.35, p.2907
IAS 19.10	Ch.35, p.2948	IAS 19.57	Ch.35, p.2908
		IAS 19.58	Ch.35, p.2928
		IAS 19.59	Ch.5, p.372

IAS 19.59	Ch.35, p.2908	IAS 19.100	Ch.35, p.2941
IAS 19.59	Ch.35, p.2924	IAS 19.101	Ch.35, p.2941
IAS 19.59	Ch.35, p.2928	IAS 19.101A	Ch.35, p.2941
IAS 19.60	Ch.35, p.2908	IAS 19.102	Ch.35, p.2942
IAS 19.60	Ch.35, p.2928	IAS 19.103	Ch.5, p.373
IAS 19.61	Ch.35, p.2912	IAS 19.103	Ch.35, p.2942
IAS 19.62	Ch.35, p.2912	IAS 19.104	Ch.35, p.2942
IAS 19.63	Ch.35, p.2929	IAS 19.105	Ch.35, p.2942
IAS 19.64	Ch.35, p.2930	IAS 19.106	Ch.35, p.2942
IAS 19.65	Ch.35, p.2929	IAS 19.107	Ch.35, p.2942
IAS 19.66	Ch.35, p.2917	IAS 19.108	Ch.35, p.2943
IAS 19.67	Ch.35, p.2917	IAS 19.109	Ch.35, p.2941
IAS 19.67	Ch.35, p.2941	IAS 19.110	Ch.35, p.2941
IAS 19.68	Ch.35, p.2917	IAS 19.111	Ch.35, p.2924
IAS 19.69	Ch.35, p.2924	IAS 19.111	Ch.35, p.2943
IAS 19.70	Ch.35, p.2918	IAS 19.112	Ch.35, p.2943
IAS 19.70	Ch.35, p.2919	IAS 19.113	Ch.35, p.2910
IAS 19.71	Ch.35, p.2918	IAS 19.114	Ch.35, p.2909
IAS 19.71-74	Ch.35, p.2920	IAS 19.115	Ch.35, p.2910
IAS 19.72	Ch.35, p.2918	IAS 19.116-118	Ch.35, p.2910
IAS 19.73	Ch.35, p.2919	IAS 19.119	Ch.35, p.2910
IAS 19.74	Ch.35, p.2922	IAS 19.120	Ch.15, p.1200
IAS 19.75	Ch.35, p.2928	IAS 19.120	Ch.35, p.2940
IAS 19.75-77	Ch.35, p.2923	IAS 19.121	Ch.35, p.2940
IAS 19.76	Ch.15, p.1201	IAS 19.122	Ch.7, p.526
IAS 19.76	Ch.35, p.2922	IAS 19.122	Ch.35, p.2940
IAS 19.76(b)	Ch.35, p.2947	IAS 19.122A	Ch.35, p.2941
IAS 19.78	Ch.35, p.2923	IAS 19.123	Ch.35, p.2945
IAS 19.79	Ch.35, p.2925	IAS 19.123A	Ch.35, p.2945
IAS 19.80	Ch.35, p.2923	IAS 19.124	Ch.35, p.2945
IAS 19.80	Ch.35, p.2928	IAS 19.125	Ch.35, p.2945
IAS 19.81	Ch.35, p.2923	IAS 19.126	Ch.35, p.2945
IAS 19.82	Ch.35, p.2923	IAS 19.127	Ch.35, p.2946
IAS 19.83	Ch.15, p.1201	IAS 19.127(b)	Ch.15, p.1200
IAS 19.83	Ch.26, p.1952	IAS 19.128	Ch.35, p.2924
IAS 19.83	Ch.35, p.2925	IAS 19.128	Ch.35, p.2946
IAS 19.83	Ch.35, p.2926	IAS 19.129	Ch.35, p.2946
IAS 19.83	Ch.35, p.2927	IAS 19.130	Ch.35, p.2946
IAS 19.84	Ch.26, p.1952	IAS 19.130	Ch.35, p.2947
IAS 19.84	Ch.35, p.2924	IAS 19.131	Ch.35, p.2940
IAS 19.85	Ch.35, p.2924	IAS 19.132	Ch.35, p.2939
IAS 19.86	Ch.26, p.1953	IAS 19.133	Ch.3, p.125
IAS 19.86	Ch.35, p.2926	IAS 19.133	Ch.35, p.2939
IAS 19.87	Ch.35, p.2913	IAS 19.134	Ch.35, p.2940
IAS 19.87	Ch.35, p.2923	IAS 19.135	Ch.35, p.2957
IAS 19.87-90	Ch.35, p.2912	IAS 19.136	Ch.35, p.2957
IAS 19.88	Ch.35, p.2913	IAS 19.136	Ch.35, p.2965
IAS 19.89	Ch.35, p.2913	IAS 19.137	Ch.35, p.2958
IAS 19.91	Ch.35, p.2913	IAS 19.137	Ch.35, p.2966
IAS 19.92	Ch.35, p.2913	IAS 19.138	Ch.35, p.2958
IAS 19.93	Ch.35, p.2913	IAS 19.139	Ch.35, p.2958
IAS 19.93	Ch.35, p.2914	IAS 19.140	Ch.35, p.2959
IAS 19.94	Ch.35, p.2916	IAS 19.141	Ch.35, p.2959
IAS 19.95	Ch.35, p.2913	IAS 19.142	Ch.35, p.2961
IAS 19.96-97	Ch.35, p.2923	IAS 19.142	Ch.35, p.2966
IAS 19.97	Ch.35, p.2923	IAS 19.143	Ch.35, p.2961
IAS 19.98	Ch.35, p.2923	IAS 19.143	Ch.35, p.2967
IAS 19.99	Ch.35, p.2941	IAS 19.143	Ch.47, p.3742

IAS 19.144	Ch.35, p.2962	IAS 20.6	Ch.24, p.1825
IAS 19.145	Ch.5, p.372	IAS 20.7	Ch.24, p.1830
IAS 19.145	Ch.35, p.2963	IAS 20.7	Ch.24, p.1843
IAS 19.146	Ch.35, p.2963	IAS 20.8	Ch.24, p.1830
IAS 19.147	Ch.35, p.2963	IAS 20.9	Ch.24, p.1824
IAS 19.148	Ch.35, p.2964	IAS 20.9	Ch.24, p.1830
IAS 19.149	Ch.35, p.2965	IAS 20.10	Ch.24, p.1831
IAS 19.150	Ch.35, p.2967	IAS 20.10A	Ch.5, p.265
IAS 19.151	Ch.35, p.2967	IAS 20.10A	Ch.24, p.1823
IAS 19.152	Ch.35, p.2967	IAS 20.10A	Ch.24, p.1827
IAS 19.153	Ch.35, p.2951	IAS 20.10A	Ch.24, p.1832
IAS 19.154	Ch.35, p.2951	IAS 20.10A	Ch.24, p.1833
IAS 19.154	Ch.35, p.2953	IAS 20.10A	Ch.24, p.1836
IAS 19.155-156	Ch.35, p.2951	IAS 20.10A	Ch.49, p.3855
IAS 19.157	Ch.35, p.2952	IAS 20.11	Ch.24, p.1830
IAS 19.158	Ch.35, p.2967	IAS 20.12	Ch.24, p.1824
IAS 19.159	Ch.35, p.2954	IAS 20.12	Ch.24, p.1832
IAS 19.160	Ch.35, p.2954	IAS 20.12	Ch.24, p.1834
IAS 19.161	Ch.35, p.2954	IAS 20.12	Ch.24, p.1836
IAS 19.162	Ch.35, p.2954	IAS 20.13	Ch.24, p.1834
IAS 19.163	Ch.35, p.2954	IAS 20.15	Ch.24, p.1834
IAS 19.164	Ch.35, p.2955	IAS 20.16	Ch.24, p.1834
IAS 19.165	Ch.35, p.2955	IAS 20.16	Ch.24, p.1835
IAS 19.165(b)	Ch.41, p.3207	IAS 20.16	Ch.24, p.1836
IAS 19.166	Ch.35, p.2955	IAS 20.17	Ch.24, p.1824
IAS 19.167	Ch.35, p.2955	IAS 20.17	Ch.24, p.1834
IAS 19.168	Ch.35, p.2955	IAS 20.17	Ch.24, p.1835
IAS 19.169	Ch.35, p.2956	IAS 20.18	Ch.24, p.1835
IAS 19.170	Ch.35, p.2956	IAS 20.19	Ch.24, p.1835
IAS 19.171	Ch.35, p.2967	IAS 20.19	Ch.24, p.1837
IAS 19.BC29	Ch.35, p.2895	IAS 20.20	Ch.24, p.1837
IAS 19.BC48-49	Ch.35, p.2901	IAS 20.20-22	Ch.24, p.1835
IAS 19.BC127	Ch.35, p.2947	IAS 20.23	Ch.17, p.1310
IAS 19.BC130	Ch.35, p.2928	IAS 20.23	Ch.17, p.1361
IAS 19.BC200	Ch.3, p.125	IAS 20.23	Ch.17, p.1367
IAS 19.BC200	Ch.35, p.2939	IAS 20.23	Ch.24, p.1825
IAS 19.BC207	Ch.35, p.2957	IAS 20.23	Ch.24, p.1830
IAS 19.BC209	Ch.35, p.2957	IAS 20.24	Ch.24, p.1840
IAS 19.BC253	Ch.35, p.2904	IAS 20.25	Ch.24, p.1840
		IAS 20.26	Ch.24, p.1840
		IAS 20.27	Ch.24, p.1840
IAS 20		IAS 20.28	Ch.24, p.1842
		IAS 20.28	Ch.40, p.3164
IAS 20.1	Ch.24, p.1826	IAS 20.29	Ch.17, p.1367
IAS 20.2	Ch.24, p.1827	IAS 20.29	Ch.24, p.1840
IAS 20.2	Ch.33, p.2462	IAS 20.30	Ch.24, p.1841
IAS 20.2(b)	Ch.24, p.1828	IAS 20.31	Ch.24, p.1841
IAS 20.2(d)	Ch.24, p.1823	IAS 20.32	Ch.24, p.1838
IAS 20.3	Ch.24, p.1823	IAS 20.33	Ch.24, p.1838
IAS 20.3	Ch.24, p.1825	IAS 20.34	Ch.24, p.1824
IAS 20.3	Ch.24, p.1826	IAS 20.34	Ch.24, p.1826
IAS 20.3	Ch.24, p.1830	IAS 20.34	Ch.24, p.1838
IAS 20.3	Ch.24, p.1831	IAS 20.35	Ch.24, p.1824
IAS 20.3	Ch.25, p.1854	IAS 20.35	Ch.24, p.1826
IAS 20.4	Ch.24, p.1824	IAS 20.35	Ch.24, p.1834
IAS 20.4	Ch.24, p.1826	IAS 20.35	Ch.24, p.1839
IAS 20.5	Ch.24, p.1824	IAS 20.36	Ch.24, p.1824
IAS 20.6	Ch.24, p.1823	IAS 20.36	Ch.24, p.1839

IAS 20.38	Ch.24, p.1826	IAS 21.22	Ch.15, p.1188
IAS 20.38	Ch.24, p.1839	IAS 21.22	Ch.15, p.1190
IAS 20.39	Ch.24, p.1843	IAS 21.23	Ch.5, p.333
IAS 20.39(b)	Ch.24, p.1834	IAS 21.23	Ch.5, p.373
IAS 20.39(b)	Ch.24, p.1839	IAS 21.23	Ch.15, p.1193
IAS 20.39(b)	Ch.24, p.1845	IAS 21.23	Ch.26, p.1959
IAS 20.41	Ch.24, p.1823	IAS 21.23	Ch.50, p.3899
IAS 20.41	Ch.24, p.1838	IAS 21.23	Ch.53, p.4325
IAS 20.43	Ch.24, p.1823	IAS 21.23(a)	Ch.53, p.4322
IAS 20.45	Ch.24, p.1830	IAS 21.24	Ch.15, p.1193
		IAS 21.25	Ch.15, p.1193
		IAS 21.25	Ch.20, p.1558

IAS 21

		IAS 21.26	Ch.15, p.1191
		IAS 21.26	Ch.15, p.1192
IAS 21.1	Ch.15, p.1180	IAS 21.27	Ch.15, p.1181
IAS 21.2	Ch.15, p.1180	IAS 21.28	Ch.15, p.1194
IAS 21.3	Ch.15, p.1180	IAS 21.28	Ch.26, p.1959
IAS 21.4	Ch.15, p.1181	IAS 21.29	Ch.15, p.1194
IAS 21.5	Ch.15, p.1181	IAS 21.30	Ch.15, p.1195
IAS 21.6	Ch.15, p.1181	IAS 21.30	Ch.15, p.1196
IAS 21.7	Ch.15, p.1181	IAS 21.31	Ch.15, p.1195
IAS 21.7	Ch.40, p.3165	IAS 21.32	Ch.5, p.304
IAS 21.8	Ch.15, p.1181	IAS 21.32	Ch.15, p.1194
IAS 21.8	Ch.15, p.1196	IAS 21.32	Ch.15, p.1217
IAS 21.8	Ch.15, p.1217	IAS 21.32	Ch.15, p.1219
IAS 21.8	Ch.16, p.1258	IAS 21.33	Ch.15, p.1219
IAS 21.8	Ch.26, p.1959	IAS 21.33	Ch.15, p.1220
IAS 21.8	Ch.53, p.4307	IAS 21.34	Ch.15, p.1204
IAS 21.8-14	Ch.5, p.373	IAS 21.35	Ch.15, p.1202
IAS 21.9	Ch.15, p.1182	IAS 21.36	Ch.15, p.1202
IAS 21.9	Ch.15, p.1183	IAS 21.36	Ch.43, p.3425
IAS 21.9	Ch.43, p.3422	IAS 21.37	Ch.15, p.1202
IAS 21.10	Ch.15, p.1183	IAS 21.38	Ch.7, p.500
IAS 21.10	Ch.43, p.3422	IAS 21.38	Ch.15, p.1204
IAS 21.11	Ch.5, p.373	IAS 21.38	Ch.16, p.1277
IAS 21.11	Ch.15, p.1183	IAS 21.39	Ch.5, p.304
IAS 21.11	Ch.43, p.3422	IAS 21.39	Ch.15, p.1205
IAS 21.12	Ch.15, p.1183	IAS 21.39	Ch.16, p.1264
IAS 21.12	Ch.43, p.3422	IAS 21.39	Ch.16, p.1278
IAS 21.13	Ch.15, p.1184	IAS 21.39(b)	Ch.15, p.1216
IAS 21.14	Ch.16, p.1254	IAS 21.39(b)	Ch.53, p.4261
IAS 21.14	Ch.16, p.1277	IAS 21.40	Ch.15, p.1206
IAS 21.15	Ch.15, p.1217	IAS 21.40	Ch.15, p.1212
IAS 21.15	Ch.53, p.4269	IAS 21.41	Ch.15, p.1206
IAS 21.15A	Ch.15, p.1220	IAS 21.41	Ch.15, p.1208
IAS 21.16	Ch.15, p.1196	IAS 21.41	Ch.15, p.1216
IAS 21.16	Ch.15, p.1197	IAS 21.41	Ch.16, p.1278
IAS 21.16	Ch.16, p.1258	IAS 21.41	Ch.16, p.1279
IAS 21.17	Ch.15, p.1182	IAS 21.42	Ch.15, p.1209
IAS 21.18	Ch.15, p.1182	IAS 21.42	Ch.16, p.1264
IAS 21.18	Ch.15, p.1204	IAS 21.42	Ch.16, p.1277
IAS 21.19	Ch.15, p.1182	IAS 21.42	Ch.16, p.1278
IAS 21.20	Ch.15, p.1187	IAS 21.42(b)	Ch.16, p.1280
IAS 21.21	Ch.5, p.333	IAS 21.42(b)	Ch.16, p.1281
IAS 21.21	Ch.5, p.373	IAS 21.43	Ch.15, p.1209
IAS 21.21	Ch.15, p.1188	IAS 21.43	Ch.15, p.1210
IAS 21.21	Ch.26, p.1959	IAS 21.43	Ch.16, p.1277
IAS 21.21	Ch.53, p.4261	IAS 21.43	Ch.16, p.1279

IAS 21.44	Ch.15, p.1204	IAS 23.4	Ch.22, p.1686
IAS 21.44	Ch.53, p.4307	IAS 23.4(a)	Ch.21, p.1647
IAS 21.45	Ch.15, p.1216	IAS 23.4(b)	Ch.21, p.1646
IAS 21.45	Ch.15, p.1217	IAS 23.4(b)	Ch.29, p.2204
IAS 21.45	Ch.15, p.1223	IAS 23.5	Ch.21, p.1646
IAS 21.46	Ch.7, p.503	IAS 23.5	Ch.21, p.1649
IAS 21.46	Ch.15, p.1225	IAS 23.5	Ch.43, p.3370
IAS 21.47	Ch.5, p.282	IAS 23.5-6	Ch.29, p.2204
IAS 21.47	Ch.15, p.1226	IAS 23.6	Ch.15, p.1195
IAS 21.48	Ch.5, p.304	IAS 23.6	Ch.21, p.1649
IAS 21.48	Ch.11, p.873	IAS 23.6(e)	Ch.21, p.1650
IAS 21.48	Ch.15, p.1227	IAS 23.6(e)	Ch.21, p.1657
IAS 21.48	Ch.53, p.4364	IAS 23.7	Ch.21, p.1646
IAS 21.48-48B	Ch.7, p.527	IAS 23.7	Ch.21, p.1648
IAS 21.48A	Ch.11, p.871	IAS 23.7	Ch.22, p.1686
IAS 21.48A	Ch.15, p.1229	IAS 23.7	Ch.29, p.2204
IAS 21.48B	Ch.7, p.534	IAS 23.7	Ch.29, p.2205
IAS 21.48B	Ch.15, p.1229	IAS 23.8	Ch.21, p.1645
IAS 21.48C	Ch.7, p.534	IAS 23.8	Ch.21, p.1650
IAS 21.48C	Ch.11, p.872	IAS 23.8	Ch.21, p.1651
IAS 21.48C	Ch.15, p.1230	IAS 23.8	Ch.22, p.1686
IAS 21.48C	Ch.15, p.1231	IAS 23.8	Ch.29, p.2204
IAS 21.48D	Ch.15, p.1230	IAS 23.8	Ch.43, p.3370
IAS 21.49	Ch.15, p.1228	IAS 23.9	Ch.21, p.1650
IAS 21.49	Ch.15, p.1230	IAS 23.9	Ch.21, p.1651
IAS 21.50	Ch.15, p.1242	IAS 23.9	Ch.21, p.1663
IAS 21.51	Ch.15, p.1243	IAS 23.9	Ch.21, p.1665
IAS 21.52	Ch.15, p.1242	IAS 23.9	Ch.43, p.3370
IAS 21.52	Ch.15, p.1243	IAS 23.10	Ch.21, p.1651
IAS 21.52	Ch.15, p.1244	IAS 23.10	Ch.21, p.1661
IAS 21.52(a)	Ch.54, p.4486	IAS 23.11	Ch.21, p.1651
IAS 21.53	Ch.15, p.1243	IAS 23.12	Ch.21, p.1651
IAS 21.54	Ch.15, p.1243	IAS 23.12	Ch.41, p.3245
IAS 21.55	Ch.15, p.1243	IAS 23.13	Ch.21, p.1651
IAS 21.56	Ch.15, p.1243	IAS 23.14	Ch.21, p.1652
IAS 21.57	Ch.15, p.1243	IAS 23.14	Ch.41, p.3245
IAS 21.BC6	Ch.15, p.1183	IAS 23.15	Ch.21, p.1652
IAS 21.BC17	Ch.15, p.1208	IAS 23.16	Ch.5, p.320
IAS 21.BC18	Ch.7, p.500	IAS 23.16	Ch.21, p.1669
IAS 21.BC18	Ch.15, p.1209	IAS 23.17	Ch.21, p.1664
IAS 21.BC18	Ch.15, p.1214	IAS 23.18	Ch.21, p.1652
IAS 21.BC19	Ch.15, p.1209	IAS 23.18	Ch.21, p.1656
IAS 21.BC20	Ch.15, p.1208	IAS 23.18	Ch.21, p.1665
IAS 21.BC27	Ch.15, p.1225	IAS 23.19	Ch.21, p.1665
IAS 21.BC30	Ch.15, p.1226	IAS 23.20	Ch.21, p.1668
IAS 21.BC31	Ch.15, p.1226	IAS 23.21	Ch.21, p.1668
IAS 21.BC32	Ch.15, p.1226	IAS 23.22	Ch.21, p.1669
IAS 21.BC33-34	Ch.11, p.872	IAS 23.23	Ch.21, p.1669
IAS 21.BC35	Ch.15, p.1230	IAS 23.24	Ch.21, p.1669
		IAS 23.25	Ch.21, p.1669
		IAS 23.25	Ch.21, p.1670
		IAS 23.26	Ch.5, p.320

IAS 23

IAS 23.1	Ch.21, p.1645	IAS 23.26	Ch.21, p.1671
IAS 23.2	Ch.21, p.1646	IAS 23.29	Ch.21, p.1645
IAS 23.3	Ch.21, p.1646	IAS 23.BC2	Ch.21, p.1645
IAS 23.3	Ch.21, p.1663	IAS 23.BC6	Ch.21, p.1646
IAS 23.4	Ch.21, p.1646	IAS 23.BC6	Ch.21, p.1647
		IAS 23.BC14B	Ch.21, p.1653

IAS 32.42	Ch.40, p.3143	IAS 32.AG22	Ch.45, p.3588
IAS 32.42	Ch.43, p.3409	IAS 32.AG23	Ch.45, p.3589
IAS 32.42	Ch.52, p.4151	IAS 32.AG25	Ch.47, p.3670
IAS 32.42	Ch.54, p.4491	IAS 32.AG25	Ch.47, p.3678
IAS 32.42	Ch.55, p.4583	IAS 32.AG25	Ch.47, p.3679
IAS 32.43	Ch.54, p.4492	IAS 32.AG26	Ch.47, p.3680
IAS 32.44	Ch.54, p.4492	IAS 32.AG27	Ch.47, p.3711
IAS 32.45	Ch.54, p.4492	IAS 32.AG27	Ch.47, p.3714
IAS 32.46	Ch.54, p.4492	IAS 32.AG27(a)	Ch.47, p.3703
IAS 32.47	Ch.54, p.4495	IAS 32.AG27(a)-(b)	Ch.47, p.3711
IAS 32.48	Ch.54, p.4495	IAS 32.AG27(b)	Ch.7, p.552
IAS 32.48	Ch.54, p.4496	IAS 32.AG27(b)	Ch.47, p.3712
IAS 32.49(a)	Ch.54, p.4497	IAS 32.AG27(c)	Ch.47, p.3711
IAS 32.49(b)	Ch.54, p.4497	IAS 32.AG27(c)	Ch.47, p.3714
IAS 32.49(c)	Ch.54, p.4497	IAS 32.AG27(d)	Ch.47, p.3707
IAS 32.49(d)	Ch.54, p.4497	IAS 32.AG27(d)	Ch.47, p.3710
IAS 32.49(e)	Ch.54, p.4497	IAS 32.AG28	Ch.47, p.3674
IAS 32.50	Ch.54, p.4495	IAS 32.AG29	Ch.7, p.546
IAS 32.96C	Ch.34, p.2661	IAS 32.AG29	Ch.7, p.555
IAS 32.AG3	Ch.45, p.3586	IAS 32.AG29	Ch.47, p.3695
IAS 32.AG4	Ch.45, p.3586	IAS 32.AG29A	Ch.7, p.546
IAS 32.AG5	Ch.45, p.3586	IAS 32.AG29A	Ch.47, p.3689
IAS 32.AG6	Ch.45, p.3586	IAS 32.AG30	Ch.47, p.3715
IAS 32.AG6	Ch.47, p.3695	IAS 32.AG30	Ch.47, p.3716
IAS 32.AG7	Ch.45, p.3585	IAS 32.AG31(b)	Ch.47, p.3717
IAS 32.AG8	Ch.45, p.3587	IAS 32.AG32	Ch.47, p.3720
IAS 32.AG9	Ch.14, p.1010	IAS 32.AG33	Ch.47, p.3722
IAS 32.AG9	Ch.45, p.3587	IAS 32.AG34	Ch.47, p.3722
IAS 32.AG10	Ch.45, p.3587	IAS 32.AG35	Ch.47, p.3725
IAS 32.AG11	Ch.45, p.3588	IAS 32.AG36	Ch.47, p.3742
IAS 32.AG12	Ch.45, p.3585	IAS 32.AG36	Ch.47, p.3743
IAS 32.AG12	Ch.45, p.3586	IAS 32.AG37	Ch.47, p.3679
IAS 32.AG13	Ch.45, p.3589	IAS 32.AG37	Ch.47, p.3715
IAS 32.AG13	Ch.45, p.3591	IAS 32.AG37	Ch.47, p.3739
IAS 32.AG13	Ch.47, p.3677	IAS 32.AG38A	Ch.54, p.4493
IAS 32.AG13	Ch.47, p.3678	IAS 32.AG38B	Ch.54, p.4493
IAS 32.AG13	Ch.47, p.3703	IAS 32.AG38C	Ch.54, p.4493
IAS 32.AG14	Ch.47, p.3678	IAS 32.AG38D	Ch.54, p.4493
IAS 32.AG14B	Ch.47, p.3690	IAS 32.AG38E	Ch.54, p.4492
IAS 32.AG14C	Ch.47, p.3690	IAS 32.AG38F	Ch.54, p.4496
IAS 32.AG14D	Ch.47, p.3690	IAS 32.AG39	Ch.54, p.4497
IAS 32.AG14E	Ch.47, p.3687	IAS 32.IE2-6	Ch.47, p.3746
IAS 32.AG14F	Ch.47, p.3692	IAS 32.IE7-11	Ch.47, p.3748
IAS 32.AG14G	Ch.47, p.3692	IAS 32.IE12-16	Ch.47, p.3752
IAS 32.AG14H	Ch.47, p.3693	IAS 32.IE17-21	Ch.47, p.3754
IAS 32.AG14I	Ch.47, p.3693	IAS 32.IE22-26	Ch.47, p.3756
IAS 32.AG14J	Ch.47, p.3692	IAS 32.IE27-31	Ch.47, p.3758
IAS 32.AG15	Ch.45, p.3589	IAS 32.IE31	Ch.47, p.3761
IAS 32.AG16	Ch.45, p.3589	IAS 32.IE32	Ch.54, p.4488
IAS 32.AG16	Ch.45, p.3590	IAS 32.IE32	Ch.54, p.4518
IAS 32.AG17	Ch.45, p.3590	IAS 32.IE33	Ch.54, p.4489
IAS 32.AG18	Ch.45, p.3590	IAS 32.IE33	Ch.54, p.4519
IAS 32.AG19	Ch.45, p.3591	IAS 32.IE34-36	Ch.47, p.3717
IAS 32.AG20	Ch.43, p.3473	IAS 32.IE37-38	Ch.47, p.3727
IAS 32.AG20	Ch.45, p.3588	IAS 32.IE39-46	Ch.47, p.3722
IAS 32.AG20	Ch.45, p.3607	IAS 32.IE47-50	Ch.47, p.3725
IAS 32.AG20	Ch.51, p.4046	IAS 32.BC4I	Ch.47, p.3709
IAS 32.AG21	Ch.45, p.3589	IAS 32.BC4K	Ch.47, p.3709

IAS 32.BC7-BC8	Ch.47, p.3686	IAS 33.27	Ch.37, p.3027
IAS 32.BC9	Ch.47, p.3682	IAS 33.28	Ch.37, p.3027
IAS 32.BC12	Ch.47, p.3711	IAS 33.29	Ch.37, p.3029
IAS 32.BC17	Ch.47, p.3674	IAS 33.29	Ch.37, p.3031
IAS 32.BC21(a)	Ch.47, p.3701	IAS 33.29	Ch.37, p.3062
IAS 32.BC67	Ch.47, p.3689	IAS 33.30	Ch.37, p.3040
IAS 32.BC68	Ch.47, p.3689	IAS 33.31	Ch.37, p.3040
IAS 32.BC77	Ch.54, p.4500	IAS 33.32	Ch.37, p.3022
IAS 32.BC80	Ch.54, p.4493	IAS 33.32	Ch.37, p.3040
IAS 32.BC83	Ch.54, p.4494	IAS 33.33	Ch.37, p.3041
IAS 32.BC84	Ch.54, p.4494	IAS 33.33	Ch.37, p.3048
IAS 32.BC94	Ch.54, p.4492	IAS 33.34	Ch.37, p.3041
IAS 32.BC94-BC100	Ch.54, p.4496	IAS 33.35	Ch.37, p.3041
IAS 32.BC101	Ch.54, p.4497	IAS 33.36	Ch.37, p.3041
IAS 32.BC103	Ch.54, p.4499	IAS 33.36	Ch.37, p.3051
IAS 32.BC105-BC111	Ch.54, p.4500	IAS 33.37	Ch.37, p.3041
		IAS 33.38	Ch.37, p.3032
		IAS 33.38	Ch.37, p.3041

IAS 33

		IAS 33.38	Ch.37, p.3051
		IAS 33.39	Ch.37, p.3042
IAS 33.1	Ch.37, p.3022	IAS 33.40	Ch.37, p.3059
IAS 33.2	Ch.37, p.3022	IAS 33.42	Ch.37, p.3043
IAS 33.3	Ch.37, p.3022	IAS 33.43	Ch.37, p.3042
IAS 33.4	Ch.37, p.3023	IAS 33.44	Ch.37, p.3043
IAS 33.4A	Ch.37, p.3061	IAS 33.44	Ch.37, p.3048
IAS 33.5	Ch.37, p.3023	IAS 33.45	Ch.37, p.3050
IAS 33.5	Ch.37, p.3040	IAS 33.45-46	Ch.37, p.3050
IAS 33.5	Ch.37, p.3042	IAS 33.46	Ch.37, p.3050
IAS 33.5	Ch.37, p.3048	IAS 33.46	Ch.37, p.3051
IAS 33.5	Ch.37, p.3055	IAS 33.47	Ch.37, p.3062
IAS 33.6	Ch.37, p.3023	IAS 33.47A	Ch.37, p.3021
IAS 33.7	Ch.37, p.3040	IAS 33.47A	Ch.37, p.3055
IAS 33.8	Ch.37, p.3021	IAS 33.48	Ch.37, p.3025
IAS 33.8	Ch.37, p.3023	IAS 33.48	Ch.37, p.3054
IAS 33.9	Ch.37, p.3023	IAS 33.48	Ch.37, p.3055
IAS 33.10	Ch.37, p.3023	IAS 33.49	Ch.37, p.3045
IAS 33.11	Ch.37, p.3022	IAS 33.50	Ch.37, p.3046
IAS 33.12	Ch.37, p.3023	IAS 33.51	Ch.37, p.3047
IAS 33.13	Ch.37, p.3023	IAS 33.52	Ch.37, p.3055
IAS 33.14(a)	Ch.37, p.3035	IAS 33.52	Ch.37, p.3062
IAS 33.14(b)	Ch.37, p.3035	IAS 33.53	Ch.37, p.3056
IAS 33.15	Ch.37, p.3035	IAS 33.54	Ch.37, p.3058
IAS 33.16	Ch.37, p.3035	IAS 33.55	Ch.37, p.3056
IAS 33.17	Ch.37, p.3035	IAS 33.56	Ch.37, p.3058
IAS 33.18	Ch.37, p.3035	IAS 33.56	Ch.37, p.3059
IAS 33.19	Ch.37, p.3024	IAS 33.57	Ch.37, p.3061
IAS 33.20	Ch.37, p.3026	IAS 33.58	Ch.37, p.3042
IAS 33.21	Ch.37, p.3024	IAS 33.59	Ch.37, p.3042
IAS 33.21	Ch.37, p.3025	IAS 33.59-60	Ch.37, p.3048
IAS 33.21(f)	Ch.37, p.3033	IAS 33.60	Ch.37, p.3042
IAS 33.22	Ch.37, p.3033	IAS 33.61	Ch.37, p.3042
IAS 33.23	Ch.37, p.3024	IAS 33.62	Ch.37, p.3053
IAS 33.24	Ch.37, p.3024	IAS 33.63	Ch.37, p.3051
IAS 33.24	Ch.37, p.3025	IAS 33.64	Ch.37, p.3027
IAS 33.26	Ch.37, p.3027	IAS 33.64	Ch.37, p.3033
IAS 33.26	Ch.37, p.3032	IAS 33.64	Ch.37, p.3036
IAS 33.26	Ch.37, p.3062	IAS 33.64	Ch.37, p.3062
IAS 33.26-27	Ch.37, p.3029	IAS 33.65	Ch.37, p.3041

IAS 33.65	Ch.37, p.3062	IAS 34.1	Ch.41, p.3196
IAS 33.65	Ch.41, p.3265	IAS 34.1	Ch.41, p.3197
IAS 33.66	Ch.37, p.3023	IAS 34.2	Ch.41, p.3196
IAS 33.66	Ch.37, p.3036	IAS 34.2	Ch.41, p.3197
IAS 33.66	Ch.37, p.3061	IAS 34.3	Ch.41, p.3197
IAS 33.66	Ch.37, p.3062	IAS 34.4	Ch.41, p.3196
IAS 33.67	Ch.37, p.3062	IAS 34.4	Ch.41, p.3208
IAS 33.67A	Ch.3, p.141	IAS 34.4	Ch.41, p.3232
IAS 33.67A	Ch.37, p.3061	IAS 34.4	Ch.41, p.3267
IAS 33.68	Ch.37, p.3061	IAS 34.5	Ch.41, p.3198
IAS 33.68	Ch.37, p.3062	IAS 34.5(f)	Ch.41, p.3240
IAS 33.68A	Ch.37, p.3061	IAS 34.6	Ch.41, p.3199
IAS 33.69	Ch.37, p.3061	IAS 34.6	Ch.41, p.3204
IAS 33.70	Ch.37, p.3063	IAS 34.7	Ch.41, p.3198
IAS 33.71	Ch.37, p.3063	IAS 34.7	Ch.41, p.3199
IAS 33.72	Ch.37, p.3063	IAS 34.7	Ch.41, p.3237
IAS 33.73	Ch.37, p.3039	IAS 34.8	Ch.41, p.3199
IAS 33.73A	Ch.37, p.3039	IAS 34.8A	Ch.41, p.3199
IAS 33.A1	Ch.37, p.3023	IAS 34.8A	Ch.41, p.3228
IAS 33.A2	Ch.37, p.3029	IAS 34.9	Ch.41, p.3198
IAS 33.A2	Ch.37, p.3030	IAS 34.10	Ch.41, p.3199
IAS 33.A3	Ch.37, p.3043	IAS 34.10	Ch.41, p.3242
IAS 33.A4	Ch.37, p.3051	IAS 34.10	Ch.41, p.3267
IAS 33.A5	Ch.37, p.3051	IAS 34.11	Ch.41, p.3203
IAS 33.A6	Ch.37, p.3052	IAS 34.11A	Ch.41, p.3203
IAS 33.A7	Ch.37, p.3048	IAS 34.14	Ch.41, p.3203
IAS 33.A7	Ch.37, p.3052	IAS 34.15	Ch.32, p.2440
IAS 33.A8	Ch.37, p.3052	IAS 34.15	Ch.41, p.3199
IAS 33.A9	Ch.37, p.3048	IAS 34.15	Ch.41, p.3204
IAS 33.A9	Ch.37, p.3053	IAS 34.15	Ch.41, p.3205
IAS 33.A10	Ch.37, p.3052	IAS 34.15	Ch.41, p.3207
IAS 33.A11	Ch.37, p.3059	IAS 34.15	Ch.41, p.3231
IAS 33.A12	Ch.37, p.3060	IAS 34.15	Ch.41, p.3236
IAS 33.A13	Ch.37, p.3036	IAS 34.15	Ch.41, p.3267
IAS 33.A14	Ch.37, p.3037	IAS 34.15	Ch.54, p.4407
IAS 33.A14	Ch.37, p.3047	IAS 34.15-15A	Ch.5, p.361
IAS 33.A15	Ch.37, p.3024	IAS 34.15A	Ch.41, p.3204
IAS 33.A16	Ch.37, p.3053	IAS 34.15A	Ch.41, p.3231
IAS 33.IE1	Ch.37, p.3035	IAS 34.15A	Ch.41, p.3236
IAS 33.IE2	Ch.37, p.3024	IAS 34.15A	Ch.54, p.4407
IAS 33.IE2	Ch.37, p.3026	IAS 34.15B	Ch.32, p.2440
IAS 33.IE3	Ch.37, p.3028	IAS 34.15B	Ch.41, p.3204
IAS 33.IE4	Ch.37, p.3030	IAS 34.15B	Ch.41, p.3205
IAS 33.IE5	Ch.37, p.3050	IAS 34.15B	Ch.54, p.4407
IAS 33.IE5A	Ch.37, p.3055	IAS 34.15B(a)	Ch.41, p.3208
IAS 33.IE6	Ch.37, p.3046	IAS 34.15B(a)	Ch.41, p.3209
IAS 33.IE7	Ch.37, p.3057	IAS 34.15B(b)	Ch.41, p.3209
IAS 33.IE8	Ch.37, p.3046	IAS 34.15B(c)	Ch.41, p.3207
IAS 33.IE9	Ch.37, p.3043	IAS 34.15B(d)	Ch.41, p.3210
IAS 33.IE10	Ch.37, p.3060	IAS 34.15B(e)	Ch.41, p.3210
IAS 33.IE11	Ch.37, p.3037	IAS 34.15B(f)	Ch.41, p.3210
IAS 33.IE12	Ch.37, p.3064	IAS 34.15B(g)	Ch.41, p.3232
		IAS 34.15B(h)	Ch.41, p.3211
		IAS 34.15B(i)	Ch.41, p.3212
		IAS 34.15B(j)	Ch.41, p.3212
		IAS 34.15B(k)	Ch.41, p.3214
IAS 34 Objective	Ch.19, p.1495	IAS 34.15B(k)	Ch.41, p.3267
IAS 34 Objective	Ch.41, p.3196	IAS 34.15B(m)	Ch.41, p.3214

IAS 34

IAS 34.15B(m)	Ch.41, p.3268	IAS 34.26	Ch.41, p.3239
IAS 34.15C	Ch.41, p.3204	IAS 34.26	Ch.41, p.3252
IAS 34.15C	Ch.41, p.3205	IAS 34.27	Ch.41, p.3237
IAS 34.15C	Ch.54, p.4407	IAS 34.28	Ch.41, p.3195
IAS 34.16A	Ch.41, p.3203	IAS 34.28	Ch.41, p.3237
IAS 34.16A	Ch.41, p.3204	IAS 34.28	Ch.41, p.3239
IAS 34.16A	Ch.41, p.3206	IAS 34.28	Ch.41, p.3242
IAS 34.16A	Ch.41, p.3207	IAS 34.28	Ch.41, p.3245
IAS 34.16A	Ch.41, p.3208	IAS 34.29	Ch.41, p.3237
IAS 34.16A(a)	Ch.41, p.3199	IAS 34.29	Ch.41, p.3238
IAS 34.16A(a)	Ch.41, p.3215	IAS 34.29	Ch.41, p.3243
IAS 34.16A(a)	Ch.41, p.3232	IAS 34.29	Ch.41, p.3253
IAS 34.16A(a)	Ch.41, p.3267	IAS 34.30(a)	Ch.41, p.3238
IAS 34.16A(b)	Ch.41, p.3216	IAS 34.30(b)	Ch.41, p.3238
IAS 34.16A(b)	Ch.41, p.3243	IAS 34.30(c)	Ch.41, p.3238
IAS 34.16A(c)	Ch.41, p.3216	IAS 34.30(c)	Ch.41, p.3249
IAS 34.16A(d)	Ch.41, p.3207	IAS 34.30(c)	Ch.41, p.3252
IAS 34.16A(d)	Ch.41, p.3239	IAS 34.31	Ch.41, p.3243
IAS 34.16A(d)	Ch.41, p.3252	IAS 34.32	Ch.41, p.3238
IAS 34.16A(d)	Ch.41, p.3267	IAS 34.32	Ch.41, p.3243
IAS 34.16A(e)	Ch.41, p.3217	IAS 34.32	Ch.41, p.3259
IAS 34.16A(f)	Ch.41, p.3218	IAS 34.33	Ch.41, p.3238
IAS 34.16A(g)	Ch.41, p.3221	IAS 34.34-36	Ch.41, p.3239
IAS 34.16A(g)	Ch.41, p.3268	IAS 34.36	Ch.41, p.3245
IAS 34.16A(g)(iv)	Ch.41, p.3268	IAS 34.37	Ch.41, p.3242
IAS 34.16A(g)(v)	Ch.41, p.3267	IAS 34.38	Ch.41, p.3242
IAS 34.16A(h)	Ch.41, p.3218	IAS 34.39	Ch.41, p.3243
IAS 34.16A(h)	Ch.41, p.3252	IAS 34.39	Ch.41, p.3260
IAS 34.16A(i)	Ch.9, p.753	IAS 34.40	Ch.41, p.3243
IAS 34.16A(i)	Ch.13, p.946	IAS 34.41	Ch.41, p.3236
IAS 34.16A(i)	Ch.41, p.3207	IAS 34.41	Ch.41, p.3265
IAS 34.16A(i)	Ch.41, p.3219	IAS 34.42	Ch.41, p.3265
IAS 34.16A(j)	Ch.41, p.3223	IAS 34.43	Ch.41, p.3239
IAS 34.16A(j)	Ch.54, p.4407	IAS 34.43	Ch.41, p.3240
IAS 34.16A(k)	Ch.13, p.946	IAS 34.43(a)	Ch.41, p.3242
IAS 34.16A(l)	Ch.32, p.2439	IAS 34.44	Ch.41, p.3239
IAS 34.19	Ch.41, p.3224	IAS 34.44	Ch.41, p.3240
IAS 34.20	Ch.41, p.3227	IAS 34.45	Ch.41, p.3240
IAS 34.20	Ch.41, p.3232	IAS 34.B1	Ch.41, p.3246
IAS 34.20	Ch.41, p.3234	IAS 34.B2	Ch.41, p.3260
IAS 34.20	Ch.41, p.3266	IAS 34.B3	Ch.41, p.3259
IAS 34.20(b)	Ch.41, p.3228	IAS 34.B4	Ch.41, p.3259
IAS 34.21	Ch.41, p.3228	IAS 34.B5	Ch.41, p.3246
IAS 34.21	Ch.41, p.3234	IAS 34.B6	Ch.41, p.3246
IAS 34.21	Ch.41, p.3243	IAS 34.B7	Ch.41, p.3260
IAS 34.22	Ch.41, p.3228	IAS 34.B8	Ch.41, p.3244
IAS 34.23	Ch.41, p.3207	IAS 34.B9	Ch.41, p.3247
IAS 34.23	Ch.41, p.3235	IAS 34.B10	Ch.41, p.3248
IAS 34.23	Ch.41, p.3236	IAS 34.B11	Ch.41, p.3260
IAS 34.24	Ch.41, p.3235	IAS 34.B12	Ch.41, p.3249
IAS 34.25	Ch.41, p.3199	IAS 34.B13	Ch.41, p.3249
IAS 34.25	Ch.41, p.3200	IAS 34.B13	Ch.41, p.3250
IAS 34.25(a)	Ch.41, p.3204	IAS 34.B13	Ch.41, p.3251
IAS 34.25	Ch.41, p.3205	IAS 34.B13	Ch.41, p.3252
IAS 34.25	Ch.41, p.3207	IAS 34.B13	Ch.41, p.3253
IAS 34.25	Ch.41, p.3235	IAS 34.B14	Ch.41, p.3250
IAS 34.25	Ch.41, p.3236	IAS 34.B14	Ch.41, p.3251
IAS 34.26	Ch.41, p.3237	IAS 34.B15	Ch.41, p.3250

IAS 34.B16	Ch.41, p.3250	IAS 36.10-11	Ch.20, p.1610
IAS 34.B17	Ch.41, p.3254	IAS 36.11	Ch.20, p.1522
IAS 34.B18	Ch.41, p.3254	IAS 36.11	Ch.20, p.1610
IAS 34.B19	Ch.41, p.3257	IAS 36.12	Ch.20, p.1523
IAS 34.B20	Ch.41, p.3255	IAS 36.12-13	Ch.20, p.1522
IAS 34.B21	Ch.41, p.3254	IAS 36.12(f)	Ch.18, p.1415
IAS 34.B22	Ch.41, p.3254	IAS 36.12(h)	Ch.8, p.599
IAS 34.B23	Ch.41, p.3249	IAS 36.13	Ch.8, p.600
IAS 34.B24	Ch.41, p.3244	IAS 36.13	Ch.20, p.1518
IAS 34.B25	Ch.41, p.3248	IAS 36.13	Ch.20, p.1628
IAS 34.B26	Ch.41, p.3248	IAS 36.14	Ch.20, p.1523
IAS 34.B28	Ch.41, p.3249	IAS 36.15	Ch.20, p.1522
IAS 34.B29	Ch.41, p.3257	IAS 36.15	Ch.20, p.1523
IAS 34.B30	Ch.41, p.3257	IAS 36.16	Ch.20, p.1525
IAS 34.B31	Ch.41, p.3257	IAS 36.16	Ch.20, p.1565
IAS 34.B32	Ch.16, p.1273	IAS 36.17	Ch.20, p.1523
IAS 34.B32	Ch.41, p.3258	IAS 36.18	Ch.19, p.1486
IAS 34.B33	Ch.16, p.1273	IAS 36.18	Ch.20, p.1544
IAS 34.B33	Ch.41, p.3258	IAS 36.18	Ch.43, p.3434
IAS 34.B34	Ch.16, p.1274	IAS 36.19	Ch.20, p.1544
IAS 34.B34	Ch.41, p.3258	IAS 36.19	Ch.43, p.3434
IAS 34.B35	Ch.41, p.3244	IAS 36.20	Ch.20, p.1544
IAS 34.B36	Ch.41, p.3244	IAS 36.20	Ch.20, p.1548
IAS 34.B36	Ch.41, p.3245	IAS 36.21	Ch.20, p.1545
IAS 34.IE A	Ch.41, p.3228	IAS 36.22	Ch.17, p.1350
IAS 34.IE C7	Ch.19, p.1495	IAS 36.22	Ch.20, p.1544
		IAS 36.22	Ch.43, p.3434
		IAS 36.23	Ch.20, p.1544

IAS 36

		IAS 36.24	Ch.20, p.1610
		IAS 36.24	Ch.20, p.1611
IAS 36.2	Ch.20, p.1521	IAS 36.28	Ch.20, p.1546
IAS 36.3	Ch.20, p.1521	IAS 36.29	Ch.20, p.1546
IAS 36.4	Ch.20, p.1521	IAS 36.30	Ch.20, p.1551
IAS 36.4	Ch.20, p.1625	IAS 36.30	Ch.20, p.1552
IAS 36.6	Ch.14, p.1051	IAS 36.30	Ch.20, p.1563
IAS 36.6	Ch.20, p.1525	IAS 36.31	Ch.20, p.1544
IAS 36.6	Ch.20, p.1544	IAS 36.31	Ch.20, p.1551
IAS 36.6	Ch.43, p.3431	IAS 36.31	Ch.43, p.3434
IAS 36.6	Ch.43, p.3432	IAS 36.32	Ch.20, p.1551
IAS 36.6	Ch.43, p.3434	IAS 36.33	Ch.20, p.1552
IAS 36.6	Ch.43, p.3440	IAS 36.33	Ch.20, p.1557
IAS 36.8-9	Ch.8, p.599	IAS 36.33(a)	Ch.43, p.3436
IAS 36.8-9	Ch.20, p.1522	IAS 36.33(b)	Ch.43, p.3435
IAS 36.8-9	Ch.42, p.3284	IAS 36.34	Ch.20, p.1552
IAS 36.8-17	Ch.43, p.3373	IAS 36.35	Ch.20, p.1553
IAS 36.9	Ch.17, p.1339	IAS 36.35	Ch.43, p.3435
IAS 36.9	Ch.20, p.1522	IAS 36.36	Ch.20, p.1553
IAS 36.9	Ch.20, p.1591	IAS 36.37	Ch.20, p.1553
IAS 36.9	Ch.20, p.1610	IAS 36.38	Ch.20, p.1553
IAS 36.10	Ch.9, p.680	IAS 36.39	Ch.20, p.1553
IAS 36.10	Ch.17, p.1319	IAS 36.39(b)	Ch.20, p.1526
IAS 36.10	Ch.17, p.1339	IAS 36.39(b)	Ch.20, p.1558
IAS 36.10	Ch.17, p.1347	IAS 36.40	Ch.20, p.1553
IAS 36.10	Ch.17, p.1350	IAS 36.41	Ch.20, p.1554
IAS 36.10	Ch.20, p.1522	IAS 36.41	Ch.20, p.1559
IAS 36.10	Ch.20, p.1595	IAS 36.42	Ch.20, p.1554
IAS 36.10	Ch.20, p.1610	IAS 36.42	Ch.43, p.3439
IAS 36.10-11	Ch.20, p.1531	IAS 36.43	Ch.20, p.1553

IAS 36.44	Ch.20, p.1554	IAS 36.78	Ch.20, p.1561
IAS 36.44	Ch.20, p.1556	IAS 36.78	Ch.43, p.3435
IAS 36.44	Ch.20, p.1559	IAS 36.79	Ch.20, p.1536
IAS 36.44	Ch.43, p.3439	IAS 36.79	Ch.20, p.1540
IAS 36.45	Ch.20, p.1556	IAS 36.79	Ch.20, p.1554
IAS 36.46	Ch.20, p.1556	IAS 36.79	Ch.43, p.3435
IAS 36.47	Ch.20, p.1556	IAS 36.80	Ch.20, p.1582
IAS 36.48	Ch.20, p.1554	IAS 36.80	Ch.20, p.1585
IAS 36.49	Ch.20, p.1555	IAS 36.80	Ch.20, p.1587
IAS 36.50	Ch.20, p.1554	IAS 36.80	Ch.20, p.1621
IAS 36.50	Ch.20, p.1584	IAS 36.80(b)	Ch.20, p.1588
IAS 36.51	Ch.20, p.1554	IAS 36.80(b)	Ch.36, p.2983
IAS 36.51	Ch.20, p.1584	IAS 36.81	Ch.20, p.1582
IAS 36.52	Ch.20, p.1556	IAS 36.81	Ch.20, p.1587
IAS 36.53	Ch.20, p.1556	IAS 36.82	Ch.20, p.1583
IAS 36.53A	Ch.20, p.1581	IAS 36.83	Ch.20, p.1583
IAS 36.53A	Ch.20, p.1582	IAS 36.84	Ch.20, p.1589
IAS 36.54	Ch.20, p.1557	IAS 36.84	Ch.20, p.1590
IAS 36.54	Ch.26, p.1959	IAS 36.84	Ch.20, p.1591
IAS 36.54	Ch.43, p.3440	IAS 36.85	Ch.20, p.1589
IAS 36.55	Ch.20, p.1564	IAS 36.86	Ch.20, p.1598
IAS 36.55	Ch.20, p.1567	IAS 36.87	Ch.20, p.1588
IAS 36.55	Ch.20, p.1577	IAS 36.87	Ch.20, p.1599
IAS 36.55	Ch.20, p.1578	IAS 36.88	Ch.20, p.1613
IAS 36.55	Ch.43, p.3436	IAS 36.89	Ch.20, p.1610
IAS 36.56	Ch.20, p.1564	IAS 36.89	Ch.20, p.1611
IAS 36.56	Ch.20, p.1568	IAS 36.90	Ch.20, p.1590
IAS 36.59	Ch.20, p.1612	IAS 36.90	Ch.20, p.1591
IAS 36.60	Ch.20, p.1612	IAS 36.96	Ch.20, p.1591
IAS 36.60	Ch.42, p.3284	IAS 36.97-98	Ch.20, p.1592
IAS 36.61	Ch.18, p.1422	IAS 36.99	Ch.20, p.1592
IAS 36.62	Ch.20, p.1612	IAS 36.100	Ch.20, p.1542
IAS 36.63	Ch.20, p.1612	IAS 36.101	Ch.20, p.1542
IAS 36.64	Ch.20, p.1613	IAS 36.102	Ch.20, p.1542
IAS 36.66	Ch.20, p.1551	IAS 36.104	Ch.17, p.1350
IAS 36.66	Ch.43, p.3431	IAS 36.104	Ch.20, p.1531
IAS 36.67	Ch.20, p.1551	IAS 36.104	Ch.20, p.1604
IAS 36.68	Ch.20, p.1525	IAS 36.104	Ch.20, p.1613
IAS 36.68-69	Ch.20, p.1528	IAS 36.105	Ch.20, p.1545
IAS 36.69	Ch.20, p.1525	IAS 36.105	Ch.20, p.1613
IAS 36.70	Ch.20, p.1534	IAS 36.105	Ch.20, p.1614
IAS 36.70	Ch.20, p.1558	IAS 36.106	Ch.20, p.1614
IAS 36.70	Ch.20, p.1620	IAS 36.107	Ch.20, p.1615
IAS 36.70	Ch.43, p.3432	IAS 36.108	Ch.20, p.1614
IAS 36.71	Ch.20, p.1534	IAS 36.108	Ch.26, p.1976
IAS 36.72	Ch.20, p.1531	IAS 36.109-123	Ch.43, p.3374
IAS 36.73	Ch.20, p.1531	IAS 36.109-125	Ch.31, p.2385
IAS 36.74	Ch.43, p.3434	IAS 36.110	Ch.20, p.1616
IAS 36.74-79	Ch.5, p.334	IAS 36.111	Ch.20, p.1616
IAS 36.75	Ch.20, p.1535	IAS 36.112	Ch.20, p.1616
IAS 36.75	Ch.43, p.3434	IAS 36.113	Ch.20, p.1616
IAS 36.76	Ch.20, p.1535	IAS 36.114-116	Ch.20, p.1617
IAS 36.76	Ch.43, p.3435	IAS 36.117	Ch.18, p.1424
IAS 36.77	Ch.20, p.1535	IAS 36.117	Ch.20, p.1617
IAS 36.78	Ch.20, p.1536	IAS 36.118	Ch.20, p.1617
IAS 36.78	Ch.20, p.1537	IAS 36.119	Ch.5, p.376
IAS 36.78	Ch.20, p.1538	IAS 36.119	Ch.20, p.1618
IAS 36.78	Ch.20, p.1546	IAS 36.119	Ch.20, p.1619

IAS 36.120	Ch.20, p.1619
IAS 36.121	Ch.20, p.1618
IAS 36.121	Ch.20, p.1619
IAS 36.122	Ch.20, p.1618
IAS 36.123	Ch.20, p.1618
IAS 36.124	Ch.20, p.1593
IAS 36.124	Ch.20, p.1615
IAS 36.124	Ch.20, p.1629
IAS 36.124	Ch.41, p.3245
IAS 36.125	Ch.20, p.1593
IAS 36.125	Ch.20, p.1615
IAS 36.126	Ch.20, p.1630
IAS 36.127	Ch.20, p.1630
IAS 36.128	Ch.20, p.1630
IAS 36.129	Ch.20, p.1630
IAS 36.130	Ch.20, p.1631
IAS 36.131	Ch.20, p.1632
IAS 36.132	Ch.20, p.1632
IAS 36.133	Ch.20, p.1632
IAS 36.134	Ch.20, p.1634
IAS 36.134(d)(i)-(ii)	Ch.43, p.3437
IAS 36.134(d)(v)	Ch.20, p.1575
IAS 36.134(e)(i)-(ii)	Ch.43, p.3437
IAS 36.134(f)	Ch.20, p.1524
IAS 36.134(f)(ii)	Ch.20, p.1635
IAS 36.135	Ch.20, p.1634
IAS 36.135	Ch.20, p.1635
IAS 36.A2	Ch.20, p.1563
IAS 36.A4	Ch.20, p.1563
IAS 36.A6	Ch.20, p.1563
IAS 36.A7	Ch.20, p.1563
IAS 36.A10	Ch.20, p.1563
IAS 36.A10-13	Ch.20, p.1564
IAS 36.A15	Ch.20, p.1578
IAS 36.A16	Ch.20, p.1564
IAS 36.A17	Ch.20, p.1564
IAS 36.A17	Ch.20, p.1580
IAS 36.A18	Ch.20, p.1565
IAS 36.A19	Ch.20, p.1565
IAS 36.A19	Ch.20, p.1579
IAS 36.A20	Ch.20, p.1565
IAS 36.A21	Ch.20, p.1565
IAS 36.C1	Ch.20, p.1602
IAS 36.C2	Ch.20, p.1602
IAS 36.C3	Ch.20, p.1604
IAS 36.C4	Ch.20, p.1604
IAS 36.C6	Ch.20, p.1602
IAS 36.C7	Ch.20, p.1602
IAS 36.C8	Ch.20, p.1604
IAS 36.IE5-10	Ch.20, p.1535
IAS 36.IE62-68	Ch.20, p.1604
IAS 36.IE69-IE79	Ch.20, p.1543
IAS 36.IE Example 1C	Ch.43, p.3433
IAS 36.BCZ28-BCZ29	Ch.20, p.1550
IAS 36.BCZ49	Ch.20, p.1557
IAS 36.BCZ49	Ch.43, p.3440
IAS 36.BCZ81	Ch.20, p.1568
IAS 36.BCZ84	Ch.20, p.1569
IAS 36.BCZ85	Ch.20, p.1567
IAS 36.BCZ85	Ch.20, p.1569
IAS 36.BCZ85	Ch.20, p.1576
IAS 36.BCZ88	Ch.20, p.1568
IAS 36.BC139	Ch.20, p.1585
IAS 36.BC156	Ch.20, p.1598
IAS 36.BC162	Ch.20, p.1591
IAS 36.BC173	Ch.20, p.1591
IAS 36.BC177	Ch.20, p.1593

IAS 37 (2022)

IAS 37(2022).68A	Ch.31, p.2357

IAS 1

IAS 37 Objective	Ch.26, p.1932
IAS 37.1	Ch.26, p.1929
IAS 37.1	Ch.26, p.1932
IAS 37.2	Ch.26, p.1935
IAS 37.3	Ch.26, p.1932
IAS 37.3	Ch.26, p.1934
IAS 37.3	Ch.26, p.1945
IAS 37.3	Ch.39, p.3122
IAS 37.5	Ch.26, p.1934
IAS 37.5	Ch.26, p.2006
IAS 37.5	Ch.33, p.2561
IAS 37.5(c)	Ch.26, p.1934
IAS 37.5(c)	Ch.26, p.1975
IAS 37.5(g)	Ch.26, p.1936
IAS 37.5(g)	Ch.26, p.1977
IAS 37.7	Ch.26, p.1936
IAS 37.8	Ch.26, p.1946
IAS 37.9	Ch.26, p.1935
IAS 37.9	Ch.26, p.1967
IAS 37.9	Ch.26, p.2012
IAS 37.10	Ch.9, p.690
IAS 37.10	Ch.13, p.978
IAS 37.10	Ch.26, p.1931
IAS 37.10	Ch.26, p.1932
IAS 37.10	Ch.26, p.1936
IAS 37.10	Ch.26, p.1938
IAS 37.10	Ch.26, p.1939
IAS 37.10	Ch.26, p.1943
IAS 37.10	Ch.26, p.1944
IAS 37.10	Ch.26, p.1965
IAS 37.10	Ch.26, p.1966
IAS 37.10	Ch.26, p.1972
IAS 37.10	Ch.26, p.1974
IAS 37.10	Ch.26, p.1979
IAS 37.10	Ch.35, p.2912
IAS 37.10	Ch.43, p.3398
IAS 37.10	Ch.55, p.4569
IAS 37.11	Ch.26, p.1936
IAS 37.11(a)	Ch.54, p.4511
IAS 37.12	Ch.26, p.1937

IAS 37.13	Ch.26, p.1937	IAS 37.34	Ch.26, p.1942
IAS 37.13	Ch.26, p.1943	IAS 37.34	Ch.26, p.1945
IAS 37.14	Ch.17, p.1361	IAS 37.35	Ch.26, p.1945
IAS 37.14	Ch.26, p.1937	IAS 37.35	Ch.33, p.2569
IAS 37.14	Ch.26, p.1943	IAS 37.35	Ch.38, p.3079
IAS 37.14	Ch.26, p.1992	IAS 37.35	Ch.38, p.3081
IAS 37.14	Ch.26, p.2005	IAS 37.36	Ch.17, p.1361
IAS 37.14	Ch.26, p.2006	IAS 37.36	Ch.26, p.1947
IAS 37.14	Ch.55, p.4547	IAS 37.36	Ch.26, p.1952
IAS 37.14	Ch.56, p.4703	IAS 37.36	Ch.26, p.1958
IAS 37.15	Ch.24, p.1830	IAS 37.36	Ch.43, p.3451
IAS 37.15	Ch.26, p.1938	IAS 37.36-37	Ch.26, p.1947
IAS 37.15	Ch.26, p.2005	IAS 37.36-47	Ch.55, p.4580
IAS 37.16	Ch.26, p.1938	IAS 37.37	Ch.17, p.1364
IAS 37.16	Ch.26, p.1939	IAS 37.37	Ch.26, p.1947
IAS 37.16	Ch.26, p.2005	IAS 37.37	Ch.43, p.3451
IAS 37.16(a)	Ch.26, p.1943	IAS 37.38	Ch.26, p.1948
IAS 37.16(b)	Ch.26, p.1943	IAS 37.39	Ch.26, p.1942
IAS 37.17	Ch.26, p.1939	IAS 37.39	Ch.26, p.1948
IAS 37.17	Ch.26, p.1963	IAS 37.39	Ch.26, p.2004
IAS 37.17	Ch.26, p.2002	IAS 37.40	Ch.26, p.1942
IAS 37.18	Ch.26, p.1939	IAS 37.40	Ch.26, p.1949
IAS 37.18	Ch.26, p.1963	IAS 37.41	Ch.26, p.1947
IAS 37.18	Ch.26, p.1964	IAS 37.42	Ch.26, p.1949
IAS 37.18	Ch.26, p.2002	IAS 37.43	Ch.26, p.1949
IAS 37.19	Ch.26, p.1940	IAS 37.43	Ch.26, p.1950
IAS 37.19	Ch.26, p.1962	IAS 37.43	Ch.26, p.1951
IAS 37.19	Ch.26, p.1963	IAS 37.44	Ch.26, p.1950
IAS 37.19	Ch.26, p.1964	IAS 37.45	Ch.26, p.1950
IAS 37.19	Ch.26, p.1966	IAS 37.46	Ch.26, p.1950
IAS 37.19	Ch.26, p.1969	IAS 37.47	Ch.26, p.1950
IAS 37.19	Ch.26, p.1975	IAS 37.47	Ch.26, p.1951
IAS 37.19	Ch.26, p.2002	IAS 37.47	Ch.26, p.1952
IAS 37.20	Ch.26, p.1941	IAS 37.47	Ch.26, p.1954
IAS 37.21	Ch.26, p.1941	IAS 37.47	Ch.26, p.1957
IAS 37.22	Ch.26, p.1941	IAS 37.48	Ch.26, p.1958
IAS 37.22	Ch.26, p.1992	IAS 37.49	Ch.26, p.1959
IAS 37.23	Ch.17, p.1301	IAS 37.50	Ch.26, p.1959
IAS 37.23	Ch.26, p.1941	IAS 37.51	Ch.26, p.1972
IAS 37.23	Ch.26, p.1943	IAS 37.51-52	Ch.26, p.1961
IAS 37.23	Ch.26, p.1945	IAS 37.53	Ch.17, p.1363
IAS 37.23	Ch.33, p.2491	IAS 37.53	Ch.26, p.1959
IAS 37.24	Ch.26, p.1941	IAS 37.53	Ch.51, p.3958
IAS 37.24	Ch.26, p.2004	IAS 37.53	Ch.51, p.3959
IAS 37.25	Ch.26, p.1942	IAS 37.54	Ch.26, p.1959
IAS 37.25	Ch.26, p.2005	IAS 37.55	Ch.26, p.1959
IAS 37.25	Ch.43, p.3429	IAS 37.56	Ch.26, p.1960
IAS 37.26	Ch.26, p.1942	IAS 37.56	Ch.55, p.4542
IAS 37.26	Ch.26, p.1943	IAS 37.57	Ch.26, p.1960
IAS 37.26	Ch.43, p.3429	IAS 37.58	Ch.26, p.1960
IAS 37.27-28	Ch.26, p.1942	IAS 37.59	Ch.26, p.1955
IAS 37.29	Ch.26, p.1960	IAS 37.59	Ch.26, p.1961
IAS 37.30	Ch.26, p.1944	IAS 37.59	Ch.26, p.1981
IAS 37.31	Ch.26, p.1942	IAS 37.60	Ch.26, p.1954
IAS 37.32	Ch.26, p.1944	IAS 37.60	Ch.26, p.1956
IAS 37.33	Ch.9, p.686	IAS 37.60	Ch.26, p.1961
IAS 37.33	Ch.26, p.1944	IAS 37.61	Ch.26, p.1961
IAS 37.33	Ch.55, p.4542	IAS 37.61	Ch.26, p.2009

IAS 37.61-62	Ch.43, p.3534
IAS 37.62	Ch.26, p.1961
IAS 37.63	Ch.26, p.1962
IAS 37.63	Ch.26, p.1966
IAS 37.63	Ch.26, p.1970
IAS 37.63	Ch.26, p.1972
IAS 37.64	Ch.26, p.1962
IAS 37.65	Ch.26, p.1963
IAS 37.66	Ch.26, p.1972
IAS 37.66	Ch.31, p.2356
IAS 37.67	Ch.26, p.1972
IAS 37.67-68	Ch.31, p.2357
IAS 37.68	Ch.26, p.1960
IAS 37.68	Ch.26, p.1972
IAS 37.68	Ch.26, p.1977
IAS 37.68A	Ch.26, p.1973
IAS 37.69	Ch.26, p.1975
IAS 37.69	Ch.31, p.2356
IAS 37.70	Ch.26, p.1967
IAS 37.71	Ch.26, p.1967
IAS 37.71	Ch.41, p.3207
IAS 37.72	Ch.26, p.1967
IAS 37.72	Ch.26, p.1969
IAS 37.73	Ch.26, p.1968
IAS 37.74	Ch.26, p.1968
IAS 37.75	Ch.26, p.1968
IAS 37.76	Ch.26, p.1969
IAS 37.77	Ch.26, p.1969
IAS 37.78	Ch.26, p.1969
IAS 37.79	Ch.26, p.1970
IAS 37.80	Ch.26, p.1970
IAS 37.80	Ch.26, p.1971
IAS 37.81	Ch.26, p.1964
IAS 37.81	Ch.26, p.1970
IAS 37.82	Ch.26, p.1972
IAS 37.83	Ch.26, p.1972
IAS 37.84	Ch.26, p.2009
IAS 37.84(e)	Ch.26, p.1957
IAS 37.85	Ch.26, p.2009
IAS 37.86	Ch.13, p.978
IAS 37.86	Ch.26, p.2012
IAS 37.86	Ch.43, p.3429
IAS 37.87	Ch.26, p.2012
IAS 37.88	Ch.26, p.2012
IAS 37.89	Ch.26, p.2013
IAS 37.90	Ch.26, p.2013
IAS 37.91	Ch.26, p.2012
IAS 37.91	Ch.26, p.2013
IAS 37.92	Ch.26, p.2013
IAS 37.94A	Ch.26, p.1973
IAS 37.105	Ch.26, p.1973
IAS 37 Appendix C	Ch.43, p.3492
IAS 37.IE Example 1	Ch.26, p.2004
IAS 37.IE Example 2A	Ch.26, p.1992
IAS 37.IE Example 2B	Ch.26, p.1938
IAS 37.IE Example 2B	Ch.26, p.1992
IAS 37.IE Example 3	Ch.26, p.1946
IAS 37.IE Example 3	Ch.26, p.1979
IAS 37.IE Example 4	Ch.26, p.1938
IAS 37.IE Example 4	Ch.26, p.2005
IAS 37.IE Example 5A	Ch.26, p.1968
IAS 37.IE Example 5B	Ch.26, p.1969
IAS 37.IE Example 6	Ch.26, p.1940
IAS 37.IE Example 7	Ch.26, p.1939
IAS 37.IE Example 10	Ch.26, p.1944
IAS 37.IE Example 11A	Ch.18, p.1396
IAS 37.IE Example 11A	Ch.26, p.1963
IAS 37.IE Example 11B	Ch.18, p.1396
IAS 37.IE Example 11B	Ch.26, p.1940
IAS 37.IE Example 11B	Ch.26, p.1963
IAS 37.IE Example 11B	Ch.43, p.3492
IAS 37.IE D Examples: disclosures Example 3	Ch.26, p.2013
IAS 37.BC7	Ch.26, p.1973

IAS 38

IAS 38.1	Ch.17, p.1294
IAS 38.2	Ch.17, p.1294
IAS 38.2	Ch.43, p.3513
IAS 38.2(c)	Ch.43, p.3336
IAS 38.2(c)-(d)	Ch.43, p.3361
IAS 38.3	Ch.17, p.1292
IAS 38.3	Ch.17, p.1294
IAS 38.3	Ch.17, p.1295
IAS 38.3	Ch.17, p.1299
IAS 38.3(a)	Ch.22, p.1677
IAS 38.3(a)	Ch.22, p.1680
IAS 38.3(a)	Ch.32, p.2407
IAS 38.3(e)	Ch.22, p.1680
IAS 38.3(g)	Ch.56, p.4868
IAS 38.3(i)	Ch.31, p.2383
IAS 38.4	Ch.17, p.1298
IAS 38.4	Ch.18, p.1391
IAS 38.5	Ch.17, p.1295
IAS 38.5	Ch.17, p.1299
IAS 38.6	Ch.17, p.1294
IAS 38.6	Ch.17, p.1299
IAS 38.7	Ch.17, p.1295
IAS 38.8	Ch.9, p.672
IAS 38.8	Ch.9, p.681
IAS 38.8	Ch.17, p.1292
IAS 38.8	Ch.17, p.1293
IAS 38.8	Ch.17, p.1295
IAS 38.8	Ch.17, p.1298
IAS 38.8	Ch.17, p.1305
IAS 38.8	Ch.17, p.1312
IAS 38.8	Ch.17, p.1320
IAS 38.8	Ch.17, p.1329
IAS 38.8	Ch.17, p.1338
IAS 38.8	Ch.17, p.1341
IAS 38.8	Ch.17, p.1347
IAS 38.8	Ch.17, p.1350
IAS 38.8	Ch.17, p.1368
IAS 38.8	Ch.17, p.1369

IAS 38.8	Ch.17, p.1374	IAS 38.33	Ch.17, p.1313
IAS 38.8	Ch.33, p.2545	IAS 38.33-35	Ch.9, p.679
IAS 38.8	Ch.43, p.3395	IAS 38.34	Ch.9, p.673
IAS 38.8	Ch.43, p.3418	IAS 38.34	Ch.9, p.679
IAS 38.9	Ch.17, p.1295	IAS 38.34	Ch.17, p.1318
IAS 38.10	Ch.17, p.1295	IAS 38.35	Ch.17, p.1314
IAS 38.11	Ch.9, p.672	IAS 38.36	Ch.9, p.678
IAS 38.11	Ch.17, p.1296	IAS 38.36	Ch.17, p.1314
IAS 38.12	Ch.9, p.672	IAS 38.37	Ch.9, p.678
IAS 38.12	Ch.17, p.1293	IAS 38.37	Ch.17, p.1314
IAS 38.12	Ch.17, p.1296	IAS 38.42	Ch.9, p.680
IAS 38.12	Ch.17, p.1313	IAS 38.42	Ch.17, p.1319
IAS 38.12(b)	Ch.17, p.1299	IAS 38.43	Ch.9, p.680
IAS 38.12(b)	Ch.17, p.1368	IAS 38.43	Ch.17, p.1319
IAS 38.13	Ch.17, p.1293	IAS 38.44	Ch.17, p.1310
IAS 38.13	Ch.17, p.1296	IAS 38.45	Ch.17, p.1311
IAS 38.13	Ch.17, p.1297	IAS 38.45	Ch.25, p.1881
IAS 38.13	Ch.17, p.1299	IAS 38.45	Ch.43, p.3402
IAS 38.13	Ch.17, p.1352	IAS 38.46	Ch.17, p.1311
IAS 38.13	Ch.17, p.1368	IAS 38.46	Ch.17, p.1312
IAS 38.13	Ch.17, p.1374	IAS 38.47	Ch.17, p.1311
IAS 38.13-14	Ch.17, p.1296	IAS 38.48	Ch.17, p.1295
IAS 38.15	Ch.17, p.1297	IAS 38.48	Ch.17, p.1319
IAS 38.15	Ch.31, p.2367	IAS 38.49	Ch.17, p.1319
IAS 38.16	Ch.17, p.1296	IAS 38.50	Ch.17, p.1319
IAS 38.16	Ch.17, p.1297	IAS 38.51	Ch.17, p.1320
IAS 38.17	Ch.17, p.1298	IAS 38.52	Ch.17, p.1320
IAS 38.17	Ch.17, p.1368	IAS 38.52	Ch.17, p.1322
IAS 38.18	Ch.17, p.1297	IAS 38.53	Ch.17, p.1320
IAS 38.18	Ch.17, p.1301	IAS 38.53	Ch.17, p.1321
IAS 38.19	Ch.17, p.1301	IAS 38.53	Ch.17, p.1322
IAS 38.20	Ch.17, p.1305	IAS 38.54	Ch.9, p.679
IAS 38.20	Ch.17, p.1326	IAS 38.54	Ch.17, p.1320
IAS 38.20	Ch.17, p.1352	IAS 38.54-55	Ch.17, p.1321
IAS 38.20	Ch.17, p.1369	IAS 38.55	Ch.17, p.1322
IAS 38.21	Ch.5, p.281	IAS 38.56	Ch.17, p.1320
IAS 38.21	Ch.9, p.679	IAS 38.56	Ch.17, p.1369
IAS 38.21	Ch.17, p.1301	IAS 38.57	Ch.9, p.679
IAS 38.21	Ch.17, p.1313	IAS 38.57	Ch.17, p.1321
IAS 38.21	Ch.17, p.1376	IAS 38.57	Ch.17, p.1369
IAS 38.21	Ch.43, p.3395	IAS 38.57(d)	Ch.24, p.1832
IAS 38.21	Ch.43, p.3398	IAS 38.58	Ch.17, p.1321
IAS 38.22	Ch.17, p.1301	IAS 38.59	Ch.17, p.1320
IAS 38.23	Ch.17, p.1301	IAS 38.60	Ch.9, p.679
IAS 38.24	Ch.17, p.1304	IAS 38.60	Ch.17, p.1321
IAS 38.24	Ch.17, p.1329	IAS 38.61	Ch.17, p.1322
IAS 38.24	Ch.43, p.3367	IAS 38.62	Ch.17, p.1322
IAS 38.25	Ch.17, p.1305	IAS 38.63	Ch.17, p.1292
IAS 38.26	Ch.17, p.1305	IAS 38.63	Ch.17, p.1305
IAS 38.27	Ch.17, p.1306	IAS 38.63-64	Ch.17, p.1326
IAS 38.28	Ch.17, p.1306	IAS 38.64	Ch.17, p.1292
IAS 38.29-30	Ch.17, p.1307	IAS 38.65	Ch.17, p.1329
IAS 38.30	Ch.17, p.1306	IAS 38.66	Ch.17, p.1330
IAS 38.31	Ch.17, p.1307	IAS 38.67	Ch.17, p.1328
IAS 38.31	Ch.17, p.1324	IAS 38.67	Ch.17, p.1330
IAS 38.32	Ch.17, p.1306	IAS 38.67(a)	Ch.26, p.1974
IAS 38.32	Ch.25, p.1892	IAS 38.68	Ch.17, p.1301
IAS 38.33	Ch.9, p.681	IAS 38.68	Ch.17, p.1329

Index of standards 101

IAS 38.68	Ch.17, p.1330
IAS 38.68-69	Ch.31, p.2367
IAS 38.69	Ch.17, p.1330
IAS 38.69	Ch.17, p.1332
IAS 38.69	Ch.25, p.1898
IAS 38.69A	Ch.17, p.1331
IAS 38.69A	Ch.17, p.1332
IAS 38.70	Ch.17, p.1331
IAS 38.71	Ch.5, p.378
IAS 38.71	Ch.17, p.1301
IAS 38.71	Ch.17, p.1329
IAS 38.71	Ch.17, p.1334
IAS 38.71	Ch.41, p.3238
IAS 38.71	Ch.41, p.3244
IAS 38.72	Ch.17, p.1333
IAS 38.72	Ch.43, p.3368
IAS 38.73	Ch.17, p.1333
IAS 38.73	Ch.17, p.1335
IAS 38.74	Ch.17, p.1333
IAS 38.75	Ch.17, p.1333
IAS 38.75	Ch.17, p.1334
IAS 38.75	Ch.17, p.1335
IAS 38.75	Ch.43, p.3368
IAS 38.76	Ch.17, p.1334
IAS 38.77	Ch.17, p.1334
IAS 38.78	Ch.17, p.1334
IAS 38.78	Ch.17, p.1335
IAS 38.79	Ch.17, p.1335
IAS 38.80	Ch.17, p.1337
IAS 38.81-82	Ch.17, p.1333
IAS 38.81-82	Ch.17, p.1334
IAS 38.82	Ch.17, p.1335
IAS 38.83	Ch.17, p.1335
IAS 38.84	Ch.17, p.1335
IAS 38.85	Ch.17, p.1335
IAS 38.86	Ch.17, p.1336
IAS 38.87	Ch.17, p.1337
IAS 38.87	Ch.27, p.2040
IAS 38.88	Ch.17, p.1338
IAS 38.88	Ch.33, p.2548
IAS 38.88	Ch.33, p.2549
IAS 38.89	Ch.17, p.1338
IAS 38.90	Ch.17, p.1339
IAS 38.91	Ch.17, p.1338
IAS 38.91	Ch.20, p.1610
IAS 38.91	Ch.33, p.2548
IAS 38.92	Ch.17, p.1338
IAS 38.92	Ch.17, p.1339
IAS 38.93	Ch.17, p.1339
IAS 38.94	Ch.17, p.1340
IAS 38.94-95	Ch.17, p.1340
IAS 38.96	Ch.17, p.1340
IAS 38.97	Ch.17, p.1341
IAS 38.97	Ch.17, p.1342
IAS 38.97	Ch.17, p.1344
IAS 38.97	Ch.25, p.1880
IAS 38.97	Ch.25, p.1881
IAS 38.97-98	Ch.17, p.1344
IAS 38.98	Ch.17, p.1342
IAS 38.98	Ch.25, p.1881
IAS 38.98	Ch.41, p.3244
IAS 38.98A	Ch.17, p.1345
IAS 38.98A	Ch.17, p.1346
IAS 38.98A	Ch.25, p.1882
IAS 38.98B	Ch.17, p.1346
IAS 38.98B	Ch.25, p.1883
IAS 38.98C	Ch.17, p.1346
IAS 38.98C	Ch.25, p.1883
IAS 38.99	Ch.17, p.1342
IAS 38.100	Ch.17, p.1348
IAS 38.101	Ch.17, p.1348
IAS 38.102	Ch.17, p.1348
IAS 38.103	Ch.17, p.1348
IAS 38.104	Ch.5, p.379
IAS 38.104	Ch.17, p.1347
IAS 38.105	Ch.17, p.1347
IAS 38.106	Ch.17, p.1347
IAS 38.107	Ch.17, p.1349
IAS 38.108	Ch.17, p.1349
IAS 38.109	Ch.17, p.1349
IAS 38.109	Ch.33, p.2549
IAS 38.110	Ch.17, p.1349
IAS 38.111	Ch.17, p.1350
IAS 38.112	Ch.17, p.1350
IAS 38.112	Ch.17, p.1365
IAS 38.112	Ch.43, p.3395
IAS 38.112	Ch.43, p.3399
IAS 38.113	Ch.17, p.1351
IAS 38.113	Ch.17, p.1357
IAS 38.113	Ch.17, p.1365
IAS 38.113	Ch.27, p.2040
IAS 38.113	Ch.43, p.3399
IAS 38.114	Ch.17, p.1350
IAS 38.114	Ch.27, p.2040
IAS 38.115	Ch.17, p.1352
IAS 38.115A	Ch.17, p.1351
IAS 38.116	Ch.17, p.1351
IAS 38.116	Ch.27, p.2040
IAS 38.116	Ch.43, p.3400
IAS 38.116	Ch.45, p.3605
IAS 38.117	Ch.17, p.1342
IAS 38.118	Ch.17, p.1353
IAS 38.118	Ch.41, p.3232
IAS 38.118(d)	Ch.17, p.1357
IAS 38.119	Ch.17, p.1333
IAS 38.119	Ch.17, p.1353
IAS 38.120	Ch.17, p.1355
IAS 38.121	Ch.17, p.1355
IAS 38.122	Ch.17, p.1356
IAS 38.122(e)	Ch.38, p.3080
IAS 38.122(e)	Ch.39, p.3123
IAS 38.123	Ch.17, p.1356
IAS 38.124	Ch.17, p.1357
IAS 38.125	Ch.17, p.1358
IAS 38.126-127	Ch.17, p.1358
IAS 38.128	Ch.17, p.1356

IAS 38.BC5 .... Ch.17, p.1295
IAS 38.BC7 .... Ch.17, p.1295
IAS 38.BC8 .... Ch.17, p.1295
IAS 38.BC10 .... Ch.17, p.1296
IAS 38.BC13 .... Ch.17, p.1296
IAS 38.BC19A Ch.17, p.1313
IAS 38.BC19B Ch.17, p.1313
IAS 38.BCZ40 .... Ch.17, p.1302
IAS 38.BCZ41 .... Ch.17, p.1302
IAS 38.BC46B Ch.17, p.1331
IAS 38.BC46D Ch.17, p.1331
IAS 38.BC46E Ch.17, p.1331
IAS 38.BC46G Ch.17, p.1332
IAS 38.BC59 .... Ch.17, p.1348
IAS 38.BC62 .... Ch.17, p.1338
IAS 38.BC72H-72I Ch.17, p.1346
IAS 38.BC74 .... Ch.33, p.2548
IAS 38.BC82 .... Ch.9, p.679
IAS 38.BC82 .... Ch.17, p.1319

IAS 39 (2006)

IAS 39(2006).BC222(v)(ii) Ch.49, p.3855

IAS 39 (2010)

IAS 39(2010).AG70 .... Ch.14, p.1114

IAS 39 (2017)

IAS 39(2017).AG84 .... Ch.14, p.1012

IAS 39

IAS 39.2(e) Ch.55, p.4539
IAS 39.9 .... Ch.51, p.4045
IAS 39.9 .... Ch.55, p.4559
IAS 39.10 .... Ch.55, p.4559
IAS 39.11 .... Ch.55, p.4560
IAS 39.39 .... Ch.55, p.4582
IAS 39.50 .... Ch.55, p.4595
IAS 39.50A(c) Ch.55, p.4595
IAS 39.72 .... Ch.53, p.4396
IAS 39.74 .... Ch.53, p.4397
IAS 39.81A Ch.53, p.4382
IAS 39.82 .... Ch.53, p.4395
IAS 39.83 .... Ch.53, p.4395
IAS 39.84 .... Ch.53, p.4395
IAS 39.86 .... Ch.53, p.4390
IAS 39.86 .... Ch.53, p.4396
IAS 39.88 .... Ch.53, p.4396
IAS 39.88(a) Ch.53, p.4395
IAS 39.89 .... Ch.53, p.4397
IAS 39.89A Ch.53, p.4382

IAS 39.91(b) Ch.53, p.4397
IAS 39.91(c) Ch.53, p.4397
IAS 39.96 .... Ch.53, p.4397
IAS 39.101(b) Ch.53, p.4397
IAS 39.101(d) Ch.53, p.4397
IAS 39.102A-102N Ch.53, p.4369
IAS 39.102B Ch.55, p.4616
IAS 39.102F Ch.53, p.4369
IAS 39.102G Ch.53, p.4369
IAS 39.102H Ch.53, p.4369
IAS 39.102M Ch.53, p.4378
IAS 39.102P(d) Ch.53, p.4378
IAS 39.102V Ch.53, p.4378
IAS 39.108G Ch.53, p.4369
IAS 39.AG4A Ch.55, p.4542
IAS 39.AG5 .... Ch.51, p.3930
IAS 39.AG30(g) Ch.55, p.4561
IAS 39.AG32 .... Ch.55, p.4563
IAS 39.AG33(g) Ch.55, p.4563
IAS 39.AG87 .... Ch.55, p.4584
IAS 39.AG88 .... Ch.55, p.4584
IAS 39.AG94 .... Ch.53, p.4236
IAS 39.AG94 .... Ch.53, p.4396
IAS 39.AG98 .... Ch.9, p.698
IAS 39.AG99F Ch.53, p.4395
IAS 39.AG99F(a) Ch.53, p.4194
IAS 39.AG99F(a) Ch.53, p.4378
IAS 39.AG100 .... Ch.53, p.4395
IAS 39.AG105(b) Ch.53, p.4396
IAS 39.AG107 .... Ch.53, p.4283
IAS 39.AG110 .... Ch.53, p.4221
IAS 39.AG114-132 .... Ch.53, p.4382
IAS 39.IG B.9 .... Ch.46, p.3625
IAS 39.IG E.4.4 .... Ch.51, p.4018
IAS 39.IG F.1.2 .... Ch.53, p.4238
IAS 39.IG F.1.3(b) Ch.53, p.4236
IAS 39.IG F.1.4 .... Ch.53, p.4248
IAS 39.IG F.1.4 .... Ch.53, p.4249
IAS 39.IG F.1.5 .... Ch.53, p.4251
IAS 39.IG F.1.6 .... Ch.53, p.4252
IAS 39.IG F.1.7 .... Ch.53, p.4252
IAS 39.IG F.1.9 .... Ch.53, p.4283
IAS 39.IG F.1.13 .... Ch.53, p.4243
IAS 39.IG F.1.14 .... Ch.53, p.4235
IAS 39.IG F.2.1 .... Ch.53, p.4220
IAS 39.IG F.2.2 .... Ch.53, p.4264
IAS 39.IG F.2.3 .... Ch.53, p.4223
IAS 39.IG F.2.3 .... Ch.53, p.4382
IAS 39.IG F.2.5 .... Ch.53, p.4265
IAS 39.IG F.2.5 .... Ch.53, p.4266
IAS 39.IG F.2.6 .... Ch.53, p.4274
IAS 39.IG F.2.8 .... Ch.53, p.4221
IAS 39.IG F.2.12 .... Ch.53, p.4218
IAS 39.IG F.2.14 .... Ch.53, p.4261
IAS 39.IG F.2.15 .... Ch.53, p.4252
IAS 39.IG F.2.17 .... Ch.53, p.4197
IAS 39.IG F.3.5 .... Ch.53, p.4262
IAS 39.IG F.3.6 .... Ch.53, p.4263

IAS 39.IG F.3.6	Ch.53, p.4264
IAS 39.IG F.3.6	Ch.53, p.4292
IAS 39.IG F.3.7	Ch.52, p.4123
IAS 39.IG F.3.7	Ch.53, p.4217
IAS 39.IG F.3.10	Ch.53, p.4202
IAS 39.IG F.3.10	Ch.53, p.4361
IAS 39.IG F.3.11	Ch.53, p.4360
IAS 39.IG F.5.2	Ch.53, p.4296
IAS 39.IG F.5.5	Ch.53, p.4319
IAS 39.IG F.5.6	Ch.53, p.4324
IAS 39.IG F.5.6	Ch.53, p.4336
IAS 39.IG F.6.1-3	Ch.53, p.4382
IAS 39.IG F.6.1-3	Ch.53, p.4385
IAS 39.BC15	Ch.51, p.4045
IAS 39.BC220O-Q	Ch.53, p.4362
IAS 39.BC220R	Ch.53, p.4362
IAS 39.BC220S	Ch.53, p.4362
IAS 39.BC222(d)	Ch.49, p.3860

IAS 40

IAS 40.1	Ch.19, p.1441
IAS 40.2	Ch.19, p.1441
IAS 40.4	Ch.19, p.1443
IAS 40.4(a)	Ch.19, p.1451
IAS 40.4(b)	Ch.43, p.3336
IAS 40.4(b)	Ch.43, p.3361
IAS 40.5	Ch.19, p.1442
IAS 40.5	Ch.19, p.1468
IAS 40.5	Ch.22, p.1695
IAS 40.5	Ch.43, p.3418
IAS 40.7	Ch.19, p.1443
IAS 40.7	Ch.19, p.1445
IAS 40.7	Ch.19, p.1446
IAS 40.8	Ch.19, p.1445
IAS 40.8	Ch.19, p.1446
IAS 40.9	Ch.19, p.1445
IAS 40.9	Ch.19, p.1446
IAS 40.10	Ch.19, p.1447
IAS 40.10	Ch.19, p.1448
IAS 40.11	Ch.9, p.657
IAS 40.11	Ch.19, p.1448
IAS 40.11-14	Ch.9, p.641
IAS 40.11-14	Ch.9, p.657
IAS 40.12-13	Ch.19, p.1449
IAS 40.13	Ch.19, p.1449
IAS 40.14	Ch.19, p.1443
IAS 40.14	Ch.19, p.1447
IAS 40.14	Ch.19, p.1448
IAS 40.14	Ch.19, p.1449
IAS 40.14A	Ch.9, p.657
IAS 40.14A	Ch.19, p.1453
IAS 40.15	Ch.19, p.1446
IAS 40.16	Ch.19, p.1451
IAS 40.17	Ch.19, p.1451
IAS 40.18	Ch.19, p.1452
IAS 40.19	Ch.19, p.1452

IAS 40.19A	Ch.19, p.1444
IAS 40.19A	Ch.19, p.1451
IAS 40.20	Ch.14, p.1052
IAS 40.20	Ch.19, p.1457
IAS 40.20	Ch.19, p.1460
IAS 40.21	Ch.19, p.1457
IAS 40.21	Ch.19, p.1476
IAS 40.23(a)	Ch.19, p.1459
IAS 40.23(b)	Ch.19, p.1459
IAS 40.23(c)	Ch.19, p.1459
IAS 40.24	Ch.19, p.1460
IAS 40.27	Ch.43, p.3402
IAS 40.27-29	Ch.19, p.1461
IAS 40.29A	Ch.19, p.1461
IAS 40.30	Ch.19, p.1467
IAS 40.31	Ch.19, p.1467
IAS 40.32	Ch.19, p.1467
IAS 40.32	Ch.19, p.1469
IAS 40.32A	Ch.19, p.1467
IAS 40.32A	Ch.55, p.4540
IAS 40.32A	Ch.56, p.4695
IAS 40.32B	Ch.19, p.1467
IAS 40.32C	Ch.19, p.1468
IAS 40.33	Ch.14, p.1020
IAS 40.33	Ch.19, p.1468
IAS 40.33	Ch.19, p.1474
IAS 40.35	Ch.19, p.1468
IAS 40.40	Ch.19, p.1469
IAS 40.40	Ch.38, p.3089
IAS 40.40A	Ch.19, p.1444
IAS 40.40A	Ch.19, p.1472
IAS 40.41	Ch.19, p.1472
IAS 40.48	Ch.19, p.1472
IAS 40.50	Ch.19, p.1473
IAS 40.50(a)	Ch.19, p.1450
IAS 40.50(a)	Ch.19, p.1477
IAS 40.50(b)	Ch.19, p.1450
IAS 40.50(b)	Ch.19, p.1477
IAS 40.50(c)	Ch.19, p.1477
IAS 40.50(d)	Ch.19, p.1479
IAS 40.52	Ch.19, p.1482
IAS 40.53	Ch.19, p.1473
IAS 40.53	Ch.19, p.1474
IAS 40.53	Ch.19, p.1475
IAS 40.53A	Ch.19, p.1475
IAS 40.53B	Ch.19, p.1475
IAS 40.54	Ch.19, p.1474
IAS 40.55	Ch.19, p.1474
IAS 40.56	Ch.19, p.1444
IAS 40.56	Ch.19, p.1483
IAS 40.56	Ch.19, p.1486
IAS 40.57	Ch.19, p.1488
IAS 40.57	Ch.19, p.1490
IAS 40.57	Ch.42, p.3277
IAS 40.57(d)	Ch.19, p.1490
IAS 40.58	Ch.19, p.1490
IAS 40.59	Ch.19, p.1461
IAS 40.59	Ch.19, p.1490

IAS 40.60	Ch.19, p.1491
IAS 40.61	Ch.19, p.1491
IAS 40.62	Ch.19, p.1491
IAS 40.63	Ch.19, p.1491
IAS 40.64	Ch.19, p.1491
IAS 40.65	Ch.19, p.1492
IAS 40.66	Ch.19, p.1492
IAS 40.67	Ch.19, p.1492
IAS 40.67	Ch.27, p.2040
IAS 40.68	Ch.19, p.1494
IAS 40.69	Ch.19, p.1493
IAS 40.69	Ch.27, p.2040
IAS 40.70	Ch.19, p.1493
IAS 40.70	Ch.27, p.2040
IAS 40.71	Ch.19, p.1493
IAS 40.72	Ch.19, p.1495
IAS 40.73	Ch.19, p.1495
IAS 40.74	Ch.19, p.1496
IAS 40.75	Ch.19, p.1497
IAS 40.76	Ch.19, p.1505
IAS 40.77	Ch.19, p.1506
IAS 40.78	Ch.19, p.1508
IAS 40.79	Ch.19, p.1509
IAS 40.79(e)	Ch.14, p.1008
IAS 40.79(e)	Ch.19, p.1467
IAS 40.79(e)(iii)	Ch.14, p.1012
IAS 40.BC19-20	Ch.19, p.1453
IAS 40.BC25	Ch.19, p.1489
IAS 40.BC26	Ch.19, p.1489
IAS 40.BC27	Ch.19, p.1489
IAS 40.BC28	Ch.19, p.1489

IAS 41 (2008)

IAS 41(2008).21	Ch.42, p.3306

IAS 41

IAS 41 Objective	Ch.42, p.3273
IAS 41.1	Ch.42, p.3277
IAS 41.1	Ch.42, p.3281
IAS 41.1(a)	Ch.24, p.1842
IAS 41.2	Ch.19, p.1443
IAS 41.2	Ch.42, p.3278
IAS 41.2(b)	Ch.42, p.3279
IAS 41.2(e)	Ch.42, p.3281
IAS 41.3	Ch.42, p.3278
IAS 41.3	Ch.42, p.3279
IAS 41.4	Ch.42, p.3275
IAS 41.5	Ch.24, p.1825
IAS 41.5	Ch.24, p.1842
IAS 41.5	Ch.42, p.3274
IAS 41.5	Ch.42, p.3275
IAS 41.5	Ch.42, p.3277
IAS 41.5	Ch.42, p.3287
IAS 41.5	Ch.42, p.3295

IAS 41.5A	Ch.18, p.1393
IAS 41.5A	Ch.42, p.3276
IAS 41.5B	Ch.18, p.1393
IAS 41.5B	Ch.42, p.3276
IAS 41.5C	Ch.18, p.1393
IAS 41.5C	Ch.42, p.3275
IAS 41.5C	Ch.42, p.3289
IAS 41.6	Ch.42, p.3274
IAS 41.7	Ch.42, p.3274
IAS 41.7	Ch.42, p.3287
IAS 41.8	Ch.42, p.3277
IAS 41.10	Ch.42, p.3281
IAS 41.10	Ch.42, p.3288
IAS 41.11	Ch.42, p.3281
IAS 41.12	Ch.19, p.1443
IAS 41.12	Ch.42, p.3282
IAS 41.13	Ch.42, p.3283
IAS 41.13	Ch.42, p.3284
IAS 41.15	Ch.42, p.3295
IAS 41.16	Ch.42, p.3297
IAS 41.22	Ch.42, p.3296
IAS 41.22	Ch.42, p.3298
IAS 41.24	Ch.42, p.3305
IAS 41.25	Ch.42, p.3300
IAS 41.25	Ch.42, p.3303
IAS 41.26	Ch.42, p.3289
IAS 41.27	Ch.42, p.3290
IAS 41.28	Ch.42, p.3290
IAS 41.29	Ch.42, p.3290
IAS 41.30	Ch.14, p.1012
IAS 41.30	Ch.42, p.3282
IAS 41.30	Ch.42, p.3290
IAS 41.30	Ch.42, p.3291
IAS 41.30	Ch.42, p.3292
IAS 41.31	Ch.42, p.3292
IAS 41.32	Ch.42, p.3283
IAS 41.33	Ch.42, p.3292
IAS 41.34	Ch.24, p.1843
IAS 41.34	Ch.42, p.3294
IAS 41.35	Ch.24, p.1843
IAS 41.35	Ch.42, p.3294
IAS 41.36	Ch.24, p.1843
IAS 41.36	Ch.42, p.3294
IAS 41.37-38	Ch.24, p.1842
IAS 41.37-38	Ch.42, p.3293
IAS 41.38	Ch.24, p.1842
IAS 41.40	Ch.42, p.3313
IAS 41.41	Ch.42, p.3315
IAS 41.42	Ch.42, p.3315
IAS 41.43	Ch.42, p.3316
IAS 41.44	Ch.42, p.3316
IAS 41.45	Ch.42, p.3316
IAS 41.46	Ch.42, p.3289
IAS 41.46	Ch.42, p.3316
IAS 41.49	Ch.42, p.3316
IAS 41.50	Ch.42, p.3316
IAS 41.51	Ch.42, p.3317
IAS 41.52	Ch.42, p.3317

IAS 41.53	Ch.42, p.3318
IAS 41.54	Ch.42, p.3322
IAS 41.55	Ch.42, p.3322
IAS 41.56	Ch.42, p.3323
IAS 41.57	Ch.42, p.3323
IAS 41.B8	Ch.42, p.3278
IAS 41.B8	Ch.42, p.3284
IAS 41.B22	Ch.42, p.3296
IAS 41.B33	Ch.42, p.3296
IAS 41.B35	Ch.42, p.3292
IAS 41.B36	Ch.42, p.3292
IAS 41.B37	Ch.42, p.3293
IAS 41.B41	Ch.42, p.3278
IAS 41.B42	Ch.42, p.3284
IAS 41.B43	Ch.42, p.3283
IAS 41.B45	Ch.42, p.3278
IAS 41.B50-B54	Ch.42, p.3297
IAS 41.B55-B57	Ch.42, p.3278
IAS 41.B58-B60	Ch.42, p.3278
IAS 41.B62	Ch.42, p.3282
IAS 41.B66	Ch.24, p.1827
IAS 41.B66	Ch.24, p.1843
IAS 41.B66	Ch.42, p.3294
IAS 41.B67	Ch.24, p.1827
IAS 41.B69	Ch.24, p.1830
IAS 41.B74-B77	Ch.42, p.3317
IAS 41.B78-B79	Ch.42, p.3313
IAS 41.B81	Ch.42, p.3296
IAS 41.B82(n)	Ch.42, p.3280
IAS 41.IE1	Ch.42, p.3308
IAS 41.IE1	Ch.42, p.3314
IAS 41.IE2	Ch.42, p.3317
IAS 41.BC3	Ch.42, p.3296
IAS 41.BC4A-D	Ch.42, p.3279
IAS 41.BC4B	Ch.42, p.3279
IAS 41.BC4C	Ch.42, p.3291
IAS 41.BC4D	Ch.42, p.3288

IFRIC 1

IFRIC 1.1	Ch.25, p.1900
IFRIC 1.1	Ch.26, p.1981
IFRIC 1.2	Ch.18, p.1406
IFRIC 1.2	Ch.26, p.1982
IFRIC 1.2	Ch.26, p.1985
IFRIC 1.3	Ch.18, p.1406
IFRIC 1.3	Ch.26, p.1982
IFRIC 1.4-6	Ch.41, p.3259
IFRIC 1.4-7	Ch.26, p.1982
IFRIC 1.5	Ch.25, p.1900
IFRIC 1.5	Ch.26, p.1957
IFRIC 1.5	Ch.26, p.1982
IFRIC 1.5	Ch.33, p.2509
IFRIC 1.5	Ch.43, p.3501
IFRIC 1.6	Ch.26, p.1983
IFRIC 1.6	Ch.26, p.1984
IFRIC 1.7	Ch.18, p.1414
IFRIC 1.7	Ch.26, p.1957
IFRIC 1.7	Ch.26, p.1982
IFRIC 1.8	Ch.25, p.1900
IFRIC 1.8	Ch.26, p.1954
IFRIC 1.8	Ch.26, p.1961
IFRIC 1.8	Ch.26, p.1982
IFRIC 1.IE1-4	Ch.26, p.1983
IFRIC 1.IE5	Ch.26, p.1957
IFRIC 1.IE5	Ch.26, p.1985
IFRIC 1.IE6-10	Ch.26, p.1984
IFRIC 1.IE7	Ch.26, p.1985
IFRIC 1.IE11-12	Ch.26, p.1984
IFRIC 1.BC23	Ch.26, p.1985
IFRIC 1.BC26	Ch.26, p.1954
IFRIC 1.BC26-27	Ch.26, p.1982

IFRIC 2

IFRIC 2.1-4	Ch.47, p.3693
IFRIC 2.5	Ch.47, p.3694
IFRIC 2.6	Ch.47, p.3694
IFRIC 2.6-8	Ch.47, p.3694
IFRIC 2.8	Ch.47, p.3694
IFRIC 2.9	Ch.47, p.3694
IFRIC 2.10	Ch.47, p.3694
IFRIC 2.11	Ch.47, p.3694
IFRIC 2.BC10	Ch.47, p.3734

IFRIC 5

IFRIC 5.1	Ch.26, p.1986
IFRIC 5.2	Ch.26, p.1987
IFRIC 5.3	Ch.26, p.1987
IFRIC 5.4	Ch.26, p.1987
IFRIC 5.5	Ch.26, p.1987
IFRIC 5.5	Ch.45, p.3606
IFRIC 5.6	Ch.26, p.1988
IFRIC 5.7	Ch.26, p.1988
IFRIC 5.7	Ch.26, p.1990
IFRIC 5.8	Ch.26, p.1988
IFRIC 5.9	Ch.26, p.1988
IFRIC 5.10	Ch.26, p.1990
IFRIC 5.11	Ch.26, p.1991
IFRIC 5.12	Ch.26, p.1991
IFRIC 5.13	Ch.26, p.1991
IFRIC 5.BC7	Ch.26, p.1990
IFRIC 5.BC8	Ch.26, p.1991
IFRIC 5.BC14	Ch.26, p.1988
IFRIC 5.BC19-20	Ch.26, p.1988
IFRIC 5.BC19-20	Ch.26, p.1989

IFRIC 6

IFRIC 6.3	Ch.26, p.1995
IFRIC 6.4	Ch.26, p.1995

IFRIC 6.5	Ch.26, p.1996	IFRIC 12.10	Ch.25, p.1917
IFRIC 6.6	Ch.26, p.1995	IFRIC 12.11	Ch.25, p.1853
IFRIC 6.7	Ch.26, p.1996	IFRIC 12.11	Ch.25, p.1858
IFRIC 6.8	Ch.26, p.1995	IFRIC 12.11	Ch.25, p.1867
IFRIC 6.9	Ch.26, p.1996	IFRIC 12.11	Ch.25, p.1879
IFRIC 6.BC5	Ch.26, p.1996	IFRIC 12.11	Ch.25, p.1890
IFRIC 6.BC6	Ch.26, p.1996	IFRIC 12.12	Ch.25, p.1868
IFRIC 6.BC7	Ch.26, p.1996	IFRIC 12.12	Ch.25, p.1884
		IFRIC 12.13	Ch.25, p.1868
		IFRIC 12.13	Ch.25, p.1869
		IFRIC 12.13	Ch.25, p.1884

IFRIC 7

IFRIC 7.3	Ch.16, p.1263	IFRIC 12.14	Ch.25, p.1853
IFRIC 7.3	Ch.16, p.1274	IFRIC 12.14	Ch.25, p.1857
IFRIC 7.3	Ch.41, p.3258	IFRIC 12.14	Ch.25, p.1867
IFRIC 7.4	Ch.16, p.1265	IFRIC 12.14	Ch.25, p.1869
IFRIC 7.5	Ch.16, p.1265	IFRIC 12.14	Ch.25, p.1875
IFRIC 7.IE1-IE6	Ch.16, p.1265	IFRIC 12.14	Ch.25, p.1879
IFRIC 7.BC21-BC22	Ch.16, p.1264	IFRIC 12.14	Ch.25, p.1890
		IFRIC 12.14	Ch.25, p.1899
		IFRIC 12.15	Ch.25, p.1853
		IFRIC 12.15	Ch.25, p.1873
		IFRIC 12.15	Ch.25, p.1879

IFRIC 10

IFRIC 10.2	Ch.41, p.3245	IFRIC 12.16	Ch.25, p.1873
IFRIC 10.8	Ch.41, p.3245	IFRIC 12.16	Ch.25, p.1875
IFRIC 10.9	Ch.41, p.3246	IFRIC 12.16	Ch.45, p.3589
IFRIC 10.BC9	Ch.41, p.3245	IFRIC 12.17	Ch.25, p.1873
		IFRIC 12.17	Ch.25, p.1879
		IFRIC 12.18	Ch.25, p.1873
		IFRIC 12.18	Ch.25, p.1885

IFRIC 12

IFRIC 12 references	Ch.2, p.47	IFRIC 12.19	Ch.25, p.1853
IFRIC 12.1	Ch.5, p.319	IFRIC 12.19	Ch.25, p.1868
IFRIC 12.1	Ch.25, p.1854	IFRIC 12.19	Ch.25, p.1873
IFRIC 12.1	Ch.25, p.1855	IFRIC 12.19	Ch.25, p.1875
IFRIC 12.1	Ch.25, p.1862	IFRIC 12.19	Ch.25, p.1879
IFRIC 12.2	Ch.5, p.319	IFRIC 12.19	Ch.25, p.1883
IFRIC 12.2	Ch.25, p.1853	IFRIC 12.19	Ch.25, p.1899
IFRIC 12.3	Ch.25, p.1853	IFRIC 12.19	Ch.25, p.1909
IFRIC 12.3	Ch.25, p.1854	IFRIC 12.19	Ch.25, p.1910
IFRIC 12.3	Ch.25, p.1892	IFRIC 12.19	Ch.25, p.1912
IFRIC 12.4	Ch.25, p.1854	IFRIC 12.19	Ch.25, p.1916
IFRIC 12.4	Ch.25, p.1858	IFRIC 12.20	Ch.25, p.1853
IFRIC 12.5	Ch.25, p.1854	IFRIC 12.20	Ch.25, p.1869
IFRIC 12.5	Ch.25, p.1857	IFRIC 12.20	Ch.25, p.1899
IFRIC 12.5	Ch.25, p.1858	IFRIC 12.20	Ch.25, p.1901
IFRIC 12.5	Ch.25, p.1869	IFRIC 12.21	Ch.25, p.1899
IFRIC 12.5(b)	Ch.25, p.1859	IFRIC 12.21	Ch.25, p.1901
IFRIC 12.6	Ch.25, p.1854	IFRIC 12.21	Ch.25, p.1906
IFRIC 12.6	Ch.25, p.1861	IFRIC 12.21	Ch.25, p.1914
IFRIC 12.7	Ch.25, p.1853	IFRIC 12.22	Ch.25, p.1876
IFRIC 12.7	Ch.25, p.1854	IFRIC 12.22	Ch.25, p.1879
IFRIC 12.7	Ch.25, p.1862	IFRIC 12.22	Ch.25, p.1916
IFRIC 12.7	Ch.25, p.1864	IFRIC 12.23	Ch.25, p.1916
IFRIC 12.8	Ch.25, p.1862	IFRIC 12.24	Ch.25, p.1876
IFRIC 12.8	Ch.25, p.1865	IFRIC 12.25	Ch.25, p.1876
IFRIC 12.9	Ch.25, p.1854	IFRIC 12.26	Ch.25, p.1881
IFRIC 12.9	Ch.25, p.1858	IFRIC 12.27	Ch.25, p.1904
		IFRIC 12.29	Ch.5, p.319
		IFRIC 12.30	Ch.5, p.319

IFRIC 12.AG2 .... Ch.25, p.1859
IFRIC 12.AG3 .... Ch.25, p.1859
IFRIC 12.AG5 .... Ch.25, p.1858
IFRIC 12.AG6 .... Ch.25, p.1858
IFRIC 12.AG6 .... Ch.25, p.1860
IFRIC 12.AG7 .... Ch.25, p.1855
IFRIC 12.AG7 .... Ch.25, p.1866
IFRIC 12.AG8 .... Ch.25, p.1866
IFRIC 12.IE15 .... Ch.25, p.1879
IFRIC 12.IE15 .... Ch.25, p.1916
IFRIC 12.IE19 .... Ch.25, p.1902
IFRIC 12.IE20 .... Ch.25, p.1902
IFRIC 12.BC7 .... Ch.2, p.47
IFRIC 12.BC11-13 .... Ch.25, p.1852
IFRIC 12.BC11-13 .... Ch.25, p.1854
IFRIC 12.BC13 .... Ch.25, p.1855
IFRIC 12.BC14 .... Ch.25, p.1858
IFRIC 12.BC15 .... Ch.25, p.1858
IFRIC 12.BC16 .... Ch.25, p.1865
IFRIC 12.BC20 .... Ch.2, p.47
IFRIC 12.BC21 .... Ch.25, p.1858
IFRIC 12.BC22 .... Ch.25, p.1858
IFRIC 12.BC31 .... Ch.25, p.1867
IFRIC 12.BC31 .... Ch.25, p.1869
IFRIC 12.BC32 .... Ch.25, p.1880
IFRIC 12.BC35 .... Ch.25, p.1884
IFRIC 12.BC44 .... Ch.25, p.1873
IFRIC 12.BC52 .... Ch.25, p.1874
IFRIC 12.BC53 .... Ch.25, p.1885
IFRIC 12.BC65 .... Ch.25, p.1881
IFRIC 12.BC66 .... Ch.25, p.1900
IFRIC 12.BC68 .... Ch.25, p.1900

IFRIC 14

IFRIC 14.1 .... Ch.35, p.2930
IFRIC 14.1-3 .... Ch.35, p.2930
IFRIC 14.2 .... Ch.35, p.2930
IFRIC 14.3 .... Ch.35, p.2930
IFRIC 14.5 .... Ch.35, p.2933
IFRIC 14.6 .... Ch.35, p.2930
IFRIC 14.7 .... Ch.35, p.2931
IFRIC 14.8 .... Ch.35, p.2931
IFRIC 14.9 .... Ch.35, p.2931
IFRIC 14.10 .... Ch.35, p.2967
IFRIC 14.11-12 .... Ch.35, p.2931
IFRIC 14.11-12 .... Ch.35, p.2932
IFRIC 14.13 .... Ch.35, p.2931
IFRIC 14.14 .... Ch.35, p.2931
IFRIC 14.14 .... Ch.35, p.2969
IFRIC 14.15 .... Ch.35, p.2932
IFRIC 14.16 .... Ch.35, p.2933
IFRIC 14.17 .... Ch.35, p.2933
IFRIC 14.18 .... Ch.35, p.2934
IFRIC 14.19 .... Ch.35, p.2934
IFRIC 14.20 .... Ch.35, p.2934
IFRIC 14.21 .... Ch.35, p.2933
IFRIC 14.21 .... Ch.35, p.2934
IFRIC 14.22 .... Ch.35, p.2934
IFRIC 14.23 .... Ch.35, p.2936
IFRIC 14.24 .... Ch.35, p.2937
IFRIC 14.IE1-2 .... Ch.35, p.2937
IFRIC 14.IE3-8 .... Ch.35, p.2937
IFRIC 14.IE9-27 .... Ch.35, p.2934
IFRIC 14.BC10 .... Ch.35, p.2932
IFRIC 14.BC30 .... Ch.35, p.2933

IFRIC 16

IFRIC 16.1 .... Ch.53, p.4266
IFRIC 16.2 .... Ch.53, p.4267
IFRIC 16.2 .... Ch.53, p.4306
IFRIC 16.3 .... Ch.53, p.4300
IFRIC 16.4 .... Ch.53, p.4266
IFRIC 16.7 .... Ch.53, p.4267
IFRIC 16.7 .... Ch.53, p.4306
IFRIC 16.8 .... Ch.53, p.4267
IFRIC 16.10 .... Ch.53, p.4267
IFRIC 16.11 .... Ch.53, p.4268
IFRIC 16.11 .... Ch.53, p.4269
IFRIC 16.12 .... Ch.53, p.4269
IFRIC 16.13 .... Ch.53, p.4269
IFRIC 16.13 .... Ch.53, p.4270
IFRIC 16.14 .... Ch.53, p.4270
IFRIC 16.14 .... Ch.53, p.4302
IFRIC 16.14 .... Ch.53, p.4303
IFRIC 16.15 .... Ch.53, p.4301
IFRIC 16.15 .... Ch.53, p.4302
IFRIC 16.16 .... Ch.53, p.4364
IFRIC 16.17 .... Ch.7, p.500
IFRIC 16.17 .... Ch.7, p.501
IFRIC 16.17 .... Ch.15, p.1214
IFRIC 16.17 .... Ch.53, p.4364
IFRIC 16.17 .... Ch.53, p.4365
IFRIC 16.AG1-3 .... Ch.53, p.4268
IFRIC 16.AG2 .... Ch.53, p.4268
IFRIC 16.AG2 .... Ch.53, p.4303
IFRIC 16.AG2 .... Ch.53, p.4304
IFRIC 16.AG4 .... Ch.53, p.4268
IFRIC 16.AG4 .... Ch.53, p.4301
IFRIC 16.AG5 .... Ch.53, p.4301
IFRIC 16.AG5 .... Ch.53, p.4302
IFRIC 16.AG6 .... Ch.53, p.4269
IFRIC 16.AG6 .... Ch.53, p.4271
IFRIC 16.AG7 .... Ch.53, p.4301
IFRIC 16.AG8 .... Ch.53, p.4365
IFRIC 16.AG10 .... Ch.53, p.4269
IFRIC 16.AG11 .... Ch.53, p.4270
IFRIC 16.AG12 .... Ch.53, p.4270
IFRIC 16.AG12 .... Ch.53, p.4302
IFRIC 16.AG13 .... Ch.53, p.4270
IFRIC 16.AG14 .... Ch.53, p.4269
IFRIC 16.AG15 .... Ch.53, p.4270
IFRIC 16.BC24A Ch.53, p.4270

IFRIC 16.BC24B Ch.53, p.4270
IFRIC 16.BC36 ....Ch.7, p.501

IFRIC 17

IFRIC 17.3 ....Ch.7, p.531
IFRIC 17.3 ....Ch.8, p.601
IFRIC 17.4 ....Ch.7, p.531
IFRIC 17.4 ....Ch.8, p.602
IFRIC 17.5 ....Ch.7, p.531
IFRIC 17.5 ....Ch.8, p.602
IFRIC 17.5 ....Ch.8, p.617
IFRIC 17.6 ....Ch.7, p.531
IFRIC 17.6 ....Ch.8, p.602
IFRIC 17.7 ....Ch.7, p.531
IFRIC 17.7 ....Ch.8, p.602
IFRIC 17.8 ....Ch.7, p.531
IFRIC 17.10 ....Ch.7, p.531
IFRIC 17.10 ....Ch.8, p.599
IFRIC 17.10 ....Ch.8, p.602
IFRIC 17.10 ....Ch.38, p.3081
IFRIC 17.11 ....Ch.7, p.532
IFRIC 17.11 ....Ch.8, p.602
IFRIC 17.12 ....Ch.7, p.532
IFRIC 17.12 ....Ch.8, p.602
IFRIC 17.13 ....Ch.7, p.532
IFRIC 17.13 ....Ch.8, p.602
IFRIC 17.14-15 ....Ch.7, p.532
IFRIC 17.14-15 ....Ch.8, p.603
IFRIC 17.16 ....Ch.7, p.533
IFRIC 17.16 ....Ch.8, p.603
IFRIC 17.17 ....Ch.7, p.533
IFRIC 17.17 ....Ch.8, p.604
IFRIC 17.17 ....Ch.38, p.3085
IFRIC 17.BC5 ....Ch.8, p.602
IFRIC 17.BC18-20 ....Ch.38, p.3081
IFRIC 17.BC22 ....Ch.45, p.3591
IFRIC 17.BC27 ....Ch.45, p.3591
IFRIC 17.BC55 ....Ch.7, p.532
IFRIC 17.BC56 ....Ch.7, p.532

IFRIC 19

IFRIC 19 references Ch.2, p.47
IFRIC 19.1 ....Ch.47, p.3737
IFRIC 19.2 ....Ch.5, p.321
IFRIC 19.2 ....Ch.47, p.3737
IFRIC 19.3 ....Ch.5, p.321
IFRIC 19.3 ....Ch.47, p.3738
IFRIC 19.5-7 ....Ch.47, p.3738
IFRIC 19.7 ....Ch.47, p.3738
IFRIC 19.8 ....Ch.47, p.3738
IFRIC 19.9 ....Ch.47, p.3738

IFRIC 19.10 ....Ch.47, p.3739
IFRIC 19.11 ....Ch.47, p.3738
IFRIC 19.13 ....Ch.5, p.321
IFRIC 19.BC16 ....Ch.2, p.47
IFRIC 19.BC22 ....Ch.47, p.3738
IFRIC 19.BC33 ....Ch.5, p.321

IFRIC 20

IFRIC 20 references Ch.2, p.47
IFRIC 20.1 ....Ch.5, p.322
IFRIC 20.2 ....Ch.43, p.3502
IFRIC 20.3 ....Ch.5, p.322
IFRIC 20.3 ....Ch.43, p.3502
IFRIC 20.5 ....Ch.5, p.322
IFRIC 20.8 ....Ch.43, p.3502
IFRIC 20.9 ....Ch.43, p.3504
IFRIC 20.10 ....Ch.43, p.3504
IFRIC 20.12 ....Ch.43, p.3505
IFRIC 20.13 ....Ch.43, p.3505
IFRIC 20.14 ....Ch.43, p.3511
IFRIC 20.15 ....Ch.43, p.3506
IFRIC 20.15 ....Ch.43, p.3511
IFRIC 20.16 ....Ch.43, p.3511
IFRIC 20 Appendix A Ch.5, p.322
IFRIC 20.BC4 ....Ch.43, p.3502
IFRIC 20.BC8 ....Ch.43, p.3510
IFRIC 20.BC10 ....Ch.43, p.3504
IFRIC 20.BC12 ....Ch.43, p.3505
IFRIC 20.BC15 ....Ch.43, p.3505
IFRIC 20.BC17 ....Ch.43, p.3510

IFRIC 21

IFRIC 21.2 ....Ch.26, p.1997
IFRIC 21.2 ....Ch.41, p.3261
IFRIC 21.3 ....Ch.26, p.1997
IFRIC 21.3 ....Ch.26, p.2000
IFRIC 21.4 ....Ch.26, p.1932
IFRIC 21.4 ....Ch.26, p.1997
IFRIC 21.4 ....Ch.26, p.1998
IFRIC 21.5 ....Ch.26, p.1997
IFRIC 21.5 ....Ch.26, p.2001
IFRIC 21.6 ....Ch.26, p.1997
IFRIC 21.6 ....Ch.41, p.3261
IFRIC 21.7 ....Ch.26, p.1997
IFRIC 21.8 ....Ch.26, p.1997
IFRIC 21.8 ....Ch.26, p.1998
IFRIC 21.8 ....Ch.41, p.3261
IFRIC 21.9 ....Ch.26, p.1998
IFRIC 21.9-10 ....Ch.41, p.3261
IFRIC 21.10 ....Ch.26, p.1998
IFRIC 21.11 ....Ch.26, p.1998
IFRIC 21.11 ....Ch.41, p.3261
IFRIC 21.12 ....Ch.26, p.1998
IFRIC 21.14 ....Ch.26, p.1998

IFRIC 21.14	Ch.26, p.2000
IFRIC 21.14	Ch.26, p.2001
IFRIC 21.31	Ch.41, p.3261
IFRIC 21.A1	Ch.26, p.1997
IFRIC 21.IE1	Ch.26, p.1999
IFRIC 21.IE1 Example 2	Ch.26, p.1998
IFRIC 21.IE1 Example 2	Ch.41, p.3261
IFRIC 21.IE1 Example 3	Ch.26, p.2000
IFRIC 21.IE1 Example 4	Ch.41, p.3262
IFRIC 21.BC4	Ch.26, p.1997
IFRIC 21.BC4	Ch.26, p.2001

IFRIC 22

IFRIC 22 references	Ch.2, p.47
IFRIC 22.4	Ch.5, p.341
IFRIC 22.4	Ch.15, p.1189
IFRIC 22.5	Ch.15, p.1189
IFRIC 22.6	Ch.15, p.1190
IFRIC 22.7	Ch.5, p.342
IFRIC 22.8	Ch.15, p.1189
IFRIC 22.8-9	Ch.5, p.342
IFRIC 22.9	Ch.15, p.1189
IFRIC 22.BC8	Ch.15, p.1190
IFRIC 22.BC17	Ch.2, p.47
IFRIC 22.BC17	Ch.15, p.1197

IFRIC 23

IFRIC 23.3	Ch.33, p.2458
IFRIC 23.3	Ch.33, p.2476
IFRIC 23.3	Ch.33, p.2542
IFRIC 23.3	Ch.33, p.2562
IFRIC 23.4	Ch.26, p.1935
IFRIC 23.4	Ch.33, p.2561
IFRIC 23.4	Ch.33, p.2568
IFRIC 23.5	Ch.33, p.2561
IFRIC 23.6	Ch.33, p.2563
IFRIC 23.8	Ch.33, p.2563
IFRIC 23.9	Ch.33, p.2564
IFRIC 23.10	Ch.33, p.2564
IFRIC 23.10	Ch.33, p.2567
IFRIC 23.11	Ch.33, p.2564
IFRIC 23.12	Ch.33, p.2563
IFRIC 23.12	Ch.33, p.2566
IFRIC 23.13	Ch.33, p.2477
IFRIC 23.13	Ch.33, p.2566
IFRIC 23.13	Ch.38, p.3090
IFRIC 23.14	Ch.33, p.2477
IFRIC 23.14	Ch.33, p.2566
IFRIC 23.14	Ch.33, p.2567
IFRIC 23.14	Ch.38, p.3078
IFRIC 23.14	Ch.38, p.3080
IFRIC 23.14	Ch.38, p.3090
IFRIC 23.A2	Ch.33, p.2566
IFRIC 23.A2	Ch.38, p.3090

IFRIC 23.A3	Ch.33, p.2567
IFRIC 23.A4(a)	Ch.33, p.2567
IFRIC 23.A4(b)	Ch.33, p.2567
IFRIC 23.A5	Ch.33, p.2567
IFRIC 23.B1	Ch.33, p.2455
IFRIC 23.B1	Ch.33, p.2561
IFRIC 23.B2	Ch.33, p.2561
IFRIC 23.IE1	Ch.33, p.2565
IFRIC 23.IE2-6	Ch.33, p.2564
IFRIC 23.IE7-10	Ch.33, p.2565
IFRIC 23.BC4	Ch.33, p.2569
IFRIC 23.BC6	Ch.33, p.2561
IFRIC 23.BC8	Ch.33, p.2562
IFRIC 23.BC9	Ch.33, p.2562
IFRIC 23.BC11	Ch.33, p.2563
IFRIC 23.BC13	Ch.33, p.2563
IFRIC 23.BC23	Ch.9, p.691
IFRIC 23.BC23	Ch.33, p.2562
IFRIC 23.BC24	Ch.9, p.692
IFRIC 23.BC24	Ch.33, p.2562

SIC-7

SIC-7.3	Ch.15, p.1241
SIC-7.4	Ch.15, p.1242
SIC-7.5	Ch.15, p.1241
SIC-7.6	Ch.15, p.1242
SIC-7.7	Ch.15, p.1242

SIC-10

SIC-10.3	Ch.24, p.1827

SIC-25

SIC-25.4	Ch.33, p.2475
SIC-25.4	Ch.33, p.2599

SIC-29

SIC-29.1	Ch.25, p.1855
SIC-29.1	Ch.25, p.1856
SIC-29.1	Ch.25, p.1917
SIC-29.2	Ch.25, p.1917
SIC-29.2(a)	Ch.25, p.1855
SIC-29.3	Ch.25, p.1917
SIC-29.4	Ch.25, p.1852
SIC-29.5	Ch.25, p.1917
SIC-29.6	Ch.25, p.1917
SIC-29.6	Ch.25, p.1918
SIC-29.6A	Ch.25, p.1918
SIC-29.7	Ch.25, p.1918

SIC-32

SIC-32.1	Ch.17, p.1326
SIC-32.2	Ch.17, p.1327
SIC-32.3	Ch.17, p.1327
SIC-32.5-6	Ch.17, p.1327
SIC-32.7	Ch.17, p.1326
SIC-32.8	Ch.17, p.1327
SIC-32.9	Ch.17, p.1327
SIC-32.10	Ch.17, p.1328

Management Commentary

MC.12	Ch.2, p.107
MC.13	Ch.2, p.107
MC.24	Ch.2, p.107
MC Appendix	Ch.2, p.106
MC.IN2	Ch.2, p.106
MC.IN3	Ch.2, p.106
MC.IN4	Ch.2, p.106
MC.IN5	Ch.2, p.107

PS 2

PS 2.2	Ch.3, p.160
PS 2.5-7	Ch.3, p.161
PS 2.8-10	Ch.3, p.161
PS 2.11-12	Ch.3, p.161
PS 2.13-23	Ch.3, p.161
PS 2.24-26	Ch.3, p.161
PS 2.28	Ch.3, p.161
PS 2.29-32	Ch.3, p.162
PS 2.35-39	Ch.3, p.162
PS 2.40-55	Ch.3, p.162
PS 2.56-59	Ch.3, p.162
PS 2.60-65	Ch.3, p.162
PS 2.66-71	Ch.3, p.162
PS 2.72-80	Ch.3, p.163
PS 2.81-83	Ch.3, p.163
PS 2.84-88	Ch.3, p.163

Index

Note: This index uses chapter number followed by section number for locators. A section number includes all its sub-sections. For example the locator Ch. 37, 2.7 will include subsections 2.7.1 and 2.7.2 in chapter 37. The locator Ch. 21, 5.3.1 will include subsections and 5.3.1.B. Where a range is indicated, for example, Ch. 3, 2–3, this means the topic starts from the beginning of section 2 to the end of section 3.

Accounting estimates
    vs. accounting policies, Ch. 3, 4.2
    changes in, Ch. 3, 4.5
    disclosures of, Ch. 3, 5.2
Accounting policies, Ch. 3, 4. *See also* IAS 1; IAS 8
    vs. accounting estimates, Ch. 3, 4.2
    accrual basis of accounting, Ch. 3, 4.1.3
    aggregation, Ch. 3, 4.1.5.A
    application of, Ch. 3, 4.3
    changes in, Ch. 3, 4.4
    consistency, Ch. 3, 4.1.4; Ch. 7, 2.6
    correction of errors, Ch. 3, 4.6
    definition of, Ch. 3, 4.2
    disclosures relating to, Ch. 3, 5.1
        changes in accounting policies, Ch. 3, 5.1.2
        changes pursuant to the initial application of an IFRS, Ch. 3, 5.1.2.A
        judgements made in applying accounting policies, Ch. 3, 5.1.1.B
        new IFRS, future impact of, Ch. 3, 5.1.2.C
        summary of significant accounting policies, Ch. 3, 5.1.1.A
        voluntary changes in accounting policy, Ch. 3, 5.1.2.B
    fair presentation, Ch. 3, 4.1.1
    general principles, Ch. 3, 4.1
    going concern, Ch. 3, 4.1.2
    interim financial reports, Ch. 41, 8.1
        measurement on a year-to-date basis, Ch. 41, 8.1.1
        new accounting pronouncements and other changes in accounting policies, Ch. 41, 8.1.2
        voluntary changes in presentation, Ch. 41, 8.1.3
    materiality, Ch. 3, 4.1.5.A
    offset, Ch. 3, 4.1.5.B
    Practice Statement 2, Ch. 3, 4.1.7
    profit or loss for the period, Ch. 3, 4.1.6
    selection of, Ch. 3, 4.3
Accounting Standards Advisory Forum (ASAF), Ch. 1, 2.8
Accounting Standards Board (AcSB), Ch. 1, 4.3.2
Accounting Standards Board of Japan (ASBJ), Ch. 1, 4.4.2
Accounting Standards Codification (ASC). *See under* ASC
Accounting Standards for Business Enterprises (ASBE), Ch. 1, 4.4.1.A
Accrual basis of accounting, Ch. 3, 4.1.3

Accrued operating lease income, Ch. 19, 6.6
    rental income and lease incentives, Ch. 19, 6.6.1
Acquired receivables, Ch. 49, 3.3.4; Ch. 54, 4.6.1
Acquirer's obligation to transfer proceeds from realisation of acquired contingent asset, Ch. 9, 5.6.4.A
Acquisition method of accounting, Ch. 9, 4. *See also* Business combinations; IFRS 3
    acquisition date determination, Ch. 9, 4.2
    business combinations under common control, application to, Ch. 10, 3.1–3.2
    identifying the acquirer, Ch. 9, 4.1
    'reverse acquisitions', Ch. 9, 4.1
Acquisition of cash flows, insurance contracts, Ch. 56, 8.2.3.E
Acquisition of insurance contracts, Ch. 56, 13
Acquisition-related costs, Ch. 9, 7.3; Ch. 40, 6.3.1
Active market, Ch. 14, 3, 8.1.1, 17; Ch. 20, 3.3
Active market identifying CGUs, Ch. 20, 3.3
Actuarial assumptions, Ch. 35, 7.5
Actuarial gains and losses, Ch. 35, 7.5
Actuarial methodology, Ch. 35, 7.3
Adjusting events, Ch. 38, 2.1.2
    determining value in use, Ch. 20, 7
    treatment of, Ch. 38, 2.2
Advisory bodies, Ch. 1, 2.9
    Accounting Standards Advisory Forum (ASAF), Ch. 1, 2.8
    Advisory Council, IFRS, Ch. 1, 2.7
    Capital Markets Advisory Committee, Ch. 1, 2.9
    Consultative Group for Rate Regulation, Ch. 1, 2.9
    Emerging Economies Group, Ch. 1, 2.9
    Global Preparers Forum, Ch. 1, 2.9
    IFRS Taxonomy Consultative Group, Ch. 1, 2.9
    Islamic Finance Consultative Group, Ch. 1, 2.9
    Management Commentary Consultative Group, Ch. 1, 2.9
    SME Implementation Group, Ch. 1, 2.9
    Transition Resource Group for IFRS 17 Insurance Contracts, Ch. 1, 2.9
    World Standard-setters Conferences, Ch. 1, 2.9
Agenda consultation 2011, Ch. 10, 6.1
Agenda consultation 2015, Ch. 10, 6.1; Ch. 43, 1.3.6, 8.4.1
Aggregated exposures, hedge accounting, Ch. 53, 2.7
Aggregation criteria, operating segments, Ch. 36, 1.3, 3.2.1

Agriculture, Ch. 42, 1–5. *See also* IAS 41
'All employee' share plans, Ch. 34, 2.2.2.D
All-in-one hedges, hedge accounting, Ch. 53, 5.2.1
Americas, IFRS adoption in, Ch. 1, 4.3
Amortisation of intangible assets, Ch. 17, 9
    assessing the useful life of an intangible asset as finite/indefinite, Ch. 17, 9.1
        factors affecting the useful life, Ch. 17, 9.1.1
        useful life of contractual/other legal rights, Ch. 17, 9.1.2
    impairment losses, Ch. 17, 9.4; Ch. 20, 11
    intangible assets with a finite useful life, Ch. 17, 9.2
        amortisation period and method, Ch. 17, 9.2.1
            amortisation of programme and other broadcast rights, Ch. 17, 9.2.1.B
            amortising customer relationships and similar intangible assets, Ch. 17, 9.2.1.A
        residual value, Ch. 17, 9.2.4
        revenue-based amortisation, Ch. 17, 9.2.2
        review of amortisation period and amortisation method, Ch. 17, 9.2.3
    intangible assets with an indefinite useful life, Ch. 17, 9.3; Ch. 20, 10
    retirements and disposals, Ch. 17, 9.5
        derecognition of parts of intangible assets, Ch. 17, 9.5.1
Amortised cost, Ch. 50, 3; Ch. 51, 14.1
    financial assets measured at, Ch. 50, 2.1; Ch. 51, 14.1
    financial liabilities measured at, Ch. 50, 2.2
    transfers of assets measured at, Ch. 52, 5.4.2
Area-of-interest method, E&E expenditure, Ch. 43, 3.2.5
ASC 310–*Receivables*, Ch. 27, 3.5.1.C
ASC 405–*Liabilities*, Ch. 27, 3.5.1.B
ASC 460–*Guarantees*, Ch. 27, 3.5.1.B
ASC 718–*Compensation Stock Compensation*, Ch. 34, 1.1
ASC 815–*Derivatives and Hedging*, Ch. 27, 3.5.1.B
ASC 860–*Transfers and Servicing*, Ch. 27, 3.5.1.B
ASC 924–*Entertainment–Casinos*, Ch. 27, 3.5.1.F
ASC 958–605–*Not-for-Profit Entities–Revenue Recognition*, Ch. 27, 3.5.1.E
Asia, IFRS adoption in, Ch. 1, 4.4
Asset swap accounts, Ch. 43, 6.3
Associates. *See also* Equity method/accounting, IAS 28; Investments in associates and joint ventures
    cash flows of, Ch. 40, 6.4
    definition, Ch. 11, 3
    disclosure, Ch. 13, 5
        nature, extent and financial effects of interests in associates, Ch. 13, 5.1
        risks associated with interests in associates, Ch. 13, 5.2
    dividends from, Ch. 8, 2.4.1
    equity accounted associate or joint venture that is not a business becomes a subsidiary in an acquisition in stages, Ch. 7,3.1.2
    first-time adoption
        assets and liabilities of, Ch. 5, 5.9
        investments in, Ch. 5, 5.8
    investments in, Ch. 11, 5.3; Ch. 20, 12.4
    loss of control – interest retained in former subsidiary is an associate, Ch. 7, 3.3.2, 7.1; Ch. 11, 7.4.1

separate financial statements and interests in, Ch. 8, 1.1.1
share-based payments to employee of, Ch. 34, 12.9
significant influence, Ch. 11, 4
    fund managers, Ch. 11, 4.6
    holdings of less than 20% of the voting power, Ch. 11, 4.3
    lack of, Ch. 11, 4.2
    potential voting rights, Ch. 11, 4.4
    severe long-term restrictions impairing ability to transfer funds to the investor, Ch. 11, 4.1
    voting rights held in a fiduciary capacity, Ch. 11, 4.5
Assurance-type warranty, Ch. 31, 3.3
Australia, IFRS adoption in, Ch. 1, 4.5
Australian Accounting Standards (AAS), Ch. 1, 4.5
'Back-to-back' forward contracts, Ch. 47, 11.1.3
Balance sheet. *See* Statement of financial position
Bank overdrafts, Ch. 40, 3.2.4
Barter transactions, Ch. 29, 2.6.2
Basel Committee on Banking Supervision, Ch. 1, 2.5
'Basic' sensitivity analysis, Ch. 54, 5.5.1
Bearer plants, Ch. 18, 3.1.7; Ch. 42, 2.3.3
    definition, Ch. 18, 2.2; Ch. 42, 2.2.1.A
    requirements for produce growing on, Ch. 42, 3.2.3
    in scope of IAS 16, Ch. 18, 2.1; Ch. 42, 3.2.3.A
Bid-ask spread, Ch. 14, 15.3.2
Binomial model, Ch. 34, 8.3.2
Biological assets, Ch. 42, 2.3.1. *See also* IAS 41–*Agriculture*
    definition of, Ch. 42, 2.2.1
    disclosure of groups of, Ch. 42, 5.1.3
    fair value measurement, Ch. 42, 4.5.2, 4.6.2.A
    leases of, Ch. 42, 2.3.5
    measurement, Ch. 42, 3.2.1
Black economic empowerment (BEE) and share-based payment, Ch. 34, 15.5
Black-Scholes-Merton formula, Ch. 34, 8.3.1
Block caving, depreciation, depletion and amortisation (mining), Ch. 43, 16.2
Bonds. *See* Convertible bonds
Borrowing costs, Ch. 21. *See also* Capitalisation of borrowing costs; IAS 23
    definition of, Ch. 21, 4
    eligible for capitalisation, Ch. 17, 6.3.2; Ch. 21, 5
        accrued costs and trade payables, Ch. 21, 5.3.3
        calculation of capitalisation rate, Ch. 21, 5.3.2
        directly attributable, Ch. 21, 5.1
        exchange differences as, Ch. 21, 5.4
        general borrowings, Ch. 21, 5.3
            completed qualifying assets, related to, Ch. 21, 5.3.1.A
            specific non-qualifying assets, related to, Ch. 21, 5.3.1.B
        group considerations, Ch. 21, 5.7
        hyperinflationary economies, Ch. 21, 5.6
        specific borrowings, Ch. 21, 5.2
    intangible assets, Ch. 17, 4.2
    interim reporting, Ch. 41, 9.1.4
    inventory, Ch. 22, 3.1.3C
    investment property, Ch. 19, 4.8
    on 'land expenditures', Ch. 21, 6.3.1
    other finance costs as, Ch. 21, 4.2, 5.5
    property, plant and equipment, Ch. 18, 4.1.2

Branches, foreign exchange, Ch. 15, 4.4
Brazil, IFRS adoption in, Ch. 1, 4.3.3
Broadcast rights, intangible assets amortisation of, Ch. 17, 9.2.1.B
Business Advisory Council (BAC), Ch. 1, 4.4.2
Business combination exemption (first-time adoption), Ch. 5, 5.2
    associates and joint arrangements, Ch. 5, 5.2, 5.2.2.A
    classification of business combinations, Ch. 5, 5.2.3
    currency adjustments to goodwill, Ch. 5, 5.2.6
    goodwill previously deducted from equity, Ch. 5, 5.2.5.C
    goodwill, restatement of, Ch. 5, 5.2.5
    measurement of deferred taxes and non-controlling interests, Ch. 5, 5.2.9
    option to restate business combinations retrospectively, Ch. 5, 5.2.2
    previously consolidated entities that are not subsidiaries, Ch. 5, 5.2.8
    previously unconsolidated subsidiaries, Ch. 5, 5.2.7
    recognition of assets and liabilities, Ch. 5, 5.2.4
    subsequent measurement under IFRSs not based on cost, Ch. 5, 5.2.4.E
Business combinations, Ch. 9, 1–16. *See also* Common control business combinations; IFRS 3; Income taxes
    achieved in stages (step acquisitions), Ch. 9, 9
    accounting for previously held interests in a joint operation, Ch. 9, 9.1
    achieved without the transfer of consideration, Ch. 9, 7.4
    acquired receivables, Ch. 54, 4.6
    acquirer and a vendor in, contracts between, Ch. 44, 3.7.2
    acquirer, identifying the, Ch. 9, 4.1
    acquirer, new entity formed to effect business combination, Ch. 9, 4.1.1
    acquirer that is not a legal entity, Ch. 9, 4.1
    acquisition method of accounting, Ch. 9, 4
        determining the acquisition date, Ch. 9, 4.2
        identifying the acquirer, Ch. 9, 4.1
    acquisition of intangible assets in, Ch. 17, 5
        customer relationship intangible assets, Ch. 17, 5.4
        in-process research and development, Ch. 17, 5.5
        intangible assets acquired, examples, Ch. 17, 5.2
        measuring the fair value of intangible assets, Ch. 17, 5.3
        recognition of intangible assets, Ch. 17, 5.1
    acquisition related costs, Ch. 9, 7.3
        presentation in statement of cash flows, Ch. 40, 6.3.1
    acquisitions of investment property in or a, Ch. 19, 3.3
    apparent immediate impairment of goodwill created by deferred tax, Ch. 33, 12.3
    assessing whether acquired process is substantive, Ch. 9, 3.2.4
        bargain purchase transactions, Ch. 9, 10
        recognising and measuring goodwill or a gain in, Ch. 9, 6
    'business' under IFRSs, definition of, Ch. 9, 3.2; Ch. 19, 3.3.1
        assessment whether acquired set of activities and assets constitutes a, Ch. 9, 3.2.2
    'capable of' from the viewpoint of a market participant, Ch. 9, 3.2.5
    common control, Ch. 10, 1–6; Ch. 56, 13.3
    concentration test, Ch. 9, 3.2.3
    consideration transferred, Ch. 9, 7
    contingent consideration, Ch. 9, 7.1

        cash flows, Ch. 40, 6.3.3
        and indemnification assets, Ch. 54, 4.6.2
        payable by an acquirer, Ch. 45, 3.7.1.A
        receivable by a vendor, Ch. 45, 3.7.1.B
    contingent liabilities recognised in a business combination, Ch. 9, 5.6.1
        changes in, Ch. 26, 4.10
    by contract alone, Ch. 9, 7.4.1
    contracts between acquirer and vendor, Ch. 45, 3.7.2
    customer relationship intangible assets acquired in, Ch. 17, 5.4
    deferred taxes, Ch. 33, 6.2.1.E, 6.2.2.E,
        arising on a business combination, Ch. 33, 12.1.2
            assets of the acquiree, Ch. 33, 12.1.2.B
            assets of the acquirer, Ch. 33, 12.1.2.A
    development stage entities, Ch. 9, 3.2.7
    disclosures, Ch. 9, 16
        combinations during current reporting period, Ch. 9, 16.1.1
        combinations effected after the end of reporting period, Ch. 9, 16.1.2
        financial effects of adjustments, Ch. 9, 16.2
        nature and financial effect, Ch. 9, 16.1
    exceptions to recognition and/or measurement principles, Ch. 9, 5.6
        assets held for sale, Ch. 9, 5.6.6
        contingent liabilities, Ch. 9, 5.6.1
        employee benefits, Ch. 9, 5.6.3
        income taxes, Ch. 9, 5.6.2
        indemnification assets, Ch. 9, 5.6.4
        insurance contracts within the scope of IFRS 17, Ch. 9, 5.6.9
        leases in which the acquiree is a lessee, Ch. 9, 5.6.8
        reacquired rights, Ch. 9, 5.6.5
        share-based payment transactions, Ch. 9, 5.6.7
    fair value of intangible assets acquired in, measuring, Ch. 17, 5.3
    goodwill, Ch. 9, 6
    identifying a, Ch. 9, 3.1
    identifying the acquirer, Ch. 9, 4.1
    in-process research and development (IPR&D) acquired in, Ch. 17, 5.5
    insurance contracts acquired in, Ch. 55, 9
    intangible assets acquired in, recognition of
        identifiability in relation to an intangible asset, Ch. 17, 5.1.3
            contractual-legal rights, Ch. 17, 5.1.3.A
            separability, Ch. 17, 5.1.3.B
        probable inflow of benefits, Ch. 17, 5.1.1
        reliability of measurement, Ch. 17, 5.1.2
    involving a Newco, Ch. 9, 4.1.1; Ch. 10, 4
    involving mutual entities, Ch. 9, 7.5
    leases, Ch. 23, 9
    loans and receivables acquired in, Ch. 49, 3.3.4
    measurement and recognition of deferred tax in, Ch. 33, 12.1
        deferred tax assets arising on a business combination, Ch. 33, 12.1.2
        deferred tax liabilities of acquired entity, Ch. 33, 12.1.3
        manner of recovery of assets and settlement of liabilities, determining, Ch. 33, 12.1.1
            changes in tax base consequent on the business combination, Ch. 33, 12.1.1.A

Business combinations—*contd*
    measurement period, Ch. 9, 12
    non-controlling interest as part of a business combination under common control, Ch. 10, 3.3.5
    non-controlling interests, measurement in, Ch. 7, 3.2, 3.1.1, 3.1.2, 5.2, 5.3
    pre-existing relationships, Ch. 9, 11.1
    process, Ch. 9, 3.2.1
    push down accounting, Ch. 9, 15
    recognition and measurement of assets acquired, liabilities assumed and non-controlling interests, Ch. 9, 5
        assembled workforce, Ch. 9, 5.5.4.A
        assets and liabilities related to contacts with customers, Ch. 9, 5.5.8
        assets with uncertain cash flows, Ch. 9, 5.5.5
        equity-accounted entities, investments in, Ch. 9, 5.5.7
        future contract renewals, Ch. 9, 5.5.4.B
        items not qualifying as assets, Ch. 9, 5.5.4.B
        liabilities assumed, Ch. 9, 5
        non-controlling interests, Ch. 9, 5.1, 7.2, 7.4.1
        reacquired rights, Ch. 9, 5.5.3
    replacement share-based payment awards in, Ch. 9, 7.2; Ch. 34, 11
    reverse acquisitions, Ch. 9, 14, 14.8, 14.9
    spin-off transaction, Ch. 9, 4.1.1
    stapling arrangements, Ch. 9, 4.1.2
    subsequent measurement and accounting, Ch. 9, 13
    tax deductions for acquisition costs, Ch. 33, 12.4
    tax deductions for replacement share-based payment awards in a business combination, Ch. 33, 12.2
    temporary differences arising from the acquisition of a group of assets that is not a business, Ch. 33, 12.5
Business combinations under common control' (BCUCC) research project
    accounting methods and disclosures, Ch. 10, 6.2
    background and scope, Ch. 10, 6.1
    next steps, Ch. 10, 6.3
'Business model' assessment, financial assets, Ch. 48, 5
    anticipated capital expenditure, Ch. 48, 5.6
    applying in practice, Ch. 48, 5.6
    credit-impaired financial assets in a hold to collect business model, Ch. 48, 5.6
    credit risk management activities, Ch. 48, 5.6
    hedging activities in a hold to collect business model, Ch. 48, 5.6
    hold to collect contractual cash flows, Ch. 48, 5.2
    hold to collect contractual cash flows and selling financial assets, Ch. 48, 5.3
    impact of sales on the assessment, Ch. 48, 5.2.1
    level at which the business model assessment should be applied, Ch. 48, 5.1
    liquidity portfolio for every day liquidity needs, Ch. 48, 5.6
    liquidity portfolio for stress case scenarios, Ch. 48, 5.6
    loans that are to be sub-participated, Ch. 48, 5.6
    opportunistic portfolio management, Ch. 48, 5.6
    other business models, Ch. 48, 5.4
    portfolio managed on a fair value basis, Ch. 48, 5.6
    replication portfolios, Ch. 48, 5.6
    sales to manage concentration risk, Ch. 48, 5.6
    securitisation, Ch. 48, 5.6
    splitting portfolios, Ch. 48, 5.6
    subsidiary that is held for sale, Ch. 48, 5.5
    transferred financial assets that are not derecognised, Ch. 48, 5.2.2
Buying reinsurance, gains/losses on, Ch. 55, 7.2.6.C
By-products, extractive industries, Ch. 43, 12.6, 14.2.1, 16.1.3.D
Call options, Ch. 7, 6.1, 6.3, 6.4, 6.5; Ch. 34, 8.2.1; Ch. 47, 11.2
    over non-controlling interests, Ch. 7, 6.1, 6.3, 6.4, 6.5; Ch. 9, 8.5
        call and put options entered into in relation to existing non-controlling interests, Ch. 7, 6.4
        call options only, Ch. 7, 6.1
        combination of call and put options, Ch. 7, 6.3
        separate financial statements, Ch. 7, 6.5
    purchased call option, Ch. 47, 11.2.1
    share-based payment, Ch. 34, 8.2.1
        intrinsic value and time value, Ch. 34, 8.2.2
    written call option, Ch. 47, 11.2.2
Canada, IFRS adoption in, Ch. 1, 4.3.2
Capital commitments, Ch. 41, 4.3.4
Capital, disclosures about, Ch. 3, 5.4; Ch. 54, 5.6.3
    general capital disclosures, Ch. 3, 5.4.1
    puttable financial instruments classified as equity, Ch. 3, 5.4.2
Capital Markets Advisory Committee, Ch. 1, 2.9
Capitalisation of borrowing costs, Ch. 21, 1–7. *See also* IAS 23
    cessation of capitalisation, Ch. 21, 6.3
        borrowing costs on 'land expenditures', Ch. 21, 6.3.1
    commencement, Ch. 21, 6.1
        expenditures on a qualifying asset, Ch. 21, 6.1.1
    disclosure requirements, Ch. 21, 7
    group considerations, Ch. 21, 5.7
        borrowings in one company and development in another, Ch. 21, 5.7.1
        qualifying assets held by joint arrangements, Ch. 21, 5.7.2
    in hyperinflationary economies, Ch. 21, 5.6
    interim financial reporting, Ch. 41, 9.1.4
    suspension of, Ch. 21, 6.2
        impairment considerations, Ch. 21, 6.2.1
Carried interests/party, extractive industries, Ch. 43, 6.1
    in E&E phase, Ch. 43, 6.1.2
    financing-type, Ch. 43, 6.1.3
    purchase/sale-type, Ch. 43, 6.1.4
Carve-out financial statements. *See* Combined financial statements
Cash and cash equivalents, Ch. 40, 3. *See also* IAS 7
    components of, Ch. 40, 3.2
        bank overdrafts, Ch. 40, 3.2.4
        client money, Ch. 40, 3.2.6
        cryptocurrencies, Ch. 40, 3.2.5
        demand deposits, Ch. 40, 3.2.1
        investments with maturities greater than three months, Ch. 40, 3.2.3
        money market funds (MMF), Ch. 40, 3.2.2
        short-term investments, Ch. 40, 3.2.1
    restrictions on the use of, Ch. 40, 3.4
    statement of financial position items, reconciliation with, Ch. 40, 3.3
Cash flow hedges, Ch. 53, 1.5, 5.2, 7.2; Ch. 54, 4.3.3
    acquisition or disposal of subsidiaries, Ch. 53, 7.2.4

acquisitions, Ch. 53, 7.2.4
all-in-one hedges, Ch. 53, 5.2.1
discontinuation, Ch. 53, 8.3
of firm commitments, Ch. 53, 5.2.2
of foreign currency monetary items, Ch. 53, 5.2.3
hypothetical derivatives, Ch. 53, 7.4.4
leased assets, CGU identification, Ch. 20, 3.2
measuring ineffectiveness, Ch. 53, 7.4.6
of a net position, Ch. 53, 2.5.3
presentation, Ch. 53, 10.1
reclassification of gains and losses, Ch. 53, 7.2.2

Cash-generating units (CGUs). *See also* Impairment of assets; Value in use (VIU)
active markets, identifying, Ch. 20, 3.2
carrying amount of, identifying, Ch. 20, 4
dividing the entity into, Ch. 20, 3
estimating the future pre-tax cash flows of, Ch. 20, 7.1
and goodwill impairment, Ch. 20, 8
impairment losses, Ch. 20, 11.2
leased assets and CGUs, Ch. 20, 3.2
reversal of impairments, Ch. 20, 11.4

Cash-settled share-based payment transaction, Ch. 34, 9; Ch. 36, 2.2.1. *See also* Equity-settled share-based payment transaction; IFRS 2; Share-based payment transactions
accounting treatment, Ch. 34, 9.3
    application of the accounting treatment, Ch. 34, 9.3.2
        market conditions and non-vesting conditions, Ch. 34, 9.3.2.D
        modification, cancellation and settlement, Ch. 34, 9.3.2.E
        non-market vesting conditions, Ch. 34, 9.3.2.C
        periodic allocation of cost, Ch. 34, 9.3.2.B
        vesting period determination, Ch. 34, 9.3.2.A
    basic accounting treatment, Ch. 34, 9.3.1
modification to or from equity-settlement, Ch. 34, 9.4
    cash-settled award modified to equity-settled award, Ch. 34, 9.4.2
    equity-settled award modified to cash-settled award, Ch. 34, 9.4.1
scope of requirements, Ch. 34, 9.1
transactions with equity and cash alternatives, Ch. 34, 10.1, 10.2, 10.3
what constitutes a cash-settled award?, Ch. 34, 9.2
    arrangements to sell employees' shares including 'broker settlement,' Ch. 34, 9.2.4
    economic compulsion for cash settlement (including unlisted company schemes), Ch. 34, 10.2.1.A
    formal and informal arrangements for the entity to purchase illiquid shares or otherwise settle in cash, Ch. 34, 9.2.1
    market purchases of own equity following equity-settlement of award, Ch. 34, 9.2.3
    market purchases of own equity to satisfy awards, Ch. 34, 9.2.2

Catastrophe provisions, Ch. 55, 7.2.1
CCIRS. *See* Cross-currency interest rate swaps (CCIRS)
CCP. *See* Central clearing party (CCP)
Cedant, Ch. 55, 2.2.1
Chief operating decision maker (CODM), Ch. 36, 1.3, 3.1
China Accounting Standards Committee (CASC), Ch. 1, 4.4.1.A

China, IFRS adoption in, Ch. 1, 4.4.1
Clawback conditions, share-based payment, Ch. 34, 3.1.1
Clean-up call options, Ch. 52, 4.2.7
Client money, Ch. 40, 3.2.6; Ch. 52, 3.7
'Closely related,' meaning of, Ch. 46, 5
Cloud computing, Ch. 17, 11.6
    implementation costs, Ch. 17, 11.6.2
    'software as a service' cloud computing arrangements, Ch. 17, 11.6.1
'Collar' put and call options, Ch. 52, 5.4.3.C
Collateral, Ch. 51, 5.8.1; Ch. 52, 5.5.2
Collectability, revenue IFRS 15, Ch. 28, 2.1.6
    assessing for a portfolio of contracts, Ch. 28, 2.1.6.A
    determining when to reassess, Ch. 28, 2.1.6.B
Combined financial statements, Ch. 6, 2.2.6
    common control, Ch. 6, 2.2.6.A
    preparation of, Ch. 6, 2.2.6.C
    purpose and users, Ch. 6, 2.2.6.B
    reporting entity in, Ch. 6, 1.1; Ch. 6, 2.2.6.B; Ch. 6, 2.2.6.C; Ch. 6, 2.2.6.E
    'special- purpose' vs 'general- purpose', Ch. 6, 2.2.6.D
Comissão de Valores Mobiliários (CVM), Ch. 1, 2.3, 4.3.3
Commencement of lease, Ch. 23, 4.2
Committee for Mineral Reserves International Reporting Standards (CRIRSCO), Ch. 43, 1.3
    International Reporting Template, Ch. 43, 2.3.1
    reporting terminology, Ch. 43, 2.3.1.B
    scope, Ch. 43, 2.3.1.A
Commodity-based contracts, extractive industries
    allocate the transaction price, Ch. 43, 12.15.4
    definition of commodity contract, Ch. 43, 12.6.1
    fixed consideration, Ch. 43, 12.15.4.B
    forward-selling to finance development, Ch. 43, 12.6
    modifications to, Ch. 43, 12.10
    multi-period, Ch. 43, 12.15
    normal purchase and sales exemption, Ch. 43, 13.1
    principal *vs.* agent considerations in, Ch. 43, 12.11
    revenue recognition, Ch. 43, 12.15.5
    take-or-pay contracts, Ch. 43, 12.16, 17.2
    trading activities, Ch. 43, 12.7
Commodity broker-traders, Ch. 45, 4.2.2
Commodity, equity-linked interest and principal payments, Ch. 46, 5.1.7
Commodity price assumptions, Ch. 43, 11.4.3, 11.5.2
Common control business combinations, Ch. 10, 1–6
    accounting for, Ch. 10, 3
        application of the acquisition method under IFRS 3, Ch. 10, 3.2
        application of the pooling of interests method, Ch. 10, 3.3
            acquisition of non-controlling interest as part of a business combination under common control, Ch. 10, 3.3.5
            carrying amounts of assets and liabilities, Ch. 10, 3.3.2
            equity reserves and history of assets and liabilities carried over, Ch. 10, 3.3.4
            general requirements, Ch. 10, 3.3.1
            restatement of financial information for periods prior to the date of the combination, Ch. 10, 3.3.3

Common control business combinations—*contd*
  accounting for—*contd*
    pooling of interests method versus acquisition method, Ch. 10, 3.1
  accounting for transactions under common control (or ownership) involving a Newco, Ch. 10, 4
    inserting a new intermediate parent within an existing group, Ch. 10, 4.3
    setting up a new top holding company, Ch. 10, 4.2
      transactions effected through issuing equity interests, Ch. 10, 4.2.1
      transactions involving consideration other than equity interests, Ch. 10, 4.2.2
    transferring businesses outside an existing group using a Newco, Ch. 10, 4.4
  accounting for transfers of associates/joint ventures under common control, Ch. 10, 5
  future developments, Ch. 10, 6
    BCUCC research project
      accounting methods and disclosures, Ch. 10, 6.2
      background and scope, Ch. 10, 6.1
      next steps, Ch. 10, 6.3
  group reorganisations, Ch. 10, 1.2
  IFRS 3 scope exclusion, Ch. 10, 2
    common control by an individual/group of individuals, Ch. 10, 2.1.1
    transitory control, Ch. 10, 2.1.2
  scope of chapter, Ch. 10, 1.3
Common control/group transactions, individual financial statements, Ch. 8, 4. *See also* Group reorganisations
  application of the principles in practice, Ch. 8, 4.4
    acquiring and selling businesses–transfers between subsidiaries, Ch. 8, 4.4.2
      accounting for a business that has been acquired, Ch. 8, 4.4.2.B
      accounting for transactions if net assets are not a business, Ch. 8, 4.4.2.D
      purchase and sale of a business for cash/equity not representative of fair value of business, Ch. 8, 4.4.2.C
    financial instruments within the scope of IFRS 9 (or IAS 39), Ch. 8, 4.4.5
      financial guarantee contracts, parent guarantee issued on behalf of subsidiary, Ch. 8, 4.4.5.B
      interest-free or non-market interest rate loans, Ch. 8, 4.4.5.A
    incurring expenses and settling liabilities without recharges, Ch. 8, 4.4.4
    transactions involving non-monetary assets, Ch. 8, 4.4.1
      acquisition of assets for shares, Ch. 8, 4.4.1.C
      contribution and distribution of assets, Ch. 8, 4.4.1.D
      parent exchanges PP&E for a non-monetary asset of the subsidiary, Ch. 8, 4.4.1.B
      sale of PP&E from parent to subsidiary for an amount of cash not representative of fair value of asset, Ch. 8, 4.4.1.A
      transfers between subsidiaries, Ch. 8, 4.4.1.E
    transfers of businesses between parent and subsidiary, Ch. 8, 4.4.3
      distributions of businesses without consideration, Ch. 8, 4.4.3.A
      legal merger of parent and subsidiary, Ch. 8, 4.4.3.B
      subsidiary as a surviving entity, Ch. 8, 4.4.3.B
  cost of investments acquired in, Ch. 8, 2.1.1.B
  disclosures, Ch. 8, 4.5
  measurement, Ch. 8, 4.3
    fair value in intra-group transactions, Ch. 8, 4.3.1
  recognition, Ch. 8, 4.2
Comparative information, Ch. 3, 2.4; Ch. 4, 4; Ch. 5, 6.1
  interim financial statements, Ch. 41, 5.1
  treatment on cessation of classification as held for sale, Ch. 4, 4.2
  treatment on initial classification as held for sale statement of comprehensive income, Ch. 4, 4.1.1
Compensation, related-party disclosures, Ch. 39. 2.6.1
Compound financial instruments, Ch. 47, 6
  background, Ch. 47, 6.1
  common forms of convertible bonds, Ch. 47, 6.6
    bond convertible into fixed percentage of equity, Ch. 47, 6.6.6
    contingent convertible bond, Ch. 47, 6.6.2
    convertible bonds with down round or ratchet features, Ch. 47, 6.6.7
    convertibles with cash settlement at the option of the issuer, Ch. 47, 6.6.5
    foreign currency convertible bond, Ch. 47, 6.6.4
    functional currency bond convertible into a fixed number of shares, Ch. 47, 6.6.1
    mandatorily convertible bond, Ch. 47, 6.6.3
  components of a compound instrument, Ch. 47, 6.4
    compound instruments with embedded derivatives, Ch. 47, 6.4.2
      issuer call option-'closely related' embedded derivatives, Ch. 47, 6.4.2.A
    determining, Ch. 47, 6.4.1
  conversion at maturity, Ch. 47, 6.3.1
    before maturity, Ch. 47, 6.3.2
      accounting treatment, Ch. 47, 6.3.2.B
      embedded derivatives, Ch. 47, 6.3.2.C
      'fixed stated principal' of a bond, Ch. 47, 6.3.2.A
  deferred tax, initial recognition exception, Ch. 33, 7.2.8
  early redemption/repurchase, Ch. 47, 6.3.3
    through exercising an embedded call option, Ch. 47, 6.3.3.B
    through negotiation with bondholders, Ch. 47, 6.3.3.A
  modification, Ch. 47, 6.3.4
  with multiple embedded derivatives, statement of financial position, Ch. 54, 4.4.7
  'split accounting', Ch. 47, 6.2
    initial recognition of a compound instrument, Ch. 47, 6.2
      accounting for the equity component, Ch. 47, 6.2.1
      temporary differences arising from, Ch. 47, 6.2.2
  treatment by holder and issuer contrasted, Ch. 47, 6.1.1
Comprehensive income, Ch. 3, 3.2
Comprehensive income statement. *See* Statement of comprehensive income
Concentration test, Ch. 9, 3.2.3
Concentrations of risk, Ch. 54, 5.6.1; Ch. 55, 11.2.4
Conceptual Framework for Financial Reporting 2010, Ch. 2, 2

Conceptual framework, IASB's, Ch. 1, 2.5; Ch. 2, 1–12. *See also* General purpose financial reporting
- contents, Ch. 2, 3.1
- derecognition, Ch. 2, 8.3
- development, Ch. 2, 2
- discussion paper on, Ch. 2, 1
- effective date, Ch. 2, 2
- enhancing qualitative characteristics, Ch. 2, 5.2
  - applying, Ch. 2, 5.2.5
  - comparability, Ch. 2, 5.2.1
  - timeliness, Ch. 2, 5.2.3
  - understandability, Ch. 2, 5.2.4
  - verifiability, Ch. 2, 5.2.2
- financial capital maintenance, Ch. 2.11.1
- financial statements, Ch. 2.6.1
  - assets, Ch. 2.7.2
  - consolidated and unconsolidated, Ch. 2.6.2.1
  - elements, Ch. 2.7
  - equity, Ch. 2.7.4
  - executory contracts, Ch. 2.7.1.2
  - going concern assumption, Ch. 2.6.1.4
  - income and expenses, Ch. 2.7.5
  - liabilities, Ch. 2.7.3
  - objective and scope, Ch. 2.6.1.1
  - perspective adopted in financial statements, Ch. 2.6.1.3
  - reporting period and comparative information, Ch. 2.6.1.2
  - substance of contractual rights and contractual obligations, Ch. 2.7.1.3
  - unit of account, Ch. 2.7.1.1
- fundamental qualitative characteristics, Ch. 2, 5.1
  - applying, Ch. 2, 5.1.3
  - cost constraint, Ch. 2, 5.3
  - faithful representation, Ch. 2, 5.1.2
  - relevance (including materiality), Ch. 2, 5.1.1
- general purpose financial reporting, Ch. 2, 4
  - economic resources, Ch. 2, 4.2.1
  - limitations, Ch. 2, 4.1.2
  - objective and usefulness, Ch. 2, 4.1.1
- management commentary, Ch. 2, 12
- measurement, Ch. 2, 9
  - bases, Ch. 2, 9.1
  - cash-flow-based measurement techniques, Ch. 2, 9.5
  - equity, Ch. 2, 9.4
  - factors to consider in selecting measurement bases, Ch. 2, 9.3
  - information provided by different measurement bases, Ch. 2, 9.2
- physical capital maintenance, Ch. 2, 11.2
- political and economic environment influences, Ch. 2, 1.2
- presentation and disclosure, Ch. 2, 10
  - aggregation, Ch. 2, 10.3
  - classification, Ch. 2, 10.2
  - objectives and principles, Ch. 2, 10.1
- purpose, Ch. 2, 3.2
- recognition criteria, Ch. 2, 8.2
  - faithful representation, Ch. 2, 8.2.2
  - relevance, Ch. 2, 8.2.1
- recognition process, Ch. 2, 8.1
- reporting entity, Ch. 2, 6.2
- scope, Ch. 2, 3
- standard settings, Ch. 2, 1.2
- status, Ch. 2, 3.2
- useful financial information, qualitative characteristics of, Ch. 2, 5

Concession agreements. *See* Service concession arrangements (SCA)
- mineral reserves and resources, Ch. 43, 2

Concessionary agreements (concessions), extractive industries, Ch. 43, 5.2

Condensed interim financial statements, Ch. 41, 3.2. *See also under* IAS 34
- disclosures in, Ch. 41, 4
  - accounting policies and methods of computation, Ch. 41, 4.3.11
  - amounts that are unusual because of their nature, size or incidence, Ch. 41, 4.3.13
  - capital commitments, Ch. 41, 4.3.4
  - changes in circumstances affecting fair values, Ch. 41, 4.3.6
  - changes in composition of the entity, Ch. 41, 4.3.17
  - compliance with IFRS, Ch. 41, 4.6
  - contingent liabilities, Ch. 41, 4.3.10
  - debt and equity securities, Ch. 41, 4.3.14
  - default or breach of loan covenants not remedied before end of interim period, Ch. 41, 4.3.7
  - dividends paid Ch. 41, 4.3.15
  - events after the interim reporting date, Ch. 41, 4.3.16
  - fair value disclosures, Ch. 41, 4.5
  - fair value hierarchy levels, transfers between, Ch. 41, 4.3.9
  - inventory write-down and reversals, Ch. 41, 4.3.1
  - litigation settlements, Ch. 41, 4.3.5
  - PP&E, acquisition and disposal of, Ch. 41, 4.3.3
  - recognition and reversal of impairment losses, Ch. 41, 4.3.2
  - related party transactions, Ch. 41, 4.3.8
  - seasonality or cyclicality of operations, Ch. 41, 4.3.12
  - segment information, Ch. 41, 4.4
  - significant events and transactions, Ch. 41, 4.1
  - transfers between different levels of fair value hierarchy, , Ch. 41, 4.3.9
- first-time presentation, Ch. 41, 11.1
- requirements for interim financial information, Ch. 41, 3.3

Consideration transferred, Ch. 9, 7. *See also* Contingent consideration
- acquisition-related costs, Ch. 9, 7.3

Consignment stock and sale and repurchase agreements, Ch. 22, 2.3.1F

Consistency in application of IFRS, Ch. 1, 5

Consistent accounting policies, Ch. 7, 2.6; Ch. 11, 7.8. *See also* Financial statements, presentation of; IAS 1

Consolidated financial statements, Ch. 6, 1–11; Ch. 8, 1.1. *See also* consolidation procedures, IFRS 10
- continuous assessment, Ch. 6, 9
- control, Ch. 6, 3
- control of specified assets, Ch. 6, 8
- employee benefit trusts, Ch. 6, 2.2.2; Ch. 34, 12.3, 12.4.1, 12.5.1
- entity no longer a parent at the end of reporting period, Ch. 6, 2.2.4
- exemption from preparing
  - consent of non-controlling shareholders, Ch. 6, 2.2.1.A

Consolidated financial statements—*contd*
  exemption from preparing—*contd*
    not filing financial statements for listing securities, Ch. 6, 2.2.1.C
    parent's IFRS financial statements are publicly available, Ch. 6, 2.2.1.D
    securities not traded in a public market, Ch. 6, 2.2.1.B
  exposure to variable returns, Ch. 6, 5
  future developments, Ch. 6, 11
  investment entities, Ch. 6, 10
  power over an investee, Ch. 6, 4
  principal-agency situations, Ch. 6, 6
  related parties and *de facto* agents, Ch. 6, 7
Consolidated statement of cash flows, preparing, Ch. 40, 6.1
Consolidation procedures, Ch. 7. *See also* non-controlling interests
  basic principles, Ch. 7, 2.1
  changes in control, Ch. 7, 3
    accounting for a loss of control Ch. 7, 3.2
    deemed disposal, Ch. 7, 3.6
    demergers and distributions of non-cash assets to owners, Ch. 7, 3.7, Ch. 8, 2.4.2. *See also* IFRIC 17
    interest retained in the former subsidiary, Ch. 7, 3.3
      associate or joint venture, Ch. 7, 3.3.2, 7.1
      financial asset, Ch. 7, 3.3.1
      joint operation, Ch. 7, 3.3.3, 7.2
    Interpretations Committee and IASB discussions about the sale of a single asset entity containing real estate, Ch. 7.3.2.1
    loss of control in multiple arrangements, Ch. 7, 3.4
    other comprehensive income, Ch. 7, 3.5
  changes in ownership interest without a loss of control, Ch. 7, 4
    contingent consideration on purchase of a noncontrolling interest, Ch. 7, 4.5
    goodwill attributable to non-controlling interests, Ch. 7, 4.2; Ch. 20, 9
    non-cash acquisition of non-controlling interests, Ch. 7, 4.3
    reattribution of other comprehensive income, Ch. 7, 4.1
    transaction costs, Ch. 7, 4.4
  commencement and cessation of consolidation, Ch. 7, 3.1
    acquisition in stages: associate or joint venture that is not a business becomes a subsidiary, Ch. 7, 3.1.2
    acquisition of a subsidiary that is not a business, Ch. 7, 3.1.1
    demergers and distributions of non-cash assets to owners, Ch. 7, 3.7
      presentation and disclosure, Ch. 7, 3.7.3
      recognition and measurement in IFRIC 17, Ch. 7, 3.7.2
      scope of IFRIC 17, Ch. 7, 3.7.1
  consistent accounting policies, Ch. 7, 2.6
  consolidating foreign operations, Ch. 7, 2.3
  intragroup eliminations, Ch. 7, 2.4
  non-coterminous accounting periods, Ch. 7, 2.5
  proportion consolidated, Ch. 7, 2.2, 5.6
Constructive obligation, Ch. 26, 3.1
  employee benefits, Ch. 37, 7.1
  provisions, Ch. 26, 3.1

Consultative Group for Rate Regulation, Ch. 1, 2.9
Contingent assets, Ch. 26, 3.2.2
  definition, Ch. 26, 3.2.2
  disclosure of, Ch. 26, 7.3
  relating to business combinations, Ch. 9, 5.5.4.B
Contingent consideration, Ch. 7, 4.5; Ch. 9, 7.1
  cash flows in business combinations, Ch. 40, 6.3.3.A
    payable by an acquirer, Ch. 45, 3.7.1.A
    receivable by a vendor, Ch. 45, 3.7.1.B
  initial recognition and measurement, Ch. 9, 7.1.1
  intangible assets acquired for, Ch. 17, 4.5
  on loss of control of a subsidiary, Ch. 7.3.2
  obligation, classification, Ch. 9, 7.1.2
  on purchase of non-controlling interest, Ch. 7, 4.5
  subsequent measurement and accounting, Ch. 9, 7.1.3
Contingent convertible bond, Ch. 47, 6.6.2
Contingent costs, investment property, Ch. 19, 4.10
Contingent liabilities, Ch. 26, 3.2.1
  business combinations, Ch. 9, 5.6.1
  definition, Ch. 26, 3.2.1
  disclosure of, Ch. 26, 7.2
  joint ventures and associates, Ch. 13, 5.2.2
Contingent resources, extractive industries, Ch. 43, 2.2.1
Contingent settlement provisions, Ch. 47, 4.3
  contingencies that are 'not genuine,' Ch. 47, 4.3.1
  liabilities that arise only on a change of control, Ch. 47, 4.3.3
  liabilities that arise only on liquidation, Ch. 47, 4.3.2
  some typical contingent settlement provisions, Ch. 47, 4.3.4
Contingently issuable shares (EPS), Ch. 37, 6.4.6
  earnings-based contingencies, Ch. 37, 6.4.6.A
  share-price-based contingencies, Ch. 37, 6.4.6.B
Continuous assessment of control, Ch. 6, 9; Ch. 12, 8
  bankruptcy filings, Ch. 6, 9.2
  changes in market conditions, Ch. 6, 9.1
  control re-assessment, Ch. 6, 9.3
  joint arrangements, Ch. 12, 8
  troubled debt restructurings, Ch. 6, 9.2
Contract asset, Ch. 32, 2.1
  presentation requirements for, Ch. 32, 2.1
Contract costs, Ch. 31, 5
  amortisation of capitalised costs, Ch. 31, 5.3
    classification and presentation of capitalised contract costs and related amortisation, Ch. 31, 5.3.6
  costs to fulfil a contract, Ch. 31, 5.2
    assets recognised from, Ch. 32, 3.2.3
  costs to obtain a contract, Ch. 31, 5.1
  impairment of capitalised costs, Ch. 31, 5.4
Contract liability, Ch. 32, 2.1
  presentation requirements for, Ch. 32, 2.1
Contract modifications, Ch. 28, 2.4
  not a separate contract, Ch. 28, 2.4.2
  represents a separate contract, Ch. 28, 2.4.1
Contractual arrangement, business combinations, Ch. 6, 4.4
  additional rights from, Ch. 6, 4.3.6
  with other vote holders, Ch. 6, 4.3.5
  structured entities, Ch. 6, 4.4.1
Contractual cash flows, financial instruments IFRS 9, Ch. 48, 6
  auction rate securities, Ch. 48, 6.4.4.B

bonds with a capped or floored interest rate, Ch. 48, 6.3.3
contractual features that may affect the classification, Ch. 48, 6.4
   de minimis and non-genuine features, Ch. 48, 6.4.1
   features that change the timing or amount of contractual cash flows, Ch. 48, 6.4.4
      prepayment – assets originated at a premium or discount, Ch. 48, 6.4.4.B
      prepayment – negative compensation, Ch. 48, 6.4.4.A
   features that modify the consideration for the time value of money, Ch. 48, 6.4.2
   features that normally do not represent payment of principal and interest, Ch. 48, 6.4.5
   regulated interest rates, Ch. 48, 6.4.3
contractual features that normally pass the test, Ch. 48, 6.3
   bonds with a capped or floored interest rate, Ch. 48, 6.3.3
   conventional subordination features, Ch. 48, 6.3.1
   features which compensate the lender for changes in tax or other related costs, Ch. 48, 6.3.6
   full recourse loans secured by collateral, Ch. 48, 6.3.2
   lender has discretion to change the interest rate, Ch. 48, 6.3.4
   unleveraged inflation-linked bonds, Ch. 48, 6.3.5
contractually linked instruments, Ch. 48, 6.6
   assessing the characteristics of the underlying pool, Ch. 48, 6.6.1
   assessing the exposure to credit risk in the tranche held, Ch. 48, 6.6.2
conventional subordination features, Ch. 48, 6.3.1
convertible debt, Ch. 48, 6.4.5
de minimis features, Ch. 48, 6.4.1.A
debt covenants, Ch. 48, 6.4.4.B
dual currency instruments, Ch. 48, 6.4.2
five-year constant maturity bond, Ch. 48, 6.4.2
fixed rate bond prepayable by the issuer at fair value, Ch. 48, 6.4.5
full recourse loans secured by collateral, Ch. 48, 6.3.2
interest rate period, Ch. 48, 6.4.2
inverse floater, Ch. 48, 6.4.5
investment in open-ended money market or debt funds, Ch. 48, 6.4.5
lender has discretion to change the interest rate, Ch. 48, 6.3.4
loan commitments, Ch. 48, 6.4.6
meaning of 'interest,' Ch. 48, 6.2
meaning of 'principal', Ch. 48, 6.1
modified time value of money component, Ch. 48, 6.4.2
multiple of a benchmark interest rate, Ch. 48, 6.4.5
non-genuine features, Ch. 48, 6.4.1.B
non-recourse assets, Ch. 48, 6.5
non-recourse loans, Ch. 48, 6.5
perpetual instruments with potentially deferrable coupons, Ch. 48, 6.4.5
prepayment, assets originated at a premium or discount, Ch. 48, 6.4.4.B
prepayment, negative compensation, Ch. 48, 6.4.4.A
prepayment options, Ch. 48, 6.4.4
regulated interest rates, Ch. 48, 6.4.3
unleveraged inflation-linked bonds, Ch. 48, 6.3.5
Contractual-legal criterion (intangible assets), Ch. 9, 5.5.2

Contractual service margin (CSM), insurance contracts, Ch. 56, 8.5
   measurement of, using the variable fee approach, Ch. 56, 11.2.2
   recognition of in profit or loss, Ch. 56, 11.2.4
   release of, Ch. 56, 10.4.1
   subsequent measurement, Ch. 56, 8.6.2
Contractually linked instruments, Ch. 48, 6.6
   assessing the characteristics of the underlying pool, Ch. 48, 6.6.1
   assessing the exposure to credit risk in the tranche held, Ch. 48, 6.6.2
Control, Ch. 6, 3; Ch. 12, 4, Ch 30
   assessing control, Ch. 6, 3.1
   changes in control (*see* Consolidation procedures)
   common control, Ch. 6, 2.2.6.A
   de facto control, Ch. 6, 4.3.3
   joint, Ch. 12, 4
   potential voting rights, Ch. 6, 4.3.4
   purpose and design of investee, Ch. 6, 3.2
   of specified assets, Ch. 6, 8
      of silo, evaluating, Ch. 6, 8.2
   transfer of, Ch 30
Controlling relationships, disclosure of, Ch. 39, 2.4
Convergence, IFRS/US GAAP, Ch. 1, 3.2
Convertible bonds, Ch. 47, 6.6
   bond convertible into fixed percentage of equity, Ch. 47, 6.6.6
   with cash settlement at the option of the issuer, Ch. 47, 6.6.5
   contingent convertible bond, Ch. 47, 6.6.2
   with down round or ratchet features, Ch. 47, 6.6.7
   foreign currency convertible bond, Ch. 47, 6.6.4
   functional currency bond convertible into a fixed number of shares, Ch. 47, 6.6.1
   issued to acquire goods/services, Ch. 34, 10.1.6
   mandatorily convertible bond, Ch. 47, 6.6.3
Convertible debt instruments, Ch. 46, 5.1.9
Convertible instruments (EPS), Ch. 37, 6.4.1
   convertible debt, Ch. 37, 6.4.1.A
   convertible preference shares, Ch. 37, 6.4.1.B
   participating equity instruments, Ch. 37, 6.4.1.C
Convertible loans, Ch. 54, 7.4.4.B
Core deposits, Ch. 43, 2.6.7
Core inventories, extractive industries, Ch. 43, 14.3
Corporate assets, Ch. 20, 4.2, Ch. 20, 3.1.1
   leased corporate assets, Ch. 20, 4.2.1
Cost approach, Ch. 18, 6.1.1.C
Cost of investment, Ch. 8, 2.1.1
   acquired for own shares or other equity instruments, Ch. 8, 2.1.1.A
   acquired in a common control transactions, Ch. 8, 2.1.1.B
   formation of a new parent, Ch. 8, 2.1.1.E–F
   reverse acquisitions in the separate financial statements, Ch. 8, 2.1.1.G
   subsidiary accounted for at cost: partial disposal, Ch. 8, 2.1.1.D
   subsidiary, associate or joint venture acquired in stages, Ch. 8, 2.1.1.C

Cost model
   investment property, Ch. 19, 7
      impairment, Ch. 19, 7.3
      incidence of use of the cost model, Ch. 19, 7.2
      initial recognition, Ch. 19, 7.1
         non-physical parts, identification of, Ch. 19, 7.1.2
         physical parts, identification of, Ch. 19, 7.1.1
   property, plant and equipment, Ch. 18, 5
      depreciable amount, Ch. 18, 5.2
      depreciation charge, Ch. 18, 5.3
      depreciation methods, Ch. 18, 5.6
      impairment, Ch. 18, 5.7
      land, Ch. 18, 5.4.2
      repairs and maintenance, Ch. 18, 5.4.1
      residual values, Ch. 18, 5.2
      significant parts of assets, Ch. 18, 5.1
      technological change, Ch. 18, 5.4.3
      useful lives, Ch. 18, 5.4
      when depreciation starts, Ch. 18, 5.5

Costs of hedging, accounting for, Ch. 53, 7.5
   foreign currency basis spreads in financial instruments, Ch. 53, 7.5.3
      measurement of the costs of hedging for, Ch. 53, 7.5.3.A
      transition, Ch. 53, 13.3.3
   forward element of forward contracts, Ch. 53, 7.5.2
      forward element in net investment hedge, Ch. 53, 7.5.2.A
      transition, Ch. 53, 13.3.2
   time value of options, Ch. 53, 7.5.1
      aligned time value, Ch. 53, 7.5.1.A
      transition, Ch. 53, 13.3.1

Council of European Securities Regulators (CESR), Ch. 1, 5
Credit break clauses, Ch. 53, 3.2.4
Credit card arrangements, Ch. 27, 3.5.1.C
   and similar arrangements which give rise to insurance risk, Ch. 45, 3.3.4
Credit card-holder rewards programmes, Ch. 27, 3.5.1.D
Credit enhancements, Ch. 51, 6.1.1; Ch. 52, 3.3.1
Credit guarantees, Ch. 52, 4.3
Credit-linked notes, Ch. 46, 5.1.8
Credit losses. *See* Expected credit losses (ECLs)
Credit risk, Ch. 54, 5.3
   changes in, calculating gain/loss attributable to, Ch. 51, 6.2.1
   counterparty
      fair value measurement, Ch. 14, 12.2.2
      valuation of derivative transactions, Ch. 14, 11.3.2
   disclosures, Ch. 55, 11.2.6.A
   exposure, Ch. 54, 5.3.4
   of financial instrument, Ch. 54, 5.3
   hedging, Ch. 53, 12.1
   illustrative disclosures, Ch. 54, 5.3.6
   impact on hedged item, Ch. 53, 6.4.2.A
   impact on hedging instrument, Ch. 53, 6.4.2.B, 7.4.9
   incorporation into valuation of derivative contracts, Ch. 14, 11.3.3
   management practices, Ch. 54, 5.3.2
   significant increases in, determining, Ch. 51, 6
      change in the risk of a default occurring, Ch. 51, 6.1
         contractually linked instruments (CLIs) and subordinated interests, Ch. 51, 6.1.2
         determining change in risk of a default under loss rate approach, Ch. 51, 6.1.3
         impact of collateral, credit enhancements and financial guarantee contracts, Ch. 51, 6.1.1
      collective assessment, Ch. 51, 6.5
         basis of aggregation for collective assessment, Ch. 51, 6.5.2
         example of collective assessment ('bottom up' and 'top down' approach), Ch. 51, 6.5.3
         example of individual assessment of changes in credit risk, Ch. 51, 6.5.1
      determining the credit risk at initial recognition of an identical group of financial assets, Ch. 51, 6.6
      factors/indicators of changes in credit risk, Ch. 51, 6.2
         concessions granted to a wide range of customers, Ch. 51, 6.2.3
         examples, Ch. 51, 6.2.1
         illustrative examples when assessing significant increases in credit risk, Ch. 51, 6.2.4
         past due status and more than 30 days past due presumption, Ch. 51, 6.2.2
         use of behavioural factors, Ch. 51, 6.2.5
      operational simplifications, Ch. 51, 6.4
         assessment at the counterparty level, Ch. 51, 6.4.4
         delinquency, Ch. 51, 6.4.2
         determining maximum initial credit risk for a portfolio, Ch. 51, 6.4.5
         low credit risk, Ch. 51, 6.4.1
         12-month risk as an approximation for change in lifetime risk, Ch. 51, 6.4.3
      revolving credit facilities, Ch. 51, 12
   in the tranche held, Ch. 48, 6.6.2

Cross-currency interest rate swaps (CCIRS), Ch. 53, 3.2.4.A, 7.3.3.B, 7.5.3
Crypto-assets
   additional disclosure requirements for, Ch. 22, 6.2
   cost model, Ch. 17, 11.5.2.A
   Cryptocurrencies as cash, Ch. 40, 3.2.5
   In scope of IAS 2, Ch. 22, 2.3.1.D
   recognition and initial measurement, Ch. 17, 11.5.1
   revaluation model, Ch. 17, 11.5.2.B
   standard setter activity, Ch. 17, 11.5.3
   subsequent measurement, Ch. 17, 11.5.2
Cryptocurrencies, Ch. 40, 3.2.5
CSM. *See* Contractual service margin
Cumulative preference shares, Ch. 11, 7.5.2
Cumulative translation differences, foreign operations, Ch. 5, 5.7
Current assets, Ch. 3, 3.1.3
Current liabilities, Ch. 3, 3.1.4
   Subsequent rectification of a covenant breach, Ch. 38, 2.3.2
Current service cost, employee benefits, Ch. 35, 5, 10.1
Current tax, Ch. 33, 5. *See also* IAS 12
   definition, Ch. 33, 3
Customer, Ch. 28, 3.6
   definition, Ch. 27, 3.3
Customer relationship intangible assets, Ch. 9, 5.5.2.B
Customer-supplier relationship, Ch. 6, 7.1
DAC. *See* Deferred acquisition costs

Date of transition to IFRSs, Ch. 5, 1.3
'Day 1' profits, Ch. 49, 3.3
De facto **agents**, Ch. 12, 4.2.5
De facto **control**, Ch. 6, 4.3.3
Death-in-service benefits, Ch. 35, 3.6
Death waivers, loans with, Ch. 45, 3.3.5
Debt, extinguishment of, Ch. 52, 6.1
    gains and losses on, Ch. 52, 6.3
Debt instruments, Ch. 45, 3.4.1.B; Ch. 48, 2.1
    convertible and exchangeable, Ch. 37, 6.4.1.A; Ch. 46, 5.1.9
    measured at fair value through other comprehensive income, Ch. 51, 9
    term extension and similar call, put and prepayment options in, Ch. 46, 5.1.4
Debt investments, foreign currency, Ch. 51, 9.2
Decommissioning, Ch. 26, 6.3; Ch. 43, 10
    accounting for changes in costs, Ch. 18, 4.3
    in extractive industries, Ch. 43, 10
        foreign exchange differences, treatment of, Ch. 43, 10.2
        indefinite life assets, Ch. 43, 10.3
        recognition and measurement issues, Ch. 43, 10.1
    provisions, Ch. 26, 6.3
Deductible temporary differences, Ch. 33, 6.2.2. *See also* Temporary differences, Deferred tax assets
    business combinations and consolidation, Ch. 33, 6.2.2.E
    definition, Ch. 33, 3
    foreign currency differences, Ch. 33, 6.2.2.F
    recognition, Ch. 33, 7.1.2
        initial recognition of goodwill, Ch. 33, 7.2.2.B
    restrictions on recognition, Ch. 33, 7.4
        and future and 'probable' taxable profit, Ch. 33, 7.4.3
        and unrealised losses, Ch. 33, 7.4.5
    revaluations, Ch. 33, 6.2.2.C
    tax re-basing, Ch. 33, 6.2.2.D
    transactions that affect, Ch. 33, 6.2.2.A
        profit/loss, Ch. 33, 6.2.2.A
        statement of financial position, Ch. 33, 6.2.2.B
Deemed cost on first-time adoption, Ch. 5, 5.5
    for assets used in operations subject to rate regulation, Ch. 5, 5.5.4
    disclosures regarding, Ch. 5, 6.5
    event-driven fair value measurement as, Ch. 5, 5.5.2
        exemption for event-driven revaluations after the date of transition, Ch. 5, 5.5.2.C
        'fresh start' accounting, Ch. 5, 5.5.2.B
        'push down' accounting, Ch. 5, 5.5.2.A
    fair value or revaluation as, Ch. 5, 5.5.1
        determining deemed cost, Ch. 5, 5.5.1.A
        before the date of transition to IFRSs, Ch. 5, 5.5.1.B
    for oil and gas assets, Ch. 5, 5.5.3
    of subsidiary, on transition to IFRS, Ch. 8, 2.1.2
    use of
        after severe hyperinflation, Ch. 5, 6.5.5
        for assets used in operations subject to rate regulation, Ch. 5, 6.5.4
        fair value as, Ch. 5, 6.5.1
        for investments in subsidiaries, joint ventures and associates, Ch. 5, 6.5.2
        for oil and gas assets, Ch. 5, 6.5.3

Deemed disposals, Ch. 7, 3.6; Ch. 11, 7.12.6
Default
    change in the risk of a default occurring, Ch. 51, 6.1
        contractually linked instruments (CLIs) and subordinated interests, Ch. 51, 6.1.2
        determining change in risk of a default under loss rate approach, Ch. 51, 6.1.3
        impact of collateral, credit enhancements and financial guarantee contracts, Ch. 51, 6.1.1
    definition of, Ch. 51, 5.1
    exposure at default, revolving facilities, Ch. 51, 12.3
    losses expected in the event of default, Ch. 51, 5.8
        cash flows from the sale of a defaulted loan, Ch. 51, 5.8.2
        credit enhancements: collateral and financial guarantees, Ch. 51, 5.8.1
        treatment of collection costs paid to an external debt collection agency, Ch. 51, 5.8.3
    probability of default (PD) and loss rate approaches, Ch. 51, 5.4
    loss rate approach, Ch. 51, 5.4.2
    probability of default approach, Ch. 51, 5.4.1
Deferred acquisition costs (DAC), Ch. 55, 9.1.1.B
Deferred tax, Ch. 33, 6–8. *See also* IAS 12; Income taxes; Tax bases; Temporary differences
    assets, Ch. 33, 6.1.1; Ch. 33, 7.1.2
    investment property held by a 'single asset' entity, Ch. 19, 6.10
    liabilities, Ch. 33, 6.1.2, 7.1.1
    measurement, Ch. 33, 8
        different tax rates applicable to retained and distributed profits, Ch. 33, 8.5
            effectively tax-free entities, Ch. 33, 8.5.1
            withholding tax/distribution tax?, Ch. 33, 8.5.2
        discounting, Ch. 33, 8.6
        expected manner of recovery of assets/settlement of liabilities, Ch. 33, 8.4
        assets and liabilities with more than one tax base, Ch. 33, 8.4.3
        carrying amount, Ch. 33, 8.4.2
        change in expected manner of recovery of an asset/settlement of a liability, Ch. 33, 8.4.11
        depreciable PP&E and intangible assets, Ch. 33, 8.4.5
        determining the expected manner of recovery of assets, Ch. 33, 8.4.4
        investment properties, Ch. 19, 6.10; Ch. 33, 8.4.7
        non-depreciable PP&E and intangible assets, Ch. 33, 8.4.6
        non-amortised or indefinite life intangible assets, Ch. 33, 8.4.6.B
        PP&E accounted for using the revaluation model, Ch. 33, 8.4.6.A
        other assets and liabilities, Ch. 33, 8.4.8
        'outside' temporary differences relating to subsidiaries, branches, associates and joint arrangements, Ch. 33, 8.4.9
        'single asset' entities, Ch. 19, 4.1.2, 6.10; Ch. 33, 8.4.10
        tax planning strategies, Ch. 33, 8.4.1
    legislation at the end of the reporting period, Ch. 33, 8.1

Deferred tax—*contd*
  measurement—*contd*
    'prior year adjustments' of previously presented tax balances and expense (income), Ch. 33, 8.3
    uncertain tax treatments, Ch. 33, 8.2, 9
    unrealised intragroup profits and losses in consolidated financial, Ch. 33, 8.7
      intragroup transfers of goodwill and intangible assets, Ch. 33, 8.7.1
        consolidated financial statements, Ch. 7, 2.4, Ch. 33, 8.7.1.C
        individual financial statements of buyer, Ch. 33, 8.7.1.A
        individual financial statements of seller, Ch. 33, 8.7.1.B
        when the tax base of goodwill is retained by the transferor entity, Ch. 33, 8.7.1.D
  recognition, Ch. 33, 7
    assets carried at fair value/revalued amount, Ch. 33, 7.3
    basic principles, Ch. 33, 7.1
      deductible temporary differences (deferred tax assets), Ch. 33, 7.1.2
      taxable temporary differences (deferred tax liabilities), Ch. 33, 7.1.1
    deferred taxable gains, Ch. 33, 7.7
    initial recognition exception, Ch. 33, 7.2
      acquisition of an investment in a subsidiary, associate, branch or joint arrangement, Ch. 33, 7.2.10
      acquisition of subsidiary that does not constitute a business, Ch. 33, 7.2.9
      changes to temporary differences after initial recognition, Ch. 33, 7.2.4
        change in carrying value due to revaluation, Ch. 33, 7.2.4.B
        change in tax base due to deductions in tax return, Ch. 33, 7.2.4.C
        depreciation, amortisation/impairment of initial carrying value, Ch. 33, 7.2.4.A
        temporary difference altered by legislative change, Ch. 33, 7.2.4.D
      initial recognition of compound financial instruments by the issuer, Ch. 33, 7.2.8
      initial recognition of goodwill, Ch. 33, 7.2.2
      initial recognition of other assets and liabilities, Ch. 33, 7.2.3
      intragroup transfers of assets with no change in tax base, Ch. 33, 7.2.5
      partially deductible and super-deductible assets, Ch. 33, 7.2.6
      tax losses, acquisition of, Ch. 33, 7.2.1
      transactions involving the initial recognition of an asset and liability, Ch. 33, 7.2.7
        decommissioning costs, Ch. 33, 7.2.7.A
        finance leases under IFRS 16 taxed as operating leases, Ch. 33, 7.2.7.B
    interpretation issues, Ch. 33, 7.1.3
      accounting profit, Ch. 33, 7.1.3.A
      taxable profit 'at the time of the transaction,' Ch. 33, 7.1.3.B
    'outside' temporary differences relating to subsidiaries, branches, associates and joint arrangements, Ch. 33, 7.5
      calculation of, Ch. 33, 7.5.1
        consolidated financial statements, Ch. 33, 7.5.1.A
        separate financial statements of investor, Ch. 33, 7.5.1.B
      deductible temporary differences, Ch. 33, 7.5.3
      foreseeable future – anticipated intragroup dividend, Ch. 33, 7.5.4
        consolidated financial statements of receiving entity, Ch. 33, 7.5.4.A
        separate financial statements of paying entity, Ch. 33, 7.5.4.B
      taxable temporary differences, Ch. 33, 7.5.2
      unpaid intragroup interest, royalties, management charges etc., Ch. 33, 7.5.5
    restrictions on recognition of deferred tax assets, Ch. 33, 7.4
      effect of disposals on recoverability of tax losses, Ch. 33, 7.4.8
        tax losses of retained entity recoverable against profits of subsidiary disposed of, Ch. 33, 7.4.8.B
        tax losses of subsidiary disposed of recoverable against profits of retained entity, Ch. 33, 7.4.8.C
        tax losses of subsidiary disposed of recoverable against profits of that subsidiary, Ch. 33, 7.4.8.A
      re-assessment of deferred tax assets, Ch. 33, 7.4.7
      restrictions imposed by relevant tax laws, Ch. 33, 7.4.1
      sources of 'probable' taxable profit, estimates of future taxable profits, Ch. 33, 7.4.3
        ignore origination of new future deductible temporary differences, Ch. 33, 7.4.3.A
        ignore reversal of existing deductible temporary differences, Ch. 33, 7.4.3.B
      sources of 'probable' taxable profit, taxable temporary differences, Ch. 33, 7.4.2
      tax planning opportunities, Ch. 33, 7.4.4
      unrealised losses on debt securities measured at fair value, Ch. 33, 7.4.5
      unused tax losses and unused tax credits, Ch. 33, 7.4.6
    'tax-transparent' ('flow-through') entities, Ch. 33, 7.6
    tax bases and temporary differences, Ch. 33, 6

Deferred tax assets, Ch. 33, 3, 7.4

Deferred tax liabilities, Ch. 33, 3

Defined benefit plans, Ch. 35, 5–11. *See also* IAS 19; IFRIC 14
  costs of administering, Ch. 35, 11
  vs. defined contribution plans, Ch. 35, 3.1
  disclosure requirements, Ch. 35, 15.2
    amounts in financial statements, Ch. 35, 15.2.2
    characteristics and risks associated with, Ch. 35, 15.2.1
    future cash flows, amount, timing and uncertainty of, Ch. 35, 15.2.3
    multi-employer plans, Ch. 35, 15.2.4
    in other IFRSs, Ch. 35, 15.2.6
    sharing risks between entities under common control, Ch. 35, 15.2.5
  and insured benefits, Ch. 35, 3.2
  and multi-employer plans, Ch. 35, 3.3
  net defined benefit liability (asset), presentation of, Ch. 35, 9

plan assets, Ch. 35, 6
    contributions to defined benefit funds, Ch. 35, 6.5
    definition of, Ch. 35, 6.1
    longevity swaps, Ch. 35, 6.6
    measurement of, Ch. 35, 6.2
    qualifying insurance policies, Ch. 35, 6.3
    reimbursement rights, Ch. 35, 6.4
plan liabilities, Ch. 35, 7
    actuarial assumptions, Ch. 35, 7.5
    actuarial methodology, Ch. 35, 7.3
    attributing benefit to years of service, Ch. 35, 7.4
    contributions by employees and third parties, Ch. 35, 7.2
    discount rate, Ch. 35, 7.6
    frequency of valuations, Ch. 35, 7.7
    legal and constructive obligations, Ch. 35, 7.1
refund from, Ch. 35, 16.2.1
sharing risks between entities under common control, Ch. 35, 3.3.2
treatment in profit/loss and other comprehensive income, Ch. 35, 10
    acquisition of a qualifying insurance policy, Ch. 35, 10.2.2
    net interest on the net defined benefit liability (asset), Ch. 35, 10.2
    past service cost, Ch. 35, 10.1.1
    remeasurements, Ch. 35, 10.3
    service cost, Ch. 35, 10.1
    settlements, Ch. 35, 10.2.3
treatment of the plan surplus/deficit in the statement of financial position, Ch. 35, 8
    assets restriction to their recoverable amounts, Ch. 35, 8.2
        economic benefits available as reduced future contributions when no minimum funding requirements for future service, Ch. 35, 8.2.2
        IFRIC 14 requirements concerning limit on defined benefit asset, Ch. 35, 8.2.1
        minimum funding requirements, IFRIC interpretation effect on economic benefit available as a reduction in future contributions, Ch. 35, 8.2.3
            when the requirement may give rise to a liability, Ch. 35, 8.2.4
        pension funding payments contingent on future events within the control of the entity, Ch. 35, 8.2.5
    net defined benefit liability (asset), Ch. 35, 8.1
Defined contribution plans, Ch. 35, 4
    accounting requirements, Ch. 35, 4.1
    vs. defined benefit plans, Ch. 35, 3.1
    disclosure requirements, Ch. 35, 15
    with vesting conditions, Ch. 35, 4.1.2
Delegated decision making, Ch. 12, 4.2.4
Delegated power, Ch. 6, 6.1
Demand deposits, Ch. 40, 3.2.1
Deposit components unbundling, Ch. 55, 5
    illustration, Ch. 55, 5.2
    practical difficulties, Ch. 55, 5.3
    requirements, Ch. 55, 5.1
Depreciation, depletion and amortisation (DD&A), extractive industries, Ch. 43, 16
    block caving, Ch. 43, 16.2
    determining when production phase commences, Ch. 43, 15.5.2
    requirements under IAS 16 and IAS 38, Ch. 43, 16.1
        assets depreciated using the straight-line method, Ch. 43, 16.1.2
        assets depreciated using the units of production method, Ch. 43, 16.1.3
            joint and by-products, Ch. 43, 16.1.3.D
            reserves base, Ch. 43, 16.1.3.B
            unit of measure, Ch. 43, 16.1.3.C
            units of production formula, Ch. 43, 16.1.3.A
        mineral reserves, Ch. 43, 16.1.1
Depreciation, property, plant and equipment (PP&E), Ch. 18, 5
    charge, Ch. 18, 5.3
    depreciable amount and residual values, Ch. 18, 5.2
    methods, Ch. 18, 5.6
        diminishing balance methods, Ch. 18, 5.6.1
        sum of the digits method, Ch. 18, 5.6.1
        unit-of-production method, Ch. 18, 5.6.2
    and useful life of asset, Ch. 18, 5.4
Derecognition, financial instruments, Ch. 52, 1–8
    accounting treatment, Ch. 52, 5
        collateral, Ch. 52, 5.5.2
        offset, Ch. 52, 5.5.1
        reassessing derecognition, Ch. 52, 5.6
        reassessment of consolidation of subsidiaries and SPEs, Ch. 52, 5.6.1
        rights/obligations over transferred assets that continue to be recognised, Ch. 52, 5.5.3
        transfers that do not qualifying for derecognition, through retention of risks and rewards, Ch. 52, 5.2
        transfers that qualify for derecognition, Ch. 52, 5.1
            servicing assets and liabilities, Ch. 52, 5.1.2
            transferred asset part of larger asset, Ch. 52, 5.1.1
        transfers with continuing involvement, Ch. 52, 5.3
            associated liability, Ch. 52, 5.3.3
            continuing involvement in part only of a larger asset, Ch. 52, 5.3.5
            guarantees, Ch. 52, 5.3.1
            options, Ch. 52, 5.3.2
            subsequent measurement of assets and liabilities, Ch. 52, 5.3.4
        transfers with continuing involvement–accounting examples, Ch. 52, 5.4
            continuing involvement in part only of a financial asset, Ch. 52, 5.4.4
            transfers of assets measured at amortised cost, Ch. 52, 5.4.2
            transfers of assets measured at fair value, Ch. 52, 5.4.3
                'collar' put and call options, Ch. 52, 5.4.3.C
                transferor's call option, Ch. 52, 5.4.3.A
                transferee's put option, Ch. 52, 5.4.3.B
            transfers with guarantees, Ch. 52, 5.4.1
    CUSIP 'netting', Ch. 52, 7
    definitions, Ch. 52, 2.1
    development of IFRS, Ch. 52, 2
    financial assets, Ch. 52, 3
        background, Ch. 52, 3.1
        client money, Ch. 52, 3.7
        contractual rights to receive cash flows from the asset, expiration of, Ch. 52, 3.4

Derecognition, financial instruments—*contd*
  financial assets—*contd*
    contractual rights to receive cash flows from the asset, expiration of—*contd*
      asset restructuring in the context of Greek government debt, Ch. 52, 3.4.2
      IBOR reform, Ch. 52, 3.4.3
      novation of contracts to intermediary counterparties, Ch. 52, 3.4.4
      renegotiation of the terms of an asset, Ch. 52, 3.4.1
      write-offs, Ch. 52, 3.4.5
    retention of rights subject to obligation to pay over to others (pass-through arrangement), Ch. 52, 3.5.2
    transfers of, Ch. 52, 3.5.1
  decision tree, Ch. 52, 3.2
    importance of applying tests in sequence, Ch. 52, 3.2.1
  groups of financial assets, Ch. 52, 3.3.2
    IASB's view and the Interpretations Committee's tentative conclusions, Ch. 52, 3.3.2.A
    similar assets, Ch. 52, 3.3.2.B
  principles, parts of assets and groups of assets, Ch. 52, 3.3
    credit enhancement through, Ch. 52, 3.3.1
    transfer of asset (or part of asset) for only part of its life, Ch. 52, 3.3.3
  securitisations, Ch. 52, 3.6
    'empty' subsidiaries or SPEs, Ch. 52, 3.6.6
    insurance protection, Ch. 52, 3.6.3
    non-optional derivatives along with a group of financial assets transfers, Ch. 52, 3.6.5
    recourse to originator, Ch. 52, 3.6.1
    short-term loan facilities, Ch. 52, 3.6.2
    treatment of collection proceeds, Ch. 52, 3.6.4
  transfer/retention of substantially all the risks and rewards of ownership, Ch. 52, 3.8
    evaluating extent to which risks and rewards are transferred, Ch. 52, 3.8.4
    transferee's 'practical ability' to sell the asset, Ch. 52, 3.9.1
    transfers, cumulative basis, Ch. 52, 3.8.5
    transfers, resulting in neither transfer nor retention of substantially all risks and rewards, Ch. 52, 3.8.3
    transfers, resulting in retention of substantially all risks and rewards, Ch. 52, 3.8.2
    transfers, resulting in transfer of substantially all risks and rewards, Ch. 52, 3.8.1
  financial liabilities, Ch. 52, 6
    derivatives that can be financial assets or financial liabilities, Ch. 52, 6.4
    exchange or modification of debt by original lender, Ch. 52, 6.2
      costs and fees, Ch. 52, 6.2.5
      examples, Ch. 52, 6.2.4
      IBOR reform, Ch. 52, 6.2.2
      loan syndications, Ch. 52, 6.2.3
      modification gains and losses, Ch. 52, 6.2.6
      settlement of financial liability with issue of new equity instrument, Ch. 52, 6.2.8
      'substantially' different, Ch. 52, 6.2.1
      through intermediary, Ch. 52, 6.2.4
    extinguishment of debt
      in exchange for transfer of assets not meeting the derecognition criteria, Ch. 52, 6.1.4
      'in-substance defeasance' arrangements, Ch. 52, 6.1.3
      legal release by creditor, Ch. 52, 6.1.2
      what constitutes 'part' of a liability, Ch. 52, 6.1.1
    gains and losses on extinguishment of debt, Ch. 52, 6.3
    supply-chain finance, Ch. 52, 6.5
  future developments, Ch. 52, 8
  off-balance sheet finance, Ch. 52, 1.1
  practical application factoring of trade receivables, Ch. 52, 4.5
  repurchase agreements ('repos') and securities lending, Ch. 52, 4.1
    agreement to repurchase at fair value, Ch. 52, 4.1.5
    agreements to return the same asset, Ch. 52, 4.1.1
    agreements with right of substitution, Ch. 52, 4.1.3
    agreements with right to return the same or substantially the same asset, Ch. 52, 4.1.2
    net cash-settled forward repurchase, Ch. 52, 4.1.4
    right of first refusal to repurchase at fair value, Ch. 52, 4.1.6
    wash sale, Ch. 52, 4.1.7
  scope, Ch. 52, 2.2
  subordinated retained interests and credit guarantees, Ch. 52, 4.3
  transfers by way of swaps, Ch. 52, 4.4
    interest rate swaps, Ch. 52, 4.4.2
    total return swaps, Ch. 52, 4.4.1
  transfers subject to put and call options, Ch. 52, 4.2
    changes in probability of exercise of options after initial transfer of asset, Ch. 52, 4.2.9
    clean-up call options, Ch. 52, 4.2.7
    deeply in the money put and call options, Ch. 52, 4.2.1
    deeply out of the money put and call options, Ch. 52, 4.2.2
    net cash-settled options, Ch. 52, 4.2.5
    option to put or call at fair value, Ch. 52, 4.2.4
    options that are neither deeply out of the money nor deeply in the money, Ch. 52, 4.2.3
    removal of accounts provision, Ch. 52, 4.2.6
    same (or nearly the same) price put and call options, Ch. 52, 4.2.8

Derivative(s), Ch. 46, 1–3. *See also* Embedded derivatives
  call and put options over non-controlling interest. Ch. 7, 6. *See also* 'Non-controlling interest'
  changes in value in response to changes in underlying, Ch. 46, 2.1
    non-financial variables specific to one party to the contract, Ch. 46, 2.1.3
    notional amounts, Ch. 46, 2.1.1
    underlying variables, Ch. 46, 2.1.2
  common derivatives, Ch. 46, 3.1
  contracts, cash flows on, Ch. 40, 4.4.12
  defining characteristics, Ch. 46, 2
    changes in value in response to changes in underlying, Ch. 46, 2.1
    future settlement, Ch. 46, 2.3
    initial net investment, Ch. 46, 2.2
  discount rates for calculating fair value of, Ch. 53, 7.4.5
  in-substance derivatives, Ch. 46, 3.2
  linked and separate transactions, Ch. 46, 8
  regular way contracts, Ch. 46, 3.3

restructuring of, Ch. 53, 3.6.3
'synthetic' instruments, Ch. 46, 8
Derivative financial instruments, Ch. 45, 2.2.8; Ch. 53, 3.2
    basis swaps, Ch. 53, 3.2.5
    credit break clauses, Ch. 53, 3.2.4
        principal resetting cross currency swaps, Ch. 53, 3.2.4.A
    embedded derivatives, Ch. 53, 3.2.3
    net written options, Ch. 53, 3.2.2
    offsetting external derivatives, Ch. 53, 3.2.1
Designation at fair value through profit or loss, Ch. 48, 7
Dilapidation provision, Ch. 26, 6.9
Diluted EPS, Ch. 37, 6. *See also* Earnings per share (EPS); IAS 33
    calculation of, Ch. 37, 6.2; Ch. 37, 8
        diluted earnings, Ch. 37, 6.2.1
        diluted number of shares, Ch. 37, 6.2.2
    contingently issuable potential ordinary shares, Ch. 37, 6.4.8
    contingently issuable shares, Ch. 37, 6.4.6
        earnings-based contingencies, Ch. 37, 6.4.6.A
        not driven by earnings or share price, Ch. 37, 6.4.6.C
        share-price-based contingencies, Ch. 37, 6.4.6.B
    convertible instruments, Ch. 37, 6.4.1
        convertible debt, Ch. 37, 6.4.1.A
        convertible preference shares, Ch. 37, 6.4.1.B
        participating equity instruments, Ch. 37, 6.4.1.C
    dilutive instruments, types, Ch. 37, 6.4
    dilutive potential ordinary shares, Ch. 37, 6.3
        judged by effect on profits from continuing operations, Ch. 37, 6.3.1
        judged by the cumulative impact of potential shares, Ch. 37, 6.3.2
    need for, Ch. 37, 6.1
    options, warrants and their equivalents, Ch. 37, 6.4.2
        forward purchase agreements, Ch. 37, 6.4.2.C
        numerator, Ch. 37, 6.4.2.A
        options over convertible instruments, Ch. 37, 6.4.2.D
        settlement of option exercise price, Ch. 37, 6.4.2.E
        specified application of option proceeds, Ch. 37, 6.4.2.F
        written call options, Ch. 37, 6.4.2.B
        written put options, Ch. 37, 6.4.2.C
    partly paid shares, Ch. 37, 6.4.4
    potentially ordinary shares of investees, Ch. 37, 6.4.7
    presentation, restatement and disclosure, Ch. 37, 7
    purchased options and warrants, Ch. 37, 6.4.3
    share-based payments, Ch. 37, 6.4.5
Diminishing balance methods, depreciation, Ch. 18, 5.6.1
Direct method of consolidation, foreign operations, Ch. 7, 2.3; Ch. 15, 6.6.3
Directly attributable borrowing costs, Ch. 21, 5.1
'Directly attributable' costs, Ch. 18, 4.1.1
'Dirty' fair values, Ch. 53, 7.4.10
Disclosure(s). *See also* individual entries for standards
    in annual financial statements, Ch. 32, 3
    business combinations, Ch. 9, 16
    capital disclosures, Ch. 3, 5.4; Ch. 54, 5.6.3
    capitalisation of borrowing costs, Ch. 21, 7
    of changes in ownership interests in subsidiaries, Ch. 13, 4.5
    common control transactions, Ch. 8, 4.3.1
    in condensed interim financial statements, Ch. 41, 4
    earnings per share (EPS), Ch. 37, 7.3
    employee benefits, Ch. 35, 15
    first-time adoption, Ch. 5, 6
    financial instruments
        qualitative disclosures, Ch. 54, 5.1
        quantitative disclosures, Ch. 54, 5.2, 5.6
    foreign exchange, Ch. 15, 10
    government assistance, Ch. 24, 6
    government grants, Ch. 24, 6
    of IFRS information before adoption of IFRSs, Ch. 5, 6.7
    of IFRS information in financial statements, Ch. 5, 6.3.1
    impairment of fixed assets and goodwill, Ch. 20, 13.3
    income taxes, Ch. 33, 14
    insurance contracts, Ch. 55, 11; Ch. 56, 16
    intangible assets, Ch. 17, 11
        additional disclosures when the revaluation model is applied, Ch. 17, 10.4
        general disclosures, Ch. 17, 10.1
        profit/loss presentation, Ch. 17, 10.3
        of research and development expenditure, Ch. 17, 10.5
        statement of financial position presentation, Ch. 17, 10.2
    inventories, Ch. 22, 6
        additional disclosure requirements for crypto-assets, Ch. 22, 6.2
        general disclosure requirements, Ch. 22, 6.1
    investment property, Ch. 19, 12
    investments in associates and joint ventures, Ch. 11, 10; Ch. 13, 5
    joint arrangements, Ch. 13, 5
    leases (IFRS 16), Ch. 23, 10.6
    of mineral reserves and resources, Ch. 43, 2.4
    objective and general requirements, Ch. 32, 3.1
    offsetting, Ch. 2, 10.2.1.A; Ch. 54, 7.4.2.D
    property, plant and equipment (PP&E), Ch. 18, 8–8.3
    provisions, contingent liabilities and contingent assets, Ch. 26, 7
    related party disclosures, Ch. 39, 1–2
    relating to accounting policies, Ch. 3, 5
        changes in accounting estimates, Ch. 3, 5.2.2
        changes in accounting policies, Ch. 3, 5.1.2
        changes pursuant to the initial application of an IFRS, Ch. 3, 5.1.2.A
        estimation uncertainty, Ch. 3, 5.2.1
        judgements made in applying accounting policies, Ch. 3, 5.1.1.B
        new IFRS, future impact of, Ch. 3, 5.1.2.C
        prior period errors, Ch. 3, 5.3
        significant accounting policies, Ch. 3, 5.1.1.A
        voluntary changes in accounting policy, Ch. 3, 5.1.2.B
    reportable segments, Ch. 36, 5
    revenue and contract cost disclosure requirements, Ch. 32, 3.2
    separate financial statements, Ch. 8, 3
    service concession arrangements (SCA), Ch. 25, 7
    share-based payment, Ch. 34, 13
Disclosure of interests in other entities, Ch. 13, 1–6. *See also* IFRS 12; Interests in joint arrangements and associates
    definitions, Ch. 13, 2.2.1
        interaction of IFRS 12 and IFRS 5, Ch. 13, 2.2.1.C
        interests in other entities, Ch. 13, 2.2.1.A
        structured entities, Ch. 13, 2.2.1.B
    interests disclosed under IFRS 12, Ch. 13, 2.2.2
    interests not within the scope of IFRS 12, Ch. 13, 2.2.3

16 Index

Disclosure of interests in other entities—*contd*
  joint arrangements and associates, Ch. 13, 5
    nature, extent and financial effects, Ch. 13, 5.1
    risks associated, Ch. 13, 5.2
      commitments relating to joint ventures, Ch. 13, 5.2.1
      contingent liabilities relating to joint ventures and associates, Ch. 13, 5.2.2
  objective, Ch. 13, 2.1
  scope, Ch. 13, 2.2
  significant judgements and assumptions, Ch. 13, 3
  subsidiaries, Ch. 13, 4
    changes in ownership interests in subsidiaries, Ch. 13, 4.5
    composition of the group, Ch. 13, 4.1
    consolidated structured entities, nature of risks, Ch. 13, 4.4
      current intentions to provide financial or other support, Ch. 13, 4.4.4
      financial or other support to with no contractual obligation, Ch. 13, 4.4.2
      terms of contractual arrangements, Ch. 13, 4.4.1
    nature and extent of significant restrictions, Ch. 13, 4.3
    non-controlling interests, Ch. 13, 4.2
  unconsolidated structured entities, Ch. 13, 6
    nature of interests, Ch. 13, 6.1
    nature of risks, Ch. 13, 6.2
      actual and intended financial and other support to structured entities, Ch. 13, 6.2.2
      disclosure of funding difficulties, Ch. 13, 6.3.6
      disclosure of liquidity arrangements, Ch. 13, 6.3.5
      disclosure of losses, Ch. 13, 6.3.2
      disclosure of ranking and amounts of potential losses, Ch. 13, 6.3.4
      disclosure of support, Ch. 13, 6.3.1
      disclosure of the forms of funding of an unconsolidated structured entity, Ch. 13, 6.3.7
      disclosure of types of income received, Ch. 13, 6.3.3
      maximum exposure to loss from those interests, Ch. 13, 6.2.1

Discontinued operation, Ch. 3, 3.2.5; Ch. 4, 3.2. *See also* IFRS 5
  cash flows of, Ch. 40, 8.1
  definition of, Ch. 4, 3.1
  presentation of, Ch. 4, 3.2
  property, plant and equipment, derecognition and disposal, Ch. 18, 7.1
  trading with continuing operations, Ch. 4, 3.3

Discount rate
  for calculating fair value of derivatives, Ch. 53, 7.4.5
  employee benefits, Ch. 35, 7.6
    high quality corporate bonds, Ch. 35, 7.6.1
    no deep market, Ch. 35, 7.6.2
  estimated cash flows to a present value (provisions), Ch. 26, 4.3
    adjusting for risk and using a government bond rate, Ch. 26, 4.3.2
    effect of changes in interest rates on the discount rate applied, Ch. 26, 4.3.6
    own credit risk is not taken into account, Ch. 26, 4.3.3
    pre-tax discount rate, Ch. 26, 4.3.4
    real *vs.* nominal rate, Ch. 26, 4.3.1
    unwinding of the discount, Ch. 26, 4.3.5
  impairment of fixed assets and goodwill, Ch. 20, 7.2
    approximations and short cuts, Ch. 20, 7.2.4
    discount rates other than WACC, Ch. 20, 7.2.9
    entity-specific WACCs and capital structure, Ch. 20, 7.2.8
    entity-specific WACCs and different project risks within the entity, Ch. 20, 7.2.7
    pre-tax discount rate, calculating, Ch. 20, 7.2.2
    pre-tax discount rates disclosing when using a post-tax methodology, Ch. 20, 7.2.5
    pre-tax rates determination taking account of tax losses, Ch. 20, 7.2.6
    VIU calculation using post-tax cash flows, Ch. 20, 7.2.3
    WACC, Ch. 20, 7.2.1
  insurance contracts, Ch. 56, 8.3
  leases, Ch. 23, 4.6
  significant financing components, Ch. 29, 2.5

Discretionary participation feature (DPF), Ch. 55, 2.2.1, 6
  definition, Ch. 55, 2.2.1
  in financial instruments, Ch. 55, 6.2
  guaranteed benefits, Ch. 55, 6
  in insurance contracts, Ch. 55, 6.1
  investment contracts with, Ch. 55, 2.2.2, 6.1, 6.2, 7.2.2.C
  practical issues, Ch. 55, 6.3
    contracts with switching features, Ch. 55, 6.3.2
    negative DPF, Ch. 55, 6.3.1

Discussion Paper (DP)–*Accounting for Dynamic Risk Management*, Ch. 53, 11.1
Discussion Paper (DP)–*Extractive Activities*, Ch. 43, 1.3
Discussion Paper (DP)–*Preliminary Views on Insurance Contracts*, Ch. 55, 1.1
Discussion Paper (DP)–*A Review of the Conceptual Framework for Financial Reporting*, Ch. 2, 1

Disposal groups held for sale/distribution, Ch. 3, 3.1.2; Ch. 4, 1–6. *See also* IFRS 5
  changes to a plan of sale/plan of distribution, Ch. 4, 2.2.5
  classification as held for sale/held for distribution to owners, Ch. 4, 2.1.2
    abandonment, Ch. 4, 2.1.2.C
    available for immediate sale, meaning of, Ch. 4, 2.1.2.A
    criteria met after the reporting period, Ch. 38, 2.1.3
    highly probable, meaning of, Ch. 4, 2.1.2.B
  comparative information, Ch. 4, 4
  concept of disposal group, Ch. 4, 2.1.1
  disclosure requirements, Ch. 4, 5
  discontinued operations, Ch. 4, 3
  future developments, Ch. 4, 6
  measurement, Ch. 4, 2.2
    impairments and reversals of impairment, Ch. 4, 2.2.3
    presentation in statement of financial position, Ch. 4, 2.2.4
  partial disposals of operations, Ch. 4, 2.1.3
    of an associate or joint venture, Ch. 4, 2.1.3.B
    loss of control of a subsidiary, Ch. 4, 2.1.3.A; Ch. 7, 3.2, 3.4, 3.5, 3.7

'Dividend blocker' clause, Ch. 47, 4.5.3.A
Dividend discount model (DDM), Ch. 20, 12.2, 12.4.2.A
'Dividend pusher' clause, Ch. 47, 4.5.3.B
Dividends, Ch. 8, 2.4; Ch. 11, 7.11.1
  declared after the reporting period, Ch. 38, 2.1.3.A

and other distributions, Ch. 8, 2.4
    distributions of noncash assets to owners (IFRIC 17), Ch. 7, 3.7; Ch. 8, 2.4.2
    dividend exceeding total comprehensive income, Ch. 8, 2.4.1
    resulting in carrying amount of an investment exceeding consolidated net assets, Ch. 8, 2.4.1.B
    returns of capital, Ch. 8, 2.4.1.C
    from subsidiaries, joint ventures or associates, Ch. 8, 2.4.1
    payable on shares classified as financial liabilities, Ch. 21, 5.5.4

Divisions, foreign exchange, Ch. 15, 4.4

Downstream activities, extractive industries, Ch. 43, 1.6

'Downstream' transactions elimination, equity accounted investments, Ch. 11, 7.6.1

Downward valuations of property, plant and equipment, reversals of, Ch. 18, 6.3

DP. *See under* Discussion Paper

DPF. *See* Discretionary participation feature (DPF)

Due Process Handbook, Ch. 1, 2.6

Dynamic hedging strategies, Ch. 53, 6.3.2

Earnings-based contingencies (EPS), Ch. 37, 6.4.6.A

Earnings per share (EPS), Ch. 37, 1–8. *See also* Diluted EPS; IAS 33
    basic EPS, Ch. 37, 3
        earnings, Ch. 37, 3.1
        number of shares, Ch. 37, 3.2
    definitions, Ch. 37, 1.1
    disclosure, Ch. 37, 7.3
    interim financial reporting, Ch. 41, 9.8
    numerator, matters affecting, Ch. 37, 5
        earnings, Ch. 37, 5.1
        other bases, Ch. 37, 5.5
        participating equity instruments, Ch. 37, 5.4
        preference dividends, Ch. 37, 5.2
        retrospective adjustments, Ch. 37, 5.3
        tax deductible dividends on, Ch. 37, 5.4.1
    outstanding ordinary shares, changes in, Ch. 37, 4
    presentation, Ch. 37, 7.1
    restatement, Ch. 37, 7.2
    reverse acquisitions, business combinations, Ch. 9, 14.5; Ch. 37, 4.6.2

EBTs. *See* Employee benefit trusts (EBTs)

Economic relationship, hedge accounting, Ch. 53, 6.4.1

EDs. *See* Exposure Drafts (EDs)

Effective interest method, Ch. 50, 3

Effective interest rate (EIR), Ch. 50, 3.1

Effective tax rate, Ch. 33, 14.2
    changes in during the year, Ch. 41, 9.5.2

Embedded derivatives, Ch. 46, 4–7; Ch. 55, 4
    cash flows, Ch. 54, 5.4.2.E
    characteristics, Ch. 55, 4
    in commodity arrangements, Ch. 43, 12.8
    compound financial instruments with multiple, Ch. 54, 4.4.7
    compound instruments with, Ch. 47, 6.4.2
    contracts for the sale of goods or services, Ch. 46, 5.2
        floors and caps, Ch. 46, 5.2.4
        foreign currency derivatives, Ch. 46, 5.2.1
        fund performance fees, Ch. 46, 5.2.5
        inflation-linked features, Ch. 46, 5.2.3
        inputs, ingredients, substitutes and other proxy pricing mechanisms, Ch. 46, 5.2.2
    decision tree, Ch. 55, 4
    derivative and, Ch. 46, 4
    exposures to market risk from, Ch. 55, 11.2.7
    extractive industries, Ch. 43, 13.2
    financial instrument hosts, Ch. 46, 5.1
        commodity-and equity-linked interest and principal payments, Ch. 46, 5.1.7
        convertible and exchangeable debt instruments, Ch. 46, 5.1.9
        credit-linked notes, Ch. 46, 5.1.8
        fallback provisions relating to interest rate benchmark reform, Ch. 46, 5.1.3
        foreign currency monetary items, Ch. 46, 5.1.1
        inflation-linked debt instruments, Ch. 46, 5.1.6
        interest rate floors and caps, Ch. 46, 5.1.5
        interest rate indices, Ch. 46, 5.1.2
        puttable instruments, Ch. 46, 5.1.10
        term extension and similar call, put and prepayment options in debt instruments, Ch. 46, 5.1.4
    foreign currency embedded derivatives, Ch. 43, 13.2.1
    gains and losses recognised in profit/loss, Ch. 54, 7.1.4
    gas markets, development of, Ch. 43, 13.2.4
    hedging instruments, Ch. 53, 3.2.3
    and host contracts, identifying the terms, Ch. 46, 6
        embedded non-option derivatives, Ch. 46, 6.1
        embedded option-based derivative, Ch. 46, 6.2
        multiple embedded derivatives, Ch. 46, 6.3
    initial measurement, Ch. 49, 3.5
    insurance contracts, Ch. 46, 5.4
    leases, Ch. 46, 5.3
        contingent rentals based on related sales, Ch. 46, 5.3.3
        contingent rentals based on variable interest rates, Ch. 46, 5.3.4
        foreign currency derivatives, Ch. 46, 5.3.1
        inflation-linked features, Ch. 46, 5.3.2
    long-term supply contracts, Ch. 43, 13.2.3
    provisionally priced contracts, Ch. 43, 13.2.2
    reassessment, Ch. 46, 7
        acquisition of contracts, Ch. 46, 7.1
        business combinations, Ch. 46, 7.2
        remeasurement issues arising from, Ch. 46, 7.3
    unit-linked features, Ch. 55, 4.1

Embedded leases, extractive industries, Ch. 43, 17.1

Embedded value (EV) of insurance contract, Ch. 55, 1.4.3

Emerging Economies Group, Ch. 1, 2.9

Emission rights, Ch. 9, 5.5.2.E; Ch. 17, 11.2
    acquired in a business combination, Ch. 9, 5.5.2.E; Ch. 17, 11.2.5
    amortisation, Ch. 17, 11.2.4
    by brokers and traders, accounting for, Ch. 17, 11.2.7
    impairment testing, Ch. 17, 11.2.4
    sale of, Ch. 17, 11.2.6

Emissions trading schemes, intangible assets, Ch. 17, 11.2
    accounting for emission rights by brokers and traders, Ch. 17, 11.2.7
    amortisation and impairment testing of emission rights, Ch. 17, 11.2.4

Emissions trading schemes, intangible assets—*contd*
    emission rights acquired in a business combination, Ch. 17, 11.2.5
    government grant approach, Ch. 17, 11.2.3
    green certificates compared to, Ch. 26, 6.6 IFRIC 3, Ch. 17, 11.2.1
    liabilities associated with, Ch. 26, 6.5
    net liability approaches, Ch. 17, 11.2.2
    sale of emission rights, Ch. 17, 11.2.6

Employee benefit(s), Ch. 35, 1–16. *See also* Defined benefit plans; Defined contribution plans; IAS 19; Long-term employee benefits, Multi-employer plans; Short-term employee benefits
    costs of administering, Ch. 35, 11
    death-in-service benefits, Ch. 35, 3.6
    defined benefit plans, Ch. 35, 5–11
    defined contribution plans, Ch. 35, 4
    disclosure requirements, Ch. 35, 15
        defined benefit plans, Ch. 35, 15.2
        defined contribution plans, Ch. 35, 15.1
        multi-employer plans, Ch. 35, 15.2.4
    future developments, Ch. 35, 16
    insured benefits, Ch. 35, 3.2
    interim financial reporting, Ch. 41, 9.3
        employer payroll taxes and insurance contributions, Ch. 41, 9.3.1
        pensions, Ch. 41, 9.3.3
        vacations, holidays and other short-term paid absences, Ch. 41, 9.3.4
        year-end bonuses, Ch. 41, 9.3.2
    long-term employee benefits, Ch. 35, 13
    multi-employer plans, Ch. 35, 3.3
    objective of IAS 19, Ch. 35, 2.1
    pensions, Ch. 35, 3
    plans that would be defined contribution plans, Ch. 35, 3.5
    post-employment benefits, Ch. 35, 3
    scope of IAS 19, Ch. 35, 2.2
    short-term employee benefits, Ch. 35, 12
    state plans, Ch. 35, 3.4
    termination benefits, Ch. 35, 14

Employee benefit plans, Ch. 6, 2.2.2; Ch. 13, 2.2.3.A

Employee benefit trusts (EBTs) and similar arrangements, Ch. 34, 12.3
    accounting for, Ch. 34, 12.3.2
    awards satisfied by shares purchased by, or issued to, an EBT, Ch. 34, 12.3.3
    background, Ch. 34, 12.3.1
    EBT as extension of parent, Ch. 34, 12.4.2.B, 12.5.2.B
    financial statements of the EBT, Ch. 34, 12.3.5
    financial statements of the parent, Ch. 34, 12.4.2, 12.5.2
    group share scheme illustrative examples
        equity-settled award satisfied by fresh issue of shares, Ch. 34, 12.5
        equity-settled award satisfied by market purchase of shares, Ch. 34, 12.4
    separate financial statements of sponsoring entity, Ch. 34, 12.3.4

Employee, definition, Ch. 34, 5.2.1

'Empty' subsidiaries, Ch. 52, 3.6.6

'End-user' contracts, Ch. 45, 4.2.4

Enhanced Disclosure Task Force (EDTF), Ch. 54, 9.2

Entity's functional currency determination, Ch. 15, 4
    branches and divisions, Ch. 15, 4.4
    documentation of judgements made, Ch. 15, 4.5
    intermediate holding companies/finance subsidiaries, Ch. 15, 4.2
    investment holding companies, Ch. 15, 4.3

EPS. *See* Earnings per share

Equalisation provisions, Ch. 55, 7.2.1

Equity instruments, Ch. 8, 2.1.1.A; Ch. 45, 2.2.7, 3.6
    classification, Ch. 48, 2.2
    contracts to issue equity instruments, Ch. 47, 4.4.2
    contracts settled by delivery of the entity's own equity instruments, Ch. 47, 5
        contracts accounted for as equity instruments, Ch. 47, 5.1
            comparison with IFRS 2–share-based payment, Ch. 47, 5.1.1
            contracts to acquire non-controlling interests, Ch. 47, 5.3.2
            contracts to purchase own equity during 'closed' or 'prohibited' periods, Ch. 47, 5.3.1
            exchange of fixed amounts of equity (equity for equity), Ch. 47, 5.1.4
            number of equity instruments issued adjusted for capital restructuring or other event, Ch. 47, 5.1.2
            stepped up exercise price, Ch. 47, 5.1.3
        contracts accounted for as financial assets/liabilities, Ch. 47, 5.2
            derivative financial instruments with settlement options, Ch. 47, 5.2.8
            fixed amount of cash denominated in a currency other than entity's functional currency, Ch. 47, 5.2.3
                rights issues with a price fixed in a currency other than entity's functional currency, Ch. 47, 5.2.3.A
            fixed amount of cash determined by reference to share price Ch. 47, 5.2.6
            fixed number of equity instruments for variable consideration, Ch. 47, 5.2.2
            fixed number of equity instruments with variable value, Ch. 47, 5.2.5
            instrument with equity settlement alternative of significantly higher value than cash settlement alternative, Ch. 47, 5.2.4
            net-settled contracts over own equity, Ch. 47, 5.2.7
            variable number of equity instruments, Ch. 47, 5.2.1
        gross-settled contracts for the sale or issue of the entity's own equity instruments, Ch. 47, 5.4
        liabilities arising from gross-settled contracts for the purchase of the entity's own equity instruments, Ch. 47, 5.3
            contracts to acquire non-controlling interests, Ch. 47, 5.3.2
            contracts to purchase own equity during 'closed' or 'prohibited' periods, Ch. 47, 5.3.1
    definition, Ch. 34, 2.2.1; Ch. 45, 2.1; Ch. 47, 3
    determining fair value of, Ch. 14, 11.2; Ch. 34, 5.5
    holder, Ch. 45, 3.6.2
    investments in, designated at fair value through OCI, Ch. 51, 9
    issued instruments, Ch. 45, 3.6.1; Ch. 47, 4.4.1

Equity method/accounting, Ch. 11, 7
   application of the equity method, Ch. 11, 7
      consistent accounting policies, Ch. 11, 7.8
      date of commencement of equity accounting, Ch. 11, 7.3
      discontinuing the use of the equity method, Ch. 11, 7.12
         deemed disposals, Ch. 11, 7.12.6
         investment in associate becomes a joint venture (or vice versa), Ch. 11, 7.12.4
         investment in associate/joint venture that is a business becoming a subsidiary, Ch. 11, 7.12.1
         investment in associate or joint venture that is not a business becoming a subsidiary, Ch. 11, 7.12.2
         partial disposals of interests in associate/joint venture, Ch. 11, 7.12.4
         retained investment in the former associate or joint venture is a financial asset, Ch. 11, 7.12.3
      distributions received in excess of the carrying amount, Ch. 11, 7.10
      equity accounting and consolidation, comparison between, Ch. 11, 7.2
      equity transactions in an associate's/joint venture's financial statements, Ch. 11, 7.11
         dividends/other forms of distributions, Ch. 11, 7.11.1
         effects of changes in parent/non-controlling interests in subsidiaries, Ch. 11, 7.11.4
         equity-settled share-based payment transactions, Ch. 11, 7.11.3
         issues of equity instruments, Ch. 11, 7.11, 7.11.2
      impairment losses, Ch. 11, 8
         general, Ch. 11, 8.1
         investment in the associate or joint venture, Ch. 11, 8.2
         other interests that are not part of the net investment in the associate or joint venture, Ch. 11, 8.3
      impairment of investments in subsidiaries, associates and joint ventures, Ch. 20, 12.4
         equity accounted investments and CGU's, Ch. 20, 12.4.5
         equity accounted investments and goodwill for impairment, Ch. 20, 12.4.6
         indicators of impairment, Ch. 20, 12.4.3, 12.4.4
      initial carrying amount of an associate/joint venture, Ch. 11, 7.4
         cost-based approach, Ch. 11, 7.4.2.A
         fair value (IFRS 3) approach, Ch. 11, 7.4.2.A
         following loss of control of an entity, Ch. 7, 3.3.2, 7.1, 3.2; Ch. 11, 7.4.1, 7.6.5
         piecemeal acquisition, Ch. 11, 7.4.2
            common control transactions involving sales of associates, Ch. 11, 7.4.2.D
            existing associate that becomes a joint venture, or vice versa, Ch. 11, 7.4.2.C
            financial instrument becoming an associate/joint venture, Ch. 11, 7.4.2.A
            step increase in an existing associate/joint venture without a change in status of the investee, Ch. 11, 7.4.2.B
      loss-making associates/joint ventures, Ch. 11, 7.9
      non-coterminous accounting periods, Ch. 11, 7.7
      overview, Ch. 11, 7.1
      share of the investee, Ch. 11, 7.5
         accounting for potential voting rights, Ch. 11, 7.5.1
         cumulative preference shares held by parties other than the investor, Ch. 11, 7.5.2
         several classes of equity, Ch. 11, 7.5.3
         where the investee is a group, Ch. 11, 7.5.5
         where the reporting entity is a group, Ch. 11, 7.5.4
      transactions between the reporting entity and its associates/joint ventures, Ch. 11, 7.6
         contributions of non-monetary assets to an associate/a joint venture, Ch. 11, 7.6.5
         commercial substance, Ch. 11, 7.6.5.A
         conflict between IAS 28 and IFRS 10, Ch. 11, 7.6.5.C
         practical application, Ch. 11, 7.6.5.B
         elimination of 'upstream' and 'downstream' transactions, Ch. 11, 7.6.1
         loans and borrowings between the reporting entity, Ch. 11, 7.6.3
         reciprocal interests, Ch. 11, 7.6.2
         statement of cash flows, Ch. 11, 7.6.4
   exemptions from applying the equity method, Ch. 11, 5.3
      investments held in associates/joint ventures held by venture capital organisations, Ch. 11, 5.3
         application of IFRS 9 (or IAS 39) to exempt, Ch. 11, 5.3.2
         entities with a mixture of activities, Ch. 11, 5.3.2.A
      investment entities exception, Ch. 11, 5.3.1
   former subsidiary that becomes an equity-accounted investee, Ch. 7, 3.3.2, 7.1
      application of partial gain recognition where the gain exceeds the carrying amount of the investment in the associate or joint venture accounted using the equity method, Ch. 7, 3.3.2.D
      conflict between IFRS 10 and IAS 28 (September 2014 amendments applied), Ch. 7, 3.3.2.B, 3.3.2.E, 7.1
      conflict between IFRS 10 and IAS 28 (September 2014 amendments not applied), Ch. 7, 3.3.2.A, 3.3.2.E
      determination of the fair value of the retained interest in a former subsidiary that is an associate or joint venture, Ch. 7, 3.3.2.F
      examples of accounting for sales or contributions to an existing associate, Ch. 7, 3.3.2.E
      presentation of comparative information for a former subsidiary that becomes an investee for using the equity method, Ch. 7, 3.3.2.G
      reclassification of items of other comprehensive income where the interest retained in the former subsidiary is an associate or joint venture accounted using the equity method, Ch. 7, 3.3.2.C
   parents exempt from preparing consolidated financial statements, Ch. 11, 5.1
   partial use of fair value measurement of associates, Ch. 11, 5.4
   subsidiaries meeting certain criteria, Ch. 11, 5.2
   transfers of associates/joint ventures between entities under common control, Ch. 10, 5

Equity-settled share-based payment transactions, Ch. 34, 2.2.1, 4–8. *See also* Cash-settled share-based payment transactions; IFRS 2; Share-based payment/transactions; Vesting, share-based payment
   accounting treatment, summary, Ch. 34, 4.1

Equity-settled share-based payment transactions—*contd*
- allocation of expense, Ch. 34, 6
  - market conditions, Ch. 34, 6.3
  - non-vesting conditions, Ch. 34, 6.4
  - overview, Ch. 34, 6.1
    - accounting after vesting, Ch. 34, 6.1.3
    - continuous estimation process of IFRS 2, Ch. 34, 6.1.1
    - vesting and forfeiture, Ch. 34, 6.1.2
  - vesting conditions other than market conditions, Ch. 34, 6.2
    - 'graded' vesting, Ch. 34, 6.2.2
    - service conditions, Ch. 34, 6.2.1
    - variable exercise price, Ch. 34, 6.2.5
    - variable number of equity instruments, Ch. 34, 6.2.4
    - variable vesting periods, Ch. 34, 6.2.3
- award modified to, or from, cash-settled, Ch. 34, 9.4
- cancellation, replacement and settlement, Ch. 34, 7.4
  - calculation of the expense on cancellation, Ch. 34, 7.4.3
  - cancellation and forfeiture, distinction between, Ch. 34, 7.4.1
    - surrender of award by employee, Ch. 34, 7.4.1.B
    - termination of employment by entity, Ch. 34, 7.4.1.A
  - cancellation and modification, distinction between, Ch. 34, 7.4.2
  - replacement awards, Ch. 34, 7.4.4
    - designation, Ch. 34, 7.4.4.A
    - incremental fair value of, Ch. 34, 7.4.4.B
    - replacement of vested awards, Ch. 34, 7.4.4.C
  - valuation requirements when an award is cancelled or settled, Ch. 34, 7.2
- cost of awards, Ch. 34, 5
  - determining the fair value of equity instruments, Ch. 34, 5.5, 8
    - reload features, Ch. 34, 5.5.1, 8.9
  - grant date, Ch. 34, 5.3
  - overview, Ch. 34, 5.1
  - transactions with employees, Ch. 34, 5.2
  - transactions with non-employees, Ch. 34, 5.4
- credit entry, Ch. 34, 4.2
- entity's plans for future modification/replacement of award, Ch. 34, 7.6
- grant date, Ch. 34, 5.3
- market conditions, Ch. 34, 6.3
  - accounting treatment summary, Ch. 34, 6.3.2
  - awards with a condition linked to flotation price, Ch. 34, 6.3.8
  - definition, Ch. 34, 6.3.1
  - hybrid/interdependent market conditions and non-market vesting conditions, Ch. 34, 6.3.7
  - independent market conditions and non-market vesting conditions, Ch. 34, 6.3.6
  - market conditions and known vesting periods, Ch. 34, 6.3.3
  - multiple outcomes depending on market conditions, Ch. 34, 6.3.5
  - transactions with variable vesting periods due to market conditions, Ch. 34, 6.3.4
- market purchases of own equity, Ch. 34, 9.2.2, 9.2.3
- modification, Ch. 34, 7.3
  - altering vesting period, Ch. 34, 7.3.3
  - decreasing the value of an award, Ch. 34, 7.3.2
    - additional/more onerous non-market vesting conditions, Ch. 34, 7.3.2.C
    - decrease in fair value of equity instruments granted, Ch. 34, 7.3.2.A
    - decrease in number of equity instruments granted, Ch. 34, 7.3.2.B
  - from equity-settled to cash-settled, Ch. 34, 7.3.5
  - increasing the value of an award, Ch. 34, 7.3.1
    - increase in fair value of equity instruments granted, Ch. 34, 7.3.1.A
    - increase in number of equity instruments granted, Ch. 34, 7.3.1.B
    - removal/mitigation of non-market vesting conditions, Ch. 34, 7.3.1.C
  - that reduces the number of equity instruments granted but maintains or increases the value of an award, Ch. 34, 7.3.4
  - share splits and consolidations, Ch. 34, 7.8
  - two awards running 'in parallel', Ch. 34, 7.7
  - valuation requirements when an award is modified, Ch. 34, 7.2
- non-vesting conditions, Ch. 34, 6.4
  - awards with no conditions other than non-vesting conditions, Ch. 34, 6.4.1
  - awards with non-vesting conditions and variable vesting periods, Ch. 34, 6.4.2
  - failure to meet non-vesting conditions, Ch. 34, 6.4.3
- reload features, Ch. 34, 5.5.1, 8.9
- termination of employment by entity, Ch. 34, 7.4.1.A
  - replacement and *ex gratia* awards, Ch. 34, 7.5
- transactions with employees, Ch. 34, 5.2
  - basis of measurement, Ch. 34, 5.2.2
  - employee definition, Ch. 34, 5.2.1
- transactions with non-employees, Ch. 34, 5.4
  - effect of change of status from employee to non-employee (or vice versa), Ch. 34, 5.4.1
- transactions with equity and cash alternatives, Ch. 34, 10.1, 10.2, 10.3
  - awards requiring cash settlement in specific circumstances (awards with contingent cash settlement), Ch. 34, 10.3
    - change in manner of settlement where award is contingent on future events outside the control of the entity and the counterparty, Ch. 34, 10.3.4
    - cash settlement on a change of control, Ch. 34, 10.3.3
    - IASB discussion, Ch. 34, 10.3.5
    - treat as cash-settled if contingency is outside entity's control, Ch. 34, 10.3.1
    - contingency outside entity's control and probable, Ch. 34, 10.3.2
  - cash settlement alternative not based on share price/value, Ch. 34, 10.4
- transactions where the counterparty has choice of settlement, Ch. 34, 10.1
  - accounting treatment, during vesting period, Ch. 34, 10.1.3.A
  - accounting treatment, settlement, Ch. 34, 10.1.3. B
  - 'backstop' cash settlement rights, Ch. 34, 10.1.5
  - cash-settlement alternative for employee introduced after grant date, Ch. 34, 10.1.4

convertible bonds issued to acquire goods/services, Ch. 34, 10.1.6
transactions in which the fair value is measured directly, Ch. 34, 10.1.1
transactions in which the fair value is measured indirectly, Ch. 34, 10.1.2
transactions where the entity has choice of settlement, Ch. 34, 10.2
    change in entity's settlement policy/intention leading to change in classification of award after grant date, Ch. 34, 10.2.3
    transactions treated as cash-settled, Ch. 34, 10.2.1
        economic compulsion for cash settlement, Ch. 34, 10.2.1.A
    transactions treated as equity-settled, Ch. 34, 10.2.2
valuation, Ch. 34, 8
    awards of equity instruments to a fixed monetary value, Ch. 34, 8.10
    awards other than options, Ch. 34, 8.7
        non-recourse loans, Ch. 34, 8.7.2
        performance rights, Ch. 34, 8.7.4
        share appreciation rights (SAR), Ch. 34, 8.7.3
        shares, Ch. 34, 8.7.1
    awards whose fair value cannot be measured reliably, Ch. 34, 8.8
        intrinsic value method, Ch. 34, 8.8.1
        modification, cancellation and settlement, Ch. 34, 8.8.2
    awards with reload features, Ch. 34, 8.9
    capital structure effects and dilution, Ch. 34, 8.6
    option-pricing model, selection of, Ch. 34, 8.3
        binomial model, Ch. 34, 8.3.2
        Black-Scholes-Merton formula, Ch. 34, 8.3.1
        Monte Carlo Simulation, Ch. 34, 8.3.3
    option-pricing model, selecting appropriate assumptions, Ch. 34, 8.5
        exercise and termination behaviour, Ch. 34, 8.5.2
        expected dividends, Ch. 34, 8.5.4
        expected term of the option, Ch. 34, 8.5.1
        expected volatility of share price, Ch. 34, 8.5.3
        risk-free interest rate, Ch. 34, 8.5.5
    option-pricing models, adapting for share-based payment, Ch. 34, 8.4
        non-transferability, Ch. 34, 8.4.1
        vesting and non-vesting conditions, treatment of, Ch. 34, 8.4.2
    options, Ch. 34, 8.2
        call options, overview, Ch. 34, 8.2.1
        call options, valuation, Ch. 34, 8.2.2
        factors specific to employee share options, Ch. 34, 8.2.3
vesting conditions other than market conditions, Ch. 34, 6.2
    'graded' vesting, Ch. 34, 6.2.2
    service conditions, Ch. 34, 6.2.1
    variable exercise price, Ch. 34, 6.2.5
    variable number of equity instruments, Ch. 34, 6.2.4
    variable vesting periods, Ch. 34, 6.2.3

Equity transactions
in an associate's/joint venture's financial statements, Ch. 11, 7.11
    dividends/other forms of distributions, Ch. 11, 7.11.1
effects of changes in parent/non-controlling interests in subsidiaries, Ch. 11, 7.11.4
equity-settled share-based payment transactions, Ch. 11, 7.11.3
issues of equity instruments, Ch. 11, 7.11.2
tax effects of, Ch. 47, 8.2
transaction costs of, Ch. 47, 8.1

Errors, prior period
correction of, Ch. 3, 4.6
disclosure of, Ch. 3, 5.3
discovery of fraud after the reporting period, Ch. 38, 3.5
impracticability of restatement, Ch. 3, 4.7.2

Estimates. *See* Accounting Estimates

Estimation uncertainty, Ch. 3, 5.2
disclosures of, Ch. 3, 5.2
sources of, Ch. 3, 5.2.1

Euro, introduction of, Ch. 15, 8

European Commission, Ch. 1, 1, 2.2–2.3, 2.5, 4.2.1

European Embedded Values (EEV), Ch. 55, 1.4.3

European Financial Reporting Advisory Group (EFRAG), Ch. 1, 4.2.1

European Securities and Markets Authority (ESMA), Ch. 1, 5

European Union
adoption of IRFS in the EU, Ch. 1, 4.2.1
EU directive on WE&EE (IFRIC 6), Ch. 26, 6.7
EU 'top up' for financial conglomerates, Ch. 1, 4.2.1
introduction of the euro, Ch. 15, 8
tax implications of UK withdrawal from the (EU), Ch. 33, 5.1.4

Events after the reporting period, Ch. 38, 1–3. *See also* IAS 10
adjusting events, Ch. 38, 2.1.2
    treatment of, Ch. 38, 2.2
extractive industries, Ch. 43, 20
    business combinations-application of the acquisition method, Ch. 43, 20.2
    completion of E&E activity after, Ch. 43, 20.3
    reserves proven after the reporting period, Ch. 43, 20.1
impairment, Ch. 20, 7.1.9
non-adjusting events, Ch. 38, 2.1.3
    dividend declaration, Ch. 38, 2.1.3.A
    treatment of, Ch. 38, 2.3
practical issues, Ch. 38, 3
    changes to estimates of uncertain tax treatments, Ch. 38, 3.6
    discovery of fraud after the reporting period, Ch. 38, 3.5
    insolvency of a debtor and IFRS 9 expected credit losses, Ch. 38, 3.3
    percentage of completion estimates, Ch. 38, 3.2
    valuation of inventory, Ch. 38, 3.1
    valuation of investment property at fair value and tenant insolvency, Ch. 38, 3.4

Evidence of power over an investee, Ch. 6, 4.5

Ex gratia **share-based payment award,** Ch. 34, 7.5

Exchanges of assets, Ch. 17, 4.7; Ch. 18, 4.4
commercial substance, Ch. 17, 4.7.2; Ch. 18, 4.4.1
measurement of assets exchanged, Ch. 17, 4.7.1
reliably measurable, Ch. 18, 4.4.2

Executory contract, Ch. 26, 2.2.1.A

Existing rights, investee
  budget approval rights, Ch. 6, 4.2.2.C
  evaluation whether rights are protective, Ch. 6, 4.2.2
  evaluation whether rights are substantive, Ch. 6, 4.2.1
  franchises, Ch. 6, 4.2.2.B
  incentives to obtain power, Ch. 6, 4.2.3
  independent directors, Ch. 6, 4.2.2.D
  veto rights, Ch. 6, 4.2.2.A

Expected credit losses (ECLs), Ch. 51, 14. *See also* Credit risk
  approaches, Ch. 51, 3
    general approach, Ch. 51, 3.1
    purchased/originated credit-impaired financial assets, Ch. 51, 3.3
    simplified approach, Ch. 51, 3.2
  background and history of impairment project, Ch. 51, 1.1
  calculations, Ch. 51, 7
    Basel guidance on accounting for ECLs, Ch. 51, 7.1
    date of derecognition and date of initial recognition, Ch. 51, 7.3.1
    Global Public Policy Committee (GPPC) guidance, Ch. 51, 7.2
    interaction between expected credit losses calculations and fair value hedge accounting, Ch. 51, 7.5; Ch. 53, 6.4.2.B
    interaction between the initial measurement of debt instruments acquired in a business combination and the impairment model of IFRS 9, Ch. 51, 7.4
    measurement dates of ECLs, Ch. 51, 7.3
    trade date and settlement date accounting, Ch. 51, 7.3.2
  derecognition of contract assets, Ch. 32, 2.1.4
  disclosures, Ch. 51, 15
  financial assets measured at fair value through other comprehensive income, Ch. 51, 9; Ch. 53, 2.6.3
    accounting treatment for debt instruments measured at fair value through other comprehensive income, Ch. 51, 9.1
    interaction between foreign currency translation, fair value hedge accounting and impairment, Ch. 51, 9.2
  financial guarantee contracts, Ch. 51, 11
  Global Public Policy Committee guidance, Ch. 51, 7.2
  IFRS Transition Resource Group for Impairment of Financial Instruments (ITG) and IASB webcasts, Ch. 51, 1.5
  impairment of contract assets, Ch. 32, 2.1.3
  impairment requirements (IFRS 9), Ch. 51, 1.2
  initial measurement of receivables, Ch. 32, 2.1.5
  intercompany loans, Ch. 51, 13
  key changes from the IAS 39 requirements and the main implications of these changes, Ch. 51, 1.3
  key differences from the FASB's requirements, Ch. 51, 1.4
  loan commitments, Ch. 51, 11
  measurement, Ch. 51, 5
    definition of default, Ch. 51, 5.1
    expected life *vs.* contractual period, Ch. 51, 5.5
    lifetime expected credit losses, Ch. 51, 5.2
    losses expected in the event of default, Ch. 51, 5.8
      cash flows from the sale of a defaulted loan, Ch. 51, 5.8.2
      credit enhancements: collateral and financial guarantees, Ch. 51, 5.8.1
      treatment of collection costs paid to an external debt collection agency, Ch. 51 5.8.3
    12-month expected credit losses, Ch. 51, 5.3
    probability of default (PD) and loss rate approaches, Ch. 51, 5.4
      loss rate approach, Ch. 51, 5.4.2
      probability of default approach, Ch. 51, 5.4.1
    probability-weighted outcome, Ch. 51, 5.6
    reasonable and supportable information, Ch. 51, 5.9
      information about past events, current conditions and forecasts of future economic conditions, Ch. 51, 5.9.3
      sources of information, Ch. 51, 5.9.2
      undue cost/effort, Ch. 51, 5.9.1
    time value of money, Ch. 51, 12.4
  modified financial assets, accounting treatment, Ch. 51, 8
    if assets are derecognised, Ch. 51, 8.1
    if assets are not derecognised, Ch. 51, 8.2
  other guidance on ECLs, Ch. 51, 1.6
  presentation of ECLs in the statement of financial position, Ch. 51, 14
    accumulated impairment amount for debt instruments measured at fair value through other comprehensive income, Ch. 51, 14.3
    allowance for financial assets measured at amortised cost, contract assets and lease receivables, Ch. 51, 14.1
      presentation of the gross carrying amount and ECL allowance for credit-impaired assets, Ch. 51, 14.1.2
      write-off, Ch. 51, 14.1.1
    provisions for loan commitments and financial guarantee contracts, Ch. 51, 14.2
  revolving credit facilities, Ch. 51, 12
    determining a significant increase in credit risk, Ch. 51, 12.5
    exposure at default, Ch. 51, 12.3
    period over which to measure ECLs, Ch. 51, 12.2
    scope of the exception, Ch. 51, 12.1
    time value of money, Ch. 51, 12.4
  scope of IFRS 9 impairment requirements, Ch. 51, 2
  trade receivables, contract assets and lease receivables, Ch. 51, 10
    lease receivables, Ch. 51, 10.2
    trade receivables and contract assets, Ch. 51, 10.1

Expenses analysis, Ch. 3, 3.2.3
  by function, Ch. 3, 3.2.3.B,
  by nature, Ch. 3, 3.2.3.A

Exploration and evaluation (E&E) assets. *See also* IFRS 6 asset swaps, Ch. 43, 6.3.3
  carried interest in E&E phase, Ch. 43, 6.1.2
  exchanges of E&E assets for other types of assets, Ch. 43, 6.3.3
  farm-in arrangements, Ch. 43, 6.2
  impairment of, Ch. 43, 3.5
    additional considerations if E&E assets are impaired, Ch. 43, 3.5.5
    cash-generating units comprising successful and unsuccessful E&E projects, Ch. 43, 3.5.3
    impairment testing 'triggers,' Ch. 43, 3.5.1

income statement treatment of E&E write downs, Ch. 43, 3.5.6
order of impairment testing, Ch. 43, 3.5.4
reversal of impairment losses, Ch. 43, 3.5.7
specifying the level at which E&E assets are assessed for impairment, Ch. 43, 3.5.2
measurement of, Ch. 43, 3.3
    capitalisation of borrowing costs in the E&E phase, Ch. 43, 3.3.2
    types of expenditure in the E&E phase, Ch. 43, 3.3.1
reclassification of, Ch. 43, 3.4.1
recognition of, Ch. 43, 3.2
    area-of-interest method, Ch. 43, 3.2.5
    changes in accounting policies, Ch. 43, 3.2.6
    developing an accounting policy under IFRS 6, Ch. 43, 3.2.1
    full cost method, Ch. 43, 3.2.4
    options for an exploration and evaluation policy, Ch. 43, 3.2.2
    successful efforts method, Ch. 43, 3.2.3

Exposure Drafts (EDs)
ED 5–*Insurance Contracts*, Ch. 55, 1.2
ED/2009/2–*Income Tax*, Ch. 33, 1.3, 8.5.1
ED/2014/4 – *Measuring Quoted Investments in Subsidiaries, Joint Ventures and Associates at Fair Value (Proposed amendments to IFRS 10, IFRS 12, IAS 27, IAS 28 and IAS 36 and Illustrative Examples for IFRS 13)*, Ch. 7, 3.3.2.F; Ch. 14, 5.1.1
ED/2017/5 – *Accounting Policies and Accounting Estimates – Proposed amendments to IAS 8*, Ch. 3, 6.2.1; Ch. 22, 3.2.2
ED/2019/5 – *Deferred Tax related to Assets and Liabilities arising from a Single Transaction: Proposed amendments to IAS 12*, Ch. 33, 7.2.7
ED/2019/6 – *Disclosure of Accounting Policies, Proposed amendments to IAS 1 and IFRS Practice Statement 2*, Ch. 3, 6.2.2
ED/2019/7 – *General Presentation and Disclosure*, Ch. 3, 6.1.2
External hedging instruments, offsetting, Ch. 53, 3.2.1
Extractive industries, Ch. 43, 1–20. *See also* IFRS 6; Mineral reserves and resources; Reserves
acquisitions, Ch. 43, 8
    accounting for land acquisitions, Ch. 43, 8.4.2
    acquisition of an interest in a joint operation that is a business, Ch. 43, 8.3
    asset acquisitions and conditional purchase consideration, Ch. 43, 8.4.1
    business combinations, Ch. 43, 8.2
        events after the reporting period, Ch. 43, 22.2
        goodwill in business combinations, Ch. 43, 8.2.1
        impairment of assets and goodwill recognised on acquisition, Ch. 43, 8.2.2
        value beyond proven and probable reserves (VBPP), Ch. 43, 8.2.3
    business combinations *vs.* asset acquisitions, Ch. 43, 8.1
        definition of a business, Ch. 43, 8.1.2
        differences between asset purchase transactions and, Ch. 43, 8.1.1
April 2010 discussion paper, extractive activities, Ch. 43, 1.3
    asset measurement, Ch. 43, 1.3.3
    asset recognition, Ch. 43, 1.3.2
    disclosure, Ch. 43, 1.3.4
    Extractive Activities project, status of, Ch. 43, 1.3.6
    project status, Ch. 43, 1.3.6
    publish what you pay proposals, Ch. 43, 1.3.5
    reserves and resources, definitions of, Ch. 43, 1.3.1
decommissioning and restoration/rehabilitation, Ch. 43, 10
    indefinite life assets, Ch. 43, 10.3
    recognition and measurement issues, Ch. 43, 10.1
    treatment of foreign exchange differences, Ch. 43, 10.2
definitions, Ch. 43, 1.1, 21
depreciation, depletion and amortisation (DD&A), Ch. 43, 16
    block caving, Ch. 43, 16.2
    determining when production phase commences, Ch. 43, 15.5.2
    requirements under IAS 16 and IAS 38, Ch. 43, 16.1
        assets depreciated using the straight-line method, Ch. 43, 16.1.2
        assets depreciated using the units of production method, Ch. 43, 16.1.3
        mineral reserves, Ch. 43, 16.1.1
events after the reporting period, Ch. 43, 22
    business combinations-application of the acquisition method, Ch. 43, 22.2
    completion of E&E activity after, Ch. 43, 22.3
    reserves proven after the reporting period, Ch. 43, 22.1
financial instruments, Ch. 43, 13
    embedded derivatives, Ch. 43, 13.2
        development of gas markets, Ch. 43, 13.2.4
        foreign currency embedded derivatives, Ch. 43, 13.2.1
        long-term supply contracts, Ch. 43, 13.2.3
        provisionally priced sales contracts, Ch. 43, 13.2.2
    hedging sales of metal concentrate (mining), Ch. 43, 13.4
    normal purchase and sales exemption, Ch. 43, 13.1
    volume flexibility in supply contracts, Ch. 43, 13.3
functional currency, Ch. 43, 9
    changes in, Ch. 43, 9.2
    determining, Ch. 43, 9.1
guidance under national accounting standards, Ch. 43, 1.5
impact of IFRS 15, Ch. 43, 12
    commodity-based contracts, modifications to, Ch. 43, 12.10
    embedded derivatives in commodity arrangements, Ch. 43, 12.8
    forward-selling contracts to finance development, Ch. 43, 12.6
    gold bullion sales (mining only), Ch. 43, 12.13
    inventory exchanges with the same counterparty, Ch. 43, 12.3
    multi-period commodity-based sales contracts, Ch. 43, 12.15
    overlift and underlift (oil and gas), Ch. 43, 12.4
    principal *vs.* agent considerations in commodity-based contracts, Ch. 43, 12.11
    production sharing contracts/arrangements (PSCs), Ch. 43, 12.5
    repurchase agreements, Ch. 43, 12.14
    royalty income, Ch. 43, 12.9
    sale of product with delayed shipment, Ch. 43, 12.2
    shipping, Ch. 43, 12.12
    take-or-pay contracts, Ch. 43, 12.16
    trading activities, Ch. 43, 12.7

Extractive industries—*contd*
- impact of IFRS 16, Ch. 43, 17, 18
  - allocating contract consideration, Ch. 43, 17.6
  - definition of a lease, Ch. 43, 17.2
  - identifying and separating lease and non-lease components, Ch. 43, 17.
  - identifying lease payments included in the measurement of the lease liability, Ch. 43, 17.5
  - interaction of IFRS 16 and IFRS 11, Ch. 43, 18
  - interaction of leases with asset retirement obligations, Ch. 43, 17.7
  - joint arrangements, Ch. 43, 18
  - land easements or rights of way, Ch. 43, 17.1.2
  - scope and scope exclusions, Ch. 43, 17.1
  - substitution rights, Ch. 43, 17.3
  - subsurface rights, Ch. 43, 17.1.3
- impairment of assets, Ch. 43, 11
  - basis of recoverable amount – value-in-use (VIU) or fair value less costs of disposal (FVLCD), Ch. 43, 11.3
  - calculation of FVLCD, Ch. 43, 11.5
  - calculation of VIU, Ch. 43, 11.4
  - cash flows from mineral reserves and resources and the appropriate discount rate, Ch. 43, 11.4.2.A
  - commodity price assumptions, Ch. 43, 11.4.3, 11.5.2
  - foreign currency cash flows, Ch. 43, 11.4.5, 11.5.4
  - future capital expenditure, Ch. 43, 11.4.4, 11.5.3
  - identifying cash-generating units (CGUs), Ch. 43, 11.2
  - impairment indicators, Ch. 43, 11.1
  - low mine or field profitability near end of life, Ch. 43, 11.6
  - projections of cash flows, Ch. 43, 11.4.2, 11.5.1
- inventories, Ch. 43, 14
  - carried at fair value, Ch. 43, 14.4
  - core inventories, Ch. 43, 14.3
  - heap leaching (mining), Ch. 43, 14.6
  - recognition of work in progress, Ch. 43, 14.1
  - sale of by-products and joint products, Ch. 43, 14.2
    - by-products, Ch. 43, 14.2.1
    - joint products, Ch. 43, 14.2.2
  - stockpiles of low grade ore (mining), Ch. 43, 14.5
- investments in the extractive industries, Ch. 43, 7
  - joint arrangements, Ch. 43, 7.1
    - assessing joint control, Ch. 43, 7.1.1
    - determining whether a manager has control, Ch. 43, 7.1.2
    - managers of joint arrangements, Ch. 43, 7.1.4
    - non-operators, Ch. 43, 7.1.5
    - parties without joint control/control, Ch. 43, 7.1.3
  - undivided interests, Ch. 43, 7.2
- legal rights to explore for, develop and produce mineral properties, Ch. 43, 5
  - concessionary agreements (concessions), Ch. 43, 5.2
  - different types of royalty interests, Ch. 43, 5.7
    - net profits interests, Ch. 43, 5.7.4
    - overriding royalties, Ch. 43, 5.7.2
    - production payment royalties, Ch. 43, 5.7.3
    - revenue and royalties: gross or net?, Ch. 43, 5.7.5
    - working interest and basic royalties, Ch. 43, 5.7.1
  - evolving contractual arrangements, Ch. 43, 5.5
  - how a mineral lease works, Ch. 43, 5.1
  - joint operating agreements, Ch. 43, 5.6
  - pure-service contract, Ch. 43, 5.4
  - traditional production sharing contracts, Ch. 43, 5.3
- long-term contracts and leases, Ch. 43, 19
  - embedded leases, Ch. 43, 19.1
  - impact of IFRS 16, Ch. 43, 19.3
  - take-or-pay contracts, Ch. 43, 19.2
    - make-up product and undertake, Ch. 43, 19.2.1
- mineral reserves and resources, Ch. 43, 2
  - disclosure of mineral reserves and resources, Ch. 43, 2.4
    - mining sector, Ch. 43, 2.4.2
    - oil and gas sector, Ch. 43, 2.4.1
    - value of reserves, Ch. 43, 2.4.3
  - international harmonisation of reserve reporting, Ch. 43, 2.1
  - mining resource and reserve reporting, Ch. 43, 2.3
    - CIRSCO International reporting template, Ch. 43, 2.3.1
  - petroleum reserve estimation and reporting, Ch. 43, 2.2
    - basic principles and definitions, Ch. 43, 2.2.1
    - classification and categorisation guidelines, Ch. 43, 2.2.2
- property, plant and equipment, Ch. 43, 15
  - care and maintenance, Ch. 43, 15.3
  - major maintenance and turnarounds/renewals and reconditioning costs, Ch. 43, 15.1
  - redeterminations, Ch. 43, 15.4.2
    - as capital reimbursements, Ch. 43, 15.4.2.A
    - decommissioning provisions, Ch. 43, 15.4.2.C
    - 'make-up' oil, Ch. 43, 15.4.2.B
  - stripping costs in the production phase of a surface mine (mining), Ch. 43, 15.5
    - determining when production phase commences, Ch. 43, 15.5.2
    - disclosures, Ch. 43, 15.5.6
    - initial recognition, Ch. 43, 15.5.4
    - recognition criteria-stripping activity asset, Ch. 43, 15.5.3
    - scope of IFRIC 20, Ch. 43, 15.5.1
    - subsequent measurement, Ch. 43, 15.5.5
  - unitisations, Ch. 43, 15.4
  - well workovers and recompletions (oil and gas), Ch. 43, 15.2
- revenue recognition, Ch. 43, 12
  - forward-selling contracts to finance development, Ch. 43, 12.6
  - inventory exchanges with the same counterparty, Ch. 43, 12.3
  - overlift and underlift (oil and gas), Ch. 43, 12.4
    - accounting for imbalances in revenue under IFRS 15, Ch. 43, 12.4.1
    - consideration of cost of goods sold where revenue is recognised in accordance with IFRS 15, Ch. 43, 12.4.2
    - facility imbalances, Ch. 43, 12.4.3
  - revenue in the development phase, Ch. 43, 12.1
    - incidental revenue, Ch. 43, 12.1.1
    - integral to development, Ch. 43, 12.1.2
  - sale of product with delayed shipment, Ch. 43, 12.2
  - trading activities, Ch. 43, 12.7
- risk-sharing arrangements, Ch. 43, 6
  - asset swaps, Ch. 43, 6.3

Index

E&E assets, Ch. 43, 6.3.1
    Exchanges of E&E assets for other types of assets, Ch. 43, 6.3.3
    PP&E, intangible assets and investment property, Ch. 43, 6.3.2
carried interests, Ch. 43, 6.1
    arrangements in E&E phase, Ch. 43, 6.1.2
    financing-type carried interest arrangements in the development phase, Ch. 43, 6.1.3
    purchase/sale-type carried interest arrangements in the development phase, Ch. 43, 6.1.4
    types of carried interests, Ch. 43, 6.1.1
farm-ins and farm-outs, Ch. 43, 6.2
    farm-in arrangements in E&E phase, Ch. 43, 6.2.1
    farm-in arrangements outside the E&E phase: accounting by the farmee, Ch. 43, 6.2.2
    farm-in arrangements outside the E&E phase: accounting by the farmor, Ch. 43, 6.2.3
status of the statement of recommended practice, UK Oil Industry Accounting Committee, June 2001 (OIAC SORP), Ch. 43, 1.4
taxation, Ch. 43, 21
    excise duties, production taxes and severance taxes, Ch. 43, 21.1
    petroleum revenue tax (or resource rent tax), Ch. 43, 21.1.2
    production-based taxation, Ch. 43, 21.1.1
    grossing up of notional quantities withheld, Ch. 43, 21.2
    tolling arrangements, Ch. 43, 20
unit of account, Ch. 43, 4
upstream versus downstream activities, Ch. 43, 1.6

Fair presentation, Ch. 3, 4.1.1
and compliance with IFRS, Ch. 3, 4.1.1.A
override, Ch. 3, 4.1.1.B

Fair value. *See also* Fair value hedges; Fair value hierarchy; Fair value less costs of disposal (FVLCD);

Fair value measurement *under* **IFRS 13.** *See also* Fair value measurement and IFRS 13 below
'clean' *vs.* 'dirty' values, Ch. 53, 7.4.10
definition, Ch. 14, 3
derivatives, discount rates for calculating, Ch. 53, 7.4.5
designation of own use contracts at fair value through profit or loss, Ch. 53, 12.2
financial assets and financial liabilities at, Ch. 50, 2.4
financial assets designated at fair value through profit/loss, Ch. 54, 4.4.3
financial liabilities designated at fair value through profit/loss, Ch. 54, 4.4.2
first-time adoption, Ch. 5, 3.3
future investment management fees in, Ch. 55, 8.2.1.B
hedged items held at fair value through profit/loss, Ch. 53, 2.6.2
hedging using instruments with non-zero fair value, Ch. 53, 7.4.3
on initial recognition of financial instrument, measurement of, Ch. 49, 3.3.2
of insurer's liabilities, Ch. 55, 9.1.1.B
of intangible assets, determining, Ch. 9, 5.5.2.F
in intra-group transactions, Ch. 8, 4.3.1
investment property, fair value model, Ch. 19, 6

deferred taxation for property held by a 'single asset' entity, Ch. 19, 6.10
estimating fair value, Ch. 19, 6.1
    comparison with value in use, Ch. 19, 6.1.3
    'double counting,' Ch. 19, 6.1.4
    methods of estimation, Ch. 19, 6.1.1
    observable data, Ch. 19, 6.1.2
fair value of investment property under construction, Ch. 19, 6.3
fair value of properties held under a lease, valuation adjustments to the, Ch. 19, 6.7
fixtures and fittings subsumed within fair value, Ch. 19, 6.5
future capital expenditure and development value ('highest and best use'), Ch. 19, 6.8
inability to determine fair value of completed investment property, Ch. 19, 6.2
negative present value, Ch. 19, 6.9
prepaid and accrued operating lease income, Ch. 19, 6.6
    accrued rental income and lease incentives, Ch. 19, 6.6.1
    prepaid rental income, Ch. 19, 6.6.2
transaction costs incurred by the reporting entity on acquisition, Ch. 19, 6.4
property, plant and equipment, revaluation model, Ch. 18, 6
meaning of fair value, Ch. 18, 6.1
    cost approach, Ch. 18, 6.1.1.C
    highest and best use, Ch. 18, 6.1.1.A
    revaluing assets under IFRS 13, Ch. 18, 6.1.1
    valuation approaches, Ch. 18, 6.1.1.B
and value in use (VIU), differences between, Ch. 20, 7.3

Fair value hedges, Ch. 53, 1.5, 5.1, 7.1; Ch. 54, 4.3.3
adjustments to the hedged item, Ch. 53, 7.1.2
discontinuing, Ch. 53, 8.3
firm commitments, Ch. 53, 5.1.1
foreign currency monetary items, Ch. 53, 5.1.2
layer components for, Ch. 53, 2.3.2
presentation, Ch. 53, 9.2

Fair value hierarchy, Ch. 14, 16
categorisation within, Ch. 14, 16.2
    over-the-counter derivative instruments, Ch. 14, 16.2.4
    significance of inputs, assessing, Ch. 14, 16.2.1
    third-party pricing services/brokers, Ch. 14, 16.2.3
    transfers between levels within, Ch. 14, 16.2.2

Fair value less costs of disposal (FVLCD), Ch. 20, 6
calculation of (extractive industries), Ch. 43, 11.5
depreciated replacement cost/current replacement cost as, Ch. 20, 6.1.2
estimating, Ch. 20, 6.1
investments in subsidiaries, associates and joint ventures, Ch. 20, 12.4.1
and unit of account, Ch. 20, 6.1.1

Fair value measurement, Ch. 14, 1–23. *See also* Fair value; Fair value hierarchy; IFRS 13; Offsetting positions; Valuation techniques
agriculture, Ch. 42, 4
    establishing what to measure, Ch. 42, 4.2
    determining costs to sell, Ch. 42, 4.4
    disclosures, Ch. 42, 5.2
        additional disclosures if fair value cannot be measured reliably, Ch. 42, 5.3

Fair value measurement—*contd*
  agriculture—*contd*
    IAS 41-specific requirements, Ch. 42, 4.5
    interaction between IAS 41 and IFRS 13, Ch. 42, 4.1
    overview of IFRS 13 requirements, Ch. 42, 4.6
    problem of measuring fair value for part-grown or immature biological assets, Ch. 42, 4.7
    when to measure fair value, Ch. 42, 4.3
  asset/liability, Ch. 14, 5
    characteristics
      condition and location, Ch. 14, 5.2.1
      restrictions on assets/liabilities, Ch. 14, 5.2.2
    unit of account
      asset's (or liability's) components, Ch. 14, 5.1.4
      and portfolio exception, Ch. 14, 5.1.2
      and PxQ, Ch. 7, 3.3.2.F; Ch. 14, 5.1.1
      vs. valuation premise, Ch. 14, 5.1.3
  of associates, partial use of, Ch. 11, 5.4
  convergence with US GAAP, Ch. 14, 22
    disclosures, Ch. 14, 22.2.4
    fair value of liabilities with demand feature, Ch. 14, 22.2.2
    IFRS 13, development of, Ch. 14, 22.1
    practical expedient for alternative investments, Ch. 14, 22.2.1
    recognition of day-one gains and losses, Ch. 14, 22.2.3
  day 1 profits, financial instruments, Ch. 54, 4.5.2
  definitions, Ch. 14, 3
  disclosures, Ch. 14, 20
    accounting policy, Ch. 14, 20.2
    objectives
      format of, Ch. 14, 20.1.1
      level of disaggregation, Ch. 14, 20.1.2
      'recurring' *vs.* 'non-recurring, Ch. 14, 20.1.3
    for recognised fair value measurements, Ch. 14, 20.3
      fair value hierarchy categorisation, Ch. 14, 20.3.3
      highest and best use, Ch. 14, 20.3.9
      level 3 reconciliation, Ch. 14, 20.3.6
      non-recurring fair value measurements, Ch. 14, 20.3.2
      recurring fair value measurements, Ch. 14, 20.3.1
      sensitivity of level 3 measurements to changes in significant unobservable inputs, Ch. 14, 20.3.8
      transfers between hierarchy levels for recurring fair value measurements, Ch. 14, 20.3.4
      of valuation processes for level 3 measurements, Ch. 14, 20.3.7
      valuation techniques and inputs, Ch. 14, 20.3.5
    regarding liabilities issued with an inseparable third-party credit enhancement, Ch. 14, 20.5
    for unrecognised fair value measurements, Ch. 14, 20.4
  effective date and transition, Ch. 14, 22
  fair value framework, Ch. 14, 4
    definition, Ch. 14, 4.1
    measurement, Ch. 14, 4.2
  financial assets and liabilities with offsetting positions, Ch. 14, 12
    criteria for using the portfolio approach for offsetting positions, Ch. 14, 12.1
      accounting policy considerations, Ch. 14, 12.1.1
      level 1 instruments in, Ch. 14, 12.1.4
      minimum level of offset, to use portfolio approach, Ch. 14, 12.1.3
      presentation considerations, Ch. 14, 12.1.2
    measuring fair value for offsetting positions, Ch. 14, 12.2
      exposure to market risks, Ch. 14, 12.2.1
      exposure to the credit risk of a particular counterparty, Ch. 14, 12.2.2
  hierarchy, Ch. 14, 16
    categorisation within, Ch. 14, 16.2
      over-the-counter derivative instruments, Ch. 14, 16.2.4
      significance of inputs, assessing, Ch. 14, 16.2.1
      third-party pricing services/brokers, Ch. 14, 16.2.3
      transfers between levels within, Ch. 14, 16.2.2
  IFRS 13, objective of, Ch. 14, 1.3
  IFRS 13, overview, Ch. 14, 1.2
  at initial recognition, Ch. 14, 13
    day 1 gains and losses, Ch. 14, 13.2
    exit price *vs.* entry price, Ch. 14, 13.1
    related party transactions, Ch. 14, 13.3
  inputs to valuation techniques, Ch. 14, 15
    broker quotes and pricing services, Ch. 14, 15.5
    general principles, Ch. 14, 15.1
    premiums and discounts, Ch. 14, 15.2
      blockage factors (or block discounts), Ch. 14, 15.2.1
    pricing within the bid-ask spread, Ch. 14, 15.3
      bid-ask spread, Ch. 14, 15.3.2
      mid-market pricing, Ch. 14, 15.3.1
    risk premiums, Ch. 14, 15.4
  of intangible assets, determining, Ch. 9, 5.5.2.F
  level 1 inputs, Ch. 14, 17
    alternative pricing methods, Ch. 14, 17.2
    quoted prices in active markets Ch. 14, 17.3
    unit of account, Ch. 14, 17.4
    use of, Ch. 14, 17.1
  level 2 inputs, Ch. 14, 18
    examples of, Ch. 14, 18.2
    making adjustments to, Ch. 14, 18.4
    market corroborated inputs, Ch. 14, 18.3
    recently observed prices in an inactive market, Ch. 14, 18.5
  level 3 inputs, Ch. 14, 19
    examples of, Ch. 14, 19.2
    use of, Ch. 14, 19.1
  liabilities and an entity's own equity, application to, Ch. 14, 11
    financial liability with demand feature, Ch. 14, 11.5
    general principles
      fair value of an entity's own equity, Ch. 14, 11.1.2
      fair value of liability, Ch. 14, 11.1.1
      settlement value *vs.* transfer value, Ch. 14, 11.1.3
    non-performance risk, Ch. 14, 11.1
      counterparty credit risk and its own credit risk, Ch. 14, 11.3.2
      derivative liabilities, Ch. 14, 11.3.4
      entity incorporate credit risk into the valuation of its derivative contracts, Ch. 14, 11.3.3
      with third-party credit enhancements, Ch. 14, 11.3.1
    not held by other parties as assets, Ch. 14, 11.2.2
    restrictions preventing the transfer of, Ch. 14, 11.4
    that are held by other parties as assets, Ch. 14, 11.2.1
  market participants, Ch. 14, 7
    assumptions, Ch. 14, 7.2
    characteristics, Ch. 14, 7.1

non-financial assets, application to, Ch. 14, 10
   highest and best use, Ch. 14, 10.1
      vs. current use, Ch. 14, 10.1.2
      vs. intended use, Ch. 14, 10.1.3
      legally permissible, Ch. 14, 10.1.1
   valuation premise, Ch. 14, 10.2
      in combination with other assets and/or liabilities, Ch. 14, 10.2.2
      liabilities association, Ch. 14, 10.2.3
      stand-alone basis, Ch. 14, 10.2.1
      unit of account *vs.*, Ch. 14, 10.2.4
for part-grown or immature biological assets, Ch. 42, 4.7
present value techniques, Ch. 14, 21
   components of, Ch. 14, 21.2
      risk and uncertainty in, Ch. 14, 21.2.2
      time value of money, Ch. 14, 21.2.1
   discount rate adjustment technique, Ch. 14, 21.3
   expected present value technique, Ch. 14, 21.4
   general principles for use of, Ch. 14, 21.1
price, Ch. 14, 9
   transaction costs, Ch. 14, 9.1
   transportation costs, Ch. 14, 9.2
principal (or most advantageous) market, Ch. 14, 6
scope, Ch. 14, 2
   exclusions, Ch. 14, 2.2
      exemptions from the disclosure requirements of IFRS 13, Ch. 14, 2.2.4
      fair value, measurements similar to, Ch. 14, 2.2.3
      lease transactions, Ch. 14, 2.2.2
      share-based payments, Ch. 14, 2.2.1
   fair value measurement exceptions, Ch. 14, 2.4
   IFRS 13, items in scope of, Ch. 14, 2.1
      fair value disclosures, Ch. 14, 2.1.1
      fair value measurements, Ch. 14, 2.1.2
      short-term receivables and payables, Ch. 14, 2.1.3
   practical expedient for impaired financial assets carried at amortised cost, Ch. 14, 2.4.2
   present value techniques, Ch. 14, 2.3
transaction, Ch. 14, 8
   estimation, Ch. 14, 8.3
   identification, Ch. 14, 8.2
   volume and level of activity for an asset/liability, Ch. 14, 8.1
unit of account, Ch. 14, 5.1
   asset's (or liability's) components, Ch. 14, 5.1.4
   level 1 assets and liabilities, Ch. 14, 17.4
   and portfolio exception, Ch. 14, 5.1.2
   and PxQ, Ch. 7, 3.3.2.F; Ch. 14, 5.1.1
   vs. valuation premise, Ch. 14, 5.1.3
valuation techniques, Ch. 14, 14
   cost approach, Ch. 14, 14.3
   income approach, Ch. 14, 14.4
   market approach, Ch. 14, 14.2
   selecting appropriate, Ch. 14, 14.1
      making changes to valuation techniques, Ch. 14, 14.1.4
      single *vs.* multiple valuation techniques, Ch. 14, 14.1.1
      using multiple valuation techniques to measure fair value, Ch. 14, 14.1.2
      valuation adjustments, Ch. 14, 14.1.3

Fair value model, investment property, Ch. 19, 6. *See also* Fair value; Investment property
   completed investment property, inability to determine fair value, Ch. 19, 6.2
   deferred taxation for property held by a 'single asset' entity, Ch. 19, 6.10
   estimating fair value, Ch. 19, 6.1
   fixtures and fittings subsumed, Ch. 19, 6.5
   future capital expenditure and development value ('highest and best use'), Ch. 19, 6.8
   negative present value, Ch. 19, 6.9
   prepaid and accrued operating lease income, Ch. 19, 6.6
   properties held under a lease, valuation adjustment to the, Ch. 19, 6.7
   property under construction, Ch. 19, 6.3
   transaction costs incurred on acquisition, Ch. 19, 6.4

Fair value through other comprehensive income (FVTOCI), Ch. 48, 8; Ch. 54, 7.2
   debt instruments, subsequent measurement accumulated impairment amount for, Ch. 51, 14.3
   financial assets measured at, Ch. 51, 9
   hedges of exposures classified as, Ch. 53, 2.6.3
   non-derivative equity investments designation at, Ch. 48, 8

Faithful representation, Ch. 2, 5.1.2

Farm-ins and farm outs, extractive industries, Ch. 43, 6.2
   farm-in arrangements in the E&E phase, Ch. 43, 6.2.1
   farm-in arrangements outside the E&E phase: accounting by the farmee, Ch. 43, 6.2.2
      farming into an asset, Ch. 43, 6.2.2.A
      farming into a business which is a joint operation or results in the formation of a joint operation, Ch. 43, 6.2.2.B
   farm-in arrangements outside the E&E phase: accounting by the farmor, Ch. 43, 6.2.3

Finance costs as a borrowing cost, Ch. 21, 5.5
   derecognition of borrowings, gains and losses on, Ch. 21, 5.5.2
   derivative financial instruments, Ch. 21, 5.5.1
   derivative financial instruments, gains or losses on termination of, Ch. 21, 5.5.3
   dividends payable on shares classified as financial liabilities, Ch. 21, 5.5.4
   unwinding discounts, Ch. 21, 4.2

Finance leases, accounting for, Ch. 23, 6.2
   accounting by lessors, Ch. 23, 6.2–6.2.4
      initial measurement, Ch. 23, 6.2.1
      presentation in the statement of cash flows, Ch. 40, 5.5.5
      remeasurement, Ch. 23, 6.2.4
      subsequent measurement, Ch. 23, 6.2.3
         unguaranteed residual values, Ch. 23, 6.2.3.A
   manufacturer/dealer lessors, Ch. 23, 6.2.2

Financial Accounting Standards Board (FASB), Ch. 1, 2.9, 3.2; Ch. 14, 22.2

Financial assets
   accounting for loss of control, interest retained in the former subsidiary is a financial asset, Ch. 7, 3.3.1
   call options over non-controlling interest, Ch. 7, 6.1, 6.3, 6.4, 6.5

Financial assets—contd
    classification and measurement on first-time adoption, Ch. 5, 4.9
    classifying, Ch. 48, 2
        debt instruments, Ch. 48, 2.1
        equity instruments and derivatives, Ch. 48, 2.2
    contractual obligation to deliver, Ch. 47, 4.2
    definition, Ch. 45, 2.1; Ch. 47, 3; Ch. 52, 2.1
    derecognition, Ch. 52, 3
    designated as measured at fair value through profit/loss, Ch. 54, 4.4.3
    at fair value through profit/loss, Ch. 50, 2.4
    held for trading, Ch. 48, 4
    and liabilities with offsetting positions, Ch. 14, 12
        criteria for using the portfolio approach for offsetting positions, Ch. 14, 12.1
        measuring fair value for offsetting positions, Ch. 14, 12.2
    measured at amortised cost, Ch. 51, 14.1
    measured at fair value through other comprehensive income, Ch. 51, 14.3
    measured at fair value through profit/loss, Ch. 51, 9.1
    modified financial assets, Ch. 51, 8.2
    offsetting, Ch. 54, 7.4.1
        cash pooling arrangements, Ch. 54, 7.4.1.E
        disclosure, Ch. 54, 7.4.2
        enforceable legal right of set-off, Ch. 54, 7.4.1.A
        intention to settle net, Ch. 54, 7.4.1.C
        master netting agreements, Ch. 54, 7.4.1.B
        offsetting collateral amounts, Ch. 54, 7.4.1.F
        situations where offset is not normally appropriate, Ch. 54, 7.4.1.D
        unit of account, Ch. 54, 7.4.1.G
    reclassifications of, Ch. 48, 9; Ch. 50, 2.7
    redesignation of, Ch. 55, 8.4
    that are either past due or impaired, Ch. 54, 5.3.3
    transfers of, Ch. 54, 6
        assets that are derecognised in their entirety, Ch. 54, 6.3
            disclosure requirements, Ch. 54, 6.3.2
            meaning of continuing involvement, Ch. 54, 6.3.1
        assets that are not derecognised in their entirety, Ch. 54, 6.2
        meaning of 'transfer,' Ch. 54, 6.1

Financial capital maintenance (framework), Ch. 2, 11.1

Financial guarantee(s), Ch. 51, 5.8.1
    to provide a loan at a below-market interest rate, Ch. 50, 2.8

Financial guarantee contracts, Ch. 45, 3.4; Ch. 49, 3.3.3; Ch. 55, 2.2.3.D
    between entities under common control, Ch. 45, 3.4.4
    definition, Ch. 45, 3.4.1; Ch. 51, 11.1
        debt instrument, Ch. 45, 3.4.1.B
        form and existence of contract, Ch. 45, 3.4.1.C
        reimbursement for loss incurred, Ch. 45, 3.4.1.A
    holders of, Ch. 45, 3.4.3
    IFRS 9 impairment requirements, Ch. 51, 1.2
    issuers of, Ch. 45, 3.4.2
    maturity analysis, Ch. 54, 5.4.2.F

Financial instrument(s). *See also* IAS 32, IAS 39, IFRS 7; IFRS 9
    contracts to buy or sell commodities and other non-financial items, Ch. 45, 4
    contracts that may be settled net, Ch. 45, 4.1
    definitions, Ch. 45, 2.1
        applying, Ch. 45, 2.2
        contingent rights and obligations, Ch. 45, 2.2.3
        derivative financial instruments, Ch. 45, 2.2.8
        dividends payable, Ch. 45, 2.2.9
        equity instruments, Ch. 45, 2.1; Ch. 45, 2.2.7
        financial asset, Ch. 45, 2.1
        financial instrument, Ch. 45, 2.1
        financial liability, Ch. 45, 2.1
        leases, Ch. 45, 2.2.4
        need for a contract, Ch. 45, 2.2.1
        non-financial assets and liabilities and contracts thereon, Ch. 45, 2.2.5
        payments for goods and services, Ch. 45, 2.2.6
        simple financial instruments, Ch. 45, 2.2.2
    discretionary participation feature in, Ch. 55, 6.2
    normal sales and purchases (or own use contracts), Ch. 45, 4.2
        commodity broker-traders and similar entities, Ch. 45, 4.2.2
        contracts containing volume flexibility, Ch. 45, 4.2.5
        electricity and similar 'end-user' contracts, Ch. 45, 4.2.4
        fair value option in IFRS 9, Ch. 45, 4.2.6
        net settlement of similar contracts, Ch. 45, 4.2.1
        written options that can be settled net, Ch. 45, 4.2.3
    scope, Ch. 45, 3
        business combinations, Ch. 45, 3.7
        contingent pricing of property, plant and equipment and intangible assets, Ch. 45, 3.8
        disposal groups classified as held for sale and discontinued operations, Ch. 45, 3.11
        employee benefit plans and share-based payment, Ch. 45, 3.9
        equity instruments, Ch. 45, 3.6
        financial guarantee contracts, Ch. 45, 3.4
        indemnification assets, Ch. 45, 3.12
        insurance and similar contracts, Ch. 45, 3.3
            contracts with discretionary participation features, Ch. 45, 3.3.2
            separating financial instrument components including embedded derivatives from insurance contracts, Ch. 45, 3.3.3
            weather derivatives, Ch. 45, 3.3.1
        leases, Ch. 45, 3.2
        loan commitments, Ch. 45, 3.5
        reimbursement rights in respect of provisions, Ch. 45, 3.10
        rights and obligations within the scope of IFRS 15, Ch. 45, 3.13
        subsidiaries, associates, joint ventures and similar investments, Ch. 45, 3.1

Financial instrument hosts, Ch. 49, 3.5

Financial instruments, classification, Ch. 48, 1–9
    'business model' assessment, Ch. 48, 5
        applying in practice, Ch. 48, 5.6
        consolidated and subsidiary accounts, Ch. 48, 5.5
        hold to collect contractual cash flows, Ch. 48, 5.2
        hold to collect contractual cash flows and selling financial assets, Ch. 48, 5.3
        impact of sales on the assessment, Ch. 48, 5.2.1
        level at which the business model assessment is applied, Ch. 48, 5.1

transferred financial assets that are not derecognised, Ch. 48, 5.2.2
contractual cash flows, Ch. 48, 6
    auction rate securities, Ch. 48, 6.4.4
    bonds with a capped or floored interest rate, Ch. 48, 6.3.3
    contractual features that change the timing or amount, Ch. 48, 6.4.4
    contractually linked instruments, Ch. 48, 6.6
    conventional subordination features, Ch. 48, 6.3.1
    convertible debt, Ch. 48, 6.4.5
    de minimis features, Ch. 48, 6.4.1.A
    debt covenants, Ch. 48, 6.4.4
    dual currency instruments, Ch. 48, 6.4.5
    five-year constant maturity bond, Ch. 48, 6.4.2
    fixed rate bond prepayable by the issuer at fair value, Ch. 48, 6.4.5
    full recourse loans secured by collateral, Ch. 48, 6.3.2
    interest rate period, Ch. 48, 6.4.2
    inverse floater, Ch. 48, 6.4.5
    investment in open-ended money market or debt funds, Ch. 48, 6.4.5
    lender has discretion to change the interest rate, Ch. 48, 6.3.4
    meaning of 'interest', Ch. 48, 6.2
    meaning of 'principal,' Ch. 48, 6.1
    modified time value of money component, Ch. 48, 6.4.2
    multiple of a benchmark interest rate, Ch. 48, 6.4.5
    non-genuine features, Ch. 48, 6.4.1.B
    non-recourse loans, Ch. 48, 6.5
    perpetual instruments with potentially deferrable coupons, Ch. 48, 6.4.5
    prepayment, assets originated at a premium or discount, Ch. 48, 6.4.4.B
    prepayment options, Ch. 48, 6.4.4
    prepayment, negative compensation, Ch. 48, 6.4.4.A
    regulated interest rates, Ch. 48, 6.4.3
    term extension options, Ch. 48, 6.4.4
    unleveraged inflation-linked bonds, Ch. 48, 6.3.5
    variable interest rate, Ch. 48, 6.4.4
designation at fair value through profit or loss, Ch. 48, 7
financial assets and liabilities held for trading, Ch. 48, 4
financial assets classification, Ch. 48, 2
    debt instruments, Ch. 48, 2.1
    equity instruments and derivatives, Ch. 48, 2.2
financial liabilities classification, Ch. 48, 3
reclassification of financial assets, Ch. 48, 9

Financial instruments, derecognition, Ch. 52, 1–8. *See also* Derecognition

Financial instruments, derivatives and embedded derivatives, Ch. 46, 1–8
call and put options over noncontrolling interests, Ch. 7, 6. *See also* Non-controlling interests
changes in value in response to changes in underlying, Ch. 46, 2.1
    non-financial variables specific to one party to the contract, Ch. 46, 2.1.3
    notional amounts, Ch. 46, 2.1.1
    underlying variables, Ch. 46, 2.1.2
common derivatives, Ch. 46, 3.1
embedded derivatives, Ch. 46, 4
contracts for the sale of goods or services, Ch. 46, 5.2
    floors and caps, Ch. 46, 5.2.4
    foreign currency derivatives, Ch. 46, 5.2.1
    fund performance fees, Ch. 46, 5.2.5
    inflation-linked features, Ch. 46, 5.2.3
    inputs, ingredients, substitutes and other proxy pricing mechanisms, Ch. 46, 5.2.2
financial instrument hosts, Ch. 46, 5.1
    commodity-and equity-linked interest and principal payments, Ch. 46, 5.1.7
    convertible and exchangeable debt instruments, Ch. 46, 5.1.9
    credit-linked notes, Ch. 46, 5.1.8
    foreign currency monetary items, Ch. 46, 5.1.1
    inflation-linked debt instruments, Ch. 46, 5.1.6
    interest rate floors and caps, Ch. 46, 5.1.5
    interest rate indices, Ch. 46, 5.1.2
    puttable instruments, Ch. 46, 5.1.10
    term extension and similar call, put and prepayment options in debt instruments, Ch. 46, 5.1.14
identifying the terms of embedded derivatives and host contracts, Ch. 46, 6
    embedded non-option derivatives, Ch. 46, 6.1
    embedded option-based derivative, Ch. 46, 6.2
    multiple embedded derivatives, Ch. 46, 6.3
insurance contracts, Ch. 46, 5.4
leases, Ch. 46, 5.3
reassessment, Ch. 46, 7
    acquisition of contracts, Ch. 46, 7.1
    business combinations, Ch. 46, 7.2
    remeasurement issues arising from reassessment, Ch. 46, 7.3
future settlement, Ch. 46, 2.3
initial net investment, Ch. 46, 2.2
in-substance derivatives, Ch. 46, 3.2
linked and separate transactions and 'synthetic' instruments, Ch. 46, 8
prepaid forward purchase of shares, Ch. 46, 2.2
prepaid interest rate swap, Ch. 46, 2.2
regular way contracts, Ch. 46, 3.3

Financial Instruments: disclosures (IFRS 7), Ch. 54, 1–9

Financial instruments, extractive industries, Ch. 43, 13
embedded derivatives, Ch. 43, 13.2
    development of gas markets, Ch. 43, 13.2.4
    foreign currency embedded derivatives, Ch. 43, 13.2.1
    long-term supply contracts, Ch. 43, 13.2.3
    provisionally priced sales contracts, Ch. 43, 13.2.2
hedging sales of metal concentrate (mining), Ch. 43, 13.4
normal purchase and sales exemption, Ch. 43, 13.1
volume flexibility in supply contracts, Ch. 43, 13.3

Financial instruments: financial liabilities and equity, Ch. 47, 1–12
background, Ch. 47, 1.1
classification of instruments, Ch. 47, 4
    consolidated financial statements, Ch. 47, 4.8.1
    contingent settlement provisions, Ch. 47, 4.3
    contractual obligation to deliver cash or other financial assets, Ch. 47, 4.2
    definition of equity instrument, Ch. 47, 4.1
    examples of equity instruments, Ch. 47, 4.4

Financial instruments: financial liabilities and equity—*contd*
   classification of instruments—*contd*
      examples of equity instruments—*contd*
         contracts to issue equity instruments, Ch. 47, 4.4.2
         issued instruments, Ch. 47, 4.4.1
         instruments redeemable
            with a 'dividend blocker,' Ch. 47, 4.5.3.A
            with a 'dividend pusher,' Ch. 47, 4.5.3.B
            mandatorily or at the holder's option, Ch. 47, 4.5.1
            only at the issuer's option or not redeemable, Ch. 47, 4.5.2
         perpetual debt, Ch. 47, 4.7
         preference shares and similar instruments, Ch. 47, 4.5
         puttable instruments and instruments repayable only on liquidation, Ch. 47, 4.6.5
      reclassification of instruments
         change of circumstances, Ch. 47, 4.9.2
         change of terms, Ch. 47, 4.9.1
      single entity financial statements, Ch. 47, 4.8.2
   compound financial instruments, Ch. 47, 6
      background, Ch. 47, 6.1
      common forms of convertible bonds, Ch. 47, 6.6
         bond convertible into fixed percentage of equity, Ch. 47, 6.6.6
         contingent convertible bond, Ch. 47, 6.6.2
         convertible bonds with down round or ratchet features, Ch. 47, 6.6.7
         convertibles with cash settlement at the option of the issuer, Ch. 47, 6.6.5
         foreign currency convertible bond, Ch. 47, 6.6.4
         functional currency bond convertible into a fixed number of shares, Ch. 47, 6.6.1
         mandatorily convertible bond, Ch. 47, 6.6.3
      components, Ch. 47, 6.4
         compound instruments with embedded derivatives, Ch. 47, 6.4.2
         determining the components of a compound instrument, Ch. 47, 6.4.1
      conversion
         at maturity, Ch. 47, 6.3.1
         before maturity, Ch. 47, 6.3.2
         early redemption/repurchase, Ch. 47, 6.3.3
            exercising an embedded call option, Ch. 47, 6.3.3.B
            through negotiation with bondholders, Ch. 47, 6.3.3.A
      initial recognition–'split accounting,' Ch. 47, 6.2
         accounting for the equity component, Ch. 47, 6.2.1
         temporary differences arising from split accounting, Ch. 47, 6.2.2
      modification, Ch. 47, 6.3.4
      treatment by holder and issuer contrasted, Ch. 47, 6.1.1
   contracts accounted for as equity instruments, Ch. 47, 5.1
   contracts accounted for as financial assets or financial liabilities, Ch. 47, 5.2
   definitions, Ch. 47, 3
   derivatives over own equity instruments, Ch. 47, 11
      call options, Ch. 47, 11.2
         purchased call option, Ch. 47, 11.2.1
         written call option, Ch. 47, 11.2.2
      forward contracts, Ch. 47, 11.1
         'back-to-back' forward contracts, Ch. 47, 11.1.3
         forward purchase, Ch. 47, 11.1.1
         forward sale, Ch. 47, 11.1.2
      put options
         purchased put option, Ch. 47, 11.3.1
         written put option, Ch. 47, 11.3.2
   future developments, Ch. 47, 12

Financial Instruments with Characteristics of Equity Research Project (FICE), Ch. 7, 7.3, 7.4, 7.5; Ch. 47, 1, 4.6.6, 5.1.2, 5.3.2A, 6.6.3B, 12
   gross-settled contracts for the sale or issue of the entity's own equity instruments, Ch. 47, 5.4
   'hedging' of instruments classified as equity, Ch. 47, 10
   interest, dividends, gains and losses, Ch. 47, 8
      tax effects, Ch. 47, 8.2
      transaction costs, Ch. 47, 8.1
   liabilities arising from gross-settled contracts for the purchase of the entity's own equity instruments, Ch. 47, 5.3
      contracts to acquire non-controlling interests, Ch. 47, 5.3.2
      contracts to purchase own equity during 'closed' or 'prohibited' periods, Ch. 47, 5.3.1
   objective, Ch. 47, 2.1
   scope, Ch. 47, 2.2
   settlement of financial liability with equity instrument, Ch. 47, 7
      debt for equity swaps with shareholders, Ch. 47, 7.3
      requirements of IFRIC 19, Ch. 47, 7.2
      scope and effective date of IFRIC 19, Ch. 47, 7.1
   treasury shares, Ch. 47, 9
      IFRS 17 Treasury share election, Ch. 47, 9.2
      transactions in own shares not at fair value, Ch. 47, 9.1

Financial instruments: hedge accounting, Ch. 53, 1–14
   accounting for the costs of hedging, Ch. 53, 7.5
      foreign currency basis spreads in financial instruments, Ch. 53, 7.5.3
      forward element of forward contracts, Ch. 53, 7.5.2
      time value of options, Ch. 53, 7.5.1
   aggregated exposures, Ch. 53, 2.7
      accounting for, Ch. 53, 2.7.3
   alternatives to hedge accounting, Ch. 53, 12
      credit risk exposures, Ch. 53, 12.1
      own use contracts, Ch. 53, 12.2
   background, Ch. 53, 1.1
   development of, Ch. 53, 1.3
   discontinuation, Ch. 53, 8.3, 14.5
      of cash flow hedges, Ch. 53, 8.3.2
      of fair value hedges, Ch. 53, 8.3.1
      hedging counterparty within the same consolidated group, Ch. 53, 8.3.7
      hedged net investment, disposal of, Ch. 53, 8.3.8
      novation to central clearing parties, Ch. 53, 8.3.5
      settle to market derivatives, Ch. 53, 8.3.6
   economic relationship, Ch. 53, 6.4.1
   effective hedges, accounting for, Ch. 53, 7
      cash flow hedges, Ch. 53, 7.2
         acquisition or disposal of subsidiaries, Ch. 53, 7.2.4
         all-in-one hedges, Ch. 53, 5.2.1
         discontinuing, Ch. 53, 8.3.2
         firm commitments, hedges of, Ch. 53, 5.2.2
         foreign currency monetary items, Ch. 53, 5.2.3

hypothetical derivatives, Ch. 53, 7.4.4
measuring ineffectiveness of, Ch. 53, 7.4.6
of a net position, Ch. 53, 2.5.3
novation of, due to central clearing regulations, Ch. 53, 8.3.5
ongoing accounting, Ch. 53, 7.2.1
presentation, Ch. 53, 10.1
reclassification of gains and losses, Ch. 53, 7.2.2
documented rollover hedging strategy, Ch. 53, 7.7
equity instrument designated at fair value through OCI, Ch. 53, 7.8
fair value hedges, Ch. 53, 1.5, 5.1, 7.1
adjustments to the hedged item, Ch. 53, 7.1.2
discontinuing, Ch. 53, 8.3.1
firm commitments, Ch. 53, 5.1.1
foreign currency monetary items, Ch. 53, 5.1.2
layer components for, Ch. 53, 2.3.2
ongoing accounting, Ch. 53, 7.1.1
presentation, Ch. 53, 10.2
hedges of a firm commitment to acquire a business, Ch. 53, 7.6
hedges of a net investment in a foreign operation, accounting for, Ch. 7, 2.3; Ch. 53, 1.5, 5.3, 7.3, 8.3.7
effective date and transition, Ch. 53, 13
limited retrospective application, Ch. 53, 13.3
prospective application in general, Ch. 53, 13.2
effectiveness assessment, Ch. 53, 8.1, 6.4
credit risk dominance, Ch. 53, 6.4.2
economic relationship, Ch. 53, 6.4.1
hedge ratio, Ch. 53, 6.4.3
effectiveness measurement, Ch. 53, 7.4
calculation of, Ch. 53, 7.4.6
'clean' vs. 'dirty' values, Ch. 53, 7.4.10
comparison of spot rate and forward rate methods, Ch. 53, 7.4.7
discount rates for calculating the change in value of the hedged item, Ch. 53, 7.4.5
effectiveness of options, Ch. 53, 7.4.11
foreign currency basis spreads, Ch. 53, 7.4.8
hedged items with embedded optionality, Ch. 53, 7.4.12
hedging instrument's impact on credit quality, Ch. 53, 7.4.9
hedging using instruments with a non-zero fair value, Ch. 53, 7.4.3
hypothetical derivatives, Ch. 53, 7.4.4
time value of money, Ch. 53, 7.4.2
hedged items, Ch. 53, 2
core deposits, Ch. 53, 2.6.7
held at fair value through profit or loss, Ch. 53, 2.6.2
held at fair value through OCI, Ch. 53, 2.6.3
firm commitment to acquire a business, Ch. 53, 7.6
forecast acquisition/issuance of foreign currency monetary items, Ch. 53, 2.6.5
general requirements, Ch. 53, 2.1
groups of items, Ch. 53, 2.5
cash flow hedge of a net position, Ch. 53, 2.5.3
general requirements, Ch. 53, 2.5.1
hedging a component of a group, Ch. 53, 2.5.2
nil net positions, Ch. 53, 2.5.4
highly probable, Ch. 53, 2.6.1
internal, Ch. 53, 4.3
nominal components. Ch. 53, 2.3
general requirement, Ch. 53, 2.3.1
layer component for fair value hedge, Ch. 53, 2.3.2
own equity instruments, Ch. 53, 2.6.6
risk components, Ch. 53, 2.2
contractually specified, Ch. 53, 2.2.2
foreign currency as, Ch. 53, 2.2.5
general requirements, Ch. 53, 2.2.1
inflation as, Ch. 53, 2.2.6
interest rate, Ch. 53, 2.2.7
non-contractually specified, Ch. 53, 2.2.3
partial term hedging, Ch. 53, 2.2.4
sub-LIBOR issue, Ch. 53, 2.4
negative interest rates, Ch. 53, 2.4.2
hedge ratio, Ch. 53, 6.4.3
hedging instruments, Ch. 53, 3
combinations of instruments, Ch. 53, 3.5
derivatives, Ch. 53, 3.2
basis swaps, Ch. 53, 3.2.5
credit break clauses, Ch. 53, 3.2.4
principal resetting cross currency swaps, Ch. 53, 3.2.4.A
embedded derivatives, Ch. 53, 3.2.3
net written options, Ch. 53, 3.2.2
offsetting external derivatives, Ch. 53, 3.2.1
embedded derivatives, Ch. 53, 3.2.3
general requirements, Ch. 53, 3.1
hedging different risks with one instrument, Ch. 53, 3.6.2
non-derivative financial instruments, Ch. 53, 3.3
of foreign currency risk, Ch. 53, 3.3.1
non-derivative liabilities, Ch. 53, 3.3
own equity instruments, Ch. 53, 3.4
portions and proportions of, Ch. 53, 3.6
different risks with one instrument, Ch. 53, 3.6.2
foreign currency basis spread, Ch. 53, 3.6.5
interest elements of forwards, Ch. 53, 3.6.5
portion of a time period, Ch. 53, 3.6.6
proportions of instruments, Ch. 53, 3.6.1
restructuring of derivatives, Ch. 53, 3.6.3
time value of options, Ch. 53, 3.6.4
hedging relationships, types of, Ch. 53, 5
cash flow hedges, Ch. 53, 5.2
all-in-one hedges, Ch. 53, 5.2.1
firm commitments hedges, Ch. 53, 5.2.2
foreign currency monetary items, Ch. 53, 5.2.3
fair value hedges, Ch. 53, 5.1
firm commitments, hedges of, Ch. 53, 5.1.1
foreign currency monetary items, hedges of, Ch. 53, 5.1.2
hedges of net investments in foreign operations, Ch. 53, 5.3
amount of the hedged item for which a hedging relationship may be designated, Ch. 53, 5.3.2
nature of the hedged risk, Ch. 53, 5.3.1
where the hedging instrument can be held, Ch. 53, 5.3.3
ineffectiveness, measuring, Ch. 53, 7.4
interbank Offered Rate Reform (IBOR), Ch. 53, 9
internal hedges and other group accounting issues, Ch. 53, 4
central clearing parties, Ch. 53, 4.1.1
external hedging instruments, offsetting, Ch. 53, 4.2

Financial instruments: hedge accounting—*contd*
    internal hedges and other group accounting issues—*contd*
        hedged item and hedging instrument held by different group entities, Ch. 53, 4.4
        internal hedged items, Ch. 53, 4.3
        internal hedging instruments, Ch. 53, 4.1
        offsetting internal hedges instruments, Ch. 53, 4.2
    macro hedging, Ch. 53, 11
        accounting for dynamic risk management, Ch. 53, 11.1
        macro hedging strategies under IFRS 9, Ch. 53, 11.2
    main differences between IFRS 9 and IAS 39 hedge accounting requirements, Ch. 53, 14
        discontinuation, Ch. 53, 14.5
        effectiveness criteria, Ch. 53, 14.4
        eligible hedged items, Ch. 53, 14.2
        eligible hedging instruments, Ch. 53, 14.3
        hedge accounting mechanisms, Ch. 53, 14.6
        objective of hedge accounting, Ch. 53, 14.1
    portfolio/macro hedging, Ch. 53, 11
    objective of, Ch. 53, 1.4
    overview, Ch. 53, 1.5
    own use contracts, Ch. 53, 12.2
    presentation, Ch. 53, 10
        cash flow hedges, Ch. 53, 10.1
        cost of hedging, Ch. 53, 10.4
        fair value hedges, Ch. 53, 10.2
        hedges of groups of items, Ch. 53, 10.3
    proxy hedges, Ch. 53, 6.2.1
    qualifying criteria, Ch. 53, 6
        credit risk dominance, Ch. 53, 6.4.2
            on the hedged item, Ch. 53, 6.4.2.B
            on the hedging instrument, Ch. 53, 6.4.2.A
        designating 'proxy hedges', Ch. 53, 6.2.1
        documentation and designation, Ch. 53, 6.3
            business combinations, Ch. 53, 6.3.1
            dynamic hedging strategies, Ch. 53, 6.3.2
            forecast transactions, Ch. 53, 6.3.3
        economic relationship, Ch. 53, 6.4.1
        general requirements, Ch. 53, 6.1
        hedge effectiveness requirements, Ch. 53, 6.4
            credit risk dominance, Ch. 53, 6.4.2
            economic relationship, Ch. 53, 6.4.1
            hedge ratio, Ch. 53, 6.4.3
        proxy hedging, Ch. 53, 6.2.1
        risk management strategy, Ch. 53, 6.2
        risk management objective, Ch. 53, 6.2
        setting the hedge ratio, Ch. 53, 6.4.3
    rebalancing, Ch. 53, 8.2
        definition, Ch. 53, 8.2.1
        mechanics of, Ch. 53, 8.2.3
        requirement to rebalance, Ch. 53, 8.2.2
    risk management, Ch. 53, 6.2, 6.3
        proxy hedges, Ch. 53, 6.2.1
        risk management objective, Ch. 53, 6.2
            change in, Ch. 53, 8.3
        risk management strategy, Ch. 53, 6.2
    standards, development of, Ch. 53, 1.3

Financial instruments: presentation and disclosure, Ch. 54, 1–9
    disclosures, structuring, Ch. 54, 3
        classes of financial instrument, Ch. 54, 3.3
        level of detail, Ch. 54, 3.1
        materiality, Ch. 54, 3.2
    effective date and transitional provisions, Ch. 54, 8
    future developments, Ch. 54, 9
    interim reports, Ch. 54, 2.3
    nature and extent of risks arising from financial instruments, Ch. 54, 5
        credit risk, Ch. 54, 5.3
            collateral and other credit enhancements obtained, Ch. 54, 5.3.5
            credit risk exposure, Ch. 54, 5.3.4
            credit risk management practices, Ch. 54, 5.3.2
            illustrative disclosures, Ch. 54, 5.3.6
            quantitative and qualitative information about amounts arising from expected credit losses, Ch. 54, 5.3.3
            scope and objectives, Ch. 54, 5.3.1
        liquidity risk, Ch. 54, 5.4
            information provided to key management, Ch. 54, 5.4.1
            management of associated liquidity risk, Ch. 54, 5.4.3
            maturity analyses, Ch. 54, 5.4.2
            puttable financial instruments classified as equity, Ch. 54, 5.4.4
        market risk, Ch. 54, 5.5
            'basic' sensitivity analysis, Ch. 54, 5.5.1
            other market risk disclosures, Ch. 54, 5.5.3
            value-at-risk and similar analyses, Ch. 54, 5.5.2
        qualitative disclosures, Ch. 54, 5.1
        quantitative disclosures, Ch. 54, 5.2, 5.6
            capital disclosures, Ch. 54, 5.6.3
            concentrations of risk, Ch. 54, 5.6.1
            operational risk, Ch. 54, 5.6.2
    presentation on the face of the financial statements and related disclosures, Ch. 54, 7
        gains and losses recognised in other comprehensive income, Ch. 54, 7.2
        gains and losses recognised in profit/loss, Ch. 54, 7.1
            embedded derivatives, Ch. 54, 7.1.4
            entities whose share capital is not equity, Ch. 54, 7.1.5
            further analysis of gains and losses recognised in profit/loss, Ch. 54, 7.1.2
            offsetting and hedges, Ch. 54, 7.1.3
            presentation on the face of the statement of comprehensive income (or income statement), Ch. 54, 7.1.1
    significance of financial instruments for an entity's financial position/performance, Ch. 54, 4
        accounting policies, Ch. 54, 4.1
        business combinations, Ch. 54, 4.6
            acquired receivables, Ch. 54, 4.6.1
            contingent consideration and indemnification assets, Ch. 54, 4.6.2
        day 1 profits, Ch. 54, 4.5.2
        fair values, Ch. 54, 4.5
        general disclosure requirements, Ch. 54, 4.5.1
        hedge accounting, Ch. 54, 4.3
            amount, timing and uncertainty of future cash flows, Ch. 54, 4.3.2
            effects of hedge accounting on financial position and performance, Ch. 54, 4.3.3

option to designate a credit exposure as measured at fair value through profit/loss, Ch. 54, 4.3.4
risk management strategy, Ch. 54, 4.3.1
uncertainty arising from interest rate benchmark (or IBOR) reform, Ch. 54, 4.3.5
income, expenses, gains and losses, Ch. 54, 4.2
fee income and expense, Ch. 54, 4.2.3
gains and losses by measurement category, Ch. 54, 4.2.1
interest income and expense, Ch. 54, 4.2.2
statement of cash flows, Ch. 54, 7.5
statement of changes in equity, Ch. 54, 7.3
statement of financial position, Ch. 54, 7.4, , Ch. 54, 4.4
assets and liabilities, Ch. 54, 7.4.3
categories of financial assets and financial liabilities, Ch. 54, 4.4.1
collateral, Ch. 54, 4.4.6
compound financial instruments with multiple embedded derivatives, Ch. 54, 4.4.7
current and non-current assets and liabilities, distinction between, Ch. 54, 7.4.4
convertible loans, Ch. 54, 7.4.4.B
debt with refinancing or roll over agreements, Ch. 54, 7.4.4.D
derivatives, Ch. 54, 7.4.4.A
A loan covenants, Ch. 54, 7.4.4.E
long-term loans with repayment on demand terms, Ch. 54, 7.4.4.C
defaults and breaches of loans payable, Ch. 54, 4.4.8
disclosure requirements, Ch. 54, 7.4.2.C
enforceable legal right of set-off, Ch. 54, 7.4.1.A
entities whose share capital is not equity, Ch. 54, 7.4.6
equity, Ch. 54, 7.4.5
financial assets designated as measured at fair value through profit/loss, Ch. 54, 4.4.3
financial liabilities designated at fair value through profit/loss, Ch. 54, 4.4.2
intention to settle net, Ch. 54, 7.4.1.C
interests in associates and joint ventures accounted for in accordance with IFRS 9, Ch. 54, 4.4.9
investments in equity instruments designated at fair value through other comprehensive income (IFRS 9), Ch. 54, 4.4.4
master netting agreements, Ch. 54, 7.4.1.B
objective, Ch. 54, 7.4.2.A
offsetting collateral amounts, Ch. 54, 7.4.1.F
offsetting financial assets and financial liabilities, Ch. 54, 7.4.1
offsetting financial assets and financial liabilities: disclosure, Ch. 54, 7.4.2
reclassification, Ch. 54, 4.4.5
scope, Ch. 54, 7.4.2.B
situations where offset is not normally appropriate, Ch. 54, 7.4.1.D
unit of account, Ch. 54, 7.4.1.G
transfers of financial assets, Ch. 54, 6
meaning of 'transfer,' Ch. 54, 6.1
transferred financial assets that are derecognised in their entirety, Ch. 54, 6.3
disclosure requirements, Ch. 54, 6.3.2
meaning of continuing involvement, Ch. 54, 6.3.1
transferred financial assets that are not derecognised in their entirety, Ch. 54, 6.2
transitional provisions, Ch. 54, 8

Financial instruments: recognition and initial measurement, Ch. 49, 1–3
initial measurement (IFRS 9), Ch. 49, 3
assets and liabilities arising from loan commitments, Ch. 49, 3.7
embedded derivatives and financial instrument hosts, Ch. 49, 3.5
general requirements, Ch. 49, 3.1
initial fair value and 'day 1' profits, Ch. 49, 3.3
financial guarantee contracts and off-market loan commitments, Ch. 49, 3.3.3
interest-free and low-interest long-term loans, Ch. 49, 3.3.1
loans and receivables acquired in a business combination, Ch. 49, 3.3.4
measurement of financial instruments following modification of contractual terms, Ch. 49, 3.3.2
regular way transactions, Ch. 49, 3.6
transaction costs, Ch. 49, 3.4
recognition (IFRS 9), Ch. 49, 2
general requirements, Ch. 49, 2.1
cash collateral, Ch. 49, 2.1.7
firm commitments to purchase/sell goods/services, Ch. 49, 2.1.2
forward contracts, Ch. 49, 2.1.3
option contracts, Ch. 49, 2.1.4
planned future/forecast transactions, Ch. 49, 2.1.5
principal versus agent, Ch. 49, 2.1.8
receivables and payables, Ch. 49, 2.1.1
transfers of financial assets not qualifying for derecognition by transferor, Ch. 49, 2.1.6
'regular way' transactions, Ch. 49, 2.2
exchanges of non-cash financial assets, Ch. 49, 2.2.5.A
financial liabilities, Ch. 49, 2.2.2
general requirements, Ch. 49, 2.2.1
settlement date accounting, Ch. 49, 2.2.4
trade date accounting, Ch. 49, 2.2.3

Financial instruments: subsequent measurement
amortised cost and the effective interest method, Ch. 50, 3
fixed interest rate instruments, Ch. 50, 3.2
floating rate instruments, Ch. 50, 3.3
inflation-linked debt, Ch. 50, 3.6
more complex financial liabilities, Ch. 50, 3.7
perpetual debt instruments, Ch. 50, 3.5
prepayment, call and similar options, Ch. 50, 3.4
revisions to estimated cash flows, Ch. 50, 3.4.1
foreign currencies, Ch. 50, 4
foreign entities, Ch. 50, 4.2
instruments, Ch. 50, 4.1
and recognition of gains and losses, Ch. 50, 2
financial assets and financial liabilities at fair value through profit/loss, Ch. 50, 2.4
financial guarantees and commitments to provide a loan at a below-market interest rate, Ch. 50, 2.8
reclassification of financial assets, Ch. 50, 2.7

Financial liabilities and equity, Ch. 47, 1–12. *See also* Equity instruments; Financial assets; IAS 32

Financial liabilities and equity—*contd*
  background, Ch. 47, 1.1
  classification, Ch. 48, 3
  classification of instruments
    consolidated financial statements, Ch. 47, 4.8.1
    contingent settlement provisions, Ch. 47, 4.3
      contingencies that are 'not genuine,' Ch. 47, 4.3.1
      liabilities that arise only on a change of control, Ch. 47, 4.3.3
      liabilities that arise only on liquidation, Ch. 47, 4.3.2
      some typical contingent settlement provisions, Ch. 47, 4.3.4
    contractual obligation to deliver cash or other financial assets, Ch. 47, 4.2
      implied contractual obligation to deliver cash or other financial assets, Ch. 47, 4.2.2
      relationship between an entity and its members, Ch. 47, 4.2.1
    definition of equity instrument, Ch. 47, 4.1
    examples of equity instruments
      contracts to issue equity instruments, Ch. 47, 4.4.2
      issued instruments, Ch. 47, 4.4.1
    IFRS development on, Ch. 47, 12
    instruments redeemable
      with a 'dividend blocker,' Ch. 47, 4.5.3.A
      with a 'dividend pusher,' Ch. 47, 4.5.3.B
      mandatorily or at the holder's option, Ch. 47, 4.5.1
      only at the issuer's option or not redeemable, Ch. 47, 4.5.2
    perpetual debt, Ch. 47, 4.7
    preference shares and similar instruments, Ch. 47, 4.5
      'change of control,' 'taxation change' and 'regulatory change' clauses, Ch. 47, 4.5.8
      economic compulsion, Ch. 47, 4.5.6
      instruments redeemable mandatorily or at the holder's option, Ch. 47, 4.5.1
      'linked' instruments, Ch. 47, 4.5.7
      perpetual instruments with a 'step-up' clause, Ch. 47, 4.5.4
      relative subordination, Ch. 47, 4.5.5
    puttable instruments and instruments repayable only on liquidation IFRIC 2, Ch. 47, 4.6.6
      instruments entitling the holder to a pro rata share of net assets only on liquidation, Ch. 47, 4.6.3
      instruments issued by a subsidiary, Ch. 47, 4.6.4.A
      instruments that substantially fix or restrict the residual return to the holder of an instrument, Ch. 47, 4.6.4.E
      issue, Ch. 47, 4.6.1
      meaning of 'identical features,' Ch. 47, 4.6.4.C
      no obligation to deliver cash or another financial asset, Ch. 47, 4.6.4.D
      puttable instruments, Ch. 47, 4.6.2
      reclassification, Ch. 47, 4.6.5
      relative subordination of the instrument, Ch. 47, 4.6.4.B
      transactions entered into by an instrument holder other than as owner of the entity, Ch. 47, 4.6.4.F
    reclassification of instruments
      change of circumstances, Ch. 47, 4.9.2
      change of terms, Ch. 47, 4.9.1
    single entity financial statements, Ch. 47, 4.8.2
  compound financial instruments, Ch. 47, 6
    background, Ch. 47, 6.1
    common forms of convertible bonds, Ch. 47, 6.6
      bond convertible into fixed percentage of equity, Ch. 47, 6.6.6
      contingent convertible bond, Ch. 47, 6.6.2
      convertible bonds with down round or ratchet features, Ch. 47, 6.6.7
      convertibles with cash settlement at the option of the issuer, Ch. 47, 6.6.5
      foreign currency convertible bond, Ch. 47, 6.6.4
      functional currency bond convertible into a fixed number of shares, Ch. 47, 6.6.1
      mandatorily convertible bond, Ch. 47, 6.6.3
    components, Ch. 47, 6.4
      compound instruments with embedded derivatives, Ch. 47, 6.4.2
      determining the components of a compound instrument, Ch. 47, 6.4.1
    conversion
      at maturity, Ch. 47, 6.3.1
      before maturity, Ch. 47, 6.3.2
    early redemption/repurchase, Ch. 47, 6.3.3
      exercising an embedded call option, Ch. 47, 6.3.3.B
      through negotiation with bondholders, Ch. 47, 6.3.3.A
    initial recognition–'split accounting,' Ch. 47, 6.2
      accounting for the equity component, Ch. 47, 6.2.1
      temporary differences arising from split accounting, Ch. 47, 6.2.2
    modification, Ch. 47, 6.3.4
    treatment by holder and issuer contrasted, Ch. 47, 6.1.1
  contracts accounted for as equity instruments, Ch. 47, 5.1
    comparison with IFRS 2–share-based payment, Ch. 47, 5.1.1
    exchange of fixed amounts of equity (equity for equity), Ch. 47, 5.1.4
    number of equity instruments issued adjusted for capital, Ch. 47, 5.1.2
    restructuring or other event, Ch. 47, 5.1.2
    stepped up exercise price, Ch. 47, 5.1.3
  contracts accounted for as financial assets or financial liabilities, Ch. 47, 5.2
    derivative financial instruments with settlement options, Ch. 47, 5.2.8
    fixed amount of cash (or other financial assets) denominated in a currency other than the entity's functional currency, Ch. 47, 5.2.3
    fixed amount of cash determined by reference to share price, Ch. 47, 5.2.6
    fixed number of equity instruments for variable consideration, Ch. 47, 5.2.2
    fixed number of equity instruments with variable value, Ch. 47, 5.2.5
    instrument with equity settlement alternative of significantly higher value than cash settlement alternative, Ch. 47, 5.2.4
    net-settled contracts over own equity, Ch. 47, 5.2.7
    variable number of equity instruments, Ch. 47, 5.2.1
  definitions, Ch. 45, 2.1; Ch. 47, 3; Ch. 52, 2.1

derecognition, Ch. 52, 6. *See also* Derecognition
   derivatives that can be financial assets or financial
      liabilities, Ch. 52, 6.4
   exchange or modification of debt by original lender,
      Ch. 52, 6.2
      costs and fees, Ch. 52, 6.2.5
      examples, Ch. 52, 6.2.7
      exchange of debt through an intermediary, Ch. 52,
         6.2.4
      Interbank Offered Rate (IBOR) Reform, Ch. 52, 6.2.2
      loan syndications, Ch. 52, 6.2.3
      modification gains and losses, Ch. 52, 6.2.6
      settlement of financial liability with issue of new equity
         instrument, Ch. 52, 6.2.8
   extinguishment of debt, Ch. 52, 6.1
      extinguishment in exchange for transfer of assets not
         meeting the derecognition criteria, Ch. 52, 6.1.4
      'in-substance defeasance' arrangements, Ch. 52, 6.1.3
      legal release by creditor, Ch. 52, 6.1.2
      what constitutes 'part' of a liability?, Ch. 52, 6.1.1
   gains and losses on extinguishment of debt, Ch. 52, 6.3
   supply-chain finance, Ch. 52, 6.5
derivatives over own equity instruments, Ch. 47, 11
   call options, Ch. 47, 11.2
      call options over non-controlling interest, Ch. 7, 6.1,
         6.3, 6.4, 6.5
      purchased call option, Ch. 47, 11.2.1
      written call option, Ch. 47, 11.2.2
   forward contracts, Ch. 47, 11.1
      'back-to-back' forward contracts, Ch. 47, 11.1.3
      forward purchase, Ch. 47, 11.1.1
      forward sale, Ch. 47, 11.2
   put options, Ch. 47, 11.3
      purchased put option, Ch. 47, 11.3.1
      put options over noncontrolling interest, Ch. 7, 6.2,
         6.3, 6.4, 6.5
      written put option, Ch. 47, 11.3.2
designated at fair value through profit/loss, Ch. 54, 4.4.2;
   Ch. 50, 2.4
dividends payable on shares classified as, Ch. 21, 5.5.4
Financial Instruments with Characteristics of Equity Research
   Project (FICE), Ch. 7, 7.3, 7.4, 7.5; Ch. 47, 1, 4.6.6,
   5.1.2, 5.3.2A, 6.6.3B, 12
future developments, Ch. 47, 12
gross-settled contracts for the sale or issue of the entity's own
   equity instruments, Ch. 47, 5.4
'hedging' of instruments classified as equity, Ch. 47, 10
held for trading, Ch. 48, 4
interest, dividends, gains and losses, Ch. 47, 8
   tax effects, Ch. 47, 8.2
   transaction costs, Ch. 47, 8.1
liabilities arising from gross-settled contracts for the purchase
   of the entity's own equity instruments, Ch. 47, 5.3
   contracts to acquire non-controlling interests, Ch. 47,
      5.3.2
   contracts to purchase own equity during 'closed' or
      'prohibited' periods, Ch. 47, 5.3.1
non-controlling interests classified as, Ch. 7, 5.5, 6.2, 6.3, 6.4
objective, Ch. 47, 2.1
offsetting, Ch. 54, 7.4.1
   cash pooling arrangements, Ch. 54, 7.4.1.E
   disclosure, Ch. 54, 7.4.2
   enforceable legal right of set-off, Ch. 54, 7.4.1.A
   intention to settle net, Ch. 54, 7.4.1.C
   master netting agreements, Ch. 54, 7.4.1.B
   offsetting collateral amounts, Ch. 54, 7.4.1.F
   situations where offset is not normally appropriate, Ch. 54,
      7.4.1.D
   unit of account, Ch. 54, 7.4.1.G
recognition, Ch. 49, 2.2.2
scope, Ch. 47, 2.2
settlement of financial liability with equity instrument,
   Ch. 47, 7
   debt for equity swaps with shareholders, Ch. 47, 7.3
   requirements of IFRIC 19, Ch. 47, 7.2
   scope and effective date of IFRIC 19, Ch. 47, 7.1
   shares/warrants issued in connection with, Ch. 34, 2.2.4.I
treasury shares, Ch. 47, 9
   IFRS 17 Treasury share election, Ch. 47, 9.2
   transactions in own shares not at fair value, Ch. 47, 9.1
Financial reporting in hyperinflationary economies, Ch. 16,
   1–12. *See also* Hyperinflation
Financial Service Agency, Japan, Ch. 1, 2.3
Financial Service Commission, Republic of Korea, Ch. 1, 2.3
Financial statements, Ch. 3, 2–3.4. *See also* IAS 1; IAS 8; IAS 10;
   Income statement; Statement of comprehensive income;
   Statement of financial position comparative information,
   Ch. 3, 2.4
   components of, Ch. 3, 2.3
   conceptual framework, IASB's, Ch. 2.6.1
      assets, Ch. 2.7.2
      consolidated and unconsolidated, Ch. 2.6.2.1
      elements, Ch. 2.7
      equity, Ch. 2.7.4
      executory contracts, Ch. 2.7.1.2
      going concern assumption, Ch. 2.6.1.4
      income and expenses, Ch. 2.7.5
      liabilities, Ch. 2.7.3
      objective and scope, Ch. 2.6.1.1
      perspective adopted in financial statements, Ch. 2.6.1.3
      reporting period and comparative information, Ch. 2.6.1.2
      substance of contractual rights and contractual obligations,
         Ch. 2.7.1.3
      unit of account, Ch. 2.7.1.1
   date when financial statements are authorised for issue,
      Ch. 38, 2.1.1
   events requiring adjustment to the amounts
      recognised/disclosures in, Ch. 38, 2.2.1
   first IFRS financial statements in scope of IFRS 1, Ch. 5, 2.1
   frequency of reporting and period covered, Ch. 3, 2.2
   identification of, Ch. 3, 2.5.1
   notes to, Ch. 3, 3.4
   purpose of, Ch. 3, 2.1
   re-issuing (dual dating), Ch. 38, 2.1.1.B
   statement of changes in equity, Ch. 3, 3.3
   statement of compliance with IFRS, Ch. 3, 2.5.2
   statement of comprehensive income and income statement,
      Ch. 3, 3.2
   statement of financial position, Ch. 3, 3.1
   structure of, Ch. 3, 3
Financial statements, presentation of, Ch. 3, 2–3. *See also* IAS 1

Financial statements, presentation of—*contd*
   comparative information, Ch. 3, 2.4
   components of a complete set of financial statements, Ch. 3, 2.3
   frequency of reporting and period covered, Ch. 3, 2.2 IAS 1, Ch. 3, 1.1
   IAS 8, Ch. 3, 1.2
   identification of, Ch. 3, 2.5.1
   purpose of, Ch. 3, 2.1
   statement of compliance with IFRS, Ch. 3, 2.5.2
   structure of financial statements, Ch. 3, 3
      notes to the financial statements, Ch. 3, 3.4
      statement of changes in equity, Ch. 3, 3.3
      statement of comprehensive income and the statement of profit or loss, Ch. 3, 3.2
         classification of expenses recognised in profit or loss by nature or function, Ch. 3, 3.2.3
         discontinued operations, Ch. 3, 3.2.5
         information required on the face of the statement of profit or loss, Ch. 3, 3.2.2
         material and extraordinary items, Ch. 3, 3.2.6
         operating profit, Ch. 3, 3.2.2.A
         profit and loss and comprehensive income, Ch. 3, 3.2.1
         statement of comprehensive income, Ch. 3, 3.2.4
      statement of financial position, Ch. 3, 3.1
         current assets, Ch. 3, 3.1.3
         current liabilities, Ch. 3, 3.1.4
         current/non-current assets and liabilities, distinction between, Ch. 3, 3.1.1
         information required either on the face of the statement of financial position or in the notes, Ch. 3, 3.1.6
         information required on the face of statement of financial position, Ch. 3, 3.1.5
         non-current assets and disposal groups held for sale/distribution, Ch. 3, 3.1.2
Financing activities, cash flows from, Ch. 40, 4.3
Firm commitments
   to acquire a business, hedges of, Ch. 53, 7.6
   hedges of, Ch. 53, 5.1.1, 5.2.2
   to purchase or sell goods or services, Ch. 49, 2.1.2
First-time adoption, Ch. 5, 1–8. *See also* IFRS 1
   actuarial assumptions, Ch. 5, 7.7.3
   authoritative literature, Ch. 5, 1.2
   business combinations, Ch. 5, 5.2
   classification and measurement of financial instruments, Ch. 5, 4.9
   compound financial instruments, Ch. 5, 5.10
   consolidated financial statements, Ch. 5, 5.8.1
   cumulative translation differences, Ch. 5, 5.7
   date of transition to IFRSs, Ch. 5, 5.5.1.B
   deemed cost, Ch. 5, 5.5
   defined terms, Ch. 5, 1.3
   derecognition of financial assets and financial liabilities, Ch. 5, 4.3
   embedded derivatives, Ch. 5, 4.11
   employee benefits, Ch. 5, 7.7
   estimates, Ch. 5, 4.2
   fair value, Ch. 5, 3.3, 5.5.1
   first IFRS financial statements, Ch. 5, 2.1
   first IFRS reporting period, Ch. 5, 7.2.1
   first-time adopter, identifying, Ch. 5, 2
      application of IFRS 1, Ch. 5, 2.2
      dual reporting entity, Ch. 5, 2.3
      first IFRS financial statements in scope of IFRS 1, Ch. 5, 2.1
      previous GAAP, determining, Ch. 5, 2.3
   full actuarial valuations, Ch. 5, 7.7.2
   full retrospective application, Ch. 5, 3.5
   government loans, Ch. 5, 4.12
   hedge accounting, Ch. 5, 4.4, 4.5, 4.6, 4.7
   insurance contracts, Ch. 5, 4.13, 5.4
   interim financial reports, Ch. 5, 6.6
   leases, Ch. 5, 5.6
   line-by-line reconciliations, Ch. 5, 6.3.2
   mandatory exceptions, Ch. 5, 3.5, 4.1
   measurement, Ch. 5, 4.9
   non-controlling interests, Ch. 5, 4.8
   objectives of, Ch. 5, 1.1
   opening IFRS statement of financial position, Ch. 5, 3
      accounting policies, applying, Ch. 5, 3.2
      timeline, Ch. 5, 3.1
   optional exemptions, Ch. 5, 5
   regulatory issues
      foreign private issuers that are SEC registrants, Ch. 5, 8.1
      International Practices Task Force (IPTF) guidance, Ch. 5, 8.1.2
   related hedges, gains and losses arising on, Ch. 5, 5.7.1
   restatement of goodwill, Ch. 5, 5.2.5
   revenue from contracts with customers, Ch. 5, 5.21
   separate financial statements, Ch. 5, 5.8.2
   timeline, Ch. 5, 3.1
   unrecognised past service costs, Ch. 5, 7.7.4
First-time presentation of interim reports, Ch. 41, 11.1
Fixed fee service contracts, Ch. 55, 3.5.1
Fixed interest rate instruments, Ch. 50, 3.2
'Fixed stated principal' of a bond, Ch. 47, 6.3.2.A
Floating interest rate instruments, Ch. 50, 3.3
Foreign currency basis spreads, Ch. 53, 3.6.5, 7.4.8, 7.5.3
   retrospective application, Ch. 53, 13.3.3
Foreign currency cash flows
   impairment, Ch. 20, 7.1.5
   statement of cash flows, Ch. 40, 5.3
Foreign currency convertible bond, Ch. 47, 6.6.4
   instrument issued by foreign subsidiary convertible into equity of parent, Ch. 47, 6.6.4.A
Foreign currency derivatives, Ch. 46, 5.2.1
   commonly used currencies, Ch. 46, 5.2.1.C
   functional currency of counterparty, Ch. 46, 5.2.1.A
   oil contract, Ch. 46, 5.2.1.D
   routinely denominated in commercial transactions, Ch. 46, 5.2.1.B
Foreign currency instruments, Ch. 50, 4.1
   debt security measured at fair value through other comprehensive income, Ch. 51, 14.3
Foreign currency translation, interim financial reporting, Ch. 41, 9.6

Foreign entities, subsequent measurement of financial instruments, Ch. 50, 4
    IFRS 9, Ch. 51, 1.2
Foreign exchange, Ch. 15, 1–11. *See also* IAS 21
    background, Ch. 15, 1.1
    change in functional currency, Ch. 15, 5.5
    change of presentation currency, Ch. 15, 7
    disclosure requirements, Ch. 15, 10
        convenience translations of financial statements/other financial information, Ch. 15, 10.3
        exchange differences, Ch. 15, 10.1
        judgements made in applying IAS 21 and related disclosures, Ch. 15, 10.4
        presentation and functional currency, Ch. 15, 10.2
    entity's functional currency determination, Ch. 15, 4
        branches and divisions, Ch. 15, 4.4
        documentation of judgements made, Ch. 15, 4.5
        general, Ch. 15, 4.1
        intermediate holding companies/finance subsidiaries, Ch. 15, 4.2
        investment holding companies, Ch. 15, 4.3
    future developments, Ch. 15, 11
    introduction of euro, Ch. 15, 8
    monetary/non-monetary determination, Ch. 15, 5.4
        deferred tax, Ch. 15, 5.4.5
        deposits and advance payments for actively traded commodities, Ch. 15, 5.4.2
        deposits/progress payments, Ch. 15, 5.4.1
        foreign currency share capital, Ch. 15, 5.4.4
        investments in preference shares, Ch. 15, 5.4.3
        post-employment benefit plans-foreign currency assets, Ch. 15, 5.4.6
        post-employment benefit plans-foreign currency plans, Ch. 15, 5.4.7
    presentation currency other than the functional currency, Ch. 15, 6
        average rate calculation, Ch. 15, 6.1.4
        disposal of a foreign operation, Ch. 15, 6.6; Ch. 7, 2.3, 3.5
            partial disposal, Ch. 15, 6.6.2; Ch. 7, 2.3, 4.1
            step-by-step and direct methods of consolidation, Ch. 15, 6.6.3; Ch. 7, 2.3
        exchange differences on intragroup balances, Ch. 15, 6.3
            becoming part of the net investment in a foreign operation, Ch. 15, 6.3.1.F
            ceasing to be part of the net investment in a foreign operation, Ch. 15, 6.3.61.G
            currency of monetary item, Ch. 15, 6.3.1.C dividends, Ch. 15, 6.3.2
            monetary items included as part of the net investment in a foreign operation, Ch. 15, 6.3.1
            transacted by other members of the group, Ch. 15, 6.3.1.E
            treatment in individual financial statements, Ch. 15, 6.3.1.D
            unrealised profits on intragroup transactions, Ch. 15, 6.3.3
        foreign operations where sub-groups exist, accounting for, Ch. 15, 6.1.5
        goodwill and fair value adjustments, Ch. 15, 6.5
        non-coterminous period ends, Ch. 15, 6.4
        partial disposal of a foreign operation, Ch. 15, 6.6.2
        translation of equity items, Ch. 15, 6.2
            equity balances resulting from income and expenses being recognised in other comprehensive income, Ch. 15, 6.2.3
            equity balances resulting from transactions with equity holders, Ch. 15, 6.2.2
            share capital, Ch. 15, 6.2.1
        translation to the presentation currency, Ch. 15, 6.1
            accounting for foreign operations where sub-groups exist, Ch. 15, 6.1.5
            calculation of average rate, Ch. 15, 6.1.4
            dual rates, suspension of rates and lack of exchangeability, Ch. 15, 6.1.3
            functional currency is not that of a hyperinflationary economy, Ch. 15, 6.1.1
            functional currency is that of a hyperinflationary economy, Ch. 15, 6.1.2; Ch. 16, 11
    reporting foreign currency transactions in the functional currency of an entity, Ch. 15, 5
        books and records not kept in functional currency, Ch. 15, 5.6
        change in functional currency, Ch. 15, 5.5
        at ends of subsequent reporting periods, Ch. 15, 5.2
        exchange differences, treatment of, Ch. 15, 5.3
            monetary items, Ch. 15, 5.3.1
            non-monetary items, Ch. 15, 5.3.2
        initial recognition, Ch. 15, 5.1
            deposits and other consideration received or paid in advance, Ch. 15, 5.1.2
            dual rates, Ch. 15, 5.1.4.A
            identifying the date of transaction, Ch. 15, 5.1.1
            suspension of rates: longer term lack of exchangeability, Ch. 15, 5.1.4.C
            practical difficulties in determining exchange rates, Ch. 15, 5.1.4
            suspension of rates: temporary lack of exchangeability, Ch. 15, 5.1.4.B
            using average rates, Ch. 15, 5.1.3
    tax effects of all exchange differences, Ch. 15, 9
Forfeiture, share-based payments, Ch. 34, 6.1.2, 7.4.1
Forward contracts, Ch. 47, 11.1; Ch. 49, 2.1.3
    'back-to-back' forward contracts, Ch. 47, 11.1.3
    forward purchase, Ch. 47, 11.1.1
    forward sale, Ch. 47, 11.1.2
Forward currency contracts, Ch. 53, 3.6.5, 7.3.3.A, 7.5.2, 13.3.2
Forward purchase agreements (EPS), Ch. 37, 6.4.2.C
Forward rate method, Ch. 53, 7.4.7
'Fresh start' accounting, Ch. 5, 5.5.2.B
Full cost method, extractive industries, Ch. 43, 3.2.4
Functional currency, Ch. 5, 7.8.1; Ch. 15, 3–6; Ch. 43, 9. *See also* Foreign exchange
    books and records not kept in, Ch. 15, 5.6
    change in, Ch. 15, 5.5; Ch. 43, 9.2
    definition of, Ch. 15, 2.3
    determining, Ch. 15, 4; Ch. 43, 9.1
    at ends of subsequent reporting periods, Ch. 15, 5.2
    exchange differences, treatment of, Ch. 15, 5.3
        monetary items, Ch. 15, 5.3.1
        non-monetary items, Ch. 15, 5.3.2
    initial recognition, Ch. 15, 5.1

Functional currency—*contd*
  initial recognition—*contd*
    deposits and other consideration received or paid in advance, Ch. 15, 5.1.2
    dual rates, Ch. 15, 5.1.4.A
    identifying the date of transaction, Ch. 15, 5.1.1
    suspension of rates: longer term lack of exchangeability, Ch. 15, 5.1.4.C
    practical difficulties in determining exchange rates, Ch. 15, 5.1.4
    suspension of rates: temporary lack of exchangeability, Ch. 15, 5.1.4.B
    using average rates, Ch. 15, 5.1.3
  monetary/non-monetary determination, Ch. 15, 5.4
    deferred tax, Ch. 15, 5.4.4
    deposits/progress payments, Ch. 15, 5.4.1
    foreign currency share capital, Ch. 15, 5.4.3
    investments in preference shares, Ch. 15, 5.4.2
    post-employment benefit plans-foreign currency assets, Ch. 15, 5.4.5
    post-employment benefit plans-foreign currency plans, Ch. 15, 5.4.6
Fund performance fees, Ch. 46, 5.2.5
FVTOCI. *See* Fair value through other comprehensive income
General price index, Ch. 16, 3
  not available for all periods, Ch. 16, 3.2
  selection of, Ch. 16, 3.1
General purpose financial reporting, Ch. 2, 4
  changes in economic resources and claims, Ch. 2, 4.2.2
  economic resources and claims, Ch. 2, 4.2.1
  information about the use of economic resources (stewardship), Ch. 2, 4.2.3
  objective and usefulness, Ch. 2, 4.1.1
  limitations, Ch. 2, 4.1.2
Global Preparers Forum, Ch. 1, 2.9
Global Public Policy Committee (GPPC) guidance, Ch. 51, 7.2
Going concern, Ch. 2, 6.1.4; Ch. 3, 4.1.2; Ch. 38, 2.2.2
  disclosure in relation to the going concern assumption, Ch. 41, 4.7
Gold bullion sales (mining), Ch. 43, 12.13
'Good leaver' arrangements, share-based payments, Ch. 34, 5.3.9
Goodwill, Ch. 9, 6
  and allocation to cash-generating units (CGUs), Ch. 20, 8.1
  attributable to non-controlling interests, changes in ownership interest without loss of control, Ch. 7, 4.2; Ch. 20, 9
  in business combinations, Ch. 9, 6;
  and fair value adjustments, foreign operations, Ch. 15, 6.5
  impairment of goodwill, Ch. 20, 8
    acquisitions by subsidiaries and determining the level at which the group tests goodwill for impairment, Ch. 20, 12.2.3
    effect of IFRS 8 – Operating Segments – on impairment tests, Ch. 20, 8.1.4
    goodwill initially unallocated to CGUs, Ch. 20, 8.1.5
    identifying synergies and CGUs/CGU groups for allocating goodwill, Ch. 20, 8.1.2, 12.2
    measuring the goodwill allocated to CGUs/GCU groups, Ch. 20, 8.1.3
    disposal of operation within a CGU to which goodwill has been allocated, Ch. 20, 8.5
    changes in composition of CGUs, Ch. 20, 8.5.1
    effect of IFRS 8 (operating segments) when allocating goodwill to CGU's in individual financial statements, Ch. 20, 12.2.2
    goodwill synergies arising outside of the reporting entity/subgroup, Ch. 20, 12.2.1
    impairment of assets and goodwill recognised on acquisition, Ch. 20, 8.3
      deferred tax assets and losses of acquired businesses, Ch. 20, 8.3.2
      testing goodwill 'created' by deferred tax for impairment, Ch. 20, 8.3.1; Ch. 33, 12.3
    impairment testing when a CGU crosses more than one operating segment, Ch. 20, 8.4
    in individual (or subgroup) financial statements and the interaction with the group financial statements, Ch. 20, 12.2
    when to test CGUs with goodwill for impairment, Ch. 20, 8.2
  internally generated, Ch. 17, 6.2
  measuring, Ch. 9, 6
  non-controlling interests (NCIs)
    goodwill attributable to, Ch. 7, 4.2, 5.2.1
    impact of impairment testing on, Ch. 20, 9
  recognising and measuring, Ch. 9, 6
    subsequent accounting for goodwill, Ch. 9, 6.1
  restatement of goodwill on first-time adoption, Ch. 5, 5.2.5
    derecognition of negative goodwill, Ch. 5, 5.2.5.B
    goodwill previously deducted from equity, Ch. 5, 5.2.5.C
    prohibition of other adjustments of goodwill, Ch. 5, 5.2.5.A
  tax deductible, Ch. 33, 7.2.2.C
  tax on initial recognition of, Ch. 33, 7.2.2
Government grants, Ch. 24, 1–6. *See also* IAS 20
  acquisition of intangible assets by way of, Ch. 17, 4.6
  acquisition of property, plant and equipment by way of, Ch. 18, 4.6
  agriculture, Ch. 42, 3.3
  definition, Ch. 24, 1.2
  disclosures, Ch. 24, 6
  presentation of grants, Ch. 24, 4
    cash flows, Ch. 24, 4.1.1
    related to assets, Ch. 24, 4.1
    related to income, Ch. 24, 4.2
  recognition and measurement, Ch. 24, 3
    forgivable loans, Ch. 24, 3.3
    general requirements of IAS 20, Ch. 24, 3.1
    government assistance, Ch. 24, 3.8
    in the income statement, Ch. 24, 3.6
    loans at lower than market rates of interest, Ch. 24, 3.4
    non-monetary grants, Ch. 24, 3.2
    repayment of government grants, Ch. 24, 3.7
  related to biological assets, IAS 41, Ch. 24, 5, Ch. 42, 3.3
  scope of IAS 20, Ch. 24, 2
Government-related entities, Ch. 39, 2.2.10
'Graded' vesting, Ch. 34, 6.2.2. *See also* Share-based payment transactions
Grant date, share-based payment, Ch. 34, 5.3

award of equity instruments to a fixed monetary value, Ch. 34, 5.3.5
awards over a fixed pool of shares (including 'last man standing' arrangements), Ch. 34, 5.3.6
awards subject to modification by entity after original grant date, Ch. 34, 5.3.8
   discretion to make further awards, Ch. 34, 5.3.8.C
   interpretation of general terms, Ch. 34, 5.3.8.B
   significant equity restructuring or transactions, Ch. 34, 5.3.8.A
awards with multiple service and performance periods, Ch. 34, 5.3.7
awards vesting or exercisable on an exit event or change of control, Ch. 34, 15.4.1
communication of awards to employees and services in advance of, Ch. 34, 5.3.2
determination of, Ch. 34, 5.3.1
exercise price paid in shares (net settlement of award), Ch. 34, 5.3.4
exercise price/performance target dependent on a formula/future share price, Ch. 34, 5.3.3
'good leaver' arrangements, Ch. 34, 5.3.9
   automatic full/pro rata entitlement on leaving employment, Ch. 34, 5.3.9.C
   discretionary awards to, Ch. 34, 5.3.9.B
   provision for 'good leavers' made in original terms of award, Ch. 34, 5.3.9.A
special purpose acquisition companies ('SPACs'), Ch. 34, 5.3.10

Gross/net presentation of cash flows, Ch. 40, 5.2

Gross-settled contracts for entity's own equity instruments, Ch. 47, 5.4

Group reorganisations, Ch. 10, 1.2
and the carrying value of investments in subsidiaries, Ch. 20, 12.3

Group share schemes, Ch. 34, 12. *See also* Employee benefit trusts (EBTs) and similar arrangements; Share-based payment transactions
accounting treatment of group share schemes, summary, Ch. 34, 12.2
   awards settled in equity of the subsidiary, Ch. 34, 12.2.5.A
   awards settled in equity of the parent, Ch. 34, 12.2.5.B
   cash-settled transactions not settled by the entity receiving goods/services, Ch. 34, 12.2.6, 12.6
   entity receiving goods or services, Ch. 34, 12.2.3
   entity settling the transaction, Ch. 34, 12.2.4
   intragroup recharges and management charges, Ch. 34, 12.2.7
   scope of IFRS 2 for group share schemes, Ch. 34, 12.2.2
cash-settled transactions not settled by the entity receiving goods/services, illustrative example, Ch. 34, 12.6
consolidated financial statements, Ch. 34, 12.6.1
employee benefit trusts ('EBTs') and similar arrangements, Ch. 34, 12.3
employee transferring between group entities, Ch. 34, 12.7
equity-settled award satisfied by fresh issue of shares, illustrative example, Ch. 34, 12.5
equity-settled award satisfied by market purchase of shares, illustrative example, Ch. 34, 12.4
features of a group share scheme, Ch. 34, 12.1
group reorganisations, Ch. 34, 12.8
joint ventures or associates, share-based payments to employees of, Ch. 34, 12.9
scope of IFRS 2 for group share schemes, Ch. 34, 12.2.2
timing of recognition of intercompany recharges, Ch. 34, 12.2.7.A

Group transactions. *See* Common control/group transactions

Group treasury arrangements, Ch. 40, 6.5.2

Groups of items, hedge accounting, Ch. 53, 2.5
cash flow hedge of a net position, Ch. 53, 2.5.3
general requirements, Ch. 53, 2.5.1
hedging a component of a group, Ch. 53, 2.5.2
layer component designation, Ch. 53, 2.3.2
macro hedging, Ch. 53, 11
   accounting for dynamic risk management, Ch. 53, 11.1
   applying hedge accounting for macro hedging strategies under IFRS 9, Ch. 53, 11.2
nil net positions, Ch. 53, 2.5.4

Guarantees, transferred assets, Ch. 52, 5.3.1, 5.4.1
parent guarantees issued on behalf of subsidiary, Ch. 8, 4.4.5.B

Heap leaching, mining, Ch. 43, 14.6

Hedge accounting
accounting for the costs of hedging, Ch. 53, 7.5
   foreign currency basis spreads in financial instruments, Ch. 53, 7.5.3
   forward element of forward contracts, Ch. 53, 7.5.2
   time value of options, Ch. 53, 7.5.1
aggregated exposures, Ch. 53, 2.7
   accounting for, Ch. 53, 2.7.3
alternatives to hedge accounting, Ch. 53, 12
   credit risk exposures, Ch. 53, 12.1
   own use contracts, Ch. 53, 12.2
background, Ch. 53, 1.1
development of, Ch. 53, 1.3
discontinuation, Ch. 53, 8.3, 14.5
   of cash flow hedges, Ch. 53, 8.3.2
   Documented hedged item no longer exists, Ch. 53, 8.3.4
   of fair value hedges, Ch. 53, 8.3.1
   hedged net investment, disposal of, Ch. 53, 8.3.8
   hedging counterparty within the same consolidated group, Ch. 53, 8.3.7
   novation to central clearing parties, Ch. 53, 8.3.5
   risk management objective, change in, Ch. 53, 8.3.3
   settle to market derivatives, Ch. 53, 8.3.6
economic relationship, Ch. 53, 6.4.1
effective hedges, accounting for, Ch. 53, 7
   cash flow hedges, Ch. 53, 7.2
      acquisition or disposal of subsidiaries, Ch. 53, 7.2.4
      all-in-one hedges, Ch. 53, 5.2.1
      discontinuing, Ch. 53, 8.3
      documented rollover hedging strategy, Ch. 53, 7.7
      equity instrument designated at fair value through OCI, Ch. 53, 7.8
   fair value hedges, Ch. 53, 1.5, 5.1, 7.1
      adjustments to the hedged item, Ch. 53, 7.1.2
      discontinuing, Ch. 53, 8.3.1
      firm commitments, Ch. 53, 5.1.1
      foreign currency monetary items, Ch. 53, 5.1.2
      layer components with prepayment risk for, Ch. 53, 2.3.2

Hedge accounting—*contd*
  effective hedges, accounting for—*contd*
    cash flow hedges—*contd*
      fair value hedges—*contd*
        ongoing accounting, Ch. 53, 7.1.1
        presentation, Ch. 53, 10.2
      firm commitments, hedges of, Ch. 53, 5.2.2
      foreign currency monetary items, Ch. 53, 5.2.3
      hedges of a firm commitment to acquire a business, Ch. 53, 7.6
      hedges of a net investment in a foreign operation, accounting for, Ch. 7, 2.3; Ch. 53, 1.5, 5.3, 7.3, 8.3.7
      hypothetical derivatives, Ch. 53, 7.4.4
      measuring ineffectiveness of, Ch. 53, 7.4
      of a net position, Ch. 53, 2.5.3
      novation of, due to central clearing regulations, Ch. 53, 8.3.5
      ongoing accounting, Ch. 53, 7.2.1
      presentation, Ch. 53, 10.1
      reclassification of gains and losses, Ch. 53, 7.2.2
    effective date and transition, Ch. 53, 13
      limited retrospective application, Ch. 53, 13.3
      prospective application in general, Ch. 53, 13.2
    effectiveness assessment, Ch. 53, 8.1, 6.4
      credit risk dominance, Ch. 53, 6.4.2
      economic relationship, Ch. 53, 6.4.1
      hedge ratio, Ch. 53, 6.4.3
    effectiveness measurement, Ch. 53, 7.4
      calculation of, Ch. 53, 7.4.6
      'clean' *vs.* 'dirty' values, Ch. 53, 7.4.10
      comparison of spot rate and forward rate methods, Ch. 53, 7.4.7
      detailed example of calculation of ineffectiveness for a cash flow hedge, Ch. 53, 7.4.6
      discount rates for calculating fair value of hypothetical derivatives, Ch. 53, 7.4.5
      effectiveness of options, Ch. 53, 7.4.11
      foreign currency basis spreads, Ch. 53, 7.4.8
      hedged items with embedded optionality, Ch. 53, 7.4.12
      hedging instrument's impact on credit quality, Ch. 53, 7.4.9
      hedging using instruments with a non-zero fair value, Ch. 53, 7.4.3
      hypothetical derivative, Ch. 53, 7.4.4
      time value of money, Ch. 53, 7.4.2
    hedge ratio, Ch. 53, 6.4.3
    hedged items, Ch. 53, 2
      core deposits, Ch. 53, 2.6.7
      firm commitment to acquire a business, Ch. 53, 7.64
      forecast acquisition/issuance of foreign currency monetary items, Ch. 53, 2.6.5
      general requirements, Ch. 53, 2.1
      groups of items, Ch. 53, 2.5
        cash flow hedge of a net position, Ch. 53, 2.5.3
        general requirements, Ch. 53, 2.5.1
        hedging a component of a group, Ch. 53, 2.5.2
        nil net positions, Ch. 53, 2.5.4
      held at fair value through profit or loss, Ch. 53, 2.6.2
      held at fair value through OCI, Ch. 53, 2.6.3
      highly probable, Ch. 53, 2.6.1
      internal, Ch. 53, 4.3
      nominal components, Ch. 53, 2.3
        general requirement, Ch. 53, 2.3.1
        layer component for fair value hedge with prepayment risk, Ch. 53, 2.3.2
      own equity instruments, Ch. 53, 2.6.6
      risk components, Ch. 53, 2.2
        contractually specified, Ch. 53, 2.2.2
        foreign currency as, Ch. 53, 2.2.5
        general requirements, Ch. 53, 2.2.1
        inflation as, Ch. 53, 2.2.6
        non-contractually specified, Ch. 53, 2.2.3
        partial term hedging, Ch. 53, 2.2.4
      sub-LIBOR issue, Ch. 53, 2.4
        negative interest rates, Ch. 53, 2.4.2
    hedging instruments, Ch. 53, 3
      combinations of instruments, Ch. 53, 3.5
      derivatives, Ch. 53, 3.2
        basis swaps, Ch. 53, 3.2.5
        credit break clauses, Ch. 53, 3.2.4
        embedded derivatives, Ch. 53, 3.2.3
        net written options, Ch. 53, 3.2.2
        offsetting external derivatives, Ch. 53, 3.2.1
      embedded derivatives, Ch. 53, 3.2.3
      general requirements, Ch. 53, 3.1
      hedging different risks with one instrument, Ch. 53, 3.7
      non-derivative financial instruments, Ch. 53, 3.3
        of foreign currency risk, Ch. 53, 3.3.1
      non-derivative liabilities, Ch. 53, 3.3
      own equity instruments, Ch. 53, 3.4
      portions and proportions of, Ch. 53, 3.6
        foreign currency basis spread, Ch. 53, 3.6.5
        interest elements of forwards, Ch. 53, 3.6.5
        notional decomposition, Ch. 53, 3.6.2
        portion of a time period, Ch. 53, 3.6.6
        proportions of instruments, Ch. 53, 3.6.1
        restructuring of derivatives, Ch. 53, 3.6.3
        time value of options, Ch. 53, 3.6.4
    hedging relationships, types of, Ch. 53, 5
      cash flow hedges, Ch. 53, 5.2
        all-in-one hedges, Ch. 53, 5.2.1
        firm commitments hedges, Ch. 53, 5.2.2
        foreign currency monetary items, Ch. 53, 5.2.3
      fair value hedges, Ch. 53, 5.1
        firm commitments, hedges of, Ch. 53, 5.1.1
        foreign currency monetary items, hedges of, Ch. 53, 5.1.2
      hedges of net investments in foreign operations, Ch. 53, 5.3
        amount of the hedged item for which a hedging relationship may be designated, Ch. 53, 5.3.2
        nature of the hedged risk, Ch. 53, 5.3.1
        where the hedging instrument can be held, Ch. 53, 5.3.3
    ineffectiveness, measuring, Ch. 53, 7.4
    internal hedges and other group accounting issues, Ch. 53, 4
      central clearing parties, Ch. 53, 4.1.1
      external hedging instruments, offsetting, Ch. 53, 4.2
      hedged item and hedging instrument held by different group entities, Ch. 53, 4.4
      internal hedged items, Ch. 53, 4.3

internal hedging instruments, Ch. 53, 4.1
offsetting internal hedges instruments, Ch. 53, 4.2
macro hedging, Ch. 53, 11
accounting for dynamic risk management, Ch. 53, 11.1
macro hedging strategies under IFRS 9, Ch. 53, 11.2
main differences between IFRS 9 and IAS 39 hedge accounting requirements, Ch. 53, 14
discontinuation, Ch. 53, 14.5
effectiveness criteria, Ch. 53, 14.4
eligible hedged items, Ch. 53, 14.2
eligible hedging instruments, Ch. 53, 14.3
hedge accounting mechanisms, Ch. 53, 14.5
objective of hedge accounting, Ch. 53, 14.1
negative interest rates, Ch. 53, 2.4.2
portfolio/macro hedging, Ch. 53, 11
presentation, Ch. 53, 10
cash flow hedges, Ch. 53, 10.1
cost of hedging, Ch. 53, 10.4
fair value hedges, Ch. 53, 10.2
hedges of groups of items, Ch. 53, 10.3
proxy hedges, Ch. 53, 6.2.1
objective of, Ch. 53, 1.4
overview, Ch. 53, 1.5
own use contracts, Ch. 53, 12.2
qualifying criteria, Ch. 53, 6
credit risk dominance, Ch. 53, 6.4.2
on the hedged item, Ch. 53, 6.4.2.B
on the hedging instrument, Ch. 53, 6.4.2.A
designating 'proxy hedges', Ch. 53, 6.2.1
documentation and designation, Ch. 53, 6.3
business combinations, Ch. 53, 6.3.1
dynamic hedging strategies, Ch. 53, 6.3.2
forecast transactions, Ch. 53, 6.3.3
economic relationship, Ch. 53, 6.4.1
general requirements, Ch. 53, 6.1
hedge effectiveness requirements, Ch. 53, 6.4
credit risk dominance, Ch. 53, 6.4.2
economic relationship, Ch. 53, 6.4.1
hedge ratio, Ch. 53, 6.4.3
proxy hedging, Ch. 53, 6.2.1
risk management strategy, Ch. 53, 6.2
risk management objective, Ch. 53, 6.2
setting the hedge ratio, Ch. 53, 6.4.3
rebalancing, Ch. 53, 8.2
definition, Ch. 53, 8.2.1
mechanics of, Ch. 53, 8.2.3
requirement to rebalance, Ch. 53, 8.2.2
risk management, Ch. 53, 6.2, 6.3
proxy hedges, Ch. 53, 6.2.1
risk management objective, Ch. 53, 6.2
change in, Ch. 53, 8.3
risk management strategy, Ch. 53, 6.2
standards, development of, Ch. 53, 1.3

Hedge ratio, setting, Ch. 53, 6.4.3
'Hedging' of instruments classified as equity, Ch. 47, 10
Hedging sales of metal concentrate (mining sector), Ch. 43, 13.4
High-Level Expert Group (HLEG), Ch. 1, 4.2.1.B
Hong Kong Accounting Standards (HKAS), Ch. 1, 4.4.1.B
Hong Kong Financial Reporting Standards (HKFRS), Ch. 1, 4.4.1.B

Hong Kong, IFRS adoption in, Ch. 1, 4.4.1.B
Hong Kong Institute of Certified Public Accountants (HKICPA), Ch. 1, 4.4.1.B
Hybrid taxes, Ch. 33, 4.1.2, 4.5
minimum based on a measure other than taxable profits, Ch. 33, 4.5.1
tax based on revenues, unless a profit measure gives a lower result, Ch. 33, 4.5.3
tax is the higher of measures based on taxable profits and revenues, Ch. 33. 4.5.2
Hyperinflation, Ch. 16, 1–12. *See also* IAS 29–*Financial Reporting in Hyperinflationary Economies*
background, Ch. 16, 1.1
capitalisation of borrowing costs, Ch. 21, 5.6
definition of, Ch. 16, 2.3
disclosures, Ch. 16, 12
general price index, selection of, Ch. 16, 3.1
hyperinflationary economies, Ch. 16, 1.2
capitalisation of borrowing costs in, Ch. 16, 4.1.4; Ch. 21, 5.6
interim financial reporting in, Ch. 16.9; Ch. 41, 9.6.2
restatement approach, Ch. 16, 1.3
restatement of comparative figures, Ch. 16, 8
restatement of the statement of cash flows, Ch. 16, 7
restatement of the statement of changes in equity, Ch. 16, 5
restatement of the statement of profit and loss and other comprehensive income, Ch. 16, 6
restatement of the statement of financial position, Ch. 16, 4
transition, Ch. 16, 10
translation to a different presentation currency, Ch. 16, 11
comparative information, Ch. 16, 11.2
Hypothetical derivative, hedge accounting, Ch. 53, 7.4.4
IAS 1–*Presentation of Financial Statements*, Ch. 3. *See also* Financial Statements, presentation of
accrual basis of accounting, Ch. 3, 4.1.3
capital disclosures, Ch. 3, 5.4.1
consistency, Ch. 3, 4.1.4
current assets criteria, Ch. 3, 3.1.3
current liabilities criteria, Ch. 3, 3.1.4
current *versus* non-current classification, Ch. 3, 3.1.1
disclosures, Ch. 3, 5.1, 5.5; Ch. 54, 5.2
capital disclosures, Ch. 3, 5.4.1; Ch. 54, 5.6.3
going concern basis, Ch. 3, 4.1.2
sources of estimation uncertainty, Ch. 3, 5.2.1
fair presentation and compliance with IFRS, Ch. 3, 4.1.1.A
fair presentation override, Ch. 3, 4.1.1.B
future developments, Ch. 3, 6
general principles, Ch. 3, 4.1
going concern basis, Ch. 3, 4.1.2
materiality concept, Ch. 3, 4.1.5; Ch. 54, 3.2
objective of, Ch. 3, 1.1 offset, Ch. 3, 4.1.5.B
profit or loss for the period, Ch. 3, 4.1.6 purpose of, Ch. 3, 2, Ch. 3, 2.1
scope of, Ch. 3, 1.1
statement of comprehensive income, Ch. 3, 3.2
IAS 2–*Inventories*, Ch. 22, 1–6
definitions, Ch. 22, 2.2
disclosure requirements of IAS 2, Ch. 22, 6
crypto-assets, Ch. 22, 6.2
measurement, Ch. 22, 3

IAS 2–*Inventories*—contd
  measurement—*contd*
    cost criteria, Ch. 22, 3.1
      borrowing costs and purchases on deferred terms, Ch. 22, 3.1.3.C
      costs of purchase, Ch. 22, 3.1.1
      costs of conversion, Ch. 22, 3.1.2
      drug production costs within the pharmaceutical industry, Ch. 22, 3.1.3.F
      forward contracts to purchase inventory, Ch. 22, 3.1.3.E
      general and administrative overheads, Ch. 22, 3.1.3.B
      other cost, Ch. 22, 3.1.3
      service providers, Ch. 22, 3.1.3.D
      storage and distribution costs, Ch. 22, 3.1.3.A
    cost formulas, Ch. 22, 3.2.2
      first-in, first-out (FIFO), Ch. 22, 3.2.2.A
      last-in, first-out (LIFO), Ch. 22, 3.2.2.C
      weighted average cost, Ch. 22, 3.2.2.B
    crypto-assets, Ch. 22, 3.4
      cost or lower net realisable value, Ch. 22, 3.4.1
      fair value less costs to sell, Ch. 22, 3.4.2
    net realisable value, Ch. 22, 3.4.1
      sale after the reporting period, Ch. 38, 3.3
    transfers of rental assets to inventory, Ch. 22, 2.3.1.E
  objective of, Ch. 22, 2
  real estate inventory, Ch. 22, 4
    classification, Ch. 22, 4.1
    costs of, Ch. 22, 4.2
      allocation to individual units in multi-unit developments, Ch. 22, 4.2.1
      property demolition and operating lease, Ch. 22, 4.2.2
  recognition in profit/loss, Ch. 22, 5
  scope and recognition issues, IAS 2/another IFRS, Ch. 22, 2.3
    crypto-assets, Ch. 22, 2.3.1.D
    broadcast rights - IAS 2/IAS 38, Ch. 22, 2.3.1.B
    consignment stock and sale and repurchase agreements, Ch. 22, 2.3.1.F
    core inventories and spare parts, Ch. 22, 2.3.1.A
    emission rights, Ch. 22, 2.3.1.C
    sales with a right of return, Ch. 22, 2.3.1.G
    transfers of rental assets to inventory, Ch. 22, 2.3.1.E
  techniques for the measurement of cost, Ch. 22, 3.2.1
    retail method, Ch. 22, 3.2.1.B
    standard cost, Ch. 22, 3.2.1.A

IAS 7–*Statement of Cash Flows*, Ch. 40, 1–8. *See also* Statement of cash flows
  additional IAS 7 considerations for financial institutions, Ch. 40, 7
    operating cash flows, Ch. 40, 7.1
    reporting cash flows on a net basis, Ch. 40, 7.2
  additional IAS 7 considerations for groups, Ch. 40, 6
    acquisitions and disposals, Ch. 40, 6.3
      acquisition-related costs, Ch. 40, 6.3.1
      contingent consideration, Ch. 40, 6.3.3
      deferred and other non-cash consideration, Ch. 40, 6.3.2
      settlement of amounts owed by the acquired entity, Ch. 40, 6.3.4
      settlement of intra-group balances on a demerger, Ch. 40, 6.3.5
    cash flows in separate financial statements, Ch. 40, 6.5
      cash flows of subsidiaries, associates and joint ventures, Ch. 40, 6.5.1
      cash pooling, Ch. 40, 6.5.4
        and cash sharing arrangements, Ch. 40, 6.5.2
        notional cash pooling, Ch. 40, 6.5.4.A
        physical cash pooling, Ch. 40, 6.5.4.B
      group treasury arrangements, Ch. 40, 6.5.3
    cash flows of subsidiaries, associates and joint ventures, Ch. 40, 6.4
      cash flows in investment entities, Ch. 40, 6.4.3
      cash flows of joint operations, Ch. 40, 6.4.2
      investments in associates and joint ventures, Ch. 40, 6.4.1
    preparing a consolidated statement of cash flows, Ch. 40, 6.1
    transactions with non-controlling interests, Ch. 40, 6.2
  background, Ch. 40, 1.1
  cash and cash equivalents, Ch. 40, 3
    cash management policies, Ch. 40, 3.1
    components of cash and cash equivalents, Ch. 40, 3.2
      bank overdrafts, Ch. 40, 3.2.4
      client money, Ch. 40, 3.2.6
      cryptocurrencies, Ch. 40, 3.2.5
      demand deposits and short-term investments, Ch. 40, 3.2.1
      investments with maturities greater than three months, Ch. 40, 3.2.3
      money market funds, Ch. 40, 3.2.2
    reconciliation with items in the statement of financial position, Ch. 40, 3.3
    restrictions on the use of cash and cash equivalents, Ch. 40, 3.4
  cash flow presentation issues, Ch. 40, 5
    exceptional and other material cash flows, Ch. 40, 5.1
    disclosure of accounting policies, Ch. 40, 5.7
    foreign currency cash flows, Ch. 40, 5.3
      entities applying the direct method, Ch. 40, 5.3.1
      entities applying the indirect method, Ch. 40, 5.3.2
      indirect method and foreign subsidiaries, Ch. 40, 5.3.2.C
      treatment of non-operating cash flows, Ch. 40, 5.3.2.B
      treatment of operating cash flows, Ch. 40, 5.3.2.A
    gross/net presentation of cash flows, Ch. 40, 5.2
    non-cash transactions and transactions on deferred terms, Ch. 40, 5.4
      asset disposals on deferred terms, Ch. 40, 5.4.2
      asset purchased on deferred terms from the supplier, Ch. 40, 5.4.1
      revenue contracts with deferred payment terms, Ch. 40, 5.4.3
      sale and leaseback transactions, Ch. 40, 5.5.4
    voluntary disclosures, Ch. 40, 5.7
      cash flows to increase and maintain operating capacity, Ch. 40, 5.7.1
      segment cash flow disclosures, Ch. 40, 5.7.2
  future developments, Ch. 40, 1.3
  liabilities arising from financing activities, changes in, Ch. 40, 5.6
  objective, Ch. 40, 2.1
  primary financial statement, Ch. 40, 1.2
  requirements of other standards, Ch. 40, 8

cash flows arising from insurance contracts, Ch. 40, 8.2
cash flows arising from interests in subsidiaries, joint
    ventures and associates, Ch. 40, 8.4
cash flows arising from the exploration of mineral
    resources, Ch. 40, 8.3
cash flows of discontinued operations, Ch. 40, 8.1
scope, Ch. 40, 2.2
terms used in IAS 7, Ch. 40, 1.5
transparency and consistency of cash flow presentation,
    Ch. 40, 1.3

IAS 8–*Accounting Policies, Changes in Accounting Estimates and Errors*, Ch. 3, 4; Ch. 5, 7.2. *See also* Accounting policies; Financial Statements
accounting policies defined by, Ch. 3, 4.2
changes in accounting estimates, Ch. 3, 4.5, 5.2.2, 6.2.2.6..C
changes in accounting policies, Ch. 3, 4.4, 6.2.2.6..C
changes in estimates, Ch. 3, 5.2.2
consistency of accounting policies, Ch. 3, 4.1.4
correction of errors, Ch. 3, 4.6
disclosure of prior period errors, Ch. 3, 5.3
during the first IFRS reporting period, Ch. 5, 7.2.1
materiality defined by, Ch. 3, 4.1.5.A
objective of, Ch. 3, 1.2
scope of, Ch. 3, 1.2

IAS 10–*Events after the Reporting Period*, Ch. 38, 1–3. *See also* Events after the reporting period
adjusting events, Ch. 38, 2.1.2
    treatment of, Ch. 38, 2.2
date when financial statements are authorised for issue,
    Ch. 38, 2.1.1
    impact of preliminary reporting, Ch. 38, 2.1.1.A
    re-issuing (dual dating) financial statements, Ch. 38, 2.1.1.B
definitions, Ch. 38, 2.1
non-adjusting events, Ch. 38, 2.1.3
    dividend declaration, Ch. 38, 2.1.3.A
    treatment of, Ch. 38, 2.3
objective, Ch. 38, 2.1
other disclosures, Ch. 38, 2.4
practical issues, Ch. 38, 3
    changes to estimates of uncertain tax treatments, Ch. 38, 3.6
    discovery of fraud after the reporting period, Ch. 38, 3.5
    insolvency of a debtor and IFRS 9 expected credit losses,
        Ch. 38, 3.3
    percentage of completion estimates, Ch. 38, 3.2
    valuation of inventory, Ch. 38, 3.1
    valuation of investment property at fair value and tenant
        insolvency, Ch. 38, 3.4
scope, Ch. 38, 2.1
treatment of adjusting events, Ch. 38, 2.2
    events indicating that the going concern basis is not
        appropriate, Ch. 38, 2.2.2
    events requiring adjustment to the amounts recognised, or
        disclosures, in the financial statements, Ch. 38, 2.2.1
treatment of non-adjusting events, Ch. 38, 2.3
    breach of a long-term loan covenant and its subsequent
        rectification, Ch. 38, 2.3.2
    declaration to distribute non-cash assets to owners, Ch. 38,
        2.3.1

IAS 12–*Income Taxes*, Ch. 33, 1–14. *See also* Deferred tax;
Income taxes

allocation of tax charge or credit, Ch. 33, 10
business combinations, Ch. 33, 12
current tax, Ch. 33, 5
deferred tax
    measurement, Ch. 33, 8
        discounting, Ch. 33, 8.6
        expected manner of recovery, Ch. 33, 8.4
    recognition, Ch. 33, 7
        assets carried at fair value or revalued amount, Ch. 33,
            7.3
        basic principles, Ch. 33, 7.1
        initial recognition exception, Ch. 33, 7.2
        'outside' temporary differences, Ch. 33, 7.5
        restriction on recognition of deferred tax assets,
            Ch. 33, 7.4
        'tax transparent' entities, Ch. 33, 7.6
    tax bases and temporary differences, Ch. 33, 6
definitions, Ch. 33, 3
development of IAS 12, Ch. 33, 1.3
disclosure, Ch. 33, 14
first-time adoption, Ch. 5, 7.3
objective, Ch. 33, 2.1
overview, Ch. 33, 2.2
presentation, Ch. 33, 13
scope, Ch. 33, 4
uncertain tax treatments, Ch. 33, 9

IAS 16–*Property, Plant and Equipment*, Ch. 18, 1–8. *See also*
Property, plant and equipment (PP&E)
definitions used in IAS 16, Ch. 18, 2.2
depreciation, Ch. 18, 5
derecognition and disposal, Ch. 18, 7
    partial disposals and undivided interests, Ch. 18, 7.3
        joint control, Ch. 18, 7.3.1
        subsidiary that is a single asset entity, Ch. 19, 6.10
        vendor retains control, Ch. 18, 7.3.2
    and replacement of insured assets, Ch. 18, 7.4
    sale of assets held for rental, Ch. 18, 7.2
disclosure requirements, Ch. 18, 8–8.3
    additional disclosures for revalued assets, Ch. 18, 8.2
    first-time adopter, Ch. 5, 7.4
    general disclosures, Ch. 18, 8.1
    other disclosures, Ch. 18, 8.3
measurement after recognition, cost model, Ch. 18, 5
    depreciable amount and residual values, Ch. 18, 5.2
    depreciation charge, Ch. 18, 5.3
    depreciation methods, Ch. 18, 5.6
        diminishing balance methods, Ch. 18, 5.6.1
        unit-of-production method, Ch. 18, 5.6.2
    impairment, Ch. 18, 5.7
    significant parts of assets, Ch. 18, 5.1
    useful lives, Ch. 18, 5.4
        land, Ch. 18, 5.4.2
        repairs and maintenance, Ch. 18, 5.4.1
        technological change, Ch. 18, 5.4.3
    when depreciation starts, Ch. 18, 5.5
        measurement after recognition, revaluation model,
            Ch. 18, 6–6.5
            accounting for valuation surpluses and deficits,
                Ch. 18, 6.2
            adopting a policy of revaluation, Ch. 18, 6.4
            assets held under finance leases, Ch. 18, 6.5

IAS 16–*Property, Plant and Equipment*—*contd*
  measurement after recognition, cost model—*contd*
    when depreciation starts—*contd*
      measurement after recognition, revaluation model—*contd*
        meaning of fair value, Ch. 18, 6.1
        reversals of downward valuations, Ch. 18, 6.3
  measurement at recognition, Ch. 18, 4
    accounting for changes in decommissioning and restoration costs, Ch. 18, 4.3
    assets acquired with the assistance of government grants, Ch. 18, 4.6
    assets held under finance leases, Ch. 18, 4.5
    elements of cost and cost measurement, Ch. 18, 4.1
      administration and other general overheads, Ch. 18, 4.1.3
      borrowing costs, Ch. 18, 4.1.2
      cessation of capitalisation, Ch. 18, 4.1.4
      deferred payment, Ch. 18, 4.1.6
      'directly attributable' costs, Ch. 18, 4.1.1
      land and buildings to be redeveloped, Ch. 18, 4.1.7
      self-built assets, Ch. 18, 4.1.5
      transfers of assets from customers (IFRIC 18), Ch. 18, 4.1.8
      variable and contingent consideration, Ch. 18, 4.1.9
    exchanges of assets, Ch. 18, 4.4
      commercial substance, Ch. 18, 4.4.1
      reliably measurable, Ch. 18, 4.4.2
    incidental and non-incidental income, Ch. 18, 4.2
      income earned while bringing the asset to the intended location and condition, Ch. 18, 4.2.1
      income received during the construction of property, Ch. 18, 4.2.2
      liquidated damages during construction, Ch. 18, 4.2.3
  and presentation of right-of-use assets, Ch. 18, 2.3
  recognition, Ch. 18, 3
    accounting for parts ('components') of assets, Ch. 18, 3.2
    aspects of recognition, Ch. 18, 3.1
      bearer plants, Ch. 18, 3.1.7, Ch. 42, 3.2.3.A
      classification of items as inventory or PP&E when minimum levels are maintained, Ch. 18, 3.1.5
      classification as PP&E/intangible asset, Ch. 18, 3.1.4
      environmental and safety equipment, Ch. 18, 3.1.2
      production stripping costs of surface mines, Ch. 18, 3.1.6
      property economic benefits and property developments, Ch. 18, 3.1.3
      spare parts and minor items, Ch. 18, 3.1.1
    initial and subsequent expenditure, Ch. 18, 3.3
      major inspections, Ch. 18, 3.3.2
      types of parts, Ch. 18, 3.3.1
  requirements of IAS 16, Ch. 18, 2
  scope, Ch. 18, 2.1

IAS 19–*Employee Benefits*, Ch. 35, 1–16. *See also* Defined benefit plans; Defined contribution plans; Employee benefits; Long-term employee benefits; short-term employee benefits
  defined contribution plans, Ch. 35, 4
    general accounting requirements, Ch. 35, 4.1
    with minimum return guarantee, Ch. 35, 3.5
    with vesting conditions, Ch. 35, 4.2
  disclosure requirements, Ch. 35, 15
    defined benefit plans, Ch. 35, 15.2
      amount, timing and uncertainty of future cash flows, Ch. 35, 15.2.3
      characteristics and risks associated with, Ch. 35, 15.2.1
      defined benefit plans that share risks between entities under common control, Ch. 35, 15.2.5
      disclosure requirements in other IFRSs, Ch. 35, 15.2.6
      explanation of amounts in financial statements, Ch. 35, 15.2.2
      multi-employer plans, Ch. 35, 15.2.4
      plans accounted for as defined benefit plans, Ch. 35, 15.2.5.A
      plans accounted for as defined contribution plans, Ch. 35, 15.2.5.B
    defined contribution plans, Ch. 35, 15.1
  first-time adopter, Ch. 5, 7.7
  future developments, Ch. 35, 16
  interpretations committee activities, Ch. 35, 16.2
    availability of refund from defined benefit plan, Ch. 35, 16.2.2
  long-term employee benefits other than post-employment benefits, Ch. 35, 13
    meaning of other long-term employee benefits, Ch. 35, 13.1
    recognition and measurement, Ch. 35, 13.2
      attribution to years of service, Ch. 35, 13.2.1
      long-term disability benefit, Ch. 35, 13.2.2
      long-term benefits contingent on a future event, Ch. 35, 13.2.3
  objective, Ch. 35, 2.1
  pensions and other post-employment benefits, defined contribution and defined benefit plans, Ch. 35, 3
    death-in-service benefits, Ch. 35, 3.6
    distinction between, Ch. 35, 3.1
    insured benefits, Ch. 35, 3.2
    multi-employer plans, Ch. 35, 3.3
    plans that would be defined contribution plans but for existence of minimum return guarantee, Ch. 35, 3.5
    state plans, Ch. 35, 3.4
  scope, Ch. 35, 2.2
    employee benefits settled by a shareholder or another group entity, Ch. 36, 2.2.2
    scope requirements of IAS 19, Ch. 35, 2.2.1
  short-term employee benefits, Ch. 35, 12
    general recognition criteria for, Ch. 35, 12.1
    profit-sharing and bonus plans, Ch. 35, 12.3
    short-term paid absences, Ch. 35, 12.2
  termination benefits, Ch. 35, 14

IAS 20–*Accounting for Government Grants and Disclosure of Government Assistance*, Ch. 24, 1–6
  definitions, Ch. 24, 1.2
  disclosures, Ch. 24, 6
    government assistance, Ch. 24, 6.2
    government grants, Ch. 24, 6.1
  government grants related to biological assets in the scope of IAS 41, Ch. 24, 5, Ch. 42, 3.3
  overview of IAS 20, Ch. 24, 1.1
  presentation of grants, Ch. 24, 4
    related to assets, Ch. 24, 4.1
      cash flows, Ch. 24, 4.1.1

    impairment testing of assets that qualified for government grants, Ch. 24, 4.1.2
    related to income, Ch. 24, 4.2
  recognition and measurement, Ch. 24, 3
    forgivable loans, Ch. 24, 3.3
    general requirements of IAS 20, Ch. 24, 3.1
    government assistance, Ch. 24, 3.7
    loans at lower than market rates of interest, Ch. 24, 3
    non-monetary grants, Ch. 24, 3.2
    recognition in the income statement, Ch. 24, 3.6
      achieving the most appropriate matching, Ch. 24, 3.6.1
      loans at lower than market rates of interest, Ch. 24, 3.6.2
      period to be benefited by the grant, Ch. 24, 3.6.3
      separating grants into elements, Ch. 24, 3.6.4
    repayment of government grants, Ch. 24, 3.7
  scope, Ch. 24, 2
    government assistance, Ch. 24, 2.1
    government grants, Ch. 24, 2.2
      definition, Ch. 24, 2.2.1
    scope exclusion, Ch. 24, 2.3
      general considerations, Ch. 24, 2.3.1
      investment tax credits, Ch. 24, 2.3.2
IAS 21–*The Effects of Changes in Foreign Exchange Rates*, Ch. 15, 1–11. *See also* Foreign exchange, Functional currency
  background, Ch. 15, 1.1
  change in functional currency, Ch. 15, 5.5
  change of presentation currency, Ch. 15, 7
  definitions of terms, Ch. 15, 2.3
  disclosure requirements, Ch. 15, 10
    entity's functional currency determination, Ch. 15, 4
    branches and divisions, Ch. 15, 4.4
    documentation of judgements made, Ch. 15, 4.5
    general, Ch. 15, 4.1
    intermediate holding companies/finance subsidiaries, Ch. 15, 4.2
    investment holding companies, Ch. 15, 4.3
  first-time adopter, Ch. 5, 7.8
  future developments, Ch. 15, 11
  introduction of euro, Ch. 15, 8
  objective of the standard, Ch. 15, 2.1
  presentation currency use other than the functional currency, Ch. 15, 6
    disposal or partial disposal of a foreign operation, Ch. 7, 2.3, 3.5, 4.1; Ch. 15, 6.6
      step-by-step and direct methods of consolidation, Ch. 7, 2.3; Ch. 15, 6.6.3
    exchange differences on intragroup balances, Ch. 15, 6.3
      monetary items included as part of the net investment in a foreign operation, Ch. 15, 6.3.1
        becoming part of the net investment in a foreign operation, Ch. 15, 6.3.1.F
        ceasing to be part of the net investment in a foreign operation, Ch. 15, 6.3.1.G
        currency of monetary item, Ch. 15, 6.3.1.C
        dividends, Ch. 15, 6.3.2
        manner of settlement of monetary, Ch. 15, 6.3.1.B
        trade receivables or payables included as part of the net investment in a foreign operation, Ch. 15, 6.3.1.A
        transacted by other members of the group, Ch. 15, 6.3.1.E
      treatment in individual financial statements, Ch. 15, 6.3.1.D
      unrealised profits on intragroup transactions, Ch. 15, 6.3.3
    goodwill and fair value adjustments, Ch. 15, 6.5
    non-coterminous period ends, Ch. 15, 6.4
    translation of equity items, Ch. 15, 6.2
      equity balances from income and expenses in OCI, Ch. 15, 6.2.3
      equity balances from transactions with equity holders, Ch. 15, 6.2.2
      share capital, Ch. 15, 6.2.1
    translation to the presentation currency, Ch. 15, 6.1
      accounting for foreign operations where sub-groups exist, Ch. 7, 2.3; Ch. 15, 6.1.5
      calculation of average rate, Ch. 15, 6.1.4
      dual rates, suspension of rates and lack of exchangeability, Ch. 15, 6.1.3
      functional currency is not that of a hyperinflationary economy, Ch. 15, 6.1.1
      functional currency is that of a hyperinflationary economy, Ch. 15, 6.1.2
  relevant pronouncements, Ch. 15, 1.2
  reporting foreign currency transactions in the functional currency of an entity, Ch. 15, 5
    books and records not kept in functional currency, Ch. 15, 5.6
    change in functional currency, Ch. 15, 5.5
    at ends of subsequent reporting periods, Ch. 15, 5.2
    exchange differences, treatment of, Ch. 15, 5.3
      monetary items, Ch. 15, 5.3.1
      non-monetary items, Ch. 15, 5.3.2
    initial recognition, Ch. 15, 5.1
      deposits and other consideration received or paid in advance, Ch. 15, 5.1.2
      dual rates, Ch. 15, 5.1.4.A
      identifying the date of transaction, Ch. 15, 5.1.1
      practical difficulties in determining exchange rates, Ch. 15, 5.1.4
      suspension of rates: longer term lack of exchangeability, Ch. 15, 5.1.4.C
      suspension of rates: temporary lack of exchangeability, Ch. 15, 5.1.4.B
      using average rates, Ch. 15, 5.1.3
    monetary/non-monetary determination, Ch. 15, 5.4
      deferred tax, Ch. 15, 5.4.5
      deposits and advance payments for actively traded commodities, Ch. 15, 5.4.2
      deposits or progress payments, Ch. 15, 5.4.1
      foreign currency share-capital, Ch. 15, 5.4.4
      investments in preference shares, Ch. 15, 5.4.3
      post-employment benefit plans-foreign currency assets, Ch. 15, 5.4.5
      post-employment benefit plans-foreign currency plans, Ch. 15, 5.4.6
  summary of approach required by IAS 21, Ch. 15, 3
  scope of IAS 21, Ch. 15, 2.2
  tax effects of all exchange differences, Ch. 15, 9
IAS 23–*Borrowing Costs*, Ch. 21, 1–7. *See also* Borrowing costs

IAS 23–*Borrowing Costs*—contd
  borrowing costs eligible for capitalisation, Ch. 21, 5
    capitalisation of borrowing costs in hyperinflationary economies, Ch. 21, 5.6
    derivative financial instruments, Ch. 21, 5.5.1
    directly attributable borrowing costs, Ch. 21, 5.1
    dividends payable on shares classified as financial liabilities, Ch. 21, 5.5.4
    exchange differences as a borrowing cost, Ch. 21, 5.4
    gains and losses on derecognition of borrowings, Ch. 21, 5.5.2
    gains/losses on termination of derivative financial instruments, Ch. 21, 5.5.3
    general borrowings, Ch. 21, 5.3
      accrued costs and trade payables, Ch. 21, 5.3.3
      assets carried below cost in the statement of financial position, Ch. 21, 5.3.4
      calculation of capitalisation rate, Ch. 21, 5.3.2
      completed qualifying assets, related to, Ch. 21, 5.3.1.A
      definition of general borrowings, Ch. 21, 5.3.1
      specific non-qualifying assets, related to, Ch. 21, 5.3.1.B
    group considerations, Ch. 21, 5.7
      borrowings in one company and development in another, Ch. 21, 5.7.1
      qualifying assets held by joint arrangements, Ch. 21, 5.7.2
    specific borrowings, Ch. 21, 5.2
  commencement, suspension and cessation of capitalisation, Ch. 21, 6
    cessation, Ch. 21, 6.3
      borrowing costs on 'land expenditures', Ch. 21, 6.3.1
    commencement, Ch. 21, 6.1
      expenditures on a qualifying asset, Ch. 21, 6.1.1
    suspension, Ch. 21, 6.2
      impairment considerations, Ch. 21, 6.2.1
  definition of borrowing costs, Ch. 21, 4
    in IAS 23, Ch. 21, 4.1
    other finance costs, Ch. 21, 4.2
  disclosure requirements, Ch. 21, 7
  qualifying assets, Ch. 21, 3
    assets measured at fair value, Ch. 21, 3.2
    constructed good, over time transfer of, Ch. 21, 3.1
    financial assets, Ch. 21, 3.3
    inventories, Ch. 21, 3.1
  requirements of, Ch. 21, 2
    core principle, Ch. 21, 2.1
    scope, Ch. 21, 2.2

IAS 24–*Related Party Disclosures*, Ch. 39, 1–2. *See also* Key management personnel; Related party
  disclosable transactions, Ch. 39, 2.5
    materiality, Ch. 39, 2.5.1
  disclosure of controlling relationships, Ch. 39, 2.4
  disclosure of expense incurred with management entity, Ch. 39, 2.8
  disclosure of key management personnel compensation, Ch. 39, 2.6
    compensation, Ch. 39, 2.6.1
      key management personnel compensated by other entities, Ch. 39, 2.6.8
    post-employment benefits, Ch. 39, 2.6.3
    reporting entity part of a group, Ch. 39, 2.6.7
    share-based payment transactions, Ch. 39, 2.6.6
    short-term employee benefits, Ch. 39, 2.6.2
    termination benefits, Ch. 39, 2.6.5
  disclosure of other related party transactions, including commitments, Ch. 39, 2.7
    disclosures required for related party transactions, including commitments, Ch. 39, 2.7.2
    related party transactions requiring disclosure, Ch. 39, 2.7.1
      aggregation of items of a similar nature, Ch. 39, 2.7.1.A
      commitments, Ch. 39, 2.7.1.B
  disclosures with government-related entities, Ch. 39, 2.9
  objective, Ch. 39, 2.1.1
  parties that are not related parties, Ch. 39, 2.3
  possible solutions, Ch. 39, 1.2
    remeasurement of related party transactions at fair values, Ch. 39, 1.2.1
  related party and related party transactions, identification of, Ch. 39, 2.2
    entities that are associates/joint ventures, Ch. 39, 2.2.3
      joint operations, Ch. 39, 2.2.3.A
    entities that are joint ventures and associates of the same third entity, Ch. 39, 2.2.5
    entities that are joint ventures of the same third party, Ch. 39, 2.2.5
    entities that are members of the same group, Ch. 39, 2.2.2
    entities under control or joint control of certain persons/close members of their family, Ch. 39, 2.2.7
    entities under significant influence of certain persons/close members of their family, Ch. 39, 2.2.8
    government-related entities, Ch. 39, 2.2.10
    key management personnel services provided by a management entity, Ch. 39, 2.2.9
    persons/close members of a person's family that are related parties, Ch. 39, 2.2.1
      control, Ch. 39, 2.2.1.A
      joint control, Ch. 39, 2.2.1.B
      key management personnel, Ch. 39, 2.2.1.D
      significant influence, Ch. 39, 2.2.1.C
    post-employment benefit plans, Ch. 39, 2.2.6
  related party issue, Ch. 39, 1.1
  scope, Ch. 39, 2.1.2

IAS 27–*Separate Financial Statements*, Ch. 8, 1–3. *See also* Separate financial statements
  definitions, Ch. 8, 1
  disclosure, Ch. 8, 3
  requirements of separate financial statements, Ch. 8, 2
  scope, Ch. 8, 1

IAS 28–*Investments in Associates and Joint Ventures*, Ch. 11, 1–11. *See also* Investments in associates and joint ventures
  application of the equity method, Ch. 11, 7
  definitions, Ch. 11, 3
  entities with no subsidiaries but exempt from applying IAS 28, Ch. 8, 3.3.1
  exemptions from applying the equity method, Ch. 11, 5
    investments held in associates/joint ventures held by venture capital organisations, Ch. 11, 5.3
      application of IFRS 9 (or IAS 39) to exempt, Ch. 11, 5.3.2

designation of investments as 'at fair value through
profit or loss', Ch. 11, 5.3.2.B
entities with a mixture of activities, Ch. 11,
5.3.2.A
investment entities exception, Ch. 11, 5.3.1
parents exempt from preparing consolidated financial
statements, Ch. 11, 5.1
partial use of fair value measurement of associates, Ch. 11,
5.4
subsidiaries meeting certain criteria, Ch. 11, 5.2
first-time adoption, Ch. 5, 7.9
and IFRS 10, conflict between, Ch. 7, 3.3.2, 7.1; Ch. 11,
7.6.5.C; Ch. 12, 8.2.3
impairment losses, Ch. 11, 8, 9.1, 10.1.2
objective, Ch. 11, 2.1
scope, Ch. 11, 2.2
significant influence, Ch. 11, 4
fund managers, Ch. 11, 4.6
holdings of less than 20% of the voting power, Ch. 11, 4.3
lack of, Ch. 11, 4.2
potential voting rights, Ch. 11, 4.4
severe long-term restrictions impairing ability to transfer
funds to the investor, Ch. 11, 4.1
voting rights held in a fiduciary capacity, Ch. 11, 4.5
IAS 29–*Financial Reporting in Hyperinflationary Economies*,
Ch. 16, 1–12. *See also* Hyperinflation
context of, Ch. 16, 2.1
definition of hyperinflation, Ch. 16, 2.3
disclosures, Ch. 16, 12
restatement of comparative figures, Ch. 16, 8
restatement of the statement of cash flows, Ch. 16, 7
restatement of the statement of changes in equity, Ch. 16, 5
restatement of the statement of profit and loss and other
comprehensive income, Ch. 16, 6
calculation of gain or loss on net monetary position,
Ch. 16, 6.2
interest and exchange differences, Ch. 16, 6.1
measurement of reclassification adjustments within equity,
Ch. 16, 6.3
restatement process, Ch. 16, 2.4
scope, Ch. 16, 2.2
selection of general price index, Ch. 16, 3.1
statement of financial position, analysis and restatement of,
Ch. 16, 4
deferred taxation, calculation of, Ch. 16, 4.4
inventories, Ch. 16, 4.2
monetary and non-monetary items, Ch. 16, 4.1
distinguishing between, Ch. 16, 4.1.1
monetary items, Ch. 16, 4.1.2
non-monetary items carried at current cost, Ch. 16,
4.1.3
non-monetary items carried at historic cost, Ch. 16,
4.1.4
restatement of associates, joint ventures and subsidiaries,
Ch. 16, 4.3
transition
economies becoming hyperinflationary, Ch. 16, 10.1
economies ceasing to be hyperinflationary, Ch. 16, 10.2
economies exiting severe hyperinflation, Ch. 16, 10.3
translation to a different presentation currency, Ch. 16, 11
comparative information, Ch. 16, 11.2

initial application and ceasing application of IAS 29,
Ch. 16, 11.1
IAS 32–*Financial Instruments: Presentation*, Ch. 44, 2; Ch. 54,
See also Financial instruments, financial liabilities and equity;
Presentation and disclosure, financial instruments
definitions, Ch. 47, 3
objective, Ch. 47, 2.1
options over puttable instruments classified as equity, Ch. 34,
2.2.4.J
presentation
compound financial instruments, Ch. 47, 6
interest, dividends, losses and gains, Ch. 47, 8
liabilities and equity
contingent settlement provisions, Ch. 47, 4.3
contracts to issue equity instruments, Ch. 47, 4.4.2
contractual obligation to deliver cash or other financial
assets, Ch. 47, 4.2
implied contractual obligation to deliver cash or other
financial assets, Ch. 47, 4.2.2
perpetual debt, Ch. 47, 4.7
preference shares, Ch. 47, 4.5
puttable instruments, Ch. 47, 4.6
offsetting a financial asset and a financial liability, Ch. 54,
7.4.1
treasury shares, Ch. 47, 9
scope, Ch. 47, 2.2
transactions in financial assets outside the scope of, Ch. 34,
2.2.3.F
transactions not in the scope of (compared with IFRS 2),
Ch. 34, 2.2.3.E
IAS 33–*Earnings per Share*, Ch. 37, 1–8. *See also* Diluted EPS
basic EPS, Ch. 37, 3
earnings, Ch. 37, 3.1
number of shares, Ch. 37, 3.2
changes in outstanding ordinary shares, Ch. 37, 4
adjustments to EPS in historical summaries, Ch. 37, 4.7
changes in ordinary shares without corresponding changes
in resources, Ch. 37, 4.3
B share schemes, Ch. 37, 4.3.4
capitalisation, bonus issues and share splits, Ch. 37,
4.3.1.A
put warrants priced above market value, Ch. 37, 4.3.5
rights issue, Ch. 37, 4.3.3
share consolidation with a special dividend, Ch. 37,
4.3.2
share consolidations, Ch. 37, 4.3.1.C
stock dividends, Ch. 37, 4.3.1.B
issue to acquire another business, Ch. 37, 4.6
acquisitions, Ch. 37, 4.6.1
establishment of a new parent undertaking, Ch. 37,
4.6.3
reverse acquisitions, Ch. 37, 4.6.2
options exercised during the year, Ch. 37, 4.4
post balance sheet changes in capital, Ch. 37, 4.5
purchase and redemption of own shares, Ch. 37, 4.2
weighted average number of shares, Ch. 37, 4.1
contingently issuable potential ordinary shares, Ch. 37, 6.4.8
contingently issuable shares, Ch. 37, 6.4.6
earnings-based contingencies, Ch. 37, 6.4.6.A
share-price-based contingencies, Ch. 37, 6.4.6.B

IAS 33—*Earnings per Share*—*contd*
- convertible instruments, Ch. 37, 6.4.1
  - convertible debt, Ch. 37, 6.4.1.A
  - convertible preference shares, Ch. 37, 6.4.1.B
  - participating equity instruments, Ch. 37, 6.4.1.C
- definitions, Ch. 37, 1.1
- disclosure, Ch. 37, 7.3
- matters affecting the numerator, Ch. 37, 5
  - earnings, Ch. 37, 5.1
  - participating equity instruments and two class shares, Ch. 37, 5.4
  - preference dividends, Ch. 37, 5.2
  - retrospective adjustments, Ch. 37, 5.3
- objective, Ch. 37, 2.1
- options, warrants and their equivalents, Ch. 37, 6.4.2
  - forward purchase agreements, Ch. 37, 6.4.2.C
  - numerator, Ch. 37, 6.4.2.A
  - options over convertible instruments, Ch. 37, 6.4.2.D
  - settlement of option exercise price, Ch. 37, 6.4.2.E
  - specified application of option proceeds, Ch. 37, 6.4.2.F
  - written call options, Ch. 37, 6.4.2.B
  - written put options, Ch. 37, 6.4.2.C
- ordinary shares of investees, Ch. 37, 6.4.7
- partly paid shares, Ch. 37, 6.4.4
- presentation, Ch. 37, 7.1
- purchased options and warrants, Ch. 37, 6.4.3
- restatement, Ch. 37, 7.2
- scope, Ch. 37, 2.2
- share based payments, Ch. 37, 6.4.5

IAS 34—*Interim Financial Reporting*, Ch. 41, 1–11; Ch. 54, 2.3
- components, form and content, Ch. 41, 3
  - complete set of interim financial statements, Ch. 41, 3.1
  - condensed interim financial statements, Ch. 41, 3.2
  - management commentary, Ch. 41, 3.4
  - requirements for both complete and condensed interim financial information, Ch. 41, 3.3
- definitions, Ch. 41, 1.1
- disclosure in annual financial statements, Ch. 41, 7
- disclosures in condensed financial statements, Ch. 41, 4
  - disclosure of compliance with IFRS, Ch. 41, 4.6
  - examples of disclosures, Ch. 41, 4.3
    - accounting policies and methods of computation, Ch. 41, 4.3.11
    - acquisition and disposal of property, plant and equipment, Ch. 41, 4.3.3
    - amounts that are unusual because of their nature, size or incidence, Ch. 41, 4.3.14
    - capital commitments, Ch. 41, 4.3.4
    - changes in circumstances affecting fair values, Ch. 41, 4.3.6
    - changes in the composition of the entity, Ch. 41, 4.3.17
    - contingent liabilities, Ch. 41, 4.3.10
    - default/breach of loan covenants not remedied before the end of interim period, Ch. 41, 4.3.7
    - dividends paid, Ch. 41, 4.3.15
    - events after the interim reporting date, Ch. 41, 4.3.16
    - inventory write-down and reversals, Ch. 41, 4.3.1
    - issues, repurchases and repayments of debt and equity securities, Ch. 41, 4.3.14
    - litigation settlements, Ch. 41, 4.3.5
    - recognition and reversal of impairment losses, Ch. 41, 4.3.3
    - related party transactions, Ch. 41, 4.3.8
    - seasonality/cyclicality of operations, Ch. 41, 4.3.12
    - transfers between different levels of fair value hierarchy, Ch. 41, 4.3.9
  - fair value disclosures for financial instruments, Ch. 41, 4.5
  - going concern assumption, disclosure in relation to, Ch. 41, 4.7
  - other disclosures required by IAS 34, Ch. 41, 4.2
  - segment information, Ch. 41, 4.4
  - significant events and transactions, Ch. 41, 4.1
  - specified disclosures, location of, Ch. 41, 4.2.1
- effective dates and transitional rules, Ch. 41, 11
  - first-time presentation of interim reports complying with IAS 34, Ch. 41, 11.1
- estimates, use of, Ch. 41, 10
- materiality, Ch. 41, 6
- objective, Ch. 41, 2.1
- periods for which interim financial statements are required to be presented, Ch. 41, 5
  - change in financial year-end, Ch. 41, 5.3
  - comparatives following a financial period longer than a year, Ch. 41, 5.4
  - length of interim reporting period, Ch. 41, 5.2
  - other comparative information, Ch. 41, 5.1
  - when the comparative period is shorter than the current period, Ch. 41, 5.5
- recognition and measurement, Ch. 41, 8
  - examples of, Ch. 41, 9
    - contingent lease payments, Ch. 41, 9.7.4
    - contractual/anticipated purchase price changes, Ch. 41, 9.4.2
    - cost of sales, Ch. 41, 9.4
    - earnings per share, Ch. 41, 9.8
    - employee benefits, Ch. 41, 9.3
    - foreign currency translation, Ch. 41, 9.6
    - interim period manufacturing cost variances, Ch. 41, 9.4.3
    - inventories, Ch. 41, 9.4.1
    - levies charged by public authorities, Ch. 41, 9.7.5
    - periodic maintenance/overhaul, Ch. 41, 9.7.3
    - property, plant and equipment and intangible assets, Ch. 41, 9.1
    - provisions, contingencies and accruals for other costs, Ch. 41, 9.7
    - reversal of impairment losses recognised in a previous interim period (IFRIC 10), Ch. 41, 9.2
    - taxation, Ch. 41, 9.5
  - same accounting policies as in annual financial statements, Ch. 41, 8.1
    - measurement on a year-to-date basis, Ch. 41, 8.1.1
    - new accounting pronouncements and other changes in accounting policies, Ch. 41, 8.1.2
    - voluntary changes in presentation, Ch. 41, 8.1.3
  - seasonal businesses, Ch. 41, 8.2
    - costs incurred unevenly during the year, Ch. 41, 8.2.2
    - revenues received seasonally, cyclically, or occasionally, Ch. 41, 8.2.1
- scope, Ch. 41, 2.2
- use of estimates, Ch. 41, 10

Index

IAS 36–*Impairment of Assets*, Ch. 20, 1–14. *See also* Goodwill; Impairment of assets; Value in use (VIU)
    carrying amount of CGU assets, identifying, Ch. 20, 4
        consistency and the impairment test, Ch. 20, 4.1
    corporate assets, Ch. 20, 4.2
        leased corporate assets, Ch. 20, 4.2.1
    developments, Ch. 20, 14
    disclosures required by IAS 36, Ch. 20, 13.3
        annual impairment disclosures for goodwill and intangible assets with an indefinite useful life, Ch. 20, 13.3
        for impairment losses or reversals, Ch. 20, 13.2.1
        material impairments, Ch. 20, 13.2.2
    dividing the entity into cash-generating units (CGUs), Ch. 20, 3
        active markets and identifying CGUs, Ch. 20, 3.3
        CGUs and intangible assets, Ch. 20, 3.1
    fair value less costs of disposal, Ch. 20, 6
        estimating, Ch. 20, 6.1
            Depreciated replacement costs or current replacement cost as FVLCD, Ch. 20, 6.1.2
            FVLCD and the unit of account, Ch. 20, 6.1.1
    first-time adopters of IAS 36, Ch. 5, 7.12
    goodwill and its allocation to CGUs, Ch. 20, 8.1
        composition of goodwill, Ch. 20, 8.1.1
        effect of IFRS 8 on impairment tests, Ch. 20, 8.1.4
            aggregation of operating segments for disclosure purposes, Ch. 20, 8.1.4.B
            changes to operating segments, Ch. 20, 8.1.4.A
        goodwill initially unallocated to CGUs, Ch. 20, 8.1.5
        identifying synergies and identifying CGUs/CGU groups for allocating goodwill, Ch. 20, 8.1.2
        measuring the goodwill allocated to CGUs/CGU groups, Ch. 20, 8.1.3
    group and separate financial statement issues, Ch. 20, 12
        goodwill in individual (or subgroup) financial statements and the interaction with the group financial statements, Ch. 20, 12.2
        group reorganisations and the carrying value of investments in subsidiaries, Ch. 20, 12.3
        VIU: relevant cash flows and non-arm's length prices, Ch. 20, 12.1
    investments in subsidiaries, associates and joint ventures, Ch. 20, 12.4
    impairment of intangible assets with an indefinite useful life, Ch. 20, 10
    impairment losses, recognising and reversing, Ch. 20, 11
        impairment losses and CGUs, Ch. 20, 11.2
        on individual assets, Ch. 20, 11.1
        reversal of impairment losses recognised in a previous interim period, Ch. 41, 9.2
            relating to goodwill prohibited, Ch. 20, 11.3
            relating to assets other than goodwill, Ch. 20, 11.4
    impairment of goodwill, Ch. 20, 8
        disposal of operation within a CGU to which goodwill has been allocated, Ch. 20, 8.5
            changes in composition of CGUs, Ch. 20, 8.5.1
        impairment of assets and goodwill recognised on acquisition, Ch. 20, 8.3
            deferred tax assets and losses of acquired businesses, Ch. 20, 8.3.2
            testing goodwill 'created' by deferred tax for impairment, Ch. 20, 8.3.1
        impairment testing when a CGU crosses more than one operating segment, Ch. 20, 8.4
        when to test CGUs with goodwill for impairment, Ch. 20, 8.2
            carry forward of a previous impairment test calculation, Ch. 20, 8.2.3
            reversal of impairment loss for goodwill prohibited, Ch. 20, 8.2.4
            sequence of impairment tests for goodwill and other assets, Ch. 20, 8.2.2
            timing of impairment tests, Ch. 20, 8.2.1
    impairment review, features of, Ch. 20, 1.2
    impairment testing requirements, Ch. 20, 2
        indicators of impairment, Ch. 20, 2.1
            (future) performance, Ch. 20, 2.1.2
            individual assets/part of CGU?, Ch. 20, 2.1.3
            interest rates, Ch. 20, 2.1.4
            market capitalisation, Ch. 20, 2.1.1
    non-controlling interests, impact on goodwill impairment testing, Ch. 7, 4.2, Ch. 20, 9
    recoverable amount, Ch. 20, 5
        impairment of assets held for sale, Ch. 20, 5.1
    scope of IAS 36, Ch. 20, 1.3
    theory behind, Ch. 20, 1.1
    value in use (VIU), determining, Ch. 20, 7
        appropriate discount rate and discounting the future cash flows, Ch. 20, 7.2
            approximations and short cuts, Ch. 20, 7.2.4
            calculating VIU using post-tax cash flows, Ch. 20, 7.2.3
            determining pre-tax rates taking account of tax losses, Ch. 20, 7.2.6
            disclosing pre-tax discount rates when using a post-tax methodology, Ch. 20, 7.2.5
            discount rates and the weighted average cost of capital, Ch. 20, 7.2.1
            entity-specific WACCs and capital structure, Ch. 20, 7.2.8
            entity-specific WACCs and different project risks within the entity, Ch. 20, 7.2.7
            pre-tax discount rate, calculating, Ch. 20, 7.2.2
            use of discount rates other than the WACC, Ch. 20, 7.2.9
        fair value and value in use, differences between, Ch. 20, 7.3
        future pre-tax cash flows of the CGU under review, estimating, Ch. 20, 7.1
            budgets and cash flows, Ch. 20, 7.1.1
            cash inflows and outflows from improvements and enhancements, Ch. 20, 7.1.2
            events after the reporting period, Ch. 20, 7.1.9
            foreign currency cash flows, Ch. 20, 7.1.5
            internal transfer pricing, Ch. 20, 7.1.6
            lease payments, Ch. 20, 7.1.8
            overheads and share-based payments, Ch. 20, 7.1.7
            restructuring, Ch. 20, 7.1.3
            terminal values, Ch. 20, 7.1.4

IAS 37–*Provisions, Contingent Liabilities and Contingent Assets*, Ch. 26, 1–7. *See also* Provisions, contingent liabilities and contingent assets
    cases in which no provision should be recognised, Ch. 26, 5
        future operating losses, Ch. 26, 5.1
        rate-regulated activities, Ch. 26, 5.4
        repairs and maintenance of owned assets, Ch. 26, 5.2
        staff training costs, Ch. 26, 5.3
    definitions, Ch. 26, 1.3
    disclosure requirements, Ch. 26, 7
        contingent assets, Ch. 26, 7.3
        contingent liabilities, Ch. 26, 7.2
        provisions, Ch. 26, 7.1
        reduced disclosure when information is seriously prejudicial, Ch. 26, 7.4
    first-time adopters, Ch. 5, 7.13
    interpretations related to the application of IAS 37, Ch. 26, 1.2
    measurement, Ch. 26, 4
        anticipating future events that may affect the estimate of cash flows, Ch. 26, 4.4
        best estimate of provision, Ch. 26, 4.1
        changes and uses of provisions, Ch. 26, 4.9
            changes in contingent liabilities recognised in a business combination, Ch. 26, 4.10
        dealing with risk and uncertainty in measuring a provision, Ch. 26, 4.2
        discounting the estimated cash flows to a present value, Ch. 26, 4.3
            adjusting for risk and using a government bond rate, Ch. 26, 4.3.2
            effect of changes in interest rates on the discount rate applied, Ch. 26, 4.3.6
            own credit risk is not taken into account, Ch. 26, 4.3.3
            pre-tax discount rate, Ch. 26, 4.3.4
            real *vs.* nominal rate, Ch. 26, 4.3.1
            unwinding of the discount, Ch. 26, 4.3.5
        joint and several liability, Ch. 26, 4.7
        provisions are not reduced for gains on disposal of related assets, Ch. 26, 4.8
        provisions that will be settled in a currency other than the entity's functional currency, Ch. 26, 4.5
        reimbursements, insurance and other recoveries from third parties, Ch. 26, 4.6
    objective of IAS 37, Ch. 26, 2.1
    recognition, Ch. 26, 3
        contingencies, Ch. 26, 3.2
            contingent assets, Ch. 26, 3.2.2
                obligations contingent on the successful recovery of, Ch. 26, 3.2.2.A
            contingent liabilities, Ch. 26, 3.2.1
            how probability determines whether to recognise or disclose, Ch. 26, 3.2.3
        determining when a provision should be recognised, Ch. 26, 3.1
            an entity has a present obligation as a result of a past event, Ch. 26, 3.1.1
            it is probable that an outflow of resources embodying economic benefits will be required to settle the obligation, Ch. 26, 3.1.2
            a reliable estimate can be made of the amount of the obligation, Ch. 26, 3.1.3
        recognising an asset when recognising a provision, Ch. 26, 3.3
    scope of IAS 37, Ch. 26, 2.2
        distinction between provisions and contingent liabilities, Ch. 26, 2.2.3
        items outside the scope of IAS 37, Ch. 26, 2.2.1
            executory contracts, except where the contract is onerous, Ch. 26, 2.2.1.A
            items covered by another standard, Ch. 26, 2.2.1.B
        provisions compared to other liabilities, Ch. 26, 2.2.2
    specific examples of provisions and contingencies, Ch. 26, 6
        decommissioning provisions, Ch. 26, 6.3
            changes in estimated decommissioning costs (IFRIC 1), Ch. 26, 6.3.1
            changes in legislation after construction of the asset, Ch. 26, 6.3.2
            funds established to meet an obligation (IFRIC 5), Ch. 26, 6.3.3
            interaction of leases with asset retirement obligations, Ch. 26.6.3.4
        dilapidation and other provisions relating to leased assets, Ch. 26, 6.9
        environmental provisions, general guidance in IAS 37, Ch. 26, 6.4
        EU Directive on 'Waste Electrical and Electronic Equipment' (IFRIC 6), Ch. 26, 6.7
        green certificates compared to emissions trading schemes, Ch. 26, 6.6
        levies imposed by governments, Ch. 26, 6.8
            payments relating to taxes other than income tax, Ch. 26, 6.8.4
            recognition and measurement of levy liabilities, Ch. 26, 6.8.2
            recognition of an asset/expense when a levy is recorded, Ch. 26, 6.8.3
            scope of IFRIC 21, Ch. 26, 6.8.1
        liabilities associated with emissions trading schemes, Ch. 26, 6.5
        litigation and other legal claims, Ch. 26, 6.11
        obligations to make donations to non-profit organisations, Ch. 26, 6.14
        onerous contracts, Ch. 26, 6.2
            contracts with customers that are, or have become, onerous, Ch. 26, 6.2.2
            onerous leases, Ch. 26, 6.2.1
        refunds policy, Ch. 26, 6.12
        restructuring provisions, Ch. 26, 6.1
            costs that can (and cannot) be included in a restructuring provision, Ch. 26, 6.1.4
            definition, Ch. 26, 6.1.1
            recognition of a restructuring provision, Ch. 26, 6.1.2
            recognition of obligations arising from the sale of an operation, Ch. 26, 6.1.3
        self insurance, Ch. 26, 6.13
        settlement payments, Ch. 26, 6.15
        warranty provisions, Ch. 26, 6.10

IAS 38–*Intangible Assets*, Ch. 17, 1–11. *See also* Intangible assets
    acquisition as part of a business combination, Ch. 17, 5
        customer relationship intangible assets, Ch. 17, 5.4

in-process research and development, Ch. 17, 5.5
intangible assets acquired, Ch. 17, 5.2
measuring the fair value of intangible assets, Ch. 17, 5.3
recognition of intangible assets acquired in a business combination, Ch. 17, 5.1
agile software development, Ch. 17, 6.2.6
amortisation of intangible assets, Ch. 17, 9
  assessing the useful life of an intangible asset as finite/indefinite, Ch. 17, 9.1
    factors affecting the useful life, Ch. 17, 9.1.1
    useful life of contractual/other legal rights, Ch. 17, 9.1.2
  impairment losses, Ch. 17, 9.4
  intangible assets with a finite useful life, Ch. 17, 9.2
    amortisation period and method, Ch. 17, 9.2.1
      amortisation of programme and other broadcast rights, Ch. 17, 9.2.1.B
      amortising customer relationships and similar intangible assets, Ch. 17, 9.2.1.A
    residual value, Ch. 17, 9.2.4
    revenue-based amortisation, Ch. 17, 9.2.2
    review of amortisation period and amortisation method, Ch. 17, 9.2.3
  intangible assets with an indefinite useful life, Ch. 17, 9.3
  retirements and disposals, Ch. 17, 9.5
    derecognition of parts of intangible assets, Ch. 17, 9.5.1
background, Ch. 17, 1.1
cloud computing, Ch. 17, 11.6
  implementation costs, Ch. 17, 11.6.2
  'software as a service' cloud computing arrangements, Ch. 17, 11.6.1
development phase, Ch. 17, 6.2.2
disclosure, Ch. 17, 10
  additional disclosures when the revaluation model is applied, Ch. 17, 10.4
  general disclosures, Ch. 17, 10.1
  profit/loss presentation, Ch. 17, 10.3
  of research and development expenditure, Ch. 17, 10.5
  statement of financial position presentation, Ch. 17, 10.2
first-time adoption, Ch. 5, 7.14
identifiability, Ch. 17, 2.1.1
  in relation to asset acquired in a business combination, Ch. 17, 5.1.3
impairment losses, Ch. 17, 9.4
intangible asset, definition, Ch. 17, 2.1–2.1.3
  control, Ch. 17, 2.1.2
  future economic benefits, Ch. 17, 2.1.3
  identifiability, Ch. 17, 2.1.1
internally generated intangible assets, Ch. 17, 6
  cost of an internally generated intangible asset, Ch. 17, 6.3
    determining the costs eligible for capitalisation, Ch. 17, 6.3.2
      establishing the time from which costs can be capitalised, Ch. 17, 6.3.1
  development phase, Ch. 17, 6.2.2
  internally generated brands, mastheads, publishing titles and customer lists, Ch. 17, 6.2.4
  internally generated goodwill, Ch. 17, 6.1
  pharmaceutical industry, research and development in, Ch. 17, 6.2.3

research phase, Ch. 17, 6.2.1
website costs (SIC-32), Ch. 17, 6.2.5
measurement, Ch. 17, 3.2
  asset exchanges, Ch. 17, 4.7.1
  assets acquired for contingent consideration, Ch. 17, 4.5
measurement after initial recognition, Ch. 17, 8
  cost model for measurement of intangible assets, Ch. 17, 8.1
  revaluation model for measurement of intangible assets, Ch. 17, 8.2
    accounting for revaluations, Ch. 17, 8.2.3
    frequency of revaluations, Ch. 17, 8.2.2
    revaluation is only allowed if there is an active market, Ch. 17, 8.2.1
objective, Ch. 17, 2
recognition, Ch. 17, 3.1
  assets acquired in a business combination, Ch. 17, 5.1
  of expense, Ch. 17, 7
    catalogues and other advertising costs, Ch. 17, 7.1
    programme and other broadcast rights, Ch. 17, 3.1.1
    separately acquired intangible assets, Ch. 17, 4.1
research and development in pharmaceutical industry, Ch. 17, 6.2.3
retirements and disposals, Ch. 17, 9.5
scope of, Ch. 17, 2
separate acquisition, Ch. 17, 4
  by way of government grant, Ch. 17, 4.6
  components of cost, Ch. 17, 4.2
  costs to be expensed, Ch. 17, 4.3
  exchanges of assets
    commercial substance, Ch. 17, 4.7.2
    measurement of assets exchanged, Ch. 17, 4.7.1
  income from incidental operations, Ch. 17, 4.4
  measurement of intangible assets acquired for contingent consideration, Ch. 17, 4.5
  recognition, Ch. 17, 4.1
specific regulatory and environmental issues regarding intangible assets, Ch. 17, 11
  accounting for green certificates/renewable energy certificates, Ch. 17, 11.3
  accounting for REACH costs, Ch. 17, 11.4
  crypto-assets, Ch. 17, 11.5
  emissions trading schemes, Ch. 17, 11.2
  rate-regulated activities, Ch. 17, 11.1
subsequent expenditure, Ch. 17, 3.3
terms used in, Ch. 17, 1.2
IAS 39–*Financial Instruments: Recognition and Measurement*, Ch. 44, 3. *See also* Financial instruments, recognition and initial measurement
  hedge accounting, Ch. 53, 1.3, 14
    requirements in IAS 39, Ch. 53, 14
IAS 40–*Investment Property*, Ch. 13, 4.3; Ch. 19, 1–12. *See also* Investment property
  cost model, Ch. 19, 7
  definitions, Ch. 19, 2
  disclosure requirements of, Ch. 19, 12
    for cost model, Ch. 19, 12.3
    direct operating expenses, Ch. 19, 12.1.3
    for fair value model, Ch. 19, 12.2
    level of aggregation for IFRS 13 disclosures, Ch. 19, 12.1.2

IAS 40–*Investment Property*—*contd*
  disclosure requirements of—*contd*
    methods and assumptions in fair value estimates, Ch. 19, 12.1.1
    presentation of changes in fair value, Ch. 19, 12.2.1
    presentation of sales proceeds, Ch. 19, 12.4
    under both fair value and cost models, Ch. 19, 12.1
    where fair value cannot be determined reliably, Ch. 19, 12.2.2
  disposal of, Ch. 19, 10
  fair value model, Ch. 19, 6
  held for sale, Ch. 19, 8
  initial measurement, Ch. 19, 4
  interim reporting, Ch. 19, 11
  measurement after initial recognition, Ch. 19, 5
  recognition, Ch. 19, 3
    business combination, Ch. 19, 3.3
      definition of business, Ch. 19, 3.3.1
    cost recognition, Ch. 19, 3.2
      allocation into parts, Ch. 19, 3.2.2
      repairs and maintenance, Ch. 19, 3.2.1
    expenditure prior to planning permissions/zoning consents, Ch. 19, 3.1
  scope, Ch. 19, 2
    group of assets leased out under a single operating lease, Ch. 19, 2.10
    investment property under construction, Ch. 19, 2.5
    land, Ch. 19, 2.2
    property held for own use ('owner-occupied'), Ch. 19, 2.4
    property held/under construction for sale in the ordinary course of business, Ch. 19, 2.6
    property interests held under a lease, Ch. 19, 2.1
    property leased to others, Ch. 19, 2.3
    property where rentals are determined by reference to the operations in the property, Ch. 19, 2.9
    property with dual uses, Ch. 19, 2.7
    property with the provision of ancillary services, Ch. 19, 2.8
  transfer of assets to/from investment property, Ch. 19, 9
IAS 41–*Agriculture*, Ch. 42, 1–5
  control, Ch. 42, 3.1.1
  definitions, Ch. 42, 2.2
    agriculture-related definitions, Ch. 42, 2.2.1
      bearer plants, Ch. 42, 2.2.1.A
    general definitions, Ch. 42, 2.2.2
  disclosure, Ch. 42, 5
    additional disclosures if fair value cannot be measured reliably, Ch. 42, 5.3
    fair value measurement disclosures, Ch. 42, 5.2
    government grants, Ch. 42, 5.4
    groups of biological assets, Ch. 42, 5.1.3
    income statement, Ch. 42, 5.1.2
    statement of financial position, Ch. 42, 5.1.1
      current *vs.* non-current classification, Ch. 42, 5.1.1.A
  government grants, Ch. 42, 3.3
  measurement, Ch. 42, 3.2
    agricultural produce, Ch. 42, 3.2.2
    biological assets within the scope of IAS 41, Ch. 42, 3.2.1
      initial and subsequent measurement, Ch. 42, 3.2.1.A
      subsequent expenditure, Ch. 42, 3.2.1.B
    gains and losses, Ch. 42, 3.2.4
    inability to measure fair value reliably, Ch. 42, 3.2.5
      cost model, Ch. 42, 3.2.5.B
      rebutting the presumption, Ch. 42, 3.2.5.A
    requirements for produce growing on a bearer plant, Ch. 42, 3.2.3
      agricultural produce growing on bearer plants, Ch. 42, 3.2.3.B
      requirements for bearer plants in the scope of IAS 16, Ch. 42, 3.2.3.A
  measurement of change, Ch. 42, 2.2.1
  measuring fair value less costs to sell, Ch. 42, 4
    determining costs to sell, Ch. 42, 4.4
    establishing what to measure, Ch. 42, 4.2
      grouping of assets, Ch. 42, 4.2.2
      unit of account, Ch. 42, 4.2.1
    interaction between IAS 41 and IFRS 13, Ch. 42, 4.1
    measuring fair value: IAS 41-specific requirements, Ch. 42, 4.5
      financing cash flows and taxation, Ch. 42, 4.5.5
      forward sales contracts, Ch. 42, 4.5.3
      obligation to re-establish a biological asset after harvest, Ch. 42, 4.5.2
      onerous contracts, Ch. 42, 4.5.4
      use of external independent valuers, Ch. 42, 4.5.1
    measuring fair value: overview of IFRS 13's requirements, Ch. 42, 4.6
      fair value measurement framework, Ch. 42, 4.6.1
      highest and best use and valuation premise, Ch. 42, 4.6.2
        biological assets attached to land, Ch. 42, 4.6.2.A
      selecting appropriate assumptions, Ch. 42, 4.6.3
        condition and location, Ch. 42, 4.6.3.A
      valuation techniques in IFRS 13, Ch. 42, 4.6.4
        cost as an approximation of fair value, Ch. 42, 4.6.4.A
    problem of measuring fair value for part-grown or immature biological assets, Ch. 42, 4.7
    when to measure fair value, Ch. 42, 4.3
  objective, Ch. 42, 2.1
  recognition, Ch. 42, 3.1
  scope, Ch. 42, 2.3
    agricultural produce before and after harvest, Ch. 42, 2.3.2
    bearer plants and produce growing on a bearer plant, Ch. 42, 2.3.3
    biological assets outside the scope of IAS 41, Ch. 42, 2.3.1
    concessions, Ch. 42, 2.3.6
    leases of biological assets (excluding bearer plants), Ch. 42, 2.3.5
    products that are the result of processing after harvest, Ch. 42, 2.3.4
Identifiable assets acquired in a business combination, Ch. 9, 5.2
  acquisition-date fair values of, Ch. 9, 5.3
  classifying, Ch. 9, 5.4
  intangible assets, Ch. 9, 5.5.2
  operating leases, recognising and measuring, Ch. 9, 5.5
  recognising, Ch. 9, 5
IFRIC 1–*Changes in Existing Decommissioning, Restoration and Similar Liabilities*, Ch. 26, 1.2.1, 6.3
  changes in estimated decommissioning costs, Ch. 26, 6.3.1

IFRIC 12–*Service Concession Arrangements*, Ch. 25, 1–7. *See also* Service concession arrangements
   accounting by the concession operator, financial asset and intangible asset models, Ch. 25, 4
      accounting for contractual payments to be made by an operator to a grantor, Ch. 25, 4.7
         under the financial asset model, Ch. 25, 4.7.2
         under the intangible asset model, Ch. 25, 4.7.3
         variable payments in a service concession, Ch. 25, 4.7.1
      accounting for residual interests, Ch. 25, 4.6
      allocating the consideration, Ch. 25, 4.1.1
         allocating the transaction price to the performance obligations in the contract, Ch. 25, 4.1.1.D
         determining the transaction price under the contract, Ch. 25, 4.1.1.C
         identifying the contract(s) with a customer, Ch. 25, 4.1.1.A
         identifying the performance obligations in the contract, Ch. 25, 4.1.1.B
      'bifurcation,' single arrangements that contain both financial and intangible assets, Ch. 25, 4.5
      determining the accounting model after the construction phase, Ch. 25, 4.1.2
      financial asset model, Ch. 25, 4.2
      intangible asset model, Ch. 25, 4.3
         amortisation of the intangible asset, Ch. 25, 4.3.1
         impairment during the construction phase, Ch. 25,4.3.2
      revenue recognition implications of the two models, Ch. 25, 4.4
   application of IFRIC 12 and interactions with IFRS 15 and IFRS 9, Ch. 26, 6
   control model, Ch. 25, 3
      assets within scope, Ch. 25, 3.3
      control of the residual interest, Ch. 25, 3.2
      partially regulated assets, Ch. 25, 3.4
      regulation of services, Ch. 25, 3.1
   definitions, Ch. 25, 1.2
   disclosure requirements, SIC-29, Ch. 25, 7
   revenue and expenditure during the operations phase, Ch. 25, 5
      accounting for the operations phase, Ch. 25, 5.2
      additional construction and upgrade services, Ch. 25, 5.1
         subsequent construction services that are part of the initial infrastructure asset, Ch. 25, 5.1.1
         subsequent construction services that comprise additions to the initial infrastructure, Ch. 25, 5.1.2
      items provided to the operator by the grantor, Ch. 25, 5.3
   scope of IFRIC 12, Ch. 25, 2
      accounting by grantors, Ch. 25, 2.5
      arrangements that are not in the scope of IFRIC 12, Ch. 25, 2.2
         outsourcing arrangements, Ch. 25, 2.2.1
      interaction of IFRS 16 and IFRIC 12, Ch. 25, 2.3
      private-to-private arrangements, Ch. 25, 2.4
      public service nature of the obligation, Ch. 25, 2.1
IFRIC 14–IAS 19–*The Limit on a Defined Benefit Asset Minimum Funding Requirements and their Interaction*, Ch. 35, 8.2

IFRIC 16–*Hedges of a Net Investment in a Foreign Operation*, Ch. 7, 2.3; Ch. 15, 6.1.5. *See also* Net investment hedges
IFRIC 17–*Distributions of Non-cash Assets to Owners*, Ch. 7, 3.7; Ch. 8, 2.4.2
   demerger and, Ch. 7, 3.7
   measurement in, Ch. 7, 3.7.2; Ch. 8, 2.4.2.B
   recognition in, Ch. 7, 3.7.2; Ch. 8, 2.4.2.B
   scope of, Ch. 7, 3.7.1; Ch. 8, 2.4.2.A
IFRIC 19–*Extinguishing Financial Liabilities with Equity Instruments*, Ch. 5, 5.16; Ch. 47, 7
   effective date, Ch. 47, 7.1
   requirements, Ch. 47, 7.2
   scope, Ch. 47, 7.1
IFRIC 20–*Stripping Costs in the Production Phase of a Surface Mine*, Ch. 5, 5.19; Ch. 18, 3.1.6; Ch. 43, 15.5
   determining when production phase commences, Ch. 43, 15.5.2
   disclosures, Ch. 43, 15.5.6
   initial recognition, Ch. 43, 15.5.4
      allocating costs between inventory and the stripping activity asset, Ch. 43, 15.5.4.A
      identifying the component of the ore body, Ch. 43, 15.5.4.B
   recognition criteria-stripping activity asset, Ch. 43, 15.5.3
   scope of IFRIC 20, Ch. 43, 15.5.1
   subsequent measurement, Ch. 43, 15.5.5
IFRIC 21–*Levies*, Ch. 26, 6.8
IFRIC 22–*Foreign Currency Transactions and Advance Consideration*, Ch. 5, 5.22
IFRIC 23–*Uncertainty over Income Tax Treatments*, Ch. 33, 9
   changes to estimates of uncertain tax treatments, Ch. 38, 3.6
   events after the reporting period
      adjusting events, Ch. 38, 2.1.2
      non-adjusting events, Ch. 38, 2.1.3
IFRS 1–*First-time Adoption of International Financial Reporting Standards*, Ch. 5, 1–8. *See also* First-time adoption accounting
   policies and practical application issues, Ch. 5, 7
   authoritative literature, Ch. 5, 1.2
   borrowing costs, Ch. 5, 5.15
   compound financial instruments, Ch. 5, 5.10
   cumulative translation differences, Ch. 5, 5.7
   decommissioning liabilities included in the cost of property, plant and equipment, Ch. 5, 5.13
   deemed cost, Ch. 5, 5.5
   designation of contracts to buy or sell a non-financial item, Ch. 5, 5.23
   designation of previously recognised financial instruments, Ch. 5, 5.11
   disclosures, Ch. 5, 5.20.6.B, 6
   embedded derivatives, Ch. 5, 4.11
   employee benefits, Ch. 5, 7.7
   exceptions to retrospective application of other IFRSs, Ch. 5, 4
   estimates, Ch. 5, 4.2
   extinguishing financial liabilities with equity instruments, Ch. 5, 5.16
   fair value measurement of financial assets and liabilities at initial recognition, Ch. 5, 5.12
   financial assets or intangible assets accounted for in accordance with IFRIC 12, Ch. 5, 5.14

IFRS 1–*First-time Adoption of International Financial Reporting Standards*—contd
  financial instruments under IFRS 9, classification and measurement of, Ch. 5, 4.9
  first-time adopter, Ch. 5, 2
  foreign currency transactions and advance consideration, Ch. 5, 5.22
  future developments, Ch. 5, 1.4
  government loans, Ch. 5, 4.12
  hedge accounting, Ch. 5, 4.4–4.7
    in opening IFRS statement of financial position, Ch. 5, 4.5
    subsequent treatment, Ch. 5, 4.6
  impairment of financial instruments, Ch. 5, 4.10
  insurance contracts, Ch. 5, 4.13, 5.4
  investment entities, Ch. 5, 5.9.5
  investments in subsidiaries, joint ventures and associates, Ch. 5, 6.5.2
  joint arrangements, Ch. 5, 5.18
  leases, Ch. 5, 5.6, 7.5
  non-controlling interests, Ch. 5, 4.8
  objectives of, Ch. 5, 1.1
  opening IFRS statement of financial position, Ch. 5, 3
    and accounting policies, Ch. 5, 3.2
    defined terms, Ch. 5, 1.3
    departures from full retrospective application, Ch. 5, 3.5
    fair value and deemed cost, Ch. 5, 3.3
    first-time adoption timeline, Ch. 5, 3.1
    hedge accounting in, Ch. 5, 4.5
    transitional provisions in other standards, Ch. 5, 3.4
  optional exemptions from the requirements of certain IFRSs, Ch. 5, 5
    business combinations and acquisitions of associates and joint arrangements, Ch. 5, 5.2
      associates and joint arrangements, Ch. 5, 5.2.2.A
    business combinations and acquisitions of associates and joint ventures asset acquisitions, Ch. 5, 5.2.1.A
      assets and liabilities excluded, Ch. 5, 5.2.4.B
      assets and liabilities to be recognised in the opening IFRS statement of financial position, Ch. 5, 5.2.4
      classification of business combinations, Ch. 5, 5.2.3
      currency adjustments to goodwill, Ch. 5, 5.2.6
      deferred taxes and non-controlling interests, measurement of, Ch. 5, 5.2.9
      definition of a 'business' under IFRS 3, Ch. 5, 5.2.1
      derecognition of negative goodwill, Ch. 5, 5.2.5.B
      goodwill previously deducted from equity, Ch. 5, 5.2.5.C
      in-process research and development, Ch. 5, 5.2.4.D
      option to restate business combinations retrospectively, Ch. 5, 5.2.2
      previous GAAP carrying amount as deemed cost, Ch. 5, 5.2.4.C
      previously consolidated entities that are not subsidiaries, Ch. 5, 5.2.8
      previously unconsolidated subsidiaries, Ch. 5, 5.2.7
      prohibition of other adjustments of goodwill, Ch. 5, 5.2.5.A
      recognition and measurement requirements, Ch. 5, 5.2.4.F
      recognition of assets and liabilities, Ch. 5, 5.2.4.B
      restatement of goodwill, Ch. 5, 5.2.5
      subsequent measurement under IFRSs not based on cost, Ch. 5, 5.2.4.E
      transition accounting for contingent consideration, Ch. 5, 5.2.10
  presentation and disclosure, Ch. 5, 6
    comparative information, Ch. 5, 6.1 designation of financial instruments, Ch. 5, 6.4
    disclosure of IFRS information before adoption of IFRSs, Ch. 5, 6.7
    disclosures regarding deemed cost use, Ch. 5, 6.5
      after severe hyperinflation, Ch. 5, 6.5.5
      for assets used in operations subject to rate regulation, Ch. 5, 6.5.4
      for investments in subsidiaries, joint ventures and associates, Ch. 5, 6.5.2
      for oil and gas assets, Ch. 5, 6.5.3
      use of fair value as deemed cost, Ch. 5, 6.5.1
    explanation of transition to IFRSs, Ch. 5, 6.3
      disclosure of reconciliations, Ch. 5, 6.3.1
      inclusion of IFRS 1 reconciliations by cross reference, Ch. 5, 6.3.4
      line-by-line reconciliations and detailed explanations, Ch. 5, 6.3.2
      recognition and reversal of impairments, Ch. 5, 6.3.3
      reconciliation by a first-time adopter that continues to publish previous GAAP financial statements, Ch. 5, 6.3.1.A
    interim financial reports, Ch. 5, 6.6
      disclosures in, Ch. 5, 6.6.2
      reconciliations in, Ch. 5, 6.6.1
  regulatory deferral accounts, Ch. 5, 5.20
  regulatory issues, Ch. 5, 8
  revenue from contracts with customers (IFRS 15), Ch. 5, 5.21; Ch. 5, 7.6
  severe hyperinflation, Ch. 5, 5.17
  share-based payment transactions, Ch. 5, 5.3
  stripping costs in the production phase of a surface mine, Ch. 5, 5.19
IFRS 2 – *Share-based payment*, Ch. 34, 1–16. *See also* Cash-settled share based payment transactions; Equity-settled share-based payment transactions; Share-based payment transactions; Vesting
  awards entitled to dividends during the vesting period, Ch. 34, 15.3
  awards vesting/exercisable on an exit event/change of control, Ch. 34, 15.4
    awards 'purchased for fair value', Ch. 34, 15.4.5
    awards requiring achievement of a minimum price on flotation/sale, Ch. 34, 15.4.4
    'drag along' and 'tag along' rights, Ch. 34, 15.4.6
    is flotation/sale a vesting condition or a non-vesting condition?, Ch. 34, 15.4.3
    grant date, Ch. 34, 15.4.1
    vesting period, Ch. 34, 15.4.2
  business combination, replacement share-based payment awards issued, Ch. 34, 11
    acquiree award not replaced by acquirer, Ch. 34, 11.3
    background, Ch. 34, 11.1
    financial statements of the acquired entity, Ch. 34, 11.4
    replacement award, Ch. 34, 11.2

Index

accounting for changes in vesting assumptions after the acquisition date, Ch. 34, 11.2.3
acquiree awards that the acquirer is not 'obliged' to replace, Ch. 34, 11.2.2
awards that the acquirer is 'obliged' to replace, Ch. 34, 11.2.1
cash-settled transactions, Ch. 34, 9
cost of awards, equity-settled transactions, Ch. 34, 5
development of IFRS 2, Ch. 34, 1.2
definitions, Ch. 34, 2.2.1
disclosures, Ch. 34, 13
equity-settled transactions
    allocation of expense, Ch. 34, 6
    cost of awards, Ch. 34, 5
    modification, cancellation and settlement, Ch. 34, 7
    overview, Ch. 34, 4
    valuation, Ch. 34, 8
first-time adoption, Ch. 34, 16.1
general recognition principles, Ch. 34, 3
grant date, Ch. 34, 5.3. *See also* Grant date
group share schemes, Ch. 34, 12. *See also* Group share schemes
loans to employees to purchase shares, Ch. 34, 15.2
market conditions, Ch. 34, 6.3
matching share awards, Ch. 34, 15.1
modification, cancellation and settlement of equity-settled transactions, Ch. 34, 7
non-compete agreements, Ch. 34, 3.2.3
Non-controlling interests in share-based payment transactions, Ch. 7, 5.1, 5.2, 5.6
objective of IFRS 2, Ch. 34, 2.1
overall approach of IFRS 2, Ch. 34, 1.4
    classification differences between IFRS 2 and IAS 32/IFRS 9, Ch. 34, 1.4.1
research project, Ch. 34, 1.2.1
scope, Ch. 34, 2.2
    definitions, Ch. 34, 2.2.1
    practical applications of scope requirements, Ch. 34, 2.2.4
        awards for which the counterparty has paid 'fair value', Ch. 34, 2.2.4.D
        awards with a foreign currency strike price, Ch. 34, 2.2.4.G
        cash bonus dependent on share price performance, Ch. 34, 2.2.4.E
        cash-settled awards based on an entity's 'enterprise value' or other formula, Ch. 34, 2.2.4.F
        equity-settled award of subsidiary with put option against the parent, Ch. 34, 2.2.4.B
        holding own shares to satisfy or 'hedge' awards, Ch. 34, 2.2.4.H
        increase in ownership interest with no change in number of shares held, Ch. 34, 2.2.4.C
        options over puttable instruments classified as equity under specific exception in IAS 32, Ch. 34, 2.2.4.J
        remuneration in non-equity shares and arrangements with put rights over equity shares, Ch. 34, 2.2.4.A
        shares/warrants issued in connection with a financial liability, Ch. 34, 2.2.4.I
        special discounts to certain categories of investor on a share issue, Ch. 34, 2.2.4.K
    transactions not within the scope of IFRS 2, Ch. 34, 2.2.3
        business combinations, Ch. 34, 2.2.3.C
        common control transactions and formation of joint arrangements, Ch. 34, 2.2.3.D
        transactions in financial assets outside the scope of IAS 32 and IFRS 9, Ch. 34, 2.2.3.F
        transactions in the scope of IAS 32 and IFRS 9, Ch. 34, 2.2.3.E
        transactions with shareholders in their capacity as such, Ch. 34, 2.2.3.A
        transfer of assets in group restructuring arrangements, Ch. 34, 2.2.3.B
    transactions within the scope of IFRS 2, Ch. 34, 2.2.2
        'all employee' share plans, Ch. 34, 2.2.2.D
        group schemes and transactions with group shareholders, Ch. 34, 2.2.2.A
        transactions where the identifiable consideration received appears to be less than the consideration given, Ch. 34, 2.2.2.C
        transactions with employee benefit trusts and similar vehicles, Ch. 34, 2.2.2.B
        vested transactions, Ch. 34, 2.2.2.E
South African black economic empowerment ('BEE') and similar arrangements, Ch. 34, 15.5
taxes related to share-based payment transactions, Ch. 34, 14
transactions with equity and cash alternatives, Ch. 34, 10
    awards requiring cash settlement in specific circumstances (awards with contingent cash settlement), Ch. 34, 10.3
        accounting for change in manner of settlement where award is contingent on future events outside the control of the entity and the counterparty, Ch. 34, 10.3.4
        cash settlement on a change of control, Ch. 34, 10.3.3
        cash-settled if contingency is outside entity's control, Ch. 34, 10.3.1
        cash-settled if contingency is outside entity's control and probable, Ch. 34, 10.3.2
        manner of settlement contingent on future events, Ch. 34, 10.3.5
    cash settlement alternative not based on share price/value, Ch. 34, 10.4
    transactions where the counterparty has choice of settlement, Ch. 34, 10.1
        accounting treatment, Ch. 34, 10.1.3
        'backstop' cash settlement rights, Ch. 34, 10.1.5
        cash-settlement alternative for employee introduced after grant date, Ch. 34, 10.1.4
        convertible bonds issued to acquire goods/services, Ch. 34, 10.1.6
        transactions in which the fair value is measured directly, Ch. 34, 10.1.1
        transactions in which the fair value is measured indirectly, Ch. 34, 10.1.2
    transactions where the entity has choice of settlement, Ch. 34, 10.2
        change in entity's settlement policy/intention leading to change in classification of award after grant date, Ch. 34, 10.2.3
        transactions treated as cash-settled, Ch. 34, 10.2.1
        transactions treated as equity-settled, Ch. 34, 10.2.2
valuation of equity-settled transactions, Ch. 34, 8
vesting conditions, Ch. 34, 3.1

IFRS 2 – Share-based payment—contd
  vesting conditions other than market conditions, Ch. 34, 6.2
  vesting period, Ch. 34, 3.3

IFRS 3–Business Combinations, Ch. 9, 1–16. *See also* Business combinations
  acquisition method of accounting, Ch. 9, 4
    acquisition date determination, Ch. 9, 4.2
    identifying the acquirer, Ch. 9, 4.1
      new entity formed to effect a business combination, Ch. 9, 4.1.1
      stapling arrangements, Ch. 9, 4.1.2
  assessing what is part of the exchange for the acquiree, Ch. 9, 11
    effective settlement of pre-existing relationships, Ch. 9, 11.1
    reimbursement for paying the acquirer's acquisition-related costs, Ch. 9, 11.3
    remuneration for future services of employees or former owners of the acquire, Ch. 9, 11.2
    restructuring plans, Ch. 9, 11.4
  bargain purchase transactions, Ch. 9, 10
  business combinations achieved in stages ('step acquisitions'), Ch. 9, 9
  consideration transferred, Ch. 9, 7
    acquisition-related costs, Ch. 9, 7.3
    business combinations achieved without the transfer of consideration, Ch. 9, 7.4
      business combinations by contract alone, Ch. 9, 7.4.1
    combinations involving mutual entities, Ch. 9, 7.5
    contingent consideration, Ch. 9, 7.1
      classification of a contingent consideration obligation, Ch. 9, 7.1.2
      initial recognition and measurement, Ch. 9, 7.1.1
      subsequent measurement and accounting, Ch. 9, 7.1.3
    replacement share-based payment awards, Ch. 9, 7; Ch. 34, 11.2, 11.3
  disclosures, Ch. 9, 16
    financial effects of adjustments recognised in the current reporting period, Ch. 9, 16.2
    illustrative example, Ch. 9, 16.4
    nature and financial effect of business combinations, Ch. 9, 16.1
      business combinations during the current reporting period, Ch. 9, 16.1.1
      business combinations effected after the end of the reporting period, Ch. 9, 16.1.2
  identifying a business combination, Ch. 9, 3.2.3
    definition of a business, Ch. 9, 3.2; Ch. 19, 3.3.1
      assessing whether an acquired process is substantive, Ch. 9, 3.2.4
      assessment whether acquired set of activities and assets constitutes a business, Ch. 9, 3.2.2
      'capable of' from the viewpoint of a market participant, Ch. 9, 3.2.5
      concentration test, Ch. 9, 3.2.3
      development stage entities, Ch. 9, 3.2.7
      identifying business combinations, Ch. 9, 3.2.6
      inputs, processes and outputs, Ch. 9, 3.2.1
  IFRS 3 (as revised in 2008) and subsequent amendments, Ch. 9, 1.1
    post-implementation review, Ch. 9, 1.1.1
  measurement period, Ch. 9, 12
    adjustments made after end of measurement period, Ch. 9, 12.2
    adjustments made during measurement period to provisional amounts, Ch. 9, 12.1
  push down accounting, Ch. 9, 15
  recognising and measuring goodwill or a gain in a bargain purchase, Ch. 9, 6
    subsequent accounting for goodwill, Ch. 9, 6.1
  recognising and measuring non-controlling interests, Ch. 7, 3.1.1, 3.1.2, 5, 6; Ch. 9, 8
    call and put options over non-controlling interests, Ch. 7, 6; Ch. 9, 8.5
    implications of method chosen for measuring non-controlling interests, Ch. 9, 8.3
    measuring qualifying non-controlling interests at acquisition-date fair value, Ch. 9, 8.1
    measuring qualifying non-controlling interests at the proportionate share of the value of net identifiable assets acquired, Ch. 9, 8.2
    measuring share-based payment and other components of non-controlling interests, Ch. 7, 5.1, 5.2, 5.6; Ch. 9, 8.4
  recognition and measurement of assets acquired, liabilities assumed and non-controlling interests, Ch. 9, 5, 5.5
    acquisition-date fair values of identifiable assets acquired and liabilities assumed, Ch. 9, 5.3
    classifying or designating identifiable assets acquired and liabilities assumed, Ch. 9, 5.4
    exceptions to recognition and/or measurement principles, Ch. 9, 5.6
      assets held for sale, Ch. 9, 5.6.6
      contingent liabilities, Ch. 9, 5.6.1; 9, 5.6.1.B
      employee benefits, Ch. 9, 5.6.3
      income taxes, Ch. 9, 5.6.2
      indemnification assets, Ch. 9, 5.6.4
      initial recognition and measurement, Ch. 9, 5.6.1.A
      insurance contracts within the scope of IFRS 17, Ch. 9, 5.6.9
      leases in which the acquiree is the lessee, Ch. 9, 5.6.8
      reacquired rights, Ch. 9, 5.6.5
      share-based payment transactions, Ch. 9, 5.6.7
    recognising and measuring particular assets acquired and liabilities assumed, Ch. 9, 5.5
      assembled workforce and other items that are not identifiable, Ch. 9, 5.5.4
      assets and liabilities related to contacts with customers, Ch. 9, 5.5.8
      assets that the acquirer does not intend to use or intends to use in a way that is different from other market participants, Ch. 9, 5.5.6
      assets with uncertain cash flows (valuation allowances), Ch. 9, 5.5.5
      combining an intangible asset with a related contract, identifiable asset or liability, Ch. 9, 5.5.2.C
      customer relationship intangible assets, Ch. 9, 5.5.2.B
      determining the fair values of intangible assets, Ch. 9, 5.5.2.F
      emission rights, Ch. 9, 5.5.2.E
      in-process research or development project expenditure, Ch. 9, 5.5.2.D

intangible assets, Ch. 9, 5.5.2.
    investments in equity-accounted entities, Ch. 9, 5.5.7
    items not qualifying as assets, Ch. 9, 5.5.4.B
    operating leases in which the acquiree is the lessor, Ch. 9, 5.5.1
    reacquired rights, Ch. 9, 5.5.3
  recognising identifiable assets acquired and liabilities assumed, Ch. 9, 5.2
  replacement awards in business combinations, Ch. 34, 11; Ch. 7, 5.2
  reverse acquisitions, Ch. 9, 14
    cash consideration, Ch. 9, 14.6
    earnings per share, Ch. 9, 14.5
    measuring goodwill, Ch. 9, 14.2
    measuring the consideration transferred, Ch. 9, 14.1
    non-controlling interest, Ch. 9, 14.4
    preparation and presentation of consolidated financial statements, Ch. 9, 14.3
    reverse acquisitions and acquirers that are not legal entities, Ch. 9, 14.9
    reverse acquisitions involving a non-trading shell company, Ch. 9, 14.8
    share-based payments, Ch. 9, 14.7
  scope of IFRS 3, Ch. 9, 2
    acquisition by an investment entity, Ch. 9, 2.3
    arrangements out of scope of IFRS 3, Ch. 9, 2.2
      acquisition of an asset or a group of assets that does not constitute a business, Ch. 9, 2.2.2, Ch. 19, 4.1.1
      arrangements under common control, Ch. 9, 2.2.3
      formation of a joint arrangement, Ch. 9, 2.2.1
    mutual entities, Ch. 9, 2.1
  subsequent measurement and accounting, Ch. 9, 13

IFRS 4–*Insurance Contracts*, Ch. 55, 1–12. *See also* Insurance contracts, IFRS 17
  development of, Ch. 55, 1.2
  objectives of, Ch. 55, 2
  scope of, Ch. 55, 2.2
    definitions, Ch. 55, 2.2.1
    product classification process, Ch. 55, 2.2.4
    transactions not within the scope of IFRS 4, Ch. 55, 2.2.3
      assets and liabilities arising from employment benefit plans, Ch. 55, 2.2.3.B
      contingent consideration payable/receivable in a business combination, Ch. 55, 2.2.3.E
      contingent rights and obligations related to non-financial items, Ch. 55, 2.2.3.C
      direct insurance contracts in which the entity is the policyholder, Ch. 55, 2.2.3.F
      financial guarantee contracts, Ch. 55, 2.2.3.D
      product warranties, Ch. 55, 2.2.3.A
    transactions within the scope of IFRS 4, Ch. 55, 2.2.2

IFRS 5–*Non-current Assets Held for Sale and Discontinued Operations*, Ch. 4, 1–6. *See also* Discontinued operation
  comparative information, Ch. 4, 4
    treatment on cessation of classification as held for sale, Ch. 4, 4.2
    treatment on initial classification as held for sale
      statement of comprehensive income, Ch. 4, 4.1.1
      statement of financial position, Ch. 4, 4.1.2
  disclosure requirements, Ch. 4, 5
  discontinued operation, Ch. 4, 3.2
    definition of, Ch. 4, 3.1
    presentation of, Ch. 4, 3.2
    trading with continuing operations, Ch. 4, 3.3
  future developments, Ch. 4, 6
  interaction with IFRS 9, Ch. 51, 7.4
  interaction of IFRS 12 and, Ch. 13, 2.2.1.C
  non-current assets (and disposal groups) held for sale/distribution, Ch. 4, 2
    classification, Ch. 4, 2.1, 2.1.1–2.1.3B
      abandonment, Ch. 4, 2.1.2.C
      classification as held for sale or as held for distribution to owners, Ch. 4, 2.1.2–2.1.2.C
      concept of a disposal group, Ch. 4, 2.1.1
      loss of control of a subsidiary, Ch. 4, 2.1.3.A; Ch. 7, 3.2, 3.7
      meaning of available for immediate sale, Ch. 4, 2.1.2.A
      meaning of highly probable, Ch. 4, 2.1.2.B
      partial disposal of an associate or joint venture, Ch. 4, 2.1.3.B
      partial disposals of operations, Ch. 4, 2.1.3
    measurement, Ch. 4, 2.2
      changes to a plan of sale/distribution, Ch. 4, 2.2.5
      impairments and reversals of impairment, Ch. 4, 2.2.3
      on initial classification as held for sale, Ch. 4, 2.2.2.A
      presentation in the statement of financial position of, Ch. 4, 2.2.4
      scope of the measurement requirements, Ch. 4, 2.2.1
      subsequent remeasurement, Ch. 4, 2.2.2.B
  objective and scope, Ch. 4, 1

IFRS 6–*Exploration for and Evaluation of Mineral Resources*, Ch. 43, 3. *See also* Extractive industries
  disclosure, Ch. 43, 3.6
  impairment, Ch. 43, 3.5
    additional considerations if E&E assets are impaired, Ch. 43, 3.5.5
    cash-generating units comprising successful and unsuccessful E&E projects, Ch. 43, 3.5.3
    impairment testing 'triggers,' Ch. 43, 3.5.1
    income statement treatment of E&E, Ch. 43, 3.5.6
    order of impairment testing, Ch. 43, 3.5.4
    reversal of impairment losses, Ch. 43, 3.5.7
    specifying the level at which E&E assets are assessed for impairment, Ch. 43, 3.5.2
  measurement of exploration and evaluation assets, Ch. 43, 3.3
    capitalisation of borrowing costs, Ch. 43, 3.3.2
    types of expenditure in, Ch. 43, 3.3.1
  objective, Ch. 43, 3.1
  presentation and classification, Ch. 43, 3.4
    reclassification of E&E assets, Ch. 43, 3.4.1
  recognition of exploration and evaluation assets, Ch. 43, 3.2
    area-of-interest method, Ch. 43, 3.2.5
    changes in accounting policies, Ch. 43, 3.2.6
    developing an accounting policy under IFRS 6, Ch. 43, 3.2.1
    full cost method, Ch. 43, 3.2.4
    options for an exploration and evaluation policy, Ch. 43, 3.2.2
    successful efforts method, Ch. 43, 3.2.3
  scope, Ch. 43, 3.1
    scope exclusions in other standards relating to the extractive industries, Ch. 43, 3.1.1

IFRS 7–*Financial Instruments: Disclosures*, Ch. 44, 4, Ch. 54, 1–9
   disclosures, structuring, Ch. 54, 3
      classes of financial instrument, Ch. 54, 3.3
      level of detail, Ch. 54, 3.1
      materiality, Ch. 54, 3.2
   future developments, Ch. 54, 9
   interim reports, Ch. 54, 2.3
   nature and extent of risks arising from financial instruments, Ch. 54, 5
      credit risk, Ch. 54, 5.3
         collateral and other credit enhancements obtained, Ch. 54, 5.3.5
         credit risk exposure, Ch. 54, 5.3.4
         credit risk management practices, Ch. 54, 5.3.2
         illustrative disclosures, Ch. 54, 5.3.6
         quantitative and qualitative information about amounts arising from expected credit losses, Ch. 54, 5.3.3
         scope and objectives, Ch. 54, 5.3.1
      liquidity risk, Ch. 54, 5.4
         information provided to key management, Ch. 54, 5.4.1
         management of associated liquidity risk, Ch. 54, 5.4.3
         maturity analyses, Ch. 54, 5.4.2
         puttable financial instruments classified as equity, Ch. 54, 5.4.4
      market risk, Ch. 54, 5.5
         'basic' sensitivity analysis, Ch. 54, 5.5.1
         other market risk disclosures, Ch. 54, 5.5.3
         value-at-risk and similar analyses, Ch. 54, 5.5.2
      qualitative disclosures, Ch. 54, 5.1
      quantitative disclosures, Ch. 54, 5.2, 5.6
         capital disclosures, Ch. 54, 5.6.3
         concentrations of risk, Ch. 54, 5.6.1
         operational risk, Ch. 54, 5.6.2
   presentation on the face of the financial statements and related disclosures, Ch. 54, 7
      gains and losses recognised in other comprehensive income, Ch. 54, 7.2
      gains and losses recognised in profit/loss embedded derivatives, Ch. 54, 7.1.4
         entities whose share capital is not equity, Ch. 54, 7.1.5
         further analysis of gains and losses recognised in profit/loss, Ch. 54, 7.1.2
         offsetting and hedges, Ch. 54, 7.1.3
         presentation on the face of the statement of comprehensive income (or income statement), Ch. 54, 7
      statement of cash flows, Ch. 54, 7.5
      statement of changes in equity, Ch. 54, 7.3
      statement of financial position, Ch. 54, 7.4
         assets and liabilities, Ch. 54, 7.4.3
         convertible loans, Ch. 54, 7.4.4.B
         current and non-current assets and liabilities, distinction between, Ch. 54, 7.4.4
         debt with refinancing or roll over agreements, Ch. 54, 7.4.4.D
         derivatives, Ch. 54, 7.4.4.A
         disclosure requirements, Ch. 54, 7.4.2.C
         enforceable legal right of set-off, Ch. 54, 7.4.1.A
         entities whose share capital is not equity, Ch. 54, 7.4.6
         equity, Ch. 54, 7.4.5
         intention to settle net, Ch. 54, 7.4.1.C
         loan covenants, Ch. 54, 7.4.4.E
         long-term loans with repayment on demand terms, Ch. 54, 7.4.4.C
         master netting agreements, Ch. 54, 7.4.1.B
         objective, Ch. 54, 7.4.2.A
         offsetting collateral amounts, Ch. 54, 7.4.1.F
         offsetting financial assets and financial liabilities, Ch. 54, 7.4.1
         offsetting financial assets and financial liabilities: disclosure, Ch. 54, 7.4.2
         scope, Ch. 54, 7.4.2.B
         situations where offset is not normally appropriate, Ch. 54, 7.4.1.D
         unit of account, Ch. 54, 7.4.1.G
   significance of financial instruments for an entity's financial position/performance, Ch. 54, 4
      accounting policies, Ch. 54, 4.1
      business combinations, Ch. 54, 4.6
         acquired receivables, Ch. 54, 4.6.1
         contingent consideration and indemnification assets, Ch. 54, 4.6.2
      fair values, Ch. 54, 4.5
         day 1 profits, Ch. 54, 4.5.2
         general disclosure requirements, Ch. 54, 4.5.1
      hedge accounting, Ch. 54, 4.3
         amount, timing and uncertainty of future cash flows, Ch. 54, 4.3.2
         effects of hedge accounting on financial position and performance, Ch. 54, 4.3.3
         option to designate a credit exposure as measured at fair value through profit/loss, Ch. 54, 4.3.4
         risk management strategy, Ch. 54, 4.3.1
         uncertainty arising from interest rate benchmark (or IBOR) reform, Ch. 54, 4.3.5
      income, expenses, gains and losses, Ch. 54, 4.2
         fee income and expense, Ch. 54, 4.2.3
         gains and losses by measurement category, Ch. 54, 4.2.1
         interest income and expense, Ch. 54, 4.2.2
      statement of financial position, Ch. 54, 4.4
         categories of financial assets and financial liabilities, Ch. 54, 4.4.1
         collateral, Ch. 54, 4.4.6
         compound financial instruments with multiple embedded derivatives, Ch. 54, 4.4.7
         defaults and breaches of loans payable, Ch. 54, 4.4.8
         financial assets designated as measured at fair value through profit/loss, Ch. 54, 4.4.3
         financial liabilities designated at fair value through profit/loss, Ch. 54, 4.4.2
         interests in associates and joint ventures accounted for in accordance with IFRS 9, Ch. 54, 4.4.9
         investments in equity instruments designated at fair value through other comprehensive income (IFRS 9), Ch. 54, 4.4.4
         reclassification, Ch. 54, 4.4.5
   transfers of financial assets, Ch. 54, 6
      meaning of 'transfer,' Ch. 54, 6.1

transferred financial assets that are derecognised in their
   entirety, Ch. 54, 6.3
      disclosure requirements, Ch. 54, 6.3.2
      meaning of continuing involvement, Ch. 54, 6.3.1
transferred financial assets that are not derecognised in
   their entirety, Ch. 54, 6.2
transitional provisions, Ch. 54, 8
IFRS 8–*Operating Segments*, Ch. 36, 1–6. *See also* Operating
segments; Reportable segments
   definition of an operating segment, Ch. 36, 3.1.3
      availability of discrete financial information, Ch. 36, 1.3
      'chief operating decision maker' and 'segment manager,'
         Ch. 36, 3.1.2
      equity accounted investment can be an operating segment,
         Ch. 36, 3.1.5
      revenue earning business activities, Ch. 36, 3.1.1
      when a single set of components is not immediately
         apparent, Ch. 36, 3.1.4
   entity-wide disclosures for all entities, Ch. 36, 6
      information about geographical areas, Ch. 36, 6.2
      information about major customers, Ch. 36, 6.3
         customers known to be under common control,
            Ch. 36, 6.3.1
      information about products and services, Ch. 36, 6.1
   externally reportable segments, identifying, Ch. 36, 3.2
      aggregation criteria, Ch. 36, 3.2.1
      'all other segments,' Ch. 36, 3.2.4
      combining small operating segments into a larger
         reportable segment, Ch. 36, 3.2.3
      'practical limit' for the number of reported operating
         segments, Ch. 36, 3.2.5
      restatement of segments reported in comparative periods,
         Ch. 36, 3.2.6
      quantitative thresholds, operating segments which are
         reportable because of their size, Ch. 36, 3.2.2
   features of IFRS 8, Ch. 36, 1.2
   measurement, Ch. 36, 4
   objective of IFRS 8, Ch. 36, 2.1
   reportable segments, information to be disclosed, Ch. 36, 5
      additional disclosures relating to segment assets,
         Ch. 36, 5.4
      disclosures required by IFRS 15, Ch. 36, 1.3
      disclosure of commercially sensitive information,
         Ch. 36, 5.8
      disclosure of other elements of revenue, income and
         expense, Ch. 36, 5.3
      explanation of the measurements used in segment
         reporting, Ch. 36, 5.5
      general information about reportable segments,
         Ch. 36, 5.1
         disclosure of how operating segments are aggregated,
            Ch. 36, 5.1.1
      measure of segment profit or loss, total assets and total
         liabilities, Ch. 36, 5.2
      reconciliations, Ch. 36, 5.6
      restatement of previously reported information,
         Ch. 36, 5.7
         changes in organisation structure, Ch. 36, 5.7.1
         changes in segment measures, Ch. 36, 5.7.2
   scope of IFRS 8, Ch. 36, 2.2
      consolidated financial statements presented with those of
         the parent, Ch. 36, 2.2.2
      entities providing segment information on a voluntary
         basis, Ch. 36, 2.2.3
      meaning of 'traded in a public market', Ch. 36, 2.2.1
   single set of operating segments, identifying, Ch. 36, 3
   terms used in IFRS 8, Ch. 36, 1.4
   transitional provisions, Ch. 36, 1.5
IFRS 9–*Financial Instruments*, Ch. 44, 5; Ch. 48, 1–9; Ch. 49,
1–3. *See also* Financial instruments, classification (IFRS 9);
Financial instruments, hedge accounting (IFRS 9); Financial
instruments, subsequent measurement (IFRS 9)
   amortised cost and the effective interest method, Ch. 50, 3
      fixed interest, fixed term instruments, Ch. 50, 3.2
      floating rate instruments, Ch. 50, 3.3
      inflation-linked debt, Ch. 50, 3.6
      modified financial assets and liabilities, Ch. 50, 3.8
      more complex financial liabilities, Ch. 50, 3.7
      perpetual debt instruments, Ch. 50, 3.5
      prepayment, call and similar options, Ch. 50, 3.4
         estimated cash flows, revisions to, Ch. 50, 3.4.1
   'business model' assessment, Ch. 48, 5
      applying in practice, Ch. 48, 5.6
      consolidated and subsidiary accounts, Ch. 48, 5.5
      hold to collect contractual cash flows, Ch. 48, 5.2
         impact of sales on the assessment, Ch. 48, 5.2.1
      hold to collect contractual cash flows and selling financial
         assets, Ch. 48, 5.3
      level at which the business model assessment is applied,
         Ch. 48, 5.1
      transferred financial assets that are not derecognised,
         Ch. 48, 5.2.2
   classification, Ch. 48, 2
   contractual cash flows, Ch. 48, 6
      auction rate securities, Ch. 48, 6.4.4
      bonds with a capped or floored interest rate, Ch. 48, 6.3.3
      contractual features that change the timing or amount,
         Ch. 48, 6.4.4
      contractually linked instruments, Ch. 48, 6.6
         assessing the characteristics of the underlying pool,
            Ch. 48, 6.6.1
         assessing the exposure to credit risk in the tranche held,
            Ch. 48, 6.6.2
         characteristics of underlying pool, assessing, Ch. 48,
            6.6.1
         exposure to credit risk in the tranche held, assessing,
            Ch. 48, 6.6.2
      conventional subordination features, Ch. 48, 6.3.1
      convertible debt, Ch. 48, 6.4.5
      de minimis features, Ch. 48, 6.4.1.A
      debt covenants, Ch. 48, 6.4.4
      dual currency instruments, Ch. 48, 6.4.5
      five-year constant maturity bond, Ch. 48, 6.4.2
      fixed rate bond prepayable by the issuer at fair value,
         Ch. 48, 6.4.5
      full recourse loans secured by collateral, Ch. 48, 6.3.2
      interest rate period, Ch. 48, 6.4.2
      inverse floater, Ch. 48, 6.4.5
      investment in open-ended money market or debt funds,
         Ch. 48, 6.4.5

IFRS 9–*Financial Instruments*—*contd*
  contractual cash flows—*contd*
    lender has discretion to change the interest rate, Ch. 48, 6.3.4
    loan commitments, Ch. 48, 6.4.6
    meaning of 'interest,' Ch. 48, 6.2
    meaning of 'principal,' Ch. 48, 6.1
    modified time value of money component, Ch. 48, 6.4.2
    multiple of a benchmark interest rate, Ch. 48, 6.4.5
    non-genuine features, Ch. 48, 6.4.1.B
    non-recourse loans, Ch. 48, 6.5
    perpetual instruments with potentially deferrable coupons, Ch. 48, 6.4.5
    prepayment, asset originated at a premium of discount, Ch. 48, 6.4.4.B
    prepayment, negative compensation, Ch. 48, 6.4.4.A
    prepayment options, Ch. 48, 6.4.4
    regulated interest rates, Ch. 48, 6.4.3
    term extension options, Ch. 48, 6.4.4
    unleveraged inflation-linked bonds, Ch. 48, 6.3.5
    variable interest rate, Ch. 48, 6.4.4
  designation at fair value through profit or loss, Ch. 48, 7
  designation of contracts to buy or sell a non-financial item, Ch. 5, 5.23
  designation of non-derivative equity investments at fair value through other comprehensive income, Ch. 48, 8
  fair value option for own use contracts, Ch. 45, 4.2.6
  financial assets and liabilities held for trading, Ch. 48, 4
  financial assets classification, Ch. 48, 2
    debt instruments, Ch. 48, 2.1
    equity instruments and derivatives, Ch. 48, 2.2
  financial instruments within the scope of, Ch. 8, 4.4.5
  financial liabilities classification, Ch. 48, 3
  IFRS 4 applying IFRS 9 with, Ch. 55, 10
    interest rate benchmark reform Ch. 55, 10.1.6
    overlay approach, Ch. 55, 10.2
    temporary exemption from IFRS 9, Ch. 55, 10.1
  impairment
    approaches, Ch. 51, 3
      general approach, Ch. 51, 3.1
      purchased/originated credit-impaired financial assets, Ch. 51, 3.3
      simplified approach, Ch. 51, 3.2
    calculation of expected credit losses (ECLs), other matters, Ch. 51, 7
      Basel guidance on accounting for ECLs, Ch. 51, 7.1
      changes in ECL methodologies – errors, changes in estimates or changes in accounting policies, Ch. 51, 7.6
      Global Public Policy Committee (GPPC) guidance, Ch. 51, 7.2
      interaction between expected credit losses calculations and fair value hedge accounting, Ch. 51, 7.5
      interaction between the initial and subsequent measurement of debt instruments acquired in a business combination and the impairment model of IFRS 9, Ch. 51, 7.4
      measurement dates of ECLs, Ch. 51, 7.3
        date of derecognition and date of initial recognition, Ch. 51, 7.3.1
        trade date and settlement date accounting, Ch. 51, 7.3.2
    determining significant increases in credit risk, Ch. 51, 6
      change in the risk of a default occurring, Ch. 51, 6.1
      collective assessment, Ch. 51, 6.5
      definition of significant, Ch. 51, 6.3
      factors/indicators of changes in credit risk, Ch. 51, 6.2
      at initial recognition of an identical group of financial assets, Ch. 51, 6.6
      multiple scenarios for 'staging' assessment, Ch. 51, 6.7
      operational simplifications, Ch. 51, 6.4
    disclosures, Ch. 51, 15
    expected credit losses measurement
      credit enhancements: collateral and financial guarantees, Ch. 51, 5.8.1
      definition of default, Ch. 51, 5.1
      expected life *vs.* contractual period, Ch. 51, 5.5
      information about past events, current conditions and forecasts of future economic conditions, Ch. 51, 5.9.3
      lifetime expected credit losses, Ch. 51, 5.2
      12-month expected credit losses, Ch. 51, 6.4.3
      probability-weighted outcome, Ch. 51, 5.6
      reasonable and supportable information, Ch. 51, 5.9
      sources of information, Ch. 51, 5.9.2
      time value of money, Ch. 51, 5.7
      undue cost/effort, Ch. 51, 5.9.1
    financial assets measured at fair value through other comprehensive income, Ch. 51, 9
      debt instruments measured at fair value through other comprehensive income, Ch. 51, 9.1
    financial guarantee contracts, Ch. 51, 11
    Global Public Policy Committee guidance, Ch. 51, 7.2
    history and background, Ch. 51, 1.1
    IFRS Transition Resource Group for Impairment of Financial Instruments (ITG), Ch. 51, 1.5
    intercompany loans, Ch. 51, 13
      determining the ECLs, Ch. 51, 13.3
      repayable on demand, Ch. 51, 13.2
      scope, Ch. 51, 13.1
    key changes from the IAS 39 impairment requirements and the main implications of these changes, Ch. 51, 1.3
    key differences from the FASB's standard, Ch. 51, 1.4 lease receivables, Ch. 51, 10.2
    lease receivables, Ch. 51, 10.2
    loan commitments and financial guarantee contracts, Ch. 51, 11
    measurement dates of expected credit losses, Ch. 51, 7.3
      date of derecognition and date of initial recognition, Ch. 51, 7.3.1
      trade date and settlement date accounting, Ch. 51, 7.3.2
    modified financial assets, Ch. 51, 8
    other guidance on expected credit losses, Ch. 51, 1.6
    presentation of expected credit losses in the statement of financial position, Ch. 51, 14
      accumulated impairment amount for debt instruments measured at fair value through other comprehensive income, Ch. 51, 14.3

allowance for financial assets measured at amortised cost, contract assets and lease receivables, Ch. 51, 14.1
    provisions for loan commitments and financial guarantee contracts, Ch. 51, 14.2
requirements, Ch. 51, 1.2
revolving credit facilities, Ch. 51, 12
scope, Ch. 51, 2
trade receivables, contract assets and lease receivables, Ch. 51, 10
    lease receivables, Ch. 51, 10.2
    trade receivables and contract assets, Ch. 51, 10.1
initial measurement, Ch. 49, 3
    acquisition of a group of assets that does not constitute a business, Ch. 49, 3.3.5
    assets and liabilities arising from loan commitments, Ch. 49, 3.7
        loan commitments outside the scope of IFRS 9, Ch. 49, 3.7.1
        loan commitments within the scope of IFRS 9, Ch. 49, 3.7. 2
    embedded derivatives and financial instrument hosts, Ch. 49, 3.5
    general requirements, Ch. 49, 3.1
    initial fair value and 'day 1' profits, Ch. 49, 3.3
        financial guarantee contracts and off-market loan commitments, Ch. 49, 3.3.3
        interest-free and low-interest long-term loans, Ch. 49, 3.3.1
        loans and receivables acquired in a business combination, Ch. 49, 3.3.4
        measurement of financial instruments following modification of contractual terms that leads to initial recognition of a new instrument, Ch. 49, 3.3.2
    regular way transactions, Ch. 49, 3.6
    trade receivables without a significant financing component, Ch. 49, 3.2
    transaction costs, Ch. 49, 3.4
interests in associates and joint ventures accounted for in accordance with IFRS 9, Ch. 54, 4.4.9
reclassification of financial assets, Ch. 48, 9
recognition, Ch. 49, 2
    general requirements, Ch. 49, 2.1
        cash collateral, Ch. 49, 2.1.7
        firm commitments to purchase/sell goods/services, Ch. 49, 2.1.2
        forward contracts, Ch. 49, 2.1.3
        option contracts, Ch. 49, 2.1.4
        planned future/forecast transactions, Ch. 49, 2.1.5
        principal *vs.* agent, Ch. 49, 2.1.8
        receivables and payables, Ch. 49, 2.1.1
        transfers of financial assets not qualifying for derecognition by transferor, Ch. 49, 2.1.6
    'regular way' transactions, Ch. 49, 2.2
        financial assets: general requirements, Ch. 49, 2.2.1
            contracts not settled according to marketplace convention: derivatives, Ch. 49, 2.2.1.B
            exercise of a derivative, Ch. 49, 2.2.1.D
            multiple active markets: settlement provisions, Ch. 49, 2.2.1.C
            no established market, Ch. 49, 2.2.1.A
        financial liabilities, Ch. 49, 2.2.2
        illustrative examples, Ch. 49, 2.2.5
        settlement date accounting, Ch. 49, 2.2.4
        trade date accounting, Ch. 49, 2.2.3

IFRS 10–*Consolidated Financial Statements*, Ch. 6, 1–11. *See also* Consolidated financial statements, consolidation procedures
continuous assessment, Ch. 6, 9
control, Ch. 6, 3
control of specified assets, Ch. 6, 8
development of IFRS 10, Ch. 6, 1.2
disclosure requirements, Ch. 6, 1.4
exposure to variable returns, Ch. 6, 5
future developments, Ch. 6, 11
investment entities, Ch. 6, 10
    accounting by a parent of an investment entity, Ch. 6, 10.4
    accounting by an investment entity, Ch. 6, 10.3
    definition, Ch. 6, 10.1
    determining whether an entity is an investment entity, Ch. 6, 10.2
        earnings from investments, Ch. 6, 10.2.3
        exit strategies, Ch. 6, 10.2.2
        fair value measurement, Ch. 6, 10.2.4
        having more than one investor, Ch. 6, 10.2.6
        holding more than one investment, Ch. 6, 10.2.5
        intermediate holding companies established for tax optimisation purposes, Ch. 6, 10.2.1.B
        investment entity illustrative examples, Ch. 6, 10.2.9
        investment-related services, Ch. 6, 10.2.1.A
        multi-layered fund structures, Ch. 6, 10.2.10
        ownership interests, Ch. 6, 10.2.8
        unrelated investors, Ch. 6, 10.2.7
objective of, Ch. 6, 2.1
power and returns, principal-agency situations, Ch. 6, 6
    application examples, Ch. 6, 6.6–6.7
    delegated power: principals and agents, Ch. 6, 6.1
    exposure to variability of returns from other interests, Ch. 6, 6.5
    remuneration, Ch. 6, 6.4
    rights held by other parties, Ch. 6, 6.3
    scope of decision-making, Ch. 6, 6.2
power over an investee, Ch. 6, 4
    contractual arrangements, Ch. 6, 4.4
    determining whether sponsoring (designing) a structured entity gives power, Ch. 6, 4.6
    existing rights, Ch. 6, 4.2
    relevant activities, Ch. 6, 4.1
    voting rights, Ch. 6, 4.3
related parties and de facto agents, Ch. 6, 7
scope, Ch. 6, 2.2
    combined and carve-out financial statements, Ch. 6, 2.2.6
    employee benefit plans and employee share trusts, Ch. 6, 2.2.2
    entity no longer a parent at the end of the reporting period, Ch. 6, 2.2.4
    exemption from preparing consolidated financial statements by an intermediate parent, Ch. 6, 2.2.1
    interaction of IFRS 10 and EU law, Ch. 6, 2.2.5
    investment entity exception, Ch. 6, 2.2.3

IFRS 11–*Joint Arrangements*, Ch. 12, 1–10. *See also* Joint arrangements
  accounting for joint operations, Ch. 12, 6
    accounting for rights and obligations, Ch. 12, 6.2
    determining the relevant IFRS, Ch. 12, 6.3
    interest in a joint operation without joint control, Ch. 12, 6.4
    not structured through a separate vehicle, Ch. 12, 6.1
    in separate financial statements, Ch. 12, 6.7
    transactions between a joint operator and a joint operation, Ch. 12, 6.6
  accounting for joint ventures, Ch. 12, 7
    contributions of non-monetary assets to a joint venture, Ch. 12, 7.2
    interest in a joint venture without joint control, Ch. 12, 7.1
    in separate financial statements, Ch. 12, 7.3
  classification of, Ch. 12, 5
    accompanying IFRS 11, illustrative examples, Ch. 12, 5.5
    contractual terms, Ch. 12, 5.3
    facts and circumstances, Ch. 12, 5.4
    legal form of the separate vehicle, Ch. 12, 5.2
    separate vehicle or not, Ch. 12, 5.1
  continuous assessment, Ch. 12, 8
    changes in ownership of a joint arrangement that does not constitute a business, Ch. 12, 8.4
    changes in ownership of a joint operation, Ch. 12, 8.3
      acquisition of an interest in a joint operation, Ch. 12, 8.3.1
      disposal of interest in a joint operation, Ch. 12, 8.3.5
      former subsidiary becomes a joint operation, Ch. 7, 3.3.3, 7.2; Ch. 12, 8.3.3
      obtaining control or joint control over a joint operation that is a business, Ch. 12, 8.3.2
      other changes in ownership of a joint operation, Ch. 12, 8.3.4
    changes in ownership of a joint venture, Ch. 12, 8.2
      acquisition of an interest, Ch. 12, 8.2.1
      becomes a financial asset (or vice versa), Ch. 12, 8.2.5
      becomes an associate (or vice versa), Ch. 12, 8.2.4
      control over a joint venture, Ch. 12, 8.3.2
      disposal of interest in, Ch. 12, 8.2.6
      former subsidiary becomes a joint venture, Ch. 7, 3.3.2, 7.1; Ch. 12, 8.3.3
      interest in a joint venture held for sale, Ch. 12, 8.2.7
    when to reassess under IFRS 11, Ch. 12, 8.1
  disclosures, Ch. 12, 9
  future developments, Ch. 12, 10
  joint control, Ch. 12, 4
    practical issues with assessing, Ch. 12, 4.4
      evaluate multiple agreements together, Ch. 12, 4.4.2
      lease/joint arrangement, Ch. 12, 4.4.1
    relevant activities in sequential activities, Ch. 12, 4.1.1
    rights to control collectively, Ch. 12, 4.2
      delegated decision-making, Ch. 12, 4.2.4
      evidence of, Ch. 12, 4.2.3
      government, role of, Ch. 12, 4.2.6
      potential voting rights and joint control, Ch. 12, 4.2.2
      protective rights, including some veto rights, Ch. 12, 4.2.1
      related parties and de facto agents, Ch. 12, 4.2.5
    sequential activities in, Ch. 12, 4.1.1
    unanimous consent, Ch. 12, 4.3
      arbitration, Ch. 12, 4.3.3
      arrangements involving passive investors, Ch. 12, 4.3.1
      statutory mechanisms, Ch. 12, 4.3.4
      ultimate voting authority, Ch. 12, 4.3.2
  nature of joint arrangements, Ch. 12, 1.1
  objective, Ch. 12, 2.1
  scope, Ch. 12, 2.2
    accounting by a joint operation, Ch. 12, 2.2.3
    application by venture capital organisations and similar entities, Ch. 12, 2.2.1
    application to joint arrangements held for sale, Ch. 12, 2.2.2

IFRS 12–*Disclosure of Interests in Other Entities*, Ch. 13, 1–6. *See also* Disclosure of interests in other entities
  definitions, Ch. 13, 2.2.1
    interaction of IFRS 12 and IFRS 5, Ch. 13, 2.2.1.C
    interests in other entities, Ch. 13, 2.2.1.A
    structured entities, Ch. 13, 2.2.1, 2.2.1.B
  interests disclosed under, Ch. 13, 2.2.2
  interests not within the scope of, Ch. 13, 2.2.3
  joint arrangements and associates, Ch. 13, 5
    nature, extent and financial effects, Ch. 13, 5.1
    risks associated with, Ch. 13, 5.2
      commitments relating to joint ventures, Ch. 13, 5.2.1
      contingent liabilities relating to joint ventures and associates, Ch. 13, 5.2.2
    significant judgements and assumptions, Ch. 13, 3
  objective, Ch. 13, 2.1
  scope, Ch. 13, 2.2
  subsidiaries, Ch. 13, 4
    changes in ownership interests in subsidiaries, Ch. 13, 4.5
    composition of the group, Ch. 13, 4.1
    consolidated structured entities, nature of risks, Ch. 13, 4.4
      current intentions to provide financial or other support, Ch. 13, 4.4.4
      financial or other support to, with no contractual obligation, Ch. 13, 4.4.2
      terms of contractual arrangements, Ch. 13, 4.4.1
    nature and extent of significant restrictions, Ch. 13, 4.3
    non-controlling interests, Ch. 13, 4.2
  unconsolidated structured entities, Ch. 13, 6
    nature of interests, Ch. 13, 6.1
      nature, purpose, size, activities and financing of structured entities, Ch. 13, 6.1.1
      sponsored structured entities for which no interest is held at the reporting date, Ch. 13, 6.1.2
    nature of risks, Ch. 13, 6.2–6.3
      actual and intended financial and other support to structured entities, Ch. 13, 6.2.2
      disclosure of funding difficulties, Ch. 13, 6.3.6
      disclosure of liquidity arrangements, Ch. 13, 6.3.5
      disclosure of losses, Ch. 13, 6.3.2
      disclosure of ranking and amounts of potential losses, Ch. 13, 6.3.4
      disclosure of support, Ch. 13, 6.3.1
      disclosure of the forms of funding of an unconsolidated structured entity, Ch. 13, 6.3.7

disclosure of types of income received, Ch. 13, 6.3.3
maximum exposure to loss from those interests, Ch. 13, 6.2.1

IFRS 13–*Fair Value Measurement*, Ch. 14, 1–23. *See also* Fair value; Fair value measurement; Valuation techniques
asset/liability, Ch. 14, 5
characteristics, Ch. 14, 5.2
condition and location, Ch. 14, 5.2.1
restrictions on assets or liabilities, Ch. 14, 5.2.2
unit of account, Ch. 14, 5.1
asset's (or liability's) components, Ch. 14, 5.1.4
and portfolio exception, Ch. 14, 5.1.2
and PxQ, Ch. 7, 3.3.2.F; Ch. 14, 5.1.1
vs. valuation premise, Ch. 14, 5.1.3
convergence with US GAAP, Ch. 14, 22
disclosures, Ch. 14, 22.2.4
fair value of liabilities with demand feature, Ch. 14, 22.2.2
practical expedient for alternative investments, Ch. 14, 22.2.1
recognition of day-one gains and losses, Ch. 14, 22.2.3
definitions, Ch. 14, 3
development of, Ch. 14, 22.1
disclosures, Ch. 14, 20
accounting policy, Ch. 14, 20.2
objectives, Ch. 14, 20.1
format of, Ch. 14, 20.1.1
level of disaggregation, Ch. 14, 20.1.2
'recurring' *vs.* 'non-recurring', Ch. 14, 20.1.3
proposed amendments resulting from the Targeted Standards-level, Ch. 14, 20.6
for recognised fair value measurements, Ch. 14, 20.3
fair value hierarchy categorisation, Ch. 14, 20.3.3
highest and best use, Ch. 14, 20.3.9
level 3 reconciliation, Ch. 14, 20.3.6
non-recurring fair value measurements, Ch. 14, 20.3.2
recurring fair value measurements, Ch. 14, 20.3.1
sensitivity of level 3 measurements to changes in significant unobservable inputs, Ch. 14, 20.3.8
transfers between hierarchy levels for recurring fair value measurements, Ch. 14, 20.3.4
of valuation processes for level 3 measurements, Ch. 14, 20.3.7
valuation techniques and inputs, Ch. 14, 20.3.5
regarding liabilities issued with an inseparable third-party credit enhancement, Ch. 14, 20.5
for unrecognised fair value measurements, Ch. 14, 20.4
fair value framework, Ch. 14, 4
definition, Ch. 14, 4.1
measurement, Ch. 14, 4.2
financial assets and liabilities with offsetting positions, Ch. 14, 12
criteria for using the portfolio approach for offsetting positions
accounting policy considerations, Ch. 14, 12.1.1
level 1 instruments in, Ch. 14, 12.1.4
minimum level of offset, to use portfolio approach, Ch. 14, 12.1.3
presentation considerations, Ch. 14, 12.1.2
measuring fair value for offsetting positions
exposure to market risks, Ch. 14, 12.2.1
exposure to the credit risk of a particular counterparty, Ch. 14, 12.2.2
hierarchy, Ch. 14, 16
categorisation within, Ch. 14, 16.2
over-the-counter derivative instruments, Ch. 14, 16.2.4
significance of inputs, assessing, Ch. 14, 16.2.1
third-party pricing services/brokers, Ch. 14, 16.2.3
transfers between levels within, Ch. 14, 16.2.2
IFRS 13, objective of, Ch. 14, 1.3
IFRS 13, overview, Ch. 14, 1.2
at initial recognition, Ch. 14, 13
day one gains and losses, Ch. 14, 13.2
losses for over-the-counter derivative transactions, Ch. 14, 13.2.1
when entry and exit markets are the same, Ch. 14, 13.2.2
exit price *vs.* entry price, Ch. 14, 13.1
related party transactions, Ch. 14, 13.3
inputs to valuation techniques, Ch. 14, 15
broker quotes and pricing services, Ch. 14, 15.5
general principles, Ch. 14, 15.1
premiums and discounts, Ch. 14, 15.2
blockage factors (or block discounts), Ch. 14, 15.2.1
pricing within the bid-ask spread bid-ask spread, Ch. 14, 15.3
mid-market pricing, Ch. 14, 15.3.1
risk premiums, Ch. 14, 15.4
level 1 inputs, Ch. 14, 17
alternative pricing methods, Ch. 14, 17.2
quoted prices in active markets that are not representative of, Ch. 14, 17.3
unit of account, Ch. 14, 17.4
use of, Ch. 14, 17.1
level 2 inputs, Ch. 14, 18
examples of, Ch. 14, 18.2
making adjustments to, Ch. 14, 18.4
market corroborated inputs, Ch. 14, 18.3
recently observed prices in an inactive market, Ch. 14, 18.5
level 3 inputs, Ch. 14, 19
examples of, Ch. 14, 19.2
use of, Ch. 14, 19.1
liabilities and an entity's own equity, application to, Ch. 14, 11
financial liability with demand feature, Ch. 14, 11.5
non-performance risk, Ch. 14, 11.3
counterparty credit risk and its own credit risk, Ch. 14, 11.3.2
derivative liabilities, Ch. 14, 11.3.4
entity incorporate credit risk into the valuation of its derivative contracts, Ch. 14, 11.3.3
with third-party credit enhancements, Ch. 14, 11.3.1
not held by other parties as assets, Ch. 14, 11.2.2
principles, Ch. 14, 11.1
fair value of an entity's own equity, Ch. 14, 11.1.2
fair value of a liability, Ch. 14, 11.1.1
settlement value *vs.* transfer value, Ch. 14, 11.1.3
restrictions preventing the transfer of, Ch. 14, 11.1
that are held by other parties as assets, Ch. 14, 11.2.1
market participants, Ch. 14, 7

IFRS 13–*Fair Value Measurement*—*contd*
  market participants—*contd*
    assumptions, Ch. 14, 7.2
    characteristics, Ch. 14, 7.1
  measurement exception to the fair value principles for financial instruments, Ch. 14, 2.5.2
  non-financial assets, application to, Ch. 14, 10
    highest and best use, Ch. 14, 10.1
      vs. current use, Ch. 14, 10.1.2
      vs. intended use, Ch. 14, 10.1.3
      legally permissible, Ch. 14, 10.1.1
    valuation premise, Ch. 14, 10.2
      in combination with other assets and/or liabilities, Ch. 14, 10.2.2
      liabilities association, Ch. 14, 10.2.3
      stand-alone basis, Ch. 14, 10.2.1 unit of account *vs.*, Ch. 14, 10.2.4
  practical expedient in, Ch. 14, 2.5.1
  present value technique, Ch. 14, 21
    components of, Ch. 14, 21.2
      risk and uncertainty in, Ch. 14, 21.2.2
      time value of money, Ch. 14, 21.2.1
    discount rate adjustment technique, Ch. 14, 21.3
    expected present value technique, Ch. 14, 21.4
    general principles for use of, Ch. 14, 21.1
  price, Ch. 14, 9
    transaction costs, Ch. 14, 9.1
    transportation costs, Ch. 14, 9.2
  principal (or most advantageous) market, Ch. 14, 6
  scope, Ch. 14, 2
    exclusions, Ch. 14, 2.2
      disclosure requirements of IFRS 13, exemptions from, Ch. 14, 2.2.4
      lease transactions, Ch. 14, 2.2.2
      measurements similar to fair value, Ch. 14, 2.2.3
      share-based payments, Ch. 14, 2.2.1
    fair value measurement exceptions, Ch. 14, 2.4
    IFRS 13, items in, Ch. 14, 2.1
      fair value disclosures, Ch. 14, 2.1.1
      fair value measurements, Ch. 14, 2.1.2
      short-term receivables and payables, Ch. 14, 2.1.3
    practical expedient for impaired financial assets carried at amortised cost, Ch. 14, 2.4.2
    present value techniques, Ch. 14, 2.3
  transaction, Ch. 14, 8
    estimation, Ch. 14, 8.3
    identification, Ch. 14, 8.2
    volume and level of activity for an asset/liability, Ch. 14, 8.1
  unit of account, Ch. 14, 5
    asset's (or liability's) components, Ch. 14, 5.1.4
    level 1 assets and liabilities, Ch. 14, 17.4
    and portfolio exception, Ch. 14, 5.1.2
    and PxQ, Ch. 7, 3.3.2.F; Ch. 14, 5.1.1
    vs. valuation premise, Ch. 14, 5.1.3
  valuation techniques, Ch. 14, 14
    cost approach, Ch. 14, 14.3
    income approach, Ch. 14, 14.4
    market approach, Ch. 14, 14.2
    selecting appropriate, Ch. 14, 14.1
    making changes to valuation techniques, Ch. 14, 14.1.4
    single *vs.* multiple valuation techniques, Ch. 14, 14.1.1
    using multiple valuation techniques to measure fair value, Ch. 14, 14.1.2
    valuation adjustments, Ch. 14, 14.1.3

IFRS 14–*Regulatory Deferral Accounts*, Ch. 5, 5.20; Ch. 26, 5.4
  changes in accounting policies, Ch. 5, 5.20.5
  continuation of previous GAAP accounting policies, Ch. 5, 5.20.3
  defined terms, Ch. 5, 5.20.1
  disclosures, Ch. 5, 5.20.7
  interaction with other standards, Ch. 5, 5.20.8
  presentation, Ch. 5, 5.20.6
  recognition of regulatory deferral account balances, Ch. 5, 5.20.4
  scope, Ch. 5, 5.20.2

IFRS 15–*Revenue recognition*, Ch. 27, 1–4; Ch. 28, 1–3; Ch. 29, 1–3; Ch. 30, 1–11; Ch. 31, 1–5; Ch. 32, 1–4. *See also* Revenue recognition
  allocate the transaction price to the performance obligations, Ch. 29, 3
    allocating a discount, Ch. 29, 3.4
    allocating variable consideration, Ch. 29, 3.3
    allocation of transaction price to components outside the scope of IFRS 15, Ch. 29, 3.6
    applying the relative stand-alone selling price method, Ch. 29, 3.2
    changes in transaction price after contract inception, Ch. 29, 3.5
    determining stand-alone selling prices, Ch. 29, 3.1
      additional considerations for determining, Ch. 29, 3.1.4
      factors to consider when estimating, Ch. 29, 3.1.1
      measurement of options that are separate performance obligations, Ch. 29, 3.1.5
      possible estimation approaches, Ch. 29, 3.1.2
      updating estimated, Ch. 29, 3.1.3
    relative stand-alone selling price method, Ch. 29, 3.2
    variable consideration allocation, Ch. 29, 3.3
  definitions, Ch. 27, 2.2
  determine the transaction price, Ch. 29, 2
    changes in the transaction price, Ch. 29, 2.9
    consideration paid/payable to a customer, Ch. 29, 2.7
      classification of different types and measurement of, Ch. 29, 2.7.3
      determining who is an entity's customer when applying the requirements for consideration payable to a customer, Ch. 29, 2.7.1
      forms of, Ch. 29, 2.7.2
      timing of recognition of, Ch. 29, 2.7.4
    non-cash consideration, Ch. 29, 2.6
    non-refundable upfront fees, Ch. 29, 2.8
    refund liabilities, Ch. 29, 2.3
    rights of return, Ch. 29, 2.4
    significant financing component, Ch. 29, 2.5
      application questions on identifying and accounting for, Ch. 29, 2.5.2
      examples of, Ch. 29, 2.5.1

financial statement presentation of financing component, Ch. 29, 2.5.3
    implementation questions on identifying and accounting for, Ch. 29, 2.5.2
variable consideration, Ch. 29, 2.2
    constraining estimates of, Ch. 29, 2.2.3
    estimating, Ch. 29, 2.2.2
    forms, Ch. 29, 2.2.1
    reassessment of, Ch. 29, 2.2.4
disposal of non-financial assets not in the ordinary course of business, Ch. 27, 4.3
    sale of assets held for rental, Ch. 27, 4.3.1
extractive industries, Ch. 43, 12
income and distributable profits, Ch. 27, 4.1
interest and dividends, Ch. 27, 4.2
identify the contract with the customer, Ch. 28, 2
    arrangements not meeting the definition of a contract under the standard, Ch. 28, 2.5
    attributes of a contract, Ch. 28, 2.1
        collectability, Ch. 28, 2.1.6
        commercial substance, Ch. 28, 2.1.5
        consideration of side agreements, Ch. 28, 2.1.1.C
        each party's rights regarding the goods/services to be transferred can be identified, Ch. 28, 2.1.3
        free trial period, Ch. 28, 2.1.1.B
        master supply arrangements (MSA), Ch. 28, 2.1.1.A
        parties have approved the contract and are committed to perform their respective obligations, Ch. 28, 2.1.2
        payment terms can be identified, Ch. 28, 2.1.4
    combining contracts, Ch. 28, 2.3
        portfolio approach practical expedient, Ch. 28, 2.3.1
    contract enforceability and termination clauses, Ch. 28, 2.2
        consideration that was received from a customer, but not recognised as revenue, when contract is cancelled, accounting for, Ch. 28, 2.2.1 E
        evaluating termination clauses, Ch. 28, 2.2.1.A
        evaluating the contract term when an entity has a past practice of not enforcing termination payments, Ch. 28, 2.2.1.C
        partial termination of a contract, accounting for, Ch. 28, 2.2.1.D
        termination payments in determining the contract term, Ch. 28, 2.2.1.A
    contract modifications, Ch. 28, 2.4
        blend-and-extend, accounting for, Ch. 28, 2.4.3.F
        decrease scope of the contract, Ch. 28, 2.4.3.E
        marketing offer, Ch. 28. 2.4.3. D
        not a separate contract, Ch. 28, 2.4.2
        reassessing criteria if contract modified, Ch. 28, 2.4.3.B
        represents a separate contract, Ch. 28, 2.4.1
identify the performance obligations in the contract, Ch. 28, 3
    consignment arrangements, Ch. 28, 3.5
    customer options for additional goods/services, Ch. 28, 3.6
        accounting for the exercise of a material right, Ch. 28, 3.6.1.J
        considering whether prospective volume discounts determined to be customer options are material rights, Ch. 28, 3.6.1.G
        customer option as a separate performance obligation when there are no contractual penalties, Ch. 28, 3.6.1.D
    customer options that provide a material right: evaluating whether there is a significant financing component, Ch. 28, 3.6.1.K
        customer options that provide a material right: recognising revenue when there is no expiration date, Ch. 28, 3.6.1.L
        Considering the class of customer when evaluating whether a customer option is a material right, Ch. 28, 3.6.1.F
        Considering whether a loyalty or reward programme is a material right, Ch. 28, 3.6.1 I
        Considering whether a renewal option is a material right, Ch. 28, 3.6.1.H
        distinguishing between a customer option and variable consideration, Ch. 28, 3.6.1.C
        nature of evaluation of customer options: quantitative *versus* qualitative, Ch. 28, 3.6.1.B
        prospective volume discounts determined to be customer options are material rights, Ch. 28, 3.6.1.F
        transactions to consider when assessing customer options for additional goods/services, Ch. 28, 3.6.1.A
        volume rebates and/or discounts on goods or services: customer options *versus* variable consideration, Ch. 28, 3.6.1.E
    determining when promises are performance obligations, Ch. 28, 3.2
        determination of 'distinct,' Ch. 28, 3.2.1
        examples, Ch. 28, 3.2.3
        series of distinct goods and services that are substantially the same and have the same pattern of transfer, Ch. 28, 3.2.2
    identifying the promised goods and services in the contract, Ch. 28, 3.1
    principal *versus* agent considerations, Ch. 28, 3.4
        control of the specified good/service, Ch. 28, 3.4.2
        examples, Ch. 28, 3.4.4
        identifying the specified good/service, Ch. 28, 3.4.1
        recognising revenue as principal/agent, Ch. 28, 3.4.3
    promised goods and services that are not distinct, Ch. 28, 3.3
    sale of products with a right of return, Ch. 28, 3.7
interaction with IFRIC 12, Ch. 25, 6
licences of intellectual property, Ch. 31, 2
    identifying performance obligations in a licensing arrangement, Ch. 31, 2.1
        application questions on, Ch. 31, 2.1.5
        contracts that grant both permission for past use of intellectual property and a licence to use the intellectual property in the future, Ch. 31, 2.1.5.B
        contractual restrictions, Ch. 31, 2.1.3
        guarantees to defend or maintain a patent, Ch. 31, 2.1.4

IFRS 15–*Revenue recognition*—*contd*
  licences of intellectual property—*contd*
    identifying performance obligations in a licensing arrangement—*contd*
      licences of intellectual property that are distinct, Ch. 31, 2.1.1
      licences of intellectual property that are not distinct, Ch. 31, 2.1.2
    licence renewals, Ch. 31, 2.4
    nature of the entity's promise in granting a licence, determining, Ch. 31, 2.2
      applying the licensing application guidance to a single (bundled) performance obligation that includes a licence of intellectual property, Ch. 31, 2.2.1
    sales-based/usage-based royalties on, Ch. 31, 2.5
      application questions on the sales-based or usage-based royalty recognition constraint, Ch. 31, 2.5.2
      transfer of control of licensed intellectual property, Ch. 31, 2.3
      recognition of royalties for a licence that provides a right to access intellectual property, Ch. 31, 2.5.1
      right to access, Ch. 31, 2.3.1
      right to use, Ch. 31, 2.3.2
      use and benefit requirement, Ch. 31, 2.3.3
  objective, Ch. 27, 2
    contract costs, Ch. 31, 5
      amortisation of capitalised costs, Ch. 31, 5.3
      costs to obtain a contract, Ch. 31, 5.1
      costs to fulfil a contract, Ch. 31, 5.2
      impairment of capitalised costs, Ch. 31, 5.4
    onerous contracts, Ch. 31, 4
    warranties, Ch. 31, 3
      assurance-type warranty, Ch. 31, 3.3
      contracts that contain both assurance and service-type warranties, Ch. 31, 3.4
      service-type warranties, Ch. 31, 3.2
  overview, Ch. 27, 2.1
  presentation and disclosure
    disclosure objective and general requirements, Ch. 32, 3.1
    disclosures in interim financial statements, Ch. 32, 4
    presentation requirements for, Ch. 32, 2.2
      presentation of income outside the scope of IFRS 15, Ch. 32, 2.2.1
      presentation requirements for contract assets and contract liabilities, Ch. 32, 2.1
        application questions on presentation of contract assets and liabilities, Ch. 32, 2.1.6
    specific disclosure requirements, Ch. 32, 3.2
      assets recognised from the costs to obtain or fulfil a contract, Ch. 32, 3.2.3
      contracts with customers, Ch. 32, 3.2.1
        contract balances, Ch. 32, 3.2.1.B
        disaggregation of revenue, Ch. 32, 3.2.1.A
        performance obligations, Ch. 32, 3.2.1.C
        use of 'backlog' practical expedient when criteria to use 'right to invoice' expedient are not met, Ch. 32, 3.2.1.D
      practical expedients, Ch. 32, 3.2.4
      significant judgements, Ch. 32, 3.2.2
        timing of satisfaction of performance obligations, Ch. 32, 3.2.2.A
        transaction price and the amounts allocated to performance obligations, Ch. 32, 3.2.2.B
  satisfaction of performance obligations, Ch. 30, 1-11
    bill-and-hold arrangements, Ch. 30, 7
    breakage and prepayments for future goods/services, Ch. 30, 11
    consignment arrangements, Ch. 30, 6
    control transferred at a point in time, Ch. 30, 4
      customer acceptance, Ch. 30, 4.2
      effect of shipping terms when an entity has transferred control of a good to a customer, Ch. 30, 4.1
    over time, Ch. 30, 2
      asset with no alternative use and right to payment, Ch. 30, 2.3
        enforceable right to payment for performance completed to date, Ch. 30, 2.3.2
        considerations when assessing the over-time criteria for the sale of a real estate unit, Ch. 30, 2.3.2.F
        determining whether an entity has an enforceable right to payment, Ch. 30, 2.3.2.A
        determining whether an entity has an enforceable right to payment for a contract priced at a loss, Ch. 30, 2.3.2.D
        enforceable right to payment: contemplating consideration an entity might receive from the potential resale of the asset, Ch. 30, 2.3.2.G
        enforceable right to payment determination when not entitled to a reasonable profit margin on standard inventory materials purchased, but not yet used, Ch. 30, 2.3.2.E
        enforceable right to payment: does an entity need a present unconditional right to payment, Ch. 30, 2.3.2.B
        enforceable right to payment: non-refundable upfront payments that represent the full transaction price, Ch. 30, 2.3.2.C
      no alternative use, Ch. 30, 2.3.1
      customer controls asset as it is created/enhanced, Ch. 30, 2.2
      customer simultaneously receives and consumes benefits as the entity performs, Ch. 30, 2.1
      measuring progress over time, Ch. 30, 3
        application questions, Ch. 30, 3.4
        examples, Ch. 30, 3.3
        input methods, Ch. 30, 3.2
        output methods, Ch. 30, 3.1
  recognising revenue for customer options for additional goods and services, Ch. 30, 10
  recognising revenue for licences of intellectual property, Ch. 30, 8
  recognising revenue when a right of return exists, Ch. 30, 9
  repurchase agreements, Ch. 30, 5
    forward/call option held by the entity, Ch. 30, 5.1
    put option held by the customer, Ch. 30, 5.2
    sales with residual value guarantees, Ch. 30, 5.3
  regulatory assets and liabilities, Ch. 27, 4.4
  scope, Ch. 27, 3

collaborative arrangements, Ch. 27, 3.4
definition of customer, Ch. 27, 3.3
interaction with other standards, Ch. 27, 3.5
    certain fee-generating activities of financial institutions, Ch. 27, 3.5.1.B
    contributions, Ch. 27, 3.5.1.E
    credit card arrangements, Ch. 27, 3.5.1.C
    credit card-holder rewards programmes, Ch. 27, 3.5.1.D
    determining whether IFRS 10 or IFRS 15 applies to the sale of a corporate wrapper to a customer, Ch. 7, 3.2.1; Ch. 27, 3.5.1.J
    equity instruments issued by an entity to a customer in connection with a revenue arrangement, Ch. 27, 3.5.1.L
    fixed-odds wagering contracts, Ch. 27, 3.5.1.F
    Islamic financing transactions, Ch. 27, 3.5.1.A
    prepaid gift cards, Ch. 27, 3.5.1.I
    pre-production activities related to long-term supply arrangements, Ch. 27, 3.5.1.G
    revenue arising from an interest in a joint operation, Ch. 27, 3.5.1.K
    sales of by-products or scrap materials, Ch. 27, 3.5.1.H
rights and obligations within, Ch. 45, 3.13

IFRS 16–*Leases*, Ch. 23, 1–10. *See also* Leases (IFRS 16)
business combinations, Ch. 23, 9, 10.5.2
    acquiree in a business combination is a lessee, Ch. 23, 9.1
    acquiree in a business combination is a lessor, Ch. 23, 9.2
commencement date of the lease, Ch. 23, 4.2
definition, Ch. 23, 3
    contract combinations, Ch. 23, 3.3
    determining whether an arrangement contains a lease, Ch. 23, 3.1
    identifying and separating lease and non-lease components of a contract, Ch. 23, 3.2
discount rates, Ch. 23, 4.6
    determination of the incremental borrowing rate by a subsidiary with centralised treasury functions, Ch. 23, 4.6.1
economic life, Ch. 23, 4.8
effective date and transition, Ch. 23, 10
    amounts previously recognised in a business combination, Ch. 23, 10.5.2
    disclosure, Ch. 23, 10.6
    effective date, Ch. 23, 10.1; Ch. 54, 8.4
    lessee transition, Ch. 23, 10.3
        full retrospective approach, Ch. 23, 10.3.1
        modified retrospective approach, Ch. 23, 10.3.2
            leases previously classified as operating leases, Ch. 23, 10.3.2.A
            leases previously classified as finance leases, Ch. 23, 10.3.2.C
            separating and allocating lease and non-lease components of a contract upon transition, Ch. 23, 10.3.2.B
    lessor transition, Ch. 23, 10.4
        subleases, Ch. 23, 10.4.1
    references to IFRS 9, Ch. 23, 10.5.3
    sale and leaseback transactions, Ch. 23, 10.5.1
    transition, Ch. 23, 10.2
fair value, Ch. 23, 4.9
inception of the lease (inception date), Ch. 23, 4.1
initial direct costs, Ch. 23, 4.7; Ch. 19, 4.9.2
    directly attributable costs other than initial direct costs incurred by lessees, Ch. 23, 4.7.1
lease liabilities under IFRS 16, Ch. 20, 4.1.2
lease payments, Ch. 23, 4.5
    amounts expected to be payable under residual value guarantees– lessees only, Ch. 23, 4.5.6
    amounts payable under residual value guarantees–lessors only, Ch. 23, 4.5.7
    exercise price of a purchase option, Ch. 23, 4.5.4 in-substance fixed lease payments, Ch. 23, 4.5.1
    lease incentives, Ch. 23, 4.5.2; Ch. 19, 4.9.1
    presentation in the statement of cash flows, Ch. 40, 5.5.3
    payments for penalties for terminating a lease, Ch. 23, 4.5.5
    reassessment of the lease liability, Ch. 23, 4.5.9
    remeasurement by lessors, Ch. 23, 4.5.13
    security deposits, Ch. 23, 4.5.9
    value added tax and property taxes, Ch. 23, 4.5.10
    variable lease payments that depend on an index/rate, Ch. 23, 4.5.3
    variable lease payments which do not depend on an index or rate, Ch. 23, 4.5.8
lease term and purchase options, Ch. 23, 4.4
    cancellable leases, Ch. 23, 4.4.1
    reassessment of lease term and purchase options–lessees, Ch. 23, 4.4.2
    reassessment of lease term and purchase options–lessors, Ch. 23, 4.4.3
lessee accounting, Ch. 23, 5
    disclosure, Ch. 23, 5.8
        additional, Ch. 23, 5.8.3
        of assets, liabilities, expenses and cash flows, Ch. 23, 5.8.2
        objective, Ch. 23, 5.8.1
    initial measurement, Ch. 23, 5.2
        lease liabilities, Ch. 23, 5.2.2
        right-of-use assets, Ch. 23, 5.2.1
    initial recognition, Ch. 23, 5.1
        leases of low-value assets, Ch. 23, 5.1.2
        short-term leases, Ch. 23, 5.1.1
    lease modifications, Ch. 23, 5.5
        amendment to IFRS 16 for covid-19 related rent concessions, Ch. 23, 5.5.4
        application of lease modification guidance to rent concessions, Ch. 23, 5.5.3
        determining whether a lease modification results in a separate lease, Ch. 23, 5.5.1
        lessee accounting for a modification that does not result in a separate lease, Ch. 23, 5.5.2
    lessee matters, Ch. 23, 5.6
        impairment of right-of-use assets, Ch. 23, 5.6.1
        income tax accounting, Ch. 23, 5.6.4
        leases denominated in a foreign currency, Ch. 23, 5.6.2
        portfolio approach, Ch. 23, 5.6.3
    presentation, Ch. 23, 5.7
    remeasurement of lease liabilities and right-of-use assets, Ch. 23, 5.4

IFRS 16–*Leases—contd*
  lessee accounting—*contd*
    subsequent measurement, Ch. 23, 5.3
      expense recognition, Ch. 23, 5.3.3
      lease liabilities, Ch. 23, 5.3.2
      right-of-use assets, Ch. 23, 5.3.1
  lessee involvement with the underlying asset before the commencement date, Ch. 23, 4.3
  lessor accounting, Ch. 23, 6
    cash flows, Ch. 40, 5.5.5
    disclosure, Ch. 23, 6.7
      for all lessors, Ch. 23, 6.7.2
      for finance leases, Ch. 23, 6.7.3
      objective, Ch. 23, 6.7.1
      for operating leases, Ch. 23, 6.7.4
    finance leases, Ch. 23, 6.2
      initial measurement, Ch. 23, 6.2.1
      manufacturer/dealer lessors, Ch. 23, 6.2.2
      remeasurement of the net investment in the lease, Ch. 23, 6.2.4
      subsequent measurement, Ch. 23, 6.2.3
      unguaranteed residual values, Ch. 23, 6.2.3.A
    lease classification, Ch. 23, 6.1
      criteria, Ch. 23, 6.1.1
      reassessment of, Ch. 23, 6.1.4
      residual value guarantees included in the lease classification test, Ch. 23, 6.1.3
      test for land and buildings, Ch. 23, 6.1.2
    lease modifications, Ch. 23, 6.4
      determining whether a modification to a finance lease results in a separate lease, Ch. 23, 6.4.1
      lessor accounting for a modification to a finance lease that does not result in a separate lease, Ch. 23, 6.4.2
      modification to an operating lease, Ch. 23, 6.4.3
    lessor matters, Ch. 23, 6.5
      portfolio approach, Ch. 23, 6.5
    operating leases, Ch. 23, 6.3
      income, Ch. 23, 6.3.1
    presentation, Ch. 23, 6.6
  objective, Ch. 23, 2.1
  recognition exemptions, Ch. 23, 2.3
  sale and leaseback transactions, Ch. 23, 8
    determining whether the transfer of an asset is a sale, Ch. 23, 8.1
    disclosures, Ch. 23, 8.4
    transactions in which the transfer of an asset is a sale, Ch. 23, 8.2
      accounting for the leaseback, Ch. 23, 8.2.2
      accounting for the sale, Ch. 23, 8.2.1
      adjustment for off-market terms, Ch. 23, 8.2.3
    transactions in which the transfer of an asset is not a sale, Ch. 23, 8.3
  scope, Ch. 23, 2.2
  service concession arrangements, Ch. 25, 2.3
  subleases, Ch. 23, 7
    definition, Ch. 23, 7.1
    disclosure, Ch. 23, 7.5
    intermediate lessor accounting, Ch. 23, 7.2
    presentation, Ch. 23, 7.4
    sublessee accounting, Ch. 23, 7.3
IFRS 17-**Insurance contracts**, Ch. 56. *See also* Insurance contracts
  acquisitions of insurance contracts, Ch. 56, 13
    cash flows acquired in a business combination within the scope of IFRS 3, Ch. 56, 13.1
    common control business combinations, Ch. 56, 13.3
    practical issues, Ch. 56, 13.4
    subsequent treatment of contracts acquired in their settlement period, Ch. 56, 13.2
  definitions in IFRS 17, Ch. 56, 2.2
  derecognition, Ch. 56, 12.2
    accounting for, Ch. 56, 12.3
  disclosure, Ch. 56, 16
    accounting policies, Ch. 56, 16.4
    explanation of recognised amounts, Ch. 56, 16.1
    nature and extent of risks arising from contracts within the scope of IFRS 17, Ch. 56, 16.5
    significant judgements in applying IFRS 17, Ch. 56, 16.3
    transition amounts, Ch. 56, 16.2
  effective date and transition, Ch. 56, 17
    effective date, Ch. 56, 17.1
    entities that have not previously applied IFRS 9, Ch. 56, 17.7
    fair value approach, Ch. 56, 17.5
    modified retrospective approach, Ch. 56, 17.4
    redesignation of financial assets – IFRS 9 previously applied, Ch. 56, 17.6
    retrospective application of transition, Ch. 56, 17.3
    transition, Ch. 56, 17.2
      disclosures about the effect of, Ch. 56, 17.2.2
  impairment of insurance acquisition cash flows, Ch. 56, 8.10
  insurance contract definition, Ch. 56, 3
    changes in the level of insurance risk, Ch. 56, 3.6
    the definition, Ch. 56, 3.1
    insurance and non-insurance contracts, Ch. 56, 3.7
    insurance risk *vs.* financial risk, Ch. 56, 3.4
    payments in kind, Ch. 56, 3.3
    significant insurance risk, Ch. 56, 3.5
    uncertain future events, Ch. 56, 3.2
  initial recognition, Ch. 56, 6
    insurance acquisition cash flows as assets, Ch. 56, 6.3
    investment components, Ch. 56, 4.2
      definition, Ch. 56, 4.2.1
      separability of, Ch. 56, 4.2.2
      measurement, Ch. 56, 4.2.3
      investment-return service, Ch. 56, 8.7.2
  level of aggregation, Ch. 56, 5
    identifying groups according to expected profitability, Ch. 56, 5.2
    identifying groups for contracts applying the premium allocation approach, Ch. 56, 5.3
    identifying portfolios, Ch. 56, 5.1
  measurement
    contracts with participation features, Ch. 56, 11
      cash flows that affect or are affected by cash flows to policyholders of other contracts (mutualisation), Ch. 56, 11.1
      direct participation features, Ch. 56, 11.2
        allocation of the contractual service margin to profit or loss, Ch. 56, 11.2.4
        definition, Ch. 56, 11.2.1
        disaggregation of finance income or expense between profit or loss and other comprehensive income, Ch. 56, 11.2.6

measurement of CSM using variable fee approach, Ch. 56, 11.2.3
risk adjustment for non-financial risk using the variable fee approach, Ch. 56, 11.2.2
risk mitigation, Ch. 56, 11.2.5
general model, Ch. 56, 8
allocation of the contractual service margin to profit or loss, Ch. 56, 8.7
contract boundary, Ch. 56, 8.1
acquisition cash flows paid on an initially written contract, Ch. 56, 8.1.4
constraints or limitations relevant in assessing repricing, Ch. 56, 8.1.2
contracts between an entity and customers of an association or bank, Ch. 56, 8.1.3
issues related to reinsurance contracts held, Ch. 56, 8.1.5
options to add insurance coverage, Ch. 56, 8.1.1
contractual service margin (CSM), Ch. 56, 8.5
allocation to profit or loss, Ch. 56, 8.7
discount rates, Ch. 56, 8.3
estimates of expected future cash flows, Ch. 56, 8.2
contract boundary, Ch. 56, 8.2.4
excluded from the contract boundary, Ch. 56, 8.2.4
market and non-market variables, Ch. 56, 8.2.1
using current estimates, Ch. 56, 8.2.2
within the contract boundary, Ch. 56, 8.2.3
impairment of assets recognised for insurance acquisition cash flows, Ch. 56, 8.10
insurance contracts issued by mutual entities, Ch. 56, 8.11
onerous contracts, Ch. 56, 8.8
other matters, Ch. 56, 8.12
impairment of insurance receivables, Ch. 56, 8.12.1
policyholder loans, Ch. 56, 8.12.2
reinsurance contracts issued, Ch. 56, 8.9
accounting for ceding commissions and reinstatement premiums, Ch. 56, 8.9.3
boundary of, Ch. 56, 8.9.1
determining the quantity of benefits for identifying coverage units, Ch. 56, 8.9.4
issued adverse loss development covers, Ch. 56, 8.9.2
risk adjustment for non-financial risk, Ch. 56, 8.4
consideration of reinsurance held, Ch. 56, 8.4.3
level, Ch. 56, 8.4.2
statement of comprehensive income, Ch. 56, 8.4.4
techniques, Ch. 56, 8.4.1
subsequent measurement, Ch. 56, 8.6
of CSM (for contracts without direct participation features), Ch. 56, 8.6.3
liability for incurred claims, Ch. 56, 8.6.2
liability for remaining coverage, Ch. 56, 8.6.1
investment contracts with discretionary participation features, Ch. 56, 11.3
contracts with switching features, Ch. 56, 11.3.1
overview of measurement, Ch. 56, 7

insurance contracts in a foreign currency, Ch. 56, 7.3
modifications to the general model, Ch. 56, 7.2
overview of general model, Ch. 56, 7.1
premium allocation approach, Ch. 56, 9
criteria for use of, Ch. 56, 9.1
applying materiality for the premium allocation approach eligibility assessment, Ch. 56, 9.1.1
main sources of difference between the premium allocation approach and the general approach, Ch. 56, 9.1.2
initial measurement, Ch. 56, 9.2
subsequent measurement, liability for incurred claims, Ch. 56, 9.4
remaining coverage, Ch. 56, 9.3
reinsurance contracts held, Ch. 56, 10
aggregation level, Ch. 56, 10.1
allocation of the CSM to profit or loss, Ch. 56, 10.5
boundary of, Ch. 56, 10.2
initial recognition, Ch. 56, 10.3
premium allocation approach for, Ch. 56, 10.6
subsequent measurement, Ch. 56, 10.4
and the variable fee approach, Ch. 56, 10.7
modification and derecognition, Ch. 56, 12
accounting for derecognition, Ch. 56, 12.3
derecognition, Ch. 56, 12.2
modification, Ch. 56, 12.1
mutual entities, Ch. 56, 3.2.2.B, 8.11
objective of IFRS 17, Ch. 56, 2.1
presentation in the statement of financial performance, Ch. 56, 15
insurance finance income or expenses, Ch. 56, 15.3
insurance revenue, Ch. 56, 15.1
and expense from reinsurance contracts held, Ch. 56, 15.1.3
related to the provision of services in a period, Ch. 56, 15.1.1
under the premium allocation approach, Ch. 56, 15.1.2
insurance service expenses, Ch. 56, 15.2
reporting the CSM in interim financial statements, Ch. 56, 15.4
presentation in the statement of financial position, Ch. 56, 14
scope of IFRS 17, Ch. 56, 2
separating components from an insurance contract, Ch. 56, 4
embedded derivatives from an insurance contract, Ch. 56, 4.1
investment components from an insurance contract, Ch. 56, 4.2
definition, Ch. 56, 4.2.1
measurement of the non-distinct, Ch. 56, 4.2.3
separable, Ch. 56, 4.2.2
a promise to provide distinct goods and non-insurance services from insurance contracts, Ch. 56, 4.3

IFRS Taxonomy, Ch. 1, 2.6, 2.9

IFRS Taxonomy Consultative Group, Ch. 1, 2.9

IFRS Transition Resource Group for Impairment of Financial Instruments (ITG), Ch. 51, 1.5

Impairment of assets, Ch. 20. *See also* IAS 36; Impairment of goodwill; Value in use (VIU)

Impairment of assets—*contd*
  basis of recoverable amount–value-in-use (VIU) or fair value less costs of disposal (FVLCD), Ch. 43, 11.3
  calculation of FVLCD, Ch. 20, 6.1, Ch. 43, 11.5
  calculation of VIU, Ch. 20, 7, Ch. 43, 11.4
  held for sale, Ch. 20, 5.1
  identifying cash-generating units (CGUs), Ch. 20, 3, Ch. 43, 11.2
    external users of processing assets, Ch. 43, 11.2.2
    fields/mines operated on a portfolio basis, Ch. 43, 11.2.4
    markets for intermediate products, Ch. 43, 11.2.1
    shared infrastructure, Ch. 43, 11.2.3
  impairment indicators, Ch. 20, 2.1, Ch. 43, 11.1
  intangible assets with an indefinite useful life, Ch. 20, 10
  low mine/field profitability near end of life, Ch. 43, 11.6
Impairment of goodwill, Ch. 20, 8 created by deferred tax, Ch. 33, 12.3
  disposal of operation within a cash-generating unit (CGU) to which goodwill has been allocated, Ch. 20, 8.5
    changes in composition of cash-generating units CGUs, Ch. 20, 8.5.1
  goodwill and its allocation to cash-generating unites, Ch. 20, 8.1
  recognised on acquisition, Ch. 20, 8.3
    deferred tax assets and losses of acquired businesses, Ch. 20, 8.3.2
    testing goodwill 'created' by deferred tax for impairment, Ch. 20, 8.3.1
  impairment testing when a CGU crosses more than one operating segment, Ch. 20, 8.4
  when to test CGUs with goodwill for impairment, Ch. 20, 8.2
    carry forward of a previous impairment test calculation, Ch. 20, 8.2.3
    reversal of impairment loss, Ch. 20, 5, 8.2.4
    sequence of tests, Ch. 20, 8.2.2
    timing of tests, Ch. 20, 8.2.1
Impairments. *See also* IAS 36; Impairment of assets; Impairment of goodwill
  associates or joint ventures, Ch. 11, 8
    in separate financial statements, Ch. 11, 9.1
  cost model, Ch. 18, 5; Ch. 19, 7.3
  of fixed assets and goodwill, Ch. 20, 1–14
    intangible assets, Ch. 17, 9.4
  of insurance assets, hierarchy exemption, Ch. 55, 7.2.6.B
  of reinsurance assets, hierarchy exemption, Ch. 55, 7.2.5
  suspension of capitalisation of borrowing costs, Ch. 21, 6.2
Income approach (fair value), Ch. 14, 14.4
  property, plant and equipment, Ch. 18, 6.1.1.B
Income, definition of, Ch. 27, 4.1
Income statement (statement of profit or loss), Ch. 3, 3.2.1. *See also* Statement of comprehensive income
  classification of expenses recognised in profit/loss, Ch. 3, 3.2.3
    analysis of expenses by function, Ch. 3, 3.2.3.B
    analysis of expenses by nature, Ch. 3, 3.2.3.A
  face of, information required on, Ch. 3, 3.2.2
Income taxes, Ch. 33, 1–14. *See also* IAS 12
  allocation between periods, Ch. 33, 1.2
    no provision for deferred tax ('flow through'), Ch. 33, 1.2.1
    provision for deferred tax (the temporary difference approach), Ch. 33, 1.2.2
  allocation of tax charge/credit, Ch. 33, 10
    change in tax status of entity/shareholders, Ch. 33, 10.9
    defined benefit pension plans, Ch. 33, 10.7
      tax on refund of pension surplus, Ch. 33, 10.7.1
    discontinued operations, Ch. 33, 10.6
    disposal of an interest in a subsidiary that does not result in a loss of control, Ch. 33, 10.11
    dividends and transaction costs of equity instruments, Ch. 33, 10.3
      dividend subject to differential tax rate, Ch. 33, 10.3.1
      dividend subject to withholding tax, Ch. 33, 10.3.2
      incoming dividends, Ch. 33, 10.3.4
      intragroup dividend subject to withholding tax, Ch. 33, 10.3.3
      tax benefits of distributions and transaction costs of equity instruments, Ch. 33, 10.3.5
    gain/loss in profit/loss and loss/gain outside profit/loss offset for tax purposes, Ch. 33, 10.5
    gains and losses reclassified ('recycled') to profit/loss, Ch. 33, 10.4
      debt instrument measured at fair value through OCI under IFRS 9, Ch. 33, 10.4.1
      recognition of expected credit losses with no change in fair value, Ch. 33, 10.4.2
    previous revaluation of PP&E treated as deemed cost on transition to IFRS, Ch. 33, 10.10
    retrospective restatements/applications, Ch. 33, 10.2
    revalued and rebased assets, Ch. 33, 10.1
      non-monetary assets with a tax base determined in a foreign currency, Ch. 33, 10.1.1
    share-based payment transactions, Ch. 33, 10.8
      allocation of tax deduction between profit/loss and equity, Ch. 33, 10.8.1
      allocation when more than one award is outstanding, Ch. 33, 10.8.3
      replacement awards in a business combination, Ch. 33, 10.8.5
      share-based payment transactions subject to transitional provisions of IFRS 1 and IFRS 2, Ch. 33, 10.8.6
      staggered exercise of awards, Ch. 33, 10.8.4
      tax base, determining, Ch. 33, 10.8.2
  business combinations, Ch. 33, 12
    apparent immediate impairment of goodwill created by deferred tax, Ch. 33, 12.3
    measurement and recognition of deferred tax in, Ch. 33, 12.1
      deferred tax assets rising on a business combination, Ch. 33, 12.1.2
      deferred tax liabilities of acquired entity, Ch. 33, 12.1.3
      manner of recovery of assets and settlement of liabilities, determining, Ch. 33, 12.1.1
    tax deductions for acquisition costs, Ch. 33, 12.4
    tax deductions for replacement share-based payment awards in a business combination, Ch. 33, 12.2
    temporary differences arising from the acquisition of a group of assets that is not a business, Ch. 33, 12.5

consolidated tax returns and offset of taxable profits and losses within groups, Ch. 33, 11
    examples of accounting by entities in a tax-consolidated group, Ch. 33, 11.1
    payments for intragroup transfer of tax losses, Ch. 33, 11.2
    recognition of deferred tax assets where tax losses are transferred in a group, Ch. 33, 11.3
current tax, Ch. 33, 5
    discounting of current tax assets and liabilities, Ch. 33, 5.4
    enacted/substantively enacted tax legislation, Ch. 33, 5.1
        changes to tax rates and laws enacted after the reporting date, Ch. 33, 5.1.3
        changes to tax rates and laws enacted before the reporting date, Ch. 33, 5.1.2
        implications of the decision by the UK's to withdrawal from the EU, Ch. 33, 5.1.4
        substantive enactment meaning, Ch. 33, 5.1.1
    intra-period allocation, presentation and disclosure, Ch. 33, 5.5
    'prior year adjustments' of previously presented tax balances and expense, Ch. 33, 5.3
    uncertain tax treatments, Ch. 33, 5.2
deferred tax, measurement, Ch. 33, 8
    different tax rates applicable to retained and distributed profits, Ch. 33, 8.5
        effectively tax-free entities, Ch. 33, 8.5.1
        withholding tax/distribution tax, Ch. 33, 8.5.2
    discounting, Ch. 33, 8.6
    expected manner of recovery of assets/settlement of liabilities, Ch. 33, 8.4
        assets and liabilities with more than one tax base, Ch. 33, 8.4.3
        carrying amount, Ch. 33, 8.4.2
        change in expected manner of recovery of an asset/settlement of a liability, Ch. 33, 8.4.11
        depreciable PP&E and intangible assets, Ch. 33, 8.4.5
        determining the expected manner of recovery of assets, Ch. 33, 8.4.4
        investment properties, Ch. 33, 8.4.7
        non-depreciable PP&E and intangible assets, Ch. 33, 8.4.6
            non-amortised or indefinite life intangible assets, Ch. 33, 8.4.6.B
            PP&E accounted for using the revaluation model, Ch. 33, 8.4.6.A
        other assets and liabilities, Ch. 33, 8.4.8
        'outside' temporary differences relating to subsidiaries, branches, associates and joint arrangements, Ch. 33, 8.4.9
        'single asset' entities, Ch. 33, 8.4.10
        tax planning strategies to reduce liabilities are not anticipated, Ch. 33, 8.4.1
    legislation at the end of the reporting period, Ch. 33, 8.1
        changes to tax rates and laws enacted after the reporting date, Ch. 33, 8.1.2
        changes to tax rates and laws enacted before the reporting date, Ch. 33, 8.1.1
            backward tracing of changes in deferred taxation, Ch. 33, 8.1.1.B
            disclosures relating to changes, Ch. 33, 8.1.1.C

            managing uncertainty in determining the effect of new tax legislation, Ch. 33, 8.1.1.A
    'prior year adjustments' of previously presented tax balances and expense (income), Ch. 33, 8.3
    uncertain tax treatments, Ch. 33, 8.2, 9
    unrealised intragroup profits and losses in consolidated financial, Ch. 33, 8.7
        intragroup transfers of goodwill and intangible assets, Ch. 33, 8.7.1
            consolidated financial statements, Ch. 33, 8.7.1.C
            individual financial statements of buyer, Ch. 33, 8.7.1.A
            individual financial statements of seller, Ch. 33, 8.7.1.B
            when the tax base of goodwill is retained by the transferor entity, Ch. 33, 8.7.1.D
deferred tax, recognition, Ch. 33, 7
    assets carried at fair value/revalued amount, Ch. 33, 7.3
    basic principles, Ch. 33, 7.1
        deductible temporary differences (deferred tax assets), Ch. 33, 7.1.2
        interpretation issues, Ch. 33, 7.1.3
            accounting profit, Ch. 33, 7.1.3.A
            taxable profit 'at the time of the transaction,' Ch. 33, 7.1.3.B
        taxable temporary differences (deferred tax liabilities), Ch. 33, 7.1.1
    gains, Ch. 33, 7.7
    initial recognition exception, Ch. 33, 7.2
        acquisition of an investment in a subsidiary, associate, branch or joint arrangement, Ch. 33, 7.2.10
        acquisition of subsidiary that does not constitute a business, Ch. 33, 7.2.9
        acquisition of tax losses, Ch. 33, 7.2.1
        changes to temporary differences after initial recognition, Ch. 33, 7.2.4
            change in carrying value due to revaluation, Ch. 33, 7.2.4.B
            change in tax base due to deductions in tax return, Ch. 33, 7.2.4.C
            depreciation, amortisation/impairment of initial carrying value, Ch. 33, 7.2.4.A
            temporary difference altered by legislative change, Ch. 33, 7.2.4.D
        initial recognition of compound financial instruments by the issuer, Ch. 33, 7.2.8
        initial recognition of goodwill, Ch. 33, 7.2.2
            deductible temporary differences, Ch. 33, 7.2.2.B
            taxable temporary differences, Ch. 33, 7.2.2.A
            tax deductible goodwill, Ch. 33, 7.2.2.C
        initial recognition of other assets and liabilities, Ch. 33, 7.2.3
        intragroup transfers of assets with no change in tax base, Ch. 33, 7.2.5
        partially deductible and super-deductible assets, Ch. 33, 7.2.6
        transactions involving the initial recognition of an asset and liability, Ch. 33, 7.2.7
            decommissioning costs, Ch. 33, 7.2.7.A
            leases under IFRS 16 taxed as operating leases, Ch. 33, 7.2.7.B

Income taxes—*contd*
  deferred tax, recognition—*contd*
    'outside' temporary differences relating to subsidiaries, branches, associates and joint arrangements, Ch. 33, 7.5
      calculation of, Ch. 33, 7.5.1
        consolidated financial statements, Ch. 33, 7.5.1.A
        separate financial statements of the investor, Ch. 33, 7.5.1.B
      deductible temporary differences, Ch. 33, 7.5.3
      foreseeable future – anticipated intragroup dividend, Ch. 33, 7.5.4
        consolidated financial statements of receiving entity, Ch. 33, 7.5.4.A
        separate financial statements of paying entity, Ch. 33, 7.5.4.B
      taxable temporary differences, Ch. 33, 7.5.2
      unpaid intragroup interest, royalties, management charges etc., Ch. 33, 7.5.5
    restrictions on recognition of deferred tax assets, Ch. 33, 7.4
      effect of disposals on recoverability of tax losses, Ch. 33, 7.4.8
        tax losses of retained entity recoverable against profits of subsidiary disposed of, Ch. 33, 7.4.8.B
        tax losses of subsidiary disposed of recoverable against profits of retained entity, Ch. 33, 7.4.8.C
        tax losses of subsidiary disposed of recoverable against profits of that subsidiary, Ch. 33, 7.4.8.A
      re-assessment of deferred tax assets, Ch. 33, 7.4.7
      restrictions imposed by relevant tax laws, Ch. 33, 7.4.1
      sources of 'probable' taxable profit, estimates of future taxable profits, Ch. 33, 7.4.3
        ignore the origination of new future deductible temporary differences, Ch. 33, 7.4.3.B
        ignore the reversal of existing deductible temporary differences, Ch. 33, 7.4.3.A
      sources of 'probable' taxable profit, taxable temporary differences, Ch. 33, 7.4.2
      tax planning opportunities, Ch. 33, 7.4.4
      unrealised losses on debt securities measured at fair value, Ch. 33, 7.4.5
      unused tax losses and unused tax credits, Ch. 33, 7.4.6
    'tax-transparent' ('flow-through') entities, Ch. 33, 7.6
  deferred tax–tax bases and temporary differences, Ch. 33, 6
    tax base, Ch. 33, 6.1
      of assets, Ch. 33, 6.1.1
      assets and liabilities whose tax base is not immediately apparent, Ch. 33, 6.1.3
      disclaimed/with no economic value, Ch. 33, 6.1.7
      equity items with a tax base, Ch. 33, 6.1.5
      of items not recognised as assets/liabilities in financial statements, Ch. 33, 6.1.4
      items with more than one tax base, Ch. 33, 6.1.6
      of liabilities, Ch. 33, 6.1.2
    temporary differences, examples, Ch. 33, 6.2
      assets and liabilities with no temporary difference, Ch. 33, 6.2.3
      business combinations and consolidation, Ch. 33, 6.2.1.E, 6.2.2.E
      deductible, Ch. 33, 6.2.2
        business combinations and consolidation, Ch. 33, 6.2.2.E
        foreign currency differences, Ch. 33, 6.2.1.F, 6.2.2.F
        hyperinflation, Ch. 33, 6.2.1.G
        revaluations, Ch. 33, 6.2.1.C, 6.2.2.C
        tax re-basing, Ch. 33, 6.2.1.D, 6.2.2.D
        transactions that affect profit of loss, Ch. 33, 6.2.2.A
        transactions that affect statement of financial position, Ch. 33, 6.2.2.B
      taxable, Ch. 33, 6.2.1
        business combinations and consolidation, Ch. 33, 6.2.1.E
        foreign currency differences, Ch. 33, 6.2.1.F
        hyperinflation, Ch. 33, 6.2.1.G
        revaluations, Ch. 33, 6.2.1.C
        tax re-basing, Ch. 33, 6.2.1.D
        transactions that affect profit of loss, Ch. 33, 6.2.1.A, 6.2.2.A
        transactions that affect statement of financial position, Ch. 33, 6.2.1.B, 6.2.2.B
  definitions, Ch. 33, 3, 4.1
    effectively tax-free entities, Ch. 33, 4.56
    hybrid taxes (including minimum taxes), Ch. 33, 4.1.2, 4.5
      minimum based on a measure other than taxable profits, Ch. 33, 4.5.1
      tax based on revenues, unless a profit measure gives a lower result, Ch. 33, 4.5.3
      tax is the higher of measures based on taxable profits and revenues, Ch. 33, 4.5.2
    interest and penalties, Ch. 33, 4.4
    investment tax credits, Ch. 33, 4.3
    levies, Ch. 33, 4.1.1, Ch. 26, 6.8
    withholding and similar taxes, Ch. 33, 4.2
  development of IAS 12, Ch. 33, 1.3
  disclosure, Ch. 33, 14
    components of tax expense, Ch. 33, 14.1
    discontinued operations–interaction with IFRS 5, Ch. 33, 14.6
    dividends, Ch. 33, 14.4
    examples, Ch. 33, 14.5
    other disclosures, Ch. 33, 14.2
      tax (or tax rate) reconciliation, Ch. 33, 14.2.1
      temporary differences relating to subsidiaries, associates, branches and joint arrangements, Ch. 33, 14.2.2
    reason for recognition of certain tax assets, Ch. 33, 14.3
  nature of taxation, Ch. 33, 1.1
  presentation, Ch. 33, 13
    statement of cash flows, Ch. 33, 13.3
    statement of comprehensive income, Ch. 33, 13.2
    statement of financial position, Ch. 33, 13.1
      offset current tax, Ch. 33, 13.1.1.A
      offset deferred tax, Ch. 33, 13.1.1.B
      no offset of current and deferred tax, Ch. 33, 13.1.1.C
  uncertain tax treatments, Ch. 33, 9

assumptions about the examination of tax treatments ('detection risk'), Ch. 33, 9.3
consideration of changes in facts and circumstances, Ch. 33, 9.5
    the expiry of a taxation authority's right to examine or re-examine a tax treatment, Ch. 33, 9.5.1
considered separately (unit of account), Ch. 33, 9.2
determining effects of, Ch. 33, 9.4
disclosures relating to, Ch. 33, 9.6
IFRIC 23, scope and definitions used, Ch. 33, 9.1
presentation of liabilities or assets for uncertain tax treatments, Ch. 33, 9.7
recognition of an asset for payments on account, Ch. 33, 9.8
transition to IFRIC 23, Ch. 33,9.9

Indemnification assets, Ch. 9, 5.6.4; Ch. 45, 3.12

India, IFRS adoption in, Ch. 1, 4.4.3

Indian Accounting Standards (Ind AS), Ch. 1, 4.4.3

Individual financial statements, Ch. 8, 1–4. *See also* Separate and individual financial statements; Separate financial statements
common control or group transactions in, Ch. 8, 4
    application of the principles in practice, Ch. 8, 4.4
        acquiring and selling businesses, transfers between subsidiaries, Ch. 8, 4.4.2
        acquisition and sale of assets for shares, Ch. 8, 4.4.1.C
        contribution and distribution of assets, Ch. 8, 4.4.1.D
        financial guarantee contracts, Ch. 8, 4.4.5.B
        financial instruments within the scope of IFRS 9, Ch. 8, 4.4.5
        incurring expenses and settling liabilities without recharges, Ch. 8, 4.4.4
        interest-free or non-market interest rate loans, Ch. 8, 4.4.5.A
        legal merger of parent and subsidiary, Ch. 8, 4.4.3.B
        parent exchanges PP&E for a non-monetary asset of the subsidiary, Ch. 8, 4.4.1.B
        sale of PP&E from the parent to the subsidiary for an amount of cash not representative of the fair value of the asset, Ch. 8, 4.4.1.A
        subsidiary transferring business to the parent, Ch. 8, 4.4.3.A
        transactions involving non-monetary assets, Ch. 8, 4.4.1
        transfers between subsidiaries, Ch. 8, 4.4.1.E
        transfers of businesses between parent and subsidiary, Ch. 8, 4.4.3
disclosures, Ch. 8, 4.5
fair value in intra-group transactions, Ch. 8, 4.3.1
measurement, Ch. 8, 4.3
put and call options in separate financial statements, Ch. 7, 6.5
recognition, Ch. 8, 4.2

Inflation-linked debt, Ch. 50, 3.6; Ch. 53, 2.2.6

Inflation risk, hedges of, Ch. 53, 2.2.6

Infrastructure assets. *See* Service concession arrangements (SCA)

Initial measurement of financial instruments, Ch. 49, 3
acquisition of a group of assets that does not constitute a business, Ch. 49, 3.3.5
business combination, loans and receivables acquired in, Ch. 49, 3.3.4

'day 1' profits, Ch. 49, 3.3
embedded derivatives, Ch. 49, 3.5
financial guarantee contracts, Ch. 49, 3.3.3
financial instrument hosts, Ch. 49, 3.5
general requirements, Ch. 49, 3.1
initial fair value, transaction price and 'day 1' profits, Ch. 49, 3.3
    interest-free and low-interest long-term loans, Ch. 49, 3.3.1
    measurement of financial instruments following modification of contractual terms that leads to initial recognition of a new instrument, Ch. 49, 3.3.2
loan commitments, assets and liabilities arising from, Ch. 49, 3.7
off-market loan commitments, Ch. 49, 3.3.3
regular way transactions, Ch. 49, 3.6
trade receivables without a significant financing component, Ch. 49, 3.2
transaction costs, Ch. 49, 3.4
transaction price, Ch. 49, 3.3

In-process research and development (IPR&D), Ch. 9, 5.5.2.D; Ch. 17, 5.5

Institute of Chartered Accountants of India (ICAI), Ch. 1, 4.4.3

In-substance defeasance arrangements, Ch. 52, 6.1.3

In-substance derivatives, Ch. 46, 3.2

Insurance acquisition cash flows, Ch. 56, 8.2.3.E

Insurance assets, Ch. 55, 2.2.2
derecognition of, Ch. 55, 7.2.6.A
impairment of, Ch. 55, 7.2.6.B
reconciliations of changes in, Ch. 55, 11.1.6

Insurance contracts, Ch. 45, 3.3; Ch. 55, 1–12; Ch. 56, 1–18. *See also* IFRS 4–*Insurance Contracts;* IFRS 17–*Insurance Contracts*
acquired in business combinations and portfolio transfers, Ch. 55, 9; Ch. 56, 13
    customer lists and relationships not connected to contractual insurance rights and obligations, Ch. 55, 9.2
    expanded presentation of insurance contracts, Ch. 55, 9.1
    practical issues, Ch. 55, 9.1.1; Ch. 56, 13.4
applying IFRS 9 with IFRS 4, Ch. 55, 1.3, 10
    overlay approach, Ch. 55, 10.2
        designation and de-designation of eligible financial assets, Ch. 55, 10.2.1
        disclosures required for entities using the overlay approach, Ch. 55, 10.2.3
        first-time adopters, Ch. 55, 10.2.2
    temporary exemption from IFRS 9, Ch. 55, 10.1
        activities that are predominantly connected with insurance, Ch. 55, 10.1.1
        disclosures required for entities using the temporary exemption, Ch. 55, 10.1.5
        first-time adopters, Ch. 55, 10.1.3
        initial assessment and reassessment of the temporary exemption, Ch. 55, 10.1.2
        interest rate benchmark reform, Ch. 55, 10.1.6
        relief from investors in associates and joint ventures, Ch. 55, 10.1.4
cash flows excluded from the contract boundary, Ch. 56, 8.2.4
cash flows within the contract boundary, Ch. 56, 8.2.3

Insurance contracts—*contd*
- changes in accounting policies, Ch. 55, 8
  - criteria for, Ch. 55, 8.1
  - practical issues, Ch. 55, 8.5
    - changes to local GAAP, Ch. 55, 8.5.1
  - redesignation of financial assets, Ch. 55, 8.4; Ch. 56, 17.6
  - shadow accounting, Ch. 55, 8.3
  - specific issues, Ch. 55, 8.2
    - continuation of existing practices, Ch. 55, 8.2.1
    - current market interest rates, Ch. 55, 8.2.2
    - future investment margins, Ch. 55, 8.2.4
    - prudence, Ch. 55, 8.2.3
- contract boundary, Ch. 56, 8.2.3
- contractual service margin (CSM), Ch. 56, 8.5
  - measurement of using the variable fee approach, Ch. 56, 11.2.2
  - recognition of in profit or loss, Ch. 56, 11.2.5
  - release of, Ch. 56, 10.4.1
  - subsequent measurement, Ch. 56, 8.6.2
- definition of, Ch. 55, 3; Ch. 56, 3
  - accounting differences between insurance and non insurance contracts, Ch. 55, 3.7
  - adverse effect on the policyholder, Ch. 55, 3.7
    - insurance of non-insurance risks, Ch. 55, 3.7.2; Ch. 56, 3.4.3
    - lapse, persistency and expense risk, Ch. 55, 3.7.1; Ch. 56, 3.4.2
  - changes in the level of insurance risk, Ch. 55, 3.3; Ch. 56, 3.6
  - examples of insurance and non-insurance contracts, Ch. 55, 3.9; Ch. 56, 3.7
  - insurable interest, Ch. 56, 3.4.1
  - insurance risk and financial risk, distinction between, Ch. 55, 3.6; Ch. 56, 3.4
  - payments in kind, Ch. 55, 3.5; Ch. 56, 3.3
  - service contracts, Ch. 55, 3.5.1
  - significant insurance risk, Ch. 55, 3.2; Ch. 56, 3.5
  - uncertain future events, Ch. 55, 3.4; Ch. 56, 3.2
- derecognition of, Ch. 56, 12
- with direct participating features, Ch. 56, 11.2
- direct participation features, Ch. 56, 11.2
  - coverage period for insurance contracts with, Ch. 56, 11.2
  - definition, Ch. 56, 11.2.1
  - disaggregation of finance income or expense between profit/loss and OCI, Ch. 56, 11.2.6
  - measurement of contractual service margin using variable fee approach, Ch. 56, 11.2.3
  - risk mitigation, Ch. 56, 11.2.5
- disclosure, Ch. 55, 11; Ch. 56, 16
  - nature and extent of risks arising from insurance contracts, Ch. 55, 11.2; Ch. 56, 16.5
    - credit risk, liquidity risk and market risk disclosures, Ch. 55, 11.2.6; Ch. 56, 16.5.2, 16.5.4-16.5.5
    - exposures to market risk from embedded derivatives, Ch. 55, 11.2.7
    - insurance risk
      - claims development information, Ch. 55, 11.2.5; Ch. 56, 16.5.3
      - concentrations of risk, Ch. 55, 11.2.4; Ch. 56, 16.5.1
      - insurance risk–general matters, Ch. 55, 11.2.2
    - sensitivity information, Ch. 55, 11.2.3; Ch. 56, 16.5.2
    - objectives, policies and processes for managing insurance contract risks, Ch. 55, 11.2.1
  - other disclosure matters, Ch. 55, 11.2.8
    - fair value disclosures, Ch. 55, 11.2.8.C
    - financial guarantee contracts, Ch. 55, 11.2.8.B
    - IAS 1 capital disclosures, Ch. 55, 11.2.8.A
    - key performance indicators, Ch. 55, 11.2.8.D
  - recognised amounts, explanation of, Ch. 55, 11.1; Ch. 56, 16.1
    - disclosure of accounting policies, Ch. 55, 11.1.1; Ch. 56, 16.4
    - effects of changes in assumptions, Ch. 55, 11.1.5
    - gains/losses on buying reinsurance, Ch. 55, 11.1.3
    - insurance finance income or expenses, Ch. 56, 16.1.3
    - premium allocation approach, accounting policies adopted for, Ch. 56, 16.1.2
    - process used to determine significant assumptions, Ch. 55, 11.1.4
    - recognised assets, liabilities, income and expense, Ch. 55, 11.1.2
    - reconciliations of changes in insurance assets and liabilities, Ch. 55, 11.1.6
    - reconciliations required for contracts applying the general model, Ch. 56, 16.1.1
    - reconciliations required for contracts applying the premium allocation approach, Ch. 56, 16.1.2
  - regulatory, Ch. 56, 16.5.6
  - significant judgements in applying IFRS 17, Ch. 56, 16.3
  - transition amounts, Ch. 56, 16.2
- discount rates, Ch. 56, 8.3
- discretionary participation feature, Ch. 55, 6; Ch. 56, 11.3
  - in financial instruments, Ch. 55, 6.2; Ch. 56, 11.2
  - in insurance contracts, Ch. 55, 6.1
  - investment contracts with, Ch. 56, 11.3
  - practical issues, Ch. 55, 6.3
    - contracts with switching features, Ch. 55, 6.3.2
    - negative DPF, Ch. 55, 6.3.1
- embedded derivatives, Ch. 55, 4
  - unit-linked features, Ch. 55, 4.1
- estimates of expected future cash flows, Ch. 56, 8.2
- existing accounting practices for, Ch. 55, 1.4
  - embedded value, Ch. 55, 1.4.3
  - life insurance, Ch. 55, 1.4.2
  - non-life insurance, Ch. 55, 1.4.1
- first-time adoption, Ch. 5, 5.4
- foreign currency, Ch. 56, 7.3
- history of the IASB's insurance project, Ch. 55, 1.1
- liability for incurred claims, Ch. 56, 8.6.2
- liability for remaining coverage, Ch. 56, 8.6.1
- modification of, Ch. 56, 12.1
- with participating features, Ch. 56, 11
- premium allocation approach, criteria and measurement, Ch. 56, 9
- risk adjustment for non-financial risk, Ch. 56, 8.4
- selection of accounting policies, Ch. 55, 7
  - hierarchy exemption, Ch. 55, 7.1
  - limits on the hierarchy exemption, Ch. 55, 7.2

accounting policy matters not addressed by IFRS 4, Ch. 55, 7.2.6
catastrophe and equalisation provisions, Ch. 55, 7.2.1
impairment of reinsurance assets, Ch. 55, 7.2.5
insurance liability derecognition, Ch. 55, 7.2.3
liability adequacy testing, Ch. 55, 7.2.2
offsetting of insurance and related reinsurance contracts, Ch. 55, 7.2.4
unbundling of deposit components, Ch. 55, 5
illustration, Ch. 55, 5.2
practical difficulties, Ch. 55, 5.3
requirements, Ch. 55, 5.1
without direct participating features, Ch. 56, 8.6.3, 17.4.2
Insurance finance income or expense, Ch. 56, 15.3, 16.1.3, 17.5.1
Insurance liability, Ch. 55, 2.2.1
derecognition, Ch. 55, 7.2.3
reconciliations of changes in, Ch. 55, 11.1.6
on undiscounted basis, measuring, Ch. 55, 8.2.1.A
Insurance mutuals, Ch. 55, 3.2.2.B; Ch. 56, 3.5.2.B
Insurance protection, Ch. 52, 3.6.3
Insurance revenue, Ch. 56, 15.1
Insurance risk
changes in the level of, Ch. 55, 3.3; Ch. 56, 3.6
claims development information, Ch. 55, 11.2.5; Ch. 56, 16.5.3
concentrations of risk, Ch. 55, 11.2.4; Ch. 56, 16.5.1
financial risk, distinction from, Ch. 55, 3.6; Ch. 56, 3.4
general matters, Ch. 55, 11.2.2
sensitivity information, Ch. 55, 11.2.3
significant insurance risk, Ch. 55, 3.2; Ch. 56, 3.5
level of assessment, Ch. 55, 3.2.2
insurance mutuals, Ch. 55, 3.2.2.B
intragroup insurance contracts, Ch. 55, 3.2.2.C
self insurance, Ch. 55, 3.2.2.A
meaning of 'significant,' Ch. 55, 3.2.1
quantity of insurance risk, Ch. 56, 3.5.1
significant additional benefits, Ch. 55, 3.2.3
Insurance service expenses, Ch. 56, 15.2
Insured benefits, employee benefits, Ch. 35, 3.2
Insured event, Ch. 55, 2.2.1
Insurer, Ch. 55, 2, 2.2.1; Ch. 56, 2
Insurer's liabilities, fair value of, Ch. 55, 9.1.1.B
Intangible asset model, service concession arrangements, Ch. 25, 4.3
Intangible assets, Ch. 9, 5.5.2; Ch. 17, 1–11. *See also* Amortisation of intangible assets; IAS 38; Internally generated intangible assets
acquisition by way of government grant, Ch. 17, 4.6
agile software development, Ch. 17, 6.2.6
as corporate assets, Ch. 20, 3.1.1
cloud computing, Ch. 17, 11.6
accounting, intangible asset, Ch. 17, 11.6.4; Ch. 17, 11.6.5
arrangement contains a lease, Ch. 17, 11.6.2
arrangement contains an intangible asset, , Ch. 17, 11.6.3
arrangements that contain an intangible asset, accounting for, Ch. 17,11.6.4
fees in the arrangement, Ch. 17, 11.6.4.A; Ch. 17, 11.6.4.B
implementation costs, Ch. 17, 11.6.4.B; Ch. 17, 11.6.5.B
types of cloud computing arrangements and determination of applicable IFRSs, Ch. 17, 11.6.1
definition, Ch. 17, 2.1
classification of programme and other broadcast rights as inventory/intangible assets, Ch. 17, 2.2.2
control, Ch. 17, 2.1.2
future economic benefits, Ch. 17, 2.1.3
identifiability, Ch. 17, 2.1.1
whether to record a tangible/intangible asset, Ch. 17, 2.2.1
disclosure, Ch. 17, 10
additional disclosures when the revaluation model is applied, Ch. 17, 10.4
general disclosures, Ch. 17, 10.1
profit/loss presentation, Ch. 17, 10.3
of research and development expenditure, Ch. 17, 10.5
statement of financial position presentation, Ch. 17, 10.2
exchanges of assets
commercial substance, Ch. 17, 4.7.2
measurement of assets exchanged, Ch. 17, 4.7.1
impairment losses, Ch. 17, 9.4
impairment of intangibles with an indefinite useful life, Ch. 20, 10
interim financial reporting, depreciation and amortisation, Ch. 41, 9.1
issues regarding, Ch. 17, 11
accounting for green certificates/renewable energy certificates, Ch. 17, 11.3
accounting for REACH costs, Ch. 17, 11.4
crypto-assets, Ch. 17, 11.5
emissions trading schemes, Ch. 17, 11.2
accounting for emission rights by brokers and traders, Ch. 17, 11.2.7
amortisation and impairment testing of emission rights, Ch. 17, 11.2.4
emission rights acquired in a business combination, Ch. 17, 11.2.5
government grant approach, Ch. 17, 11.2.3
IFRIC 3, Ch. 17, 11.2.1
net liability approaches, Ch. 17, 11.2.2
sale of emission rights, Ch. 17, 11.2.6
rate-regulated activities, Ch. 17, 11.1
measurement, Ch. 17, 3.2
acquired for contingent consideration, Ch. 17, 4.5
after initial recognition, Ch. 17, 8
cost model for measurement of intangible assets, Ch. 17, 8.1
revaluation model for measurement of intangible assets, Ch. 17, 8.2
accounting for revaluations, Ch. 17, 8.2.3
frequency of revaluations, Ch. 17, 8.2.2
revaluation is only allowed if there is an active market, Ch. 17, 8.2.1
recognising and measuring assets acquired and liabilities assumed in a business combination, Ch. 9, 5.5
combining an intangible asset with a related contract, Ch. 9, 5.5.2.C
contractual-legal, Ch. 9, 5.5.2

Intangible assets—*contd*
  recognising and measuring assets acquired and liabilities assumed in a business combination—*contd*
    customer relationship intangible assets, Ch. 9, 5.5.2.B
    emission rights, Ch. 9, 5.5.2.E
    fair values of intangible assets, determining, Ch. 9, 5.5.2.F
    in-process research or development project expenditure, Ch. 9, 5.5.2.D
    Multi Period Excess Earnings Method (MEEM), Ch. 9, 5.5.2.F
    Relief from Royalty method, Ch. 9, 5.5.2.F
    separability, Ch. 9, 5.5.2; Ch. 17, 5.1.3.B
  recognition, Ch. 17, 3.1
    PP&E components classified as, Ch. 18, 3.1.4
  separate acquisition, Ch. 17, 4
    acquisition by way of government grant, Ch. 17, 4.6
    components of cost, Ch. 17, 4.2
    costs to be expensed, Ch. 17, 4.3
    exchanges of assets, Ch. 17, 4.7
      commercial substance, Ch. 17, 4.7.2
      measurement of assets exchanged, Ch. 17, 4.7.1
    income from incidental operations, Ch. 17, 4.4
    measurement of intangible assets acquired for contingent consideration, Ch. 17, 4.5
    recognition, Ch. 17, 4.1
  subsequent expenditure, Ch. 17, 3.3
  useful life of, assessing, Ch. 17, 9.1
    with an indefinite useful life, Ch. 17, 9.3
    contractual/other legal rights, Ch. 17, 9.1.2
    factors affecting, Ch. 17, 9.1.1
    with a finite useful life, Ch. 17, 9.2
Intellectual property licences, Ch. 31, 2
  identifying performance obligations in a licensing arrangement, Ch. 31, 2.1
    application questions, Ch. 31, 2.1.5
    contracts that grant both permission for past use of intellectual property and a licence to use the intellectual property in the future, Ch. 31, 2.1.5.B
    contractual restrictions, Ch. 31, 2.1.3
    guarantees to defend or maintain a patent, Ch. 31, 2.1.4
    licences of intellectual property that are distinct, Ch. 31, 2.1.1
    licences of intellectual property that are not distinct, Ch. 31, 2.1.2
  licence renewals, Ch. 31, 2.4
  nature of the entity's promise in granting a licence, determining, Ch. 31, 2.2
    applying the licensing application guidance to a single (bundled) performance obligation that includes a licence of intellectual property, Ch. 31, 2.2.1
  recognising revenue for, Ch. 30, 8
  sales-based/usage-based royalties on, Ch. 31, 2.5
    application questions on the sales-based or usage-based royalty recognition constraint, Ch. 31, 2.5.2
    recognition of royalties for a licence that provides a right to access intellectual property, Ch. 31, 2.5.1
  transfer of control of licensed intellectual property, Ch. 31, 2.3
    right to access, Ch. 31, 2.3.1
    right to use, Ch. 31, 2.3.2
    use and benefit requirement, Ch. 31, 2.3.3

Interbank Offered Rate Reform (IBOR), Ch. 50, 3.8.3; Ch. 53,9; Ch. 54, 4.3.5, 5.7; Ch. 55, 10.1.6
Intercompany. *See* Intragroup
Interest-free long-term loans, Ch. 49, 3.3.1
Interest rate
  floors and caps, Ch. 46, 5.1.5
  indices, Ch. 46, 5.1.2
  negative, Ch. 53, 2.4.2
Interest rate risk, Ch. 54, 5
  contractually specified portions of, Ch. 53, 2.2.2
  offsetting internal hedging instruments, Ch. 53, 4.2
  sensitivity analysis, Ch. 54, 5.5.1
Interest rate swaps (IRS), Ch. 6, 5.3.1; Ch. 21, 5.5.1; Ch. 52, 4.4.2
  future settlement, Ch. 46, 2.3
  initial net investment, Ch. 46, 2.2
  at initial recognition, Ch. 14, 13.2.1
Interests in consolidated structured entities
  disclosure of risks associated with, Ch. 13, 4.4
Interests in joint arrangements and associates, disclosure of, Ch. 13, 5. *See also* IFRS 12
  extent, Ch. 13, 5.1
  financial effects, Ch. 13, 5.1
  individually immaterial joint ventures and associates, Ch. 13, 5.1.2
  joint ventures, Ch. 13, 5.2
  nature, Ch. 13, 5.1
  risks associated, Ch. 13, 5.2
  summarised financial information, Ch. 13, 5.1.1
Interests in other entities, Ch. 13, 2.2.1.A, 2.2.3.D
Interests in subsidiaries, disclosure of, Ch. 13, 4
  changes in ownership interests in subsidiaries, Ch. 13, 4.5
  composition of the group, Ch. 13, 4.1
  interests of non-controlling interests, Ch. 13, 4.2
  of nature and extent of significant restrictions, Ch. 13, 4.3
  required by investment entities, Ch. 13, 4.6
  risks associated with interests in consolidated structured entities, Ch. 13, 4.4
  terms of contractual arrangements, Ch. 13, 4.4.1
Interests in unconsolidated structured entities, disclosure of, Ch. 13, 6. *See also* IFRS 12
  nature of interests, Ch. 13, 6.1
    nature, purpose, size, activities and financing of structured entities, Ch. 13, 6.1.1
    sponsored structured entities for which no interest is held at the reporting date, Ch. 13, 6.1.2
  nature of risks, Ch. 13, 6.2–6.3
Interim financial reporting, Ch. 41, 1–11. *See also* IAS 34
Interim income tax expense, measuring, Ch. 41, 9.5.1
Internal hedges
  held by other group entities, Ch. 53, 4
  internal hedged items, Ch. 53, 4.3
    forecast intragroup transactions, Ch. 53, 4.3.2
    intragroup monetary items, Ch. 53, 4.3.1
  internal hedging instruments, Ch. 53, 4.1
    central clearing parties and ring fencing, Ch. 53, 4.1.1
  offsetting instruments, Ch. 53, 4.2
    foreign exchange risk, Ch. 53, 4.2.2
    interest rate risk, Ch. 53, 4.2.1

Internally generated intangible assets, Ch. 17, 6
- brands, Ch. 17, 6.2.4
- cost of
  - eligible for capitalisation, Ch. 17, 6.3.2
  - establishing the time from, Ch. 17, 6.3.1
- customer lists, Ch. 17, 6.2.4
- development phase, Ch. 17, 6.2.2
- goodwill, Ch. 17, 6.1
- mastheads, Ch. 17, 6.2.4
- pharmaceutical industry, research and development in, Ch. 17, 6.2.3
- publishing titles, Ch. 17, 6.2.4
- research phase, Ch. 17, 6.2.1
- website costs (SIC-32), Ch. 17, 6.2.5
  - application and infrastructure, Ch. 17, 6.2.5
  - content development, Ch. 17, 6.2.5
  - graphical design development, Ch. 17, 6.2.5
  - operating stage, Ch. 17, 6.2.5
  - planning, Ch. 17, 6.2.5

International Accounting Standards (IAS), Ch. 1, 2.1. *See also individual* IAS *entries*

International Accounting Standards Board (IASB), Ch. 1, 2.4. *See also* Conceptual framework, IASB's
- agenda consultation, Ch. 1, 2.2, 2.4, 3.1,3.2
- annual improvements , Ch. 1, 2.5
- convergence, Ch. 1, 3.2
- current priorities, Ch. 1, 3.1
- Due Process Handbook, Ch. 1, 2.5, 2.6
- future agenda, Ch. 1, 3.1
- maintenance projects, Ch. 3, 6.2
- primary financial statements, Ch. 3, 6.1.2
- Monitoring Board, Ch. 1, 2.3
- standard-setting projects, Ch. 3, 6.1
- standard setting structure, Ch. 1, 2.1
  - advisory bodies, Ch. 1, 2.9
  - IFRS Advisory Council, Ch. 1, 2.7
  - IFRS Foundation, Ch. 1, 2.2
  - IFRS Interpretations Committee, Ch. 1, 2,1-2.2, 2.5–2.7

International Financial Reporting Standards (IFRS), Ch. 1, 2.1. *See also individual* IFRS *entries*
- adoption, worldwide, Ch. 1, 4.1
  - Americas, Ch. 1, 4.3
  - Asia, Ch. 1, 4.4
  - Australia, Ch. 1, 4.5
  - Europe, Ch. 1, 4.2
  - South Africa, Ch. 1, 4.6
- consistency in application of, Ch. 1, 5

International Organisation of Securities Commissions (IOSCO), Ch. 1, 1, 2.3, 5

Interpretations Committee, Ch. 1, 2.5
- agenda decisions Ch. 1, 2.5.1

Intragroup (Intercompany)
- deferred tax on foreseeable future – anticipated intragroup dividend, Ch. 33, 7.5.4
- dividend subject to withholding tax, Ch. 33, 10.3.3
- eliminations, Ch. 7, 2.4
- insurance contracts, Ch. 56, 3.5.2.C
- transactions, Ch. 8, 4.3.1
- transfer of assets with no change in tax base, Ch. 33, 7.2.5
- transfer of tax losses, payments for, Ch. 33, 11.2
- unpaid interest, royalties, management charges etc., Ch. 33, 7.5.5
- unrealised profits and losses in consolidated financial statements, Ch. 33, 8.7

Intrinsic value method, share-based payments Ch. 34, 8.8.1

Inventories, Ch. 22, 1–6. *See also* IAS 2–*Inventories*
- disclosure requirements, Ch. 22, 6
- interim financial reporting, Ch. 41, 9.4
- measurement, Ch. 22, 3
- real estate inventory, Ch. 22, 4
- recognition in profit/loss, Ch. 22, 5

Inventories, extractive industries, Ch. 43, 14
- carried at fair value, Ch. 43, 14.4
- core inventories, Ch. 43, 14.3
- heap leaching (mining), Ch. 43, 14.6
- recognition of work in progress, Ch. 43, 14.1
- sale of by-products and joint products, Ch. 43, 14.2
  - by-products, Ch. 43, 14.2.1
  - joint products, Ch. 43, 14.2.2
- stockpiles of low grade ore (mining), Ch. 43, 14.5

Investing activities, cash flows, Ch. 40, 4.2

Investment contracts, Ch. 55, 2.2.2, 3.9.2

Investment contracts with discretionary participation features, Ch. 55, 6.1–6.2, 7.2.2.C; Ch. 56, 11.3

Investment entity, Ch. 6, 10
- accounting by a parent of an investment entity, Ch. 6, 10.4
- accounting by an investment entity, Ch. 6, 10.3
- cash flows in, Ch. 40, 6.4.3
- definition, Ch. 6, 10.1
- determining whether an entity is an investment entity, Ch. 6, 10.2
  - earnings from investments, Ch. 6, 10.2.3
  - exit strategies, Ch. 6, 10.2.2
  - fair value measurement, Ch. 6, 10.2.4
  - having more than one investor, Ch. 6, 10.2.6
  - holding more than one investment, Ch. 6, 10.2.5
  - intermediate holding companies established for tax optimization purposes, Ch. 6, 10.2.1.B
  - investment entity illustrative examples, Ch. 6, 10.2.9
  - investment-related services, Ch. 6, 10.2.1.A
  - multi-layered fund structures, Ch. 6, 10.2.10
  - ownership interests, Ch. 6, 10.2.8
  - unrelated investors, Ch. 6, 10.2.7
- disclosures required by, Ch. 13, 4.6

Investment property, Ch. 19, 1–12. *See also* IAS 40
- cost model, Ch. 19, 7
  - impairment, Ch. 19, 7.3
  - incidence of use of the cost model, Ch. 19, 7.2
  - initial recognition, Ch. 19, 7.1
    - identification of non-physical parts, Ch. 19, 7.1.2
    - identification of physical parts, Ch. 19, 7.1.1
- definitions, Ch. 19, 2
- disclosure requirements of IAS 40, Ch. 19, 12
  - additional disclosures for the cost model, Ch. 19, 12.3
  - additional disclosures for the fair value model, Ch. 19, 12.2
    - extra disclosures where fair value cannot be determined reliably, Ch. 19, 12.2.2
    - presentation of changes in fair value, Ch. 19, 12.2.1

Investment property—*contd*
  disclosure requirements of IAS 4—*contd*
    disclosures under both fair value and cost models, Ch. 19, 12.1
      disclosure of direct operating expenses, Ch. 19, 12.1.3
      level of aggregation for IFRS 13 disclosures, Ch. 19, 12.1.2
      methods and assumptions in fair value estimates, Ch. 19, 12.1.1
    presentation of sales proceeds, Ch. 19, 12.4
  disposal of investment property, Ch. 19, 10
    calculation of gain/loss on disposal, Ch. 19, 10.1
    compensation from third parties, Ch. 19, 10.4
    replacement of parts of investment property, Ch. 19, 10.3
    sale prior to completion of construction, Ch. 19, 10.2
  fair value model, Ch. 19, 6
    deferred taxation for property held by a 'single asset' entity, Ch. 19, 6.10
    estimating fair value, Ch. 19, 6.1
      comparison with value in use, Ch. 19, 6.1.3
      'double counting,' Ch. 19, 6.1.4
      methods of estimation, Ch. 19, 6.1.1
      observable data, Ch. 19, 6.1.2
    fair value of investment property under construction, Ch. 19, 6.3
    fixtures and fittings subsumed within fair value, Ch. 19, 6.5
    future capital expenditure and development value ('highest and best use'), Ch. 19, 6.8
    inability to determine fair value of completed investment property, Ch. 19, 6.2
    negative present value, Ch. 19, 6.9
    prepaid and accrued operating lease income, Ch. 19, 6.6
      accrued rental income and lease incentives, Ch. 19, 6.6.1
      prepaid rental income, Ch. 19, 6.6.2
    transaction costs incurred by the reporting entity on acquisition, Ch. 19, 6.4
    valuation adjustment to the fair value of properties held under a lease, Ch. 19, 6.7
  IFRS 5 and investment property, Ch. 19, 8
  initial measurement, Ch. 19, 4
    assets acquired in exchange transactions, Ch. 19, 4.6
    attributable costs, Ch. 19, 4.1
      acquisition of a group of assets that does not constitute a business, Ch. 19, 4.1.1
      deferred taxes when acquiring a 'single asset' entity that is not a business, Ch. 19, 4.1.2
    borrowing costs, Ch. 19, 4.8
    contingent costs, Ch. 19, 4.10
    deferred payments, Ch. 19, 4.3
    income from tenanted property during development, Ch. 19, 4.11
    initial recognition of tenanted investment property subsequently measured using the cost model, Ch. 19, 4.7
    lease incentives and initial costs of leasing a property, Ch. 19, 4.9
      initial direct costs of obtaining a lease, Ch. 19, 4.9.2
      lease incentives, Ch. 19, 4.9.1
    payments by the vendor to the purchaser, Ch. 19, 4.12
    property held under a lease, Ch. 19, 4.5
    reclassifications from property, plant and equipment ('PP&E'/from inventory, Ch. 19, 4.4
    start-up costs and self-built property, Ch. 19, 4.2
      cost of a building to be demolished in connection with the construction of a new building, Ch. 19, 4.2.1
  interim reporting and IAS 40, Ch. 19, 11
  measurement after initial recognition, Ch. 19, 5
    by insurers and similar entities, Ch. 19, 5.1
  recognition, Ch. 19, 3
  scope, Ch. 19, 2
  transfer of assets to/from investment property, Ch. 19, 9
    accounting treatment of transfers, Ch. 19, 9.2
    transfers from investment property to inventory, Ch. 19, 9.1

Investment tax credits, Ch. 24, 2.3.2; Ch. 33, 4.3

Investments in associates and joint ventures, Ch. 11, 1–11. *See also* Equity method/accounting; IAS 28; Reciprocal interests in equity accounted entities
  application of the equity method, Ch. 11, 7
    consistent accounting policies, Ch. 11, 7.8
    date of commencement of equity accounting, Ch. 11, 7.3
    discontinuing the use of the equity method, Ch. 11, 7.12
      deemed disposals, Ch. 11, 7.12.6
      investment in associate becomes a joint venture (or vice versa), Ch. 11, 7.12.4
      investment in associate/joint venture that is a business becoming a subsidiary, Ch. 11, 7.12.1
      partial disposals of interests in associate/joint venture, Ch. 11, 7.12.5
      retained investment in associate or joint venture that is not a business becoming a subsidiary, Ch. 11, 7.12.2
      retained investment in the former associate or joint venture is a financial asset, Ch. 11, 7.12.3
    distributions received in excess of the carrying amount, Ch. 11, 7.10
    equity accounting and consolidation, comparison between, Ch. 11, 7.2
    equity transactions in an associate's/joint venture's financial statements, Ch. 11, 7.11
      dividends/other forms of distributions, Ch. 11, 7.11.1
      effects of changes in parent/non-controlling interests in subsidiaries, Ch. 11, 7.11.4
      equity-settled share-based payment transactions, Ch. 11, 7.11.3
      issues of equity instruments, Ch. 11, 7.11.2
    initial carrying amount of an associate/joint venture, Ch. 11, 7.4
      applying a cost-based approach, Ch. 11, 7.4.2.A
      applying a fair value (IFRS 3) approach, Ch. 11, 7.4.2.A
      following loss of control of an entity, Ch. 7, 3.3.2, 7.1; Ch. 11, 7.4.1
      piecemeal acquisition, Ch. 11, 7.4.2
        common control transactions involving sales of associates, Ch. 11, 7.4.2.D
        existing associate that becomes a joint venture, or vice versa, Ch. 11, 7.4.2.C
        financial instrument becoming an associate/joint venture, Ch. 11, 7.4.2.A

step increase in an existing associate/joint venture without a change in status of the investee, Ch. 11, 7.4.2.B
  loss-making associates/joint ventures, Ch. 11, 7.9
  non-coterminous accounting periods, Ch. 11, 7.7
  overview, Ch. 11, 7.1
  share of the investee, Ch. 11, 7.5
    accounting for potential voting rights, Ch. 11, 7.5.1
    cumulative preference shares held by parties other than the investor, Ch. 11, 7.5.2
    several classes of equity, Ch. 11, 7.5.3
    where the investee is a group, Ch. 11, 7.5.5
    where the reporting entity is a group, Ch. 11, 7.5.4
  transactions between the reporting entity and its associates/joint ventures, Ch. 11, 7.6
    contributions of non-monetary assets to an associate/joint venture, Ch. 11, 7.6.5
      commercial substance, Ch. 11, 7.6.5.A
      conflict between IAS 28 and IFRS 10, Ch. 7, 3.3.2, 7.1; Ch. 11, 7.6.5.C
      practical application, Ch. 11, 7.6.5.B
    elimination of 'upstream' and 'downstream' transactions, Ch. 11, 7.6.1
    loans and borrowings between the reporting entity, Ch. 11, 7.6.3
    reciprocal interests, Ch. 11, 7.6.2
    statement of cash flows, Ch. 11, 7.6.4
classification as held for sale (IFRS 5), Ch. 11, 6
definitions, Ch. 11, 3
disclosures, Ch. 11, 10.2
exemptions from applying the equity method, Ch. 11, 5.3
  investments held in associates/joint ventures held by venture capital organisations, Ch. 11, 5.3
    application of IFRS 9 to exempt, Ch. 11, 5.3.2
      entities with a mixture of activities, Ch. 11, 5.3.2.A
    application of IFRS 9 to exempt investments in associates or joint ventures, Ch. 11, 5.3.2
    investment entities exception, Ch. 11, 5.3.1
future developments, Ch. 11, 11
impairment losses, Ch. 11, 8
objective, Ch. 11, 2.1
parents exempt from preparing consolidated financial statements, Ch. 11, 5.1
partial use of fair value measurement of associates, Ch. 11, 5.4
presentation, Ch. 11, 10.1
  other items of comprehensive income, Ch. 11, 10.1.3
  profit/loss, Ch. 11, 10.1.2
  statement of cash flows, Ch. 11, 10.1.4
  statement of financial position, Ch. 11, 10.1.1
scope, Ch. 11, 2.2
separate financial statements, Ch. 11, 9
significant influence, Ch. 11, 4
  fund managers, Ch. 11, 4.6
  holdings of less than 20% of the voting power, Ch. 11, 4.3
    lack of, Ch. 11, 4.2
  potential voting rights, Ch. 11, 4.4
  severe long-term restrictions impairing ability to transfer funds to the investor, Ch. 11, 4.1
  voting rights held in a fiduciary capacity, Ch. 11, 4.5
subsidiaries meeting certain criteria, Ch. 11, 5.2

transfers of associates/joint ventures between entities under common control, Ch. 10, 5

Investments in subsidiaries, associates and joint ventures, Ch. 8.2.1, Ch. 20, 12.4
  equity accounted investment and indicators of impairment, Ch. 20, 12.4.3
  equity accounted investments and CGUs, Ch. 20, 12.4.5
  equity accounted investments and long term loans, Ch. 20, 12.4.4
  equity accounted investments and testing goodwill for impairment, Ch. 20, 12.4.6
  exemptions from applying the equity method, Ch. 11, 5
  fair value less costs of disposal (FVLCD), Ch. 20, 12.4.1
  value in use (VIU) for, Ch. 20, 12.4.2
Islamic Finance Consultative Group, Ch. 1, 2.9
Islamic financial institutions (IFIs), Ch. 27, 3.5.1.A
Japan, IFRS adoption in, Ch. 1, 4.4.2
Joint arrangements, Ch. 12, 1–910. *See also* IFRS 11; Joint control; Joint operations
  accounting for joint operations, Ch. 12, 6
    accounting for rights and obligations, Ch. 12, 6.2
    determining the relevant IFRS, Ch. 12, 6.3
    interest in a joint operation without joint control, Ch. 12, 6.4
    not structured through a separate vehicle, Ch. 12, 6.1
    with a party that participates in a joint arrangement but does not have joint control, Ch. 12, 6.5
    in separate financial statements, Ch. 12, 6.7
    transactions between a joint operator and a joint operation, Ch. 12, 6.6
  accounting for joint ventures, Ch. 12, 7
    contributions of non-monetary assets to a joint venture, Ch. 12, 7.2
    interest in a joint venture without joint control, Ch. 12, 7.1
    in separate financial statements, Ch. 12, 7.3
  applications to joint arrangements held for sale, Ch. 12, 2.2.2
  cash flows of, Ch. 40, 6.4.2
  classification of, Ch. 12, 5
    contractual terms, Ch. 12, 5.3
    facts and circumstances, Ch. 12, 5.4
    illustrative examples, Ch. 12, 5.5
    legal form of the separate vehicle, Ch. 12, 5.2
    separate vehicle or not, Ch. 12, 5.1
  continuous assessment, Ch. 12, 8
    changes in ownership of a joint arrangement that is not a business, Ch. 12, 8.4
      joint operator obtains control, Ch. 7, 3.1.2; Ch. 12, 8.4.1
      parties that participate in a joint arrangement but do not have joint control obtain joint control, Ch. 12, 8.4.1
    changes in ownership of a joint operation that is a business, Ch. 12, 8.3
      acquisition of an interest in, Ch. 12, 8.3.1
      disposal of interest in, Ch. 12, 8.3.5
      former subsidiary becomes, Ch. 7, 3.3.3, 7.2; Ch. 12, 8.3.3
      obtaining control or joint control over a joint operation that is a business, Ch. 12, 8.3.2
      other changes in ownership of, Ch. 12, 8.3.4

Joint arrangements—*contd*
  continuous assessment—*contd*
    changes in ownership of a joint venture that is a business, Ch. 12, 8.2
      acquisition of an interest, Ch. 12, 8.2.1
      becomes a financial asset (or vice versa), Ch. 12, 8.2.5
      becomes an associate (or vice versa), Ch. 12, 8.2.4
      control over a former joint venture, Ch. 12, 8.2.2
      disposal of interest in, Ch. 12, 8.2.6
      former subsidiary becomes a joint venture, Ch. 7, 3.3.2, 7.1; Ch. 12, 8.2.3
      interest in a joint venture held for sale, Ch. 12, 8.2.7
      when to reassess under IFRS 11, Ch. 12, 8.1
  definition of, Ch. 12, 3; Ch. 13, 2.2.2.B
  disclosures, Ch. 12, 9
  guarantees, Ch. 12, 5.3.1
  nature of, Ch. 12, 1.1
  objective, Ch. 12, 2.1
  scope, Ch. 12, 2.2
    accounting by a joint operation, Ch. 12, 2.2.3
    application by venture capital organisations and similar entities, Ch. 12, 2.2.1
    application to joint arrangements held for sale, Ch. 12, 2.2.2
  unit of account, Ch. 12, 3.1

Joint control, Ch. 12, 4
  assessing in extractive industries, Ch. 43, 7.1.1
    meaning of unanimous consent, Ch. 43, 7.1.1.B
    relevant activities, Ch. 43, 7.1.1.A
  practical issues with assessing, Ch. 12, 4.4
    evaluate multiple agreements together, Ch. 12, 4.4.2
    undivided share/lease/joint arrangement, Ch. 12, 4.4.1
  rights to control collectively, Ch. 12, 4.2
    de facto agents, Ch. 12, 4.2.5
    delegated decision-making, Ch. 12, 4.2.4
    evidence of, Ch. 12, 4.2.3
    government, role of, Ch. 12, 4.2.6
    potential voting rights and joint control, Ch. 12, 4.2.2
    protective rights, including some veto rights, Ch. 12, 4.2.1
  sequential activities in, Ch. 12, 4.1.1
  unanimous consent, Ch. 12, 4.3
    arbitration, Ch. 12, 4.3.3
    arrangements involving passive investors, Ch. 12, 4.3.1
    ultimate voting authority, Ch. 12, 4.3.2

Joint operating agreement (JOA), Ch. 43, 5.6, 17.3.3

Joint operations
  accounting for, Ch. 12, 6
    accounting for rights and obligations, Ch. 12, 6.2
    determining the relevant IFRS, Ch. 12, 6.3
    interest in a joint operation without joint control, Ch. 12, 6.4
    not structured through a separate vehicle, Ch. 12, 6.1
    with a party that participates in a joint arrangement but does not have joint control, Ch. 12, 6.5
    in separate financial statements, Ch. 12, 6.7
    transactions between a joint operator and a joint operation, Ch. 12, 6.6
  changes in ownership of, Ch. 12, 8.3 acquisition of an interest in, Ch. 12, 8.3.1
    disposal of interest in, Ch. 12, 8.3.5
    former subsidiary becomes, Ch. 7, 3.3.3, 7.2; Ch. 12, 8.3.3
    obtaining control or joint control over a joint operation that is a business, Ch. 12, 8.3.2
  implications of controlling, Ch. 43, 7.1.2.A
  in separate financial statements, Ch. 8, 1.1.2

Joint products, extractive industries, Ch. 43, 14.2, 16.1.3.D

Joint ventures. *See also IAS 28–Investments in associates and joint ventures*
  accounting for, Ch. 12, 7
    contributions of non-monetary assets to a joint venture, Ch. 12, 7.2
    interest in a joint venture without joint control, Ch. 12, 7.1
    in separate financial statements, Ch. 8, 1.1.1; Ch. 12, 7.3
  cash flows, Ch. 40, 6.4
    arising from interests in, Ch. 40, 8.4
    cash flows of joint operations, Ch. 40, 6.4.2
    investments in associates and joint ventures, Ch. 40, 6.4.1
  changes in ownership, Ch. 12, 8.2
  disclosure of commitments relating to, Ch. 13, 5.2.1
  disclosure of contingent liabilities relating to, Ch. 13, 5.2.2
  equity transactions in, Ch. 11, 7.11
  FVLCD for investments in, Ch. 20, 12.4.1
  implications of controlling, Ch. 43, 7.1.2.B
  initial carrying amount of an associate/joint venture, Ch. 11, 7.4
  following loss of control of an entity, Ch. 7, 3.3.2, 7.1; Ch. 11, 7.4.1
  piecemeal acquisition, Ch. 11, 7.4.2
    common control transactions involving sales of associates, Ch. 11, 7.4.2.D
    existing associate that becomes a joint venture, or vice versa, Ch. 11, 7.4.2.C
    financial instrument becoming an associate/joint venture, Ch. 11, 7.4.2.A
    step increase in an existing associate/joint venture without a change in status of the investee, Ch. 11, 7.4.2.B
  investments held in, Ch. 11, 5.3
  loans and borrowings between the reporting entity and, Ch. 11, 7.6.3
  risks associated with interests in, Ch. 13, 5.2
  separate financial statements and interests in, Ch. 8, 1.1.1
  share-based payments to employees of, Ch. 34, 12.9
  transactions between the reporting entity and, Ch. 11, 7.6
  VIU for investments in, calculating, Ch. 20, 12.4.2
    based on cash flows generated by underlying assets, Ch. 20, 12.4.2.B
    using dividend discount models, Ch. 20, 12.4.2.A

Key management personnel, related party, Ch. 39, 2.2.1.D

Leases (IFRS 16), Ch. 23, 1–10. *See also IFRS 16*
  acquiree in a business combination is a lessee, Ch. 23, 9.1
  acquiree in a business combination is a lessor, Ch. 23, 9.2
  business combinations, Ch. 23, 9–9.2
  commencement date of the lease, Ch. 23, 4.2
  contract combinations, Ch. 23, 3.3
  definition, Ch. 23, 3–3.3
    determining whether an arrangement contains a lease, Ch. 23, 3.1

flowchart of the decision making process, Ch. 23, 3.1.6
identified asset, Ch. 23, 3.1.2
joint arrangements, Ch. 23, 3.1.1
reassessment of the contract, Ch. 23, 3.1.7
right to direct the use of the identified asset, Ch. 23, 3.1.5
    how and for what purpose the asset is used, Ch. 23, 3.1.5.A
    protective rights, Ch. 23, 3.1.5.D
    relevant decisions about how and for what purpose the asset is used are predetermined, Ch. 23, 3.1.5.B
    specifying the output of an asset before the period of use, Ch. 23, 3.1.5.C
right to obtain substantially all of the economic benefits from use of the identified asset, Ch. 23, 3.1.4
substantive substitution rights, Ch. 23, 3.1.3
identifying and separating lease and non-lease components of a contract, Ch. 23, 3.2
    determining and allocating the consideration in the contract– lessees, Ch. 23, 3.2.3
    determining and allocating the consideration in the contract– lessors, Ch. 23, 3.2.4
    identifying and separating lease components of a contract, Ch. 23, 3.2.1
    identifying and separating lease from non-lease components of a contract, Ch. 23, 3.2.2
        lessee reimbursements, Ch. 23, 3.2.2.A
        practical expedient–lessees, Ch. 23, 3.2.2.B
discount rates, Ch. 23, 4.6
    determination of the incremental borrowing rate by a subsidiary with centralised treasury functions, Ch. 23, 4.6.1
economic life, Ch. 23, 4.8
effective date and transition, Ch. 23, 10
    amounts previously recognised in a business combination, Ch. 23, 10.5.2
    disclosure, Ch. 23, 10.6
    effective date, Ch. 23, 10.1
    lessee transition, Ch. 23, 10.3
        full retrospective approach, Ch. 23, 10.3.1
        modified retrospective approach, Ch. 23, 10.3.2
    lessor transition, Ch. 23, 10.4
        subleases, Ch. 23, 10.4.1
    sale and leaseback transactions, Ch. 23, 10.5.1
    transition, Ch. 23, 10.2
extractive industries, impact of IFRS 16 on, Ch. 43, 17, 18
    allocating contract consideration, Ch. 43, 17.6
    definition of a lease, Ch. 43, 17.2
    identifying and separating lease and non-lease components, Ch. 43, 17.
    identifying lease payments included in the measurement of the lease liability, Ch. 43, 17.5
    interaction of IFRS 16 and IFRS 11, Ch. 43, 18
    interaction of leases with asset retirement obligations, Ch. 43, 17.7
    joint arrangements, Ch. 43, 18
    scope and scope exclusions, Ch. 43, 17.1
    substitution rights, Ch. 43, 17.3

fair value, Ch. 23, 4.9
inception of a contract, Ch. 23, 4.1
initial direct costs, Ch. 23, 4.7; Ch. 19, 4.9.2
lease liabilities under IFRS 16, Ch. 20, 4.1.2
lease payments, Ch. 23, 4.5
    amounts expected to be payable under residual value guarantees lessees only, Ch. 23, 4.5.6
    co-tenancy clauses, Ch. 23, 4.5.11
    exercise price of a purchase option, Ch. 23, 4.5.4
    in-substance fixed lease payments, Ch. 23, 4.5.1
    lease incentives, Ch. 23, 4.5.2; Ch. 19, 4.9.1
    lessors only, Ch. 23, 4.5.7
    payments for penalties for terminating a lease, Ch. 23, 4.5.5
    reassessment of the lease liability, Ch. 23, 4.5.12
    remeasurement by lessors, Ch. 23, 4.5.13
    security deposits, Ch. 23, 4.5.9
    value added tax and property taxes, Ch. 23, 4.5.10
    variable lease payments that depend on an index/rate, Ch. 23, 4.5.3
    variable lease payments which do not depend on an index or rate, Ch. 23, 4.5.8
lease term and purchase options, Ch. 23, 4.4 cancellable leases, Ch. 23, 4.4.1
    reassessment of lease term and purchase options, lessees, Ch. 23, 4.4.2
    lessors, Ch. 23, 4.4.3
lessee accounting, Ch. 23, 5
    disclosure, Ch. 23, 5.8
        additional, Ch. 23, 5.8.3
        of assets, liabilities, expenses and cash flows, Ch. 23, 5.8.2 objective, Ch. 23, 5.8.1
    initial measurement, Ch. 23, 5.2
        lease liabilities, Ch. 23, 5.2.2
        right-of-use assets, Ch. 23, 5.2.1
    initial recognition, Ch. 23, 5.1
        leases of low-value assets, Ch. 23, 5.1.2
        short-term leases, Ch. 23, 5.1.1
    lease modifications, Ch. 23, 5.5
        amendment to IFRS 16 for covid-19 related rent concessions, Ch. 23, 5.5.4
            accounting for a concession in the form of a deferral of lease payments as if the lease is unchanged (Approach 3), Ch. 23, 5.5.4.C
            accounting for a concession, in the form of forgiveness or deferral of lease payments, as a negative variable lease payment (Approach 1), Ch. 23, 5.5.4.A
            accounting for a concession in the form of forgiveness or deferral of lease payments as a resolution of a contingency that fixes previously variable lease payments (Approach 2), Ch. 23, 5.5..B
            disclosure, Ch. 23, 5.5.4.D
            transition and effective date, Ch. 23, 5.5.4.E
        application of lease modification guidance to rent concessions, Ch. 23, 5.5.3
            lessee accounting for rent concessions as lease modifications, Ch. 23, 5.5.3.B
            rent concessions that change the consideration in the contract, Ch. 23, 5.5.3.A

Leases (IFRS 16)—*contd*
  lessee accounting—*contd*
    lease modifications—*contd*
      lessee accounting for a modification that does not result in a separate lease, Ch. 23, 5.5.2
      resulting in a separate lease, Ch. 23, 5.5.1
    lessee matters, Ch. 23, 5.6
      impairment of right-of-use assets, Ch. 23, 5.6.1
      income tax accounting, Ch. 23, 5.6.4
      leases denominated in a foreign currency, Ch. 23, 5.6.2
      portfolio approach, Ch. 23, 5.6.3
    presentation, Ch. 23, 5.7
    presentation in the statement of cash flows, Ch. 40, 5.5.1
    remeasurement of lease liabilities and right-of-use assets, Ch. 23, 5.4
    subsequent measurement, Ch. 23, 5.3
      expense recognition, Ch. 23, 5.3.3
      lease liabilities, Ch. 23, 5.3.2
      right-of-use assets, Ch. 23, 5.3.1
  lessee involvement with the underlying asset before the commencement date, Ch. 23, 4.3
  lessor accounting, Ch. 23, 6
    disclosure, Ch. 23, 6.7
      for all lessors, Ch. 23, 6.7.2
      for finance leases, Ch. 23, 6.7.3
      objective, Ch. 23, 6.7.1
      for operating leases, Ch. 23, 6.7.4
    finance leases, Ch. 23, 6.2
      initial measurement, Ch. 23, 6.2.1
      manufacturer/dealer lessors, Ch. 23, 6.2.2
      remeasurement of the net investment in the lease, Ch. 23, 6.2.4
      subsequent measurement, Ch. 23, 6.2.3
    lease classification, Ch. 23, 6.1
      criteria, Ch. 23, 6.1.1
      reassessment of, Ch. 23, 6.1.4
      residual value guarantees included in the lease classification test, Ch. 23, 6.1.3
      test for land and buildings, Ch. 23, 6.1.2
    lease modifications, Ch. 23, 6.4
      determining whether a modification to a finance lease results in a separate lease, Ch. 23, 6.4.1
      lessor accounting for a modification to a finance lease that does not result in a separate lease, Ch. 23, 6.4.2
      modification to an operating lease, Ch. 23, 6.4.3
    lessor matters, Ch. 23, 6.5
      portfolio approach, Ch. 23, 6.5.1
    operating leases, Ch. 23, 6.3
      income, Ch. 23, 6.3.1
    presentation, Ch. 23, 6.6
    presentation in the statement of cash flows, Ch. 40, 5.5.5
  sale and leaseback transactions, Ch. 23, 8
    determining whether the transfer of an asset is a sale, Ch. 23, 8.1
    disclosures, Ch. 23, 8.4
    transactions in which the transfer of an asset is a sale, Ch. 23, 8.2
      accounting for the leaseback, Ch. 23, 8.2.2
      accounting for the sale, Ch. 23, 8.2.1
      adjustment for off-market terms, Ch. 23, 8.2.3
    transactions in which the transfer of an asset is not a sale, Ch. 23, 8.3
  subleases, Ch. 23, 7
    definition, Ch. 23, 7.1
    disclosure, Ch. 23, 7.5
    intermediate lessor accounting, Ch. 23, 7.2
    presentation, Ch. 23, 7.4
    sublessee accounting, Ch. 23, 7.3

Leases of land, Ch. 23, 3.2
  separating land and buildings, Ch. 23, 6.1.2

Legal obligation, Ch. 26, 1.3, 3.1.1; Ch. 35, 7.1, 12.3.1

Legal right of set-off, enforceable, Ch. 54, 7.4.1.A

Lessee accounting (IFRS 16), Ch. 23, 5
  disclosure, Ch. 23, 5.8
    additional, Ch. 23, 5.8.3
    of assets, liabilities, expenses and cash flows, Ch. 23, 5.8.2
    objective, Ch. 23, 5.8.1
  initial measurement, Ch. 23, 5.2
    lease liabilities, Ch. 23, 5.2.2
    right-of-use assets, Ch. 23, 5.2.1
  initial recognition, Ch. 23, 5.1
    leases of low-value assets, Ch. 23, 5.1.2
    short-term leases, Ch. 23, 5.1.1
  lease liabilities under IFRS 16, Ch. 20, 4.1.2
  lease modifications, Ch. 23, 5.5
    determining whether a lease modification results in a separate lease, Ch. 23, 5.5.1
    lessee accounting for a modification that does not result in a separate lease, Ch. 23, 5.5.2
  lessee matters, Ch. 23, 5.6
    impairment of right-of-use assets, Ch. 23, 5.6.1
    income tax accounting, Ch. 23, 5.6.4
    leases denominated in a foreign currency, Ch. 23, 5.6.2
    portfolio approach, Ch. 23, 5.6.3
  presentation, Ch. 23, 5.7
  remeasurement of lease liabilities and right-of-use assets, Ch. 23, 5.4
  subsequent measurement, Ch. 23, 5.3
    expense recognition, Ch. 23, 5.3.3
    lease liabilities, Ch. 23, 5.3.2
    right-of-use assets, Ch. 23, 5.3.1

Lessor accounting (IFRS 16), Ch. 23, 6
  disclosure, Ch. 23, 6.7
    for all lessors, Ch. 23, 6.7.2
    for finance leases, Ch. 23, 6.7.3
    objective, Ch. 23, 6.7.1
    for operating leases, Ch. 23, 6.4.3
  finance leases, Ch. 23, 6.2
    initial measurement, Ch. 23, 6.2.1
    manufacturer/dealer lessors, Ch. 23, 6.2.2
    remeasurement of the net investment in the lease, Ch. 23, 6.2.4
    subsequent measurement, Ch. 23, 6.2.3
  lease classification, Ch. 23, 6.1
    criteria, Ch. 23, 6.1.1
    reassessment of, Ch. 23, 6.1.4
    residual value guarantees included in the lease classification test, Ch. 23, 6.1.3
    test for land and buildings, Ch. 23, 6.1.2

lease modifications, Ch. 23, 6.4
    determining whether a modification to a finance lease results in a separate lease, Ch. 23, 6.4.1
    lessor accounting for a modification to a finance lease that does not result in a separate lease, Ch. 23, 6.4.2
    modification to an operating lease, Ch. 23, 6.4.3
  lessor matters, Ch. 23, 6.5
    portfolio approach, Ch. 23, 6.5.1
  operating leases, Ch. 23, 6.3
  presentation, Ch. 23, 6.6

Level 1, 2 and 3 inputs, fair value measurement, Ch. 14, 17, 18, 19; Ch. 19, 12.1.1

Levies, Ch. 33, 4.1.1, Ch. 26, 6.8
  charged by public authorities, interim reports, Ch. 41, 9.7.5

Liability adequacy testing, Ch. 55, 7.2.2
  investment contracts with a discretionary participation feature. Ch. 55, 7.2.2.C
  and shadow accounting, interaction between, Ch. 55, 7.2.2.D
  specified in IFRS Ch. 55, 7.2.2.B
  under existing accounting policies, Ch. 55, 7.2.2.A

LIBOR
  LIBOR replacement, Ch. 53, 8.3.5
  'sub-LIBOR issue', Ch. 53, 2.4

Life insurance, Ch. 55, 1.4.2

'Linked' instruments, Ch. 47, 4.5.7

Liquidity risk, Ch. 54, 5.4
  associated liquidity risk, management of, Ch. 54, 5.4.3
  information provided to key management, Ch. 54, 5.4.1
  maturity analyses, Ch. 54, 5.4.2
    cash flows: borrowings, Ch. 54, 5.4.2.C
    cash flows: derivatives, Ch. 54, 5.4.2.D
    cash flows: embedded derivatives, Ch. 54, 5.4.2.E
    cash flows: financial guarantee contracts and written options, Ch. 54, 5.4.2.F
    cash flows: general requirements, Ch. 54, 5.4.2.B
    examples of disclosures in practice, Ch. 54, 5.4.2.G
    time bands, Ch. 54, 5.4.2.A
  puttable financial instruments classified as equity, Ch. 54, 5.4.4

Litigation, provisions and contingencies, Ch. 26, 6.11

Loan commitments, Ch. 48, 6.4.6
  assets and liabilities from, Ch. 49, 3.7
  IFRS 9 impairment requirements, Ch. 51, 11
  off-market, Ch. 49, 3.3.3
  outside the scope of and IFRS 9, Ch. 49, 3.7.1
  within the scope of and IFRS 9, Ch. 49, 3.7.2

Loans
  acquired in business combination, Ch. 49, 3.3.4
  at a below-market interest rate, Ch. 50, 2.8
  commitment, Ch. 45, 3.5
  intercompany loans, Ch. 51, 13
  low-interest long-term, Ch. 49, 3.3.1
  payable, defaults and breaches of, Ch. 54, 4.4.8

Longevity swaps, Ch. 35, 6.6

Long-term contracts and leases, extractive industries Ch. 43, 19
  embedded leases, Ch. 43, 19.1
  impact of IFRS 16, Ch. 43, 19.3
  take-or-pay contracts, Ch. 43, 19.2
    make-up product and undertake, Ch. 43, 19.2.1

Long-term employee benefits, Ch. 35, 13
  meaning of, Ch. 35, 13.1
  other than post-employment benefits, Ch. 35, 13.1
  recognition and measurement, Ch. 35, 13.2
    attribution to years of service, Ch. 35, 13.2.1
    long-term disability benefit, Ch. 35, 13.2.2
    long-term benefits contingent on a future event, Ch. 35, 13.2.3

Long-term loans with repayment on demand terms, Ch. 54, 7.4.4.C

Loss-making associates/joint ventures, Ch. 11, 7.9

Loss-making subsidiaries, Ch. 7, 5.6.1

Low-interest long-term loans, Ch. 49, 3.3.1

Macro hedge accounting, Ch. 53, 11

'Make-up' oil, Ch. 43, 15.4.2.B

Make-up product and undertake, Ch. 43, 17.2.1

'Malus' clauses, share-based payments, Ch. 34, 3.1.1

Management commentary, Ch. 2, 12

Management Commentary Consultative Group, Ch. 1, 2.9

Mandatorily convertible bond, Ch. 47, 6.6.3
  convertible into a variable number of shares
    upon a contingent 'non-viability' event, Ch. 47, 6.6.3.B
    with option for issuer to settle early for a maximum number of shares, Ch. 47, 6.6.3.A

Mandatory tender offers, Ch. 7, 6.2.4, 7.4

Market and non-market variables, insurance contracts, Ch. 56, 8.2.1

Market approach, valuation technique, Ch. 14, 14.2

Market Consistent Embedded Value Principles (MCEV), Ch. 55, 1.4.3

Market participants, Ch. 14, 7
  assumptions, Ch. 14, 7.2
  characteristics, Ch. 14, 7.1

Market risk, Ch. 54, 5.5
  'basic' sensitivity analysis, Ch. 54, 5.5.1
  other market risk disclosures, Ch. 54, 5.5.3
  value-at-risk and similar analyses, Ch. 54, 5.5.2

Market vesting conditions, share-based payments, Ch. 34, 6.3. *See also* Cash-settled share-based payment transactions; Equity-settled share-based payment transactions; IFRS 2; Share-based payment transactions

Master netting agreements, Ch. 54, 7.4.1.B
  and non-performance risk, Ch. 14, 11.3.4

Material cash flows, Ch. 40, 5.1

Materiality, Ch. 3, 4.1.5.A; Ch. 54, 3.2
  interim financial reporting, Ch. 41, 6

Maturity analyses, liquidity risk, Ch. 54, 5.4.2
  cash flows
    borrowings, Ch. 54, 5.4.2.C
    derivatives, Ch. 54, 5.4.2.D
    embedded derivatives, Ch. 54, 5.4.2.E
    examples of disclosures in practice, Ch. 54, 5.4.2.G
    financial guarantee contracts and written options, Ch. 54, 5.4.2.F
    general requirements, Ch. 54, 5.4.2.B
    time bands, Ch. 54, 5.4.2.A

Measurement period, business combinations, Ch. 9, 12

Measurement period, business combinations—*contd*
    adjustments made during, Ch. 9, 12.1
        to provisional amounts, Ch. 9, 12.1
    after end of measurement period, Ch. 9, 12.2

Measurements based on fair value. *See* Fair value measurements

Measuring ECLs during the coronavirus (covid-19) pandemic, Ch. 51, 7.8
    calculation of ECLs, Ch. 51, 7.8.3
    determining whether there has been a significant increase in credit risk, Ch. 51, 7.8.4
    disclosures, Ch. 51, 7.8.5
    guidance, Ch. 51, 7.8.2
    introduction, Ch. 51, 7.8.1

Mineral reserves and resources, extractive industries
    disclosure of mineral reserves and resources, Ch. 43, 2.4
        associates, joint arrangements and other investments, Ch. 43, 2.4
        commodity price, Ch. 43, 2.4
        mining sector, Ch. 43, 2.4.2
        non-controlling interests, Ch. 43, 2.4
        oil and gas sector, Ch. 43, 2.4.1
        production sharing contracts and risk service contracts, Ch. 43, 2.4
        proven and probable reserves, Ch. 43, 2.4 royalties, Ch. 43, 2.4
        standardised measure of oil and gas, Ch. 43, 2.4.3.A
        value of reserves, Ch. 43, 2.4.3
    international harmonisation of reserve reporting, Ch. 43, 2.1
    legal rights to explore for, develop and produce mineral properties, Ch. 43, 5
        concessionary agreements (concessions), Ch. 43, 5.2
        different types of royalty interests, Ch. 43, 5.7
        evolving contractual arrangements, Ch. 43, 5.5
        joint operating agreements, Ch. 43, 5.6
    mineral lease agreements, Ch. 43, 5.1
    pure-service contract, Ch. 43, 5.4
        basic principles and definitions, Ch. 43, 2.2.1
        classification and categorisation guidelines, Ch. 43, 2.2.2
        mining resource and reserve reporting, Ch. 43, 2.3
        petroleum reserve estimation and reporting, Ch. 43, 2.2
        traditional production sharing contracts, Ch. 43, 5.3

Mining sector disclosures, Ch. 43, 2.4.2. *See also* Extractive industries

Ministry of Finance, People's Republic of China, Ch. 1, 2.3, 4.4.1.A

Modifications in share-based payment, Ch. 34, 7.3
    cash-settled modified to equity-settled, Ch. 34, 9.4.2
    decrease the value of an award, Ch. 34, 7.3.2
        additional/more onerous non-market vesting conditions, Ch. 34, 7.3.2.C
        decrease in fair value of equity instruments granted, Ch. 34, 7.3.2.A
        decrease in number of equity instruments granted, Ch. 34, 7.3.2.B
        distinction between cancellation and modification, Ch. 34, 7.4.2
    entity's plans for future, Ch. 34, 7.6
    equity-settled modified to cash-settled, Ch. 34, 7.3.5, 9.4.1
    'give and take', Ch. 34, 7.3.4
    increase the value of an award, Ch. 34, 7.3.1
        increase in fair value of equity instruments granted, Ch. 34, 7.3.1.A
        increase in number of equity instruments granted, Ch. 34, 7.3.1.B
        removal/mitigation of non-market vesting conditions, Ch. 34, 7.3.1.C
    reduce the number of equity instruments granted but maintain or increase the value of an award, Ch. 34, 7.3.4
    share splits and consolidations, Ch. 34, 7.8
    two awards running 'in parallel', Ch. 34, 7.7
    valuation requirements, Ch. 34, 7.2
    'value for value', Ch. 34, 7.3.4
    of vesting period, Ch. 34, 7.3.3

Modified International Standards (JMIS), Japan, Ch. 1, 4.4.2

Monetary/non-monetary determination, foreign exchange, Ch. 15, 5.4
    deferred tax, Ch. 15, 5.4.5
    deposits and advance payments for actively traded commodities, Ch. 15, 5.4.2
    deposits/progress payments, Ch. 15, 5.4.1
    foreign currency share capital, Ch. 15, 5.4.4
    insurance contracts, Ch. 56, 7.3
    investments in preference shares, Ch. 15, 5.4.3
    post-employment benefit plans-foreign currency assets, Ch. 15, 5.4.6
    post-employment benefit plans-foreign currency plans, Ch. 15, 5.4.7

Monetary/non-monetary distinction
    hyperinflationary economies, Ch. 16, 4.1.1

Money market funds (MMF), Ch. 40, 3.2.2

Monitoring Board, Ch. 1, 2.3

Monte Carlo Simulation, Ch. 34, 8.3.3

Most advantageous market, Ch. 14, 6.2

Multi-employer plans, employee benefits, Ch. 35, 3.3
    defined benefit plans sharing risks between entities under common control, Ch. 35, 3.3.2
    disclosure requirements
        other than plans sharing risks between entities under common control, Ch. 35, 3.3.1
        plans accounted for as defined benefit plans, Ch. 35, 15.2.4.A
        plans accounted for as defined contribution plans, Ch. 35, 15.2.4.B

Multi-layered fund structures, Ch. 6, 10.2.10

Multi Period Excess Earnings Method (MEEM), Ch. 9, 5.5.2.F

Multiple valuation techniques, fair value measurement, Ch. 14, 14.1.2
    vs. single valuation techniques, Ch. 14, 14.1.1

Mutual entities, Ch. 9, 2.1, 7.5

Negative compensation, Ch. 48, 6.4.4.A

Negative discretionary participation feature, Ch. 55, 6.3.1

Negative intangible assets, Ch. 55, 9.1.1.D

Net cash-settled forward repurchase, Ch. 52, 4.1.4

Net defined benefit liability (asset), employee benefits, Ch. 35, 8.1
    net interest on, Ch. 35, 10.3.2
    presentation of, Ch. 35, 9

Net finance costs, Ch. 54, 7.1.1

Net investment hedges
    combination of derivatives and non-derivatives, Ch. 53, 7.3.4
    in foreign operations, Ch. 53, 1.5, 5.3, 7.3; Ch. 54, 4.3.3
        amount of the hedged item for which a hedging relationship may be designated, Ch. 53, 5.3.2
        nature of the hedged risk, Ch. 53, 5.3.1
        where the hedging instrument can be held, Ch. 53, 5.3.3
    identifying the effective portion, Ch. 53, 7.3.1
        cross-currency interest rate swaps, Ch. 53, 7.3.3.B
        derivatives used as the hedging instrument, Ch. 53, 7.3.3
        forward currency contracts, Ch. 53, 7.3.3.A
    individual/separate financial statements, Ch. 53, 7.3.5
        non-derivative liabilities used as the hedging instrument, Ch. 53, 7.3.2
        purchased options, Ch. 53, 7.3.3.C
Net realisable value, inventories, Ch. 22, 3.3
Net-settled contracts over own equity, Ch. 47, 5.2.7
Nominal amount components, Ch. 53, 2.3
    general requirement, Ch. 53, 2.3.1
    layer components for fair value hedges with prepayment risk, Ch. 53, 2.3.2
Non-adjusting events, Ch. 38, 2.1.3, 2.3
Non-cash assets to owners, Ch. 7, 3.7; Ch. 8, 2.4.2
    declaration to distribute, Ch. 38, 2.3.1.A
    distributions of, Ch. 7, 3.7; Ch. 8, 2.4.2
Non-cash transactions and transactions on deferred terms, Ch. 40, 5.4
Non-contractually specified risk components, Ch. 53, 2.2.3
Non-controlling interests (NCI), Ch. 7, 2.1, 3.1.1, 3.1.2, 4, 5, 6; Ch. 43, 2.4
    acquisition of, as part of a business combination under common control, Ch. 10, 3.3.5
    associate holds an interest in a subsidiary, Ch. 7, 5.3
    business combinations, recognising and measuring NCIs, Ch. 7, 5.2.1; Ch. 9, 8
        call and put options over NCIs, Ch. 7, 6; Ch. 9, 8.5
        implications of method chosen for measuring NCIs, Ch. 9, 8.3
        measuring qualifying NCIs at acquisition-date fair value, Ch. 7, 5.2.1; Ch. 9, 8.1
        measuring qualifying NCIs at the proportionate share of the value of net identifiable assets acquired, Ch. 7, 5.2.1; Ch. 9, 8.2
        measuring share-based payment and other components of NCIs, Ch. 7, 5.2.1, 5.6; Ch. 9, 8.4
    call and put options over, Ch. 7, 6.5
    call and put options, combination, Ch. 7, 6.3
    call and put options entered into in relation to existing NCIs, Ch. 7, 6.4
    call options only, Ch. 7, 6.1
        options giving the acquirer present access to returns associated with that ownership interest, Ch. 7, 6.1.1
        options not giving the acquirer present access to returns associated with that ownership interest, Ch. 7, 6.1.2
    exercisable in cash or shares, Ch. 7, 6.2
    put options only, Ch. 7, 6.2
        assessing whether multiple transactions should be accounted for as a single arrangement, Ch. 7, 6.2.4

        financial liability for the NCI put, Ch. 7, 6.2.1
        full recognition of NCI, Ch. 7, 6.2.3.B
        mandatory tender offers, Ch. 7, 6.2.4
        NCI is subsequently derecognized, Ch. 7, 6.2.3.D
        NCI put does not provide a present ownership interest, Ch. 7, 6.2.3
        NCI put provides a present ownership interest, Ch. 7, 6.2.2, 6.2.3.A
        partial recognition of NCI, Ch. 7, 6.2.3.C
        separate financial statements, Ch. 7, 6.5
    changes in ownership interest without loss of control (*see* Consolidation procedures)
    classified as financial liabilities, Ch. 7, 5.5
    definition of NCI, Ch. 7, 5.1
    disclosure of interests held by, Ch. 13, 4.2
    exceptions to retrospective application of other IFRSs, Ch. 5, 4.8
    future developments, Ch. 7, 7
        financial instruments with characteristics of equity project, Ch. 7, 7.3
        mandatory purchase of NCIs, Ch. 7, 7.4
        Post-implementation Reviews of IFRS 10, IFRS 11 and IFRS 12, Ch. 7, 7.5
    goodwill impairment testing, Ch. 7, 4.2; Ch. 20, 9
        acquisitions of NCIs measured at the proportionate share of net identifiable assets, Ch. 20, 9.1.1
        testing for impairment in entities with NCIs, alternative allocation methodologies, Ch. 20, 9.3
        testing for impairment in entities with NCIs initially measured at fair value, Ch. 20, 9.2
        testing for impairment in entities with NCIs measured at the proportionate share of net identifiable assets, Ch. 20, 9.1
    initial measurement of NCIs in a business combination, Ch. 7, 5.2.1, 5.2.2
    initial measurement of NCIs in a subsidiary that is not a business combination, Ch. 7, 3.1.1, 5.2.2
    mandatory tender offers in a business combination, Ch. 7, 6.2.4
    measurement in, Ch. 7, 2.1, 2.2, 3.1.1, 3.1.2, 5
    measurement of NCI where an associate holds an interest in a subsidiary, Ch. 7, 5.3
    non-cash acquisition of, Ch. 7, 4
    not recognized, Ch. 7, 6.2.3.A
    presentation of NCIs, Ch. 7, 5.4
    reverse acquisitions, business combinations, Ch. 9, 14.4
    subsequent measurement of, Ch. 7, 5.6
        loss-making subsidiaries, Ch. 7, 5.6.1
    transactions with, IAS 7, Ch. 40, 6.2
Non-coterminous accounting periods, Ch. 7, 2.5; Ch. 11, 7.7; Ch. 15, 6.4
Non-current assets (and disposal groups) held for sale/distribution, Ch. 4, 2
    classification, Ch. 4, 2.1
        abandonment, Ch. 4, 2.1.2.C
        classification as held for sale or as held for distribution to owners, Ch. 4, 2.1.2
        concept of a disposal group, Ch. 4, 2.1.1
        loss of control of a subsidiary, Ch. 4, 2.1.3.A
        meaning of available for immediate sale, Ch. 4, 2.1.2.A

Non-current assets (and disposal groups) held for sale/distribution—*contd*
   classification—*contd*
      meaning of highly probable, Ch. 4, 2.1.2.B
      partial disposal of an associate or joint venture, Ch. 4, 2.1.3.B
      partial disposals of operations, Ch. 4, 2.1.3
   comparative information, Ch. 4, 4
   disclosure requirements, Ch. 4, 5
   discontinued operation, Ch. 4, 3.2
   future developments, Ch. 4, 6
   measurement, Ch. 4, 2.2
      changes to a plan of sale/distribution, Ch. 4, 2.2.5
      impairments and reversals of impairment, Ch. 4, 2.2.3
      on initial classification as held for sale, Ch. 4, 2.2.2.A
      presentation in the statement of financial position of, Ch. 4, 2.2.4
      scope of the measurement requirements, Ch. 4, 2.2.1
      subsequent remeasurement, Ch. 4, 2.2.2.B
   property, plant and equipment, Ch. 18, 7.1
   statement of financial position presentation, Ch. 4, 4.1.2

Non-employees, share-based payment transactions with, Ch. 34, 5.4.1

Non-financial assets
   financial instruments definition, Ch. 45, 2.2.5
   hedged item, Ch. 53, 2.2.3.A; Ch. 53, 2.2.1
   non-contractual risk components, Ch. 53, 2.2.3.A

Non-financial risk, risk adjustment for, Ch. 56, 8.4

Non insurance contracts, Ch. 55, 3.8; Ch. 56, 3.7.2

Non-life insurance, Ch. 55, 1.4.1

Non-market interest rate loans, Ch. 8, 4.4.5.A

Non-monetary assets
   to an associate/a joint venture, contributions of, Ch. 7, 3.3.2, 7.1; Ch. 11, 7.6.5.B
   transactions involving, Ch. 8, 4.4.1

Non-performance risk
   counterparty credit risk and its own credit risk, Ch. 14, 11.3.2
   derivative liabilities, Ch. 14, 11.3.4
   entity incorporate credit risk into the valuation of its derivative contracts, Ch. 14, 11.3.3
   with third-party credit enhancements, Ch. 14, 11.3.1

Non-recourse loans, Ch. 34, 8.7.2; Ch. 48, 6.5

Non-vesting conditions, share-based payment, Ch. 34, 3.2
   background, Ch. 34, 3.2.1
   cash-settled transactions, Ch. 34, 9.3.2.D
   defining non-vesting condition, Ch. 34, 3.2.2
   equity-settled transactions, Ch. 34, 6.4
   non-compete agreements, Ch. 34, 3.2.3
   option pricing models, treatment of non-vesting condition, Ch. 34, 8.4.2

Notional decomposition, hedging instruments, Ch. 53, 3.6.2

Novation of contracts to intermediary counterparties, Ch. 52, 3.4.4

Numerator (EPS), Ch. 37, 6.4.2.A

Obligating event, Ch. 26, 1.3, 3.1

Observable inputs, Ch. 14, 8.3.2

OCI. *See* Other Comprehensive Income (OCI)

Off-balance sheet finance, Ch. 52, 1.1

Off-market loan commitments, Ch. 49, 3.3.3

Offsetting and hedges, Ch. 54, 7.1.3
   external instruments, Ch. 53, 3.2.1
   internal hedging instruments, Ch. 53, 4.2
      foreign exchange risk, Ch. 53, 4.2.2
      interest rate risk, Ch. 53, 4.2.1

Offsetting financial assets and financial liabilities, Ch. 54, 7.4.1
   cash pooling arrangements, Ch. 54, 7.4.1.E
      presentation in the statement of cash flows, Ch. 40, 6.5
   collateral amounts, Ch. 54, 7.4.1.F
   disclosures, Ch. 54, 7.4.2
      examples, Ch. 54, 7.4.2.D
      objective, Ch. 54, 7.4.2.A
      requirements, Ch. 54, 7.4.2.C
      scope, Ch. 54, 7.4.2.B
   enforceable legal right of set-off criterion, Ch. 54, 7.4.1.A
   master netting agreements, Ch. 54, 7.4.1.B
   net settlement criterion, Ch. 54, 7.4.1.C
   situations where offset is not normally appropriate, Ch. 54, 7.4.1.D
   unit of account, Ch. 54, 7.4.1.G

Oil and gas sector. *See also* Extractive industries
   disclosures by, Ch. 43, 2.4.1
   IFRIC 1 exemption for oil and gas assets at deemed cost, Ch. 5, 5.13.2

Oil Industry Accounting Committee (OIAC), Statement of Recommended Practice (SORP), Ch. 43, 1.4

Onerous contracts, Ch. 26, 6.2
   onerous leases, Ch. 23, 10.3.2.A

Operating activities, cash flows from, Ch. 40, 4.1

Operating segments, Ch. 36, 1–7. *See also* IFRS 8; Reportable segments
   aggregation criteria, Ch. 36, 3.2.1
   'chief operating decision maker' and 'segment manager', Ch. 36, 3.1.2
   combining small operating segments into a larger reportable segment, Ch. 36, 3.2.3
   entity-wide disclosures for all entities, Ch. 36, 6
      information about geographical areas, Ch. 36, 6.2
      information about major customers, Ch. 36, 6.3
      information about products and services, Ch. 36, 6.1
   equity accounted investment can be an operating segment, Ch. 36, 3.1.5
   identifying externally reportable segments, Ch. 36, 3.2
   measurement, Ch. 36, 4
   operating segments which are reportable because of their size, Ch. 36, 3.2.2
      proposed amendments to IFRS 8 and IAS 34 (ED/2017/2), Ch. 36, 7.1
   reportable segments, information to be disclosed, Ch. 36, 5
      additional disclosures relating to segment assets, Ch. 36, 5.4
      disclosure of commercially sensitive information, Ch. 36, 5.8
      disclosure of other elements of revenue, income and expense, Ch. 36, 5.3
      explanation of the measurements used in segment reporting, Ch. 36, 5.5
      general information about reportable segments, Ch. 36, 5.1

disclosure of how operating segments are aggregated, Ch. 36, 5.1.1
measure of segment profit or loss, total assets and total liabilities, Ch. 36, 5.2
reconciliations, Ch. 36, 5.6
restatement of previously reported information, Ch. 36, 5.7
    changes in organisation structure, Ch. 36, 5.7.1
    changes in segment measures, Ch. 36, 5.7.2
restatement of segments reported in comparative periods, Ch. 36, 3.2.6
revenue earning business activities, Ch. 36, 3.1.1
scope, Ch. 36, 2.2
    consolidated financial statements presented with those of the parent, Ch. 36, 2.2.2
    entities providing segment information on a voluntary basis, Ch. 36, 2.2.3
    meaning of 'traded in a public market,' Ch. 36, 2.2.1
single set of operating segments, identifying, Ch. 36, 3
    definition of an operating segment, Ch. 36, 3.1
terms used in IFRS 8, Ch. 36, 1.3
transitional provisions, Ch. 36, 1.4

Operational risk, Ch. 54, 5.6.2

Option contracts, Ch. 49, 2.1.4

Option-pricing models. *See also* Share-based payment transactions
accounting for share-based payment, Ch. 34, 8.4
    market-based performance measures and non-vesting conditions, Ch. 34, 8.4.2.A
    non-market vesting conditions, Ch. 34, 8.4.2.B
    non-transferability, Ch. 34, 8.4.1
    vesting and non-vesting conditions, treatment of, Ch. 34, 8.4.2
selecting appropriate assumptions for, Ch. 34, 8.5
    binomial model and other lattice models, Ch. 34, 8.5.4.B
    Black-Scholes-Merton formula, Ch. 34, 8.5.4.A
    exercise and termination behaviour, Ch. 34, 8.5.2
    expected dividends, Ch. 34, 8.5.4
    expected term of the option, Ch. 34, 8.5.1
    expected volatility of share price, Ch. 34, 8.5.3
    risk-free interest rate, Ch. 34, 8.5.5
selection of model, Ch. 34, 8.3
    binomial model, Ch. 34, 8.3.2
    Black-Scholes-Merton formula, Ch. 34, 8.3.1
    lattice models-number of time steps, Ch. 34, 8.3.2.A
    Monte Carlo Simulation, Ch. 34, 8.3.3

Orderly transaction, Ch. 14, 8.2.2

Other Comprehensive Income (OCI), Ch. 3, 3.2.1
accounting for loss of control, Ch. 7, 2.3, 3.5
cash flow hedge accounting, Ch. 53, 7.2, 7.3
debt instrument measured at fair value through OCI under IFRS 9, Ch. 33, 10.4.1
defined benefit plans, Ch. 33, 10.7; Ch. 35, 9
    remeasurements, Ch. 35, 10.4
        actuarial gains and losses, Ch. 35, 10.4.1
        return on plan assets, excluding amounts included in net interest on the net defined benefit liability (asset), Ch. 35, 10.4.2
gains and losses recognised in, Ch. 54, 7.2
hedges of exposures affecting, Ch. 53, 2.6.3

insurance contracts, allocating finance income or expenses on, Ch. 56, 15.3
non-derivative equity investments designation at, Ch. 48, 8
reattribution of, changes in ownership interest without a loss of control, Ch. 7, 4.1
tax on items of, Ch. 3, 3.2.4.C

Outside temporary differences, deferred tax recognition, Ch. 33, 7.5
anticipated intragroup dividends in future foreseeable future, Ch. 33, 7.5.4
    consolidated financial statements of receiving entity, Ch. 33, 7.5.4.A
    separate financial statements of paying entity, Ch. 33, 7.5.4.B
calculation of, Ch. 33, 7.5.1
    consolidated financial statements, Ch. 33, 7.5.1.A
    separate financial statements, Ch. 33, 7.5.1.B
deductible temporary differences, Ch. 33, 7.5.3
other overseas income taxed only on remittance, Ch. 33, 7.5.6
taxable temporary differences, Ch. 33, 7.5.2
'tax transparent' entities, Ch. 33, 7.6
unpaid intragroup interest, royalties, management charges etc., Ch. 33, 7.5.5

Outstanding ordinary shares, changes in, Ch. 37, 4
adjustments to EPS in historical summaries, Ch. 37, 4.7
issue to acquire another business, Ch. 37, 4.6
    acquisitions, Ch. 37, 4.6.1
    establishment of a new parent undertaking, Ch. 37, 4.6.3
    reverse acquisitions, Ch. 37, 4.6.2
new parent undertaking, establishment of, Ch. 37, 4.6.3
options exercised during the year, Ch. 37, 4.4
ordinary shares without corresponding changes in resources, changes in, Ch. 37, 4.3
    B share schemes, Ch. 37, 4.3.4
    bonus issue, Ch. 37, 4.3.1.A
    capitalisation, Ch. 37, 4.3.1.A
    put warrants priced above market value, Ch. 37, 4.3.5
    rights issue, Ch. 37, 4.3.3
    share consolidation, Ch. 37, 4.3.1.C
    share consolidation with a special dividend, Ch. 37, 4.3.2
    share consolidations, Ch. 37, 4.3.1.C
    share split, Ch. 37, 4.3.1.A
    stock dividends, Ch. 37, 4.3.1.B
post balance sheet changes in capital, Ch. 37, 4.5
purchase and redemption of own shares, Ch. 37, 4.2
weighted average number of shares, Ch. 37, 4.1

Overlift and underlift (oil and gas), Ch. 43, 12.4

Over-the-counter (OTC) derivatives
categorisation, Ch. 14, 16.2.4

Own equity instruments, Ch. 53, 3.4

Own use contracts, Ch. 53, 12.2

Owner-occupied property, Ch. 19, 2.4. *See also* IAS 16; Property, plant and equipment

Ownership changes in a joint venture, Ch. 12, 8.2
acquisition of an interest in a joint venture, Ch. 12, 8.2.1
control over a joint venture, Ch. 12, 8.3.2
demergers and distributions of non-cash assets to owners, Ch. 7, 3.7
disposal of interest in a joint venture, Ch. 12, 8.2.6

Ownership changes in a joint venture—*contd*
   former subsidiary becomes a joint venture, Ch. 7, 3.3.2, 7.1; Ch. 12, 8.3.3
   interest in a joint venture held for sale, Ch. 12, 8.2.7
   joint venture becomes a financial asset (or vice versa), Ch. 12, 8.2.5
   joint venture becomes an associate (or vice versa), Ch. 12, 8.2.4

Ownership interests, changes in, Ch. 7, 3, 4, 5.2, 6
   accounting for a loss of control, Ch. 7 3.2, 3.3, 3.4, 3.5, 3.6, 3.7, 7.1, 7.2
   acquisition of a subsidiary that is not a business, Ch. 7, 3.1.1, 3.1.2
   deemed disposal, Ch. 7, 3.6. *See also* IFRIC 17
   interest retained in the former subsidiary, Ch. 7, 3.3
      interest retained in the former subsidiary-associate or joint venture, Ch. 7, 3.3.2, 7.1
      interest retained in the former subsidiary–financial asset, Ch. 7, 3.3.1
      interest retained in the former subsidiary–joint operation, Ch. 7, 3.3.3, 7.2
   loss of control in multiple arrangements Ch. 7, 3.4
   mandatory tender offers in a business combination, Ch. 7, 6.2.4, 7.4
   multiple arrangements, loss of control in, Ch. 7, 3.4
   non-cash assets to owners, Ch. 7, 3.5
   other comprehensive income, Ch. 7, 2.3, 3.5, 4.1
   without a loss of control, Ch. 7, 4.1, 4.2, 4.3, 4.4, 4.5

Partial disposals. *See also* Ownership interests, changes in
   of an associate or joint venture, Ch. 4, 2.1.3.B; Ch. 11, 7.12.5
   of foreign operation, Ch. 15, 2.3, 4.1, 6.6.2.
   of interests in associate/joint venture, Ch. 11, 7.12.5
   of operations, Ch. 4, 2.1.3
   of property, plant and equipment, Ch. 18, 7.3

Partial term hedging, Ch. 53, 2.2.4

Parts (components) approach, assets, accounting for, Ch. 18, 3.2

Past service cost, employee benefits, Ch. 35, 10.2.1

Payables, Ch. 49, 2.1.1

Pension, Ch. 35, 3. *See also* Defined benefit plans; Defined contribution plans; IAS 19; IFRIC 14
   defined benefit plans, Ch. 35, 3.1, 5
      funding payments contingent on future events within the control of the entity, Ch. 35, 8.2.5
   insured benefits, Ch. 35, 3.2

Performance condition, share-based payment, Ch. 34, 3.1, 6.2, 6.3

Performance obligation, IFRS 15, Ch. 28, 3

Performance rating, share-based payment, Ch. 34, 3.1.2

Performance target, share-based payment, Ch. 34, 3.1, 5.3.3

Perpetual debt, Ch. 47, 4.7; Ch. 50, 3.5

Perpetual instruments with a 'step-up' clause, Ch. 47, 4.5.4

Persistency risk, insurance contracts, Ch. 55, 3.7.1

Petroleum reserve estimation and reporting, Ch. 43, 2.2
   basic principles and definitions, Ch. 43, 2.2.1
   classification and categorisation guidelines, Ch. 43, 2.2.2

Phantom options, share-based payment, Ch. 34, 9.1

Physical capital maintenance (framework), Ch. 2, 11.2

Piecemeal acquisition of an associate/joint venture, Ch. 11, 7.4.2

   common control transactions involving sales of associates, Ch. 11, 7.4.2.D
   cost-based approach, Ch. 11, 7.4.2.A
   existing associate that becomes a joint venture, or vice versa, Ch. 11, 7.4.2.C
   fair value (IFRS 3) approach, Ch. 11, 7.4.2.A
   financial instrument becoming an associate/joint venture, Ch. 11, 7.4.2.A
   step increase in an existing associate/joint venture without a change in status of the investee, Ch. 11, 7.4.2.B

Plan assets, employee benefits, Ch. 35, 6
   contributions to defined benefit funds, Ch. 35, 6.5
   definition of, Ch. 35, 6.1
   longevity swaps, Ch. 35, 6.6
   measurement of, Ch. 35, 6.2
   qualifying insurance policies, Ch. 35, 6.3
   reimbursement rights, Ch. 35, 6.4

Plan liabilities, employee benefits, Ch. 35, 7
   actuarial assumptions, Ch. 35, 7.5
   actuarial methodology, Ch. 35, 7.3
   attributing benefit to years of service, Ch. 35, 7.4
   contributions by employees and third parties, Ch. 35, 7.2
   discount rate, Ch. 35, 7.6
   frequency of valuations, Ch. 35, 7.7
   legal and constructive obligations, Ch. 35, 7.1

Policy administration and maintenance costs (insurance contracts), Ch. 56, 8.2.3.H

Policyholder, Ch. 55, 2.2.1
   adverse effect on, Ch. 55, 3.7
      insurance of non-insurance risks, Ch. 55, 3.7.2
      lapse, persistency and expense risk, Ch. 55, 3.7.1
   of direct insurance contracts, Ch. 55, 2.2.3.F

Policyholder loans, Ch. 55, 7.2.6.F; Ch. 56, 8.12.2

Pooling of interests method, Ch. 10, 3.1, 3.3

Post-employment benefits, Ch. 35, 3. *See also* Pension
   defined benefit plans, Ch. 35, 3.1
   defined contribution plans, Ch. 35, 3.1
   disclosure of key management personnel compensation, Ch. 39, 2.6.3
   insured benefits, Ch. 35, 3.2
   multi-employer plans, Ch. 35, 3.3
   related parties, Ch. 39, 2.2.6
   state plans, Ch. 35, 3.4

Post-tax cash flows, VIU calculation using, Ch. 20, 7.2.3

Power and returns, principal-agency situations, Ch. 6, 6
   application examples in IFRS 10, Ch. 6, 6.6–6.7
   available replacements, Ch. 6, 6.3.1.A
   decision-making, scope of, Ch. 6, 6.2
   delegated power: principals and agents, Ch. 6, 6.1
   exercise period, Ch. 6, 6.3.1.B
   exposure to variability of returns from other interests, Ch. 6, 6.5
   liquidation rights and redemption rights, Ch. 6, 6.3.2
   remuneration, Ch. 6, 6.4
   rights held by other parties, Ch. 6, 6.3

Power over an investee, Ch. 6, 4. *See also* Existing rights, investee; Voting rights, investee
   contractual arrangements, Ch. 6, 4.4
   determining whether sponsoring (designing) a structured entity gives power, Ch. 6, 4.6

existing rights, Ch. 6, 4.2
management of defaults on assets, Ch. 6, 4.1.4
more than one relevant activity, Ch. 6, 4.1.1
no relevant activities, Ch. 6, 4.1.2
relevant activities, Ch. 6, 4.1
single asset, single lessee vehicles, Ch. 6, 4.1.3
voting rights, Ch. 6, 4.3

PP&E. *See* Property, Plant and Equipment

Pre-existing relationships, business combination, Ch. 9, 11.1
assessing part of exchange for the acquiree, Ch. 9, 11
contingent payments, arrangements for, Ch. 9, 11.2.1
effective settlement of, Ch. 9, 11.1
reimbursement for paying acquirer's acquisition-related costs, Ch. 9, 11.3
remuneration for future services, Ch. 9, 11.2
restructuring plans, Ch. 9, 11.4
share-based payment awards, Ch. 9, 7.2

Preference dividends (EPS), Ch. 37, 5.2

Preference shares, Ch. 47, 4.5
'change of control,' 'taxation change' and 'regulatory change' clauses, Ch. 47, 4.5.8
economic compulsion, Ch. 47, 4.5.6
instruments redeemable
    with a 'dividend blocker,' Ch. 47, 4.5.3.A
    with a 'dividend pusher,' Ch. 47, 4.5.3.B
    mandatorily or at the holder's option, Ch. 47, 4.5.1
    only at the issuer's option or not redeemable, Ch. 47, 4.5.2
'linked' instruments, Ch. 47, 4.5.7
perpetual instruments with a 'step-up' clause, Ch. 47, 4.5.4
relative subordination, Ch. 47, 4.5.5

Premium allocation approach, insurance contracts, Ch. 56, 9
accounting policies adopted for contracts applying, Ch. 56, 16.1.2.A
aggregation for contracts applying, Ch. 56, 5.3
allocating insurance finance income/expenses for incurred claims when applying, Ch. 56, 15.3.2
criteria for use of, Ch. 56, 9.1
derecognition contracts, Ch. 56, 12.3.4
initial measurement, Ch. 56, 9.2
insurance revenue under, Ch. 56, 15.1.2
reconciliations required for contracts applying, Ch. 56, 16.1.1
for reinsurance contracts held, Ch. 56, 10.7
subsequent measurement
    liability for incurred claims, Ch. 56, 9.4
    liability for remaining coverage, Ch. 56, 9.3

Premium cash flows, Ch. 56, 8.2.3.A

Prepaid and accrued operating lease income, Ch. 19, 6.6

Prepayment, negative compensation, Ch. 48, 6.4.4.A

Present value of future profits (PVFP), Ch. 55, 9.1

Present value of in-force business (PVIF), Ch. 55, 9.1

Presentation and disclosure, financial instruments, Ch. 54, 1–9
disclosures, structuring, Ch. 54, 3
    classes of financial instrument, Ch. 54, 3.3
    level of detail, Ch. 54, 3.1
    materiality, Ch. 54, 3.2
effective date and transitional provisions, Ch. 54, 8
future developments, Ch. 54, 9
interim reports, Ch. 54, 2.3
nature and extent of risks arising from financial instruments, Ch. 54, 5
    qualitative disclosures, Ch. 54, 5.1
    quantitative disclosures, Ch. 54, 5.2
    'basic' sensitivity analysis, Ch. 54, 5.5.1
    capital disclosures, Ch. 54, 5.6.3
    cash flows, Ch. 54, 5.4.2
    concentrations of risk, Ch. 54, 5.6.1
    credit risk, Ch. 54, 5.3
    credit risk exposure, Ch. 54, 5.3.4
    credit risk management practices, Ch. 54, 5.3.2
    illustrative disclosures, Ch. 54, 5.3.6
    information provided to key management, Ch. 54, 5.4.1
    liquidity risk, Ch. 54, 5.4
    management of associated liquidity risk, Ch. 54, 5.4.3
    market risk, Ch. 54, 5.5
    maturity analyses, Ch. 54, 5.4.2
    operational risk, Ch. 54, 5.6.2
    puttable financial instruments classified as equity, Ch. 54, 5.4.4
    quantitative and qualitative information about amounts arising from expected credit losses, Ch. 54, 5.3.3
    scope and objectives, Ch. 54, 5.3.1
    time bands, Ch. 54, 5.4.2.A
    value-at-risk and similar analyses, Ch. 54, 5.5.2
presentation on the face of the financial statements and related disclosures, Ch. 54, 7
    gains and losses recognised in other comprehensive income, Ch. 54, 7.2
    gains and losses recognised in profit/loss embedded derivatives, Ch. 54, 7.1.4
    entities whose share capital is not equity, Ch. 54, 7.1.4
    further analysis of gains and losses recognised in profit/loss, Ch. 54, 7.1.2
    offsetting and hedges, Ch. 54, 7.1.3
    presentation on the face of the statement of comprehensive income (or income statement), Ch. 54, 7.1.1
statement of cash flows, Ch. 54, 7.5
statement of changes in equity, Ch. 54, 7.3
statement of financial position, Ch. 54, 7.4
    assets and liabilities, Ch. 54, 7.4.3
    convertible loans, Ch. 54, 7.4.4.B
    current and non-current assets and liabilities, distinction between, Ch. 54, 7.4.4
    debt with refinancing or roll over agreements, Ch. 54, 7.4.4.D
    derivatives, Ch. 54, 7.4.4.A
    disclosure requirements, Ch. 54, 7.4.2.C
    enforceable legal right of set-off, Ch. 54, 7.4.1.A
    entities whose share capital is not equity, Ch. 54, 7.4.6
    equity, Ch. 54, 7.4.5
    intention to settle net, Ch. 54, 7.4.1.C
    loan covenants, Ch. 54, 7.4.4.E
    long-term loans with repayment on demand terms, Ch. 54, 7.4.4.C
    master netting agreements, Ch. 54, 7.4.1.B
    objective, Ch. 54, 7.4.2.A
    offsetting collateral amounts, Ch. 54, 7.4.1.F

Presentation and disclosure, financial instruments—*contd*
  presentation on the face of the financial statements and related disclosures—*contd*
    statement of financial position—*contd*
      offsetting financial assets and financial liabilities, Ch. 54, 7.4.1
      offsetting financial assets and financial liabilities: disclosure, Ch. 54, 7.4.2
      scope, Ch. 54, 7.4.2.B
      situations where offset is not normally appropriate, Ch. 54, 7.4.1.D
      unit of account, Ch. 54, 7.4.1.G
  significance of financial instruments for an entity's financial position/performance, Ch. 54, 4
    accounting policies, Ch. 54, 4.1
    business combinations, Ch. 54, 4.6
      acquired receivables, Ch. 54, 4.6.1
      contingent consideration and indemnification assets, Ch. 54, 4.6.2
    fair values, Ch. 54, 4.5
      day 1 profits, Ch. 54, 4.5.2
      general disclosure requirements, Ch. 54, 4.5.1
    hedge accounting, Ch. 54, 4.3
      amount, timing and uncertainty of future cash flows, Ch. 54, 4.3.2
      effects of hedge accounting on financial position and performance, Ch. 54, 4.3.3
      option to designate a credit exposure as measured at fair value through profit/loss, Ch. 54, 4.3.4
      risk management strategy, Ch. 54, 4.3.1
      uncertainty arising from interest rate benchmark (or IBOR) reform, Ch. 54, 4.3.5
    income, expenses, gains and losses, Ch. 54, 4.2
      fee income and expense, Ch. 54, 4.2.3
      gains and losses by measurement category, Ch. 54, 4.2.1
      interest income and expense, Ch. 54, 4.2.2
    statement of financial position, Ch. 54, 4.4
      categories of financial assets and financial liabilities, Ch. 54, 4.4.1
      collateral, Ch. 54, 4.4.6
      compound financial instruments with multiple embedded derivatives, Ch. 54, 4.4.7
      defaults and breaches of loans payable, Ch. 54, 4.4.8
      financial assets designated as measured at fair value through profit/loss, Ch. 54, 4.4.3
      financial liabilities designated at fair value through profit/loss, Ch. 54, 4.4.2
      interests in associates and joint ventures accounted for in accordance with IFRS 9, Ch. 54, 4.4.9
      investments in equity instruments designated at fair value through other comprehensive income (IFRS 9), Ch. 54, 4.4.4
      reclassification, Ch. 54, 4.4.5
  transfers of financial assets, Ch. 54, 6
    meaning of 'transfer,' Ch. 54, 6.1
    transferred financial assets that are derecognised in their entirety, Ch. 54, 6.3
      disclosure requirements, Ch. 54, 6.3.2
      meaning of continuing involvement, Ch. 54, 6.3.1
    transferred financial assets that are not derecognised in their entirety, Ch. 54, 6.2
  transitional provisions, Ch. 54, 8
Presentation currency. *See also* IAS 21
  average rate calculation, Ch. 15, 6.1.4
  change of, Ch. 15, 7
  disposal of a foreign operation, Ch. 15, 6.6
    step-by-step and direct methods of consolidation, Ch. 7, 2.3; Ch. 15, 6.6.3
  exchange differences on intragroup balances, Ch. 15, 6.3
    becoming part of the net investment in a foreign operation, Ch. 15, 6.3.1.F
    ceasing to be part of the net investment in a foreign operation, Ch. 15, 6.3.1.G
    currency of monetary item, Ch. 15, 6.3.1.C
    dividends, Ch. 15, 6.3.2
    manner of settlement of monetary, Ch. 15, 6.3.1.B
    monetary items included as part of the net investment in a foreign operation, Ch. 15, 6.3.1
    net investment in a foreign operation, Ch. 15, 6.3.1.F
    transacted by other members of the group, Ch. 15, 6.3.1.E
    treatment in individual financial statements, Ch. 15, 6.3.1.D
    unrealised profits on intragroup transactions, Ch. 15, 6.3.3
  foreign operations where sub-groups exist, accounting for, Ch. 15, 6.1.5
  goodwill and fair value adjustments, Ch. 15, 6.5
  non-coterminous period ends, Ch. 15, 6.4
  partial disposal of foreign operation, Ch. 7, 4.1 Ch. 15, 6.6.2
  translation of equity items, Ch. 15, 6.2
    equity balances resulting from income and expenses being recognised in other comprehensive income, Ch. 15, 6.2.3
    equity balances resulting from transactions with equity holders, Ch. 15, 6.2.2
    share capital, Ch. 15, 6.2.1
  translation to, Ch. 15, 6.1
    accounting for foreign operations where sub-groups exist, Ch. 15, 6.1.5
    calculation of average rate, Ch. 15, 6.1.4
    dual rates, suspension of rates and lack of exchangeability, Ch. 15, 6.1.3
    where functional currency is not that of a hyperinflationary economy, Ch. 15, 6.1.1
    where functional currency is that of a hyperinflationary economy, Ch. 15, 6.1.2
  use other than the functional currency, Ch. 15, 6
Presentation of financial statements and accounting policies, Ch. 3, 1–6. *See also* IAS 1; IAS 8
Previous GAAP, Ch. 5, 2.3
  carrying amount as deemed cost, Ch. 5, 5.2.4.C
  definition of, Ch. 5, 1.3
  determining, Ch. 5, 2.3
    transition to IFRSs from a similar GAAP, Ch. 5, 2.3.1
  restatement of costs recognised under, Ch. 5, 5.3.2
Price, fair value measurement, Ch. 14, 9
  transaction costs, Ch. 14, 9.1
  transportation costs, Ch. 14, 9.2
Price risk, Ch. 54, 5

Principal-agency situations, IFRS 10, Ch. 6, 6, IFRS 15, Ch. 28, 3.4
   application examples in IFRS 10, Ch. 6, 6.6–6.7
   delegated power: principals and agents, Ch. 6, 6.1
   exposure to variability of returns from other interests, Ch. 6, 6.5
   liquidation rights, Ch. 6, 6.3.2
   redemption rights, Ch. 6, 6.3.2
   remuneration, Ch. 6, 6.4
   rights held by other parties, Ch. 6, 6.3.
   scope of decision-making, Ch. 6, 6.2
Principal market, Ch. 14, 6
   entity-specific volume, Ch. 14, 6.1.2
   market-based volume and activity, Ch. 14, 6.1.2
   most advantageous market, Ch. 14, 6.2
Prior period errors
   correction of, Ch. 3, 4.6
   disclosure of, Ch. 3, 5.3
Probability-weighted outcome, Ch. 51, 5.6
Production sharing contracts (PSCs), Ch. 43, 5.3; Ch. 43, 12.5
Property, plant and equipment (PP&E), Ch. 18, 1–8. *See also* IAS 16; Investment property
   administration and other general overheads, Ch. 18, 4.1.3
   borrowing costs, Ch. 18, 4.1.2
   decommissioning and restoration costs, Ch. 18, 4.3
   deferred payment, Ch. 18, 4.1.6
   definitions, Ch. 18, 2.2
   depreciation, cost model, Ch. 18, 5
      charge, Ch. 18, 5.3
      depreciable amount, Ch. 18, 5.2
      methods, Ch. 18, 5.6
      significant 'parts' of asset, Ch. 18, 5.1
      start and finish, Ch. 18, 5.5
      and useful life of asset, Ch. 18, 5.4
   derecognition and disposal, Ch. 18, 7
      held for sale and discontinued operations (IFRS 5), Ch. 18, 7.1
      partial disposals and undivided interests, Ch. 18, 7.3
      of parts ('components') of an asset, Ch. 18, 3.2
      sale of assets held for rental, Ch. 18, 7.2
   disclosure, Ch. 18, 8
   environmental and safety equipment, Ch. 18, 3.1.2
   exchanges of assets, Ch. 18, 4.4
   extractive industries, Ch. 43, 15
      care and maintenance, Ch. 43, 15.3
      major maintenance and turnarounds/renewals and reconditioning costs, Ch. 43, 15.1
      redeterminations, Ch. 43, 15.4.2
         as capital reimbursements, Ch. 43, 15.4.2.A
         decommissioning provisions, Ch. 43, 15.4.2.C
         'make-up' oil, Ch. 43, 15.4.2.B
      stripping costs in the production phase of a surface mine (mining), Ch. 43, 15.5
         determining when production phase commences, Ch. 43, 15.5.2
         disclosures, Ch. 43, 15.5.6
         initial recognition, Ch. 43, 15.5.4
         recognition criteria-stripping activity asset, Ch. 43, 15.5.3
         scope of IFRIC 20, Ch. 43, 15.5.1
         subsequent measurement, Ch. 43, 15.5.5
      unitisations, Ch. 43, 15.4
      well workovers and recompletions (oil and gas), Ch. 43, 15.2
   fair value, Ch. 18, 6.1
   finance leases, assets held under, Ch. 18, 6.5
   first-time adoption, Ch. 5, 7.4
      depreciation method and rate, Ch. 5, 7.4.1
      IFRIC 1 exemptions, Ch. 5, 5.13.1
      parts approach, Ch. 5, 7.4.4
      residual value and useful life estimation, Ch. 5, 7.4.2
      revaluation model, Ch. 5, 7.4.3
   government grants, assets acquired with, Ch. 18, 4.6
   impairment, Ch. 18, 5.7
   income, Ch. 18, 4
      earned while bringing the asset to the intended location and condition, Ch. 18, 4.2.1
      received during the construction of property, Ch. 18, 4.2.2
   interim financial reporting, Ch. 41, 9.1
   inventory, classification as, Ch. 18, 3.1.5
   land, Ch. 18, 5.4.2
   measurement after recognition
      cost model, Ch. 18, 5
      revaluation model, Ch. 18, 6
   residual values, Ch. 18, 5.2
   revaluation
      assets held under finance leases, Ch. 18, 4.5
      revaluation policy, adopting, Ch. 18, 6.4
      reversals of downward valuations, Ch. 18, 6.3
      valuation surpluses and deficits, accounting for, Ch. 18, 6.2
   sale of assets held for rental, Ch. 18, 7.2 scope, Ch. 18, 2.1
   significant parts of assets, Ch. 18, 5.1
   spare parts and minor items, Ch. 18, 3.1.1
   technological change, Ch. 18, 5.4.3
   unit of production method, Ch. 18, 5.6.2
   useful lives, Ch. 18, 5.4
Prospective resources, Ch. 43, 2.2.1
Provisions, Contingent Liabilities and Contingent Assets, Ch. 26, 1–7. *See also* IAS 37; Restructuring provisions
   cases in which no provision should be recognised, Ch. 26, 5
      future operating losses, Ch. 26, 5.1
      rate-regulated activities, Ch. 26, 5.4
      repairs and maintenance of owned assets, Ch. 26, 5.2
      staff training costs, Ch. 26, 5.3
   disclosure requirements, Ch. 26, 7
      contingent assets, Ch. 26, 7.3
      contingent liabilities, Ch. 26, 7.2
      provisions, Ch. 26, 7.1
      reduced disclosure when information is seriously prejudicial, Ch. 26, 7.4
   examples of provisions and contingencies, Ch. 26, 6
      decommissioning provisions, Ch. 26, 6.3
         changes in estimated decommissioning costs (IFRIC 1), Ch. 26, 6.3.1
         changes in legislation after construction of the asset, Ch. 26, 6.3.2
         funds established to meet an obligation (IFRIC 5), Ch. 26, 6.3.3
      dilapidation and other provisions relating to leased assets, Ch. 26, 6.9

Provisions, Contingent Liabilities and Contingent Assets—*contd*
  examples of provisions and contingencies—*contd*
    environmental provisions–general guidance in IAS 37, Ch. 26, 6.4
    EU Directive on 'Waste Electrical and Electronic Equipment' (IFRIC 6), Ch. 26, 6.7
    green certificates compared to emissions trading schemes, Ch. 26, 6.6
    levies imposed by governments, Ch. 26, 6.8
      payments relating to taxes other than income tax, Ch. 26.6.8.4
      recognition and measurement of levy liabilities, Ch. 26, 6.8.2
      recognition of an asset/expense when a levy is recorded, Ch. 26, 6.8.3
      scope of IFRIC 21, Ch. 26, 6.8.1
    liabilities associated with emissions trading schemes, Ch. 26, 6.5
    litigation and other legal claims, Ch. 26, 6.11
    obligations to make donations to non-profit organisations, Ch. 26, 6.14
    onerous contracts, Ch. 26, 6.2
    refunds policy, Ch. 26, 6.12
    restructuring provisions, Ch. 26, 6.1
    self insurance, Ch. 26, 6.13
    settlement payments, Ch. 26.6.15
    warranty provisions, Ch. 26, 6.10
  measurement, Ch. 26, 4
    anticipating future events that may affect the estimate of cash flows, Ch. 26, 4.4
    best estimate of provision, Ch. 26, 4.1
    changes and uses of provisions, Ch. 26, 4.9
    changes in contingent liabilities recognised in a business combination, Ch. 26, 4.10
    dealing with risk and uncertainty in measuring a provision, Ch. 26, 4.2
    discounting the estimated cash flows to a present value, Ch. 26, 4.3
      adjusting for risk and using a government bond rate, Ch. 26, 4.3.2
      effect of changes in interest rates on the discount rate applied, Ch. 26, 4.3.6
      own credit risk is not taken into account, Ch. 26, 4.3.3
      pre-tax discount rate, Ch. 26, 4.3.4
      real *vs.* nominal rate, Ch. 26, 4.3.1
      unwinding of the discount, Ch. 26, 4.3.5
    disposal of related assets, Ch. 26, 4.8
    joint and several liability, Ch. 26, 4.7
    provisions are not reduced for gains on disposal of related assets, Ch. 26, 4.8
    provisions that will be settled in a currency other than the entity's functional currency, Ch. 26, 4.5
    reimbursements, insurance and other recoveries from third parties, Ch. 26, 4.6
    settlement in a foreign currency, Ch. 26, 4.5
  recognition, Ch. 26, 3
    contingencies, Ch. 26, 3.2
      contingent assets, Ch. 26, 3.2.2
        obligations contingent on the successful recovery of, Ch. 26, 3.2.2.A
      contingent liabilities, Ch. 26, 3.2.1
      how probability determines whether to recognise or disclose, Ch. 26, 3.2.3
    determining when a provision should be recognised, Ch. 26, 3.1
      an entity has a present obligation as a result of a past event, Ch. 26, 3.1.1
      it is probable that an outflow of resources embodying economic benefits will be required to settle the obligation, Ch. 26, 3.1.2
      a reliable estimate can be made of the amount of the obligation, Ch. 26, 3.1.3
    recognising an asset when recognising a provision, Ch. 26, 3.3

'Proxy hedges,' designating, Ch. 53, 6.2.1
Prudence, Ch. 55, 8.2.3
Public Company Accounting Oversight Board, Ch. 2, 1.2
Publicly accountable enterprises, Ch. 1, 4.3.2
Purchased options
  call option (EPS), Ch. 37, 6.4.3
  hedge accounting, Ch. 53, 3.2.2, 7.3.3.C
  put option (EPS), Ch. 37, 6.4.3
  and warrants (EPS), Ch. 37, 6.4.3
Pure-service contract, Ch. 43, 5.4
Push down accounting, Ch. 5, 5.5.2.A; Ch. 9, 15
Put option(s)
  held by the customer, Ch. 30, 5.2
  over non-controlling interests, Ch. 7, 6.2, 6.3, 6.4, 6.5, 6.6, 7.3, 7.4, 7.5;; Ch. 9, 8.5 (*see also* Noncontrolling interests, call and put options over)
  purchased put option, Ch. 47, 11.3.1
  written put option, Ch. 47, 11.3.2
Puttable instruments, Ch. 47, 4.6.2
  classified as equity, Ch. 3, 5.4.2; Ch. 47, 4.6; Ch. 54, 5.4.4
  options over, IAS 32 specific exception, Ch. 34, 2.2.4.J
  definitions, Ch. 47, 3
  embedded derivatives, Ch. 46, 5.1.10
  entitling the holder to a pro rata share of net assets only on liquidation, Ch. 47, 4.6.3
  IFRIC 2, Ch. 47, 4.6.6
  issue, Ch. 47, 4.6.1
  issued by a subsidiary, Ch. 47, 4.6.4.A
  meaning of 'identical features,' Ch. 47, 4.6.4.C
  no obligation to deliver cash or another financial asset, Ch. 47, 4.6.4.D
  reclassification, Ch. 47, 4.6.5
  relative subordination of the instrument, Ch. 47, 4.6.4.B
  substantially fix or restrict the residual return to the holder of an instrument, Ch. 47, 4.6.4.E
  transactions entered into by an instrument holder other than as owner of the entity, Ch. 47, 4.6.4.F
Qualifying assets, Ch. 21, 3. *See also* IAS 23
  assets measured at fair value, Ch. 21, 3.2
  constructed good, over time transfer of, Ch. 21, 3.4
  financial assets, Ch. 21, 3.3
  inventories, Ch. 21, 3.1
Qualitative disclosures, financial instruments, Ch. 54, 5.1
Quantitative disclosures, financial instruments, Ch. 54, 5.2, 5.6
  capital disclosures, Ch. 54, 5.6.3
  concentrations of risk, Ch. 54, 5.6.1
  operational risk, Ch. 54, 5.6.2

Quantitative thresholds, operating segments, Ch. 36, 1.3, 3.2.2
Quoted prices in active markets, Ch. 14, 17.3
    consideration of an entry price in measuring a liability or entity's own equity not held as an asset, Ch. 14, 11.2.2.B
    fair value of a liability or an entity's own equity, measuring when quoted prices for the liability or equity instruments are not available, Ch. 14, 11.2
    liabilities or an entity's own equity not held by other parties as assets, Ch. 14, 11.2.2
    liabilities or an entity's own equity that are held by other parties as assets, Ch. 14, 11.2.1
    use of present value techniques to measure fair value for liabilities and an entity's own equity instruments not held by other parties as asset, Ch. 14, 11.2.2.A
Rate-regulated activities, intangible assets, Ch. 17, 11.1
Reacquired rights, Ch. 9, 5.5.3
Real estate inventory, Ch. 22, 4
    classification of, Ch. 22, 4.1
    costs of, Ch. 22, 4.2
        individual units in multi-unit developments, Ch. 22, 4.2.1
        property demolition and operating lease costs, Ch. 22, 4.2.2
Real Estate Investment Trusts (REITs), Ch. 55, 6
Rebalancing, hedge accounting, Ch. 53, 8.2
    definition, Ch. 53, 8.2.1
    mechanics of, Ch. 53, 8.2.3
    requirement to rebalance, Ch. 53, 8.2.2
Receivables
    acquired in business combination, Ch. 49, 3.3.4; Ch. 54, 4.6.1
    distinction between contract assets and, Ch. 32, 2.1.1
    initial measurement of, Ch. 32, 2.1.5
    lease receivables, measurement of expected credit losses, Ch. 51, 10.2
    recognition, Ch. 49, 2.1.1
    trade receivables, measurement of expected credit losses, Ch. 51, 10.1
    trade receivables with no significant financing component initial measurement, Ch. 49, 3.2
Reciprocal interests in equity accounted entities, Ch. 11, 7.6.2
    measurement of noncontrolling interests where an associate holds and interest in a subsidiary, Ch. 7, 5.3
    in reporting entity accounted for, Ch. 11, 7.6.2.A
    in reporting entity not accounted for, Ch. 11, 7.6.2.B
Reclassification adjustments, financial statements, Ch. 3, 3.2.4.B
Recognition of financial instruments, Ch. 49, 2
    general requirements, Ch. 49, 2.1
        cash collateral, Ch. 49, 2.1.7
        firm commitments to purchase/sell goods/services, Ch. 49, 2.1.2
        forward contracts, Ch. 49, 2.1.3
        option contracts, Ch. 49, 2.1.4
        planned future/forecast transactions, Ch. 49, 2.1.5
        principal *vs.* agent, Ch. 49, 2.1.8
        receivables and payables, Ch. 49, 2.1.1
        transfers of financial assets not qualifying for derecognition by transferor, Ch. 49, 2.1.6
    'regular way' transactions, Ch. 49, 2.2
        exchanges of non-cash financial assets, Ch. 49, 2.2.5.A
        financial assets: general requirements, Ch. 49, 2.2.1

        contracts not settled according to marketplace convention: derivatives, Ch. 49, 2.2.1.B
        exercise of a derivative, Ch. 49, 2.2.1.D
        multiple active markets: settlement provisions, Ch. 49, 2.2.1.C
        no established market, Ch. 49, 2.2.1.A
    financial liabilities, Ch. 49, 2.2.2
    illustrative examples, Ch. 49, 2.2.5
    settlement date accounting, Ch. 49, 2.2.4
    trade date accounting, Ch. 49, 2.2.3
Recompletions, oil and gas wells, Ch. 43, 15.2
Reconciliation on first-time adoption, Ch. 5, 6.3.1.A
    inclusion of IFRS 1 reconciliations by cross reference, Ch. 5, 6.3.4
    line-by-line reconciliations, Ch. 5, 6.3.2
Recoverable amount, Ch. 20, 5. *See also* IAS 36.
Redesignation of financial assets, Ch. 55, 8.4; Ch. 56, 17.6
Redeterminations, Ch. 43, 15.4.2
Reduced Disclosure Requirements (RDRs), Ch. 1, 4.5
Registration, Evaluation, Authorisation and Restriction of Chemicals (REACH), Ch. 17, 11.4
Regression analysis, Ch. 53, 6.4.1
Regular way contracts, derivatives, Ch. 46, 3.3
'Regular way' transactions, Ch. 49, 2.2
    financial assets: general requirements, Ch. 49, 2.2.1
        contracts not settled according to marketplace convention: derivatives, Ch. 49, 2.2.1.B
        exercise of a derivative, Ch. 49, 2.2.1.D
        multiple active markets: settlement provisions, Ch. 49, 2.2.1.C
        no established market, Ch. 49, 2.2.1.A
    financial liabilities, Ch. 49, 2.2.2
    illustrative examples, Ch. 49, 2.2.5
    initial measurement, Ch. 49, 3.6
    settlement date accounting, Ch. 49, 2.2.4
    subsequent measurement exceptions, Ch. 50, 2.9.2
    trade date accounting, Ch. 49, 2.2.3
Reimbursement rights, Ch. 45, 3.10
Reinsurance assets
    definition, Ch. 55, 2.2.1
    impairments of, Ch. 55, 7.2.5; Ch. 56, 10.3
Reinsurance contract, Ch. 55, 2.2.1, 2.2.2, 3.7.2, 7.2.4; Ch. 56, 2.2, 2.3, 8.9
Reinsurance contracts held, Ch. 56, 10
    aggregation level, Ch. 56, 10.1
    allocation of the CSM to profit or loss, Ch. 56, 10.5
    boundary of, Ch. 56, 10.2
    measurement - initial recognition, Ch. 56, 10.3, 10.4
    premium allocation approach for, Ch. 56, 10.6
    subsequent measurement, Ch. 56, 10.4
    and the variable fee approach, Ch. 56, 10.7
Reinsurance contracts issued, Ch. 56, 8.9
    accounting for ceding commissions and reinstatement premiums, Ch. 56, 8.9.3
    boundary of, Ch. 56, 8.9.1
    determining the quantity of benefits for identifying coverage units, Ch. 56, 8.9.4
    issued adverse loss development covers, Ch. 56, 8.9.2

Reinsurer, Ch. 55, 2.2.1
Reissuing (dual dating) financial statements, Ch. 38, 2.1.1.B
Related party disclosures, Ch. 39. *See also* IAS 24
    compensation, defined, Ch. 39, 2.6.1
    disclosure
        of controlling relationships, Ch. 39, 2.4
        expense incurred with management entity, Ch. 39, 2.8
        with government-related entities, Ch. 39, 2.9
        key management personnel compensation, Ch. 39, 2.6
        other related party transactions, including commitments, Ch. 39, 2.7
        transactions, Ch. 39, 2.5
    identification of a related party and related party transactions, Ch. 39, 2.2
        entities that are associates/joint ventures, Ch. 39, 2.2.3
        entities that are joint ventures and associates of the same third entity, Ch. 39, 2.2.5
        entities that are joint ventures of the same third party, Ch. 39, 2.2.4
        joint operations (IFRS 11), Ch. 39, 2.2.3.A
        entities that are members of same group, Ch. 39, 2.2.2
        entities under control/joint control of certain persons/close members of their family, Ch. 39, 2.2.7
        entities under significant influence of certain persons/close members of their family, Ch. 39, 2.2.8
        government-related entities, Ch. 39, 2.2.10
        persons/close members of a person's family that are related parties, Ch. 39, 2.2.1
            control, Ch. 39, 2.2.1.A
            joint control, Ch. 39, 2.2.1.B
            key management personnel, Ch. 39, 2.2.1.D
            significant influence, Ch. 39, 2.2.1.C
        post-employment benefit plans, Ch. 39, 2.2.6
    parties that are not related parties, Ch. 39, 2.3
    post-employment benefits, Ch. 39, 2.6.3
    related party issue, Ch. 39, 1.1
    reporting entity part of a group, Ch. 39, 2.6.7
    share-based payment transactions, Ch. 39, 2.6.6
    short-term employee benefits, Ch. 39, 2.6.2
    termination benefits, Ch. 39, 2.6.5
    transactions requiring disclosure, Ch. 39, 2.7.1
Relative subordination, Ch. 47, 4.5.5, 4.6.4.B
    preference shares, Ch. 47, 4.5.5
    of puttable instrument, Ch. 47, 4.6.4.B
Relevant activities, investee
    management of defaults on assets, Ch. 6, 4.1.4
    more than one relevant activity, Ch. 6, 4.1.1
    no relevant activities, Ch. 6, 4.1.2
    single asset, single lessee vehicles, Ch. 6, 4.1.3
Renewable energy certificates (RECs), Ch. 17, 11.3
Rental assets transferred to inventory, Ch. 22, 2.3.1.E
Rental income, Ch. 19, 6.6.1. *See also* IFRS 16
Replacement share-based payment awards, Ch. 34, 7.4.4, 11. *See also* Equity-settled share-based payment transactions
    in a business combination, Ch. 7, 5.2.1; Ch. 9, 7.2; Ch. 34, 11
        accounted for under IFRS 3, Ch. 34, 11.2
            accounting for changes in vesting assumptions after the acquisition date, Ch. 34, 11.2.3
            acquiree awards the acquirer is not 'obliged' to replace, Ch. 34, 11.2.2
            awards that the acquirer is 'obliged' to replace, Ch. 34, 11.2.1
        acquiree award not replaced by acquirer, Ch. 34, 11.3
        background, Ch. 34, 11.1
        financial statements of the acquired entity, Ch. 34, 11.4
    designation of award as, Ch. 34, 7.4.4.A
    incremental fair value of, Ch. 34, 7.4.4.B
    replacement of vested awards, Ch. 34, 7.4.4.C
    tax deductions for, Ch. 33, 12.2
    on termination of employment, Ch. 34, 7.5
Reportable segments. *See also* IFRS 8; Operating segments
    externally reportable segments, identifying, Ch. 36, 3.2
        aggregation criteria, Ch. 36, 3.2.1
        'all other segments,' Ch. 36, 3.2.4
        combining small operating segments into a larger reportable segment, Ch. 36, 3.2.3
        'practical limit' for the number of reported operating segments, Ch. 36, 3.2.5
        restatement of segments reported in comparative periods, Ch. 36, 3.2.6
        quantitative thresholds, operating segments which are reportable because of their size, Ch. 36, 3.2.2
    information to be disclosed about, Ch. 36, 5
        commercially sensitive information, Ch. 36, 5.8
        explanation of measurements used in segment reporting, Ch. 36, 5.5
        general information, Ch. 36, 5.1
        other elements of revenue, income and expense, Ch. 36, 5.3
        reconciliations, Ch. 36, 5.6
        restatement of previously reported information, Ch. 36, 5.7
            organisation structure, changes in, Ch. 36, 5.7.1
            segment measures, changes in, Ch. 36, 5.7.2
        segment profit or loss, measure of, Ch. 36, 5.2
        total assets and total liabilities, measure of, Ch. 36, 5.2
Repurchase agreements ('repos')
    agreement to repurchase at fair value, Ch. 52, 4.1.5
    agreements to return the same asset, Ch. 52, 4.1.1
    agreements with right of substitution, Ch. 52, 4.1.3
    agreements with right to return the same or substantially the same asset, Ch. 52, 4.1.2
    derecognition criteria, securities lending, Ch. 52, 4.1
    inventory, Ch. 22, 2.3.1.F
    net cash-settled forward repurchase, Ch. 52, 4.1.4
    revenue from contracts with customers (IFRS 15)
        forward/call option held by the entity, Ch. 30, 5.1
        put option held by the customer, Ch. 30, 5.2
        sales with residual value guarantees, Ch. 30, 5.3
    right of first refusal to repurchase at fair value, Ch. 52, 4.1.6
    sale and leaseback transactions, Ch. 23, 7.3
    wash sale, Ch. 52, 4.1.7
Reserves and resources. *See also* Extractive industries
    definitions, Ch. 43, 1.3.1
    disclosure, Ch. 43, 2.4
        mining sector, Ch. 43, 2.4.2
        oil and gas sector, Ch. 43, 2.4.1
        standardised measure of oil and gas, Ch. 43, 2.4.3.A
        value of reserves, Ch. 43, 2.4.3
    reporting, Ch. 43, 2.1–2.3

Residual values
  definition, Ch. 23, 6.1.3
  finance lease accounting, Ch. 23, 6.2.3
  property, plant and equipment, Ch. 18, 5.2
Restatement
  hyperinflation, Ch. 16, 8
  of prior periods, impracticability of, Ch. 3, 4.7
    for change in accounting policy, Ch. 3, 4.7.1
    for a material error, Ch. 3, 4.7.2
Restatement of goodwill on first-time adoption, Ch. 5, 5.2.5
  derecognition of negative goodwill, Ch. 5, 5.2.5.B
  previously deducted from equity, Ch. 5, 5.2.5.C
  prohibition of other adjustments of goodwill, Ch. 5, 5.2.5.A
Restructuring of derivatives, hedging instruments, Ch. 53, 3.6.3
Restructuring provisions, Ch. 26, 6.1
  costs that can (and cannot) be included in, Ch. 26, 6.1.4
  definition, Ch. 26, 6.1.1
  recognition of, Ch. 26, 6.1.2
  recognition of obligations arising from the sale of an operation, Ch. 26, 6.1.3
Retrospective application, first-time adoption
  departures from, Ch. 5, 3.5
  estimates, Ch. 5, 4.2
  exceptions to, Ch. 5, 4
  financial assets and liabilities, derecognition of, Ch. 5, 4.3
Returns of capital, Ch. 8, 2.4.1.C
Revaluation model
  assets held under finance leases, Ch. 18, 6.5
  downward valuations, reversals of, Ch. 18, 6.3
  fair value before the adoption of IFRS 13, Ch. 18, 6.1.1.A
  first-time adopter, Ch. 5, 7.4.3
  for intangible assets measurement, Ch. 17, 8.2
    accounting for revaluations, Ch. 17, 8.2.3
    frequency of revaluations, Ch. 17, 8.2.2
    revaluation is only allowed if there is an active market, Ch. 17, 8.2.1
  meaning of fair value, Ch. 18, 6.1
  policy of revaluation, adopting, Ch. 18, 6.4
  revalued assets, disclosures for, Ch. 18, 8.2
  revaluing assets under IFRS 13, Ch. 18, 6.1.1
    cost approach, Ch. 18, 6.1.1.C
    highest and best use, Ch. 18, 6.1.1.A
    income approach, Ch. 18, 6.1.1.B
    market approach, Ch. 18, 6.1.1.B
    valuation approaches, Ch. 18, 6.1.1.B
  valuation surpluses and deficits, accounting for, Ch. 18, 6.2
Revenue from contracts with customers. *See* IFRS 15
Revenue recognition, Ch. 28, 1–3, Ch. 30, 1–11. *See also* IFRS 15; IFRS 17
  and agency relationships, Ch. 28, 3.4
  disclosure, Ch. 32
  extractive industries, Ch. 43, 12
    accounting for imbalances in revenue under IFRS 15, Ch. 43, 12.4.2
      consideration of cost of goods sold where revenue is recognised in accordance with IFRS 15, Ch. 43, 12.4.3
      facility imbalances, Ch. 43, 12.4.4
      future developments, Ch. 43, 12.1.2.A
      historical industry practice, Ch. 43, 12.4.1
      incidental revenue, Ch. 43, 12.1.1
      integral to development, Ch. 43, 12.1.2
      revenue in the development phase, Ch. 43, 12.1
    forward-selling contracts to finance development, Ch. 43, 12.6
      accounting by the investor, Ch. 43, 12.6.2
      accounting by the producer, Ch. 43, 12.6.1
    impact of IFRS 15, Ch. 43, 12
    inventory exchanges with the same counterparty, Ch. 43, 12.3
    overlift and underlift (oil and gas), Ch. 43, 12.4
    sale of product with delayed shipment, Ch. 43, 12.2
    trading activities, Ch. 43, 12.7
  insurance revenue, Ch. 56, 15.1
Reversal of impairment losses, Ch. 20, 11
Reverse acquisitions, Ch. 9, 14
  cash consideration, Ch. 9, 14.6
  earnings per share, Ch. 9, 14.5
  measuring goodwill, Ch. 9, 14.2
  measuring the consideration transferred, Ch. 9, 14.1
  non-controlling interest, Ch. 9, 14.4
  preparation and presentation of consolidated financial statements, Ch. 9, 14.3
  reverse acquisitions and acquirers that are not legal entities, Ch. 9, 14.9
  reverse acquisitions involving a non-trading shell company, Ch. 9, 14.8
  share-based payments, Ch. 9, 14.7
Reverse factoring, *See* Supply-chain finance
Reverse indemnification liabilities, Ch. 9, 5.6.4.A
Rights issue, Ch. 37, 4.3.3
Risk components, hedge accounting, Ch. 53, 2.2
Risk, concentrations of, Ch. 54, 5.6.1; Ch. 55, 11.2.4
Risk management objective, hedge accounting, Ch. 53, 6.2
Risk management strategy, hedge accounting, Ch. 53, 6.2; Ch. 54, 4.3.1
Risk service contracts, Ch. 43, 5.5.1
Risk-sharing arrangements, extractive industries, Ch. 43, 6
  asset swaps, Ch. 43, 6.3
  carried interests, Ch. 43, 6.1
  E&E assets, Ch. 43, 6.3.1
  exchanges of E&E assets for other types of assets, Ch. 43, 6.3.3
  farm-ins and farm-outs, Ch. 43, 6.2
  PP&E, intangible assets and investment property, Ch. 43, 6.3.2
Rollover hedging strategy, Ch. 53, 7.7
Royalties
  extractive industries, Ch. 43, 5.7, 12.9
Russia, IFRS adoption in, Ch. 1, 4.2.2
Russian Accounting Principles (RAP), Ch. 1, 4.2.2
Sale and leaseback transactions, Ch. 23, 7; Ch. 23, 8–8.4
  determining whether the transfer of an asset is a sale, Ch. 23, 8.1
  disclosures, Ch. 23, 8.4
  finance leaseback, Ch. 23, 7.2
  operating leaseback, Ch. 23, 7.2

Sale and leaseback transactions—*contd*
   presentation in the statement of cash flows, Ch. 40, 5.4.3
   repurchase agreements and options, Ch. 23, 8.1
   transactions in which the transfer of an asset is a sale, Ch. 23, 8.2
      accounting for the leaseback, Ch. 23, 8.2.2
      accounting for the sale, Ch. 23, 8.2.1
      adjustment for off-market terms, Ch. 23, 8.2.3
   transactions in which the transfer of an asset is not a sale, Ch. 23, 8.3

Sale of goods
   sale and repurchase agreements, Ch. 30, 5.3

Sale of a mineral interest and a contract to provide extraction services, Ch. 43, 12.1.2

SARs. *See* Share appreciation rights

Seasonal businesses, Ch. 41, 8.2
   costs incurred, Ch. 41, 8.2.2
   revenues received, Ch. 41, 8.2.1

Seasonality or cyclicality of operations, Ch. 41, 4.3.12

Securities and Exchange Board of India (SEBI), Ch. 1, 4.4.3

Securities and Exchange Commission (SEC), US, Ch. 1, 2.3, 3.2
   first-time adoption by foreign private issuers, Ch. 5, 8.1

Securities lending, Ch. 52, 4.1

Securitisations, Ch. 52, 3.6
   'business model' assessment, Ch. 48, 5.6
   'empty' subsidiaries or SPEs, Ch. 52, 3.6.6
   group of assets transfer, Ch. 52, 3.6.5
   insurance protection, Ch. 52, 3.6.3
   recourse to originator, Ch. 52, 3.6.1
   short-term loan facilities, Ch. 52, 3.6.2
   treatment of collection, Ch. 52, 3.6.4
   vehicles, Ch. 13, 2.2.1.B

Securitisations and special purpose entities (SPEs), Ch. 51, 7.7
   accounting for a financial liability issued, Ch. 51, 7.7.2
   ECL requirements for the SPE, Ch. 51, 7.7.1

Segment cash flow disclosures, Ch. 40, 5.6.2

Segment manager, Ch. 36, 3.1.2

Self-built assets, Ch. 18, 4.1.5

Self insurance, Ch. 26, 6.13; Ch. 55, 3.2.2.A; Ch. 56, 3.5.2.A

Separability criterion
   intangible assets, Ch. 9, 5.5.2; Ch. 17, 5.1.3.B

Separate and individual financial statements, Ch. 8, 1
   consolidated financial statements and, Ch. 8, 1.1
      associates and joint ventures, separate financial statements and interests in, Ch. 8, 1.1.1
      joint operation, separate financial statements and interests in, Ch. 8, 1.1.2
      publishing without consolidated financial statements or financial statements in which investments in associates or joint ventures are equity accounted, Ch. 8, 1.1.3
   disclosure, Ch. 8, 3
   entities incorporated in EU and consolidated and separate financial statements, Ch. 8, 1.2
   entities with no subsidiaries but exempt from applying IAS 28, Ch. 8, 3.3.1
   prepared by an entity other than a parent electing not to prepare consolidated financial statements, Ch. 8, 1.2
   prepared by parent electing not to prepare consolidated financial statements, Ch. 8, 3.1
   put and call options in separate financial statements, Ch. 7, 6.5

Separate financial statements, Ch. 8, 1–3; Ch. 13, 2.2.3.B. *See also* Separate and individual financial statements; Individual financial statements
   disclosure, Ch. 8, 3
   requirements of, Ch. 8, 2
      cost method, Ch. 8, 2.1
         cost of investment, Ch. 8, 2.1.1
         cost of investment in subsidiary, associate or joint venture acquired in stages, Ch. 8, 2.1.1.C
         deemed cost on transition to IFRS, Ch. 8, 2.1.2
         formation of a new parent, Ch. 8, 2.1.1.E formation of a new parent: calculating the cost and measuring equity, Ch. 8, 2.1.1.F
         investment in a subsidiary accounted for at cost: partial disposal, Ch. 8, 2.1.1.D
         investments acquired for own shares or other equity instruments, Ch. 8, 2.1.1.A
         investments acquired in common control transactions, Ch. 8, 2.1.1.B
         reverse acquisitions in the separate financial statements, Ch. 8, 2.1.1.G
      dividends and other distributions, Ch. 8, 2.4
         carrying amount of investment exceeds the consolidated net assets, Ch. 8, 2.4.1.B
         distributions of non-cash assets to owners (IFRIC 17), Ch. 8, 2.4.2
            recognition, measurement and presentation, Ch. 8, 2.4.2.B
            scope, Ch. 8, 2.4.2.A
         dividend exceeds the total comprehensive income, Ch. 8, 2.4.1.A
         dividends from subsidiaries, joint ventures or associates, Ch. 8, 2.4.1
         returns of capital, Ch. 8, 2.4.1.C
      equity method, Ch. 8, 2.3
      IFRS 9 method, Ch. 8, 2.2

Service concession arrangements (SCA), Ch. 25, 1–7. *See also* IFRIC 12
   accounting by grantors, Ch. 25, 2.5
   additional construction and upgrade services, Ch. 25, 5.1
      that comprise a new infrastructure asset, Ch. 25, 5.1.2
      that are part of the initial infrastructure asset, Ch. 25, 5.1.1
   bifurcation, Ch. 25, 4.5
   cash flows for, Ch. 40, 4.4.9
   consideration for services provided, Ch. 25, 4.1
      allocating, Ch. 25, 4.1.1
      determining accounting model, Ch. 25, 4.1.2
   construction phase, impairment during, Ch. 25, 4.3.2
   contract acquisition and mobilisation costs, Ch. 25, 4.8
   contractual payments made by an operator to a grantor, Ch. 25, 4.7
      under financial asset model, Ch. 25, 4.7.2
      under intangible asset model, Ch. 25, 4.7.3
      variable payments, Ch. 25, 4.7.1
   control model, Ch. 25, 3
      assets within scope, control model, Ch. 25, 3.3
      partially regulated assets, Ch. 25, 3.4
      residual interest, control of, Ch. 25, 3.2
      regulation of services, Ch. 25, 3.1
   disclosure requirements, Ch. 25, 7
   expenditure during operations phase, Ch. 25, 5

financial asset model, Ch. 25, 4.2
grantor, Ch. 25, 5.3
intangible asset model, Ch. 25, 4.3
    amortisation of, Ch. 25, 4.3.1
    impairment during construction phase, Ch. 25, 4.3.2
interaction of IFRS 16 and IFRIC 12, Ch. 25, 2.3
Interpretations Committee's approach to, Ch. 25, 1.1
operations phase, accounting for, Ch. 25, 5.2
operations services, Ch. 25, 4.1.1
outsourcing arrangements and, Ch. 25, 2.2.1
previously held assets, Ch. 25, 3.3.3
private-to-private arrangements, Ch. 25, 2.4
public service nature of the obligation, Ch. 25, 2.1
residual interests
    accounting for, Ch. 25, 4.6
    control of, Ch. 25, 3.2
revenue recognition, Ch. 25, 4.4
upgrade services, Ch. 25, 5.1

Service condition, share-based payment, Ch. 34, 3.1

Service cost, defined benefit pension plans, Ch. 35, 10.1
    current service cost, Ch. 35, 10.1
    past service cost, Ch. 35, 10.2.1
    settlements, Ch. 35, 10.2.3

Service-type warranties, Ch. 31, 3.2

Set-off, enforceable legal right of, financial assets and liabilities, Ch. 54, 7.4.1.A

Settlement date accounting, Ch. 49, 2.2.4; Ch. 51, 7.3.2
    exchange of non-cash financial assets, Ch. 49, 2.2.5.A

Shadow accounting, insurance contracts, Ch. 55, 7.2.2.D, 8.3

Share appreciation rights (SARs), Ch. 34, 8.7.3, 9.1

Share-based payment arrangement, Ch. 34, 2.2.1

Share-based payment transactions, Ch. 34, 2.2.1. *See also* Cash-settled share-based payment transactions; Equity-settled share-based payment transactions; IFRS 2; Vesting, share-based payment
    allocation of expense for equity-settled transactions, overview, Ch. 34, 6.1
    awards entitled to dividends or dividend equivalents during the vesting period, Ch. 34, 15.3
    awards exchanged for awards held by acquiree's employees, Ch. 9, 11.2.2
    awards vesting/exercisable on an exit event/change of control, Ch. 34, 15.4
    cash-settled transactions, Ch. 34, 9
        accounting, Ch. 34, 9.3
        modification of award from equity-settled to cash-settled (or vice versa), Ch. 34, 9.4
    cost of awards, equity-settled, Ch. 34, 5
        determining the fair value of equity instruments, Ch. 34, 5.5
        grant date, Ch. 34, 5.3
        transactions with employees, Ch. 34, 5.2
        transactions with non-employees, Ch. 34, 5.4
    disclosures, Ch. 34, 13
        impact of share-based payment transactions on financial statements, Ch. 34, 13.3
        of key management personnel compensation, Ch. 39, 2.6.6
        nature and extent of share-based payment arrangements, Ch. 34, 13.1
        valuation of share-based payment arrangements, Ch. 34, 13.2
    equity-settled transactions, allocation of expense, Ch. 34, 6
        cost of awards, Ch. 34, 5
        modification, cancellation and settlement, Ch. 34, 7
        overview, Ch. 34, 4
        valuation, Ch. 34, 8
    first-time adoption, Ch. 34, 16.1
    group share schemes, Ch. 34, 12
    loans to employees to purchase shares (limited recourse and full recourse loans), Ch. 34, 15.2
    matching share awards, Ch. 34, 15.1
        cancellation and settlement, Ch. 34, 7.4
        future modification or replacement of award, Ch. 34, 7.6
        modification, cancellation and settlement of equity-settled transactions, Ch. 34, 7
    modifications, Ch. 34, 7.3
        replacement and ex-gratia awards on termination of employment, Ch. 34, 7.5
        share splits and consolidations, Ch. 34, 7.8
        two awards running 'in parallel', Ch. 34, 7.7
        valuation requirements, Ch. 34, 7.2
    recognition, general principles of, Ch. 34, 3
        non-vesting conditions, Ch. 34, 3.2
        vesting conditions, Ch. 34, 3.1
            market conditions, Ch. 34, 6.3
            non-vesting conditions, Ch. 34, 6.4
        vesting conditions other than market conditions, Ch. 34, 6.2
        vesting period, Ch. 34, 3.3
    replacement awards in business combination, Ch. 34, 11; Ch. 7, 5.2.1; Ch. 9, 7.2
        accounted for under IFRS 3, Ch. 34, 11.2
        acquiree award not replaced by acquirer, Ch. 34, 11.3
        financial statements of the acquired entity, Ch. 34, 11.4
    South African black economic empowerment ('BEE') and similar arrangements, Ch. 34, 15.5
    tax base, determining, Ch. 33, 10.8.2
    taxes related to, Ch. 33, 10.8; Ch. 34, 14
        employment taxes of the employer, Ch. 34, 14.2
        income tax deductions for the entity, Ch. 34, 14.1
        sale or surrender of shares by employee to meet employee's tax liability ('sell to cover' and net settlement), Ch. 34, 14.3
    transactions with equity and cash alternatives, Ch. 34, 10
        awards requiring cash or equity settlement in specific circumstances (awards with contingent cash or contingent equity settlement), Ch. 34, 10.3
        cash settlement alternative not based on share price or value, Ch. 34, 10.4
        transactions where counterparty has choice of settlement, Ch. 34, 10.1
        transactions where entity has choice of settlement, Ch. 34, 10.2
    valuation of equity-settled transactions, Ch. 34, 8
        adapting option-pricing models, Ch. 34, 8.4
        appropriate assumptions for option-pricing models, Ch. 34, 8.5
        awards to a fixed monetary value, Ch. 34, 8.10
        awards whose fair value cannot be measured reliably, Ch. 34, 8.8

Share-based payment transactions—*contd*
   valuation of equity-settled transactions—*contd*
      awards with reload features, Ch. 34, 8.9
      option-pricing model selection, Ch. 34, 8.3
      other awards requiring the use of option valuation models, Ch. 34, 8.7
Share option, Ch. 34, 2.2
Share price-based contingencies, Ch. 37, 6.4.6.B
Share splits and consolidations, Ch. 37, 4.3.1
Shipping of commodities, Ch. 43, 12.12
   identification of performance obligations, Ch. 43, 12.12.1
   sale of product with delayed shipment, Ch. 43, 12.2
   satisfaction of performance obligations – control assessment, Ch. 43, 12.12.2
Short-term employee benefits, Ch. 35, 12
   disclosure of key management personnel compensation, Ch. 39, 2.6.2
   general recognition criteria for, Ch. 35, 12.1
   profit-sharing and bonus plans, Ch. 35, 12.3
      present legal or constructive obligation, Ch. 35, 12.3.1
      reliable estimate of provision, Ch. 35, 12.3.2
      statutory profit-sharing based on taxable profit, Ch. 35, 12.3.3
   short-term paid absences, Ch. 35, 12.2
      accumulating absences, Ch. 35, 12.2.1
      non-accumulating absences, Ch. 35, 12.2.2
Short-term loan facilities, Ch. 52, 3.6.2
Short-term receivables and payables, Ch. 14, 2.1.3
SIC-5–*Classification of Financial Instruments–Contingent Settlement Provisions*, Ch. 47, 4.3.1
SIC-7–*Introduction of the Euro*, Ch. 15, 1.2, 8
SIC-10–*Government Assistance-No Specific Relation to Operating Activities*, Ch. 24, 2.2.2
SIC-12–*Consolidation–Special Purpose Entities*, Ch. 6,
SIC-16–*Share Capital – Reacquired Own Equity Instruments (Treasury Shares)*, Ch. 47, 9.1
SIC-21–*Income Taxes–Recovery of Revalued Non-Depreciable Assets*, Ch. 33, 8.4.6
SIC-25–*Income Taxes– Changes in the Tax Status of an Entity or its Shareholders*, Ch. 33, 10.9
SIC-29–*Service Concession Arrangements: Disclosures*, Ch. 25.1–7
SIC-32–*Intangible Assets-Web Site Costs*, Ch. 17, 6.2.5
Significant estimates and judgements, disclosure of, Ch. 13, 3
Significant influence, Ch. 11, 4
   fund managers, Ch. 11, 4.6
   holdings of less than 20% of the voting power, Ch. 11, 4.3
   lack of, Ch. 11, 4.2
   potential voting rights, Ch. 11, 4.4
   severe long-term restrictions impairing ability to transfer funds to the investor, Ch. 11, 4.1
   voting rights held in a fiduciary capacity, Ch. 11, 4.5
Significant insurance risk, Ch. 55, 3.2; Ch. 56, 3.5
   changes in level of, Ch. 56, 3.6
   level of assessment, Ch. 55, 3.2.2; Ch. 56, 3.5.2
      insurance mutuals, Ch. 55, 3.2.2.B; Ch. 56, 3.5.2.B
      intragroup insurance contracts, Ch. 55, 3.2.2.C; Ch. 56, 3.5.2.C
      self insurance, Ch. 55, 3.2.2.A; Ch. 56, 3.5.2.A
   meaning of 'significant', Ch. 55, 3.5.1
   quantity of insurance risk, Ch. 56, 3.5.1
   significant additional amounts, Ch. 56, 3.5.3
   significant additional benefits, Ch. 55, 3.5.3
Silo, Ch. 6, 8
   consolidation of, Ch. 6, 8.3
   evaluating control of, Ch. 6, 8.2
   identifying, Ch. 6, 8.1
      in insurance industry, Ch. 6, 8.1.1
      in investment funds industry, Ch. 6, 8.1.2
Simplified Disclosure Standard (SDS), Ch. 1, 4.5
SME Implementation Group, Ch. 1, 2.9
South Africa, IFRS adoption in, Ch. 1, 4.6
SPACs. *See* Special purpose acquisition companies (SPACs)
Special purpose acquisition companies (SPACs), Ch. 34, 5.3.10
Special purpose entities (SPEs), Ch. 52, 3.6.6, 5.6.1
Split accounting, compound financial instruments, Ch. 47, 6.2
   accounting for the equity component, Ch. 47, 6.2.1
   temporary differences arising from split accounting, Ch. 47, 6.2.2
Standing Interpretations Committee (SIC), Ch. 1, 2.1
Start-up costs, investment properties, Ch. 19, 4.2
   intangible assets, Ch. 17, 7
Statement of cash flows, Ch. 40, 1–8. *See also* IAS 7
   acquisition-related costs, Ch. 40, 6.3.1
   acquisitions, Ch. 40, 6.3
   classification, Ch. 40, 4
      allocating items to operating, investing and financing activities, Ch. 40, 4.4
         cash flows for service concession arrangements, Ch. 40, 4.4.9
         cash flows from factoring of trade receivables, Ch. 40, 4.4.5
         cash flows from supply-chain financing (reverse factoring), Ch. 40, 4.4.6
         cash flows on derivative contracts, Ch. 40, 4.4.12
         cash flows related to the costs of a share issue, Ch. 40, 4.4.11
         classification of cash flows-future developments, Ch. 40, 4.4.11
         compensation for an insured loss, Ch. 40, 4.4.8
         contributions to a log-term employee benefit fund, Ch. 40, 4.4.4
         debt instrument issued at a discount or redeemed at a premium, Ch. 40, 4.4.13
         early settlement of a debt instrument, Ch. 40, 4.4.14
         interest and dividends, Ch. 40, 4.4.1
         property, plant and equipment held for rental, Ch. 40, 4.4.7
         sales taxes and other non-income tax cash flows, Ch. 40, 4.4.3
         taxes on income, Ch. 40, 4.4.2
         treasury shares, Ch. 40, 4.4.10
   cash flows from financing activities, Ch. 40, 4.3
   cash flows from investing activities, Ch. 40, 4.2
   cash flows from operating activities, Ch. 40, 4.1
      direct method, Ch. 40, 4.1.1
      indirect method, Ch. 40, 4.1.2
   consolidated statement of cash flows, preparing, Ch. 40, 6.1

contingent consideration, Ch. 40, 6.3.3
deferred and other non-cash consideration, Ch. 40, 6.3.2
disposals, Ch. 40, 6.3
first-time adopter, Ch. 5, 7.1
foreign currency cash flows, Ch. 40, 5.3
    entities applying the direct method, Ch. 40, 5.3.1
    entities applying the indirect method, Ch. 40, 5.3.2
gross/net presentation of cash flows, Ch. 40, 5.2
group treasury arrangements, Ch. 40, 6.5.2
non-cash transactions and transactions on deferred terms, Ch. 40, 5.4
    asset disposals on deferred terms, Ch. 40, 5,4,2
    asset purchased on deferred terms from the supplier, Ch. 40, 5.4.1
    revenue contracts with deferred payment terms, Ch. 40, 5.4.3
    sale and leaseback transactions, Ch. 40, 5.5.4
operating, investing and financing activities, allocating items to, Ch. 40, 4.4
    accounting as lessee, Ch. 40, 5.5.1
    accounting as lessor, Ch. 40, 5.5.5
    cash flows for service concession arrangements, Ch. 40, 4.4.9
    cash flows from factoring of trade receivables, Ch. 40, 4.4.5
    cash flows from leasing transactions, Ch. 40, 5.5
    cash flows from supply-chain financing (reverse factoring), Ch. 40, 4.4.6
    cash flows on derivative contracts, Ch. 40, 4.4.12
    cash flows related to the costs of a share issue, Ch. 40, 4.4.11
    contributions to a log-term employee benefit fund, Ch. 40, 4.4.4
    debt instrument issued at a discount or redeemed at a premium, Ch. 40, 4.4.13
    interest and dividends, Ch. 40, 4.4.1
    lease incentives, Ch. 40, 5.5.3
    payments made by the lessee before commencement date, Ch. 40, 5.5.2
    property, plant and equipment held for rental, Ch. 40, 4.4.7
    received as compensation for an insured loss, Ch. 40, 4.4.9
    sales taxes, Ch. 40, 4.4.3
    taxes on income, Ch. 40, 4.4.2
    treasury shares, Ch. 40, 4.4.10
settlement of amounts owed by the acquired entity, Ch. 40, 6.3.4
settlement of intra-group balances on a demerger, Ch. 40, 6.3.5
in subsidiaries, associates and joint ventures, Ch. 40, 6.5.1
transactions with non-controlling interests, Ch. 40, 6.2
voluntary disclosures, Ch. 40, 5.7
    cash flows to increase and maintain operating capacity, Ch. 40, 5.7.1
    segment cash flow disclosures, Ch. 40, 5.7.2

Statement of changes in equity, Ch. 3, 3.3

Statement of comprehensive income, Ch. 3, 3.2
    cash flow hedges, Ch. 54, 4.3.3
    comparative information, Ch. 4, 4
    for co-operative, Ch. 54, 7.1.5
    discontinued operations, Ch. 3, 3.2.5
    expenses analysis, Ch. 3, 3.2.3
        by function, Ch. 3, 3.2.3.B
        by nature, Ch. 3, 3.2.3.A
    extraordinary items, Ch. 3, 3.2.6.B
    face of, information required on, Ch. 3, 3.2.2
    fair value hedges, Ch. 54, 4.3.3
    material items, Ch. 3, 3.2.6.A
    for mutual fund, Ch. 54, 7.1.5
    operating profit, Ch. 3, 3.2.2.A
    ordinary activities, Ch. 3, 3.2.6.B
    presentation on face of, Ch. 54, 7
    reclassification adjustments, Ch. 3, 3.2.4.B
    tax on items of other comprehensive income, Ch. 3, 3.2.4.C

Statement of financial position, Ch. 3, 3.1. *See also* IAS 1
    comparative information, Ch. 3, 2.4; Ch. 4, 4.2
    current assets, Ch. 3, 3.1.3
    current liabilities, Ch. 3, 3.1.4
    current/non-current assets and liabilities, distinction between, Ch. 3, 3.1.1
    hyperinflation, Ch. 16, 4
    IFRS statement of financial position, opening, Ch. 5, 3
        and accounting policies, Ch. 5, 3.2
        assets and liabilities to be recognised in, Ch. 5, 5.2.4
        defined terms, Ch. 5, 1.3
        departures from full retrospective application, Ch. 5, 3.5
        fair value and deemed cost, Ch. 5, 3.3
        first-time adoption timeline, Ch. 5, 3.1
        hedge accounting in, Ch. 5, 4.5
        transitional provisions in other standards, Ch. 5, 3.4
    information required either on the face of the statement of financial position or in the notes, Ch. 3, 3.1.6
    information required on the face of statement of financial position, Ch. 3, 3.1.5
    non-current assets and disposal groups held for sale, Ch. 3, 3.1.2
    plan surplus or deficit in, treatment of, Ch. 35, 8
        assets restriction to their recoverable amounts, Ch. 35, 8.2
        net defined benefit liability (asset), Ch. 35, 8.1

Step acquisitions, Ch. 9, 9

Step-by-step method, Ch. 7, 2.3; Ch. 15, 6.6.3
    in consolidating foreign operations, Ch. 7, 2.3

Step-disposal of a subsidiary, Ch. 7, 3.4
    advance payment, Ch. 7, 3.4
    immediate disposal, Ch. 7, 3.4

'Step-up' clause, perpetual instruments, Ch. 47, 4.5.4

Stepped up exercise price, Ch. 47, 5.1.3

Stewardship, Ch. 2, 4.2.3

Straight-line method, assets depreciated using, Ch. 43, 16.1.2

Streaming arrangements, forward-selling contracts to finance development, Ch. 43, 12.6

Stripping costs in the production phase of a surface mine, Ch. 43, 15.5
    determining when production phase commences, Ch. 43, 15.5.2
    disclosures, Ch. 43, 15.5.6
    initial recognition, Ch. 43, 15.5.4
        allocating costs between inventory and the stripping activity asset, Ch. 43, 15.5.4.A
        identifying components of the ore body, Ch. 43, 15.5.4.B

Stripping costs in the production phase of a surface mine—*contd*
   recognition criteria-stripping activity asset, Ch. 43, 15.5.3
   scope of IFRIC 20, Ch. 43, 15.5.1
   subsequent measurement, Ch. 43, 15.5.5
Structured entities, Ch. 13, 2.2.1, 2.2.1.B
   disclosure of interests in unconsolidated, Ch. 13, 6
   disclosure of the nature of the risks associated with
      consolidated, Ch. 13, 4.4
   unconsolidated, Ch. 13, 2.2.2.D
Subleases, Ch. 23, 7
   definition, Ch. 23, 7.1
   disclosure, Ch. 23, 7.5
   intermediate lessor accounting, Ch. 23, 7.2
   presentation, Ch. 23, 7.4
   sublessee accounting, Ch. 23, 7.3
Sub-LIBOR issue, Ch. 53, 2.4
Subordinated financial support, Ch. 13, 2.2.1.B
Subordinated retained interests, Ch. 52, 4.3
Subrogation, Ch. 55, 7.2.6.E
Subsequent measurement, financial instruments, Ch. 50, 1–4.
   See also Impairments
   amortised cost and the effective interest method, Ch. 50, 3
      effective interest rate, Ch. 50, 3.1
      fixed interest rate instruments, Ch. 50, 3.2
      floating interest rate instruments, Ch. 50, 3.3
      inflation-linked debt instruments, Ch. 50, 3.6
      modified financial assets and liabilities, Ch. 50, 3.8
         accounting for modifications that do not result in
            derecognition, Ch. 50, 3.8.1, 5.1.1
         treatment of modification fees, Ch. 50, 3.8.2
      more complex financial liabilities, Ch. 50, 3.7
      perpetual debt instruments, Ch. 50, 3.5
      prepayment, call and similar options, Ch. 50, 3.4
         revisions to estimated cash flows, Ch. 50, 3.4.1
   estimated cash flows, revisions to, Ch. 50, 3.4.1
   exceptions to the general principles, Ch. 50, 2.9
      hedging relationships, Ch. 50, 2.9.1
      liabilities arising from 'failed derecognition' transactions,
         Ch. 50, 2.9.3
      regular way transactions, Ch. 50, 2.9.2
   financial assets and financial liabilities at fair value through
      profit/loss, Ch. 50, 2.4
   financial guarantees and commitments to provide a loan at a
      below-market interest rate, Ch. 50, 2.8
   floating interest rate instruments, Ch. 50, 3.3
   foreign currencies
      foreign entities, Ch. 50, 4.2
      instruments, Ch. 50, 4.1
   impairment, Ch. 51, 1–15
      approaches, Ch. 51, 3
      for corporates, Ch. 51, 4
      disclosures, Ch. 51, 15
      financial assets measured at fair value through other
         comprehensive income, Ch. 51, 9
      general approach, Ch. 51, 6
      intercompany loans, Ch. 51, 13
      introduction, Ch. 51, 1
      loan commitments and financial guarantee contracts,
         Ch. 51, 11
      measurement of ECL's, Ch. 51, 5
      modified financial assets, Ch. 51, 8
      presentation of credit losses, Ch. 51, 14
      revolving credit facilities, Ch. 51, 12
      scope, Ch. 51, 2
      trade receivables, contract assets and lease receivables,
         Ch. 51, 10
   reclassification of financial assets, Ch. 50, 2.7
   and recognition of gains and losses, Ch. 50, 2
      debt financial assets measured at amortised cost, Ch. 50,
         2.1
      debt financial assets measured at fair value through other
         comprehensive income, Ch. 50, 2.3
      exceptions to the general principles, Ch. 50, 2.9
         hedging relationships, Ch. 50, 2.9.1
         liabilities arising from 'failed derecognition'
            transactions, Ch. 50, 2.9.3
         regular way transactions, Ch. 50, 2.9.2
      financial assets and financial liabilities at fair value through
         profit/loss, Ch. 50, 2.4
      financial guarantees and commitments to provide a loan at
         a below-market interest rate, Ch. 50, 2.8
      financial liabilities measured at amortised cost, Ch. 50, 2.2
      reclassification of financial assets, Ch. 50, 2.7
      unquoted equity instruments and related derivatives,
         Ch. 50, 2.6
   unquoted equity instruments and related derivatives, Ch. 50, 2.6
Subsidiaries, Ch. 7; Ch. 13, 2.2.2.A. *See also* Ownership interests,
   changes in
   acquired in stages, cost of, Ch. 7, 3.1.1, 3.1.2; Ch. 8, 2.1.1.C
   acquisition, Ch. 8, 4.4.2
      deferred tax exemption, Ch. 33, 7.2.9
   becoming a first-time adopter later than its parent, Ch. 5,
      5.9.1
   dividends from, Ch. 8, 2.4.1
   former subsidiary
      comparative information for, Ch. 7, 3.3.2.G
      interest retained in, Ch. 7, 3.3.1
   investments in, Ch. 5, 5.8; Ch. 20, 12.4
   parent becoming a first-time adopter later than, Ch. 5, 5.9.2
Substantive rights, Ch. 6, 4.2.1
Substantively enacted tax legislation, Ch. 33, 5.1
Successful efforts method, E&E expenditure, Ch. 43, 3.2.3
Super-deductible assets (tax), Ch. 33, 7.2.6
Supply-chain finance, Ch. 52, 6.5; Ch. 40, 4.4.6
'Synthetic' instruments, Ch. 46, 8
Take-or-pay contracts, Ch. 43, 12.7.14, 17.2
Tax bases, Ch. 33, 6.1
   of assets, Ch. 33, 6.1.1
   assets and liabilities whose tax base is not immediately
      apparent, Ch. 33, 6.1.3
   disclaimed or with no economic value, Ch. 33, 6.1.7
   equity items with, Ch. 33, 6.1.5
   of items not recognised as assets/liabilities in financial
      statements, Ch. 33, 6.1.4
   items with more than one tax base, Ch. 33, 6.1.6
   of liabilities, Ch. 33, 6.1.2
Tax expense (tax income)
   definition, Ch. 33, 3
Tax planning opportunities, Ch. 33, 7.4.4, 8.4.1

Taxable profit (tax loss)
　definition, Ch. 33, 3
Taxable temporary differences
　definition, Ch. 33, 3
Taxation, Ch. 33. *See also* Deferred tax; IAS 12–*Income taxes*; Income taxes
　extractive industries, Ch. 43, 19
　interim financial reporting, Ch. 41, 9.5
　　changes in the effective tax rate during the year, Ch. 41, 9.5.2
　　difference in financial year and tax year, Ch. 41, 9.5.3
　　measuring interim income tax expense, Ch. 41, 9.5.1
　　tax credits, Ch. 41, 9.5.5
　　tax loss and tax credit carrybacks and carryforwards, Ch. 41, 9.5.4
Taxes related to share-based payment transactions, Ch. 34, 14
　employment taxes of the employer, Ch. 34, 14.2
　　applicable standards, Ch. 34, 14.2.1
　　holding of own shares to 'hedge' employment tax liabilities, Ch. 34, 14.2.3
　　recovery of employer's taxes from employees, Ch. 34, 14.2.2
　income tax deductions for the entity, Ch. 34, 14.1
　sale or surrender of shares by employee to meet employee's tax liability ('sell to cover' and net settlement), Ch. 34, 14.3
　　net settlement feature for withholding tax obligations, Ch. 34, 14.3.1
Temporal method, Ch. 15, 1.1
Temporary differences, Ch. 33, 6, 6.2, 7. *See also* Deferred tax
　changes after initial recognition Ch. 33, 7.42.4
　　altered by legislative change, Ch. 33, 7.2.4.D
　　amortisation, Ch. 33, 7.2.4.A
　　in carrying value due to revaluation, Ch. 33, 7.2.4.B
　　depreciation, Ch. 33, 7.2.4.A
　　in tax base due to deductions in tax return, Ch. 33, 7.2.4.C
　deductible, Ch. 33, 3, 6, 6.1, 6.2.2, 7.2.2.B, 7.5.3
　　business combinations and consolidation, Ch. 33, 6.2.2.E
　　foreign currency differences, Ch. 33, 6.2.2.F
　　revaluations, Ch. 33, 6.2.2.C
　　tax re-basing, Ch. 33, 6.2.2.D
　　transactions that affect profit of loss, Ch. 33, 6.2.2.A
　　transactions that affect statement of financial position, Ch. 33, 6.2.2.B
　definition, Ch. 33, 3
　taxable, Ch. 33, 6.2.1
　　business combinations and consolidation, Ch. 33, 6.2.1.E
　　foreign currency differences, Ch. 33, 6.2.1.F
　　hyperinflation, Ch. 33, 6.2.1.G
　　revaluations, Ch. 33, 6.2.1.C
　　tax re-basing, Ch. 33, 6.2.1.D
　　transactions that affect profit of loss, Ch. 33, 6.2.1.A
　　transactions that affect statement of financial position, Ch. 33, 6.2.1.B
Termination benefits, employee benefits, Ch. 35, 14
　measurement, Ch. 35, 14.3
　recognition, Ch. 35, 14.2
　statutory termination indemnities, Ch. 35, 14.1
Third-party credit enhancement, liabilities issued with
　by the issuer, Ch. 14, 11.3.1
　by a third-party, Ch. 14, 11.3.1.A

Time-period related hedged item, Ch. 53, 7.5.1
Time value of money, Ch. 51, 5.7
　hedge effectiveness, measurement of, Ch. 53, 7.4.2
Time value of options, Ch. 53, 3.6.4, 7.5.1
　aligned time value, Ch. 53, 7.5.1.A
　and effectiveness of options, Ch. 53, 7.4.12
　hedged items with embedded optionality, Ch. 53, 3.6.4
　retrospective application, Ch. 53, 12.3.1
Tolling arrangements, mining sector, Ch. 43, 20
Total Distributable Income (TDI), Ch. 55, 6
Total return swaps, Ch. 52, 4.4.1
Trade date accounting, Ch. 49, 2.2.3; Ch. 51, 7.3.2
　exchange of non-cash financial assets, Ch. 49, 2.2.5.A
Trade receivables. *See* Receivables
'Traded in a public market,' meaning of, Ch. 6, 2.2.1.B; Ch. 36, 2.2.1
Transaction-based taxes, Ch. 56, 8.2.3.I
Transaction costs
　changes in ownership interest without loss of control, Ch. 7, 4.4
　equity instruments, tax benefits, Ch. 33, 10.3.5
　equity transactions, Ch. 47, 8.1
　fair value measurement, Ch. 14, 9.1
　financial instruments, Ch. 49, 3.4
　　accounting treatment, Ch. 49, 3.4.1
　identifying, Ch. 49, 3.4.2
　incurred by the reporting entity on acquisition of investment property, Ch. 19, 6.4
Transaction price, IFRS 15
　allocation of, Ch. 29, 3
　determination of, Ch. 29, 2
　initial measurement, Ch. 49, 3.3
Transaction related hedged item, Ch. 53, 7.5.1
Transfer of control, Ch 30. 2-4
Transferee's put option, Ch. 52, 5.4.3.B
Transferor's call option, Ch. 52, 5.4.3.A
Transfers of financial assets, Ch. 54, 6
　disclosure requirements, Ch. 54, 6.3.2
　meaning of continuing involvement, Ch. 54, 6.3.1
　meaning of 'transfer,' Ch. 54, 6.1
　transferred financial assets
　　that are derecognised in their entirety, Ch. 54, 6.3
　　that are not derecognised in their entirety, Ch. 54, 6.2
Transition Resource Group for Impairment of Financial Instruments, IFRS, Ch. 1, 2.9
Transition Resource Group for Insurance Contracts, Ch. 1, 2.9
Transition Resource Group for Revenue Recognition, Ch. 1, 2.9, 27, 28, 29, 30, 31, 32
Transportation costs, Ch. 14, 9.2
Treasury shares, Ch. 47, 9
　cash flow statement, Ch. 40, 4.4.10
　IFRS 17 Treasury share election, Ch. 47, 9.2
　transactions in own shares not at fair value, Ch. 47, 9.1
Trustees, IFRS Foundation, Ch. 1, 2,2–2.8, 3.2, 5
Unanimous consent, joint control, Ch. 12,4.3; Ch. 43, 7.1.1.B
Unbundling of deposit components, Ch. 55, 5
　illustration, Ch. 55, 5.2

Unbundling of deposit components—*contd*
   practical difficulties, Ch. 55, 5.3
   requirements, Ch. 55, 5.1
Uncertain future events, insurance contracts, Ch. 55, 3.4; Ch. 56, 3.2
Uncertain tax treatments, Ch. 33, 5.2, 8.2, 9
   assumptions about the examination of tax treatments ('detection risk'), Ch. 33, 9.3
   consideration of changes in facts and circumstances, Ch. 33, 9.5
   considered separately (unit of account), Ch. 33, 9.2
   determining effects of, Ch. 33, 9.4
   disclosures relating to, Ch. 33, 9.6
   IFRIC 23
      changes in estimates, Ch. 38, 3.6
      scope and definitions used, Ch. 33, 9.1
   presentation of liabilities or assets for, Ch. 33, 9.7
   recognition of an asset for payments on account, Ch. 33, 9.8
Unconsolidated structured entities, Ch. 13, 2.2.2.D
   disclosure of interests, Ch. 13, 6
   financial or other support to, Ch. 13, 4.4.3
Undivided interests, Ch. 18, 7.3; Ch. 43, 7.2
Unit of account, Ch. 14, 5.1
   extractive industries, Ch. 43, 4
   fair value measurement
      asset's (or liability's) components, Ch. 14, 5.1.4
      and portfolio exception, Ch. 14, 5.1.2
      and PxQ, Ch. 7, 3.3.2.F; Ch. 14, 5.1.1
      vs. valuation premise, Ch. 14, 5.1.3
   and FVLCD estimation, Ch. 20, 6.1.1
Unit of production method, Ch. 18, 5.6.2
United Kingdom (UK) adopted- IAS, Ch. 1, 4,.2.3
United Kingdom (UK), IFRS adoption in, Ch. 1, 4.2.3
United States of America (US), IFRS adoption in, Ch. 1, 3.2, 4.3.1
Unitisations, mineral properties, Ch. 43, 15.4.1
Unit-linked features, Ch. 55, 4.1
Units of production method, assets depreciated using, Ch. 43, 16.1.3
   joint and by-products, Ch. 43, 16.1.3.D
   reserves base, Ch. 43, 16.1.3.B
   unit of measure, Ch. 43, 16.1.3.C
   units of production formula, Ch. 43, 16.1.3.A
Unquoted equity instruments
   and related derivatives, Ch. 50, 2.6
Upstream activity phases, extractive industries, Ch. 43, 1.6.1
   acquisition of mineral rights, Ch. 43, 1.6.1
   appraisal/evaluation, Ch. 41, 1.6.1
   closure and decommissioning, Ch. 43, 1.6.1
   construction, Ch. 43, 1.6.1
   development, Ch. 43, 1.6.1
   exploration, Ch. 43, 1.6.1
   production, Ch. 43, 1.6.1
   prospecting, Ch. 43, 1.6.1
'Upstream' transactions elimination, equity accounted entities, Ch. 11, 7.6.1
US GAAP, convergence with IFRS, Ch. 1, 3.2
US, IFRS adoption in, Ch. 1, 3.2
Useful life, intangible assets, Ch. 17, 9.1.1
   contractual/other legal rights, Ch. 17, 9.1.2
   with a finite useful life, Ch. 17, 9.2
   with an indefinite useful life, Ch. 17, 9.3
Valuation techniques, fair value measurement, Ch. 14, 14
   cost approach, Ch. 14, 14.3
      use of depreciated replacement cost to measure fair value, Ch. 14, 14.3.1
   disclosure of, Ch. 14, 20.3.5
   income approach, Ch. 14, 14.4
   inputs to, Ch. 14, 15
      broker quotes and pricing services, Ch. 14, 15.5
      central clearing organisations, values from, Ch. 14, 15.5.1
         general principles, Ch. 14, 15.1
      premiums and discounts, Ch. 14, 15.2
         blockage factors (or block discounts), Ch. 14, 15.2.1
      pricing within the bid-ask spread, Ch. 14, 15.3
         bid-ask spread, Ch. 14, 15.3.2
         mid-market pricing, Ch. 14, 15.3.1
      risk premiums, Ch. 14, 15.4
   market approach, Ch. 14, 14.2
   property, plant and equipment, Ch. 18, 6.1.1.B
   selecting appropriate, Ch. 14, 14.1
      making changes to valuation techniques, Ch. 14, 14.1.4
      single *vs.* multiple valuation techniques, Ch. 14, 14.1.1
      using multiple valuation techniques to measure fair value, Ch. 14, 14.1.2
      valuation adjustments, Ch. 14, 14.1.3
Value-at-risk and similar analyses, Ch. 54, 5.5.2
Value beyond proven and probable reserves (VBPP), Ch. 43, 8.2.3
Value in use (VIU). *See also* IAS 36
   calculation of (extractive industries), Ch. 43, 11.4
      commodity price assumptions, Ch. 43, 11.4.3
      consistency in cash flows and book values attributed to the CGU, Ch. 43, 11.4.1
         environmental provisions and similar provisions and liabilities, Ch. 43, 11.4.1.A
      foreign currency cash flows, Ch. 43, 11.4.5
      future capital expenditure, Ch. 43, 11.4.4
      projections of cash flows, Ch. 43, 11.4.2
         cash flows from mineral reserves and resources and the appropriate discount rate, Ch. 43, 11.4.2.A
   differences between fair value and VIU, Ch. 20, 7.3
   estimating the future pre-tax cash flows of the CGU under review, Ch. 20, 7.1
      budgets and cash flows, Ch. 20, 7.1.1
      cash inflows and outflows from improvements and enhancements, Ch. 20, 7.1.2
      events after the reporting period, Ch. 20, 7.1.9
      foreign currency cash flows, Ch. 20, 7.1.5
      internal transfer pricing, Ch. 20, 7.1.6
      lease payments, Ch. 20, 7.1.8
      overheads and share-based payments, Ch. 20, 7.1.7
      restructuring, Ch. 20, 7.1.3
      terminal values, Ch. 20, 7.1.4
   identifying appropriate discount rate and discounting future cash flows, Ch. 20, 7.2
      approximations and short cuts, Ch. 20, 7.2.4
      calculating VIU using post-tax cash flows, Ch. 20, 7.2.3
      determining pre-tax rates taking account of tax losses, Ch. 20, 7.2.6

disclosing pre-tax discount rates when using a post-tax methodology, Ch. 20, 7.2.5
discount rates and the weighted average cost of capital, Ch. 20, 7.2.1
entity-specific WACCs and capital structure, Ch. 20, 7.2.8
entity-specific WACCs and different project risks within the entity, Ch. 20, 7.2.7
pre-tax discount rate, calculating, Ch. 20, 7.2.2
use of discount rates other than the WACC, Ch. 20, 7.2.9
for investment in subsidiaries, associates and joint ventures, Ch. 20, 12.4.2
based on cash flows generated by underlying assets, Ch. 20, 12.4.2.B
using dividend discount models, Ch. 20, 12.4.2.A
relevant cash flows and non-arm's length prices (transfer pricing), Ch. 20, 12.1

Value of business acquired (VOBA), Ch. 55, 9.1

Variable interest entity (VIE), Ch. 13, 2.2.1.B

Variable returns, exposure to
evaluating derivatives, Ch. 6, 5.3
as indicator of power, Ch. 6, 5.1
interest rate swaps, Ch. 6, 5.3.1
plain vanilla foreign exchange swaps, Ch. 6, 5.3.1
returns, Ch. 6, 5.2
total return swaps, Ch. 6, 5.3.2

Vested transactions, share-based payment, Ch. 34, 2.2.2.E

Vesting, share-based payment, Ch. 34, 3.1, 6.1, 9.3.2. *See also* Cash-settled share-based payment transactions; Equity-settled share-based payment transactions
market conditions, Ch. 34, 6.3
non-vesting conditions, Ch. 34, 3.2, 3.4, 6.4
background, Ch. 34, 3.2.1
defining, Ch. 34, 3.2.2
non-compete agreements Ch. 34, 3.2.3
treatment of, option-pricing models, Ch. 34, 8.4.2
overview, Ch. 34, 6.1
accounting after vesting, Ch. 34, 6.1.3
continuous estimation process of IFRS 2, Ch. 34, 6.1.1
vesting and forfeiture, Ch. 34, 6.1.2
shares used as a currency of payment, Ch. 34, 15.6
awards assessed on the market value of a subsidiary or business unit and settled by reference to the fair value of shares in the parent entity, Ch. 34, 15.6.1
vesting conditions, Ch. 34, 3.1, 3.4
employee's performance rating, Ch. 34, 3.1.2
'malus' clauses and clawback conditions, Ch. 34, 3.1.1
other than market conditions, Ch. 34, 6.2
service condition, Ch. 34, 6.2.1
vesting period, Ch. 34, 3.3
awards entitled to dividends during, Ch. 34, 15.3
determining, Ch. 34, 9.3.2.A
market conditions and known vesting periods, Ch. 34, 6.3.3
modifications with altered vesting period, Ch. 34, 7.3.3
non-vesting conditions and, Ch. 34, 6.4.2
variable vesting periods due to market conditions, Ch. 34, 6.3.4
variable vesting periods due to non-market vesting conditions, Ch. 34, 6.2.3
vesting in instalments ('graded vesting'), Ch. 34, 6.2.2

Veto rights, Ch. 6, 4.2.2.A

Voluntary changes of accounting policy, Ch. 3, 4.4; Ch. 41, 8.1.2.B
disclosures relating to, Ch. 3, 5.1.2

Voting power, Ch. 11, 4.3

Voting rights
held in fiduciary capacity, Ch. 11, 4.5
significant influence, potential, Ch. 11, 4.4

Voting rights, investee
additional rights from other contractual arrangements, Ch. 6, 4.3.6
contractual arrangement with other vote holders, Ch. 6, 4.3.5
de facto control, Ch. 6, 4.3.3
majority without power, Ch. 6, 4.3.3
potential voting rights, Ch. 6, 4.3.4
power with a majority, Ch. 6, 4.3.1

Warranties, Ch. 31, 3
assurance-type warranties, Ch. 31, 3.3
contracts that contain both assurance and service-type warranties, Ch. 31, 3.4
determining whether warranty is an assurance-type or service-type warranty, Ch. 31, 3.1
customer's return of defective item in exchange for compensation: right of return *vs.* assurance type warranty, Ch. 31, 3.1.3
evaluating whether a product warranty is a service-type warranty (i.e. a performance obligation) when it is not separately priced, Ch. 31, 3.1.1
how would an entity account for repairs provided outside the warranty period?, Ch. 31, 3.1.2
service-type warranties, Ch. 31, 3.2

Warranty provisions (IAS 37), Ch. 26, 6.10

Waste electrical and electronic equipment (WE&EE), EU directive, Ch. 26, 6.7

Weather derivatives, Ch. 45, 3.3.1

Website costs, Ch. 17, 6.2.5
application and infrastructure, Ch. 17, 6.2.5
content development, Ch. 17, 6.2.5
graphical design development, Ch. 17, 6.2.5
operating stage, Ch. 17, 6.2.5
planning, Ch. 17, 6.2.5

Weighted average cost of capital (WACC), Ch. 20, 7.2
discount rates and, Ch. 20, 7.2.1
entity-specific WACCs
and capital structure, Ch. 20, 7.2.8
and different project risks, Ch. 20, 7.2.7

Weighted average number of shares, Ch. 37, 4.1

Work in progress, recognition of, Ch. 43, 14.1

Workovers, oil and gas wells, Ch. 43, 15.2

World Standard-setters Conferences, Ch. 1, 2.9

Worldwide adoption of IFRS, Ch. 1, 4.1

Written options
call option, Ch. 37, 6.4.2.B; Ch. 47, 11.2.2
maturity analysis, Ch. 54, 5.4.2.F
net settlement, Ch. 45, 4.2.3
net written options, Ch. 53, 3.2.2
put option, Ch. 7, 6.2, 6.3, 6.4, 6.5, 7.3, 7.4; Ch. 37, 6.4.2.C; Ch. 47, 11.3.2

Notes

Notes

Notes

Notes

Notes

Notes

Notes

Notes

Notes

Notes

Notes

Notes

Notes

Notes

Notes

Notes

Notes